THE NEW INTERNATIONAL
WEBSTER'S
COLLEGIATE
DICTIONARY
OF THE ENGLISH LANGUAGE

◆ ◆ ◆

INTERNATIONAL
ENCYCLOPEDIC EDITION

MRZYGŁÓD

THE NEW INTERNATIONAL

WEBSTER'S COLLEGIATE DICTIONARY

OF THE ENGLISH LANGUAGE

$$\blacklozenge \blacklozenge \blacklozenge$$

INTERNATIONAL ENCYCLOPEDIC EDITION

SIDNEY I. LANDAU
EDITOR IN CHIEF

TRIDENT PRESS INTERNATIONAL
2002 EDITION

Published by

TRIDENT PRESS INTERNATIONAL

Copyright © 2002
Typhoon International

ISBN 1582794499 Standard
ISBN 1582794375 Special
ISBN 1582793891 Padded

Contents

Dictionary Advisory Committee

Albert H. Marckwardt *Chairman*
Professor Emeritus of English and Linguistics
Princeton University

Harold B. Allen
Professor Emeritus of English and Linguistics
University of Minnesota

S. I. Hayakawa
President Emeritus
San Francisco State University

Rudolph C. Troike
Director
Center for Applied Linguistics

H. Rex Wilson
Associate Professor of English (Linguistics)
University of Western Ontario

Editorial Staff

EDITOR IN CHIEF
Sidney I. Landau

MANAGING EDITOR
Ronald J. Bogus

EDITORS
Sheila C. Brantley, Samuel Davis,
Barbara Nolan, Kathleen D. Shafer

CONTRIBUTING EDITORS
Myrna Breskin, Olga Coren, Helene MacLean,
Harold A. Rodgers, Karin Whiteley

CLERICAL ASSISTANTS
Lurlene Scott, Lynn Tricarico, Martha Adams

ART DIRECTOR
Marian Hurd Manfredi

CARTOGRAPHER
Rafael Palacios

ARTISTS
Robert Byrd, Kiyoshi Kanai, Mary Suzuki, Jean Taylor

Special acknowledgment is gratefully made of the contributions of Diana Klemin, Associate Art Director of Doubleday & Company, Inc., in acquiring new illustrations for this work.

THE NEW INTERNATIONAL
WEBSTER'S
COLLEGIATE
DICTIONARY
OF THE ENGLISH LANGUAGE

◆◆◆

INTERNATIONAL
ENCYCLOPEDIC EDITION

TRIDENT PRESS INTERNATIONAL
NAPLES, FLORIDA

Pronunciation Key

The primary stress mark (′) is placed after the syllable bearing the heavier stress or accent; the secondary stress mark (′) follows a syllable having a somewhat lighter stress, as in com·men·da·tion (kom′ən·dā′shən).

a	add, map	g	go, log	o	odd, hot	t	talk, sit	v	vain, eve
ā	ace, rate	h*	hope, hate	ō	open, so	th	thin, both	w	win, away
â(r)	care, air			ô	order, jaw	th	this, bathe	y*	yet, yearn
ä	palm, father	i	it, give	oi	oil, boy	u	up, done	z	zest, muse
		ī	ice, write	ou	pout, now	û(r)	burn, term	zh	vision, pleasure
b	bat, rub			ŏŏ	took, full	yŏŏ	fuse, few		
ch	check, catch	j	joy, ledge	ōō	pool, food				
d	dog, rod	k	cool, take			ə	the schwa, an unstressed vowel		
e	end, pet	l	look, rule	p	pit, stop		representing the sound of		
ē	even, tree	m	move, seem	r	run, poor		*a* in *above*	o	in *melon*
f	fit, half	n	nice, tin	s	see, pass		*e* in *sicken*	u	in *focus*
		ng	ring, song	sh	sure, rush		*i* in *clarity*		

* Superscript *h*, as in *white* (ʰwīt) or *whale* (ʰwāl), and *y*, as in *due* (dyōō) or *Tuesday* (tyōōz′dā) represent sounds that commonly occur in certain regions but are commonly omitted in others.

FOREIGN SOUNDS

à as in French *ami, patte*. This is a vowel midway in quality between (a) and (ä).

œ as in French *peu*, German *schön*. Round the lips for (ō) and pronounce (ā).

ü as in French *vue*, German *grün*. Round the lips for (ōō) and pronounce (ē).

kh as in German *ach*, Scottish *loch*. Pronounce a strongly aspirated (h) with the tongue in position for (k) as in *cool* or *keep*.

ṅ This symbol indicates that the preceding vowel is nasal. The nasal vowels in French are œṅ *(brun)*, aṅ *(main)*, äṅ *(chambre)*, ôṅ *(dont)*.

′ This symbol indicates that a preceding (l) or (r) is voiceless, as in French *débâcle* (dā·bä′kl') or *fiacre* (fyà′kr'), or that a preceding (y) is pronounced consonantly in a separate syllable followed by a slight schwa sound, as in French *fille* (fē′y').

Formation of Plurals and Participles

Basically, plurals in English are formed by the addition of -*s* or -*es* (depending on the preceding sound) to the complete word; past participles are formed by the addition of -*ed*, and present participles by adding -*ing*. There are, however, many exceptions. In this dictionary, all such exceptions (the "irregular" inflected forms) are indicated within the entry, in boldface immediately following the part-of-speech label.

fly (flī) *n. pl.* **flies** . . .
sheep (shēp) *n. pl.* **sheep** . . .
cal·ci·fy (kal′sə·fī) *v.t. & v.i.* **-fied, ·fy·ing** . . .
go (gō) *v.* **went, gone, go·ing** . . .

Some rules for the spelling of these forms (with the exception of nouns which form their plurals by some internal change and the so-called strong verbs) are listed below:

PLURALS

1. Nouns ending in *y* preceded by a consonant change *y* to *i* and add -*es*.
   baby babies   story stories
2. Nouns ending in *y* preceded by a vowel add -*s* without change.
   chimney chimneys   valley valleys
   Note, however, that *money* may have either form in the plural—*moneys, monies*.
3. Some nouns ending in *f* or *fe* change this to *v* and add -*es*.
   knife knives   shelf shelves
   But: roof roofs   safe safes
   Some words may have alternate plural forms.
   scarf scarfs or scarves
4. Most words ending in *o* add -*s* without change.
   cameo cameos folio folios

A few words ending in *o* (*echo, hero, Negro*, etc.) form the plural only in -*oes* (*echoes, heroes, Negroes*), but many others in this category have alternative plurals in both forms.
   mosquito   mosquitos or mosquitoes
   volcano   volcanoes or volcanos

PAST AND PRESENT PARTICIPLES

1. The final consonant is doubled for monosyllables or words accented on the final syllable when they end in a *single* consonant preceded by a *single* vowel.
   control, controlled, controlling
   hop, hopped, hopping
   occur, occurred, occurring
   But: help, helped, helping *(two consonants)*
   seed, seeded, seeding *(two vowels)*

Some words *not* accented on the final syllable have a variant participial form with a doubled consonant; the single consonant form is preferred in the United States.
   travel, traveled or travelled, traveling or travelling
   worship, worshiped or worshipped, worshiping or worshipping

2. Words ending in silent or mute *e* drop the *e* before -*ed* and -*ing*, unless it is needed to avoid confusion with another word.
   change, changed, changing   love, loved, loving
   singe, singed, singeing   dye, dyed, dyeing

3. Verbs ending in *ie* usually change this to *y* before adding -*ing*.
   die, died, dying   lie, lied, lying

4. Verbs ending in *c* add a *k* before -*ed* and -*ing*.
   mimic, mimicked, mimicking
   picnic, picnicked, picnicking

ix

Terms Used in the Guide to the Use of This Dictionary

cross-reference to illustration —— **ser·rate** (ser′āt, -it) *adj.* Having sawlike teeth, as the margins of certain leaves. Also **ser′rat·ed.** [< L *serra* a saw] • See LEAF.

inflected forms —— **skin·ny** (skin′ē) *adj.* ·ni·er, ·ni·est 1 Consisting of or like skin. 2 Without sufficient flesh; too thin. 3 Lacking the

skip (skip) *v.* skipped, skip·ping *v.i.* 1 To move with springing steps, esp. by a series of light hops on alternate feet.

homographs —— **skip·per¹** (skip′ər) *n* 1 One who or that which skips. 2 Any of various insects that make erratic, skipping movements.

definition number —— **skip·per²** (skip′ər) *n.* 1 The master or captain of a vessel, esp. of a small ship or boat. 2 One who is in charge of any endeavor. —*v.t.* To act as the skipper of (a vessel, etc.) [< Du. *schip* ship]

abbreviation —— **Skt.** Sanskrit.

variant form —— **sku·a** (skyōō′ə) *n.* A predatory sea bird. Also skua gull. [< ON *skūfr*]

slice (slīs) *n.* 1 A thin, broad piece cut off from a larger

*   *   *

such a course. —*v.* sliced, slic·ing *v.t.* 1 To cut or remove

usage information —— from a larger piece: often with *off, from,* etc. 2 To cut,

cross-reference —— **slide fastener** ZIPPER.

splen·did (splen′did) *adj.* 1 Magnificent; imposing. 2 Conspicuously great or illustrious; glorious: a *splendid* achievement. 3 Giving out or reflecting brilliant light;

*   *   *

synonym list —— *n.* —Syn. 1 majestic, dazzling, sublime, superb, grand. 2 outstanding, renowned, celebrated, marvelous.

part-of-speech labels —— **splin·ter** (splin′tər) *n.* 1 A thin, sharp piece of wood, glass, metal, etc., split or torn off lengthwise; a sliver. 2 SPLINTER GROUP. —*v.t. & v.i.* 1 To split into thin sharp pieces or

usage note —— **split infinitive** A verbal phrase in which the sign of the infinitive "to" is separated from its verb by an intervening word, usu. an adverb, as in "to quickly return." • Although this construction is often condemned by purists, it is sometimes justified to avoid ambiguity or awkwardness.

syllabic dots —— **stra·to·cu·mu·lus** (strāt′ō·kyōō′myə·ləs, strat′-) *n. pl.* ·li
subject label —— (-lī) *Meteorol.* A type of dark, low-lying cloud, characterized by horizontal bases and high, rounded summits.

main entry —— **strength** (strength) *n.* 1 The quality or property of being physically strong: the *strength* of a weight lifter. 2 The capacity to sustain the application of force without yielding or breaking. 3 Effectiveness: the *strength* of an argument. 4 Binding force or validity, as of a law. 5 Vigor or force of style: a drama of great *strength.* 6 Available numerical force in a military unit or other organization. 7 Degree of intensity, as of color, light, or sound. 8 Potency, as of a drug, chemical, or liquor; concentration. 9 A support; aid: He is our *strength.* —on the strength of Relying on; on the basis of. [< OE *strang* strong] —Syn. 1 force, power, vigor. 2 solidity, tenacity, toughness.

illustrative example ——

idiomatic phrase ——

run-on derivatives —— **stren·u·ous** (stren′yōō·əs) *adj.* Necessitating or marked by strong effort or exertion. [< L *strenuus*] —stren′u·ous·ly *adv.* —stren′u·ous·ness *n.*

pronunciation —— **strep·to·coc·cus** (strep′tə·kok′əs) *n. pl.* ·coc·ci (-kok′sī, -sē, -ī, -ē) Any of a large group of spherical bacteria that

strep·to·my·cin (strep′tō·mī′sin) *n.* A potent antibiotic isolated from a mold. [< Gk. *streptos* twisted + *mykēs* fungus]

etymology ——

cross-reference to map —— **Swit·zer·land** (swit′sər·lənd) *n.* A republic of CEN. Europe, 15,940 sq. mi., cap. Bern. • See map at ITALY.

Guide to the Use
of This Dictionary

1. Main entries are in large, bold-faced type and are listed alphabetically by letter, regardless of whether composed of one or more words.

> **blue·jack·et**
> **blue jay**

2. Syllabication is indicated by syllabic dots dividing main-entry words. **blue·jack·et** may be hyphenated at the end of a line after *blue-* or after *bluejack-*. Phrasal entries are not syllabified when each element is entered elsewhere.

3. Homographs These words, identical in spelling but differing in meaning and origin (and sometimes in pronunciation), are separately entered and differentiated by a superior figure, as **bear¹** (to support or endure) and **bear²** (the animal).

4. Pronunciations are shown in parentheses immediately following the main entry, as **di·chot·o·my** (dī·kot′ə·mē). When more than one pronunciation is recorded, the first given is usually the most widely used wherever it has been possible to determine extent of usage; often, however, usage may be almost equally divided. The order of the pronunciations is not intended to be an indication of preference; all pronunciations shown are valid for educated American speech.

The syllabication of the pronunciations follows, in general, the syllabic breaks heard in speech rather than the conventional division of the main entry, as **ju·di·cial** (jōō·dish′əl), **an·es·the·tize** (ə·nes′thə·tīz).

When a variant pronunciation differs merely in part from the first pronunciation recorded, only the differing syllable or syllables are shown, provided that there is no possibility of misinterpretation, as **eq·ua·ble** (ek′wə·bəl, ē′kwə-). Phrasal entries are not pronounced if the individual elements are separately entered in proper alphabetical place.

5. Part-of-speech labels are shown in italics following the pronunciation for main entries, and are abbreviated as follows: *n.* (noun), *v.* (verb), *pron.* (pronoun), *adj.* (adjective), *adv.* (adverb), *prep.* (preposition), *conj.* (conjunction), *interj.* (interjection). When more than one part of speech is entered under a main entry, the additional labels are run in and preceded by a bold-faced dash, as **cor·ner** (kôr′nər) *n.* . . . —*v.t.* . . . —*v.i.* . . . —*adj.* . . .

Verbs used transitively are identified as *v.t.,* those intransitively as *v.i.;* those used both transitively and intransitively in all senses are designated *v.t. & v.i.*

6. Inflected forms include the past tense, past participle, and present participle of verbs, the plural of nouns, and the comparative and superlative of adjectives and adverbs. The inflected forms are entered wherever there is some irregularity in spelling or form. They are shown in bold-faced type with syllabication immediately after the part-of-speech label. Only the syllable affected is shown, provided there is no ambiguity possible, as **com·pute** (kəm·pyōōt′) *v.t.* **·put·ed, ·put·ing.** An inflected form that requires pronunciation or is alphabetically distant from the main entry may also be separately entered and pronounced in its proper vocabulary place.

a *Principal parts of verbs* The order in which the principal parts are shown is past tense, past participle, and present participle, as **come** (kum) *v.* **came, come, com·ing.** Where the past tense and past participle are identical, only two forms are entered, as **bake** (bāk) *v.* **baked, bak·ing.** When alternative forms are given, the first form indicated is usually the one preferred, as **grov·el** (gruv′əl, grov′-) *v.i.* **grov·eled** or **grov·elled, grov·el·ing** or **grov·el·ling.** Variant forms not in the standard vocabulary are shown in parentheses and labeled, as **drink** (dringk) *v.* **drank** (*Archaic* **drunk**), **drunk** (*Archaic* **drunk·en**), **drink·ing.** Principal parts entirely regular in formation—those that add *-ed* and *-ing* directly to the infinitive without spelling modification—are not shown.

b *Plural of nouns* Irregular forms are here preceded by the designation *pl.,* as **a·lum·nus** (ə·lum′·nəs) *n. pl.* **·ni** (-nī); **deer** (dir) *n. pl.* **deer.** When alternative plurals are given, the first shown is the preferred form, as **buf·fa·lo** (buf′ə·lō) *n. pl.* **·loes** or **·los** or **·lo.**

c *Comparison of adjectives and adverbs* The comparatives and superlatives of adjectives and adverbs are shown immediately after the part of speech when there is some spelling modification or a complete change of form, as **mer·ry** (mer′ē) *adj.* **·ri·er, ·ri·est; bad** (bad) *adj.* **worse, worst.**

7. Definition In entries for words having several senses, the order in which the definitions appear is, wherever possible, that of frequency of use, rather than semantic evolution. Each such definition is distinguished by a bold-faced number, the numbering starting anew after each part-of-speech label when it is followed by more than one sense. Closely related meanings, especially those within a specific field or area of study, may be defined under the same number and set apart by small bold-faced letters. Illustrative examples are provided when necessary to supplement definitions.

> **strength** (strength) *n.* **1** The quality or property of being physically strong: the *strength* of a weight lifter.

8. Restrictive labels Entries or particular senses of words and terms having restricted application are variously labeled according to:

a usage level, as *Slang, Informal* (colloquial)

b localization, as *Regional* (restricted in usage to a particular region of the U.S.), *Brit.* (British), *Can.* (Canadian), *Austral.* (Australian), etc.; *U.S.* (United States) is used only to avoid confusion with another meaning of the same word not restricted to the U.S. It is understood that many unlabeled definitions are current chiefly or only in the U.S.

c field or subject, as *Astron.* (astronomy), *Ecol.* (ecology), *Med.* (medicine), *Naut.* (nautical), etc.

d language of origin, as *French, German, Latin,* etc. These entries, although used in English speech and writing, have not yet undergone the process of Anglicization of pronunciation, meaning, or usage, and are usually italicized in writing.

e *Nonstand.* (nonstandard) is applied to those usages which are not accepted as standard English by most native speakers.

Restrictive labels that apply to only one sense of a word are entered after the definition number. Restrictive labels entered immediately after the part-of-speech label apply to all the senses for that part of speech; those shown before the first part-of-speech label refer to the entire entry.

9. Cross-references Small capital letters are used to identify:

a A cross-reference from a variant form to the entry where the term is defined.

> **es·thet·ic** (es·thet′ik) *adj.* AESTHETIC.

b A cross-reference to a synonymous meaning or term where a full definition will be found.

> **slide fastener** ZIPPER.

c A cross-reference to an illustration, map, or usage note. These cross-references are preceded by •.

d A cross-reference in an etymology. See *Etymologies* below.

Variant forms that do not require cross-reference are shown after the definition or definitions to which they apply, and appear in bold-faced type with syllabication, stress marks, and, when necessary, pronunciation. When they apply to one sense only of an

entry having more than one definition, they are linked to the appropriate definition with a colon.

10. Spelling variations between U.S. and British usage are noted by the label *Brit. sp.,* followed by the usual British spelling or that part of it that differs from the U.S. spelling.

> **hon·or** . . . *Brit. Sp.* **·our.**

11. Idiomatic phrases, as those formed by a verb and preposition or adverb (*carry on, put down, set off,* etc.) appear in bold-faced type within the entry for the principal word in the phrase, following the definitions for the principal part of speech involved.

> **car·ry** . . . *v.t.* . . . *v.i.* **19** . . . **20** . . . **21** . . . —**carry on 1** To keep going; continue. **2** To behave in a free, frolicsome manner. **3** To continue, as a tradition. . . . —*n.* . . . .

12. Etymologies are shown in brackets after the definitions. The following examples show the manner of entry and the use of cross-references:

a **special** [< L *species* kind, species] means: ultimately derived from (<) the Latin (L) word *species,* meaning "kind, species."

b **arroyo** [Sp.] means that *arroyo* was borrowed directly from a Spanish (Sp.) word of the same form and meaning.

c **cloche** [F, lit., bell]; like *arroyo* above, *cloche* exists in the same form and meaning in another language, French (F), from which English borrowed it, but in this case the foreign word has a literal meaning (lit.), "bell," that elucidates its English meaning.

d **hassle** [?< HAGGLE + TUSSLE] means: possibly (?) derived from (<) a blending of "haggle" and (+) "tussle."

e **decency** [< L *decens.* See DECENT.]; "See" directs attention to the etymology under "decent" for further information.

13. Run-on derivatives Words that are actually or ostensibly derived from other words by the addition or replacement of a suffix, and whose sense can be inferred from the meaning of the main word, are run on in smaller bold-faced type at the end of the appropriate main entries. The run-on derivatives are preceded by a heavy dash and followed by a part-of-speech label. They are syllabified and stressed, and, when necessary, a full or partial pronunciation is provided.

14. Usage information, when an integral part of definition, is included, following a colon, after the particular sense of a word to which it applies, as:

> **slice** . . . *v.t.* **1** To cut or remove from a larger piece: often with *off, from,* etc.

More extensive notes consisting of supplementary information on accepted usage, style, grammar, status of variant forms, etc., are entered at the end of the relevant entries and prefaced with the symbol •. (See *anyone, Asia, shop, split infinitive.*)

15. Synonym lists are appended to many entries following the abbreviation **Syn.** In entries having more than one sense, synonyms are keyed by definition number, and, if necessary, by part of speech, to the appropriate sense.

16. Word lists The meaning of many combinations of words is easily apparent by combining the senses of their component parts. Such self-explaining compounds have been entered in six lists under the respective first elements: *in-*, *multi-*, *non-*, *over-*, *re-*, and *un-*. These lists serve to indicate the preferred form of a compound—whether written solid, with a hyphen, or as a two-word phrase. The listings are not intended to be all-inclusive; the prefixes and combining forms so entered combine freely in English in the formation of new compounds based on existing forms.

17. Trade names Some words used to identify trademarked or proprietary articles, drugs, processes, and services have been entered and defined because these terms are so familiar that their omission would be remarkable. In every case the word is identified with the notation "a trade name," and no treatment of any such term should be construed as affecting its status as a trademark.

18. Abbreviations commonly used in English are entered in their respective alphabetic places in the main section of this dictionary.

Usage

BY ALBERT H. MARCKWARDT

Every society places its stamp of approval upon certain forms or modes of social behavior and looks askance upon deviations from them. In our culture, applause for a fine musical performance would be considered out of place at a church service, but entirely appropriate and in fact praiseworthy in a concert hall. The particular mode of behavior which is accorded such prestige may vary according to geography and social class. The English and European continentals recognize one manner of manipulating a knife and fork to convey food to the mouth; Americans employ a quite different technique. The American way seems needlessly awkward to the European; the European way seems crude to the Americans. When they entertain at dinner, upper middle-class Americans are likely to eat by candlelight and to have flowers on the table. This is regarded as ostentatious, or at best superfluous, in working-class circles.

The use of language is one of many kinds of social behavior. Here, as in other matters, certain forms of speech and writing have acquired prestige, whereas others are looked upon with disfavor. Moreover, differentiations on the basis of geography and social class are readily apparent. The past tense of the verb *eat (et)*, used by many speakers of British English of unquestioned social standing, would be considered rustic or uneducated by most Americans; conversely, the Americanism *donate* has not yet gained thorough acceptance in Britain. "Bring them crates over here," is a sentence calculated to produce cooperation and a speedy result when addressed to a group of factory workmen; the substitution of *those containers* in that particular social context would produce suspicion, resentment, and probably not the desired result.

Standard English

That form of the English language which has acquired prestige from its use by those educated persons who are carrying on the affairs of the English-speaking community (whether narrowly or broadly conceived) is known as Standard English. In short, the standard language is that which possesses social utility and social prestige. History bears out this observation with remarkable fidelity. All we know of the earliest stage of our language, that which we refer to as Old English, spoken on the island between the mid-fifth century incursions of Germanic-speaking Angles, Saxons, and Jutes and the mid-11th century Norman Conquest, was that there were decided regional differences, resulting in four major dialects. During the first two of these six centuries the center of power was clearly in the kingdom of Northumbria, and that dialect constituted the standard. At the time of the powerful King Offa, political and cultural influence shifted southward, and the dialect of Mercia acquired prestige. From the mid-ninth century onward, the West Saxon dynasty assumed political leadership; King Alfred fathered a cultural renaissance and a major educational program; and this time the standard moved westward, remaining there through the period of religious reform, also centered in the same area. Thus it is that most of the Old English literature which has come down to us is in West Saxon. Even the early selections originally written in other dialects were finally recopied in the prestige dialect.

The development of the language during the Middle English period (1050–1475) bears out the same principle. By the time the English language had recovered from its temporary subjugation to Norman French, London was firmly established as the political, economic, and cultural center of the island. It is interesting to observe that by the end of the 14th century the dialect of London was used by many of the major literary figures irrespective of where they were born. Chaucer, a native Londoner, employed it in his poetry, which is possibly no surprise, but so too did Gower, born in Kent, and Wycliffe, who hailed from Lincolnshire. One acute observer has pointed out that Standard English had its origin in the kind of language employed in the courts of law and the governmental offices at Westminster, that it was essentially administrative English. This is another telling bit of evidence of the close relationship between the standard language and the bases of influence.

The emergence of the London dialect as a standard for the entire country first won formal recognition in

Puttenham's *The Arte of English Poesie* (1589) in which the language of London and of the shires within a radius of sixty miles, "and not much beyond," was recommended as a model for aspiring writers to follow. This was accompanied by the statement that educated gentlemen in the outlying portions of England had adopted London English as a standard and were speaking it as well as people living in the capital.

It was just at this point in time that the English language entered on its worldwide career. It was transported first across the Atlantic to the American mainland and the Caribbean islands. The spread to the Asian subcontinent followed in the 18th century; to Australia and South Africa in the 19th. At the outset the colonies were generally willing and eager to follow the standard of the mother country, even though it was at times less than ideally suited to all aspects of the local situation, but as they acquired more and more independence, economic and cultural as well as political, new national forms of the language tended to emerge and to develop their own standard norms.

Today English is spoken as a native language by vast numbers of people—approximately 275,000,000 —distributed over four continents of the globe. The standard reveals a considerable amount of variation from one country to another, and even in one part of some countries as compared with another. Thus, Standard West Indian English differs from both Standard British and Standard American English, and Standard South African differs from all of these. Standard Canadian English is distinct from Standard Australian. It is even possible to speak of standard forms of English in areas where it is not the native language, notably India and the Philippines. In the United Kingdom itself there is a standard form of Scots and a standard Northern English, both of which differ from the Received Standard of the London area.

The Role of the Dictionary

Ideally a dictionary is an accurate record of a language as it is employed by those who speak and write it. But as we have already seen, the English language, even in terms of just its present use, to say nothing of its past, exists on such a vast scale that no single work is likely to do justice to it in its entirety. Inevitably the task has had to be broken up into smaller segments. Some dictionaries deal with pronunciation only, at times even confined to a particular country—England or America. Others confine themselves to particular segments of the language: dialect, slang, or one or another technical vocabulary. More ambitious is the attempt by the historical dictionary to include within the bounds of a single work evidence of both the present and earlier stages of the language, although sometimes a dictionary may be confined to just one early period—Old or Middle English, for example. There are dictionaries which concentrate on the language as it is, and has been, used in England, in Scotland, in the United States, and in Canada. Consequently, in the face of this inescapable specialization and division of labor, a dictionary which purports to be general in its purpose must of necessity exercise a high degree of selective reporting on those aspects of the language which will best serve the needs of those who consult it.

The editors of this dictionary have assumed that it will be used principally in the United States, by persons who are familiar with American English. Only rarely have they felt it necessary to identify features of the language which are characteristic of this country. For example, the past participial form *gotten* is identified in a note as an American usage, and the peculiarly American use of *integrate* as used in "to integrate schools" bears the label *U.S.* The editors have taken on the responsibility of identifying usages peculiar to Britain, Canada, or Australia, indicating these with the appropriate label. Any item not so identified is in current use in the United States. In this connection it should be realized that despite all that has been said here about differences throughout the world, the unity of the English language in the many countries in which it is spoken far outweighs the diversity.

The obligation of the dictionary to record the state of the language or some segment of it as accurately as possible has already been mentioned. This may properly be termed a descriptive function, and it reflects the way in which the editors approach their task. But the nonprofessional, the layman who consults the dictionary, does so from other motives. Either he is seeking information on some particular facet of the language about which he knows nothing—the most obvious instance being the meaning of a word he has not previously encountered—or to discover which of several possible uses of the language, relative to spelling, pronunciation, word division, word meaning, or grammatical form, has acquired a sufficient degree of prestige and propriety to justify his employment of it. In short, his view of the dictionary function is essentially prescriptive. He hopes to be told what to say and to write, or more accurately perhaps, how to say and how to write.

In the light of all that has been said up to this point, these two concepts, the descriptive and the prescriptive, should not be in conflict with each other. It has already been pointed out that the standard language *is* the language of the socially and culturally dominant group within a speech community. There can be no other source upon which to base it. Accordingly, if the dictionary records that language accurately and faithfully, it should constitute a reliable guide and preceptor.

Unfortunately, the problem is not so simple as it seems on the surface. For a number of reasons too complicated to explain here, many people, Americans in particular, are reluctant to accept this simple and straightforward view of the matter. For one thing, experience has taught them that some persons of position and influence have little feeling for or command of the niceties of the language, and accordingly they are led to question the reliability and usefulness of an accurate exercise of the descriptive technique. Second, they are committed to a rigid and monolithic view of what constitutes the standard language and expect to find a single answer as to what is linguistically approved or appropriate, irrespective of the circumstances in which it may occur. The facts of the case are quite at variance with this assumption. Again, language like any form of social behavior varies in response to the demands of the particular social situation. Many of us would not hesitate to pick up a chicken drumstick with our fingers at a picnic but would feel constrained to use a knife and fork at a formal dinner. Neither form of behavior is superior or inferior to the other; it is a question of adaptation to the circumstances. Differences in regional standards prevail as well. In some parts of the country, for the host at a cocktail party to employ a bartender smacks of ostentation, whereas a hired caterer is accepted as the norm. Elsewhere just the reverse set of values prevails.

Varieties of Usage

It is precisely for this reason that dictionaries find it necessary to employ various kinds of labels to indicate the sphere of usage in which a particular word or expression is or is not acceptable. Those labels which are most often misunderstood have to do with the degree of formality which characterizes the communication. No dictionary has found it possible to recognize more than a dichotomy here, namely a formal and an informal type of speech. Clearly, each one of us in the course of a day's use of the language communicates much more in an informal manner than in a formal. The differences are pervasive, including pronunciation and structure as well as vocabulary. To take just a few obvious instances: the clipped form *dorm* is a frequent informal equivalent for *dormitory;* the phrase *all in* often serves for *exhausted, catch on* for *understand,* to cover at least three of the four major parts of speech. There is a whole battery of adverbs such as *consequently* and *accordingly* which may find *so* as their normal equivalent in less formal discourse. The same distinction extends to such phrase structures as *at all events* and *needless to say.* In the negative-interrogative form of the verb, *isn't he, can't he, won't he* are the informal expressions corresponding to *is he not, can he not, will he not,* a consideration affecting both syntax and pronunciation.

Actually we are faced with more than a dichotomy here. Some observers recognize at least four distinct linguistic styles, including the formal *(This is not the man whom we seek),* the consultative *(This is not the man we're looking for),* the casual *(He's not our man)* and the intimate *('Fraid you picked a lemon).* It is beyond the bounds of practicality or serviceability for the dictionary to recognize more than two broad types of situation, the formal and the informal. Moreover, in terms of the expectations of most of the people who consult a dictionary, it is more to the point to label the justifiably informal than it would be to signalize the formal. Generally the length and stylistic aura of a word will identify it as being primarily confined to formal use.

Distinctions drawn on the basis of formality often cut across differences in the mode of communication, speech or writing. Much, but not all, of our speech activity in the course of a day is informal. Some of our writing at least is more likely to be formal, although many personal letters, memoranda, the private writing contained in diaries and journals, may well fall into the informal category.

The point is that these are matters of the function of language, not of acceptability or correctness. A person whose informal speech may be characterized as "talking like a book" or "talking as if he had swallowed the dictionary," has simply failed to sort out the styles properly. One may rest assured that whatever a dictionary labels as *informal* is not less correct than an unlabeled item but that it is appropriate to an informal situation or purpose. Dictionaries usually do not affix a label to those words appropriate only for formal use on the ground that the social penalties for excessive formality of speech, though very real, seem somehow less onerous than those for misplaced informality.

Slang

Somewhat akin to informality, but differing from it in several important respects, is the use of language we have come to call slang. Slang is difficult to define, partly because the term itself has changed in meaning over the centuries. Originally it referred to thieves' argot, and today the term is still applied to the special terminology of certain occupations and other groups, including oil drillers, baseball players, rock or jazz musicians, college students, shoe salesmen, tramps, drug addicts, and prison inmates, but it has also taken on a much broader application. It includes clipped forms like *benny* and *frag,* echoic terms like *slurp,* meaningless tag phrases of the class of *twenty-three skidoo* from the early years of the century, *so's your old man, and how, you better believe it,* all of which have had their fleeting currency, only to be replaced by what will undoubtedly be the equally temporary *got to (He's got to be the best ball player in the league)* and the interjection *Wow!* which appears to be the stock in trade of the younger generation and the mindless consumer pictured on television commercials.

Not included in the concept of slang are dialect, localisms, profanity, and the so-called four-letter words once taboo in polite society, now increasingly accepted. It is also important to recognize that most slang is colloquial in nature in that it occurs in speech much more frequently than in writing; on the other hand, it would be a grave error to think of all colloquial or informal language as slang. Nor is slang to be confused with nonstandard language; it is at times consciously employed for a particular effect by persons of unquestioned cultivation.

Dictionaries are far from uniform in what they label as slang; even the special dictionaries of slang include many entries which do not at all fit the concept as it has been set forth here. The label *slang* after a word or a particular meaning of a word is an indication of its general unsuitability for formal communication; it suggests moreover that when used informally, it may have something of a slight shock value in a serious context; at the very least it will call attention to itself. This would be true, for example, of *boss* used adjectivally in the sense of "great, wonderful," of *bug off* for "go away!" and of *bug out,* "to escape, run away." Each country where English is a native language has its own variety of slang. *Wizard* is often used in England as a blanket term of approval; *dinkum* is confined to Australia. Both are relatively unknown in the United States. In this dictionary, slang terms found in other English-speaking countries will be labeled as to their place of origin. If an item is simply characterized as *slang* with no additional qualifying term, it may be assumed to be current in this country.

Regional Variation

In no English-speaking country is the language uniform over the entire area. In certain fields of the vocabulary, terminology differs from one part of the country to the other. This is especially true of words having to do with the more homelike and intimate aspects of life: the physical environment, the home, foods and cooking, the farm and farm operations, the fauna and flora. The literary term *earthworm* is called an *angleworm* in certain regions and a *fishworm* or *fishing worm* in others, and in addition there are several terms which have a much more restricted currency: *eaceworm, angle dog,* and *dewworm. Skillet* and *spider,* though now somewhat old-fashioned, are still used for *frying pan* or *fry pan* in some areas. Limited access highways have developed a highly varied terminology: *turnpike, freeway, expressway, parkway,* to mention only a few.

It is impossible in a general dictionary such as this to include all such variants, nor would it be helpful to label as *Regional* every term limited to extensive regions. Nevertheless, in terms of its function as an accurate recorder of the language, the dictionary must inform its users when a term, limited geographically, differs from a more commonly preferred synonym. There is a problem here in that dialect research in this country is still going on and that reliable information about the regional incidence of many terms is not yet readily available. In general the policy of this dictionary will be to indicate that a word is regional when that is known to be the case and when the word is not likely to be familiar to others outside the region of its use, but there will be no attempt to delimit the precise areas of its occurrence.

Nonstandard English

The very fact that a painstaking attempt has been made to clarify the concept of Standard English should be evidence in itself that there are features of the language which do not meet these requirements. Most of the aberrations are matters of grammatical form: *hisself* instead of *himself, hisn* instead of *his, growed* instead of *grew* or *grown, anyways* instead of *anyway,* and so on. Occasionally these are matters which pertain wholly to the vocabulary, like *irregardless,* or to the pronunciation, as with the dropping of the first *r* in *secretary* and *library.*

At one time it was the custom for dictionaries to employ the label *illiterate* for such deviations from standard usage. For several reasons the term is far from satisfactory. The percentage of actual illiterates in the United States is relatively small, even if so-called functional illiteracy is to be used as a criterion. The type of expressions so labeled often extended to many persons who had experienced some schooling. Because of these and other considerations dictionaries have recently tended to use *nonstandard* as the preferred designation for deviations from the linguistic norm which tend to be matters of social rather than regional dialect. It is rare, of course, for anyone to consult the dictionary for the meanings of words so labeled. The principal service that the dictionary performs is to indicate their status.

Usage Notes

It must be recognized, however, that there is no immediately definable hard-and-fast line separating the standard from the nonstandard. There is, indeed, a gray area, a zone of disputed items about which there may be considerable difference of opinion, even among authorities of equal experience and eminence. In connection with some of the locutions falling within this zone of uncertainty, not only must the extent of use by speakers of the standard language be considered but also the attitude toward the word or construction in question. For example, there can be no doubt about the extent to which the verb *finalize* has been used in American English by speakers and writers of unquestioned prestige. It is by no means a new coinage. It has appeared in magazines and newspapers with high editorial standards. It conforms to an active and long-standing pattern of converting adjectives to verbs by the addition of the *-ize* suffix, one which has been present in the language for some four centuries, evident in words like *fertilize, brutalize,* and *solemnize,* the propriety of which is never questioned. Yet the fact remains that a fair number of persons who can use the language with skill and discrimination react negatively to this single *-ize* formation. To them it suggests the awkwardness and bombast of bureaucratic language, administrators' jargon. Logical or illogical, informed or uninformed, this fairly widespread feeling is part of the total record, the total history of the word, and as such, it is the function of the dictionary to take note of that fact. Clearly no single label would suffice in this instance; an explanation of some sort is called for. This dictionary, along with many other reference works on language, copes with problems such as this through the device of a usage note, which, though necessarily brief and concise, does explain the nature of the problem that has arisen in connection with this particular word.

Further issues about usage may arise from mistaken grammatical analysis on the one hand, or the failure to distinguish what is current in informal as opposed to the formal standard language on the other. An instance of the latter is the use of *like* as a conjunction introducing a subordinate clause ("He didn't work like his father worked."). Reliable measures of the incidence of this construction indicate that it has a high frequency in informal English but that it occurs only rarely in the formal written language. But again there are some who are reluctant to accept it. Labeling the construction *informal* would probably satisfy the purely factual requirements of the situation, but it would fail to warn the reader of the dictionary that his use of the construction might give offense in some quarters. Again a brief statement is more helpful than a single unmodified categorization.

The usual ground for objecting to *hopefully* in a context such as "Hopefully, the project will be finished by the end of the year," is that *hopefully* as an adverb cannot properly modify the verb phrase *will be finished* and is therefore grammatically unacceptable. Again the facts are simple enough. The word, used in this manner, is widely current among those who employ Standard English. Moreover, the grammatical argument is unsound since in this instance the word modifies the entire clause and not just the verb phrase. This time the usage note serves to clarify a grammatical misconception.

As one compares the usage notes in various dictionaries, he is likely to find a wide divergence of attitude and philosophy, ranging from a fairly broad permissiveness to a nervous reluctance to admit any deviation from the most rigid adherence to approved formal usage of a century ago. It is the considered opinion of the editors of this work that neither of these extremes is well calculated to serve the needs of those who look to the dictionary for help in matters of this kind.

Language changes from century to century and from generation to generation. To the extent that these changes have affected the usage of Standard English it is the responsibility of the dictionary to acknowledge them. There is often a discrepancy, as well, between what is in actual fact current as Standard English and what many opinionated or ill-informed persons believe that usage to be. The responsibility of the dictionary here is to set the record straight, to report and interpret the facts as accu-

rately as possible. At the same time the dictionary must be equally perceptive in distinguishing, for the person who consults it, between standard usage which is acceptable beyond a shadow of doubt and that about which there is some qualification or question. Unfortunately, there is a great lack of awareness on the part of the general public about the services which dictionaries do perform with respect to matters of usage. As dictionaries improve in their faithfulness to fact and the nicety of their discrimination, it is reasonably certain that readers will take fuller advantage of the service which only a carefully and conscientiously edited dictionary is capable of offering.

Punctuation

BY HAROLD B. ALLEN

Punctuation is the art of using special marks to make written or printed material more easily understood, just as pause and stress and intonation or pitch change are needed to make speech understood.

Punctuation uses can be grouped, somewhat loosely, into two kinds. The first kind is structural, since it principally includes those uses that reveal the external structure of what is written, that show how its parts relate meaningfully to one another. In these uses punctuation marks do often correspond to the spoken signals of pause and intonation, so that generally that relationship is a useful clue to choice of punctuation. But it is not safe to rely unthinkingly upon that correspondence. A person who habitually pauses for emphasis after the adversative conjunctions *but* and *yet* can thus be misled into inserting an unnecessary comma, as in *We expected the shipment yesterday but, it did not come* or *Yet, the weather has remained too wet for planting.* A safer reliance is upon correspondence between the punctuation and the grammatical structure.

In ordinary communication the structural uses of punctuation typically conform to accepted conventions, although it is true that, as with the comma, options exist that the skilled writer can utilize in order to indicate more precisely his particular emphasis and shades of meaning. But punctuation is one area where individualism is likely to be self-defeating. Since the purpose of writing is to communicate, punctuation should help and not hinder the attainment of the objective—communication.

The second kind of punctuation use is essentially arbitrary, like that of a period after an abbreviation. Although some variation does occur in printers' styles, once a writer has memorized the arbitrary uses they should cause no problems.

Some marks are employed in different ways in other countries and in other languages. The uses described here are those common in the United States and Canada. They are treated in the following order. Three punctuation marks serve principally to end sentences. These are the period (.), called full stop in Britain; the question mark or interrogation point (?); and the exclamation point (!). The others are the comma (,); the semicolon (;); the quotation marks, both single and double, (' ') and (" "); parentheses, known as brackets in Britain, ( ); the brackets, known as square brackets in Britain, ([ ]); the hyphen (-); the apostrophe ('); and the virgule, also called the slant, slash, diagonal, or solidus (/). In each section structural uses are given first, under 1, and arbitrary uses next, under 2.

THE PERIOD

1. Put a period at the end of every sentence not signaled by a question word or intonation pattern as a question or exclamation.

> The faucet leaked all night.
> Please ship the remaining goods at once.
> The chairman asked us to be seated.

Sometimes the sentence intonation justifies the use of a period with a word or words constituting less than a complete grammatical sentence.

> No, sir.   Thanks.
> Just as you like.   All right.

Especially in business correspondence a request in the form of a question may be followed by a period instead of a question mark. Spoken, such a request has a falling intonation pattern.

> May we obtain a list of possible suppliers.

2. Use three periods in a row, called an ellipsis, to show omission within a quoted passage.

> Housewares include a wide range of items from silverware to . . . stainless steel fixtures. . . .

The second ellipsis of three periods is followed by a fourth period to denote the end of the sentence.

Use a period after an abbreviation.

> J. O. Morton, M.D.   etc.   Ms. Anne Janis

Omission of the period is common with frequent and familiar abbreviations.

> YMCA   rpm   FBI

In Britain the period is now generally omitted after these:

> Dr   Mr   Mrs

A period after an abbreviation may be followed by any other required punctuation mark except another period.

B. D., our dog, is a three-year-old schnauzer.
But: We named our dog B.D.

Use a period with decimals, with cents, when the dollar sign is present, and with parts or divisions, as in a section of a book.

7.3% $9.46   Section 3.7

THE QUESTION MARK

1. Use a question mark at the end of any sentence signaled as a question

By a question word, i.e., a *wh-* word.
When will the meeting be held?

By inverted word order.
Are nonmembers allowed to attend?

By rising intonation.
You said Harry won the election?

Use a question mark after a nonsentence marked by a *wh-* word or a rising question intonation.
Why not?
What if the truth were known?
At three-thirty then?

2. Use a question mark to indicate doubt about a specific item, such as a spelling or a number.
Cyrus was born in (?)424 B.C.

Use only one question mark if a question ends with a quoted question, and put it inside the quotation marks.
Did he actually ask, "Is your mother married?"

After a quoted question within a sentence, use no other punctuation such as a comma or semicolon.
Because the manager asked her specifically, "Why weren't you at work yesterday?" Miss Fleming felt that she had a just complaint.

If a question ends with a quoted declarative sentence, put the question mark outside the quotation marks.
Who said, "All the world's a stage"?

THE EXCLAMATION POINT

Use an exclamation point after heavily stressed, often high-pitched, short sentences, commands, phrases, or single words and interjections that convey intense feeling.
Yes, and a damnable war it was!
"How exquisite!" Jean exclaimed sarcastically.

Use only the exclamation point when otherwise a comma or semicolon would be required.
Before she is finished there are shouts of "Thunder!" "Lightning!" "Twister!"

THE COMMA

Although most of its uses are conventional, the comma responds more sensitively than other punctuation marks to the needs of the individual writer. Its use or nonuse in certain situations enables a writer to communicate subtle meanings and relationships not readily shown in words alone. But generally its uses are governed by accepted basic principles common in ordinary social and business writing. The structural uses of the comma usually correlate in speech with the level or the rising intonation accompanied by pause, and in writing with definable grammatical structures.

1. A major structural use of the comma is to set off certain language units from the rest of the sentence. If any such unit is at the beginning or the end of a sentence, usually one comma is needed; if it is within the sentence, then usually two commas are needed.

Use commas to set off nonrestrictive elements. A nonrestrictive element is one that adds information without limiting or cutting down the idea of the main clause. It may be identified by your supplying the testing clue, "and by the way," as well as by the pause following level or rising intonation. Suppose you have written "Suburban residents who object to the wheelage tax are expected to petition the metropolitan council." If you can say to yourself, "Suburban residents—and, by the way, they object to the wheelage tax—are expected to petition the metropolitan council," then you have a nonrestrictive clause, and you should set it off with commas, representing the intonation pattern and pause. But if you find that now the sentence does not say what you mean it to say, and if you can say to yourself, "Those particular residents who object to the wheelage tax, etc.," then the included element restricts the meaning of the main clause and no commas are needed, and, spoken aloud, the sentence would not have a pause both after "residents" and after "tax."

Use commas to set off a nonrestrictive clause.
William James, who was a pioneer in psychology, developed the philosophical idea of pragmatism.

But not a restrictive clause:
Only staff members who are teachers will go to the convention.

Use commas to set off a nonrestrictive phrase.
It was also raining here when the senator's plane landed, at the end of his trip.

But not a restrictive phrase:
Other members of the senator's party were making different kinds of news on his first morning back.

Use commas to set off that special nonrestrictive word or phrase usually called an appositive.
I called the press officer, David Kelsey.

Do not use commas with close apposition, which is not marked by the intonation plus pause.
I called press officer David Kelsey.

Use commas to set off a negative appositive.
It is paid for in local currency, not gold.

Use commas to set off parenthetical words and phrases.
Had he been back home, of course, he would have gone by jet or car.

Use commas to set off transitional words and phrases.
Nevertheless, man still has not learned to fly like a bird.
Consider, for example, the invention of one of the world's all-time best-selling games.

But not when a transitional word or phrase is an integral part of the sentence.
The next man to speak was a local politician.

Use commas to set off an adverbial clause at the beginning or in the middle of a sentence.
It also seems very likely that, where obscenity laws continue to be constitutionally applicable, the Supreme Court will give the law relatively broad scope.

However, a short introductory clause may occur without the comma if the meaning is quite clear, as when both clauses have the same subject.
When he saw the sun he shouted for joy.

Use commas to set off an adverbial phrase out of its expected position after the verb.

The doors slid silently shut, and, without so much as a slight jerk, the train sped away.

Use commas to set off words in direct address.

"Can you spare him for a few minutes, Shirley?"

Use commas to prevent ambiguity or misunderstanding.

What is needed are investment funds to start up the service network, and assured means for paying for continuing home service.

(The comma prevents the reader from taking both "network" and "means" as objects of "start up.")

2. Commas are often used to separate coordinate or correlative sentence parts, especially when such separation is indicated in speech by level or rising intonation pattern plus pause.

Except when the clauses are short and the meaning quite clear, use a comma before a conjunction that precedes the second clause of a compound sentence. The comma is most necessary before *for*.

It's very hard work, for the children have led quite pampered lives up till now.
The public schools have been open to all since before the Civil War, and some public colleges have admitted virtually all applicants.

But not in:

Karla withdrew the doll and the child released it with a sigh.

Between short main clauses you may use a comma without a conjunction when it represents a rising or level intonation with pause. Note that this use is not the objectionable "sentence fault" or "comma splice" that occurs with a falling intonation.

Décor is part of the dining experience. People like it, people demand it.
She left early, she had such a bad headache.

Use commas to separate words, phrases, and clauses that constitute a series.

I had a lunch of sauerbraten, red cabbage, lentils, pumpernickel, and dark beer.

Newspapers and some other publications tend to omit the comma before *and* on the assumption that the comma represents the absence of a conjunction and thus is not needed when the conjunction is present. Actually, it represents a perceptible rising or level intonation pattern with pause, which occurs before the final member of the series regardless of the presence or absence of *and*. It is best to use a comma there consistently, so that inadvertently you do not produce such a result as this:

Berle can sing, dance, juggle, act, do card tricks, imitations and acrobatics, ride a unicycle and mug under water.

You may use a comma to separate long predicative constructions even when a conjunction is present.

Even the newest bones were now crusted with moss and lichen, and were scarred with the teeth marks of foxes.

Use a comma to separate two or more adjectives that independently modify a noun, as would be signaled by an intonation pattern with pause.

Please enclose a stamped, self-addressed envelope.
They were not like the lounging, bossy owners.

The owners were both lounging and bossy. Compare a "bright blue dress," with punctuation indicating a dress that is bright blue, not a dress that is both bright and blue.

Use a comma to indicate the omission of an element that, if present, would parallel the same element in a preceding part of the sentence.

Most of the young climbers had come by motor scooters; the older ones, by train.

3. Certain uses of the comma are nonstructural—arbitrary and mechanical rather than related to the syntax.

Use a comma to set off a direct quotation.

"I eat too much," Adler confessed.

Use commas to separate place names.

Bernard came from Astoria, Oregon.
My new address is 1737 Fillmore Avenue, Philadelphia, PA 19146.

No punctuation mark is used between the official post office abbreviation and the ZIP code number.

Use commas in dates.

On September 3, 1939, the judge offered him the choice between prison and the Army.

There is a tendency not to use the comma when the date of the month is not given, and also to omit it after the year even if the date is given.

Steller and his companions abandoned ship on Bering Island in November 1741.

THE SEMICOLON

The semicolon is essentially a mark of coordination. Its use indicates that the grammatical construction before it is equivalent to the construction after it. It correlates with rising, sometimes level, intonation pattern with pause.

1. Use a semicolon between main clauses when no conjunction is present and the clauses are not very short.

I was unprepared for the sight of the main dining room without its bright bustle and white linen; the place looked as forlorn as an abandoned house with windows broken and shutters hanging loose.

Use a semicolon between main clauses when the second clause is introduced by a conjunctive adverb, such as *however, moreover, nevertheless, furthermore, consequently*.

The strike left a residue of ill feeling on both sides; moreover, the terms of the settlement were bound to cause trouble in the future.

2. Use a semicolon between main clauses when commas break up one or both of them, even if a conjunction is present.

They wandered over the dunes, hand in hand, often shouting in sheer exuberance as the salt breezes whipped their hair; and then, suddenly overwhelmed by the emptiness of the island, they sat on the top of a dune and looked around for a long time, silent and somewhat sad.

3. Use a semicolon between clauses or other constructions in a series when the constructions themselves are subdivided by commas.

Schools may make you suspicious, not curious; cynical, not skeptical; passive and bored, not calm.

4. Use a semicolon before a word or phrase, abbreviated or not, such as *namely, i.e., for example, e.g., for instance*, that introduces an illustration, example, or explanation.

Most student clubs can't survive without a strong leader; for example, the Ornithology Club folded when its founder graduated.

THE COLON

1. Structurally the colon indicates suspense in anticipation of something to follow and hence corresponds to a level intonation pattern with a long pause. It is more common in formal writing than in informal writing, where its function is often assumed by the dash.

Use a colon to introduce a long statement or question, whether quoted or not.

As the certifying agent from the Maine Board of Education put it: "We can't figure out exactly what you folks are up to, but I reckon you should have a right to try."

Use a colon to introduce a series of formal items or phrases.

Karate can be done at three speeds: slow for grace, medium for skill, and fast for the kill.

Use a colon before a long explanatory passage.

Seismologists disagree on the significance of creep: some believe that it reduces the strain on faults, reducing the likelihood of a major quake.

2. The colon has several purely arbitrary functions.

Use a colon at the end of a formal salutation in a letter.

Dear Dr. Fenton: Gentlemen: Dear Madam:

Use a colon between the numerals for the hour and the minutes.

If you get the 7:30 flight, you'll be home in time.

Use a colon in the title of a book or article before a supplementary phrase.

Rattlesnakes: Their Habits, Life Histories, and Influence on Mankind

Use a colon after the name of a speaker in a play or other long dialogue.

HAMLET: Are you fair?
OPHELIA: What means your lordship?

QUOTATION MARKS

Quotation marks, both single and double, are essentially arbitrary rather than structural; certain uses, however, such as those denoting a sarcastic or humorous repetition of another's word, do correspond with a special intonation pattern.

1. The primary function of quotation marks is to indicate matter that is taken verbatim from some source, spoken or written.

Use double quotation marks to set off a simple direct quotation.

"Wait a minute," the girl said.

Do not enclose an indirect quotation. Compare:
Jim asked what she was doing.

If the quotation is longer than a single paragraph, use quotation marks at the beginning of each paragraph but at the end of the last quoted paragraph only.

Use quotation marks to designate words or phrases quoted directly within a sentence. Some editors prefer single quotation marks for this purpose.

The manufacturers prefer to describe the effect as a "tingling sensation."

Use single quotation marks to indicate quoted material within other quoted material. In England the reverse practice is common, the double marks occurring within the single marks.

"What does 'decisional' mean?" the boy asked.

Use quotation marks to set off words or phrases quoted derisively or humorously or with other special attitudinal meaning associated with the source of the word or phrase. This device should not be overused.

The owners of the Lobster were "the boys"—two very tall men in their early fifties.

2. Several conventional uses of quotation marks do not correspond with written or spoken structural units.

Quotation marks are used, usually double, to distinguish titles of stories, articles, plays, songs, and the like incorporated in a longer work, such as a book or opera.

Oddly enough, the editor has seen fit to omit "Macbeth" from the anthology.

Some editors use double quotation marks or, less frequently, italics (indicated by underlining the typewritten copy) for the title of the entire work.

The opera "Der Junge Lord," first performed in Berlin, in 1965. . . .

Use double quotation marks to designate names of trains, ships, planes, and the like. Italics may serve the same purpose.

Now ships like the "Volendam" are devoted to the cruise business.

Use single or double quotation marks to set off words considered as items. In books italics often serve this function.

But "nice" is a double-edged word.

3. Use quotation marks appropriately with other marks.

For aesthetic reasons American printers customarily put the period and the comma inside the closing quotation marks, illogical though the practice is.

Harris put on a new recording he had bought of Mahler's "Songs of a Wayfarer."
"It's raining," he said.

Other punctuation marks are put either before or after the closing marks, according to whether they are required by the quoted passage or by the entire sentence.

"Do you like that?" we asked. "Others imitating you?"
He asked, "Have you read 'The Necklace'?"
"What a riot!" a girl exclaimed.

If you put a terminal punctuation mark before closing quotation marks, do not put another one after them. No period is required with the following:

She couldn't compare with Carol Burnett in "Who's Been Sleeping in My Bed?"
"I saw a flying saucer! It was—" She interrupted him, her hands still in the water.

THE DASH

Structurally, the dash represents some kind of break or interference in the normal flow of language and hence corresponds usually to a level intonation, sometimes rising, plus pause, with the implication that more is to follow. With a typewriter a dash is made with two unspaced hyphens.

1. Use a dash to set off with emphasis any parenthetical material considered so close or relevant to the thought that commas are inadequate.

Some are mainly for hauling oil; others—known as LNG carriers—are for liquefied natural gas.

Use a dash to set off appositional elements more emphatically or more clearly than could be done with commas.

> Actually, there were only two—a pair of good-sized corn snakes.

Use a dash to mark an abrupt break in speech, as denoting an unfinished or interrupted sentence.

> CLARA: But she—
> ROBERT: I will never believe it.

Use a dash to mark an abrupt break in the grammatical structure.

> I've heard of cases—What am I saying?—I've known them: cases of immorality. . . .

Somewhat less formally, use a dash instead of a colon before a list or explanation.

> The Ashanti have kept their gold sculptures largely within the tribe, bringing them out only for the most solemn ceremonies—coronations, weddings, funerals.

Informally, use a dash after the salutation in a personal letter.

> Dear Connie—   Hi, Dad—

2. Use a dash to indicate omission of letters, euphemistically to avoid spelling out a possibly offensive term, to withhold information, or to indicate lack of information.

> The h— you say!
> The mysterious Lawrence M— who brought the letter has never been identified.

PARENTHESES

1. Use parentheses to set off an element that supplies comment or additional information and that is usually less relevant to the main thought than would be suggested by commas.

> The idiocy is made worse by journalists and politicians (also divines, academics, bank presidents, and union organizers) who, for reasons of their own, require an opaque use of the language.

Use parentheses to enclose an explanatory element that is not structurally a part of the sentence.

> On the day in 1853 on which they were introduced, Robert Schumann noted in his diary: "Brahms to see me (a genius)."

2. Use parentheses to enclose letters or numbers in a series or outline. The use of only the closing parenthesis, common in Europe and sometimes found in the United States, is illogical and in a sentence context can lead to misunderstanding.

> The Committee's functions will be (1) to facilitate the orderly consideration of proposals and (2) to make an equitable apportionment of available time for discussion.

Use parentheses to enclose a numeral equivalent to a preceding spelled-out number.

> As an initial payment I enclose a check for thirty-five dollars ($35.00).

3. Use no punctuation before an opening parenthesis.

Put a comma, semicolon, or colon only after the closing parenthesis. Put a question mark, exclamation point, or quotation marks inside the closing parenthesis only if the parenthetical element requires their use.

> She is forced to wade in Scots dialect ("I dinna ken the wor-rd").
> (Why should one minor blunder disqualify him forever from holding public office?)

BRACKETS

1. Use brackets to set off an explanatory word or phrase inserted by a writer or editor into context written by someone else.

> It was a spring evening [1908].
> The integrity and authority of the Supreme Court has been flaunted [sic!].

Use brackets to enclose a word or phrase inserted to complete the syntax of quoted material.

> ". . . special instruments and techniques [are] taken to be the method itself."

2. Use brackets as parentheses within a parenthesis. This use is largely restricted to bibliographical entries and footnotes.

> *Problems in Lexicography.* (RCAFL-P 21; IJAL, 28[2], Part IV, Bloomington.)

THE HYPHEN

The first two uses of the hyphen listed below are structural insofar as they relate to word or phrase structure and do correspond to a level intonation pattern with slight pause. The remaining uses are arbitrary printers' conventions.

1. Use hyphens to separate words in a phrase that functions as a single adjective before a noun.

> A 51-foot-long, 65,000-pound prototype is now being tested.

Use a hyphen after the first part of a compound when the second part is to be inferred from its occurrence in a following compound in the same construction.

> The hotel never used anything brighter than 40- and 60-watt bulbs.

2. Use a hyphen to separate the parts of spelled-out fractions and the parts of both cardinal and ordinal numerals between twenty-one and ninety-nine.

> That makes twenty-eight present already. When the twenty-ninth comes, we'll have a quorum.

You may use a hyphen to separate the parts of a compound noun when it is so treated in this dictionary or other current dictionaries. The punctuation of compounds is too inconsistent to be generalized in a rule; dictionaries themselves vary with respect to particular compounds. Some compounds appear with a space between the parts, as *income tax, appropriations committee, measuring cup, surprise party;* some appear with a hyphen, as *hanky-panky, one-sided, awe-inspiring;* and some are written solid, as *football, typewriter, secondhand.* The modern tendency, stronger in America than in Britain, is to avoid the use of the hyphen.

Use a hyphen to distinguish two similarly spelled words having different pronunciations and different meanings. Usually the word requiring the hyphen is a recent formation.

> I commend James Lawton for his bravery in rescuing a four-year-old child from a burning house and re-commend him for rescuing and resuscitating an invalid overcome by gas fumes, and therefore recommend him for the department's citation for valor in the line of duty.

Use a hyphen to represent a missing part of a word, one element of which is treated as an item.

> He was such a poor speller that he could never get beyond the *Miss-* in "Mississippi" without making a mistake.

Use a hyphen at the end of a line to indicate that part of a word is at the beginning of the next line. Always divide at a syllable break. Consult your dictionary if you are uncertain about the syllabication.

Use hyphens to indicate the letter-by-letter spelling of a word.

Ron carefully spelled it for her: "p-t-a-r-m-i-g-a-n."

Use hyphens to indicate stammering or hesitation or prolongation of a sound.

"I never s-s-stuttered b-b-before," he said.

Use a hyphen after a prefix when otherwise confusion or misreading might result, as with similar letters or an internal capital letter.

semi-inspired   un-American   non-English

Use a hyphen to indicate a time stretch between two inclusive dates.

The conference is scheduled for May 14-18.

In printed matter, a slightly longer dash (en-dash) is often used in place of the hyphen between numerals.

His dates were 1841–1903.

THE APOSTROPHE

The apostrophe is structural only in that the uses under 1 are related to grammatical functions, but without correspondence with a spoken feature.
1. Use an apostrophe in the singular possessive or genitive form of a noun or indefinite pronoun. This use reflects an early loss of *e* from the *-es* ending some genitives had. Illogically, the personal pronouns *hers, its, ours, yours,* and *theirs* are not written with an apostrophe.

the chairman's prerogative
someone's coat
the river's edge
It was John's money, not hers.

If the addition of the possessive *-s* to a noun already ending in the sound of *s* or *z* makes too much hissing, some speakers prefer not to pronounce it and hence omit it in spelling. The present tendency, however, is both to pronounce the added *s* and to add the letter.

Harry Sparks's car (*or* Harry Sparks' car)
Jesus's parables (*or* Jesus' parables)

Use only an apostrophe at the end of a regular plural noun to denote the possessive or genitive

case, since the pronounced *-s* of the possessive has merged with the *-s* of the plural.

the players' unanimous vote

However, if the plural is irregular, not ending in *-s,* then use the apostrophe with *-s.*

Where is the men's room?

Note these special uses.

her father-in-law's present
both fathers-in-law's presents
someone else's idea
Gilbert and Sullivan's popularity

Use the apostrophe with *-s* in forming the plural of letters, numerals, symbols, abbreviations, and words used as items. The current trend, however, is to omit the apostrophe when no loss of clarity results.

She never dots her i's.
(*but compare* . . . adding "t"s and "s"s . . .)
In the 1730's (*or* 1730s)
The reporter asked how many ICBM's are in the nation's stockpile.

2. Use an apostrophe to show the omission of a letter or letters and the omission of numerals.

two o'clock (two of the clock)
it's (it is)
Class of '34 (1934)

THE VIRGULE

1. You may use a virgule as equivalent to a hyphen in indicating a correspondence between two terms used as a single modifier.

Price/earnings ratios show equally glaring disparities.

2. Use a virgule to indicate a contrasting or alternative relation between two or more words.

An Art/Information/Science Issue

3. You may use a virgule to show a choice between an alternative and an additive relationship.

For sale: pick-up truck and/or house trailer.

4. You may use a virgule between year dates to indicate overlapping.

Post-Impressionist exhibits of 1910/1911 and 1912/1913.

5. Use a virgule when in quoting poetry or a long prose passage you want to indicate a line-ending in the original.

Do you remember what comes after "Stone walls do not a prison make / Nor iron bars a cage"?

Canadian English

BY H. REX WILSON

As the language of the greatest colonizing nation in modern times, English has spread to widely separated parts of the world and has evolved on its own as the first language of the dominant peoples of several now-independent nations. The largest of these is the United States, but just as inhabitants of both sides of the Atlantic recognize the difference between American English and that of the Old Country, so Canadians are conscious of respectable varieties of English within their boundaries which differ in various degrees and ways from the language used by the residents of Great Britain or the United States.

Scholarly interest in Canadian English has developed real strength only since World War II, although the bibliography of writings on the English spoken in Canada goes back over a hundred years. This literature is disproportionately loaded with alarm and indignation over the unfortunate spread of "Americanisms." Because Canada evolved by gradual stages from a group of colonies to an independent nation, the long-held British connection has led to false linguistic expectations on the part of some Englishmen and Canadians, and even of a few residents of the United States. To the majority of visitors from the U.S. who come from the states just south of the border from New York and on westward, Canadians speak "just like us." And indeed even the most exacting students of Canadian English would have to admit that superficially this remark is justified.

Origins of Canadian English

In its origins Canadian English is predominantly American. It descends directly from the language of pre-Revolutionary War settlers on the seaboard and immediate hinterland of the present United States. In the uprootings, both forced and voluntary, which followed the Revolution, Canada received an English-speaking population drawn almost entirely from the old American colonies. It is estimated that by 1830 eighty percent of the English-speaking population of Canada could be traced back to the United States. Upon the language of this majority the relative handful of governors, administrators, military officers and clergy of English origin could not be expected to make any substantial impression, although as members of a highly prestigious group they were bound to have some effect.

Some time before the settlement of the American colonies, some groups in England began to lose the r-sound between a vowel and a following consonant (as in art). This sort of pronunciation and the one which retained the older r were rivals both in England and in some of the settlement areas of the U.S. The "r-droppers" prevailed in eastern New England and in the coastal South, but the r-sound was retained throughout the rest of the colonies, and it was largely from these areas that the basic post-Revolutionary population of Canada was drawn. Meanwhile, the r-dropping became the dominant speech fashion in England. These easily-noted features are the main ones which cause superficial observers from England to identify Canadian speakers as "American" and U.S. visitors to find that Canadians talk "just like us."

But subsequent settlement, independent patterns of pronunciation, the distinctive experience of the physical environment, contact with other linguistic groups, and the prestige of the colonial administration have imposed upon Canadian English features which set it off from other types of English.

Pronunciation

The first difference in language that most people notice when they meet someone from another speech area is in pronunciation. Strangers have accents. But this is just what Canadians seem to lack when they are first heard by many residents of the U.S., and even visitors from the South and Southwest will find Canadian speech little different from that of the "Yankees." The origins of Canadian English just mentioned will help account for this.

Sooner or later the visitor to Canada will notice that Canadians say oot and aboot for out and about, but if he asks about it Canadians will deny it. And, strictly speaking, they are right. However, what has been heard is something different from the vowel in down and mountain. This tendency to have a different vowel before sounds like t and s than before sounds like *d, z, n* is very widespread. In the verb *house* (where the vowel is followed by a *z* sound) the vowel sound will be the same as the one in *down,* and although it may sound different in various places in Canada the range of difference will be about the same as in the U.S. But the vowel sound of the noun *house* (where the vowel is followed by an *s* sound) is different. This pronunciation varies quite a bit from place to place and even in the pronunciations of one speaker, but the general characteristic of most Canadian speech is to have a difference between the vowels in these different situations, and Americans are left with the impression that Canadians say *oot* and *aboot.*

The pronunciation of vowels varying on the basis of the following sound is not unique and can be found in scattered parts of the United States. In these areas and in Canada the vowels of *write* and *ride* show a similar pattern.

The pronunciation of a few individual words may also catch the visitor's ear. The words *either* and *neither* have first syllables which rhyme with *eye* with far greater frequency than is found in the United States. Some longer words, such as *controversy,* may have the main stress on the second rather than the first syllable, reflecting the prestige of British pronunciation supported by private schools set up on the British model and by returning Canadians who have studied at British universities. Although not unknown before World War II, the British pronunciation of *schedule* (shed′yōōl) has gained ground in recent years, apparently under the influence of the Canadian Broadcasting Corporation.

The pronunciation of the word *clerk* like that of the family name *Clark,* once a striking feature of Ontario speech, has now died out except in official usage *(County Clerk)* and in the Presbyterian Church *(Clerk of Session).*

Regional accents are not prominent in Canada, probably because of a large amount of movement within the country and relatively few isolated homogeneous settlements of native speakers of English. The island provinces of Newfoundland and Prince Edward Island are notable exceptions, while the imprint of New England continues to set parts of Nova Scotia and New Brunswick off from Ontario and from the Scottish-settled areas of Nova Scotia. Some areas originally settled by non-English-speakers have produced distinctive varieties of English as the result of earlier bilingualism.

Spelling Differences

For the most part, differences in spelling between England and the United States are traceable to Noah Webster, America's first great lexicographer. Canadians understandably did not come under the influence of Webster's spelling reforms in the early 19th century, and British spelling conventions have persisted. Words like *traveller* and *jeweller* continued to have double *l,* and *-our* spellings persisted in words like *honour* and *flavour.* The noun *practice* continued to be set off from the verb *practise.* Today these spellings are no longer insisted upon in most school systems, although consistency in usage by the individual is expected. This "loss of standards," especially in the *-our* spellings, can still raise furious condemnation in the editorial pages of some newspapers

in Canada. In their own style these pages and the advertisements in the paper may tend to be conservative, while the news columns tend toward "American" spellings.

The spellings *tyre* and *kerb(stone)* are as strange to Canadians as to Americans and must be explained in Canadian dictionaries as *Brit.* for *tire* and *curb-(stone).* The spelling *gaol* for *jail* was once common in newspapers but began disappearing even before World War II.

Vocabulary

The words which a nation uses to conduct its business are great reflectors of its discovery of its environment and its historical development. In 1967 a group of scholars under Professor Walter S. Avis produced *A Dictionary of Canadianisms on Historical Principles* which provides a comprehensive view of the growing and changing vocabulary of Canadian life. This vocabulary has been drawn from many sources, and much of it belongs to experiences shared with settlers of the northern states in the common development of North America. It is not surprising, therefore, that many words reflecting this early experience have passed out of use or are found only in writings referring to specific historical periods.

An American would be puzzled, to say the least, by a reference to an alligator in the forests of Ontario. In the movement of logs by water the lumber industry was greatly helped by *alligators,* amphibious paddle-wheel scows, equipped with a winching arrangement for travel overland.

An equally puzzling term, but in this case a contemporary one, might be found in the statement, "We went to separate schools together." In many parts of Canada religious groups have the legal right to set up their own schools supported by public funds. These are usually referred to as *separate schools,* and a statement such as the one mentioned may be made without suspicion of humorous intent or mental deficiency.

In the Arctic (usually pronounced *Artic*) the term *white-out* has been formed on the model of *black-out* to describe a condition where reflected light from snow or haze or fine blowing snow obscures the horizon and features of the landscape.

Canadian coiners of words have sometimes shown a fine sense of irony as in the now obsolete *Nova Scotia nightingale* for a "singing" marsh frog, and *CPR strawberries* for prunes, which were a prominent item of diet during the building of the Canadian Pacific Railway. On the whole, Canadians have not been distinguished in coining regional names. Most are obviously derivative, like Winipegger or Newfie (Newfoundlander), but Maritimers may be called *Bluenoses* (from Nova Scotia), *Herringchokers* (from New Brunswick) and *Spud Islanders* (a reference to the importance of the potato in the economy of Prince Edward Island).

The *Dictionary of Canadianisms* shows a surprising number of words which have long been accepted in the United States but apparently first gained currency in Canada. In recent times the most striking exports have been in the vocabulary of lacrosse and hockey. *Lacrosse* is of Canadian French origin from a fancied resemblance between the stick used in the game and a Bishop's crozier. While U.S. fans are familiar with the whole standard terminology of hockey, including the penitential seat known as the *penalty box*, they may not know the journalistic coinage *sin bin*.

Because of an administrative history different from that of the United States, Canadian government offers a large number of distinctive terms of British origin. The title *Prime Minister* is, of course, widely used in other countries, but the names of some other positions may be surprising and even a little quaint, such as the term *Reeve* for the council chairman of a village, township, or municipal district council in Ontario and the West. In Ontario the County Council composed of Reeves and Deputy Reeves is presided over by a *Warden*. The familiar title *Sheriff* in Canada signifies a court officer and not a man charged with general law enforcement and peacekeeping duties. A Lieutenant- (pronounced *leftenant*) Governor is not a person who acts for a Governor but the official and ceremonial head of the government of a Province, representing the Crown.

Since colonial times Canadian English has imported virtually its whole technological vocabulary from the United States. Visitors from England have problems in discussing automobile maintenance until they have learned the American words for parts of their motor cars. Canadian railroading, established in large part by American engineers, uses the terminology they brought augmented by later imports. The term *sleeper* for a railway tie held its own until the 1920's at least, but now is rarely heard and one Canadian dictionary labels it *British*.

Canada made its first contribution to the jet age in 1854 by the invention and naming of kerosene in Nova Scotia. Oddly, in Ontario a term of apparent Pennsylvania origin, *coal oil*, is preferred. So widely accepted has *kerosene* become in the U.S. that it has even raised objections in New Zealand as an "Americanism" displacing the British *paraffin (oil)*.

Canadians have borrowed words from languages with which they have had contact. *Woodchuck*, although it looks and sounds English, is derived from an Algonquian word which was first imitated by English speakers as *wejack*. The Canada jay has a name that goes one step further. A Cree name was first imitated as *Whisky John* and then familiarized to *whisky-jack*.

Naturally the long French sojourn in Canada before English settlement has left its marks and, as far as place names go, this extends beyond the border of Canada. The word *portage* is classically representative of the early years, and it has never been displaced by *carry* or *carrying place*. In politics the old terms *Bleu* (or *Parti Bleu*, Conservative) and *Rouge* (or *Parti Rouge*, Liberal) may occasionally appear in English newspaper accounts of politics in Quebec. Sometimes these are Anglicized to *Blue* and *Red*.

Influenced by the special economics of printing in a bilingual country, no passenger train of the Canadian National Railways has "left" its station for many years, although most have "departed" fairly close to schedule. The abbreviations *Arr.* and *Dep.* in the timetable require no translation. Similarly, the two telegraph companies in the country have settled on *telecommunications* in their names.

In its modest space program Canada has named its first communications satellite *Alouette* (French, lark) and a more recent one *anik* (Eskimo, brother).

Abbreviations and Symbols
Used in This Dictionary

abbr.	abbreviation	Gram.	Grammar	Paleontol.	Paleontology
abl.	ablative	Heb.	Hebrew	Pers.	Persian
A.D.	year of our Lord	Her.	Heraldry	Pg.	Portuguese
adj.	adjective	HG	High German	Philos.	Philosophy
adv.	adverb	Hind.	Hindustani	Phonet.	Phonetics
Aeron.	Aeronautics	Hung.	Hungarian	Phot.	Photography
AF	Anglo-French	Icel.	Icelandic	Physiol.	Physiology
Agric.	Agriculture	Illit.	Illiterate	pl.	plural
Alg.	Algebra	imit.	imitative	Pol.	Polish
Algon.	Algonquian	incl.	including	p.p., pp.	past participle
alt.	alternative	infl.	influence, influenced	prec.	preceding
alter.	alteration	intens.	intensive	prep.	preposition
Amer.	American	interj.	interjection	pres.	present
Am. Ind.	American Indian	Ir.	Irish	prob.	probably
Am. Sp.	American Spanish	Ital.	Italian	pron.	pronoun
Anat.	Anatomy	Jap.	Japanese	Prov.	Provençal
Anthropol.	Anthropology	L, Lat.	Latin (Classical, 80	pr.p.	present participle
appar.	apparently		B.C.–A.D. 200)	pseud.	pseudonym
Ar.	Arabic	LG	Low German	Psychoanal.	Psychoanalysis
Archeol.	Archeology	LGk.	Late Greek (200–600)	Psychol.	Psychology
Archit.	Architecture	Ling.	Linguistics	pt.	preterit
Astron.	Astronomy	lit.	literally	p.t.	past tense
aug.	augmentative	LL	Late Latin (200–600)	redupl.	reduplication
Austral.	Australian	M	Middle	ref.	reference
b.	born	masc.	masculine	Rom.	Roman
Bacteriol.	Bacteriology	Math.	Mathematics	Russ.	Russian
B.C.	before Christ	MD, MDu.	Middle Dutch	s	south
Belg.	Belgian	ME	Middle English (1150–	S. Am. Ind.	South American In-
Biochem.	Biochemistry		1500)		dian
Biol.	Biology	Mech.	Mechanics	Scand.	Scandinavian
Bot.	Botany	Med.	Medicine, Medieval	Scot.	Scottish
Brit.	British	Med. Gk.	Medieval Greek (600–	Scot. Gael.	Scottish Gaelic
c.	century		1500)	SE	southeast
ca.	circa	Med. L	Medieval Latin (600–	sing.	singular
Can.	Canadian		1500)	Skt.	Sanskrit
cap.	capital, capitalized	Metall.	Metallurgy	Sociol.	Sociology
CEN.	central	Meteorol.	Meteorology	sp.	spelling
cf.	compare	MF	Middle French (1400–	Sp.	Spanish
Chem.	Chemistry		1600)	sq. mi.	square miles
Chin.	Chinese	MHG	Middle High German	Stat.	Statistics
compar.	comparative		(1100–1450)	superl.	superlative
conj.	conjunction	Mil.	Military	Surg.	Surgery
d.	died	Mineral.	Mineralogy	Sw.	Swedish
Dan.	Danish	MLG	Middle Low German	sw	southwest
def(s).	definition(s)		(1100–1450)	syn.	synonyms
Dent.	Dentistry	Myth.	Mythology	Technol.	Technology
dial.	dialect, dialectal	n.	noun	Telecom.	Telecommunication
dim.	diminutive	N	north	Theol.	Theology
Du.	Dutch	N. Am. Ind.	North American In-	trans.	translation
E	east		dian	Trig.	Trigonometry
E	English	Naut.	Nautical	ult.	ultimate, ultimately
Eccl.	Ecclesiastical	Nav.	Naval	U.S.	United States
Ecol.	Ecology	NE	northeast	usu.	usually
Econ.	Economics	neut.	neuter	v.	verb
Egypt.	Egyptian	NF	Norman French	var.	variant
Electr.	Electricity	NL	New Latin (after 1500)	v.i.	verb intransitive
Eng.	English	Nonstand.	Nonstandard	v.t.	verb transitive
Engin.	Engineering	Norw.	Norwegian	w	west
Entomol.	Entomology	NW	northwest	WGmc.	West Germanic
esp.	especially	O	Old	Zool.	Zoology
F	French	Obs.	Obsolete		
fem.	feminine	ODan.	Old Danish (before		
Fr.	French		1400)		
freq.	frequentative	OE	Old English (before		
G	German		1150)		
Gael.	Gaelic	OF	Old French (before		
Geog.	Geography		1400)		
Geol.	Geology	OHG	Old High German		
Geom.	Geometry		(before 1100)		
Ger.	German	ON	Old Norse (before 1500)		
Gk.	Greek, Greek (Homer–	orig.	original, originally		
	A.D. 200)	Ornithol.	Ornithology		
Gmc.	Germanic	OSp.	Old Spanish (before		
Govt.	Government		1500)		

• Introduces a usage note or marks a cross-reference to a note, illustration, or map

< means "from"

+ means "plus"

? (preceding etymology) means "possibly"; (preceding date) means "approximately"

[?] means "origin uncertain or un-known"

Biblical abbreviations are listed alphabetically in the main section. Abbreviations used in the Gazetteer are listed at the beginning of that section.

THE NEW INTERNATIONAL
WEBSTER'S
COLLEGIATE
DICTIONARY
OF THE ENGLISH LANGUAGE

◆◆◆

INTERNATIONAL
ENCYCLOPEDIC EDITION

A Dictionary
of the English Language

A

A, a (ā) *n. pl.* **A's, a's, As, as** (āz) **1** The first letter of the English alphabet. **2** Any spoken sound representing the letter *A* or *a*. **3** First in a series, class, or order. **4** The highest grade in quality. **5** *Music* The sixth tone in the diatonic scale of C major. **6** Something shaped like an A. —*adj.* Shaped like an A.

a¹ (ə, *stressed* ā) *indefinite article or adj.* In each; to each; for each: twice *a* year. [< OE *an, on* in, on, at]

a² (ə, *stressed* ā) *indefinite article or adj.* **1** One; one type or kind of: I saw *a* bird. **2** Each; any: *A* fish swims. **3** Some: to have *a* fear of height. **4** The same: birds of *a* feather. [Reduced form of AN] • **a, an** *A* is used before a word beginning with a consonant or a consonant sound, now including *h* when pronounced: *a* history. *a* hotel (*Brit.* often *an* hotel). Before a vowel sound or silent *h, an* is used: *an* egg, *an* opera, *an* honor. Before an unaccented syllable beginning with *h* some writers prefer the older usage: *an* historical novel, *an* hysterical cry.

a-¹ *prefix* On; in; at: *aboard, atop.* [< OE *an, on* in, on, at]

a-² *prefix* Used as an intensive or without added meaning: *arise, abide.* [< OE *ā-*]

a-³ *prefix* Of; from: *athirst, akin, anew.* [< OE *of* off, of]

a-⁴ *prefix* **1** Without; not: *achromatic.* **2** Apart from; unconcerned with: *amoral.* [Reduced form of AN- used before consonant sounds]

a. about; alto; ampere; are (measure); area; before (L *ante*); in the year (L *anno*).

AA, A.A. Alcoholics Anonymous.

AAA, A.A.A. American Automobile Association.

aard·vark (ärd′värk′) *n.* A burrowing, ant-eating African mammal about the size of the pig. Also **ant bear.** [< Afrikaans, lit., earth pig]

aard·wolf (ärd′woolf′) *n.* A hyenalike, nocturnal mammal of southern Africa. [< Afrikaans, lit., earth wolf]

Aar·on (âr′ən, ar′ən) The first Jewish high priest; brother of Moses.

Aardvark

ab- *prefix* Off; from; away: *absolve, abduct.* [< L *ab* from]

A.B. Bachelor of Arts (L *Artium Baccalaureus*).

A.b., a.b. able-bodied (seaman).

a·ba (ä′bə) *n.* **1** Fabric woven of camel's or goat's hair. **2** A sleeveless garment worn in Arabia, Syria, etc. [< Ar. *'abā'*]

ABA American Bar Association.

ab·a·ca (ab′ə·kä, ä′bə·kä′) *n.* **1** A bananalike Philippine plant. **2** The inner fiber of this plant, used for cordage. Also **ab′a·ka.** [< Tagalog]

a·back (ə·bak′) *adv.* So as to be pressed or blown backward against the mast: said of sails. — **taken aback** Startled, surprised, or disconcerted. [< OE *on bæc* to or on the back]

ab·a·cus (ab′ə·kəs) *n. pl.* **cus·es** or **·ci** (-sī) **1** A calculating device with counters sliding on wires or in grooves. **2** *Archit.* A slab forming the top of a capital. [L < Gk. *abax* counting table]

Abacus def. 1

a·baft (ə·baft′, ə·bäft′) *adv.* At or toward the stern. —*prep.* Behind; to the rear of. [< OE *on* on, at + *be* about + *æftan,* adv., behind, back]

ab·a·lo·ne (ab′ə·lō′nē) *n.* An edible shellfish having an ear-shaped shell lined with mother-of-pearl. [< Sp.]

a·ban·don (ə·ban′dən) *v.t.* **1** To desert; forsake. **2** To surrender or give up. **3** To yield (oneself) without restraint, as to a feeling or pastime. —*n.* Utter surrender to one's feelings or natural impulses. [< OF *a bandon* under one's own control]. —**a·ban′don·er, a·ban′don·ment** *n.*

a·ban·doned (ə·ban′dənd) *adj.* **1** Deserted; forsaken. **2** Unrestrained. **3** Immoral; dissolute.

a·base (ə·bās′) *v.t.* **a·based, a·bas·ing** To humiliate, humble, or degrade. [< L *ad-* to + LL *bassus* low] —**a·bas·ed·ly** (ə·bā′sid·lē) *adv.* —**a·bas′ed·ness, a·base′ment, a·bas′er** *n.*

a·bash (ə·bash′) *v.t.* To make ashamed, confused, or ill at ease. [< L *ex-* out of + *batare* to gape] —**a·bash·ed·ly** (ə·bash′id·lē) *adv.* —**a·bash′ment** *n.* —**Syn.** disconcert, discompose, bewilder, embarrass.

a·bate (ə·bāt′) *v.* **a·bat·ed, a·bat·ing** *v.t.* **1** To make less; reduce in quantity, degree, force, etc. **2** To deduct. **3** *Law* **a** To put an end to. **b** To annul. —*v.i.* **4** To become less, as in strength, degree, force, etc.: After six hours, the storm *abated.* [< L *ad-* to + *batuere* to beat] —**a·bat′a·ble** *adj.* —**a·bate′ment, a·bat′er** *n.*

ab·at·toir (ab′ə·twär′) *n.* A slaughterhouse. [F]

ab·ba·cy (ab′ə·sē) *n. pl.* **·cies** The office, term, or jurisdiction of an abbot.

ab·bé (ab′ā, *Fr.* á·bā′) *n.* In France, a title of respect given to any male entitled to wear ecclesiastical dress. [< LL *abbas* abbot]

ab·bess (ab′is) *n.* A female superior of a community of nuns connected with an abbey.

ab·bey (ab′ē) *n. pl.* **ab·beys 1** A monastery under the jurisdiction of an abbot or a convent under an abbess. **2** The church or buildings of an abbey.

ab·bot (ab′ət) *n.* The superior of a community of monks. [< LGk. *abbas* < Aramaic *abba* father] —**ab′bot·cy, ab′·bot·ship** *n.*

abbr., abbrev. abbreviation.

ab·bre·vi·ate (ə·brē′vē·āt) *v.t.* **·at·ed, ·at·ing 1** To condense or make briefer. **2** To shorten, as a word or expression, esp. by omission or contraction. [< L *ad-* to + *breviare* shorten] —**ab·bre′vi·a′tor** *n.*

ab·bre·vi·a·tion (ə·brē′vē·ā′shən) *n.* **1** A shortened form

Abbreviation *def. 3*

or contraction, as of a word or phrase. **2** A making shorter, or the state of being shortened. **3** *Music* A notation indicating repeated notes, chords, etc., by a single symbol.

ABC (ā′bē′sē′) *pl.* **ABC's** *Usu. pl.* **1** The alphabet. **2** The rudiments, elements, or basic facts (of a subject).

ABC American Broadcasting Company.

ab·di·cate (ab′də·kāt) *v.* **·cat·ed, ·cat·ing** *v.t.* **1** To give up formally; renounce, as a throne, power, or rights. —*v.i.* **2** To surrender or relinquish a throne, a right, responsibility, etc. [< L *ab-* away + *dicare* proclaim] —**ab·di·ca·ble** (ab′di·kə·bəl), **ab′di·ca′tive** *adj.* —**ab′di·ca′tion, ab′di·ca′tor** *n.*

ab·do·men (ab′də·mən, ab·dō′mən) *n.* 1 In mammals, the visceral cavity between the diaphragm and the pelvic floor; the belly. 2 In vertebrates other than mammals, the region or cavity that contains the viscera. 3 In insects, crabs, etc., the hindmost part of the body. [< L] —**ab·dom·i·nal** (ab·dom′ə·nəl) *adj.* —**ab·dom′i·nal·ly** *adv.*

Abdomen def. 3

ab·duct (ab·dukt′) *v.t.* 1 To carry away wrongfully, as by force or fraud; kidnap. 2 To draw (a part of the body) away from the median axis of the body or from a neighboring part. [< L *ab-* away + *ducere* lead] —**ab·duc′tion, ab·duc′tor** *n.*

a·beam (ə·bēm′) *adv.* At right angles to the line of a vessel's keel.

a·bed (ə·bed′) *adv.* In bed; on a bed; to bed.

A·bel (ā′bəl) Second son of Adam.

ab·er·rant (ab·er′ənt, ab′ər·ənt) *adj.* 1 Straying from the right way or usual course. 2 Varying from type; abnormal; deviant. [< L *ab-* from + *errare* wander] —**ab·er′rance, ab·er′ran·cy** *n.*

ab·er·ra·tion (ab′ə·rā′shən) *n.* 1 Deviation from a right, customary, prescribed, or natural course or condition. 2 Partial mental derangement.

a·bet (ə·bet′) *v.t.* **a·bet·ted, a·bet·ting** To encourage and support, esp. to support wrongdoing. [< OF *abeter* incite, arouse] —**a·bet′ment, a·bet′tal, a·bet′ter, a·bet′tor** *n.*

a·bey·ance (ə·bā′əns) *n.* Suspension or temporary inaction. Also **a·bey′an·cy.** [< OF *abaer* to gape at, yearn for]. —**a·bey′ant** *adj.*

ab·hor (ab·hôr′) *v.t.* **ab·horred, ab·hor·ring** To regard with repugnance, horror, or disgust. [< L *ab-* from + *horrere* shrink] —**ab·hor′rer** *n.* —Syn. loathe, detest, despise, abominate.

ab·hor·rence (ab·hôr′əns, -hor′-) *n.* 1 The act of abhorring. 2 That which is abhorred.

ab·hor·rent (ab·hôr′ənt, -hor′-) *adj.* 1 Detestable or horrible. 2 Feeling abhorrence: with *of.* 3 Opposed; not in accord: with *to.* —**ab·hor′rent·ly** *adv.*

a·bide (ə·bīd′) *v.* **a·bode** or **a·bid·ed, a·bid·ing** *v.i.* 1 To continue, last, or endure. 2 To continue in a place; stay; dwell; reside. —*v.t.* 3 To look for; wait for. 4 To endure; put up with. —**abide by** 1 To behave in accordance with, as a promise or rule. 2 To accept the consequences of; submit to. [< OE *abidan*] —**a·bid′ance, a·bid′er** *n.* —**a·bid′ing** *adj.* —**a·bid′ing·ly** *adv.*

a·bil·i·ty (ə·bil′ə·tē) *n. pl.* **·ties** 1 The condition or power of being able. 2 Talent or skill. [< L *habilitas*]

ab·i·o·gen·e·sis (ab′ē·ō·jen′ə·sis) *n.* The springing up of living from nonliving matter. [< A-⁴ + BIO- + GENESIS]

ab·ir·ri·tant (ab·ir′ə·tənt) *n.* A soothing agent; a medicine that eases irritation. —*adj.* Relieving irritation; soothing.

ab·ir·ri·tate (ab·ir′ə·tāt) *v.t.* **·tat·ed, ·tat·ing** To diminish sensibility in; relieve irritation in. —**ab·ir′ri·ta′tion** *n.*

ab·ject (ab′jekt, ab·jekt′) *adj.* 1 Of the lowest kind or degree; wretched. 2 Servile; cringing. [< L *ab-* away + *jacere* throw] —**ab·jec′tive** *adj.* —**ab′ject·ly** *adv.* —**ab′ject·ness, ab·jec′tion** *n.*

ab·jure (ab·jŏŏr′) *v.t.* **ab·jured, ab·jur·ing** 1 To renounce under oath; forswear. 2 To retract or recant, as an opinion. [< L *abjurare* deny on oath] —**ab·jur·a·to·ry** (ab·jŏŏr′ə·tôr′ē, -tō′rē) *adj.* —**ab′ju·ra′tion, ab·jur′er** *n.*

abl. ablative.

ab·la·tion (ab·lā′shən) *n.* The act or process of wearing away or eroding. [< L *ablatus* carried away]

ab·la·tive (ab′lə·tiv) *Gram. adj.* In Latin, Sanskrit, and certain other languages, designating a grammatical case expressing separation, deprivation, direction away from, or instrumentality. —*n.* 1 The ablative case. 2 A word in this case. [< L *ablatus* carried away]

a·blaze (ə·blāz′) *adj.* 1 On fire. 2 Brilliantly glowing with light. 3 Zealous; ardent.

a·ble (ā′bəl) *adj.* **a·bler** (ā′blər), **a·blest** (ā′blist) 1 Having adequate power; competent. 2 Having superior abilities; talented. [< L *habilis* manageable, fit < *habere* have, hold] —**a′bly** *adv.*

-able *suffix* 1 Given to; tending to: *changeable.* 2 Fit to; able to; capable of; worthy of: *eatable, solvable.* Also **-ble, -ible.** [< L *-abilis*]

a·ble-bod·ied (ā′bəl·bod′ēd) *adj.* Having a sound, strong body; robust.

able-bodied seaman An experienced and skilled seaman. Also **able seaman.**

a·bloom (ə·blŏŏm′) *adj. & adv.* Blooming.

ab·lu·tion (ab·lŏŏ′shən) *n.* 1 A washing or cleansing of the body; a bath. 2 *Eccl.* **a** A washing of the priest's hands or of the chalice during the Mass. **b** The liquid used to do this. [< L *abluere* wash away] —**ab·lu′tion·ar′y** *adj.*

-ably *suffix* Like; in the manner of: *peaceably.*

ABM antiballistic missile.

ab·ne·gate (ab′nə·gāt) *v.t.* **·gat·ed, ·gat·ing.** To renounce or give up, as a right or privilege. [< L *ab-* away + *negare* deny] —**ab′ne·ga′tion, ab′ne·ga′tor** *n.*

ab·nor·mal (ab·nôr′məl) *adj.* Not according to what is normal, usual, or average; unnatural; irregular. [< Gk. *anōmalos* irregular] —**ab·nor′mal·ly** *adv.*

ab·nor·mal·i·ty (ab′nôr·mal′ə·tē) *n. pl.* **·ties** 1 The state of being abnormal. 2 That which is abnormal.

a·board (ə·bôrd′, ə·bōrd′) *adv.* 1 On board; into, in, or on a ship, airplane, etc. 2 Alongside. —**all aboard!** Get on board or in!: a warning to passengers. —*prep.* On board of; upon or within.

a·bode (ə·bōd′) *p.t. & p.p.* of ABIDE. —*n.* 1 A place of abiding; dwelling; home. 2 A sojourn; stay. [< ME *abiden* to abide]

a·bol·ish (ə·bol′ish) *v.t.* To do away with; put an end to. [< L *abolere* destroy] —**a·bol′ish·a·ble** *adj.* —**a·bol′ish·er, a·bol′ish·ment** *n.* —Syn. destroy, eradicate, annul, end.

ab·o·li·tion (ab′ə·lish′ən) *n.* 1 The act of abolishing or the state of being abolished. 2 *Sometimes cap.* The abolishing of slavery in the United States. —**ab′o·li′tion·al, ab′o·li′tion·ar′y** *adj.* —**ab′o·li′tion·ism, ab′o·li′tion·ist** *n.*

ab·o·ma·sum (ab′ə·mā′səm) *n. pl.* **·sa** (-sə) The fourth or true digestive stomach of a ruminant. [< L *ab-* away from + *omasum* bullock's tripe]

A-bomb (ā′bom′) *n.* ATOMIC BOMB.

a·bom·i·na·ble (ə·bom′ə·nə·bəl) *adj.* 1 Very hateful; loathsome. 2 Very bad or unpleasant. —**a·bom′i·na·bly** *adv.*

a·bom·i·nate (ə·bom′ə·nāt) *v.t.* **·nat·ed, ·nat·ing** 1 To regard with horror or loathing; abhor. 2 To dislike strongly. [< L *abominari* abhor as an ill omen] —**a·bom′i·na′tion, a·bom′i·na′tor** *n.*

ab·o·rig·i·nal (ab′ə·rij′ə·nəl) *adj.* 1 Of or pertaining to aborigines. 2 Existing from the beginning; indigenous; primitive. —*n. pl.* **·nes** (-nēz) An aborigine. —**ab′o·rig′i·nal·ly** *adv.*

ab·o·rig·i·ne (ab′ə·rij′ə·nē) *n.* 1 One of the original native inhabitants of a country. 2 *pl.* Flora and fauna indigenous to a geographical area. [< L *ab origine* from the beginning]

a·bort (ə·bôrt′) *v.i.* 1 To bring forth young prematurely; miscarry. 2 To remain rudimentary. 3 To conclude prematurely or fail, as a mission. —*v.t.* 4 To cause to have a miscarriage. 5 To bring to a premature or unsuccessful conclusion. [< L *aboriri* miscarry < *ab-* off, away + *oriri* arise, be born]

a·bor·tion (ə·bôr′shən) *n.* 1 The expulsion of a fetus prematurely; miscarriage. 2 The defective result of a premature birth; a monstrosity. 3 A person or thing that fails to progress or develop normally or as expected. —**a·bor′tion·al** *adj.* —**a·bor′tion·ist** *n.*

a·bor·tive (ə·bôr′tiv) *adj.* 1 Brought forth or born prematurely. 2 Imperfectly developed. 3 Coming to naught; failing, as an effort. 4 Causing abortion. —**a·bor′tive·ly** *adv.* —**a·bor′tive·ness** *n.*

a·bound (ə·bound′) *v.i.* 1 To be in abundance; be plentiful. 2 To have plenty of; be rich: with *in.* 3 To be full of; teem: with *with.* [< L *abundare* overflow]

a·bout (ə·bout′) *adv.* 1 In every direction; on every side: Look *about.* 2 In any direction; here and there: to wander *about.* 3 Almost: *about* finished. 4 Nearly; approximately: in *about* an hour. 5 To a reversed position; around: It turned *about.* 6 In the area; near. 7 In rotation: spinning *about* on its axis. —*prep.* 1 On every side of; encircling. 2 Here and there in or upon. 3 Somewhere near or within:

Stay *about* the house. **4** Attached to as an attribute: an aura of sanctity *about* him. **5** Approximating to, as in measure: *about* 500 miles. **6** Engaged in; concerned with: Go on *about* your business. **7** In reference to; concerning: a book *about* Napoleon. **8** With: I have no money *about* me. —*adj. Used only predicatively* **1** Astir; moving: to be up and *about*. **2** Nearby. [< OE *onbūtan, abūtan*]

a·bout-face (ə·bout′fās′) *n.* **1** A pivoting about to face in exactly the opposite direction. **2** A sudden reversal, as of opinion or point of view. —*v.i.* (ə·bout′fās′) **-faced, -fac·ing** To perform an about-face.

a·bove (ə·buv′) *adv.* **1** To or in a higher place; overhead; up. **2** Superior in rank, position, etc. **3** In a previous place of something written. **4** In heaven. —*adj.* Given, said, placed, etc., in what is above: the *above* names. —*n.* Something above. —*prep.* **1** Vertically over; higher than. **2** Beyond or farther north than: the town *above* ours. **3** In excess of; more than. **4** In preference to; over: We chose her *above* all others. **5** Surpassing or superior to in any way. [< OE *abufen*]

a·bove·board (ə·buv′bôrd′ -bōrd′) *adj. & adv.* Without concealment, fraud, or trickery; honest.

abr. abridged; abridgment.

ab·ra·ca·dab·ra (ab′rə·kə·dab′rə) *n.* **1** A word used as a preventive or curative charm. **2** A spell. **3** Any jargon or nonsensical words. [< LL]

a·brade (ə·brād′) *v.t.* **a·brad·ed, a·brad·ing** To rub or wear off; scrape away. [< L *ab-* away + *radere* scrape] —**a·bra′dant** *adj., n.* —**a·brad′er** *n.*

A·bra·ham (ā′brə·ham) The progenitor of the Hebrews.

a·bran·chi·ate (ə·brang′kē·it, -āt′) *adj. Zool.* Without gills. Also **a·bran·chi·al** (ə·brang′kē·əl). [< A-⁴ without + Gk. *branchia* gills]

a·bra·sion (ə·brā′zhən) *n.* **1** The act or result of abrading. **2** An abraded place, as on the skin.

a·bra·sive (ə·brā′siv, -ziv) *adj.* **1** Abrading or tending to abrade. **2** Harshly irritating: an *abrasive* person. —*n.* An abrasive substance.

a·breast (ə·brest′) *adv.* Side by side. —**abreast of (or with)** Side by side with.

a·bridge (ə·brij′) *v.t.* **a·bridged, a·bridg·ing** **1** To give the substance of in fewer words; condense. **2** To shorten, as in time. **3** To curtail or lessen, as rights. [< L *abbreviare.* See ABBREVIATE.] —**a·bridg′a·ble, a·bridge′a·ble** *adj.*

a·bridg·ment (ə·brij′mənt) *n.* **1** The act of abridging or the state of being abridged. **2** A condensation, as of a book. Also **a·bridge′ment.**

a·broad (ə·brôd) *adv.* **1** Out of one's home; outdoors. **2** Out of one's own country; in or to foreign lands. **3** Broadly; widely. **4** At large; in circulation. —**from abroad** From a foreign country or countries.

ab·ro·gate (ab′rə·gāt) *v.i.* **·gat·ed, ·gat·ing** To annul by authority, as a law. [< L *ab-* away + *rogare* ask, propose] — **ab·ro·ga·ble** (ab′rə·gə·bəl), **ab′ro·ga′tive** *adj.* —**ab′ro·ga′tion, ab′ro·ga′tor** *n.* —**Syn.** abolish, repeal, cancel, nullify.

a·brupt (ə·brupt′) *adj.* **1** Beginning, ending, or happening suddenly. **2** Brusque or curt, as in speech. **3** Changing subject suddenly; unconnected, as style. **4** Steep, as a cliff. [< L *ab-* off + *rumpere* break] —**a·brupt′ly** *adv.* —**a·brupt′ness** *n.* —**Syn. 1** sudden, unexpected. **4** sheer, precipitous.

abs. absent; absolute; absolutely; abstract.

Ab·sa·lom (ab′sə·ləm) The favorite and rebellious son of David.

ab·scess (ab′ses) *n.* A collection of pus within a body tissue, usu. painfully inflamed. —*v.i.* To form an abscess. [< L *abscedere* go away]

ab·scis·sa (ab·sis′ə) *n. pl.* **ab·scis·sas** or **ab·scis·sae** (-ē) The distance of any point from the Y-axis in a two-dimensional coordinate system, measured on a line parallel to the X-axis. [< L *(linea) abscissa* (line) cut off]

Abscissa
AB: axis of abscissas
(X-axis). AC: axis of
ordinates (Y-axis).
df or Ae: abscissa
of point f.

ab·scond (ab·skond′) *v.i.* To depart suddenly and secretly, esp. to hide oneself. [< L *ab-* away + *condere* store] —**ab·scond′er** *n.*

ab·sence (ab′səns) *n.* **1** The state, fact, or time of being absent. **2** Lack; want.

ab·sent (ab′sənt) *adj.* **1** Not present. **2** Nonexistent; missing. **3** Inattentive; absentminded. —*v.t.* (ab·sent′) To take or keep (oneself) away; not be present. [< L *ab-* away + *esse* be] —**ab·sent′er, ab′sent·ness** *n.* —**ab′sent·ly** *adv.*

ab·sen·tee (ab′sən·tē′) *n.* One who is absent, as from a job. —*adj.* **1** Designating or for a person qualified to vote by mail. **2** Nonresident. —**ab′sen·tee′ism** *n.*

ab·sent-mind·ed (ab′sənt·mīn′did) *adj.* **1** Inattentive to one's immediate environment or duties because the mind is occupied elsewhere. **2** Constantly forgetful. —**ab′-sent-mind′ed·ly** *adv.* —**ab′sent-mind′ed·ness** *n.*

ab·sinthe (ab′sinth) *n.* **1** A green, bitter liqueur having the flavor of licorice and wormwood. **2** Wormwood. Also **ab′sinth.** [< L *absinthium* wormwood]

ab·so·lute (ab′sə·lōōt) *adj.* **1** Free from restriction; unlimited; unconditional. **2** Complete or perfect. **3** Unadulterated; pure. **4** Positive; unquestionable. **5** Not dependent on or relative to anything else; independent. **6** Relating to or describing a form of government in which the power of the ruler is complete and unchecked, as by any constitutional restraint: *absolute* monarchy. **7** *Gram.* **a** Free from the usual relations of syntax, as *It being late* in *It being late, we started home.* **b** Of a transitive verb, having no object expressed but implied, as *She is one who really gives.* **c** Of an adjective or pronoun, standing alone with the noun understood, as *Ours is first.* **8** *Physics* **a** Not dependent on any arbitrary standard. **b** Of, pertaining to, or measured on the absolute temperature scale. —*n.* That which is absolute or perfect. —**the Absolute** The ultimate basis of all being. [< L *absolvere.* See ABSOLVE.] —**ab′so·lute·ly** *adv.* —**ab′so·lute′ness** *n.*

absolute pitch 1 The pitch of a musical tone determined by its frequency. **2** The ability to remember pitch.

absolute temperature Temperature reckoned from absolute zero.

absolute zero That temperature at which a body would be wholly deprived of heat, equivalent to about –273°C. or –459°F.

ab·so·lu·tion (ab′sə·lōō′shən) *n.* **1** An absolving, or a being absolved; forgiveness. **2** *Eccl.* In certain churches: **a** The sacramental remission of sin, or the penalties attached to it. **b** The formula pronounced by a priest declaring the sins to be remitted.

ab·so·lu·tism (ab′sə·lōō·tiz′əm) *n.* In government, the doctrine or practice of unlimited authority and control; despotism. —**ab′so·lu′tist** *n.* —**ab′so·lu·tis′tic** *adj.*

ab·solve (ab·solv′, -zolv′) *v.t.* **ab·solved, ab·solv·ing** **1** To pronounce free from the penalties or consequences of an action. **2** To release from an obligation, liability, or promise. **3** *Eccl.* To grant a remission of sin. [< L *ab-* from + *solvere* loosen] —**ab·solv′a·ble** *adj.* —**ab·sol′vent** *adj., n.* —**ab·solv′er** *n.*

ab·sorb (ab·sôrb′, -zôrb′) *v.t.* **1** To drink in or suck up, as through or into pores. **2** To engross completely; occupy wholly. **3** *Physics* To take up or in with no reflection or transmission. **4** To take in and incorporate; assimilate. **5** To assume or defray (costs). **6** To receive the force or action of; intercept. [< L *ab-* from + *sorbere* suck in] —**ab·sorb′a·bil′i·ty, ab·sorb′er** *n.* —**ab·sorb′a·ble, ab·sorb′ing** *adj.* —**ab·sorb′ing·ly** *adv.*

ab·sorbed (ab·sôrbd′, -zôrbd′) *adj.* **1** Deeply engrossed; rapt. **2** Sucked up, assimilated, etc.

ab·sor·bent (ab·sôr′bənt, -zôr′-) *adj.* Absorbing or tending to absorb. —*n.* A substance, duct, etc., that absorbs. —**ab·sor′ben·cy** *n.*

ab·sorp·tion (ab·sôrp′shən, -zôrp′-) *n.* **1** The act of absorbing or the condition of being absorbed. **2** Engrossment of the mind; preoccupation. **3** Assimilation, as by the digestive process. —**ab·sorp′tive** *adj.* —**ab·sorp′tive·ness, ab′sorp·tiv′i·ty** *n.*

ab·stain (ab·stān′) *v.i.* To refrain voluntarily; with *from*. [< L *ab-* from + *tenere* hold] —**ab·stain′er** *n.*

ab·ste·mi·ous (ab·stē′mē·əs) *adj.* 1 Eating and drinking sparingly. 2 Characterized by abstinence. [< L *abstemius* temperate] —**ab·ste′mi·ous·ly** *adv.* —**ab·ste′mi·ous·ness** *n.*

ab·sten·tion (ab·sten′shən) *n.* An abstaining. —**ab·sten′·tious** *adj.*

ab·sti·nence (ab′stə·nəns) *n.* The act or practice of abstaining, as from alcoholic beverages, food, pleasure, etc. —**ab′sti·nent** *adj.* —**ab′sti·nent·ly** *adv.* —Syn. continence, self-denial, temperance, fasting.

abstr. abstract.

ab·stract (ab·strakt′, ab′strakt) *adj.* 1 Considered apart from particular examples or concrete objects; general, as opposed to particular. 2 Theoretical; ideal, as opposed to practical. 3 Expressing a quality or relation that is thought of apart from any specific object or particular instance: Redness is an *abstract* noun. 4 Difficult to understand; abstruse. 5 Designating art that uses as subject matter the relationship of formal elements rather than the depiction or representation of recognizable objects. — *n.* (ab′strakt) 1 A summary or epitome, as of an article, book, report, etc. 2 Something abstract. —**in the abstract** Apart from actual, concrete examples or experience. — *v.t.* (ab·strakt′) 1 To take away; remove. 2 To take away secretly or dishonestly; steal. 3 To withdraw or disengage (the attention, interest, etc.). 4 To consider apart from particular or material instances. 5 (ab′strakt) To make an abstract of, as a book or treatise; summarize. [< L *abaway* + *trahere* draw] —**ab·stract′er, ab·stract′ness** *n.* —**ab·stract′ly** *adv.*

ab·stract·ed (ab·strak′tid) *adj.* 1 Absentminded; preoccupied. 2 Separated from all else; apart. —**ab·stract′ed·ly** *adv.* —**ab·stract′ed·ness** *n.*

ab·strac·tion (ab·strak′shən) *n.* 1 The act of removing or summarizing; also, the result of this. 2 The forming of an idea or concept without reference to actual objects or specific examples. 3 An abstract idea or a term to express it. 4 Absence of mind; preoccupation. 5 An abstract work of art. —**ab·strac′tive** *adj.* —**ab·strac′tive·ly** *adv.* —**ab·strac′tive·ness** *n.*

ab·struse (ab·strōōs′) *adj.* Hard to understand. [< L *abstrudere* to hide] —**ab·struse′ly** *adv.* —**ab·struse′ness** *n.*

ab·surd (ab·sûrd′, -zûrd′) *adj.* 1 Irrational; preposterous; ridiculous. 2 Of or pertaining to the absurd. —*n.* The state of man's existence in what appears to be an unreasonable, meaningless universe: a thesis dealing with the literature of the *absurd.* [< L *absurdus* out of tune, incongruous]— **ab·surd′ism, ab·surd′ness** *n.* —**ab·surd′ist** *adj., n.* —**ab·surd′ly** *adv.*

ab·surd·i·ty (ab·sûr′də·tē, -zûr′-) *n. pl.* **·ties** 1 The quality of being absurd. 2 Something absurd.

a·bun·dance (ə·bun′dəns) *n.* 1 A plentiful supply. 2 Affluence; wealth.

a·bun·dant (ə·bun′dənt) *adj.* 1 More than enough; ample. 2 Well supplied; abounding. [< L *abundare* to overflow] —**a·bun′dant·ly** *adv.*

a·buse (ə·byōōz′) *v.t.* **a·bused, a·bus·ing** 1 To use improperly or injuriously; misuse. 2 To hurt by treating wrongly; injure. 3 To speak in coarse or bad terms of or to; revile; malign. —*n.* (ə·byōōs′) 1 Improper or injurious use; misuse. 2 Ill-treatment; injury. 3 An immoral or dishonest practice or act. 4 Harsh, abusive language. [< L *abuti* misuse] —**a·bus′er** *n.*

a·bu·sive (ə·byōō′siv) *adj.* 1 Of or characterized by abuse or misuse; mistreating. 2 Insulting or vituperative. —**a·bu′sive·ly** *adv.* —**a·bu′sive·ness** *n.*

a·but (ə·but′) *v.* **a·but·ted, a·but·ting** *v.i.* 1 To touch or join at the end or side; border: with *on, upon,* or *against.* —*v.t.* 2 To border on; end at. [< OF *abouter* to border on] —**a·but′ter** *n.* —**a·but′ting** *adj.*

a·but·ment (ə·but′mənt) *n.* 1 The act of abutting. 2 That which abuts. 3 The point at which one thing abuts another thing. 4 A supporting structure or buttress, as at the end of a bridge or wall.

Abutments

a·bysm (ə·biz′əm) *n.* An abyss. [< L *abyssus* abyss]

a·bys·mal (ə·biz′məl) *adj.* 1 Bottomless. 2 Immeasurably great or terrible: *abysmal* ignorance. —**a·bys′mal·ly** *adv.*

a·byss (ə·bis′) *n.* 1 A deep chasm or gulf. 2 Any bottomless void or depth: the *abyss* of infinity. 3 The lowest depths of the sea. [< Gk. *a-* without + *byssos* bottom] —**a·bys′sal** *adj.*

Ab·ys·sin·i·a (ab′ə·sin′ē·ə) ETHIOPIA. —**Ab′ys·sin·i·an** *adj., n.* •See map at AFRICA.

-ac *suffix* 1 Having; affected by: *demoniac.* 2 Like or pertaining to: *cardiac.* [< Gk. *-akos* or L *-acus* or F *-aque*]

A.C., a.c. alternating current.

A/C, a/c account; account current.

Ac actinium.

a·ca·cia (ə·kā′shə) *n.* 1 Any of a genus of usu. evergreen leguminous trees and shrubs found in warm regions, having yellow or white flowers. 2 GUM ARABIC. 3 The common locust tree. [< Gk. *akakia* a thorny tree of Egypt]

acad. academic; academy.

ac·a·dem·i·a (ak′ə·dē′mē·ə) *n. Often cap.* Academic institutions, collectively; the academic world. [L]

ac·a·dem·ic (ak′ə·dem′ik) *adj.* 1 Pertaining to an academy, college, or university. 2 In education, classical and literary rather than technical or vocational. 3 Theoretical rather than practical: What he might have done is *academic.* 4 Scholarly; pedantic. 5 Conventional; traditional. Also **ac′a·dem′i·cal.** —*n.* A college or university teacher or student. —**ac′a·dem′i·cal·ly** *adv.*

a·cad·e·mi·cian (ə·kad′ə·mish′ən, ak′ə·də-) *n.* A member of a society for the advancement of an art or science.

a·cad·e·my (ə·kad′ə·mē) *n. pl.* **·mies** 1 A secondary school, usu. private. 2 A school for special studies, as in art or music. 3 A learned society for the advancement of arts or sciences. [< Gk. *Akadēmeia,* name of the grove in Athens where Plato taught]

A·ca·di·a (ə·kā′dē·ə) A former French colony that settled in 1604 in what are now the Canadian provinces of Nova Scotia and New Brunswick. —**A·ca′di·an** *adj., n.*

a·can·thus (ə·kan′thəs) *n. pl.* **·thus·es** or **·thi** (-thī) 1 Any of several related plants having large, lobed, usu. spiny leaves, common in the Mediterranean region. 2 *Archit.* A decorative representation of its leaf, characteristic of the Corinthian capital. Also **acanthus leaf.** [< Gk. *akanthos* < *akē* thorn]

a cap·pel·la (ä′ kə·pel′ə, *Ital.* ä′ käp·pel′lä) *Music* Without instrumental accompaniment. [< L *ad* according to + *cappella* chapel]

Acanthus
def. 2

acc. accompanied; account; accountant; accusative.

ac·cede (ak·sēd′) *v.i.* **ac·ced·ed, ac·ced·ing** 1 To give one's consent or adherence; agree; assent: with *to.* 2 To come into or enter upon an office or dignity: with *to.* [< L *ad-* to + *cedere* yield, go]

ac·cel·er·an·do (ak·sel′ə·ran′dō; *Ital.* ät·che′le·rän′dō) *adj. & adv. Music* With a gradually accelerating tempo. [Ital., lit., accelerating]

ac·cel·er·ate (ak·sel′ə·rāt) *v.* **·at·ed, ·at·ing** *v.t.* 1 To cause to act or move faster; increase the speed of. 2 *Physics* To increase or change the velocity of. 3 To hasten the natural or usual course of: to *accelerate* a schedule. 4 To cause to happen ahead of time. —*v.i.* 5 To move or become faster: The car suddenly *accelerated.* [< L *ad-* to + *celerare* hasten] —**ac·cel′er·a′tive** *adj.*

ac·cel·er·a·tion (ak·sel′ə·rā′shən) *n.* 1 The act of accelerating, or the process of being accelerated. 2 *Physics* The rate at which the velocity of a body changes per unit of time.

ac·cel·er·a·tor (ak·sel′ə·rā′tər) *n.* 1 One who or that which accelerates. 2 The throttle control of an automobile, etc. 3 *Physics* Any of several devices for accelerating various subatomic particles, as a cyclotron.

ac·cent (ak′sent) *n.* 1 A vocal stress or emphasis given to a word. 2 A mark used to indicate such stress: the **primary accent** (′), noting the chief stress, and the **secondary accent** (′), noting a weaker stress. 3 In certain languages, a mark used to indicate the quality of a vowel or diphthong, as in French, the acute (´), grave (`), and circumflex (ˆ) accents. **4** *Music* **a** Rhythmic prominence, as of a tone. **b** A characteristic, esp. greater loudness, that causes this. **5** A modulation of the voice. **6** A particular manner of speech or pronunciation: a British *accent.* **7** *pl. Archaic* Speech. **8** In prosody, the stress determining the rhythm of poetry. **9** A distinguishing feature or characteristic. **10** An object, color, etc., that provides interest or contrast. **11** Special emphasis: He put an *accent* on clarity. —*v.t.* (ak′sent, ak·sent′) **1** To speak, pronounce, or produce with an accent; stress. **2** To write or print with a mark indicating accent or stress. **3** To call attention to; emphasize. [< L *accentus*, lit., song added to speech]

ac·cen·tu·al (ak·sen′chōō·əl) *adj.* Of, pertaining to, having, or made by accent. —**ac·cen′tu·al·ly** *adv.*

ac·cen·tu·ate (ak·sen′chōō·āt) *v.t.* ·**at·ed**, ·**at·ing 1** To strengthen or heighten the effect of; emphasize. **2** To speak or pronounce with an accent. [< L *accentus.* See ACCENT.] —**ac·cen′tu·a′tion** *n.*

ac·cept (ak·sept′) *v.t.* **1** To receive with favor or willingness, as a gift. **2** To give an affirmative answer to. **3** To agree to; admit: to *accept* an apology. **4** To take with good grace; submit to: to *accept* the inevitable. **5** To agree to pay, as a draft. **6** To believe in. —*v.i.* **7** To agree or promise to fulfill an engagement; receive favorably. [< L *ad-* to + *capere* take] —**ac·cept′er** *n.*

ac·cept·a·ble (ak·sep′tə·bəl) *adj.* Worthy or capable of being accepted. —**ac·cept′a·ble·ness, ac·cept′a·bil′i·ty** *n.* —**ac·cept′a·bly** *adv.* —**Syn.** adequate, satisfactory, agreeable.

ac·cep·tance (ak·sep′təns) *n.* **1** The act of accepting or the state of being accepted. **2** Approval. **3** Belief in something. **4** A written agreement to pay; also, the paper itself when endorsed "accepted." Also **ac·cep′tan·cy.** —**ac·cep′tant** *adj.*

ac·cep·ta·tion (ak′sep·tā′shən) *n.* The accepted meaning of a word or expression.

ac·cept·ed (ak·sep′tid) *adj.* Commonly recognized, believed, approved, etc.

ac·cess (ak′ses) *n.* **1** The act of approaching; approach. **2** A means of approaching, using, knowing, etc. **3** The right to approach, use, etc. **4** Increase. **5** An attack; onset, as of a disease. **6** An outburst. [< L *accedere.* See ACCEDE.]

ac·ces·si·ble (ak·ses′ə·bəl) *adj.* **1** Capable of being approached or reached. **2** Easy to approach or reach. **3** That can be obtained or used: *accessible* funds. **4** Open to the influence of: with *to*: *accessible* to pity. —**ac·ces′si·bil′i·ty** *n.* —**ac·ces′si·bly** *adv.*

ac·ces·sion (ak·sesh′ən) *n.* **1** The attainment of or the succession to an office, throne, right, etc. **2** Assent; agreement; consent. **3** An increase by adding something; also, that which is added. —*v.t.* To record, as additions to a library or museum. [< L *accedere.* See ACCEDE.] —**ac·ces′sion·al** *adj.*

ac·ces·so·ry (ak·ses′ər·ē) *n. pl.* ·**ries 1** Something added as an aid, convenience, decorative item, etc. **2** *Law* A person who, even if not present during the perpetration of a felony, knowingly instigates or assists the felony beforehand (**accessory before the fact**) or assists or conceals the felon afterwards (**accessory after the fact**). —*adj.* **1** Aiding the principal design, or assisting subordinately the chief agent, as in the commission of a crime. **2** Supplemental; additional. Also, esp. in law, **ac·ces′sa·ry.** [< L *accessus* access] —**ac·ces′so·ri·ly** *adv.* —**ac·ces′so·ri·ness** *n.*

ac·ci·dent (ak′sə·dənt) *n.* **1** Anything that happens unexpectedly, undesignedly, or without known cause. **2** Any unpleasant or unfortunate occurrence involving injury, loss, suffering, or death. **3** Chance; fortune. **4** Any nonessential circumstance or attribute. [< L *ad-* upon + *cadere* fall]

ac·ci·den·tal (ak′sə·den′təl) *adj.* **1** Happening or coming by chance or without design. **2** Nonessential; subordinate; incidental. **3** *Music* Of or indicating an accidental. —*n.* **1** A casual, incidental, or nonessential feature or property. **2** *Music* A sharp, flat, or natural elsewhere than in the signature. —**ac′ci·den′tal·ly** *adv.* —**ac′ci·den′tal·ness** *n.*

ac·claim (ə·klām′) *v.t.* **1** To proclaim or receive with ap-

proval; hail. **2** To show enthusiasm for; welcome with applause or praise. **3** *Can.* To elect by acclamation. —*v.i.* **4** To applaud or shout approval. —*n.* Great approval, demonstrated by applause, shouting, etc. [< L *ad-* to + *clamare* shout] —**ac·claim′a·ble** *adj.* —**ac·claim′er** *n.*

ac·cla·ma·tion (ak′lə·mā′shən) *n.* **1** An expression of approval, as by applause, shouting, etc. **2** An enthusiastic vocal vote. **3** *Can.* An election in which the candidate has no opposition. —**ac·clam·a·to·ry** (ə·klam′ə·tôr′ē, -tō′rē) *adj.*

ac·cli·mate (ak′lə·māt, ə·klī′mit) *v.t. & v.i.* ·**mat·ed**, ·**mat·ing** To adapt or become adapted to a different climate, environment, or situation. [< F *à* to + *climat* climate] — **ac·cli·ma·ta·ble** (ə·klī′mə·tə·bəl) *adj.* —**ac·cli·ma·tion** (ak′lə·mā′shən), **ac·cli·ma·ta·tion** (ə·klī′mə·tā′shən) *n.*

ac·cli·ma·tize (ə·klī′mə·tīz) *v.t. & v.i.* ·**tized**, ·**tiz·ing** To acclimate. —**ac·cli′ma·tiz′a·ble** *adj.* —**ac·cli′ma·ti·za′tion** *n.*

ac·cliv·i·ty (ə·kliv′ə·tē) *n. pl.* ·**ties** An upward slope. [< L *acclivitas* steepness] —**ac·cliv′i·tous, ac·cli·vous** (ə·klī′vəs) *adj.*

ac·co·lade (ak′ə·lād′, -läd′) *n.* **1** Anything done or given to show praise, honor, or approval. **2** *Archit.* A curved ornamental molding. **3** In conferring knighthood, the light blow with a sword. [< Ital. *accollare* embrace about the neck]

Accolade *def. 2*

ac·com·mo·date (ə·kom′ə·dāt) *v.* ·**dat·ed**, ·**dat·ing** *v.t.* **1** To do a favor for; oblige; help. **2** To provide for; give lodging to. **3** To be suitable or have space for. **4** To adapt or modify; adjust. **5** To reconcile or settle, as conflicting opinions. —*v.i.* **6** To be or become adjusted or conformed, as the eye to distance. [< L *ad-* to + *commodare* make fit, suit] —**ac·com′mo·da′tive** *adj.* —**ac·com′mo·da′tive·ness** *n.*

ac·com·mo·dat·ing (ə·kom′ə·dā′ting) *adj.* Disposed to accommodate; obliging. —**ac·com′mo·dat′ing·ly** *adv.*

ac·com·mo·da·tion (ə·kom′ə·dā′shən) *n.* **1** An adaptation or adjustment. **2** A reconciliation, as of conflicts. **3** *pl.* Lodging, board, etc. **4** *pl.* A seat, berth, etc., on a train, airplane, or the like. **5** A disposition to help or oblige. **6** A loan. **7** A convenience. **8** The adjustment of the eye to vision at different distances.

ac·com·pa·ni·ment (ə·kum′pə·ni·mənt, ə·kump′ni-) *n.* **1** Anything that accompanies. **2** *Music* A part that sounds along with a main or leading part.

ac·com·pa·nist (ə·kum′pə·nist, ə·kump′nist) *n.* A musician who provides an accompaniment.

ac·com·pa·ny (ə·kum′pə·nē) *v.t.* ·**nied**, ·**ny·ing 1** To go with; attend; escort. **2** To be or occur with; coexist with: Weakness often *accompanies* disease. **3** To supplement with. **4** *Music* **a** To provide with an accompaniment. **b** To be the accompaniment to or for. [< LL *ad-* to + *companio* companion] —**ac·com′pa·ni·er** *n.*

ac·com·plice (ə·kom′plis) *n.* An associate in wrong or crime, whether as principal or accessory. [< *a,* indefinite article + LL *complex* accomplice]

ac·com·plish (ə·kom′plish) *v.t.* To do, perform, effect, or finish. [< L *ad-* to + *complere* fill up, complete] —**ac·com′·plish·a·ble** *adj.* —**ac·com′plish·er** *n.*

ac·com·plished (ə·kom′plisht) *adj.* **1** Completed; finished. **2** Skilled; proficient. **3** Socially polished or polite.

ac·com·plish·ment (ə·kom′plish·mənt) *n.* **1** A completion or fulfillment. **2** Something acquired or attained, as a skill. **3** Something done, as a task.

ac·cord (ə·kôrd′) *v.t.* **1** To render as due; grant; concede. **2** To bring into agreement, as opinions. —*v.i.* **3** To agree; harmonize. —*n.* **1** Harmony, agreement, or conformity. **2** An agreement between governments. —**of one's own accord** By one's own choice; voluntarily. [< LL *accordare* be of one mind, agree] —**ac·cord′a·ble** *adj.* —**ac·cord′er** *n.*

ac·cord·ance (ə·kôr′dəns) *n.* Agreement; conformity. — **ac·cord′ant** *adj.* —**ac·cord′ant·ly** *adv.*

ac·cord·ing (ə·kôr′ding) *adj.* Being in agreement; harmonizing. —*adv.* Accordingly. —**according as 1** In proportion as. 2 Depending on whether. —**according to** 1 In accordance with. 2 As stated or believed by; on the authority of. 3 In proportion to.

ac·cord·ing·ly (ə·kôr′ding·lē) *adv.* 1 In a conformable manner; suitably. 2 Consequently.

ac·cor·di·on (ə·kôr′dē·ən) *n.* A portable reed organ using air from a self-contained bellows operated by the performer. [< Ital. *accordare* accord, harmonize] —**ac·cor·di·on·ist** *n.*

ac·cost (ə·kôst′, ə·kost′) *v.t.* To speak to first; address. [< LL *accostare* be side to side]

ac·couche·ment (ə·kōōsh′· mənt, *Fr.* à·kōōsh·män′) *n.* The act of childbirth; confinement. [F < *accoucher* put to bed, give birth]

Accordion

ac·count (ə·kount′) *v.t.* 1 To hold to be; consider; estimate. —*v.i.* 2 To provide a reckoning, as of funds paid or received: with *to* or *with* (someone) *for* (something). 3 To give a rational explanation: with *for.* 4 To be responsible; answer: with *for.* 5 To cause death, capture, or incapacitation: with *for.* —*n.* 1 An explanation, statement, report, or description. 2 Importance; value. 3 A reckoning or calculation. 4 A record of financial transactions, as of debits, credits, etc. 5 A bank account. 6 A charge account. 7 A customer or client. —**give a good account of oneself** To do well. —**on account** 1 On credit. 2 As partial payment. —**on account of** Because of; for the sake of. —**on no account** Under no circumstances. — **take into account** To take into consideration. [< L *ad-* to + *computare* count]

ac·count·a·ble (ə·koun′tə·bəl) *adj.* 1 Liable to be called to account; responsible. 2 Capable of being accounted for or explained. —**ac·count′a·bil′i·ty** *n.* —**ac·count′a·bly** *adv.*

ac·count·ant (ə·koun′tənt) *n.* One whose business is to keep or examine accounts, as of a business or bank. —**ac· count′an·cy** *n.*

ac·count·ing (ə·koun′ting) *n.* The occupation or system of recording, classifying, and interpreting financial accounts; also, an item so recorded, classified, etc.

ac·cou·ter (ə·kōō′tər) *v.t.* To outfit or equip, esp. for military service. [< F *accoutrer*]

ac·cou·ter·ment (ə·kōō′tər·mənt) *n.* Equipment or furnishings, esp. the equipment of a soldier other than arms and dress.

ac·cou·tre (ə·kōō′tər) *v.t.* **·tred, ·tring** (ə·kōō′tə·ring, -kōō′. tring) ACCOUTER. —**ac·cou′tre·ment** (-trə·mənt, -tər-) *n.*

ac·cred·it (ə·kred′it) *v.t.* 1 To furnish or send with credentials, as an ambassador. 2 To certify as fulfilling requirements. 3 To give credit for. 4 To attribute to. 5 To accept as true; believe. 6 To confer acceptance or favor on. [< F *à* to + *crédit* credit]

ac·cre·tion (ə·krē′shən) *n.* 1 Growth or increase in size, as by external additions. 2 The result of such growth or increase; also, that which is added to effect such a result. 3 An accumulation, as of soil on a seashore. [< L *accrescere* to grow to] —**ac·cre′tive** *adj.*

ac·crue (ə·krōō′) *v.i.* **·crued, ·cru·ing** 1 To come as a natural result or increment, as by growth: with *to.* 2 To accumulate, as the interest on money: with *from.* [< L *accrescere* to grow to] —**ac·cru′al, ac·crue′ment** *n.*

ac·cu·mu·late (ə·kyōōm′yə·lāt) *v.t. & v.i.* To gather; collect; heap or pile up. [< L < *ad-* to + *cumulare* heap] —**ac· cu·mu·la·ble** (ə·kyōōm′yə·lə·bəl) *adj.*

ac·cu·mu·la·tion (ə·kyōōm′yə·lā′shən) *n.* 1 The act or process of accumulating. 2 That which has accumulated.

ac·cu·mu·la·tive (ə·kyōōm′yə·lā′tiv) *adj.* 1 Tending to accumulate. 2 Resulting from accumulation. —**ac·cu′mu· la′tive·ly** *adv.* —**ac·cu′mu·la′tive·ness** *n.*

ac·cu·mu·la·tor (ə·kyōōm′yə·lā′tər) *n.* 1 A person that accumulates. 2 *Brit.* A storage battery.

ac·cu·ra·cy (ak′yər·ə·sē) *n.* The quality or condition of being accurate. —**Syn.** correctness, precision, exactness.

ac·cu·rate (ak′yər·it) *adj.* 1 Conforming exactly to truth or to a standard; without error: an *accurate* measurement. 2 Careful; precise. [< L *accurare* take care of] —**ac′cu· rate·ly** *adv.* —**ac′cu·rate·ness** *n.*

ac·cursed (ə·kûr′sid, ə·kûrst′) *adj.* 1 Doomed to be un-

der a curse. 2 Deserving a curse; detestable. Also **ac·curst′.** —**ac·curs′ed·ly** *adv.* —**ac·curs′ed·ness** *n.*

ac·cu·sa·tion (ak′yōō·zā′shən) *n.* 1 The act of accusing or the state of being accused. 2 The crime or act of which one is accused. Also **ac·cu·sal** (ə·kyōō′zəl). —**ac·cu·sa·to·ry** (ə·kyōō′zə·tôr′ē, -tō′rē) *adj.*

ac·cu·sa·tive (ə·kyōō′zə·tiv) *Gram. adj.* Denoting, in inflected languages, the case of the noun, pronoun, etc., that is the direct object of a verb or preposition. —*n.* 1 The accusative case. 2 A word in this case. [< L *(casus) accusativus* (the case) indicating accusation] —**ac·cu′sa·tive· ly** *adv.*

ac·cuse (ə·kyōōz′) *v.t.* **ac·cused, ac·cus·ing** 1 To charge with fault or error; blame. 2 To bring charges against, as of a crime or an offense: with *of.* [< L *accusare* call to account] —**ac·cus′er** *n.* —**ac·cus′ing·ly** *adv.*

ac·cused (ə·kyōōzd′) *n. Law* The defendant or defendants in a criminal case.

ac·cus·tom (ə·kus′təm) *v.t.* To make familiar by use; habituate or inure: with *to.* [< OF *a-* to + *costume* custom]

ac·cus·tomed (ə·kus′təmd) *adj.* 1 Habitual; usual: his *accustomed* haunts. 2 Used; wont: with *to:* He is *accustomed* to rising early.

ace (ās) *n.* 1 A playing card, die, etc., marked with a single spot; also, the single spot. 2 One who excels in any field. 3 A military pilot who has destroyed five or more enemy aircraft. 4 In tennis and similar games, a point won by a single serve; also, such a serve. —*adj. Informal* First-rate; excellent. —*v.t.,* **aced** (āst), **ac·ing** To score an ace against, as in tennis. [< L *as* unity, unit]

-acea *suffix Zool.* Used in forming names of classes and orders of animals. [< L]

-aceae *suffix Bot.* Used in forming names of families of plants. [< L]

a·cen·tric (ā·sen′trik) *adj.* Without a center; off-center.

-aceous *suffix* Of the nature of; belonging or pertaining to; like: used in botany and zoology to form adjectives corresponding to nouns in *-acea, -aceae.* [< L *-aceus* of the nature of]

ac·er·bate (as′ər·bāt) *v.t.* **·bat·ed, ·bat·ing** To exasperate.

a·cerb·ic (ə·sûr′bik) *adj.* 1 Sour and astringent to the taste, as unripe fruit. 2 Harsh or sharp in tone: an *acerbic* rejoinder. Also **a·cerb** (ə·sûrb′). [< L *acerbus* sharp] — **a·cer′bi·ty** *n.*

ac·e·tab·u·lum (as′ə·tab′yə·ləm) *n. pl.* **·la** (-lə) The socket in the hip into which the thighbone fits. [< L, a small vinegar cup < *acetum* vinegar]

ac·et·an·i·lide (as′ə·tan′ə·līd, -lid) *n.* A derivative of aniline, used as an analgesic and antipyretic.

ac·e·tate (as′ə·tāt) *n.* A salt or ester of acetic acid.

a·ce·tic (ə·sē′tik, ə·set′ik) *adj.* Pertaining to or like vinegar; sour. [< L *acetum* vinegar]

acetic acid A colorless sour liquid, found in vinegar.

a·cet·i·fy (ə·set′ə·fī) *v.t. & v.i.* **·fied, ·fy·ing** To make into or become acid or vinegar. —**a·cet′i·fi·ca′tion, a·cet′i·fi′er** *n.*

aceto- *combining form* Of, pertaining to, or from acetic acid. Also, before vowels, **acet-.** [< L *acetum* vinegar]

ac·e·tone (as′ə·tōn) *n.* A clear, flammable liquid produced industrially and used as a solvent. [< ACET(O)- + -ONE] —**ac·e·ton·ic** (as′ə·ton′ik) *adj.*

a·cet·y·lene (ə·set′ə·lēn) *n.* A colorless hydrocarbon gas, used as an illuminant and for welding. [< ACET- + -YL + -ENE]

a·ce·tyl·sal·i·cyl·ic acid (ə·set′əl·sal′ə·sil′ik, ə·sē′təl-) Aspirin.

A·chae·an (ə·kē′ən) *adj.* Pertaining to Achaea, its people, or their culture. —*n.* 1 A member of one of the four major tribes of ancient Greece. 2 A Greek. Also **A·cha′. ian** (ə·kā′ən, -kī′-).

ache (āk) *v.i.* **ached** (ākt), **ach·ing** 1 To suffer dull, continued pain. 2 To feel sympathy or distress: with *for.* 3 To be anxious or distressed. 4 To yearn; be eager: followed by *for* or the infinitive. —*n.* A local, dull, and protracted pain. [< OE *ācan*]

a·chene (ə·kēn′) *n.* A small, dry fruit having one seed, as the dandelion. [< A-⁴ not + Gk. *chainein* to gape, recoil]

Achenes
of dandelion

Ach·e·ron (ak′ə·ron) *Gk. & Rom. Myth.* 1 The river of woe, one of the five rivers surrounding Hades. 2 HADES.

a·chieve (ə·chēv′), *v.* **a·chieved, a·chiev·ing** *v.t.* 1 To accomplish; do successfully. 2 To win or attain, as by effort or skill. —*v.i.* 3 To accomplish something; to attain an object. [< LL *ad caput (venire)* (come) to a head] —**a·chiev′a·ble** *adj.* —**a·chiev′er** *n.*

a·chieve·ment (ə·chēv′mənt) *n.* 1 The act of achieving. 2 Something achieved.

A·chil·les (ə·kil′ēz) In the *Iliad,* the foremost Greek hero of the Trojan War, who killed Hector and was killed by the arrow Paris shot into his right heel, the only vulnerable spot on his body.

Achilles' heel A vulnerable point.

Achilles tendon The tendon that connects the muscles of the calf of the leg to the bone of the heel.

ach·ro·mat·ic (ak′rə·mat′ik) *adj.* 1 *Optics* Transmitting light without separating it into its constituent colors, as a lens. 2 Having lightness or darkness only, with no hue, as a gray color. [< Gk. *a-* without + *chrōma* color] —**ach′·ro·mat′i·cal·ly** *adv.*

ac·id (as′id) *adj.* 1 Sharp and biting to the taste, as vinegar; sour. 2 *Chem.* Having properties of or pertaining to an acid. 3 Sharp; biting; sarcastic. —*n.* 1 *Chem.* A compound which in aqueous solution produces hydrogen ions which have a sour taste, turn blue litmus red, and may be replaced by another positive ion to form a salt. 2 Any sour substance. 3 *Slang* LSD. [< L *acidus* sour] —**ac′id·ly** *adv.* —**ac′id·ness** *n.*

acid head *Slang* A habitual user of LSD.

a·cid·ic (ə·sid′ik) *adj.* 1 Tending to form acid. 2 Acid.

a·cid·i·fy (ə·sid′ə·fī) *v.t. & v.i.* **·fied, ·fy·ing** To make or become acid. —**a·cid′i·fi′a·ble** *adj.* —**a·cid′i·fi·ca′tion, a·cid′i·fi′er** *n.*

a·cid·i·ty (ə·sid′ə·tē) *n.* 1 The state or quality of being acid; sourness; tartness. 2 Degree of acid strength. 3 HYPERACIDITY. Also **ac′id·ness.**

ac·i·do·sis (as′ə·dō′sis) *n.* A deficiency of sodium bicarbonate in the blood, characteristic of certain diseases. —**ac·i·dot·ic** (as′ə·dot′ik) *adj.*

acid test A final, severe test revealing the genuineness or worth of something.

a·cid·u·late (ə·sij′oo·lāt) *v.t.* **·lat·ed, ·lat·ing** To make somewhat acid or sour. —**a·cid·u·la′tion** *n.*

a·cid·u·lous (ə·sij′oo·ləs) *adj.* Slightly acid, as in taste or manner. Also **a·cid′u·lent.** —**Syn.** sour, biting, caustic, tart.

-acious *suffix of adjectives* Abounding in; characterized by; given to: *pugnacious, vivacious.* [< L *-ax, -acis* + OUS]

-acity *suffix* Quality or state of: used to form abstract nouns corresponding to adjectives in *-acious.* [< L *-acitas*]

ack-ack (ak′ak′) *n. Slang* Antiaircraft fire. [British radio operator's code for *A.A.* (antiaircraft)]

ac·knowl·edge (ak·nol′ij) *v.t.* **·edged, ·edg·ing** 1 To own or admit as true; confess. 2 To declare or admit the validity of, as a claim or right. 3 To show appreciation of; thank for. 4 To recognize and respond to, as a greeting. 5 To respond to the arrival of: to *acknowledge* a letter. [< OE *oncnāwan* recognize] —**ac·knowl′edge·a·ble** *adj.* —**ac·knowl′edg·er** *n.*

ac·knowl·edg·ment (ak·nol′ij·mənt) *n.* 1 The act of acknowledging. 2 Something done, given, or said in acknowledging a greeting, favor, etc. 3 A legal certificate or avowal. Also **ac·knowl′edge·ment.**

ac·me (ak′mē) *n.* The highest point or summit. [< Gk. *akmē* point]

ac·ne (ak′nē) *n.* A skin disease causing pimples on the face, chest, and back, and caused by clogging or inflammation of the sebaceous glands. [Alter. of Gk. *akmē* point]

ac·o·lyte (ak′ə·līt) *n.* 1 An attendant or assistant. 2 ALTAR BOY. 3 In the Roman Catholic Church, a member of the highest of the four minor orders. [< Gk. *akolouthos* follower, attendant]

ac·o·nite (ak′ə·nīt) *n.* 1 Any of a genus of usu. poisonous plants with a helmet-shaped petal on the flowers, as monkshood. 2 An extract made from an aconite, formerly used in medicine. [< Gk. *akoniton*]

a·corn (ā′kôrn, ā′kərn) *n.* The fruit of the oak, a one-seeded nut, fixed in a woody cup. [< OE *æcern*]

a·cous·tic (ə·koos′tik) *adj.* 1 Pertaining to the act or sense of hearing, sound, or the science of sound. 2 Adapted for modifying sound or hearing. Also **a·cous′ti·cal.** [< Gk. *akoustikos* < *akouein* hear] —**a·cous′ti·cal·ly** *adv.*

Acorns

a. red oak. b. pin oak.
c. black oak.

ac·ous·ti·cian (ak′oos·tish′ən) *n.* A specialist in acoustics.

a·cous·tics (ə·koos′tiks) *n. pl.* (*construed as sing. in def. 1*) 1 The branch of physics that deals with the phenomena of sound. 2 The sound-transmitting properties of a place, as an auditorium.

ac·quaint (ə·kwānt′) *v.t.* 1 To make familiar or conversant; inform: with *with: Acquaint* yourself with the court routine. 2 To cause to know, esp. socially. [< LL *adcognitare* make known]

ac·quain·tance (ə·kwān′təns) *n.* 1 Knowledge of any person or thing. 2 A person whom one knows, but not closely. 3 The state of being acquainted. —**ac·quain′tance·ship** *n.*

ac·qui·esce (ak′wē·es′) *v.i.* **·esced (-est′), esc·ing** To consent or concur quietly or passively; comply: usu. with *in:* The candidate *acquiesced* in all his party's plans. [< L *acquiescere* to remain at rest] —**ac′qui·es′cence** *n.* —**ac′qui·es′cent** *adj.* —**ac′qui·es′cent·ly** *adv.*

ac·quire (ə·kwīr′) *v.t.* **·quired, ·quir·ing** 1 To obtain by one's own endeavor or purchase. 2 To gain or possess as one's own. [< L *ad-* to + *quaerere* seek] —**ac·quir′a·ble** *adj.* —**ac·quir′er** *n.*

ac·quire·ment (ə·kwīr′mənt) *n.* 1 The act of acquiring. 2 Something acquired, as a skill.

ac·qui·si·tion (ak′wə·zish′ən) *n.* 1 The act of acquiring. 2 Anything acquired, as by purchase or trade.

ac·quis·i·tive (ə·kwiz′ə·tiv) *adj.* Eager or inclined to acquire; greedy. —**ac·quis′i·tive·ly** *adv.* —**ac·quis′i·tive·ness** *n.*

ac·quit (ə·kwit′) *v.t.* **ac·quit·ted, ac·quit·ting** 1 To free or clear, as from an accusation. 2 To relieve, as of an obligation. 3 To conduct (oneself): He *acquitted* himself nobly. [< L *ad-* to + *quietare* settle, quiet] —**ac·quit′ter** *n.*

ac·quit·tal (ə·kwit′l) *n.* 1 The act of setting free or the state of being set free by legal process. 2 The performance of a duty.

ac·quit·tance (ə·kwit′əns) *n.* Release or discharge from indebtedness or obligation.

a·cre (ā′kər) *n.* 1 A measure of area equal to 4,840 square yards. 2 *pl.* Lands. 3 *pl. Informal* A great many; lots. [< OE *æcer* field]

a·cre·age (ā′kər·ij) *n.* Area in acres; acres collectively.

ac·rid (ak′rid) *adj.* 1 Sharp, burning, or bitter to the taste or smell. 2 Bitterly sarcastic or satirical. [< L *acer*] —**a·crid·i·ty** (ə·krid′ə·tē), **ac′rid·ness** *n.* —**ac′rid·ly** *adv.*

ac·ri·mo·ni·ous (ak′rə·mō′nē·əs) *adj.* Bitterly sarcastic; caustic; sharp. —**ac′ri·mo′ni·ous·ly** *adv.* —**ac′ri·mo′ni·ous·ness** *n.*

ac·ri·mo·ny (ak′rə·mō′nē) *n.* Sharpness or bitterness of speech or temper. [< L *acrimonia* < *acer* sharp] —**Syn.** acridity, acerbity, sharpness, tartness.

acro- *combining form* 1 At the top, tip, or end of. 2 Pertaining to the extremities of the body. [< Gk. *akros* at the top or end]

ac·ro·bat (ak′rə·bat) *n.* One who is skilled in feats requiring muscular coordination, as in tightrope walking, tumbling, trapeze performing, etc.; a gymnast. [< Gk. *akrobatos* walking on tiptoe] —**ac′ro·bat′ic** or **·i·cal** *adj.* —**ac′·ro·bat′i·cal·ly** *adv.*

ac·ro·bat·ics (ak′rə·bat′iks) *n. pl* (*construed as sing. or pl.*) 1 The art or feats of an acrobat. 2 Anything requiring or demonstrating unusual agility.

ac·ro·gen (ak′rə·jən) *n.* A plant growing at the tip only, as ferns, mosses, etc. [< ACRO- + -GEN] —**ac′ro·gen′ic** *adj.*

ac·ro·meg·a·ly (ak′rō·meg′ə·lē) *n. Pathol.* A pituitary disorder characterized by enlargement of the extremities, thorax, and face. [< ACRO- + Gk. *megas, megalon* big] — **ac·ro·me·gal·ic** (ak′rō·mi·gal′ik) *adj.*

ac·ro·nym (ak′rə·nim) *n.* A word formed by the combining of initial letters *(UNESCO)* or syllables and letters *(radar, sonar)* of a series of words or a compound term. [< ACRO- + *-nym* name, as in HOMONYM]

ac·ro·pho·bi·a (ak′rə·fō′bē·ə) *n.* A fear of high places.

a·crop·o·lis (ə·krop′ə·lis) *n.* The fortified upper section of various ancient Greek cities. —**the Acropolis** Such a section in Athens, site of the Parthenon and other temples. [< Gk. *akros* top, highest part + *polis* city]

a·cross (ə·krôs′, ə·kros′) *adv.* 1 From one side to the other. 2 On or at the other side. 3 Crosswise; crossed. — *prep.* 1 From one side to the other side of. 2 On or to the other side of. 3 Into an encounter with or discovery of: I came *across* the book today. [< A-¹ on, in + CROSS]

a·cross-the-board (ə·krôs′thə·bôrd′, ə·kros′-, -bôrd′) *adj.* 1 In horse racing, designating a bet in which equal amounts are placed on the same horse to win, place, or show. 2 That includes or affects all people, categories, etc.

a·cros·tic (ə·krôs′tik, ə·kros′-) *n.* A poem or other composition in which initial or other letters, taken in order, form a word or phrase. [< Gk. *akros* end + *stichos* line of verse] —**a·cros′ti·cal·ly** *adv.*

a·cryl·ic (ə·kril′ik) *adj.* Pertaining to or derived from an organic acid that polymerizes to form various commercially important transparent resins and plastics. —*n.* 1 Any of a class of clear, transparent resins and plastics derived from acrylic acid, as lucite, plexiglass, etc. 2 A substance derived from an acrylic resin, as a paint medium, a fiber, etc. 3 A painting done in such a medium. [< ACR(ID + OLEIN) + -YL + -IC]

act (akt) *v.t.* 1 To play the part of; impersonate. 2 To perform on the stage, as a play. 3 To perform as if on a stage; feign: Don't *act* the martyr. 4 To behave as suitable to: *Act* your age. —*v.i.* 5 To behave or conduct oneself: He knows how to *act* in society. 6 To carry out a purpose or function: The test *acted* as a check. 7 To do something: You must *act* immediately. 8 To produce an effect: often with *on:* The poison *acted* on his stomach at once. 9 To serve temporarily or as a substitute, as in some office or capacity: with *for.* 10 To perform on or as on the stage: She *acts* for a living. 11 To pretend so as to appear: She concealed her real feelings and *acted* friendly. —**act up** *Informal* 1 To behave mischievously. 2 To become troublesome, painful, etc. —*n.* 1 Something done; a deed. 2 An action; a doing: caught in the *act.* 3 An enactment, law, decree, or edict, as of a legislative body. 4 A formal written statement, as of a law or decree. 5 A main section or division of a play or opera. 6 A separate, specialty performance: a circus *act.* 7 Insincere behavior; pose. [< L *actus* a doing, and *actum* a thing done < *agere* do]

act·a·ble (ak′tə·bəl) *adj.* That can be acted, as a role in a play. —**act′a·bil′i·ty** *n.*

ACTH A pituitary hormone that stimulates hormone production in the cortical area of the adrenal glands; adrenocorticotropic hormone.

act·ing (ak′ting) *adj.* 1 Operating or officiating, esp. in place of another: *acting* secretary. 2 Functioning; in working order. 3 Containing directions for actors: the *acting* script. —*n.* The art or occupation of an actor.

ac·tin·i·a (ak·tin′ē·ə) *n. pl.* **·i·ae** (-i·ē) or **·i·as** A sea anemone. [< Gk. *aktis* ray] —**ac·tin′i·an** *adj., n.*

ac·tin·ic (ak·tin′ik) *adj.* Of or exhibiting actinism. Also **ac·tin′i·cal.** —**ac·tin′i·cal·ly** *adv.*

ac·ti·nide series (ak′ti·nīd) A series of chemically similar radioactive elements within the periodic table, from actinium, element 89, through lawrencium, element 103. • See PERIODIC TABLE OF ELEMENTS.

ac·tin·ism (ak′tin·iz′əm) *n.* 1 The property of radiant energy which effects chemical changes. 2 The production of such change. [< Gk. *aktis* ray + -ISM]

ac·tin·i·um (ak·tin′ē·əm) *n.* A radioactive element (symbol Ac) occurring in pitchblende.

ac·ti·noid (ak′ti·noid) *adj.* Having the form of rays; radiate, as a starfish.

ac·ti·no·zo·an (ak′ti·nə·zō′ən) *n.* ANTHOZOAN.

ac·tion (ak′shən) *n.* 1 The doing of something by the use of power, movement, energy, etc. 2 The thing done; deed.

3 *pl.* Behavior; conduct. 4 Energy, initiative, and decisiveness: a man of *action.* 5 The result or effect of something: the medicine's *action.* 6 The movement or manner of movement of a body organ, mechanism, etc.: the *action* of the heart. 7 The parts that move in a mechanism, as in a gun, piano, etc. 8 An event or series of events in a novel, play, etc. 9 *Law* A lawsuit. 10 A military conflict or encounter. 11 *Slang* Lively or exciting social activity; excitement: to find out where the *action* is. [< L *actio* < *agere* do]

ac·tion·a·ble (ak′shən·ə·bəl) *adj. Law* Affording ground or cause for a lawsuit.

ac·ti·vate (ak′tə·vāt) *v.t.* **·vat·ed, ·vat·ing** 1 To make active. 2 To put into action, as a military unit. 3 To make radioactive. 4 To promote chemical reaction in. 5 To make pure by aeration, as sewage. —**ac′ti·va′tion, ac′ti·va′tor** *n.*

ac·tive (ak′tiv) *adj.* 1 Abounding in action; busy. 2 Being in or capable of action, movement, performance, etc.: an *active* volcano. 3 Causing or promoting action, change, movement etc. 4 Agile; lively; quick. 5 Characterized by actual participation, contribution, etc.: an *active* member. 6 Producing profit or bearing interest: *active* funds. 7 *Gram.* **a** Designating a voice of the verb which indicates that the subject of the sentence is performing the action. **b** Describing verbs expressing action as distinguished from being and state, as *run, hit, jump.* —*n. Gram.* The active voice. [< L *activus* < *agere* do] —**ac′tive·ly** *adv.* — **ac′tive·ness** *n.*

active duty Full military or naval duty. Also **active service.**

ac·tiv·ism (ak′tə·viz′əm). The doctrine or practice of active engagement in pursuit of a social or political goal. — **ac′tiv·ist** *adj., n.*

ac·tiv·i·ty (ak·tiv′ə·tē) *n. pl.* **·ties** 1 The state or quality of being active; action. 2 Lively action or movement. 3 A specific action, project, pursuit, etc.: school *activities.* 4 *Physics* The degree of emission from a radioactive source.

act of God *Law* An event occurring by reason of the operations of nature unmixed with human agency or human negligence.

ac·tor (ak′tər) *n.* 1 A performer on the stage, in motion pictures, etc. 2 Any person who actively participates in something.

ac·tress (ak′tris) *n.* A woman who acts, as on the stage, in television, motion pictures, etc.

Acts of the Apostles The fifth book of the New Testament. Also **Acts.**

ac·tu·al (ak′chōō·əl) *adj.* 1 Existing in fact; real. 2 Being in existence or action now; existent; present. [< LL *actualis* < L *actus* a doing. See ACT.]

ac·tu·al·i·ty (ak′chōō·al′ə·tē) *n. pl.* **·ties** 1 The quality of being actual; reality. 2 *pl.* Actual facts or conditions.

ac·tu·al·ize (ak′chōō·əl·īz) *v.t.* **·ized, ·iz·ing** 1 To make real; realize in action, as a possibility. 2 To make seem real; represent realistically. —**ac′tu·al·i·za′tion** *n.*

ac·tu·al·ly (ak′chōō·əl·ē) *adv.* As a matter of fact; in reality; really; truly.

ac·tu·ar·y (ak′chōō·er′ē) *n. pl.* **·ar·ies** One who specializes in the mathematics of insurance; esp., an official statistician of an insurance company. [< L *actuarius* clerk < *actus.* See ACT.] —**ac·tu·ar·i·al** (ak′chōō·âr′ē·əl) *adj.* —**ac′tu·ar′i·al·ly** *adv.*

ac·tu·ate (ak′chōō·āt) *v.t.* **·at·ed, ·at·ing** 1 To set into action or motion. 2 To incite or influence to action: [< Med.L *actuare* < L *actus* a doing. See ACT.] —**ac′tu·a′tion, ac′tu·a′tor** *n.*

a·cu·i·ty (ə·kyōō′ə·tē) *n.* Acuteness; sharpness. [< L *acus* needle]

a·cu·men (ə·kyōō′mən, ak′yōō·mən) *n.* Quickness of insight or discernment; keenness of intellect. [< L, sharpness (of the mind) < *acuere* sharpen] —**Syn.** acuteness, cleverness, keenness, insight.

a·cu·mi·nate (ə·kyōō′mə·nāt) *v.t.* **·nat·ed, ·nat·ing** To sharpen; make pointed. —*adj.* (ə·kyōō′mə·nit, -nāt) Ending in a long tapering point, as a leaf, feather, fin, etc. Also **a·cu′mi·nat′ed.** [< L *acumen.* See ACUMEN.] —**a·cu′mi·na′tion** *n.* • See LEAF.

ac·u·punc·ture (ak′yōō·pungk′chər) *n.* The Chinese art of traditional medicine in which needles are inserted at specific points through the skin to treat disease and induce anesthesia. [<L *acus* needle + PUNCTURE]

a·cute (ə-kyo͞ot′) *adj.* **1** Keenly discerning or sensitive. **2** Affecting keenly; poignant; intense. **3** Critical; crucial: an *acute* lack of power. **4** Coming to a crisis quickly: *acute* appendicitis. **5** Shrill; of high pitch. **6** Less than 90° in measure: an *acute* angle. **7** Sharply pointed; not blunt. [< L *acuere* sharpen] **—a·cute′ly** *adv.* **—a·cute′ness** *n.* • See ANGLE.

acute accent A mark (′) used to indicate: **1** Primary stress of a sound or syllable. **2** Rhythmical stress, as in poetry. **3** Vowel quality or length.

-acy *suffix* Quality, state or condition: *fallacy, celibacy.* [<L *-acia,* or <Gk. *-ateia*]

a·cy·clo·vir (ā-sī′klə-vir) *n.* An antiviral drug used in the treatment of genital herpes.

ad (ad) *n. Informal* **1** An advertisement. **2** In tennis, advantage.

ad- *prefix* To; toward; near: *adhere, advert.* Also **a-, ab-, ac-, af-, ag-, al-, an-, ap-, ar-, as-, at-,** before various consonants. [<L *ad-* <*ad* to]

A.D. year of our Lord (L *anno Domini*).

A.D.A. American Dental Association; Americans for Democratic Action.

ad·age (ad′ij) *n.* A saying or proverb. [<L *adagium*]

a·da·gio (ə-dä′jō, -zhē-ō) *Music adj.* Slow. **—n.** An adagio composition, movement, etc. **—adv.** Slowly. [<Ital. *adagio,* lit., at ease]

Ad·am (ad′əm) The first man, progenitor of the human race. **—the old Adam** Unregenerate or depraved human nature. **—A·dam·ic** (ə-dam′ik) *adj.*

ad·a·mant (ad′ə·mant, -mənt) *n.* In legends, a very hard but imaginary mineral. **—adj. 1** Very hard. **2** Immovable and unyielding, as in purpose. [<Gk *adamas* the hardest metal (hence, unyielding)] **—ad·a·man·tine** (ad′ə·man′tin, -tēn, -tin, at ease)

Adam's apple The projection of the thyroid cartilage at the front of the neck, conspicuous in men.

a·dapt (ə-dapt′) *v.t.* **1** To make suitable, as by changing: to *adapt* a novel for the theater. **2** To modify (oneself) to conform to a situation or environment. **—v.i. 3** To become adjusted to a circumstance or environment. [<L *ad-* to + *aptare* fit]

a·dapt·a·ble (ə·dap′tə·bəl) *adj.* **1** Capable of being adapted. **2** Able to adapt, as to new circumstances. **—a·dapt′a·bil′i·ty, a·dapt′a·ble·ness** *n.*

ad·ap·ta·tion (ad′ap·tā′shən) *n.* **1** The act of adapting or the state of being adapted. **2** Something adapted.

a·dapt·er (ə·dap′tər) *n.* **1** A person or thing that adapts. **2** Any device designed to connect two pieces of apparatus, or to broaden the use or application of another device. Also **a·dap′tor.**

a·dap·tive (ə·dap′tiv) *adj.* Capable of, fit for, or manifesting adaptation. **—a·dap′tive·ly** *adv.* **—a·dap′tive·ness** *n.*

A.D.C., a.d.c., aide-de-camp.

add (ad) *v.t.* **1** To join or unite, so as to increase the importance, size, quantity or number: with *to.* **2** To find the sum of, as a column of figures; unite in a total. **3** To say or write further. **—v.i. 4** To produce an increase in: with *to:* His new duties *added* to his worries. **5** To perform the arithmetical operation of addition. **—add up 1** To accumulate to a total. **2** *Informal.* To make sense. **—add up to** *Informal* To signify; mean. [<L *ad-* to + *dare* give] **—add′a·ble, add′i·ble** *adj.*

add. addendum; addition; additional; address.

ad·dax (ad′aks) *n.* A North African and Arabian antelope. [<L <native African word]

ad·dend (ad′end, ə·dend′) *n. Math.* A number or element to be added to another.

ad·den·dum (ə·den′dəm) *n. pl.* **·da** (-də) A thing added, or to be added. [<L *addere* add]

ad·der¹ (ad′ər) *n.* **1** A viper, esp. the common European viper. **2** One of various other snakes, as the puff adder, the milk snake, etc. [<OE *nædre* (*a nadder* in ME becoming *an adder*)]

add·er² (ad′ər) *n.* One who or that which performs addition, esp. a computer circuit.

ad·der's-tongue (ad′ərz·tung′) *n.* **1** Any of a genus of ferns having a single sterile frond and a spore-bearing spike. **2** Dog's-tooth violet.

ad·dict (ə·dikt′) *v.t.* **1** To give or devote (oneself) persistently or habitually: usu. used in the passive voice with *to:* He is *addicted* to drugs. **2** To cause to pursue or practice continuously: with *to:* This task *addicted* him to obscure research. **—n.** (ad′ikt) One who is addicted to some habit, esp. to the use of narcotic drugs. [<L *addicere* assign, devote to] **—ad·dict′ed·ness** *n.*

ad·dic·tion (ə·dik′shən) *n.* The state of being addicted to a habit, as to the taking of narcotic drugs.

ad·dic·tive (ə·dik′tiv) *adj.* Of, pertaining to, causing, or characterized by addiction.

ad·di·tion (ə·dish′ən) *n.* **1** The act of adding. **2** That which is added, esp. a room, annex, etc. **3** *Math.* An operation defined for every pair of elements or numbers of a set, whereby each pair is associated with a unique element of the same set called the sum. **—ad·di′tion·al** *adj.* **—ad·di′· tion·al·ly** *adv.*

ad·di·tive (ad′ə·tiv) *n.* A substance added or to be added to a product or device. **—adj. 1** That is to be added. **2** *Math.* Pertaining to addition. **—ad′di·tive·ly** *adv.*

ad·dle (ad′l) *v.t.* & *v.i.* **ad·dled, ad·dling 1** To make or become spoiled. **2** To make or become muddled or mixed up. **—adj. 1** Spoiled, as eggs; rotten. **2** Confused; mixed up. [<OE *adela* liquid filth]

ad·dle·brained (ad′l·brānd′) *adj.* Confused; mixed up. Also **ad′dle·head′ed, ad′dle·pat′ed.**

ad·dress (ə·dres′) *v.t.* **ad·dressed, ad·dress·ing 1** To speak to. **2** To deliver a set discourse to. **3** To direct, as spoken or written words, to the attention of: with *to:* He *addressed* his prayers to his God. **4** To direct the attention, energy, or force of (oneself): with *to:* He *addressed* himself to the task. **5** To mark with a destination, as a letter. **6** To consign, as a cargo to a merchant. **7** To aim or direct the club at (a golf ball). **—n.** (ə·dres′, *esp. for defs. 3 & 4* ad′. res) **1** The act of addressing or speaking to a person or persons. **2** A formal speech. **3** The writing on an envelope, etc., directing something to a person or place. **4** The name, place, residence, etc., of a person. **5** Consignment, as of a vessel or cargo. **6** Conversational manner or delivery. **7** *Usu. pl.* Any courteous or devoted attention; wooing. **8** Adroitness; tact. **9** In the memory or storage element of a computer, a particular location or its designation. [<L *ad-* to + *directus* straight] **—ad·dress′er, ad·dres′sor** *n.*

ad·dress·ee (ad′res·ē′, ə·dres·ē′) *n.* One to whom mail, etc., is addressed.

ad·duce (ə·d(y)o͞os′) *v.t.* **ad·duced, ad·duc·ing** To bring forward for proof or consideration, as an example. [<L *ad-* to + *ducere* lead] **—ad·duce′a·ble, ad·duc′i·ble** *adj.* **—Syn.** cite, allege, advance.

ad·duct (ə·dukt′) *v.t. Physiol.* To draw a part of the body toward the median axis of the body or toward a neighboring part. [<L *adducere.* See ADDUCE.] **—ad·duc′tion** *n.* **— ad·duc′tive** *adj.*

ad·duc·tor (ə·duk′tər) *n. Physiol.* An adducting muscle.

-ade *suffix of nouns* **1** Act or action of: *cannonade.* **2** A person or group concerned in an action or process: *cavalcade.* **3** Product of: *pomade.* **4** Drink made from: *lemonade.* [<L *-ata,* fem. pp. ending]

A·den (äd′en, ād′n) A former British colony, part of the People's Democratic Republic of Yemen since 1968.

ad·e·noid (ad′ə·noid) *adj.* Of or like a gland; glandular: also **ad′e·noi′dal.** **—n.** *Usu. pl.* An enlarged lymphoid growth behind the pharynx. [<Gk. *adēn* gland + -OID]

ad·e·no·ma (ad′ə·nō′mə) *n.* A usu. benign tumor of glandular origin or structure. [<Gk. *adēn* gland + -OMA]

a·dept (ə·dept′) *adj.* Highly skillful; proficient. —**ad·ept** (ad′ept, ə·dept′) *n.* One fully skilled in any art; an expert. [< L *adeptus* pp. of *adipisci* attain] —**a·dept′ly** *adv.* —**a·dept′ness** *n.*

ad·e·quate (ad′ə·kwit) *adj.* 1 Equal to what is required; suitable; sufficient. 2 Barely acceptable or sufficient. [< L *ad-* to + *aequus* equal] —**ad·e·qua·cy** (ad′ə·kwə·sē), **ad′e·quate·ness** *n.* —**ad′e·quate·ly** *adv.*

ad·here (ad·hir′) *v.i.* **ad·hered, ad·her·ing** 1 To stick fast or together. 2 To be attached or devoted, as to a party or faith. 3 To follow closely or without deviation. [< L *ad-* to + *haerere* stick] —**ad·her′ence** *n.*

ad·her·ent (ad·hir′ənt) *adj.* Clinging or sticking fast. —*n.* One who is devoted or attached, as to a cause or leader; a follower: also **ad·her′er.** —**ad·her′ent·ly** *adv.*

ad·he·sion (ad·hē′zhən) *n.* 1 The act of sticking together or the state of being stuck together. 2 Assent; concurrence. 3 Close connection, as of ideas. 4 *Physics* The force of attraction between molecules of unlike substances in contact. 5 *Med.* Abnormal surface union of dissimilar tissues as a result of inflammation, etc. [< L *adhaerere.* See ADHERE.]

ad·he·sive (ad·hē′siv) *adj.* 1 Tending to adhere; sticky; clinging. 2 Prepared to adhere; gummed. —*n.* A substance that promotes adhesion. —**ad·he′sive·ly** *adv.* —**ad·he′sive·ness** *n.*

ad hoc (ad hok′, hōk′) With respect to this (particular thing); for this purpose. [L]

ad·i·a·bat·ic (ad′ē·ə·bat′ik, ā′dē·ə-) *adj. Physics* Without gain or loss of heat, as a thermodynamic system or reaction. [< Gk. *adiabatos* impassable]

a·dieu (ə·dyōō′; *Fr.* à·dyœ′) *n. pl.* **a·dieus,** *Fr.* **a·dieux** (ə·dyōō′) A farewell. —*interj.* Good-by; farewell: literally, "to God (I commend you)." [< F < à to + *dieu* God]

ad in·fi·ni·tum (ad in′fə·nī′təm) Endlessly; limitlessly. [L]

ad in·ter·im (ad in′tər·im) In the meantime. [L]

a·di·os (ä′dē·ōs′, ad′ē·ōs′; *Sp.* ä·dyōs′) *interj.* Farewell; good-by: literally, "to God (I commend you)." [Sp. < *a* to + *dios* God]

ad·i·pose (ad′ə·pōs) *adj.* Of or pertaining to fat; fatty: also **ad·i·pous** (ad′ə·pəs). —*n.* Fat. [< L *adeps* fat] —**ad′i·pose′ness, ad·i·pos·i·ty** (ad′ə·pos′ə·tē) *n.*

adj. adjective; adjunct; adjustment; adjutant.

ad·ja·cent (ə·jā′sənt) *adj.* Lying near or close at hand. [< L *ad-* near + *jacere* lie] —**ad·ja′cence, ad·ja′cen·cy,** *n.* —**ad·ja′cent·ly** *adv.* —**Syn.** adjoining, contiguous, abutting, bordering.

adjacent angle Either of a pair of angles having a common vertex and a common side. See ANGLE.

ad·jec·ti·val (aj′ik·tī′vəl, aj′ik·ti·vəl) *adj.* Of or like an adjective. —**ad′jec·ti′val·ly** *adv.*

ad·jec·tive (aj′ik·tiv) *n.* 1 *Gram.* A word used to limit or qualify a noun or other substantive. 2 A phrase or clause used similarly. —*adj.* Of, pertaining to, or functioning as an adjective. [< L *adjectivus* that is added < *adjicere* add to] —**ad′jec·tive·ly** *adv.*

ad·join (ə·join′) *v.t.* 1 To be next to; border upon. 2 To join to; append; unite: with *to.* —*v.i.* 3 To lie close together; be in contact. [< L *ad-* to + *jungere* join]

ad·join·ing (ə·join′ing) *adj.* Lying next; contiguous.

ad·journ (ə·jûrn′) *v.t.* 1 To put off to another day or place, as a meeting or session; postpone. —*v.i.* 2 To postpone or suspend proceedings for a specified time. 3 *Informal* To move or go to another place. [< LL *adjurnare* set a day] —**ad·journ′ment** *n.*

ad·judge (ə·juj′) *v.t.* 1 To determine or decide judicially, as a case. 2 To pronounce or order by law; find; rule. 3 To condemn or sentence: with *to.* 4 To award by law, as damages. 5 To deem; regard. [< L *ad-* to + *judicare* judge]

ad·ju·di·cate (ə·jōō′də·kāt) *v.* **·cat·ed, ·cat·ing** *v.t.* 1 To determine judicially, as a case; adjudge. —*v.i.* 2 To act as a judge. [< L *adjudicare.* See ADJUDGE.] —**ad·ju′di·ca′tion, ad·ju′di·ca′tor** *n.*

ad·junct (aj′ungkt) *n.* 1 Something connected to another thing but in a subordinate position. 2 A person associated with another person in an auxiliary or subordinate relation; an associate; assistant. 3 *Gram.* A modifier. 4 Any nonessential quality or property. —*adj.* Joined subordi-

nately; auxiliary. [< L *adjungere.* See ADJOIN.] —**ad·junc·tive** (ə·jungk′tiv) *adj.* —**ad·junc′tive·ly** *adv.*

ad·jure (ə·jōōr′) *v.t.* **ad·jured, ad·jur·ing** 1 To charge or entreat solemnly, as under oath or penalty. 2 To appeal to earnestly. [< L *ad-* to + *jurare* swear] —**ad·ju·ra·tion** (aj′ōō·rā′shən), **ad·jur′er, ad·ju′ror** *n.* —**ad·jur·a·to·ry** (ə·jōōr′ə·tor′ē, -tō′rē) *adj.*

ad·just (ə·just′) *v.t.* 1 To arrange or regulate so as to produce a desired accuracy, condition, fit, etc. 2 To harmonize or compose, as differences. 3 To arrange in order; systematize. 4 To determine an amount to be paid, as in settling an insurance claim. —*v.i.* 5 To adapt oneself; conform, as to a new environment: to *adjust* to civilian life. [< L *ad-* to + *juxta* near] —**ad·just′a·ble** *adj.* —**ad·just′er, ad·jus′tor** *n.* —**ad·jus′tive** *adj.*

ad·just·ment (ə·just′mənt) *n.* 1 The act of adjusting or the condition of being adjusted. 2 A means or device whereby something may be adjusted. 3 A determining of an amount to be paid, as in an insurance claim.

ad·ju·tant (aj′ə·tənt) *n.* 1 *Mil.* A staff officer who assists and issues the administrative orders of a commanding officer. 2 A large stork of India and Africa. [< L *adjutare* to assist] —**ad′ju·tan·cy, ad′ju·tant·ship** *n.*

adjutant general *pl.* **adjutants general** The adjutant of a division or larger military unit.

ad·lib (ad′lib′) *Informal v.t. & v.i.* **-libbed, -lib·bing** To improvise, as words, gestures, or music not called for in the original script or score. —*n.* An instance of this. [< AD LIBITUM]

ad lib·i·tum (ad lib′ə·təm) 1 At will; as one pleases. 2 *Music* Freely; at the discretion of the performer: also **ad lib.** [L]

Adm. Admiral; Admiralty.

ad·meas·ure (ad·mezh′ər) *v.t.* **·ured, ·ur·ing** To apportion. [< LL *ad-* to + *mensurare.* See MEASURE.] —**ad·meas′ure·ment, ad·meas′ur·er** *n.*

ad·min·is·ter (ad·min′is·tər) *v.t.* 1 To have the charge or direction of; manage. 2 To provide with; apply, as medicine or treatment. 3 To inflict; dispense, as punishment. 4 *Law* To act as executor of, as an estate. 5 To tender, as an oath. —*v.i.* 6 To be helpful; minister: with *to.* 7 To carry out the functions of an administrator. [< L *administrare* minister to] —**ad·min·is·te·ri·al** (-min′is·tir′ē·əl), **ad·min·is·tra·ble** (-min′is·trə·bəl) *adj.* —**ad·min′is·trant** *adj., n.*

ad·min·is·trate (ad·min′is·trāt) *v.t.* **·trat·ed, ·trat·ing** To administer.

ad·min·is·tra·tion (ad·min′is·trā′shən) *n.* 1 The act of administering, or the state of being administered. 2 a The executive department of a government, school, etc. b Their policies. c Their term of office.

ad·min·is·tra·tive (ad·min′is·trā′tiv) *adj.* Pertaining to administration; executive. —**ad·min′is·tra′tive·ly** *adv.*

ad·min·is·tra·tor (ad·min′is·trā′tər) *n.* 1 One who administers something; an executive. 2 *Law* One commissioned by a competent court to administer the personal property of a deceased or incompetent person. —**ad·min′is·tra′tor·ship** *n.* —**ad·min·is·tra·trix** (ad·min′is·trā′triks) *n. Fem.* (*pl.* **·tra·trix·es** or **·tra·tri·ces**)

ad·mi·ra·ble (ad′mər·ə·bəl) *adj.* Worthy of admiration or praise; excellent. [< L *admirari.* See ADMIRE.] —**ad′mi·ra·bil′i·ty, ad′mi·ra·ble·ness** *n.* —**ad′mi·ra·bly** *adv.*

ad·mi·ral (ad′mər·əl) *n.* See GRADE. [< Ar. *amir-al* commander of the]

ad·mi·ral·ty (ad′mər·əl·tē) *n. pl.* **·ties** 1 The office or functions of an admiral. 2 The branch of the judiciary in charge of maritime affairs.

ad·mi·ra·tion (ad′mə·rā′shən) *n.* 1 Wonder combined with pleasure and approval in view of anything rare, great, excellent, etc. 2 That which excites pleased approval.

ad·mire (ad·mīr′) *v.* **ad·mired, ad·mir·ing** *v.t.* 1 To regard with wonder, pleasure, and approval. 2 To have respect or esteem for. —*v.i.* 3 To feel or express admiration. [< L *ad-* + *mirari* wonder] —**ad·mir′er** *n.* —**ad·mir′ing** *adj.* —**ad·mir′ing·ly** *adv.* —**Syn.** 1 approve, applaud, enjoy. 2 honor, revere.

ad·mis·si·ble (ad·mis′ə·bəl) *adj.* 1 Such as may be admitted; allowable. 2 Worthy of being considered. —**ad·mis′si·bil′i·ty** *n.* —**ad·mis′si·bly** *adv.*

admission 11 advantage

ad·mis·sion (ad-mish′ən) *n.* **1** The act of admitting, or the state of being admitted. **2** A right to enter. **3** An entrance fee. **4** An acknowledging or confessing. **5** That which is acknowledged or confessed. —**ad·mis′sive** *adj.*

ad·mit (ad-mit′) *v.* **ad·mit·ted, ad·mit·ting** *v.t.* **1** To grant entrance to. **2** To be the means or channel of admission to; let in: This key will *admit* you. **3** To have room for; contain. **4** To leave room for; permit: His impatience *admits* no delay. **5** To concede or grant. **6** To acknowledge or avow. **7** To allow to join. —*v.i.* **8** To give scope or warrant: with *of*: This problem *admits* of several solutions. **9** To afford entrance; open on: with *to*. [< L *ad-* to + *mittere* send, let go]

ad·mit·tance (ad-mit′əns) *n.* **1** The act of admitting or the state or fact of being admitted. **2** The right or permission to enter.

ad·mit·ted·ly (ad-mit′id-lē) *adv.* Confessedly.

ad·mix (ad-miks′) *v.t.* **ad·mixed** or **ad·mixt, ad·mix·ing** To mix with something else.

ad·mix·ture (ad-miks′chər) *n.* **1** A mixture. **2** The thing added in mixing.

ad·mon·ish (ad-mon′ish) *v.t.* **1** To scold or reprove gently. **2** To caution against danger or error; warn. **3** To exhort; urge. [< L *ad-* to + *monere* warn] —**ad·mon′ish·er** *n.* —**Syn. 1** rebuke, reprimand, censure. **2** counsel, advise.

ad·mo·ni·tion (ad′mə·nish′ən) *n.* **1** The act of admonishing. **2** A gentle reproof. Also **ad·mon′ish·ment.**

ad·mon·i·tor (ad·mon′ə·tər) *n.* One who admonishes. —**ad·mon′i·to·ry** (-tôr′ē, -tō′rē) *adj.*

ad nau·se·am (ad nô′zē·əm, -sē-) So as to nauseate or produce disgust. [L]

a·do (ə·dōō′) *n.* Bustling activity; fuss; trouble. [ME *at do* to do]

a·do·be (ə·dō′bē) *n.* **1** A sun-dried brick. **2** The mixed earth or clay of which such bricks are made. **3** A building made of such bricks. —*adj.* Composed of adobe. [< Sp. *adobar* to plaster]

Adobe house

ad·o·les·cence (ad′ə·les′əns) *n.* **1** The condition or quality of being adolescent. **2** The period of growth from puberty to maturity.

ad·o·les·cent (ad′ə·les′ənt) *adj.* **1** Approaching maturity. **2** Characteristic of or pertaining to youth. —*n.* A person in the period of adolescence. [< L *adolescere* grow up]

A·don·is (ə·don′is, ə·dō′nis) *Gk. Myth.* A youth beloved by Venus for his beauty. —*n.* Any very handsome youth or man.

a·dopt (ə·dopt′) *v.t.* **1** To take into a new relationship, esp. to take legally and raise as one's own child. **2** To take (a course of action) and follow as one's own. **3** To use as one's own, as a phrase, practice, etc. **4** To vote to accept. [< L *ad-* to + *optare* choose] —**a·dopt′a·ble** *adj.* —**a·dopt′er, a·dop·tion** (ə·dop′shən) *n.*

a·dop·tive (ə·dop′tiv) *adj.* **1** Pertaining to adoption. **2** Related by adoption. —**a·dop′tive·ly** *adv.*

a·dor·a·ble (ə·dôr′ə·bəl, ə·dōr′-) *adj. Informal* Attractive; pretty; charming. —**a·dor′a·bil′i·ty, a·dor′a·ble·ness** *n.* —**a·dor′a·bly** *adv.*

ad·o·ra·tion (ad′ə·rā′shən) *n.* **1** The act of worshiping a divine being. **2** Profound love and devotion.

a·dore (ə·dôr′, ə·dōr′) *v.t.* **a·dored, a·dor·ing** **1** To worship as divine. **2** To love or honor with intense devotion. **3** *Informal* To like very much. [< L *ad-* to + *orare* speak, pray] —**a·dor′er** *n.*

a·dorn (ə·dôrn′) *v.t.* **1** To be an ornament to; increase the beauty of. **2** To decorate with ornaments. [< L *ad-* to + *ornare* furnish] —**a·dorn′er, a·dorn′ment** *n.*

a·dre·nal (ə·drē′nəl) *adj.* **1** Near the kidneys. **2** Of or from the adrenal glands. —*n.* An adrenal gland. [< AD- + L *renes* kidneys]

adrenal gland Either of two small ductless glands situated above each kidney.

Ad·ren·a·lin (ə·dren′ə·lin) *n.* EPINEPHRINE: a trade name. Also **ad·ren′a·lin, ad·ren′a·line.**

ad·re·no·cor·ti·co·tro·pic (ə·drē′nō·kôr′ti·kō·trō′pik) *adj.* Acting on the cortex of the adrenal gland.

Adrenal glands

a·drift (ə·drift′) *adv. & adj.* **1** Without moorings. **2** Without a goal or purpose.

a·droit (ə·droit′) *adj.* Skillful; dexterous; expert. [< F *à* to + *droit* right] —**a·droit′ly** *adv.* —**a·droit′ness** *n.* —**Syn.** clever, deft, apt, handy.

ad·sorb (ad·sôrb′, -zôrb′) *v.t.* To hold by adsorption. [< AD- + L *sorbere* suck in] —**ad·sor′bent** *n.*

ad·sorp·tion (ad·sôrp′shən, -zôrp′-) *n.* Retention of a gas or soluble substance upon the surface of a solid. [< AD-SORB] —**ad·sorp′tive** *adj.*

ad·u·late (aj′ə·lāt) *v.t.* **-lat·ed, -lat·ing** To flatter or praise extravagantly. [< L *adulari* to fawn] —**ad′u·la′tion, ad′u·la′tor** *n.* —**ad·u·la·to·ry** (aj′ə·lə·tôr′ē, -tō′rē) *adj.*

a·dult (ə·dult′, ad′ult) *n.* **1** A person who has attained the age of maturity or legal majority. **2** *Biol.* A fully developed animal or plant. —*adj.* **1** Pertaining to mature life; full-grown. **2** Of or for adults. [< L *adolescere* grow up] —**a·dult′hood, a·dult′ness** *n.*

a·dul·ter·ant (ə·dul′tər·ənt) *n.* An adulterating substance. —*adj.* Adulterating.

a·dul·ter·ate (ə·dul′tər·āt) *v.t.* **-at·ed, -at·ing** To make impure or inferior by adding other or baser ingredients; corrupt. —*adj.* (ə·dul′tər·it) **1** Adulterated; corrupted. **2** Adulterous. [< L *adulterare* corrupt < *ad-* to + *alter* other, different] —**a·dul′ter·a′tion, a·dul′ter·a′tor** *n.*

a·dul·ter·ous (ə·dul′tər·əs) *adj.* Of, pertaining to, or given to adultery; illicit. —**a·dul′ter·ous·ly** *adv.*

a·dul·ter·y (ə·dul′tər·ē) *n. pl.* **·ter·ies** The voluntary sexual intercourse of two persons, either or both of whom are married but not to each other. [< L *adulterare* to adulterate] —**a·dul′ter·er** *n.* —**a·dul′ter·ess** *n. Fem.*

ad·um·brate (ad′əm·brāt, ə·dum′-) *v.t.* **·brat·ed, ·brat·ing** **1** To outline sketchily. **2** To foreshadow; prefigure. **3** To obscure or overshadow. [< L *ad-* to + *umbrare* shade] —**ad′um·bra′tion** *n.* —**ad·um′bra·tive** (-brə·tiv) *adj.*

adv. adverb; adverbial; advertisement.

ad va·lo·rem (ad və·lôr′əm, -lō′rəm) According to value. [L]

ad·vance (ad·vans′, -väns′) *v.* **ad·vanced, ad·vanc·ing** *v.t.* **1** To move forward in position or place. **2** To put in a better or more advantageous situation. **3** To further; promote. **4** To make occur earlier; accelerate. **5** To offer; propose. **6** To raise in rate or price. **7** To pay (money) before due. **8** To lend. —*v.i.* **9** To move or go forward: The armies *advance* on all fronts. **10** To make progress; rise or improve. —*adj.* Being ahead or before in time or place. —*n.* **1** The act of advancing. **2** Progress; improvement. **3** An increase or rise, as of prices. **4** Anything paid beforehand; also, a loan. **5** An overture; proposal: His *advances* were rejected. —**in advance 1** In front. **2** Before due; beforehand. [< L *ab-* away + *ante* before] —**ad·vanc′er** *n.*

ad·vanced (ad·vanst′, -vänst′) *adj.* **1** Being in advance of others, as in progress, degree of difficulty, thought, etc. **2** Far on, as in time. **3** Higher: *advanced* prices.

ad·vance·ment (ad·vans′mənt, -väns′-) *n.* **1** The act of advancing, or the state of being advanced. **2** Progression; furtherance; promotion. **3** A payment of money before it is due.

ad·van·tage (ad·van′tij, -vän′-) *n.* **1** Anything favorable to success. **2** Superiority, as of position, rank, etc. **3** Gain or benefit. **4** In tennis, the first point scored after deuce. —**take advantage of 1** To use so as to benefit. **2** To use or impose upon for selfish purposes. —**to advantage** So as to bring about the best results. —*v.t.* **·taged, ·tag·ing** To be a benefit or service to. [< OF *avant* before < L *ab ante* from before]

---

add, āce, câre, pälm; end, ēven; it, īce; odd, ōpen, ôrder; tŏŏk, pōōl; up, bûrn; ə = *a* in *above, u* in *focus;* yŏŏ = *u* in *fuse;* oil; pout; check; go; ring; thin; this; zh, *vision.* < derived from; ? origin uncertain or unknown.

ad·van·ta·geous (ad'vən·tā'jəs) *adj.* Affording advantage; profitable; beneficial. —**ad'van·ta'geous·ly** *adv.* —**ad'van·ta'geous·ness** *n.*

ad·vent (ad'vent) *n.* A coming or arrival. [<L *ad-* to + *venire* come]

Ad·vent (ad'vent) *n.* **1** The birth of Christ. **2** The second coming of Christ. **3** The season including the four Sundays before Christmas.

Ad·vent·ist (ad'ven·tist, ad·ven'-) *n.* A member of a religious sect that believes the second coming of Christ is near at hand. —**Ad'vent·ism** *n.*

ad·ven·ti·tious (ad'vən·tish'əs) *adj.* Not inherent; extrinsic; accidental. [<L *adventicius* coming from abroad, foreign] —**ad'ven·ti'tious·ly** *adv.* —**ad'ven·ti'tious·ness** *n.*

ad·ven·ture (ad·ven'chər) *n.* **1 a** A hazardous or exciting experience. **b** A daring feat. **2** A commercial venture; a speculation. —*v.i.* **·tured, ·tur·ing** To run risks. [<L *adventura (res)* (a thing) about to happen <*advenire* to come to]

ad·ven·tur·er (ad·ven'chər·ər) *n.* **1** A seeker of adventures. **2** A speculator in finance. **3** A person who tries to gain wealth, social position, etc., by questionable means.

ad·ven·tur·ism (ad·ven'chər·iz'əm) *n.* Aggressive and incautious action or conduct often involving grave risk, esp. in the execution of national policy. —**ad·ven'tur·ist** *adj., n.*

ad·ven·tur·ous (ad·ven'chər·əs) *adj.* **1** Disposed to seek adventures or take risks. Also **ad·ven'ture·some** (-səm). **2** Attended with risk; hazardous. —**ad·ven'tur·ous·ly** *adv.* —**ad·ven'tur·ous·ness** *n.*

ad·verb (ad'vûrb) *n.* Any of a class of words used to modify the meaning of a verb, adjective, or other adverb, in regard to time, place, manner, means, cause, degree, etc. [<L *ad-* to + *verbum* verb] —**ad·ver·bi·al** (ad·vûr'bē·əl) *adj.* —**ad·ver'bi·al·ly** *adv.*

ad·ver·sar·y (ad'vər·ser'ē) *n. pl.,* **·sar·ies** An opponent or enemy. [<L *adversarius,* lit., one turned towards]

ad·ver·sa·tive (ad·vûr'sə·tiv) *adj.* Expressing opposition or antithesis. —**ad·ver'sa·tive·ly** *adv.*

ad·verse (ad·vûrs', ad'vûrs) *adj.* **1** Opposing or opposed. **2** Unfriendly. **3** Harmful; detrimental. **4** Opposite. [<L *ad-* to + *vertere* turn] —**ad·verse'ly** *adv.* —**ad·verse'ness** *n.*

ad·ver·si·ty (ad·vûr'sə·tē) *n. pl.,* **·ties 1** A condition of hardship or misfortune. **2** *Usu. pl.* An instance of misfortune. —**Syn. 2** calamity, disaster, mishap, affliction, blow.

ad·vert (ad·vûrt') *v.i.* To take notice; refer: with *to.* [<L *ad-* to + *vertere* turn] —**ad·ver'tence, ad·ver'ten·cy** *n.*

ad·ver·tent (ad·vûr'tənt) *adj.* Giving attention; heedful. —**ad·ver'tent·ly** *adv.*

ad·ver·tise (ad'vər·tīz, ad'vər·tīz') *v.* **·tised, ·tis·ing** *v.t.* **1** To or proclaim the qualities of, as by publication or broadcasting, generally in order to sell. **2** To call attention to. —*v.i.* **3** To inquire by public notice, as in a newspaper: with *for:* to *advertise* for a house. **4** To distribute or publish advertisements. [<MF *advertir* warn, give notice to <L *advertere.* See ADVERT.] —**ad'ver·tis'er** *n.*

ad·ver·tise·ment (ad'vər·tīz'mənt, ad·vûr'tis·mənt, -tiz-) *n.* A public notice, as of products for sale, events, etc.

ad·ver·tis·ing (ad'vər·tī'zing) *n.* **1** Any system or method of attracting public notice to an event or product. **2** The business of preparing advertisements. Also **ad'ver·tiz'ing.**

ad·ver·tor·i·al (ad·vər·tôr'ē·əl, -to·re-) *n.* An editorial that includes elements of a commercial advertising message. [ADVERT(ISING)+(EDIT)ORIAL]

ad·vice (ad·vīs') *n.* **1** Counsel or a suggestion as to a course of action. **2** *Often pl.* Information; notification. [<L *ad-* to + *visum,* p.p. of *videre* see]

ad·vis·a·ble (ad·vī'zə·bəl) *adj.* Recommended; expedient. —**ad·vis'a·bil'i·ty, ad·vis'a·ble·ness** *n.* —**ad·vis'a·bly** *adv.*

ad·vise (ad·vīz') *v.* **ad·vised, ad·vis·ing** *v.t.* **1** To give advice to; counsel. **2** To recommend: to *advise* a course of action. **3** To notify; inform, as of a transaction: with *of.* —*v.i.* **4** To take counsel: with *with: He advised* with his lawyer. **5** To give advice. —**ad·vis'er, ad·vis'or** *n.*

ad·vised (ad·vīzd') *adj.* **1** Done with deliberation and forethought. **2** Counseled. **3** Informed.

ad·vis·ed·ly (ad·vī'zid·lē) *adv.* With forethought or advice; not hastily.

ad·vise·ment (ad·vīz'mənt) *n.* Consultation; deliberation.

ad·vi·so·ry (ad·vī'zər·ē) *adj.* **1** Having power to advise. **2**

Containing or given as advice.

ad·vo·ca·cy (ad'və·kə·sē) *n.* The act of advocating or pleading a cause; a defense.

ad·vo·cate (ad'və·kāt) *v.t.* **·cat·ed, ·cat·ing** To speak or write in favor of. —*n.* (ad'və·kit, -kāt) One who defends or supports something or someone. [<L *advocatus* one summoned to another] —**ad'vo·ca'tor** *n.* —**ad·vo·ca·to·ry** (ad·vok'ə·tôr'ē, -tō'rē) *adj.*

advt. advertisement.

adz (adz) *n.* A hand cutting tool having its usu. curved blade at right angles with its handle, used for dressing timber, etc. Also **adze.** [<OE *adesa*]

ae- For words not entered below, see under E-.

æ A ligature of Latin origin, sometimes retained in Greek and Latin proper names and used in certain scientific terms, but in modern spelling usu. represented by *e.*

Adzes
a. sculptor's.
b. cooper's.
c. carpenter's.

AEC, A.E.C. Atomic Energy Commission.

AEF, A.E.F. American Expeditionary Force.

ae·gis (ē'jis) *Gk. Myth.* The shield of Zeus, used also by Athena. —*n.* **1** Any protection. **2** Patronage; sponsorship.

-aemia -EMIA.

Ae·ne·as (i·nē'əs) *Gk. & Rom. Myth.* A Trojan who, after the sack of Troy, wandered for seven years before settling in Italy.

Ae·ne·id (i·nē'id) *n.* A Latin epic poem by Virgil narrating the adventures of Aeneas.

ae·o·li·an (ē·ō'lē·ən) *adj.* EOLIAN.

aeolian harp A stringed instrument constructed to produce musical sounds when exposed to a current of air.

ae·on (ē'on, ē'on) *n.* EON.

aer- AERO-.

aer·ate (âr'āt, ā'ə·rāt) *v.t.* **·at·ed, ·at·ing 1** To supply or charge with air or gas. **2** To purify by exposure to air. **3** To oxygenate, as blood. [<AER(O)-] —**aer·a'tion, aer'a·tor** *n.*

aeri- AERO-.

aer·i·al (âr'ē·əl, ā·ir'ē·əl) *adj.* **1** Of, in, or by the air. **2** Like air; atmospheric. **3** Growing in the air: an *aerial* root. **4** Not real; imaginary; unsubstantial. **5** Existing or performed in the air. **6** Of, by, or for aircraft: *aerial* bombardment. —*n.* (âr'ē·əl) ANTENNA (def. 2). [<L *aer* air] —**aer'i·al·ly** *adv.* • See AIRPLANE.

aer·i·al·ist (âr'ē·əl·ist, ā·ir'ē·əl-) *n.* One who performs on a tightrope, trapeze, etc.

aer·ie (âr'ē, ir'ē) *n.* **1** The nest of a predatory bird, as the eagle, on a crag. **2** The brood or young of such a bird. **3** A house or fortress built on a high place. [<L *area* open space] —**aer'ied** *adj.*

aer·i·fy (âr'ə·fī, ā'ər·ə·fī) *v.t.* **·fied, ·fy·ing 1** To aerate. **2** To change into a gaseous form. —**aer'i·fi·ca'tion** *n.*

aero- *combining form* **1** Air; of the air: *aerodynamics.* **2** Of aircraft or flying. **3** Gas; of gases. [<Gk. *aēr* air]

aer·obe (âr'ōb, ā'ər·ōb) *n.* A microorganism which cannot live without free oxygen. [<AERO- + Gk. *bios* life] —**aer·o'bic** *adj.*

aer·o·bics (âr'ō'biks) *n.pl.* Exercises that involve a workout for the lungs and heart.

aer·o·dy·nam·ics (âr'ō·dī·nam'iks, ā'ər·ō-) *n.pl. (construed as sing.)* The branch of physics that deals with the motion of gases, esp. with the effects of bodies moving through the atmosphere. —**aer'o·dy·nam'ic** *adj.*

aer·o·foil (âr'ə·foil, ā'ər·ə-) *n.* AIRFOIL.

aer·o·me·chan·ics (âr'ō·mə·kan'iks, ā'ər·ō-) *n. pl. (construed as sing.)* The mechanics of air and gases. —**aer'o·me·chan'ic** *adj., n.*

aer·o·naut (âr'ə·nôt, ā'ər·ə-) *n.* The pilot of any aircraft. [<AERO- + Gk. *nautēs* sailor]

aer·o·nau·tics (âr'ə·nô'tiks, ā'ər·ə-) *n.pl. (construed as sing.)* The science and technology that deal with the design, construction, and operation of aircraft. —**aer'o·nau'tic or ·ti·cal** *adj.*

aer·o·pause (âr'ə·pôz, ā'ər·ə-) *n. Meteorol.* The uppermost region of the atmosphere.

aer·o·plane (âr'ə·plān, ā'ər·ə-) *Chiefly Brit.* AIRPLANE.

aer·o·sol (âr′ə·sŏl, -sol, ā′ər·ə-) *n.* A colloidal dispersion of a solid or liquid in a gas. —*adj.*
1 Pertaining to a method of packaging a product under pressure in a valved container so that on release of the valve the contents escape in a spray or foam. 2 Describing a product so packaged: an *aerosol* disinfectant. [< AERO- + SOL(UTION)]

gas under pressure

solution of propellant and active ingredients

Aerosol bomb

aer·o·space (âr′ō·spās, ā′ər-ō-) *n.* 1 The earth's atmosphere and the space beyond it. 2 The science and technology of aeronautics and space flight.

aer·o·stat (âr′ə·stat, ā′ər-ə-) *n.* Any aircraft which is lighter than air, as a balloon or dirigible. [< AERO- + Gk. *statos* standing] —**aer′o·stat′ic** or ·**i·cal** *adj.*

aer·o·stat·ics (âr′ə·stat′iks, ā′ər·ə) *n. pl. (construed as sing.)* The branch of physics that deals with air and gases not in motion.

aer·y (âr′ē, ir′ē) *n.* AERIE.

Aes·cu·la·pi·us (es′kyə·lā′pē·əs) *Rom. Myth.* The god of medicine. —**Aes′cu·la′pi·an** *adj.*

aes·thete (es′thēt) *n.* 1 A person who appreciates beauty, culture, and art. 2 A person possessing an excessive refinement of taste and a pretentious sensibility to art and culture. —**aes·thet·i·cism** (es·thet′ə·siz′əm) *n.*

aes·thet·ic (es·thet′ik) *adj.* 1 Of aesthetics. 2 Of, pertaining to, or appreciating beauty and art. 3 Having or characterized by fine taste. [< Gk. *aisthētikos* of sense perception] Also **aes·thet′i·cal.** —**aes·thet′i·cal·ly** *adv.*

aes·thet·ics (es·thet′iks) *n. pl. (construed as sing.)* The philosophy or study of beauty and art, and the responses they engender. —**aes·the·ti·cian** (es′thə·tish′ən) *n.*

af- AD-.

AF Anglo-French.

AF, A.F. Air Force.

AF, A.F. a.f., a-f audio frequency.

a·far (ə·fär′) *adv.* At, from, or to a distance; remotely.

a·feard (ə·fird′) *adj. Regional* Afraid. Also **a·feared**′.

af·fa·ble (af′ə·bəl) *adj.* Easy and courteous in manner; friendly; approachable. [< L *affabilis*, lit., able to be spoken to] —**af′fa·bil′i·ty, af′fa·ble·ness** *n.* —**af′fa·bly** *adv.* —**Syn.** amicable, cordial, genial, sociable, kind.

af·fair (ə·fâr′) *n.* 1 Anything done or to be done; business. 2 *pl.* Matters of business or concern. 3 Any matter, event, or thing. 4 A social event. 5 An object or device. 6 A romantic and usu. sexual relationship between two people not married to each other.

af·fect[1] (ə·fekt′) *v.t.* 1 To act upon or have an effect upon. 2 To touch or move emotionally. —*n.* (af′ekt) *Psychol.* Emotion, as distinguished from thought or perception. [< L *afficere* influence, attack < *ad-* to + *facere* do] • **affect**[1], **effect** To *effect* means to produce, accomplish, or bring about a definite, specific result, whereas to *affect* means merely to influence or act upon: The disease *affected* the patient's eyesight until her doctor *effected* a cure.

af·fect[2] (ə·fekt′) *v.t.* 1 To have a liking for; show a preference for. 2 To imitate or counterfeit for effect or show: to *affect* a British accent. [< L *affectare* aim at, freq. of *afficere.* See AFFECT[1].]

af·fec·ta·tion (af′ek·tā′shən) *n.* 1 A studied pretense; shallow display: with *of.* 2 Artificiality of manner. [< L < *affectare.* See AFFECT[2].]

af·fect·ed[1] (ə·fek′tid) *adj.* 1 Acted upon, as by a drug. 2 Moved emotionally; influenced. 3 Attacked, as by disease. [p.p. of AFFECT[1]]

af·fect·ed[2] (ə·fek′tid) *adj.* 1 Artificial or mannered, as in behavior. 2 Assumed falsely or for outward show only. [p.p. of AFFECT[2]] —**af·fect′ed·ly** *adv.* —**af·fect′ed·ness** *n.*

af·fect·ing (ə·fek′ting) *adj.* Having power to move the feelings. —**af·fect′ing·ly** *adv.*

af·fec·tion (ə·fek′shən) *n.* 1 Good, kind, or loving feelings, as towards another. 2 A particular mental state or disposition. 3 A disease. 4 A property or attribute. [< L *afficere* to influence, affect]

af·fec·tion·ate (ə·fek′shən·it) *adj.* Having or expressing affection; loving; fond. —**af·fec′tion·ate·ly** *adv.* —**af·fec′tion·ate·ness** *n.*

af·fec·tive (ə·fek′tiv) *adj. Psychol.* Of or arising from emotion rather than from thought.

af·fer·ent (af′ər·ənt) *adj.* Conducting inward: said of those nerve processes which transmit sensory stimuli to the central nervous system. [< L *ad-* to + *ferre* bear]

af·fi·ance (ə·fī′əns) *v.t.* ·**anced, ·anc·ing** To promise in marriage; betroth. [< L *ad-* to + *fidus* faithful]

af·fi·da·vit (af′ə·dā′vit) *n.* A sworn declaration, in writing, made before an official authority. [< Med.L, he has stated on oath]

af·fil·i·ate (ə·fil′ē·āt) *v.* ·**at·ed, ·at·ing** *v.t.* 1 To associate or unite, as a member or branch: with *to* or *with.* 2 To join or associate (oneself): with *with.* 3 To determine the origins of. —*v.i.* 4 To associate or ally oneself: with *with.* —*n.* (ə·fil′ē·it) An affiliated person or thing. [< L *affiliare* adopt] —**af·fil′i·a′tion** *n.*

af·fin·i·ty (ə·fin′ə·tē) *n. pl.* ·**ties** 1 Any natural liking or inclination. 2 Likenesses indicating a common origin. 3 Physical or chemical attraction. 4 Connection through certain relations formed, as by marriage. 5 An attraction held to exist between certain persons. [< L *affinis* adjacent, related]

af·firm (ə·fûrm′) *v.t.* 1 To declare positively; assert to be true. 2 To confirm or ratify, as a judgment or law. —*v.i.* 3 *Law* To make a formal judicial declaration, but not under oath. [< L *ad-* to + *firmare* make firm] —**af·firm′a·ble** *adj.* —**af·firm′a·bly** *adv.* —**af·firm′ant** *adj., n.* —**af·firm′er** *n.* —**Syn.** 1 maintain, propound, avow, advance, insist.

af·fir·ma·tion (af′ər·mā′shən) *n.* 1 The act of affirming. 2 That which is affirmed. 3 A solemn declaration made before a competent officer, in place of a judicial oath.

af·firm·a·tive (ə·fûr′mə·tiv) *adj.* 1 Asserting or confirming that something is so. 2 Positive. Also **af·firm·a·to·ry** (ə·fûr′mə·tôr′ē, -tō′re). —*n.* 1 A word or expression of affirmation or assent. 2 That side in a debate which affirms the proposition debated. —**af·firm′a·tive·ly** *adv.*

af·fix (ə·fiks′) *v.t.* 1 To fix or attach; fasten. 2 To put at the end; append, as a signature. 3 To attribute, as blame. —*n.* (af′iks) 1 That which is attached, appended, or added. 2 *Ling.* A prefix, suffix, or infix. [< L *ad-* to + *figere* fasten]

af·fla·tus (ə·flā′təs) *n.* Any creative inspiration or impulse. [< L *afflare* blow on]

af·flict (ə·flikt′) *v.t.* To distress with continued suffering; trouble. [< L *affligere* dash against, strike down] —**af·flict′er** *n.* —**af·flic′tive** *adj.* —**af·flic′tive·ly** *adv.*

af·flic·tion (ə·flik′shən) *n.* 1 The state of being afflicted. 2 A misfortune; calamity.

af·flu·ence (af′lōō·əns, ə·flōō′-) *n.* Riches; wealth. [< L *affluere.* See AFFLUENT.]

af·flu·ent (af′lōō·ənt, ə·flōō′-) *adj.* 1 Abounding; abundant. 2 Wealthy; opulent. —*n.* A stream that flows into another. [< L *ad-* to + *fluere* flow] —**af′flu·ent·ly** *adv.*

af·ford (ə·fôrd′, ə·fōrd′) *v.t.* 1 To have sufficient means for: usu. preceded by *can* or *be able to.* 2 To be able to do, say, etc., without detriment: usu. preceded by *can:* He can *afford* to laugh now. 3 To provide or furnish: It *affords* me great delight. [< OE *geforthian* further, promote] —**af·ford′a·ble** *adj.*

af·fray (ə·frā′) *n.* A public brawl or fight; a disturbance of the peace. [< OF *esfrei*]

af·fri·cate (af′ri·kit) *n. Phonet.* A sound consisting of a stop followed by the fricative release of breath at the point of contact, as *ch* in *match.* [< L *ad-* against + *fricare* rub] —**af·fric·a·tive** (ə·frik′ə·tiv) *adj., n.*

af·front (ə·frunt′) *v.t.* 1 To insult openly; offend by word or act. 2 To confront in defiance; accost. —*n.* An open insult or indignity. [< OF *afronter* strike on the forehead] —**af·front′er** *n.* —**af·fron′tive** *adj.* —**Syn.** 1 aggravate, annoy, provoke, irritate, vex.

Afg., Afgh. Afghanistan.

af·ghan (af′gən, -gan) *n.* A soft wool coverlet, knitted or crocheted.

Af·ghan (af′gən, -gan) *adj.* Of or pertaining to Afghanistan, its people, or their language. —*n.* 1 A native or citizen of Afghanistan. 2 The language spoken by the Afghans.

Af·ghan·i·stan (af·gan'ə·stan) *n.* A republic of sw Asia, 250,000 sq. mi., cap. Kabul.

a·fi·cio·na·do (ə·fish'ə·nä'dō, ə·fis'ē·ə-, ə·fē'sē·ə-, *Sp.* äfē·thyō·nä'tho, -fē·syō-) *n. pl.* **·dos** (-dōz, *Sp.* -thōs) An avid follower or fan, as of a sport or activity; devotee. [Sp.]

a·field (ə·fēld') *adv.* 1 In or to the field. 2 Away; abroad. 3 Off the track; astray.

a·fire (ə·fīr') *adv. & adj.* On fire.

AFL, A.F.L., A.F. of L. American Federation of Labor.

a·flame (ə·flām') *adv. & Adj.* 1 Flaming; glowing. 2 Very much excited or aroused.

AFL-CIO, A.F.L.-C.I.O. American Federation of Labor-Congress of Industrial Organizations: a labor organization formed by a merger in 1955.

a·float (ə·flōt') *adv. & adj.* 1 On the water. 2 In circulation, as a rumor. 3 Adrift. 4 Flooded, as the deck of a ship. 5 Out of trouble or difficulties.

a·foot (ə·foŏt') *adv.* 1 On foot. 2 Able to walk. 3 In motion or progress; on the move. [ME *on fot*]

a·fore (ə·fôr', ə·fōr') *adv., prep., & conj. Chiefly Naut.* Before [<OE *onforan*]

a·fore·men·tioned (ə·fôr'men'shənd, ə·fōr'-) *adj.* Mentioned before.

a·fore·said (ə·fôr'sed', ə·fōr'-) *adj.* Said or mentioned before.

a·fore·thought (ə·fôr'thôt', ə·fōr'-) *adj.* Intended or planned beforehand.

a·fore·time (ə·fôr'tīm', ə·fōr'-) *adv.* At a previous time.

a for·ti·o·ri (ä fôr'tē·ôr'ē, ā fôr'tē·ō'rī, ä fôr'shē·ôr'ī, -ôr'ē) For a stronger reason; all the more. [L]

a·foul (ə·foul') *adv. & adj.* In collision; entangled. —**run** (or **fall**) **afoul of** To get into difficulties with.

Afr. Africa; African.

a·fraid (ə·frād') *adj.* Filled with fear or apprehension. [<ME *affrayen* to fear <OF *esfrei* affray]

A-frame (ā'frām') *n.* A framework in the shape of the letter A, as that supporting a slanted roof.

a·fresh (ə·fresh') *adv.* Once more; anew; again.

Af·ri·ca (af'ri·kə) *n.* The second largest continent, located

[Map of Africa]

in the E hemisphere south of Europe and joined to Asia by the Sinai peninsula, 11,500,000 sq. mi.

Af·ri·can (af'ri·kən) *adj.* Of Africa, its peoples and their languages, culture, etc. —*n.* 1 A native or naturalized inhabitant of Africa. 2 One of the indigenous peoples of Africa, esp. a Negro.

African American An American of black African descent.

Af·ri·can·ize (af'rə·kən·īz') *v.t.* **·ized, ·iz·ing** 1 To make African in character. 2 To place under the control of Africans, esp. black Africans. —**Af'ri·can·i·za'tion** *n.*

Af·ri·kaans (af'ri·käns', -känz') *n.* A language spoken in South Africa, evolved from 17th-century Dutch.

Af·ri·ka·ner (af'ri·kä'nər) *n.* An Afrikaans-speaking South African descended from the early Dutch settlers.

Af·ro (af'rō) *n. pl.* **Af·ros** A hair style in which bushy hair is shaped into a full, rounded mass. —*adj.* Of, pertaining to, or influenced by African culture, style, etc. Also **af'ro.**

Afro- *combining form* Africa; African.

Af·ro-Amer·i·can (af'rō·ə·mer'ə·kən) *adj.* Of or pertaining to Americans of black African descent. —*n.* An Afro-American person.

aft (aft, äft) *adj.* Of or near the stern, or rear, of a vessel. —*adv.* Toward the rear; astern. [<OE *æftan* behind]

A.F.T. American Federation of Teachers.

af·ter (af'tər, äf'-) *prep.* 1 In the rear of; following. 2 At a later period. 3 In succession to; following repeatedly. 4 As a result of; subsequently to. 5 Notwithstanding. 6 Next below in order or importance. 7 In search or pursuit of: to strive *after* wisdom. 8 According to the nature, wishes, or customs of. 9 In the manner of: a painting *after* Vermeer. 10 In honor, remembrance, or observance of: I was named *after* Lincoln. 11 In relation to: to inquire *after* someone's health. —*conj.* Following the time that. —*adj.* 1 Following in time or place. 2 *Naut.* Farther aft. —*adv.* 1 At a later time. 2 In the rear; behind. [<OE *æfter* behind]

af·ter·birth (af'tər·bûrth', äf'-) *n.* The placenta and fetal membranes expelled from the uterus after childbirth.

af·ter·burn·er (af'tər·bûr'nər, äf'-) *n. Aeron.* A device that injects extra fuel into the exhaust of a jet engine to increase its thrust.

af·ter·deck (af'tər·dek', äf'-) *n. Naut.* That part of a deck toward the stern.

af·ter·ef·fect (af'tər·ə·fekt', äf'-) *n.* An effect succeeding its cause after an interval.

af·ter·glow (af'tər·glō, äf'-) *n.* 1 A glow left after a light has disappeared. 2 An agreeable feeling occurring after a pleasant or profitable experience.

af·ter·im·age (af'tər·im'ij, äf'-) *n.* An image or sensation that persists after the direct stimulation has been withdrawn.

af·ter·math (af'tər·math, äf'-) *n.* Results; consequences. [<AFTER + OE *mæth* a mowing]

af·ter·most (af'tər·mōst, äf'-) *adj.* 1 *Naut.* Nearest the stern: also **aft'most.** 2 Last.

af·ter·noon (af'tər·nōōn', äf'-) *n.* That part of the day between noon and sunset. —*adj.* Of, for, or occurring in the afternoon.

af·ter·taste (af'tər·tāst', äf'-) *n.* 1 A taste persisting in the mouth, as after eating or drinking. 2 A feeling or reaction that comes after an experience.

af·ter·thought (af'tər·thôt', äf'-) *n.* 1 A later or more deliberate thought, as after decision or action. 2 A thought occurring too late to affect action.

af·ter·ward (af'tər·wərd, äf'-) *adv.* In time following; subsequently. Also **af'ter·wards.**

AG, A.G. Adjutant General; Attorney General.

Ag silver (L *argentum*).

Ag. August.

a·gain (ə·gen', *esp. Brit.* ə·gān') *adv.* 1 Once more; anew. 2 Once repeated: half as much *again.* 3 In or to the same or former place or condition: to be ill *again.* 4 Further; moreover. 5 On the other hand; from another point of view. [<OE *ongegn*]

a·gainst (ə·genst', *esp. Brit.* ə·gänst') *prep.* 1 In contact with and pressing upon. 2 In collision with. 3 In front of; directly opposite: *against* a background. 4 In anticipation of; in preparation for. 5 In opposition to; contrary to. 6 In a counter or opposite direction to. 7 In hostility to. 8 To the debit of. **9** In comparison with; contrasted with. [< OE *ongegn* again]

Ag·a·mem·non (ag′ə-mem′non, -nən) *Gk. Myth.* The king of Mycenae and leader of the Greek army in the Trojan War.

a·gape (ə-gāp′, ə-gap′) *adv. & adj.* **1** In a state of wonder or astonishment, usu. with the mouth wide open. **2** Wide open; gaping.

a·gar (ä′gär, ā′gär, ag′ər) *n.* A gelatinous substance obtained from seaweed, employed as a laxative, emulsifier, and bacterial culture medium. [< Malay *agar-agar*]

ag·a·ric (ag′ə-rik, ə-gar′ik) *n.* Any fungus of the mushroom group. [< Gk. *agarikon* • See MUSHROOM.

ag·ate (ag′it) *n.* **1** A variegated, waxy, usu. banded quartz or chalcedony. **2** A child's playing marble. **3** *Printing* 5½ point type [< Gk. *achatēs*]

a·ga·ve (ə-gä′vē) *n.* An American desert plant with fleshy leaves and a single spike of flowers; the century plant. [< Gk. *agauos* noble]

age (āj) *n.* **1** The entire period of life or existence, as of a person, thing, nation, etc. **2** A period or stage of life: a good *age* to be married. **3** The closing period of life. **4** A generation or lifetime. **5** *Often cap.* Any great or distinct period in history: the Atomic *Age.* **6** *Often pl. Informal* A long time. —**of age** To or at the age of full legal responsibility: to be *of age.* —*v.* **aged, ag·ing** or **age·ing** *v.t.* **1** To cause to become mature. **2** To cause to grow or seem to grow old. —*v.i.* **3** To become or seem to become old. **4** To ripen or mature. [< L *aetas* age, a span of life]

-age *suffix of nouns* **1** Collection or aggregate of: *baggage.* **2** Condition, office, service, or other relation or connection of: *pilgrimage.* [< L *-aticum*, neut. adj. suffix]

a·ged (ā′jid *for defs. 1 & 2;* ājd *for def. 3*) *adj.* **1** Advanced in years; old. **2** Of, like, or characteristic of old age. **3** Of or at the age of: a child, *aged* five. —**a′ged·ness** *n.*

age·ism (ā′jiz·əm) *n.* Discrimination or prejudice, esp. as directed against elderly people. —**age′ist** *n., adj.*

age·less (āj′lis) *adj.* **1** Not seeming to grow old. **2** Having no limits of duration.

age·long (āj′lông′) *adj.* Lasting a long time.

a·gen·cy (ā′jən·sē) *n. pl.* **·cies 1** Active power or force. **2** Means; instrumentality. **3** Any establishment where business is done for others. **4** The office or offices of such an establishment. **5** A specific division of governmental administration. [< L *agere* do]

a·gen·da (ə-jen′də) *n. pl.* **·das** A list or program of things to be done, as at a meeting. [< L < *agere* to do]

a·gen·dum (ə-jen′dəm) *n. pl.* **·dums** or **·da** An agenda.

a·gent (ā′jənt) *n.* **1** One who acts or has power to act. **2** Any force or substance having power to cause change: a chemical *agent.* **3** A person, business, etc., who represents or acts for another: an actor's *agent.* **4** A means by which something is done. **5** *Informal* A traveling salesman. [< L *agere* do] —**a·gen·tial** (ā·jen′shəl) *adj.* —**Syn. 1** actor, doer, operator, mover. **3** representative, proxy, deputy. **4** factor, cause, instrument.

age of consent The age at which a girl may legally consent to have sexual intercourse.

a·ge·ra·tum (aj′ə-rā′təm, ə-jer′ə-təm) *n.* Any of a genus of plants having long-lasting, usu. blue, composite flowers. [< Gk. *agēraton*, a kind of plant < *agēratos* ageless]

ag·gior·na·men·to (ə-jôr′nə-men′tō, *It.* ä-jôr′nä-men′-tō) *n.* A bringing up to date, esp. of the ideas, rituals, or policies of the Roman Catholic Church. [It.]

ag·glom·er·ate (ə-glom′ə-rāt) *v.t. & v.i.* **·at·ed, ·at·ing** To gather, form, or grow into a ball or rounded mass. —*adj.* (ə-glom′ər·it, -ə-rāt) Gathered into a mass or heap; clustered densely. —*n.* (ə-glom′ər·it, -ə-rāt) A heap or mass of things thrown together indiscriminately. [< L *ad-* to + *glomerare* gather into a ball] —**ag·glom′er·a′tion** *n.*

ag·glu·ti·nant (ə-glōō′tə-nənt) *adj.* Tending to cause adhesion; uniting. —*n.* Any sticky substance.

ag·glu·ti·nate (ə-glōō′tə-nāt) *v.t. & v.i.* **·nat·ed, ·nat·ing 1** To unite, as with glue; join by adhesion. **2** *Ling.* To form (words) by combining into compounds. **3** *Biol.* To come together in clumps, as blood corpuscles, etc. —*adj.* (ə-glōō′-

tə-nit, -nāt) Joined by adhesion. [< L *ad-* to + *glutinare* to glue] —**ag·glu′ti·na′tion** *n.* —**ag·glu′ti·na′tive** *adj.*

ag·gran·dize (ə-gran′dīz, ag′rən-dīz) *v.t.* **·dized, ·diz·ing 1** To make great or greater. **2** To make appear greater; exalt. [< L *ad-* to + *grandire* make great or large] —**ag·gran′dize·ment, ag·gran′diz·er** *n.*

ag·gra·vate (ag′rə-vāt) *v.t.* **·vat·ed, ·vat·ing 1** To make worse. **2** To make heavier or more burdensome, as a duty. **3** *Informal* To provoke or exasperate. [< L *ad-* to + *gravare* make heavy] —**ag′gra·vat′ing, ag′gra·va′tive** *adj.* —**ag′gra·vat′ing·ly** *adv.* —**ag′gra·va′tion** *n.*

ag·gre·gate (ag′rə-gāt) *v.t.* **·gat·ed, ·gat·ing 1** To bring or gather together, as into a mass, sum, or body. **2** To amount to; form a total of. —*adj.* (ag′rə-git) Collected into a sum, mass, or total; gathered into a whole. —*n.* (ag′rə-git) **1** The entire number, sum, mass, or quantity of something; amount; total. **2** Material, as sand or pebbles, used in making concrete. —**in the aggregate** Collectively; as a whole. [< L *aggregare*, lit. bring to the flock] —**ag′gre·ga′tive** *adj.* —**ag′gre·ga′tion, ag′gre·ga′tor** *n.*

ag·gress (ə-gres′) *v.i.* To undertake an attack; begin a quarrel. [< L *aggredi* approach, attack]

ag·gres·sion (ə-gresh′ən) *n.* **1** An unprovoked attack. **2** Aggressive action or practices.

ag·gres·sive (ə-gres′iv) *adj.* **1** Characterized by or inclined to begin an attack or encroachment; hostile. **2** Disposed to vigorous activity; energetic and forceful. —**ag·gres′sive·ly** *adv.* —**ag·gres′sive·ness** *n.*

ag·gres·sor (ə-gres′ər) *n.* One who commits an aggression or begins a quarrel.

ag·grieve (ə-grēv′) *v.t.* **ag·grieved, ag·griev·ing 1** To cause sorrow to; distress or afflict. **2** To give cause for just complaint. [< L *aggravare.* See AGGRAVATE.]

a·ghast (ə-gast′, ə-gäst′) *adj.* Struck with horror or amazement; shocked. [< ᴀ-² + *gæstan* terrify]

ag·ile (aj′əl, aj′īl) *adj.* **1** Able to move quickly and easily; nimble. **2** Alert; lively: an *agile* mind. [< L *agilis* < *agere* do, move] —**ag′ile·ly** *adv.* —**ag′ile·ness, a·gil·i·ty** (ə-jil′ə-tē) *n.*

ag·i·tate (aj′ə-tāt) *v.* **·tat·ed, ·tat·ing** *v.t.* **1** To shake or move irregularly. **2** To set or keep moving, as a fan. **3** To excite or endeavor to excite, as a crowd. **4** To discuss publicly and incessantly, as a controversial question. —*v.i.* **5** To excite public interest in a cause by continuous discussion, writing, etc. [< L *agitare* set in motion, freq. of *agere* do, move] —**ag′i·ta′tion** *n.*

ag·i·ta·tor (aj′ə-tā′tər) *n.* **1** One who or that which agitates. **2** One who seeks to stimulate public opinion and response to controversial issues: usu. derogatory.

ag·it·prop (aj′it-prop′) *n.* **1** Communist political propaganda, esp. in a play, film, etc. **2** Any political propaganda. —*adj.* Pertaining to or of the nature of agitprop. [Russ., Communist Party agency for agitation and propaganda]

a·gleam (ə-glēm′) *adv. & adj.* Bright; gleaming.

a·glow (ə-glō′) *adv. & adj.* In a glow; glowing.

ag·no·men (ag-nō′mən) *n. pl.* **ag·nom·i·na** (ag-nom′ə-nə) A nickname. [< L *ad-* to + (*g*)*nomen* name]

ag·nos·tic (ag-nos′tik) *adj.* Of or pertaining to agnosticism or agnostics. —*n.* One who believes in agnosticism. [< Gk. *agnōstos* unknowing, unknown]

ag·nos·ti·cism (ag-nos′tə-siz′əm) *n.* The theory that man can neither prove nor disprove the existence of God nor know with certainty the nature of ultimate truth.

Ag·nus De·i (ag′nəs dē′ī, dā′ē) **1** A figure of a lamb, as an emblem of Christ. **2** *Eccl.* **a** A prayer in the Mass, beginning with the words *Agnus Dei.* **b** A musical setting for this prayer. [LL, Lamb of God]

a·go (ə-gō′) *adv.* In the past; since. —*adj.* Gone by; past. [OE *āgān* past, gone away]

a·gog (ə-gog′) *adv. & adj.* In a state of eager interest or expectation. [< MF *en gogues* in a merry mood]

à go-go (ä gō′gō) *adj.* GO-GO. Also **a go′-go′, a-go′go′.** [F, lit., joyfully]

-agogue *combining form* Leading, promoting, or inciting; *demagogue, pedagogue.* Also **-agog.** [< Gk. *agōgos* leading]

---

add, āce, câre, pälm; end, ēven; it, īce; odd, ōpen, ôrder; tŏŏk, pōōl; up, bûrn; ə = *a* in *above*, *u* in *focus*; yōō = *u* in *fuse*; oil; pout; check; go; ring; thin; this; zh, *vision*. < derived from; ? origin uncertain or unknown.

ag·o·nize (ag′ə·nīz) v. **·nized**, **·niz·ing** v.i. 1 To be in or suffer extreme pain or anguish. 2 To make convulsive efforts, as in wrestling; strive. —v.t. 3 To subject to agony; torture. [<Gk. agōnizesthai contend, strive]

ag·o·ny (ag′ə·nē) n. pl. **·nies** 1 Intense suffering of body or mind. 2 Any violent emotion. 3 Violent striving or effort. 4 The struggle that sometimes precedes death. [<Gk. agōnia <agon contest]

a·go·ra (ag′ər·ə) n. pl. **ag·o·rae** (-ər·ē) or **ag·o·ras** 1 In ancient Greece, a popular assembly. 2 A place of popular assembly.

a·gou·ti (ə·gōō′tē) n. pl. **·tis** or **·ties** A large, burrowing rodent of tropical America with dark, gray-flecked fur. Also **a·gou′ty.**[<Sp.aguti<Tupian]

agr. agricultural; agriculture; agriculturist.

a·grar·i·an (ə·grâr′ē·ən) adj. 1 Pertaining to land or its distribution. 2 Agricultural. —n. One who advocates a more equitable distribution of land or farm income. [<L ager field] —**a·grar′i·an·ism** n.

Agouti

a·gree (ə·grē′) v. **a·greed**, **a·gree·ing** v.i. 1 To give consent; accede: with to. 2 To be in harmony or in accord. 3 To be of one mind; concur: with with. 4 To come to terms, as in the details of a transaction: with about or on. 5 To be acceptable; suit: with with. 6 Gram. To correspond in person, number, case, or gender. —v.t. 7 To grant as a concession: with a noun clause: I agree that it is difficult. [<L ad to + gratus pleasing] —**Syn.** 1 acquiesce, assent. 2 coincide, harmonize. 3 approve, accept.

a·gree·a·ble (ə·grē′ə·bəl) adj. 1 Pleasing; pleasurable. 2 Ready or inclined to agree: He is agreeable to your proposal. 3 Being in accordance or conformity. —**a·gree′a·bil′i·ty, a·gree′a·ble·ness** n. —**a·gree′a·bly** adv.

a·greed (ə·grēd′) adj. 1 In agreement; united. 2 Settled by consent or contract. 3 Admitted or conceded; granted.

a·gree·ment (ə·grē′mənt) n. 1 The act of agreeing. 2 The state of being agreed or in accord; conformity. 3 An arrangement or understanding between two or more people, countries, etc. 4 A contract. 5 Correspondence between words as to number, person, gender, or case.

ag·ri·bus·i·ness (ag′rə·biz′·nis, -niz) n. All those commercial activities associated with agriculture, including the production, processing, and distribution of farm products and the manufacture of farm equipment. [<AGRI(CULTURE) + BUSINESS]

ag·ri·cul·ture (ag′rə·kul′chər) n. The act or science of cultivating the soil and of raising food crops and livestock; farming. [<L ager field + cultura cultivation] —**ag′ri·cul′tur·al** adj. —**ag′ri·cul′tur·al·ly** adv.

ag·ri·cul·tur·ist (ag′rə·kul′chər·ist) n. One who studies or practices agriculture. Also **ag′ri·cul′tur·al·ist.**

ag·ri·mo·ny (ag′rə·mō′nē) n. pl. **·nies** A perennial herb with small yellow flowers and bristly fruit. [<Gk. argemōnē]

agro- combining form Of or pertaining to fields or agriculture: agronomy. [<Gk. <agros field]

a·gron·o·my (ə·gron′ə·mē) n. The application of scientific principles to the cultivation of land. [<Gk. agronomos an overseer of lands] —**ag·ro·nom·ic** (ag′rə·nom′ik) or **·i·cal** adj. —**a·gron′o·mist** n.

a·ground (ə·ground′) adv. & adj. On the shore or bottom, as a vessel; stranded.

agt. agent; agreement.

a·gue (ā′gyōō) n. Intermittent fever or chills and fever. [<L (febris) acuta an acute fever] —**a′gu·ish** adj.

ah (ä) interj. An exclamation expressive of various emotions, as surprise, triumph, satisfaction, contempt, etc.

a·ha (ä·hä′) interj. An exclamation expressing surprise, triumph, or mockery.

a·head (ə·hed′) adv. 1 At the head or front. 2 In advance. 3 Onward; forward. —**ahead of** In advance of. —**get ahead** To succeed socially, financially, etc.

a·hoy (ə·hoi′) interj. Ho there! a call used in hailing: ship ahoy! [<AH + HOY]

aid (ād) v.t. & v.i. To render assistance (to). —n. 1 Help; assistance. 2 A person or thing that helps. 3 An aide. [<

L adjuvare give help to] —**aid′er** n.

aide (ād) n. 1 An assistant. 2 AIDE-DE-CAMP. [F]

aide-de-camp (ād′də·kamp′) n. pl. **aides-de-camp** An officer in the army, navy, etc., acting as a confidential assistant to a superior officer. Also **aid′-de-camp′.** [<F aide de camp, lit., field assistant]

AIDS (ādz) n. An infectious disease that attacks the human immune system, caused by a retrovirus, spread by transfer of infected blood or by sexual contact, usually fatal. [<A(CQUIRED) I(MMUNO) D(EFICIENCY) S(YNDROME)]

ai·gret (ā′gret, ā·gret′) n. An ornamental tuft of feathers or gems. Also **ai′grette.** [<F aigrette an egret]

ail (āl) v.t. 1 To cause uneasiness or pain to; trouble; make ill. —v.i. 2 To be somewhat ill; feel pain. [<OE eglan] —**ail′ing** adj.

ai·lan·thus (ā·lan′thəs) n. Any of several tall deciduous trees of Asiatic origin; tree of heaven. [<native Indonesian name]

ai·le·ron (ā′lə·ron) n. Any of several types of control surfaces of an airplane, usu. near the trailing edge of the wing, used to produce rolling on the longitudinal axis. [<L ala wing] • See AIRPLANE.

ail·ment (āl′mənt) n. Any illness of body or mind, esp. a minor one.

aim (ām) v.t. 1 To direct, as a missile, blow, weapon, word, or act, toward or against some thing or person. —v.i. 2 To have a purpose; endeavor: with an infinitive: to aim to please. 3 To direct a missile, weapon, etc. —n. 1 The act of aiming. 2 The line of direction of anything aimed. 3 Design; purpose; intention. [<L ad- to + aestimare estimate] —**Syn.** n. 3 goal, end, aspiration, endeavor, intent.

aim·less (ām′lis) adj. Wanting in aim or purpose. —**aim′less·ly** adv. —**aim′less·ness** n.

ain't (ānt) Nonstand. & Regional Contraction of am not; also used for are not, is not, has not, and have not.

Ai·nu (ī′nōō) n. 1 One of a primitive, aboriginal people of Japan, now found only in the northern parts. 2 The language of the Ainu.

air (âr) n. 1 The gaseous envelope of the earth, consisting chiefly of nitrogen and oxygen; the atmosphere. 2 The open space around and above the earth. 3 A wind; breeze. 4 Utterance or publicity: to give air to one's opinions. 5 Peculiar or characteristic appearance or impression: an air of mystery. 6 pl. Artificial manners or affectations: to put on airs. 7 Travel or transportation by aircraft. 8 Music A melody or tune. —**in the air** 1 Prevalent; abroad, as gossip. 2 Not finally decided or settled: also **up in the air.** —v.t. 1 To expose to the air, so as to dry, ventilate, etc. 2 To make public; display; exhibit. [<Gk. aēr air, mist] —Syn. n. 5 demeanor, look, mien, manner, way.

air base A base for operations by aircraft.

air bladder A sac filled with air, found in many aquatic animals and plants. Also **air cell.**

air·borne (âr′bôrn′, -bōrn′) adj. 1 Transported through the air, esp. in aircraft. 2 Not on the ground; aloft.

air brake A brake operated by compressed air.

air·brush (âr′brush′) n. An implement for spraying liquids, esp. paint, by compressed air.

air·burst (âr′bûrst′) n. An explosion in the air, as of a bomb or projectile.

air·bus (âr′bus′) n. A large airplane designed to accommodate several hundred passengers.

air-con·di·tion (âr′kən·dish′ən) v.t. To equip with or ventilate by air conditioning. —**air′-con·di·tioned** adj.

air conditioner A machine to provide air conditioning.

air conditioning A system for controlling the temperature, purity, and humidity of air in buildings, cars, etc.

air-cool (âr′kōōl′) v.t. To cool, as engine cylinders, with a flow of air. —**air′-cooled′** adj.

air·craft (âr′kraft′, -kräft′) n. Any form of craft designed for flight through the air, as airplanes, dirigibles, etc.

aircraft carrier A large ship designed to carry aircraft, with a level upper flight deck usu. extending beyond the bow and stern.

air·drome (âr′drōm′) n. An airport.

air·drop (âr′drop′) n. Personnel, food, equipment, and other supplies dropped by parachute from an aircraft. —v.t. & v.i. **dropped**, **·drop·ping** To drop (personnel, supplies, etc.) by parachute from an aircraft.

Aire·dale (âr′dāl) *n.* A large terrier with a wiry tan coat and black markings. [< *Airedale,* the valley of the Aire River in Yorkshire, England]

air·field (âr′fēld′) *n.* An airport or landing strip.

air·foil (âr′foil′) *n.* A part of an aircraft, as a wing, rudder, etc., designed to produce or be subject to certain forces when in motion through the air.

Airedale

air force The air arm of a country's defense forces.

air gun 1 A gun impelling a missile by compressed air. **2** A device for spraying liquids by compressed air.

air hole 1 A hole for the flow of air. **2** An opening in the ice over a body of water. **3** AIR POCKET.

air·i·ly (âr′ə·lē) *adv.* In a light or airy manner; jauntily.

air·i·ness (âr′ē·nis) *n.* The quality of being airy.

air·ing (âr′ing) *n.* **1** An exposure to the air, as for drying. **2** Public exposure or discussion. **3** A walk or drive outdoors.

air lane An established route for air traffic.

air·less (âr′lis) *adj.* **1** Destitute of air. **2** Destitute of fresh air, a breeze, etc.; close. —**air′less·ness** *n.*

air letter 1 An airmail letter. **2** An international airmail letter consisting of a single folded sheet.

air·lift (âr′lift′) *n.* The operation of transporting foodstuffs, other commodities, and personnel by airplane during land blockade. —*v.t. & v.i.* To transport (food and supplies) by airplane.

air·line (âr′līn′) *n.* **1** A regular route traveled by aircraft carrying freight and passengers. **2** The business organization operating such a system. —*adj.* Of or for an airline.

air·lin·er (âr′lī′nər) *n.* A large, passenger aircraft operated by an airline.

air·lock (âr′lok′) *n.* An airtight chamber for adjusting the air pressure between regions of different atmospheric pressure.

air·mail (âr′māl′) *n.* **1** Mail carried by airplane. **2** A postal system of carrying mail by airplane. —*v.t.* To send by airmail.

air·man (âr′mən) *n. pl.* **air·men 1** Any person who is occupied with flying, maintaining, or servicing aircraft. **2** An enlisted man or woman in the U.S. Air Force.

air mass *Meteorol.* Any large portion of the atmosphere having little variation of temperature, pressure, moisture, etc.

air mile A nautical mile by air.

air·plane (âr′plān′) *n.* A heavier-than-air flying craft,

cabin cockpit   aerial mast   aerial   fin   rudder   elevator   spinner   cowling   stabilizer   fuselage   trailing edge of wing   exhaust   propeller   retractable undercarriage   aileron   leading edge of wing

Airplane

supported by aerodynamic forces and propelled by an engine or engines.

air pocket An atmospheric condition that causes an airplane to have a sudden brief drop in altitude.

air·port (âr′pôrt′, -pōrt′) *n.* An area for aircraft takeoffs and landings, together with buildings for maintenance, storage, and passenger service.

air pressure The pressure of the atmosphere or of compressed air.

air raid An attack by military aircraft, esp. bombers.

air rifle A rifle utilizing compressed air to propel a pellet.

air sac Any of the hollow cavities in the body and bones of a bird and communicating with its lungs.

air shaft A shaft intended to secure ventilation of a building, tunnel, etc.

air·ship (âr′ship′) *n.* A lighter-than-air aircraft having means for propulsion and steering; dirigible.

air·sick·ness (âr′sik′nis) *n.* Nausea due to varied motions of an aircraft in which one is traveling. —**air′sick′** *adj.*

air·space (âr′spās′) *n.* The part of the atmosphere over a designated geographical area that is subject to territorial jurisdiction or international law in respect to use by aircraft, rockets, etc.

air speed The speed of an aircraft with respect to the air rather than to the ground.

air·strip (âr′strip′) *n.* A runway for airplanes, usu. for temporary use.

air·tight (âr′tīt′) *adj.* **1** Not allowing air to escape or enter. **2** Having no weak places; flawless: an *airtight* argument.

air·waves (âr′wāvz′) *n. pl.* The medium for transmitting radio or television signals.

air·way (âr′wā′) *n.* **1** Any passageway for air, as an air shaft. **2** AIR LANE. **3** *pl.* AIRWAVES.

air·wor·thy (âr′wûr′thē) *adj.* Being in fit condition for flight. —**air′wor′thi·ness** *n.*

air·y (âr′ē) *adj.* **air·i·er, air·i·est 1** Of the air. **2** In the air. **3** Open to the air; breezy. **4** Light or delicate, as air. **5** Vivacious; gay. **6** Lightly nonchalant or flippant. **7** Without reality; visionary.

aisle (īl) *n.* **1** A passageway to or between rows of seats. **2** A similar passageway, as between trees. **3** An interior division of a church, alongside the main part or nave. [< OF *aile, ele* wing (of a building)] —**aisled** (īld) *adj.*

a·jar¹ (ə·jär′) *adv. & adj.* Partly open, as a door. [ME *a-* on + *char* a turning]

a·jar² (ə·jär′) *adv. & adj.* In a jarring or discordant condition; wanting in harmony.

AK Alaska (P.O. abbr.).

a·kim·bo (ə·kim′bō) *adv.* With the hands on hips and the elbows outward. [ME *in kenebowe* in a sharp bow]

a·kin (ə·kin′) *adj. & adv.* **1** Of the same kin; related by blood. **2** Of similar nature or qualities.

al-¹ *prefix* The Arabic definite article, as in *algebra.*

al-² Var. of AD-.

-al¹ *suffix of adjectives and nouns* Of or pertaining to; characterized by: *personal, musical.* [< L *-alis*]

-al² *suffix of nouns* The act or process of: used with a verb stem, as in *betrayal, refusal.* [< L *-alia,* neut. pl. of *-alis*]

AL Alabama (P.O. abbr.).

Al aluminum.

à la (ä′lä, ä′lə; *Fr.* à là) After the manner or in the style of. Also **a la.** [F]

Ala. Alabama.

al·a·bas·ter (al′ə·bas′tər, -bäs′-) *n.* **1** A white or delicately tinted fine-grained gypsum. **2** A banded variety of calcite. —*adj.* **1** Made of or like alabaster. **2** Smooth and white. [< Gk. *alabast(r)os*] —**al′a·bas′trine** (-trin) *adj.*

à la carte (ä′ lə kärt′) According to the menu: said of meals, menus, etc., in which each item of food has a separate price. [F, lit., by the bill of fare]

a·lack (ə·lak′) *interj. Archaic* An exclamation of regret or sorrow. Also **a·lack·a·day** (ə·lak′ə·dā′). [< *ah* oh + *lack* failure, lack]

a·lac·ri·ty (ə·lak′rə·tē) *n.* **1** Cheerful willingness: She accepted the challenging assignment with *alacrity.* **2** Prompt and lively action: to respond to the taunt with *alacrity.* [< L *alacer* lively] —**a·lac′ri·tous** *adj.*

à la mode (ä′ lə mōd′, al′ə mōd′) **1** According to the mode; in the fashion. **2** Served with ice cream: pie *à la mode.* **3** Cooked in a rich sauce with vegetables: beef *à la mode.* [F, lit., in the fashion]

a·larm (ə·lärm′) *n.* **1** Sudden fear or apprehension. **2** Any sound or signal to warn of danger or arouse from sleep. **3** A mechanism, as of a clock, giving such a signal. —*v.t.* **1**

To strike with sudden fear. **2** To arouse to a sense of danger; give warning to. [< Ital. *all' arme* to arms]

alarm clock A clock that can be set to sound an alarm at a predetermined hour.

a·larm·ing (ə·lär'ming) *adj.* Causing alarm or apprehension. —**a·larm'ing·ly** *adv.*

a·larm·ist (ə·lär'mist) *n.* One who needlessly excites or tries to excite alarm. —*adj.* Provoking unnecessary alarm. —**a·larm'ism** *n.*

a·las (ə·las', ə·läs') *interj.* An exclamation of disappointment, regret, sorrow, etc. [< OF *a* ah! + *las* wretched]

Alas. Alaska.

alb (alb) *n. Eccl.* A white linen vestment, reaching to the ankles and girded at the waist, worn by a priest celebrating Mass. [< L *alba (vestis)* white (garment)]

Alb. Albania; Albanian.

al·ba·core (al'bə·kôr, -kōr) *n.* Any of various tunas or related fish. [< Ar. *al* the + *bukr* young camel]

Al·ba·ni·a (al·bā'nē·ə, -bān'yə) *n.* A Balkan republic s of Yugoslavia, 10,629 sq. mi., cap. Tirana. —**Al·ba'ni·an** *adj., n.* • See map at BALKAN STATES.

al·ba·tross (al'bə·trôs, -tros) *n. pl.* **·tross·es** or **·tross** A large, web-footed sea bird with long narrow wings and a hooked beak. [< Pg. *alcatraz* pelican]

al·be·it (ôl·bē'it) *conj.* Even though; although. [ME *al be it* although it be completely]

al·bi·no (al·bī'nō) *n. pl.* **·nos** **1** A person having a genetic deficiency of normal pigmentation, resulting in a very pale skin, whitish hair, and a pale or pinkish eye coloration. **2** An animal or plant lacking normal pigmentation. [< L *albus* white] —**al·bin·ic** (al·bin'ik) *adj.* —**al·bin·ism** (al'bə·niz'əm) *n.*

al·bum (al'bəm) *n.* **1** A blank book for holding photographs, autographs, stamps, etc. **2** A long-playing phonograph record or records encased in a jacket or box. **3** A booklike container for a number of phonograph records. **4** A bound anthology, as of musical compositions. [< L, white tablet]

Albatross

al·bu·men (al·byōō'mən) *n.* **1** The white of an egg. **2** The nutritive material surrounding the embryo in a seed. **3** ALBUMIN. [< L *albus* white]

al·bu·min (al·byōō'mən) *n.* Any of a class of protein substances found in many animal and vegetable fluids and tissues. [< L *albumen*. See ALBUMEN.] —**al·bu'mi·nous** (-nəs), **al·bu'mi·nose** (-nōs) *adj.*

al·caz·ar (al·kaz'ər, al'kə·zär; *Sp.* äl·kä'thär) *n.* A Moorish castle in Spain; esp. **the Alcazar**, a Moorish palace in Seville. [< Sp. < Ar. *al-qasr* the castle]

al·che·my (al'kə·mē) *n.* **1** The primitive chemistry of the Middle Ages, characterized by the search for a way to change base metals into gold. **2** Any mysterious changing of the structure or appearance of things. Also **al'chy·my.** [< Ar. *al-kīmiyā* < L Gk. *chēmeia* transmutation of metals] —**al·chem·ic** (al·kem'ik) *adj.* —**al·chem'i·cal·ly** *adv.* —**al·che·mist** (al'kə·mist) *n.*

al·co·hol (al'kə·hôl, -hol) *n.* **1** A volatile, flammable, colorless, potable but intoxicating liquid obtained from fermentation of the sugars in grain, grapes, etc., by yeast; ethyl alcohol. **2** Any potable liquor containing ethyl alcohol, as brandy, gin, etc. **3** A very toxic liquid similar chemically to ethyl alcohol, obtained from wood tar or synthetically; methanol. **4** Any of a large group of organic compounds in which one or more hydrogen atoms in a hydrocarbon have been replaced by a hydroxyl group. [< Med.L, orig., fine powder < Ar. *al-koh'l* the powdered antimony]

al·co·hol·ic (al'kə·hôl'ik, -hol'-) *adj.* **1** Of or containing alcohol. **2** Caused by alcohol or alcoholism. **3** Suffering from alcoholism. —*n.* One who suffers from alcoholism.

al·co·hol·ism (al'kə·hôl'iz·əm, -hol'-) *n.* The habitual and compulsive use of alcoholic beverages.

al·cove (al'kōv) *n.* **1** A recess connected with or at the side of a larger room. **2** Any embowered or secluded spot.

3 A niche in the face of a cliff or the wall of a building. [< Ar. *al-qobbah* the vaulted chamber]

Al·deb·a·ran (al·deb'ə·rən) *n.* A bright, red, double star in the constellation Taurus. [< Ar. *al-dabarān* the follower (i.e., of the Pleiades)]

al·de·hyde (al'də·hīd) *n.* Any of a group of organic compounds derived from the alcohols by gentle oxidation. [< AL(COHOL) + DEHYD(ROGENIZED)]

al·der (ôl'dər) *n.* Any of various shrubs or small trees related to the birch. [< OE *alor*]

al·der·man (ôl'dər·mən) *n. pl.* **·men** **1** A member of a municipal legislative body who often exercises certain judicial functions. **2** In England and Ireland, a member of the higher branch of a town council. [< OE *ealdorman* head man] —**al'der·man·ic** (-man'ik) *adj.*

Al·der·ney (ôl'dər·nē) *n.* One of a breed of cattle originally peculiar to the island of Alderney of the Channel Islands.

ale (āl) *n.* A beverage resembling beer made from a fermented infusion of malt, usu. flavored with hops. [< OE *ealu*]

a·le·a·tor·ic (ā'lē·ə·tôr'ik, -tō'rik) *adj.* **1** Based on chance or on improvisation: *aleatoric* music. **2** ALEATORY.

a·le·a·to·ry (ā'lē·ə·tôr'ē, -tō'rē) *adj.* Of or dependent upon chance or luck. —*n.* Aleatoric music. [< L *aleator* gambler < *alea* a die, chance]

ale·house (āl'hous') *n.* A saloon or tavern.

a·lert (ə·lûrt') *adj.* **1** Keenly watchful; vigilant. **2** Lively; nimble. **3** Intelligent. —*n.* **1** A warning or warning signal against sudden attack or danger. **2** The time such a warning is in effect. —**on the alert** On the lookout; ready. —*v.t.* To warn, as of a threatened attack or danger. [< Ital. *all' erta* on the watch] —**a·lert'ly** *adv.* —**a·lert'ness** *n.* —Syn. *adj.* **1** prepared, ready. **2** quick, brisk. **3** active, quick, perceptive, responsive.

A·leut (ə·lōōt') *n. pl.* **A·leuts** or **A·leut 1** A native of the Aleutian Islands. **2** A subfamily of the Eskimo-Aleut family of languages. —**A·leu·tian** (ə·lōō'shən) *adj., n.*

ale·wife (āl'wīf') *n. pl.* **·wives** A small North American fish related to the herring. [?]

Al·ex·an·dri·an (al'ig·zan'drē·ən, -zän'-) *adj.* **1** Of or pertaining to Alexander the Great. **2** Of or pertaining to Alexandria. **3** ALEXANDRINE. —*n.* **1** A native or inhabitant of Alexandria. **2** An Alexandrine verse.

Al·ex·an·drine (al'ig·zan'drin, -drēn, -zän'-) *n.* A line of verse having six iambic feet with the caesura generally after the third. —*adj.* Composed of Alexandrines.

al·fal·fa (al·fal'fə) *n.* A cloverlike plant used as forage. [< Sp. < Ar. *al-fasfasah* the best kind of fodder]

al·fres·co (al·fres'kō) *adv.* In the open air. —*adj.* Occurring outdoors, as a meal. Also **al fresco.** [< Ital.]

Alg. Algeria; Algerian.

alg. algebra.

al·ga (al'gə) *n. pl.* **·gae** (-jē) Any of a large variety of primitive chlorophyll-bearing plants widely distributed in aquatic and moist habitats, and including the seaweeds, kelps, diatoms, etc. [< L, seaweed] —**al·gal** (al'gəl) *adj.*

al·ge·bra (al'jə·brə) *n.* **1** A generalized arithmetic in which symbols representing any of a set of numbers are used in calculations. **2** A defined set of elements with various operations defined on the set. [< Ital. < Ar. *al-jebr* the reunion of broken parts, bone-setting] —**al'ge·bra'ic** (-brā'ik) *adj.* —**al'ge·bra'i·cal·ly** *adv.* —**al'ge·bra'ist** *n.*

Al·ge·ri·a (al·jir'ē·ə) *n.* A republic of NW Africa, 919,352 sq. mi., cap. Algiers. —**Al·ge'ri·an** *adj., n.* • See map at AFRICA.

-algia *suffix* Pain or disease of: *neuralgia.* [< Gk. *algos* pain]

Algon. Algonquian.

Al·gon·qui·an (al·gong'kē·ən, -kwē·ən) *n.* **1** A large family of languages used by many tribes of North American Indians, including the Algonquin, Blackfoot, Cheyenne, Cree, Ojibwa, Shawnee and other tribes. **2** A member of one of the tribes belonging to this language family. —*adj.* Of or pertaining to the Algonquian family of languages.

Al·gon·quin (al·gong'kin, -kwin) *n.* **1** A member of a tribe of Algonquin Indians. **2** The language spoken by this tribe. Also **Al·gon·kin** (al·gong'kin).

Al·ham·bra (al·ham′brə) *n.* The medieval palace of the Moorish kings at Granada, Spain. [< Ar. *al-hamrā'* the red (house)]

a·li·as (ā′lē·əs) *n. pl.* **a·li·as·es** An assumed name: She used an *alias* to cash the stolen checks. —*adv.* Called by the assumed name of: Horace Jones, *alias* Howard Smith. [L, at another time or place]

al·i·bi (al′ə·bī) *n. pl.* **·bis** 1 A form of defense by which the accused undertakes to show that he was elsewhere when the crime was committed. 2 *Informal* Any excuse. —*v.i.* **·bied, ·bi·ing** *Informal* To make excuses for oneself. [< L, elsewhere]

al·i·en (ā′lē·ən, āl′yən) *adj.* 1 Of another country or people; foreign. 2 Opposed; contrary; inconsistent: with *to:* actions *alien* to his character. —*n.* 1 A foreign-born person who is not a citizen of the country in which he resides. 2 A person of another race, country, religion, etc. 3 One excluded; an outsider. [< L *alienus*] —**Syn.** *adj.* 2 contradictory, foreign, unlike.

al·ien·a·ble (āl′yən·ə·bəl, ā′lē·ən-) *adj.* That can be transferred, as property, to the ownership of another. —**al′ien·a·bil′i·ty** *n.*

al·ien·ate (āl′yən·āt, ā′lē·ən-) *v.t.* **·at·ed, ·at·ing** 1 To make indifferent or unfriendly; estrange. 2 To cause to feel estranged or withdrawn from society. 3 To transfer, as property, to the ownership of another. —**al′ien·a′tion, al′ien·a′tor** *n.*

a·light¹ (ə·līt′) *v.i.* **a·light·ed** or **a·lit, a·light·ing** 1 To descend and come to rest, as after flight. 2 To dismount. 3 To come by accident: with *on* or *upon.* [< OE *ā-* out, off + *līhtan* alight, orig., make light]

a·light² (ə·līt′) *adj. & adv.* Lighted; on fire. [ME *alihten* light up]

a·lign (ə·līn′) *v.t.* 1 To place or bring into a straight line. 2 To bring (oneself, a group, etc.) to the support of an idea, cause, etc. —*v.i.* 3 To come into line. [< F *a-* to + *ligne* line] —**a·lign′ment** *n.*

a·like (ə·līk′) *adj.* Having resemblance; like one another. —*adv.* In like manner. [< OE *gelīc*] —**a·like′ness** *n.*

al·i·ment (al′ə·mənt) *n.* Nourishment; food. [< L *alimentum < alere* nourish] —**al·i·men·tal** (al′ə·men′təl) *adj.* —**al′i·men′tal·ly** *adv.*

al·i·men·ta·ry (al′ə·men′tər·ē) *adj.* 1 Supplying nourishment. 2 Of or pertaining to food or nutrition.

alimentary canal The digestive tract between the mouth and the anus, including esophagus, stomach, and intestines.

al·i·men·ta·tion (al′ə·men·tā′shən) *n.* 1 The act or process of supplying nutrition. 2 Maintenance; support. —**al′·i·men′ta·tive** (-men′tə·tiv) *adj.*

al·i·mo·ny (al′ə·mō′nē) *n.* The allowance made to a woman from her husband's estate or income, for her maintenance after her divorce or legal separation. [< L *alimonia* food, support < *alere* nourish]

a·line (ə·līn′) *v.* **a·lined, a·lin·ing** ALIGN. —**a·line′ment** *n.*

a·lit (ə·lit′) A *p.t. & p.p.* of ALIGHT¹.

a·live (ə·līv′) *adj.* 1 In a living state; having life. 2 In existence, operation, etc. 3 In an animated state; lively. —**alive to** Aware of; alert to. —**alive with** Abounding in (living things). [< OE *on līfe* in life] —**Syn.** 3 active, alert, vivacious.

a·liz·a·rin (ə·liz′ə·rin) *n.* An orange-red synthetic compound formerly obtained from madder, used as a red dye and to manufacture other dyes. Also **a·liz·a·rine** (ə·liz′ə·rin, -rēn). [< F *alizari* madder]

al·ka·li (al′kə·lī) *n. pl.* **·lis** or **·lies** 1 Any of various highly reactive compounds that dissolve readily in water to form hydroxyl ions, neutralize acids, saponify fats, and turn red litmus blue. 2 Any compound that will neutralize an acid, as sodium carbonate, magnesia, etc. 3 Mineral matter found in soil and natural water and capable of neutralizing acid. [< Ar. *al-qalīy* the ashes of saltwort] —**al·ka·line** (al′kə·lin, -līn) *adj.* —**al′ka·lin′i·ty** (-lin′ə·tē) *n.*

al·ka·lize (al′kə·līz) *v.t. & v.i.* **·lized, ·liz·ing** To make or become like an alkali. —**al′ka·li·za′tion** *n.*

al·ka·loid (al′kə·loid) *n.* A nitrogenous organic base, usu.

of vegetable origin, toxic in effect on animals and man, as strychnine, caffeine, morphine, etc. —**al′ka·loi′dal** *adj.*

Al·ko·ran (al′kō·rän′, -ran′) *n.* The Koran. —**Al′ko·ran′ic** (-ran′ik) *adj.*

all (ôl) *adj.* 1 The entire substance or extent of: *all* wisdom. 2 The entire number of. 3 The greatest possible: in *all* haste. 4 Any whatever: beyond *all* doubt. 5 Every: used in phrases with *manner, sorts,* and *kinds.* 6 Nothing except; only: He was *all* skin and bones. —*n.* 1 Everything that one has. 2 Whole being; totality. —*pron.* 1 Everyone: *All* are condemned. 2 Each one. 3 Everything: *All* is in readiness. 4 Every part, as of a whole: *All* of it is gone. —**above all** Primarily. —**after all** 1 On the other hand. 2 In spite of everything. —**all in all** All things considered. —**at all** 1 In any way: I can't come *at all.* 2 To any degree or extent: no luck *at all.* —**for all** To the degree that: *For all* I care, you can go without me. —**in all** Including everything; all told. —*adv.* 1 Wholly; entirely; traveling *all* through the night. 2 Exclusively; only: That portion is *all* for me. 3 For each; on each side: a score of three *all.* —**all along** All the time: I knew it *all along.* —**all but** 1 Almost: I was *all but* drowned. 2 Every one except: He took *all but* six. —**all in** *Informal* Wearied. —**all of** No less than; quite: It's *all of* ten miles. —**all out** Making every effort. —**all over** 1 Finished; past and gone. 2 Everywhere. 3 *Informal* Typically; in every way: That's George *all over.* —**all the** (**better, more,** etc.). So much the (better, more, etc.) [< OE]

Al·lah (al′ə, ä′lə) In the Muslim religion, the one supreme being; God. [< Ar.]

all-A·mer·i·can (ôl′ə·mer′ə·kən) *adj.* 1 Composed of or considered as representing the best in America: an *all-American* football team; an *all-American* boy. 2 Of or composed of Americans or products made in America. —*n.* 1 A hypothetical team, as of football players, selected from U.S. college players considered best in a season. 2 A player selected for such a team.

all-a·round (ôl′ə·round′) *adj.* 1 Having many uses. 2 Excelling in many things; versatile.

al·lay (ə·lā′) *v.t.* 1 To lessen the violence or reduce the intensity of. 2 To lay to rest, as fears; pacify; calm. [< OE *ā-* away + *lecgan* lay] —**al·lay′er** *n.*

all-clear (ôl′klir′) *n.* The signal indicating that an air raid is over. Also **all clear.**

al·le·ga·tion (al′ə·gā′shən) *n.* 1 The act of alleging. 2 That which is alleged. 3 Something alleged without proof. 4 *Law* The assertion that a party to a suit undertakes to prove.

al·lege (ə·lej′) *v.t.* **al·leged, al·leg·ing** 1 To assert to be true without proving; affirm. 2 To plead as an excuse, in support of or in opposition to a claim or accusation. [? < L *allegare* to send on a mission, dispatch] —**al·lege′a·ble** *adj.* —**al·leg′er** *n.*

al·leged (ə·lejd′, ə·lej′id) *adj.* So represented but not proven: his *alleged* crime. —**al·leg′ed·ly** (-lej′id-) *adv.*

al·le·giance (ə·lē′jəns) *n.* Loyalty, or an obligation of loyalty, to a government, a superior, a cause, etc. [< OF *ligeance < liege.* See LIEGE.]

al·le·gor·ic (al′ə·gôr′ik, -gor′-) *adj.* Pertaining to or containing allegory. Also **al′le·gor′i·cal.** —**al′le·gor′i·cal·ly** *adv.*

al·le·go·rize (al′ə·gə·rīz) *v.* **·rized, ·riz·ing** *v.t.* 1 To relate or explain as or in the manner of an allegory. —*v.i.* 2 To make or use allegory. —**al·le·go·ri·za·tion** (al′ə·gôr′ə·zā′·shən, -gor′-), **al′le·go·riz′er** *n.*

al·le·go·ry (al′ə·gôr′ē, -gō′rē) *n. pl.* **·ries** 1 A story or narrative that teaches a moral or truth by using people, animals, events, etc., as symbols of that moral or truth. 2 Any symbolic representation in literature or art. [< Gk. *allēgoria,* lit., a speaking otherwise] —**al′le·go′rist** (-gôr′ist, -gō′rist, -gər·ist) *n.*

al·le·gret·to (al′ə·gret′ō, *Ital.* ä′lā·gret′tō) *adj. & adv. Music* Somewhat slower than allegro. —*n. pl.* **·tos** An allegretto movement or passage. [Ital.]

al·le·gro (ə·lā′grō, ə·leg′rō; *Ital.* äl·lā′grō) *adj. & adv. Music* Quick; lively. —*n. pl.* **·gros** An allegro passage or movement. [Ital.]

---

add, āce, câre, pălm; end, ēven; it, īce; odd, ōpen, ôrder; tŏŏk, pōōl; up, bûrn; ə = a in *above*, u in *focus;* yōō = u in *fuse;* oil; pout; check; go; ring; thin; ţhis; zh, *vision.* < derived from; ? origin uncertain or unknown.

al·le·lu·ia (al'ə·lōō'yə) n. & interj. HALLELUJAH.

al·ler·gen (al'ər·jən) n. Any substance capable of producing allergy. —**al·ler·gen·ic** (al'ər·jen'ik) adj.

al·ler·gic (ə·lûr'jik) adj. 1 Of or caused by allergy. 2 Highly susceptible to. 3 Informal Having an aversion.

al·ler·gist (al'ər·jist) n. A doctor specializing in allergies.

al·ler·gy (al'ər·jē) n. pl. ·gies A condition of heightened susceptibility to a substance, as smoke or pollen. [< G Allergie, lit., altered reaction]

al·le·vi·ate (ə·lē've·āt) v.t. ·at·ed, ·at·ing To make lighter or easier to bear; relieve. [< L alleviare < ad- to + levis light] —**al·le'vi·a'tion, al·le'vi·a'tor** n. —**al·le·vi·a·tive** (ə·lē've·ā'tiv, ə·lē've·ə·tiv) adj. —**Syn.** allay, assuage, lessen, mitigate.

al·ley (al'ē) n. pl. ·leys 1 A narrow passageway, esp. one behind or between city buildings. 2 A walk or lane bordered by trees, flowers, etc. 3 A bowling lane. [< OF alee a going, passage < aler go]

al·ley·way (al'ē·wā') n. An alley (def. 1).

All Fools' Day APRIL FOOLS' DAY.

all fours The four legs of a quadruped, or the arms and legs of a person.

All·hal·lows (ôl'hal'ōz) n. All Saints' Day, Nov. 1.

al·li·ance (ə·lī'əns) n. 1 A formal treaty or agreement between countries, states, parties, etc; also, those involved in such an agreement. 2 Any union or relationship, as by blood, marriage, interests, etc. 3 Any similarity or affinity. [< L alligantia < alligare. See ALLY.]

al·lied (ə·līd') adj. 1 United, as by treaty, relationship, etc. 2 Similar in nature or qualities.

Al·lies (al'īz, ə·līz') 1 In World War I, Russia, France, Great Britain, and, later, the U.S., Italy, Japan, etc., the nations allied against Germany, Austria-Hungary, Bulgaria, and Turkey. 2 In World War II, Great Britain, the U.S.S.R., the U.S., and the other nations that fought the Axis. —**Al'lied** adj.

al·li·ga·tor (al'ə·gā'tər) n. 1 A large crocodilian reptile, found only in the southern U.S. and in China, having a shorter, blunter snout than the crocodile. 2 Leather made from the skin of the alligator. [< Sp. el lagarto the lizard < L lacertus]

alligator pear AVOCADO.

all-im·por·tant (ôl'im·pôr'tənt) adj. Very important; crucial; necessary.

all-in·clu·sive (ôl'in·klōō'siv) adj. Including everything.

al·lit·er·ate (ə·lit'ə·rāt) v. ·at·ed, ·at·ing v.i. 1 To use alliteration. 2 To constitute alliteration. —v.t. 3 To make alliterative. [< L ad- to + littera a letter (of the alphabet)]

al·lit·er·a·tion (ə·lit'ə·rā'shən) n. The use or repetition of a succession of words with the same initial letter or sound, as in "The river running round the rock." —**al·lit·er·a·tive** (ə·lit'ər·ə·tiv, ə·rā'tiv) adj. —**al·lit'er·a·tive·ly** adv.

al·lo·cate (al'ə·kāt) v.t. ·cat·ed, ·cat·ing 1 To set apart for a special purpose, as funds. 2 To apportion; assign, as a share or in amount. 3 To locate or localize, as a person or event. [< L ad- to + locare to place] —**al'lo·ca'tion** n.

al·lo·path (al'ə·path) n. One who practices or approves of allopathy. Also **al·lop·a·thist** (ə·lop'ə·thist).

al·lop·a·thy (ə·lop'ə·thē) n. The system of treating disease by producing conditions different from or incompatible with the effects of the disease. [< Gk. allos other + pathos suffering] —**al·lo·path·ic** (al'ə·path'ik) adj. —**al'lo·path'i·cal·ly** adv.

al·lot (ə·lot') v.t. **al·lot·ted, al·lot·ting** 1 To assign or distribute by lot. 2 To apportion or assign: with to. [< OF a- to + lot a portion, lot]

al·lot·ment (ə·lot'mənt) n. 1 The act of allotting or that which is allotted. 2 A portion or share.

al·lo·trope (al'ə·trōp) n. Any of the forms assumed by an allotropic element.

al·lot·ro·py (ə·lot'rə·pē) n. The occurrence of certain chemical elements, as carbon, oxygen, etc., in two or more forms exhibiting different properties. Also **al·lot'ro·pism'** (-rə·piz'əm). —**al·lo·trop·ic** (al'ə·trop'ik) adj. —**al·lo·trop'i·cal·ly** adv. [< Gk. allotropia variation < allos other + tropos turn, manner]

all-out (ôl'out') adj. Done with maximum effort; unrestrained. —adv. Without stint; with maximum effort.

al·low (ə·lou') v.t. 1 To permit to occur, do, have, enter, etc. 2 To admit; acknowledge as true or valid. 3 To make

provision for: Allow one yard for waste. 4 To grant; allot, as a share or portion. 5 Regional To maintain; declare. —**allow for** To make provision for; bear in mind: Allow for traffic. —**allow of** To permit or be subject to: Your remark allows of several interpretations. [< OF alouer place, use, assign < Med.L allocare to allocate and OF alouer, aloer approve < L allaudare extol] —**al·lowed'** adj.

al·low·a·ble (ə·lou'ə·bəl) adj. Permissible; admissible. —**al·low'a·ble·ness** n. —**al·low'a·bly** adv.

al·low·ance (ə·lou'əns) n. 1 The act of allowing. 2 That which is allowed. 3 An amount or portion, as of money or food, granted at regular intervals, for a specific purpose, etc. 4 A discount given, as for buying in volume, exchanging a used article, etc. 5 A compensation or consideration, as for circumstances, etc.: an allowance for late delivery. —v.t. ·anced, ·anc·ing 1 To put on an allowance. 2 To supply in limited or meager quantities.

al·low·ed·ly (ə·lou'id·lē) adv. Admittedly.

al·loy (al'oi, ə·loi') n. 1 A substance having metallic properties and consisting of a metal and at least one other element, usu. another metal. 2 Anything that reduces purity. —v.t. (ə·loi') 1 To reduce the purity of, as a metal, by mixing with an alloy. 2 To mix (metals) so as to form into an alloy. 3 To modify or debase, as by mixture with something inferior. [< L alligare to bind to]

all-pur·pose (ôl'pûr'pəs) adj. Generally useful; answering every purpose.

all-right (ôl'rīt') adj. Slang Honest, good, excellent, etc.: an all-right guy.

all right 1 Satisfactory: His work is all right. 2 Correct. 3 Uninjured; not hurt. 4 Informal Certainly; without a doubt: I'll be there all right! 5 Yes: usu. in answer to a question: May I leave now? All right.

all-round (ôl'round') adj. ALL-AROUND.

All Saints' Day A Christian festival commemorative of all saints, occurring Nov. 1.

All Souls' Day In certain Christian churches, a day of commemoration for the dead, usu. Nov. 2.

all·spice (ôl'spīs') n. 1 The berry of a West Indian tree; the pimento. 2 The fragrant spice made from it. 3 The tree itself. [So called because it seems to combine the flavors of several spices]

all-star (ôl'stär') adj. Consisting wholly of star performers, as the cast of a play.

all-time (ôl'tīm') adj. Of or for all time.

al·lude (ə·lōōd') v.i. **al·lud·ed, al·lud·ing** To make indirect or casual reference: with to. [< L alludere play with, joke] —**Syn.** hint, imply, insinuate, intimate, suggest.

al·lure (ə·lōōr') v.t. & v.i. **al·lured, al·lur·ing** To attract attention and interest; entice. —n. The ability to attract or fascinate. [< OF a- to + leurre a lure] —**al·lur'er, al·lure'·ment** n.

al·lur·ing (ə·lōōr'ing) adj. Attractive; fascinating. —**al·lur'ing·ly** adv. —**al·lur'ing·ness** n.

al·lu·sion (ə·lōō'zhən) n. 1 The act of alluding. 2 An indirect reference or mention. [< L allusus, p.p. of alludere. See ALLUDE.]

al·lu·sive (ə·lōō'siv) adj. Containing allusions. —**al·lu'sive·ly** adv. —**al·lu'sive·ness** n.

al·lu·vi·al (ə·lōō'vē·əl) adj. Pertaining to or composed of alluvium. —n. Alluvial soil.

al·lu·vi·um (ə·lōō'vē·əm) n. pl. ·vi·a (-vē-ə) or ·vi·ums Geol. Any deposit, as of sand or mud, transported and left by flowing water. [< L]

al·ly (ə·lī') v. **al·lied, al·ly·ing** v.t. 1 To unite or combine by some relationship: usu. used in the passive or reflexively. —v.i. 2 To enter into alliance; become allied. —n. (al'ī, ə·lī') pl. **al·lies** 1 A country, sovereign, group, etc., leagued with another or others, as by treaty. 2 Any friend, associate, or helper. [< L ad- to + ligare bind]

al·ma ma·ter (al'mə mä'tər, al'mə mā'tər, äl'mə mä'tər) The institution of learning that one has attended. [L, fostering mother]

al·ma·nac (ôl'mə·nak) n. 1 A yearly calendar giving weather forecasts, astronomical information, times of high and low tides, and other data. 2 An annual book containing facts and statistics on a large variety of subjects. [< Ar. al-manākh]

al·might·y (ôl·mī'tē) adj. 1 Able to do all things; omnipo-

tent. **2** *Informal* Great; extreme: an *almighty* defeat. —
adv. Slang Exceedingly: *almighty* mad. —**the Almighty**
God. [< OE < *eall* all + *mihtig* mighty] —**al·might'i·ly** *adv.*
—**al·might'i·ness** *n.*

al·mond (ä'mənd, am'ənd) *n.* **1** A small tree related to
the plum, cultivated in warm regions. **2** The edible, nutlike kernel of the fruit of this tree. [< Gk. *amygdalē*]

al·mon·er (al'mən·ər, ä'mən-) *n.* An official dispenser of
alms. [< L *eleemosyna* alms]

al·most (ôl'mōst, ôl·mōst') *adv.* Approximately; very
nearly; all but: *Almost* everyone attended; *almost* time for
supper. [< OE *eall* all + *mæst* most]

alms (ämz) *n. sing. & pl.* Money or gifts for the poor. [<
Gk. *eleēmosynē* < *eleos* pity]

alms·house (ämz'hous') *n.* A poorhouse.

al·oe (al'ō) *n. pl.* **·oes** Any of various liliaceous plants with
fleshy leaves, mostly native to Africa. [< Gk. *aloē*]

al·oes (al'ōz) *n. pl. (construed as sing.)* A bitter cathartic
made from certain species of aloe.

a·loft (ə·lôft', ə·loft') *adv.* **1** In or to a high or higher place;
on high; high up. **2** *Naut.* At or to the higher parts of a
ship's rigging. [< ON *a lopt* in (the) air]

a·lo·ha (ə·lō'ə, ä·lō'hä) *n. Hawaiian* Love: used also as a
salutation and a farewell.

a·lone (ə·lōn') *adv. & adj.* **1** Without company; solitary.
2 Without equal; unique. **3** Excluding all other people or
things; only: She *alone* understood. [ME *al* all + *one* one]

a·long (ə·lông', ə·long') *adv.* **1** Following the length of;
lengthwise. **2** Progressively onward. **3** In company or association: with *with*: I came *along* with my cousins. **4** As
a companion, necessary object, etc.: Bring a sweater
along. **5** Advanced: well *along* in years. **6** *Informal* Near;
approaching: with *about*: *along* about sundown. —**all
along** The whole time; from the outset. —**get along 1** To
go forward. **2** To manage in spite of difficulties. **3** To be
successful. **4** To exist together in harmony. **5** *Informal* To
go away. —*prep.* **1** In the line of; through or over the
length of: *along* the coast. **2** In agreement or harmony
with: *along* certain principles. [< OE *andlang*]

a·long·shore (ə·lông'shôr', ə·long'-, -shôr') *adv.* Along
the shore.

a·long·side (ə·lông'sīd', ə·long'-) *adv.* Close to or along
the side. —*prep.* Side by side with.

a·loof (ə·lōōf') *adj.* Distant or reserved, as in manner, interest, etc. —*adv.* At a distance. [< A-¹ + earlier *loof* luff]
—**a·loof'ly** *adv.* —**a·loof'ness** *n.*

a·loud (ə·loud') *adv.* Loudly or audibly.

alp (alp) *n.* **1** Any peak of the Alps. **2** A high mountain.
[< L *Alpes* the Alps]

al·pac·a (al·pak'ə) *n.* **1** A domesticated ruminant of
South America, resembling the
llama. **2** Its long, silky wool. **3** A
cloth made of this wool. [< Sp.]

al·pen·horn (al'pən·hôrn') *n.* A
very long, wooden horn, used by
herdsmen in the Alps.

al·pen·stock (al'pən·stok') *n.* A
long, iron-pointed staff, used by
mountain-climbers. [< G, lit.,
alps stick]

al·pha (al'fə) *n.* **1** The first letter
and vowel of the Greek alphabet
(A, α). **2** The beginning or first of
anything.

Alpaca

al·pha·bet (al'fə·bet) *n.* **1** The letters that form the elements of written language, in an order as fixed by usage.
2 Any system of characters or symbols representing the
sounds of speech. **3** The simplest elements of anything. [<
Gk. *alpha* alpha + *bēta* beta]

al·pha·bet·i·cal (al'fə·bet'i·kəl) *adj.* **1** Of or expressed by
an alphabet. **2** Arranged in the order of the alphabet. Also
al'pha·bet'ic. —**al'pha·bet'i·cal·ly** *adv.*

al·pha·bet·ize (al'fə·bə·tīz') *v.t.* **·ized, ·iz·ing 1** To put in
alphabetical order. **2** To express by or furnish with an
alphabet. —**al·pha·bet·i·za·tion** (al'fə·bet'ə·zā'shən) *n.*

Alpha Cen·tau·ri (sen·tôr'ē) *Astron.* The stellar system

nearest to the solar system, a bright double star about 4.4
light-years away.

al·pha·nu·mer·ic (al'fə·nʸōō·mer'ik) *adj.* Consisting of
or using the letters of the alphabet and numerals, as in
a computer code. Also **al'pha·nu·mer'i·cal.** [< ALPHA(BET) +
NUMERIC(AL)] —**al'pha·nu·mer'i·cal·ly** *adv.*

alpha particle *Physics* The nucleus of a helium atom,
consisting of two protons and two neutrons.

alpha ray *Physics* A stream of alpha particles.

al·pine (al'pīn, -pin) *adj.* **1** Like an alp or mountain; lofty
and towering. **2** *Biol.* Inhabiting or growing in mountain
regions.

Al·pine (al'pīn, -pin) *adj.* Pertaining to or characteristic
of the Alps. [< L *Alpinus*]

al·read·y (ôl·red'ē) *adv.* Before or by this time; even now:
He has *already* left.

al·right (ôl·rīt') All right: a spelling not yet considered
acceptable.

Al·sa·tian (al·sā'shən) *adj.* Of or pertaining to Alsace. —
n. **1** A native or citizen of Alsace. **2** A German shepherd
dog.

al·so (ôl'sō) *adv. & conj.* **1** Besides; in addition. **2** In like
manner; likewise. [< OE *alswā, ealswā* all so]

al·so-ran (ôl'sō·ran') *n. Informal* One who loses a race,
election, or any competition.

alt. alteration; alternate; altitude; alto.

Alta. Alberta (Canada).

Al·ta·ir (al·tä'ir, al·târ') A double star, one of the 20
brightest stars. [< Ar. *al-tā'ir* the bird]

al·tar (ôl'tər) *n.* **1** Any raised place or structure on which
sacrifices may be offered or incense burned as an act of
worship. **2** *Eccl.* The structure of wood or stone on which
the elements are consecrated in the Eucharist. —**lead to
the altar** To marry. [< L *altare*]

altar boy A boy or man who assists the celebrant of a
religious service.

al·tar·piece (ôl'tər·pēs') *n.* A painting, mosaic, or bas-
relief for display over or behind an altar.

al·ter (ôl'tər) *v.t.* **1** To cause to be different; change;
modify. **2** To fit (a garment) by recutting, resewing, etc. **3**
To castrate. —*v.i.* **4** To change, as in character or appearance. [< Med.L *alterare* < L *alter* other] —**al'ter·a·ble** *adj.*
—**al'ter·a·bly** *adv.*

al·ter·a·tion (ôl'tə·rā'shən) *n.* **1** The act of altering or the
state of being altered. **2** The result of this; change.

al·ter·a·tive (ôl'tə·rā'tiv, -tər·ə·tiv) *adj.* **1** Tending to produce change. **2** *Med.* Gradually returning the body to a
normal state. —*n. Med.* An alterative medicine. Also **al·ter-
ant** (ôl'tər·ənt).

al·ter·cate (ôl'tər·kāt, al'-) *v.i.* **·cat·ed, ·cat·ing** To dispute
vehemently; wrangle. [< L *altercari* to dispute with one
another < *alter* other]

al·ter·ca·tion (ôl'tər·kā'shən, al'-) *n.* Angry controversy;
disputing; wrangling.

al·ter e·go (ôl'tər ē'go, al'tər eg'ō) **1** Another self; a
double. **2** An intimate friend. [L, lit., other I]

al·ter·nate (ôl'tər·nāt, al'-) *v.* **·nat·ed, ·nat·ing** *v.t.* **1** To arrange, use, or perform by turns. **2** To cause to follow in
turns. —*v.i.* **3** To occur or appear in turns. **4** To take turns:
to *alternate* on a job. **5** To pass repeatedly back and forth
from one thing or condition to another —*adj.* (ôl'tər·nit,
al'-) **1** Existing, occurring, or following by turns; reciprocal. **2** Referring to every second or every other (of a series).
3 Alternative: an *alternate* method. **4** *Bot.* **a** Placed singly
at intervals on either side of the stem, as leaves. **b** Disposed at intervals between other parts. —*n.* (ôl'tər·nit,
al'-) A substitute or second. [< L *alternare* < *alternus* every second one < *alter* other] —**al'ter·nate·ly** *adv.* —**al'ter·
nate·ness** *n.*

alternating current An electric current that undergoes cyclic changes in direction or polarity.

al·ter·na·tion (ôl'tər·nā'shən, al'-) *n.* Occurrence or
change from one place, state, or condition to another and
back again.

al·ter·na·tive (ôl·tûr'nə·tiv, al-) *adj.* Being or affording a
choice between two or, loosely, more than two things. —

---

add, āce, câre, pälm; end, ēven; it, īce; odd, ōpen, ôrder; tōōk, pōōl; up, bûrn; ə = *a* in *above, u* in *focus;*
yōō = *u* in *fuse;* oil; pout; check; go; ring; thin; this; zh, *vision.* < derived from; ? origin uncertain or unknown.

n. **1** A choice between two things or, loosely, more than two. **2** One of the things to be chosen. **3** Something still to be chosen or decided: What is the *alternative* to war? —**al·ter'na·tive·ly** *adv.* —**al·ter·na·tive·ness** *n.*

al·ter·na·tor (ôl'tər·nā'tər, al'-) *n.* A mechanical generator of alternating current.

al·though (ôl·thō') *conj.* Admitting or granting that; though. Also **al·tho'**. [< ALL + THOUGH]

al·tim·e·ter (al·tim'ə·tər, al'tə·mē'tər) *n.* Any of various instruments for measuring altitude, esp. of aircraft.

al·ti·tude (al'tə·tᵊood) *n.* **1** Vertical elevation above any given reference point, esp. above mean sea level; height. **2** *Astron.* Angular elevation above the horizon. **3** *Geom.* The vertical distance from the base of a figure to its highest point. **4** A high or the highest point. [< L *altus* high] —**al'ti·tu'di·nal** (-də·nəl) *adj.*

al·to (al'tō) *adj.* Having a range immediately below the highest or between soprano and tenor: an *alto* saxaphone. —*n. pl.* **·tos** **1** The lowest female voice; contralto. **2** The highest male voice; countertenor. **3** An alto singer, instrument, or part. [< Ital. < L *altus* high]

al·to·geth·er (ôl'tə·geth'ər, ôl'tə·geth'ər) *adv.* **1** Completely; wholly; entirely. **2** With everything included; all told. —*n.* A whole.

al·tru·ism (al'trᵊoo·iz'əm) *n.* Unselfish devotion to the welfare of others. [< L *alter* other] —**al'tru·ist** *n.* —**al'tru·is'tic** *adj.* —**al'tru·is'ti·cal·ly** *adv.*

al·um (al'əm) *n.* **1** A double sulfate of aluminum and potassium, used as a styptic and astringent. **2** Any of a class of double sulfates containing both a univalent and a trivalent metal. [< L *alumen*]

a·lu·mi·na (ə·lᵊoo'mə·nə) *n.* An oxide of aluminum occurring abundantly in clay and bauxite and as corundum in emery, sapphires, rubies, etc. [< L *alumen* alum]

a·lu·mi·num (ə·lᵊoo'mə·nəm) *n.* A lightweight, silvery, metallic element (symbol Al) very abundant in minerals in the earth's crust and having countless technological uses, esp. as a structural and packaging material. *Brit. sp.* **al·u·min·i·um** (al'yə·min'ē·əm). [< L *alumen* alum] —**a·lu'mi·nous** *adj.*

a·lum·na (ə·lum'nə) *n. pl.* **·nae** (-nē) A woman who has attended or graduated from a college or school. [< L, fem. of ALUMNUS.] • See ALUMNUS.

a·lum·nus (ə·lum'nəs) *n. pl.* **·ni** (-nī) A person, esp. a male, who has attended or graduated from a college or school. [< L, foster son < *alere* nourish] • In referring to graduates or former students of a coeducational school, the plural form *alumni* often is used to include both men and women.

al·ve·o·lar (al·vē'ə·lər) *adj.* **1** Denoting that part of the jaws in which the teeth are set. **2** *Phonet.* Formed with the tongue touching or near the alveolar ridge, as (t), (d), and (s) in English. —*n. Phonet.* A sound so produced.

alveolar ridge *Anat.* The bony ridge of the jaw just above the upper front teeth.

al·ve·o·late (al·vē'ə·lit, al'vē·ə-) *adj.* Deeply pitted. —**al·ve'o·la'tion** *n.*

al·ve·o·lus (al·vē'ə·ləs) *n. pl.* **·li** (-lī) **1** A small cavity or pit, as an air cell of a lung, a tooth socket, etc. **2** *Usu. pl.* The alveolar ridge. [< L, dim. of *alveus* a hollow]

al·ways (ôl'wāz, -wiz) *adv.* **1** Perpetually; for all time. **2** At every time; on all occasions. [< OE *ealne weg* all the way]

a·lys·sum (ə·lis'əm) *n.* Any of a large genus of plants related to mustard and often grown in gardens, as sweet alyssum. [< Gk. *alysson*, name of a plant]

am (am, *unstressed* əm) Present tense, first person singular, of BE. [< OE *eom, am*]

AM, A.M., a.m., a-m, amplitude modulation.

A.M. Air Mail; Master of Arts (L *Artium Magister*).

A.M., a.m. before noon (L *ante meridiem*).

Am americium.

Am. America; American.

A.M.A. American Medical Association.

a·mah (ä'mə, am'ə) *n.* In India and the Orient, a female attendant for children. Also **a'ma**.

a·mal·gam (ə·mal'gəm) *n.* **1** An alloy of mercury with another metal. **2** Any mixture or combination. [< Med.L *amalgama*]

a·mal·ga·mate (ə·mal'gə·māt) *v.t. & v.i.* **·mat·ed, ·mat·ing** **1** To form an amalgam. **2** To unite or combine: to *amalgamate* several small government agencies. —**a·mal'ga·ma'tion, a·mal'ga·ma'tor** or **a·mal'ga·ma'ter** *n.*

a·man·u·en·sis (ə·man'yᵊoo·en'sis) *n. pl.* **·ses** (-sēz) One who copies manuscript or takes dictation; a secretary. [< L *ab-* from, by + *manus* hand]

am·a·ranth (am'ə·ranth) *n.* **1** Any of various plants with dry flowers that do not readily fade. **2** An imaginary, never-fading flower. **3** A purplish red. [< Gk. *amarantos*, lit., unfading] —**am·a·ran·thine** (am'ə·ran'thin) *adj.*

am·a·ryl·lis (am'ə·ril'is) *n.* A bulbous South African plant with large white, red, or purplish flowers, superficially resembling the lily. [< Gk. *Amaryllis*, fem. personal name]

a·mass (ə·mas') *v.t.* To heap up; accumulate, esp. wealth or possessions. [< OF *a-* to + *masser* pile up] —**a·mass'a·ble** *adj.* —**a·mass'er, a·mass'ment** *n.* —**Syn.** collect, gather, acquire.

am·a·teur (am'ə·chŏor, -tᵊʏoor, -tər, am'ə·tûr') *n.* **1** One who practices an art, science, skill, etc., for his own pleasure and not as a paid professional. **2** An athlete who has not used any athletic skill or fame as a means of profit. **3** One who does something without professional skill or ease. —*adj.* **1** Of, pertaining to, or done by an amateur or amateurs. **2** Not expert. [< L *amator* lover < *amare* love] —**am'a·teur·ism** *n.*

am·a·teur·ish (am'ə·chŏor'ish, -tᵊʏoor'-, -tûr'-) *adj.* Lacking the skill or perfection of an expert or professional. —**am'a·teur'ish·ly** *adv.* —**am'a·teur'ish·ness** *n.*

am·a·to·ry (am'ə·tôr'ē, -tō'rē) *adj.* Of, characterized by, or exciting love, esp. sexual love. [< L *amare* love]

a·maze (ə·māz') *v.t.* **a·mazed, a·maz·ing** To overwhelm, as by wonder or surprise; astonish greatly: explorers *amazed* to discover a flourishing civilization. [< OE *āmasian*] —**a·maz·ed·ly** (ə·mā'zid·lē), **a·maz'ing·ly** *adv.*

a·maze·ment (ə·māz'mənt) *n.* Wonder; surprise; astonishment.

Am·a·zon (am'ə·zon, -zən) *Gk. Myth.* One of a race of female warriors. —*n.* Any large, strong, or athletic woman or girl: also **am'a·zon**.

am·bas·sa·dor (am·bas'ə·dər, -dôr) *n.* **1** An accredited diplomatic agent of the highest rank, appointed as the representative of one government to another. **2** Any personal representative or messenger. **3** A person considered as a representative, as of his homeland: visiting athletes serving as *ambassadors* of good will. [< Ital. *ambasciatore*] —**am·bas·sa·do·ri·al** (am·bas'ə·dôr'ē·əl, -dō'rē-) *adj.* —**am·bas'sa·dor·ship** *n.* —**am·bas'sa·dress** (-drəs) *n. Fem.*

am·ber (am'bər) *n.* **1** A translucent, yellow or brownish yellow fossil resin, used in the arts, jewelry, etc. **2** The color of amber. —*adj.* Pertaining to, like, or of the color of amber. [< Ar. *'anbar* ambergris]

am·ber·gris (am'bər·grēs, -gris) *n.* An opaque, gray, waxy secretion from the intestines of the sperm whale, used in certain perfumes. [< F *ambre gris* gray amber]

ambi- *combining form* Both: *ambidextrous*. [< L *ambo* both]

am·bi·ance (am'bē·əns, *Fr.* än·byäns') *n.* The environment or pervading atmosphere of a place, situation, etc. Also **am·bi·ence**. [F < L *ambi-* around + *ire* go]

am·bi·ant (am'bē·ənt) *adj.* Surrounding; encompassing. Also **am'bi·ent**.

am·bi·dex·ter·i·ty (am'bə·dek·ster'ə·tē) *n.* **1** The state or quality of being ambidextrous. **2** Duplicity; trickery.

am·bi·dex·trous (am'bə·dek'strəs) *adj.* **1** Able to use both hands equally well. **2** Very dexterous or skillful. **3** Dissembling; double-dealing. —**am'bi·dex'trous·ly** *adv.* —**am'bi·dex'trous·ness** *n.*

am·bi·gu·i·ty (am'bə·gyᵊoo'ə·tē) *n. pl.* **·ties** **1** The quality of being ambiguous. **2** Something ambiguous.

am·big·u·ous (am·big'yᵊoo·əs) *adj.* **1** Capable of being understood in more senses than one. **2** Doubtful or uncer-

Amaryllis
a. bulb. b. flower.

ambition   23   amidst

tain. [< L *ambigere* wander about] —**am·big′u·ous·ly** *adv.*
—**am·big′u·ous·ness** *n.*

am·bi·tion (am-bish′ən) *n.* **1** A strong desire to achieve something, as success, power, wealth, etc. **2** An object so desired or striven for. **3** A desire to work, or energy for work. [< L *ambitio* a going about (to solicit votes) < *ambire* to go about]

am·bi·tious (am-bish′əs) *adj.* **1** Actuated or characterized by ambition. **2** Greatly desiring; eager for: with *of* or the infinitive. **3** Demanding; difficult: an *ambitious* plan. —**am·bi′tious·ly** *adv.* —**am·bi′tious·ness** *n.*

am·biv·a·lence (am-biv′ə-ləns) *n.* The existence of contradictory emotions or ideas about a person or thing. [< AMBI- + L *valere* be strong, be worth] —**am·biv′a·lent** *adj.*

am·ble (am′bəl) *v.i.* **am·bled** (-bəld), **am·bling 1** To move, as a horse, by lifting the two feet on one side together, alternately with the two feet on the other. **2** To proceed leisurely. —*n.* An ambling movement, like that of a horse. [< L *ambulare* walk] —**am′bler** *n.* —**am′bling·ly** *adv.*

am·bro·sia (am-brō′zhə, -zhē-ə) *n.* **1** *Gk. & Rom. Myth.* The food of the gods, giving immortality. **2** Any very delicious food or drink. [< Gk. *ambrotos* immortal] —**am·bro′sial, am·bro′sian** *adj.* —**am·bro′sial·ly** *adv.*

am·bu·lance (am′byə-ləns) *n.* A vehicle for conveying the sick and wounded. [< F *(hôpital) ambulant* walking (hospital)]

am·bu·lant (am′byə-lənt) *adj.* Walking or moving about. [< L *ambulare* walk]

am·bu·late (am′byə-lāt) *v.i.* **·lat·ed, ·lat·ing** To walk about; move from place to place. [< L *ambulare* walk] —**am′bu·la′tion** *n.* —**am·bu·la·tive** (am′byə-lā′tiv, -lə-tiv) *adj.*

am·bu·la·to·ry (am′byə-lə-tôr′ē, -tō′rē) *adj.* **1** Of or for walking or walkers. **2** Able to walk, as an invalid. **3** Shifting; not fixed or stationary.

am·bus·cade (am′bəs·kād′, am′bəs·kād′) *n.* AMBUSH. —*v.t. & v.i.* **·cad·ed, ·cad·ing** AMBUSH. [< Ital. *imboscata* an ambush]

am·bush (am′boosh) *n.* **1** The act of lying in wait to surprise or attack an enemy. **2** The hiding place or the persons hidden. Also **am′bush·ment.** —*v.t. & v.i.* To hide in or attack from ambush. [< Ital. *imboscare* place in a bush, set an ambush] —**am′bush·er** *n.*

a·me·ba (ə-mē′bə) *n. pl.* **·bas** or **·bae** (-bē) AMOEBA.
a·me·boid (ə-mē′boid) *adj.* AMOEBOID.
a·meer (ə-mir′) *n.* EMIR.

a·mel·io·rate (ə-mēl′yə-rāt) *v.t & v.i.* **·rat·ed, ·rat·ing** To make or become better; improve. [< L *ad-* to + *miliorare* to better] —**a·mel′io·rant** (-rənt), **a·mel′io·ra′tion** *n.* —**a·mel·io·ra·tive** (ə-mēl′yə-rā′tiv, -rə-tiv) *adj.*

a·men (ā′men′, ä′-) *interj.* So it is; so be it; used at the end of a prayer or to express agreement. —*adv.* Verily; truly. —*n.* The word *amen* or its use. [< Heb. *āmēn* verily]

A·men (ä′mən) *Egypt. Myth.* The god of life and procreation. Also **A′men-Ra′** (-rä′).

a·me·na·ble (ə-mē′nə-bəl, ə-men′ə-) *adj.* **1** Agreeable; tractable. **2** Accountable or responsible, as to authority. **3** Capable of being tested by rule or law. [< L *ad-* to + *minare* drive (with threats)] —**a·me′na·bil′i·ty, a·me′na·ble·ness** *n.* —**a·me′na·bly** *adv.*

a·mend (ə-mend′) *v.* t. **1** To change for the better; improve. **2** To free from faults. **3** To change or alter by authority; to *amend* a bill. —*v.i.* **4** To become better in conduct. [< L *emendare* to free from faults] —**a·mend′a·ble, a·mend′a·to′ry** *adj.* —**a·mend′a·ble·ness, a·mend′er** *n.* —**Syn. 1** ameliorate, better, mitigate. **2** correct, rectify, reform, repair, restore.

a·mend·ment (ə-mend′mənt) *n.* **1** Change for the better. **2** A removal of faults; correction. **3** The changing, as of a law, bill, or motion. **4** The statement of such a change.

a·mends (ə-mendz′) *n. pl.* Reparation, as in satisfaction for loss, insult, etc.

a·men·i·ty (ə-men′ə-tē, ə-mēn′-) *n. pl.* **·ties 1** Agreeableness; pleasantness. **2** *Usu. pl.* Any of the pleasant acts and courtesies of polite behavior. [< L *amoenus* pleasant]

Amer. America; American.
Am·er·a·sian (am′ər-ā′zhən, -shən) *adj.* Of American and

Asian descent. —*n.* A person of mixed American and Asian parentage.

a·merce (ə-mûrs′) *v.t.* **a·merced, a·merc·ing 1** To punish by an assessment or fine. **2** To punish, as by deprivation. [< AF *a merci* at the mercy of] —**a·merce′a·ble** *adj.*

A·mer·i·ca (ə-mer′ə-kə) *n.* **1** The United States of America. **2** North America. **3** South America. **4** Both of these continents considered together: also **the Americas.**

A·mer·i·can (ə-mer′ə-kən) *adj.* **1** Of or pertaining to the United States of America, its history, government, people, etc. **2** Of, in, near, or pertaining to North America or South America. —*n.* **1** A native or citizen of the U.S. **2** English as used in the U.S.; American English.

A·mer·i·ca·na (ə-mer′ə-kä′nə, -kan′ə, -kā′nə) *n. pl.* Things or materials relating to or characteristic of America, its history, traditions, etc.

American cheese Any of several mild Cheddar cheeses popular in the U.S.

American English The English language as used in the U.S.

American Expeditionary Forces The U.S. Army troops sent to Europe during World War I.

American Federation of Labor A federation of trade unions, founded in 1886, which merged in 1955 with the Congress of Industrial Organizations.

American Indian 1 A member of one of the aboriginal races of North or South America or the West Indies. **2** Any of the native languages spoken by American Indians.

A·mer·i·can·ism (ə-mer′ə-kən-iz′əm) *n.* **1** A word, phrase, usage, or a trait, custom, or tradition peculiar to the people of the U.S. **2** Attachment to America, its institutions and traditions.

A·mer·i·can·ize (ə-mer′ə-kən-īz) *v.t. & v.i.* **·ized, ·iz·ing** To become or cause to become American in spirit, speech, customs, etc. —**A·mer′i·can·i·za′tion** *n.*

American Legion An organization of U.S. war veterans, founded in 1919.

American plan At a hotel, a system in which meals and services are included in the price for the room.

American Revolution The war (1775–83) by which the British colonies in North America won their independence.

American Spanish The Spanish language as it is used in the Western Hemisphere.

am·er·ic·i·um (am′ə-rish′ē·əm) *n.* An artificially produced radioactive element (symbol Am). [< *America*]

Am·er·ind (am′ə-rind) *n.* An American Indian or Eskimo. —**Am′er·in′di·an** *adj., n.* —**Am′er·in′dic** *adj.*

am·e·thyst (am′ə-thist) *n.* **1** Quartz with purple or violet color; a semiprecious stone. **2** A purple variety of sapphire or corundum used as a gem. **3** A purplish violet color. [< Gk. *amethystos* not intoxicated, from the ancient belief that the stone prevented intoxication]

Am·har·ic (am-har′ik, äm-hä′rik) *n.* A Semitic language, the official language of Ethiopia.

a·mi (á·mē′) *n. pl.* **a·mis** (á·mē′) *French* A friend.

a·mi·a·ble (ā′mē-ə-bəl) *adj.* Friendly and good-natured. [< L *amicus* friend.] —**a′mi·a·bil′i·ty, a′mi·a·ble·ness** *n.* —**a′mi·a·bly** *adv.* —**Syn.** agreeable, kind, pleasant, pleasing.

am·i·ca·ble (am′i·kə·bəl) *adj.* Friendly; peaceable. [< L *amicus* friend] —**am·i·ca·bil′i·ty** (am·i·kə·bil′ə·tē), **am′i·ca·ble·ness** *n.* —**am′i·ca·bly** *adv.*

am·ice (am′is) *n.* A rectangular piece of white linen worn around the shoulders by a priest celebrating Mass. [< L *amictus* cloak]

a·mid (ə-mid′) *prep.* In the midst of; among. [< OE *on middan* in the middle]

am·ide (am′īd, -id) *n.* A derivative of ammonia having one or more hydrogen atoms replaced by an organic radical or a metal. Also **am·id** (am′id). [< AM(MONIA) + -IDE] —**am·ic** (am′ik), **a·mid·ic** (ə-mid′ik) *adj.*

am·i·dol (am′ə-dol, -dōl) *n.* A white crystalline powder used in photography as a developer.

a·mid·ships (ə-mid′ships) *adv. Naut.* Halfway between stem and stern of a ship.

a·midst (ə-midst′) *prep.* AMID.

---

add, āce, câre, pälm; end, ēven; it, īce; odd, ōpen, ôrder; tŏŏk, pōōl; up, bûrn; ə = *a* in *above*, *u* in *focus*; yōō = *u* in *fuse*; oil; pout; check; go; ring; thin; ᵺis; zh, *vision.* < derived from; ? origin uncertain or unknown.

a·mi·go (ə·mē′gō) *n. pl.* **-gos** *Spanish* A friend.

Am. Ind. American Indian.

am·ine (am′ēn, ə·mēn′) *n.* One of numerous organic compounds derived from ammonia by replacement of hydrogen by one or more univalent hydrocarbon radicals. [< AM-(MONIA) + -INE]

a·mi·no (ə·mē′nō, am′ə·nō) *adj.* Pertaining to an amine or amines.

amino acid Any of a group of amines having both acidic and basic properties and forming the constituents of protein molecules.

a·mir (ə·mir′) *n.* EMIR.

Am·ish (am′ish, ä′mish) *n.* A sect of Mennonites, founded in the 17th century. —*adj.* Of this sect. [after Jacob *Ammann,* the founder]

a·miss (ə·mis′) *adj.* Out of order; wrong; improper: used predicatively: Something is *amiss.* —*adv.* In a wrong, improper, or defective way or manner. —**take amiss** To take offense at. [< ME *a-* at + *missen* to miss]

am·i·to·sis (ā′mī·tō′sis) *n.* Cell division without preliminary formation of chromosomes. [< A-⁴ without + MITO-SIS] —**am·i·tot·ic** (ā′mī·tot′ik) *adj.* —**am′i·tot′i·cal·ly** *adv.*

am·i·ty (am′ə·tē) *n. pl.* **-ties** Peaceful relations; friendship. [< L *amicus* friend]

am·me·ter (am′mē′tər) *n. Electr.* An instrument for measuring an electric current. [< AM(PERE) + -METER]

am·mo·nia (ə·mōn′yə, ə·mō′nē·ə) *n.* **1** A colorless, pungent, suffocating gas composed of nitrogen and hydrogen. **2** A solution of this gas in water: also **ammonia water.** [< SAL AMMONIAC] —**am·mo′ni·ac, am·mo·ni·a·cal** (am′ə·nī′ə·kəl) *adj.*

am·mo·ni·ac (ə·mō′nē·ak) *n.* A gum resin obtained from a plant related to the carrot. [< Gk. *ammōniakon,* a resinous gum said to come from a plant growing near the temple of *Amen* in Libya]

am·mon·ite (am′ən·īt) *n.* A spiral fossil cephalopod shell, commonly found in Mesozoic rocks. [< L *cornu Ammonis* horn of Amen]

am·mo·ni·um (ə·mō′nē·əm) *n.* The univalent cation formed by the solution of ammonia in water.

ammonium chloride A white, crystalline, soluble compound formed by the replacement of hydrogen in hydrochloric acid by ammonium; sal ammoniac, used in medicine and industry.

Ammonite

ammonium hydroxide The alkaline solution of ammonia in water.

am·mu·ni·tion (am′yə·nish′ən) *n.* **1** Any one of various articles used in the discharge of firearms and ordnance, as cartridges, shells, rockets, grenades, etc. **2** Any resources for attack or defense. [< L *munitio* < *munire* fortify]

am·ne·sia (am·nē′zhə, -zhē·ə) *n.* Loss or impairment of memory. [< Gk. *amnēsia* forgetfulness] —**am·ne′si·ac** (-zhē·ak′, -zē-) *adj., n.* —**am·ne′sic** (-sik, -zik), **am·nes′tic** (-nes′tik) *adj.*

am·nes·ty (am′nəs·tē) *n. pl.* **-ties** An act of pardon on the part of a government or authority, absolving offenders or groups of offenders. —*v.t.* **-tied, -ty·ing** To grant amnesty to. [< Gk. *amnēstia* < *a-* not + *mnasthai* remember]

am·ni·o·cen·te·sis (am′nē·ō·sen·tē′sis) *n. Med.* The sampling of amniotic fluid of a pregnant woman, as to detect chromosomal anomalies or determine the sex of the fetus. [< AMNION + Gk. *kentein* to prick]

am·ni·on (am′nē·ən) *n. pl.* **-ni·ons** or **-ni·a** (-nē·ə) *Biol.* A membranous sac enclosing the embryo in mammals, birds, and reptiles. [< Gk. *amnion* sac] —**am·ni·on·ic** (am′·nē·on′ik), **am·ni·ot·ic** (am′nē·ot′ik) *adj.*

a·mok (ə·muk′) *adj.* Possessed with murderous frenzy. —*adv.* In a violent or frenzied manner. —**run** (or **go**) **amok 1** To run around attacking everybody one meets. **2** To exceed all bounds of restraint; go wild. Also **a·mock′.** [< Malay *amoq* engaging furiously in battle]

a·moe·ba (ə·mē′bə) *n. pl.* **-bas** or **-bae** (bē) Any of a genus of unicellular organisms found in soil, water, and as parasites in other animals, of an indefinite shape that changes in the process of moving. [< Gk. *amoibē* change] —**a·moe′bic, a·moe′boid** *adj.*

A·mon (ä′mən) AMEN.

a·mong (ə·mung′) *prep.* **1** In the midst of. **2** In the class, number, or company of: She is *among* the best. **3** In company or association with: working *among* the poor. **4** Of or with a number of: a custom *among* the French. **5** In portions for each of: Divide this *among* the sick. **6** In comparison with: He was just one *among* hundreds. **7** Reciprocally with or between: quarrels *among* friends. **8** Through the joint effort of: *Among* us, we can get the money. Also **a·mongst′.** [< OE *on gemang* in the crowd] • See BETWEEN.

a·mon·til·la·do (ə·mon′tə·lä′dō, *Sp.* ä·môn′tē·lyä′thō) *n.* A pale, dry sherry. [< *Montilla,* a town in southern Spain]

a·mor·al (ā·môr′əl, ā·mor′əl) *adj.* **1** Not subject to or concerned with moral or ethical distinctions. **2** Lacking a sense of right and wrong. —**a·mo·ral·i·ty** (ā′mə·ral′ə·tē) *n.* —**a·mor′al·ly** *adv.* • See UNMORAL.

am·o·rous (am′ə·rəs) *adj.* **1** Full of or desiring love, esp. sexual love. **2** Showing, springing from, or exciting to love or sexual desire: an *amorous* look. **3** In love; enamored: usu. with *of.* [< OF < LL *amorosus* < L *amor* love] —**am′o·rous·ly** *adv.* —**am′o·rous·ness** *n.*

a·mor·phous (ə·môr′fəs) *adj.* **1** Without definite form or shape; structureless. **2** Without definite characteristics or organization; anomalous. **3** Lacking definite crystalline structure. [< Gk. *a-* without + *morphē* form] —**a·mor′phism, a·mor′phous·ness** *n.* —**a·mor′phous·ly** *adv.*

am·or·tize (am′ər·tīz, ə·môr′tīz) *v.t.* **-tized, -tiz·ing** To pay off (a debt) by installments or by payments to a sinking fund. *Brit. sp.* **-tise.** [< OF *amortir* extinguish < L *ad-* to + *mors* death] —**am·or·tiz·a·ble** (am′ər·tīz′ə·bəl, a·môr′·tiz·ə·bəl) *adj.* —**am·or·ti·za·tion** (am′ər·tə·zā′shən, ə·môr′·tə·zā′shən), **a·mor·tize·ment** (ə·môr′tiz·mənt) *n.*

A·mos (ā′məs) A minor Hebrew prophet of the eighth century B.C. —*n.* The Old Testament book bearing his name.

a·mount (ə·mount′) *n.* **1** A sum of two or more quantities; total. **2** The principle sum with the interest included, as in a loan. **3** The entire significance, value, or effect. **4** Quantity: a considerable *amount* of discussion. —*v.i.* **1** To total or add up: with *to:* to *amount* to ten dollars. **2** To be equivalent in effect or importance: with *to:* Their actions *amounted* to nothing. [< OF *amont* upward < *a mont* to the mountain]

a·mour (ə·mŏor′) *n.* A love affair. [F]

amp. ampere; amperage.

am·pe·lop·sis (am′pə·lop′sis) *n.* Any of a genus of ornamental woody vines related to the grape. [< Gk. *ampelos* vine + *opsis* appearance]

am·per·age (am′pər·ij, am·pir′ij) *n.* The measure of an electric current in amperes.

am·pere (am′pir, am·pir′) *n.* A unit of electric current, defined as the steady current that produces a force of 2×10^{-7} newtons per meter of length when flowing through parallel wires of negligible cross section and infinite length one meter apart in free space. [< A. M. *Ampère,* 1775–1836, French physicist]

am·per·sand (am′pər·sand, am′pər·sand′) *n.* The character (usu. &) meaning *and.* [< *and per se and,* lit., & by itself equals and]

am·phet·a·mine (am·fet′ə·mēn, -min) *n.* A synthetic organic compound used as a stimulant. [< A(LPHA)-M(ETHYL)-PH(ENYL)-ET(HYL)-AMINE]

amphi- *prefix* **1** On both or all sides: amphitheater. **2** Of both kinds; in two ways: *amphibious.* [< Gk. *amphi* around]

am·phib·i·an (am·fib′ē·ən) *n.* **1** One of a class of cold-blooded, chiefly egg-laying, scaleless vertebrates that breathe with lungs or gills or both at different stages of development, as salamanders, newts, frogs, and toads. **2** An amphibious plant. **3** An airplane constructed to rise from and land on water or land. **4** A vehicle capable of operating on land and water. —*adj.* Of or pertaining to an amphibian. [< Gk. *amphibios.* See AMPHIBIOUS.]

am·phib·i·ous (am·fib′ē·əs) *adj.* **1** Living or adapted to life both on land and in water. **2** Capable of operating on or from land or water, as a vehicle or aircraft. **3** Of a mixed nature. [< Gk. *amphibios* having a double life] —**am·phib′·i·ous·ly** *adv.* —**am·phib′i·ous·ness** *n.*

am·phi·bole (am′fə·bōl) *n. Mineral.* Any of a class of var-

iously colored silicate minerals, as asbestos or horn-
blende. [< Gk. *amphibolos* ambiguous]

am·phi·the·a·ter (am'fə·thē'ə·tər) *n.* **1** A round or oval
structure consisting of tiers of seats rising upward from
a central open space or arena. **2** Any structure of similar
shape. **3** Any arena or place of contest.

am·pho·ra (am'fə·rə) *n. pl.* **·rae** (-rē) In ancient Greece, a
tall, two-handled earthenware
jar for wine or oil, narrow at the
neck and the base. [< Gk. *am-*
phoreus < AMPHI- + *phoreus*
bearer] —**am'pho·ral** *adj.*

am·ple (am'pəl) *adj.* **1** Large in
size, capacity, amount, etc. **2**
More than enough; abundant. **3**
Sufficient to meet all needs or requirements; adequate. [< L *am-*
plus large, abundant] —**am'ple·**
ness *n.*

am·pli·fi·ca·tion (am'plə·fi·kā'-
shən) *n.* **1** An amplifying or being
amplified. **2** Details or other mat-
ter added to amplify a subject, statement, etc. **3** An increase in the power of a signal, esp. an electric signal.

am·pli·fi·er (am'plə·fī'ər) *n.* **1** One who or that which
amplifies or increases. **2** Any device that increases the
power of a signal, esp. an electric signal.

am·pli·fy (am'plə·fī) *v.* **·fied**, **·fy·ing** *v.t.* **1** To enlarge or
increase in scope, significance, or power. **2** To add to so as
to make more complete, as by examples, data, etc. **3** To
exaggerate; magnify. **4** To increase the power of a signal,
esp. an electric signal. —*v.i.* **5** To make additional remarks; expatiate. [< L *amplus* large + *facere* make] —**am-**
pli·fi·ca·tive (am'plə·fi·kā'tiv, am·plif'i·kə·tiv), **am·plif·i·ca-**
to·ry (am·plif'i·kə·tôr'ē, -tō'rē) *adj.*

am·pli·tude (am'plə·tyōōd) *n.* **1** The quality of being ample; largeness; breadth. **2** Fullness or completeness; abundance; richness. **3** Broad range or scope, as of mental capacity. **4** *Physics* The difference between the peak and
mean values of an oscillating variable. [< L *amplus* large]

amplitude modulation Modulation of a carrier wave
so that its amplitude is at any instant proportional to the
value of another signal, as in radio transmission.

am·ply (am'plē) *adv.* In an ample manner; largely; liberally; sufficiently.

am·poule (am·pōōl') *n.* A sealed glass vial used as a sterile container for one dose of a hypodermic injection. Also
am·pule (am'pyōōl), **am·pul** (am'pul). [< L *ampulla* ampulla (def. 2)]

am·pul·la (am·pul'ə) *n. pl.* **am·pul·lae** (-pul'ē) **1** *Eccl.* The
cruet used for the wine or water at Mass. **2** An ancient
Roman bottle used to hold perfumes, oils, or wine. [< L,
dim. of *amphora* amphora] —**am·pul'lar** *adj.*

am·pu·tate (am'pyōō·tāt) *v.t.* **·tat·ed**, **·tat·ing** To remove by
cutting, as a limb. [< L *ambi-* around + *putare* trim,
prune] —**am'pu·ta'tion**, **am'pu·ta'tor** *n.*

am·pu·tee (am'pyōō·tē') *n.* One who has had a limb or
limbs removed by amputation.

amt. amount.

Am·trak (am'trak) *n.* A private corporation, administered
by the Federal Government, that manages passenger
service on selected U.S. railroads.

amu atomic mass unit.

a·muck (ə·muk') *adj. & adv.* AMOK.

am·u·let (am'yə·lit) *n.* Anything worn about one's person
to protect from accident or ill luck; a charm. [< L *amule-*
tum charm]

a·muse (ə·myōōz') *v.t.* **a·mused**, **a·mus·ing** **1** To occupy
pleasingly; entertain; divert. **2** To cause to laugh or smile.
[< OF *a* to + *muser* to muse] —**a·mus'er** *n.*

a·muse·ment (ə·myōōz'mənt) *n.* **1** The state of being
amused. **2** That which amuses.

a·mus·ing (ə·myōō'zing) *adj.* **1** Entertaining. **2** Arousing
laughter. —**a·mus'ing·ly** *adv.*

am·yl (am'il) *n.* A univalent radical composed of carbon
and hydrogen. [< Gk. *amylon* starch + -YL]

Amphorae

am·y·la·ceous (am'ə·lā'shəs) *adj.* Pertaining to or like
starch; starchy.

am·y·lase (am'ə·lās) *n.* Any of several digestive enzymes
that promote the conversion of starch into simple sugars.
[< AMYL + -ASE]

am·y·loid (am'ə·loid) *n.* A starchlike substance. —*adj.*
Like or containing starch. —**am'y·loi'dal** *adj.*

am·y·lum (am'ə·ləm) *n.* Starch. [< Gk. *amylon*]

Am·y·tal (am'ə·tal, -tôl) *n.* A barbiturate: a trade name.

an (an, *unstressed* ən) *indefinite article & adj.* **1** Each or
any. **2** One; one kind of. **3** For each: The price is ten cents
an apple. [< OE *ān* one] • See A[2].

an-[1] *prefix* Without; not: *anastigmatic.* [< Gk.]

an-[2] Var. of ANA-: *anode.*

an-[3] Var. of AD-.

-an *suffix* Used to form adjectives and nouns denoting connection with a country, person, group, doctrine, etc., as
follows: **1** Pertaining to; belonging to: *human, sylvan.* **2**
Originating in; living in: *Italian.* **3** Adhering to; following:
Lutheran. **4** *Zool.* Belonging to a class or order: *am-*
phibian. [< L -*anus*]

an. anonymous; in the year (L *anno*).

ana- *prefix* **1** Up; upward: *anadromous.* **2** Back; backward:
anapest. **3** Anew: sometimes capable of being rendered *re-*,
as *Anabaptism.* **4** Throughout; thoroughly: *analysis.* [<
Gk. *ana* on]

-ana *suffix* Pertaining to: added to the names of notable
persons, places, etc., to indicate a collection of materials,
such as writings or anecdotes, about the subject:
Americana. Also *-iana.* [< L *-anus*]

An·a·bap·tist (an'ə·bap'tist) *n.* One of a 16th-century,
Protestant sect that opposed infant baptism, believing
only adults could validly be baptized. [< Gk. *ana-* anew +
baptizein baptize] —**An'a·bap'tism** *n.*

a·nab·o·lism (ə·nab'ə·liz'əm) *n.* Constructive metabolism; the process by which nutrients are built up into the
living organism. [< ANA- up + (META)BOLISM] —**an·a·bol·ic**
(an'ə·bol'ik) *adj.*

a·nach·ro·nism (ə·nak'rə·niz'əm) *n.* **1** The representation of something existing or occurring out of its proper
time. **2** Anything placed out of its proper time. [< Gk.
anachronizein refer to a wrong time] —**a·nach'ro·nis'tic,**
a·nach'ro·nis'ti·cal, a·nach'ro·nous *adj.*

an·a·con·da (an'ə·kon'də) *n.* **1** A very large nonvenomous tropical serpent that
crushes its prey in its coils. **2** Any
similar snake, as the boa constrictor or python. [?]

a·nad·ro·mous (ə·nad'rə·məs)
adj. Running up: said of fishes, as
the salmon, that go up rivers to
spawn. [< Gk. *ana-* up + *dromos*
a running]

a·nae·mi·a (ə·nē'mē·ə) *n.* ANE-
MIA.

Anaconda *def. 1*

an·aer·obe (an'ə·rōb, an·âr'ōb,
an·ā'ə·rōb) *n.* A microorganism which flourishes without
free oxygen. [See ANAEROBIUM] —**an·aer·o·bic** (an'âr·ō'bik,
-ob'ik, an·ā'ə·rō'bik, -rob'ik) *adj.*

an·aer·o·bi·um (an'âr·ō'bē·əm, an'ā·ə·rō'-) *n. pl.* **·bi·a**
(-bē·ə) An anaerobe. [< AN-[1] without + AERO- + Gk. *bios*
life]

an·aes·the·sia (an'is·thē'zhə, -zhē·ə) *n.* ANESTHESIA.

an·a·gram (an'ə·gram) *n.* **1** A word or phrase formed by
transposing the letters of another word or phrase. **2** *pl.*
(*construed as sing.*) A game in which the players make
words by transposing or adding letters. [< ANA- back +
Gk. *gramma* a letter] —**an·a·gram·mat·ic** (an'ə·grə·mat'ik)
or **·i·cal** *adj.* —**an'a·gram·mat'i·cal·ly** *adv.*

a·nal (ā'nəl) *adj.* Of, pertaining to, or situated in the region of the anus. —**a'nal·ly** *adv.*

an·al·ge·si·a (an'əl·jē'zē·ə, -sē·ə) *n.* Insensibility to pain.
[< Gk. *an-* without + *algos* pain]

an·al·ge·sic (an'əl·jē'zik, -sik) *n.* A drug that alleviates
pain. —*adj.* Pertaining to or promoting analgesia.

a·nal·o·gous (ə·nal'ə·gəs) *adj.* **1** Similar in certain respects. **2** *Biol.* Having a similar function but different in origin and structure. —**a·nal′o·gous·ly** *adv.*

an·a·logue (an′ə·lôg, -log) *n.* Anything analogous to something else. Also **an′a·log.**

a·nal·o·gy (ə·nal′ə·jē) *n. pl.* **·gies 1** A similarity or resemblance between things not otherwise identical. **2** *Biol.* A similarity in function but not in origin or structure. **3** *Logic* The assumption that things similar in some respects are probably similar in others.

a·nal·y·sis (ə·nal′ə·sis) *n. pl.* **·ses** (-sēz) **1** The separation of a whole into its parts or elements. **2** A statement of the results of this. **3** A method of determining or describing the nature of a thing by separating it into its parts. **4** *Chem.* The identification of some or all constituents forming a compound or substance. **5** PSYCHOANALYSIS. [<Gk. *analysis* a releasing]

an·a·lyst (an′ə·list) *n.* One who analyzes or is skilled in analysis. **2** PSYCHOANALYST.

an·a·lyt·ic (an′ə·lit′ik) *adj.* **1** Pertaining to, skilled in, or proceeding by analysis. **2** Separating into constituents or first principles. Also **an′a·lyt′i·cal.** —**an′a·lyt′i·cal·ly** *adv.*

an·a·lyt·ics (an′ə·lit′iks) *n. pl. (construed as sing.)* The science or use of logical analysis.

an·a·lyze (an′ə·līz) *v.t.* **·lyzed, ·lyz·ing 1** To separate into constituent parts or elements. **2** To make an analysis of, as a chemical compound. **3** *Gram.* To separate (a sentence) into its grammatical elements. **4** To examine minutely or critically, as a text. *Brit. sp.* **an′a·lyse.** —**an′a·lyz·a·ble** *adj.* —**an′a·ly·za′tion, an′a·lyz′er** *n.*

an·a·pest (an′ə·pest) *n.* **1** In prosody, a metrical foot consisting of two short or unaccented syllables followed by one long or accented syllable. **2** A line of verse made up of or characterized by such feet. Also **an′a·paest.** [<Gk. *anapaistos*<*ana-* back + *paiein* strike] —**an′a·pes′tic** *adj.*

an·a·phy·lac·tic (an′ə·fə·lak′tik) *adj.* Of or pertaining to a severe reaction to a usually harmless drug when injected the second time, often resulting in shock or death. [<Gk. *ana* on + *phylaxis* a guarding]

an·ar·chism (an′ər·kiz′əm) *n.* **1** The theory that all forms of government are incompatible with individual and social liberty and should be replaced by voluntary cooperation and mutual aid. **2** The methods, esp. terroristic ones, of anarchists.

an·ar·chist (an′ər·kist) *n.* **1** One who believes in anarchism. **2** One who encourages or furthers anarchy. —**an′·ar·chis′tic** *adj.*

an·ar·chy (an′ər·kē) *n. pl.* **·chies 1** Absence of government. **2** Lawless confusion and political disorder. **3** General disorder. [<Gk. *an-* without + *archos* leader] —**an·ar·chic** (an·är′kik), **an·ar′chi·cal** *adj.* —**an·ar′chi·cal·ly** *adv.*

an·as·tig·mat·ic (an·as′tig·mat′ik) *adj.* Not astigmatic; esp., corrected for astigmatism, as a lens. [<AN-¹ + ASTIGMATIC]

anat. anatomical; anatomy.

a·nath·e·ma (ə·nath′ə·mə) *n. pl.* **·mas** or **·ma·ta** (-mə·tə) **1** A formal ecclesiastical ban or curse, excommunicating a person or damning something, as a book or heresy. **2** A person or thing so banned or cursed. **3** Any curse or imprecation. **4** A person or thing greatly disliked or detested. [<Gk. *anathema* an offering]

a·nath·e·ma·tize (ə·nath′ə·mə·tīz) *v.* **·tized, ·tiz·ing** *v.t.* To pronounce an anathema against. —*v.i.* To utter or express anathemas. —**a·nath′e·ma·ti·za′tion** *n.*

an·a·tom·i·cal (an′ə·tom′i·kəl) *adj.* **1** Of or pertaining to anatomy. **2** Structural. Also **an′a·tom′ic.** —**an′a·tom′i·cal·ly** *adv.*

a·nat·o·mist (ə·nat′ə·mist) *n.* One skilled in or a student of anatomy.

a·nat·o·mize (ə·nat′ə·mīz) *v.t.* **·mized, ·miz·ing 1** To dissect (an animal or plant) for the purpose of investigating its structure. **2** To examine critically or minutely; analyze.

a·nat·o·my (ə·nat′ə·mē) *n. pl.* **·mies 1** The structure of a plant or animal. **2** The science of the structure of organisms. **3** The art or practice of dissection in order to investigate structure. **4** The human body. [<Gk. *anatomē* dissection]

-ance *suffix of nouns* Forming nouns of action, quality, state, or condition from adjectives in *-ant*, and also from verbs, as in *ignorance, resistance, forbearance*. [<L *-antia*]

an·ces·tor (an′ses·tər) *n.* **1** One from whom a person is descended; progenitor; forebear. **2** Anything regarded as an earlier model or forerunner. **3** An earlier organism from which later organisms have been derived. [<L *ante-* before + *cedere* go] —**an·ces·tress** (an′ses·tris) *n. Fem.*

an·ces·tral (an·ses′trəl) *adj.* Of, pertaining to, or inherited from an ancestor. —**an·ces′tral·ly** *adv.*

an·ces·try (an′ses·trē) *n. pl.* **·tries 1** Ancestors collectively. **2** Descent; ancestral lineage.

an·chor (ang′kər) *n.* **1** A heavy implement, usu. metal, attached to a chain or cable and used, when lowered into the water, to hold a ship or boat in place by its weight or its hooks or flukes that grip the bottom. **2** Anything or anyone giving support or security. —**at anchor** Anchored, as a ship. —**cast (or drop) anchor** To put down the anchor in order to hold fast a vessel. —**ride at anchor** To be anchored, as a ship. —**weigh anchor** To take up the anchor so as to sail away. —*v.t.* **1** To secure or make secure by an anchor. **2** To fix firmly. —*v.i.* **3** To lie at anchor, as a ship. **4** To be or become fixed. [<Gk. *ankyra*]

Anchor

an·chor·age (ang′kər·ij) *n.* **1** A place used for anchoring. **2** A lying at anchor. **3** The fee charged for anchoring. **4** Any means of support or security.

an·cho·rite (ang′kə·rīt) *n.* A religious recluse or hermit. Also **an′cho·ret** (-rit, -ret). [<Gk. *anachōreein* retire, retreat] —**an·cho·rit·ic** (ang′kə·rit′ik) *adj.*

anchor man 1 An athlete, as in a relay race, who competes last for his team. **2** A television or radio broadcaster who coordinates the coverage of an event or program.

an·cho·vy (an′chō·vē, -chə·vē, an·chō′vē) *n. pl.* **·vies** Any of several small, herringlike fish found in warm seas, used as food. [<Sp., Pg. *anchova,?* <Basque *anchua*]

an·cient (ān′shənt) *adj.* **1** Existing or occurring in times long gone by, esp. before the fall of the Roman Empire. **2** Having existed a long time; of great age. —*n.* **1** One who lived in ancient times. **2** A very old person. —**an′cient·ly** *adv.*

an·cil·lar·y (an′sə·ler′ē) *adj.* Subordinate; auxiliary. [<L *ancilla* maidservant]

an·con (ang′kon) *n. pl.* **an·co·nes** (ang·kō′nēz) *Archit.* An elbow-shaped projection. Also **an·cone** (ang′kōn). [<Gk. *ankōn* a bend, the elbow]

-ancy Var. of **-ANCE**: *infancy*. [<L *-antia*]

and (and, *unstressed* ənd, ən) *conj.* **1** Also; added to; as well as. **2** As a result or consequence: Speak one word *and* you are a dead man! **3** Although; but: One day is cold *and* the next is warm. **4** *Informal* To: Try *and* stop me. [<OE]

and. andante.

an·dan·te (an·dan′tē, än·dän′tä) *adj. & adv. Music* Moderately slow or slowly. —*n.* An andante passage, movement, etc. [<Ital., lit., walking]

an·dan·ti·no (an′dan·tē′nō, än′dän-) *adj. & adv. Music* Slightly quicker than andante. —*n.* An andantino passage, movement, etc. [<Ital., dim. of *andante*]

and·i·ron (and′ī′ərn) *n.* One of two metal supports for wood to be burned in an open fireplace. [<OF *andier*]

and/or Either *and* or *or*, according to the meaning intended.

An·dor·ra (an·dôr′ə, -dor′ə) *n.* A principality located in the Pyrenees between France and Spain, 179 sq. mi., cap. Andorra la Vella.

andro- *combining form* **1** Man; male; *androgen*. **2** *Bot.* Stamen; anther: *androecium*. [<Gk. *anēr, andros* man]

an·droe·ci·um (an·drē′shē·əm, -sē·əm) *n. pl.* **·ci·a** (-shē·ə, -sē·ə) The stamens of a flower collectively. [<ANDRO- + Gk. *oikos* house] —**an·droe·cial** (an·drē′shəl) *adj.*

an·dro·gen (an′drə·jən) *n.* Any of various hormones that control the appearance and development of male characteristics. —**an·dro·gen·ic** (an′drə·jen′ik) *adj.*

an·drog·y·nous (an·droj′ə·nəs) *adj.* **1** Uniting the characteristics of both sexes; hermaphrodite. **2** Having male and female flowers on the same spike. Also **an·drog′y·nal, an·dro·gyn·ic** (an′drə·jin′ik). [<Gk.<ANDRO- + *gynē* woman] —**an·drog′y·ny** (-drə·nē) *n.*

An·drom·a·che (an·drom′ə·kē) *Gk. Myth.* The wife of Hector, taken captive after the fall of Troy.

An·drom·e·da (an-drom'ə-də) *Gk. Myth.* An Ethiopian princess rescued from a sea monster and married by Perseus. —*n.* A northern constellation.

an·dros·ter·one (an-dros'tə-rōn) *n.* An androgen present in the urine of men and women. [< ANDRO- + STER(OL) + -ONE]

-androus *suffix Bot.* Having a stamen or stamens. [< Gk. *anēr, andros* man]

-ane *suffix Chem.* Denoting a hydrocarbon compound of the methane series.

an·ec·do·tal (an'ik-dōt'l) *adj.* Pertaining to, characterized by, or consisting of anecdotes. —**an'ec·do'tal·ly** *adv.*

an·ec·dote (an'ik-dōt) *n.* A short narrative of an interesting or entertaining nature. [< Gk. *anekdotos* unpublished] —**an'ec·dot'ic** (-dot'ik) or **·i·cal** *adj.* —**an'ec·dot'ist** (-dō'tist) *n.*

a·ne·mi·a (ə-nē'mē-ə) *n.* A deficiency in the amount or quality of red blood corpuscles or of hemoglobin in the blood. [< Gk. *an-* without + *haima* blood] —**a·ne'mic** *adj.*

a·nem·o·graph (ə-nem'ə-graf, -gräf) *n. Meteorol.* An anemometer that produces a graphic record. [< Gk *anemos* wind + -GRAPH] —**an·em'o·graph'ic** *adj.*

an·e·mom·e·ter (an'ə-mom'ə-tər) *n. Meteorol.* An instrument for measuring the force or velocity of wind. [< Gk. *anemos* wind + -METER] —**an·e·mo·met·ric** (an'ə-mō-met'rik) or **·ri·cal** *adj.*

a·nem·o·ne (ə-nem'ə-nē) *n.* **1** Any of various small herbs related to buttercups, having flowers with no petals but showy sepals. **2** SEA ANEMONE. [< Gk. *anemos* wind]

Anemometer

an·er·oid barometer (an'ə-roid) An instrument that indicates atmospheric pressure by the movements of the elastic top of a chamber from which almost all the air has been removed. [< Gk. *a-* not + *nēron* water + -OID]

an·es·the·sia (an'is-thē'zhə, -zhē-ə) *n.* **1** Partial or total loss of physical sensation, due to disease. **2** Local insensibility to pain or general unconsciousness induced by an anesthetic. Also **an·es·the·sis** (an'is-thē'sis). [< Gk. *an-* without + *aisthēsis* sensation]

an·es·thet·ic (an'is-thet'ik) *adj.* **1** Pertaining to or like anesthesia. **2** Producing anesthesia; making insensible to pain. —*n.* A drug that causes unconsciousness or deadens sensation, as during surgery, etc.

an·es·the·tist (ə-nes'thə-tist) *n.* A person trained to administer anesthetics.

an·es·the·tize (ə-nes'thə-tīz) *v.t.* **·tized, ·tiz·ing** To render insensible, esp. to pain, by means of an anesthetic. —**an·es·the·ti·za·tion** (ə-nes'thə-tə-zā'shən, an'is-thet'ə-) *n.*

an·eu·rysm (an'yə-riz'əm) *n.* A sac formed by localized dilation of the wall of an artery, due to disease or injury. Also **an'eu·rism.** [< Gk. *ana-* throughout + *eurys* wide] —**an·eu·rys·mal** (an'yə-riz'məl) or **·ris'mal** *adj.*

a·new (ə-n^yo͞o') *adv.* **1** Again. **2** Again in a different way.

an·gel (ān'jəl) *n.* **1** *Theol.* **a** One of an order of spiritual beings attendant upon the Deity; a heavenly messenger. **b** A fallen spiritual being. **2** A conventional representation of an angel, usu. a youthful winged human figure in white robes with a halo. **3** A person thought of as being angelically beautiful, pure, kind, etc. **4** A guardian spirit or attendant. **5** *Informal* The financial backer of a play or of any enterprise. [< Gk. *angelos* messenger]

an·gel·fish (ān'jəl·fish') *n.* **1** A raylike shark of temperate seas, having very large winglike pectoral fins. **2** A fish of warm seas having brilliant coloration, as the porgy.

Angelfish *def. 2*

angel food cake A delicate, spongy cake made with egg whites and no shortening. Also **angel cake.**

an·gel·ic (an·jel'ik) *adj.* **1** Pertaining to, of, or consisting of angels. **2** Like an angel; pure; beautiful; saintly. Also **an·gel'i·cal. —an·gel'i·cal·ly** *adv.*

an·gel·i·ca (an·jel'i·kə) *n.* **1** Any of various aromatic plants related to celery. **2** The stalks of this plant, often candied and used as a flavoring. [< Med.L *(herba) angelica* the angelic (herb)]

an·ge·lus (an'jə-ləs) *n.* **1** A prayer to commemorate the Annunciation. **2** A bell rung at morning, noon, and night as a call to recite this prayer. Also **An'ge·lus.** [< L, angel]

an·ger (ang'gər) *n.* Violent and strong displeasure, as a result of opposition, mistreatment, etc.; wrath; ire. —*v.t.* **1** To make angry; enrage. —*v.i.* **2** To become angry. [< ON *angr* grief]

an·gi·na (an·jī'nə, an'jə-nə) *n.* **1** Inflammation of the throat characterized by spasmodic suffocation, as quinsy, croup, etc. **2** Angina pectoris. [< L, quinsy]

angina pec·to·ris (pek'tə-ris) A condition characterized by pain in the chest and usu. the left arm, due to insufficient blood supply to the heart muscle. [< NL, angina of the chest]

an·gi·o·ma (an'jē-ō'mə) *n. pl.* **·mas** or **·ma·ta** (-mə-tə) A tumor composed of dilated blood or lymph vessels. [< Gk. *angeion* vessel + *ōma,* a noun ending] —**an·gi·om·a·tous** (an'jē-ōm'ə-təs) *adj.*

an·gi·o·sperm (an'jē-ə-spûrm') *n.* One of a class comprising all flowering plants, in which the seeds are contained within a pericarp. [< Gk. *angeion* vessel + SPERM] —**an'gi·o·sper'mal, an'gi·o·sper'ma·tous** (-spûr'mə-təs), **an'·gi·o·sper'mous** *adj.*

Angl. Anglican; Anglicized.

an·gle[1] (ang'gəl) *v.i.* **an·gled, an·gling 1** To fish with a hook and line. **2** To seek deviously; fish: to *angle* for compliments. [< OE *angel* fish hook]

an·gle[2] (ang'gəl) *n.* **1** *Geom.* **a** The figure formed by the intersection of two lines or of two planes. **b** The inclination of either of these lines or planes with respect to the other. **2** A corner or sharp bend. **3** A position from which something may be regarded; viewpoint. —*v.t. & v.i.* **an·gled, an·gling 1** To move or turn at an angle or by angles. **2** To present with or show a particular bias or interpretation, as a story or report. [< L *angulus* a corner, angle] —**an'gled** *adj.*

Angle
ADB: acute, adjacent.
ADC: right. BDE:
obtuse.

An·gle (ang'gəl) *n.* A member of a Germanic tribe that migrated from southern Denmark to Britain in the fifth and sixth centuries and founded the kingdoms of East Anglia, Mercia, and Northumbria. [< L *Anglus,* sing. of *Angli* < Gmc.]

angle iron A piece of metal in the form of an angle, especially a right angle, for joining or strengthening beams, girders, etc.

angle of incidence *Physics* The angle between a beam of radiant energy and a perpendicular to a surface at the point of incidence.

an·gler (ang'glər) *n.* **1** One who fishes by angling. **2** An anglerfish.

an·gler·fish (ang'glər·fish') *n., pl.* **·fish** or **·fish·es** One of a family of fishes having antennalike filaments attached to the head with which it lures its prey.

an·gle·worm (ang'gəl·wûrm') *n.* An earthworm, esp. one used as fishing bait.

An·gli·can (ang'glə-kən) *adj.* **1** Of or pertaining to the Church of England or the churches derived from it. **2** Of or pertaining to England; English. —*n.* A member of the Church of England or of any church derived from it. [< Med.L *Anglicus* English] —**An'gli·can·ism'** *n.*

An·gli·cism (ang'glə-siz'əm) *n.* **1** A word, phrase, or idiom typical of English, esp. British English. **2** A typically English trait, quality, etc.

An·gli·cize (ang'glə-sīz) *v.t. & v.i.* **·cized, ·ciz·ing** To give or acquire a characteristically English use, style, quality, etc. *Brit. sp.* **An'gli·cise. —An·gli·ci·za·tion** (ang'glə-sə-zā'· shən, -sī-zā'shən) *n.*

an·gling (ang'gling) *n.* The act or art of fishing with a hook, line, and rod.

An·glo (ang'glō) *n. pl.* **·glos** An Anglo-American.

Anglo- *combining form* English; English and: *Anglo- American.* [< L *Angli* the English]

An·glo-A·mer·i·can (ang'glō-ə-mer'ə-kən) *adj.* Of, per- taining to, or between England and America. —*n.* A U.S. citizen of English origin.

An·glo-French (ang'glō-french') *adj.* Of, pertaining to, or between England and France or the English and French. —*n.* The Norman dialect of Old French current in England from the Norman Conquest to the end of the 13th century.

An·glo·ma·ni·a (ang'glō-mā'nē-ə) *n.* A passion for Eng- lish customs, speech, etc. —**An·glo·ma·ni·ac** (-ak) *n.*

An·glo-Nor·man (ang'glō-nôr'mən) *adj.* Pertaining to the Normans who settled in England after the Norman Conquest in 1066. —*n.* 1 One of the Norman settlers in England after the Norman Conquest. 2 Anglo-French.

An·glo·phile (ang'glə-fīl, -fil) *n.* A devotee of England and its people, institutions, etc. —*adj.* Of or like Anglo- philes. Also **An'glo·phil** (-fil).

An·glo·phobe (ang'glə-fōb) *n.* One who dislikes or dis- trusts England or its people, institutions, etc. —*adj.* Of or like Anglophobes. Also **An·glo·pho·bi·ac** (ang'glə-fō'bē- ak). —**An·glo·pho·bi·a** (ang'glə-fō'bē-ə) *n.* —**An'glo·pho'bic** (-fō'bik, -fob'ik) *adj.*

An·glo-Sax·on (ang'glō-sak'sən) *n.* 1 A member of one of the Germanic tribes that conquered Britain in the fifth and sixth centuries. 2 A member of the nation descended from these peoples. 3 Their West Germanic language. See OLD ENGLISH. 4 One of English origin or descent. 5 The simple, earthy elements of modern English retained from Old English. —*adj.* Of or pertaining to the Anglo-Saxons, their language, customs, or descendants. —**An'glo-Sax'on· ism** *n.*

An·go·la (ang-gō'lə) *n.* A Portuguese colony in sw Africa, 481,351 sq. mi., cap. Luanda. • See map at AFRICA.

An·go·ra (ang-gôr'ə, -gō'rə) *n.* 1 A type of goat bred for its long, silky hair. 2 The long, silky hair of this goat, or cloth made from it. 3 A type of cat having long hair. [< *Angora,* former name of Ankara]

an·gos·tu·ra bark (ang'gəs-t $\overline{oo}$ r'ə) The bark of a South American tree used in the preparation of a tonic and as a flavoring in bitters. Also **angostura.** [< *Angostura,* former name of Ciudad Bolivar]

an·gry (ang'grē) *adj.* **an·gri·er, an·gri·est** 1 Feeling, show- ing, or excited by anger. 2 Appearing to threaten: *angry* skies. 3 Badly inflamed: an *angry* sore. —**an·gri·ly** (ang'grə- lē) *adv.* —**an·gri·ness** *n.* —**Syn.** 1 furious, enraged, irate, wrathful. 2 stormy, turbulent. 3 sore, painful, burning.

angst (ängst) *n.* Anxiety; dread. [G]

ang·strom (ang'strəm) *n. Often cap.* A unit of length equal to 10⁻⁸ meter. Also **Ångstrom, angstrom unit.** [< A. J. *Ångström,* 1814–74, Swedish physicist]

an·guish (ang'gwish) *n.* Severe mental or physical dis- tress. [< L *angustus* narrow, tight] —**an·guished** *adj.* —**Syn.** agony, torment, torture, suffering.

an·gu·lar (ang'gyə-lər) *adj.* 1 Of, having, or forming an angle or angles. 2 Measured by an angle: *angular* motion. 3 Bony; gaunt. 4 Awkwardly stiff: *angular* gestures. —**an'· gu·lar·ly** *adv.*

an·gu·lar·i·ty (ang'gyə-lar'ə-tē) *n. pl.* **·ties** 1 The state or condition of being angular. 2 *pl.* Angular contours. Also **an'gu·lar·ness.**

an·hy·dride (an-hī'drīd, -drid) *n.* 1 Any compound from which the elements of water have been removed. 2 An oxide which reacts with water to form an acid or a base. [See ANHYDROUS]

an·hy·drous (an-hī'drəs) *adj.* Without water, esp. water of crystallization. [< Gk. *anydros* waterless]

an·il (an'il) *n.* 1 A West Indian plant. 2 The indigo dye made from it. [< Ar. *al-nīl*]

an·ile (an'īl, ā'nīl, an'il) *adj.* Like an old woman; infirm. [< L *anus* old woman] —**a·nil·i·ty** (ə-nil'ə-tē) *n.*

an·i·line (an'ə-lin, -līn) *n.* A colorless oily compound derived from benzene, used in the production of many

dyes, resins, and varnishes. —*adj.* Of, derived from, or pertaining to aniline. Also **an·i·lin** (an'ə-lin). [< ANIL + -INE]

an·i·mad·ver·sion (an'ə-mad-vûr'zhən, -shən) *n.* An un- favorably critical comment: with *on* or *upon.* [See ANIMAD- VERT.] —**an'i·mad·ver'sive** (-siv) *adj.* —**an'i·mad·ver'sive· ness** *n.*

an·i·mad·vert (an'ə-mad-vûrt') *v.i.* To comment with ad- verse criticism: with *on* or *upon.* [< L *animadvertere* take notice of]

an·i·mal (an'ə-məl) *n.* 1 Any member of a primary sub- division of organisms distinguished from plants by inabil- ity to produce nutrients by photosynthesis and by various other characteristics. 2 Any such creature as distin- guished from man, esp. a mammal. 3 A bestial human being. —*adj.* 1 Of or pertaining to animals. 2 Like an animal; bestial. [< L *animalis* living < *animus* breath]

an·i·mal·cule (an'ə-mal'kyōol) *n.* A microscopically small animal. —**an'i·mal'cu·lar** (-kyə-lər) *adj.*

animal husbandry The breeding, raising, and care of farm animals.

an·i·mal·ism (an'ə-məl-iz'əm) *n.* 1 Existence dominated by animal instincts, appetites, etc. 2 The doctrine that man is entirely animal, having no soul or spirit. —**an'i· mal·ist** *n.* —**an'i·mal·is'tic** *adj.*

an·i·mal·i·ty (an'ə-mal'ə-tē) *n.* 1 Animal nature or quali- ties. 2 Animal life.

an·i·mal·ize (an'ə-məl-īz') *v.t.* **·ized, ·iz·ing** To make bes- tial, inhuman, etc.; brutalize. —**an·i·mal·i·za·tion** (an'ə-məl- ə-zā'shən) *n.*

animal kingdom One of the three divisions of nature, embracing all animals.

animal magnetism 1 MESMERISM. 2 Magnetic personal qualities.

animal spirits Vivaciousness or buoyancy of good health.

an·i·mate (an'ə-māt) *v.t.* **·mat·ed, ·mat·ing** 1 To impart life to; make alive. 2 To make lively, energetic, vivacious, etc. 3 To move to action; incite; inspire. 4 To impart lifelike motion to. —*adj.* (an'ə-mit) 1 Possessing animal life; liv- ing. 2 Animated. [< L *animare* to fill with breath, make alive] —**an'i·ma'tor, an'i·ma'ter** *n.*

an·i·mat·ed (an'ə-māt'id) *adj.* Full of life, spirit, etc. — **an'i·mat'ed·ly** *adv.* —**Syn.** lively, spirited, vivacious, ener- getic.

animated cartoon A motion-picture film made by photographing a series of drawings, each changed slightly from the preceding one to produce an effect of motion.

an·i·ma·tion (an'ə-mā'shən) *n.* 1 The act or process of animating. 2 The state of being animated; liveliness; vivacity. 3 The process and technique of preparing draw- ings for an animated cartoon.

a·ni·ma·to (ä'nē-mä'tō) *adv. Music* With animation; in an animated manner. [< Ital.]

an·i·mism (an'ə-miz'əm) *n.* The belief that inanimate ob- jects and natural phenomena possess a personal life or soul. [< L *anima* soul] —**an'i·mist** *n.* —**an'i·mis'tic** *adj.*

an·i·mos·i·ty (an'ə-mos'ə-tē) *n. pl.* **·ties** Active, intense enmity or hostility. [< L *animositas* high spirit, boldness < *animus* soul, spirit]

an·i·mus (an'ə-məs) *n.* 1 Hostile feeling; animosity. 2 Ani- mating purpose or intention. [< L mind, soul]

an·i·on (an'ī'ən) *n.* A negatively charged ion; the ion mi- grating to the anode in electrolysis. [< Gk. *anion* (thing) going up]

an·ise (an'is) *n.* 1 A plant related to parsley, having small white or yellow flowers and seeds with a flavor like lico- rice. 2 Aniseed. [< Gk. *anison*]

an·i·seed (an'i·sēd) *n.* The fragrant seed of the anise plant, used in cookery and medicine.

an·i·sette (an'ə-zet', -set') *n.* A cordial flavored with ani- seed. [F]

an·kle (ang'kəl) *n.* 1 The joint connecting the foot and the leg. 2 The part of the leg between the foot and the calf near the ankle joint. [< OE *anclēow*]

an·kle·bone (ang'kəl·bōn') *n.* TALUS.

an·klet (ang'klit) *n.* 1 An ornament or fetter for the an- kle. 2 A short sock reaching just above the ankle.

an·ky·lose (ang'kə-lōs) *v.t. & v.i.* **·losed, ·los·ing** To unite or join together into a single unit.

an·ky·lo·sis (ang'kə·lō'sĭs) n. 1 The consolidation of two bones or other parts. 2 The abnormal cohesion of bones, esp. those forming a joint; stiffening of a joint. [<Gk. *ankylōsis* joint stiffening] —**an'ky·lot'ic** (-lot'ĭk) adj.

ann. annals; annual; annuity.

an·na (an'ə) n. A former monetary unit and copper coin of India, equal to ¹⁄₁₆ of a rupee. [<Hind. *ānā*]

an·nals (an'əlz) n. pl. 1 A year-by-year record of events in chronological order. 2 History or records in general. 3 A periodical publication of discoveries, transactions, etc. [<L *annales* (*libri*) yearly (record)] —**an'nal·ist** n.

an·neal (ə·nēl') v.t. To toughen (brittle metal, glass, etc.) by heating and then slowly cooling. [<OE *onælan* to burn] —**an·neal'er** n.

an·ne·lid (an'ə·lid) n. Any of a phylum of worms having bodies segmented into a series of rings, including earthworms, leeches, etc. —adj. Of or pertaining to this phylum. [<F *anneler* arrange in rings] —**an·nel·i·dan** (ə·nel'ə·dən) adj., n.

an·nex (ə·neks') v.t. 1 To add or append, esp. to something larger. 2 To incorporate as territory. 3 To attach, as an attribute, condition, etc. —n. (an'eks) 1 An addition to a building, or a nearby auxiliary building. 2 An addition to a document. Brit. sp. **annexe** (n.) [<L *annectere* tie together] —**an·nex'a·ble, an·nex'ive** adj.

an·nex·a·tion (an'ek·sā'shən) n. 1An annexing or being annexed. 2 That which is annexed. Also **an·nex'ment**.

An·nie Oak·ley (an'ē ōk'lē) Slang A free ticket or pass to a theater, etc. [From resemblance of a punched ticket to a target used by *Annie Oakley*, 1860–1926, U.S. markswoman]

an·ni·hi·late (ə·nī'ə·lāt) v.t. ·lat·ed, ·lat·ing To destroy absolutely. [<L *ad-* to + *nihil* nothing] —**an·ni·hi·la·ble** (ə·nī'ə·lə·bəl) adj. —**an·ni'hi·la'tion, an·ni'hi·la'tor** n. —Syn. demolish, wipe out, exterminate.

an·ni·ver·sa·ry (an'ə·vûr'sər·ē) n. pl. ·ries 1 A day or occasion recurring on the same date each year as a past event. 2 An observance or celebration on such a day. —adj. 1 Recurring on the same date every year. 2 Of or marking an anniversary. [<L *annus* year + *versus*, p.p. of *vertere* turn]

Anniversary Day Australia Day.

an·no Dom·i·ni (an'ō dom'ə·nī) Latin In the year of the Lord; in a specified year of the Christian era.

an·no·tate (an'ō·tāt) v.t. & v.i. ·tat·ed, ·tat·ing To make explanatory or critical notes on or provide a commentary for (a text, etc.). [<L *ad-* to + *notare* note, mark<*nota* a mark] —**an'no·ta'tion, an'no·ta'tor** n. —**an'no·ta'tive** adj.

an·nounce (ə·nouns') v.t. **an·nounced, an·nounc·ing** 1 To make known publicly or officially. 2 To give notice of the approach or appearance of, as by a signal. 3 To serve as the announcer for, as a radio program [<L<*ad-* to + *nuntiare* report]

an·nounce·ment (ə·nouns'mənt) n. 1 An announcing or being announced. 2 That which is announced. 3 A printed declaration or publication.

an·nounc·er (ə·noun'sər) n. One who announces, esp. one who introduces performers, provides station identification, etc., on radio or television broadcasts.

an·noy (ə·noi') v.t. To be troublesome to; bother; vex. [< LL *inodiare* to make odious] —**an·noy'er** n. —Syn. irk, irritate, harass, pester, bedevil, plague.

an·noy·ance (ə·noi'əns) n. 1 An annoying or being annoyed. 2 One who or that which annoys.

an·noy·ing (ə·noi'ing) adj. Vexatious; troublesome. —**an·noy'ing·ly** adv. —**an·noy'ing·ness** n.

an·nu·al (an'yōo·əl) adj. 1 Returning, performed, or occurring every year. 2 Of or for a year; reckoned by the year. 3 Bot. Lasting or living only one year. —n. 1 A book or pamphlet issued once a year. 2 Bot. A plant living for a single year or season. [<L *annus* year] —**an'nu·al·ly** adv.

an·nu·i·ty (ə·n'yōo'ə·tē) n. pl. ·ties 1 a An annual allowance or income. b The right to receive such an allowance. c The duty to pay it. 2 The return from an investment of capital, in a series of yearly payments. [<L *annus* year]

an·nul (ə·nul') v.t. **an·nulled, an·nul·ling** To make or declare

void or invalid, as a law or marriage. [<L *ad-* to + *nullus* none] —**an·nul'la·ble** adj. —**an·nul'ment** n.

an·nu·lar (an'yə·lər) adj. Formed like a ring; ring-shaped. [<L *annulus* ring] —**an'nu·lar·ly** adv.

annular eclipse Astron. A solar eclipse in which a circular strip of the sun is visible.

an·nu·lus (an'yə·ləs) n. pl. ·li (-lī) or ·lus·es A ringlike part, marking, etc. [<L, a ring]

an·nun·ci·ate (ə·nun'shē·āt, -sē-) v.t. ·at·ed, ·at·ing To announce [<L *annuntiare*. See ANNOUNCE.]

an·nun·ci·a·tion (ə·nun'sē·ā'shən, -shē-) n. The act of announcing; a proclamation.

An·nun·ci·a·tion (ə·nun'sē·ā'shən, -shē-) n. 1 The announcement of the Incarnation to the Virgin by an angel. Luke 1:28–38. 2 The festival (March 25) commemorating this event.

an·nun·ci·a·tor (ə·nun'shē·ā'tər, -sē-) n. An electrical indicator that identifies the caller when a bell is rung.

an·ode (an'ōd) n. 1 The electrode of a polarized device through which current enters. 2 In an electrolytic cell, the positive pole at which oxidation of anions occurs. [<Gk. *anodos* a way up] —**an·od·ic** (an·od'ĭk) adj.

an·o·dize (an'ə·dīz) v.t. ·dized, ·diz·ing To treat the surface of (a metal) by making it the anode of an electrolytic bath.

an·o·dyne (an'ə·dīn) adj. Having power to allay pain; soothing. —n. Anything that relieves pain or soothes. [< Gk. *an-* without + *odynē* pain]

a·noint (ə·noint') v.t. 1 To rub with oil, ointment, etc. 2 To put oil on as a sign of consecration. [<L *inungere*<*in-* on + *ungere* smear] —**a·noint'er, a·noint'ment** n.

a·nom·a·lous (ə·nom'ə·ləs) adj. Deviating from the usual or normal; irregular; abnormal. [<Gk. *an-* not + *homalos* even] —**a·nom'a·lous·ly** adv. —**a·nom'a·lous·ness** n.

a·nom·a·ly (ə·nom'ə·lē) n. pl. ·lies 1 Deviation from rule, type, or form; irregularity; abnormality. 2 Something anomalous. [<Gk. *anōmalos* uneven] —**a·nom'a·lism** n. —**a·nom·a·lis·tic** (ə·nom'ə·lis'tik) or ·ti·cal adj.

an·o·mie (an'ə·mē) n. An anxious awareness of the irrelevance of society's values to oneself; also, a condition of society marked by the absence of moral standards. Also **an'o·my**. [F<Gk. *anomia* lawlessness] —**a·nom·ic** (ə·nom'ik) adj.

a·non (ə·non') adv. 1 In a little while; soon; presently. 2 At another time; again. —**ever and anon** From time to time; now and then. [<OE *on ān* in one]

Anon., anon. anonymous.

an·o·nym (an'ə·nim) n. 1 An anonymous person or writer. 2 A pseudonym.

a·non·y·mous (ə·non'ə·məs) adj. 1 Of unknown authorship or agency. 2 Bearing no name. [<Gk. *an-* without + *onoma, onyma* name] —**an·o·nym·i·ty** (an'ə·nim'ə·tē), **a·non'y·mous·ness** n. —**a·non'y·mous·ly** adv.

a·noph·e·les (ə·nof'ə·lēz) n. Any of a genus of mosquitoes that carry the malaria parasite. [<Gk. *anōphelēs* harmful] —**a·noph·e·line** (ə·nof'ə·līn, -lin) adj.

an·o·rex·i·a (an'ə·rek'sē·ə) n. Med. A chronic condition marked by extreme avoidance of food, often resulting in near-starvation.

an·oth·er (ə·nuth'ər) adj. 1 An additional; one more. 2 Not the same; different. —pron. 1 One more. 2 A different one; a substitute. 3 One of the same or similar character. [<ME *an other*]

an·ox·i·a (an·ok'sē·ə) n. Oxygen deficiency; insufficient oxidation of body tissues. [<AN-¹ + OX(YGEN)]

ans. answer.

an·ser·ine (an'sə·rīn, -sər·in) adj. Of or like a goose; gooselike. [<L *anser* a goose]

an·swer (an'sər, än'-) v.i. 1 To reply or respond, as by words or actions. 2 To prove successful. 3 To be accountable: with *for:* I will *answer* for his honesty. 4 To correspond or match, as in appearance: with *to:* He *answers* to your description. —v.t. 5 To speak, write, or act in response or reply to: to *answer* a letter. 6 To be sufficient for; fulfill: This rod *answers* the purpose. 7 To conform or correspond to: to *answer* a description. —**answer back** To talk back, as in contradiction. —n. A reply, as to a question, message, request, etc. **2** Any action in return or in kind; retaliation. **3** The result or solution, as of a problem in mathematics. **4** *Music* The restatement of a musical theme or phrase by a different voice or instrument. [<OE *andswaru* an answer] —**an'swer·er** *n.* —*Syn. v.* reply, respond, react. *n.* **1** response, rejoinder, acknowledgment. **2** reaction.

an·swer·a·ble (an'sər·ə·bəl, än'-) *adj.* **1** Responsible; accountable. **2** Capable of being answered. **3** Adequate; suitable. —**an'swer·a·ble·ness** *n.* —**an'swer·a·bly** *adv.*

answering service A business that answers telephone calls and takes messages for its clients.

ant (ant) *n.* Any of a large family of typically wingless insects living in colonies having an elaborate social organization. [<OE *æmete*]

-ant *suffix* **1** In the act or process of doing: *exultant.* **2** One who or that which does: *servant.* [<L *-ans (-antis)* present participial suffix]

ant. antenna; antonym.

Ant

ant·ac·id (ant·as'id) *adj.* Counteracting acidity. —*n.* An antacid substance. Also **an'ti·ac'id.**

an·tag·o·nism (an·tag'ə·niz'əm) *n.* Mutual opposition or hostility.

an·tag·o·nist (an·tag'ə·nist) *n.* **1** An adversary; opponent. **2** Anything that acts in an opposite direction, as a muscle, drug, etc.

an·tag·o·nis·tic (an·tag'ə·nis'tik) *adj.* **1** Opposed; hostile. **2** Counteractive. Also **an·tag'o·nis'ti·cal.—an·tag'o·nis'ti·cal·ly** *adv.*

an·tag·o·nize (an·tag'ə·nīz) *v.t.* **·nized, ·niz·ing 1** To oppose, contend with, or struggle against. **2.** To make unfriendly; to make an antagonist of. [<Gk. *antagōnizesthai* struggle against]

Ant·arc·tic (ant·ärk'tik, -är'tik) *n.* **1** The region south of the Antarctic Circle: used with *the.* **2** The Antarctic Ocean. —*adj.* Of, in, or pertaining to the Antarctic or the Antarctic Ocean, [<Gk. *antarktikos* southern <*anti-* opposite + *arktos* the Bear (a northern constellation), the north]

antartic circle *Often cap.* The parallel at about 66.5 south latitude that encircles the southern frigid zone.

An·tar·es (an·târ'ēz) *n.* A bright giant red star in the constellation Scorpio.

ant bear (ant' bâr') **1** A giant anteater of tropical America having a shaggy, black-banded coat. **2.** AARDVARK.

an·te (an'tē) *v.t. & v.i.* **an·teed** or **an·ted, an·te·ing 1** To put up (a poker stake) before the cards are dealt. **2** *Slang* To pay (one's share). —**ante up** *Slang* To ante. —*n.* **1** The stake put up in a game of poker. **2** *Slang* The share one must pay. [<L, before]

ante- *prefix* Before in time, order, or position: *antedate, anteroom.* [<L *ante* before]

ant·eat·er (ant'ē'tər) *n.* Any of several mammals that have a long snout and sticky tongue adapted to feeding on ants, as the echidna, aardvark, etc.

an·te·bel·lum (an'tē·bel'əm) *adj.* Before the war, esp. the U.S. Civil War. [<L *ante bellum* before the war]

Anteater

an·te·cede (an'tə·sēd') *v.t. & v.i.* **·ced·ed, ·ced·ing** To go or come before; precede. [<L *ante* before + *cedere* go]

an·te·ce·dence (an'tə·sēd'əns) *n.* **1** Precedence; priority. **2** *Astron.* The apparent retrograde motion of a planet. Also **an'te·ce'den·cy.**

an·te·ce·dent (an'tə·sēd'ənt) *adj.* Going before; prior in time, place, or order. —*n.* **1** One who or that which precedes or goes before. **2.** *pl.* One's ancestry or past background. **3** *Gram.* The word, phrase, or clause referred to by a pronoun. **4** *Math.* The first term of a ratio; numerator. —**an'te·ce'dent·ly** *adv.*

an·te·cham·ber (an'ti·chām'bər) *n.* A room serving as an entranceway to another.

an·te·date (an'ti·dāt') *v.t.* **·dat·ed, ·dat·ing 1** To come before in time; precede. **2** To assign to a date earlier than the actual one.

an·te·di·lu·vi·an (an'ti·di·lōō've·ən) *adj.* **1** Of the times,

events, etc., before the Flood. **2** Antiquated; primitive. —*n.* Someone or something antediluvian. [<ANTE- + L *diluvium* deluge]

an·te·lope (an'tə·lōp) *n. pl.* **·lope** or **·lopes 1** Any of various swift-running, long-horned bovines, including the gazelle, chamois, gnu, etc. **2** Leather made from the hide of such an animal. **3** PRONGHORN. [<LGk. *antholops*]

an·te me·rid·i·em (an'tē mə·rid'ē·em) *Latin* Before noon.

an·ten·na (an·ten'ə) *n. pl.* **·ten·nae** (-ten'ē) *for def. 1,* **·ten'nas** *for def. 2.* **1** One of the paired, movable, sensory appendages on the head of an insect or other arthropod; a feeler. **2** Any of various devices designed to project or receive electromagnetic waves, as in television or radio. [<L, a yard on which a sail is spread] • See INSECT.

an·te·pe·nult (an'ti·pē'nult, -pi·nult') *n.* The syllable before the next to the last syllable, as *pol* in *anthropology.*

an·te·pe·nul·ti·mate (an'ti·pi·nul'tə·mit) *adj.* The last but two of any series. —*n.* ANTEPENULT.

an·te·ri·or (an·tir'ē·ər) *adj.* **1** In front or forward. **2** Preceding in time; earlier. [<L, compar. of *ante* before] —**an·te'ri·or·ly** *adv.* —*Syn.* **1** front, fore, forward, foremost. **2** prior, preceding, antecedent.

an·te·room (an'ti·rōōm', -rōōm') *n.* A waiting room; antechamber.

an·them (an'thəm) *n.* **1** A song of praise or triumph, as one officially adopted by a nation. **2** A choral composition, usually on a religious text. [<Gk. *antiphōna,* lit., things sounding in response]

an·ther (an'thər) *n.* The pollen-bearing part of a stamen. [<Gk. *anthēros* flowery <*anthos* flower] • See STAMEN.

an·ther·id·i·um (an'thə·rid'ē·əm) *n. pl.* **·i·a** (-ē·ə) The organ in which male cells are developed in mosses, fungi, etc., the analog of the anther in flowering plants. [<Gk. *anthēros* flowery] —**an'ther·id'i·al** *adj.*

ant hill The earth heaped by ants or termites at the entrance to their nest.

an·thol·o·gize (an·thol'ə·jīz) *v.i. & v.t.* **·gized, ·giz·ing** To make or include in an anthology. —**an·thol'o·gist** *n.*

an·thol·o·gy (an·thol'ə·jē) *n. pl.* **·gies** A collection of selected poems, stories, etc. [<Gk. *anthologia* a garland, collection of poems] —**an·tho·log·i·cal** (an'thə·loj'i·kəl) *adj.*

an·tho·zo·an (an'thə·zō'ən) *n.* One of a class of sessile marine coelenterates, including the sea anemones and corals; a polyp. —*adj.* Of or pertaining to anthozoans. Also **an'tho·zo'on** (-on). [<Gk. *anthos* flower + *zōon* animal] —**an'tho·zo'ic** *adj.*

an·thra·cene (an'thrə·sēn) *n.* A fluorescent crystalline compound derived from coal tar and used in the manufacture of dyes and to detect radiation. [<Gk. *anthrax* coal + -ENE]

an·thra·cite (an'thrə·sīt) *n.* Coal that burns with much heat and little flame; hard coal. [<Gk. *anthrax* coal] —**an·thra·cit·ic** (an'thrə·sit'ik) *adj.*

an·thrac·nose (an·thrak'nōs) *n.* Any one of many plant diseases often producing dark lesions or blisters. [<Gk. *anthrax* coal+*nosos* disease]

an·thrax (an'thraks) *n. pl.* **·thra·ces** (-thrə·sēz) **1** A malignant febrile disease of sheep, swine, and other animals, sometimes transmitted to man by the resistant spores of the causative bacillus. **2** A pustule due to the disease. [<Gk., coal, carbuncle]

anthropo- *combining form* Man; human: *anthropology.* [<Gk. *anthrōpos* man]

an·thro·po·cen·tric (an'thrə·pō·sen'trik) *adj.* Regarding mankind and human values as the central fact or focus of the universe, life, etc. -**an'thro·po·cen'tri·cal·ly** *adv.*

an·thro·pog·e·ny (an'thrə·poj'ə·nē) *n.* The branch of anthropology that deals with the origin and development of human beings. Also **an·thro·po·gen·e·sis** (an'thrə·pō·jen'ə·sis).

an·thro·poid (an'thrə·poid) *adj.* **1** Resembling a human being: said of the highest apes, as the gorilla, chimpanzee, and orang-utan. **2** Apelike: long, *anthropoid* arms. Also **an'thro·poid'al.** —*n.* An anthropoid ape.

an·thro·pol·o·gy (an'thrə·pol'ə·jē) *n.* The scientific study of human beings and their physiscal, social, material, and cultural development. —**an·thro·po·log·i·cal** (an'thrə·pə·loj'i·kəl) or **·log'ic** *adj.* —**an'thro·po·log'i·cal·ly** *adv.* —**an'thro·pol'o·gist** *n.*

an·thro·pom·e·try (an'thrə·pom'ə·trē) *n.* The science and technique of measuring anatomical and physiological features of human beings. —**an·thro·po·met·ric** (an'thrə·pō·met'rik) or **·met'ri·cal** *adj.*

an·thro·po·mor·phism (an'thrə·pō·môr'fiz·əm) n. The ascription of human attributes, feelings, motives, or characteristics to nonhuman objects, beings, or phenomena. — **an'thro·po·mor'phic** adj. —**an'thro·po·mor'phi·cal·ly** adv. — **an'thro·po·mor'phist** n.

an·thro·po·mor·phize (an'thrə·pō·môr'fīz) v.t. & v.i. ·phized, ·phiz·ing To attribute human characteristics (to).

an·thro·po·mor·phous (an'thrə·pō·môr'fəs) adj. Having or resembling human form.

an·thro·poph·a·gous (an'thrə·pof'ə·gəs) adj. Feeding on human flesh; cannibalistic. [< Gk. anthrōpos man + phagein eat] —**an·thro·poph·a·gy** (an'thrə·pof'ə·jē) n.

an·ti (an'tī, an'tē) n. pl. ·tis Informal One opposed to a policy, group, etc.

anti- prefix 1 Against; opposed to: anti-Semitic. 2 Opposite to; reverse: antisocial. 3 Rivaling; spurious: Antichrist. 4 Counteracting: antibiotic. [< Gk. anti against]

an·ti·air·craft (an'tē·âr'kraft', -âr'kräft') adj. Used defensively against aircraft.

an·ti·bal·lis·tic missile (an'tē·bə·lis'tik) A missile designed to intercept and destroy hostile ballistic missiles as soon as possible.

an·ti·bi·ot·ic (an'ti·bī·ot'ik) n. Any of certain substances, as penicillin and streptomycin, produced by various fungi, bacteria, etc., that destroy or arrest the growth of other microorganisms, used in the treatment of infectious diseases. —adj. Of or acting as an antibiotic. [< ANTI- + Gk. bios mode of life]

an·ti·bod·y (an'ti·bod'ē) n. pl. ·bod·ies A protein in the blood serum formed in response to a specific foreign protein and conferring immunity to that foreign protein.

an·tic (an'tik) n. A ludicrous or clownish action; a prank; caper. —adj. Odd; ludicrous; incongruous. —v.i. an·ticked, an·tick·ing To perform antics. [< Ital. antico old, grotesque]

An·ti·christ (an'ti·krīst') n. An opponent or enemy of Christ.

an·tic·i·pate (an·tis'ə·pāt) v.t. ·pat·ed, ·pat·ing 1 To count on in advance; expect; foresee. 2 To be in advance of or earlier than. 3 To act so as to prevent; forestall. 4 To foresee and act on beforehand. 5 To take or make use of beforehand, as income not yet available. [< L ante- before + capere take] —**an·tic'i·pa'tor** n. —**an·tic·i·pa·to·ry** (-tis'ə·pə·tôr'ē, -tō'rē) adj.

an·tic·i·pa·tion (an·tis'ə·pā'shən) n. 1 The act of anticipating. 2 Something anticipated or expected. 3 The act of awaiting expectantly; expectation. 4 A presentiment; foretaste.

an·ti·cler·i·cal (an'ti·kler'i·kəl) adj. Opposed to clerical influence, esp. that of the Roman Catholic Church.

an·ti·cli·max (an'ti·klī'maks) n. 1 A sudden shift from the serious, lofty, etc., to the trivial or ludicrous. 2 Any sudden and disappointingly contrasting shift. —**an'ti·cli·mac'tic** (-klī·mak'tik) adj. —**an'ti·cli·mac'ti·cal·ly** adv.

an·ti·cline (an'ti·klīn) n. A rock stratum or group of strata forming a bend with the convex side upward. [< ANTI- + Gk. klinein to slope]— **an'ti·cli'nal, an'ti·clin'ic** (-klin'ik) adj.

an·ti·cy·clone (an'ti·sī'klōn) n. An atmospheric condition of high pressure relative to the surrounding area, with clockwise

Anticline

horizontal currents in the northern hemisphere, and counterclockwise ones in the southern. —**an·ti·cy·clon·ic** (an'ti·sī·klon'ik) adj.

an·ti·dote (an'ti·dōt) n. 1 Anything that neutralizes or counteracts the effects of a poison. 2 Something that counteracts a harmful effect. [< Gk antidotos given against] — **an'ti·do'tal** adj. —**an'ti·do'tal·ly** adv.

an·ti·freeze (an'ti·frēz') n. A liquid added to or substituted for the water in a cooling or heating system to prevent freezing.

an·ti·gen (an'tə·jən) n. Any substance that stimulates the development of antibodies. Also **an'ti·gene** (-jēn). —**an·ti·gen·ic** (an'tə·jen'ik) adj.

An·tig·o·ne (an·tig'ə·nē) Gk. Myth. A daughter of Oedipus who was sentenced to death for performing forbidden funeral rites for her brother.

an·ti·he·ro (an'tē·hē'rō, an'tī-) n. A protagonist, as of a novel or play, who lacks traditional qualities attributed to a hero, as courage, gallantry, etc. —**an·ti·he·ro·ic** (an'tē·hi·rō'ik, an'tī-) adj.

an·ti·his·ta·mine (an'ti·his'tə·mēn, -min) n. Any of certain drugs that neutralize the action of histamine in allergic conditions and colds. —**an'ti·his'ta·min'ic** (-min'ik) adj.

an·ti·knock (an'ti·nok') adj. Preventing detonation in an engine. —n. An agent, as tetraethyl lead, that prevents knock or detonation when added to the fuel of an internal-combustion engine.

an·ti·log·a·rithm (an'ti·lôg'ə·rith'əm, -log'-) n. The number corresponding to a given logarithm.

an·ti·ma·cas·sar (an'ti·mə·kas'ər) n. A small covering to prevent soiling of the backs or arms of chairs or sofas. [< ANTI- + Macassar a kind of hair oil]

an·ti·mat·ter (an'ti·mat'ər) n. A theoretical form of matter composed of antiparticles.

an·ti·mo·ny (an'tə·mō'nē) n. A metallic element (symbol Sb) used chiefly in alloys, as type metal, etc. [< Med. L antimonium]

an·ti·par·ti·cle (an'ti·par'ti·kəl) n. Either of a pair of subatomic particles, as an electron and positron, that are equal in mass but opposite in charge and in magnetic properties. Contact between a particle and its opposite results in mutual annihilation and the release of energy.

an·ti·pas·to (än·tē·päs'tō) n. An appetizer of assorted meats, fish, vegetables, etc. [< Ital. anti- before + pasto food]

an·ti·pa·thet·ic (an·tip'ə·thet'ik, an'ti·pə-) adj. Having antipathy; opposed; averse. Also **an·tip'a·thet'i·cal.** —**an·tip'a·thet'i·cal·ly** adv.

an·tip·a·thy (an·tip'ə·thē) n. pl. ·thies 1 A feeling of aversion or dislike. 2 The cause of such feeling. [< Gk. anti- against + pathein feel, suffer] —**Syn.** repugnance, abhorrence, antagonism, hostility.

an·ti·per·son·nel (an'ti·pûr'sə·nel') adj. Used as a weapon against individuals rather than against defenses or equipment.

an·ti·per·spi·rant (an'ti·pûr'spə·rənt) n. A preparation applied to the skin to retard or prevent perspiration. — adj. Preventing or retarding perspiration.

an·ti·phon (an'tə·fon) n. 1 A hymn or liturgical chant sung by alternating choirs. 2 A versicle chanted before, and often after, a psalm or canticle. [< Gk. antiphona. See ANTHEM.] —**an·tiph·o·nal** (an·tif'ə·nəl), **an'ti·phon'ic** or ·i·cal adj. —**an·tiph'o·nal·ly** adv.

an·tiph·o·ny (an·tif'ə·nē) n. Antiphonal singing, form, etc.

an·ti·pode (an'ti·pōd) n. An exact opposite.

an·tip·o·des (an·tip'ə·dēz) n. pl. 1 A place or region on the opposite side of the earth. 2 (often construed as sing.) Something diametrically opposed to another; an opposite extreme. [< Gk. antipous having the feet opposite] —**an·tip'o·dal, an·tip'o·de'an** adj.

an·ti·py·ret·ic (an'ti·pī·ret'ik) adj. Alleviating fever. — n. A medicine to allay fever. [< ANTI- + Gk. pyretos fever]

an·ti·quar·i·an (an'ti·kwâr'ē·ən) adj. Pertaining to antiquity or to expertise in antiquities. —n. An antiquary. —**an'ti·quar'i·an·ism** n.

an·ti·quar·y (an'ti·kwer'ē) n. pl. ·quar·ies One who collects, deals in, or studies antiquities. [< L antiquarius < antiquus ancient]

an·ti·quate (an'ti·kwāt) v.t. ·quat·ed, ·quat·ing 1 To make old or obsolete. 2 To cause to appear old-fashioned. —**an'ti·qua'tion** n.

an·ti·quat·ed (an'ti·kwā'tid) adj. 1 Out of date; obsolete. 2 Ancient. —**Syn.** old-fashioned, passé, superannuated, archaic.

an·tique (an·tēk') adj. 1 Of or pertaining to ancient

times, esp. ancient Greece or Rome. **2** Of or in the style of an earlier time. **3** Old; ancient. —*n.* **1** An object, esp. a work of art or handicraft, valued because of its age. **2** The style of ancient art. —*v.t.* **an·tiqued, an·ti·quing** To cause to resemble an antique. [< L *antiquus* ancient] —**an·tique′ly** *adv.* —**an·tique′ness** *n.*

an·tiq·ui·ty (an·tik′wə·tē) *n. pl.* **·ties 1** The condition of being ancient; great age. **2** Ancient times. **3** *Usu. pl.* A relic of ancient times.

an·ti·scor·bu·tic (an′ti·skôr·byōō′tik) *adj.* Relieving or preventing scurvy. —*n.* A remedy for scurvy.

an·ti·Sem·i·tism (an′ti·sem′ə·tiz′əm) *n.* Hostility toward or prejudice against Jews. —**an′ti-Sem′ite** *n.* —**an′ti-Se·mit′ic** (-sə·mit′ik) *adj.* —**an′ti-Se·mit′i·cal·ly** *adv.*

an·ti·sep·sis (an′tə·sep′sis) *n.* The prevention of infection by destroying the causative organisms. [< ANTI- + Gk. *sēpsis* putrefaction]

an·ti·sep·tic (an′tə·sep′tik) *adj.* **1** Of, pertaining to, or used in antisepsis. **2** Destructive of organisms causing infection, fermentation, or putrefaction. Also **an′ti·sep′ti·cal.** —*n.* An antiseptic substance. —**an′ti·sep′ti·cal·ly** *adv.*

an·ti·slav·er·y (an′ti·slā′vər·ē, -slāv′rē) *adj.* Opposed to human slavery.

an·ti·so·cial (an′ti·sō′shəl) *adj.* **1** Opposed to or disruptive of social order. **2** Avoiding social contact; not sociable. —**an′ti·so′cial·ly** *adv.*

an·tis·tro·phe (an·tis′trə·fē) *n.* In ancient Greek dramatic poetry, the verses sung by the chorus while moving from left to right in answer to the strophe. [< Gk. *antistrephein* turn against.] —**an·ti·stroph·ic** (an′ti·strof′ik) *adj.*

an·ti·tank (an′ti·tangk′) *adj.* Designed to combat mechanized equipment, as tanks.

an·tith·e·sis (an·tith′ə·sis) *n. pl.* **·ses** (-sēz) **1** The balancing of contrasted words, ideas, etc., against each other. **2** The direct contrary or opposite. [< Gk. *antitithenai* oppose] —**an·ti·thet·i·cal** (an′tə·thet′i·kəl), **an′ti·thet′ic** *adj.* —**an′ti·thet′i·cal·ly** *adv.*

an·ti·tox·in (an′ti·tok′sin) *n.* **1** An antibody formed in response to a specific toxin. **2** A preparation of a serum containing an antitoxin, used in treating certain diseases. —**an′ti·tox′ic** *adj.*

an·ti·trades (an′ti·trādz′) *n. pl.* The upper air currents in the tropics, moving contrary to the trade winds.

an·ti·trust (an′ti·trust′) *adj.* Regulating or opposing trusts, monopolies, etc., that are in restraint of trade.

ant·ler (ant′lər) *n.* One of the paired, deciduous, solid, bony outgrowths on the head of various members of the deer family. [< OF *antoillier,* < L *ante-* before + *oculus* eye] —**ant′lered** *adj.*

ant lion An insect resembling a dragonfly, esp. its louselike larva, which preys on ants and other insects.

Antlers

an·to·nym (an′tə·nim) *n.* A word opposite to another in meaning. [< Gk. *anti-* opposite + *onoma, onyma* name]

an·trum (an′trəm) *n. pl.* **·tra** (-trə) A cavity, usu. in a bone. [< Gk. *antron* cave]

a·nus (ā′nəs) *n.* The opening at the lower end of the alimentary canal. [< L, orig. a ring]

an·vil (an′vil) *n.* **1** A heavy block of iron or steel on which metal may be forged. **2** *Anat.* The incus of the inner ear. [< OE *anfilt*]

anx·i·e·ty (ang·zī′ə·tē) *n. pl.* **·ties 1** Distress of mind; uneasiness; worry. **2** Strained or intent eagerness. **3** A neurotic state of great tension or dread. —**Syn. 1** concern, misgiving, apprehension, disquiet, care. [< L *anxius* anxious]

anx·ious (angk′shəs, ang′-) *adj.* **1** Troubled in mind; uneasy; worried. **2** Fraught with or causing anxiety: an *anxious* wait. **3** Intently eager or desirous: *anxious* to succeed. [< L *anxius* < *angere* choke, distress] —**anx′ious·ly** *adv.* —**anx′ious·ness** *n.*

anxious seat *U.S.* The bench at a revival meeting for those who fear they may not be saved.

an·y (en′ē) *adj.* **1** One or some of several or many: Choose *any* item. Have *any* eggs hatched? **2** Some, no matter

what: at *any* price. **3** Every: *Any* fool knows that. —*pron.* One or more persons, things, etc., of a number. —*adv.* At all: Are you *any* better today? [< OE *ān* one]

an·y·bod·y (en′i·bod′ē, -bud′ē) *pron.* Any person; anyone. —*n.* A person of importance: He isn't *anybody.*

an·y·how (en′i·hou′) *adv.* **1** In any way whatever; by any means. **2** Notwithstanding; in any case. **3** Carelessly.

an·y·more (en′ē·môr′, -mōr′) *adv.* Now; at present: used only in the negative and in questions: He's not welcome *anymore.* Do you see her *anymore?* Also **any more.**

an·y·one (en′i·wun′, -wən) *pron.* Any person. • **any one,** anyone *Any one* is used to distinguish one individual from others in the same group or class: *Any one* of these men may be guilty. *Anyone* means any person at all: Can *anyone* identify the culprit?

any·place (en′ē·plās′) *adv.* In or to any place.

an·y·thing (en′i·thing′) *pron.* Any thing or matter of any sort. —*n.* A thing of any kind. —*adv.* At all; in any way: not *anything* like that. —**anything but** By no means: *anything but* safe.

an·y·way (en′i·wā′) *adv.* **1** No matter what happens; in any event. **2** Nevertheless; anyhow. **3** Carelessly.

an·y·where (en′i·hwâr′) *adv.* In, at, or to any place.

an·y·wise (en′i·wīz′) *adv.* In any manner.

An·zac (an′zak) *n.* A soldier from Australia or New Zealand.

A/O, a/o account of.

A-OK (ā′ō·kā′) *adj. Informal* Perfectly all right; just fine. Also **A′-o·kay′.**

A-one (ā′wun′) *adj. Informal* Excellent; first-rate. Also **A-1.**

a·or·ta (ā·ôr′tə) *n. pl.* **·tas** or **·tae** (-tē) The great artery leading from the left ventricle of the heart and distributing oxygenated blood to the body. [< NL < Gk. *aortē* < *aeirein* to raise, heave] —**a·or′tal, a·or′tic** *adj.* • See HEART.

a·ou·dad (ä′ōō·dad) *n.* A wild sheep of northern Africa. [< Berber *audad*]

AP, A.P. Associated Press.

a·pace (ə·pās′) *adv.* Rapidly; swiftly. [< *a-* on + PACE]

a·pache (ə·päsh′, ə·pash′; *Fr.* á·pásh′) *n.* A Parisian hoodlum or gangster. [< *Apache*]

A·pach·e (ə·pach′ē) *n. pl.* **A·pach·es** or **A·pach·e** A member of a tribe of North American Indians of Athapascan stock.

ap·a·nage (ap′ə·nij) *n.* APPANAGE.

a·part (ə·pärt′) *adv.* **1** At a distance or interval: placed two feet *apart.* **2** So as to be isolated or separated: set *apart.* **3** Away or aside: held *apart.* **4** Separately; independently: considered *apart.* **5** In or to pieces: torn *apart.* —**apart from** Other than; with the exception of. —*adj.* Separated. [< L *ad* to + *pars* part]

a·part·heid (ə·pärt′hīt, -hāt) *n.* The racial segregation decreed by law in the Republic of South Africa. [Afrikaans, apartness]

a·part·ment (ə·pärt′mənt) *n.* One of several rooms or suites of rooms in one building, equipped for housekeeping. [< Ital. *appartamento*]

apartment house A multiple-dwelling building divided into a number of apartments.

ap·a·thet·ic (ap′ə·thet′ik) *adj.* Feeling or showing no emotion, interest, etc.; indifferent. Also **ap′a·thet′i·cal.** —**ap′a·thet′i·cal·ly** *adv.* —**Syn.** unfeeling, unconcerned, sluggish, listless, spiritless.

ap·a·thy (ap′ə·thē) *n.* **1** Lack of emotion, motivation, etc. **2** Lack of concern; indifference. [< Gk. *a-* without + *pathos* feeling]

ape (āp) *n.* **1** A large, tailless primate, as a gorilla or chimpanzee. **2** Loosely, any monkey. **3** A mimic. —*v.t.* **aped, ap·ing** To imitate; mimic. [< OE *apa*]

a·pe·ri·ent (ə·pir′ē·ənt) *adj.* Acting as a laxative. —*n.* An aperient remedy. Also **a·per′i·tive** (ə·per′ə·tiv). [< L *aperire* open]

a·pe·ri·tif (ä′per·ə·tēf′, ə·per-, *Fr.* á·pā·rē·tēf′) *n.* An alcoholic drink, esp. of fortified wine, taken as an appetizer. [< F *apéritif*]

ap·er·ture (ap′ər·chŏŏr, -chər) *n.* **1** An opening; hole. **2** An opening through which radiation is captured, as by a lens or antenna. [< L *apertus,* pp. of *aperire* open] —**ap′er·tur·al** *adj.* —**ap′er·tured** *adj.*

a·pet·al·ous (ā·pet′əl·əs) *adj.* Without petals.

a·pex (ā′peks) *n. pl.* **a·pex·es** or **ap·i·ces** (ap′ə·sēz, ā′pə-) **1** The highest point; tip; top. **2** The vertex of an angle. **3** Climax. [< L]

a·pha·sia (ə·fā′zhə, -zhē-ə) *n.* Partial or total loss of the power to use language, due to brain injury or disease. [< Gk. *aphatos* speechless] —**a·pha·sic** (ə·fā′zik, -sik), **a·pha·si·ac** (ə·fā′zē·ak) *adj., n.*

a·phe·li·on (ə·fē′lē·ən) *n. pl.* **·li·a** (-lē·ə) The point in an orbit, as of a planet, farthest from the sun. [< Gk. *apo* away from + *hēlios* sun] —**a·phe′li·an** (-ən) *adj.*

a·phid (ā′fid, af′id) *n.* Any of a family of numerous, small, juice-sucking insects, injurious to plants; a plant louse.

a·phis (ā′fis, af′is) *n. pl.* **aph·i·des** (af′ə·dēz) APHID.[?]

aph·o·rism (af′ə·riz′əm) *n.* A brief, pithy statement of a truth or principle; maxim. [< Gk. *aphorismos* definition] —**aph·o·rist** (af′ə·rist) *n.* —**aph·o·ris′tic** or **·ti·cal** *adj.* —**aph·o·ris′ti·cal·ly** *adv.*

Aphid

aph·ro·dis·i·ac (af′rə·diz′ē·ak) *adj.* Arousing or increasing sexual desire or potency. —*n.* An aphrodisiac drug, food, etc. [< Gk. *Aphroditē* goddess of love]

Aph·ro·di·te (af′rə·dī′tē) *Gk. Myth.* The goddess of love and beauty, identified with the Roman Venus.

a·pi·an (ā′pē·ən) *adj.* Of or pertaining to bees.

a·pi·ar·i·an (ā′pē·âr′ē·ən) *adj.* Of or relating to bees or beekeeping. —*n.* An apiarist.

a·pi·a·rist (ā′pē·ə·rist) *n.* One who tends bees and collects honey.

a·pi·ar·y (ā′pē·er′ē) *n. pl.* **·ar·ies** A place where bees are kept. [< L *apis* bee]

ap·i·cal (ap′i·kəl, ā′pi-) *adj.* Of, at, or forming an apex. [< L *apex* tip] —**ap′i·cal·ly** *adv.*

ap·i·ces (ap′ə·sēz, ā′pə-) *n.pl.* of APEX.

a·pi·cul·ture (ā′pi·kul′chər) *n.* The raising and care of bees, esp. on a large scale. [< L *apis* bee + CULTURE]

a·piece (ə·pēs′) *adv.* For or to each one; each.

ap·ish (ā′pish) *adj.* **1** Of or like an ape. **2** Foolishly imitative. **3** Sly; tricky. —**ap′ish·ly** *adv.* —**ap′ish·ness** *n.*

a·plen·ty (ə·plen′tē) *adv. Informal* In plentiful supply.

a·plomb (ə·plom′, ə·plum′) *n.* Assurance; self-confidence. [F, perpendicularity, assurance] —**Syn.** poise, self-assurance, self-possession, equanimity.

apo- *prefix* Off; from; away: *apogee.* [< Gk. *apo* from, off]

APO, A.P.O. Army Post Office.

Apoc. Apocalypse; Apocrypha; Apocryphal.

a·poc·a·lypse (ə·pok′ə·lips) *n.* A prophetic revelation. [< L < Gk. *apokalyptein* disclose] —**a·poc′a·lyp′tic** (-lip′tik) or **·ti·cal** *adj.* —**a·poc′a·lyp′ti·cal·ly** *adv.*

A·poc·a·lypse (ə·pok′ə·lips) *n.* The book of Revelation, the last book of the New Testament.

á·poc·o·pe (ə·pok′ə·pē) *n.* A cutting off or elision of the last sound or syllable of a word. [< Gk. *apokoptein* cut off]

a·poc·ry·pha (ə·pok′rə·fə) *n. pl.* Any writings or accounts of questionable authorship or doubtful authenticity. [< Gk. *apokryphos* hidden]

A·poc·ry·pha (ə·pok′rə·fə) *n. pl.* **1** Fourteen books of the Septuagint, eleven of which are accepted in the Roman Catholic canon, but none of which is accepted by Protestants or included in the Hebrew Scriptures. **2** Any of various unauthenticated early Christian writings. —**A·poc′ry·phal** *adj.*

a·poc·ry·phal (ə·pok′rə·fəl) *adj.* Of doubtful authenticity. —**a·poc′ry·phal·ly** *adv.*

ap·o·gee (ap′ə·jē) *n.* **1** The point in the orbit of the moon or of an artificial satellite that is farthest from the earth. **2** The highest point; climax. [< Gk. < *apo* away from + *gē, gaia* earth] —**ap·o·ge·al** (ap′ə·jē′əl), **ap·o·ge·an** *adj.*

a. apogee. p. perigee.

a·po·lit·i·cal (ā′pə·lit′i·kəl) *adj.* Not associated with or interested in politics. —**a′po·lit′i·cal·ly** *adv.*

A·pol·lo (ə·pol′ō) *Gk. & Rom. Myth.* The god of music, poetry, prophecy, and medicine. —*n.* Any handsome young man.

A·pol·lyon (ə·pol′yən) The devil. *Rev.* 9:11.

a·pol·o·get·ic (ə·pol′ə·jet′ik) *adj.* **1** Making or implying an apology. **2** Defending or explaining. Also **a·pol′o·get′i·cal.** [< Gk. *apologia* a speech in defense] —**a·pol′o·get′i·cal·ly** *adv.*

a·pol·o·get·ics (ə·pol′ə·jet′iks) *n. pl. (construed as sing.)* The branch of theology that deals with the defense of Christianity.

ap·o·lo·gi·a (ap′ə·lō′jē·ə) *n.* A justification or defense. [< Gk.]

a·pol·o·gist (ə·pol′ə·jist) *n.* One who argues in defense of a person or cause.

a·pol·o·gize (ə·pol′ə·jīz) *v.i.* **·gized, ·giz·ing 1** To express regret for an offense or wrongdoing. **2** To make a formal justification or defense. —**a·pol′o·giz′er** *n.*

ap·o·logue (ap′ə·lôg) *n.* A moral tale; a fable. Also **ap′o·log.** [< Gk. *apologos* < *apo-* from + *logos* speech]

a·pol·o·gy (ə·pol′ə·jē) *n. pl.* **·gies 1** A formal expression of regret for an offense, incivility, etc. **2** A poor substitute. [< Gk. *apologia* a speech in defense < *apo-* from + *logos* speech]

ap·o·phthegm (ap′ə·them) *n.* APOTHEGM.

ap·o·plec·tic (ap′ə·plek′tik) *adj.* **1** Of, affected with, or tending toward apoplexy. **2** Causing or likely to cause apoplexy. **3** Wildly excited, as with rage; beside oneself. Also **ap′o·plec′ti·cal.** —*n.* A person subject to apoplexy. —**ap′o·plec′ti·cal·ly** *adv.*

ap·o·plex·y (ap′ə·plek′sē) *n.* Sudden loss of sensation and voluntary motion, due to hemorrhage or impaired circulation in the brain; a stroke. [< Gk. *apoplēxia* < *apoplēssein* disable by a stroke]

a·port (ə·pôrt′, ə·pōrt′) *adv. Naut.* On or toward the port or left side.

a·pos·ta·sy (ə·pos′tə·sē) *n. pl.* **·sies** Desertion of one's religious faith, party, or principles, etc. [< Gk. *apostasia* a standing off, desertion]

a·pos·tate (ə·pos′tāt, -tit) *n.* One guilty of apostasy. —*adj.* Guilty of apostasy.

a·pos·ta·tize (ə·pos′tə·tīz) *v.i.* **·tized, ·tiz·ing** To forsake one's faith, principles, etc.

a pos·te·ri·o·ri (ā′ pos·tir′ē·ôr′ī, -ō′rī) **1** Reasoning from facts to principles or from effect to cause. **2** Inductive; empirical. [L, from what comes after]

a·pos·tle (ə·pos′əl) *n.* **1** *Often cap.* One of the twelve disciples originally chosen by Christ to preach the gospel. **2** A missionary or preacher in the early Christian church. **3** A Christian missionary who first evangelizes a nation or place. **4** An early or chief advocate of a cause. [< Gk. *apostolos* one sent forth, a messenger] —**a·pos′tle·ship,** **a·pos·to·late** (ə·pos′tə·lit, -lāt) *n.*

Apostles' Creed A traditional Christian confession of faith.

ap·os·tol·ic (ap′ə·stol′ik) *adj.* **1** Of or pertaining to an apostle, the Apostles, or their times. **2** According to the doctrine or practice of the Apostles. **3** *Often cap.* Papal. Also **ap′os·tol′i·cal.** —**ap′os·tol′i·cal·ly** *adv.* —**ap′os·tol′i·cism** (-ə·siz′əm) *n.*

Apostolic See The see of Rome, regarded as having been founded by St. Peter.

a·pos·tro·phe[1] (ə·pos′trə·fē) *n.* A symbol (′) shown above the line, to indicate the omission of a letter or letters, the possessive case, or certain plurals, esp. of numbers *(4's)* or letters *(i's).* [< Gk. *(prosōidia) apostrophos* (accent) of turning away] —**ap′os·troph′ic** (ap′ə·strof′ik) *adj.*

a·pos·tro·phe[2] (ə·pos′trə·fē) *n.* A digression from a discourse, esp. to speak to an imaginary or absent person. [< Gk. *apostrophē* a turning away] —**ap·os·troph·ic** (ap′ə·strof′ik) *adj.*

a·pos·tro·phize[1] (ə·pos′trə·fīz) *v.t. & v.i.* **·phized, ·phiz·ing** To mark with or use the apostrophe in writing.

a·pos·tro·phize[2] (ə·pos′trə·fīz) *v.t. & v.i.* **·phized, ·phiz·ing** To address by or use a rhetorical apostrophe.

apothecaries' measure A system of liquid measure used in pharmacy. • See MEASURE.

apothecaries' weight A system of weights used in pharmacy. • See MEASURE.

a·poth·e·car·y (ə·poth′ə·ker′ē) n. pl. ·car·ies A druggist; pharmacist. [< Gk. apothēkē storehouse]

ap·o·thegm (ap′ə·them) n. A terse, instructive, practical saying; a maxim. [< Gk. apophthegma a thing uttered] — **ap·o·theg·mat·ic** (ap′ə·theg·mat′ik) or **-i·cal** adj.

a·poth·e·o·sis (ə·poth′ē·ō′sis, ap′ə·thē′ə·sis) n. pl. ·ses (-sēz) 1 Elevation to divine status; deification. 2 Supreme exaltation or idealization; essence. [< Gk. apo- from + theos a god]

a·poth·e·o·size (ə·poth′ē·ə·sīz′, ap′ə·thē′ə·sīz) v.t. ·sized, ·siz·ing 1 To deify. 2 To glorify.

app. apparatus; appendix; apprentice.

ap·pall (ə·pôl′) v.t. ap·palled, ap·pal·ling To fill with dismay or horror; horrify; shock. Also ap·pal (ap·palled, ap·pal·ling). [< OF apallir become or make pale]

ap·pal·ling (ə·pô′ling) adj. Causing dismay; shocking; frightful. —**ap·pall′ing·ly** adv.

ap·pa·loo·sa (ap′ə·lōō′sə) n. Often cap. A breed of western saddle horses having a mottled appearance. [Prob. after Palouse Indians of the NW U.S.]

ap·pa·nage (ap′ə·nij) n. 1 Land, property, etc., for the maintenance of a ruler's younger offspring. 2 One's due; a perquisite. 3 A natural attribute or adjunct. [< OF apaner nourish]

ap·pa·rat (ap′ə·rat, äp′ə·rät′) n. APPARATUS (def. 4). [Russ.]

ap·pa·rat·chik (äp′ə·rä′chik) n. pl. ·ra·tchi·ki (-rä′chə·kē) or ·ra·tchiks A political functionary in a Communist bureaucracy. [Russ.]

ap·pa·ra·tus (ap′ə·rā′təs, -rat′əs) n. pl. ·tus or ·tus·es 1 A complex device or machine for a particular purpose. 2 An assembly of devices designed to achieve a specified result. 3 The organs and parts of the body involved in a specific function. 4 The organization or bureaucratic formula for accomplishing a political purpose, as maintaining a party in power. [L, preparation]

ap·par·el (ə·par′əl) n. Garments; clothing. —v.t. ·eled or ·elled, ·el·ing or ·el·ling To clothe; dress. [< OF apareiller prepare] —Syn. n. dress, attire, raiment, garb.

ap·par·ent (ə·par′ənt, ə·pâr′-) adj. 1 Evident; obvious. 2 Seeming rather than actual. [< OF aparoir appear] —**ap·par′ent·ly** adv. —**ap·par′ent·ness** n.

ap·pa·ri·tion (ap′ə·rish′ən) n. 1 A specter; phantom; ghost. 2 An eerie or startlingly unusual sight. 3 An appearance. [< L apparere to appear] —**ap′pa·ri′tion·al** adj.

ap·peal (ə·pēl′) n. 1 An earnest entreaty for aid, sympathy, etc. 2 A quality or manner that attracts. 3 A resort to some higher power or final means. 4 Law a The carrying of a cause from a lower to a higher tribunal for a rehearing. b The right or request to do this. c A case so carried. —v.i. 1 To make an earnest supplication or request. 2 To be interesting or attractive. 3 To resort or have recourse: to appeal to reason. 4 Law To request that a case be moved to a higher court. —v.t. 5 To refer or transfer (a case) to a higher court. [< L appellare call upon] —**ap·peal′a·ble** adj. —**ap·peal′er** n. —**ap·peal′ing·ly** adv.

ap·pear (ə·pir′) v.i. 1 To become visible; come into view. 2 To seem: He appeared tired and out of sorts. 3 To be on public view. 4 To be published or issued, as a book. 5 To present oneself formally in a law court. [< L ad- to + parere come forth, appear]

ap·pear·ance (ə·pir′əns) n. 1 The act of appearing; a coming into view, notice, etc. 2 External aspect: her stern appearance. 3 Semblance: an appearance of diligence. 4 pl. Circumstances or indications. 5 A visible phenomenon, as an apparition.

ap·pease (ə·pēz′) v.t. ap·peased, ap·peas·ing 1 To placate or pacify, as by yielding to demands. 2 To satisfy; allay. [< OF a- to + pais peace] —**ap·peas′a·ble** adj. —**ap·peas′a·bly**, **ap·peas′ing·ly** adv. —**ap·peas′er** n. —Syn. 1 calm, soothe, mollify, propitiate. 2 relieve, assuage, alleviate, quench.

ap·pease·ment (ə·pēz′mənt) n. 1 An appeasing or being appeased. 2 The policy of making concessions to a potential aggressor in order to maintain peace.

ap·pel·lant (ə·pel′ənt) adj. Law Of or pertaining to an appeal. —n. One who appeals.

ap·pel·late (ə·pel′it) adj. Law Pertaining to or having jurisdiction of appeals: an appellate court. [< L appellare to entreat, appeal to]

ap·pel·la·tion (ap′ə·lā′shən) n. 1 A name or title. 2 The act of calling or naming.

ap·pel·la·tive (ə·pel′ə·tiv) adj. Serving to designate or name. —n. A title; appellation. —**ap·pel′la·tive·ly** adv.

ap·pend (ə·pend′) v.t. 1 To add, as something supplemental. 2 To attach; affix. [< L ad- to + pendere hang]

ap·pend·age (ə·pen′dij) n. 1 Anything appended. 2 Biol. A part attached to the main body, as a limb, tail, leaf, etc.

ap·pen·dant (ə·pen′dənt) adj. 1 Attached; adjunct. 2 Associated by cause; consequent. —n. Something attached or appended. Also **ap·pen′dent**.

ap·pen·dec·to·my (ap′ən·dek′tə·mē) n. pl. ·mies Surgical excision of the vermiform appendix. Also **ap·pen·di·cec·to·my** (ə·pen′də·sek′tə·mē). [< APPENDIX + Gk. ex- out + -tomos a cutting]

ap·pen·di·ci·tis (ə·pen′də·sī′tis) n. Inflammation of the vermiform appendix.

ap·pen·dix (ə·pen′diks) n. pl. ·dix·es or ·di·ces (-də·sēz) 1 An addition, as of supplementary matter at the end of a book. 2 An outgrowth or prolongation, esp. the vermiform appendix. [< L, an appendage] • See INTESTINE.

ap·per·cep·tion (ap′ər·sep′shən) n. 1 Perception in which the mind is conscious of perceiving. 2 The ability to acquire and utilize knowledge; understanding. [< L ad- to + percipere perceive] —**ap′per·cep′tive** adj. —**ap′per·cep′tive·ly** adv.

ap·per·tain (ap′ər·tān′) v.i. To relate or be relevant; pertain; belong: with to. [< LL ad- to + pertinere pertain]

ap·pe·tence (ap′ə·təns) 1 Strong craving or desire. 2 Natural propensity or tendency. Also **ap′pe·ten·cy**. [< L appetere. See APPETITE.] —**ap′pe·tent** adj.

ap·pe·tite (ap′ə·tīt) n. 1 A desire for food or drink. 2 Any strong liking or desire. [< L appetitus < appetere strive for] —**ap·pe·ti·tive** (ap′ə·tī′tiv, ə·pet′ə·tiv) adj.

ap·pe·tiz·er (ap′ə·tī′zər) n. 1 A food or drink served before a meal to stimulate the appetite. 2 A sample, foretaste, etc., that stimulates further desire or interest. Brit. sp. **ap′pe·tis′er**.

ap·pe·tiz·ing (ap′ə·tī′zing) adj. 1 Arousing the appetite. 2 Temptingly attractive. Brit. sp. **ap′pe·tis′ing**. —**ap′pe·tiz′ing·ly** adv.

ap·plaud (ə·plôd′) v.t. & v.i. 1 To express approval (of) by clapping the hands. 2 To commend; praise. [< L ad- to + plaudere clap hands, strike] —**ap·plaud′a·ble** adj. —**ap·plaud′a·bly**, **ap·plaud′ing·ly** adv. —**ap·plaud′er** n.

ap·plause (ə·plôz′) n. 1 Approval shown by clapping the hands. 2 General acclaim. [< L applaudere to applaud]

ap·ple (ap′əl) n. 1 The fleshy, edible, round fruit of any variety of a widely cultivated tree. 2 A tree that bears apples. 3 Any of various fruits or plants with more or less resemblance to the apple. [< OE æppel]

ap·ple·jack (ap′əl·jak′) n. Brandy made from fermented cider.

ap·ple-pie order (ap′əl·pī′) Informal Neat or excellent condition.

apple polisher Slang One who seeks favor by obsequious behavior, flattery, etc.

ap·ple·sauce (ap′əl·sôs′) n. 1 Apples sweetened and stewed to a pulp. 2 Slang Nonsense; bunk.

ap·pli·ance (ə·plī′əns) n. A machine or device, esp. one used in the home. [< APPLY]

ap·pli·ca·ble (ap′li·kə·bəl, ə·plik′ə-) adj. Capable of or suitable for application; relevant; fitting. —**ap′pli·ca·bil′i·ty**, **ap′pli·ca·ble·ness** n. —**ap′pli·ca·bly** adv.

ap·pli·cant (ap′li·kənt) n. One who applies, as for employment or admission.

ap·pli·ca·tion (ap′li·kā′shən) n. 1 The act of applying. 2 That which is applied, as a medical remedy. 3 That by which one applies, as a written request or form. 4 Appropriation or relevance to a particular use. 5 Close and continuous attention. —**ap·pli·ca·tive** (ap′li·kā′tiv), **ap′pli·ca·to′ry** adj.

Appliance
(electric skillet)

applications software Computer software for a specific job or problem, such as word processing.

ap·pli·ca·tor (ap'li·kā'tər) *n.* An object used to apply medication, adhesives, etc.

ap·plied (ə·plīd') *adj.* Put in practice; used practically: *applied* science.

ap·pli·qué (ap'li·kā') *n.* Ornamentation made from pieces cut out from one material and sewed or fastened to the surface of another. —*v.t.* **·quéd** (-kād'), **·qué·ing** (-kā'ing) To decorate with appliqué. [F < L *applicare* apply]

ap·ply (ə·plī') *v.* **ap·plied, ap·ply·ing** *v.t.* 1 To put or spread on: to *apply* paint. 2 To put to a particular use: to *apply* steam to navigation. 3 To connect, as an epithet, with a person or thing. 4 To devote (oneself): to *apply* oneself to study. —*v.i.* 5 To make a formal request, as for employment or admission. 6 To be relevant or appropriate. [< L *applicare* join to < *ad-* to + *plicare* fold]

ap·pog·gia·tu·ra (ə·poj'ə·t'yōōr'ə, *Ital.* äp·pôd'jä·tōō'rä) *n. Music* An accented ornamental tone followed, usu. stepwise, by a tone that fits the harmony. [Ital. < *appoggiare* lean upon, rest]

ap·point (ə·point') *v.t.* 1 To designate or select, as a person for a position. 2 To name or decide upon, as a time or place for a meeting. 3 To ordain; decree. 4 To fit out; equip: a *well-appointed* office. [< OF *apointer* arrange, lit., bring to a point]

ap·point·ee (ə·poin'tē') *n.* One appointed to an office or position.

ap·poin·tive (ə·poin'tiv) *adj.* Filled by appointment: *appointive* office.

ap·point·ment (ə·point'mənt) *n.* The act of appointing or the condition of being appointed, as to a position. 2 A position to which one may be appointed. 3 An agreement to meet at a given time; an engagement. 4 *pl.* Accessories; equipment.

ap·por·tion (ə·pôr'shən, ə·pōr'-) *v.t.* To divide and assign proportionally; allot. [< L *ad-* to + *portio* position] —**ap·por'tion·ment** *n.*

ap·pose (ə·pōz') *v.t.* **ap·posed, ap·pos·ing** 1 To apply or put one thing to another. 2 To arrange side by side. [< F *à-* to + *poser* put] —**ap·pos'a·ble** *adj.*

ap·po·site (ap'ə·zit) *adj.* Appropriate; pertinent. [< L *apponere* put near to] —**ap'po·site·ly** *adj.* —**ap'po·site·ness** *n.*

ap·po·si·tion (ap'ə·zish'ən) *n.* 1 *Gram.* A construction in which one substantive is placed beside another to add to or explain the first, as in *John, president* of the class. 2 A placing or being in contact or side by side. —**ap'po·si'tion·al** *adj.* —**ap'po·si'tion·al·ly** *adv.*

ap·pos·i·tive (ə·poz'ə·tiv) *adj.* In or of apposition. —*n.* A word or phrase in apposition. —**ap·pos'i·tive·ly** *adv.*

ap·prais·al (ə·prā'zəl) *n.* 1 An appraising. 2 An official valuation. Also **ap·praise'ment.**

ap·praise (ə·prāz') *v.t.* **ap·praised, ap·prais·ing** 1 To make an official valuation of. 2 To estimate the amount, quality, or worth of; judge. [< AD- + PRAISE] —**ap·prais'er** *n.*

ap·pre·ci·a·ble (ə·prē'shē·ə·bəl, -sha·bəl) *adj.* Sufficient to be noticed and evaluated. —**ap·pre'ci·a·bly** *adv.*

ap·pre·ci·ate (ə·prē'shē·āt) *v.* **·at·ed, ·at·ing** *v.t.* 1 To be fully aware of the worth of; regard or value highly. 2 To be keenly sensitive to. 3 To enjoy deeply or fully. 4 To be grateful for. 5 To raise the price or value of. —*v.i.* 6 To rise in value. [< L *appretiare* appraise] —**ap·pre'ci·a·tor** *n.* —**Syn.** 1 value, esteem, prize, treasure.

ap·pre·ci·a·tion (ə·prē'shē·ā'shən) *n.* 1 High or adequate valuation or regard. 2 Keen awareness or enjoyment. 3 Recognition or gratitude. 4 Increase in value.

ap·pre·ci·a·tive (ə·prē'shē·ə'tiv, -shə'tiv, -shē·ā'-) *adj.* Feeling or showing appreciation. Also **ap·pre·ci·a·to·ry** (ə·prē'shē·ə·tôr'ē, -tô'rē, -shə-). —**ap·pre'ci·a·tive·ly** *adv.* —**ap·pre'ci·a·tive·ness** *n.*

ap·pre·hend (ap'ri·hend') *v.t.* 1 To seize; arrest. 2 To grasp mentally; understand. 3 To expect with fear or anxiety. [< L *ad-* to + *prehendere* seize] —**ap'pre·hend'er** *n.*

ap·pre·hen·si·ble (ap'ri·hen'sə·bəl) *adj.* Capable of being apprehended. —**ap'pre·hen'si·bil'i·ty** *n.* —**ap'pre·hen'si·bly** *adv.*

ap·pre·hen·sion (ap'ri·hen'shən) *n.* 1 Fearful anxiety; foreboding. 2 Seizure; arrest. 3 Ability to apprehend; understanding. 4 An estimate; opinion. [< L *apprehendere* to seize]

ap·pre·hen·sive (ap'ri·hen'siv) *adj.* 1 Anxiously fearful. 2 Of or pertaining to understanding or perception. —**ap'pre·hen'sive·ly** *adv.* —**ap'pre·hen'sive·ness** *n.*

ap·pren·tice (ə·pren'tis) *n.* 1 One who is legally bound to serve another in order to learn a trade or business. 2 Any learner or beginner. —*v.t.* **·ticed, ·tic·ing** To place as an apprentice. [< OF *aprendre* teach < L *apprehendere* comprehend] —**ap·pren'tice·ship** *n.*

ap·prise (ə·prīz') *v.t.* **ap·prised, ap·pris·ing** To notify, as of an event; inform. [< F *apprendre* teach, inform] —**ap·prise'ment, ap·pris'er** *n.*

ap·proach (ə·prōch') *v.i.* 1 To draw near or nearer. —*v.t.* 2 To draw near or nearer to. 3 To come close to; approximate. 4 To begin to treat or deal with: to *approach* a new subject. 5 To make a proposal, advances, etc., to. —*n.* 1 The act of approaching. 2 Nearness; approximation. 3 A way of approaching; access. 4 A way of treating or dealing with something: Try a new *approach.* 5 A golf stroke made toward the putting green after teeing off. [< LL *appropiare* < L *ad-* to + *prope* near]

ap·proach·a·ble (ə·prōch'ə·bəl) *adj.* 1 Capable of being approached. 2 Easy to speak to or get to know. —**ap·proach'a·bil'i·ty** *n.*

ap·pro·ba·tion (ap'rə·bā'shən) *n.* 1 Approval; commendation. 2 Official approval; sanction. [< L *approbare* approve] —**ap·pro·ba·tive** (ap'rə·bā'tiv), **ap·pro'ba·to·ry** (ə·prō'bə·tôr'ē) *adj.*

ap·pro·pri·ate (ə·prō'prē·it) *adj.* Suitable; fitting; proper; relevant. —*v.t.* (ə·prō'prē·āt) **·at·ed, ·at·ing** 1 To set apart for a particular use. 2 To take for one's own use. [< L *appropriare* to make one's own] —**ap·pro'pri·ate·ly** *adv.* —**ap·pro'pri·ate·ness, ap·pro'pri·a'tor** *n.* —**ap·pro'pri·a'tive** *adj.*

ap·pro·pri·a·tion (ə·prō'prē·ā'shən) *n.* 1 The act of appropriating. 2 Funds, etc., set apart for a special use.

ap·prov·al (ə·prōō'vəl) *n.* 1 An approving or being approved; approbation. 2 Official consent; sanction. 3 Favorable opinion; praise. —**on approval** For a customer's examination without obligation to purchase.

ap·prove (ə·prōōv') *v.* **ap·proved, ap·prov·ing** *v.t.* 1 To regard as worthy, proper, or right. 2 To confirm formally or authoritatively. 3 To show or state approval: often with *of.* [< L *ad-* to + *probare* approve, prove] —**ap·prov'er** *n.* —**ap·prov'ing·ly** *adv.*

approx. approximate; approximately.

ap·prox·i·mate (ə·prok'sə·mit) *adj.* Nearly exact, accurate, complete, etc. —*v.* (ə·prok'sə·māt) **·mat·ed, ·mat·ing** *v.t.* 1 To be almost the same as or very close to. 2 To bring close to or cause to approach closely. 3 *Math.* To calculate an approximation of. —*v.i.* 4 To come close; be similar. [< L *approximare* come near] —**ap·prox'i·mate·ly** *adv.*

ap·prox·i·ma·tion (ə·prok'sə·mā'shən) *n.* 1 The process or result of approximating. 2 *Math.* A result sufficiently exact for a specified purpose.

ap·pur·te·nance (ə·pûr'tə·nəns) *n.* 1 Something added or attached as an accessory or adjunct. 2 *pl.* Accessory equipment, fittings, etc. [< L *appertinere* to pertain to]

ap·pur·te·nant (ə·pûr'tə·nənt) *adj.* Appertaining or belonging. —*n.* APPURTENANCE.

Apr, Apr. April.

a·pri·cot (ā'pri·kot, ap'ri·kot) *n.* 1 A yellowish, cultivated fruit resembling a small peach. 2 The tree bearing this fruit. 3 A yellow-orange color. [< Ar. *al-barqūq* < Med. Gk. *praikokion* early ripe]

A·pril (ā'prəl) *n.* The fourth month of the year, containing 30 days. [< L *Aprilis*]

April Fools' Day April 1, traditionally a day for playing practical jokes.

a pri·o·ri (ā'prī·ō'rī, ā' prē·ôr'ē) 1 Proceeding from cause to effect, or from an assumption to its logical conclusion. 2 Based on theory and not supported by experience. [L, from what is before] —**a'pri·or'i·ty** *n.*

a·pron (ā′prən, ā′pərn) *n.* **1** A garment, usu. tied at the waist, worn to cover the front of a person's clothes. **2** Any of various pieces protecting parts of machines. **3** A paved area surrounding a hangar or aircraft shelter. **4** The part of a theater stage in front of the curtain. [< OF *naperon*, dim. of *nape* cloth]

ap·ro·pos (ap′rə·pō′) *adj.* Suited to the time, place, or occasion; pertinent. —*adv.* **1** With reference or regard: with *of.* **2** Pertinently; appropriately. **3** By the way; incidentally. [< F *à* to + *propos* purpose]

apse (aps) *n.* A usu. semicircular recess with a half dome, forming the eastern or altar end of a church. [< Gk. *hapsis* a fastening, loop, wheel]

apt (apt) *adj.* **1** Likely; liable; **2** Quick to learn. **3** Pertinent; appropriate. [< L *aptus* fitted, suited] —**apt′ly** *adv.* —**apt′ness** *n.*

apt. (*pl.* **apts.**) apartment.

ap·ter·ous (ap′tər·əs) *adj.* Lacking wings or winglike expansions. [< Gk. *a-* without + *pteron* wing]

ap·ter·yx (ap′tər·iks) *n.* A New Zealand bird, the kiwi. [< Gk. *a-* without + *pteryx* wing]

ap·ti·tude (ap′tə·tyōōd) *n.* **1** A natural ability or gift. **2** Quickness in learning or understanding. **3** Fitness; suitability. [< L *aptus* fitted, suited] —**Syn. 1** endowment, talent, skill.

aptitude test A test designed to gauge ability to learn or to perform a skill.

aq·ua (ak′wə·, äk′-, ä′kwə) *n. pl.* **aq·uas,** or *for def. 1* **aq·uae** (ak′wē, ä′kwē) **1** Water. **2** A light bluish green color. —*adj.* Light bluish green. [L]

aqua for·tis (fôr′tis) Commercial nitric acid. [L, strong water]

Aq·ua-lung (ak′wə·lung′) *n.* An underwater breathing apparatus or scuba: a trade name. Also **aq′ua·lung′.**

aq·ua·ma·rine (ak′wə·mə·rēn′) *n.* **1** A bluish green variety of precious beryl. **2** A bluish green color. —*adj.* Bluish green. [< L *aqua marina* sea water]

aq·ua·naut (ak′wə·nôt) *n.* One trained and equipped to live, work, or explore underwater over a period of time. [< L *aqua* water + *-naut* < Gk. *nautēs* sailor]

aq·ua·plane (ak′wə·plān′) *n.* A board on which one stands while being towed over water by a motorboat. —*v.i.* **·planed, ·plan·ing** To ride an aquaplane.

aqua re·gi·a (rē′jē·ə) A mixture of concentrated nitric and hydrochloric acids which dissolves gold and platinum. [L, royal water]

a·quar·i·um (ə·kwâr′ē·əm) *n. pl.* **·i·ums** or **·i·a** (-ē·ə) **1** A tank, pond, etc., for the exhibition or study of aquatic animals or plants. **2** A public building containing such an exhibition. [< L *aquarius* pertaining to water]

A·quar·i·us (ə·kwâr′ē·əs) *n.* A constellation and the eleventh sign of the zodiac; the Water Bearer. —**A·quar′i·an** *adj., n.* • See ZODIAC.

a·quat·ic (ə·kwat′ik, ə·kwot′-) *adj.* **1** Of, living, or growing in water. **2** Done in or on water: *aquatic* sports. —*n.* **1** An aquatic animal or plant. **2** *pl.* Aquatic sports. [< L *aqua* water] —**a·quat′i·cal·ly** *adv.*

aq·ua·tint (ak′wə·tint′) *n.* **1** A form of engraving differing from an etching in which spaces instead of, or as well as, lines are etched by acid. **2** An engraving printed from a plate so prepared. —*v.t.* To etch by this process. [< Ital. *acqua tinta* dyed water]

a·qua·vit (ä′kwə·vēt) *n.* A colorless Scandinavian liquor flavored with caraway seed. Also **ak·va·vit** (äk′vä·vēt).

aqua vi·tae (vī′tē) **1** Alcohol. **2** Whiskey, brandy, etc. [< L, water of life]

aq·ue·duct (ak′wə·dukt) *n.* **1** A water conduit, esp. one for supplying a community from a distance. **2** A structure supporting such a conduit across a river or over low ground. **3** *Anat.* Any of several canals through which body liquids are conducted. [< L *aqua* water + *ductus,* p.p. of *ducere* lead]

Aqueduct

a·que·ous (ā′kwe·əs, ak′we-) *adj.* Of, resembling, or containing water. [< L *aqua* water]

aqueous humor The limpid fluid that fills the anterior chamber of the eye from the cornea to the crystalline lens.

aq·ui·line (ak′wə·līn, -lin) *adj.* **1** Of or like an eagle. **2** Hooked like an eagle's beak: an *aquiline* nose. [< L *aquila* eagle]

-ar *suffix* **1** Pertaining to; like: *regular, singular.* **2** A person having to do with: *scholar.* [< L *-aris*]

AR Arkansas (P.O. abbr.).

Ar Argon.

Ar., Arab. Arabian; Arabic.

Ar·ab (ar′əb) *n.* **1** A native or inhabitant of Arabia. **2** One of an Arabic-speaking people. **3** One of a Semitic people inhabiting Arabia from ancient times. **4** A horse of a swift-running, graceful breed originally native to Arabia. —*adj.* Arabian.

ar·a·besque (ar′ə·besk′) *n.* **1** An ornament or design of intertwined scrollwork, conventionalized leaves or flowers, etc. **2** In ballet, a position in which the dancer extends one leg straight backward, one arm forward, and the other arm backward. —*adj.* Of, resembling, or forming an arabesque. [< F < Ital. *arabesco,* lit., Arabic]

A·ra·bi·an (ə·rā′bē·ən) *adj.* Of or pertaining to Arabia or the Arabs. —*n.* **1** A native or inhabitant of Arabia. **2** An Arab horse.

Arabian Nights A collection of stories from Arabia, India, Persia, etc., dating from the tenth century A.D.

Ar·a·bic (ar′ə·bik) *adj.* Of or pertaining to Arabia, the Arabs, their language, culture, etc. —*n.* The Semitic language of the Arabians.

Arabic numerals The characters 0, 1, 2, 3, 4, 5, 6, 7, 8, 9.

ar·a·ble (ar′ə·bəl) *adj.* Capable of being plowed or cultivated. [< L *arare* plow] —**ar′a·bil′i·ty** *n.*

Arab League A confederation formed originally by Egypt, Iraq, Jordan, Lebanon, Saudi Arabia, Syria, and Yemen, and later joined by Kuwait, Libya, Morocco, Sudan, and Tunisia.

Ar·a·by (ar′ə·bē) *n. Archaic* Arabia.

a·rach·nid (ə·rak′nid) *n.* Any of a class of eight-legged arthropods, including the spiders, scorpions, mites, etc. [< NL < Gk. *arachnē* spider] —**a·rach′ni·dan** *adj., n.*

Aram. Aramaic.

Ar·a·ma·ic (ar′ə·mā′ik) *n.* Any of a group of Semitic languages, including the language of the Jews in Palestine at the time of Jesus.

ar·ba·lest (är′bə·list) *n.* A medieval crossbow having a steel bow. Also **ar′ba·list.** [< L *arcus* a bow + *ballista* < Gk. *ballein* throw] —**ar′ba·lest′er** *n.*

ar·bi·ter (är′bə·tər) *n.* **1** A person chosen to settle a dispute. **2** One who is authorized to judge or decide or whose decisions are considered final. [< L, one who goes to see, a witness] —**Syn. 1** judge, referee, umpire, moderator. **2** authority, expert, master, specialist.

ar·bi·tra·ment (är·bit′rə·mənt) *n.* **1** The act of arbitration. **2** The decision of an arbitrator. **3** The power or right to make such decision. Also **ar·bit′re·ment.**

ar·bi·trar·y (är′bə·trer′ē) *adj.* **1** Based on mere opinion or prejudice; capricious. **2** Absolute; despotic. [< L *arbiter.* See ARBITER.] —**ar′bi·trar′i·ly** *adv.* —**ar′bi·trar′i·ness** *n.*

ar·bi·trate (är′bə·trāt) *v.t. & v.i.* **·trat·ed, ·trat·ing 1** To submit (a dispute) to or have (a dispute) settled by an arbiter. **2** To act as arbiter in (a dispute). [< L *arbiter.* See ARBITER.] —**ar′bi·tra·ble** (är′bə·trə·bəl) *adj.* —**ar′bi·tra′tive** *adj.*

ar·bi·tra·tion (är′bə·trā′shən) *n.* The hearing and settlement of a dispute between two parties by the decision of a third party to whom the matter is referred.

ar·bi·tra·tor (är′bə·trā′tər) *n.* **1** A person chosen to decide a dispute, as in arbitration. **2** An arbiter (def. 2). [< L]

ar·bor¹ (är′bər) *n.* A bower, as of latticework, supporting vines or trees; a place shaded by trees. [< L *herbarium* a collection of herbs]

ar·bor² (är′bər) *n. pl.* **ar·bo·res** (är′bər·ēz) *for def. 1,* **ar·bors** *for def. 2.* **1** A tree: used chiefly in botanical names. **2** *Mech.* **a** A shaft, mandrel, spindle, or axle for a rotary part. **b** A support for a cutting tool. [< L, tree]

Arbor Day A U.S. spring holiday observed in some States by planting trees.

ar·bo·re·al (är·bôr′ē·əl, -bō′rē) *adj.* 1 Of or pertaining to a tree or trees; arborescent. 2 Living or situated among trees. Also **ar·bor′e·ous.**

ar·bo·res·cent (är′bə·res′ənt) *adj.* Treelike in appearance or growth. —**ar′bo·res′cence** *n.*

ar·bo·re·tum (är′bə·rē′təm) *n. pl.* **·tums** or **·ta** (-tə) A botanical garden exhibiting trees for their scientific and educational value. [< L *arbor* tree]

ar·bor·vi·tae (är′bər·vī′tē) *n.* An evergreen shrub or tree of the pine family. [< L, tree of life]

ar·bu·tus (är·byōō′təs) *n.* 1 Any of several evergreen trees or shrubs related to heath. 2 TRAILING ARBUTUS. [< L, strawberry tree]

arc (ärk) *n.* 1 Anything in the shape of an arch, of a curve, or of a part of a circle. 2 A part of any curve, esp. of a circle. 3 *Electr.* The light caused by an electric discharge in a gas. —*v.i.* **arcked** or **arced** (ärkt), **arck·ing** or **arc·ing** (är′king) *Electr.* To form an arc. [< L *arcus* bow, arch]

ARC, A.R.C. American Red Cross

ar·cade (är·kād′) *n.* 1 A series of arches with their supporting columns or piers. 2 An arched or covered passageway or street, esp. one having shops, etc. opening from it. —*v.t.* **·cad·ed, ·cad·ing** To furnish with or form into an arcade. [< L *arcus,* arch]

Ar·ca·di·a (är·kā′dē·ə) *n.* 1 An ancient pastoral region in the Peloponnesus. 2 Any region of rustic simplicity and peace. Also **Ar·ca·dy** (är′kə·dē). —**Ar·ca′di·an** *adj., n.*

ar·cane (är·kān′) *adj.* Secret; hidden; mysterious. [< L *arcanus.* See ARCANUM.]

ar·ca·num (är·kā′nəm) *n. pl.* **·na** (-nə) A secret or mystery. [< L *arcanus* hidden < *arca* chest]

arch[1] (ärch) *n.* 1 A curved structure spanning an opening, formed of wedge-shaped parts resting on supports at the two extremities. 2 Any similarly shaped structure, object, or part: the dental *arch.* 3 The form of an arch; a bowlike curve. —*v.t.* 1 To cause to form into an arch. 2 To furnish with an arch or arches. —*v.i.* 3 To form an arch or arches. [< L *arcus* bow, arch]

arch[2] (ärch) *adj.* 1 Roguish; sly. 2 Artificially playful; forced. 3 Most eminent; chief. [< ARCH-] —**arch′·ly** *adv.* —**arch′ness** *n.*

Arch

arch- *prefix* Chief; principal: *archbishop.* [< Gk. *archos* ruler]

Arch., Archbp. Archbishop.

arch. archaic; archipelago; architect; architecture.

ar·chae·ol·o·gy (är′kē·ol′ə·jē) The scientific search for and study of artifacts and relics of past human cultures. [< Gk. *archaios* ancient + -LOGY] —**ar·chae·o·log·i·cal** (är′kē·ə·loj′i·kəl) or **·log·ic** *adj.* —**ar′chae·ol′o·gist** (-jist) *n.*

Ar·chae·o·zo·ic (är′kē·ə·zō′ik) ARCHEOZOIC.

ar·cha·ic (är·kā′ik) *adj.* 1 Belonging to a former period; ancient or antiquated. 2 Characterizing a verbal form or phrase no longer in current use except for special purposes, as poetry, the law, and church ritual. Also **ar·cha′·i·cal.** [< Gk. *archaios* ancient]

ar·cha·ism (är′kē·iz′əm, -kā-) *n.* 1 An archaic word, idiom, or expression. 2 Archaic style or usage. —**ar′cha·ist** *n.* —**ar′cha·is′tic** *adj.*

arch·an·gel (ärk′ān′jəl) *n.* An angel of highest rank. —**arch·an·gel·ic** (ärk′an·jel′ik) or **·i·cal** *adj.*

arch·bish·op (ärch′bish′əp) *n.* The chief bishop of an ecclesiastical province.

arch·bish·op·ric (ärch′bish′əp·rik) *n.* The office, rank, term of office, or jurisdictional province of an archbishop.

arch·dea·con (ärch′dē′kən) *n.* A church official next in rank below a bishop. —**arch′dea·con·ate** (ärch′dē′kən·it), **arch′dea′con·ship** *n.*

arch·dea·con·ry (ärch′dē′kən·rē) *n. pl.* **·ries** The office, rank, jurisdiction, or residence of an archdeacon.

arch·di·o·cese (ärch′dī′ə·sis, -sēs′) *n.* The diocese of an archbishop.

arch·du·cal (ärch′dyōō′kəl) *adj.* Of or pertaining to an archduke or an archduchy.

arch·duch·ess (ärch′duch′is) *n.* 1 A princess of the former imperial family of Austria. 2 The wife or widow of an archduke.

arch·duch·y (ärch′duch′ē) *n. pl.* **·duch·ies** The territory under the control of an archduke or an archduchess. Also **arch′duke′dom.**

arch·duke (ärch′dyōōk′) *n.* A sovereign prince, esp. a prince of the former imperial family of Austria.

arch·en·e·my (ärch′en′ə·mē) *n. pl.* **·mies** 1 A chief enemy. 2 Satan.

ar·che·ol·o·gy (är′kē·ol′ə·jē) *n.* ARCHAEOLOGY. —**ar·che·o·log·i·cal** (är′kē·ə·loj′i·kəl) or **·log′ic** *adj.* —**ar′che·ol′o·gist** (-jist) *n.*

Ar·che·o·zo·ic (är′kē·ə·zō′ik) *n. & adj.* See GEOLOGY. [< Gk. *archaios* ancient + *zōion* animal]

arch·er (är′chər) *n.* One who shoots with a bow and arrow. [< L *arcus* bow]

Arch·er (är′chər) *n.* SAGITTARIUS.

arch·er·y (är′chər·ē) *n.* 1 The art or sport of shooting with bow and arrow. 2 The gear of the archer. 3 Archers collectively.

ar·che·type (är′kə·tīp) *n.* An original or standard pattern or model. [< Gk. *arche-* first + *typos* stamp, pattern] —**ar′che·typ′al** *adj.* —**ar′che·typ′ic** (-tip′ik) or **·i·cal** *adj.* — Syn. prototype, example, ideal, paradigm.

arch·fiend (ärch′fēnd′) *n.* A chief fiend; specifically, Satan.

archi- *prefix* Principal; chief: *architrave.*

ar·chi·e·pis·co·pal (är′kē·i·pis′kə·pəl) *adj.* Of or pertaining to an archbishop.

ar·chi·pel·a·go (är′kə·pel′ə·gō) *n. pl.* **·goes** or **·gos** A sea studded with many islands, or the islands collectively. [< ARCHI- + *pelagos* sea] —**ar·chi·pe·lag·ic** (är′kə·pə·laj′ik) *adj.*

ar·chi·tect (är′kə·tekt) *n.* 1 One whose profession is to design and draw up the plans for buildings, etc., and supervise their construction. 2 A planner; creator; designer. [< Gk. *archi-* chief + *tektōn* worker]

ar·chi·tec·ton·ics (är′kə·tek·ton′iks) *n. pl. (construed as sing.)* 1 The science of architecture. 2 *Philos.* The scientific arrangement and construction of systems of knowledge. 3 Structural design, as in works of art.

ar·chi·tec·ture (är′kə·tek′chər) *n.* 1 The science, art, or profession of designing and constructing buildings or other structures. 2 A style or system of building. 3 Construction or structure generally; any ordered arrangement of the parts of a system. 4 A building, or buildings collectively. —**ar′chi·tec′tur·al** *adj.* —**ar′chi·tec′tur·al·ly** *adv.*

ar·chi·trave (är′kə·trāv) *n. Archit.* 1 A chief beam; that part of an entablature which rests upon the column heads and supports the frieze. 2 A molded ornament, as that skirting the head and sides of a door or window. [< ARCHI- + L *trabs* beam] • See ENTABLATURE, FRIEZE.

ar·chives (är′kīvz) *n. pl.* 1 A place where public records and historical documents are kept. 2 The records and documents themselves. [< Gk. *archeion* a public office < *archē* government] —**ar·chi′val** *adj.* —**ar′chi·vist** (-kə·vist) *n.*

arch·priest (ärch′prēst′) *n.* Formerly, the priest serving as chief assistant to a bishop. —**arch′priest′hood, arch′priest′ship** *n.*

arch·way (ärch′wā′) *n.* A passage under an arch.

-archy *combining form* Rule; government: *patriarchy.* [< Gk. *archos* ruler]

arc light A lamp in which intense light is produced directly by a continuous electric discharge. Also **arc lamp.**

arc·tic (ärk′tik, är′tik) *adj.* Extremely cold; frigid. —*n.* A warm, waterproof overshoe.

Arc·tic (ärk′tik, är′tik) *adj.* 1 The region north of the Arctic Circle: used with *the.* 2 The Arctic Ocean. —*adj.* Of, in, or pertaining to the Arctic or the Arctic Ocean. [< Gk. *artikos* of the Bear (the northern constellation *Ursa Major*) < *arktos* bear]

Arc·tu·rus (ärk·tyŏŏr′əs) *n.* A bright, orange star located in the constellation Boötes. [< Gk. *Arktouros* guardian of the bear]

-ard *suffix of nouns* One who does something to excess or who is to be disparaged: *drunkard.* Also **-art:** *braggart.* [< G *-hard, -hart* hardy]

ar·dent (är′dənt) *adj.* 1 Passionate; zealous; intense. 2 Red; glowing; flashing. 3 Fiery; burning. [< L *ardere* burn] —**ar′den·cy** n. —**ar′dent·ly** *adv.*

ar·dor (är′dər) *n.* 1 Warmth or intensity of feeling; eagerness; zeal. 2 Great heat, as of fire, sun, or fever. *Brit. sp.* **ar′dour.** [< L, a flame, fire]

ar·du·ous (är′jōō-əs) *adj.* 1 Involving great labor or hardship; difficult. 2 Toiling strenuously; energetic. 3 Steep. [< L *arduus* steep] —**ar′du·ous·ly** *adv.* —**ar′du·ous·ness** *n.*

are[1] (är) *v.* First, second, and third person plural, present indicative, of the verb BE; also used as second person singular. [< OE *aron*]

are[2] (âr, är) *n.* A metric unit of area equal to one hundred square meters. [< L *area* area]

ar·e·a (âr′ē·ə) 1 An open space, often devoted to a special purpose. 2 A tract or portion of the earth's surface; region; section. 3 The measure of a surface. 4 A yard of a building; areaway. 5 Extent; scope. [< L, an open space of level ground] —**ar′e·al** *adj.*

ar·e·a·way (âr′ē·ə·wā) *n.* 1 A small sunken passageway to a basement door. 2 A passageway, as from one building to another.

a·re·na (ə·rē′nə) *n.* 1 The central space for contestants in a Roman amphitheater. 2 Any place like this: the boxing *arena.* 3 A sphere of action or contest. [< L, sand, sandy place]

ar·e·na·ceous (ar′ə·nā′shəs) *adj.* Sandy.

aren't (ärnt) Contraction of *are not.*

a·re·o·la (ə·rē′ə·lə) *n. pl.* **·lae** (-lē) or **·las** 1 A small space in a network of veins or vessels, as on leaves. 2 *Anat.* The colored circle about a nipple or about a vesicle. Also **ar·e·ole** (âr′ē·ōl). [< L, dim. of *area* open space] —**a·re′o·lar** *adj.*

Ar·es (âr′ēz) *Gk. Myth.* The god of war.

Arg. Argentina.

ar·ga·li (är′gə·lē) *n. pl.* **·lis** or **·li** An Asiatic wild sheep with large, curved horns [< Mongolian]

ar·gent (är′jənt) *n. Archaic* Silver. —*adj.* Silvery: also **ar·gen·tal** (är·jen′təl). [< L *argentum* silver]

Ar·gen·ti·na (är′jən·tē′nə) *n.* A republic of sw South America, 1,084,362 sq. mi., cap. Buenos Aires.

ar·gen·tine (är′jən·tin, -tīn) *n.* Silver. —*adj.* Silvery. [< L *argentum* silver]

Ar·gen·tine (är′jən·tēn′, -tīn′) *adj.* Of or pertaining to Argentina. —*n.* A native or citizen of Argentina: also **Ar·gen·tin·e·an** (är′jən·tin′ē·ən). —**the Argentine** *Brit.* Argentina.

ar·gil (är′jil) *n.* Potters' clay; white clay. [< L *argos* white]

Ar·go (är′gō) *Gk. Myth.* The ship in which Jason sailed for the Golden Fleece.

ar·gon (är′gon) *n.* A colorless, odorless, chemically inactive, gaseous element (symbol Ar), constituting almost one percent of the atmosphere, and used chiefly to fill electric light bulbs. [< Gk. *argos* idle, inert]

ar·go·sy (är′gə·sē) *n. pl.* **·sies** 1 A large merchant ship. 2 A fleet of merchant vessels. [< *Ragusa,* Italian name of Dubrovnik]

ar·got (är′gō, -gət) *n.* The specialized or secret language peculiar to a class or group, as to the underworld. [< F] —**ar·got·ic** (är·got′ik) *adj.*

ar·gue (är′gyōō) *v.* **ar·gued, ar·gu·ing** *v.i.* 1 To give reasons to support or contest a measure or opinion. 2 To dispute or quarrel. —*v.t.* 3 To give reasons for or against; discuss. 4 To contend or maintain. 5 To prove or indicate, as from evidence. 6 To influence or convince, as by argument. [< L *arguere* make clear, prove] —**ar′gu·a·ble** *adj.* —**ar′gu·er** *n.*

ar·gu·ment (är′gyə·mənt) *n.* 1 A reason offered for or against something. 2 The act of reasoning to establish or

refute a position. 3 A disagreement, dispute, or quarrel. 4 A summary or synopsis of a plot, subject, etc. [< L *arguere* make clear, prove]

ar·gu·men·ta·tion (är′gyə·men·tā′shən) *n.* 1 The methodical setting forth of premises and the drawing of conclusions therefrom. 2 Discussion; debate.

ar·gu·men·ta·tive (är′gyə·men′tə·tiv) *adj.* 1 Consisting of or marked by argument. 2 Given to arguing. —**ar′gu·ment′a·tive·ly** *adv.* —**ar′gu·men′ta·tive·ness** *n.* —**Syn.** 1 controversial, debatable, disputable, controvertible. 2 disputatious, contentious, quarrelsome, combative.

ar·gyle (är′gīl) *n.* 1 A design of varicolored diamonds on a solid-color background. 2 A knit sock of this design. Also **Ar′gyle, ar′gyll, Ar′gyll.** [from the tartan of the clan Campbell of *Argyll,* Scotland] • See PLAID.

a·ri·a (ä′rē·ə, âr′ē·ə) *n.* 1 An air; melody. 2 An elaborate solo for voice, as in an opera. [< L *aer* air]

-aria *suffix* Used in forming new Latin names, esp. in zoological and botanical classifications. [< L *-arius*]

Ar·i·ad·ne (ar′ē·ad′nē) *Gk. Myth.* The daughter of Minos, who gave Theseus the thread by which he found his way out of the Labyrinth.

Ar·i·an (âr′ē·ən, ar′-, är-, är′yən) *adj., n.* ARYAN.

-arian *suffix* Used in forming adjectives and adjectival nouns denoting occupation, age, sect, beliefs, etc.: *nonagenarian, seminarian.* [< L *-arius -ary* + *-anus -an*]

ar·id (ar′id) *adj.* 1 Lacking enough moisture to support vegetation; barren. 2 Without interest; dull. [< L *arere* be dry] —**a·rid·i·ty** (ə·rid′ə·tē), **ar′id·ness** *n.* —**ar′id·ly** *adv.*

Ar·ies (âr′ēz, âr′ē·iz) *n.* A constellation and the first sign of the zodiac; the Ram. [< L, the Ram] • See ZODIAC.

a·right (ə·rīt′) *adv.* In a right way; correctly.

-arious *suffix of adjectives* Connected with; pertaining to: *gregarious.* [< L *-arius -ary* + *-ous*]

a·rise (ə·rīz′) *v.i.* **a·rose** (ə·rōz′), **a·ris·en** (ə·riz′ən), **a·ris·ing** 1 To get up, as from a prone position. 2 To rise; ascend. 3 To come into being; originate. 4 To result or proceed: with *from.* [OE *ā-* up + *rīsan* rise]

ar·is·toc·ra·cy (ar′is·tok′rə·sē) *n. pl.* **·cies** 1 A hereditary nobility or privileged class. 2 Government by a privileged upper class. 3 A country having such a government. 4 Any group made up of the best: an *aristocracy* of musicians. [< Gk. *aristos* best + *-CRACY*]

a·ris·to·crat (ə·ris′tə·krat, ar′is·tə·krat′) *n.* 1 A member of an aristocracy. 2 A person who has the tastes, ideas, manners, etc., associated with the aristocracy. —**a·ris′to·crat′ic** or **·i·cal** *adj.* —**a·ris′to·crat′i·cal·ly** *adv.*

Ar·is·to·te·li·an (ar′is·tə·tē′lē·ən, -tə·tēl′yən, ə·ris′tə-) *adj.* Of or pertaining to Aristotle or his philosophy. —*n.* An adherent of Aristotle. —**Ar′is·to·te′li·an·ism′** *n.*

a·rith·me·tic (ə·rith′mə·tik) *n.* The use and study of integers under the operations of addition, subtraction, multiplication, division. [< Gk. *(hē) arithmetikē (technē)* (the) counting (art)] —**a·rith·met·ic** (ar′ith·met′ik) or **·i·cal** *adj.* —**ar′ith·met′i·cal·ly** *adv.*

a·rith·me·ti·cian (ə·rith′mə·tish′ən, ar′ith-) *n.* One who uses or is skilled in arithmetic.

arithmetic mean The sum of a set of measures, observations, scores, etc., divided by the number of items in the set.

arithmetic progression A sequence of terms such that each except the first is equal to the sum of its predecessor and a given constant, as 3, 7, 11, 15, 19, etc.

-arium *suffix of nouns* 1 A place for: *herbarium.* 2 Connected with: *honorarium.* [< L< *-arius.* See -ARY.]

Ariz. Arizona.

ark (ärk) *n.* 1 In the Bible: **a** The ship of Noah (*Gen.* 6). **b** The chest containing the stone tablets on which were inscribed the Ten Commandments: also **ark of the covenant** (*Ex.* 25:10). 2 A place of refuge. 3 A large, usu. flat-bottomed boat. [< L *arca* chest]

Ark. Arkansas.

arm[1] (ärm) *n.* 1 The upper limb of the human body, from the shoulder to the hand or wrist. 2 The fore limb of vertebrates other than man. 3 An armlike part or appendage. 4 The part in contact with or covering the human arm: *arm* of a chair. 5 Anything branching out like an arm, usu. considered as a distinct part or branch: an *arm* of the sea. 6 Strength; might: the *arm* of the law. —**at**

arm's length At a distance, so as to preclude intimacy. [< OE *arm, earm*]

arm[2] (ärm) *n.* 1 *Usu. pl.* A weapon. 2 A distinct branch of the naval or military service: the air *arm.* —*v.t.* 1 To supply with instruments of warfare. 2 To provide with whatever is necessary for action, struggle, protection, etc. —*v.i.* 3 To equip oneself with weapons. 4 To supply oneself with the means necessary for an undertaking. [See ARMS]

Arm. Armenia; Armenian.

ar·ma·da (är·mä'də, -mā'-) *n.* A fleet of war vessels or war planes. —**the Armada** The fleet sent against England by Spain in 1588 and defeated by the English navy: also **Spanish Armada.** [< L < *armare* to arm]

ar·ma·dil·lo (är'mə·dil'ō) *n. pl.* **·los** An American burrowing nocturnal mammal having an armorlike covering of jointed plates. [< Sp. *armado* armed]

Ar·ma·ged·don (är'mə·ged'n) *n.* 1 In the Bible, the scene of a great battle between the forces of good and evil, to occur at the end of the world. *Rev.* 16:16. 2 Any great or decisive conflict. [< Heb. *Megiddon* the plain of Megiddo, a battlefield]

Armadillo

ar·ma·ment (är'mə·mənt) *n.* 1 *Often pl.* The whole of a nation's military forces and equipment. 2 The guns, munitions, and other military equipment of a fortification, military unit, airplane, etc. 3 The body of naval, air, and ground forces equipped for war. 4 The act of arming for war. [< L *armamenta* implements < *armare* to arm]

ar·ma·ture (är'mə·chŏŏr) *n.* 1 A piece of soft iron joining the poles of a magnet to prevent the loss of magnetic power. 2 *Electr.* **a** The rotor of a generator or motor, carrying coils of insulated wire on iron cores. **b** The part of a relay, buzzer, or bell that moves when activated. 3 *Biol.* Protective devices for defense or offense, as quills, thorns, etc. 4 In sculpture, a framework to support the clay or other modeling substance. 5 Arms; armor. —*v.t.* **·tured, ·tur·ing** To furnish with an armature. [< L *armatura* armor]

arm·band (ärm'band') *n.* A band worn around the upper arm to identify the wearer, indicate bereavement, etc.

arm·chair (ärm'châr') *n.* A chair with side supports for the arms or elbows. —*adj.* Describing one who offers opinions or advice about matters with which he is not involved or not conversant: an *armchair* critic.

armed (ärmd) *adj.* Provided with that which aids in an offensive action, affords defense, gives security, etc.

armed forces The combined military and naval forces of a nation.

Ar·me·ni·a (är·mē'nē·ə, -mēn'yə) *n.* A former country of w Asia, now in Turkey, Iran, and the Soviet Union. —**Ar·me·ni·an** *adj., n.*

arm·ful (ärm'fŏŏl) *n. pl.* **·fuls** That which is held, or as much as can be held, in the arm.

arm·hole (ärm'hōl') *n.* An opening for the arm in a garment.

ar·mi·stice (är'mə·stis) *n.* A temporary cessation, by mutual agreement, of hostilities; a truce. [< L *arma* arms + -*stitium* a stoppage]

Armistice Day VETERANS DAY.

arm·let (ärm'lit) *n.* 1 A little arm, as of the sea. 2 An ornamental band worn around the upper arm.

ar·moire (är·mwär') *n.* A large, movable wardrobe or cabinet. [< L *armarium* a chest, orig., place to store arms]

ar·mor (är'mər) *n.* 1 A defensive covering, as of mail for a warrior, or of metallic plates for a war vessel, a tank, etc. 2 *Biol.* Any protective covering on a plant or animal. —*v.t. & v.i.* To furnish with or put on armor. *Brit. sp.* **ar'mour.** [< L *armatura < armare* to arm] • See MAIL[2].

ar·mored (är'mərd) *adj.* 1 Protected by armor. 2 Equipped with armored vehicles, as a military unit.

ar·mor·er (är'mər·ər) *n.* 1 A maker or repairer of armor. 2 A manufacturer of arms. 3 *Mil.* An enlisted man in charge of small arms. *Brit. sp.* **ar'mour·er.**

ar·mo·ri·al (är·môr'ē·əl, -mō'rē-) *adj.* Pertaining to heraldry or heraldic arms.

armor plate A protective covering of a special steel alloy, used on warships, tanks, etc. —**ar'mor-plat'ed** *adj.*

ar·mor·y (är'mər·ē) *n. pl.* **·mor·ies** 1 A place for the storage of arms. 2 A building for the use of a body of militia, including storage for arms and equipment, drill-rooms, etc. 3 A factory for making firearms. *Brit. sp.* **ar'mour·y.** [< ARMOR]

arm·pit (ärm'pit') *n.* The cavity under the arm at the shoulder; axilla.

arms (ärmz) *n. pl.* 1 Weapons collectively. 2 Warfare. 3 The official insignia or device of a state, person, or family. 4 Heraldic symbols. —**under arms** Ready for war. —**up in arms** Aroused and ready to fight. [< L *arma* weapons]

ar·my (är'mē) *n. pl.* **·mies** 1 A large organized body of men armed for military service on land. 2 The whole of the military land forces of a country. [< L *armata < armare* to arm]

ar·ni·ca (är'ni·kə) *n.* 1 Any of a genus of plants bearing heads of yellow-rayed composite flowers. 2 A tincture prepared from this plant, once used for sprains and bruises. [< NL]

a·ro·ma (ə·rō'mə) *n.* 1 Fragrance, as from plants; agreeable odor. 2 Characteristic quality or style. [< Gk. *arōma* spice]

ar·o·mat·ic (ar'ə·mat'ik) *adj.* Having an aroma; fragrant; spicy. Also **ar'o·mat'i·cal.** —*n.* Any vegetable or drug of agreeable odor. —**ar'o·mat'i·cal·ly** *adv.*

a·ro·ma·tize (ə·rō'mə·tīz) *v.t.* **·tized, ·tiz·ing** To make fragrant or aromatic.

a·rose (ə·rōz') *p.t.* of ARISE.

a·round (ə·round') *adv.* 1 On all sides; in every direction. 2 In a circle or a circular manner or course. 3 In or to the opposite way, belief, attitude, etc. 4 From place to place; here and there. 5 From beginning to end: the year *around.* 6 For every person, part, etc.: enough to go *around.* 7 *Informal* To a usual or desired condition. 8 *Informal* Nearby; in the vicinity: Wait *around* until I call. 9 In or to a particular place: Come *around* to see us again. —**have been around** *Informal* To be experienced in the ways of the world. —*prep.* 1 About the circumference or outer part of; encircling. 2 On all or many sides of. 3 So as to encircle or envelop. 4 In or to various parts of. 5 On the other side of: *around* the corner. 6 About the center or axis of: to rotate *around* a shaft. 7 Close to: We leave *around* midnight. [< A-[1] on + ROUND]

a·rouse (ə·rouz') *v.* **a·roused, a·rous·ing** *v.t.* 1 To stir from or as if from sleep. 2 To excite, as to a state of high emotion. —*v.i.* 3 To become aroused from or as if from sleep. [< ROUSE, on analogy with *arise*] —**a·rous'al, a·rous'er** *n.* —**Syn.** 1, 3 wake, waken, awake, awaken. 2 incite, provoke, stimulate, stir up.

ar·peg·gi·o (är·pej'ē·ō, -pej'ō) *n. pl.* **·gi·os** *Music* 1 The sounding or playing of the notes of a chord in rapid succession instead of simultaneously. 2 A chord so played. [< Ital. *arpeggiare* play on a harp]

written   played

Arpeggio

ar·que·bus (är'kwə·bəs) *n.* HARQUEBUS.

arr. arranged; arrangement(s); arrival; arrive.

ar·rack (ar'ək) *n.* A strong Oriental liquor distilled from rice, molasses, etc. [< Ar. *'araq* sweat, juice]

ar·raign (ə·rān') *v.t.* 1 To call into court to answer to an indictment. 2 To call upon for an answer; accuse. [< LL *arrationare* call to account] —**ar·raign'ment** *n.*

ar·range (ə·rānj') *v.* **ar·ranged, ar·rang·ing** *v.t.* 1 To put in definite or proper order. 2 To adjust, as a conflict or dispute; settle. 3 To make plans or prepare for. 4 To change or adapt, as a musical composition, for performers other than those originally intended. —*v.i.* 5 To come to an agreement or understanding: often with *with.* 6 To see about the details; make plans. [< OF *a-* to + *rangier* put in order]

ar·range·ment (ə·rānj'mənt) *n.* 1 An arranging or a being arranged. 2 That which is arranged. 3 *Usu. pl.* A preparation or plan. 4 The style or manner in which something is arranged. 5 Settlement, as of a dispute. 6 *Music* a The adaptation of a composition to performers or instruments other than those originally intended. b The composition so adapted.

ar·rant (ar'ənt) *adj.* Notoriously bad; unmitigated. [Var. of ERRANT] —**ar'rant·ly** *adv.*

ar·ras (ar'əs) *n.* 1 A tapestry. [*Arras,* France]

ar·ray (ə·rā') *n.* 1 Regular or proper order, esp. of troops. 2 A military force. 3 Clothing; fine dress. 4 An impressive gathering or arrangement, as of people or things. —*v.t.* 1 To draw up in order of battle, as troops. 2 To adorn; dress, as for display. [<OF <*a-* to + *rei* order]

ar·ray·al (ə·rā'əl) *n.* 1 The act or process of arraying. 2 Anything arrayed; an array.

ar·rear·age (ə·rir'ij) *n.* 1 The state of being in arrears. 2 The amount in arrears.

ar·rears (ə·rirz') *n. pl.* Debts, obligations, etc., not met on time. —**in arrears** (or **arrear**) Behind in meeting payment, fulfilling an obligation, etc. [<L *ad-* to + *retro* backward]

ar·rest (ə·rest') *v.t.* 1 To stop suddenly; check, as the course, movement, or development of. 2 To take into custody by legal authority. 3 To attract and fix, as the attention; engage. —*n.* 1 An arresting or being arrested. 2 A device for arresting motion, as in a machine. [<L *ad-* to + *restare* stop, remain] —**ar·rest'er, ar·res'tor** *n.*

ar·rest·ing (ə·res'ting) *adj.* Notable; compelling attention. —**ar·rest'ing·ly** *adv.*

ar·rhyth·mi·a (ə·rith'mē·ə) *n.* Variation from the normal heartbeat. —**ar·rhyth'mic** *adj.*

ar·ri·val (ə·rī'vəl) *n.* 1 The act of arriving. 2 One who or that which arrives or has arrived.

ar·rive (ə·rīv') *v.i.* **ar·rived, ar·riv·ing** 1 To reach or come to a destination or place. 2 To come at length, by any stage or process; often with *at:* to *arrive* at an idea. 3 To attain worldly success or fame. [<LL *arripare* come to shore <L *ad-* to + *ripa* shore]

ar·ri·viste (a.rē·vēst', *Fr.* ȧ-) One newly arrived at social position, wealth, etc., disparaged as an upstart. [F]

ar·ro·gance (ar'ə·gəns) *n.* The quality or state of being arrogant. Also **ar'ro·gan·cy.**

ar·ro·gant (ar'ə·gənt) *adj.* Full of or characterized by excessive pride or self-esteem; overbearing; haughty. [<L *arrogare.* See ARROGATE.] —**ar'ro·gant·ly** *adv.*

ar·ro·gate (ar'ə·gāt) *v.t.* **·gat·ed, ·gat·ing** 1 To claim, demand, or take presumptuously; assume; usurp. 2 To attribute or ascribe without reason. [<L *arrogare* claim for oneself] —**ar'ro·ga'tion** *n.*

ar·row (ar'ō) *n.* 1 A straight, slender shaft, usu. feathered at one end and with a pointed head at the other, to be shot from a bow. 2 Anything resembling an arrow in shape, speed, etc. 3 A sign or figure in the shape of an arrow, used to indicate directions. [<OE *earh, arwe*] —**ar'row·y** *adj.*

ar·row·head (ar'ō·hed') *n.* 1 The sharp-pointed head of an arrow. 2 Something resembling an arrowhead. 3 Any of various water plants with arrow-shaped leaves.

ar·row·root (ar'ō·rōōt', -rŏŏt') *n.* 1 A starch obtained from the roots of a tropical American plant. 2 The plant.

ar·roy·o (ə·roi'ō) *n. pl.* **·os** (-ōz) *sw U.S.* 1 A brook. 2 A dry gully. [Sp.]

ar·se·nal (är'sə·nəl) *n.* 1 A place for making or storing arms and munitions. 2 Any supply or stock. [<Ar. *dār aṣ-ṣinā'ah* workshop]

ar·se·nic (är'sə·nik) *n.* 1 An element (symbol As) chemically similar to phosphorus, used chiefly to make insecticides. 2 The highly poisonous, white, crystalline trioxide of arsenic: also **ar·sen·ic** (är·sen'ik) *adj.* Of or containing arsenic: also **ar·sen'i·cal.** [<L *arsenicum*]

ar·son (är'sən) *n.* The crime of deliberately setting fire to another's building, property, etc., or to one's own, esp. for a criminal or fraudulent purpose. [<L *arsus,* pp. of *ardere* burn] —**ar'son·ist** *n.*

art¹ (ärt) *n.* 1 The ability of man to arrange or adapt natural things or conditions to his own uses. 2 The creation of works that are, in form, content, and execution, esthetically pleasing and meaningful, as in music, painting, sculpture, literature, architecture, dance, etc. 3 The principles and techniques governing the creation of such works. 4 The works so created, esp. paintings, drawings, and sculpture. 5 Skilled workmanship; craft. 6 Any specific skill, craft, trade, or profession: the *art* of cooking; a teacher's *art.* 7 *Printing* Any illustrative or decorative material that accompanies the text. 8 *Usu. pl.* The liberal arts. 9 Craft; cunning. 10 *Usu. pl.* A trick, stratagem, or wile. —*adj.* Of or for artists or their works. [<L *ars* skill]

art² (ärt) Archaic or poetic second person singular present tense of BE: used with *thou.* [<OE *eart*]

-art *suffix* Var. of -ARD.

Ar·te·mis (är'tə·mis) *Gk. Myth.* The goddess of the chase and of the moon; twin sister of Apollo.

ar·te·ri·al (är·tir'ē·əl) *adj.* 1 Of, like, or carried in the arteries. 2 Pertaining to the bright red blood which has been aerated in the lungs. 3 Constituting a main channel or route: an *arterial* highway.

ar·te·ri·o·scle·ro·sis (är·tir'ē·ō·sklə·rō'sis) *n.* Thickening and loss of elasticity of the walls of an artery, as in old age. —**ar·te'ri·o·scle·rot'ic** (-rot'ik) *adj.*

ar·ter·y (är'tər·ē) *n. pl.* **·ter·ies** 1 Any of the numerous muscular vessels and their branches that convey blood from the heart to every part of the body. • See HEART. 2 Any main channel or route. [<L *arteria* artery, windpipe]

ar·te·sian well (är·tē'zhən) A well bored down to a water-bearing stratum in which the water pressure is great enough to force a flow of water to the surface. [<F *artésien,* from *Artois,* town in France]

art·ful (ärt'fəl) *adj.* 1 Crafty; cunning. 2 Artificial; imitative. 3 Skillful; ingenious. —**art'ful·ly** *adv.* —**art'ful·ness** *n.*

ar·thri·tis (är·thrī'tis) *n.* Inflammation of a joint or joints. [<Gk. *arthron* joint + -ITIS] —**ar·thrit·ic** (är·thrit'ik) *adj.*

ar·thro·pod (är'thrə·pod) *n.* Any of a large group of invertebrate animals characterized by jointed legs and segmented body parts, as insects, spiders, crabs, etc. [<Gk. <*arthron* joint + *podos* foot] —**ar·throp·o·dous** (är·throp'ə·dəs), **ar·throp'o·dal** *adj.*

ar·thro·scope (är'thrə·skōp) *n.* A small endoscope for the examination and repair of a shoulder or knee joint. [<ARTHRO- + SCOPE]

Ar·thur (är'thər) A legendary British king of the sixth century A.D., hero of the Round Table. —**Ar·thu·ri·an** (är·thŏŏr'ē·ən) *adj.*

ar·ti·choke (är'tə·chōk) *n.* 1 A thistlelike garden plant. 2 Its succulent flower head, used as a vegetable. 3 The Jerusalem artichoke. [<Ar. *al-kharshūf*]

ar·ti·cle (är'ti·kəl) *n.* 1 A particular object or thing. 2 A member of a class of things. 3 A composition written for or appearing in a newspaper, magazine, etc. 4 A distinct proposition, statement, or stipulation in a series of such, as in a constitution, treaty, etc. 5 A complete item of religious belief; a point of doctrine. 6 *Gram.*

Artichoke def. 2

One of the three words *a, an* (**indefinite articles**) or *the* (**definite article**), used as modifiers. —*v.* **·cled, ·cling** *v.t.* 1 To bind to service by a written contract. 2 To specify. 3 To accuse by formal articles. —*v.i.* 4 To make accusations: with *against.* [<L *articulus,* dim. of *artus* a joint]

ar·tic·u·lar (är·tik'yə·lər) *adj.* Pertaining to a joint or the joints.

ar·tic·u·late (är·tik'yə·lit) *adj.* 1 Jointed; segmented: also **ar·tic'u·lat'ed** (-lā'tid). 2 Able to speak. 3 Able to speak clearly, easily, and effectively. 4 Divided into syllables or words so as to be intelligible. 5 Clear and logically coherent. —*v.* (är·tik'yə·lāt) **·lat·ed, ·lat·ing** *v.t.* 1 To utter distinctly; enunciate. 2 To express clearly in words. 3 *Phonet.* To produce, as a speech sound, by the movement of the organs of speech. 4 To unite by joints. —*v.i.* 5 To speak distinctly. 6 *Phonet.* To produce a speech sound. 7 *Anat.* To form a joint: used with *with.* [<L *articulare* divide into joints, utter distinctly] —**ar·tic'u·late·ly** *adv.* —**ar·tic'u·late·ness, ar·tic'u·lat·or** *n.* —**ar·tic'u·la·tive** *adj.*

ar·tic·u·la·tion (är·tik'yə·lā'shən) *n.* 1 A jointing or being jointed together; also the manner or method of this. 2 A joint between two bones. 3 The utterance of articulate sounds; enunciation. 4 A speech sound, esp. a consonant. 5 *Bot.* A joint between two separable parts; a node.

ar·ti·fact (är′tə·fakt) n. Anything made by human work or art. Also **ar′te·fact**. [<L ars art, skill + factus, p.p. of facere make]

ar·ti·fice (är′tə·fis) n. 1 Subtle or deceptive craft; trickery. 2 Skill; ingenuity. 3 An ingenious expedient; stratagem. [<L artificium handicraft, skill]

ar·tif·i·cer (är·tif′ə·sər) n. 1 A skilled craftsman. 2 An inventor or designer of things.

ar·ti·fi·cial (är′tə·fish′əl) adj. 1 Produced by human art rather than by nature. 2 Made in imitation of or as a substitute for something natural. 3 Not genuine or natural; affected. [See ARTIFICE.] —ar′ti·fi·ci·al′i·ty, ar′ti·fi′cial·ness n. —ar′ti·fi′cial·ly adv.

artificial insemination Impregnation of the female with semen from the male without direct sexual contact.

ar·til·ler·y (är·til′ər·ē) n. 1 Guns of larger caliber than machine guns. 2 Military units armed with such guns. 3 Branches of the U.S. Army composed of such units. 4 Informal Any small firearm. 5 The science of gunnery. [<OF artiller fortify] —ar·til′ler·y·man n. (pl. -men)

ar·ti·san (är′tə·zən) n. A trained or skilled workman. [<L ars art]

art·ist (är′tist) n. 1 One who is skilled in or who makes a profession of any of the fine arts or the performing arts. 2 One who does anything with artistry. [<L ars art]

ar·tiste (är·tēst′) n. A professional entertainer: usu. a humorous usage. [<F]

ar·tis·tic (är·tis·tik) adj. 1 Of or pertaining to art or artists. 2 Esthetically pleasing; tastefully executed. 3 Fond of or sensitive to art. —ar·tis·ti·cal·ly adv.

art·ist·ry (är′tis·trē) n. Artistic ability, quality, or workmanship. —Syn. talent, skill, invention, genius.

art·less (ärt′lis) adj. 1 Without guile or deceit; innocent. 2 Natural; simple. 3 Without art or skill; clumsy. 4 Without taste; ignorant. —art′less·ly adv. —art′less·ness n.

Art Nou·veau (ärt nōō·vō′, Fr. är nōō·vō′) A style of art and design of the late 19th and early 20th centuries characterized by curved and twisting shapes often representing natural objects. [F, lit., new art]

art·y (är′tē) adj. art·i·er, art·i·est Affectedly or ostentatiously artistic. —art′i·ness n.

ar·um (âr′əm) n. Any of various plants having small flowers on a thick spike surrounded by a spathe, as the jack-in-the-pulpit. [<Gk. aron]

-ary suffix of adjectives and nouns 1 Connected with or pertaining to what is expressed in the root word: elementary. 2 A person engaged in: apothecary. 3 A thing connected with or a place dedicated to: dictionary. [<L -arius, -arium]

Ar·y·an (âr′ē·ən, ar′-, är′yən) n. 1 A member or descendant of a prehistoric people who spoke Indo-European. 2 In Nazi ideology, a Caucasian gentile, esp. one of Nordic stock. —adj. Of or pertaining to Aryans. [<Skt. ārya noble]

as (az, unstressed əz) adv. 1 To the same extent or degree; equally: Do I look as pretty? 2 For instance; thus: to release, as prisoners, from confinement. —conj. 1 To the same amount or degree that: He became gentler as he grew older. 2 In the way that: Do as I tell you. 3 At the same time that; while: They sang as we left. 4 Because: As the weather was bad, the game was postponed. 5 However; though: Bad as it was, it might have been worse. 6 That the result is: The play is so bad as not to merit discussion. 7 Informal That: I don't know as I told you. —prep. 1 In the role, capacity, or sense of: I'll act as referee. 2 In the manner of; like: to dress as a witch. — pron. 1 That: used after such and same: the same pen as you have. 2 A fact that: She is a genius, as everyone knows. —as . . . as A correlative construction that indicates identity or equality of two things: as much as, as good as. —as for Concerning; in the case of. —as if (or as though) 1 As it would if. 2 That: It seems as if he'll never win. —as is Informal Just as it is: said of an article somewhat damaged. —as it were So to speak. —as to Concerning. —As yet Up to the present time. [<OE eallswa entirely so, also] • See LIKE.

AS, A.S., AS. Anglo-Saxon.

As arsenic.

as·a·fet·i·da (as′ə·fet′ə·də) n. A fetid gum resin obtained from certain plants related to parsley, formerly used in medicine. [<Med.L àsa mastic + L foetida ill-smelling]

as·bes·tos (as·bes′təs, az-) n. A white or gray mineral silicate of calcium and magnesium which may be woven or shaped into acid-resisting, nonconducting, and fireproof articles. —adj. Of asbestos. [<Gk., unquenchable]

ASCAP, A.S.C.A.P. American Society of Composers, Authors, and Publishers.

as·cend (ə·send′) v.i. 1 To go or move upward; rise. 2 To go from a lower to a higher degree, pitch, etc. 3 To slope upward. —v.t. 1 To move or climb upward on. 5 To succeed to (a throne). [<L ad- to + scandere climb] —as·cend′a·ble or -i·ble adj. —as·cen′der n.

as·cen·den·cy (ə·sen′dən·sē) n. The state of being in the ascendent; domination; supremacy. Also **as·cen′dan·cy**.

as·cen·dent (ə·sen′dənt) adj. 1 Ascending; rising. 2 Superior; dominant. —n. 1 A position of supreme power; preeminence. 2 In astrology, the sign of the zodiac that is rising above the eastern horizon at any given instant. Also **as·cen′dant**. —**in the ascendent** Approaching or having controlling power, fame, influence, etc.

as·cen·sion (ə·sen′shən) n. The act of ascending —**the Ascension** Theol. The bodily ascent of Christ into heaven after the Resurrection, commemorated on **Ascension Day**, the fortieth day after Easter. —as·cen′sion·al adj.

as·cent (ə·sent′) n. 1 The act of ascending, rising, or climbing. 2 The method or way of ascending. 3 The measure or degree of upward slope: an ascent of 30°. 4 A rise in rank or station; advancement [<ASCEND]

as·cer·tain (as′ər·tān′) v.t. To learn with certainty about; find out. [<OF a- to + certain certain] — **as′cer·tain′a·ble** adj. —as′cer·tain′a·bly adv. —as′cer·tain′ment n.

as·cet·ic (ə·set′ik) n. 1 A religious hermit or recluse. 2 One who leads a very austere and self-denying life. —adj. Given to or involving severe self-denial and austerity: also **as·cet′i·cal**. [<Gk. askētēs one who exercises (self-denial), a monk] —as·cet′i·cal·ly adv.

as·cet·i·cism (ə·set′ə·siz′əm) n. Ascetic practices and conduct, esp. as a way to greater spirituality.

ASCII (as′kē) n. American Standard Code for Information Interchange, a coding scheme for representing information digitally so that different kinds of computers can communicate with each other.

a·scor·bic acid (ə·skôr′bik) A white, odorless, crystalline compound, present in citrus fruits and other foods, and also made synthetically; vitamin C. [<Gk. a- not + SCORB(UT)IC]

as·cot (as′kət, -kot) n. A kind of scarf or necktie, knotted so that the broad ends are laid one across the other. [<Ascot, England]

as·cribe (ə·skrīb′) v.t. as·cribed, as·crib·ing 1 To attribute, as to a cause, source, author, etc. 2 To assign as a quality or attribute. [<L ad- to + scribere write] —as·crib·a·ble (ə·skrī′bə·bəl) adj.

as·crip·tion (ə·skrip′shən) n. An ascribing or being ascribed.

-ase suffix Chem. Used in naming enzymes; sometimes added to the name of the compound which the enzyme decomposes: amylase, casease, etc. [<(DIAST)ASE]

a·sep·sis (ə·sep′sis, ā-) n. 1 An aseptic condition. 2 The prevention of infection by maintaining sterile conditions. [A- (not) + SEPSIS]

a·sep·tic (ə·sep′tik, ā-) adj. Free from or doing away with microorganisms that produce disease or putrefaction. — a·sep′ti·cal·ly adv.

a·sex·u·al (ā·sek′shōō·əl) adj. 1 Having no distinct sexual organs; without sex. 2 Occurring or performed without union of the sexes. —a·sex·u·al′i·ty (ā·sek′shōō·al′ə·tē) n. — a·sex′u·al·ly adv.

Ascot

---

add, āce, dâre, pälm; end, ēven; it, īce; odd, ōpen, ôrder; tōōk, pōōl; up; bûrn; ə = a in above, u in focus; yōō = u in fuse; oil; pout; check; go; ring; thin; this; zh, vision. < derived from; ? origin uncertain or unknown.

ash¹ (ash) *n.* The powdery, whitish gray residue of a substance that has been burnt. [< OE *asce*]

ash² (ash) *n.* 1 Any of a genus of hardy deciduous trees related to the olive and valued as a shade and timber tree. 2 Its light, tough, elastic wood. —*adj.* Made of ash wood. [< OE *æsc*]

a·shamed (ə-shāmd′) *adj.* 1 Feeling shame. 2 Deterred by the anticipation of shame. [< obs. *ashame* to shame or feel shame] —**a·sham·ed·ly** (ə-shā′mid-lē) *adv.* —**Syn.** 1 embarrassed, mortified, abashed, humiliated.

ash·en¹ (ash′ən) *adj.* 1 Of, pertaining to, or like ashes. 2 Pale and grayish in color.

ash·en² (ash′ən) *adj.* Pertaining to or made of the wood of the ash tree.

ash·es (ash′iz) *n. pl.* 1 The grayish white, powdery particles remaining after something has been burned. 2 The remains of the human body after cremation. 3 Any dead body; corpse. 4 Remains or ruins, as after destruction.

ash·lar (ash′lər) *n.* 1 A rough-hewn block of stone. 2 A thin, dressed, squared stone, used for facing a wall. 3 Masonwork made of ashlar. Also **ash′ler.** [< L *axilla*, dim. of *axis* board, plank]

a·shore (ə-shôr′, ə-shōr′) *adv.* 1 To or on the shore. 2 On land; aground.

Ash Wednesday The first day of Lent.

ash·y (ash′ē) *adj.* **ash·i·er, ash·i·est** 1 Of, pertaining to, or like ashes. 2 Very pale.

A·sia (ā′zhə, ā′shə) *n.* The world's largest continent, bounded by Europe and the Pacific, Arctic, and Indian Oceans; 16,900,000 square miles. —**A′sian, A·si·at·ic** (ā′zhē-at′ik, ā′shē-) *adj., n.* • In most cases, esp. in the ethnic sense, *Asian* is now preferred to *Asiatic*.

Asia Minor The peninsula of extreme western Asia between the Black and the Mediterranean seas, comprising most of Turkey in Asia.

Asiatic cholera An acute, infectious, often epidemic disease marked by severe diarrhea and high mortality.

a·side (ə-sīd′) *adv.* 1 On or to one side; apart. 2 Out of thought or use. 3 Notwithstanding; apart: all kidding *aside.* 4 In reserve. —**aside from** 1 Excepting. 2 Apart from. —*n.* 1 The words spoken by an actor and supposed to be heard by the audience but not by the other actors. 2 A digression. [< A- on + SIDE]

as·i·nine (as′ə-nīn) *adj.* 1 Of or like an ass. 2 Silly, thoughtless, stupid, etc. [< L *asinus* ass] —**as′i·nine′ly** *adv.* —**as·i·nin·i·ty** (as′ə-nin′ə-tē) *n.*

ask (ask, äsk) *v.t.* 1 To put a question to. 2 To put a question about; inquire after. 3 To make a request for; solicit. 4 To need or require: This job *asks* too much of me. 5 To state the price of; demand. 6 To invite: Were many guests *asked?* —*v.i.* 7 To make inquiries: with *for, after,* or *about.* 8 To make a request. 9 To act as if inviting something: with *for:* to *ask* for trouble. [< OE *āscian*] —**ask′er** *n.* **ask′ing** *n.*

a·skance (ə-skans′) *adv.* 1 With a side glance; sidewise. 2 Disdainfully; distrustfully. Also **a·skant′.** [< A- on + SKEW]

a·skew (ə-skyōō′) *adj.* Oblique. —*adv.* In an oblique position or manner; to one side. [< A- on + SKEW]

a·slant (ə-slant′, ə-slänt′) *adj.* Slanting; oblique. —*adv.* In a slanting direction or position; obliquely. —*prep.* Across or over in a slanting direction or position.

a·sleep (ə-slēp′) *adj.* 1 Sleeping. 2 Dormant; inactive. 3 Numb or prickly. 4 Dead. —*adv.* Into a sleeping condition.

a·slope (ə-slōp′) *adj.* Sloping. —*adv.* In a sloping position.

a·so·cial (ā-sō′shəl) *adj.* Avoiding society; not gregarious.

asp¹ (asp) *n.* Any of several small poisonous snakes of Africa and Europe, as the horned viper. [< Gk. *aspis*]

asp² (asp) *n.* ASPEN.

as·par·a·gus (ə-spar′ə-gəs) *n.* 1 The edible shoots of a cultivated plant of the lily family. 2 Any plant of this genus. [< Gk. *asparagos, aspharogos*]

as·pect (as′pekt) *n.* 1 The look a person has; expression of countenance. 2 Appearance presented to the eye by something; look. 3 Appearance presented to the mind by circumstances, etc.; interpretation. 4 A facing in a given direction. 5 The side or surface facing in a certain direction. 6 In astrology, the configuration of the planets in relation to each other or to the observer, as a supposed influence on human affairs. [< L *aspicere* to look at]

asp·en (as′pən) *n.* Any of several kinds of poplar with leaves that flutter in the slightest breeze. —*adj.* 1 Of the aspen. 2 Quivering; shaking. [< OE *aspe*]

as·per·i·ty (as·per′ə·tē) *n. pl.* **·ties** 1 Roughness or harshness, as of surface, sound, weather, etc. 2 Bitterness or sharpness of temper [< L *asper* rough]

as·perse (ə-spûrs′) *v.t.* **as·persed** (ə-spûrst′), **as·pers·ing** To spread false charges against; slander. [< L *aspergere* sprinkle on] —**as·pers′er, as·per′sor** *n.*

as·per·sion (ə-spûr′zhən, -shən) *n.* 1 A slandering. 2 Slander; a slanderous report or charge.

as·phalt (as′fôlt) *n.* 1 A dark brown, semisolid, bituminous substance obtained from natural deposits or as a residue in refining petroleum; mineral pitch. 2 A mixture of this with sand or gravel, used for paving, etc. Also **as·phal·tum** (as·fôl′təm). —*v.t.* To pave or cover with asphalt. [< Gk. *asphaltos*] —**as·phal·tic** (as·fôl′tik) *adj.*

as·pho·del (as′fə-del) *n.* A plant of the lily family, bearing white or yellow flowers. [< Gk. *asphodelos*]

as·phyx·i·a (as-fik′sē-ə) *n.* Loss of consciousness, usu. resulting from suffocation caused by too little oxygen and too much carbon dioxide in the blood. [< Gk. *asphyxia* stopping of the pulse] —**as·phyx′i·ant** *adj., n.*

as·phyx·i·ate (as-fik′sē-āt) *v.* **·at·ed, ·at·ing** *v.t.* 1 To cause asphyxia in. 2 To suffocate, as by drowning or breathing noxious gases. —*v.i.* 3 To undergo asphyxia. —**as·phyx′i·a′tion, as·phyx′i·a′tor** *n.*

as·pic (as′pik) *n.* A savory jelly of meat or vegetable juices, served as a relish or mold for meat, vegetables, etc. [< F]

as·pi·dis·tra (as′pə-dis′trə) *n.* Any of a small genus of stemless Asian plants of the lily family, with large, glossy, evergreen leaves. [< Gk. *apis* shield + *astron* star]

as·pir·ant (as′pər-ənt, ə-spīr′ənt) *n.* One who aspires after something. —*adj.* Aspiring.

as·pi·rate (as′pə-rāt) *v.t.* **·rat·ed, ·rat·ing** 1 To utter with a breathing or as if preceded by the letter *h.* 2 To follow (a consonant, esp. (p), (t), and (k)) with an explosive release of breath. 3 To draw off by suction. —*n.* An aspirated sound. —*adj.* (as′pər-it) Uttered with an aspirate: also **as′pi·rat·ed.** [< L *aspirare* to breathe on]

as·pi·ra·tion (as′pə-rā′shən) *n.* 1 Exalted desire; high ambition. 2 The act of breathing. 3 The use of an aspirator. 4 *Phonet.* **a** The pronunciation of a consonant with an aspirate. **b** An aspirate.

as·pi·ra·tor (as′pə-rā′tər) *n.* An appliance producing suction, as for drawing off fluid matter or gases from the body.

as·pi·ra·to·ry (ə-spīr′ə-tôr′ē, -tō′rē) *adj.* Of, pertaining to, or adapted for breathing or suction.

as·pire (ə-spīr′) *v.i.* **as·pired, as·pir·ing** 1 To have an earnest desire or ambition: with *to.* 2 To long for: with *after.* [< L *aspirare* breathe on, attempt to reach] —**as·pir′er** *n.*

as·pi·rin (as′pər-in) *n.* A white crystalline synthetic compound, used to allay pain and fever and to treat rheumatism. [< A(CETYL) + *spir(aeic acid)* former name of salicylic acid + -IN]

a·squint (ə-skwint′) *adj. & adv.* With sidelong glance.

ass¹ (as) *n. pl.* **ass·es** 1 Any of a genus of animals, including the donkey, resembling but smaller than the horse, and with longer ears. 2 A stubborn or stupid person. [< L *asinus*]

ass² (as) *n.* The buttocks: *usu. considered vulgar.* [ME < OE *assa*]

ass. assistant; association.

as·sail (ə-sāl′) *v.t.* 1 To attack violently, as by force, argument, or censure; assault. [< L *assalire* leap upon] —**as·sail′a·ble** *adj.* —**as·sail′a·ble·ness, as·sail′er** *n.*

as·sail·ant (ə-sā′lənt) *n.* One who assails or attacks.

as·sas·sin (ə-sas′in) *n.* A murderer, esp. one who murders a politically prominent person. [< Ar. *hashshāshīn* hashish-eaters, from hashish-eating Muslims who murdered Christians during the Crusades]

as·sas·si·nate (ə-sas′ə-nāt) *v.t.* **·nat·ed, ·nat·ing** 1 To kill by secret assault. 2 To destroy or harm by treachery, as a reputation. —**as·sas′si·na′tion, as·sas′si·na′tor** *n.*

as·sault (ə-sôlt′) *n.* 1 Any violent physical or verbal attack. 2 *Law* An unlawful attempt or offer to do bodily injury to another. 3 A rape. 4 *Mil.* A violent attack by troops, as upon a fortified place. —*v.t. & v.i.* To make an assault (upon). [< L *ad*- to + *salire* leap] —**as·sault'er** *n.*

assault and battery *Law* The carrying out of an assault with force and violence; a beating.

as·say (ə·sā′, as′ā) *n.* **1** The analysis of an alloy, etc., to ascertain the ingredients and their proportions. **2** The substance to be so examined. **3** The result of such a test. **4** Any examination or testing. —*v.t.* (ə·sā′) **1** To make an assay of. **2** To test. —*v.i.* **3** To show by analysis a certain value or proportion, as of a precious metal. [< L *exagium* a weighing < *exigere* prove] —**as·say'er** *n.*

as·sem·blage (ə·sem′blij) *n.* **1** An assembling or being assembled. **2** Any gathering of persons or things; assembly. **3** A fitting together, as parts of a machine. **4** A work of art created by assembling materials and objects; also, the technique of making such works.

as·sem·ble (ə·sem′bəl) *v.t. & v.i.* **·bled, ·bling 1** To collect or convene; congregate. **2** To fit together, as the parts of a mechanism. [< L *assimulare* < *ad*- to + *simul* together] —**as·sem′bler** *n.*

as·sem·bly (ə·sem′blē) *n. pl.* **·blies 1** An assembling or being assembled. **2** A number of persons met together for a common purpose. **3** The act or process of fitting together the parts of a machine, etc.; also, the parts themselves. **4** *Mil.* The signal calling troops to form ranks.

As·sem·bly (ə·sem′blē) *n.* In some states of the U.S., the lower house of the legislature.

assembly line In some factories, an arrangement in which workers perform specialized operations on a unit of work as it passes before them.

as·sem·bly·man (ə·sem′blē·mən) *n. pl.* **·men** (-men′, -mən) *U.S.* A member of a legislative assembly.

as·sent (ə·sent′) *v.i.* To express agreement; concur: usu. with *to.* —*n.* Concurrence or agreement. [< L *assentire* < *ad*- to + *sentire* feel] —**as′sen·ta′tion, as·sent′er** *n.*

as·sert (ə·sûrt′) *v.t.* **1** To state positively; affirm. **2** To maintain as a right or claim. —**assert oneself** To state and defend firmly one's rights, opinions, etc. [< L *asserere* bind to, claim] —**as·sert′er, as·ser′tor** *n.*

as·ser·tion (ə·sûr′shən) *n.* **1** The act of asserting. **2** A positive statement or declaration.

as·ser·tive (ə·sûr′tiv) *adj.* Characterized by confidence and positiveness, often excessively so. —**as·ser′tive·ly** *adv.* —**as·ser′tive·ness** *n.* —**Syn.** positive, decided, dogmatic, aggressive.

as·sess (ə·ses′) *v.t.* **1** To charge with a tax, fine, etc., as a person or property. **2** To determine the amount of, as a tax or fine, on a person or property. **3** To put a value on, as property, for taxation. **4** To take stock of; evaluate. [< LL *assessare* fix a tax] —**as·sess′a·ble** *adj.*

as·sess·ment (ə·ses′mənt) *n.* **1** An assessing. **2** The amount assessed.

as·ses·sor (ə·ses′ər) *n.* One who makes assessments, as for taxation. [< L, lit., one who sits beside as assistant judge] —**as·ses·so·ri·al** (as′ə·sôr′ē·əl, -sō′rē·əl) *adj.*

as·set (as′et) *n.* **1** An item of property. **2** A person, thing, or quality regarded as useful or valuable to have. **3** *pl.* In accounting, the entries in a balance sheet showing all the property or resources of a person or business, as cash, accounts receivable, equipment, etc. **4** *pl. Law* **a** The property of a deceased person which can be used to pay debts or legacies. **b** All the property, real or personal, of a person or corporation. [< L *ad*- to + *satis* enough]

as·sev·er·ate (ə·sev′ə·rāt) *v.t.* **·at·ed, ·at·ing** To affirm or aver emphatically or solemnly. [< L < *ad*- to + *severus* serious] —**as·sev′er·a′tion** *n.*

as·si·du·i·ty (as′ə·dyōō′ə·tē) *n.* The quality or state of being assiduous; diligence.

as·sid·u·ous (ə·sij′ōō·əs) *adj.* Carefully attentive and diligent. [< L *assidere* sit by] —**as·sid′u·ous·ly** *adv.* —**as·sid′u·ous·ness** *n.*

as·sign (ə·sīn′) *v.t.* **1** To set apart, as for a particular function; designate. **2** To appoint, as to a post. **3** To give out or allot, as a lesson. **4** To ascribe or attribute, as a motive. **5** *Law* To make over or transfer, as personal property, to another. —*n. Law Usu. pl.* Assignee. [< L *ad*- to + *signare* make a sign] —**as·sign′a·bil′i·ty, as·sign′er,** *Law* **as·sign′or** *n.* —**as·sign′a·ble** *adj.*

as·sig·na·tion (as′ig·nā′shən) *n.* **1** An appointment for meeting, esp. a secret or illicit one as made by lovers; a tryst. **2** An assignment.

as·sign·ee (ə·sī′nē′, as′ə·nē′) *n. Law* A person to whom property, rights, or powers are transferred by another.

as·sign·ment (ə·sīn′mənt) *n.* **1** An assigning or being assigned. **2** Anything assigned, as a lesson or task. **3** *Law* **a** The transfer of a claim, right, or property or the instrument or writing of transfer. **b** The claim, right, or property transferred.

as·sim·i·la·ble (ə·sim′ə·lə·bəl) *adj.* Capable of being assimilated. —**as·sim′i·la·bil′i·ty** *n.*

as·sim·i·late (ə·sim′ə·lāt) *v.* **·lat·ed, ·lat·ing** *v.t.* **1** To absorb and incorporate (food) into the body. **2** To make part of one's own thinking. **3** To absorb (a different culture, group, etc.) into the main social or cultural body. **4** To make alike; cause to resemble. —*v.i.* **5** To become alike or similar. **6** To become absorbed or assimilated. [< L *ad*- to + *similare* make like] —**as·sim′i·la′tion** *n.* —**as·sim′i·la′tive, as·sim·i·la·to·ry** (ə·sim′ə·lə·tôr′ē, -tō′rē) *adj.*

as·sist (ə·sist′) *v.t.* **1** To give succor or support to; help; relieve. **2** To act as an assistant to. —*v.i.* **3** To give help or support. **4** In baseball, to aid a teammate or partner in a play. —**assist at** To be present at (a ceremony, etc.). —*n.* **1** An act of helping. **2** In baseball, a play that helps to put out a runner. [< L *ad*- to + *sistere* cause to stand] —**as·sist′er** *n.*

as·sis·tance (ə·sis′təns) *n.* Help; aid; support.

as·sis·tant (ə·sis′tənt) *n.* A subordinate or helper. —*adj.* **1** Holding a subordinate or auxiliary place, office, or rank. **2** Affording aid; assisting.

as·size (ə·sīz′) *n.* In England, one of the regular sessions of a superior court. [< L *assidere* sit at, settle]

assn. association.

assoc. associate; association.

as·so·ci·ate (ə·sō′shē·it, -āt, -sē-) *n.* **1** A companion. **2** A co-worker; colleague. **3** Anything that accompanies or is associated with something else; a concomitant. **4** One admitted to partial membership in an association, society, etc. —*adj.* **1** Joined with another or others; united; allied. **2** Having subordinate or secondary status: an *associate* professor. —*v.* (ə·sō′shē·āt) **·at·ed, ·at·ing** *v.t.* **1** To bring into company or relation; combine together. **2** To unite (oneself) with another or others, as in friendship. **3** To connect mentally: to *associate* poetry with madness. —*v.i.* **4** To join or be in company or relation: with *with.* **5** To unite, as nations. [< L *associare* join to]

as·so·ci·a·tion (ə·sō′sē·ā′shən, -shē-) *n.* **1** The act of associating. **2** The state of being associated; fellowship; companionship. **3** A body of persons associated for some common purpose. **4** *Ecol.* A grouping of many plant species over a wide area, sharing a common habitat and similar geographic conditions. **5** A connection or relation in the mind of ideas, feelings, etc., with each other or with external objects or symbols. —**as·so′ci·a′tion·al** *adj.*

association football SOCCER.

as·so·ci·a·tive (ə·sō′shē·ā′tiv, -shē·ə-, -sē-) *adj.* **1** Of, pertaining to, or characterized by association. **2** Causing association. —**as·so′ci·a′tive·ly** *adv.*

as·so·nance (as′ə·nəns) *n.* Resemblance in sound; specifically, in prosody, correspondence of the accented vowels, but not of the consonants, as in *main, came.* [< L *assonare* sound to, respond to] —**as′so·nant** *adj., n.*

as·sort (ə·sôrt′) *v.t.* **1** To distribute into groups or classes according to kinds; classify. **2** To furnish, as a warehouse, with a variety of goods, etc. —*v.i.* **3** To fall into groups or classes of the same kind. **4** To associate; consort: with *with.* [< OF *a*- to + *sorte* sort, kind] —**as·sort′a·tive** (ə·sôr′tə·tiv) *adj.*

as·sort·ed (ə·sôr′tid) *adj.* **1** Varied; miscellaneous. **2** Sorted out; classified. **3** Matched; suited.

as·sort·ment (ə·sôrt′mənt) *n.* **1** The act of assorting; classification. **2** A collection or group of various things; miscellany.

---

add, āce, câre, pälm; end, ēven; it, īce; odd, ōpen, ôrder; tŏŏk, pōōl; up, bûrn; ə = a in above, u in focus; yōō = u in fuse; oil; pout; check; go; ring; thin; this; zh, vision. < derived from; ? origin uncertain or unknown.

asst. assistant.

as·suage (ə·swāj′) v. **as·suaged, as·suag·ing** v.t. **1** To lessen or reduce the intensity of. **2** To reduce to a quiet or peaceful state. **3** To end by satisfying. [< L ad- to + suavis sweet] —**as·suage′ment** n. —**Syn. 1** ease, alloy, mitigate. **2** calm, pacify, mollify. **3** appease, slake, quench.

as·sume (ə·sōōm′) v.t. **as·sumed, as·sum·ing 1** To take up or adopt, as a style of dress, aspect, or character. **2** To undertake, as an office or duty. **3** To arrogate to oneself; usurp, as powers of state. **4** To take for granted; suppose to be true. **5** To affect; pretend to have. [< L assumere to take up, adopt] —**as·sum·a·ble** (ə·sōō′mə·bəl) adj.

as·sumed (ə·sōōmd′) adj. **1** Taken for granted. **2** Pretended; fictitious.

as·sum·ing (ə·sōō′ming) adj. Presumptuous; arrogant.

as·sump·tion (ə·sump′shən) n. **1** The act of assuming. **2** Something taken for granted; supposition. **3** Presumption; arrogance. —**the Assumption 1** The doctrine that the Virgin Mary was bodily taken up into heaven at her death. **2** A church feast, observed on August 15, commemorating this event. —**as·sump′tive** adj.

as·sur·ance (ə·shŏŏr′əns) n. **1** The act of assuring. **2** A positive or encouraging declaration. **3** Full confidence; certainty. **4** Self-confidence; firmness of mind. **5** Boldness; effrontery. **6** Brit. Insurance.

as·sure (ə·shŏŏr′) v.t. **as·sured, as·sur·ing 1** To make sure or secure; establish. **2** To give confidence to; convince. **3** To guarantee, as something risky. **4** To promise confidently. **5** Brit. To insure. [< L ad- to + securus safe] —**as·sur′a·ble** adj.

as·sured (ə·shŏŏrd′) adj. **1** Made certain and sure. **2** Self-possessed; confident. **3** Insured. —n. An insured person or persons. —**as·sur·ed·ly** (ə·shŏŏr′id·lē) adv. —**as·sur′ed·ness** n.

As·syr·i·a (ə·sir′ē·ə) n. An ancient empire of western Asia, cap. Nineveh. —**As·syr′i·an** adj., n.

As·tar·te (as·tär′tē) In Phoenician mythology, the goddess of love and fertility.

as·ta·tine (as′tə·tēn, -tin) n. An artificially produced radioactive element (symbol At) chemically similar to iodine. [< Gk. astatos unstable + -INE]

as·ter (as′tər) n. Any of a large group of related plants having composite flowers with white, purple, or blue rays and yellow disk. [< Gk. astēr star]

-aster suffix A contemptuous diminutive: poetaster, criticaster. [< L]

as·ter·isk (as′tər·isk) n. A starlike figure (*) used to indicate omissions, footnotes, references, etc. —v.t. To mark with an asterisk. [< Gk. astēr star]

a·stern (ə·stûrn′) adv. Naut. **1** In or at the stern. **2** In the rear; at any point behind a vessel. **3** To the rear; backward.

as·ter·oid (as′tə·roid) n. **1** Any of several hundred small, planetlike bodies with orbits mainly between Mars and Jupiter. **2** A starfish. —adj. Resembling a star. [< Gk. astēr star + -OID] —**as′ter·oi′dal** adj.

asth·ma (az′mə, as′-) n. A chronic disorder characterized by recurrent breathing difficulty and bronchial spasms. [< Gk. azein breathe hard] —**asth·mat·ic** (az·mat′ik, as-) adj., n. —**asth·mat′i·cal** adj. —**asth·mat′i·cal·ly** adv.

a·stig·ma·tism (ə·stig′mə·tiz′əm) n. A defect of the eye or a lens such that the rays of light from an object do not converge to a perfect focus. [< A-⁴ without + Gk. stigma mark] —**as·tig·mat·ic** (as′tig·mat′ik) adj.

a·stir (ə·stûr′) adv. & adj. Stirring; moving about.

a·ston·ish (ə·ston′ish) v.t. To affect with wonder and surprise; amaze; confound. [< L ex- out + tonare thunder] —**a·ston′ish·ing** adj. —**a·ston′ish·ing·ly** adv.

a·ston·ish·ment (ə·ston′ish·mənt) n. **1** The state of being astonished; surprise; amazement. **2** An object or cause of such emotion.

a·stound (ə·stound′) v.t. To overwhelm or shock with wonder or surprise; confound. [ME astoned stunned, pp. of astonien astonish] —**a·stound′ing** adj. —**a·stound′ing·ly** adv.

a·strad·dle (ə·strad′l) adv. & adj. Astride.

as·tra·khan (as′trə·kan, -kən) n. **1** The pelts of very young lambs, with tightly curled wool, from the region near Astrakhan. **2** A fabric imitating this.

as·tral (as′trəl) adj. **1** Of, coming from, or like the stars. **2** In theosophy, pertaining to or consisting of a supersensible substance supposed to pervade all space. [< Gk. astron star] —**as′tral·ly** adv.

a·stray (ə·strā′) adv. **1** Away from the right path. **2** Wandering in or into error or evil. [< L extra- beyond + vagare wander]

a·stride (ə·strīd′) adv. **1** With one leg on each side. **2** With the legs far apart. —prep. With one leg on each side of.

as·trin·gent (ə·strin′jənt) adj. **1** Causing contraction of body tissue; styptic. **2** Harsh; stern; austere. —n. A substance that arrests perspiring or bleeding. [< L astringere bind together] —**as·trin′gen·cy** n. —**as·trin′gent·ly** adv.

astro- combining form Star: astrophysics. [< Gk. astron star]

astrol. astrologer; astrological; astrology.

as·tro·labe (as′trə·lāb) n. An ancient instrument for determining altitudes of planets and stars. [< Gk. astrolabon, orig., star-taking]

as·trol·o·gy (ə·strol′ə·jē) n. **1** Originally, the practical application of astronomy to human uses. **2** The study professing to interpret the influence of the heavenly bodies upon the destinies and behavior of men. [< Gk. < ASTRO- + -LOGY] —**as·trol′o·ger** n. —**as·tro·log·ic** (as′trə·loj′ik), **as·tro·log′i·cal** adj. —**as′tro·log′i·cal·ly** adv.

astron. astronomer; astronomy.

as·tro·naut (as′trə·nôt) n. One who travels in space. [< ASTRO- + Gk. nautēs sailor]

as·tro·nau·tics (as′trə·nô′tiks) n. pl. (construed as sing.) The science of space travel.

as·tron·o·mer (ə·stron′ə·mər) n. One learned or expert in astronomy.

as·tro·nom·ic (as′trə·nom′ik) adj. **1** Of or pertaining to astronomy. **2** Enormously or inconceivably large. Also **as·tro·nom′i·cal.** —**as′tro·nom′i·cal·ly** adv.

astronomical year Solar year.

as·tron·o·my (ə·stron′ə·mē) n. The science that studies stars, planets, and other bodies in space and the phenomena that involve them. [< Gk. astronomia < astron star + nomos law]

as·tro·phys·ics (as′trō·fiz′iks) n. pl. (construed as sing.) The branch of astronomy that deals with the physical constitution and properties of bodies in space. —**as′tro·phys′i·cal** adj. —**as·tro·phys·i·cist** (as′trō·fiz′ə·sist) n.

as·tute (ə·st^yōōt′) adj. Having or showing keen intelligence or shrewdness: an astute businessman. [< L astus cunning] —**as·tute′ly** adv. —**as·tute′ness** n. —**Syn.** acute, sagacious, cunning, crafty.

a·sun·der (ə·sun′dər) adv. **1** In or into a different place or direction. **2** Apart; into pieces. [< OE on sundran]

a·sy·lum (ə·sī′ləm) n. **1** An institution for the care of the aged, the mentally disturbed, the poor, etc. **2** A place of refuge. **3** An inviolable shelter from arrest or punishment, as a temple or church in ancient times. **4** The protection afforded by a sanctuary or refuge. [< Gk. a- without + sylon right of seizure]

a·sym·met·ric (ā′si·met′rik, as′i-) adj. Not symmetrical. Also **a′sym·met′ri·cal.** —**a′sym·met′ri·cal·ly** adv.

a·sym·me·try (ā·sim′ə·trē) n. Lack of symmetry or proportion. [< Gk. a- without + symmetria symmetry]

as·ymp·tote (as′im·tōt) n. Math. A straight line which is a limit of the set of lines tangent to a curve as the point of tangency approaches infinity. [< Gk. asymptōtos not falling together] —**as′ymp·tot′ic** (-tot′ik) or **·i·cal** adj. —**as′ymp·tot′i·cal·ly** adv.

at (at, unstressed ət) prep. **1** On; in; near; upon: at the door; at the center. **2** On or near the age or time of: the train leaving at two; a man at sixty. **3** During the course or lapse of: at the moment. **4** To or toward: Look at that sunset! **5** Through; by way of: smoke coming out at the windows. **6** From: Get gas at the pump. **7** Engaged or occupied in: to be at work. **8** Attending: He was at the party. **9** In the state or condition of: a nation at war. **10** Viewed from; with an interval of: a target at sixty paces. **11** As a result of: He winced at the thought. **12** In the manner of: at a trot. **13** In pursuit or quest of; in the direction of: to catch at straws. **14** Dependent upon: to be at an enemy's mercy. **15** According to: Proceed at your discretion. **16** To or for the extent, amount, degree, price, etc., of: pencils at a dime apiece. 17 With reference to: to be good *at* baking cakes. [< OE *æt*]

At·a·brine (at′ə·brin, -brēn) *n.* A synthetic antimalarial drug: a trade name.

at·a·vism (at′ə·viz′əm) *n.* 1 Reversion to an earlier or primitive type. 2 *Biol.* **a** The occurrence in an individual of a characteristic present in remote ancestors. **b** An instance of such an occurrence. [< L *atavus* ancestor] —**at′· a·vist** *n.* —**at′a·vis′tic** *adj.*

a·tax·i·a (ə·tak′sē·ə) *n.* 1 Absence or failure of muscular coordination. 2 Locomotor ataxia. Also **a·tax·y** (ə·tak′sē). [< Gk. *ataxia* lack of order] —**a·tax′ic** *adj.*, *n.*

ate (āt, *chiefly Brit.* et) *p.t.* of EAT.

-ate[1] *suffix* Forming: 1 Participial adjectives equivalent to those in *-ated*: *separate*. 2 Adjectives meaning "possessing or characterized by": *foliate*. 3 Verbs formed by analogy: *assassinate*. 4 *Chem.* Verbs with the meaning "combine or treat with": *chlorinate*. [< L *-atus*, pp. ending of 1st conjugation verbs]

-ate[2] *suffix* Forming: 1 Nouns denoting office, function, or agent: *magistrate*. 2 Nouns denoting the object or result of an action: *mandate*. [< L *-atus*, suffix of nouns]

-ate[3] *suffix Chem.* Used to form the names of salts and esters derived from acids whose names end in *-ic*: *carbonate, nitrate*. [< L *-atum*, neut. of *-atus* -ATE[1]]

at·el·ier (at′əl·yā, *Fr.* á·tə·lyā′) *n.* A workshop; studio. [< F, orig., pile of chips]

a tem·po (ä tem′pō) *Music* In the tempo originally indicated. [< Ital.]

a·the·ism (ā′thē·iz′əm) *n.* The belief that there is no God. [< Gk. *a-* without + *theos* god] —**a′the·ist** *n.* —**a′the·is′tic** or **-ti·cal** *adj.* —**a′the·is′ti·cal·ly** *adv.*

A·the·na (ə·thē′nə) *Gk. Myth.* The goddess of wisdom, war, and patroness of arts and crafts. Also **A·the·ne** (ə·thē′nē). [< Gk. *Athēnē*]

ath·e·ne·um (ath′ə·nē′əm) *n.* 1 A literary or scientific club. 2 A reading room or library. Also **ath′e·nae′um**. [< Gk. *Athēnaion* the temple of Athena]

A·the·ni·an (ə·thē′nē·ən) *adj.* Of or pertaining to Athens, or to its art or culture. —*n.* A native or citizen of Athens.

a·thirst (ə·thûrst′) *adj.* 1 Wanting water; thirsty. 2 Having a strong desire. —Syn. 2 eager, anxious, avid, longing.

ath·lete (ath′lēt) *n.* A person trained or skilled in acts or games requiring physical strength, agility, speed, etc. [< Gk. *athlētēs* a contestant in the games]

athlete's foot Ringworm of the foot.

ath·let·ic (ath·let′ik) *adj.* 1 Of, pertaining to, or like an athlete. 2 Strong; vigorous; muscular. —**ath·let′i·cal·ly** *adv.* —**ath·let·i·cism** (ath·let′ə·siz′əm) *n.*

ath·let·ics (ath·let′iks) *n. pl. (sometimes construed as sing.)* Athletic games and exercises collectively.

at-home (ət·hōm′) *n.* An informal party or reception given at one's home.

a·thwart (ə·thwôrt′) *adv.* 1 From side to side; across. 2 So as to thwart; perversely. —*prep.* 1 Across the course of; from side to side of. 2 Contrary to; in opposition to. [< *a-* on + THWART]

-atic *suffix* Of; of the kind of: *erratic*. [< Gk. *-atikos*]

a·tilt (ə·tilt′) *adv. & adj.* Tilted.

-ation *suffix* 1 Act or process of: *creation*. 2 Condition or quality of: *affectation*. 3 Result of: *reformation*. [< L *-atio, -ationis*]

-ative *suffix* 1 Of, like, or pertaining to: *qualitative* 2 Tending to: *talkative*. [< L *-ativus*]

At·lan·tic (at·lan′tik) *adj.* 1 Of, near, in, or pertaining to the Atlantic Ocean. 2 Of, near, on, or pertaining to the E coast of the U.S. —*n.* The Atlantic Ocean. [< Gk. *Atlantikos* pertaining to Atlas]

Atlantic Charter A statement issued in August 1941 by Churchill and Roosevelt, setting forth the basic aims of the Allied Nations for peace after World War II.

At·lan·tis (at·lan′tis) *n.* A legendary island continent supposed to have existed west of Gibraltar and to have been engulfed by the Atlantic Ocean.

at·las (at′ləs) *n.* 1 A book of maps. 2 A collection of charts, tables, etc. illustrating any subject.

At·las (at′ləs) 1 *Gk. Myth.* A Titan supporting the pillars of heaven on his shoulders. 2 *n.* An intercontinental ballistic missile of the U.S. Air Force. [< Gk. *Atlas* < *tlaein* bear]

atm. atmosphere; atmospheric.

at·mos·phere (at′məs·fir) *n.* 1 The envelope of gases that surrounds the earth or any body in space. 2 The particular climatic condition of any place or region regarded as dependent on the air. 3 Any surrounding or pervasive element or influence: an *atmosphere* of gloom. 4 *Physics* A unit of pressure equal to 14.69 pounds per square inch or 1.01325 x 10⁵ newtons per square meter. [< Gk. *atmos* vapor + *sphaira* sphere]

at·mos·pher·ic (at′məs·fer′ik) *adj.* 1 Of, pertaining to, or existing in atmosphere. 2 Dependent on, caused by, or producing atmosphere. Also **at′mos·pher′i·cal.** —**at′mos·pher′i·cal·ly** *adv.*

at. no. atomic number.

at·oll (at′ôl, -ol, ə·tol′) *n.* A ring-shaped coral island and its associated reef, nearly or totally enclosing a lagoon. [< Malayalam *atolu*]

at·om (at′əm) *n.* 1 The smallest unit of an element capable of existing, consisting of the electrically neutral combination of a nucleus and its complement of electrons. 2 An exceedingly small quantity or particle; iota. [< Gk. *atomos* indivisible]

Atoll
a. islet. b. reef. c. lagoon.

a·tom·ic (ə·tom′ik) *adj.* 1 Of or pertaining to an atom or atoms: also **a·tom′i·cal.** 2 Minute; infinitesimal. 3 Nuclear: an *atomic* power plant. —**a·tom′i·cal·ly** *adv.*

atomic bomb A bomb whose explosive power is derived from nuclear fission.

atomic energy The energy released from an atom, as by nuclear fission or nuclear fusion.

atomic mass unit A unit of mass, equal to 1/12 of the mass of an atom of the most abundant isotope of carbon, or about 1.6604×10^{-24} gram.

atomic number A number which represents the unit positive charges (protons) in the atomic nucleus of each element.

atomic theory The concept that all matter is composed of atoms, and that the properties of matter are ultimately to be understood in terms of the properties and interactions of the component atoms.

atomic weight The weight of an atom of an element relative to that of an atom of carbon, expressed in atomic mass units.

at·om·ize (at′əm·īz) *v.t.* **·ized, ·iz·ing** 1 To reduce to or separate into atoms; pulverize. 2 To reduce to a spray.

at·om·iz·er (at′əm·ī′zər) *n.* An apparatus for reducing a liquid, esp. medicine or perfume, to a spray.

a·to·nal (ā·tō′nəl) *adj. Music* Without tonality; lacking key. —**a·to·nal·i·ty** (ā′tō·nal′ə·tē) *n.* —**a·to′nal·ly** *adv.*

a·tone (ə·tōn′) *v.* **a·toned, a·ton·ing** *v.i.* To make amends, as for sin. [< earlier *at one* in accord, short for *to set at one, reconcile*] —**a·ton′a·ble, a·tone′a·ble** *adj.* —**a·ton′er** *n.*

a·tone·ment (ə·tōn′mənt) *n.* 1 Satisfaction made, as for wrong or injury. 2 *Theol. Usu. cap.* The reconciliation between God and man effected by Christ's life, passion, and death. —Syn. 1 reparation, amends, compensation.

a·top (ə·top′) *adv. & adj.* On or at the top. —*prep.* On the top of.

-atory *suffix* Of or pertaining to; produced by, characterized by: *exclamatory*. [< L *-atorius* adj. suffix]

at·ra·bil·ious (at′rə·bil′yəs) *adj.* 1 Disposed to melancholy; gloomy. 2 Peevish; surly. Also **at′ra·bil′i·ar** (-bil′ē·ər) [< L *atra bilis* black bile] —**at′ra·bil′ious·ness** *n.*

a·tri·um (ā′trē·əm) *n. pl.* **a·tri·a** (ā′trē·ə) 1 In ancient Roman houses, the central hall or court. 2 A hall or open court. 3 *Anat.* A chamber or sac, esp. one of the upper chambers of the heart through which venous blood is transmitted to the ventricles. [< L] • See HEART.

a·tro·cious (ə·trō′shəs) *adj.* 1 Outrageously wicked, criminal, cruel, etc. 2 *Informal.* Very bad or in bad taste: an *atrocious* remark. [< L *atrox* harsh, cruel < *ater* black] —**a·tro′cious·ly** *adv.* —**a·tro′cious·ness** *n.*

a·troc·i·ty (ə·tros′ə·tē) *n. pl.* ·**ties** 1 The state or quality of being atrocious. 2 An atrocious deed or act; cruelty, wickedness, etc. 3 *Informal.* Something that is very bad or in bad taste.

at·ro·phy (at′rə·fē) *n. pl.* ·**phies** 1 A wasting away of the body or any of its parts. 2 A stoppage of growth or development, as of a part. —*v.* ·**phied**, ·**phy·ing** *v.t.* 1 To affect with atrophy. —*v.i.* 2 To waste away; wither. [< Gk. *atrophas* poorly nourished] —**a·troph·ic** (ə·trof′ik).

at·ro·pine (at′rə·pēn, -pin) *n.* A poisonous alkaloid found in belladonna and other plants, used in medicine as an antispasmodic, to enlarge the pupil of the eye, etc. [< Gk. *atropos* inflexible]

att. attorney.

at·tach (ə·tach′) *v.t.* 1 To make fast to something; fasten on. 2 To connect, join on, or bind: He *attached* himself to the expedition. 3 To add or append, as a word or signature. 4 To attribute; ascribe: to *attach* great importance to the outcome of an event. 5 *Law* To secure for legal jurisdiction; seize or arrest by legal process: to *attach* an employee's salary. 6 *Mil.* To order to serve temporarily or as a nonintegral part: The regiment *attached* a medical officer. —*v.i.* 7 To belong, as a quality or circumstance; be incidental: with *to:* Much interest *attaches* to this opinion. [< OF *atachier* < *a-* to + *tache* nail] —**at·tach′a·ble** *adj.*

at·ta·ché (at′ə·shā′, *esp. Brit.* ə·tash′ā) *n.* A person assigned to a diplomatic mission or staff. [< F *attacher* attach]

attaché case A slender rectangular case with a hard exterior, for carrying papers, documents, etc.

at·tach·ment (ə·tach′mənt) *n.* 1 An attaching or a being attached. 2 Something that is attached, as an accessory for an appliance. 3 That by which anything is attached. 4 Affection; devoted regard. 5 *Law* a Seizure of a person or property. b The writ commanding this.

at·tack (ə·tak′) *v.t.* 1 To set upon suddenly; assault or begin conflict with. 2 To assail with hostile words; criticize, censure. 3 To begin work on, esp. with vigor. 4 To begin to affect seriously or injuriously: Acid *attacks* metal; Disease *attacks* a person. —*v.i.* 5 To make an attack. —*n.* 1 The act of attacking. 2 The first movement toward any undertaking. 3 Any hostile, offensive movement or action, as with troops. 4 A seizure, as by disease. [< Ital. *attaccare*]

at·tain (ə·tān′) *v.t.* 1 To achieve, accomplish or gain. 2 To come to; arrive at. —**attain to** To arrive at with effort; succeed in reaching. [< L *attingere* reach] —**at·tain′a·bil′i·ty, at·tain′a·ble·ness** *n.* —**at·tain′a·ble** *adj.*

at·tain·der (ə·tān′dər) *n.* The loss of all civil rights of a person sentenced to death or outlawed. [< OF *ataindre* attain, strike, accuse]

at·tain·ment (ə·tān′mənt) *n.* 1 The act of attaining. 2 That which is attained, as a skill. —**Syn.** 1, 2 accomplishment, acquisition, acquirement, achievement.

at·taint (ə·tānt′) *v.t.* 1 To inflict attainder upon; condemn. 2 To disgrace; taint; sully. —*n.* Attainder.

at·tar (at′ər) *n.* A perfume or essential oil extracted from the petals of flowers, esp. roses. [< Ar. *'itr* perfume]

at·tempt (ə·tempt′) *v.t.* To make an effort to perform, get, etc.; endeavor; try. —*n.* 1 A putting forth of effort; trial; endeavor; essay. 2 An attack. [< L *attemptare* try] —**at·tempt′a·bil′i·ty** *n.* —**at·tempt′a·ble** *adj.*

at·tend (ə·tend′) *v.t.* 1 To wait upon; minister to; visit or care for professionally. 2 To be present at or in, as a meeting. 3 To follow as a result. 4 To accompany. 5 *Archaic* To give heed; listen. [< L *attendere* give heed to, consider]

at·ten·dance (ə·ten′dəns) *n.* 1 An attending. 2 Those who attend; an audience or congregation; retinue.

at·ten·dant (ə·ten′dənt) *n.* 1 One who attends, as a servant. 2 One who is present at a ceremony. 3 A concomitant; consequent. —*adj.* Following or accompanying; waiting upon.

at·ten·tion (ə·ten′shən) *n.* 1 The act or faculty of concentrating on something. 2 Observation; notice: to get some-

one's *attention.* 3 *Usu. pl.* An act of courtesy, gallantry, or devotion. 4 Practical or thoughtful consideration or care. 5 *Mil.* a The prescribed position of readiness to obey orders. b The order to assume this position. [< L *attendere* to attend]

at·ten·tive (ə·ten′tiv) *adj.* 1 Giving or showing attention; observant. 2 Courteous; gallant; polite. —**at·ten′tive·ly** *adv.* —**at·ten′tive·ness** *n.*

at·ten·u·ate (ə·ten′yōō·āt) *v.* ·**at·ed**, ·**at·ing** *v.t.* 1 To make thin, small, or fine. 2 To reduce in value, quantity, severity, strength, etc.; weaken. 3 To reduce in density; rarefy, as a liquid or gas. 4 To weaken the virulence of a microorganism. —*v.i.* 5 To become thin, weak, rarefied, etc. —*adj.* (ə·ten′yōō·it) Attenuated. [< L *ad-* + *tenuare* make thin] —**at·ten′u·a·ble** *adj.* —**at·ten′u·a′tion** *n.*

at·test (ə·test′) *v.t.* 1 To confirm as accurate, true, or genuine; vouch for. 2 To certify, as by signature or oath. 3 To be proof of. 4 To put upon oath. —*v.i.* 5 To bear witness; testify: with *to.* [< L *ad-* to + *testari* bear witness]

at·tes·ta·tion (at′es·tā′shən) *n.* 1 The act of attesting. 2 Testimony.

at·tic (at′ik) *n.* 1 A usu. low story or room beneath the roof; a garret. 2 A low structure above a cornice or entablature. [< F *attique* Attic (in style)]

At·tic (at′ik) *adj.* 1 Of Attica. 2 Of or characteristic of Athens or the Athenians. —*n.* The dialect of Attica.

At·ti·ca (at′i·kə) An ancient Greek kingdom that included Athens.

at·tire (ə·tīr′) *v.t.* **at·tired**, **at·tir·ing** To dress; array; adorn. —*n.* Dress or clothing. [< OF *atirer* arrange, adorn]

at·ti·tude (at′ə·t(y)ōōd) *n.* 1 Position of the body, as suggesting some thought, feeling, or action. 2 State of mind, behavior, or conduct, as indicating one's feelings, opinion, or purpose. [< LL *aptitudo* fitness, aptitude] —**at·ti·tu·di·nal** (at′ə·t(y)ōō′də·nəl) *adj.*

at·ti·tu·di·nize (at′ə·t(y)ōō′də·nīz) *v.i.* ·**nized**, ·**niz·ing** To pose for effect; strike an attitude. *Brit. sp.* **at′ti·tu′di·nise.**

at·tor·ney (ə·tûr′nē) *n. pl.* ·**neys** A person empowered by another to act in his stead, esp. a lawyer. —**by attorney** By proxy. —**power of attorney** Legal written authority to transact business for another. [< OF *atorner* turn to, assign] —**at·tor′ney·ship** *n.*

attorney at law A lawyer.

attorney general *pl.* **attorneys general, attorney generals** The chief law officer of a state or national government.

Attorney General The head of the U.S. Department of Justice and a member of the President's cabinet.

at·tract (ə·trakt′) *v.t.* 1 To draw to or cause to come near by some physical force, without apparent mechanical connection. 2 To draw the admiration, attention, etc. of. [< L *ad-* toward + *trahere* draw, drag] —**at·tract′a·ble** *adj.* —**at·tract′a·ble·ness, at·tract·a·bil′i·ty, at·tract′er, at·trac′tor** *n.*

at·trac·tion (ə·trak′shən) *n.* 1 The act of attracting. 2 Power to attract. 3 Something that attracts. 4 A physical force exerted between or among bodies, tending to draw them together or prevent their separation.

at·trac·tive (ə·trak′tiv) *adj.* 1 Having the power or quality of attracting. 2 Pleasing, winning, pretty, etc. —**at·trac′tive·ly** *adv.* —**at·trac′tive·ness** *n.*

attrib. attribute; attributive; attributively.

at·trib·ute (ə·trib′yōōt) *v.t.* ·**ut·ed**, ·**ut·ing** To ascribe as belonging to, resulting from, or created or caused by. —*at·tri·bute* (at′rə·byōōt) *n.* 1 A quality or characteristic. 2 *Gram.* An adjective or its equivalent. 3 In art and mythology, a distinctive mark or symbol. [< L *ad-* to + *tribuere* allot, give over] —**at·trib′u·ta·ble** *adj.* —**Syn.** *v.* assign, impute, associate. *n.* 1 property, trait, feature, peculiarity.

at·tri·bu·tion (at′rə·byōō′shən) *n.* 1 An attributing or being attributed. 2 An ascribed characteristic or quality; attribute.

at·trib·u·tive (ə·trib′yə·tiv) *adj.* 1 Pertaining to or of the nature of an attribute. 2 So ascribed, as a work of art: That canvas is an *attributive* Vermeer. 3 *Gram.* Designating an adjective or its equivalent which stands before the noun it modifies. —*n. Gram.* An attributive word or phrase. —**at·trib′u·tive·ly** *adv.* —**at·trib′u·tive·ness** *n.*

at·tri·tion (ə·trish′ən) *n.* 1 A rubbing out or grinding down, as by friction. 2 A gradual wearing down or weakening. [< L *atterere* rub away]

at·tune (ə·tʸo͞on′) v.t. **at·tuned, at·tun·ing 1** To bring into accord with; harmonize. **2** To adjust to the right pitch; tune. [<AD- + TUNE]

at·ty. attorney.

at. wt. atomic weight.

a·typ·i·cal (ā·tip′i·kəl) adj. Not typical. Also **a·typ′ic.** —**a·typ′i·cal·ly** adv.

A.U., A.u., a.u. angstrom unit.

Au gold (L aurum).

au·burn (ô′bûrn) adj. & n. Reddish brown. [<LL alburnus whitish]

au cou·rant (ō ko͞o·räN′) Up to date; well or fully informed. [F, lit., in the current]

auc·tion (ôk′shən) n. **1** A public sale in which the price offered for individual items is increased by bids, until the highest bidder becomes the purchaser. **2** The bidding in bridge. —v.t. To sell by or at auction: usu. with off. [<L auctio an increase, a public sale (with increasing bids)]

auc·tion·eer (ôk′shən·ir′) n. One who conducts an auction, usu. as a business. —v.t. To sell by auction.

au·da·cious (ô·dā′shəs) adj. **1** Fearless; bold. **2** Defiant of convention, decorum, etc.; brazen; insolent. [<L audax bold] —**au·da′cious·ly** adv. —**au·da′cious·ness** n.

au·dac·i·ty (ô·das′ə·tē) n. pl. **·ties 1** Boldness; fearlessness. **2** Insolence; shamelessness. **3** An audacious act, remark, etc. [<L audax bold, rash <audere dare]

au·di·bil·i·ty (ô′də·bil′ə·tē) n. Capability of being heard.

au·di·ble (ô′də·bəl) adj. Perceptible by the ear. [<L audire hear] —**au′di·ble·ness** n. —**au′di·bly** adv.

au·di·ence (ô′dē·əns) n. **1** An assembly gathered to hear and see, as at a concert. **2** Those who are reached by a book, television program, etc. **3** A formal hearing, interview, or conference. **4** Opportunity to be heard. [<L audientia a hearing]

au·di·o (ô′dē·ō) adj. Telecom. **1** Of or pertaining to characteristics, esp. frequency, associated with sound waves. **2** Designating devices used in transmission or reception of sound. [<L audire hear]

au·di·o·cas·ette (ô′dē·ō·kə·set′, -ka·set′) adj. A cassette for the storage of audio material.

audio frequency A frequency of electrical, sound, or other wave vibrations coming within the range of normal human hearing, or from about 20 to 20,000 hertz.

au·di·o·vis·u·al (ô′dē·ō·vizh′o͞o·əl) adj. **1** Relating to both hearing and sight. **2** Pertaining to instructional materials other than books, as filmstrips, motion pictures, television, and recordings.

au·dit (ô′dit) v.t. **1** To examine, adjust, and certify, as accounts. **2** To attend (a college course) as a listener only without receiving credit. —n. **1** An examination of financial accounts to establish their correctness. **2** A prepared statement concerning such an examination. **3** An adjustment and settlement of accounts. [<L auditus a hearing]

au·di·tion (ô·dish′ən) n. **1** The act or sense of hearing. **2** A trial test or hearing, as of an actor or singer. —v.t. **1** To give an audition to. —v.i. **2** To give an audition. [<L auditio a hearing]

au·di·tor (ô′də·tər) n. **1** One who audits accounts. **2** One who listens. **3** One who audits classes.

au·di·to·ri·um (ô′də·tôr′ē·əm, -tō′rē·əm) n. pl. **·to·ri·ums** or **·to·ri·a** (-tôr′ē·ə, -tō′rē·ə) **1** The room or part of a building, as a church, theater, etc., occupied by the audience. **2** A building for concerts, public meetings, etc. [<L, lecture room, courtroom]

au·di·to·ry (ô′də·tôr′ē, -tō′rē) adj. Of or pertaining to hearing or the organs or sense of hearing. [<L audire hear] —**au′di·to′ri·ly** adv.

auditory canal Anat. The passage in the ear leading from the auricle to the tympanic membrane. • See EAR.

Aug. August.

au·gend (ô′jend) n. Math. A number or element to which another is to be added. [<L augere to increase]

Auger

au·ger (ô′gər) n. A large tool with a spiral groove for boring holes in wood, etc. [<OE nafugār, lit., nave-borer]

aught¹ (ôt) n. Anything; any part or item. —adv. By any chance; at all. [<OE ā ever + wiht thing]

aught² (ôt) n. The figure 0; cipher; nothing. [a naught taken as an aught]

aug·ment (ôg·ment′) v.t. & v.i. To make or become greater, as in size, number, or amount. [<L augere to increase] —**aug·ment′a·ble** adj. —**aug·ment′er** n. —Syn. enlarge, intensify, increase, expand.

aug·men·ta·tion (ôg′men·tā′shən) n. **1** An augmenting or being augmented. **2** An addition or increase.

aug·men·ta·tive (ôg·men′tə·tiv) adj. **1** Having the quality or power of augmenting. **2** Gram. Denoting greater size or intensity. —n. Gram. An augmentative suffix, prefix, etc. Also **aug·men′tive.**

au gra·tin (ō grät′n, grat′n; Fr. ō grá·taN′) Sprinkled with bread crumbs or grated cheese and baked until brown. [F, lit., with the burnt part]

au·gur (ô′gər) n. A prophet; soothsayer. —v.t. **1** To be an omen of. —v.i. **2** To be an augury or omen. [<L]

au·gu·ry (ô′gʸə·rē) n. pl. **·ries 1** The art or practice of divination. **2** A portent or omen.

au·gust (ô·gust′) adj. Majestic; grand; imposing. [<L augere increase, exalt] —**au·gust′ly** adv. —**au·gust′ness** n.

Au·gust (ô′gəst) n. The eighth month of the year, containing 31 days. [<L, after Augustus Caesar, 63 B.C.-A.D. 14, Roman emperor]

Au·gus·tan (ô·gus′tən) adj. **1** Of or pertaining to Augustus Caesar or to his times. **2** Classical; refined.

Augustan age 1 The period of the reign of Augustus Caesar, the golden age of Roman literature. **2** A period in English literature during the reign of Queen Anne in the early 18th century.

Au·gus·tin·i·an (ô′gəs·tin′ē·ən) adj. **1** Of or pertaining to St. Augustine or his doctrines. **2** Belonging to a monastic order named after St. Augustine or following his rule.

auk (ôk) n. Any of various short-winged, web-footed diving birds of northern seas. [<ON ālka]

au lait (ō le′) With milk. [F]

auld lang syne (ôld′ lang sīn′, zīn′) Literally, old long since; hence, long ago. [Scot.]

aunt (ant, änt) n. The sister of one's father or mother, or the wife of one's uncle. [<L amita paternal aunt]

aunt·ie (an′tē, än′-) n. A familiar, diminutive form of aunt. Also **aunt′y.**

au pair (ō pâr) Chiefly Brit. **1** An arrangement whereby one receives room and board in a foreign household in exchange for doing certain chores: often used attributively: au pair girls. **2** Informal A girl participating in such an arrangement. [<F, lit., at par]

au·ra (ôr′ə) n. pl. **au·ras** or **au·rae** (ôr′ē) **1** An invisible emanation or exhalation. **2** A distinctive air or quality enveloping or characterizing a person or thing. [<Gk. aurē breath] —**au′ral** adj.

au·ral (ôr′əl) adj. Pertaining to the ear or the sense of hearing. [<L auris ear + -AL]

au·re·ate (ôr′ē·it) adj. **1** Of the color of gold; golden. **2** Florid, grandiloquent. [<L aurum gold]

au·re·ole (ôr′ē·ōl) n. **1** A halo that appears to surround the image of a brilliant body, as the corona of the sun. **2** A radiant glow around the head or body, as of a saint. Also **au·re·o·la** (ô·rē′ə·lə). [<L aureolus golden]

Au·re·o·my·cin (ôr′ē·ō·mī′sin) n. An antibiotic effective against bacteria and certain viruses: a trade name.

au re·voir (ō rə·vwär′) Good-by; till we meet again. [F, lit., to the seeing again]

au·ri·cle (ôr′i·kəl) n. **1** The external ear. **2** Any ear-shaped appendage or part. **3** An atrium of the heart. [<L auris ear] —**au′ri·cled** adj.

au·ric·u·lar (ô·rik′yə·lər) adj. **1** Of or pertaining to the ear or the sense of hearing. **2** Intended for the ear; confidential. **3** Ear-shaped. **4** Of or pertaining to an auricle.

au·rif·er·ous (ô·rif′ər·əs) adj. Containing gold. [<L aurum gold + ferre bear] —**au·rif′er·ous·ly** adv.

au·ri·form (ôr′ə·fôrm) adj. Ear-shaped. [<L auris ear + -FORM]

au·rochs (ôr′oks) n. **1** The extinct European wild ox. **2** A rare or extinct bison of Europe. [< OHG *ūr* bison + *ohso* ox]

au·ro·ra (ô·rôr′ə, ô·rō′rə) *n.* **1** The dawn. **2** *Meteorol.* A luminous display seen in the skies of high northern and southern latitudes, caused by electrical disturbances in the atmosphere. [< L, dawn]

Au·ro·ra (ô·rôr′ə, ô·rō′rə) *Rom. Myth.* The goddess of the dawn.

aurora aus·tra·lis (ôs·trā′lis) *Meteorol.* The aurora as seen in far southern latitudes. [< NL, southern aurora]

aurora bo·re·al·is (bôr′ē·al′is, -ā′lis, bō′rē-) *Meteorol.* The aurora as seen in the high northern latitudes. [< NL, northern aurora]

au·ro·ral (ô·rôr′əl, ô·rō′rəl) *adj.* **1** Pertaining to or like the dawn. **2** Of, like, or caused by an aurora. Also **au·ro·re·an** (ô·rôr′ē·ən, ô·rō′rē-), **au·ro′ric.** —**au·ro′ral·ly** *adv.*

aus·cul·tate (ôs′kəl·tāt) *v.t. & v.i.* **·tat·ed, ·tat·ing** *Med.* To examine by listening, as with a stethoscope, for sounds produced in the chest, abdomen, etc. [< L *auscultare* listen, give ear to] —**aus·cul·ta·tion** (ôs′kəl·tā′shən) *n.* —**aus·cul·ta·tive** (ôs′kul′tə·tiv), **aus·cul′ta·to′ry** *adj.*

aus·pice (ôs′pis) *n. pl.* **aus·pi·ces** (ôs′pə·sēz) **1** *Usu. pl.* Patronage; sponsorship: under the *auspices* of the alumni association. **2** An omen or sign. [< L *auspex* a bird augur]

aus·pi·cious (ôs·pish′əs) *adj.* **1** Favoring or conducive to future success. **2** Attended by good fortune; fortunate; successful. —**aus·pi′cious·ly** *adv.* —**aus·pi′cious·ness** *n.* —**Syn. 1** propitious, favorable, hopeful, promising.

aus·tere (ô·stir′) *adj.* **1** Severe, grave, or stern, as in look or conduct. **2** Abstemious; ascetic. **3** Severely simple; unadorned. [< Gk. *austēros* harsh, bitter] —**aus·tere′ly** *adv.*

aus·ter·i·ty (ô·ster′ə·tē) *n. pl.* **·ties 1** The quality or condition of being austere. **2** An austere act, practice, or manner. **3** Extreme or rigid economy. Also **aus·tere′ness.**

aus·tral (ôs′trəl, os′-) *adj.* Southern; southerly. [< L *auster* south wind]

Aus·tral·a·sian (ôs′trəl·ā′zhən, -ā′shən) *n.* An inhabitant of Australasia. —*adj.* Of Australasia or its people.

Aus·tra·lia (ô·strāl′yə, o-) *n.* A country, a member of the Commonwealth of Nations, occupying a continent SE of Asia, 2,971,081 sq. mi., cap. Canberra.

Australia Day January 26, an Australian holiday marking the landing of the British in 1788.

Aus·tra·lian (ô·strāl′yən, o-) *n.* A native or citizen of Australia. —*adj.* Of or pertaining to Australia or its people.

Australian ballot A ballot bearing the names of all the candidates of all parties, given out only at the polls where it is marked in secret by the voter.

Aus·tri·a (ôs′trē·ə) *n.* A republic of CEN. Europe, 32,375 sq. mi., cap. Vienna. —**Aus′tri·an** *adj., n.*

Aus·tri·a-Hun·ga·ry (ôs′trē·ə·hung′gə·rē) *n.* A former monarchy of CEN. Europe. —**Aus·tro-Hun·gar·i·an** (ôs′trō·hung·gâr′ē·ən) *adj.*

Aus·tro·ne·sian (ôs′trō·nē′zhən, -shən) *adj.* Of or pertaining to Austronesia, its inhabitants, or their languages. —*n.* A family of languages spoken throughout the Pacific and divided into three subfamilies: Indonesian or Malayan, Oceanic (including the Melanesian and Micronesian languages), and Polynesian.

au·tar·chy (ô′tär·kē) *n.* **1** Absolute rule or sovereignty or a country under such rule. **2** Self-government. **3** AUTARKY. [< Gk. *autarchos* absolute ruler] —**au·tar·chic** (ô·tär′kik) or **·chi·cal** *adj.*

au·tar·ky (ô′tär·kē) *n.* National economic self-sufficiency. [< Gk. *autarkeia* self-sufficiency] —**au·tar·ki·cal** (ô·tär′ki·kəl) *adj.*

au·teur (ō·tœr′) *n.* A film director whose work is the product of personal vision and total production control. [F, lit., author]

au·then·tic (ô·then′tik) *adj.* **1** Authoritative; trustworthy; reliable. **2** Genuine; real. **3** *Law* Duly executed

before the proper officer. Also **au·then′ti·cal.** [< Gk. *authentikos*] —**au·then′ti·cal·ly** *adv.*

au·then·ti·cate (ô·then′ti·kāt) *v.t.* **·cat·ed, ·cat·ing 1** To make genuine, credible, or authoritative. **2** To give legal force or validity to. **3** To establish or certify as genuine or authentic. —**au·then′ti·ca′tion, au·then′ti·ca′tor** *n.*

au·then·tic·i·ty (ô′thən·tis′ə·tē, ô′then′-) *n.* The state or quality of being authentic or authoritative.

au·thor (ô′thər) *n.* **1** The writer of a book, article, etc. **2** A person who writes as a profession. **3** A person who originates or creates something. —*v.t. Informal* To be the author of. [< L *auctor* originator, producer] —**au′thor·ess** *n. Fem.* —**au·tho·ri·al** (ô·thôr′ē·əl, ô·thō′rē-) *adj.*

au·thor·i·tar·i·an (ô·thor′ə·târ′ē·ən, -thôr′-, ə-) *adj.* Encouraging and upholding absolute obedience to some authority as against individual freedom. —*n.* A person who favors or enforces such obedience. —**au·thor′i·tar′i·an·ism** *n.*

au·thor·i·ta·tive (ô·thor′ə·tā′tiv, ô·thôr′-, ə-) *adj.* **1** Possessing or proceeding from proper or reliable authority; duly sanctioned. **2** Exercising authority, esp. in a dictatorial manner. —**au·thor′i·ta′tive·ly** *adv.* —**au·thor′i·ta′tive·ness** *n.*

au·thor·i·ty (ə·thor′ə·tē, ə·thôr′-, ô-) *n. pl.* **·ties 1** The right to command, enforce obedience, make decisions, etc. **2** Such a right given to another; authorization. **3** *pl.* Persons having the right to command or govern. **4** Personal power or expertness that commands influence, respect, or confidence. **5** That which may be appealed to in support of action or belief, as an author, volume, etc. **6** One who has special skill, knowledge, etc.; expert. **7** An authoritative opinion, decision, or precedent. [< L *auctoritas* power, authority < *augere* increase]

au·thor·i·za·tion (ô′thər·ə·zā′shən) *n.* **1** The act of conferring legality. **2** Formal legal power; sanction.

au·thor·ize (ô′thər·īz) *v.t.* **·ized, ·iz·ing 1** To confer authority upon; empower; commission. **2** To warrant; justify. **3** To sanction; approve. —**au′thor·i·za′tion, au′thor·iz′er** *n.*

au·thor·ized (ô′thər·īzd) *adj.* **1** Endowed with authority; accepted as authoritative. **2** Formally or legally sanctioned.

au·thor·ship (ô′thər·ship) *n.* **1** The profession or occupation of an author. **2** Origin or source, esp. of a literary work.

au·tism (ô′tiz·əm) *n. Psychol.* A mental disorder, esp. in children, marked by lack of response to external activities. [< AUT(O)- + -ISM] —**au·tis·tic** (ô·tis′tik) *adj.*

au·to (ô′tō) *Informal n. pl.* **·tos** An automobile. —*v.i.* To ride in or travel by an automobile.

auto-¹ *combining form* **1** Arising from some process or action within; as in *autism.* **2** Acting, directed upon, or of the self; as in *autobiography, autosuggestion.* Also, before vowels, **aut-.** [< Gk. *autos* self]

auto-² *combining form* Self-propelled. [< AUTOMOBILE]

au·to·bi·og·ra·phy (ô′tə·bī·og′rə·fē, -bē·og′-) *n. pl.* **·phies** The story of a person's life written by that same person. —**au′to·bi·og′ra·pher** *n.* —**au·to·bi·o·graph·ic** (ô′tə·bī′ə·graf′ik) or **·i·cal** *adj.* —**au′to·bi′o·graph′i·cal·ly** *adv.*

au·to·clave (ô′tə·klāv) *n.* A container designed to contain superheated steam under pressure, used for the sterilization of surgical instruments, etc. [< AUTO-¹ + L *clavis* a key]

au·toc·ra·cy (ô·tok′rə·sē) *n. pl.* **·cies 1** Absolute government or rule by an autocrat. **2** A state ruled by an autocrat. **3** Complete power or dominance over others.

au·to·crat (ô′tə·krat) *n.* **1** A supreme ruler of unrestricted power. **2** An arrogant, dictatorial person. [< Gk. *autokratēs* self-ruling, independent] —**au′to·crat′ic** or **·i·cal** *adj.* —**au′to·crat′i·cal·ly** *adv.*

au·to-da-fé (ô′tō·də·fā′, ou′-) *n. pl.* **au·tos-da-fé** (ô′tōz-, ou′tōz-) The public announcement and execution of the sentence of the Inquisition, as the burning of heretics at the stake, etc. [< Pg., lit., act of the faith]

au·to·gi·ro (ô′tə·jī′rō) *n. pl.* **·ros** An aircraft that is propelled forward by a propeller, but which receives its lift and support from freely revolving, horizontal rotors. Also **au′to·gy′ro.** [< *Autogiro* former trade name]

au·to·graph (ô′tə·graf, -gräf) *n.* **1** A person's own handwriting or signature. **2** Something written in a person's own handwriting, as a manuscript. —*v.t.* **1** To write one's name in or affix one's signature to. **2** To write in one's own handwriting. —*adj.* Written by one's own hand, as a will. [<Gk. *autographos* written with one's own hand] —**au′to·graph′ic** or **·i·cal** *adj.* —**au′to·graph′i·cal·ly** *adv.*

au·to·im·mune (ô′tō·i·myoon) *adj.* Caused by antibodies that operate against the body's own tissues: *autoimmune diseases.* —**au′to·im·mu′ni·ty** *n.*

au·to·in·tox·i·ca·tion (ô′tō·in·tok′sə·kā′shən) *n.* The poisoning of an organism by a toxin produced within the organism.

au·to·mat (ô′tə·mat) *n.* U.S. A restaurant in which certain foods are automatically made available from a receptacle when money is deposited in a slot alongside.

au·to·mate (ô′tə·māt) *v.t.* **·mat·ed, ·mat·ing** To operate or adapt (a factory, process, etc.) for automation.

au·to·mat·ic (ô′tə·mat′ik) *adj.* **1** Done as from force of habit or without conscious intent or volition; involuntary; reflex. **2** Capable of moving, operating, etc., at least partly, without human control or attention, as a machine. **3** Accomplished by such movements or operations. Also **au′to·mat′i·cal, au·tom·a·tous** (ô·tom′ə·təs). —*n.* An automatic machine, device, or firearm. [<Gk. *automatos* acting of oneself] —**au′to·mat′i·cal·ly** *adv.*

automatic pilot A device that automatically keeps a moving aircraft or other vehicle on a stable course.

au·to·ma·tion (ô′tə·mā′shən) *n.* **1** The automatic performance or control of an operation, system, device, etc. **2** The equipment or devices used to accomplish this. **3** The design and installation of such devices. [<AUTOM(ATIC) + (OPER)ATION] —**au′to·ma′tive** *adj.*

au·tom·a·tism (ô·tom′ə·tiz′əm) *n.* **1** The state or quality of being automatic. **2** The functioning or action of muscular or other processes independent of conscious control. —**au·tom′a·tist** *n.*

au·tom·a·ton (ô·tom′ə·ton, -tən) *n. pl.* **·tons** or **·ta** (-tə) **1** A contrivance or apparatus that functions automatically, esp. a robot. **2** Any living being whose actions are or appear to be involuntary or mechanical. **3** Anything capable of spontaneous movement or action. [<Gk. *automatos* acting of oneself, independent]

au·to·mo·bile (ô′tə·mə·bēl′, ô′tə·mə·bēl′, ô′tə·mō′bēl) *n.* A usu. four-wheeled vehicle for a small number of passengers, driven by an engine or motor and independent of rails or tracks; a motorcar. —*adj.* (ô′tə·mō′bil) Of or for automobiles. [<F]

au·to·mo·tive (ô′tə·mō′tiv) *adj.* **1** Self-propelling. **2** Of or for automobiles or similar vehicles.

au·to·nom·ic (ô′tə·nom′ik) *adj.* **1** Autonomous. **2** *Biol.* Functioning spontaneously or independently. Also **au′to·nom′i·cal.** —**au′to·nom′i·cal·ly** *adv.*

autonomic nervous system The part of the nervous system that activates and controls tissues and organs not subject to voluntary control, as the heart, blood vessels, smooth muscle, glands, stomach, and intestines.

au·ton·o·mous (ô·ton′ə·məs) *adj.* **1** Functioning or existing independently. **2** Of or having self-government, as a state, group, etc. [<Gk. *autos* self + *nomos* law, rule] —**au·ton′o·mous·ly** *adv.*

au·ton·o·my (ô·ton′ə·mē) *n. pl.* **·mies 1** The condition or quality of being autonomous; esp., the power or right of self-government. **2** A self-governing state, community, or group. —**au·ton′o·mist** *n.* —**Syn.** 1 independence, freedom, self-rule, self-determination.

au·top·sy (ô′top·sē, ô′tə·p-) *n. pl.* **·sies** Post-mortem examination of a human body, esp. to determine the cause of death. [<Gk. *autopsia* a seeing for oneself]

au·to·sug·ges·tion (ô′tō·səg·jes′chən, -sə·jes′-) *n.* The process of dwelling upon an idea to induce a change in one's behavior or physical condition. —**au′to·sug·ges′tive** *adj.*

au·tumn (ô′təm) *n.* **1** The season between summer and winter; fall. **2** A time of maturity and incipient decline. —*adj.* Of, in, or like autumn. [<L *autumnus*] —**au·tum·nal** (ô·tum′nəl) *adj.* —**au·tum′nal·ly** *adv.*

autumnal equinox The equinox that occurs near the end of September.

aux·il·ia·ry (ôg·zil′yər·ē, -zil′ər-) *adj.* **1** Giving or furnishing aid. **2** Subsidiary; subordinate. **3** Supplementary; additional. —*n. pl.* **·ries 1** An auxiliary person, group, ship, etc. **2** *pl.* Foreign troops helping those of a nation at war. **3** AUXILIARY VERB. [<L *auxilium* a help]

auxiliary verb A verb that helps to express the tense, mood, voice, or aspect of another verb, as *be, have, do, will, shall, can, may, must.*

A.V. Authorized Version (of the Bible).

A/V, a.v., a/v according to value (L *ad valorem*).

av. average; avoirdupois.

a·vail (ə·vāl′) *n.* **1** Use or advantage; benefit; good. **2** *pl.* Proceeds. —*v.t.* **1** To assist or aid; profit. —*v.i.* **2** To be of value or advantage; suffice. —**avail oneself of** To take advantage of; utilize. [<L *ad-* to + *valere* be strong] —**a·vail′ing** *adj.* —**a·vail′ing·ly** *adv.*

a·vail·a·ble (ə·vā′lə·bəl) *adj.* **1** At hand or at one's disposal, as funds. **2** That can be contacted, had, used, etc. —**a·vail′a·bil′i·ty, a·vail′a·ble·ness** *n.* —**a·vail′a·bly** *adv.*

av·a·lanche (av′ə·lanch, -länch) *n.* **1** A large mass of snow, ice, rocks, etc., sliding down a mountain slope. **2** Something like an avalanche, as in power, destructiveness, etc. —*v.* **·lanched, ·lanch·ing** —*v.i.* **1** To fall or slide like an avalanche. —*v.t.* **2** To fall or come down upon like an avalanche. [F]

a·vant-garde (ə·vänt′gärd′, *Fr.* à·vän·gàrd′) *n.* A group, as of artists or writers, who support or use the most advanced or unconventional ideas, techniques, etc.; vanguard. —*adj.* Of this group or their ideas, techniques, etc. [<F, lit., advance guard] —**a·vant-gard′ism** *n.* —**a·vant-gard′ist** *adj., n.*

av·a·rice (av′ə·ris) *n.* Passion for riches; covetousness; greed. [<L *avarus* greedy] —**av·a·ri·cious** (av′ə·rish′əs) *adj.* —**av′a·ri′cious·ly** *adv.* —**av′a·ri′cious·ness** *n.*

a·vast (ə·vast′, ə·väst′) *interj.* Naut. Stop! hold! cease! [<Du. *hou' vast, houd vast* hold fast]

av·a·tar (av′ə·tär′) *n.* **1** In Hindu mythology, the incarnation of a god. **2** Any embodiment or manifestation, as of a quality. [<Skt. *avatāra* descent]

a·ve (a′vē, ä′vā) *interj.* **1** Hail! **2** Farewell! —*n.* The salutation *ave.* [<L, hail or farewell]

ave. avenue.

A·ve Ma·ri·a (ä′vä mə·rē′ə, ä′vē) **1** A prayer to the Virgin Mary. **2** Hail Mary, the first words of this prayer. [<Med. L, hail Mary]

a·venge (ə·venj′) *v.t.* **a·venged, a·veng·ing 1** To take vengeance or exact punishment for (a crime, insult, etc.) or on behalf of (a person or persons). —*v.i.* **2** To take vengeance. [<L *ad-* to + *vindicare* avenge] —**a·veng′er** *n.*

av·e·nue (av′ə·n'yōō) *n.* **1** A broad street. **2** A way of approach, as to an estate, often bordered with trees or statues. **3** A way of attaining something. [<F *avenir* to approach]

a·ver (ə·vûr′) *v.t.* **a·verred, a·ver·ring 1** To declare confidently as fact; affirm. **2** *Law* To assert formally; prove or justify (a plea). [<L *ad-* to + *verus* true] —**a·ver′ment** *n.* —**a·ver′ra·ble** *adj.*

av·er·age (av′rij, av′ər·ij) *n.* **1** *Math.* A number representing a set of numbers of which it is a function, esp. an arithmetic mean. **2** A symbol, ratio, etc., representing such a number: a B *average.* **3** The normal or ordinary quality, amount, kind, degree, etc.: This meal is above *average.* **4** In marine law: **a** The loss arising by damage to a ship or cargo. **b** The proportion of such loss falling to a single person in an equitable distribution among those interested. —*adj.* **1** Obtained by calculating the mean of several. **2** Normal; ordinary. —*v.* **·aged, ·ag·ing** *v.t.* **1** To fix or calculate as the mean. **2** To amount to or obtain an average of: He *averages* three dollars profit every hour. **3** To apportion on the average. —*v.i.* **4** To be or amount to an average. **5** To sell or purchase more of something so as to increase the average price. [<OF *avarie* damage to a ship or its cargo] —**av′er·age·ly** *adv.*

a·verse (ə·vûrs′) *adj.* Opposed; unfavorable; reluctant: with *to.* [<L *avertere* turn aside] —**a·verse′ly** *adv.* —**a·verse′ness** *n.*

a·ver·sion (ə-vûr′zhən, -shən) *n.* **1** Extreme dislike; repugnance; antipathy. **2** A cause of extreme dislike. —**a·ver′sive** *adj.*

a·vert (ə-vûrt′) *v.t.* **1** To turn or direct away: to *avert* one's eyes. **2** To prevent or ward off, as a danger. [< L *avertere* turn aside] —**a·vert′ed·ly** *adv.* —**a·vert′i·ble, a·vert′a·ble** *adj.*

A·ves·ta (ə-ves′tə) *n.* The sacred writings of Zoroastrianism, written in an ancient Iranian language, **A·ves·tan** (ə-ves′tən).

avg. average.

a·vi·ar·y (ā′vē·er′ē) *n. pl.* **·ar·ies** An enclosure or large cage for birds. [< L *avis* bird] —**a·vi·ar·ist** (ā′vē·er′ist, -ər ist) *n.*

a·vi·a·tion (ā′vē·ā′shən, av′ē-) *n.* The operation or production of heavier-than-air aircraft. [< L *avis* bird]

a·vi·a·tor (ā′vē·ā′tər, av′ē-) *n.* One who flies airplanes or similar aircraft; a pilot. —**a·vi·a′tress** (-tris) or **a·vi·a·trix** (ā′vē·ā′triks, av′ē-) *n. Fem.*

av·id (av′id) *adj.* Having or showing an intense desire or interest. [< L *avere* crave] —**av′id·ly** *adv.* —**av′id·ness, a·vid·i·ty** (ə-vid′ə·tē) *n.* —**Syn.** desirous, greedy, eager, anxious.

a·vi·on·ics (ā·vē·on′iks, av′ē-) *n. pl.* (*construed as sing.*) The study of the applications of electricity and electronics to aviation. [< AVI(ATION ELECTR)ONICS] —**a′vi·on′ic** *adj.*

av·o·ca·do (av′ə·kä′dō, ä′və-) *n. pl.* **·dos** **1** A pear-shaped, edible fruit with a green skin and buttery flesh; alligator pear. **2** The tree bearing this fruit. [< Nahatl *ahuacatl*]

av·o·ca·tion (av′ə·kā′shən) *n.* An occupation or hobby that one has in addition to one's regular work or profession. [< L *ab-* away + *vocare* to call]

av·o·cet (av′ə·set) *n.* A long-legged shore bird having webbed feet and slender up-curved bill. Also **av′o·set.** [< Ital. *avocetta*]

a·void (ə-void′) *v.t.* **1** To keep away or at a distance from; shun; evade. **2** *Law* To make void. [< L *ex-* out + *viduare* empty, deprive] —**a·void′a·ble** *adj.* —**a·void′a·bly** *adv.* —**a·void′ance, a·void′er** *n.*

av·oir·du·pois (av′ər·də·poiz′) *n.* **1** Avoirdupois weight. **2** *Informal.* Weight; corpulence. —*adj.* Measured or expressed in avoirdupois weight. [< OF *avoir de pois* goods of (i.e., sold by) weight]

avoirdupois weight The ordinary U.S. system of weight in which 16 ounces make a pound. • See MEASURE.

a·vouch (ə-vouch′) *v.t.* **1** To vouch for; guarantee. **2** To affirm positively; proclaim. **3** To acknowledge; avow. [< L *advocare* call to one's aid, summon]

a·vow (ə-vou′) *v.t.* To declare openly, as facts; own; acknowledge. [< L *advocare* summon] —**a·vow′a·ble** *adj.* —**a·vow′a·bly** *adv.* —**a·vow′er** *n.*

a·vow·al (ə-vou′əl) *n.* Frank admission or acknowledgment.

a·vowed (ə-voud′) *adj.* Openly acknowledged; plainly declared. —**a·vow·ed·ly** (ə-vou′id·lē) *adj.* —**a·vow′ed·ness** *n.*

a·vun·cu·lar (ə-vung′kyə·lər) *adj.* Of or pertaining to an uncle. [< L *avunculus* maternal uncle]

a·wait (ə-wāt′) *v.t.* **1** To wait for; expect. **2** To be ready or in store for. [< OF *awaitier* watch for]

a·wake (ə-wāk′) *adj.* **1** Not asleep. **2** Alert; vigilant. —*v.* **a·woke** (or **a·waked**), **a·waked** (or **a·woke** or **a·wok·en**), **a·wak·ing** *v.t.* **1** To arouse from sleep. **2** To stir up; excite. —*v.i.* **3** To cease to sleep; become awake. **4** To become alert or aroused. **5** To become aware of something: with *to.* [< OE ǎ- A-² + *wacian* watch]

a·wak·en (ə-wā′kən) *v.t. & v.i.* To awake. [< OE *onwæcnan* arise] —**a·wak′en·er** *n.*

a·wak·en·ing (ə-wā′kən·ing) *adj.* Stirring; exciting. —*n.* **1** The act of waking. **2** An arousing of attention or interest.

a·ward (ə-wôrd′) *v.t.* **1** To adjudge as due, as by legal decisions. **2** To bestow as the result of a contest or examination, as a prize. —*n.* **1** A decision, as by a judge or arbitrator. **2** That which is awarded. [< OF *es-* out + *guarder* watch] —**a·ward′a·ble** *adj.* —**a·ward′er** *n.*

a·ware (ə-wâr′) *adj.* Knowing or conscious of something; cognizant. [< OE *gewær* watchful] —**a·ware′ness** *n.*

a·wash (ə-wosh′, ə-wôsh′) *adv. & adj.* **1** Level with or just above the surface of the water. **2** Tossed or washed about by waves. **3** Covered or flooded with water.

a·way (ə-wā′) *adv.* **1** From a given place; off. **2** Far; at or to a distance. **3** In another direction; aside. **4** Out of existence; at an end. **5** On and on continuously: to peg *away* at a task. **6** From one's keeping, attention, or possession. **7** At once, without hesitation: Fire *away!* —**do** (or **make**) **away with** **1** To get rid of. **2** To kill. —*adj.* **1** Absent. **2** At a distance. —*interj.* Begone! [< OE *on weg* on (one's) way]

awe (ô) *n.* **1** Wonder and veneration somewhat mixed with fear. **2** Overwhelming admiration or appreciation. —*v.t.* **awed, aw·ing** or **awe·ing** to fill with awe. [< ON *agi* fear]

a·weigh (ə·wā′) *adv. Naut.* Hanging with the flukes just clear of the bottom: said of an anchor. [< A- (on) + WEIGH]

awe·some (ô′səm) *adj.* **1** Inspiring awe: an *awesome* display of strength. **2** Characterized by or expressing awe. —**awe′some·ly** *adv.* —**awe′some·ness** *n.*

awe·struck (ô′struk′) *adj.* Filled with awe. Also **awe·strick·en** (ô′strik′an).

aw·ful (ô′fəl) *adj.* **1** Exceedingly bad, unpleasant, etc.: an *awful* man. **2** Terrible; dreadful: an *awful* accident. **3** Great: an *awful* egotist. **4** Very bad, as in quality, performance, taste, etc.: an *awful* play. —**aw′ful·ness** *n.*

aw·ful·ly (ô′fəl·ē) *adv.* **1** In an awful manner. **2** (ô′flē) *Informal* Excessively; very.

a·while (ə·ʰwīl′) *adv.* For a brief time. • Since the word "for" is part of the meaning of *awhile*, it is redundant to say or write "He will be here for awhile." The correct sentence would be either "He will be here awhile" or "He will be here for a while."

awk·ward (ôk′wərd) *adj.* **1** Ungraceful in bearing. **2** Unskillful in action; bungling. **3** Embarrassing or perplexing. **4** Difficult or dangerous to deal with, as an opponent. **5** Inconvenient for use; uncomfortable. [< ON *afug* turned the wrong way + -WARD] —**awk′ward·ly** *adv.* —**awk′ward·ness** *n.* —**Syn. 1** ungainly, gawky. **2** clumsy, inept.

awl (ôl) *n.* A pointed instrument for making small holes. [< OE *al, awel*]

awn (ôn) *n.* A bristlelike appendage of certain grasses; beard, as of barley, etc. [< ON *ögn* chaff]

Awl

awn·ing (ô′ning) *n.* A rooflike cover, as of canvas, for protection from sun or rain. [?]

a·woke (ə-wōk′) *p.t.* of AWAKE.

a·wok·en (ə-wō′kən) A *p.p.* of AWAKE.

AWOL (*as an acronym pronounced* ā′wôl) *Mil.* Absent or absence without leave. Also **awol, A.W.O.L., a.w.o.l.**

a·wry (ə-rī′) *adj. & adv.* **1** Toward one side; crooked; askew. **2** Out of the right course; erroneously. [< A- (on) + WRY]

ax (aks) *n. pl.* **ax·es** A tool with a bladed head mounted on a handle, used for chopping, hewing, etc. —**get the ax** *Informal* **1** To be beheaded. **2** To be fired from one's job. —**have an ax to grind** *Informal* To have a private purpose or interest to promote. —*v.t.* **1** To cut or shape with an ax. **2** *Informal* To dismiss or delete. Also **axe.** [OE *æx, eax*]

ax·es¹ (ak′sēz) *n.* Plural of AXIS.

ax·es² (ak′siz) *n.* Plural of AX.

ax·i·al (ak′sē·əl) *adj.* **1** Of, pertaining to, or constituting an axis. **2** On or along an axis.

ax·il (ak′sil) *n.* The angle between the upper side of a leafstalk, branch, etc., and a stem or branch. [< L *axilla* armpit] —**ax′il·lar′y** *adj.*

ax·il·la (ak-sil′ə) *n. pl.* **ax·il·las** or **ax·il·lae** (-sil′ē) The armpit [< L] —**ax′il·lar′y** *adj.*

ax·i·om (ak′sē·əm) *n.* **1** A self-evident or universally recognized truth. **2** An established principle or rule. **3** *Logic & Math.* A proposition assumed to be true. [< Gk. *axiōma* a thing thought worthy]

ax·i·o·mat·ic (ak′sē·ə·mat′ik) *adj.* **1** Of, pertaining to, or resembling an axiom. **2** Full of axioms; aphoristic, as a literary style. Also **ax′i·o·mat′i·cal.** —**ax′i·o·mat′i·cal·ly** *adv.*

ax·is (ak′sis) *n. pl.* **ax·es** (ak′sēz) **1** A line around which a turning body rotates or may be supposed to rotate. **2** *Geom.* **a** A straight line through the center of a figure, esp. one with respect to which the figure is symmetrical. **b** A line along which distances are measured or to which positions are referred. **3** A real or imaginary central line about which things or parts are symmetrically arranged.

Axes
a. common.
b. fireman's.
c. double-bitted.

4 An affiliation or coalition of two or more nations to promote mutual interest, cooperation, etc. **—the Axis** In World War II, the coalition between Germany, Italy, and later Japan and other countries that opposed the United Nations. [<L, axis, axle]

ax·le (ak′səl) *n.* **1** A shaft or spindle on which a wheel is mounted and on or with which it turns. **2** AXLETREE. [<ON *öxull*] **—ax′led** *adj.*

ax·le·tree (ak′səl·trē) *n.* A crossbar that connects the opposite wheels of an automobile, wagon, etc., and on which the wheels revolve.

ax·man (aks′man) *n. pl.* **·men** (-mən) One who wields an ax; a woodman. Also **axe′man.**

ax·on (ak′sän) *n.* A nerve-cell structure that usu. conducts impulses away from the cell body.

a·yah (ä′yə) *n.* India, a native nurse or lady's maid. [<Hind. *āya* <Pg. *aia* nurse]

a·ya·tol·lah (ä′yə·tō′lə) *n.* Title of the highest-ranking teacher of religion in Iran. [<Ar., sign of God]

aye (ī) *n.* An affirmative vote or voter. *—adv.* Yes; yea. Also **ay.** [?]

AZ Arizona (P.O. abbr.).

a·zal·ea (ə·zāl′yə) *n.* Any of various usu. deciduous shrubs with showy flowers, related to rhododendrons. [<Gk. *azein* parch, from its preference for dry soil]

az·i·muth (az′ə·məth) *n.* Direction to or toward an object, measured as an angle in the horizontal plane. [<Ar. *as-sumūt* the ways] **—az·i·muth·al** (az′ə·muth′əl) *adj.* **—az′i·muth′al·ly** *adv.*

az·o (az′ō, ā′zō) *adj.* Containing nitrogen. [<F *azote* nitrogen]

Az·tec (az′tek) *n.* **1** A member of a tribe of Mexican Indians, founders of an empire at its height when Cortés invaded the country in 1519. **2** NAHUATL. *—adj.* Of or pertaining to the Aztec Indians, their language, culture, or empire: also **Az·tec·an** (az′tek·ən).

az·ure (azh′ər, ā′zhər) *adj.* Sky-blue. *—n.* **1** A clear sky-blue color or pigment. **2** The sky. [<Ar. *al-lāzward* lapis lazuli]

az·u·rite (azh′ə·rīt) *n.* A blue, glassy, mineral carbonate of copper sometimes used as a gem.

az·y·gous (az′i·gəs, ā·zī′gəs) *adj.* Having no mate; not paired. [<Gk. *azygos* unpaired]

B

B, b (bē) *n. pl.* **B's, b's, Bs, bs** (bēz) **1** The second letter of the English alphabet. **2** Any spoken sound representing the letter *B* or *b.* **3** Second in a series, class, or order. **4** Something shaped like a B. **5** *Music* The seventh tone in the diatonic scale of C. *—adj.* **1** Shaped like a B. **2** Second-class.

B *chess* bishop; boron.

B. bacillus; Bible; British; Brotherhood.

B., b. bachelor; base; bass; basso; bat; battery; book; born.

b, B. base; base hit; baseman.

B.A. Bachelor of Arts; British Academy.

Ba barium.

baa (bä, ba) *v.i.* **baaed, baa·ing** To bleat, as a sheep. *— n.* The bleat, as of a sheep. [Imit.]

Ba·al (bā′əl, bāl) *n. pl.* **Ba·al·im** (bā′əl·im) **1** Any of several ancient Semitic gods of fertility. **2** An idol or false god. [<Heb. *Ba'al* lord] **—Ba′al·ish** *adj.*

Bab·bitt metal (bab′it) A soft, white, antifriction alloy of tin, copper, and antimony, used in making bearings. [after Isaac *Babbitt,* 1799–1862, U.S. metallurgist]

bab·ble (bab′əl) *n.* **1** A murmuring sound, as of a stream. **2** Prattle, as of an infant. **3** A confusion of sounds, as of a crowd. *—v.* **bab·bled, bab·bling** *—v.t.* **1** To utter unintelligibly. **2** To blurt out thoughtlessly *—v.i.* **3** To utter inarticulate or meaningless noises. **4** To murmur, as a brook. **5** To talk unwisely or foolishly. [ME *babelen*] **—bab′bler** *n.*

babe (bāb) *n.* **1** A baby. **2** *Informal* One lacking worldly experience. **3** *Slang* A girl. [ME]

ba·bel (bā′bəl, bab′əl) *n.* A confusion of many voices or languages; tumult. Also **Ba′bel.**

Ba·bel (bā′bəl, bab′əl) *n.* In the Bible, an ancient city now thought to be Babylon. **—Tower of Babel** A tower built in Babel and intended to reach to heaven. God punished such presumption by preventing the workers from understanding each other and from completing the tower. *Gen.* 11:1–9.

ba·bies' breath BABY'S BREATH.

ba·boon (ba·bōōn′) *n.* A large, terrestrial monkey of Africa and Asia having large bare callosities on the buttocks, and usu. a short tail. [<OF *babuin*] **—ba·boon′ish** *adj.*

Baboon

ba·bush·ka (bə·bōōsh′kə) *n.* A woman's scarf for the head. [<Russ., grandmother]

ba·by (bā′bē) *n. pl.* **ba·bies 1** An infant. **2** The youngest or smallest member of a family or group. **3** A very timid person. **4** *Slang* **a** A girl or woman. **b** Anything one likes or is interested in. *—adj.* **1** For a baby. **2** Childish; infantile. **3** Small; diminutive. *—v.t.* **ba·bied, ba·by·ing** To treat or handle with care or affection. **—ba′by·hood** *n.* **—ba′by·like′** *adj.* [ME]

baby carriage A padded carriage for a baby, often with a collapsible top.

ba·by·ish (bā′bē·ish) *adj.* Childish; infantile **—ba′by·ish·ly** *adv.* **—ba′by·ish·ness** *n.*

Bab·y·lon (bab′ə·lən, -lon) **1** An ancient city of Mesopotamia, capital of Babylonia and celebrated as a seat of wealth, luxury, and vice. **2** Any city or place of great wealth, luxury, or vice.

Bab·y·lo·ni·a (bab′ə·lō′nē·ə) An ancient empire (*circa* 2100–538 B.C.) of sw Asia; capital, Babylon. **—Bab′y·lo′ni·an** *adj., n.*

baby's breath 1 A tall plant with clusters of small, white or pink, fragrant flowers. **2** Any of several similar plants.

ba·by·sit (bā′bē·sit′) *v.* **-sat, sit·ting** To act as a baby sitter.

baby sitter A person employed to take care of young children during the hours when the parents are absent.

baby tooth Any of the first, temporary set of teeth in children, normally 20 in all; milk tooth.

bac·ca·lau·re·ate (bak′ə·lôr′ē·it) *n.* **1** The degree of bachelor of arts, bachelor of science, etc. **2** An address to a graduating class at commencement; also **baccalaureate sermon.** [<Med. L *baccalaurius* a squire]

bac·ca·rat (bak′ə·rä′, bak′ə·rä) *n.* A card game of chance. Also **bac′ca·ra′.** [<F *baccara*]

Bac·chae (bak′ē, -ī) *n. pl.* The female followers or priestesses of the god Bacchus; BACCHANAL (def. 1).

bac·cha·nal (bak′ə·nəl) *n.* **1** A votary of Bacchus. **2** A drunken reveler. **3** *pl.* BACCHANALIA. *—adj.* Bacchanalian. [<L *bacchanalis* of Bacchus]

bac·cha·na·li·a (bak′ə·nā′lē·ə, -nāl′yə) *n. pl.* **1** Drunken revelries; orgies. **2** *Usu. cap.* An ancient Roman festival in honor of Bacchus. **—bac′cha·na′li·an** *adj., n.*

Bac·chus (bak′əs) *Rom. Myth.* The god of wine and revelry.

bach·e·lor (bach′ələr, bach′lər) *n.* **1** An unmarried man. **2** One who has a baccalaureate degree. *—adj.* Of or for a bachelor. [<Med. L *baccalaurius* a squire] **—bach′e·lor·hood′, bach′e·lor·ship′** *n.*

Bachelor of Arts (of Science, of Engineering, etc.) **1** A degree given by a college or university to a person who has completed a four-year course or its equivalent in one of the (specified) academic disciplines. **2** A person who has received this degree.

bachelor's button Any of several plants with composite flowers having a flasklike involucre, esp. the cornflower.

ba·cil·lus (bə·sil′əs) n. pl. **ba·cil·li** (-sil′ī) **1** Any of a genus of aerobic, rod-shaped, spore-forming bacteria often growing linked together. **2** Any rod-shaped bacterium. [< L *baculum* rod] —**ba·cil′lar, bac·il·ar·y** (bas′ə·ler′ē) adj. • See BACTERIUM.

bac·i·tra·cin (bas′ə·trā′sin) n. An antibiotic produced from a bacillus, used in the treatment of some bacterial skin infections.

back[1] (bak) n. **1** The part of the body nearest the spine; in man the hinder, in quadrupeds the upper part, extending from the neck to the base of the spine. **2** The backbone or spine. **3** A part touching or supporting the back: the *back* of a dress. **4** The rear or posterior part: the *back* of the car. **5** The part opposite in position to the part most used, seen, etc.: the *back* of a knife; the *back* of the hand. **6** The part of the pages of a book stitched or glued together; also, the part of the binding around this part. **7** In certain sports: **a** A position behind the front line of players. **b** A player in this position. **8** Physical strength or energy. —**at one's back** Following closely. —**behind one's back 1** Secretly. **2** Treacherously. —**be (flat) on one's back** To be helplessly ill. —**in back of** Behind; to the rear of. —**turn one's back on 1** To turn away from, as in contempt or criticism. **2** To ignore or refuse to help. **3** To renounce. —**with one's back to the wall** Cornered. —v.t. **1** To cause to move or go backwards or to the rear: often with *up*. **2** To form the back of. **3** To strengthen at the back. **4** To support, assist, or uphold: often with *up*. **5** To bet on the success or chances of. —v.i. **6** To move or go backward: often with *up*. **7** To have the back facing in a certain direction: It *backs* onto the woods. **8** To shift counterclockwise: said of the wind. —**back down** To withdraw from a position, abandon a claim, etc. —**back off** To retreat, as from contact. —**back out (of)** To withdraw from or refuse to carry out an engagement, contest, etc. —adj. **1** In the rear; behind: a *back* room. **2** Distant; remote: the *back* country. **3** Of or for a previous date. **4** In arrears; overdue, as a debt. **5** In a backward direction: a *back* thrust. [< OE *bæc* back]

back[2] (bak) adv. **1** At, to, or toward the rear. **2** In, to, or toward a former place, condition, etc. **3** To or towards times past. **4** In return or retort: to talk *back*. **5** In reserve or concealment: to keep something *back* [< ABACK]

back·bench·er (bak′ben′chər) n. A new, inexperienced, or unimportant member of a legislature, esp. of the British House of Commons or the Canadian Parliament.

back·bite (bak′bīt) v.t. & v.i. **·bit, ·bit·ten** (or Informal **·bit**), **·bit·ing** To revile behind one's back; slander. —**back′bit′er, back′bit′ing** n.

back·blocks (bak′bloks′) n.pl. Austral. Inland farming areas.

back·bone (bak′bōn′) n. **1** The spine or vertebral column. **2** Any main support. **3** Firmness; resolution; courage.

back·break·ing (bak′brā′king) adj. Physically exhausting; fatiguing.

back·door (bak′dôr′, -dōr′) adj. Underhand; indirect; secret.

back·drop (bak′drop′) n. The curtain hung at the rear of a stage, often painted to represent a scene. Also **back cloth**.

backed (bakt) adj. Having a specified kind of back or backing: used in combination: *low-backed; steel-backed*.

back·er (bak′ər) n. **1** One who supports with money; a patron. **2** One who bets on a contestant.

back·field (bak′fēld′) n. In football, the players behind the line of scrimmage, including the quarterback.

back·fill (bak′fil′) n. Soil and other material used to refill an excavation. —v.t. To refill (an excavation).

back·fire (bak′fīr′) n. **1** A fire built to check an advancing forest or prairie fire by creating a barren area in its path. **2** Premature explosion in the cylinder of an internal-combustion engine. —v.i. **·fired, ·fir·ing 1** To set or use a backfire. **2** To explode in a backfire. **3** To have an unexpected and unfavorable result or conclusion.

back formation Ling. **1** The creation, by analogy, of one word from another in cases where the original word would seem to be the derivative, as *emote* from *emotion*. **2** A word so formed.

back·gam·mon (bak′gam′ən, bak′gam′ən) n. **1** A board game for two players, the moves of the pieces being determined by dice throws. **2** A victory in this game. —v.t. To win a backgammon from. [ME *back gamen* back game]

back·ground (bak′ground′) n. **1** That part in a picture which forms a setting for the main elements. **2** The surface, area, object, etc. that is behind something, usu. of a contrasting color, texture, or shape. **3** A subordinate or obscure place or position. **4** The whole of one's experiences, training, cultural environment, etc. **5** Music or sound effects accompanying a motion picture, play, etc. **6** The events leading up to or causing a situation. **7** Information explaining a situation, person, etc.

back·hand (bak′hand′) adj. Backhanded. —n. **1** Handwriting that slopes toward the left. **2** A stroke, as in tennis, made with the back of the hand moving forward. —adv. With a backhand.

back·hand·ed (bak′han′did) adj. **1** In sports: **a** Made with the back of the hand moving forward. **b** Made with the back of the hand turned toward the body, as a catch in baseball. **2** Having elements of criticism and sarcasm: a *backhanded* compliment. —adv. With a backhand. —**back′hand′ed·ly** adv. —**back′hand′ed·ness** n.

back·ing (bak′ing) n. **1** Support or assistance given to a person, cause, etc. **2** Supporters collectively. **3** Something added at the back for extra support or strength. **4** Informal Musical accompaniment.

back·lash (bak′lash′) n. **1** A sudden, usu. violent backward movement. **2** In angling, a snarl or tangle of the line on a reel. **3** A sudden, violent reaction, as of public opinion.

back·log (bak′lôg, -log′) n. U.S. **1** A large log at the back of a fireplace. **2** Any reserve or accumulation, as of funds, business orders, etc.

back number 1 An old issue of a magazine or newspaper. **2** Informal An old-fashioned person or thing.

back·pack (bak′pak′) n. A pack or knapsack carried on the back, as by campers. —v.t. & v.i. To carry (equipment) in a backpack. —**back′pack′er** n.

back seat Status or position of little or no importance.

back-seat driver (bak′sēt′) A passenger in a vehicle who, unasked, offers advice about driving.

back·side (bak′sīd′) n. **1** The back part. **2** The rump or buttocks.

back·slide (bak′slīd′) v.i. **·slid, ·slid** or **slid·den, ·slid·ing** To return to former ways or opinions after reformation or conversion; relapse. —**back′slid′er** n.

back·spin (bak′spin′) n. Reverse rotation of a round object that is moving forward, causing it to rebound.

back·stage (bak′stāj′) adv. In or toward the portion of a theater behind the stage, including the wings, dressing rooms, etc. —n. The back portion of the stage. —adj. (bak′stāj′) Placed backstage, so as to be hidden.

back·stop (bak′stop′) n. A fence or screen to stop the ball from going too far in certain games, as baseball, tennis, etc.

back·stretch (bak′strech′) n. That part of a race course farthest from the spectators and opposite the homestretch.

back·stroke (bak′strōk′) n. In swimming, a stroke executed while on one's back.

back talk Impudent answering back.

back·track (bak′trak′) v.i. **1** To retrace one's steps. **2** To withdraw from a position.

back·up (bak′up′) adj. **1** Held in readiness for use as a substitute: a *backup* plan. **2** Supporting. —n. A substitute.

back·ward (bak′wərd) adj. **1** Turned to the back or rear; reversed. **2** Done the reverse way. **3** Shy; bashful. **4** Slow in growth or development; retarded. —adv. **1** In the direction of the back; to the rear. **2** Into time past; toward earlier times. **3** With the back foremost. **4** In reverse order. **5** From better to worse. —**back′ward·ly** adv. —**back′ward·ness** n.

back·wards (bak′wardz) adv. Backward.

back·wash (bak′wosh′, -wôsh′) n. **1** The water moved

backward, as by a boat, oars, etc. **2** A backward current of air, as set up by aircraft propellers. **3** An aftermath.

back·wa·ter (bak′wô′tər, -wot′ər) n. **1** Water set, thrown, or held back, as by a dam. **2** Any place or condition regarded as stagnant, backward, etc.

back·woods (bak′wo͝odz′) n.pl. Remote, heavily wooded, or sparsely settled districts. —adj. In, from, or like the backwoods: also **back′wood′**. —**back′woods′man** n.

ba·con (bā′kən) n. The salted and dried or smoked back and sides of the hog. —**bring home the bacon** Informal **1** To provide a living. **2** To succeed. [< OF]

bact., bacteriol. bacteriologist; bacteriology.

bac·te·ri·a (bak·tir′ē·ə) Plural of BACTERIUM.

bac·te·ri·cide (bak·tir′ə·sīd) n. An agent destructive of bacteria. —**bac·te′ri·ci′dal** adj.

bac·te·ri·ol·o·gy (bak·tir′ē·ol′ə·jē) n. The branch of science that deals with bacteria. —**bac·te·ri·o·log·i·cal** (bak·tir′ē·ə·loj′i·kəl) adj. —**bac·te′ri·o·log′i·cal·ly** adv. —**bac·te′ri·ol′o·gist** n.

bac·te·ri·o·phage (bak·tir′ē·ə·fāj′) n. A virus having the power to destroy bacteria. [< BACTERIA + Gk. phagein eat]

bac·te·ri·um (bak·tir′ē·əm) n. pl. **·te·ri·a** (-tir′ē·ə) One of numerous unicellular microorganisms that exhibit both plant and animal characteristics, and range from the harmless and beneficial to the intensely virulent and lethal. [< Gk. baktērion, dim. of baktron staff, stick] —**bac·te′ri·al** adj. —**bac·te′ri·al·ly** adv.

Bacteria
a. staphylococcus. b. species of spirochete. c. bacillus typhosus.

bad (bad) adj. **worse, worst 1** Not good in any manner or degree. **2** Inadequate or defective: bad lighting. **3** Lacking skill or proficiency: a bad musician. **4** Disagreeable; unpleasant: a bad odor; bad manners. **5** Rotten; decomposed. **6** Incorrect: bad grammar. **7** Immoral; corrupt; wicked. **8** Naughty: a bad child. **9** Injurious; harmful: a bad habit. **10** Severe: a bad sprain. **11** Sick; in poor health. **12** Sorry: to feel bad about it. —**in bad** Informal **1** In difficulty. **2** In disfavor. —**not bad** Rather good: also **not half bad, not so bad.** —n. **1** That which is bad. **2** Those who are bad. **3** A bad state or condition; wickedness. —adv. Informal Badly. [ME badde] —**bad′ness** n. —Syn. adj. **2** imperfect, unsatisfactory. **3** inferior, mediocre. **4** offensive, displeasing, nasty, disgusting, revolting, repulsive. **7** evil, vile, sinful. **8** mischievous, disobedient, troublesome. **9** hurtful, detrimental. • Bad is an adjective and badly an adverb. Their use is confusing only when they come after one of the linking verbs, as feel, seem, appear, look, etc. It is correct to say I feel bad (ill), because bad describes or refers back to the pronoun I and not to the verb. I feel badly is correct only if one's sense of touch is defective. In like manner, it is correct to say That egg smells bad; This meat tastes bad, because bad is obviously describing the noun in each case and not the verb. However, because badly is so often, although incorrectly, used in such instances, it is becoming somewhat acceptable, esp. in casual, informal speech.

bade (bad) p.t. of BID.

badge (baj) n. **1** A token, decoration, or emblem of office, rank, attainment, etc. **2** Any distinguishing mark or symbol. —v.t. **badged, badg·ing** To decorate or provide with a badge. [ME bagge]

badg·er (baj′ər) n. **1** A small, burrowing, nocturnal, carnivorous mammal, with a broad body, short legs, and long clawed forefeet. **2** The fur of a badger. —v.t. To worry persistently; nag. [?]

bad·i·nage (bad′ə·näzh′, bad′ə·nij) n. Playful raillery; banter. —v.t. **·naged, ·nag·ing** To tease with badinage. [< F badin silly, jesting]

bad·lands (bad′landz′) n. A barren area characterized by numerous ridges, peaks, and mesas cut into unusual shapes by erosion.

Bad·lands (bad′landz′) n. The badlands of western U.S., esp. in sw South Dakota. Also **Bad Lands.**

bad·ly (bad′lē) adv. **1** Improperly; imperfectly; incorrectly. **2** Unpleasantly. **3** Harmfully. **4** Informal Very much; greatly. • See BAD.

bad·min·ton (bad′min·tən) n. A game played by batting a shuttlecock back and forth over a high narrow net with a light racket. [< Badminton, an estate in England.]

bad·tem·pered (bad′tem′pərd) adj. Irritable.

baf·fle (baf′əl) v. **baf·fled, baf·fling** v.t. **1** To confuse or perplex. **2** To thwart or frustrate; defeat. **3** To block with or as with a baffle. —v.i. **4** To struggle to no avail. —n. A plate or partition acting as a barrier to sound, motion of a fluid, etc. —**baf′fling** adj. —**baf′fling·ly** adv. —**baf′fle·ment, baf′fler** n.

bag (bag) n. **1** A flexible container open at one end and made of paper, plastic, etc.; a sack or pouch. **2** A purse. **3** A suitcase. **4** A bagful. **5** The amount of game caught or killed. **6** A bulging, wrinkled, or puffy condition: bags under one's eyes. **7** An animal sac or udder. **8** Slang An interest, skill, profession, etc.: What's your bag? **9** In baseball, a base. —**a mixed bag** Informal A heterogeneous collection. —**be in the bag** Informal To be assured of a success. —**be left holding the bag** Informal To be left to assume full responsibility. —v. **bagged, bag·ging** v.t. **1** To put into a bag or bags. **2** To cause to bulge like a bag. **3** To capture or kill, as game. —v.i. **4** To bulge or swell like a bag. **5** To hang loosely. [< ON baggi pack, bundle]

ba·gasse (bə·gas′) n. The dry refuse of sugarcane after the juice has been expressed. Also **ba·gass′.** [< Sp. bagazo refuse, dregs]

bag·a·telle (bag′ə·tel′) n. **1** A trifle. **2** A game similar to billiards. [< Ital. bagatella]

ba·gel (bā′gəl) n. A doughnut-shaped hard-baked roll of unsalted yeast dough. [< Yiddish]

bag·ful (bag′fo͝ol′) n. pl. **·fuls** The amount a bag will hold.

bag·gage (bag′ij) n. **1** The trunks, packages, etc., of a traveler. **2** Archaic A prostitute. [< OF bague bundle]

bag·ging (bag′ing) n. A coarse material for making bags.

bag·gy (bag′ē) adj. **bag·gi·er, bag·gi·est 1** Loose or ill-fitting. **2** Wrinkled. **3** Puffy. —**bag′gi·ly** adv. —**bag′gi·ness** n.

bag·pipe (bag′pīp′) n. Often pl. A reed musical instrument in which the several drone pipes and the melody pipe with its finger stops are supplied with air from a windbag filled by the player's breath. —**bag′pip′er** n.

ba·guette (bag·get′) n. **1** A gem cut in long, narrow, rectangular form. **2** This form. Also **ba·guet′.** [< Ital. bacchetta, dim. of bacchio staff, stick]

bah (bä, ba) interj. A scornful exclamation.

Bagpipe

Bah·rain (bä·rān′) n. A sheikdom under British protection, located on an archipelago in the Persian Gulf, 213 sq. mi., cap. Manama. Also **Bah·rein′, Bah·rayn′.** • See map at SAUDI ARABIA.

bail¹ (bāl) n. A scoop or bucket for dipping out fluids, as from a boat. —v.t. & v.i. **1** To dip (water), as from a boat. **2** To clear (a boat) of water by dipping out. —**bail out** To parachute from an aircraft. [< OF baille] —**bail′er** n.

bail² (bāl) n. In cricket, one of the crosspieces of the wicket. [< OF baile barrier]

bail³ (bāl) Law n. **1** Money or security given to a court to secure the release of an arrested person on the proviso that the person will be present later to stand trial. **2** Such a release. **3** The person or persons who give such money or security. —v.t. **1** To release (an arrested person) on bail: often with out. **2** To obtain the release of (an arrested person) on bail: usu. with out. **3** To help out of any difficulty: usu. with out. —**go (or stand) bail for** To provide bail for. [< OF baillier guard, carry] —**bail′a·ble** adj.

bail⁴ (bāl) n. **1** The semicircular handle of a pail, kettle, etc. **2** An arch-shaped support, as for a canopy. [ME baile]

bai·liff (bā′lif) n. **1** An officer of court having custody of prisoners under arraignment. **2** A sheriff's deputy. **3** A custodian of an estate; overseer. **4** *Brit.* A subordinate magistrate. [< L *bajulus* porter, manager]

bai·li·wick (bā'lə·wik) *n.* **1** The office, jurisdiction, or district of a bailiff. **2** One's own special place. [< OF *baillif* bailiff + OE *wic* village]

bails·man (bālz'mən) *n. pl.* **·men** (-mən) One who provides bail for another.

bait (bāt) *n.* **1** Food or other lure in a trap, on a hook, etc. **2** Any allurement or enticement. —*v.t.* **1** To put food or some other lure on or in. **2** To torment, as by setting dogs upon, for sport: to *bait* a bear. **3** To harass; heckle. **4** To lure; entice. [< ON *beita* food] —**bait'er** *n.*

baize (bāz) *n.* A cotton or woolen feltlike, usu. green fabric, used to cover pool tables, etc. [< OF *baies,* fem. pl. of *bai* chestnut-brown]

bake (bāk) *v.* **baked, bak·ing** *v.t.* **1** To cook by dry heat, as in an oven. **2** To harden or vitrify by heat, as bricks or pottery. —*v.i.* **3** To bake bread, pastry, meat, or other food. **4** To become baked or hardened by heat, as soil. —*n.* A baking or the amount baked. [< OE *bacan*] —**bak'er** *n.*

Ba·ke·lite (bā'kə·līt) *n.* Any of a group of thermosetting plastics derived from phenol and formaldehyde: a trade name.

baker's dozen Thirteen.

bak·er·y (bā'kər·ē, bāk'rē) *n. pl.* **·er·ies 1** A place for baking bread, cake, etc. **2** A shop where baked goods are sold: also **bake'shop'.**

bak·ing powder (bā'king) A mixture of baking soda and an acid salt, acting as a leavening agent by releasing carbon dioxide when moistened in a batter.

baking soda SODIUM BICARBONATE.

bal. balance; balancing.

Ba·laam (bā'ləm) A prophet, reproached by the ass he rode for cursing the Israelites. *Num. 22–24.*

bal·a·lai·ka (bal'ə·lī'kə) *n.* A Russian instrument with a triangular body, a guitar neck, and three strings.

bal·ance (bal'əns) *n.* **1** An instrument for measuring weights, often a bar pivoted on a central point with matched pans at either end; scales. **2** The imaginary scales of destiny; a symbol of justice. **3** The power to decide fate, value, etc., as by a balance. **4** A state of equilibrium or equality, as in value, importance, etc. **5** Equilibrium of the body. **6** Mental or emotional stability; sanity. **7** Harmonious proportion, as in the design or arrangement of parts. **8** Something used to produce an equilibrium; counteracting influence; counterpoise. **9** The act of balancing. **10 a** Equality between the credit and debit totals of an account. **b** A difference between such totals; the excess on either the debit or credit side. **11** *Informal* Whatever is left over; remainder: the *balance* of the week. **12** A balance wheel. —**in the balance** Being judged; not yet settled. —**strike a balance** To compromise. —*v.* **·anced, ·anc·ing** *v.t.* **1** To bring into or keep in equilibrium; poise. **2** To weigh in a balance. **3** To compare or weigh in the mind. **4** To offset or counteract. **5** To bring into harmony, proportion, etc. **6** To be equal to. **7** To compute the difference between the debit and credit sides of (an account). **8** To reconcile, as by making certain entries, the debit and credit sides of (an account). **9** To adjust (an account) by paying what is owed. —*v.i.* **10** To be or come into equilibrium. **11** To be equal. **12** To hesitate or waver; tilt: to *balance* on the edge of a chasm. [< L *bilanx* having two plates or scales < *bis* two + *lanx* plate] —**bal'ance·a·ble** *adj.* —**bal'an·cer** *n.*

Balalaika

balance of payments The difference in payments made and received between a country and other countries, including costs of exports and imports of goods and services and the exchange of gold and capital.

balance of power A distribution of forces among nations such that no single nation or combination of nations will dominate or endanger any other.

balance of trade The difference in value between exports and imports of a country.

balance sheet A statement in tabular form to show

assets and liabilities, profit and loss, etc., of a business at a specified date.

balance wheel The oscillating wheel of a watch or chronometer, which determines its rate of motion.

bal·brig·gan (bal·brig'ən) *n.* **1** A fine, knitted cotton fabric, used for hosiery, underwear, etc. **2** Clothing made of this. [< *Balbriggan,* Ireland]

bal·co·ny (bal'kə·nē) *n. pl.* **·nies 1** A platform with balustrade or railing projecting from a wall of a building. • See BALUSTRADE. **2** A projecting gallery inside a theater, auditorium, etc. [< Ital. *balco* a beam]

bald (bôld) *adj.* **1** Without hair on the head. **2** Without natural growth, as a mountain. **3** Unadorned; without embellishments; plain. **4** Without disguise: *bald* jealousy. **5** Having white feathers or fur on the head: the *bald* eagle. [ME *balled*] —**bald'ly** *adv.* —**bald'ness** *n.*

bald eagle A large eagle of N America, dark brown, with the head, neck, and tail white.

Bal·der (bôl'dər) *Norse Myth.* The god of sunlight, spring, and joy. Also **Bal'dr.**

bal·der·dash (bôl'dər·dash) *n.* A meaningless flow of words; nonsense. [?]

bald·head (bôld'hed') *n.* One whose head is bald. —**bald'head'·ed** *adj.*

Bald eagle

bald·pate (bôld'pāt') *n.* A baldheaded person. —**bald'·pat'ed** *adj.*

bal·dric (bôl'drik) *n.* A belt worn over one shoulder to support a sword, bugle, etc. [< OF *baudrei*]

Bald·win (bôld'win) *n.* A red winter apple. [< Col. L. *Baldwin,* 1740–1807, U.S. soldier]

bale (bāl) *n.* A large package of bulky material, as hay or cotton, corded or otherwise prepared for transportation. —*v.t.* **baled, bal·ing** To make into a bale or bales. [< OF] —**bal'er** *n.*

ba·leen (bə·lēn') *n.* Whalebone. [< L *balaena whale*]

bale·ful (bāl'fəl) *adj.* Hurtful; malignant; **2** Sorrowful: a *baleful* look. [< OE *bealu* evil + -FUL] —**bale'ful·ly** *adv.* —**bale'ful·ness** *n.*

balk (bôk) *v.t.* **1** To render unsuccessful; thwart; frustrate. —*v.i.* **2** To stop short and refuse to proceed. **3** To refuse to consider or act upon: with *at:* He *balked* at every idea. **4** In baseball, to make a balk. —*n.* **1** a hindrance, disappointment, defeat, etc. **2** An error; blunder. **3** In baseball, an illegal, uncompleted motion by a pitcher when there are men on base. **4** A ridge left unplowed between furrows. **5** A squared beam or timber. [< OE *balca* bank, ridge]

Bal·kan (bôl'kən) *adj.* **1** Of or pertaining to the Balkan Peninsula, to the people of this region, their customs, etc. **2** Of or pertaining to the Balkan Mountains.

bal·kan·ize (bôl'kən·īz) *v.t.* **·ized, ·iz·ing** *Often cap.* To subdivide (a nation or region) into small and often incompatible units, as the Balkans after World War I. —**bal'kan·i·za'tion** *n.*

Balkan Peninsula A peninsula of SE Europe, bounded by the Black, Aegean, Mediterranean, Ionian, and Adriatic Seas.

Balkan States The countries occupying the Balkan Peninsula; Albania, Bulgaria, Greece, Romania, Yugoslavia, and the western part of Turkey. Also **the Balkans.** • See map next page.

balk·y (bô'kē) *adj.* **balk·i·er, balk·i·est** Disposed to stop suddenly or refuse to go: a *balky* mule. —**balk'i·ly** *adv.* —**balk'i·ness** *n.*

ball¹ (bôl) *n.* **1** A spherical body. **2** Such a body, of any size and made of various substances, used in a number of games. **3** Any of several such games, esp. baseball. **4** The manner of throwing or pitching a ball: a slow *ball.* **5** In baseball, a pitch in which the ball fails either to pass over home plate or between the batter's shoulder and knees and is not struck at by him. **6** A roundish part of something: the *ball* of the foot. **7** A planet or star, esp. the earth. —*v.t. & v.i.* To form into a ball. [< ON *böllr*]

ball² (bôl) *n.* **1** A large, formal gathering for dancing. **2** *Slang* A very good time. —*v.i. Slang* To have a very good time. [< LL *ballare* dance]

bal·lad (bal'əd) *n.* **1** A narrative poem or song of popular

Balkan States

origin in short stanzas, often with a refrain. **2** A popular song, usu. slow in tempo and sentimental in nature. [< OF *ballade* dancing song] —**bal·lad·eer** (bal'ə·dir'), **bal'lad·ry** *n.*

bal·lade (bə·läd', ba-) *n.* **1** A verse form. **2** A musical composition of romantic nature, usu. for piano. [< OF *ballade* dancing song]

bal·last (bal'əst) *n.* **1** Any heavy substance carried in a vessel or vehicle to stablize it or, in a balloon, to control altitude. **2** Gravel or broken stone laid down as a railroad bed. **3** That which gives stability to character, morality, etc. —*v.t.* **1** To provide with ballast. **2** To stabilize. [< ODan. *barlast* bare load]

ball bearing *Mech.* **1** A bearing in which the shaft rests upon small metal balls that turn freely as it revolves. **2** Any of the metal balls in such a bearing.

bal·le·ri·na (bal'ə·rē'nə) *n.* A female ballet dancer. [< LL *ballare* to dance]

bal·let (bal'ā, ba·lā') *n.* **1** An elaborate group dance using conventionalized movements, often for narrative effects. **2** This style of dancing. **3** Music for a ballet. **4** A company of ballet dancers. [< LL *ballare* to dance] —**bal·let·ic** (ba·let'ik) *adj.*

ball game **1** A game played with a ball, esp. a baseball game. **2** *Informal* **a** Any collective effort or its purpose. **b** A set of circumstances; situation: It's a whole new *ball game.*

bal·lis·ta (bə·lis'tə) *n. pl.* **·tae** (-tē) An engine used in ancient and medieval warfare for hurling missiles. [< Gk. *ballein* throw]

bal·lis·tic (bə·lis'tik) *adj.* Pertaining to projectiles or to ballistics.

ballistic missile A missile that is powered and guided at launch and through the early part of its trajectory, and in free fall thereafter.

bal·lis·tics (bə·lis'tiks) *n. pl. (construed as sing.)* The science that deals with the motion of projectiles. —**bal·lis·ti·cian** (bal'ə·stish'ən) *n.*

bal·loon (bə·lōōn') *n.* **1** A large, airtight bag, inflated with gas lighter than air, designed to rise and float in the atmosphere, often carrying passengers, instruments, etc. **2** A small inflatable rubber bag, used as a toy. **3** In comic strips, the outline containing the dialogue. —*v.i.* **1** To increase quickly in scope or magnitude; expand. **2** To swell out like a balloon. **3** To ascend in a balloon. —*v.t.* **4** To

inflate or swell with air. [< Ital. *balla* ball, sphere] —**bal·loon'ist** *n.*

bal·lot (bal'ət) *n.* **1** A written or printed slip or ticket used in secret voting. **2** The total number of votes cast in an election. **3** The act or system of voting secretly by ballots or by voting machines. **4** The list of candidates in an election. —*v.* **bal·lot·ed, bal·lot·ing** —*v.i.* **1** To vote or decide by ballot. —*v.t.* **2** To vote for or decide on by means of a ballot: to *ballot* the players in selecting a captain. [< Ital. *ballotta,* dim. of *balla* ball]

ball·play·er (bôl'plā'ər) *n.* A baseball player.

ball-point pen (bôl'point') A pen having for a point a ball bearing that rolls against an ink cartridge. Also **ball'point', ball point.**

ball·room (bôl'rōōm', -rōōm') *n.* A large room or public hall for dancing.

bal·ly·hoo (bal'ē·hōō) *n. Informal* **1** Noisy talk or patter. **2** Immoderate or sensational advertising or propaganda. —*v.t. & v.i.* **·hooed, ·hoo·ing** To publicize sensationally or with much fanfare. [?]

balm (bäm) *n.* **1** An aromatic gum resin from various trees or shrubs. **2** Any of a genus of fragrant herbs. **3** Any oil or resin used as ointment, esp. if fragrant. **4** Anything that soothes or heals. [< L *balsamum* balsam]

balm of Gilead **1** Any of several Asian evergreen trees. **2** The fragrant resin obtained from them. **3** The balsam fir.

balm·y (bä'mē) *adj.* **balm·i·er, balm·i·est** **1** Very pleasant and mild. **2** Soothing. **3** *Slang* Insane; crazy; foolish. —**balm'i·ly** *adv.* —**balm'i·ness** *n.*

ba·lo·ney (bə·lō'nē) *n.* **1** *Slang* Nonsense. **2** Bologna sausage. [< BOLOGNA]

bal·sa (bôl'sə, bäl'-) *n.* **1** A tree of tropical America; also, its very lightweight wood. **2** A raft. [< Sp. *balza*]

bal·sam (bôl'səm) *n.* **1** Any of a group of fragrant oleoresins obtained from various trees. **2** Any such tree. **3** Any fragrant ointment. **4** The balsam fir. —*v.t.* To anoint with balsam; salve. [< L *balsamum* < Gk. *balsamon* balsam tree]

balsam fir A North American tree of the pine family, yielding Canada balsam.

Bal·tic (bôl'tik) *adj.* Of or pertaining to the Baltic Sea or the Baltic States.

Bal·ti·more oriole (bôl'tə·môr, -mōr) An American oriole with orange and black feathers in the male. [< George Calvert, Lord *Baltimore's* coat-of-arms' colors]

Baltimore oriole

bal·us·ter (bal'əs·tər) *n.* One of a set of small pillars that support a hand rail. [< Ital. < *balaustra* pomegranate flower < the resemblance in shape of the post]

bal·us·trade (bal'ə·strād') *n.* A hand rail supported by balusters.

bam·bi·no (bam·bē'nō) *n. pl.* **·ni** (-nē) *Ital.* **1** A little child; a baby. **2** A figure of the child Jesus.

bam·boo (bam·bōō') *n.* **1** A tall shrubby grass of tropical and semi-tropical regions. **2** The tough, hollow, jointed stem of this plant. [< Malay *bambu*]

Balustrade on balcony

bam·boo·zle (bam·bōō'zəl) *v.* **·zled, ·zling** *v.t. Informal* **1** To mislead; cheat. **2** To perplex. —*v.i.* **3** To practice deception. [?] —**bam·boo'zle·ment** *n.* —**bam·boo'zler** *n.*

ban (ban) *v.t.* To forbid or prohibit, esp. officially. —*n.* **1** An official prohibition. **2** Disapproval or prohibition, as by public opinion. **3** An ecclesiastical edict of excommunication or interdiction. [< ME *bannen* to summon & OF *ban* a summoning]

ba·nal (bā'nəl, bə·nal', ban'əl) *adj.* Trite; commonplace. [< OF, ordinary, common] —**ba·nal·i·ty** (bə·nal'ə·tē) *n.* —**ba'nal·ly** *adv.* —**Syn.** hackneyed, stale, boring, dull.

ba·nan·a (bə·nan'ə) *n.* **1** A large, tropical, treelike plant cultivated for its fruit. 2 The edible, pulpy fruit of this plant. [< native w African name]

banana oil Amyl acetate, a sweet-smelling, colorless liquid, used as a solvent and a flavoring.

band[1] (band) n. 1 A flat flexible strip of any material, used for binding, securing, etc. 2 Any strip of fabric used to finish, strengthen, or trim an article of dress: a *neckband.* 3 *pl.* A pair of linen strips hanging from the front of the neck, worn with certain clerical or academic garments. 4 Any broad stripe of contrasting color, material, or surface. 5 *Physics* An interval of some variable, such as frequency, wavelength, energy, etc. 6 A ring. —*v.t.* 1 To unite or tie with a band; encircle. 2 To mark with a band, as birds. [< OF *bande* ribbon]

band[2] (band) n. 1 A company of persons associated together for some purpose. 2 A group of musicians performing together, esp. on wind and percussion instruments. 3 A drove of animals wandering together. 4 *Can.* A group of Indians living as a recognized unit on a reservation. —*v.t.* To join or unite, as in a league or company: often with *together.* —*v.i.* To confederate. [< OF *bande* a troop]

band·age (ban′dij) n. A strip, usu. of soft cloth, used in dressing wounds, etc. —*v.t.* **·aged, ·ag·ing** To bind or cover with a bandage. [< F *bande* band]

Band-Aid (band′ād′) n. A gauze patch attached to an adhesive strip, used to cover minor wounds: a trade name. —*adj.* Makeshift or improvised. Also **band′-aid′.**

ban·dan·na (ban·dan′ə) n. A large, bright-colored handkerchief with spots or figures. Also **ban·dan′a.** [< Hind. *bāndhnū* method of dyeing]

band·box (band′boks′) n. A light round or oval box, for carrying hats, collars, etc.

ban·deau (ban·dō′) n. *pl.* **·deaux** (-dōz′) 1 A narrow band, esp. one worn about the hair. 2 A brassiere. [< OF *bande* ribbon]

ban·di·coot (ban′di·kōot) n. 1 A very large rat of India and Ceylon. 2 A small marsupial of Australia, Tasmania, etc. [< Telugu *pandikokku*]

ban·dit (ban′dit) n. *pl.* **ban·dits** or **ban·dit·ti** (ban·dit′ē) 1 A robber. 2 Any outlaw. [< Ital. *bandire* to join together in a band] —**ban′dit·ry** n.

band·mas·ter (band′mas′tər, -mäs′tər) n. The conductor of a musical band.

ban·do·leer (ban′də·lir′) n. A broad, canvas band, with loops for holding cartridges, worn over the shoulder. Also **ban′do·lier′.** [< F *bandoulière*]

band saw *Mech.* A saw consisting of a toothed endless belt on wheels.

band shell A concave, hemispherical bandstand for concerts.

band·stand (band′stand′) n. An outdoor or indoor platform for a band of musicians.

band·wag·on (band′wag′ən) n. A high, decorated wagon to carry a band in a parade. —**climb (get, hop, etc.) on the bandwagon** To support those principles, candidates, etc., that are most popular or most likely to succeed.

ban·dy (ban′dē) *v.t.* **ban·died, ban·dy·ing** 1 To give and take; exchange, as blows, quips, or words. 2 To pass along; circulate: to *bandy* stories. [?]

ban·dy-leg·ged (ban′dē·leg′id, -legd′) *adj.* Bowlegged. [< earlier *bandy* crooked]

bane (bān) n. 1 Anything destructive or ruinous. 2 A deadly poison. [< OE *bana* murderer, destruction]

bane·ful (bān′fəl) *adj.* Injurious; deadly; ruinous. — **bane′ful·ly** *adv.* —**bane′ful·ness** n.

bang[1] (bang) n. 1 A sudden or noisy blow, thump, whack, or explosion. 2 *Informal* A sudden spurt of energy, activity, etc. 3 *Slang* Thrill; excitement. —*v.t.* 1 To beat, slam, or strike loudly. —*v.i.* 2 To make a heavy, loud sound. 3 To strike noisily. —*adv.* 1 Loudly and with force. 2 Suddenly. [< ON *banga* hammer, beat]

bang[2] (bang) n. Usu. *pl.* Front hair cut straight across. [?< BANG[1]]

bang[3] (bang) n. BHANG.

Bang·la Desh (bäng′glä·desh′) A nation situated on the NE part of the Indian subcontinent, coextensive with the former East Pakistan, 55,126 sq. mi., cap. Dacca. Also **Bang′la·desh′.** • See map at INDIA.

ban·gle (bang′gəl) n. A decorative bracelet or anklet. [< Hind. *bangrī* glass bracelet]

bang-up (bang′up′) *adj. Slang* Excellent.

ban·ish (ban′ish) *v.t.* 1 To compel to leave a country by political decree; exile. 2 To expel; drive away; dismiss, as a thought from one's mind. [< LL *banire*] —**ban′ish·er, ban′ish·ment** n.

ban·is·ter (ban′is·tər) n. Often *pl.* The railing on a staircase. [Alter. of BALUSTER]

ban·jo (ban′jō) n. *pl.* **·jos** A long-necked, stringed musical instrument having a circular body covered on top with stretched skin and played by plucking. [Alter. of *mbanza,* a similar instrument of Africa] — **ban′jo·ist** n.

Banjo

bank[1] (bangk) n. 1 Any mound-like formation or mass, as of ground, clouds, etc. 2 A steep rising, as of ground. 3 The slope of land at the edge of a body of water. 4 A large, raised portion of the bed of an ocean; also, a shallow; sandbar; shoal. 5 An upward lateral slope, as on the curve of a race track. 6 The cushioned edge of a billiard table. 7 *Aeron.* The sidewise inclination of an airplane in making a turn. —*v.t.* 1 To enclose, cover, or protect by a bank, dike, or border; embank. 2 To heap up into a bank or mound. 3 To cover (a fire) with fuel, ashes, etc., to keep it alive but burning low. 4 To give an upward lateral slope to, as the curve of a road. 5 To incline (an airplane) laterally. 6 In billiards and pool, to cause (a ball) to rebound at an angle from a cushion. — *v.i.* 7 To form or lie in banks. 8 To incline an airplane laterally. [ME *banke*]

bank[2] (bangk) n. 1 An institution for lending, borrowing, exchanging, issuing, or storing money. 2 An office or building used for such purposes. 3 The funds of a gaming establishment or the fund held by the dealer or banker in some gambling games. 4 A reserve supply of anything needed for future use: a blood *bank.* —*v.t.* 1 To deposit in a bank. —*v.i.* 2 To do business as or with a bank or banker. 3 In gambling, to keep the bank. —**bank on** *Informal* To rely or count on. [< Ital. *banca* money-changer's table] — **bank′er, bank′ing** n.

bank[3] (bangk) n. 1 A set of like articles grouped together in a line. 2 A rowers' bench in a galley. 3 A horizontal row of keys, as on a typewriter or organ. 4 In journalism, a subhead under a headline; deck. —*v.t.* To bring together in a bank. [< OF *banc* bench]

bank account Money deposited in a bank and subject to the withdrawal of the depositor.

bank·book (bangk′bŏŏk′) n. A book held by the depositor and serving as a record of deposits; passbook.

bank·note (bangk′nōt′) n. A promissory note, issued by a bank, payable on demand, and serving as a form of currency.

bank·rupt (bangk′rupt) n. 1 A person unable to pay his debts. 2 *Law* One judicially declared insolvent, whose property is administered for and divided among his creditors. 3 A person who has failed in or totally lacks something. —*adj.* 1 Being a bankrupt; insolvent. 2 Destitute or depleted: spiritually *bankrupt.* 3 Utterly ruined. —*v.t.* To make bankrupt. [< Ital. *banca rotta* bankruptcy, lit., broken counter] —**bank′rupt·cy** n. (*pl.* **·cies**)

ban·ner (ban′ər) n. 1 A piece of cloth, often long, bearing a design, motto, advertisement, etc. 2 Any flag or standard. 3 In journalism, a headline extending across a newspaper page. —*v.t.* To furnish with a banner. —*adj.* Leading; foremost; outstanding. [< LL *bandum* banner]

ban·nis·ter (ban′is·tər) n. BANISTER.

banns (banz) n. *pl. Eccl.* A public announcement of an intention to marry, usu. made on three successive Sundays. [< BAN]

ban·quet (bang′kwit) n. 1 A sumptuous feast. 2 A formal or ceremonial dinner, often followed by speeches. —*v.t. & v.i.* To entertain at a banquet; feast sumptuously. [< F *banc* bench, table] —**ban′quet·er** n.

ban·quette (bang·ket′) n. 1 *Mil.* A gunner's raised platform behind an earthwork. 2 An upholstered bench along a wall, as in a restaurant. **3** s *U.S.* A sidewalk. [<F *banc* bench]

ban·shee (ban'shē, ban·shē') *n.* In Gaelic folklore, a supernatural being whose wailing foretold a death. Also **ban'shie.**

ban·tam (ban'təm) *n.* **1** Any of various breeds of small domestic fowl. Also **Ban'tam. 2** A small, pugnacious person. —*adj.* Like a bantam; small; combative. [<*Bantam,* a town in Java]

ban·tam·weight (ban'təm·wāt') *n.* A boxer who weighs between 113 and 118 pounds.

ban·ter (ban'tər) *n.* Good-humored joking or repartee. — *v.t.* **1** To tease good-naturedly. —*v.i.* **2** To exchange good-natured repartee.[?] —**ban'ter·er** *n.* —**ban'ter·ing·ly** *adv.* — **Syn.** *n.* badinage, raillery.

Ban·tu (ban'tōō) *n. pl.* **Ban·tu** or **Ban·tus** (-tōōz) **1** A member of any of numerous Negro tribes of central and southern Africa. **2** A family of languages spoken by these tribes.

ban·tu·stan (ban'tōō·stan) *n. Usu. cap.* One of a number of enclaves for black South Africans within the Republic of South Africa.

ban·yan (ban'yən) *n.* An East Indian fig-bearing tree which sends down from its branches roots that become new trunks. [<Skt. *vanija* merchant, from the use of the ground under the tree as a market place]

ba·o·bab (bā'ō·bab, bä'ō-) *n.* An African tree with a thick trunk, bearing edible, gourdlike fruit. [<native African name]

bap·tism (bap'tiz·əm) *n.* **1** The act of baptizing or of being baptized. **2** Any initiatory or purifying experience. [<Gk. *baptismos* immersion] —**bap·tis·mal** (bap.tiz'məl) *adj.* —**bap·tis'mal·ly** *adv.*

Bap·tist (bap'tist) *n.* A member of a Protestant denomination holding that baptism should be given only to adult believers, and by immersion rather than by sprinkling. — **the Baptist** John the Baptist.

bap·tis·ter·y (bap'tis·tər·ē, -tis·trē) *n. pl.* **·ter·ies** A part of a church set apart for baptism. Also **bap'tis·try** (-trē).

bap·tize (bap·tīz', bap'tīz) *v.* **·tized, ·tiz·ing** *v.t.* **1** *Eccl.* To immerse in water or pour water on, symbolizing purification and admission into a specific church. **2** To christen or name at baptism. **3** To purify or cleanse. **4** To initiate. — *v.i.* **5** To administer baptism. [<Gk. *baptizein* immerse, wash] —**bap·tiz'er** *n.*

bar (bär) *n.* **1** A piece of solid material, evenly shaped and long in proportion to its width and thickness. **2** Any barrier or obstruction. **3** Any hindrance. **4** A sandbar. **5** The enclosed place in court occupied by counsel; also, the place where a prisoner stands to plead. **6** A court or any place of justice. **7** Lawyers collectively or the legal profession. **8** A room, establishment, or a counter where liquors or refreshments are dispensed. **9** A stripe; a band, as of color. **10** *Mil.* Small metal or cloth strips showing rank. **11** *Music* **a** Any of the vertical lines that mark off measures. **b** A double bar. **c** The unit of music between two bars; measure. **12** A handrail for certain ballet exercises; also, the exercises done at a bar. —*v.t.* **barred, bar·ring 1** To fasten, lock, or secure with or as with a bar. **2** To confine or shut out with or as with bars. **3** To obstruct or hinder. **4** To exclude or except. **5** To mark with bars. —*prep.* Excluding; excepting: *bar* none. [<LL *barra* bar] —**Syn.** *v.* **3** block, impede, thwart, check. **4** prohibit, reject, prevent, boycott.

BAR, B.A.R. Browning automatic rifle.

bar. barometer; barometric; barrel; barrister.

barb (bärb) *n.* **1** A backward-projecting point on a sharp weapon, as on an arrow, fish hook, etc. **2** A beard, as in certain grains and grasses; awn. **3** One of the threadlike outgrowths from the shaft of a feather. **4** A cutting remark. **5** Sting: the *barb* of his wit. —*v.t.* To provide with a barb or barbs. [<L *barba* beard] —**barbed, bar'bate** *adj.*

bar·bar·i·an (bär·bâr'ē·ən, -bar'-) *n.* **1** A member of a tribe or race thought of as uncivilized. **2** Any rude, brutal, or coarse person. **3** A person lacking culture. **4** Originally, a non-Greek, non-Roman, or non-Christian. —*adj.* **1** Uncivilized; cruel; barbarous. **2** Foreign; alien.

bar·bar·ic (bär·bar'ik) *adj.* **1** Of or characteristic of bar-

barians. **2** Wild; crude; uncouth.

bar·ba·rism (bär'bə·riz'əm) *n.* **1** The use of words or forms not standard in a language; also, an instance of this. **2** Rudeness, cruelty, or coarseness of manner, speech, acts, etc.; also, an instance of this. **3** An uncivilized state or condition.

bar·bar·i·ty (bär·bar'ə·tē) *n. pl.* **·ties 1** Brutal or barbarous conduct. **2** A cruel deed. **3** Crudeness or coarseness in taste or behavior; also, an instance of this.

bar·ba·rize (bär'bə·rīz) *v.* **·rized, ·riz·ing** *v.t.* To make barbarous; corrupt, as language. —*v.i.* To become barbarous.

bar·ba·rous (bär'bər·əs) *adj.* **1** Uncivilized. **2** Uncultivated; crude. **3** Cruel; savage. **4** Marked by barbarisms in speech; unpolished. **5** Rude or harsh in sound. [<Gk. *barbaros* non-Hellenic, foreign, rude] —**bar'ba·rous·ly** *adv.* —**bar'ba·rous·ness** *n.* —**Syn. 2** uncouth, unrefined, vulgar, coarse, gross. **3** brutal, inhuman, ferocious.

Barbary ape A tailless monkey of North Africa and Gibraltar.

bar·be·cue (bär'bə·kyōō) *n.* **1** An outdoor meal for which the food is roasted over an open fire. **2** Any meat roasted over an open fire. —*v.t.* **·cued, ·cu·ing 1** To roast (meat, fowl, etc.) over an open fire or in a trench. **2** To cook (meat) with a highly seasoned sauce. [<Taino *barbacoa* framework of sticks]

barbed wire Fence wire having sharp points or barbs at intervals.

bar·bel (bär'bəl) *n.* **1** One of the threadlike appendages on the jaws and mouth of certain fishes: an organ of touch. **2** A European fish having such appendages. [<L *barba* beard]

bar·bell (bär'bel') *n.* A bar with circular weights attached to each end, used for weightlifting exercises.

bar·ber (bär'bər) *n.* One who cuts the hair, shaves the beard, etc., as a business. —*v.t.* To cut or dress the hair of; shave or trim the beard of. [<L *barba* beard]

bar·ber·ry (bär'ber'ē, -bər·ē) *n.* **1** A thorny shrub bearing yellow flowers and red berries. **2** Its fruit. [<Ar. *barbārīs*]

bar·ber·shop (bär'bər·shop') *n.* The place of business of a barber. —*adj.* Characterized by close harmony, esp. of male voices in sentimental songs.

bar·bit·u·rate (bär·bich'ər·it, bär'bə·t'yōōr'it) *n.* Any of various derivatives of barbituric acid used in medicine to induce sedation or sleep.

bar·bi·tu·ric acid (bär'bə·t'yōōr'ik) A synthetic organic compound from which barbiturates are derived.[?]

bar·ca·role (bär'kə·rōl) *n.* **1** A Venetian gondolier's song. **2** A melody in imitation of this. Also **bar'ca·rolle.** [<F< Ital. *barca* boat]

bar code A code made up of a set of short vertical lines and spaces printed on something, designed to be machine-readable to yield a price, an address, etc.

bard (bärd) *n.* **1** A Celtic poet and minstrel. **2** A poet. — **bard'ic** *adj.*

bare[1] (bâr) *adj.* **1** Lacking its natural or usual covering. **2** Without clothes; naked. **3** Poorly supplied or unfurnished. **4** Destitute: *bare* of all comforts. **5** Without arms or equipment: with his *bare* hands. **6** Unadorned; undisguised: *bare* facts. **7** Not more than just suffices; mere. **8** Threadbare. —*v.t.* **bared, bar·ing** To make or lay bare; reveal; expose. [<OE *bær*] —**bare'ness** *n.*

bare[2] (bâr) Obsolete *p.t.* of BEAR.

bare·back (bâr'bak') *adj.* Riding a horse without a saddle. —*adv.* Without a saddle. —**bare'backed'** *adj.*

bare·faced (bâr'fāst') *adj.* **1** Having the face bare. **2** Unconcealed; open. **3** Impudent; audacious. —**bare·fac·ed·ly** (bâr'fā'sid·lē, -fāst'lē) *adv.* —**bare'fac'ed·ness** *n.*

bare·foot (bâr'fŏŏt') *adj. & adv.* With the feet bare. Also **bare'foot·ed** *adj.*

bare·hand·ed (bâr'han'did) *adj. & adv.* **1** With the hands uncovered. **2** Without weapons, tools, etc.

bare·head·ed (bâr'hed'id) *adj. & adv.* With the head bare.

bare·leg·ged (bâr'leg'id, -legd') *adj. & adv.* With the legs bare.

bare·ly (bâr′lē) *adv.* **1** Only just; scarcely. **2** Meagerly. **3** Openly; boldly; plainly.

bar·gain (bär′gən) *n.* **1** An agreement between persons, esp. one to buy or sell goods. **2** That which is agreed upon or the terms of the agreement. **3** The agreement as it affects one of the parties: a bad *bargain*. **4** An article bought or offered at a price favorable to the buyer. —*v.i.* **1** To discuss terms for selling or buying. **2** To make a bargain; reach an agreement. —*v.t.* **3** To barter or sell by bargaining. —**bargain for** (or **on**) To expect; count on: usu. in the negative: We didn't *bargain on* getting twins. [< OF *bargaine*]

barge (bärj) *n.* **1** A flat-bottomed freight boat for harbors and inland waters. **2** A large boat, for pleasure, state occasions, etc. —*v.* **barged, barg·ing** *v.t.* **1** To transport by barge. —*v.i.* **2** To move clumsily and slowly. **3** *Informal* To collide with: with *into.* **4** *Informal* To intrude; enter rudely: with *in* or *into.* [< OF] —**barge′man** *n.*

bar graph A graph in which parallel bars represent, by their lengths, numerical variations in a set of data.

bar·ite (bâr′īt, bâr′-) *n.* A crystalline barium sulfate mineral.

bar·i·tone (bar′ə·tōn) *n.* **1** A male voice higher than bass and lower than tenor. **2** One having such a voice. **3** A small tuba, used chiefly in military bands. —*adj.* **1** Of, like, or pertaining to a baritone. **2** Having the range of a baritone. [< Gk. *barytonos* deepsounding]

Bar graph

bar·i·um (bâr′ē·əm) *n.* A metallic element (symbol Ba) similar in properties to calcium but forming certain compounds that are poisonous.

barium sulfate An insoluble white salt, used in paints and in X-ray diagnosis.

bark[1] (bärk) *n.* **1** The short, explosive sound made by a dog. **2** Any sound like this. —*v.i.* **1** To utter a bark, as a dog, or to make a sound like a bark. **2** *Informal* To cough. **3** To speak loudly and sharply. **4** *Slang* To announce the attractions of a show at its entrance. —*v.t.* **5** To say roughly and curtly. [< OE *beorcan* to bark]

bark[2] (bärk) *n.* The covering of the stems, branches, and roots of a woody plant. —*v.t.* **1** To remove the bark from. **2** To rub off the skin of. **3** To tan or treat with an infusion of bark. [< Scand.]

bark[3] (bärk) *n.* **1** A three-masted vessel square-rigged except for the mizzenmast, which is foreand-aft rigged. **2** Any vessel or boat. [< LL *barca* boat]

bar·keep·er (bär′kē′pər) *n.* **1** One who owns or manages a bar where alcoholic liquors are served. **2** A bartender. Also **bar′·keep′.**

Bark

bar·ken·tine (bär′kən·tēn) *n.* A three-masted vessel square-rigged on the foremast and fore-and-aft rigged on the other two masts. [? < BARK[3] + (BRIG)ANTINE]

bark·er (bär′kər) *n.* **1** One who barks. **2** A person stationed at the entrance to a store, a show, etc., to attract patrons by loud, animated patter.

bar·ley (bär′lē) *n.* **1** A hardy, bearded cereal grass. **2** Its grain. [< OE *bærlic*]

bar·ley·corn (bär′lē·kôrn) *n.* A grain of barley. —**John Barleycorn** A humorous personification of intoxicating liquors.

barm (bärm) *n.* The froth rising on fermented malt liquors. [< OE *beorma* yeast]

bar·maid (bär′mād) *n.* A woman who tends bar.

bar mitz·vah (bär mits′və) *Often cap.* In Judaism, a boy commencing his thirteenth year, the age of religious duty; also, the ceremony celebrating this. Also **bar miz′vah.**

barm·y (bär′mē) *adj.* **barm·i·er, barm·i·est 1** Full of barm; frothy. **2** *Brit. Slang* Silly.

barn (bärn) *n.* A building for storing hay, stabling livestock, etc. [< OE *bern*]

bar·na·cle (bär′nə·kəl) *n.* **1** A marine shellfish that attaches itself firmly to rocks, ship bottoms, etc. **2** Something or someone that clings tenaciously. [ME *bernacle*] —**bar′na·cled** *adj.*

barn dance A party, originally held in a barn, for square dancing, etc.

barn owl An owl with brownish back and white breast flecked with black, often found in barns.

barn·storm (bärn′stôrm′) *v.i.* To tour rural districts, giving plays, making political speeches, giving exhibitions of stunt flying, etc. —**barn′storm′er, barn′storm′ing** *n.*

barn swallow A common swallow that frequently nests in the eaves of barns.

barn·yard (bärn′yärd′) *n.* An enclosed space adjoining a barn.

baro- *combining form* Pressure, esp. atmospheric pressure: *barometer.* [< Gk. *baros* weight]

Barn owl

bar·o·gram (bar′ə·gram) *n.* The record of a barograph.

bar·o·graph (bar′ə·graf, -gräf) *n.* A recording barometer. —**bar′o·graph′ic** *adj.*

ba·rom·e·ter (bə·rom′ə·tər) *n.* **1** An instrument for measuring atmospheric pressure. **2** Anything that indicates changes. —**bar·o·met·ric** (bar′ə·met′rik) or **·ri·cal** *adj.* —**bar′o·met′ri·cal·ly** *adv.* —**ba·rom′e·try** *n.*

bar·on (bar′ən) *n.* **1** A member of the lowest order of hereditary nobility in Great Britain, Japan, and several European countries; also, the dignity or rank itself. **2** One who has great power in a commercial field: a coal *baron.* [< LL *baro*] —**ba·ro·ni·al** (bə·rō′nē·əl) *adj.*

bar·on·age (bar′ən·ij) *n.* **1** Barons collectively. **2** The dignity or rank of a baron.

bar·on·ess (bar′ən·is) *n.* **1** The wife or widow of a baron. **2** A woman holding a barony.

bar·on·et (bar′ən·it, -ə·net) *n.* **1** An inheritable English title, below that of baron. **2** The bearer of the title, who is not a member of the nobility. —**bar′on·et·cy** (-sē) *n.*

bar·o·ny (bar′ə·nē) *n. pl.* **·nies** The rank, dignity, or domain of a baron.

ba·roque (bə·rōk′) *adj.* **1** Of, like, or characteristic of a style of art, architecture, and music that flourished in 16th- and 17th-century Europe, characterized by elaboration and profuse ornamentation. **2** Excessively elaborate and decorative. **3** Irregularly shaped: said of pearls. —*n.* **1** The baroque style. **2** An object, composition, or design in this style. [< Ital. *barroco*]

ba·rouche (bə·rōōsh′) *n.* A four-wheeled, low-bodied carriage with folding top, two inside seats, and an outside seat for the driver. [< Ital. *baroccio*]

barque (bärk) *n.* BARK[3].

bar·quen·tine (bär′kən·tēn) *n.* BARKENTINE.

bar·rack (bar′ək) *n.* **1** *pl.* A structure or group of structures for the housing of soldiers. **2** *pl.* A temporary or rough shelter for a gang of laborers, etc. —*v.t. & v.i.* To house in barracks. [< Ital. *baracca* soldiers' tent]

barracks bag A soldier's cloth bag for holding clothing and equipment. Also **barrack bag.**

bar·ra·cu·da (bar′ə·kōō′də) *n. pl.* **·da** or **·das** A voracious fish of tropical seas. [< Sp.]

bar·rage (bə·räzh′) *n.* **1** A curtain of artillery fire designed to prevent enemy advancement, protect one's own advancing troops, etc. **2** Any overwhelming attack, as of words or blows. —*v.t. & v.i.* **raged, rag·ing** To lay down a barrage (against) or subject to a barrage. [< F *(tir de) barrage* barrage (fire)]

bar·ran·ca (bə·rang′kə) *n. sw U.S.* A deep ravine or gorge. [< Sp.]

bar·ra·tor (bar′ə·tər) *n.* One guilty of barratry. Also **bar′ra·ter.**

bar·ra·try (bar′ə·trē) *n. pl.* **·tries 1** Any willful and unlawful act committed by the master or crew of a ship, whereby the owners suffer a loss. **2** *Law* The offense of habitually exciting lawsuits, quarrels, etc. [< OF *barat* fraud] —**bar′ra·trous** *adj.*

barred (bärd) *adj.* **1** Having or made of bars. **2** Obstructed by bars. **3** Striped. **4** Prohibited; not allowed.

bar·rel (bar′əl) *n.* **1** A large, round, wooden vessel, made with staves and hoops, having a flat base and top and slightly bulging sides. **2** As much as a barrel will hold; in liquid measure varying from 31 to 42 U.S. gallons. **3** Something resembling a barrel, as the rotating drum of a windlass, capstan, etc. **4** In firearms, the tube through which the projectile is discharged. • See REVOLVER. —*v.* **·reled** or **·relled, ·rel·ing** or **·rel·ling** —*v.t.* **1** To put or pack in a barrel. —*v.i.* **2** *Slang* To move at high speed. [< OF *baril*]

barrel organ HAND ORGAN.

bar·ren (bar′ən) *adj.* **1** Incapable of producing offspring; sterile. **2** Not producing crops, fruit, etc. **3** Unprofitable, as an enterprise. **4** Lacking in interest or attractiveness; dull. **5** Devoid; lacking: *barren* of any new ideas. —*n. Usu. pl.* A tract of level, usu. sandy, barren land. [< OF *baraigne*] —**bar′ren·ly** *adv.* —**bar′ren·ness** *n.*

Barren Grounds The tundra of northern Canada. Also **Barren Lands, Barrens.**

bar·rette (bə·ret′) *n.* A small bar or comb with a clasp, used for keeping a girl's or woman's hair in place. [< F *barre* bar]

bar·ri·cade (bar′ə·kād, bar′ə·kād′) *n.* **1** A barrier hastily built for obstruction or for defense. **2** Any obstruction or barrier closing a passage. —*v.t.* **·cad·ed, ·cad·ing** To enclose, obstruct, or defend with a barricade. [< Sp. *barricada* barrier < *barrica* barrel]

bar·ri·er (bar′ē·ər) *n.* **1** Something that prevents entrance, obstructs passage, etc., as a fence. **2** Anything that tends to separate or retard progress: a language *barrier*. **3** A boundary or limit. [< OF *barre* bar]

barrier reef A long, narrow ridge of rock or coral parallel to the coast and close to or above the surface of the sea.

bar·ring (bär′ing) *prep.* Excepting; apart from.

bar·ri·o (bär′rē·ō) *n. pl.* **·os** **1** In Spanish-speaking countries, a district or ward of a town or city. **2** *U.S.* A section of a city or town populated largely by Spanish-speaking people. [Sp.]

bar·ris·ter (bar′is·tər) *n.* In English law, a member of the legal profession who argues cases in the courts, as distinguished from a solicitor, who prepares them. [< BAR]

bar·room (bär′rŏŏm′, -rŏŏm′) *n.* A room where alcoholic liquors are served across a bar.

bar·row¹ (bar′ō) *n.* **1** WHEELBARROW. **2** HANDBARROW. **3** A two-wheeled pushcart, as that of a street vendor. [< OE *bearwe*]

bar·row² (bar′ō) *n.* **1** A burial mound. **2** A hill. [< OE *beorg*]

bar sinister BEND SINISTER.

Bart. Baronet.

bar·tend·er (bär′ten′dər) *n.* One who serves liquors over a bar.

bar·ter (bär′tər) *v.i.* **1** To exchange goods or services without use of money. —*v.t.* **2** To trade (one thing) for another of equal value. —*n.* **1** The act of bartering. **2** Something bartered. [< OF *barater* exchange] —**bar′ter·er** *n.*

bar·ti·zan (bär′tə·zən, bär′tə·zan′) *n.* A small turret jutting out from a tower or wall. [Alter. of *bratticing,* planking]

Bart·lett (bärt′lit) *n.* A variety of large, juicy pear. Also **Bartlett pear.** [< E. *Bartlett,* 1779–1860, U.S. merchant]

ba·ry·tes (bə·rī′tēz) *n.* BARITE.

ba·sal (bā′səl) *adj.* **1** Of, at, or being the base. **2** Basic; fundamental. —**ba′sal·ly** *adv.*

basal metabolism The energy, measured in calories, used by the body at rest in maintaining essential vital activities.

ba·salt (bə·sôlt′, bas′ôlt) *n.* A fine-grained, volcanic rock of high density and dark color. [< L *basaltes*] —**ba·sal′tic** *adj.*

bas·cule (bas′kyōōl) *n.* A mechanical apparatus of which each end counterbalances

Bartizan

the other, used in a kind of drawbridge (**bascule bridge**) operated by a counterpoise. [< F, see-saw]

base¹ (bās) *n.* **1** The lowest or supporting part of anything; bottom; foundation. **2** The essential or main part or element of anything: the *base* of our plan. **3** The essential ingredient or bottom layer of something: a tar *base*. **4** Any point, line, or quantity from which a measurement, inference, or conclusion is made; basis. **5** In certain games, a starting point or goal; esp. in baseball, any one of the four points of the diamond. **6** A place from which operations proceed, supplies are stored, etc.: a military *base*. **7** The point of attachment of a bodily organ. **8** *Archit.* The lowest part of a column, wall, etc. **9** *Chem.* **a** A compound capable of reacting with an acid to form a salt. **b** Any molecule or radical that takes up positive ions. **10** *Geom.* The side or face of a figure on which it appears to rest. **11** *Math.* A number whose powers are used as the various orders of units in a numeration system. **12** *Ling.* The form of a word used in making derivatives, as by adding prefixes or suffixes; root. **13** *Her.* The lower part of a shield. —**off base** **1** In baseball, not on the base one should be on. **2** *Informal* In error. —*v.t.* **based, bas·ing** **1** To put on a logical basis, as an argument, decision, or theory: with *on* or *upon.* **2** To make or form a base for. **3** To assign to a base: with *in* or *at.* —*adj.* Serving as a base. [< Gk. *basis* step, pedestal]

base² (bās) *adj.* **1** Vile; low; contemptible: *base* conduct. **2** Menial; degrading: *base* employment. **3** Inferior, as in quality. **4** Debased or counterfeit, as money. **5** Having comparatively little value: said of metals. [< LL *bassus* low] —**base′ly** *adv.* —**base′ness** *n.* —**Syn. 1** ignoble, infamous, mean, sordid, despicable. **2** miserable, wretched.

base·ball (bās′bôl′) *n.* **1** A game played with a wooden bat and a hard ball by two teams of nine players each, one team being at bat and the other in the field, alternately, for a minimum of nine innings. The game is played on a field having four bases in a diamond formation. **2** The ball used in this game.

base·board (bās′bôrd′, -bōrd′) *n.* **1** A board skirting the wall of a room, next to the floor. **2** A board forming a base.

base·born (bās′bôrn′) *adj.* **1** Born out of wedlock. **2** Of low birth. **3** Mean.

base hit In baseball, a hit by which the batter reaches base without help of an opposing player's error or without forcing out a runner previously on base.

base·less (bās′lis) *adj.* Without foundation in fact; unfounded; groundless. —**base′less·ness** *n.*

base line **1** In baseball, a path of a certain width connecting the bases. **2** In tennis, the line behind which the players serve. **3** Any line acting as a base.

base·ment (bās′mənt) *n.* **1** The lowest floor of a building, usu. underground. **2** The substructure of any building, structure, or member.

base runner In baseball, a member of the team at bat who has reached base.

bas·es¹ (bā′siz) *n.pl.* of BASE¹.

ba·ses² (bā′sēz) *n.pl.* of BASIS.

bash (bash) *v.t. Informal* To strike heavily; smash in. —*n.* **1** *Informal* A smashing blow. **2** *Slang* A gala party or gathering. [?]

bash·ful (bash′fəl) *adj.* Shy; timid; modest. [< ABASH + -FUL] —**bash′ful·ly** *adv.* —**bash′ful·ness** *n.*

ba·sic (bā′sik) *adj.* **1** Pertaining to, forming, or like a base or basis. **2** Essential; fundamental. **3** *Chem.* Having properties of a base; alkaline. —*n. Usu. pl.* The essential or fundamental principles, techniques, etc.: to learn the *basics* of good design. —**ba′si·cal·ly** *adv.*

bas·il (baz′əl) *n.* Any of certain aromatic plants of the mint family, used as a culinary herb. [< Gk. *basilikon (phyton)* royal (plant), basil]

bas·i·lar (bas′ə·lər) *adj.* At the base, esp. of the skull. Also **bas·i·lar·y** (bas′ə·ler′ē).

ba·sil·i·ca (bə·sil′i·kə) *n.* **1** In ancient Rome, a rectangular building divided into nave and aisles, used as a hall of justice, etc. **2** A church shaped like a Roman basilica. **3** A Roman Catholic church accorded certain liturgical privileges. [< Gk. *basilikos* royal] —**ba·sil′i·can** *adj.*

bas·i·lisk (bas′ə·lisk) *n.* **1** A fabled reptile whose breath and look were supposedly fatal. **2** A tropical American lizard having an erectile crest. [< Gk. *basiliskos,* dim. of *basileus* king]

ba·sin (bā′sən) *n.* **1** A round, wide, shallow vessel for holding liquids. **2** The amount that a basin will hold. **3** A sink or wash bowl. **4** A depression in the earth's surface, as a valley. **5** The region drained by a river. **6** A partially enclosed harbor or bay. **7** A bowllike depression in the floor of the ocean. [< LL *bacca*] **—ba′sined** *adj.*

Basilisk *def. 2*

ba·sis (bā′sis) *n. pl.* **ba·ses** (bā′sēz) **1** That on which anything rests; support; foundation. **2** Fundamental principle. **3** The main component of a thing. [< Gk., base, pedestal] **—Syn. 1** base, groundwork. **2** theory, premise.

bask (bask, bäsk) *v.i.* **1** To lie in and enjoy a pleasant warmth, as of the sun. **2** To enjoy a pleasing circumstance: to *bask* in the affection of a friend. [< Scand.]

bas·ket (bas′kit, bäs′-) *n.* **1** A container made of interwoven twigs, rushes, strips, etc. **2** Something resembling a basket, as the structure under a balloon for carrying passengers or ballast. **3** The amount a basket will hold. **4** In basketball, either of the goals, consisting of a cord net suspended from a metal ring; also, the point or points made by throwing the ball through the basket. [ME]

bas·ket·ball (bas′kit·bôl′, bäs′-) *n.* **1** A game played by two teams of five players each, in which the object is to throw the ball through the elevated goal (basket) at the opponent's end of a zoned, oblong court. **2** The inflated ball used in this game.

bas·ket·ry (bas′kit·rē, bäs′-) *n.* **1** Baskets collectively. **2** The art of making baskets.

bas·ket·weave (bas′kit·wēv′, bäs′-) *n.* A fabric weave that resembles the plaiting of a basket.

bas·ket·work (bas′kit·wûrk′, bäs′-) *n.* Work that is woven or textured like a basket; wickerwork.

basque (bask) *n.* A woman's closely fitting bodice, separate from the skirt. [F]

Basque (bask) *n.* **1** One of a people of unknown origin living in the w Pyrenees. **2** The language of the Basque people, unrelated to any other language. *—adj.* Of or pertaining to the Basques.

bas-re·lief (bä′ri·lēf′) *n.* Sculpture in which the figures project only slightly from the background. [F< Ital. *basso* low + *rilievo* relief]

bass[1] (bas) *n.* Any of various unrelated marine and freshwater food fishes having spiny fins. [< OE *bærs*]

bass[2] (bās) *n.* **1** The lowest-pitched male singing voice. **2** A deep, low sound, as of this voice or of low-pitched instruments. **3** The lowest of two or more musical parts. **4** A low-pitched musical instrument, esp. a double bass. *—adj.* **1** Low in pitch or range. **2** Pertaining to, for, or able to play bass. [< OE *bas* low, base]

bass[3] (bas) *n.* **1** LINDEN. **2** BAST. [Alter. of BAST]

bass drum (bās) A large drum producing a sound of low frequency. • See DRUM.

bas·set (bas′it) *n.* A hound with a long, low body, long head and nose, and short, heavy, crooked forelegs. Also **bas′set·hound′** (-hound′). [< OF *bas* low]

basset horn A tenor clarinet. [< Ital. < *bassetto,* dim. of *basso* low + *corno* horn]

bass horn (bās) TUBA.

bas·si·net (bas′ə·net′) *n.* **1** A partly hooded basket, used as a cradle. **2** A small basket for holding the clothing of an infant. [< F *bassin* basin]

bas·so (bas′ō, *Ital.* bäs′sō) *n. pl.* **bas·sos** (bas′ōz) or *Ital.* **bas·si** (bäs′sē) **1** A bass singer. **2** The bass part. [Ital., low]

bas·soon (ba·sōōn′, bə-) *n.* A large, double-reed woodwind instrument with a long, curved mouthpiece. [< F *bas* low]

bass viol (bās vī′əl) *Music* DOUBLE BASS.

Bassoon

bass·wood (bas′wŏŏd′) *n.* LINDEN.

bast (bast) *n. Bot.* **1** The food-conducting tissue of vascular plants; phloem. **2** Fibrous vegetable material used for making cordage, etc. [< OE *bæst*]

bas·tard (bas′tərd) *n.* **1** An illegitimate child. **2** Any hybrid plant, tree, or animal. **3** Any irregular, inferior, or counterfeit thing. *—adj.* **1** Born out of wedlock. **2** False; spurious. **3** Resembling but not typical of the genuine thing. **4** Abnormal or irregular in size, shape, or proportion. [< OF *fils de bast* packsaddle child] **—bas′tard·ly** *adv.* **—bas′tar·dy** *n.*

bas·tard·ize (bas′tər·dīz) *v.* **·ized, ·iz·ing** *v.t.* **1** To prove to be, or stigmatize as, a bastard. **2** To debase. *—v.i.* **3** To become debased. **—bas′tard·i·za′tion** *n.*

baste[1] (bāst) *v.t.* **bast·ed, bast·ing** To sew together with long, temporary stitches. [< OF *bastir*]

baste[2] (bāst) *v.t.* **bast·ed, bast·ing** To moisten (meat or fish) with drippings, butter, etc., while cooking. [?]

baste[3] (bāst) *v.t. Informal.* **1** To thrash. **2** To attack verbally; abuse. [prob. < Scand.]

bas·tille (bas·tēl′) *n.* A prison. Also **bas·tile′.** **—the Bastille** A fortress in Paris serving as a prison until its destruction July 14, 1789 in the French Revolution. [< OF]

bas·ti·na·do (bas′tə·nā′dō) *n. pl.* **·does** **1** A beating with a stick, usu. on the soles of the feet. **2** A stick or cudgel. *—v.t.* **·doed, ·do·ing** To beat with a stick, usu. on the soles of the feet. Also **bas′ti·nade′.** [< Sp. *bastón* cudgel]

bast·ing (bās′ting) *n.* **1** The act of sewing loosely together. **2** *pl.* Loose, temporary stitches. **3** The thread used. [< BASTE[1]]

bas·tion (bas′chən, -tē·ən) *n.* **1** In fortifications, a projecting part. **2** Any fortified or strongly defended place or position. [< Ital. *bastione*] **—bas′tioned** *adj.*

Ba·su·to·land (bə·sōō′tō·land′) *n.* A former British colony in s Africa, now the nation of Lesotho. • See map at AFRICA.

bat[1] (bat) *n.* **1** In baseball, cricket, and other games: **a** A stick or club for batting the ball. **b** The act of batting. **c** A turn at batting. **d** A racket or paddle, as in table tennis, badminton, etc. **e** The batsman, as in cricket. **2** Any heavy club or cudgel. **3** *Informal* A blow, as with a stick. **4** *Slang* A drunken spree. **—go to bat for** *Informal* To defend or advocate the cause of. *—v.* **bat·ted, bat·ting** *—v.i.* **1** In baseball, cricket, and other games: **a** To use a bat. **b** To take a turn at bat. *—v.t.* **2** To strike with or as with a bat. **3** To have a batting average of. **—bat around** *Slang* **1** To travel about. **2** To discuss. [< OE *batt* cudgel]

bat[2] (bat) *n.* A nocturnal flying mammal having elongated forelimbs and digits that support a thin wing membrane. [< Scand.]

bat[3] (bat) *v.t. Informal* To wink; flutter. **—not bat an eye** or **eyelash** *Informal* To fail to show surprise. [< F *battre* to beat (as wings)]

batch (bach) *n.* **1** The quantity of bread, etc., baked at one time. **2** The amount of material required for one operation. **3** The amount produced at one operation. **4** Persons or things in a group; lot. [< OE *bacan* to bake]

bate (bāt) *v.t.* **bat·ed, bat·ing** To lessen; moderate. [Var. of ABATE]

ba·teau (ba·tō′) *n. pl.* **·teaux** (-tōz′) **1** A light, flat-bottomed boat. **2** A pontoon for a floating bridge. [F < OE *batel,* ult. < Gmc.]

bat·fish (bat′fish′) *n.* Any of various marine fishes having broad, flat bodies suggestive of a bat's wings.

bath (bath, bäth) *n. pl.* **baths** (bathz, bäthz; baths, bäths) **1** The act of washing or immersing something, esp. the body, in water or other liquid. **2** The liquid used for this. **3** The container for such a liquid, as a bathtub. **4** A bathroom. **5** *Often pl.* A set of rooms or a building for bathing. **6** *Often pl.* A resort where bathing is part of a medical treatment. *—v.t. Brit.* To bathe. [< OE *bæth*]

bathe (bāth) *v.* **bathed, bath·ing** *v.t.* **1** To place in liquid; immerse. **2** To wash; wet. **3** To apply liquid to, as for comfort or healing. **4** To cover or suffuse as with liquid: The hill was *bathed* in light. *—v.i.* **5** To take a bath. **6** To go into or remain in water so as to swim or cool off. **7** To be covered or suffused as if with liquid: to *bathe* photographic prints in a fixer solution. *—n. Brit.* The act of bathing, as in the sea. [< OE *bathian*] **—bath′er** *n.*

bath·house (bath′hous′, bäth′-) *n.* **1** A building for taking baths. **2** A dressing room or rooms for bathers.

bath·ing suit (bāth′ing) A garment worn for swimming.

ba·thos (bā′thos) *n.* **1** A descent from the lofty to the trite in discourse. **2** Insincere pathos; sentimentality. [< Gk. *bathys* deep] —**ba·thet·ic** (bə·thet′ik) *adj.*

bath·robe (bath′rōb′, bäth′-) *n.* A long, loose garment for wear before and after bathing.

bath·room (bath′rōōm′, -rōōm′, bäth′-) *n.* **1** A room in which to bathe. **2** A toilet.

bath·tub (bath′tub′, bäth′-) *n.* A tub in which to bathe, esp. one in a bathroom.

bathy- *combining form* Deep: of the ocean depths: *bathysphere*. [< Gk. *bathys* deep]

bath·y·scaph (bath′ə·skaf) *n.* A self-propelled diving ship for deep-sea exploration. Also **bath·y·scaphe** (-skaf, -skāf). [< BATHY- + Gk. *skaphē* bowl]

bath·y·sphere (bath′ə·sfir) *n.* A spherical, cable-lowered, diving chamber with windows for deep-sea observations. [< BATHY- + SPHERE]

ba·tik (bə·tēk′, bat′ik) *n.* **1** A process for dyeing fabrics in which those areas not to be dyed are covered with wax. **2** A fabric so dyed. —*adj.* Of batik. [< Malay]

ba·tiste (bə·tēst′) *n.* A sheer, cotton fabric. [< Jean *Baptiste*, 13th c. French linen weaver]

ba·ton (bə·ton′, ba·ton′) *n.* **1** A short staff borne as an emblem of authority or privilege. **2** *Music* A slender stick or rod used for conducting. **3** A short stick passed from one runner to another in relay racing. **4** A hollow metal rod, knobbed at one end, twirled as by a drum majorette. [< LL *bastum* stick]

ba·tra·chi·an (bə·trā′kē·ən) *adj.* Of frogs and toads. [< Gk. *batrachos* frog]

bat·tal·ion (bə·tal′yən) *n.* **1** *Mil.* **a** A regimental unit, consisting of a headquarters and two or more companies, batteries, or comparable units. **b** A body of troops. **2** *Usu. pl.* A large group or number. [< Ital. *battaglione*]

bat·ten[1] (bat′n) *v.i.* **1** To grow fat or thrive. **2** To live well, esp. at another's expense. —*v.t.* **3** To make fat, as cattle. [< ON *batna* grow better, improve]

bat·ten[2] (bat′n) *n.* **1** A narrow strip of wood, often nailed across parallel boards as reinforcement. **2** *Naut.* A thin strip of wood placed in a sail to keep it flat or used to fasten down a tarpaulin covering on a hatchway. —*v.t.* To strengthen or fasten with battens. [Var. of BATON]

bat·ter[1] (bat′ər) *v.t.* **1** To strike with repeated, violent blows. **2** To break or injure with or as with such blows. — *v.i.* **3** To beat with blow after blow. [< L *battuere* beat]

bat·ter[2] (bat′ər) *n.* In baseball and cricket, the player whose turn it is to bat.

bat·ter[3] (bat′ər) *n.* A liquid mixture of eggs, flour, milk, etc., used for making pancakes, cakes, etc. [< OF *battre* beat]

bat·ter·ing-ram (bat′ər·ing·ram′) *n.* **1** A long, stout beam, used in ancient warfare for forcing gates and making breaches in walls. **2** Any similar device used to make forced entrance.

bat·ter·y (bat′ər·ē) *n. pl.* **·ter·ies** **1** Any group or array of similar things used or connected together to serve a common end or purpose. **2** *Electr.* **a** An array of similar parts or devices, esp. primary or secondary cells, connected together. **b** A primary cell: a flashlight *battery*. **3** *Mil.* **a** A unit of an artillery regiment equivalent to an infantry company. **b** A group of heavy artillery, as guns, missiles, etc. **4** *Law* The illegal beating or touching of another person. **5** In baseball, the pitcher and catcher together. **6** *Music* The percussion instruments of an orchestra. [< F *battre* beat]

bat·tik (bə·tēk′, bat′ik) *n.* BATIK.

bat·ting (bat′ing) *n.* Wadded cotton or other fiber prepared in sheets or rolls.

bat·tle (bat′l) *n.* **1** An extensive combat between hostile armies or fleets. **2** Any fighting, dispute, or conflict. —*v.* **bat·tled, bat·tling** —*v.i.* **1** To contend in or as in battle; struggle. —*v.t.* **2** To fight. [< LL *battuere* beat] —**bat′tler** *n.* — **Syn.** *n.* **1** engagement, encounter. *v.* **1** vie.

bat·tle-ax (bat′l·aks′) *n.* **1** A large ax formerly used in battle; a broad-ax. **2** *Slang* An aggressively contentious woman. Also **bat′tle-axe′**.

battle cruiser A war vessel less heavily armored but faster than a battleship.

battle cry **1** A shout used by troops in battle. **2** A rallying slogan or identifying phrase.

bat·tle·dore (bat′l·dôr, -dōr) *n.* **1** A paddle or bat, used to drive a shuttlecock. **2** The game in which a shuttlecock is so batted: also **battledore and shuttlecock**. [? < Provençal *batedor* an implement for beating]

battle fatigue A psychoneurotic condition occurring among soldiers engaged in prolonged combat.

bat·tle·field (bat′l·fēld′) *n.* The ground on which a battle is fought. Also **bat′tle·ground′** (-ground′).

bat·tle·ment (bat′l·mənt) *n.* A parapet indented along its upper line. —**bat·tle·ment·ed** (bat′l·men′tid) *adj.* [< OF *batailler* fortify]

battle royal **1** A fight involving numerous combatants. **2** A protracted, rigorous dispute.

bat·tle·ship (bat′l·ship′) *n. Nav.* A large warship having heavy armor and powerful guns.

bat·ty (bat′ē) *adj.* **·ti·er, ·ti·est** *Slang* Crazy; odd.

Battlement

bau·ble (bô′bəl) *n.* A worthless, showy trinket or trifle. [< OF *baubel* toy]

baulk (bôk) *v.* BALK.

baux·ite (bôk′sīt, bō′zīt) *n.* A claylike mineral of varying composition, the principal ore of aluminum. [< Les *Baux*, town in southern France]

bawd (bôd) *n.* The keeper of a brothel; a procuress. [ME *bawde*]

bawd·y (bô′dē) *adj.* **bawd·i·er, bawd·i·est** Obscene; indecent. —**bawd′i·ly** adv. —**bawd′i·ness** *n.* —**Syn.** improper, lewd, immodest, salacious, lascivious.

bawd·y-house (bô′dē·hous′) *n.* A brothel.

bawl (bôl) *v.t.* **1** To proclaim or call out noisily; bellow. — *v.i.* **2** To weep or sob noisily. —**bawl out** *Slang* To scold; berate. —*n.* A loud outcry. [< Scand.] —**bawl′er** *n.*

bay[1] (bā) *n.* A body of water partly enclosed by land; an inlet of a sea or lake. [< LL *baia*]

bay[2] (bā) *n.* **1** A space or compartment separated from others in a structure, as in an aircraft. **2** *Archit.* **a** BAY WINDOW. **b** A wing of a building. [< F *baie* < *bayer* gape]

bay[3] (bā) *adj.* Reddish brown: said esp. of horses. —*n.* **1** A horse or other animal of this color. **2** This color. [< L *badius*]

bay[4] (bā) *n.* **1** A deep bark or cry, as of dogs in hunting. **2** The situation of or as of a hunted creature compelled to turn on its pursuers. —**at bay** **1** Cornered; with no escape. **2** Held off: He kept his attackers *at bay*. —**bring to bay** To force into a position from which there is no escape. —*v.i.* **1** To utter a deep-throated, prolonged bark, as a hound. —*v.t.* **2** To utter as with this bark: to *bay* defiance. **3** To bring to bay. [< OF *abai* a barking]

bay[5] (bā) *n.* **1** A laurel wreath, bestowed as a token of honor. **2** *pl.* Fame; poetic renown. **3** BAYBERRY. **4** Any of several trees and shrubs resembling the laurels. [< L *baca* berry]

bay·ber·ry (bā′ber′ē, -bər·ē) *n. pl.* **·ber·ries** **1** Any of various trees, as the wax myrtle or laurel, or its fruit. **2** A tropical American tree whose leaves are used in making bay rum. [< BAY[5] + BERRY]

bay·o·net (bā′ə·nit, -net′, bā′ə·net′) *n.* A daggerlike weapon attachable to the muzzle of a rifle, for close fighting. — *v.t.* **·net·ed, ·net·ing** To stab or pierce with a bayonet. [< *Bayonne*, France, where first made]

Bayonets

bay·ou (bī′ōō) *n.* A marshy inlet or outlet of a lake, bay, river, etc. [< Choctaw *bayuk* small stream]

bay rum An aromatic liquid used in medicines and cosmetics. [< BAY⁵]

bay window 1 A window structure projecting from the wall of a building. 2 *Slang* A protruding abdomen.

ba·zaar (bə-zär′) *n.* 1 An Oriental market place or range of shops. 2 A shop or store for the sale of miscellaneous wares. 3 A sale of miscellaneous articles, as for charity. Also **ba·zar′.** [< Pers. *bāzār* market]

ba·zoo·ka (bə-zōō′kə) *n. Mil.* A long, tubular launcher which fires an explosive rocket at short range. [< the *bazooka,* a comical musical instrument]

BB A standard, commercial size of lead shot, 0.18 in. in diameter.

B.B.A., B. Bus. Ad. Bachelor of Business Administration.

BBC, B.B.C. British Broadcasting Corporation.

bbl, bbl. barrel; barrels.

B.C. before Christ; British Columbia.

bch. bunch.

B.D. Bachelor of Divinity.

B/D., b.d. bank draft; bills discounted.

bd. board; bond; bound; bundle.

bd. ft. board feet.

bdl., bdle. bundle.

be (bē, *unstressed* bi) *v.i.* **been, be·ing** Present indicative: I **am,** he, she, it **is,** we, you, they **are;** past indicative: I, he, she, it **was,** we, you, they **were;** present subjunctive: **be;** past subjunctive: **were;** archaic forms: thou **art** (present); thou **wast** or **wert** (past). 1 As a substantive verb, *be* is used to mean: **a** To have existence, truth, or actuality: There *are* bears in the zoo. **b** To take place; happen: The party *is* next week. **c** To stay or continue: She *was* here for one week. **d** To belong; befall: often with *to* or *unto:* Joy *be* unto you. 2 As a copulative verb, *be* forms a link between the subject and the predicate noun, pronoun, or adjective: This *is* Charles; I *am* he; they both *are* sick; it also forms infinitive and participial phrases: the pleasure of *being* here. 3 As an auxiliary verb, *be* is used: **a** With the present participle of other verbs to express continuous or progressive action: I *am* working. **b** With the past participle of transitive verbs to form the passive voice: He *was* injured. **c** With the past participle of intransitive verbs to form the perfect tense: I *am* finished. **d** With the infinitive or present participle to express purpose, duty, possibility, futurity, etc.: We *are* to start on Monday. [< OE *bēon*]

be- *prefix* Used to form words from nouns, adjectives, and verbs with the following meanings: 1 (from verbs) Around; all over; throughout: *besmudge, besprinkle.* 2 (from verbs) Completely; thoroughly: *bemuddle; beset.* 3 (from verbs) Off; away: *behead.* 4 (from intransitive verbs) About; at; on; over; against; for: *beswarm; beweep.* 5 (from adjectives and nouns) To make; cause to be: *befoul.* 6 (from nouns) To provide with; affect by; cover with: *bejewel; begloom.* 7 (from adjectives usu. in past participial forms) Furnished or covered with, usu. excessively: *bespangled; beribboned.* [< OE *be-, bi-*]

B.E. Bachelor of Education; Bachelor of Engineering; Bank of England; Board of Education.

BE, B/E bill of exchange.

Be beryllium.

beach (bēch) *n.* 1 The shore of a body of water, as of a lake or sea, esp. when covered with sand or pebbles. 2 Loose pebbles on the shore; shingle. —*v.t. & v.i.* To drive or haul up (a boat or ship) on a beach; strand. [?]

beach·comb·er (bēch′kō′mər) *n.* 1 A vagrant living on what he can find or beg around the wharves and beaches of ports. 2 A long wave rolling upon the beach.

beach·head (bēch′hed′) *n. Mil.* A landing position on a hostile shore established by an advance invasion force.

bea·con (bē′kən) *n.* 1 A signal fire or light on a hill, tower, or the like. 2 A lighthouse or other warning signal on a coast or shoreline. 3 Something that serves as a conspicuous warning or a guide. 4 *Aeron.* A radio device used to establish and plot flight courses. —*v.t.* 1 To furnish with a beacon. —*v.i.* 2 To shine or serve as a beacon. [< OE *bēacen* sign, signal]

bead (bēd) *n.* 1 Any small, usu. round piece of glass, wood, stone, etc., perforated and intended to be strung or attached to a fabric. 2 *pl.* A string of beads. 3 *pl.* A rosary.

4 Froth; foam. 5 A liquid drop, as of sweat. 6 A small spherical knob used as the front sight of a gun. 7 *Archit.* A molding composed of a row of half-oval ornaments. — **draw a bead on** To take careful aim at. —*v.t.* 1 To decorate with beads or beading. —*v.i.* 2 To collect in beads or drops. [< OE *gebed* prayer]

bead·ing (bē′ding) *n.* 1 Ornamentation of beads. 2 Any narrow trimming. 3 A decorative work made with beads.

bea·dle (bēd′l) *n.* In the Church of England, a minor parish officer who ushers, etc. [< OE *bydel* messenger]

beads·man (bēdz′mən) *n. pl.* **·men** (-mən) One who prays for another, esp. when hired to do so. —**beads′wom′an** *n. Fem.*

bead·y (bē′dē) *adj.* **bead·i·er, bead·i·est** 1 Small and glittering, like beads. 2 Decorated with beads. 3 Foamy.

bea·gle (bē′gəl) *n.* A small, short-coated hound with short legs and drooping ears. [ME *begle*]

Beagle

beak (bēk) *n.* 1 The horny projecting mouth parts of birds; the bill. 2 A beaklike part or organ, as the horny jaws of turtles. 3 *Slang* The nose of a person. 4 Something shaped like a beak, as the spout of a pitcher. [< L *beccus*] —**beaked** (bēkt, bē′kid) *adj.*

beak·er (bē′kər) *n.* 1 A large, wide-mouthed cup or goblet. 2 A cylindrical, flat-bottomed vessel with a pouring lip, used in laboratories. 3 The contents or capacity of a beaker. [< ON *bikarr*]

beam (bēm) *n.* 1 A long, horizontal piece of material forming part of a structure. 2 *Naut.* **a** One of the heavy pieces of timber or iron set transversely across a vessel. **b** The greatest width of a vessel. 3 The widest part of anything. 4 The bar of a balance; also, the balance. 5 *Slang* The hips. 6 A ray or a group of nearly parallel rays of light or other radiant energy. 7 A radiant smile. 8 *Aeron.* A continuous radio signal used as a beacon: also **radio beam.** —**off the beam** 1 *Aeron.* Not following the radio beam. 2 *Informal* On the wrong track; wrong. —**on the beam** 1 *Aeron.* Following the radio beam. 2 *Informal* **a** Functioning well or quickly. **b** In the right direction; correct. —*v.t.* 1 To send out in or as in beams or rays. 2 *Telecom.* To aim or transmit (a signal) in a specific direction. 3 *Aeron.* To guide (an airplane) by a radio beam. —*v.i.* 4 To emit light. 5 To smile or grin radiantly. [< OE *bēam* tree]

beam·ing (bē′ming) *adj.* Radiant; bright; cheerful. — **beam′ing·ly** *adv.*

beam·y (bē′mē) *adj.* **beam·i·er, beam·i·est** 1 Sending out beams of light; radiant. 2 Like a beam; massive; broad.

bean (bēn) *n.* 1 The oval edible seed of various leguminous plants. 2 A plant that bears beans. 3 One of several beanlike seeds or plants. 4 *Slang* The head. —*v.t. Slang* To hit on the head. [< OE *bēan*]

bear[1] (bâr) *v.* **bore** (*Archaic* **bare**), **borne** or **born, bear·ing** *v.t.* 1 To support; hold up. 2 To carry; convey. 3 To show visibly; carry: to *bear* a scar. 4 To conduct or guide. 5 To spread: to *bear* tales. 6 To hold in the mind: to *bear* a grudge. 7 To suffer or endure; undergo. 8 To accept or assume, as responsibility. 9 To give birth to (see note below). 10 To conduct or comport (oneself). 11 To manage or carry (oneself or a part of oneself). 12 To render; give: to *bear* witness. 13 To be able to withstand; allow: His story will not *bear* investigation. 14 To have or stand (in comparison or relation): with *to:* What relation does this *bear* to the other? 15 To possess as a right or power: to *bear* title. —*v.i.* 16 To carry burdens; convey. 17 To rest heavily; lean; press. 18 To endure patiently; suffer: often with *with.* 19 To produce fruit or young. 20 To move, point, or lie in a certain direction: Later, we *bore* west. 21 To be relevant; have reference: with *on* or *upon.* —**bear down upon** 1 To approach. 2 To put pressure on. —**bear out** To confirm; justify. [< OE *beran*] • In def. 9, meaning *to give birth to, borne* is the participle used when speaking of the mother or when followed by *by:* She has *borne* twins; The twins were *borne* by her. When speaking of the offspring, *born* is used: He was *born* today. In all other meanings, the participle *borne* is the only one used: They have *borne* their troubles well; *air-borne* bacteria.

bear[2] (bâr) *n.* 1 Any of various large carnivorous or omnivorous mammals with massive thick-furred body and short tail. 2 An ill-mannered, grumpy, or clumsy person. 3 A speculator who sells shares of stock, etc., in the belief that prices will decline and he can buy later at a profit. — *adj.* Of or favorable to bears (def. 3). [< OE *bera*]

Bear

Bear (bâr) *n.* Either of two constellations, the Great Bear or the Little Bear.

bear·a·ble (bâr′ə·bəl) *adj.* Capable of being borne or endured. —**bear′a·ble·ness** *n.* —**bear′a·bly** *adv.*

beard (bird) *n.* 1 The hair on a man's face, esp. on the chin. 2 The long hair on the chin of some animals, as the goat. 3 Any similar growth or appendage. 4 *Bot.* A tuft of hairlike processes; an awn. • See WHEAT. —*v.t.* 1 To defy courageously. 2 To furnish with a beard. [< OE] —**beard′ed** *adj.*

bear·er (bâr′ər) *n.* 1 One who or that which bears, carries, or has in possession. 2 A person who presents a check, money order, etc., for payment. 3 A tree or vine producing fruit. 4 PALLBEARER.

bear·ing (bâr′ing) *n.* 1 Manner of conducting or carrying oneself. 2 The act, capacity, or period of producing. 3 That which is produced; yield. 4 Endurance. 5 A direction in relation to the compass or another point or place. 6 *Usu. pl.* The position or attitude of something relative to that of another. 7 *pl.* An awareness of one's position or surroundings. 8 Relevance; connection. 9 *Mech.* That part of a machine on which something moves, turns, etc.

bear·ish (bâr′ish) *adj.* 1 Like a bear; rough; surly. 2 Tending to depress the price of stocks by offering to sell. —**bear′ish·ly** *adv.* —**bear′ish·ness** *n.*

bear·skin (bâr′skin′) *n.* The skin of a bear or a garment or rug made of it.

beast (bēst) *n.* 1 Any animal except man. 2 Any large quadruped. 3 Animal characteristics or animal nature. 4 A cruel, rude, or filthy person. [< L *bestia* beast]

beast·ly (bēst′lē) *adj.* **beast·li·er, beast·li·est** 1 Resembling a beast; brutish; vile. 2 *Informal* Disagreeable or unpleasant; nasty; abominable. —*adj. Brit. Slang* Very. —**beast′·li·ness** *n.*

beat (bēt) *v.* **beat, beat·en** (*Informal* **beat**), **beat·ing** *v.t.* 1 To strike repeatedly; pound. 2 To punish in this way; thrash. 3 To dash or strike against. 4 To make, as a path, by repeated walking, blows, pushing, etc. 5 To forge or shape by hammering. 6 To walk on for a long time. 7 To defeat or outdo. 8 To flap; flutter, as wings. 9 *Music* To mark (time or rhythm) with or as with a baton. 10 To hunt over; search. 11 To sound (a signal) as on a drum. 12 To whip (ingredients) so as to make lighter or frothier. 13 *Informal* To baffle; perplex: It *beats* me. 14 *Slang* To defraud; swindle. —*v.i.* 15 To strike repeated blows. 16 To strike or pound as with blows. 17 To throb; pulsate. 18 To give forth sound, as when struck. 19 To sound a signal, as on a drum. 20 *Physics* To fluctuate periodically in intensity. 21 To be adaptable to beating: The yolk *beats* well. 22 To hunt through underbrush, etc., as for game. 23 To win a victory or contest. —**beat around the bush** To be evasive. —**beat it** *Slang* To go hastily. —**beat up** *Informal* To thrash thoroughly. —*n.* 1 A stroke or blow. 2 A pulsation or throb, as of the pulse. 3 *Physics* A periodic reinforcement and cancellation that results when waves of slightly different frequencies interact. 4 *Naut.* A tack. 5 *Music* a One of a series of pulses used to mark time in music. b The gesture or symbol for this. 6 A round, line, or district regularly traversed, as by a sentry or a policeman. 7 *Slang* A scoop for a newspaper. 8 *Slang* A deadbeat. 9 *Informal* A beatnik. —*adj.* 1 *Informal* Fatigued; worn out. 2 Of or pertaining to the Beat Generation. [< OE *bēatan*]

beat·en (bēt′n) *adj.* 1 Struck by repeated blows; thrashed. 2 Shaped or made thin by beating. 3 Worn by use or much travel. 4 Defeated. 5 Utterly discouraged or fatigued.

Beat Generation A group of young people who, esp. in the 1950's, expressed a growing social disillusionment by adopting unconventional modes of dress and behavior, Eastern philosophies, etc.

be·a·tif·ic (bē′ə·tif′ik) *adj.* Showing or imparting great joy or blessedness. —**be·a·tif′i·cal·ly** *adv.*

be·at·i·fy (bē·at′ə·fī) *v.t.* **·fied, ·fy·ing** 1 To make supremely happy. 2 In the Roman Catholic Church, to declare as blessed and worthy for public honor by an act of the Pope. 3 To exalt above others. [< L *beatus* happy, blessed + *facere* make] —**be·at·i·fi·ca·tion** (bē·at′ə·fi·kā′shən) *n.*

beat·ing (bē′ting) *n.* 1 The action of one who or that which beats. 2 A flogging. 3 Pulsation; throbbing. 4 A defeat.

be·at·i·tude (bē·at′ə·tyōod) *n.* Supreme blessedness. —**the Beatitudes** The declarations of special blessedness in the Sermon on the Mount. *Matt.* 5:3–11. [< L *beatitudo* blessedness]

beat·nik (bēt′nik) *n.* A member of the Beat Generation. [< BEAT, *adj.* def. 2 + -NIK]

beau (bō) *n. pl.* **beaus** or **beaux** (bōz) 1 A lover or suitor of a girl or woman. 2 An escort. [< F < L *bellus* fine, pretty]

Beau·fort scale (bō′fərt) *Meteorol.* A scale of wind velocities, ranging from 0 (calm) to 12 (hurricane). [< Sir Francis *Beaufort*, 1774–1857, British admiral]

beau·te·ous (byōo′tē·əs) *adj.* Beautiful. —**beau′te·ous·ly** *adv.* —**beau′te·ous·ness** *n.*

beau·ti·cian (byōo·tish′ən) *n.* One who works in a beauty parlor, or a person trained in hairdressing, manicuring, massaging, etc.

beau·ti·ful (byōo′tə·fəl) *adj.* Possessing beauty. —**beau′ti·ful·ly** *adv.* —**Syn.** attractive, comely, exquisite, fair, handsome, lovely, pretty.

beau·ti·fy (byōo′tə·fī) *v.t. & v.i.* **·fied, ·fy·ing** To make or grow beautiful; embellish; adorn. —**beau′ti·fi·ca′tion, beau′ti·fi′er** *n.*

beau·ty (byōo′tē) *n. pl.* **·ties** 1 Any of those attributes of form, sound, color, execution, character, behavior, etc., which give pleasure and gratification to the senses or to the mind. 2 A person or thing that is beautiful, esp. a woman. 3 Physical attractiveness. 4 Any special or compelling feature. [< OF *beaute* < L *bellus* handsome, fine, pretty]

beauty parlor A place for the hairdressing, manicuring, cosmetic treatment, etc., of women. Also **beauty salon, beauty shop.**

beauty spot 1 A small black patch put on the face to enhance the brilliance of the complexion. 2 A mole or other natural mark resembling this.

beaux (bōz) *n.pl.* of BEAU.

beaux-arts (bō·zàr′) *n. pl. French* The fine arts, as music, painting, sculpture, etc.

bea·ver[1] (bē′vər) *n.* 1 An aquatic rodent with a scaly, broad tail and webbed hind feet, noted for skill in damming shallow streams. 2 The fur of the beaver. 3 A high silk hat, originally made of this fur. [< OE *beofor*]

bea·ver[2] (bē′vər) *n.* 1 A movable piece of medieval armor covering the lower part of the face. 2 The visor of a helmet. 3 *Slang* A beard. [< OF *bavière* child's bib]

bea·ver·board (bē′vər·bôrd′, -bōrd′) *n.* A light, stiff building material made of compressed or laminated wood pulp, used chiefly for walls and partitions. [< *Beaverboard,* a trade name]

be-bop (bē′bop′) *n.* A variety of jazz; bop.

Beaver

be·calm (bi·käm′) *v.t.* 1 To make quiet or calm; still. 2 To cause to be motionless for lack of wind, as a ship: used in the passive: *becalmed* off the coast of Spain.

be·came (bi·kām′) *p.t.* of BECOME.

be·cause (bi·kôz′) *conj.* For the reason that; since. —

—because of On account of; by reason of. [ME *bi cause* by cause]

be·chance (bi-chans′, -chäns′) *v.t.* & *v.i.* **be-chanced, be-chanc-ing** To befall; happen by chance.

Bech·u·a·na·land (bech′ōō·ä′nə·land, bek′yōō-) A former British protectorate in s Africa, now the nation of Botswana. • See map at AFRICA.

beck (bek) *n.* A nod or other gesture of summons. **—at one's beck and call** Subject to one's slightest wish. [Var. of BECKON]

beck·on (bek′ən) *v.t.* & *v.i.* **1** To signal, direct, or summon by sign or gesture. **2** To entice or lure. **—n.** A summoning gesture; beck. [<OE *biecnan, beacnian* to make signs]

be·cloud (bi-kloud′) *v.t.* **1** To make cloudy; darken. **2** To confuse, as an issue.

be·come (bi·kum′) *v.* **be·came, be·come, be·com·ing** *v.i.* **1** To grow to be: The chick *becomes* the chicken. **2** To come to be: The land *became* dry. **—v.t. 3** To suit or befit. **4** To show to advantage: Your dress *becomes* you. **—become of** To be the fate of: What *became* of him? [<OE *becuman* happen, come about]

be·com·ing (bi·kum′ing) *adj.* **1** Appropriate; suitable. **2** Pleasing; adorning. **—be·com′ing·ly** *adv.*

bed (bed) *n.* **1** An article of furniture to rest or sleep in or on, usu. consisting of the bedstead, springs, mattress, and bedclothes. **2** Any place or thing used for resting or sleeping. **3** Conjugal cohabitation or the right to it. **4** The ground at the bottom of a body of water. **5** Something serving as a foundation or support: a *bed* of gravel. **6** A garden plot or the plants, etc., growing therein. **7** A pile of something resembling a bed. **8** *Geol.* Any layer in a mass of stratified rock; a seam. **—bed and board 1** Accommodations for sleeping and for meals. **2** The marriage state. **—put** (or **go**) **to bed 1** To prepare for sleeping. **2** To prepare (a newspaper, etc.) for printing; go to press. **—v. bed·ded, bed·ding** *v.t.* **1** To furnish with a sleeping place. **2** To put to bed. **3** To set out or plant in a bed of earth. **4** To have sexual intercourse with. **5** To lay flat or arrange in layers: to *bed* oysters. **6** EM-BED. **—v.i. 7** To go to bed. **8** To form a closely packed layer; stratify. **—bed down** To prepare a sleeping place for: to *bed down* cattle. [<OE] **—bed′der** *n.*

be·daub (bi·dôb′) *v.t.* **1** To smear or oil. **2** To load with vulgar ornament or flattery.

be·daz·zle (bi·daz′əl) *v.t.* **·zled, ·zling 1** To blind by too much light. **2** To bewilder; stun.

bed·bug (bed′bug′) *n.* A flat, wingless, bloodsucking insect of reddish brown color, infesting houses, esp. beds, and usu. active only at night.

bed·cham·ber (bed′chām′bər) *n.* A bedroom.

bed·clothes (bed′klōz′, -klōthz′) *n.pl.* Covering for a bed, as sheets, blankets, quilts, etc.

bed·ding (bed′ing) *n.* **1** Mattress and bedclothes. **2** Straw or other litter for animals to sleep on. **3** That which forms a bed or foundation. **4** *Geol.* Stratification of rocks.

be·deck (bi·dek′) *v.t.* To deck; adorn.

be·dev·il (bi·dev′əl) *v.t.* **·iled** or **·illed, ·il·ing** or **·il·ling 1** To harass; worry. **2** To torment diabolically; plague. **3** To spoil; corrupt. **4** To bewitch. **—be·dev′il·ment** *n.*

be·dew (bi·d′ōō′) *v.t.* To moisten with or as with dew.

bed·fel·low (bed′fel′ō) *n.* **1** One who shares a bed with another. **2** A companion, cohort, etc.

be·dight (bi·dīt′) *adj. Archaic* Adorned.

be·dim (bi·dim′) *v.t.* **be·dimmed, be·dim·ming** To make dim; obscure.

be·di·zen (bi·dī′zən, -diz′ən) *v.t.* To dress or adorn in a gaudy way. **—be·di′zen·ment** *n.*

bed·lam (bed′ləm) *n.* **1** An excited crowd. **2** An incoherent uproar. **3** A lunatic asylum. [<*Bedlam*, a former London asylum]

bed linen Sheets, pillow cases, etc., for beds.

Bed·ou·in (bed′ōō·in, -ēn) *n.* **1** One of the nomadic Arabs of Syria, Arabia, etc. **2** Any nomad or vagabond. **—adj. 1** Of or pertaining to the Bedouins. **2** Roving; nomadic. [<Ar. *badāwī* desert dweller]

bed·pan (bed′pan′) *n.* **1** A vessel used for urination or defecation by a bedridden person. **2** A warming pan.

be·drag·gle (bi·drag′əl) *v.t.* & *v.i.* **·gled, ·gling** To make or become wet or soiled, as by dragging through mire.

bed·rid·den (bed′rid′ən) *adj.* Confined to bed, as by

sickness. Also **bed′rid′**. [<OE *bed* bed + *rida* rider]

bed·rock (bed′rok′) *n.* **1** The solid rock underlying the looser materials of the earth's surface. **2** Any solid foundation. **3** The bottom or lowest limit. **4** Basic principles; fundamentals.

bed·roll (bed′rōl′) *n.* Bedding compactly rolled to facilitate carrying.

bed·room (bed′rōōm′, -rŏŏm′) *n.* A room for sleeping in.

bed·side (bed′sīd′) *n.* The space beside a bed. **—adj. 1** Beside a bed. **2** Suitable for the sick: a *bedside* manner.

bed·sit·ter (bed′sit′ər) *n. Brit.* A one-room apartment consisting of a combined bedroom and living room. Also **bed′-sit′ting room.**

bed·sore (bed′sôr′, -sōr′) *n.* An ulcer due to prolonged pressure on a small area of a bedridden person's body.

bed·spread (bed′spred′) *n.* A piece of fabric, usu. ornamental, for covering a bed.

bed·spring (bed′spring′) *n.* The framework of springs supporting the mattress of a bed.

bed·stead (bed′sted′) *n.* A framework for supporting the springs and mattress of a bed.

bed·time (bed′tīm′) *n.* The time for retiring to bed. **—adj.** Of or for this time.

bed·wet·ting (bed′wet′ing) *n.* Involuntary urination during sleep.

bee (bē) *n.* **1** Any of a large number of hymenopterous insects that feed largely upon nectar and pollen, esp. the common honeybee. **2** A social gathering for work or competitive activity. [<OE *bēo*]

bee·bread (bē′bred′) *n.* A mixture of pollen and honey, made and stored by bees for food.

beech (bēch) *n.* **1** Any of a family of trees of temperate regions with smooth, ash-gray bark, and bearing an edible nut. **2** The wood of this tree. [<OE *bēce*] **—beech′en** *adj.*

beech·mast (bēch′mast′) *n.* Beechnuts.

beech·nut (bēch′nut′) *n.* The edible nut of the beech.

beef (bēf) *n. pl.* **beeves** (bēvz) or **beefs** for def. 2; **beefs** for def. 4 **1** The flesh of a slaughtered adult bovine animal. **2** Any adult bovine animal, as an ox, cow, steer, bull, etc., fattened for the butcher. **3** *Informal* Muscular power; brawn. **4** *Slang* A complaint. **—v.i.** *Slang* To complain. **—beef up** *Slang* To strengthen. [<L *bos, bovis* ox]

beef·cake (bēf′kāk′) *n. Slang* The display of a male's legs or torso, as in photographs.

beef·steak (bēf′stāk′) *n.* A slice of beef suitable for broiling or frying.

beef tea A beverage made by boiling lean beef or from a beef extract.

beef·y (bē′fē) *adj.* **beef·i·er, beef·i·est 1** Like an ox; fat; dull. **2** *Informal* Brawny; muscular. **—beef′i·ness** *n.*

bee·hive (bē′hīv′) *n.* **1** A hive for a colony of honeybees. **2** A place of great activity.

bee·keep·er (bē′kē′pər) *n.* APIARIST. **—bee′keep′ing** *n.*

bee·line (bē′līn′) *n.* The shortest course from one place to another, as of a bee to its hive.

Be·el·ze·bub (bē·el′zə·bub) The devil. **—n.** Any devil.

been (bin, *Brit.* bēn) *p.p.* of BE.

beep (bēp) *n.* A short, usu. high-pitched mechanical or electronic sound used as a signal or warning. **—v.i. 1** To make such a sound. **—v.t. 2** To sound (a horn). **3** To transmit (a message) by a beep or beeps. [Imit.]

beer (bir) *n.* **1** An undistilled alcoholic liquor made from fermented grain, esp. from malted barley flavored with hops. **2** A beverage made from the roots, etc., of plants, as sassafras, ginger, etc. [<OE *bēor*]

beer·y (bir′ē) *adj.* **beer·i·er, beer·i·est 1** Affected by beer. **2** Like beer in taste or smell. **3** Maudlin. **—beer′i·ly** *adv.* **—beer′i·ness** *n.*

beest·ings (bēs′tingz) *n.pl. (construed as sing.)* The first milk from a cow after calving. [<OE *bēost*]

bees·wax (bēz′waks′) *n.* A wax secreted by honey bees, from which they make their honeycomb. **—v.t.** To smear with beeswax; wax.

beet (bēt) *n.* **1** The fleshy red or white root of a biennial herb, eaten as a vegetable and used as a source of sugar. **2** The plant. [<OE *bēte* <L *beta*]

bee·tle[1] (bēt′l) *n.* **1** Any of a large order of insects having biting mouth parts and hard front wings that cover the membranous hind wings

Carpet beetle

when at rest. 2 Loosely, any insect resembling a beetle. —
adj. Shaggy; overhanging: a *beetle* brow: also **bee'tling.** —
v.i. **·tled, ·tling** To jut out; overhang. [< OE *bitula* < *bītan*
bite]

bee·tle² (bēt'l) *n.* 1 A heavy wooden hammer or mallet.
2 A pestle or mallet for pounding, mashing, etc. —*v.t.* **·tled,
·tling** To beat or stamp with or as with a beetle. [< OE
bīetel mallet]

bee·tle-browed (bēt'l·broud') *adj.* 1 Having prominent, overhanging eyebrows. 2 Scowling; frowning. [<
BEETLE¹]

beeves (bēvz) A *n.pl.* of BEEF.

be·fall (bi·fôl') *v.* **be·fell, be·fall·en, be·fall·ing** *v.i.* 1 To come
about; happen. —*v.t.* 2 To happen to. [< OE *bef(e)allan*
fall]

be·fit (bi·fit') *v.t.* **be·fit·ted, be·fit·ting** To be suited to; be
appropriate for. —**be·fit'ting** *adj.* —**be·fit'ting·ly** *adv.*

be·fog (bi·fôg', -fog') *v.t.* **be·fogged, be·fog·ging** 1 To envelop in or as in fog. 2 To confuse; obscure.

be·fore (bi·fôr', -fōr') *adv.* 1 In front; ahead. 2 Preceding
in time; previously. 3 Earlier; sooner. —*prep.* 1 In front of;
ahead of, as in time, place, rank, sequence, etc. 2 In or into
the presence, sight, attention, etc. of: He stood *before* the
court. 3 Under the judgment or consideration of: The bill
is *before* the senate. 4 In preference to; rather than. —
conj. 1 Previous to the time when. 2 Sooner than: They
would die *before* they yielded. [< OE *beforan* in front of]

be·fore·hand (bi·fôr'hand', -fōr'-) *adv. & adj.* In anticipation or advance; ahead of time.

be·foul (bi·foul') *v.t.* 1 To make foul or dirty. 2 To slander;
defame.

be·friend (bi·frend') *v.t.* 1 To be a friend to; stand by. 2
To become a friend to; make friends with.

be·fud·dle (bi·fud'l) *v.t.* **·dled, ·dling** To confuse, as with
liquor or glib arguments.

beg (beg) *v.* **begged, beg·ging** *v.t.* 1 To ask for or solicit in
charity. 2 To entreat of; beseech. —*v.i.* 3 To ask alms or
charity. 4 To entreat politely or humbly. —**beg off** To ask
to be excused from. —**beg the question** 1 To take for
granted the matter in dispute. 2 To avoid the question or
issue; equivocate. [?] —**Syn.** 2 implore, plead, supplicate.

be·gan (bi·gan') *p.t.* of BEGIN.

be·get (bi·get') *v.t.* **be·got** (*Archaic* **be·gat**), **be·got·ten** or
be·got, be·get·ting 1 To procreate; be the father of. 2 To
cause to be; occasion. [< OE *begitan*] —**be·get'ter** *n.*

beg·gar (beg'ər) *n.* 1 One who asks alms, esp. one who
lives by begging. 2 An impoverished person. 3 A fellow;
rogue. —*v.t.* 1 To impoverish. 2 To exhaust the resources
of: It *beggars* analysis. —**beg'gar·dom, beg'gar·hood** *n.*

beg·gar·ly (beg'ər·lē) *adj.* Miserably poor, mean, sordid,
etc. —**beg'gar·li·ness** *n.*

beg·gar's-lice (beg'ərz·līs') *n.* Any of various plants
bearing burs which adhere to clothes. Also **beg·gar·ticks**
(beg'ər·tiks'), **beg'gar's-ticks'.**

be·gin (bi·gin') *v.* **be·gan, be·gun, be·gin·ning** *v.i.* 1 To take
a first step in doing something; start. 2 To come into being;
arise. 3 To have the essentials or the ability: It doesn't
begin to compare with the original painting. —*v.t.* 4 To
enter upon; commence. 5 To give origin to; start. [< OE
beginnan]

be·gin·ner (bi·gin'ər) *n.* 1 A founder; originator. 2 One
beginning to learn a new skill, subject, etc.; a novice.

be·gin·ning (bi·gin'ing) *n.* 1 The starting point in space,
time, or action; origin. 2 The first stage or part. 3 The
source or first cause. 4 *Usu. pl.* An early phase.

be·gone (bi·gôn', -gon') *interj.* Go away!

be·gon·ia (bi·gōn'yə) *n.* Any of various tropical plants
widely cultivated for their showy leaves and flowers. [<
Michel *Begon*, 1638-1710, French colonial administrator]

be·got (bi·got') *p.t. & p.p.* of BEGET.

be·got·ten (bi·got'n) A *p.p.* of BEGET.

be·grime (bi·grīm') *v.t.* **be·grimed, be·grim·ing** To soil;
make dirty with grime.

be·grudge (bi·gruj') *v.t.* **be·grudged, be·grudg·ing** 1 To
envy one the possession of (something). 2 To give or grant
reluctantly. —**be·grudg'ing·ly** *adv.*

be·guile (bi·gīl') *v.t.* **be·guiled, be·guil·ing** 1 To deceive;
mislead by guile. 2 To cheat; defraud: with *of* or *out of.* 3
To while away pleasantly, as time. 4 To charm; divert. —
be·guile'ment, be·guil'er *n.* —**be·guil'ing·ly** *adv.*

be·gum (bē'gəm) *n.* A Muslim princess, or woman of
rank in India.

be·gun (bi·gun') *p.p.* of BEGIN.

be·half (bi·haf', -häf') *n.* The interest or defense (of anyone): preceded by *in, on,* or *upon.* [< OE *be healfe* by the
side (of)]

be·have (bi·hāv') *v.* **be·haved, be·hav·ing** *v.i.* 1 To comport
oneself properly. 2 To act; conduct itself or itself: The
car *behaves* well. 3 To react to stimuli or environment. —
v.t. 4 To conduct (oneself) properly or suitably. [ME *be-*
thoroughly + *haven* hold oneself, have]

be·hav·ior (bi·hāv'yər) *n.* 1 Manner of one's conduct; deportment. 2 Manner or action of a machine, substance,
organism, etc. 3 Any observable response of an organism
to stimuli. *Brit. sp.* **be·hav'iour.** —**be·hav'ior·al** (-yər·əl) *adj.*
—**Syn.** 1 comportment, manner, actions, ways.

behavioral science Any science dealing with some
aspect of human activity, as psychology, sociology, anthropology, etc.

be·hav·ior·ism (bi·hāv'yər·iz'əm) *n.* A school of psychology that confines its studies to observable phenomena, holding that subjective factors, as thought and feelings, are beyond scientific investigation. —**be·hav'ior·ist**
adj., n. —**be·hav'ior·is'tic** *adj.*

be·head (bi·hed') *v.t.* To cut off the head of; decapitate.
—**be·head'ing** *n.*

be·held (bi·held') *p.t. & p.p.* of BEHOLD.

be·he·moth (bi·hē'məth, bē'ə-) *n.* 1 In the Bible, a colossal beast. 2 Anything huge. [< Heb. *behēmāh* beast]

be·hest (bi·hest') *n.* An authoritative request; command.
[< OE *behæs* promise, vow]

be·hind (bi·hīnd') *adv.* 1 In, toward, or at the rear. 2 In
a previous place, condition, etc.: They left their regrets
behind. 3 In time gone by. 4 In arrears. 5 Retarded in time,
as a train or clock. —*prep.* 1 At the back or farther side
of. 2 To or toward the rear. 3 No longer existing for: His
troubles are *behind* him. 4 Remaining after. 5 Later than.
6 Sustaining; supporting. 7 Inferior to, as in rank, achievement, etc. 8 Not yet revealed or made known about: something strange *behind* that remark. —*adj.* 1 Following: the
car *behind.* 2 In arrears. —*n. Informal* The buttocks. [<
OE *behindan*]

be·hind·hand (bi·hīnd'hand') *adv. & adj.* 1 Behind
time; late. 2 In arrears. 3 In a backward state; not sufficiently advanced.

be·hold (bi·hōld') *v.t.* **be·held, be·hold·ing** To look at or
upon. —*interj.* Look! See! [< OE *beh(e)aldan* hold] —**be·
hold'er** *n.*

be·hold·en (bi·hōl'dən) *adj.* Under obligation; indebted.

be·hoof (bi·hōōf') *n.* That which benefits; advantage; use.
[< OE *behōf* advantage]

be·hoove (bi·hōōv') *v.t.* **be·hooved, be·hoov·ing** To be fit,
needful, or right for: used impersonally: It *behooves* me to
leave. *Brit. sp.* **be·hove** (bi·hōv'). [< OE *behōfian*]

beige (bāzh) *n.* The light, grayish tan color of natural
wool. —*adj.* Of this color. [F]

be·ing (bē'ing) *p.p.* of BE. —*n.* 1 The state or quality of
existing, either materially or immaterially: when art
came into *being.* 2 One who exists or is conceived of as
existing. 3 Any living thing. 4 Essential nature or substance: His whole being is musical.

Be·ing (bē'ing) *n.* God: the Supreme *Being.*

be·la·bor (bi·lā'bər) *v.t.* 1 To beat; thrash soundly. 2 To
assail verbally. 3 To repeat, explain, etc., endlessly.

be·lat·ed (bi·lā'tid) *adj.* Late; tardy. —**be·lat'ed·ly** *adv.* —
be·lat'ed·ness *n.*

be·lay (bi·lā') *v.* **be·layed, be·lay·ing** *v.t.* 1 *Naut.* To make
fast (a rope) by winding on a pin (**belaying pin**), cleat, etc.
—*v.i.* 2 *Informal* To stop or hold; cease: *Belay* there. [< OE
belecgan]

belch (belch) *v.t. & v.i.* 1 To eject forcibly or violently. 2
To eject (gas) noisily from the stomach through the

mouth. —*n.* The act of belching or the thing belched. [< OE *bealcian*] —**belch′er** *n.*

bel·dam (bel′dəm) *n.* An old woman, esp. a hag or crone. Also **bel·dame** (bel′dəm, -dām′). [ME, grandmother]

be·lea·guer (bi-lē′gər) *v.t.* 1 To surround or shut in with an armed force. 2 To harass or annoy, as if from all directions at once. [< Du. *belegeren*] —**be·lea′guered** *adj.*

bel·fry (bel′frē) *n. pl.* **·fries** 1 A tower in which a bell is hung. 2 The part of such a tower containing the bell. [< OF *berfrei*] —**bel′fried** *adj.*

Belg. *n.* Belgian; Belgium.

Bel·gium (bel′jəm, -jē·əm) *n.* A constitutional monarchy of northwestern Europe, 11,775 sq. mi., cap. Brussels. —**Bel′gian** (-jən) *adj., n.*

be·lie (bi·lī′) *v.t.* **be·lied, be·ly·ing** 1 To misrepresent; disguise. 2 To contradict: Her actions *belied* her words. 3 To fail to fulfill: to *belie* hopes. 4 To slander. [< OE *belēogan*] —**be·li′er** *n.*

be·lief (bi·lēf′) *n.* 1 The acceptance of something as true or actual. 2 That which is believed true, as a creed. 3 Religious faith. 4 Confidence; trust. 5 An opinion.

be·lieve (bi·lēv′) *v.* **be·lieved, be·liev·ing** *v.t.* 1 To accept as true or real. 2 To accept the word of (someone). 3 To think; assume: with a clause as object. —*v.i.* 4 To accept the truth, existence, worth, etc., of something: with *in.* 5 To have confidence: with *in:* The country *believes* in you. 6 To have religious faith. [< OE *gelēfen* believe] —**be·liev′a·ble** *adj.* —**be·liev′a·bly** *adv.* —**be·liev′er** *n.*

be·lit·tle (bi·lit′l) *v.t.* **·tled, ·tling** To cause to seem small or less; disparage; minimize. —**Syn.** run down, depreciate, deride, ridicule, malign, criticize, sneer at.

bell (bel) *n.* 1 A hollow, usu. cuplike metallic instrument which rings when struck. 2 The sound of a bell. 3 Anything in the shape of or suggesting a bell. 4 The flaring end of a tubular musical instrument. 5 *Naut.* **a** A stroke on a bell to mark the time on shipboard. **b** *pl.* With a numeral prefixed, the time so marked in half-hours. —*v.t.* 1 To put a bell on. 2 To shape like a bell. —*v.i.* 3 To flare out, as a bell. [< OE *belle*]

bel·la·don·na (bel′ə·don′ə) *n.* 1 A poisonous plant with purple-red flowers and shining black berries; deadly nightshade. 2 A drug derived from this plant; atropine. [< Ital. *bella donna* beautiful lady]

bell·boy (bel′boi′) *n.* BELLMAN.

belle (bel) *n.* 1 A beautiful woman or girl. 2 The reigning beauty of a city, social function, etc. [F, beautiful]

belles-let·tres (bel′let′rə) *n. pl. (construed as sing.)* Literary works, as poetry, drama, fiction, etc., as distinguished from technical or didactic writings. [F, fine letters] —**bel·let·rist** (bel′let′rist) *n.* —**bel·le·tris·tic** (bel′lə·tris′tik) *adj.*

bel·li·cose (bel′ə·kōs) *adj.* Pugnacious; warlike. [< L *bellum* war] —**bel′li·cose′ly** *adv.* —**bel′li·cos′i·ty** (-kos′ə·tē) *n.*

bel·lig·er·ent (bə·lij′ər·ənt) *adj.* 1 Warlike. 2 Engaged in or pertaining to war. 3 Aggressively quarrelsome. —*n.* A belligerent nation or person. [< L *belligare* wage war] —**bel·lig′er·ence, bel·lig′er·en·cy,** *n.* —**bel·lig′er·ent·ly** *adv.*

bell·man (bel′mən) *n. pl.* **·men** (-mən) A man or boy employed by a hotel to carry luggage, run errands, etc., for the guests. Also **bell·hop** (bel′hop′).

bel·low (bel′ō) *v.i.* 1 To utter a loud, hollow sound; roar, as a bull. 2 To roar, usu. with anger. —*v.t.* 3 To utter with a loud, roaring voice. —*n.* A loud, hollow cry or roar. [ME *belwen*] —**bel′low·er** *n.*

bel·lows (bel′ōz, *earlier* bel′əs) *n.* 1 An instrument with flexible sides, for drawing in air and expelling it under pressure through a tube. 2 The expansible portion of a camera. 3 *Informal* The lungs. [< OE *belg, ·belig* bag]

Bellows *def. 1*

bell·weth·er (bel′weth′ər) *n.* 1 The male sheep that wears a bell and leads a flock of sheep. 2 One who leads a group, esp. a sheeplike group.

bel·ly (bel′ē) *n. pl.* **bel·lies** 1 The soft ventral part of a vertebrate body between ribs and pelvis; abdomen. 2 The thick, middle part of a muscle. 3 The stomach. 4 Anything resembling a belly: the *belly* of a flask; the *belly* of a wind-filled sail. 5 The front surface of the sounding box of a violin, viola, etc. —*v.t. & v.i.* **bel·lied, bel·ly·ing** To swell out or fill, as a sail. [< OE *belg, belig* bag]

bel·ly·ache (bel′ē·āk′) *n.* Pain in the abdomen; colic. —*v.i.* **·ached, ·ach·ing** *Slang* To complain petulantly.

bel·ly·band (bel′ē·band′) *n.* A strap passing beneath a draft animal, as to fasten the saddle, harness, etc.

bel·ly·but·ton (bel′ē·but′n) *n. Informal* The navel.

be·long (bi·lông′, -long′) *v.i.* 1 To be in the possession of someone: with *to.* 2 To be a part of or an appurtenance to something: with *to:* The screw *belongs* to this fan. 3 To be suitable: That lamp *belongs* in this room. 4 To have relation or be a member: with *to.* [< ME *be-* completely + *longen* to suit, go along with]

be·long·ing (bi·lông′ing, -long′-) *n.* 1 That which belongs to a person or thing. 2 *pl.* Possessions; effects. 3 Rapport; relationship: a sense of *belonging.*

be·lov·ed (bi·luv′id, -luvd′) *adj.* Greatly loved; dear to the heart. —*n.* One greatly loved.

be·low (bi·lō′) *adv.* 1 In or to a lower place. 2 To a place under the floor or deck: Get *below!* 3 Farther along, as on a page, list, etc. 4 On earth. 5 In or to hell. 6 Lower in rank or authority. —*prep.* 1 Farther or lower down than. 2 Inferior to in degree, rank, value, etc. 3 Unworthy of. [< BY- + LOW]

belt (belt) *n.* 1 A band worn around the waist, as to hold up clothing, secure tools, etc. 2 Any encircling band, highway, etc. 3 *Mech.* **a** A flexible band passing over two or more wheels and serving to transmit motion from one part to another. **b** A moving assembly line in a factory. 4 *Ecol.* A zone or stretch of country having some distinct characteristic: a corn *belt.* 5 A girdle of armor plates protecting a warship along the water line. 6 *Informal* A blow, as with the fist. 7 *Slang* A drink of liquor. —**below the belt** Unfairly. —*v.t.* 1 To gird with or as with a belt. 2 To fasten with a belt. 3 *Informal* To strike with force. 4 *Informal* To sing or play loudly: usu. with *out.* 5 *Slang* To have one or more drinks of liquor: usu. with *down.* [< OE] —**belt′ed** *adj.* —**belt′er** *n.*

belt·ing (bel′ting) *n.* 1 Belts collectively, or the material for belts. 2 *Slang* A beating.

be·lu·ga (bə·lōō′gə) *n. pl.* **·ga** or **·gas** 1 A large, white dolphin of arctic seas. 2 The great white sturgeon of the Caspian Sea and the Black Sea; its roe is **beluga caviar.** [< Russ., whale, white whale]

be·mire (bi·mīr′) *v.t.* **be·mired, be·mir·ing** 1 To soil with mud or mire. 2 To stall in mud.

be·moan (bi·mōn′) *v.t. & v.i.* To mourn or lament. [< OE *bemænan*]

be·muse (bi·myōōz′) *v.t.* **·mused, ·mus·ing** 1 To muddle or stupefy. 2 To engross; preoccupy. —**be·mused′** *adj.*

bench (bench) *n.* 1 A long, wooden seat, with or without a back. 2 A stout worktable. 3 The judges' seat in court. 4 The judge or the judges collectively; also, the court. 5 The office or status of a judge. 6 In sports: **a** The seat or seats for the players not playing. **b** Such players collectively. —**on the bench** 1 Presiding, as a judge. 2 In sports, not playing, as a substitute player. —*v.t.* 1 To furnish with benches. 2 To seat on a bench. 3 In sports, to remove (a player) from a game. [< OE *benc*]

bench·mark (bench′märk′) *n.* 1 A permanent reference mark fixed in the ground for use in surveys, tidal observations, etc. 2 A reference point serving as a standard for comparing or judging other things. Also **bench mark.**

bench warrant A warrant issued by a presiding judge for the arrest of a person.

bend[1] (bend) *v.* **bent** (*Archaic* **bend·ed**), **bend·ing** *v.t.* 1 To make curved or different in shape. 2 To direct or turn, as one's course, in a certain direction. 3 To subdue; cause to yield, as to one's will. 4 To direct or concentrate, as the mind. 5 To resolve: used in the passive: with *on:* They were *bent* on winning. 6 *Naut.* To tie; make fast. —*v.i.* 7 To take or assume a new or different shape. 8 To take a new or different direction; swerve. 9 To bend over; stoop. 10 To yield or conform. —*n.* 1 A curve or crook. 2 A bending or being bent. 3 Any of various knots used to fasten a rope to something. [< OE *bendan*]

bend² (bend) *n. Her.* A band drawn diagonally from the upper left to the lower right of a shield. [< OE *bend* band]

bend·er (ben′dər) *n.* **1** A person or thing that bends. **2** *Slang* A drinking spree.

bends (bendz) *n.pl.* DECOMPRESSION SICKNESS.

bend sinister *Her.* A band drawn diagonally from the lower left to the upper right of a shield, a mark of bastardy.

Bend

be·neath (bi-nēth′) *adv.* **1** At a lower point; below. **2** On the underside of; underneath. —*prep.* **1** In a lower place or position than. **2** Underneath. **3** Influenced or controlled by. **4** Inferior to or lower in rank, quality, etc., than. **5** Unworthy of. [< OE *beneathan*]

Ben·e·dic·tine (ben′ə-dik′tin, -tēn) *adj.* Of St. Benedict or his order. —*n.* **1** A monk or nun following St. Benedict's monastic rules. **2** A liqueur originally made by Benedictines in France.

ben·e·dic·tion (ben′ə-dik′shən) *n.* **1** The act of blessing. **2** The invocation of divine favor upon a person. **3** Any of various formal ecclesiastical ceremonies of blessing. [< L *benedicere* bless] —**ben′e·dic′tive, ben′e·dic′to·ry** *adj.*

ben·e·fac·tion (ben′ə-fak′shən) *n.* **1** The act of giving or doing something for charitable reasons. **2** That which is given or done. [< L *benefacere* do well]

ben·e·fac·tor (ben′ə-fak′tər, ben′ə-fak′-) *n.* A friendly and generous helper; a patron. —**ben′e·fac′tress** *n. Fem.*

ben·e·fice (ben′ə-fis) *n.* **1** A church office, as for a rector, parson, etc., endowed with funds or property. **2** The revenue from such funds or property. —*v.t.* ·ficed, ·fic·ing To invest with a benefice. [< L *beneficium* favor] —**ben′e·ficed** *adj.*

be·nef·i·cence (bə-nef′ə-səns) *n.* **1** The quality of being charitable and good. **2** A charitable act or gift. [< L *beneficus* generous] —**be·nef′i·cent** *adj.* —**be·nef′i·cent·ly** *adv.*

ben·e·fi·cial (ben′ə-fish′əl) *adj.* Benefiting or tending to benefit; advantageous; helpful; useful; salutary. [< L *beneficium* favor] —**ben′e·fi′cial·ly** *adv.*

ben·e·fi·ci·ar·y (ben′ə-fish′ē-er′ē, -fish′ər-ē) *n. pl.* ·ar·ies **1** One who receives benefit. **2** The holder of a benefice or church living. **3** The person designated to receive the income from an insurance policy, annuity, inheritance, etc. [< L *beneficium* favor]

ben·e·fit (ben′ə-fit) *n.* **1** Something helpful; profit; advantage. **2** A special public event, as a performance, bazaar, etc., the proceeds of which are donated to a charitable cause. **3** *Usu. pl.* Payments made by a government, employer, insurance company, etc., to the aged, unemployed, sick, etc. —*v.* ·fit·ed, ·fit·ing *v.t.* **1** To be helpful or useful to. —*v.i.* **2** To profit; gain advantage. [< L *benefacere* do well] —**Syn.** *v.* **1** help, serve, assist, profit, improve, aid, better.

benefit of clergy Churchly approval or sanction: married without *benefit of clergy.*

Ben·e·lux (ben′ə-luks) *n.* The economic union of Belgium, the Netherlands, and Luxembourg. [< BE(LGIUM) + NE(THERLANDS) + LUX(EMBOURG)]

be·nev·o·lence (bə-nev′ə-ləns) *n.* **1** Good will; charitableness. **2** Any act of kindness or charity.

be·nev·o·lent (bə-nev′ə-lənt) *adj.* **1** Characterized by benevolence. **2** Kindly; charitable. [< L *bene* well + *volens,* pr.p. of *velle* wish] —**be·nev′o·lent·ly** *adv.*

Beng. Bengal; Bengali.

Ben·ga·li (ben-gô′lē, beng-) *adj.* Of or pertaining to Bengal. —*n.* **1** A native of Bengal. **2** The modern Indic language of Bengal.

ben·ga·line (beng′gə-lēn, beng′gə-lēn′) *n.* A ribbed fabric of silk, wool, etc. [< BENGAL]

be·night·ed (bi-nī′tid) *adj.* **1** Morally or intellectually unenlightened; ignorant. **2** Overtaken by nightfall. —**be·night′ed·ness** *n.*

be·nign (bi-nīn′) *adj.* **1** Kindly; genial. **2** Mild; temperate. **3** Beneficial; favorable. **4** *Pathol.* Not likely to worsen; harmless: a *benign* tumor. [< L *benignus* kindly] —**be·nign′ly** *adv.* —**Syn. 1** kind, gentle, gracious, amiable, affable. **3** salutary, salubrious, wholesome.

be·nig·nant (bi-nig′nənt) *adj.* **1** Gentle; gracious. **2** Beneficial; benign. [< BENIGN] —**be·nig′nant·ly** *adv.*

be·nig·ni·ty (bi-nig′nə-tē) *n. pl.* ·ties Benign quality, influence, behavior, etc. Also **be·nig·nan·cy** (bi-nig′nən-sē).

Be·nin (be-nēn′) *n.* A republic of w Africa, 44,696 sq. mi., cap. Porto-Novo. • See map at Africa.

ben·i·son (ben′ə-zən, -sən) *n.* A benediction; blessing [< LL *benedictio* benediction]

Ben·ja·min (ben′jə-mən) In the Old Testament, the youngest son of Jacob and Rachel. —*n.* The tribe of Israel descended from him.

ben·ny (ben′ē) *n. pl.* ·nies *Slang* An amphetamine pill or capsule. [< BENZEDRINE]

bent¹ (bent) *p.t. & p.p.* of BEND. —*adj.* **1** Not straight; crooked. **2** Set; determined: *bent* on having her own way. —*n.* Inclination; tendency; penchant: following one's natural *bent.* —**to** (or **at**) **the top of one's bent** To the limit of capacity or endurance.

bent² *n.* **1** Any of various grasses having flower heads of branched spikelets: also **bent grass. 2** The stiff flower stalk of various grasses. [< OE *beonet*]

Ben·tham·ism (ben′thəm-iz′əm) *n.* The philosophy of Jeremy Bentham, which equates good with happiness and maintains that the greatest good for the greatest number is the chief social and moral goal. [< Jeremy *Bentham,* 1748–1832, English philosopher] —**Ben′tham·ite** *n.*

be·numb (bi-num′) *v.t.* **1** To make numb. **2** To make incapable of feeling or responding; deaden: He was *benumbed* with grief. [< OE *benumen,* p.p. of *benuman* deprive]

Ben·ze·drine (ben′zə-drēn, -drin) *n.* A brand of amphetamine: a trade name.

ben·zene (ben′zēn, ben-zēn′) *n.* A flammable liquid hydrocarbon obtained from coal tar and used in the manufacture of various synthetic chemicals. [< BENZOIN]

ben·zine (ben′zēn, ben-zēn′) *n.* A mixture of hydrocarbons derived from petroleum by fractional distillation and used as a solvent and fuel. [< BENZOIN]

ben·zo·ate (ben′zō-it, -āt) *n.* A salt of benzoic acid.

ben·zo·caine (ben′zo-kān′) *n.* A white compound used in some ointments as a local anesthetic for minor burns.

ben·zo·ic (ben-zō′ik) *adj.* Pertaining to or derived from benzoin.

benzoic acid An aromatic compound used as a food preservative and antiseptic.

ben·zo·in (ben′zō-in, -zoin) *n.* **1** A resin from various East Indian plants used in medicine and as a perfume. **2** A crystalline chemical compound. [< Ar. *lubān jāwī* incense of Java]

ben·zol (ben′zōl, -zol) *n.* A grade of crude benzene.

Be·o·wulf (bā′ə-woolf′) The hero of the eighth-century Anglo-Saxon epic poem of the same name.

be·queath (bi-kwēth′, -kwēth′) *v.t.* **1** *Law* To give (personal property) by will. **2** To hand down, as to posterity. [< OE *becwethan*] —**be·queath′al, be·queath′ment** *n.*

be·quest (bi-kwest′) *n.* **1** The act of bequeathing. **2** Something bequeathed. [ME *biqueste*]

be·rate (bi-rāt′) *v.t.* ·rat·ed, ·rat·ing To scold harshly. —**Syn.** upbraid, castigate, revile.

Ber·ber (bûr′bər) *n.* **1** A member of a group of Muslim tribes inhabiting northern Africa. **2** The Hamitic language of the Berbers. —*adj.* Of or pertaining to the Berbers or their language.

ber·ceuse (bâr·sœz′) *n. pl.* ·ceuses (-sœz′) A cradle song; a lullaby. [F]

be·reave (bi-rēv′) *v.t.* ·reaved or ·reft (bi-reft′), ·reav·ing **1** To leave saddened by someone's death. **2** To deprive, as of hope or happiness. [< OE *berēafian*] —**be·reave′ment** *n.*

be·reft (bi-reft′) A *p.t. & p.p.* of BEREAVE. —*adj.* Deprived: *bereft* of all hope.

be·ret (bə-rā′, ber′ā) *n.* A soft, flat, visorless cap, usu. of wool or felt. [F]

Beret

berg (bûrg) *n.* An iceberg.

ber·ga·mot (bûr′gə·mot) *n.* **1** A citrus tree bearing pear-shaped fruit. **2** Its fruit, furnishing an oil used as a perfume. **3** Any of several herbs of the mint family. [<Ital. *bergamotta*]

Berg·son·ism (berg′sən·iz′əm) *n.* The philosophy of Henri Bergson, which holds that reality is the expression of the creative or vital force inherent in all organisms. [< Henri Bergson, 1859–1941, French philosopher] —**Berg′·son·ist** *adj., n.*

ber·i·ber·i (ber′ē·ber′ē) *n.* A disease affecting the nervous system and due to a deficiency of thiamine in the diet. [<Singhalese *beri* weakness]

berke·li·um (bûrk′lē·əm) *n.* An artificially produced radioactive element (symbol Bk) of atomic number 97. [< *Berkeley,* California]

Berk·shire (bûrk′shir, -shər) *n.* One of a breed of medium-sized black swine from Berkshire, England.

berm (burm) *n.* A ledge or bank along the side of a road, canal, etc. Also **berme.** [<F *berme*]

Ber·mu·da onion (bər·myŏŏ′də) A large, mild-flavored variety of onion.

Bermuda shorts Shorts reaching to just above the knees.

ber·ry (ber′ē) *n. pl.* **ber·ries 1** Any small, succulent fruit, as the blackberry or strawberry. **2** *Bot.* A fruit with seeds in a juicy pulp, as the grape or tomato. **3** A dry seed or kernel of various plants, as the coffee bean. —*v.i.* ·**ried,** ·**ry·ing 1** To form or bear berries. **2** To gather berries. [< OE *berie*]

ber·serk (bər·sûrk′, -zûrk′) *adj. & adv.* In or into a violent, destructive frenzy. —*n.* BERSERKER. [<BERSERKER]

ber·serk·er (bər·sûrk′ər, -zûrk′-) *n.* In Norse legend, a warrior who battled with frenzied fury. [<ON *berserkr* bearskin]

berth (bûrth) *n.* **1** A bunk or bed in a ship, sleeping car, etc. **2** A place where a ship may anchor or dock. **3** A job; employment. —**give a wide berth to** To keep out of the way of. —*v.t.* **1** To bring (a ship) to a berth. **2** To provide with a berth. —*v.i.* **3** To come to or occupy a berth. [?]

ber·tha (bûr′thə) *n.* A deep, capelike collar. [<Queen *Bertha,* Charlemagne's mother]

Ber·til·lon system (bûr′tə·lon, *Fr.* ber·tē·yôṅ′) A system of coded physical measurements and personal characteristics used as a means of identifying people, esp. criminals. [<Alphonse *Bertillon,* 1853–1914, French anthropologist]

ber·yl (ber′əl) *n.* A vitreous mineral of various colors, consisting of silicate of aluminum and beryllium, and used as a gem, esp. in the green and blue varieties. [<Gk. *bēryllos*] —**ber′yl·line** (ber′ə·lin, -lin) *adj.*

Bertha

be·ryl·li·um (bə·ril′ē·əm) *n.* A rigid, lightweight, metallic element (symbol Be), having important technological uses in alloys, etc. [<L *beryllus* beryl]

be·seech (bi·sēch′) *v.t.* ·**sought,** ·**seech·ing** To entreat or beg for earnestly; implore. [<OE *besēcan*] —**be·seech′er** *n.* —**be·seech′ing·ly** *adv.* —**Syn.** entreat, implore, plead, supplicate.

be·seem (bi·sēm′) *v.t.* To be fitting or appropriate to; befit.

be·set (bi·set′) *v.t.* ·**set,** ·**set·ting 1** To trouble persistently; plague. **2** To attack on all sides. **3** To hem in; encircle. **4** To set or stud, as with gems. [<OE *besettan*] —**be·set′ment** *n.* —**Syn. 1** harass, annoy, pester.

be·set·ting (bi·set′ing) *adj.* Constantly present and troublesome; a *besetting* sin.

be·shrew (bi·shrōō′) *v.t. Archaic* To curse. [<ME *be-shrewen* to curse]

be·side (bi·sid′) *prep.* **1** At the side of; close to. **2** In comparison with. **3** Away or apart from: This discussion is *beside* the point. **4** Other than. —**beside oneself** Out of one's senses, as from anger, fear, etc. —*adv.* In addition; besides. [<OE *be sīdan* by the side (of)]

be·sides (bi·sīdz′) *adv.* **1** In addition; as well. **2** Moreover; furthermore. **3** Otherwise; else. —*prep.* **1** In addition to. **2** Except for; apart from.

be·siege (bi·sēj′) *v.t.* ·**be·sieged, be·sieg·ing 1** To lay siege to, as a castle or city. **2** To crowd around; block. **3** To overwhelm, as with requests. —**be·siege′ment, be·sieg′er** *n.*

be·smirch (bi·smûrch′) *v.t.* **1** To soil; stain. **2** To sully; dishonor. —**be·smirch′er, be·smirch′ment** *n.*

be·som (bē′zəm) *n.* **1** A bundle of twigs used as a broom. **2** The broom plant. [<OE *besma*]

be·sot (bi·sot′) *v.t.* ·**sot·ted,** ·**sot·ting 1** To stupefy, as with drink. **2** To make foolish or stupid. **3** To infatuate. —**be·sot′ted** *adj.* —**be·sot′ted·ly** *adv.* —**be·sot′ted·ness** *n.*

be·sought (bi·sôt′) *p.t. & p.p.* of BESEECH.

be·spat·ter (bi·spat′ər) *v.t.* **1** To soil by spattering. **2** To sully; dishonor.

be·speak (bi·spēk′) *v.t.* ·**spoke** (*Archaic* ·**spake**), ·**spoke** or ·**spo·ken,** ·**speak·ing 1** To give evidence of; indicate. **2** To arrange for in advance; reserve. **3** To foretell; foreshadow.

be·spec·ta·cled (bi·spek′tə·kəld) *adj.* Wearing eyeglasses.

be·spoke (bi·spōk′) *p.t. & a p.p.* of BESPEAK. —*adj. Brit.* Made to order, as clothing.

Bes·se·mer converter (bes′ə·mər) A large pear-shaped container for molten iron to be converted into steel by the Bessemer process.

Bessemer process A process for oxidizing excess carbon, silicon, etc. in pig iron and converting it to steel by forcing a blast of air through the molten metal. [<Sir Henry *Bessemer,* 1813–98, British engineer]

best (best) Superlative of GOOD and WELL. —*adj.* **1** Excelling all others. **2** Most advantageous, suitable, desirable, etc. **3** Largest; greatest: the *best* part of an hour. —*adv.* **1** In the best way or with the best result. **2** To the greatest degree; most. —**had best** Ought to; should. —*n.* **1** One who or that which is best. **2** Best condition, effort, etc. **3** One's best clothes. —**at best** Given the most favorable conditions, interpretation, etc. —**get** (or **have**) **the best of** To defeat or outwit. —**make the best of** To do as well as one can under the circumstances. —*v.t.* To defeat or outdo. [<OE *betst*]

bes·tial (bes′chəl, bēs′-, best′yəl, bēst′-) *adj.* **1** Of or typical of a beast. **2** Having the undesirable qualities of an animal; brutish. [<L *bestia* beast] —**bes′ti·al′i·ty** (-chē·al′·ə·tē, -tē·al′-) *n.* —**bes′tial·ly** *adv.*

bes·tial·ize (bes′chəl·īz, bēs′-, best′yəl-, bēst′-) *v.t.* ·**ized,** ·**iz·ing** To make bestial; brutalize.

bes·ti·ar·y (bes′tē·er′ē) *n. pl.* ·**ar·ies** A medieval allegory or treatise on animals.

be·stir (bi·stûr′) *v.t.* ·**stirred,** ·**stir·ring** To rouse to activity.

best man The bridegroom's chief attendant at a wedding.

be·stow (bi·stō′) *v.t.* **1** To present as a gift or honor; confer: with *on* or *upon.* **2** To expend; apply. **3** To give in marriage. [ME *bi-* to, upon + *stowen* place] —**be·stow′al, be·stow′ment** *n.*

be·strew (bi·strōō′) *v.t.* ·**strewed,** ·**strewed** or ·**strewn,** ·**strew·ing 1** To cover or strew (a surface). **2** To scatter about. **3** To lie scattered over. [<OE *bestreowian*]

be·stride (bi·strīd′) *v.t.* ·**strode,** ·**strid·den,** ·**strid·ing 1** To stand or sit astride of; straddle. **2** To stride over or across.

best-sell·er (best′sel′ər) *n.* A product, esp. a book, that sells better than most others of its kind. —**best′-sell′er·dom** *n.* —**best′-sell′ing** *adj.*

bet (bet) *n.* **1** An offer or agreement to risk winning or losing money or something of value on an uncertain outcome. **2** The wager thus risked. **3** A contestant, event, etc. on which a bet is made. **4** Anything to be risked or chanced. —*v.* **bet** or **bet·ted, bet·ting** *v.t.* **1** To stake or pledge (money, etc.) in a bet. **2** To declare as in a bet: I'll *bet* he doesn't come. —*v.i.* **3** To place a wager. —**you bet** *Informal* Certainly. [?]

bet. between.

be·ta (bā′tə, bē′-) *n.* **1** The second letter of the Greek alphabet (B, β). **2** The second in a series.

beta blocker A drug useful in slowing the heartbeat by blocking the effect of adrenal hormones on the heart's action.

be·take (bi·tāk′) *v.t.* ·**took,** ·**tak·en,** ·**tak·ing 1** To take (oneself); go: used reflexively with *to.* **2** To resort or have recourse: used reflexively with *to.*

beta particle An electron.

beta rays A stream of high-energy electrons, esp. as emitted by radioactive substances.

be·ta·tron (bā'tə·tron) *n.* An accelerator designed to operate on electrons, raising them to high velocities. [<BETA (RAY) + (ELEC)TRON]

be·tel (bēt'l) *n.* An Asian plant of the pepper family, the leaves of which are chewed in some parts of Asia. [<Pg. *betel* <Malay *vettila*]

Be·tel·geuse (bē'təl·jōōz, bet'əl·jœz) *n.* A giant red star in the constellation Orion. Also **Be'tel·geux.** [<Ar. *bat al-jauza,* shoulder of the giant]

be·tel·nut (bēt'l·nut') *n.* The seed of an East Indian palm, the **betel palm,** used for chewing with betel leaves.

bête noire (bāt'nwär', *Fr.* bet nwär') An object of hate or dread. [<F, black beast]

beth·el (beth'əl) *n.* 1 A seamen's church or chapel. 2 A hallowed place. [<Heb. *bēth-ēl* house of God]

be·think (bi·thingk') *v.t.* ·thought, ·think·ing To remind (oneself); remember: used reflexively.

be·tide (bi·tīd') *v.t. & v.i.* ·tid·ed, ·tid·ing To happen (to); befall.

be·times (bi·tīmz') *adv.* In good time; soon enough. [ME *betymes* in time, seasonably]

be·to·ken (bi·tō'kən) *v.t.* 1 To be a sign of; indicate. 2 To portend. —**be·to'ken·er** *n.* —Syn. 1 signify, denote, bespeak. 2 bode, presage, foreshadow, augur.

be·took (bi·tŏŏk') *p.t.* of BETAKE.

be·tray (bi·trā') *v.t.* 1 To commit treason against; be a traitor to. 2 To be faithless or disloyal to. 3 To disclose, as secret information. 4 To reveal unwittingly. 5 To seduce and desert; wrong. 6 To indicate; show. [<ME *bi* over, to + OF *trair* <L *tradere* deliver, give up] —**be·tray'al, be·tray'er** *n.*

be·troth (bi·trōth', -troth') *v.t.* 1 To engage to marry. 2 To contract to give in marriage. [<ME *bi* to + *treuthe* truth]

be·troth·al (bi·trō'thəl, -trôth'əl) *n.* The state of being betrothed; an engagement to marry. Also **be·troth'ment.**

be·trothed (bi·trōthd', -trôtht') *adj.* Engaged to be married. —*n.* A person engaged to be married.

bet·ter[1] (bet'ər) Comparative of GOOD and WELL. —*adj.* 1 Of greater excellence. 2 More advantageous, suitable, desirable, etc. 3 Larger; greater: the *better* part of a week. 4 Improved in health. —*adv.* 1 In a better way or with a better result. 2 To a greater degree. 3 More usually, correctly, etc. 4 More: lasted *better* than a day. —**better off** In more advantageous circumstances. —**had better** Should. —**think better of** To reconsider and change one's mind. —*n.* 1 That which is better. 2 *Usu. pl.* A superior, as in ability, rank, etc. —**get** (or **have**) **the better of** 1 To gain an advantage over. 2 To overcome. —*v.t.* 1 To improve. 2 To surpass. —*v.i.* 3 To grow better. [<OE *betera*]

bet·ter[2] (bet'ər) *n.* BETTOR.

bet·ter·ment (bet'ər·mənt) *n.* Improvement.

bet·tor (bet'ər) *n.* One who bets.

betw. between.

be·tween (bi·twēn') *prep.* 1 In a space or interval separating two persons, things, times, events, etc. 2 In an intermediate state, quantity, etc. 3 From one point to another in time or space. 4 In joint or reciprocal relationship or action. 5 One or the other of. 6 As a combined result of. —**between you and me** Confidentially. —*adv.* In an intervening space, position, relationship, etc. —**in between** In an intermediate state or relationship. [<OE *betwēonan*] • **between, among** In strict usage, the preposition *between* is used only of two objects, *among* of more than two: Divide the money *between* the two, *among* the three. *Between,* however, may be used of more than two when some reciprocal relation is denoted: a treaty *between* the three powers.

be·twixt (bi·twikst') *adv. & prep. Archaic* Between. —**betwixt and between** In an intermediate state; neither one nor the other. [<OE *betwēohs* twofold]

bev·el (bev'əl) *n.* 1 An inclination of two surfaces other than 90°, as the edge of a timber, etc. 2 An adjustable instrument for measuring angles: also **bevel square.** —*adj.* Oblique; slanting; beveled. —*v.* **bev·eled** or **bev·elled, bev·el·**

ing or **bev·el·ling** *v.t.* To cut or form a bevel on. —*v.i.* To slant. [?]

bevel gear A gear having beveled teeth.

bev·er·age (bev'rij, bev'ər·ij) *n.* Any kind of drink. [<L *bibere* to drink]

beverage room *Can.* A public room in a hotel licensed to sell only beer.

bev·y (bev'ē) *n. pl.* ·ies 1 A flock of quail, grouse, etc. 2 A small group, usu. of girls or women. [ME]

be·wail (bi·wāl') *v.t. & v.i.* To lament.

be·ware (bi·wâr') *v.t. & v.i.* To be wary (of); look out (for): used in the imperative and infinitive. [ME *be ware* be on guard, be wary]

be·wil·der (bi·wil'dər) *v.t.* To confuse utterly; perplex. [<BE- + archaic English *wilder*] —**be·wil'dered·ly, be·wil'der·ing·ly** *adv.* —**be·wil'der·ment** *n.*

be·witch (bi·wich') *v.t.* 1 To gain power over by witchcraft. 2 To charm; fascinate. —**be·witch'ment, be·witch'er·y** *n.* —Syn. 2 captivate, entrance, enchant, beguile.

be·witch·ing (bi·wich'ing) *adj.* Charming; captivating. —**be·witch'ing·ly** *adv.*

bey (bā) *n.* 1 The governor of a Turkish province or district. 2 Formerly, a ruler of Tunis. 3 A Turkish title of respect. [<Turkish *beg* lord]

be·yond (bi·yond') *prep.* 1 Farther than; on or to the far side of. 2 Extending past. 3 After; later than. 4 Out of the reach or scope of. 5 Surpassing; exceeding: *beyond* description. —*adv.* Farther on or away. —**the** (**great**) **beyond** Whatever comes after death. [<OE *begeondan*]

bez·el (bez'əl) *n.* 1 A bevel on the edge of a cutting tool. 2 The upper part of a cut gem. 3 A groove and flange made to receive a beveled edge. [?]

be·zique (bə·zēk') *n.* A game of cards similar to pinochle. [<F *bésigue*]

B/F, b.f. brought forward.

bf., b.f. *Printing* bold face.

bhang (bang) *n.* 1 The hemp plant. 2 The dried leaves and capsules of hemp, used as an intoxicant and narcotic. [<Skt. *bhangā* hemp]

Bhu·tan (bōō·tän') *n.* A small state in the E Himalayas, associated with India in its external affairs, 18,000 sq. mi., cap. Thimpu. —**Bhu'tan·ese'** *adj., n.* • See map at INDIA.

bi- *prefix* 1 Two; doubly: *bicycle; bifurcate.* 2 Occurring twice or at intervals of two: *biannual; bicentennial.* 3 *Chem.* **a** Having two equivalents of: *bichloride.* **b** Indicating the named component in double the ordinary proportion, or the doubling of a radical, etc., in an organic compound. [<L *bis* twice]

Bi bismuth.

bi·a·ly (bē·ä'lē) *n. pl.* ·lys A flat, onion-topped roll. [<*Byalystok,* city in Poland]

bi·an·nu·al (bī·an'yŏŏ·əl) *adj.* Occurring twice a year; semiannual. —**bi·an'nu·al·ly** *adv.*

bi·as (bī'əs) *n. pl.* **bi·as·es** 1 A line crossing the weave of a fabric obliquely: sewn on the *bias.* 2 A personal inclination, esp. one based on fixed attitudes unresponsive to persuasion or influence. 3 A personal preference. 4 A fixed or steady force, voltage, current, etc., impressed on a device or system to set its conditions of operation. —*adj.* Diagonal; slanting: *bias* seams. —*adv.* Diagonally. —*v.t.* **bi·ased** or **bi·assed, bi·as·ing** or **bi·as·sing** 1 To influence unduly or unfairly; prejudice. 2 To impose a fixed condition of operation on. [<F *biais* oblique]

bi·ath·lon (bī·ath'lon) *n.* A contest in the winter Olympics that combines cross-country ski racing with rifle marksmanship. [<BI- + Gk. *athlon* a contest]

Bib

bib (bib) *n.* 1 A cloth worn under the chin by children while eating to protect against spillage. 2 The upper portion of an apron, overalls, etc. [<L *bibere* to drink]

Bib. Bible; Biblical.

bib and tucker *Informal* Clothes.

bib·cock (bib′kok′) *n.* A faucet having the nozzle bent downward.

bibe·lot (bib′lō, *Fr.* bēb·lō′) *n.* A small, decorative or valued object; a curio or trinket. [F]

Bibl., bibl. Biblical; bibliographical.

bi·ble (bī′bəl) *n.* Any authoritative text or writing.

Bi·ble (bī′bəl) *n.* 1 The sacred writings of Christianity; the Old Testament and the New Testament. 2 The Holy Scriptures of Judaism; the Old Testament. 3 The sacred text or writings of any religion. [<Gk. *biblion* book]

bib·li·cal (bib′li·kəl) *adj. Often cap.* 1 Of, in, or derived from the Bible. 2 In harmony with the Bible. —**bib′li·cal·ly** *adv.*

Bib·li·cist (bib′lə·sist) *n.* 1 One well versed in the Bible. 2 A literal adherent of the Bible.

biblio- *combining form* Of or pertaining to books or to the Bible; *bibliophile.* [<Gk. *biblion* book]

bib·li·og·ra·phy (bib′lē·og′rə·fē) *n. pl.* ·phies 1 a A list of the works of an author. b A list of writings on a particular subject, esp. one of sources consulted by an author. 2 The study of books, their history, authorship, etc. —**bib′li·og′· ra·pher** *n.* —**bib·li·o·graph·ic** (bib′lē·ō·graf′ik) or **·i·cal** *adj.*

bib·li·o·ma·ni·a (bib′lē·ō·mā′nē·ə) *n.* A passion for acquiring books. —**bib′li·o·ma′ni·ac** (-ak) *n., adj.*

bib·li·o·phile (bib′lē·ə·fīl′, -fil′) *n.* One who loves books. Also **bib·li·oph·i·list** (bib′lē·of′ə·list). —**bib′li·oph′i·lism** *n.*

bib·u·lous (bib′yə·ləs) *adj.* 1 Given to drinking alcoholic liquor. 2 Absorbent. [<L *bibere* to drink]

bi·cam·er·al (bī·kam′ər·əl) *adj.* Consisting of two chambers or houses, as a legislature. [<BI- + L *camera* chamber]

bi·car·bo·nate (bī·kär′bə·nit, -nāt) *n.* A salt of carbonic acid in which one of the hydrogen atoms is replaced by a metal: sodium *bicarbonate.*

bicarbonate of soda SODIUM BICARBONATE.

bi·cen·ten·ni·al (bī′sen·ten′ē·əl) *adj.* 1 Of a 200th anniversary. 2 Occurring once in 200 years. —*n.* A 200th anniversary. Also **bi·cen·ten·a·ry** (bī′sen·ten′ər·ē, bī·sen′tə· ner′ē) (*pl.* ·ries)

bi·ceps (bī′seps) *n. pl.* **bi·ceps** A muscle having two points or origin, esp. the large flexor muscle of the upper arm or of the back of the thigh. [<L, two headed]

bi·chlo·ride (bī·klôr′īd, -id, -klō′rīd, -rid) *n.* 1 A salt having two atoms of chlorine per atom of another element. 2 Bichloride of mercury, or corrosive sublimate.

bick·er (bik′ər) *v.i.* 1 To dispute petulantly; wrangle. 2 To flow noisily, as a brook. —*n.* A petulant dispute; a petty squabble. [ME *bikeren*] —**bick′er·er** *n.*

bi·coast·al (bī′kō′stəl) *adj.* Of or pertaining to both the east and west coasts of the United States: a *bicoastal* production company.

bi·col·or (bī′kul′ər) *adj.* Having two colors. Also **bi′col′· ored.**

bi·con·cave (bī·kon′kāv, -kong′-, bī′kon·kāv′) *adj.* Concave on both sides. • See LENS.

bi·con·vex (bī·kon′veks, bī′kon·veks′) *adj.* Convex on both sides. • See LENS.

bi·cron (bī′kron) *n.* The one-billionth part of a meter.

bi·cus·pid (bī·kus′pid) *adj.* Having two cusps or points. Also **bi·cus′pi·dal** (-dəl), **bi·cus′pi·date** (-dāt). —*n.* Any of the eight teeth with two cusps in the normal human jaw. [< L *bi-* two + *cuspis* point] • See TOOTH.

bi·cy·cle (bī′sik·əl) *n.* A two-wheeled vehicle with the wheels in tandem, a seat or seats, a steering handle, and propelled by pedals or a motor. —*v.i.* ·cled, ·cling To ride a bicycle. [<BI- + Gk. *kyklos* wheel] —**bi′cy·cler, bi′cy·clist** *n.* • See TANDEM.

bid (bid) *v.* **bade** (bad, bād) *for defs. 1,2,3* or **bid** *for defs. 4,5,6* **bid·den** (bid′ən), **bid·ding** *v.t.* 1 To command; order. 2 To invite. 3 To say (to) in greeting or farewell. 4 To offer (a price), as in an auction. 5 In card games, to declare the number of tricks one intends to make in a specified trump suit. —*v.i.* 6 To make a bid, as in cards or at an auction. —**bid fair** To seem probable. —**bid up** To increase the price of by offering higher bids. —*n.* 1 a An offer to pay or accept a price. b The amount offered. 2 a In card games, the number of tricks or points that a player engages to

make. b A player's turn to bid. 3 An effort to win or attain. 4 An invitation to join. [Fusion of OE *biddan* ask, demand and *bēodan* proclaim, command] —**bid′der** *n.*

bid·da·ble (bid′ə·bəl) *adj.* 1 Of sufficient value to bid on. 2 Docile; obedient.

bid·ding (bid′ing) *n.* 1 A behest; command. 2 A request or invitation. 3 The making of a bid or bids.

bid·dy (bid′ē) *n. pl* ·dies 1 A hen. 2 A gossipy woman. [?]

bide (bīd) *v.* **bid·ed** or **bode** (bōd), **bid·ing** —*v.i.* 1 To remain; stay. 2 To dwell; abide. —*v.t.* 3 To await. —**bide one's time** To await the most favorable opportunity. [<OE *bīdan* wait, stay]

bi·den·tate (bī·den′tāt) *adv.* Having two teeth or tooth-like processes.

bi·det (bē·dā′) *n.* A fountainlike fixture used for washing the anus and genitals. [<F]

bi·en·ni·al (bī·en′ē·əl) *adj.* 1 Occurring every second year. 2 Lasting or living for two years. —*n.* 1 A plant that normally dies after two seasons of growth. 2 An event occurring once in two years. [<L *bi-* two + *annus* year] —**bi· en′ni·al·ly** *adv.*

bien·ve·nue (byan·və·nü′) *n. French* A welcome.

bier (bir) *n.* A framework for supporting a corpse or coffin. [<OE *bǣr*]

biff (bif) *Slang v.t.* To give a blow. —*n.* A whack; blow. [Imit.]

bi·fid (bī′fid) *adj.* Cleft in two; forked. [<L *bifidus]*

bi·fo·cal (bī·fō′kəl) *adj.* Having two foci; said of a lens ground for both near and far vision. [<BI- + L *focus* hearth, focus of a lens]

bi·fo·cals (bī·fō′kəlz, bī′fō·kəlz) *n. pl.* Eyeglasses with bifocal lenses ground for distant and near vision.

bi·fur·cate (bī′fər·kāt, bī·fûr′kāt) *v.t. & v.i.* ·cat·ed, ·cat· ing To divide into two branching parts; fork. —*adj.* (bī′· fər·kāt, bī·fûr′kit) Forked: also **bi′fur·cat′ed.** [<BI- + L *furca* fork] —**bi′fur·cate·ly** (-kit·lē) *adv.* —**bi′fur·ca′tion** *n.*

big (big) *adj.* **big·ger, big·gest** 1 Of great size, amount, etc.; large. 2 Of great intensity, degree, etc. 3 Fully grown. 4 Pregnant. 5 Important. 6 Pompous; self-important. 7 Generous; magnanimous. 8 Loud. —*adv. Informal* 1 Boastfully; extravagantly; to talk *big.* 2 On a grand scale. [ME] —**big′gish** *adj.* —**big′ly** *adv.* —**big′ness** *n.*

big·a·my (big′ə·mē) *n.* The crime of marrying another person while still legally married. [<BI- + Gk. *gamos* wedding] —**big′a·mist** *n.* —**big′a·mous** *adj.* —**big′a·mous·ly** *adv.*

Big Ben 1 The bell of a clock which strikes the hour in the tower of the Houses of Parliament, London. 2 The clock itself.

Big Dipper A dipper-shaped group of seven stars in the constellation Ursa Major.

big game 1 Large wild animals hunted for sport. 2 *Informal* An important objective, esp. if difficult.

big-heart·ed (big′här′tid) *adj.* Generous; charitable. — **big′heart′ed·ly** *adv.* —**big′heart′ed·ness** *n.*

big·horn (big′hôrn′) *n. pl.* ·horns or ·horn A wild sheep of the Rocky Mountains, having large horns.

bight (bīt) *n.* 1 A loop or turn in a rope. 2 A bend in a shoreline, river, etc. 3 A shallow bay formed by such a bend. —*v.t.* To secure with a bight. [<OE *byht* corner, bay]

big·no·ni·a (big·nō′nē·ə) *n.* Any of a genus of tropical American vines bearing large, trumpet-shaped flowers. [<A. J. *Bignon,* 1711-72, librarian to Louis XV]

Bighorn

big·ot (big′ət) *n.* One intolerant of or prejudiced against those of differing religious beliefs, political opinions, etc. [<F] —**big′ot·ed** *adj.* —**big′ot·ed·ly** *adv.* —**big′ot·ry** *n.*

big shot *Slang* A person of importance.

big time *Slang* The highest or best-paid level in an occupation or field. —**big′time′** *adj.* —**big′tim′er** *n.*

big top *Informal* 1 The main tent of a circus. 2 The circus.

big tree The giant sequoia of California.

big wheel *Slang* A person of importance.

big·wig (big′wig′) *n. Informal* A person of importance.

bi·jou (bē′zhōō, bē·zhōō′) *n. pl.* **bi·joux** (bē′zhōōz, bē·zhōōz′) A jewel; trinket. [F]

bike (bīk) *n. Informal* A bicycle.

bi·ki·ni (bi·kē′nē) *n. pl.* **·nis** A very scanty two-piece bathing suit for women. [< *Bikini* atoll in the Pacific]

bi·la·bi·al (bī·lā′bē·əl) *adj.* 1 Articulated with both lips, as certain consonants. 2 Having two lips. —*n.* A bilabial speech sound. —**bi·la′bi·al·ly** *adv.*

bi·la·bi·ate (bī·lā′bē·āt, -it) *adj.* Two-lipped: said of a flower.

bi·lat·er·al (bī·lat′ər·əl) *adj.* 1 Two-sided. 2 On or of two corresponding sides. 3 Undertaken by two sides: a *bilateral* agreement. —**bi·lat′er·al·ly** *adv.* —**bi·lat′er·al·ness** *n.*

bil·ber·ry (bil′ber′ē, -bər·ē) *n. pl.* **·ries** 1 A European shrub with edible blue-black berries; whortleberry. 2 Its fruit. [< Scand.]

bile (bīl) *n.* 1 A bitter, golden brown or greenish digestive fluid secreted by the liver. 2 Anger; peevishness. [< L *bilis* bile, anger] —**bil·i·ar·y** (bil′ē·er′ē) *adj.*

bilge (bilj) *n.* 1 The lower, rounded part of a ship's bottom. 2 The foul water that collects there: also **bilge water.** 3 The bulge of a barrel. 4 *Slang* Stupid nonsense. —*v.t. & v.i.* **bilged, bilg·ing** To leak or cause to leak in the bilge. [Var. of BULGE] —**bilg′y** *adj.* (**·i·er, ·i·est**)

bi·lin·gual (bī·ling′gwəl) *adj.* 1 Written or expressed in two languages. 2 Fluent in two languages. —**bi·lin′gual·ism** *n.* —**bi·lin′gual·ly** *adv.*

bil·ious (bil′yəs) *adj.* 1 Suffering from malaise attributed to a disorder of the liver. 2 Of or suggestive of bile. 3 Ill-natured; cross. [< L *bilis* bile] —**bil′ious·ly** *adv.* —**bil′ious·ness** *n.*

bilk (bilk) *v.t.* To cheat; swindle. —*n.* 1 A swindler. 2 A trick; a hoax. [?] —**bilk′er** *n.*

bill¹ (bil) *n.* 1 A statement of payment due for goods or services. 2 A piece of paper money. 3 A list of items: a *bill* of fare. 4 The draft of a proposed law. 5 An advertising poster. 6 A theater program. 7 *Law* A formal statement of a case, charge, etc. —**fill the bill** *Informal* To meet the needs. —**foot the bill** *Informal* To pay the costs. —*v.t.* 1 To enter in a bill; charge. 2 To present a bill to. 3 To advertise by bills or placards. [< L *bulla* document, seal] —**bill′er** *n.*

bill² (bil) *n.* A beak, as of a bird. —*v.i.* To join bills, as birds. —**bill and coo** To kiss and murmur lovingly. [< OE *bile*]

bill³ (bil) *n.* 1 A hook-shaped gardening instrument: also **bill′hook.** 2 A weapon with a hook-shaped blade. [< OE *bill* sword, ax]

bil·la·bong (bil′ə·bong) *n. Austral.* A stagnant pool or backwater. [< native Australian *billa* water + *bong* dead]

bill·board (bil′bôrd′, -bōrd′) *n.* A board or panel for displaying posters or placards.

bil·let¹ (bil′it) *n.* 1 A lodging for soldiers in a household or nonmilitary building. 2 A requisition for such lodging. 3 A job; position. —*v.t. & v.i.* To lodge (soldiers) in a private household or other billet. [< L *bulla* seal, document] —**bil′let·er** *n.*

bil·let² (bil′it) *n.* 1 A short, thick stick, as of firewood. 2 A mass of iron or steel forming a small bar. [< OF *bille* log]

bil·let-doux (bil′ā·dōō′, -ē·dōō′, *Fr.* bē·ye·dōō′) *n. pl.* **bil·lets-doux** (bil′ā·dōōz′, -ē·dōōz′, *Fr.* bē·ye·dōō′) A love letter. [F, lit., sweet note]

bill·fold (bil′fōld′) *n.* A folding wallet.

bill·head (bil′hed′) *n.* 1 A heading on paper used for making out bills. 2 A sheet of such paper.

bil·liard (bil′yərd) *adj.* Of or pertaining to billiards. —*n.* A carom in billiards.

bil·liards (bil′yərdz) *n.* A game played with a cue and hard balls (**billiard balls**) on an oblong, cloth-covered table with cushioned edges. [< OF *bille* log] —**bil′liard·ist** *n.*

bill·ing (bil′ing) *n.* The order in which performers or acts are listed on a theater billboard, playbill, etc.

bil·lings·gate (bil′ingz·gāt) *n.* Vulgar and abusive language. [< *Billingsgate* fish market, London]

bil·lion (bil′yən) *n.* See NUMBER. [< F] —**bil·lionth** (bil′yənth) *adj., n.*

bil·lion·aire (bil′yən·âr′) *n.* One who owns wealth worth a billion dollars.

bill of attainder Formerly, a legal act making certain actions punishable by attainder.

bill of exchange A written order to pay a particular amount of money to a specified person.

bill of fare A menu.

bill of health An official certificate of the crew's health issued to a ship's master on departure from a port.

bill of lading A written acknowledgment of goods received for transportation.

bill of rights 1 A formal summary and declaration of the fundamental rights of individuals. 2 *Often cap.* The first ten amendments to the U.S. Constitution.

bill of sale A document transferring title to personal property by sale.

bil·low (bil′ō) *n.* 1 A great wave or surge of the sea. 2 A swell or surge, as of sound. —*v.i.* To form billows; surge. [< ON *bylgja*] —**bil′low·y** *adj.* —**bil′low·i·ness** *n.*

bill·post·er (bil′pōs′tər) *n.* One who posts advertising bills on walls, fences, etc. —**bill′post′ing** *n.*

bil·ly¹ (bil′ē) *n. pl.* **bil·lies** A short bludgeon, esp. a policeman's club. [< *Billy*, a nickname for William]

bil·ly² (bil′ē) *n. Austral.* A can used for heating water. [< native Australian *billa* water]

billy goat A male goat.

bi·lo·bate (bī·lō′bāt) *adj.* Divided into or having two lobes. Also **bi·lo′bat·ed.**

bi·man·u·al (bī·man′yōō·əl) *adj.* Employing both hands. —**bi·man′u·al·ly** *adv.*

bi·me·tal·lic (bī′mə·tal′ik) *adj.* 1 Consisting of or relating to two metals. 2 Of or pertaining to bimetallism. [< F *bimétallique*]

bi·met·al·lism (bī·met′əl·iz′əm) *n.* The concurrent use of both gold and silver as the standard of currency and value. —**bi·met′al·list** *n.*

bi·month·ly (bī·munth′lē) *adj.* 1 Occurring once every two months. 2 Semimonthly. —*adv.* 1 Every two months. 2 Semimonthly. —*n.* A publication issued bimonthly. • In strict usage, *bimonthly, biweekly,* and *biyearly* are used only to mean once in every interval of two months, two weeks, etc., while *semimonthly, semiweekly,* etc., are used to mean twice a month, twice a week, etc.

bin (bin) *n.* An enclosed place for holding foods, coal, etc. —*v.t.* **binned, bin·ning** To store or deposit in a bin. [< OE *binn* basket, crib]

bi·na·ry (bī′nə·rē) *adj.* 1 Of, characterized by, or consisting of two; double; paired. 2 Denoting a pair of stars revolving about a common center. 3 Of or denoting the binary numeration system. —*n. pl.* **·ries** A paired or double entity, esp. a binary star. [< L *bini* two, double]

binary numeration system A system of numeration based on two, capable of expressing any integer as a numeral using only the characters 0 and 1.

bi·nate (bī′nāt) *adj.* Growing in pairs. [< L *bini* double, two by two] —**bi′nate·ly** *adv.* • See LEAF.

bin·au·ral (bī·nôr′əl, bin·ôr′əl) *adj.* 1 Hearing with both ears. 2 Designating a device for presenting sounds, esp. different sounds simultaneously to both ears. —**bin·au′ral·ly** *adv.*

bind (bīnd) *v.* **bound, bind·ing** *v.t.* 1 To tie together; make fast by tying; secure. 2 To encircle, as with a belt. 3 To bandage. 4 To cause to cohere or adhere. 5 To strengthen or ornament at the edge, as in sewing. 6 To fasten together within a cover, as a book. 7 To make irrevocable, as a bargain. 8 To oblige, as by moral or legal authority. 9 To make constipated. —*v.i.* 10 To tie up anything. 11 To cohere; stick together. 12 To have binding force; be obligatory. 13 To become stiff, hard, or tight. —**bind over** *Law* To hold under bond for appearance at a future time. —*n.* 1 *Informal* A difficult or constraining situation. 2 That which fastens, ties, or binds. [< OE *bindan*]

bind·er (bīn′dər) *n.* 1 One who binds, esp. a bookbinder. 2 Something that binds; a device, substance, etc., used for binding. 3 A loose-leaf notebook cover. 4 A payment or written statement given as a pledge pending the completion of a contract. **5** A device on a reaper for binding grain.

bind·er·y (bīn′dər·ē) n. pl. **·er·ies** A place where books are bound.

bind·ing (bīn′ding) adj. **1** Something that binds or is used to bind. **2** The act of one who or that which binds. **3** The cover holding together the pages of a book. **4** A strip sewed or fastened over an edge for protection. —adj. **1** Obligatory. **2** Uncomfortably tight or confining.

bind·weed (bīnd′wēd′) n. Any of various plants with twining stems.

bine (bīn) n. **1** A twining or climbing stem. **2** A plant with such stems, as the hop, woodbine, etc. [<ME binden to bind]

Bi·net·Si·mon scale (bi·nā′sī′mən, Fr. bē·ne′sē·môn′) A system of rating the mental development of children according to norms established by a series of tests given previously to many children at given ages. [<Alfred Binet, 1857–1911, and Théodore Simon, 1873–1961, French psychologists]

binge (binj) n. Slang **1** A drunken carousal. **2** Any uncontrolled bout; a spree. [?]

bin·go (bing′gō) n. A game in which players cover numbers on a printed card as they are called out, the first to cover five numbers in a row being the winner. [?]

bin·na·cle (bin′ə·kəl) n. A stand or case for a ship's compass, usu. placed before the steering wheel. [<Pg. bitacola <LL habitaculum little house]

bin·oc·u·lar (bə·nok′yə·lər, bī-) adj. Of, for, or using eyes at once. —n. Often pl. A telescope, opera glass, etc., adapted for use by both eyes at once. [<BI + OCULAR] —bin·oc′u·lar′l·ty (-lar′ə·tē) n. —bin·oc′u·lar·ly adv.

bi·no·mi·al (bī·nō′mē·əl) adj. Consisting of or using two names or terms. —n. Math. An algebraic expression in the form of a sum of two terms. [<Med. L binomius having two names] —bi·no′mi·al·ly adv.

bio- combining form Life: biology. [<Gk. bios life]

Binoculars

bi·o·chem·is·try (bī′ō·kem′is·trē) n. The branch of chemistry relating to life processes, their mode of action, and their products. —bi′o·chem′i·cal adj. —bi′o·chem′i·cal·ly adv. —bi′o·chem′ist n.

bi·o·de·grad·a·ble (bī′ō·di·grā′də·bəl) adj. Capable of being broken down by natural processes, such as bacterial action, etc. [<BIO- + DEGRADABLE]

bi·o·e·col·o·gy (bī′ō·ē·kol′ə·jē) n. That branch of ecology having to do with the mutual relationships between organisms and the environment.

bi·o·e·lec·tric·i·ty (bī′ō·i·lek′tris′ə·tē) n. Electric phenomena associated with and characteristic of living matter. —bi′o·e·lec′tri·cal adj.

bi·o·eth·ics (bī′ō·eth′iks) n. pl. (construed as sing.) The study of the ethical implications of medical practice, esp. in regard to the preservation of human life. —bi′o·eth′i·cal adj. —bi′o·eth′i·cist (-eth′ə·sist) n.

bi·o·feed·back (bī′ō·fēd′bak) n. Voluntary control by feedback of involuntary functions, as heart rate.

biog. biographer; biographical; biography.

bi·o·gen·e·sis (bī′ō·jen′ə·sis) n. **1** The doctrine that life is generated from living organisms only. **2** Such generation itself. Also **bi·og·e·ny** (bī·oj′ə·nē). —bi·o·ge·net·ic (bī′ō·jə·net′ik) or **·i·cal** adj. —bi′o·ge·net′i·cal·ly adv.

bi·og·ra·phy (bī·og′rə·fē, bē-) n. pl. **·phies 1** A written account of a person's life. **2** Such writing as a literary form or practice. [<Gk. bios life + graphein write] —bi·og′raph·er n. —bi·o·graph·ic (bī′ə·graf′ik) or **·i·cal** adj. —bi′o·graph′i·cal·ly adv.

biol. biological; biologist; biology.

bi·o·log·i·cal (bī′ə·loj′i·kəl) adj. **1** Of or pertaining to vital functions, structures, and processes. **2** Used for or produced by research in biology. Also **bi′o·log′ic.** —bi′o·log′i·cal·ly adv.

biological warfare The use of disease-producing microorganisms, toxins, etc., in waging war.

bi·ol·o·gy (bī·ol′ə·jē) n. The science of life and the origin, structure, reproduction, growth, and development of liv-

ing organisms. [<BIO- + -LOGY] —bi·ol′o·gist n.

bi·o·lu·mi·nes·cence (bī′ō·lōō′mə·nes′əns) n. **1** The emission of light by living organisms. **2** The light so emitted. —bi′o·lu′mi·nes′cent adj.

bi·o·mass (bī′ō·mas′) n. All the plant material in a given area, esp. when considered as an energy source.

bi·ome (bī′ōm) n. Any major ecosystem, such as a desert, that has its own particular climate and plant and animal life.

bi·om·e·try (bī·om′ə·trē) n. The application of statistics to biological data. Also **bi·o·met·rics** (bī′ə·met′riks). [<BIO + -METRY] —bi′o·met′ric or **·ri·cal** adj.

bi·o·phys·ics (bī′ō·fiz′iks) n. pl. (construed as sing.) The study of the physics of living organisms. —bio′o·phys′i·cal adj. —bi′o·phys′i·cist n.

bi·op·sy (bī′op·sē) n. pl. **·sies** The excision and examination of tissue from a living subject for diagnostic purposes. [<BIO- + Gk. opsis sight] —bi·op·sic (bī·op′sik) adj.

bi·o·sphere (bī′ə·sfir) n. The envelope of soil, water, and air to which life on earth is confined.

bi·o·ta (bī·ō′tə) n. The combined fauna and flora of an area or period. [<Gk. biotē life <bios life]

bi·o·tech·nol·o·gy (bī′ō·tek·nol·ə·jē) n. **1** The use of technology in biological science. **2** The use of microorganisms in the production of valuable products.

bi·ot·ic (bī·ot′ik) adj. Of or pertaining to living organisms.

bi·o·tin (bī′ə·tin) n. A constituent of the vitamin B complex. [<Gk. bios life]

bi·par·ti·san (bī·pär′tə·zən) adj. Of or supported by two political parties. —bi·par′ti·san·ship n.

bi·par·tite (bī·pär′tīt) adj. Consisting of two usu. corresponding parts. —bi·par′tite·ly adv.

bi·ped (bī′ped) n. A two-footed animal. —adj. Two-footed: also **bi·pe·dal** (bī·ped′əl, bī′pə·dəl). [<L bipes two-footed]

bi·pin·nate (bī·pin′āt) adj. Twice or doubly pinnate, as a leaf. Also **bi·pin′nat·ed.** —bi·pin′nate·ly adv.

bi·plane (bī′plān) n. Aeron. An airplane having two parallel wings, one above the other.

bi·po·lar (bī·pō′lər) adj. **1** Relating to or having two poles. **2** Found in both polar regions of the earth.

birch (bûrch) n. **1** Any of a genus of hardy trees and shrubs usu. having the outer bark separable in thin layers. **2** A rod from such a tree, used as a whip. **3** The tough, close-grained wood of the birch. —v.t. To whip with a birch rod. [<OE birce] —birch·en (bûr′chən) adj.

bird (bûrd) n. **1** Any of a class of warm-blooded, feathered, egg-laying vertebrates having the forelimbs modified as wings. **2** GAME BIRD. **3** A shuttlecock used in the game of badminton. **4** CLAY PIGEON. **5** Slang A peculiar or remarkable person. **6** Slang A derisive sound of disapproval. —for the birds Slang Worthless. —v.i. **1** To be a bird watcher. **2** To trap or shoot birds. [<OE bridd]

bird·call (bûrd′kôl′) n. A bird's characteristic note or song. **2** A device for imitating this.

bird dog A dog trained to assist in hunting game birds.

bird·ie (bûr′dē) n. **1** Informal A small bird. **2** In golf, a score of one stroke less than par in playing a hole.

bird·lime (bûrd′līm′) n. A sticky substance smeared on twigs to catch small birds.

bird of paradise A bird of New Guinea noted for its colorful plumage.

bird of prey Any of various predacious birds, as an eagle, hawk, etc.

bird·seed (bûrd′sēd′) n. A mixture of seeds used to feed birds.

bird's-eye (bûrdz′ī) adj. **1** Marked with spots resembling birds' eyes: bird's-eye maple. **2** Seen at a distance and from above: a bird's-eye view. —n. A fabric woven in a pattern of small, eyelike indentations.

bird watcher One who observes birds in their natural state, esp. as a hobby. —bird watching.

bi·reme (bī′rēm) n. An ancient galley having two banks of oars. [<L bi- two + remus oar]

bi·ret·ta (bī·ret′ə) n. A stiff, square cap with three or four upright projections on the crown, worn by clerics of the Roman Catholic Church. [<LL birretum cap]

birl (bûrl) v.t. **1** To rotate (a floating log) rapidly with the feet. —v.i. **2** To spin with a humming sound. [Blend of earlier birr, whirring sound + WHIRL] —birl′er n.

birl·ing (bûr′ling) n. A contest in which opponents try to outstay each other while balanced on a floating log rotated by their feet. [?]

birth (bûrth) *n.* 1 The act or fact of being born. 2 The bringing forth of offspring; parturition. 3 Beginning; origin. 4 Ancestry or descent. 5 Inborn or inherent tendency. —**give birth to** 1 To bear as offspring. 2 To give rise to. [<ON *byrth*]

birth control The use of preventive methods or devices to regulate conception; contraception.

birth·day (bûrth′dā′) *n.* The day of one's birth or its anniversary.

birth·mark (bûrth′märk′) *n.* A mark or blemish existing on the body from birth.

birth·place (bûrth′plās′) *n.* 1 The place of one's birth. 2 A place of origin: the *birthplace* of freedom.

birth rate The number of births in a given population during a given time, usu. births per 1,000 persons per year.

birth·right (bûrth′rīt′) *n.* A right or privilege due by virtue of one's birth or origin.

birth·stone (bûrth′stōn′) *n.* A jewel identified with the particular month of one's birth.

bis·cuit (bis′kit) *n.* 1 Bread in the form of a small cake leavened with baking powder or soda. 2 *Brit.* A cracker or cooky. 3 Fired, unglazed pottery. 4 A pale brown. [<L *bis* twice + *coquere* to cook]

bi·sect (bī′sekt, bī·sekt′) *v.t.* 1 To cut into two parts; halve. 2 *Geom.* To divide into two equal parts. —*v.i.* 3 To fork, as a road. [<BI- + L *sectus* cut] —**bi·sec′tion, bi·sec′tor** *n.* —**bi·sec′tion·al** *adj.* —**bi·sec′tion·al·ly** *adv.*

bi·sex·u·al (bī·sek′shōō·əl) *adj.* 1 Pertaining to both sexes. 2 Having both male and female organs; hermaphroditic. 3 Attracted sexually by both sexes. —**bi·sex′u·al·ism, bi·sex′u·al′i·ty** (-shōō·al′ə·tē) *n.* —**bi·sex′u·al·ly** *adv.*

bish·op (bish′əp) *n.* 1 In various Christian churches, a clergyman of the highest order, usu. head of a diocese. 2 A chessman which may be moved only diagonally. [<LL *episcopus*]

bish·op·ric (bish′əp·rik) *n.* The office or diocese of a bishop.

bis·muth (biz′məth) *n.* A brittle, reddish white metallic element (symbol Bi) of atomic number 83, used chiefly as a constituent of alloys. [G] —**bis′muth·al** *adj.*

bi·son (bī′sən, -zən) *n. pl.* **bi·son** 1 A bovine mammal of western North America, having a dark, shaggy mane; buffalo. 2 A similar European animal. [<L *bison* wild ox]

bisque¹ (bisk) *n.* A thick, rich, cream soup made from shellfish, vegetables, etc. [F]

bisque² (bisk) *n.* BISCUIT (def. 3). [<BISCUIT]

North American bison

bis·sex·tile (bi·seks′təl, -tīl) *adj.* 1 Pertaining to the extra day occurring in a leap year. 2 Pertaining to a leap year. —*n.* A leap year. [<L *bisextilis* intercalary day in the Julian calendar]

bis·ter (bis′tər) *n.* 1 A yellowish brown pigment made from soot. 2 A dark brown. Also **bis′tre.** [F *bistre* dark brown] —**bis′tered** *adj.*

bis·tro (bis′trō, Fr. bē·strō′) *n. pl.* **·tros** *Informal* A small night club, bar, or café. [F]

bi·sul·fate (bī·sul′fāt) *n.* An acid sulfate.

bit¹ (bit) *n.* 1 A small piece, amount, etc. 2 A short time: Wait a *bit.* 3 A very small part, as in a play. 4 *Informal* An amount worth 12½ cents: now used mostly in the expression *two bits.* —**a bit of** To some degree; somewhat: *a bit of* a nuisance. —**do one's bit** To contribute one's share of work, money, etc. [<OE *bita* piece bitten off] —**Syn.** 1 morsel, fragment, scrap, mite, iota.

bit² (bit) *n.* 1 A boring tool adapted to be used with a stock or brace. • See BRACE. 2 The metallic mouthpiece of a bridle. 3 Something that curbs or restrains. 4 The part of a key that engages the bolt or tumblers of a lock. —*v.t.* **bit·ted, bit·ting** 1 To put a bit in the mouth of. 2 To curb; restrain. [<OE *bite* a biting]

bit³ (bit) *p.t. & alt. p.p.* of BITE.

bit⁴ (bit) *n.* 1 A binary digit; a 0 or 1. 2 A unit of informa-

tion equivalent to the choice between a pair of alternatives of equal probability. [<B(INARY) + (DIG)IT]

bitch (bich) *n.* 1 A female dog, coyote, etc. 2 *Slang* A woman regarded as hateful, sluttish, mean, etc. 3 *Slang* Something difficult or troublesome to accomplish. —*v.i. Slang* To complain. —**bitch up** *Slang* To botch. [<OE *bicce*]

bitch·y (bich′ē) *adj.* **bitch·i·er, bitch·i·est** *Slang* 1 Quick to find fault or complain; captious. 2 Mean-spirited; malicious; spiteful. —**bitch′i·ly** *adv.* —**bitch′i·ness** *n.*

bite (bīt) *v.* **bit, bit·ten** (bit′n) or **bit, bit·ing** *v.t.* 1 To seize, cut, tear, or wound with the teeth. 2 To cut, tear, etc., as if with teeth. 3 To pierce with a sting, fangs, etc. 4 To cause to smart; sting. 5 To corrode, as acid. 6 To grip or hold, as by traction. —*v.i.* 7 To seize or cut into something with or as if with the teeth. 8 To have a stinging effect. 9 To take firm hold. 10 To take bait, as fish. 11 To be taken in by a trick. —**bite the dust** To fall dead or wounded, as in battle. —*n.* 1 The act of biting. 2 An injury inflicted by biting. 3 A smarting sensation or effect. 4 An amount taken by or as by biting. 5 A quick, light meal; snack. 6 A grip or hold, as of a tool. 7 The way in which the jaws meet. [<OE *bītan*] —**bit′a·ble, bite′a·ble** *adj.* —**bit′er** *n.*

bit·ing (bī′ting) *adj.* 1 Sharp; stinging. 2 Mordant; sarcastic. —**bit′ing·ly** *adv.* —**bit′ing·ness** *n.* —**Syn.** 2 caustic, cutting, incisive, acrimonious.

bitt (bit) *n.* A post on a ship's deck, to which cables, etc., are made fast. —*v.t.* To wind (a cable) around a bitt. [?]

bit·ter (bit′ər) *adj.* 1 Having an acrid, usu. unpleasant taste. 2 Causing acute physical discomfort or mental anguish. 3 Feeling or showing resentment, animosity, etc. 4 Hard to bear or accept. —*v.t. & v.i.* To make or become bitter. [<OE *biter*] —**bit′ter·ly** *adv.* —**bit′ter·ness** *n.*

bit·tern (bit′ərn) *n.* Any of various small herons noted for sounding a booming note in the breeding season. [<OF *butor*]

bit·ter·root (bit′ər·rōōt′, -rōōt′) *n.* A perennial herb of w North America with showy flowers and an edible root.

bit·ters (bit′ərs) *n. pl.* A usu. alcoholic liquor containing bitter herbs, bark, roots, etc., used as a tonic or flavoring agent.

bit·ter·sweet (bit′ər·swēt′) *n.* 1 A climbing shrub having orange seed pods that open to display a red aril. 2 A trailing plant of the nightshade family, having poisonous red berries. —*adj.* Both bitter and sweet or pleasant and unpleasant.

bi·tu·men (bi·t′yōō′mən, bich′ōō·mən) *n.* A mixture of solid and semisolid hydrocarbons, as naphtha or asphalt. [<L] —**bi·tu·mi·noid** (bi·t′yōō′mə·noid), **bi·tu′mi·nous** *adj.*

bi·tu·mi·nize (bi·t′yōō′mi·nīz) *v.t.* **·ized, ·iz·ing** To treat with bitumen. —**bi·tu′mi·ni·za′tion** *n.*

bituminous coal Coal containing volatile hydrocarbons and burning with a smoky flame.

bi·va·lent (bī·vā′lənt, biv′ə-) *adj.* 1 *Chem.* a Having a valence of two. b Having two valences. 2 *Biol.* Composed of or characterizing two similar chromosomes joined together or in close proximity. —*n.* A double chromosome. [<BI- + L *valens,* pr.p. of *valere* have power] —**bi·va′lence, bi·va′len·cy** *n.*

bi·valve (bī′valv′) *n.* A mollusk having a shell of two hinged valves. —*adj.* Having two valves, as a mollusk: also **bi′valved′, bi·val·vous** (bī·val′vəs), **bi·val·vu·lar** (bī·val′vyə·lər).

biv·ou·ac (biv′ōō·ak, biv′wak) *n.* A temporary field encampment with little or no shelter, esp. for soldiers. —*v.i.* **biv·ou·acked, biv·ou·ack·ing** To encamp in a bivouac. [<G *Beiwacht* guard]

bi·week·ly (bī·wēk′lē) *adj.* 1 Occurring every two weeks. 2 Semiweekly. —*adv.* 1 Every two weeks. 2 Semiweekly. —*n.* A biweekly publication. • See BIMONTHLY.

bi·year·ly (bī·yir′lē) *adj.* 1 Occurring once every two years. 2 Biannual. —*adv.* 1 Every two years. 2 Biannually. • See BIMONTHLY.

bi·zarre (bi·zär′) *adj.* Startlingly odd. [F] —**bi·zarre′ly** *adv.* —**bi·zarre′ness** *n.* —**Syn.** outré, outlandish, fantastic, grotesque, freakish.

add, āce, câre, pälm; end, ēven; it, īce; odd, ōpen, ôrder; tŏŏk, pŏŏl; up, bûrn; ə = a in *above*, u in *focus*; yŏŏ = u in *fuse*; oil; pout; check; go; ring; thin; this; zh, *vision.* < derived from; ? origin uncertain or unknown.

Bk berkelium.

bk. blank; block; book.

bkg. banking.

B.L., B.LL. Bachelor of Laws.

B/L, b.l. bill of lading.

bl. bale; barrel; black; blue.

blab (blab) *v.t. & v.i.* **blabbed, blab·bing 1** To reveal (a secret or confidence) indiscreetly. **2** To prattle. —*n.* **1** One who blabs. **2** Idle chatter. [ME *blabblen*]

blab·ber (blab′ər) *v.i.* To chatter; babble —*n.* One who blabs.

blab·ber·mouth (blab′ər·mouth′) *n. Informal* One who talks too much and can't be trusted to keep secrets.

black (blak) *adj.* **1** Reflecting little or no light; of the darkest color, as of coal or jet. **2** Without light; very dark. **3 a** Belonging to a dark-skinned ethnic group; esp., Negroid. **b** Of or relating to members of such a group: *black* power; *black* studies. **4** Soiled; stained. **5** Gloomy; dismal. **6** Disastrous; unlucky. **7** Indicating or deserving disgrace, censure, etc. **8** Evil; wicked. **9** Angry; scowling. **10** Dressed in black clothing. **11** Without cream or milk: *black* coffee. —*n.* **1** The darkest of all colors. **2** Something black, esp. black clothing. **3** A dark-skinned person, esp. a Negro. —**in the black** Ahead in business or finance; prospering. —*v.t. & v.i.* **1** To make or become black. **2** To polish with blacking. —**black out 1** To extinguish or screen all light. **2** To become temporarily unconscious. **3** To delete by scoring through. [< OE *blæc*] —**black′ish** *adj.* —**black′ly** *adv.* —**black′ness** *n.*

black·a·moor (blak′ə·moŏr′) *n. Archaic* A dark-skinned person, esp. a Negro.

black-and-blue (blak′ən·bloō′) *adj.* Discolored: said of skin that has been bruised.

black and white Writing or printing.

black art Necromancy; magic.

black·ball (blak′bôl′) *v.t.* **1** To vote against and ban from membership. **2** To exclude or ostracize. —*n.* **1** A negative vote resulting in the rejection of an application for membership. **2** A willful act of ostracism. [< BLACK + BALL, a black ball to signify a negative vote during balloting] —**black′ball′er** *n.*

black bass Any of a genus of fresh-water fishes of the eastern United States and Canada.

black bear 1 The common North American bear. **2** A dark-colored bear of Asia.

black·ber·ry (blak′ber′ē, -bər·ē) *n. pl.* **·ries 1** The black, edible fruit of certain shrubs of the rose family. **2** Any of the plants producing it.

black·bird (blak′bûrd′) *n.* **1** One of various black or blackish North American birds related to the orioles. **2** A common European thrush, the male of which is black.

black·board (blak′bôrd′, -bōrd′) *n.* A slate or black surface on which chalk is used to write or draw.

Blackberries

black body An ideal body that is uniformly and completely absorptive of radiation at all frequencies.

black·cap (blak′kap′) *n.* **1** Any of several birds having a black crown. **2** A variety of raspberry bearing black fruit.

Black Death A bubonic plague of exceptional virulence prevalent in the 14th century.

black·en (blak′ən) *v.t.* **1** To make black or dark. **2** To slander; defame. —*v.i.* **3** To become black; darken. —**black′·en·er** *n.*

black eye 1 A discolored bruise near the eye. **2** *Informal* A bad reputation.

black-eyed Susan (blak′īd′) A composite flower having a dark, conical center and yellow ray florets.

black·face (blak′fās′) *n.* **1** Dark, often grotesquely exaggerated make-up worn by someone portraying a Negro, esp. in a minstrel show. **2** Someone so made up.

Black·foot (blak′foŏt) *n. pl.* **·feet** or **·foot** A member of a confederacy of Algonquian North American Indian tribes

formerly living E of the Rocky Mountains, now on reservations in Alberta and Montana.

black·guard (blag′ərd, -ärd) *n.* A despicable scoundrel. —*v.t.* To vilify. —*v.i.* **2** To act like a blackguard. —*adj.* Of or like a blackguard: also **black′guard·ly.** [< *black guard*, orig., a group of low menials.] —**black′guard·ism** *n.*

Black Hand A secret organization in the U.S., esp. of Sicilians, for the purpose of vengeance or blackmail.

black·head (blak′hed′) *n.* **1** A plug of fatty material in a pore of the skin. **2** SCAUP, a duck. **3** An infectious disease of domestic fowl.

black·heart·ed (blak′här′tid) *adj.* Villainous; wicked.

black hole A hypothetical region characterized by an intense gravitational field that causes infinite curvature of the space within it allowing no matter or electromagnetic energy to escape, believed to result as the final stage of gravitational collapse of stellar material too massive to reach any stable state short of infinite density.

black·ing (blak′ing) *n.* A black polish used on shoes, stoves, etc.

black·jack (blak′jak′) *n.* **1** A small bludgeon with a flexible handle. **2** JOLLY ROGER. **3** A card game won by the player holding cards whose face value totals 21 or less but is higher than that of the dealer, popular as a gambling game. **4** A large drinking cup, formerly of leather. —*v.t.* **1** To strike with a blackjack. **2** To coerce by threat.

black·leg (blak′leg′) *n.* **1** An infectious, often fatal disease of cattle and sheep. **2** A professional swindler or gambler; sharper. **3** *Brit.* A strikebreaker.

black letter A type face with heavy, angular letters.

This line is in black letter

black·list (blak′list′) *n.* A list of persons or groups to be censured, refused membership, excluded from employment, etc. —*v.t.* To place on a blacklist.

black lung disease A form of pneumoconiosis caused by prolonged exposure to and inhalation of coal dust.

black magic Sorcery with an evil intention.

black·mail (blak′māl′) *n.* **1** The extortion of payment by threats of public exposure. **2** Money, etc. obtained by such extortion. —*v.t.* **1** To subject to blackmail. **2** To coerce, as by threats. [< BLACK + obs. *mail* tribute] —**black′mail′er** *n.*

Black Ma·ri·a (mə·rī′ə) *Informal* A police patrol wagon.

black market A place or business in which merchandise is sold in amounts or at prices contrary to legal restrictions. —**black mar·ket·eer** (mar′kə·tir′)

Black Muslim A member of a U.S. Negro sect (the **Nation of Islam**) which follows the practices of Islam and rejects integration with whites.

black nightshade The common nightshade, having black, poisonous berries.

black·out (blak′out′) *n.* **1** The hiding or extinguishing of all lights, esp. as a precautionary measure against air attack. **2** A temporary loss of consciousness or vision. **3** The sudden darkening of the stage in a theatrical performance. **4** A ban or suppression, as of news, a television broadcast, etc.

black sheep A person regarded as a disreputable member of a family or group.

Black Shirt A member of a fascist group having uniforms with black shirts, as the Italian Fascist Party.

black·smith (blak′smith′) *n.* One who shapes metal using an anvil and forge, esp. one who makes horseshoes and shoes horses.

black·snake (blak′snāk′) *n.* **1** Any of various black or nearly black snakes. **2** A heavy, pliant whip of braided leather or rawhide.

black spruce 1 A small conifer abundant in boggy northern areas of North America. **2** Its soft wood.

black·thorn (blak′thôrn′) *n.* **1** A thorny European shrub of the rose family; the sloe. **2** A cane made from its wood.

black tie 1 A black bow tie. **2** A dinner jacket and its correct accessories.

black walnut 1 A large walnut tree native to North America, having hard, dark brown wood. **2** Its wood. **3** Its oily, edible nut. • See WALNUT.

black widow An American spider of which the venom-ous female has a black body marked with red.

Black widow

blad·der (blad′ər) n. 1 A disten-sible sac for the temporary reten-tion of urine. 2 Any similar part or organ for retaining fluid or gas. 3 An air vessel or float in some seaweeds. [< OE *blædre*] —**blad′-der·y** adj.

blad·der·wort (blad′ər·wûrt′) n. Any of a genus of usu. aquatic plants having little bladders in which minute or-ganisms are trapped and digested.

blade (blād) n. 1 The flat cutting part of an edged tool or weapon. 2 A thin, flat part, as of an oar, propeller, plow, etc. 3 a The expanded part of a leaf. b A narrow leaf having no petiole: a *blade* of grass. 4 a A sword. b A swordsman. 5 A rakish young man. [< OE *blæd* blade of a leaf] —**blad′ed** adj.

blah (blä) *Slang* n. Blather; nonsense. —adj. Lacking in-terest or animation.

blain (blān) n. A small inflamed area; a blister. [< OE *blegen*]

blam·a·ble (blā′mə·bəl) adj. Deserving blame; culpable. —**blam′a·bly** adv.

blame (blām) v.t. **blamed, blam·ing** 1 To accuse of fault: often with *for*. 2 To find fault with; reproach. 3 To hold responsible for something undesirable. —**be to blame** To be at fault. —n. 1 Responsibility for a fault, error, wrong-doing, etc. 2 Censure; condemnation. [< OF *blasmer* < LL *blasphemare* revile, reproach] —**blame′ful** adj. —**blame′ful-ly** adv. —**blame′ful·ness** n. —**blame′less** adj. —**blame′less·ly** adv. —**blame′less·ness** n. —Syn. v. 1 censure, condemn, damn, charge, indict.

blamed (blāmd) adj. & adv. *Regional* Damned: a *blamed* fool; *blamed* hot.

blame·wor·thy (blām′wûr′thē) adj. Deserving of blame. —**blame′wor′thi·ness** n.

blanch (blanch, blänch) v.t. 1 To remove the color from; bleach. 2 To cause to turn pale. 3 To plunge (food) briefly into boiling water, as to remove the skin or in preparation for freezing. —v.i. 4 To turn or become white or pale. [< F *blanc* white] —**blanch′er** n.

blanc·mange (blə·mänzh′, -mänzh′) n. A whitish, jelly-like dessert of milk, eggs, sugar, cornstarch, flavoring, etc. [< OF *blanc-manger* white food]

bland (bland) adj. 1 Smooth; suave; unctuous. 2 Mild; gen-tle; temperate. 3 Not stimulating or irritating. 4 Insipid; flat. [< L *blandus* mild] —**bland′ly** adv. —**bland′ness** n.

blan·dish (blan′dish) v.t. To wheedle; flatter; cajole. [< OF *blandir* flatter] —**blan′dish·er, blan′dish·ment** n.

blank (blangk) adj. 1 Having no writing, printing, decora-tion, etc. 2 Not completed or filled out: a *blank* check. 3 Vacant; empty: a *blank* stare. 4 Utter; complete: *blank* terror. 5 Useless; fruitless: *blank* efforts. 6 Not finished, as with cuts or grooves: a *blank* key. —n. 1 An empty area, condition, etc.; a void. 2 A space left empty, as in printed matter. 3 A printed form to be filled out. 4 A piece, as of metal or wood, ready to be formed into a finished object, as a key, button, etc. 5 A cartridge loaded with powder only: also **blank cartridge.** —**draw a blank** 1 To draw a lottery ticket that does not win. 2 *Informal* To fail in an effort. —v.t. 1 To delete; invalidate: often with *out*. 2 In games, to prevent (an opponent) from scoring. [< OF *blanc* white] —**blank′ly** adv. —**blank′ness** n.

blan·ket (blang′kit) n. 1 A large cloth covering used esp. for warmth, as on a bed. 2 Any thick, extensive covering: a *blanket* of snow. —adj. Covering a wide range of condi-tions, needs, items, etc.: a *blanket* injunction. —v.t. 1 To cover with or as with a blanket. 2 To have uniform ap-plication to. 3 To obscure or suppress as with a blanket. [< OF *blankete,* dim. of *blanc* white]

blank verse Unrhymed verse, esp. of iambic pentameter as used in English epic and dramatic poetry.

blare (blâr) v.t. & v.i. **blared, blar·ing** 1 To sound loudly and harshly, as a trumpet. 2 To exclaim loudly and stridently. —n. 1 A loud, brazen sound. 2 Brightness or glare, as of color. [Prob. imit.]

blar·ney (blär′nē) n. Coaxing flattery. —v.t. & v.i. To flatter or cajole. [< BLARNEY STONE]

Blarney Stone A stone in a castle in Blarney, Ireland, which, when kissed, reputedly endows one with invincible eloquence.

bla·sé (blä·zā′, blä′zā) adj. Sated or bored, as by excessive indulgence, experience, etc. [< F *blaser* satiate]

blas·pheme (blas·fēm′) v. **·phemed, ·phem·ing** —v.t. 1 To speak in an impious or irreverent manner of (God or sa-cred things). 2 To speak ill of; malign. —v.i. 3 To utter blasphemy. [< Gk. *blasphēmeein* revile] —**blas·phem′er** n.

blas·phe·my (blas′fə·mē) n. pl. **·mies** 1 Words or action showing impious irreverence toward God or sacred things. 2 Any irreverent act or utterance. —**blas′phe·mous** adj. —**blas′phe·mous·ly** adv.

blast (blast, bläst) n. 1 To shatter, destroy, etc., by or as by explosion. 2 To cause to wither or fail to mature. 3 To attack or criticize with intense force. —v.i. 4 To make a loud, harsh sound. —**blast off** To begin a flight with ex-plosive force, as a rocket. —n. 1 A strong or sudden wind. 2 The strong jet of air in a blast furnace. 3 The discharge of an explosive, or its effect. 4 A loud, sudden sound, as of a trumpet. 5 A blight or blighting influence —**at full blast** At maximum speed or capacity. [< OE *blæst* a blow-ing] —**blast′er** n.

blast·ed (blas′tid, bläs′-) adj. 1 Withered or destroyed. 2 Damned; confounded: a euphemistic oath.

blast furnace A smelting furnace in which the fire is intensified by an air blast.

blast·off (blast′ôf, -of) n. The launching of a rocket, space vehicle, etc.

blas·tu·la (blas′chŏŏ·lə) n. pl. **·lae** (-lē) or **·las** An early stage of embryonic development, consisting of a hollow sphere enclosed by one or more layers of cells. [< Gk. *blastos* sprout] —**blas′tu·lar** adj.

blat (blat) v. **blat·ted, blat·ting** v.t. 1 *Informal* To blurt out. —v.i. 2 To bleat, as a sheep. [Imit.]

bla·tant (blā′tənt) adj. 1 Offensively loud or clamorous. 2 Obtrusively obvious; glaring: a *blatant* lie. [? < L *blatire* babble] —**bla′tan·cy** n. —**bla′tant·ly** adv.

blath·er (blath′ər) v.t. & v.i. To talk or say foolishly. —n. Foolish talk. [< ON *blathra* talk stupidly]

blath·er·skite (blath′ər·skīt) n. A blustering, noisy fel-low. [< BLATHER + SKATE (fish)]

blaze¹ (blāz) v.i. **blazed, blaz·ing** 1 To burn brightly. 2 To burn as with emotion: to *blaze* with anger. 3 To shine; be resplendent. —**blaze away** 1 To keep on firing. 2 To at-tack persistently. —n. 1 A brightly burning fire. 2 Intense light or glare. 3 A brilliant display. 4 A burst, as of emo-tion. 5 pl. Hell: a euphemism in oaths. [< OE *blæse* fire-brand] —**blaz′ing·ly** adv.

blaze² (blāz) v.t. **blazed, blaz·ing** 1 To mark (a tree) by chip-ping off a piece of bark. 2 To indicate (a trail) by making such marks. —n. 1 A white spot on the face of an animal. 2 A mark made by blazing a tree. [?]

blaze³ (blāz) v.t. **blazed, blaz·ing** To publicize or noise about. [< ON *blāsa* blow]

blaz·er (blā′zər) n. A lightweight jacket, often vividly col-ored or patterned.

bla·zon (blā′zən) n. 1 A coat of arms. 2 A technical de-scription or a graphic representation of a coat of arms. 3 Ostentatious display. —v.t. 1 To inscribe or adorn, as with names or symbols. 2 To describe technically or paint (coats of arms). 3 To proclaim; publish. [< OF *blason* coat of arms, shield] —**bla′zon·er, bla′zon·ment, bla′zon·ry** n.

bldg., blg. building.

bleach (blēch) v.t. & v.i. To make or become colorless, pale, or white. —n. 1 An act of bleaching. 2 A fluid or powder used as a bleaching agent. [< OE *blæcean*]

bleach·er (blē′chər) n. 1 One who or that which bleach-es. 2 pl. Outdoor, uncovered seats or benches for specta-tors, as of a sports event.

bleak (blēk) adj. 1 Exposed to wind and weather; bare. 2

Cold; cutting. **3** Dreary; gloomy. [<ON *bleikja* pale] — **bleak·ly** *adv.* —**bleak′ness** *n.* —**Syn. 1** barren, unsheltered, windswept, withered. **3** melancholy, miserable.

blear (blir) *adj.* Bleary. —*v.t.* **1** To dim or inflame (the eyes). **2** To obscure; blur. [ME *blere*]

blear·y (blir′ē) *adj.* ·i·er, ·i·est **1** Made dim, as by tears. **2** Blurry; hazy: *bleary* vision. —**blear′i·ly** *adv.* —**blear′i·ness** *n.*

blear·y-eyed (blir′ē·īd′) *adj.* Having bleary eyes or vision. Also **blear′-eyed′**.

bleat (blēt) *v.i.* **1** To cry, as a sheep or goat. **2** To speak with such a sound, as in complaint. —*v.t.* **3** To utter with the sound of a bleat. **4** To babble foolishly; prate. —*n.* The act or sound of bleating. [<OE *blǣtan*] —**bleat′er** *n.*

bleed (blēd) *v.* **bled, bleed·ing** *v.i.* **1** To lose or shed blood. **2** To exude sap or other fluid. **3** To suffer wounds or die, as in battle. **4** To feel grief or sympathy. —*v.t.* **5** To draw blood from. **6** To exude (sap, blood, etc.). **7** To draw sap or other fluid from. **8** *Informal* To extort money from. — **bleed white** To deplete of all resources, as if by draining of blood. [<OE *blēdan*]

bleed·er (blē′dər) *n.* A person who bleeds profusely, esp. a hemophiliac.

bleeding heart 1 Any of various plants having pink, drooping flowers. **2** *Informal* One whose political views are unduly influenced by sympathy for alleged suffering.

blem·ish (blem′ish) *v.t.* To mar the perfection of; sully. —*n.* **1** A spot or surface defect, as on the skin. **2** A fault or shortcoming. [<OF *blemir* make livid] —**blem′ish·er** *n.*

blench[1] (blench) *v.i.* To shrink back; flinch. [<OE *blencan* deceive] —**blench′er** *n.*

blench[2] (blench) *v.t.* & *v.i.* To make or become pale; blanch.

blend (blend) *v.* **blend·ed** or **blent, blend·ing** *v.t.* **1** To mix or combine so as to obtain a product of a desired quality, taste, color, or consistency. —*v.i.* **2** To mix; intermingle. **3** To pass or shade imperceptibly into each other, as colors. **4** To harmonize. —*n.* The act or result of blending. [<ON *blanda* mingle]

blende (blend) *n.* Any of several shiny minerals, esp. a compound of sulfur with a metal. [<G *blendendes erz* deceptive ore]

blend·er (blen′dər)*n.* **1** One who or that which blends. **2** Any of various electrical devices that mix and blend substances, as foods, paints, cement, etc.

blen·ny (blen′ē) *n. pl.* **blen·nies** Any of various small, elongated marine fishes. [<Gk. *blennos* slime]

bless (bles) *v.t.* **blessed** or **blest, bless·ing 1** To consecrate; make holy by religious rite. **2** To glorify. **3** To make the sign of the cross over or upon. **4** To invoke divine favor upon (a person or thing). **5** To make happy. **6** To endow, as with a gift: She was *blessed* with a beautiful face. **7** To guard; protect: *Bless* me! [<OE *blētsian* consecrate (with blood)] —**bless′er** *n.*

bless·ed (bles′id, blest) *adj.* **1** Made holy by a religious rite. **2** In heavenly bliss; beatified. **3** Characterized by or causing great happiness. **4** Confounded; damned: used euphemistically or ironically: not a *blessed* cent. Also **blest** (blest). —**bless′ed·ly** *adv.* —**bless′ed·ness** *n.* —**Syn. 1** consecrated, sanctified, sacred. **3** joyous, joyful, rapturous.

blessed event *Informal* The birth of a baby.

bless·ing (bles′ing) *n.* **1** A benediction. **2** A grace said at mealtime. **3** Approval. **4** Good wishes. **5** Anything that gives happiness, prosperity, etc.

blest (blest) A *p.t.* & *p.p.* of BLESS. —*adj.* Blessed.

bleu (blœ) *Can. n.* A member of the Conservative party in Quebec. —*adj.* Of or pertaining to the Conservative party.

blew (blōō) *p.t.* of BLOW.

blight (blīt) *n.* **1** Any of a number of destructive plant diseases, as rust, smut, etc. **2** An environmental factor injurious to a specific group or groups of plants or animals. **3** A person or thing that withers hopes, destroys prospects, etc. **4** A blighted condition. —*v.t.* **1** To cause to decay. **2** To ruin; frustrate. —*v.i.* **3** To suffer blight. [?]

blimp (blimp) *n. Informal* A small, nonrigid dirigible. [< Type *B-Limp*, a kind of British dirigible]

blind (blīnd) *adj.* **1** Without the power of seeing. **2** Of or for blind persons. **3** Lacking in perception, sound judgment, or logic. **4** Done without preparation, plan, or con-

trol: a *blind* effort. **5** Impossible to control or foresee: *blind* fate. **6** Having no opening or outlet: a *blind* ditch. **7** Open at one end only: a *blind* alley. **8** Hard to see; hidden: a *blind* driveway. **9** Using instruments only: *blind* flying. — *n.* **1** Something that obstructs vision or shuts off light, as a window shade. **2** A person or thing meant to deceive; decoy. **3** A hiding place, esp. for hunters. —**the blind** Blind people. —*v.t.* **1** To make blind. **2** To dazzle. **3** To deprive of judgment. **4** To darken; obscure. **5** To outshine; eclipse. —*adv.* **1** By using instruments only. **2** So as to be insensible. [<OE] —**blind′ly** *adv.* —**blind′ness** *n.*

blind date 1 A social engagement arranged for a man and woman who have not previously met. **2** Either of the two persons involved.

blind·er (blīn′dər) *n.* **1** One who or that which blinds. **2** A flap on both sides of a horse's bridle, used to obstruct his side view.

blind·fold (blīnd′fōld′) *v.t.* **1** To cover or bandage the eyes of. **2** To hoodwink; mislead. —*n.* A bandage, etc., over the eyes. —*adj.* **1** Having the eyes bandaged. **2** Reckless; rash. [<ME *blind* blind + *fellen* to strike]

Blinders

blind spot 1 A small area on the retina occupied by optic nerve connections and hence insensible to light. **2** A subject or area of thought about which one is ignorant or prejudiced.

blink (blingk) *v.i.* **1** To wink rapidly. **2** To squint, as in sunlight. **3** To twinkle; glimmer; also, to flash on and off. **4** To ignore or disregard something: He *blinked* at the corruption in politics. —*v.t.* **5** To cause to wink. **6** To shut the eyes to; evade. **7** To send (a message) by a flashing light. —*n.* **1** A blinking of the eye. **2** A gleam of light. — **on the blink** *Informal* Out of order; not working. [ME *blinken*]

blink·er (blingk′ər) *n.* **1** A light that flashes on and off, used as a warning, to send messages, etc. **2** *pl.* Goggles. **3** A horse's blinder.

blin·tze (blin′tsə) *n.* A thin pancake folded about a filling, as of cheese. Also **blintz** (blints). [Yiddish]

blip (blip) *n.* **1** *Telecom.* A visual display of a radar echo. **2** A short, sharp sound. —*v.i.* **blipped, blip·ping 1** To make blips. —*v.t.* **2** To delete (speech) from a videotape, as in censoring, thus creating a discontinuity. [Imit.]

bliss (blis) *n.* **1** Superlative happiness and joy. **2** A cause of delight. [<OE *bliths*] —**bliss′ful** *adj.* —**bliss′ful·ly** *adv.*

blis·ter (blis′tər) *n.* **1** A raised sac under the epidermis, containing watery matter, as from a burn or irritation. **2** Something that resembles a blister, as on a plant, on a painted surface, etc. —*v.t.* **1** To produce a blister or blisters upon. **2** To rebuke harshly. —*v.i.* **3** To become blistered. [OF *blestre*] —**blis′ter·y** *adj.*

blithe (blīth) *adj.* Joyous; gay; carefree. [<OE] —**blithe′ly** *adv.* —**blithe′ness** *n.*

blithe·some (blīth′səm) *adj.* Blithe; merry. —**blithe′· some·ly** *adv.* —**blithe′some·ness** *n.*

blitz (blits) *v.t.* To attack with sudden and overwhelming force. —*n.* A sudden, overwhelming attack. [G, lightning]

blitz·krieg (blits′krēg) *n.* A sudden, overwhelming attack. [G, lit., lightning war]

bliz·zard (bliz′ərd) *n.* **1** A severe storm with heavy snow. **2** Anything resembling a blizzard, as in the swirl or rush of great numbers of things. [?]

blk. black; block; bulk.

bloat (blōt) *v.t.* **1** To cause to swell, as with fluid or gas. **2** To make proud or vain. —*v.i.* **3** To swell; become puffed up. [<ME *blout* swollen]

blob (blob) *n.* A soft, globular mass, as of viscous liquid. —*v.t.* **blobbed, blob·bing** To smear with ink or color. [Imit.]

bloc (blok) *n.* A group, as of politicians, nations, etc., combined to foster special interests. [F]

block (blok) *n.* **1** A solid piece of wood, stone, etc., usu. with flat

Blocks *def.* 8
a. tackle. b. gin.

surfaces. **2** An obstacle, obstruction, or hindrance. **3** The act of obstructing or the condition of being obstructed. **4** A wooden log or cube on which chopping is done: a butcher's *block;* a headsman's *block.* **5** In sports, an interference with an opponent's movements. **6** An auctioneer's stand. **7** The mold on which something is shaped: a hat *block.* **8** A pulley, or set of pulleys, in a frame or shell. **9** A toy building cube, usu. of wood. **10** A piece of wood, linoleum, etc., for engraving a design to be printed. **11** A city square bounded by streets; also, the distance along any of such streets. **12** A large group of adjacent buildings. **13** A group acting or considered as a unit: a *block* of theater seats; the Asian *block* of nations. **14** A section of a railroad track controlled by signals. **15** An interruption of normal physical or mental functioning: a nerve *block;* a memory *block.* **16** *Austral.* An area of farming land. —*v.t.* **1** To obstruct; impede the progress of. **2** To fill (an area or space) so as to prevent movement into or through. **3** In sports: **a** To hinder the movements of (an opposing player). **b** To stop (a ball, etc.) with the body. **4** To shape on a block, as a hat. **5** To put up on blocks. —*v.i.* **6** To act so as to hinder. — **block out 1** To obscure from view. **2** To plan broadly without details: to *block out* a design. [< OF *bloc*] —**block'age,** **block'er** *n.*

block·ade (blo·kād′) *n.* **1** A military or naval closing of an enemy port, coast, etc., to traffic or communication. **2** The forces that set up a blockade. **3** Any hindrance or obstruction to action or traffic. —**run the blockade** To elude a blockade. —*v.t.* **·ad·ed, ·ad·ing** To subject to a blockade. [< F *bloquer* obstruct]

block and tackle An arrangement of pulleys and ropes for hoisting heavy objects.

block·bust·er (blok′bus′tər) *n.* **1** An aerial bomb capable of devastating a large area. **2** *U.S.* One who engages in blockbusting.

block·bust·ing (blok′bust′ing) *n.* *U.S.* The practice of inducing home owners to sell hastily and often at a loss by arousing the fear that the sale of nearby homes to members of a minority group will lower the values of their houses.

block·head (blok′hed′) *n.* A stupid person. —**Syn.** ass, dolt, dunce, fool.

block·house (blok′hous′) *n.* **1** A fortification, formerly of logs and heavy timbers, having loopholes from which to fire guns. **2** A heavily reinforced shelter offering protection and observation at missile launchings, nuclear bomb testings, etc. **3** *U.S.* A house made of hewn logs set square.

block·ish (blok′ish) *adj.* Like a block; stupid; dull. — **block'ish·ly** *adv.* —**block'ish·ness** *n.*

block·y (blok′ē) *adj.* **·i·er, ·i·est** **1** Unequally shaded, as if printed in blocks. **2** Short and stout; stocky.

bloke (blōk) *n.* *Brit. Slang* A fellow; guy.

blond (blond) *adj.* **1** Having flaxen or yellowish brown hair, fair skin and light eyes. **2** Flaxen, golden, or yellowish brown: said of hair. **3** Light-colored. —*n.* A blond person. [< Med.L *blondus*]

blonde (blond) *adj.* *(feminine only)* BLOND (def. 1). —*n.* A blond woman or girl. • In modern usage the final *-e* is usu. kept in the noun when it refers to a fair-haired woman or girl and in the adjective describing such a woman or girl.

blood (blud) *n.* **1** The usu. red fluid that circulates throughout the bodies of vertebrates, delivering oxygen and nutrients to the cells and tissues and removing waste products. **2** A fluid resembling blood, as in certain invertebrates. **3** The shedding of blood, esp. murder. **4** Temperament; disposition: cool *blood.* **5** Vitality; life; lifeblood. **6** Relationship by descent from a common ancestor; kinship. **7** Ancestry; lineage. **8** Royal or noble lineage. —**in cold blood** Without passion or mercy; deliberately. —**make one's blood boil** To make one very angry. —**make one's blood run cold** To terrify one. [< OE *blōd*]

blood bank A reserve of processed blood from various donors for clinical use.

blood bath A massacre; slaughter.

blood count The number and proportion of red cells, platelets, etc., in a given sample of blood.

blood·cur·dling (blud′kurd′ling) *adj.* Terrifying; horrible; chilling.

blood·ed (blud′id) *adj.* **1** Having blood or temper of a specified character: cold-*blooded.* **2** Having pure blood or lineage; thoroughbred.

blood group One of several classes to which any sample of human blood is assignable according to genetic factors identified by agglutination reactions.

blood·hound (blud′hound′) *n.* **1** A large hound with an unusual ability to follow a scent, often used to track fugitives, etc. **2** A person who pursues relentlessly.

Bloodhound

blood·less (blud′lis) *adj.* **1** Having no blood. **2** Without bloodshed. **3** Without vitality; lifeless. **4** Cold-hearted. —**blood'less·ly** *adv.* —**blood'less·ness** *n.*

blood·let·ting (blud′let′ing) *n.* **1** Drawing blood for a therapeutic purpose. **2** Bloodshed.

blood money 1 Money paid to a hired murderer. **2** Money paid as compensation to the next of kin of a murdered man. **3** Money obtained at the expense of another's death, suffering, etc.

blood plasma The liquid part of blood in which corpuscles and other particles are suspended.

blood platelet One of the minute circular bodies found in the blood of higher vertebrates, essential to clotting.

blood poisoning The presence of bacteria in the blood; septicemia.

blood pressure The pressure of the blood on the walls of the arteries.

blood relation A person related by birth.

blood·root (blud′rōōt′, -rŏŏt′) *n.* A perennial North American herb having a fleshy rootstalk with red sap.

blood·shed (blud′shed′) *n.* The shedding of blood; slaughter; carnage.

blood·shot (blud′shot′) *adj.* Red and inflamed or irritated: said of the eye.

blood·stained (blud′stānd′) *adj.* Stained or spotted with blood.

blood·stone (blud′stōn′) *n.* A green chalcedony flecked with red jasper, often cut as a gem.

blood stream The blood in motion in a living body.

blood·suck·er (blud′suk′ər) *n.* **1** An animal that sucks blood, as a leech. **2** A person who takes excessively from or sponges on others.

blood·thirst·y (blud′thûrs′tē) *adj.* Thirsting for blood; murderous; cruel. —**blood'thirst'i·ly** *adv.* —**blood'thirst'i·ness** *n.*

blood type BLOOD GROUP.

blood vessel Any tubular canal in which the blood circulates; an artery, vein, or capillary.

blood·y (blud′ē) *adj.* **blood·i·er, blood·i·est** **1** Covered or stained with blood: also **blood'ied. 2** Of, containing, or mixed with blood. **3** Involving bloodshed. **4** Bloodthirsty. **5** Red like blood. **6** *Brit. Slang* Damned; confounded. — *adv. Brit. Slang* Very; exceedingly. —*v.t.* **blood·ied, blood·y·ing** To smear or stain with blood. —**blood'i·ly** *adv.* — **blood'i·ness** *n.*

bloom (blōōm) *n.* **1** A flower; blossom. **2** Flowers collectively. **3** The state of being in flower. **4** A time of freshness, vigor, and health; prime. **5** A fresh flush or glow, as on the cheeks. **6** A whitish, powdery coating on certain fruits and leaves. —*v.i.* **1** To bear flowers; blossom. **2** To glow with health and vigor. **3** To flourish; be in a prime condition. — *v.t.* **4** To bring into bloom; cause to flourish. [< ON *blōm* flower, blossom] —**bloom'er** *n.*

bloom·er (blōō′mər) *n.* **1** Formerly, a woman's costume of loose trousers gathered at the ankles and worn under a short skirt. **2** *pl.* Loose, wide knickerbockers gathered at the knees, formerly worn by women in athletic practice; also, an undergarment resembling this. [< Amelia *Bloomer,* 1818–94, U.S. feminist reformer who first proposed it]

bloom·ing (blōō'ming) *adj.* 1 Coming into flower. 2 Fresh and vigorous. 3 Flourishing. 4 *Brit. Informal* Utter; veritable. —**Syn.** 3 prosperous, successful, thriving.

bloop·er (blōō'pər) *n. Slang* 1 An error or blunder. 2 In baseball: a A weakly hit fly ball reaching just beyond the infield. b A high, softly thrown pitch. [Imit.]

blos·som (blos'əm) *n.* 1 A flower, esp. one of a plant yielding edible fruit. 2 The state or period of flowering; bloom. —*v.i.* 1 To come into blossom; bloom. 2 To prosper; thrive. [OE *blōstma*] —**blos'som·y** *adj.*

blot (blot) *n.* 1 A spot or stain, as of ink. 2 A moral fault or disgrace. 3 Something unattractive; blemish. —*v.* **blot·ted, blot·ting** *v.t.* 1 To spot, as with ink; stain. 2 To disgrace; sully. 3 To obliterate, as writing, a memory, etc.: often with *out.* 4 To dry with blotting paper. 5 To obscure; darken: usu. with *out.* —*v.i.* 6 To spread in a blot or blots, as ink. 7 To become blotted; acquire spots. 8 To absorb: This paper *blots* well. [ME *blotte*]

blotch (bloch) *n.* 1 A spot or blot. 2 An eruption on the skin. —*v.t.* To mark or cover with blotches. [Blend of BLOT and BOTCH] —**blotch'y** *adj.* (-i·er, -i·est)

blot·ter (blot'ər) *n.* 1 A sheet or pad of blotting paper. 2 The daily record of arrests and charges in a police station.

blotting paper Unsized paper for absorbing excess ink.

blouse (blous, blouz) *n.* 1 A loose garment extending from the neck to the waist or below, worn by women and children. 2 A loose, knee-length shirt usu. belted at the waist, worn chiefly by French workmen. 3 A U.S. Army service coat. —*v.t. & v.i.* **bloused** (bloust, blouzd), **blous·ing** To drape at the waistline. [F]

blow¹ (blō) *v.* **blew, blown, blow·ing** *v.t.* 1 To move by a current of air. 2 To cause air to be released from (a bellows, etc.). 3 To emit, as air or smoke, from the mouth. 4 To force air upon, as for cooling, drying, warming, etc. 5 To empty or clear by forcing air through, as pipes. 6 To cause to sound, as a bugle or horn. 7 To sound (a signal) by blowing. 8 To form or shape, as by inflating: to *blow* glass. 9 To put out of breath, as a horse. 10 To shatter or destroy by or as by explosion: usu. with *up, down, out, through,* etc.: to *blow* a hole through a wall; to *blow* up a house. 11 To melt (a fuse). 12 To lay eggs in, as flies in meat. 13 *Informal* To spend (money) lavishly; also, to treat or entertain: I'll *blow* you to a meal. 14 *Informal* To forget (one's lines) in a play, etc. 15 *Slang* To leave; go out of. 16 *Slang* To handle badly; bungle. —*v.i.* 17 To be in motion, usu. with some force: said of wind or air. 18 To move in a current of air; be carried by the wind. 19 To emit a current or jet of air, water, steam, etc. 20 To sound by being blown: The bugle *blew* at dawn. 21 To fail or become useless, as by melting: The fuse *blew.* 22 To explode: usu. with *up, down, to,* etc. 23 To pant; gasp for breath. 24 *Informal* To talk boastfully. 25 *Slang* To leave; go. —**blow hot and cold** *Informal* To vacillate. —**blow off** 1 To let off steam, as from a boiler. 2 *Informal* To speak in anger, as to relieve pent-up emotion. —**blow out** 1 To extinguish (a fire or flame) by blowing. 2 To be extinguished by air or wind. 3 To explode, as a tire. 4 To subside: The storm will *blow* itself *out.* —**blow over** 1 To overturn by blowing. 2 To be forgotten. 3 To pass, as a storm; subside. —**blow up** 1 To inflate. 2 To enlarge, as a photographic print. 3 To explode. 4 *Informal* To lose self-control; become enraged. 5 To arise, as a storm. 6 To exaggerate (an incident, etc.). —*n.* 1 The act of blowing. 2 A gale. 3 *Slang* Boastfulness. 4 *Slang* A braggart. [< OE *blāwan*]

blow² (blō) *n.* 1 A hard hit or punch, as with the fist or a weapon. 2 A sudden misfortune. 3 A hostile or combative act. —**come to blows** To start fighting. [< ME *blaw*]

blow·er (blō'ər) *n.* 1 One who or that which blows. 2 A device for forcing a draft of air through a building, furnace, machinery, etc.

blow·fly (blō'flī') *n. pl.* **·flies** Any of several flies that lay eggs in carrion or in open wounds.

blow·gun (blō'gun') *n.* A long tube through which a missile may be blown by the breath.

blow·hole (blō'hōl') *n.* 1 The breathing opening in the heads of whales, etc. 2 A vent for the release of gas or air. 3 A hole in the ice to which seals, etc., come to breathe.

blown¹ (blōn) *p.p.* of BLOW¹. —*adj.* 1 Winded from overexertion. 2 Spoiled, as food, by exposure to flies or other organisms. 3 Inflated or swollen. 4 Made with a blowpipe: *blown* glass.

blown² (blōn) *adj.* In full flower or bloom.

blow-out (blō'out') *n.* 1 *Electr.* The opening of a fuse due to excess current. 2 *Slang* An elaborate social function or meal. 3 A sudden bursting of a tire. 4 A flameout.

blow·pipe (blō'pīp') *n.* 1 A tube by which air or gas is blown through a flame to increase its temperature. 2 BLOWGUN.

blow·torch (blō'tôrch') *n.* A device that burns a jet of air and gasoline vapor to make an intensely hot flame.

blow·up (blō'up') *n.* 1 An explosion. 2 An enlarged photograph, page of print, etc. 3 *Informal* Loss of self-control.

blow·y (blō'ē) *adj.* **blow·i·er, blow·i·est** Windy.

blowz·y (blou'zē) *adj.* **·i·er, ·i·est** 1 Unkempt; slovenly. 2 Coarse, fat, and ruddy-faced. Also **blows·y** (blou'zē). [?]

blub·ber¹ (blub'ər) *v.t.* 1 To utter sobbingly. —*v.i.* 2 To weep and sob noisily. [ME *blubren*] —**blub'ber·er** *n.*

blub·ber² (blub'ər) *n.* The layer of fat beneath the skin of whales and other sea mammals. [ME *bluber*] —**blub'ber·y** *adj.*

bludg·eon (bluj'ən) *n.* A short club, commonly loaded at one end, used as a weapon. —*v.t.* 1 To strike with or as with a bludgeon. 2 To coerce; bully. [?]

blue (blōō) *adj.* **blu·er, blu·est** 1 Having the color of the clear, daytime sky. 2 Livid: said of the skin. 3 Sad; melancholy. 4 Depressing; discouraging. 5 Puritanic; strict: *blue* laws. 6 *Informal* Risqué. 7 *Can.* BLEU. —*n.* 1 The color of the clear, daytime sky; azure. 2 Any blue coloring matter or pigment. 3 BLUING. 4 *Often pl.* Blue clothing. 5 *Sometimes cap.* A person who wears a blue uniform. 6 *pl.* See BLUES. 7 *Can.* BLEU. —**out of the blue** From an unsuspected source; completely unforeseen. —*v.t.* **blued, blu·ing** 1 To make blue. 2 To treat with bluing. [< OF *bleu*] —**blue'ly** *adv.* —**blue'ness** *n.*

Blue·beard (blōō'bird') In folklore, a man who married and then murdered one wife after another.

blue·bell (blōō'bel') *n.* Any of various plants that bear blue, bell-shaped flowers.

blue·ber·ry (blōō'ber'ē; -bər·ē) *n. pl.* **·ries** 1 A many-seeded, edible, blue-black berry. 2 The plant that bears it.

blue·bird (blōō'bûrd') *n.* Any of various small North American songbirds with blue plumage.

blue blood 1 Descent from a noble or aristocratic family. 2 A person of noble or aristocratic family. Also **blue'blood'.** —**blue'-blood·ed** *adj.*

blue·bon·net (blōō'bon'it) *n.* 1 A lupine with blue flowers. 2 Any of various herbs having blue flowers.

blue book 1 A government report or register: also **Blue Book.** 2 A register of socially prominent persons. 3 A blue-covered, blank notebook for writing college examinations.

blue·bot·tle (blōō'bot'l) *n.* 1 A large blowfly with a metallic-blue or -green abdomen. 2 Any of various blue flowers with bottle-shaped parts, as the cornflower.

blue cheese A cheese marbled with bluish mold.

blue·coat (blōō'kōt') *n.* A policeman.

blue·col·lar (blōō'kol'ər) *adj.* Of, pertaining to, or designating employees engaged in physical or manual work that requires them to wear rough-textured, dark, or special clothing for protection or as a uniform.

blue·fish (blōō'fish') *n. pl.* **·fish** or **·fish·es** A food fish common along the Atlantic Coast of North America.

blue flag An iris having blue flowers.

blue·grass (blōō'gras', -gräs') *n.* Any of a genus of forage and lawn grasses.

blue·gum (blōō'gum') *n.* A species of eucalyptus tree.

blue·ing (blōō'ing) BLUING.

blue·ish (blōō'ish) BLUISH.

blue·jack·et (blōō'jak'it) *n.* An enlisted man in the U.S. Navy.

blue jay A crested corvine bird of North America.

blue law Any of various puritanical laws, esp. one prohibiting certain activities and entertainments on Sunday.

blue·nose (blōō'nōz') *n.* A puritanical person.

blue-pen·cil (blōō'pen'səl) *v.t.* 1 To edit or revise. 2 *Informal* To veto or censor.

· Blue jay

blue·print (bloo′print′) n. 1 A photographic print of a plan or drawing showing in white lines on a blue ground. 2 Any detailed plan. —v.t. To make a blueprint of.
blue ribbon In competitions, a first prize.
blues (blooz) n.pl. (construed as sing. or pl.) 1 Depression; melancholy: with the. 2 A type of song written in minor keys, and characterized by slow jazz rhythms and melancholy words: usu. with the.
blue-sky (bloo′skī′) adj. 1 Without value; worthless. 2 Informal Highly speculative in nature; impractical. —v. -skied, -sky·ing Informal v.i. 1 To engage in impractical or visionary speculation. —v.t. 2 To speculate about impractically.
blue-sky laws Laws enacted to prevent the sale of worthless stocks and bonds.
blue·stock·ing (bloo′stok′ing) n. A learned or literary woman, usu. pretentiously so.
blu·et (bloo′it) n. Any of various plants with blue flowers.
bluff[1] (bluf) v.t. 1 To deceive by putting on a bold front. 2 To frighten with empty threats. —v.i. 3 To pretend to knowledge, ability, strength, etc., which one does not have. —**bluff one's way** To obtain (an objective) by bluffing. —n. 1 The act of bluffing. 2 One who bluffs. [?< Du. bluffen deceive, mislead] —**bluff′er** n.
bluff[2] (bluf) n. A high, steep cliff or bank. —adj. 1 Blunt, frank, and hearty. 2 Having an upright, broad, flattened front. [?< Du. blaf flat, as in blaf aensicht broad flat face] —**bluff′ly** adv. —**bluff′ness** n. —Syn. 1 abrupt, brusque, open, plain-spoken.
blu·ing (bloo′ing) n. The blue coloring matter used in laundering white fabrics to counteract yellowing.
blu·ish (bloo′ish) adj. Somewhat blue. —**blu′ish·ness** n.
blun·der (blun′dər) n. A stupid mistake. —v.t. 1 To move carelessly or awkwardly. 2 To make a stupid and awkward mistake. —v.t. 3 To say clumsily or thoughtlessly: often with out. 4 To bungle. [ME blondren mix up, confuse] —**blun′der·er** n. —**blun′der·ing·ly** adv.
blun·der·buss (blun′dər·bus) n. 1 An old-fashioned, short gun with a large bore and flaring mouth. 2 One who blunders. [Blend of BLUNDER and Du. donderbus thunder box]
blunt (blunt) adj. 1 Having a thick or dull end or edge. 2 Abrupt and plain-spoken in manner. 3 Slow of wit; dull. —v.t. & v.i. 1 To make or become blunt or dull. 2 To make or become less keen or poignant. [ME blunt; origin unknown] —**blunt′ly** adv. —**blunt′ness** n.
blur (blûr) n. 1 A smeared or indistinct marking. 2 Something vague or indistinct to the sight or mind. —v.t. & v.i. blurred, blur·ring v.t. 1 To stain, smear, or smudge. 2 To make or become obscure or indistinct in outline. 3 To make or become dim or cloudy. [?] —**blur′ry** adj. (·ri·er, ·ri·est)
blurb (blûrb) n. A brief, commendatory statement, as on a book jacket, that serves as publicity for a book, author, etc. [Coined by Gelett Burgess, 1866–1951, U.S. humorist]
blurt (blûrt) v.t. To utter abruptly, as if on impulse: usu. with out. [?]
blush (blush) v.i. 1 To redden in the face, as from embarrassment. 2 To be or become red or rosy. 3 To feel shame or regret: usu. with at or for. —v.t. 4 To make red. —n. 1 A reddening of the face, as from modesty, etc. 2 A red or rosy tint; flush. [< OE blyscan redden] —**blush′er** n. —**blush′ful** adj.
blus·ter (blus′tər) n. 1 Boisterous talk or swagger. 2 A noisy blowing of the wind. —v.i. 1 To blow gustily, as the wind. 2 To act or speak noisily and aggressively. —v.t. 3 To utter noisily and boisterously. 4 To force or bully by blustering. [ME blusteren] —**blus′ter·er** n. —**blus′ter·y**, **blus′ter·ous** adj.
blvd. boulevard.
Bn., bn. battalion.
b.o. box office; branch office.
bo·a (bō′ə) n. pl. **bo·as** 1 Any of several nonvenomous serpents that crush their prey, as the anaconda, python, and esp. the **boa constrictor.** 2 A long feather or fur neckpiece for women. [< L]

boar (bôr, bōr) n. pl. **boars** or **boar** 1 An uncastrated male hog. 2 The wild hog of Europe, North Africa, and Asia. [< OE bār]

Boar def. 2

board (bôrd, bōrd) n. 1 A flat piece of sawed wood whose length is much greater than its width. 2 A slab of wood or other material prepared for a specific purpose: a diving board. 3 Pasteboard or other material, often used for book covers. 4 A table, spread for serving food. 5 Meals regularly furnished for pay. 6 An organized official body: a board of directors. 7 A table around which meetings are held. —**on board** On or. in a vessel or other conveyance. —**tread the boards** To appear as an actor. —v.t. 1 To cover or enclose with boards: often with up. 2 To furnish with meals or meals and lodging for pay. 3 To place (someone) where meals are provided, as in a boarding school. 4 Naut. To come alongside or go on board of (a ship). 5 To enter, as a ship or train. —v.i. 6 To take meals or meals and lodging for pay. (< OE bord]
board·er (bôr′dər, bōr′-) n. 1 A person who receives regular meals, or meals and lodging, for pay. 2 One detailed to board an enemy's ship.
board foot pl. **board feet** The measure of a board 1 foot square and 1 inch thick; 144 cubic inches.
board·ing (bôr′ding, bōr′-) n. 1 Boards collectively. 2 A structure of boards.
boarding house A house for keeping boarders.
boarding school A school in which pupils are boarded.
board measure A system of measure for boards, based on the board foot.
board·walk (bôrd′wôk′, bōrd′-) n. 1 A promenade along a beach, usu. raised and made of boards. 2 Any walk made of boards.
boast (bōst) v.i. 1 To extol the deeds or abilities of oneself or of another; brag. 2 To be excessively proud: with of. —v.t. 3 To brag about. 4 To be proud to possess; take pride in. —n. 1 A boastful speech. 2 A source of pride. [ME bosten] —**boast′er** n. —Syn. v. 1 crow, flaunt, swagger, vaunt.
boast·ful (bōst′fəl) adj. Tending to brag. —**boast′ful·ly** adv. —**boast′ful·ness** n.
boat (bōt) n. 1 A small, open watercraft propelled by oars, sails, or an engine. 2 A large, seagoing vessel; ship: a nautically incorrect usage. 3 A dish resembling a boat. —**be in the same boat** To be in the same situation. —v.i. 1 To travel by boat. 2 To go boating for pleasure. —v.t. 3 To transport or place in a boat. [< OE bāt]
boat·house (bōt′hous′) n. A building for storing boats.
boat·ing (bō′ting) n. Rowing, cruising, or sailing.
boat·load (bōt′lōd′) n. 1 The full amount that a boat can hold. 2 The load carried by a boat.
boat·man (bōt′mən) n. pl. **·men** One who manages, rows, or works on a boat. —**boat′man·ship** n.
boat·swain (bō′sən, rarely bōt′swān′) n. On a ship, a warrant officer or petty officer in charge of the deck crew, the rigging, anchors, etc.
bob[1] (bob) n. 1 In fishing: a A cork or float on a line. b A ball-shaped bait of angleworms, rags, etc. 2 A small, pendent object or weight: a plumb bob. 3 A jerky bow or curtsy. 4 Any short, jerky movement. 5 A short style of haircut. 6 The docked tail of a horse. —v. bobbed, bob·bing v.t. 1 To move up and down: to bob the head. 2 To cut short, as hair. —v.i. 3 To move up and down with an irregular motion. 4 To curtsy. 5 To fish with a bob. —**bob up** To appear or emerge suddenly. [ME bobbe a hanging cluster] —**bob′·ber** n.
bob[2] (bob) v.t. bobbed, bob·bing To strike lightly; tap. [ME bobben]
bob[3] (bob) n. pl. **bob** Brit. Informal A shilling. [?]
bob·bin (bob′in) n. A spool or reel to hold weft or thread in spinning, weaving, or in machine sewing. [F bobine]
bob·ble (bob′əl) n. 1 A bobbing motion. 2 One of the small decorative balls forming an edge of a tablecloth, etc. 3 Informal A blunder; esp., in sports, the mishan-

dling of a ball upon trying to field or catch it. —v. **bob·bled**, **bob·bling** v.i. 1 To move with a bobbing motion. —v.t. Informal To mishandle; fumble. [Freq. of BOB[1]] —**bob'·bler** n.

bob·by (bob'ē) n. pl. **·bies** Brit. Informal A policeman. [after Sir Robert (Bobby) Peel, 1788–1850, Brit. statesman]

bobby pin A metal hairpin so shaped as to hold the hair tightly. Also **bobbie pin.**

bobby socks Informal Ankle-length socks worn by girls.

bob·by-sox·er (bob'ē·sok'sər) n. Informal An adolescent girl, esp. in the 1940's.

bob·cat (bob'kat') n. The American lynx.

bob·o·link (bob'ə·lingk) n. An American songbird with black and white or buff plumage. [Imit. of its call]

bob·sled (bob'sled') n. 1 A racing sled having a set of runners in front, another set in back, and controlled by a steering apparatus and brakes. 2 A sled made of two short sleds or pairs of runners connected tandem by a top plank. —v.i. **·sled·ded**, **·sled·ding** To ride on a bobsled.

bob·tail (bob'tāl') n. 1 A short tail or a tail cut short. 2 An animal with such a tail. —adj. 1 Having the tail docked. 2 Incomplete. —v.t. To cut the tail of; dock. —**bob'·tailed'** adj.

bob·white (bob'hwīt') n. A small North American quail. [Imit. of its call]

bock beer (bok) An extra strong beer brewed in the winter and served in early spring. Also **bock.** [< Einbeck, town in Germany]

bode[1] (bōd) Archaic p.t. & p.p. of BIDE.

bode[2] (bōd) v. **bod·ed**, **bod·ing** v.t. 1 To be a token of; presage, as good, evil, etc. —v.i. 2 To presage good or ill. [< OE bodian announce] —**bode'ment** n. —**Syn.** 1, 2 augur, forebode, foretell, predict.

bod·ice (bod'is) n. 1 The part of a woman's dress from waist to shoulder. 2 A woman's ornamental laced waist. [Var. of bodies, pl. of BODY]

bod·ied (bod'ēd) adj. 1 Having a body. 2 Having a specified kind of body: used in combination: able-bodied.

bod·i·less (bod'i·lis) adj. Having no body; incorporeal.

bod·i·ly (bod'ə·lē) adj. 1 Of or pertaining to the body. 2 Physical rather than mental. —adv. 1 In the body; in person. 2 All together; wholly; completely.

bod·kin (bod'kin) n. 1 A thick needle for drawing tape through a hem. 2 A pointed instrument for piercing holes in cloth, etc. 3 A pin for fastening the hair. 4 Obs. A stiletto. [ME boydekin dagger]

bod·y (bod'ē) n. pl. **bod·ies** 1 The entire physical structure of a person, animal, or plant. 2 A corpse. 3 The trunk of a person or animal. 4 Informal A person. 5 A collection of persons or things considered as a unit. 6 The principal part or mass of anything. 7 Any mass of matter: a celestial body; a body of water. 8 Density or substance: a fabric with body. 9 Fullness and richness, as of a wine. —v.t. **bod·ied**, **bod·y·ing** To give shape or form to; embody; represent: usu. with forth. [< OE bodig]

bod·y·guard (bod'ē·gärd') n. A person or persons designated to guard or protect someone.

body politic The people of a state or nation viewed as an organized political body.

Boe·o·tia (bē·ō'shə, -shē·ə) n. An ancient province of Greece, cap. Thebes. —**Boe·o'tian** adj., n.

Boer (bōr, bôr, bōōr) n. A Dutch colonist, or person of Dutch descent in South Africa. [Du., farmer]

bog (bog, bôg) n. Wet and spongy ground; marsh; morass, —v.t. & v.i. **bogged**, **bog·ging** To sink or stick in or as in a bog: often with down. [< Ir., soft] —**bog'gish** adj.

bo·gey (bō'gē) n. pl. **bo·geys** In golf: 1 An estimated standard score. 2 One stroke over par on a hole. Also **bo'gie.** [?]

bog·gle (bog'əl) v. **bog·gled**, **bog·gling** v.i. 1 To hesitate, as from doubt or scruples: often with at. 2 To be startled or amazed. 3 To bungle. —v.t. 4 To startle. 5 To bungle. [?]

bog·gy (bog'ē, bôg'ē) adj. **bog·gi·er**, **bog·gi·est** Swampy; miry. —**bog'gi·ness** n.

bo·gus (bō'gəs) adj. Counterfeit; spurious; fake. [?]

bo·gy (bō'gē) n. pl. **bo·gies** A goblin; bugbear. Also **bo'gie, bo'gey.** [?]

Bo·he·mi·an (bō·hē'mē·ən) adj. 1 Of or pertaining to Bohemia. 2 Leading the life of a Bohemian; unconventional. —n. 1 A native or inhabitant of Bohemia. 2 A gypsy. 3 A person, usu. of artistic or literary tastes, who lives in a more or less unconventional manner. Also (for adj. def. 2 and n. def. 3) **bo·he'mi·an.** —**Bo·he'mi·an·ism** n.

boil[1] (boil) v.i. 1 To be agitated, as a liquid when heated, by gaseous bubbles rising to the surface. 2 To reach the boiling point. 3 To undergo the action of a boiling liquid. 4 To be agitated: The water boiled with sharks. 5 To be stirred, as by violent anger. —v.t. 6 To bring to the boiling point. 7 To cook or cleanse by boiling. —**boil away** 1 To evaporate in boiling. —**boil down** 1 To reduce in bulk by boiling. 2 To condense; edit. —**boil over** 1 To overflow while boiling. 2 To become enraged. —n. The act or state of boiling. [< L bullire to boil]

boil[2] (boil) n. A pussy and painful swelling in the skin, of bacterial origin. [< OE bȳl, bȳle]

boil·er (boi'lər) n. 1 A utensil in which food or liquid is boiled. 2 A closed vessel generating steam, as for motive power. 3 A receptacle for heating and storing hot water.

boiling point The temperature at which the vapor pressure in a liquid equals the external pressure; at normal atmospheric pressure the boiling point of water is 212°F or 100°C.

bois·ter·ous (bois'tər·əs) adj. 1 Noisy; rowdy; unrestrained. 2 Violent; turbulent. [ME boistous] —**bois'ter·ous·ly** adv. —**bois'ter·ous·ness** n.

bo·la (bō'lə) n. A weapon consisting of balls fastened to cords and used, when thrown, to entangle the legs of cattle and large game. Also **bo·las** (bō'ləs). [< Sp., a ball]

Bola

bold (bōld) adj. 1 Possessing courage; fearless. 2 Showing or requiring courage. 3 Shameless; forward; brazen. 4 Striking; vigorous, as language. 5 Clear; prominent: bold outlines. 6 Abrupt; steep, as a cliff. —**make bold** To take the liberty; venture. [< OE bald] —**bold'ly** adv. —**bold'ness** n. —**Syn.** 1 audacious, brave, daring, valiant. 3 brassy, immodest, impudent.

bold·face (bōld'fās') n. Printing A type in which the lines have been thickened to give a very heavy impression. —**bold'-faced'** adj.

bole (bōl) n. The trunk of a tree. [< ON bolr]

bo·le·ro (bō·lâr'ō) n. pl. **·ros** 1 A short jacket open at the front. 2 A Spanish dance, usu. accompanied by castanets; also, the music for it. [Sp.]

bol·i·var (bol'ə·vər, Sp. bō·lē'vär) n. pl. **bol·i·vars**, Sp. **bo·li·va·res** (bō'lē·vä'räs) A monetary unit of Venezuela. [< Simón Bolivar, 1783–1830, South American liberator]

Bo·liv·i·a (bə·liv'ē·ə) n. A republic of CEN. South America, 424,162 sq. mi., caps. Sucre and La Paz. —**Bo·liv'·i·an** adj. & n. • See map at BRAZIL.

boll (bōl) n. A round seed capsule, as of flax or cotton. —v.i. To form pods. [< MDu. bolle]

boll weevil A small weevil whose larvae destroy cotton bolls.

boll·worm (bōl'wûrm') n. The very destructive moth larva that feeds on cotton bolls, corn ears, and other plants.

bo·lo (bō'lō) n. pl. **·los** (-lōz) A heavy, single-edged weapon used in the Philippine Islands. [Sp.]

bo·lo·gna (bə·lō'nē, -lo'nə, -lōn'yə) Sometimes cap. A highly seasoned sausage of mixed meats. Also **bologna sausage.** [< Bologna, Italy]

bo·lo·ney (bə·lō'nē) n. BALONEY.

Bol·she·vik (bōl'shə·vik, bol'-) n. pl. **Bol·she·viks** or **Bol·she·vi·ki** (bōl'shə·vē'kē, bol'-) 1 A member of the dominant branch of the Russian Social Democratic Party or, since the 1917 Revolution, of the Russian Communist Party. 2 A Communist. 3 Loosely, any radical. Also **bol'she·vik.** [Russ., a member of the majority (group in the party)]

Bol·she·vism (bōl′shə·viz′əm, bol′-) n. 1 The Marxian doctrines and policies of the Bolsheviki. 2 A government based on these policies. Also **bol′she·vism.** —**Bol′she·vist** n. —**Bol′she·vis′tic** adj.

bol·ster (bōl′stər) n. 1 A long, narrow pillow as wide as a bed. 2 A pad used as a support or for protection. 3 Anything shaped like or used as a bolster. —v.t. To prop up, as something ready to fall. [< OE] —**bol′ster·er** n.

bolt[1] (bōlt) n. 1 A sliding bar or piece for fastening a door, etc. 2 In a lock, the movable bar or piece that is operated by the key. 3 A metal pin or rod usu. threaded and having a head at one end, used with a nut for holding anything in its place. 4 A sliding bar that closes the breech in certain firearms. 5 An arrow for a crossbow. 6 A lightning flash. 7 A sudden start or departure. 8 A roll of cloth, wall paper, etc. —**bolt from the blue** A sudden and wholly unexpected event. —v.i. 1 To move, go, or spring suddenly: usu. with *out* or *from*: He *bolted* from the room. 2 U.S. To break away, as from a political party. —v.t. 3 To fasten with or as with bolts. 4 U.S. To break away from, as a political party. 5 To gulp, as food. 6 To blurt out. —adv. Rigidly; erectly: to sit *bolt* upright. [< OE, arrow for a crossbow]

bolt[2] (bōlt) v.t. 1 To sift. 2 To examine as by sifting. [< OF *buleter*]

bo·lus (bō′ləs) n. pl. **bo·lus·es** 1 A large pill. 2 Any rounded mass. [< Gk. *bōlos* clod of earth, lump]

bomb (bom) n. 1 A hollow projectile containing explosive, incendiary, or chemical material to be discharged by concussion or by a time fuse. 2 An unexpected occurrence. 3 *Slang* A flop; failure; dud. 4 *Informal* In football, a long forward pass. —v.t. 1 To attack or destroy with or as with bombs. —v.i. 2 *Slang* To fail utterly. [< L *bombus* loud sound]

bom·bard (bom·bärd′) v.t. 1 To attack with bombs or shells. 2 To attack or press as with bombs: to *bombard* with questions. 3 To expose to the effect of radiation or to the impact of high-energy atomic particles. [< MF *bombarde* a cannon] —**bom·bard′er, bom·bard′ment** n.

bom·bar·dier (bom′bər·dir′) n. The member of the crew of a bomber who operates the bombsight and releases bombs.

bom·bast (bom′bast) n. Pompous, high-flown language. [< OF *bombace* cotton padding] —**bom·bas′tic, bom·bas′ti·cal** adj. —**bom·bas′ti·cal·ly** adv. —**Syn.** grandiloquence, prolixity, verbosity, wordiness.

bomb bay A compartment in military aircraft in which bombs are carried and from which they are dropped.

bombed (bombd) adj. *Slang* Drunk.

bomb·er (bom′ər) n. 1 One who attacks with bombs. 2 An airplane employed in bombing.

bomb·proof (bom′proof′) adj. So constructed as to resist damage from bombs.

bomb·shell (bom′shel′) n. **bomb** (def. 1). 2 *Informal* Something astounding or shocking.

bomb·sight (bom′sīt′) n. An instrument for aiming aerial bombs.

bo·na fide (bō′nə·fīd′, -fī′dē) 1 Acting or carried out in good faith. 2 Authentic; real. [< L, in good faith]

bo·nan·za (bə·nan′zə) n. 1 A rich mine, vein, or find of ore. 2 Any profitable operation. [Sp., success]

bon·bon (bon′bon′, Fr. bôṅ·bôṅ′) n. A small piece of candy coated with fondant or chocolate. [< F *bon* good]

bond (bond) n. 1 Something that binds, holds, or fastens. 2 The union thus formed. 3 A tie, link, or union: a family *bond*. 4 An obligation, promise, or agreement. 5 pl. A Fetters. b Captivity. 6 An interest-bearing certificate sold by a government or business to raise money and carrying the promise to repay the purchaser by a specified date. 7 An insurance policy covering losses suffered through the acts of an employee. 8 The condition of goods stored in a warehouse until duties are paid. 9 *Law* a An obligation in writing under seal. b One who furnishes bail. c Bail. 10 *Chem.* A force that holds together the atoms of a molecule. — **bottled in bond** Bottled after storage in a bonded warehouse for a specified amount of time, as some whiskies. —

v.t. 1 To put a certified debt upon; mortgage. 2 To furnish bond for; be surety for (someone). 3 To place, as goods or an employee, under bond. 4 To unite or bind tightly together. —v.i. 5 To hold or cohere with or as with a bond. [< ON *band*]

bond·age (bon′dij) n. 1 Compulsory servitude; slavery. 2 Subjection to any force or influence. —**Syn.** 1 captivity, serfdom, thralldom.

bond·ed (bon′did) adj. 1 Subject to a bond. 2 Stored in a warehouse until duties are paid. 3 Held close together, as by a strong adhesive or by chemical action.

bond·hold·er (bond′hōl′dər) n. One owning or holding bonds. —**bond′hold′ing** adj., n.

bond paper A strong paper of superior fiber, used in printing bonds and paper money, for business letters, etc.

bond·ser·vant (bond′sûr′vənt) n. One in servitude without wages; slave. Also **bond′slave′.**

bonds·man (bondz′mən) n. pl. **·men** (-mən) A person who furnishes bond or surety for another.

bone (bōn) n. 1 A separate piece of the skeleton of a vertebrate animal. 2 The hard tissue of which a skeleton is composed. 3 One of various objects made of bone or similar material, as a corset stay. 4 A material resembling bone, as whalebone. 5 pl. *Slang* Dice. —**feel in (one's) bones** To have an intuition of. —**have a bone to pick** To have grounds for complaint or dispute. —**make no bones about** To be totally frank or honest about. —v. **boned, bon·ing** v.t. 1 To remove the bones from. 2 To stiffen with whalebone. —v.i. 3 *Slang* To study intensely: often with *up*. [< OE *bān*]

bone·head (bōn′hed′) n. *Informal* A slow-witted, stupid person. —**bone′head′ed** adj.

bone meal Pulverized bone, used as fertilizer or animal feed.

bon·er (bō′nər) n. *Slang* An error; faux pas.

bone·set (bōn′set′) n. Any of various herbs of the composite family thought to have curative properties.

bon·fire (bon′fīr′) n. A large fire in the open air. [< BONE + FIRE; formerly a fire for calcining bones]

bon·go drums (bong′gō) A pair of drums played with the hands, originally from Africa. Also **bon′gos.** [Am. Sp.] • See DRUM.

bo·ni·to (bə·nē′tō) n. pl. **·tos** or **·toes** Any of various large, tunalike marine food and game fishes. [Sp., beautiful]

bon jour (bôṅ zhoor′) *French* Good day.

bon mot (bôṅ mō′) pl. **bons mots** (bôṅ mōz′, Fr. mō′) A clever saying; terse witticism. [F]

Bonito

bon·net (bon′it) n. 1 An outdoor headdress for women and children, usu. tied under the chin. 2 A brimless cap for men and boys, worn esp. in Scotland. 3 An American Indian headdress of feathers. 4 Any of various metal hoods protecting machinery, etc. 5 *Brit.* The hood of an automobile. —v.t. To cover with or as with a bonnet. [< OF *bonet*]

bon·ny (bon′ē) adj. **·ni·er, ·ni·est** *Chiefly Brit. & Scot.* 1 Pretty and sweet. 2 Robust; healthy. 3 Fine; good. Also **bon′nie.** [< F *bon* good] —**bon′ni·ly** adv. —**bon′ni·ness** n.

bon·sai (bon′sī, bōn′-) n. pl. **·sai** 1 A decorative dwarfed tree grown in a pot. 2 The art of creating such trees. [Jap.]

bon soir (bôṅ swär′) *French* Good evening.

bo·nus (bō′nəs) n. pl. **bo·nus·es** Something given, as a sum of money, over and above what is usual, current, or stipulated. [L, good]

bon vi·vant (bôṅ vē·vän′) pl. **bons vi·vants** (bôṅ vē·vän′) A person who enjoys the pleasurable things of life. [F] — **Syn.** sybarite, voluptuary, epicure.

bon vo·yage (bôṅ vwä·yàzh′) *French* A phrase wishing a traveler a pleasant voyage or trip.

bon·y (bō′nē) adj. **bon·i·er, bon·i·est** 1 Of, like, or consisting of bone. 2 Having prominent bones. 3 Thin; gaunt. — **bon′i·ness** n.

boo (boo) n. & interj. A vocal sound made to indicate contempt or frighten. —*v.* **booed, boo·ing** *v.i.* To utter boos. —*v.t.* To shout boo at.

boob (bōōb) *n. Slang* A stupid or gullible person, simpleton. [Short for BOOBY]

boo-boo (bōō'bōō') *n. pl.* **-boos** *Slang* A mistake or blunder. Also **boo'boo'**.

boob tube *Slang* Television or a television set.

boo·by (bōō'bē) *n. pl.* **boo·bies** 1 A dull fellow; dunce. 2 In some games, the person who makes the poorest score. 3 Any of several gannets of warm seas. [Sp. *bobo* fool <L *balbus* stammering]

booby prize A mock award for the worst score or performance in a contest, game, etc.

booby trap 1 A concealed bomb, mine, etc., designed to explode when inadvertently disturbed. 2 Any scheme for catching a person off guard.

boo·dle (bōōd'l) *n. Slang* 1 A bribe; graft. 2 Loot; plunder. 3 A crowd; caboodle. —*v.i.* **·dled, ·dling** To bribe or receive bribes. [<Du. *boedel* property] —**boo'dler** *n.*

boog·ie-woog·ie (bōōg'ē·wōōg'ē) *n.* A style of jazz piano playing characterized by a repeated, rhythmic bass with melodic inventions in the treble. —*adj.* Of, in, or pertaining to this style. [?]

boo·hoo (bōō'·hōō') *v.i.* **·hooed, ·hoo·ing** To weep loudly. —*n. pl.* **·hoos** Noisy sobbing. [Imit.]

book (bōōk) *n.* 1 A number of printed or written sheets of paper bound together, usu. between covers. 2 A literary or other written composition or treatise so bound and usu. of some length. 3 A subdivision of a literary composition or treatise: one of the *books* of the Bible. 4 A business record or ledger. 5 LIBRETTO. 6 A script for a play, musical comedy, etc. 7 A booklike pack of matches, etc. 8 A list of bets made. —**by the book** According to rule. —**like a book** Thoroughly. —**the Book** The Bible. —*v.t.* 1 To enter or list in a book. 2 To arrange for beforehand, as accommodations or seats. 3 To engage, as actors or a play, for performance. 4 To make a record of charges against (someone) on a police blotter. [<OE *bōc*]

book·bind·ing (bōōk'bīn'ding) *n.* The art or trade of binding books. —**book'bind'er** *n.*

book·case (bōōk'kās') *n.* A case containing shelves for holding books.

book club An organisation that sells books at reduced prices to its members.

book·end (bōōk'end') *n.* A support or prop used to hold upright a row of books.

book·ie (bōōk'ē) *n. Informal* BOOKMAKER (def. 2).

book·ish (bōōk'ish) *adj.* 1 Fond of reading and learning. 2 Pedantic. —**book'ish·ly** *adv.* —**book'ish·ness** *n.*

book jacket DUST JACKET.

book·keep·ing (bōōk'kē'ping) *n.* The art, method, or practice of recording business transactions systematically. —**book'keep'er** *n.*

book·let (bōōk'lit) *n.* A small, thin book.

book·mak·er (bōōk'mā'kər) *n.* 1 One who compiles, prints, or binds books. 2 One whose business is accepting and paying off bets, esp. in horse racing.

book·mark (bōōk'märk') *n.* Any object to be placed between the leaves of a book to mark a place.

book·plate (bōōk'plāt') *n.* A printed label placed in a book to indicate ownership.

book·rack (bōōk'rak') *n.* 1 A frame to hold an open book: also **book'rest'**. 2 A framework to hold books, as on a table.

book review An article or essay discussing or critically examining a book.

book·sel·ler (bōōk'sel'ər) *n.* One who sells books.

book·stack (bōōk'stak') *n.* A tall rack containing shelves for books, as in a library.

book·stall (bōōk'stôl) *n.* A stall or stand where books are sold.

book·stand (bōōk'stand') *n.* 1 A rack for books. 2 BOOKSTALL.

book·store (bōōk'stôr', -stōr') *n.* A store for the sale of books.

book·worm (bōōk'wûrm') *n.* 1 A person devoted to books and study. 2 Any of various insect larvae destructive to books.

boom[1] (bōōm) *n.* 1 A spar used to extend or support the foot of a sail. 2 A chain of logs to intercept or retard the advance of a vessel, to confine timbers, sawlogs, etc. 3 A long mobile beam projecting upward from the foot of a derrick to carry or guide a load suspended from its outer end. 4 A long, mobile arm with a microphone attached at one end. [<Du. *boom* tree, beam]

boom[2] (bōōm) *v.i.* 1 To emit a deep, resonant sound, as cannon. 2 To grow rapidly; flourish. —*v.t.* 3 To utter or sound in a deep, resonant tone. 4 To praise or advertise vigorously. —*n.* 1 A deep, reverberating sound, as of a cannon. 2 Any sudden or rapid growth or popularity. [Imit.] —**Syn.** *v.* 1 resound, reverberate, roar. 2 increase, prosper, succeed, thrive.

boom box (bōōm'boks') *n. Slang* A portable combination of radio and tape player.

boom·e·rang (bōō'mə·rang) *n.* 1 A curved, wooden missile weapon originated in Australia, one form of which will return to the thrower. 2 Any act or statement that works to the disadvantage of its originator. —*v.i.* To react harmfully on the doer or user. [<native Australian name]

Boomerangs

boom town A town that has suddenly increased in population, as from a discovery of gold or oil.

boon[1] (bōōn) *n.* 1 A good thing; blessing. 2 *Archaic* A petition. [<ON *bōn* petition]

boon[2] (bōōn) *adj.* Genial; jovial: now only in **boon companion**. [<L *bonus* good]

boon·docks (bōōn'doks') *n. pl. Informal* An out-of-the-way or backwoods area: used with *the*. [<Tagalog *bundok* mountain]

boon·dog·gle (bōōn'dôg'əl) *v.i.* **·dog·gled, ·dog·gling** *Informal* To work on wasteful or unnecessary projects. —*n.* A wasteful or worthless project. [?] —**boon'dog'gler, boon'dog'gling** *n.*

boor (bōōr) *n.* A rude, coarse, or unpleasant person. [<Du. *boer* farmer, rustic] —**boor'ish** *adj.* —**boor'ish·ly** *adv.* —**boor'ish·ness** *n.*

boost (bōōst) *v.t.* 1 To raise by or as by pushing from beneath or behind. 2 To speak in praise of; help by speaking well of. 3 To increase: to *boost* prices. —*n.* 1 A lift; help. 2 An increase. [?]

boost·er (bōōs'tər) *n.* 1 Any device for increasing the output of another device or system. 2 One who gives enthusiastic support to a person, organization, community, or cause. 3 The first stage of a multistage rocket, the source of thrust during takeoff. 4 BOOSTER SHOT.

booster shot Another injection, as of a vaccine, to reinforce immunity, administered at an interval after the initial dose.

boot[1] (bōōt) *n.* 1 A shoelike covering, as of leather, rubber, etc., for the foot and all or part of the leg. 2 A shoe reaching to or above the ankle. 3 An overshoe. 4 A medieval instrument of torture for crushing the foot and leg. 5 A kick. 6 *Informal* In the U.S. Navy or Marine Corps, a new recruit. —**die with one's boots on** To die fighting or working. —**get the boot** *Slang* To be discharged. —*v.t.* 1 To put boots on. 2 To kick; also, in football, to punt. 3 *Slang* To dismiss; fire. —*v.i.* To load a program into a computer. [<OF *bote*]

boot[2] (bōōt) *n. Obs.* Advantage; resource. —**to boot** In addition; over and above. [<OE *bōt* profit]

boot·black (bōōt'blak') *n.* One who cleans and shines shoes or boots.

boot camp The primary training station for naval or marine recruits.

boo·tee (bōō·tē', bōō'tē) *n.* 1 A woman's or child's short, light boot. 2 A knitted woolen boot for a baby.

Bo·ö·tes (bō·ō'tēz) *n.* A northern constellation, whose brightest star is Arcturus.

booth (bōōth, bōōth) *n.* 1 A stall at a fair, market, etc. 2 A small compartment or enclosure: a voting *booth*. 3 A stationary table and seating compartment, as in a restaurant. [<Scand.]

boot·jack (bōōt'jak') *n.* A forked device for holding the heel of a boot while the wearer withdraws his foot.

boot·leg (bōōt'leg') *v.t. & v.i.* **·legged, ·leg·ging** To make, sell, or carry for sale (liquor, etc.) illegally; smuggle. —*adj.* Unlawful: *bootleg* whisky. —*n.* 1 The part of a boot above the instep. **2** Something bootlegged, esp. liquor. [With ref. to the smuggling of liquor in bootlegs] —**boot'·leg'ger, boot'leg'ging** *n.*

boot·less (bo͞ot'lis) *adj.* Profitless; useless; unavailing. —**boot'less·ly** *adv.* —**boot'less·ness** *n.*

boot·lick (bo͞ot'lik') *v.t. & v.i.* To flatter servilely; to toady. —**boot'lick'er** *n.* —**boot'lick'ing** *adj., n.*

boo·ty (bo͞o'tē) *n. pl.* **boo·ties 1** The spoils of war. **2** Any plunder. **3** Any prize or gain. [< MLG *būte* exchange]

booze (bo͞oz) *n. Informal* **1** Strong drink; liquor. **2** A drunken spree. —*v.i.* **boozed, booz·ing** To drink to excess. [< MDu. *busen* drink, tipple] —**booz'er** *n.*

booz·y (bo͞o'zē) *adj.* Somewhat intoxicated. —**booz'i·ly** *adv.* —**booz'i·ness** *n.*

bop¹ (bop) *v.t.* **bopped, bop·ping** *Slang* To hit or strike. [Imit.]

bop² (bop) *n.* A type of jazz having characteristically complex harmony and rhythm and in which nonsense syllables are often used in singing. [Short for BE-BOP]

bo·rac·ic (bə·ras'ik) *adj.* BORIC.

bor·age (bûr'ij, bôr'-, bor'-) *n.* An edible herb with blue flowers and hairy leaves. [< Med. L *borrago*]

bo·rate (bôr'āt, bō'rāt) *n.* A salt of boric acid. —**bo'rat·ed** *adj.*

bo·rax (bôr'aks, bō'raks) *n.* A white crystalline borate of sodium having various uses, as in soap and glass manufacture. [< Ar. *bōraq* < Pers. *būrah*]

Bor·deaux (bôr·dō') *n.* A white or red wine produced in the vicinity of Bordeaux, France.

Bordeaux mixture A fungicide composed of copper sulfate, water, and lime.

bor·der (bôr'dər) *n.* **1** A margin or edge. **2** The peripheral line or district of a country or state; a boundary or frontier. **3** A surrounding or enclosing strip or edge. **4** A decorative edge or margin. —*adj.* Of, on, forming, or pertaining to a border. —*v.t.* **1** To put a border or edging on. **2** To lie next to; form a boundary to. —**border on** (or **upon**) **1** To resemble; have the appearance: That *borders on* piracy. **2** To touch or abut. [< OF *bord* edge] —**bor'der·er** *n.*

bor·der·land (bôr'dər·land') *n.* **1** Land on or near the border of two adjoining countries. **2** A debatable or indeterminate area or condition.

bor·der·line (bôr'dər·līn') *n.* **1** A boundary line. **2** An indeterminate line or condition. Also **border line.** —*adj.* Difficult to classify; indeterminate.

bore¹ (bôr, bōr) *v.* **bored, bor·ing** *v.t.* **1** To make a hole in or through, as with a drill. **2** To make (a tunnel, hole, well, etc.) by or as by drilling. **3** To advance or force (one's way). **4** To weary by monotony, dullness, etc. —*v.i.* **5** To make a hole, etc., by or as by drilling. **6** To admit of being drilled: This wood *bores* easily. **7** To force one's way. —*n.* **1** A hole made by or as if by boring. **2** The interior diameter of a firearm or cylinder. **3** A tiresome person or thing. [< OE *borian*]

bore² (bôr, bōr) *n.* A high crested wave caused by the rush of flood tide up a river. [< ON *bāra* billow]

bore³ (bôr, bōr) *p.t.* of BEAR.

bo·re·al (bôr'ē·əl, bō'rē-) *adj.* Pertaining to the north or the north wind. [< LL *borealis* < BOREAS]

Bo·re·as (bôr'ē·əs, bō'rē-) *n. Gk. Myth.* The north wind.

bore·dom (bôr'dəm, bōr'-) *n.* The condition of being bored; fatigue. —**Syn.** ennui, tedium, weariness.

bor·er (bôr'ər, bō'rər) *n.* **1** One who or that which bores. **2** A larva or worm that burrows in plants, wood, etc.

bo·ric (bôr'ik, bō'rik) *adj.* Of, pertaining to, or derived from boron.

boric acid A white crystalline compound of hydrogen, boron, and oxygen, used as a mild antiseptic.

born (bôrn) *adj.* **1** Brought forth or into being, as offspring. **2** Natural; innate: a *born* musician. [< OE *boren,* p.p. of *beran* bear]

borne (bôrn, bōrn) *p.p.* of BEAR.

bo·ron (bôr'on, bō'ron) *n.* A nonmetallic element (symbol B), occurring in nature only in compounds, as borax. [< BOR(AX) + (CARB)ON]

bor·ough (bûr'ō) *n.* **1** An incorporated village or town. **2** One of the five administrative divisions of New York, N.Y. **2** *Brit.* **a** A town having a municipal corporation endowed by royal charter with certain privileges. **b** A town, whether corporate or not, entitled to representation in Parliament. [< OE *burg, burh* fort, town]

bor·row (bôr'ō, bor'ō) *v.t. & v.i.* **1** To take or obtain (something) on a promise to return it or its equivalent. **2** To adopt for one's own use: to *borrow* an idea. **3** *Math.* In subtraction, to perform the operation inverse of carrying, in addition. [< OE *borgian* give a pledge, borrow] —**bor'row·er** *n.*

borscht (bôrsht) *n.* A Russian beet soup, often served with sour cream and eaten hot or cold. Also **borsch** (bôrsh). [Russ.]

bor·stal (bôr'stəl) *n. Often cap.* Any of a number of correctional schools for delinquent boys and girls in England. [after *Borstal,* an English village]

bort (bôrt) *n.* A poor diamond, used for cutting and polishing. Also **bortz** (bôrts). [?< OF *bort* bastard]

bor·zoi (bôr'zoi) *n.* A breed of Russian hounds, generally resembling the greyhound, but with a long, silky coat; a Russian wolfhound. [< Russ., swift]

bosh (bosh) *n. Informal* Empty words; nonsense. [< Turkish, empty, worthless]

bo's'n (bō'sən) *n.* BOATSWAIN.

Bos·ni·an (boz'nē·ən) *adj.* Of or belonging to Bosnia: also **Bos·ni·ac** (boz'nē·ak). —*n.* **1** A native of Bosnia, esp. one inhabiting the region on the northern Adriatic. **2** Their Serbo-Croatian language.

bos·om (bo͞oz'əm, bo͞o'zəm) *n.* **1** The breast of a human being, esp. of a woman. **2** That portion of a garment covering the breast, as a shirt front. **3** The breast thought of as the seat of emotion or thought. **4** The central part; midst. —*adj.* Close; intimate; cherished: a *bosom* friend. —*v.t.* **1** To have or cherish in the bosom; embrace. **2** To hide; conceal. [< OE *bōsm*]

boss¹ (bôs, bos) *n.* **1** A person who employs workers or supervises their work. **2** One who controls a political party or organization. —*v.t.* **1** To control or supervise. **2** *Informal* To order or control in a domineering manner: often with *around.* —*adj.* **1** *Informal* Chief. **2** *Slang* Great; excellent. [< Du. *baas* master]

boss² (bôs, bos) *n.* **1** A circular prominence; a knob. **2** A raised ornament on a surface. **3** *Mech.* An enlargement of a shaft to couple with a wheel or another shaft. —*v.t.* To ornament with bosses. [< OF *boce* bump, knob]

boss·ism (bôs'iz·əm, bos'-) *n.* Political control or management by bosses.

boss·y (bôs'ē, bos'ē) *adj.* **boss·i·er, boss·i·est** *Informal* Domineering; dictatorial. —**boss'i·ly** *adv.* —**bos'si·ness** *n.*

Boston terrier Any of a breed of small terriers having a smooth dark-brown or black coat with white markings. Also **Boston bull.**

bo·sun (bō'sən) *n.* BOATSWAIN.

bot (bot) *n.* The larva of a botfly. [?]

bot. botanical; botanist; botany; bottle.

bo·tan·i·cal (bə·tan'i·kəl) *adj.* Of or pertaining to botany or plants. Also **bo·tan'ic.** [< Gk. *botanē* plant] —**bo·tan'i·cal·ly** *adv.*

Boston terrier

bot·a·nist (bot'ə·nist) *n.* A specialist in botany.

bot·a·nize (bot'ə·nīz) *v.* **·nized, ·niz·ing** *v.i.* **1** To study botanical specimens. **2** To gather plants for study. —*v.t.* **3** To explore in search of botanical specimens. —**bot'a·niz'er** *n.*

bot·a·ny (bot'ə·nē) *n. pl.* **·nies 1** That division of biology which treats of plants with reference to their structure, functions, classification, etc. **2** The plant life of a region. **3** The common characteristics of a group of plants: the *botany* of orchids.

botch (boch) *v.t.* **1** To patch or mend clumsily. **2** To do ineptly; bungle. —*n.* A bungled piece of work. [ME *bocchen*]—**botch′er** *n.* —**botch′er·y** *n.*

botch·y (boch′ē) *adj.* **botch·i·er, botch·i·est** Imperfect; botched; poorly done. —**botch′i·ly** *adv.* —**botch′i·ness** *n.*

bot·fly (bot′flī) *n.* Any of various flies whose larvae are parasitic in horses, sheep and other animals.

both (bōth) *adj. & pron.* The two; the one and the other: *Both* girls laughed; *Both* were there. —*adv. & conj.* Equally; as well: with *and:* He is *both* thin and pale. [< ON *badhir*]

bother (both′ər) *v.t.* **1** To give trouble to; pester; annoy. **2** To confuse; fluster. —*v.i.* **3** To trouble or concern oneself. —*n.* A source or condition of annoyance. [?]

both·er·a·tion (both′ə-rā′shən) *n. Informal* Annoyance; vexation.

both·er·some (both′ər·səm) *adj.* Causing bother.

Bot·swa·na (bot′swä′nä) *n.* A republic in s Africa, 222,000 sq. mi., cap. Gaberones. • See map at AFRICA.

bott (bot) *n.* BOT.

bot·tle (bot′l) *n.* **1** A vessel for holding, carrying, and pouring liquids, having a relatively narrow neck and mouth. **2** As much as a bottle will hold: also **bot′tle·ful.** —**hit the bottle** *Slang* To drink alcoholic beverages to excess. —*v.t.* **·tled, ·tling 1** To put into a bottle or bottles. **2** To restrain; shut in: with *up.* [< LL *buticula* flask, dim. of *butis* vat, vessel] —**bot′tler** *n.*

bot·tle·neck (bot′l·nek′) *n.* **1** A narrow or congested way. **2** Any condition that retards progress.

bot·tle·nose (bot′l·nōz′) . One of various dolphins.

bot·tom (bot′əm) *n.* **1** The lowest part of anything. **2** The undersurface or base of something. **3** The last or lowest place. **4** The seat of a chair. **5** The ground beneath a body of water. **6** *Often pl.* BOTTOM LAND. **7** The real meaning, cause, or source of something. **8** The part of a ship's hull below the water line. **9** *Informal* The buttocks. **10** Endurance; stamina; grit. —**at bottom** Basically; fundamentally. —*adj.* Lowest; fundamental; basal. —*v.t.* **1** To provide with a bottom. **2** To base or found: with *on* or *upon.* **3** To fathom; comprehend. —*v.i.* **4** To be founded; rest. **5** To touch or rest upon the bottom. [< OE *botm*]

bottom land Lowland along a river.

bottom line 1 *Informal* The line of a business accounting statement showing net profit or loss: with *the.* **2** *Slang* The condition or status of any enterprise after assets and liabilities have been calculated: with *the.*

bot·tom·ry (bot′əm·rē) *n.* A contract whereby the owner of a ship borrows money, pledging the vessel as security.

bot·u·lism (boch′ōō·liz′əm) *n.* An often fatal form of food poisoning due to a toxin formed by a species of anaerobic bacteria. [< L *botulus* sausage; the bacteria were first isolated from spoiled sausage]

bou·clé (bōō·klā′) *n.* **1** A curly yarn of wool, silk, or cotton. **2** Fabric made with such yarn. Also **bou′cle.** [< F *boucler* to buckle, curl]

bou·doir (bōō′dwär, bōō·dwär′) *n.* A lady's private dressing room or bedroom. [< F, lit., pouting room]

bough (bou) *n.* A limb of a tree. [< OE *bog* shoulder, bough]

bought (bôt) *p.t. & p.p.* of BUY.

bought·en (bôt′n) *adj. Regional* Bought at a store rather than being homemade.

bouil·la·baisse (bōōl′yə·bās′, *Fr.* bōō·yá·bes′) *n.* A chowder made of several varieties of fish. [< Prov. *boui* boil + *abaisso* settle, go down]

bouil·lon (bōōl′yon, ·yən; *Fr.* bōō·yôn′) *n.* Clear broth made from meat, as beef or chicken. [< F *bouillir* boil]

boul·der (bōl′dər) *n.* A large stone moved, as by a glacier, from its original location. [< Scand.]

boul·e·vard (bōōl′ə·värd, bōō′lə·) *n.* A broad avenue, often planted with trees. [< MHG *bolwerc* bulwark]

bounce (bouns) *v.* **bounced, bounc·ing** *v.t.* **1** To cause to bound or rebound. **2** *Slang* To eject forcibly. **3** *Slang* To discharge from employment. —*v.i.* **4** To bound or rebound. **5** To move suddenly and violently; jump or spring. **6** *Informal* To be returned because of insufficient funds: said of a check. —*n.* **1** A sudden spring or leap. **2** A bounding or elastic motion; rebound. [ME *bunsen*]

bounc·er (boun′sər) *n. Informal* A strong man employed in a bar, etc., to throw out objectionable customers.

bounc·ing (boun′sing) *adj.* **1** Strong and active. **2** Large; strapping.

bound[1] (bound) *v.i.* **1** To strike and spring back from a surface, as a ball. **2** To leap. —*v.t.* **3** To cause to bound. —*n.* **1** A leap or spring. **2** A rebound. [< F *bondir* leap]

bound[2] (bound) *v.t.* **1** To set limits to; restrict. **2** To form the boundary of. **3** To describe or name the boundaries of. —*v.i.* **4** To adjoin. —*n.* **1** A limit or boundary. **2** *pl.* An area near or within a boundary. [< LL *bodina* limit]

bound[3] (bound) *p.t. & p.p.* of BIND. —*adj.* **1** Made fast; tied. **2** Obligated legally or morally. **3** Connected; related. **4** Certain: *bound* to fail. **5** Having a cover or binding. **6** *Informal* Determined; resolved.

bound[4] (bound) *adj.* Having one's course directed; on the way: with *for* or *to.* [< ON *būinn* < *būa* prepare]

bound·a·ry (boun′də·rē, -drē) *n. pl.* **·ries** Anything forming or serving to indicate a limit or end. —**Syn.** border, confines, edge, margin.

bound·en (boun′dən) *adj.* **1** Obligatory; necessary: *bounden* duty. **2** Under obligations; obliged. [Obs. p.p. of BIND]

bound·er (boun′dər) *n. Chiefly Brit. Informal* A man whose behavior is offensive; cad.

bound·less (bound′lis) *adj.* Having no limit; measureless; infinite. —**bound′less·ly** *adv.* —**bound′less·ness** *n.*

boun·te·ous (boun′tē·əs) *adj.* **1** Bountiful; generous. **2** Plentiful. —**boun′te·ous·ly** *adv.* —**boun′te·ous·ness** *n.*

boun·ti·ful (boun′tə·fəl) *adj.* **1** Giving freely; generous. **2** Abundant; plentiful. —**boun′ti·ful·ly** *adv.*

boun·ty (boun′tē) *n. pl.* **·ties 1** Liberality in giving. **2** Gifts or favors generously bestowed. **3** A reward paid by a government for the killing of predatory animals, raising certain crops, etc. [< L *bonitas* goodness]

bou·quet (bō·kā′, bōō·kā′ *for def. 1;* bōō·kā′ *for def. 2)* *n.* **1** A bunch of flowers. **2** The distinctive aroma of a wine. [< OF *boschet,* dim. of *bosc* wood]

bour·bon (bûr′bən) *n.* A whiskey distilled from corn or partly from corn. Also **bourbon whiskey.** [< *Bourbon* County, Ky., where originally made]

Bour·bon (bōōr′bən) **1** A ruling family of French origin which ruled, for certain periods, over France, Spain, Naples, and Sicily. **2** One who is stubbornly conservative in politics. —**Bour′bon·ism, Bour′bon·ist** *n.*

bour·geois (bōōr′zhwä, bōōr·zhwä′) *n. pl* **·geois** A member of the middle class as distinguished from the aristocracy or the working class. —*adj.* **1** Of the middle class. **2** Regarded as typically middle-class; conventional, smug, etc. [< OF *burgeis*]—**bour·geoise** (-zhwäz′) *n. Fem.*

bour·geoi·sie (bōōr′zhwä·zē′) *n.* **1** The middle class as distinguished from the aristocracy or the working class. **2** In Marxist philosophy, the social class in conflict with the proletariat. [< F *bourgeois* middle class]

bourn[1] (bôrn, bōrn, bōōrn) *n.* **1** A boundary; limit. **2** An end; goal. **3** Realm; domain. Also **bourne.** [< LL *bodina* limit]

bourn[2] (bôrn, bōrn, bōōrn) *n.* A brook or rivulet. Also **bourne.** [< OE *burna* spring]

bourse (bōōrs) *n. Often cap.* An exchange or money market, esp. the Paris stock exchange. [< LL *bursa* bag]

bout (bout) *n.* **1** A contest or match, as in boxing. **2** An active period; spell: a *bout* of illness [Var. of ME *bought* bending, turn]

bou·tique (bōō·tēk′) *n.* A small shop in which dress accessories, gifts, etc., are sold. [F]

bou·ton·niere (bōō′tə·nyâr′) *n.* A flower or small bouquet worn in the button hole of a lapel. [< F *bouton* button] Also **bou·ton·nière.**

bou·zou·ki (bə·zōō′kē) *n.* A mandolinlike instrument with a very long neck. [< New Gk. *mpouzouki*]

bo·vine (bō′vīn, -vin) *adj.* **1** Of, related to, or characteristic of cattle, oxen, etc. **2** Patient and dull; stolid. —*n.* A bovine animal, as an ox, cow, etc. [< L *bos* ox]

bow[1] (bou) *v.i.* **1** To bend the body or head, as in greeting, reverence, assent, etc. **2** To bend or incline downward. **3** To submit; yield. —*v.t.* **4** To bend (the head, knee, etc.) in reverence, assent, etc. **5** To express by bowing. **6** To escort or direct while bowing. **7** To cause to bend, stoop, etc., as by weighting down. **8** To cause to yield or submit. —**bow out** To withdraw or resign. —*n.* **1** A bending of the body

off

on

or head, as in greeting. **2** An indication of polite acknowledgment. [< OE *bugan* bow, bend, flee] **—Syn.** *v.* **3** capitulate, surrender, acquiesce. *n.* **1** obeisance, curtsey, salaam.

bow² (bō) *n.* **1** A weapon for shooting arrows, made from a flexible strip of wood, etc., strung from end to end with a cord. **2** A rod with hairs stretched between the ends, used to vibrate the strings of a violin, cello, etc., by friction. **3** A knot tied with a loop or loops. **4** Something bent or curved. **5** A rainbow. —*adj.* Bent; curved. —*v.t. & v.i.* **1** To bend into the shape of a bow. **2** To play (a stringed instrument) with a bow. [< OE *boga*]

Bow *def. 1*

bow³ (bou) *n.* **1** The forward part of a ship or boat. **2** The forward oarsman of a boat. [< MLG *boog*]

bowd·ler·ize (boud′lər·īz) *v.t.* **·ized, ·iz·ing** To expurgate or edit prudishly. [< Thomas *Bowdler*, 1754–1825, Brit. editor of a "family" edition of Shakespeare] **—bowd′ler·ism, bowd′ler·i·za′tion** *n.*

bow·el (bou′əl, boul) *n.* **1** An intestine. **2** *pl.* The intestines collectively. **3** *pl.* The inner part of anything: the *bowels* of the earth. **4** *pl. Archaic* Inmost or deepest feelings. — *v.t.* **·eled** or **·elled, ·el·ing** or **·el·ling** To disembowel. [< L *botellus*, dim. of *botulus* sausage]

bow·er (bou′ər) *n.* **1** A shady, usu. leafy shelter. **2** *Archaic* A private apartment; boudoir. —*v.t.* To enclose in or as in a bower. [< OE *būr* chamber] **—bow′er·y** *adj.*

Bow·er·y (bou′ər·ē), **the** A street in downtown New York City noted for its seedy bars, hotels, etc.

bow·fin (bō′fin′) *n.* A freshwater fish of eastern North America, having a long dorsal fin.

bow·ie knife (bō′ē, boo′ē) A hunting knife with a long, single-edged blade. [< James Bowie, died 1836, American soldier]

bow·knot (bō′not′) *n.* An ornamental slipknot with one or more loops. • See KNOT.

Bowie knife

bowl¹ (bōl) *n.* **1** A deep, rounded container or dish. **2** The amount held by a bowl. **3** Something rounded and hollow that resembles a bowl. **4** A bowl-shaped amphitheater or stadium. [< OE *bolla*]

bowl² (bōl) *v.i.* **1** To engage in the game of bowling. **2** To roll a ball or similar object in or as in this game. **3** To move swiftly and smoothly. —*v.t.* **4** To throw (a ball) with a rolling motion. —**bowl over 1** To knock down. **2** To dumbfound; astound. —*n.* **1** A large ball used for bowling or similar games. **2** A throw of the ball in or as in bowling. [< F *boule* ball]

bowl·der (bōl′dər) *n.* BOULDER.

bow·leg (bō′leg′) *n.* A leg bent in an outward curve. — **bow′leg′ged** (-leg′id) *adj.*

bowl·er¹ (bō′lər) *n.* One who bowls.

bowl·er² (bō′lər) *n. Brit.* A derby hat. [< John *Bowler*, 19th c. Brit. hatter]

bow·line (bō′lin, -līn′) *n.* **1** A knot that forms a loop and that does not slip. Also **bowline knot. 2** A rope to keep the edge of a vessel's square sail forward when sailing close-hauled.

bowl·ing (bō′ling) *n.* **1** A game played on a narrow lane along which a ball is rolled in an attempt to knock down ten pins at the far end of the lane. **2** Any of various similar games. **3** The playing of any of these games.

bowling alley 1 A narrow, wood-surfaced lane used in the game of bowling. **2** A building containing such alleys.

bowls (bōlz) *n.pl. (construed as sing.)* Any of various bowling games, esp. one played outdoors with weighted balls rolled at a stationary ball.

bow·man (bō′mən) *n. pl.* **·men** (-mən) An archer.

bow·shot (bō′shot′) *n.* The distance which an arrow may be shot from a bow.

bow·sprit (bou′sprit′, bō′-) *n.* A spar projecting forward from the bow of a vessel.

bow·string (bō′string′) *n.* The string of a bow.

bow·tie (bō′tī′) *n.* A necktie tied in a bow.

bow window (bō) A projecting curved window.

box¹ (boks) *n.* **1** A container of wood, cardboard, metal, etc., usu. rectangular and having a cover or top. **2** The amount held by a box. **3** Something resembling a box, as a rectangular space or enclosed compartment. **4** A separate, enclosed seating space, as in a theater. **5** A raised seat for the driver of a coach or carriage. **6** A casing or enclosure for a mechanical part or device. **7** A space on a baseball field designated for the pitcher, batter, etc. —*v.t.* **1** To put or enclose in a box. **2** To confine as if in a box; trap or block, esp. to impede movement: often with *in* or *up*. — **box the compass 1** To recite in order the 32 points of the compass. **2** To make a complete turn or revolution. [< OE < LL *buxis*] **—box′er** *n.* **—box′ful** *adj.*

box² (boks) *v.t.* **1** To hit with the hand; cuff. **2** To engage in a boxing match with. —*v.i.* **3** To fight with one's fists; engage in boxing. —*n.* A cuff or blow, esp. on the ear. [ME]

box³ (boks) *n.* **1** An evergreen shrub with small, glossy leaves, often used for hedges. **2** Its hard wood. [< OE < L *buxus*]

box·car (boks′kär′) *n.* An enclosed railway car for carrying freight.

box elder A maple tree having compound leaves.

box·er¹ (bok′sər) *n.* A man who fights in boxing matches; pugilist.

box·er² (bok′sər) *n.* A breed of medium-sized dog related to the bulldog. [< G < E BOXER¹]

Box·er (bok′sər) *n.* A member of a Chinese secret society, active in 1900, which aimed to rid China of foreigners by force. [From their practice of traditional posture boxing]

box·ing (bok′sing) *n.* The sport or practice of fighting with one's fists; pugilism.

boxing glove A thickly padded leather mitten used for boxing.

box office 1 The ticket office of a theater, etc. **2** Success rated according to volume of tickets sold.

box score A tabular record of a baseball game, giving statistical information for each player.

box seat A seat in a box at a theater, stadium, etc.

box·wood (boks′wŏŏd′) *n.* **1** The hard, close-grained, durable wood of the box shrub. **2** The shrub.

boy (boi) *n.* **1** A male child or youth. **2** *Informal* A fellow; man. **3** A male servant or worker. —*interj. Informal* An exclamation of pleasure, wonder, etc. [ME *boi*] **—boy′ish** *adj.* **—boy′ish·ly** *adv.* **—boy′ish·ness** *n.*

boy·cott (boi′kot) *v.t.* **1** To combine together in refusing to deal or associate with, so as to punish or coerce. **2** To refuse to use or buy. —*n.* An act or instance of boycotting. [< Capt. C. *Boycott*, 1832–1897, Irish landlord's agent]

boy friend *Informal* **1** A girl's or woman's sweetheart, favorite male companion, etc. **2** A male friend. Also **boy′·friend′.**

boy·hood (boi′hŏŏd′) *n.* **1** The state or period of being a boy. **2** Boys collectively.

boy scout A member of the **Boy Scouts,** an organization giving boys training and experience in self-reliance, citizenship, outdoor activities, etc.

boy·sen·ber·ry (boi′zən·ber′ē) *n. pl.* **·ries 1** A hybrid plant obtained by crossing the blackberry, raspberry, and loganberry. **2** Its edible fruit. [< Rudolph *Boysen*, 20th c. U.S. horticulturist, the originator]

B/P, b.p. bill of parcels; bills payable.

bp, b.p. boiling point.

bp. birthplace; bishop.

B.P.O.E. Benevolent and Protective Order of Elks.

B/R, b.r. bills receivable.

Br bromine.

Br. Breton; Britain; British.

br. branch; brand; bridge; bronze; brother.

bra (brä) *n.* A brassiere.

brace (brās) *v.* **braced, brac·ing** *v.t.* **1** To make firm or steady; strengthen with or as with a prop or support. **2** To make ready to withstand pressure, impact, assault, etc. **3** To stimulate; enliven. —*v.i.* **4** To strain against pressure. —**brace up** *Informal* To rouse one's courage or resolution. —*n.* **1** A support, as of wood or metal, to hold something firmly in place. **2** A clasp or clamp used for connecting, fastening, etc. **3** A cranklike handle for turning a bit or other boring tool. **4** *Often pl.* A wire device attached to the teeth to correct malformation. **5** A pair: a *brace of ducks*. **6** A doubly curved line, { }, used to connect printed or written lines, staves of music, etc. **7** *pl. Brit.* Suspenders. [< L *brachia*, pl. of *brachium* arm] —**Syn.** *v.* **1** support, prop, shore, buttress.

Brace *(def. 3)* and bits
a. brace. b. drill bit.
c. screwdriver bit.
d. auger bit.

brace·let (brās′lit) *n.* **1** An ornamental band worn around the wrist or arm. **2** *Informal* A handcuff. [< L *brachium* arm]

brac·er (brā′sər) *n.* **1** One who or that which braces or steadies. **2** *Informal* A stimulating drink.

bra·ce·ro (brə-sâr′ō) *n. pl.* **·ros** A Mexican laborer brought into the U.S. under contract for seasonal farm work. [< Sp., day laborer]

bra·chi·o·pod (brā′kē-ə·pod′, brak′ē-) *n.* Any of a phylum of marine animals having a bivalve shell and a pair of armlike appendages near the mouth. [< Gk. *brachiōn* arm + *pous* foot]

bra·chi·um (brā′kē·əm, brak′ē-) *n. pl.* **·chi·a** (brā′kē·ə, brak′ē-) **1** The upper arm, or a homologous part. **2** Any armlike appendage. [< L] —**bra′chi·al** *adj.*

brach·y·ce·phal·ic (brak′i·sə·fal′ik) *adj.* Having a short, relatively broad skull; round-headed. Also **brach·y·ceph·a·lous** (brak′ē·sef′ə·ləs). [< Gk. *brachys* short + *kephalē* head] —**brach′y·ceph′a·lism, brach′y·ceph′a·ly** *n.*

brac·ing (brā′sing) *adj.* Invigorating.

brack·en (brak′ən) *n.* **1** A large, coarse, weedy fern. **2** A place covered with such ferns. [< Scand.]

brack·et (brak′it) *n.* **1** A piece projecting from a wall to support a shelf or other weight. **2** A projecting fixture, as for a lamp. **3** A brace used to strengthen an angle. **4** One of two marks, [ ], used to enclose part of a text. **5** A part within a graded grouping or category: the high-income *bracket*. —*v.t.* **1** To provide or support with a bracket. **2** To enclose within brackets. **3** To group or categorize together. [< L *bracae*, pl., breeches]

brack·ish (brak′ish) *adj.* **1** Somewhat saline; briny. **2** Unpleasant to taste. [< Du. *brak* salty] —**brack′ish·ness** *n.*

bract (brakt) *n.* A modified leaf growing near and sometimes seemingly part of a flower. [< L *bractea* thin metal plate] —**brac·te·al** (brak′tē·əl), **brac′te·ate** (-tē·it, -āt) *adj.*

brad (brad) *n.* A slender nail with a small head. [< ON *broddr* spike]

brad·awl (brad′ôl′) *n.* A short awl with a chisellike end.

brag (brag) *v.* **bragged, brag·ging** *v.t. & v.i.* To say or talk boastfully. —*n.* **1** Boastfulness; boastful language. **2** Something bragged of. **3** A person who brags. [ME *braggen*] —**brag′ger** *n.*

brag·ga·do·ci·o (brag′ə·dō′shē·ō) *n. pl.* **·ci·os** **1** Pretentious boasting. **2** A swaggering braggart. [< *Braggadochio*, a boastful character in Spenser's *Faerie Queene*]

brag·gart (brag′ərt) *n.* A bragging showoff. —*adj.* Boastful.

Brah·ma (brä′mə) *n.* In Hinduism: **1** The supreme soul of the universe. **2** The supreme creator conceived of as forming a trinity together with Vishnu and Siva. [< Skt. *Brahmā*]

Brah·man (brä′mən) *n. pl.* **·mans** **1** A member of the highest, or priestly, Hindu caste. **2** One of a breed of humped cattle developed from stock from India. [< Skt. *brahman* praise, worship] —**Brah·man·i** (brä′mən·ē) *n. Fem.* —**Brah·man·ic** (brä·man′ik) or **·i·cal** *adj.*

Brah·man·ism (brä′mən·iz′əm) *n.* The religious and social system of the Brahmans. —**Brah′man·ist** *n.*

Brah·min (brä′min) *n.* **1** BRAHMAN. **2** An aristocratic, highly cultured person, esp. one of an old New England family. —**Brah′min·ism** *n.*

braid (brād) *v.t.* **1** To interweave or intertwine several strands of; plait. **2** To form by braiding: to *braid* a mat. **3** To ornament with braid. —*n.* **1** Anything braided or plaited: a *braid* of hair. **2** A flat tape or strip for binding or ornamenting fabrics. [< OE *bregdan* brandish, weave, braid] —**braid′er, braid′ing** *n.*

Braille (brāl) *n.* **1** A system of printing or writing for the

Braille alphabet

blind in which the characters consist of raised dots to be read by feeling with the fingers. **2** The characters themselves. Also **braille.** [< Louis *Braille*, 1809–52, French educator, who invented it]

brain (brān) *n.* **1** The mass of nerve tissue contained within the cranium of vertebrates and continuous with the spinal cord. **2** The chief focal area of the nervous system in any animal. **3** *Often pl.* Mind; intellect. **4** *Informal* A notably intelligent person. —**have on the brain** To be obsessed by —*v.t.* **1** To dash out the brains of. **2** *Slang* To strike on the head. [< OE *brægen*]

brain·child (brān′chīld′) *n.* An idea, project, or other product of the mind considered as belonging to its creator.

brain·less (brān′lis) *adj.* Lacking brains or intelligence; senseless. —**brain′less·ly** *adv.* —**brain′less·ness** *n.*

brain·pan (brān′pan′) *n.* The part of the skull enclosing the brain; cranium.

brain·sick (brān′sik′) *adj.* Mentally disordered. —**brain′·sick′ness** *n.*

brain·storm (brān′stôrm′) *n. Informal* A burst of inspiration.

brain trust *Informal* A group of experts who advise, plan policy, etc.

brain·wash (brān′wosh′, -wôsh′) *v.t.* To alter the convictions, beliefs, etc., of by systematic indoctrination. —**brain′wash·ing** *n.*

brain wave **1** A rhythmic fluctuation of electrical potential in the brain. **2** *Informal* A sudden inspiration.

brain·y (brā′nē) *adj.* **brain·i·er, brain·i·est** *Informal* Intelligent; smart. —**brain′i·ly** *adv.* —**brain′i·ness** *n.*

braise (brāz) *v.t.* **braised, brais·ing** To cook by browning quickly and then simmering in a covered pan. [< F *braise* charcoal]

brake[1] (brāk) *n.* **1** A device for retarding or arresting the motion of a vehicle, a wheel, etc. **2** *Often pl.* Anything that checks or slows an action or process. **3** An instrument for separating the fiber of flax, hemp, etc., by bruising. —*v.* **braked, brak·ing** *v.t.* **1** To apply a brake to. **2** To bruise and crush, as flax. —*v.i.* **3** To operate a brake or brakes. **4** To be retarded or stopped by a brake. [< MDu. *braeke* brake for flax]

brake[2] (brāk) *n.* A fern; bracken.

brake[3] (brāk) *n.* A thicket. [< OE *(fearn) braca* bed of (fern)]

brake[4] (brāk) *Archaic p.t. of* BREAK.

brake·man (brāk′mən) *n. pl.* **·men** (-mən) A railroad employee who assists the conductor on a train.

brake shoe A part that presses on a wheel or associated structure in order to stop or slow it.

bram·ble (bram′bəl) *n.* A prickly plant or shrub, as the raspberry, blackberry, etc. [< OE *bræmble*] —**bram′bly** *adj.* (**·bli·er, ·bli·est**)

bran (bran) *n.* The coarse, outer coat of cereals, separated from the flour. [< OF *bran, bren*]

branch (branch, bränch) *n.* **1** A secondary stem growing from the trunk or main limb of a tree, shrub, etc. **2** A similar division or part, as of a deer's antler. **3** A part or subdivision of a comprehensive whole. **4** A separate unit, department, etc., as of a business organization or institution. **5** A division of a family, tribe, etc. **6** A subdivision of a linguistic family. **7** A tributary of a river or main stream. **8** A small stream or creek. —*v.i.* **1** To put forth branches. **2** To divide into branches or subdivisions; diverge. —*v.t.* **3** To separate into branches. —**branch out** To extend or diversify, as one's business or interests. [< LL *branca* paw]

bran·chi·a (brang'kē·ə) *n. pl.* **·chi·ae** (-kī·ē) *Zool.* A gill or gill-like respiratory organ. [< Gk. *branchia*, pl., gills] — **bran'chi·al, bran'chi·ate** (-kē·it, -āt) *adj.*

brand (brand) *n.* **1** A name or trademark used to identify a product. **2** A product so identified: a popular *brand* of toothpaste. **3** A distinctive type or kind. **4** A mark burned with a hot iron, as on cattle for identification. **5** A mark of disgrace or shame. **6** A burning stick of wood. —*v.t.* **1** To mark with or as with a hot iron. **2** To mark or label, as with disgrace; stigmatize: to *brand* someone a traitor. [< OE, torch, sword] —**brand'er** *n.*

bran·dish (bran'dish) *v.t.* To wave or flourish triumphantly, menacingly, etc. —*n.* A flourish, as with a weapon. [< OF *brand* sword] —**brand'ish·er** *n.*

brand-new (bran'nyōō') *adj.* Quite new; not yet used. Also **bran-new** (bran'-).

bran·dy (bran'dē) *n. pl.* **·dies** An alcoholic liquor distilled from the fermented juice of grapes or other fruits. —*v.t.* **·died, dy·ing** To mix, flavor, or preserve with brandy. [< Du. *brandewijn* brandy, lit., distilled wine]

brant (brant) *n. pl.* **brants** or **brant** A small, dark, wild goose of Europe and North America. [? < Scand.]

brash[1] (brash) *adj.* **1** Hasty and thoughtless; rash. **2** Impudent; bold. [?] —**brash'ly** *adv.* —**brash'ness** *n.* —Syn. **1** reckless, impetuous. **2** impertinent, pert, cheeky, saucy.

brash[2] (brash) *adj.* Brittle: said of wood or timber. [?]

bra·sier (brā'zhər) *n.* BRAZIER.

brass (bras, bräs) *n.* **1** A yellow alloy of copper and zinc. **2** *Sometimes pl.* Brass ornaments, utensils, etc. **3** The brass wind instruments of an orchestra or band, collectively. **4** *Informal* Impudence; effrontery. **5** *Slang* High-ranking military officers, executives, etc. —*adj.* Made of brass. [< OE *bræs*]

bras·sard (bras'ärd, brə·särd') *n.* **1** A cloth arm band worn as a badge. **2** A piece of armor for the arm: also **bras·sart** (bras'ərt). [< F *bras* arm]

brass band A band of musicians using mostly brass instruments.

brass hat *Slang* A high-ranking military officer or official.

brass·ie (bras'ē, bräs'ē) *n.* A wooden golf club with a brass plate on the sole. Also **brass'y.**

bras·siere (brə·zir') *n.* A woman's undergarment shaped to support the breasts. Also **bras·sière'.** [< F *brassière* shoulder strap < *bras* arm]

brass knuckles A metal device that slips over the fingers and is used as a weapon in fist fighting.

brass tacks *Informal* Concrete or essential facts.

brass winds *Music* The wind instruments that sound by a buzzing of the player's lips into a mouthpiece, as the trumpet, horn, trombone, and tuba.

brass·y (bras'ē, bräs'ē) *adj.* **brass·i·er, brass·i·est** **1** Of or decorated with brass. **2** Resembling brass. **3** Blaring; harsh-sounding. **4** Flashy; tawdry. **5** Bold and shameless. —**brass'i·ly** *adv.* —**brass'i·ness** *n.*

brat (brat) *n.* An objectionable child. [?] —**brat'ti·ness** *n.* —**brat'ty** *adj.*

bra·va·do (brə·vä'dō) *n. pl.* **·dos** or **·does** **1** Affectation of reckless bravery; bluster. **2** A show of false courage or daring. [< Sp. *bravo* brave]

brave (brāv) *adj.* **brav·er, brav·est** **1** Having or showing courage. **2** Showy; splendid. —*v.t.* —**braved, brav·ing 1** To face with courage and fortitude. **2** To defy; challenge. —*n.* A North American Indian warrior. [< L *barbarus* wild,

fierce] —**brave'ly** *adv.* —**brave'ness** *n.* —Syn. *adj.* **1** courageous, fearless, bold, intrepid, valorous.

brav·er·y (brā'vər·ē) *n.* **1** Courage; valor. **2** Showy or splendid appearance.

bra·vo[1] (brä'vō) *interj.* Good! well done! —*n. pl.* **·vos** A shout of "bravo!" [< Ital., brave]

bra·vo[2] (brä'vō) *n. pl.* **·voes** or **·vos** A hired assassin or ruffian. [< Ital., brave]

bra·vu·ra (brə·vyŏŏr'ə, *Ital.* brä·vōō'rä) *n.* **1** A brilliant style of musical execution. **2** Any dashing or daring style. [< Ital., dash, daring < *bravo* brave]

brawl (brôl) *n.* **1** A noisy quarrel or fight; a row. **2** *Slang* A noisy celebration. —*v.i.* **1** To quarrel or fight noisily. **2** To move noisily, as water. [ME *braulen*] —**brawl'er** *n.*

brawn (brôn) *n.* **1** Strong, well-developed muscles. **2** Muscular strength; physical power. [< OF *braon* slice of flesh] —**brawn'y** *adj.* (**·i·er, ·i·est**) —**brawn'i·ness** *n.*

bray (brā) *v.i.* **1** To utter a loud, harsh cry, as a donkey. **2** To sound harshly, as a trumpet. —*v.t.* **3** To utter loudly and harshly. —*n.* **1** The loud, harsh cry of a donkey. **2** A sound resembling this. [< OF *braire* cry out] —**bray'er** *n.*

Braz. Brazil; Brazilian.

braze (brāz) *v.t.* **brazed, braz·ing** To join the surfaces of metals with a solder that melts at a high temperature. [< F *braser* to solder] —**braz'er** *n.*

bra·zen (brā'zən) *adj.* **1** Made of or resembling brass. **2** Trumpetlike; blaring. **3** Bold and shameless. —*v.t.* To face with bold or defiant self-assurance: with *out.* —**bra'zen·ly** *adv.* —**bra'zen·ness** *n.*

bra·zier[1] (brā'zhər) *n.* An open pan for holding burning coals. [< F *braise* hot coals]

bra·zier[2] (brā'zhər) *n.* A worker in brass.

Bra·zil (brə·zil') *n.* A republic of CEN. and E South America, 3,287,951 sq.mi., cap. Brasilia. — **Bra·zil'ian** *adj., n.*

Brazil nut An oily, hard-shelled, edible seed of a South American tree.

breach (brēch) *n.* **1** Violation or infraction of a law, legal obligation, promise, etc. **2** A gap or break, as in a wall. **3** A break in friendly relations; an estrangement. —*v.t.* To make a breach in; break through. [< OE *bryce* a breaking]

bread (bred) *n.* **1** A food made with flour or meal mixed with a liquid, usu. raised with yeast, kneaded, and baked. **2** Food in general. **3** The necessities of life. **4** *Slang* Money. —*v.t.* To coat with bread crumbs before cooking. [< OE *bread*]

bread-and-but·ter (bred'ən·but'ər) *adj.* Expressing thanks for hospitality: a *bread-and-butter* letter.

bread and butter *Informal* Subsistence; livelihood

bread-fruit (bred'frōōt') *n.* The fruit of a tree of the South Sea Islands which, when roasted, resembles bread. **2** The tree.

bread line A line of persons waiting for charitable donations of food.

bread·stuff (bred'stuf') *n.* **1** Grain, flour, etc., for making bread. **2** Bread.

breadth (bredth, bretth) *n.* **1** Measure or distance from side to side; width. **2** A piece of something, as cloth, of full or standard width. **3** Comprehensive range or scope. **4** Freedom from bias or restriction. [< OE *brad* broad]

breadth·wise (bredth'wīz', bretth'-) *adv.* In the direction of the breadth. Also **breadth'ways'** (-wāz').

bread·win·ner (bred'win'ər) *n.* One whose earnings support one's wife, husband, or family.

break (brāk) *v.* **broke** (*Archaic* **brake**), **bro·ken** (*Archaic* **broke**), **break·ing** *v.t.* **1** To separate into pieces by or as by force, a blow, etc. **2** To crack; fracture. **3** To pierce or part the surface of. **4** To cause to burst. **5** To make useless or inoperative. **6** To make a way through by force. **7** To escape from: to *break* jail. **8** To end by force or opposition: to *break* a strike. **9** To destroy the order, continuity, or completeness of: to *break* step; to *break* the silence. **10** To diminish the force of; moderate: to *break* a fall. **11** To interrupt (an electric circuit, a journey, etc.). **12** To violate: to *break* a law. **13 a** To discontinue (a habit). **b** To cause to discontinue a habit. **14** To train or tame, as a horse. **15** To demote in rank. **16** To subdue or destroy; crush. **17** To surpass; excel: to *break* a record. **18** To make known, as news. **19** To exchange for smaller units: to *break* a dollar. **20** To invalidate (a will) by court action. **21** To solve or decipher. **22** To bankrupt. **23** To overwhelm with grief: It *broke* his heart. —*v.i.* **24** To become separated into pieces or fragments; come or fall apart. **25** To burst. **26** To become unusable or inoperative. **27** To move apart or away; disperse: The crowd *broke*. **28** To move or escape suddenly: He *broke* from the crowd. **29** To come into being or evidence: Dawn *broke*. **30** To collapse or crash. **31** To diminish or fall abruptly: The fever *broke*. **32** To change suddenly, as the voice. **33** To be overwhelmed with grief: Her heart *broke*. **34** In baseball, to curve near the plate, as a pitched ball. —**break down 1** To become inoperative. **2** To have a physical or nervous collapse. **3** To give way, as to grief. **4** To decompose. **5** To analyze. — **break in 1** To enter by force. **2** To interrupt. **3** To train. **4** To adapt to use or wear. —**break off 1** To stop suddenly, as in speaking. **2** To sever relations. —**break out 1** To start suddenly. **2** To develop a rash, pimples, etc. —**break up 1** To disperse. **2** To bring or come to an end. **3** *Informal* To overwhelm or be overwhelmed, as with distress or laughter. —**break with** To sever connection with. —*n.* **1** An instance or result of breaking; a fracture, crack, etc. **2** An opening, rift, gap, etc. **3** A breach or interruption of continuity. **4** A pause or interval. **5** A beginning; start: the *break* of day. **6** A dash or run, esp. to escape. **7** A severing of connection or friendly relations. **8** A sudden change or decline. **9** *Informal* An opportunity or piece of luck. **10** A point where there is a change of register of a voice or instrument. [< OE *brecan*] —**break'a·ble** *adj.* —**Syn.** *v.* **1** shatter, smash, fragment, shiver, disintegrate, splinter, dash.

break·age (brā'kij) *n.* **1** A breaking, or the state of being broken. **2** Articles broken. **3** Loss or damage due to breaking. **4** Compensation for this.

break·down (brāk'doun') *n.* **1** The act of breaking down; a failure, as of a machine, one's health, etc. **2** A systematic analysis. **3** *Chem.* Decomposition or analysis of compounds.

break·er (brā'kər) *n.* **1** One who or that which breaks. **2** A wave that breaks into foam on the shore, on rocks, etc. **3** *Can.* ICEBREAKER.

break·fast (brek'fəst) *n.* The first meal of the day. —*v.i.* To eat breakfast. —**break'fast·er** *n.*

break·front (brāk'frunt') *n.* A high, wide bookcase or cabinet with a slightly projecting center part.

break·neck (brāk'nek') *adj.* Headlong and recklessly dangerous: *breakneck* speed.

break·through (brāk'throō') *n.* **1** A decisive or dramatic advance, as in research, knowledge, etc. **2** An attack that penetrates an enemy's defensive system.

break·up (brāk'up') *n.* **1** The act or process of breaking up. **2** A rift or dissolution, as of a relationship.

break·wa·ter (brāk'wô'tər, -wot'ər) *n.* A structure for protecting a harbor or beach from the force of waves.

bream (brēm) *n. pl.* **breams** or **bream 1** A European freshwater fish. **2** Any of various freshwater sunfishes. [< OF *bresme*]

breast (brest) *n.* **1** The front of the body from the neck to the abdomen. **2** One of the two milk-secreting organs on the upper front part of a woman's torso. **3** A similar organ in any mammal. **4** The part of a garment that covers the breast. **5** The seat of the emotions. **6** Anything likened to the human breast. —**make a clean breast of** To confess. —*v.t.* To face or advance against boldly or resolutely. [< OE *brēost*]

breast·bone (brest'bōn') *n.* STERNUM.

breast-feed (brest'fēd') *v.t. & v.i.* **-fed, -feed·ing** To feed (a baby) with milk from the breast; suckle.

breast·plate (brest'plāt') *n.* A piece of armor covering and protecting the breast.

breast stroke A swimming stroke in which the arms are simultaneously thrust forward from the breast, then brought laterally back to the sides.

breast·work (brest'wûrk') *n.* A low, temporary defensive structure, usu. breast-high.

Breastplate

breath (breth) *n.* **1** Air inhaled or exhaled in respiration. **2** An act of respiration, esp. an inhalation. **3** Ability to breathe or breathe freely. **4** The moisture of exhaled air condensed by cooling. **5** The time of a single respiration; an instant. **6** A slight breeze or motion of air. **7** A slight indication, suggestion, etc. **8** A whisper. —**hold one's breath** To prevent oneself from breathing temporarily. —**in the same breath** At the same moment. —**out of breath** Panting, as from exertion. —**take one's breath away** To awe, astonish, etc. — **under one's breath** In a whisper. [< OE *bræth* vapor]

breath·a·lyz·er (breth'ə·lī'zər) *n.* A device that measures the alcoholic content of blood, used esp. to test motorists for intoxication. *Brit. sp.* **·lys·er.** [< BREATH + (AN)ALYZER]

breathe (brēth) *v.* **breathed** (brēthd), **breath·ing** *v.i.* **1** To inhale and exhale air. **2** To be alive; live. **3** To pause for breath. **4** To move gently, as a breeze. **5** To allow air to penetrate: said of a fabric or garment. —*v.t.* **6** To inhale and exhale, as air. **7** To take in or emit by inhaling or exhaling. **8** To infuse or impart, as by breathing. **9** To evince; manifest. **10** To utter; whisper. **11** To allow to rest. [ME *brethren* < *breth* breath] —**breath'a·ble** *adj.*

breath·er (brē'thər) *n. Informal* A brief rest period.

breath·less (breth'lis) *adj.* **1** Out of breath. **2** Intense or eager, as if holding the breath. **3** Causing or filled with tension or excitement. **4** Dead. **5** Having no breeze; oppressive. —**breath'less·ly** *adv.* —**breath'less·ness** *n.*

breath·tak·ing (breth'tā'king) *adj.* Very exciting, moving, etc. —**breath'tak'ing·ly** *adv.*

breath·y (breth'ē) *adj.* **breath·i·er, breath·i·est** Characterized by audible breathing.

bred (bred) *p.t. & p.p.* of BREED.

breech (brēch) *n.* **1** The buttocks. **2** The rear end of a gun barrel, cannon bore, etc. —*v.t.* (brēch, brich) *Archaic* To clothe with breeches. [< OE *brec*, pl., breeches]

breech·cloth (brēch'klôth, -kloth') *n.* LOINCLOTH. Also **breech'clout'** (-klout').

breech·es (brich'iz) *n. pl.* **1** Trousers, usu. close-fitting, that reach to or just below the knee. **2** *Informal* Trousers. [< OE *brec*]

breeches buoy A life-saving apparatus consisting of canvas breeches attached to a life buoy and run upon a rope stretched from a ship to the shore or another ship.

breech·load·er (brēch'lō'dər) *n.* A firearm that is loaded at the breech. —**breech'load'ing** *adj.*

breed (brēd) *v.* **bred, breed·ing** *v.t.* **1** To produce (offspring). **2** To control the reproduction of (animals or plants), often to develop new strains in. **3** To cause; give rise to. **4** To bring up; train. —*v.i.* **5** To procreate. **6** To originate or be caused. —*n.* **1** A strain or type, esp. of an animal, produced by selective mating. **2** A sort or kind. [< OE *brēdan*] —**breed'er** *n.*

Breeches buoy

breeder reactor A nuclear reactor that produces power and acts on nonfissionable elements to produce more fissionable material than it uses.

breed·ing (brē'ding) *n.* **1** The production of offspring. **2** Ancestry; descent. **3** Training, as in good manners; upbringing. **4** The selective production of desired strains of animals or plants.

breeze (brēz) *n.* **1** A moderate current of air; a gentle wind. **2** *Informal* An easily accomplished thing or action. —*v.i.* **breezed, breez·ing** *Informal* To go quickly and blithely. [< Sp. and Pg. *brisa, briza* northeast wind]

breeze·way (brēz'wā') *n.* A roofed, open passageway between two buildings, as a house and a garage.

breez·y (brē′zē) *adj.* **breez·i·er, breez·i·est 1** Having a breeze; slightly windy. **2** Jaunty; light-hearted. **—breez′i·ly** *adv.* **—breez′i·ness** *n.*

breth·ren (breth′rən) *n. Alternative pl. of* BROTHER: now used chiefly in formal and religious contexts.

Bret·on (bret′n) *adj.* Of or pertaining to Brittany, its inhabitants, or their language. **—***n.* **1** A native of Brittany. **2** The Celtic language of the Bretons.

breve (brev, brēv) *n.* **1** A mark (˘) placed over a vowel to indicate that it has a short sound. **2** *Music* A note equal in time to two whole notes. [< L *brevis* short]

bre·vet (brə·vet′, *esp. Brit.* brev′it) *n.* A commission advancing an officer in honorary rank without advance in pay. **—***v.t.* **bre·vet·ted** or **bre·vet·ed, bre·vet·ting** or **bre·vet·ing** To raise in rank by brevet. **—***adj.* Held or conferred by brevet. [< OF *brevet,* dim. of *bref* letter, document] **—bre·vet′cy** *n.*

bre·vi·ar·y (brē′vē·er′ē, brev′ē-) *n. pl.* **·ar·ies** A book of daily prayers, etc., for the canonical hours. [< LL *breviarium* abridgment]

brev·i·ty (brev′ə·tē) *n.* **1** Shortness of duration or time. **2** Condensation of language; conciseness. [< L *brevis* short]

brew (bro͞o) *v.t.* **1** To make, as beer or ale, by steeping, boiling, and fermentation of malt, hops, etc. **2** To make (a beverage) by boiling, steeping, etc. **3** To concoct; devise. **—***v.i.* **4** To make ale, beer, etc. **5** To be imminent. **—***n.* A beverage, etc., made by brewing. [< OE *breōwan*] **—brew′·er** *n.*

brew·er·y (bro͞o′ər·ē) *n. pl.* **·er·ies** An establishment for brewing beer, etc.

brew·ing (bro͞o′ing) *n.* **1** The process of making beer, ale, etc. **2** An amount brewed at one time.

bri·ar[1] (brī′ər) *n.* **1** A European shrub of the heath family, having a hard, woody root. **2** A tobacco pipe made from this root. [< F *bruyère*]

bri·ar[2] (brī′ər) *n.* BRIER[1].

bri·ar·root (brī′ər·ro͞ot′, -ro͝ot′) *n.* The woody root of the briar.

bri·ar·wood (brī′ər·wo͝od′) *n.* The wood of the briarroot.

bribe (brīb) *n.* **1** Something of value given or offered as an inducement to do something wrong. **2** Anything that seduces or allures. **—***v.* **bribed, brib·ing** *v.t.* **1** To offer or give a bribe to. **2** To gain or influence by means of bribery. **—***v.i.* **3** To give bribes. [< OF, piece of bread given a beggar] **—brib′a·ble** *adj.* **—brib′er** *n.*

brib·er·y (brī′bər·ē) *n. pl.* **·er·ies** The giving, offering, or accepting of a bribe.

bric-a-brac (brik′ə·brak) *n.* Small objects displayed as ornaments; knickknacks. Also **bric-à-brac.** [F]

brick (brik) *n.* **1** A molded block of baked or fired clay, used for building, paving, etc. **2** Bricks collectively. **3** An object shaped like a brick. **4** *Informal* An admirable fellow. **—***v.t.* **1** To build or line with bricks. **2** To cover or close with bricks: with *up* or *in.* [< OF *brique* fragment, bit]

brick·bat (brik′bat′) *n.* **1** A piece of a brick, esp. when used as a missile. **2** A critical or unflattering comment.

brick·lay·er (brik′lā′ər) *n.* One who builds walls, etc., with bricks. **—brick′lay′ing** *n.*

brick red Dull brownish red. **—brick-red** (brik′red′) *adj.*

brick·work (brik′wûrk′) *n.* Construction with or a structure of bricks.

brick·yard (brik′yärd′) *n.* A place where bricks are made.

bri·dal (brīd′l) *adj.* Of a bride or a wedding; nuptial. **—***n.* A wedding. [< OE *brȳdeala* wedding feast]

bri·dal·wreath (brīd′l·rēth′) *n.* A cultivated shrub with small white flowers.

bride (brīd) *n.* A woman newly married or about to be married. [< OE *brȳd*]

bride·groom (brīd′gro͞om′, -gro͝om′) *n.* A man newly married or about to be married. [< OE *brȳd* bride + *guma* man]

brides·maid (brīdz′mād′) *n.* A usu. young, unmarried woman who attends a bride at her wedding.

bridge[1] (brij) *n.* **1** A structure built to span and afford passage across a waterway, railroad, ravine, etc. **2** Something that spans or connects in the manner of a bridge. **3** An observation platform across and above a ship's deck for the use of the officers, the pilot, etc. **4** The bony upper portion of the nose. **5** The part of a pair of eyeglasses resting on this part of the nose. **6** A block for raising the strings of a musical instrument, as a violin or guitar. • See VIOLIN. **7** A mounting for holding false teeth, attached to adjoining teeth on each side. **8** *Music* A transitional passage. **—burn one's bridges (behind one)** To cut off all possibility of retreat. **—***v.t.* **bridged, bridg·ing 1** To construct a bridge over. **2** To span or connect as by a bridge. [< OE *brycg*] **—bridge′a·ble** *adj.*

bridge[2] (brij) *n.* A card game derived from whist, in which a trump suit is determined by bidding. [?]

bridge·head (brij′hed′) *n.* An advance military position on or near a river bank, pass, etc., in enemy territory.

bridge·work (brij′wûrk′) *n.* A dental bridge or bridges.

bri·dle (brīd′l) *n.* **1** The head harness of a horse, including bit and reins. **2** Anything that restrains or checks. **—***v.* **bri·dled, bri·dling** *v.t.* **1** To put a bridle on. **2** To check or control with or as with a bridle. **—***v.i.* **3** To raise the head and draw in the chin, as in resentment, pride, etc. [< OE *brīdel*] **—bri′dler** *n.*

bri·dle·path (brīd′l·path′, -päth′) *n.* A path for horseback riding.

brief (brēf) *adj.* **1** Short in duration or extent. **2** Of few words; concise. **3** Curt; abrupt. **—***n.* **1** A concise statement or summary. **2** A written summary of the relevant facts, points of law, etc., in a legal case. **3** *pl.* Short, close-fitting underpants. **—in brief** Briefly; in short. **—hold a brief for** To champion. **—***v.t.* **1** To make a summary of. **2** To instruct or advise in advance. [< L *brevis* short] **—brief′ly** *adv.* **—brief′ness** *n.* **—Syn.** *adj.* **2** condensed, succinct, terse, laconic.

brief·case (brēf′kās′) *n.* A soft-sided case, as of leather, for carrying papers, books, etc.

brief·ing (brē′fing) *n.* Final instructions, advice, etc., given in preparation for an action or undertaking.

bri·er[1] (brī′ər) *n.* A prickly bush or shrub, esp. of the rose family. [< OE *brēr*] **—bri′er·y** *adj.*

bri·er[2] (brī′ər) *n.* BRIAR[1].

bri·er·root (brī′ər·ro͞ot′, -ro͝ot′) *n.* BRIARROOT.

bri·er·wood (brī′ər·wo͝od′) *n.* BRIARWOOD.

brig[1] (brig) *n.* A two-masted ship, square-rigged on both masts. [Short for BRIGANTINE]

brig[2] (brig) *n.* **1** A prison on shipboard. **2** *Slang* A guardhouse. [?< BRIG[1]]

Brig. brigade; brigadier.

bri·gade (bri·gād′) *n.* **1** A U.S. Army unit of varying size, together with its headquarters and supporting units. **2** Any of various large military units. **3** A group of persons organized to work together: a fire *brigade.* **—***v.t.* **·gad·ed, ·gad·ing** To form into a brigade. [< Ital. *brigata* crew < *brigare* to brawl]

brig·a·dier (brig′ə·dir′) *n.* BRIGADIER GENERAL.

brigadier general See GRADE.

brig·and (brig′ənd) *n.* A bandit; esp. one of a roving band of outlaws. [< Ital. *brigare* to brawl, fight] **—brig′and·age** (-ij), **brig′and·ism** *n.*

brig·an·tine (brig′ən·tēn, -tīn) *n.* A two-masted vessel, square-rigged on the foremast, and fore-and-aft rigged on the mainmast. [< MF *brigandin* a fighting vessel < Ital. *brigare* to fight]

Brig. Gen. Brigadier General.

bright (brīt) *adj.* **1** Emitting or reflecting much light; shining. **2** Full of light. **3** Brilliant, as in color or tone; vivid. **4** Intelligent; quick-witted. **5** Cheerful; gay. **6** Promising; auspicious. **—***adv.* In a bright manner. [< OE *beorht, briht*] **—bright′ly** *adv.* **—bright′ness** *n.* **—Syn. 1** radiant, luminous, glowing, gleaming, effulgent.

bright·en (brīt′n) *v.t.* & *v.i.* To make or become bright or brighter. **—bright′en·er** *n.*

Bright's disease Any of various forms of nephritis, an inflammation of the kidney. [< Richard *Bright,* 1789–1858, English physician]

bril·liant (bril′yənt) *adj.* **1** Very bright or vivid: a *brilliant*

light. **2** Splendid; dazzling: a *brilliant* performance. **3** Strikingly intelligent or extraordinarily able or talented. —*n.* A diamond cut with many facets. [< MF *briller* to sparkle] —**bril′liance, bril′lian·cy** *n.* —**bril′liant·ly** *adv.*

bril·lian·tine (bril′yən·tēn) *n.* A perfumed hair oil. [< F *brillant* brilliant]

brim (brim) *n.* **1** The rim or uppermost edge of a cup, bowl, etc. **2** A projecting rim, as of a hat. —*v.t. & v.i.* **brimmed, brim·ming** To fill or be filled to the brim. —**brim over** To overflow. [ME *brimme*]

brim·ful (brim′fŏŏl′) *adj.* Full to the brim.

brim·stone (brim′stōn′) *n.* SULFUR. [< OE *brynstān*, lit., burning stone]

brin·dle (brin′dəl) *adj.* BRINDLED. —*n.* **1** A brindled color. **2** A brindled animal.

brin·dled (brin′dəld) *adj.* Tawny or grayish with darker streaks or spots. [< ME *brende*]

brine (brīn) *n.* **1** Water saturated with salt. **2** The sea; the ocean. —*v.t.* **brined, brin·ing** To steep in brine. [< OE *brӯne*] —**brin′i·ness** *n.* —**brin′y** *adj.* (**·i·er, ·i·est**)

bring (bring) *v.t.* **brought, bring·ing 1** To convey or cause (a person or thing) to come with oneself to or toward a place. **2** To cause to come about; result in. **3** To cause to appear, come to mind, etc. **4** To persuade or induce, as to a course of action. **5** To sell for: The house *brought* a good price. **6** To institute (a lawsuit, charge, etc.). —**bring about 1** To cause to happen. **2** *Naut.* To turn, as a ship. —**bring around** (or **round) 1** To cause to adopt an opinion, course of action, etc. **2** To restore to consciousness. —**bring down 1** To cause to fall. **2** To fell. —**bring forth 1** To give birth to. **2** To produce. —**bring in 1** To render or submit (a verdict). **2** To yield or produce, as profits. —**bring off** To do successfully. —**bring on** To cause; lead to. —**bring out 1** To reveal; cause to be evident. **2** To publish or produce. **3** To introduce, as a young girl to society. —**bring to 1** To restore to consciousness. **2** *Naut.* To cause (a ship) to lie to. —**bring up 1** To raise and train during childhood; rear. **2** To mention or introduce, as a subject. **3** To cough or vomit up. [< OE *bringan*] —**bring′er** *n.* • In strict usage, *bring* (def. 1) means to convey or accompany to a place, while *take* means to remove or go with from a place: *Take* the books from the shelf and *bring* them to the office.

brink (bringk) *n.* **1** The upper edge of a steep place. **2** The edge; verge: the *brink* of despair. [< Scand.]

brink·man·ship (bringk′mən·ship) *n.* A policy of following a course of action to a point bordering on disaster.

bri·oche (brē·ōsh′, -osh′) *n.* A soft, sweet roll. [F]

bri·quette (bri·ket′) *n.* A block of compressed coal dust or charcoal, used as fuel. Also **bri·quet′.** [< F *brique* brick]

brisk (brisk) *adj.* **1** Quick; energetic; spirited. **2** Zestful; stimulating. **3** Active: *brisk* sales. [? < F *brusque* abrupt, sudden] —**brisk′ly** *adv.* —**brisk′ness** *n.*

bris·ket (bris′kit) *n.* **1** The breast of an animal. **2** A cut of meat from this part. [? < Scand.]

bris·tle (bris′əl) *n.* A short, stiff hair or similar part. —*v.* **·tled, ·tling** —*v.i.* **1** To erect the bristles. **2** To stand up stiffly, as bristles. **3** To be thickly set as if with bristles. **4** To show anger, irritation, etc. —*v.t.* **5** To erect as or like bristles. [< OE *byrst*] —**bris·tli·ness** (bris′lē·nis) *n.* —**bris·tly** (bris′lē) *adj.* (**·i·er, ·i·est**)

Brit. Britain; British.

Brit·ain (brit′n) *n.* GREAT BRITAIN.

Bri·tan·ni·a (bri·tan′yə, -tan′ē·ə) *n.* **1** Great Britain or the British Empire. **2** A female personification of Great Britain or the British Empire. [< L]

Bri·tan·nic (bri·tan′ik) *adj.* Of Great Britain; British.

britch·es (brich′iz) *n. pl. Informal* BREECHES.

Brit·i·cism (brit′ə·siz′əm) *n.* A verbal usage characteristic of the British.

Brit·ish (brit′ish) *adj.* Of or pertaining to Great Britain or the United Kingdom. —*n.* **1** The people of Great Britain: used with *the.* **2** The English language as used in Great Britain.

British America 1 Canada: also **British North America. 2** Sometimes, all British possessions in or near North or South America.

Brit·ish·er (brit′ish·ər) *n.* A native or subject of Great Britain.

British thermal unit The quantity of heat required to

raise the temperature of one pound of water one degree Fahrenheit.

Brit·on (brit′n) *n.* **1** A member of one of the Celtic tribes of ancient Britain. **2** A native or subject of Great Britain.

brit·tle (brit′l) *adj.* **1** Likely to break or snap; fragile. **2** Stiff or tense in manner. —*n.* A crisp candy made with sugar and nuts. [ME *britel*] —**brit′tle·ness** *n.*

bro. (*pl.* **bros.**) brother.

broach (brōch) *v.t.* **1** To introduce or mention for the first time, as a subject. **2** To pierce (a cask, etc.) to draw off liquid. —*n.* A pointed, tapering tool for boring or reaming. [< OF *broche* a spit] —**broach′er** *n.*

broad (brôd) *adj.* **1** Extended in lateral dimensions; wide. **2** Extensive; spacious. **3** Clear; full: *broad* daylight. **4** Wide in scope or range; comprehensive. **5** Liberal; tolerant. **6** Obvious; plain: a *broad* hint. **7** Not detailed or specific; general. **8** Coarse; ribald. **9** Strongly dialectal. **10** *Phonet.* Formed with the oral passage wide open and the tongue low and flat, as the *a* in *calm.* —*n.* **1** The broad part of anything. **2** *Slang* A woman: a disparaging term. —*adv.* Completely; fully. [< OE *brād*] —**broad′ly** *adv.* —**broad′ness** *n.*

broad·ax (brôd′aks′) *n.* An ax with a broad edge and short handle. Also **broad′axe′.**

broad·cast (brôd′kast′, -käst′) *v.* **·cast** or **·casted, ·cast·ing** *v.t.* **1** To transmit over an area by radio or television. **2** To make known; disseminate. **3** To scatter, as seed, over a wide area. —*v.i.* **4** To transmit or take part in a broadcast program. —*adj.* **1** Of or for transmission by broadcasting. **2** Scattered widely, as seed. —*n.* **1** The transmitting of a radio or television program. **2** A program so transmitted. —*adv.* Over an extended area. —**broad′cast′er** *n.*

broad·cloth (brôd′klôth′, -kloth′) *n.* **1** A fine, smooth-surfaced wool cloth. **2** A closely woven fabric of silk, cotton, etc.

broad·en (brôd′n) *v.t. & v.i.* To make or become broad or broader.

broad·gauge (brôd′gāj′) *adj.* Having railroad tracks more than the standard 56½ inches apart. Also **broad′-gauged′.**

broad jump A jump for distance in an athletic contest.

broad·loom (brôd′lōōm′) *n.* Carpeting woven on a wide loom. —*adj.* Woven on a wide loom.

broad·mind·ed (brôd′mīn′did) *adj.* Liberal or tolerant in beliefs and opinions. —**broad′-mind′ed·ly** *adv.* —**broad′-mind′ed·ness** *n.*

broad·side (brôd′sīd′) *n.* **1 a** All the guns on one side of a man-of-war. **b** The simultaneous firing of such guns. **2** An abusive attack or denunciation. **3** A ship's side above the water line. **4** A large sheet of paper printed on one side: also **broad′sheet′.** —*adv.* With the side facing or turned toward something: The shell struck the ship *broadside.*

broad·sword (brôd′sôrd′, -sōrd′) *n.* A sword with a broad cutting blade.

broad·tail (brôd′tāl′) *n.* Fur made from the flat, glossy pelts of very young karakul lambs.

Broad·way (brôd′wā′) *n.* A street running north from lower Manhattan through New York City, famous for its entertainment district.

bro·cade (brō·kād′) *n.* A rich fabric with a raised interwoven design. —*v.t.* **·cad·ed, ·cad·ing** To weave (cloth) with a raised design. [< Med. L *broccare* embroider]

broc·co·li (brok′ə·lē) *n.* A plant related to cauliflower, having green, edible buds and stalks. [< Ital., pl. of *broccolo* cabbage sprout]

bro·chure (brō·shŏŏr′) *n.* A pamphlet. [< F *brocher* to stitch]

bro·gan (brō′gən) *n.* A heavy ankle-high shoe. [< Ir. *brōg* shoe]

brogue¹ (brōg) *n.* A dialectal accent, esp. an Irish accent, in speaking English. [? < BROGUE²]

brogue² (brōg) *n.* **1** A heavy oxford shoe with decorative perforations. **2** A shoe of untanned hide formerly worn in Ireland and Scotland. [< Ir. *brōg* brogue (def. 2)]

broil¹ (broil) *v.t.* **1** To cook, as meat, by subjecting to direct heat. **2** To expose to great heat. —*v.i.* **3** To become cooked by broiling. **4** To be exposed to great heat. —*n.* **1** Something broiled. **2** A broiling heat. [< OF *bruller*]

broil² (broil) *n.* A noisy quarrel; brawl. —*v.i.* To engage in a broil; brawl. [< OF *brouiller* confuse]

broil·er (broi′lər) *n.* 1 A device for broiling. 2 A chicken suitable for broiling.

broke (brōk) *p.t. & archaic p.p.* of BREAK. —*adj. Informal* Without money; bankrupt.

bro·ken (brō′kən) *p.p.* of BREAK. —*adj.* 1 Shattered; fractured. 2 Not working; out of order. 3 Violated; disregarded: *broken* oaths. 4 Not continuous; interrupted. 5 Incomplete: a *broken* set. 6 Disordered; disrupted. 7 Rough or irregular. 8 Crushed, as in spirit. 9 Weakened; infirm. 10 Tamed; trained. 11 Imperfectly spoken: *broken* English. —**bro′ken·ly** *adv.* —**bro′ken·ness** *n.*

bro·ken-heart·ed (brō′kən-här′tid) *adj.* Overwhelmed by grief, despair, etc. —**bro′ken-heart′ed·ly** *adv.*

bro·ker (brō′kər) *n.* One who acts as a commissioned agent in negotiating contracts, buying and selling stocks, real estate, etc.

bro·ker·age (brō′kər·ij) *n.* The business or commission of a broker.

bro·mide (brō′mīd, -mid) *n.* 1 Any of various compounds of bromine with a metallic or organic radical, used in medicine, photography, anti-knock gasoline, etc. 2 A medicine, esp. a sedative, containing a bromide. 3 *Informal* A dull remark; platitude. —**bro·mid·ic** (brō-mid′ik) *adj.* [< BROM(INE) + -IDE]

bro·mine (brō′mēn) *n.* A reddish brown, heavy, liquid element (symbol Br) of the halogen group, with irritating fumes. [< Gk. *brōmos* stench + -INE] —**bro′mic** *adj.*

bron·chi (brong′kī) *pl.* of BRONCHUS.

bron·chi·al (brong′kē·əl) *adj.* Of or pertaining to the chief air passages of the lungs.

bronchial tubes The subdivisions of the trachea conveying air into the lungs.

bron·chi·tis (brong·kī′tis) *n.* Inflammation of the bronchial tubes, or, loosely, of the bronchi or trachea. [< Gk. *bronchos* windpipe + -ITIS] —**bron·chit·ic** (brong·kit′ik) *adj.*

bron·cho·scope (brong′kə·skōp) *n.* An instrument for inspecting or treating the interior of the bronchi.

bron·chus (brong′kəs) *n. pl.* **·chi** (-kī) One of the two forked branches of the trachea. [< Gk. *bronchos* windpipe]

bron·co (brong′kō) *n. pl.* **·cos** A small, wild, or partly broken horse of the w U.S. Also **bron′cho.** [< Sp., rough]

bron·co-bust·er (brong′kō·bus′tər) *n. Informal* One who breaks a bronco to the saddle. Also **bron′cho·bust′er.**

bron·to·sau·rus (bron′tə·sôr′əs) *n.* A huge, herbivorous

Brontosaurus

dinosaur of the Jurassic period. Also **bron′to·saur′.** [< Gk. *brontē* thunder + *sauros* lizard]

Bronx cheer *Slang* A derisive sound made by sticking out the tongue and vibrating the nearly closed lips by forcibly expelling breath.

bronze (bronz) *n.* 1 A reddish brown alloy of copper, esp. with tin. 2 The color of bronze. 3 A sculpture cast in bronze. —*v.* **bronzed, bronz·ing** *v.t.* 1 To color like or cover with bronze. —*v.i.* 2 To become brown or tan. [< Ital. *bronzo*] —**bronz′y** *adj.* (**·i·er, ·i·est**)

Bronze Age A period between the Stone Age and the Iron Age during which implements were made of bronze.

Bronze Star A U.S. military decoration awarded for heroic or meritorious achievement.

brooch (brōch, brōoch) *n.* An ornamental pin fastened with a clasp. [Var. of BROACH, *n.*]

brood (brōōd) *n.* 1 All the young birds of a single hatching. 2 The children of a household. —*v.t.* 1 To sit upon or incubate (eggs). 2 To protect (young) by or as by covering with the wings. —*v.i.* 3 To sit on eggs; incubate. 4 To think about gloomily and persistently; ponder moodily. —*adj.* Kept for breeding: a *brood* mare. [< OE *brod*]

brood·er (brōō′dər) *n.* 1 A warmed shelter for chicks reared without a hen. 2 One who broods.

brood·y (brōō′dē) *adj.* **brood·i·er, brood·i·est** 1 Inclined to sit on eggs, as a hen. 2 Moody.

brook¹ (brōōk) *n.* A small, natural stream. [< OE *brōc*]

brook² (brōōk) *v.t.* To put up with; tolerate: He will *brook* no disobedience. [< OE *brūcan* use, enjoy]

brook·let (brōōk′lit) *n.* A little brook.

brook trout A speckled freshwater game fish of North America.

broom (brōōm, brōom) *n.* 1 A brush with a long handle, used for sweeping. 2 Any of various leguminous shrubs with flexible shoots and usu. yellow flowers. —*v.t.* To sweep with a broom. [< OE *brōm*]

broom·corn (brōōm′kôrn′, brōom′-) *n.* A grass used to make brooms and brushes.

broom·stick (brōōm′stik′, brōom′-) *n.* The handle of a broom.

broth (brôth, broth) *n.* Thin soup consisting of the water in which meat, vegetables, etc., have been boiled. [< OE]

broth·el (broth′əl, brôth′-, brôth′əl, brôth′-) *n.* A house of prostitution. [< OE *brēothan* to ruin, decay]

broth·er (bruth′ər) *n. pl.* **broth·ers** or esp. *in formal or religious use* **breth·ren** 1 A male person having the same parents as another person. 2 A male of the lower animals having one parent in common with another. 3 **a** HALF BROTHER. **b** BROTHER-IN-LAW. **c** A foster brother. 4 A fellow man. 5 A man or boy allied to another or others by race, creed, membership in a society, etc. 6 A lay member of a male Christian religious order. [< OE *brōthor*]

broth·er·hood (bruth′ər·hōod) *n.* 1 The condition or relationship of being brothers. 2 A group or organization of men having a close relationship, common interests, etc.

broth·er-in-law (bruth′ər·in·lô′) *n. pl.* **broth·ers-in-law** 1 The brother of one's husband or wife. 2 One's sister's husband. 3 The husband of one's husband's or wife's sister.

broth·er·ly (bruth′ər·lē) *adj.* Of or typical of a brother or brothers; fraternal; affectionate. —**broth′er·li·ness** *n.*

brougham (brōōm, brōō′əm, brō′əm) *n.* A closed, four-wheeled carriage or automobile with an uncovered driver's seat. [< Lord Henry *Brougham,* 1778–1868, British statesman]

brought (brôt) *p.t. & p.p.* of BRING.

Brougham

brow (brou) *n.* 1 The forehead. 2 An eyebrow. 3 The countenance in general. 4 The upper edge of a cliff, precipice, etc. [< OE *brū*]

brow·beat (brou′bēt′) *v.t.* **·beat, ·beat·en, ·beat·ing** To intimidate by an overbearing manner. —**Syn.** cow, bully, hector.

brown (broun) *n.* 1 A color, as of coffee or chocolate, combining red, yellow, and black. 2 A pigment, dye, etc., of this color. —*adj.* 1 Of the color brown. 2 Tanned by the sun. —*v.t. & v.i.* 1 To make or become brown. 2 To cook until brown. [< OE *brūn*] —**brown′ish** *adj.* —**brown′ness** *n.*

brown Betty A baked pudding made with bread crumbs, apples, sugar, etc.

Brown·i·an movement (brou′nē·ən) The rapid random movement of small particles suspended in fluids. Also **Brownian motion.** [< Robert *Brown,* 1773–1858, English botanist, who discovered it]

brown·ie (brou′nē) *n.* 1 A good-natured elflike sprite. 2 A small, flat, usu. square chocolate cake. [< BROWN]

Brown·ie (brou′nē) *n.* A junior girl scout of the age group seven through nine.

brown-out (broun′out′) *n.* A partial dimming of lights or loss of electric power.

brown rice Unpolished rice grains.

Brown Shirt 1 A member of the storm troops in Germany under Hitler. 2 A Nazi.

---

add, āce, câre, pālm; end, ēven; it, īce; odd, ōpen, ôrder; tōōk, pōōl; up, bûrn; ə = *a* in *above, u* in *focus;* yōō = *u* in *fuse;* oil; pout; check; go; ring; thin; this; zh, *vision.* < derived from; ? origin uncertain or unknown.

brown·stone (broun′stōn′) *n.* **1** A brownish red sandstone. **2** A house built of or faced with this.

brown study A state of deep, preoccupied thought.

brown sugar Partly or wholly unrefined sugar.

browse (brouz) *v.* **browsed, brows·ing** —*v.i.* **1** To feed on leaves, twigs, etc. **2** To read or inspect casually. —*v.t.* **3** To nibble at (leaves, twigs, etc.). —*n.* Leaves, twigs, etc., eaten by animals. [< MF *broust* bud, sprout] —**brows′er** *n.*

bru·in (brōō′in) *n.* A bear. [< Du., brown]

bruise (brōōz) *v.* **bruised, bruis·ing** *v.t.* **1** To injure, as by a blow, without breaking the surface of the skin. **2** To dent or mar the surface of. **3** To hurt or offend slightly, as feelings. **4** To crush, as with a mortar and pestle. —*v.i.* **5** To become discolored as the result of a blow. —*n.* A surface injury, usu. with discoloration of the skin. [Fusion of OE *brȳsan* crush and OF *bruisier* break, shatter]

bruis·er (brōō′zər) *n.* A powerfully built fellow.

bruit (brōōt) *v.t.* To noise abroad; talk about. [< OF *bruit* noise]

brunch (brunch) *n.* A meal combining breakfast and lunch. [Blend of BREAKFAST and LUNCH]

Bru·nei (brōō·nī′) *n.* A sultanate under British protection on the N part of Borneo, 2,226 sq. mi., cap. Brunei.

bru·net (brōō·net′) *adj.* **1** Dark in color, as the hair or complexion. **2** Having dark hair and often dark complexion and eyes. —*n.* A man or boy with dark hair, complexion, etc. [< F *brun* brown]

bru·nette (brōō·net′) *adj.* BRUNET. —*n.* A woman or girl with dark hair, complexion, etc. [< F *brun* brown]

brunt (brunt) *n.* The main force or impact of a blow, attack, etc. [?]

brush¹ (brush) *n.* **1** An implement having bristles, hair, wires, etc., fixed in a handle or a back, and used for applying paint, removing dirt, grooming the hair, etc. **2** The act of brushing. **3** A light, grazing touch. **4** A short, brisk fight; skirmish. **5** Something resembling a brush, as the bushy tail of a fox. **6** An electrical conductor bearing on the commutator of a dynamo or motor. —*v.t.* **1** To sweep, polish, smooth, paint, etc., with a brush. **2** To remove with or as with a brush. **3** To touch lightly in passing. **4** To refuse to consider; dismiss: used with *aside, away,* or *off.* —*v.i.* **5** To move with a slight contact: to *brush* past someone. —**brush up** To refresh one's knowledge or skill. [< OF *brosse*]

brush² (brush) *n.* **1** A growth of small trees and shrubs. **2** Wooded country sparsely settled; backwoods. **3** Cut or broken-off branches; brushwood. [< OF *broche*]

brush-off (brush′ôf′, -of′) *n. Informal* An abrupt or contemptuously quick refusal or dismissal.

brush·wood (brush′wōōd′) *n.* **1** Cut or broken-off branches. **2** A dense, thicketlike growth.

brusque (brusk, *esp. Brit.* brōōsk) *adj.* Blunt or gruff, esp. so as to cause offense; rudely abrupt. Also **brusk.** [< Ital. *brusco* rough, rude] —**brusque′ly** *adv.* —**brusque′ness** *n.* — Syn. curt, short, bluff.

Brus·sels sprouts (brus′əlz) **1** A cultivated variety of cabbage having stems covered with sprouts like little cabbages. **2** The small edible heads of this plant.

bru·tal (brōōt′l) *adj.* **1** Of or typical of a brute; savagely cruel; unfeeling. **2** Harsh; insufferable; punishing: *brutal* weather; He maintained a *brutal* pace. [< L *brutus* stupid] —**bru′tal·ly** *adv.* —Syn. bestial, barbarous, inhuman, savage.

bru·tal·i·ty (brōō·tal′ə·tē) *n. pl.* **·ties 1** The state or quality of being brutal. **2** A brutal act.

bru·tal·ize (brōōt′əl·īz) *v.t. & v.i.* **·ized, ·iz·ing** To make or become brutal. —**bru′tal·i·za′tion** *n.*

brute (brōōt) *n.* **1** An animal as distinguished from a human being. **2** A brutal person. —*adj.* **1** Of or typical of a brute; animal. **2** Merely physical: *brute* force. [< L *brutus* stupid] .

brut·ish (brōō′tish) *adj.* Resembling or characteristic of a brute; gross; coarse. —**brut′ish·ly** *adv.* —**brut′ish·ness** *n.*

bry·ol·o·gy (brī·ol′ə·jē) *n.* The branch of botany that treats of bryophytes. [< Gk. *bryon* moss + -LOGY] —**bry·o·log·i·cal** (brī′ə·loj′i·kəl) *adj.* —**bry·ol′o·gist** *n.*

bry·o·phyte (brī′ə·fīt) *n.* Any moss or liverwort. [< Gk. *bryon* moss + *phyton* plant] —**bry′o·phyt′ic** (-fit′ik) *adj.*

B.S., B. Sc. Bachelor of Science.

B/S bags; bales.

B/S, b.s. bill of sale.

b.s. balance sheet.

B.S.A. Boy Scouts of America.

B.S. Ed. Bachelor of Science in Education.

B.T., B. Th. Bachelor of Theology.

Bt. Baronet.

Btry. Battery.

BTU, B.T.U., Btu, B.th.u. British thermal unit.

bu. bureau; bushel; bushels.

bub·ble (bub′əl) *n.* **1** A rounded film of cohesive liquid filled with air or other gas. **2** A globule of air or other gas confined in a liquid or solid. **3** A usu. transparent glass or plastic dome. **4** Something insubstantial or delusive. **5** The process or sound of bubbling. —*v.* **·bled, ·bling** *v.i.* **1** To form or rise in bubbles. **2** To move or flow with a gurgling sound. **3** To behave in a lively, irrepressible manner. —*v.t.* **4** To cause to bubble. **5** To utter as by bubbling. [ME *buble*] —**bub′bly** *adj.* (**·i·er, ·i·est**)

bubble gum Chewing gum that can be blown into bubbles.

bu·bo (byōō′bō) *n. pl.* **bu·boes** An inflammatory swelling of a lymph gland, esp. in the groin or armpit. [< Gk. *boubōn* groin] —**bu·bon·ic** (byōō·bon′ik) *adj.*

bubonic plague A contagious, often fatal disease, characterized by fever, vomiting, diarrhea, and buboes, caused by a bacterium transmitted by fleas from infected rats.

buc·cal (buk′əl) *adj.* Of or pertaining to the cheek or mouth cavity. [< L *bucca* cheek]

buc·ca·neer (buk′ə·nir′) *n.* A pirate or freebooter. [< F *boucanier*]

buck¹ (buk) *n.* **1** A male deer, rabbit, etc. **2** A sudden upward leap, as of a horse. **3** A dashing young fellow. —*v.i.* **1** To leap upward suddenly, as a horse trying to dislodge a rider. **2** To charge with the head down. **3** To move with jerks and jolts. —*v.t.* **4** To throw by bucking. **5** To butt with the head. **6** To resist stubbornly; struggle against. **7** To charge into (the opposing line in football). —**buck for** *Slang* To strive for (a raise, promotion, etc.). —**buck up** *Informal* To cheer up. —*adj.* Being of the lowest grade within a class: *buck* sergeant. [Fusion of OE *buc* he-goat and *bucca* male deer] —**buck′er** *n.*

buck² (buk) *n. Slang* A dollar. [< BUCKSKIN]

buck³ (buk) *n.* A marker formerly used in poker to indicate the next dealer. —**pass the buck** *Informal* To shift responsibility, blame, etc., to someone else. [?]

buck and wing An intricate, fast tap dance.

buck·a·roo (buk′ə·rōō′, buk′ə·rōō) *n.* A cowboy. [< Sp. *vaquero* cowboy]

buck·board (buk′bôrd′, -bōrd′) *n.* A four-wheeled open carriage with the seat resting on a flexible floorboard. [< BUCK, *v.* + BOARD]

buck·et (buk′it) *n.* **1** A cylindrical container with a curved handle at the top; a pail. **2** As much as a bucket will hold: also **buck′et·ful.** **3** A scooplike part, as of a steam shovel. —*v.t.* **1** To draw or carry in a bucket. —*v.i.* **2** To move along rapidly. —**kick the bucket** *Slang* To die. [< OF *buket* kind of tub]

bucket seat A single seat with a rounded, usu. padded back, as in a sports car or airplane.

buck·eye (buk′ī′) *n.* **1** Any of several North American species of horse chestnut. **2** The glossy brown nut of such a tree. [< BUCK¹ + EYE]

buck·le¹ (buk′əl) *n.* **1** A metal clasp for fastening together ends of a strap, belt, etc. **2** An ornament resembling this, as on a shoe. —*v.t. & v.i.* **·led, ·ling** To fasten or be fastened with a buckle. —**buckle down** To apply oneself vigorously or industriously. [< F *boucle* cheek strap, boss of a shield]

buck·le² (buk′əl) *v.t. & v.i.* **·led, ·ling 1** To bend, warp, or crumple, as under pressure. **2** To give way; collapse. —*n.* A bend, bulge, wrinkle, etc. [< F *boucler* bulge]

buck·ler (buk′lər) *n.* **1** A small, round shield. **2** Something that defends or protects. [< OF *boucler* having a boss]

buck private *Informal* A private of the lowest rank in the U.S. Army.

buck·ram (buk′rəm) *n.* A coarse, stiffened cotton fabric, used for bookbinding, lining garments, etc. [< OF *boquerant*]

buck·saw (buk'sô') *n.* A saw set in an adjustable H-shaped frame.

buck·shot (buk'shot') *n.* Shot of a large size, used in hunting deer and other large game.

buck·skin (buk'skin') *n.* 1 Soft, strong, yellowish leather made from the skins of deer or sheep. 2 *pl.* Breeches, etc., made from this leather.

Bucksaw

buck·thorn (buk'thôrn') *n.* Any of several sometimes thorny trees and shrubs with small greenish flowers.

buck·tooth (buk'tōōth') *n. pl.* **·teeth** A projecting front tooth. **—buck'toothed'** *adj.*

buck·wheat (buk'hwēt') *n.* 1 A plant with triangular seeds used as fodder and for flour. 2 Its seeds. 3 The flour. [< OE *bōc* beech + WHEAT]

bu·col·ic (byōō·kol'ik) *adj.* 1 Of or concerning shepherds; pastoral. 2 Rustic; rural. —*n.* A pastoral poem. [< Gk. *boukolos* herdsman] **—bu·col'i·cal·ly** *adv.*

bud (bud) *n.* 1 a An undeveloped stem, branch, or shoot of a plant, with rudimentary leaves or unexpanded flowers. b The state or stage of budding. 2 A budlike projection or part. 3 An early or undeveloped state. **—nip in the bud** To stop in the initial stage. —*v.* **bud·ded, bud·ding** *v.i.* 1 To put forth buds. 2 To begin to grow or develop. —*v.t.* 3 To cause to bud. 4 To graft by inserting a bud of (a plant) into another plant. [ME *budde*] **—bud'der** *n.*

Bud·dhism (bōōd'iz·əm, bōō'diz-) *n.* A mystical and ascetic religious faith of E Asia, founded in northern India by Buddha in the sixth century B.C., teaching that the ideally perfect and happy state of Nirvana can be attained by mental and sensory discipline and purification. **—Bud'dhist** *adj., n.* **—Bud·dhis'tic** or **·ti·cal** *adj.*

bud·dy (bud'ē) *n. pl.* **·dies** *Informal* Pal; chum.

budge (buj) *v.t. & v.i.* **budged, budg·ing** 1 To move or stir slightly. 2 To give in or cause to give in. [< F *bouger* stir, move]

budg·et (buj'it) *n.* 1 A statement of probable revenue and expenditure and of financial proposals for the ensuing year. 2 A summary of probable income for a given period, with approximate allowances for certain expenditures. 3 A collection or stock of items. —*v.t.* 1 To determine in advance the expenditure of (time, money, etc.) over a period of time. 2 To put on or into a budget. —*v.i.* 3 To make a budget. [< L *bulga* leather bag] **—budg·et·ar·y** (buj'ə·ter'ē) *adj.* **—budg'et·er** *n.*

buff[1] (buf) *n.* 1 A soft, flexible, undyed leather, made from the skins of buffalo, elk, oxen, etc. 2 Its color, a light yellow. 3 A coat made of buff leather. 4 *Informal* The bare skin; the nude. 5 A stick or wheel covered with leather, velvet, etc., and used in polishing. —*adj.* 1 Made of buff. 2 Light brownish yellow. —*v.t.* To clean or polish with or as with a buff. [< OF *buffle* buffalo]

buff[2] (buf) *v.t.* 1 To deaden the shock of. —*v.i.* 2 To act as a buffer; absorb or reduce shock. [< OF *buffe* blow]

buff[3] (buf) *n.* *Informal* An enthusiast or devotee: a theater *buff.* [< BUFF[1], after the buff coats worn by certain volunteer firemen]

buf·fa·lo (buf'ə·lō) *n. pl.* **·loes** or **·los** or **·lo** 1 Any of several wild or domesticated oxlike mammals, as the water buffalo, etc. 2 The North American bison. —*v.t.* *Slang* To overawe; hoodwink. [< Gk. *boubalos* buffalo]

buffalo grass A low, creeping, prairie grass, used for forage.

Cape buffalo

buff·er[1] (buf'ər) *n.* One who or that which cleans or polishes with a buff.

buff·er[2] (buf'ər) *n.* 1 Something that lessens or absorbs the shock of an impact. 2 A person or thing that reduces friction, as between antagonists. 3 A substance that tends to prevent change in acidity or alkalinity. —*v.t.* To stabilize (a solution) by adding a buffer. **—buff'ered** *adj.*

buffer state A small country situated between two larger rival powers and regarded as lessening the possibility of open hostilities between them.

buf·fet[1] (bōō·fā', bə·fā', *Brit.* buf'it) *n.* 1 A sideboard for china, glassware, etc. 2 A counter for serving refreshments. 3 An informal meal in which guests serve themselves from a table or buffet. [F]

buf·fet[2] (buf'it) *v.t.* 1 To strike or cuff, as with the hand. 2 To strike again and again; knock about, as if by blows: *buffeted* by high winds. 3 To force (a way) by pushing or striking. —*v.i.* 4 To struggle. 5 To force a way. —*n.* A blow; cuff. [< OF *buffe* blow, slap] **—buf'fet·er** *n.*

buf·foon (bu·fōōn', bə-) *n.* 1 One given to jokes, coarse pranks, etc.; a clown. 2 A loutish or inept person. [< Ital. *buffone* clown] **—buf·foon'er·y** *n.* **—buf·foon'ish** *adj.*

bug (bug) *n.* 1 Any of a large variety of insects with piercing and sucking mouth parts. 2 Loosely, any insect. 3 *Informal* A pathogenic microorganism. 4 *Informal* Any small but troublesome defect in a motor, machine, etc. 5 *Slang* An enthusiast. 6 *Informal* A miniature electronic microphone, used in wiretapping, etc. —*v.* **bugged, bug·ging** *v.i.* 1 To stare; stick out: said of eyes. —*v.t.* 2 *Informal* To fix an electronic eavesdropping device in (a room, etc.) or to (a wire, etc.). 3 *Slang* To annoy or anger; also to bewilder or puzzle. **—bug off** *Slang* Go away! Get lost! **—bug out** *Slang* To quit, esp. hastily or ignominiously. [?]

bug·a·boo (bug'ə·bōō) *n. pl.* **·boos** BUGBEAR. [< ME *bugge* scarecrow + BOO]

bug·bear (bug'bâr') *n.* An imaginary object of terror; a specter. [< ME *bugge* scarecrow + BEAR[2]]

bug·gy[1] (bug'ē) *n. pl.* **·gies** 1 A light, horse-drawn vehicle. 2 A baby carriage. [?]

bug·gy[2] (bug'ē) *adj.* **·gi·er, ·gi·est** 1 Infested with bugs. 2 *Slang* Crazy. **—bug'gi·ness** *n.*

bug·house (bug'hous') *Slang* *n.* An asylum for the insane. —*adj.* Crazy; insane.

bu·gle (byōō'gəl) *n.* A brass, trumpetlike instrument, usu. without keys or valves. —*v.t. & v.i.* **bu·gled, bu·gling** 1 To summon with a bugle. 2 To sound a bugle. [< L *buculus*, dim. of *bos* ox; because first made from the horns of oxen] **—bu'gler** *n.*

buhl (bōōl) *n.* Metal or tortoise shell inlaid in furniture; also, cabinetwork so decorated. Also **buhl'work'**. [< A. C. Boule, 1642–1732, French cabinetmaker]

build (bild) *v.* **built** (*Archaic* **build·ed**), **build·ing** *v.t.* 1 To construct, erect, or make by assembling separate parts or materials. 2 To establish and increase: often with *up*: to *build* up a business. 3 To make a basis for; found: immigrants who *built* a new life. —*v.i.* 4 To construct a house, building, etc. 5 To be in the business of building. 6 To grow in intensity, force, etc.: often with *up*. 7 To base or form an idea, theory, etc.: with *on* or *upon*. **—build up** 1 To renew or strengthen, as health. 2 To fill, as an area, with houses. —*n.* The manner in which a person or thing is shaped or formed; form; figure: a good *build;* a slight or husky *build*. [< OE *byldan*]

build·er (bil'dər) *n.* 1 One who or that which builds. 2 One whose occupation is building.

build·ing (bil'ding) *n.* 1 A structure, usu. having walls and a roof, as a house, a place of work, etc. 2 The occupation, business, or art of constructing.

build·up (bild'up') *n.* 1 A gradual accumulation or increase. 2 *Informal* An enhancement of reputation, as by praise or favorable publicity. Also **build'-up'**.

built-in (bilt'in') *adj.* 1 Part of or permanently attached to the structure: *built-in* bookcases. 2 By the nature of things; inherent: a *built-in* advantage.

bulb (bulb) *n.* 1 An underground plant stem having a cluster of thickened leaves above and sending down roots, as in the onion, lily, etc. 2 An underground stem resembling a bulb, as a corm, tuber, or rhizome. 3 An enlargement resembling a plant bulb, as the end of a thermometer tube. 4 An incandescent electric lamp. [< Gk. *bolbos* bulbous root] **—bul·ba·ceous** (bul·bā'shəs), **bul'bar, bul'bous** *adj.* • See INCANDESCENT.

Bul·gar·i·a (bul·gâr'ē·ə, bŏŏl-) *n.* A republic of SE Europe, 42,796 sq. mi., cap. Sofia. • See map at BALKAN STATES.

Bul·gar·i·an (bul·gâr'ē·ən, bŏŏl-) *adj.* Of or pertaining to Bulgaria, its people, or their language. *—n.* 1 A native or citizen of Bulgaria. 2 The Slavic language of Bulgaria.

bulge (bulj) *v.t. & v.i.* **bulged, bulg·ing** To swell out; make or be protuberant. *—n.* Something that swells out or protrudes. [<OF *boulge*] **—bulg'y** *adj.* **—bulg'i·ness** *n.*

bu·lim·i·a (byŏŏ·lim'ē·ə) *n.* A psychological disorder marked by alternating periods of uncontrolled eating and induced vomiting. [<Gk. *boulimia* great hunger]

bulk (bulk) *n.* 1 Mass, volume, or size, esp. if large or great. 2 A large body, esp. a human body. 3 The largest or principal part. **—in bulk** Loose; not boxed or packaged. *—v.i.* 1 To have an appearance of largeness or weight. 2 To be of importance: to *bulk* large in his thought. *—v.t.* 3 To cause to expand or grow large. [<ON *būlki* heap, cargo]

bulk·head (bulk'hed') *n.* 1 Any of various partitions in a ship, airplane, etc., used as a protection against the spread of water, fire, etc. 2 A partition of stone or wood to keep back earth, gas, etc., as in a mine. 3 A framework opening into a staircase or shaft. **—bulk'head·ed** *adj.*

bulk·y (bul'kē) *adj.* **bulk·i·er, bulk·i·est** 1 Marked by great bulk; massive. 2 Clumsy; ungainly.

bull¹ (bŏŏl) *n.* 1 The male of cattle or of some other animals, as of the elephant, moose, giraffe, whale, seal, etc. 2 A dealer who seeks or expects higher prices, and buys stocks or bonds accordingly. 3 One whose actions or looks suggest a bull. 4 *Slang* A policeman. 5 *Slang* Exaggerated or nonsensical talk. *—v.t.* 1 To attempt to raise the price of or in. 2 To push or force (a way). *—v.i.* 3 To go up in price: said of stocks, etc. *—adj.* 1 Male. 2 Large; bull-like. 3 Going up or advancing: a *bull* market. [OE *bola*]

bull² (bŏŏl) *n.* An official edict or decree issued by the Pope. [<L *bulla* edict, seal]

Bull (bŏŏl) *n.* TAURUS.

bull·dog (bŏŏl'dôg', -dog') *n.* A medium-sized, short-haired, powerful dog, originally bred to bait bulls. *—adj.* Resembling a bulldog; tenacious. *—v.t. Informal* To throw (a steer) by gripping its horns and twisting its neck.

bull·doze (bŏŏl'dōz') *v.t.* **·dozed, ·doz·ing** 1 *Slang* To intimidate; bully. 2 To clear, dig, scrape, etc., with a bulldozer. 3 *Slang* To force in a coarse, pushing manner. [?< BULL, *adj.* + DOSE]

bull·doz·er (bŏŏl'dō'zər) *n.* 1 A powerful tractor with a heavy plowing blade, used for moving soil, cleaning debris, etc. 2 *Slang* One who bulldozes.

bul·let (bŏŏl'it) *n.* 1 A small projectile for a firearm. 2 Any small ball. [<F *boule* ball]

bul·le·tin (bŏŏl'ə·tən) *n.* 1 A brief news item, usu. of special or immediate interest. 2 A periodical publication, as of the proceedings of a society. *—v.t.* To make public by bulletin. [<L *bulla* edict] **—bul'le·tin·ist** *n.*

bul·let·proof (bŏŏl'it·prŏŏf') *adj.* Not penetrable by bullets: a *bulletproof* vest.

bull·fight (bŏŏl'fīt') *n.* A spectacle held in an arena and marked by combat between men and a bull, which is goaded and usu. killed, traditional in Hispanic countries. **—bull'fight'ing, bull'fight'er** *n.*

bull·finch (bŏŏl'finch') *n.* A European songbird having a short, stout bill and red breast. [<BULL, *adj.* + FINCH]

bull·frog (bŏŏl'frog', -frôg') *n.* A large frog with a deep hoarse voice.

bull·head (bŏŏl'hed') *n.* 1 Any of various catfishes, as the horned pout. 2 An obstinate person.

bull·head·ed (bŏŏl'hed'id) *adj.* Obstinate; stubborn.

bull·horn (bŏŏl'hôrn') *n.* An electrical, hand-held voice amplifier resembling a megaphone.

bul·lion (bŏŏl'yən) *n.* Gold or silver uncoined or in mass, as in ingots. [<AF *bullion*]

bull·ish (bŏŏl'ish) *adj.* 1 Like a bull, as in size. 2 Characterized by or suggesting a trend toward higher prices, as in the stock market; also, hopeful of such a trend. 3 Confidently optimistic. **—bull'ish·ly** *adv.* **—bull'ish·ness** *n.*

bul·lock (bŏŏl'ək) *n.* A gelded bull; a steer or an ox. [<OE *bulluc*]

bull·pen (bŏŏl'pen') *n.* 1 An enclosure for bulls. 2 *Informal* A large room for temporary detention of prisoners. 3 In baseball, an area near the playing field where pitchers who may be called upon to enter a game can practice.

bull·ring (bŏŏl'ring') *n.* A circular enclosure for bullfights.

bull session *Informal* An informal discussion.

bull's-eye (bŏŏlz'ī') *n.* 1 The center of a target, or a shot that hits it. 2 Anything that exactly achieves a specific goal or result. 3 A thick, circular, glass window.

bull terrier A short-haired white terrier crossbred from bulldog, terrier, and pointer breeds.

bull·whip (bŏŏl'ʰwip') *n.* A long, tough whip used by teamsters.

bul·ly¹ (bŏŏl'ē) *n. pl.* **bul·lies** A person who likes to hurt or intimidate those weaker than himself. *—adj.* **bul·li·er, bul·li·est** 1 *Informal* Excellent, admirable, 2 Jolly; dashing; gallant. *—interj.* Well done! *—v.* **bul·lied, bul·ly·ing** *v.t.* 1 To coerce by threats; intimidate. *—v.i.* 2 To be quarrelsome and blustering. [?]

bul·ly² (bŏŏl'ē) *n.* Canned or pickled beef. Also **bul'ly·beef'** (-bēf'). [?<F *bouillir* boil]

bul·rush (bŏŏl'rush') *n.* 1 Any of various tall marsh plants having brown spikes of tiny flowers, as the cattail and certain sedges. 2 Papyrus. *Exodus* 2:3. [<BULL¹, *adj.* + RUSH]

bul·wark (bŏŏl'wərk) *n.* 1 A defensive wall or rampart. 2 A person or thing considered as a strong support or defense. 3 *Usu. pl.* The raised side of a ship, above the upper deck. *—v.t.* To fortify with, or as with, a bulwark. [<MHG *bolwerc*]

bum (bum) *n. Informal* 1 A shiftless, often drunken loafer or beggar. 2 A hobo; tramp. 3 An irresponsible devotee: a ski *bum*. *—adj.* **bum·mer, bum·mest** *Slang* 1 Bad; inferior. 2 Ailing. *—v.* **bum·med, bum·ming** *Informal v.i.* 1 To live by sponging from others. 2 To loaf. *—v.t.* 3 To get by begging. [Short for *bummer*, alter. of G *bummler* loafer, dawdler] **—bum'mer** *n.*

bum·ble·bee (bum'bəl·bē') *n.* Any of certain large, hairy, social bees.

bum·bling (bum'bling) *adj.* Awkward and inept. [<BUNGLE]

Bumblebee

bump (bump) *v.t.* 1 To come into contact with; knock into. 2 To cause to knock into or against. 3 *Informal* To displace, as from a position or seat. *—v.i.* 4 To come into contact; collide. 5 To move with jerks and jolts. 6 *Slang* To do a bump (def. 3). *—n.* 1 An impact or collision; a jolt. 2 A swelling, protuberance, or rough part. 3 *Slang* A sharp forward movement of the pelvis, as in a striptease. [Imit.]

bump·er¹ (bum'pər) *n.* A guard on the front or rear of an automobile to absorb the shock of collision.

bump·er² (bum'pər) *n.* A cup or glass filled to the brim. *—adj.* Unusually full or large: a *bumper* crop. [?]

bump·kin (bump'kin) *n.* An awkward, unsophisticated person from the country. [?<Du. *boomkin* little tree, block]

bump·tious (bump'shəs) *adj.* Aggressively and offensively conceited.[?] **—bump'tious·ly** *adj.* **—bump'tious·ness** *n.*

bump·y (bum'pē) *adj.* **bump·i·er, bump·i·est** 1 Having bumps. 2 Producing jolts or bounces: a *bumpy* ride. — **bump'i·ly** *adv.* **—bump'i·ness** *n.*

bun (bun) *n.* 1 A small bread roll, usu. sweetened or spiced. 2 A roll of hair worn at the nape of the neck. [ME *bunne*]

bunch (bunch) *n.* 1 A group of usu. like objects growing or fastened together. 2 *Informal* A group or cluster, as of people. *—v.t. & v.i.* 1 To make into or form bunches or groups. 2 To gather, as in pleats or folds. [ME *bonche, bunche*]

bun·co (bung'kō) *n. pl.* **·cos** *Informal* A swindling game in which confederates join to rob a stranger. *—v.t.* **·coed, ·co·ing** To swindle or bilk. [Prob.<Sp. *banco*, a card game]

bun·combe (bung'kəm) *n.* Empty, bombastic talk or speechmaking; humbug. [<*Buncombe* County, N.C., whose Congressman (1819–21) often insisted on making empty, unimportant speeches "for Buncombe"]

bun·dle (bun'dəl) n. 1 A number of things or a quantity of anything bound together. 2 A parcel or package. 3 A group; collection. 4 *Slang* A large sum of money. —v. ·dled, ·dling v.t. 1 To tie, roll, or otherwise secure in a bundle. 2 To send away in haste: with *away, off, out,* or *into.* —v.i. 3 To leave or move hastily. 4 To practice bundling. — **bundle up** To dress warmly for outdoors. [< MDu. *bond* group] —**bun'dler** n.

bun·dling (bun'dling) n. An old courting custom, prevalent in New England, in which sweethearts lay or slept together in bed without undressing.

bung (bung) n. 1 A stopper for the hole in a keg, barrel, etc. 2 BUNGHOLE. —v.t. 1 To close with or as with a bung. 2 *Slang* To damage; maul: with *up.* [< MDu. *bonghe*]

bun·ga·low (bung'gə·lō) n. 1 In India, a one-storied house with wide verandas. 2 A small house or cottage. [< Hind. *banglā* Bengalese]

bung·hole (bung'hōl') n. A hole in a keg or barrel from which liquid is tapped.

bun·gle (bung'gəl) v.t. & v.i. ·gled, ·gling To do (something) badly; botch. —n. An imperfect job or performance; botch. —**bun'gler** n. [? < Scand.]

bun·ion (bun'yən) n. A painful swelling of the bursa at the base of the great toe. [? < OF *bugne* swelling]

bunk[1] (bungk) n. 1 A small compartment, shelf, or recess, used as a sleeping place. 2 *Informal* Any bed, esp. a small one. —v.i. 1 To sleep in a bunk or bed. 2 *Informal* To sleep overnight, esp. in makeshift accommodations. —v.t. 3 To provide with a bunk or place to sleep. [?]

bunk[2] (bungk) n. *Slang* Inflated or empty speech; balderdash. [Short for BUNCOMBE]

bun·ker (bung'kər) n. 1 A large bin or tank, as for fuel on a ship. 2 In golf, a sandy hollow or a mound of earth serving as an obstacle. 3 A steel and concrete fortification, usu. underground. —v.i. 1 To fill the bunkers of a ship. — v.t. 2 In golf, to drive (a ball) into a bunker. [?]

bunk·house (bungk'hous') n. A structure used as sleeping quarters.

bun·ko (bung'kō) n. pl. ·kos BUNCO.

bun·kum (bung'kəm) n. BUNCOMBE.

bun·ny (bun'ē) n. pl. ·nies A rabbit. [?]

Bun·sen burner (bun'sən) An adjustable gas burner used in laboratories to produce a small, hot flame. [< R. W. E. *Bunsen,* 1811–99, German inventor]

bunt (bunt) v.t. & v.i. 1 To butt, as with horns. 2 In baseball, to bat (the ball) lightly to the infield, without swinging the bat. —n. 1 A push or butt. 2 In baseball: a The act of bunting. b A bunted ball. [? < Celtic]

bunt·ing[1] (bun'ting) n. 1 A light fabric used for flags. 2 Flags. 3 Lengths of fabric decorated as a flag. 4 A hooded, outer garment for a baby. [?]

bunt·ing[2] (bun'ting) n. Any of various brightly colored, small birds related to the finches. [ME *bountyng*]

Bunsen burner
a. flame.
b. air. c. gas.

buoy (boi, boo'ē) n. 1 A float moored near a dangerous rock or shoal or at the edge of a channel, as a guide to navigators. 2 LIFE BUOY. —v.t. 1 To keep from sinking in a liquid; keep afloat. 2 To sustain the courage or heart of; encourage: usu. with *up.* 3 To mark, as a channel, with buoys. [< MDu. *boeie*]

buoy·an·cy (boi'ən·sē, boo'yən·sē) n. 1 The property of being able to float in liquid or air. 2 The power of a liquid or gas to keep an object afloat. 3 Cheerfulness; liveliness. Also **buoy'ance.**

buoy·ant (boi'ənt, boo'yənt) adj. 1 Having buoyancy. 2 Vivacious; cheerful; hopeful. [Prob. < Sp. *boyar* float] — **buoy'ant·ly** adv.

bur[1] (bûr) n. 1 A rough, prickly, clinging seedcase, as of the chestnut or burdock. 2 A plant that bears burs. 3 Something resembling a bur. 4 A dentist's drilling bit. —v.t. **burred, bur·ring** To remove burs from. [< Scand.]

bur[2] (bûr) 1 BURR[1] (defs. 1 and 2). 2 BURR[2].

bur·ble (bûr'bəl) v.i. ·bled, ·bling 1 To bubble; gurgle. 2 To talk excitedly and confusedly. [ME]

bur·bot (bûr'bət) n. pl. ·bots or ·bot A freshwater fish with barbels on the nose and chin. [< L *barbata* bearded]

bur·den[1] (bûr'dən) n. 1 Something carried; a load. 2 Something difficult to bear, as a worry, responsibility, etc. 3 The carrying of loads: beasts of *burden.* 4 *Naut.* a The carrying capacity of a vessel. b The weight of the cargo. —v.t. 1 To load or overload. 2 To oppress, as with care. [< OE *byrthen* load]

bur·den[2] (bûr'dən) n. 1 The prevailing idea or tone: the *burden* of a speech. 2 A refrain of a song. [< F *bourdon* bass]

burden of proof The obligation to prove something to be true or genuine.

bur·den·some (bûr'dən·səm) adj. Hard or heavy to bear; oppressive. —**bur'den·some·ly** adv. —**bur'den·some·ness** n.

bur·dock (bûr'dok) n. A coarse weed having large leaves and prickly burs. [< BUR[1] + DOCK]

bu·reau (byoor'ō) n. pl. **bu·reaus** or **bu·reaux** (byoor'ōz) 1 A chest of drawers for clothing. 2 A government department or subdivision of a department. 3 Any agency providing specialized information and services: travel *bureau.* [< F, cloth-covered desk]

bu·reauc·ra·cy (byoo·rok'rə·sē) n. pl. ·cies 1 Government by bureaus managed by officials who are appointed rather than elected. 2 Such officials collectively. 3 Excessively rigid and arbitrary governmental regulations and routines.

bu·reau·crat (byoor'ə·krat) n. 1 A member of a bureaucracy. 2 An official who governs by rigid routine. —**bu'reau·crat'ic** or **·i·cal** adj. —**bu'reau·crat'i·cal·ly** adv.

bu·reau·cra·tize (byoo·rok'rə·tīz) v.t. ·tized, ·tiz·ing To make into a bureaucracy. —**bu·reau'cra·ti·za'tion** n.

bu·rette (byoo·ret') n. A graduated glass tube with a stopcock for drawing off precise quantities of liquid. Also **bu·ret'.** [< F *buire* vase]

burg (bûrg) n. *Informal* A town or city, usu. considered somewhat backward. [< OE *burg*]

bur·geon (bûr'jən) v.t. & v.i. 1 To put forth buds; sprout. 2 To grow or develop rapidly. [< OF *burjon* a bud]

bur·gess (bûr'jis) n. 1 A citizen or officer of a borough. 2 In colonial Maryland and Virginia, a member of the lower house of the legislature. [< OF *bourg* town]

burgh (bûrg, *Scot.* bûr'ō, -ə) n. A chartered town or borough in Scotland. [Var. of BOROUGH] —**burgh·al** (bûr'gəl) adj.

burgh·er (bûr'gər) n. An inhabitant of a borough or town. [< Du. *burg* town]

bur·glar (bûr'glər) n. One who commits a burglary. [< Med.L *burglator*]

bur·glar·ize (bûr'glə·rīz) v.t. ·ized, ·iz·ing To commit burglary in or upon.

bur·gla·ry (bûr'glər·ē) n. pl. ·ries The breaking and entering of a building to steal something or commit some other felony.

bur·gle (bûr'gəl) v.t. & v.i. ·gled ·gling *Informal* To burglarize or commit burglary. [Back formation < BURGLAR]

bur·go·mas·ter (bûr'gə·mas'tər, -mäs'-) n. A mayor in the Netherlands, Germany, or Austria. [< Du. *burgemeester*]

Bur·gun·dy (bûr'gən·dē) n. pl. ·dies 1 A red or white wine made in Burgundy. 2 A similar wine made elsewhere.

bur·i·al (ber'ē·əl) n. The burying of a dead body. [< OE *byrgels* tomb]

bu·rin (byoor'in) n. A pointed engraver's tool. [F]

burl (bûrl) n. 1 A knot or lump in yarn or cloth. 2 A large, wartlike excrescence, formed on the trunks of trees. 3 A veneer made from wood having burls. —v.t. To dress (cloth) by removing burls. [< LL *burra* shaggy hair] — **burled** adj. —**burl'er** n.

bur·lap (bûr'lap) n. A coarse fabric of jute or hemp, used for wrapping, bagging, etc. [?]

bur·lesque (bər·lesk') n. 1 Broad, satirical imitation or caricature; parody. 2 A product of such imitation, as a literary work. **3** A theatrical entertainment marked by low comedy, striptease, etc. —*v.* **·lesqued, ·les·quing** *v.t.* **1** To imitate or parody by using burlesque. —*v.i.* **2** To use burlesque. [< Ital. *burla* joke] —**bur·les′quer** *n.*

bur·ley (bûr′lē) *n. Often cap.* A fine, light tobacco grown principally in Kentucky. [? < *Burley,* name of a grower]

bur·ly (bûr′lē) *adj.* **bur·li·er, bur·li·est 1** Large and muscular of body; stout. **2** Rough and lusty in manner. [ME *borlich*] —**bur′li·ly** *adv.* —**bur′li·ness** *n.*

Bur·ma (bûr′mə) *n.* A republic of SE Asia, 261,789 sq. mi., cap. Rangoon. —**Bur·mese** (bər·mēz′, -mēs′) *adj., n.* • See map at INDOCHINA.

burn (bûrn) *v.* **burned** or **burnt, burn·ing** *v.t.* **1** To destroy or consume by fire. **2** To set afire; ignite. **3** To injure or kill by fire. **4** To injure or damage by friction, heat, steam, etc.; scald; wither. **5** To produce by fire, as a hole in a suit. **6** To brand; also, to cauterize. **7** To finish or harden by intense heat; fire. **8** To use or employ so as to give off light, heat, etc. **9** To cause a feeling of heat in. **10** To sunburn. **11** To transform into energy, as fat in body tissues. **12** *Slang* To electrocute. **13** *Slang* To cheat. —*v.i.* **14** To be on fire; blaze. **15** To be destroyed, damaged, or changed by fire. **16** To give off light, heat, etc.; shine. **17** To die by fire. **18** To appear or feel hot. **19** To be eager, excited, or inflamed. **20** To oxidize; undergo combustion. **21** *Slang* To be electrocuted. —**burn out 1** To become extinguished through lack of fuel. **2** To destroy or wear out by heat, friction, etc. —**burn up 1** To consume by fire. **2** *Slang* To make or become irritated or enraged. —*n.* **1** An effect or injury from burning; a burnt place. **2** The process or result of burning. **3** *Aerospace* A single firing of a space rocket. [Fusion of OE *beornan* be on fire and OE *bærnan* set afire]

burn·er (bûr′nər) *n.* **1** One who or that which burns. **2** The light-giving or heat-giving part of a lamp, stove, etc.

burn·ing (bûr′ning) *adj.* **1** Consuming or being consumed by fire. **2** Extremely important or controversial.

bur·nish (bûr′nish) *v.t. & v.i.* To polish by friction; make or become brilliant or shiny. —*n.* Polish; luster. [< OF *burnir* polish] —**bur′nish·er, bur′nish·ment** *n.*

bur·noose (bər·nōōs′, bûr′nōōs) *n.* A cloak with hood, worn by Arabs and Moors. Also **bur·nous′.** [< Ar. *burnus*]

burn·sides (bûrn′sīdz) *n. pl.* Side whiskers and mustache worn with closely shaven chin. [< Ambrose E. *Burnside,* 1824–81, U.S. major general]

burnt (bûrnt) A *p.t. & p.p.* of BURN.

burp (bûrp) *n. Informal* BELCH. —*v.i.* **1** *Informal* BELCH. —*v.t.* **2** To cause (a baby) to belch, esp. after a meal, by rubbing or patting the back. [Imit.]

burr¹ (bûr) **1** A roughness or rough edge, esp. one left on metal in casting or cutting. **2** A rotary cutting tool. **3** BUR¹. —*v.t.* **1** To form a rough edge on. **2** To remove a rough edge from. [Var. of BUR¹]

burr² (bûr) *n.* **1** A rough guttural sound of *r* caused by the vibration of the uvula, as in the dialectal pronunciation of Scotland. **2** A whirring sound; a buzz. —*v.t.* **1** To pronounce with a burr. —*v.i.* **2** To speak with a burr. **3** To whir. [Imit.]

bur·ro (bûr′ō, bŏŏr′ō) *n. pl.* **·ros** A small donkey, used as a pack animal. [Sp.]

bur·row (bûr′ō) *n.* A hole or tunnel made in the ground, as by an animal, for shelter, etc. —*v.t.* **1** To make by burrowing. **2** To perforate with burrows. —*v.i.* **3** To live or hide in or as in a burrow. **4** To make a burrow. [ME *borow*] —**bur′row·er** *n.*

bur·sa (bûr′sə) *n. pl.* **·sas** or **·sae** (-sē) A closed sac within the body, esp. one containing a viscid fluid and located at a joint. [< Med. L, sack, pouch] —**bur′sal** *adj.*

bur·sar (bûr′sər, -sär) *n.* A treasurer, as of a college. [< Med. L *bursarius* treasurer] —**bur·sar·i·al** (bər-sâr′ē-əl) *adj.*

bur·sa·ry (bûr′sər·ē) *n. pl.* **·ries 1** The treasury, as of a public institution. **2** A grant; scholarship.

bur·si·tis (bər·sī′tis) *n.* Inflammation of a bursa.

burst (bûrst) *v.* **burst, burst·ing** *v.i.* **1** To break open or come apart suddenly and violently; explode, as from internal force. **2** To be full of something to the breaking point. **3** To issue forth or enter suddenly or violently. **4** To appear or begin; become audible or evident, etc. **5** To give sudden expression to passion, grief, etc. —*v.t.* **6** To cause to break open suddenly or violently; puncture. **7** To fill or cause to

swell to the point of breaking open. —*n.* **1** The act or result of bursting. **2** A sudden eruption, as of feeling. **3** A sudden effort; spurt. **4** A series of shots fired. [< OE *berstan*] —**burst′er** *n.* —**Syn.** *v.* **1, 6** rupture, shatter, tear, rip, rend.

Bu·run·di (bŏŏ·rōōn′dē) *n.* A republic in CEN. Africa, 10,-747 sq. mi., cap. Usumbura. • See map at AFRICA.

bury (ber′ē) *v.t.* **bur·ied, bur·y·ing 1** To put (a dead body) in a grave, etc.; inter. **2** To conceal in the ground. **3** To cover, as for concealment. **4** To sink or embed. **5** To end; put out of mind: to *bury* a quarrel. **6** To occupy deeply; engross: He *buried* himself in study. [< OE *byrgan*]

burying ground A cemetery.

bus (bus) *n. pl.* **bus·es** or **bus·ses 1** A large motor vehicle that carries passengers; an omnibus. **2** *Informal* An automobile. —*v.* **bused** or **bussed, bus·ing** or **bus·sing** *v.t.* **1** To transport by bus. —*v.i.* **2** To go by bus. **3** *Informal* To do the work of a bus boy. [Short form of OMNIBUS]

bus boy A waiter's helper who sets and clears tables, fills water glasses, etc.

bus·by (buz′bē) *n. pl.* **·bies** A tall fur cap worn as part of the full-dress uniform of British hussars, artillerymen, and engineers. [?]

bush¹ (bŏŏsh) *n.* **1** A low, thickly branching shrub. **2** A thick growth of shrubs. **3** Land that is unsettled, remote, often arid, and covered with a scrubby undergrowth, esp. such land in Australia: with *the*. **4** A bushy tail. —*v.i.* **1** To grow or branch like a bush. —*v.t.* **2** To protect or support with bushes. —*adj. Slang* Bush-league; small-time. [ME *bussche*]

bush² (bŏŏsh) *v.t.* To line with a bushing, as an axle bearing, a pivot hole, etc. —*n.* BUSHING. [< MDu. *busse* box]

Busby

bushed (bŏŏsht) *adj. Informal* **1** Exhausted; worn out. **2** *Austral.* Lost; confused.

bush·el (bŏŏsh′əl) *n.* **1** A measure of capacity; four pecks, 35.238 liters, or 2150.42 cubic inches. **2** A vessel holding that amount. **3** *Informal* A large amount. [< OF *boissel*]

bu·shi·do (bŏŏ′shē·dō) *n. Often cap.* The code of conduct for the medieval Japanese samurai.

bush·ing (bŏŏsh′ing) *n.* **1** A protective lining for a hole, as in the hub of a wheel. **2** A tube for insertion into another to reduce the diameter.

bush league *Slang* **1** In baseball, a minor league. **2** Anything minor or second-rate. —**bush′-league′** *adj.* —**bush′-lea′guer** *n.*

bush·man (bŏŏsh′mən) *n. pl.* **·men** (-mən) *Austral.* A dweller or farmer in the bush.

Bush·man (bŏŏsh′mən) *n. pl.* **·men** (-mən) **1** One of a nomadic people of South Africa, related to the Pygmies. **2** The language of the Bushmen, characterized by clicks.

bush·mas·ter (bŏŏsh′mas′tər, -mäs′-) *n.* A large, poisonous viper of Central and South America.

bush·rang·er (bŏŏsh′rān′jər) *n.* **1** One who lives in the bush. **2** *Austral.* A robber.

bush·whack (bŏŏsh′ʰwak′) *v.i.* **1** To cut one's way through bushes or underbrush. **2** To ride or range in the bush. **3** To fight from ambush, as a guerrilla. —*v.t.* **4** To ambush. [< Du. *boschwachter* forest-keeper; infl. by WHACK] —**bush′whack′er, bush′whack′ing** *n.*

bush·y (bŏŏsh′ē) *adj.* **bush·i·er, bush·i·est 1** Covered with or full of bushes. **2** Thick and shaggy. —**bush′i·ly** *adv.* —**bush′i·ness** *n.*

bus·ied (biz′ēd) *p.t. & p.p.* of BUSY.

bus·i·ly (biz′ə·lē) *adv.* In a busy manner.

busi·ness (biz′nis, -niz) *n.* **1** One's occupation, trade, or profession. **2** A function or province. **3** Legitimate interest or concern. **4** An activity, matter, or affair. **5** Commercial affairs in general. **6** A commercial enterprise or establishment, as a store. **7** Amount of commercial trade or patronage. **8** Commercial policy or practices. **9** The actions on a stage, in a movie, etc., other than dialogue. —*adj.* Of or for business. [< OE *bysignis* < *bysig* active] —**Syn. 1** employment, work, calling, vocation, career. **5** commerce, industry. **7** volume, traffic.

busi·ness·like (biz′nis·līk′, -niz-) *adj.* Methodical and efficient, as in matters of business.

busi·ness·man (biz′nis·man′, -niz-) *n. pl.* **·men** (-men′)

One engaged in commerical business. —**busi′ness·wom′an** *n. Fem. (pl. ·wom′en)*

bus·ing (bus′ing) *n.* The transporting of pupils in school-buses from one school district to another to approximate racial balance in schools.

bus·kin (bus′kin) *n.* **1** A high shoe or half boot reaching halfway to the knee, esp. one worn in ancient times by actors in Greek or Roman tragedies. **2** Tragedy.[?]

buss (bus) *Informal n.* A kiss; smack. —*v.t. & v.i.* To kiss heartily. [Imit.]

buss·es (bus′iz) A plural of BUS.

bust¹ (bust) *n.* **1** The human chest or breast. **2** A statue of the human head, shoulders, and breast. [<Ital. *busto* trunk of the body]

bust² (bust) *Slang v.t.* **1** To burst. **2** To tame; train, as a horse. **3** To make bankrupt or short of funds. **4** To reduce in rank; demote. **5** To arrest. **6** To hit; strike. —*v.i.* **7** To burst. **8** To become bankrupt or short of funds. —*n.* **1** Failure; bankruptcy. **2** A spree. **3** An arrest. [Alter. of BURST]

bus·tard (bus′tərd) *n.* Any of a family of large Old World game birds related to the plovers and cranes. [<OF *bistarde, oustarde*<L *avis tarda*, lit., slow bird]

bus·tle¹ (bus′əl) *n.* Excited activity; noisy stir; fuss. —*v.t. & v.i.* ·tled, ·tling To hurry noisily; make a stir or fuss.[?]

bus·tle² (bus′əl) *n.* A frame or pad formerly worn by women on the back below the waist to distend the skirts.[?]

bus·y (biz′ē) *adj.* bus·i·er, bus·i·est **1** Intensely active; constantly occupied. **2** Temporarily engaged; not at leisure. **3** Prying; meddling. **4** In use, as a telephone. **5** Full of varied designs, colors, etc., usu. excessively so. —*v.t.* **bus·ied, bus·y·ing** To make or be busy. [<OE *bysig* active]

bus·y·bod·y (biz′ē·bod′ē) *n. pl.* ·bodies One who intrudes upon others′ privacy or interferes with their affairs.

but (but, *unstressed* bət) *conj.* **1** However; yet: He seemed honest, *but* he was lying. **2** Unless; if not: It never rains *but* it pours. **3** Excepting: Nothing would satisfy him *but* I come along. **4** Other than; otherwise than: I cannot choose *but* hear. **5** On the other hand: You are right, *but* he′s also right. **6** That: We don′t doubt *but* matters will improve. **7** That . . . not: He is not so strong *but* a little exercise will do him good. —*prep.* Except for; save: owning nothing *but* his clothes. —*adv.* **1** Only; just: If I had *but* thought. **2** Merely: She is *but* a child. —**all but** Almost: He is *all but* well. —**but for** Were it not for: *But for* me, how would you have succeeded? —*n.* An objection; exception; condition: without any ifs or *buts* [<OE *būten*]

bu·ta·di·ene (byōō′tə·dī′ēn, -dī·ēn′) *n.* A hydrocarbon obtained from petroleum and used to manufacture synthetic rubber. [<BUTA(NE) + DI- + -ENE]

bu·tane (byōō′tān, byōō·tān′) *n.* A flammable, gaseous hydrocarbon. [<L *butyrum* butter]

butch (bōoch) *adj. Slang* Masculine, as in appearance or manner: said of one who adopts a masculine role, esp. a female homosexual. —*n.* **1** A closely cropped haircut for boys or men. **2** *Slang* A butch woman, esp. a lesbian. [Prob.<*Butch*, a boy′s nickname]

butch·er (bōoch′ər) *n.* **1** One who slaughters animals or deals in meats for food. **2** A bloody or cruel murderer. **3** A vendor of candy, cigarettes, etc., on trains, in theaters, etc. —*v.t.* **1** To slaughter or dress (animals) for market. **2** To kill (people or game) barbarously or brutally. **3** *Slang* To botch. [<OF *bouchier*<*boc* buck, he-goat]

butch·er·bird (bōoch′ər·bûrd′) *n.* Any of various shrikes.

butch·er·broom (bōoch′ər·brōom′, -brōōm′) *n.* A low, evergreen shrub with leathery stems bearing scarlet berries: also **butch′er′s-broom′**.

butch·er·y (bōoch′ər·ē) *n. pl.* ·er·ies **1** Wanton slaughter. **2** A slaughterhouse. **3** The trade of a butcher.

but·ler (but′lər) *n.* The chief male servant in a household, usu. in charge of the dining room, wine, plate, etc. [<OF *bouteillier* bottle-bearer<Med. L] —**but′ler·ship** *n.*

butler′s pantry A serving room between the kitchen and the dining room.

butt¹ (but) *v.t.* **1** To strike with or as with the head or horns; ram. **2** To touch or bump against. **3** To cause to abut. **4** To abut on. **5** To make a butting motion. **6** To

project; jut out. **7** To abut. —*n.* **1** A stroke, thrust, or push with or as with the head. **2** A thrust in fencing. [<OF *abouter* strike]

butt² (but) *n.* **1** A target, as for a rifle range. **2** *Often pl.* The range itself. **3** The retaining wall placed behind a target to stop the bullets. **4** A target for ridicule or criticism. [< OF *but* end, goal]

butt³ (but) *n.* **1** The larger or thicker end of anything, as of a rifle stock. **2** The remaining end or edge of something, esp. the unused end of a cigar or cigarette. **3** *Slang* The buttocks. [ME *butte*]

butt⁴ (but) *n.* **1** A large cask. **2** A measure of wine, 126 U.S. gallons. [<OF *boute*]

butte (byōōt) *n.* An isolated hill, esp. one with steep sides and a flattened top. [<F]

but·ter (but′ər) *n.* **1** The fatty constituent of milk, separated by churning into a soft, whitish yellow solid, processed for cooking and table use. **2** A substance like butter. —*v.t.* **1** To put butter on. **2** *Informal* To flatter: usu. with *up*. [<OE *butere*, ult.<Gk. *boutyron* lit. cow cheese]

butter bean Wax bean.

but·ter·cup (but′ər·kup′) *n.* **1** A species of crowfoot with yellow, cup-shaped flowers. **2** The flower.

but·ter·fat (but′ər·fat′) *n.* The fat component of milk of which butter is made.

but·ter·fin·gers (but′ər·fing′gərz) *n. pl. (construed as sing.)* One who drops things easily. —**but′ter·fin′gered** *adj.*

but·ter·fish (but′ər·fish′) *n. pl.* ·fish or ·fish·es One of various marine food fishes of the North Atlantic.

but·ter·fly (but′ər·flī′) *n. pl.* ·flies **1** A diurnal lepidopterous insect with large, often brightly colored wings, knobbed antennae, and slender body. **2** One who lives frivolously. [<OE *buttor flēoge*]

butter knife A small, blunt-edged knife for cutting or spreading butter.

but·ter·milk (but′ər·milk′) *n.* The sour liquid left after the butterfat has been separated from milk or cream.

but·ter·nut (but′ər·nut′) *n.* **1** The oily, edible nut of the North American white walnut. **2** The tree, or its inner bark.

but·ter·scotch (but′ər·skoch′) *n.* **1** Hard, sticky candy made with brown sugar, butter, and flavoring. **2** A syrup having a butterscotch flavor. —*adj.* Made of or flavored with butterscotch.

but·ter·y¹ (but′ər·ē) *adj.* Containing, like, flavored, or smeared with butter.

but·ter·y² (but′ər·ē, but′rē) *n. pl.* ·ter·ies A pantry or a wine cellar. [<LL *botaria*<*butta* bottle]

but·tock (but′ək) *n.* **1** Either of the two fleshy prominences that form the rump, on which a person sits. **2** *pl.* The rump. [?<OE *buttuc* end]

but·ton (but′n) *n.* **1** A knob or disk, as of bone, metal, leather, etc., used as an ornament or fastening. **2** Anything like a button. **3** A knob or protuberance, as for operating an electric switch, etc. **4** *Slang* The point of the jaw. —*v.t.* **1** To fasten with or as with a button or buttons. **2** To provide with buttons. —*v.i.* **3** To admit of being buttoned. [<OF *boton* button, bud] —**but′ton·er** *n.*

but·ton·hole (but′n·hōl′) *n.* A slit to receive and hold a button. —*v.t.* ·holed, ·hol·ing **1** To work buttonholes in. **2** To detain by conversation. —**but′ton·hol′er** *n.*

but·ton·wood (but′n·wŏŏd′) *n.* The sycamore or plane tree of the U.S.; also, its wood. Also **but′ton·ball′**.

but·tress (but′ris) *n.* **1** A structure built against a wall to strengthen it. **2** Any support or prop. **3** Any formation suggesting a buttress. —*v.t.* **1** To support with a buttress. **2** To prop up; sustain. [<OF *bouter* push, thrust] • See FLYING BUTTRESS.

bu·tyr·ic (byōō·tir′ik) *adj.* Of, pertaining to, or derived from butter or butyric acid. [<L *butyrum* butter]

butyric acid Either of two isomeric acids, esp. one found as an ester in butter and certain oils, and free in rancid butter, perspiration, etc.

bux·om (buk′səm) *adj.* **1** Attractively plump and well-proportioned: said of women. **2** Having a large bosom. [< OE *būhsum* pliant] —**bux′om·ly** *adv.* —**bux′om·ness** *n.*

---

add, āce, câre, pälm; end, ēven; it, īce; odd, ōpen, ôrder; tŏŏk, pōōl; up, bûrn; ə = *a* in *above, u* in *focus;* yōō = *u* in *fuse;* oil; pout; check; go; ring; thin; this; zh, *vision.* < derived from; ? origin uncertain or unknown.

buy (bī) *v.* **bought, buy·ing** *v.t.* **2** To obtain for a price; purchase. **2** To be a price for. **3** To obtain by an exchange or sacrifice: to *buy* wisdom with experience. **4** To bribe; corrupt. **5** *Slang* To accept as true, possible, etc. —*v.i.* **6** To make purchases; be a purchaser. —**buy off** To bribe. —**buy out** To purchase the stock, interests, etc., of, as in a business. —*n.* *Informal* **1** A purchase. **2** A bargain. [<OE *bycgan*] —**buy′a·ble** *adj.* —**buy′er** *n.*

buy out (bī′out′) *n.* The purchase of a business or stock shares in it by its management or its employees.

buzz (buz) *v.i.* **1** To make a vibrating hum, as a bee. **2** To discuss or gossip excitedly. **3** To bustle about. —*v.t.* **4** To utter or gossip about in a buzzing manner. **5** To cause to buzz, as wings. **6** To fly an airplane low over. **7** To summon with a buzzer. **8** *Informal* To telephone. —*n.* **1** A low vibrating hum, as of bees, of talk, or of distant sounds. **2** Rumor; gossip. **3** Activity; bustle. **4** The sound of a buzzer. **5** *Informal* A telephone call. [Imit.]

buzzard (buz′ərd) *n.* **1** One of several large, slow-flying hawks. **2** TURKEY BUZZARD. [<OF *busart* <L *buteo* hawk]

buzz bomb A self-propelled, guided missile used by the Germans in World War II.

buzz·er (buz′ər) *n.* An electric signal making a buzzing sound.

buzz saw A motor-driven, circular saw.

by (bī) *prep.* **1** Next to; near: the house *by* the road. **2** Toward: west *by* north. **3** Past or beyond: The train flashed *by* us. **4** In the course of; during: birds flying *by* night. **5** Not later than: Be here *by* four tomorrow. **6** For the period of; according to: They work *by* the day. **7** As a result of the effort, means, or action of: a play written *by* Shakespeare. **8** With the perception of: a loss felt *by* all. **9** By means of: leading a child *by* the hand. **10** In consequence of: a case won *by* default. **11** As a means of conveyance; via: Mail your letters *by* air. **12** To the extent or amount of: insects *by* the thousands. **13** On the basis of: four miles long *by* actual measurement. **14** Considered according to: advancing step *by* step; reading word *by* word. **15** With reference to: to do well *by* one's friends. **16** And; and in another dimension: used in numerical measurements and processes: to divide 9 *by* 3; a room ten *by* twelve. **17** In the name of: swearing *by* all that is sacred. —*adv.* **1** At hand; near: to keep one's sword *by*. **2** Up to and beyond something; past: the train roared *by*. **4** Apart; aside: to lay something *by*. **4** At or into a person's house, store, etc.: to stop *by*. —*adj. & n.* BYE. [<OE *bī* near, about]

by- *combining form* **1** Secondary; inferior; incidental: *by-product.* **2** Near; close: *bystander.* **3** Aside; out of the way: *byway.*

bye (bī) *n.* **1** Something of minor or secondary importance. **2** The position of a person who is assigned no opponent and automatically advances to the next round, as in the preliminary pairings of a tennis tournament. —*adj.* Not principal or main; secondary. [Var. of BY]

bye-bye (bī′bī′) *interj.* Good-bye.

by-e·lec·tion (bī′i·lek′shən) *n. Brit.* A parliamentary election between general elections, held to fill a vacancy.

Bye·lo·rus·sian (byel′ō·rush′ən) *adj.* Of or pertaining to the Byelorussian SSR, its people, or their language.

—*n.* **1** A native or citizen of the Byelorussian SSR. **2** The Slavic language of the Byelorussian SSR. Also **Be·lo·rus·sian** (bel′ō·rush′ən).

by·gone (bī′gôn′, -gon′) *adj.* Gone by; former. —*n. Usu. pl.* Something past; that which has gone by.

by·law (bī′lô) *n.* A rule or law adopted by an association, a corporation, etc., which is subordinate to a constitution or charter. [ME *by, bi* village + *lawe* law]

by-line (bī′līn′) *n.* The line at the head of a newspaper article, giving the name of the writer.

by-pass (bī′pas′, -päs′) *n.* Any road, channel, duct, or route that is auxiliary to the one normally used; a detour. —*v.t.* **1** To go around (an obstacle). **2** To provide with a bypass. **3** To pay no attention to.

by-path (bī′path′, -päth′) *n.* A side, secluded, or secondary path.

by-play (bī′plā′) *n.* Any action that is secondary or incidental to the main action, as in a play.

by-prod·uct (bī′prod′əkt) *n.* **1** Any material or product produced in the making of something else. **2** A secondary result or effect.

by-road (bī′rōd′) *n.* A secondary road.

by-stand·er (bī′stan′dər) *n.* One who stands by; an onlooker.

by-street (bī′strēt′) *n.* A side street; a byway.

byte (bīt) *n.* A group of eight bits in a computer memory that form a character symbol, or keyboard function. [<B(INAR)Y (DIGI)T E(IGHT)]

by·way (bī′wā′) *n.* A side road.

by·word (bī′wûrd′) *n.* **1** A proverb, common saying, etc. **2** Something that has become an object of derision. [<OE *biword* proverb]

Byz·an·tine (biz′ən·tēn, -tīn, bi·zan′tin) *adj.* **1** Of or per-

Byzantine architecture

taining to Byzantium. **2** Of or designating a style of architecture developed in the Byzantine Empire, characterized by round arches, domes, and colorful mosaics. —*n.* A native or inhabitant of Byzantium. [<L *Byzantinus* <*Byzantium*]

Byzantine Empire The eastern part of the later Roman Empire (395–1453).

By·zan·ti·um (bi·zan′shē·əm, -tē·əm) *n.* **1** An ancient city on the site of what is now Istanbul. **2** BYZANTINE EMPIRE.

C

C, c. (sē) *n. pl.* **C's, c's, Cs, cs** (sēz) **1** The third letter of the English alphabet. **2** Any spoken sound representing the letter *C* or *c*. **3** In Roman notation, the symbol for 100. **4** *Music* The first tone in the diatonic scale of C major. **5** Something shaped like a C. **6** A grade of average in quality. **7** *Slang* One hundred dollars. —*adj.* Shaped like a C.

C Carbon.

C, C., c, c. Celsius or centigrade; centimeter.

C. Catholic; Chancellor; Congress; Conservative; Church; Court.

C., c. capacity; carton; cent; century; chapter; church; circa; copyright.

CA California (P.O. abbr.).

Ca calcium.

ca. circa; cathode.

cab (kab) *n.* **1** TAXICAB. **2** A one-horse public carriage. **3** The part of a locomotive, truck, crane, etc., where the controls are operated. [Short form of CABRIOLET]

CAB Civil Aeronautics Board.

ca·bal (kə·bal′) *n.* **1** A number of persons secretly united, as in a plot or conspiracy. **2** Intrigue; conspiracy. —*v.i.* **ca·balled, ca·bal·ling** To form a cabal; plot. [<Med. L *cabbala* cabala]

cab·a·la (kab′ə·lə, kə·bä′lə) *n.* **1** The mystic theosophy of the Hebrews. **2** Any secret, occult, or mystic system. [<Heb. *qabbālāh* tradition] —**ca·bal′ic, cab′a·lis′tic** *adj.* —**cab·a·lism** (kab′ə·liz′əm), **cab′a·list** *n.*

cab·al·le·ro (kab′əl·yâr′ō) *n. pl.* **·ros** A Spanish gentleman; cavalier; knight.

ca·ba·na (kə·bä′nə, -ban′ə) *n.* **1** A small cabin. **2** A small bathhouse, as on a beach. Also **ca·ba′ña** (-bän′yə, -ban′yə). [< Sp.]

cab·a·ret (kab′ə·rā′) *n.* **1** A restaurant or café with singing, dancing, etc., as entertainment. **2** Entertainment of this type.

cab·bage (kab′ij) *n.* **1** A plant having a rounded, dense head of leaves eaten as a vegetable. **2** The head of such a plant. **3** *Slang* Money, esp. paper money. —*v.i.* **·baged, ·baging** To form a head, as cabbage. [< OF *caboche*]

cabbage palm A palm with a terminal leaf bud used as a vegetable.

cab·by (kab′ē) *n. pl.* **·bies** *Informal* A taxicab driver.

cab·in (kab′in) *n.* **1** A small, crudely built house; hut. **2** A compartment in a vessel, aircraft, etc., for crew or passengers. —*v.t. & v.i.* To shut up or dwell in or as in a cabin. [< LL *capanna*]

cabin boy A boy who waits on the officers and passengers of a vessel.

cabin cruiser A powerboat with an equipped cabin.

cab·i·net (kab′ə·nit) *n.* **1** A piece of furniture, case, etc., with shelves, drawers, or compartments. **2** *Often cap.* The body of official advisers of a chief of state. **3** A private council room or study. —*adj.* Of or suitable for a cabinet. [< OF *cabinet*]

cab·i·net·mak·er (kab′ə·nit·mā′kər) *n.* A craftsman who makes fine wooden furniture, etc.

cab·i·net·work (kab′ə·nit·wûrk′) *n.* The work of a cabinetmaker; expert woodwork.

ca·ble (kā′bəl) *n.* **1** A heavy rope of wire strands, hemp, etc. **2** A unit of nautical measure, 720 feet in the U.S. and 608 feet in England. Also **cable length, cable's length. 3** An insulated electrical conductor or group of conductors protected by an outer covering. **4** CABLEGRAM. —*v.* **·bled, ·bling** *v.t.* **1** To send a cablegram to. **2** To fasten with a cable. —*v.i.* **3** To send a cablegram. [< LL *capulum* rope]

cable car A car pulled along rails by a cable.

ca·ble·gram (kā′bəl·gram) *n.* A telegraphic message sent by undersea cable.

ca·ble-tel·e·vi·sion (kā′bəl·tel′ə·vizh′ən) *n.* A system utilizing cables or wires to transmit television signals. Also **cable-TV** (kā′bəl·tē′vē′).

cab·man (kab′mən) *n. pl.* **·men** (-mən) The driver of a cab.

cab·o·chon (kab′ə·shon, *Fr.* ká·bô·shôn′) *n.* **1** An unfaceted gemstone cut convex and highly polished. **2** This style of cutting. [< F *caboche* head]

ca·boo·dle (kə·bōōd′l) *n. Informal* Lot; collection: usu. in the phrase **the whole (kit and) caboodle.** [Prob. < KIT + BOODLE]

ca·boose (kə·bōōs′) *n.* A railroad car, usu. the last of a freight train, equipped for the use of the crew. [< MDu. *cabuse* cook's galley]

cab·ri·o·let (kab′rē·ə·lā′, -let′) *n.* **1** An automobile of the coupé type, having a collapsible top. **2** A one-horse carriage with two seats and a usu. collapsible top. [< L *capreolus* wild goat]

cab·stand (kab′stand′) *n.* A place where cabs are stationed for hire.

ca·ca·o (kə·kā′ō, -kä′ō) *n. pl.* **·ca·os 1** A tropical American tree bearing large seed pods. **2** The seeds of this tree, from which chocolate and cocoa are obtained. [< Nah. *cacauatl* cacao]

cach·a·lot (kash′ə·lot, -lō) *n.* SPERM WHALE. [F]

cache (kash) *v.t.* **cached, cach·ing** To store or hide in a secret place. —*n.* **1** A place for hiding or storing provisions. **2** Supplies stored or hidden in such a place. [< F *cacher* hide]

ca·chet (ka·shā′, kash′ā) *n.* **1** A seal, as on a document or letter. **2** A distinctive mark of individuality. **3** A mark, slogan, etc., stamped or printed on mail. [< F *cacher* hide]

cach·in·nate (kak′ə·nāt) *v.i.* **·nat·ed, ·nat·ing** To laugh immoderately or noisily. [< L *cachinnare*] —**cach′in·na′tion** *n.*

ca·cique (kə·sēk′) *n.* An Indian chief of the West Indies or Latin America. [< Sp. < Arawakan]

cack·le (kak′əl) *v.* **·led, ·ling** *v.i.* **1** To make a shrill cry, as a hen that has laid an egg. **2** To laugh or talk with a sound resembling this. —*v.t.* **3** To utter in a cackling manner. —*n.* **1** The shrill, broken cry made by a hen after laying an egg. **2** A laugh or sound resembling this. **3** Idle talk. [Imit.] —**cack′ler** *n.*

caco- *combining form* Bad; unpleasant. [< Gk. *kakos* bad]

ca·cog·ra·phy (kə·kog′rə·fē) *n.* Bad handwriting or spelling.

ca·coph·o·ny (kə·kof′ə·nē) *n. pl.* **·nies** A harsh, disagreeable, discordant sound. —**ca·coph′o·nous** *adj.* —**ca·coph′on·ous·ly** *adv.*

cac·tus (kak′təs) *n. pl.* **·tus·es** or **·ti** (-tī) Any of a family of plants native to arid regions of America, having fleshy, usu. leafless and spiny stems and often showy flowers. [< Gk. *kaktos* a prickly plant]

Cactus

cad (kad) *n.* A contemptible, ungentlemanly man. [Short form of CADDIE] —**cad′·dish** *adj.* —**cad′dish·ly** *adv.* —**cad′dish·ness** *n.* —Syn. bounder, rotter, scoundrel, heel.

ca·dav·er (kə·dav′ər, -dā′vər) *n.* A dead body, esp. a human corpse intended for dissection. [< L]

ca·dav·er·ous (kə·dav′ər·əs) *adj.* Of or resembling a corpse; pale; ghastly; gaunt. —**ca·dav′er·ous·ly** *adv.* —**ca·dav′er·ous·ness** *n.*

cad·die (kad′ē) *n.* One paid to carry clubs for golf players. —*v.i.* **·died, ·dy·ing** To act as a caddie. [< CADET]

cad·dis fly (kad′is) Any of certain four-winged insects having an aquatic larva, the **caddis worm,** enclosing itself in a cylindrical case covered with sand, gravel, etc. [?]

cad·dy¹ (kad′ē) *n. pl.* **·dies** A small box or receptacle, esp. for tea. [< Malay *kati,* a measure of weight]

cad·dy² (kad′ē) *n. pl.* **·dies** CADDIE. —*v.i.* **·died, ·dy·ing** CADDIE.

ca·dence (kād′ns) *n.* **1** Rhythmic flow, as of poetry. **2** Rhythmic beat or measure, as of marching. **3** Modulation or inflection, as of the voice. **4** A formula for ending a phrase, section, etc. Also **ca′den·cy.** [< LL *cadentia* a falling]

ca·den·za (kə·den′zə, *Ital.* kä·dent′sä) *n. Music* An elaborate display passage, often improvised, inserted into a composition for a solo voice or instrument. [Ital.]

ca·det (kə·det′) *n.* **1** A student at a military or naval school who is training for commissioning as an officer. **2** A younger son or brother. [F, ult. < dim. of L *caput* head, chief] —**ca·det′ship** *n.*

cadge (kaj) *v.t.* **cadged, cadg·ing** *Informal* To get by begging or sponging. [?] —**cadg′er** *n.*

ca·di (kä′dē, kā′-) *n. pl.* **·dis** A Muslim judge or magistrate. [< Ar. *qādī*]

cad·mi·um (kad′mē·əm) *n.* A bluish white metallic element (symbol Cd), occurring in small quantities in ores of zinc and used in fusible alloys, in electroplating, etc. [< L *cadmia* zinc ore] —**cad′mic** *adj.*

cad·re (kad′rē) *n.* **1** A framework. **2** The nucleus of trained personnel necessary to establish and manage a larger organization, as a military unit. [< Ital. *quadro* < L *quadrum* square]

ca·du·ce·us (kə·dʸōō′sē·əs) *n. pl.* **·ce·i** (-sē·ī) The winged, snake-entwined staff of the god Hermes, now used as a symbol of the medical profession. [< Gk. *karykion* herald's staff] —**ca·du′ce·an** *adj.*

Caduceus

cae·cum (sē′kəm) *n.* CECUM.

Cae·sar (sē′zər) **1** The title of the Roman emperors from Augustus to Hadrian. **2** A dictator or despot.

Cae·sar·e·an (si·zâr′ē·ən) *adj.* Pertaining to Caesar. —*n.* CAESAREAN SECTION. Also **Cae·sar′i·an.**

Caesarean section The delivery of a child through a surgical incision in the abdominal wall. Also **Caesarean operation.**

cae·si·um (sē′zē·əm) n. CESIUM.

cae·su·ra (si·zhōōr′ə, -zyōōr′ə) n. pl. **·su·ras** or **·su·rae** (-zhōōr′ē, -zyōōr′ē) 1 A pause within a line or foot of verse, usu. near the middle. 2 *Music* A pause at a division point of an air or melody. [< L, a cutting, caesura < *caedere* to cut] —**cae·su′ral** adj.

ca·fé (ka·fā′, ka-) n. 1 A coffee house, restaurant, bar-room, etc. 2 Coffee. Also **ca·fe.** [F]

ca·fé au lait (kå·fā′ ō lā′) *French* 1 Coffee with scalded milk. 2 A light brown.

ca·fé noir (kå·fā′ nwår′) *French* Black coffee.

caf·e·te·ri·a (kaf′ə·tir′ē·ə) n. A restaurant where the patrons wait upon themselves. [< Am. Sp., coffee store]

caf·feine (kaf′ēn, ka·fēn′, kaf′ē·in) n. An alkaloid found in coffee, tea, and cola and used as a stimulant. Also **caf′fein.** [< F *café* coffee]

caf·tan (kaf′tən, käf·tän′) n. A loose, long-sleeved robe worn in E Mediterranean countries. [< Turkish *qaftān*]

cage (kāj) n. 1 A structure enclosed with bars or wires, for confining birds, animals, etc. 2 A structure or enclosure resembling this. 3 In baseball, a backstop used for batting practice. 4 In hockey, the frame and network forming the goal. 5 In basketball, the basket. —v.t. **caged, cag·ing** To confine in or as in a cage. [< L *cavea* an enclosure < *cavus* empty, hollow]

ca·gey (kā′jē) adj. **·gi·er, ·gi·est** *Informal* Shrewd; wary. Also **ca′gy.** —**ca′gi·ly** adv. —**ca′gi·ness** n.

ca·hoots (kə·hōōts′) n. pl. *Informal* Partnership; collusion: used in the phrase **in cahoots.**

cai·man (kā′mən) n. A tropical American crocodilian related to the alligator. [< Cariban]

Cain (kān) The eldest son of Adam and slayer of his brother Abel. —n. A murderer. —**raise Cain** *Slang* To make a noisy disturbance.

ca·ique (kä·ēk′) n. A long, narrow skiff used on the Bosporus. [< Turkish *qāyiq*]

cairn (kârn) n. A mound of stones placed as a memorial or marker. [< Celtic] —**cairned** adj.

cais·son (kā′sən, -son) n. 1 An ammunition chest. 2 A two-wheeled vehicle carrying such a chest. 3 A watertight chamber within which work is done under water, as on a bridge pier. 4 A watertight box or other apparatus for floating a sunken vessel. [< F *caisse* box, chest]

caisson disease DECOMPRESSION SICKNESS.

cai·tiff (kā′tif) n. A base wretch or coward. —adj. Vile or cowardly. [< AF *caitif* weak, wretched < L *captivus* captive]

ca·jole (kə·jōl) v.t. & v.i. **·joled, ·jol·ing** To persuade or coax with flattery; wheedle. [< F *cajoler*] —**ca·jole′ment, ca·jol′er, ca·jol′er·y** n. —**ca·jol′ing·ly** adv.

Ca·jun (kā′jən) n. A descendant of the Acadian French in Louisiana. [Alter. of ACADIAN]

cake (kāk) n. 1 A baked mixture of flour, eggs, milk, sugar, etc. 2 A thin mass of dough or batter, etc., baked or fried: *pancake.* 3 A patty or shaped mass, as of fish or meat. 4 A hardened mass: a *cake* of soap, etc. —**take the cake** *Informal* To deserve a prize; be the best. —v.t. & v.i. **caked, cak·ing** To form into a hardened mass. [< ON *kaka*]

cakes and ale A carefree way of life.

cake·walk (kāk′wôk′) n. 1 Originally, a promenade in which the couple performing the most original dance steps won a cake as a prize. 2 a A dance based on this. b Music for such a dance. —v.i. To do a cakewalk. —**cake′walk′er** n.

Cal calorie (large).

Cal. California.

cal calorie (small).

cal. calendar; caliber.

cal·a·bash (kal′ə·bash) n. 1 A tropical American tree bearing gourdlike fruit. 2 A vine of Africa and Asia having bottle-shaped, hard-shelled fruit. 3 The fruit of a calabash tree or vine. 4 An object, as a pipe, rattle, etc., made from a calabash gourd. [< Sp. *calabaza* pumpkin]

cal·a·boose (kal′ə·bōōs) n. *Slang* A jail. [< Sp. *calaboza*]

ca·la·di·um (kə·lā′dē·əm) n. A tropical American plant with large, variegated leaves. [< NL < Malay *kēlādy*]

cal·a·mine (kal′ə·mīn, -min) n. 1 A white zinc silicate mineral, often colored by impurities. 2 A native zinc car-

bonate, a pink powder used in lotions and ointments. —v.t. **·mined, ·min·ing** To apply calamine to. [< LL *calamina* < L *cadmia* zinc ore]

ca·lam·i·tous (kə·lam′ə·təs) adj. Causing or resulting in a calamity. —**ca·lam′i·tous·ly** adv. —**ca·lam′i·tous·ness** n. —Syn. disastrous, catastrophic, ruinous.

ca·lam·i·ty (kə·lam′ə·tē) n. pl. **·ties** 1 An event causing great suffering, grief, or misery; disaster. 2 A state or time of affliction, distress, etc. [< L *calamitas*]

cal·a·mus (kal′ə·məs) n. pl. **·mi** (-mī) 1 SWEET FLAG. 2 The quill of a feather. [< Gk. *kalamos* reed]

ca·lash (kə·lash′) n. 1 A low-wheeled carriage with a folding top. 2 A folding carriage top. 3 A folding hoodlike bonnet of the 18th century. [< F *calèche*]

cal·ca·ne·us (kal·kā′nē·əs) n. pl. **·ne·i** (-nē·ī) The heel bone. Also **cal·ca′ne·um.** [< L < *calx* heel]

cal·car·e·ous (kal·kâr′ē·əs) adj. Composed of, containing, or of the nature of limestone; chalky. [< L *calx* lime]

cal·ces (kal′sēz) n.pl. of CALX.

calci- combining form Lime. [< L *calx, calcis* lime]

cal·cif·er·ol (kal·sif′ər·ōl, -ol) n. Vitamin D as formed by the irradiation of ergosterol. [< CALCIFER(OUS) + (ERGOSTER)OL]

Calash def. 3

cal·cif·er·ous (kal·sif′ər·əs) adj. Yielding or containing calcium carbonate, as rocks.

cal·ci·fi·ca·tion (kal′sə·fi·kā′shən) n. 1 Hardening of tissue by deposition of calcium salts, as in bone formation. 2 Such hardened tissue.

cal·ci·fy (kal′sə·fī) v.t. & v.i. **·fied, ·fy·ing** To make or become hard by the deposit of lime salts.

cal·ci·mine (kal′sə·mīn, -min) n. A white or tinted wash of zinc white, glue, and water, for ceilings, walls, etc. —v.t. **·mined, ·min·ing** To apply calcimine to. [< L *calx* lime]

cal·cine (kal′sīn, -sin) v. **·cined, ·cin·ing** v.t. 1 To expel volatile matter from (a substance) by heat. 2 To reduce to powder by roasting. —v.i. 3 To become changed by the action of heat into a powder. [< L *calx* lime] —**cal·ci·na·tion** (kal′sə·nā′shən) n.

cal·cite (kal′sīt) n. Any of various mineral forms of calcium carbonate, usu. colorless or whitish, as chalk, limestone, and marble. —**cal·cit·ic** (kal·sit′ik) adj.

cal·ci·um (kal′sē·əm) n. A silver-white, malleable, metallic element (symbol Ca) widely distributed in combination, as in chalk, gypsum and limestone. [< L *calx* lime]

calcium carbide A compound of calcium and carbon which when treated with water yields acetylene.

calcium carbonate The chief natural compound of calcium, occurring as chalk, marble, limestone, etc., and as a constituent of bones, teeth, shells, etc.

calcium chloride A white, deliquescent salt, used as a drying agent, refrigerant, etc.

calcium hydroxide A white, crystalline powder used to make bleaches, cement, etc.; slaked lime.

calcium phosphate Any of a class of phosphates found in various animal tissues and prepared commercially for use as an antacid, polishing agent, etc.

cal·cu·la·ble (kal′kyə·lə·bəl) adj. 1 Capable of being calculated. 2 Reliable. —**cal′cu·la·bly** adv.

cal·cu·late (kal′kyə·lāt) v. **·lat·ed, ·lat·ing** v.t. 1 To determine by arithmetical means. 2 To ascertain beforehand; determine by estimation. 3 To adapt to a purpose; intend: used chiefly in the passive: *calculated* to carry a two-ton load. 4 *Regional* To suppose; believe. —v.i. 5 To compute. 6 *Informal* To rely; depend. [< LL *calculatus*, pp. of *calculare* reckon < *calculus* a pebble used in reckoning] —Syn. 1 compute, figure, reckon. 2 estimate, surmise, presume, conjecture.

cal·cu·lat·ed (kal′kyə·lā′tid) adj. 1 Arrived at by calculation. 2 Thoughtfully estimated: a *calculated* risk. 3 Intentional; deliberate: a *calculated* insult.

cal·cu·lat·ing (kal′kyə·lā′ting) adj. 1 Shrewdly self-interested; scheming. 2 Designed for computation: a *calculating* machine. —**cal′cu·lat′ing·ly** adv.

cal·cu·la·tion (kal′kyə·lā′shən) n. 1 The act, process, or

calculator

101

callus

result of calculating. **2** A shrewd forethought; prudence.

cal·cu·la·tor (kal′kyə·lā·tər) *n.* **1** One who calculates. **2** A mechanical or electronic device, usu. having a keyboard, for doing mathematical computations.

cal·cu·lus (kal′kyə·ləs) *n. pl.* **·li** (-lī) or **·lus·es 1** *Pathol.* Any abnormal hard mass formed in the body. **2** *Math.* **a** A method of calculating by the use of a highly specialized system of symbols. **b** Analysis based on determination of rates of change of functions and the determination of a set of functions having a given rate of change, and their study and application. [<L, a pebble (used in counting)]

cal·de·ra (kôl·dir′ə, kal-) *n.* Crater formed by the collapse of, or outward explosion from, the cone of a volcano [<Sp.]

cal·dron (kôl′drən) *n.* A large kettle or boiler. [<L *caldaria* kettle <*calidus* hot]

ca·lèche (kà·lesh′) *n.* CALASH.

Cal·e·do·ni·a (kal′ə·dō′nē·ə, -dōn′yə) *n.* Scotland. —**Cal′·e·do′ni·an** *adj., n.*

cal·en·dar (kal′ən·dər) *n.* **1** A systematic arrangement of subdivisions of time, as years, months, days, weeks, etc. **2** A table showing such subdivisions, esp. of a single year. **3** A schedule or list: *a calendar of events.* —*v.t.* To register in a calendar or list. [<L *calendae* calends]

cal·en·der (kal′ən·dər) *n.* A machine for giving a gloss to cloth, paper, etc., by pressing between rollers. —*v.t.* To press (cloth, paper, etc.) in a calender. [<Gk. *kylindros* roller] —**cal′en·der·er** *n.*

cal·ends (kal′əndz) *n. pl. (often construed as sing.)* The first day of the month in the ancient Roman calendar. [<L *calendae*]

ca·len·du·la (kə·len′jōō·lə) *n.* A plant related to the daisies, having yellow or orange flowers. [<NL *calendae* calends; because it blooms almost every month]

calf¹ (kaf, käf) *n. pl.* **calves** (kavz, kävz) **1** The young of cattle. **2** The young of certain mammals, as the elephant, whale, etc. **3** Leather made from the skin of a calf. **4** *Informal* An awkward young fellow. [<OE *cealf*]

calf² (kaf, käf) *n. pl.* **calves** (kavz, kävz) The muscular back part of the human leg below the knee. [<ON *kálfi*]

calf·skin (kaf′skin′, käf′-) *n.* **1** The skin of a calf. **2** Leather made from this.

cal·i·ber (kal′ə·bər) *n.* **1** The internal diameter of a tube or of the barrel of a gun, cannon, etc. **2** The diameter of a bullet, shell, etc. **3** Degree of personal ability or quality. Also **cal′i·bre.** [<Ar. *qālib* mold, form]

cal·i·brate (kal′ə·brāt) *v.t.* **·brat·ed, ·brat·ing 1** To graduate or adjust (a measuring instrument). **2** To ascertain the caliber of. —**cal′i·bra′tion** *n.* —**cal′i·bra′tor** *n.*

cal·i·co (kal′i·kō) *n. pl.* **·coes** or **·cos** A cotton cloth printed in bright colors. —*adj.* **1** Made of calico. **2** Resembling calico; dappled or spotted: *a calico cat.* [<*Calicut*, India]

Calif. California.

Cal·i·for·nia poppy (kal′ə·fôrn′yə, -fôr′nē·ə) A plant of the poppy family, having finely divided leaves and usu. yellow-orange flowers.

cal·i·for·ni·um (kal′ə·fôr′nē·əm) *n.* An artificially produced radioactive element (symbol Cf). [<the University of *California*, where first produced]

cal·i·per (kal′ə·pər) *n. Usu. pl.* Any of various instruments for making precise measurements of dimensions. —*v.t. & v.i.* To measure by using calipers. [Var. of CALIBER]

ca·liph (kā′lif, kal′if) *n.* The spiritual and civil head of a Muslim state. Also **ca′lif.** [<Ar. *khalīfah* successor] —**cal·i·phate** (kal′ə·fāt, -fit) *n.*

cal·is·then·ics (kal′is·then′iks) *n. pl.* **1** Light gymnastic exercises to promote physical fitness. **2** *(construed as sing.)* The art of practice of such exercises. [<Gk. *kallos* beauty + *sthenos* strength] —**cal′is·then′ic** *adj.*

calk¹ (kôk) *v.t.* CAULK.

calk² (kôk) *n.* **1** A spur on a horse's shoe to prevent slipping. **2** A plate with sharp points worn on the sole of a boot or shoe to prevent slipping. —*v.t.* To furnish with calks. [<L *calx* heel]

call (kôl) *v.t.* **1** To utter loudly. **2** To address or appeal to by such utterance. **3** To read or enumerate aloud: *to call* the roll. **4** To summon. **5** To communicate with by telephone. **6** To waken. **7** To convoke; convene. **8** To bring to action or being, as by order. **9** To name or designate. **10** To consider to be; estimate as. **11** To insist on payment of: to *call* a loan. **12** To predict in advance, as a shot in pool. **13** To stop or suspend (a game). **14** To judge on (a play, pitched ball, etc.), as in baseball. **15** In poker, to demand that (a player) show his hand by equaling his bet. —*v.i.* **16** To shout or raise the voice, as to attract attention. **17** To telephone. **18** To make a brief visit: often with *on.* **19** In poker, to demand a show of hands by equaling an opponent's bet. —**call down 1** To invoke. **2** *Informal* To reprimand. —**call for 1** To go to get; stop by for. **2** To require; demand. —**call forth** To evoke. —**call in** To remove from circulation, as currency. —**call off** To cancel. —**call on 1** To ask to speak. **2** To visit briefly. —**call up 1** To telephone. **2** To summon for active military service. **3** To bring to memory. —*n.* **1** A shout or cry. **2** A summons, appeal, or command. **3** A telephone communication or message. **4** A sounded signal: a bugle *call.* **5** A brief visit. **6** A demand; need. **7** Occasion; reason: no *call* for such behavior. **8** A claim or obligation. **9** A religious vocation. **10 a** The characteristic cry of a bird or animal. **b** A device for imitating such a sound. **11** A sports decision, as by an umpire. —**on call 1** Ready when summoned or requested. **2** Payable on demand. [<ON *kalla*]

cal·la (kal′ə) *n.* Any of several plants of the arum family, having a showy, usu. white petallike leaf surrounding a club-shaped flower stalk. Also **calla lily.** [<NL *calla*, a plant name]

call·board (kôl′bôrd′, -bōrd′) *n.* A backstage theater bulletin board for posting notices.

call·boy (kôl′boi′) *n.* **1** A boy who calls actors to go on stage. **2** BELLMAN.

call·er (kô′lər) *n.* **1** One who calls, esp. one who calls out the steps in square dancing. **2** One making a brief visit.

call girl *Informal* A prostitute who makes assignations in response to telephone calls.

cal·lig·ra·phy (kə·lig′rə·fē) *n.* **1** Beautiful penmanship. **2** The art of fine handwriting. [<Gk. *kalos* beautiful + -GRAPHY] —**cal·lig′ra·pher, cal·lig′ra·phist** *n.* —**cal·li·graph·ic** (kal′ə·graf′ik) *adj.*

call·ing (kô′ling) *n.* **1** A profession or occupation. **2** A vocation or inner urge, esp. of a religious nature.

calling card A small card bearing one's name, used when paying a business or social call, etc.

cal·li·o·pe (kə·lī′ə·pē, kal′ē·ōp) *n.* A musical instrument having steam whistles played by means of a keyboard. [<L<Gk. *Kalliopē* Calliope, lit., the beautiful-voiced]

Cal·li·o·pe (kə·lī′ə·pē) *Gk. Myth.* The Muse of eloquence and epic poetry.

cal·li·per (kal′ə·pər) *n.* CALIPER.

call letters The code letters identifying a radio or television transmitting station.

call number A number employed by libraries to classify and locate a book.

cal·los·i·ty (kə·los′ə·tē) *n. pl.* **·ties 1** A thickened, hardened area of skin, produced by or as by pressure or friction. **2** Hardness; insensibility.

cal·lous (kal′əs) *adj.* **1** Thickened and hardened, as the skin by friction or pressure. **2** Coldly or cruelly unfeeling. —*v.t. & v.i.* To make or become callous. [<L *callus* hard skin] —**cal′lous·ly** *adv.* —**cal′lous·ness** *n.* —**Syn. 2** insensitive, thick-skinned, hard, heartless, hardhearted.

cal·low (kal′ō) *adj.* **1** Inexperienced; youthful. **2** Unfledged, as a bird. [<OE *calu* bare, bald] —**cal′low·ness** *n.*

cal·lus (kal′əs) *n. pl.* **·lus·es 1** A thickened; hardened area of skin. **2** The new tissue formed around the ends of a broken bone when reuniting. —*v.t. & v.i.* To develop callus (on). [<L, hard skin]

add, āce, câre, pălm; end, ēven; it, īce; odd, ōpen, ôrder; tōōk, pōōl; up, bûrn; ə = a in above, u in focus; yōō = u in fuse; oil; pout; check; go; ring; thin; this; zh, vision. < derived from; ? origin uncertain or unknown.

calm (käm) *adj.* 1 Free from agitation; unruffled; composed. 2 Not turbulent; quiet; still. —*n.* 1 Lack of turbulence, wind, or motion. 2 Serenity; peacefulness. —*v.t. & v.i.* To make or become calm. [<LL *cauma* heat of the day, rest at midday] —**calm′ly** *adv.* —**calm′ness** *n.* —**Syn.** *adj.* 1 tranquil, serene, placid, peaceful, untroubled.

cal·o·mel (kal′ə·mel, -məl) *n.* A white, tasteless compound of mercury and chlorine, a strong purgative now used chiefly in prophylactic ointments. [<Gk. *kalos* beautiful + *melas* black]

ca·lor·ic (kə·lôr′ik, -lor′-) *adj.* Of or pertaining to heat. [<L *calor* heat]

cal·o·rie (kal′ə·rē) *n.* 1 One of two units of heat. The **great, large,** or **kilogram calorie** is the amount of heat required to raise the temperature of one kilogram of water 1°C. The **small** or **gram calorie** is the amount of heat required to raise one gram of water 1° C. 2 The large calorie, used as a measure of the energy value of foods or the heat output of organisms. [<F *calorie* <L *calor* heat]

cal·o·rif·ic (kal′ə·rif′ik) *adj.* Of or producing heat. [<L *calorificus* heat-producing]

cal·o·rim·e·ter (kal′ə·rim′ə·tər) *n.* Any apparatus for measuring heat. [<L *calor* heat + -METER] —**cal·or·i·met·ric** (kə·lôr′ə·met′rik, -lor′-) *adj.* —**cal′o·rim′e·try** *n.*

cal·u·met (kal′yə·met, kal′yə·met′) *n.* A tobacco pipe with a long, ornamented stem, used by American Indians in various ceremonies. [<L *calamus* reed]

Calumet

ca·lum·ni·ate (kə·lum′nē·āt) *v.t.* **·at·ed, ·at·ing** To make false and damaging statements about; slander. [<L *calumnia* slander] —**ca·lum′ni·a′tion, ca·lum′ni·a′tor** *n.*

ca·lum·ni·ous (kə·lum′nē·əs) *adj.* Slanderous; defamatory. —**ca·lum′ni·ous·ly** *adv.*

cal·um·ny (kal′əm·nē) *n. pl.* **·nies** 1 A false accusation or report made with malicious or injurious intent. 2 The making of such statements; defamation. [<L *calumnia* slander]

Cal·va·ry (kal′vər·ē) *n.* The place where Christ was crucified; Golgotha. *Luke* 23:33. [<L *calvaria* skull]

calve (kav, käv) *v.t. & v.i.* **calved, calv·ing** To give birth to (a calf). [<OE *cealf* calf]

calves (kavz, kävz) *n. pl.* of CALF.

Cal·vin·ism (kal′vin·iz′əm) *n.* The religious system or doctrines of John Calvin, characterized by an austere moral code. —**Cal′vin·ist** *adj., n.* —**Cal′vin·is′tic** or **·ti·cal** *adj.* —**Cal′vin·is′ti·cal·ly** *adv.*

calx (kalks) *n. pl.* **calx·es** or **cal·ces** (kal′sēz) The residue from the calcination of minerals. [<L, lime]

ca·lyp·so (kə·lip′sō) *n. pl.* **·sos** A type of improvised, often topical song that originated in Trinidad. [<Calypso]

Ca·lyp·so (kə·lip′sō) In the *Odyssey,* a nymph who detained Odysseus for seven years on an island.

ca·lyx (kā′liks, kal′iks) *n. pl.* **ca·lyx·es** or **cal·y·ces** (kal′ə·sēz, kā′lə-) *Bot.* The outermost part of a flower, made up of usu. green, leaflike sepals. [<Gk. *kalyx* husk, pod]

cam (kam) *n.* A rotating wheel of irregular shape, used to change the direction of the motion of another part moving against it. [? <F *came*]

ca·ma·ra·de·rie (kä′mə·rä′dər·ē) *n.* Friendly good will; comradeship. [F]

cam·a·ril·la (kam′ə·ril′ə, *Sp.* kä′mä·rē′lyä) *n.* A group or clique of unofficial political advisers; a cabal. [<Sp. *camara* chamber]

cam·as (kam′əs) *n.* Any of several North American plants related to lilies, having an edible bulb. Also **cam′ass.** [<Chinook jargon]

cam·ber (kam′bər) *v.t. & v.i.* To shape with or have a slight upward convex curve. —*n.* A slight upward bend or convex curve. [<L *camera* curved roof, vault]

cam·bi·um (kam′bē·əm) *n.* A layer of growing and dividing cells between the phloem and xylem in the stems and roots of many plants, from which new tissues are developed. [<LL, exchange]

Cam·bo·di·a (kam·bō′dē·ə) *n.* A country of sw Indochina, 69,844 sq. mi., cap. Phnom Penh. • See map at INDOCHINA.

Cam·bri·a (kam′brē·ə) *n.* The Latin name for Wales.

Cam·bri·an (kam′brē·ən) *n. & adj.* See GEOLOGY.

cam·bric (kām′brik) *n.* A fine white linen or cotton fabric. [<Flemish *Kameryk* Cambrai, city in France]

cambric tea A drink made of sweetened hot water, milk, and often a little tea.

cam·cor·der (kam′kôr′dər) *n.* A combination of a portable TV camera and a videotape recorder.

came (kām) *p.t.* of COME.

cam·el (kam′əl) *n.* Either of two species of domesticated ruminants used as beasts of burden in arid regions of Africa and Asia: the **Arabian camel,** or dromedary, having one hump on the back, and the **Bactrian camel,** having two. [<Gk. *kamēlos* <Semitic]

Bactrian camel

ca·mel·lia (kə·mēl′yə, -mēl′ē·ə) *n.* A tropical tree or shrub with glossy evergreen leaves and showy flowers. [<George Joseph *Kamel,* 1661–1706, Jesuit missionary]

ca·mel·o·pard (kə·mel′ə·pärd) *n. Archaic* The giraffe. [<Gk. *kamēlos* camel + *pardalis* leopard]

Cam·e·lot (kam′ə·lot) In Arthurian legend, the seat of King Arthur's court.

camel's hair 1 The hair of a camel. 2 A warm, soft, usu. yellowish-tan cloth made from this. Also **camel hair.** —**cam′el-hair′, cam′el's-hair′** *adj.*

Cam·em·bert (kam′əm·bâr, *Fr.* kà·mäN·bâr′) *n.* A rich, creamy, soft, cheese. [<*Camembert,* town in NW France]

cam·e·o (kam′ē·ō) *n. pl.* **·e·os** 1 A gem of onyx, agate, shell, etc., carved in relief with design and background of different colors. 2 A small part, as in a movie or TV show, played by a well-known performer. [<Ital. *cammeo*]

cam·er·a (kam′ər·ə, kam′rə) *n. pl.* **·er·as** for defs. *1 & 2,* **·er·ae** for def. *3* 1 A device for exposing a sensitized plate or film to light that forms an image thereon. 2 A device that converts optical images into electrical impulses for television transmission. 3 *Law* A judge's private room. —**in camera** *Law* Not in public court; privately. [<Gk. *kamara* vault]

cam·er·a·man (kam′ər·ə·man′, kam′rə-) *n. pl.* **·men** (-men′) The operator of a camera, esp. a motion-picture camera.

Cam·e·roon (kam′ə·rōōn′) *n.* A republic of CEN. Africa, 183,376 sq. mi., cap. Yaoundé. Also **Cam′e·roun′.** • See map at AFRICA.

cam·i·sole (kam′ə·sōl) *n.* A woman's sleeveless, often lace-trimmed undergarment. [<Sp. *camisa* shirt]

cam·o·mile (kam′ə·mīl) *n.* CHAMOMILE.

cam·ou·flage (kam′ə·fläzh) *n.* 1 A protective disguise that matches, blends in with, or imitates natural surroundings. 2 Any disguise or pretense. —*v.t.* **·flaged, ·flag·ing** To hide or obscure with or as with camouflage. [<F *camoufler* disguise] —**cam′ou·flag′er** *n.*

camp¹ (kamp) *n.* 1 **a** A place where a group of people, soldiers, hunters, miners, or vacationers, live in tents or other temporary or informal shelters. **b** The tents or shelters of such a place. 2 A body of persons who support a doctrine or cause: the opposing political *camp.* —*v.i.* 1 To set up a camp. 2 To live temporarily in or as in a camp. 3 To sleep outdoors in a tent: often with *out.* —*v.t.* 4 To shelter or station in a camp. [<L *campus* level plain]

camp² (kamp) *n.* Something so banal, flamboyant, out-of-date, or artificial as to be thought humorous or appealing. —*adj.* Characterized by camp: also **camp′y (·i·er, ·i·est).** [?]

cam·paign (kam·pān′) *n.* 1 A series of military operations conducted for a particular objective. 2 A series of related political or other activities designed to bring about a result. —*v.i.* To conduct or take part in a campaign. [<L *campus* open field] —**cam·paign′er** *n.*

cam·pa·ni·le (kam′pə·nē′lē, *Ital.* -nē′lā) *n. pl.* **·les** or **·li** (-lē) A tower that houses and supports a bell, esp. a tower near but not attached to a church. [<LL *campana* bell]

cam·pan·u·la (kam·pan′yə·lə) *n.* Any of a genus of plants having flowers with a bell-shaped, usu. blue corolla. [<LL *campana* bell]

camp chair A light, folding chair.

camp·er (kamp'ər) n. 1 One who camps out or stays in a summer camp, as for children. 2 A vehicle equipped as a shelter for travelers, vacationers, etc.

camp·fire (kamp'fīr') n. 1 A fire in an outdoor camp, for cooking, warmth, etc. 2 A gathering around such a fire.

camp follower 1 A civilian who follows an army about, esp. a prostitute. 2 An adherent or hanger-on who is not officially a member of a group.

camp·ground (kamp'ground') n. An area used for a camp or a camp meeting.

cam·phor (kam'fər) n. A crystalline compound with a penetrating odor and pungent taste, obtained synthetically or from the wood of an Asian tree, and used as a moth repellant, in medicine, etc. [< Ar. *kāfūr* < Malay *kāpūr*] —**cam·phor·ic** (kam·fôr'ik, -for'-) adj.

cam·phor·ate (kam'fə·rāt) v.t. ·at·ed, ·at·ing To treat or saturate with camphor.

camphor ball A moth ball.

camphor ice An ointment containing camphor, used for chapped skin, etc.

camp·ing (kamp'ing) n. The act or practice of living outdoors, as in tents or without shelter, esp. for recreation.

cam·pi·on (kam'pē·ən) n. One of various flowering plants related to the pinks. [?]

camp meeting A series of religious meetings held outdoors or in a tent.

camp·site (kamp'sīt') n. An outdoor site for camping.

camp stool A light, folding stool or seat.

cam·pus (kam'pəs) n. The grounds of a school, college, etc. [L, field, plain]

can[1] (kan, *unstressed* kən) v., *present* **can**, *past* **could** 1 To be able to. 2 To know how to. 3 To have the right to. 4 *Informal* To be permitted to; may. [< OE *cunnan* know, be able] • Although there is a formal distinction made between *can* to express ability to do something and *may* to express permission, in informal usage *can* is generally acceptable to express permission, esp. in questions or negative statements.

can[2] (kan) n. 1 A usu. metal container in which foods, beverages, etc., are sealed for preserving. 2 A usu. large metal container for garbage, milk, etc. 3 The contents of a can. 4 *Slang* a A jail. b A toilet. c The backside. —v.t. **canned, can·ning** 1 To preserve in a sealed can, jar, etc. 2 *Slang* To dismiss; fire. 3 *Informal* To record the sound of. [< OE *canne* cup] —**can'ner** n.

Can. Canada; Canadian.

Ca·naan (kā'nən) n. The part of Palestine between the Jordan and the Mediterranean; the Promised Land of the Israelites.

Ca·naan·ite (kā'nən·īt) n. A dweller in Canaan prior to the Israelite conquest.

Can·a·da (kan'ə·də) n. A member of the Commonwealth

of Nations in N North America, 3,851,809 sq. mi., cap. Ottawa. —**Ca·na·di·an** (kə·nā'dē·ən) adj., n.

Canada goose A grayish wild goose of North America, having a black head and neck.

Canadian bacon Bacon from the loin of a pig, having the flavor of ham.

Ca·na·di·en (kə·nā'dē·en', *Fr.* kä·nä·dyen') n. FRENCH CANADIAN.

ca·naille (kə·nāl', *Fr.* kȧ·nä'y') n. The rabble; mob. [< Ital. *canaglia* pack of dogs < L *canis* dog]

ca·nal (kə·nal') n. 1 An artificial waterway for navigation, irrigation, etc. 2 *Anat.* A duct, tube, or groove. 3 One of the faint lines visible on the planet Mars. 3 *Zool.* A groove. —v.t. **ca·nalled** or **ca·naled, ca·nal·ling** or **ca·nal·ing** To make a canal in or through. [< L *canalis* groove.]

ca·nal·ize (kə·nal'īz, kan'əl·īz) v.t. ·ized, ·iz·ing 1 To convert into a canal. 2 To furnish with a canal or canals. 3 To furnish with an outlet. —**ca·nal·i·za·tion** (kə·nal'ə·zā'shən, kan'ə·lə-) n.

can·a·pé (kan'ə·pē, -pā; *Fr.* kȧ·nȧ·pā') n. A piece of bread, cracker, etc., topped with any of various relishes. [< F, lit., couch]

ca·nard (kə·närd', *Fr.* kȧ·när') n. A false or baseless story or rumor. [F, lit., duck]

ca·nar·y (kə·nâr'ē) n. pl. ·nar·ies 1 A small, usu. yellow songbird native to the Canary Islands, popular as a cage bird. 2 A bright yellow color: also **canary yellow**. 3 A sweet, white wine from the Canary Islands. [< L *Canaria (Insula)* Dog (Island) < the dogs found there]

ca·nas·ta (kə·nas'tə) n. A card game similar to rummy, using two decks. [< Sp., basket]

canc. cancel; cancellation; canceled.

can·can (kan'kan', *Fr.* kän·kän') n. A lively dance characterized by high kicking. [F]

can·cel (kan'səl) v.t. **can·celed** or **·celled, can·cel·ing** or **·cel·ling** 1 To strike out, as by marking lines through; cross off. 2 To countermand or call off. 3 To stamp or mark, as a postage stamp, to prevent reuse. 4 To make up for; counterbalance. 5 *Math.* To eliminate (a common factor) by dividing the numerator and denominator of a fraction, or both sides of an equation. —v.i. 6 To be canceled or counterbalanced: with *out*. —n. A cancellation. [< L *cancellare* cross out] —**can'cel·a·ble, can'cel·la·ble** adj. —**can'cel·er, can'cel·ler** n. —**Syn.** 1 delete, expunge, obliterate. 2 repeal, annul, abrogate.

can·cel·la·tion (kan'sə·lā'shən) n. 1 The act of canceling. 2 That which is canceled. 3 A mark that cancels.

can·cer (kan'sər) n. 1 A malignant neoplasm, as carcinoma, sarcoma, etc. 2 Any baneful and spreading evil. [< L, crab, ulcer] —**can'cer·ous** adj.

Can·cer (kan'sər) n. A constellation and the fourth sign of the zodiac; the Crab. • See TROPIC and ZODIAC.

can·de·la (kan·del'ə) n. A unit of luminous intensity, equal to that of 1/60 of one square centimeter of the surface of a black body radiating at 1773.5°C.

can·de·la·brum (kan'də·lä'brəm, -lā'-) n. pl. ·bra (-brə) or ·brums A large, branched candlestick. [< L *candela* candle]

can·des·cence (kan·des'əns) n. INCANDESCENCE. [< L *candere* to glow] —**can·des'cent** adj.

can·did (kan'did) adj. 1 Frank, open, and sincere. 2 Impartial; fair. 3 Unposed; natural or informal: a *candid* snapshot. [< L *candidus* white, pure] —**can'did·ly** adv. —**can'did·ness** n. —**Syn.** 1 straightforward, outspoken, ingenuous, guileless.

can·di·date (kan'də·dāt, -dit) n. One seeking or considered for an elective office, position, honor, etc. [< L *candidatus* wearing white < the white togas of Roman candidates] —**can·di·da·cy** (kan'də·də·sē), **can·di·da·ture** (kan'də·də·chōor, -dā'chər) n.

candid camera A small camera with a fast lens, used for taking informal pictures of unposed subjects.

can·died (kan'dēd) adj. Cooked, glazed or permeated with sugar, syrup, etc.

can·dle (kan'dəl) n. 1 A usu. cylindrical stick of wax, tallow, etc., containing a wick providing to give light. 2 Something resembling this. 3 CANDELA. —**burn the candle at both ends** To expend one's energy or resources excessively. —**hold a candle to** To compare with favorably: usu. used in the negative. —v.t. **·dled, ·dling** To test (eggs) for freshness by holding between the eye and a light. [< L *candela* < *candere* shine, gleam] —**can'dler** n.

can·dle·ber·ry (kan′dəl·ber′ē) n. pl. **·ries** BAYBERRY.

can·dle·light (kan′dəl·līt′) n. 1 Light given by a candle. 2 Early evening; dusk.

Can·dle·mas (kan′dəl·məs) n. February 2, a church festival marking the purification of the Virgin and the presentation of Christ in the temple. [OE *candel* candle + *mæsse* mass]

can·dle·pow·er (kan′dəl·pou′ər) n. Illuminating power as expressed in candelas.

can·dle·stick (kan′dəl·stik′) n. A holder for a candle or candles.

can·dor (kan′dər) n. 1 Openness; frankness. 2 Freedom from prejudice; impartiality; fairness. *Brit. sp.* **can′dour.** [< L, sincerity, purity, whiteness]

can·dy (kan′dē) n. pl. **·dies** 1 Any of numerous confections made from sugar, syrup, etc., often combined with chocolate, fruit, nuts, etc. 2 A single piece of this. 3 Sugar or syrup crystallized by boiling or evaporation. —v. **·died, ·dy·ing** v.t. 1 To cook, coat, or preserve with sugar or syrup. 2 To cause to form sugar crystals. 3 To make pleasant; sweeten. —v.i. 4 To form sugar crystals; turn to sugar. [< Ar. *qandī* made of sugar]

can·dy·tuft (kan′dē·tuft′) n. A garden plant with white, pink, or purple flowers.

cane (kān) n. 1 A stick carried or used as an aid in walking. 2 A similar rod, esp. one used for flogging. 3 A plant, as bamboo, rattan, or sugar cane, having jointed, woody stems. 4 The stem of certain of these plants, often split and woven, as for furniture. 5 The woody stem of a raspberry, blackberry, rose, etc. —v.t. **caned, can·ing** 1 To strike or beat with a cane. 2 To weave or repair with cane, as a chair seat. [< Gk. *kanna* reed < Semitic] —**can′er** n.

cane·brake (kān′brāk′) n. An area densely overgrown with canes.

cane sugar Sucrose made from sugar cane.

ca·nine (kā′nīn) adj. Of, resembling, or characteristic of a dog or related animal. —n. 1 A dog or related animal, as a wolf, coyote, etc. 2 Any of the four conical teeth adjoining the incisors at the front of the upper and lower jaws: also **canine tooth.** [< L < *canis* dog] • See TOOTH.

Ca·nis Ma·jor (kā′nis mā′jər) A northern constellation that contains the bright star Sirius.

Canis Mi·nor (mī′nər) A northern constellation containing the star Procyon.

can·is·ter (kan′is·tər) n. 1 An usu. metal container, as for tea, coffee, or spices. 2 A metal cylinder containing shot, etc., that shatters when fired, as from a cannon. [< L *canistrum* basket]

can·ker (kang′kər) n. 1 An ulcerous sore in the mouth. 2 A plant disease marked by dead tissue. 3 Any secret or spreading evil. —v.t. 1 To infect with canker. 2 To decay or corrupt. —v.i. 3 To be affected by a canker. [< L *cancer* crab, ulcer] —**can′ker·ous** adj.

can·ker·worm (kang′kər·wûrm′) n. Any of several moth larvae that destroy trees.

can·na (kan′ə) n. Any of a genus of tropical plants with broad leaves and red or yellow irregular flowers. [< Gk. *kanna* reed]

can·na·bis (kan′ə·bis) n. MARIHUANA. [< Gk. *kannabis* hemp]

canned (kand) adj. 1 Preserved in a can or jar. 2 *Informal* Recorded: *canned* music.

can·nel (kan′əl) n. A bituminous coal that burns with a bright flame. Also **cannel coal.** [Alter. of *candle coal*]

can·ner·y (kan′ər·ē) n. pl. **·ner·ies** A processing plant where foods are canned.

can·ni·bal (kan′ə·bəl) n. 1 A human being who eats human flesh. 2 An animal that devours members of its own species. [< Sp. *Canibales*, var. of *Caribes* Caribs] —**can′ni·bal·ism** n. —**can′ni·bal·is′tic** adj. —**can′ni·bal·is′ti·cal·ly** adv.

can·ni·bal·ize (kan′ə·bəl·īz′) v.t. **·ized, ·iz·ing** To take parts from (inoperative equipment) to repair other equipment and vehicles. —**can′ni·bal·i·za′tion** n.

can·ni·kin (kan′ə·kin) n. A small can or drinking cup.

can·ning (kan′ing) n. The process or business of preserving food, etc., in sealed cans or jars.

can·non (kan′ən) n. pl. **·nons** or **·non** 1 A large, usu. mounted tubular weapon for discharging a heavy projectile. 2 The large bone between the fetlock and knee of a

horse or related animal: also **cannon bone. 3** *Brit.* CAROM. —v.t. & v.i. 1 To fire or attack with cannon. 2 *Brit.* To carom or cause to carom.

can·non·ade (kan′ən·ād′) v. **·ad·ed, ·ad·ing** v.t. 1 To attack with cannon shot. —v.t. 2 To fire cannon repeatedly. —n. A continued attack with or discharge of cannon.

cannon ball A large spherical shot for firing from a cannon.

can·non·eer (kan′ən·ir′) n. An artillery man.

cannon fodder Soldiers regarded as expendable in warfare.

can·non·ry (kan′ən·rē) n. 1 Artillery. 2 Cannon fire.

can·not (ka′not) v.i. Can not. —**cannot but** Have no alternative except to.

can·ny (kan′ē) adj. **can·ni·er, can·ni·est** 1 Shrewd; astute. 2 Prudent; thrifty. [< CAN (to know how)] —**can′ni·ly** adv. —**can′ni·ness** n. —**Syn.** 1 clever, sharp, smart, wise.

ca·noe (kə·nōō′) n. A light, narrow boat, pointed at both ends and propelled by paddles. —v.t. & v.i. To travel or convey by canoe. [< Sp. *canoa* boat] —**ca·noe′ist** n.

Canoe

can·on[1] (kan′ən) n. 1 A law, rule, or body of rules of a church. 2 An established rule or principle; standard; criterion. 3 Writings, as books of the Bible, considered holy or authoritative by a church, sect, etc. 4 An official list or catalogue. 5 *Often cap.* A portion of the Mass following the Sanctus. 6 *Music* A composition in which each voice or part in turn takes up the melody and all combine in counterpoint. [< Gk. *kanōn* rule, straight rod]

can·on[2] (kan′ən) n. A clergyman belonging to the chapter of a cathedral or collegiate church. [< LL *canon* rule]

cañ·on (kan′yən, *Sp.* kä·nyôn′) n. CANYON.

ca·non·i·cal (kə·non′i·kəl) adj. 1 Of or according to church law. 2 Accepted or approved; authoritative. Also **ca·non′ic.** —**ca·non′i·cal·ly** adv.

canonical hours The seven daily periods fixed by church rule for prayer and devotion.

ca·non·i·cals (kə·non′i·kəlz) n. pl. Garments prescribed by canon for wear by officiating members of the clergy.

can·on·ize (kan′ən·īz′) v.t. **·ized, ·iz·ing** 1 To declare (a dead person) to be a saint by official church ruling. 2 To glorify. 3 To make or regard as canonical or authoritative. —**can′on·i·za′tion** n.

canon law The body of ecclesiastical laws governing a Christian church.

can·on·ry (kan′ən·rē) n. pl. **·ries** The office or benefice of a canon. Also **can′on·ship.**

Ca·no·pus (kə·nō′pəs) n. A very bright star in the southern sky. [L]

can·o·py (kan′ə·pē) n. pl. **·pies** 1 A covering or shelter suspended or supported over a throne, bed, entrance, etc. 2 Any similar overhead covering. —v.t. **·pied, ·py·ing** To cover with or as with a canopy. [< Gk. *kōnōpeion* bed with mosquito net < *kōnōps* mosquito]

Canopy

canst (kanst) *Archaic* Second person singular present tense of CAN[1]: used with *thou.*

cant[1] (kant) n. 1 A slant, slope, or tilt. 2 A motion that tilts or tips. 3 A slanted surface. —v.t. & v.i. 1 To slant or tilt. 2 To move or cause to move with a sudden, swerving motion. [< L *cantus,* rim of a wheel]

cant[2] (kant) n. 1 Hypocritically pious talk. 2 Any specialized or esoteric jargon or vocabulary: thieves' *cant;* legal *cant.* 3 Whining speech, as of beggars. —v.i. To use or speak in cant. [< L *cantus* song] —**cant′er** n.

can't (kant, känt) Contraction of *cannot.*

Cantab. of Cambridge (Univ.) (L *Cantabrigiensis*).

can·ta·bi·le (kän·tä′bē·lā) *Music* adj. & adv. In a flowing, songlike style. —n. A composition or passage in this style. [Ital.]

can·ta·loupe (kan′tə·lōp′) n. A variety of muskmelon with a hard, rough rind and orange flesh. Also **can′ta·loup.** [< *Cantalupo,* a villa near Rome]

can·tank·er·ous (kan-tang′kər-əs) *adj.* Bad-tempered; quarrelsome. [ME *contak* strife] —**can·tank′er·ous·ly** *adv.* —**can·tank′er·ous·ness** *n.* —**Syn.** irritable, irascible, snappish, testy, cranky.

can·ta·ta (kən-tä′tə) *n.* A vocal composition in several movements. [Ital. < *cantare* to sing]

can·teen (kan-tēn′) *n.* 1 A usu. metal flask for carrying drinking water, etc. 2 A shop at a military base where soldiers buy provisions, refreshments, etc. 3 A cafeteria, recreation center, etc., usu. operated by an institution. [< Ital. *cantina* cellar]

can·ter (kan′tər) *n.* A moderate, easy gallop. —*v.t. & v.i.* To ride or go at a canter. [Short for *Canterbury gallop*; with ref. to the pace of pilgrims riding to Canterbury]

Can·ter·bur·y bells (kan′tər-ber′ē) A garden plant having bell-shaped usu. blue flowers.

cant hook A pole with a hinged hook, used for handling logs.

can·ti·cle (kan′ti-kəl) *n.* A chant or hymn, esp. one with words taken directly from the Bible. [< L *cantus* song]

can·ti·lev·er (kan′tə-lev′ər) *n.* 1 A projecting structural member supported at only one end. 2 A similar arrangement consisting of a projecting part supported only at its point of balance. —*v.t.* To build or design (a structural part) to extend as a cantilever. [?]

cantilever bridge A bridge formed by two counterbalanced projecting parts each supported at one end.

can·tle (kan′təl) *n.* The upward-curving rear part of a saddle. [< LL *cantus* corner]

can·to (kan′tō) *n. pl.* **·tos** A division of an extended poem. [< L *cantus* song]

can·ton (kan′tən, -ton, kan-ton′) *n.* A political division of Switzerland. —*v.t.* 1 To divide into cantons. 2 To assign to quarters, as military troops. [< LL *cantus* corner] —**can·ton·al** (kan′tən-əl) *adj.*

Can·ton·ese (kan′tən-ēz′, -ēs′) *n. pl.* **·ese** 1 A native of Canton, China. 2 The Chinese language spoken in and around Canton. —*adj.* Of Canton.

can·ton·ment (kan-ton′mənt, -tōn′-) *n.* 1 A group of buildings used as temporary housing for troops. 2 The assignment or troops to such housing.

can·tor (kan′tər, -tôr) *n.* 1 A liturgical singer serving as soloist and leader of prayer in a synagogue. 2 A leader of church choral music. [< L]

Ca·nuck (kə-nuk′) *n. Slang* 1 A Canadian. 2 FRENCH CANADIAN. *Sometimes disparaging.*

can·vas (kan′vəs) *n.* 1 Strong, close-woven cloth of cotton, flax, or hemp, used for sails, tents, etc. 2 A piece of such cloth used for a painting. 3 A painting on such cloth. 4 A sail or sails. —**under canvas** 1 With sails set. 2 In tents. [< L *cannabis* hemp]

can·vas·back (kan′vəs-bak′) *n.* A North American wild duck with a grayish white back.

can·vass (kan′vəs) *v.t.* 1 To go about (an area) or to (persons) to solicit opinions, votes, orders, etc. 2 To examine or discuss thoroughly. —*v.i.* 3 To go about seeking votes, information, etc. —*n.* 1 A survey, poll, etc., as to ascertain opinion or solicit votes. 2 A detailed examination or discussion. [< CANVAS] —**can′vass·er** *n.*

can·yon (kan′yən) *n.* A deep gorge or narrow valley with high, steep sides. [< Sp. *cañón*]

caout·chouc (kou·chook′, koo′chook) *n.* Rubber; esp. crude rubber. [F]

cap (kap) *n.* 1 A close-fitting head covering, usu. with a visor or brimless. 2 A distinctive head covering denoting status, occupation, etc. 3 A cover, top part, etc., resembling or suggestive of a cap. 4 A metal case, small paper container, etc., enclosing an explosive. —**set one's cap for** To try to win as a suitor or husband. —*v.t.* **capped, cap·ping** 1 To put a cap or cover on. 2 To cover as with a cap; top. 3 To add the final touch to. 4 To surpass. [< LL *cappa* hooded cloak, cap]

cap. (*pl.* **caps.**) capacity; capital; capitalize.

ca·pa·bil·i·ty (kā′pə·bil′ə·tē) *n. pl.* **·ties** 1 The quality of being capable; ability. 2 *Often pl.* A feature, quality, etc., that may be used or developed; potential.

ca·pa·ble (kā′pə-bəl) *adj.* Having suitable ability; competent. —**capable of** 1 Having the required ability or capacity for. 2 Open to; susceptible of. [< LL *capabilis* < L *capere* take, receive] —**ca′pa·ble·ness** *n.* —**ca′pa·bly** *adv.*

ca·pa·cious (kə·pā′shəs) *adj.* Able to contain or receive much. [< L *capax* able to hold, roomy < *capere* take] —**ca·pa′cious·ly** *adv.* —**ca·pa′cious·ness** *n.* —**Syn.** ample, roomy, commodious, spacious.

ca·pac·i·tance (kə·pas′ə·təns) *n.* The ratio of electrical charge on a system of conductors to the resulting potential. [< CAPACI(TY) + (REAC)TANCE] —**ca·pac′i·tive** *adj.*

ca·pac·i·tate (kə·pas′ə·tāt) *v.t.* **·tat·ed, ·tat·ing** To render capable or qualified.

ca·pac·i·ty (kə·pas′ə·tē) *n. pl.* **·ties** 1 Ability to receive or contain. 2 A measure of the ability to receive or contain; volume. 3 Maximum ability to contain, perform, etc. 4 Ability to do something; power. 5 Specific position, role, etc. 6 Legal qualification. 7 *Electr.* **a** CAPACITANCE. **b** The maximum output of an electric generator. [< L *capax* able to hold]

cap-a-pie (kap′ə-pē′) *adv.* From head to foot. Also **cap′-à-pie′**. [< OF]

ca·par·i·son (kə·par′ə·sən) *n.* 1 A decorative covering for a horse. 2 Showy or sumptuous apparel. —*v.t.* 1 To put ornamental trappings on. 2 To clothe richly. [< OF *caparasson* < Sp. *caparazón* < LL *cappa* cape]

cape[1] (kāp) *n.* A point of land extending into the sea or other body of water. [< L *caput* head]

cape[2] (kāp) *n.* A sleeveless outer garment falling loosely over the shoulders. [< LL *cappa*]

cap·e·lin (kap′ə-lin) *n. pl.* **·lin** or **·lins** A small, edible, smeltlike fish of northern seas. [< F *capelan*]

ca·per[1] (kā′pər) *v.i.* To leap or skip playfully; frisk. —*n.* 1 A playful skip or jump. 2 A prank; antic. —**cut a caper** (or **capers**) To caper; frolic. [Short for CAPRIOLE] —**ca′per·er** *n.* —**Syn.** *v.* gambol, frolic, prance, cavort.

ca·per[2] (kā′pər) *n.* 1 The flower bud of a Mediterranean shrub, pickled and used as a condiment. 2 The shrub. [< Gk. *kapparis*]

cape·skin (kāp′skin′) *n.* Leather made from sheepskins, used esp. for gloves. [< *Cape* of Good Hope]

ca·pi·as (kā′pē·əs, kap′ē·əs) *n. Law* A judicial writ ordering an arrest by an officer. [< L, you may take]

cap·il·lar·i·ty (kap′ə·lar′ə·tē) *n.* 1 The state or quality of being capillary. 2 *Physics* The interaction between adjoining surfaces of a liquid and a solid that constrains it.

cap·il·lar·y (kap′ə·ler′ē) *n. pl.* **·lar·ies** 1 Any of the microscopic blood vessels connecting the arterial and venous systems. 2 Any tube with a fine, hairlike bore. —*adj.* 1 Of or resembling a hair; fine; slender. 2 Having a slender, hairlike opening, as a tube or vessel. 3 Of capillarity. [< L *capillus* hair]

cap·i·tal[1] (kap′ə·təl) *n.* 1 A city that is the seat of government of a country, state, etc. 2 CAPITAL LETTER. 3 Wealth or property assets available for producing more wealth, as through investment. 4 The assets of a business after deduction of liabilities. 5 Capitalists or wealthy people as a class. 6 A quality, resource, etc., that can be used to advantage. —*adj.* 1 Chief; principal; foremost. 2 Serving as the seat of government. 3 Excellent; first-rate. 4 Of or pertaining to financial capital. 5 Involving or punishable by the death penalty. [< MF < L *caput* head]

cap·i·tal[2] (kap′ə·təl) *n.* The top part of a column or pillar. [< L *caput* head]

capital gain Profit from the sale of capital investments, such as stocks, real estate, etc.

cap·i·tal·ism (kap′ə·təl·iz′əm) *n.* 1 An economic system in which the means of production and distribution are privately owned and operated for private profit. 2 The principles, power, results, etc., of this system.

Capitals. a. Doric. b. Ionic. c. Corinthian.

cap·i·tal·ist (kap′ə·təl·ist) n. 1 An owner of capital, esp. one with considerable wealth invested in business. 2 A supporter of capitalism. 3 Loosely, any very wealthy person. —**cap′i·tal·is′tic** adj. —**cap′i·tal·is′ti·cal·ly** adv.

cap·i·tal·ize (kap′ə·təl·īz) v.t. ·**ized**, ·**iz·ing** 1 To begin with a capital letter, or write or print in capital letters. 2 To convert into capital or cash. 3 To invest for profit; use to provide capital. 4 To organize on a basis of capital. 5 To profit by: used with on. —**cap′i·tal·i·za′tion** n.

capital letter A letter, as A, B, or Z, printed or written larger than and often in different form from that of the corresponding small letter.

cap·i·tal·ly (kap′ə·təl·ē) adv. Excellently; very well.

capital punishment The death penalty for a crime.

capital ship A large warship, as an aircraft carrier.

capital stock The amount of negotiable shares of stock owned by an individual or a corporation.

cap·i·ta·tion (kap′ə·tā′shən) n. An individual assessment or tax; a poll tax. [< LL capitatio poll tax < L caput head]

cap·i·tol (kap′ə·təl) n. The building in which a State legislature convenes.

Cap·i·tol (kap′ə·təl) n. 1 The official building of the U.S. Congress in Washington. 2 The temple of Jupiter in ancient Rome. [< L Capitolium]

Capitol Hill 1 The site of the Capitol in Washington, D.C. 2 The U.S. Congress. —**on Capitol Hill** or **on the Hill** In the U.S. Congress.

ca·pit·u·late (kə·pich′ōō·lāt) v.i. ·**lat·ed**, ·**lat·ing** 1 To surrender on stipulated conditions. 2 To give in; yield. [< L capitulare draw up in chapters, arrange terms] —**ca·pit′· u·la′tor** n. —**ca·pit′u·la·to′ry** adj.

ca·pit·u·la·tion (kə·pich′ōō·lā′shən) n. 1 The act of capitulating; surrender. 2 A statement of the terms of surrender. 3 A summary or outline of main points.

ca·pon (kā′pon, -pən) n. A rooster castrated and raised for eating. [< OE < L capo, -onis]

ca·pote (kə·pōt′) n. 1 A hooded coat or cloak. 2 A bonnet. [F cape cape, hood]

ca·pric·ci·o (kə·prē′chē·ō, Ital. kä·prēt′chō) n. pl. ·**ci·os** or Ital. **ca·pric·ci** (kä·prēt′chē) 1 A lively musical composition of irregular form. 2 A prank or whim. [Ital., caprice]

ca·price (kə·prēs′) n. 1 A sudden, unreasonable impulse or change of mind; a whim. 2 A tendency to such acts or impulses. 3 Music CAPRICCIO. [< Ital. capriccio]

ca·pri·cious (kə·prish′əs) adj. 1 Characterized by or resulting from caprice. 2 Liable to sudden changes or impulses; fickle. —**ca·pri′cious·ly** adv. —**ca·pri′cious·ness** n.

Cap·ri·corn (kap′rə·kôrn) n. A constellation and the tenth sign of the zodiac; the Goat. [< L caper goat + cornu horn] • See TROPIC and ZODIAC.

cap·ri·ole (kap′rē·ōl) n. An upward leap in place with feet off the ground, made by a trained horse. —v.i. ·**oled**, ·**ol·ing** To do a capriole. [< Ital. capriola leap of a goat]

cap·si·cum (kap′si·kəm) n. 1 Any of various plants of the nightshade family producing many-seeded pods from which red pepper is obtained. 2 The fruit of these plants. [< L capsa box (from the shape of the fruit)]

cap·size (kap′sīz, kap·sīz′) v.t. & v.i. ·**sized**, ·**siz·ing** To upset or overturn. [?]

cap·stan (kap′stən) n. A drumlike apparatus for hoisting anchors, etc., by exerting traction upon a cable. [< L capistrum halter < capere to hold]

capstan bar A lever used in turning a capstan.

cap·stone (kap′stōn′) n. COPESTONE.

cap·sule (kap′səl, -syōōl) n. 1 A small gelatinous case for containing a dose of a drug. 2 Bot. A dry seed vessel or spore case, esp. one that splits open when ripe. 3 A membrane enclosing an organ or structure. 4 The cargo or passenger container of a space vehicle. [< L capsula, dim. of capsa box] —**cap′su·lar** adj.

Capt. Captain.

cap·tain (kap′tən, -tin) n. 1 One at the head of or in command; chief; leader. 2 The master or commander of a vessel. 3 See GRADE. —v.t. To be captain of; command; [< LL capitaneus < L caput head] —**cap′tain·cy** (-sē), **cap′tain·ship** n.

cap·tion (kap′shən) n. 1 A heading of a chapter, section, document, etc. 2 The title and explanatory material accompanying an illustration. 3 A subtitle in a motion picture. —v.t. To provide a caption for. [< L captio deception, sophism < capere take]

cap·tious (kap′shəs) adj. 1 Apt to find fault. 2 Intended to confuse or trip up: captious questions. [< L captiosus fallacious] —**cap′tious·ly** adj. —**cap′tious·ness** n. —Syn. 1 critical, carping, caviling.

cap·ti·vate (kap′tə·vāt) v.t. ·**vat·ed**, ·**vat·ing** To charm; fascinate. [< L captivus. See CAPTIVE.] —**cap′ti·vat′ing·ly** adv. —**cap′ti·va′tion**, **cap′ti·va′tor** n.

cap·tive (kap′tiv) n. 1 One captured and held; a prisoner. 2 One who is captivated or enthralled. —adj. 1 Taken or held as a prisoner. 2 Held under constraint or control. 3 Unable to avoid being present or listening: a captive audience. 4 Captivated; enthralled. [< L captivus < capere take]

cap·tiv·i·ty (kap·tiv′ə·tē) n. pl. ·**ties** The state of being held captive.

cap·tor (kap′tər) n. One who takes or holds a captive.

cap·ture (kap′chər) v.t. ·**tured**, ·**tur·ing** 1 To seize and hold, as by force, skill, etc. 2 To win possession of; gain. 3 To succeed in preserving an impression or image of. —n. 1 The act of capturing or of being captured. 2 One who or that which is captured. [< L captura < capere take]

cap·u·chin (kap′yōō·chin, -shin) n. 1 A hooded cloak. 2 A long-tailed South American monkey with a hoodlike growth of hair. [< Ital. cappuccino hooded one]

Cap·u·chin (kap′yōō·chin, -shin) n. A monk of a Franciscan order wearing a habit with a pointed hood.

cap·y·ba·ra (kap′i·bä′rə) n. A large, short-tailed aquatic rodent of South America. [< Tupi]

car (kär) n. 1 An automobile. 2 A wheeled vehicle that moves on rails. 3 An enclosure for passengers, as of an elevator. 4 A chariot. [< L carrus wagon]

ca·ra·ba·o (kä′rə·bä′ō) n. pl. ·**ba·os** WATER BUFFALO. [< Malay karbau]

car·a·bin (kar′ə·bin), **car·a·bine** (-bīn) n. CARBINE.

car·a·bin·eer, **car·a·bin·ier** (kar′ə·bin·ir′) n. CARBINEER.

car·a·cal (kar′ə·kal) n. A wild cat of sw Asia and Africa, having light brown fur and pointed, black-tipped ears. [< Turkish qarah black + qulaq ear]

Caracal

ca·ra·ca·ra (kä′rə·kä′rə) n. A large, vulturelike hawk of South America. [< Tupian]

car·a·cole (kar′ə·kōl) n. A sudden half turn to the right or left made by a horse and rider. —v.i. ·**coled**, ·**col·ing** To make a caracole or caracoles. [< Ital. caracollo]

car·a·cul (kar′ə·kəl) n. KARAKUL.

ca·rafe (kə·raf′, -räf′) n. A glass bottle for serving water, wine, etc. [< Ar. gharafa draw water]

car·a·mel (kar′ə·məl, -mel, kär′məl) n. 1 A chewy candy made with butter, sugar, etc. 2 A brown syrup made by heating sugar, used to flavor and color foods. [Prob. < L calamus reed]

car·a·pace (kar′ə·pās) n. The hard, horny shield on the back of a turtle, lobster, etc. [< Sp. carapacho]

car·at (kar′ət) n. 1 A unit of weight for gems, equal to 200 milligrams, or 3.086 grains. 2 Loosely, a karat. [< Ar. qī·rāt weight of 4 grains < Gk. keration seed, small weight]

car·a·van (kar′ə·van) n. 1 A company of people traveling together, as across a desert. 2 A group of vehicles traveling together. 3 VAN¹ (def. 1). 4 Brit. TRAILER (def. 3). [< Pers. kārwān caravan]

car·a·van·sa·ry (kar′ə·van′sə·rē) n. pl. ·**ries** A hostelry or inn. [< Pers. kārwān caravan + sarāī inn]

car·a·vel (kar′ə·vel) n. A fleet vessel of Spain and Portugal in the 15th and 16th centuries. [< Gk. korabus light ship]

car·a·way (kar′ə·wā) n. 1 A biennial herb related to parsley. 2 Its small aromatic seeds (**caraway seeds**) used for flavoring. [< Sp. *alcarahueya* < Arabic *al* the + *karwīyā* caraway < Gk. *karon*]

car·bide (kär′bid, -bid) *n.* A compound of carbon with a metal or other element.

car·bine (kär′bīn, -bēn) *n.* 1 A light short-barreled rifle originally devised for mounted troops. 2 A magazine-fed, gas-operated .30-caliber rifle used by the U.S. armed forces in World War II. [< F *carabine*] —**car′bi·neer′** *n*

carbo- *combining form* Carbon: *carbohydrate.* Also **carb-**.

car·bo·hy·drate (kär′bō·hī′drāt) *n.* Any of a group of compounds synthesized by plants from carbon dioxide and water, including sugars, starches, and cellulose.

car·bol·ic acid (kär·bol′ik) A poisonous, caustic organic compound with a distinctive odor, derived from coal tar and used as a disinfectant. [< CARB- + L *oleum* oil]

car·bon (kär′bən) *n.* 1 A nonmetallic element (symbol C) that occurs in three allotropic forms and as a constituent of all organisms and in many inorganic minerals and in atmospheric gases. 2 *Electr.* A rod of carbon, used as an electrode in an arc light. 3 A piece of carbon paper. 4 CARBON COPY. —*adj.* 1 Of, pertaining to, or like carbon. 2 Treated with carbon. [< L *carbo* coal]

car·bo·na·ceous (kär′bə·nā′shəs) *adj.* Of, pertaining to, or yielding carbon.

car·bon·ate (kär′bə·nāt) *v.t.* **-at·ed**, **-at·ing** 1 To charge with carbonic acid. 2 CARBONIZE. —*n.* (kär′bə·nāt, -nit) A salt or ester of carbonic acid. —**car′bo·na′tion** *n.*

carbon copy 1 A copy of a typewritten letter, etc., made by means of carbon paper. 2 Someone or something closely resembling another.

carbon dating The assignment of approximate age to fossils by measuring the residual radioactivity of the carbon 14 incorporated in a specimen during its lifetime.

carbon dioxide A heavy, colorless, nonflammable gas, comprising about 0.04 percent of the atmosphere, utilized by plants in photosynthesis of carbohydrates, and released by respiration of plants and animals.

carbon 14 A radioactive isotope of carbon, having a half-life of 5,700 years.

car·bon·ic (kär·bon′ik) *adj.* Of, pertaining to, or obtained from carbon.

carbonic acid A weak, unstable acid, existing only in solution and readily dissociating into water and carbon dioxide.

car·bon·ic-ac·id gas (kär·bon′ik·as′id) CARBON DIOXIDE.

car·bon·if·er·ous (kär′bə·nif′ər·əs) *adj.* Of, pertaining to, containing, or yielding carbon or coal.

Car·bon·if·er·ous (kär′bə·nif′ər·əs) *adj. & n.* See GEOLOGY.

car·bon·ize (kär′bən·īz) *v.t.* **-ized**, **-iz·ing** 1 To reduce to carbon; char. 2 To coat with carbon, as paper. 3 To combine with carbon. —**car′bon·i·za′tion** *n.*

carbon monoxide A colorless, odorless, poisonous gas, formed by the incomplete oxidation of carbon.

carbon paper A tissuelike paper coated on one side with carbon or other material for transferring impressions made, as by a typewriter, from a sheet placed over it to another facing the carbon, etc.

carbon tetrachloride A colorless, nonflammable, volatile, poisonous liquid.

Car·bo·run·dum (kär′bə·run′dəm) *n.* An abrasive of silicon carbide: a trade name.

car·boy (kär′boi) *n.* A large glass bottle enclosed in a crate or in wickerwork, used as a container for corrosive acids, etc. [< Pers. *qarāba* demijohn]

car·bun·cle (kär′bung·kəl) *n.* 1 A skin eruption resembling a boil but larger and more painful. 2 A garnet or other red gemstone cut without facets. [< L *carbunculus,* dim. of *carbo* coal] —**car·bun·cu·lar** (kär·bung′kyə·lər) *adj.*

car·bu·re·tor (kär′byə·rā′tər) *n.* A device for mixing a liquid fuel with air to form an explosive mixture, as in internal-combustion engines, *Brit. sp.* **car·bu·ret·tor** (kär′·byə·ret′ər).

car·ca·jou (kär′kə-jōō, -zhōō) *n.* WOLVERINE. [< native Algon. name]

car·cass (kär′kəs) *n.* 1 The dead body of an animal. 2 The human body: a contemptuous use. 3 Something lifeless or worthless. 4 A framework or skeleton, Also **car′case**. [< MF *carcasse* a corpse]

car·cin·o·gen (kär′sin′ə·jen) *n.* A cancer-producing substance. —**car′cin·o·gen′ic** *adj.*

car·ci·no·ma (kär′sə·nō′mə) *n. pl.* **-ma·ta** (-mə·tə) or **-mas** A malignant tumor; cancer. [< Gk. *karkinos* cancer] —**car′ci·nom′a·tous** (-nom′ə·təs, -nōm′ə-) *adj.*

card[1] (kärd) *n.* 1 A usu. small and rectangular piece of stiff paper or cardboard. 2 One of a pack of playing cards. 3 *pl.* Any of various games played with cards. 4 CALLING CARD. 5 GREETING CARD. 6 POSTAL CARD. 7 A card used for identification, supplying information, etc.: a library *card.* 8 A program of events: a boxing *card.* 9 *Informal* A witty or humorous person. —*v.t.* 1 To put or list on a card or cards. 2 To provide with a card. [< F *carte* < Ital. *carta* card, sheet of paper < L *charta* paper < Gk. *chartēs*]

card[2] (kärd) *n.* 1 A wire-toothed brush for combing and cleansing fibers, as wool. 2 A similar instrument for currying cattle and horses. —*v.t.* To comb, dress, or cleanse with a card. [< MF *carde* < Ital. *carda* < Med. L *cardus* < L *carduus* thistle] —**card′er** *n.*

car·da·mom (kär′də·məm) *n.* 1 An Asian plant related to ginger. 2 Its aromatic seeds, used as a flavoring. Also, **car′da·mon** (-mən), **car′da·mum**. [< Gk. *kardamon* cress + *amōmon* spice]

card·board (kärd′bôrd′, -bōrd′) *n.* A thin, stiff pasteboard used for making cards, boxes, etc.

car·di·ac (kär′dē·ak) *adj.* 1 Of or pertaining to the heart. 2 Of or designating the upper part of the stomach. —*n.* 1 One suffering from a heart disease. 2 A cardiac stimulant. [< Gk. *kardia* heart]

car·di·gan (kär′də·gən) *n.* A knitted sweater opening down the front. [< the seventh Earl of *Cardigan*, 1797–1868]

car·di·nal (kär′də·nəl) *adj.* 1 Of prime importance. 2 Of a deep scarlet color. —*n.* 1 In the Roman Catholic Church, a member of the Sacred College whose members elect and advise the Pope. 2 A North American, bright red, crested finch. 3 A deep scarlet. 4 CARDINAL NUMBER. [< L *cardinalis* important < *cardo* hinge] —**car′di·nal·ly** *adv.*

Cardinal

car·di·nal·ate (kär′də·nəl·āt′) *n.* The rank, diginity, or term of office of a cardinal.

cardinal flower A perennial North American lobelia having scarlet flowers.

cardinal number A number, esp. an integer, indicating how many (as ten, 48, etc.).

cardinal point Any one of the four principal points of the compass, north, south, east, or west.

card·ing (kär′ding) *n.* The combing of wool, flax, or cotton fibers before spinning.

cardio- *combining form* Heart: *cardiogram.* Also **cardi-**. [< Gk. *kardia* heart]

car·di·o·gram (kär′dē·ə·gram′) *n.* The record produced by a cardiograph.

car·di·o·graph (kär′dē·ə·graf′, -gräf′) *n.* An instrument for recording the activity of the heart. —**car′di·o·graph′ic** *adj.* —**car·di·og·ra·phy** (kär′dē·og′rə·fē) *n.*

car·di·o·pul·mo·nar·y (kär′dē·ō·pŏŏl′mə·ner′ē) *adj.* Pertaining to or affecting the heart and lungs.

card·sharp (kärd′shärp′) *n.* One who cheats at cards, esp. as a profession.

care (kâr) *v.i.* **cared, car·ing** 1 To have or show regard, interest or concern. 2 To mind or be concerned. —*v.t.* 3 To want; desire: used with an infinitive: Do you *care* to go? 4 To be interested in or concerned about: I don't *care* what he said. —**care for** 1 To protect or provide for; watch over. 2 To feel love or affection for. 3 To want; desire. 4 To be interested in: to *care* for music. —*n.* 1 Anxiety, concern, or worry. **2** A cause of anxiety or worry. **3** Watchful attention or regard; heed. **4** Charge; custody. **5** An object of solicitude or guardianship. [< OE *carian*] —**car'er** *n.* — **Syn.** *n.* **1** solicitude. **3** precaution, forethought, vigilance, watchfulness, prudence.

CARE Cooperative for American Relief Everywhere.

ca·reen (kə-rēn') *v.i.* **1** To lurch or twist from side to side. **2** To lean sideways. —*v.t.* **3** To cause (a ship) to turn over to one side, as for repairing. **4** To clean, repair, or calk (a careened ship). **5** To tilt; tip. —*n.* A careening. [< L *carina* keel of a ship]

ca·reer (kə-rir') *n.* **1** One's lifework or employment. **2** The course or progress of one's life or lifework. **3** A swift course or run. —*adj.* Pursuing the (stated) occupation as a lifework: a *career* diplomat. **2** To move with a swift, free, and headlong motion. [< LL *carraria (via)* road for carriages] —**ca·reer'er** *n.*

ca·reer·ist (kə-rir'ist) *n.* A person chiefly or excessively concerned with advancing himself professionally. —**ca·reer'ism** *n.*

care·free (kâr'frē') *adj.* Free of troubles or responsibilities; light-hearted.

care·ful (kâr'fəl) *adj.* **1** Exercising, marked by, or done with care and attention. **2** Prudent; circumspect. —**care'·ful·ly** *adv.* —**care'ful·ness** *n.* —**Syn.** **1** heedful, thoughtful, painstaking, particular. **2** guarded, cautious, alert.

care·less (kâr'lis) *adj.* **1** Not attentive or careful. **2** Done without attention, precision, etc. **3** Indifferent; unconcerned: *careless* about his appearance. **4** Not studied or constrained; easy: a *careless* attitude. **5** Free from worry or anxiety. —**care'less·ly** *adv.* —**care'less·ness** *n.*

ca·ress (kə-res') *n.* An expression of affection by patting, embracing, or stroking. —*v.t.* To touch or handle lovingly. [< L *carus* dear] —**ca·ress'er** *n.* —**ca·ress'ive** *adj.* —**Syn.** *v.* fondle, embrace, pet, cuddle.

car·et (kar'ət) *n.* A sign (∧) placed below a line to denote an omission. [< L, it is missing]

care·tak·er (kâr'tā'kər) *n.* One who takes care of a place, thing, or person.

care·worn (kâr'wôrn') *adj.* Harassed with troubles or worries.

car·fare (kär'fâr') *n.* The charge for a ride on a bus, subway train, etc.

car·go (kär'gō) *n. pl.* **·goes** or **·gos** Goods and merchandise taken on board a vessel, aircraft, etc. [< LL *carricum* load]

car·hop (kär'hop') *n. Informal* A waiter or waitress at a drive-in restaurant.

Car·ib (kar'ib) *n.* One of an Indian people of N South America and the Lesser Antilles. —*adj.* Of or pertaining to the Caribs.

Car·ib·an (kar'ə-bən) *n.* The language family comprising the languages of the Caribs. —*adj.* Of or pertaining to Cariban.

Car·ib·be·an (kar'ə-bē'ən, kə-rib'ē-ən) *n.* The Caribbean Sea and the islands in it. —*adj.* Of, in, or pertaining to the Caribbean Sea or its islands.

Caribbean Sea An arm of the Atlantic between the West Indies and Central and South America.

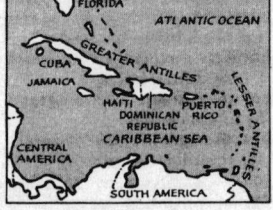

Caribbean Sea

car·i·bou (kar'ə·bōō) *n.* Any of several large North American deer having antlers projecting forward in both sexes. [< Algon.]

car·i·ca·ture (kar'i·kə·chŏŏr, -chər) *n.* **1** A picture or description using gross exaggeration or distortion, as for humorous effect or in ridicule. **2** The act or art of caricaturing. **3** A poor imitation. —*v.t.* **·tured, ·tur·ing** To represent so as to make ridiculous; travesty. [< Ital. *caricatura*, lit., an overloading] —**car'i·ca·tur'al** *adj.* —**car'i·ca·tur'ist** *n.*

car·ies (kâr'ēz, -i·ēz) *n.* Decay of a bone or tooth. [< L]

car·il·lon (kar'ə·lon) *n.* **1** A set of bells sounding the tones of the chromatic scale, now usu. played by a keyboard. **2** A tune played on such bells. —*v.i.* **·lonned, ·lon·ning** To play a carillon. [< Med. L *quadrilio* set of four bells]

car·il·lon·neur (kar'ə·lə·nûr') *n.* One who plays a carillon. [F]

car·i·ole (kar'ē·ōl) *n.* A small carriage. [< F < Ital. *carra* wagon]

car·i·ous (kâr'ē·əs) *adj.* Affected with caries; decayed. Also **ca·ri·ose** (-ēd). —**car'i·os'i·ty** (-os'ə·tē), **car'i·ous·ness** *n.*

car·load (kär'lōd') *n.* The amount a car can carry or is carrying.

Car·mel·ite (kär'məl·īt) *n.* A member of the religious order of Our Lady of Mt. Carmel.

car·min·a·tive (kär·min'ə·tiv, kär'mə·nā'tiv) *adj.* Tending to relieve flatulence. —*n.* A remedy for flatulence. [< L *carminare* cleanse]

car·mine (kär'min, -mīn) *n.* A rich purplish red pigment prepared mainly from cochineal. —*adj.* Having the color of carmine. [< Med. L *carminium*]

car·nage (kär'nij) *n.* Extensive and bloody slaughter; massacre. [< L *caro* flesh, meat]

car·nal (kär'nəl) *adj.* **1** Pertaining to bodily appetites; not spiritual. **2** Sensual; sexual. [< L *caro, carnis* flesh] —**car'·nal·ist, car·nal·i·ty** (kär·nal'ə·tē) *n.* —**car'nal·ly** *adv.*

car·na·tion (kär·nā'shən) *n.* **1** Any of many cultivated varieties of plants related to the pink, having fragrant, usu. double, flowers. **2** A light pink, bright rose, or scarlet color. [< L *carnatio* fleshiness < *caro* flesh]

car·nel·ian (kär·nēl'yən) *n.* A clear red chalcedony, often cut as a gem. [< MF *corneline*]

car·ni·val (kär'nə·vəl) *n.* **1** A period of festival and gaiety immediately preceding Lent. **2** Any gay festival, esp. one featuring sports contests or other amusements. **3** A traveling amusement show. [< Ital. *carnivale*, lit., the putting away of flesh]

car·ni·vore (kär'nə·vôr, -vōr) *n.* **1** A flesh-eating mammal. **2** An insectivorous plant.

car·niv·o·rous (kär·niv'ə·rəs) *adj.* Eating or living on flesh. [< L *caro* flesh + *vorare* eat, devour] —**car·niv'o·rous·ly** *adv.* —**car·niv'o·rous·ness** *n.*

car·ol (kar'əl) *v.* **·oled** or **·olled, ·ol·ing** or **·ol·ling** *v.t.* **1** To sing, as a bird. **2** To celebrate in song. —*v.i.* **3** To sing, esp. in a joyous strain. —*n.* A song of joy; esp., a Christmas song. [< L *choraules* a flutist] —**car'ol·er, car'ol·ler** *n.*

car·om (kar'əm) *v.t. & v.i.* To make or cause to make a rebounding movement. —*n.* In billiards, the impact of one ball against two others in succession. [< Sp. *carambola* a kind of fruit]

car·o·tene (kar'ə·tēn) *n.* A deep yellow plant pigment that is changed in the body to vitamin A. Also **car'o·tin** (-tin). [< L *carota* carrot]

ca·rot·id (kə·rot'id) *adj.* Of, pertaining to, or near one of the two major arteries on each side of the neck. Also **ca·rot'i·dal.** [< Gk. *karoein* stupefy; so called because pressure on them can cause unconsciousness]

ca·rou·sal (kə·rou'zəl) *n.* A boisterous or drunken party.

ca·rouse (kə·rouz') *v.i.* **ca·roused, ca·rous·ing** To drink heavily and boisterously with others. —*n.* CAROUSAL. [< G *gar aus (trinken)* (drink) all out] —**ca·rous'er** *n.*

car·ou·sel (kar'ə·sel', -zel') *n.* MERRY-GO-ROUND (def. 1). [< F *carrousel* < Ital. *carosello* tournament]

carp[1] (kärp) *v.i.* To nag or find fault excessively. [< ON *karpa* boast] —**carp'er** *n.*

carp[2] (kärp) *n. pl.* **carp** or **carps** **1** Any of a group of related freshwater food fish. **2** Any of various similar fishes, as minnows and goldfish. [< LL *carpa*]

-carp *combining form* Fruit; fruit (or seed) vessel: *pericarp.* [< Gk. *karpos* fruit]

car·pal (kär'pəl) *adj.* Of, to, or near the wrist. —*n.* A wrist bone. [< L *carpus* wrist]

Carp *def. 1*

car·pel (kär'pəl) *n.* A simple pistil or one member of a compound pistil. [< Gk. *karpos* fruit] —**car·pel·lar·y** (kär'pə·ler'ē) *adj.*

car·pen·ter (kär'pən·tər) *n.* One who builds or repairs houses, ships, etc., with timber or wood. —*v.t.* **1** To make by carpentry. —*v.i.* **2** To work with wood. [< LL *carpentarius* carpenter, wagon-maker] —**car'pen·try** (-trē) *n.*

car·pet (kär′pit) n. 1 A heavy, usu. ornamental fabric for covering a floor. 2 Any smooth surface upon which one may walk. —v.t. To cover with or as with a carpet. [< LL carpita thick woolen covering < L carpere pluck]

car·pet·bag (kär′pit·bag′) n. A suitcase of carpeting.

car·pet·bag·ger (kär′pit·bag′ər) n. Any of the Northern political or profit-seeking adventurers in the South after the Civil War.

carpet beetle A beetle whose larvae feed on fur and woolen fabrics. • See BEETLE.

car·pet·ing (kär′pit·ing) n. 1 Fabric used for carpets. 2 Carpets collectively.

carpet sweeper A hand-operated apparatus for sweeping carpets.

carp·ing (kär′ping) adj. Apt to find fault or criticize without sufficient cause. —carp′ing·ly adv.

car·port (kär′pôrt′, -pōrt′) n. A roof projecting from the side of a building, used as a shelter for motor vehicles.

car·pus (kär′pəs) n. pl. ·pi (-pī) The wrist. [< Gk. karpos wrist]

car·riage (kar′ij) n. 1 A wheeled, usu. horse-drawn vehicle for carrying persons. 2 BABY CARRIAGE. 3 A wheeled or moving mechanical part for supporting or carrying something. 4 One's physical posture; bearing. 5 The act or cost of transporting something. [< AF carier to carry]

car·ri·er (kar′ē·ər) n. 1 One who or that which carries something, as a mailman, bus, airplane, etc. 2 A device, mechanical part, conduit, etc., in or on which something is carried. 3 AIRCRAFT CARRIER. 4 A person or animal who is immune to a disease but transmits it to others. 5 Telecom. A flow of energy that changes in some way with time, so as to carry information.

carrier pigeon HOMING PIGEON.

car·ri·ole (kar′ē·ōl) n. CARIOLE. [F]

car·ri·on (kar′ē·ən) n. Dead and putrefying flesh. —adj. 1 Feeding on carrion. 2 Like or pertaining to carrion; putrefying. [< L caro flesh]

car·rom (kar′əm) n. CAROM.

car·rot (kar′ət) n. 1 A widely cultivated plant related to parsley. 2 Its reddish yellow edible root. [< L carota < Gk. karōton]

car·rot·y (kar′ət·ē) adj. 1 Like a carrot, esp in color. 2 Having red hair.

car·rou·sel (kar′ə·sel′, -zel′) n. MERRY-GO-ROUND (def. 1). [F]

car·ry (kar′ē) v. ·ried, ·ry·ing v.t. 1 To bear from one place to another; transport; convey. 2 To have or bear upon or about one's person or in one's mind. 3 To serve as a means of conveyance or transportation: The wind carries sounds. 4 To lead; urge; move; influence: Love for art carried him abroad. 5 To have or bear as a feature, quality, consequence, etc. 6 To bear up; hold in position. 7 To conduct (oneself) or move or hold (oneself) in a specified manner. 8 To transfer, as a number or figure, to the column of next highest order, as in adding. 9 To keep on the account books. 10 To have or keep on hand: We carry a full stock. 11 To have as part of its program, contents, etc.: This radio station does not carry the news. 12 To win, as an election; also, to win the majority of votes in (a state, city, etc.). 13 To win the support of (a group, audience, etc.). 14 To gain the acceptance or adoption of (a cause, law, etc.). 15 To support or sustain, esp. financially. 16 To be pregnant with. 17 To extend or continue: to carry a joke too far. 18 Music To sing or play (a melody or part). —v.i. 19 To act as bearer or carrier. 20 To have a specified range, propelling power, etc.: The sound carried nearly a mile. 21 To gain acceptance or adoption. —carry off 1 To cause to die. 2 To win, as a prize or honor. 3 To face or handle (an embarrassment, etc.) well. —carry on 1 To keep going; continue. 2 To behave in a free, frolicsome manner. 3 To continue, as a tradition. —carry out To accomplish; bring to completion. —carry through 1 To carry to completion or success. 2 To sustain or support to the end. —n. pl. ·ries 1 The act or manner of carrying. 2 A portage, as between navigable steams. 3 The range of, or the distance covered by, a gun, projectile, golf ball, etc. [< LL carricare

L carrus cart] —Syn. v. 1 move, transfer, haul, ship. 4 impel. 5 show, display, harbor.

carrying charge In installment buying, the interest charged on the unpaid balance.

carrying place Can. PORTAGE (def. 2).

car·ry·o·ver (kar′ē·ō′vər) n. Something left over or repeated, as an entry brought forward in bookkeeping.

cart (kärt) n. 1 A two-wheeled vehicle, for carrying loads. 2 Loosely, any two- or four-wheeled vehicle. —v.t. 1 To convey or carry in or as in a cart. —v.i. 2 To drive or use a cart. [< OE cræt] —cart′er n.

cart·age (kär′tij) n. The act or cost of carting.

carte blanche (kärt′ blänsh′, Fr. kärt blänsh′) n. pl. cartes blanches (kärts′ blänsh′, Fr. kärt blänsh′) Unrestricted authority or freedom to act. [F, white card]

car·tel (kär·tel′, kär′təl) n. 1 An association of businesses aiming at monopolistic control of the market. 2 A written official agreement between governments at war, as for the exchange of prisoners. [< Ital. carta paper]

Car·te·sian (kär·tē′zhən) adj. Of or pertaining to Descartes, or to his philosophy, doctrines, and methods. —n. A follower of Descartes. [< NL Cartesius, Latinized form of Descartes] —Car·te′sian·ism n.

Car·thage (kär′thij) n. An ancient city-state in North Africa near modern Tunis, destroyed by the Romans in 146 B.C. —Car·tha·gin·i·an (kär′thə·jin′ē·ən) adj., n.

Car·thu·sian (kär·thōō′zhən) n. A monk or nun of a religious order founded in 1086 in Chartreuse in the French Alps. —adj. Of or pertaining to this order. [< Med. L Carturissium Chartreuse]

car·ti·lage (kär′tə·lij) n. 1 A tough, elastic supporting tissue in animals; gristle. 2 A structure or part consisting of cartilage. [< L cartilago gristle]

car·ti·lag·i·nous (kär′tə·laj′ə·nəs) adj. 1 Of or like cartilage; gristly. 2 Having a gristly skeleton, as sharks.

car·tog·ra·phy (kär·tog′rə·fē) n. The science or art of drawing or compiling maps or charts. [< L charta + -GRAPHY] —car·tog′ra·pher n. —car′to·graph′ic or ·i·cal adj.

car·ton (kär′tən) n. 1 A pasteboard box. 2 A heavyweight paper container for liquids. [< L charta paper]

car·toon (kär·tōōn′) n. 1 A humorously critical or satirical drawing or caricature, as in a periodical. 2 A sketch for a fresco or mosaic. 3 COMIC STRIP. 4 ANIMATED CARTOON. —v.t. 1 To make a caricature or cartoon of; satirize pictorially. —v.i. 2 To make cartoons. [< Ital. cartone pasteboard < carta card] —car·toon′ist n.

car·tridge (kär′trij) n. 1 An explosive charge for a small arm, consisting of primer, gunpowder, cardboard or metal case, and projectile or projectiles. 2 Phot. A roll of protected sensitized films. 3 A small case attached to the arm of a phonograph and containing the stylus and pickup. 4 CASSETTE. [< F cartouche]

Cartridge
a. powder. b. wad. c. shot.

cart·wheel (kärt′ʰwēl′) n. 1 Informal A silver dollar. 2 A sideways handspring.

carve (kärv) v. carved, carv·ing v.t. 1 To cut figures or designs upon. 2 To make by cutting or chiseling. 3 To cut up, as cooked meat. —v.i. 4 To make carved work or figures. 5 To cut up meat. [< OE ceorfan] —carv′er, carv′ing n.

car·vel (kär′vəl) n. CARAVEL.

car·y·at·id (kar′ē·at′id) n. pl. ·ids or ·i·des (-ə·dēz) Archit. A supporting column in the form of a sculptured female figure. [< Gk. Karyatis a priestess of Artemis at Karyai, town of Laconia, Greece]

ca·sa·ba (kə·sä′bə) n. A melon with sweet white flesh and yellow rind. Also casaba melon. [< Kasaba, in w Turkey]

ca·sa·va (kə·sä′və) n. CASSAVA.

Cas·bah (käz′bä) n. The native quarter of Algiers or of other cities with a large Arab population.

cas·cade (kas·kād′) n. 1 A fall of water over steeply slanting rocks, or one of a series of such falls. 2 Anything resembling a waterfall. —*v.i.* **·cad·ed, ·cad·ing** To fall in the form of a waterfall; form cascades. [< Ital. *cascare* to fall]

cas·car·a (kas·kâr′ə) *n.* A buckthorn of the NW U.S. whose bark yields **cascara sa·gra·da** (sə·grä′də), used as a laxative. Also **cascara buckthorn.** [< Sp. *cáscara* bark]

case¹ (kās) *n.* **1** An instance, example, or condition: a *case* of fraud. **2** The actual fact or facts: Such is not the *case*. **3** A person or matter being given aid, undergoing investigation, treatment, etc. **4** *Law* **a** A suit or action. **b** The facts or arguments presented in a legal action. **5** Any facts or arguments that support a belief or action. **6** A question or dilemma: a *case* of conscience. **7** *Gram.* **a** The syntactical relationship of a noun, pronoun, or adjective to other words in a sentence. **b** The form of a word indicating this relationship. **8** *Informal* A peculiar or exceptional person. **9** *Informal* An infatuation. —**in any case** No matter what; regardless. —**in case** In the event that; if. —**in no case** Not under any circumstances. [< L *casus* event < *cadere* fall]

case² (kās) *n.* **1** A box, sheath, bag, etc., in which something is or may be kept. **2** A box and the items contained in it. **3** A protective cover. **4** A set or pair, as of pistols. **5** The frame for a door or window. **6** *Printing* A tray, with compartments for holding type. —*v.t.* **cased, cas·ing 1** To cover with a case; incase. **2** *Slang* To look over; inspect, esp. secretly. [< F *caisse* box < *capere* take, hold]

case·hard·en (kās′här′dən) *v.t.* **1** *Metall.* To harden the surface of (iron). **2** To make callous or unfeeling.

case history The record of an individual, as compiled by hospitals, social agencies, insurance companies, etc.

ca·se·in (kā′sē·in, -sēn) *n.* The protein found in milk and constituting the principal ingredient in cheese, also used in manufacturing adhesives, plastics, etc. [< L *caseus* cheese] —**ca·se·ic** (kā′sē·ik) *adj.*

case·mate (kās′māt) *n.* **1** A bombproof shelter from which guns fire through openings. **2** An armored bulkhead on shipboard, with openings for guns. [< F < Ital. *casamatta*, ? < Gk. *chasmata*, pl. of *chasma* opening]

case·ment (kās′mənt) *n.* **1** A window arranged to open on hinges at the side. **2** A case; covering. [< OF *encassement*] —**case′ment·ed** *adj.*

ca·se·ous (kā′sē·əs) *adj.* Of or like cheese; cheesy.

case·work (kās′wûrk′) *n.* The investigation and guidance by a social worker of maladjusted individuals and families. —**case′work′er** *n.*

cash (kash) *n.* **1** Current money in hand or readily available. **2** Money paid down; immediate payment. —*v.t.* To convert into ready money, as a check. —**cash in 1** In gambling, to receive cash in exchange for. **2** *Slang* To die. —**cash in on** *Informal* To turn to advantage; make a profit from. [< F *caisse* cash box, cash < L *capsa* box]

cash-and-car·ry (kash′ən·kar′ē) *adj.* Operated on a system of cash purchase and no delivery.

cash·book (kash′bŏŏk′) *n.* A book in which money received or paid out is recorded.

cash discount A discount from a purchase price contingent on payment within a stipulated period.

cash·ew (kash′ŏŏ, kə·shŏŏ′) *n.* **1** A tropical evergreen tree. **2** Its small, kidney-shaped, edible fruit, the **cashew nut.** [< Tupi]

cash·ier¹ (ka·shir′) *n.* **1** A person who has charge of accepting and recording the payment of bills, as in a restaurant. **2** A bank official who has charge of the receipts, disbursements, cash on hand, etc.

cash·ier² (ka·shir′) *v.t.* **1** To dismiss in disgrace, as a military officer. **2** To discard. [< L *quassare* destroy]

cash·mere (kash′mir) *n.* **1** A fine wool obtained from goats native to Kashmir. **2** A soft fabric made from this. **3** Something made of cashmere. [< *Kashmir*, India]

cash register A mechanical device having a cash drawer and recording, adding, and displaying the amount of each sale.

cas·ing (kā′sing) *n.* **1** A protective cover or covering. **2** The framework around a door or window. **3** The outer covering of an automobile tire. **4** *pl.* The intestines of cattle, hogs, etc., used as sausage containers.

ca·si·no (kə·sē′nō) *n. pl.* **·nos** **1** A room or building for public amusement, dancing, gambling, etc. **2** A game of cards. [Ital., dim. of *casa* house]

cask (kask, käsk) *n.* **1** A barrel made of staves, used for liquids, nails, etc. **2** The quantity a cask will hold. [< Sp. *casco* skull, cask]

cas·ket (kas′kit, käs′-) *n.* **1** A coffin. **2** A small box or chest. —*v.t.* To enclose in or as in a casket. [< F *casse* chest]

casque (kask) *n.* A helmet.

cas·sa·ba (kə·sä′bə) *n.* CASABA.

Cas·san·dra (kə·san′drə) *Gk. Myth.* A daughter of Priam whose prophecies were never believed. —*n.* Anyone who utters unheeded prophecies of disaster.

cas·sa·va (kə·sä′və) *n.* **1** One of several tropical American plants cultivated for their edible roots. **2** The root or starch made from it, used to make tapioca, bread, etc. [< native West Indian language]

cas·se·role (kas′ə·rōl) *n.* **1** A baking dish of earthenware, glass, etc., in which food may be baked and served. **2** The food so prepared and served. [F]

cas·sette (kə·set′, ka-) *n.* **1** A lightproof, quick-loading case for holding film in a camera. **2** A small cartridge containing magnetic tape for use in a tape recorder. [F, lit., small box]

cas·sia (kash′ə) *n.* **1** A variety of cinnamon obtained from a species of Asian laurel. **2** The tree yielding it. **3** Any of a genus of usu. tropical leguminous shrubs or herbs yielding pods whose pulp contains a laxative. [< Gk. *kasia*]

cas·si·no (kə·sē′nō) *n.* CASINO (def. 2).

cas·sock (kas′ək) *n.* A close-fitting garment, reaching to the feet, worn by many clergymen, altar boys, or choristers. [< Ital. *casacca* greatcoat] —**cas·socked** (kas′əkt) *adj.*

cas·so·war·y (kas′ə·wer′ē) *n. pl.* **·war·ies** Any of a genus of large, flightless, ostrichlike birds of Australia and New Guinea. [< Malay *kasuārī*]

cast (kast, käst) *v.* **cast, cast·ing** *v.t.* **1** To throw with force; fling; hurl. **2** To place with violence or force, as by the sea. **3** To throw up, as with a shovel. **4** To put into some form or system; formulate. **5** To deposit; give: He *cast* his vote. **6** To draw by chance; throw, as dice. **7** To cause to fall upon or over; direct: to *cast* a shadow. **8** To throw out or forth; get rid of. **9** To let down; put out; let drop: to *cast* anchor. **10** To discard or shed, as in the process of growth. **11** To give birth to, esp. prematurely; drop. **12** *Metall.* To shape in a mold; make a cast of; found. **13** *Printing* To stereotype or electroplate. **14** To assign roles, as in a play; assign to a part. **15** To add; total, as a column of figures. **16** To calculate (a horoscope, tides, etc.). **17** *Naut.* To veer. —*v.i.* **18** To throw or throw out something, as dice or a fishing line. **19** To calculate a horoscope, tides, etc. **20** To take shape in a mold. **21** To add up a column of figures. **22** *Naut.* To veer; tack. —**cast about 1** To consider ways and means; scheme. **2** To search for. —**cast away** To discard; reject. —**cast down 1** To overthrow; destroy. **2** To discourage; depress. —**cast off 1** To reject or discard. **2** To let go, as a ship from a dock. —*n.* **1** The act of throwing or casting. **2** The manner of casting; also the distance thrown or cast. **3** A throw of dice; also, the number or total thrown. **4** Anything thrown out or off, as an insect's skin. **5** The material run into molds at one operation. **6** An object formed in a mold; also, the mold. **7** An impression taken of something and usu. forming a mold. **8** An electrotype plate. **9** A hardened plaster support for a broken limb. **10** An appearance or type: a man of his *cast.* **11** Shade; tinge: a bluish *cast.* **12** A twisting of the eye to one side. **13** A glance; look. **14** The actors in a play, movie, etc. [< ON *kasta* throw]

cas·ta·net (kas′tə·net′) *n.* One of a pair of small concave disks of wood or ivory, clapped together with the fingers, as an accompaniment to song or dance. [< L *castanea* chestnut]

cast·a·way (kast′ə·wā′, käst′-) *adj.* **1** Adrift; shipwrecked. **2** Thrown away; discarded. —*n.* **1** One who is shipwrecked. **2** An outcast.

caste (kast, käst) *n.* **1** One of the hereditary classes into which Hindu society is traditionally divided in India. **2** Any rigidly exclusive social class. **3** Any system of such class distinctions. **4** Social standing or prestige. [< L *castus* pure]

Castanets

cas·tel·lat·ed (kas'tə·lā'tid) *adj.* Having battlements and turrets. —**cas'tel·la'tion** *n.*

cast·er (kas'tər, käs'-) *n.* **1** One who or that which casts. **2** A cruet for condiments. **3** A swiveling, wheellike roller fastened under an article of heavy furniture, etc.

cas·ti·gate (kas'tə·gāt) *v.t.* **·gat·ed, ·gat·ing** To punish or scold severely; chastise. [< L *castigare* chasten] —**cas'ti·ga'tion, cas'ti·ga'tor** *n.* —**cas·ti·ga·to·ry** (kas'ti·gə·tôr'ē, -tō'rē) *adj.*

Cas·tile soap (kas·tēl', kas'tēl) A pure, mild soap made with olive oil. [< *Castile*, Spain]

Cas·til·ian (kas·til'yən) *n.* **1** A citizen of Castile. **2** The official and literary form of Spanish. —*adj.* Pertaining to Castile, its language, and inhabitants.

cast·ing (kas'ting, käs'-) *n.* **1** The act of one who or that which casts. **2** Something cast in a mold.

cast·i·ron (kast'ī'ərn, käst'-) *adj.* **1** Made of cast iron. **2** Like cast iron; rigid; unyielding. **3** Tough; strong: a *cast-iron* stomach.

cast iron A hard, brittle iron produced in a blast furnace and containing a large proportion of carbon, manganese, silicon, and other impurities.

cas·tle (kas'əl, käs'-) *n.* **1** The fortified dwelling of a feudal noble. **2** Any massive or imposing dwelling. **3** Any place of security or refuge. **4** In chess, a rook. —*v.t. & v.i.* **·tled, ·tling** In chess, to move (the king) two squares to the right or left, at the same time bringing the rook to the square over which the king has passed. [< L *castellum*, dim. of *castrum* camp, fort]

castle in the air A fanciful, impractical scheme. Also **castle in Spain.**

cast-off (kast'ôf', -of', käst'-) *adj.* Thrown aside; discarded. —*n.* A person or thing no longer wanted or used.

cas·tor¹ (kas'tər, käs'-) *n.* **1** A hat of beaver or other fur. **2** An oily, odorous secretion of beavers, used in perfumery: also **cas·to·re·um** (kas·tôr'ē·əm, -tō'rē·əm). [< Gk. *kastōr* beaver]

cas·tor² (kas'tər, käs'-) *n.* CASTER (defs. 2 & 3).

Cas·tor (kas'tər, käs'-) *Gk. Myth.* The mortal twin of Pollux. —*n.* One of the two brightest stars in the constellation Gemini.

castor bean The seed of the castor-oil plant.

castor oil A viscous oil extracted from castor beans, used as a cathartic and lubricant.

cas·tor-oil plant (kas'tər·oil', käs'-) A herbaceous plant of warm climates, yielding the castor bean.

cas·trate (kas'trāt) *v.t.* **·trat·ed, ·trat·ing 1** To remove the testicles from; emasculate; geld. **2** To remove the ovaries from; spay. **3** To make less vigorous, forceful, significant, etc. [< L *castrare*] —**cas'trat·er, cas·tra'tion** *n.*

cas·u·al (kazh'ōō·əl) *adj.* **1** Occurring by chance; not planned; accidental. **2** Irregular; occasional. **3** Nonchalant. **4** Careless; haphazard. **5** Slight: a *casual* acquaintance. **6** Informal: *casual* clothes. —*n.* **1** A casual laborer. **2** *pl.* Informal clothes and accessories. [< L *casus* accident < *cadere* fall] —**cas'u·al·ly** *adv.* —**cas'u·al·ness** *n.* —*Syn. adj.* **1** random; incidental. **2** haphazard, cursory. **3** dispassionate, unconcerned, offhand. **4** negligent, slovenly.

cas·u·al·ty (kazh'ōō·əl·tē) *n. pl.* **·ties 1** A fatal or serious accident. **2** A person killed or severely injured in an accident. **3** Any person or thing badly harmed or damaged. **4** *Mil.* **a** A soldier missing in action or removed from active duty by death, wounds, or capture. **b** *pl.* Losses arising from death, etc.

cas·u·ist (kazh'ōō·ist) *n.* A person given to casuistry. [< L *casus* event, case] —**cas·u·is·tic** (kazh'ōō·is'tik) or **·ti·cal** *adj.* —**cas'u·is'ti·cal·ly** *adv.*

cas·u·ist·ry (kazh'ōō·is·trē) *n. pl.* **·ries 1** The resolving of questions of right and wrong according to standard ethical principles. **2** Overly refined or false reasoning, esp. about matters of conscience.

cat (kat) *n.* **1** A small, domesticated, carnivorous mammal with retractile claws. **2** Any animal of the cat family, as a lion, tiger, lynx, ocelot, etc. **3** *Informal* A spiteful woman given to gossip. **4** CAT-O'-NINE-TAILS. **5** *Slang* CATERPILLAR. **6** *Slang* **a** A person, esp. a man. **b** A jazz musician or devo-

tee. **7** *Naut.* A device used for hoisting an anchor. [< OE]

cat. catalog; catechism.

cata- *prefix* **1** Down; against; upon. **2** Back; over. Also **cat-.** [< Gk. *kata* down, against, back]

ca·tab·o·lism (kə·tab'ə·liz'əm) *n.* The destructive aspect of metabolism, by which living matter breaks down into simpler substances. [< Gk. *katabolē* destruction] —**cat·a·bol·ic** (kat'ə·bol'ik) *adj.* —**cat'a·bol'i·cal·ly** *adv.*

cat·a·chre·sis (kat'ə·krē'sis) *n.* The misuse of a word. [< Gk. *katachrēsis*] —**cat·a·chres·tic** (kat'ə·kres'tik) or **·ti·cal** *adj.* —**cat'a·chres'ti·cal·ly** *adv.*

cat·a·clysm (kat'ə·kliz'əm) *n.* **1** An overwhelming flood. **2** Any violent change or upheaval, as a war or earthquake. [< Gk. *kataklysmos* flood] —**cat·a·clys·mal** (kat'ə·kliz'məl), **cat'a·clys'mic** *adj.*

cat·a·comb (kat'ə·kōm) *n. Usu. pl.* A long underground gallery with excavations in its sides for tombs or human remains. [< LL *catacumbas*]

cat·a·falque (kat'ə·falk) *n.* A temporary raised structure that supports the coffin of a deceased personage lying in state. [< Ital. *catafalco*]

Cat·a·lan (kat'ə·lan, -lən) *adj.* Of Catalonia, its people, or their language. —*n.* **1** One of Catalonian descent or blood. **2** The Romance language of Catalonia and Valencia.

cat·a·lep·sy (kat'ə·lep'sē) *n.* An abnormal condition of muscular rigidity and lack of response to stimuli. [< Gk. *kata-* upon + *lēpsis* seizure] —**cat'a·lep'tic** (-lep'tik) *adj., n.*

cat·a·log (kat'ə·lôg, -log) *n.* **1** A systematic list or enumeration of names, persons, or things, bound in book form, printed on cards, etc. **2** A publication listing wares for sale by a commercial establishment. —*v.* **·loged, ·log·ing** *v.t.* **1** To make a catalog of. —*v.i.* **2** To work on or make a catalog. [< Gk. *kata-* down + *legein* select, choose] —**cat'a·log'er, cat'a·log'ist** *n.*

cat·a·logue (kat'ə·lôg, -log) *n., v.t. & v.i.* **·logued, ·logu·ing** CATALOG. —**cat'a·logu'er, cat'a·logu'ist** *n.*

ca·tal·pa (kə·tal'pə) *n.* A hardy, deciduous tree having large, ovate leaves, large, fragrant bell-shaped flowers, and long slender pods. [< N. Am. Ind.]

ca·tal·y·sis (kə·tal'ə·sis) *n. pl.* **·ses** (-sēz) An alteration in the speed of a chemical reaction effected by an agent that itself remains unchanged. [< Gk. *katalysis* dissolution] —**cat·a·lyt·ic** (kat'ə·lit'ik) *adj., n.*

cat·a·lyst (kat'ə·list) *n.* **1** A substance that effects catalysis. **2** Any factor providing impetus for change.

cat·a·lyze (kat'ə·līz) *v.t.* **·lyzed, ·lyz·ing** To submit (a reaction) to catalysis. —**cat'a·lyz'er** *n.*

cat·a·ma·ran (kat'ə·mə·ran') *n. Naut.* **1** A boat having twin hulls. **2** A long, narrow raft of logs, often with an outrigger. [< Tamil *katta-maram* tied wood]

Catamaran

cat·a·mount (kat'ə·mount) *n.* Any of various wildcats, as a cougar or lynx. [Short form of *cat of the mountain*]

cat·a·pult (kat'ə·pult, -pŏolt) *n.* **1** An engine of ancient warfare for throwing stones, spears, or arrows. **2** A slingshot. **3** *Aeron.* A device for launching an airplane at flight speed, as from the deck of a ship. —*v.t.* **1** To hurl from or as from a catapult. —*v.i.* **2** To hurtle through the air as if from a catapult. [< Gk. *kata-* down + *pallein* to hurl]

cat·a·ract (kat'ə·rakt) *n.* **1** A waterfall. **2** *Pathol.* Opacity of the crystalline lens of the eye. **3** A deluge; downpour. [< Gk. *kata-* down + *arassein* fall headlong]

ca·tarrh (kə·tär') *n.* Inflammation of mucous membrane, esp. of the throat and nose. [< Gk. *kata-* down + *rheein* flow] —**ca·tarrh'al, ca·tarrh'ous** *adj.*

ca·tas·tro·phe (kə·tas'trə·fē) *n.* **1** Any great and sudden misfortune; disaster. **2** A sudden, violent change. **3** A ruinous failure. [< Gk. *kata-* over, down + *strephein* turn] —**cat·a·stroph·ic** (kat'ə·strof'ik) *adj.* —*Syn.* **1** calamity, mishap, débacle. **2** cataclysm, convulsion, upheaval.

Ca·taw·ba (kə·tô′bə) *n.* **1** One of a tribe of North American Indians. **2** An American red grape. **3** A dry white wine made from it.

cat·bird (kat′bûrd′) *n.* A small slate-colored North American songbird, having a catlike cry.

cat·boat (kat′bōt′) *n. Naut.* A small sailboat, having its mast well forward and carrying a single fore-and-aft sail.

cat·call (kat′kôl′) *n.* A shrill, discordant call or whistle indicating impatience or derision. —*v.t.* & *v.i.* To deride with or utter catcalls.

catch (kach) *v.* **caught, catch·ing** *v.t.* **1** To take or seize; capture. **2** To entrap; ensnare. **3** To captivate, gain, or hold. **4** To apprehend or perceive clearly. **5** To surprise; detect, as in a misdeed. **6** To contract; incur, as a disease. **7** To arrive at or take, as a train or boat. **8** To arrest the motion of; entangle. **9** To grasp and retain. **10** To perceive, as something fleeting: to *catch* sight of. **11** To reach, as a person, with a blow: She *caught* him a box on the ear. — *v.i.* **12** To close and remain fastened: The lock didn't *catch.* **13** In baseball, to act as catcher. **14** To become entangled or fastened. **15** To be communicated or communicable, as a disease or enthusiasm. **16** To take fire; kindle; ignite. — **catch on** *Informal* **1** To understand. **2** To become popular or fashionable. —**catch up 1** To seize or snatch quickly. **2** To discover (someone) to be in error. **3** To overtake. **4** To regain lost ground, as by extra work. **5** To become involved or engrossed in something: *caught up* in his studies. **6** To fasten loosely or with loops. —*n.* **1** The act of catching. **2** That which catches or fastens. **3** A person or thing caught. **4** The amount caught. **5** A person worth obtaining, as in marriage. **6** A brief bit or scrap, as of a song. **7** *Informal* Something deceitful or misleading: a *catch* in that bargain sale. **8** An impediment; a break, as in the voice or breathing. —*adj.* **1** Attracting or meant to attract notice: a *catch* phrase. **2** Meant to test or trick: a *catch* question. [<LL *captiare,* freq. of L *capere* take, hold]

catch-all (kach′ôl′) *n.* A bag or other container to hold odds and ends.

catch·er (kach′ər) *n.* **1** One who or that which catches. **2** In baseball, the player stationed behind home plate to catch balls that pass the batter.

catch·ing (kach′ing) *adj.* **1** Infectious. **2** Captivating; attractive.

catch·pen·ny (kach′pen′ē) *adj.* Cheap, poor, and showy. —*n. pl.* **·nies** An inferior article.

catch·up (kach′əp, kech′-) *n.* KETCHUP.

catch·word (kach′wûrd′) *n.* **1** A much-repeated word, phrase, or slogan. **2** A word at the head of a page or column, as of a dictionary, encyclopedia, etc.

catch·y (kach′ē) *adj.* **·i·er, ·i·est 1** Interesting; infectious. **2** Deceptive; puzzling. **3** Broken; fitful. —**catch′i·ness** *n.*

cat·e·chet·ic (kat′ə·ket′ik) *adj.* Of or pertaining to oral instruction by question and answer. Also **cat·e·chet′i·cal.**

cat·e·chism (kat′ə·kiz′əm) *n.* **1** A short manual of instruction in religious doctrine, usu. in the form of questions and answers. **2** Any similar manual of instruction. [<Gk. *katēchizein* instruct]

cat·e·chist (kat′ə·kist) *n.* One who catechizes. —**cat·e·chis·tic** (kat′ə·kis′tik) or **·ti·cal** *adj.*

cat·e·chize (kat′ə·kīz) *v.t.* **·chized, ·chiz·ing 1** To teach, esp. religious doctrine, by questions and answers. **2** To question closely and fully. Also **cat′e·chise.** [<Gk. *katēchizein* to instruct] —**cat·e·chi·za′tion** *n.*

cat·e·chu·men (kat′ə·kyōō′mən) *n.* **1** One who is under instruction in the elements of Christianity. **2** One learning the elements of any subject or skill. [<Gk. *katēchoumenos*]

cat·e·gor·i·cal (kat′ə·gôr′i·kəl, -gor′-) *adj.* **1** Without qualification; absolute; unequivocal. **2** Of, relating to, or in a category. —**cat′e·gor′i·cal·ly** *adv.* —**cat′e·gor′i·cal·ness** *n.*

cat·e·go·rize (kat′ə·gə·rīz′) *v.t.* **·rized, ·riz·ing** To put into a category; classify.

cat·e·go·ry (kat′ə·gôr′ē, -gō′rē) *n. pl.* **·ries** A class, division, or group in any system of classification. [<Gk. < *katēgoreein* allege, predicate]

ca·ter (kā′tər) *v.i.* **1** To furnish food or entertainment. **2** To provide for the gratification of any need or taste. —*v.t.* **3** To furnish food for. [<LL *acceptare* buy, procure, accept] —**ca′ter·er** *n.*

cat·er-cor·nered (kat′ər·kôr′nərd) *adj.* Diagonal. —*adv.* Diagonally. Also **cat′er-cor′ner.** [<F *quatre* four + CORNERED]

cat·er·pil·lar (kat′ər·pil′ər) *n.* The larva of certain insects, esp. of a butterfly or moth. [<L *catta* cat + *pilum* hair]

Cat·er·pil·lar (kat′ər·pil′ər) *n.* A tractor whose wheels drive continuous treads or tracks: a trade name.

cat·er·waul (kat′ər·wôl) *v.i.* **1** To utter the discordant cry peculiar to cats at rutting time. **2** To make any discordant screeching. —*n.* Such a sound. [ME *caterwawen*]

cat·fish (kat′fish′) *n. pl.* **·fish** or **·fish·es** Any of various fishes having no scales and having barbels around the mouth suggestive of a cat's whiskers.

Catfish

cat·gut (kat′gut′) *n.* A very tough cord made from the intestines of certain animals and used for stringing musical instruments, making surgical ligatures, etc.

ca·thar·sis (kə·thär′sis) *n.* **1** *Med.* A purgation, esp. of the alimentary canal. **2** A purifying or relieving of the emotions. [<Gk. <*katharos* pure] —**ca·thar′tic** *adj., n.*

ca·the·dral (kə·thē′drəl) *n.* **1** The church containing the official chair of the bishop. **2** Any large or important church. —*adj.* Of, pertaining to, or like a cathedral. [< Gk. *kata*- down + *hedra* seat]

cath·e·ter (kath′ə·tər) *n.* A slender tube for drawing off fluid from a body cavity, esp. urine from the bladder. [< Gk. *kata*- down + *hienai* send, let go]

cath·e·ter·ize (kath′ə·tər·īz′) *v.t.* **·ized, ·iz·ing** To introduce a catheter into.

cath·ode (kath′ōd) *n. Electr.* The electrode through which negative charges leave a nonmetallic conductor and toward which positive ions flow from the anode. [< Gk. *kata*- down + *hodos* road, way]

cathode rays *Physics* A stream of electrons that pass from a cathode of an electron tube.

cath·ode-ray tube (kath′ōd-rā′) *Electronics* A type of electron tube in which a beam of electrons is focused and deflected so as to make a trace or image on a screen, as in a television receiver.

cath·o·lic (kath′ə·lik, kath′lik) *adj.* **1** Broadminded, as in belief, tastes, or views; liberal; comprehensive. **2** Universal in reach; general. [<Gk. *katholikos* universal] —**ca·thol·i·cal·ly** (kə·thol′ik·lē) *adv.* —**cath·o·lic·i·ty** (kath′ə·lis′ə·tē) *n.*

Cath·o·lic (kath′ə·lik, kath′lik) *adj.* **1** Of or pertaining to the Roman Catholic Church. **2** Of or pertaining to the ancient, undivided Christian Church or its later divisions, as the Anglican or Eastern Orthodox. —*n.* A member of any Catholic Church. —**Cath·o·lic·i·ty** (kath′ə·lis′ə·tē) *n.*

Catholic Church 1 ROMAN CATHOLIC CHURCH. **2** Any of several Christian churches, as the Anglican or Eastern Orthodox.

Ca·thol·i·cism (kə·thol′ə·siz′əm) *n.* The doctrine, system, and practice of a Catholic Church, esp. the Roman Catholic Church.

ca·thol·i·cize (kə·thol′ə·sīz) *v.t.* & *v.i.* **·cized, ·ciz·ing** To make or become catholic or Catholic.

cat·house (kat′hous′) *n. Slang* A house of prostitution.

cat·i·on (kat′ī′ən) *n. Chem.* A positive ion. [<Gk. *kata*-down + *ienai* go] —**cat·i·on·ic** (kat′ī·on′ik) *adj.*

cat·kin (kat′kin) *n.* A dense, deciduous scaly spike of flowers, as in the willow, birch, etc. [<MDu. *katteken* kitten]

cat·nap (kat′nap′) *n.* A short doze.

cat·nip (kat′nip) *n.* An aromatic herb of the mint family, of which cats are fond. Also **cat′mint′** (-mint′).

cat-o′-nine-tails (kat′ə·nīn′tālz′) *n.* A whip with nine lashes.

CAT scan An electronic scanning procedure in which the body is x-rayed from many angles as it revolves.

cat's-eye (kats′ī′) *n.* A gemstone that shows a line of light across the dome resembling that in the eye of a cat.

cat's-paw (kats′pô′) *n.* **1** A person used as a tool or dupe. **2** A light wind that barely ruffles the water. Also **cats′. paw′.**

cat·sup (kat′səp, kech′əp) *n.* KETCHUP.

cat·tail (kat′tāl′) *n.* A tall, marsh plant with long, strap-like leaves and flowers in dense, brown terminal spikes.

cat·tle (kat′l) *n.* **1** Domesticated cows, bulls, steers, and oxen. **2** Formerly, all livestock. **3** Human beings: a contemptuous term. [< L *capitale* capital, wealth]

cat·tle·man (kat′l·mən) *n. pl.* **-men** (-mən) One who raises cattle.

cat·ty (kat′ē) *adj.* **-ti·er, -ti·est** **1** Of cats. **2** Malicious; spiteful. —**cat′ti·ly** *adv.* —**cat′ti·ness** *n.*

CATV community antenna television.

cat·walk (kat′wôk′) *n.* Any narrow walking space, as at the side of a bridge, in an aircraft, near the ceiling of the stage in a theater, etc.

Cau·ca·sian (kô·kā′zhən) *n.* **1** A Caucasoid person. **2** A native of the Caucasus region. —*adj.* **1** Of the Caucasus region, its inhabitants, or their languages. **2** CAUCASOID. Also **Cau·cas·ic** (kô·kas′ik). [< *Caucasus*, the region where the "white" race was once thought to have originated]

Cau·ca·soid (kô′kə·soid) *adj.* Of or pertaining to the so-called white race, believed to have originally inhabited Europe, N Africa, India, and parts of E Asia, and characterized by a skin color varying from very light to dark brown. —*n.* A member of this racial group.

cau·cus (kô′kəs) *n.* A meeting of members of a political party to select candidates or plan a campaign. —*v.i.* **cau·cused** or **-cussed, -cus·ing** or **-cus·sing** To meet in or hold a caucus. [< Algon.]

cau·dal (kôd′l) *adj.* **1** Of, pertaining to, or near the tail or posterior part of the body. **2** Resembling a tail. [< L *cauda* tail] —**cau′dal·ly** *adj.*

cau·date (kô′dāt) *adj.* Having a tail or taillike appendage. Also **cau′dat·ed.** [< L *cauda* tail]

cau·dle (kôd′l) *n.* A warm drink of gruel with wine, eggs, etc., for invalids. [< Med. L *caldum, calidum* warm, hot]

caught (kôt) *p.t. & p.p.* of CATCH.

caul (kôl) *n.* The amniotic sac, esp. if it envelops the head of a newborn child. [Prob. < OF *cale* cap]

caul·dron (kôl′drən) *n.* CALDRON.

cau·li·flow·er (kô′lə·flou′ər, kol′i-) *n.* **1** A vegetable consisting of the dense, white, flower head of a plant related to cabbage. **2** The plant bearing this. [< NL *cauliflora* flowering cabbage]

caulk (kôk) *v.t.* To make watertight, as a boat, window frame, pipe, etc., by using some waterproof substance. [< L *calcare* to tread] —**caulk′er** *n.*

caus·al (kô′zəl) *adj.* **1** Of, being, or expressing a cause. **2** Having to do with cause and effect. —**caus′al·ly** *adv.*

cau·sal·i·ty (kô·zal′ə·tē) *n. pl.* **-ties** **1** The principle that all that exists or happens depends upon a cause. **2** Causal action or agency.

cau·sa·tion (kô·zā′shən) *n.* **1** The act of causing. **2** That which causes an effect. **3** CAUSALITY.

caus·a·tive (kô′zə·tiv) *adj.* **1** Effective as a cause. **2** *Gram.* Expressing cause or agency. —*n.* A causative word or form. —**caus′a·tive·ly** *adv.* —**caus′a·tive·ness** *n.*

cause (kôz) *n.* **1** Any person, thing, event, etc., that produces an effect or result. **2** Any rational ground for choice or action; reason. **3** Any great enterprise, movement, principle, or aim. **4** *Law* An action or suit to be settled in court. —*v.t.* **caused, caus·ing** To be the cause of; produce; effect; induce; compel. [< L *causa* cause, legal case] —**caus′a·ble** *adj.* —**caus′er** *n.* —**Syn.** **1** agent, principle, origin, source.

cause cé·lè·bre (kōz′sə·leb′r′, *Fr.* kōz′sā·leb′r′) **1** A famous legal case. **2** A controversial issue or event. [F, lit., celebrated case]

cause·way (kôz′wā′) *n.* **1** A raised road or way, as over marshy ground. **2** A highway. [< LL *calciata* paved]

caus·tic (kôs′tik) *adj.* **1** Capable of corroding or eating away tissue. **2** Stinging; biting; sarcastic. —*n.* A caustic substance. [< Gk. *kausos* burning < *kaiein* to burn] — **caus′ti·cal·ly** *adv.* —**caus·tic′i·ty** (-tis′ə·tē) *n.*

caustic potash POTASSIUM HYDROXIDE.

caustic soda SODIUM HYDROXIDE.

cau·ter·ize (kô′tər·īz) *v.t.* **-ized, -iz·ing** To destroy dead or abnormal tissue by applying a caustic, intense heat or cold, etc. [< L *cauterium* branding iron] —**cau′ter·i·za′tion** *n.*

cau·ter·y (kô′tər·ē) *n. pl.* **-ter·ies** **1** The process of cauterizing. **2** A cauterizing substance or instrument. [< L *cauterium* branding iron] .

cau·tion (kô′shən) *n.* **1** Care to avoid injury or misfortune; prudence; wariness. **2** An admonition or warning. **3** *Informal* A person or thing that alarms, astonishes, provokes, etc. —*v.t.* To advise to be prudent; warn. [< L *cautio* < *cavere* beware, take heed]

cau·tion·ar·y (kô′shən·er′ē) *adj.* Constituting or conveying a warning; admonitory.

cau·tious (kô′shəs) *adj.* Exercising or manifesting caution; wary; prudent. —**cau′tious·ly** *adv.* —**cau′tious·ness** *n.* —**Syn.** careful, discreet, circumspect, heedful, chary.

cav·al·cade (kav′əl·kād, kav′əl·kād′) *n.* **1** A procession or parade, esp. of horsemen. **2** A series or procession of events. [< Ital. *cavalcare* to ride on horseback]

cav·a·lier (kav′ə·lir′) *n.* **1** A horseman; knight. **2** GALLANT. —*adj.* **1** Free and easy; offhand. **2** Haughty; supercilious. —**cav′a·lier′ly** *adj., adv.*

cav·al·ry (kav′əl·rē) *n. pl.* **-ries** Mobile ground troops, originally mounted on horses, but now using mechanized or motorized units. [< LL *caballarius* horseman < L *caballus* horse] —**cav′al·ry·man** *n.*

cave (kāv) *n.* A natural cavity beneath the earth's surface or in a mountain. —*v.i.* **caved, cav·ing** To fall in or down; give way, as ground. —**cave in** **1** To fall in or down, as by undermining. **2** *Informal* To yield utterly; give in. [< L *cava* < *cavus* hollow]

ca·ve·at (kā′vē·at, kav′ē·at, käv′-) *n.* **1** *Law* A formal notification to a court or officer not to take a certain step until the person giving notice can be heard. **2** A caution, esp. to avoid misinterpretation. [< L, let him beware]

cave-in (kāv′in′) *n.* A collapse or falling in, as of a mine or tunnel; also, the site of such a collapse.

cave man **1** A cave dweller, esp. of prehistoric times. **2** *Informal* A rough and brutal man.

cav·ern (kav′ərn) *n.* A large cave.

cav·ern·ous (kav′ər·nəs) *adj.* **1** Full of caverns. **2** Like a cavern, esp. hollow. —**cav′ern·ous·ly** *adv.*

cav·i·ar (kav′ē·är, kä′vē-) *n.* The salted roe of sturgeon or other related fish, considered a delicacy. Also **cav′i·are.** [< Turkish *khavyar*]

cav·il (kav′əl) *v.i.* **cav·iled** or **-illed, cav·il·ing** or **-il·ling** To pick flaws or raise trivial objections; quibble: with *at* or *about*. —*n.* A trivial objection. [< L *cavilla* a jeering, a scoffing] —**cav′il·er, cav′il·ler** *n.*

cav·i·ty (kav′ə·tē) *n. pl.* **-ties** **1** A hollow or depression. **2** A natural hollow in the body. **3** A hollow place in a tooth, esp. one caused by decay. [< L *cavus* hollow, empty]

ca·vort (kə·vôrt′) *v.i.* **1** To act up; cut up. **2** To prance and show off, as a horse. [?]

CAVU ceiling and visibility unlimited.

ca·vy (kā′vē) *n. pl.* **-vies** Any of various South American burrowing rodents, as the guinea pig. [< Cariban]

caw (kô) *n.* The harsh cry of crows, ravens, etc. —*v.i.* To make this cry. [Imit.]

cay (kā, kē) *n.* A coastal reef or sandy islet. [< Sp. *cayo* shoal]

cay·enne pepper (kī·en′, kā-) A hot, red pepper made from the fruit of various pepper plants; red pepper. Also **cay·enne′.**

cay·man (kā′mən) *n. pl.* **-mans** CAIMAN.

Ca·yu·ga (kā·yōō′gə, kī-) *n. pl.* **-ga** or **-gas** A member of a tribe of North American Indians of Iroquoian linguistic stock formerly dwelling in w New York State.

cay·use (kī·yōōs′) *n.* A small horse native to w U.S. [< the *Cayuse* Indians, formerly living in Oregon.]

Cb columbium.

CBC Canadian Broadcasting Corporation.

CBS Columbia Broadcasting System.

C.C., c.c. carbon copy; cashier's check; city council; county clerk.

Cattail

---

add, āce, câre, pälm; end, ēven; it, īce; odd, ōpen, ôrder; tŏŏk, pōōl; up, bûrn; ə = a in *above*, u in *focus*;
yōō = u in *fuse*; oil; pout; check; go; ring; thin; this; zh, *vision.* < derived from; ? origin uncertain or unknown.

cc, cc., c.c. cubic centimeter(s).

CCCP A Russian acronym for SSSR, Soyuz (Union) Soviet Socialist Republic.

C clef See CLEF.

Cd cadmium.

cd candela.

c.d. cash discount, compact disc.

Ce cerium.

cease (sēs) v. ceased, ceas·ing v.t. 1 To leave off or discontinue. —v.i. 2 To come to an end; stop; desist. —Without cease Without end. [<L *cessare* stop <*cedere* withdraw, yield] —cease′less adj. —cease′less·ly adv. —cease′less·ness n. —Syn. v. 1 conclude, end, finish, terminate, quit, stop, break off.

cease-fire (sēs′fīr′) n. A temporary truce, esp. in warfare.

ce·cum (sē′kəm) n. pl. ce·ca (sē′kə) A cavity with a single opening, esp. the blind pouch between the large and small intestines. [<L *caecus* blind] —ce′cal adj.

ce·dar (sē′dər) n. 1 Any of a genus of large, Old World conifers, having needlelike leaves and fragrant wood. 2 Any of a large variety of similar evergreen trees. 3 The wood of any of these trees. —adj. Pertaining to or made of cedar. [<Gk *kedros*]

ce·dar·bird (sē′dər·bûrd′) n. A common American waxwing. Also cedar waxwing. • See WAXWING.

cede (sēd) v.t. ced·ed, ced·ing 1 To yield or give up: to *cede* disputed territory to avoid war. 2 To surrender title to; transfer. [<L *cedere* withdraw, yield]

ce·dil·la (si·dil′ə) n. A mark put under the letter c (ç) to indicate that it is to be sounded as (s). [<Sp., dim of *ceda*, the letter *z*]

ceil·ing (sē′ling) n. 1 The overhead covering of a room. 2 The top limit or maximum, as of prices, wages, etc. 3 *Aeron.* a The maximum height attainable by a given aircraft. b The upward limit of visibility for flying. [ME *celing*]

cel·an·dine (sel′ən·dīn) n. Any of several weedy plants with yellow flowers. [<Gk. *chelidōn* a swallow]

cel·e·brant (sel′ə·brənt) n. 1 One who celebrates. 2 The officiating priest at a mass.

cel·e·brate (sel′ə·brāt) v. ·brat·ed, ·brat·ing v.t. 1 To observe, as a festival or occasion: to *celebrate* an anniversary. 2 To make known or famous; extol. 3 To perform a ceremony publicly and as ordained: to *celebrate* the mass. —v.i. 4 To observe or commemorate a day or event. 5 *Informal* To have a lively and happy time. [<L *celebrare* <*celeber* famous] —cel′e·brat′er or ·bra′tor n. —Syn. v. 1 commemorate, keep. 2 glorify, exalt, commend. 3 solemnize. 5 rejoice, make merry.

cel·e·brat·ed (sel′ə·brā′tid) adj. 1 Famous; renowned. 2 Performed or observed with customary rites.

cel·e·bra·tion (sel′ə·brā′shən) n. 1 The act or an instance of celebrating. 2 Things done in commemoration of any event.

ce·leb·ri·ty (sə·leb′rə·tē) n. pl. ·ties 1 A famous or much publicized person. 2 Fame; renown.

ce·ler·i·ty (sə·ler′ə·tē) n. Quickness of motion; speed; rapidity. [<L *celer* swift]

cel·er·y (sel′ər·ē) n. An herb related to parsley, having long, crisp, edible leafstocks. [<Gk *selinon* parsley]

ce·les·ta (sə·les′tə) n. A musical instrument having a keyboard of five octaves and hammers that strike steel plates. [<F *celeste* celestial]

ce·les·tial (sə·les′chəl) adj. 1 Of or pertaining to the sky or heavens. 2 Heavenly; divine. [<L *caelum* sky, heaven] —ce·les′tial·ly adv.

celestial equator *Astron.* The great circle in which the plane of the earth's equator cuts the celestial sphere.

celestial sphere The spherical surface on which the positions of bodies in space are projected.

ce·li·ac (sē′lē·ak) adj. Of or pertaining to the abdomen. [<Gk. *koilia* belly, abdomen]

cel·i·ba·cy (sel′ə·bə·sē) n. 1 The state of being unmarried, esp. in accordance with religious vows. 2 Abstinence from sexual intercourse. [<L *caelebs* unmarried]

cel·i·bate (sel′ə·bit, -bāt) adj. Unmarried or sexually abstinent, esp. by vow. —n. One who practices celibacy.

cell (sel) n. 1 A small room, as in a prison or monastery.

2 Any small area or space, as a chamber in a seedcase, a single compartment in a honeycomb, an area bounded by veins on an insect's wing. 3 *Biol* One of the fundamental structural units of which all living tissue is composed, typically consisting of a cell membrane enclosing a mass of cytoplasm that contains a nucleus and various ultramicroscopic structures. 4 *Electr.* A device consisting of electrodes in contact with an electrolyte. 5 A body of persons forming a single unit in an organization of similar groups. —dry cell A voltaic cell with its electrolyte in the form of a paste. [<L *cella*]

Cell. a. cell wall.
b. nucleus.
c. cell body.

cel·lar (sel′ər) n. 1 An underground room usu. under a building. 2 A room for storing wines. 3 The wines so stored. —v.t. To put or keep in or as in a cellar. [<L *cellarium* pantry <*cella*, small room]

cel·lar·er (sel′ər·ər) n. The keeper of a cellar, as in a monastery.

cel·lo (chel′ō) n. pl. ·los A stringed instrument of the violin family, usu. tuned an octave below the viola and held between the knees when played; violoncello. Also 'cel'lo. [Short for VIOLONCELLO] —cel′list n.

cel·lo·phane (sel′ə·fān) n. A specially treated cellulose in transparent sheets, used as a wrapping. [<CELL(ULOSE) + -PHANE]

cel·lu·lar (sel′yə·lər) adj. 1 Of, pertaining to, or like a cell or cells. 2 Consisting of or containing cells.

cellular telephone A portable radiotelephone, as in an automobile, connected to the regular telephone system. A system of cells, each equipped with a radiotransmitter and a receiver, allows the phone to operate as it moves from one place to another.

cel·lule (sel′yōōl) n. A very small cell.

Cel·lu·loid (sel′yə·loid) n. A flammable synthetic solid derived from cellulose: a trade name.

cel·lu·lose (sel′yə·lōs) n. A complex carbohydrate forming the cell walls of plants and the principal component of wood, paper, cotton, etc. [<L *cella* cell]

ce·lom (sē′ləm) n. COELOM.

Cel·si·us (sel′sē·əs) adj. Of or designating a temperature scale in which the freezing point of water is 0° and the boiling point 100°. [<Anders *Celsius*, 1701–44, Swedish astronomer]

Celt (selt, kelt) n. A person of Celtic linguistic stock, now represented by the Irish, Welsh, Highland Scots, Manx, Cornish, and Bretons.

Celt·ic (sel′tik, kel′-) n. A subfamily of the Indo-European family of languages, including Cornish, Welsh, Breton, Irish, Scottish Highland Gaelic, and Manx. —adj. Of or pertaining to the Celtic peoples, their languages, or culture.

ce·ment (si·ment′) n. 1 A powdery substance, usu. of burned lime and clay, that when mixed with water or with water, sand, and gravel produces mortar or concrete. 2 Any gluelike substance. 3 A dental filling for cavities. • See TOOTH. 4 Any bond or union, as between persons. —v.t. 1 To unite or join with or as with cement. 2 To cover or coat with cement. —v.t. 3 To become united by cement; cohere. [<L *caementum* rough stone, stone chip <*caedere* cut] —ce·men·ta·tion (sē′mən·tā′shən, sem′ən-), ce·ment′er n. • *Cement* is often used as a synonym for *concrete*. This is technically incorrect, since cement is only one, although the principal, ingredient of concrete.

cem·e·ter·y (sem′ə·ter′ē) n. pl. ·ter·ies A place for the burial of the dead. [<Gk. *koimaein* put to sleep]

cen., cent. central; century.

-cene suffix Recent; new; pleistocene. [Gk. *kainos* new]

cen·o·taph (sen′ə·taf, -täf) n. A monument to a dead person whose remains are elsewhere. [<Gk. *kenos* empty + *taphos* tomb]

Ce·no·zo·ic (sē′nə·zō′ik, sen′ə-) adj. & n. See GEOLOGY. [<Gk. *kainos* new + *zōē* life]

cen·ser (sen′sər) n. A vessel for burning incense. [<Med. L *incensum* incense]

cen·sor (sen′sər) n. 1 An official examiner of manuscripts, plays, movies, etc., empowered to delete or suppress whatever is considered offensive or objectionable. **2** An official who deletes from letters, dispatches, etc., any secret or forbidden information. **3** Anyone who censures or criticizes. **4** In Ancient Rome, one of two magistrates who took the census and supervised public morals. —*v.t.* To act as censor of. [<L *censere* judge] —**cen·so·ri·al** (sen·sôr'ē·əl, -sō'rē-) *adj.*

cen·so·ri·ous (sen·sôr'ē·əs, -sō'rē-) *adj.* Given to or expressing censure; critical. —**cen·so'ri·ous·ly** *adv.* —**cen·so'ri·ous·ness** *n.*

cen·sor·ship (sen'sər·ship) *n.* **1** The office or power of a censor. **2** The act or process of censoring.

cen·sur·a·ble (sen'shər·ə·bəl) *adj.* Deserving censure; blameworthy. —**cen'sur·a·bly** *adv.*

cen·sure (sen'shər) *n.* Condemnation or blame; disapproval. —*v.t.* **·sured, ·sur·ing** To express disapproval of; condemn. [<L *censere* judge] —**cen'sur·er** *n.*

cen·sus (sen'səs) *n. pl.* **cen·sus·es** An official count of the people of a country or district, including age, sex, employment, etc. [<L *censere* assess]

cent (sent) *n.* **1** The hundredth part of a dollar. **2** The hundredth part of a standard unit of other money systems. **3** A coin of this value. [<L *centum* hundred]

cent. centered; centigrade; centimeter; century.

cen·taur (sen'tôr) *Gk. Myth.* One having the head, arms, and torso of a man and the body and legs of a horse.

cen·ta·vo (sen·tä'vō) *n. pl.* **·vos** (-vōz, *Sp.* -vōs) A small coin of the Philippines, Mexico, and other Latin American countries, usu. equal to the hundredth part of a peso. [*Sp.*]

cen·te·nar·i·an (sen'tə·nâr'ē·ən) *n.* One who is one hundred or more years old.

cen·te·nary (sen'tə·ner'ē, sen·ten'ə·rē) *n. pl.* **·nar·ies** **1** A hundredth anniversary. **2** A period of a hundred years. [<L *centum* hundred]

cen·ten·ni·al (sen·ten'ē·əl) *adj.* Of a hundred or a hundredth anniversary. —*n.* A hundredth anniversary. [<L *centum* hundred + *annus* a year] —**cen·ten'ni·al·ly** *adv.*

cen·ter (sen'tər) *n.* **1** *Geom.* The point within a circle or sphere equally distant from any point on the circumference or surface. **2** The middle: the *center* of the town. **3** The point, object, person, or place about which things cluster or revolve or from which they emanate: a *center* of interest. **4** Any hub of a specified activity: a manufacturing *center*. **5** *Mech.* A point on or by which an object is secured or rotated. **6** The person who takes the middle position in certain games, as football, basketball, etc. **7** *Often cap.* **a** The moderate position of a political group neither conservative nor liberal but sharing some views with both. **b** Such a group. —*v.t.* **1** To place in or at the center. **2** To supply with a center. **3** To draw to or direct toward one place; concentrate. —*v.i.* **4** To be in or at the center. **5** To have a focal point; concentrate. —*adj.* Central; middle. [<Gk. *kentron* point (i.e., around which a circle is described)]

center of gravity That point, if it exists, at which the weight of a body appears to be concentrated regardless of the position of the body.

cen·ter·piece (sen'tər·pēs') *n.* **1** An ornament for the center of a table. **2** Any object conspicuously displayed.

cen·tes·i·mal (sen·tes'ə·məl) *adj.* **1** Hundredth. **2** Divided into hundredths. [<L *centesimus* hundredth]

centi- combining form **1** Hundred: *centipede*. **2** Hundredth. [<L *centum* hundred]

cen·ti·grade (sen'tə·grād) *adj.* **1** Graduated to a scale of a hundred. **2** CELSIUS. [<L *centum* hundred + *gradus* step, degree]

cen·til·lion (sen·til'yən) *n.* See NUMBER.

cen·time (sän'tēm, *Fr.* sän·tēm') *n.* A hundredth of a franc. [F < OF *centisme* < L *centesimus* hundredth]

cen·ti·me·ter (sen'tə·mē'tər) *n.* The hundredth part of a meter.

cen·ti·pede (sen'tə·pēd) *n.* Any of a class of elongated arthropods having a pair of legs to each segment. [<L *centum* hundred + *pes, pedis* foot]

Centipede

cen·tral (sen'trəl) *adj.* **1** Of, in, near, or from the center. **2** Being the center. **3** Being a dominant or controlling factor, element, point, etc.; chief. —*n. Informal.* **1** A telephone exchange. **2** The operator in charge of it. [<L *centrum* center] —**cen'tral·ly** *adv.* —**cen·tral·i·ty** (sen'tral'ə·tē), **cen'tral·ness** *n.*

Central African Republic A republic in CEN. Africa, 238,234 sq. mi., cap. Bangui. • See map at AFRICA.

Central America A narrow, winding strip of land between Mexico and South America.

Central America

cen·tral·ize (sen'trəl·īz) *v.* **·ized, ·iz·ing** *v.t.* **1** To make central; bring to a center. **2** To concentrate (power or control) in one authority. —*v.i.* **3** To come to a center. —**cen·tral·i·za'tion, cen'tral·iz'er** *n.*

central processing unit A microprocessor that directs a computer to execute instructions and performs basic mathematical functions.

cen·tre (sen'tər) *n., adj., v.t. & v.i.* **·tred, ·tring** *Brit.* CENTER.

cen·tric (sen'trik) *adj.* **1** In, at, or near the center. **2** Being or having a center. Also **cen'tri·cal.** —**cen'tri·cal·ly** *adv.* —**cen·tric·i·ty** (sen·tris'ə·tē) *n.*

cen·trif·u·gal (sen·trif'yə·gəl, -ə·gəl) *adj.* **1** Directed or tending away from a center; radiating. **2** Employing centrifugal force: a *centrifugal* pump. [<L *centrum* center + *fugere* flee] —**cen·trif'u·gal·ly** *adv.*

centrifugal force *Physics* The force that makes a rotating body tend to pull away from the center around which it rotates.

cen·tri·fuge (sen'trə·fyōōj) *n.* A rotary machine employing centrifugal force to separate substances having different densities.

cen·trip·e·tal (sen·trip'ə·təl) *adj.* **1** Directed, tending, or drawing toward a center. **2** Employing centripetal force: a *centripetal* pump. [<L *centrum* center + *petere* seek]

centripetal force *Physics* A force attracting a body toward a center around which it revolves.

cen·tro·some (sen'trə·sōm) *n. Biol.* A small body situated near the nucleus. [<Gk *kentron* center + *sōma* body]

cen·tro·sphere (sen'trə·sfir') *n.* **1** *Geol.* The central portion of the earth. **2** *Biol.* The sphere which surrounds the centrosome.

cen·tu·ple (sen'tə·pəl, sen·t'ōō'pəl) *v.t.* **·pled, ·pling** To increase a hundredfold. —*adj.* Increased a hundredfold. [<L *centuplus* hundredfold]

cen·tu·ri·on (sen·t'ōōr'ē·ən) *n.* The commander of a century in the ancient Roman army. [<L *centurio*]

cen·tu·ry (sen'chə·rē) *n. pl.* **·ries** **1** A period of 100 years in any system of chronology, esp. in reckoning from the first year of the Christian era. **2** A body of Roman foot soldiers (at one time 100 men). [<L *centum* hundred]

century plant An American agave that flowers after twenty to thirty years and then dies.

ce·phal·ic (sə·fal'ik) *adj.* Of, pertaining to, on, in, or near the head. [<Gk. *kephalē* head]

cephalic index The ratio of the greatest breadth of the skull to the greatest length, multiplied by 100.

ceph·a·lo·pod (sef'ə·lə·pod') *n.* Any of a class of mollusks such as squids, cuttlefishes, octopuses, etc., having a clearly defined head and eyes, ink sac, and tentacles or arms. —*adj.* Of or pertaining to cephalopods. [<Gk. *kephalē* head + *pous, podis* foot]

-cephalous combining form Headed; *hydrocephalous*. [<Gk. *kephalē* head]

ce·ram·ic (sə·ram'ik) *adj.* Of or pertaining to earthenware, pottery, porcelain, etc., or to their manufacture. —*n.* An article of ceramic manufacture. [<Gk. *keramos* potters' clay]

ce·ram·ics (sə·ram′iks) *n.pl.* *(construed as sing.)* The art or technique of making ceramic articles. —**ce·ra′mist, ce·ram′i·cist** *n.*

Cer·ber·us (sûr′bər·əs) *Gk. & Rom. Myth.* The three-headed dog guarding the portals of Hades.

cere (sir) *n.* In parrots, eagles, etc., a waxlike, fleshy area about the bill. [< L *cera* wax]

ce·re·al (sir′ē·əl) *n.* 1 The grain of certain grasses used as food, as rice, wheat, etc. 2 Any of the plants yielding such grains. 3 A breakfast food made from a cereal —*adj.* Pertaining to edible grain. [< CERES]

cer·e·bel·lum (ser′ə·bel′əm) *n. pl.* **·bel·lums** or **·bel·la** (-bel′ə) The part of the brain that acts as the coordination center of voluntary movement, posture, and equilibrium. [< L *cerebrum* brain] —**cer′e·bel′lar** *adj.*

cer·e·bral (ser′ə·brəl, sə·rē′-) *adj.* 1 Of or pertaining to the cerebrum or the brain. 2 Appealing to or requiring the intellect; intellectual.

cerebral palsy Paralysis and inability to control movement due to brain injury.

Cerebellum

cer·e·brate (ser′ə·brāt) *v.i.* **·brat·ed, ·brat·ing** To think. [< L *cerebrum* brain] —**cer′e·bra′tion** *n.*

cer·e·bro·spi·nal (ser′ə·brō·spī′nəl) *adj.* Of the brain and the spinal cord.

cer·e·brum (sə·rē′brəm, ser′ə·brəm) *n. pl.* **·bra** (-brə) The upper part of the brain consisting of two hemispheres connected at the base. [< L] —**cer·e·bric** (sə·rē′brik, ser′ə-) *adj.*

cere·cloth (sir′klôth′, -kloth′) *n.* A cloth treated with wax, formerly used to cover the dead. [< obs. *cere* to cover with wax < L *cera* wax]

cere·ment (sir′mənt) *n. Usu. pl.* SHROUD.

cer·e·mo·ni·al (ser′ə·mō′nē·əl) *adj.* Of, pertaining to or characterized by ceremony; ritual; formal. —*n.* 1 A system of rules of ceremony; ritual. 2 A ceremony. —**cer′e·mo′ni·al·ism, cer′e·mo′ni·al·ist** *n.* —**cer′e·mo′ni·al·ly** *adv.*

cer·e·mo·ni·ous (ser′ə·mō′nē·əs) *adj.* 1 Observant of or conducted with ceremony; formal. 2 Studiously polite. —**cer′e·mo′ni·ous·ly** *adv.* —**cer′e·mo′ni·ous·ness** *n.*

cer·e·mo·ny (ser′ə·mō′nē) *n. pl.* **·nies** 1 A formal act, or a series of them, as on religious and state occasions. 2 The performance of such acts. 3 Mere outward form. 4 Formal civility; formality. [< L *caerimonia* awe, veneration]

Ce·res (sir′ēz) *Rom. Myth.* The goddess of grain and harvests.

ce·rise (sə·rēz′, -rēs′) *adj., n.* Bright, cherry red. [< F, cherry]

ce·ri·um (sir′ē·əm) *n.* A shiny, gray, rare-earth element (symbol Ce). [< the asteroid *Ceres*]

cert. certificate; certify; certified.

cer·tain (sûr′tən) *adj.* 1 Established as fact or truth; beyond doubt or question; true. 2 Absolutely sure; convinced. 3 Definitely settled; fixed; determined. 4 Inevitable: Death is *certain*. 5 Sure in its workings or results; reliable. 6 Appreciable; limited: to a *certain* extent. 7 Indefinite, but assumed to be determinable: a *certain* man. —**for certain** Without doubt. [< L *certus*, p.p. of *cernere* determine] —**Syn.** 1 undeniable, indisputable, incontestable, irrefutable. 2 positive. 3 assured, decided. 4 unavoidable.

cer·tain·ly (sûr′tən·lē) *adv.* Without a doubt; surely.

cer·tain·ty (sûr′tən·tē) *n. pl.* **·ties** 1 The quality or fact of being certain. 2 Something definite and certain.

cer·tif·i·cate (sər·tif′ə·kit) *n.* A document or written statement declaring something to be true, genuine, or legally valid. —*v.t.* (-kāt) **·cat·ed, ·cat·ing** To furnish with or attest by a certificate. [< Med.L *certificare* certify]

cer·ti·fi·ca·tion (sûr′tə·fi·kā′shən) *n.* 1 The act of certifying. 2 The state of being certified. 3 A certified statement.

certified check A check drawn on an account having sufficient funds for the bank to guarantee in writing its payment.

cer·ti·fy (sûr′tə·fī) *v.t.* **·fied, ·fy·ing** 1 To guarantee (something) to be true, genuine, etc., usu. in a formal,

written statement. 2 To issue a certificate to. 3 To give assurance of; vouch for. 4 To declare to be legally insane. [< L *certus* certain + *facere* make] —**cer′ti·fi′er** *n.*

cer·ti·o·ra·ri (sûr′shē·ə·râr′ē, -rār′ī) *n. Law* A writ from a superior to an inferior court, directing that a record of a designated case be sent up for review. [< LL, to be certified]

cer·ti·tude (sûr′tə·t³ōōd) *n.* Perfect assurance; certainty. [< L *certus* certain]

ce·ru·le·an (sə·rōō′lē·ən) *n.* Sky blue. —*adj.* Sky-blue. [< L *caeruleus* dark blue]

cer·vi·cal (sûr′vi·kəl) *adj. Anat.* Of or pertaining to the neck or a necklike part. [< L CERVIX]

cer·vine (sûr′vīn, -vin) *adj.* Of or similar to deer. [< L *cervus* deer]

cer·vix (sûr′viks) *n. pl.* **cer·vix·es** or **cer·vi·ces** (sər·vī′sēz, sûr′və·sēz) 1 The neck. 2 Any necklike part, as the constricted end of the uterus, etc. [< L]

Ce·sar·e·an (si·zâr′ē·ən) *adj.* CAESAREAN. Also **Ce·sar′i·an.**

ce·si·um (sē′zē·əm) *n.* A soft, silvery, and very reactive metallic element (symbol Cs) chemically similar to potassium and used in photoelectric cells. [< L *caesius* bluish gray]

ces·sa·tion (se·sā′shən) *n.* A ceasing; stop; pause. [< L *cessare* stop]

ces·sion (sesh′ən) *n.* The act of ceding; surrender. [< L *cessus* p.p. of *cedere* yield]

cess·pool (ses′pōōl′) *n.* 1 A covered well or pit for the drainage from sinks, etc. 2 Any repository of filth. [?]

ce·su·ra (si·zhōōr′ə, -zyōōr′ə) *n.* CAESURA.

ce·ta·cean (sə·tā′shən) *adj.* Of or belonging to an order of aquatic mammals, as the whales, dolphins, and porpoises. Also **ce·ta′ceous.** —*n.* A cetacean mammal. [< Gk. *kētos* whale]

Cey·lon (si·lon′) *n.* SRI LANKA.

C.F., c.f. cost and freight.

C/F, c/f carried forward.

Cf californium.

cf. compare (L *confer*).

C.F.I., c.f.i. cost, freight, and insurance.

cfm., c.f.m. cubic feet per minute.

cfs., c.f.s. cubic feet per second.

C.G. Coast Guard.

cg, cg., cgm. centigram(s).

cgs, c.g.s., C.G.S. centimeter-gram-second.

C.H., c.h. courthouse; customhouse.

Ch. Chaldean; Chaldea; China; Chinese.

ch. champion; chapter; check; chief; children; church.

cha·blis (sha·blē′) *n.* 1 A dry, white, Burgundy wine made in the region of Chablis, France. 2 Any of various similar wines.

Chad (chad) *n.* A republic in CEN. Africa, 495,752 sq. mi., cap. Fort-Lamy. • See map at AFRICA.

chafe (chāf) *v.* **chafed, chaf·ing** *v.t.* 1 To abrade or make sore by rubbing. 2 To make warm by rubbing. 3 To irritate; annoy. —*v.i.* 4 To rub. 5 To be irritated; fret. —*n.* 1 Soreness or wear from friction. 2 Irritation or vexation. [< OF *chaufer* warm < L *calere* be warm + *facere* make] —**chaf′er** *n.*

chaf·er (chā′fər) *n.* The cockchafer or other scarabaeid beetle. Also **chaf·fer** (chaf′ər). [< OE *ceafor*]

chaff[1] (chaf, chäf) *n.* 1 The husks of grain. 2 Worthless matter; refuse. [OE *ceaf*] —**chaff′y** *adj.*

chaff[2] (chaf, chäf) *v.t.* To poke fun at; ridicule. —*n.* Good-natured banter. [?]

chaf·fer (chaf′ər) *v.i.* To haggle about price; bargain. —*n.* The act of chaffering; bargaining. [< OE *cēap* bargain + *faru* going] —**chaf′fer·er** *n.*

chaf·finch (chaf′inch) *n.* A European song finch, popular as a cage bird. [< CHAFF[1] + FINCH]

chaf·ing dish (chā′fing) *n.* A vessel with a heating apparatus beneath, to cook or keep hot its contents at table.

cha·grin (shə·grin′) *n.* Distress or embarrassment caused by disappointment, failure, etc.; mortification. —*v.t.* To humiliate; mortify. [F, sad] —**Syn.** *n.* confusion, dismay, humiliation, vexation.

chain (chān) *n.* 1 A series of connected rings or links, serving to bind, drag, hold, or ornament. **2** *pl.* Shackles; bonds. **3** *pl.* Bondage; captivity. **4** Any connected series: a *chain* of events. **5** A range of mountains. **6** A unit of linear measure equal to 66 or 100 feet. **7** *Chem.* A series of atoms linked together. **8** A series of associated stores, banks, etc. —*v.t.* **1** To fasten, as with a chain. **2** To bring into or hold in subjection. [< L *catena*]

chain gang A gang of convicts chained together while doing hard labor.

chain mail Flexible armor made of joined metal links. • See MAIL².

chain of command A hierarchy of persons in command according to rank.

chain reaction A series of reactions each of which develops from the energy or products released by its predecessor.

chain stitch A sewing stitch of loops connected in a chain, used in embroidery, etc.

chain store A retail store that is a member of a chain of stores.

chair (châr) *n.* **1** A seat, usu. with four legs and a back and for one person. **2** A seat of office, as of a professor or moderator. **3** A person holding such an office. **4** A chairman. **5** ELECTRIC CHAIR. —*v.t.* **1** To put into a chair; install in office. **2** To preside over (a meeting). [< F *chaiere* < L *cathedra*]

chair·man (châr′mən) *n.* *pl.* ·men (-mən) One who presides over an assembly, committee, etc. —**chair′man·ship** *n.*

chair·per·son (châr′pûr′sən) *n.* *pl.* ·sons One who presides over an assembly, committee, etc.

chair·wom·an (châr′wŏŏm′ən) *n.* *pl.* ·wom·en (-wim′ən) A woman who presides over an assembly, committee, etc.

chaise (shāz) *n.* **1** A light, four-wheeled carriage, usu. with an open top. **2** CHAISE LONGUE. [F, var. of *chair* chair]

chaise longue (shāz′ lông′, *Fr.* shez lôṅg′) *n.* A chair having a backrest at one end and the seat prolonged to support the sitter's outstretched legs. [F, lit., long chair]

cha·la·za (kə·lā′zə) *n.* *pl.* ·zas or ·zae (-zē) Either of the two ropes of dense albumen attached to the lining membrane of an egg. [< Gk., hailstone, small lump]

chal·ced·o·ny (kal·sed′ə·nē, kal′sə·dō′nē) *n.* *pl.* ·nies A waxy, translucent variety of quartz. [< *Chalcedon*, an ancient Greek port]

Chal·de·a (kal·dē′ə) *n.* In Biblical geography, the southernmost part of the valley of the Tigris and the Euphrates, sometimes extended to include Babylonia. Also **Chal·dae′a.** —**Chal·de′an** *adj.* & *n.*

cha·let (sha·lā′, shal′ā) *n.* **1** A Swiss cottage having a gently sloping and projecting roof. **2** Any house built in this style. [F]

chal·ice (chal′is) *n.* **1** A consecrated cup used in the celebration of the Eucharist. **2** Any cup or goblet. **3** A cup-shaped flower. [< L *calix* cup]

chalk (chôk) *n.* **1** A soft, grayish white or yellowish limestone, largely composed of minute sea shells. **2** A piece of chalk or chalklike material used for marking or drawing. **3** A score or reckoning, as one recorded with chalk. —*v.t.* **1** To mark or draw with chalk. **2** To put chalk on or in. **3** To make pale. —**chalk up 1** To score. **2** To give credit. —*adj.* Made with chalk. [< OE *cealc* < L *calx* limestone] —**chalk′i·ness** *n.* —**chalk′y** *adj.* (·i·er, ·i·est)

chalk·board (chôk′bôrd′, -bōrd′) *n.* A hard, flat surface for writing on with chalk, used for classroom instruction.

chal·lenge (chal′ənj) *v.* ·lenged, ·leng·ing *v.t.* **1** To dare or invite to a duel, contest, etc. **2** To stop and demand identification. **3** To call in question; object to: to *challenge* a decision, voter, juror, etc. **4** To stimulate: to *challenge* the imagination. **5** To call for; claim as due. —*v.i.* **6** To utter or make a challenge. —*n.* **1** A call or dare to fight, esp. to fight a duel. **2** A formal objection or exception to a person or thing. **3** A sentry's call, requiring one to halt and give identification. **4** Something that stimulates a person or persons to greater effort, dedication, etc. [< LL *calumniare* accuse falsely < *calumnia* slander] —**Syn.** *v.* **3** dispute, query, contest, doubt. **4** excite, arouse, animate, spur, stir. —**chal′lenge·a·ble** *adj.* —**chal′leng·er** *n.*

chal·lis (shal′ē) *n.* A light printed dress fabric. [?]

cham·ber (chām′bər) *n.* **1** A room in a house, esp. a bedroom. **2** *pl.* A suite of rooms or offices for the use of one person, as a judge's office. **3 a** A hall where an assembly or council meets. **b** The council or assembly itself. **4** An enclosed space, as one of the cavities in the cartridge cylinder of a revolver. **5** *Anat.* A cavity or compartment, as in the heart, eyeball, etc. —*v.t.* To make chambers in, as a gun. [< L *camera* vaulted room < Gk. *kamara*]

cham·ber·lain (chām′bər·lin) *n.* **1** A high court official. **2** An official who manages a royal household. **3** A treasurer. [< L *camera*. See CHAMBER.]

cham·ber·maid (chām′bər·mād′) *n.* A woman who cleans bedrooms in a hotel.

chamber music Music for a small ensemble.

chamber of commerce An association of businessmen for the protection and regulation of commerce.

chamber pot A portable receptacle used in a bedroom as a toilet.

cham·bray (sham′brā) *n.* A cotton fabric woven with colored warp crossed by white threads. [< *Cambrai*, France]

cha·me·le·on (kə·mē′lē·ən, -mēl′yən) *n.* **1** Any of various lizards having the power to change its color. **2** A person of changeable character or habits. [< Gk. < *chamai* on the ground + *leōn* lion] —**cha·me·le·on·ic** (kə·mē′lē·on′ik) *adj.*

Chameleon

cham·fer (cham′fər) *v.t.* **1** To cut a channel or groove in. **2** To bevel. —*n.* A groove or channel. [< F *chanfrein* < OF *chanfraindre* to cut off an edge]

cham·ois (sham′ē, *Fr.* sha·mwä′) *n.* *pl.* ·ois **1** A small mountain antelope of Europe and western Asia. **2** A soft leather originally prepared from the skin of the chamois, now from sheep, goats, deer, etc. [F]

cham·o·mile (kam′ə·mīl) *n.* A strongly scented, bitter herb with daisylike flowers, used to make a medicinal tea. [< Gk. *chamai* on the ground + *mēlon* apple]

champ¹ (champ) *v.t.* **1** To crush and chew noisily; munch. **2** To bite upon restlessly. —*n.* The action of champing.

champ² (champ) *n.* *Slang* Champion.

cham·pagne (sham·pān′) *n.* **1** A sparkling white wine made in the region of Champagne, France. **2** Any sparkling white wine. **3** A pale, tawny or greenish yellow.

cham·paign (sham·pān′) *n.* Flat and open country; a plain. —*adj.* Level and open. [< L *campus*, plain, field]

cham·pi·on (cham′pē·ən) *n.* **1** The victor in a contest. **2** One who defends a person, principle, etc. —*adj.* Acknowledged superior to all competitors; holding the first prize. —*v.t.* To stand up for the rights of; defend. [< LL *campio* fighter < L *campus* field]

cham·pi·on·ship (cham′pē·ən·ship′) *n.* **1** A contest held to determine a champion. **2** The position of a champion. **3** The act of championing; advocacy.

chance (chans, chäns) *n.* **1** The unknown or the undefined cause of events; luck; fortune. **2** An unknown agency, assumed to be the cause of events. **3** The likelihood of something; probability. **4** A fortuitous event; an accident. **5** An opportunity. **6** A risk. **7** A ticket in a lottery, raffle, etc. —*v.* **chanced, chanc·ing** *v.i.* **1** To occur accidentally; happen. —*v.t.* **2** To risk; hazard. —*adj.* Occurring by chance. [< LL *cadentia* < L *cadere* to fall]

chan·cel (chan′səl, chän′-) *n.* The space in a church for the clergy and choir, often separated from the rest of the church by a screen or railing. [< LL < *cancelli*, pl., lattice]

chan·cel·ler·y (chan′sə·lər·ē, chän′-, chans′lər·ē, chäns′-) *n.* *pl.* ·ries **1** The office or position of a chancellor. **2** The building or room in which a chancellor has his office. **3** The office of an embassy or legation.

chan·cel·lor (chan′sə·lər, chän′-, chans′lər, chäns′-) *n.* **1** In certain universities, the president. **2** In certain countries, the head of state or prime minister. **3** A judicial officer sitting in a court of chancery or equity. [< LL *cancellarius* one who stands at the bar in a court < *cancelli*, pl., railing] —**chan′cel·lor·ship′** *n.*

---

add, āce, câre, pälm; end, ēven; it, īce; odd, ōpen, ôrder; tŏŏk, pōōl; up, bûrn; ə = a in *above*, u in *focus*; yŏŏ = u in *fuse*; oil; pout; check; go; ring; thin; ṯẖis; zh, *vision*. < derived from; ? origin uncertain or unknown.

chan·cer·y (chan'sər·ē, chän'-) *n. pl.* **·cer·ies 1** In the U.S., a court of equity. **2** In Great Britain, one of the five divisions of the High Court of Justice. **3** A court of records; archives. **4** CHANCELLERY (def. 3). **—in chancery 1** Pending in a court of chancery. **2** In a hopeless predicament. [< LL *cancellarius*. See CHANCELLOR.]

chan·cre (shang'kər) *n.* A primary syphilitic lesion. [< L *cancer* crab, ulcer] **—chan·crous** (shang'krəs) *adj.*

chan·croid (shang'kroid) *n.* A nonsyphilitic venereal sore.

chan·cy (chan'sē, chän'-) *adj.* **·i·er, ·i·est** *Informal.* Subject to chance; risky.

chan·de·lier (shan'də·lir') *n.* A branched light fixture. [< L *candela* candle]

chan·dler (chan'dlər, chän'-) *n.* **1** A retailer or supplier of groceries, provisions, etc. **2** One who makes or sells candles. [< F *chandelier* chandler, candlestick]

change (chānj) *v.* **changed, chang·ing** *v.t.* **1** To make different; alter. **2** To exchange; interchange: to *change* places. **3** To replace, substitute, or abandon (something) for another thing: to *change* plans. **4** To give or get the equivalent of, as money. **5** To put other garments, coverings, etc., on: to *change* the bed. **—v.i. 6** To become different; vary. **7** To make an exchange. **8** To transfer from one train to another. **9** To put on other garments. **—n. 1** The act or result of changing. **2** A substitution or something used in substitution: a *change* of clothes. **3** Something different or varied. **4** The money returned to a purchaser who has given a bill or coin of greater value than his purchase. **5** Money of smaller denomination given in exchange for money of larger denomination. **6** Small coins. **7** An exchange for the transaction of business: also **'change. — ring the changes 1** To operate a chime of bells so as to produce a variety of tuneful combinations. **2** To repeat something with much variation. [< LL *cambiare* exchange] **—change'ful** *adj.* **—change'ful·ly** *adv.* **—chang'er, change'ful·ness** *n.* **—Syn. v. 1** transmute, transform, vary, modify.

change·a·ble (chān'jə·bəl) *adj.* **1** Capable of being changed; alterable. **2** Likely to change or vary; inconstant. **3** Reflecting light so as to appear of different color from different points of view. **—change·a·bil·i·ty** (chān'jə·bil'ə·tē), change'a·ble·ness *n.* **—change'a·bly** *adv.*

change·less (chānj'lis) *adj.* Without change; constant; enduring. **—change'less·ly** *adv.* **—change'less·ness** *n.*

change·ling (chānj'ling) *n.* A child believed to have been substituted secretly for another.

change of life MENOPAUSE.

chan·nel (chan'əl) *n.* **1** The bed of a stream. **2** A wide strait: the English *Channel.* **3** The deep part of a river, harbor, strait, etc. **4** A groove or tubular passage, as for liquids. **5** *pl.* A usu. official course or route through which communications, requests, etc., are handled or transmitted. **6** *Telecom.* **a** A path for the transmission of telegraph, telephone, and radio communications. **b** A wave band of specified frequency over which radio and television programs are transmitted. **—v.t.** **chan·neled** or **·nelled, chan·nel·ing** or **·nel·ling 1** To cut or wear channels in. **2** To convey through or as through a channel. [< L *canalis* groove]

chant (chant, chänt) *n.* **1** A vocal melody sung in free rhythm, usu. unaccompanied, and with a series of words sung at a single pitch. **2** A psalm or canticle so recited. **3** A song; melody. **4** Any measured monotonous singing or speaking. **—v.t. 1** To sing to a chant. **2** To celebrate in song. **3** To say repetitiously and monotonously. **—v.i. 4** To sing chants. **5** To sing. **6** To talk monotonously and continuously. [< L *cantare*, freq. of *canere* sing] **—chant'er** *n.*

chant·ey (shan'tē, chan'-) *n. pl.* **·eys** A rhythmical working song of sailors. [Alter. of F *chantez*, imperative of *chanter* sing]

chan·ti·cleer (chan'tə·klir') *n.* COCK[1] (defs. 1, 2). [< OF < *chanter* sing, crow + *cler* aloud]

Cha·nu·kah (khä'noo·kä) *n.* HANUKKAH.

cha·os (kā'os) *n.* **1** A condition of utter disorder and confusion. **2** *Often cap.* The primal, formless condition said to have existed before the creation of the universe. [< Gk., abyss < *chainein* gape, yawn]

cha·ot·ic (kā·ot'ik) *adj.* Of or like chaos; completely disordered. **—cha·ot'i·cal·ly** *adv.*

chap[1] (chap) *n. Informal* A fellow; lad. [< OE *cēap* trade + *man*]

chap[2] (chap) *v.t. & v.i.* **chapped** or **chapt, chap·ping** To split, crack, or redden. **—n.** A chapped place in the skin. [ME *chappen*]

chap[3] (chap, chop) *n.* A jaw or cheek.

chap. chaplain; chapter.

cha·pa·re·jos (chä'pä·rā'hos) *n. pl.* CHAPS. Also **cha·pa·ra·jos** (chä'pä·rä'hōs) [< Sp.]

chap·ar·ral (chap'ə·ral') *n.* A thicket of dwarf oak, low thorny shrubs, etc. [< Sp. *chaparra* evergreen oak]

chap·book (chap'book') *n.* A cheap popular book formerly sold on the street.

cha·peau (sha·pō', *Fr.* shä·pō') *n. pl.* **·peaux** (-pōz', *Fr.* -pō') or **·peaus** (-pōz') A hat. [F < LL *cappa* head covering]

chap·el (chap'əl) *n.* **1** A building for Christian worship, but smaller than a church. **2** A room for worship, as in a hospital, etc. **3** A building for religious services on a campus; also, the services. **4** A compartment or recess in a church where independent services may be held. [< Med. L *cappa* cloak; orig., a sanctuary where the cloak of St. Martin was kept as a relic]

chap·er·on (shap'ə·rōn) *n.* **1** A woman who acts as attendant to a young unmarried woman in public. **2** An older person who attends a social function to maintain its decorum and propriety. **—v.t.** To act as chaperon to. Also **chap'er·one.** [F < *chape* cape; because she protects her charges from harm] **—chap·er·on·age** (shap'ə·rō'nij) *n.*

chap·lain (chap'lin) *n.* A clergyman authorized to conduct religious services in a legislative assembly, in a regiment, on board a ship, at court, etc. [< Med. L *cappella* CHAPEL] **—chap'lain·cy, chap'lain·ship** *n.*

chap·let (chap'lit) *n.* **1** A wreath for the head. **2** A string of beads. **3** A third of a rosary. [< LL *cappa* hooded cape]

chaps (shaps, chaps) *n. pl.* Leather overalls without a seat, worn over trousers by cowboys to protect the legs. [Short for CHAPAREJOS]

chap·ter (chap'tər) *n.* **1** A division of a book or treatise, usu. marked by a number and heading. **2** Any period or a sequence of episodes. **3** The canons of a cathedral or other collegiate church. **4** A meeting of such canons or of monks or nuns. **5** A branch of a club, fraternity, etc. **—v.t.** To divide into chapters, as a book. [< L *caput* head, capital, chapter]

Chaps

char[1] (chär) *n. Brit.* A chore; an odd job. **—v.i.** **charred, char·ring** To clean and scrub for pay. [OE *cerr* turn of work]

char[2] (chär) *v.* **charred, char·ring** *v.t.* **1** To burn or scorch. **2** To convert into charcoal. **—v.i. 3** To become charred. **—n.** Charcoal. [? < CHARCOAL]

char. character; charter.

char·ac·ter (kar'ik·tər) *n.* **1** The combination of qualities or traits distinguishing any person or class of persons. **2** Any distinguishing or essential quality or property. **3** Moral excellence. **4** A good reputation. **5** Position; status. **6** A person in a novel, play, etc. **7** A person of note. **8** Any person. **9** A humorous or eccentric person. **10** A written or printed figure, as a letter, mark, sign, etc. **11** *Genetics* A structural or functional trait in a plant or animal. **—v.t. 1** To write or print. **2** To describe. [< Gk. *charaktēr* stamp, mark < *charassein* engrave]

char·ac·ter·is·tic (kar'ik·tə·ris'tik) *adj.* Distinguishing or distinctive; typical. **—n. 1** A distinctive feature; peculiarity. **2** The integral part of a logarithm; index. **— char'ac·ter·is'ti·cal·ly** *adv.*

char·ac·ter·ize (kar'ik·tə·rīz') *v.t.* **·ized, ·iz·ing 1** To describe or portray by qualities or peculiarities. **2** To be a mark or peculiarity of; distinguish. **—char'ac·ter·i·za'tion, char'ac·ter·iz'er** *n.*

cha·rade (shə·rād') *n.* A guessing game in which a word or each syllable of a word is acted in pantomime. [< Prov. *charrado* chatter]

char·coal (chär'kōl') *n.* **1** An impure carbon obtained by driving off volatile compounds of organic matter, as of wood, used as a fuel, a filter, etc. **2** A drawing pencil or crayon of charcoal. **3** A drawing made in charcoal. **—v.t.** To write, draw, or mark with charcoal. [ME *charcole*]

chard (chärd) *n.* A variety of beet having large leaves and leafstalks, which are used as a vegetable. [< L *carduus* thistle]

chare (char) *n. & v.* CHARE¹.

charge (chärj) *v.* **charged, charg·ing** *v.t.* **1** To lay or impose a load, burden, responsibility, etc. upon. **2** To put something into or upon. **3** To put carbon dioxide into (water, etc.). **4** *Electr.* To replenish, as a storage battery. **5** To load (a firearm, etc.). **6** To command or instruct authoritatively: to *charge* a jury. **7** To accuse: with *with*. **8** To make an onset against or attack upon, as a fort. **9** To set or state, as a price. **10** To set down or record, as a debt to be paid later; also, to purchase (something) by this method. —*v.i.* **11** To demand or fix a price. **12** To make an onset: *Charge!* —**charge off** To regard or write off as a loss. —*n.* **1** The quantity of gunpowder, fuel, etc., put or to be put into a firearm, a furnace etc. **2** A quantity of electricity, as in a storage battery or carried by an atomic particle. **3** Care, custody, responsibility, etc. **4** The person or thing for which one is responsible. **5** Instruction or command: the *charge* to a jury. **6** An accusation. **7** A price or cost. **8** A debt; expense. **9** An entry in an account of indebtedness. **10** A charge account. **11** An attack or onslaught; also, the signal for it. [< LL *carricare* carry] —**charge′a·ble** *adj.*

charge account An account against which the purchase of merchandise in a store is charged.

char·gé d'af·faires (shär·zhā′ də·fâr′, *Fr.* shär·zhä′ da·fâr′) *pl.* **char·gés d'af·faires** (shär·zhāz′də·fâr′, *Fr.* shär·zhä′ da·fâr′) **1** A person who temporarily assumes the command of a diplomatic mission. **2** A diplomat ranking below an ambassador or minister.

charg·er (chär′jər) *n.* **1** One who or that which charges. **2** A horse used for battle and in parades. **3** An apparatus for charging electric storage batteries.

char·i·ly (châr′ə·lē) *adv.* In a chary manner; warily.

char·i·ness (châr′ē·nis) *n.* The quality of being chary.

char·i·ot (char′ē·ət) *n.* An ancient two-wheeled vehicle used in war and in racing. —*v.t. & v.i.* To convey, ride, or drive in a chariot. [< L *carrus* cart, wagon] —**char′i·o·teer′** *n.*

Chariot

cha·ris·ma (kə·riz′mə) *n.* A quality that enables a person, esp. a leader, to capture the interest, devotion, and confidence of others. [< Gk., grace, favor] —**char·is·mat·ic** (kar′iz·mat′ik) *adj.*

char·i·ta·ble (char′ə·tə·bəl) *adj.* **1** Of or characterized by charity. **2** Generous in giving gifts to the poor. **3** Tolerant; benevolent; kindly. —**char′i·ta·ble·ness** *n.* —**char′i·ta·bly** *adv.*

char·i·ty (char′ə·tē) *n. pl.* **·ties 1** The giving of aid to the poor. **2** The aid given. **3** An institution, organization, or fund for the help of the needy. **4** A feeling of good will or kindness towards others. **5** An act of good will or kindness. **6** Tolerance; leniency. [< L *caritas* love < *carus* dear]

char·la·tan (shär′lə·tən) *n.* A person who claims to possess a knowledge or skill he does not have; a fake; quack. —**char′la·tan·ry, char′la·tan·ism** *n.* [< Ital. *ciarlatano* babbler]

Charles·ton (chärlz′tən) *n.* A fast dance in four-four time. [< *Charleston*, S.C.]

char·ley horse (chär′lē) *Informal* A cramp in the muscles of the leg or arm, caused by excessive exertion. [?]

char·lock (chär′lək) *n.* Wild mustard, often a troublesome weed. [< OE *cerlic*]

charm (chärm) *v.t.* **1** To attract irresistibly; delight; enchant. **2** To influence as by magic power. **3** To protect as by a spell: a *charmed* life. —*v.i.* **4** To be pleasing or fascinating. **5** To act as a charm; work as a spell. —*n.* **1** The power to allure or delight; fascination. **2** Something that delights or fascinates. **3** A small ornament worn on a bracelet, etc. **4** Something worn or used to avert evil or bring good luck. [< L *carmen* song, incantation] —**charm′· er** *n.* —**Syn.** *v.* 1 bewitch, captivate, entrance, fascinate.

charm·ing (chär′ming) *adj.* Enchanting; fascinating; bewitching. —**charm′ing·ly** *adv.* —**charm′ing·ness** *n.*

char·nel house (chär′nəl) A room or building where bones or bodies of the dead are placed. [< L *caro, carnis* flesh]

Char·on (kâr′ən) *Gk. Myth.* The ferryman who carried the dead over the river Styx to Hades.

chart (chärt) *n.* **1** A map; esp., one for the use of navigators, aviators, and meteorologists. **2** A sheet showing facts graphically or in tabular form. —*v.t.* To map out; lay out on a chart. [< Gk. *chartē* leaf of paper]

char·ter (chär′tər) *n.* **1** A document, given by a ruler or government, granting special rights or privileges to a person, institution, etc. **2** *Usu. cap.* A document outlining the aims or purposes of a group: *Charter* of the United Nations. **3** A permit to establish a branch or chapter of a society. **4** The leasing or renting of a vessel, airplane, bus, etc. —*v.t.* **1** To hire or rent. **2** To give a charter to. [< L *charta* paper] —**char′ter·er** *n.*

charter member An original member of an organization or society.

char·treuse (shär·trœz′) *n.* **1** A yellow, pale green, or white liqueur made by the Carthusian monks. **2** (*also* shär·trōōz′) A pale yellowish green. —*adj.* Pale, yellowish green. [< *Chartreuse*, a monastery in France.]

char·wom·an (chär′wŏŏm′ən) *n. pl.* **·wom·en** A woman employed to do cleaning, scrubbing, etc., as in office buildings.

char·y (châr′ē) *adj.* **char·i·er, char·i·est 1** Cautious; wary. **2** Slow to give; sparing. [< OE *cearig* sorrowful, sad]

Cha·ryb·dis (kə·rib′dis) *Gk. Myth.* A whirlpool off the Sicilian coast opposite the rock Scylla.

chase¹ (chās) *v.* **chased, chas·ing** *v.t.* **1** To pursue with intent to catch, capture, or molest. **2** To drive away; dispel: often with *away, out* or *off.* **3** To hunt, as deer. —*v.i.* **4** To follow in pursuit. **5** *Informal* To rush; go hurriedly. —*n.* **1** Earnest pursuit. **2** That which is pursued. **3** The sport of hunting: usu. with *the.* [< LL *captiare,* freq. of *capere* take, hold]

chase² (chās) *n.* **1** *Printing* A metal frame into which pages of type are fastened for printing. **2** A groove or slot. —*v.t.* **chased, chas·ing** To ornament by embossing, indenting, etc. [< L *capsa* box]

chas·er (chā′sər) *n.* **1** One who chases or pursues. **2** *Informal* Water or some mild beverage taken with or after a drink of liquor.

chasm (kaz′əm) *n.* **1** A deep gorge. **2** A gap or void. **3** A difference, as of opinions, feelings, etc. [< Gk. *chasma* < *chainein* gape] —**chas·mal** (kaz′məl) *adj.*

Chas·si·dim (khä·sē′dim) *n. pl.* of **Chas·sid** (khä′sid) A sect of Jewish mystics. [< Heb., pious] —**Chas·si·dic** (khä·sē′dik) *adj.*

chas·sis (shas′ē, chas′ē) *n. pl.* **chas·sis** (shas′ēz, chas′-) **1** The frame, suspension, wheels, brakes, and steering assembly of an automobile or similar vehicle. **2** The landing gear of an aircraft. **3 a** The metal framework supporting the parts of a radio, television set, etc. **b** The assembled framework and components. [< L *capsa* box]

chaste (chāst) *adj.* **1** Free from unlawful sexual activity; virtuous. **2** Sexually abstinent. **3** Pure and modest, as in conduct. **4** Pure and simple in style; not ornate. [< L *castus* pure] —**chaste′ly** *adv.* —**chaste′ness** *n.*

chast·en (chās′sən) *v.t.* **1** To discipline by punishment or affliction; chastise. **2** To moderate; soften; temper. [< L *castigare* castigate] —**chast′en·er** *n.* —**chast′en·ing** *n.*

chas·tise (chas·tīz′) *v.t.* **·tised, ·tis·ing 1** To punish, esp. by whipping. **2** To scold sharply. [< L *castigare* castigate] —**chas·tise·ment** (chas′tiz·mənt, chas·tīz′-), **chas·tis′er** *n.*

chas·ti·ty (chas′tə·tē) *n.* The state or quality of being chaste. [< L *castus* pure]

chas·u·ble (chaz′yə·bəl, chas′-) *n.* The sleeveless, outer vestment worn by a priest in celebrating the Mass or Eucharist. [< Med. L *casula* cloak < L, dim. of *casa* house]

chat (chat) *v.i.* **chat·ted, chat·ting** To converse in an easy, familiar manner. —*n.* **1** An informal conversation. **2** Any of several singing birds. [Short for CHATTER]

---

cha·teau (sha·tō′, *Fr.* shä·tō′) *n. pl.* **·teaux** (-tōz′, *Fr.* -tō′) 1 A French castle or manor house. 2 A house on a country estate. [F< L *castellum* CASTLE]

chat·e·laine (shat′ə·lān) *n.* 1 The mistress of a chateau or castle. 2 A clasp or chain hung from a woman's belt to hold small articles. [F]

chat·tel (chat′l) *n.* An article of personal property that is movable, such as furniture, livestock, etc. [< L *capitale* property < *caput* head]

chat·ter (chat′ər) *v.i.* 1 To click together rapidly, as the teeth in shivering. 2 To talk rapidly and trivially. 3 To make rapid and indistinct sounds, as a monkey or squirrel. —*v.t.* 4 To utter in a trivial or chattering manner. —*n.* 1 Idle prattle. 2 Jabbering, as of a monkey. [Imit.] —**chat′ter·er** *n.*

chat·ter·box (chat′ər·boks′) *n.* A person who talks incessantly.

chat·ty (chat′ē) *adj.* **·ti·er, ·ti·est** 1 Given to chatting. 2 Familiar; informal: a *chatty* writing style. —**chat′ti·ly** *adv.* —**chat′ti·ness** *n.*

chauf·feur (shō′fər, shō·fûr′) *n.* One employed to drive an automobile for someone else. —*v.t.* To serve as a chauffeur for. [F< *chauffer* warm]

chaunt (chônt, chänt) *n. & v.* CHANT.

chau·vin·ist (shō′vən·ist) *n.* One who believes excessively and often belligerently in the superiority of his own country, race, sex, etc.: a male *chauvinist*. [< Nicolas *Chauvin,* an overzealous supporter of Napoleon Bonaparte] —**chau′vin·ism** *n.* —**chau′vin·is′tic** *adj.* —**chau′vin·is′ti·cal·ly** *adv.*

chaw (chô) *v.t. & n. Regional* CHEW.

Ch.E., Che.E. Chemical Engineer.

cheap (chēp) *adj.* 1 Low in price; inexpensive. 2 Lower in price than the going rate or the real value. 3 Demanding little effort: a *cheap* victory. 4 Of little value. 5 Inferior in quality. 6 Low; vulgar; contemptible. 7 Stingy; tight. 8 Embarrassed; sheepish. 9 *Econ.* Obtainable at a low interest rate; also, depreciated: said of money. —*adv.* 1 At a low cost. 2 In a cheap manner. [Earlier *good cheap* a bargain < OE *ceap* business, trade] —**cheap′ly** *adv.* —**cheap′ness** *n.*

cheap·en (chē′pən) *v.t. & v.i.* To make or become cheap or cheaper. —**cheap′en·er** *n.*

cheap·skate (chēp′skāt′) *n. Slang* A miserly person.

cheat (chēt) *v.t.* 1 To deceive or defraud. 2 To delude; trick. 3 To elude or escape; foil: to *cheat* the hangman. —*v.i.* 4 To practice fraud or act dishonestly. —**cheat on** *Slang* To be sexually unfaithful to. —*n.* 1 An act of cheating. 2 One who cheats. [ME *chete,* short for *achete* escheat] —**cheat′er** *n.* —**cheat′ing·ly** *adv.*

check (chek) *n.* 1 A sudden stopping or halt. 2 Any control or restraint. 3 Any person or thing that controls or restrains. 4 Any examination, test, comparison, etc., for quality, verification, or identification. 5 A mark to show verification, approval, identification, etc. 6 A numbered tag used in duplicate to identify the owner of something. 7 A bill, as in a restaurant. 8 A written order for money drawn upon one's account in a bank. 9 A single square in a checkered surface. 10 A checkered pattern or a fabric having a checkered pattern. 11 In chess, an attack upon or menace to a king. 12 A slight crack. —**check in** 1 To register, as at a hotel. 2 To report, as for work. —**check into** To investigate. —**check out** 1 To vacate one's lodging and settle the bill, as at a hotel. 2 To calculate the cost of and collect payment for (merchandise), as in a supermarket. 3 To examine and approve. 4 To prove, upon examination, to be accurate, in good condition, etc. —**in check** 1 Under control. 2 In danger: said of the king in chess. —*v.t.* 1 To stop or restrain forcibly or suddenly. 2 To curb; hold in restraint. 3 To ascertain the correctness, completeness, etc., of. 4 To investigate. 5 To mark with a check or checks. 6 To mark with a pattern of squares, as cloth. 7 To cause to crack; to make checks or chinks in. 8 To rebuke; rebuff; repulse: They *checked* the attack. 9 In chess, to put (an opponent's king) in check. 10 To deposit temporarily for safekeeping: to *check* one's luggage. —*v.i.* 11 To agree item for item: My figures *check* with yours. 12 To investigate: often with *on.* 13 To crack, as paint. 14 In chess, to put an opponent's king in check. —*interj.* 1 In chess, an exclamation proclaiming that the opponent's

king is in check. 2 Correct; I understand; OK. —*adj.* 1 Having a checked pattern. 2 Serving to verify or confirm. [< Ar. *shāh* king (in chess) < Pers.] —**check′a·ble** *adj.*

check·book (chek′bŏŏk′) *n.* A book of blank bank checks.

checked (chekt) *adj.* 1 Marked with squares: *checked* gingham. 2 Kept in check; restrained. 3 Stopped.

check·er (chek′ər) *n.* 1 A piece in the game of checkers, usu. a small disk. 2 One of the squares in a checkered surface. 3 One who checks, esp. one who inspects, counts, or supervises the disposal of merchandise. —*v.t.* 1 To mark with squares or crossed lines. 2 To vary or diversify, as with changes in fortune, etc. [< OF *eschequier* chessboard < Ar. *shāh* king (in chess)]

check·er·board (chek′ər·bôrd′, -bōrd′) *n.* A board divided into 64 squares, used in playing checkers or chess.

check·ered (chek′ərd) *adj.* 1 Divided into squares. 2 Showing alternating spaces of color or of light and darkness. 3 Varied or diversified, as by changes in fortune.

check·ers (chek′ərz) *n. pl. (construed as sing.)* A game played by two persons with 24 pieces on a checkerboard.

checking account A bank account against which a depositor may draw checks.

check·mate (chek′māt′) *v.t.* **·mat·ed, mat·ing** 1 In chess, to put (an opponent's king) in check from which no escape is possible, thus winning the game. 2 To defeat by a skillful maneuver. —*n.* 1 The act of checkmating. 2 The situation of a king that has been checkmated. 3 Complete defeat. [< Ar. *al-shāh māt* the king is dead]

check·off (chek′ôf′, -of′) *n.* The collection of trade-union dues by deduction from the pay of each employee.

check·out (chek′out′) *n.* The action or an instance of checking out.

check·rein (chek′rān′) *n.* A rein from the bit of the bridle to the saddle of a harness to keep a horse's head up.

check·up (chek′up′) *n.* 1 A medical examination. 2 Any examination or investigation.

Ched·dar (ched′ər) *n.* Any of several types of mild or sharp, white to yellow, hard, smooth cheese. Also **ched′-dar.** [< *Cheddar,* Somersetshire, England]

cheek (chēk) *n.* 1 Either side of the face below the eye and above the mouth. 2 A side or part analogous to the side of a face. 3 *Informal* Impudent boldness. [< OE *cēce, cēace*]

cheek·bone (chēk′bōn′) *n.* Either of two bones in the upper cheek, just below the eye.

cheek·y (chē′kē) *adj.* **cheek·i·er, cheek·i·est** *Informal* Impudent; brazen. —**cheek′i·ly** *adv.* —**cheek′i·ness** *n.*

cheep (chēp) *v.t. & v.i.* To chirp faintly or shrilly. —*n.* A weak chirp, as of a young bird. [Imit.] —**cheep′er** *n.*

cheer (chir) *n.* 1 A shout of approval or encouragement. 2 Cheerfulness; gaiety. 3 Something that promotes cheerfulness. 4 Food or drink. —*v.t.* 1 To make cheerful; comfort: often with *up.* 2 To applaud or salute with cheers. 3 To encourage; incite: often with *on.* —*v.i.* 4 To become cheerful, happy or glad: with *up.* 5 To utter cheers. [< OF *chere* face, countenance < LL *cara*] —**cheer′er** *n.*

cheer·ful (chir′fəl) *adj.* 1 Joyous; happy. 2 Willing. 3 Attractively bright, sunny, etc. —**cheer′ful·ly** *adv.* —**cheer′ful·ness** *n.*

cheer·i·o (chir′ē·ō) *interj. & n. Brit.* 1 Hello! 2 Goodbye!

cheer·less (chir′lis) *adj.* Bleak; gloomy. —**cheer′less·ly** *adv.* —**cheer′less·ness** *n.*

cheer·y (chir′ē) *adj.* **cheer·i·er, cheer·i·est** Joyous; bright; cheerful. —**cheer′i·ly** *adv.* —**cheer′i·ness** *n.*

cheese (chēz) *n.* 1 The pressed curd of milk, variously prepared and flavored. 2 A cake or mass of this substance. [< L *caseus* cheese]

cheese·cake (chēz′kāk′) *n.* 1 A cake containing cheese, sugar, eggs, milk, etc.: also **cheese cake.** 2 *Slang* A photograph of a pretty girl's legs or figure.

cheese·cloth (chēz′klôth′, -kloth′) *n.* A thin, loosely woven, white cotton fabric.

chees·y (chē′zē) *adj.* **·i·er, ·i·est** 1 Like cheese, as in texture, taste, etc. 2 *Slang* Of inferior quality; second-rate.

chee·tah (chē′tə) *n.* A swift feline resembling the leopard, native to Asia and Africa. [< Hind. *chītā* leopard]

chef (shef) *n.* 1 A head cook. 2 Any cook. [< OF *chef* chief]

chef-d'oeu·vre (she·dœ′vr′) *n. pl.* **chefs-d'oeu·vre** (she-) *French* A masterpiece, as of an artist, writer, etc.

che·la (kē′lə) *n. pl.* **·lae** (-lē) *Zool.* A terminal pincerlike claw, as in lobsters and scorpions. [< Gk. *chēlē* claw] **—che·late** (kē′lāt) *adj.*

Chelae of scorpion

chem. chemical; chemist; chemistry.

chem·i·cal (kem′i·kəl) *adj.* 1 Of or pertaining to chemistry. 2 Obtained by or used in chemistry. **—***n.* A substance obtained by or used in a chemical process. **— chem′i·cal·ly** *adv.*

chemical energy Energy released from substances by chemical reaction, as in the detonation of explosives, burning of fuel, etc.

chemical engineering The application of chemistry to industrial processes.

chemical warfare The military use of chemical agents, such as poisonous gases, incendiary materials, etc.

che·mise (shə·mēz′) *n.* 1 A woman's undergarment resembling a short slip. 2 A dress that hangs straight from the shoulders. [< LL *camisia* shirt]

chem·ist (kem′ist) *n.* 1 One versed in chemistry. 2 *Brit.* A druggist. [< Med. L *alchymista* alchemist]

chem·is·try (kem′is·trē) *n.* 1 That science which treats of the structure, composition, and properties of substances and of the transformations which they undergo. 2 Chemical composition or processes.

chem·o·ther·a·py (kem′ō·ther′ə·pē) *n.* The treatment of disease with chemicals. Also **chem′o·ther′a·peu′tics. — chem′o·ther′a·peu′tic** *adj.* **—chem′o·ther′a·pist** *n.*

chem·ur·gy (kem′ər·jē) *n.* The utilization of organic raw materials, esp. agricultural products, in the development of new products. **—chem·ur·gic** (kem·ûr′jik) or **·gi·cal** *adj.*

che·nille (shə·nēl′) *n.* 1 A soft, fluffy cord or yarn having a fuzzy pile on all sides, used for embroidery, tassels, etc. 2 Any fabric made with such yarn. [F, lit., caterpillar < L *canicula*, dim. of *canis* dog]

cheque (chek) *n. Brit.* CHECK (def. 8). **—cheq′uer** *n.*

cher·ish (cher′ish) *v.t.* 1 To care for kindly. 2 To hold dear. 3 To entertain fondly, as a hope or an idea. [< F *cher* dear < L *carus*] **—cher′ish·er** *n.*

Cher·o·kee (cher′ə·kē, cher′ə·kē′) *n. pl.* **·kee** or **·kees** 1 A member of a tribe of Iroquoian Indians now dwelling in Oklahoma. 2 The language of this tribe.

Cherokee rose An evergreen, trailing rose having large, fragrant white flowers.

che·root (shə·rōōt′) *n.* A cigar cut square at both ends. [< Tamil *shuruttu* roll, cigar]

cher·ry (cher′ē) *n. pl.* **·ries** 1 Any of various trees related to the plum and bearing small, round or heart-shaped drupes enclosing a smooth pit. 2 The wood or fruit of a cherry tree. 3 A bright red color: also **cherry red. —***adj.* 1 Bright red. 2 Made of cherry wood. 3 Made with or from cherries. 4 Having a cherrylike flavor. [< Gk. *kerasos* cherry tree]

cher·ub (cher′əb) *n. pl.* **cher·ubs** for defs. 1 & 2, **cher·u·bim** (cher′yə·bim) for def. 3. 1 In art, the representation of a beautiful winged child. 2 Any beautiful child or infant. 3 One of an order of angelic beings ranking second to the seraphim. [< Heb. *kerūbh*, an angelic being] **—che·ru·bic** (chə·rōō′bik) *adj.* **—che·ru′bi·cal·ly** *adv.*

cher·vil (chûr′vəl) *n.* A garden herb related to parsley. [< Gk. *chairephyllon*]

chess (ches) *n.* A game played by two persons on a checkered board, with

Chess game in progress. The horizontal rows are *ranks;* the vertical rows are *files.*

16 pieces on each side, the object being to checkmate an opponent's king. [< OF *eschec* check (at chess)]

chest (chest) *n.* 1 The part of the body enclosed by the ribs; the thorax. 2 A box usu. having a hinged lid, used for tools, personal possessions, etc. 3 A chest of drawers. 4 a A public treasury or fund. b The funds contained there. [< Gk. *kistē* basket, box]

ches·ter·field (ches′tər·fēld) *n.* A single-breasted topcoat, usu. with concealed buttons and a velvet collar. [< an Earl of *Chesterfield* of the 19th c.]

chest·nut (ches′nut′, -nət) *n.* 1 A smooth-shelled, edible nut. 2 Any of various trees related to the beech that bear this nut. 3 One of certain other trees: the horse *chestnut.* 4 A reddish brown. 5 A horse of this color. 6 *Informal* a A trite joke. b Anything trite. **—***adj.* Reddish brown. [< Gk. *kastanea* + NUT]

chest of drawers A piece of furniture containing a set of drawers for storing linens, wearing apparel, etc.

chest·y (ches′tē) *adj.* **chest·i·er, chest·i·est** *Informal* 1 Having a large chest. 2 Proud; self-important.

che·tah (chē′tə) *n.* CHEETAH.

chev·a·lier (shev′ə·lir′) *n.* 1 A French knight or nobleman. 2 A gallant gentleman. 3 A member of the French Legion of Honor. [< LL *caballarius* cavalier]

chev·i·ot (shev′ē·ət) *n.* A sturdy woolen or cotton cloth of twill weave, used for suits, overcoats, etc.

Chev·i·ot (chev′ē·ət, chē′vē-) *n.* One of a breed of sheep, much esteemed for their wool.

chev·ron (shev′rən) *n.* A V-shaped insignia worn on the sleeve of a military or police uniform to show rank or length of service. [< Med. L *capro* rafter < L *caper* goat]

chev·y (chev′ē) *v.t.* **chev·ied, chev·y·ing** CHIVY.

Chevrons

chew (chōō) *v.t. & v.i.* 1 To cut or grind with the teeth. 2 To consider carefully. **—chew out** *Slang* To scold or reprimand severely. **—***n.* 1 The act of chewing. 2 Something chewed or made for chewing. [< OE *cēowan*] **—chew′er** *n.*

chewing gum A sweetened, gummy substance, usu. chicle, for chewing.

che·wink (chi·wingk′) *n.* A towhee having red-brown sides and a black hood and back.

chew·y (chōō′ē) *adj.* **chew·i·er, chew·i·est** Relatively soft and requiring chewing: Caramels are *chewy.*

Chey·enne (shī·en′) *n. pl.* **·enne** or **·ennes** 1 A member of an Algonquian tribe of North American Indians now dwelling in Montana and Oklahoma. 2 The language of this tribe.

chg. change.

chgd. charged.

chi (kī) The twenty-second letter of the Greek alphabet (Χ, χ), transliterated into English by *ch.*

Chian·ti (kyän′tē) *n.* A dry, red Italian wine; also, any similar wine. [< Monti *Chianti*, a region in Italy]

chi·a·ro·scu·ro (kē·är′ə·skyŏŏr′ō) *n. pl.* **·ros** 1 The distribution and treatment of light and shade in a picture. 2 A technique of painting or drawing using only light and shade to achieve its effects. 3 A painting or drawing using this technique. Also **chi·a·ro·o·scu·ro** (kē·är′ə·ō·skyŏŏr′ō). [Ital. < *chiaro* clear + *oscuro* dim, obscure]

chic (shēk, shik) *adj.* Smart; stylish; elegant. **—***n.* Elegance and taste; style. [F < G *Schick* skill]

chi·can·er·y (shi·kā′nər·ē) *n. pl.* **·er·ies** 1 The use of tricky or deceptive talk or action. 2 An instance of this. [< F *chicaner* to quibble]

Chi·ca·no (chi·kä′nō) *n. pl.* **·nos** A Mexican-American.

chi·chi (shē′shē) *adj. Informal* Ostentatiously chic, elegant, or sophisticated. [F]

chick (chik) *n.* 1 A young chicken or other bird. 2 *Slang* A young woman.

chick·a·dee (chik′ə·dē) *n.* A North American titmouse with the top of the head and the throat dark-colored. [Imit. of its cry]

Chick·a·saw (chik′ə·sô) *n. pl.* **·saw** or **·saws** 1 A member of a tribe of Muskhogean North American Indians now dwelling in Oklahoma. 2 The language of this tribe.

chick·en (chik′ən) n. 1 The young of the common domestic fowl. 2 Loosely, a fowl of any age. 3 Its flesh used as food. 4 *Informal* A young or inexperienced person. —*adj.* 1 Of chicken. 2 Small. 3 *Slang* Cowardly. [< OE *cȳcen*]

chick·en-heart·ed (chik′ən-här′tid) *adj.* Timid or cowardly; faint-hearted.

chicken pox An infectious, viral disease of childhood, characterized by skin eruptions.

chick·weed (chik′wēd′) n. Any of several common low-growing weeds related to pinks.

chic·le (chik′əl) n. 1 The milky juice of the sapodilla tree. 2 A gum prepared from it, used in making chewing gum. Also **chicle gum**. [< Nah. *chictli*]

chic·o·ry (chik′ə-rē) n. pl. ·ries 1 Any of several species of perennial edible salad herbs of the composite family. 2 The dried, ground roots of a chicory plant, sometimes used with or instead of coffee. [< Gk. *kichora*]

chide (chīd) v.t. & v.i. **chid·ed** or **chid** (chid), **chid·ed** or **chid·den** (chid′n), **chid·ing** To scold or reprove. [< OE *cidan*] —**chid′er** n. —**chid′ing·ly** *adv.*

chief (chēf) n. 1 A ruler, leader, head, etc., of an organization, group, or establishment. 2 *Usu. cap. Naut.* a A chief petty officer. b A chief engineer. 3 *Slang* A boss. —*adj.* 1 Highest in rank or authority. 2 Principal, most important, or most eminent. [< L *caput* head]

Chief Executive The President of the U.S.

chief justice The presiding judge of a court composed of several justices.

Chief Justice The official head of the U.S. Supreme Court.

chief·ly (chēf′lē) *adv.* 1 Most of all or above all. 2 Generally; mostly.

Chief of Staff The ranking officer of a staff, assisting the officer in command, as, in the U.S. Army or Air Force, the officer immediately under the Secretary of his department.

chief·tain (chēf′tən) n. 1 The head of a tribe or clan. 2 Any chief.

chif·fon (shi·fon′) n. A sheer fabric of silk, nylon, etc. [F < *chiffe* rag]

chif·fo·nier (shif′ə·nir′) n. A high chest of drawers. Also **chif′fon·nier′**. [F < *chiffon* chiffon]

chig·ger (chig′ər) n. 1 The tiny larvae of certain mites that burrow under the skin. 2 CHIGOE (def. 1). [Alter. of CHIGOE]

chi·gnon (shēn′yon, Fr. shē·nyôn′) n. A roll of hair worn at the back of a woman's head. [F< OF *chaignon* chain]

chig·oe (chig′ō) n. 1 A flea of tropical Africa and South America whose female causes sores by burrowing under the skin. 2 CHIGGER (def. 1). [< Cariban]

Chi·hua·hua (chi·wä′wä) n. One of an ancient Mexican breed of very small, smooth-coated dogs with large, pointed ears. [< *Chihuahua*, Mexico]

chil·blain (chil′blān) n. A painful inflamed area on the hands or feet, due to exposure to cold. [< CHILL + BLAIN] —**chil′blained** *adj.*

child (chīld) n. pl. **chil·dren** 1 An offspring of either sex of human parents. 2 A young person, usu. one between infancy and youth. 3 A descendant. 4 A childish or immature person. 5 A person or thing considered as an offspring or product: Poems are the *children* of fancy. [< OE *cild*]

child·bear·ing (chīld′bâr′ing) n. The act or process of bearing children. —*adj.* Of or relating to childbearing.

child·birth (chīld′bûrth′) n. The act of bearing a child; parturition.

child·hood (chīld′hŏŏd′) n. The state or time of being a child.

child·ish (chīl′dish) *adj.* 1 Of, pertaining to, or characteristic of a child. 2 Immature; petty. —**child′ish·ly** *adv.* — **child′ish·ness** n. —Syn. 2 babyish, infantile, puerile, foolish, trivial, silly. • See CHILDLIKE.

child·like (chīld′līk′) *adj.* 1 Like a child. 2 Innocent; naive. • The word *childish*, when applied to an adult, is never complimentary. If one wishes to describe a grown-up who possesses a certain innocence, charm, candor, etc., ascribed to children, the word to use is *childlike*.

chil·dren (chil′drən) n. pl. of CHILD.

chil·e (chil′ē) n. CHILI.

Chil·e (chil′ē, Sp. chē′lä) n. A republic of w South America, 286,397 sq. mi., cap. Santiago. —**Chil′e·an** *adj.*, n. • See map at ARGENTINA.

Chile saltpeter A mineral sodium nitrate found in Chile and Peru.

chil·i (chil′ē) n. pl. **chil·ies** 1 A tropical species of capsicum. 2 The dried pod of this plant, used in red pepper. 3 CHILI CON CARNE. Also **chile, chilli**. [< Nah. *chilli*]

chil·i con car·ne (chil′ē kon kär′nē) A Mexican dish of red peppers, with meat, beans, spices, etc. Also **chile con car′ne**.

chili sauce A spicy sauce made with tomatoes, sweet peppers, etc. Also **chile sauce**.

chill (chil) n. 1 A sensation of cold, often with shivering or shaking. 2 A disagreeable feeling of coldness, as from fear. 3 A dampening of enthusiasm, joy, etc. 4 A distant or unfriendly manner. —*v.t.* 1 To reduce to a low or lower temperature. 2 To make chilly; seize with a chill. 3 To discourage; dampen, as joy. —*v.i.* 4 To become cold. 5 To be stricken with a chill. —*adj.* CHILLY. [< OE *ciele, cyle*] —**chill′er, chill′ness** n. —**chill′ing·ly** *adv.*

chill·y (chil′ē) *adj.* **chill·i·er, chill·i·est** 1 Producing or feeling cold. 2 Disheartening; depressing. 3 Not genial; unfriendly. —**chill′i·ly** *adv.* —**chill′i·ness** n.

chime (chīm) n. 1 *Often pl.* A set of bells tuned to a scale. 2 A single bell, as in a clock. 3 *Often pl.* The sounds produced by a chime or chimes. 4 Accord; harmony. —*v.* **chimed, chim·ing** *v.t.* 1 To cause to ring musically, as by striking. 2 To announce, as the hour, by the sound of bells. 3 To summon, welcome, or send by chiming. 4 To recite in unison or cadence. —*v.i.* 5 To ring musically, as bells. 6 To harmonize; agree: with *with*. 7 To recite or intone in cadence. [< L *cymbalum* cymbal] —**chim′er** n.

chi·me·ra (kə·mir′ə, kī-) n. 1 An impractically fanciful or absurd hope, plan, or conception. 2 Any fabulous creature composed of incongruous parts 3 *Biol.* An organism or mass of living cells incorporating diverse genetic patterns. Also **chi·mae′ra**. [See CHIMERA.]

Chi·me·ra (kə·mir′ə, kī-) *Gk. Myth.* A fire-breathing monster having a lion's head, a goat's body, and a serpent's tail. [< Gk. *chimaira* she-goat]

chi·mer·i·cal (kə·mer′i·kəl, kī-) *adj.* 1 Not realizable or possible; impractical; visionary. 2 Imaginary; fanciful. Also **chi·mer′ic**. —**chi·mer′i·cal·ly** *adv.*

chim·ney (chim′nē) n. pl. ·neys 1 A pipe or tube for the escape of smoke or gases from a fire. 2 A structure containing such a pipe or tube, often extending above a roof. 3 A tube for enclosing a flame, as of a lamp. 4 *Geol.* A rock formation or a volcano vent resembling a chimney. [< Gk. *kaminos* furnace]

chimney corner The space between the sides of a large, old-fashioned fireplace and the fire, where one might sit.

chim·ney·sweep (chim′nē·swēp′) n. One who cleans the soot from chimneys.

chimney swift A swift with dark plumage that nests in chimneys and hollow trees. • See SWIFT.

chim·pan·zee (chim′pan·zē′, chim·pan′zē) n. An African anthropoid ape with large ears and black hair, smaller than the gorilla. [< native w African name]

chin (chin) n. The central part of the lower jaw; the part of the face below the mouth. —*v.* **chinned, chin·ning** *v.t.* 1 To grasp an overhead horizontal support and lift (oneself) until the chin is level with the hands. —*v.i.* 2 To chin oneself. 3 *Informal* To talk idly. [< OE *cin*]

Chin. Chinese.

chi·na (chī′nə) n. 1 Porcelain or similar pottery, originally from China. 2 Dishes, etc., made of such ware. Also **chi′na·ware′** (-wâr′).

Chi·na (chī′nə) n. 1 A republic of E and CEN. Asia, 3,768,377 sq. mi., cap. Peking. 2 A republic located on Taiwan and nearby islands, 13,890 sq. mi., cap. Taipei. • See map next page.

chi·na·ber·ry (chī′nə·ber′ē) n. pl. ·ries 1 A tree common in s North America, having purple flowers and yellowish, ball-like fruit. Also **China tree**. 2 The fruit of this tree.

Chi·na·town (chī′nə·toun′) n. The Chinese quarter of any city outside China.

chin·ca·pin (ching′kə·pin) n. CHINQUAPIN.

China

chinch (chinch) *n.* BEDBUG. [<L *cimex* bug]

chinch bug A small black and white insect destructive to grain.

chin·chil·la (chin·chil′ə) *n.* **1** A small South American rodent having soft pearl-gray fur. **2** Its highly valued fur. **3** A heavy wool fabric with a nubbed surface, used esp. for overcoats. [<Sp.]

chine (chīn) *n.* **1** The spine, backbone, or back. **2** A cut of meat including vertebrae. [<OF *eschine* backbone]

Chi·nese (chī·nēz′, -nēs′) *n. pl.* **·nese 1** A native or citizen of China. **2** A person whose ancestry is Chinese. **3** Any of a group of related languages spoken in China, esp. the official language. —*adj.* Of or pertaining to China, its peoples, or any of their languages.

Chinese lantern A collapsible lantern made of thin, usu. brightly colored paper.

chink¹ (chingk) *n.* A small, narrow cleft; crevice. —*v.t.* **1** To make cracks or fissures in. **2** To fill the cracks of, as a wall. [?<OE *cine* crack]

chink² (chingk) *n.* A short, sharp, metallic sound. —*v.t. & v.i.* To make or cause to make such a sound. [Imit.]

chi·no (chē′nō) *n. pl.* **·nos 1** A strong, twilled cotton fabric. **2** *pl.* Trousers made of this fabric. [<Sp., toasted; with ref. to the original tan color]

chi·nook (chi·nōōk′, -nōōk′) *n.* **1** A warm, moist wind of the Oregon and Washington coasts. **2** A warm, dry wind that descends the eastern slopes of the Rocky Mountains in the NW United States and W Canada.

Chi·nook (chi·nōōk′, -nōōk′) *n. pl.* **·nook** or **·nooks 1** A member of a tribe of North American Indians formerly occupying the Columbia River valley. **2** The language of this tribe. —**Chi·nook′an** *adj., n.*

Chinook jargon A language comprised of words from Chinook and other Indian languages, mixed with English and French, once used by traders and Indians from Oregon to Alaska.

chin·qua·pin (ching′kə·pin) *n.* **1** A dwarf chestnut tree of the E U.S. **2** A related tall tree of NW North America. **3** The edible nut of any of these trees. Also **chink′a·pin.** [<N.Am. Ind.]

chintz (chints) *n.* A usu. glazed, brightly printed cotton fabric. [<Skt. *chitra* variegated]

chintz·y (chint′sē) *adj.* **chintz·i·er, chintz·i·est 1** Of or like chintz. **2** *Informal* Tacky; cheap.

chip (chip) *n.* **1** A small piece cut or broken off. **2** A mark where such a piece has broken off. **3** A small disk used as a counter in games, as poker. **4** A thin crisp morsel: potato *chips*. **5** *pl. Brit.* French-fried potatoes. **6** An integrated circuit in a computer. —**a chip off the old block** A child who closely resembles either parent. —**a chip on one's shoulder** A tendency to quarrel. —*v.* **chipped, chip·ping** *v.t.* **1** To break or cut a small piece or pieces from. —*v.i.* **2** To become broken in this way. —**chip in** To contribute, as money. [<OE *cippe* piece cut off a beam]

chip·munk (chip′mungk) *n.* Any of various squirrellike striped North American rodents. [<N.Am. Ind.]

chipped beef Smoked beef sliced thin.

Chip·pen·dale (chip′ən·dāl) *adj.* Of or designating a rococo style of 18th-century furniture. [<Thomas *Chippendale*, 1718–79, English cabinetmaker]

chip·per (chip′ər) *adj.* Brisk; cheerful. [<earlier *chip* chirp] —**Syn.** lively, spry, sprightly, cheery.

Chipmunk

Chip·pe·wa (chip′ə·wä, -wā, -wə) *n. pl.* **·wa** or **·was** OJIBWA. Also **Chip·pe·way** (chip′ə·wā).

chiro- *combining form* Hand. [<Gk. *cheir* hand]

chi·rog·ra·phy (kī·rog′rə·fē) *n.* Handwriting; penmanship. —**chi·rog′ra·pher** *n.*

chi·rop·o·dy (kə·rop′ə·dē, kī-) *n.* PODIATRY. [<CHIRO- + Gk. *pous, podos* foot] —**chi·rop′o·dist** *n.*

chi·ro·prac·tic (kī′rə·prak′tik) *n.* Therapeutic treatment involving manipulation of the body, esp. the spine. [<CHIRO + Gk. *praktikos* effective<*prattein* do, act] —**chi′ro·prac′tor** *n.*

chirp (chûrp) *v.i.* **1** To give a short, sharp cry, as a small bird or cricket. **2** To talk in a quick, high-pitched manner. —*v.t.* **3** To utter with a quick, sharp sound. —*n.* A sound made by chirping. [ME *chirpen*, var. of *chirken*]

chirr (chûr) *v.i.* To make a sharp trilling sound, as of a grasshopper. —*n.* The sound of chirring. [Imit.]

chir·rup (chir′əp) *v.i.* To chirp continuously or repeatedly. —*n.* A series of chirps. [<CHIRP]

chis·el (chiz′əl) *n.* A tool with a sharp, beveled edge, used for cutting or shaping metal, stone, or wood. —*v.t. & v.i.* **chis·eled** or **·elled, chis·el·ing** or **·el·ling 1** To cut, engrave, or carve with or as with a chisel. **2** *Informal.* To cheat; swindle. [<L *caesus* pp. of *caedere* cut] —**chis′el·er** or **chis′el·ler** *n.*

chit¹ (chit) *n.* A voucher of a small sum owed, as for food. [<Hind. *chitthī* note]

chit² (chit) *n.* A pert girl. [ME *chitte*]

chit-chat (chit′chat′) *n.* Informal talk or gossip. [Redupl. of CHAT]

chi·tin (kī′tin) *n.* A tough, horny substance forming the principal constituent of the hard covering of insects, crustaceans, etc. [<Gk. *chitōn* tunic] —**chi′tin·ous** *adj.*

chit·ter·lings (chit′ər·lingz) *n. pl.* The small intestines of pigs, prepared as food. Also **chit′lings, chit′lins.** [ME *chiterling*]

chiv·al·rous (shiv′əl·rəs) *adj.* **1** Having the qualities of the ideal knight; courteous, honorable, brave, etc. **2** Of or pertaining to chivalry. Also **chi·val·ric** (shi·val′rik, shiv′.əl-). —**chiv′al·rous·ly** *adv.* —**chiv′al·rous·ness** *n.* —**Syn.** gallant, knightly, courtly, valiant.

chiv·al·ry (shiv′əl·rē) *n.* **1** The system or spirit of medieval knighthood. **2** The idealized qualities of knighthood, as courtesy, magnanimity, bravery, etc. **3** An instance of such qualities. [<LL *caballarius* cavalier]

chive (chīv) *n.* An herb related to the onion, having slender, hollow leaves used as flavoring in cooking. [<L *cepa* onion]

chiv·y (chiv′ē) *v.t.* **chiv·ied, chiv·y·ing** To harass; hound. Also **chiv′vy.** [<*Chevy* Chase, old English ballad]

chla·myd·i·a (klə·mid′ē·ə) *n.* A venereal disease affecting the genitals and urinary tract, caused by a parasitic organism. [<NL<Gk. *chlamys* short cloak]

chlo·ral (klôr′əl, klō′rəl) *n.* **1** A colorless, oily liquid with a penetrating odor, obtained by the action of chlorine on alcohol. **2** A white, toxic, crystalline compound, used medicinally as a hypnotic, etc.: also **chloral hydrate.** [<CHLOR(INE) + AL(COHOL)]

chlor·am·phen·i·col (klôr′am·fen′i·kol, -kol, klō′ram-) *n.* An antibiotic used in the treatment of typhoid fever and various other diseases. [<CHLOR- + AM(IDE) + PHE-(NOL) + NI(TROGEN) + (GLY)COL]

chlo·rate (klôr′āt, klō′rāt) *n.* A salt of chloric acid.

chlor·dane (klôr′dān, klôr′-) *n.* A colorless, odorless, poisonous liquid compound, used as an insecticide.

chlo·ric (klôr′ik, klō′rik) *adj.* Of, pertaining to, or combined with chlorine: said specifically of relatively unstable compounds containing oxygen.

chloric acid An unstable acid with great oxidizing power.

chlo·ride (klôr′īd, -id, klō′rīd, -rid) *n.* A compound of chlorine with another element or radical. —**chlo·rid·ic** (klə·rid′ik) *adj.*

chloride of lime A disinfecting and bleaching agent made by the action of chlorine gas on slaked lime.

chlo·rin·ate (klôr′ə·nāt, klō′rə-) *v.t.* **·at·ed, ·at·ing** To treat, impregnate, or cause to combine with chlorine, as in disinfecting sewage, etc. —**chlo′rin·a′tion, chlo′rin·a′tor** *n.*

chlo·rine (klôr′ēn, -in, klō′rēn, -rin) *n.* A greenish yellow, poisonous, gaseous element (symbol Cl) of the halogen group, occurring abundantly in combination with other elements and widely used in industry, medicine, etc. [< Gk. *chlōros* green]

chloro- *combining form* **1** Light green: *chlorophyll.* **2** Chlorine: *chloroform.* Also **chlor-**. [< Gk. *chlōros* green]

chlo·ro·form (klôr′ə·fôrm, klō′rə-) *n.* A colorless, volatile, sweetish liquid compound, used as an anesthetic and a solvent. —*v.t.* To anesthetize or kill with chloroform. [< CHLORO- + FORM(YL)]

Chlo·ro·my·ce·tin (klôr′ə·mī·sē′tən, klō′rə-) *n.* CHLORAMPHENICOL: a trade name.

chlo·ro·phyll (klôr′ə·fil, klō′rə-) *n.* The green pigment of plants, essential to photosynthesis. Also **chlo′ro·phyl**. [< CHLORO- + Gk. *phyllon* leaf] —**chlo′ro·phyl′lose** (-fil′ōs), **chlo′ro·phyl′lous** (-fil′əs) *adj.*

chlo·ro·plast (klôr′ə·plast, klō′rə-) *n.* One of the small chlorophyll-bearing bodies found in the cytoplasm of plant cells. [< CHLORO- + Gk. *plastos* molded]

chlor·pro·ma·zine (klôr·prō′mə·zēn, -zin, klôr-) *n.* A synthetic drug used as a tranquilizer in treating mental illness. [A composite word from di*methyl* amino*propyl* *chlor*ophenothi*azine* hydrochloride]

chm., chmn. chairman.

chock (chok) *n.* **1** A block or wedge placed so as to prevent or limit motion. **2** *Naut.* A heavy piece of metal or wood fastened to a deck, etc., and having jaws through which a rope or cable may pass. —*v.t.* To wedge or hold in place with or as with chocks. —*adv.* As completely or as close as possible. [< AF *choque* log]

chock-a-block (chok′ə·blok′) *adj.* Close together; crowded. —*adv.* Close; very near.

chock-full (chok′fŏŏl′) *adj.* Completely full. [ME *chokkeful*]

choc·o·late (chôk′lit, chôk′ə·lit, chok′-) *n.* **1** Roasted and ground cacao seeds, often sweetened or flavored. **2** A beverage or confection made from this. **3** A dark brown. —*adj.* **1** Flavored or made with chocolate. **2** Dark brown. [< Nah. *chocólatl*]

Choc·taw (chok′tô) *n. pl.* **·taw** or **·taws 1** A member of a tribe of North American Indians of Muskhogean linguistic stock now dwelling in Oklahoma. **2** The language of this tribe.

choice (chois) *n.* **1** The act of choosing; selection. **2** The right or power to choose; option. **3** Something or someone chosen. **4** A number or a variety from which to choose. **5** An alternative. **6** The best or preferred part. —*adj.* **choic·er, choic·est 1** Of special quality; excellent. **2** Carefully selected. [< OF *choisir* choose] —**choice′ly** *adv.* —**choice′ness** *n.*

choir (kwīr) *n.* **1** A body of trained singers, esp. in a church. **2** The part of a church used by such a group. **3** A group of musicians, as instrumentalists. —*v.t. & v.i.* To sing in a choir or in chorus. [< L *chorus* chorus]

choke (chōk) *v.* **choked, chok·ing** *v.t.* **1** To stop or obstruct the breathing of; strangle. **2** To keep back; suppress. **3** To obstruct or close up by filling. **4** To retard the progress, growth, or action of. **5** To lessen the air intake in order to enrich the fuel mixture of (a gasoline engine). —*v.i.* **6** To become suffocated or stifled. **7** To have difficulty in breathing. **8** To be so affected by emotion, fright, etc., that one's behavior is noticeably constrained or one's speech falter-

ing: usu. with *up*. **9** To become clogged or obstructed. —*n.* **1** The act or sound of choking. **2** A device to control the supply of air to a gasoline engine. [< OE *acēocian*]

choke·cher·ry (chōk′cher′ē) *n. pl.* **·ries** A North American wild cherry bearing astringent fruit.

choke·damp (chōk′damp′) *n.* A choking carbon dioxide gas that collects in mines.

chok·er (chō′kər) *n.* A necklace, collar, etc., that fits closely around the neck.

chol·er (kol′ər) *n.* Anger or sharpness of temper. [< L *cholera* jaundice]

chol·er·a (kol′ər·ə) *n.* An acute, infectious, epidemic disease, characterized by serious intestinal disorders. [< Gk. < *cholē* bile, gall]

chol·er·ic (kol′ər·ik, kə·ler′ik) *adj.* Easily aroused to anger; bad-tempered. —**Syn.** irascible, irritable, cranky.

cho·les·ter·ol (kə·les′tə·rōl, -rōl) *n.* A fat-soluble, solid alcohol found in the blood, brain and nerve tissue, etc., and in deposits constricting blood vessels in arteriosclerosis. [< Gk. *cholē* bile + *stereos* solid + -OL]

chomp (chomp) *v.t. & v.i.* To chew or bite upon (something). [Alter. of CHAMP¹] —**chomp′er** *n.*

choose (chōōz) *v.* **chose, cho·sen, choos·ing** *v.t.* **1** To select among others or as an alternative. **2** To desire or prefer (to do something). —*v.i.* **3** To make a selection or decision. [< OE *cēosan*] —**choos′er** *n.*

choos·y (chōō′ze) *adj.* **choos·i·er, choos·i·est** *Informal* Particular or fussy in one's choices. —**choos′i·ness** *n.*

chop¹ (chop) *v.* **chopped, chop·ping** *v.t.* **1** To cut or make by strokes of a sharp tool; hew. **2** To cut up in small pieces; mince. **3** To utter jerkily. —*v.i.* **4** To make cutting strokes, as with an ax. **5** To move with a sudden, jerky motion. —*n.* **1** A small cut of meat, usu. containing a rib. **2** The act of chopping. **3** A short, swift blow. **4** A sudden choppy motion, as of a wave. [ME *choppen* var. of *chappen* to chap]

chop² (chop) *v.i.* To veer suddenly; shift, as the wind. [< OE *cēapian* to barter, exchange]

chop·house (chop′hous′) *n.* A restaurant specializing in steaks and chops.

chop·per (chop′ər) *n.* **1** One who or that which chops. **2** *pl. Slang* Teeth. **3** *Slang* A helicopter.

chop·py (chop′ē) *adj.* **·pi·er, ·pi·est 1** Full of short, rough waves. **2** Jerky; irregular; shifting. —**chop′pi·ly** *adv.* —**chop′pi·ness** *n.*

chops (chops) *n. pl.* **1** The jaws. **2** The mouth, or the area of the face near the mouth. [?]

chop·sticks (chop′stiks′) *n. pl.* Paired, slender sticks used as eating implements in China, Japan, etc. [< Pidgin English *chop* quick + STICK]

chop su·ey (chop′ sōō′ē) A Chinese-American dish of meat and vegetables cooked together and served with rice. [< Chin. *tsa-sui*, lit., mixed pieces]

cho·ral (kôr′əl, kō′rəl) *adj.* **1** Of a chorus or choir. **2** Written for or sung by a chorus. —**cho′ral·ly** *adv.*

cho·rale (kə·ral′) *n.* A hymn, esp. a German Protestant hymn. Also **cho·ral′**. [< G *choral* choral]

chord¹ (kôrd) *n.* A combination of three or more musical tones sounded together. [Earlier *cord*, short for ACCORD]

chord² (kôrd) *n.* **1** A string of a musical instrument. **2** An emotional response or reaction. **3** *Geom.* A straight line connecting the ends of an arc. **4** *Anat.* A cordlike structure, as a tendon or ligament. [< Gk. *chordē* string of a musical instrument] —**chord′al** *adj.*

Chord²
AB and CB
are chords.

chore (chôr, chōr) *n.* **1** A small or routine task. **2** An unpleasant or hard task. [Var. of CHAR¹]

cho·re·a (kô·rē′ə, kō-) *n.* A nervous disease characterized by involuntary spasms of muscular contraction. [< Gk. *choreia* dance] —**cho·re′al** *adj.*

cho·re·o·graph (kôr′ē·ə·graf, kō′rē-, -gräf) *v.t.* To devise dance steps and movements for (a ballet, etc.). —**cho·re·og·ra·pher** (kôr′ē·og′rə·fər, kō′rē-) *n.*

cho·re·og·ra·phy (kôr′ē·og′rə·fē, kō′rē-) *n.* **1** The art of devising ballets and dances. **2** The art of dancing, esp. for theatrical performance. **3** The written representation of figures and steps of dancing. [< Gk. *choreia* dance + -GRAPHY] —**cho·re·o·graph·ic** (kôr′ē·ə·graf′ik, kō′rē-) *adj.*

cho·ric (kôr′ik) *adj.* Of or pertaining to a chorus, as in Greek drama.

chor·is·ter (kôr′is·tər, kor′-) *n.* A singer in a choir.

cho·roid (kôr′oid, kō′roid) *adj.* Of or pertaining to certain highly vascular membranes. —*n.* The middle or vascular layer covering the eyeball. Also **cho·ri·oid** (kôr′ē·oid, kō′rē-). [< Gk. *chorion* afterbirth, membrane]

chor·tle (kôr′təl) *v.t. & v.i.* **·tled, ·tling** To utter or say with a loud, exuberant, chuckling sound. —*n.* A loud, exuberant chuckle. [Blend of CHUCKLE and SNORT; coined by C. L. Dodgson (Lewis Carroll), 1832–98, Eng. author]

cho·rus (kôr′əs, kō′rəs) *n.* **1** A group of singers who perform together. **2** A musical composition or section for such a group. **3** A group of dancers and singers who perform together in supporting roles in musical comedy, etc. **4** Any group uttering something simultaneously. **5** Something uttered by such a group. **6** A repeated section of a song; refrain. **7** In Greek drama, a body of actors who comment upon and sometimes take part in the main action of a play. —**in chorus** All together; in unison. —*v.t. & v.i.* **chorused** or **·russed, ·rus·ing** or **·rus·sing** To sing or utter in chorus. [< L < Gk. *choros* dance]

chorus girl A woman in the chorus of a musical comedy, cabaret, etc.

chose (chōz) *p.t.* of CHOOSE.

cho·sen (chō′zən) *p.p.* of CHOOSE. —*adj.* Accorded or worthy of special choice or preference.

chow (chou) *n.* **1** A medium-sized dog having a thick brownish or black coat and a blue-black tongue: also **chow chow.** **2** *Slang* Food. [< Pidgin English]

chow·chow (chou′chou′) *n.* A relish of chopped pickles in mustard. [< Pidgin English]

chow·der (chou′dər) *n.* A thick soup of clams, other seafood, or vegetables, often with milk. [< L *caldaria* cauldron]

chow mein (chou′mān′) A Chinese-American dish of pieces of meat and various vegetables served with fried noodles. [< Chin. *ch'ao mien* fried noodles]

Chr. Christ; Christian.

chrism (kriz′əm) *n.* Oil used for anointing at baptism, confirmation, unction, etc. [< Gk. *chrisma* < *chriein* anoint]

Christ (krīst) *n.* **1** The founder of Christianity; Jesus. **2** MESSIAH (def. 1). [< Gk. *Christos* < *chriein* anoint] —**Christ′li·ness** *n.* —**Christ′ly** *adj.* • The *Christ* means the Anointed, or the divinely chosen one, and was originally used as a title identifying Jesus as the Messiah. Now it is commonly used as part of the name *Jesus Christ.*

chris·ten (kris′ən) *v.t.* **1** To name in baptism. **2** To baptize. **3** To give a name to in some ceremony: to *christen* a ship. **4** *Informal* To use for the first time. [< OE *cristnian* < *cristen* Christian]

Chris·ten·dom (kris′ən·dəm) *n.* **1** Christians collectively. **2** The Christian world.

chris·ten·ing (kris′ən·ing) *n.* A baptismal ceremony, esp. the baptizing of an infant.

Chris·tian (kris′chən) *adj.* **1** Professing or following the religion of Christ. **2** Of or derived from Christ or his doctrine. **3** Manifesting the spirit of Christ or of his teachings. **4** Of Christianity or Christendom. **5** *Informal* Human; decent. —*n.* **1** One who believes in or professes belief in Jesus as the Christ; a member of a Christian church. **2** *Informal* A civilized, decent, or respectable person. [< LL *christianus* < *Christus* Christ] —**Chris′tian·ly** *adv.*

Christian era The period beginning with the birth of Christ.

Chris·ti·an·i·ty (kris′chē·an′ə·tē) *n.* **1** The Christian religion. **2** Christians collectively. **3** The state of being a Christian.

Chris·tian·ize (kris′chən·īz) *v.* **·ized, ·iz·ing** *v.t.* **1** To convert to Christianity. **2** To imbue with Christian ideas, principles, and faith. —*v.i.* **3** To adopt Christianity. — **Chris′tian·i·za′tion** *n.* —**Chris′tian·iz′er** *n.*

Christian name A baptismal name; first or given name.

Christian Science A religious system embodying metaphysical healing, founded in 1866 by Mary Baker Eddy, and practiced in the *Church of Christ, Scientist.* — **Christian Scientist**

Christ·like (krīst′līk′) *adj.* **1** Resembling Christ. **2** Having or showing the spirit of Christ. —**Christ′like′ness** *n.*

Christ·mas (kris′məs) *n.* December 25, a holiday marking the birth of Jesus Christ. Also **Christmas Day.** [< CHRIST + MASS]

Christmas Eve The evening or day before Christmas.

Christ·mas·tide (kris′məs·tīd) *n.* The Christmas season, esp. from December 24 to January 6.

Christmas tree An evergreen or artificial tree decorated with ornaments at Christmas.

chro·ma (krō′mə) *n.* The shade and intensity of a color other than white, black, or gray. [< Gk. *chrōma* color]

chro·mate (krō′māt) *n.* A salt of chromic acid.

chro·mat·ic (krō·mat′ik) *adj.* **1** Of color or colors. **2** *Music* Using or proceeding by semitones. —**chro·mat′i·cal·ly** *adv.*

chro·mat·ics (krō·mat′iks) *n. pl. (construed as sing.)* The science of colors.

chromatic scale The musical scale made up of semitones. • See SCALE.

chro·ma·tin (krō′mə·tin) *n.* The deeply staining material in the nucleus of a living cell, that forms the chromosomes during cell division. [< Gk. *chrōma, -atos* color]

chro·ma·tog·ra·phy (krō′mə·tog′rə·fē) *n.* A method of separating the constituents of a solution by their differing adsorption by various substances. —**chro·mat·o·graph·ic** (krō·mat′ə·graf′ik) *adj.*

chrome (krōm) *n.* **1** Chromium, or an alloy of chromium, esp. as used in plating. **2** Any of certain chromium compounds used as pigments. —*v.t.* **chromed, chrom·ing** To plate with chromium. [< Gk. *chrōma* color]

chro·mic (krō′mik) *adj.* Of, from, or pertaining to chromium, esp. in its higher valency.

chromic acid A hypothetical acid known only in solution and forming chromates.

chro·mi·um (krō′mē·əm) *n.* A hard, gray, metallic element (symbol Cr) having resistance to corrosion and forming highly colored compounds. [< Gk. *chrōma* color]

chro·mo (krō′mō) *n. pl.* **·mos** CHROMOLITHOGRAPH.

chromo- *combining form* **1** Color. **2** Chromium. [< Gk. *chrōma* color]

chro·mo·lith·o·graph (krō′mō·lith′ə·graf, -gräf) *n.* A print reproduced in color by lithography. —**chro·mo·li·thog·ra·pher** (krō′mō·li·thog′rə·fər), **chro′mo·li·thog′ra·phy** *n.* —**chro′mo·lith′o·graph′ic** *adj.*

chro·mo·some (krō′mə·sōm) *n.* One of the rodlike bodies formed from chromatin in the nucleus during cell division, acting as a carrier of the genes or units of heredity. [< CHROMO- + Gk. *sōma* body]

chro·mo·sphere (krō′mə·sfir′) *n.* The envelope of incandescent gas surrounding the sun beyond the photosphere. —**chro·mo·spher·ic** (krō′mə·sfer′ik) *adj.*

Chron. Chronicles.

chron., chronol. chronological; chronology.

chron·ic (kron′ik) *adj.* **1** Continuing for a long period, as a disease. **2** Inveterate; habitual: a *chronic* complainer. [< Gk. *chronos* time] —**chron′i·cal·ly** *adv.*

chron·i·cle (kron′i·kəl) *n.* A record of events chronologically arranged. —*v.t.* **·cled, ·cling** To record in or as a chronicle. [< Gk. *chronikos* of time] —**chron′i·cler** *n.*

Chron·i·cles (kron′i·kəlz) *n. pl.* Either of two books of the Old Testament, I and II Chronicles.

chrono- *combining form* Time. [< Gk. *chronos* time]

chron·o·log·i·cal (kron′ə·loj′i·kəl) *adj.* **1** Occurring or recorded in sequential time order. **2** Of the science of time. Also **chron′o·log′ic.** —**chron′o·log′i·cal·ly** *adv.*

chro·nol·o·gy (krə·nol′ə·jē) *n. pl.* **·gies 1** The science that treats of the measurement of time or the order of events. **2** An arrangement of events in the order of the time of their occurrence. **3** A table or list so arranged. [< CHRONO- + -LOGY] —**chro·nol′o·ger, chro·nol′o·gist** *n.*

chro·nom·e·ter (krə·nom′ə·tər) *n.* A timekeeping instrument of high precision and accuracy. [< CHRONO- + -METER] —**chron·o·met·ric** (kron′ə·met′rik) or **·ri·cal** *adj.* —**chron′o·met′ri·cal·ly** *adv.*

chro·nom·e·try (krə·nom′ə·trē) *n.* The science, method, or process of measuring time.

chrys·a·lid (kris′ə·lid) *n.* CHRYSALIS. —*adj.* Of or like a chrysalis.

chrys·a·lis (kris′ə·lis) *n. pl.* **chrys·a·lis·es** or **chry·sal·i·des** (kri·sal′ə·dēz) 1 The capsule-enclosed pupal stage of a butterfly or moth, from which the winged adult emerges. 2 Anything in an undeveloped stage. [< Gk. *chrysallis* < *chrysos* gold]

chrys·an·the·mum (kri·san′thə·məm) *n.* 1 Any of several varieties of plants cultivated for their showy, composite flowers. 2 The flower. [< Gk. *chrysanthemon*, lit., golden flower]

chrys·o·lite (kris′ə·līt) *n.* A vitreous, olive-green mineral used as a gem. [< Gk. *chrysolithos*, lit., gold stone]

chrys·o·prase (kris′ə·prāz) *n.* A green variety of chalcedony, used as a gem. [< Gk. *chrysos* gold + *prason* leek]

chub (chub) *n. pl.* **chub** or **chubs** 1 A freshwater fish related to the carp. 2 One of various other fishes. [ME *chubbe*]

Chrysalis

chub·by (chub′ē) *adj.* **·bi·er**, **·bi·est** Plump. [< CHUB] —**chub′bi·ness** *n.*

chuck[1] (chuk) *v.t.* 1 To pat or tap lightly, esp. under the chin. 2 To throw; toss. 3 *Informal* To throw out or away. —*n.* 1 A playful pat. 2 A throw or toss. [?]

chuck[2] (chuk) *n.* 1 A cut of beef extending from the neck to the shoulder blade. 2 A clamp, etc., used to hold a tool or piece of work. [Var. of CHOCK]

chuck-full (chuk′fŏŏl′) *adj.* CHOCK-FULL.

chuck·le (chuk′əl) *v.i.* **·led**, **·ling** 1 To laugh quietly, as to oneself. 2 To cluck, as a hen. —*n.* A low, quiet laugh. [? Imit.] —**chuck′ler** *n.*

chuck·le·head (chuk′əl·hed′) *n. Informal* A stupid person; blockhead. —**chuck′le·head′ed** *adj.*

chuck wagon A wagon that carries provisions and cooking equipment for cowboys, harvest hands, etc.

chug (chug) *n.* A short, dull, explosive sound, as of an engine. —*v.i.* **chugged**, **chug·ging** To make or move with such sounds. [Imit.]

chuk·ker (chuk′ər) *n.* One of the periods of play in a polo game. Also **chuk′kar.** [< Hind. *chakkar* circle]

chum[1] (chum) *n.* An intimate companion. —*v.i.* **chummed**, **chum·ming** To be close friends. [? Short for *chamber fellow* (roommate)] —**Syn.** *n.* crony, pal, buddy.

chum[2] (chum) *n.* Cut-up fish, etc., scattered as bait. —*v.i.* **chummed**, **chum·ming** To fish with chum. [?]

chum·my (chum′ē) *adj.* **·mi·er**, **·mi·est** *Informal* Friendly; intimate. —**chum′mi·ly** *adv.* —**chum′mi·ness** *n.*

chump (chump) *n. Informal* A gullible person; fool. [? Var. of CHUNK]

chunk (chungk) *n.* 1 A thick piece, lump, etc. 2 A goodly amount. [Var. of CHUCK[2]]

chunk·y (chung′kē) *adj.* **chunk·i·er**, **chunk·i·est** 1 Short and thickset; stocky. 2 In a chunk or chunks. —**chunk′i·ly** *adv.* —**chunk′i·ness** *n.*

church (chûrch) *n.* 1 A building for Christian worship. 2 Religious services in a church. 3 A congregation of Christians. 4 *Usu. cap.* A body of Christians having a common faith; a denomination. 5 Christians collectively. 6 Ecclesiastical organization and authority: separation of *church* and state. 7 The clerical profession. [< Gk. *kyriakon (dōma)* the Lord's (house)]

church·go·er (chûrch′gō′ər) *n.* One who goes to church regularly. —**church′go′ing** *adj., n.*

church·ly (chûrch′lē) *adj.* Of or suitable for a church. —**church′li·ness** *n.*

church·man (chûrch′mən) *n. pl.* **·men** (-mən) 1 A clergyman. 2 A male member of a church. —**church′man·ly** *adj.* —**church′man·ship** *n.*

Church of Christ, Scientist The official name of the Christian Science Church.

Church of England The national church of England.

Church of Jesus Christ of Latter-Day Saints The official name of the Mormon Church.

church·war·den (chûrch′wôr′dən) *n.* 1 In the Church of England or the Protestant Episcopal Church, a lay officer who assists in the administration of a parish. 2 A long-stemmed clay pipe.

church·wom·an (chûrch′wŏŏm′ən) *n. pl.* **·wom·en** (wim′in) A female member of a church.

church·yard (chûrch′yärd′) *n.* Ground adjacent to a church, esp. a graveyard.

churl (chûrl) *n.* 1 A surly, boorish fellow. 2 A peasant, esp. in medieval England. [< OE *ceorl*] —**churl′ish** *adj.* —**churl′ish·ly** *adv.* —**churl′ish·ness** *n.*

churn (chûrn) *n.* A vessel in which milk or cream is agitated to produce butter. —*v.t.* 1 To stir or agitate (cream or milk) in or as in a churn. 2 To make (butter) in a churn. 3 To agitate violently. —*v.i.* 4 To use a churn. 5 To be in violent agitation. [< OE *cyrin*] —**churn′er** *n.*

churr (chûr) *n.* The whirring sound made by certain birds or insects. —*v.i.* To make such a sound. [Imit.]

chute (shoot) *n.* 1 An inclined trough, slide, or passageway, as for grain, ore, coal, etc. 2 A waterfall or a rapid in a river. 3 *Informal* A parachute.

chut·ney (chut′nē) *n.* A piquant relish of fruit, spices, etc. Also **chut′nee.** [< Hind. *chatnī*]

chutz·pah (hŏŏts′pə, khŏŏts′-) *n. Informal* Brazen effrontery; gall. [Yiddish] —**Syn.** nerve, cheek, impudence.

chyle (kīl) *n.* The milky emulsion of lymph and fat taken up from the intestines by the lacteals during digestion. [< Gk. *chylos* juice < *cheein* pour] —**chy·la·ceous** (kī·lā′shəs), **chy·lous** (kī′ləs) *adj.*

chyme (kīm) *n.* Partly digested food in liquid form as it passes from the stomach into the small intestine. [< Gk. *chymos* juice < *cheein* pour] —**chy·mous** (kī′məs) *adj.*

CIA Central Intelligence Agency.

ci·bo·ri·um (si·bôr′ē·əm, -bō′rē-) *n. pl.* **·bo·ri·a** (-bôr′ē·ə, -bō′rē·ə) 1 An arched canopy over an altar. 2 A receptacle for the wafers of the Eucharist. [< Gk. *kibōrion* cup]

ci·ca·da (si·kā′də, -kä′-) *n. pl.* **·das** or **·dae** (-dē) A large transparent-winged insect of which the male has vibrating membranes that produce a loud, shrill sound. [< L]

cic·a·trix (sik′ə·triks) *n. pl.* **cic·a·tri·ces** (sik′ə·trī′sēz) 1 A scar remaining after a wound has healed. 2 A scar marking a former attachment of a leaf, etc. [< L] —**cic·a·tri·cial** (sik′ə·trish′əl) *adj.*

Cicada

cic·a·trize (sik′ə·trīz) *v.t. & v.i.* **·trized**, **·triz·ing** To heal or become healed by the formation of a scar. —**cic·a·tri·za·tion** (sik′ə·trə·zā′shən) *n.*

cic·e·ro·ne (sis′ə·rō′nē, *Ital.* chē′chā·rô′nä) *n. pl.* **·nes**, *Ital.* **·ni** (-nē) A guide for sightseers. [< Ital., Cicero]

-cide *combining form* 1 Killer or destroyer of: *insecticide.* 2 Murder or killing of: *suicide.* [< L *caedere* kill]

ci·der (sī′dər) *n.* The juice of apples, used to make vinegar and as a beverage before fermentation (**sweet cider**) or after fermentation (**hard cider**). [< OF *sidre* < LL *sicera* strong drink < Heb. *shēkār*]

ci·gar (si·gär′) *n.* A small roll of tobacco leaves prepared for smoking. [< Sp. *cigarro*]

cig·a·rette (sig′ə·ret′, sig′ə·ret) *n.* A small roll of finely cut tobacco in thin paper, used for smoking. Also **cig′a·ret′.** [< F *cigare* cigar]

cil·i·a (sil′ē·ə) *n. pl.* of CILIUM.

cil·i·ar·y (sil′ē·er′ē) *adj.* Of, pertaining to, or like cilia.

cil·i·ate (sil′ē·it, -āt) *adj.* Having cilia. Also **cil′i·at′ed.** —*n.* One of a class of microscopic, single-celled organisms possessing cilia.

cil·i·um (sil′ē·əm) *n. pl.* **cil·i·a** (sil′ē·ə) 1 *Biol.* A microscopic, hairlike process on the surface of a cell, organ, plant, etc., capable of a vibrating or whiplike movement. 2 EYELASH. [< L, eyelid]

Cim·me·ri·an (si·mir′ē·ən) *adj.* Densely dark; gloomy. —*n.* A member of a mythical people said by Homer to live in perpetual darkness.

CINC, C in C, C. in C. Commander in Chief.

cinch (sinch) *n.* 1 A saddle girth. 2 *Slang* A sure or easy thing. —*v.t.* 1 To fasten a saddle girth around. 2 *Slang* To make sure of. [< L *cingula* girdle < *cingere* bind] • See SADDLE.

cin·cho·na (sin·kō′nə, -chō′-) *n.* 1 Any of various South

American trees and shrubs widely cultivated as a source of quinine and related alkaloids. **2** The bark of any of these trees. [< the Countess of *Chinchón*, 1576–1639, wife of the viceroy of Peru] —**cin·chon′ic** *adj.*

cin·cho·nize (sin′kə·nīz) *v.t.* **-nized, -niz·ing** To dose with cinchona or quinine. —**cin′cho·ni·za′tion** *n.*

cinc·ture (singk′chər) *n.* **1** A belt, girdle, etc. **2** Anything that encircles or encloses. —*v.t.* **-tured, -tur·ing** To gird with or as with a cincture. [< L *cingere* gird]

cin·der (sin′dər) *n.* **1** Any partly burned combustible substance not completely reduced to ashes. **2** A charred bit of wood, coal, etc. **3** *pl.* Ashes. [< OE *sinder*] —**cin′der·y** *adj.*

cinder block A hollow building block of concrete mixed with cinders.

Cin·der·el·la (sin′dər·el′ə) *n.* A fairy-tale heroine who is treated as a household drudge but who eventually marries a prince.

cin·e·ma (sin′ə·mə) *n.* **1** A theater exhibiting motion-picture films. **2** A motion-picture film. —**the cinema 1** Motion-picture films collectively. **2** The art or business of making such films. [Short for CINEMATOGRAPH] —**cin·e·mat·ic** (sin′-ə·mat′ik) *adj.* —**cin′e·mat·i·cal·ly** *adv.*

cin·e·mat·o·graph (sin′ə·mat′ə·graf, -gräf) *n.* **1** A camera for taking motion-picture films. **2** A projector for showing such films. [< Gk. *kinēma, -atos* movement + -GRAPH]

cin·e·ma·tog·ra·phy (sin′ə·mə·tog′rə·fē) *n.* The art and process of making motion-picture films. —**cin′e·ma·tog′ra·pher** *n.* —**cin·e·mat·o·graph·ic** (sin′ə·mat′ə·graf′ik) *adj.* —**cin′e·mat′o·graph′i·cal·ly** *adv.*

cin·e·rar·i·a (sin′ə·râr′ē·ə) *n.* A plant with showy clusters of blue, reddish, or white flowers widely grown as a house plant. [< L *cineraria* ashy < *cinis* ash]

cin·e·rar·i·um (sin′ə·râr′ē·əm) *n. pl.* **-rar·i·a** (-râr′ē·ə) A place for the ashes of a cremated body. [L]

cin·na·bar (sin′ə·bär) *n.* **1** A crystallized red mercuric sulfide, an ore of mercury. **2** A mixture formed by subliming mercury and sulfur, used esp. as a pigment. [< Gk. *kinnabari*]

cin·na·mon (sin′ə·mən) *n.* **1** The aromatic inner bark of any of several tropical trees of the laurel family, used as a spice. **2** Any tree that yields cinnamon. **3** A light reddish brown. —*adj.* **1** Made with cinnamon. **2** Light reddish brown. [< Gk. *kinnamōmon* < Heb. *qinnāmōn*]

cinque·foil (singk′foil) *n.* **1** Any of several related plants having leaves with usu. five leaflets. **2** An architectural ornament composed of five converging arcs. [< L *quinque* five + *folium* leaf]

CIO, C.I.O. Congress of Industrial Organizations.

ci·on (sī′ən) *n.* SCION (def. 2).

ci·pher (sī′fər) *n.* **1** The character 0; zero. **2** Any Arabic numeral. **3 a** A written code in which letters of the alphabet are substituted for others or represented by symbols. **b** The key for solving such a code. **4** A person or thing of no significance. **5** A monogram. —*v.i.* **1** To do arithmetic. —*v.t.* **2** To calculate arithmetically. **3** To put into cipher; encode.[< Ar. *sifr*]

cir., circ. circa; circular; circumference.

cir·ca (sûr′kə) *prep.* About; around: used to indicate approximate dates, etc. [L]

Cir·cas·sian (sər·kash′ən, -kash′ē·ən) *n.* A member of a group of tribes of the Caucasus region. —*adj.* Of or pertaining to Circassia, the Circassians, or their language.

Cir·ce (sûr′sē) In the *Odyssey*, an enchantress who turned Odysseus's men into swine.

cir·cle (sûr′kəl) *n.* **1** A plane figure bounded by a curved line everywhere equally distant from a fixed point. **2** Something having the form of such a figure, as a ring, round object or enclosure, etc. **3** A course, cycle, series, etc., that ends at the starting point. **4** A group of persons sharing a common interest, occupation, or other tie. **5** A sphere or area of influence. **6** A tier of seats in a theater.

Cinquefoil

—*v.* **·cled, ·cling** *v.t.* **1** To enclose with or as with a circle. **2** To move around, or over, as in a circle. —*v.i.* **3** To move in a circle. [< L *circulus,* dim. of *circus* ring] —**cir′cler** *n.* —**Syn.** *n.* **4** set, crowd, coterie, clique.

cir·clet (sûr′klit) *n.* A small ring or ring-shaped object, esp. an ornament.

cir·cuit (sûr′kit) *n.* **1** A more or less circular route, course, etc.; a round. **2** A journey from place to place through such a course, as by a judge or clergyman. **3** A district visited by or within the jurisdiction of one having such a route, esp. a judge. **4** An association, as of theaters or teams, in which performances, contests, etc., take place in turn. **5** A curve forming a closed circumference. **6 a** The entire course traversed by an electric current. **b** An assembly of parts and components that function together in an electric or electronic device or system. **7** A radio transmission and reception system. —*v.t. & v.i.* To go or move through in a circuit. [< F < L *circuitus,* pp of < *circumire* go around]

circuit breaker *Electr.* A switch or relay for breaking a circuit under specified or abnormal conditions of current flow.

circuit court A court that holds sessions at different places within its jurisdiction.

cir·cu·i·tous (sər·kyōō′ə·təs) *adj.* Roundabout; indirect. —**cir·cu′i·tous·ly** *adv.* —**cir·cu′i·tous·ness** *n.*

circuit rider A minister who preaches at churches on a circuit or district route.

cir·cuit·ry (sûr′kit·rē) *n.* The design or component parts of an electric circuit.

cir·cu·lar (sûr′kyə·lər) *adj.* **1** Shaped like a circle; round. **2** Of, forming, or moving in a circle. **3** Ending at the point of beginning. **4** Circuitous; indirect. —*n.* A communication or notice for general circulation. [< L *circulus* CIRCLE] —**cir·cu·lar·i·ty** (sûr′kyə·lar′ə·tē) *n.* —**cir′cu·lar·ly** *adv.*

cir·cu·lar·ize (sûr′kyə·lə·rīz′) *v.t.* **·ized, ·iz·ing 1** To issue circulars to. **2** To publicize with circulars. —**cir′cu·lar·i·za′·tion, cir′cu·lar·iz′er** *n.*

circular saw A disk-shaped saw having a toothed edge, rotated at high speed by a motor.

cir·cu·late (sûr′kyə·lāt) *v.* **·lat·ed, ·lat·ing** —*v.i.* **1** To move in a closed course. **2** To move or travel about. **3** To move or flow freely, as air. —*v.t.* **4** To cause to circulate. [< L *circulari*] —**cir′cu·la·tive, cir·cu·la·to·ry** (sûr′kyə·lə·tôr′ē, -tō′rē) *adj.* —**cir′cu·la·tor** *n.*

cir·cu·la·tion (sûr′kyə·lā′shən) *n.* **1** The act of circulating or the state of being circulated. **2** Motion in a closed course. **3** Transmission or dissemination, as from person to person. **4** The extent or amount of distribution, as the number of copies issued of a periodical.

circum- *prefix* About; around; on all sides: *circumscribe*. [< L *circus* circle]

cir·cum·am·bi·ent (sûr′kəm·am′bē·ənt) *adj.* Surrounding; encompassing. —**cir′cum·am′bi·ence, cir′cum·am′bi·en·cy** *n.*

cir·cum·cise (sûr′kəm·sīz) *v.t.* **·cised, ·cis·ing** To cut off the prepuce or clitoris of. [< L *circum-* around + *caedere* cut] —**cir′cum·cis′er** *n.* —**cir′cum·ci′sion** (-sizh′ən) *n.*

cir·cum·fer·ence (sər·kum′fər·əns) *n.* **1** The boundary line of a circle. **2** Distance or measurement around something. [< L *circumferentia* < *circum-* around + *ferre* bear] —**cir·cum·fer·en·tial** (sər·kum′fər·en′shəl) *adj.*

cir·cum·flex (sûr′kəm·fleks) *n.* A mark (û) used over a vowel to indicate a pronunciation. —*adj.* **1** Pronounced or marked with the circumflex accent. **2** Bent or curved. —*v.t.* To mark with a circumflex. [< L *circum-* around + *flectere* bend]

cir·cum·flu·ent (sər·kum′flōō·ənt) *adj.* Flowing around; surrounding. Also **cir·cum′flu·ous.** [< L pr.p. of *circum-fluere* < *circum-* around + *fluere* flow]

cir·cum·fuse (sûr′kəm·fyōōz′) *v.t.* **·fused, ·fus·ing 1** To pour or spread about. **2** To surround, as with a liquid. [< L *circum-* around + *fundere* pour] —**cir·cum·fu·sion** (-fyōō′zhən) *n.*

cir·cum·lo·cu·tion (sûr′kəm·lō·kyōō′shən) *n.* A long, roundabout way of saying or expressing something. [< L *circum-* around + *loqui* speak] —**cir·cum·loc·u·tory** (sûr'·kəm·lok'yə·tôr'ē, -tō'rē) *adj.*

cir·cum·nav·i·gate (sûr'kəm·nav'ə·gāt) *v.t.* -gat·ed, -gat·ing To sail around. —**cir'cum·nav'i·ga'tion, cir'cum·nav'i·ga'tor** *n.*

cir·cum·po·lar (sûr'kəm·pō'lər) *adj.* 1 Near or surrounding one of the terrestrial poles. 2 Revolving about a celestial pole without setting, as a star.

cir·cum·scribe (sûr'kəm·skrīb') *v.t.* -scribed, -scrib·ing 1 To draw a line around; encircle. 2 To confine within bounds; restrict. 3 *Geom.* a To surround with a figure that coincides at every possible point: to *circumscribe* a triangle with a circle. b To cause to surround a figure thus: to *circumscribe* a circle about a triangle. [< L *circum-* around + *scribere* write] —**cir'cum·scrib'er, cir·cum·scrip·tion** (sûr'·kəm·skrip'shen) *n.*

cir·cum·spect (sûr'kəm·spekt) *adj.* Attentive to all possibilities; cautious. [< L *circum-* around + *specere* look] —**cir'cum·spec'tion, cir·cum·spect'ness** *n.* —**cir'cum·spec'tive** *adj.* —**cir'cum·spect'ly** *adv.* —**Syn.** prudent, wary.

cir·cum·stance (sûr'kəm·stans) *n.* 1 A related or concomitant condition, fact, occurrence, etc. 2 Any condition, fact, etc. 3 *pl.* The situation a person is in relative to certain conditions, esp. financial conditions. 4 Formal display; ceremony: pomp and *circumstance.* —**under no circumstances** Never; under no conditions. —**under the circumstances** Such being the case or conditions. [< L *circum-* around + *stare* stand] —**cir'cum·stanced** *adj.*

cir·cum·stan·tial (sûr'kəm·stan'shəl) *adj.* 1 Pertaining to or dependent on circumstances. 2 Incidental; not essential. 3 Complete and detailed; minute. —**cir'cum·stan'ti·al'i·ty** (-shē·al'ə·tē) *n.* —**cir'cum·stan'tial·ly** *adv.*

circumstantial evidence *Law* Evidence based on circumstances which form reasonable grounds for determining facts relevant to a case.

cir·cum·stan·ti·ate (sûr'kəm·stan'shē·āt) *v.t.* -at·ed, -at·ing To establish by circumstances or in detail. —**cir'cum·stan'ti·a'tion** *n.*

cir·cum·vent (sûr'kəm·vent') *v.t.* 1 To avoid by or as by going around; bypass. 2 To get the better of by strategy or craft; outwit. [< L *circum-* around + *venire* come] —**cir'cum·vent'er, cir'cum·vent'or, cir'cum·ven'tion** *n.* —**cir'cum·ven'tive** *adj.*

cir·cus (sûr'kəs) *n.* 1 A show in which acrobats, trained animals, clowns, etc., perform. 2 The circular, often tented enclosure in which such a show is held. 3 The members of such a show. 4 A large arena with tiers of seats around it, used in ancient Rome for contests or public spectacles. 5 *Brit.* A circular intersection of several streets. 6 *Informal* Something uproariously entertaining. [< L, a ring, racecourse]

cir·rho·sis (si·rō'sis) *n.* A chronic disease of the liver or other organ, marked by degeneration of tissue. [< Gk. *kirrhos* tawny < the color of the cirrhotic liver] —**cir·rhot·ic** (si·rot'ik) *adj.*

cirro- *combining form* CIRRUS: *cirrostratus.* [< L *cirrus* curl]

cir·ro·cu·mu·lus (sir'ō·kyōō'myə·ləs) *n.* A mass of small, fleecy clouds at an average height of 5 miles.

cir·ro·stra·tus (sir'ō·strā'təs) *n.* A fine, whitish cloud at an average height of 6 miles.

cir·rus (sir'əs) *n. pl.* **cir·ri** (sir'ī) A type of white, wispy cloud at an average height of 7 miles, seen in tufts or feathery bands. [< L, ringlet]

cis·co (sis'kō) *n. pl.* **·coes** or **·cos** A North American freshwater fish related to the whitefish. [< N. Am. Ind.]

Cis·ter·cian (sis·tûr'shən) *n.* A monk of a Benedictine order founded in France in 1098. —*adj.* Of this order. [< Med. L *Cistercium,* French abbey site]

cis·tern (sis'tərn) *n.* 1 A tank or receptacle for storing water. 2 *Anat.* A large lymph space; a sac. [< L *cisterna* < *cista* chest]

cit. citation; cited; citizen.

cit·a·del (sit'ə·dəl, -del) *n.* 1 A fortress commanding a city. 2 Any fortress. [< Ital. *cittadella,* dim. of *citta* city]

ci·ta·tion (sī·tā'shən) *n.* 1 The act of citing. 2 A passage or source cited. 3 A public commendation for exceptional achievement, bravery, etc. 4 A summons to appear in a law court. —**ci·ta·to·ry** (sī'tə·tôr'ē, -tō'rē) *adj.*

cite (sīt) *v.t.* **cit·ed, cit·ing** 1 To quote or refer to for proof, support, etc. 2 To mention specifically, esp. in official commendation. 3 To summon to appear in a court of law. [< L *citare,* freq. of *ciēre* call] —**cit·a·ble, cite·a·ble** *adj.*

cith·a·ra (sith'ə·rə) *n.* An ancient Greek stringed instrument similar to a lyre. [< Gk. *kithara*]

cith·er (sith'ər) *n.* CITTERN. Also **cith·ern** (sith'ərn).

cit·i·fied (sit'i·fīd) *adj.* Considered typical of city dwellers or city life.

cit·i·zen (sit'ə·zən) *n.* 1 A native or naturalized person owing allegiance to, and entitled to protection from, a government. 2 A member of a state. 3 A resident of a city or town. 4 One who is not a member of the military, police, etc.; a civilian. [< OF *citeain* < *cité* CITY] • The word *citizen* is generally applied to one whose national government derives its power from the people, as in a republic. A *subject* is one who owes allegiance to a monarch or other sovereign.

Cithara

cit·i·zen·ry (sit'ə·zən·rē) *n.* Citizens collectively.

cit·i·zen·ship (sit'ə·zən·ship') *n.* 1 The status of a citizen. 2 The activities or attitudes of a citizen, esp. with regard to obligations, rights, etc.

cit·rate (sit'rāt, -rit, sī'trāt) *n.* A salt of citric acid.

cit·ric (sit'rik) *adj.* Derived from citrus fruits.

citric acid A white, crystalline, organic acid found in various fruits and also made synthetically.

cit·rine (sit'rin) *n.* A light yellow variety of quartz resembling topaz. [< F *citrin*]

cit·ron (sit'rən) *n.* 1 A fruit like a lemon, but larger and less acid. 2 The tree producing this fruit. 3 A variety of watermelon with hard-fleshed fruit: also **citron melon.** 4 The candied rind of either of these fruits. [< L *citrus* citron tree]

cit·ron·el·la (sit'rə·nel'ə) *n.* A s Asian grass yielding **citronella oil,** which is used in perfumery, insect repellents, etc. Also **citronella grass.** [< CITRON]

cit·rus (sit'rəs) *adj.* Of or pertaining to a genus of fruit-bearing trees or shrubs including the orange, lemon, lime, grapefruit, etc. Also **cit'rous.** —*n. pl.* **·rus·es** A citrus tree or fruit. [< L, citron tree]

cit·tern (sit'ərn) *n.* A 16th- to 17th-century musical instrument resembling a lute or guitar. [Blend of CITHER and GITTERN.]

cit·y (sit'ē) *n. pl.* **cit·ies** 1 A place inhabited by a large, permanent, organized community. 2 In the U.S. and Canada, a municipality of the first class. 3 The people of a city, collectively. [< L *civitas* < *civis* citizen]

city hall 1 The municipal building of a city. 2 A municipal government. 3 Bureaucratic procedures or officials characterized as obstinately unresponsive: Go fight *city hall.*

city manager An administrator appointed to manage the municipal affairs of a city.

cit·y·scape (sit'ē·skāp') *n.* 1 A view of a city. 2 The plan or arrangement of elements in a city.

cit·y·state (sit'ē·stāt') *n.* A sovereign state consisting of a city and adjacent territories, as in ancient Greece.

civ. civil; civilian.

civ·et (siv'it) *n.* 1 Any of several catlike mammals of Africa and Asia, having scent glands secreting a fluid with a musky odor: also **civet cat.** 2 The musky secretion of such an animal, used in perfume. [< Ar. *zabād*]

civ·ic (siv'ik) *adj.* Of or pertaining to a city, citizens, or citizenship. [< L *civis* citizen]

civ·ics (siv'iks) *n.pl. (construed as sing.)* The branch of social science dealing with government, citizens' rights and duties, etc.

civ·ies (siv'ez) *n.pl.* CIVVIES.

civ·il (siv'əl) *adj.* 1 Of or pertaining to citizens, esp. in relation to the state. 2 Of or pertaining to general public life as distinguished from military or ecclesiastical activities. 3 Of or involving internal relationships and affairs of a country. 4 Socially acceptable; polite. [< L *civis* citizen] —**civ'il·ly** *adv.* —**Syn.** 4 courteous, well-bred, civilized, proper, well-mannered, attentive.

civil defense A civilian program of action by civilians for general protection and maintenance of essential services in case of enemy attack or widespread disaster.

civil disobedience Passive resistance to offensive laws or official policies.

civil engineer An engineer trained to design and build roads, bridges, tunnels, etc. —**civil engineering**

ci·vil·ian (sə·vil′yən) n. One who is not a member of the armed forces. —adj. Of civilians or civil life.

ci·vil·i·ty (sə·vil′ə·tē) n. pl. **·ties** 1 Courtesy; politeness. 2 A courteous act, expression, etc.

civ·i·li·za·tion (siv′ə·lə·zā′shən, -lī·zā′-) n. 1 A condition of human society characterized by a comparatively high degree of cultural and technical development. 2 A region or people considered to be in this stage. 3 A stage in the cultural development of a people, region, or period. 4 The process of civilizing or of becoming civilized. Brit. sp. **civ′·i·li·sa′tion.**

civ·i·lize (siv′ə·līz) v.t. **·lized**, **·liz·ing** 1 To bring from a primitive to a culturally advanced state. 2 To train in social amenities. Brit. sp. **civ′i·lise.**

civ·i·lized (siv′ə·līzd) adj. 1 Having or characteristic of a state of civilization. 2 Cultured; refined.

civil law The branch of law dealing with the rights of citizens.

civil liberty A right, as freedom of speech or thought, guaranteed to individuals by law.

civil rights Private, nonpolitical rights of citizens, as those established by the 13th and 14th amendments to the U.S. Constitution.

civil servant One employed in the civil service.

civil service 1 The branches of government service that are neither military, legislative, or judicial. 2 The persons employed in these branches.

civil war War between factions or sections of a nation.

Civil War In the U.S., a war between the North (the Union) and the South (the Confederacy), 1861–65.

civ·vies (siv′ēz) n. pl. Slang Civilian dress as distinguished from military uniform.

ck. cask; check; cook.

Cl chlorine.

c.l. carload; center line; civil law.

cl. centiliter(s); claim; class; classification; clause; clearance; clergyman; clerk; cloth.

clab·ber (klab′ər) n. Milk curdled by souring. —v.t. & v.i. To curdle, as milk. [Short for earlier bonnyclabber < Ir. bainne clabair curdled milk]

clack (klak) v.t. & v.i. 1 To make or cause to make the sound of a short, sharp impact. 2 To chatter. —n. 1 A sharp, short sound. 2 Chatter. [Imit.] —**clack′er** n.

clad (klad) A p.t. & pp. of CLOTHE. —adj. Clothed.

claim (klām) v.t. 1 To demand as a right; assert ownership or title to. 2 To hold to be true. 3 To require or deserve. —n. 1 A demand for something due; assertion of a right. 2 The basis for such a demand or assertion. 3 An assertion, as of a fact. 4 Something claimed, as a piece of land for use by a settler or miner. [< L clamare declare] —**claim′a·ble** adj. —**claim′er** n.

claim·ant (klā′mənt) n. One who makes a claim.

clair·voy·ant (klâr·voi′ənt) adj. Having the ability to see or know things not perceptible to normal human senses. —n. A clairvoyant person. [F, lit., clear-seeing] —**clair·voy′ance** n.

clam (klam) n. 1 Any of numerous often edible bivalve mollusks. 2 Informal An uncommunicative person. —v.i. **clammed**, **clam·ming** To hunt for or dig clams. —**clam up** Slang To become silent. [< OE clamm a clamp]

clam·bake (klam′bāk′) n. A seashore picnic where clams and other food are baked.

clam·ber (klam′bər) v.t. & v.i. To climb clumsily or laboriously as by using the hands and feet. —n. A difficult climb. [< ON klimbra to grip] —**clam′ber·er** n.

clam·my (klam′ē) adj. **·mi er**, **·mi·est** Damp and sticky or cold. [< OE clæman to stick] —**clam′mi·ly** adv. —**clam′mi·ness** n.

clam·or (klam′ər) n. 1 A loud, persistent outcry or noise. 2 A vehement general demand or protest. —v.i. 1 To make a clamor. —v.t. 2 To utter with loud outcry. Brit. sp. **clam′our.** [< L clamare cry out] —**clam′or·er** n. —Syn. n. 1 din, uproar, hubbub, racket.

clam·or·ous (klam′ər·əs) adj. Making or made with clamor; noisy. —**clam′or·ous·ly** adv. —**clam′or·ous·ness** n.

clamp (klamp) n. A device for holding or pressing together two or more parts. —v.t. To join or press with or as with a clamp. [< MDu. klampe]

clan (klan) n. 1 A group of families having a common ancestor, as in the Scottish Highlands. 2 A group of related or closely associated persons. [< Scot. Gael. clänn]

clan·des·tine (klan·des′tin) adj. Kept secret; surreptitious. [< L clandestinus < clam in secret] —**clan·des′tine·ly** adv. —**clan·des′tine·ness** n.

clang (klang) v.t. & v.i. 1 To make or cause to make a loud, ringing, metallic sound. 2 To strike together with such a sound. —n. A loud, ringing sound, as of metal struck. [< L clangere]

clan·gor (klang′gər, klang′ər) n. Repeated clanging. —v.i. To ring noisily; clang. Brit. sp. **clan′gour.** [< L clangere clang] —**clan′gor·ous** adj. —**clan′gor·ous·ly** adv.

clank (klangk) n. A short, harsh, metallic sound. —v.t. & v.i. To make or cause to make a clank. [Blend of CLANG and CLINK]

clan·nish (klan′ish) adj. 1 Of or typical of a clan. 2 Tending to associate only with members of the same group. —**clan′nish·ly** adv. —**clan′nish·ness** n.

clans·man (klanz′mən) n. pl. **·men** (-mən) A male member of a clan. —**clans′wom′an** (pl. **·wom′en**) n. Fem.

clap[1] (klap) v. **clapped**, **clap·ping** v.i. 1 To strike the palms of the hands together with a short, sharp sound. 2 To strike or come together with a sharp, explosive sound. —v.t. 3 To strike together, as the hands, with a sharp, explosive sound. 4 To applaud by striking the hands together. 5 To strike briskly. 6 To put quickly or suddenly: to clap someone into jail. —n. 1 The act of clapping, esp. the hands. 2 A loud, sudden noise, as of thunder. 3 A slap. [< OE clæppan]

clap[2] (klap) n. Slang Gonorrhea: usu. with the. [< OF clapoir a venereal sore]

clap·board (klab′ərd, klap′bôrd′, -bōrd′) n. An overlapping board, usu. with one edge thicker than the other, used on the outside of buildings. —v.t. To cover with clapboards. [< MDu klappen to split]

clap·per (klap′ər) n. 1 The tongue of a bell. 2 One who or that which claps.

clap·trap (klap′trap) n. Cheap, sensational, pretentious language, trappings, etc.

claque (klak) n. 1 People hired to applaud in a theater. 2 Any group of fawning followers. [< F claquer clap]

clar·et (klar′ət) n. 1 A red wine, esp. a Bordeaux. 2 A deep purplish red. [< OF (vin) claret clear (wine)]

clar·i·fy (klar′ə·fī) v. **·fied**, **·fy·ing** v.t. 1 To make clear or understandable. 2 To free from impurities, as fats. —v.i. 3 To become clear. [< L clarus clear + facere make] —**clar·i·fi·ca·tion** (klar′ə·fə·kā′shən) n. —**clar′i·fi′er** n.

clar·i·net (klar′ə·net′) n. A cylindrical woodwind instrument with a bell mouth, having a single reed mouthpiece, finger holes, and keys. [< F clarine bell < L clarus clear] —**clar′i·net′ist** or **clar′i·net′tist** n.

Clarinet

clar·i·on (klar′ē·ən) n. 1 A small trumpet. 2 The sound of a trumpet or a similar sound. —adj. Shrill and clear. [< L clarus clear]

clar·i·ty (klar′ə·tē) n. The state or fact of being clear; clearness.

clash (klash) v.i. 1 To collide with a harsh, metallic sound. 2 To be in opposition; conflict. —v.t. 3 To strike together with a harsh, metallic sound. —*n.* 1 A loud, harsh sound, as of metal objects striking. 2 A marked conflict. [Imit.]

clasp (klasp, kläsp) *n.* 1 A fastener by which things are held together. 2 A firm grasp or embrace. —*v.t.* 1 To fasten with or as with a clasp. 2 To embrace. 3 To grasp firmly in or with the hand. [ME *claspe*] —**clasp′er** *n.*

class (klas, kläs) *n.* 1 A group having something in common; category. 2 A grouping based on social or economic status. 3 A rating according to quality, rank, etc. 4 **a** A group of students under one teacher or pursuing a study together. **b** A meeting of such a group. **c** A group of students of the same graduating year. 5 *Biol.* A group of plants or animals ranking below a phylum and above an order. 6 *Slang* Superiority; elegance. —*v.t.* To assign to a class; classify. [< L *classis* group, class] —**Syn.** 1 kind, sort, type, set.

clas·sic (klas′ik) *adj.* 1 Regarded as best or exemplary of its kind. 2 Of or pertaining to the art, literature, etc., of ancient Greece and Rome. 3 Considered typical of such art or literature; formal; regular. 4 Founded or celebrated in tradition. 5 Fashionable because of the simplicity of its style: said of wearing apparel, furniture, etc. —*n.* 1 An author, artist, or creative work generally regarded as of the highest excellence. 2 A traditional event, as in sports. 3 Something that is classic (def. 5). —**the classics** Ancient Greek and Roman literature. [< L *classicus* of the first rank < *classis* order, class]

clas·si·cal (klas′i·kəl) *adj.* 1 Of, pertaining to, or based on the art, literature, or culture of ancient Greece and Rome. 2 Of, in, or pertaining to the style of European music of the late 18th century. 3 Highly regarded, authoritative, or traditional; standard. 4 *Physics* Pertaining to or describing theories based upon or derived from Newtonian mechanics, esp. as distinguished from relativity theory and quantum mechanics. —**clas′si·cal′i·ty** *n.* —**clas′si·cal·ly** *adv.*

clas·si·cism (klas′ə·siz′əm) *n.* 1 Aesthetic qualities and principles characterized by formality, balance, restraint, etc., regarded as typical of ancient Greek and Roman art, literature, and culture. 2 Application of these principles. 3 Classical scholarship. 4 An idiom or expression typical of the classics. Also **clas′si·cal·ism.**

clas·si·cist (klas′ə·sist) *n.* 1 One versed in the classics. 2 A user of classical style.

clas·si·fi·ca·tion (klas′ə·fə·kā′shən) *n.* 1 The act, process, or result of classifying. 2 A category; class. 3 TAXONOMY. —**clas·si·fi·ca·to·ry** (klas′ə·fə·kə·tôr′ē, -tō′rē, klas′ə·fə·kā′tər·ē, klə·sif′ə·kə·tôr′ē, -tō′rē) *adj.*

classified advertisement One of a listing of brief advertisements printed under a variety of headings.

clas·si·fy (klas′ə·fī) *v.t.* **·fied, ·fy·ing** 1 To arrange systematically on the basis of class or category. 2 To restrict as to circulation or use, as a specially designated document or item of information. [< L *classis* class + -FY] —**clas′si·fi′a·ble** *adj.* —**clas′si·fi′er** *n.*

class·mate (klas′māt′, kläs′-) *n.* A member of the same class in school or college.

class·room (klas′rōōm′, -rōŏm′, kläs′-) *n.* A room where classes are held, as in a school.

class·y (klas′ē) *adj.* *Slang* **class·i·er, class·i·est** Elegant.

clat·ter (klat′ər) *v.i.* 1 To make or move with a rattling noise. 2 To chatter noisily. —*v.t.* 3 To cause to make a rattling noise. —*n.* 1 A rattling noise. 2 Noisy chatter. [< OE *clatrung* a clattering noise] —**clat′ter·er** *n.*

clause (klôz) *n.* 1 *Gram.* A group of words containing a subject and predicate and usu. forming part of a compound or complex sentence. 2 A separate statement or proviso in a legal document, treaty, etc. [< L *clausus,* pp. of *claudere* close] —**claus′al** *adj.*

claus·tro·pho·bi·a (klôs′trə·fō′bē·ə) *n.* Morbid fear of enclosed or confined places. [< L *claustrum* a closed place + -PHOBIA] —**claus′tro·pho′bic** *adj.*

clav·i·chord (klav′ə·kôrd) *n.* A keyboard musical instrument whose tones are produced by brass pins striking horizontal strings. [< L *clavis* key + *chorda* string]

clav·i·cle (klav′ə·kəl) *n.* The bone connecting the shoulder blade and breastbone. [< L *clavicula,* dim. of *clavis* key] —**cla·vic·u·lar** (klə·vik′yə·lər) *adj.*

clav·i·er (klav′ē·ər, klə·vir′) *n.* Any keyboard stringed in-strument, as a clavichord, piano, etc. [F, keyboard < L *clavis* key]

claw (klô) *n.* 1 A sharp, curved, horny nail on the toe of a bird, mammal, or reptile. 2 A pincer or chela at the end of an appendage, as in certain insects and crustaceans. 3 Anything sharp and hooked. —*v.t. & v.i.* To tear, scratch, pull, etc., with or as with claws. [< OE *clawu*]

claw hammer A hammer with one end of its head forked and curved for drawing nails. • See HAMMER.

clay (klā) *n.* 1 A fine-textured earth that is plastic when wet but hard and compact when dry, used to make ceramic ware, bricks, etc. 2 Earth in general. 3 The human body. [< OE *clæg*] —**clay·ey** (klā′ē) *adj.*

clay·more (klā′môr, -mōr) *n.* A double-edged sword used formerly by Scottish Highlanders. [< Scot. Gael. *claidheamh* sword + *mor* great]

clay pigeon A saucer-shaped disk of baked clay or other brittle material, projected as a flying target in trapshooting.

clean (klēn) *adj.* 1 Free from dirt, stain, impurity, etc. 2 Unblemished; pure. 3 Habitually avoiding dirt; neat. 4 Not marked; blank: *clean* paper. 5 Not rough, uneven, or irregular. 6 Complete; thorough. 7 Clear; unencumbered: a *clean* title to land. 8 Dexterous; skillful. 9 Sportsmanlike; fair. 10 Producing little radioactive contamination: a *clean* nuclear test. —*v.t.* 1 To free from dirt, impurities, etc. 2 To prepare (fowl, fish, etc.) for cooking. —*v.i.* 3 To undergo or perform the act of cleaning. —**clean out** 1 To empty (a place) of contents or occupants. 2 *Informal.* To leave without money. —**clean up** *Informal.* To win a large amount or make large profits. —*adv.* 1 In a clean manner. 2 *Informal* Completely; wholly. [< OE *clæne* clear, pure] —**clean′a·ble** *adj.* —**clean′ness** *n.*

clean-cut (klēn′kut′) *adj.* 1 Clear in outline; sharply defined. 2 Neat and pleasing in appearance: a *clean-cut* young man.

clean·er (klē′nər) *n.* 1 One who cleans, esp. one who does dry cleaning. 2 A substance or device that removes dirt.

clean·ly (klen′lē) *adj.* **·li·er, ·li·est** Habitually and carefully clean; neat. —*adv.* (klēn′lē) In a clean manner. —**clean·li·ness** (klen′lē·nis) *n.*

cleanse (klenz) *v.t.* **cleansed, cleans·ing** To free from dirt or defilement; clean; purge. [< OE *clænsian* < *clæne* clean]

cleans·er (klenz′ər) *n.* A substance, as a soap or abrasive, used for cleaning.

clean·up (klēn′up′) *n.* 1 A thorough cleaning. 2 *Informal* A sweeping profit.

clear (klir) *adj.* 1 Not clouded, dimmed, or obscured. 2 Transparent. 3 Free from obstruction. 4 Free from blemish. 5 Readily perceived; distinct. 6 Readily understood; intelligible. 7 Plain; evident. 8 Free from confusion or doubt. 9 Free from guilt. 10 Free from hindrance or entanglement. 11 Without deductions; net. —*v.t.* 1 To make clear; brighten. 2 To free from impurities, blemishes, etc. 3 To remove, as obstructions, in making clear. 4 To remove obstructions from. 5 To free of guilt or blame. 6 To free from doubt or ambiguity. 7 To free from debt by payment. 8 To pass by or over without touching: to *clear* a fence. 9 To obtain or give clearance, as for a ship or cargo. 10 To net or gain over and above expenses. 11 To pass through a clearing house, as a check. —*v.i.* 12 To become clear. 13 To pass away, as mist or fog. 14 To settle accounts by exchange of bills and checks, as in a clearinghouse. —**clear out** *Informal.* To leave; depart. —**clear the air** To dispel emotional tensions, misunderstanding, etc. —**clear up** 1 To grow fair, as the weather. 2 To free from confusion or mystery. 3 To tidy. —*adv.* 1 Clearly; plainly. 2 *Informal* Completely; entirely. —*n.* An unobstructed space. —**in the clear** 1 Free from limitations or obstructions. 2 Not open to blame or accusation. [< L *clarus* clear, bright] —**clear′a·ble** *adj.* —**clear′ly** *adv.* —**clear′ness** *n.* —**Syn.** *adj.* 2 limpid, crystalline, pellucid. 7 obvious, apparent, manifest.

clear·ance (klir′əns) *n.* 1 The act or process of clearing. 2 The space by which a moving vehicle, part, etc., clears something. 3 A sale to dispose of accumulated merchandise. 4 Permission for a vessel, aircraft, etc., to proceed. 5 Authorization, as for access to information.

clear-cut (klir′kut′) *adj.* **1** Distinctly and sharply outlined. **2** Clearly evident; definite.

clear cutting Nonselective felling of all trees in a stand of timber.

clear-head·ed (klir′hed′id) *adj.* Having a clear perception or understanding; not mentally confused; sensible. —**clear′-head′ed·ly** *adv.* —**clear′-head′ed·ness** *n.*

clear·ing (klir′ing) *n.* A tract of land cleared of trees, underbrush, etc.

clear·ing·house (klir′ing-hous′) *n.* An office where bankers exchange drafts and checks and adjust balances.

clear-sight·ed (klir′sī′tid) *adj.* **1** Having keen eyesight. **2** Having accurate perception and good judgment. —**clear′-sight′ed·ly** *adv.* —**clear′-sight′ed·ness** *n.*

clear-sto·ry (klir′stôr′ē, -stō′rē) *n. pl.* **·ries** CLERESTORY.

cleat (klēt) *n.* **1** A piece of wood, metal, etc., fastened to a surface to strengthen, support, or prevent slipping. **2** *Naut.* A piece of metal or wood on which to belay a rope. —*v.t.* **1** To furnish or strengthen with a cleat or cleats. **2** *Naut.* To fasten (rope, etc.) to or with a cleat. [ME *clete*]

cleav·age (klē′vij) *n.* **1** A cleaving or being cleft. **2** A split, cleft, or division. **3** A tendency in certain rocks or crystals to split in certain directions. **4** The hollowed space between a woman's breasts, esp. when exposed by a low-cut neckline.

cleave[1] (klēv) *v.* **cleft** or **cleaved** or **clove, cleft** or **cleaved** or **clo·ven, cleav·ing** *v.t.* **1** To split or sunder, as with an ax or wedge. **2** To make or achieve by cutting. **3** To pass through; penetrate. —*v.i.* **4** To split or divide. **5** To make one's way, as by cutting: with *through.* [< OE *clēofan*] —**cleav′a·ble** *adj.*

cleave[2] (klēv) *v.i.* **cleaved, cleaved, cleav·ing 1** To stick fast; adhere. **2** To be faithful: with *to.* [< OE *cleofian*]

cleav·er (klē′vər) *n.* A heavy, hatchetlike knife used by butchers.

clef (klef) *n. Music* A symbol placed upon the staff to de-

Clefs
Showing position of middle C on each.
1. Treble or G clef. 2. Bass or F clef.
3, 4. C clefs (alto, tenor).

termine the pitch of the notes, namely, the **treble** or **G clef, bass** or **F clef,** and the **C clef.** [< L *clavis* key]

cleft (kleft) *v.* A *p.t. & p.p.* of CLEAVE[1]. —*adj.* Divided partially or completely. —*n.* A fissure; crevice; crack.

cleft lip A congenital fissure of the upper lip.

cleft palate A congenital gap from front to back of the hard palate.

clem·a·tis (klem′ə·tis) *n.* A perennial shrub or woody vine related to the crowfoot. [< Gk. *klēma* vine]

clem·en·cy (klem′ən·sē) *n. pl.* **·cies 1** Leniency; mercy. **2** An act of leniency. **3** Mildness, as of weather. [< L *clemens* mild]

clem·ent (klem′ənt) *adj.* **1** Lenient; merciful. **2** Mild: said of weather. [< L *clemens* mild, merciful] —**clem′ent·ly** *adv.*

clench (klench) *v.t.* **1** To grasp or grip firmly. **2** To close tightly or lock, as the fist or teeth. **3** To clinch, as a nail. —*n.* **1** A firm grip. **2** A device that clenches. [< OE *beclencan* hold fast]

clere·sto·ry (klir′stôr′ē, -stō′rē) *n. pl.* **·ries 1** The highest story of the nave and choir of a church, with windows opening above the aisle roofs, etc. **2** A similar story in other structures. Also **clere′sto′rey.** [< earlier *clere* clear + STORY]

cler·gy (klûr′jē) *n. pl.* **·gies** The group of people ordained for service in a Christian church. [< OF *clerc* clerk, cleric < LL *clericus*]

cler·gy·man (klûr′jē·mən) *n. pl.* **·men** (-mən) One of the clergy; an ordained minister.

cler·ic (kler′ik) *adj.* CLERICAL (def. 1). —*n.* A member of the clergy.

cler·i·cal (kler′i·kəl) *adj.* **1** Of, pertaining to, or character-

istic of a clergyman or the clergy. **2** Of or pertaining to workers or clerks in an office or to their work. —*n.* **1** A clergyman. **2** *pl.* The garb of a clergyman. —**cler′i·cal·ly** *adv.*

cler·i·cal·ism (kler′i·kəl·iz′əm) *n.* The policy of favoring or increasing the power of the clergy, esp. in politics. —**cler′i·cal·ist** *adj. & n.*

clerk (klûrk, *Brit.* klärk) *n.* **1** A person employed in an office to take care of records, filing, correspondence, etc. **2** An employee of a court, legislative body, etc. who has charge of records and accounts. **3** A salesperson in a store. **4** A hotel employee who assigns guests to their rooms. —*v.i.* To work or act as clerk. [< Gk. *klērikos* < *klēros* lot, portion] —**clerk′li·ness** *n.* —**clerk′ly** *adj.*

clev·er (klev′ər) *adj.* **1** Physically skillful; dexterous; adroit. **2** Mentally quick and intelligent; bright; keen; able. **3** Marked by ingenuity and originality. [? < Scand.] —**clev′er·ly** *adv.* —**clev′er·ness** *n.* —**Syn. 1** adept, expert, handy, deft. **2** sharp, shrewd, knowing, smart, talented. **3** inventive, ingenious, felicitous.

clev·is (klev′is) *n.* A U-shaped piece of iron with holes at both ends for a bolt, used to attach things together for hauling, pulling, etc. [? < Scand.]

clew (kloō) *n.* **1** In legends, a thread that guides through a maze. **2** A clue. **3** *pl.* The cords by which a hammock is slung. [< OE *cliewen* to roll into a ball]

cli·ché (klē·shā′) *n.* A trite saying, idea, etc. —*adj.* Being a cliché. [< F *clicher* to stereotype]

click (klik) *n.* **1** A short, sharp, metallic sound, as that made by the latch of a door. **2** *Phonet.* A speech sound occurring in certain African languages, produced by the sudden withdrawal of the tip of the tongue from the teeth or palate. —*v.t.* **1** To cause to make a click or clicks. —*v.i.* **2** To produce a click or clicks. **3** *Slang* To succeed. **4** *Slang* To agree or be in accord. [Imit.] —**click′er** *n.*

cli·ent (klī′ənt) *n.* **1** One in whose interest a lawyer acts. **2** One who engages the services of any professional adviser. **3** A customer. [< L *cliens* follower] —**cli·en·tal** (klī′en·təl, klī′ən·təl) *adj.*

cli·en·tele (klī′ən·tel′) *n.* A body of clients; a following.

cliff (klif) *n.* A high steep face of rock; a precipice. [< OE *clif*]

cliff-hang·er (klif′hang′ər) *n.* **1** A situation marked by suspense or uncertainty of outcome. **2** A serialized drama marked by suspense at the end of each episode. Also **cliff′-hang′er.** —**cliff′hang′ing** *adj., n.*

cli·mac·ter·ic (klī·mak′tər·ik, klī′mak·ter′ik) *n.* **1** A period of life characterized by physiological changes, esp. the menopause in women. **2** Any critical period of marked changes. —*adj.* Of or pertaining to a critical period of change: also **cli·mac·ter·i·cal** (klī′mak·ter′i·kəl). [< Gk. *klimaktēr* rung of a ladder]

cli·mac·tic (klī·mak′tik) *adj.* Of or constituting a climax. Also **cli·mac′ti·cal.** —**cli·mac′ti·cal·ly** *adv.*

cli·mate (klī′mit) *n.* **1** The weather and other meteorological conditions characteristic of a locality or region over an extended period of time. **2** A region as characterized by such conditions. **3** A prevailing or dominant trend in social affairs: *climate* of opinion. [< Gk. *klima* region, zone] —**cli·mat·ic** (klī·mat′ik) or **·i·cal** *adj.* —**cli·mat′i·cal·ly** *adv.*

cli·ma·tol·o·gy (klī′mə·tol′ə·jē) *n.* The science of climate. —**cli·ma·to·log·ic** (klī′mə·tə·loj′ik) or **·i·cal** *adj.* —**cli′·ma·tol′o·gist** *n.*

cli·max (klī′maks) *n.* **1** The highest point of intensity, interest, activity, etc.; culmination. **2** ORGASM. —*v.t. & v.i.* To reach or bring to a climax. [< Gk. *klimax* ladder]

climb (klīm) *v.t.* **1** To ascend or descend (something), esp. by means of the hands and feet. —*v.i.* **2** To mount, rise, or go up, esp. by using the hands and feet. **3** To rise, as in position or status: to *climb* to the top of one's profession. **4** To incline or slope upward. **5** To rise during growth, as certain vines, by clinging to a support. —*n.* **1** The act or process of climbing. **2** A place ascended by climbing. [< OE *climban*] —**climb′a·ble** *adj.* —**climb′er** *n.*

clime (klīm) *n.* A country; region; climate. [< L *clima* climate]

clinch (klinch) *v.t.* **1** To secure firmly, as a nail or staple, by bending down the protruding point. **2** To fasten together by this means. **3** To confirm or settle, as a bargain or agreement. —*v.i.* **4** To grip or grapple, as combatants. **5** *Slang* To embrace or hug. —*n.* **1** The act of clinching. **2** That which clinches; a clamp. **3** A grip or struggle at close quarters, as in boxing. **4** *Slang* A close embrace. [Var. of CLENCH]

clinch·er (klin′chər) *n.* **1** One who or that which clinches. **2** A nail made for clinching. **3** *Informal* A decisive argument, proof, etc.

cling (kling) *v.i.* **clung, cling·ing 1** To hold on to something firmly, as by grasping, embracing, or winding round. **2** To resist separation: with *together.* **3** To stick to tenaciously, as in the memory. [< OE *clingan*] —**cling′er** *n.* —**cling′y** *adj.* (**·i·er, ·i·est**)

cling·stone (kling′stōn′) *adj.* Having a stone to which the fleshy pulp adheres, as certain kinds of peach, plum, etc. —*n.* A fruit of this kind.

clin·ic (klin′ik) *n.* **1** The teaching of medicine and surgery by treatment of patients in the presence of a class. **2** A class receiving such instruction. **3** A medical establishment, often connected with a hospital, for the treatment of nonresident patients. **4** An organization that offers advice or instruction on certain problems: a drug *clinic.* [< Gk. *klinē* bed < *klinein* recline]

clin·i·cal (klin′i·kəl) *adj.* **1** Of or pertaining to a clinic or to the treatment of patients in clinics. **2** Scientific and impersonal; detached. —**clin′i·cal·ly** *adv.*

cli·ni·cian (kli·nish′ən) *n.* One who practices or is qualified to practice clinical medicine, psychiatry, or psychology.

clink¹ (klingk) *v.t. & v.i.* To make or cause to make a short, slight, ringing sound. —*n.* A short, slight, ringing sound. [< MDu. *klinken*]

clink² (klingk) *n. Slang* A prison. [< the *Clink*, a prison in London]

clink·er (kling′kər) *n.* **1** The stonelike residue left by coal in burning. **2** *Slang* **a** A mistake. **b** A failure. —*v.t. & v.i.* To form or cause to form a clinker. [< Du. *klinckaerd*, kind of brick]

cli·nom·e·ter (klī·nom′ə·tər, kli-) *n.* An instrument for determining angular inclination, as of guns, slopes, etc. [< Gk. *klinein* to bend + -METER]

Cli·o (klī′ō) *Gk. Myth.* The Muse of history.

clip¹ (klip) *n.* Any device that clasps, grips, or holds fast. —*v.t.* **clipped, clip·ping** To grip, fasten, or hold tightly. [< OE *clyppan* to clasp]

clip² (klip) *v.t.* **clipped, clip·ping 1** To cut or trim with shears or scissors, as hair. **2** To cut short; curtail: to *clip* the ends of words. **3** *Informal* To strike with a sharp blow. **4** *Slang* To cheat or defraud. —*v.i.* **5** To cut or trim. **6** *Informal* To run or move swiftly. —*n.* **1** The act of clipping, or that which is clipped. **2** The wool yielded at one shearing or season. **3** *Informal* A blow with the hand or fist. **4** *Informal* A quick pace. [< ON *klippa*]

clipped form A shortened form of a polysyllabic word, as *bus* for *omnibus.*

clip·per (klip′ər) *n.* **1** One who clips. **2** *Usu. pl.* An instrument for cutting or clipping hair, fleece, etc. **3** *Naut.* A 19th-century sailing vessel built for speed, with tall, raking masts: also **clipper ship.**

clip·ping (klip′ing) *n.* **1** The act of one who or that which clips. **2** That which is cut off or cut by clipping: a newspaper *clipping.* —*adj.* That cuts or clips.

Clipper ship

clique (klēk, klik) *n.* An exclusive or clannish group of people; coterie. —*v.i.* **cliqued, cli·quing** To unite in a clique; act clannishly. [< F *cliquer* click, clap]

cli·quish (klē′kish, klik′ish) *adj.* Inclined to form cliques;

exclusive. Also **cli′quey, cli′quy.** —**cli′quish·ly** *adv.* —**cli′quish·ness** *n.*

cli·to·ris (klit′ə·ris, klī′tə-) *n.* A small, erectile organ at the upper part of the vulva, corresponding to the penis. [< Gk. *kleitoris*]

clk. clerk; clock.

clo·a·ca (klō·ā′kə) *n. pl.* **·cae** (-kē, -sē) **1** The common cavity into which the urinary, genital, and intestinal tracts lead in certain fishes, reptiles, birds, insects, etc. **2** A sewer or cesspool. [< L, a drain] —**clo·a′cal** *adj.*

cloak (klōk) *n.* **1** A loose outer garment. **2** Something that covers or hides; a pretext; disguise. —*v.t.* **1** To cover with a cloak. **2** To disguise; conceal. [< OF *cloque*, bell, cape]

cloak·room (klōk′rōōm′, -room′) *n.* A room where hats, coats, luggage, etc., are cared for temporarily.

clob·ber (klob′ər) *v.t. Slang* **1** To beat or trounce. **2** To defeat badly. [?]

cloche (klōsh) *n.* **1** A woman's closefitting, bell-shaped hat. **2** A portable translucent cover for the protection and forcing of young plants. [F, lit., bell]

clock¹ (klok) *n.* **1** An instrument for measuring and indicating time by mechanical movements; a timepiece. **2** Any clocklike recording device. **3** TIME CLOCK. —*v.t.* To time or measure by or as by means of a stopwatch. [< Med. L *cloca* bell]

clock² (klok) *n.* An embroidered ornament on the side of a stocking or sock. [?]

clock·wise (klok′wīz′) *adj. & adv.* In the direction traveled by the hands of a clock.

clock·work (klok′wûrk′) *n.* The machinery of a clock, or any similar mechanism.

clod (klod) *n.* **1** A lump of earth, clay, etc. **2** A dull, stupid fellow. [< OE *clott* lump, clot] —**clod′dish, clod′dy** *adj.*

clod·hop·per (klod′hop′ər) *n.* **1** *Informal* A hick; rustic. **2** *pl.* Large, heavy shoes.

clog (klog) *n.* **1** Anything that impedes motion, as a block attached to an animal or a vehicle. **2** An obstruction or hindrance. **3** A wooden-soled shoe. **4** CLOG DANCE. —*v.* **clogged, clog·ging** —*v.t.* **1** To choke up or obstruct. **2** To hinder. **3** To fasten a clog to; hobble. —*v.i.* **4** To become choked up. **5** To adhere in a mass; coagulate. **6** To perform a clog dance. [ME *clogge* block of wood] —**clog′gi·ness** *n.*

clog dance A dance performed by a person who wears clogs, using them to beat out a rhythm on the floor.

cloi·son·né (kloi′zə·nā′) *n.* **1** A method of producing designs in enamel by laying out the pattern with strips of flat wire and filling the interstices with enamel paste, which is then fused in place. **2** The ware so produced. —*adj.* Of, pertaining to, or made by this method. [< F *cloison* a partition]

clois·ter (klois′tər) *n.* **1** A covered walk along the inside walls of buildings enclosing a courtyard, as in a monastery or college. **2** A monastery or convent. **3** Monastic life. —*v.t.* **1** To seclude; confine, as in a cloister. **2** To provide with cloisters. [< L *claustrum* enclosed place] —**clois′ter·ed, clois′tral** *adj.*

clomb (klōm) *Archaic p.t. & p.p.* of CLIMB.

clone (klōn) *n.* **1** A group of organisms derived from a single individual by asexual means. **2** an exact genetic replica of an organism. Also **clon** (klōn, klon). —*v.t.* **cloned, clon·ing** To produce in the form of a clone. [< Gk. *klōn* sprout, twig] —**clon′al** *adj.* —**clon′al·ly** *adv.*

clon·ing (klōn′ing) *n.* The production of progeny that is genetically identical with a single progenitor.

clo·nus (klō′nəs) *n. Pathol.* A series of violent muscular spasms. [< Gk. *klonos* motion] —**clon·ic** (klon′ik) *adj.*

close (klōs) *adj.* **clos·er, clos·est 1** Near or near together in space, time, order, etc. **2** Compact; dense: a *close* weave. **3** Tight: a *close* fit. **4** Near to the surface; very short. **5** Affectionately associated; intimate: a *close* friend. **6** Near to the original; exact; literal: a *close* copy. **7** Thorough; strict: a *close* search. **8** Accurate. **9** Nearly even or equal in score, performance, etc.: said of contests or contestants. **10** Shut in or about. **11** Confined or encompassed by limits, walls, etc.: *close* quarters. **12** Carefully watched or guarded: *close* custody. **13** Secretive; reticent. **14** Not liberal; stingy. **15** Ill-ventilated; warm; stifling. **16** Difficult to obtain; tight: said of money, credit, etc. **17** Not open or free; restricted. **18** *Phonet.* Describing those vowels pronounced with a part of the tongue relatively near to the palate, as the (ē) in *seat.* —*v.* (klōz) **closed, clos·ing** *v.t.* **1** To shut, as a door. **2** To fill or obstruct, as an opening or passage. **3** To bring together; unite; join. **4** To bring to an end; terminate. **5** To shut in; enclose. —*v.i.* **6** To become shut or closed. **7** To come to an end. **8** To come to close quarters. **9** To join; coalesce; unite. **10** To come to an agreement. **11** To be worth at the end of a business day: Stocks *closed* three points higher. —*n.* (klōz) **1** The act of closing. **2** An end; conclusion. **3** (klōs) *Chiefly Brit.* Any place shut in or enclosed, esp. such a place adjoining a cathedral or abbey. —*adv.* (klōs) In a close manner or position. [< L *claudere* to close] —**close·ly** (klōs′lē) *adv.* —**close·ness** (klōs′nis) *n.* —**clos·er** (klō′zər) *n.*

close call (klōs) *Informal* A narrow escape. Also **close shave.**

closed circuit (klōzd) A system of transmitting a television program by cable only to those receivers connected to a special circuit. —**closed′-cir′cuit** *adj.*

closed shop An establishment in which all the employees are union members.

close·fist·ed (klōs′fis′tid) *adj.* Stingy; miserly. —**close′fist′ed·ness** *n.*

close·fit·ting (klōs′fit′ing) *adj.* Fitting tightly.

close·hauled (klōs′hôld′) *adj. & adv. Naut.* With the sails set for sailing as close to the wind as possible.

close·mouthed (klōs′mouthd′, -moutht′) *adj.* Not given to imparting information; taciturn; uncommunicative.

clos·et (kloz′it) *n.* **1** A small room or recess for storage of clothes, linen, etc. **2** A room for privacy, esp. one used by a monarch as a council chamber. **3** WATERCLOSET. —*v.t.* **clos·et·ed, clos·et·ing** To shut up or conceal in or as in a closet: usu. used reflexively. —*adj.* **1** Private; confidential. **2** Based on theory rather than practice: *closet* strategy. [< L *clausus* closed]

close-up (klōs′up′) *n.* **1** In motion pictures and television, a picture taken at close range. **2** A personal or intimate look or view.

clo·sure (klō′zhər) *n.* **1** A closing or shutting up. **2** Something that closes or shuts. **3** A conclusion. **4** CLOTURE. —*v.t.* **clo·sured, clo·sur·ing** To cloture.

clot (klot) *n.* A thickened or coagulated mass, as of blood. —*v.t. & v.i.* **clot·ted, clot·ting** To form clots; coagulate. [< OE *clott* lump, mass] —**clot′ty, clot′ted** *adj.*

cloth (klôth, kloth) *n. pl.* **cloths** (klôthz, klothz, klôths, kloths) **1** A woven, knitted, or felted fabric of wool, cotton, rayon, etc. **2** A piece of cloth for a special use, as a table-cloth. —**the cloth** Clerical attire; also, the clergy. [< OE *clath*]

clothe (klōth) *v.t.* **clothed** or **clad, cloth·ing 1** To cover or provide with clothes. **2** To cover as if with clothing; invest. [< OE *clathian*]

clothes (klōz, klōthz) *n. pl.* **1** Wearing apparel; garments. **2** BEDCLOTHES. [< OE *clath* cloth]

clothes·horse (klōz′hôrs′, klōthz′-) *n.* **1** A frame on which to hang or dry clothes. **2** *Slang* A person excessively concerned with dress.

clothes·line (klōz′līn′, klōthz′-) *n.* A cord, rope, or wire on which to hang clothes to dry.

clothes·pin (klōz′pin′, klōthz′-) *n.* A peg or clamp with which to fasten clothes on a line.

clothes·press (klōz′pres′, klōthz′-) *n.* A closet for clothes; wardrobe.

clothes tree An upright pole having arms or hooks on which to hang hats, coats, etc.

cloth·ier (klōth′yər) *n.* One who makes or sells cloths or clothing.

cloth·ing (klō′thing) *n.* **1** Dress collectively; apparel. **2** A covering.

clo·ture (klō′chər) *n.* A procedure to stop debate in a legislative body in order to secure a vote. —*v.t.* **·tured, ·tur·ing** To apply cloture to (a debate). [< OF *closure* closed]

cloud (kloud) *n.* **1** A mass of visible vapor or an aggregation of watery or icy particles floating in the atmosphere. **2** Any cloudlike mass, as of birds, dust, steam, etc. **3** Some-

thing that darkens, obscures, or threatens. **4** A milkiness or murkiness, as in a liquid. —**under a cloud 1** Under suspicion. **2** Unhappy; depressed. —*v.t.* **1** To cover with or as with clouds; dim; obscure. **2** To render gloomy or troubled. **3** To bring disgrace on. —*v.i.* **4** To become overcast with clouds. **5** To be or appear sad or troubled. [< OE *clūd* rocky mass, hill] —**cloud′less** *adj.*

cloud·burst (kloud′bûrst′) *n.* A sudden, heavy rainfall.

cloud chamber A chamber containing a super-saturated vapor from which droplets condense along the tracks of charged atomic particles.

cloud·y (klou′dē) *adj.* **cloud·i·er, cloud·i·est 1** Overspread with clouds. **2** Of or like a cloud or clouds. **3** Obscure; vague; confused. **4** Gloomy; troubled. **5** Not limpid or clear. **6** Marked with cloudlike spots. —**cloud′i·ly** *adv.* —**cloud′i·ness** *n.*

clout (klout) *n.* **1** *Informal* A heavy blow or cuff with the hand. **2** *Informal* In baseball, a long hit. **3** *Slang* Influence or power; pull. —*v.t. Informal* **1** To hit or strike; cuff. **2** To hit (a ball) hard. [< OE *clūt*]

clove[1] (klōv) *n.* A dried flower bud of a tropical evergreen tree, used as a spice. [< OF *clou (de girofle)* nail (of clove)]

clove[2] (klōv) *n.* A small, individual section of a bulb, as of garlic. [< OE *clufu*]

clo·ven (klō′vən) A *p.p.* of CLEAVE[1]. —*adj.* Parted; split.

cloven hoof 1 A divided hoof, as in cattle. **2** A symbol for Satan. Also **cloven foot.** —**clo′ven-hoofed′, clo′ven-foot′ed** (-fŏŏt′id) *adj.*

clo·ver (klō′vər) *n.* Any of several leguminous plants having dense flower heads and leaves divided into three leaflets; esp. the **red clover** used for forage. [< OE *clǣfre*]

clo·ver·leaf (klō′vər·lēf′) *n.* A highway intersection with curving ramps in the form of a four-leaf clover, designed to route traffic in four directions without interference.

Cloverleaf

clown (kloun) *n.* **1** A professional buffoon in a play or circus who entertains by antics, jokes, tricks, etc. **2** A person who behaves like a clown. —*v.i.* To behave like a clown. [? < Scand.] —**clown′er·y, clown′ish·ness** *n.* —**clown′ish** *adj.* —**clown′ish·ly** *adv.*

cloy (kloi) *v.t.* **1** To satiate with too much of something; surfeit. —*v.i.* **2** To cause satiation. [Var. of earlier *accloy* < OF *encloyer* nail up, block, overload] —**cloy′ing·ly** *adv.* —**cloy′ing·ness** *n.*

C.L.U. Chartered Life Underwriter.

club[1] (klub) *n.* **1** A stout stick or staff; cudgel. **2** In certain sports, a stick used to hit a ball, esp. a golf club. **3 a** A three-lobed spot used to identify one of the four suits in a deck of playing cards. **b** A card so marked. **c** *pl.* The suit so identified. —*v.* **clubbed, club·bing** *v.t.* To beat, as with a club. [< ON *klubba*]

club[2] (klub) *n.* **1** A group of persons organized for a particular purpose or activity. **2** A house or room reserved for the use of such a group. —*v.* **clubbed, club·bing** *v.t.* **1** To contribute for a common purpose. —*v.i.* **2** To unite for a particular purpose or activity: often with *together.* —*adj.* Of, pertaining to, or belonging to a club. [Special meaning of CLUB[1]]

club·by (klub′ē) *adj.* **·bi·er, ·bi·est** *Informal* Characteristic of a social club; friendly, congenial, or exclusive. —**club′bi·ness** *n.*

club car A railroad passenger car furnished with easy chairs, tables, a bar, etc.

club·foot (klub′fŏŏt′) *n. pl.* **·feet 1** Congenital distortion of the foot; talipes. **2** A foot so affected. —**club′foot′ed** *adj.*

club·house (klub′hous′) *n.* **1** The building occupied by a club. **2** A dressing room or rooms for athletes.

club sandwich A sandwich containing three or more

slices of bread or toast filled with meat, lettuce, tomatoes, mayonnaise, etc.

club steak A small beefsteak cut from the loin.

cluck (kluk) *v.i.* **1** To make the noise of a hen calling her chicks. **2** To make any sound similar to a cluck. —*v.t.* **3** To call by clucking. **4** To express by clucking: to *cluck* disapproval. —*n.* The sound of clucking. [Imit.]

clue (kloo) *n.* A fact, object, idea, etc., that leads to the solution of a problem or mystery. —*v.t.* **clued, clu·ing** *Informal* To give a clue or information to: often with *in.* [Var. of CLEW]

clump (klump) *n.* **1** A thick cluster. **2** A heavy sound, as of tramping. **3** A lump or mass. —*v.t.* **1** To place or plant in a cluster or group. —*v.i.* **2** To walk clumsily and noisily. **3** To form clumps. [< LG] —**clump′y** (·i·er, ·i·est), **clump′ish** *adj.*

clum·sy (klum′zē) *adj.* **·si·er, ·si·est 1** Lacking physical dexterity, ease, or grace; awkward. **2** Badly constructed; unwieldy. **3** Awkwardly worded, delivered, etc.; inept. [< ME *clumsen* be numb (with cold) < Scand.] —**clum′si·ly** *adv.* —**clum′si·ness** *n.* —**Syn. 1** ungainly, unhandy, maladroit. **2** heavy, cumbersome, ungainly. **3** bungling, heavy-handed, gauche.

clung (klung) *p.t. & p.p. of* CLING.

clus·ter (klus′tər) *n.* **1** A group or bunch of objects or things joined together. **2** A group or assembly of persons or things close together. —*v.t. & v.i.* To be, form, or grow in a cluster or clusters. [< OE *clyster*] —**clus′tered** *adj.*

clutch[1] (kluch) *v.t.* **1** To snatch, as with hands or talons. **2** To grasp and hold firmly. —*v.i.* **3** To attempt to seize, snatch, or reach: with *at.* —*n.* **1** The act of clutching. **2** A tight, powerful grasp. **3** *pl.* Control; power: to fall into the *clutches* of an enemy. **4** *Mech.* **a** Any of various devices for coupling two working parts. **b** A pedal or lever for operating such a device. **5** A device for seizing and holding. **6** *Informal* A crisis or emergency. [< OE *clyccan* to grasp]

clutch[2] (kluch) *n.* **1** A nest of eggs. **2** A brood of chickens. **3** A tightly bunched group or cluster: a *clutch* of reporters. —*v.t.* To hatch. [< ON *klekja* hatch]

clut·ter (klut′ər) *n.* A disordered state or collection; litter. —*v.t.* **1** To make disordered; litter: often with *up.* —*v.i.* **2** To run or move with bustle. [ME *clotteren* to clot]

Clydes·dale (klīdz′dāl) *n.* A breed of draft horses originating in the valley of the Clyde, Scotland.

clyp·e·ate (klip′ē·āt) *adj.* Shield-shaped. Also **clyp′e·at′· ed.** [< L *clypeus* a shield]

clys·ter (klis′tər) *n. Med.* ENEMA. [< Gk. *klystēr* < *klyzein* wash out, rinse]

Cly·tem·nes·tra (klī′təm·nes′trə) *Gk. Myth.* The wife of Agamemnon who killed her husband and was herself killed by her son Orestes.

Cm. curium.

cm, cm. centimeter(s).

Cmdr. Commander.

cml. commercial.

CNO Chief of Naval Operations.

co- *prefix* **1** With; together; joint or jointly: *coexistence; coauthor.* **2** Of, pertaining to, or being the complement of an angle: *cosine.* [< L *cum* with]

CO Colorado (P.O. abbr.).

C.O. commanding officer; conscientious objector.

C/O, c/o, c.o. care of; carried over; cash order.

Co cobalt.

Co., co. (*pl.* **Cos., cos.**) company; county.

coach (kōch) *n.* **1** A large four-wheeled closed carriage; stagecoach. **2** A passenger bus. **3** The lowest-priced accommodations on a passenger train or airplane. **4** A trainer or director, as of athletes, singers, actors, etc. **5** A private tutor. —*v.t.* **1** To train or direct (athletes, singers, etc.). —*v.i.* **2** To study with or be trained by a coach. **3** To act as coach. [< *Kocs*, a Hungarian village where first used] —**coach′er** *n.*

coach-and-four (kōch′ən·fôr′, -fōr′) *n.* A coach drawn by four horses.

coach dog DALMATIAN.

coach·man (kōch′mən) *n. pl.* **·men** (-mən) One who drives a coach or a carriage.

co·ad·ju·tant (kō·aj′ə·tənt) *adj.* Cooperating. —*n.* An assistant. [< CO- + L *adjutare* to help]

co·ad·ju·tor (kō·aj′ə·tər, kō′ə·jōō′tər) *n.* **1** An assistant. **2** A bishop's assistant, usu. another bishop.

co·ag·u·late (kō·ag′yə·lāt) *v.t. & v.i.* **·lat·ed, ·lat·ing** To change from a liquid state into a clot or jelly, as blood. [< L *coagulare* curdle] —**co·ag′u·la′tion, co·ag′u·la′tor** *n.* —**co·ag′u·la·ble, co·ag′u·la′tive** *adj.*

coal (kōl) *n.* **1** A black, brittle, amorphous mineral, resulting from the carbonization of prehistoric vegetation, used as fuel. **2** A piece of coal. **3** A glowing piece of wood, charcoal, or similar substance. —*v.t.* **1** To supply with coal. —*v.i.* **2** To take in coal. [< OE *col*]

co·a·lesce (kō′ə·les′) *v.i.* **·lesced, ·lesc·ing** To grow or come together into one; fuse; blend. [< L *coalescere* unite] —**co′a·les′cence** *n.* —**co′a·les′cent** *adj.*

coal gas 1 The poisonous fumes produced by incomplete combustion of coal. **2** A fuel gas made by the distillation of bituminous coal.

co·a·li·tion (kō′ə·lish′ən) *n.* **1** An alliance, often temporary, of persons, parties, or states, usu. for a specific purpose. **2** A fusion or union. [< L *coalitio* < *coalescere* to coalesce] —**co′a·li′tion·ist** *n.*

coal oil 1 KEROSENE. **2** Crude petroleum.

coal tar A black viscid pitch obtained by heating bituminous coal in the absence of air and yielding a variety of compounds used in making dyestuffs, explosives, drugs, plastics, etc. —**coal′-tar′** *adj.*

coarse (kôrs, kōrs) *adj.* **coars·er, coars·est 1** Composed of somewhat large or rough pairs or particles. **2** Not fine or delicate in form, texture, etc. **3** Vulgar; indelicate; crude. [Adjectival use of COURSE, *n.*, def. 2] —**coarse′ly** *adv.* —**coarse′ness** *n.*

coarse-grained (kôrs′grānd′, kōrs′-) *adj.* **1** Having a coarse texture. **2** Crude; indelicate.

coars·en (kôr′sən, kōr′-) *v.t. & v.i.* To make or become coarse.

coast (kōst) *n.* **1** The land next to the sea; the seashore. **2** A slope suitable for sliding, as on a sled; also, a slide down it. —**the Coast** That part of the United States bordering on the Pacific Ocean. —*v.i.* **1** To sail or travel along, as a coast or border. —*v.i.* **2** To slide or ride down a slope by force of gravity alone, as on a sled. **3** To continue moving on momentum after the source of power has been stopped. **4** To move or behave aimlessly. [< L *costa* rib, flank] —**coast′al** *adj.*

coast·er (kōs′tər) *n.* **1** One who or that which coasts. **2** A sled or toboggan. **3** A small disk on which to set a drinking glass.

coaster brake A clutch brake on a bicycle, operated by reversing the pressure on the pedals.

coast guard Any force used to guard or police the coasts of a country.

coast·line (kōst′līn′) *n.* The boundary or shape of a coast.

coast·ward (kōst′wərd) *adj.* Directed or facing toward the coast. —*adv.* Toward the coast: also **coast′wards.**

coast·wise (kōst′wīz′) *adj.* Along the coast. —*adv.* Along the coast: also **coast′ways′.**

coat (kōt) *n.* **1** A sleeved outer garment opening down the front, as an overcoat, suit jacket, etc. **2** Any outer covering, as the fur of an animal. **3** An outer layer, as of paint, ice, etc. —*v.t.* To cover with or as with a coat, as of paint. [< OF *cote*] —**coat′ed** *adj.*

coat·dress (kōt′dres′) *n.* A dress buttoned along the full length of the front like a coat.

coat hanger A device of wood, plastic, etc., shaped to fit inside the shoulders of a coat or other garment, for hanging clothes when not in use.

co·a·ti (kō·ä′tē) *n. pl.* **·tis** A small, tree-dwelling, carnivorous, raccoonlike mammal of tropical America. Also **co·a′ti·mon′di, co·a′ti·mun′di** (-mun′dē). [< Tupi]

coat·ing (kō′ting) *n.* **1** A covering layer; coat. **2** Cloth for coats.

coat of arms The special armorial emblems and symbols of a person or family, as on a shield. • See CREST.

coat of mail *pl.* **coats of mail** A protective outer garment made of interlinked metal rings or scales; a hauberk.

coat·tail (kōt′tāl′) *n.* **1** The back part of a coat below the waist. **2** *Usu. pl.* The divided, tapering, rear part of a man's formal or dress coat.

co·au·thor (kō-ô′thər) n. One who collaborates with another or others in writing a book, article, etc. —v.t. Informal To be a coauthor of.

coax (kōks) v.t. 1 To persuade or seek to persuade by gentleness, flattery, etc.; wheedle. 2 To obtain by coaxing. —v.i. 3 To use persuasion or cajolery. —n. One who coaxes. —coax′er n. [< earlier cokes a fool]

co·ax·i·al (kō-ak′sē-əl) adj. Having a common axis or coincident axes: also **co·ax·al** (kō-ak′səl).

coaxial cable An electric cable consisting of two insulated conductors, one of which surrounds the other.

cob (kob) n. 1 CORNCOB. 2 A male swan. 3 A thickset, short-legged horse. 4 A lump. [ME cobbe]

co·balt (kō′bôlt) n. A hard, gray, metallic element (symbol Co) related to iron and nickel, used in alloys and pigments. [< G kobalt, var. of kobold goblin]

cobalt blue 1 A deep blue pigment made from the oxides of cobalt and aluminum. 2 Dark blue.

cobalt 60 A radioactive isotope of cobalt emitting gamma rays, used chiefly in radiotherapy.

cob·ble[1] (kob′əl) n. COBBLESTONE. —v.t. **·bled**, **·bling** To pave with cobblestones. [< ME cobbe lump, cob]

cob·ble[2] (kob′əl) v.t. **·bled**, **·bling** 1 To make or repair, as boots or shoes. 2 To put together roughly. [?]

cob·bler[1] (kob′lər) n. 1 A shoemaker. 2 A clumsy workman. [< COBBLE[2]]

cob·bler[2] (kob′lər) n. 1 An iced drink made of wine, sugar, fruit juices, etc. 2 A deep-dish fruit pie with no bottom crust. [?]

cob·ble·stone (kob′əl·stōn′) n. A rounded stone formerly used for paving. [See COBBLE[1]]

cob coal Large round pieces of coal.

co·bel·lig·er·ent (kō′bə·lij′ər·ənt) n. A country fighting on the side of another or others but not bound by alliance.

co·bra (kō′brə) n. Any of various poisonous snakes of Asia and Africa that when excited dilate the loose skin at their necks into a hood. [< L colubra snake]

cob·web (kob′web′) n. 1 The network of fine thread spun by a spider; also, a single thread of this. 2 Anything finespun or ensnaring. —v.t. **cob·webbed**, **cob·web·bing** To cover with or as with cobwebs. [< ME coppe spider + WEB] —**cob′web′by** adj.

Cobra

co·ca (kō′kə) n. 1 The dried leaves of a South American shrub yielding cocaine and other alkaloids. 2 The shrub itself. [< Quechua]

co·caine (kō·kān′, kō′kān) n. A white, bitter, crystalline alkaloid, obtained from coca and used as a local anesthetic and as a narcotic. Also **co·cain′**. [< COCA]

-coccal combining form Of or produced by (a specified form of) coccus. Also **-coccic**.

coc·cus (kok′əs) n. pl. **coc·ci** (kok′sī) Any bacterium having an ovoid or spherical shape. [< Gk. kokkos berry] —**coc·coid** (kok′oid) adj.

-coccus combining form Ovoid or spherical in shape: used to indicate bacteria so shaped: streptococcus.

coc·cyx (kok′siks) n. pl. **coc·cy·ges** (kok·sī′jēz) The small, triangular bone at the caudal end of the spine. [< Gk. kokkyx cuckoo; from a fancied resemblance to a cuckoo's bill] —**coc·cyg·e·al** (kok·sij′ē·əl) adj. ● See PELVIS.

coch·i·neal (koch′ə·nēl′, kōch′ə·nēl) n. A brilliant scarlet dye made from the dried bodies of the female of a scale insect. [< L coccineus scarlet < coccus a berry, grain of kermes]

coch·le·a (kok′lē·ə) n. pl. **·le·ae** (-li·ē) Anat. A spiral passage in the internal ear, containing the auditory nerve endings. [< L, snail] —**coch′le·ar** adj. ● See EAR.

coch·le·ate (kok′lē·āt) adj. Spirally twisted like a snail shell. Also **coch′le·at′ed**.

cock[1] (kok) n. 1 A full-grown male of the domestic fowl. 2 Any male bird. 3 A leader; champion. 4 WEATHERCOCK. 5 A faucet, often with the nozzle bent downward. 6 In a

firearm, the hammer; also, its position when ready to fire. 7 A jaunty, upward turn or position, as of a hat brim, the ears, eyes, etc. —v.t. 1 To raise the cock or hammer of (a firearm) preparatory to firing. 2 To turn up or to one side alertly, jauntily, or inquiringly, as the head, eye, ears, etc. —v.i. 3 To raise the hammer of a firearm. 4 To stick up; be prominent. —adj. Male. [< OE cocc]

cock[2] (kok) n. A small conical pile of straw or hay. —v.t. To arrange in cocks, as hay. [< OE cocc]

cock·ade (kok·ād′) n. A knot of ribbon, or the like, worn on the hat as a badge. [< MF coq cock] —**cock·ad′ed** adj.

cock·a·too (kok′ə·tōō′, kok′ə·tōō) n. pl. **·toos** Any of various bright-colored, crested parrots of the East Indies or Australia. [< Malay kākatūa]

cock·a·trice (kok′ə·tris) n. A legendary serpent, said to be hatched from a cock's egg, deadly to those who felt its breath or met its glance. [< Med. L calcatrix]

cock·boat (kok′bōt′) n. A small boat, esp. a ship's tender. [< OF coque cockboat + BOAT]

cock·chaf·er (kok′chā′fər) n. A large, European beetle destructive to vegetation. [< COCK[1] + CHAFER]

cock·crow (kok′krō′) n. The early morning. Also **cock′crow′ing**.

cocked hat (kokt) A three-cornered hat with the brim turned up.

Cockatoo

cock·er·el (kok′ər·əl) n. A rooster less than a year old. [Dim. of COCK[1]]

cock·er spaniel (kok′ər) A small, sturdy spaniel having long, silky hair of solid or various coloring and drooping ears.

cock·eye (kok′ī′) n. A squinting eye.

cock·eyed (kok′īd′) adj. 1 Cross-eyed. 2 Slang Off center; askew. 3 Slang Absurd; preposterous. 4 Slang Drunk.

cock·fight (kok′fīt′) n. A battle between gamecocks, usu. equipped with metal spurs on their legs. —**cock′·fight′ing** adj. & n.

cock·horse (kok′hôrs′) n. A child's rockinghorse or hobbyhorse.

cock·le[1] (kok′əl) n. 1 An edible European bivalve mollusk. 2 COCKLESHELL. 3 A wrinkle; pucker. —v.t. & v.i. **cock·led**, **cock·ling** To wrinkle; pucker. [< L conchylium shell]

cock·le[2] (kok′əl) n. Any of various weeds that grow among grain. [< OE coccel]

cock·le·boat (kok′əl·bōt′) n. COCKBOAT.

cock·le·bur (kok′əl·bûr′) n. A low-branching weed with burs about an inch long.

cock·le·shell (kok′əl·shel′) n. 1 The shell of a cockle. 2 A scallop shell. 3 A small, light boat.

cock·ney (kok′nē) n. pl. **·neys** 1 One born in the East End of London and speaking a characteristic dialect. 2 The characteristic dialect or accent of East End Londoners: also **cock′ney·ese′** (-ēz′, -ēs′). —adj. Of or like cockneys or their speech. [ME cokeney, lit., cock's egg, later, a soft or effeminate person, a city man] —**cock′ney·ish** adj.

cock·pit (kok′pit′) n. 1 A space in small airplanes for the pilot and a passenger or, in large airplanes, for the pilot and his crew. 2 A pit or ring for cockfighting. 3 In small ships or yachts, a space near the stern lower than the rest of the deck.

cock·roach (kok′rōch′) n. Any of a large group of swift-running, chiefly nocturnal insects having long feelers and flat, oval bodies, several species of which are household pests. [< Sp. cucaracha]

cocks·comb (koks′kōm′) n. 1 The comb of a rooster. 2 A plant with red or yellowish flowers. 3 COXCOMB.

cock·sure (kok′shoor′) adj. 1 Absolutely sure. 2 Presumptuously self-confident or sure. —**cock′sure′ness** n.

cock·swain (kok′sən, -swān′) n. COXSWAIN.

cock·tail (kok′tāl′) n. 1 Any of various mixed alcoholic drinks. 2 Any of various appetizers, as diced fruits, fruit juices, sea food, etc. [?]

cock·y (kok′ē) adj. **cock·i·er**, **cock·i·est** Informal Jaunty

---

add, āce, câre, pälm; end, ēven; it, īce; odd, ōpen, ôrder; tŏŏk, pōōl; up, bûrn; ə = a in above, u in focus; yōō = u in fuse; oil; pout; check; go; ring; thin; this; zh, vision. < derived from; ? origin uncertain or unknown.

and confident, esp. in a swaggering or conceited way. — **cock′i·ly** *adv.* —**cock′i·ness** *n.*

co·co (kō′kō) *n. pl.* ·**cos** 1 The coconut palm tree. 2 Its fruit. [< Pg., coconut shell]

co·coa (kō′kō) *n.* 1 A powder made from the roasted, husked seed kernels of the cacao. 2 A beverage made from it. 3 A reddish brown color. [Alter. of CACAO]

co·co·nut (kō′kə·nut′, -nət) *n.* The fruit of the coconut palm, containing white meat enclosed in a hard shell, and a milky liquid. Also **co′coa·nut′**.

coconut oil Oil obtained from coconut meat, used in soaps, etc. Also **coco palm.**

coconut palm A tropical palm tree that produces coconuts. Also **coco palm.**

co·coon (kə·kōōn′) *n.* The envelope spun by the larvae of certain insects in which they are enclosed during the pupa stage. [< F *coque* shell]

cod (kod) *n. pl.* **cod** or **cods** An important food fish of the North Atlantic. [ME]

C.O.D., c.o.d. cash on delivery; collect on delivery.

co·da (kō′də) *n.* A musical passage used to conclude a movement. [< L *cauda* tail]

cod·dle (kod′l) *v.t.* ·**dled**, ·**dling** 1 To cook gently in water. 2 To pamper, as a baby or an invalid. [? < CAUDLE] — **cod′dler** *n.*

code (kōd) *n.* 1 A systematized body of law. 2 Any system of rules or regulations. 3 A system of signals, characters, or symbols used in communication. 4 A set of prearranged symbols used for purposes of secrecy or brevity in transmitting messages. —*v.t.* **cod·ed, cod·ing** 1 To systematize as laws; make a digest of. 2 To put into the symbols of a code. [< L *codex* writing tablet]

co·deine (kō′dēn, kō′dē·in) *n.* An alkaloid derived from opium: used as an analgesic and in cough medicines. Also **co·de·in.** [< Gk. *kōdeia* head of a poppy]

co·dex (kō′deks) *n. pl.* **co·di·ces** (kō′də·sēz, kod′ə-) An ancient or medieval manuscript, as of the Scriptures or classics. [< L, writing tablet]

cod·fish (kod′fish′) *n.* COD.

codg·er (koj′ər) *n. Informal* A testy or eccentric old man. [Prob. var. of *cadger* < CADGE.]

cod·i·cil (kod′ə·səl) *n.* 1 A supplement to a will. 2 Any supplement or appendix. [< L *codex* writing tablet] — **cod·i·cil·la·ry** (kod′ə·sil′ə·rē) *adj.*

cod·i·fy (kod′ə·fī, kō′də-) *v.t.* ·**fied**, ·**fy·ing** To systematize, as laws. —**cod′i·fi·ca′tion, cod′i·fi′er** *n.*

cod·ling[1] (kod′ling) *n.* 1 A young cod. 2 HAKE.

cod·ling[2] (kod′ling) *n.* 1 One of a variety of cooking apples, elongated and tapering. 2 A green or defective apple. Also **cod·lin** (kod′lin). [ME *querdling*]

codling moth A moth whose larvae bore into and feed on apples, pears, walnuts, etc. Also **codlin moth.**

cod-liv·er oil (kod′liv′ər) Oil from the livers of cod, esp. rich in vitamins A and D.

co·ed (kō′ed′) *Informal n.* A young woman being educated at a coeducational institution. —*adj.* Of, pertaining to, or devoted to coeducation. Also **co′-ed′.**

co·ed·u·ca·tion (kō′ej·ōō·kā′shən) *n.* The education of both sexes in the same classes or institution. —**co′ed·u·ca′tion·al** *adj.*

coef., coeff. coefficient.

co·ef·fi·cient (kō′ə·fish′ənt) *n.* 1 *Math.* A number or symbol by which an algebraic expression is multiplied. 2 *Physics* A number indicating the degree of magnitude, or the kind and amount of change under given conditions.

coe·la·canth (sē′lə·kanth) *n.* Any of an order of primitive fossil fishes of which a few living specimens have been found. [< Gk. *koilos* hollow + *akantha* spine]

coe·li·ac (sē′lē·ak) CELIAC.

coe·lom (sē′ləm) *n.* The body cavity occupied by the viscera. Also **coe·lome** (sē′lōm). [< Gk. *koilos* hollow]

Coelacanth

coe·no·bite (sen′ə·bīt, sē′nə-) *n.* CENOBITE.

co·e·qual (kō-ē′kwəl) *adj.* Of the same value, age, size, importance, etc. —*n.* The equal of another or others.

co·erce (kō-ûrs′) *v.t.* **co·erced, co·erc·ing** 1 To constrain or force to do something. 2 To bring under control by force; repress. 3 To bring about by coercion: to *coerce* obedience. [< L *co-* together + *arcere* shut up, restrain] —**co·er′cer** *n.* —**co·er′ci·ble** *adj.*

co·er·cion (kō-ûr′shən) *n.* 1 Forcible constraint or restraint, moral or physical. 2 Government by force.

co·er·cive (kō-ûr′siv) *adj.* Serving or tending to coerce. —**co·er′cive·ly** *adv.* —**co·er′cive·ness** *n.*

co·e·val (kō-ē′vəl) *adj.* Of or belonging to the same age, time, or duration. —*n.* A contemporary. [< L *co-* together + *aevus* age] —**co·e′val·ly** *adv.*

co·ex·ist (kō′ig·zist′) *v.i.* To exist together, in the same place or at the same time. —**co′ex·ist′ence** *n.* —**co′ex·ist′ent** *adj.*

C. of C. Chamber of Commerce.

cof·fee (kôf′ē, kof′ē) *n.* 1 The seeds (**coffee beans**) of a tropical evergreen shrub. 2 The shrub itself. 3 A beverage made from the roasted and ground seeds of this shrub. 4 The color of coffee containing cream. [< Turkish *qahveh* < Ar. *qahwah*]

coffee break A recess from work for the purpose of taking coffee or other refreshments.

coffee cake Any of several kinds of cake, usu. containing nuts, raisins, etc., and meant to be eaten with coffee.

coffee house A café where coffee and other refreshments are served.

coffee mill A hand mill for grinding roasted coffee beans. Also **coffee grinder.**

coffee pot A covered vessel in which coffee is prepared or served.

coffee shop A small restaurant, often in a hotel, where coffee and food are served. Also **coffee room.**

coffee table A low table, usu. placed in front of a sofa, for serving refreshments, etc.

cof·fer (kôf′ər, kof′-) *n.* 1 A chest or strongbox for valuables. 2 *pl.* Financial resources; funds. 3 A decorative, sunken panel in a dome or vault. 4 COFFERDAM. —*v.t.* 1 To place in a coffer. 2 To adorn with coffers, as a ceiling. [< L *cophinus*]

cof·fer·dam (kôf′ər·dam′, kof′-) *n.* A temporary enclosing dam or structure placed or built in the water and pumped dry, to protect workmen.

cof·fin (kôf′in, kof′-) *n.* The case or chest in which a corpse is buried. —*v.t.* To put into or as into a coffin. [< Gk. *kophinos* basket]

C. of S. Chief of Staff.

cog (kog) *n.* 1 A tooth or one of a series of teeth projecting from the surface of a wheel or gear to impart or receive motion. 2 COGWHEEL. 3 A person regarded as making a minor contribution to a large organization or process. [< Scand.]

co·gent (kō′jənt) *adj.* Compelling belief, assent, or action; forcible; convincing. [< L *cogere* compel] —**Syn.** forceful, persuasive, weighty, compelling, trenchant.

cog·i·tate (koj′ə·tāt) *v.t.* & *v.i.* ·**tat·ed**, ·**tat·ing** To think carefully (about); ponder. [< L *co-* together + *agitare* consider] —**cog·i·ta·ble** (koj′ə·tə·bəl) *adj.* —**cog′i·ta′tor** *n.*

cog·i·ta·tion (koj′ə·tā′shən) *n.* Consideration; reflection; thought. —**cog′i·ta·tive** *adj.* —**cog′i·ta·tive·ly** *adv.* —**cog′i·ta·tive·ness** *n.*

co·gnac (kōn′yak, kon′-) *n.* 1 Brandy produced in the area of Cognac, France. 2 Any brandy.

cog·nate (kog′nāt) *adj.* 1 Allied by blood; kindred. 2 Belonging to the same stock or root: English *cold* and Latin *gelidus* are *cognate* words. 3 Having the same nature or quality. —*n.* A cognate person or thing. [< L *co-* together + (*g*)*natus*, pp. of (*g*)*nasci* be born] —**cog·na′tion** *n.*

cog·ni·tion (kog·nish′ən) *n.* 1 The act or faculty of apprehending, knowing, or perceiving. 2 Something known or perceived; a perception. [< L *co-* together + (*g*)*noscere* know] —**cog·ni′tion·al, cog·ni·tive** (kog′nə·tiv) *adj.*

cog·ni·zance (kog′nə·zəns) *n.* 1 Knowledge; perception; awareness. 2 *Law* a The hearing of a case in court. b Jurisdiction. [< L *cognoscere* to know]

cog·ni·zant (kog′nə·zənt) *adj.* Having knowledge; aware: with *of.*

cog·no·men (kog-nō′mən, kog′nə-) *n. pl.* **·no·mens** or **·nom·i·na** (-nom′ə·nə) **1** One's family name; surname. **2** Any name or nickname. [< L *co-* together + (*g*)*nomen* name] —**cog·nom·i·nal** (kog·nom′ə·nəl) *adj.*

cog·wheel (kog′ʰwēl′) *n.* A wheel with cogs.

co·hab·it (kō-hab′it) *v.i.* To live together as husband and wife, esp. without legal marriage. [< L *co-* together + *habitare* live] —**co·hab′i·tant, co·hab′it·er, co·hab′i·ta′tion** *n.*

co·here (kō-hir′) *v.i.* **co·hered, co·her·ing 1** To stick or hold firmly together. **2** To be logically consistent or connected, as a piece of writing. [< L *co-* together + *haerere* stick]

b

a

Cogwheels
a. spur gears.
b. bevel gears.

co·her·ence (kō-hir′əns) *n.* **1** A sticking together; union; cohesion. **2** The quality of being consistent and intelligible, as in logic, thought, etc. **3** *Physics* That relation between two sets of waves, as light or sound waves, in which the phase of either can be determined from the other. Also **co·her′en·cy.**

co·her·ent (kō-hir′ənt) *adj.* **1** Cleaving or sticking together. **2** Logical, intelligible, or articulate, as in thought, speech, etc. **3** *Physics* Exhibiting coherence. —**co·her′ent·ly** *adv.*

co·he·sion (kō-hē′zhən) *n.* **1** The act or state of cohering. **2** *Physics* That force by which molecules of the same kind or of the same body are held together so that the substance or body resists separation.

co·he·sive (kō-hē′siv) *adj.* Having or causing cohesion. —**co·he′sive·ly** *adv.* —**co·he′sive·ness** *n.*

co·hort (kō′hôrt) *n.* **1** The tenth of an ancient Roman military legion, 300 to 600 men. **2** A band of soldiers. **3** A companion, colleague, or follower. [< L *cohors*]

coif (koif) *n.* **1** A close-fitting cap, hood, or headdress: a nun's *coif.* **2** (kwäf) A hair style. —*v.t.* **1** To cover with or as with a coif. **2** (kwäf) To style (hair). [< LL *cofia*]

coif·feur (kwä·fœr′) *n.* A male hairdresser. [F] —**coif·feuse** (kwä·fœz′) *n. Fem.*

coif·fure (kwä·fyŏor′, *Fr.* kwá·für′) *n.* **1** A style of arranging the hair. **2** HEADDRESS. —*v.t.* **·fured, ·furing** To style (hair). [F< OF *coiffe* coif]

coign (koin) *n.* A projecting angle or corner. Also **coigne.** [< OF, wedge]

coign of vantage An advantageous position.

coil (koil) *n.* **1** A single ring or spiral, or a series of rings or spirals, formed by winding. **2** A series of pipes connected in rows or reversed windings. **3** An induction coil. —*v.t.* **1** To wind spirally or in rings. —*v.i.* **2** To form rings or coils. [< L *colligere* to collect] —**coil′er** *n.*

coin (koin) *n.* **1** A piece of metal stamped by government authority, for use as money. **2** Metal currency, collectively. **3** A corner; quoin. —*v.t.* **1** To stamp or mint (coins) from metal. **2** To make into coins, as metal. **3** To originate or invent, as a word or phrase. [< F, wedge, die < L *cuneus* wedge] —**coin′a·ble** *adj.* —**coin′er** *n.*

coin·age (koi′nij) *n.* **1** The making of coins or the coins made. **2** The system of coins of a country. **3** The act of fabricating or creating something, esp. a word or phrase. **4** An artificially created word or phrase.

co·in·cide (kō′in·sīd′) *v.i.* **·cid·ed, ·cid·ing 1** To be alike in parts, shape, space occupied, or position. **2** To agree exactly, as in opinions, interests, etc. **3** To occur at the same time. [< L *co-* together + *incidere* to happen]

co·in·ci·dence (kō·in′sə·dəns) *n.* **1** The fact or condition of coinciding; correspondence. **2** A remarkable occurrence of events, ideas, etc., at the same time or in the same way, apparently by mere accident.

co·in·ci·dent (kō·in′sə·dənt) *adj.* **1** Occurring at the same time. **2** Having the same shape, position, etc. **3** Exactly corresponding; identical. —**co·in′ci·dent·ly** *adv.*

co·in·ci·den·tal (kō·in′sə·den′təl) *adj.* Characterized by or involving coincidence. —**co·in′ci·den′tal·ly** *adv.*

coir (koir) *n.* Coconut-husk fiber, used in making ropes, matting, etc. [< Malay *kāyar* rope]

co·i·tus (kō′i·təs, kō·ēt′əs) *n.* Sexual intercourse. Also **co·i·tion** (kō·ish′ən). [< L *co-* together + *ire* go] —**co′i·tal** *adj.*

coke (kōk) *n.* A solid fuel obtained by heating coal so as to remove its gases. —*v.t. & v.i.* **coked, cok·ing** To change into coke. [ME]

Col. Colombia; Colonel; Colorado; Colossians.

col. collected; collector; college; colonial; colony; color; colored; column.

co·la (kō′lə) *n.* **1** A small, tropical tree bearing nuts which yield an extract used in the preparation of beverages and medicines. **2** A carbonated beverage flavored with this extract. **3** The extract itself. [< *kola* native African name]

col·an·der (kul′ən·dər, kol′-) *n.* A perforated vessel for draining off liquids. [< L *colare* strain]

cold (kōld) *adj.* **1** Of a relatively low temperature as compared with a normal or standard temperature. **2** Feeling chilled; chilly. **3** Without sufficient heat: *cold* coffee. **4** Dead. **5** Without feeling or enthusiasm; unmoved; indifferent. **6** Not cordial; unfriendly. **7** Without sexual desire; frigid. **8** Depressing or discouraging. **9** Objective; impersonal; detached: *cold* reasoning. **10** Lacking freshness, odor, etc.: a *cold* trail. **11** *Informal* Unconscious: to be out *cold.* **12** Distant from the object or answer sought: said of a guesser, etc. **13** In art, suggesting cold, as bluish or grayish colors. **14** *Informal* Unprepared. **15** *Slang* Perfectly prepared. —*adv. Slang* Completely; absolutely. —*n.* **1** A low temperature, esp. one below freezing. **2** Lack of heat, or the sensation caused by it. **3** A common viral infection marked by inflammation of the upper respiratory tract, chills, nasal discharge, etc. [< OE *cald*] —**cold′ly** *adv.* —**cold′ness** *n.*

cold-blood·ed (kōld′blud′id) *adj.* **1** Deliberately cruel; heartless. **2** Unfeeling; matter-of-fact. **3** Very sensitive to cold. **4** *Zool.* Having a temperature that fluctuates with that of the surrounding medium, as a fish or reptile. —**cold′blood′ed·ly** *adv.* —**cold′blood′ed·ness** *n.*

cold chisel A chisel of tempered steel for cutting cold metal.

cold cream A cleansing and soothing ointment for the skin.

cold front The forward edge of a cold air mass advancing against a warmer mass.

cold-heart·ed (kōld′här′tid) *adj.* Without sympathy, pity, or understanding; unfeeling. —**cold′heart′ed·ly** *adv.* —**cold′heart′ed·ness** *n.*

cold pack 1 *Med.* A wrapping of cold, wet blankets or sheets about a patient as a means of therapy. **2** A canning process in which raw food is packed in cans or jars, which are then heated for cooking and to destroy bacteria.

cold sore An eruption of small blisters, usu. about the mouth and accompanying a cold or fever.

cold turkey *Slang* **1** The abrupt and total deprivation of a substance, as a narcotic drug or cigarettes, from one addicted to its use. **2** Blunt, candid talk.

cold war Intense rivalry between nations in diplomacy, economic strategy, etc., falling just short of armed conflict.

cold wave A spell of unusually cold weather.

cole (kōl) *n.* Any of various plants related to cabbage, esp. rape. Also **cole·wort** (kōl′wûrt′). [< L *caulis* cabbage]

co·le·op·ter·ous (kō′lē·op′tər·əs, kol′ē) *adj.* Belonging to a large order of insects, including beetles and weevils, in which the front wings are modified to form a hard sheath. [< Gk. *koleos* sheath + *pteron* wing] —**co′le·op′ter, co′le·op′ter·an** *n.*

cole·slaw (kōl′slô′) *n.* A salad made of shredded, raw cabbage. [< Du. *kool sla* cabbage salad]

col·ic (kol′ik) *n.* Acute spasmodic pain in the abdomen. —*adj.* Pertaining to or like colic. [< Gk. *kolon* colon] —**col′ick·y** *adj.*

col·i·se·um (kol′ə·sē′əm) *n.* A large building or stadium for sports events, exhibitions, etc.

co·li·tis (kə·lī′tis) *n.* Inflammation of the colon.

coll. colleague; collect; collection; collector; college; colloquial.

col·lab·o·rate (kə·lab′ə·rāt) *v.i.* **·rat·ed, ·rat·ing 1** To labor or cooperate with another, esp. in literary or scientific pursuits. **2** To be a collaborationist. [< L *com-* with + *laborare* work] —**col·lab′o·ra′tion, col·lab′o·ra′tor** *n.* —**col·lab′o·ra′tive** *adj.*

col·lab·o·ra·tion·ist (kə·lab′ə·rā′shən·ist) *n.* A citizen of a country invaded or occupied by foreign troops who cooperates with the enemy.

col·lage (kə·läzh′) *n.* An artistic composition of objects and materials pasted on a surface. [< Gk. *kolla* glue]

col·lapse (kə·laps′) *v.* **·lapsed, ·laps·ing** *v.i.* **1** To give way; cave in. **2** To fail utterly. **3** To become compact by the folding in of parts. **4** To lose health, strength, value, etc., suddenly and completely. —*v.t.* **5** To cause to collapse. — *n.* **1** The act of collapsing. **2** Extreme prostration. **3** Utter failure; ruin. [< L *collapsus*, pp. of *collabi* fall together] — **col·laps′i·ble** or **·a·ble** *adj.* —**col·laps′i·bil′i·ty** *n.*

col·lar (kol′ər) *n.* **1** The part of a garment that circles the neck. **2** An article worn about the neck. **3** A band, part of a harness, etc., for the neck of an animal. **4** A growth of fur or ring of color about the neck of an animal. **5** *Mech.* Any of various cylindrical or ring-shaped devices used to limit or control motion. —*v.t.* **1** To grasp by the collar. **2** To provide with a collar. **3** *Informal* To detain or to capture. [< L *collum* neck]

col·lar·bone (kol′ər·bōn′) *n.* CLAVICLE.

col·lard (kol′ərd) *n.* A variety of cabbage with leaves that do not form a head. [Alter. of *colewort* < COLE]

collat. collateral.

col·late (kə·lāt′, kol′āt, kō′lāt) *v.t.* **·lat·ed, ·lat·ing 1** To compare critically, as writings or facts. **2** To examine (pages, as those of an unbound book) to see that none are missing or out of order. **3** To assemble (mimeographed pages, etc.) in proper or consecutive order. [< L *collatus* carried together] —**col·la′tor** *n.*

col·lat·er·al (kə·lat′ər·əl) *adj.* **1** Subordinate; secondary. **2** Corroborating; confirmatory. **3** Being or lying alongside; parallel. **4** Descended from the same ancestor but in a different line. **5** Guaranteed by property, as stocks or bonds, deposited as security: a *collateral* loan. —*n.* **1** Property, stocks, bonds, etc. deposited as security for a loan or the like. **2** A collateral relative. [< L *com-* together + *latus, -eris* side] —**col·lat′er·al·ly** *adv.*

col·la·tion (kə·lā′shən, ko-, kō-) *n.* **1** The act or process of collating. **2** A light meal.

col·league (kol′ēg) *n.* A fellow worker, as in an office, or a fellow member of the same profession, etc. [< L *collega* one chosen simultaneously with another]

col·lect¹ (kə·lekt′) *v.t.* **1** To gather together; assemble. **2** To bring together as for a hobby. **3** To gather or obtain (payments of money). **4** To regain control of: to *collect* one's wits. —*v.i.* **5** To assemble or congregate, as people. **6** To accumulate, as dust. **7** To gather payments or donations. —*adj.* To be paid for by the receiver. —*adv.* So that the receiver pays. [< L *com-* together + *legere* gather] — **col·lect′a·ble** or **·i·ble** *adj.*

col·lect² (kol′ekt) *n.* In certain church services, a brief prayer varying with the season or occasion. [< L *collecta* a gathering together]

col·lect·ed (kə·lek′tid) *adj.* **1** Assembled; gathered. **2** Composed; self-possessed. —**col·lect′ed·ly** *adv.* —**col·lect′·ed·ness** *n.*

col·lec·tion (kə·lek′shən) *n.* **1** The act of collecting. **2** A group of collected objects or individuals. **3** An accumulation. **4** A sum of money that has been collected.

col·lec·tive (kə·lek′tiv) *adj.* **1** Formed or brought together by collecting. **2** Of, involving, or accomplished by a group of persons rather than individuals. —*n.* **1** A collective enterprise. **2** The people involved in such an enterprise. **3** COLLECTIVE NOUN. —**col·lec′tive·ly** *adv.* —**col·lec′·tive·ness, col·lec·tiv′i·ty** *n.*

collective bargaining Negotiation between organized workers and employers for reaching an agreement on working conditions, wages, hours, etc.

collective noun A singular noun naming a collection, or group of persons or things, as *jury, family, flock,* etc. • A *collective noun* takes either a singular or plural verb, according as it refers to the objects composing it as an aggregate or as separate individuals: The audience *was* large; The audience *were* divided in opinion.

col·lec·tiv·ism (kə·lek′tiv·iz′əm) *n.* An economic theory or system in which the people as a whole own or control the material and means of production and distribution. — **col·lec′tiv·ist** *adj., n.* —**col·lec′tiv·is′tic** *adj.*

col·lec·tiv·ize (kə·lek′tiv·īz) *v.t.* **·ized, ·iz·ing** To organize (an agricultural settlement, industry, economy, etc.) under a system of collectivism. —**col·lec′tiv·i·za′tion** *n.*

col·lec·tor (kə·lek′tər) *n.* One who or that which collects, as a person who receives taxes, duties, etc.

col·leen (kol·ēn′, ko·lēn′) *n.* An Irish girl.

col·lege (kol′ij) *n.* **1** A school of higher learning, as an undergraduate school at a university, that offers a four-year course of study leading to a bachelor's degree. **2** A school, often a graduate school in a university, offering instruction in a specialized course of study: a *college* of medicine. **3** A building or buildings used by a college. **4** A body of associates or colleagues engaged in some definite work or duty: electoral *college.* [< L *collegium* body of associates] —**col·le·gi·al** (kə·lē′jē·əl) *adj.*

College of Cardinals In the Roman Catholic Church, the body of cardinals who elect the Pope, act as his council, and, in his absence, administer the Holy See.

col·le·gi·al·i·ty (kə·lē′jē·al′i·tē) *n.* **1** The relationship between colleagues. **2** In the Roman Catholic Church, the sharing of the power of government between the bishops and the Pope.

col·le·gian (kə·lē′jən, -jē·ən) *n.* A college student.

col·le·giate (kə·lē′jit, -jē·it) *adj.* Of, like, or for a college or college student.

col·lide (kə·līd′) *v.i.* **·lid·ed, ·lid·ing 1** To come together with violent impact; crash. **2** To come into conflict; clash. [< L *com-* together + *laedere* strike]

col·lie (kol′ē) *n.* A breed of shepherd dogs which originated in Scotland, characterized by a long, narrow head and an abundant long-haired coat. [Prob. < Scot. Gael. *cuilean* puppy]

col·lier (kol′yər) *n. Chiefly Brit.* **1** A coal miner. **2** A vessel employed in carrying coal. [ME *colier* < *col* coal]

col·lier·y (kol′yər·ē) *n. pl.* **·lier·ies** *Chiefly Brit.* **1** A coal mine. **2** The coal trade.

col·li·mate (kol′ə·māt) *v.t.* **·mat·ed, ·mat·ing 1** To bring into line. **2** To adjust the line of sight of, as of a telescope. **3** To make parallel, as refracted rays of light. [< L *com-* together + *lineare* align] —**col′li·ma′tion, col′li·ma′tor** *n.*

col·li·sion (kə·lizh′ən) *n.* **1** A violent impact or crash. **2** A conflict, as of views, interests, etc. [< L *collidere* to collide]

col·lo·cate (kol′ō·kāt) *v.t.* **·cat·ed, ·cat·ing** To place or arrange in certain order, as side by side. [< L *com-* together + *locare* place] —**col′lo·ca′tion** *n.*

col·lo·di·on (kə·lō′dē·ən) *n.* A flammable, quick-drying solution of cellulose, used to coat wounds, photographic plates, etc. Also **col·lo·di·um** (kə·lō′dē·əm). [< Gk. *kollōdēs* gluelike]

col·loid (kol′oid) *n.* Any system of mutually insoluble gaseous, liquid, or solid substances in which one component in very finely divided form remains dispersed in the other. —*adj.* Of, like, or pertaining to a colloid: also **col·loi·dal** (kə·loid′l). [< Gk. *kollōdēs* gluelike] —**col·loi·dal·i·ty** (kol′oi·dal′ə·tē) *n.*

colloq. colloquial.

col·lo·qui·al (kə·lō′kwē·əl) *adj.* **1** Characteristic of or suitable to the informal language of ordinary conversation or writing. **2** Of or pertaining to conversation; conversational. —**col·lo′qui·al·ly** *adv.* —**col·lo′qui·al·ness** *n.*

col·lo·qui·al·ism (kə·lō′kwē·əl·iz′əm) *n.* A colloquial style, usage, word, or expression.

col·lo·quy (kol′ə·kwē) *n. pl.* **·quies** A more or less formal conversation or conference. [< L *colloquium* conversation] —**col′lo·quist** *n.*

col·lude (kə·lood′) *v.i.* **·lud·ed, ·lud·ing** To cooperate secretly; conspire; connive. [< L *com-* together + *ludere* play, trick] —**col·lud′er** *n.*

col·lu·sion (kə·loo′zhən) *n.* Secret cooperation in fraud or in illegal activities. [< L *colludere* to collude] —**col·lu′sive** *adj.* —**col·lu′sive·ly** *adv.* —**col·lu′sive·ness** *n.*

co·logne (kə·lōn′) *n.* A toilet water consisting of alcohol scented with aromatic oils. Also **Cologne water.** [< *Cologne,* Germany]

Co·lom·bi·a (kə·lum'bē·ə, *Sp.* kō·lōm'byä) *n.* A republic in NW South America, 439,519 sq. mi., cap. Bogotá. —**Co·lom'bi·an** *adj., n.* • See map at VENEZUELA.

co·lon¹ (kō'lən) *n.* A punctuation mark (:) used to introduce a series or catalog of things, a speech, quotation, example, etc., and after the salutation in a formal letter. [<Gk. *kōlon* member, limb, clause]

co·lon² (kō'lən) *n. pl.* **co·lons** or **co·la** (kō'lə) The large intestine between the cecum and the rectum. [<Gk. *kolon*] —**co·lon·ic** (kə·lon'ik) *adj.* • See INTESTINE.

co·lon² (kō·lōn') *n. pl.* **co·lons** (kō·lōnz'), *Sp.* **co·lo·nes** (kō·lō'nās) The monetary unit of Costa Rica and El Salvador.

co·lo·nel (kûr'nəl) *n.* See GRADE. [<Ital. *colonna* column of soldiers] —**colo'nel·cy, colo'nel·ship** *n.*

co·lo·ni·al (kə·lō'nē·əl) *adj.* 1 Of, possessing, like, or forming a colony or colonies. 2 *Often cap.* Of the Colonies. 3 *Often cap.* Of or like a style of architecture prevalent in the American colonies. —*n.* A citizen or inhabitant of a colony. —**co·lo'ni·al·ly** *adv.*

co·lo·ni·al·ism (kə·lō'nē·əl·iz'əm) *n.* The policy of a nation seeking to acquire, extend, or retain overseas dependencies. —**co·lo'ni·al·ist** *adj., n.* —**co·lo'ni·al·is'tic** *adj.*

col·o·nist (kol'ə·nist) *n.* 1 A member or inhabitant of a colony. 2 A founder of a colony.

col·o·nize (kol'ə·nīz) *v.* **·nized, ·niz·ing** *v.t.* 1 To settle a colony or colonies in. 2 To establish as colonists. —*v.i.* 3 To establish or unite in a colony or colonies. *Brit. sp.* **col'o·nise.** —**col'o·ni·za'tion, col'o·niz'er** *n.*

col·on·nade (kol'ə·nād') *n. Archit.* A series of columns, usu. topped by an entablature. [<F *colonne* column] —**col'on·nad'ed** *adj.*

col·o·ny (kol'ə·nē) *n. pl.* **·nies** 1 A body of emigrants who settle in a remote region but remain under the control of a parent country. 2 The region thus settled. 3 Any group of people having common ethnic backgrounds, interests, etc., and living in a particular area or region: the movie *colony.* 4 The area or region in which they live. 5 A discrete group of microorganisms growing in a culture medium. 6 A group of related plants or animals living or growing together. —**the Colonies** The British colonies that became the original thirteen states of the U.S.: Va., N.Y., Mass., Conn., R.I., N.H., Md., N.J., N.C., S.C., Pa., Del., and Ga. [<L *colonus* farmer]

col·o·phon (kol'ə·fon, ·fən) *n.* A publisher's distinctive emblem, usu. printed on the title page of a book. [<Gk. *kolophon* summit]

col·or (kul'ər) *n.* 1 A visual attribute of bodies or substances distinct from their spatial characteristics and depending upon the spectral composition of the light emitted or reflected by them. 2 Any coloring matter, as a paint or pigment. 3 The hue or pigmentation of the human skin. 4 The pigmentation of the skin of a Negro or other non-Caucasian. 5 The complexion of the human face, esp. if ruddy or flushed. 6 *pl.* A flag or banner, as of a nation, military unit, etc. 7 *Usu. pl.* Any identifying color, ribbon, badge, etc.: our college *colors.* 8 *pl.* One's personal opinions, beliefs, etc.: Stick to your *colors.* 9 An outward appearance or semblance, often deceptive or false: under the *color* of truth. 10 General nature or character: the *color* of her thinking. 11 Liveliness or animation; vividness. 12 Justification; plausibility. 13 In art and literature, the use of realistic or characteristic details and effects. 14 In art, the effect produced by color. 15 *Music* TIMBRE. —*v.t.* 1 To apply or give color to, as by painting, staining, or dyeing. 2 To misrepresent by distortion or exaggeration. 3 To modify in nature or character. —*v.i.* 4 To take on or change color, as ripening fruit. 5 To blush or flush. *Brit. sp.* **col'our** [<L] —**col'or·er** *n.*

col·or·a·ble (kul'ər·ə·bəl) *adj.* 1 Capable of being colored. 2 Seemingly valid or plausible but actually specious; deceptive. —**col'or·a·bil'i·ty, col'or·a·ble·ness** *n.* —**col'or·a·bly** *adv.*

col·or·a·tion (kul'ə·rā'shən) *n.* 1 The state of being colored. 2 The choice or use of colors. 3 Arrangement or depth of color, as in an animal or plant.

col·or·a·tu·ra (kul'ər·ə·t⁽ȳ⁾ŏŏr'ə) *n.* 1 Grace notes, runs, trills, or other florid decoration in vocal music. 2 A so-

prano who specializes in singing such music: also **coloratura soprano.** [<Ital., coloration]

col·or-blind (kul'ər·blīnd') *n.* Totally or partially unable to distinguish between certain colors. —**col'or-blind'ness** *n.* or **color blindness**

col·ored (kul'ərd) *adj.* 1 Having color. 2 Of a (specified) color. 3 Of a race other than the Caucasoid race, esp. Negro. 4 Exaggerated, prejudiced, or influenced in some way: views *colored* by years of poverty.

col·or·fast (kul'ər·fast', ·fäst') *adj.* Resistant to fading or running: *colorfast* fabrics.

col·or·ful (kul'ər·fəl) *adj.* 1 Full of colors, esp. contrasting colors. 2 Full of interest; picturesque: a *colorful* life. —**col'or·ful·ly** *adv.* —**col'or·ful·ness** *n.*

color guard The flagbearers and guards who conduct the colors in a ceremony.

col·or·ing (kul'ər·ing) *n.* 1 The imparting of color. 2 A source of color. 3 ˝.he natural color of something. 4 The effect produced by colors. 5 The tone, quality or style of something. 6 False or specious appearance.

col·or·ist (kul'ər·ist) *n.* 1 One who uses color. 2 An artist skilled in the use of color.

col·or·ize (kul'ər·īz) *v.t.* **·ized, ·iz·ing** To add color to movies that were originally black-and-white by means of computer-enhanced techniques. —**col'or·i·za'tion** *n.*

col·or·less (kul'ər·lis) *adj.* 1 Without color. 2 Dull; uninteresting. —**col'or·less·ly** *adv.* —**col'or·less·ness** *n.*

color line A social, political, or economic distinction drawn between the white and other races.

col·los·sal (kə·los'əl) *adj.* 1 Enormous; huge. 2 *Informal* Unbelievable; extraordinary: a *colossal* bore. —**co·los'sal·ly** *adv.*

Col·os·se·um (kol'ə·sē'əm) *n.* An amphitheater in Rome, built by Vespasian and Titus in A.D. 75–80.

Co·los·sian (kə·losh'ən) *n.* 1 A native or inhabitant of Colossae. 2 *pl.* Saint Paul's epistle to the Colossians, a book of the New Testament.

co·los·sus (kə·los'əs) *n. pl.* **co·los·si** (kə·los'ī) or **co·los·sus·es** 1 A gigantic statue. 2 Any strikingly huge or important person or object. [<Gk. *kolossos*]

colt (kōlt) *n.* 1 A young horse, ass, etc., esp. a young male horse. 2 A frisky person. 3 An inexperienced person. [<OE] —**colt'ish** *adj.*

col·ter (kōl'tər) *n.* A blade or disk on the beam of a plow, to cut the sod. [<L *culter* knife]

col·um·bar·i·um (kol'əm·bâr'ē·əm) *n. pl.* **·bar·i·a** (·bâr'ē·ə) 1 A vault with recesses for urns containing ashes of the dead. 2 Such a recess. 3 DOVECOTE. [<L *columba* dove]

Co·lum·bi·a (kə·lum'bē·ə) *n.* The personification of the U.S. as a woman. [<Christopher *Columbus*]

col·um·bine (kol'əm·bīn) *n.* A herbaceous plant with variously colored flowers of five petals; esp. the **Colorado columbine.** [<L *columba* dove]

Columbus Day The second Monday in October, a U.S. holiday marking the discovery of America by Christopher Columbus in 1492, formerly celebrated October 12.

col·umn (kol'əm) *n.* 1 A vertical shaft or pillar, usu. having a base and a capital, and used as a support or as ornamentation. 2 Any object or structure resembling a column: the spinal *column.* 3 A vertical, usu. narrow section of printed matter separated from similar sections by a rule or a blank space. 4 A unit of troops, vehicles, ships, etc., arranged in single file or several abreast. 5 An article by a special writer or on a specific subject that appears regularly in a newspaper or periodical. [<L *columna*] —**co·lum·nar** (kə·lum'nər), **col·umned** (kol'əmd) *adj.*

co·lum·ni·a·tion (kə·lum'nē·ā'shən) *n.* The use or the grouping of columns, as in a building.

col·um·nist (kol'əm·nist, ·əm·ist) *n.* A person who writes or conducts a special column for a newspaper or periodical.

Column

col·za (kol′zə) n. The summer rape whose seeds yield rape oil. [< Du. *kool* cabbage + *zaad* a seed]

com- prefix With; together: *combine, compare.* Also: *col-* before *l*, as in *collide; con-* before *c, d, f, g, j, n, q, s, t, v*, as in *concur, confluence, connect, conspire; cor-* before *r*, as in *correspond.* [< L *cum* with]

Com. commander; commission; commissioner; committee; commodore; Communist.

com. comedy; comma; commerce; commercial; common; commonly; communication.

co·ma¹ (kō′mə) n. pl. **co·mas** 1 A state of deep, prolonged unconsciousness caused by disease, injury, etc. 2 Stupor; lethargy. [< Gk. *kōma* deep sleep] —**co′ma·tose** (-tōs) adj. —**co′ma·tose′ly** adv. —**co′ma·tose′ness** n.

co·ma² (kō′mə) n. pl. **co·mae** (kō′mē) 1 Astron. The nebulous mass surrounding the nucleus and constituting the head of a comet. 2 Bot. A tuft, as of hairs, at the end of certain seeds, etc. [< Gk. *komē* hair]

Co·man·che (kō-man′chē) n. pl. **·ches** A member of a tribe of North American Indians, formerly roaming between Kansas and northern Mexico, now in Oklahoma.

comb (kōm) n. 1 A firm piece of hard rubber, plastic, etc., with teeth, for dressing or fastening the hair. 2 Something resembling a comb, as a currycomb or card for dressing wool. 3 The fleshy crest on the head of a fowl. 4 The crest of a hill or wave. 5 HONEYCOMB. —v.t. 1 To dress, disentangle, etc., with or as with a comb. 2 To search carefully and exhaustively. —v.i. 3 To crest and break: said of waves. [< OE *camb*]

comb. combination; combining.

com·bat (kom′bat, kum′-) n. A battle or fight; struggle. —v. (kəm-bat′) **·bat·ed** or **·bat·ted, ·bat·ing** or **·bat·ting** v.t. 1 To fight or contend with. 2 To resist. —v.i. 3 To do battle; struggle: with *with* or *against*. [< L *com-* with + *battuere* fight, beat] —**com·bat′a·ble** adj. —**com·bat′er** n.

com·bat·ant (kəm·bat′ənt, kom′bə·tənt) n. One engaged in or prepared for combat. —adj. 1 Fighting; battling. 2 Ready for combat.

combat fatigue Severe anxiety, depression, etc., that can occur after prolonged exposure to combat in war.

com·bat·ive (kəm·bat′iv, kom′bə·tiv) adj. Inclined or eager to fight; pugnacious. —**com·bat′ive·ly** adv. —**com·bat′· ive·ness** n. —Syn. warlike, bellicose, belligerent, hostile.

comb·er (kō′mər) n. 1 One who combs. 2 A long crested wave; a breaker.

com·bi·na·tion (kom′bə·nā′shən) n. 1 A combining or being combined. 2 That which is formed by combining. 3 A group of people, businesses, etc., allied for a common activity or purpose. 4 The series of numbers or letters used to open a combination lock. 5 pl. Underwear made in one piece. 6 Math. A set in which the order of elements is immaterial. [< LL *combinare* to combine]

combination lock A lock opened by turning a dial to a set sequence of letters or numbers.

com·bine (kəm·bīn′) v.t. & v.i. **·bined, ·bin·ing** 1 To bring or come into a close union; join; unite. 2 To unite chemically to form a compound. —n. (kom′bīn) 1 An association of persons united for political or business control, often by dishonest means. 2 A farm machine which combines the heading, threshing, and cleaning of grain while harvesting it. [< LL *com-* together + *bini* two by two] —**com·bin′· a·ble** adj. —**com·bin′er** n.

combining form A word element used in combination with words or other forms to create compounds, as *over-* in *overeat.*

com·bo (kom′bō) n. pl. **·bos** Informal 1 A small group of jazz musicians performing together. 2 A combination.

com·bus·ti·ble (kəm·bus′tə·bəl) adj. 1 That burns easily. 2 Excitable; fiery. —n. Any substance that burns easily. —**com·bus′ti·ble·ness, com·bus′ti·bil′i·ty** n.

com·bus·tion (kəm·bus′chən) n. 1 The action or operation of burning. 2 The rapid combination of a substance with oxygen, accompanied by heat and usu. light. 3 Slow oxidation, as of food in the body. 4 Disturbance; tumult. [< LL *comburere* burn up] —**com·bus′tive** adj.

come (kum) v. **came, come, com·ing** v.i. 1 To move or go to or toward a position, place, or person. 2 To exist or occur at a specific place or point: Youth *comes* before maturity. 3 To occur mentally: A solution *came* to him. 4 To arrive as the result of motion or progress: They *came* to land. 5 To attain to a specific result or end. 6 To arrive at some state or condition; develop. 7 To appear: The static *comes* and goes. 8 To occur in time: when Christmas *comes.* 9 To become: The chain *came* loose. 10 To proceed or emanate as from a source. 11 To exist as an effect or result: This *comes* of trifling. 12 To happen or befall: *Come* what may, I'll do it. 13 To prove to be; become: The sign *came* true. 14 To reach or extend: with *to.* 15 To be offered, obtainable, or produced: The car *comes* in many colors. 16 To be descended. 17 To have lived or been born in: to *come* from Greece. 18 To amount: with *to:* This *comes* to two dollars. —**come about** To take place; happen. —**come across** To find or meet accidentally. —**come around** (or **round**) 1 To recover or revive. 2 To acquiesce or accede. —**come down** 1 To oppose or criticize: with *on* or *upon.* 2 To become ill: with *with.* —**come into** To inherit. —**come off** Informal 1 To occur; happen. 2 To be effective or successful. —**come out** 1 To become evident; transpire. 2 To make a debut in society. 3 To prove to be; turn out. 4 To declare oneself, esp. publicly: often with *for.* —**come through** To do what is wanted or needed. —**come to** To recover consciousness. —**come up** 1 To be mentioned or considered, as in discussion. 2 To occur. —**come up with** To suggest, propose, or produce: They had better *come up with* a new plan soon. [< OE *cuman*]

come·back (kum′bak′) n. 1 Informal A return to a former state or position. 2 Slang A smart retort.

co·me·di·an (kə·mē′dē·ən) n. 1 A comic actor or entertainer. 2 One who writes comedies. 3 One who is or tries to be amusing. —**co·me·di·enne** (kə·mē′dē·en′) n. Fem.

come·down (kum′doun′) n. A descent to a lower condition or position; downfall.

com·e·dy (kom′ə·dē) n. pl. **·dies** 1 Originally, a literary work with a nontragic view of life and a happy ending. 2 A play, motion picture, etc., characterized by a humorous treatment of characters, situation, etc., and having a happy ending. 3 Comedies collectively, esp. as a branch of the drama. 4 Any comic or ludicrous incident or series of incidents. [< Gk. *kōmos* revel + *aeidein* sing]

come·hith·er (kum′hith′ər) adj. Slang Alluring; inviting; able to attract: a *come-hither* look.

come·ly (kum′lē, kōm′lē) adj. **·li·er, ·li·est** Pleasing in appearance; attractive. [< OE *cymlic*] —**come′li·ness** n.

come·on (kum′on′) n. Slang Someone or something that attracts, interests, etc.

com·er (kum′ər) n. 1 One who comes or arrives. 2 Informal One showing great promise.

co·mes·ti·ble (kə·mes′tə·bəl) adj. Edible. —n. Usu. pl. Something that is eatable. [< L *comedere* to eat up]

com·et (kom′it) n. Astron. A celestial body consisting of a nucleus of condensed material surrounded by a luminous coma and accompanied by an elongated, luminous tail that always points away from the sun. [< Gk. *kometēs* long-haired] —**com·et·ar·y** (kom′ə·ter′ē), **co·met·ic** (kə·met′· ik) adj.

come·up·pance (kum′up′əns) n. Informal Deserved punishment; deserts: to get one's *comeuppance.*

com·fit (kum′fit, kom′-) n. A sweetmeat; confection. [< L *confectus.* See CONFECTION]

com·fort (kum′fərt) n. 1 Freedom from pain, annoyance, want, etc. 2 Anything that contributes to such relief. 3 Relief from sorrow or distress. 4 One who or that which helps relieve sorrow or distress. 5 A bed comforter. —v.t. To give cheer or ease to; console; solace. [< LL *confortare* strengthen] —**com′fort·ing** adj. —**com′fort·ing·ly** adv.

com·fort·a·ble (kum′fər·tə·bəl, kumf′tə·bəl) adj. 1 Marked by or providing ease and comfort. 2 Informal Providing or enjoying security, well-being, etc.: a *comfortable* income. —**com′fort· a·ble·ness** n. —**com′fort·a·bly** adv.

com·fort·er (kum′fər·tər) n. 1 One who or that which comforts. 2 A thick, quilted bedcover.

comfort station A public restroom.

com·ic (kom′ik) adj. 1 Of, like, or connected with comedy. 2 Amusing, funny, ludicrous, etc. 3 Acting in or composing comedy. —n. 1 A comedian. 2 A comic book or comic strip. 3 The humorous side of art, life, etc. 4 pl. A newspaper section devoted to comic strips. [< Gk. *kōmos* revelry]

com·i·cal (kom′i·kəl) *adj.* Causing amusement, laughter, etc. —**com′i·cal·ly** *adv.* —**com′i·cal·ness** *n.*

comic book A magazine of comic strips.

comic strip A series of cartoons printed in a strip in newspapers, magazines, etc., and picturing a sequence of comic or adventurous incidents.

com·ing (kum′ing) *adj.* 1 Approaching; next: the *coming* year. 2 On the way to fame or note. —*n.* Arrival; advent.

com·i·ty (kom′ə·tē) *n.* Friendliness; good will; courtesy. [< L *comitas* courtesy]

com·ma (kom′ə) *n.* 1 A punctuation mark (,) indicating a slight separation in ideas or construction within a sentence. 2 Any pause or separation. [< Gk. *komma* short phrase < *koptein* cut]

comma bacillus The comma-shaped causative agent of Asiatic cholera.

com·mand (kə·mand′, -mänd′) *v.t.* 1 To order, require or enjoin with authority. 2 To control or direct; rule. 3 To have at one's disposal or use. 4 To overlook, as from a height. 5 To exact as being due or proper. —*v.i.* 6 To be in authority; rule. 7 To overlook, as from a height. —*n.* 1 The right to command; authority. 2 An order. 3 The troops or district under the command of one person. 4 Dominating power; control. 5 Mastery. 6 Range of view. [< L *com-* thoroughly + *mandare* order, charge]

com·man·dant (kom′ən·dant′, -dänt′) *n.* COMMANDING OFFICER.

com·man·deer (kom′ən·dir′) *v.t.* 1 To force into military service. 2 To take possession of for public use, esp. under military necessity. 3 To take over by force or by threat of force. [< Afrikaans *kommandeeren* command]

com·mand·er (kə·man′dər, -män′-) *n.* 1 One in command; a leader. 2 In the U.S. Army, the commanding officer of a post or unit. 3 See GRADE.

commander in chief *pl.* **commanders in chief** 1 Often *cap.* The officer commanding all the armed forces of a nation; in the U.S., the President. 2 The officer commanding all the armed forces in a certain area of war.

com·mand·ing (kə·man′ding, -män′-) *adj.* 1 Having power; in command. 2 Authoritative; impressive; dignified. 3 Having a wide, overlooking view or position. —**com·mand′ing·ly** *adv.*

commanding officer An officer in command, as of an army installation.

com·mand·ment (kə·mand′mənt, -mänd′-), *n.* An authoritative mandate, order, or law, esp. one of the Ten Commandments.

command module *Aerospace* A part of a space vehicle that houses the crew and navigational systems and is equipped for reentry.

com·man·do (kə·man′dō, -män′-) *n. pl.* **·dos** or **·does** 1 A special fighting force trained for quick raids into enemy territory. 2 A member of such a unit.

com·mem·o·rate (kə·mem′ə·rāt) *v.t.* **·rat·ed**, **·rat·ing** To celebrate the memory of, as with a ceremony. [< L *com-* together + *memorare* remember] —**com·mem·o·ra·ble** (kə·mem′ə·rə·bəl), **com·mem′o·ra′tive**, **com·mem′o·ra·to·ry** (kə·mem′ə·rə·tôr′ē, -tō′rē) *adj.* —**com·mem′o·ra′tion** *n.*

com·mence (kə·mens′) *v.t. & v.i.* **·menced**, **·menc·ing** To begin; initiate; start. [< L *com-* together + *initiare* begin]

com·mence·ment (kə·mens′mənt) *n.* 1 A beginning; origin. 2 A ceremony held at the completion of a school or college course, when degrees are conferred. 3 The day of such a ceremony.

com·mend (kə·mend′) *v.t.* 1 To express a favorable opinion of; praise. 2 To recommend. 3 To present the regards of. 4 To entrust. [< L *com-* thoroughly + *mandare* order, charge] —**com·mend′a·ble** *adj.* —**com·mend′a·bly** *adv.*

com·men·da·tion (kom′ən·dā′shən) *n.* 1 The act of commending; approbation. 2 Something that commends.

com·mend·a·to·ry (kə·men′də·tôr′ē, -tō′rē) *adj.* Expressing approval.

com·men·su·ra·ble (kə·men′shər·ə·bəl, -sər·ə-) *adj.* 1 Measurable by a common unit. 2 In proper proportion; proportionate. [< LL *com-* together + *mensurabilis* measurable] —**com·men′su·ra·bil′i·ty** *n.* —**com·men′su·ra·bly** *adv.*

com·men·su·rate (kə·men′shə·rit, -sə·rit) *adj.* 1 In proper proportion; proportionate. 2 COMMENSURABLE. 3 Equal in size or extent. [< LL *com-* together + *mensurare* measure] —**com·men′su·rate·ly** *adv.* —**com·men′su·rate·ness, com·men′su·ra′tion** *n.*

com·ment (kom′ent) *n.* 1 A note in explanation or criticism. 2 A remark made in observation or criticism. 3 Talk; conversation; gossip. —*v.i.* To make a comment or comments: with *on* or *upon*. [< L *comminisci* contrive]

com·men·tar·y (kom′ən·ter′ē) *n. pl.* **·tar·ies** 1 A series or body of comments; exposition. 2 Anything explanatory or illustrative.

com·men·ta·tor (kom′ən·tā′tər) *n.* 1 A writer of commentaries; an expounder. 2 One who discusses or analyzes news, politics, etc., as on television or radio.

com·merce (kom′ərs) *n.* 1 Exchange of goods, products, or property, as between states or nations. 2 Social intercourse. 3 SEXUAL INTERCOURSE. [< L *com-* together + *merx, mercis* wares]

com·mer·cial (kə·mûr′shəl) *adj.* 1 Of or belonging to trade or commerce; mercantile. 2 Made in large quantities for the market. 3 Having financial gain or popular appeal as an object: a *commercial* novel. —*n.* In radio and television, a paid advertisement. —**com·mer′cial·ly** *adv.*

com·mer·cial·ism (kə·mûr′shəl·iz′əm) *n.* The spirit, methods, or principles of commerce, esp. an excessive interest in profits.

com·mer·cial·ize (kə·mûr′shəl·īz) *v.t.* **·ized**, **·iz·ing** 1 To put on a commercial basis. 2 To make or do mainly for profit. —**com·mer′cial·i·za′tion** *n.*

com·min·gle (kə·ming′gəl) *v.t. & v.i.* **·gled**, **·gling** To mix together; mingle.

com·mi·nute (kom′ə·nyo̅o̅t) *v.t.* **·nut·ed**, **·nut·ing** To reduce to minute particles; pulverize. [< L *com-* thoroughly + *minuere* lessen] —**com′mi·nu′tion** *n.*

com·mis·er·ate (kə·miz′ə·rāt) *v.* **·at·ed**, **·at·ing** *v.t.* 1 To feel or manifest pity for; sympathize. —*v.i.* 2 To condole: with *with.* [< L *com-* with + *miserari* feel pity] —**com·mis′er·a·tive** *adj.* —**com·mis′er·a′tive·ly** *adv.* —**com·mis′er·a′tion, com·mis′er·a′tor** *n.*

com·mis·sar (kom′ə·sär, kom′ə·sär′) *n.* Formerly, an official in charge of a commissariat of the Soviet government. [< L *committere*. See COMMIT.]

com·mis·sar·i·at (kom′ə·sâr′ē·ət) *n.* 1 An army department supplying food and other necessaries. 2 Formerly, a major department of the government of the U.S.S.R.

com·mis·sar·y (kom′ə·ser′ē) *n. pl.* **·sar·ies** 1 A store selling food, supplies, etc., as at an army or lumber camp. 2 A restaurant for the employees of a movie studio, etc.

com·mis·sion (kə·mish′ən) *n.* 1 The act of entrusting or giving authority to perform certain acts or duties. 2 The acts or duties so entrusted. 3 An authorization or order to do something; also, a document conferring this. 4 *Mil.* a A document conferring rank and authority. b The rank or authority so conferred. 5 A body of persons authorized to perform certain duties. 6 The fee given an agent or salesperson for his or her services. 7 The act of committing or perpetrating, as a crime. —*v.t.* 1 To give rank or authority to, as an officer. 2 To put into active service, as a ship of war. 3 To give a commission to. 4 To appoint; delegate. 5 To order to be done: to *commission* a painting. [< L *committere*. See COMMIT.]

com·mis·sion·er (kə·mish′ən·ər) *n.* 1 A person commissioned to have certain powers or to perform certain acts. 2 A member of a commission. 3 A public official appointed as head of a state or municipal department. —**com·mis′sion·er·ship′** *n.*

com·mit (kə·mit′) *v.t.* **·mit·ted**, **·mit·ting** 1 To do; perpetrate. 2 To place in an institution or prison. 3 To entrust or consign to any person, place, or use. 4 To devote or pledge (oneself) to the doing of something. 5 To consign for future reference, preservation, etc.: to *commit* a speech to memory. 6 To refer, as to a committee, for consideration or report. [< L *com-* together + *mittere* send]

com·mit·ment (kə·mit′mənt) *n.* 1 The act of committing, or the state of being committed. 2 An official order committing someone to a prison or asylum. **3** A pledge; promise. Also **com·mit'tal** (kə·mit'l). —**Syn. 3** guarantee, word, obligation, compact, warrant.

com·mit·tee (kə·mit'ē) *n.* A group of persons organized or appointed to act upon some matter. [< COMMIT]

com·mit·tee·man (kə·mit'ē·mən) *n. pl.* **·men** (-mən) A member of a committee. —**com·mit'tee·wom'an** *n. Fem.*

com·mode (kə·mōd')
n. **1** A low chest of drawers. **2** A covered washstand. **3** A low chair or cabinet enclosing a chamber pot. **4** A toilet. [< L *commodus* convenient]

Commode
def. 1

com·mo·di·ous (kə·mō'dē·əs) *adj.* Spacious; roomy. [< L *commodus* convenient] —**com·mo'di·ous·ly** *adv.* —**com·mo'di·ous·ness** *n.*

com·mod·i·ty (kə·mod'ə·tē) *n. pl.* **·ties 1** Something bought and sold. **2** Something useful. [< L *commoditas* convenience]

com·mo·dore (kom'ə·dôr, -dōr) *n.* **1** In the U.S. Navy, an officer next below a rear admiral, a rank no longer in use since World War II. **2** In the British Navy, the commander of a squadron or division of a fleet. **3** A title given to the presiding officer of a yacht club. [< Du. *kommandeur* commander]

com·mon (kom'ən) *adj.* **1** Not unusual; ordinary; regular. **2** Of, pertaining to, or participated in by all or by others. **3** Belonging to the public: *common* facilities. **4** Widespread; general: *common* knowledge. **5** Coarse; vulgar; low. **6** Notorious: a *common* thief. **7** Having no special rank or privilege; not of the upper classes: the *common* people. **8** Having no rank: a *common* soldier. **9** *Gram.* **a** Of either gender. **b** Applicable to any individual of a class. **10** *Math.* Referring to a number or element related in a particular way to two or more other numbers or elements: a *common* denominator. —*n. Often pl.* Land owned by a town and open to the use of all. —**in common** Equally; jointly. [< L *communis* common] —**com'mon·ly** *adv.* —**com'mon·ness** *n.*

com·mon·al·ty (kom'ən·əl·tē) *n. pl.* **·ties 1** The common people, as opposed to persons of title or rank. **2** The possession of qualities, characteristics, etc., in common.

common carrier An individual or company which, for a fee, provides public transportation.

com·mon·er (kom'ən·ər) *n.* One of the common people.

common fraction A fraction whose numerator and denominator are integers.

common law Law based on custom, usage, and legal precedent.

com·mon-law marriage (kom'ən·lô') A marriage in which both parties agree to live as man and wife but without a church or civil ceremony.

Common Market EUROPEAN ECONOMIC COMMUNITY.

common noun A noun that represents any or all members of its class, as *plant, dog.*

com·mon·place (kom'ən·plās') *adj.* Not remarkable or interesting; ordinary. —*n.* **1** A trite remark; platitude; truism. **2** Anything ordinary or common.

com·mons (kom'ənz) *n. pl.* **1** The common people; commonalty. **2** *(Often construed as sing.)* **a** Food served for many people. **b** The dining facilities for such food, as at a college.

Com·mons (kom'ənz) *n. pl.* HOUSE OF COMMONS.

common sense Practical understanding; sound judgment. —**com'mon-sense'** *adj.*

common stock Stock which entitles the owner to dividends only after all other obligations have been met and dividends paid to owners of preferred stock.

com·mon·weal (kom'ən·wēl') *n.* The general welfare.

com·mon·wealth (kom'ən·welth') *n.* **1** The people of a state or nation. **2** A state or nation in which the people rule; a republic. **3** Loosely, any State of the U.S. **4** A body of persons united by some common interest.

Commonwealth of Nations A political association comprising the United Kingdom, its dependencies, and

certain of its former colonies that are now sovereign states.

com·mo·tion (kə·mō'shən) *n.* **1** A disturbance; fuss. **2** Violent agitation; tumult. [< L *com-* thoroughly + *movere* move]

com·mu·nal (kom'yə·nəl, kə·myōō'nəl) *adj.* **1** Of or pertaining to a commune. **2** Common; public. **3** Belonging to a community. —**com·mu'nal·ly** *adv.*

com·mune[1] (kə·myōōn') *v.i.* **·muned, ·mun·ing 1** To converse or confer intimately. **2** To partake of the Eucharist. —*n.* (kom'yōōn) Intimate conversation. [< OF *comun* common]

com·mune[2] (kom'yōōn) *n.* **1** A small political division, as in France, Italy, and Spain. **2** A self-governing community. [< L *communis* common]

com·mu·ni·ca·ble (kə·myōō'nə·kə·bəl) *adj.* Capable of being communicated or transmitted. —**com·mu'ni·ca·bil'i·ty** *n.* —**com·mu'ni·ca·ble·ness** *n.* —**com·mu'ni·ca·bly** *adv.*

com·mu·ni·cant (kə·myōō'nə·kənt) *n.* **1** One who communicates or imparts, as information. **2** One who partakes of the Eucharist. —*adj.* Communicating.

com·mu·ni·cate (kə·myōō'nə·kāt) *v.* **·cat·ed, ·cat·ing** *v.t.* **1** To impart; transmit, as news, a disease, or an idea. —*v.i.* **2** To make or hold communication. **3** To be connected, as rooms. **4** To partake of the Eucharist. [< L *communicare* share < *communis* common] —**com·mu'ni·ca'tor** *n.*

com·mu·ni·ca·tion (kə·myōō'nə·kā'shən) *n.* **1** The act of communicating; exchange of ideas, conveyance of information, etc. **2** That which is communicated, as a letter or message. **3** *pl.* Means of communicating, as a highway, telephone, radio, television, etc.

com·mu·ni·ca·tive (kə·myōō'nə·kā'tiv, -kə·tiv) *adj.* **1** Ready to communicate; frank; talkative. **2** Of communication. —**com·mu'ni·ca'tive·ly** *adv.* —**com·mu'ni·ca'tive·ness** *n.*

com·mun·ion (kə·myōōn'yən) *n.* **1** The act of communing or sharing. **2** A sympathetic, intimate relationship or conversation. **3** A body of Christians having a common faith and discipline. **4** *Usu. cap.* The Eucharist, or the act of celebrating or partaking of it.

com·mu·ni·qué (kə·myōō'nə·kā) *n.* An official message, announcement, etc. [F]

com·mu·nism (kom'yə·niz'əm) *n.* **1** A social system in which there are no classes and no private ownership of the means of production. **2** The theory of social change on which such a system is based. **3** *Often cap.* The system based on this theory in force in any state.

Com·mu·nist (kom'yə·nist) *n.* **1** A member of the Communist party. **2** Any person who endorses, supports, or advocates communism: also **communist.** —**com'mu·nis'tic** *adj.*

Communist party Any political party advocating communism.

com·mu·ni·ty (kə·myōō'nə·tē) *n. pl.* **·ties 1** The people who reside in one locality and are subject to the same laws, have the same interests, etc. **2** The locality of such a group. **3** The public; society at large. **4** A group of plants and animals mutually reacting to create common habitat. **5** Common sharing, participation, or ownership. **6** Similarity or likeness: *community* of interest. [< L *communis* common]

community antenna television A television reception service in which a signal received at a master antenna is distributed to subscribers by cable.

com·mu·tate (kom'yə·tāt) *v.t.* **·tat·ed, ·tat·ing** *Electr.* To alter or reverse the direction of (a current). —**com'mu·ta'tor** *n.*

com·mu·ta·tion (kom'yə·tā'shən) *n.* **1** A substitution, as of one kind of payment or service for another. **2** The payment or service substituted. **3** A reduction or change of a penalty. **4** *Electr.* The reversal of the direction of a current. **5** Daily or periodic travel on a commutation ticket. [< L *com-* thoroughly + *mutare* change]

commutation ticket A ticket issued at a reduced rate for a specified number of trips within a certain period of time.

com·mute (kə·myōōt') *v.* **·mut·ed, ·mut·ing** *v.t.* **1** To exchange reciprocally for something else. **2** To change to something less severe: to *commute* a sentence. —*v.i.* **3** To serve as or be a substitute. **4** To travel as a commuter. —

n. Informal A commuter's trip, or its duration or distance: a two-hour *commute*. [<L *commutare*. See COMMUTATION] —**com·mut′a·ble** *adj.* —**com·mut′a·ble·ness, com·mut′a·bil′i·ty** *n.*

com·mut·er (kə·myōō′tər) *n.* One who daily or regularly travels for some distance between his or her home and place of work, school, etc.

comp. companion; comparative; compare; comparison; compiled; complete; composer; composition; compositor; compound; comprising.

com·pact[1] (kəm·pakt′, kom′pakt) *adj.* **1** Closely and firmly united, pressed together; solid; dense. **2** Condensed; brief; terse. **3** Composed; made up: with *of.* **4** Relatively small: a *compact* car. —*v.t.* (kəm·pakt′) To pack or press closely; condense. —*n.* (kom′pakt) **1** A small, hinged box for face powder and sometimes rouge. **2** A compact car. [<L *compactus*, pp. of *compangere* fasten together] —**com·pact′ly** *adv.* —**com·pact′ness** *n.*

com·pact[2] (kom′pakt) *n.* A covenant, agreement, or contract. [<L *compactus*, pp. of *compacisci* agree together]

compact disc A small digital disc on which recorded sound has been encoded so as to be replayed on an electronic device that utilizes a laser beam to reproduce the original sound with a very high level of fidelity.

com·pan·ion (kəm·pan′yən) *n.* **1** One who or that which accompanies; a comrade; associate. **2** One hired to live or travel with another. **3** A mate; one of a pair. —*v.t.* To be a companion to; accompany. [<LL *companio* <L *com-* together + *panis* bread] —**com·pan′ion·ship** *n.*

com·pan·ion·a·ble (kəm·pan′yən·ə·bəl) *adj.* Fitted for companionship; friendly. —**com·pan′ion·a·bil′i·ty** *n.* —**com·pan′ion·a·bly** *adv.*

com·pan·ion·ate (kəm·pan′yən·it) *adj.* Of companionship or association.

com·pan·ion·way (kəm·pan′yən·wā′) *n.* A staircase from the deck of a ship to its cabins.

com·pa·ny (kum′pə·nē) *n. pl.* **·nies 1** The society or presence of another or others. **2** One or more guests or visitors. **3** A business firm or corporation. **4** A number of persons associated for some common purpose. **5** The person or persons with whom one often associates: keeping bad *company.* **6** A body of soldiers, usu. a unit made up of two or more platoons and a headquarters. **7** A ship's crew, including officers. **8** A group of performers who work together: a ballet *company.* [<OF *compagnon* companion] —**Syn.** *n.* **1** companionship, fellowship. **4** assembly, group. **8** troupe.

compar. comparative; comparison.

com·pa·ra·ble (kom′pər·ə·bəl, kəm·par′-) *adj.* **1** Capable of being compared. **2** Worthy of comparison —**com′pa·ra·ble·ness, com′pa·ra·bil′i·ty** *n.* —**com′pa·ra·bly** *adv.*

com·par·a·tive (kəm·par′ə·tiv) *adj.* **1** Of, using, or resulting from comparison. **2** Not total or absolute; relative. **3** *Gram.* Expressing a degree of an adjective or adverb higher than the positive and lower than the superlative: "Better" is the *comparative* of "good." —*n. Gram.* The comparative degree. —**com·par′a·tive·ly** *adv.*

com·pare (kəm·pâr′) *v.* **·pared, ·par·ing** *v.t.* **1** To represent or speak of as similar, analogous, or equal: with *to.* **2** To examine so as to perceive and note similarity or dissimilarity: with *with.* **3** *Gram.* To form the degrees of comparison of (an adjective or adverb). —*v.i.* **4** To be worthy of comparison: with *with.* —*n.* Comparison: usu. in the phrase *beyond compare.* [<L *comparare* <*com-* together + *par* equal] • **compare to; compare with** Formal usage requires that one use *compare to* when noting a striking similarity between two things: The industrial potential of Japan *compares to* that of many larger nations. If the things being compared are similar in some aspects but dissimilar in others, *compare with* is preferred: to *compare* the physical discipline demanded of a classical ballet dancer *with* that required of a gymnast.

com·par·i·son (kəm·par′ə·sən) *n.* **1** An estimate or statement of relative likeness or unlikeness. **2** Similarity. **3** *Gram.* That inflection of adjectives or adverbs which indicates the positive, comparative, and superlative degrees.

com·part·ment (kəm·pärt′mənt) *n.* **1** One of the divi-

sions or sections into which an enclosed space is subdivided. **2** Any separate section, category, division, etc. [<L *com-* together + *pars* a part]

com·pass (kum′pəs) *n.* **1** An instrument for determining direction, as from the earth's magnetic field. **2** *Often pl.* Any of various instruments having two legs hinged at the top, used for drawing circles, taking measurements, etc. **3** An enclosed area. **4** A boundary or circumference. **5** A range or scope, esp. the range of a voice or instrument. —*v.t.* **1** To go around; make a circuit of. **2** To surround; encompass. **3** To grasp mentally; comprehend. **4** To plot or scheme. **5** To attain or accomplish. [<L *com-* together + *passus* step] —**com′pass·a·ble** *adj.*

Compass
def. 2

compass card The circular card or dial resting on the pivot of a mariner's compass, on which the 32 points of the compass and 360 degrees of the circle are marked. Also **compass dial.**

com·pas·sion (kəm·pash′ən) *n.* Pity for suffering, with desire to help; sympathy. [<L *com-* together + *pati* feel, suffer] —**Syn.** mercy, commiseration, empathy, clemency, charity.

com·pas·sion·ate (kəm·pash′ən·it) *adj.* Feeling compassion or pity; sympathetic. —*v.t.* (kəm·pash′ən·āt) **·at·ed, ·at·ing** To have compassion for; to pity. —**com·pas′sion·ate·ly** *adv.* —**com·pas′sion·ate·ness** *n.*

com·pat·i·ble (kəm·pat′ə·bəl) *adj.* **1** Capable of existing or living together; congruous; congenial. **2** Describing a television system in which broadcasts in color may be received in black and white on sets not adapted for color reception. [<L *com-* together + *pati* suffer] —**com·pat′i·bil′i·ty, com·pat′i·ble·ness** *n.* —**com·pat′i·bly** *adv.*

com·pa·tri·ot (kəm·pā′trē·ət, -pat′rē·ət) *n.* **1** A fellow countryman. **2** *Informal* A colleague.

com·pel (kəm·pel′) *v.t.* **·pelled, ·pel·ling 1** To drive or urge irresistibly; constrain. **2** To get or obtain by force. [<L *com-* together + *pellere* drive] —**com·pel′la·ble** *adj.* —**com·pel′la·bly** *adv.* —**com·pel′ler** *n.*

com·pel·ling (kəm·pel′ing) *adj.* Convincing; cogent: *compelling* evidence. —**com·pel′ling·ly** *adv.*

com·pen·di·ous (kəm·pen′dē·əs) *adj.* Briefly stated; succinct. [<L *compendiosus* brief] —**com·pen′di·ous·ly** *adv.* —**com·pen′di·ous·ness** *n.*

com·pen·di·um (kəm·pen′dē·əm) *n. pl.* **·di·ums** or **·di·a** (-dē·ə) A brief, comprehensive summary; abridgment. [<L *com-* together + *pendere* weigh]

com·pen·sa·ble (kəm·pen′sə·bəl) *adj.* Entitled to be or capable of being compensated.

com·pen·sate (kom′pən·sāt) *v.* **·sat·ed, ·sat·ing** *v.t.* **1** To make suitable amends to or for; remunerate. **2** To counterbalance or make up for; offset. —*v.i.* **3** To make compensation or amends: often with *for.* [<L *com-* together + *pensare*, freq. of *pendere* weigh] —**com·pen′sa·tive** (kəm·pen′sə·tiv), **com·pen·sa·to·ry** (kəm·pen′sə·tôr′ē, -tō′rē) *adj.* —**com′pen·sa′tor** *n.*

com·pen·sa·tion (kom′pən·sā′shən) *n.* **1** The act of compensating. **2** That which compensates or makes amends, as wages, unemployment benefits, etc. **3** *Biol.* The correction or counterbalancing of some organic defect or malfunction by a new or heightened activity in a different organ or an unimpaired part of the same organ. **4** *Psychol.* A mechanism by which a person attempts to compensate for feelings of inferiority or frustration in one area by achievement in another. —**com′pen·sa′tion·al** *adj.*

com·pete (kəm·pēt′) *v.i.* **·pet·ed, ·pet·ing** To contend with another or others for a prize, superiority, etc.; vie. [<L *com-* together + *petere* seek]

com·pe·tence (kom′pə·təns) *n.* **1** The state of being competent. **2** Sufficient means for comfortable living. Also **com′pe·ten·cy.**

com·pe·tent (kom′pə·tənt) *adj.* **1** Sufficiently able or qualified; fit: a *competent* physician. **2** Sufficient; adequate. **3** Legally capable or qualified: *competent* to stand

---

add, āce, câre, pälm; end, ēven; it, īce; odd, ōpen, ôrder; tōōk, pōōl; up, bûrn; ə = *a* in ˈabove, *u* in *focus*; yōō = *u* in *fuse*; oil; pout; check; go; ring; thin; this; zh, vision. < derived from; ? origin uncertain or unknown.

trial. [<L *com-* together + *petere* go, seek] —**com′pe·tent·ly** *adv.* —**com′pe·tent·ness** *n.*

com·pe·ti·tion (kom′pə·tish′ən) *n.* **1** The act of competing; rivalry, as in business, athletics, etc. **2** The quality or degree of competitiveness or opposition. **3** Those persons against whom one competes. **4** A specific contest.

com·pet·i·tive (kəm·pet′ə·tiv) *adj.* Of or marked by competition. —**com·pet′i·tive·ly** *adj.* —**com·pet′i·tive·ness** *n.*

com·pet·i·tor (kəm·pet′ə·tər) *n.* One who competes; a rival: a business *competitor.*

com·pile (kəm·pīl′) *v.t.* **·piled, ·pil·ing 1** To compose (a literary work, etc.) from other works or sources. **2** To gather (facts, data, etc.) into a volume or into orderly form. [<L *com-* thoroughly + *pilare* strip, plunder] —**com·pi·la·tion** (kom′pə·lā′shən) *n.*

com·pil·er (kəm·pī′lər) *n.* A computer program that translates instruction programs into machine language.

com·pla·cen·cy (kəm·plā′sən·sē) *n. pl.* **·cies 1** Satisfaction, esp. with oneself. **2** EQUANIMITY. Also **com·pla′cence.**

com·pla·cent (kəm·plā′sənt) *adj.* Feeling or showing complacency, esp. smugly self-satisfied. [<L *com-* thoroughly + *placere* to please] —**com·pla′cent·ly** *adv.*

com·plain (kəm·plān′) *v.i.* **1** To express a sense of ill-treatment or of pain, grief, etc. **2** To find fault. **3** To make a formal accusation. [<L *com-* thoroughly + *plangere* beat (the breast in grief)] —**com·plain′er** *n.* —**com·plain′ing·ly** *adv.* —**Syn. 1** murmur, whine, lament. **2** grumble, deplore, gripe.

com·plain·ant (kəm·plā′nənt) *n.* One who complains, esp. before a magistrate or other authority.

com·plaint (kəm·plānt′) *n.* **1** A statement of wrong, grievance, or injury. **2** The paper setting forth the plaintiff's cause of action. **3** A grievance. **4** A physical ailment; disease.

com·plai·sant (kəm·plā′sənt, -zənt) *adj.* Showing a desire to please; obliging. [<L *complacere* to please thoroughly] —**com·plai′sance** *n.* —**com·plai′sant·ly** *adv.*

com·plect·ed (kəm·plek′tid) *adj. Informal or Regional* COMPLEXIONED.

com·ple·ment (kom′plə·mənt) *n.* **1** That which fills up, completes, or makes perfect. **2** The number needed to fill or make complete. **3** Either of two parts that together form a whole; a counterpart. **4** Full number: the vessel has her *complement* of men. **5** *Geom.* The amount by which an angle or arc falls short of 90 degrees. **6** *Gram.* A word or phrase used after a verb to complete the meaning of the predicate, as *happy* in *She is happy.* —*v.t.* To supply a lack in; make complete; supplement. [<L *complere* complete] —**com·ple·men·tal** (kom′plə·men′təl) *adj.* ● See SUPPLEMENT.

com·ple·men·ta·ry (kom′plə·men′tər·ē, -trē) *adj.* **1** Serving as a complement; completing. **2** Mutually providing each other's needs.

com·plete (kəm·plēt′) *adj.* **·plet·er, ·plet·est 1** Having all needed or normal parts, elements, or details; lacking nothing; entire. **2** Thoroughly wrought; finished. **3** Perfect. —*v.t.* **·plet·ed, ·plet·ing 1** To make entire or whole. **2** To make perfect. **3** To finish; fulfill; end. [<L *com-* thoroughly + *plere* fill] —**com·plete′ly** *adv.* —**com·plete′ness** *n.* —**com·ple′tive** *adj.*

com·ple·tion (kəm·plē′shən) *n.* **1** The act of completing or the state of being completed. **2** Accomplishment; fulfillment.

com·plex (kəm·pleks′, kom′pleks) *adj.* **1** Consisting of various parts or elements; composite. **2** Complicated; involved; intricate. —*n.* (kom′pleks) **1** A whole made up of interrelated parts or units. **2** *Psychoanal.* A group of interrelated and usu. repressed ideas with strong emotional content which distorts patterns of thought and behavior. **3** Loosely, an extreme or exaggerated fear or dislike. [<L *complexus,* pp. of *complectere* twist together] —**com·plex′ly** *adv.* —**com·plex′ness** *n.*

complex fraction A fraction having a fraction in its numerator or denominator, or in each.

com·plex·ion (kəm·plek′shən) *n.* **1** The color and appearance of the skin, esp. of the face. **2** General aspect; character; quality. [<L *complexio* the constitution of a body, a combination < *complectere* twist together] —**com·plex′ion·al** *adj.*

com·plex·ioned (kəm·plek′shənd) *adj.* Having a (specified) facial complexion.

com·plex·i·ty (kəm·plek′sə·tē) *n. pl.* **·ties 1** The state of being complex. **2** Something complex.

complex number A number of the form $a + bi$ in which a and b are real numbers and i is the square root of -1.

complex sentence A sentence having one main clause and one or more subordinate clauses.

com·pli·ance (kəm·plī′əns) *n.* **1** The act of complying, yielding, or acting in accord. **2** The disposition or willingness to please. Also **com·pli′an·cy.**

com·pli·ant (kəm·plī′ənt) *adj.* Disposed or willing to comply. —**com·pli′ant·ly** *adv.*

com·pli·cate (kom′plə·kāt) *v.t.* & *v.i.* **·cat·ed, ·cat·ing** *v.t.* To make or become complex, difficult, or perplexing. —*adj.* (kom′plə·kit) Complicated; complex. [<L *com-* together + *plicare* to fold] —**com·pli·ca′tive** *adj.*

com·pli·cat·ed (kom′plə·kā′tid) *adj.* **1** Containing many parts or elements; intricate. **2** Difficult to analyze, understand, solve, etc. —**com·pli·cat′ed·ly** *adv.* —**com·pli·cat′ed·ness** *n.*

com·pli·ca·tion (kom′plə·kā′shən) *n.* **1** The act of complicating or the state of being complicated. **2** Anything that complicates, as an abnormal condition that aggravates a preexisting but unrelated disease.

com·plic·i·ty (kəm·plis′ə·tē) *n. pl.* **·ties** The act or state of being an accomplice, as in a crime.

com·pli·ment (kom′plə·mənt) *n.* **1** An expression of admiration, praise, congratulation, etc. **2** *pl.* A formal greeting or remembrance. —*v.t.* (kom′plə·ment) **1** To pay a compliment to. **2** To show regard for, as by a gift or other favor. [<Sp. *cumplimiento,* lit., completion of courtesy <L *complementum* completion]

com·pli·men·ta·ry (kom′plə·men′tər·ē, -trē) *adj.* **1** Expressing a compliment. **2** Given free. —**com′pli·men′ta·ri·ly** *adv.*

com·plin (kom′plin) *n.* The last of the canonical hours.

com·ply (kəm·plī′) *v.i.* **·plied, ·ply·ing** To act in conformity; consent; obey: with *with.* [<Sp. *cumplir* complete an act of courtesy <L *complere* to complete] —**com·pli′er** *n.*

com·po·nent (kəm·pō′nənt) *n.* A constituent part. —*adj.* Forming a part or ingredient. [<L *componere* to place together]

com·port (kəm·pôrt′, -pōrt′) *v.t.* To conduct (oneself). —*v.i.* To be compatible; agree. [<L *com-* together + *portare* carry]

com·port·ment (kəm·pôrt′mənt, -pōrt′-) *n.* Behavior; deportment.

com·pose (kəm·pōz′) *v.* **·posed, ·pos·ing** *v.t.* **1** To be the constituent elements or parts of; constitute; form. **2** To tranquilize; calm. **3** To reconcile, arrange, or settle, as differences. **4** To create artistically, as a literary or musical work. **5** To arrange (type) in lines; set. —*v.i.* **6** To engage in composition, as of a literary or musical work. **7** To set type. [<L *com-* together + *poser* to put]

com·posed (kəm·pōzd′) *adj.* Free from agitation; calm. —**com·pos·ed·ly** (kəm·pō′zid·lē) *adv.* —**com·pos′ed·ness** *n.*

com·pos·er (kəm·pō′zər) *n.* One who composes, esp. one who composes music.

com·pos·ite (kəm·poz′it) *adj.* **1** Made up of separate parts or elements. **2** *Bot.* Belonging to a large family of plants, as the aster, sunflower, etc., having massed heads of modified florets that resemble single flowers. —*n.* That which is composed of parts; a compound. [<L *compositus,* pp. of *componere* to put together] —**com·pos′ite·ly** *adv.*

com·po·si·tion (kom′pə·zish′ən) *n.* **1** The act or art of composing a literary, musical, or artistic work. **2** The work so composed or its general arrangement or style. **3** Any putting together of separate elements or parts to form a whole; also, the whole so formed. **4** The general nature or makeup of a thing or person. **5** The act or skill of setting type.

com·pos·i·tor (kəm·poz′ə·tər) *n.* One who sets type; typesetter.

com·post (kom′pōst) *n.* A mixture of decomposed vegetable matter, used as fertilizer. [<L *compositus.* See COMPOSITE.]

com·po·sure (kəm·pō′zhər) *n.* Tranquility, as of manner; calmness; serenity.

com·pote (kom′pōt, *Fr.* kôn·pôt′) *n.* 1 Fruit stewed or preserved in syrup. 2 A dish for holding fruits, etc. [< L *compositus* put together. See COMPOSITE.]

com·pound[1] (kom′pound) *n.* 1 A combination of two or more elements, ingredients, or parts. 2 *Chem.* A substance composed of two or more elements combined chemically in definite proportions by weight. —*v.* (kom·pound′, kəm-) *v.t.* 1 To make by the combination of various elements or ingredients. 2 To mix (elements or parts); combine. 3 To settle for less than the sum due: to *compound* a debt. 4 To make more serious or complicated. 5 To compute (interest) on the principal and the interest that has accrued. —*v.i.* 6 To compromise or agree. —*adj.* (kom′pound, kom·pound′) Composed of or produced by the union of two or more elements, ingredients, or parts. [< L *componere* put together] —**com·pound′a·ble** *adj.* —**com·pound′er** *n.*

com·pound[2] (kom′pound) *n.* An enclosed area of dwellings, as for prisoners of war. [< Malay *kampong*]

compound fracture A bone fracture in which a broken end of bone penetrates the skin.

compound interest Interest computed not only on the principal but also on the unpaid interest that has accrued.

compound sentence A sentence having at least two independent clauses.

com·pre·hend (kom′pri·hend′) *v.t.* 1 To grasp mentally; understand fully. 2 To include, take in, or comprise. [< L *com-* together + *prehendere* seize] —**com′pre·hend′i·ble** *adj.*

com·pre·hen·si·ble (kom′pri·hen′sə·bəl) *adj.* That can be comprehended; understandable. —**com′pre·hen′si·bil′i·ty, com′pre·hen′si·ble·ness** *n.* —**com′pre·hen′si·bly** *adv.*

com·pre·hen·sion (kom′pri·hen′shən) *n.* 1 The act of comprehending or understanding. 2 The ability to do this. 3 The knowledge so gained. 4 The state or quality of being comprehensive.

com·pre·hen·sive (kom′pri·hen′sive) *adj.* 1 Large in scope or content; broadly inclusive. 2 Able to understand fully. —**com′pre·hen′sive·ly** *adv.* —**com′pre·hen′sive·ness** *n.*

com·press (kəm·pres′) *v.t.* To press together or into smaller space; compact. —*n.* (kom′pres) 1 A device for compressing. 2 *Med.* A soft pad for applying pressure, heat, moisture, etc. to a part of the body. [< LL *compressare*, freq. of *comprimere* press together] —**com·press′i·ble, com·press′ive** *adj.* —**com·press′i·bil′i·ty, com·press′i·ble·ness** *n.*

com·pres·sion (kəm·presh′ən) *n.* The act of compressing or the state of being compressed.

com·pres·sor (kəm·pres′ər) *n.* 1 One who or that which compresses. 2 *Mech.* A machine for compressing a gas.

com·prise (kəm·prīz′) *v.t.* ·prised, ·pris·ing To include and contain; consist of. [< L *comprehendere* comprehend] —**com·pris′a·ble** *adj.* —**com·pri′sal** *n.*

com·pro·mise (kom′prə·mīz) *n.* 1 A settlement by arbitration and mutual concession. 2 An adjustment or concession between conflicting courses, ideas, desires, etc. 3 An imperiling or surrender, as of character or reputation. —*v.* ·mised, ·mis·ing *v.t.* 1 To adjust or settle by concessions. 2 To imperil or surrender. —*v.i.* 3 To make a compromise. [< L *com-* together + *promittere* promise] —**com′pro·mis′er** *n.*

comp·trol·ler (kən·trō′lər) *n.* CONTROLLER (def. 2). —**comp·trol′ler·ship** *n.*

com·pul·sion (kəm·pul′shən) *n.* 1 The act of compelling or the state of being compelled. 2 *Psychol.* An irresistible urge to perform some act without rational purpose. —**com·pul′sive** *adj.* —**com·pul′sive·ly** *adv.* —**com·pul′sive·ness** *n.*

com·pul·so·ry (kəm·pul′sər·ē) *adj.* 1 Employing compulsion; coercive. 2 Required by law or other rule. —**com·pul′so·ri·ly** *adv.* —**com·pul′so·ri·ness** *n.*

com·punc·tion (kəm·pungk′shən) *n.* 1 Self-reproach for wrong-doing; guilt. 2 A feeling of slight regret. [< L *com-* greatly + *pungere* to prick, sting] —**com·punc′tious** *adj.*

com·pu·ta·tion (kom′pyə·tā′shən) *n.* 1 The act of computing; calculation. 2 A computed amount or number.

com·pute (kəm·pyōōt′) *v.t.* ·put·ed, ·put·ing To estimate numerically; calculate. [< L *com-* together + *putare* reckon] —**com·put′a·bil′i·ty** *n.* —**com·put′a·ble** *adj.*

com·put·er (kəm·pyōō′tər) *n.* 1 One who or that which computes. 2 An electronic machine capable of accepting data, manipulating or performing arithmetic on such data at high speed, and showing or printing the results.

com·put·er·ize (kəm·pyōō′tər·īz) *v.t.* ·ized, ·iz·ing 1 To operate or process by or as if by computer. 2 To equip with computers. *Brit. sp.* ·ise. —**com·put′er·i·za′tion** *n.*

Comr. Commissioner.

com·rade (kom′rad, -rid) *n.* 1 A friend or close companion. 2 A fellow member, as of a political party, esp. the Communist party. [< Sp. *camarada* roommate < L *camera* room] —**com′rade·ship** *n.*

com·sat (kom′sat′) *n.* Any of various artificial satellites employed to relay radio or television signals, etc. [< COM(MUNICATIONS) + SAT(ELLITE)]

con[1] (kon) *v.t.* **conned, con·ning** To peruse carefully; study. [< OE *cunnan* to know]

con[2] (kon) *adv.* Against. —*n.* Something opposed, as a reason, position, etc. [< L *contra* against]

con[3] (kon) *Slang adj.* Confidence: a *con* game. —*v.t.* **conned, con·ning** 1 To defraud; swindle. 2 To persuade, as by flattery.

con[4] (kon) *n. Slang* A convict.

con. against (L *contra*); concerto; conclusion; connection; conduct; consolidated; continued; wife (L *conjunx*).

con·cat·e·nate (kon·kat′ə·nāt) *v.t.* ·nat·ed, ·nat·ing To join or link together; connect in a series. [< L *com-* together + *catena* chain] —**con·cat′e·na′tion** *n.*

con·cave (kon·kāv′, kon′kāv, kong′-) *adj.* Hollow and rounded, as the interior of a sphere or circle. —*n.* (kon′·kāv, kong′-) A concave surface. [< L *com-* thoroughly + *cavus* hollow] —**con·cave′ly** *adv.* • See CONVEX.

con·cav·i·ty (kon·kav′ə·tē) *n. pl.* ·ties 1 The state of being concave. 2 A concave surface, object, line, etc.

con·ceal (kən·sēl′) *v.t.* To keep from sight, discovery, or knowledge; hide. [< L *com-* thoroughly + *celare* hide] —**con·ceal′a·ble** *adj.* —**con·ceal′er, con·ceal′ment** *n.*

con·cede (kən·sēd′) *v.* ·ced·ed, ·ced·ing *v.t.* 1 To grant as a right or privilege. 2 To acknowledge as true, correct, or proper; admit. —*v.i.* 3 To make a concession. [< L *com-* thoroughly + *cedere* yield, go away] —**con·ced′er** *n.*

con·ceit (kən·sēt′) *n.* 1 Excessive self-esteem or vanity. 2 A fanciful or elaborate idea, expression, or metaphor. 3 Imagination. 4 A small, ingenious article or design. [< CONCEIVE]

con·ceit·ed (kən·sē′tid) *adj.* Having an excessively fine opinion of oneself; vain. —**con·ceit′ed·ly** *adv.* —**con·ceit′ed·ness** *n.* —**Syn.** immodest, egotistic, haughty, arrogant.

con·ceive (kən·sēv′) *v.* ·ceived, ·ceiv·ing *v.t.* 1 To become pregnant with. 2 To form in the mind; think of. 3 To believe or suppose. 4 To express in words. —*v.i.* 5 To form an idea or conception: with *of.* 6 To become pregnant. [< L *com-* thoroughly + *capere* take] —**con·ceiv′a·ble** *adj.* —**con·ceiv′a·bil′i·ty, con·ceiv′a·ble·ness, con·ceiv′er** *n.* —**con·ceiv′a·bly** *adv.*

con·cen·trate (kon′sən·trāt) *v.* ·trat·ed, ·trat·ing *v.t.* 1 To bring or draw to a common center; focus. 2 To increase the strength or density of, as by condensation. 3 To fix or focus (one's thoughts, actions, etc.). —*v.i.* 4 To converge toward a center. 5 To fix or focus one's thoughts, actions, etc.: with *on* or *upon.* —*n.* A product of concentration. [< L *com-* together + *centrum* center] —**con·cen·tra·tive** (kon′sən·trā′tiv, kən·sen′trə·tiv) *adj.* —**con′cen·tra′tor** *n.*

con·cen·tra·tion (kon′sən·trā′shən) *n.* 1 The act of concentrating or the state of being concentrated. 2 That which is concentrated. 3 The amount of one substance contained per unit volume of another substance; density.

concentration camp A place of detention for prisoners of war, political prisoners, aliens, etc.

con·cen·tric (kən·sen′trik) *adj.* Having a common center: *concentric* circles. Also **con·**

Concentric
tree rings

cen·tri·cal. —**con·cen'tri·cal·ly** *adv.* —**con·cen·tric·i·ty** (kon'·sen·tris'ə·tē) *n.*

con·cept (kon'sept) *n.* An idea, thought, or opinion. [< L *conceptus* a conceiving]

con·cep·tion (kən·sep'shən) *n.* **1** The act of becoming pregnant. **2** An embryo or fetus. **3** The act of conceiving ideas or notions. **4** An idea, thought, or concept. —**con·cep'·tion·al, con·cep'tive** *adj.*

con·cep·tu·al (kən·sep'chōō·əl) *adj.* Of conception or a concept. —**con·cep'tu·al·ly** *adv.*

con·cern (kən·sûrn') *v.t.* **1** To be of interest, relevance, or importance to. **2** To cause to be anxious or troubled. —*n.* **1** That which concerns one; something affecting one's interest or welfare. **2** Interest or regard. **3** Anxiety; worry. **4** Relation; reference. **5** A business establishment. [< Med. L. *com-* thoroughly + *cernere* to see, discern]

con·cerned (kən·sûrnd') *adj.* **1** Involved or implicated. **2** Anxious; uneasy.

con·cern·ing (kən·sûr'ning) *prep.* In relation to; regarding; about.

con·cern·ment (kən·sûrn'mənt) *n.* **1** Bearing; importance. **2** Anxiety; solicitude. **3** Affair; concern; business.

con·cert (kon'sûrt) *n.* **1** A performance, as by a solo musician, an orchestra, dance group, etc. **2** Harmony; unity. —**in concert** Together. —*adj.* Of or for concerts. —*v.* (kən·sûrt') *v.t. & v.i.* To arrange or contrive by mutual agreement. [< Ital. *concertare* agree]

con·cert·ed (kən·sûr'tid) *adj.* Arranged or agreed upon in concert. —**con·cert'ed·ly** *adv.*

con·cer·ti·na (kon'sər·tē'nə) *n.* A small, simple accordion. [< Ital. *concerto* a concert]

con·cert·mas·ter (kon'sərt·mas'tər, -mäs'-) *n.* The leader of the first violin section of an orchestra, who often serves as assistant to the conductor.

con·cer·to (kən·cher'tō) *n. pl.* **-tos, -ti** (-tē) A composition, usu. having three movements, for performance by a solo instrument or instruments accompanied by an orchestra. [< Ital., concert]

con·ces·sion (kən·sesh'ən) *n.* **1** The act of conceding, or that which is conceded. **2** A privilege granted by a government, as the right to use land. **3** The right or a lease to operate a small business, as selling food, newspapers, etc., in office buildings, railroad stations, etc. **4** The space, land, etc., so leased, or the activity carried on there. [< L *concessus,* pp. of *concedere* to concede]

con·ces·sion·aire (kən·sesh'ən·âr') *n.* One who holds a concession. Also **con·ces·sion·er** (kən·sesh'ən·ər).

conch (kongk, konch) *n. pl.* **conchs** (kongks) or **conch·es** (kon'chiz) The large, spiral shell of various marine mollusks. [< Gk. *konchē* shell]

con·ci·erge (kon'sē·ûrzh', *Fr.* kôn·syârzh') A doorkeeper or attendant, as of an apartment house or hotel, esp. in France. [F]

con·cil·i·ate (kən·sil'ē·āt) *v.t.* **·at·ed, ·at·ing** **1** To overcome the enmity or hostility of; placate. **2** To secure or attract by reconciling measures; win. [< L *concilium* council] —**con·cil'i·a'tion, con·cil'i·a'tor** *n.* —**con·cil'i·a·to·ry** (kən·sil'ē·ə·tôr'ē, -tō'rē), **con·cil'i·a'tive** *adj.* —**con·cil'i·a·to'ri·ly** *adv.*

con·cise (kən·sīs') *adj.* Expressing much in brief form; compact. [< L *concisus,* pp. of *concidere* to cut thoroughly] —**con·cise'ly** *adv.* —**con·cise'ness** *n.* —**Syn.** brief, terse, pithy, short, compact.

con·clave (kon'klāv, kong'-) *n.* **1** A secret council or meeting. **2 a** The apartments in the Vatican in which the college of cardinals meets to choose a pope. **b** The meeting itself. [< L, a place which can be locked up]

con·clude (kən·klōōd') *v.* **·clud·ed, ·clud·ing** *v.t.* **1** To come to a decision about; decide or determine. **2** To infer or deduce as a result or effect. **3** To arrange or settle finally. **4** To terminate. —*v.i.* **5** To come to an end. **6** To come to a decision. [< L *com-* thoroughly + *claudere* close, shut off] —**con·clud'er** *n.*

con·clu·sion (kən·klōō'zhən) *n.* **1** The act or an instance of concluding; termination. **2** A conviction reached by reasoning, inference, etc. **3** The last or closing part of something. **4** A result or outcome.

con·clu·sive (kən·klōō'siv) *adj.* **1** Putting an end to doubt; decisive. **2** Leading to a conclusion; final. —**con·clu'sive·ly** *adv.* —**con·clu'sive·ness** *n.*

con·coct (kon·kokt', kən-) *v.t.* **1** To make by mixing ingredients, as a drink or soup. **2** To contrive; devise. [< L *com-* together + *coquere* to cook, boil] —**con·coct'er, con·coc'tor** *n.*

con·coc·tion (kon·kok'shən, kən-) *n.* **1** The act of concocting. **2** Something concocted.

con·com·i·tant (kon·kom'ə·tənt, kən-) *adj.* Existing or occurring together; attendant. —*n.* An attendant circumstance. [< L *com-* with + *comitari* accompany] —**con·com'·i·tance, con·com'i·tan·cy** *n.* —**con·com'i·tant·ly** *adv.*

con·cord (kon'kôrd, kong'-) *n.* **1** Unity of feeling or interest; agreement; accord. **2** A peace treaty. **3** *Music* A harmonious combination of simultaneous tones. **4** *Gram.* AGREEMENT (def. 5). [< L *concors* agreeing < *com-* together + *cor* heart]

con·cor·dance (kon·kôr'dəns, kən-) *n.* **1** An alphabetical list of the important words in a book or books, with reference to the passages in which each word is found. **2** Concord; agreement; harmony.

con·cor·dant (kon·kôr'dənt, kən-) *adj.* Harmonious; agreeing. —**con·cor'dant·ly** *adv.*

con·cor·dat (kon·kôr'dat) *n.* **1** An agreement between the papal see and a secular power for the settlement and regulation of ecclesiastical affairs. **2** Any public agreement.

con·course (kon'kôrs, -kōrs, kong'-) *n.* **1** An assembling or moving together; confluence. **2** An assembly; throng. **3** A large area for the passage of crowds, as a boulevard or a long passageway in a railroad station, subway, etc. [< L *concurrere* to run together]

con·crete (kon'krēt, kon·krēt') *adj.* **1** Not general or abstract; specific. **2** Actually existing; real. **3** Made of concrete. **4** Joined into or being a solid mass. —*n.* **1** A material made of sand and gravel that is united by cement into a hardened mass, used for roads, foundations, etc. • See CEMENT. **2** Something concrete, as an idea, circumstance, etc. —*v.* (kon·krēt'; *usu. for def. 2* kon'krēt) **·cret·ed, ·cret·ing** *v.t.* **1** To unite together in one mass or body. **2** To treat or cover with concrete. —*v.i.* **3** To solidify. [< L *concretus,* pp. of *concrescere* to grow together] —**con·crete'ly** *adv.* —**con·crete'ness** *n.*

con·cre·tion (kon·krē'shən) *n.* **1** The act or an instance of concreting. **2** A solid mass. **3** *Geol.* An aggregate of rounded masses found in sedimentary rocks. —**con·cre'·tive** *adj.* —**con·cre'tive·ly** *adv.*

con·cre·tize (kon'kri·tīz, kong'-) *v.t.* **·tized, ·tiz·ing** To present in concrete terms; make actual or specific. —**con·cre·ti·za'tion** *n.*

con·cu·bine (kong'kyə·bīn, kon'-) *n.* **1** A woman who cohabits with a man without a marriage bond. **2** In certain polygamous societies, a secondary wife. [< L *com-* with + *cumbere* lie] —**con·cu'bi·nage** *n.*

con·cu·pis·cence (kon·kyōō'pə·səns) *n.* **1** Sexual desire; lust. **2** Any inordinate appetite or desire. [< L *com-* thoroughly + *cupere* to desire] —**con·cu'pis·cent** *adj.*

con·cur (kən·kûr') *v.i.* **·curred, ·cur·ring** **1** To agree, as in opinion or action: Three justices *concurred* in the finding. **2** To happen at the same time; coincide. **3** To act together: Many facts *concurred* to defeat him. [< L *com-* together + *currere* to run] —**con·cur'rence** *n.*

con·cur·rent (kən·kûr'ənt) *adj.* **1** Occurring or acting together. **2** In agreement. **3** Meeting at the same point. —**·cur'rent·ly** *adv.*

con·cus·sion (kən·kush'ən) *n.* **1** A violent shaking; shock. **2** Injury to soft tissue, esp. the brain, due to a violent shock or blow. [< L *concussus,* pp. of *concutere* to beat together] —**con·cus·sive** (kən·kus'iv) *adj.*

con·demn (kən·dem') *v.t.* **1** To hold or prove to be wrong; censure. **2** To prove to be wrong or guilty, esp. to pronounce judicial sentence against. **3** To forbid the use of, commonly by official order, as something unfit. **4** To appropriate for public use by judicial decree. **5** To doom. [< L *com-* thoroughly + *damnare* condemn] —**con·dem·na·ble** (kən·dem'nə·bəl), **con·dem·na·to·ry** (kən·dem'nə·tôr'ē, -tō'rē) *adj.* —**con·demn·er** (kən·dem'ər) *n.* —**Syn. 1** blame, denounce, rebuke, vilify.

con·dem·na·tion (kon'dem·nā'shən) *n.* **1** The act of condemning or the state of being condemned. **2** The cause for condemning.

con·den·sa·tion (kon′den·sā′shən) *n.* **1** The act of condensing or the state of being condensed. **2** The reduction of a vapor or gas to a liquid or solid, or of a liquid to a solid or semisolid. **3** Any product of condensing.

con·dense (kən·dens′) *v.* **-densed, -dens·ing** *v.t.* **1** To compress or make dense; subject to condensation. **2** To abridge or make concise. —*v.i.* **3** To become condensed. [< L *condensus* thick < *com-* together + *densus* crowded, close] —**con·dens′a·bil′i·ty** *n.* —**con·dens′a·ble** or **con·dens′i·ble** *adj.*

condensed milk Cow's milk, sweetened, and thickened by evaporation.

con·dens·er (kən·den′sər) *n.* **1** One who or that which condenses. **2** Any device for condensing a vapor. **3** *Electr.* A capacitor. **4** *Optics* A combination of lenses for focusing light rays.

con·de·scend (kon′di·send′) *v.i.* **1** To come down voluntarily to equal terms with a supposed inferior so as to do something; deign. **2** To behave towards others in a patronizing manner. [< L *com-* thoroughly + *descendere* to descend] —**con′de·scen′dence** *n.* —**con′de·scend′ing** *adj.* —**con′de·scend′ing·ly** *adv.*

con·de·scen·sion (kon′di·sen′shən) *n.* **1** An act or instance of condescending. **2** A patronizing manner.

con·dign (kən·dīn′) *adj.* Merited; deserved: said of punishment. [< L *com-* thoroughly + *dignus* worthy]

con·di·ment (kon′də·mənt) *n.* A sauce, relish, spice, etc. [< L *condimentum*]

con·di·tion (kən·dish′ən) *n.* **1** The state or mode in which a person or thing exists. **2** State of health. **3** A sound state of health or fitness. **4** *Informal* An ailment. **5** A modifying circumstance. **6** An event, circumstance, or fact necessary to the occurrence, completion, or fulfillment of something else: Luck is often a *condition* of success. **7** *Usu. pl.* Any circumstances that affect a person or activity: good working *conditions*. **8** Rank or social position. —**on condition that** Provided that; if. —*v.t.* **1** To place a stipulation upon; prescribe. **2** To be the prerequisite to. **3** To specify as a requirement. **4** To render fit. **5** *Psychol.* To train to a behavior pattern or conditioned response. **6** To accustom (a person or animal) to something. —*v.i.* **7** To stipulate. [< L *com-* together + *dicere* say] —**con·di′tion·er** *n.*

con·di·tion·al (kən·dish′ən·əl) *adj.* **1** Expressing or imposing conditions. **2** Not certain; indefinite. —**con·di·tion·al·i·ty** (kən·dish′ən·al′ə·tē) *n.* —**con·di′tion·al·ly** *adv.*

conditioned response *Psychol.* A learned response elicited by a stimulus which, though originally ineffective, has replaced the normal or natural stimulus after a period of close and repeated juxtaposition with it. Also **conditioned reflex.**

con·do (kon′dō) *n. U.S. Colloq.* Condominium (def. 3).

con·dole (kən·dōl′) *v.i.* **-doled, -dol·ing** To grieve or express sympathy with *with.* [< L *com-* together + *dolere* grieve] —**con·do·la·to·ry** (kən·dō′lə·tôr′ē, -tō′rē) *adj.* —**con·dol′er** *n.* —**con·dol′ing·ly** *adv.*

con·do·lence (kən·dō′ləns) *n.* Expression of sympathy with a person in pain, sorrow, or misfortune.

con·dom (kon′dəm, kun′-) *n.* A thin, impermeable sheath that is fitted over the penis to prevent conception and venereal disease. [? Alter. of *Conton,* an 18th c. English physician said to have invented it.]

con·do·min·i·um (kon′də·min′ē·əm) *n. U.S.* An apartment house in which the units are owned separately by individuals and not by a corporation or cooperative; also, an apartment in such a building. [< L *com-* together + *dominium* rule]

con·done (kən·dōn′) *v.t.* **-doned, -don·ing** To overlook or forgive. [< L *com-* thoroughly + *donare* give] —**con·do·na·tion** (kon′dō·nā′shən), **con·don′er** *n.*

con·dor (kon′dər) *n.* **1** A very large vulture of the high Andes characterized by a bare head and white neck ruff. **2** A California vulture. [< Quechua *cuntur*]

con·duce (kən·dyōōs′) *v.i.* **-duced, -duc·ing** To help toward a result; contribute; with *to.* [< L *com-* together + *ducere* lead] —**con·duc′er** *n.*

con·du·cive (kən·dyōō′siv) *adj.* Contributing; helping; with *to.* —**con·duc′ive·ly** *adv.* —**con·du′cive·ness** *n.*

con·duct (kən·dukt′) *v.t.* **1** To accompany and show the way; guide; escort. **2** To manage or control. **3** To direct and lead the performance of. **4** To serve as a medium of transmission for, as electricity. **5** To act or behave: used reflexively. —*v.i.* **6** To serve as a conductor. **7** To direct or lead. —*n.* (kon′dukt) **1** One's course of action; behavior. **2** Direction; control. **3** The act of leading. [< L *com-* together + *ducere* lead] —**con·duct′i·bil′i·ty** *n.* —**con·duct′i·ble, con·duct′ive** *adj.*

con·duc·tance (kən·duk′təns) *n. Electr.* The reciprocal of resistance.

con·duc·tion (kən·duk′shən) *n.* **1** *Physics* The transmission of heat, sound, or electricity through matter without motion of the conducting body as a whole. **2** Transmission or conveyance in general.

con·duc·tiv·i·ty (kon′duk·tiv′ə·tē) *n.* The capacity to transmit energy, as light, heat, or electricity.

con·duc·tor (kən·duk′tər) *n.* **1** One who conducts or leads. **2** One in charge of a railroad car, bus, etc. **3** The director of an orchestra or chorus. **4** Any medium, material, or device that conducts electricity, heat, etc. —**con·duc′tor·ship** *n.*

con·duit (kon′dit, -dōō·it) *n.* **1** A means for conducting something, as a tube or pipe for a fluid. **2** A passage for electric wires, underground cables, gas and water pipes, etc. [< L *conducere.* See CONDUCT.]

cone (kōn) *n.* **1** A solid figure that tapers uniformly from a circular base to a point. **2** *Geom.* A surface generated by a straight line passing always through a fixed point, called the *vertex,* and tracing a plane curve. **3** Something shaped like a cone, as a machine part or a pastry shell for ice cream. **4** *Bot.* A dry multiple fruit composed of scales, as of the pine or fir tree. —*v.t.* **coned, con·ing** To shape conically. [< Gk. *kōnos*]

Cones. a. stone pine. b. California big tree. c. Eastern hemlock.

con·el·rad (kon′əl·rad) *n.* A technique for arranging radio signals from separate stations so as to prevent enemy aircraft from using the signals as a navigation aid or for information. [< *con(trol of) el(ectromagnetic) rad(iation)*]

Con·es·to·ga wagon (kon′is·tō′gə) A covered wagon with broad wheels. [< *Conestoga,* Pa., where first made]

co·ney (kō′nē, kun′ē) *n.* CONY.

con·fab (kon′fab) *Informal v.i.* **-fabbed, -fab·bing** To chat. —*n.* A chat. [< CONFABULATE]

con·fab·u·late (kən·fab′yə·lāt) *v.i.* **-lat·ed, -lat·ing** To chat; gossip; converse. [< L *com-* together + *fabulari* chat < *fabula* story] —**con·fab′u·la′tion** *n.*

con·fec·tion (kən·fek′shən) *n.* Any sweet, such as candy. [< L *confectus,* pp. of *conficere* to prepare, make together] —**con·fec′tion·ar′y** *adj.*

con·fec·tion·er (kən·fek′shən·er) *n.* One who makes or sells confectionery.

con·fec·tion·er·y (kən·fek′shən·er′ē) *n. pl.* **-er·ies 1** Candies, sweetmeats, etc., collectively. **2** A confectioner's shop or the business of a confectioner: sometimes **confectionary.**

Confed. Confederate; Confederation.

con·fed·er·a·cy (kən·fed′ər·ə·sē) *n. pl.* **-cies 1** A number of states or persons in league with each other; league. **2** An unlawful conspiracy. —**the Confederacy** The 11 southern States that seceded from the U.S. in 1860–61.

con·fed·er·ate (kən·fed′ər·it) *n.* One united with another or others in an enterprise, plot, etc.; an associate; accomplice. —*adj.* Associated in a confederacy. —*v.t. & v.i.* (kən·fed′·ə·rāt) **-at·ed, -at·ing** To form or join in a confederacy. [< LL *confoederare* join in a league < L *com-* together + *foedus* league] —**con·fed′er·a′tive** *adj.*

Con·fed·er·ate (kən·fed′ər·it) *adj.* Of or pertaining to the Confederacy. —*n.* An adherent of the Confederacy.

con·fed·er·a·tion (kən·fed′ə·rā′shən) *n.* **1** The act of confederating. **2** CONFEDERACY. —**the Confederation** The union of the American colonies, 1781–89, under the Articles of Confederation.

Con·fed·er·a·tion (kən·fed'ə·rā'shən) *n.* The union of Ontario, Quebec, Nova Scotia, and New Brunswick in 1867.

con·fer (kən·fûr') *v.* **·ferred, ·fer·ring** *v.t.* **1** To give or grant; bestow. —*v.i.* **2** To hold a conference; consult. [< L *com-* together + *ferre* bring, carry] —**con·fer'ment, con·fer'rer** *n.* —**con·fer'ra·ble** *adj.*

con·fer·ee (kon'fə·rē') *n.* **1** One who participates in a discussion. **2** One upon whom some honor, degree, etc., is conferred.

con·fer·ence (kon'fər·əns, ·frəns) *n.* **1** A formal meeting for counsel or discussion. **2** A discussion or consultation. **3** A league or association, as of churches, schools, athletic teams, etc. [< L *conferre* to confer]

con·fess (kən·fes') *v.t.* **1** To acknowledge or admit, as a fault, guilt, or debt. **2** To acknowledge belief or faith in. **3 a** To admit or make known (one's sins) to a priest, to obtain absolution. **b** To hear the confession of: said of a priest. **4** To concede or admit to be true. —*v.i.* **5** To make acknowledgment of, as a fault, crime, or error. **6** To make confession to a priest. [< L *confessus*, pp. of *confiteri* declare thoroughly] —**con·fess'ed·ly** *adv.*

con·fes·sion (kən·fesh'ən) *n.* **1** An avowal or admission, as of guilt. **2** That which is confessed or admitted. **3** *Eccl.* A contrite acknowledgment of one's sins to a priest in order to obtain absolution. **4** A formal declaration of belief or faith.

con·fes·sion·al (kən·fesh'ən·əl) *n.* A private booth in a church where a priest hears confessions. —*adj.* Of confession.

con·fes·sor (kən·fes'ər) *n.* **1** A priest who hears confessions. **2** One who confesses. Also **con·fess'er.**

con·fet·ti (kən·fet'ē) *n.pl.* (*construed as sing.*) Small pieces of brightly colored paper thrown about at weddings, etc. [< Ital. *confetto* confection]

con·fi·dant (kon'fə·dant', ·dänt', kon'fə·dant', ·dänt') *n.* A person to whom secrets are entrusted. [< L *confidere* to confide] —**con'fi·dante'** *n. Fem.*

con·fide (kən·fīd') *v.* **·fid·ed, ·fid·ing** *v.t.* **1** To reveal in trust or confidence. **2** To put into one's trust or keeping. —*v.i.* **3** To reveal secrets in trust: often with *in.* [< L *com-* thoroughly + *fidere* to trust] —**con·fid'er** *n.*

con·fi·dence (kon'fə·dəns) *n.* **1** Trust in or reliance upon something or someone. **2** Assurance. **3** Self-reliance; courage or boldness. **4** A private conversation or a secret. **5** A relationship of trust: take into one's *confidence.*

confidence game A swindle in which the swindler first wins the confidence of his victim and then defrauds him.

confidence man One who practices or promotes a confidence game.

con·fi·dent (kon'fə·dənt) *adj.* Having or showing confidence; assured. —*n.* A confidant. —**con'fi·dent·ly** *adv.*

con·fi·den·tial (kon'fə·den'shəl) *adj.* **1** Trusted with secret or private information. **2** Imparted in confidence; secret: *confidential* information. **3** Of or marked by trust in others; confiding: a *confidential* manner. —**con'fi·den'tial·ly** *adv.* —**con'fi·den'tial·ness** *n.*

con·fid·ing (kən·fī'ding) *adj.* Trustful. —**con·fid'ing·ly** *adv.*

con·fig·u·ra·tion (kən·fig'yə·rā'shən) *n.* Structural arrangement; contour. —**con·fig'u·ra'tion·al** *adj.*

con·fine (kən·fīn') *v.* **·fined, ·fin·ing** *v.t.* **1** To shut within an enclosure; imprison. **2** To restrain or oblige to stay within doors. **3** To keep within limits; restrict: to *confine* remarks. —*n. Usu. pl.* A boundary; limit; border. [< L *confinis* bordering < *com-* together + *finis* border] —**con·fin'a·ble** *adj.* —**con·fin'er** *n.*

con·fine·ment (kən·fīn'mənt) *n.* **1** The state of being confined. **2** Childbirth.

con·firm (kən·fûrm') *v.t.* **1** To assure by added proof; verify; make certain. **2** To strengthen. **3** To ratify, as a bill, law, etc. **4** To receive into the church by confirmation. [< L *confirmare* strengthen < *com-* thoroughly + *firmus* strong] —**con·firm'a·ble, con·firm'a·tive, con·firm·a·to·ry** (kən·fûr'mə·tôr'ē, ·tō'rē) *adj.* —**con·firm'er, con·firm'or** *n.* —**Syn. 1** corroborate, prove, settle, substantiate, establish.

con·fir·ma·tion (kon'fər·mā'shən) *n.* **1** The act of confirming. **2** That which confirms; proof. **3** A rite adminis-

tered to baptized persons, confirming or strengthening their faith, and admitting them to all the privileges of the church.

con·firmed (kən·fûrmd') *adj.* **1** Verified; made certain. **2** Ratified. **3** Having received religious confirmation. **4** Firmly established; inveterate: a *confirmed* drunkard.

con·fis·cate (kon'fis·kāt) *v.t.* **·cat·ed, ·cat·ing** **1** To appropriate as forfeited to the public use or treasury, usu. as a penalty. **2** To appropriate by or as by authority. [< L *confiscare* < *com-* together + *fiscus* chest, treasury] —**con'fis·ca'tion** *n.* —**con'fis·ca'tor** *n.*

con·fla·gra·tion (kon'flə·grā'shən) *n.* A great or disastrous fire. [< L *com-* thoroughly + *flagrare* to burn]

con·flict (kon'flikt) *n.* **1** A struggle; battle. **2** A state or condition of opposition; antagonism. **3** Emotional disturbance due to opposed and contradictory impulses. —*v.i.* (kən·flikt') **1** To come into collision; be in mutual opposition; clash. **2** To battle; struggle. [< L *com-* together + *fligere* strike] —**con·flic'tion** *n.* —**con·flic'tive** *adj.*

conflict of interest A situation in which the disinterested performance of official duties may be unduly influenced by considerations of private interest.

con·flu·ence (kon'floo·əns) *n.* **1** The flowing together of streams or the place where they meet. **2** The body of water so formed. **3** A flocking together, as of people; throng.

con·flu·ent (kon'floo·ənt) *adj.* Flowing together so as to form one. [< L *com-* together + *fluere* flow]

con·flux (kon'fluks) *n.* CONFLUENCE.

con·form (kən·fôrm') *v.t.* **1** To make like or similar in form or character: with *to.* **2** To bring into agreement: often used reflexively. —*v.i.* **3** To be or act in accord; comply: with *to.* **4** To hold to or comply with the accepted modes of behavior, prevailing opinions, etc. [< L *com-* together + *formare* shape] —**con·form'er** *n.*

con·form·a·ble (kən·fôr'mə·bəl) *adj.* **1** In agreement. **2** Similar, as in form or character. **3** Adapted; suited. **4** Obedient; submissive. —**con·form'a·bil'i·ty, con·form'a·ble·ness** *n.* —**con·form'a·bly** *adv.*

con·form·ance (kən·fôr'məns) *n.* CONFORMITY.

con·for·ma·tion (kon'fôr·mā'shən) *n.* **1** The manner of formation of a body; general structure, form, or outline. **2** A symmetrical arrangement of parts.

con·form·ist (kən·fôr'mist) *n.* One who conforms or complies.

con·form·i·ty (kən·fôr'mə·tē) *n. pl.* **·ties 1** Correspondence in form, manner, or use; agreement; harmony. **2** The act or habit of conforming; acquiescence.

con·found (kon·found', kən-) *v.t.* **1** To amaze, confuse, or perplex. **2** To mingle or mix up (elements, things, ideas, etc.) indistinguishably. **3** (kon'found') To damn: used as a mild oath. [< L *confundere.* See CONFUSE.] —**con·found'er** *n.*

con·found·ed (kon·foun'did, kən-) *adj.* **1** DAMNED (def. 2). **2** Perplexed; confused. —**con·found'ed·ly** *adv.*

con·front (kən·frunt') *v.t.* **1** To stand face to face with. **2** To place or put face to face: with *with: Confront* him with the evidence. **3** To face defiantly. [< L *com-* together + *frons* face, forehead] —**con·front'er** *n.*

con·fron·ta·tion (kon'frən·tā'shən) *n.* **1** The act of confronting, or the state of being confronted. **2** A direct challenge, or the crisis resulting from it.

Con·fu·cian·ism (kən·fyoo'shən·iz'əm) *n.* The ethical system based on the teachings of Confucius and emphasizing ancestor worship, devotion to family and friends, and the maintenance of justice and peace. —**Con·fu·cian** *adj., n.* —**Con·fu·cian·ist** *n.*

con·fuse (kən·fyooz') *v.t.* **·fused, ·fus·ing 1** To perplex; confound; bewilder. **2** To mix indiscriminately. **3** To mistake (a person or thing) for another. **4** DISCONCERT. [< L *confusus*, pp. of *confundere* to pour together] —**con·fus·ed·ly** (kən·fyoo'zid·lē) *adv.* —**con·fus'ed·ness** *n.* —**con·fus'ing·ly** *adv.*

con·fu·sion (kən·fyoo'zhən) *n.* **1** The act of confusing or the state of being confused. **2** A state of disorder; jumble. —**con·fu'sion·al** *adj.*

con·fute (kən·fyoot') *v.t.* **·fut·ed, ·fut·ing 1** To prove to be false or invalid; refute successfully. **2** To prove (a person) to be in the wrong. [< L *confutare* check, restrain] —**con'fu·ta'tion** *n.* —**con·fut'er** *n.*

Cong. Congress; Congressional.

con·ga (kong′gə) *n.* **1** A Latin-American dance in which the dancers form a winding line. **2** The music for this dance. —*v.i.* To dance the conga. [< Am. Sp.]

con·geal (kən·jēl′) *v.t.* **1** To solidify or thicken, as by cooling. **2** To curdle or coagulate. —*v.i.* **3** To become hard, stiff, or viscid. [< L *com*- together + *gelare* freeze < *gelum* frost] —con·geal′a·ble *adj.* —con·geal′er, con·geal′ment *n.*

con·gen·ial (kən·jēn′yəl) *adj.* **1** Having similar character or tastes. **2** Suited to one's disposition. [< CON- + GE-NIAL] —con·ge·ni·al·i·ty (kən·jē′nē·al′ə·tē) *n.* —con·gen′ial·ly *adv.* —**Syn. 1** Sympathetic, kindred, congenial. **2** Agreeable, gratifying, pleasant.

con·gen·i·tal (kən·jen′ə·təl) *adj.* Existing at or from birth. [< L *com*- together + *genitus*, pp. of *gignere* bear, produce] —con·gen′i·tal·ly *adv.*

con·ger (kong′gər) *n.* Any of a family of large marine eels. Also **conger eel.** [< Gk. *gongros*]

Conger

con·gest (kən·jest′) *v.t.* **1** To collect or crowd together; overcrowd. **2** To cause excessive accumulation of blood in (an organ or tissue). —*v.i.* **3** To become congested. [< L *congestum*, pp. of *congerere* to carry together] —con·ges′tion *n.* —con·ges′tive *adj.*

con·glom·er·ate (kən·glom′ər·it) *adj.* **1** Massed or clustered. **2** *Geol.* Consisting of loosely cemented heterogeneous material. —*n.* **1** A heterogeneous collection. **2** *Geol.* A rock composed of fragments loosely cemented together. **3** A large corporation formed by merging a number of separate companies, often in unrelated fields. —*v.t. & v.i.* (kən·glom′ə·rāt) ·at·ed, ·at·ing To gather into a cohering mass. [< L *com*- together + *glomus, glomeris* ball] —con·glom′er·a′tion *n.*

con·glu·ti·nate (kən·glōō′tə·nāt) *v.t. & v.i.* ·nat·ed, ·nat·ing To glue or stick together; adhere. —*adj.* Glued together. [< L *com*- together + *glutinare* stick < *gluten* glue] —con·glu′ti·na′tion *n.*

con·go (kong′gō) *n.* An eellike salamander with rudimentary limbs, found in swamps of the SE U.S. Also **congo eel, congo snake.**

Con·go (kong′gō) *n.* A republic of CEN. Africa, 132,000 sq. mi., capital Brazzaville: also **Congo (Brazzaville).** —Con·go·lese (kong′gō·lēz′,-lēs′) *adj., n.* • See map at AFRICA.

con·grat·u·late (kən·grach′ōō·lāt) *v.t.* ·lat·ed, ·lat·ing To express sympathetic pleasure in the joy, success, or good fortune of (another). [< L *com*- together + *gratulari* rejoice] —con·grat′u·lant, con·grat′u·la·to′ry *adj.* —con·grat′u·la′tor *n.*

con·grat·u·la·tion (kən·grach′ōō·lā′shən) *n.* **1** The act of congratulating. **2** *pl.* Expressions of pleasure and good wishes on another's fortune or success.

con·gre·gant (kong′grə·gənt) *n.* A member of a congregation.

con·gre·gate (kong′grə·gāt) *v.t. & v.i.* ·gat·ed, ·gat·ing To bring or come together into a crowd; assemble. —*adj.* (kong′grə·git) Gathered together; collected. [< L *com*- together + *gregare* crowd, collect < *grex* flock] —con′gre·ga′tive *adj.* —con′gre·ga′tor *n.*

con·gre·ga·tion (kong′grə·gā′shən) *n.* **1** The act of congregating. **2** An assemblage of people or of things. **3** A group of people gathered for worship. **4** The body of persons who regularly attend a place of worship. —con′gre·ga′tion·al *adj.*

Con·gre·ga·tion·al (kong′grə·gā′shən·əl) *adj.* Belonging or pertaining to the **Congregational Christian Churches,** an evangelical Protestant denomination.

con·gre·ga·tion·al·ism (kong′grə·gā′shən·əl·iz′əm) *n.* A form of church polity in which each local congregation is autonomous in all ecclesiastical matters.

Con·gre·ga·tion·al·ism (kong′grə·gā′shən·əl·iz′əm) *n.* The beliefs and organizational form of an evangelical Protestant denomination that recognizes each member church as self-governing. —Con′gre·ga′tion·al·ist *n., adj.*

con·gress (kong′gris) *n.* **1** An assembly or conference; a gathering. **2** A coming together. [< L *congressus* a coming together < *congredi* to move together] —con·gres·sive (kən·gres′iv) *adj.*

Con·gress (kong′gris) *n.* The national legislative body of the U.S., consisting of the Senate and the House of Representatives. —Con·gres·sion·al (kən·gresh′ən·əl) *adj.*

con·gres·sion·al (kən·gresh′ən·əl) *adj.* Of or pertaining to a congress.

con·gress·man (kong′gris·mən) *n. pl.* ·men (-mən) *Often cap.* A member of Congress, esp. of the House of Representatives.

Congress of Industrial Organizations A former affiliation of trade unions now merged with the American Federation of Labor.

con·gress·wom·an (kong′gris·wŏŏm′ən) *n. pl.* ·wom·en (-wim′in) *Often cap.* A female member of Congress, esp. of the House of Representatives.

con·gru·ence (kong′grōō·əns) *n.* Harmony; conformity; agreement. Also **con′gru·en·cy.**

con·gru·ent (kong′grōō·ənt) *adj.* **1** Having mutual agreement or conformity. **2** *Geom.* Describing two geometric figures that are identical part for part. [< L *congruere* agree] —con′gru·ent·ly *adv.*

con·gru·i·ty (kən·grōō′ə·tē) *n. pl.* ·ties **1** Agreement; harmoniousness. **2** An example or case of harmoniousness.

con·gru·ous (kong′grōō·əs) *adj.* **1** Harmoniously related or combined. **2** Appropriate; consistent. **3** *Geom.* CONGRUENT. [< L *congruere* agree] —con′gru·ous·ly *adv.* —con′gru·ous·ness *n.*

con·ic (kon′ik) *adj.* **1** Cone-shaped. **2** Relating to or formed by or upon a cone. Also **con′i·cal.** —*n.* CONIC SECTION. —con′i·cal·ly *adv.*

conic section *Math.* A curve formed by the intersection of a plane with a right circular cone; a circle, ellipse, parabola, or hyperbola.

co·nid·i·um (kō·nid′ē·əm) *n. pl.* co·nid·i·a (kō·nid′ē·ə) An asexual spore produced by certain fungi. Also **co·nid·i·o·spore** (kō·nid′ē·ə·spôr′, -spōr′). [< Gk. *konis* dust] —co·nid′i·al *adj.*

con·i·fer (kon′ə·fər, kō′nə-) *n.* Any of an order of cone-bearing, usu. evergreen shrubs and trees, including pine, spruce, fir, cedar, etc. [< L *conus* cone + *ferre* bear] —co·nif·er·ous (kō·nif′ər·əs) *adj.*

conj. conjugation; conjunction; conjunctive.

con·jec·tur·al (kən·jek′chər·əl) *adj.* **1** Of or based on conjecture. **2** Given to conjecturing. —con·jec′tur·al·ly *adv.*

con·jec·ture (kən·jek′chər) *n.* ·tured, ·tur·ing **1** To conclude or suppose from incomplete evidence; guess. —*v.i.* **2** To make a conjecture. —*n.* **1** An indecisive opinion; a guess. **2** The act of conjecturing. [< L *conjectura* < *conjicere* to throw together] —con·jec′tur·a·ble *adj.* —con·jec′tur·a·bly *adv.* —con·jec′tur·er *n.*

con·join (kən·join′) *v.t. & v.i.* To join together. —**Syn.** associate, connect, unite, combine.

con·joint (kən·joint′) *adj.* **1** Associated; conjoined. **2** Joint. —con·joint′ly *adv.*

con·ju·gal (kon′jōō·gəl) *adj.* Of or pertaining to marriage; matrimonial. [< L *conjungere* join in marriage] —con·ju·gal·i·ty (kon′jōō·gal′ə·tē) *n.* —con′ju·gal·ly *adv.*

con·ju·gate (kon′jōō·gāt, *for adj. & n., usu.* -git) *v.* ·gat·ed, ·gat·ing *v.t.* **1** To give the inflections of: said of verbs. **2** To unite or join together. —*adj.* Joined in pairs; coupled; paired. —*n.* **1** A word closely related to another or others. **2** A member of a conjugate pair. [< L *com*- together + *jugare* to yoke] —con′ju·ga·tive *adj.* —con′ju·ga′tor *n.*

con·ju·ga·tion (kon′jōō·gā′shən) *n.* **1** CONJUNCTION (def. 1). **2** *Gram.* The inflection of a verb or the expression of such inflection. **3** A class of verbs with a similar inflection. —con′ju·ga′tion·al *adj.*

con·junc·tion (kən·jungk′shən) *n.* **1** The act of joining or the state of being joined together. **2** *Astron.* The position of a planet when it, the earth, and the sun lie on the same straight line. **3** Simultaneous occurrence of events. **4** *Gram.* A word used to connect words, phrases, clauses, or sentences. [< L *com*- together + *jungere* join]

---

add, āce, câre, pälm; end, ēven; it, īce; odd, ōpen, ôrder; tŏŏk, pōōl; up, bûrn; ə = a in *above*, u in *focus*; yōō = u in *fuse*; oil; pout; check; go; ring; thin; this; zh, *vision*. < derived from; ? origin uncertain or unknown.

con·junc·ti·va (kon'jungk·tī'və) n. pl. **·vas** or **·vae** (-vē) The mucous membrane lining the eyelids and covering the front of the eyeball. [< NL *(membrana) conjunctiva* connective (membrane)] —**con·junc·ti'val** adj.

con·junc·tive (kən·jungk'tiv) adj. **1** Joining; connective. **2** Joined together. **3** *Gram.* Serving as a conjunction: a *conjunctive* adverb. —n. *Gram.* A conjunctive word. —**con·junc'tive·ly** adv.

con·junc·ti·vi·tis (kən·jungk'tə·vī'tis) n. Inflammation of the conjunctiva.

con·junc·ture (kən·jungk'chər) n. **1** A combination of circumstances. **2** A crisis. **3** The act of joining; union.

con·ju·ra·tion (kon'jōō·rā'shən) n. **1** INCANTATION. **2** Magic or a magical expression used in incantation.

con·jure (*for def. 1*, kon'jər, kun'- *for defs. 2–5*) v. **·jured**, **·jur·ing** v.t. **1** To appeal to solemnly. **2** To summon, bring, or drive away by incantation or spell, as a devil or spirit. **3** To accomplish or effect by or as by magic. —v.i. **4** To practice magic. **5** To summon a devil or spirit by incantation. [< L *com-* together + *jurare* swear] —**con'jur·er** n.

conk (kongk) *Slang* n. A blow, esp. on the head. —v.t. To hit on the head. —**conk out 1** To stall or fail, as a motor. **2** *Slang* To fall asleep, faint, or die.

con man (kon) *Slang* A confidence man.

Conn. Connecticut.

con·nect (kə·nekt') v.t. **1** To join together, as by links; combine. **2** To associate mentally. **3** To close or complete, as an electric circuit or telephone connection. —v.i. **4** To unite or join; be in close relation. **5** To meet as scheduled, as buses or trains, for transference of passengers. [< L *com-* together + *nectere* bind] —**con·nect'er, con·nect'or** n.

connecting rod *Mech.* A rod that transmits motion by connecting a rotary with a reciprocating part.

con·nec·tion (kə·nek'shən) n. **1** The act of connecting or the state of being connected. **2** The means or place of connection. **3** That which connects or serves to connect. **4** *Often pl.* A relative, associate, or friend. **5** A direct transfer from one route to another, as in railway service. **6** Logical coherence or consistency. **7** *Slang* A contact for acquiring narcotics. *Brit. sp.* **con·nex'ion.**

con·nec·tive (kə·nek'tiv) adj. Capable of connection or serving to connect. —n. **1** That which connects. **2** *Gram.* A connecting word or particle, as a conjunction. —**con·nec'tive·ly** adv. —**con'nec·tiv'i·ty** n.

connective tissue The cellular tissue that serves to support muscle, nerve and epithelial tissues in the body, as cartilage, bone, tendon, etc.

con·ning tower (kon'ing) **1** The armored pilothouse on the deck of a warship. **2** In submarines, an observation tower serving also as an entrance.

con·nip·tion (kə·nip'shən) n. *Informal* A fit of hysteria, rage, etc. [?]

con·ni·vance (kə·nī'vəns) n. **1** The act of conniving. **2** *Law* Knowledge of a wrongful or criminal act during its occurrence. Also **con·ni'van·cy.**

con·nive (kə·nīv') v.i. **·nived**, **·niv·ing 1** To encourage or assent to a wrong by silence or feigned ignorance: with *at*. **2** To be in collusion: with *with*. [< L *conivere* shut the eyes] —**con·niv'er** n.

con·nois·seur (kon'ə·sûr') n. A competent critical judge, esp. in matters of art and taste. [F< L *cognoscere* know thoroughly] —**con'nois·seur'ship** n.

con·no·ta·tion (kon'ə·tā'shən) n. **1** The emotional content or significance of a word in addition to its explicit literal meaning; implication. **2** The act of connoting. **3** The quality or qualities connoted. —**con'no·ta'tive** adj.

con·note (kə·nōt') v.t. **·not·ed**, **·not·ing** To indicate or imply along with the literal meaning. [< L *com-* together + *notare* mark]

con·nu·bi·al (kə·nᵞōō'bē·əl) adj. Pertaining to matrimony. [< L *com-* together + *nubere* marry] —**con·nu·bi·al·i·ty** (kə·nᵞōō'bē·al'ə·tē) n. —**con·nu'bi·al·ly** adv.

co·noid (kō'noid) adj. Cone-shaped. —n. Something having the form of a cone. —**co·noi'dal** adj.

con·quer (kong'kər) v.t. **1** To overcome or subdue by force, as in war. **2** To acquire or gain control of by or as by force. **3** To overcome by mental or moral force. —v.i. **4** To be victorious. [< L *conquirere* < *com-* thoroughly +

quaerere seek] —**con'quer·a·ble, con'quer·ing** adj. —**con'quer·ing·ly** adv. —**con'quer·or** n.

con·quest (kon'kwest, kong'-) n. **1** The act of conquering. **2** That which is conquered by force. **3 a** The winning of the favor of a person. **b** The person whose favor is won. [< OF, pp. of *conquerre* conquer]

con·quis·ta·dor (kon·kwis'tə·dôr, *Sp.* kōng·kēs'tä·thōr') n. pl. **·dors**, *Sp.* **·do·res** (-thō'rās) A conqueror, esp. any of the Spanish conquerors of Mexico and Peru in the 16th century. [< Sp. *conquistar* conquer]

Cons., cons. constable, constitution; consul.

cons. consonant.

con·san·guin·e·ous (kon'sang·gwin'ē·əs) adj. Descended from the same parent or ancestor; related. Also **con·san·guine** (kon·sang'gwin). [< L *com-* together + *sanguis* blood] —**con'san·guin'e·ous·ly** adv. —**con'san·guin'i·ty** n.

con·science (kon'shəns) n. The faculty by which distinctions are made between right and wrong; ethical judgment or sensibility. —**in (all) conscience 1** In reason and honesty. **2** Certainly; assuredly. [< L *conscientia* < *com-* together + *scire* know]

con·sci·en·tious (kon'shē·en'shəs) adj. **1** Governed or dictated by conscience. **2** Characterized by or done with care and attention. —**con'sci·en'tious·ly** adv. —**con'sci·en'tious·ness** n. —Syn. **1** scrupulous, honest, principled, moral. **2** careful, thorough, meticulous, attentive.

conscientious objector One who refuses to perform military service on grounds of religious or moral convictions.

con·scion·a·ble (kon'shən·ə·bəl) adj. Conforming to conscience. —**con'scion·a·bly** adv.

con·scious (kon'shəs) adj. **1** Mentally aware of one's inner thoughts and feelings and also of things external to oneself. **2** In possession of one's mental faculties; awake. **3** Able to think, will, perceive, etc.; rational. **4** Felt or acknowledged by oneself: *conscious* guilt. **5** Self-conscious. **6** Deliberate; intentional: a *conscious* lie. —n. *Psychoanal.* That part of mental life of which an individual is aware. [< L *conscius* < *com-* together + *scire* know] —**con'scious·ly** adv.

con·scious·ness (kon'shəs·nis) n. **1** The state of being conscious. **2** The aggregate of the conscious states in an individual or a group of persons.

con·script (kon'skript) n. One who is compulsorily enrolled for military service; a draftee. —v.t. (kən·skript') To force into military service; draft. —adj. (kon'skript) Compulsorily enlisted; drafted. [< L *conscriptus*, pp. of *conscribere* enroll < *com-* together + *scribere* write] —**con·scrip'tion** n.

con·se·crate (kon'sə·krāt) v.t. **·crat·ed**, **·crat·ing 1** To set apart as sacred; dedicate to sacred uses. **2** To dedicate solemnly or devote: *consecrate* one's life to a cause. **3** To make reverend; hallow. [< L *com-* thoroughly + *sacer* holy] —**con'se·cra'tion, con'se·cra'tor** n. —**con·se·cra·to·ry** (kon'sə·krə·tôr'ē, -tō'rē) adj.

con·sec·u·tive (kən·sek'yə·tiv) adj. **1** Following in uninterrupted succession; successive. **2** Characterized by logical sequence. [< L *consequi* follow together] —**con·sec'u·tive·ly** adv. —**con·sec'u·tive·ness** n.

con·sen·sus (kən·sen'səs) n. A collective opinion; general agreement. [< L *com-* together + *sentire* feel, think]

con·sent (kən·sent') v.i. To yield or accede; agree. —n. **1** A voluntary yielding to what is proposed or desired by another; acquiescence. **2** Agreement in opinion or sentiment. [< L *consentire*. See CONSENSUS.] —**con·sent'er** n.

con·se·quence (kon'sə·kwens, -kwəns) n. **1** That which naturally follows from a preceding action or condition; result. **2** A logical conclusion of an inference; deduction. **3** Distinction; note: a woman of *consequence*. **4** Significance; moment: an event of no *consequence*.

con·se·quent (kon'sə·kwent, -kwənt) adj. **1** Following as a natural result; resulting. **2** Characterized by correctness of reasoning; logical. —n. **1** That which follows something else. **2** An inference or conclusion.

con·se·quen·tial (kon'sə·kwen'shəl) adj. **1** Having or showing importance. **2** Self-important. **3** Following logically; consequent. —**con·se·quen·ti·al·i·ty** (kon'sə·kwen'shē·al'ə·tē), **con'se·quen'tial·ness** n. —**con'se·quen'tial·ly** adv.

con·se·quent·ly (kon′sə·kwent′lē, -kwənt·lē) adv. As a result; therefore.

con·ser·va·tion (kon′sər·vā′shən) n. 1 The act of keeping or protecting from loss of injury. 2 The preservation of natural resources. [< L *conservare*. See CONSERVE] —**con′ser·va′tion·al** adj. —**con′ser·va′tion·ist** n.

conservation of energy *Physics* The principle that in any closed material system the total amount of energy remains constant.

con·ser·va·tism (kən·sûr′və·tiz′əm) n. Conservative principles and practices.

con·ser·va·tive (kən·sûr′və·tiv) adj. 1 Adhering to and tending to preserve the existing order of things; opposed to change. 2 *Often cap.* Of, pertaining to, or characterizing a political party or philosophy that favors the preservation of the status quo and is critical of proposals for change. 3 Conserving; preservative. 4 Moderate; cautious: a *conservative* estimate or statement. —n. 1 A conservative person. 2 *Often cap.* A member of a conservative political party. —**con·ser′va·tive·ly** adv. —**con·ser′va·tive·ness** n.

con·ser·va·to·ry (kən·sûr′və·tôr′ē, -tō′rē) n. pl. **·ries** 1 A glass-enclosed room in which plants are grown and displayed. 2 A school of art, music, etc.

con·serve (kən·sûrv′) v.t. **·served, ·serv·ing** 1 To keep from loss, decay, or depletion; supervise and protect. 2 To preserve with sugar. —n. (kon′sûrv, kən·sûrv′) Often *pl.* A preserve made of several fruits stewed together in sugar, often with nuts, raisins, etc. [< L *com-* thoroughly + *servare* keep, save] —**con·serv′a·ble** adj. —**con·serv′er** n.

con·sid·er (kən·sid′ər) v.t. 1 To think about or deliberate upon. 2 To think to be. 3 To make allowance for. 4 To take into account: *consider* the feelings of others. —v.i. 5 To think closely; cogitate. [< L *considerare*, lit., to observe the stars]

con·sid·er·a·ble (kən·sid′ər·ə·bəl) adj. 1 Somewhat large in amount, extent, etc. 2 Worthy of consideration; significant. —**con·sid′er·a·bly** adv.

con·sid·er·ate (kən·sid′ər·it) adj. Showing consideration. —**con·sid′er·ate·ly** adv. —**con·sid′er·ate·ness** n. —Syn. mindful, thoughtful, kind, charitable.

con·sid·er·a·tion (kən·sid′ə·rā′shən) n. 1 The act of considering. 2 Something resulting from deliberation; a thought. 3 Thoughtful and kindly feeling or treatment. 4 A circumstance to be taken into account. 5 Something given in return for a service. 6 Importance; consequence.

con·sid·er·ing (kən·sid′ər·ing) prep. In view of. —adv. *Informal.* Taking all the facts into account: He came out quite well, *considering*.

con·sign (kən·sīn′) v.t. 1 To entrust or commit to the care of another. 2 To make over or relegate. 3 To forward or deliver, as merchandise, for sale or disposal. 4 To set apart, as for a specific purpose or use. [< L *com-* with + *signum* a seal] —**con·sign′a·ble** adj. —**con·sign·or** (kən·sī′nər, kon·sī′nôr′), **con·sign′er** n.

con·sign·ee (kon′sī·nē′) n. A person to whom property has been consigned.

con·sign·ment (kən·sīn′mənt) n. 1 The act of consigning. 2 The property consigned. —**on consignment** Sent to or in the possession of a retailer who pays the shipper after sale: said of merchandise.

con·sist (kən·sist′) v.i. 1 To be made up or constituted: with *of*. 2 To have as substance, quality, or nature: with *in*. 3 To exist in agreement: with *with*. [< L *com-* together + *sistere* stand]

con·sis·ten·cy (kən·sis′tən·sē) n. pl. **·cies** 1 Compatibility or harmony, as between things, acts, or statements. 2 Agreement with what has been previously done, expressed, etc. 3 Firmness, or density, as of a liquid. 4 Degree of firmness, thickness, or density. Also **con·sis′tence**.

con·sis·tent (kən·sis′tənt) adj. 1 Characterized by consistency. 2 In accord; compatible. —**con·sis′tent·ly** adv.

con·sis·to·ry (kən·sis′tər·ē) n. pl. **·ries** 1 A church council, esp. the council of Roman Catholic cardinals usu. presided over by the Pope. 2 The place where such a council meets, or the meeting itself. [< LL *consistorium* place of

assembly] —**con·sis·to·ri·al** (kon′sis·tôr′ē ·əl, -tō′rē-), **con′·sis·to′ri·an** adj.

con·so·la·tion (kon′sə·lā′shən) n. 1 The act of consoling or the state of being consoled; solace. 2 A comforting thought, person, or fact.

con·sol·a·to·ry (kən·sol′ə·tôr′ē, -tō′rē) adj. Providing comfort or solace.

con·sole[1] (kən·sōl′) v.t. **·soled, ·sol·ing** To comfort (a person) in grief or sorrow; solace. [< L *com-* together + *solari* solace] —**con·sol′a·ble** adj. —**con·sol′er** n.

con·sole[2] (kon′sōl) n. 1 A bracket, esp. an ornamental one. 2 CONSOLE TABLE. 3 The portion of an organ containing the manuals and stops. 4 A cabinet for a radio, phonograph, or television set, designed to rest on the floor. [F]

console table A table supported by consoles or whose legs have the appearance of consoles.

con·sol·i·date (kən·sol′ə·dāt) v. **·dat·ed, ·dat·ing** v.t. 1 To make solid, firm, or coherent. 2 *Mil.* To secure and strengthen, as a newly captured position. 3 To form a union of. —v.i. 4 To become united, solid, or firm. [< L *com-* together + *solidus* solid] —**con·sol′i·da′tion, con·sol′i·da′tor** n.

consolidated school A school usu. consisting of several rural elementary schools merged into one.

Console *def. 1*

con·som·mé (kon′sə·mā′, *Fr.* kôn·sô·mā′) n. A clear soup made from meat and sometimes vegetables boiled in water. [< F, pp. of *consommer* to concentrate]

con·so·nance (kon′sə·nəns) n. 1 Agreement; harmony. 2 *Music* A combination of tones regarded as pleasing and not requiring resolution. Also **con′so·nan·cy**.

con·so·nant (kon′sə·nənt) adj. 1 Being in agreement or harmony; consistent. 2 CONSONANTAL. 3 Having the quality of musical consonance. —n. 1 *Phonet.* A sound produced by partial blockage of the breath stream. 2 A letter representing such a sound. [< L *com-* together + *sonare* to sound] —**con′so·nant·ly** adv.

con·so·nan·tal (kon′sə·nan′təl) adj. Of the nature of ôr having a consonant or consonants.

con·sort (kon′sôrt) n. 1 A companion or associate. 2 A husband or wife; mate. 3 An accompanying vessel. —v.t. (kən·sôrt′) 1 To join; associate. —v.i. 2 To keep company; associate. 3 To be in agreement; harmonize. [< L *consors,* lit., one who shares the same fate]

con·sor·ti·um (kən·sôr′shē·əm) n. pl. **·ti·a** (-shē·ə) An association or agreement, often one entered into for international business or financial purposes. [L, fellowship]

con·spic·u·ous (kən·spik′yŏŏ·əs) adj. 1 Clearly visible; prominent; obvious. 2 Unusual; striking. [< L *com-* together + *specere* look at] —**con·spic′u·ous·ly** adv. —**con·spic′u·ous·ness** n.

con·spir·a·cy (kən·spir′ə·sē) n. pl. **·cies** 1 The act of conspiring. 2 A plot, esp. one to do something harmful, illegal, or treasonable. 3 The persons engaged in such a plot. 4 A striking concurrence, as of circumstances or tendencies. —**con·spir·a·tor** (kən·spir′ə·tər) n. —**con·spir·a·to·ri·al** (kən·spir′ə·tôr′ē·əl, -tō′rē-) adj.

con·spire (kən·spīr′) v. **·spired, ·spir·ing** v.t. 1 To plot. —v.i. 2 To form a plot, especially secretly, for evil or unlawful purposes. 3 To concur in action or endeavor, as circumstances. [< L *com-* together + *spirare* breathe] —**con·spir·ant** (kən·spī′rənt) adj., n. —**con·spir′er** n.

con·sta·ble (kon′stə·bəl, kun′-) n. 1 An officer of the peace; a policeman. 2 A high military officer in medieval monarchies. [< LL *comes stabuli* count of the stable] —**con′sta·ble·ship′** n.

con·stab·u·lar·y (kən·stab′yə·ler′ē) n. pl. **·lar·ies** 1 Constables of an area, collectively. 2 A military police force.

con·stant (kon′stənt) adj. 1 Steady in purpose; resolute; persevering. 2 Steady in faithfulness; loyal. 3 Continually recurring. 4 Invariable; unchanging. —n. 1 That which is permanent or invariable. 2 *Math.* A quantity which retains a fixed value throughout a given discussion. **3** In the sciences, any characteristic of a substance, event, or phenomenon, numerically determined, that remains always the same under specified conditions, as gravitation, the velocity of light, etc. [< L *com-* together + *stare* stand] — **con·stan·cy** *n.* —**con'stant·ly** *adv.*

con·stel·late (kon'stə-lāt) *v.t. & v.i.* **·lat·ed, ·lat·ing** To group in constellations. [< LL *constellatus* studded with stars]

con·stel·la·tion (kon'stə-lā'shən) *n.* **1** *Astron.* Any of 88 apparent clusters of stars, each named for a mythological person, an animal, or some object that it suggests; also, the area in the heavens covering such a group. **2** Any assemblage of things or persons. **3** In astrology, the position of the planets, esp. at the time of one's birth.

CONSTELLATIONS

Explanation: GROUP N includes all constellations within 45 degrees of the North Pole. GROUP E includes all constellations within 45 degrees of each side of the equator. GROUP S includes all constellations within 45 degrees of the South Pole.

Name	Group	On the Meridian at 9 p.m.	Name	Group	On the Meridian at 9 p.m.
Andromeda	E	Nov.	Indus	S	Oct.
Antlia	E	April	Lacerta	N	Oct.
Apus	S	July	Leo	E	April
Aquarius	E	Oct.	Leo Minor	E	April
Aquila	E	Aug.	Lepus	E	Jan.
Ara	S	July	Libra	E	June
Aries	E	Dec.	Lupus	E	June
Auriga	E	Feb.	Lynx	N	Feb.
Boötes	E	June	Lyra	E	Aug.
Cælum	E	Jan.	Mensa	S	Jan.
Camelopardalis	N	March	Microscopium	E	Sept.
			Monoceros	E	March
Cancer	E	March	Musca	S	May
Canes			Norma	S	July
Venatici	E	May	Octans	S	.....
Canis Major	E	Feb.	Ophiuchus	S	July
Canis Minor	E	March	Orion	E	Jan.
Capricornus	E	Sept.	Pavo	S	Aug.
Carina	S	March	Pegasus	E	Oct.
Cassiopeia	N	Nov.	Perseus	N	Dec.
Centaurus	E	May	Phœnix	S	Nov.
Cepheus	N	Nov.	Pictor	S	Jan.
Cetus	E	Dec.	Pisces	E	Nov.
Chameleon	S	April	Piscis		
Columba	E	Feb.	Austrinus	E	Oct.
Coma			Puppis	E	Feb.
Berenices	E	May	Pyxis	E	March
Corona			Reticulum	S	Jan.
Australis	E	Aug.	Sagitta	E	Aug.
Corona			Sagittarius	E	Aug.
Borealis	E	July	Scorpius	E	July
Corvus	E	May	Sculptor	E	Nov.
Crater	E	April	Scutum	E	Aug.
Crux	S	May	Serpens	E	July
Cygnus	E	Sept.	Sextans	E	April
Delphinus	E	Sept.	Taurus	E	Jan.
Dorado	S	Jan.	Telescopium	S	Aug.
Draco	N	June	Triangulum	E	Dec.
Equuleus	E	Sept.	Triangulum		
Eridanus	E	Dec.	Australe	S	July
Fornax	E	Dec.	Tucana	S	Oct.
Gemini	E	Feb.	Ursa Major	N	April
Grus	S	Oct.	Ursa Minor	N	.....
Hercules	E	July	Vela	E	March
Horologium	S	Dec.	Virgo	E	June
Hydra	E	April	Volans	S	March
Hydrus	S	Dec.	Vulpecula	E	Sept.

The four constellations Carina, Puppis, Pyxis, and Vela were formerly considered as a single one, called Argo Navis.

---

con·ster·na·tion (kon'stər-nā'shən) *n.* Complete confusion or dismay. [< L *consternare* to stretch out, perplex] — **Syn.** amazement, astonishment, shock, distraction.

con·sti·pate (kon'stə-pāt) *v.t.* **·pat·ed, ·pat·ing** To cause constipation in. [< L *com-* together + *stipare* press, crowd] —**con'sti·pat'ed** *adj.*

con·sti·pa·tion (kon'stə-pā'shən) *n.* Infrequent or difficult evacuation of the bowels.

con·stit·u·en·cy (kən-stich'o͞o-ən-sē) *n. pl.* **·cies** **1** The voters or residents in an electoral district. **2** An electoral district.

con·stit·u·ent (kən-stich'o͞o-ənt) *adj.* **1** Serving to form or compose as a necessary part; constituting. **2** Entitled to

vote for a public officer or representative. **3** Having the power to frame or modify a constitution. —*n.* **1** One represented politically; a voter. **2** An essential part; a component. [< L *constituere*. See CONSTITUTE.]

con·sti·tute (kon'stə-to͞ot) *v.t.* **·tut·ed, ·tut·ing** **1** To form or be the substance of; make up. **2** To establish or found, as a school. **3** To set up or enact, as a law. **4** To depute or appoint, as to an office or function. [< L *constituere* < *com-* together + *statuere* place, station] —**con'sti·tut'er** *n.*

con·sti·tu·tion (kon'stə-tyo͞o'shən) *n.* **1** The act of constituting. **2** A system of related parts; composition, esp. bodily make-up. **3** The fundamental laws and practices that normally govern the operation of a state or association. **4** A document containing these laws. —**the Constitution** The document drawn up in 1787 containing the laws by which the United States of America is governed.

con·sti·tu·tion·al (kon'stə-tyo͞o'shən-əl) *adj.* **1** Of, inherent in, or affecting the constitution of a person or thing. **2** Acting under and controlled by a constitution: a *constitutional* monarchy. **3** Loyal to the constitution of a government. **4** For one's health. —*n.* A walk taken for one's health. —**con·sti·tu·tion·al·i·ty** (kon'stə-tyo͞o'shən-al'ə-tē) *n.* —**con'sti·tu'tion·al·ly** *adv.*

constr. construction, construed.

con·strain (kən-strān') *v.t.* **1** To compel; oblige. **2** To confine, as by bonds. **3** To restrain. [< L *com-* together + *stringere* bind tight] —**con·strain'a·ble** *adj.* —**con·strain'er** *n.*

con·strained (kən-strānd') *adj.* Resulting from constraint; compulsory. —**con·strain'ed·ly** (-strā'nid-lē) *adv.*

con·straint (kən-strānt') *n.* **1** The act of constraining or the state of being constrained. **2** Embarrassment. **3** Anything that constrains.

con·strict (kən-strikt') *v.t.* To compress or draw together at some point; bind. [< L *constrictus,* pp. of *constringere* to bind together] —**con·stric'tive** *adj.*

con·stric·tion (kən-strik'shən) *n.* **1** A constricting. **2** That which constricts or is constricted. **3** A feeling of tightness, as in the chest.

con·stric·tor (kən-strik'tər) *n.* **1** That which constricts. **2** A muscle which contracts a part or organ of the body. **3** A snake that crushes its prey by coiling around it and squeezing.

con·struct (kən-strukt') *v.t.* To put together and set up; build. —*n.* (kon'strukt) Anything systematically constructed or composed from simple elements, as a concept. [< L *constructus,* pp. of *construere* See CONSTRUE.] —**con·struct'er,** **con·struc'tor** *n.*

con·struc·tion (kən-struk'shən) *n.* **1** The act of constructing. **2** That which is constructed. **3** Style of building or composing. **4** An interpretation arrived at or deduced. **5** The arrangement of grammatical forms, as in sentences. —**con·struc'tion·al** *adj.*

con·struc·tion·ist (kən-struk'shən-ist) *n.* One who explains or interprets an instrument, as the Constitution, in a specified manner: a strict *constructionist.*

con·struc·tive (kən-struk'tiv) *adj.* **1** Involving the act or process of construction. **2** Tending toward or resulting in positive conclusions; affirmative. **3** *Law* Assumed or inferred. —**con·struc'tive·ly** *adv.* —**con·struc'tive·ness** *n.*

con·strue (kən-stro͞o') *v.* **·strued, ·stru·ing** *v.t.* **1** To analyze the grammatical structure of (a clause or sentence) so as to determine the use and function of each word. **2** To translate orally. **3** To explain or interpret the meaning of. —*v.i.* **4** To construe a clause or sentence, esp. in translating. [< L *com-* together + *struere* build up] —**con·stru'a·ble** *adj.* —**con·stru'er** *n.*

con·sul (kon'səl) *n.* **1** An officer appointed to reside in a foreign city, chiefly as a representative of his country's commercial interests. **2** Either of two chief magistrates ruling in Ancient Rome. **3** Any of the three chief magistrates of the French republic, 1799-1804. [< L] —**con·su·lar** *adj.* —**con'sul·ship** *n.*

con·su·late (kon'sə-lit) *n.* **1** The offices and residence of a consul. **2** The position, duties and authority of a consul. **3** A consul's term of office.

consul general *pl.* **consuls general** A consular officer of the first rank.

con·sult (kən-sult') *v.t.* **1** To ask advice or information of.

2 To consider. —*v.i.* **3** To ask advice. **4** To compare views: with *with.* [< L *consultare,* freq. of *consulere* seek advice] —con·sult′a·ble *adj.* —con·sult′er *n.*

con·sult·ant (kən·sul′tənt) *n.* **1** A person referred to for expert or professional advice. **2** One who consults.

con·sul·ta·tion (kon′səl·tā′shən) *n.* **1** The act of consulting. **2** A meeting for conference.

con·sume (kən·sΰōm′) *v.* ·sumed, ·sum·ing *v.t.* **1** To destroy, as by burning. **2** To eat or drink up. **3** To squander; use up, as money or time. **4** To hold the interest of; engross. —*v.i.* **5** To be wasted or destroyed. [< L *com-* thoroughly + *sumere* take up, use] —con·sum′a·ble *adj.*

con·sum·er (kən·sΰōm′ər) *n.* **1** One who or that which consumes. **2** One who uses economic goods or services.

con·sum·er·ism (kən·sΰōm′ər·iz′əm) *n.* The policy or program of protecting the interests of the consumer. [< CONSUMER + -ISM, on analogy with *capitalism,* etc.] —con·sum′er·ist *adj., n.*

con·sum·mate (kon′sə·māt) *v.t.* ·mat·ed, ·mat·ting **1** To bring to completion or perfection; achieve. **2** To fulfill, as a marriage by the first act of sexual intercourse. —*adj.* (kən·sum′it) Of the highest degree; perfect. [< L *com-* together + *summa* sum, total] —con·sum′mate·ly *adv.* —con′sum·ma′tion, con′sum·ma′tor *n.* —con′sum·ma′tive *adj.*

con·sump·tion (kən·sump′shən) *n.* **1** The act or process of consuming. **2** The amount used up. **3** The using up of goods by consumers. **4** A wasting disease; specifically, pulmonary tuberculosis.

con·sump·tive (kən·sump′tiv) *adj.* **1** Tending to, causing, or designed for consumption. **2** Connected with or affected by pulmonary tuberculosis. —*n.* A person affected with pulmonary tuberculosis. —con·sump′tive·ly *adv.* —con·sump′tive·ness *n.*

cont. containing; contents; continent; continued.

con·tact (kon′takt) *n.* **1** The coming together, meeting, or touching of two bodies. **2** *Electr.* **a** The touching or joining of points or surfaces of conductors, permitting the passage or flow of a current. **b** One of two or more conductors that touch in this way. **3** Immediate proximity or association. **4** A useful or helpful acquaintance. —*v.t.* **1** To bring or place in contact; touch. **2** *Informal* To get or be in touch with (a person); communicate with. —*v.i.* **3** To be or come in contact. [< L *com-* together + *tangere* touch]

contact lens A thin, corrective lens of hard or soft plastic that fits against the eyeball.

contact print *Phot.* A positive print obtained by exposure of a photosensitive surface in direct contact with the negative.

con·ta·gion (kən·tā′jən) *n.* **1** The communication of disease by contact, direct or indirect. **2** A disease communicated in this way. **3** The medium of transmission of a disease. **4** A poison. **5** The transmission of an emotion, idea, etc., from person to person. [< L < *contingere*]

con·ta·gious (kən·tā′jəs) *adj.* **1** Transmissible by contact, as a disease. **2** Transmitting disease; pestilential. **3** Communicable from one person to another; catching; spreading. —con·ta′gious·ly *adv.* —con·ta′gious·ness *n.*

con·tain (kən·tān′) *v.t.* **1** To hold or enclose. **2** To include or comprise. **3** To be able to hold. **4** To keep within bounds; restrain. **5** *Math.* To have as an exact factor. [< L *com-* together + *tenere* hold] —con·tain′a·ble *adj.* —con·tain′er *n.*

con·tain·er·i·za·tion (kən·tān′ər·i·zā′shən) *n.* The packing and shipping of freight in very large, sealed containers. —con·tain′er·ized *adj.*

con·tain·er·ship (kən·tān′ər·ship′) *n.* A ship equipped to handle containerized cargo. Also container ship.

con·tain·ment (kən·tān′mənt) *n.* The forestalling or offsetting of territorial or ideological extension by an inimical power.

con·tam·i·nate (kən·tam′ə·nāt) *v.t.* ·nat·ed, ·nat·ing To make impure by contact or admixture. [< L *com-* together + *tangere* touch] —con·tam′i·nant, con·tam′i·na′tion, con·tam′i·na′tor *n.* —con·tam′i·na′tive *adj.* —Syn. taint, defile, pollute, debase.

contd. continued.

con·temn (kən·tem′) *v.t.* To despise; scorn. [< L *com-*

thoroughly + *temnere* slight, scorn] —con·temn·er (kən·tem′ər, -tem′nər), con·tem·nor (kən·tem′nər) *n.*

con·tem·plate (kon′təm·plāt) *v.* ·plat·ed, ·plat·ing *v.t.* **1** To look at attentively; gaze at. **2** To consider thoughtfully; ponder. **3** To intend or plan. **4** To treat as possible. —*v.i.* **5** To meditate; muse. [< L *contemplari* < *com-* together + *templum* temple; with ref. to the art of divination] —con·tem·pla·ble (kən·tem′plə·bəl) *adj.* —con′tem·pla′tion, con′tem·pla′tor *n.*

con·tem·pla·tive (kən·tem′plə·tiv, kon′təm·plā′-) *adj.* Of or given to contemplating; meditative, thoughtful, etc. —con′tem·pla′tive·ly *adv.*

con·tem·po·ra·ne·ous (kən·tem′pə·rā′nē·əs) *adj.* Living or occurring at the same time. [< L *com-* together + *tempus, temporis* time] —con·tem·po·ra·ne·i·ty (kən·tem′pə·rə·nē′ə·tē), con·tem′po·ra′ne·ous·ness *n.* —con·tem′po·ra′ne·ous·ly *adv.*

con·tem·po·rar·y (kən·tem′pə·rer′ē) *adj.* **1** Contemporaneous. **2** Having the same age. **3** Modern. —*n. pl.* ·rar·ies A person or thing that is contemporary.

con·tempt (kən·tempt′) *n.* **1** Disdain; scorn. **2** *Law* Willful disregard of authority, as of a court. **3** The state of being despised; disgrace; shame. [< L *contemptus* < *contemnere* despise, disdain. See CONTEMN.]

con·tempt·i·ble (kən·temp′tə·bəl) *adj.* Deserving of contempt; despicable; vile. —con·tempt′i·bil′i·ty, con·tempt′i·ble·ness *n.* —con·tempt′i·bly *adv.*

con·temp·tu·ous (kən·temp′chōō·əs) *adj.* Disdainful; scornful. —con·temp′tu·ous·ly *adv.* —con·temp′tu·ous·ness *n.*

con·tend (kən·tend′) *v.t.* **1** To maintain or assert in argument. —*v.i.* **2** To debate earnestly; dispute. **3** To strive in competition: to *contend* for a prize. **4** To struggle or fight in opposition or combat. [< L *com-* together + *tendere* strive, strain] —con·tend′er *n.*

con·tent¹ (kon′tent) *n.* **1** *Usu. pl.* All that a thing contains or deals with. **2** The significance or basic meaning, as of a literary work. **3** Holding capacity; size. **4** Included area or space. **5** The quantity of a specified part: the silver *content* of a ton of ore. [< L *continere* contain]

con·tent² (kən·tent′) *adj.* Satisfied with things as they are. —*v.t.* To satisfy. —*n.* Contentment; satisfaction. [< L *continere* contain]

con·tent·ed (kən·ten′tid) *adj.* Satisfied; content. —con·tent′ed·ly *adv.* —con·tent′ed·ness *n.*

con·ten·tion (kən·ten′shən) *n.* **1** The act of contending; strife, conflict, struggle, dispute, argument, etc. **2** An object or point in debate or controversy.

con·ten·tious (kən·ten′shəs) *adj.* **1** Of, pertaining to, or fond of contention; quarrelsome. **2** Full of or marked by contention. —con·ten′tious·ly *adv.* —con·ten′tious·ness *n.*

con·tent·ment (kən·tent′mənt) *n.* The condition or fact of being content.

con·ter·mi·nous (kən·tûr′mə·nəs) *adj.* **1** Having a common boundary line. **2** Having the same boundaries. [< L *com-* together + *terminus* limit]

con·test (kon′test) *n.* **1** A struggle to determine a winner; a competition. **2** Verbal conflict; controversy. —*v.t.* (kən·test′) **1** To fight about; contend for; strive to win, keep, or control. **2** To argue about or challenge: to *contest* an election. —*v.i.* **3** To contend, struggle, or vie: with *with* or *against.* [< L *contestari* bring legal action against] —con·test′a·ble *adj.* —con·test′er *n.*

con·test·ant (kən·tes′tənt) *n.* One who enters a contest; a competitor.

con·text (kon′tekst) *n.* The portions of a discourse, treatise, etc., preceding and following a passage quoted or considered. [< L *com-* together + *texere* weave] —con·tex·tu·al (kən·teks′chōō·əl) *adj.* —con·tex′tu·al·ly *adv.*

con·ti·gu·i·ty (kon′tə·gyōō′ə·tē) *n.* The state of being contiguous.

con·tig·u·ous (kən·tig′yōō·əs) *adj.* **1** Touching or joining at the edge or boundary. **2** Adjacent; close. [< L *contingere* to contact] —con·tig′u·ous·ly *adv.* —con·tig′u·ous·ness *n.*

con·ti·nence (kon′tə·nəns) *n.* **1** Self-restraint; **2** Moderation, esp. in sexual passion; chastity. Also con′ti·nen·cy.

con·ti·nent (kon′tə·nənt) *n.* One of the great bodies of land on the globe, generally regarded as Africa, Antarctica, Asia, Australia, Europe, North America, and South America. —**the Continent** Europe, exclusive of the British Isles. —*adj.* Self-restrained; abstinent; chaste. [<L *continere* contain] —**con·ti·nen·tal** (kon′tə·nen′təl) *adj.* —**con′ti·nent·ly** *adv.*

Con·ti·nen·tal (kon′tə·nen′təl) *adj.* 1 European. 2 Pertaining to the United States during the Revolutionary War. —*n.* 1 A European. 2 A soldier of the regular forces under the control of Congress in the Revolutionary War. 3 A note of the rapidly depreciated paper money issued by Congress during the Revolution.

Continental Congress Either of two American legislative assemblies convened during the period 1774–1781.

Continental Divide In North America, the great ridge of Rocky Mountain summits separating westward-flowing streams from eastward-flowing streams.

continental drift *Geol.* The gradual alteration of the relative position of the land masses of the earth.

continental shelf *Geog.* The submerged border of a continent, of varying width and degree of slope, which separates the land mass from the ocean depths.

con·tin·gen·cy (kən·tin′jən·sē) *n. pl.* ·**cies** 1 The condition of being contingent. 2 An unexpected, possible, or chance occurrence or condition. 3 Something incidental.

con·tin·gent (kən·tin′jənt) *adj.* 1 Not certain to happen; possible. 2 Accidental; fortuitous. 3 Dependent upon an uncertain occurrence or condition. —*n.* A contingency. 2 A representational group: the American *contingent* at the conference. 3 A quota of troops, laborers, etc. [<L *contingere* to contact] —**con·tin′gent·ly** *adv.*

con·tin·u·al (kən·tin′yo̅o̅·əl) *adj.* 1 Renewed in regular succession; often repeated. 2 Continuous (in time); uninterrupted. —**con·tin′u·al·ly** *adv.* • In careful usage *continual* refers to that which happens at intervals, *continuous* to that which goes on without interruption: the *continual* ticking of a clock; a *continuous* flow of oil.

con·tin·u·ance (kən·tin′yo̅o̅·əns) *n.* 1 The act of continuing. 2 The time during which something lasts; duration. 3 Uninterrupted succession. 4 A postponement of court proceedings to a future date. 5 A sequel, as of a novel.

con·tin·u·a·tion (kən·tin′yo̅o̅·ā′shən) *n.* 1 The act or state of continuing. 2 Something which continues, extends, increases, or carries on.

con·tin·ue (kən·tin′yo̅o̅) *v.* ·**tin·ued**, ·**tin·u·ing** *v.t.* 1 To extend or prolong in space or time. 2 To persist in. 3 To cause to last or remain, as in a position or office. 4 To take up again after an interruption. 5 *Law* To postpone, as a judicial proceeding. —*v.i.* 6 To last; endure. 7 To keep on or persist. 8 To remain, as in a place or position. 9 To resume after an interruption. 10 To extend. [<L *continere* hold together, contain] —**con·tin′u·a·ble** *adj.* —**con·tin′u·er** *n.*

con·ti·nu·i·ty (kon′tə·n̄o̅o̅′ə·tē) *n.* 1 The state or quality of being continuous. 2 That which has or exhibits such a state or quality; an unbroken sequence or whole.

con·tin·u·ous (kən·tin′yo̅o̅·əs) *adj.* Connected, extended, prolonged, or going on without a break. —**con·tin′u·ous·ly** *adv.* —**con·tin′u·ous·ness** *n.* • See CONTINUAL.

con·tin·u·um (kən·tin′yo̅o̅·əm) *n. pl.* ·**tin·u·a** (-tin′yo̅o̅·ə) 1 A total that is continuous and uninterrupted. 2 *Math.* A set of numbers or points such that between any two of them a third may be interpolated.

con·tort (kən·tôrt′) *v.t.* To twist or wrench out of shape or place. [<L *com-* together + *torquere* twist] —**con·tor′tion** *n.* —**con·tor′tive** *adj.* —Syn. bend, distort, deform.

con·tor·tion·ist (kən·tôr′shən·ist) *n.* An acrobat trained to contort his limbs into unusual positions.

con·tour (kon′to̅o̅r) *n.* The line bounding a figure, land, etc.; outline. —*v.t.* To make or draw in outline or contour. —*adj.* Following the contour lines of land so as to avoid erosion. [<LL *com-* together + *tornare* make round]

Contour map

contour map A map designed to show the comparative elevation of topographic features.

contr. contract; contraction; control.

con·tra (kon′trə, kôn′-) *n.* A rebel counter- revolutionary, especially in Central America; guerrilla. [<Sp. *contra(revolucionario)*]

contra- *prefix* Against; opposite: *contraception*. [<L *contra* against]

con·tra·band (kon′trə·band) *adj.* Forbidden or excluded, as by law or treaty. —*n.* 1 Illegal or forbidden trade. 2 Contraband goods. 3 CONTRABAND OF WAR. [< LL *contra* against + *bannum* law, proclamation] —**con′·tra·band′ist** *n.*

contraband of war Anything furnished by a neutral to a belligerent that is by the laws of war subject to seizure.

con·tra·bass (kon′trə·bās) *n.* DOUBLE BASS. —*adj.* Having its pitch an octave lower than a bass instrument of the same class; of deeper range: a *contrabass* horn.

con·tra·bas·soon (kon′trə·bə·so̅o̅n′) *n.* DOUBLE BASSOON.

con·tra·cep·tion (kon′trə·sep′shən) *n.* The prevention of conception. [<CONTRA- + (CON)CEPTION]

con·tra·cep·tive (kon′trə·sep′tiv) *adj.* 1 Used to prevent conception. 2 Of or pertaining to contraception. —*n.* Any device or substance that inhibits conception.

con·tract (kən·trakt′ *for v. defs. 1, 3–6;* kon′trakt, kən·trakt′ *for v. def. 2) v.t.* 1 To reduce in size; shrink; narrow. 2 To arrange or settle by agreement; enter upon with reciprocal obligations. 3 To acquire or become affected with, as a disease or habit. 4 To shorten, as a word, by omitting or combining medial letters or sounds. —*v.i.* 5 To shrink. 6 To make a contract. —*n.* (kon′trakt) 1 An agreement between two or more parties, esp. when legally enforceable. 2 A formal document containing the terms of such an agreement. 3 The act of marriage. 4 A formal agreement of marriage; betrothal. 5 CONTRACT BRIDGE. 6 The highest bid in a hand of contract bridge. [<L *contractus*, pp. of *contrahere* pull together] —**con·tract′ed** *adj.* —**con·tract′i·bil′i·ty** *n.* **con·tract′a·ble** *adj.*

contract bridge A form of bridge in which the declarer, if successful, scores toward game only the tricks named in the bid.

con·trac·tile (kən·trak′təl) *adj.* Having the power to contract or inducing contraction. —**con·trac·til·i·ty** (kən·trak′til′ə·tē) *n.*

con·trac·tion (kən·trak′shən) *n.* 1 The act of contracting or the state of being contracted. 2 That which is contracted, as a word. 3 A shortening and thickening of a muscle in action.

con·trac·tor (kon′trak·tər, kən·trak′-) *n.* 1 One of the parties to a contract. 2 One who agrees to supply labor or materials or both.

con·trac·tu·al (kən·trak′cho̅o̅·əl) *adj.* Of, pertaining to, or implying a contract. —**con·trac′tu·al·ly** *adv.*

con·tra·dict (kon′trə·dikt′) *v.t.* 1 To maintain the opposite of (a statement); deny. 2 To be inconsistent with or opposed to. 3 To disagree with (someone). —*v.i.* 4 To dispute, deny, or maintain the opposite of something. [<L *contra-* against + *dicere* say, speak] —**con′tra·dict′a·ble, con′tra·dic′tive** *adj.* —**con′tra·dict′er** or **con′tra·dic′tor, con′·tra·dic′tion** *n.*

con·tra·dic·to·ry (kon′trə·dik′tər·ē) *adj.* 1 Involving or of the nature of a contradiction. 2 Given or inclined to contradiction. —**con′tra·dic′to·ri·ly** *adv.*

con·tra·dis·tinc·tion (kon′trə·dis·tingk′shən) *n.* Distinction by contrast or by contrasting qualities. —**con′·tra·dis′tinc′tive** *adj.*

con·trail (kon′trāl) *n.* The vapor trail sometimes left by an airplane flying at high altitudes, caused by the condensation of moisture from exhaust gases. [<CON(DENSATION) + TRAIL]

con·tra·in·di·cate (kon′trə·in′də·kāt) *v.t.* ·**cat·ed**, ·**cat·ing** *Med.* To make (a given drug or method of treatment) dangerous or inadvisable. —**con′tra·in′di·ca′tion** *n.*

con·tral·to (kən·tral′tō) *n. pl.* ·**tos** or ·**ti** (-tē) 1 The lowest female voice, intermediate between soprano and tenor. 2 A part written for such a voice. 3 A singer with such a voice. —*adj.* Of or for a contralto. [<Ital.]

con·trap·tion (kən·trap′shən) *n. Informal* A contrivance or gadget. [?<CONTRIVE]

con·tra·pun·tal (kon′trə-pun′təl) *adj.* 1 Of, pertaining to, or according to the rules of counterpoint. 2 Characterized by the use of counterpoint. [< Ital. *contrapunto* counterpoint] —**con′tra·pun′tal·ly** *adv.* —**con′tra·pun′tist** *n.*

con·trar·i·wise (kon′trer-ē-wīz′; *for def. 3, also* kən-trâr′ē-wīz′) *adv.* 1 On the contrary; on the other hand. 2 In the reverse order; conversely. 3 In a contrary manner.

con·trar·y (kon′trer-ē; *for adj. def. 4, also* kən-trâr′ē) *adj.* 1 Totally different; opposed. 2 Adverse: *contrary* winds. 3 Opposite or other. 4 Inclined to opposition or contradiction; perverse —*n. pl.* **·trar·ies** 1 One of two opposing things. 2 The opposite. —**on the contrary** 1 On the other hand. 2 Just the opposite of what has been said. —**to the contrary** To the opposite effect. —*adv.* In a contrary manner. [< L *contra* against] —**con′trar·i·ly** *adv.* —**con′trar·i·ness** *n.*

con·trast (kən-trast′) *v.t.* 1 To place or set in opposition so as to show dissimilarities. —*v.i.* 2 To show dissimilarities when set in opposition. —*n.* (kon′trast) 1 The dissimilarity between two or more things or persons, as revealed by comparison. 2 A person or thing that contrasts with another. [< L *contra-* against + *stare* stand] —**con′trast′a·ble** *adj.*

con·tra·vene (kon′trə-vēn′) *v.t.* **·vened, ·ven·ing** 1 To act against or infringe upon, as a law. 2 To argue or disagree with. [< L *contra-* against + *venire* come] —**con′tra·ven′er, con·tra·ven·tion** (kon′trə-ven′shən) *n.* —**Syn.** 1 disregard, violate, disobey, defy. 2 dispute, contradict, contest, refute.

con·tre·danse (kôṅ′trə-däṅs′) *n.* COUNTRY-DANCE. Also **con·tre·dance** (kon′trə-dans′, -däns′). [< Alter. of COUNTRY-DANCE]

con·tre·temps (kôṅ′trə-taṅ′) *n. pl.* **·temps** (-täṅz′, *Fr.* -täṅ′) An embarrassing occurrence; awkward incident. [F, lit., against time]

con·trib·ute (kən-trib′yo͞ot) *v.* **·ut·ed, ·ut·ing** *v.t.* 1 To give or furnish (money, ideas, etc.), as for a common purpose. 2 To furnish, as an article or story, to a magazine or other publication. —*v.i.* 3 To share in effecting a result. 4 To make or give a contribution. [< L *com-* together + *tribuere* grant, allot] —**con·trib′ut·a·ble, con·trib′u·tive** *adj.* —**con·trib′u·tive·ly** *adv.* —**con·trib′u·tive·ness, con·trib′u·tor** *n.*

con·tri·bu·tion (kon′trə-byo͞o′shən) *n.* 1 The act of contributing. 2 Something contributed, as money, knowledge, etc. —**con′tri·bu′tion·al** *adj.*

con·trib·u·to·ry (kən-trib′yə-tôr′ē, -tō′rē) *adj.* 1 Contributing, as toward a result or action. 2 Involving or like a contribution. —*n. pl.* **·ries** One who or that which contributes.

con·trite (kən-trīt′, kon′trīt) *adj.* 1 Remorseful or guilty because of one's sins or shortcomings. 2 Proceeding from or showing remorse or guilt. [< L *contritus* bruised, pp. of *conterere* to rub together] —**con·trite′ly** *adv.* —**con·trite′·ness, con·tri′tion** (-trish′ən) *n.*

con·tri·vance (kən-trī′vəns) *n.* 1 The act or manner of contriving. 2 Something contrived, as a device, tool, etc.

con·trive (kən-trīv′) *v.* **·trived, ·triv·ing** *v.t.* 1 To scheme or plan; devise. 2 To plot or conspire. 3 To make ingeniously; improvise; invent. 4 To manage or carry through, as by some device or scheme. —*v.i.* 5 To plan or plot. [< LL *contropare* represent figuratively] —**con·triv′a·ble** *adj.* —**con·triv′er** *n.*

con·trived (kən-trīvd′) *adj.* Overly planned or ingenious; artificial; labored.

con·trol (kən-trōl′) *v.t.* **·trolled, ·trol·ling** 1 To exercise authority over; govern. 2 To restrain; curb. 3 To direct, guide, or regulate, as a machine. 4 To verify, as an experiment, by comparison with a parallel experiment or other standard. 5 To check, as an account, by means of a duplicate register; verify or rectify. —*n.* 1 The act of controlling. 2 The power or ability to govern, regulate, or direct. 3 The condition of being controlled: The machine was out of *control.* 4 Something that directs, guides, or regulates, as a mechanical device. 5 A standard of comparison against which to check the results of an experiment. [< Med. L *contrarotulus* a check list < L *contra-* against +

rotulus list] —**con·trol′la·bil′i·ty, con·trol′la·ble·ness** *n.* —**con·trol′la·ble** *adj.*

con·trol·ler (kən-trō′lər) *n.* 1 One who or that which controls. 2 An officer to examine and verify accounts; comptroller. —**con·trol′ler·ship** *n.*

con·tro·ver·sial (kon′trə-vûr′shəl) *adj.* 1 Of, causing, or characterized by controversy. 2 Given to controversy; disputatious. —**con′tro·ver′sial·ist** *n.* —**con′tro·ver′sial·ly** *adv.*

con·tro·ver·sy (kon′trə-vûr′sē) *n. pl.* **·sies** 1 Debate or disputation arising from conflicting attitudes and opinions. 2 A quarrel or dispute. [< L *contra-* against + *versus,* pp. of *vertere* turn]

con·tro·vert (kon′trə-vûrt, kon′trə-vûrt′) *v.t.* 1 To endeavor to disprove; argue against. 2 To argue about. [< L *controversus* turned against] —**con′tro·vert′er** *n.* —**con′tro·vert′i·ble** *adj.* —**con′tro·vert′i·bly** *adv.*

con·tu·ma·cy (kon′t^yo͞o-mə-sē) *n. pl.* **·cies** Contemptuous disregard of authority; insolent and stubborn disobedience. Also **con·tu·mac·i·ty** (kon′t^yo͞o-mas′ə-tē). [< L *contumax* stubborn] —**con·tu·ma·cious** (kon′t^yo͞o-mā′shəs) *adj.* —**con′tu·ma′cious·ly** *adv.* —**con′tu·ma′cious·ness** *n.*

con·tu·me·ly (kon′t^yo͞o-mə-lē, -mē′lē; kən-t^yo͞o′mə-lē) *n. pl.* **·lies** 1 Insulting rudeness in speech or manner; scornful insolence. 2 An example of this. [< L *contumelia* reproach] —**con·tu·me·li·ous** (kon′t^yo͞o-mē′lē-əs) *adj.* —**con′tu·me′li·ous·ly** *adv.* —**con′tu·me′li·ous·ness** *n.*

con·tuse (kən-t^yo͞oz′) *v.t.* **·tused, ·tus·ing** To bruise by a blow. [< L *com-* together + *tundere* beat] —**con·tu·sive** (kən-t^yo͞o′siv) *adj.*

con·tu·sion (kən-t^yo͞o′zhən) *n.* A bruise.

co·nun·drum (kə-nun′drəm) *n.* 1 A riddle, often depending on a pun. 2 Any perplexing question or thing. [?]

con·va·lesce (kon′və-les′) *v.i.* **·lesced ·lesc·ing** To regain health after illness. [< L *com-* thoroughly + *valere* be strong] —**con·va·les·cent** (kon′və-les′ənt) *adj., n.*

con·va·les·cence (kon′və-les′əns) *n.* 1 Gradual recovery from illness. 2 The period of such recovery. Also **con′va·les′cen·cy.**

con·vec·tion (kən-vek′shən) *n.* 1 The act of conveying. 2 *Physics* **a** The diffusion of heat through a liquid or gas by motion of its parts. **b** A process whereby atmospheric circulation is maintained through the transfer of air masses of different temperature. [< L *convectus,* pp. of *convehere* carry together] —**con·vec′tion·al, con·vec′tive** *adj.* —**con·vec′tive·ly** *adv.* —**con·vec′tor** *n.*

con·vene (kən-vēn′) *v.* **·vened, ·ven·ing** *v.t.* 1 To cause to assemble; convoke. 2 To summon to appear, as by judicial authority. —*v.i.* 3 To assemble. [< L *com-* together + *venire* come] —**con·ven′a·ble** *adj.* —**con·ven′er** *n.*

con·ven·ience (kən-vēn′yəns) *n.* 1 The quality of being convenient. 2 Personal comfort and ease. 3 Something which gives ease or comfort, as a labor-saving device.

con·ven·ient (kən-vēn′yənt) *adj.* 1 Conducive to comfort or ease; serviceable; handy. 2 Easy to get to; nearby. [< L *convenire.* See CONVENE.] —**con·ven′ient·ly** *adv.*

con·vent (kon′vent, -vənt) *n.* 1 A religious community, esp. of nuns. 2 The building or buildings occupied by such a body. [< L *conventus* meeting]

con·ven·ti·cle (kən-ven′ti·kəl) *n.* 1 A religious meeting, esp. a secret one. 2 The building in which such meetings are held. [< L *conventus.* See CONVENT.] —**con·ven′ti·cler** *n.*

con·ven·tion (kən-ven′shən) *n.* 1 A formal meeting of delegates, esp. for political or professional purposes. 2 The delegates themselves. 3 A generally accepted social custom or mode of behavior. 4 An established rule, form, or principle, as in art. 5 A formal agreement or compact.

con·ven·tion·al (kən-ven′shən-əl) *adj.* 1 Of or established by convention or custom; customary. 2 According to rule or custom; not natural, spontaneous, or unusual. 3 In art, stylized or simplified. 4 Nonnuclear: *conventional* warfare. 5 Of or pertaining to a convention of delegates. —**con·ven′tion·al·ism, con·ven′tion·al·ist** *n.* —**con·ven′tion·al·ly** *adv.*

con·ven·tion·al·i·ty (kən-ven·shən-al′ə-tē) *n. pl.* **·ties** 1 Adherence to established forms, customs, or usages. 2 A conventional act, principle, form, etc.

con·ven·tion·al·ize (kən·ven′shən·əl·īz) v.t. **·ized, ·iz·ing** **1** To make conventional. **2** Art To represent in a conventional manner. —**con·ven′tion·al·i·za′tion** n.

con·ven·tu·al (kən·ven′chōō·əl) adj. Belonging to a convent. —n. One who belongs to a convent.

con·verge (kən·vûrj′) v. **·verged, ·verg·ing** v.t. **1** To cause to tend toward one point. —v.i. **2** To move toward one point; come together by gradual approach. **3** To tend toward the same conclusion or result. [< L com- together + vergere bend]

con·ver·gence (kən·vûr′jəns) n. **1** The act or condition of converging. **2** Degree or point of convergence. Also **con·ver′gen·cy**. —**con·ver′gent** adj.

con·ver·sant (kon′vər·sənt, kən·vûr′sənt) adj. Familiar, as a result of study, experience, etc.: with with [< L conversari. See CONVERSE¹] —**con′ver·sant·ly** adv.

con·ver·sa·tion (kon′vər·sā′shən) n. **1** The informal, verbal exchange of ideas, information, etc. **2** An instance of such an exchange. —**con′ver·sa′tion·al** adj. —**con′ver·sa′tion·al·ly** adv. —Syn. 1,2 talk, communication, chat, dialogue.

con·ver·sa·tion·al·ist (kon′vər·sā′shən·əl·ist) n. A person skilled in conversation. Also **con′ver·sa′tion·ist**.

conversation piece Any article of furniture, decoration, etc., that arouses comment.

con·verse¹ (kən·vûrs′) v.i. **·versed, ·vers·ing** To speak together informally; engage in conversation. —n. (kon′· vûrs) **1** Conversation. **2** Close fellowship. [< L conversari, freq. of convertere to turn together] —**con·vers′a·ble** adj. —**con·vers′a·bly** adv. —**con·vers′er** n.

con·verse² (kən·vûrs′, kon′vûrs) adj. Turned about so that two parts are interchanged; transposed; reversed. —n. (kon′vûrs) That which exists in a converse relation; opposite. [< L convertere to turn around] —**con·verse·ly** (kən·vûrs′lē, kon′vûrs·lē) adv.

con·ver·sion (kən·vûr′zhən, -shən) n. **1** The act of converting, or the state of being converted, in any sense. **2** A change in one's opinions, way of life, etc., esp. the adoption of a religious belief. —**con·ver′sion·al** adj.

con·vert (kən·vûrt′) v.t. **1** To change into another state, form, or substance; transform. **2** To apply or adapt to a new or different purpose or use. **3** To change from one belief, doctrine, creed, opinion, or course of action to another. **4** To exchange for an equivalent value, as goods for money. **5** To exchange for value of another form, as preferred for common stock. **6** Law To assume possession of illegally. —v.i. **7** To become changed in character. **8** In football, to score the extra point after touchdown, as by kicking a field goal. —n. (kon′vûrt) A person who has been converted, as from one opinion, creed, etc., to another. [< L convertere to turn around]

con·vert·er (kən·vûr′tər) n. **1** One who or that which converts. **2** An apparatus for converting direct into alternating current. Also **con·ver′tor**.

con·vert·i·ble (kən·vûr′tə·bəl) adj. Capable of being converted. —n. **1** A convertible thing. **2** An automobile with a top that can be removed or folded back. —**con·vert′i·bil′· i·ty, con·vert′i·ble·ness** n. —**con·vert′i·bly** adv.

con·vex (kon·veks′, kon′veks) adj. Curving outward like a segment of a globe or of a circle viewed from outside; bulging out. —n. (kon′veks) A convex surface, body, line, etc. [< L convexus vaulted, curved] —**con·vex′i·ty, con· vex′ness** n. —**con·vex′ly** adv.

con·vey (kən·vā′) v.t. **1** To carry from one place to another; transport. **2** To serve as a medium or path for; transmit. **3** To make known or impart; communicate. **4** To transfer ownership of, as real estate. [< L com- together + via road, way] —**con·vey′· a·ble** adj.

a. convex lens. b. concave lens.

con·vey·ance (kən·vā′əns) n. **1** The act of conveying. **2** That by which anything is conveyed. **3** A vehicle. **4** Law **a** The transference of property ownership, esp. of real estate. **b** The document by which such transference is effected; deed. —**con·vey′anc·er, con·vey′anc·ing** n.

con·vey·er (kən·vā′ər) n. **1** One who or that which conveys. **2** A mechanical device, as a moving belt, that conveys materials. Also (esp. for def. 2) **con·vey′or** n.

con·vict (kən·vikt′) v.t. To prove or find guilty, esp. after a judicial trial. —n. (kon′vikt) One found guilty of or undergoing punishment for crime; a criminal. [< L convictus, pp. of convincere. See CONVINCE.] —**con·vic′tive** adj.

con·vic·tion (kən·vik′shən) n. **1** The act of convicting or the state of being convicted. **2** The act of convincing or the state of being convinced. **3** Something one firmly believes. **4** Fixed belief: He spoke with conviction. —**con·vic′tion·al** adj.

con·vince (kən·vins′) v.t. **·vinced, ·vinc·ing** To satisfy by evidence; persuade by argument. [< L com- thoroughly + vincere overcome, conquer] —**con·vinc′er** n. —**con·vinc′i·ble** adj.

con·vinc·ing (kən·vin′sing) adj. Having or marked by persuasive or satisfying evidence, arguments, or authority. —**con·vinc′ing·ly** adv.

con·viv·i·al (kən·viv′ē·əl) adj. Pertaining to or fond of feasting, drinking, or sociability; festive; jovial. [< L convivium a feast, banquet < com- together + vivere live] —**con·viv′i·al·ist, con·viv·i·al·i·ty** (kən·viv′ē·al′ə·tē) n. —**con· viv′i·al·ly** adv.

con·vo·ca·tion (kon′vō·kā′shən) n. **1** The act of summoning together an assembly. **2** The assembly thus summoned. [< L convocare. See CONVOKE.] —**con′vo·ca′tion·al** adj. —**con′vo·ca′tor** n.

con·voke (kən·vōk′) v.t. **·voked, ·vok·ing** To call together, as for a meeting. [< L com- together + vocare summon] — **con·vok′er** n. —Syn. summon, assemble, gather, muster.

con·vo·lute (kon′və·lōōt) adj. Rolled or coiled with one part turning inward upon another. —v.t. & v.i. **·lut·ed, ·lut·ing** To coil or twist around. [< L convolvere. See CON-VOLVE.] —**con′vo·lute′ly** adv.

con·vo·lu·tion (kon′və·lōō′shən) n. **1** The act of convolving. **2** The state of being convolved. **3** A coil, twist, or fold, esp. one of the folds of the surface of the brain.

con·volve (kən·volv′) v. **·volved, ·volv·ing** v.t. To roll, twist, or wind around something. —v.i. To turn or wind upon itself. [< L com- together + volvere spin, twist]

con·vol·vu·lus (kən·vol′vyə·ləs) n. Any of a genus of twining herbs, as the morning glory, with trumpet-shaped flowers. [< L, bindweed]

con·voy (kon′voi) n. **1** A protecting force, as for accompanying ships at sea. **2** A group of vehicles, ships, etc., traveling together for protection. **3** The act of convoying. [< MF convoi < convoyer] —v.t. (kən·voi′, kon′voi) To act as convoy to. [< L com- together + via road]

con·vulse (kən·vuls′) v.t. **·vulsed, ·vuls·ing** **1** To affect with violent movements; agitate violently. **2** To cause to laugh violently. [< L convulsus, pp. of convellere to pull together] —**con·vul′sive** (kən·vul′siv) adj. —**con·vul′sive·ly** adv. —**con·vul′sive·ness** n.

con·vul·sion (kən·vul′shən) n. **1** A violent and abnormal muscular contraction of the body; spasm; fit. **2** An uncontrollable fit of laughter. **3** Any violent disturbance. —**con· vul·sion·ar·y** (kən·vul′shən·er′ē) adj., n.

co·ny (kō′nē, kun′ē) n. pl. **co·nies** **1** A rabbit. **2** Rabbit fur. [< L cuniculus rabbit]

coo (kōō) v. **cooed, coo·ing** v.t. **1** To utter with the soft murmuring sound of a dove or pigeon. —v.i. **2** To utter the coo of a dove, or a similar sound. **3** To speak in low, amorous tones: to bill and coo. —n. A murmuring sound, as of a dove. [Imit.] —**coo′er** n. —**coo′ing·ly** adv.

cook (kōōk) v.t. **1** To prepare (foodstuff) for eating by the action of heat. **2** Slang To ruin. —v.i. **3** To do the work of a cook. **4** To undergo cooking. —**cook up** Informal To concoct or invent, as a plot. [< L coquere] —n. One who prepares food for eating. —**cook′er** n.

cook·book (kōōk′bōōk′) n. A book containing recipes and instructions for cooking.

cook·er·y (kōōk′ər·ē) n. pl. **·er·ies** **1** The art or practice of cooking. **2** A place for cooking.

cook·out (kōōk′out′) n. Informal A picnic at which the meal is cooked out-of-doors; also, the meal itself.

cook·y (kōōk′ē) n. pl. **cook·ies** A small, flat, usu. crisp sweet cake. Also **cook′ey, cook′ie.** [< Du. koek cake]

cool (kōōl) adj. **1** Not warm; somewhat cold. **2** Serving to produce the effect of coolness: cool colors; a cool dress. **3** Self-controlled; self-possessed. **4** Slang Not involved or committed emotionally; detached. **5** Not friendly; chilling.

6 *Informal* Actual; not exaggerated: a *cool* million dollars. **7** *Slang* Very good; well done. —*v.t.* **1** To make cool. **2** To allay, as passion; calm. —*v.i.* **3** To become cool. **4** To become less ardent, angry, zealous, etc. —**cool it** *Slang* To become less angry, excited, emotional, etc.; calm down. — *n.* **1** A time, place, etc. that is cool. **2** *Slang* Self-possession: to lose one's *cool*. [< OE *col*] —**cool'ish** *adj.* —**cool'ly** *adv.* —**cool'ness** *n.*

cool·ant (kōō'lənt) *n.* Any substance used as a cooling medium, as for an internal-combustion engine.

cool·er (kōō'lər) *n.* **1** That which cools, as a vessel to cool liquids. **2** *Slang* A jail.

coo·lie (kōō'lē) *n.* **1** In the Orient, an unskilled laborer. **2** Any such person doing heavy work for low wages. Also **coo'ly**. [Prob. < Hind. *Kuli*, an aboriginal Gujarat tribe]

coon (kōōn) *n.* RACCOON.

coop (kōōp, kŏŏp) *n.* **1** An enclosure, as for fowls or rabbits. **2** *Slang* A jail; prison. —**fly the coop** *Slang* To flee or escape. —*v.t.* To put into a coop; confine. [< MLG *kūpe* cask, basket]

co-op (kō'op, kō-op') *n.* *Informal* A cooperative enterprise, as for a store or apartment.

coop·er (kōō'pər, kŏŏp'ər) *n.* One who makes or mends casks, barrels, etc. —*v.t. & v.i.* To make or mend (casks, barrels, etc.) [? < MLG *kūpe* a cask]

coop·er·age (kōō'pər·ij, kŏŏp'ər-) *n.* The work of the cooper or the cost of such work.

co·op·er·ate (kō-op'ə·rāt) *v.i.* **·at·ed, ·at·ing** To work or operate together for a common purpose, effect, etc. —**co·op'er·a'tor** *n.*

co·op·er·a·tion (kō-op'ə·rā'shən) *n.* **1** Joint action or effort. **2** A union of laborers, farmers, small capitalists, etc., for mutual benefit. —**co·op'er·a'tion·ist** *n.*

co·op·er·a·tive (kō-op'ə·rə·tiv, -op'rə-, -op'ə·rā'tiv) *adj.* **1** Working together or inclined to work together. **2** Of, pertaining to, or set up as a cooperative. —*n.* An organization, store, apartment house, etc., owned in common by persons who use its services, facilities, etc. —**co·op'er·a·tive·ly** *adv.* —**co·op'er·a·tive·ness** *n.*

co·opt (kō-opt') *v.i.* **1** To elect to fill a vacant membership. **2** To take or win over. [< L *co-* together + *optare* choose] —**co·op·ta·tive** (kō-op'tə·tiv) *adj.* —**co·op'tion, co'op·ta'tion** *n.* —**Syn. 2** appropriate, preempt, assimilate, absorb, persuade, influence.

co·or·di·nate (kō-ôr'də·nit, -nāt) *adj.* **1** Of the same order, importance, or rank. **2** *Math.* Of or pertaining to coordinates. —*n.* **1** One who or that which is of the same order, rank, power, etc. **2** *Math.* Any of an ordered set of numbers that define the position of a point. —*v.* (kō-ôr'də·nāt) **·nat·ed, ·nat·ing** *v.t.* **1** To put in the same rank, class, or order. **2** To bring into harmonious relation or action. —*v.i.* **3** To be of the same order or rank. **4** To act in harmonious or reciprocal relation. [< L *co-* together + *ordinare* set in order] —**co·or'di·nate·ly** *adv.* —**co·or'di·nate·ness, co·or'di·na'tor** *n.* —**co·or'di·na'tive** *adj.*

co·or·di·na·tion (kō-ôr'də·nā'shən) *n.* **1** The act of coordinating. **2** The state of being coordinate. **3** The harmonious action of the various parts of a system.

coot (kōōt) *n.* **1** A dark, short-billed water bird. **2** *Informal* A simple-minded, usu. elderly fellow. [ME *cote*]

coot·ie (kōō'tē) *Slang* A body louse. [? < Indonesian *kutu*, parasitic insect]

cop (kop) *n.* *Informal* A policeman. —*v.t.* **copped, cop·ping** *Slang* **1** To steal. **2** To seize; take. —**cop out** *Slang* **1** To back down; renege. **2** To quit; give up. [Var. of *cap* to catch, take]

cop. copyright; copyrighted.

co·pal (kō'pəl) *n.* A hard, transparent resin exuded by various tropical trees, used in varnishes. [< Nah. *copalli* incense]

co·part·ner (kō-pärt'nər) *n.* An equal partner, as in a business. —**co·part'ner·ship** *n.*

cope¹ (kōp) *v.i.* **coped, cop·ing** To contend or deal successfully: often with *with*. [< OF *coup, colp* a blow < L *cola-phus*]

cope² (kōp) *n.* **1** A semicircular ecclesiastical mantle worn on ceremonial occasions. **2** Something that arches or forms a canopy overhead.

Co·per·ni·can (kō-pûr'nə·kən) *adj.* Of or pertaining to the astronomical theories of Copernicus, who stated that the earth revolves on its axis and, with the other planets, revolves around the sun.

cope·stone (kōp'stōn') *n.* **1** A top stone of a wall, as in a coping. **2** The finishing touch; culmination.

cop·i·er (kop'ē·ər) *n.* One who or that which copies.

co·pi·lot (kō'pī'lət) *n.* The assistant or relief pilot of an aircraft.

cop·ing (kō'ping) *n.* The top, usu. sloping course of a wall, roof, etc.

coping saw A narrow-bladed saw set in a frame and used for cutting curves in wood.

co·pi·ous (kō'pē·əs) *adj.* Ample in quantity; abundant. [< L *copia* abundance] —**co'pi·ous·ly** *adv.* —**co'pi·ous·ness** *n.* —**Syn.** plentiful, plenteous, profuse.

cop-out (kop'out') *n.* *Slang* An act of or excuse for copping out; a quitting or backing down.

cop·per¹ (kop'ər) *n.* **1** A heavy, reddish metallic element (symbol Cu) with high thermal and electrical conductivity. **2** A coin made of this metal. **3** *Brit.* A large metal vat or pot. **4** A reddish brown. —*v.t.* To coat with copper. [< L *(aes) cyprium* Cyprian (metal)] —**cop'per·y** *adj.*

cop·per² (kop'ər) *n.* *Slang* A policeman. [< COP]

cop·per·as (kop'ər·əs) *n.* A green ferrous sulfate used in dyeing, inkmaking, photography, etc. [< Med. L *(aqua) cuprosa* copper (water)]

cop·per·head (kop'ər·hed') *n.* A venomous North American snake with reddish brown markings.

Cop·per·head (kop'ər·hed') *n.* During the Civil War, a Northerner who sympathized with the Confederate States.

cop·per·plate (kop'ər·plāt') *n.* **1** An engraved or etched copper printing plate. **2** An impression printed from it.

cop·per·smith (kop'ər·smith') *n.* One who makes utensils of copper.

Copperhead

co·pra (kop'rə) *n.* Dried coconut meat, yielding coconut oil. Also **cop·per·ah** (kop'ər·ə), **cop'rah**. [< Malayalam *koppara*]

copse (kops) *n.* A thicket of small trees or bushes. Also **cop·pice** (kop'is) [< OF *coper* to cut]

Copt (kopt) *n.* **1** A native Egyptian descended from ancient Egyptian stock. **2** A member of the Coptic Church.

cop·ter (kop'tər) *n.* *Informal* HELICOPTER.

Cop·tic (kop'tik) *adj.* Of or pertaining to the Copts, or to their language. —*n.* The Hamitic language of the Copts, the liturgical language of the Coptic Church.

Coptic Church The principal Christian sect of Egypt, a separate body after 451.

cop·u·la (kop'yə·lə) *n. pl.* **·las** or **·lae** (-lē) *Gram.* A verb, as a form of *be, seem*, etc., that connects subject and predicate; a linking verb. [< L, a link, band] —**cop'u·lar** *adj.*

cop·u·late (kop'yə·lāt) *v.i.* **·lat·ed, ·lat·ing** To unite in sexual intercourse. [< L *copulare* fasten, link] —**cop'u·la'tion** *n.* —**cop·u·la·to·ry** (kop'yə·lə·tôr'ē, -tō'rē) *adj.*

cop·u·la·tive (kop'yə·lā'tiv) *adj.* **1** *Gram.* **a** Connecting coordinate words, clauses, etc., as a conjunction. **b** Serving as a copula. **2** Of or pertaining to copulation. —*n.* A copulative word. **cop'u·la'tive·ly** *adv.*

cop·y (kop'ē) *n. pl.* **cop·ies 1** Something made to reproduce or imitate an original. **2** A single example of a printed edition, issue, etc. **3** Manuscript or other material to be reproduced in print. **4** A newsworthy or suitable subject for writing about. —*v.* **cop·ied, cop·y·ing** *v.t.* **1** To make a copy of; reproduce. **2** To follow as a model; imitate. —*v.i.* **3** To make a copy. [< L, supply, abundance]

cop·y·book (kop'ē·bŏŏk') *n.* A book containing examples to be imitated in penmanship. —*adj.* Unimaginative; trite.

copy boy An errand boy in a newspaper office who carries copy.

cop·y·cat (kop′ē·kat′) *n. Informal* One who apes or imitates.

copy desk A desk in a newspaper office where copy is edited.

cop·y·ist (kop′ē·ist) *n.* **1** One who makes copies. **2** An imitator.

cop·y·right (kop′ē·rīt′) *n.* The exclusive statutory right to publish and dispose of a literary, musical, artistic, or dramatic work for a specified time. —*v.t.* To secure copyright for. —**cop′y·right′a·ble** *adj.* —**cop′y·right′er** *n.*

cop·y·writ·er (kop′ē·rī′tər) *n.* One who writes copy for advertisements. —**cop′y·writ′ing** *n.*

co·quet (kō·ket′) *v.* **co·quet·ted, co·quet·ing** *v.i.* **1** To flirt; play the coquette. **2** To act in a trifling manner; dally. [< F *coq* a cock; with ref. to its strutting] —**co·quet·ry** (kō′kə·trē, kō·ket′rē) *n.* (*pl.* **·ries**)

co·quette (kō·ket′) *n.* A woman or girl who flirts, esp. to gratify her vanity. [F< *coq* a cock] —**co·quet′tish** *adj.* — **co·quet′tish·ly** *adv.* —**co·quet′tish·ness** *n.*

co·qui·na (kō·kē′nə) *n.* **1** Any of a genus of small marine clams with varicolored shells. **2** A soft, porous limestone containing fragments of marine shells, used as building material. [Sp., shellfish]

Cor. Corinthians.

cor. corner; coroner; corpus; correct.

cor·a·cle (kôr′ə·kəl, kor′-) *n.* A small, rounded fishing boat of hide, etc., stretched on a wicker frame. [< Welsh *corwg* boat]

cor·al (kôr′əl, kor′-) *n.* **1** The calcareous skeletons secreted by various marine polyps and deposited in various forms and colors. **2** Any of numerous marine polyps that secrete coral. **3** A yellowish pink or red. —*adj.* **1** Made of coral. **2** Yellowish pink or red. [< Gk. *korallion*]

coral reef A reef formed by the gradual deposit of coral skeletons.

coral snake A venomous snake of tropical America and the s U.S., having brilliant red, black, and yellow markings.

cor·bel (kôr′bəl, -bel) *n.* A bracketlike projection from the face of a wall, supporting a cornice or similar part. —*v.t.* **cor·beled** or **·belled, cor·bel·ing** or **·bel·ling** To supply or support with corbels. [< L *corvus* crow; from its shape]

Corals
a. bud. b. mushroom.

cord (kôrd) *n.* **1** A string or thin rope of intertwined strands. **2** A flexible insulated electrical wire usu. having a plug at one end. **3** *Anat.* A cordlike structure: the spinal *cord.* **4** A measure for cut firewood equal to a pile of 128 cubic feet. **5 a** A raised rib in a fabric. **b** A fabric having such ribs. **6** *pl.* Corduroy trousers. **7** A force or influence acting as a bond. —*v.t.* **1** To bind or secure with cord. **2** To pile (firewood) by the cord. [< Gk. *chordē* string of a musical instrument] —**cord′ed** *adj.* —**cord′er** *n.*

cord·age (kôr′dij) *n.* **1** Ropes and cords collectively, esp. in the rigging of a ship. **2** The amount of wood in cords in a given area.

cor·date (kôr′dāt) *adj.* Heart-shaped. [< L *cor, cordis* heart] —**cor′date·ly** *adv.*

cor·dial (kôr′jəl) *adj.* Warm and sincere. —*n.* **1** A liqueur. **2** A medicine, etc., that stimulates or invigorates. [< L *cor, cordis* heart] —**cor·dial·i·ty** (kôr·jal′ə·tē, -jē·al′-, -dē·al′-), **cor′dial·ness** *n.* —**cor′dial·ly** *adv.* —**Syn.** *adj.* hearty, heartfelt, genial.

cor·dil·le·ra (kôr·dil·yâr′ə, kôr·dil′ər·ə) *n.* A system of mountain ranges extending through a large land mass. [< OSp. *cordilla,* dim. of *cuerda* rope, chain] —**cor′dil·le′ran** *adj.*

cord·ite (kôr′dīt) *n.* A smokeless explosive. [< CORD; with ref. to its appearance]

cor·don (kôr′dən) *n.* **1** An extended line, as of men, ships, etc., enclosing or guarding an area. **2** A cord, ribbon, etc., esp. worn as a badge of honor. [< F *corde* cord]

cor·do·van (kôr′də·vən) *n.* A fine leather, usu. of split horsehide. —*adj.* Made of this leather. [< Sp. *Cordobán,* of Cordoba]

cor·du·roy (kôr′də·roi, kôr′də·roi′) *n.* **1** A durable usu. cotton fabric with ribs or wales of cut pile. **2** *pl.* Trousers made of corduroy. —*adj.* **1** Made of corduroy. **2** Formed from logs laid transversely; a *corduroy* road. [?]

cord·wood (kôrd′wŏŏd′) *n.* Cut wood piled into cords or sold by the cord.

core (kôr, kōr) *n.* **1** The hard or fibrous central part of certain fruits, usu. containing the seeds. **2** The innermost or most important part of something. **3 a** The insulated conducting wires of an electric cable. **b** A ferromagnetic mass used to intensify or hold the magnetic field of a wire. —*v.t.* **cored, cor·ing** To remove the core of. [?]

CORE (kôr, kōr) Congress of Racial Equality.

co·re·lig·ion·ist (kō′ri·lij′ən·ist) *n.* A person having the same religion as another.

co·re·op·sis (kō′rē·op′sis, kō′rē-) *n.* A plant of the composite family, having daisylike yellow or red and yellow flowers. [< Gk. *koris* bedbug + *opsis* appearance; with ref. to the shape of the seed]

cor·er (kôr′ər, kō′rər) *n.* A utensil for removing the cores of apples and other fruit.

co·re·spon·dent (kō′ri·spon′dənt) *n. Law* One charged with committing adultery with the husband or wife from whom a divorce is being sought. —**co′re·spon′den·cy** *n.*

co·ri·an·der (kôr′ē·an′dər, kō′rē-) *n.* **1** A plant related to parsley, having aromatic seeds used for seasoning. **2** The seeds of this plant. [< Gk. *koriannon*]

Co·rin·thi·an (kə·rin′thē·ən) *adj.* **1** Of or pertaining to Corinth, Greece. **2** Of or denoting an architectural order characterized by fluted columns having capitals decorated with stylized acanthus leaves. • See CAPITAL. —*n.* **1** A native or inhabitant of Corinth. **2** *pl.* Either of two books of the New Testament written by the apostle Paul as epistles to the Christians of Corinth. **3** A worldly, fashionable man. **4** An amateur yachtsman.

cork (kôrk) *n.* **1** The light, porous, elastic outer bark of a tree, the **cork oak,** of the Mediterranean region. **2** Something, esp. a bottle stopper, made from this bark. **3** A similar stopper, as of rubber. **4** *Bot.* The outer protective layer of the stems of woody plants. —*v.t.* **1** To stop with a cork. **2** To restrain; check. **3** To blacken with burnt cork. [< OSp. *alcorque* a cork slipper] —**cork′y** *adj.* (**·i·er, ·i·est**)

cork·er (kôr′kər) *n. Slang* An excellent or extraordinary person or thing.

cork·ing (kôr′king) *adj. Slang* Fine; excellent.

cork·screw (kôrk′skrōō′) *n.* A spiral implement for drawing corks from bottles. —*v.t. & v.i.* To move or cause to move in a spiral; twist. —*adj.* Shaped like a corkscrew; twisted; spiral.

corm (kôrm) *n.* A bulblike underground enlargement of a plant stem. [< Gk. *kormos* tree trunk]

cor·mo·rant (kôr′mər·ənt) *n.* **1** A web-footed diving bird with dark plumage and a hooked bill. **2** A greedy or rapacious person. [< L *corvus marinus* sea crow]

corn¹ (kôrn) *n.* **1** A tall, widely cultivated cereal grass native to the New World, bearing edible kernels on large ears. **2** The kernels or ears of this plant. **3** *Brit.* **a** Any widely grown cereal plant, as wheat or rye. **b** The seeds of such a plant. **4** *Slang* Something regarded as trite, mawkish, etc. —*v.t.* To preserve in salt or in brine: to *corn* beef. [< OE]

Cormorant

corn² (kôrn) *n.* A horny thickening of the skin, esp. on a toe. [< L *cornu* horn]

corn borer A moth larva that infests and destroys corn and other plants.

corn bread Bread made from cornmeal.

corn·cob (kôrn′kob′) *n.* The hard central part of an ear of corn, on which the kernels grow.

corncob pipe A pipe whose bowl is cut from a corncob.

corn cockle A plant with purplish red flowers, often growing in grain fields.

cor·ne·a (kôr′nē·ə) *n.* The transparent outer coat of the eyeball, covering the iris and pupil. [< Med. L *cornea* horny] —**cor′ne·al** *adj.* • See EYE.

cor·nel (kôr′nəl) *n.* Any of several shrubs, trees, or plants belonging to the genus that includes the dogwood. [< L *cornus* cornel tree]

cor·nel·ian (kôr·nēl′yən) *n.* CARNELIAN.

cor·ner (kôr′nər) *n.* 1 The point or angle formed by the meeting of two lines or surfaces. 2 A space adjacent to the angle formed by converging surfaces or lines. 3 A place where two streets meet. 4 An area or region. 5 A remote or secluded place. 6 A position from which escape or extrication is difficult. 7 A piece placed on a corner for protection, decoration, etc. 8 Control of a commodity, stock, etc., acquired by buying up to force higher prices. —**cut corners** To reduce expenses; economize. —*v.t.* 1 To force or drive into a corner or difficult position. 2 To acquire control of (a commodity, stock, etc.) —*v.i.* 3 To turn a corner or corners, as a vehicle. 4 To form or abut with a corner. —*adj.* 1 Located at a corner. 2 Designed for a corner. [< L *cornu* horn, point]

cor·ner·stone (kôr′nər·stōn′) *n.* 1 A stone uniting two walls at the corner of a building. 2 Such a stone, often inscribed, laid ceremonially in a foundation. 3 Something fundamental or of primary importance.

cor·ner·wise (kôr′nər·wīz) *adv.* 1 With a corner in front. 2 Diagonally.

cor·net (kôr·net′) *n.* 1 A wind instrument like the trumpet but having a more flaring tube. 2 A cone-shaped paper wrapper, pastry shell, etc. [< L *cornu* a horn] —**cor·net′ist** or **cor·net′ist** *n.*

corn·flow·er (kôrn′flou′ər) *n.* A plant of the composite family having usu. blue flowers.

corn·husk·ing (kôrn′hus′king) *n.* A social gathering for the purpose of husking corn. —**corn′husk·er** *n.*

cor·nice (kôr′nis) *n.* 1 A horizontal projecting molding at the top of a wall, column, etc. 2 A framework or molding to conceal curtain rods, etc. —*v.t.* **·niced, ·nic·ing** To provide with a cornice. [< Gk. *korōnis* wreath, garland]

Cor·nish (kôr′nish) *adj.* Of or pertaining to Cornwall, England, or its people. —*n.* The Celtic language formerly spoken in Cornwall. —**Corn′ish·man** *n.* (*pl.* **·men**)

corn·meal (kôrn′mēl′) *n.* Meal made from corn. Also **corn meal.**

corn pone Bread made from cornmeal, usu. without milk and eggs. *Cornice*

corn silk The pale, lustrous, elongated styles which hang from an ear of corn.

corn·stalk (kôrn′stôk′) *n.* A stalk of the corn plant. Also **corn stalk.**

corn·starch (kôrn′stärch′) *n.* Starch obtained from corn, used in cooking, etc.

corn sugar Glucose obtained from cornstarch.

corn syrup Syrup obtained from cornstarch, containing glucose, maltose, etc.

cor·nu·co·pi·a (kôr′nə·kō′pē·ə) *n.* 1 A stylized representation of a goat's horn filled with fruit, grain, etc., symbolizing plenty or prosperity. 2 A cone-shaped container. [< L *cornu copiae* horn of plenty] —**cor′nu·co′pi·an** *adj.*

corn whiskey Whiskey made from corn.

corn·y (kôr′nē) *adj.* **corn·i·er, corn·i·est** *Slang* Trite, banal, sentimental, etc. —**corn′i·ness** *n.*

co·rol·la (kə·rol′ə) *n.* The inner envelope of a flower, consisting of separate petals or a single often tubelike or flaring part. [< L, dim. of *corona* crown]

cor·ol·lar·y (kôr′ə·ler′ē, kor′-; *Brit.* kə·rol′ər·ē) *n. pl.* **·lar·ies** 1 A proposition following so obviously from another that it requires little or no demonstration. 2 An inference; deduction. 3 A natural consequence. —*adj.* Deduced; resultant. [< L *corollarium* gift, orig. money paid for a garland]

co·ro·na (kə·rō′ə) *n. pl.* **·nas** or **·nae** (-nē) 1 A crownlike part, structure, or process. 2 *Astron.* A luminous circle around one of the heavenly bodies. 3 The luminous discharge at the surface of an electrical conductor under very high voltage. 4 *Bot.* A crownlike extension of the corolla, as in daffodils. [< L, crown]

cor·o·nar·y (kôr′ə·ner′ē, kor′-) *adj.* Pertaining to the two arteries that supply blood to the heart muscle. —*n. pl.* **·nar·ies** 1 A coronary artery. 2 CORONARY THROMBOSIS. [< L *corona* crown]

coronary thrombosis Blockage of a coronary artery by a blood clot.

cor·o·na·tion (kôr′ə·nā′shən, kor′-) *n.* The act or ceremony of crowning a monarch. [< L *coronare* to crown]

cor·o·ner (kôr′ə·nər, kor′-) *n.* A public officer who seeks to determine the cause of deaths not clearly due to natural causes. [< AF *coruner* officer of the crown]

cor·o·net (kôr′ə·net, -nit, kor′-) *n.* 1 A small crown, denoting noble rank below that of sovereign. 2 An ornamental band, wreath, etc., worn on the head. [< L *corona* crown]

corp., corpn. corporation.

cor·po·ral[1] (kôr′pər·əl) *adj.* Of or relating to the body: *corporal* punishment. [< L *corpus* body] —**cor·po·ral·i·ty** (kôr′pə·ral′ə·tē) *n.* —**cor′po·ral·ly** *adv.* —Syn. physical, bodily. *Coronet*

cor·po·ral[2] (kôr′pər·əl) *n.* See GRADE. [< Ital. *caporale* < *capo* head]

cor·po·rate (kôr′pər·it) *adj.* 1 Constituting a corporation; incorporated. 2 Of or belonging to a corporation. 3 Combined; collective. [< L *corporare* make into a body < *corpus* body] —**cor′po·rate·ly** *adv.*

cor·po·ra·tion (kôr′pə·rā′shən) *n.* 1 A group of people having a legal charter that empowers them to transact business as a single body. 2 *Informal* A protuberant abdomen. —**cor·po·ra·tive** (kôr′pə·rā′tiv, -pər·ə·tiv′) *adj.* —**cor·po·ra·tor** (kôr′pə·rā′tər) *n.*

cor·po·re·al (kôr·pôr′ē·əl, -pō′rē·əl) *adj.* 1 Of or of the nature of the body. 2 Having physical or material existence. [< L *corpus* body] —**cor·po·re·al·i·ty** (kôr·pôr′ē·al′ə·tē, -pō′rē-), **cor·po′re·al·ness** *n.* —**cor·po′re·al·ly** *adv.*

corps (kôr, kōr) *n. pl.* **corps** (kôrz, kōrz) 1 *Mil.* a A special department or subdivision: the Quartermaster *Corps.* b A tactical unit consisting of two or more divisions. 2 An organized group of persons acting together. [< L *corpus* body]

corps de bal·let (kôr′də ba·lā′, *Fr.* bá·le′) The dancers of a ballet company who perform as a group rather than as soloists. [F]

corpse (kôrps) *n.* A dead body, esp. of a human being. [< L *corpus* body].

cor·pu·lent (kôr′pyə·lənt) *adj.* Having a fat body. [< L *corpulentus* < *corpus* body] —**cor′pu·lence, cor′pu·len·cy,** *n.* —**cor′pu·lent·ly** *adv.* —Syn. fat, obese, fleshy, stout.

cor·pus (kôr′pəs) *n. pl.* **·po·ra** (-pər·ə) 1 A large body or collection of written material of a specific nature. 2 The main mass or substance of anything. 3 A body of a person or animal. [L, body]

Cor·pus Chris·ti (kôr′pəs kris′tē, -tī) The first Thursday following Trinity Sunday, a Roman Catholic Church festival in honor of the Eucharist. [L, lit., body of Christ]

cor·pus·cle (kôr′pəs·əl, -pus·əl) *n.* 1 One of the particles forming part of the blood of vertebrates; an erythrocyte (**red corpuscle**) or a leukocyte (**white corpuscle**). 2 A minute particle. Also **cor·pus·cule** (kôr′pus·kyōol). [< L *corpusculum,* dim. of *corpus* body] —**cor·pus·cu·lar** (kôr·pus′kyə·lər) *adj.*

corpus de·lic·ti (də·lik′tī) 1 *Law* The essential fact or material evidence proving the commission of a crime. 2 Loosely, the body of a murder victim. [L, lit., the body of the offense]

corr. corrected; correction; correspondence; correspondent.

cor·ral (kə·ral′) *n.* 1 An enclosed space or pen for livestock. 2 A space enclosed by wagons for protection against attack. —*v.t.* **·ralled, ·ral·ling** 1 To drive into and enclose in a corral. 2 *Informal* To seize or capture; secure. [Sp.]

cor·rect (kə·rekt′) *v.t.* 1 To remove errors from; make right. 2 To mark or indicate the errors of. 3 To rebuke or chastise. **4** To remedy or counteract, as a malfunction. **5** To make conformable to a standard: to *correct* a lens. —*adj.* **1** Free from fault or mistake. **2** True; right; accurate. **3** Proper; acceptable. [< L *com-* together + *regere* make straight] —cor·rect′a·ble or ·i·ble *adj.* —cor·rect′ly *adv.* — cor·rect′ness, cor·rec′tor *n.* —Syn. *v.* **1** rectify, right, redress. **5** adjust, regulate.

cor·rec·tion (kə·rek′shən) *n.* **1** The act of correcting. **2** Something offered or substituted to correct an error. **3** Chastisement; punishment. —cor·rec′tion·al *adj.*

cor·rec·tive (kə·rek′tiv) *adj.* Tending or intended to correct. —*n.* Something that corrects or is intended to correct. —cor·rec′tive·ly *adv.*

correl. correlative.

cor·re·late (kôr′ə·lāt, kor′-) *v.* ·lat·ed, ·lat·ing *v.t.* **1** To place or put in reciprocal relation. —*v.i.* **2** To be mutually or reciprocally related. —*adj.* Having mutual or reciprocal relations. —*n.* CORRELATIVE (def. 1). [< COM- + RELATE]

cor·re·la·tion (kôr′ə·lā′shən, kor′-) *n.* **1** Mutual or reciprocal relation. **2** The act or process of correlating. —cor′re·la′tion·al *adj.*

cor·rel·a·tive (kə·rel′ə·tiv) *adj.* **1** Having a corresponding or reciprocal relationship. **2** Used together and indicating a grammatical or logical relationship, as the conjunctions *either* and *or.* —*n.* **1** Either of two things in correlation. **2** A correlative term, as in grammar. —cor·rel′a·tive·ly *adv.* —cor·rel′a·tive·ness, cor·rel′a·tiv′i·ty *n.*

cor·re·spond (kôr′ə·spond′, kor′-) *v.i.* **1** To be in agreement, or conformity. **2** To be similar, equivalent, or analogous. **3** To communicate by letters. [< Med. L *com-* together + *respondere* to answer]

cor·re·spon·dence (kôr′ə·spon′dəns, kor′-) *n.* **1** Conformity; agreement. **2** Similarity; analogous relationship. **3 a** Communication by letters. **b** The letters themselves.

correspondence school A school that gives courses of instruction by mail.

cor·re·spon·dent (kôr′ə·spon′dənt, kor′-) *n.* **1** One who communicates by means of letters. **2** A reporter or writer, as for a newspaper, who sends news or articles from a distant place. **3** Something having a corresponding relationship. —*adj.* Having a corresponding relationship.

cor·re·spond·ing (kôr′ə·spon′ding, kor′-) *adj.* Reciprocal, analogous, or equivalent. —cor′re·spond′ing·ly *adv.*

cor·ri·dor (kôr′ə·dər, -dôr, kor′-) *n.* **1** A hallway or passageway usu. having rooms opening on it. **2** A strip of land belonging to one country crossing the territory of another. **3** A densely populated strip of territory including major cities. [< Ital. *corridore* < *correre* to run]

cor·ri·gen·dum (kôr′ə·jen′dəm, kor′-) *n. pl.* ·da (-də) **1** An error to be corrected in a printed work. **2** *pl.* A list of corrected errors included in a book. [< L, gerundive of *corrigere.* See CORRECT.]

cor·ri·gi·ble (kôr′ə·jə·bəl, kor′-) *adj.* Capable of being corrected or reformed. [< L *corrigere* to correct] —cor′ri·gi·bil′i·ty *n.* —cor′ri·gi·bly *adv.*

cor·rob·o·rate (kə·rob′ə·rāt) *v.t.* ·rat·ed, ·rat·ing To confirm or support (evidence, a statement, etc.) [< L *com-* together + *robur* strength] —cor·rob′o·ra′tor, cor·rob′o·ra′tion *n.* —cor·rob·o·ra·tive (kə·rob′ə·rā·tiv, -rob′ər·ə·tiv), cor·rob·o·ra·to·ry (kə·rob′ər·ə·tôr′ē, -tō′rē) *adj.* —cor·rob′o·ra′tive·ly *adv.*

cor·rode (kə·rōd′) *v.t. & v.i.* ·rod·ed, ·rod·ing To wear away gradually, esp. by chemical action such as rusting. [< L *com-* thoroughly + *rodere* gnaw] —cor·rod′i·ble, cor·ro·si·ble (kə·rō′sə·bəl) *adj.*

cor·ro·sion (kə·rō′zhən) *n.* **1** The process of corroding. **2** A product of corrosive action.

cor·ro·sive (kə·rō′siv) *adj.* **1** Having the power of corroding. **2** Caustic; scathing. —*n.* Something that causes corrosion. —cor·ro′sive·ly *adv.* —cor·ro′sive·ness *n.*

corrosive sublimate MERCURIC CHLORIDE.

cor·ru·gate (kôr′ə·gāt, kor′-) *v.t. & v.i.* ·gat·ed, ·gat·ing To form into alternating ridges and furrows. [< L *com-* together + *ruga* a wrinkle] —cor′ru·ga′tion *n.*

cor·rupt (kə·rupt′) *adj.* **1** Viciously immoral; depraved. **2** Capable of being bribed, improperly influenced, etc.; dishonest. **3** Altered or debased by errors, changes, etc., as a text. **4** Rotten; putrid. —*v.t. & v.i.* To make or become corrupt. [< L *com-* thoroughly + *rumpere* to break] —cor·

rupt′er, cor·rup′tor, cor·rupt′ness *n.* —cor·rupt′ly *adv.* —cor·rup′tive *adj.*

cor·rupt·i·ble (kə·rup′tə·bəl) *adj.* Capable of being corrupted, as by bribery or improper influence. —cor·rup′ti·bil′i·ty, cor·rup′ti·ble·ness. *n.* —cor·rup′ti·bly *adv.*

cor·rup·tion (kə·rup′shən) *n.* **1** The act or process of corrupting or the condition of being corrupt. **2** An influence or action that corrupts, as bribery. **3** An alteration, as of a word or text, often to an incorrect or debased form.

cor·sage (kôr·säzh′) *n.* **1** A small bouquet of flowers for a woman to wear at the shoulder, waist, etc. **2** The bodice or waist of a woman's dress. [< OF < *cors* body < L]

cor·sair (kôr′sâr) *n.* **1** A pirate. **2** A pirate's vessel. **3** A privateer. [< Med. L *cursarius* < *cursus* inroad, raid]

corse·let (kôrs′lit *for def. 1;* kôr′sə·let′ *for def. 2)* **1** Armor for the upper part of the body: also **cors′let. 2** A light corset: also **cor′se·lette′.** [< MF, dim. of *cors* body]

cor·set (kôr′sit) *n.* A close-fitting under-garment, usu. reinforced by stays and sometimes tightened with laces, worn esp. by women to shape and support the body. —*v.t.* To enclose or dress in a corset. [< OF, dim. of *cors* body]

Corselet

cor·tege (kôr·tezh′, -tāzh′) *n.* **1** A train of attendants. **2** A ceremonial procession. Also **cor·tège′.** [< Ital. *corte* court]

cor·tex (kôr′teks) *n. pl.* ·ti·ces (-tə·sēz) **1** *Bot.* An outer layer, as the bark of trees or the rind of fruits. **2** *Anat.* **a** A distinctive outer layer of an organ, as the brain, kidney, etc. **b** The external portion of the adrenal glands. [< L, bark] • See KIDNEY.

cor·ti·cal (kôr′ti·kəl) *adj.* **1** Of, pertaining to, or consisting of a cortex. **2** Caused by or associated with the cerebral cortex. —cor′ti·cal·ly *adv.*

cor·ti·sone (kôr′tə·sōn, -zōn) *n.* A hormone secreted by the cortex of the adrenal gland and also made synthetically. [Short for *corticosterone* < L *cortex, -icis* cortex + STER(OID) + (HORM)ONE]

co·run·dum (kə·run′dəm) *n.* A hard aluminum oxide mineral occurring as sapphire or ruby and also used as an abrasive. [< Skt. *kuruvinda* ruby]

cor·us·cate (kôr′ə·skāt, kor′-) *v.i.* ·cat·ed, ·cat·ing To sparkle; glitter; flash. [< L *coruscare* to glitter] —cor′us·ca′tion *n.*

cor·vette (kôr·vet′) *n.* **1** A small armed ship used chiefly as an antisubmarine escort vessel. **2** Formerly, a warship having sails and a single tier of guns. Also **cor·vet** (kôr′vet′, kôr′vet). [< MF]

cor·vine (kôr′vīn, -vin) *adj.* Of, related to, or resembling the crow. [< L *corvus* crow]

cor·ymb (kôr′imb, -im, kor′-) *n.* A flower cluster having stalks of different lengths growing to the same level. [< Gk. *korymbos* flower cluster] —co·rym·bose (kə·rim′bōs), co·rym·bous (kə·rim′bəs) *adj.* —co·rym′bose·ly *adv.*

co·ry·za (kə·rī′zə) *n.* Congestion of the nose and connecting sinuses; a cold in the head. [< Gk. *koryza* catarrh]

cos cosine.

cosec cosecant.

co·se·cant (kō·sē′kənt) *n. Trig.* The reciprocal of the sine of an angle.

co·sig·na·to·ry (kō·sig′nə·tor′ē, -tō′rē) *n. pl.* ·ries One of two or more joint signers of a treaty, contract, or other document.

co·sine (kō′sīn) *n. Trig.* The sine of the complement of a given angle or arc.

cos·met·ic (koz·met′ik) *n.* A preparation applied to the skin, hair, etc., to beautify or improve appearance. —*adj.* **1** Used to beautify physical appearance. **2** Intended to improve appearance: *cosmetic* surgery. [< Gk. *kosmos* order, ornament] —cos·met′i·cal·ly *adv.*

cos·mic (koz′mik) *adj.* **1** Of or pertaining to the universe as a whole. **2** Immense; vast. Also **cos′mi·cal.** [< Gk. *kosmos* the universe] —cos′mi·cal·ly *adv.*

cosmic dust Fine particles of matter in or from space.

cosmic rays High-energy radiation that reaches the earth from space.

cosmo- *combining form* The universe: *cosmogony.* [< Gk. *kosmos* the universe]

cos·mog·o·ny (koz·mog′ə·nē) *n. pl.* **·nies 1** The origin of the universe. **2** A theory of the origin or creation of the world or universe. —**cos·mo·gon·ic** (koz′mə·gon′ik) or **·i·cal, cos·mog′o·nal** *adj.* —**cos·mog′o·nist** *n.*

cos·mog·ra·phy (koz·mog′rə·fē) *n. pl.* **·phies.** The science that describes the universe. —**cos·mog′ra·pher, cos·mog′ra·phist** *n.* —**cos·mo·graph·ic** (koz′mə·graf′ik) or **·i·cal** *adj.*

cos·mol·o·gy (koz·mol′ə·jē) *n. pl.* **·gies** The general science or philosophy of the universe. —**cos·mo·log·ic** (koz′mə·loj′ik) or **·i·cal** *adj.* —**cos·mol′o·gist** *n.*

cos·mo·naut (koz′mə·nôt) *n.* ASTRONAUT. [< COSMO- + Gk. *nautēs* sailor]

cos·mo·pol·i·tan (koz′mə·pol′ə·tən) *adj.* **1** Common to all the world; not local or limited. **2** At home in all parts of the world. **3** *Biol.* Widely distributed, as a plant or animal. —*n.* A cosmopolitan person. —**cos′mo·pol′i·tan·ism** *n.*

cos·mop·o·lite (koz·mop′ə·līt) *n.* **1** A cosmopolitan person. **2** *Biol.* A plant or animal widely distributed over the world. [< Gk. *kosmopolites* world citizen]

cos·mos (koz′məs, -mos) *n.* **1** The world or universe considered as an orderly system. **2** Any orderly and complete system. **3** A plant with daisylike flowers of various colors. [< Gk. *kosmos* order, universe]

Cos·sack (kos′ak, -ək) *n.* One of a people of the s U.S.S.R., famous as cavalrymen.

cos·set (kos′it) *v.t.* To treat indulgently; pamper. —*n.* A pet, esp. a pet lamb. [?]

cost (kôst, kost) *v.* cost (*for def. 3, also* cost·ed), cost·ing *v.t.* **1** To have or require as a price. **2** To cause to pay, lose, suffer, or exert. **3** To estimate the cost of production of. —*n.* **1** The price paid for anything. **2** Loss; suffering; detriment. **3** *pl.* The charges in a lawsuit. —**at all costs** (or **at any cost**) No matter what price or effort is involved. [< L *constare* to stand at, cost]

cos·tal (kos′təl) *adj.* Of, pertaining to, or near a rib or ribs. [< L *costa* rib]

Cos·ta Ri·ca (kos′tə rē′kə, kôs′tə) A republic of Central America, 19,690 sq. mi., cap. San José. —**Costa Rican** • See map at CENTRAL AMERICA.

cos·ter·mon·ger (kos′tər·mung′gər, -mong′-, kôs′-) *n. Brit.* A street hawker of vegetables, fruits, etc. Also **cos′ter.** [Earlier *costardmonger* apple seller]

cos·tive (kos′tiv, kôs′-) *adj.* Constipated. [< L *constipare* constipate] —**cos′tive·ly** *adv.* —**cos′tive·ness** *n.*

cost·ly (kôst′lē, kost′-) *adj.* **·li·er, ·li·est 1** Of great cost; expensive. **2** Resulting in great loss, sacrifice, etc. **3** Splendid; sumptuous. —**cost′li·ness** *n.* —**Syn. 1** dear, high-priced, valuable, precious.

cost of living The average cost of the necessities of life, as food, clothing, shelter, etc.

cos·tume (kos′t(y)ōōm) *n.* **1** Clothing or style of dress characteristic of a particular country, period, etc. **2** Such clothing, or other distinctive dress, worn by a theatrical performer, to a masquerade, etc. **3** A set of clothing; ensemble; outfit. —*v.t.* (kos·t(y)ōōm′) **·tumed, ·tum·ing** To furnish with costumes. [< Ital. *costuma* fashion, guise < L *consuetudo* custom]

costume jewelry Inexpensive jewelry made from nonprecious materials.

cos·tum·er (kos·t(y)ōō′mər) *n.* One who makes or furnishes costumes, as for stage wear. Also **cos·tum·ier** (kos·t(y)ōōm′yər; *Fr.* kôs·tü·myâ′).

co·sy (kō′zē) *adj.* **·si·er, ·si·est** COZY. —**co′si·ly** *adv.* —**co′si·ness** *n.*

cot¹ (kot) *n.* A light, narrow bed, usu. with a folding frame. [< Skt. *khatvā*]

cot² (kot) *n.* **1** A small house; cottage. **2** A protective sheath for a finger. [< OE]

cot cotangent.

co·tan·gent (kō·tan′jənt) *n. Trig.* The tangent of the complement of an angle. —**co·tan·gen·tial** (kō′tan·jen′shəl) *adj.*

cote (kōt) *n.* A small shelter for sheep or birds. [< OE]

co·te·rie (kō′tə·rē) *n.* A closely knit group of persons with shared interests. [< OF, group of landholding peasants < *cote* hut]

co·ter·mi·nous (kō·tûr′mə·nəs) *adj.* CONTERMINOUS.

co·til·lion (kō·til′yən, kə-) *n.* **1** A ballroom dance with many different figures. **2** A formal ball, esp. for debutantes. Also **co·til·lon** (kō·til′yən, kə-; *Fr.* kô·tē·yôn′). [< OF *cotillon* petticoat.]

cot·tage (kot′ij) *n.* **1** A small, unpretentious house. **2** A usu. small temporary residence, as at a vacation resort. [< OE *cote* hut]

cottage cheese A soft, white cheese made of strained milk curds.

cottage pudding Plain cake served with a sweet sauce.

cot·tag·er (kot′ij·ər) *n.* One who lives in a cottage.

cot·ter (kot′ər) *n.* A key or wedge used to fasten parts of machinery together. [?]

cotter pin A split metal pin for insertion in a nut, bolt, etc., to hold it in place.

cot·ton (kot′n) *n.* **1** A plant of warm regions cultivated for the fibrous material surrounding its seeds. **2** The soft, downy white fibers of this plant, used for textiles, etc. **3** Cloth or thread made from these fibers. —*adj.* Of or made from cotton. —*v.i. Informal* To become friendly; take a liking: used with *to.* —**cotton up to** *Informal* To flatter or make friendly overtures to. [< Ar. *quṭun*] —**cot′ton·y** *adj.*

cotton gin A machine used to separate the seeds from the fiber of cotton.

cot·ton·mouth (kot′n·mouth′) *n.* WATER MOCCASIN.

cot·ton·seed (kot′n·sēd′) *n.* The seed of the cotton plant, pressed to produce a yellow oil, **cottonseed oil,** used in cooking, paints, etc.

cot·ton·tail (kot′n·tāl′) *n.* Any of several common American rabbits having a tail with fluffy white fur.

cot·ton·wood (kot′n·wŏŏd′) *n.* Any of several American poplar trees having seeds covered with cottony fibers.

cotton wool 1 Raw cotton. **2** A mass of cotton fibers used for padding, surgical dressing, etc.

cot·y·le·don (kot′ə·lēd′n) *n.* An embryonic leaf within a seed, often one of a pair appearing as the first sprouting leaves of a seedling plant. [< Gk. *kotylēdōn* socket] —**cot′y·le·do·nal; cot′y·le′do·nous** *adj.*

Cotyledons of Norway maple

couch (kouch) *n.* **1** A long, usu. upholstered piece of furniture on which one may sit or lie. **2** Any place for repose. —*v.t.* **1** To cause to recline. **2** To put into words; phrase. **3** To hold in readiness for use, as a spear. —*v.i.* **4** To lie down; recline. [< F *coucher* put to bed < L *collocare* to set, place] —**couch′er** *n.*

couch·ant (kou′chənt) *adj. Her.* Reclining with head uplifted. [F< *coucher* to put to bed]

couch grass (kouch, kōōch) A weedy grass that spreads rapidly by means of long rootstocks. [< OE *cwice* couch grass + GRASS]

cou·gar (kōō′gər) *n.* MOUNTAIN LION. [< Tupian]

cough (kôf, kof) *v.i.* **1** To expel air from the lungs in a noisy or spasmodic manner. —*v.t.* **2** To expel by coughing. —**cough up 1** To expel (phlegm, etc.) by coughing. **2** *Slang* To hand over, as money. —*n.* **1** A sudden, harsh expulsion of breath. **2** An illness characterized by much coughing. [ME *coughen*] —**cough′er** *n.*

cough drop A small, medicated lozenge to relieve coughing.

could (kŏŏd) *p.t.* of CAN¹.

could·n't (kŏŏd′nt) Contraction of *could not.*

cou·lee (kōō′lē) *n.* **1** A deep, usu. dry gulch. **2** A sheet of solidified lava. [< F *couler* to flow]

cou·lomb (kōō′lom, -lōm, kōō·lom′) *n.* The unit of electric charge, the amount carried by a constant current of one ampere in one second. [< C. A. de *Coulomb,* 1736–1806, French physicist]

---

add, āce, câre, pälm; end, ēven; it, īce; odd, ōpen, ôrder; tŏŏk, pōōl; up, bûrn; ə = *a* in *above,* u in *focus;* yōō = *u* in *fuse;* oil; pout; check; go; ring; thin; this; zh, *vision.* < derived from; ? origin uncertain or unknown.

coul·ter (kōl′tər) n. COLTER.

coun·cil (koun′səl) n. 1 An assembly of persons convened for consultation or deliberation. 2 A body of persons elected or appointed to assist in the administration of government. 3 Deliberation or consultation among the members of a council. [< L *concilium*] • See COUNSEL.

coun·cil·man (koun′səl·mən) n. pl. ·men (-mən) A member of a council, esp. the governing council of a city. — **coun′cil·wom′an** n. Fem. (pl. ·wom′en)

coun·cil·or (koun′səl·ər, -slər) n. A council member. Also **coun′cil·lor.** —**coun′cil·or·ship′** n.

coun·sel (koun′səl) n. 1 Consultation for exchange of advice, opinions, etc. 2 Advice; opinion. 3 A lawyer or lawyers engaged for legal advice. —**keep one's (own) counsel** To keep one's ideas, plans, etc., to oneself. —v. ·seled or ·selled, ·sel·ing or ·sel·ling v.t. 1 To advise; give advice to. 2 To advise in favor of; recommend. —v.i. 3 To confer; deliberate. [< L *consilium*] • The nouns *counsel* (def. 2) and *council* (def. 1) have related meanings, but are not interchangeable. *Council* in this sense is used chiefly in the phrase *in council*, while *counsel* is used in such expressions as *take counsel, heed someone's counsel*, etc.

coun·sel·or (koun′səl·ər, -slər) n. 1 One who gives counsel; an adviser. 2 An attorney. 3 One who supervises at a children's camp. Also **coun′sel·lor.**

count[1] (kount) v.t. 1 To list or call off the units of (a set or collection) in correspondence with a sequence of natural numbers. 2 To list numbers in a progressive sequence to: count *ten*. 3 To include in a reckoning. 4 To consider to be. —v.i. 5 To list numbers in sequence. 6 To rely; depend: with *on*. 7 To have importance; merit consideration. —**count in** To include. —**count out** 1 To exclude. 2 To count to ten over (a downed boxer). —n. 1 The act of counting. 2 A number reached by counting. 3 A relevant item or point. 4 *Law* One of the charges in an indictment. 5 In boxing, the ten counted seconds during which a downed contestant must get up or lose the bout. [< L *computare*] —**count′a·ble** adj.

count[2] (kount) n. In some European countries, a nobleman having a rank corresponding to that of an earl in England. [< L *comes* an associate]

count·down (kount′doun′) n. A specified interval of time before an intended action, measured in descending units to zero.

coun·te·nance (koun′tə·nəns) n. 1 The face or features. 2 Expression; appearance. 3 Approval; support. 4 Composure; aplomb —**out of countenance** Disconcerted; abashed. —v.t. ·nanced, ·nanc·ing To approve; give sanction to. [< L *continentia* behavior < *continere* to contain] —**coun′te·nanc·er** n. —**Syn.** v. condone, sanction, favor, abet.

coun·ter[1] (koun′tər) adv. In a contrary manner or direction. —adj. Opposing; opposite; contrary. —v.t. 1 To act so as to oppose or offset. 2 To return or parry, as a blow. —v.i. 3 To make an opposing or offsetting move or action. —n. 1 That which counters or opposes. 2 A parrying blow. 3 An outer piece of shoe leather that stiffens the heel. [< L *contra* against]

coun·ter[2] (koun′tər) n. 1 A narrow table or surface on which sales are transacted, food is served, etc. 2 A piece of wood, ivory, etc., used in counting or keeping score. [< L *computare*, to compute]

count·er[3] (koun′tər) n. One who or that which counts, esp. a machine for counting.

counter- *combining form* 1 In opposition; contrary: *counterclockwise.* 2 In exchange or retaliation: *counterattack.* 3 Complementing or corresponding: *counterpart.*

coun·ter·act (koun′tər·akt′) v.t. To act in opposition to; have an offsetting effect on. —**coun′ter·ac′tion** n. —**coun′ter·ac′tive** adj. —**coun′ter·ac′tive·ly** adv.

coun·ter·at·tack (koun′tər·ə·tak′) n. An attack in response to a previous attack. —v.t. & v.i. To attack in response to a previous attack.

coun·ter·bal·ance (koun′tər·bal′əns) v.t. ·anced, ·anc·ing To oppose with an equal weight or force; offset. —n. (koun′tər·bal′əns) 1 Any power equally opposing another. 2 A weight that balances another.

coun·ter·claim (koun′tər·klām′) n. A claim, esp. a legal claim, made in opposition to another claim. —v.t. & v.i. To make or offer as a counterclaim. —**coun′ter·claim′ant** n.

coun·ter·clock·wise (koun′tər·clok′wīz′) adj. & adv. Contrary to the direction in which the hands of a clock move.

coun·ter·cul·ture (koun′tər·kul′chər) n. 1 The effort and methods used by certain alienated people to create a life style different from that of the Establishment. 2 The life style thus created. 3 The people who follow it.

coun·ter·es·pi·o·nage (koun′tər·es′pē·ə·nij, -näzh′) n. Activities intended to counteract enemy spying.

coun·ter·feit (koun′tər·fit) v.t. 1 To make a copy or imitation of (money, etc.) with intent to defraud. 2 To pretend; feign. 3 To imitate; resemble closely. —v.i. 4 To practice deception; dissemble. 5 To make counterfeits. —n. 1 A copy or imitation fraudulently intended to pass as genuine. 2 An imitation or close resemblance. —adj. 1 Fraudulently made to resemble something genuine. 2 Pretended; feigned. [< L *contra*- against + *facere* make] —**coun′ter·feit′er** n. —**Syn.** adj. false, spurious, fake, bogus.

coun·ter·in·tel·li·gence (koun′tər·in·tel′ə·jens) n. Activities intended to counteract or prevent espionage, subversion, sabotage, etc.

coun·ter·ir·ri·tant (koun′tər·ir′ə·tənt) n. An agent used to produce mild surface irritation so as to relieve more serious irritation elsewhere.

coun·ter·mand (koun′tər·mand′, -mänd′, koun′tər·mand, -mänd) v.t. 1 To cancel or revoke (an order, command, etc.). 2 To recall by a contradictory order. —n. (koun′tər·mand, -mänd) An order contrary to or revoking a previous one. [< L *contra*- against + *mandare* to order]

coun·ter·mea·sure (koun′tər·mezh′ər) n. An action taken to offset another.

coun·ter·of·fen·sive (koun′tər·ə·fen′siv, koun′tər·ə·fen′siv) n. A large-scale military action designed to stop an enemy offensive.

coun·ter·pane (koun′tər·pān′) n. A coverlet or quilt for a bed. [Alter. of obs. *counterpoint* < L *culcita puncta* a quilted coverlet]

coun·ter·part (koun′tər·pärt′) n. One having a close resemblance or corresponding relationship to another.

coun·ter·plot (koun′tər·plot′) n. A plot to oppose or frustrate another. —v.t. & v.i. (koun′tər·plot′) ·plot·ted, ·plot·ting To oppose (a plot) by another plot.

coun·ter·point (koun′tər·point′) n. 1 The art of adding to a melody a part or parts related to but independent of it, according to fixed rules. 2 The part or parts so arranged. [< Med. L *(cantus) contrapunctus* (a melody) with contrasting notes]

coun·ter·poise (koun′tər·poiz′) v.t. ·poised, ·pois·ing To balance by opposing with an equal weight or force; counterbalance. —n. (koun′tər·poiz) 1 A counterbalancing weight. 2 A force, influence, etc., that offsets another. 3 A state of equilibrium. [< L *contra*- against + *pensare* weigh]

coun·ter·pro·duc·tive (koun′tər·prə·duk′tiv) adj. Producing an effect opposite from that intended: The slurs on his opponent proved to be *counterproductive.*

coun·ter·rev·o·lu·tion (koun′tər·rev′ə·lōō′shən) n. An uprising against the government, policies, etc., established by a previous revolution. —**coun′ter·rev′o·lu′tion·ar′y** adj., n. —**coun′ter·rev′o·lu′tion·ist** n.

coun·ter·shaft (koun′tər·shaft′, -shäft′) n. Mech. An intermediate shaft driven by the main shaft and driving other parts.

coun·ter·sign (koun′tər·sīn′) v.t. To add one's signature to (a signed document) as authentication. —n. A password or secret signal to be given, as to a sentry. —**coun·ter·sig·na·ture** (koun′tər·sig′nə·chər) n.

coun·ter·sink (koun′tər·singk′) v.t. ·sank or ·sunk, ·sunk, ·sink·ing 1 To shape the opening of (a hole) to hold the head of a screw or bolt level with or below the surface. 2 To sink a bolt, screw, etc. into such a hole. —n. 1 A tool for countersinking. 2 A hole made by countersinking.

coun·ter·ten·or (koun′tər·ten′ər) n. 1 A man's voice with a range higher than that of a tenor. 2 A singer with such a voice.

coun·ter·weight (koun′tər·wāt′) n. Any counterbalancing weight, force, or influence. —**coun′ter·weight′ed** adj.

count·ess (koun′tis) n. 1 The wife or widow of a count, or, in Great Britain, of an earl. 2 A woman ranking equally with a count or earl.

count·ing·house (koun'ting·hous') *n.* An office or building used by a business establishment for bookkeeping, correspondence, etc. Also **counting house, counting room.**

count·less (kount'lis) *adj.* Too numerous to be counted; innumerable. —**count'less·ly** *adv.*

coun·tri·fied (kun'tri·fīd) *adj.* Considered typical of country life; rural or rustic. Also **coun'try·fied.**

coun·try (kun'trē) *n. pl.* **·tries 1** A land with its own government and geographic limits; a nation. **2** The land of one's birth or citizenship. **3** The people of a nation. **4** A tract or region of a specified nature. **5** A rural region. — *adj.* Of, pertaining to, or typical of rural regions. [<L *contra* on the opposite side]

country club A suburban club with facilities for outdoor sports and social activities.

coun·try-dance (kun'trē·dans', -däns') *n.* A folk dance in which partners are ranged in opposite lines.

coun·try·man (kun'trē·mən) *n. pl.* **·men** (-mən) **1** A man of the same country as another. **2** RUSTIC. —**coun'try·wom'an** *n. Fem.* (*pl.* **·wom'en**)

coun·try·side (kun'trē·sīd') *n.* **1** A rural area. **2** Its inhabitants.

coun·ty (koun'tē) *n. pl.* **·ties 1** A civil division of a nation or territory. **2** In most of the U.S., an administrative division of a state. **3** The inhabitants of a county. [<L *comes* count, companion]

county seat A municipality that is a county's center of government.

coup (kōō) *n. pl.* **coups** (kōōz, *Fr.* kōō) **1** A sudden and successful action; a masterstroke. **2** A coup d'état. [<L *colaphus* a blow with the fist]

coup de grâce (kōō'də gräs') **1** A death stroke, as to one mortally wounded or suffering. **2** A finishing stroke. [F, lit., stroke of mercy]

coup d'é·tat (kōō' dā·tä')A forceful, unexpected political move, esp. a sudden overthrow of government and seizure of power. [F, lit., stroke of state]

cou·pé (kōō·pā') *n.* **1** A small, closed, two-door automobile: also **coupe** (kōōp). **2** A closed carriage with two passenger seats and an outside seat. [<F *couper* to cut]

coup·le (kup'əl) *n.* **1** Two of a kind; a pair. **2** Two persons of opposite sex, married or otherwise paired. **3** *Informal* A few. —*v.* **coup·led, coup·ling** *v.t.* **1** To join, as one thing to another; link. **2** *Electr.* **a** To connect (two circuits). **b** To transfer (electricity), as by such connection. —*v.i.* **3** To copulate. **4** To form a pair or pairs. [<L *copula* a band, a bond]

coup·ler (kup'lər) *n.* **1** One who or that which couples. **2** A mechanical device by which objects are connected. **3** *Telecom.* A device for transferring signals from one circuit to another.

coup·let (kup'lit) *n.* Two successive lines of verse, usu. rhymed and of the same meter and length. [<F, dim. of *couple* a pair]

coup·ling (kup'ling) *n.* **1** The act of joining together. **2** A device for linking or connecting objects; a coupler.

cou·pon (kyōō'pon) *n.* **1** One of a number of dated certificates attached to a bond, representing interest payable at stated periods.

Coupling

2 A certificate, detachable form, etc., entitling one to something in exchange. [<F *couper* to cut]

cour·age (kûr'ij) *n.* The capacity to meet danger or difficulty with firmness; bravery. [<L *cor* heart]

cou·ra·geous (kə·rā'jəs) *adj.* Possessing or characterized by courage. —**cou·ra'geous·ly** *adv.* —**cou·ra'geous·ness** *n.* —Syn. brave, fearless, intrepid, valorous, valiant.

cou·ri·er (kōōr'ē·ər, kûr'-) *n.* **1** A messenger, esp. one of official business. **2** An attendant who makes arrangements for travelers. [<Ital. *corriere* < *corre* to run]

course (kôrs, kōrs) *n.* **1** Onward motion or progress. **2** The way, direction, or duration of such progress. **3** A customary or expected procedure or development. **4** A line of conduct or action; policy. **5** A series of connected acts or

events. **6 a** A series of prescribed studies, as for a degree. **b** A series of classes in a specific subject. **7** A tract or area used for golf, racing, etc. **8** A part of a meal served at one time. **9** A row or layer, as of bricks. —**of course 1** As one might expect; naturally. **2** Certainly. —*v.* **coursed, cours·ing** —*v.i.* **1** To move swiftly; run; race. **2** To hunt with hounds. —*v.t.* **3** To pursue, as in hunting. **4** To cause (hounds) to pursue game. **5** To traverse swiftly. [<L *cursus* a running)

cours·er (kôr'sər, kōr'-) *n.* A spirited or swift horse.

course·ware (kôrs'wâr', kōrs'wâr') *n.* Computer software used in teaching a subject, a skill, etc.

court (kôrt, kōrt) *n.* **1** An area enclosed by walls or buildings; a courtyard. **2** A short street or walled alley. **3 a** A level area laid out for a game, as tennis or basketball. **b** A division of such an area. **4** The residence of a sovereign; palace. **5** The household, retinue, advisers, etc., of a sovereign. **6** A formal assembly held by or as by a sovereign. **7 a** A tribunal for administering justice. **b** A judge or judges presiding at such a tribunal. **c** The place where such a tribunal meets. **d** A session of such a tribunal. **8** Attention paid to another to win affection, favor, etc. —**out of court** Without holding a trial. —*v.t.* **1** To attempt to acquire as a mate or lover; woo. **2** To try to get in the good graces of. **3** To attempt to gain: to *court* applause. **4** To invite, often unwisely: to *court* trouble. —*v.i.* **5** To conduct a courtship. —*adj.* Of or pertaining to a court. [<L *cohors, cohortis* yard, troop of soldiers]

cour·te·ous (kûr'tē·əs) *adj.* Showing courtesy; polite. —**cour'te·ous·ly** *adv.* —**cour'te·ous·ness** *n.*

cour·te·san (kôr'tə·zən, kōr'-, kûr'-) *n.* A prostitute who consorts with men of wealth or high status. Also **cour'te·zan.** [<Ital. *cortigiana* courtier]

cour·te·sy (kûr'tə·sē) *n. pl.* **·sies 1** Gracious or considerate behavior; habitual politeness. **2** A courteous act. **3** Custom or indulgence rather than strict usage: He was called "Colonel" by *courtesy.* [<OF *corteisie*]

court·house (kôrt'hous', kōrt'-) *n.* **1** A public building occupied by judicial courts. **2** A building for the offices of a county government.

court·i·er (kôr'tē·ər, -tyər, kōr'-) *n.* **1** An attendant at or frequenter of a royal court. **2** One who seeks favor by flattery.

court·ly (kôrt'lē, kōrt'-) *adj.* **·li·er, ·li·est 1** Of or befitting a royal court. **2** Ceremonious and polite. —*adv.* In a courtly manner. —**court'li·ness** *n.*

court-mar·tial (kôrt'mär'shəl, kōrt'-) *n. pl.* **courts-mar·tial 1** A military court convened to try persons subject to military law. **2** A trial by such a court. —*v.t.* —**mar·tialed** or **·tialled, ·mar·tial·ing** or **·tial·ling** To try by court-martial.

court plaster An adhesive covering slight cuts, etc.

court·room (kôrt'rōōm', -rōōm', kōrt'-) *n.* A room in which judicial proceedings are held.

court·ship (kôrt'ship, kōrt'-) *n.* The act or period of courting or wooing.

court·yard (kôrt'yärd', kōrt'-) *n.* An enclosed yard adjoining a building or surrounded by buildings.

cous·in (kuz'ən) *n.* **1** A child of one's aunt or uncle. **2** One collaterally related by descent from a common ancestor. **3** One of a kindred people or kind. [<L *consobrinus* child of a maternal aunt] —**cous'in·hood, cous'in·ship** *n.* —**cous'in·ly** *adj. adv.*

cou·tu·ri·er (kōō·tü·ryā') *n.* A man who designs women's clothes. [F, lit., dressmaker] —**cou·tu·ri·ère** (kōō·tü·ryâr') *n. Fem.*

cove¹ (kōv) *n.* **1** A small, sheltered bay or inlet. **2** A recess or sheltered place. [OE *cofa* chamber, cave]

cove² (kōv) *n. Brit. Slang* A man; fellow. [<Romany *covo* that man]

cov·en (kuv'ən) *n.* An assembly of witches. [?<MF *covin* band]

cov·e·nant (kuv'ə·nənt) *n.* **1** A formal and binding agreement entered into by two or more persons or parties; a compact. **2** God's promises to mankind as set forth in the Bible. —*v.t. & v.i.* To promise by or in a covenant. [<L *convenire* meet together, agree] —**cov'e·nant·er** *n.*

cov·er (kuv′ər) v.t. 1 To place something over or upon, as to protect, conceal, etc. 2 To occupy the surface of. 3 To spread; overlay. 4 To clothe. 5 To hide; conceal. 6 To extend over. 7 To travel over. 8 To protect, as with insurance. 9 To provide for payment of (an expense, debt, etc.). 10 To treat of; include. 11 To keep within aim, as with a gun. 12 To report details of, as for a newspaper. 13 In sports, to guard (an opponent or position). 14 To incubate or sit on, as eggs. —v.i. 15 To substitute during someone's absence: with for. 16 To conceal an error, wrongdoing, crime, etc.: with up. —n. 1 Something that covers. 2 Shelter; protection. 3 Dense plant growth, underbrush, etc. 4 Something that masks, conceals, etc. 5 A table setting for one person. 6 COVER CHARGE. —break cover To come out from a hiding place. —take cover To seek shelter for protection. —under cover in secrecy; under concealment. [< L cooperire to hide thoroughly] —cov′er·er n.

cov·er·age (kuv′ər·ij) n. 1 The protection against risks extended by an insurance policy. 2 The extent to which a news story is covered.

cov·er·all (kuv′ər·ôl) n. Often pl. A one-piece garment worn over clothing as protection.

cover charge A fixed charge added to that for food and drink at a restaurant, nightclub, etc.

covered wagon A large wagon covered with canvas secured over arched supports, used esp. by American pioneers.

cov·er·ing (kuv′ər·ing) n. Something that covers, conceals, etc.

cov·er·let (kuv′ər·lit) n. A bedspread.

cov·ert (kuv′ərt, kō′vərt) adj. 1 Concealed; secret. 2 Sheltered. —n. 1 A place of shelter or concealment, as for

Covered wagon

hunters or game. 2 Any of the feathers overlying the bases of the quills of a bird's wings and tail. 3 A closely woven twilled cloth used for suits, coats, etc: also **covert cloth.** [< OF covrir to cover] —cov′ert·ly adv. —cov′ert·ness n.

cov·er-up (kuv′ər·up′) n. 1 An act or effort designed to prevent the facts or truth, as of an embarrassing or illegal activity, from becoming known. 2 A means of covering up or concealing something.

cov·et (kuv′it) v.t. & v.i. To have an inordinate desire for (esp. something belonging to another). [< L cupere to desire] —cov′et·a·ble adj. —cov′et·er n.

cov·et·ous (kuv′ə·təs) adj. Overly desirous of something; greedy. —cov′et·ous·ly adv. —cov′et·ous·ness n.

cov·ey (kuv′ē) n. pl. ·eys 1 A small flock of quails, partridges, etc. 2 A small group or band. [< OF cover hatch]

cow[1] (kou) n. pl. cows (Archaic kine) 1 The mature female of cattle and of some other animals, as the elephant. 2 Any domestic bovine regardless of sex or age. [< OE cū]

cow[2] (kou) v.t. To intimidate, as by instilling fear or awe; daunt. [< ON kūga]

cow·ard (kou′ərd) n. One lacking in courage; esp., one who gives in ignobly to fear. —adj. Cowardly. [< L cauda tail; with ref. to a dog with its tail between its legs]

cow·ard·ice (kou′ər·dis) n. Lack of courage; abject fearfulness.

cow·ard·ly (kou′ərd·lē) adj. 1 Lacking courage; abjectly fearful. 2 Of or typical of a coward. —adv. In the manner of a coward. —cow′ard·li·ness n.

cow·bell (kou′bel′) n. A bell hung from the neck of a cow to show where she is by its sound.

cow·bird (kou′bûrd′) n. An American blackbird that lays its eggs in the nests of other species of birds.

cow·boy (kou′boi′) n. A man, usu. working on horseback, who herds and tends cattle, esp. in the w U.S. Also **cow′hand′.** —**cow′girl′** n. Fem.

cow·catch·er (kou′kach′ər) n. A metal frame on the front of a locomotive to remove obstructions from the track.

cow·er (kou′ər) v.i. To crouch or draw back tremblingly as in fear. [Prob. < Scand.] —Syn. cringe, quail, shrink, grovel.

cow·herd (kou′hûrd′) n. One who herds cattle.

cow·hide (kou′hīd′) n. 1 The hide of a cow. 2 Leather made from this. 3 A heavy, flexible leather whip. —v.t. ·hid·ed, ·hid·ing To whip with or as with a cowhide.

cowl (koul) n. 1 A monk's hood or similar hooded garment. 2 A hood-shaped top for a chimney. 3 Aeron. COWLING. 4 The part of an automobile body to which the windshield, dash board, and the rear of the hood are attached. —v.t. To cover with or as with a cowl. [< L cucullus hood]

cow·lick (kou′lik′) n. A tuft of hair that stands up stubbornly.

cowl·ing (kou′ling) n. Aeron. A metal covering for an airplane engine, etc. • See AIRPLANE.

cow·man (kou′mən) n. pl. ·men (-mən) One who owns a cattle ranch.

co-work·er (kō′wûr′kər) n. A fellow worker.

cow·pea (kou′pē′) n. 1 A twining leguminous plant cultivated in the s U.S. 2 The edible seed of this plant.

cow·poke (kou′pōk′) n. Informal A cowboy.

cow pony A small horse used in herding cattle.

cow·pox (kou′poks′) n. A contagious disease of cows, forming pustules containing a virus that is the source of vaccine for smallpox.

cow·punch·er (kou′pun′chər) n. Informal A cowboy.

cow·ry (kou′rē) n. pl. ·ries Any of various tropical marine mollusks having a glossy shell. Also **cow′rie.** [< Hind. kaurī]

cow·slip (kou′slip′) n. 1 A European wildflower related to the primrose. 2 MARSH MARIGOLD. [< OE cū cow + slyppe dung]

cox (koks) Informal n. COXSWAIN. —v.t. & v.i. To act as coxswain (for).

cox·comb (koks′kōm′) n. 1 A vain, pretentious fellow; fop. 2 COCKSCOMB. [Var. of cockscomb] —cox·comb·i·cal (koks·kom′i·kəl, -kō′mi-) adj.

cox·swain (kok′sən, kok′swān′) n. One who steers or has charge of a small boat or a racing shell. [< F coque small boat + SWAIN]

coy (koi) adj. 1 Shy; diffident. 2 Pretending shyness or reluctance. [< L quietus quiet] —coy′ly adv. —coy′ness n.

coy·o·te (kī·ō′tē, kī′ōt) n. A wolflike North American animal common in the w U.S. [< Nah.]

coy·pu (koi′pōō) n. pl. ·pus or ·pu NUTRIA (def. 1). Also **coy′pou.** [Am. Sp.]

coz·en (kuz′ən) v.t. & v.i. To cheat in a petty way. [F cousiner deceive by claiming kinship < cousin cousin] —coz·en·age (kuz′ən·ij), coz′en·er n.

co·zy (kō′zē) adj. co·zi·er, co·zi·est Snug; comfortable. —n. pl. ·zies A padded cover for a teapot to prevent the heat from escaping. [Scot. cosie] —co′zi·ly adv. —co′zi·ness n.

CP Command Post.

C.P. Chief Patriarch; Common Pleas; Common Prayer; Communist Party.

cp. compare.

cp., c.p. candlepower.

c.p. chemically pure.

C.P.A. Certified Public Accountant.

cpd. compound.

Cpl. corporal.

cpm, c.p.m. cycles per minute.

CPO, C.P.O. Chief Petty Officer.

cps, c.p.s. cycles per second.

C.R. Costa Rica.

Cr chromium.

cr. credit; creditor; crown.

crab[1] (krab) n. 1 Any of various crustaceans having eight legs, two pincers, a small abdomen, a flattened carapace, and short antennae. 2 HERMIT CRAB. 3 HORSESHOE CRAB. —v. crabbed, crab·bing v.i. To take or fish for crabs. [< OE crabba]

crab[2] (krab) n. 1 CRAB APPLE. 2 An ill-tempered person. —v. crabbed, crab·bing Informal v.i. 1 To complain; grumble. —v.t. 2 To ruin or spoil. [? < Scand.]

Crab def. 1

Crab n. CANCER.

crab apple 1 Any of various kinds of small, sour apples. 2 A tree bearing crab apples: also **crab tree.**

crab·bed (krab'id) *adj* **1** Sour-tempered; cross; peevish. **2** Hard to understand; abstruse. **3** Irregular in form; cramped. [< CRAB¹, *n.* (def. 1)] —**crab'bed·ly** *adv.* —**crab'·bed·ness** *n.*

crab·by (krab'ē) *adj.* **·bi·er**, **·bi·est** Cross; ill-tempered. — **crab'bi·ly** *adv.* —**crab'bi·ness** *n.*

crab·grass (krab'gras', -gräs') *n.* A low-growing grass with freely rooting stems, a lawn pest.

crack (krak) *v.t.* **1** To cause to break open partially or completely. **2** To cause to give forth a sharp, sharp sound: to *crack* a whip. **3** *Slang* To open in order to drink, read, etc.: to *crack* a bottle or book. **4** *Informal* To break into, as a safe or building, in order to rob. **5** To solve, as a puzzle, crime, or code. **6** *Slang* To tell (a joke). **7** To destroy or crush: to *crack* one's spirit. **8** To cause (the voice) to break or change register. **9** *Informal* To strike sharply or with a sharp sound: He *cracked* him on the jaw. —*v.i.* **10** To split or break, esp. with suddenness. **11** To make a sharp snapping sound, as a whip or pistol. **12** To have a break in tone or to change register suddenly: said of the voice. **13** To become impaired or broken, as the spirit or will. — **crack down** To introduce severe disciplinary or corrective action. —**crack up 1** To crash, as an airplane. **2** *Informal* To have a breakdown, nervous or physical. **3** *Informal* To break or cause to break into laughter. —*n.* **1** An incomplete separation into two or more parts; a fissure. **2** A narrow space, as between two boards. **3** A sudden sharp or loud sound. **4** *Informal* A blow that resounds. **5** A mental or physical defect or flaw. **6** A break in tone or change of register in the voice. **7** *Informal* An attempt. **8** An exact instant: the *crack* of dawn. **9** *Informal* A witty or sarcastic remark. —*adj. Informal* Of superior excellence; first-class. [< OE *cracian*]

crack·brain (krak'brān') *n.* A weak-minded person. — *adj.* Weak-minded; crazy; odd: also **crack'-brained'**.

crack·down (krak'doun') *n. Informal* Summary disciplinary or corrective action.

cracked (krakt) *adj.* **1** Having a crack or cracks; broken or split. **2** Hoarse or broken in tone, as the voice. **3** *Informal* Crazy; mentally unsound.

crack·er (krak'ər) *n.* **1** A person or thing that cracks. **2** A firecracker. **3** A thin brittle biscuit. **4** An impoverished white inhabitant of parts of the SE U.S.: a contemptuous term.

crack·er·jack (krak'ər·jak') *Slang adj.* Of or pertaining to a person or thing of worth, merit, or the like. —*n.* A person or thing of exceptional skill or value. Also **crack'a·jack'**.

crack·ing (krak'ing) *n.* The process of splitting complex hydrocarbon molecules by heat, catalysts, etc., as in the production of gasoline from petroleum.

crack·le (krak'əl) *v.* **·led**, **·ling** *v.i.* **1** To crack or snap repeatedly with light, sharp noises. —*v.t.* **2** To crush with such sounds. **3** To cover, as china, with a delicate network of cracks. —*n.* **1** A succession of light, cracking sounds. **2** The appearance produced in china, porcelain, etc., by the cracking of the glaze in all directions. **3** Such ware: also **crack'le·ware'**. [Freq. of CRACK] —**crack'ly** *adj.*

crack·ling (krak'ling) *n.* **1** The giving out of small sharp sounds. **2** The crisp browned skin of roasted pork. **3** *pl.* The crisp remains of rendered fat.

crack·pot (krak'pot') *Slang n.* A weak-minded or eccentric person; crank. —*adj.* Eccentric; foolish; insane.

crack·up (krak'up') *n.* **1** A serious accident in an aircraft or motor vehicle. **2** A mental or physical breakdown.

-cracy *combining form* Government or authority: *democracy.* [< Gk. *krateein* to rule]

cra·dle (krād'l) *n.* **1** A rocking or swinging bed for an infant. **2** A place of birth or origin. **3** A scythe with fingers that catch the grain when cut. **4** A frame or device for supporting an object or structure. **5** A support or holder for a handset telephone. —*v.* **·dled**, **·dling** *v.t.* **1** To rock in or as in a cradle; soothe. **2** To cut or reap, as grain, with a cradle. **3** To place or support in or as in a cradle. —*v.i.* **4** To cut or reap with a cradle. [< OE *cradol*]

craft (kraft, kräft) *n.* **1** Any skill or art. **2** An occupation

or trade demanding skill, esp. a manual skill. **3** The members of such a trade; guild. **4** Cunning or skill in deceiving; guile. **5** (*pl.* **craft**) A boat, ship, or airplane. [< OE *cræft* skill, art, strength, courage] —**Syn. 1** expertness, artistry, mastery, facility. **2** business, job, employment. **4** trickery, deceitfulness, craftiness.

-craft *combining form* Skill; trade; art of: *woodcraft.*

crafts·man (krafts'mən, kräfts'-) *n. pl.* **·men** (-mən) A skilled workman or artist. —**crafts'man·ship** *n.*

craft union A labor union in which membership is limited to workers having the same trade or occupation.

craft·y (kraf'tē, kräf'-) *adj.* **craft·i·er**, **craft·i·est** Skillful in deception; cunning. —**craft'i·ly** *adv.* —**craft'i·ness** *n.*

crag (krag) *n.* A rough, steep, or broken rock rising or jutting out prominently. [ME *cragg* < Celtic]

crag·ged (krag'id) *adj.* Having numerous crags. Also **crag'gy.** —**crag'gi·ness** *n.*

crake (krāk) *n.* Any of several small, short-billed birds related to the rail. [< ON *krāka* crow]

cram (kram) *v.* **crammed**, **cram·ming** *v.t.* **1** To press or pack tightly together; crowd. **2** To feed to satiety. **3** To prepare hurriedly for an examination. —*v.i.* **4** To eat greedily; stuff oneself with food. **5** To force knowledge into the mind by hurried study. —*n.* **1** The act of cramming. **2** A crowded condition. [< OE *crammian* to stuff] —**cram'mer** *n.*

cramp¹ (kramp) *n.* **1** A metal bar with both ends bent into right angles, for holding together two stones, pieces of timber, etc.: also **cramp iron. 2** An adjustable clamp. **3** Something that restrains or confines. —*v.t.* **1** To restrain or confine the action of; hinder. **2** To make fast; hold tightly, as with a cramp. **3** To turn (the wheels of an automobile, etc.) sharply to one side. [< MDu. *krampe* hook]

cramp² (kramp) *n.* **1** An involuntary, sudden, painful muscular contraction. **2** *pl.* Acute abdominal pains. —*v.t.* To affect with cramps. [< OF *crampe*]

cram·pon (kram'pən) *n.* A device of metal spikes attached to the shoe for walking on ice or to aid in climbing.

cran·ber·ry (kran'ber'ē, -bər·ē) *n. pl.* **·ries 1** The edible, scarlet, acid berry of a woody, evergreen plant growing in marshy land. **2** The plant itself. [< Du. *kranebere*, lit., crane berry]

cranberry tree A shrub or small tree related to honeysuckle, having sour, edible fruit similar to the cranberry. Also **cranberry bush.**

crane (krān) *n.* **1** One of a family of large, long-necked, long-legged, heronlike birds allied to the rails. **2** Any of various similar birds, as a heron, stork, etc. **3** A hoisting machine having a movable arm for lifting, lowering, or shifting heavy weights. **4** An iron arm, swinging horizontally, attached to a fireplace, used for suspending pots or kettles. — *v.t. & v.i.* **craned**, **cran·ing 1** To stretch out; elongate or be elongated. **2** To elevate or lift by or as if by a crane. [< OE *cran*]

Crane *def. 1*

crane fly A fly with very long, slender legs resembling a large mosquito.

cra·ni·ol·o·gy (krā'nē·ol'ə·jē) *n.* The branch of anatomy and medicine that treats of the structure and characteristics of skulls. [< ML *cranium* cranium + -LOGY] —**cra·ni·o·log·i·cal** (krā'nē·ə·loj'i·kəl) *adj.* —**cra·ni·ol'o·gist** *n.*

cra·ni·om·e·ter (krā'nē·om'ə·tər) *n.* An instrument for measuring skulls. —**cra·ni·o·met·ric** (krā'nē·ə·met'rik) or **·ri·cal** *adj.* —**cra·ni·o·met'ri·cal·ly** *adv.* —**cra·ni·om'e·try** *n.*

cra·ni·um (krā'nē·əm) *n. pl.* **·ni·ums** or **·ni·a** (-nē·ə) The skull, esp. the part that encloses the brain. [< Gk. *kranion* skull] —**cra'ni·al** *adj.*

crank (krangk) *n.* **1** A device, as a handle attached at right angles to a shaft, for transmitting motion or for converting reciprocating motion into rotary motion, or vice versa. **2** *Informal* **a** A person given to odd notions or actions; an eccentric. **b** A grouchy, ill-tempered person. — *v.t.* **1** To bend into the shape of a crank. **2** To operate or start by a crank. —*v.i.* **3** To turn a crank. [<OE *cranc*, as in *crancstæf* a weaving comb]

crank·case (krangk′kās′) *n.* The case enclosing an engine crankshaft.

crank·shaft (krangk′shaft′, -shäft′) *n.* A shaft that bears one or more cranks or piston rods.

crank·y (krang′kē) *adj.* **crank·i·er, crank·i·est 1** Irritable; peevish. **2** Eccentric; odd. **3** Loose and rickety. —**crank′i·ly** *adv.* —**crank′i·ness** *n.*

cran·ny (kran′ē) *n. pl.* **·nies** A narrow opening, fissure. [<OF *cran*, *cren* notch] —**cran′nied** *adj.*

crape (krāp) *n.* **1** CREPE (def. 1). **2** A piece of black crepe worn or hung as a sign of mourning. [Var. of CRÊPE]

crape myrtle A shrub having bright, rose-colored, purple, or white crumpled petals, native to China but often grown in the southeastern United States. Also *crepe myrtle*.

crap·pie (krap′ē) *n. pl.* **·pies** or **·pie** Any of a genus of edible freshwater sunfish.[?]

craps (kraps) *n. pl. (construed as sing.)* A game of chance, played with two dice. Also **crap game, crap shoot′ing.** [obs. *crabs*, the lowest throw (two aces) in hazard]

crap·shoot·er (krap′shōō′tər) *n.* One who plays the game of craps.

crap·u·lence (krap′yōō·ləns) *n.* **1** Sickness by intemperance in eating or drinking. **2** Gross intemperance, as in drinking. [<Gk. *kraipalē* drunken headache]

crash[1] (krash) *v.t.* **1** To break in pieces noisily and with violence. **2** To proceed noisily and with violence: He *crashed* his way through the jungle. **3** *Informal* To enter uninvited or without paying admission: to *crash* a dance. **4** To cause, as an airplane, truck, or train, to fall to the earth or strike an obstacle with force. —*v.i.* **5** To break or fall in pieces with a violent sound. **6** To make a noise of clashing or breaking. **7** To move with such a noise. **8** To fall to the earth or violently strike an obstacle, as an airplane or automobile. **9** To fail or collapse; come to ruin. —*n.* A loud noise, as of something falling and breaking. **2** A breaking, colliding, or crashing. **3** A failure or collapse; ruin. [Imit.]

crash[2] (krash) *n.* A coarse fabric woven of thick uneven yarns: used for towels, curtains, etc. [<Russ. *krashenina*]

crash program An intensive emergency undertaking.

crass (kras) *adj.* Coarse or thick in structure; dense. **2** Dull; stupid. [<L *crassus* thick] —**crass′ly** *adv.* —**crass′· ness** *n.*

-crat *combining form* A supporter or member of a social class or a type of government: *democrat, aristocrat.* [<Gk. *krateein* govern]

crate (krāt) *n.* **1 a** A large hamper or packing box for shipping or storing. **b** Its contents. **2** *Slang* An old or decrepit vehicle or airplane. —*v.t.* **crat·ed, crat·ing** To pack, store, or send in a crate. [<L *cratis* wickerwork]

cra·ter (krā′tər) *n.* **1** The bowl-shaped depression forming the outlet of a volcano or of a hot spring. **2** A pit made by an explosion or impact. **3** Any large bowl or cavity. [<Gk. *kratēr* bowl]

cra·vat (krə·vat′) *n.* **1** A neckcloth or scarf. **2** A necktie. [<F *Cravate* a Croatian, with ref. to the neckcloths worn by Croatian soldiers]

crave (krāv) *v.* **craved, crav·ing** *v.t.* **1** To beg for humbly and earnestly. **2** To long for; desire greatly. **3** To be in need of; require. —*v.i.* **4** To desire or long: with *for* or *after.* [< OE *crafian*] —**crav′er** *n.* —**Syn.** **1** ask, solicit, seek, request, beseech, petition. **2** yearn for, wish, wish for, want.

cra·ven (krā′vən) *adj.* Lacking in courage; cowardly. — *n.* A base coward. [<L *crepare* to break] —**cra′ven·ly** *adv.*

crav·ing (krā′ving) *n.* An intense longing or need.

craw (krô) *n.* **1** The crop of a bird. **2** The stomach of any animal. [ME *crawe*]

craw·fish (krô′fish′) *n. pl.* **·fish** or **·fish·es** CRAYFISH. [Var. of CRAYFISH]

crawl (krôl) *v.i.* **1** To move by dragging the body along a surface; creep. **2** To move slowly, feebly, or cautiously. **3** To have a sensation of crawling things upon the body.

4 To have crawling things in or on the body, as a dead body. **5** To act with servility. —*n.* **1** The act of crawling. **2** An overarm swimming stroke. [<ON *krafla*] —**crawl′er** *n.* —**crawl′ing·ly** *adv.*

crawl·y (krô′lē) *adj.* **crawl·i·er, crawl·i·est** *Informal* Covered or filled with crawling things.

cray·fish (krā′fish′) *n. pl.* **·fish** or **·fish·es** **1** A marine crustacean resembling a lobster but without claws. **2** Any of various small, fresh-water crustaceans resembling the lobster. [Earlier *crevice*<OF; infl. in form by *fish*]

cray·on (krā′ən, -on) *n.* **1** A small cylinder of colored wax, chalk, etc., used for coloring or drawing. **2** A drawing made with crayons. —*v.t.* To sketch or draw with a crayon or crayons. [<L *creta* chalk] —**cray′on·ist** *n.*

craze (krāz) *v.* **crazed, craz·ing** *v.t.* **1** To cause to become mentally ill. **2** To make full of minute cracks, as the glaze of pottery. —*v.i.* **3** To become insane. **4** To become full of minute cracks. —*n.* **1** A fad; rage. **2** An intense enthusiasm. **3** A flaw in the glaze of pottery. [<Scand. Cf. Sw. *krasa* break.] —**crazed** *adj.*

cra·zy (krā′zē) *adj.* **cra·zi·er, cra·zi·est 1** Insane; mentally unbalanced. **2** Excessively emotional or disturbed as with rage. **3** *Informal* Impractical, illogical, etc.: a *crazy* plan. **4** *Informal* Inordinately eager or enthusiastic: *crazy* about jazz. —**cra′zi·ly** *adv.* —**cra′zi·ness.** *n.*

crazy bone FUNNY BONE.

crazy quilt A patchwork bed quilt made of pieces of various sizes, shapes, and colors.

creak (krēk) *n.* A sharp, squeaking sound, as from friction. —*v.t.* & *v.i.* To make, or cause to make, a creak. [Imit.] —**creak′i·ly** *adv.* —**creak′i·ness** *n.* —**creak′y** *adj.* (·i·er, ·i·est)

cream (krēm) *n.* A thick, oily, light-yellow liquid contained in milk. **2** A food, candy, etc., containing or resembling cream. **3** A soft, oily cosmetic for the skin. **4** The best or choicest part. **5** A light yellow color. —*v.t.* **1** To skim cream from. **2** To take the best part from. **3** To add cream to, as coffee. **4** To beat (butter) until soft enough for mixing. **5** To cook or prepare (food) with cream or cream sauce. **6** *Slang* To defeat thoroughly. **7** To froth. **8** To form cream. [<LL *chrisma* ointment] —**cream′i·ness** *n.* **cream′y** *adj.* (·i·er, ·i·est)

cream cheese Soft, unripened cheese made of cream or a mixture of cream and milk.

cream·er (krē′mer) *n.* **1** A cream pitcher. **2** Any dish or machine in which cream is separated from milk.

cream·er·y (krē′mər·ē) *n. pl.* **·er·ies 1** A store that sells mainly dairy products. **2** A place where butter and cheese are made, milk and cream are pasteurized, separated, bottled, etc.

cream of tartar A potassium salt of tartaric acid, used in baking powder.

cream puff 1 A shell of pastry filled with whipped cream or custard. **2** *Slang* An ineffectual or inconsequential person or thing.

crease[1] (krēs) *n.* **1** The mark of a wrinkle, fold, or the like. **2** In cricket, any of the lines limiting the position of the bowler or batsman. —*v.* **creased, creas·ing** *v.t.* **1** To make a crease or fold in; wrinkle. **2** To wound by a shot that grazes the flesh. —*v.i.* **3** To become wrinkled. [Var. of ME *creste* a crest, ridge] —**creas′er** *n.* —**creas′y** *adj.*

crease[2] (krēs) KRIS

cre·ate (krē·āt′) *v.* **·at·ed, ·at·ing** *v.t.* **1** To cause to come into existence; originate. **2** To be the cause of; bring about: *create* interest. **3** To invest with a new rank, office, etc. **4** To be the first to portray, as a character in a play. [<L *creare*] —**Syn.** **1** fashion, make, form, produce, conceive, invent, build.

cre·a·tion (krē·ā′shən) *n.* **1** The act of creating or the fact of being created. **2** That which is created. **3** The universe or all things in it. —**the Creation** The act of God in creating the world. —**cre·a′tion·al** *adj.*

cre·a·tion·ism (krē·ā′shən·iz′əm) *n.* The belief that the Biblical story of the Creation in Genesis is as valid a theory as the theory of evolution.

cre·a·tive (krē·ā′tiv) *adj.* **1** Having the ability to create. **2** Having or characterized by imagination, originality, artistic skill, etc. **3** Productive: with *of.* —**cre·a′tive·ly** *adv.* —**cre·a′tive·ness, cre·a′tiv′i·ty** (-ə·tē) *n.*

cre·a·tor (krē·ā′tər) n. One who or that which creates. — **the Creator** God.

crea·ture (krē′chər) n. 1 Anything created. 2 Something living, esp. an animal. 3 A human being. 4 An imaginary being.

creature comfort Anything contributing to bodily comfort, as food and drink.

crèche (kresh, krāsh) n. 1 A group of figures representing the Nativity. 2 A foundling hospital. 3 *Brit.* A day nursery. [< F, crib]

cre·dence (krēd′ns) n. Confidence based upon external evidence; belief. [< L *credere* believe]

cre·den·tial (kri·den′shəl) n. 1 That which certifies one's authority, credit, or claim to confidence. 2 *pl.* Testimonials certifying a person's authority or claim to confidence or consideration.

cred·i·bil·i·ty (kred′ə·bil′ə·tē) n. 1 Capacity of being believed. 2 The capacity, as of a government or a public official, of maintaining the public's confidence that its report of the conduct of its affairs is worthy of belief. — **credibility gap** 1 A lessening or loss of credibility, as in a government or public official. 2 The extent or degree of a decline in credibility: *The official statement only widened the* credibility gap.

cred·i·ble (kred′ə·bəl) adj. Capable of being believed; reliable. [< L *credibilis* < *credere* believe] —**cred′i·ble·ness** n. —**cred′i·bly** adv.

cred·it (kred′it) n. 1 Belief; trust; confidence. 2 Reputation for trustworthiness; character; repute. 3 Influence derived from trustworthiness, good opinion of others, etc. 4 Approval; praise: *Give him* credit *for telling the truth.* 5 One who or that which adds honor or reputation: a *credit* to his class. 6 *Usu. pl.* Acknowledgement of work done, as in the making of a motion picture. 7 In an account, the balance in one's favor. 8 An amount made available by a bank, against which a person or business may draw. 9 In bookkeeping: a The entry of any amount paid by a debtor. b The amount so entered. c The right-hand side of an account where such amounts are recorded. 10 Confidence in a firm's or person's solvency or ability to meet payments. 11 The time allowed for payment of a debt. 12 The amount to which a person or business may be financially trusted. 13 In education, official certification that a course of study has been finished; also, a recognized unit of school or college work. —**on credit** With a promise to pay later. —v.t. 1 To give credit for; accept as true. 2 To ascribe, as intelligence or honor, to: with *with.* 3 In bookeeping, to give credit for or enter as credit to. 4 In education, to give educational credits to (a student). [< L *credere* believe, trust] —**cred′it·a·bil′i·ty, cred′it·a·ble·ness** n. —**cred′it·a·ble** adj. —**cred′it·a·bly** adv.

credit card A card issued by a business, bank, etc., giving the owner the privilege to charge bills at certain stores, restaurants, etc.

cred·i·tor (kred′i·tər) n. One who gives credit or to whom another is indebted.

credit rating A rating given a person or business regarding financial status, reputation for paying bills, etc.

credit union A cooperative group for making loans to its members at low rates of interest.

cre·do (krē′dō, krā′-) n. pl. ·**dos** CREED. [L, I believe; the opening word of the Nicene Creed.]

cre·du·li·ty (krə·dyōō′lə·tē) n. A disposition to believe on slight evidence. [< L *credulus* credulous]

cred·u·lous (krej′ōō·ləs) adj. 1 Apt or disposed to believe on slight evidence. 2 Arising from credulity. [< L *credere* believe] —**cred′u·lous·ly** adv. —**cred′u·lous·ness** n.

Cree (krē) n. pl. **Cree** or **Crees** 1 One of a tribe of the Algonquian stock of North American Indians. 2 The language of this tribe.

creed (krēd) n. 1 A formal summary of religious belief. 2 Any statement of things believed, principles held, etc. [< L *credo* I believe]

creek (krēk, krik) n. 1 A stream between a brook and a river in size. 2 *Chiefly Brit.* A small inlet, bay, or cove. [< Scand.]

creel (krēl) n. 1 An angler's basket for carrying fish. 2 A cage for catching lobsters, etc. [< L *cratis* wickerwork]

creep (krēp) v.i. **crept, creep·ing** 1 To move with the body close to a surface; crawl. 2 To move or change imperceptibly, slowly, secretly, or stealthily. 3 To exhibit servility; cringe. 4 To feel as if covered with creeping things. 5 To grow along a surface or support: *creeping* plants. 6 To slip out of place. —n. 1 The act of creeping. 2 *pl.* A sensation of uneasy apprehensiveness. 3 *Slang* A distasteful or obnoxious person. [< OE *crēopan*]

creep·er (krēp′ər) n. 1 One who or that which creeps. 2 A plant that trails on the ground or climbs on a support. 3 *pl.* A device worn on shoes to prevent one's slipping. 4 *pl.* A baby's one-piece garment.

creep·y (krē′pē) adj. **creep·i·er, creep·i·est** Having or producing a feeling of apprehension or disgust. —**creep′i·ly** adv. —**creep′i·ness** n.

creese (krēs) n. KRIS.

cre·mate (krē′māt, kri·māt′) v.t. **·mat·ed, ·mat·ing** To burn (a dead body) to ashes. [< L *cremare* burn to ashes] —**cre·ma′tion, cre′ma·tor** n.

cre·ma·to·ry (krē′mə·tôr′ē, -tō′rē, krem′-) adj. Related to cremation. —n. pl. ·**ries** A place for cremating. Also **cre′ma·to′ri·um** (-tôr′ē·əm, -tō′rē-).

crème de ca·ca·o (də kə·kā′ō, -kä′ō) A sweet, chocolate-flavored liqueur. [F, lit., cream of cocoa]

crème de menthe (də mänt, menth) A green or white cordial with a strong flavor of mint. [F, lit., cream of mint]

cre·nate (krē′nāt) adj. Having a margin of rounded projections, as certain leaves. Also **cre′nat·ed.** [< LL *crena* a notch] —**cre·na′tion** n.

cren·e·late (kren′ə·lāt) v.t. **·lat·ed, ·lat·ing** To fortify or decorate with battlements. Also **cren′el·late.** [< LL *crena* notch] —**cren′e·la′tion, cren′el·la′tion** n.

cre·ole (krē′ōl) adj. Cooked with a savory sauce of peppers, tomatoes, onions, etc.

Cre·ole (krē′ōl) n. 1 A native of Spanish America or the West Indies, of European parentage. 2 A descendant of French, Spanish, or Portuguese settlers of the Gulf States. 3 The French patois of Louisiana. 4 Any person of both Creole and Negro descent. —adj. Of or relating to the Creoles.

cre·o·sol (krē′ə·sōl, -sol) n. A colorless, aromatic, oily compound derived from certain resins. [< CREOS(OTE) + -OL²]

cre·o·sote (krē′ə·sōt) n. An oily liquid mixture of phenols or hydrocarbons, obtained by the distillation of wood or coal tar, used to preserve timber. —v.t. **·sot·ed, ·sot·ing** To treat or impregnate with creosote, as shingles, etc. [< Gk. *kreas* flesh + *sōtēr* preserver]

crepe (krāp, def. 4 also krep) n. 1 A thin, crinkled fabric of silk, cotton, wool, etc. 2 Crape (def. 2). 3 CREPE PAPER. 4 A thin pancake. Also **crêpe.** [< F *crêpe* < L *crispus* curled]

crepe paper A crinkled, decorative paper.

crept (krept) p.t. of CREEP.

cre·pus·cu·lar (kri·pus′kyə·lər) adj. Of, pertaining to, or active during twilight. [< L *creper* dark, dusky]

cres., cresc. crescendo.

cres·cen·do (krə·shen′dō, -sen′-) n. pl. ·**dos** *Music* A gradual increase in loudness. —adj. Slowly increasing in loudness. [< Ital. *crescere* to increase]

cres·cent (kres′ənt) n. 1 The visible part of the moon in its first quarter, having one concave edge and one convex edge. 2 Something crescent-shaped. —adj. 1 Increasing: said of the moon in its first quarter. 2 Shaped like the moon in its first quarter. [< L *crescere* to increase] • See MOON.

cre·sol (krē′sōl, -sol) n. Any one of three isomeric compounds obtained by the distillation of coal tar. [Var. of CREOSOL]

cress (kres) n. One of various plants of the mustard family having a pungent taste and used in salads. [< OE *cressa*] —**cress′y** adj.

cres·set (kres′it) n. An incombustible frame or vessel mounted to hold a torch or its fuel. [< OF *craicet, craisset*]

crest (krest) n. 1 A comb or tuft on the head of an animal or bird. 2 The decoration on the top of a helmet; a plume; tuft. 3 The ridge of a wave or of a mountain. 4 The highest point or maximum degree of anything. 5 A heraldic device placed above the shield in a coat of arms and also used on stationery, silverware, etc. —v.t. 1 To serve as a crest for; cap. 2 To furnish with or as with a crest. 3 To reach the crest of. 4 To adorn with a crest. —v.i. 5 To come to a crest, as a wave prior to breaking. [< L crista tuft] — **crest'ed** adj.

Crest def. 5
above coat of arms

crest·fall·en (krest'fô'lən) adj. 1 Dejected; depressed. 2 Having the crest lowered.

cre·ta·ceous (kri·tā'shəs) adj. Of or like chalk; chalky. [< L creta chalk]

Cre·ta·ceous (kri·tā'shəs) n. & adj. See GEOLOGY.

cre·tin (krē'tin) n. A person afflicted with cretinism. [< F crétin, var. of chrétien Christian, human being, i.e., not an animal] —**cre'tin·ous** adj.

cre·tin·ism (krē'tən·iz'əm) n. A condition associated with thyroid deficiency during early development, marked by physical deformities and mental retardation.

cre·tonne (kri·ton', krē'ton) n. A heavy, unglazed patterned fabric used for draperies, chair coverings, etc. [< Creton, a village in Normandy]

cre·vasse (krə·vas') n. 1 A deep fissure, as in a glacier. 2 A break in a levee. —v.t. ·vassed, ·vass·ing To split with crevasses. [< OF crevace crevice] —**cre·vassed'** adj.

crev·ice (krev'is) n. A small fissure or crack. [< L crepare to crack, creak] —**crev'iced** adj.

crew¹ (krōō) n. 1 All of the seamen manning a specific ship, usu. excluding officers. 2 All those manning an aircraft. 3 Any group of people organized for a particular work project. 4 A company of people in general; crowd. 5 The oarsmen and coxswain of a racing shell. [< OF creue an increase]

crew² (krōō) p.t. of CROW.

crew cut A closely cropped haircut.

crew·el (krōō'əl) n. A slackly twisted worsted yarn, used in fancywork. [?]

crew·el·work (krōō'əl·wûrk') n. Embroidery with crewel.

crib (krib) n. 1 A manger for fodder. 2 A stall for cattle. 3 A child's bed, with side railings. 4 A box, bin, or small building for grain. 5 A frame of wood or metal, used to support or retain earth, etc., as in a mine. 6 Informal PLAGIARISM. 7 A translation or other unauthorized aid in study. —v. cribbed, crib·bing v.t. 1 To enclose in or as in a crib; confine closely. 2 Informal To take and pass off as one's own, as an answer; plagiarize. 3 Informal To steal. 4 Informal To translate with a crib. —v.i. 5 Informal To use a crib in translating. [< OE cribb] —**crib'ber** n.

crib·bage (krib'ij) n. A game of cards for two, three, or four players in which the score is kept on a pegboard. [? < CRIB]

crick (krik) n. A spasmodic cramping of the muscles, as of the neck. —v.t. To turn or twist so as to produce a crick. [?]

crick·et¹ (krik'it) n. A leaping insect related to the grasshopper but having long antennae, the male of which makes a chirping sound by friction of the forewings. [< OF criquet]

crick·et² (krik'it) n. 1 An outdoor game played with bats, a ball, and wickets, between two opposing sides of eleven players each. 2 Informal Fair, gentlemanly behavior; sportsmanship. [< F criquet bat, stick] —**crick'et·er** n.

crick·et³ (krik'it) n. FOOTSTOOL. [?]

cried (krīd) p.t. & p.p. of CRY.

cri·er (krī'ər) n. 1 One who cries. 2 One who makes public announcements in the street.

crime (krīm) n. 1 Law An act that subjects the doer to legal punishment. 2 Any grave offense against morality or social order. 3 Informal Any unjust or shameful action. [< L crimen accusation, charge]

crim·i·nal (krim'ə·nəl) adj. 1 Law a Of, relating to, or being a crime. b Dealing with penal as opposed to civil law. 2 Guilty of or involving crime. 3 Informal Regrettable; shameful. —n. One convicted of or guilty of a crime. —**crim·i·nal·i·ty** (krim'ə·nal'ə·tē), **crim'i·nal·ness** n. —**crim'i·nal·ly** adv.

crim·i·nol·o·gy (krim'ə·nol'ə·jē) n. The scientific study and investigation of crime and criminals. —**crim·i·no·log·i·cal** (krim'ə·nə·loj'i·kəl) adj. —**crim'i·nol'o·gist** n.

crimp (krimp) v.t. 1 To bend or press into ridges or folds; corrugate; flute. 2 To curl or wave: to crimp the hair. 3 To fold one edge of (paper, etc.) over another edge and press tightly together. 4 Informal To hinder or obstruct. —n. 1 The act of crimping. 2 Anything crimped. 3 Informal An obstruction or hindrance. [< MDu. crimpen wrinkle, draw together] —**crimp'er** n. —**crimp'y** adj.

crim·son (krim'zən) n. A deep red color. —adj. 1 Of a deep red color. 2 Bloody. —v.t. & v.i. To make or become crimson. [< Ar. qirmiz kermes (insect used in making a red dye)]

cringe (krinj) v.i. cringed, cring·ing 1 To crouch, wince, draw back, etc., as in fear. 2 To seek favor in a servile or flattering manner. —n. The act of cringing. [ME cringen, crengen] —**cring'er** n.

crin·kle (kring'kəl) v.t. & v.i. ·kled, ·kling 1 To be or cause to be full of wrinkles or twists. 2 To make a crackling sound. —n. A wrinkle; ripple. [ME < crenklen] —**crin'kly** adj. (·kli·er, ·kli·est)

cri·noid (krī'noid, krin'oid) adj. Of or pertaining to various small, flowerlike sea animals attached by stalks to the sea bottom: also **cri·noi·dal** (kri·noid'l). —n. One of these animals. [< Gk. krinon lily + -OID]

crin·o·line (krin'ə·lin, -lēn) n. 1 A highly sized, stiff fabric, used in hems, interlinings, etc. 2 A skirt stiffened with such fabric. 3 HOOP SKIRT. [< L crinis hair + linum flax, thread]

crip·ple (krip'əl) n. A lame person or animal or one lacking the natural use of a limb or the body. —v.t. ·pled, ·pling 1 To lame. 2 To impair or disable in some way. [< OE crypel] —**crip'pler** n.

cri·sis (krī'sis) n. pl. cri·ses (-sēz) 1 A decisive or crucial turning point in the progress of a series of events. 2 A dangerous or critical moment or development. 3 Pathol. A decisive change, favorable or unfavorable, in the course of a disease. [< Gk. krisis < krinein decide]

crisp (krisp) adj. 1 Firm and fresh. 2 Brittle or crumbling readily, as pastry. 3 Clean and neat. 4 Terse or pithy: a crisp reply. 5 Fresh and bracing. 6 Tightly curled or waved. —v.t. & v.i. To make or become crisp. [< L crispus curled] —**crisp'er, crisp'ness** n. —**crisp'ly** adv. —**crisp'y** adj.

criss·cross (kris'krôs', -kros') v.t. 1 To cross with interlacing lines. —v.i. 2 To move in crisscrosses. —adj. Characterized by crossing lines. —n. 1 The cross of one who cannot write. 2 A pattern of intersecting lines. —adv. Across; crosswise. [Alter. of Christ-cross]

crit. critic; critical; criticism.

cri·te·ri·on (krī·tir'ē·ən) n. pl. ·te·ri·a (-tir'ē·ə) or ·te·ri·ons A standard, rule, or test by which a correct judgment can be made. [< Gk. kritēs a judge]

crit·ic (krit'ik) n. 1 One who judges anything by some standard or criterion. 2 One whose profession is to judge or evaluate literary, theatrical, musical, or other artistic productions. 3 A faultfinder. —adj. Pertaining to criticism; critical. [< Gk. kritēs a judge]

crit·i·cal (krit'i·kəl) adj. 1 Faultfinding; censorious. 2 Characterized by careful, precise analysis or examination. 3 Of critics or criticism. 4 Risky; perilous. 5 Of, being, or contributing to a crisis; decisive. 6 Pathol. Of a crisis in a disease. 7 Physics Designating a value or point indicating a decisive change in a specified condition. —**crit'i·cal·ly** adv. —**crit'i·cal·ness** n. —Syn. 1 condemnatory, captious, carping, disapproving. 5 grave, serious, urgent, pressing.

crit·i·cism (krit'ə·siz'əm) n. 1 The act or art of criticizing. 2 A discriminating judgment; an evaluation. 3 A severe or unfavorable judgment. 4 The principles or rules for judging anything, esp. works of literature or art. 5 A review, article, etc., expressing a critical judgment.

crit·i·cize (krit'ə·sīz) v.t. & v.i. ·cized, ·ciz·ing 1 To examine and judge as a critic. 2 To judge severely; censure. *Brit. sp.* **crit'i·cise.** —**crit'i·ciz'a·ble** *adj.* —**crit'i·ciz'er** *n.*

cri·tique (kri·tēk') *n.* 1 A critical review. 2 The art of criticism.

crit·ter (krit'ər) *n. Regional* 1 A domestic animal. 2 Any living creature. [Var. of CREATURE]

croak (krōk) *v.i.* 1 To utter a hoarse, low-pitched cry, as a frog or raven. 2 To speak in a low, hoarse voice. 3 To forbode evil; grumble. 4 *Slang* To die. —*v.t.* 5 To utter with a croak. 6 *Slang* To kill. —*n.* A hoarse vocal sound. [Imit.] —**croak'y** *adj.*

croak·er (krō'kər) *n.* 1 Any of various animals that croak. 2 One who forebodes evil.

Cro·at (krō'ăt, -ət) *n.* 1 A native or citizen of Croatia. 2 The language of the Croats; Serbo-Croatian. —**Cro·a·tian** (krō·ā'shən) *n., adj.*

cro·chet (krō·shā') *v.t. & v.i.* ·cheted (-shād'), ·chet·ing (-shā'ing) To form or ornament (a fabric) by interlacing thread with a hooked needle. —*n.* A kind of fancywork produced by crocheting. [< F *croche* a hook]

crock (krok) *n.* A earthenware pot or jar. [< OE *crocca*]

crock·er·y (krok'ər·ē) *n.* Earthenware; earthen vessels collectively.

croc·o·dile (krok'ə·dīl) *n.* A large, lizardlike, aquatic reptile of tropical re-gions, having the head longer and narrower than that of an alliga-tor. [< Gk. *krokodilos* lizard, crocodile.] — **croc·o·dil·i·an** (krok'ə-dil'ē·ən), **croc'o·dil'e·an** *adj., n.*

Crocodile

crocodile   tears
Simulated weeping; hypocritical grief.

cro·cus (krō'kəs) *n. pl.* **cro·cus·es** or **cro·ci** (krō'sī) 1 Any of a genus of plants related to the iris with long grasslike leaves and large flowers. 2 The flower of this plant. 3 An orange-yellow or saffron color. [< Gk. *krokos* saffron]

crois·sant (krwä·sän') *n.* A small, buttery, crescent-shaped roll. [F]

Croix de Guerre (krwä də gâr') A French military decoration for bravery. [F lit., cross of war]

Cro-Mag·non (krō-mag'non, -man'yən) *n.* A member of a prehistoric race of men whose remains were found in France. —*adj.* Pertaining or relating to the Cro-Magnon race. [< *Cro-Magnon*, a cave in s France]

crom·lech (krom'lek) *n.* 1 DOLMEN. 2 An ancient monu-ment of standing stones arranged in a circle. [< Welsh *crom* bent + *llech* flat stone]

crone (krōn) *n.* A withered old woman. [< OF *carogne* carcass]

cro·ny (krō'nē) *n. pl.* ·nies A familiar friend. [< Gk. *chronios* long-lasting]

crook (krŏok) *n.* 1 A bend or curve. 2 The curved or bent part of a thing: the *crook* of a branch. 3 An implement with a crook in it: a shepherd's *crook*. 4 *Informal* A crimi-nal; swindler; cheat. [< ON *krōkr*]

crook·ed (krŏok'id) *adj.* 1 Not straight; having angles or curves. 2 Tricky; dishonest. —**crook'ed·ly** *adv.* —**crook'ed·ness** *n.*

crook·neck (krŏok'nek') *n.* Any of several varieties of squash with a long, curved neck.

croon (krŏon) *v.t. & v.i.* To sing or hum in a soft or roman-tic manner. —*n.* A low, humming sound. [< MDu. *krōnen* sing softly, lament] —**croon'er** *n.*

crop (krop) *n.* 1 Cultivated plants, grains, fruits, etc., col-lectively. 2 The plant product of a particular kind, place, or season. 3 The entire yield of anything. 4 A short hair-cut. 5 The first stomach of a bird; craw. 6 A hunting or riding whip with a leather loop for a lash. 7 A collection of things: a *crop* of lies. —*v.* **cropped, crop·ping** *v.t.* 1 To cut or eat off the stems or ends of. 2 To pluck or reap. 3 To cut off closely, as hair; trim, as a dog's ears or tail. 4 To raise a crop or crops on; cause to bear crops. —*v.i.* 5 To appear above the surface; sprout: with *up* or *out.* 6 To develop or

come up unexpectedly: with *up* or *out:* A new problem *cropped* up. [< OE *cropp*]

crop·per¹ (krop'ər) *n.* 1 One who or that which crops. 2 SHARECROPPER.

crop·per² (krop'ər) *n.* A fall, as from a horse. —**come a cropper** 1 To fall headlong. 2 To fail disastrously. [? < *neck and crop* completely, thoroughly]

cro·quet (krō·kā') *n.* An outdoor game played by knock-ing wooden balls through a series of wire arches by means of mallets. [< F *croquet*]

cro·quette (krō·ket') *n.* A ball or cake of previously cooked, minced food, fried in deep fat or baked. [F < *croquer* crunch]

cro·sier (krō'zhər) *n.* A staff surmounted by a crook or cross, borne by or before a bishop or archbishop on occa-sions of ceremony. [< Med. L *crocia* bishop's crook]

cross (krôs, kros) *n.* 1 A vertical post intersected by a horizontal bar near the top, used as an instrument of torture and death by the ancient Romans. 2 A representation of the cross on which Christ was crucified, a symbol of Christianity. 3 Any rep-resentation of a cross, used as a badge of honor, a grave marker, etc. 4 Any suffering, trial, or tribulation. 5 Any mark or design composed of two inter-secting lines. 6 Such a mark used as a signature by one who cannot write. 7 Anything that combines the qualities of characteristics of two other things: a *cross* between poetry and prose. 8 The act of crossing, as from one side to another. 9 *Biol.* a A mixing of varieties or breeds of plants or animals. b The product of any such mixing; a hybrid. —**the Cross** 1 The cross on which Christ was crucified. 2 Christianity. —*v.t.* 1 To pass or move from one side to the other side of. 2 To extend from side to side of; span. 3 To intersect, as streets or lines. 4 To draw or put a line across. 5 To lay or place over or across: to *cross* the legs. 6 To transport across. 7 To make the sign of the cross upon or over. 8 To meet and pass: Your letter *crossed* mine. 9 To obstruct or hinder; thwart. 10 To cause, as plants or animals, to interbreed; hybridize. —*v.i.* 11 To intersect; lie across. 12 To pass, move, or extend from side to side. 13 To meet and pass. 14 To breed together; inter-breed. —*adj.* 1 Lying or moving across or through; trans-verse: *cross* streets. 2 Contrary; opposed: *cross* purposes. 3 Ill-tempered; peevish. 4 HYBRID. —*adv.* Across; crosswise; traversely. [< L *crux*] —**cross'ly** *adv.* —**cross'ness** *n.*

Crosses
a. Celtic. b. Latin.
c. Maltese.

cross·bar (krôs'bär, kros'-) *n.* A transverse bar or line. —*v.t.* To secure or mark with transverse bars.

cross·beam (krôs'bēm', -kros'-) *n.* 1 A beam extending from wall to wall. 2 A beam that crosses another.

cross·bill (krôs'bil', kros'-) *n.* A finchlike bird having mandibles that cross each other when the beak is closed.

cross·bones (krôs'bōnz', kros'-) *n.* A symbol of death consisting of two arm or leg bones crossing each other, usu. surmounted by a skull.

cross·bow (krôs'bō', kros'-) *n.* A medieval missile weapon consisting of a bow fixed transversely on a grooved stock.

cross·breed (krôs'brēd', kros'-) *v.t. & v.i.* ·bred, ·breed·ing *Biol.* HYBRIDIZE —*n.* A strain or animal so produced. —**cross'bred'** *adj.*

cross·coun·try (krôs'kun'trē, kros'-) *adj. & adv.* Across open country instead of by roads.

cross·cut (krôs'kut', kros'-) *v.t.* ·cut, ·cut·ting To cut crosswise or through. —*adj.* Used or made for the purpose of cutting something across: a *crosscut* saw. —*n.* A cut across or a shortcut.

cross-ex·am·ine (krôs'ig·zam'in, kros'-) *v.t.* ·ined, ·in·ing 1 To question anew (a witness already called by the opposing party) to test the reliability of his previous testi-mony. 2 To question thoroughly. —**cross'-ex·am'i·na'tion, cross'-ex·am'in·er** *n.*

cross-eye (krôs'ī', kros'-) *n.* STRABISMUS. —**cross'-eyed'** *adj.*

cross·fer·ti·li·za·tion (krôs′fûr′tə·lə·zā′shən, kros′-) *n.*
1 The union of male and female gametes from different
individuals. 2 The fertilization of one plant or flower by
the pollen from another.

cross·fer·ti·lize (krôs′fûr′tə·līz, kros′-) *v.t. & v.i.* **-lized,**
·liz·ing To fertilize or be fertilized by cross-fertilization.

cross-grained (krôs′grānd′, kros′-) *adj.* 1 Having the
grain run across or irregularly: said of wood. 2 Difficult;
stubborn; perverse.

cross·hatch (krôs′hach′, kros′-) *v.t.* To shade, as a picture, by crossed lines, either diagonal or rectangular. —
cross′·hatch′ing *n.*

cross-in·dex (krôs′in′deks, kros′-) *v.t. & v.i.* To insert
cross references in (an index, etc.).

cross·ing (krôs′ing, kros′-) *n.* 1 The place where a road,
river, etc., may be crossed. 2 An intersection, as of roads.
3 The act of crossing.

cross·patch (krôs′pach′, kros′-) *n.* A cranky, ill-tempered person.

cross·piece (krôs′pēs′, kros′-) *n.* A piece of material of
any kind crossing another.

cross·pol·li·nate (krôs′pol′ə·nāt, kros′-) *v.t.* **·nat·ed, ·nat·**
ing To subject to cross-fertilization (def. 2). —**cross′·pol′li·**
na′tion *n.*

cross·pur·pose (krôs′pûr′pəs, kros′-) *n.* A purpose
which is contrary to or conflicts with another. —**at cross-**
purposes In conflict as to means and aims.

cross·ques·tion (krôs′kwes′chən, kros′-) *v.t.* CROSS-
EXAMINE.

cross-re·fer (krôs′ri·fûr′, kros′-) *v.* **·ferred, ·fer·ring** *v.t.*
To refer to another passage or part. —*v.i.* To make a
cross-reference.

cross-ref·er·ence (krôs′ref′rəns, kros′-) *n.* 1 A reference from one passage in a text to another in the same
work. 2 In a library catalog, and in research and documentation, reference from one subject to another.

cross·road (krôs′rōd, kros′-) *n.* A road that crosses another, or that crosses from one main road to another. Also
cross′way.

cross·roads (krôs′rōdz′, kros′-) *n. pl. (construed as*
sing.) 1 A place where roads cross. 2 A juncture in time
where two cultures, eras, etc., meet. 3 A critical time or
decision.

cross section 1 A section of any object cut at right
angles to its length. 2 Any specimen or example typical
of the whole.

cross-stitch (krôs′stich′, kros′-) *n.* 1 A double stitch in
the form of an X. 2 Needlework made with this stitch. —
v.t. To make or mark with a cross-stitch.

cross-town (krôs′toun′, kros′-) *adj.* Going across a city:
a *cross-town* bus. —*adv.* Across a city: to go *cross-town.*

cross·tree (krôs′trē′, kros′-) *n. Usu. pl. Naut.* One of the
pieces of wood or iron set crosswise at the head of a mast.

cross·walk (krôs′wôk′, kros′-) *n.* Any lane marked off,
usu. by white lines, to be used by pedestrians in crossing
a street.

cross·wise (krôs′wīz′, kros′-) *adv.* Across. Also **cross′·**
ways.

cross·word puzzle (krôs′wûrd′, kros′-) A puzzle consisting of black and white squares, the latter of which are
numbered and are to be filled in with letters forming
words to which clues are given in lists of definitions, synonyms, etc.

crotch (kroch) *n.* 1 A point of division or divergence; a
fork. 2 The region of the human body where the legs
separate from the pelvis. 3 A forked pole or stick. [?]

crotched (krocht) *adj.* Having a crotch.

crotch·et (kroch′it) *n.* 1 A whimsical notion; an eccentricity. 2 A small hook. [< OF *crochet* a hook]

crotch·et·y (kroch′ə·tē) *adj.* 1 Perverse; cantankerous;
eccentric. 2 Like a crotchet. —**crotch′et·i·ness** *n.*

cro·ton (krōt′n) *n.* 1 Any of a genus of widely dispersed
trees and shrubs of the spurge family. 2 An ornamental
plant with variegated foliage. [< Gk. *krotōn* a kind of
plant]

Croton bug GERMAN COCKROACH. [< *Croton* River, New
York]

croton oil A purgative obtained from the seeds of an
East Indian croton.

crouch (krouch) *v.i.* 1 To stoop or bend low. 2 To cringe;
cower. —*v.t.* 3 To bend low. —*n.* A crouching or the position taken in crouching. [< OF *croc* a hook]

croup¹ (krōōp) *n.* A disease characterized by hoarse
coughing, laryngeal spasm, and difficulty in breathing.
[Imit.] —**croup′ous, croup′y** *adj.*

croup² (krōōp) *n.* The rump of a horse, etc. Also **croupe.**
[< OF *croupe*] • See HORSE.

crou·pi·er (krōō′pē·ər, *Fr.* krōō·pyā′) *n.* One in charge of
collecting or paying out money at a gambling table. [F, lit.,
one who rides on the croup, an assistant]

crou·ton (krōō′ton, krōō·ton′; *Fr.* krōō·tôn′) *n.* Any of the
small, toasted or fried cubes of bread used in soups, salads,
etc. [< F *croûte* crust]

crow¹ (krō) *n.* 1 Any of various omnivorous, raucous birds
with glossy black plumage. 2 Loosely, a rook or raven. [<
OE *crāwe*]

crow² (krō) *v.i.* **crowed** or *(for def. 1) Chiefly Brit.* **crew,**
crowed, crow·ing 1 To utter the cry of a rooster. 2 To exult;
boast. 3 To utter sounds expressive of delight, as an infant.
—*n.* A crowing sound of a rooster, infant, etc. [< OE *crā-*
wan]

Crow (krō) *n. pl.* **Crow** or **Crows** 1 A North American Indian of a Siouan tribe. 2 The language of this tribe.

crow·bar (krō′bär′) *n.* A straight iron or steel bar, with
the point flattened and sometimes set at an angle, used as
a lever.

crowd (kroud) *n.* 1 A large number of persons or things
gathered closely together. 2 The populace in general; the
masses. 3 *Informal* A particular set of people; a clique. —
v.t. 1 To shove or push. 2 To fill to overflowing, as with a
crowd; fill to excess. 3 To cram together; force into a confined space. 4 *Informal* To put pressure upon (a person),
as by mental harassment. —*v.i.* 5 To gather in large numbers; throng together. 6 To push forward; force one's way.
7 To shove or push. [< OE *crūdan*] —**crowd′er** *n.*

crow·foot (krō′fŏŏt′) *n. pl.* **·foots** Any of numerous
plants having variously lobed leaves and usu. yellow flowers.

crown (kroun) *n.* 1 A decorative circlet for the head, esp.
as a mark of sovereign power. 2 *Often cap.*
A sovereign ruler; also, sovereignty: with
the. 3 A wreath or garland for the head. 4
A reward or prize for excellence or merit.
5 A complete or perfect state or type;
acme. 6 The top or summit; crest. 7 The top
of the head: a bald *crown.* 8 The head itself. 9 The upper portion of a hat. 10 *Dent.*
a The part of a tooth exposed beyond the
gum. **b** An artificial substitute for this. • See TOOTH. 11 **a**
A coin stamped with a crown or crowned head. **b** Formerly, a British five-shilling piece. 12 *Naut.* The outer
point of junction of the two arms of an anchor. —*v.t.* 1 To
place a crown or garland on the head of. 2 To enthrone;
make a monarch of. 3 To be the topmost part of. 4 To form
the ultimate ornament to or aspect of. 5 To endow with
honor or dignity. 6 To bring to completion; consummate.
7 *Dent.* To put a crown on (a tooth). 8 *Slang* To hit, as a
person, on the head. 9 In checkers, to make into a king.
[< L *corona*] —**crown′er** *n.*

Crown

crown colony A colonial dependency of Great Britain
in which the crown retains control of legislation.

crown glass Very hard, clear glass used in optical instruments.

crown land In some British dominions or colonies, land
held under government control.

crown prince The heir apparent to a crown, a monarch's oldest living son.

crown princess 1 The wife of a crown prince. 2 The
female heir apparent to a throne.

crow's-foot (krōz′fŏŏt′) *n. pl.* **-feet** One of the wrinkles
diverging from the outer corner of the eye.

crow's-nest (krōz′nest′) *n.* 1 *Naut.* A small platform at
a ship's masthead, used by the lookout. 2 Any similar
lookout ashore.

cro·zier (krō′zhər) *n.* CROSIER.

crs. credits; creditors.

CRT cathode-ray tube.

cru·ces (krōō′sēz) A *n.pl.* of CRUX.

cru·cial (krōō′shəl) *adj.* 1 Of immense and decisive importance; critical. 2 Severely difficult and trying. [< L *crux*, *crucis* cross, torture] —**cru′cial·ly** *adv.*

cru·ci·ble (krōō′sə·bəl) *n.* 1 A pot or vessel made of a substance that will stand extreme heat. 2 The hollow place in the bottom of an ore furnace. 3 A trying and purifying test. [< Med. L *crucibulum* earthen pot]

cru·ci·fix (krōō′sə·fiks) *n.* A cross bearing an effigy of Christ crucified. [< L *crucifixus* one hanged on a cross]

cru·ci·fix·ion (krōō′sə·fik′shən) *n.* The act of crucifying or the state of being crucified. 2 Any representation of Christ's death. —**the Crucifixion** The death of Christ on the cross.

cru·ci·form (krōō′sə·fôrm) *adj.* Having the shape of a cross: a *cruciform* church. [< L *crux* cross + -FORM]

cru·ci·fy (krōō′sə·fī) *v.t.* **·fied, ·fy·ing** 1 To put to death by nailing or binding to a cross. 2 To torture; torment. [< L *crucifigere* fasten to a cross] —**cru′ci·fi′er** *n.*

Crucifix

crud (krud) 1 *Brit. Dial.* Curd. 2 A deposit or accretion of an undesirable substance, as grit. 3 *Slang* Worthless rubbish. —**crud′dy** *adj.* (**·di·er, ·di·est**)

crude (krōōd) *adj.* **crud·er, crud·est** 1 Not in a state ready for use; raw; unrefined: *crude* oil. 2 Lacking refinement, tact, good taste, etc. 3 Rough in workmanship, design, etc. 4 Not disguised; bare: a *crude* truth. [< L *crudus*] —**crude′ly** *adv.* —**crude′ness** *n.* —**Syn.** 2 coarse, gross, vulgar.

cru·di·ty (krōō′də·tē) *n. pl.* **·ties** 1 The state or quality of being crude. 2 A crude act, remark, etc.

cru·el (krōō′əl) *adj.* 1 Disposed to inflict suffering, pain, etc., on others. 2 Causing suffering, distress, etc.: a *cruel* fate. [< L *crudelis* severe] —**cru′el·ly** *adv.* —**Syn.** 1 pitiless, inhuman, merciless, sadistic, ruthless.

cru·el·ty (krōō′əl·tē) *n. pl.* **·ties** 1 The quality or condition of being cruel. 2 Something cruel, as an action.

cru·et (krōō′it) *n.* A small glass bottle, as for vinegar. [< OF *crue* pot]

cruise (krōōz) *v.* **cruised, cruis·ing** *v.i.* 1 To sail about, as for pleasure. 2 To drive about, as a taxi or police patrol car. 3 To move or proceed at a speed suitable for sustained travel. —*v.t.* 4 To cruise over or about. —*n.* The act of cruising, esp. at sea. [< Du. *kruisen*]

cruise missile A guided missile that flies like an airplane at low altitudes.

cruis·er (krōō′zər) *n.* 1 A person, vehicle, or ship that cruises. 2 A fast, maneuverable warship, having a long cruising radius. 3 CABIN CRUISER.

crul·ler (krul′ər) *n.* A small, twisted cake of sweetened fried dough. [< Du. *krullen* to curl]

crumb (krum) *n.* 1 A small bit, as of crumbled bread. 2 The soft inner part of a loaf. 3 A morsel. —*v.t.* 1 To break into small pieces. 2 In cooking, to cover with bread crumbs. [< OE *cruma*] —**crumb′y** *adj.* (**·i·er, ·i·est**)

crum·ble (krum′bəl) *v.t. & v.i.* **·bled, ·bling** To fall or cause to fall into small pieces; disintegrate. —*n.* 1 A crumb. 2 Any crumbly material. [Freq. of CRUMB, *v.*] —**crum′bly** *adj.*

crum·my (krum′ē) *adj.* **crum·mi·er, crum·mi·est** *Slang* Inferior, shoddy, cheap, etc. [< CRUMB] —**crum′mi·ness** *n.*

crum·pet (krum′pit) *n.* A thin, leavened batter cake baked on a griddle and then toasted. [< ME *crompid cake* curled cake]

crum·ple (krum′pəl) *v.t. & v.i.* **·pled, ·pling** 1 To become or cause to become wrinkled; rumple. 2 *Informal* To collapse. —*n.* A wrinkle, as in cloth or the earth. [Freq. of obs. *crump*, var. of CRIMP]

crunch (krunch) *v.t.* 1 To chew with a brittle, crushing sound. 2 To crush or grind noisily. —*v.i.* 3 To chew noisily. 4 To move or advance with a crushing sound. —*n.* 1 The act or sound of crunching. 2 *Slang* A critical time, as the moment of decision. [Imit.] —**crunch′y** *adj.* (**·i·er, ·i·est**)

crup·per (krup′ər) *n.* 1 The looped strap that goes under a horse's tail. 2 The rump of a horse; croup. [< OF *croupe*, *croup*, *rump*]

cru·sade (krōō·sād′) *n.* 1 Any of the military expeditions undertaken by Christians from the 11th through the 13th century to recover the Holy Land from the Muslims. 2 Any similar expedition sanctioned by a church. 3 Any movement or cause conducted aggressively and vigorously, esp. against public evil. —*v.i.* **·sad·ed, ·sad·ing** To go on or engage in a crusade. [< Med. L *cruciare* mark with a cross] —**cru·sad′er** *n.*

cruse (krōōz, krōōs) *n.* A small bottle, flask, or jug; cruet.

crush (krush) *v.t.* 1 To press or squeeze out of shape; mash. 2 To smash or grind into particles. 3 To obtain or extract by pressure. 4 To press upon; crowd. 5 To put down; subdue; overwhelm. 6 To oppress. —*v.i.* 7 To become broken or misshapen by pressure. 8 To crowd: with *into*, *against*, etc. —*n.* 1 The act of crushing. 2 A pressing or crowding together. 3 A fruit drink. 4 *Informal* An infatuation. [< OF *croissir* break] —**crush′er** *n.*

crust (krust) *n.* 1 A hard, thin coating over something softer. 2 a The outer part of bread. b A bit of stale, hard bread. 3 The pastry envelope of a pie or the like. 4 The cold, exterior portion of the earth. 5 *Slang* Insolence; impertinence. —*v.t. & v.i.* To cover with or acquire a crust. [< L *crusta*]

crus·ta·cean (krus·tā′shən) *n.* One of a class of arthropods having a hard shell, two pairs of antennae, and usu. gills, including lobsters, crabs, shrimps, etc. —*adj.* Of or pertaining to these animals. [< L *crusta* crust, shell]

crus·tal (krus′təl) *adj.* Of or derived from a crust, esp. of the moon, earth, or other planet.

crust·y (krus′tē) *adj.* **crust·i·er, crust·i·est** 1 Like a crust. 2 Having or hard as a crust. 3 Morosely curt in manner or speech; surly. —**crust′i·ly** *adv.* —**crust′i·ness** *n.*

crutch (kruch) *n.* 1 Any of various devices used as a support in walking, esp. a staff with a crosspiece fitting in the armpit. 2 Anything one feels to be necessary as a support or aid. 3 *Naut.* A forked support for a swinging boom when not in use. —*v.t.* To prop up, as on crutches. [< OE *crycc*]

crux (kruks) *n. pl.* **crux·es** or **cru·ces** (krōō′sēz) 1 A pivotal, fundamental, or vital point. 2 A tormenting or baffling problem. [L, a cross]

cry (krī) *v.* **cried, cry·ing** *v.t.* 1 To utter loudly or shout out; exclaim. 2 To proclaim loudly and publicly; advertise loudly. 3 To affect (one) in some specified way by weeping: to *cry* oneself to sleep. —*v.i.* 4 To speak, call, or appeal loudly; shout; yell. 5 To utter sounds of grief and sorrow; weep; sob. 6 To have or show a great need: with *for*. 7 To make characteristic calls: said of animals. —*n. pl.* **cries** 1 A loud call; shout; yell. 2 The act of weeping. 3 An earnest appeal; entreaty. 4 Advertisement by outcry. 5 General report or rumor; public opinion. 6 A word or phrase to rally men to action. 7 Public demand; outcry: a *cry* for clean streets. 8 The characteristic call of a bird or an animal. [< L *quiritare* call out]

cry·ba·by (krī′bā′bē) *n. pl.* **·bies** A person, esp. a child, given to crying or complaining over his circumstances.

cry·ing (krī′ing) *adj.* Calling for immediate action or redress: a *crying* shame.

cryo- *combining form* Cold; frost: *cryogenic.* [< Gk. *kyros* frost]

cry·o·gen·ic (krī′ə·jen′ik) *adj.* Pertaining to very low temperatures or their study. [< CRYO- + -GENIC]

cry·o·gen·ics (krī′ə·jen′iks) *n. pl.* (construed as *sing.*) The branch of physics dealing with very low temperatures.

cry·o·lite (krī′ō·līt) *n.* A vitreous, snow-white, translucent mineral fluoride of sodium and aluminum. [< CRYO- + Gk. *lithos* stone]

cry·o·sur·ger·y (krī′ō·sûr′jər·ē) *n.* Surgery utilizing extreme cold to destroy tissue. —**cry′o·sur′gi·cal** *adj.*

crypt (kript) *n.* A recess or vault, esp. one under some churches, used for burial, etc. [< Gk. *kryptos* hidden]

cryp·tic (krip′tik) *adj.* 1 Puzzling; ambiguous; mysterious. 2 Secret; arcane. Also **cryp′ti·cal.** [< Gk. *kryptos* hidden] —**cryp′ti·cal·ly** *adv.*

crypto- *combining form* Hidden; secret: *cryptogram.* [< Gk. *kryptos* hidden]

cryp·to·gam (krip'tə·gam) *n.* A plant having no flowers, but propagating by spores, as algae, fungi, lichens, and mosses. Also **cryp'to·phyte** (-fīt). [< CRYPTO- + Gk. *gamos* marriage] —**cryp'to·gam'ic, cryp·tog·a·mous** (krip·tog'ə·məs) *adj.*

cryp·to·gram (krip'tə·gram) *n.* A message whose meaning is hidden, as by use of a code.

cryp·to·graph (krip'tə·graf, -gräf) *n.* 1 CRYPTOGRAM. 2 A system of secret writing; a cipher. —**cryp·tog·ra·pher** (krip·tog'rə·fər), **cryp·tog'ra·phist** *n.* —**cryp'to·graph'ic** *adj.*

cryp·tog·ra·phy (krip·tog'rə·fē) *n.* The art or process of writing in secret characters.

cryst. crystalline; crystals.

crys·tal (kris'təl) *n.* 1 The solid form assumed by many minerals, esp. color-less transparent quartz, or rock crystal. 2 *Physics* A definite and symmetrical structure, based on a recurring unit cell, assumed by the atoms, molecules, or ions of a solid. 3 Flint glass, or any fine glass; also, tableware and decorative pieces made of

Crystals
a. tetragonal pyramid.
b. dodecahedron.

such glass. 4 The transparent cover for a watch face. 5 Anything clear and transparent. —*adj.* 1 Composed of crystal. 2 Like crystal; extremely clear; limpid. [< Gk. *krystallos*] —**crys·tal·lic** (kris·tal'ik) *adj.*

crys·tal·line (kris'tə·lin, -līn, -lēn) *adj.* 1 Of, pertaining to, or like crystal or crystals. 2 Transparent; clear.

crystalline lens A transparent, biconvex body situated behind the iris of the eye, serving to focus light on the retina. Also **crystalline humor.**

crys·tal·lize (kris'tə·līz) *v.* **-lized, ·liz·ing** *v.t.* 1 To cause to form crystals or become crystalline. 2 To bring to definite and permanent form. —*v.i.* 3 To assume the form of crystals. 4 To assume permanent form. —**crys'tal·liz'a·ble** *adj.* —**crys'tal·li·za'tion** *n.*

crys·tal·log·ra·phy (kris'tə·log'rə·fē) *n.* The science of crystals. —**crys'tal·log'ra·pher** *n.*

crys·tal·loid (kris'tə·loid) *adj.* Like, of, or pertaining to a crystal or crystals. —*n.* One of a class of substances, usu. crystallizable, whose solutions pass readily through animal or vegetable membranes. —**crys'tal·loi'dal** *adj.*

C.S. Christian Science; Christian Scientist.

C.S., c.s. capital stock; civil service.

Cs cesium.

CSC Civil Service Commission.

csc cosecant.

csk. cask.

CST, C.S.T., c.s.t. central standard time.

CT Connecticut (P.O. abbr.).

ct. cent; county; court.

ctn. carton, cotangent.

ctr. center.

cts. centimes; cents.

Cu copper (L *cuprum*).

cu, cu. cubic.

cub (kub) *n.* 1 The young of the bear, fox, wolf, and certain other carnivores; a whelp. 2 An awkward youth. 3 A beginner or learner. —*adj.* Young; inexperienced: a *cub* reporter; *cub* pilot. [?]

Cu·ba (kyoo'bə) *n.* A republic on an island in the Caribbean Sea, 44,217 sq. mi., cap. Havana. —**Cu'ban** *adj., n.*

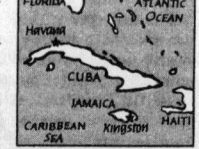

cub·by·hole (kub'ē·hōl') *n.* A small, enclosed space. [< *cubby,* dim. of dial. E *cub* shed + HOLE]

cube (kyoob) *n.* 1 *Geom.* A solid bounded by six equal squares and having all its angles right angles. 2 *Math.* The third power of a quantity; the product of three equal factors. —*v.t.* **cubed, cub·ing** 1 To raise (a number or quantity) to the third power. 2 To find the cubic capacity of. 3 To form or cut into cubes or cubelike shapes. [< Gk. *kybos* cube, die²]

cu·beb (kyoo'beb) *n.* The berry of an East Indian species of pepper, formerly used to treat urinary and bronchial disorders. [< Ar. *kabābah*]

cube root A number which, taken three times as a factor, produces a given number.

cu·bic (kyoo'bik) *adj.* 1 Formed like a cube. 2 Being, or equal to, a cube whose edge is a given unit: a *cubic* foot. 3 *Math.* Of the third power or degree. Also **cu'bi·cal.** —**cu'bi·cal·ly** *adv.* —**cu'bi·cal·ness** *n.*

cu·bi·cle (kyoo'bi·kəl) *n.* 1 A partially enclosed section of a dormitory. 2 Any small, partially enclosed place, as a partitioned space for study. [< L *cubiculum* < *cubare* lie down]

cubic measure A unit or system of units for measuring volume.

cu·bism (kyoo'biz·əm) *n.* An early 20th-century school of art concerned with an abstract and geometric, rather than realistic, representation of things. —**cu'bist** *adj., n.*

cu·bit (kyoo'bit) *n.* An ancient measure equal to about 18 to 20 inches. [< L *cubitum* elbow]

cuck·old (kuk'əld) *n.* The husband of an unfaithful wife. —*v.t.* To make a cuckold of. [< OF *cucu* cuckoo, which lays its eggs in another bird's nest] —**cuck'old·ry** (-əl·drē) *n.*

cuck·oo (kook'oo) *n.* 1 Any of a large family of slender birds with slightly curved bills, long, narrow tails, and a call like the sound of its name. 2 A cuckoo's cry. 3 An imitation of this sound. —*v.* **·ooed, ·oo·ing** *v.t.* 1 To repeat without cessation. —*v.i.* 2 To utter or imitate the cry of the cuckoo. —*adj.* (also kook'koo) *Slang* Slightly deranged mentally. [< OF *cucu, coucou;* imit.]

cuckoo clock A clock in which a mechanical cuckoo announces the hours.

cu·cum·ber (kyoo'kum·bər) *n.* 1 The long, hard-rinded fruit of a creeping plant of the gourd family cultivated as a vegetable. 2 The plant. [< L *cucumis*]

cud (kud) *n.* Food forced up into the mouth from the first stomach of a ruminant and chewed over again. [< OE *cudu, cwidu*]

cud·dle (kud'l) *v.* **·dled, ·dling** *v.t.* 1 To protect and caress fondly within a close embrace; hug. —*v.i.* 2 To hug one another; nestle together. —*n.* An embrace; caress. [?] —**cud'dle·some, cud·dly** (kud'lē) *adj.* (**·dli·er, ·dli·est**)

cudg·el (kuj'əl) *n.* A short, thick stick used as a club. —*v.t.* **·eled** or **·elled, ·el·ing** or **·el·ling** To beat with a cudgel. [< OE *cycgel*] —**cudg'el·er** or **cudg'el·ler** *n.*

cue¹ (kyoo) *n.* 1 A long, tapering rod, used to strike the cue ball in billiards, pool, etc. 2 A queue or line of persons. —*v.t.* **cued, cu·ing** 1 In billiards, etc., to hit with a cue. —*v.i.* 2 To form a line of persons: usu. with *up.* [< F *queue* tail]

cue² (kyoo) *n.* 1 In the performing arts: **a** Any of various signals for an actor to speak or do something, as another actor's words or actions, a bit of music, etc. **b** Anything that initiates some action or change: a music *cue;* a lighting *cue.* 2 Any hint or suggestion. —*v.t.* **cued, cu·ing** To give a cue to. [?]

cue ball A white or whitish yellow ball struck by the cue in billiards or pool.

cuff¹ (kuf) *n.* 1 A band about the wrist, as a part of a sleeve. 2 The part of a long glove covering the wrist. 3 A turned-up hem on a trouser leg. 4 HANDCUFF. —**off the cuff** *Informal* Extemporaneous; unrehearsed. [ME *cuffe*]

cuff² (kuf) *v.t.* 1 To strike, as with the open hand; buffet. —*v.i.* 2 To scuffle or fight; box. —*n.* A blow, esp. with the open hand. [?]

cuff links A pair of linked buttons, etc., used to fasten shirt cuffs.

cu. ft. cubic foot; cubic feet.

cu. in. cubic inch(es).

cui·rass (kwi·ras') *n.* 1 A piece of defensive armor consisting of a plate covering the breast and back. 2 The breastplate alone. [< OF *cuirasse*]

Cuirass

cui·sine (kwi·zēn') *n.* 1 A particular style or manner of cooking. 2 The food prepared. [F < LL *coquina* kitchen]

cul-de-sac (kul'də·sak', kool'-; *Fr.* kü'də·såk') *n. pl.* **cul-de-sacs,** *Fr.* **culs-de-sac** (kü'-) 1 A passage open only at one end; blind alley. **2** Something having no way out. [F, lit., bottom of the bag]

-cule *suffix of nouns* Small; little: *animalcule*. [< L *-culus*]

cu·li·nar·y (kyōō′lə·ner′ē, kul′ə-) *adj.* Of or pertaining to cooking or the kitchen. [< L *culina* kitchen]

cull (kul) *v.t.* **culled, cull·ing 1** To pick or sort out; collect. **2** To select and gather. —*n.* Something picked or sorted out and rejected. [< L *colligere* collect] —**cull′er** *n.*

culm[1] (kulm) *n. Bot.* The jointed, usu. hollow, stem of certain grasses. [< L *culmus* stalk] —**cul·mif·er·ous** (kul·mif′ər·əs) *adj.*

culm[2] (kulm) *n.* **1** Coal dust. **2** An inferior anthracite coal. [ME *colme*]

cul·mi·nate (kul′mə·nāt) *v.i.* **·nat·ed, ·nat·ing 1** To attain the highest point or degree. **2** To come to a complete result; reach a final effect. [< L *culmen* top, highest point] —**cul′mi·nal** *adj.*

cul·mi·na·tion (kul′mə·nā′shən) *n.* The highest point, condition, or degree.

cu·lottes (kyōō·lots′) *n.pl.* A woman's garment having trouser legs cut full to resemble a skirt. [F]

cul·pa·ble (kul′pə·bəl) *adj.* Deserving of blame or censure. [< L *culpa* fault] —**cul′pa·bil′i·ty, cul′pa·ble·ness** *n.* —**cul′pa·bly** *adv.*

cul·prit (kul′prit) *n.* **1** A guilty person. **2** A person charged with crime, but not yet convicted. [< AF *cul prit*, short for *culpable* guilty + *prit* ready for trial]

cult (kult) *n.* **1** A system of religious observances. **2** Extravagant devotion to a person, cause, or thing. **3** The object of such devotion. **4** A group of persons having an excessive interest in something. [< L *cultus*, pp. of *colere* worship]

cul·ti·va·ble (kul′tə·və·bəl) *adj.* Capable of cultivation. Also **cul′ti·vat′a·ble.** —**cul′ti·va·bil′i·ty** *n.*

cul·ti·vate (kul′tə·vāt) *v.t.* **·vat·ed, ·vat·ing 1** To prepare and use (land), as by plowing, fertilizing, sowing, etc. **2** To loosen the soil under (growing plants) with a cultivator, hoe, etc. **3** To plant and tend. **4** To improve or develop by study, exercise, training, etc.: to *cultivate* the mind. **5** To study carefully; pay special attention to: to *cultivate* philosophy. **6** To try to make friends with: to *cultivate* one's teacher. [< L *cultus*, pp. of *colere* care for, worship]

cul·ti·va·tion (kul′tə·vā′shən) *n.* **1** The act or result of cultivating. **2** Refinement; culture.

cul·ti·va·tor (kul′tə·vā′tər) *n.* **1** One who cultivates. **2** A tool or machine used to loosen the ground and destroy weeds.

cul·tur·al (kul′chər·əl) *adj.* **1** Of, pertaining to, or developing culture. **2** Resulting from breeding or artificial cultivation, as certain varieties of fruits or plants. —**cul′tur·al·ly** *adv.*

cul·ture (kul′chər) *n.* **1** The sum total of the attainments and activities of any specific period, race, or people; civilization: the *culture* of the ancient Greeks. **2** The knowledge, good taste, refinement, etc., acquired by training the mind and faculties. **3** Development or improvement, as of the mind or body, by special care, training, etc.: physical *culture;* voice *culture.* **4** *Bacteriol.* **a** The proliferation of a specific microorganism in a specially prepared nutrient, or **culture medium. b** The organisms so developed. **5** The cultivation or raising of a plant or animal. **6** Cultivation of the soil; tillage. —*v.t.* **·tured, ·tur·ing 1** CULTIVATE. **2** *Bacteriol.* To produce in a culture. [< L *cultura* < *cultus*. See CULTIVATE.]

cul·tured (kul′chərd) *adj.* **1** Having or characterized by culture and refinement. **2** Produced by cultivation; cultivated. —**Syn. 1** civilized, refined, polished, enlightened.

cul·vert (kul′vərt) *n.* An artificial, covered channel for water, as under a road. [?]

cum·ber (kum′bər) *v.t.* **1** To hinder, hamper, obstruct, or burden. **2** To trouble or inconvenience. [?< OF *encombrer* hinder]

cum·ber·some (kum′bər·səm) *adj.* Clumsy, unwieldy, or burdensome. —**cum′ber·some·ly** *adv.* —**cum′ber·some·ness** *n.*

cum·brance (kum′brəns) *n.* ENCUMBRANCE.

cum·brous (kum′brəs) *adj.* CUMBERSOME. —**cum′brous·ly** *adv.* —**cum′brous·ness** *n.*

cum·in (kum′in) *n.* **1** A small plant related to parsley. **2** Its aromatic seeds, used as flavoring. Also **cum′min.** [< Gk. *kyminon*]

cum lau·de (kum lô′dē, kŏŏm lou′de) With praise: to be graduated *cum laude.* [L]

cum·mer·bund (kum′ər·bund) *n.* A broad sash worn as a waistband. [< Pers. *kamar* loin + *band* band]

cum·quat (kum′kwot) *n.* KUMQUAT.

cu·mu·late (kyōō′myə·lāt) *v.t.* **·lat·ed, ·lat·ing** To collect into a heap; accumulate. —*adj.* (*also* kyōō′myə·lit) Massed; heaped; accumulated. [< L *cumulus* a heap] —**cu′mu·la′tion** *n.*

cu·mu·la·tive (kyōō′myə·lə·tiv, -lā′-) *adj.* **1** Gathering volume, strength, value, etc., by successive additions. **2** Increasing or accruing, as unpaid interest or dividends, to be paid in the future. —**cu′mu·la·tive·ly** *adv.*

cu·mu·lo·nim·bus (kyōō′myə·lō·nim′bəs) *n.* A massive cloud rising vertically to great heights; thundercloud.

cu·mu·lus (kyōō′myə·ləs) *n. pl.* **·li** (-lī) **1** A mass; pile. **2** A dense cloud formation with a horizontal base and dome-shaped upper surfaces. [L] —**cu′mu·lous** *adj.*

cu·ne·ate (kyōō′nē·it, -āt) *adj.* Wedge-shaped. [< L *cuneus* wedge] —**cu′ne·ate·ly** *adv.*

cu·ne·i·form (kyōō·nē′ə·fôrm, kyōō′nē·ə·fôrm′) *adj.* Wedge-shaped, as the characters in some ancient Assyrian, Babylonian, and Persian inscriptions. —*n.* Cuneiform writing. [< L *cuneus* wedge + -FORM]

cun·ni·lin·gus (kun′ə·ling′gəs) *n.* Oral stimulation of the vulva or clitoris. [L, lit., one who licks the vulva]

cun·ning (kun′ing) *n.* **1** Skill in deception; guile; artifice. **2** Proficiency; skill; dexterity. —*adj.* **1** Crafty; tricky; artful; guileful. **2** Appealing because of prettiness, charm, smallness, etc. **3** Showing ingenuity, skill, dexterity, etc. [< OE *cunnung* < *cunnan* know] —**cun′ning·ly** *adv.* —**cun′ning·ness** *n.*

cup (kup) *n.* **1** A small open vessel, usu. with a handle, used chiefly for drinking. **2** CUPFUL. **3** The contents of a cup: another *cup* of tea. **4** The ornamental vessel used in administering wine at the Eucharist; also, the wine itself. **5** One's lot in life; portion. **6** A cup-shaped vessel awarded as a prize. **7** In golf, a hole, or its metal lining, into which the ball drops. **8** Any cup-shaped object or part. **9** A usu. iced beverage, as of wine mixed with fruit and spices. —*v.t.* **cupped, cup·ping 1** To subject to or treat by cupping. **2** To shape like or place in or as in a cup. [< LL *cuppa*]

cup·board (kub′ərd) *n.* **1** A closet or cabinet with shelves, as for tableware. **2** Any small cabinet or closet.

cup·cake (kup′kāk′) *n.* A small cake baked in a cup-shaped mold.

cup·ful (kup′fŏŏl) *n. pl.* **·fuls 1** The quantity held by a cup. **2** In cooking, half a pint.

cu·pid (kyōō′pid) *n.* A representation of Cupid as a naked, winged boy with a bow and arrow.

Cu·pid (kyōō′pid) *Rom. Myth.* The god of love.

cu·pid·i·ty (kyōō·pid′ə·tē) *n.* An inordinate wish for possession, esp. of wealth; avarice. [< L *cupidus* desirous]

cu·po·la (kyōō′pə·lə) *n.* **1** A dome-shaped roof or ceiling. **2** A small structure, often with a dome-shaped top, built on a roof. —*v.t.* **·laed, ·la·ing** To provide with a cupola. [< L *cupula*, dim. of *cupa* tub, cask]

cup·ping (kup′ing) *n.* The therapeutic application of a partial vacuum to an area of skin in order to draw blood to the surface.

cu·pre·ous (kyōō′prē·əs) *adj.* Of, pertaining to, containing, or like copper. [< L *cuprum* copper]

Cupola *def. 2*

cu·pric (kyōō′prik) *adj.* Of, pertaining to, or containing bivalent copper.

cu·prous (kyōō′prəs) *adj. Chem.* Of, pertaining to, or containing univalent copper.

---

add, āce, câre, pälm; end, ēven; it, īce; odd, ōpen, ôrder; tŏŏk, pōōl; up, bûrn; ə = a in *above, u* in *focus;* yōō = u in *fuse;* oil; pout; check; go; ring; thin; ṯhis; zh, *vision.* < derived from; ? origin uncertain or unknown.

cu·prum (kyōō′prəm) n. COPPER. [L]

cur (kûr) n. 1 A mongrel dog. 2 A mean or malicious person. [Short for earlier kur-dogge snarling dog]

cur. currency; current.

cur·a·ble (kyōōr′ə·bəl) adj. Capable of being cured. — **cur′a·bil′i·ty, cur′a·ble·ness** n. —**cur′a·bly** adv.

cu·ra·cao (kyōōr′ə·sō′) n. A liqueur flavored with orange peel. [< Curacao, of the Netherlands Antilles]

cu·ra·cy (kyōōr′ə·sē) n. pl. ·cies The position, duties, or term of office of a curate.

cu·ra·re (kyōō·rä′rē) n. 1 A toxic resinous extract of certain South American plants, originally used as an arrow poison, and in modern medicine as a muscle relaxant. 2 The plant from which this extract is obtained. Also **cu·ra·ra** (kyōō·rä′rə), **cu·ra′ri.** [< Tupian]

cu·rate (kyōōr′it) n. A clergyman assisting a parish priest, rector, or vicar. [< Med. L cura care or cure (of souls)] —**cu′rate·ship** n.

cur·a·tive (kyōōr′ə·tiv) adj. Pertaining to or used in the curing of disease. —**cur′a·tive·ly** adv.

cu·ra·tor (kyōō·rā′tər, kyōō′rā′tər) n. A person having charge, as of a museum or library; a superintendent. [< L curare care for < cura care] —**cu·ra·to·ri·al** (kyōōr′ə·tôr′· ē·əl, -tō′rē-) adj. —**cu·ra′tor·ship** n.

curb (kûrb) n. 1 A chain or strap to brace a bit against a horse's lower jaw, used to check the horse when the reins are pulled. 2 Anything that restrains or controls. 3 A raised border or edge, as that which forms a gutter along a street. 4 A market dealing in securities not listed on a stock exchange. —v.t. 1 To hold in check; control, with or as with reins. 2 To provide with a curb. 3 To lead (a dog) off a curb for defecation in the street. [< OF courbe curved < L curvus] —**Syn.** v. 1 restrain, subdue, repress, manage.

curb·ing (kûr′bing) n. 1 Material for making a curb. 2 A curb or a part of a curb.

curb·stone (kûrb′stōn′) n. A stone or a row of stones making up a curb.

curd (kûrd) n. Often pl. The solids separated from the watery whey of milk. —v.t. & v.i. CURDLE. [Metathetic var. of CRUD] —**curd′i·ness** n. —**curd′ly, curd′y** adj.

cur·dle (kûrd′l) v.t. & v.i. ·dled, ·dling 1 To change or turn to curds. 2 To thicken; congeal. 3 To turn sour. [Freq. of CURD, v.]

cure (kyōōr) n. 1 A recovery from an unhealthy condition. 2 That which effects such a recovery, as a drug, treatment, etc. 3 Spiritual care: the cure of souls. 4 A manner of preserving something, as meat or fish. —v. **cured, cur·ing** v.t. 1 To restore to a healthy condition. 2 To remedy or eradicate, as a disease or bad habit. 3 To preserve, as by salting or smoking. 4 To vulcanize, as rubber. —v.i. 5 To bring about recovery. 6 To be preserved, as meat. [< L cura care]

cu·ré (kyōō·rā′) n. In France, a parish priest. [F, curate]

cure-all (kyōōr′ôl′) n. That which is asserted to cure all diseases or evils; a panacea.

cur·few (kûr′fyōō) n. 1 A regulation that specified persons leave the streets or that specified establishments close at a designated time. 2 The sounding of a signal at such a time. 3 The time at which a curfew goes into effect. 4 The length of time a curfew is in effect. [< OF couvrir to cover + feu fire]

cu·ri·a (kyōōr′ē·ə) n. pl. ·ae (-ē) 1 A feudal court of justice. 2 Often cap. The collective body of officials that aids the pope in the government and administration of the Roman Catholic Church. [L] —**cu′ri·al** adj.

cu·rie (kyōōr′ē, kyōō·rē′) n. Physics A unit of radioactivity, equal to 3.70 x 10¹⁰ nuclear disintegrations per second. [< Marie Curie, 1867–1934, Polish-born Fr. chemist]

cu·ri·o (kyōōr′ē·ō) n. pl. ·os An object considered rare or unusual. [Short for CURIOSITY]

cu·ri·os·i·ty (kyōōr′ē·os′ə·tē) n. pl. ·ties 1 A desire for knowledge. 2 Inquisitive interest in things which are not of proper concern; nosiness. 3 A person or thing that excites interest or inquiry. [< L curiosus. See CURIOUS.]

cu·ri·ous (kyōōr′ē·əs) adj. 1 Eager for knowledge. 2 Too inquisitive; prying. 3 Novel; odd; strange; mysterious. [< L curiosus < cura care] —**cu′ri·ous·ly** adv. —**cu′ri·ous·ness** n. —**Syn.** 1 inquiring, inquisitive, questioning. 2 meddlesome, nosy, intrusive.

cu·ri·um (kyōōr′ē·əm) n. An artificially produced radioactive element (symbol Cm). [< Marie Curie, 1867–1934, and Pierre Curie, 1859–1906, Fr. chemists]

curl (kûrl) v.t. 1 To twist into ringlets or curves, as the hair. 2 To form into a curved or spiral shape. —v.i. 3 To become curved; take a spiral shape. 4 To play at the game of curling. —n. 1 Anything coiled or spiral, as a ringlet. 2 The act of curling or the condition of being curled. [< MDu. crulle curly]

cur·lew (kûr′lyōō) n. Any of a genus of shore birds with long legs and down-curved bills. [< OF corlieu]

curl·i·cue (kûr′li·kyōō) n. An odd or fancy curl or twist, as a flourish with a pen. Also **curl′y·cue.** [< CURLY + CUE¹]

curl·ing (kûr′ling) n. A game in which the players slide a heavy, round weight, or **curling stone,** along a narrow strip of ice toward a target circle.

curling iron An implement of metal, used when heated for curling the hair. Also **curling irons.**

curl·y (kûr′lē) adj. curl·i·er, curl·i·est 1 Having curls. 2 Tending to curl, as hair. 3 Marked by a wavy grain. —**curl′i·ness** n.

Curlew

cur·mudg·eon (kər·muj′ən) n. A bad-tempered, ill-mannered man. [?] —**cur·mudg′eon·ly** adj.

cur·rant (kûr′ənt) n. 1 A small, round, acid berry, used for making jelly. 2 Any of a genus of hardy shrubs whose fruit is the red, white, or black currant. 3 A small seedless raisin from the Levant. [< AF (raisins de) Corauntz (raisins from) Corinth]

cur·ren·cy (kûr′ən·sē) n. pl. ·cies 1 The money in general use in any country. 2 A circulation or passing from person to person. 3 General acceptance; prevalence; use.

cur·rent (kûr′ənt) adj. 1 Belonging to the present time; now in progress or in effect. 2 Generally accepted. 3 Circulating; going around. —n. 1 That part of any body of water or air which has a more or less steady flow in a definite direction. 2 Electr. a A flow of electricity through a conductor. b The measure of this flow. 3 Any general course, tendency, trend, or drift. [< L currere to run] —**cur′rent·ly** adv. —**cur′rent·ness** n.

cur·ric·u·lum (kə·rik′yə·ləm) n. pl. ·lums or ·la (-lə) 1 A regular or particular course of study, as in a college. 2 All of the courses offered by an educational institution. [< L, a race < currere run] —**cur·ric′u·lar** adj.

cur·rish (kûr′ish) adj. Like a cur; mean; nasty. —**cur′rish·ly** adv. —**cur′rish·ness** n.

cur·ry¹ (kûr′ē) v.t. ·ried, ·ry·ing 1 To rub down and clean with a currycomb or other implement; groom (a horse, dog, etc.). 2 To prepare (tanned hides) for use, as by soaking, beating, etc. —**curry favor** To seek favor, as by adulation and subserviency. [< OF carreier, conreder make ready, prepare]

cur·ry² (kûr′ē) n. pl. ·ries 1 A cooked dish consisting of meats, fish, etc., seasoned with curry powder. 2 CURRY POWDER. 3 A sauce flavored with curry powder. —v.t. ·ried, ·ry·ing To flavor with curry. [< Tamil kari sauce]

cur·ry·comb (kûr′ē·kōm′) n. A comb consisting of a series of upright serrated ridges, for grooming horses. —v.t. To comb with a currycomb.

curry powder A powdered condiment, prepared from turmeric, coriander, and other spices.

curse (kûrs) v. cursed or curst, curs·ing v.t. 1 To invoke evil or injury upon; damn. 2 To swear at. 3 To cause evil or injury to. —v.i. 4 To utter curses; swear; blaspheme. —n. 1 A blasphemous or profane oath. 2 A calling on a god to visit trouble or evil upon some person or thing. 3 A source of trouble or evil. 4 The evil which comes as a result of a curse. 5 A person or thing that is cursed. [< OE cursian]

curs·ed (kûr′sid, kûrst) adj. 1 Under a curse. 2 Deserving a curse; hateful; detestable. —**curs·ed·ly** (kûr′sid·lē) adv. —**curs′ed·ness** n.

cur·sive (kûr′siv) adj. Running; flowing; said of writing in which the letters are joined. —n. 1 A letter or character used in cursive writing. **2** In printing, a type face that resembles handwriting. [<L *cursus* < *currere* to run] — **cur′sive·ly** *adv.* —**cur′sive·ness** *n.*

cur·sor (kûr′sər) *n.* A pointer on a computer screen that shows the position where an operation is taking place.

cur·so·ry (kûr′sər·ē) *adj.* Rapid and superficial; hasty, with no attention to detail. [<L *cursor* a runner < *currere* run] —**cur′so·ri·ly** *adv.* —**cur′so·ri·ness** *n.*

curst (kûrst) A *p.t.* & *p.p.* of CURSE. —*adj.* Cursed.

curt (kûrt) *adj.* **1** Concise; brief; terse. **2** Short and sharp in manner; brusque; abrupt. [<L *curtus* shortened] —**curt′ly** *adv.* —**curt′ness** *n.*

cur·tail (kər·tāl′) *v.t.* To cut off or cut short; abbreviate; lessen; reduce. [<obs. *curtal* short; infl. in form by TAIL] —**cur·tail′er, cur·tail′ment** *n.*

cur·tain (kûr′tən) *n.* **1** A piece of fabric, often adjustable, hung for decoration, concealment, or to shut out light, as before a wall, window, doorway, etc. **2** Something that conceals, covers, or separates like a curtain. **3** In a theater, the drapery hanging at the front of a stage, drawn up or aside to reveal the stage. **4** *pl. Slang* The end; death. —*v.t.* **1** To supply or adorn with or as with a curtain or curtains. **2** To conceal or shut off as with a curtain; cover. [<LL *cortina*]

curtain call The appearance of a performer or performers to acknowledge applause from an audience.

curtain raiser A short play, sketch, etc., presented before a longer or more important work.

curt·sy (kûrt′sē) *n. pl.* **·sies** A gesture of civility or respect, made esp. by women, consisting of a slight lowering of the body with a bending of the knees. —*v.i.* **·sied, ·sy·ing** To make such a gesture. Also **curt′sey.** [Var. of COURTESY]

cur·va·ceous (kûr·vā′shəs) *adj. Informal* Having voluptuous curves; shapely in form: said of a woman.

cur·va·ture (kûr′və·chər) *n.* **1** The act of curving or the state of being curved. **2** A curve or curved part, often an abnormal one: *curvature* of the spine.

curve (kûrv) *n.* **1** A line continuously bent so that no portion of it is straight, as the arc of a circle. **2** The form, movement, or path of a curve. **3** Something having the form of a curve. **4** An instrument for drawing curves, used by draftsmen. **5** *Math.* A set of connected points having only length as a variable measure. **6** In baseball, a pitched ball so thrown that it veers to one side before crossing the plate. —*v.* **curved, curv·ing** *v.t.* **1** To cause to assume the form of a curve. —*v.i.* **2** To assume the form of a curve. **3** To move in a curve, as a projectile or ball; bend. [<L *curvus* bent]

cur·vet (kûr′vit) *n.* A light, low leap of a horse, with the forelegs and hind legs lifted and brought down an instant apart. —*v.t.* & *v.i.* (also kər·vet′) **·vet·ted** or **·vet·ed, ·vet·ting** or **·vet·ing** To make or cause to make a curvet. [<Ital. *corva* bent]

cur·vi·lin·e·ar (kûr′və·lin′ē·ər) *adj.* Formed or enclosed by curved lines. Also **cur·vi·lin′e·al.**

cush·ion (koo͝osh′ən) *n.* **1** A flexible bag or casing filled with some soft or elastic material, as feathers, air, etc. **2** Anything resembling a cushion in appearance, construction, or application, as a device to deaden the jar or impact of parts. **3** The elastic rim of a billiard table. —*v.t.* **1** To place, seat, or arrange on or as on a cushion. **2** To provide with a cushion. **3** To cover or hide as with a cushion. **4** To absorb the shock or effect of. [<OF *coissin*]

Cush·it·ic (koo͝osh·it′ik) *n.* A group of Hamitic languages spoken in Ethiopia and Somaliland. —*adj.* Of this group of languages.

cush·y (koo͝osh′ē) *adj. Slang* **cush·i·er, cush·i·est** Comfortable; agreeable; easy; pleasant. [<CUSHION]

cusp (kusp) *n.* **1** A point or pointed end. **2** *Astron.* Either point of a crescent moon. **3** A prominence or point, as on the crown of a tooth. [<L *cuspis* a point]

cus·pate (kus′pāt, kus′pit) *adj.* **1** Having a cusp or cusps. **2** Cusp-shaped. Also **cus′pat·ed, cusped** (kuspt).

cus·pid (kus′pid) *n.* A canine tooth. —*adj.* CUSPIDATE.

cus·pi·date (kus′pə·dāt) *adj.* Having a cusp or cusps. Also **cus′pi·dat·ed, cus·pi·dal** (kus′pə·dəl).

cus·pi·dor (kus′pə·dôr) *n.* A spittoon. [<Pg. *cuspir* to spit <L *conspuere*]

cuss (kus) *Informal v.t.* & *v.i.* To curse. —*n.* **1** A curse. **2** A person or animal, often one that is odd or perverse. [Var. of CURSE]

cuss·ed (kus′id) *adj. Informal* **1** Cursed. **2** Mean; perverse. —**cuss′ed·ly** *adv.* —**cuss′ed·ness** *n.*

cus·tard (kus′tərd) *n.* A mixture of milk, eggs, sugar, and flavoring, either boiled or baked. [Alter. of earlier *crustade* a type of pie <L *crusta* crust]

cus·to·di·an (kus·tō′dē·ən) *n.* A guardian, caretaker, or janitor. —**cus·to′di·an·ship′** *n.*

cus·to·dy (kus′tə·dē) *n. pl.* **·dies** **1** A keeping; guardianship. **2** The state of being held in keeping or under guard; imprisonment. [<L *custos* guardian] —**cus·to·di·al** (kus·tō′dē·əl) *adj.*

cus·tom (kus′təm) *n.* **1** An ordinary or usual manner of doing or acting. **2** The habitual practice of a community or people; common usage. **3** *Law* An old and general usage that has obtained the force of law. **4** Business support; patronage. **5** *pl.* **a** A tariff or duty by a government upon goods imported or exported. **b** The government agency which collects such tariffs or duties. —*adj.* **1** Made to order. **2** Specializing in made-to-order goods: a *custom* tailor. [<L *consuetudo*]

cus·tom·ar·y (kus′tə·mer′ē) *adj.* **1** Conforming to or established by custom; habitual. **2** *Law* Holding or held by custom. —*n. pl.* **·ar·ies** A group of laws established by custom, as for a manor, district, etc. —**cus·tom·ar·i·ly** (kus′tə·mer′ə·lē) *adv.* —**cus′tom·ar′i·ness** *n.*

cus·tom-built (kus′təm·bilt′) *adj.* Built to individual specifications.

cus·tom·er (kus′təm·ər) *n.* **1** One who gives his custom or trade; a purchaser. **2** *Informal* A person to be dealt with; a fellow: an ugly *customer.*

cus·tom·house (kus′təm·hous′) *n.* The place where entries of imports are made, vessels cleared, and duties collected.

cus·tom-made (kus′təm·mād′) *adj.* Made to order.

cut (kut) *v.* **cut, cut·ting** *v.t.* **1** To pierce, gash, or pass through with or as with a sharp edge. **2** To strike sharply, as with a whip. **3** To affect deeply; hurt the feelings of. **4** To divide, sever, or carve into parts or segments. **5** To fell, hew, or chop down, as a tree or timber: often with *down.* **6** To mow or reap, as grain. **7** To shape, prepare, or make, as gems or clothing. **8** To hollow out; excavate. **9** To trim, shear, or pare. **10** To excise; edit out. **11** To reduce or lessen: to *cut* prices. **12** To dilute or weaken: to *cut* whisky. **13** To dissolve or break down, as fat globules: to *cut* grease. **14** To cross or intersect. **15** *Slang* To discontinue; stop. **16** *Informal* **a** To ignore socially; snub. **b** To stay away from willfully, as work or classes. **17** To divide, as a pack of cards before dealing. **18** In racket sports, to chop (the ball) so it will spin and bound sharply and irregularly. **19** To turn the wheels of, as an automobile, so as to make the vehicle turn sharply. **20** To perform; present: to *cut* a caper. **21** To grow or acquire: to *cut* a tooth. —*v.i.* **22** To cut, cleave, or make an incision; do the work of a sharp edge. **23** To admit of being severed or cut. **24** To use an instrument for cutting. **25** To cause physical or mental distress: winds that *cut; cut* by his nastiness. **26** To divide a card pack before dealing. **27** In sports, to chop the ball. **28** To move or pass through by the shortest or most direct route. —**cut a figure 1** To make a fine appearance. **2** To be of importance. **3** To make an impression. —**cut back 1** To shorten by removing the end. **2** To curtail or cancel, as a contract, before fulfillment. **3** To run or dash erratically; change direction suddenly. —**cut down** To reduce the length or amount of; shorten; curtail. —**cut in 1** To interrupt a dancing couple in order to take the place of one partner. **2** To interrupt, as a conversation. **3** To move into (a line or queue) out of turn. —**cut it fine** To make precise calculations or distinctions. —**cut loose** To speak or behave without restraint. —**cut off 1** To put an end to; stop or shut off. **2** To interrupt. **3** To intercept. **4** To sever. **5** To disinherit. —**cut out 1** *Informal* To leave quickly. **2**

To displace (another); supplant, as a rival. **3** To quit or renounce, as smoking. **4** To form or make by or as if by cutting. —**cut up 1** To slice or cut into pieces. **2** *Slang* To behave in an unruly manner. —*n.* **1** The act of cutting. **2** An opening, cleft, or wound made by an edged instrument. **3** A groove, channel, or passage, as a road through a mountain. **4** A cutting motion or stroke. **5** A part or section removed by cutting. **6** That which cuts or hurts the feelings. **7** A direct way or route. **8** Fashion, form, or style: the *cut* of a suit. **9** An engraved block or plate used in printing; also, an impression made from it. **10** A reduction or decrease. **11** A refusal to recognize an acquaintance; snub. **12** *Informal* An intentional failure to attend a class, etc. **13** *Informal* A share. —*adj.* **1** That has been cut. **2** Formed or affected by cutting. **3** Reduced. [ME *cutten*]

cu·ta·ne·ous (kyōō·tā′nē·əs) *adj.* Of, pertaining to, affecting, or on the skin. [< L *cutis* skin]

cut·a·way (kut′ə·wā′) *n.* A man's coat with the front corners cut slopingly away from the waist down to the back. Also **cutaway coat.**

cut·back (kut′bak′) *n.* A reduction or cessation, as of production or in supply: a *cutback* in fuel.

cute (kyōōt) *adj.* **cut·er, cut·est** *Informal* **1** Pretty or dainty; attractive. **2** Clever or sharp. **3** Artificially striving for effect. [Var. of ACUTE] —**cute′ly** *adv.* —**cute′ness** *n.*

cut glass Glass ornamented by cutting or grinding and polishing.

cu·ti·cle (kyōō′ti·kəl) *n.* **1** The outer layer of cells that protect the true skin; epidermis. **2** The crescent of toughened skin around the base of a fingernail or toenail. [< L *cutis* skin] —**cu·tic′u·lar** *adj.*

cu·tin (kyōō′tin) *n.* A waxy, waterproof film on the leaves, stems, etc., of plants [< L *cutis* skin + -IN]

cut·lass (kut′ləs) *n.* A short, swordlike weapon, often curved, formerly used by sailors. Also **cut′·las.** [< F *couteau* knife]

cut·ler (kut′lər) *n.* One who manufactures or deals in cutlery. [< L *culter* knife]

cut·ler·y (kut′lər·ē) *n.* **1** Cutting instruments, as knives and shears, esp. those for use at the dinner table. **2** The occupation of a cutler. [< OF *coutelier* cutler]

Cutlasses
a. British, 10th century.
b. German, 15th century.

cut·let (kut′lit) *n.* **1** A thin piece of meat from the ribs or leg, for broiling or frying. **2** A flat croquette of chopped meat, fish, etc. [< F *côte* rib < L *costa*]

cut·off (kut′ôf′, -of′) *n.* **1** The act of cutting off or terminating; cessation. **2** SHORT CUT. **3** A mechanism that cuts off the flow of a fuel or fluid. **3** The point at which flow is thus cut off. —*adj.* Terminating; ending.

cut·out (kut′out′) *n.* **1** *Electr.* A switch or other device for bypassing an element of a circuit. **2** A device to let the exhaust gases from an internal-combustion engine pass directly to the air without passing through the muffler. **3** Something that is or may be cut out of something else.

cut·o·ver (kut′ō′vər) *adj.* Having the timber cut: *cutover* land.

cut·purse (kut′pûrs′) *n.* A pickpocket.

cut-rate (kut′rāt′) *adj.* **1** Available at a reduced price or rate. **2** Offering goods or services at reduced prices or rates.

cut·ter (kut′ər) *n.* **1** One who cuts, shapes, or fits anything by cutting. **2** That which cuts, as a tool or a machine. **3** A boat carried by a large ship to transport passengers and supplies. **4** A small armed boat, esp. one in government service. **5** A sailboat or yacht having a single mast. **6** A small sleigh usu. drawn by one horse.

Cutter *def.* 6

cut·throat (kut′thrōt′) *adj.* **1** Murderous. **2** Ruinous; merciless: *cut-throat* competition. —*n.* A murderer.

cut·ting (kut′ing) *adj.* **1** Adapted to cut; sharp. **2** Piercing; penetrating; chilling. **3** Tending to wound the feelings; sarcastic; bitter. —*n.* **1** Something cut off or out. **2** *Bot.* A plant shoot cut off for rooting or grafting. **3** *Chiefly Brit.* A clipping from a newspaper or magazine.

cut·tle·bone (kut′l·bōn′) *n.* The internal calcareous plate of a cuttlefish, used as a dietary supplement for birds and, when powdered, as a polishing agent.

cut·tle·fish (kut′l·fish′) *n. pl.* **·fish** or **·fish·es** Any of various marine mollusks with lateral fins, ten sucker-bearing arms, and an internal calcareous skeleton. [< OE *cudele* + FISH]

cut·worm (kut′wûrm′) *n.* The larva of various moths that feeds on young plants, destroying the stems at ground level.

CWO, C.W.O. Chief Warrant Officer.

C.W.O., c.w.o. cash with order.

CWS Chemical Warfare Service.

cwt. hundredweight.

-cy *suffix* **1** Quality, state, or condition of being: *bankruptcy.* **2** Rank, order, or position of: *chaplaincy, baronetcy.* [< L *-cia* or < Gk. *-kia*]

cy·a·nate (sī′ə·nāt) *n.* A salt or ester of cyanic acid.

cy·an·ic (sī·an′ik) *adj.* **1** Of, pertaining to, or containing cyanogen. **2** Blue or bluish.

cyanic acid A volatile liquid compound with a pungent odor and caustic properties, that is stable at low temperatures only.

cy·a·nide (sī′ə·nīd) *n.* A compound of cyanogen with a metallic element or radical: potassium *cyanide.* —*v.t.* **·nid·ed, ·nid·ing** To subject to the action of cyanide: to extract gold by *cyaniding* the ore. —**cy′a·ni·da′tion** *n.*

cy·an·o·gen (sī·an′ə·jən) *n. Chem.* **1** A colorless, poisonous, gaseous compound of carbon and nitrogen, having an almondlike odor. **2** The univalent radical composed of carbon and nitrogen. [< Gk. *kyanos* dark blue + -GEN]

cy·a·no·sis (sī′ə·nō′sis) *n.* A blue color of the skin due to inadequate aeration of the blood. [< Gk. *kyanos* dark blue + -OSIS] —**cy·a·not·ic** (sī′ə·not′ik) *adj.*

cy·ber·nate (sī′bər·nāt) *v.t.* **·nat·ed, ·nat·ing** To subject to cybernation.

cy·ber·na·tion (sī′bər·nā′shən) *n.* Automation combined with computer control, requiring little or no human intervention. [< CYBERN(ETICS) + -ATION]

cy·ber·net·ics (sī′bər·net′iks) *n. pl. (construed as sing.)* The study of the control processes in physical and biological systems. [< Gk. *kybernētēs* steersman] —**cy′ber·net′ic** *adj.*

cy·cla·mate (sī′klə·māt) *n.* A synthetic organic salt, usu. of sodium or calcium, used as a nonnutritive sweetener.

cyc·la·men (sik′lə·mən, -men, sīk′-) *n.* An Old World plant related to the primrose, with showy white, pink, or crimson flowers. [< Gk. *kyklaminos*]

cy·cle (sī′kəl) *n.* **1** A period of time during which one sequence of a succession of regularly recurring phenomena or events is completed. **2** A sequence of phenomena or events that recur regularly in the same order. **3** A very long period of time; eon; age. **4** All of the legends, poems, romances, etc., relating to one period, person, event, etc. **5** A series of poems, songs, etc., dealing with a single theme. **6** A bicycle, tricycle, etc. —*v.i.* **cy·cled, cy·cling 1** To pass through or occur in cycles. **2** To ride a bicycle, tricycle, or the like. —*v.t.* **3** To put through a cycle or process. [< Gk. *kyklos* circle]

cy·clic (sī′klik, sik′lik) *adj.* **1** Of, pertaining to, or recurring in cycles. **2** *Chem.* Characterized by a closed chain or ring formation, as benzene. Also **cy′cli·cal.** —**cy′cli·cal·ly** *adv.*

cy·clist (sī′klist) *n.* One who rides a cycle, as a bicycle.

cyclo- *combining form* Circle or circular: *cyclometer.* [< Gk. *kyklos* circle]

cy·cloid (sī′kloid) *adj.* Circular. —**cy·cloi′dal** *adj.*

cy·clom·e·ter (sī·klom′ə·tər) *n.* An instrument for recording the rotations of a wheel, used to show the distance traveled by a vehicle. [< CYCLO- + -METER]

cy·clone (sī′klōn) *n.* **1** *Meteorol.* A storm or system of winds rotating clockwise in the southern hemisphere or counterclockwise in the northern hemisphere, about a center of low atmospheric pressure. 2 Loosely, any violent and destructive whirling windstorm. [<Gk. *kykloein* move in a circle] —cy·clon·ic (sī-klon′ĭk) or ·i·cal *adj.* —cy·clon′i·cal·ly *adv.*

cy·clo·pe·an (sī′klə-pē′ən) *adj.* 1 *Usu. cap.* Pertaining to the Cyclopes. 2 Huge; gigantic.

cy·clo·pe·di·a (sī′klə-pē′dē-ə) *n.* ENCYCLOPEDIA. Also cy′clo·pae′di·a. [Short for ENCYCLOPEDIA] —cy′clo·pe′dic, cy′clo·pae′dic *adj.* —cy′clo·pe′dist, cy′clo·pae′dist *n.*

Cy·clops (sī′klops) *pl.* Cy·clo·pes (sī-klō′pēz) *Gk. Myth.* Any of a race of one-eyed giants.

cy·clo·ram·a (sī′klə-ram′ə, -rä′mə) *n.* 1 A series of pictures on the interior of a cylindrical surface, appearing as in natural perspective to a spectator standing in the center. 2 A backdrop curtain or wall, often concave, used on theater stages to give the illusion of unlimited space. [< CYCLO- + Gk. *horama* a view] —cy′clo·ram′ic *adj.*

cy·clo·spo·rine (sī′klə-spôr′ĕn, -spōr′-) *n.* A drug useful in reducing the body's natural rejection of organ transplants by partially repressing the immune system.

cy·clo·tron (sī′klə-tron) *n.* *Physics* An apparatus for accelerating charged particles to high energies in spiral paths by means of a fluctuating magnetic field. [<CYCLO- + (ELEC)TRON]

cyg·net (sig′nĭt) *n.* A young swan. [<Gk. *kyknos*]

Cyg·nus (sig′nəs) *n.* The Swan, a N constellation.

cyl. cylinder; cylindrical.

cyl·in·der (sil′in-dər) *n.* 1 *Geom.* A solid described by the circumference of a circle as its center moves along a straight line, the ends of the solid being parallel, equal circles. 2 Any object, container, etc., having this shape. 3 Any cylindrical portion of a machine, esp. one of a motor in which a piston moves. 4 The rotating chamber that holds the cartridges of a revolver. • See REVOLVER. [<Gk. *kylindros*<*kylindein* to roll]

cy·lin·dri·cal (si-lin′dri-kəl) *adj.* 1 Of or pertaining to a cylinder. 2 Having the form or shape of a cylinder. Also cy·lin′dric.—cy·lin′dri·cal·ly *adv.*—cy·lin·dri·cal·i·ty (si-lin′dri-kal′ə-tē) *n.*

cym·bal (sim′bəl) *n.* A platelike metallic musical instrument, played by being struck with a drumstick or brush or by striking one against another. [<Gk. *kymbē* cup, hollow of a vessel] —cym′bal·ist *n.*

cyme (sīm) *n.* A flat-topped flower cluster in which the central flowers bloom first. [<L *cyma* a wave, a sprout] — cy·mose (sī′mōs, sī-mōs′) *adj.*

Cym·ric (kim′rik, sim′-) *adj.* Relating to the Cymry. —*n.* The Welsh language.

Cym·ry (kim′rē, sim′-) *n.* A collective name for the Welsh and their Cornish and Breton kin.

cyn·ic (sin′ik) *n.* A person who tends to question the virtues, values, and sincerity of others. —*adj.* CYNICAL. [< Gk. *kynikos* doglike]

Cyn·ic (sin′ik) *n.* One of a sect of ancient Greek philosophers who held that virtue was the ultimate goal of life, their doctrine gradually coming to symbolize insolent self-righteousness. —*adj.* Belonging to or like the Cynics: also Cyn′i·cal.

cyn·i·cal (sin′i·kəl) *adj.* 1 Given to questioning people's virtues, values, and sincerity; skeptical; pessimistic. 2 Mocking; sarcastic; sneering. —cyn′i·cal·ly *adv.*

cyn·i·cism (sin′ə·siz′əm) *n.* 1 The state or quality of being cynical. 2 A cynical act, remark, etc.

cy·no·sure (sī′nə-shōor, sin′ə-) *n.* An object of general interest or attention. [<Gk. *kynosoura* the constellation Ursa Minor<*kynos* dog + *oura* tail]

cy·pher (sī′fər) *n.* CIPHER.

cy·press (sī′prəs) *n.* 1 Any of a genus of evergreen conifers growing in warm climates. 2 Any of various similar trees, as the white cedar. 3 The wood of these trees. [<Gk. *kyparissos*]

Cyp·ri·an (sip′rē-ən) *adj.* Of or pertaining to Cyprus, its people, or their language. —*n.* CYPRIOT.

cyp·ri·noid (sip′rə-noid, si-prī′-) *adj.* Carplike. —*n.* Any of numerous freshwater fishes related to carp, as the minnow, dace, goldfish, etc. Also cyp′ri·nid (-nid). [<Gk. *kyprinos* carp]

Cyp·ri·ot (sip′rē-ət) *n.* A native or citizen of Cyprus. — *adj.* Of or pertaining to Cyprus. Also Cyp′ri·ote (-ōt).

Cy·prus (sī′prəs) *n.* A republic located on an island in the Mediterranean s of Turkey, 3,572 sq. mi., cap. Nicosia. • See map at TURKEY.

Cy·ril·lic (si-ril′ik) *adj.* Of or pertaining to the alphabet used in the Soviet Union, Bulgaria, and other Slavic countries.

cyst (sist) *n.* A saclike structure in a plant or animal containing liquid or semisolid material. [<Gk. *kystis* bladder] —cys′tic *adj.*

cystic fibrosis A hereditary disease marked by copious mucous secretion, breathing difficulty, enzyme deficiencies, and loss of weight.

cys·to·scope (sis′tə-skōp) *n.* A catheter with a device for viewing the interior of the urinary bladder. [<Gk. *kystis* bladder + -SCOPE] —cys·to·scop·ic (sis′tə-skop′ik) *adj.* —cys·tos·co·py (sis-tos′kə-pē) *n.*

-cyte *combining form* Cell: *phagocyte.* [<Gk. *kytos* hollow vessel]

cyto- *combining form* Cell: *cytology.* [<Gk. *kytos* hollow vessel]

cy·tol·o·gy (sī-tol′ə-jē) *n.* The branch of biology concerned with the structure and functions of cells. —cy·to·log·ic (sī′tə-loj′ik) or ·i·cal *adj.* —cy′to·log′i·cal·ly *adv.* —cy·tol′o·gist *n.*

cy·to·plasm (sī′tə-plaz′əm) *n.* The colloidal substance surrounding the nucleus and other structures in living cells. —cy′to·plas′mic *adj.*

cy·to·plast (sī′tə-plast) *n.* The cytoplasm in a single cell. —cy′to·plas′tic *adj.*

C.Z. Canal Zone.

czar (zär) *n.* 1 An emperor or absolute monarch; esp., one of the former emperors of Russia. 2 A person having great power or authority. [<Russ. *tsare*, ult. <L *Caesar* Caesar] —czar′ism *n.* —czar′ist *adj.*, *n.*

czar·e·vitch (zär′ə-vich) *n.* The eldest son of a czar of Russia.

cza·ri·na (zä-rē′nə) *n.* The wife of a czar of Russia. Also cza·rit·za (zä-rit′sə).

Czech (chek) *n.* 1 A native or citizen of Czechoslovakia. 2 The language of Czechoslovakia. — *adj.* Of Czechoslovakia, its people, or their language.

Czech·o·slo·va·ki·a (chek′ə-slō-vä′kē-ə, -vak′ē-ə) *n.* A republic of CEN. Europe, 49,368 sq. mi., cap. Prague. — Czech′o·slo′vak, Czech′o·slo·va′ki·an *adj.*, *n.*

D

D, d (dē) *n. pl.* **D's, d's, Ds, ds** (dēz) **1** The fourth letter of the English alphabet. **2** Any spoken sound representing the letter *D* or *d*. **3** *Music* The second tone in the diatonic scale of C major. **4** Something shaped like a D. **5** In Roman notation, the symbol for 500. —*adj.* Shaped like a D.

D deuterium.

D. December; Democrat(ic); Dutch.

d. date; daughter; day(s); dead; degree; delete; died; dose; *Brit.* penny (L *denarius*) or pence (L *denarii*).

D.A. District Attorney.

dab[1] (dab) *n.* **1** One of various small flounders. **2** Any flatfish. [?]

dab[2] (dab) *n.* **1** A gentle blow; a pat. **2** A small amount of something. —*v.t. & v.i.* **dabbed, dab·bing 1** To strike softly; tap. **2** To peck. **3** To pat with something soft and damp. **4** To apply (paint, etc.) with light strokes. [Prob. < MDu. *dabben* fumble, dabble] —**dab'ber** *n.*

dab·ble (dab'əl) *v.* **·bled, ·bling** *v.i.* **1** To play, as with the hands, in a liquid; splash gently. **2** To do superficially or without serious involvement; to *dabble* in art. —*v.t.* **3** To wet slightly; bespatter. [Freq. of DAB[2]] —**dab'bler** *n.*

dab·chick (dab'chik) *n.* **1** A small grebe of Europe. **2** The pied-billed grebe of North America. [< DAB[2] + CHICK]

da ca·po (dä kä'pō) *Music* From the beginning. [Ital.]

dace (dās) *n. pl.* **dac·es** or **dace** Any of a genus of small freshwater fishes related to the carp. [< OF *dars*]

dachs·hund (däks'hŏŏnt', daks'hŏŏnd', dash'-) *n.* A breed of dog native to Germany, of medium size, with long, compact body and short legs, and reddish brown or black coat. [G < *Dachs* badger + *Hund* dog]

Da·cron (dā'kron, dak'ron) *n.* A strong synthetic fiber or washable fabric, resistant to stretching and wrinkling: a trade name. Also **da'cron.**

Dachshund

dac·tyl (dak'təl) *n.* In prosody, a measure consisting of one accented syllable followed by two short or unaccented ones (ōŏŏ). [< Gk. *daktylos* finger, dactyl] —**dac·tyl'ic** *adj.*

dad (dad) *n. Informal* Father: used familiarly, as by children. Also **dad'dy.**

da·da (dä'dä, -də) *n. Often cap.* An antirational movement in art and literature, about 1916–20, that rejected traditional aesthetic values and endorsed the absurd and incongruous. Also **da'da·ism.** [F] —**da'da·ist** *n.*

dad·dy-long·legs (dad'ē-lông'legz', -long'-) *n.* **1** A long-legged, insect-eating arachnid resembling a spider. **2** CRANE FLY.

da·do (dā'dō) *n. pl.* **da·does** *Archit.* **1** A plain, flat surface at the base of a wall, as of a room, often decorated. **2** That part of a pedestal between the base and the surbase. [Ital., a die, a cube]

Daed·a·lus (ded'ə-ləs, *Brit.* dē'də-) *Gk. Myth.* An architect and inventor who devised the Cretan Labyrinth in which he was later imprisoned with his son Icarus and from which they escaped by means of artificial wings.

Daddy-longlegs def. 1

dae·mon (dē'mən) *n.* DEMON.

daf·fo·dil (daf'ə-dil) *n.* A species of narcissus having yellow flowers with a long, trumpet-shaped corona. Also **daf'fa·dil'ly, daf'fa-down-dil'ly** (-doun-dil'ē), **daf'fy-down-dil'ly.** [< L *asphodelus* asphodel]

daf·fy (daf'ē) *adj.* **·fi·er, ·fi·est** *Informal* Crazy; daft. [Prob. < DAFT]

daft (daft, däft) *adj.* **1** Silly; frolicsome. **2** Insane; crazy. [< OE *gedæfte* mild, meek] —**daft'ly** *adv.* —**daft'ness** *n.*

dag·ger (dag'ər) *n.* **1** A short, edged, and pointed weapon, for stabbing. **2** *Printing* A reference mark (†). —**double**

dagger *Printing* A mark of reference (‡). —*v.t.* **1** To pierce with a dagger; stab. **2** *Printing* To mark with a dagger. [< OF *dague* dagger]

da·guerre·o·type (də·ger'ə·tīp, -ē·ə·tīp') *n.* **1** An early photographic process using light-sensitive metallic plates. **2** A picture made by this process. [< Louis J. M. *Daguerre*, 1789–1851, French inventor] —**da·guerre'o·typ'er, da·guerre'o·typ'ist** *n.* —**da·guerre'o·typ'y** *n.*

dahl·ia (dal'yə, däl'-, dāl'-) *n.* **1** A perennial plant having tuberous roots and large, composite flower heads of various colors. **2** Its flower or root. [< Anders *Dahl*, 18th c. Swedish botanist]

Dail Ei·reann (dôl âr'ən) The lower house of the legislature of Ireland.

dai·ly (dā'lē) *adj.* Occurring, appearing, or pertaining to every day. —*n. pl.* **·lies** A daily publication. —*adv.* Day after day; on every day. [< OE *dæg* day]

dain·ty (dān'tē) *adj.* **·ti·er, ·ti·est 1** Charmingly pretty or graceful. **2** Refined or delicate in tastes, manners, etc. **3** Overly nice or fastidious. **4** Delicious; tasty. —*n. pl.* **·ties** A choice bit of food. [< L *dignitas* dignity] —**dain'ti·ly** *adv.* —**dain'ti·ness** *n.*

dair·y (dâr'ē) *n. pl.* **dair·ies 1** A building or room where milk and cream are kept and made into butter and cheese. **2** A place for the sale of milk products. **3** DAIRY FARM. **4** DAIRY CATTLE. **5** DAIRYING. [< OE *dæge* dairymaid]

dairy cattle Cows of a breed adapted for milk production.

dairy farm A farm devoted to producing milk or milk products.

dair·y·ing (dâr'ē·ing) *n.* The business of conducting a dairy farm or a dairy.

dair·y·maid (dâr'ē·mād') *n.* A woman or girl who works in a dairy.

dair·y·man (dâr'ē·mən) *n. pl.* **·men** (-mən) A man who works in, or for, or keeps a dairy.

da·is (dā'is, dās) *n. pl.* **da·is·es** A raised platform in a room where speakers, distinguished guests, etc., may sit or stand. [< OF *deis* < LL *discus* disk]

dai·sy (dā'zē) *n. pl.* **dai·sies** Any of various small plants having composite flowers consisting of a yellow disk with white or rose-colored rays. [< OE *dæges ēage* day's eye]

Da·ko·ta (də·kō'tə) *n.* **1** A member of the largest division of the Siouan linguistic stock of North American Indians; a Sioux. **2** The Siouan language of the Dakotas. —**Da·ko'tan** *adj., n.*

Da·lai La·ma (dä·lī' lä'mə) The principal priest of Lamaism in Tibet and Mongolia.

dale (dāl) *n.* A small valley. [< OE *dæl*]

dal·li·ance (dal'ē·əns) *n.* The act of dallying; frivolous or flirtatious action.

dal·ly (dal'ē) *v.* **dal·lied, dal·ly·ing** *v.i.* **1** To make love sportively; frolic. **2** To toy with; trifle; flirt: to *dally* with disaster. **3** To waste time. —*v.t.* **4** To waste (time): with *away.* [< OF *dalier* converse, chat] —**dal'li·er** *n.*

Dal·ma·tian (dal·mā'shən) *n.* **1** A native or citizen of Dalmatia. **2** A large, short-haired dog, white with black spots.

Dalmatian

dam[1] (dam) *n.* **1** A barrier to check the flow of a body of water. **2** The water held up by a dam. **3** Any obstruction. —*v.t.* **dammed, dam·ming 1** To erect a dam in; obstruct by a dam. **2** To restrain: with *up* or *in.* [< MDu. *damm*]

dam[2] (dam) *n.* A female parent: said of animals. [Var. of *dame*]

dam·age (dam'ij) *n.* **1** Destruction, injury, or harm to a person or thing. **2** *pl. Law* Money recoverable for a wrong or an injury. **3** *pl. Informal* Cost. —*v.* **dam·aged, dam·ag·ing**

v.t. **1** To cause damage to; impair the usefulness or value of. —*v.i.* **2** To be susceptible to damage. [< L *damnum* loss] —**dam′age·a·ble** *adj.* —**Syn.** *n.* **1** impairment, deterioration, loss. *v.* **1** injure, harm, ruin.

dam·as·cene (dam′ə·sēn, dam′ə·sēn′) *v.t.* **·cened, ·cen·ing** To ornament (metal, iron, steel, etc.) with wavy or variegated patterns. Also **dam·as·keen** (dam′ə·skēn, dam′·ə·skēn′). —*adj.* Relating to damascening. —*n.* Work ornamented by damascening.

Da·mas·cus steel (də·mas′kəs) A steel decorated with wavy patterns, formerly used in making swords at Damascus.

dam·ask (dam′əsk) *n.* **1** A rich silk, linen, or wool fabric woven in elaborate patterns. **2** A fine, ornamentally patterned table linen. **3** Damascus steel or its patterns. **4** A deep-pink or rose color. —*adj.* **1** Of or from Damascus. **2** Made of damask steel or fabric. **3** Of the color of damask. —*v.t.* **1** DAMASCENE. **2** To weave with rich patterns. [< *Damascus,* Syria]

damask rose A large white, pink, or red rose noted for its fragrance.

dame (dām) *n.* **1** A married or mature woman. **2** *Slang* Any woman. **3** In Great Britain: **a** A title of address for a woman upon whom an order of knighthood has been conferred: used with the given name. **b** The title of the wife of a baronet or knight. [< L *domina* lady]

damn (dam) *v.t.* **1** To pronounce worthless, unfit, bad, a failure, etc. **2** To curse or swear at. **3** *Theol.* To condemn to eternal punishment. **4** To pronounce guilty; doom. —*v.i.* **5** To swear; curse. —**damn with faint praise** To praise so reluctantly as to imply adverse criticism. —*n.* **1** The saying of "damn" as an oath or curse. **2** *Informal* The least bit: not worth a *damn.* —*interj.* An expression of anger, disappointment, etc. —*adj. & adv. Informal* DAMNED. [< L *damnare* condemn to punishment]

dam·na·ble (dam′nə·bəl) *adj.* Meriting damnation; detestable; outrageous. [< OF < L *damnabilis* < *damnare* condemn] —**dam′na·ble·ness** *n.* —**dam′na·bly** *adv.*

dam·na·tion (dam·nā′shən) *n.* The act of damning or the state of the damned. —*interj.* DAMN. —**dam′na·to·ry** (-tôr′ē, -tō′rē) *adj.*

damned (damd) *adj.* **1** Judicially condemned; doomed, as to eternal punishment. **2** Damnable; detestable. —*adv. Informal* Very; extremely: *damned* funny.

Dam·o·cles (dam′ə·klēz) *Gk. Myth.* A courtier who was forced to sit at a banquet under a sword suspended by a single hair to show him the perilous nature of a ruler's life. —**sword of Damocles** Any impending danger or calamity. —**Dam·o·cle·an** (dam′ə·klē′ən) *adj.*

Da·mon and Pyth·i·as (dā′mən; pith′ē·əs) *Rom. Myth.* Two friends so devoted that when the condemned Pythias wished to visit his home before dying, Damon volunteered to remain as hostage.

damp (damp) *n.* **1** Moisture; humidity; mist. **2** Foul air or gas, esp. in coal mines. **3** *Archaic* Depression of spirits. —*adj.* **1** Somewhat wet; moist. **2** Depressed in spirit. —*v.t.* **1** To moisten; make damp. **2** To check or lessen (energy, sound, flames, etc.). [< MDu., vapor, steam] —**damp′er,** **damp′ness.** *n.* —**damp′ly** *adv.*

damp·en (dam′pən) *v.t.* **1** To make or become damp; moisten. **2** To check; reduce, as ardor, sound, etc. —*v.i.* **3** To become damp. —**damp′en·er** *n.*

dam·sel (dam′zəl) *n. Archaic* A young girl; maiden. [< OF *dameisele,* ult. < L *domina* lady]

dam·son (dam′zən) *n.* **1** A small, purple plum. **2** The tree producing it. Also **damson plum.** [< L *(prunum) Damascenum* plum of Damascus]

Dan (dan) One of the twelve tribes of Israel.

Dan. Daniel; Danish.

Dan·a·id (dan′ē·id) *Gk. Myth.* One of the Danaides.

Da·na·i·des (də·nā′ə·dēz) *Gk. Myth.* The fifty daughters of a king, Danaus. All but one murdered their husbands at their father's command and were punished by having to draw water in a sieve forever.

dance (dans, däns) *v.* **danced, danc·ing** *v.i.* **1** To move the body and feet rhythmically, esp. to music. **2** To move excit-edly; quiver. **3** To move about lightly and quickly. —*v.t.* **4** To perform or take part in the steps or figures of (a dance). **5** To cause to dance. —*n.* **1** A series of specified movements, usu. done to music. **2** A dancing party; ball. **3** A piece of music for dancing. **4** The art of dancing. [< OF *danser*] —**danc′er** *n.*

dan·de·li·on (dan′də·lī′ən) *n.* A weed with composite yellow flower heads and deeply toothed, edible leaves. [< F *dent de lion* lion's tooth; with ref. to the shape of the leaves]

dan·der (dan′dər) *Informal* Ruffled temper; anger. —**get one's dander up** *Informal* To become angry. [?]

dan·di·fy (dan′də·fī) *v.t.* **·fied, ·fy·ing** To cause to resemble a dandy. —**dan′di·fi·ca′tion** *n.*

dan·dle (dan′dəl) *v.t.* **·dled, ·dling** **1** To move up and down lightly on the knees, as an infant. **2** To fondle; caress. [?]

dan·druff (dan′drəf) *n.* Dead, scaly skin shed by the scalp; scurf. [?]

dan·dy (dan′dē) *n. pl.* **·dies** **1** A man overly refined in dress and affected in manner; a fop. **2** *Informal* A particularly fine specimen. —*adj.* **1** Like a dandy. **2** *Informal* Excellent; very fine. [?] —**dan′dy·ish** *adj.* —**dan′dy·ism** *n.*

Dane (dān) *n.* A native or citizen of Denmark.

dan·ger (dān′jər) *n.* **1** Exposure to chance of evil, injury, or loss; risk. **2** A cause of peril or risk. [< OF *dangier* power] —**Syn.** **1, 2** peril, jeopardy, hazard.

dan·ger·ous (dān′jər·əs) *adj.* **1** Attended with danger; hazardous; perilous; unsafe. **2** Likely to or capable of causing injury or harm: a *dangerous* man. —**dan′ger·ous·ly** *adv.* —**dan′ger·ous·ness** *n.*

dan·gle (dang′gəl) *v.* **·gled, ·gling** *v.i.* **1** To hang loosely; swing to-and-fro. **2** To follow someone as a suitor or hanger-on. **3** *Gram.* To lack clear connection as a modifier in sentence construction: a *dangling* participle. —*v.t.* **4** To hold so as to swing loosely. [< Scand.] —**dan′gler** *n.*

Dan·iel (dan′yəl) A Hebrew prophet, saved by faith when imprisoned in a lion's den. —*n.* A book of the Old Testament attributed to him.

Dan·ish (dā′nish) *adj.* Of or pertaining to Denmark, the Danes, or their language. —*n. pl.* **Dan·ish** *for def.* **3** **1** The North Germanic language of the Danes. **2** DANISH PASTRY. **3** A piece of Danish pastry.

Danish pastry A rich pastry made with raised dough.

dank (dangk) *adj.* Unpleasantly damp and chilly. [< Scand.] —**dank′ish** *adj.* —**dank′ish·ness** *n.* —**dank′ly** *adv.*

dan·seuse (dän·sœz′) *n. pl.* **·seus·es** (-sœ′ziz, *Fr.* -sœz′) Female dancer; esp., a ballerina. [F]

Daph·ne (daf′nē) *Gk. Myth.* A nymph who eluded Apollo by becoming a laurel tree.

dap·per (dap′ər) *adj.* **1** Smartly dressed; natty. **2** Small and active. [< MDu., strong, energetic] —**dap′per·ly** *adv.* —**dap′per·ness** *n.*

dap·ple (dap′əl) *v.t.* **·pled, ·pling** To spot or vary in color. —*adj.* Spotted; variegated: also **dap′pled.** —*n.* **1** A spot or dot, as on a horse. **2** A spotted animal. [?]

DAR, D.A.R. Daughters of the American Revolution.

dare (dâr) *v.* **dared** (*Archaic* **durst**), **dar·ing** *v.t.* **1** To have the courage or boldness for; venture on. **2** To challenge (someone) to do something dangerous or difficult. **3** To defy; oppose and challenge. —*v.i.* **4** To have the courage or boldness to do or attempt something; venture. —**I dare say** I am reasonably certain. —*n.* A challenge. [< OE *durran*] —**dar′er** *n.*

dare·dev·il (dâr′dev′əl) *n.* One who is recklessly bold. —*adj.* Venturesome; reckless. —**dare′dev′il·try** *n.*

dar·ing (dâr′ing) *adj.* Having or showing courage and boldness; lacking or putting aside restraints, as of fear or prudence. —*n.* Courage; boldness. —**dar′ing·ly** *adv.* —**dar′ing·ness** *n.* —**Syn.** *adj.* courageous, fearless, venturesome.

dark (därk) *adj.* **1** Having or giving off little or no light. **2** Of a deep shade; black or almost black. **3** Of brunette complexion. **4** Not easily understood; obscure. **5** Ignorant; unenlightened. **6** Gloomy; dismal. **7** Angry; glum. **8** Evil; wicked. **9** Not known; hidden. **10** Deep and full in tone. —*n.* **1** Lack of light. **2** A place or state where there is little or no light. **3** Night. **4** A dark color or shade. —**in the**

dark Ignorant; uninformed. [<OE *deorc*] —**dark′ish** *adj.* —**dark′ly** *adv.* —**dark′ness** *n.*

Dark Ages 1 The period in European history from the fall of the Western Roman Empire in 476 to about 1000. 2 The Middle Ages, esp. the early part.

dark·en (där′kən) *v.t.* 1 To make dark or darker. 2 To obscure; confuse. —*v.i.* 3 To become dark or darker. —**dark′en·er** *n.*

dark horse One who unexpectedly wins a race, political nomination, etc.

dar·kling (därk′ling) *adj.* 1 Dim; obscure. 2 Occurring or being in the dark. —*adv.* In the dark.

dark·room (därk′rōōm′, -rŏŏm′) *n.* A room equipped for developing and treating photographic films, etc., in comparative darkness.

dar·ling (där′ling) *n.* 1 One tenderly beloved: often a term of direct address. 2 A favorite. —*adj.* Tenderly beloved; very dear. [<OE *dēor* dear]

darn[1] (därn) *v.t. & v.i.* To repair (a garment or a hole or rent) by filling the gap with interlacing stitches. —*n.* A place so mended. [<F *darner*] —**darn′er** *n.*

darn[2] (därn) *v.t., adj., n., & interj. Informal* Damn: a euphemism.

dar·nel (där′nəl) *n.* A weedy grass similar to rye, often found in grain fields. [ME]

darning needle 1 DRAGONFLY. 2 A large-eyed needle used in darning.

dart (därt) *n.* 1 A small, arrowlike, pointed missile, usu. thrown or shot. 2 Something resembling this. 3 A sudden and rapid motion. 4 A tapering tuck made in a garment to fit it to the figure. —*v.t. & v.i.* 1 To emit swiftly or suddenly. 2 To move swiftly and suddenly. [<OF]

dart·er (där′tər) *n.* 1 Any of various small American perchlike fish. 2 SNAKEBIRD.

darts (därts) *n. pl. (construed as sing.)* A game of skill in which small darts are thrown at a bull's-eye target.

Dar·win·ism (där′win·iz′əm) *n.* The biological theory of evolution by natural selection with variation, advanced by Charles Darwin. —**Dar·win·i·an** (där·win′ē·ən), **Dar′win·ist** *adj., n.* —**Dar′win·is′tic** *adj.*

dash (dash) *v.t.* 1 To strike with violence, esp. so as to break or shatter. 2 To throw, thrust, or knock suddenly and violently; usu. with *away, out, down,* etc. 3 To splash; bespatter. 4 To do, write, etc., hastily: with *off* or *down.* 5 To frustrate; confound: to *dash* hopes. 6 To daunt or discourage. 7 To put to shame; abash. 8 To adulterate; mix: with *with.* —*v.i.* 9 To strike; hit: The waves *dashed* against the shore. 10 To rush or move impetuously. —*n.* 1 A sudden advance or rush. 2 A short race. 3 A small addition or bit: a *dash* of humor. 4 Impetuosity; spirit; vigor. 5 Striking or ostentatious display. 6 A check or hindrance. 7 An impact or collision or its sound. 8 A quick stroke, as with a pen. 9 A horizontal line (—), as a mark of punctuation, etc. 10 The long element of the Morse code. 11 DASHBOARD. [<Scand.] —**dash′er** *n.*

dash·board (dash′bôrd′, -bōrd′) *n.* 1 A panel containing gauges and instruments, as in an automobile. 2 An upright screen on the front of a vehicle to intercept mud, etc.

da·shi·ki (dä·shē′kē) *n. pl.* **-kis** A loose-fitting garment of varying length, worn by men and women in West Africa and elsewhere. [<Yoruba]

dash·ing (dash′ing) *adj.* 1 Full of verve and spirit. 2 Stylishly showy or gay. —**dash′ing·ly** *adv.*

dash·y (dash′ē) *adj.* **dash·i·er, dash·i·est** Stylish; showy.

das·tard (das′tərd) *n.* A base coward; a sneak. [ME]

das·tard·ly (das′tərd·lē) *adj.* Contemptibly mean; base; cowardly. —**das′tard·li·ness** *n.*

dat. dative

da·ta (dā′tə, dat′ə, dä′tə) *n. pl.* of **da·tum** Facts or figures from which conclusions may be drawn. [L. neut. pl. of *datus,* pp. of *dare* give] • *Data,* although plural, is so frequently used with either a plural or singular verb that both forms have become acceptable, as in *Very little data is yet in; These data are not to be released.*

data bank An electronic library that contains information in database form.

da·ta base (dā′tə·bās′) *n.* An extensive body of information organized and stored in a computer's memory for the quick retrieval of data in response to particular queries.

data processing The preparing, storing, or otherwise handling of information for or by computers.

date[1] (dāt) *n.* 1 A point of time, esp. the time of some event. 2 That part of a writing, inscription, coin, etc., which tells when it was written, published, etc. 3 The duration of something. 4 The day of the month. 5 A social engagement with a person, or the person with whom one has it. 6 An appointment: a *date* with a dentist. —**to date** Up to the present day or time; until now. —*v.* **dat·ed, dat·ing** *v.t.* 1 To furnish or mark with a date. 2 To ascertain the time or era of. 3 To reveal or betray as of a certain time or era. 4 To make an appointment with, as a member of the opposite sex. —*v.i.* 5 To have origin in or be in existence since an era or time: usu. with *from.* 6 To become obsolete or old-fashioned. 7 To have social engagements with persons of the opposite sex. [<L *datum* <*dare* give; from first word of Latin formula giving a letter's date and place of writing] —**dat′a·ble, date′a·ble** *adj.* —**dat′er** *n.*

date[2] (dāt) *n.* 1 The oblong, sweet, fleshy fruit of the date palm. 2 A lofty palm bearing this fruit: also **date palm.** [<Gk. *daktylos* finger; with ref. to its shape]

dat·ed (dā′tid) *adj.* 1 Marked with a date. 2 Antiquated; old-fashioned.

date·less (dāt′lis) *adj.* 1 Bearing no date. 2 Without end or limit. 3 Being beyond memory; immemorial. 4 Of permanent interest.

date·line (dāt′līn′) *n.* The line containing the date and place of issue or publication, as of a newspaper, letter, etc.

date line A line approximately congruent with 180° longitude from Greenwich, separating points on the earth's surface which are by agreement a day apart in time. Also **International Date Line.**

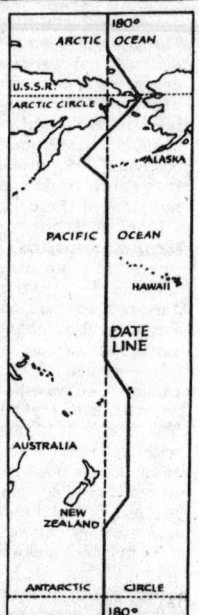

da·tive (dā′tiv) *n. Gram.* 1 In inflected Indo-European languages, that case of a noun, pronoun, or adjective denoting the indirect object. It is expressed in English by *to* or *for* with the objective or by word order, as in *I told the story to him, I told him the story.* 2 A word in this case. —*adj.* Pertaining to or designating the dative case or a word in this case. [<L (*casus*) *dativus* (the case of) giving] —**da′tive·ly** *adv.*

da·tum (dā′təm, dat′əm, dä′təm) Sing. of DATA. • See DATA.

daub (dôb) *v.t. & v.i.* 1 To smear or coat (something), as with plaster, grease, mud, etc. 2 To paint without skill or taste. —*n.* 1 Any sticky application. 2 A smear or spot. 3 A coarse, amateurish painting. 4 An instance or act of daubing. [<L *dealbare* whitewash] —**daub′er** *n.*

daugh·ter (dô′tər) *n.* 1 A female child considered in her relationship to one parent or both. 2 Any female descendant. 3 One who occupies the place of a daughter, as by adoption, marriage, or regard. 4 Any female regarded with reference to her origin: a *daughter* of Israel. [<OE *dohtor*] —**daugh′ter·ly** *adj.*

daugh·ter-in-law (dô′tər·in·lô′) *n. pl.* **daugh·ters-in-law** The wife of one's son.

daunt (dônt, dänt) *v.t.* To dishearten or intimidate; cow; abash. [<L *domitare,* freq. of *domare* tame]

daunt·less (dônt′lis, dänt-) *adj.* Fearless; intrepid. —**daunt′less·ly** *adv.* —**daunt′less·ness** *n.*

dau·phin (dô′fin, *Fr.* dō·fan′) *n.* The eldest son of a king of France. [F, lit., a dolphin, from a heraldic device]

dav·en·port (dav′ən·pôrt, -pōrt) *n.* A large sofa, often one that can be used as a bed. [Prob. after the name of the first manufacturer]

Da·vid (dā′vid) In the Old Testament, second king of Israel, reputed writer of the *Psalms.*

dav·it (dav'it, dā'vit) *n.* One of a pair of small cranes on a ship's side for hoisting its boats, stores, etc. [< *David,* proper name]

Da·vy Jones (dā'vē jōnz') Sailors' name for the spirit of the sea.

Davy Jones's locker The bottom of the ocean, esp. as the grave of the drowned.

daw·dle (dôd'l) *v.t. & v.i.* **·dled, ·dling** To waste (time) in slow trifling; loiter. [Prob. var. of earlier *daddle* < DIDDLE] **—daw'dler** *n.* **—Syn.** linger, dally, trifle.

dawn (dôn) *v.i.* 1 To begin to grow light at the start of day. 2 To begin to be understood: with *on* or *upon.* 3 To begin to expand or develop. —*n.* 1 DAYBREAK. 2 An awakening or beginning. [Back formation < *dawning,* earlier *dawe-nyng* daybreak < Scand.]

day (dā) *n.* 1 The period of light from the sun's rising to its setting. 2 DAYLIGHT. 3 The 24-hour interval represented by one revolution of the earth upon its axis; also, this interval as a unit in computing time. 4 The period of rotation about its axis of any heavenly body. 5 A time or period; era; age: in Caesar's *day.* 6 A period of success, vigor, power, etc.: to have one's *day.* 7 A contest or battle: The liberals won the *day.* 8 The hours one works. 9 *Often cap.* A specified date: Independence *Day.* **—day after day** Every day. **—day by day** Each day. **—day in, day out** Every day. **—(from) day to day** From one day to the next; not long-range. [< OE *dæg*]

day·bed (dā'bed') *n.* A lounge or couch convertible into a bed at night.

day·book (dā'bŏŏk') *n.* 1 In bookkeeping, the book in which transactions are recorded in the order of occurrence. 2 DIARY.

day·break (dā'brāk') *n.* The time of the sun's rising at the beginning of a day; dawn.

day-care center (dā'kâr') A place for the care of young children during the day.

day coach A railroad car equipped for day-time travel only, as opposed to a sleeping-car.

day·dream (dā'drēm') *n.* A usu. hopeful, dreamlike play of the imagination while awake; a reverie. —*v.i.* To have daydreams or indulge in wishful thinking. **—day'dream'er** *n.*

day laborer One who works for pay by the day, as at unskilled manual tasks.

day·light (dā'līt') *n.* 1 Sunlight; the light of day. 2 The period of light during the day. 3 Insight; comprehension. 4 Exposure to view; publicity. 5 The end, as of a task.

day·light-sav·ing time (dā'līt'sā'ving) Time in which clocks are set one hour ahead of standard time.

day nursery DAY-CARE CENTER.

Day of Atonement YOM KIPPUR.

day school 1 A school that holds classes during the daytime only. 2 A private school attended by pupils living outside the school.

day·time (dā'tīm') *n.* The time of daylight.

daze (dāz) *v.t.* **dazed, daz·ing** To stupefy or bewilder; stun. —*n.* The state of being dazed. [ME *dasen* < Scand.] **—daz'ed·ly** (dā'zid·lē) *adv.*

daz·zle (daz'əl) *v.* **·zled, ·zling** *v.t.* 1 To blind or dim the vision of by excess of light. 2 To bewilder or charm, as with brilliant display. —*v.i.* 3 To be blinded by lights or glare. 4 To excite admiration. —*n.* 1 The act of dazzling; dazzled condition. 2 Something that dazzles. [Freq. of DAZE] **—daz'zler** *n.* **—daz'zling·ly** *adv.*

db, db., decibel(s).

D. Bib. Douay Bible.

DC District of Columbia (P.O. abbr.).

DC, D.C. dc, d.c. direct current.

D.C. District of Columbia.

D.D. Doctor of Divinity.

D/D, d.d. demand draft.

D-day (dē'dā') *n.* The unspecified day of the launching of a military attack, esp. June 6, 1944, the day France was invaded by the Allies in World War II. [< D, initial letter of DAY]

D.D.S. Doctor of Dental Surgery.

DDT A highly toxic derivative of chloral, widely used as an insecticide. [< *d(ichloro-)d(iphenyl-)t(richloroethane)*]

de- *prefix* 1 Away; off: *decapitate.* 2 Down: *decline.* 3 Completely: *denude.* 4 The reversing or ridding of (the action or condition expressed by the main element): *decoding, decentralization.* [< L *de* from, away, down]

DE Delaware (P.O. abbr.)

dea·con (dē'kən) *n.* 1 A lay church officer or subordinate minister. 2 In the Anglican, Greek, and Roman Catholic churches, a clergyman ranking next below a priest. [< Gk. *diakonos* servant, minister] **—dea'con·ry, dea'con·ship** *n.*

dea·con·ess (dē'kən·is) *n.* A woman appointed or chosen as a lay church worker or officer.

de·ac·ti·vate (dē·ak'tə·vāt) *v.t.* **·vat·ed, ·vat·ing** 1 To render inoperative or ineffective, as a bomb. 2 To release (a military unit, etc.) from active duty; demobilize. **—de·ac'ti·va'tion, de·ac'ti·va·tor** *n.*

dead (ded) *adj.* 1 Having ceased to live; lifeless. 2 In a state or condition resembling death. 3 Inanimate: *dead* rocks. 4 Without interest, effectiveness, vitality, brillance, resonance, etc.: a *dead* color; a *dead* sound; a *dead* passage in a book. 5 Unresponsive; insensible: *dead* to feeling. 6 Motionless and unfeeling; numb: My arm felt *dead.* 7 Extinguished: *dead* cinders. 8 No longer productive or operative: *dead* capital; *dead* ground. 9 No longer used; obsolete: a *dead* language. 10 Without elasticity or resilience: These tennis balls are *dead.* 11 Unfailing; certain; sure: a *dead* shot. 12 Complete; absolute; utter: a *dead* stop; *dead* level. 13 *Informal* Exhausted; worn-out. 14 Not transmitting an electric current: a *dead* wire. 15 In sports, no longer in play: a *dead* ball. —*n.* 1 The part of most intense cold, darkness, etc.: the *dead* of night. 2 Dead persons collectively: with *the.* —*adv.* To the last degree; wholly; absolutely; exactly: *dead* right; *dead* straight. [< OE *dēad*] **—dead'ness** *n.*

dead·beat (ded'bēt') *n.* 1 *Informal.* One who is notorious for not paying his bills. 2 *Slang* A sponger.

dead center *Mech.* Either of two positions of a crank and connecting rod in which the alignment is so perfect that the connecting rod has no power to turn the crank.

dead·en (ded'n) *v.t.* 1 To diminish the sensitivity, force, or intensity of. 2 To lessen or impede the velocity of; retard. 3 To render soundproof. 4 To make dull or less brilliant in color. —*v.i.* 5 To become dead. **—dead'en·er** *n.*

dead end 1 An end of a street, road, etc., having no outlet. 2 A proposal, plan, or program that cannot develop or lead into something else. **—dead'-end'** *adj.*

dead·fall (ded'fôl') *n.* A trap designed to drop a heavy weight upon its prey.

dead·head (ded'hed') *n.* 1 One who receives gratis any service, admittance, or accommodation. 2 *Slang* A stupid person or a bore. —*v.i.* To make a trip, esp. by commercial carrier, without cargo.

dead heat A race in which two or more competitors finish together; a tie.

dead letter 1 A letter which can neither be delivered nor returned because of inadequate information on the envelope. 2 A statute or law not formally repealed but no longer enforced or active.

dead·line (ded'līn') *n.* The time limit by which one must complete an assignment, a payment, etc.

dead·lock (ded'lok') *n.* A cessation of activity or progress caused by the refusal of opposing parties to cooperate. —*v.t. & v.i.* To cause or come to a deadlock.

dead·ly (ded'lē) *adj.* **·li·er, ·li·est** 1 Liable or certain to cause death; fatal. 2 Mortal; implacable: *deadly* enemies. 3 Resembling death; deathly. 4 Excessive; extreme. 5 Extremely accurate or effective: a *deadly* wit; *deadly* aim. —*adv.* 1 In a way that suggests death. 2 Extremely; totally. **—dead'li·ness** *n.*

deadly nightshade BELLADONNA.

dead pan *Slang* A completely expressionless face. **—dead'-pan'** *adj., adv.*

dead point DEAD CENTER.

dead reckoning The determination of position by

means of log and compass without astronomical observations.

dead·weight (ded'wāt') n. 1 A completely inert weight or load. 2 The weight of a vehicle, as a railroad car, exclusive of its load.

dead·wood (ded'wŏŏd') n. 1 A useless or burdensome person or thing. 2 Wood dead upon the tree.

deaf (def) adj. 1 Partially or entirely unable to hear. 2 Determined not to listen or be persuaded. [<OE dēaf] — **deaf'ly** adv. —**deaf'ness** n.

deaf·en (def'ən) v.t. 1 To make deaf. 2 To stupefy or overwhelm, as with noise. 3 To drown (a sound) by a louder sound. 4 To make soundproof.

deaf-mute (def'myŏŏt') n. A person who is deaf and cannot speak. Also **deaf mute.**

deal (dēl) v. dealt (delt), deal·ing v.t. 1 To distribute; mete out, as playing cards. 2 To apportion to (one person) as a share. 3 To deliver, as a blow. —v.i. 4 To conduct oneself; behave towards: with with: to deal with an angry child. 5 To be concerned or occupied: with in or with: I deal in facts. 6 To consider, discuss, or administer; take action: with with: The court will deal with him. 7 To trade; do business: with in, with, or at. 8 In card games, to distribute the cards. —n. 1 In card games: a The act of distributing cards. b The cards so distributed. c The right or turn to distribute cards. d A single round of play. 2 An indefinite quantity, degree, or extent: a great deal of trouble. 3 A transaction or agreement, often secret: a political deal. 4 Treatment given or received: a square deal. [<OE dǣlan to divide] —deal'er n. —Syn. n. 3 scheme, arrangement, accommodation, understanding.

deal·ing (dē'ling) n. 1 Usu. pl. Any transaction with others. 2 The act of one who deals. 3 The method or manner of treatment.

dean (dēn) n. 1 The chief officer of a cathedral or of a collegiate church. 2 A college or university official having jurisdiction over a particular group of students, field of study, or acting as head of a faculty. 3 The senior or preeminent member of a group: the dean of American composers. [<LL decanus head of ten men <L decem ten] —dean'ship n.

dean·er·y (dē'nər·e) n. pl. ·er·ies The office, jurisdiction, or place of residence of a dean.

dear (dir) adj. 1 Beloved; precious. 2 Esteemed: used in letter salutations: Dear Sir. 3 Expensive; costly. 4 Characterized by high prices. 5 Intense; earnest. —n. A beloved person. —adv. 1 With great affection. 2 At great cost. — interj. An exclamation of regret, surprise, etc. [<OE dēore] —dear'ly adv. —dear'ness n.

dearth (dûrth) n. Scarcity; lack; famine. [ME derthe costliness <dere dear] —Syn. paucity, want, absence, need.

death (deth) n. 1 The permanent cessation of physical life in a person, animal, or plant. 2 The condition of being dead. 3 Extinction of anything; destruction. 4 A cause or occasion of death. 5 Something similar to dying or being dead. 6 Usu. cap. The personification of death, usu. a skeleton holding a scythe. 7 Slaughter; bloodshed. —to death Very much: He frightened me to death. —put to death To kill; execute. [<OE dēath]

death·bed (deth'bed') n. 1 The bed on which one dies. 2 The last hours of life.

death·blow (deth'blō') n. 1 A fatal blow or shock. 2 Anything that causes something to end.

death-cup (deth'kup') n. A poisonous mushroom with a cuplike structure at the base of the stem.

death house The part of a prison in which prisoners condemned to death are confined. Also **death row.**

death·less (deth'lis) adj. Not liable to die; immortal; perpetual. —death'less·ly adv. —death'less·ness n.

death·ly (deth'lē) adj. 1 Like or suggestive of death: also death'like'. 2 Pertaining to death. 3 Deadly. —adv. In the manner of one dead or dying. —death'li·ness n.

death mask A cast of the face taken just after death.

death rate The number of persons per thousand of population dying in a given unit of time.

death's-head (deths'hed') n. A human skull or a representation of it, as a symbol of death.

death·trap (deth'trap') n. 1 An unsafe structure. 2 Any place or situation involving great peril.

death warrant 1 An official order for the execution of a person. 2 That which destroys, puts an end to hope, etc.

death·watch (deth'woch', -wôch') n. 1 The last vigil with the dying or with the body of one dead. 2 A guard set over a condemned man before his execution.

deb (deb) n. Informal A debutante.

de·ba·cle (dā-bä'kəl, -bak'əl, di-) n. 1 A sudden and disastrous overthrow or collapse; ruin. 2 The breaking up of ice in a river, etc. 3 A violent flood. [<F débâcler unbar, set free]

de·bar (di-bär') v.t. -barred, -bar·ring 1 To shut out; exclude: usu. with from. 2 To prohibit; hinder. [<F dé- away + barrer to bar] —de·bar'ment n.

de·bark (di-bärk') v.t. & v.i. To put or go ashore from a ship or aircraft; disembark. [<F dé- away, from + barque a ship] —de·bar·ka·tion (dē'bär·kā'shən) n.

de·base (di-bās') v.t. de·based, de·bas·ing To lower in character, purity, value, etc.; degrade. [<DE- + ABASE] — de·base'ment, de·bas'er n. —Syn. abase, demean, devalue, cheapen.

de·bate (di-bāt') v. de·bat·ed, de·bat·ing v.t. 1 To discuss or argue about, as in a public meeting. 2 To discuss in formal argument. 3 To consider; deliberate upon in the mind. — v.i. 4 To argue; discuss. 5 To engage in formal argument. 6 To deliberate mentally; consider. —n. 1 The discussing of any question; dispute. 2 A formal argument conducted as a contest between opposing sides, usu. on a specific question. [<L de- down + batuere to strike] —de·bat'a·ble adj. —de·bat'er n.

de·bauch (di-bôch') v.t. To corrupt in morals; deprave. —v.i. 2 To indulge in depravity. —n. 1 DEBAUCHERY. 2 An act or occasion of debauchery, as an orgy. [<F débaucher to lure from work <OF desbaucher] —de·bauch'ed·ly (-id-lē) adv. —de·bauch'er, de·bauch'ed·ness n.

de·bau·chee (deb'ô·chē', -shē') n. One habitually profligate, drunken, or lewd; a libertine.

de·bauch·er·y (di-bô'chər·ē) n. pl. ·er·ies 1 Excessive gratification of all one's sensual appetites. 2 pl. Orgies. 3 Archaic Seduction from virtue, morality, fidelity, etc. Also de·bauch'ment.

de·ben·ture (di-ben'chər) n. An instrument, as a certificate, given as an acknowledgment of debt owed by the signer. [<L debere owe]

de·bil·i·tate (di-bil'ə·tāt) v.t. -tat·ed, -tat·ing To make feeble; weaken. [<L debilis weak] —de·bil'i·ta'tion n. —de·bil'i·ta'tive adj.

de·bil·i·ty (di-bil'ə·tē) n. pl. ·ties Bodily weakness; feebleness. [<L debilis weak]

deb·it (deb'it) n. 1 Something owed; a debt. 2 An item of debt. 3 The left-hand side of an account where debts are listed. —v.t. 1 To enter (a debt) in an account. 2 To charge (a customer) for goods. [<L debitum, p.p. of debere owe]

deb·o·nair (deb'ə·nâr') adj. 1 Suavely courteous and affable. 2 Carefree; gay. Also deb'o·naire', deb'on·naire'. [<OF de bon aire of good mien] —deb'o·nair'ly adv.

de·bouch (di-bouch', -bōōsh') v.i. 1 Mil. To emerge from a defile or a wood into the open. 2 To come forth. —v.t. 3 To cause to emerge. [<F dé from + bouche a mouth] — de·bouch'ment n.

de·brief (dē'brēf') v.t. To question or instruct (a pilot, agent, etc.) at the end of a mission or period of service. —de'brief'ing n.

de·bris (də·brē', dā'brē; Brit. deb'rē) n. 1 Accumulated fragments; rubbish; rubble. 2 An aggregation of detached fragments of rocks. Also dé·bris'. [<OF des- away + brisier to break]

debt (det) n. 1 That which one owes. 2 An obligation. 3 The condition of being indebted. 4 Theol. A sin. [<L debitum. See DEBIT.]

debt·or (det'ər) n. One who owes a debt. [<L debitor < debere owe]

de·bug (dē·bug') v.t. -bugged, -bug·ging To get rid of errors or other malfunctions in a computer or its software.

de·bunk (di-bungk') v.t. Informal To reveal the sham, false pretensions, etc., of [<BUNK[2]]

de·but (di·byōō', dā-, dā'byōō) n. 1 A first appearance, as in society or on the stage. 2 An opening or beginning. —v.i. Informal 1 To appear in a debut. 2 To open, as a show. Also dé·but'. [<F débuter begin, lead off]

deb·u·tante (deb′yo͞o·tänt, -yə-, -tant, deb′yo͞o·tänt′) *n.* A girl who makes a social debut. Also **dé′bu·tante′**. [< F *débuter* begin] —**deb′u·tant′** *n. Masc.*

Dec, Dec. December.

dec. deceased; decimeters; declension.

deca- *combining form* **1** Ten: *decapod.* **2** In the metric system, ten times (a specific unit of measure). Also **dec-**. [< Gk. *deka* ten]

dec·ade (dek′ād, de·kād′) *n.* **1** A period of ten years. **2** A group or set of ten. [< L *decas* a group of ten]

dec·a·dence (dek′ə·dəns, di·kād′ns) *n.* **1** A process of deterioration; decay. **2** A condition or period of decline, as in literature, art, morals, etc. [< L *de-* down + *cadere* to fall]

dec·a·dent (dek′ə·dənt, di·kād′nt) *adj.* Characterized by decadence. —*n.* A decadent person, esp. a decadent painter, writer, composer, etc. —**dec′a·dent·ly** *adv.*

dec·a·gon (dek′ə·gon) *n.* A plane figure with ten sides and ten angles. [< Gk. *deka* ten + -GON] —**de·cag·o·nai** (di·kag′ə·nəl) *adj.* —**de·cag′o·nal·ly** *adv.*

Decagon

dec·a·gram (dek′ə·gram) *n.* A measure of weight equal to ten grams. Also *dec·a·gramme.*

dec·a·he·dron (dek′ə·hē′drən) *n.* A solid bounded by ten plane faces. [< DECA- + Gk. *hedra* seat] —**dec′a·he′dral** *adj.*

de·cal (dē′kal, di·kal′) *n.* A decorative picture or design on paper that is transferable, as to glass. [Short for DECALCOMANIA]

de·cal·ci·fy (dē·kal′sə·fī) *v.t.* ·fied, ·fy·ing To deprive of calcium, as bones, teeth, etc. —**de·cal′ci·fi·ca′tion, de·cal′ci·fi·er** *n.*

Decahedron

de·cal·co·ma·ni·a (di·kal′kə·mā′nē·ə, -mān′yə) *n.* **1** A transferring of decorative pictures or designs from paper to glass, porcelain, etc. **2** DECAL. [< F *décalquer* transfer a tracing + -*manie* -MANIA]

Dec·a·logue (dek′ə·lôg, -log) *n.* TEN COMMANDMENTS. Also **Dec′a·log.** [< Gk. *deka* ten + *logos* word]

de·camp (di·kamp′) *v.i.* **1** To break camp or leave camp. **2** To leave suddenly or secretly. —**de·camp′ment** *n.*

de·cant (di·kant′) *v.t.* **1** To pour off gently so as not to disturb the sediment. **2** To pour from one container into another. [< L *de-* from + *canthus* lip of a jug] —**de·can·ta·tion** (dē′kan·tā′shən) *n.*

de·cant·er (di·kan′tər) *n.* An ornamental bottle for wine.

de·cap·i·tate (di·kap′ə·tāt) *v.t.* ·tat·ed, ·tat·ing To cut off the head of; behead. [< L *de-* down + *caput* head] —**de·cap′i·ta′tion, de·cap′i·ta′tor** *n.*

dec·a·pod (dek′ə·pod) *adj.* Ten-footed or ten-armed. —*n.* **1** A crustacean having five pairs of legs, as a crab, lobster, etc. **2** A ten-armed cephalopod, as a cuttlefish or squid. [< Gk. *deka* ten + *pous* foot] —**de·cap·o·dal** (di·kap′ə·dəl), **de·cap′o·dous** *adj.*

de·car·bon·ize (dē·kär′bə·nīz) *v.t.* ·ized, ·iz·ing To remove carbon from (molten steel, the cylinders of an internal-combustion engine, etc.). —**de·car′bon·i·za′tion, de·car′bon·iz′er** *n.*

de·car·bu·rize (dē·kär′byə·rīz) *v.t.* ·rized, ·riz·ing DECARBONIZE. —**de·car′bu·ri·za′tion** *n.*

dec·a·syl·la·ble (dek′ə·sil′ə·bəl) *n.* A line of verse having ten syllables. —**dec·a·syl·lab·ic** (dek′ə·si·lab′ik) *adj.*

de·cath·lon (di·kath′lon) *n.* An athletic contest consisting of ten different track and field events in all of which each contestant participates. [< DEC(A)- + Gk. *athlon* a contest]

de·cay (di·kā′) *v.i.* **1** To diminish slowly in health, power, beauty, quality, etc. **2** To rot; decompose. —*v.t.* **3** To cause to decay. —*n.* **1** A slow deterioration or weakening. **2** Decomposition; rottenness. **3** *Physics* The disintegration of a radioactive element. [< L *de-* down + *cadere* to fall]

decd. deceased.

de·cease (di·sēs′) *v.i.* de·ceased, de·ceas·ing To die. —*n.* Death. [< L *decessus* < *decedere* go away]

de·ceased (di·sēst′) *adj.* Dead. —**the deceased** The dead person or persons.

de·ce·dent (di·sēd′nt) *n.* A person deceased.

de·ceit (di·sēt′) *n.* **1** The act of deceiving. **2** A lie or other dishonest action. **3** The quality of being deceptive. [< OF *deceveir* deceive]

de·ceit·ful (di·sēt′fəl) *adj.* Characterized by deception; false; tricky; fraudulent. —**de·ceit′ful·ly** *adv.* —**de·ceit′ful·ness** *n.* —Syn. dishonest, disingenuous, two-faced.

de·ceive (di·sēv′) *v.* de·ceived, de·ceiv·ing *v.t.* **1** To mislead by or as by falsehood; delude. —*v.i.* **2** To practice deceit. [< L *decipere* < *de-* away, down + *capere* to take] —**de·ceiv′a·ble** *adj.* —**de·ceiv′a·bly** *adv.* —**de·ceiv′er** *n.*

de·cel·er·ate (dē·sel′ə·rāt) *v.t. & v.i.* ·at·ed, ·at·ing To diminish in speed. [< DE- + L *celerare* hasten < *celer* quick] —**de·cel′er·a′tion, de·cel′er·a′tor** *n.*

De·cem·ber (di·sem′bər) *n.* The twelfth month of the year, having 31 days. [< L *decem* ten; because December was the tenth month in the old Roman calendar]

de·cen·cy (dē′sən·sē) *n. pl.* ·cies **1** Propriety in conduct, speech, dress, etc. **2** *pl.* Actions that are socially proper or seemly. **3** *pl.* Things required for a proper manner of life. [< L *decens.* See DECENT.]

de·cen·ni·al (di·sen′ē·əl) *adj.* Continuing for or consisting of ten years; occurring every ten years. —*n.* A tenth anniversary. [< L *decem* ten + *annus* year] —**de·cen′ni·al·ly** *adv.*

de·cent (dē′sənt) *adj.* **1** Characterized by propriety of conduct, speech, manners, or dress; proper; respectable. **2** Modest; chaste. **3** Moderately good; satisfactory. **4** Kind; generous. **5** *Informal* Adequately clothed. [< L *decens,* pr.p. of *decere* be fitting, be proper] —**de′cent·ly** *adv.* —**de′cent·ness** *n.*

de·cen·tral·ize (dē·sen′trəl·īz) *v.t.* ·ized, ·iz·ing To reorganize (a government, school system, etc.) by distributing authority to smaller or local units. —**de·cen′tral·i·za′tion** *n.*

de·cep·tion (di·sep′shən) *n.* **1** The act of deceiving. **2** The state of being deceived. **3** Anything deceptive; a delusion.

de·cep·tive (di·sep′tiv) *adj.* Having power or tendency to deceive. —**de·cep′tive·ly** *adv.* —**de·cep′tive·ness** *n.* —Syn. misleading, delusive, false.

dec·i·bel (des′ə·bel) *n.* A logarithmic unit defined so that an increase of 1 decibel represents multiplication of sound or signal power by about 1.258, with, for sound, 0 decibels representing a pressure of 0.0002 microbar. [< L *decem* ten + E *bel,* logarithmic unit < Alexander Graham *Bell,* 1847–1922, U.S. inventor]

de·cide (di·sīd′) *v.* ·cid·ed, ·cid·ing *v.t.* **1** To determine; settle, as a dispute, contest, etc.; arbitrate. **2** To cause the outcome of; settle. **3** To bring (someone) to a decision. —*v.i.* **4** To give a decision. **5** To make a decision. [< MF *décider* < L *decidere* < *de-* down, away + *caedere* cut] —**de·cid′a·ble** *adj.* —**de·cid′er** *n.*

de·cid·ed (di·sī′did) *adj.* **1** Free from uncertainty; unquestionable. **2** Determined; resolute; emphatic. —**de·cid′ed·ly** *adv.* —**de·cid′ed·ness** *n.*

de·cid·u·ous (di·sij′o͞o·əs) *adj.* **1** Falling off or shed at specific seasons, as petals or leaves. **2** Characterized by such a falling off; not evergreen. [< L *de-* down, away + *cadere* to fall] —**de·cid′u·ous·ly** *adv.* —**de·cid′u·ous·ness** *n.*

de·cil·lion (de·sil′yən) *n. & adj.* See NUMBER. [< DEC(A)- + (M)ILLION]

dec·i·mal (des′ə·məl) *adj.* **1** Founded on the number 10. **2** Proceeding by powers of 10 or of one tenth. —*n.* A decimal fraction. [< L *decem* ten] —**dec′i·mal·ly** *adv.*

decimal fraction A fraction whose denominator is ten or a power of ten and is expressed by using a decimal point, as .8 = 8/10 or .08 = 8/100.

dec·i·mal·ize (des′ə·məl·īz) *v.t.* ·ized, ·iz·ing To change to a decimal system, as currency. *Brit. sp.* ·ise. —**dec′i·mal·i·za′tion** *n.*

decimal point A dot or period used before a decimal fraction.

dec·i·mate (des′ə·māt) *v.t.* ·mat·ed, ·mat·ing **1** To destroy or kill a large proportion of. **2** To select by lot and kill one out of every ten of. [< L *decimare* take a tenth part from < *decem* ten] —**dec′i·ma′tion, dec′i·ma′tor** *n.*

de·ci·pher (di·sī′fər) *v.t.* **1** To figure out the sense of, as hieroglyphics, a scribble, etc. ⁊ To translate from cipher into ordinary characters; decode. [< DE- + CIPHER] —**de·ci′pher·a·ble** *adj.* —**de·ci′pher·er, de·ci′pher·ment** *n.*

de·ci·sion (di·sizh′ən) *n.* 1 The act of deciding or making up one's mind. 2 The result or conclusion arrived at by deciding. 3 The quality of being positive and firm; determination. 4 In boxing, a victory determined by points rather than by a knockout.

de·ci·sion-mak·ing (di·sizh′ən·mā′king) *n.* 1 The process by which decisions are made, esp. important decisions affecting others and made by virtue of one's office or position: a study of presidential *decision-making.* 2 The power or ability to make decisions of consequence: agitating for a voice in *decision-making.* —*adj.* Of, relating to, or requiring decision-making. —**de·ci′sion-mak′er** *n.*

de·ci·sive (di·sī′siv) *adj.* 1 Putting an end to uncertainty or debate; conclusive. 2 Prompt; positive; decided. 3 Crucially important; critical. —**de·ci′sive·ly** *adv.* —**de·ci′sive·ness** *n.*

deck (dek) *n.* 1 A platform covering or extending horizontally across a vessel. 2 Any similar flat surface. 3 A pack of cards. —**clear the deck** To prepare for activity. —**hit the deck** 1 *Slang* To rise from bed quickly. 2 *Slang* To prepare for activity. 3 *Slang* To drop to a prone position. —**on deck** 1 Present and available for action. 2 Next at bat in a baseball game. —*v.t.* 1 To array; adorn. 2 To put a deck on. [< MDu. *dek* roof, covering]

deck hand A sailor employed about the deck.

deck·le (dek′əl) *n.* 1 In papermaking by hand, a frame to confine the pulp to a definite width. 2 The ragged edge of hand-made paper: also **deckle edge.** Also **deck′el.** [< G *decke* cover]

de·claim (di·klām′) *v.i.* 1 To speak loudly and in a rhetorical manner. 2 To give a recitation. 3 To condemn or attack verbally and vehemently: with *against.* —*v.t.* 4 To utter aloud in a rhetorical manner. [< L *de-* completely + *clamare* shout] —**de·clam·a·to·ry** (di·klam′ə·tôr′ē, -tō′rē) *adj.* —**de·claim′er, dec·la·ma·tion** (dek′lə·mā′shən) *n.*

dec·la·ra·tion (dek′lə·rā′shən) *n.* 1 The act of declaring. 2 That which is declared. 3 In law, a formal presentation of facts by the plaintiff. 4 A statement of goods that can be taxed. 5 In bridge: a A meld. b The final or winning bid.

Declaration of Independence The manifesto of the Continental Congress adopted July 4, 1776, giving the reasons why the American colonies had declared their independence.

de·clar·a·tive (di·klar′ə·tiv) *adj.* Making a declaration or statement. Also **de·clar·a·to·ry** (di·klar′ə·tôr′ē, -tō′rē).

de·clare (di·klâr′) *v.* **·clared, ·clar·ing** *v.t.* 1 To assert positively or emphatically. 2 To announce or state formally and solemnly. 3 To reveal; manifest. 4 To make full statement of, as dutiable goods. 5 In bridge, to name, as a trump suit. —*v.i.* 6 To make a declaration. 7 To proclaim a choice or decision. [< L *de-* completely + *clarare* make clear < *clarus* clear] —**de·clar′er** *n.*

de·clas·si·fy (dē·klas′ə·fī) *v.t.* **·fied, ·fy·ing** To remove secrecy restrictions from (government documents, etc.).

de·clen·sion (di·klen′shən) *n.* 1 *Gram.* a The inflection of nouns, pronouns, and adjectives to indicate case, number, and gender. b A class of words similarly inflected. 2 A slope or descent. 3 A decline; deterioration. [< L *declinare.* See DECLINE.] —**de·clen′sion·al** *adj.*

dec·li·na·tion (dek′lə·nā′shən) *n.* 1 The act of inclining or sloping downward; descent; slope. 2 Deviation, as from a course or action. 3 A courteous refusal. 4 The angular distance of a heavenly body north or south from the celestial equator. 5 The angle between the direction in which a magnetic needle points and the true meridian: also **magnetic declination.**

de·cline (di·klīn′) *v.* **·clined, ·clin·ing** *v.i.* 1 To refuse to accept, comply with, or do something, esp. politely. 2 To lessen or fail, as in health. 3 To come to an end; wane. 4 To bend or incline downward or aside. 5 To degrade oneself, as to an unworthy action. —*v.t.* 6 To refuse to accept, comply with, or do, esp. politely. 7 To cause to bend or incline downward or aside. 8 To give the inflected forms of (a noun, pronoun, or adjective). —*n.* 1 The act or result of declining; deterioration; decay. 2 The period of such declining. 3 Any enfeebling disease, as tuberculosis. 4 A

declivity; a slope. [< L *declinare* lean down] —**de·clin′a·ble** *adj.* —**de·clin′er** *n.*

de·cliv·i·ty (di·kliv′ə·tē) *n. pl.* **·ties** A downward slope; descending surface. [< L *de-* down + *clivus* hill, slope] —**de·cliv′i·tous, de·cli′vous** (-klī′vəs) *adj.*

de·coct (di·kokt′) *v.t.* To extract by boiling; condense. [< L *de-* down + *coquere* to cook] —**de·coc′tion** *n.*

de·code (dē·kōd′) *v.t.* **·cod·ed, ·cod·ing** To convert (a coded message) into plain language. —**de·cod′er** *n.*

dé·col·le·té (dā′kol·tā′, *Fr.* dā·kôl·tā′) *adj.* 1 Cut low in the neck, as a gown. 2 Wearing a low-necked gown. [< F *décolleter* bare the neck] —**dé·col·le·tage** (-täzh′) *n.*

de·com·pose (dē′kəm·pōz′) *v.t. & v.i.* **·posed, ·pos·ing** 1 To separate into constituent elements. 2 To decay. —**de′·com·pos′a·ble** *adj.* —**de′com·pos′er, de′com·po·si′tion** *n.*

de·com·press (dē′kəm·pres′) *v.t.* 1 To free of pressure. 2 To lessen the pressure on (caisson workers, etc.), as in an airlock. —**de′com·pres′sion** *n.*

decompression sickness A painful, sometimes fatal condition due to bubbles of nitrogen formed in the blood when a rapid reduction in pressure occurs, as when a diver returns directly to the surface after a period deep under water.

de·con·tam·i·nate (dē′kən·tam′ə·nāt) *v.t.* **·nat·ed, ·nat·ing** To rid of a noxious or dangerous substance. —**de′con·tam′i·na′tion** *n.*

de·con·trol (dē′kən·trōl′) *v.t.* **·trolled, ·trol·ling** To remove from control, esp. from government controls. —*n.* The removal of controls.

dé·cor (dā′kôr, dā·kôr′) *n.* 1 The plan or arrangement of furnishings and colors in an interior space, as a home or office. 2 In the theater, scenery. Also **de′cor.** [< F *décorer* decorate]

dec·o·rate (dek′ə·rāt) *v.t.* **·rat·ed, ·rat·ing** 1 To adorn; ornament. 2 To furnish, paint, refurbish (a dwelling, room, etc.). 3 To devise a décor, as for a home, and supervise its execution. 4 To confer a medal or decoration upon: *decorated* for valor. [< L *decorare* < *decus* embellishment] —**dec′o·ra′tor** *n.*

dec·o·ra·tion (dek′ə·rā′shən) *n.* 1 The act, process, or art of decorating. 2 Ornamentation; an ornament. 3 A badge or emblem conferred as a mark of honor; a medal.

Decoration Day MEMORIAL DAY.

dec·o·ra·tive (dek′ər·ə·tiv, dek′rə-, dek′ə·rā′-) *adj.* Of the nature of or used as decoration; ornamental. —**dec′o·ra·tive·ly** *adv.* —**dec′o·ra·tive·ness** *n.*

dec·o·rous (dek′ər·əs, di·kôr′əs, -kō′rəs) *adj.* Characterized by proper behavior and good taste. [< L *decus* grace, embellishment] —**dec′o·rous·ly** *adv.* —**dec′o·rous·ness** *n.* —Syn. becoming, suitable, seemly, correct.

de·co·rum (di·kôr′əm, -kō′rəm) *n.* 1 Propriety, as in manner, conduct, etc.; seemliness. 2 An act demanded by social custom. [< L *decorus* decorous]

de·coy (dē′koi, di·koi′) *n.* 1 A person or thing that lures others into danger or a snare. 2 A bird or animal, or the likeness of one, used to lure game within gunshot. 3 An enclosed place into which game may be lured. —*v.t. & v.i.* (dē′koi) To lure or be lured into danger, a snare, etc. [< Du. *de kooi* the cage] —**de′coy·er** *n.*

Decoy *def.* 2

de·crease (di·krēs′) *v.t. & v.i.* **·creased, ·creas·ing** To grow or cause to grow gradually less or smaller; abate; reduce. —*n.* (*usu.* dē′krēs) 1 The act, process, or state of decreasing. 2 The amount or degree of decreasing. [< L *decrescere* < *de-* down + *crescere* grow] —**de·creas′ing·ly** *adv.*

de·cree (di·krē′) *n.* 1 A formal order or ordinance, as of a civil or an ecclesiastical body. 2 Anything unalterably ordained. —*v.t.* 1 To order, adjudge, ordain, or appoint by law or edict. —*v.i.* 2 To issue an edict or decree. [< L *decretum*, neut. pp. of *decernere* decide]

dec·re·ment (dek′rə·mənt) *n.* 1 A decreasing; waning. 2 Amount of loss by decrease or waste. [< L *decrementum* < *decrescere.* See DECREASE.]

de·crep·it (di·krep′it) *adj.* Enfeebled by old age or overuse; broken down. [< L *decrepitus* < *de-* completely + *crepare* to creak] —**de·crep′it·ly** *adv.*

de·crep·i·tude (di·krep′ə·t$\overline{oo}$d) *n.* Enfeeblement through infirmity or old age.

de·cre·scen·do (dē′krə·shen′dō) *adj., adv., n.* DIMINUENDO. [< L *decrescere*. See DECREASE]

de·cre·tal (di·krēt′l) *n.* A decree, esp. one of the Pope determining some point in ecclesiastical law. —*adj.* Of or pertaining to a decree. [< L *decretum*. See DECREE.]

de·crim·i·nal·ize (dē·krim′ə·nəl·īz) *v.t.* ·ized, ·iz·ing To abstain from applying criminal penalties to; regard as nonpunishable. —**de·crim′i·nal·i·za′tion** *n.*

de·cry (di·krī′) *v.t.* ·cried, ·cry·ing 1 To condemn or disparage openly. 2 To depreciate, as foreign or obsolete coins. [< F *dé-* down + *crier* to cry] —**de·cri′al, de·cri′er** *n.*

de·cum·bent (di·kum′bənt) *adj.* 1 Lying down; recumbent. 2 *Bot.* Prostrate: said of stems, shoots, etc., growing along the ground. [< L *de-* down + *cumbere* lie, recline] —**de·cum′bence, de·cum′ben·cy** *n.*

ded·i·cate (ded′ə·kāt) *v.t.* ·cat·ed, ·cat·ing 1 To set apart for sacred uses; consecrate. 2 To set apart for any special use, duty, or purpose. 3 To devote (oneself) to some special work, action, etc. 4 To open (a new building, park, etc.) with ceremonies. 5 To preface with a dedication, as a book. —*adj.* Dedicated; devoted. [< L *de-* down + *dicare* proclaim] —**ded′i·ca′tive** *adj.* —**ded′i·ca′tor** *n.*

ded·i·ca·tion (ded′ə·kā′shən) *n.* 1 A dedicating or being dedicated. 2 An inscription in a book, etc., as to a friend or cause.

de·duce (di·d$\overline{oo}$s′) *v.t.* ·duced, ·duc·ing 1 To derive as a conclusion; infer. 2 To trace, as derivation or origin. [< L *deducere* < *de-* down + *ducere* to lead] —**de·duc′i·ble** *adj.*

de·duct (di·dukt′) *v.t.* To subtract; take away. [< L *deductus,* pp. of *deducere.* See DEDUCE.]

de·duct·i·ble (di·duk′tə·bəl) *adj.* That can be deducted, esp. in calculating taxable income. —*n.* In an insurance policy, a specified amount of damage or loss that the insured is responsible for before the insurer's coverage takes effect; also, such a provision in a policy. —**de′duct·i·bil′i·ty** *n.*

de·duc·tion (di·duk′shən) *n.* 1 The act of deducting or the sum or amount deducted. 2 Reasoning from stated premises to the formally valid conclusion; reasoning from the general to the particular. 3 An inference; conclusion. —**de·duc′tive** *adj.* —**de·duc′tive·ly** *adv.*

deed (dēd) *n.* 1 Anything done; an act. 2 A notable achievement or action. 3 Action performed, as opposed to words. 4 *Law* A written instrument under seal, whether a bond, agreement, or contract, but most frequently used in the conveyance of real estate. —**in deed** In fact; actually. —*v.t.* To convey or transfer by deed. [< OE *dǣd*]

deem (dēm) *v.t. & v.i.* To judge; think; regard; believe. [< OE *dēman* judge]

de·em·pha·size (dē·em′fə·sīz) *v.t.* ·sized, ·siz·ing To place less emphasis on. —**de·em′pha·sis** (-sis) *n.*

deep (dēp) *adj.* 1 Extending or situated far below the surface. 2 Extending or situated far back, far in, or far from either side. 3 Having a (specified) depth, thickness, or distance: a box ten feet *deep.* 4 Far distant in time or space. 5 Hard to understand; abstruse. 6 Intellectually penetrating; profound. 7 Heartfelt and earnest: *deep* regrets. 8 Profound or great in degree, intensity, etc.: a *deep* coma. 9 Scheming; sly. 10 Of intense or dark hue. 11 Low in pitch; sonorous: a *deep* voice. —*n.* 1 That which has great depth; the sea. 2 The most profound part: the *deep* of night. —*adv.* 1 In a deep way or to a deep extent; deeply. 2 Far on; for a long time: *deep* into the night. [< OE *dēop*] —**deep′ly** *adv.* —**deep′ness** *n.*

deep·en (dē′pən) *v.t. & v.i.* To make or become deep or deeper.

deep-freeze (dēp′frēz′) *v.t.* ·troze or ·freezed, ·fro·zen or ·freezed, ·freez·ing To freeze (foods) quickly to preserve natural flavor.

Deep-freeze (dēp′frēz′) *n.* A refrigerator for deep-freezing foods: a trade name.

deep-fry (dēp′frī′) *v.t.* ·fried, ·fry·ing To fry while submerged in fat or oil.

deep-root·ed (dēp′r$\overline{oo}$′tid, -r$\overline{oo}$t′id) *adj.* 1 Having

deeply situated roots. 2 Firmly entrenched; hard to get rid of, overcome, etc.

deep-seat·ed (dēp′sē′tid) *adj.* 1 Deeply situated. 2 Difficult to overcome, get rid of, etc.

deer (dir) *n. pl.* **deer** A ruminant with deciduous antlers, usu. in the male only, as the moose, elk, and reindeer. [< OE *dēor* beast]

deer·hound (dir′hound′) *n.* A Scottish breed of sporting dog with a long, flat head, pointed muzzle, and a shaggy coat.

deer·skin (dir′skin′) *n.* A deer's hide, or leather made from it; buckskin.

Deer

de·es·ca·late (dē·es′kə·lāt) *v.t. & v.i.* ·lat·ed, ·lat·ing To decrease or be decreased gradually, as in a conflict: to *de-escalate* a war. —**de·es′ca·la′tion** *n.*

def. defendant; defense; deferred; definition.

de·face (di·fās′) *v.t.* ·faced, ·fac·ing To mar or disfigure the surface of. [< OF *des-* down, away + *face* face] —**de·face′a·ble** *adj.* —**de·face′ment, de·fac′er** *n.*

de fac·to (dē fak′tō) Actually or really existing, with or without legal sanction. [L]

de·fal·cate (di·fal′kāt) *v.i.* ·cat·ed, ·cat·ing To embezzle money. [< Med. L *defalcare* lop off] —**de·fal·ca·tion** (dē′fal·kā′shən), **de·fal′ca·tor** *n.*

de·fame (di·fām′) *v.t.* ·famed, ·fam·ing To attack the good name or reputation of. [< L *dis-* away, from + *fama* a report, reputation] —**def·a·ma·tion** (def′ə·mā′shən), **de·fam′er** *n.* —**de·fam·a·to·ry** (di·fam′ə·tôr′ē) *adj.* —Syn. revile, besmirch, slander, libel.

de·fault (di·fôlt′) *n.* A failure to fulfill an obligation or duty; failure to appear, as in a contest or a legal suit. —**in default of** Owing to lack or failure of. —*v.i.* 1 To fail or neglect to fulfill or do a duty, obligation, etc. 2 To fail to meet financial obligations. 3 *Law* To fail to appear in court. 4 In sports, to fail to compete or complete a game, etc. —*v.t.* 5 To fail to perform or pay. 6 In sports, to fail to compete in, as a game; also, to forfeit by default. [< L *de-* down + *fallere* deceive] —**de·fault′er** *n.*

de·feat (di·fēt′) *v.t.* 1 To overcome in any contest; vanquish. 2 To thwart or frustrate, as plans. 3 *Law* To make void; annul. —*n.* 1 The act of defeating. 2 A failure to win or succeed. [< OF *defaire* undo]

de·feat·ism (di·fē′tiz·əm) *n.* A too ready acceptance or anticipation of defeat. —**de·feat′ist** *adj., n.*

def·e·cate (def′ə·kāt) *v.* ·cat·ed, ·cat·ing *v.i.* 1 To discharge excrement from the bowels. 2 To become free of dregs or impurities. —*v.t.* 3 To clear of dregs or impurities; purify. —*adj.* Clarified; refined. [< L *de-* down, away + *faex* dregs] —**def′e·ca′tion, def′e·ca′tor** *n.*

de·fect (di·fekt′, dē′fekt) *n.* 1 Lack or absence of something essential; deficiency. 2 An imperfection; failing; fault. —*v.i.* (di·fekt′) To desert; go over to the enemy or opposition. [< L *deficere* fail] —**de·fec′tor** *n.* —Syn. *n.* 2 blemish, flaw, drawback.

de·fec·tion (di·fek′shən) *n.* Abandonment of allegiance or duty; desertion.

de·fec·tive (di·fek′tiv) *adj.* 1 Incomplete or imperfect; faulty. 2 *Gram.* Lacking one or more of the normal declensional or conjugational forms: Can is a *defective* verb. 3 *Psychol.* Having less than normal intelligence. —*n.* 1 One who is physically or mentally subnormal. 2 *Gram.* A defective word. —**de·fec′tive·ly** *adv.* —**de·fec′tive·ness** *n.*

de·fend (di·fend′) *v.t.* 1 To shield from attack; protect. 2 To justify or vindicate; support. 3 *Law* **a** To act in behalf of (an accused). **b** To contest, as a claim, charge, or suit. 4 In sports, to try to keep one's opponent from scoring at (a goal, etc.). —*v.i.* 5 To make a defense. [< L *de-* down, away + *fendere* to strike] —**de·fend′a·ble** *adj.* —**de·fend′er** *n.*

de·fen·dant (di·fen′dənt) *n. Law* A person against whom an action is brought. —*adj.* Defending.

de·fense (di·fens′) *n.* 1 The act of defending or guarding.

2 The state of being defended. **3** Anything that defends. **4** A plea or statement that supports or justifies something. **5** *Law* **a** The arguments brought forth by a defendant or his legal counsel. **b** A defendant and his lawyer or lawyers. **6** Protection of oneself, as in boxing, or of one's goal, as in team sports. **7** Any group that is defending, as in sports. *Brit. sp.* **de·fence.** —**de·fense′·less** *adj.* —**de·fense′·less·ly** *adv.* —**de·fense′·less·ness** *n.*

defense mechanism 1 *Psychoanal.* An unconscious process for protecting the personality against unpleasant emotions, impulses, etc. **2** Any self-protective reaction of an organism.

de·fen·si·ble (di·fen′sə·bəl) *adj.* Capable of being defended or justified. —**de·fen′si·bil′i·ty, de·fen′si·ble·ness** *n.* —**de·fen′si·bly** *adv.*

de·fen·sive (di·fen′siv) *adj.* **1** Intended or suitable for defense. **2** Done in defense. **3** Excessively inclined to defend or justify one's conduct, opinions, etc. —*n.* An attitude or position of defense. —**de·fen′sive·ly** *adv.* —**de·fen′·sive·ness** *n.*

de·fer[1] (di·fûr′) *v.t. & v.i.* **·ferred, ·fer·ring** To delay; put off to some other time; postpone. [< L *differre* to distract] —**de·fer′ra·ble** *adj.* —**de·fer′ment** *n.*

de·fer[2] (di·fûr′) *v.i.* **·ferred, ·fer·ring** To yield to the opinions or decisions of another. [< L *de-* down + *ferre* bear, carry] —**de·fer′rer** *n.*

def·er·ence (def′ər·əns) *n.* **1** Respectful yielding. **2** Polite respect; regard. —**def′er·ent** *adj.*

def·er·en·tial (def′ə·ren′shəl) *adj.* Marked by deference; respectful; courteous. —**def′er·en′tial·ly** *adv.*

de·fi·ance (di·fī′əns) *n.* **1** Bold opposition; disposition to oppose or resist. **2** The act of defying.

de·fi·ant (di·fī′ənt) *adj.* Showing or characterized by defiance; resisting boldly. [< OF, pr.p. of *defier*. See DEFY.] —**de·fi′ant·ly** *adv.*

de·fib·ril·late (dē·fib′rə·lāt, dē·fī′brə-) *v.t.* **·lat·ed, ·lat·ing** To stop fibrillation of (the heart muscle), as by jolting with an electric current. —**de·fib′ril·la′tion, de·fib′ril·la′tor** *n.*

de·fi·cien·cy (di·fish′ən·sē) *n. pl.* **·cies 1** The state of being deficient. **2** A lack; insufficiency. Also **de·fi′cience.**

de·fi·cient (di·fish′ənt) *adj.* **1** Lacking an adequate or proper supply; insufficient. **2** Lacking some essential; incomplete. [< L *deficere* to lack] —**de·fi′cient·ly** *adv.*

def·i·cit (def′ə·sit) *n.* The amount of money lacking in a required or expected sum. [L, it is lacking]

de·fi·er (di·fī′ər) *n.* One who defies.

de·file[1] (di·fīl′) *v.t.* **·filed, ·fil·ing 1** To make foul or dirty; pollute. **2** To corrupt the purity of. **3** To sully; profane (a name, reputation, etc.). **4** To render ceremonially unclean. [< OF *de-* down + *fouler* trample] —**de·file′ment, de·fil′er** *n.*

de·file[2] (di·fīl′, dē′fīl) *v.i.* **·filed, ·fil·ing** To march in a line. —*n.* **1** A long narrow pass or gorge, as between mountains. **2** A marching in file. [< MF *dé-* down + *file* a line, file]

de·fine (di·fīn′) *v.t.* **·fined, ·fin·ing 1** To state the meaning of (a word, etc.). **2** To describe or give the characteristics of. **3** To determine and specify the limits of. **4** To determine and fix the boundaries of. **5** To show or bring out the form or outline of. [< L *de-* down + *finire* finish] —**de·fin′·a·ble** *adj.* —**de·fin′er** *n.*

def·i·nite (def′ə·nit) *adj.* **1** Having precise limits. **2** Precise; clear, as in meaning. **3** Certain; sure. **4** *Gram.* Limiting; particularizing: The *definite* article in English is "the". —**def′i·nite·ly** *adv.* —**def′i·nite·ness** *n.*

def·i·ni·tion (def′ə·nish′ən) *n.* **1** A defining or being defined. **2** A statement of the meaning of a word, phrase, etc. **3** A statement describing or making clear an object, process, etc. **4** The state of being clear, definite, etc. **5** The determining of the outline, character, or limits of anything. **6** *Optics* The power of a lens to give a distinct image at whatever magnification. **7** In television and radio, the clarity of detail in the transmitted images or sounds.

de·fin·i·tive (di·fin′ə·tiv) *adj.* **1** Decisive and final; conclusive. **2** Most nearly accurate, complete, etc.: a *definitive* study. **3** Sharply defining or limiting; explicit. —**de·fin′i·tive·ly** *adv.* —**de·fin′i·tive·ness** *n.*

de·flate (di·flāt′) *v.t. & v.i.* **·flat·ed, ·flat·ing 1** To collapse or cause to collapse by the removal of contained air or gas. **2** To take the conceit, confidence, or self-esteem out of. **3** To devaluate; lessen (currency or prices). [< L *de-* down + *flare* blow] —**de·fla′tor** *n.*

de·fla·tion (di·flā′shən) *n.* **1** The act of deflating or the condition of being deflated. **2** A decrease in the amount of currency in circulation in a country, resulting in a decline in prices. —**de·fla·tion·ar·y** (di·flā′shən·er′ē) *adj.*

de·flect (di·flekt′) *v.t. & v.i.* To turn aside; swerve or cause to swerve from a course. [< L *de-* down + *flectere* bend] —**de·flec′tion, de·flec′tor** *n.* —**de·flec′tive** *adj.*

de·flow·er (di·flou′ər) *v.t.* **1** To deprive (a woman) of virginity. **2** To violate; rob of beauty.

de·fo·li·ate (dē·fō′lē·āt) *v.t.* **·at·ed, ·at·ing** To deprive or strip of leaves. [< L *de-* down + *folium* leaf] —**de·fo′li·a′tion, de·fo′li·a′tor** *n.*

de·for·est (dē·fôr′ist, -for′-) *v.t.* To clear of forests or trees. —**de·for′es·ta′tion, de·for′est·er** *n.*

de·form (di·fôrm′) *v.t.* **1** To distort the form or shape of. **2** To make ugly or dishonorable. —*v.i.* **3** To become deformed or disfigured. —**def′or·ma′tion** (def′ər·mā′shən) *n.*

de·formed (di·fôrmd′) *adj.* **1** Misshapen; warped. **2** Unattractive; ugly. —**de·form·ed·ly** (di·fôr′mid·lē) *adv.*

de·form·i·ty (di·fôr′mə·tē) *n. pl.* **·ties 1** A deformed or misshapen condition or part. **2** Unsightliness; ugliness. **3** Moral depravity. **4** One who or that which is deformed.

de·fraud (di·frôd′) *v.t.* To take or withhold property, etc., from by fraud; cheat. —**de·fraud·a·tion** (dē′frô·dā′shən), **de·fraud′er** *n.*

de·fray (di·frā′) *v.t.* To pay for; bear the expense of. [< OF *de-* away + *frai* cost, charge] —**de·fray′a·ble** *adj.* —**de·fray′al, de·fray′ment, de·fray′er** *n.*

de·frock (dē·frok′) *v.t.* UNFROCK.

de·frost (dē·frôst′, -frost′) *v.t.* **1** To remove ice or frost from. —*v.i.* **2** To be rid of ice or frost.

de·frost·er (dē·frôs′tər, -fros′-) *n.* A device for defrosting, as in a refrigerator.

deft (deft) *adj.* Skillful; adroit; dexterous. [< OE *gedæfte* meek, gentle] —**deft′ly** *adv.* —**deft′ness** *n.*

de·funct (di·fungkt′) *adj.* Having passed out of existence or life; no longer functioning or alive: a *defunct* publication. [< L *de-* not + *fungi* perform]

de·fy (di·fī′) *v.t.* **·fied, ·fy·ing 1** To resist openly or boldly. **2** To challenge; dare: to *defy* a rival politician to make public his tax returns. **3** To resist successfully; baffle; obstruct: to *defy* definition. [< OF *defier* < Med. L *dis-* not + *fidare* be faithful]

deg. degree(s).

de·gauss (di·gous′) *v.t.* To neutralize, cancel, or destroy the magnetic field of. [< DE- + GAUSS]

de·gen·er·a·cy (di·jen′ər·ə·sē) *n.* **1** The state of being degenerate, or the process of degenerating. **2** Degenerate behavior.

de·gen·er·ate (di·jen′ə·rāt) *v.i.* **·at·ed, ·at·ing 1** To become worse or inferior. **2** *Biol.* To revert to a lower type; deteriorate. —*adj.* (di·jen′ər·it) **1** Having become worse or inferior; deteriorated. **2** Morally depraved or perverted. —*n.* (-it) **1** A deteriorated or degraded animal or human. **2** A morally depraved or perverted person. [< L *de-* down, away + *generare* create] —**de·gen′er·ate·ly** *adv.* —**de·gen′·er·a′tive** *adj.* —**de·gen′er·ate·ness** *n.*

de·gen·er·a·tion (di·jen′ə·rā′shən) *n.* **1** The process of degenerating. **2** A degenerate condition. **3** Progressive deterioration of an organ, tissue, or part.

de·grad·a·ble (di·grā′də·bəl) *adj.* *Chem.* Capable of being degraded, as a compound.

deg·ra·da·tion (deg′rə·dā′shən) *n.* **1** The act of degrading. **2** The state of being reduced in rank, honor, etc.

de·grade (di·grād′) *v.* **·grad·ed, ·grad·ing** *v.t.* **1** To reduce in rank, status, quality, etc. **2** To debase or lower in character, morals, etc. **3** To bring into contempt; dishonor. **4** *Geol.* To reduce the height of by erosion. **5** *Chem.* To break down (an organic compound) into simpler parts. —*v.i.* **6** To degenerate; become of a lower type. [< L *de-* down + *gradus* position, step]

de·grad·ing (di·grā′ding) *adj.* Debasing; humiliating.

de·gree (di·grē′) *n.* **1** One of a succession of steps, grades, or stages. **2** Relative rank, position, or dignity: an executive of high *degree*. **3** Relative extent, amount, or intensity: burns of the first *degree*. **4** Relative manner, condition, ability, etc. **5** *Gram.* One of the forms in which an adjective or adverb is compared: "Worst" is the superlative *degree* of "bad." **6** An academic rank or title conferred by an institution of learning. **7** One remove in the direct line of descent. **8** A subdivision or unit on a scale, as for temperature. **9** The 360th part of a circle. **10** *Math.* The power to which an algebraic quantity is raised. **11** *Music* **a** A line or space of a staff. **b** The interval between two such lines or spaces. **12** *Law* A grade of seriousness: murder in the first *degree.* —**by degrees** Little by little; gradually. —**to a degree 1** Extremely. **2** Somewhat. [< L *de-* down + *gradus* a step]

de·hisce (di·his′) *v.i.* **·hisced, ·hisc·ing** *Biol.* To burst open, as a cocoon or a seed pod. [< L *de-* down + *hiscere* to gape, yawn] —**de·his′cence** *n.* —**de·his′cent** *adj.*

de·hu·man·ize (dē-ʰyoo′mən·īz) *v.t.* **·ized, ·iz·ing** To divest or deprive of human qualities or attributes; make abstract or mechanical. —**de·hu′man·i·za′tion** *n.*

de·hu·mid·i·fi·er (dē′ʰyoo·mid′ə·fī′ər) *n.* An apparatus for removing moisture from the air.

de·hu·mid·i·fy (dē′ʰyoo·mid′ə·fī) *v.t.* **·fied, ·fy·ing** To render less humid; remove moisture from. —**de′hu·mid′i·fi·ca′tion** *n.*

de·hy·drate (dē-hī′drāt) *v.* **·drat·ed, ·drat·ing** *v.t.* **1** To deprive of water. **2** To remove water from. —*v.i.* **3** To suffer loss of water. —**de′hy·dra′tion, de·hy′dra·tor** *n.*

de-ice (dē-īs′) *v.t. & v.i.* **·iced, ·ic·ing 1** To remove ice from. **2** To prevent ice forming on. —**de-ic′er** *n.*

de·i·fy (dē′ə·fī) *v.t.* **·fied, ·fy·ing 1** To make a god of; rank as a deity. **2** To regard or worship as a god. [< L *deus* god + *facere* make] —**de·if′ic** (-if′ik) *adj.* —**de·i·fi·ca·tion** (dē′ə·fə·kā′shən), **de′i·fi′er** *n.*

deign (dān) *v.i.* **1** To think it befitting or suitable (to do something). —*v.t.* **2** To condescend to grant or allow. [< L *dignari* to deem worthy]

de·ism (dē′iz·əm) *n.* The belief, based on the testimony of reason, that God created the world and set it in motion, subject to natural laws, but takes no interest in it or in its inhabitants. [< L *deus* a god + -ISM] —**de′ist** *n.* —**de·is′tic** or **·ti·cal** *adj.* —**de·is′ti·cal·ly** *adv.*

de·i·ty (dē′ə·tē) *n. pl.* **·ties 1** A god, goddess, or divine person. **2** Divine nature or status; godhead; divinity. —**the Deity** GOD. [< L *deus* a god]

dé·jà vu (dā·zhä voo′, dā·zhä vü′) *Psychol.* A distortion of memory in which a new situation or experience is regarded as having happened before. [F, lit., already seen]

de·ject (di·jekt′) *v.t.* To depress in spirit; make unhappy. [< L *de-* down + *jacere* throw] —**de·jec′tion** *n.*

de·ject·ed (di·jek′tid) *adj.* In low spirits; depressed; disheartened. —**de·ject′ed·ly** *adv.* —**de·ject′ed·ness** *n.*

dé·jeu·ner (dā·zhœ·nā′) *n.* **1** A late breakfast. **2** A luncheon. [F, breakfast]

de ju·re (dē joor′ē) By right; rightfully or legally. [L]

deka- *combining form* DECA-. Also **dek-**.

Del. Delaware.

del. delegate; delete; deliver.

de·lay (di·lā′) *v.t.* **1** To put off to a later time; postpone; defer. **2** To cause to be late; detain. —*v.i.* **3** To linger; procrastinate. —*n.* **1** The act of delaying or the condition of being delayed. **2** The period of time during which a thing or person is delayed. [< L *de-* off + *laxare* to slacken] —**de·lay′er** *n.* —Syn. *n.* **1** deferment, postponement, stop, stay.

de·le (dē′lē) *v.t.* **de·led, de·le·ing** *Printing* To take out; delete. [< L *delere* erase]

de·lec·ta·ble (di·lek′tə·bəl) *adj.* Giving pleasure; delightful; charming. [< L *delectare* to please] —**de·lec′ta·bil′i·ty, de·lec′ta·ble·ness** *n.* —**de·lec′ta·bly** *adv.*

de·lec·ta·tion (dē′lek·tā′shən) *n.* **1** Delight; enjoyment. **2** Amusement; entertainment.

del·e·ga·cy (del′ə·gə·sē) *n. pl.* **·cies 1** The act of delegating or the condition of being delegated. **2** The authority given a delegate. **3** A body of delegates.

del·e·gate (del′ə·gāt, -git) *n.* **1** A person empowered to act for others; deputy; representative. **2** *U.S.* A nonvoting participant representing a Territory in the House of Representatives. **3** A member of the House of Delegates. —*v.t.* (-gāt) **·gat·ed, ·gat·ing 1** To send as a representative, with

authority to act; depute. **2** To commit or entrust (powers, authority, etc.) to another. —*adj.* (-gāt, -git) Sent as a deputy. [< L *de-* down + *legare* send]

del·e·ga·tion (del′ə·gā′shən) *n.* **1** The act of delegating. **2** A group of delegates; also, delegates collectively.

de·lete (di·lēt′) *v.t.* **·let·ed, ·let·ing** To take out or otherwise cancel (written or printed matter). [< L *delere* erase, destroy] —**de·le′tion** *n.*

del·e·te·ri·ous (del′ə·tir′ē·əs) *adj.* Causing moral or physical injury. [< Gk. *dēlētērios* harmful] —**del′e·te′ri·ous·ly** *adv.* —**del′e·te′ri·ous·ness** *n.*

delft (delft) *n.* **1** A glazed earthenware, usu. blue and white, made first at Delft, Netherlands. **2** Any tableware resembling this. Also **delf** (delf), **delft′ware′** (-wâr′). [< *Delft,* a town in the Netherlands]

del·i (del′ē) *n. pl.* **·is** *Informal* DELICATESSEN.

de·lib·er·ate (di·lib′ə·rāt) *v.* **·at·ed, ·at·ing** *v.i.* **1** To consider carefully and at length. **2** To consider reasons or arguments so as to reach a decision. —*v.t.* **3** To think about or consider carefully; weigh. —*adj.* (di·lib′ər·it) **1** Acting with or characterized by deliberation; not hasty. **2** Done after deliberation; intentional. **3** Slow and careful, as in movement. [< L *de-* completely + *librare* weigh] —**de·lib′er·ate·ly** *adv.* —**de·lib′er·ate·ness** *n.* —Syn. *adj.* **1** careful, thoughtful. **2** studied. **3** measured, unhurried.

de·lib·er·a·tion (di·lib′ə·rā′shən) *n.* **1** The act of deliberating. **2** *Often pl.* Discussion or consideration of all sides of a problem or issue. **3** Thoughtfulness and care in deciding or acting.

de·lib·er·a·tive (di·lib′ə·rā′tiv, -ər·ə·tiv) *adj.* Of, resulting from, or involved in deliberation. —**de·lib′er·a′tive·ly** *adv.* —**de·lib′er·a′tive·ness** *n.*

del·i·ca·cy (del′ə·kə·sē) *n. pl.* **·cies 1** The quality of being delicate. **2** Fragility or frailty, as of health. **3** Need for careful or subtle treatment: a question of great *delicacy.* **4** Refinement of feeling, appreciation, etc. **5** Sensitiveness of touch, response, performance, etc. **6** A fine consideration for others. **7** A choice bit of food.

del·i·cate (del′ə·kit) *adj.* **1** Nicely light, mild, subtle, etc., as in flavor or color. **2** Exceedingly fine in quality, construction, texture, etc. **3** Very subtle: a *delicate* distinction. **4** Frail; fragile. **5** Easily injured or disordered: a *delicate* stomach. **6** Requiring cautious or subtle handling or treatment. **7** Nicely sensitive in feeling, appreciating, discriminating, etc: a *delicate* ear for music. **8** Extremely accurate or sensitive, as an instrument. **9** Finely skillful in touch or technique. **10** Tactful and considerate of others. [< L *delicatus* pleasing] —**del′i·cate·ly** *adv.* —**del′i·cate·ness** *n.*

del·i·ca·tes·sen (del′ə·kə·tes′ən) *n.* A store that sells cooked or preserved foods, as cooked meats, salads, cheeses, pickles, etc. [< G *Delicatesse* dainty food]

de·li·cious (di·lish′əs) *adj.* Extremely pleasant or enjoyable, esp. to the taste. [< L *delicia* a delight] —**de·li′cious·ly** *adv.* —**de·li′cious·ness** *n.*

De·li·cious (di·lish′əs) *n.* A variety of sweet winter apple.

de·light (di·līt′) *n.* **1** Great pleasure; joyful satisfaction. **2** That which affords extreme enjoyment. **3** The quality of delighting; charm. —*v.i.* **1** To take great pleasure; rejoice: with *in* or the infinitive. **2** To give great enjoyment. —*v.t.* **3** To please or gratify highly. [< L *de-* away + *lacere* entice] —**de·light′ed** *adj.* —**de·light′ed·ly** *adv.*

de·light·ful (di·līt′fəl) *adj.* Affording delight; very pleasing; charming. —**de·light′ful·ly** *adv.* —**de·light′ful·ness** *n.*

De·li·lah (di·lī′lə) In the Bible, the mistress of Samson, who betrayed him to the Philistines. *Judges* 16:4-20.

de·lim·it (di·lim′it) *v.t.* To prescribe the limits of; bound. —**de·lim′i·ta′tion** *n.* —**de·lim′i·ta′tive** *adj.*

de·lin·e·ate (di·lin′ē·āt) *v.t.* **·at·ed, ·at·ing 1** To draw in outline; trace out. **2** To portray pictorially. **3** To describe verbally. [< L *de-* completely + *linea* a line] —**de·lin′e·a′tion** *n.* —**de·lin′e·a′tor** *n.* —**de·lin′e·a′tive** *adj.*

de·lin·quen·cy (di·ling′kwən·sē) *n. pl.* **·cies 1** Neglect of duty. **2** A fault; offense. **3** Illegal or antisocial behavior of a juvenile.

de·lin·quent (di·ling′kwənt) *adj.* **1** Neglectful of or failing in duty or obligation; faulty. **2** Due and unpaid, as taxes. —*n.* A person who is delinquent, esp. a young person who engages in illegal or antisocial behavior. [< L *de-* down, away + *linquere* leave] —**de·lin'quent·ly** *adv.*

del·i·quesce (del'ə·kwes') *v.i.* **·quesced, ·quesc·ing 1** To become liquid by absorption of moisture from the air, as certain salts. **2** To melt or pass away gradually. [< L *de-* completely + *liquescere* melt] —**del'i·ques'cence** *n.* —**del'i·ques'cent** *adj.*

de·lir·i·ous (di·lir'ē·əs) *adj.* **1** Suffering from delirium. **2** Pertaining to or caused by delirium. **3** Extremely excited. —**de·lir'i·ous·ly** *adv.* —**de·lir'i·ous·ness** *n.*

de·lir·i·um (di·lir'ē·əm) *n.* **1** A temporary mental disturbance associated with fever, intoxication, etc., and marked by agitation, hallucinations, and incoherence. **2** Intense excitement; frenzy. [< L *delirare* to deviate from a straight line]

delirium tre·mens (trē'mənz) Delirium caused by excessive use of alcoholic liquors. [NL, trembling delirium]

de·liv·er (di·liv'ər) *v.t.* **1** To hand over; transfer possession of. **2** To carry and distribute: to *deliver* mail. **3** To utter; say: to *deliver* a speech. **4** To assist (a female) in the birth of (a child). **5** To free from evil, danger, etc.; rescue. **6** To send forth; discharge; emit. **7** To give; strike, as a blow. **8** To throw or pitch, as a ball. **9** *Informal* To bring (votes, etc.) to the support of a political candidate. —*v.i.* **10** *Informal* To achieve good or proper results; perform well. [< L *de-* down, away + *liberare* set free] —**de·liv'er·a·ble** *adj.* —**de·liv'er·er** *n.*

de·liv·er·ance (di·liv'ər·əns) *n.* **1** The act of delivering or state of being delivered. **2** An opinion or judgment publically uttered.

de·liv·er·y (di·liv'ər·ē) *n. pl.* **·er·ies 1** The act of delivering. **2** Something delivered. **3** The act of releasing or setting free. **4** The act or manner of giving a speech, pitching a ball, etc. **5** Childbirth.

dell (del) *n.* A small, secluded valley, esp. a wooded one. [< OE]

de·louse (dē·lous') *v.t.* **·loused, ·lous·ing** To remove lice from.

Del·phi (del'fī) *n.* An ancient city in Greece, famous for its oracle of Apollo. —**Del·phi·an** (del'fē·ən) *adj., n.* —**Del'phic** *adj.*

del·phin·i·um (del·fin'ē·əm) *n.* Any of a genus of perennial plants having spikes of spurred flowers, usu. blue. [< Gk. *delphinion* larkspur]

del·ta (del'tə) *n.* **1** The fourth letter in the Greek alphabet. (Δ, δ). **2** An alluvial silt deposit, usu. triangular, at or in the mouth of a river. —**del·ta·ic** (del·tā'ik) *adj.*

del·toid (del'toid) *n.* The large shoulder muscle which contracts to move the arm sideways. —*adj.* **1** Triangular. **2** Of or pertaining to the deltoid. [< Gk. *delta* the letter Δ + *eidos* form]

de·lude (di·lōōd') *v.t.* **·lud·ed, ·lud·ing** To mislead the mind or judgment of; deceive. [< L *de-* down, away + *ludere* to play] —**de·lud'er** *n.*

del·uge (del'yōōj) *v.t.* **·uged, ·ug·ing 1** To flood with water; inundate. **2** To overwhelm: He *deluged* her with compliments. —*n.* **1** A great flood; inundation. **2** Anything that comes like a flood. —**the Deluge** The flood in the time of Noah. *Gen.* 7. [< L *diluere* wash away]

de·lu·sion (di·lōō'zhən) *n.* **1** The act of deluding or the state of being deluded. **2** A false, irrational, and persistent belief. —**de·lu'sion·al** *adj.*

de·lu·sive (di·lōō'siv) *adj.* Tending to delude; misleading; deceptive. Also **de·lu·so·ry** (di·lōō'sər·ē) —**de·lu'sive·ly** *adv.* —**de·lu'sive·ness** *n.*

de luxe (di lōōks', di luks', di lōōks') Luxurious; of superior quality. [F, lit., of luxury]

delve (delv) *v.* **delved, delv·ing** *v.i.* To make careful investigation for facts, knowledge, etc.: to *delve* into a crime. [< OE *delfan*] —**delv'er** *n.*

Dem. Democrat; Democratic.

de·mag·net·ize (dē·mag'nə·tīz) *v.t.* **·ized, ·iz·ing** To deprive of magnetism. —**de·mag'net·i·za'tion, de·mag'net·iz'er** *n.*

dem·a·gogue (dem'ə·gôg, -gog) *n.* One who attempts to gain power by arousing the prejudices and passions of the people. Also **dem'a·gog.** [< Gk. *dēmos* people + *agein* lead] —**dem'a·gog'ic** (-goj'ik) or **·i·cal** *adj.* —**dem'a·gog'i·cal·ly** *adv.* —**dem'a·gog'ism** (-gog'iz·əm) or **dem'a·gogu·ism, dem'·a·gogu'er·y** (-gog'ər·ē), **dem·a·go·gy** (dem'ə·gō'jē, -gôg'ē, -gog'ē) *n.*

de·mand (di·mand', -mänd') *v.t.* **1** To ask for boldly; insist upon. **2** To claim as due; ask for authoritatively. **3** To ask to know; inquire formally. **4** To have need for; require. **5** *Law* a To summon to court. **b** To make formal claim to (property). —*v.i.* **6** To make a demand. —*n.* **1** The act of demanding, or that which is demanded. **2** A requirement; claim; need. **3** *Econ.* a The desire to possess combined with the ability to purchase. **b** The amount of a given commodity people will buy at a certain price. —**in demand** Desired; sought after. —**on demand** On presentation: a note payable *on demand*. [< L *de-* down, away + *mandare* to command; order] —**de·mand'a·ble** *adj.* —**de·mand'er** *n.*

de·mand·ing (di·mand'ing, -mänd') *adj.* Making many difficult demands on one's energy, time, patience, etc. —**de·mand'ing·ly** *adv.*

de·mar·cate (di·mär'kāt, dē'mär·kāt) *v.t.* **·cat·ed, ·cat·ing 1** To mark the bounds or limits of; delimit. **2** To distinguish; separate. [Back formation < DEMARCATION]

de·mar·ca·tion (dē'mär·kā'shən) *n.* **1** The fixing of boundaries or limits. **2** The boundaries or limits fixed. **3** Limitation; discrimination. Also **de'mar·ka'tion.** [< Sp. *de-* down + *marcar* mark a boundary]

dé·marche (dā·märsh') *n.* **1** A manner of approach or mode of procedure. **2** In diplomacy, a change in plan of action. [F]

de·mean¹ (di·mēn') *v.t.* To behave or conduct (oneself). [< OF *de-* down + *mener* lead]

de·mean² (di·mēn') *v.t.* To lower in character or reputation; degrade; debase. [< DE- + MEAN²]

de·mean·or (di·mē'nər) *n.* **1** Behavior; deportment **2** Appearance; mien.

de·ment·ed (di·men'tid) *adj.* Deprived of reason; insane. —**de·ment'ed·ly** *adv.* —**de·ment'ed·ness** *n.*

de·men·tia (di·men'shə, -shē·ə) *n.* Impairment or deterioration of mental capacity. [L, madness]

dementia pre·cox (prē'koks) *Obs.* SCHIZOPHRENIA. [NL, premature dementia] Also **dementia prae'cox.**

de·mer·it (di·mer'it) *n.* **1** In schools, etc., a mark for failure or misconduct. **2** Censurable conduct. [< L *demerere* deserve]

de·mesne (di·mān', -mēn') *n.* **1** *Law* Real estate held in one's own right. **2** A lord's manor house and adjoining lands. **3** Any landed estate. **4** A region or domain. [< OF *demaine* domain]

De·me·ter (di·mē'tər) *Gk. Myth.* The goddess of agriculture, marriage, and fertility.

demi- *prefix* **1** Half: *demisemiquaver.* **2** Inferior or less in size, quality, etc.; partial: *demigod.* [< L *dimidius* half]

dem·i·god (dem'ē·god') *n.* **1** An inferior deity. **2** A man with the attributes of a god. —**dem'i·god'dess** *n. Fem.*

dem·i·john (dem'ē·jon') *n.* A large, juglike glass or crockery vessel enclosed in wickerwork. [< F *dame-jeanne*, lit., Lady Jane]

de·mil·i·ta·rize (dē·mil'ə·tə·rīz') *v.t.* **·rized, ·riz·ing 1** To remove the military control of; free from militarism. **2** To remove military equipment and troops from and declare neutral, as an area or zone. —**de·mil'i·ta·ri·za'tion** *n.*

dem·i·mon·daine (dem'ē·mon·dān') *n.* A woman of the demimonde. [F]

dem·i·monde (dem'ē·mond, dem'ē·mond') *n.* **1** A class of women who are kept as the mistresses of wealthy patrons. **2** Prostitutes collectively. **3** Any class of people whose behavior or attainments are somewhat questionable. [F < *demi-* half, partial + *monde* world]

de·mise (di·mīz') *n.* **1** Death. **2** *Law* A transfer or conveyance of rights or estate. —*v.* **·mised, ·mis·ing** *v.t.* **1** To bestow (sovereign power) by death or abdication. **2** *Law* To lease (an estate) for life or for a term of years. —*v.i.* **3** To pass by will or inheritance. [< OF *demettre* send away] —**de·mis'a·ble** *adj.*

dem·i·sem·i·qua·ver (dem'ē·sem'ē·kwā'vər) *n. Music* A thirty-second note.

dem·i·tasse (dem'ē·tas', -täs') *n.* **1** A small cup in which after-dinner coffee is served. **2** The coffee itself. [F]

de·mo·bil·ize (dē·mō′bəl·īz) v.t. ·ized, ·iz·ing 1 To disband (troops). 2 To discharge (a person) from military service. —**de·mo′bil·i·za′tion** n.

de·moc·ra·cy (di·mok′rə·sē) n. pl. ·cies 1 Government in which political control is shared by all the people, either directly or by representatives whom they elect. 2 A state so governed. 3 Political, legal, or social equality. [< Gk. dēmos people + krateein to rule]

dem·o·crat (dem′ə·krat) n. 1 One who favors a democracy. 2 One who believes in political and social equality.

Dem·o·crat (dem′ə·krat) n. A member of the Democratic party in the U.S.

dem·o·crat·ic (dem′ə·krat′ik) adj. 1 Of, pertaining to, or characterized by the principles of democracy. 2 Of, for, or appealing to all or most people. 3 Practicing social equality; not snobbish. —**dem′o·crat′i·cal·ly** adv.

Democratic Party One of the two major political parties in the U.S.

de·moc·ra·tize (di·mok′rə·tīz) v.t. & v.i. ·tized, ·tiz·ing To make or become democratic. —**de·moc′ra·ti·za′tion** n.

dé·mo·dé (dā·mô·dā′) adj. Old-fashioned; outmoded; out of style. [F]

de·mod·u·late (dē·moj′ŏŏ·lāt) v.t. ·lat·ed, ·lat·ing To restore (a modulated radio signal) to intelligible form. —**de·mod′u·la′tion** n.

de·mod·u·la·tor (de·moj′ŏŏ·lāt′ər) n. A device for receiving a modulated radio signal.

de·mog·ra·phy (di·mog′rə·fē) n. The science dealing with vital and social statistics. [< Gk. dēmos people + -GRAPHY] —**de·mog′ra·pher, de·mog′ra·phist** n. —**dem·o·graph·ic** (dem′ə·graf′ik) or **·i·cal** adj. —**dem′o·graph′i·cal·ly** adv.

de·mol·ish (di·mol′ish) v.t. 1 To tear down; raze, as a building. 2 To destroy utterly; ruin. [< L de- down + moliri build] —**de·mol′ish·er, de·mol′ish·ment** n.

dem·o·li·tion (dem′ə·lish′ən) n. The act or result of demolishing; destruction. —**dem′o·li′tion·ist** n.

demolition bomb A bomb with a high explosive charge used to demolish buildings.

de·mon (dē′mən) n. 1 An evil spirit; devil. 2 A wicked or cruel person. 3 A person of great energy, skill, etc. [< Gk. daimōn] —**de·mon·ic** (di·mon′ik) adj. —**de·mon′i·cal·ly** adv.

de·mon·e·tize (dē·mon′ə·tīz) v.t. ·tized, ·tiz·ing 1 To deprive (currency) of standard value. 2 To withdraw from use as currency. —**de·mon′e·ti·za′tion** n.

de·mo·ni·ac (di·mō′nē·ak) adj. 1 Of, like, or befitting a demon; devilish. 2 Possessed by or as by demons. 3 Mad; violent; frenzied. Also **de·mo·ni·a·cal** (dē′mə·nī′ə·kəl) —n. One possessed of a demon. —**de′mo·ni′a·cal·ly** adv.

de·mon·ism (dē′mən·iz′əm) n. 1 Belief in demons. 2 DEMONOLATRY. 3 DEMONOLOGY. —**de′mon·ist** n.

de·mon·ol·a·try (dē′mən·ol′ə·trē) n. Worship of demons. [< DEMON + Gk. latreia worship] —**de′mon·ol′a·ter** n.

de·mon·ol·o·gy (dē′mən·ol′ə·jē) n. The study of demons. —**de′mon·ol′o·gist** n.

de·mon·stra·ble (di·mon′strə·bəl) adj. Capable of being proved or demonstrated. —**de·mon′stra·ble·ness, de·mon′·stra·bil′i·ty** n. —**de·mon′stra·bly** adv.

dem·on·strate (dem′ən·strāt) v. ·strat·ed, ·strat·ing v.t. 1 To explain or describe by use of experiments, examples, etc. 2 To explain or show the operation or use of. 3 To prove or show by logic; make evident. 4 To exhibit; make clear, as emotions. —v.i. 5 To take part in a public demonstration. 6 To make a show of military force. [< L de- completely + monstrare show, point out]

dem·on·stra·tion (dem′ən·strā′shən) n. 1 The act of making known. 2 Cogent proof by the use of facts, principles, and arguments. 3 A presentation of how something operates or is done. 4 An organized public exhibition of welcome, approval, or condemnation, as by a mass meeting or procession. 5 A show of military force or invincibility. —Syn. 2 evidence, testimony, substantiation.

de·mon·stra·tive (di·mon′strə·tiv) adj. 1 Demonstrating or pointing out. 2 Convincing and conclusive. 3 Showing feelings openly or expressively. 4 Gram. Indicating the person or object referred to: This and that are demon-

strative pronouns and adjectives. —n. A demonstrative pronoun or adjective. —**de·mon′stra·tive·ly** adv. —**de·mon′·stra·tive·ness** n.

dem·on·stra·tor (dem′ən·strā′tər) n. 1 One who demonstrates, as a salesman offering a new product. 2 A participant in a mass demonstration. 3 Something, as a new product, used for demonstration.

de·mor·al·ize (di·môr′əl·īz, -mor′-, dē′-) v.t. ·ized, ·iz·ing 1 To undermine the morale of. 2 To throw into disorder. —**de·mor′al·i·za′tion, de·mor′al·iz′er** n.

de·mote (di·mōt′) v.t. ·mot·ed, ·mot·ing To reduce to a lower grade or rank. [< DE- + (PRO)MOTE] —**de·mo′tion** n.

de·mul·cent (di·mul′sənt) adj. Soothing. —n. A soothing medication. [< L de- down + mulcere soothe]

de·mur (di·mûr′) v.i. ·murred, ·mur·ring 1 To offer objections. 2 To delay; hesitate. 3 Law To interpose a demurrer. —n. 1 A delay. 2 An objection. [< L de- completely + morari to delay]

de·mure (di·myŏŏr′) adj. 1 Sedate; modest. 2 Affecting modesty; coy. [< OF demore] —**de·mure′ly** adv. —**de·mure′·ness** n.

de·mur·rage (di·mûr′ij) n. 1 The delaying of a vessel, truck, etc., beyond the specified time for departure because of loading or unloading. 2 Compensation for such delay. [< OF demourer to delay]

de·mur·rer (di·mûr′ər) n. 1 Law A plea for the dismissal of a suit on the grounds that the facts presented by the opposition, although true, do not validly support the claim. 2 Any objection. 3 One who demurs.

de·my·thol·o·gize (dē·mə·thol′ə·gīz) v.t. ·gized, ·giz·ing 1 To strip away the myth from. 2 Theol. To reinterpret (the Bible, religious subjects, etc.) without mythology. —**de·my·thol′o·gi·za′tion** n.

den (den) n. 1 A cavern occupied by animals; a lair. 2 A squalid residence or gathering place. 3 A room where one can work, read, etc., in private. —v.i. denned, den·ning To dwell in, or as in, a den. [< OE denn]

Den. Denmark.

de·nar·i·us (di·nâr′ē·əs) n. pl. ·nar·i·i (-nâr′ē·ī) 1 A silver coin of ancient Rome; the penny of the New Testament. 2 A gold coin of ancient Rome. [< L denarius of ten; because it was worth ten asses]

de·na·tion·al·ize (dē·nash′ən·əl·īz′) v.t. ·ized, ·iz·ing To deprive of national character, status, rights, etc. —**de·na′·tion·al·i·za′tion** n.

de·nat·u·ral·ize (dē·nach′ər·əl·īz′, -nach′rəl-) v.t. ·ized, ·iz·ing 1 To render unnatural. 2 To deprive of citizenship. —**de·nat′u·ral·i·za′tion** n.

de·na·ture (dē·nā′chər) v.t. ·tured, ·tur·ing 1 To alter the nature of. 2 To make (alcohol, fat, etc.) unfit for drinking or eating without destroying other useful properties. —**de·na′tur·ant, de·na′tur·a′tion** n.

den·drite (den′drīt) n. 1 Any mineral crystallizing in a branching, treelike form or having treelike markings. 2 Physiol. One of the branching processes of a nerve cell. —**den·drit′ic** (-drit′ik) or **·i·cal** adj. —**den·drit′i·cal·ly** adv. [< Gk. dendron tree]

den·drol·o·gy (den·drol′ə·jē) n. The science of trees. [< Gk. dendron tree + -LOGY] —**den·drol′o·gist** n.

-dendron combining form Tree; treelike formation: philodendron. [< Gk. dendron tree]

Dendrite def. 2

den·gue (deng′gē, -gā) n. An infectious tropical disease transmitted by mosquitoes and characterized by fever, rash, and pain in the joints. [< Swahili]

de·ni·al (di·nī′əl) n. 1 A refusal to grant a request. 2 A declaration that a statement is untrue; contradiction. 3 A disowning or disavowal; rejection. 4 A refusal to agree with or believe in a doctrine, proposal, etc. —Syn. 1 declining, rebuff. 3 repudiation, renunciation.

de·nic·o·tin·ize (dē·nik′ə·tin·īz′) v.t. ·ized, ·iz·ing To remove nicotine from.

---

add, āce, câre, pälm; end, ēven; it, īce; odd, ōpen, ôrder; tŏŏk, pōōl; up, bûrn; ə = a in above; u in focus; yŏŏ = u in fuse; oil; pout; check; go; ring; thin; this; zh, vision. < derived from; ? origin uncertain or unknown.

de·ni·er[1] (di·nī′ər) *n.* One who makes denial.

den·ier[2] (den′yər, də·nir′) *n.* A unit of weight for measuring the fineness of rayon, nylon, or silk thread. [< L *denarius* of ten]

den·i·grate (den′ə·grāt) *v.t.* ·grat·ed, ·grat·ing To slander; defame. [< L *de-* completely + *nigrare* blacken] —**den′i·gra′tion, den′i·gra′tor** *n.* —**den·i·gra·to·ry** (den′ə·grə·tôr′ē, -tō′rē) *adj.*

den·im (den′əm) *n.* A sturdy twilled cotton used for overalls, uniforms, etc. [< F *(serge) de Nîmes* (serge) of Nîmes, where first made]

den·i·zen (den′ə·zən) *n.* 1 A resident; inhabitant. 2 A person who frequents a place. 3 A person, animal, or thing at home in a region, although not a native. —*v.t. Brit.* NATURALIZE. [< AF *deinz* inside] —**den′i·zen·a′tion** *n.*

Den·mark (den′märk) *n.* A kingdom in NW Europe, 16,-619 sq. mi., cap. Copenhagen.

denom. denomination.

de·nom·i·nate (di·nom′ə·nāt) *v.t.* ·nat·ed, ·nat·ing To give a name to; call. [< L *denominare*] —**de·nom′i·na·ble** (-ə·nə·bəl) *adj.*

de·nom·i·na·tion (di·nom′ə·nā′shən) *n.* 1 The act of naming. 2 The name or designation of a class of things. 3 A specific unit of value: coins of all *denominations.* 4 A religious sect or group having a specific name. —**de·nom′i·na′tion·al** *adj.* —**de·nom′i·na′tion·al·ism, de·nom′i·na′tion·al·ist** *n.* —**de·nom′i·na′tion·al·ly** *adv.*

de·nom·i·na·tive (di·nom′ə·nā·tiv, -nā′tiv) *adj.* 1 That gives or constitutes a name; appellative. 2 Derived from a noun or adjective. —*n.* A word, esp. a verb, derived from a noun or adjective, as *to garden.* —**de·nom′i·na·tive·ly** *adv.*

de·nom·i·na·tor (di·nom′ə·nā′tər) *n.* 1 One who or that which names. 2 That term of a fraction which expresses the number of equal parts into which the numerator is divided; divisor.

de·no·ta·tion (dē′nō·tā′shən) *n.* 1 The act of denoting. 2 The actual, explicit meaning or object denoted by a word. 3 That which indicates; a sign.

de·note (di·nōt′) *v.t.* ·not·ed, ·not·ing 1 To mark; point out or make known. 2 To signify; indicate. 3 To designate; mean: said of words, symbols, etc. [< L *de-* down + *notare* to mark] —**de·not′a·ble, de·no·ta·tive** (di·nō′tə·tiv, dē′nō·tā′tiv) *adj.* —**de·no′ta·tive·ly** *adv.*

de·noue·ment (dā·nōō·män′) *n.* 1 The final unraveling or outcome of the plot of a play, novel, etc. 2 Any final solution. Also **dé·noue·ment′.** [< F *dénouement* < *dénouer* to untie]

de·nounce (di·nouns′) *v.t.* ·nounced, ·nounc·ing 1 To condemn openly and vehemently; inveigh against. 2 To inform against; accuse. 3 To give formal notice of the termination of (a treaty, truce, etc.). [< L *de-* down + *nuntiare* proclaim, announce] —**de·nounce′ment, de·nounc′er** *n.* — **Syn.** 1 decry, charge, attack, censure, curse.

de no·vo (dē nō′vō) Once again; anew. [L]

dense (dens) *adj.* **dens·er, dens·est** 1 Having its parts crowded closely together; compact; 2 Hard to penetrate. 3 Stupid; dull-witted. [< L *densus*] —**dense′ly** *adv.* —**dense′ness** *n.*

den·si·ty (den′sə·tē) *n. pl.* ·ties 1 The state or quality of being dense; compactness. 2 Stupidity. 3 *Physics* The mass of a substance per unit of its volume. 4 The number of units, as persons, families, etc., per specified area.

dent (dent) *n.* A small depression made by striking or pressing; indentation. —*v.t.* To make a dent in. —*v.i.* To become dented. [Var. of DINT]

dent. dental; dentist; dentistry.

den·tal (den′təl) *adj.* 1 Of or pertaining to the teeth. 2 Of or pertaining to dentistry. 3 *Phonet.* Produced with the tip of the tongue against or near the upper front teeth. —*n. Phonet.* A dental consonant. [< L *dens, dentis* a tooth]

den·tate (den′tāt) *adj.* 1 Having teeth or toothlike processes; toothed. 2 *Bot.* Serrated, as certain leaves. —**den′tate·ly** *adv.* —**den·ta′tion** *n.*

den·ti·frice (den′tə·fris) *n.* A preparation for cleaning the teeth. [< L *dens, dentis* tooth + *fricare* rub]

den·tine (den′tēn, -tin) *n.* The bonelike substance forming the body of a tooth beneath the enamel. Also **den′tin** (-tin). —**den′tin·al** *adj.* • See TOOTH.

den·tist (den′tist) *n.* One who practices dentistry. [< F *dent* a tooth]

den·tist·ry (den′tis·trē) *n.* 1 The medical science concerned with preserving, treating, and repairing the teeth and their associated structures. 2 The work of a dentist.

den·ti·tion (den·tish′ən) *n.* 1 The process or period of teething. 2 The kind, number, and arrangement of the teeth in the mouth. [< L *dentire* cut teeth]

den·ture (den′chər) *n.* A block or set of teeth, esp. artificial ones. [< F *dent* tooth] —**den′tur·al** *adj.*

de·nu·date (di·n^yōō′dāt, den′yōō·dāt) *adj.* Naked; stripped, as of foliage. —*v.t.* ·dat·ed, ·dat·ing DENUDE.

de·nude (di·n^yōōd′) *v.t.* ·nud·ed, ·nud·ing 1 To strip the covering from. 2 *Geol.* To wear away and expose by erosion. [< L *de-* down, completely + *nudare* to strip] —**den·u·da·tion** (den′yōō·dā′shən, dē′n^yōō-) *n.*

de·nun·ci·ate (di·nun′sē·āt) *v.t. & v.i.* ·at·ed, ·at·ing DENOUNCE. [< L *denuntiare.* See DENOUNCE.] —**de·nun′ci·a′tor** *n.* —**de·nun·ci·a·to·ry** (di·nun′sē·ə·tôr′ē, -tō′rē) *adj.*

de·nun·ci·a·tion (di·nun′sē·ā′shən) *n.* 1 The act of denouncing, esp. a vehement and public condemnation. —**de·nun′ci·a′tive** *adj.* —**de·nun′ci·a′tive·ly** *adv.*

de·ny (di·nī′) *v.t.* ·nied, ·ny·ing 1 To declare to be untrue; contradict. 2 To reject (a doctrine, etc.) as false or not real. 3 To refuse to give; withhold. 4 To refuse (someone) a request. 5 To refuse to acknowledge; disown; repudiate. 6 To refuse access to. —**deny oneself** To refuse oneself a gratification. [< L *de-* completely + *negare* refuse]

de·o·dar (dē′ə·där) *n.* 1 A large Himalayan cedar, prized for its fragrant wood. 2 This wood. [< Skt. *devadāru* divine tree]

de·o·dor·ant (dē·ō′dər·ənt) *adj.* Destroying, absorbing, or disguising bad odors. —*n.* A deodorant substance, as a cream, spray, etc. [< DE- + L *odorare* have an odor]

de·o·dor·ize (dē·ō′dər·īz) *v.t.* ·ized, ·iz·ing To modify, destroy, or disguise the odor of. —**de·o′dor·i·za′tion, de·o′dor·iz′er** *n.*

de·ox·i·dize (dē·ok′sə·dīz) *v.t.* ·dized, ·diz·ing To remove oxygen, esp. chemically combined oxygen, from. —**de·ox′i·di·za′tion, de·ox′i·diz′er** *n.*

de·ox·y·ri·bo·nu·cle·ic acid (dē·ok′sē·rī·bō·n^yōō·klē′ik, -klā′ik) A complex compound present in the nucleus of every living cell, consisting of units whose sequence in a spiral configuration determines the unique genetic make-up of the organism.

dep. depart; department; departure; deponent; deposed; deposit; depot; deputy.

de·part (di·pärt′) *v.i.* 1 To go away; leave. 2 To deviate; differ; vary: with *from.* 3 To die. —*v.t.* 4 To leave: to *depart* this life. [< OF *de-* away + *partir* divide]

de·part·ment (di·pärt′mənt) *n.* 1 A separate and distinct part, division, or subdivision of a government, business, school, etc.: the accounting *department;* French *department.* 2 A special area of activity, skill, etc.: Cooking is my *department.* 3 In France, a government administrative district. [< OF *departir* divide] —**de·part·men·tal** (dē′pärt·men′təl) *adj.* —**de′part·men′tal·ly** *adv.* —**de′part·men′tal·ism** *n.*

department store A retail store where a wide variety of merchandise is sold in separate departments.

de·par·ture (di·pär′chər) *n.* 1 The act of departing or leaving. 2 The act of deviating from a method, set of ideas, etc.: with *from.* 3 A starting out, as on a new venture.

de·pend (di·pend′) *v.i.* 1 To trust; have full reliance: with *on* or *upon.* 2 To be determined by or contingent on something else: with *on* or *upon.* 3 To rely for maintenance, support, etc.: with *on* or *upon.* 4 To hang down: with *from.* [< L *de-* down + *pendere* hang]

de·pend·a·ble (di·pen′də·bəl) *adj.* That can be depended upon; trustworthy. —**de·pend′a·bil′i·ty, de·pend′a·ble·ness** *n.* —**de·pend′a·bly** *adv.*

de·pend·ence (di·pen′dəns) *n.* 1 The condition of being determined by or dependent on some one or something else. 2 Reliance on another person or thing. 3 Subordination. 4 Reciprocal reliance; trust. Also **de·pen′dance.**

de·pen·den·cy (di·pen′dən·sē) *n. pl.* ·cies 1 DEPENDENCE.

2 Something subordinate. 3 A territory or state that is subject to another state.

de·pen·dent (di-pen′dənt) *adj.* 1 Depending or contingent upon something else: often with *on* or *upon.* 2 Needing support or aid from another: with *on.* 3 Subordinate. 4 Hanging down: with *from.* —*n.* One who looks to another for support, aid, etc. Also, esp. for noun, **de·pen′dant.**

de·per·son·al·ize (dē-pûr′sən-ə-līz′) *v.t.* ·ized, ·iz·ing 1 To deprive of distinctive character or personality. 2 To make impersonal: to *depersonalize* history. —**de·per′son·al·i·za′·tion** *n.*

de·pict (di-pikt′) *v.t.* 1 To portray or represent by drawing, sculpturing, painting, etc. 2 To describe verbally. [< L *depictus,* pp. of *depingere* to paint] —**de·pic′ter, de·pic′. tion** *n.*

dep·i·late (dep′ə-lāt) *v.t.* ·lat·ed, ·lat·ing To remove hair from.[< L *de-* away + *pilus* hair]—**dep′i·la′tion, dep′i·la′tor** *n.*

de·pil·a·to·ry (di-pil′ə-tôr′ē, -tō′rē) *adj.* Having the power to remove hair. —*n.* A preparation for removing hair, wool, etc., from skin or hides.

de·plane (di-plān′) *v.i.* ·planed, ·plan·ing To disembark from an aircraft.

de·plete (di-plēt′) *v.t.* ·plet·ed, ·plet·ing 1 To reduce or lessen, as by use, exhaustion, or waste. 2 To empty wholly or partially. [< L *de-* not + *plere* to fill]—**de·ple′tion** *n.* —**de·ple′tive** *adj.*

de·plor·a·ble (di-plôr′ə-bəl, -plō′rə-) *adj.* Lamentable; regrettable. —**de·plor′a·bil′i·ty** *n.* —**de·plor′a·bly** *adv.*

de·plore (di-plôr′, -plōr′) *v.t.* ·plored, ·plor·ing To feel or express deep regret or concern for; lament. [< L *de-* completely + *plorare* bewail]

de·ploy (di-ploi′) *v.t.* 1 To spread out (troops, etc.) strategically or in a line of battle. 2 To use or arrange in a strategic manner. —*v.i.* 3 To be deployed. [< LL *displicare* scatter]—**de·ploy′ment** *n.*

de·po·lar·ize (dē-pō′lə-rīz) *v.t.* ·ized, ·iz·ing 1 To break up or remove the polarization of. 2 To deprive of polarity. — **de·po′lar·i·za′tion, de·po′lar·iz′er** *n.*

de·po·lit·i·cize (dē-pə-lit′ə-sīz′) *v.t.* ·cized, ·ciz·ing To make nonpolitical. Also **de·po·lit′i·cal·ize** (-kəl·īz′).

de·po·nent (di-pō′nənt) *adj.* In Latin and Greek grammar, denoting a verb that has the form of the passive but is active in meaning. —*n.* 1 A deponent verb. 2 *Law* One who gives sworn testimony, esp. in writing. [< L *deponere* lay aside]

de·pop·u·late (dē-pop′yə-lāt) *v.t.* ·lat·ed, ·lat·ing To remove the inhabitants from, by massacre, famine, etc. [< L *de-* away + *populus* people]—**de·pop′u·la′tion, de·pop′u·la′tor** *n.*

de·port (di-pôrt′, -pōrt′) *v.t.* 1 To banish or expel from a country. 2 To behave or conduct (oneself). [< L *de-* away + *portare* carry]—**de′por·ta′tion** *n.*

de·port·ment (di-pôrt′mənt, -pōrt′-) *n.* The manner in which one behaves or conducts oneself.

de·pose (di-pōz′) *v.* ·posed, ·pos·ing *v.t.* 1 To deprive of official rank or office; oust, as a king. 2 To state on oath. —*v.i.* 3 To bear witness. [< OF *de-* down + *poser* put]—**de·pos′a·ble** *adj.*

de·pos·it (di-poz′it) *v.t.* 1 To give in trust or for safekeeping. 2 To give as part payment or as security. 3 To set down; put. 4 To cause, as sediment, to form a layer. —*n.* 1 Money deposited, as in a bank. 2 Something, as money, given as security or first payment. 3 The act of depositing. 4 In Canada, money put up as evidence of good faith by a candidate for Parliament or a Legislature. 5 A depositary. 6 Something, as sediment, deposited. 7 An accumulated mass of iron, oil, salt, etc. —**on deposit** Placed for safekeeping. [< L *deponere* lay aside]

de·pos·i·tar·y (di-poz′ə-ter′ē) *n. pl.* ·tar·ies 1 A person entrusted with anything for safekeeping; a trustee. 2 A place where things are stored; depository.

dep·o·si·tion (dep′ə-zish′ən, dē′pə-) *n.* 1 The act of depositing. 2 That which is deposited; esp. an accumulation. 3 The written testimony of a sworn witness. 4 Allegation; evidence. 5 The act of deposing, as from office.

de·pos·i·tor (di-poz′ə-tər) *n.* One who makes a deposit, esp. of money in a bank.

de·pos·i·to·ry (di-poz′ə-tôr′ē, -tō′rē) *n. pl.* ·ries 1 A place where things are put for safekeeping. 2 A person to whom something is entrusted for safekeeping.

de·pot (dē′pō, *Mil. & Brit.* dep′ō) *n.* 1 A warehouse or storehouse. 2 A railroad or bus station. 3 *Mil.* A storehouse or collecting station for personnel or materiel. [< L *depositum* a pledge, deposit]

de·prave (di-prāv′) *v.t.* ·praved, ·prav·ing To render bad or worse, esp. in morals; corrupt; pervert. [< L *de-* completely + *pravus* corrupt, wicked] —**de·praved′** *adj.* —**de· prav′er, dep·ra·va·tion** (dep′rə-vā′shən) *n.*

de·prav·i·ty (di-prav′ə-tē) *n. pl.* ·ties 1 The state of being depraved; wickedness. 2 A depraved act or habit.

dep·re·cate (dep′rə-kāt) *v.t.* ·cat·ed, ·cat·ing 1 To express disapproval of or regret for. 2 To belittle; depreciate. [< L *de-* away + *precari* pray]—**dep′re·cat′ing·ly** *adv.* —**dep′re·ca′tion, dep′re·ca′tor** *n.* • The use of *deprecate* as a synonym for *depreciate* is regarded as incorrect by many, but it is increasingly common: While not wishing to *deprecate* their motives, he did question their judgement.

dep·re·ca·to·ry (dep′rə-kə-tôr′ē, -tō′rē) *adj.* 1 Belittling; apologetic. 2 Tending to deprecate; disparaging. Also **dep′. re·ca′tive** (-kā′tiv) *adj.*

de·pre·ci·a·ble (di-prē′shē·ə·bəl) *adj.* That can be depreciated in value.

de·pre·ci·ate (di-prē′shē·āt) *v.* ·at·ed, ·at·ing *v.t.* 1 To lessen the worth of; lower the price or rate of. 2 To disparage; belittle. —*v.i.* 3 To become less in value, etc. [< L *de-* down + *pretium* price]—**de·pre′ci·a′tor** *n.* —**de·pre′ci·a·to′· ry** *adj.* • See DEPRECATE.

de·pre·ci·a·tion (di-prē′shē·ā′shən) *n.* 1 A loss in value of equipment, etc., through usage or wear. 2 A loss in the purchasing power of money. 3 A belittling or disparagement of something.

dep·re·date (dep′rə·dāt) *v.t. & v.i.* ·dat·ed, ·dat·ing To prey upon; pillage; plunder. [< L *de-* completely + *praeda* booty, prey]—**dep′re·da′tion, dep′re·da′tor** *n.*

de·press (di-pres′) *v.t.* 1 To lower the spirits of; sadden. 2 To lessen in vigor, force, or energy. 3 To lessen the price or value of. 4 To press or push down. [< L *de-* down + *primere* to press]—**de·press′ing** *adj.* —**de·press′ing·ly** *adv.* —**de·pres′sor** (-ər) *n.*

de·pres·sant (di-pres′ənt) *adj.* Lessening vital activity. —*n.* 1 A drug that reduces the rate or intensity of vital functions. 2 A sedative.

de·pressed (di-prest′) *adj.* 1 Sad; dejected. 2 Pressed down. 3 Flattened from above; sunk below the surface. 4 Reduced in amount, degree, value, etc. 5 *Biol.* Broader than high; flat. —**Syn.** 1 downcast, low, blue, downhearted, forlorn, desolate.

depressed area A region characterized by unemployment, a low standard of living, etc.

de·pres·sion (di-presh′ən) *n.* 1 The act of depressing, or the state of being depressed. 2 Low spirits or vitality. 3 A low or hollow place. 4 A period marked by a severe decline in business or trade, unemployment, etc. 5 Low atmospheric pressure; also, a region of low atmospheric pressure. 6 *Psychiatry* A profound, immobilizing dejection and despair. —**de·pres′sive** *adj.* —**de·pres′sive·ly** *adv.*

dep·ri·va·tion (dep′rə-vā′shən) *n.* 1 The act of depriving, or the state of being deprived. 2 Loss; want.

de·prive (di-prīv′) *v.t.* ·prived, ·priv·ing 1 To take something away from; divest. 2 To keep from acquiring, using, or enjoying. [< L *de-* completely + *privare* strip, remove] —**de·priv′a·ble** *adj.*

de·pro·gram (dē-prō′gram) *v.t.* ·gramed or ·grammed, ·gram·ing or ·gram·ming To try to convince (one) to forsake something learned well, esp. a religious belief.

dept. department; deponent; deputy.

depth (depth) *n.* 1 The state or quality of being deep. 2 Extent or distance downward, inward, or backward. 3 *Usu. pl.* The deepest part. 4 *Usu. pl.* The innermost part. 5 *Usu. pl.* The part of greatest intensity: the *depths* of despair. 6 Profundity of thought or feeling. 7 Intensity of color or shade. **8** Lowness of pitch. —**in depth** In a thorough and extensive manner. [ME *depthe*]

depth charge An explosive charge so engineered that it explodes at a certain depth under water. Also **depth bomb.**

dep·u·ta·tion (dep'yə·tā'shən) *n.* **1** A person or persons acting for another; a delegation. **2** The act of deputing, or the state of being deputed.

de·pute (di·pyōōt') *v.t.* **·put·ed, ·put·ing** **1** To appoint as an agent, deputy, or delegation. **2** To transfer, as authority, to another. [<L *de-* away + *putare* think]

dep·u·tize (dep'yə·tīz) *v.* **·tized, ·tiz·ing** *v.t.* **1** To appoint as a deputy. —*v.i.* **2** To act as a deputy.

dep·u·ty (dep'yə·tē) *n. pl.* **·ties** **1** One appointed to act for another; representative agent. **2** A member of a legislative assembly in certain countries. [<OF *deputer* depute]

der., deriv. derivation; derivative; derived.

de·rail (dē·rāl') *v.t.* **1** To cause to leave the rails, as a train. —*v.i.* **2** To leave the rails. —**de·rail'ment** *n.*

de·rail·leur (di·rā'lər) *n.* A spring-powered mechanism on a bicycle that allows the rider to change gears by transferring the drive chain from one to another size of sprocket wheels. [<F *dérailleur*]

de·range (di·rānj') *v.t.* **·ranged, ·rang·ing** **1** To disturb the arrangement of; disorder. **2** To make insane. [<F *déranger*]

de·range·ment (di·rānj'mənt) *n.* **1** The act of deranging, or state of being deranged. **2** Any severe mental disorder.

der·by (dûr'bē) *n. pl.* **·bies** A stiff, felt hat with curved brim and round crown. [<DERBY]

Der·by (dûr'bē, *Brit.* där'bē) **1** An annual horse race for three-year-olds run, since 1780, at Epsom Downs in Surrey, England. **2** Any important horse race, esp. the Kentucky Derby. [Founded by the 12th Earl of *Derby*, d. 1834]

der·e·lict (der'ə·likt) *adj.* **1** Neglectful of obligation; remiss. **2** Deserted or abandoned. —*n.* **1** That which is deserted or abandoned, as a ship at sea. **2** A person considered as socially outcast; a vagrant. [<L *de-* completely + *relinquere* abandon]

Derby

der·e·lic·tion (der'ə·lik'shən) *n.* **1** Neglect or failure in duty. **2** Voluntary abandonment of something. **3** The state or fact of being abandoned.

de·ride (di·rīd') *v.t.* **·rid·ed, ·rid·ing** To treat or laugh at with contempt; ridicule. [<L *de-* completely + *ridere* laugh, mock] —**de·rid'er** *n.* —**de·rid'ing·ly** *adv.*

de ri·gueur (də rē·gœr') *French* **1** Necessary according to etiquette; required by good form. **2** Fashionable.

de·ri·sion (di·rizh'ən) *n.* **1** The act of deriding; ridicule; scorn. **2** An object of ridicule or scorn.

de·ri·sive (di·rī'siv) *adj.* Expressive of or characterized by derision. Also **de·ri·so·ry** (di·rī'sər·ē). —**de·ri'sive·ly** *adv.* —**de·ri'sive·ness** *n.*

der·i·va·tion (der'ə·vā'shən) *n.* **1** The act of deriving, or the condition of being derived. **2** Something derived; a derivative. **3** Origin; source. **4** The tracing of a word from its origins; also, a statement of this. **5** The formation of a word from another word, as by the addition of a prefix or suffix. —**der'i·va'tion·al** *adj.*

de·riv·a·tive (di·riv'ə·tiv) *adj.* Derived; not original or basic. —*n.* **1** That which is derived. **2** A word developed from a basic word, as by the addition of a prefix or suffix. **3** *Chem.* A compound formed or regarded as being formed from another. —**de·riv'a·tive·ly** *adv.* —**de·riv'a·tive·ness** *n.*

de·rive (di·rīv') *v.* **·rived, ·riv·ing** *v.t.* **1** To draw or receive, as from a source, principle, or root; be descended from. **2** To deduce; draw, as a conclusion. **3** To trace the derivation of (a word). **4** *Chem.* To obtain (a compound) from another. —*v.i.* **5** To have derivation; originate. [<L *de-* from + *rivus* stream] —**de·riv'a·ble** *adj.* —**de·riv'er** *n.*

derm (dûrm) *n.* DERMIS. [<Gk. *derma* skin]

der·ma (dûr'mə) *n.* DERMIS. —**der'mal** *adj.*

der·ma·tol·o·gy (dûr'mə·tol'ə·jē) *n.* The branch of medical science that relates to the skin and its diseases. [<Gk. *derma, dermatos* skin + -LOGY] —**der·ma·to·log·i·cal** (dûr'mə·tə·loj'i·kəl) *adj.* —**der'ma·tol'o·gist** *n.*

der·mis (dûr'mis) *n.* The layer of skin just below the epidermis; true skin. [<Gk. *derma* skin]

der·o·gate (der'ə·gāt) *v.* **·gat·ed, ·gat·ing** *v.i.* **1** To take away; detract, as from reputation: with *from.* **2** To do something that causes one to lose the esteem of others. [<L *de-* away + *rogare* ask, propose a law] —**der'o·ga'tion** *n.*

de·rog·a·tive (der'og'ə·tiv) *adj.* Tending to derogate or detract; derogatory. —**de·rog'a·tive·ly** *adv.*

de·rog·a·to·ry (di·rog'ə·tôr'ē, -tō'rē) *adj.* Harmful to the reputation or esteem of a person or thing; disparaging. —**de·rog'a·to'ri·ly** *adv.*

der·rick (der'ik) *n.* **1** An apparatus with a hinged boom for hoisting heavy objects into place. **2** The framework over the mouth of an oil well or similar drill hole. [<*Derrick,* 17th c. London hangman]

der·ri·ere (der'ē·er') *n.* The buttocks. Also **der·ri·ère.** [<F, lit., rear, back part]

Derricks
a. hoisting. b. oil well.

der·ring-do (der'ing·dōō') *n.* Daring deeds; reckless courage. [<ME *dorrying don* daring to do; mistaken for a noun phrase]

der·rin·ger (der'in·jər) *n.* A short-barreled pistol with a large bore. [<Henry *Derringer,* 19th c. U.S. gunsmith, who invented it]

der·vish (dûr'vish) *n.* A member of any of several Mohammedan religious orders, some of whom practice whirling as a religious exercise. [<Pers. *darvish*]

Derringer

de·sal·i·nate (dē·sal'ə·nāt, -sāl'ə-) *v.t.* **·nat·ed, ·nat·ing** To remove salt from, esp. from sea water to make it drinkable. —**de·sal'i·na'tion** *n.*

de·salt (dē·sôlt') *v.t.* To remove the salt from.

desc. descendant.

des·cant (des'kant) *n.* **1** A discourse or a series of remarks. **2** *Music* **a** A varied melody or song. **b** An ornamental variation of the main melody. **c** A counterpoint above the plain song. **d** The upper part in part music. —*v.t.* (des'kant', dis-) **1** To discourse at length: with *on* or *upon.* **2** *Music* **a** To make a descant. **b** To sing. [<L *dis-* away + *cantus* a song]

de·scend (di·send') *v.i.* **1** To move from a higher to a lower point. **2** To slope or incline downward. **3** To stoop; lower oneself. **4** To come down by inheritance; be inherited. **5** To be derived by heredity: with *from.* **6** To come overwhelmingly, as in an attack or visit: with *on* or *upon.* **7** To pass, as from the general to the particular. **8** *Astron.* To move southward or toward the horizon, as a star. —*v.t.* **9** To move from an upper to a lower part of; go down. [<L *de-* down + *scandere* climb] —**de·scend'er** *n.*

de·scen·dant (di·sen'dənt) *n.* **1** One who is an offspring of a particular ancestor, group, etc. **2** Anything derived from something earlier.

de·scen·dent (di·sen'dənt) *adj.* **1** Descending. **2** Issuing by descent, as from an ancestor.

de·scend·i·ble (di·sen'də·bəl) *adj.* **1** That can be descended. **2** That can pass by descent; inheritable. Also **de·scend'a·ble.**

de·scent (di·sent') *n.* **1** The act of descending. **2** Decline; deterioration. **3** A declivity; slope. **4** Lineage; ancestry. **5** A genealogical generation. **6** A hostile raid or invasion. **7** The transmission of an estate by inheritance.

descr. descriptive.

de·scribe (di·skrīb') *v.t.* **·scribed, ·scrib·ing** **1** To give an account of; represent with spoken or written words. **2** To draw the figure of; trace; outline. [<L *de-* down + *scribere* write] —**de·scrib'a·ble** *adj.* —**de·scrib'er** *n.* —**Syn. 1** narrate, relate, recount, portray, characterize.

de·scrip·tion (di·skrip'shən) *n.* **1** The act of describing.

2 An account, statement, or report that describes. 3 A drawing or tracing. 4 Sort; kind; nature.

de·scrip·tive (di·skrip′tiv) adj. Characterized by or containing description; serving to describe. —**de·scrip′tive·ly** adv. —**de·scrip′tive·ness** n.

de·scry (di·skrī′) v.t. ·scried, ·scry·ing 1 To discover with the eye; discern; detect. 2 To discover by observation. [< OF des- away + crier to cry] —**de·scri′er** n.

des·e·crate (des′ə·krāt) v.t. ·crat·ed, ·crat·ing To divert from a sacred to a common use; profane. [< DE- + L sacrare make holy] —**des′e·crat′er** or **des′e·cra′tor**, **des′e·cra′tion** n.

de·seg·re·gate (dē·seg′rə·gāt) v.t. ·gat·ed, ·gat·ing To eliminate racial segregation in. —**de′seg·re·ga′tion** n.

de·sen·si·tize (dē·sen′sə·tīz) v.t. ·tized, ·tiz·ing To make less sensitive. —**de·sen′si·ti·za′tion, de·sen′si·tiz′er** n.

des·ert¹ (dez′ərt) n. 1 An arid, usu. sandy region abnormally deficient in rainfall or natural moisture. 2 Any uncultivated and desolate region. —adj. Of, from, or like a desert. [< LL desertum < L deserere abandon]

de·sert² (di·zûrt′) n. 1 The state of deserving reward or punishment. 2 Often pl. That which is deserved or merited. [< OF deservir deserve]

de·sert³ (di·zûrt′) v.t. 1 To forsake or abandon. 2 To forsake in violation of one's oath or orders. —v.i. 3 To abandon one's post, duty, etc. [< L deserere abandon] —**de·sert′. er, de·ser′tion** n.

des·ert·i·fi·ca·tion (dez′ər·tə·fə·kā′shən) n. The process of becoming a desert.

de·serve (di·zûrv′) v. ·served, ·serv·ing v.t. 1 To be entitled to or worthy of. —v.i. 2 To be worthy. [< L de- completely + servire serve] —**de·serv′er** n.

de·served (di·zûrvd′) adj. Earned; merited. —**de·serv· ed·ly** (di·zûr′vid·lē) adv. —**de·serv′ed·ness** n.

des·ha·bille (dez′ə·bēl′) n. DISHABILLE.

des·ic·cant (des′ə·kənt) adj. Producing dryness. —n. A desiccant agent or substance.

des·ic·cate (des′ə·kāt) v. ·cat·ed, ·cat·ing v.t. 1 To remove the moisture from, as for preserving. 2 To dry thoroughly. —v.i. 3 To become dry. [< L de- completely + siccare dry out] —**des′ic·ca′tion, des′ic·ca′tor** n. —**des′ic·ca′tive** adj., n.

de·sid·er·a·tum (di·sid′ə·rā′təm, -zid′-, -rā′təm) n. pl. ·ta (-tə) Something desirable. [< L desiderare to desire]

de·sign (di·zīn′) v.t. 1 To make, draw, or prepare preliminary plans or sketches of. 2 To plan and make with art or skill. 3 To form or make (plans, schemes, etc.) in the mind; invent. 4 To intend; purpose. —v.i. 5 To make drawings or plans; be a designer. 6 To plan mentally; conceive. —n. 1 A plan, sketch or pattern for making something. 2 A decorative or artistic arrangement of forms, colors, etc.: a floral design. 3 Any arrangement of parts, shapes, etc., that forms a complete and functioning unit: the new car designs. 4 The act or art of designing. 5 A purpose or pattern: to seek a design in the chaos of history. 6 Often pl. A plot, scheme, or intention, usu. secret or sinister: with on, upon, or against. 7 Any plan, undertaking, or objective: a design to achieve better living conditions. [< L designare designate] —**de·sign′a·ble** adj.

des·ig·nate (dez′ig·nāt) v.t. ·nat·ed, ·nat·ing 1 To indicate by some mark, sign, or name. 2 To name; characterize. 3 To select or appoint for a specific purpose, duty, office, etc. —adj. (dez′ig·nit, -nāt) Designated; selected. [< L de- completely + signare to mark] —**des′ig·na′tor** n.

des·ig·na·tion (dez′ig·nā′shən) n. 1 An indicating or pointing out. 2 An appointment or nomination. 3 A distinguishing mark, name, or title.

de·sign·ed·ly (di·zī′nid·lē) adv. By design; purposely; intentionally.

de·sign·er (di·zī′nər) n. 1 One who creates useful, decorative, or artistic designs. 2 A contriver; schemer.

de·sign·ing (di·zī′ning) n. 1 The act or art of making designs or sketches. 2 The act of plotting or scheming. —adj. 1 Artful; scheming. 2 That makes designs, patterns, etc. —**de·sign′ing·ly** adv.

de·sir·a·ble (di·zīr′ə·bəl) adj. 1 Worth having or seeking; beneficial. 2 Arousing desire; attractive. —**de·sir′a·bil′i·ty, de·sir′a·ble·ness** n. —**de·sir′a·bly** adv.

de·sire (di·zīr′) v.t. ·sired, ·sir·ing 1 To wish or long for; crave. 2 To ask for; request. —n. 1 A longing; craving; yearning. 2 A request; wish. 3 Something desired. 4 Sexual appetite; passion. [< L desiderare] —**de·sir′er** n. —Syn. v. 1 want, covet, thirst after, yearn for, aspire after.

de·sir·ous (di·zīr′əs) adj. Having or characterized by desire: often with of.

de·sist (di·zist′) v.i. To cease; stop: often with from. [< L de- from + sistere stop, cease] —**de·sis′tance** n.

desk (desk) n. 1 A table, usu. with drawers, etc., specially adapted for writing or studying. 2 A lectern. 3 A place in a public building, hotel, etc., which provides specific services: information desk. 4 A department in a newspaper office: the society desk. 5 A music stand in an orchestra; also, the musicians who use it. [< LL discus disk]

des·o·late (des′ə·lit) adj. 1 Uninhabited; deserted. 2 Laid waste; devastated. 3 Lonely; solitary. 4 Without friends; forlorn; sorrowful. —v.t. (des′ə·lāt) ·lat·ed, ·lat·ing 1 To deprive of inhabitants. 2 To lay waste; devastate. 3 To make sorrowful or forlorn. 4 To abandon. [< L de- completely + solus alone] —**des′o·late·ly** adv. —**des′o·late·ness, des′o·lat′er, des′o·la′tor** n.

des·o·la·tion (des′ə·lā′shən)n. 1 Loneliness; dreariness. 2 Sadness; grief. 3 A laying waste; devastation. 4 A desolate condition or place.

de·spair (di·spâr′) v.t. To lose or abandon hope: with of. —n. 1 Utter hopelessness and discouragement. 2 That which causes despair or which is despaired of. [< L de- away + sperare to hope] —**de·spair′ing** adj. —**de·spair′ing·ly** adv.

des·patch (di·spach′) v. & n. DISPATCH.

des·per·a·do (des′pə·rä′dō, -rā′dō) n. pl. ·does or ·dos A desperate, dangerous outlaw or criminal.

des·per·ate (des′pər·it) adj. 1 Without care for danger; reckless, as from despair. 2 Resorted to in a last extremity; drastic. 3 In frantic need, desire, etc.: desperate for money. 4 Hopelessly bad or critical: in desperate circumstances. [< L desperare. See DESPAIR.] —**des′per·ate·ly** adv. —**des′. per·ate·ness** n. —Syn. 1 rash, foolhardy, imprudent, risky. 2 extreme, severe.

des·per·a·tion (des′pə·rā′shən) n. 1 The state of being desperate. 2 The recklessness of despair.

des·pi·ca·ble (des′pi·kə·bəl, di·spik′ə·bəl) adj. Despised; contemptible; mean; vile. [< L despicari despise] —**des′pi·ca·bil′i·ty, des′pi·ca·ble·ness** n. —**des′pi·ca·bly** adv.

de·spise (di·spīz′) v.t. ·spised, ·spis·ing To regard as contemptible or worthless; scorn. [< L de- down + specere look at] —**de·spis′er** n.

de·spite (di·spīt′) prep. In spite of; notwithstanding. —n. 1 An act of defiance or contempt. 2 Extreme malice; hatred; spite. —**in despite of** Notwithstanding; in spite of. [< L despectus a looking down, contempt]

de·spoil (di·spoil′) v.t. To deprive of something by force; plunder. [< L de- completely + spoliare rob] —**de·spoil′er, de·spoil′ment, de·spo·li·a·tion** (di·spō′lē·ā′shən) n.

de·spond (di·spond′) v.i. To lose spirit, courage, or hope; be depressed. —n. Archaic DESPONDENCY. [< L de- away + spondere to promise] —**de·spond′ing·ly** adv.

de·spon·den·cy (di·spon′dən·sē) n. Loss of spirit, courage, or hope. Also **de·spon′dence**.

de·spon·dent (di·spon′dənt) adj. Dejected in spirit; disheartened. —**de·spon′dent·ly** adv.

des·pot (des′pət, -pot) n. 1 An absolute monarch; autocrat. 2 A hard master; tyrant. [< Gk. despotēs a master]

des·pot·ic (de·spot′ik, di-) adj. Of or like a despot; tyrannical. —**des·pot′i·cal·ly** adv.

des·pot·ism (des′pə·tiz′əm) n. 1 Absolute power; autocracy. 2 Any tyrannical control.

des·sert (di·zûrt′) n. Something served at the close of a meal, as pastry, pudding, fruit, cheese, etc. [< F desservir clear a table]

des·ti·na·tion (des′tə·nā′shən) n. 1 The final place or point toward which a journey, letter, etc., is directed. 2 The ultimate purpose or goal of anything.

des·tine (des′tin) v.t. ·tined, ·tin·ing 1 To design or set apart for a distinct purpose or end. 2 to determine the future of, as by destiny or fate. **—destined for 1** Bound for; directed toward. **2** Fated or set apart for. [< L *destinare* make fast]

des·ti·ny (des′tə·nē) *n. pl.* **·nies 1** That to which any person or thing is destined. **2** Inevitable necessity; fate.

des·ti·tute (des′tə·t⁄ōōt) *adj.* **1** Entirely lacking: with *of*. **2** Being in want; extremely poor. [< L *destituere* abandon] **—des′ti·tu′tion** *n.*

de·stroy (di·stroi′) *v.t.* **1** To ruin utterly; consume. **2** To demolish; tear down. **3** To put an end to; do away with. **4** To kill. **5** To make ineffective; counteract. [< L *de-* down + *struere* build]

de·stroy·er (di·stroi′ər) *n.* **1** One who or that which destroys. **2** A small, speedy, heavily armed warship.

de·struct (di·strukt′) *n.* The act of deliberately destroying a defective missile, rocket, etc., after launch. —*v.i.* To undergo deliberate destruction.

de·struc·ti·ble (di·struk′tə·bəl) *adj.* Capable of being destroyed. **—de·struc′ti·bil′i·ty, de·struc′ti·ble·ness** *n.*

de·struc·tion (di·struk′shən) *n.* **1** The act of destroying, or state of being destroyed. **2** That which destroys. [< L *destruere* destroy]

de·struc·tive (di·struk′tiv) *adj.* **1** Causing destruction: with *of* or *to*. **2** Tending to negate, discourage, make ineffective, etc. **—de·struc′tive·ly** *adv.* **—de·struc′tive·ness** *n.*

des·ue·tude (des′wə·t⁄ōōd) *n.* A condition of disuse. [< L *desuescere* put out of use]

des·ul·to·ry (des′əl·tôr′ē, -tō′rē) *adj.* **1** Aimless; changeable; unmethodical. **2** Not connected or relevant; random. [< L *de-* down + *salire* to leap, jump] **—des′ul·to′ri·ly** *adv.* **—des′ul·to′ri·ness** *n.*

det. detach; detachment; detail.

de·tach (di·tach′) *v.t.* **1** To unfasten and make separate; disconnect. **2** To send off for a special service, duty, etc., as a regiment or a ship. [< F *détacher*] **—de·tach′a·bil′i·ty** *n.* **—de·tach′a·ble** *adj.*

de·tached (di·tacht′) *adj.* **1** Separated; disconnected. **2** Not involved emotionally or intellectually; unbiased; disinterested. **—de·tach′ed·ly** (-tach′id·lē) *adv.* **—de·tach′ed·ness** *n.*

de·tach·ment (di·tach′mənt) *n.* **1** The act of detaching. **2** The condition of being detached; separation. **3** *Mil.* A unit of troops sent, organized, or trained for special duty. **4** A disinterestedness, aloofness, or impartiality.

de·tail (di·tāl′, dē′tāl) *n.* **1** A small part, item, or particular of a whole. **2** A dealing with or attending to such items or particulars: to go into too much *detail*. **3** *Mil.* **a** A small detachment assigned to some particular task. **b** The person or persons assigned. **4** In art and architecture, a minor but essential component of the finished work. **—in detail** Item by item. —*v.t.* (di·tāl′) **1** To report minutely; give the details of. **2** (*often* dē′tāl) To select for a special service, duty, etc. [< F *dé-* completely + *tailler* cut up]

de·tain (di·tān′) *v.t.* **1** To restrain from going; stop; delay. **2** To keep back; withhold. **3** To hold in custody. [< L *de-* away + *tenere* hold] **—de·tain′er, de·tain′ment** *n.*

de·tect (di·tekt′) *v.t.* **1** To discover. **2** To expose or uncover, as a crime, fault, or a criminal. **3** *Telecom.* DEMODULATE. [< L *de-* away + *tegere* to cover] **—de·tect′a·ble** *or* **·i·ble** *adj.* **—de·tect′er** *n.* **—Syn. 1** perceive, find, discern. **2** reveal, disclose, unearth.

de·tec·tion (di·tek′shən) *n.* **1** The act of detecting or the condition of being detected. **2** *Telecom.* Any method of demodulation.

de·tec·tive (di·tek′tiv) *n.* A person, often a policeman, whose work is to investigate crimes, discover evidence, etc. —*adj.* **1** Of or pertaining to detectives or their work. **2** Of or for detection.

de·tec·tor (di·tek′tər) *n.* **1** One who or that which detects. **2** *Telecom.* DEMODULATOR.

dé·tente (dā·tänt′) *n.* An easing, as of discord between nations. [F]

de·ten·tion (di·ten′shən) *n.* **1** The act of detaining or keeping in custody. **2** The state of being detained. **—de·ten′tive** *adj.*

de·ter (di·tûr′) *v.t.* **·terred, ·ter·ring** To prevent or restrain (someone) from acting or proceeding, as by reminding of difficulties, dangers, etc. [< L *de-* away + *terrere* frighten] **—de·ter′ment** *n.*

de·terge (di·tûrj′) *v.t.* **·terged, ·terg·ing 1** To cleanse, as a wound. **2** To wipe off. [< L *de-* away + *tergere* wipe]

de·ter·gent (di·tûr′jənt) *adj.* Having cleansing qualities. —*n.* A cleansing substance, esp. a synthetic substitute for soap. **—de·ter′gence, de·ter′gen·cy** *n.*

de·te·ri·o·rate (di·tir′ē·ə·rāt′) *v.t. & v.i.* **·rat·ed, ·rat·ing** To make or become worse; reduce in quality, value, etc. [< L *deterior* worse] **—de·te′ri·o·ra′tion** *n.* **—de·te′ri·o·ra′tive** *adj.* **—Syn.** decline, degenerate, ebb, fall off, wane.

de·ter·mi·nant (di·tûr′mə·nənt) *adj.* DETERMINATIVE. —*n.* Something that determines.

de·ter·mi·nate (di·tûr′mə·nit) *adj.* **1** Definitely limited or fixed; specific; distinct. **2** Settled; conclusive. **3** Resolute; decisive. **—de·ter′mi·nate·ly** *adv.* **—de·ter′mi·nate·ness** *n.*

de·ter·mi·na·tion (di·tûr′mə·nā′shən) *n.* **1** The act of or determining or the condition of being determined. **2** A firm resolve or intention. **3** The quality of being firmly resolute. **4** The fixing of the size, quality, amount, etc., of anything; also, the result of this.

de·ter·mi·na·tive (di·tûr′mə·nā′tiv, -mə·nə·tiv) *adj.* Tending or having power to determine. —*n.* That which determines. **—de·ter′mi·na′tive·ly** *adv.* **—de·ter′mi·na′tive·ness** *n.*

de·ter·mine (di·tûr′min) *v.* **·mined, ·min·ing** *v.t.* **1** To settle or decide, as an argument or question. **2** To ascertain or fix, as after investigation or observation. **3** To cause to reach a decision. **4** To influence or affect: Demand *determines* supply. **5** To give purpose or direction to. **6** To set bounds to; limit. **7** *Law* To limit; terminate. —*v.i.* **8** To decide; resolve. **9** *Law* To come to an end. [< L *de-* completely + *terminare* to end] **—de·ter′min·er** *n.*

de·ter·mined (di·tûr′mind) *adj.* **1** Settled; resolved. **2** Of firm purpose; resolute. **—de·ter′mined·ly** *adv.* **—de·ter′mined·ness** *n.*

de·ter·min·ism (di·tûr′mə·niz′əm) *n. Philos.* The doctrine that man's decisions and actions are determined not by free choice but by antecedent causes acting upon his character. **—de·ter′min·ist** *n.,* **—de·ter′min·is′tic** *adj.*

de·ter·rent (di·tûr′ənt) *adj.* Tending or serving to deter. —*n.* Something that deters. **—de·ter′rence** *n.*

de·test (di·test′) *v.t.* To hate; abhor. [< L *detestari* denounce] **—de·test′er** *n.* **—Syn.** despise, dislike, abominate.

de·test·a·ble (di·tes′tə·bəl) *adj.* Extremely hateful; abhorrent; odious. **—de·test′a·bil′i·ty, de·test′a·ble·ness** *n.* **—de·test′a·bly** *adv.*

de·tes·ta·tion (dē′tes·tā′shən) *n.* **1** Extreme hatred; abhorrence. **2** A person or thing detested.

de·throne (dē·thrōn′) *v.t.* **·throned, ·thron·ing** To remove from the throne; depose.

det·o·nate (det′ə·nāt) *v.t. & v.i.* **·nat·ed, ·nat·ing** To explode or cause to explode suddenly and with violence. [< L *de-* down + *tonare* to thunder] **—det′o·na′tion, det′o·na′tor** *n.*

de·tour (dē′tŏŏr, di·tŏŏr′) *n.* **1** A roundabout way or deviation from a direct route or course of action. **2** A road substituted for part of a main route temporarily impassable. —*v.t. & v.i.* To go or cause to go by a detour. [< F *dé-* away + *tourner* to turn]

de·tract (di·trakt′) *v.t.* **1** To take away; withdraw. —*v.i.* **2** To take away a part, as from a reputation, enjoyment, etc.: with *from*. [< L *de-* away + *trahere* draw, pull] **—de·trac′tion, de·trac′tor** *n.* **—de·trac′tive** *adj.*

det·ri·ment (det′rə·mənt) *n.* **1** Something that impairs, injures, or causes loss. **2** Injury or loss. [< L *deterere* rub away] **—det′ri·men′tal** *adj.* **—det′ri·men′tal·ly** *adv.*

de·tri·tus (di·trī′təs) *n.* **1** *Geol.* Fragments or particles of rock resulting from erosion, glacial action, etc. **2** Any debris. [< L *deterere* rub away] **—de·tri′tal** *adj.*

deuce[1] (d⁄ōōs) *n.* **1** Two; esp. a card or side of a die having two spots. **2** In tennis, a score tied at 40 or at five games each, requiring that either side win two successive points for the game or two successive games for the set. [< L *duo* two]

deuce[2] (d⁄ōōs) *n. Informal* The devil; damn: a mild oath. [Prob. < LG *de duus* the deuce (lowest throw at dice)]

deu·ced (d⁄ōō′sid, d⁄ōōst) *adj.* Devilish; exceeding. —*adv.* Devilishly. **—deu′ced·ly** *adv.*

De·us (dā′ōōs, dē′əs) *n.* God [L].

Deut. Deuteronomy.

deu·te·ri·um (dᵞo͞o·tir′ē·əm) *n.* The isotope of hydrogen having twice the mass of ordinary hydrogen. [< Gk. *deuteros* second]

deuterium oxide HEAVY WATER.

deu·ter·on (dᵞo͞o′tər·on) *n.* The nucleus of a deuterium atom.

Deu·ter·on·o·my (dᵞo͞o′tər·on′ə·mē) *n.* The fifth book of the Old Testament. [< Gk. *deuteros* second + *nomos* law]

de·val·ue (dē·val′yo͞o) *v.t.* **·val·ued, ·val·u·ing** 1 To reduce or annul the value of. 2 To fix the value of (a currency) at a point below par. Also **de·val′u·ate** (-yo͞o·āt). —**de·val′u·a′tion** *n.*

dev·as·tate (dev′ə·stāt) *v.t.* **·tat·ed, ·tat·ing** 1 To lay waste, as by war, fire, etc. 2 To crush; overwhelm. [< L *de-* completely + *vastare* lay waste] —**dev′as·tat′ing·ly** *adv.* —**dev′· as·ta′tion, dev′as·ta′tor** *n.*

devel. development.

de·vel·op (di·vel′əp) *v.t.* 1 To expand or bring out the potentialities, capabilities, etc., of. 2 To expand; enlarge upon; work out, as a plot or idea. 3 To increase the strength, effectiveness, etc., of: to *develop* one's body. 4 To make more extensive or productive, as atomic power. 5 *Phot.* **a** To bring (a picture) to view by subjecting an exposed photographic film or plate to a developer. **b** To subject (a plate or film) to a developer. 6 *Music* To elaborate on (a theme). —*v.i.* 7 To increase in capabilities, maturity, etc. 8 To advance from a lower to a higher state; grow; evolve. 9 To disclose itself; become apparent: The plot of a novel *develops.* [< OF *de-* + *voluper* to fold] —**de·vel′op·a·ble** *adj.*

de·vel·op·er (di·vel′əp·ər) *n.* 1 One who or that which develops. 2 One who builds housing, shopping centers, etc., on a speculative basis. 3 *Phot.* A chemical solution for developing photographs.

de·vel·op·ment (di·vel′əp·mənt) *n.* 1 The act of developing or the state or condition of being developed. 2 Something that has been developed. 3 An event; happening; occurrence. —**de·vel·op·men·tal** (di·vel′əp·men′təl) *adj.* — **de·vel′op·men·tal·ly** *adv.*

de·vi·ate (dē′vē·āt) *v.* **·at·ed, ·at·ing** *v.i.* 1 To turn aside from a course or a norm; diverge. 2 To differ, as in thought or belief. —*v.t.* 3 To cause to turn aside. —*n.* (dē′vē·it) One who deviates, esp. in sexual behavior: also **de·vi·ant** (dē′vē·ənt). [< L *de-* from + *via* a road] —**de′vi·a′tion, de′vi·a′tor** *n.*

de·vice (di·vīs′) *n.* 1 Something invented and constructed for special use; contrivance. 2 A plan or scheme, esp. a sly or tricky one. 3 A means to obtain an artistic effect. 4 A fanciful design or pattern, as in ornamentation. 5 A motto or emblem, as on a shield. —**leave to one's own devices** To allow (a person) to follow his own wishes, without help, guidance, etc. [< OF *devis* intention, will]

dev·il (dev′əl) *n.* 1 *Sometimes cap.* In theology, the prince and ruler of the kingdom of evil; Satan. 2 Any subordinate evil spirit; a demon. 3 A wicked person. 4 A wretched fellow: poor *devil.* 5 A person of great energy, daring, or effrontery. 6 Any of various toothed machines, as for cutting or tearing up rags. 7 PRINTER'S DEVIL. 8 Something difficult to do, understand, solve, etc. —**between the devil and the deep blue sea** In a dilemma. —**give the devil his due** To acknowledge the virtues of even a bad or disliked person. —**the devil to pay** Trouble to be expected as a consequence. —*v.t.* **dev·iled** or **·illed, dev·il·ing** or **·il·ling** 1 To prepare (food) by seasoning highly. 2 To cut up, as cloth, in a devil. 3 To harass; tease; bedevil. [< Gk. *diabolos* slanderer]

dev·il·fish (dev′əl·fish′) *n.* *pl.* **·fish** or **·fish·es** Any of various large marine animals of grotesque appearance, as an octopus and certain large rays.

dev·il·ish (dev′əl·ish, dev′lish) *adj.* 1 Having the qualities of the devil; diabolical; malicious. 2 Challenging; complex. 3 Mis-

Devilfish

chievous; impish. 4 *Informal* Excessive; extreme. —*adv.* Excessively; very. —**dev′il·ish·ly** *adv.* —**dev′il·ish·ness** *n.*

dev·il-may-care (dev′əl·mā·kâr′) *adj.* Careless; reckless; heedless of consequences.

dev·il·ment (dev′əl·mənt) *n.* 1 Mischief; impish action or tricks. 2 Wickedness; evil.

devil's advocate 1 A Roman Catholic official whose duty is to raise objections to a candidate for beatification or canonization. 2 One who takes an unpopular or indefensible side in an argument in order to provoke discussion or test the validity of accepted views.

dev·il's-food cake (dev′əlz·fo͞od′) A rich chocolate cake.

dev·il·try (dev′əl·trē) *n.* *pl.* **·tries** 1 Wanton and malicious mischief. 2 Evil magic or art. Also **dev′il·ry** (-rē).

de·vi·ous (dē′vē·əs) *adj.* 1 Winding or deviating from a straight course; rambling. 2 Straying from the proper or usual way. 3 Not straightforward or honest. [< L *de-* from + *via* way] —**de′vi·ous·ly** *adv.* —**de′vi·ous·ness** *n.*

de·vise (di·vīz′) *v.* **·vised, ·vis·ing** *v.t.* 1 To form in the mind; invent; contrive. 2 *Law* To transmit (real estate) by will. —*v.i.* 3 To form a plan. —*n.* *Law* 1 A gift of lands by will. 2 The act of bequeathing lands. 3 A will, or a clause in a will, conveying real estate. [< OF *deviser* divide, distinguish, contrive] —**de·vis′a·ble** *adj.* —**de·vis′er** *n.* —**Syn.** *v.* 1 produce, plan, fashion, concoct.

de·vi·see (di·vī′zē′, dev′ə·zē′) *n.* *Law* The person to whom a devise is made.

de·vi·sor (di·vī′zər, -zôr) *n.* *Law* One who gives by will.

de·vi·tal·ize (dē·vī′təl·īz) *v.t.* **·ized, ·iz·ing** 1 To deprive of life; kill. 2 To weaken; enfeeble. —**de·vi′tal·i·za′tion** *n.*

de·void (di·void′) *adj.* Not possessing; destitute: with *of.* [< OF *devoidier* empty out]

de·voir (də·vwär′, dev′wär) *n.* 1 Duty. 2 *pl.* Respectful words of greeting or courtesy. [< L *debere* owe]

de·volve (di·volv′) *v.* **·volved, ·volv·ing** *v.t.* 1 To cause (powers, obligations, etc.) to pass to a successor or substitute. —*v.i.* 2 To pass from a possessor to a successor or substitute: with *to, on,* or *upon.* [< L *de-* down + *volvere* roll] — **de·volve′ment, dev·o·lu·tion** (dev′ə·lo͞o′shən) *n.*

De·vo·ni·an (di·vō′nē·ən) *adj.* & *n.* See GEOLOGY.

de·vote (di·vōt′) *v.t.* **·vot·ed, ·vot·ing** 1 To give or apply (attention, time, or oneself) completely to a purpose, activity, another person, etc. 2 To set apart; dedicate; consecrate. [< L *de-* away + *vovere* vow]

de·vot·ed (di·vō′tid) *adj.* 1 Feeling or showing devotion; ardent; devout. 2 Set apart, as by a vow; consecrated. — **de·vot′ed·ly** *adv.* —**de·vot′ed·ness** *n.*

dev·o·tee (dev′ə·tē′, -tā′, di·vō′tē′) *n.* 1 One intensely devoted to something or someone. 2 A religious zealot.

de·vo·tion (di·vō′shən) *n.* 1 The quality or condition of being devoted. 2 Strong attachment or affection. 3 *Usu. pl.* An act of worship; prayer. 4 Piety. 5 The act of devoting. —**de·vo′tion·al** *adj.* —**de·vo′tion·al·ly** *adv.*

de·vour (di·vour′) *v.t.* 1 To eat up greedily. 2 To destroy; lay waste to. 3 To take in greedily with the mind or senses: He *devoured* the book. 4 To engross the attention of. 5 To engulf; absorb. [< L *de-* down + *vorare* to gulp, swallow] —**de·vour′er** *n.*

de·vout (di·vout′) *adj.* 1 Earnestly religious; pious. 2 Heartfelt; sincere. 3 Containing or expressing devotion. [< L *devovere* devote] —**de·vout′ly** *adv.* —**de·vout′ness** *n.*

dew (dᵞo͞o) *n.* 1 Moisture condensed from the atmosphere in small drops upon cool surfaces. 2 Anything suggesting the freshness of dew: the *dew* of youth. 3 Moisture generally, esp. when in minute drops, as perspiration, tears, etc. —*v.t.* To wet with or as with dew; bedew. [< OE *dēaw*]

dew·ber·ry (dᵞo͞o′ber′ē, -bər·ē) *n.* *pl.* **·ries** Any of various low-growing blackberries.

dew·claw (dᵞo͞o′klô′) *n.* A rudimentary toe, claw, or hoof on the feet of certain animals, as dogs, hogs, deer, etc. — **dew′clawed′** *adj.*

dew·drop (dᵞo͞o′drop′) *n.* A drop of dew.

Dew·ey decimal system (do͞o′ē) A numerical system for classifying books, used in libraries, etc. [< Melvil *Dewey,* 1851–1931, U.S. librarian]

---

add, āce, cåre, påim; end, ēven; it, īce; odd, ōpen, ôrder; to͞ok, po͞ol; up, bûrn; ə = *a* in *above; u* in *focus;* yo͞o = *u* in *fuse;* oil; pout; check; go; ring; thin; this; zh, *vision.* < derived from; ? origin uncertain or unknown.

dew·lap (dyōō′lap′) *n.* The pendulous skin under the throat of cattle and certain other animals. [ME *dewlappe*] —**dew′lapped′** *adj.*

DEW line (dyōō) A chain of radar stations in North America at about the 70th parallel, maintained by the U.S. in cooperation with Canada. [< *D(istant) E(arly) W(arning)*]

dew point The temperature at which the water vapor in the air condenses to a liquid.

dew·y (dyōō′ē) *adj.* **dew·i·er, dew·i·est** **1** Moist, as with dew. **2** Of or like dew. **3** Refreshing. —**dew′i·ly** *adv.* —**dew′i·ness** *n.*

Dewlap

dex·ter (dek′stər) *adj.* **1** Of, pertaining to, or situated on the right side or hand. **2** *Her.* On the wearer's right, the spectator's left. [L]

dex·ter·i·ty (dek·ster′ə·tē) *n.* **1** Manual skill; adroitness. **2** Mental quickness or skill. [< L *dexteritas* skill < *dexter* on the right]

dex·ter·ous (dek′strəs, -stər·əs) *adj.* **1** Possessing dexterity; adroit. **2** Done with dexterity. Also **dex·trous** (dek′strəs). —**dex′ter·ous·ly, dex′trous·ly** *adv.* —**dex′ter·ous·ness, dex′trous·ness** *n.*

dex·tral (dek′strəl) *adj.* **1** Of, pertaining to, or situated on the right side. **2** Right-handed. —**dex′tral·ly** *adv.* —**dex·tral·i·ty** (dek·stral′ə·tē) *n.*

dex·trin (dek′strin) *n.* A water-soluble carbohydrate formed by the partial breakdown of starch, used as an adhesive, filler, etc. Also **dex·trine** (dek′strin, -strēn). [< DEXTR(O)- + IN]

dextro- *combining form* Turned or turning to the right: used esp. in chemistry and physics: *dextrin, dextrose.* Also **dextr-**. [< L *dexter* right]

dex·trose (dek′strōs) *n.* The common isomeric form of glucose, occurring in animals and plants. [< DEXTR(O)- + (GLUC)OSE]

DF., D.F., Df direction finding.

DFC, D.F.C. Distinguished Flying Cross.

D.G. by the grace of God (L *Dei gratia*).

dg, dg. decigram(s).

DHQ Division Headquarters.

di- *prefix* **1** Twice; double. **2** *Chem.* Containing two atoms, molecules, etc.: *dioxide.* [< Gk. *dis* twice]

di., dia. diameter.

dia- *prefix* Through; across; between: *diagonal.* Also **di-**. [< Gk. *dia-* through]

di·a·be·tes (dī′ə·bē′tēz, -tis) *n.* **1** Any of several diseases characterized by thirst and excessive urinary secretion. **2** DIABETES MELLITUS. [< Gk. *dia-* through + *bainein* go] —**di·a·bet·ic** (dī′ə·bet′ik, -bē′tik) *adj., n.*

diabetes mel·li·tus (mə·lī′təs) A chronic form of diabetes in which glucose accumulates in the blood and is excreted in the urine. [NL, lit., honey diabetes < L *mel* honey]

di·a·bol·ic (dī′ə·bol′ik) *adj.* **1** Of, pertaining to, or coming from the devil; satanic. **2** Fiendishly wicked or cruel. Also **di·a·bol′i·cal.** [< Gk. *diabolos* devil] —**di·a·bol′i·cal·ly** *adv.* —**di·ab·o·lism** (dī·ab′ə·liz′əm) *n.* —**Syn. 2** malevolent, infernal, demoniacal.

di·ac·o·nate (dī·ak′ə·nit, -nāt) *n.* **1** The office, rank, or tenure of a deacon. **2** Deacons collectively. —**di·ac′o·nal** *adj.*

di·a·crit·ic (dī′ə·krit′ik) *n.* DIACRITICAL MARK. —*adj.* DIACRITICAL. [< Gk. *dia-* between + *krinein* distinguish]

di·a·crit·i·cal (dī′ə·krit′i·kəl) *adj.* Marking a difference; distinguishing. —**di·a·crit′i·cal·ly** *adv.*

diacritical mark A mark, point, or sign attached to a letter to indicate its pronunciation.

di·a·dem (dī′ə·dem) *n.* **1** A crown worn as a symbol of royalty. **2** Regal power; sovereignty. [< Gk. *diadēma*]

di·aer·e·sis (dī·er′ə·sis) *n.* DIERESIS.

diag. diagram.

di·ag·nose (dī′əg·nōs′, -nōz′) *v.* **·nosed, ·nos·ing** *v.t.* To perceive or distinguish by diagnosis. —*v.i.* To make a diagnosis.

di·ag·no·sis (dī′əg·nō′sis) *n.* **1** The art or act of identifying diseases, disorders, etc., by their characteristic symptoms. **2** An examination of the facts in any situation in

order to understand its nature: a *diagnosis* of city traffic. **3** The conclusions reached by diagnosing. [< Gk. *diagignōskein* discern] —**di·ag·nos·tic** (dī′əg·nos′tik) *adj.* —**di·ag·nos′ti·cal·ly** *adv.*

di·ag·nos·ti·cian (dī′əg·nos·tish′ən) *n.* One who is versed in diagnosis.

di·ag·o·nal (dī·ag′ə·nəl) *adj.* **1** Crossing or moving obliquely; slanting. **2** Marked by oblique lines or the like. **3** *Geom.* **a** Joining two nonadjacent vertices of a figure. **b** Joining two nonadjacent edges of a solid. —*n.* **1** *Geom.* A diagonal line or plane. **2** Anything running diagonally. [< L *dia-* across + *gonia* angle] —**di·ag′o·nal·ly** *adv.*

di·a·gram (dī′ə·gram) *n.* **1** A drawing, plan, or outline that illustrates or explains an object, area, concept, etc. **2** A figure drawn to demonstrate a geometrical proposition or relationship. **3** A graph or chart. —*v.t.* **·gramed** or **·grammed, ·gram·ing** or **·gram·ming** To represent or illustrate by a diagram. [< Gk. *dia-* across + *graphein* write] —**di·a·gram·mat·ic** (dī′ə·grə·mat′ik) or **·i·cal** *adj.* —**di′a·gram·mat′i·cal·ly** *adv.*

di·al (dī′əl, dīl) *n.* **1** A graduated circular plate or face on which an amount, a direction, or degree are indicated by a moving pointer. **2** The face of a watch or clock. **3** A disk or knob used to indicate and change frequencies in a radio or television set. **4** A rotating disk, as on a telephone, used to indicate a number. **5** SUNDIAL. —*v.t. & v.i.* **di·aled** or **di·alled, di·al·ing** or **·al·ling** **1** To measure or survey with a dial. **2** To indicate on a dial. **3** To telephone by means of a dial. **4** To adjust a radio or television set to (a station, program, etc.). [< Med. L *dialis* daily] —**di′al·er, di′al·ler** *n.*

dial. dialect; dialectic; dialectical.

di·a·lect (dī′ə·lekt) *n.* **1** The aggregate variations from standard language of the speech peculiar to a local region: the Southern *dialect* of American English. **2** Loosely, the speech adopted by a particular class, trade, or profession; jargon. **3** An imperfect use of the standard language by those to whom another language is native. **4** A language or group of languages with distinguishing characteristics but related in their origins: The Romance languages are *dialects* of Latin. —*adj.* Of or in a dialect. [< Gk. *dialektos* discourse, way of speaking]

di·a·lec·tal (dī′ə·lek′təl) *adj.* Of or characterized by a dialect. —**di′a·lec′tal·ly** *adv.*

di·a·lec·tic (dī′ə·lek′tik) *n.* **1** *Usu. pl.* The art or practice of examining ideas logically, as by a method of question and answer. **2** Any method of logical argument. **3** *Often pl.* The philosophic mode of argumentation used by Hegel and adapted to socialist ideology by Marx. —*adj.* **1** Pertaining to or using dialectic. **2** DIALECTAL. [< Gk. *dialektika (technē)* (art) of discourse]

di·a·lec·ti·cal (dī′ə·lek′ti·kəl) *adj.* **1** Of, pertaining to, or using dialectic. **2** DIALECTAL. —**di′a·lec′ti·cal·ly** *adv.*

di·a·lec·ti·cian (dī′ə·lek·tish′ən) *n.* **1** A logician. **2** One who specializes in dialects.

di·a·logue (dī′ə·lôg, -log) *n.* **1** A conversation. **2** A literary work in which the characters are represented as conversing. **3** An open exchange of different points of view for the purpose of mutual understanding. **4** Those sections of a play, story, etc., devoted to conversation. —*v.* **·logued, ·logu·ing** *v.t.* **1** To express in dialogue form. —*v.i.* **2** To carry on a dialogue. Also **di′a·log.** [< Gk. *dialegesthai* converse] —**di′a·log′ic** (dī′ə·loj′ik) or **·i·cal** *adj.* —**di·al·o·gist** (dī·al′ə·jist, dī′ə·log′ist, -lôg′-) *n.*

di·al·y·sis (dī·al′ə·sis) *n. pl.* **·ses** (-sēz) **1** *Chem.* The separation of dissolved substances from colloids in a liquid by their unequal permeation through a membrane. **2** *Med.* Removal by dialysis of toxic substances in the blood as a result of inadequate kidney function. [< Gk. *dia-* completely + *lyein* loosen] —**di·a·lyt·ic** (dī′ə·lit′ik) *adj.* —**di′a·lyt′i·cal·ly** *adv.*

diam. diameter.

di·a·mag·net·ic (dī′ə·mag·net′ik) *adj. Physics* Of or designating the property of forming an induced magnetic field opposite to and weaker than the inducing field. —*n.* A diamagnetic substance. —**di′a·mag′net·ism** (-mag′nə·tiz′əm) *n.* —**di′a·mag·net′i·cal·ly** *adv.*

di·am·e·ter (dī·am′ə·tər) *n.* **1** A straight line passing through the center of a circle, sphere, figure, etc., and reaching from one boundary to the other. **2** The length of such a line. **3** The width or thickness of an object as measured by such a line. [< Gk. *dia-* through + *metron* measure]

di·a·met·ri·cal (dī′ə·met′ri·kəl) *adj.* **1** Of or pertaining to a diameter. **2** Directly and totally opposite, different, contrary, etc.: also **di·a·met′ric.** —**di′a·met′ri·cal·ly** *adv.*

dia·mond (dī′mənd, dī′ə-) *n.* **1** A colorless, crystalline, extremely hard form of carbon, valued as a gem and as an abrasive or cutting tool. **2** *Geom.* A plane figure bounded by four equal straight lines, and having two of the angles acute and two obtuse; a lozenge or rhombus. **3** In card games: **a** A lozenge-shaped, red spot on a playing card. **b** A card having such a mark. **c** *pl.* A suit so marked. **4** The square enclosed by the lines between the bases on a baseball field; also, loosely, the field itself. —*adj.* Of or like diamonds. —*v.t.* To adorn with or as with diamonds. [< LL *daimas*]

diamond anniversary A 60th or 75th anniversary. Also **diamond jubilee.**

dia·mond·back (dī′mənd·bak′, dī′ə-) *n.* **1** An edible turtle inhabiting salt marshes of the s U.S., having diamond-shaped markings on the shell: also **diamondback terrapin. 2** A large rattlesnake of the SE U.S., having a diamond pattern on the back: also **diamondback rattlesnake.**

Di·an·a (dī·an′ə) *Rom. Myth.* Goddess of the hunt, virginity, and the moon.

di·a·pa·son (dī′ə·pā′zən, -sən) *n.* **1** Either of two principal stops in a pipe organ, extending throughout the instrument's entire range and producing its characteristic tone quality. **2** The complete range of a musical instrument or voice. [< Gk. *dia pasōn (chordōn)* through all (the notes)]

di·a·per (dī′pər, dī′ə-) *n.* **1** A soft, absorbent cloth or other material, folded and placed between a baby's legs and fastened around the waist. **2** A repeated, usu. geometric design. —*v.t.* **1** To put a diaper on (an infant). **2** To decorate with a repeated design. [< Med. Gk. *dia-* completely + *aspros* white]

di·aph·a·nous (dī·af′ə·nəs) *adj.* **1** Transparent or translucent, as a sheer fabric. **2** Vague or insubstantial. [< Gk. *dia-* through + *phainein* show] —**di·aph′a·nous·ly** *adv.* —**di·aph′a·nous·ness** *n.*

di·a·pho·re·sis (dī′ə·fə·rē′sis) *n.* Copious perspiration. [< Gk. *dia-* across, through + *phorein* carry] —**di·a·pho·ret·ic** (dī′ə·fə·ret′ik) *adj., n.*

di·a·phragm (dī′ə·fram) *n.* **1** The muscular partition between the thoracic and abdominal cavities; the midriff. **2** Any dividing membrane or partition. **3** Something resembling a diaphragm in shape or elasticity, as the thin, vibrating disk of a telephone. **4** A perforated mechanism which regulates the amount of light entering the lens of a camera, telescope, etc. **5** A contraceptive device consisting of a flexible rubber cap inserted in the vagina to cover the uterine cervix. —*v.t.* To act upon or furnish with a diaphragm. [< Gk. *dia-* across + *phragma* a fence] —**di·a·phrag·mat·ic** (dī′ə·frag·mat′ik) *adj.* —**di′a·phrag·mat′i·cal·ly** *adv.*

Diaphragm *def. 1*

di·a·rist (dī′ə·rist) *n.* One who keeps a diary.

di·ar·rhe·a (dī′ə·rē′ə) *n.* Abnormally frequent and fluid evacuation of the bowels. Also **di′ar·rhoe′a.** [< Gk. *dia-* through + *rheein* to flow] —**di′ar·rhe′al** or **·rhoe′al, di′ar·rhe′ic** or **·rhoe′ic, di′ar·rhet′ic** or **·rhoet′ic** (-ret′ik) *adj.*

di·a·ry (dī′ə·rē) *n. pl.* **·ries 1** A written, daily record of the writer's experiences, feelings, activities, etc. **2** A book for keeping such a record. [< LL *diarium* < L *dies* a day]

di·as·po·ra (dī·as′pə·rə) *n.* **1** *Usu. cap.* **a** The dispersion of the Jews among the Gentiles after the Babylonian exile. **b** The Jews so dispersed. **c** Jews or Jewish communities outside Palestine or the state of Israel. **2** Any dispersion of a people having a common heritage.

di·a·stase (dī′ə·stās) *n.* A vegetable enzyme that converts starch into maltose and dextrose. [< Gk. *diastasis* a separation]

di·as·to·le (dī·as′tə·lē) *n.* **1** The rhythmic relaxation and dilation of the heart between contractions. **2** In classical prosody, the lengthening of a syllable naturally short. [< Gk. *diastolē* a separation, lengthening] —**di·as·tol·ic** (dī′ə·stol′ik) *adj.*

di·as·tro·phism (dī·as′trə·fiz′əm) *n.* The process by which the earth's crust is reshaped, producing continents and ocean beds, plateaus, mountains, valleys, etc. [< Gk. *dia-* across + *strephein* to turn] —**di·a·stroph·ic** (dī′ə·strof′·ik) *adj.*

di·a·ther·my (dī′ə·thûr′mē) *n.* Medical treatment by means of heat generated in the body by high-frequency radiation. [< Gk. *dia-* through + *thermē* heat] —**di′a·ther′·mic** *adj.*

di·a·tom (dī′ə·təm, -tom) *n.* Any of numerous species of microscopic green algae having siliceous walls. [< Gk. *dia-* through + *temnein* to cut] —**di·a·to·ma·ceous** (dī′ə·tə·mā′shəs) *adj.*

di·a·ton·ic (dī′ə·ton′ik) *adj. Music* Of or designating the regular tones of a major or minor scale. [< Gk. *dia-* throughout + *teinein* stretch]

di·a·tribe (dī′ə·trīb) *n.* An abusive denunciation; invective. [< Gk. *diatribē* a wearing away]

di·ba·sic (dī·bā′sik) *adj.* Containing two atoms of hydrogen replaceable by basic radicals or atoms to form a salt. —**di·ba·sic·i·ty** (dī′bā·sis′ə·tē) *n.*

dib·ble (dib′əl) *n.* A pointed tool for planting seeds, setting slips, etc. Also **dib·ber** (dib′ər). —*v.t.* **·bled ·bling** To make holes in (soil) with a dibble. [?]

dice (dīs) *n. pl. of* **die 1** Small cubes of bone, ivory, plastic, etc., having the sides marked with spots from one to six. **2** A game of chance played with such cubes. **3** Any small cubes. —*v.* **diced, dic·ing** *v.t.* **1** To cut into small cubes. **2** To gamble away or win with dice. —*v.i.* **3** To play at dice. —**dic′er** *n.*

di·cey (dī′sē) *adj.* **dic·i·er, dic·i·est** *Informal* Risky; chancy. [< DICE + -Y¹]

di·chot·o·my (dī·kot′ə·mē) *n. pl.* **·mies 1** Division into two, usu. opposing parts, viewpoints, etc. **2** *Logic* The division of a class into two mutually exclusive subclasses, as minerals into gold and not-gold. **3** *Biol.* A forking in pairs; successive bifurcation. [< Gk. *dicho-* in two + *temnein* to cut] —**di·chot′o·mous** *adj.* —**di·chot′o·mous·ly** *adv.*

di·chro·mat·ic (dī′krō·mat′ik) *adj.* **1** Having two colors. **2** *Zool.* Having two kinds of coloration not due to age or sex. **3** Colorblind; able to see only two of the three primary colors. —**di·chro·ma·tism** (dī·krō′mə·tiz′əm) *n.*

dick·ens (dik′ənz) *n. Informal* The devil: a euphemistic oath. [?]

dick·er (dik′ər) *v.t. & v.i.* To trade, haggle, or barter, esp. on a small scale. —*n.* The act of dickering. [ME *dyker*]

dick·ey (dik′ē) *n.* **1** A detachable shirt or blouse front. **2** A detachable collar. **3** A bib or pinafore. **4** A small bird: also **dickey bird. 5** An outside seat on a carriage, as for the driver. Also **dick′y.** [< *Dicky*, dim. of the name *Richard*]

di·cot·y·le·don (dī′kot·ə·lēd′n, dī·kot′-) *n.* A flowering plant having seeds with two cotyledons. —**di′cot·y·le′do·nous** *adj.*

dict. dictation; dictator; dictionary.

dic·ta (dik′tə) *n.pl. of* DICTUM.

Dic·ta·phone (dik′tə·fōn) *n.* A type of instrument that records and reproduces spoken words, as for transcription by a stenographer: a trade name.

dic·tate (dik′tāt, dik·tāt′) *v.* **·tat·ed, ·tat·ing** *v.t.* **1** To utter or read aloud (something) to be recorded by another. **2** To prescribe authoritatively, as commands, terms, rules, etc. —*v.i.* **3** To utter aloud something to be recorded by another. **4** To give orders. —*n.* (dik′tāt) **1** An authoritative suggestion, rule, or command. **2** A precept or prompting. [< L *dictare,* freq. of *dicere* say, speak]

dic·ta·tion (dik·tā′shən) *n.* **1** The act of dictating. **2** The matter or material dictated. —**dic·ta′tion·al** *adj.*

dic·ta·tor (dik′tā·tər, dik·tā′tər) *n.* **1** A political ruler with absolute power. **2** One who orders, commands, or prescribes. **3** A person who dictates words. —**dic′ta·tor·ship′** *n.*

dic·ta·to·ri·al (dik′tə·tôr′ē·əl, -tō′rē-) *adj.* **1** Given to dictating; overbearing; autocratic. **2** Of or pertaining to a dictator or his rule. —**dic′ta·to′ri·al·ly** *adv.* —**Syn.** **1** dogmatic, arbitrary, despotic, opinionated, arrogant.

dic·tion (dik′shən) *n.* **1** The use, choice and arrangement of words and modes of expression. **2** The manner of enunciating words in speaking or singing. [<L *dicere* say]

dic·tion·ar·y (dik′shən·er′ē) *n. pl.* **·ar·ies** **1** A book containing the words of a language arranged alphabetically, usu. with their syllabication, pronunciation, definition, and etymology. **2** A similar work having definitions or equivalents in another language. **3** Any list of specialized words or terms arranged alphabetically and defined. [<Med. L *dictionarium* a collection of words and phrases]

dic·tum (dik′təm) *n. pl.* **dic·ta** (-tə) or **·tums** **1** An authoritative, dogmatic, or positive utterance; a pronouncement. **2** A popular saying; a maxim. [<L *dicere* say]

did (did) *p.t.* of DO[1].

di·dac·tic (dī·dak′tik, di-) *adj.* **1** Intended to instruct; expository. **2** Morally instructive; preceptive. **3** Overly inclined to teach; pedantic. Also **di·dac′ti·cal.** [<Gk. *didaskein* teach] —**di·dac′ti·cal·ly** *adv.* —**di·dac′ti·cism** *n.*

di·dac·tics (dī·dak′tiks, di-) *n. pl.* (*construed as sing.*) The science or art of instruction or education.

did·dle[1] (did′l) *v.* **·dled,** **·dling** *Informal v.t.* **1** To cheat. —*v.i.* **2** To dawdle; pass time idly. [?] —**did′dler** *n.*

did·dle[2] (did′l) *v.i.* **·dled,** **·dling** *Informal* To jerk up and down or back and forth; jiggle. [<ME *diddiren* quiver, shake, tremble]

did·n′t (did′nt) Contraction of *did not.*

di·do (dī′dō) *n. pl.* **·dos** or **·does** *Informal* An extravagant caper; antic. [?]

Di·do (dī′dō) *Rom. Myth.* The founder and queen of Carthage. In the *Aeneid,* she falls in love with Aeneas and kills herself when he leaves her.

didst (didst) *Archaic* Second person singular past tense of DO[1]: used with *thou.*

die[1] (dī) *v.i.* **died, dy·ing** **1** To suffer death; expire. **2** To suffer the pains of death: The coward *dies* a thousand deaths. **3** To lose energy, force, importance, etc.: with *away, down,* or *out.* **4** To fade away: The smile *died* on his lips. **5** To become extinct: with *out* or *off.* **6** To become indifferent or insensible: with *to:* to *die* to the world. **7** *Informal* To desire exceedingly, as if to death: He's *dying* to meet her. **8** To stop functioning, as an engine. **9** To faint or swoon. [<ON *deyja*]

die[2] (dī) *n. pl.* **dice** *for defs. 1 and 2,* **dies** *for def. 3* **1** A small cube used in games. See DICE. **2** A cast, as in playing dice; stake; hazard. **3** Any of various tools, mechanisms, patterns, etc., for cutting, molding, shaping, or stamping. —**the die is cast** The irrevocable choice has been made. —*v.t.* To cut or stamp with or as with a die. [<L *datum* something given]

die-hard (dī′härd′) *n.* **1** One who fights to the last. **2** One who obstinately refuses to modify his views; esp., a rigid conservative. —*adj.* Strongly resistent to change; unyielding. Also **die′hard′.**

di·e·lec·tric (dī′ə·lek′trik) *Electri. adj.* Nonconducting. Also **di′e·lec′tri·cal.** —*n.* A dielectric substance, medium, or material. —**di′e·lec′tri·cal·ly** *adv.*

di·er·e·sis (dī·er′ə·sis) *n. pl.* **·ses** (-sēz) Two dots (¨) placed over the second of two adjacent vowels that are to be pronounced separately; often replaced by a hyphen: *reëlect, re-elect.* [<Gk. *diairesis* a division] —**di·e·ret·ic** (dī′ə·ret′ik) *adj.*

die·sel engine (dē′zəl) An internal-combustion engine in which fuel oil is ignited by the heat resulting from the high compression of air in the cylinder. Also **Diesel engine.** [<R. *Diesel,* 1858–1913, German inventor]

Di·es I·rae (dē′ez, dē′as; ir′ā, ir′ē) A medieval Latin hymn about the Day of Judgment, often used in certain masses for the dead. [L, day of wrath]

di·e·sis (dī′ə·sis) *n. Printing* The double dagger (‡), a reference mark for the third in a series. [<L, semitone]

di·et[1] (dī′ət) *n.* **1** Limited or prescribed food and drink, as for losing weight, for controlling disease, etc. **2** One's daily or normal food and drink. —*v.t.* **1** To regulate or restrict

the food and drink of. —*v.i.* **2** To take food and drink according to a regimen. [<Gk. *diaita* a way of living] —**di′et·er** *n.*

di·et[2] (dī′ət) *n.* **1** An official assembly. **2** *Usu. cap.* In certain countries, a legislative assembly. [<L *dies* a day]

di·e·tar·y (dī′ə·ter′ē) *n. pl.* **·tar·ies** **1** A system or regimen of dieting. **2** A daily or regulated allowance of food. —*adj.* Of or relating to diet: also **di·e·tet·ic** (dī′ə·tet′ik), **di′e·tet′i·cal.** —**di′e·tet′i·cal·ly** *adv.*

di·e·tet·ics (dī′ə·tet′iks) *n. pl.* (*construed as sing.*) The study of diet in relation to health.

di·e·ti·tian (dī′ə·tish′ən) *n.* One skilled in dietetics or in planning menus for large numbers of people. Also **di′e·ti′cian.**

diff. difference; different; differential.

dif·fer (dif′ər) *v.i.* **1** To be dissimilar; be distinct, as in kind or appearance: often with *from.* **2** To hold contrary or unlike views; disagree: often with *with.* [<L *dis-* apart + *ferre* carry] —**Syn. 1** vary, contrast. **2** dissent, clash.

dif·fer·ence (dif′ər·əns, dif′rəns) *n.* **1** The state, quality, or an instance of being different. **2** The way in which persons or things are different. **3** A distinguishing characteristic. **4** A disagreement, controversy, or quarrel. **5** Distinction; discrimination. **6** *Math.* The result obtained by subtraction. —**make a difference 1** To change or have an effect on something. **2** To distinguish or discriminate: with *between.* —*v.t.* **·enced, ·enc·ing** To make or mark as different; distinguish.

dif·fer·ent (dif′ər·ənt, dif′rənt) *adj.* **1** Not the same; distinct; other. **2** Not alike; dissimilar. **3** Not ordinary; unusual. **4** Various. [<L *differre* differ] —**dif′fer·ent·ly** *adv.* —**dif′fer·ent·ness** *n.* • In American usage, *from* is established as the idiomatic preposition to follow *different;* when, however, a clause follows the connective, *than* is gaining increasing acceptance: a result *different than* (= *from that which* or *from what*) had been expected.

dif·fer·en·tial (dif′ə·ren′shəl) *adj.* **1** Relating to, showing, or marked by a difference. **2** Being or making a difference; distinctive; distinguishing. **3** *Mech.* Characterized by a construction in which a movement is obtained by the difference in two motions in the same direction. —*n. Mech.* A differential gear. —**dif′fer·en′tial·ly** *adv.*

differential gear *Mech.* An arrangement of gears that has an input shaft and two output shafts and is set up so that the sum of the speeds of the output shafts is proportional to the speed of the input shaft.

dif·fer·en·ti·ate (dif′ə·ren′shē·āt) *v.* **·at·ed, ·at·ing** *v.t.* **1** To constitute a difference between; mark off. **2** To perceive and indicate the differences of or between. —*v.i.* **3** To discriminate; perceive a difference. **4** To acquire a distinct character; become specialized. —**dif′fer·en′ti·a′tion** *n.*

dif·fi·cult (dif′ə·kult, -kəlt) *adj.* **1** Hard to do or be done; arduous. **2** Hard to understand; perplexing. **3** Hard to persuade or overcome; stubborn. **4** Hard to please, deal with, or satisfy. —**dif′fi·cult·ly** *adv.* —**Syn. 1** onerous, irksome, laborious. **2** troublesome, complicated. **4** trying, perverse.

dif·fi·cul·ty (dif′ə·kul′tē, -kəl-) *n. pl.* **·ties** **1** The state or quality of being difficult. **2** Something difficult, as a problem, obstacle, objection, or hindrance. **3** *Often pl.* A distressing or embarrassing state of affairs. **4** A quarrel. [<L *dis-* away, not + *facilis* easy]

dif·fi·dent (dif′ə·dənt) *adj.* Showing or characterized by a lack of self-confidence; timid; shy. [<L *dis-* away + *fidere* to trust] —**dif′fi·dence** *n.* —**dif′fi·dent·ly** *adv.*

dif·fract (di·frakt′) *v.t.* **1** To separate into parts. **2** To subject to diffraction. [<L *dis-* away + *frangere* break] —**dif·frac′tive** *adj.* —**dif·frac′tive·ly** *adv.* —**dif·frac′tive·ness** *n.*

dif·frac·tion (di·frak′shən) *n. Physics* A change in the path of light or other wave motion, as sound, when passing near the edge of an obstacle, through slits, etc.

dif·fuse (di·fyōōz′) *v.t. & v.i.* **·fused, ·fus·ing** **1** To pour or send out so as to spread in all directions; permeate. **2** To subject to or spread by diffusion. —*adj.* (di·fyōōs′) **1** Excessively wordy. **2** Widely spread out. [<L *dis-* away, from + *fundere* pour] —**dif·fuse′ly** (-fyōōs′-) *adv.* —**dif·fuse′ness, dif·fus·er** or **dif·fus·or** (di·fyōō′zər) *n.* —**dif·fus′i·ble** *adj.*

dif·fu·sion (di-fyoō′zhən) n. 1 The act or process of diffusing, or the state of being diffused. 2 Wordiness; verbosity. 3 The scattering of light rays. 4 *Physics* The intermingling of the atoms or molecules of two substances initially unmixed but in contact.

dif·fu·sive (di-fyoō′siv) adj. 1 Tending to diffuse. 2 Characterized by diffusion. —**dif·fu′sive·ly** adv. —**dif·fu′sive·ness** n.

dig (dig) v. dug (*Archaic* digged), dig·ging v.t. 1 To break up, turn up, or remove (earth, etc.), as with a spade, claws, or the hands. 2 To make or form by or as by digging. 3 To obtain by digging: to *dig* clams. 4 To thrust into or against, as a tool, heel, or elbow. 5 To uncover by effort or study: often with *up* or *out*: to *dig* up evidence. 6 *Slang* To understand or like. —v.i. 7 To break or turn up earth, etc. 8 To force or make a way by or as by digging. 9 *Informal* To work hard and steadily; plod. —**dig in** 1 To dig trenches. 2 To entrench (oneself). 3 *Informal* To begin to work intensively. —n. *Informal* 1 A thrust; poke. 2 A sarcastic remark; slur. 3 An archeological excavation. 4 *pl.* Living quarters. [<OF *diguer* <Gmc.]

di·gest (di·jest′, dī-) v.t. 1 To convert (food) into forms that can be assimilated by the body. 2 To take in or assimilate mentally. 3 To arrange in systematic form, usu. by condensing. 4 To tolerate patiently; endure. 5 *Chem.* To soften or decompose by subjecting to heat or moisture. —v.i. 6 To be assimilated, as food. 7 To assimilate food. 8 To be subjected to heat, moisture, chemical agents, etc. —n. (dī′jest) A systematic, classified, and abridged collection of writings, as of news, scientific material, legal statutes, etc. [<L *dis-* away + *gerere* carry] —**di·gest′er** n.

di·gest·i·ble (di·jes′tə·bəl, dī-) adj. Capable of being digested or assimilated. —**di·gest′i·bil′i·ty** n.

di·ges·tion (di·jes′chən, dī-) n. 1 The process of digesting food. 2 The power to digest food. 3 The reception and assimilation of ideas.

di·ges·tive (di·jes′tive, dī-) adj. Pertaining or conducing to digestion. —n. Something to aid digestion.

dig·ger (dig′ər) n. 1 One who or that which digs. 2 Any implement or machine for digging.

dig·gings (dig′ingz) n. pl. 1 A mining or excavation site. 2 Materials dug out of such a site. 3 *Informal* Lodgings.

dig·it (dij′it) n. 1 A finger or toe. 2 Any one of the ten Arabic numeral symbols, 0 to 9. [<L *digitus* finger]

dig·i·tal (dij′ə·təl) adj. 1 Of, pertaining to, or like the fingers or digits. 2 DIGITATE. 3 Of, like, or pertaining to a digital computer. 4 Of or pertaining to a recording system in which sounds are transcribed as binary digits, to be replayed electronically with a very high degree of fidelity. —**dig′i·tal·ly** adv.

digital audio tape An audio tape recorded by means of digital recording, so that the sound is reproduced with little or no distortion.

digital computer An electronic computing machine which receives problems and processes the answers in numerical form.

dig·i·tal·is (dij′ə·tal′is, -tā′lis) n. 1 FOXGLOVE. 2 The dried leaves of foxglove. 3 A medicine obtained from these leaves, used as a heart stimulant. [<L, finger-shaped]

dig·i·tate (dij′ə·tāt) adj. 1 Having digits on the feet or hands. 2 Resembling a finger. 3 *Bot.* Having fingerlike leaflets. Also **dig′i·tat·ed** adj. —**dig′i·tate·ly** adv. • See LEAF.

dig·i·tize (dij′ə·tīz) v. ·tized, ·tiz·ing To represent musical sounds or factual data in digital form for computerized processing.

dig·ni·fied (dig′nə·fīd) adj. Having or characterized by dignity; stately. —**dig′ni·fied·ly** adv.

dig·ni·fy (dig′nə·fī) v.t. ·fied, ·fy·ing 1 To impart or add dignity to. 2 To give a high-sounding name to. [<L *dignus* worthy + *facere* make]

dig·ni·tar·y (dig′nə·ter′ē) n. pl. ·tar·ies One having an important position or office.

dig·ni·ty (dig′nə·tē) n. pl. ·ties 1 A grave or lofty stateliness, as of manner or language. 2 High rank, title, or position. 3 The state or quality of being excellent, worthy, or honorable: the *dignity* of work. 4 Pride or self-respect: beneath one's *dignity*. [<L *dignus* worthy]

di·graph (dī′graf, -gräf) n. Two characters representing a

single sound, as *oa* in *boat*. —**di·graph′ic** adj.

di·gress (di·gres′, dī-) v.i. To turn aside from the main subject in speaking or writing; ramble; wander. [<L *di-* away, apart + *gradi* go, step] —**di·gres′sion** n.

di·gres·sive (di·gres′iv, dī-) adj. Given to or marked by digression. —**di·gres′sive·ly** adv. —**di·gres′sive·ness** n.

di·he·dral (dī-hē′drəl) adj. Two-sided; formed by or having two plane faces. —n. 1 DIHEDRAL ANGLE. 2 The inclination of aircraft or bird wings. [<DI- + Gk. *hedra* base]

dihedral angle An angle formed by two intersecting planes.

dik-dik (dik′dik′) n. A small NE African antelope. [<native African name]

dike¹ (dīk) n. 1 An embankment to protect low land from being flooded. 2 A bank or dirt formed by the excavation of a ditch. 3 A protective obstruction; barrier. 4 A ditch. 5 A raised causeway. 6 *Brit.* A low wall for enclosing land. 7 *Geol.* A mass of igneous rock filling a fissure in other rocks. —v.t. diked, dik·ing 1 To furnish with a dike. 2 To drain by ditching. [<OE *dīc*] —**dik′er** n.

dike² (dīk) n. *Slang* LESBIAN. [?]

dil. dilute.

di·lap·i·date (di·lap′ə·dāt) v.t. & v.i. ·dat·ed, ·dat·ing To fall or cause to fall into partial ruin or decay. [<L *dis-* away + *lapidare* throw stones] —**di·lap′i·da′tion** n.

di·lap·i·dat·ed (di·lap′ə·dāt′id) adj. Being in a state of partial ruin or decay; run-down.

di·la·ta·tion (dil′ə·tā′shən, dī′lə-) n. 1 DILATION. 2 *Med.* An excessive enlargement of an organ, orifice, or part.

di·late (dī·lāt′, dī′-) v. ·lat·ed, ·lat·ing v.t. 1 To make wider, larger or expanded. —v.i. 2 To expand; become larger or wider. 3 To speak or write diffusely; enlarge; expatiate: with *on* or *upon*. [<L *dis-* apart + *latus* wide] —**di·lat′a·bil′i·ty** n. —**di·lat′a·ble** adj. —**di·la′tive** adj.

di·la·tion (dī·lā′shən, di-) n. 1 The process of dilating or the state of being dilated. 2 That which is dilated.

dil·a·to·ry (dil′ə·tôr′ē, -tō′rē) adj. 1 Given to or characterized by delay; tardy; slow. 2 Causing delay. —**dil′a·to′ri·ly** adv. —**dil′a·to′ri·ness** n.

dil·do (dil′dō) n. pl. ·dos A device used as an artificial penis for sexual stimulation. Also **dil′doe**. [?]

di·lem·ma (di·lem′ə) n. 1 A necessary choice between equally undesirable alternatives. 2 A situation requiring a choice but apparently lacking a satisfactory resolution. 3 *Logic* An argument presenting two (or more) alternatives, equally conclusive against the antagonist. —**the horns of a dilemma** The equally undesirable alternatives between which a choice must be made. [<Gk. *di-* two + *lēmma* a premise] —**dil·em·mat·ic** (dil′ə·mat′ik) adj. —Syn. 2 predicament, quandary.

dil·et·tan·te (dil′ə·tänt′, -tän′tē, -tan′tē, dil′ə·tänt′) n. pl. ·tantes, ·tan·ti (-tän′tē, -tan′tē) 1 A person whose interest in a subject is merely superficial or for amusement. 2 A person who loves the arts. —adj. Pertaining to or like a dilettante. [<Ital. *dilettare* to delight] —**dil′et·tan′tish** adj. —**dil′et·tan′te·ism, dil′et·tan′tism** n.

dil·i·gence¹ (dil′ə·jəns) n. 1 Assiduous application; industry. 2 Meticulous care or attention.

dil·i·gence² (dil′ə·jəns, *Fr.* dē·lē·zhäns′) n. A public stagecoach used esp. in 18th-century France.

dil·i·gent (dil′ə·jənt) adj. 1 Having or showing careful and sustained effort or application; industrious; hard-working. 2 Done or pursued painstakingly: *diligent* search. [<L *diligens* attentive] —**dil′i·gent·ly** adv.

dill (dil) n. 1 Any of various plants related to parsley and having aromatic, pungent seeds and leaves used as a flavoring. 2 The seeds or leaves. [<OE *dile*]

dill pickle A dill-flavored, pickled cucumber.

dil·ly-dal·ly (dil′ē-dal′ē) v.i. ·dal·lied, ·dal·ly·ing To waste time, esp. in indecision or vacillation. [Redupl. of DALLY]

di·lute (di·loōt′, dī′-) v.t. ·lut·ed, ·lut·ing 1 To make weaker or less concentrated by admixture. 2 To reduce the intensity, strength, or purity of (a color, drug, etc.) by admixture. —adj. Weak; diluted. [<L *dis-* away + *luere* wash] —**di·lute′ness** n.

di·lu·tion (di·loō′shən, dī-) n. 1 The act of diluting. 2 The state or degree of being diluted. 3 Something diluted.

di·lu·vi·al (di·loō′vē·əl) adj. Of, produced by, or pertaining to a flood. Also **di·lu′vi·an**. [<L *diluere* wash away]

dim (dim) adj. dim·mer, dim·mest 1 Obscure or somewhat

dark from faintness of light. **2** Not distinctly seen; shadowy. **3** Not clearly perceived or remembered; vague. **4** Not perceiving or understanding clearly; obtuse. **5** Faint, as a sound. **6** Lacking luster or brightness; dull. **7** Not encouraging or hopeful: *dim* prospects. —*v.t. & v.i.* **dimmed, dim·ming** To render or grow dim. [< OE *dim(m)]* —**dim′ly** *adv.* —**dim′ness** *n.*

dim. dimension; diminuendo; diminutive.

dime (dīm) *n.* A coin of the U.S. and Canada, equal to ten cents or one tenth of a dollar. [< L *decima* a tenth part]

di·men·sion (di·men′shən) *n.* **1** Any measurable extent or magnitude, as length, breadth, or thickness. **2** *pl.* Actual measurements, as of length or breadth. **3** *Often pl.* Scope; importance; magnitude. [< L *dimensio]* —**di·men′· sion·al** *adj.* —**di·men′sion·al·ly** *adv.*

dimin. diminuendo; diminutive.

di·min·ish (di·min′ish) *v.t.* **1** To make smaller or less; decrease, as in size, rank, importance, etc. **2** *Music* To lessen (an interval) by a half-step. —*v.i.* **3** To become smaller or less; dwindle; decrease. [< OF *diminuer* < OF *menusier* make smaller] —**di·min′ish·a·ble** *adj.* —**di·min′ish· ment** *n.*

di·min·u·en·do (di·min′yŏŏ·en′dō) *Music adj. & adv.* Gradually lessening in volume of sound: expressed by the sign >. —*n. pl.* **·dos** A diminuendo passage. [< L *diminuere* diminish]

dim·i·nu·tion (dim′ə·n(y)ŏŏ′shən) *n.* The act of diminishing, or the condition of being diminished.

di·min·u·tive (di·min′yə·tiv) *adj.* **1** Of relatively small size; tiny; little. **2** Expressing diminished size: said of certain suffixes. —*n.* **1** A word formed from another to express diminished size, or familiarity, affection, etc., as: *Johnny, piglet, babykin.* **2** A very small variety or form of anything.

dim·i·ty (dim′ə·tē) *n. pl.* **·ties** A sheer cotton fabric, usu. with a figured weave, used for dresses, curtains, etc. [< Gk. *dimitos* a double thread]

dim·mer (dim′ər) *n.* **1** Anything that dims. **2** A control for varying the brightness of one or more electric lights.

dim-out (dim′out′) *n.* A reduction of night lighting in a city or certain area.

dim·ple (dim′pəl) *n.* **1** A slight, natural depression on a surface of the body, as on the cheek or chin. **2** A similar depression on any smooth surface. —*v.t. & v.i.* **dim·pled, dim·pling** To mark with dimples; form dimples. [ME *dympull]* —**dim′ply** *adj.*

dim-wit (dim′wit′) *n. Slang* A stupid or simple-minded person. —**dim′wit′ted** *adj.* —**dim′wit′ted·ly** *adv.* —**dim′wit′· ted·ness** *n.*

din (din) *n.* A loud continuous noise or clamor; a rattling or clattering sound. —*v.* **dinned, din·ning** *v.t.* **1** To assail with confusing noise. **2** To urge or press insistently. —*v.i.* **3** To make a din. [< OE *dyne]*

dine (dīn) *v.* **dined, din·ing** *v.i.* **1** To eat dinner. **2** To eat: with *on* or *upon.* —*v.t.* **3** To entertain at dinner. [< OF *disner]*

din·er (dī′nər) *n.* **1** One who dines. **2** A railroad dining car. **3** An informal restaurant usu. with booths and an eating counter and having a relatively long, narrow shape.

di·nette (dī·net′) *n.* A small dining area; dining alcove.

ding (ding) *v.t.* **1** To ring; sound, as a bell. **2** *Informal* To instill by constant repetition; din. —*v.i.* **3** To ring or sound. **4** *Informal* To speak with constant repetition. —*n.* The sound of a bell or a sound like it. [Imit.]

ding·dong (ding′dong′, -dông′) *n.* The repeated, ringing sound of a bell. —*adj. Informal* Energetically and closely contested, as a race. —*v.i.* To make the sound of ding-dong. [Imit.]

din·ghy (ding′gē, ding′ē) *n. pl.* **·ghies** **1** Any of various small rowing boats, as a small skiff, a ship's boat, etc. **2** An inflatable rubber life raft. Also **din′gey.** [< Hind. *dīngī* boat]

din·go (ding′gō) *n. pl.* **din·goes** The native wild dog of Australia. [< native Australian name]

din·gy (din′jē) *adj.* **din·gi·er, din·gi·est** **1.** Of a drab color, as if soiled; dull. **2** Grimy; shabby. [?] —**din′gi·ly** *adv.* —**din′gi· ness** *n.*

dining car A railway car in which meals are served.

dining room A room in which meals are served.

dink·ey (ding′kē) *n. Informal* A small engine used for shunting freight. [< DINKY]

dink·y (ding′kē) *adj.* **dink·i·er, dink·i·est** *Informal* Tiny; insignificant. [?]

din·ner (din′ər) *n.* **1** The principal meal of the day. **2** A banquet in honor of a person or event. **3** A formal feast. [< OF *disner* dine]

dinner jacket A tuxedo jacket.

din·ner·ware (din′ər·wâr′) *n.* The dishes used in a household for serving food.

di·no·saur (dī′nə·sôr) *n.* Any of a group of four-limbed, in some species gigantic, reptiles that became extinct by the end of the Mesozoic period. [< Gk. *deinos* terrible + *sauros* lizard] —**di′no·sau′ri·an** *adj., n.*

dint (dint) *n.* **1** A dent. **2** Active force; effort: now chiefly in the phrase **by dint of.** —*v.t.* **1** To make a dent in. **2** To drive in forcibly. [< OE *dynt* blow]

dioc. diocesan; diocese.

di·o·cese (dī′ə·sēs, -sis) *n.* The territory or the churches under a bishop's jurisdiction. [< Gk. *dioikēsis,* orig. management of a house] —**di·oc·e·san** (dī·os′ə·sən, dī′ə·sē′sən) *adj.*

di·ode (dī′ōd) *n. Electronics* A circuit element which permits current to pass in one direction only; a rectifier. [< DI(A)- + Gk. *hodos* a road, way]

di·oe·cious (dī·ē′shəs) *adj. Bot.* Having separate male and female flowers. [< DI- + Gk. *oikia* house, dwelling] — **di·oe′cious·ly** *adv.* —**di·oe′cious·ness** *n.*

Di·o·ny·sus (dī′ə·nī′səs) *Gk. Myth.* The god of wine and fertility. Also **Di′o·ny′sos.** —**Di·o·nys·ian** (dī′ə·nish′ən, -nis′ē·ən, -nī′sē·ən), **Di′o·nys′i·ac** (-nis′ē·ak) *adj.*

di·op·ter (dī·op′tər) *n. Optics* The unit for measuring the refractive power of a lens, mirror, etc., determined by the reciprocal of its focal length in meters. Also **di·op′tre.** [< Gk. *dioptra* an optical instrument] —**di·op′tric** or **·tri·cal** *adj.*

di·o·ra·ma (dī′ə·rä′mə, -ram′ə) *n.* **1** A miniature scene painted on cloth transparencies and so lit that changes in the scene are produced in view of the spectators. **2** A group of modeled figures, for exhibition, set in a naturalistic foreground against a painted background. [< Gk. *dia-* through + *horama* a sight] —**di·o·ram·ic** (dī′ə·ram′ik) *adj.*

di·ox·ide (dī·ok′sīd, -sid) *n.* An oxide containing two atoms of oxygen to the molecule.

dip (dip) *v.* **dipped, dip·ping** *v.t.* **1** To put or let down into a liquid momentarily. **2** To lift up and out by scooping, bailing, etc. **3** To lower and then raise, as a flag in salute. **4** To baptize by immersion. **5** To plunge (animals) into a disinfectant. **6** To dye by immersion. **7** *Chem.* To coat (a metallic surface) by immersion. **8** To make (candles) by repeatedly immersing wicks in wax or tallow. —*v.i.* **9** To plunge into and come out of water or other liquid, esp. quickly. **10.** To plunge one's hand or a receptacle into water, etc., so as to take something out. **11** To withdraw or take part of something saved, etc.: with *into.* **12** To sink or go down suddenly. **13** To go down; decline. **14** To engage in or inquire into something slightly or superficially. —*n.* **1** The act of dipping. **2** A liquid or sauce into which something is to be dipped. **3** An amount removed by dipping. **4** An object used for dipping. **5** A brief swim. **6** A sloping downward or inclination; also, the amount of this. **7** A slight depression or hollow. **8** An abrupt downward movement; drop. **9** A candle made by dipping. **10** *Slang* A pickpocket. [< OE *dyppan]*

diph·the·ri·a (dif·thir′ē·ə, dip-) *n.* An acute contagious disease caused by a bacillus and characterized by the formation of a false membrane in the upper air passages. [< Gk. *diphthera* leather, membrane] —**diph·the·rit·ic** (dif′thə· rit′ik, dip′-), **diph′the′ri·al, diph·the′ric** *adj.*

diph·thong (dif′thông, -thong, dip′-) *n.* A combination of two vowel sounds in one syllable, as *oi* in *coil* and *ou* in *doubt,* or as *i* in *fine* and *a* in *name.* [< Gk. *di-* two + *phthongos* sound] —**diph·thon′gal** *adj.*

diph·thong·ize (dif′thông·īz, -thong-, dip′-) *v.* **·ized, ·iz· ing** *v.t.* **1** To pronounce as a diphthong. —*v.i.* **2** To become a diphthong. —**diph′thong·i·za′tion,** *n.*

dipl. diplomatic; diplomatic.

di·plo·ma (di·plō′mə) *n.* **1** A certificate bestowed by a school, college, or university on those who have completed

diplomacy   201   disability

a course of study or have earned a degree. **2** A certificate bestowing some honor or privilege. [< Gk. *diplōma* paper folded double, a letter]

di·plo·ma·cy (di·plō′mə·sē) *n. pl.* **·cies 1** The art, science, or practice of conducting negotiations between nations. **2** Tact or skill in dealing with people.

dip·lo·mat (dip′lə·mat) *n.* **1** A person who represents his country in its official relations with other countries. **2** A person who is skilled and tactful in dealing with others. Also **di·plo·ma·tist** (di·plō′mə·tist). [< L *diploma* a document]

dip·lo·mat·ic (dip′lə·mat′ik) *adj.* **1** Of or pertaining to diplomats or to diplomacy. **2** Skillful and tactful in dealing with people. —**dip′lo·mat′i·cal·ly** *adv.*

dip·per (dip′ər) *n.* **1** A person employed in dipping. **2** A long-handled, cup-shaped utensil for dipping liquids, etc. **3** Any of several American diving birds, esp. the water ouzel.

Dip·per (dip′ər) *n.* Either of two constellations, the Big Dipper or the Little Dipper.

dip·so·ma·ni·a (dip′sə·mā′nē·ə) *n.* An uncontrollable craving for alcoholic drink. [< Gk. *dipsa* thirst + -MANIA] —**dip′so·ma′ni·ac** (-ak) *n.* —**dip·so·ma·ni·a·cal** (dip′sə·mə·nī′ə·kəl) *adj.*

dip·ter·ous (dip′tər·əs) *adj.* **1** Of or pertaining to an order of insects having a single pair of membranous wings, including the flies, gnats, mosquitoes, etc. **2** *Bot.* Two-winged, as certain seeds and fruits. [< Gk. *dipteros* two-winged]

dip·tych (dip′tik) *n.* **1** A pair of writing tablets hinged together and used in ancient Greece and Rome. **2** A double picture or design on a pair of hinged panels. [< Gk. *diptycha* pair of tablets]

dir. director.

dire (dīr) *adj.* **dir·er, dir·est 1** Extremely calamitous; dreadful; terrible. **2** Urgent; exigent: *dire* necessity. [< L *dirus* fearful] —**dire′ly** *adv.* —**dire′ness** *n.*

di·rect (di·rekt′, dī-) *v.t.* **1** To control or conduct the affairs of; manage; govern. **2** To order or instruct with authority; command. **3** *Music* To lead as a conductor. **4** To tell (someone) the way. **5** To cause to move, face, or go in a desired direction; aim: He *directed* his gaze toward her. **6** To indicate the destination of, as a letter. **7** To intend, as remarks to be heard by a person; address: Did you *direct* that remark at me? **8 a** To supervise the filming or staging of (a play, motion picture, etc.). **b** To supervise the performance of (actors, etc.). —*v.i.* **9** To give commands or guidance. **10** To supervise the production of a play, motion picture, etc. —*adj.* **1** Having or being the straightest course; shortest; nearest. **2** Free from intervening agencies or conditions; immediate; first-hand. **3** Unbroken in the line of descent; lineal. **4** Complete; total: the *direct* opposite. **5** Straightforward; candid; plain. **6** *Electr.* Flowing in one direction only: *direct* current. —*adv.* In a direct manner; directly. [< L *dis-* apart + *regere* set straight] —**di·rect′ness** *n.* —**Syn.** **1** supervise, run, guide, oversee.

direct discourse Language quoted in the exact words of the speaker or writer.

di·rec·tion (di·rek′shən, dī-) *n.* **1** The act of directing; supervision. **2** *Usu. pl.* Information or instructions for doing something, going somewhere, etc. **3** An order or command. **4** The position or course of movement of a point or object in its spatial relationship to something else: to go in a northerly *direction*. **5** Trend, tendency, way, etc.: a new *direction* in medicine. **6** The art or act of directing actors, musicians, films, plays, etc.

di·rec·tion·al (di·rek′shən·əl, dī-) *adj.* **1** Of, pertaining to, or indicating a direction in space. **2** *Telecom.* Of or having a preferred direction or directions of radiation or reception, as an antenna.

direction finder *Telecom.* A device with which the direction of radio signals may be determined.

di·rec·tive (di·rek′tiv, dī-) *n.* An official order or regulation. —*adj.* That directs or points out, rules, or governs.

di·rect·ly (di·rekt′lē, dī-) *adv.* **1** In a direct line or manner. **2** Without medium, agent, or go-between. **3** Immedi-

ately; as soon as possible. **4** Exactly; precisely. —*conj. Brit.* As soon as.

direct mail Mail sent directly to individuals that promotes the sale of merchandise or services or solicits contributions. —**di·rect′-mail′** *adj.*

direct object The word or words that indicate the person or thing receiving the action of a transitive verb, as *ball* in *She threw him the ball.*

di·rec·tor (di·rek′tər, dī-) *n.* **1** One who or that which directs. **2** A member of a governing body, as of a club or corporation. **3** A conductor of an orchestra. **4** One who directs or stages a film, play, etc. —**di·rec′tor·ship′** *n.* —**di·rec′tress** *n. Fem.*

di·rec·tor·ate (di·rek′tər·it, dī-) *n.* **1** A body of directors. **2** The office of a director.

di·rec·to·ri·al (di·rek′tôr′ē·əl, -tō′rē-, dī-) *adj.* **1** That directs; directive. **2** Pertaining to a director or directorate.

di·rec·to·ry (di·rek′tər·ē, dī-) *n. pl.* **·ries 1** An alphabetical or classified list, as of the names and addresses of the inhabitants of a city. **2** A book of rules. **3** A body of directors; directorate. —*adj.* Containing directions.

direct primary A primary election in which candidates for office are nominated directly by the voters and not by a body of delegates.

direct tax A tax, as on income or property, levied directly on the taxpayer.

dire·ful (dīr′fəl) *adj.* Most dire; dreadful; terrible. —**dire′ful·ly** *adv.* —**dire′ful·ness** *n.*

dirge (dûrj) *n.* **1** A song or melody expressing grief and mourning. **2** A funeral hymn. [< L *dirige* direct (imperative), the first word of the antiphon (*Psalms* 5:8) of matins in the Latin burial office]

dir·i·gi·ble (dir′ə·jə·bəl) *n.* A lighter-than-air aircraft

Dirigible *(rigid type)*

equipped with means for propulsion and steering. —*adj.* That may be directed or controlled. [< L *dirigere* to direct + -IBLE]

dirk (dûrk) *n.* A dagger or poniard. —*v.t.* To stab with a dirk. [?]

dirn·dl (dûrn′dəl) *n.* **1** A dress with a full skirt gathered to a tight bodice. **2** Such a skirt without the bodice: also **dirndl skirt.** [< G *Dirne* girl]

dirt (dûrt) *n.* **1** Any foul or filthy substance, as mud, grime, etc.; filth. **2** Loose earth or soil. **3** Something mean or contemptible. **4** Obscenity in speech, writing, or pictures. **5** Obscene gossip. **6** In mining, washed-down soil, gravel, etc., containing precious metal. —*adj.* Made of earth. [< ON *drit*]

dirt-cheap (dûrt′chēp′) *adj. Informal* Very inexpensive. —*adv.* At a low cost.

dirt farmer *Informal* A farmer who does his own work.

dirt·y (dûr′tē) *adj.* **dirt·i·er, dirt·i·est 1** Unclean; filthy. **2** Causing one to be covered with dirt: a *dirty* job. **3** Not clear; clouded; muddy: said of colors. **4** Obscene. **5** Despicable; base; contemptible. **6** Not sportsmanlike or fair. **7** Conveying anger or annoyance: a *dirty* look. **8** Producing excessive fallout: said of nuclear explosions. **9** Stormy; foul, as weather. —*v.t. & v.i.* **dirt·ied, dirt·y·ing** To make or become dirty or soiled. —**dirt′i·ly** *adv.* —**dirt′i·ness** *n.*

Dis (dis) *Rom. Myth.* **1** The god of the lower world. **2** The kingdom of the dead.

dis-¹ *prefix* **1** Apart; away from: *dismiss.* **2** The reverse of or the undoing of: *disarm.* **3** Deprivation of some quality, power, rank, etc.: *disable.* **4** Not: *distasteful.* **5** Completely; thoroughly (with a negative word): *disannul.* [< L]

dis-² *prefix* Var. of DI- [< Gk. *dis* twice]

dis. distance, distant.

dis·a·bil·i·ty (dis′ə·bil′ə·tē) *n. pl.* **·ties 1** That which disables; an infirmity or handicap. **2** Lack of ability; inability. **3** Legal incapacity or inability to act.

add, āce, câre, pälm; end, ēven; it, īce; odd, ōpen, ôrder; tŏŏk, pōōl; up, bûrn; ə = a in *above*; u in *focus*; yōō = u in *fuse*; oil; pout; check; go; ring; thin; this; zh, *vision*. < derived from; ? origin uncertain or unknown.

dis·a·ble (dis-ā′bəl) v.t. ·a·bled, ·a·bling 1 To render incapable or unable; cripple. 2 To render legally incapable, as of inheriting property, etc. —**dis·a′ble·ment** n.

dis·a·buse (dis′ə-byōōz′) v.t. ·a·bused, ·a·bus·ing To rid of a false notion or impression.

dis·ad·van·tage (dis′əd-van′tij, -vän′-) n. 1 An unfavorable condition, element, or circumstance; drawback; hindrance. 2 Loss; detriment. —v.t. ·taged, ·tag·ing To injure the interest of; prejudice; hinder.

dis·ad·van·taged (dis′əd-van′təjd) adj. Having less than what is regarded as basic or minimal for decent living, as money, social equality, etc.; underprivileged.

dis·ad·van·ta·geous (dis-ad′van-tā′jəs) adj. Attended with disadvantage; detrimental; inconvenient. —**dis·ad′·van·ta′geous·ly** adv.

dis·af·fect (dis′ə-fekt′) v.t. To destroy or weaken the affection or loyalty of; alienate. —**dis′af·fec′tion** n.

dis·af·fect·ed (dis′ə-fek′tid) adj. Alienated in feeling or loyalty; estranged. —**dis′af·fect′ed·ly** adv.

dis·a·gree (dis′ə-grē′) v.i. ·a·greed, ·a·gree·ing 1 To vary in opinion; differ; dissent. 2 To quarrel. 3 To fail to agree or harmonize, as facts. 4 To produce an unfavorable effect, as food or climate: with with.

dis·a·gree·a·ble (dis′ə-grē′ə-bəl) adj. 1 Repugnant to taste, sentiment, opinion, or the senses; displeasing. 2 Not pleasant or agreeable; bad-tempered. —**dis′a·gree′a·ble·ness**, **dis′a·gree′a·bil′i·ty** n. —**dis′a·gree′a·bly** adv.

dis·a·gree·ment (dis′ə-grē′mənt) n. 1 Failure to agree; disparity; variance. 2 A difference of opinion. 3 A quarrel; altercation.

dis·al·low (dis′ə-lou′) v.t. 1 To refuse to allow or permit. 2 To reject as untrue or invalid. —**dis′al·low′ance** n.

dis·ap·pear (dis′ə-pir′) v.i. 1 To pass from sight or view; fade away; vanish. 2 To cease to exist: His anger disappeared. —**dis′ap·pear′ance** n.

dis·ap·point (dis′ə-point′) v.t. 1 To fail to fulfill the expectation, hope, or desire of. 2 To prevent the fulfillment of (a hope or plan); frustrate. [< OF des- away + appointer arrange, appoint] —**dis′ap·point′ing·ly** adv.

dis·ap·point·ment (dis′ə-point′mənt) n. 1 The state, condition, or sense of being disappointed. 2 A person or thing that disappoints.

dis·ap·pro·ba·tion (dis-ap′rə-bā′shən) n. Disapproval; unfavorable judgment.

dis·ap·prove (dis′ə-prōōv′) v. ·proved, ·prov·ing v.t. 1 To regard with disfavor or censure; condemn. 2 To refuse assent to; decline to approve. —v.i. 3 To have or express an unfavorable opinion: often with of. —**dis′ap·prov′al** n. —**dis′ap·prov′ing·ly** adv. —**Syn.** 1 dislike, object to, frown upon, denounce, disparage.

dis·arm (dis-ärm′) v.t. 1 To deprive of weapons. 2 To render harmless. 3 To allay or reduce suspicion, aloofness, or hostility. —v.i. 4 To lay down arms. 5 To reduce or restrict the size of armed forces.

dis·ar·ma·ment (dis-är′mə-mənt) n. 1 The act of disarming. 2 The reduction or limitation of armed forces or of certain types of weapons.

dis·arm·ing (dis-är′ming) adj. Removing suspicion, aloofness, hostility, etc.: a disarming smile. —**dis·arm′ing·ly** adv.

dis·ar·range (dis′ə-rānj′) v.t. ·ranged, ·rang·ing To disturb the arrangement of. —**dis′ar·range′ment** n.

dis·ar·ray (dis′ə-rā′) n. 1 Lack of order or tidiness; confusion. 2 Disordered or insufficient dress. —v.t. To throw into disorder, as an army.

dis·as·sem·ble (dis′ə-sem′bəl) v.t. ·bled, ·bling To take apart. —**dis′as·sem′bly** n.

dis·as·so·ci·ate (dis′ə-sō′shē-āt) v.t. ·at·ed, ·at·ing To separate from association: He wished to disassociate himself from the government's policy. —**dis′as·so′ci·a′tion** n.

dis·as·ter (di-zas′tər, -zäs′-) n. Any sudden event that causes great damage; a great misfortune or calamity. [< MF des- away + astre a star]

dis·as·trous (di-zas′trəs, -zäs′-) adj. Causing or accompanied by disaster; calamitous. —**dis·as′trous·ly** adv. —**dis·as′trous·ness** n.

dis·a·vow (dis′ə-vou′) v.t. To disclaim responsibility for or approval of; repudiate. —**dis′a·vow′al**, **dis′a·vow′er** n.

dis·band (dis-band′) v.t. 1 To break up (an organization,

etc.). 2 To remove from military service. —v.i. 3 To cease to be an organization. —**dis·band′ment** n.

dis·bar (dis-bär′) v.t. ·barred, ·bar·ring To deprive of the status of a lawyer; expel from the bar. —**dis·bar′ment** n.

dis·be·lief (dis′bi-lēf′) n. A lack of belief.

dis·be·lieve (dis′bi-lēv′) v.t. & v.i. ·lieved, ·liev·ing To refuse to believe; deem false. —**dis′be·liev′er** n.

dis·bur·den (dis-bûr′dən) v.t. 1 To relieve (someone or something) of a burden; unload. 2 To get rid of (a burden). —v.i. 3 To put off a burden.

dis·burse (dis-bûrs′) v.t. ·bursed, ·burs·ing To pay out; expend. [< OF des- away + bourse a purse] —**dis·burs′a·ble** adj. —**dis·burse′ment**, **dis·burs′er** n.

disc (disk) n. 1 A phonograph record. 2 DISK. [Var. of DISK]

disc. discount; discover; discovered.

dis·card (dis-kärd′) v.t. 1 To cast aside as useless or undesirable; reject. 2 In card games, to throw out (a card or cards) from one's hand; also, to play (a card, other than a trump, of a different suit from the suit led). —v.i. 3 In card games, to throw out a card or cards from one's hand. —n. (dis′kärd) 1 The act of discarding. 2 A card or cards discarded. 3 A person or thing cast off.

dis·cern (di-sûrn′, di-zûrn′) v.t. 1 To perceive, as with sight or mind; apprehend. 2 To discriminate mentally; recognize subtle differences. —v.i. 3 To distinguish; discriminate. [< L dis- apart + cernere to separate] —**dis·cern′er**, **dis·cern′ment** n. —**dis·cern′i·ble** adj. —**Syn.** 1 recognize, detect, discover. 2 distinguish.

dis·cern·ing (di-sûr′ning, -zûr′-) adj. Quick to discern; discriminating; penetrating. —**dis·cern′ing·ly** adv.

dis·charge (dis-chärj′) v. ·charged, ·charg·ing v.t. 1 To unload; remove the contents of: to discharge a ship. 2 To remove or send forth: to discharge passengers. 3 To send forth; emit (fluid). 4 To shoot or fire, as a gun, bow, shot, or arrow. 5 To dismiss from office; fire. 6 To release, as a prisoner, soldier, or patient. 7 To relieve of duty: to discharge a jury. 8 To perform or fulfill the functions and duties of (a trust, office, etc.). 9 To pay (a debt) or meet (an obligation or duty). 10 Electr. To free of an electrical charge. —v.i. 11 To get rid of a load, burden, etc. 12 To go off, as a cannon. 13 To give or send forth contents. 14 Electr. To lose a charge of electricity. —n. (also dis′chärj) 1 The act of discharging or the state or condition of being discharged. 2 That which discharges, as a certificate releasing one from military service. 3 That which is discharged, as blood from a wound. 4 Electr. a The equalization of potential between terminals of a charged capacitor when connected by a conductor. b A disruptive flow of current through a dielectric, esp. through a gas. —**dis·charge′a·ble** adj. —**dis·charg′er** n.

dis·ci·ple (di-sī′pəl) n. 1 A student or follower of a teacher or a doctrine. 2 One of the 12 chosen companions and apostles of Jesus. [< L discipulus] —**dis·ci′ple·ship** n.

dis·ci·pli·nar·i·an (dis′ə-plə-nâr′ē-ən) n. One who is strict in disciplining others.

dis·ci·pli·nar·y (dis′ə-plə-ner′ē) adj. 1 Of, relating to, or having the nature of discipline. 2 Used in discipline.

dis·ci·pline (dis′ə-plin) n. 1 Systematic and rigorous training of the mental, moral, and physical powers by instruction and exercise. 2 The result of this. 3 Self-control. 4 Control over others, as by enforcing obedience. 5 Orderly conduct, etc., resulting from such control. 6 Punishment; chastisement. 7 A specific branch of learning or knowledge. 8 A system of rules, as of a church. 9 A small, penitential whip or scourge. —v.t. ·plined, ·plin·ing 1 To train to obedience or subjection. 2 To drill; educate. 3 To punish or chastise. [< L disciplina instruction < discipulus disciple] —**dis′ci·plin·er** n.

disc jockey A person who conducts and announces a radio or television program that presents recorded music, usu. interspersed with comments and commercials.

dis·claim (dis-klām′) v.t. 1 To deny; repudiate; disavow. 2 To renounce a right or claim to.

dis·claim·er (dis-klā′mər) n. A disclaiming act, notice, or instrument.

dis·close (dis-klōz′) v.t. ·closed, ·clos·ing 1 To lay bare; uncover. 2 To make known; divulge. —**dis·clos′er** n.

dis·clo·sure (dis-klō′zhər) n. 1 The act or process of disclosing. 2 Anything disclosed.

dis·co (dis'kō) *n. pl.* **·cos** *Informal* DISCOTHÈQUE.

dis·coid (dis'koid) *adj.* Pertaining to or like a disk or disks. —*n.* A disk or disklike object.

dis·col·or (dis·kul'ər) *v.t.* **1** To give an unnatural color to; stain. —*v.i.* **2** To become stained, faded, or of a changed color. —**dis·col'or·a'tion, dis·col'or·ment** *n.*

dis·com·fit (dis·kum'fit) *v.t.* **1** To defeat the plans or purposes of; frustrate. **2** To embarrass. **3** To vanquish. [< OF *des-* away + *confire* prepare] —**dis·com'fi·ture** *n.*

dis·com·fort (dis·kum'fərt) *n.* **1** The state of being uncomfortable; uneasiness. **2** That which causes an uncomfortable condition. —*v.t.* To make uneasy; trouble.

dis·com·mode (dis'kə·mōd') *v.t.* **·mod·ed, ·mod·ing** To cause inconvenience to. [< DIS + L *commodus* convenient] —Syn. bother, trouble, disturb.

dis·com·pose (dis'kəm·pōz') *v.t.* **·posed, ·pos·ing** **1** To disturb the composure of; make uneasy. **2** To disorder or disarrange.

dis·com·po·sure (dis'kəm·pō'zhər) *n.* The state of being discomposed.

dis·con·cert (dis'kən·sûrt') *v.t.* **1** To cause to lose one's composure or confidence; confuse; upset. **2** To frustrate, as a plan. [< MF *dis-* apart + *concerter* agree] —**dis·con·cert'ing** *adj.* —**dis'con·cert'ing·ly** *adv.*

dis·con·nect (dis'kə·nekt') *v.t.* To undo or break the connection of; detach; separate.

dis·con·nect·ed (dis'kə·nek'tid) *adj.* **1** Not connected; disjointed. **2** Incoherent; rambling. —**dis'con·nect'ed·ly** *adv.* —**dis'con·nect'ed·ness** *n.*

dis·con·so·late (dis·kon'sə·lit) *adj.* **1** Without consolation; inconsolable; sad. **2** Gloomy; cheerless. [< L *dis-* not + *consolari* console] —**dis·con'so·late·ly** *adv.* —**dis·con'so·late·ness, dis·con'so·la'tion** *n.*

dis·con·tent (dis'kən·tent') *n.* Lack of contentment; dissatisfaction: also **dis'con·tent'ment.** —*v.t.* To made discontented.

dis·con·tent·ed (dis'kən·tent'əd) *adj.* Dissatisfied; not content. —**dis'con·tent'ed·ly** *adv.* —**dis'con·tent'ed·ness** *n.*

dis·con·tin·ue (dis'kən·tin'yōō) *v.* **·tin·ued, ·tin·u·ing** *v.t.* **1** To break off or cease from; stop. **2** To cease using, receiving, etc. —*v.i.* **3** To come to an end; stop. —**dis'con·tin'u·ance, dis'con·tin'u·a'tion** *n.*

dis·con·ti·nu·i·ty (dis'kon·tə·nyōō'ə·tē) *n.* **1** Lack of continuity. **2** A gap or interruption.

dis·con·tin·u·ous (dis'kən·tin'yōō·əs) *adj.* Not continuous; interrupted; broken. —**dis'con·tin'u·ous·ly** *adv.* —**dis'con·tin'u·ous·ness** *n.*

dis·cord (dis'kôrd) *n.* **1** Lack of agreement; contention; strife. **2** *Music* A dissonant combination of tones; dissonance. **3** Harsh or disagreeable noises. —*v.i.* To be out of accord or harmony; clash. [< L *dis-* away + *cor, cordis* heart]

dis·cor·dant (dis·kôr'dənt) *adj.* **1** Contradictory; inconsistent. **2** Quarrelsome. **3** Not harmonious; dissonant. —**dis·cor'dance, dis·cor'dan·cy** *n.* —**dis·cor'dant·ly** *adv.*

dis·co·thèque (dis'kə·tek, dis·kə·tek') *n.* A night club or other public place offering recorded music for dancing. [F, lit., record library]

dis·count (dis'kount) *n.* **1** An amount deducted from a sum to be paid. **2** In lending money, the interest deducted in advance. **3** The act of discounting. **4** The rate of discount. —**at a discount** At less than the face value or amount regularly charged. —*v.t.* (dis'kount, dis·kount') **1** To deduct, as a portion of an amount owed. **2** To buy or sell (a bill or note) for face value less interest. **3** To fail to heed; disregard. **4** To believe only part of. **5** To take into account beforehand so as to lessen value, effect, enjoyment, etc. —*v.i.* **6** To lend money, deducting the interest beforehand. [< L *dis-* away + *computare* compute] —**dis'count·a·ble** *adj.* —**dis'count·er** *n.*

dis·coun·te·nance (dis·koun'tə·nəns) *v.t.* **·nanced, ·nanc·ing** **1** To look upon with disfavor. **2** To abash; disconcert. [< MF *des-* away + *contenancer* to favor]

dis·cour·age (dis·kûr'ij) *v.t.* **·aged, ·ag·ing** **1** To deprive of courage; dispirit; dishearten. **2** To deter or dissuade: with *from.* **3** To obstruct; hinder. **4** To attempt to prevent by

disapproval. —**dis·cour'age·ment, dis·cour'ag·er** *n.* —**dis·cour'ag·ing** *adj.* —**dis·cour'ag·ing·ly** *adv.*

dis·course (dis'kôrs, dis·kôrs') *n.* **1** Familiar conversation; talk. **2** Formal expression of thought, oral or written. —*v.i.* (dis·kôrs') **·coursed, ·cours·ing** **1** To set forth one's thoughts and conclusions concerning a subject: with *on* or *upon.* **2** To converse; confer. [< L *dis-* apart + *cursus* a running] —**dis·cours'er** *n.*

dis·cour·te·ous (dis·kûr'tē·əs) *adj.* Showing discourtesy; rude. —**dis·cour'te·ous·ly** *adv.* —**dis·cour'te·ous·ness** *n.*

dis·cour·te·sy (dis·kûr'tə·sē) *n. pl.* **·sies** **1** Rudeness; impoliteness. **2** An impolite act or remark.

dis·cov·er (dis·kuv'ər) *v.t.* To come upon, find out, make known, or realize, esp. for the first time. [< OF *des-* away + *covrir* to cover] —**dis·cov'er·a·ble** *adj.* —**dis·cov'er·er** *n.*

dis·cov·er·y (dis·kuv'ər·ē) *n. pl.* **·er·ies** **1** The act of discovering. **2** Something discovered.

dis·cred·it (dis·kred'it) *v.t.* **1** To disbelieve. **2** To injure the credit or reputation of. **3** To show to be unworthy of belief or confidence. —*n.* **1** Distrust or disbelief. **2** Dishonor or disgrace. **3** Something that causes distrust or disgrace. —**dis·cred'it·a·ble** *adj.* —**dis·cred'it·a·bly** *adv.*

dis·creet (dis·krēt') *adj.* Showing consideration of the privacy or trust of others, as by suppressing curious inquiry; prudent; circumspect. [< LL *discretus* pp. of *discernere* discern] —**dis·creet'ly** *adv.* —**dis·creet'ness** *n.*

dis·crep·an·cy (dis·krep'ən·sē) *n. pl.* **·cies** **1** Disagreement or difference; inconsistency. **2** An example of this. [< L < *dis-* away + *crepare* creak] —**dis·crep'ant** *adj.* —**dis·crep'ant·ly** *adv.*

dis·crete (dis·krēt') *adj.* **1** Distinct or separate. **2** Made up of distinct parts or separate units. [< LL *discretus.* See DISCREET.] —**dis·crete'ly** *adv.* —**dis·crete'ness** *n.*

dis·cre·tion (dis·kresh'ən) *n.* **1** The quality of being discreet; prudence; caution. **2** Liberty of action; freedom in the exercise of judgment. —**at one's discretion** According to one's own judgment.

dis·cre·tion·ar·y (dis·kresh'ə·ner'ē) *adj.* Left to one's own judgment. Also **dis·cre'tion·al.**

dis·crim·i·nate (dis·krim'ə·nāt) *v.* **·nat·ed ·nat·ing** *v.i.* **1** To act with partiality. **2** To observe a difference. —*v.t.* **3** To discern the difference in or between. **4** To make or constitute a difference in or between. —*adj.* (-nit) Noting or involving differences. [< L *dis-* apart + *crimen* a judgment] —**dis·crim'i·nat'ing** *adj.* —**dis·crim'i·nat'ing·ly** *adv.* —**dis·crim'i·nat'or** *n.*

dis·crim·i·na·tion (dis·krim'ə·nā'shən) *n.* **1** The act of discriminating or the ability to discriminate. **2** Biased or unfair judgments or treatment.

dis·crim·i·na·tive (dis·krim'ə·nā'tiv) *adj.* Having or practicing discrimination. Also **dis·crim'i·na·to'ry** (-nə·tôr'ē, -tō'rē). —**dis·crim'i·na·tive·ly** *adv.*

dis·cur·sive (dis·kûr'siv) *adj.* Wandering from one subject or point to another; digressive. [< L *discursus* a running to and fro] —**dis·cur'sive·ly** *adv.* —**dis·cur'sive·ness** *n.*

dis·cus (dis'kəs) *n.* **1** A circular plate, usu. of metal, thrown for distance as a test of strength in athletic contests. **2** Such a contest. [< Gk. *diskos*]

dis·cuss (dis·kus') *v.t.* To treat of in conversation or in writing. [< L *discutere*] —**dis·cuss'er** *n.* —**dis·cuss'i·ble** *adj.* —Syn. argue, debate, deliberate, examine.

dis·cus·sion (dis·kush'ən) *n.* The act of discussing.

dis·dain (dis·dān') *v.t.* To consider unworthy of one's regard or notice; scorn. —*n.* A feeling of superiority and dislike; proud contempt. [< OF *des-* away + *deignier* deign] —**dis·dain'ful** *adj.* —**dis·dain'ful·ly** *adv.*

Discus thrower

dis·ease (di·zēz') *n.* **1** Any disturbed or abnormal condition in the living organism. **2** A specific ailment or illness.

3 Any disturbed or harmful condition. —*v.t.* **-eased, -eas-ing** To cause disease in; disorder; derange. [<OF *des-* away + *aise* ease] —**dis-eased'** *adj.*

dis·em·bark (dis'im·bärk') *v.t.* & *v.i.* **1** To put or go ashore from a ship. **2** To get off or land: to *disembark* from an airplane at San Francisco. —**dis·em'bar·ka'tion, dis'em·bark'ment** *n.*

dis·em·bod·y (dis'im·bod'ē) *v.t.* **-bod·ied, -bod·y·ing** To free from the body or from physical existence. —**dis·em·bod'i·ment** *n.*

dis·em·bow·el (dis'im·bou'əl, -boul') *v.t.* **-bow·eled** or **-bow·elled, -bow·el·ing** or **-bow·el·ling 1** To take out the bowels of; eviscerate. **2** To remove the contents of.

dis·en·chant (dis'in·chant', -chänt') *v.t.* To free from enchantment or illusion. —**dis'en·chant'ment** *n.*

dis·en·cum·ber (dis'in·kum'bər) *v.t.* To free from encumbrance or burden.

dis·en·fran·chise (dis'in·fran'chīz) *v.t.* **-chised, -chis·ing** DISFRANCHISE.

dis·en·gage (dis'in·gāj') *v.t.* & *v.i.* **-gaged, -gag·ing** To set free or be free, as from engagement, attachment, etc. —**dis'en·gage'ment** *n.*

dis·en·tan·gle (dis'in·tang'gəl) *v.t.* **-gled, -gling** To free or relieve of entanglement or complications. —**dis'en·tan'gle·ment** *n.*

dis·es·tab·lish (dis'ə·stab'lish) *v.t.* To deprive of established status or character, esp. to withdraw state patronage from a church.

dis·es·teem (dis'ə·stēm') *v.t.* To feel a lack of esteem for. —*n.* Lack of esteem.

dis·fa·vor (dis·fā'vər) *n.* **1** Lack of favor; disapproval; dislike. **2** The state of being disliked or opposed. **3** An unkind act. —*v.t.* To treat or regard without favor.

dis·fig·ure (dis·fig'yər) *v.t.* **-ured, -ur·ing** To mar or destroy the figure or beauty of; render unsightly; deform. —**dis·fig'ure·ment, dis·fig'u·ra'tion** *n.*

dis·fran·chise (dis·fran'chīz) *v.t.* **-chised, -chis·ing 1** To deprive of a privilege, right, or grant. **2** To deprive of a right of citizenship, esp. the right to vote. —**dis·fran'chis·er, dis·fran'chise·ment** *n.*

dis·gorge (dis·gôrj') *v.t.* & *v.i.* **-gorged, -gorg·ing 1** To throw out, as from the throat or stomach; eject; vomit. **2** To give up unwillingly. [<OF *des-* from + *gorge* throat]

dis·grace (dis·grās') *v.t.* **-graced, -grac·ing 1** To bring reproach or shame upon. **2** To put out of favor. —*n.* **1** The state of a person who has lost respect or favor. **2** Loss of respect or favor. **3** That which disgraces. [<Ital. < *dis-* away + *grazia* favor] —**dis·grac'er** *n.*

dis·grace·ful (dis·grās'fəl) *adj.* Characterized by or causing disgrace; shameful. —**dis·grace'ful·ly** *adv.* —**dis·grace'ful·ness** *n.* —**Syn.** infamous, scandalous, ignoble.

dis·grun·tle (dis·grun'təl) *v.t.* **-gruntled, -grun·tling** To disappoint and make discontended.

dis·guise (dis·gīz') *v.t.* **-guised, -guis·ing 1** To hide or change the appearance of. **2** To misrepresent or cover up the actual nature or character of. —*n.* **1** The act of disguising, or the state of being disguised. **2** Something that disguises. [<OF *des-* down + *guise* guise] —**dis·guis'ed·ly** (-id·lē) *adv.* —**dis·guis'er** *n.*

dis·gust (dis·gust') *v.t.* **1** To offend the senses of. **2** To affect with loathing or aversion. —*n.* Strong aversion or repugnance. [<MF *des-* away + *gouster* to taste] —**dis·gust'ed** *adj.* —**dis·gust'ed·ly** *adv.*

dis·gust·ing (dis·gus'ting) *adj.* Provoking disgust; revolting. —**dis·gust'ing·ly** *adv.*

dish (dish) *n.* **1** A concave or hollow vessel for serving or holding food; also, anything of similar shape. **2** The amount of food served in a dish; also **dish'ful. 3** Prepared food: my favorite *dish.* —*v.t.* **1** To serve as food: often with *up* or *out.* **2** To make concave. —*v.i.* **3** To become concave; sink in. [<L *discus* disk]

dis·ha·bille (dis'ə·bēl') *n.* **1** A state of being partially or negligently dressed, as in night clothes. **2** The clothes worn in this state. [<F *des-* away + *habiller* to dress]

dis·har·mo·ny (dis·här'mə·nē) *n. pl.* **-nies** Lack of harmony; incongruity; discord. —**dis·har·mo·ni·ous** (dis'här-mō'nē·əs) *adj.*

dish·cloth (dish'klôth', -kloth') *n.* A cloth used in washing dishes. Also **dish'rag'** (-rag').

dis·heart·en (dis·här'ten) *v.t.* To weaken the spirit or courage of; discourage. —**dis·heart'en·ing** *adj.* —**dis·heart'en·ing·ly** *adv.* —**dis·heart'en·ment** *n.*

di·shev·el (di·shev'əl) *v.t.* **-eled** or **-elled, -el·ing** or **-el·ling 1** To disarrange, as hair or clothing. **2** To disarrange the hair, clothing, etc. of (a person). [<MF *des-* away + *chevel* hair]

di·shev·eled (di·shev'əld) *adj.* Disarranged or disorderly; untidy. Also **di·shev'elled.**

dis·hon·est (dis·on'ist) *adj.* **1** Lacking in honesty; untrustworthy. **2** Characterized by fraudulence. —**dis·hon'es·ty** *n.* —**dis·hon'est·ly** *adv.*

dis·hon·or (dis·on'ər) *v.t.* **1** To disgrace or insult. **2** To seduce. **3** To decline or fail to pay, as a note. —*n.* **1** Lack or loss of honor or respect. **2** Something that causes such a lack or loss. **3** Refusal or failure to pay a note, etc., when due. *Brit. sp.* **-our.**

dis·hon·or·a·ble (dis·on'ər·ə·bəl) *adj.* Characterized by or bringing dishonor or reproach. —**dis·hon'or·a·bly** *adv.*

dis·il·lu·sion (dis'i·loo'zhən) *v.t.* To free from illusion or delusion. —*n.* The act of freeing or the state of being freed from illusion. Also **dis'il·lu'sion·ment.**

dis·in·cen·tive (dis'in·sen'tiv) *n.* Something tending to discourage a course of action; deterrent.

dis·in·cli·na·tion (dis·in'klə·nā'shən) *n.* Lack of disposition, as to do something; unwillingness.

dis·in·cline (dis'in·klīn') *v.t.* & *v.i.* **-clined, -clin·ing** To make or be unwilling or averse.

dis·in·fect (dis'in·fekt') *v.t.* **1** To free from infection, harmful bacteria, etc. **2** To clean with a disinfectant. —**dis'in·fec'tion** *n.*

dis·in·fec·tant (dis'in·fek'tənt) *adj.* Disinfecting. —*n.* A substance used to destroy harmful bacteria.

dis·in·for·ma·tion (dis·in'fər·mā'shən) *n.* False, misleading information deliberately disseminated.

dis·in·gen·u·ous (dis'in·jen'yoō·əs) *adj.* Not sincere or candid; artful; deceitful. —**dis'in·gen'u·ous·ly** *adv.*

dis·in·her·it (dis'in·her'it) *v.t.* To deprive of an inheritance or of a right or privilege. —**dis'in·her'i·tance** *n.*

dis·in·te·grate (dis·in'tə·grāt, di·zin'-) *v.t.* & *v.i.* **-grat·ed, -grat·ing** To reduce or become reduced into parts or particles. —**dis·in'te·gra·ble** (-grə·bəl) *adj.* —**dis·in'te·gra'tion** *n.*

dis·in·ter (dis'in·tûr') *v.t.* **-terred, -ter·ring 1** To dig up, as from a grave. **2** To bring to light. —**dis'in·ter'ment** *n.*

dis·in·ter·est (dis·in'tər·ist, -trist) *n.* **1** Lack of interest; indifference. **2** Freedom from bias; impartiality.

dis·in·ter·est·ed (dis·in'tər·is·tid, -tris·tid, -tə·res'-) *adj.* **1** Free from self-interest or bias. **2** Lacking interest; uninterested. —**dis·in'ter·est·ed·ly** *adv.* —**dis·in'ter·est·ed·ness** *n.* —**Syn. 1** unselfish, impartial, detached, **2** apathetic, unconcerned, indifferent. • **disinterested, uninterested** *Disinterested* and *uninterested* are widely used interchangeably, but in precise usage *disinterested* refers to a lack of special or personal interest (the arbiter's *disinterested* decision) and *uninterested* to a lack of any interest whatsoever (an *uninterested* spectator, nodding through the performance).

dis·join (dis·join') *v.t.* To separate; undo; part. —*v.i.* To become divided or separated.

dis·joint (dis·joint') *v.t.* **1** To put out of joint. **2** To take apart. **3** To destroy the coherence, connections, or sequence of. —*v.i.* **4** To break into parts. —**dis·joint'ed** *adj.* —**dis·joint'ed·ly** *adv.* —**dis·joint'ed·ness** *n.*

dis·junc·tion (dis·jungk'shən) *n.* A disjoining or separation. Also **dis·junc'ture** (-chər).

dis·junc·tive (dis·jungk'tiv) *adj.* **1** Helping or serving to disjoin. **2** *Gram.* Expressing separation or disjoining, as certain conjunctions, as *either/or, else, otherwise*, etc. —*n. Gram.* A disjunctive conjunction. [<L *disjungere* disjoin]

disk (disk) *n.* **1** A flat, more or less circular plate of any material. **2** Any surface that is flat and circular. **3** A quoit or discus. **4** A phonograph record. **5** A round, flat, magnetically-coated plate on which computer data and programs may be stored.

disk brake A brake in which a durable pad is pressed against a metal disk to provide a retarding force.

disk drive An electronic device that writes information from computer memory onto disks, and reads information from disks.

disk harrow A harrow consisting of a series of disks set on edge, used for plowing.

disk jockey DISC JOCKEY.

Disk harrow

dis·like (dis·līk′) v.t. ·liked, ·lik·ing To regard with aversion or antipathy. —n. Distaste; repugnance; aversion. —dis·lik′a·ble, dis·like′a·ble adj. —dis·lik′er n.

dis·lo·cate (dis′lō·kāt, dis·lō′kāt) v.t. ·cat·ed, ·cat·ing 1 To put out of joint, as a bone. 2 To put out of proper place or order. —dis′lo·ca′tion n.

dis·lodge (dis·loj′) v. ·lodged, ·lodg·ing v.t. 1 To remove or drive out, as from an abode. —v.i. 2 To leave a place of abode; move. —dis·lodg′ment, n.

dis·loy·al (dis·loi′əl) adj. False to one's allegiance; faithless. —dis·loy′al·ly adv.

dis·loy·al·ty (dis·loi′əl·tē) n. pl. ·ties 1 The state of being disloyal. 2 A disloyal act.

dis·mal (diz′məl) adj. 1 Gloomy; cheerless; mournful. 2 Calamitous; horrible. [< L dies mali evil or unpropitious days] —dis′mal·ly adv. —dis′mal·ness n.

dis·man·tle (dis·man′təl) v.t. ·tled, ·tling 1 To strip of furniture, equipment, clothing, etc. 2 To take apart; reduce to pieces. [< ME des- away + manteller cover with a cloak] —dis·man′tle·ment n.

dis·may (dis·mā′) v.t. To put at a loss, as from surprise, fear, or disappointment; cause to lose spirit or confidence. —n. A state of being dismayed. [ME dismayen]

dis·mem·ber (dis·mem′bər) v.t. 1 To cut or pull limb from limb. 2 To separate into parts and distribute. [< L dis- apart + membrum a limb] —dis·mem′ber·ment n.

dis·miss (dis·mis′) v.t. 1 To put out of office or service; discharge. 2 To cause or allow to depart. 3 To put aside; reject. [< L dis- away + mittere send] —dis·mis′sal n. —dis·miss′i·ble adj.

dis·mount (dis·mount′) v.i. 1 To get off a horse, etc. —v.t. 2 To remove from a mounting, as a jewel. 3 To dismantle (a machine). 4 To cause to dismount; unseat. —n. The act or manner of dismounting.

dis·o·be·di·ent (dis′ə·bē′dē·ənt) adj. Neglecting or refusing to obey; refractory. —dis′o·be′di·ence n. —dis′o·be′di·ent·ly adv.

dis·o·bey (dis′ə·bā′) v.t. & v.i. To refuse or fail to obey. —dis′o·bey′er n.

dis·o·blige (dis′ə·blīj′) v.t. 1 To neglect or refuse to oblige. 2 To inconvenience. 3 To slight; affront.

dis·or·der (dis·ôr′dər) n. 1 The state of being disarranged. 2 Disregard or neglect of orderliness. 3 A disturbance of the peace; breach of public order. 4 A derangement of bodily or mental function; illness. —v.t. 1 To throw out of order; disarrange. 2 To disturb the natural functions of, as body or mind.

dis·or·der·ly (dis·ôr′dər·lē) adj. & adv. 1 Being in or causing disorder; not orderly. 2 Lawless; disreputable. —dis·or′der·li·ness n.

dis·o·ri·ent (dis·ôr′ē·ənt, -ō′rē-) v.t. 1 To cause to lose the sense of direction or location. 2 Psychol. To cause confusion in regard to spatial, temporal, or human relationships. —dis·o′ri·en·ta′tion n.

dis·own (dis·ōn′) v.t. To refuse to acknowledge responsibility for or ownership of; repudiate.

dis·par·age (dis·par′ij) v.t. ·aged, ·ag·ing 1 To speak of slightingly; undervalue. 2 To bring discredit or dishonor upon. [< OF des- down, away + parage equality, rank] —dis·par′age·ment, dis·par′ag·er n. —dis·par′ag·ing·ly adv. —Syn. 1 belittle, depreciate, decry, discredit.

dis·pa·rate (dis·par′it, dis′pə·rit) adj. That cannot be compared; dissimilar. [< L dis- apart + parare make ready] —dis′pa′rate·ly adv. —dis′pa′rate·ness n.

dis·par·i·ty (dis·par′ə·tē) n. pl. ·ties The state of being dissimilar; difference. [< L dis- apart + paritas equality]

dis·pas·sion (dis·pash′ən) n. Freedom from passion, emotion, or bias.

dis·pas·sion·ate (dis·pash′ən·it) adj. Free from passion, prejudice, or personal interest; detached. —dis·pas′sion·ate·ly adv. —dis·pas′sion·ate·ness n.

dis·patch (dis·pach′) v.t. 1 To send off, esp. on official business. 2 To transact with promptness. 3 To kill summarily. —n. 1 The act of dispatching. 2 A message, news story, etc., sent with haste. 3 Speed; promptness; expedition. 4 The act of killing. [< Ital. dispacciare]

dis·patch·er (dis·pach′ər) n. One who dispatches, esp., one who directs the movement of trains, trucks, etc.

dis·pel (dis·pel′) v.t. ·pelled, ·pel·ling To scatter; drive away; disperse. [< L dis- away + pellere to drive]

dis·pen·sa·ble (dis·pen′sə·bəl) adj. 1 That can be dispensed with; unnecessary. 2 That can be distributed to others. —dis·pen′sa·bil′i·ty, dis·pen′sa·ble·ness n.

dis·pen·sa·ry (dis·pen′sər·ē) n. pl. ·ries A place where medicines or medical treatment is dispensed.

dis·pen·sa·tion (dis′pən·sā′shən) n. 1 A dealing out; distribution. 2 Something dealt out or distributed. 3 Special exemption granted from the requirements of a law, rule, or obligation. 4 Theol. Any of the systems in which God has revealed his mind and will to man. —dis′pen·sa′tion·al adj. —dis′pen·sa′tion·al·ly adv.

dis·pen·sa·to·ry (dis·pen′sə·tôr′ē, -tō′rē) n. pl. ·ries A manual describing medicinal preparations.

dis·pense (dis·pens′) v. ·pensed, ·pens·ing v.t. 1 To give or deal out in portions; distribute. 2 To compound and give out (medicines). 3 To administer, as laws. 4 To relieve or excuse; absolve. —v.i. 5 To grant exemption or dispensation. —dispense with To do without; relinquish; forgo. [< L dis- away + pendere weigh] —dis·pens′er n.

dis·perse (dis·pûrs′) v. ·persed, ·pers·ing v.t. 1 To cause to scatter and go off in various directions. 2 To dispel; dissipate: The sun dispersed the mists. 3 To separate (light) into its component spectral colors. —v.i. 4 To scatter and go off in various directions. [< L dis- away + spargere scatter] —dis·per′sal, dis·pers′er n. —dis·pers′i·ble, dis·per′sive adj.

dis·per·sion (dis·pûr′zhən, -shən) n. 1 The act of dispersing or the state of being dispersed. 2 The separation of light rays of different colors by the action of a prism or lens.

dis·pir·it (dis·pir′it) v.t. To cause to lose heart or hope; weaken the spirit of; depress. —dis·pir′it·ed adj. —dis·pir′it·ed·ly adv. —dis·pir′it·ed·ness n.

dis·place (dis·plās′) v.t. ·placed, ·plac·ing 1 To move from the proper place. 2 To take the place of; supplant. 3 To remove from a position or office; discharge.

displaced person A person forced to flee his country or home.

dis·place·ment (dis·plās′mənt) n. 1 The act of displacing, or the state of being displaced. 2 The weight, volume, or mass of a fluid displaced by a body floating in it. 3 The difference between the original position of an object and its position at some later time.

dis·play (dis·plā′) v.t. 1 To show; make apparent to the eye or the mind. 2 To reveal, as ignorance. —n. 1 The act of displaying. 2 The thing or things displayed. 3 Ostentatious show. [< LL displicare scatter]

dis·please (dis·plēz′) v.t. & v.i. ·pleased, ·pleas·ing To annoy, vex, or offend.

dis·pleas·ure (dis·plezh′ər) n. The state of being displeased. —Syn. dissatisfaction, vexation, annoyance.

dis·port (dis·pôrt′, -pōrt′) v.i. 1 To play; gambol. —v.t. 2 To amuse (oneself). [< L dis- away + portare carry]

dis·pos·a·ble (dis·pō′zə·bəl) adj. 1 Subject to disposal. 2 Easily discarded after use. —dis·pos′a·bil′i·ty n.

dis·pos·al (dis·pō′zəl) n. 1 Orderly arrangement or distribution. 2 A getting rid of, as by gift or sale. 3 Power of control, management, or distribution. 4 A settling of affairs. —at one's disposal Ready at one's convenience.

dis·pose (dis·pōz′) v. ·posed, ·pos·ing v.t. 1 To put in order; arrange properly. 2 To incline or influence the mind of. 3 To put or set in a particular place or location. 4 To settle (affairs). —v.i. **5** To arrange or settle something. —**dis-pose of 1** To settle; finish. **2** To throw away. **3** To get rid of by selling or giving. [< OF *dis-* apart + *poser* put, pose] —**dis·pos′er** n.

dis·po·si·tion (dis′pə·zish′ən) n. **1** The act of disposing; arrangement, as of troops. **2** Final settlement or management. **3** Control; power. **4** Natural tendency or temperament; bent; propensity. **5** A selling or giving away.

dis·pos·sess (dis′pə·zes′) v.t. To deprive (someone) of possession, as of a house or land. —**dis′pos·ses′sion, dis′·pos·ses′sor** n.

dis·praise (dis·prāz′) v.t. ·**praised,** ·**prais·ing** To speak of with disapproval; disparage. —n. The expression of unfavorable opinion.

dis·proof (dis·proōf′) n. **1** The act or process of disproving. **2** A fact or evidence that disproves.

dis·pro·por·tion (dis′prə·pôr′shən, -pōr′-) n. Lack of proportion or symmetry. —v.t. To make disproportionate. —**dis′pro·por′tion·al** adj. —**dis′pro·por′tion·al·ly** adv.

dis·pro·por·tion·ate (dis′prə·pôr′shən·it, -pōr′-) adj. Out of proportion with regard to size, form, or value. —**dis′pro·por′tion·ate·ly,** adv. —**dis′pro·por′tion·ate·ness** n.

dis·prove (dis·proōv′) v.t. ·**proved,** ·**prov·ing** To prove to be false or erroneous; refute. —**dis·prov′a·ble** adj.

dis·put·a·ble (dis·pyoō′tə·bəl, dis′pyoō′tə·bəl) adj. That can be disputed; controvertible. —**dis·put′a·bil′i·ty** n. —**dis·put′a·bly** adv.

dis·pu·tant (dis·pyoō′tənt, dis′pyoō·tənt) adj. Disputing. —n. One who disputes; a party to a dispute.

dis·pu·ta·tion (dis′pyoō·tā′shən) n. **1** The act of disputing; controversy; argumentation. **2** A controversy or debate, often a formal one.

dis·pu·ta·tious (dis′pyoō·tā′shəs) adj. Inclined to dispute. Also **dis·put·a·tive** (dis·pyoō′tə·tiv). —**dis′pu·ta′tious·ly** adv. —**dis′pu·ta′tious·ness** n.

dis·pute (dis·pyoōt′) v. ·**put·ed,** ·**put·ing** v.t. **1** To argue about; discuss. **2** To question the validity, genuineness, etc., of. **3** To strive for, as a prize. **4** To resist; oppose. —v.i. **5** To argue. **6** To quarrel; wrangle. —n. **1** A controversial discussion. **2** A wrangle; quarrel. [< L *dis-* away + *putare* think] —**dis·put′er** n.

dis·qual·i·fi·ca·tion (dis·kwol′ə·fə·kā′shən) n. **1** The state of being disqualified. **2** That which disqualifies.

dis·qual·i·fy (dis·kwol′ə·fī) v.t. ·**fied,** ·**fy·ing 1** To render unqualified or unfit; incapacitate; disable. **2** To pronounce unqualified or ineligible, esp. in sports.

dis·qui·et (dis·kwī′ət) n. Restlessness; uneasiness. Also **dis·qui′e·tude** (-kwī′ə·t/oōd). —v.t. To make anxious or uneasy.

dis·qui·si·tion (dis′kwi·zish′ən) n. A systematic treatise or discourse. [< L *dis-* from + *quaerere* seek, ask]

dis·re·gard (dis′ri·gärd′) v.t. **1** To pay no attention to; ignore. **2** To treat without respect or attention; slight. —n. Want of regard; neglect; slight. —**dis′re·gard′ful** adj.

dis·re·pair (dis′ri·pâr′) n. The state of being out of repair.

dis·rep·u·ta·ble (dis·rep′yə·tə·bəl) adj. Being in or causing ill repute; disgraceful. —**dis·rep′u·ta·ble·ness** n. —**dis·rep′u·ta·bly** adv.

dis·re·pute (dis′ri·pyoōt′) n. Lack or loss of reputation; ill repute.

dis·re·spect (dis′ri·spekt′) n. Lack of respect; discourtesy. —v.t. To treat or regard with lack of respect. —**dis′re·spect′ful** adj. —**dis′re·spect′ful·ly** adv. —**dis′re·spect′·ful·ness** n.

dis·robe (dis·rōb′) v.t. & v.i. ·**robed,** ·**rob·ing** To undress. —**dis·robe′ment** n.

dis·rupt (dis·rupt′) v.t. & v.i. **1** To burst or break asunder. **2** To act to interrupt the normal or proper course of (a meeting, etc.). [< L *dis-* apart + *rumpere* burst] —**dis·rupt′er** or **dis·rup′tor, dis·rup′tion** n.

dis·rup·tive (dis·rup′tiv) adj. **1** Acting or tending to disrupt. **2** Marked by disruption. —**dis·rup′tive·ly** adv. —**dis·rup′tive·ness** n.

dis·sat·is·fac·tion (dis′sat·is·fak′shən) n. **1** A dissatisfied state or feeling; discontent. **2** Something that dissatisfies.

dis·sat·is·fac·to·ry (dis′sat·is·fak′tər·ē) adj. Creating dissatisfaction or discontent.

dis·sat·is·fy (dis·sat′is·fī) v.t. ·**fied,** ·**fy·ing** To fail to satisfy; disappoint; displease.

dis·sect (di·sekt′, dī-) v.t. **1** To separate the disparate tissues of (an organism.) **2** To analyze critically; examine. [< L < *dis-* apart + *secare* to cut] —**dis·sec′tion, dis·sec′tor** n.

dis·sect·ed (di·sek′tid) adj. **1** Cut in pieces. **2** Deeply cut into lobes or segments, as a leaf.

dis·sem·ble (di·sem′bəl) v. ·**bled,** ·**bling** v.t. **1** To conceal the true nature of (intentions, feelings, etc.) so as to deceive. **2** To pretend to feel: to *dissemble* shock. —v.i. **3** To conceal one's true nature, intentions, etc.; act hypocritically. [< OF *dis-* not, away + *sembler* seem] —**dis·sem′· blance, dis·sem′bler** n.

dis·sem·i·nate (di·sem′ə·nāt) v.t. ·**nat·ed,** ·**nat·ing** To spread about; scatter; promulgate. [< L *dis-* away + *seminare* to sow] —**dis·sem′i·na′tion, dis·sem′i·na′tor** n.

dis·sen·sion (di·sen′shən) n. Angry or violent difference of opinion. —**Syn.** discord, strife, conflict, disagreement.

dis·sent (di·sent′) v.i. **1** To differ in thought or opinion; disagree. **2** To refuse adherence to an established church. —n. The act or state of dissenting. [< L *dis-* apart + *sentire* think, feel] —**dis·sent′er** n.

dis·sen·tient (di·sen′shənt) adj. Dissenting; disagreeing. —n. One who dissents.

dis·ser·ta·tion (dis′ər·tā′shən) n. An extended treatise or discourse; thesis. [< L *dissertare* examine, discuss]

dis·serv·ice (dis·sûr′vis) n. An ill turn; a slight injury.

dis·sev·er (di·sev′ər) v.t. **1** To divide; separate. **2** To separate into parts. —v.i. **3** To separate; part. —**dis·sev′er·ance, dis·sev′er·ment** n.

dis·si·dence (dis′ə·dəns) n. Disagreement; dissent.

dis·si·dent (dis′ə·dənt) adj. Dissenting; differing. —n. One who dissents; dissenter. [< L *dis-* apart + *sedere* sit]

dis·sim·i·lar (di·sim′ə·lər) adj. Unlike; different. —**dis·sim′i·lar′i·ty** n. —**dis·sim′i·lar·ly** adv.

dis·sim·i·la·tion (di·sim′ə·lā′shən) n. The act or process of becoming dissimilar.

dis·si·mil·i·tude (dis′si·mil′ə·t/oōd) n. Lack of resemblance or likeness. [< L *dis-* not + *similis* alike]

dis·sim·u·late (di·sim′yə·lāt) v.t. & v.i. ·**lat·ed,** ·**lat·ing** To conceal (intentions, feelings, etc.) by pretense; dissemble. [< L *dissimulare* to feign] —**dis·sim′u·la′tion, dis·sim′u·la′tor** n.

dis·si·pate (dis′ə·pāt) v. ·**pat·ed,** ·**pat·ing** v.t. **1** To disperse or drive away. **2** To disintegrate or dissolve utterly. **3** To squander: to *dissipate* a fortune. —v.i. **4** To become dispersed; scatter. **5** To engage in excessive or dissolute pleasures. [< L *dissipare*]

dis·si·pat·ed (dis′ə·pā′tid) adj. Given to or showing dissipation. —**dis′si·pat′ed·ly** adv. —**dis′si·pat′ed·ness** n.

dis·si·pa·tion (dis′ə·pā′shən) . n. **1** The act of dissipating or the state of being dissipated. **2** Excessive indulgence, esp. in pleasures. **3** Idle distraction or amusement.

dis·so·ci·ate (di·sō′shē·āt) v. ·**at·ed,** ·**at·ing** v.t. **1** To separate from association or connection; detach. **2** *Chem.* To resolve by dissociation. —v.i. **3** To break an association. **4** *Chem.* To undergo dissociation. [< L *dis-* apart + *sociare* join together] —**dis·so′ci·a′tive** adj.

dis·so·ci·a·tion (di·sō′sē·ā′shən, -shē·ā′-) n. **1** The act of dissociating; state of separation. **2** *Chem.* The reversible separation of the constituents of a compound.

dis·sol·u·ble (di·sol′yə·bəl) adj. Capable of being dissolved. —**dis·sol′u·bil′i·ty, dis·sol′u·ble·ness** n.

dis·so·lute (dis′ə·loōt) adj. Dissipated; immoral; profligate. [< L *dissolutus,* loose, pp. of *dissolvere* dissolve] —**dis′so·lute·ly** adv. —**dis′so·lute·ness** n.

dis·so·lu·tion (dis′ə·loō′shən) n. **1** The act or state of dissolving or breaking up into parts; disintegration. **2** An ending or breaking up, as of an assembly, business, or partnership. **3** Death.

dis·solve (di·zolv′) v.t. & v.i. ·**solved,** ·**solv·ing 1** To change or make change from a solid to a fluid condition. **2** To pass or cause to pass into or combine with a solution. **3** To end or conclude; terminate, as a meeting or marriage. **4** To fade or cause to fade into or out of view, as a motion-picture or television scene. **5** To vanish or make vanish. —n. In films and television, the slow emergence of one scene out of another. [< L *dis-* apart + *solvere* loosen] —**dis·solv′a·ble** adj. —**dis·sol′vent** adj., n. —**dis·solv′er** n.

dis·so·nance (dis′ə-nəns) *n.* **1** A discordant mingling of sounds. **2** *Music* A combination of tones that give a harsh or unpleasant effect when sounded together. **3** Harsh disagreement. Also **dis′so·nan·cy.**

dis·so·nant (dis′ə-nənt) *adj.* **1** Having the quality of dissonance. **2** Naturally hostile; incongruous. [< L *dis-* away + *sonare* to sound] —**dis′so·nant·ly** *adv.*

dis·suade (di-swād′) *v.t.* **·suad·ed, ·suad·ing** To change the plans of (a person) by persuasion or advice: with *from.* [< L *dis-* away + *suadere* persuade] —**dis·suad′er, dis·sua′sion** (-swā′zhən) *n.* —**dis·sua′sive** (-swā′siv) *adj.*

dis·syl·la·ble (di·sil′ə-bəl, dī-, dis·sil′ə-bəl, dī′-) *n.* A word of two syllables. Also **di·syl′la·ble.**

dist. distance; distant; distinguished; district.

dis·taff (dis′taf, -täf) *n.* **1** A staff that holds the flax or wool for use in spinning. **2** Woman; also, woman's work or domain. [< OE *dis* bundle of flax + *stæf* staff]

Distaff

distaff side The maternal branch of a family.

dis·tal (dis′təl) *adj.* Remote from the point of attachment; peripheral. [< DISTANT] —**dis′tal·ly** *adv.*

dis·tance (dis′təns) *n.* **1** The space or interval separating two objects, points, or places. **2** The length of a line segment connecting two points **3** The period between two points of time. **4** The state of being separated in space or time. **5** A distant place or point. **6** Reserve; haughtiness; coldness. **7** *Music* The interval between two tones. —*v.t.* **·tanced, ·tanc·ing** To leave behind, as in a race; outstrip; excel.

dis·tant (dis′tənt) *adj.* **1** Separated in space or time; far apart. **2** Not closely related in qualities, relationship, or in position; remote. **3** Reserved or unapproachable; formal. **4** Indistinct; faint. **5** Not obvious or plain; indirect. [< L *dis-* apart + *stare* to stand] —**dis′tant·ly** *adv.*

dis·taste (dis·tāst′) *n.* Aversion; dislike.

dis·taste·ful (dis·tāst′fəl) *adj.* Causing or denoting distaste. —**dis·taste′ful·ly** *adv.* —**dis·taste′ful·ness** *n.* —**Syn.** disagreeable, offensive, unpleasant, disgusting.

Dist. Atty. District Attorney.

dis·tem·per[1] (dis·tem′pər) *n.* **1** Any of several infectious diseases of animals. **2** Ill humor. **3** Civil disturbance. —*v.t.* **1** To disturb or derange the functions of; disorder. **2** To ruffle; disturb. [< Med. L < *dis-* away + *temperare* regulate, mix]

dis·tem·per[2] (dis·tem′pər) *n.* **1** A pigment mixed with yolk of eggs or glue, used chiefly for murals. **2** The art of painting with such materials, or a painting executed in them. —*v.t.* **1** To mix, as colors, for distemper painting. **2** To color or paint with distemper. —*adj.* Of or pertaining to decoration done with distemper. [< Med. L *dis-* apart + *temperare* mix, mingle, soak]

dis·tend (dis·tend′) *v.t. & v.i.* To expand; swell; dilate, as by pressure from within. [< L *dis-* apart + *tendere* to stretch] —**dis·ten′si·ble** *adj.* —**dis·ten′sion, dis·ten′tion** *n.*

dis·tich (dis′tik) *n.* In prosody, a couplet. [< Gk. *di-* two + *stichos* row, line]

dis·till (dis·til′) *v.* **·tilled, ·til·ling** *v.t.* **1** To subject to or as to distillation. **2** To extract or produce by distillation: to *distill* whiskey. **3** To give forth —*v.i.* **4** To undergo distillation. **5** To exude in drops. Also **dis·til′.** [< L *de-* down + *stillare* to drop, trickle] —**dis·til′la·ble** *adj.*

dis·til·late (dis′tə·lit, -lāt) *n.* The condensed product separated by distillation.

dis·til·la·tion (dis′tə-lā′shən) *n.* **1** Separation of the volatile parts of a mixture by vaporizing and subsequently condensing. **2** The parts so separated and condensed; distillate. **3** The essential quality of anything.

dis·til·ler (dis·til′ər) *n.* **1** One who or that which distills. **2** A maker and seller of distilled liquors.

dis·til·ler·y (dis·til′ər-ē) *n. pl.* **·ler·ies** An establishment for distilling, esp. alcoholic liquors.

dis·tinct (dis·tingkt′) *adj.* **1** Clear to the senses or mind; plain; unmistakable; definite. **2** Clearly standing apart from other objects; unconnected; separate. **3** Decidedly different; not alike. [< L *distinctus*, pp. of *distinguere* distinguish] —**dis·tinct′ly** *adv.* —**dis·tinct′ness** *n.*

dis·tinc·tion (dis·tingk′shən) *n.* **1** A distinguishing mark or quality; a characteristic difference. **2** The act of distinguishing; discrimination. **3** Fame; eminent reputation. **4** Excellence; superiority. **5** A mark of honor or regard.

dis·tinc·tive (dis·tingk′tiv) *adj.* Characteristic; distinguishing. —**dis·tinc′tive·ly** *adv.* —**dis·tinc′tive·ness** *n.*

dis·tin·gué (dis′tang-gā′, *Fr.* dĕs-tań-gā′) *adj.* Distinguished. [F] —**dis′tin·guée′** *adj. Fem.*

dis·tin·guish (dis·ting′gwish) *v.t.* **1** To indicate or constitute the differences of or between. **2** To recognize as separate or distinct; discriminate. **3** To divide into classes; classify. **4** To bring fame or credit upon. **5** To perceive by one of the physical senses. —*v.i.* **6** To make or discern differences. [< L *distinguere* to separate] —**dis·tin′guish·a·ble** *adj.* —**dis·tin′guish·a·bly** *adv.*

dis·tin·guished (dis·ting′gwisht) *adj.* **1** Famous; eminent. **2** Having an air of distinction; dignified.

dis·tort (dis·tôrt′) *v.t.* **1** To twist or bend out of shape. **2** To twist the meaning of; misrepresent. [< L *dis-* apart + *torquere* to twist] —**dis·tort′er, dis·tort′ed·ness** *n.* —**Syn. 2** misconstrue, mislead, falsify, misquote.

dis·tor·tion (dis·tôr′shən) *n.* **1** The act of distorting. **2** The quality of being distorted. **3** Something distorted. —**dis·tor′tion·al** *adj.*

distr. distribute; distribution; distributor.

dis·tract (dis·trakt′) *v.t.* **1** To divert (the mind, etc.) in a different direction. **2** To bewilder; confuse. **3** To make frantic; craze. [< L *dis-* away + *trahere* to draw] —**dis·tract′er** *n.* —**dis·tract′i·ble, dis·tract′ing, dis·trac′tive** *adj.*

dis·tract·ed (dis·trak′tid) *adj.* **1** Bewildered or harassed. **2** Mentally deranged; mad. —**dis·tract′ed·ly** *adv.*

dis·trac·tion (dis·trak′shən) *n.* **1** A drawing off or diversion of the mind. **2** Confusion; perplexity. **3** Strong agitation, distress, or grief. **4** Mental aberration; madness. **5** Anything that distracts or diverts.

dis·train (dis·trān′) *v.t. Law* **1** To take and detain (personal property) as security for a debt, claim, etc. **2** To subject (a person) to distress. —*v.i.* **3** To impose a distress. [< L *dis-* completely + *stringere* draw tight] —**dis·train′a·ble** *adj.* —**dis·train′er** or **dis·train′or** *n.*

dis·traint (dis·trānt′) *n. Law* The act or process of distraining.

dis·trait (dis·trā′) *adj.* Absent-minded. [F]

dis·traught (dis·trôt′) *adj.* **1** Distracted or bewildered, as by anxiety; upset. **2** Maddened; tormented. [< L *distrahere*, distract]

dis·tress (dis·tres′) *v.t.* **1** To cause to be anxious or worry. **2** To inflict suffering upon; subject to pain or agony. —*n.* **1** The state of being distressed; pain, trouble, worry, etc. **2** Anything causing such a condition. **3** A condition requiring immediate help: a ship in *distress.* **4** *Law* **a** DISTRAINT. **b** Goods taken by distraint. [< OF < L *distringere* draw asunder] —**dis·tress′ful** *adj.* —**dis·tress′ful·ly** *adv.* —**dis·tress′ful·ness** *n.*

dis·tressed (dis·trest′) *adj.* **1** Feeling distress; troubled, anxious, pained, etc. **2** Deliberately marred so as to look antique: a *distressed* commode.

dis·trib·ute (dis·trib′yŏŏt) *v.t.* **·ut·ed, ·ut·ing** **1** To divide and deal out in shares. **2** To classify; categorize. **3** To scatter, as in an area or over a surface. **4** To put or arrange into distinctive parts or places. [< L *dis-* away + *tribuere* give, allot] —**dis·trib′ut·a·ble** *adj.*

dis·tri·bu·tion (dis′trə-byŏŏ′shən) *n.* **1** The act of distributing. **2** That which is distributed. **3** The arrangement in number and place of a set of things: the *distribution* of doctors throughout the U.S. **4** In commerce, all the steps involved in the delivery of goods from producer to consumer.

dis·trib·u·tive (dis·trib′yə·tiv) *adj.* **1** Serving or tending to distribute. **2** Pertaining to distribution. **3** *Gram.* Referring to the members of a group separately. —*n.* A distributive pronoun or adjective, as *each, every,* etc. **—dis·trib′u·tive·ly** *adv.* **—dis·trib′u·tive·ness** *n.*

dis·trib·u·tor (dis·trib′yə·tər) *n.* 1 One who or that which distributes. 2 A device that connects the spark plugs of an engine in turn to a high-voltage source.

dis·trict (dis′trikt) *n.* 1 A division of territory specially defined, as for judicial, political, educational, or other purposes. 2 Any region of space; a tract. *—v.t.* To divide into districts. [< Med. L *districtus* jurisdiction]

district attorney The elected or appointed prosecuting officer of a specific judicial district.

dis·trust (dis·trust′) *v.t.* To feel no trust for or confidence in. *—n.* A lack of trust or confidence. **—dis·trust′ful** *adj.* **—dis·trust′ful·ly** *adv.* **—Syn.** *v.* suspect, mistrust, doubt. *n.* doubt, suspicion, disbelief.

dis·turb (dis·tûrb′) *v.t.* 1 To interfere with or destroy the peace or quiet of. 2 To trouble mentally or emotionally; ruffle or annoy. 3 To upset the order or system of. 4 To interrupt. 5 To cause inconvenience to. [< L *dis-* completely + *turbare* to disorder] **—dis·turb′er** *n.*

dis·tur·bance (dis·tûr′bəns) *n.* 1 The act of disturbing or the condition of being disturbed. 2 That which disturbs. 3 A public commotion.

dis·u·nite (dis′yōō·nīt′) *v.* **·nit·ed, ·nit·ing** *v.t.* 1 To break the union of; separate. 2 To alienate; estrange, as friends. *—v.i.* 3 To come apart. **—dis·un′ion** (-yōōn′yən) *n.*

dis·use (dis·yōōs′) *n.* The state of no longer being used. *—v.t.* (dis·yōōz′) **·used, ·us·ing** To cease to use or practice.

ditch (dich) *n.* A narrow trench in the ground, as for drainage. *—v.t.* 1 To dig a ditch in. 2 To run or throw into a ditch; derail. 3 *Slang* To abandon; get rid of. *—v.i.* 4 To make a ditch. [< OE *dīc*] **—ditch′er** *n.*

dith·er (dith′ər) *n.* A state of nervousness or anxiety. [Var. of earlier *didder* tremble, shake] **—dith′er·y** *adj.*

dith·y·ramb (dith′ə·ram, -ramb) *n.* 1 In ancient Greece, a passionate hymn to Dionysus. 2 Any wild or vehement speech or writing. [< Gk. *dithyrambos*] **—dith′y·ram′bic** (-ram′bik) *adj.*

dit·to (dit′ō) *n. pl.* **·tos** The same thing repeated, often expressed by two inverted commas, called **ditto marks,** beneath the word intended to be duplicated. *—adv.* As before; likewise. *—v.t.* **·toed, ·to·ing** To copy; duplicate. [Ital. < L *dictum*]

dit·ty (dit′ē) *n. pl.* **·ties** A short, simple song; lay. [< L *dictatum* a thing said]

dit·ty-bag (dit′ē·bag′) *n.* A sailor's bag for needles, thread, personal belongings, etc. [?]

dit·ty-box (dit′ē·boks′) *n.* A small box used in place of a ditty-bag.

di·u·ret·ic (dī′yōō·ret′ik) *adj.* Stimulating the secretion of urine. *—n.* A diuretic medicine. [< Gk. *dia-* thoroughly + *ourēsis* urination]

di·ur·nal (dī·ûr′nəl) *adj.* 1 Happening every day; daily. 2 Done in or pertaining to the daytime. [< L *diurnus* daily] **—di·ur′nal·ly** *adv.*

Div. Divinity.

div. divided; dividend; division; divisor; divorced.

di·va (dē′və) *n. pl.* **·vas** or **·ve** (-vā) PRIMA DONNA (def. 1). [Ital.< *divo* divine]

di·va·lent (dī·vā′lənt) *adj.* BIVALENT.

di·van (di·van′, dī′van) *n.* A couch or sofa. [< Pers. *dēvān*]

dive (dīv) *v.* **dived** or **dove, dived, div·ing** *v.i.* 1 To plunge, usually headfirst, into water, etc. 2 To submerge, as a submarine. 3 To plunge the body, hand, or an object into something. 4 To enter suddenly or abruptly: He *dived* into the forest. 5 To descend at a steep angle and at high speed. 6 To become engrossed or deeply involved. *—v.t.* 7 To plunge (the body, hand, or an object) into something. 8 To cause (an airplane) to descend at a steep angle. *—n.* 1 A plunge head foremost into water. 2 A steep plunge, as of an airplane. 3 *Informal* A disreputable resort; den. [< OE *dūfan* dive and *dyfan* immerse]

dive bomber An airplane which dives toward its target to drop its bombs at close range.

div·er (dī′vər) *n.* 1 One whose work is to explore or gather objects under water. 2 A bird that dives.

di·verge (di·vûrj′, dī-) *v.i.* **·verged, ·verg·ing** 1 To extend or lie in different directions from the same point. 2 To vary from a typical form; differ. 3 *Math.* To approach no finite

limit. [< L *dis-* apart + *vergere* to incline] **—di·ver′gence, di·ver′gen·cy** *n.* **—di·ver′gent** *adj.* **—di·ver′gent·ly** *adv.*

di·vers (dī′vərz) *adj.* More than one, but not a great number. [< L *diversus* different] **—Syn.** several, sundry, various.

di·verse (di·vûrs′, dī-, dī′vûrs) *adj.* 1 Differing one from another; distinct. 2 Varied. [< L *diversus,* pp. of *divertere* divert] **—di·verse′ly** *adv.* **—di·verse′ness** *n.*

di·ver·si·fy (di·vûr′sə·fī, dī-) *v.t.* **·fied, ·fy·ing** To make diverse; impart variety to; vary. **—di·ver′si·fi·ca′tion** *n.*

di·ver·sion (di·vûr′zhən, -shən, dī-) *n.* 1 The act of diverting or turning aside. 2 *Mil.* An attack or feint intended to divert enemy troops from the point where a full scale attack is to be made. 3 That which diverts; amusement; recreation. **—di·ver′sion·ar·y** *adj.*

di·ver·si·ty (di·vûr′sə·tē, dī-) *n. pl.* **·ties** 1 The state of being diverse; dissimilitude. 2 Variety: a *diversity* of interests.

di·vert (di·vûrt′, dī-) *v.t.* 1 To turn aside; deflect, as in direction, interest, or purpose. 2 To amuse; entertain. [< L *dis-* apart + *vertere* turn] **—di·vert′er** *n.* **—di·vert′ing** *adj.* **—di·vert′ing·ly** *adv.*

di·ver·tisse·ment (di·vûr′tis·mənt, *Fr.* dē·ver·tēs·män′) *n.* 1 A brief performance, often a ballet, between the acts of a play. 2 Amusement. [F, lit., diversion]

di·vest (di·vest′, dī-) *v.t.* 1 To strip, as of clothes. 2 To deprive, as of office, rights, or honors. [< L *dis-* apart + *vestire* clothe]

di·vest·i·ture (di·ves′tə·chər, dī-) *n.* The act of divesting, or the state of being divested. Also **di·vest′ment.**

di·vide (di·vīd′) *v.* **·vid·ed, ·vid·ing** *v.t.* 1 To cut or separate into parts. 2 To distribute in shares; portion out. 3 To separate into classes; categorize. 4 To separate; keep apart. 5 To form the boundary between. 6 To graduate with lines; calibrate. 7 *Math.* a To subject to division. b To be an exact divisor of. 8 To cause to disagree. *—v.i.* 9 To be or come apart; separate. 10 To disagree. 11 To vote in two groups, one for and one against a measure. 12 To share. *—n. Geol.* A ridge of land separating one drainage system from another. [< L *dividere* separate] **—di·vid′a·ble** *adj.* **—di·vid′er** *n.*

di·vid·ed (di·vī′did) *adj.* 1 Parted; disunited. 2 *Bot.* Having deep incisions.

div·i·dend (div′ə·dend) *n.* 1 *Math.* A number or quantity on which division is performed. 2 A sum of money to be distributed according to some fixed scheme, as profit on shares. [< L *dividendum* thing to be divided]

div·i·na·tion (div′ə·nā′shən) *n.* 1 The act of trying to foretell the future. 2 A forecast; augury. 3 A successful or clever guess. **—di·vin·a·to·ry** (di·vin′ə·tôr′ē, -tō′rē) *adj.*

di·vine (di·vīn′) *adj.* 1 Pertaining to, proceeding from, or of the nature of God or of a god; sacred. 2 Addressed or offered up to God. 3 Altogether excellent or admirable. *—n.* A theologian or clergyman. *—v.* **·vined, ·vin·ing** *v.t.* 1 To foretell or prophesy. 2 To surmise; guess. *—v.i.* 3 To practice divination. [< L *divinus*] **—di·vine′ly** *adv.* **—di·vine′ness, di·vin′er** *n.*

diving bell A vessel, open below and supplied with air under pressure, in which divers can work under water.

diving board A springboard extending over water, as a swimming pool, used for performing dives.

diving suit A garment designed to protect a diver and supply him with air while under water.

divining rod A forked twig believed to bend downward when carried over underground water, mineral deposits, etc.

di·vin·i·ty (di·vin′ə·tē) *n. pl.* **·ties** 1 The quality or character of being divine. 2 A divine being; deity. 3 Theology. 4 A divine attribute, virtue, or quality. **—the Divinity** The Deity; God.

di·vis·i·ble (di·viz′ə·bəl) *adj.* Capable of being divided, esp. with a zero remainder. **—di·vis′i·bil′i·ty** *n.* **—di·vis′i·bly** *adv.*

di·vi·sion (di·vizh′ən) *n.* 1 The act of dividing. 2 A part, section, or particular category. 3 A disagreement; discord. 4 That which separates, divides, or makes different. 5 The act of sharing; distribution. 6 *Math.* The operation of finding the factor by which a divisor must be multiplied to produce a given dividend. 7 *Mil.* A major tactical and administrative unit that can function independently, in the army commanded by a major general. **8** A separation into opposing groups of voters in a legislative body. —**di·vi′sion·al** *adj.*

di·vi·sive (di·vī′siv, di·vis′iv, -viz′-) *adj.* Provoking dissension, discord, or disunity. —**di·vi′sive·ly** *adv.* —**di·vi′sive·ness** *n.*

di·vi·sor (di·vī′zər) *n. Math.* A number by which another number or quantity is divided.

di·vorce (di·vôrs′, -vōrs′) *n.* **1** The legal dissolution of a marriage. **2** Severance; separation. —*v.* **·vorced, ·vorc·ing** *v.t.* **1** To free legally from a marriage relationship. **2** To sunder; sever; separate. **3** To obtain a legal divorce from. —*v.i.* **4** To get a divorce. [< L *divortium* < *divertere* separate, divert] —**di·vorce′ment** *n.*

di·vor·cee (di·vôr′sē′, -vōr′-) *n.* A divorced person.

di·vor·cée (di·vôr′sā′, -vōr′-, di·vôr′sā, -vōr′-) *n.* A divorced woman. —**di·vor′cé′** *n. Masc.* [F]

div·ot (div′ət) *n.* A piece of turf cut from the sod by the stroke of a golf club. [< Scot. *devat*]

di·vulge (di·vulj′, dī-) *v.t.* **·vulged, ·vulg·ing** To tell, as a secret; disclose; reveal. [< L *dis-* away + *vulgare* make public] —**di·vulge′ment, di·vul′gence** (-jəns), **di·vulg′er** *n.*

div·vy (div′ē) *Slang n. pl.* **·vies** A share; dividend. —*v.t.* **·vied, ·vy·ing** To divide; often with *up*. [Short for DIVIDE]

Dix·ie (dik′sē) *n.* The southern United States: also **Dixie Land.**

Dix·ie·land (dik′sē·land′) *n.* A style of jazz originally played in New Orleans.

diz·zy (diz′ē) *adj.* **·zi·er, ·zi·est 1** Having a feeling of whirling and confusion; giddy. **2** Causing or caused by giddiness. **3** *Informal* Thoughtless; capricious; silly; stupid. —*v.t.* **·zied, ·zy·ing** To make giddy; confuse. [< OE *dysig* foolish] —**diz′zi·ly** *adv.* —**diz′zi·ness** *n.*

dkg, dkg. dekagram(s).

dkl, dkl. dekaliter(s).

dkm, dkm. dekameter(s).

dks, dks. dekastere(s).

D/L demand loan.

dl, dl. deciliter(s).

D.Lit., D.Litt. Doctor of Letters (Literature) (L *Doctor Lit(t)erarum*).

dlr. dealer.

D.L.S. Doctor of Library Science.

DM., Dm. Deutsche mark.

dm, dm. decameter(s); decimeter(s).

D.M.D. Doctor of Dental Medicine (L *Dentariae Medicinae Doctor*).

D.Mus. Doctor of Music.

DMZ demilitarized zone.

D.N. our Lord (L *Dominus noster*).

DNA deoxyribonucleic acid.

do¹ (dōō) *v.* **did, done, do·ing, does** *v.t.* **1** To perform, as an action; execute, as a piece of work. **2** To finish; complete. **3** To deal with or take care of: to *do* chores. **4** To cause or produce; bring about: to *do* good. **5** To exert; put forth: He *did* his best. **6** To work at as one's occupation. **7** To translate. **8** To present (a play, etc.): to *do* Hamlet. **9** To play the part of: to *do* Ophelia. **10** To cover; travel: to *do* a mile in four minutes. **11** To visit: to *do* the Louvre. **12** To serve; be sufficient for: Five dollars will *do* me. **13** To extend; render: to *do* homage. **14** To solve; work out, as a problem. **15** To serve, as a term in prison. **16** *Informal* To cheat; swindle. —*v.i.* **17** To exert oneself; strive: to *do* or die. **18** To conduct or behave oneself. **19** To fare; get along: I *did* badly in the race. **20** To suffice; serve the purpose. —**do away with 1** To throw away; discard. **2** To kill; destroy. —**do by** To act toward. —**do for 1** To provide for; care for. **2** *Informal* To ruin; kill. —**do in** *Slang* To kill. —**do over** To redecorate. —**do up 1** To tie up, as a parcel. **2** To roll up or arrange, as the hair. **3** To clean; repair. **4** To tire out. —**make do** To get along with whatever is available. — *auxiliary* As an auxiliary, *do* is used: **1** Without specific meaning in negative, interrogative, and inverted constructions: I *do* not want it; *Do* you want to leave?; Little *did* he know. **2** To add force to imperatives: *Do* hurry. **3**

To express emphasis: I *do* believe you. **4** As a substitute for another verb: Did he come? Yes, he *did*. —*n. pl.* **do's** or **dos** *Informal* A social gathering; festivity. [< OE *dōn*]

do² (dō) *n. Music* In solmization, the tone C or the first tone of a diatonic scale. [Ital. See GAMUT.]

D.O. Doctor of Osteopathy.

do. ditto.

D.O.A. dead on arrival.

do·a·ble (dōō′ə·bəl) *adj.* Capable of being done.

dob·bin (dob′in) *n.* A horse, esp. a plodding or patient one. [Var. of *Robin* < *Robert*]

Do·ber·man pin·scher (dō′bər·mən pin′shər) One of a breed of large, short-haired dogs, usu. black with rusty brown markings. [< L. *Doberman*, 19th c. Ger. breeder]

Doberman pinscher

doc. document.

doc·ile (dos′əl, *Brit.* dō′sīl) *adj.* **1** Easy to train; teachable. **2** Easy to manage or handle. [< L *docilis* able to be taught] —**doc′ile·ly** *adv.* —**do·cil·i·ty** (do·sil′ə·tē, dō-) *n.* — Syn. **2** tractable, complaint, obedient, pliant.

dock¹ (dok) *n.* **1** An artificial basin for ships. **2** The water between two adjoining piers. **3** A pier or wharf. —*v.t.* **1** To bring (a ship or boat) into a dock. —*v.i.* **2** To come into a dock. [< MDu. *docke*]

dock² (dok) *n.* **1** The solid part of an animal's tail. **2** An animal's tail when clipped or bobbed. —*v.t.* **1** To cut off the end of (a tail, etc.); clip. **2** To clip short the tail of. **3** To take a part from (wages, etc.). **4** To take a part from the wages of. [ME *dok*]

dock³ (dok) *n.* An enclosed space for prisoners on trial in court. [< Flemish *dok* cage]

dock⁴ (dok) *n.* A large-leaved weed of the buckwheat family. [< OE *docce*]

dock·age¹ (dok′ij) *n.* **1** A charge for docking. **2** Provision for docking. **3** The act of docking.

dock·age² (dok′ij) *n.* **1** Curtailment, as of wages; reduction. **2** Waste matter in grain.

dock·et (dok′it) *n.* **1** A condensed statement of a document. **2** *Law.* A record of the principal steps taken in a case; also, the register of such records. **3** A calendar of the cases to be tried in a court. **4** Any calendar of business. **5** A tag or label attached to a parcel ready for delivery. — *v.t.* **1** To place on a docket. **2** To attach a docket or label to. [?]

dock·yard (dok′yärd′) *n.* **1** A place for building or repairing ships. **2** *Brit.* A navy yard.

doc·tor (dok′tər) *n.* **1** A qualified practitioner of medicine or surgery in any of its branches. **2** A person who has received the highest academic degree, as a Ph.D., or has had a high honorary degree conferred on him. **3** A medicine man, wizard, or conjurer. —*v.t. Informal* **1** To prescribe for or treat medicinally. **2** To repair. **3** To alter; falsify, as evidence. —*v.i. Informal* **4** To practice medicine. **5** To take medicine or undergo medicinal treatment. [L, a teacher] —**doc′tor·al** *adj.*

doc·tor·ate (dok′tər·it) *n.* The degree, status, or title of one who holds a doctor's degree.

doc·tri·naire (dok′trə·nâr′) *adj.* Theoretical; visionary. —*n.* One whose views are derived from theories rather than from facts.

doc·trine (dok′trin) *n.* That which is set forth for acceptance or belief, esp., in religion, a belief or precept; dogma. [< L *doctrina* teaching]

doc·u·dra·ma (dok′yə·drä′mə, -drä′-) *n.* A television drama or series based on fact, presented in documentary style.

doc·u·ment (dok′yə·mənt) *n.* Written or printed matter conveying authoritative information, records, or evidence. —*v.t.* **1** To prove by documentary evidence. **2** To supply with notes and references to authoritative material: to *document* a text. [< L *documentum* a lesson] — **doc′u·men·ta′tion** *n.*

doc·u·men·ta·ry (dok′yə·men′tər·ē) *adj.* **1** Of, pertaining to, supported by, or based upon documents: also

doc·u·men·tal. 2 Of, pertaining to, or of the nature of a presentation, as in a film, that purports to record with little or no fictionalization the action displayed. —*n. pl.* **·ries** A documentary film, television show, etc.

dod·der (dod′ər) *v.i.* To tremble or totter, as from age. [ME *dadiren*]

dodeca- *combining form* Twelve; of or having twelve: *dodecagon.* Also, **dodec-.** [< Gk. *dōdeka*]

do·dec·a·gon (dō·dek′ə·gon) *n. Geom.* A figure, esp. a plane figure, with twelve sides and twelve angles. [< Gk. *dōdekagōnon*]

do·dec·a·he·dron (dō′dek·ə·hē′drən) *n. pl.* **·drons** or **·dra** (-drə) A solid bounded by twelve plane faces. —**do′dec·a·he′dral** *adj.*

dodge (doj) *v.* **dodged, dodg·ing** *v.t.* **1** To avoid by a sudden turn or twist. **2** To evade by cunning or trickery. —*v.i.* **3** To move or change position suddenly, as to avoid a blow. **4** To practice trickery; be deceitful. —*n.* **1** An act of dodging. **2** A trick to deceive or cheat. [?]

Dodecahedron

dodg·er (doj′ər) *n.* **1** One who dodges. **2** A tricky fellow. **3** A small handbill. **4** A cooked cake of Indian meal.

do·do (dō′dō) *n. pl.* **·does** or **·dos** An extinct bird of Mauritius about the size of a turkey. [< Pg. *doudo* foolish]

doe (dō) *n.* The female of the deer, antelope, hare, rabbit, or kangaroo. [< OE *dā*]

do·er (dōō′ər) *n.* One who does something, esp., one who accomplishes a lot.

does (duz) Present tense, third person singular, of DO.

Dodo

doe·skin (dō′skin′) *n.* **1** The skin of a doe. **2** A heavy, twilled, cotton fabric napped on one side; also, a woolen fabric resembling doeskin.

does·n't (duz′ənt) Contraction of *does not.*

doff (dof, dôf) *v.t.* **1** To take off, as clothing. **2** To take off (the hat) in salutation. **3** To discard. [Contraction of DO OFF]

dog (dôg, dog) *n.* **1** A carnivorous, domesticated mammal of worldwide distribution and many varieties, related to the wolf. **2** Any of a family (*Canidae*) of animals including the dog, wolf, jackal, etc. **3** The male of the dog and similar animals: a *dog* fox. **4** PRAIRIE DOG. **5** *Mech.* Any small device that holds or grips. **6** ANDIRON. **7** A fellow; man-about-town: a gay dog. **8** A scoundrel; rascal. **9** *Slang* HOT DOG. **10** *pl. Slang* Feet. —**go to the dogs** *Informal* To be ruined; degenerate. —**put on the dog.** *Slang* To make a pretentious display. —*adv.* Very; utterly: *dog-tired.* —*v.t.* **dogged, dog·ging** To follow persistently; hound; hunt. [< OE *dogga*]

dog biscuit A hard biscuit for feeding dogs.

dog-cart (dôg′kärt′, dog′-) *n.* **1** A one-horse vehicle with two seats set back to back. **2** A cart hauled by dogs.

dog days The hot, sultry season in July and August.

doge (dōj) *n.* The elective chief magistrate in the former republics of Venice and Genoa. [Ital.] —**doge′dom, doge′·ship** *n.*

dog-ear (dôg′ir′, dog′-) *n.* The corner of a page turned down to mark a place. —*v.t.* To turn or fold down the corner of (a page). —**dog′eared** *adj.*

dog·fight (dôg′fīt′, dog′-) *n.* **1** A fight between or as between dogs. **2** *Mil.* Combat at close quarters between aircraft or tanks.

dog·fish (dôg′fish′, dog′-) *n. pl.* **·fish** or **·fish·es** One of various small sharks.

dog·ged (dôg′id, dog′-) *adj.* Persistent; stubborn. —**dog′ged·ly** *adv.* —**dog′ged·ness** *n.*

dog·ger·el (dôg′ər·əl, dog′-) *n.* Trivial, awkwardly written verse. —*adj.* Of or composed of such verse. Also **dog′·grel.** [ME]

dog·gish (dôg′ish, dog′-) *adj.* **1** Like a dog; snappish. **2** *Informal* Stylish; chic. —**dog′gish·ly** *adv.* —**dog′gish·ness** *n.*

dog-gone (dôg′gôn′, dog′gon′) *v.t.* **-goned, -gon·ing** *Informal* DAMN. —*adj. & adv.* DAMN. [Euphemism for *God damn*]

dog·gy (dôg′ē, dog′-) *adj.* **·gi·er, ·gi·est** Of or pertaining to dogs: a *doggy* smell. —*n. pl.* **·gies** A pet dog. Also **dog′gie.**

dog house A shelter for a dog; kennel. —**in the dog house** *Slang* Out of favor.

do·gie (dō′gē) *n.* In the w U.S., a stray or motherless calf. [?]

dog·ma (dôg′mə, dog′-) *n. pl.* **·mas** or **·ma·ta** (-mə·tə) **1** *Theol.* A system of teachings of religious truth as maintained by the Christian church or any portion of it. **2** Any doctrine asserted and adopted on authority. **3** Any accepted principle, maxim, or tenet. [< Gk. *dogma* opinion]

dog·mat·ic (dôg·mat′ik, dog-) *adj.* **1** Stating opinions without evidence. **2** Overly positive or arrogant. **3** Of, like, or pertaining to dogma. Also **dog·mat′i·cal.** —**dog·mat′i·cal·ly** *adv.* —**dog·mat′i·cal·ness** *n.* —**Syn. 2** opinionated, overbearing, dictatorial. **3** doctrinal.

dog·ma·tism (dôg′mə·tiz′əm, dog′-) *n.* Positive or arrogant assertion, as of belief, without proof.

dog·ma·tize (dôg′mə·tīz, dog′-) *v.* **·tized, ·tiz·ing** *v.i.* **1** To express oneself dogmatically. —*v.t.* **2** To declare or assert as a dogma. —**dog′ma·tist, dog′ma·ti·za′tion, dog′ma·tiz′er** *n.*

dog·nap (dôg′nap′) *v.t.* **·napped** or **·naped, ·nap·ping** or **·nap·ing** To steal (a dog), esp. for sale to a medical research laboratory. [< DOG + (KID)NAP] —**dog′nap′per, dog′nap′er** *n.*

do-good·er (dōō′gŏŏd′ər) *n.* A well-meaning but naive reformer or social activist whose efforts are futile or foolish.

dog rose The wild brier of Europe, bearing pink flowers.

dog sled A sled drawn by dogs. Also **dog sledge.**

dog's life *Informal* A wretched existence.

Dog star The star Sirius.

dog's-tooth violet (dôgz′tōōth′, dogz′-) *n.* Any of various small, spring-flowering herbs of the lily family. Also **dog′tooth′ violet.**

dog tag 1 A small plate for a dog, usu. indicating ownership. **2** *Informal* A soldier's identification tag.

dog·tooth (dôg′tōōth′, dog′-) *n.* A human canine tooth or eyetooth. Also **dog tooth.**

dog-trot (dôg′trot′, dog′-) *n.* A regular and easy trot.

dog-watch (dôg′woch′, -wôch′, dog′-) *n. Naut.* One of the two watches aboard ship, each of two hours, from 4 to 6 and 6 to 8 P.M.

dog·wood (dôg′wŏŏd′, dog′-) *n.* Any of certain trees or shrubs, as the **flowering** or **Virginia dogwood,** with large decorative pinkish white flowers.

do·gy *n.* (dō′gē) *n.* DOGIE.

doi·ly (doi′lē) *n. pl.* **·lies** A matlike napkin, used under dishes, as a decoration, etc. [< *Doily* or *Doyley,* 17th c. English draper]

do·ings (dōō′ingz) *n. pl.* Proceedings; acts; course of conduct.

Dogwood blossoms

do-it-your·self (dōō′it·yər·self′) *adj.* Of, pertaining to, used in, or engaged in construction, repair, or other work that an amateur does without professional help.

dol. (*pl.* **dols.**) dollar.

dol·drums (dol′drəmz) *n. pl.* **1** Those parts of the ocean near the equator where calms or fitful winds prevail. **2** A dull, depressed, or bored condition of mind; the dumps. [?]

dole (dōl) *n.* **1** Something given to the needy, as food or money. **2** A sum of money officially paid to an unemployed person for sustenance. **3** Something given out in small portions. —*v.t.* **doled, dol·ing** To dispense in small quantities; distribute: usu. with *out.* [< OE *dāl*]

dole·ful (dōl′fəl) *adj.* Melancholy; mournful. Also **dole′some** (-səm). [< LL *dolium* grief] —**Syn.** dismal, sad, sorrowful, woeful. —**dole′ful·ly** *adv.* —**dole′ful·ness** *n.*

dol·i·cho·ce·phal·ic (dol′i·kō·sə·fal′ik) *adj.* Having a long skull, the breadth less than one third of the length. Also **dol′i·cho·ceph′a·lous** (-sef′ə·ləs). [< Gk. *dolichos* long + *kephalē* head]

doll (dol) *n.* **1** A child's toy representing a person. **2** A pretty but superficial woman. **3** *Slang* Any girl or woman. **4** *Slang* Any person warmly regarded. —*v.t. & v.i. Slang* To dress elaborately: with *up.* [< *Doll,* a nickname for Dorothy]

dol·lar (dol′ər) *n.* **1** The basic monetary unit of the United States, having the legal value of 100 cents. **2** The basic monetary unit of various other countries, as Canada and Argentina. **3** A U.S. legal coin or paper greenback worth 100 cents. **4** A loose term for the peso, the Haitian gourde, and other coins. [< G *Taler*]

dollar diplomacy The policy of utilizing the financial power of a country to strengthen its foreign relations or to promote private commercial interests abroad.

dollar sign The sign ($) meaning dollar or dollars before a number. Also **dollar mark.**

dol·ly (dol′ē) *n. pl.* **·lies 1** DOLL (def. 1). **2** A light hand truck, with wheels or rollers, used for moving heavy loads. **3** A low, wheeled platform on which a motion-picture or television camera is set. —*v.i.* **·lied, ly·ing** To move a television or motion-picture camera toward a scene or subject: with *in.* [< *Dolly,* a nickname for Dorothy]

dol·man (dol′mən) *n. pl.* **dol·mans** A woman's coat with dolman sleeves. [< Turkish *dōlāmān* long robe]

dolman sleeve A sleeve tapering from a wide opening at the armhole to a narrow one at the wrist.

dol·men (dol′men) *n.* A monument of large stones set on end and capped with a single huge stone or stones. [< Cornish *tolmen* hole of stone]

dol·o·mite (dol′ə·mīt) *n.* A brittle mineral form of calcium magnesium carbonate. [< D. de *Dolomieu,* 1750–1801, French geologist]

do·lor (dō′lər) *n.* Sorrow; anguish. [L]

do·lor·ous (dō′lər·əs, dol′ər-) *adj.* Expressing or causing sorrow or pain. —**do′lor·ous·ly** *adv.* —**do′lor·ous·ness** *n.*

dol·phin (dol′fin) *n.* **1** Any of various members of the whale family, having beaklike snouts. **2** *Naut.* A spar or buoy for mooring boats. [< Gk. *delphis*]

Dolphin

dolt (dōlt) *n.* A stupid person. [< ME *dold* stupid] —**dolt′·ish** *adj.*

-dom *suffix of nouns* **1** State or condition of being: *freedom.* **2** Domain of: *kingdom.* **3** All those having a certain rank, state, or condition: *Christendom.* [< OE *dōm* state]

dom. domestic; dominion.

do·main (dō·mān′) *n.* **1** A territory over which dominion is exercised. **2** A department, as of knowledge. **3** Land owned by one person; estate. [< L < *dominus* lord]

dome (dōm) *n.* **1** A vaulted, hemispherical roof; a cupola. **2** Any cuplike top or covering. —*v.* **domed, dom·ing** *v.t.* **1** To furnish or cover with a dome. **2** To shape like a dome. —*v.i.* **3** To rise or swell upward like a dome. [< Ital. *duomo* cupola]

do·mes·tic (də·mes′tik) *adj.* **1** Belonging to the family, house, or household. **2** Fond of family life, duties, or housekeeping. **3** Domesticated; tame. **4** Produced in one's own country. —*n.* A household servant. [< L *domus* house] —**do·mes′ti·cal·ly** *adv.*

do·mes·ti·cate (də·mes′tə·kāt) *v.* **·cat·ed, ·cat·ing** *v.t.* **1** To train for domestic use; tame. **2** To make domestic. —*v.i.* **3** To become domestic. —**do·mes′ti·ca′tion** *n.*

do·mes·tic·i·ty (dō′mes·tis′ə·tē) *n. pl.* **·ties 1** Fondness of home and family. **2** A household.

domestic science HOME ECONOMICS.

dom·i·cile (dom′ə·səl, -sīl) *n.* A home, house, or dwelling. —*v.t. & v.i.* **·ciled, ·cil·ing** *v.t.* To settle in a domicile. Also **dom′i·cil.** [< L *domus* house]

dom·i·cil·i·ar·y (dom′ə·sil′ē·er′ē) *adj.* Pertaining to a fixed or a private residence.

dom·i·nance (dom′ə·nəns) *n.* The state or condition of being dominant. Also **dom′i·nan·cy.**

dom·i·nant (dom′ə·nənt) *adj.* **1** Ruling; governing; prevailing. **2** Having a masking effect on a contrasting or recessive factor in the genetic endowment of an organism. —*n. Music* The tone a perfect fifth above the tonic. —**dom′i·nant·ly** *adv.*

dom·i·nate (dom′ə·nāt) *v.* **·nat·ed, ·nat·ing** *v.t.* **1** To control; govern. **2** To have supreme or masterful power or influ-

ence over. **3** To tower above; loom over: The city *dominates* the plain. —*v.i.* **4** To have control; hold sway. [< L *dominare* rule, dominate] —**dom′i·na′tion, dom′i·na′tor** *n.*

dom·i·neer (dom′ə·nir′) *v.t. & v.i.* **1** To tyrannize; bully. **2** To tower or loom (over or above). [< L *dominus* lord]

dom·i·neer·ing (dom′ə·nir′ing) *adj.* Overbearing; arrogant. —**dom′i·neer·ing·ly** *adv.* —**Syn.** authoritative, despotic, imperious, tyrannical.

Do·min·i·can (də·min′i·kən) *adj.* **1** Of or pertaining to St. Dominic or a monastic order following his rule. **2** Of or pertaining to the Dominican Republic or its people. —*n.* **1** A member of a Dominican order. **2** A citizen or native of the Dominican Republic.

Dominican Republic A republic on the E part of Hispaniola in the Caribbean, 18,700 sq. mi., cap. Santo Domingo.

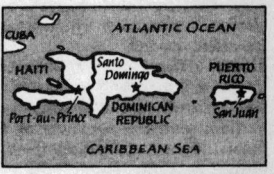

dom·i·nie (dom′ə·nē) **1** In Scotland, a schoolmaster. **2** *Informal* Any minister. [< L *dominus* lord]

do·min·ion (də·min′yən) *n.* **1** Sovereign authority; sway. **2** A country under a particular government. **3** Formerly, a self-governing member of the Commonwealth of Nations. [< L *dominus* lord]

Dominion Day July 1, the anniversary of the federation of Canada into a dominion (July 1, 1867), a legal holiday in Canada.

dom·i·no[1] (dom′ə·nō) *n. pl.* **·noes** or **·nos 1** A small mask for the eyes. **2** A loose robe, hood, and mask worn at masquerades. [< MF, a clerical garment] • See MASK.

dom·i·no[2] (dom′ə·nō) *n. pl.* **·noes** or **·nos 1** A small oblong piece of wood, etc., divided on one side into halves left blank or marked with dots. **2** *pl. (construed as sing.)* A game played with such pieces. —*adj.* Describing the view or political theory that a series of events is unavoidably contingent on the occurrence of an initial event, as a row of dominoes collapses when the first is toppled.

don[1] (don) *n.* **1** A Spanish gentleman or nobleman. **2** An important personage. **3** *Informal* In English universities, a head, fellow, or tutor of a college. [Sp. < L *dominus* lord]

don[2] (don) *v.t.* **donned, don·ning** To put on, as a garment. [Contraction of *do on*]

Don (don) *n.* Mr.; sir: a title of respect in Spain and Spanish-speaking countries.

do·ña (dō′nyä) *n.* A Spanish lady. [Sp. < L *domina* lady]

Do·ña (dō′nyä) *n.* Lady; madam: a title of respect in Spain and Spanish-speaking countries.

do·nate (dō′nāt, dō·nāt′) *v.t.* **·nat·ed, ·nat·ing** To bestow as a gift, esp. to a cause; present; contribute. [< L *donare* give < *donum* a gift] —**do′na·tor** *n.*

do·na·tion (dō·nā′shən) *n.* **1** The act of donating. **2** That which is donated; a gift.

done (dun) *p.p.* of DO[1]. —*adj.* **1** Completed. **2** Cooked sufficiently. —**done for 1** Without hope; destined to worsen, die, etc. **2** In a hopeless condition; ruined, defeated, etc.

do·nee (dō·nē′) *n.* One who receives a gift.

don·jon (dun′jən, don′-) *n.* The principal tower or keep of a medieval castle. [Var. of DUNGEON]

Don Juan (don ʰwän′, don jōō′ən, *Sp.* dôn hwän′) **1** A legendary Spanish nobleman and seducer of women. **2** Any seducer.

don·key (dong′kē, dung′-) *n.* **1** Any of a domesticated species of the ass. **2** A stupid or stubborn person. [?]

don·na (don′ə, *Ital.* dôn′nä) *n.* An Italian lady. [Ital. < L *domina* lady]

Don·na (don′ə, *Ital.* dôn′nä) *n.* Lady; madam: a title of respect, used in Italy and Italian-speaking countries.

don·nish (don′ish) *adj.* **1** Of or like an English don. **2** Formal; pedantic.

do·nor (dō′nor) *n.* **1** A giver; donator. **2** One from whom blood is taken for transfusion or from whom tissue, an organ, etc., is obtained for another. [< L *donare* give]

do-noth·ing (dōō′nuth′ing) *n.* An idler.

Don Quix·ote (don kwik′sət, ki·hō′tē; *Sp.* dôn kē·hō′tä) The hero of Cervantes' romance of that name, a satire on chivalry. Also **Don Qui·jo′te.**

don't (dōnt) Contraction of *do not.* • The use of *don't* for *doesn't* (She don't care) is now nonstandard in speech and writing. However, it is still used informally in educated conversation in parts of the U.S.

doo·dad (dōō′dad) *n. Informal* 1 DOOHICKEY. 2 A small ornament; bauble.

doo·dle (dōōd′l) *v.i. Informal* To draw pictures, symbols, etc., while the mind is otherwise occupied. —*n.* A drawing so made. [dial. E *doodle* be idle]

doo·dle·bug (dōōd′l·bug′) *n.* 1 The larva of the ant lion. 2 Loosely, any droning insect. [? < DOODLE + BUG]

doo·hick·ey (dōō′hik′ē) *n. Informal* Any contrivance or device, the name of which is not known or immediately recalled; doodad.

doom (dōōm) *v.t.* 1 To pronounce judgment upon; condemn. 2 To destine to disaster. 3 To decree as a penalty. —*n.* 1 Death; ruin. 2 Destiny. 3 Judicial decision; condemnation; sentence. —**crack of doom** The signal for the Last Judgment. [< OE *dōm*] —**Syn.** *n.* 1 destruction, downfall, end. 2 fate, lot, portion.

dooms·day (dōōmz′dā′) *n.* The day of the Last Judgment, or of any final judgment.

door (dôr, dōr) *n.* 1 A hinged, sliding, or revolving frame used for closing or opening an entrance or exit. 2 DOORWAY. 3 Any means or avenue of exit or entrance. 4 The house or room to which a door is attached: three *doors* down the street. [< OE *duru* pair of doors and *dor*]

door·bell (dôr′bel′, dōr′-) *n.* A device at a door to sound a signal that someone wishes admittance.

door·jamb (dôr′jam′, dōr′-) *n.* The vertical piece at the side of a doorway.

door·keep·er (dôr′kē′pər, dōr′) *n.* A guardian or keeper of a door.

door·knob (dôr′nob′, dōr′-) *n.* The handle for turning the catch to open a door.

door·man (dôr′man′, dōr′-) *n. pl.* **·men** (-men′, -mən) An attendant at the door of a hotel, apartment house, etc., who assists persons entering and leaving the building.

door·mat (dôr′mat′, dōr′-) *n.* A mat placed at an entrance for wiping off the shoes.

door·nail (dôr′nāl′, dōr′-) *n.* A nail or stud with a large head formerly used to ornament doors. —**dead as a doornail** Quite dead.

door·sill (dôr′sil′, dōr′-) *n.* The sill or threshold of a door: also **door sill.**

door·step (dôr′step′, dōr′-) *n* A step or one of a series of steps leading to a door.

door·stop (dôr′stop′, dōr′-) *n.* A device to keep a door open.

door·way (dôr′wā′, dōr′-) *n.* 1 Any opening closed by a door. 2 Any access.

door·yard (dôr′yärd′, dōr′-) *n.* A yard around, or esp. in front of the door of, a house.

dope (dōp) *n.* 1 *Slang* Any drug used for inducing euphoria. 2 *Slang* A drug addict. 3 *Slang* Any information or forecast. 4 Any thick liquid or semifluid, as a lubricant, etc. 5 Any substance used in treating a cloth surface, as of an airplane wing, to increase strength or produce tautness. 6 *Slang* A stupid person. —*v.t.* **doped, dop·ing** 1 To give dope to. 2 *Slang* To stupefy or exhilarate as by a drug: often with *up.* —**dope out** *Slang* 1 To plan. 2 To figure out; solve. [< Du. *doop* dipping sauce < *doopen* dip]

do·pey (dō′pē) *adj.* **·pi·er, ·pi·est** *Slang* 1 Stupefied from narcotics. 2 Stupid; dull. —**do′pi·ly** *adv.* —**do′pi·ness** *n.*

Dop·pler effect (dop′lər) *Physics* The change in the observed frequency of a wave due to the relative motion of the observer and the source. [< C. J. *Doppler*, 1803–1853, Austrian physicist and mathematician]

Dor·ic (dôr′ik, dor′-) *adj. Archit.* Of or constructed in the earliest and simplest of the three orders of Greek architecture, characterized by thick, fluted columns and plain capitals. [< Gk. *Dōris*, a district of ancient Greece] • See CAPITAL.

dorm (dôrm) *n. Informal* DORMITORY.

dor·mant (dôr′mənt) *adj.* 1 Sleeping. 2 Quiet; motionless. 3 Sleeping or resting, as certain animals and plants in winter. 4 Not erupting: said of a volcano. 5 Inactive; unused. [< L *dormire* to sleep] —**dor′man·cy** *n.*

dor·mer (dôr′mər) *n. Archit.* 1 A vertical window in a small gable rising from a sloping roof: also **dormer window.** 2 The gable in which this window is set. [< OF *dormeor* < *dormir* to sleep]

Dormer

dor·mi·to·ry (dôr′mə·tôr′ē, -tō′rē) *n. pl.* **·ries** 1 A large room in which many persons sleep. 2 A building providing sleeping and living accommodations, esp. at a school or college. [< L *dormire* to sleep]

dor·mouse (dôr′mous′) *n. pl.* **·mice** One of various small, Old World, squirrel-like rodents. [? < OF *dormir* to sleep + MOUSE]

dor·sal (dôr′səl) *adj.* Of, pertaining to, on, or near the back. [< L *dorsum* back] —**dor′sal·ly** *adv.*

do·ry (dôr′ē, dō′rē) *n. pl.* **·ries** A deep, flat-bottomed rowboat with a sharp prow and flat stern, adapted for rough weather. [< native Honduran name]

dos·age (dō′sij) *n.* 1 The administering of medicine in prescribed quantity. 2 The total dose to be given, as medicine, X-rays, etc.

Dormouse

dose (dōs) *n.* 1 The quantity of medicine prescribed to be taken at one time; also, the degree of exposure to X-rays or other radiation in a certain period of time. 2 Anything disagreeable given as a prescription or infliction. —*v.* **dosed, dos·ing** *v.t.* 1 To give medicine to in a dose. 2 To give, as medicine or drugs, in doses. —*v.i.* 3 To take medicines. [< L *dosis* < Gk., orig., a giving] —**dos′er** *n.*

do·sim·e·ter (dō·sim′ə·tər) *n. Med.* An instrument for measuring exposure to X-rays or other radiation. [< DOSE + -METER]

dos·si·er (dos′ē·ā, dôs′-, dô·syā′) *n.* A collection of documents, etc., relating to a particular matter or person. [F]

dost (dust) *Archaic* second person singular, present tense of DO: used with *thou.*

dot[1] (dot) *n.* 1 A minute, round, or nearly round mark. 2 *Music* A point, written after a note or rest, which lengthens its value by half; also, a staccato mark. 3 A precise moment of time: on the *dot.* 4 A signal of shorter duration than the dash, used in the transmission of messages. —*v.* **dot·ted, dot·ting** *v.t.* 1 To mark with a dot or dots. 2 To spread or scatter like dots. 3 To cover with dots. —*v.i.* 4 To make a dot or dots. [< OE *dott* head of a boil] —**Syn.** *n.* 1 flake, fleck, speck, spot.

dot[2] (dot) *n.* A woman's marriage dowry. [< L *dos, dotis*] —**do·tal** (dōt′l) *adj.*

do·tage (dō′tij) *n.* 1 Feebleness of mind, as a result of old age; senility. 2 Foolish and extravagant affection. [< DOTE + -AGE]

do·tard (dō′tərd) *n.* A senile old person.

dote (dōt) *v.t.* **dot·ed, dot·ing** 1 To lavish extreme fondness: with *on* or *upon.* 2 To be in one's dotage. [< MDu. *doten* be silly] —**dot′er** *n.* —**dot′ing·ly** *adv.*

doth (duth) *Archaic* third person singular, present tense of DO.

dot·ty (dot′ē) *adj.* **·ti·er, ·ti·est** 1 Consisting of or marked with dots. 2 *Informal* Of unsteady or feeble gait. 3 *Brit. Informal* Slightly demented; odd; eccentric. —**dot′ti·ly** *adv.* —**dot′ti·ness** *n.*

Dou·ay Bible (dōō·ā′) An English translation of the Latin Vulgate edition of the Bible for use in the Roman Catholic Church. Also **Douay Version.**

dou·ble (dub′əl) *adj.* 1 Having two of a sort together; being in pairs; coupled. 2 Twice as large, much, strong, heavy, valuable, or many. 3 Consisting of two unlike parts: a *double* standard. 4 Ambiguous, deceitful, or two-faced. 5 Doubled; folded. 6 *Bot.* Having the petals increased in number. —*n.* 1 Something that is twice as much. 2 A fold or plait. 3 A person or thing that closely resembles another. **4** An apparition or wraith. **5** A turning about or shift in direction. **6** A stand-in for an actor. **7** *pl.* A tennis game between two pairs of players; also, two successive faults in tennis. **8** In baseball, a two-base hit. **9** In card playing, the act of doubling. See DOUBLE (*v. def.* 7). —**on** (or **at**) **the double** In double-time: a military command. —*v.* **doub·led, doub·ling** *v.t.* **1** To make twice as great in number, size, value, force, etc. **2** To fold or bend one part of upon another: usually with *over, up, back,* etc. **3** To do over again; repeat. **4** To be twice the quantity or number of. **5** To act or be the double of. **6** *Naut.* To sail around: to *double* a cape. **7** In bridge, to increase the value of (an opponent's bid) if the contract is fulfilled, or to increase the penalty if the contract is not fulfilled. —*v.i.* **8** To become double. **9** To turn and go back on a course: often with *back.* **10** To act or perform in two capacities. **11** In baseball, to hit a double. **12** In bridge, to double a bid. —**double up 1** To bend over or cause to bend over, as from pain or laughter. **2** To share one's quarters, bed, etc., with another. **3** In baseball, to complete a double play upon. — *adv.* **1** Twice. **2** In twice the quantity. Also **doub′ly** (dub′lē) *adv.* [< L *duplus* double] —**doub′ler** *n.*

doub·le-bar·reled (dub′əl·bar′əld) *adj.* **1** Having two barrels, as a shotgun. **2** Doubly effective. **3** Ambiguous in meaning.

doub·le-bass (dub′əl·bās′) *n.* The largest and deepest-toned of the stringed instruments played with a bow.

double bed A bed wide enough for two people.

double boiler A cooking utensil consisting of two pots, one fitting into the other.

doub·le-breast·ed (dub′əl·bres′tid) *adj.* Having two rows of buttons and a double thickness of cloth across the breast, as the jacket of a suit.

double chin A fat, fleshy fold under the chin.

doub·le-cross (dub′əl·krôs′, -kros′) *Slang v.t.* To betray by not acting as promised; cheat. —*n.* (-krôs′, -kros′) The act of or an instance of betrayal. —**doub′le-cross′er** *n.*

double dagger See DAGGER.

doub·le-date (dub′əl·dāt′) *v.t. & v.i.* **-dat·ed, -dat·ing** To make or go out on a double date (with).

double date *Informal* A social appointment made by two couples.

doub·le-deal·ing (dub′əl·dē′ling) *adj.* Treacherous; deceitful. —*n.* Duplicity. —**doub′le-deal′er** *n.*

doub·le-deck·er (dub′əl·dek′ər) *n.* **1** Any structure, vehicle, or vessel having two decks or levels. **2** A sandwich made with three slices of bread and two layers of filling.

doub·le-edged (dub′əl·ejd′) *adj.* **1** Having two cutting edges. **2** Applicable both for as well as against.

dou·ble-en·ten·dre (dōō·blän·tän′dr′, dub′əl än·tän′drə) *n.* A word or phrase of double meaning, the less obvious one often risqué. [F]

double entry A method of bookkeeping in which every transaction is made to appear as both a debit and a credit. —**doub′le-en′try** *adj.*

doub·le-faced (dub′əl·fāst′) *adj.* **1** Having two faces. **2** Deceitful; hypocritical.

double feature A program of two full-length motion pictures.

doub·le-head·er (dub′əl·hed′ər) *n.* Two games, esp. of baseball, played in succession on the same day by the same two teams.

double indemnity A clause in a life insurance policy by which a payment of double the face value of the policy is made in the event of accidental death.

doub·le-joint·ed (dub′əl·join′tid) *adj.* Having a joint in which the bones have unusual freedom of movement.

doub·le-park (dub′əl·pärk′) *v.t. & v.i.* To park (a motor vehicle) alongside another already parked along the curb. —**doub′le-park′ing** *n.*

double play In baseball, a play in which two base runners are put out.

double pneumonia Pneumonia in both lungs.

doub·le-quick (dub′əl·kwik′) *n. & v.* DOUBLE-TIME.

doub·le-reed (dub′əl·rēd′) *n. Music* A wind instrument

with a reed of two segments joined at one end. —*adj.* Having such a reed.

double standard A code of conduct permitting more sexual liberty to men than to women.

doub·let (dub′lit) *n.* **1** One of a pair of like things. **2** A pair or couple. **3** A short, close-fitting, outer garment, worn by men in the 15th to 17th centuries. **4** One of a pair of words derived from the same source but entering a language through different routes, as *regal* and *royal.* [< OF, something folded]

Doublet *def. 3*

doub·le-take (dub′əl·tāk′) *n.* The delayed reaction, with visible evidence of surprise, to a joke or situation, used as a comic device.

double talk 1 Speech in which meaningless syllable combinations are substituted for expected words. **2** Ambiguous talk meant to deceive.

doub·le-think (dub′əl·thingk′) *n.* **1** The capacity to hold contradictory opinions in full knowledge of their contradiction. **2** Confused thought. Also **dou′ble-think′.**

doub·le-time (dub′əl·tīm′) *n.* In the U.S. Army, a rate of march of 180 steps a minute. —*v.t. & v.i.* **-timed, -tim·ing** To march or cause to march at this pace.

doub·loon (du·blōōn′) *n.* A former Spanish gold coin. [< Sp. *doblón*]

doubt (dout) *v.t.* **1** To hesitate to believe; question. **2** To hold as uncertain. —*v.i.* **3** To be uncertain or unconvinced. **4** To be mistrustful. —*n.* **1** Lack of certain knowledge; uncertainty. **2** A matter or case of indecision. **3** A question, objection, or difficulty. [< L *dubitare*] —**doubt′a·ble** *adj.* —**doubt′er** *n.* —**doubt′ing·ly** *adv.* —**Syn.** *v.* **1** distrust, mistrust, suspect. *n.* **1** hesitancy, misgiving.

doubt·ful (dout′fal) *adj.* **1** Subject to doubt; not definite. **2** Uncertain; undecided. **3** Indistinct; ambiguous. **4** Questionable; dubious. —**doubt′ful·ly** *adv.* —**doubt′ful·ness** *n.*

doubt·less (dout′lis) *adv.* **1** Without doubt; unquestionably. **2** Probably. Also **doubt′less·ly.** —*adj.* Having no doubt.

douche (dōōsh) *n.* **1** A jet of water or vapor sprayed on or into the body for medicinal or hygienic reasons. **2** The instrument for administering it. **3** A bath using these facilities. —*v.t. & v.i.* **douched, douch·ing** To give or take a douche. [< Ital. *doccia* a water pipe]

dough (dō) *n.* **1** A soft mass of flour, liquid, and other ingredients mixed for baking into bread, cake, etc. **2** Any soft pasty mass. **3** *Slang* Money. [< OE *dāh*] —**dough′y** *adj.*

dough·boy (dō′boi′) *n. Informal* Formerly, an infantry soldier.

dough·nut (dō′nut) *n.* A small, usu. ring-shaped cake, fried in deep fat.

dough·ty (dou′tē) *adj.* **·ti·er, ·ti·est** *Archaic* Brave; valiant: now chiefly in humorous use. [< OE *dohtig*] —**dough′ti·ly** *adv.* —**dough′ti·ness** *n.*

Douglas fir A large tree of the pine family, found in w U.S. Also **Douglas hemlock, Douglas pine, Douglas spruce.** [< David *Douglas,* 1798–1834, Scottish botanist]

dour (dour, dōōr) *adj.* **1** Gloomy; sullen. **2** Aloof; forbidding. **3** Unyielding. [< L *durus*] —**dour′ly** *adv.* —**dour′ness** *n.*

douse[1] (dous) *v.* **doused, dous·ing** *v.t.* **1** To plunge into liquid. **2** To drench with water or other liquid. **3** To put out quickly: to *douse* a light. —*v.i.* **4** To become drenched or immersed. —*n.* A ducking or drenching. [?]

douse[2] (dous) *v.* DOWSE[2].

dove[1] (duv) *n.* **1** A pigeon. **2** A symbol of the Holy Spirit. **3** A symbol of peace. **4** One who favors conciliation and negotiation rather than military, as in a dispute. **5** Any gentle creature. [ME] —**dov′ish** *adj.*

dove[2] (dōv) *p.t.* of DIVE.

dove·cote (duv′kōt′, kot′) *n.* A small house, often raised and divided into compartments, for domestic pigeons. Also **dove′cot′** (-kot′).

---

add, āce, câre, pălm; end, ēven; it, īce; odd, ōpen, ôrder; tŏŏk, pōōl; up, bûrn; ə = a in above; u in .focus; yōō = u in fuse; oil; pout; check; go; ring; thin; this; zh, vision. < derived from; ? origin uncertain or unknown.

dove·tail (duv′tāl′) *n.* **1** A manner of joining boards, timbers, etc., by interlocking wedge-shaped tenons and spaces. **2** The joint so made. — *v.t. & v.i.* **1** To join by means of a dovetail or dovetails. **2** To fit in closely or aptly.

dow·a·ger (dou′ə-jər) *n.* **1** In English law, a widow holding property or title from her late husband. **2** Any elderly lady of dignified bearing. [< OF *douage* a dower]

dow·dy (dou′dē) *adj.* **·di·er, ·di·est** Not neat or fashionable; shabby. Also **dow′dy·ish.** —*n. pl.* **·dies** **1** A slatternly woman. **2** A fruit pie baked in a deep dish. [< ME *doude* a slut] —**dow′di·ly** *adv.* —**dow′di·ness** *n.*

dow·el (dou′əl) *n.* A pin or peg that fits into a corresponding hole, used for joining together two adjacent pieces. —*v.t.* **·eled** or **·elled, ·el·ing** or **·el·ling** To fasten with dowels. [< MLG *dovel* plug]

Dovetail joint

dow·er (dou′ər) *n.* **1** A widow's life portion of her husband's property. **2** The sum of one's natural gifts; endowment. —*v.t.* **1** To provide with a dower. **2** To endow, as with a talent. [< L *dos, dotis* a dowry]

down[1] (doun) *adv.* **1** From a higher to a lower place, level, position, etc. **2** In or into a lower place, position, etc. **3** On or to the ground. **4** To or toward the south. **5** From a former or earlier time or owner. **6** To a smaller bulk, diminished volume, greater density, etc.: to boil syrup *down.* **7** To or into a less active state. **8** To a lower rate, price, demand or amount. **9** Into or in an attitude of intensity, earnestness, etc.: to get *down* to work. **10** In or into ill health. **11** In or into subjection: His competitors kept him *down.* **12** Completely; entirely: loaded *down* with honors. **13** In cash, as at the time of purchase. **14** On or as on paper: Take *down* his words. —*adj.* **1** Going or facing toward a lower position or place: a *down* elevator. **2** In a lower place: The wires are *down.* **3** Gone, brought, or paid down. **4** Downcast; dejected. **5** Sick in bed. **6** In games, behind an opponent's score by (a number of) points, goals, etc. **7** In football, not in play. —**down and out** Disabled, destitute, or socially outcast. —**down on** Opposed to, as from anger, ill will, or enmity. —*v.t.* **1** To knock, throw, or put down; subdue. **2** To swallow: to *down* a beer. —*prep.* **1** In a descending direction along, upon, or in. **2** From an earlier to a later period in the duration of: —*n.* **1** A downward movement; a descent. **2** A reverse of fortune: the ups and *downs* of life. **3** In football, any of the four consecutive plays during which a team must advance the ball at least ten yards in order to maintain possession of it. [< OE *adūne* < *of dune* from the hill]

down[2] (doun) *n.* **1** The fine, soft feathers of birds. **2** Anything resembling soft fine hair or feathers. [< ON *dūnn*]

down[3] (doun) *n.* **1** A hill having a broad, treeless, grass-grown top. **2** *pl.* Turf-covered, undulating upland. **3** A dune. [< OE *dūn*]

down·cast (doun′kast′, -käst′) *adj.* **1** Directed downward. **2** Low in spirits; dejected; despondent.

down·er (doun′ər) *n. Slang* Any of various drugs that depress the central nervous system, as barbiturates.

down·fall (doun′fôl′) *n.* **1** A sudden, heavy fall of rain or snow. **2** A fall; disgrace. —**down′fall′en** *adj.*

down·grade (doun′grād′) *n.* A descending slope. —**on the downgrade** Declining in health, reputation, status, etc. —*adj. & adv.* DOWNHILL. —*v.t.* **·grad·ed, ·grad·ing** To reduce in status, salary, etc.

down·heart·ed (doun′här′tid) *adj.* Dejected; discouraged. —**down′heart′ed·ly** *adv.*

down·hill (doun′hil′, doun′hil′) *adj.* Descending; sloping. —*adv.* Toward the bottom of a hill. —**go downhill** To decline, as in success, health, etc.

down·play (doun′plā′) *v.t.* To play down; minimize.

down·pour (doun′pôr′, -pōr′) *n.* A heavy fall of rain.

down·right (doun′rīt′) *adj.* **1** Frank; plain; outspoken. **2** Thorough; utter; absolute. —*adv.* In the extreme; utterly.

Down's syndrome (dounz) Congenital mental and physical retardation due to a chromosomal anomaly, accompanied by variable signs including a flat face and pronounced epicanthic folds. [< J. L. H. *Down,* 1828–96, Eng. physician]

down·stairs (doun′stârz′) *adj.* On a lower floor or level. —*n.* The downstairs region of a building. —*adv.* **1** Down the stairs. **2** Toward a lower floor.

down·stream (doun′strēm′) *adj. & adv.* In the direction of the current; down the stream.

down·town (doun′toun′) *adj.* **1** Of or in the part of a city geographically lower than the other parts. **2** Of, in, or characteristic of the business section of a city. —*adv.* To, toward, or in the downtown part of a city. —*n.* The chief business section of a city.

down·trod·den (doun′trod′n) *adj.* **1** Trodden under foot. **2** Oppressed; subjugated. Also **down′trod′.**

down·turn (doun′tûrn′) *n.* A downward turn or decline, as in popularity or in a state's economy.

down·ward (doun′wərd) *adj. & adv.* **1** From a higher to a lower position. **2** From that which is more remote, as in place or time. Also **down′ward·ly, down′wards** *adv.*

down·y (doun′ē) *adj.* **down′i·er, down′i·est** Of, like, or covered with down. **2** Soft; soothing. —**down′i·ness** *n.*

dow·ry (dou′rē) *n. pl.* **·ries** **1** The property a wife brings to her husband in marriage. **2** Any endowment or gift. [< L *dos, dotis*]

dowse[1] (dous) *v. & n.* DOUSE[1].

dowse[2] (douz) *v.i.* **dowsed, dows·ing** To search for water, minerals, etc., with a divining rod. [?] —**dows′er** *n.*

dowsing rod DIVINING ROD.

dox·ol·o·gy (dok·sol′ə-jē) *n. pl.* **·gies** A hymn of praise to God, esp. the one beginning "Praise God, from whom all blessings flow." —**greater doxology** The Gloria in Excelsis. —**lesser doxology** The Gloria Patri. [< Gk. *doxa* praise + *legein* speak]

doz, doz. dozen(s).

doze (dōz) *v.* **dozed, doz·ing** *v.i.* **1** To sleep lightly; nap. —*v.t.* **2** To spend (time) napping. —**doze off** To drift into a light sleep. —*n.* A light, unsound sleep. [< Scand.]

doz·en (duz′ən) *n. pl.* **doz·ens** or **doz·en** **1** A group or set of 12. **2** A large unspecific number: *dozens* of errands. [< L < *duo* two + *decem* ten] —**doz′enth** *adj.*

do·zy (dō′zē) *adj.* **·zi·er, ·zi·est** DROWSY. —**do′zi·ly** *adv.*

DP, DP. displaced person.

dpt. department; deponent.

Dr. doctor; drive.

dr. debtor; dram(s).

drab[1] (drab) *adj.* **1** Dull; colorless. **2** Dull, yellowish gray. **3** Made of heavy, yellowish gray cloth. —*n.* **1** A yellowish gray color. **2** A heavy cloth so colored. [< OF *drap* cloth] —**drab′ly** *adv.* —**drab′ness** *n.*

drab[2] (drab) *n.* A slattern; a slut. [< Celtic]

drach·ma (drak′mə) *n. pl.* **·mas** or **·mae** (-mē) **1** The modern basic monetary unit of Greece. **2** An ancient Greek silver coin. [< Gk. *drachmē*]

Dra·co·ni·an (drā·kō′nē·ən) *adj.* Severe; merciless. [< *Draco,* 7th-cent. B.C. Athenian, reputed author of an inflexible code of laws] Also **dra·co′ni·an.**

draft (draft, dräft) *n.* **1** A current of air. **2** The act of drinking or inhaling; also, that which is so taken in, as water or air. **3** *Naut.* The depth to which a vessel sinks in the water. **4** The act of drawing a load, etc.; also, that which is drawn. **5** A plan, outline or sketch, as of a piece of writing, work to be done, etc. **6** A written order for money drawn by one person, bank, etc., and payable to another. **7** A device for controlling the airflow in a furnace, stove, etc. **8** A military or naval conscription; also, those so conscripted. **9** A drain or lessening: a *draft* on one's time. —**on draft** Ready to be drawn, as beer, etc., from a cask or the like. —*v.t.* **1** To outline in writing; sketch; delineate. **2** To select and draw off, as for military service; conscript. **3** To draw off or away. —*adj.* **1** Suitable or used for pulling heavy loads: a *draft* animal. **2** Drawn from a cask, as beer. [< OE *dragan* to draw] —**draft′er, draft′i·ness** *n.*

draft·ee (draf·tē′, dräf-) *n.* A person drafted for service in the armed forces.

drafts·man (drafts′mən, dräfts′-) *n. pl.* **·men** (-mən) **1** One who prepares drawings, plans, etc., as in architecture and engineering. **2** One who plans and draws up legal documents, speeches, etc. —**drafts′man·ship** *n.*

draft·y (draf′tē, dräf′-) *adj.* **draft·i·er, draft·i·est** Having or exposed to drafts. —**draft′i·ly** *adv.* —**draft′i·ness** *n.*

drag (drag) *v.* **dragged, drag·ging** *v.t.* **1** To pull along by main force. **2** To sweep or search the bottom of, as with a net; dredge. **3** To catch or recover, as with a net. **4** To pull along heavily and wearily. **5** To harrow (land). **6** To continue tediously: often with *on* or *out.* —*v.i.* **7** To be pulled along the ground. **8** To move heavily or slowly. **9** To pass slowly, as time. **10** To operate a dredge. —*n.* **1** The act of dragging. **2** That which drags or is dragged, as a grapple, a dredge, a dragnet. **3** A heavy four-wheeled carriage. **4** Something that impedes motion, as the brake on a wagon wheel. **5** A slow or difficult movement: to walk with a *drag.* **6** *Slang* Influence; pull. **7** *Slang* A puff of a cigarette. **8** *Slang* A dull, boring person or thing. **9** *Slang* Women's clothing worn by a man. [<OE *dragan*]

drag·gle (drag'əl) *v.* **·gled, ·gling** *v.t. & v.i.* To make or become soiled or wet by dragging in mud or over damp ground. [Freq. of DRAG]

drag·net (drag'net') *n.* **1** A net drawn along the bottom of the water or along the ground, for taking fish or small animals. **2** Organized measures for capturing criminals.

drag·o·man (drag'ə·mən) *n. pl.* **·mans** (-mənz) or **·men** (-mən) An interpreter for travelers in the Near East. [<LGk. *dragoumanos* <Ar. *tarjumān* translator]

drag·on (drag'ən) *n.* **1** A mythical, serpentlike, winged monster. **2** A fierce or overbearing person. [<Gk. *drakōn* serpent]

drag·on·fly (drag'ən·flī') *n. pl.* **·flies** Any of various large insects having a long, slender body and four narrow wings.

drag·goon (drə·gōōn') *n.* In some European armies, a cavalryman. —*v.t.* **1** To harass by dragoons. **2** To coerce; browbeat. [<F *dragon* a firearm, dragon]

drag race An automobile race, esp. of hot rods, in which contestants strive for minimum elapsed time over a straight course.

Dragonfly

drain (drān) *v.t.* **1** To draw off gradually, as a fluid. **2** To draw water or fluid from: to *drain* a swamp. **3** To empty. **4** To exhaust; use up. —*v.i.* **5** To flow off or leak away gradually. **6** To become empty. —*n.* **1** The act of draining. **2** Continuous strain, leak, or outflow. **3** A pipe, trench, tube, etc., for draining. [<OE *drēahnian* strain out] —**drain'er** *n.*

drain·age (drā'nij) *n.* **1** The act of draining. **2** A system of drains. **3** That which is drained off. **4** The area drained.

drain·pipe (drān'pīp') *n.* Pipe used for draining.

drake (drāk) *n.* A male duck. [ME]

dram (dram) *n.* **1** A unit of apothecaries' weight equal to one eighth of an ounce. Also **fluid dram. 2** A unit of avoirdupois weight equal to one sixteenth of an ounce. **3** A drink of alcoholic liquor. **4** A small portion; a bit. [<L <Gk. *drachmē*]

dra·ma (drä'mə, dram'ə) *n.* **1** A literary composition to be performed upon the stage; a play. **2** The art or profession of writing, acting, or producing plays: often with *the.* **3** A series of striking actions or events like those in a play. [Gk., a deed, an action]

dra·mat·ic (drə·mat'ik) *adj.* **1** Of, connected with, or like the drama. **2** Vivid, intense, etc. —**dra·mat'i·cal·ly** *adv.*

dra·mat·ics (drə·mat'iks) *n.pl.* **1** A dramatic performance, esp. by amateurs. **2** *(construed as sing. or pl.)* The art of staging or acting plays.

dra·ma·tis per·so·nae (dram'ə·tis pər·sō'nē) *Latin* The characters of a play.

dra·ma·tist (dram'ə·tist) *n.* One who writes plays.

dra·ma·ti·za·tion (dram'ət·ə·zā'shən, dräm-) *n.* **1** The act of dramatizing. **2** A dramatized version (of a novel). A dramatized re-creation of an actual event.

dram·a·tize (dram'ə·tīz) *v.t.* **·tized, ·tiz·ing 1** To convert for stage use. **2** To tell, represent, or interpret (events; one's personality, etc.) in a theatrical manner. *Brit. sp.* **·tise.** —**dram'a·ti·za'tion** (-ə·tə·zā'shən) *n.*

dram·a·tur·gy (dram'ə·tûr'jē) *n.* The art of making or producing dramas. [<G <Gk. <*drama* + *ergein* work] —**dram'a·tur'gic** or **·i·cal** *adj.* —**dram'a·turge** (-tûrj), **dram'a·tur'gist** *n.*

drank (drangk) *p.t.* of DRINK.

drape (drāp) *v.* **draped, drap·ing** *v.t.* **1** To cover or adorn in a graceful fashion, as with drapery or clothing. **2** To arrange in graceful folds. —*v.i.* **3** To hang in folds. —*n.* **1** *Usu. pl.* Drapery; curtain. **2** The way in which cloth hangs, as in clothing. [<OF *draper* to weave <*drap* cloth]

drap·er·y (drā'pər·ē) *n. pl.* **·er·ies 1** Decorative fabric hung in loose folds, usu. in an artistic arrangement. **2** *pl.* Curtains.

dras·tic (dras'tik) *adj.* **1** Acting vigorously. **2** Extreme; severe. [<Gk. *drastikos* effective] —**dras'ti·cal·ly** *adv.*

drat(drat') *interj.* DAMN (interj.), a mild oath.

draught (draft, dräft) *n., v., & adj. Chiefly Brit.* DRAFT.

draughts (drafts, dräfts) *n.pl. Brit.* CHECKERS.

draughts·man (drafts'mən, dräfts'-) *n. pl.* **·men** (-mən) DRAFTSMAN. —**draughts'man·ship** *n.*

draw (drô) *v.* **drew, drawn, draw·ing 1** To cause to move to or with the mover; pull; haul. **2** To acquire or obtain: to *draw* water. **3** To cause to flow forth: to *draw* blood. **4** To induce: to *draw* praise. **5** To take off, on, or out, as gloves or a sword. **6** To earn, as a salary or interest. **7** To remove, as money from a bank. **8** To deduce; formulate: to *draw* a conclusion. **9** To attract; allure. **10** To close, as curtains, a bag, etc. **11** To elicit; bring out, as truth. **12** To stretch out tightly; also, to manufacture by stretching or hammering, as wire. **13** DISEMBOWEL: to *draw* a chicken. **14** To take in; inhale, as breath. **15** To drain of contents, as a pond. **16** To win or obtain, as by chance. **17** *Naut.* To require (a specified depth) to float: said of vessels. **18** To depict or sketch; delineate, as with lines or words. **19** To write out as a check or deed: often with *up.* **20** To leave undecided, as a game or contest. —*v.i.* **21** To exert a pulling force. **22** To come or go: to *draw* near. **23** To exercise an attracting influence. **24** To pull out a weapon. **25** To shrink; become contracted, as a wound. **26** To cause pus or blood to gather in one spot, as a poultice. **27** To obtain money, supplies, etc., from some source. **28** To produce a current of air: The fire *draws* well. **29** To end a contest without decision; tie. **30** *Naut.* To fill or swell out with wind. **31** To sketch; delineate: he *draws* well. **32** To steep, as tea. —**draw down** To reduce or deplete by using; expend. —**draw on 1** To rely upon: He *drew on* his reputation. **2** To lure or entice. **3** To approach its end. —**draw out 1** To protract; prolong. **2** To cause (someone) to give information or express opinions. —**draw the line** To fix the limit. —**draw up 1** To put in required legal form, as a will. **2** To bring or come to a halt. **3** To straighten (oneself); stiffen, as in anger. —*n.* **1** An act of drawing or state of being drawn; also, that which is drawn. **2** A tie game. **3** Anything that draws or attracts. **4** A drawn chance or ticket. [<OE *dragan*]

draw·back (drô'bak') *n.* **1** Anything that checks or hinders progress, success, etc. **2** REBATE.

draw·bridge (drô'brij') *n.* A bridge that can be raised,

Drawbridge

let down, or drawn aside.

draw·ee (drô'ē') *n.* One on whom an order for the payment of money is drawn.

draw·er (drô'ər) *n.* **1** One who draws. **2** One who draws a bill of exchange, money order, etc. **3** (drôr) A sliding receptacle, as in a bureau, table, etc.

draw·ers (drôrz) *n. pl.* A trouserlike undergarment.

draw·ing (drô'ing) n. 1 The act of one who or that which draws. 2 A picture, sketch, delineation, or design. 3 The art of representing objects by lines. 4 A lottery.

draw·ing-card (drô'ing-kärd') n. Any feature that attracts a crowd.

draw·ing-room (drô'ing-room', -room') n. 1 A room for reception of company. 2 The company assembled in such a room. 3 A small private room in a sleeping car on a train. [< WITHDRAWING ROOM]

draw-knife (drô'nīf') n. pl. ·knives (-nīvz') A knife with a handle at each end, used for shaving off wood surfaces. Also **draw'ing knife.**

drawl (drôl) v.t. & v.i. To speak or pronounce slowly, esp. vowels. —n. The act of drawling. [?] —**drawl'er** n. —**drawl'-ing·ly** adv. —**drawl'y** adj.

drawn (drôn) adj. 1 Tied or undecided, as a game. 2 Eviscerated: a drawn fowl. 3 Haggard; showing strain: His face looked drawn.

drawn butter Butter melted and prepared as a sauce.

drawn work Ornamental openwork made by pulling out threads of fabric and embroidering or hemstitching the edges of the openings.

draw·string (drô'string') n. A string or cord run through a hem, which pulls together or closes an opening.

dray (drā) n. A low, heavy vehicle for carrying heavy articles. —v.t. To transport by means of a dray. [< OE dræge dragnet]

dray·age (drā'ij) n. 1 The act of conveying in a dray. 2 The charge for draying.

dray·man (drā'mən) n. pl. ·men (-mən) A man who drives a dray.

dread (dred) v.t. & v.i. To anticipate with great fear or anxiety. —adj. 1 Causing great fear; terrible. 2 Exciting awe. —n. 1 Unconquerable fright or terror. 2 Fear joined to awe. [< OE drǣdan to fear]

dread·ful (dred'fəl) adj. 1 Inspiring dread or awe; terrible. 2 Informal Disagreeable; very bad; revolting. —**dread'-ful·ly** adv. —**dread'ful·ness** n.

dread·nought (dred'nôt') n. Any battleship of great size. Also **dread'naught'.**

dream (drēm) n. 1 A train of thoughts or images passing through the mind in sleep. 2 A mental condition similar to that of one sleeping; daydreaming. 3 A visionary idea or fancy. 4 Something so beautiful, pleasant, etc., as to seem possible only in a dream. —v. **dreamed** or **dreamt** (dremt), **dream·ing** v.t. 1 To see or imagine in a dream. 2 To imagine as in a dream. 3 To while away, as in idle reverie. —v.i. 4 To have a dream or dreams. 5 To have a vague idea or conception of something. —**dream up** Informal To concoct or create. [< OE drēam] —**dream'er** n. —**dream'ful** adj. —**dream'ful·ly** adv. —Syn. n. 2 fancy, fantasy, reverie. v. 2 muse, meditate, reflect.

dream·y (drē'mē) adj. **dream·i·er, dream·i·est** 1 Given to dreams. 2 Appropriate to dreams; shadowy. 3 Soothing; soft: dreamy music. 4 Filled with dreams; visionary. —**dream'i·ly** adv. —**dream'i·ness** n.

drear (drir) adj. DREARY.

drear·y (drir'ē) adj. **drear·i·er, drear·i·est** 1 Gloomy; sad; dismal. 2 Monotonous; lifeless; dull. [< OE drēorig sad, bloody] —**drear'i·ly** adv. —**drear'i·ness** n. —**drear'i·some** adj.

dredge¹ (drej) n. A device for bringing up mud, silt, etc., from under water. —v. **dredged, dredg·ing** v.t. 1 To clear or widen by means of a dredge. 2 To remove, catch, or gather by a dredge. —v.i. 3 To use a dredge. [?] —**dredg'er** n.

dredge² (drej) v.t. 1 To sprinkle or dust with flour before cooking. 2 To sift; sprinkle. [?]

dreg·gy (dreg'ē) adj. **·gi·er, ·gi·est** Containing dregs; full of dregs; foul. —**dreg'gi·ness** n. —**dreg'gish** adj.

dregs (dregz) n. pl. 1 The sediment of liquids. 2 The worthless or coarse part: the dregs of society.

drench (drench) v.t. 1 To wet thoroughly; soak. 2 In veterinary science, to force (an animal) to swallow, as medicine. —n. 1 A liquid medicine, administered to an animal. 2 A water solution for soaking. 3 The act of drenching. [< OE drencan cause to drink] —**drench'er** n.

dress (dres) v.t. 1 To clothe; supply with clothing. 2 To trim or decorate; adorn. 3 To treat medicinally, as a wound. 4 To comb and arrange (hair). 5 To prepare (stone,

timber, leather, etc.) for use or sale. 6 To clean (fowl, game, fish, etc.) for cooking. 7 To till, trim, or prune. 8 To put in proper alignment, as troops. 9 Informal To scold: usu. with down. —v.i. 10 To put on or wear clothing, esp. formal clothing. 11 To come into proper alignment. — **dress up** To put on or wear clothing more elaborate than that usually worn. —n. 1 Clothes; apparel. 2 A gown or frock of a woman or child. 3 Formal attire. 4 External appearance; guise. —adj. 1 Of, pertaining to, or suitable for making dresses: dress goods. 2 To be worn on formal occasions: a dress suit. [< OF dresser arrange]

dress circle Seats in a theater or concert hall, usu. the first gallery behind and above the orchestra, originally reserved for patrons in evening dress.

dress·er¹ (dres'ər) n. 1 One who dresses something, as shop windows, leather, etc. 2 One who assists another to dress. 3 One who dresses well: a fancy dresser.

dress·er² (dres'ər) n. 1 A chest of drawers for clothing supporting a swinging mirror. 2 A cupboard for dishes. [OF dresseur < dresser to dress]

dress goods Fabrics for dresses.

dress·ing (dres'ing) n. 1 The act of one who dresses. 2 That with which anything, as a wound, is dressed. 3 A seasoned sauce served with salads and vegetables. 4 A seasoned stuffing of bread, rice, etc., for fowl or meats.

dress·ing-down (dres'ing·doun') n. Informal A reprimand; scolding.

dressing gown A loose gown worn while dressing or relaxing.

dress·ing-room (dres'ing·room', -room') n. A room used for dressing, as in a theater.

dress·ing-ta·ble (dres'ing·tā'bəl) n. A small table equipped with a mirror; a vanity.

dress·mak·er (dres'mā'kər) n. One who makes women's dresses, etc. —adj. Not severely tailored, but having soft, feminine lines. —**dress'ma·king** adj., n.

dress parade A formal military parade.

dress rehearsal The last rehearsal of a play before the public performance, in full costume.

dress suit A man's formal evening suit.

dress·y (dres'ē) adj. **dress·i·er, dress·i·est** Informal 1 Fond of dress. 2 Showy; elegant. —**dress'i·ness** n.

drew (drōō) p.t. of DRAW.

drib·ble (drib'əl) v.t. & v.i. **·bled, ·bling** 1 To fall or let fall in drops; drip. 2 To drool; slobber. 3 In certain games, to propel (the ball) by bouncing or kicking. —n. 1 A dripping or trickle of liquid. 2 In basketball and soccer, the act of dribbling. [Freq. of earlier drib < DRIP] —**drib'bler** n.

drib·let (drib'lit) n. A small amount. Also **drib'blet.**

dried (drīd) p.t. & p.p. of DRY.

dri·er¹ (drī'ər) n. 1 One who or that which dries. 2 An additive for paints, etc., used to speed drying. 3 A mechanical device for drying.

dri·er² (drī'ər) Comparative of DRY.

dri·est (drī'ist) Superlative of DRY.

drift (drift) n. 1 That which is carried onward by a current: a drift of clouds. 2 A heap of any matter piled up by wind or sea. 3 A tendency, trend, or meaning: the drift of a discourse. 4 A number of objects moving onward by one force, as logs in a river. 5 The distance a ship or airplane is driven from its course by wind, etc. 6 An ocean current. 7 Geol. Material transported by moving masses of ice or by running water. 8 Mining A horizontal passage in a mine. —v.t. 1 To carry along, as on a current. 2 To cause to pile up in heaps, as snow, or sand. —v.i. 3 To float or be carried along, as by a current. 4 To wander aimlessly. 5 To accumulate in heaps. [< OE drīfan to drive]

drift·age (drif'tij) n. 1 The act of drifting. 2 Anything that has drifted. 3 Deviation due to drifting.

drift·er (drif'tər) n. Informal A person having no settled home or occupation.

drift·wood (drift'wood') n. Wood floated or drifted by water, esp. by the sea.

drill¹ (dril) n. 1 A tool for boring metal or other hard substance. 2 The art or action of training in military exercises. 3 Thorough and regular exercises in any branch of knowledge, activity, or industry. 4 A snail that feeds on

Drills
a. metal.
b. wood.

oysters through holes it drills in their shells. —*v.t.* **1** To bore a hole in. **2** To bore (a hole). **3** To train or teach by methodical exercises. —*v.i.* **4** To use a drill. **5** To engage in an exercise or exercises. [Du. *dril* < *drillen* to bore] —**drill'er** *n.*

drill² (dril) *n.* **1** A machine for planting seeds in rows. **2** A small furrow in which seeds are sown. **3** A row of seeds so planted. —*v.t.* To plant in rows. [?]

drill³ (dril) *n.* Heavy, twilled linen or cotton cloth. Also **drill'- ing.** [< G *Drilich* cloth with three threads]

drill·mas·ter (dril'mas'tər, -mäs'tər) *n.* A trainer in military or other exercises.

drill press An upright drilling machine.

dri·ly (drī'lē) *adv.* DRYLY.

drink (dringk) *v.* **drank** (*Archaic* **drunk**), **drunk** (*Archaic* **drunk·en**), **drink·ing** *v.t.* **1** To swallow, as water. **2** To absorb (a liquid or moisture). **3** To take in eagerly through the senses or the mind: with *in.* **4** To make a toast. **5** To swallow the contents of. —*v.i.* **6** To swallow a liquid. **7** To consume alcoholic liquors, esp. to excess. **8** To drink a toast: with *to.* —*n.* **1** Any beverage. **2** Alcoholic liquor. **3** The practice of drinking to excess. [< OE *drincan*] —**drink'a·ble** *adj.* —**drink'er** *n.*

drip (drip) *n.* **1** A falling in drops. **2** That which drips. **3** *Slang* A person regarded as socially inept. —*v.t.* & *v.i.* **dripped, drip·ping** To fall or let fall in drops. [< OE *dryppan* to drip]

drip-dry (drip'drī') *v.i.* **-dried, -dry·ing** To dry after being hung while dripping wet, as fabrics requiring little or no ironing. —*adj.* Designed to be drip-dried, as a fabric or garment.

drip·ping (drip'ing) *n.* **1** That which falls in drops. **2** *Usu. pl.* Fat exuded from meat in cooking. **3** The act of falling in drops.

drive (drīv) *v.* **drove, driv·en, driv·ing** *v.t.* **1** To propel onward or forward. **2** To force to act or work. **3** To bring to a state or condition. **4** To cause to penetrate: often with *in:* to *drive* in a nail. **5** To form by penetrating or passing through: to *drive* a well. **6** To control the movements of: to *drive* an automobile. **7** To transport in a vehicle. **8** To carry on or complete (trade, a bargain, etc.) with energy. **9** In sports, to strike and propel (a ball) with force. **10** *Mech.* To provide power for. —*v.i.* **11** To move forward rapidly or with force. **12** To operate or travel in a vehicle. **13** To have an object or intention: with *at:* What are you *driving* at? **14** To aim a blow: with *at.* —**let drive at** To aim or discharge a blow, missile, etc. —*n.* **1** The act of driving. **2** A road for driving. **3** A journey in a vehicle. **4** A basic need, longing, or pressure. **5** Energy; vitality. **6** A hunt or round-up, as of cattle. **7** An organized campaign to achieve a certain goal. **8** A hard, swift stroke or thrust. **9** *Mech.* A system for transmitting mechanical power. **10** A mass of floating logs. [< OE *drīfan*] —**Syn.** *v.* **1** impel, push, press, thrust.

drive-in (drīv'in') *n.* A restaurant, motion-picture theater, etc., serving patrons in their automobiles. —*adj.* So constructed as to be a drive-in.

driv·el (driv'əl) *v.* **driv·eled** or **driv·elled, driv·el·ing** or **driv·el·ling** *v.i.* **1** To let saliva flow from the mouth; slobber. **2** To flow like saliva. **3** To talk in a foolish manner. —*v.t.* **4** To let flow from the mouth. **5** To say in a foolish manner. —*n.* **1** A flow of saliva from the mouth. **2** Senseless talk. [< OE *dreflian*] —**driv'el·er** or **driv'el·ler** *n.*

driv·en (driv'ən) *p.p.* of DRIVE.

driv·er (drī'vər) *n.* **1** One who or that which drives, as the operator of any vehicle. **2** Any of various machine parts which transmit motion. **3** A wooden-headed golf club for driving from the tee. • See GOLF. **4** A demanding boss or overseer.

drive·way (drīv'wā') *n.* A private road providing access to a building or house.

driz·zle (driz'əl) *v.t.* & *v.i.* **-zled, -zling** To rain in fine drops. —*n.* A light rain. [?] —**driz'zly** *adj.*

drogue (drōg) *n.* A parachute or similar device used to slow or stabilize an aircraft or spacecraft. [? Related to DRAG]

droll (drōl) *adj.* Odd in a humorous or quaint way. —*n.* A droll person. [MF *drôle* jester] —**droll'ly** *adv.*

droll·er·y (drō'lər·ē) *n. pl.* **·er·ies** **1** Comical speech or manners. **2** The quality of being droll. **3** A facetious or amusing story.

-drome *combining form* Racecourse: hippodrome. [< Gk. *dromos* a running]

drom·e·dar·y (drom'ə·der'ē) *n. pl.* **·dar·ies** The one-humped Arabian camel trained for riding. [< LL < Gk. *dromas, dromad-* a dromedary, a running]

drone¹ (drōn) *v.* **droned, dron·ing** *v.i.* **1** To make a dull, humming sound; hum. **2** To speak in a slow, dull tone. —*v.t.* **3** To say in a slow, dull tone. —*n.* **1** A dull, humming sound, as of a bee. **2** One of the pipes of the bagpipe that plays a single tone. **3** BAGPIPE. [< ME *drone* a male bee]

Dromedary

drone² (drōn) *n.* **1** A stingless male bee that gathers no honey. **2** A loafer; idler. —*v.i.* **droned, dron·ing** To live in idleness. [< OE *drān*]

drool (drool) *v.t.* & *v.i.* **1** To drivel; slaver. **2** To speak foolishly. —*n.* **1** SPITTLE. **2** *Informal* Foolish talk. [Alter. of DRIVEL]

droop (droop) *v.i.* **1** To sink down. **2** To lose vigor or vitality. **3** To become dejected. —*v.t.* **4** To allow to hang or sink down. —*n.* A hanging down. [< ON *drūpa*] —**droop'ing** *adj.* —**droop'ing·ly** *adv.*

droop·y (droo'pē) *adj.* **droop·i·er, droop·i·est** Tending to droop. —**droop'i·ness** *n.*

drop (drop) *n.* **1** A globule of liquid. **2** A very small quantity of anything, as of a liquid. **3** Anything that resembles a drop of liquid. **4** A fall, or the distance fallen. **5** A sudden change of level. **6** Any of various contrivances that drop or hang, as a drop curtain in a theater. **7** A trap door. **8** *pl.* Any liquid medicine given by the drop. **9** A slot for letters. **10** A fall in prices. —*v.* **dropped, drop·ping** *v.t.* **1** To let fall in drops. **2** To let fall in any way. **3** To give birth to: said of animals. **4** To say in a casual way. **5** To write (a note, etc.) **6** To bring down or cause to fall. **7** To stop, have done with, or give up. **8** To leave at a specific place. **9** To omit (a syllable, letter, or word). **10** *Slang* To lose (money), as in gambling. **11** To discharge or dismiss. —*v.i.* **12** To fall in drops. **13** To fall rapidly; come down. **14** To fall down exhausted, injured, or dead. **15** To crouch, as a hunting dog at sight of game. **16** To come to an end; cease; stop. **17** To fall into some state or condition. **18** To fall behind: often with *behind* or *back.* —**drop in** To pay an unexpected call. —**drop out** To leave; withdraw from. [< OE *dropa*]

drop curtain A theater curtain lowered in front of the stage between the acts.

drop·forge (drop'fôrj') *v.t.* **·forged, ·forg·ing** To forge (metal) between dies by using a drop hammer.

drop hammer A machine for forging, stamping, etc., in which a heavy weight sliding between vertical guides strikes the metal.

drop·kick (drop'kik') *n.* In football, a kick given the ball just as it is rebounding after being dropped.

drop-kick (drop'kik') *v.t.* & *v.i.* To kick (a football) in the manner of a dropkick.

drop·let (drop'lit) *n.* A little drop.

drop·out (drop'out') *n.* **1** A student who leaves school or college before graduation. **2** One who abandons any undertaking before completing it.

drop·per (drop'ər) *n.* **1** One who or that which drops. **2** A glass tube with a suction bulb at one end for dispensing a liquid in drops.

drop·ping (drop'ing) *n.* **1** The act of falling or letting fall in drops. **2** *pl.* Animal dung.

drop·si·cal (drop'si·kəl) *adj.* Of or afflicted by dropsy.

drop·sy (drop'sē) *n.* An abnormal accumulation of watery fluid in body tissues or cavities. [ME *dropesie,* ult. < Gk. *hydōr* water] —**drop·si·cal** (drop'si·kəl), **drop'sied** *adj.*

---

add, āce, câre, pälm; end, ēven; it, īce; odd, ōpen, ôrder; tŏŏk, pōōl; up, bûrn; ə = *a* in *above*; *u* in *focus*; yōō = *u* in *fuse*; oil; pout; check; go; ring; thin; this; zh, *vision.* < derived from; ? origin uncertain or unknown.

drosh·ky (drosh'kē, drôsh'kē) n. pl. ·kies A light, open, four-wheeled Russian carriage. Also **dros'ky**. [< Russ. *drozhki*]

dro·soph·i·la (drō·sof'ə·lə, drə-) n. pl. ·lae (-lē) Any of a genus of fruit flies, used for research in genetics. [< Gk. *drosos* dew + *phileein* to love]

dross (drôs, dros) n. 1 Refuse or impurity in melted metal. 2 Waste matter; refuse. [< OE *drōs*] —**dross'i·ness** n. —**dross'y** adj. —Syn. 2 debris, junk, remains, rubbish.

drought (drout) n. Long-continued dry weather; want of rain. Also **drouth** (drouth). [< OE *drūgoth*] —**drought'y** adj.

drove[1] (drōv) p.t. of DRIVE.

drove[2] (drōv) n. 1 A number of animals driven or herded for driving. 2 A moving crowd of human beings. —v.t. ·droved, drov·ing To drive (cattle, etc.) for some distance. [< OE *drāf*] —**drov'er** n.

drown (droun) v.t. 1 To kill by suffocation in water or other liquid. 2 To flood; deluge. 3 To overwhelm; overpower; extinguish. —v.i. 4 To die by suffocation in water or other liquid. [< Scand.]

drowse (drouz) v. drowsed, drows·ing v.i. 1 To be sleepy; doze. —v.t. 2 To make sleepy. 3 To pass (time) in drowsing. —n. The state of being half asleep. [< OE *drūsian* become sluggish]

drow·sy (drou'zē) adj. ·si·er, ·si·est 1 Almost asleep; sleepy. 2 Lulling; soporific: *drowsy* music. —**drow'si·ly** adv. —**drow'si·ness** n.

drub (drub) v.t. drubbed, drub·bing 1 To beat, as with a stick. 2 To vanquish; overcome. —n. A blow; thump. [< Ar. *darb* a beating] —**drub'ber** n.

drub·bing (drub'ing) n. A thorough beating or one-sided defeat.

drudge (druj) v.i. drudged, drudg·ing To toil; work hard at menial tasks. —n. One who toils at menial tasks. [ME *druggen*]

drudg·er·y (druj'ər·ē) n. pl. ·er·ies Dull, wearisome, or menial work.

drug (drug) n. 1 Any substance used in or as a medicine. 2 Any narcotic. 3 An overabundant commodity: a *drug* on the market. —v.t. drugged, drug·ging 1 To mix drugs with (food, drink, etc.). 2 To administer drugs to. 3 To stupefy or poison with or as with drugs. [< MF *drogue*]

drug addict One addicted to a habit-forming drug.

drug·gist (drug'ist) n. One who compounds prescriptions and sells drugs; a pharmacist.

drug·store (drug'stôr', -stōr') n. A place where prescriptions are compounded, and drugs and miscellaneous merchandise are sold.

dru·id (drōō'id) n. One of an order of priests in ancient Gaul, Britain, and Ireland. [< L *druidae, druides* < Celtic] —**dru·id'ic, dru·id'i·cal** adj. —**dru'id·ism** n.

drum (drum) n. 1 A percussion instrument consisting of a hollow, usu. cylindrical object with skin or vellum stretched over each end, played by beating with drumsticks or the hands. 2 The sound produced by beating this instrument. 3 Anything resembling a drum in shape, as a cylindrical receptacle. 4 Any mechanical device shaped like a drum. 5 TYMPANIC MEMBRANE —v. drummed, drum·ming v.t. 1 To perform on or as on a drum. 2 To expel in disgrace: usu. with *out*. 3 To summon by beating a drum. 4 To force upon the attention by constant repetition. —v.i. 5 To beat a drum. 6 To beat on anything continuously. —**drum up** To seek: to *drum up* trade. [Prob. < MDu. *tromme*]

Drums
a. snare. b. bass. c. bongo.

drum·beat (drum'bēt') n. The sound of a drum; also, the action of beating a drum.

drum·head (drum'hed') n. 1 The membrane stretched over the end of a drum. 2 *Naut.* The top of a capstan.

drum ma·jor·ette (mā'jə·ret') A woman who leads or precedes a marching band or accompanies such a band while twirling a baton. —**drum major** *Masc.*

drum·mer (drum'ər) n. 1 One who plays a drum. 2 *Informal* A traveling salesman.

drum·stick (drum'stik') n. 1 A stick for beating a drum. 2 The lower segment of the leg of a cooked fowl.

drunk (drungk) p.p. of DRINK; former p.t.. —adj. 1 Being in a state of altered consciousness by the effect of alcoholic liquor, in which motor ability, mental acuity, and judgment are impaired; intoxicated. 2 Saturated; glutted: *drunk* with victory. 3 DRUNKEN (def. 3). —n. *Informal* 1 A drunk person. 2 A fit of drunkenness.

drunk·ard (drungk'ərd) n. One who habitually drinks to intoxication; a sot.

drunk·en (drungk'ən) adj. 1 DRUNK (def. 1). 2 Habitually drunk. 3 Resulting from or characterized by excessive drinking. 4 Occurring while intoxicated: *drunken* driving. —**drunk'en·ly** adv. —**drunk'en·ness** n.

drupe (drōōp) n. A soft, fleshy fruit enclosing a stone or seed, as the peach or cherry. [< Gk. *druppa* overripe olive] —**dru·pa·ceous** (drōō·pā'shəs) adj.

drupe·let (drōōp'lit) n. A little drupe, as the individual parts of a raspberry.

dry (drī) adj. dri·er, dri·est 1 Lacking moisture; not wet or damp. 2 Not covered by water: *dry* land. 3 Not green, as wood. 4 Having little or no rain: the *dry* season. 5 Lacking lubrication, as. bearings. 6 Thirsty. 7 Lacking interest; lifeless; dull. 8 Slyly shrewd, as wit. 9 Free from sweetness: said of wines. 10 Subject to or in favor of a prohibitory liquor law: a *dry* town. 11 Not giving milk: a *dry* cow. 12 Not liquid; solid: said of merchandise, etc. 13 Tearless: said of the eyes. 14 Characterized by absence of bloodshed. 15 Without butter: said of toast. 16 Wanting in cordiality; not genial. —v.t. & v.i. dried, dry·ing To make or become dry. —**dry up** 1 To cease or cause to cease flowing. 2 *Informal* To stop talking. —n. pl. dries The state or condition of being dry. [< OE *dryge*] **dry'a·ble** adj. —**dry'ly, dri'ly** adv. —**dry'ness** n.

dry·ad (drī'əd, -ad) *Gk. Myth.* WOOD NYMPH. [< Gk. < *drys, dryos* an oak tree] —**dry·ad'ic** (drī·ad'ik) adj.

dry battery Two or more dry cells connected together.

dry cell A sealed primary electric cell with a moist paste as its electrolyte.

dry-clean (drī'klēn') v.t. To clean (clothing, etc.) with solvents other than water, such as carbon tetrachloride, etc. —**dry'clean'er, dry'clean'ing** n.

dry-dock (drī'dok') n. A dock constructed so that the water can be pumped out when building or repairing ships. —v.t. & v.i. To put in or go into drydock.

dry·er (drī'ər) n. DRIER[1] (def. 3).

dry-eyed (drī'īd') adj. Not weeping.

dry farming In an arid country, the raising of crops without irrigation, mainly by reducing evaporation and by raising drought-resisting crops. —**dry farmer**

dry goods Textile fabrics, as distinguished from groceries, hardware, etc.

Dry Ice Solid carbon dioxide, used as a refrigerant: a trade name.

dry measure A system of units for measuring the volume of dry commodities, as fruits, grain, etc.

dry nurse A nurse who cares for an infant without suckling it. —**dry'-nurse'** v. (·nursed, ·nurs·ing)

dry-point (drī'point') n. 1 An etching needle used to cut lines in copperplate without the use of acid. 2 A work thus engraved or the method thus used.

dry rot 1 A fungous disease causing timber to crumble into powder. 2 A disease of vegetables, fruits, etc.

dry run 1 *Mil.* Practice in aiming and firing weapons without using live ammunition. 2 Any rehearsal or practice exercise.

d.t. delirium tremens: also **d.t.'s**; double-time.

Du. Dutch.

du·al (dyōō'əl) adj. 1 Of or pertaining to two. 2 Composed of two. [< L *duo* two] —**du·al·i·ty** (dyōō·al'ə·tē) n. —**du'al·ly** adv.

du·al·ism (dyōō'əl·iz'əm) 1 The state of being dual. 2 Any of various theories which assert that there are two fundamental elements or principles in the nature of man, reality, the universe, etc., as the principles of good and evil or mind and matter. —**du'al·ist** n. —**du'al·is'tic** adj. —**du'al·is'ti·cal·ly** adv.

dub[1] (dub) v.t. dubbed, dub·bing 1 To confer knighthood upon by tapping on the shoulder with a sword. 2 To call or honor by a title, description, epithet, etc. [< OE *dub-bian*] —Syn. 2 name, nickname, term, style.

dub² (dub) *Slang n.* A clumsy, second-rate player in any game. —*v.t.* dubbed, dub·bing To bungle (a golf stroke, etc.). [?]

dub³ ((dub) *v.t.* dubbed, dub·bing To insert or blend (dialogue, music, etc.) into the sound track of a film, or into a radio or television broadcast. —*n.* That which is so inserted. [Short for DOUBLE] —dub′bing *n.*

du·bi·e·ty (dʸōō·bī′ə·tē) *n. pl.* ·ties 1 The quality of being doubtful. 2 Something doubtful. [< L *dubius* doubtful]

du·bi·ous (dʸōō′bē·əs) *adj.* 1 In a state of doubt; doubtful. 2 Causing doubt. 3 Of uncertain result. 4 Questionable; suspect: a *dubious* person. [< L *dubium* doubt] —du′bi·ous·ly *adv.* —du′bi·ous·ness *n.*

du·cal (dʸōō′kəl) *adj.* Of or pertaining to a duke or a duchy. [< LL *ducalis* of a leader] —du′cal·ly *adv.*

duc·at (duk′ət) *n.* 1 One of several European coins. 2 *Slang* A ticket. [< LL *ducatus*, orig., a duchy]

du·ce (dōō′chä) *n. Ital.* A leader; commander. —il Duce The title assumed by Benito Mussolini as leader of the Italian Fascists.

duch·ess (duch′is) *n.* 1 The wife or widow of a duke. 2 The female sovereign of a duchy. [< LL *ducissa*]

duch·y (duch′ē) *n. pl.* duch·ies The territory or dominion of a duke or duchess; a dukedom. [< LL *ducatus*]

duck¹ (duk) *n.* 1 A web-footed, short-legged, broad-billed water bird. 2 The female of this bird. 3 The flesh of this bird. 4 *Informal* A dear; darling. 5 *Slang* A person; a fellow. [< OE *dūce*, lit. diver]

duck² (duk) *v.t. & v.i.* 1 To plunge briefly under water. 2 To lower quickly, as the head. 3 To dodge; evade (a blow or punishment). 4 To avoid (a duty, person, etc.). —*n.* The act of ducking. [ME *duken* to dive, ult. < Gmc.]

Mallard duck

duck³ (duk) *n.* 1 A strong, tightly woven fabric, as of linen or cotton. 2 *pl.* Trousers made of this fabric. [Du. *doek* cloth]

duck·bill (duk′bil′) *n.* PLATYPUS.

duck·pin (duk′pin′) *n.* A pin 9 inches high and 3½ inches in diameter at the body, used in **duckpins**, a game of tenpins.

duck·weed (duk′wēd′) *n.* Any of several small, floating aquatic plants common in streams and ponds.

duck·y (duk′ē) *adj. Slang* Delightful; darling.

duct (dukt) *n.* 1 Any tube or passage by which a fluid is conveyed. 2 *Anat.* A tubular passage for fluid: the bile *duct.* 3 *Electr.* A tubular channel for carrying wires or cables. [L *ductus* a leading < *ducere* to lead]

duc·tile (duk′til, -tīl′) *adj.* 1 Capable of being hammered thin or drawn out, as certain metals. 2 Easily led; tractable. [< L *ducere* lead] —duc·til′i·ty, duc′tile·ness *n.*

duct·less gland (dukt′lis) Any of several hormone-producing glands whose secretions are released directly into the blood or lymph.

dud (dud) *n.* 1 A shell or bomb that fails to explode. 2 *Informal* Any person or thing that fails. [Du. *dood* dead]

dude (dʸōōd) *n.* 1 A fop; dandy. 2 In the w U.S., a city person, esp. one from the E U.S. who is vacationing on a ranch. 3 *Slang* A man; fellow. [?] —dud′ish *adj.*

dude ranch A ranch operated for tourists.

dudg·eon (duj′ən) *n.* Sullen displeasure. [?]

duds (dudz) *n.pl. Informal* 1 Clothing. 2 Belongings in general. [ME *dudde* a cloak]

due (dʸōō) *adj.* 1 Owing and demandable; payable. 2 That should be given; appropriate. 3 Suitable; sufficient: *due* cause for alarm. 4 Appointed or expected to arrive. 5 Ascribable; owing: with *to:* The delay was *due* to rain. —*n.* 1 That which is due. 2 *pl.* Fee: club *dues.* —*adv.* Directly; exactly: *due* east. [< OF *deu*, pp. of *devoir* owe] • *Due to* as a preposition, though widely used, is still questioned by some, who would substitute for it *because of* or *on account of: Because of* (not *due to*) rain, we were delayed.

du·el (dʸōō′əl) *n.* 1 A prearranged combat between two persons, usu. fought with deadly weapons. 2 A struggle between two parties. —*v.t. & v.i.* du·eled or ·elled, du·el·ing or ·el·ling To fight or fight with, in a duel. [< L *duellum*, var. of *bellum* war] —du′el·er or du′el·ler, du′el·ist or du′el·list *n.*

du·en·na (dʸōō·en′ə) *n.* 1 An elderly woman who watches over a young woman in Spanish and Portuguese families. 2 A governess or chaperon. [Sp. < L *domina* lady]

du·et (dʸōō·et′) *n.* 1 A musical composition for two voices or instrumentalists. 2 The performance of such a composition; also, the two persons who perform. [< L *duo* two]

duff (duf) *n.* A thick flour pudding boiled in a bag. [Var. of DOUGH]

duf·fel bag (duf′əl) A sack, usu. of canvas or duck, used to carry clothing and personal possessions. [< *Duffel*, a town near Antwerp]

duf·fer (duf′ər) *n. Informal* One who performs in an incompetent manner. [?]

dug¹ (dug) *p.t. & p.p.* of DIG.

dug² (dug) *n.* A teat or udder. [?]

du·gong (dōō′gong) *n.* A whalelike, herbivorous sea mammal of the East Indies and Australia. [< Malay *duyong*]

dug·out (dug′out′) *n.* 1 A canoe formed of a hollowed log. 2 An underground shelter against bombs, tornadoes, etc. 3 In baseball, a low, boxlike structure to shelter the players when not at bat or in the field.

duke (dʸōōk) *n.* 1 An English peer of the highest rank, below a prince or an archbishop. 2 A Continental noble of corresponding rank. 3 A prince ruling over a duchy or a small state. [< L *dux* leader]

duke·dom (dʸōōk′dəm) *n.* DUCHY.

dukes (dʸōōks) *n. pl. Slang* The fists. [Short for *Duke of Yorks*, orig. rhyming slang for forks; later fingers, fists]

dul·cet (dul′sit) *adj.* Pleasant to the ear. [< L *dulcis* sweet] —Syn. sweet, soothing, agreeable, melodious.

dul·ci·mer (dul′sə·mər) *n.* A stringed musical instrument played with two padded hammers. [? < L *dulcis* sweet + *melos* a song]

dull (dul) *adj.* 1 Having a blunt edge or point. 2 Not acute or intense: *dull* pain. 3 Not quick, as in thought. 4 Lacking perception or sensibility. 5 Depressed; sad. 6 Boring: a *dull* affair. 7 Not brisk or active; sluggish. 8 Not bright or vivid, as colors. 9 Cloudy; overcast; a *dull* day. 10 Muffled; indistinct, as sounds. —*v.t. & v.i.* To make or become dull. [ME *dul* < MLG] —dull′ish *adj.* —dull′ly *adv.* —dull′ness or dul′ness *n.*

dull·ard (dul′ərd) *n.* A dull or stupid person.

dulse (duls) *n.* A reddish brown, edible seaweed. Also **dulce.** [< Ir. *duileasg*]

du·ly (dʸōō′lē) *adv.* 1 In accordance with what is due; fitly. 2 In due time or manner. 3 When due.

dumb (dum) *adj.* 1 Having no power of speech. 2 Not using words or sounds; silent. 3 *Informal* Stupid. [OE] —dumb′ly *adv.* —dumb′ness *n.*

dumb·bell (dum′bel′) *n.* 1 A gymnastic device consisting of a handle with a weighted ball at each end. 2 *Slang* A stupid person.

dumb·found (dum′found′) *v.t.* To strike dumb with amazement. Also **dumb′found.** [Blend of DUMB and CONFOUND] —Syn. confuse, confound, amaze, astonish.

dumb show 1 Gestures without words. 2 In early English drama, part of a play done in pantomime.

dumb·wait·er (dum′wā′tər) *n.* 1 A movable serving table. 2 An elevator for carrying food, etc., between floors.

dum·my (dum′ē) *n. pl.* dum·mies 1 *Informal* A stupid person. 2 A figure made to represent a human being: a ventriloquist's *dummy;* a *dummy* for displaying clothes. 3 A stuffed figure used in bayonet or tackling practice. 4 In certain card games, an exposed hand played by the opposite player; also, the player to whom that hand has been dealt. 5 A person who represents another in a transaction, but who poses as acting for himself. 6 *Printing* A model book, usu. blank, made up as a pattern. —*adj.* 1 Sham; counterfeit. 2 Supposedly acting for oneself while really acting for another. **3** Made to resemble some object, but having no real use; artificial: a *dummy* door. —*v.t.* **dum·mied**, **·my·ing** To lay out (printed matter) as a guide for making up a column or page. [<DUMB]

dump (dump) *v.t.* **1** To drop or throw down abruptly. **2** To empty out, as from a container. **3** To empty (a container), as by overturning. **4** To throw (goods) on a market in quantity and at low prices. **5** To get rid of. —*v.i.* **6** To fall or drop. **7** To unload commodities. **8** To unload refuse. — *n.* **1** A dumping ground, as for refuse. **2** That which is dumped. **3** A place where ammunition, supplies, etc. are held for rapid distribution. **4** *Slang* A poor, ill-kept dwelling or place. [<Scand.] —**dump′er** *n.*

dump·ling (dump′ling) *n.* **1** A small piece of dough filled with fruit, meat, or vegetables, and cooked by baking, steaming, or frying. **2** A small mass of dough dropped into boiling soup or stew.

dumps (dumps) *n. pl.* A gloomy state of mind; melancholy. [?<MDu. *domp* mental haze]

Dump·ster (dump′stər) *n.* a large metal container for garbage, fitted with a lid and a mechanism for dumping into a garbage truck: a trade name.

dump truck A truck which unloads by tilting back the cargo bin and opening the tailgate.

dump·y[1] (dump′ē) *adj.* **dump·i·er**, **dump·i·est** Sullen or discontented; sulky; gloomy.

dump·y[2] (dump′ē) *adj.* **dump·i·er**, **dump·i·est** Short and thick; stocky. —**dump′i·ly** *adv.* —**dump′i·ness** *n.*

dun[1] (dun) *v.t. & v.i.* **dunned**, **dun·ning** To press (a debtor) for payment. —*n.* **1** One who duns. **2** A demand for payment. [?]

dun[2] (dun) *adj.* Grayish or reddish brown. —*n.* Dun color. —*v.t.* **dunned**, **dun·ning** To make dun-colored. [<OE *dunn*]

dunce (duns) *n.* A stupid or ignorant person. [<Johannes *Duns* Scotus, 13th-century theologian]

dunce cap A conical paper cap formerly placed on the head of a dull-witted pupil.

dune (dʸoon) *n.* A hill of loose sand heaped up by the wind. [<MDu. *dūne*]

dung (dung) *n.* **1** Animal excrement; manure. **2** Anything foul. —*v.t.* To cover or enrich with dung. [<OE]

dun·ga·ree (dung′gə·rē′) *n.* **1** A coarse cotton cloth, used for working clothes, tents, sails, etc. **2** *pl.* Working clothes made of this fabric. [<Hind. *dungrī*]

dun·geon (dun′jən) *n.* **1** A dark underground prison. **2** DONJON. [<OF *donjon*]

dung·hill (dung′hil′) *n.* **1** A heap of manure. **2** Figuratively, a vile abode or condition.

dunk (dungk) *v.t. & v.i.* To dip or sop (bread, doughnuts, etc.) into tea, coffee, soup, etc. [<OHG *dunkōn*]

dun·nage (dun′ij) *n.* **1** Loose packing used to protect cargo on board ship or goods in a container from damage. **2** BAGGAGE. [?]

du·o (dʸoo′ō) *n. pl.* **du·os** DUET. [L, two]

duo- *combining form* Two. [<L *duo* two]

du·o·dec·i·mal (dʸoo′ō·des′ə·məl) *adj.* Of, pertaining to, or based on twelve. —*n.* A twelfth. [<L *duodecim* twelve]

du·o·dec·i·mo (dʸoo′ō·des′ə·mō) *n. pl.* **·mos** **1** The size of pages made from a printer's sheet folded into twelve leaves, approximately 5 × 7½ inches. **2** A book made up of pages of this size. —*adj.* Made up of pages of this size.

du·o·de·num (dʸoo′ō·dē′nəm, dʸoo·od′ə·nəm) *n. pl.* **·na** (-nə) or **·nums** That part of the small intestine next to the stomach. [<Med. L *duodenum (digitorum)* of twelve (fingers): with ref. to its length] —**du′o·de′nal** *adj.* • See INTESTINE.

dup. duplicate

dupe (dʸoop) *n.* A victim of deception. —*v.t.* **duped**, **dup·ing** To make a dupe of. [<L *upupa* a hoopoe (a bird thought to be stupid)] —**dup′a·ble** *adj.* —**dup′er·y** *n.* —**Syn.** *n.* gull, fool, ninny, victim. *v.* fool, deceive, trick, hoodwink.

du·ple (dʸoo′pəl) *adj.* **1** Double. **2** *Music* Having two beats to a measure. [<L *duplus* double]

du·plex (dʸoo′pleks) *adj.* Double; twofold. —*n.* A duplex house or apartment. [<L *duo* two + stem of *plicare* fold]

duplex apartment An apartment having rooms on two floors with an interior stairway.

duplex house A house having two one-family units.

du·pli·cate (dʸoo′plə·kit) *adj.* **1** Made or done exactly like an original. **2** Double. **3** Designating a way of playing a card game in which, for purposes of comparing scores, the same hands are played by different players. —*n.* **1** An exact copy of an original. **2** A double or counterpart. **3** A duplicate game of cards. —*v.t.* (dʸoo′plə·kāt) **·cat·ed**, **·cat·ing 1** To make an exact copy of. **2** To double; make twofold. **3** To repeat, as an effort. [<L *duplicare* to double] —**du′pli·cate·ly** *adv.* —**du′pli·ca′tion** *n.* —**du′pli·ca′tive** *adj.*

du·pli·ca·tor (dʸoo′plə·kā′tər) *n.* A device for making duplicates, as of written or typewritten matter.

du·plic·i·ty (dʸoo·plis′ə·tē) *n. pl.* **·ties** Deception in speech or conduct. [<L *duplex* twofold] —**Syn.** deceitfulness, double-dealing, dissimulation, hypocrisy.

du·ra·ble (dʸoor′ə·bəl) *adj.* Able to continue long in the same state. [<L *durus* hard] —**du′ra·bil′i·ty**, **du′ra·ble·ness** *n.* —**du′ra·bly** *adv.* —**Syn.** lasting, strong, enduring, stable.

du·ra ma·ter (dʸoor′ə mā′tər, mā′tər) The tough fibrous membrane enclosing the brain and spinal cord. [<L *dura* hard + *mater* mother] —**du′ral** *adj.*

du·ra·men (dʸoo·rā′min) *n.* The heartwood of a tree trunk. [L, hardness]

dur·ance (dʸoor′əns) *n.* Confinement in prison. [<L *durare* last, endure]

du·ra·tion (dʸoo·rā′shən) *n.* **1** The period of time during which anything lasts. **2** Continuance in time. [<L *durare* endure]

dur·bar (dûr′bär) *n.* **1** In India, a reception formerly given by a native ruler or high British officer. **2** The room in which this is held. [<Pers. *darbār* court]

du·ress (dʸoo·res′, dʸoor′is) *n.* **1** Compulsion by force or fear. **2** Restraint, as by confinement in prison. [<OF *duresse* hardness, constraint <L *durus* hard]

dur·ing (dʸoor′ing) *prep.* **1** Throughout the time, existence, or action of. **2** In the course of; at some period in. [<L *durare* endure]

durst (dûrst) *Archaic p.t.* of DARE.

du·rum (dʸoor′əm) *n.* A species of wheat widely grown for macaroni and spaghetti products. [<L *durus* hard]

dusk (dusk) *n.* **1** The dark period of twilight. **2** Partial darkness; semidarkness. —*adj.* Dusky. —*v.t. & v.i.* To make or grow dim. [<OE *dox* dark]

dusk·y (dus′kē) *adj.* **dusk·i·er**, **dusk·i·est 1** Somewhat dark in color, esp. swarthy. **2** Shadowy; dim. **3** Gloomy. —**dusk′i·ly** *adv.* —**dusk′i·ness** *n.*

dust (dust) *n.* **1** Any substance, as earth, reduced to powder. **2** A cloud of this substance. **3** GOLD DUST. **4** A dead body; remains. **5** The earth. **6** Confusion; controversy. — **bite the dust** To fall wounded or dead. —*v.t.* **1** To wipe or brush dust from. **2** To sprinkle with powder, etc. **3** To soil with dust. —*v.i.* **4** To wipe dust from furniture, etc. [<OE *dūst*] —**dust′less** *adj.*

dust bowl A region where topsoil has been blown away by dust storms during periods of drought.

dust·er (dus′tər) *n.* **1** One who or that which dusts. **2** A cloth or brush for removing dust. **3** A garment or covering to protect from dust.

dust jacket A removable covering for a book, usu. of paper.

dust·pan (dust′pan′) *n.* A shovellike implement into which rubbish from a floor is swept.

dust storm A windstorm carrying clouds of dust along with it.

dust·y (dus′tē) *adj.* **dust·i·er dust·i·est 1** Covered with dust. **2** Dull or grayish. **3** Powdery. —**dust′i·ness** *n.*

Dutch (duch) *adj.* **1** Of or pertaining to the Netherlands, its people, or their language. **2** *Slang* German. —*n.* **1** The people of the Netherlands: with *the.* **2** *Slang* Germans: with *the.* **3** The language of the Netherlands. — **in Dutch** *Slang* In trouble or disfavor. — **go Dutch** *Informal* To have each participant pay his own expenses.

Dutch door A door divided horizontally in the middle, thus allowing either half to be opened separately.

Dutch door

Dutch·man (duch′mən) *n. pl.* **·men** (-mən) **1** A citizen or native of the Netherlands. **2** *Slang* A German.

Dutch oven 1 A brick oven that cooks after the source of fire is removed. **2** A heavy pot with a tight-fitting lid. **3** A metal oven used in front of an open fire.

Dutch treat *Informal* Entertainment at which each person pays his own bill.

Dutch uncle A very frank and severe critic.

du·te·ous (dᵞōō′tē·əs) *adj.* Obedient; dutiful. —**du′te·ous·ly** *adv.* —**du′te·ous·ness** *n.*

du·ti·a·ble (dᵞōō′tē·ə·bəl) *adj.* Subject to impost duty.

du·ti·ful (dᵞōō′ti·fəl) *adj.* **1** Submissive; obedient. **2** Showing respect or a sense of duty; respectful. —**du′ti·ful·ly** *adv.* —**du′ti·ful·ness** *n.*

du·ty (dᵞōō′tē) *n. pl.* **·ties 1** Something which one is legally or morally bound to pay, do, or perform. **2** A specific obligatory service or function: to do sea *duty.* **3** A moral obligation; right action; also, a sense of this: *duty* calls. **4** Respectful or obedient conduct, as to one's parents. **5** A tax, as upon goods imported, exported, or consumed. [<OF *deu* DUE]

du·ty-free (dᵞōō′tē·frē′) *adj. & adv.* Free from customs duties.

du·vet (dᵞōō·vē′, dᵞōō′-) *n.* COMFORTER (def. 2).

du·ve·tyn (dōō′və·tēn, duv′tēn′) *n.* A fabric with a velvetlike surface. Also **du′ve·tine, du′ve·tyne.** [<F *duvet* down]

D.V., D.v. God willing (L *Deo volente*).

dwarf (dwôrf) *n.* A person, animal, or plant that is unusually small. —*v.t.* **1** To stunt development of. **2** To cause to appear small by comparison. —*v.i.* **3** To become stunted. —*adj.* Smaller than others of its kind; stunted. [<OE *dweorh*] —**dwarf′ish** *adj.* —**dwarf′ish·ly** *adv.* —**dwarf′ish·ness** *n.*

dwell (dwel) *v.i.* **dwelt** or **dwelled, dwell·ing 1** To have a fixed abode; reside. **2** To linger, as on a subject: with *on* or *upon.* [<OE *dwellan* hinder, stay] —**dwell′er** *n.*

dwell·ing (dwel′ing) *n.* A place used for residence. —*Syn.* domicile, abode, habitation, house, home.

dwin·dle (dwin′dəl) *v.t. & v.i.* **·dled, ·dling** To make or become smaller or less; diminish; decline. [<OE *dwinan* waste away]

dwt. pennyweight.

DX, D.X. distance; distant.

Dy dysprosium.

dy·ad (dī′ad, -əd) *n.* A pair, as of things or persons.

dyb·buk (dib′ək) *n.* In Jewish folklore, a wandering soul believed to possess a living person's body.

dye (dī) *v.* **dyed, dye·ing** *v.t.* **1** To fix a color in (fabric, hair, etc.) by soaking in liquid coloring matter. **2** To stain; color; tint. —*v.i.* **3** To take or give color by dyeing. —*n.* A fluid or coloring matter used for dyeing; also, the color or hue produced by dyeing. [<OE *deag* dye, color] —**dy′er** *n.*

dyed-in-the-wool (dīd′in·thə·wōōl′) *adj.* **1** Dyed before being woven. **2** Thoroughgoing; complete.

dye·ing (dī′ing) *n.* The act, process, or trade of fixing colors in cloth or the like.

dye-stuff (dī′stuf′) *n.* Any material used for dyeing.

dy·ing (dī′ing) *adj.* **1** Near to death; expiring. **2** About to end or disappear. **3** Of, pertaining to, or at the time of death. —*n.* Death.

dyke[1] (dīk) *n. & v.* DIKE[1].

dyke[2] *n.* DIKE[2].

dy·nam·ic (dī·nam′ik) *adj.* **1** Of or pertaining to motion or unbalanced forces. **2** Of or pertaining to dynamics. **3** Mentally or spiritually energetic, forceful, or powerful: a *dynamic* leader. Also **dy·nam′i·cal.** [<Gk. *dynamis* power]

—**dy·nam′i·cal·ly** *adv.*

dy·nam·ics (dī·nam′iks) *n. pl. (construed as sing. in defs. 1 and 3)* **1** The branch of physics that treats of the motion or equilibrium of bodies or of the forces that produce such motion or equilibrium. **2** The forces producing or governing activity or movement of any kind: spiritual *dynamics.* **3** *Music* The production of varying degrees of loudness; also, the words, symbols, etc., indicating this.

dy·na·mism (dī′nə·miz′əm) *n.* The quality of being dynamic, vital, or enthusiastic.

dy·na·mite (dī′nə·mīt) *n.* **1** An explosive composed of nitroglycerin held in an absorbent substance. **2** *Slang* Anything wonderful or spectacular. —*v.t.* **·mit·ed, ·mit·ing** To blow up or shatter with dynamite. [<Gk. *dynamis* power] —**dy′na·mit′er** *n.*

dy·na·mo (dī′nə·mō) *n. pl.* **·mos 1** A machine for changing mechanical energy into electrical energy by electromagnetic induction. **2** A vital, energetic person. [Short for DYNAMOELECTRIC machine]

dynamo- *combining form* Force; power: *dynamometer.* [<Gk. *dynamis* power]

dy·na·mo·e·lec·tric (dī′nə·mō·i·lek′trik) *adj.* Pertaining to the relation between electricity and mechanical energy. Also **dy′na·mo·e·lec′tri·cal.**

dy·na·mom·e·ter (dī′nə·mom′ə·tər) *n.* An instrument for measuring force exerted or power expended. [DYNAMO- + -METER] —**dy·na·mo·met·ric** (dī′nə·mō·met′rik) or **·ri·cal** *adj.* —**dy′na·mom′e·try** *n.*

dy·nast (dī′nast, -nəst) *n.* A monarch; ruler. [<Gk. *dynasthai* be powerful]

dy·nas·ty (dī′nəs·tē, *esp. Brit.* din′ə·stē) *n. pl.* **·ties 1** A succession of sovereigns in one line of family descent. **2** The length of time during which one family is in power. —**dy·nas·tic** (dī·nas′tik) or **·ti·cal** *adj.* —**dy·nas′ti·cal·ly** *adv.*

dyne (dīn) *n. Physics* A unit of force equal to 10^{-5} newton. [<Gk. *dynamis* power]

dys- *combining form* Bad; defective; difficult: *dyspepsia.* [Gk., bad, difficult]

dys·en·ter·y (dis′ən·ter′ē) *n.* A severe inflammation of the large intestine, marked by bloody evacuations. [<Gk. *dys-* bad + *enteron* intestine] —**dys′en·ter′ic** or **·i·cal** *adj.*

dys·func·tion (dis·fungk′shən) *n.* Deterioration of proper functioning, as of some bodily organ —**dys·func′tion·al** *adj.*

dys·lex·i·a (dis·lek′sē·ə) *n.* An impairment or loss of the ability to read. [<Gk. *dys-* bad + *lexis* speech]

dys·pep·sia (dis·pep′shə, -sē·ə) *n.* Difficult or painful digestion. [<Gk. *dys-* hard + *peptein* cook, digest]

dys·pep·tic (dis·pep′tik) *adj.* **1** Relating to or suffering from dyspepsia. **2** Gloomy; cross. Also **dys·pep′ti·cal.** —*n.* A dyspeptic person. —**dys·pep′ti·cal·ly** *adv.*

dys·pha·sia (dis·fā′zhə, -zhē·ə) *n.* Difficulty in understanding or using speech due to disease of or injury to the brain. [<Gk. *dys-* hard + *phasis* utterance]

dys·pro·si·um (dis·prō′sē·əm, -shē-) *n.* A highly magnetic element (symbol Dy) of the rare-earth series. [<Gk. *dys-* hard + *prosienai* to approach]

dys·to·pia (dis·tō′pē·ə) *n.* An imaginary place with an inhuman regime or intolerable conditions, the opposite of a utopia.

dys·tro·phy (dis′trə·fē) *n. pl.* **·phies 1** Defective or faulty nutrition. **2** Any of various neurological or muscular disorders. [<Gk. *dys-* hard, defective + *trophē* nourishment]

dz. dozen.

---

add, āce, câre, pälm; end, ēven; it, īce; odd, ōpen, ôrder; tŏŏk, pōōl; up, bûrn; ə = *a* in *above, u* in *focus;* yōō = *u* in *fuse;* oil; pout; check; go; ring; thin; this; zh, *vision.* < derived from; ? origin uncertain or unknown.

E

E, e (ē) *n. pl.* **E's, e's, Es, es** (ēz) **1** The fifth letter of the English alphabet. **2** Any spoken sound representing the letter *E* or *e.* **3** *Music* The third tone in the diatonic scale of C major. **4** Something shaped like an E. **5** *Math.* The number used as the base of the natural logarithms, roughly 2.718. —*adj.* Shaped like an E.

E, E. English.

E, E., e, e. east; eastern.

E. earl; earth.

ea. each.

each (ēch) *adj.* Being one of two or more individuals somehow loosely associated: *Each* shoe was muddy. —*pron.* Every one of any number or group considered individually; each one. —*adv.* For or to each person, article, etc.; apiece: one dollar *each.* [< OE *ælc*]

each other Each of two or more in reciprocal relation or action; one another: We saw *each other* at the theater last night but didn't speak.

ea·ger (ē′gər) *adj.* Having or showing an intense desire for something. [< L *acer* sharp] —**ea′ger·ly** *adv.* —**ea′ger·ness** *n.* —**Syn.** avid, desirous, keen, zealous.

ea·gle (ē′gəl) *n.* **1** A large diurnal bird of prey with powerful wings and keen eyesight. **2** A former gold coin of the United States, value $10. **3** A picture or design of an eagle, used as an emblem on a seal, flag, etc. **4** In golf, two strokes less than par in playing a hole. [< L *aquila*]

ea·gle-eyed (ē′gəl·īd′) *adj.* Keen-sighted.

ea·glet (ē′glit) *n.* A young eagle.

ear[1] (ir) *n.* **1** The organ of hearing in man and other mammals. **2** The external part of this organ. **3** The sense of hearing. **4** A discriminating perception of sounds. **5** Attentive consideration; heed. **6** Anything like the external ear, as a projecting piece, handle, etc. —**be all ears** *Informal* To pay eager attention to. —**have** (or **keep**) **an ear to the ground** To be or keep aware of public opinion, current trends, etc. —**up to the ears** *Informal* Almost overwhelmed, as by work. [< OE *ēare*] —**eared** *adj.*

Ear
a. auditory canal.
b. middle ear.
c. semicircular canals.
d. cochlea.

ear[2] (ir) *n.* The grain-bearing part of a cereal plant. —*v.i.* To form ears, as grain. [< OE *ēar*]

ear·ache (ir′āk′) *n.* Pain inside the ear.

ear·drum (ir′drum′) *n.* TYMPANIC MEMBRANE.

eared (ird) *adj.* **1** Having an ear or ears: an *eared* cup. **2** Having a specified kind or number of ears: used in combination: *floppy-eared.*

earl (ûrl) *n.* A member of the British nobility ranking below a marquess and above a viscount. [< OE *eorl* nobleman] —**earl′dom, earl′ship** *n.*

ear·ly (ûr′lē) *adj.* ·**li·er,** ·**li·est 1** Near the beginning of any stated period of time or of a movement, series, etc. **2** Ancient. **3** Being or occurring sooner than is usual or necessary. **4** About to be or happen. —*adv.* **1** At or near the beginning of a period of time or of a movement, series, etc. **2** Before the expected or ordinary time. **3** In ancient times. —**early on** Near the beginning. [< OE *ær* sooner + -*līce* -ly] —**ear′li·ness** *n.*

ear·mark (ir′märk′) *v.t.* **1** To make a mark of identification on. **2** To mark an animal's ear. **3** To set aside for special purposes, as money. —*n.* **1** An owner's mark on an animal's ear. **2** Any mark of identification.

ear·muff (ir′muf′) *n.* One of a pair of coverings for the ears, worn as a protection against cold.

earn (ûrn) *v.t.* **1** To receive, as salary or wages, for labor. **2** To merit as a result, reward, or punishment. **3** To bring in (interest, etc.) as gain or profit. [< OE *earnian*] —**earn′·er** *n.*

ear·nest[1] (ûr′nist) *adj.* **1** Intent and direct in purpose; zealous. **2** Marked by deep feeling or conviction; heartfelt. **3** Serious; important. —*n.* Seriousness. —**in earnest** With full and serious intent. [< OE *eorneste*] —**ear′nest·ly** *adv.* —**ear′nest·ness** *n.*

ear·nest[2] (ûr′nist) *n.* **1** Money paid in advance to bind a bargain. **2** A pledge. [< Heb. *ērābōn*]

earn·ings (ûr′ningz) *n.pl.* **1** Wages; salary. **2** Profits.

ear·phone (ir′fōn′) *n.* A device for converting electrical energy, as from a radio or telephone, into audible sound.

ear·ring (ir′ring′) *n.* An ear ornament.

ear·shot (ir′shot′) *n.* The distance at which sounds may be heard.

earth (ûrth) *n.* **1** *Often cap.* The planet on which man lives; the planet of the solar system third in distance from the sun. • See PLANET. **2** The people who inhabit this planet. **3** The abode of man, considered as distinct from heaven and hell. **4** The dry land portion of the surface of the globe. **5** Soil; dirt; ground. **6** The hole of a burrowing animal. **7** Worldly interests and pursuits. —**down to earth** Realistic. —**run to earth** To hunt down and find, as a fox. —*v.t.* **1** To protect with earth. **2** To chase, as a fox, into a burrow or hole. —*v.i.* **3** To burrow or hide in the earth, as a fox. [< OE *eorthe*]

earth·en (ûr′thən) *adj.* **1** Made of earth or baked clay. **2** EARTHLY.

earth·en·ware (ûr′thən·wâr′) *n.* **1** A kind of slightly porous baked clay. **2** Ceramics made from such clay.

earth·ly (ûrth′lē) *adj.* **1** Of or pertaining to the earth. **2** Secular; worldly. **3** *Informal* Possible; imaginable. —**earth′li·ness** *n.*

earth·quake (ûrth′kwāk′) *n.* A tremor of a portion of the earth's crust, caused by volcanic or other disturbances below the earth's surface.

earth·shine (ûrth′shīn′) *n. Astron.* Sunlight reflected by earth that dimly illuminates parts of the moon not exposed to direct sunlight.

earth·ward (ûrth′wərd) *adv.* Toward the earth: also **earth′wards.** —*adj.* Moving toward the earth.

earth·work (ûrth′wûrk′) *n.* **1** *Mil.* A fortification made of earth. **2** *Engin.* An operation requiring the removal of or filling in with earth.

earth·worm (ûrth′wûrm′) *n.* A burrowing worm that lives in and enriches the soil.

earth·y (ûr′thē) *adj.* **earth·i·er, earth·i·est 1** Of or like earth or soil; made of earth. **2** Unrefined; coarse. **3** Simple; natural; robust; lusty. —**earth′i·ness** *n.*

ear·wax (ir′waks′) *n.* A waxy substance found in the passages of the external ear.

ear·wig (ir′wig′) *n.* A beetlelike insect erroneously believed to enter the human ear. —*v.t.* ·**wigged,** ·**wig·ging** To influence by secret and stealthy counsel. [< OE *ēarwicga*]

ease (ēz) *n.* **1** Freedom from pain, agitation, or worry; comfort. **2** Freedom from or absence of apparent effort; facility. **3** Freedom from affectation, formality, etc.; naturalness. —*v.* **eased, eas·ing** *v.t.* **1** To relieve the mental or physical pain or oppression of; comfort. **2** To make less painful or oppressive. **3** To lessen the pressure, weight, tension, etc., of. **4** To move, lower, or put in place carefully. —*v.i.* **5** To diminish in severity, speed, etc.: often with *up* or *off.* [< OF *aise* < LL *adjacens, -entis* neighboring] —**ease′ful** *adj.* —**ease′ful·ly** *adv.* —**ease′ful·ness, eas′er** *n.* —**Syn.** *n.* **1** rest, luxury, repose, content. **2** expertness.

ea·sel (ē′zəl) *n.* A folding frame for supporting a picture, panel, etc. [< Du. *ezel* easel, orig., an ass]

ease·ment (ēz′mənt) *n.* **1** An easing or being eased. **2** Anything that gives ease or relief. **3** *Law* The privilege or right of making limited use of another's adjacent property.

eas·i·ly (ē′zə·lē) *adv.* **1** In an easy manner. **2** Without question: *easily* the winner. **3** Possibly.

eas·i·ness (ē′zi·nis) *n.* The state of being at ease, or of being easy to do or accomplish.

east (ēst) *n.* 1 The general direction in which the sun appears at sunrise. 2 The point of the compass at 90°, directly opposite west. 3 Any direction, region, or part of the horizon near that point. —**the East** 1 Asia, esp. China, Japan, and the other countries of E Asia. 2 In the U.S., the region east of the Allegheny Mountains and north of Maryland. —*adj.* 1 To, toward, facing, or in the east. 2 Coming from the east. —*adv.* In or toward the east; in an easterly direction. [< OE *ēast*]

east·bound (ēst′bound′) *adj.* Going eastward. Also **east′-bound′.**

East·er (ēs′tər) *n.* 1 A Christian festival commemorating the resurrection of Christ. 2 The day on which this festival is celebrated, the Sunday immediately after the first full moon that occurs on or after March 21: also **Easter Sunday.** [< OE *Ēastre* goddess of spring]

east·er·ly (ēs′tər·lē) *adj.* 1 Of, in, or toward the east; eastward. 2 From the east: said of winds. —*adv.* Toward the east: also **east′ern·ly.** —*n.* A storm from the east.

east·ern (ēs′tərn) *adj.* 1 Of, pertaining to, from or situated in the east. 2 *Usu. cap.* Pertaining to the East. 3 Moving to or from the east; easterly.

Eastern Church 1 The Christian Church of the Byzantine Empire. 2 The Eastern Orthodox Church.

east·ern·er (ēs′tərn·ər) *n. Often cap.* One who dwells in the eastern part of the U.S.

Eastern Hemisphere See HEMISPHERE.

Eastern Orthodox Church Any of the modern Christian Churches employing the Byzantine rite and honoring the primacy of the patriarch of Constantinople, as the Russian and Greek Orthodox Churches.

Eastern (Roman) Empire The Byzantine Empire.

East·er·tide (ēs′tər·tīd′) *n.* The season of Easter; a period extending in various churches from Easter to Ascension Day, Whitsunday, or Trinity Sunday.

East Germany See GERMANY.

east·ward (ēst′wərd) *adj.* To, toward, or in the east. —*adv.* Toward the east: also **east′wards.** Also **east′ward·ly.**

eas·y (ē′zē) *adj.* **eas·i·er, eas·i·est** 1 Involving little effort, discomfort, or difficulty. 2 Causing no pain, anxiety, or distress. 3 Relaxed and unpretentious: an *easy* manner. 4 Not harsh or stern; lenient; indulgent. 5 Unresisting; tractable: *easy* prey. 6 Comfortable; pleasant: in *easy* circumstances. 7 Gentle; moderate: an *easy* pace. 8 Undemanding; reasonable: *easy* terms. 9 *Econ.* a In little demand: said of commodities. b Plentiful, therefore obtainable at low interest rates: said of money. —*adv. Informal* 1 Easily. 2 Slowly and cautiously. —**go easy on** *Informal* 1 To use cautiously. 2 To be lenient or indulgent toward. —**take it easy** *Informal* 1 To relax. 2 To stay calm. [< OE *aise* EASE] —Syn. *adj.* 1 effortless, simple. 3 natural.

eas·y·go·ing (ē′zē·gō′ing) *adj.* Not inclined to effort or worry; complacently unconcerned.

easy mark *Informal* A person easily fooled.

eat (ēt) *v.* **ate** (āt or *Brit.* et) or *Regional* **eat** (et), **eat·en, eat·ing** *v.t.* 1 To take (food) into the mouth and swallow. 2 To consume or destroy as if by eating: to *eat* away one's savings. 3 To wear into or away; corrode; rust. 4 To make (a way or hole) by or as by gnawing or chewing. —*v.i.* 5 To take in food; have a meal. —**eat one's words** To retract what one has said. [< OE *etan*] —**eat′a·ble** *n., adj.* —**eat′er** *n.*

eats (ēts) *n. pl. Informal* Food.

eau de Co·logne (ō′də kə·lōn′) *n. pl.* **eaux** (ō′-) A toilet water; cologne. [F, lit., water of Cologne]

eaves (ēvz) *n. pl.* The projecting edge of a roof. [< OE *efes* edge]

eaves·drop (ēvz′drop′) *v.i.* **·dropped, ·drop·ping** To listen secretly, as to a private conversation. [With ref. to one who listens while standing outside under dripping eaves] —**eaves′drop′per, eaves′drop′-ping** *n.*

Eaves

ebb (eb) *v.i.* 1 To recede, as the tide. 2 To decline; fail. —*n.* 1 The flowing away of tidewater to the ocean; low tide: also **ebb tide.** 2 A condition or period of decline. [< OE *ebbian*]

eb·on·ite (eb′ən·īt) *n.* Hard rubber; vulcanite. [< EBONY]

eb·on·y (eb′ən·ē) *n. pl.* **·on·ies** 1 A hard, heavy wood, usu. black, used for cabinetwork, etc. 2 A hardwood tree of Ceylon and s India. —*adj.* 1 Made of ebony. 2 Black. [< Gk. *ebenos* ebony < Egyptian *hebni*]

e·bul·lient (i·bul′yənt) *adj.* 1 Bubbling over with enthusiasm. 2 In a boiling condition. [< L *ex-* out + *bullire* boil] —**e·bul′lient·ly** *adv.* —**e·bul′lience, e·bul′lien·cy** *n.*

eb·ul·li·tion (eb′ə·lish′ən) *n.* 1 The bubbling of a liquid; boiling. 2 Any sudden or violent agitation.

ec·cen·tric (ek·sen′trik) *adj.* 1 Not having the same center: *eccentric* circles. 2 Not having the axis or support exactly in the center: an *eccentric* wheel. 3 Deviating from a circular form or path: *eccentric* orbit. 4 Erratic; odd; unconventional: *eccentric* behavior. —*n.* 1 A person characterized by unusual or erratic behavior. 2 *Mech.* A disk mounted out of center on a driving shaft in order to produce reciprocating motion. [< Gk. *ek-* out, away + *kentron* center] —**ec·cen′tri·cal·ly** *adv.* —Syn. *adj.* 4 peculiar, strange, bizarre, singular.

ec·cen·tric·i·ty (ek′sen·tris′ə·tē) *n. pl.* **·ties** 1 An odd or capricious act. 2 The state or quality of being eccentric.

Eccl., Eccles. Ecclesiastes.

eccl., eccles. ecclesiastical.

Ec·cle·si·as·tes (i·klē′zē·as′tēz) *n.* A book of the Old Testament. [< Gk. *ekklēsia* assembly]

ec·cle·si·as·tic (i·klē′zē·as′tik) *adj.* Ecclesiastical. —*n.* A cleric; churchman. [< Gk. *ekklēsia* assembly]

ec·cle·si·as·ti·cal (i·klē′zē·as′ti·kəl) *adj.* Of or pertaining to the church, esp. considered as an organized and governing power. —**ec·cle′si·as′ti·cal·ly** *adv.*

Ecclus. Ecclesiasticus.

ech·e·lon (esh′ə·lon) *n.* 1 A steplike troop, fleet, or airplane formation, in which each rank, ship, or airplane is behind and to the right or left of the one preceding. 2 A military unit described according to its position or function: rear *echelon;* command *echelon.* 3 A level of responsibility or power, as in an organization. 4 The persons at such a level. —*v.t.* & *v.i.* To form in echelon. [< F *échelle* ladder < L *scala*]

e·chid·na (i·kid′nə) *n.* An egg-laying mammal of Australia, etc.; a spiny anteater. [< Gk., viper, adder]

e·chi·no·derm (i·kī′nə·dûrm) *n.* An invertebrate marine animal such as a starfish or sea urchin, characterized by a spiny exterior and radially arranged body parts. [< Gk. *echinos* hedgehog + *derma* skin] —**e·chi′no·der′ma·tous** (-dûr′mə·təs) *adj.*

Echidna

ech·o (ek′ō) *n. pl.* **·oes** 1 The sound or repetition of sound produced by the reflection of sound waves from an opposing surface. 2 A close imitation of another's views or thoughts. 3 A response or reaction, esp. sympathetic. 4 A suggestion or trace; reminder: an *echo* of the past. —*v.t.* 1 To repeat or send back (sound) by echo. 2 To repeat the words, opinions, etc., of. 3 To repeat (words, opinions, etc.) in imitation of another. —*v.i.* 4 To resound or reverberate by or as by echo. [< Gk. *ēchō*] —**ech′o·er** *n.*

ech·o·lo·ca·tion (ek′ō·lō·kā′shən) *n.* Determination of the position and form of objects by means of sound waves reflected by them. [ECHO + LOCATION] —**ech′o·lo·cate′** *v.* (**·cat·ed, ·cat·ing**)

é·clair (ā·klâr′, i·klâr′) *n.* A small pastry filled with custard or whipped cream and usu. iced with chocolate. [F, lit., flash of lightning]

é·clat (ā·klä′, i·klä′) *n.* 1 Brilliant or ostentatious achievement. 2 Dazzling style; stunning effect. 3 Renown; celebrity; glory. [< F *éclater* burst out]

ec·lec·tic (ek·lek′tik, ik-) *adj.* 1 Selecting from various sources. 2 Composed of selections from various sources. —*n.* One who uses an eclectic method. [< Gk. *ek-* out +

legein select] —**ec·lec′ti·cal·ly** *adv.* —**ec·lec′ti·cism** (-tə·siz′·əm) *n.*

e·clipse (i·klips′) *n.* **1** *Astron.* The dimming or elimina-

Solar eclipse
a. sun. b. moon. c. earth.

tion of light reaching an observer from a heavenly body. A **lunar eclipse** is caused by the passage of the moon through the earth's shadow; a **solar eclipse** by the passage of the moon between the sun and the observer. **2** Any dimming or passing into obscurity, as of fame. —*v.t.* **e·clipsed, e·clips·ing 1** To cause an eclipse of; darken. **2** To dim or obscure: Age *eclipsed* her beauty. **3** To outshine; surpass. [< Gk. *ek-* out + *leipein* leave] —**Syn.** *v.* **1** obscure, hide, conceal. **3** overshadow.

e·clip·tic (i·klip′tik, ē-) *n. Astron.* **1** That plane, passing through the center of the sun, which contains the orbit of the earth: also **plane of the ecliptic. 2** The great circle in which this plane intersects the celestial sphere. —*adj.* Pertaining to eclipses or to the ecliptic. —**e·clip′ti·cal** *adj.* —**e·clip′ti·cal·ly** *adv.* • See ZONE.

ec·logue (ek′lôg, -log) *n.* A poem containing discourses or dialogues, with shepherds as principal speakers. Also **ec′log.** [< Gk *eklogē* selection]

e·col·o·gy (i·kol′ə·jē) *n.* **1** That division of biology which treats of the relations between organisms and their environment. **2** The system of relationships between organisms and their environments. [< Gk. *oikos* home + -LOGY] —**ec′o·log′ic** (ek′ə·loj′ik) or **·i·cal** *adj.* —**ec′o·log′i·cal·ly** *adv.* —**e·col′o·gist** *n.*

econ. economic; economics; economy.

ec·o·nom·ic (ek′ə·nom′ik, ē′kə-) *adj.* **1** Of or relating to the production, distribution, or management of wealth. **2** Of or pertaining to the financial matters of a country, household, etc. **3** Of or pertaining to the science of economics. **4** Of practical utility: *economic* botany. [< Gk. *oikonomia.* See ECONOMY.]

ec·o·nom·i·cal (ek′ə·nom′i·kəl, ē′kə-) *adj.* **1** Careful in management; frugal; saving. **2** Not exaggerated or excessive: an *economical* style of writing. **3** ECONOMIC. —**ec′o·nom′i·cal·ly** *adv.*

ec·o·nom·ics (ek′ə·nom′iks, ē′kə-) *n. pl.* (construed as *sing.*) **1** The science that treats of the production, distribution, and consumption of wealth. **2** Financial matters.

e·con·o·mist (i·kon′ə·mist) *n.* **1** One who is proficient in economics. **2** A frugal person.

e·con·o·mize (i·kon′ə·mīz) *v.* **·mized, ·miz·ing** *v.t.* **1** To use thriftily. —*v.i.* **2** To be frugal. —**e·con′o·miz′er** *n.*

e·con·o·my (i·kon′ə·mē) *n. pl.* **·mies 1** The management of the financial and other resources of a country, community, etc. **2** Care and frugality in the use of money, time, resources, etc.; also, an instance of this. **3** A particular system of producing or managing material resources: an industrial *economy.* **4** Any practical organization of parts in a system. [< Gk. *oikonomia* < *oikos* house + *nemein* manage]

e·con·o·my-sized (i·kon′ə·mē·sīzd′) *adj.* Large-sized: a term used in consumer advertising. Also **e·con′o·my-size′** (-sīz′).

ec·o·sys·tem (ē′kō·sis′təm, ek′ō-) *n. Ecol.* A community of organisms and their nonliving environment. [< Gk. *oikos* habitat + SYSTEM]

ec·ru (ek′rōō, ā′krōō) *adj.* Light brown; tan; beige. [< OF *escru* < L *ex-* thoroughly + *crudus* raw]

ec·sta·sy (ek′stə·sē) *n. pl.* **·sies 1** The state of being beside oneself through overpowering emotion or mental exaltation. **2** Intense joy; rapture. **3** A state of trance. [< Gk. *ekstasis* distraction] —**Syn. 1** frenzy, transport. **2** bliss.

ec·stat·ic (ek·stat′ik) *adj.* Of, pertaining to, like, or in a state of ecstasy. —*n.* A person subject to ecstasies or trances. —**ec·stat′i·cal·ly** *adv.*

ecto- *combining form* Without; outside; external: *ectoderm.* [< Gk. *ektos* outside]

ec·to·derm (ek′tə·dûrm) *n.* The outer layer of the embryo, from which the epithelium and the nervous system develop. —**ec′to·der′mal, ec′to·der′mic** *adj.*

-ectomy *combining form* Removal of a part by cutting out: used in surgical terms to indicate certain kinds of operations: *appendectomy.* [< Gk. *ek-* out + *temnein* to cut]

ec·to·plasm (ek′tə·plaz′əm) *n.* The luminous substance alleged to emanate from the body of a spiritualist medium during a trance. —**ec′to·plas′mic** *adj.*

Ec·ua·dor (ek′wə·dôr) *n.* A republic in NW South America; 104,306 sq. mi., cap. Quito. —**Ec′·ua·do′re·an, Ec′ua·do′·ri·an** *adj., n.*

ec·u·men·i·cal (ek′·yōō·men′i·kəl) *adj.* **1** General; universal. **2** Of or pertaining to ecumenism. **3** Belonging to or accepted by the Christian church everywhere. [< Gk. *oikoumenē (gē)* the inhabited (world) < *oi-keein* dwell] —**ec′u·men′i·cal·ly** *adv.*

ec·u·men·ism (e·kyōō′mə·niz′əm, ek′yōō·men′iz·əm) *n.* The beliefs or practices of those who desire worldwide unity and cooperation among all Christian churches. Also **ec·u·men·i·cal·ism** (ek′yōō·men′ə·kəl·iz·əm).

ec·ze·ma (ek′sə·mə, eg′zə·mə, eg·zē′mə) *n.* An inflammatory skin disease often attended by itching, watery discharge, and lesions. [< Gk. *ek-* out + *zeein* to boil]

-ed[1] *suffix* Used to form the past tense of regular verbs: *walked, played.* [< OE *-ede, -ode, -ade*]

-ed[2] *suffix* Used to form the past participles of regular verbs: *clothed, washed.* [< OE *-ed, -ad, -od*]

-ed[3] *suffix* **1** Having; possessing; characterized by: *toothed, green-eyed.* **2** Like; resembling: *bigoted.* [< OE *-ede*]

ed. edited; edition; editor.

E·dam cheese (ē′dəm, ē′dam) A mild curd cheese, originally Dutch, made in round balls. [< *Edam,* a town in the NW Netherlands]

Ed·da (ed′ə) *n.* Either of two collections of Old Icelandic or Old Norse literature. [< ON] —**Ed·da·ic** (e·dā′ik), **Ed′dic** *adj.*

ed·dy (ed′ē) *n. pl.* **·dies** A circling current of water, air, or other fluid. —*v.t. & v.i.* **·died, ·dy·ing** To move, or cause to move, in or as in an eddy. [< ON *idha*]

e·del·weiss (ā′dəl·vīs) *n.* A small perennial alpine herb with white woolly leaves. [< G *edel* noble + *weiss* white]

e·de·ma (i·dē′mə) *n.* A morbid accumulation of fluid in various parts of the body. [< Gk. *oidēma* a tumor]

E·den (ēd′n) *n.* **1** In the Bible, the garden that was the first home of Adam and Eve. **2** Any delightful place.

e·den·tate (ē·den′tāt, i·den′-) *adj.* **1** Toothless. **2** Of or pertaining to an order of mammals some of which lack teeth, including sloths, anteaters, and armadillos. —*n.* A creature without teeth. [< L *ex-* without + *dens, dentis* tooth]

edge (ej) *n.* **1** The thin, sharp cutting part of a blade. **2** Sharpness; keenness: the *edge* of her wit. **3** An abrupt border or margin; verge; brink: the *edge* of a cliff; on the *edge* of tears. **4** A bounding or dividing line: the *edge* of a plain. **5** *Informal* Advantage. —**on edge 1** Nervous; irritable. **2** Keenly eager. —*v.* **edged, edg·ing** *v.t.* **1** To sharpen. **2** To put an edging or border on. **3** To move cautiously sidewise. **4** To move by degrees; inch. **5** *Informal* To defeat by a slight margin: often with *out.* —*v.i.* **6** To move sidewise. **7** To move by degrees. [< OE *ecg*]

edge·ways (ej′wāz′) *adv.* **1** With the edge forward. **2** On, by, with, along, or in the direction of the edge. Also **edge′wise** (-wīz′).

edg·ing (ej′ing) *n.* Anything serving as or attached to an edge; trimming.

edg·y (ej′ē) *adj.* **edg·i·er, edg·i·est 1** Having an edge or edges. **2** Irritable; on edge. —**edg′i·ness** *n.*

ed·i·ble (ed′ə·bəl) *adj.* Fit to eat. —*n. Usu. pl.* Something suitable for food. [< L *edere* eat] —**ed′i·bil′i·ty** *n.*

e·dict (ē′dikt) *n.* An official proclamation or decree. [< L < *ex-* out + *dicere* say]

ed·i·fice (ed′ə·fis) *n.* A building or other structure, esp. if large or imposing. [< L *aedes* building + *facere* make]

ed·i·fy (ed′ə·fī) *v.t.* **fied, fy·ing** To strengthen morally; enlighten. [< L *aedes* building + *facere* make] —**ed′i·fi·ca′· tion, ed′i·fi′er** *n.* —**ed′i·fy′ing** *adj.* —**ed′i·fy′ing·ly** *adv.*

ed·it (ed′it) *v.t.* **1** To manage the preparation and publication of (a newspaper, etc.). **2** To compile, arrange and emend for publication. **3** To correct and prepare for publication. **4** To prepare (a film, recording tape, etc.) for showing or hearing by cutting, splicing, or rearranging. [< L *editus,* p.p. of *edere* publish, give out]

edit. edited; edition; editor.

e·di·tion (i·dish′ən) *n.* **1** A published form of a literary work, or a copy of the form so published. **2** The total number of copies of a book, magazine, etc., issued at one time.

ed·i·tor (ed′i·tər) *n.* **1** One who prepares manuscripts, copy, etc., for publication. **2** One who writes editorials. —**ed′i·tor·ship′** *n.*

ed·i·to·ri·al (ed′i·tôr′ē·əl, -tō′rē-) *adj.* **1** Of, pertaining to, or emanating from an editor. **2** Of, pertaining to, being, or like an editorial. —*n.* A magazine or newspaper article, radio or television commentary, etc., that expresses the opinions of the editors or publishers, or of management. —**ed′i·to′ri·al·ly** *adv.*

ed·i·to·ri·al·ize (ed′i·tôr′ē·əl·īz′, -tō′rē-) *v.i.* **·ized, ·iz·ing 1** To express opinions in editorial form. **2** To insert editorial opinions into the reporting of facts.

editor in chief *pl.* **editors in chief** The chief editor of a publication.

E.D.T., e.d.t. eastern daylight time.

ed·u·ca·ble (ej′ŏŏ·kə·bəl) *adj.* Capable of being educated. —**ed′u·ca·bil′i·ty** *n.*

ed·u·cate (ej′ŏŏ·kāt) *v.t.* **·cat·ed, ·cat·ing 1** To develop or train the mind, capabilities, and character of by or as by formal schooling or instruction; teach. **2** To train for some special purpose. **3** To develop and train (taste, special ability, etc.). **4** To provide schooling for. [< L *educare* bring up] —**ed′u·ca′tor** *n.*

ed·u·cat·ed (ej′ŏŏ·kā′tid) *adj.* **1** Developed and informed by education. **2** Having a cultivated mind, speech, manner, etc.

ed·u·ca·tion (ej′ŏŏ·kā′shən) *n.* **1** The development and training of one's mind, character, skills, etc., as by instruction, study, or example. **2** Instruction and training in an institution of learning. **3** The knowledge and skills resulting from such instruction and training. **4** Teaching as a system, science, or art; pedagogy. —**ed′u·ca′tion·al** *adj.* —**ed′u·ca′tion·al·ly** *adv.*

ed·u·ca·tive (ej′ŏŏ·kā′tiv) *adj.* **1** Tending or helping to educate; instructive. **2** Of or pertaining to education.

e·duce (i·dyŏŏs′) *v.t.* **e·duced, e·duc·ing 1** To call forth; draw out; evoke. **2** To develop or formulate, as from data. [< L *ex-* out + *ducere* to lead] —**e·duc′i·ble** *adj.* —**e·duc·tion** (i·duk′shən) *n.*

-ee *suffix of nouns* **1** A person who undergoes the action or receives the benefit of the main element: *payee.* **2** A person who is described by the main element: *absentee.* [< L *-atus*]

E.E. Electrical Engineer.

E.E.C. European Economic Community.

eel (ēl) *n. pl.* **eels** or **eel** A fish having an elongated snakelike body without scales or pelvic fins. [< OE *æl*] —**eel′y** *adj.*

American eel

eel·grass (ēl′gras′, -gräs′) *n.* A plant of grasslike appearance that grows under water.

e′en (ēn) *adv.* Even. —*n. Regional* Evening.

e′er (âr) *adv.* Ever.

-eer *suffix* **1** One who is concerned with, works with, or produces the thing mentioned: *engineer.* **2** To be concerned with: *electioneer.* [< L *-arius*]

ee·rie (ē′rē, ir′ē) *adj.* **1** Inspiring fear or awe; weird. **2** Affected by fear; awed. Also **ee′ry.** [< OE *earg* timid] —**ee′ri·ly** *adv.* —**ee′ri·ness** *n.*

ef·face (i·fās′) *v.t.* **·faced, ·fac·ing 1** To rub out, as written characters; erase; cancel. **2** To obliterate or destroy. **3** To make (oneself) inconspicuous or insignificant. [< L *ex-* out + *facies* face] —**ef·face′a·ble** *adj.* —**ef·face′ment, ef·fac′er** *n.*

ef·fect (i·fekt′) *n.* **1** A result or consequence of some cause or agency. **2** The power or capacity to produce a result; efficacy. **3** The condition of being in actual operation: When does the ruling go into *effect?* **4** Actual meaning: usu. with *to:* They wrote to this *effect.* **5** An impression or reaction resulting from something seen, done, or experienced: the *effect* of a play. **6** Something causing a particular impression or reaction: many weird *effects.* **7** *pl.* Movable goods or property; belongings. —**in effect 1** In fact; actually. **2** In essence; virtually. **3** In operation or force. —**take effect** To begin to show results; become operative. —*v.t.* **1** To bring about; cause. **2** To achieve; accomplish. [< L *ex-* out + *facere* do, make] —**ef·fect′er** *n.* — Syn. *n.* **1** upshot, outcome, conclusion. • See AFFECT[1].

ef·fec·tive (i·fek′tiv) *adj.* **1** Producing a desired effect or result. **2** Impressive; striking. **3** In force, as a law. **4** Ready, as an army. —*n.* A soldier or military unit ready for active duty. —**ef·fec′tive·ly** *adv.* —**ef·fec′tive·ness** *n.*

ef·fec·tu·al (i·fek′chŏŏ·əl) *adj.* **1** Possessing or exercising power to produce a desired effect. **2** In force; legal. —**ef· fec′tu·al′i·ty** (-al′ə·tē) *n.* —**ef·fec′tu·al·ly** *adv.*

ef·fec·tu·ate (i·fek′chŏŏ·āt) *v.t.* **·at·ed, ·at·ing** To bring about; effect. —**ef·fec′tu·a′tion** *n.*

ef·fem·i·nate (i·fem′ə·nit) *adj.* **1** Having womanish traits or qualities inappropriate to a man; unmanly. **2** Characterized by weakness, a lack of dynamism, overrefinement, etc.: an *effeminate* culture. [< L *ex-* out + *femina* a woman] —**ef·fem′i·na·cy** (-nə·sē) *n.* —**ef·fem′i·nate·ly** *adv.*

ef·fer·ent (ef′ər·ənt) *adj.* Carrying or carried outward, as impulses from the central nervous system to muscles, etc. —*n.* An efferent part, as a nerve or blood vessel. [< L *ex-* out + *ferre* carry]

ef·fer·vesce (ef′ər·ves′) *v.i.* **·vesced, ·vesc·ing 1** To give off bubbles of gas, as carbonated water. **2** To issue forth in bubbles, as a gas. **3** To show exhilaration or lively spirits. [< L *ex-* out + *fervescere* to boil.] —**ef′fer·ves′cence, ef′fer· ves′cen·cy** *n.* —**ef′fer·ves′cent** *adj.* —**ef′fer·ves′cent·ly** *adv.*

ef·fete (i·fēt′) *adj.* **1** Incapable of further production; exhausted; barren. **2** Characterized by weakness, self-indulgence, decadence, etc. [< L *ex-* out + *fetus* a breeding] —**ef· fete′ness** *n.*

ef·fi·ca·cious (ef′ə·kā′shəs) *adj.* Producing or capable of producing an intended effect. [< L *efficere* to effect] —**ef′fi· ca′cious·ly** *adv.* —**ef′fi·ca′cious·ness** *n.*

ef·fi·ca·cy (ef′ə·kə·sē) *n. pl.* **·cies** Power to produce a desired result or effect.

ef·fi·cien·cy (i·fish′ən·sē) *n. pl.* **·cies 1** The character of being efficient; effectiveness. **2** The ratio of the output energy of an organism or machine to input energy.

ef·fi·cient (i·fish′ənt) *adj.* **1** Acting or operating effectively with little waste of energy, effort, or material. **2** Productive of effects or results; causative. [< L *efficere* to effect] —**ef·fi′cient·ly** *adv.* —Syn. **1** skillful, competent. **2** operative, effectual.

ef·fi·gy (ef′ə·jē) *n. pl.* **·gies 1** A figure representing a person, as in sculpture or numismatics. **2** A representation of a despised person. —**burn (or hang) in effigy** To burn or hang publicly an image of a person who is hated. [< L *effigies* image]

ef·flo·resce (ef′lô·res′, -lō-) *v.i.* **·resced, ·resc·ing 1** *Bot.* To bear flowers. **2** *Chem.* To become powdery through loss of water of crystallization. [< L *ex-* thoroughly + *florescere* to bloom]

ef·flo·res·cence (ef′lô·res′əns, -lō-) *n.* **1** *Bot.* The time or act of flowering. **2** The process or result of efflorescing. —**ef′flo·res′cent** *adj.*

---

add, āce, câre, pälm; end, ēven; it, īce; odd, ōpen, ôrder; tŏŏk, pōōl; up, bûrn; ə = a in *above,* u in *focus;* yŏŏ = u in *fuse;* oil; pout; check; go; ring; thin; this; zh, *vision.* < derived from; ? origin uncertain or unknown.

ef·flu·ent (ef′lŏŏ·ənt) *adj.* Flowing out. —*n.* An outflow, as of water from a lake or stream. [< L < *ex-* out + *fluere* to flow] —**ef′flu·ence** *n.*

ef·flu·vi·um (i·flŏŏ′vē·əm) *n. pl.* **·vi·a** (-vē·ə) or **·vi·ums** 1 An invisible emanation. 2 A noxious or ill-smelling exhalation, as from decaying matter. [< L, a flowing out] —**ef·flu′·vi·al, ef·flu′vi·ous** *adj.*

ef·fort (ef′ərt) *n.* 1 A voluntary exertion of mental or physical power in order to accomplish something. 2 An endeavor; attempt. 3 A result or display of power; an achievement. [< L *ex-* out + *fortis* strong] —**Syn.** 1 strain, stress, exertion.

ef·fort·less (ef′ərt·lis) *adj.* Showing or making no effort; easy. —**ef′fort·less·ly** *adv.* —**ef′fort·less·ness** *n.*

ef·front·er·y (i·frun′tər·ē) *n. pl.* **·er·ies** Insolent assurance; audacity; impudence. [< L *ex-* out + *frons, frontis* forehead, face]

ef·ful·gence (i·ful′jəns) *n.* A shining forth brilliantly; beaming brightness; radiance. [< L *ex-* out + *fulgere* to shine] —**ef·ful′gent** *adj.* —**ef·ful′gent·ly** *adv.*

ef·fuse *v.* (i·fyōōz′) **·fused, ·fus·ing** *v.t.* 1 To pour forth; shed. —*v.i.* 2 To emanate; exude. —*adj.* (i·fyōōs′) 1 *Bot.* Spread loosely or flat. 2 *Zool.* Having the lips separated, as a shell. [< L *effusus,* pp. of *effundere* to pour out]

ef·fu·sion (i·fyōō′zhən) *n.* 1 The act or product of pouring forth. 2 An outpouring, as of fancy or sentiment. 3 *Pathol.* The escape of blood or other fluid, as into the cellular tissue.

ef·fu·sive (i·fyōō′siv) *adj.* 1 Overflowing with sentiment; overly demonstrative; gushing. 2 Pouring forth. —**ef·fu′·sive·ly** *adv.* —**ef·fu′sive·ness** *n.*

Eg. Egypt; Egyptian.

e.g. for example (L *exempli gratia*).

e·gad (i·gad′, ē·gad′) *interj.* By God!: a mild oath. [Prob. alter. of *ah, God!*]

e·gal·i·tar·i·an (i·gal′ə·târ′ē·ən) *adj.* Of, believing in, or characterized by the doctrine of political and social equality. —*n.* A person who advocates this doctrine. [< F *égalité* equality] —**e·gal′i·tar′i·an·ism** *n.*

egg[1] (eg) *n.* 1 A reproductive body containing the germ and the food yolk of birds, insects, reptiles, or fishes, enclosed in a membranous or shell-like covering. 2 Such a body, esp. that of domestic fowl, used as food. 3 The female reproductive cell; an ovum. 4 Something like a hen's egg in shape. 5 *Slang* Person: a good *egg.* —*v.t.* 1 To mix or cover with eggs. 2 *Informal* To pelt with eggs. —**lay an egg** *Slang* To fail: said of a play, joke, etc. [< ON]

egg[2] *v.t.* To instigate or incite; urge: usu. with *on.* [< ON *eggja*]

egg·head (eg′hed′) *n. Slang* An intellectual; a highbrow: usu. slightly derisive.

egg·nog (eg′nog′) *n.* A drink made of eggs, milk, sugar, and nutmeg, and sometimes with alcoholic liquor.

egg·plant (eg′plant′, -plänt′) *n.* 1 A widely cultivated herb of the nightshade family, with large, egg-shaped, edible fruit. 2 The fruit, used as a vegetable.

egg·shell (eg′shel′) *n.* 1 The brittle outer envelope of a bird's egg. 2 A light ivory color. 3 A thin and delicate porcelain.

e·gis (ē′jis) *n.* AEGIS.

eg·lan·tine (eg′lən·tīn, -tēn) *n.* SWEETBRIER. [< OF *aiglent,* ult. < L *acus* needle]

e·go (ē′gō, eg′ō) *n. pl.* **e·gos** 1 The conscious self. 2 *Psychoanal.* The superficial conscious part of the psyche, developed in response to environment. 3 Self-centeredness; egotism; conceit. [L, I]

e·go·cen·tric (ē′gō·sen′trik, eg′ō-) *adj.* Caring excessively or only for one's self or personal interests; self-centered. —*n.* An egocentric person. —**e′go·cen·tric′i·ty** (-sen·tris′ə·tē) *n.*

e·go·ism (ē′gō·iz′əm, eg′ō-) *n.* 1 Excessive interest in or concern about one's self; self-centeredness; conceit. 2 The doctrine that the goal of human conduct is the perfection or happiness of the ego or self. —**e′go·ist** *n.* —**e·go·ist′ic** or **·i·cal** *adj.* —**e′go·is′ti·cal·ly** *adv.* • See EGOTISM.

e·go·ma·ni·a (ē′gō·mā′nē·ə, -mān′yə, eg′ō-) *n.* Abnormal or excessive egotism. —**e′go·ma′ni·ac** *n.* —**e′go·ma·ni′a·cal** (-mə·nī′ə·kəl) *adj.*

e·go·tism (ē′gə·tiz′əm, eg′ə-) *n.* 1 The excessive and habitual practice of talking only about oneself or one's concerns. 2 CONCEIT. 3 EGOISM. —**e′go·tist** *n.* —**e′go·tis′tic** or **·ti·cal** *adj.* —**e′go·tis′ti·cal·ly** *adv.* • *Egoism* and *egotism* are often used interchangeably. However, *egoism* is felt by many to manifest itself in more self-centered thought and inner concern, whereas *egotism* is outwardly revealed in speech and actions.

e·gre·gious (i·grē′jəs, -jē·əs) *adj.* Unusually or conspicuously bad; flagrant. [< L *ex-* out + *grex, gregis* the herd] —**e·gre′gious·ly** *adv.* —**e·gre′gious·ness** *n.*

e·gress (ē′gres) *n.* 1 A going out, as from a building. 2 A place of exit. 3 The right to exit. Also **e·gres′sion.** [< L *ex-* out + *gradi* go] —**Syn.** 1 emergence, exit.

e·gret (ē′grit) *n.* A heron characterized, in the breeding season, by long and loose plumes drooping over the tail and, usu., white plumage. [< OF *aigrette*]

E·gypt (ē′jipt) *n.* A republic of NE Africa, 386,198 sq. mi., capital Cairo. • See also map at AFRICA.

Egypt. Egyptian.

E·gyp·tian (i·jip′shən) *adj.* Of or pertaining to Egypt, its people, or their culture. —*n.* 1 One of the people of Egypt, ancient or modern. 2 The Hamitic language of the ancient Egyptians.

E·gyp·tol·o·gy (ē′jip·tol′ə·jē) *n.* The science or study of the antiquities of Egypt. —**E′gyp·tol′o·gist** *n.*

eh (ā, e) *interj.* What: used as an interrogative.

ei·der (ī′dər) *n.* A large sea duck of northern regions. Also **eider duck.** [< ON *æðhr*]

ei·der·down (ī′dər·doun′) *n.* 1 The down of the eider used for stuffing pillows and quilts. 2 A quilt so stuffed.

ei·det·ic (ī·det′ik) *adj. Psychol.* Of or pertaining to exceptionally clear and detailed visualization. [< Gk. *eidētikos* pertaining to images]

Eif·fel Tow·er (ī′fəl) An iron tower in Paris, 984 feet high, designed for the Exposition of 1889. [< A. G. *Eiffel,* 1832–1923, French engineer]

eight (āt) *n.* 1 The sum of seven plus one; 8; VIII. 2 A set or group of eight members. [< OE *eahta*] —**eight** *adj., pron.*

eight·een (ā′tēn′) *n.* 1 The sum of 17 plus 1; 18; XVIII. 2 A set or group of 18 members. —**eight′een′** *adj., pron.*

eight·eenth (ā′tēnth′) *adj. & adv.* Next in order after the 17th. —*n.* 1 The element of an ordered set that corresponds to the number 18. 2 One of 18 equal parts.

eight·fold (āt′fōld′) *adv.* So as to be eight times as many or as great. —*adj.* 1 Consisting of eight parts. 2 Eight times as many or as great.

eighth (ātth, āth) *adj. & adv.* Next in order after the seventh. —*n.* 1 The element of an ordered set that corresponds to the number 8. 2 One of eight equal parts.

eighth note *Music* A note having one eighth of the time value of a whole note. • See NOTE.

eight·i·eth (ā′tē·ith) *adj. & adv.* Tenth in order after the 70th. —*n.* 1 The element of an ordered set that corresponds to the number 80. 2 One of 80 equal parts.

eight·y (ā′tē) *adj.* Consisting of ten more than 70. —*n. pl.* **·ties** 1 The product of eight and ten; 80; LXXX. 2 A set or group of 80 members. 3 *pl.* The numbers, years, etc. between 80 and 90. —**eight′y** *adj., pron.*

ein·stein·i·um (īn·stīn′ē·əm) *n.* An artificially produced radioactive element (symbol Es). [< Albert *Einstein,* 1879–1955, German-born U.S. physicist]

ei·ther (ē′thər, ī′-) *adj.* 1 One or the other of two: Use *either* foot on the pedal. 2 Each of two; one and the other: on *either* side. —*pron.* One of two; one or the other. —*conj.* In one of two or more cases: used as a correlative introducing a first alternative, the second and any other being preceded by *or: Either* I shall go *or* he will come. —*adv.* Also; any more so: used as an intensifier after negative statements: He could not speak, and I could not *either.* [< OE *ǣgther*]

e·jac·u·late (i·jak′yə·lāt) v. ·lat·ed, ·lat·ing v.t. 1 To utter suddenly. 2 To eject suddenly, as semen. —v.i. 3 To eject semen. [< L ex- out + jaculari to throw] —e·jac′u·la′tion, e·jac′u·la′tor n. —e·jac′u·la·to′ry adj.

e·ject (i·jekt′) v.t. 1 To throw or drive out by sudden force; expel. 2 EVICT. [< L ex- out + jacere to throw] —e·jec′tion, e·ject′ment n. —e·jec′tive adj. —e·jec′tive·ly adv. —Syn. 1 banish, oust, exile, deport.

eke (ēk) v.t. eked, ek·ing 1 To supplement; piece out: usu. with out. 2 To obtain or produce (a living) with difficulty: usu. with out. [< OE ēcan]

EKG electrocardiogram.

e·kis·tics (i·kis′tiks) n. pl. (construed as sing.) The study of human settlements, including area planning and the relationship between communities. [< Gk. oikos habitat + -ics] —e·kis′tic adj.

el (el) n. Informal ELEVATED RAILROAD.

e·lab·o·rate (i·lab′ə·rāt) v. ·rat·ed, ·rat·ing v.t. 1 To create and work out with care and in detail. 2 To produce by labor; make. —v.i. 3 To speak or write so as to embellish a matter, subject, etc., with additional details: with on or upon. —adj. (-ər·it) 1 Developed in detail and with care: an elaborate plan. 2 Ornate; complicated, as a design. 3 PAINSTAKING. [< L ex- out + laborare to work] —e·lab′o·rate·ly adv. —e·lab′o·rate·ness, e·lab′o·ra′tion n. —e·lab′o·ra′tive adj. —Syn. v. 1 develop, devise. 2 execute. —adj. 2 showy, extravagant, fancy.

é·lan (ā·län′) n. Verve; dash; vivacity. [F < élancer to dart, throw out]

e·land (ē′lənd) n. A large oxlike African antelope with twisted horns. [Du., elk]

e·lapse (i·laps′) v.i. e·lapsed, e·laps·ing To slip by; pass away: said of time. [< L elapsus, pp. of elabi glide away]

e·las·mo·branch (i·las′mō- brangk, i·laz′-) n. Any of a class of fishes having lamellar gills and cartilaginous skeletons, includ- ing sharks and rays. [< Gk. elas- mos metal plate + branchia gill]

Eland

e·las·tic (i·las′tik) adj. 1 Sponta- neously returning to a former size, shape, etc., after being al- tered from it. 2 Capable of quick recovery, as from misfor- tune. 3 Changing or adapting readily in response to new circumstances or demands. —n. 1 A stretchable fabric having rubber or rubberlike threads woven therein. 2 A garter, suspender, etc., made of this fabric. 3 RUBBER BAND. [< Gk. elastikos driving] —e·las′ti·cal·ly adv.

e·las·tic·i·ty (i·las′tis′ə·tē, ē′las·) n. The quality or condi- tion of being elastic.

e·late (i·lāt′) v.t. ·lat·ed, ·lat·ing To raise the spirits of; ex- cite. —adj. Exalted or triumphant; exultant. [< L elatus lifted up] —e·lat′ed adj. —e·lat′ed·ly adv. —e·lat′ed·ness n.

e·la·tion (i·lā′shən) n. Exalted feeling, as from pride or joy; exultation.

el·bow (el′bō) n. 1 The joint at the bend of the arm be- tween the upper and lower arm, esp. the knoblike outer projection of this joint. 2 A similar joint in the foreleg of a quadruped. 3 Anything resembling an elbow, as a short angular pipe fitting. —v.t. 1 To push or jostle with or as with the elbows. 2 To make (one's way) by such pushing. —v.i. 3 To move ahead in such a manner. [< OE elnboga]

el·bow·room (el′bō·rōōm′, -rŏŏm′) n. Room enough to move or function without hindrance.

el·der[1] (el′dər) n. 1 A shrub of the honeysuckle family, with white flowers and purple-black or red berries. 2 Any of various unrelated shrubs and trees, as the box elder. [OE ellærn]

eld·er[2] (el′dər) adj. 1 Having lived longer; earlier born; older. 2 Having superior or prior rank, position, validity, etc. 3 Earlier in time; former. —n. 1 An older or aged person. 2 ANCESTOR. 3 An older person having a certain position of authority, as in a community. 4 Any of various officers in certain Christian churches. [< OE eldra]

el·der·ber·ry (el′dər·ber′ē, -bər·ē) n. pl. ·ber·ries The drupe of the common elder.

eld·er·ly (el′dər·lē) adj. Somewhat old; approaching old age. —eld′er·li·ness n.

eld·est (el′dist) adj. First-born; oldest.

El Do·ra·do (el də·rä′dō) 1 A legendary South American realm rich in gold and jewels. 2 Any region rich in gold or opportunity. Also El′do·ra′do.

elec., elect. electric; electrical; electricity.

e·lect (i·lekt′) v.t. 1 To choose for an office by vote. 2 To take by choice or selection. 3 Theol. To choose or set aside for eternal life. —v.i. 4 To make a choice. —adj. 1 Elected to office, but not yet in charge: used in compounds, as president-elect. 2 Theol. Chosen of God for salvation. 3 Selected; chosen; picked out. —n. An elect person. [< L ex- out + legere choose]

e·lec·tion (i·lek′shən) n. 1 The selecting of a person or persons for office, as by ballot. 2 Any choice or act of choosing. 3 In Calvinism, the predestination of some in- dividuals to be saved by God.

e·lec·tion·eer (i·lek′shən·ir′) v.i. 1 To endeavor to win an election. 2 To canvass for votes.

e·lec·tive (i·lek′tiv) adj. 1 Of or pertaining to a choice by vote. 2 Obtained or resolved by election. 3 Exerting the privilege of choice. 4 Subject to choice; optional. —n. An optional study in a school or college curriculum. —e·lec′- tive·ly adv. —e·lec′tive·ness n.

e·lec·tor (i·lek′tər) n. 1 One who elects; a qualified voter. 2 A member of the electoral college. 3 One of the German princes who had the right of electing the Holy Roman Emperor. —e·lec′tor·al adj.

electoral college The body of electors chosen by the voters of the states and the District of Columbia to elect formally the president and vice president of the U.S. Each elector is traditionally expected but not legally bound to reflect the popular vote of his state.

e·lec·tor·ate (i·lek′tər·it) n. 1 The entire body of qualified voters. 2 The rank or territory of an elector in the Holy Roman Empire.

E·lec·tra (i·lek′trə) Gk. Myth. The daughter of Agamem- non and Clytemnestra and sister of Orestes.

e·lec·tric (i·lek′trik) adj. 1 Relating to, derived from, pro- duced, or operated by electricity. 2 Containing, producing, or carrying electricity. 3 Dynamic; exciting; electrifying; also, tense, as if electrified. —n. A street car, train, or other vehicle run by electricity. [< Gk. ēlektron amber: in ref. to static charge produced when amber is rubbed]

e·lec·tri·cal (i·lek′tri·kəl) adj. 1 ELECTRIC. 2 Of or skilled in the use or science of electricity. —e·lec′tri·cal·ly adv.

electrical energy Readily transportable energy pro- duced industrially by transforming other forms of energy; electricity.

electric cell Any of various devices consisting of two dis- similar metals or materials immersed in an electrolyte, capable of generating electricity by chemical action.

electric chair 1 A chair used for electrocuting crimi- nals. 2 The sentence of death by electrocution.

electric eel An eellike fish of tropical America, capable of delivering powerful electric shocks.

electric eye PHOTOELECTRIC CELL.

e·lec·tri·cian (i·lek′trish′ən, ē′lek-) n. One skilled in the installation and repair of electrical equipment.

e·lec·tric·i·ty (i·lek′tris′ə·tē, ē′lek-) n. 1 A property of matter associated with atomic particles that are capable of attracting and repelling each other over relatively long distances, and which can be made to perform work. 2 A flow of such particles, usu. electrons, used as a source of power or energy. 3 The science dealing with electricity.

electric ray A ray fish having an electric organ with which it stuns its prey.

e·lec·tri·fy (i·lek′trə·fī) v.t. ·fied, ·fy·ing 1 To charge with, or subject to electricity. 2 To equip for the use of or opera- tion by electricity. 3 To supply with electricity. 4 To arouse; startle; thrill. —e·lec′tri·fi·ca′tion n.

electro- combining form Electric; by, with, or of elec- tricity: electrocardiogram.

---

add, āce, cāre, pălm; end, ēven; it, īce; odd, ōpen, ôrder; tŏŏk, pōōl; up, bûrn; ə = a in above, u in focus; yōō = u in fuse; oil; pout; check; go; ring; thin; this; zh, vision. < derived from; ? origin uncertain or unknown.

e·lec·tro·car·di·o·gram (i·lek′trō-kär′dē-ə-gram′) *n.* A graph showing electrical activity of the heart.

e·lec·tro·car·di·o·graph (i·lek′trō-kär′dē-ə-graf′, -gräf′) *n.* An instrument for recording the electrical activity of the heart, used in the diagnosis of heart diseases. —**e·lec·tro·car·di·og·ra·phy** (i·lek′trō-kär′dē-og′rə-fē) *n.*

e·lec·tro·chem·is·try (i·lek′trō-kem′is-trē) *n.* The science of electrical and chemical interactions. —**e·lec′tro·chem′i·cal** *adj.* —**e·lec′tro·chem′i·cal·ly** *adv.*

e·lec·tro·cute (i·lek′trə-kyōōt) *v.t.* **·cut·ed**, **·cut·ing 1** To kill by electricity. **2** To execute in an electric chair. [<ELECTRO- + (EXE)CUTE] —**e·lec′tro·cu′tion** *n.*

e·lec·trode (i·lek′trōd) *n. Electr.* A conducting element through which an electric charge leaves or enters an electrolytic cell, vacuum tube, electric arc, furnace, etc.

e·lec·tro·dy·nam·ics (i·lek′trō-dī-nam′iks) *n. pl.* (*construed as sing.*) The branch of physics which deals with the interactions of magnetic fields and electric currents. —**e·lec′tro·dy·nam′ic** or **·i·cal** *adj.*

e·lec·tro·en·ceph·a·lo·gram (i·lek′trō-en-sef′ə-lə-gram′) *n.* A record of electric activity in the brain.

e·lec·tro·en·ceph·a·lo·graph (i·lek′trō-en-sef′ə-lə-graf′) *n.* A device for recording electric activity in the brain.

e·lec·trol·y·sis (i·lek′trol′ə-sis) *n.* **1** The decomposing of an electrolyte by an electric current. **2** The use of an electrified needle to destroy the roots of unwanted body hair.

e·lec·tro·lyte (i·lek′trə-līt) *n.* A substance composed of ions and capable of conducting electricity when dissolved or molten. [<ELECTRO- + Gk. *lytos* loosened] —**e·lec·tro·lyt·ic** (i·lek′trə-lit′ik) or **·i·cal** *adj.* —**e·lec′tro·lyt′i·cal·ly** *adv.*

e·lec·tro·lyze (i·lek′trə-līz) *v.t.* **·lyzed**, **·lyz·ing** To decompose by electric current.

e·lec·tro·mag·net (i·lek′trō-mag′nit) *n.* A core of soft iron or the like, which temporarily becomes a magnet during the passage of an electric current through a coil of wire surrounding it.

electromagnetic spectrum The total range of electromagnetic waves comprising, in order of increasing wavelength, cosmic, gamma, and X-rays, ultraviolet, visible light, infrared, and radio waves.

electromagnetic wave A wave which is propagated through space by simultaneously alternating magnetic and electric fields.

e·lec·tro·mag·net·ism (i·lek′trō-mag′nə-tiz′əm) *n.* **1** Magnetism developed by electricity. **2** The branch of physics concerned with the relation between electricity and magnetism. —**e·lec′tro·mag·net′ic** (-mag·net′ik) or **·i·cal** *adj.* —**e·lec′tro·mag·net′i·cal·ly** *adv.*

e·lec·tro·mo·tive (i·lek′trə-mō′tiv) *adj.* Producing or tending to produce an electric current.

electromotive force That which tends to produce the flow of electricity from one point to another; voltage.

e·lec·tron (i·lek′tron) *n.* An atomic particle having a negative electric charge equal to 1.602×10^{-19} coulomb and a mass equal to 1/1837 that of a proton. [<Gk. *ēlektron* amber. See ELECTRIC.]

e·lec·tro·neg·a·tive (i·lek′trō-neg′ə-tiv) *adj.* **1** Bearing a charge like that of an electron; electrically negative. **2** Tending to form a chemical bond or bonds by attracting electrons.

e·lec·tron·ic (i·lek′tron′ik, ē′lek-) *adj.* **1** Of or pertaining to electrons or electronics. **2** Operating or produced by the movement of electrons or other carriers of electric charge, as in an electron tube or semiconductor device. —**e·lec′·tron′i·cal·ly** *adv.*

electronic mail 1 The transmission of text between computers, either by wire or by satellite transmission. **2** Text information sent by this system.

electronic music Music based on an arrangement of electronically produced, organized, or altered sounds, recorded on tape.

e·lec·tron·ics (i·lek′tron′iks, ē′lek-) *n. pl.* (*construed as sing.*) The study of the properties and behavior of electrons and other carriers of electric charge, esp. with reference to technical and industrial applications.

electron microscope A microscope which uses high-energy streams of electrons in order to magnify objects too small to reflect the relatively large wavelengths of visible light.

electron tube A sealed tube in which a flow of electrons from a cathode to an anode is controlled or influenced by the voltages on one or more grids through which it must pass.

electron volt A unit of energy equal to that acquired by an electron which passes through a potential difference of one volt, approximately 1.602×10^{-19} joule.

e·lec·tro·plate (i·lek′trə-plāt′) *v.t.* —**plat·ed**, **plat·ing** To coat with metal by electrolysis. —*n.* An electroplated article. —**e·lec′tro·plat′er** *n.*

e·lec·tro·pos·i·tive (i·lek′trō-poz′ə-tiv) *adj.* **1** Bearing a charge like that of a proton; electrically positive. **2** Tending to form a chemical bond or bonds by losing electrons.

e·lec·tro·scope (i·lek′trə-skōp) *n.* An instrument for detecting an electric charge by the attraction or repulsion of pith balls or strips of metal foil. —**e·lec′tro·scop′ic** (-skop′ik) *adj.*

e·lec·tro·stat·ic (i·lek′trō-stat′ik) *adj.* Of, pertaining to, produced by, or caused by electric charges at rest.

e·lec·tro·stat·ics (i·lek′trō-stat′iks) *n. pl.* (*construed as sing.*) The branch of physics that treats of electric charges at rest.

e·lec·tro·ther·a·py (i·lek′trō-ther′ə-pē) *n.* The treatment of disease by electricity. —**e·lec′tro·ther′a·pist** *n.*

e·lec·tro·type (i·lek′trō-tīp′) *n.* **1** A facsimile plate of any surface made by the electric deposition of metal on the surface, esp. such a plate made of a page of type for printing. **2** An impression made from such a plate. **3** The process of electrotyping. —*v.t.* **·typed**, **·typ·ing** To make an electrotype. —**e·lec′tro·typ′er** *n.*

el·ee·mos·y·nar·y (el′ə-mos′ə-ner′ē, el′ē-ə-) *adj.* **1** Of or pertaining to charity or alms. **2** Charitable; nonprofit: *eleemosynary* institutions. **3** Aided by or dependent upon charity. —*n. pl.* **·nar·ies** A recipient of charity. [<Med. L *eleemosyna* alms]

el·e·gance (el′ə-gəns) *n.* **1** The state or quality of being elegant or refined. **2** Anything elegant. Also **el′e·gan·cy**.

el·e·gant (el′ə-gənt) *adj.* **1** Characterized by a tasteful luxuriousness and grace of style, design, content, etc. **2** Possessing or exhibiting a refined taste and gracefulness of manner, dress, etc. **3** *Informal* Excellent; capital. **4** Marked by appropriateness and simplicity: an *elegant* solution. [<L *elegans* fastidious] —**el′e·gant·ly** *adv.* —**Syn. 2** refined, polished.

el·e·gi·ac (el′ə-jī′ək, i·lē′jē-ak) *adj.* **1** Pertaining to elegies. **2** Of the nature of an elegy; sad; plaintive. **3** In ancient prosody, written in couplets consisting of one hexameter and one pentameter line. Also **el′e·gi′a·cal**. —*n. pl.* Verse composed in the elegiac spirit or form.

el·e·gize (el′ə-jīz) *v.t. & v.i.* **·gized**, **·giz·ing** To mourn or commemorate in elegiac form. —**el·e·gist** (el′ə·jist) *n.*

el·e·gy (el′ə-jē) *n. pl.* **·gies 1** A meditative poem with sorrowful theme. **2** A classical poem written in elegiac verse. **3** A musical composition of a sad or meditative character. [<Gk. *elegos* a song]

el·e·ment (el′ə-mənt) *n.* **1** A component or essential part, esp. of anything complex. **2** *pl.* First principles or fundamental ideas; rudiments. **3** One of the four substances (earth, air, fire, and water) anciently supposed to make up all things. **4** *pl.* Atmospheric conditions or powers, as rain, wind, etc. **5** An essential or determining factor. **6** A group or class having certain characteristics in common: the *rowdy* element in the crowd. **7** The natural or appropriate sphere or environment for a person or thing. **8** *Eccl.* The bread and wine of the Lord's Supper. **9** Any of a number of substances composed entirely of atoms having identical nuclear charges, as gold, carbon, sodium, etc. **10** One of the primary parts of an organism; a cell. **11** *Geom.* One of the forms or data which together compose a figure, as a line, a point, a plane, a space. **12 a** Any one of the members of a set. **b** A term in an algebraic expression. [<L *elementum* first principle]

el·e·men·tal (el′ə-men′təl) *adj.* **1** Of or pertaining to an element or elements. **2** Having to do with rudiments or first principles; basic. **3** Of or like the basic, powerful forces or drives in man or nature. —**el′e·men′tal·ly** *adv.*

el·e·men·ta·ry (el′ə-men′tər-ē) *adj.* **1** ELEMENTAL. **2** Rudi-

CHEMICAL ELEMENTS

Each weight in parentheses represents the mass number
of the most stable isotope of the element so designated.

	Symbol	Atomic Number	Atomic Weight		Symbol	Atomic Number	Atomic Weight
actinium	Ac	89	(227)	mercury	Hg	80	200.59
aluminum	Al	13	26.9815	molybdenum	Mo	42	95.94
americium	Am	95	(243)	neodymium	Nd	60	144.24
antimony	Sb	51	121.75	neon	Ne	10	20.183
argon	Ar	18	39.948	neptunium	Np	93	(237)
arsenic	As	33	74.9216	nickel	Ni	28	58.71
astatine	At	85	(210)	niobium	Nb	41	92.906
barium	Ba	56	137.34	nitrogen	N	7	14.0067
berkelium	Bk	97	(248)	nobelium	No	102	(254)
beryllium	Be	4	9.0122	osmium	Os	76	190.2
bismuth	Bi	83	208.980	oxygen	O	8	15.9994
boron	B	5	10.811	palladium	Pd	46	106.4
bromine	Br	35	79.904	phosphorus	P	15	30.9738
cadmium	Cd	48	112.40	platinum	Pt	78	195.09
calcium	Ca	20	40.08	plutonium	Pu	94	(244)
californium	Cf	98	(251)	polonium	Po	84	(209)
carbon	C	6	12.01115	potassium	K	19	39.102
cerium	Ce	58	140.12	praseodymium	Pr	59	140.907
cesium	Cs	55	132.905	promethium	Pm	61	(145)
chlorine	Cl	17	35.453	protactinium	Pa	91	(231)
chromium	Cr	24	51.996	radium	Ra	88	(226)
cobalt	Co	27	58.9332	radon	Rn	86	(222)
copper	Cu	29	63.546	rhenium	Re	75	186.2
curium	Cm	96	(247)	rhodium	Rh	45	102.905
dysprosium	Dy	66	162.50	rubidium	Rb	37	85.47
einsteinium	Es	99	(254)	ruthenium	Ru	44	101.07
erbium	Er	68	167.26	samarium	Sm	62	150.35
europium	Eu	63	151.96	scandium	Sc	21	44.956
fermium	Fm	100	(257)	selenium	Se	34	78.96
fluorine	F	9	18.9984	silicon	Si	14	28.086
francium	Fr	87	(223)	silver	Ag	47	107.868
gadolinium	Gd	64	157.25	sodium	Na	11	22.9898
gallium	Ga	31	69.72	strontium	Sr	38	87.62
germanium	Ge	32	72.59	sulfur	S	16	32.064
gold	Au	79	196.967	tantalum	Ta	73	180.948
hafnium	Hf	72	178.49	technetium	Tc	43	(97)
helium	He	2	4.0026	tellurium	Te	52	127.60
holmium	Ho	67	164.930	terbium	Tb	65	158.924
hydrogen	H	1	1.00797	thallium	Tl	81	204.37
indium	In	49	114.82	thorium	Th	90	232.038
iodine	I	53	126.9044	thulium	Tm	69	168.934
iridium	Ir	77	192.2	tin	Sn	50	118.69
iron	Fe	26	55.847	titanium	Ti	22	47.90
krypton	Kr	36	83.80	tungsten	W	74	183.85
lanthanum	La	57	138.91	uranium	U	92	238.03
lawrencium	Lr	103	(257)	vanadium	V	23	50.942
lead	Pb	82	207.19	xenon	Xe	54	131.30
lithium	Li	3	6.939	ytterbium	Yb	70	173.04
lutetium	Lu	71	174.97	yttrium	Y	39	88.905
magnesium	Mg	12	24.312	zinc	Zn	30	65.37
manganese	Mn	25	54.9380	zirconium	Zr	40	91.22
mendelevium	Md	101	(256)				

mentary; basic; fundamental. **3** Simple. —**el·e·men·ta·ri·ly** *adv.* —**el·e·men·tar·i·ness** *n.*

elementary particle Any of the subatomic particles, as the electron, neutron, proton, etc., which are not a composite of other more fundamental entities.

elementary school A school giving a course of education in the first six or eight grades.

el·e·phant (el′ə·fənt) *n.* A massively built, almost hairless mammal of Asia or Africa having a flexible trunk and tusks valued as the chief source of ivory. [< Gk. *elephas*] —**el′e·phan′tine** (-fan′tēn, -tin, -tīn) *adj.*

el·e·phan·ti·a·sis (el′ə·fən·tī′ə·sis) *n.* A disease characterized by massive swelling

African elephant

due to obstruction of lymph vessels by a parasitic worm. [< ELEPHANT + -IASIS]

El·eu·sin·i·an (el′yōō·sin′ē·ən) *adj.* Of or pertaining to Eleusis or the Eleusinian mysteries.

Eleusinian mysteries The secret religious rites celebrated each spring in the ancient Greek city of Eleusis.

el·e·vate (el′ə·vāt) *v.t.* **·vat·ed, ·vat·ing 1** To raise; lift up. **2** To raise in rank, status, position, etc. **3** To raise the spirits of; inspire. **4** To raise the moral or intellectual level of. [< L *ex-* out, up + *levare* lighten] —**Syn. 1** heighten. **2** promote, advance. **3** exalt, cheer.

el·e·vat·ed (el′ə·vā′tid) *adj.* **1** Raised, esp. above the ground. **2** Exalted morally or intellectually. —*n. Informal* ELEVATED RAILROAD.

elevated railroad A railroad that operates principally on an elevated framework so as to allow the passage of traffic and pedestrians below it. Also **elevated railway**.

el·e·va·tion (el′ə·vā′shən) *n.* **1** The act of elevating or the condition of being elevated. **2** An elevated place. **3** Height above sea level or the earth's surface. **4** *Astron.* The angular distance of a celestial body above the horizon. **5** In dancing, the ability to perform leaps. **6** *Eccl.* The raising of the eucharistic elements: also **elevation of the Host**.

add, āce, câre, pälm; end, ēven; it, īce; odd, ōpen, ôrder; tŏŏk, pōōl; up, bûrn; ə = a in above, u in focus; yōō = u in fuse; oil; pout; check; go; ring; thin; this; zh, vision. < derived from; ? origin uncertain or unknown.

el·e·va·tor (el'ə·vā'tər) n. 1 One who or that which elevates. 2 A hoisting mechanism for grain. 3 A warehouse where grain is elevated, stored, and distributed. 4 A movable platform or cage for carrying freight or passengers up or down, as in a building. 5 Aeron. A movable airfoil used to control an aircraft's ascent or descent. • See AIRPLANE.

e·lev·en (i·lev'ən) n. 1 The sum of ten plus one; 11; XI. 2 A set or group of 11 members. [< OE endleofan] —e·lev'en adj., pron.

e·lev·enth (i·lev'ənth) adj. & adv. Next in order after the tenth. —n. 1 The element of an ordered set that corresponds to the number 11. 2 One of eleven equal parts.

eleventh hour The last opportunity.

elf (elf) n. pl. **elves** (elvz) 1 A dwarfish, mischievous sprite. 2 A small person or child. [< OE ælf]

elf·in (el'fin) adj. Of or like an elf; esp. tiny, mischievous, etc. —n. ELF.

elf·ish (el'fish) adj. ELFIN. —elf'ish·ly adv. —elf'ish·ness n.

elf·lock (elf'lok') n. Usu. pl. A lock of hair, matted as if by elves.

e·lic·it (i·lis'it) v.t. To draw out or forth, as by some attraction or inducement; bring to light. [< L ex- out + lacere entice] —e·lic'i·ta'tion, e·lic'i·tor n.

e·lide (i·līd') v.t. **e·lid·ed, e·lid·ing** 1 To omit (a vowel or syllable) in writing or pronouncing a word. 2 To omit; ignore. [< L ex- out + laedere to strike] —e·lid'i·ble adj.

el·i·gi·ble (el'ə·jə·bəl) adj. 1 Capable of being chosen or elected. 2 Worthy of acceptance. —n. One who is eligible. [< L eligere to select, elect] —el'i·gi·bil'i·ty n. —el'i·gi·bly adv. —Syn. 1 qualified, fitted. 2 suitable, desirable.

e·lim·i·nate (i·lim'ə·nāt) v.t. ·nat·ed, ·nat·ing 1 To get rid of. 2 To disregard as irrelevant or incorrect; ignore. 3 Physiol. To void; excrete. [< L ex- out + limen a threshold] —e·lim'i·na'tion, e·lim'i·na'tor n. —e·lim'i·na'tive adj.

e·li·sion (i·lizh'ən) n. The eliding or striking out of a part of a word, as in "o'er" for "over."

e·lite (i·lēt') n. 1 The choicest part, as of a society. 2 A small but powerful group. 3 A size of typewriter type, equivalent to 10-point, with 12 characters to the inch. Also é·lite'. [< F < L electa choice]

e·lit·ism (i·lēt'iz·əm) n. Rule by an elite, or advocacy of such rule. —e·lit'ist adj., n.

e·lix·ir (i·lik'sər) n. 1 A sweetened alcoholic medicinal preparation. 2 A substance which alchemists believed would change base metals to gold. 3 A cordial alleged to prolong youth. 4 The essential principle of something. 5 A cure-all; panacea. [< Ar. al-iksīr < Gk. xērion medicated powder]

E·liz·a·be·than (i·liz'ə·bē'thən, -beth'ən) adj. Relating to Elizabeth I of England, or to her era. —n. An Englishman who lived during the reign of Elizabeth I.

Elizabethan sonnet A sonnet which has the rhyme scheme abab cdcd efef gg.

elk (elk) n. pl. **elks** or **elk** 1 A large deer of N Europe and Asia, with broad antlers. 2 A large N. American deer; wapiti. [< ON elgr]

elk·hound (elk'hound') n. A hunting dog of Norwegian origin, of medium size, with a short, robust body and thick gray coat. Also **Norwegian elkhound.**

American elk

ell (el) n. Anything shaped like the letter L, as an addition at right angles to one side of a house.

el·lipse (i·lips') n. Geom. A plane curve such that the sum of the distances from any point of the curve to two fixed points is a constant. [< ELLIPSIS]

el·lip·sis (i·lip'sis) n. pl. ·ses (-sēz) 1 The omission of a word or words necessary to complete a sentence or expression. 2 A sudden jump from one thought or subject to another without the inclusion of logical connectives. 3 Marks indicating omission, as . . . , or * * *. [< Gk. elleipsis a falling short]

el·lip·ti·cal (i·lip'ti·kəl) adj. 1 Of, pertaining to, or shaped like an ellipse. 2 Characterized by ellipsis; shortened by the omission of a word or words. Also **el·lip'tic.** —el·lip'ti·cal·ly adv.

elm (elm) n. 1 A tall, graceful, deciduous shade tree of America, Europe, and Asia. 2 Its wood. [< OE]

el·o·cu·tion (el'ə·kyōō'shən) n. 1 The art of speaking or reading in public. 2 Manner of utterance. [< L ex- out + loqui speak] —el'o·cu'tion·ar'y adj. —el'o·cu'tion·ist n.

E·lo·him (e·lō·him', -lō'him) n. God: Hebrew name in the Old Testament. [< Heb. 'Elōhim, pl. of 'Elōah God]

e·lon·gate (i·lông'gāt, i·long'-) v.t. & v.i. ·gat·ed, ·gat·ing To make or grow longer; lengthen. —adj. 1 Made longer; lengthened. 2 Long and slender. —e'lon·ga'tion n.

e·lope (i·lōp') v.i. **e·loped, e·lop·ing** To run away, esp. to get married in secret. [< ME alepen run away] —e·lope'ment, e·lop'er n.

el·o·quence (el'ə·kwəns) n. 1 Graceful, articulate, and convincing expression; also, the art or forcefulness of such expression. 2 The quality of being forceful or persuasive.

el·o·quent (el'ə·kwənt) adj. 1 Having or exhibiting eloquence. 2 Expressive; affecting: an eloquent glance. [< L < ex- out + loqui speak] —el'o·quent·ly adv.

El Sal·va·dor (el sal'və·dôr, Sp. el säl'vä·thôr') n. A republic of w Central America, 8,260 sq. mi., cap. San Salvador. • See map at CENTRAL AMERICA.

else (els) adv. 1 In a different place, time, or way. 2 If the case or facts were different; otherwise. —adj. 1 In addition. 2 Other: It was someone else. [< OE elles]

else·where (els'hwâr') adv. In or to another place or places; somewhere or anywhere else.

e·lu·ci·date (i·lōō'sə·dāt) v.t. ·dat·ed, ·dat·ing To clarify by explaining. [< L ex- out + lucidus clear] —e·lu'ci·da'tion n. —e·lu'ci·da'tive adj.

e·lude (i·lōōd') v.t. **e·lud·ed, e·lud·ing** 1 To avoid or escape from by swiftness or cleverness. 2 To escape the notice or understanding of. [< L ex- out + ludere to play] —e·lud'i·ble adj. —e·lu·sion (i·lōō'zhən) n.

e·lu·sive (i·lōō'siv) adj. 1 Tending to elude. 2 Difficult to understand. —e·lu'sive·ly adv. —e·lu'sive·ness n.

elves (elvz) n.pl. of ELF.

elv·ish (el'vish) adj. ELFISH. —elv'ish·ly adv.

E·ly·sian (i·lizh'ən, -ē·ən) adj. 1 Of Elysium. 2 Supremely happy; blissful.

E·ly·si·um (i·lizh'ē·əm, i·liz'-) Gk. Myth. The abode of the blessed dead: also **Elysian Fields.** —n. A place or a condition of supreme delight.

em (em) n. 1 The thirteenth letter in the English alphabet, written M or m. 2 Printing The square of the body size of a type, used as a standard unit of measurement.

em- prefix Var. of EN-¹: embody.

EM enlisted man (men); Electrician's Mate.

e·ma·ci·ate (i·mā'shē·āt) v.t. ·at·ed, ·at·ing To make abnormally thin, as from starvation. [< L emaciare waste away] —e·ma'ci·a'tion n.

e·ma·ci·at·ed (i·mā'shē·ā'tid) adj. Very thin; wasted away, as from disease or starvation.

em·a·nate (em'ə·nāt) v.i. ·nat·ed, ·nat·ing To come or flow forth, as from a source. [< L ex- out + manare to flow]

em·a·na·tion (em'ə·nā'shən) n. 1 The act of emanating. 2 That which flows from an origin or source. —em'a·na'tive adj. —em'a·na'tive·ly adv.

e·man·ci·pate (i·man'sə·pāt) v.t. ·pat·ed, ·pat·ing 1 To release from bondage or slavery. 2 To release from any oppression or restraint. [< L ex- out + manus hand + capere take] —e·man'ci·pa'tion, e·man'ci·pa'tor n. —e·man'ci·pa·to'ry (-pə·tôr'ē, -tō'rē) adj.

e·mas·cu·late (i·mas'kyə·lāt) v.t. ·lat·ed, ·lat·ing 1 To castrate. 2 To deprive of force or effectiveness. [< L ex- away + masculus male] —e·mas'cu·la'tion, e·mas'cu·la'tor n.

em·balm (im·bäm') v.t. 1 To treat (a dead body) so as to preserve from quick decay. 2 To perfume. 3 To preserve the memory of. [< OF < em- in + basme balm] —em·balm'er, em·balm'ment n.

em·bank (im·bangk') v.t. To confine or protect by a bank, dike, or the like.

em·bank·ment (im·bangk'mənt) n. 1 A protecting or supporting bank of earth or stones. 2 The process of strengthening by a bank.

Ellipse
DE major axis
BC minor axis
$FA + AF' = FA' + A'F'$

em·bar·go (im·bär′gō) n. pl. ·goes 1 A prohibition by a government temporarily restraining vessels from leaving or entering its ports. 2 Authoritative stoppage of any commerce. 3 Any imposed impediment or hindrance. —v.t. ·goed, ·go·ing To lay an embargo upon. [< Sp. embargar to restrain]

em·bark (im·bärk′) v.i. 1 To go aboard a ship, airplane, etc., as for a voyage. 2 To get started, as with a venture: usu. with on or upon. —v.t. 1 To put or take aboard a ship, airplane, etc. 2 To invest (money) or involve (a person) in a venture. [< LL in- in + barca boat] —em′bar·ka′tion, em·bark′ment n.

em·bar·rass (im·bar′əs) v.t. 1 To make ill at ease, self-conscious, and uncomfortable. 2 To involve in difficulties, esp. in business. 3 To hamper; encumber. 4 To render difficult; complicate. [< F embarrasser] —em·bar′rass·ing adj. —em·bar′rass·ing·ly adv. —em·bar′rass·ment n. —Syn. 1 abash, discomfit, disconcert, rattle.

em·bas·sy (em′bə·sē) n. pl. ·sies 1 The mission or office of an envoy or ambassador. 2 The official residence of an ambassador and his staff. 3 An ambassador and his associates. [< Med. L ambactia service]

em·bat·tle (em·bat′l) v.t. ·tled, ·tling 1 To prepare or equip for battle or conflict. 2 To fortify, as a town.

em·bat·tled (em·bat′ld) adj. Ready for battle or conflict: embattled politicians.

em·bed (im·bed′) v.t. ·bed·ded, ·bed·ding 1 To set firmly in surrounding matter. 2 To keep in the mind, memory, etc. —em·bed′ment n.

em·bel·lish (im·bel′ish) v.t. 1 To add ornamental features to. 2 To heighten the interest of, as a story, by adding details that are often fictitious. [< OF embellir beautify] —em·bel′lish·ment n.

em·ber (em′bər) n. 1 A live coal or glowing brand. 2 pl. A dying fire. [< OE æmerge]

Ember days Eccl. A three-day period of fasting and prayer observed quarterly by Roman Catholics and some other denominations. [< OE ymbrendæg a recurring day]

em·bez·zle (im·bez′əl) v.t. ·zled, ·zling To appropriate fraudulently for one's own use; steal. [< AF embesiler] —em·bez′zle·ment, em·bez′zler n.

em·bit·ter (im·bit′ər) v.t. To render bitter, unhappy, or resentful. —em·bit′ter·ment n.

em·bla·zon (em·blā′zən) v.t. 1 To adorn with or as with heraldic designs; decorate. 2 To set off in resplendent colors. —em·bla′zon·er, em·bla′zon·ment, em·bla′zon·ry (-rē) n.

em·blem (em′bləm) n. 1 A figurative representation or symbol of an idea, organization, or object. 2 A distinctive badge. [< L emblema inlaid work]

em·blem·at·ic (em′blə·mat′ik) adj. Of or serving as an emblem. Also em′blem·at′i·cal. —em′blem·at′i·cal·ly adv.

em·bod·i·ment (im·bod′i·mənt) n. 1 The act of embodying, or the state of being embodied. 2 Something that embodies or exemplifies; incarnation.

em·bod·y (im·bod′ē) v.t. ·bod·ied, ·bod·y·ing 1 To invest with or as with a body. 2 To collect into one whole; incorporate. 3 To express concretely.

em·bold·en (em·bōl′dən) v.t. To give courage to.

em·bo·lism (em′bə·liz′əm) n. The stopping up of a blood vessel by an embolus. [< Gk. embolismos insertion] —em·bo·lis′mic adj.

em·bo·lus (em′bə·ləs) n. pl. ·li (-lī) A body carried by the blood stream, as a clot or bubble, capable of obstructing blood flow. [< Gk. embolos something inserted]

em·bos·om (em·bŏŏz′əm, -bōō′zəm) v.t. 1 To take to the bosom; embrace. 2 To shelter.

em·boss (im·bôs′, -bos′) v.t. 1 To cover or adorn (a surface) with raised figures, designs, etc. 2 To raise or represent (designs, figures, etc.) from or upon a surface. 3 To decorate sumptuously. [< OF embocer] —em·boss′er, em·boss′ment n.

em·bou·chure (äm·bŏŏ·shŏŏr′) n. 1 The point of discharge of a river or stream. 2 Position or adjustment of the lips, tongue, and associated organs in playing a wind instrument. 3 A mouthpiece, esp. of a wind instrument. [< OF em- in + bouche mouth]

em·bour·geoise·ment (äm·bŏŏr·zhwäz·môn′) n. The fact or process of becoming bourgeois. [F]

em·bow·er (em·bou′ər) v.t. To place in a shelter, as of foliage.

em·brace (im·brās′) v. ·braced, ·brac·ing v.t. 1 To put one's arms around in greeting or affection. 2 To accept willingly; adopt. 3 To avail oneself of: to embrace an offer. 4 To encircle. 5 To include; contain. 6 To take in visually or mentally. —v.i. 7 To hug each other. —n. The act of embracing; a clasping in the arms. [< L in- in + bracchia arm] —em·brace′a·ble adj. —em·brace′ment, em·brac′er n. —Syn. 1 hug, caress, hold. 2 espouse, endorse.

em·bra·sure (em·brā′zhər) n. 1 An opening in a wall, as for a cannon. 2 Archit. The sloping of an opening in a wall, as of a window, so as to enlarge its interior profile. [F]

em·bro·cate (em′brō·kāt) v.t. ·cat·ed, ·cat·ing To moisten and rub, as with liniment or oil. [< Med. L < embrocha an ointment] —em·bro·ca′tion n.

em·broi·der (im·broi′dər) v.t. 1 To ornament with designs in needlework. 2 To execute in needlework. 3 To exaggerate, as a narrative, with usu. fictitious details. —v.i. 4 To make embroidery. [< EN-¹ + obs. broider < MF brouder to stitch] —em·broi′der·er n.

em·broi·der·y (im·broi′dər·ē) n. pl. ·der·ies 1 Ornamental needlework. 2 The art of producing such work. 3 Embellishing details, as of a story.

em·broil (em·broil′) v.t. 1 To involve in dissension or conflict. 2 To throw into uproar or confusion. [< OF em- in + brouiller confuse] —em·broil′ment n.

em·bry·o (em′brē·ō) n. pl. ·os 1 An animal in the early stages of development of the fertilized ovum. 2 The fertilized human ovum during two months following implantation in the uterus. 3 A rudimentary plant within the seed. 4 Anything in process of developing its distinctive form. —in embryo In an undeveloped or incipient stage. —adj. Pertaining to an embryo; rudimentary: also em′bry·al. [< Gk. en- in + bryein to swell]

Seed showing embryo
a. seed coat.
b. embryo. c. endosperm.

em·bry·ol·o·gy (em′brē·ol′ə·jē) n. The science which deals with the origin, structure, and development of the embryo. —em′bry·o·log′ic (-ə·loj′ik) or ·i·cal adj. —em′bry·o·log′i·cal·ly adv. —em′bry·ol′o·gist n.

em·bry·on·ic (em′brē·on′ik) adj. 1 Of, pertaining to, or like an embryo. 2 Undeveloped. Also em·bry·o·nal (em′brē·ə·nəl, em·brī′-).

em·cee (em′sē′) Informal n. Master of ceremonies. —v.i. & v.t. em·ceed, em·cee·ing To act or direct as master of ceremonies. [< m(aster of) c(eremonies)]

e·mend (i·mend′) v.t. To make corrections or changes in (a literary work, etc.). Also e·men·date (ē′men·dāt). [< L ex- out + menda a fault] —e·mend′a·ble adj.

e·men·da·tion (ē′men·dā′shən, em′ən-) n. 1 A correction or alteration. 2 The act of emending. —e′men·da′tor n. —e·mend·a·to·ry (i·men′də·tôr′ē, -tō′rē) adj.

em·er·ald (em′ər·əld, em′rəld) n. A bright green precious stone, a variety of beryl. —adj. 1 Of or like the emerald. 2 Of a rich green color. [< OF emeraude, esmeraldus]

e·merge (i·mûrj′) v.i. e·merged, e·merg·ing 1 To come forth into view or existence. 2 To become noticeable or apparent: The truth emerged. [< L ex- out + mergere to dip] —e·mer·gent (i·mûr′jənt) adj. —e·mer′gence n.

e·mer·gen·cy (i·mûr′jən·sē) n. pl. ·cies A sudden, unexpected state of affairs calling for immediate action.

e·mer·i·tus (i·mer′ə·təs) adj. Retired from active service but retained in an honorary position. [< L emereri earn, deserve]

e·mer·sion (ē·mûr′zhən, -shən) n. The act or process of emerging.

em·er·y (em′ər·ē, em′rē) n. A very hard variety of corundum that occurs mixed with other minerals, used as an abrasive. [< Gk. smuris emery powder]

emery board A small, flat board covered with powdered emery, used in manicuring.

add, āce, câre, pälm; end, ēven; it, īce; odd, ōpen, ôrder; tŏŏk, pōōl; up, bûrn; ə = a in above, u in focus; yŏŏ = u in fuse; oil; pout; check; go; ring; thin; this; zh, vision. < derived from; ? origin uncertain or unknown.

e·met·ic (i·met′ik) *adj.* Causing vomiting. —*n.* A medicine used to induce vomiting. [< Gk. *emeein* to vomit]

EMF, E.M.F., emf, e.m.f. electromotive force.

-emia *combining form* Blood; used in names of diseases: *leukemia.* [< Gk. *haima* blood]

em·i·grant (em′ə·grənt) *adj.* Leaving one country or region to settle in another. —*n.* One who emigrates.

em·i·grate (em′ə·grāt) *v.i.* **·grat·ed, ·grat·ing** To go from one country, or section of a country, to settle in another. [< L *ex-* out + *migrare* to move] —**em·i·gra′tion** *n.*

é·mi·gré (em′ə·grā, *Fr.* ā·mē·grā′) *n.* An emigrant; esp. a political refugee. Also **e·mi·gré.** [F]

em·i·nence (em′ə·nəns) *n.* **1** An outstanding rank or degree. **2** A lofty place, as a hill. **3** *Usu. cap.* A title of honor applied to cardinals of the Roman Catholic Church. Also **em′i·nen·cy.**

ém·i·nence grise (ā·mē·näns grēz′) One who secretly exercises great power. [F, lit., gray eminence]

em·i·nent (em′ə·nənt) *adj.* **1** Standing out from others by achievement or station; outstanding. **2** Rising above other things: an *eminent* tower. [< L *eminere* stand out, project] —**em′i·nent·ly** *adv.* —**Syn. 1** distinguished, prominent.

eminent domain *Law* The right of a state to take private property for public use, usu. giving compensation.

e·mir (ə·mir′) *n.* A prince or commander in certain Muslim lands, esp. Arabia. Also **e·meer′.** [< Ar. *amīr* ruler] —**e·mir′ate** *n.*

em·is·sar·y (em′ə·ser′ē) *n. pl.* **·sar·ies 1** A person sent on a special mission, often as a representative of a government. **2** A secret agent. [< L *emittere* send out]

e·mis·sion (i·mish′ən) *n.* **1** Something emitted. **2** The act of emitting. **3** *Electronics* The ejection of electrons from a surface. —**e·mis′sive** *adj.*

e·mit (i·mit′) *v.t.* **e·mit·ted, e·mit·ting 1** To send or give out; discharge. **2** To utter (cries, etc.). **3** To put into circulation, as money. [< L *ex-* out + *mittere* send] —**e·mit′ter** *n.*

Em·my (em′ē) *n. pl.* **Em·mys** or **Em·mies** A gold-plated statuette awarded annually for exceptional performances and productions on television.

e·mol·lient (i·mol′yənt, -ē·ənt) *adj.* Softening or soothing. —*n. Med.* A soothing preparation for the skin or mucous membranes. [< L *ex-* thoroughly + *mollis* soft]

e·mol·u·ment (i·mol′yə·mənt) *n.* The compensation, gain, or profit arising from an office or employment. [< L *ex-* out + *molere* to grind]

e·mote (i·mōt′) *v.i.* **e·mot·ed, e·mot·ing** *Informal* To exhibit an exaggerated emotion, as in acting a melodramatic role. [Back formation < EMOTION]

e·mo·tion (i·mō′shən) *n.* **1** Any feeling, esp. a strong or intense feeling, as of love, joy, fear, etc., often accompanied by complex physiological changes. **2** Such feelings collectively, or the power of experiencing them. [< L *ex-* out + *movere* to stir, move]

e·mo·tion·al (i·mō′shən·əl) *adj.* **1** Of or pertaining to emotion. **2** Marked by a disposition to express emotion: an *emotional* person. **3** Expressing emotion and often designed to arouse emotion in others: an *emotional* speech. —**e·mo′tion·al·ism, e·mo·tion·al·i·ty** (i·mō′shə·nal′ə·tē) *n.* —**e·mo′tion·al·ly** *adv.*

e·mo·tion·a·lize (i·mō′shən·əl·īz′) *v.t.* **·ized, ·iz·ing** To make emotional. —**e·mo′tion·al·i·za′tion** *n.*

e·mo·tive (i·mō′tiv) *adj.* Expressing or tending to excite emotion. —**e·mo′tive·ly** *adv.*

em·pan·el (im·pan′əl) *v.t.* **·eled** or **·elled, ·el·ing** or **·el·ling** IMPANEL.

em·pa·thize (em′pə·thīz) *v.t. & v.i.* **·thized, ·thiz·ing** To regard with or feel empathy.

em·pa·thy (em′pə·thē) *n.* The identification of oneself with another and the resulting capacity to feel or experience sensations, emotions, or thoughts similar to those being experienced by the other. [< Gk. *en-* in + *pathos* feeling] —**em·pa·thet·ic** (em′pə·thet′ik), **em·path·ic** (impath′ik) *adj.*

em·per·or (em′pər·ər) *n.* The ruler of an empire. [< L *imperare* to order]

em·pha·sis (em′fə·sis) *n. pl.* **·ses** (-sēz) **1** Special attention, importance, or stress: to place *emphasis* on discipline. **2** Forceful expression. **3** A stress laid upon some spoken or written words. [< Gk. *en-* in + *phainein* to show]

em·pha·size (em′fə·sīz) *v.t.* **·sized, ·siz·ing** To make especially distinct or prominent.

em·phat·ic (im·fat′ik) *adj.* **1** Conveying or expressing emphasis. **2** Forceful and decisive. —**em·phat′i·cal·ly** *adv.*

em·phy·se·ma (em′fə·sē′mə, -zē′mə) *n.* An inflated condition of the lungs marked by breathlessness due to loss of elasticity of the air sacs. [< Gk. *emphysēma* an inflation] —**em′phy·sem′a·tous** *adj.*

em·pire (em′pīr) *n.* **1** A state, or union of states, governed by an emperor. **2** Any vast organization or enterprise under unified control. [< L *imperium* rule]

Em·pire (äm·pir′, em′pīr) *adj.* Of or designating a style, as of clothing, furniture, or architecture, characteristic of the first French Empire, 1804–1815, under Napoleon I.

Empire Day VICTORIA DAY.

em·pir·ic (em·pir′ik) *n.* **1** One who believes experience is the source of knowledge. **2** *Archaic* A quack or charlatan. —*adj.* Empirical. [< Gk. *empeiria* experience]

em·pir·i·cal (em·pir′i·kəl) *adj.* Relating to or based on experience and observation rather than on theory or principle. —**em·pir′i·cal·ly** *adv.*

em·pir·i·cism (em·pir′ə·siz′əm) *n.* **1** Empirical character, method, or practice. **2** Belief in experiment alone. **3** *Philos.* The doctrine that all knowledge is derived from experience through the senses. —**em·pir′i·cist** *n.*

em·place·ment (im·plās′mənt) *n.* **1** The position assigned to guns or other military equipment. **2** A setting in place. **3** Position; location.

em·plane (im·plān′) *v.i.* **·planed, ·plan·ing** To board an airplane.

em·ploy (im·ploi′) *v.t.* **1** To engage the services of; hire. **2** To provide work and livelihood for. **3** To make use of: to *employ* cunning. **4** To devote or apply: to *employ* all one's energies. —*n.* The state of being employed. [< L *implicare* involve, fold in]

em·ploy·a·ble (im·ploi′ə·bəl) *adj.* Capable of being employed. —*n.* An employable person. —**em′ploy·a·bil′i·ty** *n.*

em·ploy·ee (im·ploi′ē, em′ploi·ē′) *n.* One who works for another or for a private or public organization in return for salary or wages. Also **em·ploy′e.**

em·ploy·er (im·ploi′ər) *n.* **1** A person or business firm that employs people for salary or wages. **2** One who employs.

em·ploy·ment (im·ploi′mənt) *n.* **1** The act of employing, or the state of being employed. **2** The work or duties of an employee. —**Syn. 1** use. **2** occupation, trade, business, job, profession.

em·po·ri·um (em·pôr′ē·əm, -pō′rē-) *n. pl.* **·ri·ums** or **·ri·a** (-ē·ə) **1** A large store carrying a variety of merchandise. **2** A market place. [< Gk *emporion* a market]

em·pow·er (im·pou′ər) *v.t.* **1** To delegate authority to. **2** To enable or permit.

em·press (em′pris) *n.* **1** A woman who rules an empire. **2** The wife or widow of an emperor.

emp·ty (emp′tē) *adj.* **·ti·er, ·ti·est 1** Having nothing or no one within. **2** Without value or meaning; insincere: *empty* promises. **3** Senseless; frivolous; idle: *empty* talk. **4** *Informal* Hungry. —*v.* **emp·tied, emp·ty·ing** *v.t.* **1** To make empty. **2** To transfer the contents of: to *empty* a bucket. **3** To transfer or remove (the contents) of a container: to *empty* water. —*v.i.* **4** To become empty. **5** To discharge or pour out. —*n. pl.* **emp·ties** Something empty, as a bottle, freight car, etc. [< OE *ǣmetig*] —**emp′ti·ly** *adv.* —**emp′ti·ness** *n.* —**Syn. 1** vacant, void, unoccupied, bare. **2** vain.

emp·ty-hand·ed (emp′tē·han′did) *adj.* Having or carrying nothing.

emp·ty-head·ed (emp′tē·hed′id) *adj.* Foolish.

em·pyr·e·al (em·pir′ē·əl, em′pərē′əl, -pī-) *adj.* Of the empyrean; heavenly. [< Gk. *empyros* in the fire]

em·py·re·an (em′pə·rē′ən, -pī-) *n.* **1** Among the ancients, the region of pure fire, the highest heaven. **2** The sky; firmament. —*adj.* EMPYREAL.

Emu

e·mu (ē′myoō) *n.* An Australian flightless bird, related to but somewhat smaller than the ostrich. [< Pg. *ema*]

E.M.U., emu, e.m.u. electromagnetic units.

em·u·late (em′yə·lāt) v.t. ·lat·ed, ·lat·ing 1 To try to equal or surpass, esp. by imitating or copying. 2 To rival with some success. [< L *aemulari* to rival < *aemulus* jealous] —**em′u·la′tion, em′u·la′tor** n. —**em′u·la′tive** adj.

em·u·lous (em′yə·ləs) adj. Eager or striving to equal or excel another. —**em′u·lous·ly** adv.

e·mul·si·fy (i·mul′sə·fī) v.t. ·fied, ·fy·ing To make or convert into an emulsion. —**e·mul′si·fi·ca′tion, e·mul′si·fi′er** n.

e·mul·sion (i·mul′shən) n. 1 A liquid mixture in which a substance is suspended in minute globules, as butterfat in milk. 2 *Phot.* A substance sensitive to light, used to coat films. [< L *emulgere* to drain out] —**e·mul′sive** adj.

en (en) n. 1 The fourteenth letter in the English alphabet, written N or n. 2 *Printing* A space half the width of an em.

en-¹ prefix 1 To cover or surround with; to place into or upon: *encircle.* 2 To make; cause to be: *enable.* 3 (used as an intensifier) *encompass.* [< L *in* in, into]

en-² prefix In, into; on: *endemic.* [< Gk. *en* in, into]

-en¹ suffix 1 To cause to be or become: *harden.* 2 To cause to have; gain: *strengthen.* [< OE *-nian*]

-en² suffix Made of; resembling: *woolen.* [< OE]

-en³ suffix (used in the past participles of many strong verbs): *broken.* [< OE]

-en⁴ suffix (used in the plural of certain nouns): *oxen, children.* [< OE *-an*, pl. ending of the weak declension]

-en⁵ suffix Small; little: *kitten.* [< OE]

en·a·ble (in·ā′bəl, en-) v.t. ·bled, ·bling 1 To make able; give means or power to. 2 To make possible or more easy.

en·act (in·akt′, en-) v.t. 1 To make into a law. 2 To represent in or as in a play.

en·act·ment (in·akt′mənt, en-) n. 1 A law enacted; statute. 2 The act of establishing a law.

en·am·el (in·am′əl) n. 1 A vitreous material fused to metals, porcelain, and other materials for protection or decoration. 2 A work executed in such material. 3 A glossy lacquer or varnish used for leather, paper, etc. 4 Any hard, glossy coating. 5 The layer of hard, glossy material forming the exposed outer covering of the teeth. • See TOOTH. —v.t. ·eled or ·elled, ·el·ing or ·el·ling 1 To cover or inlay with enamel. 2 To surface with or as with enamel. 3 To adorn with different colors, as if with enamel. [< AF *en-* on + OF *esmail* enamel] —**en·am′el·er, en·am′el·ler, en·am′el·ist, en·am′el·list, e·nam′el·work** n.

en·am·el·ware (in·am′əl·wâr′) n. Enameled kitchen utensils.

en·am·or (in·am′ər, en-) v.t. To inspire with ardent love: usu. followed by *of* or *with: He was much enamored of her.* *Brit. sp.* **en·am′our.** [< L *in-* in + *amor* love]

en bloc (en blok′, *Fr.* äṅ blôk′) In one piece; as a whole. [F]

enc. enclosed, enclosure.

en·camp (in·kamp′, en-) v.i. To stay in or set up a camp. —v.t. To place in a camp. —**en·camp′ment** n.

en·cap·su·late (in·kap′sə·lāt′, -syə-, en-) v.t. ·lat·ed, ·lat·ing 1 To enclose in or as if in a capsule. 2 To summarize. Also **en·cap′sule** (-səl, -syəl). —**en·cap′su·la′tion** n.

en·case (in·kās′, en-) v.t. ·cased, ·cas·ing To place or enclose in or as in a case. —**en·case′ment** n.

en·caus·tic (in·kôs′tik, en-) adj. 1 Painted in wax and having the hues fixed by heat. 2 Processed or fixed by heat: *encaustic tile.* —n. The art of encaustic painting. [< Gk. *enkaustikos*]

-ence suffix Action, quality, state, or condition: *prominence.* [< L *-entia*, suffix used to form nouns from present participles]

en·ceinte (äṅ·saṅt′) adj. French With child; pregnant.

en·ceph·a·li·tis (en′sef·ə·lī′tis, in·sef′-) n. Inflammation of the brain. —**en′ceph·a·lit′ic** (-lit′ik) adj.

encephalo- combining form Brain: *encephalitis.* Also **encephal-.** [< Gk. *enkephalos*]

en·ceph·a·lon (in·sef′ə·lon, en-) n. pl. ·la (-lə) The brain. [< Gk. *enkephalos*] —**en·ceph′a·lous, en·ce·phal′ic** adj.

en·chain (in·chān′, en-) v.t. 1 To bind with or as with a chain. 2 To hold captive, as attention. —**en·chain′ment** n.

en·chant (in·chant′, -chänt′, en-) v.t. 1 To put a magic

spell upon. 2 To delight or charm completely. [< L *in-* in + *cantare* sing] —**en·chant′er, en·chant′ment** n. —**en·chant′ress** (-tris) n. *Fem.*

en·chant·ing (in·chant′ing, en-) adj. Fascinating; delightful; charming. —**en·chant′ing·ly** adv.

en·chi·la·da (en′chi·lä′də) n. A rolled tortilla stuffed with meat or cheese and flavored with chile. [Sp.]

en·ci·pher (in·sī′fər, en-) v.t. To convert (a message) from plain text into cipher.

en·cir·cle (in·sûr′kəl, en-) v.t. ·cled, ·cling 1 To form a circle around. 2 To go around; make a circuit of. —**en·cir′cle·ment** n.

encl. enclosed, enclosure

en·clave (en′klāv, än′-) n. 1 A part of a country surrounded by the territory of a foreign government. 2 Any area of distinct character enclosed within a larger area. [F < L *in-* in + *clavis* key]

en·close (in·klōz′, en-) v.t. ·closed, ·clos·ing 1 To surround or fence in. 2 To place in a cover, envelope, etc., often in addition to a letter or message. 3 To contain. [< OF *enclore* shut in] —**en·clos′er** n.

en·clo·sure (in·klō′zhər, en-) n. 1 Something enclosed, as in a letter or parcel. 2 An enclosed area. 3 That which encloses, as a fence. 4 The act of enclosing, or the state of being enclosed.

en·code (in·kōd′, en-) v.t. ·cod·ed, ·cod·ing To transform (a message) from plain text into code. —**en·cod′er** n.

en·co·mi·ast (in·kō′mē·ast, en-) n. One who writes or speaks encomiums. —**en·co′mi·as′tic** or ·ti·cal adj.

en·co·mi·um (in·kō′mē·əm, en-) n. pl. ·mi·ums or ·mi·a (-mē·ə) A formal expression of praise; eulogy. [< Gk. *enkōmion* eulogy]

en·com·pass (in·kum′pəs, -kom′-, en-) v.t. 1 To form a circle around; encircle. 2 To surround; hem in. 3 To include; embrace. —**en·com′pass·ment** n.

en·core (äṅ′kôr, -kōr, än′-) n. 1 A request by an audience for the repetition of a performance, usu. indicated by sustained applause. 2 The performance given in response to the audience. —v.t. ·cored, ·cor·ing To call for an encore by (a performer) or of (a performance). [< F, again]

en·coun·ter (in·koun′tər, en-) n. 1 A coming together, esp. when casual or unexpected. 2 A hostile meeting; contest. —v.t. 1 To meet accidentally; come upon. 2 To meet in conflict; face in battle. 3 To be faced with (opposition, difficulties, etc.). —v.i. 4 To meet accidentally or in battle. [< L *in-* in + *contra* against]

encounter group A relatively unstructured group of persons whose aim is to express their feelings as deeply and spontaneously as possible, using a variety of techniques such as unrestrained verbalization and physical contact.

en·cour·age (in·kûr′ij, en-) v.t. ·aged, ·ag·ing 1 To inspire with courage, hope, or confidence. 2 To help or be favorable toward. [< OF *en-* in + *corage* courage] —**en·cour′ag·er** n. —Syn. 1 hearten, embolden, rally. 2 foster, abet.

en·cour·age·ment (in·kûr′ij·mənt, en-) n. 1 The act of encouraging, or the state of being encouraged. 2 A person or thing that encourages.

en·croach (in·krōch′, en-) v.i. 1 To intrude upon the possessions or rights of another, esp. by stealth: with *on* or *upon.* 2 To make inroads beyond the proper or usual limits. [< OF *encrochier* to seize with a hook] —**en·croach′er, en·croach′ment** n.

en·crust (in·krust′, en-) v.t. 1 To cover with a crust or hard coat. 2 To decorate, as with jewels. [< OF < L < *in-* on + *crustare* form a crust] —**en′crus·ta′tion** n.

en·cum·ber (in·kum′bər, en-) v.t. 1 To obstruct or hinder in action or movement, as with a burden. 2 To make hard to use; block. 3 To weigh down or burden, as with duties. [< OF *encombrer*]

en·cum·brance (in·kum′brəns, en-) n. 1 That which encumbers. 2 *Law* Any lien or liability attached to real property.

-ency suffix Var. of -ENCE: *urgency.*

ency., encyc., encycl. encyclopedia.

en·cyc·li·cal (in·sik′li·kəl, -sī′kli-, en-) adj. Intended for general circulation. Also **en·cyc'lic.** —*n. Eccl.* A circular letter addressed by the pope to all the bishops. [< Gk. *enkyklios* circular]

en·cy·clo·pe·di·a (in·sī'klə·pē'dē·ə, en-) *n.* A work containing information on all subjects, or exhaustive of one subject. Also **en·cy·clo·pae'di·a.** [< Gk. *enkyklios paideia* a general education] —**en·cy·clo·pe'dic, en·cy·clo·pae'dic** *adj.*

en·cyst (in·sist', en-) *v.t. & v.i.* To envelop or become enclosed in a cyst, sac, etc. —**en'cys·ta·tion, en·cyst'ment** *n.*

end (end) *n.* **1** The terminal point or part of any object having length; extremity. **2** The point in time at which some process ceases. **3** The last part; conclusion; the *end* of the game. **4** The farthest limit of the space occupied by an object; edge or boundary. **5** A desired purpose; intention. **6** A result; consequence. **7** Death. **8** The extent or limit; the *end* of his strength. **9** In football, a player stationed at the end of a line. —**at loose ends** In an unsettled or confused state. —**in the end** At last. —**no end** *Informal* A great deal: *no end* of trouble. —*v.t.* **1** To bring to a finish or termination; conclude. **2** To be the end of. —*v.i.* **3** To come to an end. [< OE *ende*]

en·dan·ger (in·dān'jər, en-) *v.t.* To expose to danger; imperil. —**en·dan'ger·ment** *n.*

en·dear (in·dir', en-) *v.t.* To make dear or beloved. —**en·dear'ing** *adj.* —**en·dear'ing·ly** *adv.*

en·dear·ment (in·dir'mənt, en-) *n.* **1** An act or utterance that expresses affection. **2** The act of endearing.

en·deav·or (in·dev'ər, en-) *n.* An earnest attempt or effort to do or accomplish a desired end. —*v.t.* **1** To make an effort to do or bring about; try: usu. used with an infinitive. —*v.i.* **2** To make an effort; strive. *Brit. sp.* **en·deav·our.** [ME *endeveren* to exert oneself] —**en·deav'or·er** *n.*

en·dem·ic (en·dem'ik) *adj.* Occurring or existing only in a particular country or area or among a certain group: an *endemic* plant or disease. Also **en·dem'i·cal.** [< Gk. *en-* in + *dēmos* people]

end·ing (en'ding) *n.* **1** The final or concluding part. **2** An end or extremity. **3** One or more letters or syllables added to the base of a word, esp. to indicate an inflection.

en·dive (en'dīv, än'dēv) *n.* **1** Any of various herbs related to chicory and commonly used as salad greens. **2** The blanched head of a young chicory plant, used in salads. [< L *entibus* endive]

end·less (end'lis) *adj.* **1** Having no end; boundless. **2** Lasting or seeming to last forever; interminable. **3** Forming a closed loop or circle. —**end'less·ly** *adv.* —**end'less·ness** *n.*

end·most (end'mōst') *adj.* Placed or being at the extreme end; most remote.

endo- *combining form* Within; inside: *en·docarp.* Also **end-.** [< Gk. *endon* within]

Endive *def.* 2

en·do·carp (en'dō·kärp) *n. Bot.* The inner layer of a pericarp, as the hard part of a cherry stone.

en·do·crine (en'dō·krin, -krīn, -krēn) *adj.* **1** Denoting an organ or gland that produces one or more hormones that pass directly into the blood. **2** Pertaining to a hormonal secretion. —*n.* The secretion of a ductless gland. [< ENDO- + Gk. *krinein* separate] —**en'do·cri'nal** (-krī'nəl) *adj.*

en·do·cri·nol·o·gy (en'dō·kri·nol'ə·jē, -krī-) *n.* The branch of medicine dealing with the structure and function of the endocrine glands and their hormones. —**en'do·cri·nol'o·gist** *n.*

en·dog·e·nous (en·doj'ə·nəs) *adj.* Originating or growing within something, as cells within the wall of the parent cell. —**en·dog'e·nous·ly** *adv.*

en·dor·phin (en·dôr'fin) *n.* Any of a group of substances made up of amino acids, produced by the brain, that suppress pain naturally. [< END(O)- + (M)ORPHIN(E)]

en·dorse (in·dôrs', en-) *v.t.* **·dorsed, ·dors·ing 1** To write, esp. one's name, on the back of, as a check or other document. **2** To support: to *endorse* a policy or candidate. [< L *in*-on + *dorsum* back] —**en·dors'a·ble** *adj.*

en·dor·see (in·dôr·sē', en-) *n.* One to whom an endorsed document or its value is transferred.

en·do·skel·e·ton (en'dō·skel'ə·tən) *n.* The internal supporting structure of an animal, characteristic of all vertebrates. —**en'do·skel'e·tal** *adj.*

en·do·sperm (en'dō·spûrm) *n. Bot.* The protein nutrient within the embryo of a seed. • See EMBRYO.

en·dow (in·dou', en-) *v.t.* To provide with a permanent fund or income. **2** To furnish or equip, as with talents or natural gifts: usu. with *with.* [< OF *en-* in + *douer* to provide with a dowry]

en·dow·ment (in·dou'mənt, en-) *n.* **1** Money or property given to provide an institution or person with an income. **2** Any natural gift, as beauty. **3** The act of endowing.

end product The result or outcome.

end table A small table to be placed beside chairs, at the end of a sofa, etc.

en·due (in·dᵕᵒᵒ', en-) *v.t.* **·dued, ·du·ing** To provide or endow: with *with.* [Fusion of OF *enduire* introduce and OF *enduire* clothe]

en·dur·ance (in·dᵕᵒᵒr'əns, en-) *n.* **1** The capacity to bear pain, distress, or prolonged hardship. **2** The ability to continue or to carry on. **3** The act of enduring.

en·dure (in·dᵕᵒᵒr', en-) *v.* **·dured, ·dur·ing** *v.t.* **1** To bear or undergo, as pain, grief, or injury, esp. without yielding. **2** To tolerate; put up with. —*v.i.* **3** To last; continue to be. **4** To suffer without yielding; hold out. [< L *in*-in + *durare* harden] —**en·dur'a·ble** *adj.*

en·dur·ing (in·dᵕᵒᵒr'ing, en-) *adj.* **1** Lasting; permanent. **2** Long-suffering. —**en·dur'ing·ly** *adv.* —**en·dur'ing·ness** *n.*

end·wise (end'wīz') *adv.* **1** With the end foremost or uppermost. **2** On end. **3** Lengthwise. Also **end'ways'** (-wāz').

-ene *suffix Chem.* Denoting an open-chain, unsaturated hydrocarbon having at least one double bond: *ethylene.*

ENE, E.N.E., ene, e.n.e. east-northest.

en·e·ma (en'ə·mə) *n.* **1** A liquid injected into the rectum as a purgative or for diagnostic purposes. **2** Such an injection. [< Gk. *en-* in + *hienai* send]

en·e·my (en'ə·mē) *n. pl.* **·mies 1** One who hates or bears ill will toward another; foe. **2** One hostile to an organization, idea, etc. **3** A hostile nation or military force; also, a member of a hostile nation or force. —*adj.* Of a hostile army or power. [< L *in*-not + *amicus* friend]

en·er·get·ic (en'ər·jet'ik) *adj.* Having, acting with, or displaying energy; vigorous. [< Gk. *energein* be active] —**en'er·get'i·cal·ly** *adv.*

en·er·gize (en'ər·jīz) *v.* **·gized, ·giz·ing** *v.t.* To give energy or power to; activate. —**en'er·giz'er** *n.*

en·er·gy (en'ər·jē) *n. pl.* **·gies 1** The power by which anything acts effectively. **2** The power to be physically or mentally active, often without the normal attendant fatigue. **3** Force or power in activity: *His singing lacks energy.* **4** *Physics* The ability to do work. See also ATOMIC ENERGY, CHEMICAL ENERGY, ELECTRICAL ENERGY, GEOTHERMAL ENERGY, KINETIC ENERGY, MECHANICAL ENERGY, POTENTIAL ENERGY, SOLAR ENERGY. **5** The motive power essential to modern technology, derived from various natural sources. —*adj.* Of, for, caused by, or relating to energy or the lack of it: the *energy* crisis; *energy* needs. [< Gk. *en-* on, at + *ergon* work]

en·er·gy-in·ten·sive (en'ər·jē·in·ten'siv) *adj.* Representing a heavy investment of energy to produce or manufacture, as a material.

en·er·vate (en'ər·vāt) *v.t.* **·vat·ed, ·vat·ing** To deprive of energy or strength; weaken. —*adj.* (i·nûr'vit) Enervated. [< L *enervare* weaken] —**en·er·va'tion, en'er·va'tor** *n.*

en fa·mille (än fà·mē'y') *French* Within the family; at home; informally.

en·fant ter·ri·ble (än·fän'te·rē'bl') A person whose unconventional speech, behavior, attitudes, etc., causes embarrassment or controversy. [F, lit., terrible child]

en·fee·ble (in·fē'bəl, en-) *v.t.* **·bled, ·bling** To make feeble. —**en·fee'ble·ment, en·fee'bler** *n.*

en·fi·lade (en'fə·lād', -läd') *Mil. v.t.* **·lad·ed, ·lad·ing** To fire down the length of, as a column of troops. —*n.* **1** Gunfire that can rake lengthwise a line of troops, etc. **2** A position exposed to a raking fire. [F < *enfiler* to thread]

en·fold (in·fōld, en-) *v.t.* **1** To wrap in layers. **2** To clasp in the arms; embrace. —**en·fold'er** *n.*

en·force (in·fôrs', -fōrs', en-) *v.t.* **·forced, ·for·ing 1** To compel obedience to, as laws. **2** To compel (performance, obedience, etc.) by physical or moral force. **3** To make convincing, as an argument. [< L *in*-in + *fortis* strong] —**en·force'a·ble** *adj.* —**en·force'·ment, en·forc'er** *n.*

en·fran·chise (in-fran'chīz, en-) *v.t.* ·chised, ·chis·ing 1 To endow with a franchise, as the right to vote. 2 To set free, as from bondage. [< OF *en-* in + *franc* free] —**en·fran'chise·ment** *n.*

Eng. England; English.

eng. engine; engineer; engineering; engraved.

en·gage (in-gāj', en-) *v.* ·gaged, ·gag·ing *v.t.* 1 To bind by a promise, pledge, etc. 2 To promise to marry: usu. in the passive. 3 To hire, as a lawyer, or his services; secure the use of, as a room. 4 To hold the interest or attention of. 5 To hold (interest or attention); occupy. 6 To begin a battle with. 7 To mesh or interlock, as gears. —*v.i.* 8 To bind oneself by a promise, pledge, etc. 9 To devote or occupy oneself: to *engage* in research. 10 To begin a battle. 11 To mesh, as gears. [< OF *en-* in + *gager* to pledge]

en·gaged (in-gājd', en-) *adj.* 1 Pledged to be married. 2 Occupied or busy. 3 Partially sunk or built into another structure, as columns. 4 Meshed or interlocked, as gears. 5 Involved in a contest or conflict.

en·gage·ment (in-gāj'mənt, en-) *n.* 1 Something that engages or binds, as an appointment, promise, or obligation. 2 The condition of being engaged; a betrothal. 3 The act of engaging. 4 An entering into battle; also, the battle itself. 5 *pl.* Pecuniary obligations. 6 A salaried position.

en·gag·ing (in-gā'jing, en-) *adj.* Attracting interest; charming; winning. —**en·gag'ing·ly** *adv.*

en garde (än gärd') On guard: a fencing term. [F]

en·gen·der (in-jen'dər, en-) *v.t.* To cause to exist; produce. [< L *ingenerare* to generate in]

engin. engineering.

en·gine (en'jin) *n.* 1 A machine that uses energy, esp. energy from a fuel, to perform work. 2 A railroad locomotive. 3 Any apparatus: the *engines* of war. [< L *ingenium* talent, skill]

en·gi·neer (en'jə·nir') *n.* 1 One practicing any branch of engineering. 2 One who runs or manages an engine. 3 A manager; inventor; plotter. 4 A member of the division of an army which constructs bridges, clears and builds roads and airfields, etc. —*v.t.* 1 To put through or manage by contrivance: to *engineer* a scheme. 2 To plan and superintend as an engineer.

en·gi·neer·ing (en'jə·nir'ing) *n.* The application of scientific knowledge to the solution of practical problems, as in designing structures and apparatus.

Eng·land (ing'glənd) *n.* 1 The s part and largest political division of Great Britain, 50,237 sq. mi., cap. London. 2 Loosely, Great Britain, or the United Kingdom of Great Britain and Northern Ireland. • See map at UNITED KINGDOM.

Eng·lish (ing'glish) *adj.* Of, pertaining to, or derived from England, its people, or their language. —*n.* 1 The people of England: with *the.* 2 The Germanic language spoken by the people of the British Isles, most of the Commonwealth, and of the United States. 3 The English language as used in a particular region or time or by a specified group: American *English.* 4 In billiards, bowling, etc., a spin imparted to the ball by the manner of striking it or releasing it. —*v.t.* 1 To translate into English. 2 To Anglicize, as a foreign word.

English horn A woodwind instrument, with a pitch a fifth lower than an oboe.

Eng·lish·man (ing'glish·mən) *n. pl.* ·men (-mən) A native or citizen of England. —**Eng·lish·wom·an** (-wŏŏm'ən) *n. Fem.* (*pl.* ·wom·en) (-wim'in)

English muffin A round flat roll of unsweetened, raised dough baked on a griddle.

English setter One of a breed of dogs, usu. white marked with black or tan, trained to point to game.

English sparrow HOUSE SPARROW.

en·gorge (in-gôrj', en-) *v.t.* ·gorged, ·gorg·ing 1 To congest (an organ) with blood or other fluid. 2 To devour or swallow greedily. [< F *engorger*] —**en·gorge'ment** *n.*

engr. engineer; engraved; engraver; engraving.

en·graft (in-graft', -gräft', en-) *v.t.* 1 To graft (a piece cut from a plant or tree) to another tree or plant for propagation. 2 To implant. —**en·graft'ment** *n.*

en·grave (in-grāv', en-) *v.t.* ·graved, ·grav·ing 1 To carve or etch figures, letters, etc., into (a surface). 2 To impress deeply. 3 To cut (pictures, lettering, etc.) into metal, stone, or wood, for printing. 4 To print from plates made by such a process. [< EN-¹ + GRAVE³] —**en·grav'er** *n.*

en·grav·ing (in-grā'ving, en-) *n.* 1 The act or art of cutting designs on a plate. 2 An engraved design on a plate. 3 A picture or design printed from an engraved plate.

en·gross (in-grōs', en-) *v.t.* 1 To occupy completely; absorb. 2 To copy in large writing; make a formal transcript of. 3 To monopolize, as the supply of a product. [< LL *ingrossare* write large] —**en·gross'er, en·gross'ment** *n.* —**en·gross'ing** *adj.*

en·gulf (in-gulf', en-) *v.t.* To swallow up; bury or overwhelm.

en·hance (in-hans', -häns', en-) *v.t.* ·hanced, ·hanc·ing To make higher or greater, as in reputation, cost, beauty, quality, etc. [< L *in-* in + *altus* high] —**en·hance'ment** *n.* — Syn. heighten, intensify, strengthen, improve.

e·nig·ma (i·nig'mə) *n.* 1 An obscure or ambiguous saying; a riddle. 2 A baffling or inexplicable circumstance, person, etc. [< Gk. *ainissesthai* speak in riddles]

en·ig·mat·ic (en'ig·mat'ik, ē'nig-) *adj.* Of or like an enigma; ambiguous; puzzling. Also **en'ig·mat'i·cal.** —**en'ig·mat'i·cal·ly** *adv.*

en·join (in·join', en-) *v.t.* 1 To order authoritatively and emphatically. 2 To impose (a condition, course of action, etc.) on a person or group: to *enjoin* compliance. 3 To forbid or prohibit, esp. by judicial order. [< L *in-* + *jungere* join] —**en·join'er** *n.*

en·joy (in·joi', en-) *v.t.* 1 To experience joy or pleasure in; receive pleasure from the possession or use of. 2 To have the use or benefit of. [< L *in-* + *gaudere* rejoice] —**en·joy'·a·ble** *adj.* —**en·joy'a·ble·ness** *n.* —**en·joy'a·bly** *adv.*

en·joy·ment (in·joi'mənt, en-) *n.* 1 The act or state of enjoying; pleasure. 2 Something that gives joy or pleasure.

en·kin·dle (in·kin'dəl, en-) *v.t.* ·dled, ·dling 1 To set on fire; kindle. 2 To stir up; excite. —**en·kin'dler** *n.*

en·lace (in·lās', en-) *v.t.* ·laced, ·lac·ing 1 To bind with or as with laces. 2 To intertwine; entangle. —**en·lace'ment** *n.*

en·large (in·lärj', en-) *v.* ·larged, ·larg·ing *v.t.* 1 To make greater or larger; increase the amount or extent of; expand. —*v.i.* 2 To become greater or larger; increase; widen. 3 To express oneself in greater detail: with *on* or *upon.* —**en·larg'er** *n.*

en·large·ment (in·lärj'mənt, en-) *n.* 1 The act of enlarging, or the state of being enlarged. 2 Something enlarged, as a photograph made larger than its original negative.

en·light·en (in·līt'n, en-) *v.t.* 1 To impart knowledge to; cause to know or understand; teach. 2 To convey information to; inform. —**en·light'en·er** *n.*

en·light·en·ment (in·līt'n·mənt, en-) *n.* The act of enlightening or the state of being enlightened. —**the En·lightenment** A philosophical movement of the 18th century characterized by a belief in the paramount value of reason as an instrument of progress and the use of the empirical method in scientific inquiry.

en·list (in·list', en-) *v.t.* 1 To engage for service, as in the army or navy. 2 To gain the help or interest of (a person or his services). —*v.i.* 3 To enter military services voluntarily. 4 To join in some venture, cause, etc.

enlisted man A member of the armed forces ranking below a noncommissioned officer or petty officer.

en·list·ment (in·list'mənt, en-) *n.* 1 The act of enlisting, or the state of being enlisted. 2 The term for which one enlists.

en·li·ven (in·lī'vən, en-) *v.t.* 1 To make lively, cheerful, or sprightly. 2 To make active or vigorous; stimulate. —**en·li'ven·er, en·li'ven·ment** *n.*

en masse (än mas', en) In a mass or body; all together. [F]

en·mesh (in·mesh', en-) *v.t.* To ensnare or entangle in or as in a net.

en·mi·ty (en'mə·tē) *n. pl.* ·ties 1 The spirit of an enemy; hostility. 2 The state of being an enemy; a hostile condition. [< L *inimicus* hostile]

en·no·ble (i·nō′bəl, en-) *v.t.* **·bled, ·bling** **1** To make honorable or noble in nature, quality, etc. **2** To confer a title of nobility upon. —**en·no′ble·ment, en·no′bler** *n.*

en·nui (än′wē, än·wē′) *n.* A feeling of listless weariness resulting from satiety, inactivity, etc.; lassitude. [F]

e·nor·mi·ty (i·nôr′mə·tē) *n. pl.* **·ties** **1** The state of being outrageous or extremely wicked. **2** A flagrant instance of depravity; an atrocity. **3** Great size or extent; enormousness. • Traditionally, *enormity* refers to great wickedness, not to great size or extent, whereas *enormousness* means greatness in any sense. One speaks of the *enormity* of a crime but the *enormousness* of an Olympic stadium. However, *enormity* (def. 3) is now often used, esp. to express great extent, complexity, difficulty, etc.: *The enormity of the task filled him with awe.*

e·nor·mous (i·nôr′məs) *adj.* **1** Excessive or extraordinary in size, amount, or degree. **2** Wicked above measure; atrocious. [< L *enormis* immense] —**e·nor′mous·ly** *adv.* —**e·nor′mous·ness** *n.* • See ENORMITY.

e·nough (i·nuf′) *adj.* Adequate for demand or need; sufficient. —*n.* An ample supply. —*adv.* So as to be sufficient. —*interj.* It is enough; stop. [< OE *genoh, genog*]

en·plane (in·plān′, en-) *v.i.* **·planed, ·plan·ing** To board an airplane.

en·quire (in·kwīr′, en-) *v.* **·quired, ·quir·ing** INQUIRE.

en·quir·y (in·kwīr′ē, in′kwə·rē) *n. pl.* **·quir·ies** INQUIRY.

en·rage (in·rāj′, en-) *v.t.* **·raged, ·rag·ing** To throw into a rage; infuriate.

en rap·port (än ra·pôr′) In accord. [F]

en·rap·ture (in·rap′chər, en-) *v.t.* **·tured, ·tur·ing** To bring into a state of rapture; delight.

en·rich (in·rich′, en-) *v.t.* **1** To make rich; increase the wealth of. **2** To make fertile, as soil. **3** To increase or enhance the quality of. **4** To increase the food value of, as bread. **5** To adorn. [< OF *en-* in + *riche* rich] —**en·rich′er, en·rich′ment** *n.*

en·roll (in·rōl′, en-) *v.* **·rolled, ·roll·ing** *v.t.* **1** To write or record (a name) in a roll; register. **2** To enlist. **3** To place on record, as a document. **4** To roll up; wrap. —*v.i.* **5** To place one's name on a list. Also **en·rol′**. [< OF *enroller*]

en·roll·ment (en·rōl′mənt) *n.* **1** The act of enrolling. **2** An enrolled entry; a record. **3** The number enrolled. Also **en·rol′ment.**

en route (än rōōt′, en) On the way. [F]

Ens. Ensign.

en·sconce (in·skons′, en-) *v.t.* **·sconced, ·sconc·ing** **1** To fix securely or comfortably in some place; settle snugly. **2** To shelter; hide.

en·sem·ble (än·säm′bəl) *n.* **1** The parts of a thing viewed as a whole; general effect. **2** A combination of clothing and accessories that match or harmonize. **3** *Music* **a** A group of performers. **b** Music for such a group. **c** Collective accuracy of balance and style by such a group. **4** Any group of actors or dancers who perform together, usu. excluding the star performers; also, the performance of such a group. [< L *in-* in + *simul* at the same time]

en·shrine (in·shrīn′, en-) *v.t.* **·shrined, ·shrin·ing** **1** To place in or as in a shrine. **2** To cherish devoutly; hold sacred. —**en·shrine′ment** *n.*

en·shroud (in·shroud′) *v.t.* To cover with or as with a shroud; conceal.

en·sign (en′sən, -sīn) *n.* **1** A flag or banner, esp. a national standard or naval flag. **2** (en′sən) See GRADE. **3** In the British Army, until 1871, a commissioned officer who carried the flag of his regiment or company. **4** A badge or symbol, as of office. [< L *insignia* insignia]

en·si·lage (en′sə·lij) *n.* **1** The process of preserving succulent fodder in closed pits or silos. **2** The fodder thus preserved. —*v.t.* **·laged, ·lag·ing** ENSILE. [< F *en-* in + *silo* silo]

en·sile (in·sīl′, en-) *v.t.* **·siled, ·sil·ing** To store in a silo for preservation, as fodder.

en·slave (in·slāv′, en-) *v.t.* **·slaved, ·slav·ing** To make a slave of; dominate. —**en·slave′ment, en·slav′er** *n.*

en·snare (in·snâr′, en-) *v.t.* **·snared, ·snar·ing** To catch in a snare; trick.

en·sue (in·s^yōō′, en-) *v.i.* **·sued, ·su·ing** **1** To occur afterward or subsequently; follow. **2** To follow as a consequence; result. [< L *in-* on, in + *sequi* follow]

en·sure (in·shoor′, en-) *v.t.* **·sured, ·sur·ing** To make safe

or secure; provide protection: with *against* or *from:* to *ensure* against tyranny. **2** To make sure or certain; guarantee: to *ensure* fairness. **3** INSURE (def. 1). [< ME *insuren, ensuren* to insure]

-ent *suffix* **1** Having the quality of (the main element): *potent.* **2** One who or that which performs the action of (the main element): *superintendent.* [< L *-ens,* suffix of present participle]

en·tab·la·ture (in·tab′lə·chər, en-) *n. Archit.* The uppermost part of a columnar system, consisting of the architrave, frieze, and cornice. [< Ital. *intavolatura*]

en·tail (in·tāl′, en-) *v.t.* **1** To impose or result in as a necessary consequence. **2** *Law* To restrict the inheritance of (real property) to an unalterable succession of heirs. —*n.* **1** Anything transmitted as an inalienable inheritance. **2** An estate limited to a particular class of heirs, as eldest sons. [ME *entailen*] —**en·tail′ment** *n.*

Entablature
a. cornice.
b. frieze.
c. architrave.

en·tan·gle (in·tang′gəl, en-) *v.t.* **·gled, ·gling** **1** To catch in or as in a snare; hamper. **2** To make tangled; complicate. **3** To involve in difficulties. —**en·tan′gle·ment, en·tan′gler** *n.*

en·tente (än·tänt′) *n.* **1** An understanding between two or more nations in regard to a cooperative policy or action. **2** The parties to such an understanding. [F]

entente cor·diale (kôr·dyal′) Friendliness between governments. [F, lit., cordial understanding]

en·ter (en′tər) *v.t.* **1** To come or go into: to *enter* a room; The thought never *entered* my head. **2** To set or insert in: to *enter* a nail. **3** To become a member or members of; join. **4** To begin: often with *upon:* to *enter* upon a new career. **5** To gain admission for. **6** To write or record, as in a list. **7** To report (goods, a vessel, etc.) to the customhouse. **8** *Law* To place on the records of a court, as evidence. —*v.i.* **9** To come or go inward. **10** To become a member or members; join. —**enter into 1** To begin; start. **2** To engage in. **3** To consider or discuss. [< L *intrare* < *intra* within]

en·ter·ic (en·ter′ik) *adj.* **1** Of or pertaining to the intestine. **2** Having an intestine. [< Gk. *enteron* intestine < *entos* within]

en·ter·i·tis (en′tə·rī′tis) *n.* Inflammation of the intestines, esp. of the small intestine.

entero- *combining form* Intestine. Also **enter-.** [< Gk. *enteron* intestine]

en·ter·prise (en′tər·prīz) *n.* **1** Any projected task or work; esp., a risky or bold undertaking. **2** Boldness, energy, and invention in practical affairs. [< F *entre-* between + *prendre* take]

en·ter·pris·ing (en′tər·prī′zing) *adj.* Energetic and adventuresome; showing initiative. —**en′ter·pris′ing·ly** *adv.*

en·ter·tain (en′tər·tān′) *v.t.* **1** To hold the attention of; amuse; divert. **2** To extend hospitality to; receive as a guest. **3** To take into consideration, as a proposal. **4** To keep or bear in mind: to *entertain* a grudge. —*v.i.* **5** To receive and care for guests. [< OF *entretenir* to hold between] —**en′ter·tain′er** *n.*

en·ter·tain·ing (en′tər·tā′ning) *adj.* Of a character to entertain; amusing; diverting. —**en′ter·tain′ing·ly** *adv.*

en·ter·tain·ment (en′tər·tān′mənt) *n.* **1** The state of being entertained; pleasure or amusement. **2** A source or means of amusement. **3** The act of entertaining.

en·thrall (in·thrôl′, en-) *v.t.* **·thralled, ·thral·ling** **1** To keep spellbound; fascinate; charm. **2** ENSLAVE. Also **en·thral′.** —**en·thrall′ment, en·thral′ment** *n.*

en·throne (in·thrōn′, en-) *v.t.* **·throned, ·thron·ing** **1** To put upon a throne; invest with power, as a king. **2** To seat or place in a position of authority. **3** To exalt; revere. —**en·throne′ment** *n.*

en·thuse (in·thōōz′, en-) *v.t. & v.i.* **·thused, ·thus·ing** *Informal* To make or become enthusiastic. [Back formation from ENTHUSIASM]

en·thu·si·asm (in·thōō′zē·az′əm, en-) *n.* **1** Earnest and intense feeling; zeal. **2** A source or cause of such feeling. [< Gk. *enthusiasmos* inspiration]

en·thu·si·ast (in·thōō′zē·ast, en-) *n.* **1** One moved by enthusiasm, as for a cause or activity. **2** A religious zealot.

en·thu·si·as·tic (in·thōō′zē·as′tik, en-) *adj.* Characterized by or showing enthusiasm; ardent; zealous. —**en·thu'·si·as'ti·cal·ly** adv.

en·tice (in·tīs', en-) v.t. **·ticed, ·tic·ing** To lead on or attract by arousing hope of pleasure, profit, etc. [< OF enticier arouse] —**en·tice'ment, en·tic'er** n. —**en·tic'ing·ly** adv.

en·tire (in·tīr', en-) adj. **1** Complete in all its parts; whole. **2** Consisting of only one piece; not broken or divided. **3** Pure; unalloyed. **4** Uncastrated: an entire horse. **5** Bot. Having a smooth margin, as a leaf. [< L integer whole, intact] —**en·tire'ly** adv. —**en·tire'ness** n. —**Syn. 2** intact, of a piece, undivided.

en·tire·ty (in·tī'rət·ē, en-) n. pl. **·ties 1** The state of being entire; completeness; wholeness. **2** That which is entire.

en·ti·tle (in·tīt'l, en-) v.t. **·tled, ·tling 1** To give a right or legal authority to; authorize or qualify. **2** To give a name or designation to. **3** To give (a person) a title.

en·ti·ty (en'tə·tē) n. pl. **·ties 1** Anything that exists or may be supposed to exist. **2** Being; existence, esp. when complete or self-contained. [< L entitas < ens, pr.p. of esse be]

en·tomb (in·tōōm', en-) v.t. **1** To place in or as in a tomb; bury. **2** To serve as a tomb for. —**en·tomb'er, en·tomb·ment** n.

en·to·mol·o·gy (en'tə·mol'ə·jē) n. The branch of zoology dealing with insects. [< Gk. entomon insect] —**en·to·mo·log·i·cal** (en'tə·mə·loj'i·kəl) or **·log'ic** adj. —**en'to·mo·log'i·cal·ly** adv. —**en·to·mol'o·gist** n.

en·tou·rage (än'tōō·räzh') n. **1** Associates, companions, or attendants. **2** Environment. [< OF entourer surround]

en·tr'acte (än·trakt', Fr. äṅ·trakt') n. **1** The time between any two acts of a play or opera. **2** A musical interlude, dance, or the like, performed between acts. [F]

en·trails (en'trālz, -trəlz) n. pl. The internal parts, esp. the intestines, of an animal. [< LL intralia]

en·train (in·trān', en-) v.t. & v.i. To put or go aboard a railway train.

en·trance¹ (en'trəns) n. **1** The act of entering. **2** A passage into a house or other enclosed space. **3** The right or power of entering; entrée. [< OF entrer enter]

en·trance² (in·trans', -träns', en-) v.t. **·tranced, ·tranc·ing 1** To fill with rapture or wonder; delight; charm. **2** To put into a trance. —**en·trance'ment** n. —**en·tranc'ing** adj. —**en·tranc'ing·ly** adv.

en·trant (en'trənt) n. One who enters, esp. one who enters a contest or competition.

en·trap (in·trap', en-) v.t. **·trapped, ·trap·ping 1** To catch in or as in a trap. **2** To trick into danger or difficulty; deceive; ensnare. —**en·trap'ment** n.

en·treat (in·trēt', en-) v.t. & v.i. To ask earnestly or abjectly; beseech; implore. [< OF entraiter to deal with, treat] —**en·treat'ment** n.

en·treat·y (in·trē'tē, en-) n. pl. **·treat·ies** An earnest request; supplication.

en·trée (än'trā, än·trā') n. **1** The act or privilege of entering; access. **2** The principal course at a dinner or luncheon. Also **en·tree'**. [F]

en·trench (in·trench', en-) v.t. **1** To fortify or protect with or as with a trench. **2** To establish firmly: The idea was entrenched in his mind. —v.i. **3** To encroach or trespass: with on or upon. —**en·trench'ment** n.

en·tre nous (än'tr' nōō') French Between ourselves; confidentially.

en·tre·pre·neur (än'trə·prə·nûr') n. One who undertakes to start and conduct an enterprise or business, assuming full control and risk. [F < entreprendre to undertake] —**en'tre·pre·neur'i·al** (-ē·əl) adj.

en·tro·py (en'trə·pē) n. **1** Physics A measure of the degree to which the energy of a system is unavailable for work. **2** In information theory, an analogous measure reflecting uncertainty of knowledge. [< Gk. entropē a turning]

en·trust (in·trust', en-) v.t. **1** To place something, as a duty or responsibility, in the care or trust of. **2** To give over for care, safekeeping, or performance.

en·try (en'trē) n. pl. **·tries 1** The act of coming or going in; entrance. **2** A place of entrance; a small hallway. **3** The act of entering an item in a register or list. **4** An item entered in such a list. **5** The reporting at a customhouse of a ship's

arrival and the nature of her cargo. **6** Law The act of assuming actual possession of property by entering upon it. **7** A contestant entered in a race or competition. [< F entrer to enter]

en·twine (in·twīn', en-) v.t. & v.i. **·twined, ·twin·ing** To twine around; twine or twist together.

e·nu·mer·ate (i·nyōō'mə·rāt) v.t. **·at·ed, ·at·ing 1** To name one by one; list. **2** To count or ascertain the number of. [< L ex- out + numerare count] —**e·nu'mer·a'tion, e·nu'mer·a'tor** n. —**e·nu'mer·a'tive** adj.

e·nun·ci·ate (i·nun'sē·āt, -shē-) v. **·at·ed, ·at·ing** v.t. **1** To pronounce or articulate (words), esp. clearly and distinctly. **2** To state with exactness, as a theory. **3** To announce or proclaim. —v.i. **4** To utter or pronounce words. [< L ex- out + nunciare announce] —**e·nun'ci·a'tion, e·nun'·ci·a'tor** n. —**e·nun'ci·a'tive** adj.

en·u·re·sis (en'yə·rē'sis) n. Pathol. Involuntary urination, esp. during sleep. [< Gk. en- in + oureein urinate]

env. envelope.

en·vel·op (in·vel'əp) v.t. **·oped, ·op·ing 1** To wrap or enclose completely. **2** To hide or obscure, as by enclosing: to envelop in fog. **3** To surround. [< OF en- in + voluper to wrap, fold] —**en·vel'op·er, en·vel'op·ment** n.

en·ve·lope (en'və·lōp, än'-) n. **1** A folded wrapper of paper, usu. with gummed edges, for enclosing a letter or the like. **2** Anything that encloses completely or wraps around. [< OF enveloper to envelop]

en·ven·om (in·ven'əm) v.t. **1** To impregnate with venom; poison. **2** To make vindictive; embitter. [< OF < en- in + venim venom]

en·vi·a·ble (en'vē·ə·bəl) adj. Of a nature to cause envy or admiration. —**en'vi·a·ble·ness** n. —**en'vi·a·bly** adv.

en·vi·ous (en'vē·əs) adj. Having, showing, or caused by envy. —**en'vi·ous·ly** adv. —**en'vi·ous·ness** n.

en·vi·ron (in·vī'rən, en-) v.t. To be or extend around; encircle; surround. [< OF, around, about]

en·vi·ron·ment (in·vī'rən·mənt, -ərn-, en-) n. **1** The aggregate of all conditions affecting the existence, growth, and welfare of an organism or group of organisms. **2** Surroundings or external circumstances. —**en·vi'ron·men'tal** adj. —**en·vi'ron·men'tal·ly** adv.

en·vi·ron·ment·al·ist (in·vī'rən·men'təl·ist, -ərn-) n. **1** One who advocates preservation of the environment, as from commercial exploitation. **2** One who attaches more importance to environment than to heredity as a determinant in the development of a person or a group. —**en·vi'ron·ment'al·ism** n.

en·vi·rons (in·vī'rənz, en-) n. pl. The surrounding region; outskirts; suburbs.

en·vis·age (in·viz'ij, en-) v.t. **·aged, ·ag·ing 1** To form a mental image of; visualize. **2** To form an idea about; conceptualize. —**en·vis'age·ment** n.

en·vi·sion (in·vizh'ən, en-) v.t. To see or foresee in the imagination: to envision the future.

en·voy (en'voi, än'-) n. **1** A diplomatic agent of a government, ranking next below an ambassador. **2** One sent on a mission. [< F < envoier to send on the way]

en·vy (en'vē) n. **1** A feeling of resentment and jealousy over the possessions, achievements, etc., of another. **2** Desire for something belonging to another. **3** An object of envy. —v.t. **vied, vy·ing 1** To regard with envy. **2** To feel envy because of. [< L invidia] —**en'vi·er** n. —**en'vy·ing·ly** adv. —**Syn. n. 2** greed, covetousness, cupidity.

en·wrap (in·rap', en-) v.t. **·wrapped, ·wrap·ping** To wrap or envelop. —**en·wrap'ment** n.

en·zyme (en'zīm, -zim) n. A proteinlike substance produced by cells and having the power to initiate or accelerate specific biochemical reactions in an organism. [< Gk. < en- in + zymē leaven] —**en·zy·mat·ic** (en'zī·mat'ik, -zi-) adj.

E·o·cene (ē'ə·sēn) n. & adj. See GEOLOGY. [< Gk. ēōs dawn + kainos new]

e·o·li·an (ē·ō'lē·ən) adj. Pertaining to or caused by the winds; wind-borne. [< L Aeolus, god of the winds]

E·o·lith·ic (ē'ə·lith'ik) adj. Anthropol. Of or pertaining to a period of primitive human culture, known by crude tools of bone and chipped stone. [< Gk. *ēōs* dawn + *lithos* stone]

e·on (ē′on) *n.* **1** An incalculable period of time; an eternity. **2** *Geol.* A time interval including two or more eras. [< Gk. *aiōn* age] —**e·o·ni·an** (ē·ō′nē·ən) *adj.*

E·os (ē′əs) *Gk. Myth.* The goddess of the dawn.

-eous *suffix* Of the nature of: *gaseous.* [< L *-eus*]

ep·au·let (ep′ə·let) *n.* A shoulder ornament, as on uniforms. Also **ep′au·lette.** [F, dim. of *épaule* shoulder]

é·pée (ā·pā′) *n.* A sharp-pointed dueling sword with no cutting edge. [F < L *spatha* a broad, flat blade] —**é·pée′ist** *n.*

Epaulet

Eph, Eph., Ephes. Ephesians.

e·phed·rine (e·fed′rin) *n.* An alkaloid having various physiological effects, used mainly to reduce nasal congestion and relieve asthma. Also **e·phed′rin.** [< NL *Ephedra,* a genus of plants + -INE]

e·phem·er·al (i·fem′ər·əl) *adj.* **1** Living one day only, as certain insects. **2** Short-lived; transitory. —*n.* Anything lasting for a very short time. [Gk. *ephēmeros* < *epi-* on + *hēmera* day] —**e·phem′er·al·ly** *adv.* —**e·phem′er·al·ness** *n.* —**Syn.** *adj.* **2** transient, passing, temporal, temporary.

e·phem·er·id (i·fem′ər·id) *n.* Any of an order of insects characterized by a short-lived, fragile, adult phase, as the mayfly. [< NL < Gk. *ephēmeros* EPHEMERAL.]

E·phe·sian (i·fē′zhən) *adj.* Of or pertaining to Ephesus. —*n.* A citizen of Ephesus.

E·phe·sians (i·fē′zhənz) *n. pl. (construed as sing.)* The New Testament epistle to the church at Ephesus.

Eph·e·sus (ef′ə·səs) *n.* An ancient Greek city in w Asia Minor.

eph·or (ef′ôr, -ər) *n. pl.* **·ors** or **·o·ri** (-ə·rī) In ancient Sparta, one of a body of elected, supervising magistrates. [< Gk. *ephoran* to oversee]

E·phra·im (ē′frē·əm, ē′frəm) **1** In the Old Testament, Joseph's second son. **2** The tribe descended from him.

E·phra·im·ite (ē′frē·əm·īt) *n.* A descendant of Ephraim or a member of his tribe.

epi- *prefix* **1** Upon; above; among; outside: *epidermis.* **2** Besides; over; in addition to: *epilogue.* **3** Near; close to; beside. [< Gk. *epi* upon, on]

ep·ic (ep′ik) *n.* **1** A long, narrative poem celebrating in stately, formal verse heroic or grandiose events or achievements. **2** Any novel, play, historical event, etc., having a heroic or grandiose quality or theme. —*adj.* **1** Of, pertaining to, or like an epic. **2** Grand, noble, legendary, or heroic: also **ep′i·cal.** [< Gk. < *epos* song, word]

ep·i·ca·lyx (ep′ə·kā′liks, -kal′iks) *n. pl.* **·ca·lyx·es** or **·ca·ly·ces** (-kā′lə·sēz) *Bot.* A ring of bracts resembling the calyx of a flower, located near the true calyx.

ep·i·can·thic fold (ep′ə·kan′thik) A vertical fold of skin at the inner corner of the eyelid, found chiefly in certain Asian peoples. Also **ep′i·can′thus.** [< Gk. *epi-* upon + *kanthos* corner of the eye]

ep·i·carp (ep′ə·kärp) *n. Bot.* The outer layer of a pericarp.

ep·i·cene (ep′ə·sēn) *adj.* Belonging to or partaking of the characteristics of both sexes. —*n.* An epicene person. [< Gk. *epi-* upon + *koinos* common] —**ep′i·cen′ism** *n.*

ep·i·cen·ter (ep′ə·sen′tər) *n. Geol.* **1** The point on the earth's surface above the point of origin of an earthquake. **2** A focus or central point. —**ep′i·cen′tral** *adj.*

ep·i·cure (ep′ə·kyŏŏr) *n.* A person who enjoys and is knowledgeable about good food and drink; gourmet. [< *Epicurus,* 342?–370 B.C., Greek philosopher] —**ep′i·cu·re′an** (-kyŏŏ·rē′ən) *adj., n.* —**ep′i·cu·re′an·ism, ep′i·cur·ism** *n.*

Ep·i·cu·re·an (ep′ə·kyŏŏ·rē′ən) *adj.* Pertaining to the Greek philosopher Epicurus or to his doctrine that the chief goods of life are freedom from pain and peace of mind. —*n.* A follower of Epicurus. —**Ep′i·cu·re′an·ism′** *n.*

ep·i·dem·ic (ep′ə·dem′ik) *adj.* Affecting many in a large area or community at once: also **ep′i·dem′i·cal.** —*n.* **1** A disease temporarily prevalent in a community or throughout a large area. **2** A circumstance that suddenly becomes widespread: an *epidemic* of business failures. [< Gk. *epi-* upon + *dēmos* people] —**ep′i·dem′i·cal·ly** *adv.*

ep·i·der·mis (ep′ə·dûr′mis) *n.* The outer covering of the skin; the cuticle. [< Gk. *epi-* upon + *derma* skin] —**ep′i·der′mal, ep′i·der′mic** *adj.*

ep·i·glot·tis (ep′ə·glot′is) *n.* The leaf-shaped piece of cartilage, at the base of the tongue, that closes the trachea, or windpipe, during the act of swallowing. [< NL < Gk. *epi-* upon + *glōtta* tongue] —**ep′i·glot′tal** *adj.*

ep·i·gram (ep′ə·gram) *n.* **1** A pithy, caustic, or thought-provoking saying. **2** A short, witty, usu. satiric poem. [< Gk. *epigramma* an inscription] —**ep′i·gram·mat′ic** or **·i·cal** *adj.* —**ep′i·gram·mat′i·cal·ly** *adv.* —**ep′i·gram′ma·tist** *n.*

a. epiglottis.
b. esophagus.
c. trachea.

ep·i·graph (ep′ə·graf, -gräf) *n.* **1** A carved inscription on a monument, tomb, etc. **2** A quotation prefixed to a book, chapter, etc. [< Gk. < *epi-* upon + *graphein* write] —**ep′i·graph′ic** or **·i·cal** *adj.* —**ep′i·graph′i·cal·ly** *adv.*

ep·i·graph·y (i·pig′rə·fē) *n.* **1** Inscriptions collectively. **2** The deciphering, study, interpretation, etc., of inscriptions. —**e·pig′ra·pher, e·pig′ra·phist** *n.*

ep·i·lep·sy (ep′ə·lep′sē) *n. Pathol.* A chronic nervous affection characterized by sudden interruption of consciousness, sometimes accompanied by convulsions. Also **ep′i·lep′si·a.** [< Gk. *epi-* upon + *lambanein* seize]

ep·i·lep·tic (ep′ə·lep′tik) *adj.* Pertaining to or affected with epilepsy. —*n.* One who has epilepsy. —**ep′i·lep′ti·cal·ly** *adv.*

ep·i·logue (ep′ə·lôg, -log) *n.* **1** A concluding section, as of a novel or play, that rounds out or comments on the work. **2** A short speech to the audience delivered by an actor after the conclusion of a play. **3** The actor who delivers such a speech. Also **ep′i·log.** [< Gk. *epi-* upon, in addition + *legein* say]

ep·i·neph·rine (ep′ə·nef′rin, -rēn) *n.* An adrenal hormone, used to raise blood pressure and as a heart stimulant, etc. Also **ep′i·neph′rin** (-rin). [< EPI- + Gk. *nephros* kidney]

e·piph·a·ny (i·pif′ə·nē) *n. pl.* **·nies** A sudden recognition of or insight into the meaning, reality, or significance of something. [< Gk. *epiphainein* to manifest]

E·piph·a·ny (i·pif′ə·nē) *n.* January 6, a festival commemorating the manifestation of Christ to the Gentiles, represented by the Magi.

ep·i·phyte (ep′ə·fīt) *n. Bot.* A plant growing nonparasitically upon another. [< EPI- + Gk. *phyton* plant] —**ep′i·phyt′ic** (-fit′ik) or **·i·cal** *adj.* —**ep′i·phyt′i·cal·ly** *adv.*

Epis., Episc. Episcopal; Episcopalian.

Epis., Epist. Epistle.

e·pis·co·pa·cy (i·pis′kə·pə·sē) *n. pl.* **·cies** **1** Government of a church by bishops. **2** A bishop's state or office. **3** A body of bishops collectively. [< LL *episcopus* bishop]

e·pis·co·pal (i·pis′kə·pəl) *adj.* **1** Of or pertaining to bishops. **2** Having a government vested in bishops. [< LL < *episcopus* bishop] —**e·pis′co·pal·ly** *adv.*

E·pis·co·pal (i·pis′kə·pəl) *adj.* Belonging or pertaining to the Protestant Episcopal Church, or to any church in the Anglican communion.

Episcopal Church PROTESTANT EPISCOPAL CHURCH.

e·pis·co·pa·li·an (i·pis′kə·pā′lē·ən, -pāl′yən) *n.* An advocate of episcopacy. —*adj.* Pertaining to or favoring episcopal government.

E·pis·co·pa·li·an (i·pis′kə·pā′lē·ən, i·pāl′yən) *n.* A member of the Protestant Episcopal Church. —*adj.* EPISCOPAL. —**E·pis′co·pa′li·an·ism** *n.*

e·pis·co·pate (i·pis′kə·pit, -pāt) *n.* **1** The office, dignity, or term of office of a bishop. **2** A bishop's see. **3** Bishops collectively.

ep·i·sode (ep′ə·sōd) *n.* **1** An incident or story in a literary work, separable from, yet related to it. **2** A notable incident or action occurring as a break in the regular course of events. **3** An installment of a serial. [< Gk. *epi-* upon + *eisodos* entrance] —**ep′i·sod′ic** (-sod′ik) or **·i·cal, ep′i·so′dal** or **·di·al** *adj.* —**ep′i·sod′i·cal·ly** *adv.*

e·pis·te·mol·o·gy (i·pis′tə·mol′ə·jē) *n. pl.* **·gies** That department of philosophy which investigates critically the nature, methods, limits, and validity, of human knowledge. [< Gk. *epistēmē* knowledge + -LOGY] —**e·pis·te·mo·log·i·cal** (i·pis′tə·mə·loj′i·kəl) *adj.* —**e·pis′te·mo·log′i·cal·ly** *adv.* —**e·pis′te·mol′o·gist** *n.*

e·pis·tle (i·pis′əl) *n.* **1** A letter; esp., a long, formal letter that instructs. **2** *Usu. cap.* One of the letters of an apostle. **3** *Usu. cap.* A selection from an apostle's letter, read in certain church services. [< Gk. *epi-* on + *stellein* send]

e·pis·to·lar·y (i·pis′tə·ler′ē) *adj.* **1** Belonging or suitable to a letter or correspondence by letter. **2** Included in or maintained by letters. Also **ep·is·tol·ic** (ep′is·tol′ik), **ep′is·tol′i·cal.**

ep·i·taph (ep′ə·taf, -täf) *n.* An inscription on a tomb or monument in honor or in memory of the dead. [< Gk. *epi-* upon, at + *taphos* a tomb] —**ep′i·taph′ic** (-taf′ik) *adj.*

ep·i·the·li·um (ep′ə·thē′lē·əm) *n. pl.* **·li·ums** or **·li·a** (-lē·ə) The membranous tissue covering the inner and outer surfaces of the body [< EPI- + Gk. *thēlē* nipple]

ep·i·thet (ep′ə·thet) *n.* A word or phrase, often disparaging, used to describe or to substitute for the name of a person or thing. [< L < Gk. < *epi-* upon + *tithenai* place] —**ep′i·thet′ic** or **·i·cal** *adj.*

e·pit·o·me (i·pit′ə·mē) *n.* **1** A typical example; essence; embodiment: the *epitome* of arrogance. **2** A concise summary; abridgement. [< Gk. *epitomē*] —**ep·i·tom·ic** (ep′ə·tom′ik) or **·i·cal** *adj.*, **e·pit′o·mist**, **e·pit′o·miz′er** *n.*

e·pit·o·mize (i·pit′ə·mīz) *v.t.* **·mized**, **·miz·ing** **1** To abridge. **2** To be an epitome of.

ep·i·zo·ot·ic (ep′ə·zō·ot′ik) *adj.* Common to or affecting many animals at one time. —*n.* An epizootic disease: also **ep′i·zo′o·ty** (-zō′ə·tē). [< EPI- + Gk. *zōion* animal]

e plu·ri·bus u·num (ē plŏŏr′ə·bəs yōō′nəm) *Latin* One out of many: a motto of the U.S.

ep·och (ep′ək, *Brit.* ē′pok) *n.* **1** A point in time which marks the beginning of some new development, condition, discovery, etc. **2** An interval of time regarded in terms of extraordinary events and far-reaching results. **3** *Geol.* A time interval shorter than a period. **4** *Astron.* An arbitrarily chosen moment of time, used as a reference point. [< Gk. *epochē* a stoppage, point of time] —**ep′och·al** *adj.*

ep·ode (ep′ōd) *n.* **1** That part of a Greek ode following the strophe and antistrophe. **2** A species of lyric poem, in which a longer line is followed by a shorter one. [< Gk. *epi-* in addition + *aidein* sing]

ep·o·nym (ep′ə·nim) *n.* **1** A person from whose name the name of a nation, epoch, etc., is derived or supposedly derived. **2** A person whose name is identified with some epoch, movement, etc. [< Gk. *epi-* upon + *onyma* name] —**ep′o·nym′ic** (-nim′ik), **e·pon·y·mous** (i·pon′ə·məs) *adj.*

e·pox·y (i·pok′sē) *adj.* Designating an oxygen-carbon bond characteristic of certain durable resins used for varnishes and adhesives. [< EP(I-) + OXY-]

ep·si·lon (ep′sə·lon) *n.* The fifth letter of the Greek alphabet (E, ε).

Epsom salts A bitter, white salt, magnesium sulfate, used as a cathartic. Also **Epsom salt.** [< *Epsom*, England]

eq. equal; equation; equivalent.

eq·ua·ble (ek′wə·bəl, ē′kwə-) *adj.* **1** Of uniform condition or movement; steady; even. **2** Not readily disturbed. [< L *aequare* make equal] —**eq′ua·bil′i·ty** (-bil′ə·tē) *n.* —**eq′ua·bly** *adv.*

e·qual (ē′kwəl) *adj.* **1** Of the same size, quantity, intensity, value, etc. **2** Having the same rank, rights, importance, etc. **3** Fair; impartial; just: *equal* laws. **4** Having the strength, ability, requirements, etc., that are needed: with *to.* **5** Balanced; level; even. —*v.t.* **e·qualed** or **e·qualled**, **e·qual·ing** or **e·qual·ling 1** To be or become equal to. **2** To do or produce something equal to. —*n.* A person or thing equal to another. [< L *aequus* even] —**e′qual·ly** *adv.* —**e′qual·ness** *n.*

e·qual·i·tar·i·an (i·kwol′ə·târ′ē·ən) *adj. & n.* EGALITARIAN.

e·qual·i·ty (i·kwol′ə·tē) *n. pl.* **·ties 1** The state or an instance of being equal. **2** An equation.

e·qual·ize (ē′kwəl·īz) *v.t.* **·ized**, **·iz·ing 1** To make equal. **2** To render uniform. *Brit. sp.* **e′qual·ise.** —**e′qual·i·za′tion**, **e′qual·iz′er** *n.*

e·qua·nim·i·ty (ē′kwə·nim′ə·tē, ek′wə-) *n.* Evenness of mind or temper; composure; calmness. [< L *aequus* even + *animus* mind] —**Syn.** repose, serenity, self-possession, poise, tranquility.

e·quate (i·kwāt′) *v.t.* **e·quat·ed**, **e·quat·ing 1** To make equal. **2** To treat, consider, or express as equivalent. **3** *Math.* To indicate the equality of.

e·qua·tion (i·kwā′zhən, -shən) *n.* **1** The process or act of making equal. **2** The state of being equal. **3** A complex of interrelated and variable elements or factors: the human *equation.* **4** A mathematical statement expressing the equality of two quantities. **5** *Chem.* A quantitative, symbolic representation of a chemical reaction. —**e·qua′tion·al** *adj.* —**e·qua′tion·al·ly** *adv.*

e·qua·tor (i·kwā′tər) *n.* **1** A circle around the earth, at right angles to its axis and equidistant from the poles. **2** Any similar circle, as of the sun, a planet, etc. **3** CELESTIAL EQUATOR. [< LL *(circulus) aequator* equalizer (circle)]

e·qua·to·ri·al (ē′kwə·tôr′ē·əl, -tō′rē-) *adj.* **1** Of, pertaining to, or near an equator. **2** Pertaining to conditions at or near the earth's equator.

Equatorial Guinea (gin′ē) *n.* A republic in w Africa, 9,828 sq. mi., cap. Santa Isabel. • See map at AFRICA.

eq·uer·ry (ek′wə·rē) *n. pl.* **·ries 1** An officer having charge of the horses of a prince or nobleman. **2** An attendant upon a member of a royal household, as in England. Also **eq′uer·y.** [< OF *escuier* riding master]

e·ques·tri·an (i·kwes′trē·ən) *adj.* **1** Pertaining to horses or horsemanship. **2** On horseback. —*n.* One skilled in horsemanship. [< L *equus* a horse] —**e·ques′tri·enne′** (-en′) *n. Fem.*

equi- *combining form* Equal; equally: *equidistant.* [< L *aequus* equal]

e·qui·an·gu·lar (ē′kwē·ang′gyə·lər) *adj.* Having angles that are all equal.

e·qui·dis·tant (ē′kwə·dis′tənt) *adj.* Equally distant. —**e′qui·dis′tance** *n.*

e·qui·lat·er·al (ē′kwə·lat′ər·əl) *adj.* Having all the sides equal. —**e·qui·lat′er·al·ly** *adv.*

e·qui·li·brate (ē′kwə·lī′brāt, i·kwil′ə-) *v.t. & v.i.* **·brat·ed**, **·brat·ing 1** To bring into or be in a state of equilibrium. **2** To balance or counterbalance. [< L *aequus* equal + *libratus* level] —**e′qui·li·bra′tion**, **e′qui·li′·bra·tor** *n.*

Equilateral triangle

e·qui·lib·ri·um (ē′kwə·lib′rē·əm) *n.* **1** A state of balance produced by the counteraction of two or more forces or influences in a system. **2** Bodily balance. **3** Mental or emotional balance or poise. Also **e′qui·lib′ri·ty.** [< L *aequus* equal + *libra* a balance]

e·quine (ē′kwīn, ek′wīn) *adj.* Of, pertaining to, or like a horse. —*n.* A horse. [< L *equus* horse]

e·qui·noc·tial (ē′kwə·nok′shəl) *adj.* **1** Of, occurring at, or pertaining to either equinox.

e·qui·nox (ē′kwə·noks) *n.* **1** One of the two times in each year when the sun crosses the celestial equator, making day and night of equal length all over the earth. The **vernal** or **spring equinox** takes place about Mar. 21, the **autumnal equinox** about Sept. 21. **2** Either of two opposite points at which the sun crosses the celestial equator on these dates. [< L *aequus* equal + *nox* night]

e·quip (i·kwip′) *v.t.* **e·quipped**, **e·quip·ping 1** To furnish or prepare with whatever is needed for any purpose or undertaking. **2** To dress or attire; array. [< OF *equiper*]

eq·ui·page (ek′wə·pij) *n.* **1** The equipment for a camp, army, etc. **2** A carriage, with its horses, attendants, etc.

e·quip·ment (i·kwip′mənt) *n.* **1** The act or process of equipping. **2** The state of being equipped or furnished. **3** Those things with which a person, group, or thing is equipped for some special purpose or service.

e·qui·poise (ē′kwə·poiz, ek′wə-) *n.* **1** Equality or equal distribution, as of weight and power; equilibrium. **2** COUNTERPOISE.

eq·ui·ta·ble (ek′wə·tə·bəl) *adj.* **1** Characterized by equity, or fairness and just dealing; impartial. **2** *Law* Of, pertaining to, or valid in equity, as distinguished from common law or statute law. —**eq′ui·ta·ble·ness** n. —**eq′ui·ta·bly** adv.

eq·ui·ty (ek′wə·tē) n. pl. **·ties** 1 Fairness or impartiality; justness. 2 Something that is fair or equitable. 3 Law a Justice based on natural reason or ethical judgment. b That field of jurisprudence superseding statute law and common law when these are considered inadequate or inflexible for the purposes of justice. 4 The value of property in excess of mortgage or other liens. [< L aequus equal]

e·quiv·a·lence (i·kwiv′ə·ləns) n. The state of being equivalent. Also **e·quiv′a·len·cy.**

e·quiv·a·lent (i·kwiv′ə·lənt) adj. 1 Equal in value, force, meaning, etc. 2 Chem. Having the same valence or the same combining weight. —n. 1 That which is equivalent; something equal in value, power, effect, etc. 2 Chem. The weight of an element which combines with or displaces eight grams of oxygen or one gram of hydrogen. [< L aequus equal + valere be worth] —**e·quiv′a·lent·ly** adv. — **Syn.** adj. 1 alike, analogous, reciprocal, tantamount, same.

e·quiv·o·cal (i·kwiv′ə·kəl) adj. 1 Having two or more meanings or interpretations. 2 Uncertain; doubtful. 3 Suspicious; questionable; dubious. [< L aequus equal + vox voice] —**e·quiv′o·cal·ly** adv. —**e·quiv′o·cal·ness** n.

e·quiv·o·cate (i·kwiv′ə·kāt) v.i. **·cat·ed, ·cat·ing** To use ambiguous language with intent to deceive. —**e·quiv′o·ca′tion, e·quiv′o·ca′tor** n.

-er¹ suffix 1 A person or thing that performs the action of the root verb: checker. 2 A person concerned with or practicing a trade or profession: glover. 3 One who lives in or comes from: New Yorker. 4 A person, thing, or action related to or characterized by: three-decker. [< OE -ere, -are]

-er² suffix More: used in the comparative degree of adjectives and adverbs: harder, later. [< OE -ra, -or]

-er³ suffix Repeatedly: used in frequentative verbs: stutter. [< OE -rian]

Er erbium.

e·ra (ir′ə, ē′rə) n. 1 A system of chronological notation reckoned from some fixed point of time. 2 A period of time dating from an important date, occurrence, etc. 3 A period of time characterized by certain social, intellectual, or physical conditions, etc. 4 A date or event from which time is reckoned: the Christian era. 5 Any of the major divisions of geological time. [< L aera counters for reckoning]

e·rad·i·cate (i·rad′ə·kāt) v.t. **·cat·ed, ·cat·ing** 1 To pull up by the roots; root out. 2 To destroy utterly. [< L e- out + radix a root] —**e·rad′i·ca·ble** (-ə·kə·bəl) adj. —**e·rad′i·ca′tion, e·rad′i·ca′tor** n. —**Syn.** 2 abolish, extirpate, blot out, erase, eliminate. —**e·rad′i·ca′tive** adj.

e·rase (i·rās′) v.t. **e·rased, e·ras·ing** 1 To remove or wipe out. 2 To remove all signs or traces of; obliterate. 3 To remove (recorded matter) from (a tape). 4 Slang To kill. [< L e- out + radere scrape] —**e·ras′a·ble** adj.

e·ras·er (i·rā′sər) n. Something that erases, as a piece of rubber, felt, etc.

e·ra·sure (i·rā′shər, -zhər) n. 1 The act of erasing or the state of being erased. 2 Anything erased. 3 The place where something has been erased.

Er·a·to (er′ə·tō) Gk. Myth. The Muse of lyric and love poetry.

er·bi·um (ûr′bē·əm) n. A soft metallic element (symbol Er) of the rare-earth series. [< (Ytt)erby, town in Sweden where first found]

ere (âr) prep. Archaic Prior to; before in time. —conj. 1 Earlier than; before. 2 Sooner than; rather than. [< OE ǣr]

Er·e·bus (er′ə·bəs) Gk. Myth. A dark region under the earth through which the dead pass on their way to Hades.

e·rect (i·rekt′) v.t. 1 To construct, as a house; build. 2 To assemble the parts of; set up. 3 To set upright; lift up: to erect a flagpole. 4 To construct or formulate, as a theory. 5 To establish or cause to exist. —adj. 1 Upright in position, form, or posture; vertical. 2 Sticking upward or outward; bristling. [< L e- out + regere make straight] — **e·rect′ly** adv. —**e·rect′ness** n.

e·rec·tile (i·rek′təl, -tīl) adj. Capable of becoming erect. —**e′rec·til′i·ty** n.

e·rec·tion (i·rek′shən) n. 1 Something erected, as a building. 2 The act of erecting or the state of being erected. 3

The raising up or stiffening of a body part, as the penis, through the accumulation of blood in erectile tissue; also, the state of being so raised and stiffened.

e·rec·tor (i·rek′tər) n. 1 One who or that which erects. 2 Anat. Any of various muscles which stiffen or hold up a part of the body.

ere·long (âr′lông′, -long′) adv. Before much time has passed; soon.

er·e·mite (er′ə·mīt) n. HERMIT. [< Gk. erēmitēs] —**er·e·mit·ic** (er′ə·mit′ik) or **-i·cal,** adj.

erg (ûrg) n. Physics A unit of work or energy equal to 10^{-7} joule. [< Gk. ergon work]

er·go (ûr′gō) conj. & adv. Hence; therefore. [L]

er·gos·ter·ol (ûr·gos′tə·rōl) n. A sterol, first obtained from ergot, which is converted by ultraviolet light into vitamin D. [< ERGO(T) + STEROL]

er·got (ûr′gət) n. 1 A parasitic fungus that infects rye and other grasses and which yields several biologically potent alkaloids. 2 The disease caused by this fungus. [< OF argot spur of a cock] —**er·got·ic** (ər·got′ik), **er′got·ed** adj.

E·rie (ir′ē) n. pl. **E·rie** or **E·ries** A member of a tribe of North American Indians of Iroquoian stock, formerly inhabiting the s shores of Lake Erie.

Er·in (âr′in, ir′in) n. Ireland.

erl·king (ûrl′king′) n. In Germanic folklore, the king of the elves, malicious toward children.

er·mine (ûr′min) n. 1 A weasel of the N hemisphere, having brown fur that in winter turns white with a black tip on the tail. 2 Its fur, used in Europe for the facings of official robes, as of judges. 3 The position, rank, or functions of a judge. [< OF ermine] —**er′mined** adj.

erne (ûrn) n. SEA EAGLE. [< OE earn]

Ermine

e·rode (i·rōd′) v. **e·rod·ed, e·rod·ing** v.t. 1 To eat or wear into or away. 2 Geol. To wear down by the action of wind, water, etc. 3 To form, as a canyon, by such action. —v.i. 4 To become eroded. [< L e- off + rodere gnaw]

e·rog·e·nous (i·roj′ə·nəs) adj. Producing erotic feeling; exciting sexual desire. Also **er·o·gen·ic** (er′ə·jen′ik). [< Gk. erōs love + -GENOUS]

Er·os (ir′os, er′os) Gk. Myth. The god of love, son of Aphrodite.

e·ro·sion (i·rō′zhən) n. The act of eroding, or the state of being eroded.

e·rot·ic (i·rot′ik) adj. 1 Of, pertaining to, or tending to arouse sexual love or desire. 2 Easily aroused sexually. — n. An erotic person. [< Gk. erōs love] —**e·rot′i·cal·ly** adv. — **e·rot′i·cism** n.

e·rot·i·ca (i·rot′i·kə) n. pl. (often construed as sing.) Erotic pictures, books, etc. [< Gk. erōtikos < erōs love]

err (ûr) v.i. **erred, err·ing** 1 To make a mistake; be wrong. 2 To go astray morally; sin. [< L errare wander]

er·rand (er′ənd) n. 1 A trip made to carry a message, to purchase something, to attend to personal business, etc. 2 The reason for such a trip. [< OE ǣrende message, news]

er·rant (er′ənt) adj. 1 Roving or wandering. 2 Straying from a course that is considered proper, moral, etc. [< L iter a journey] —**er′rant·ly** adv.

er·rant·ry (er′ənt·rē) n. The vocation, conduct, or career of a knight errant.

er·rat·ic (i·rat′ik) adj. 1 Not conforming to rules or standards; queer; eccentric. 2 Irregular, as in course or direction; wandering; straying. —n. An erratic person or thing. Also **er·rat′i·cal.** [< L errare wander] —**er·rat′i·cal·ly** adv. — **Syn.** 1 odd, peculiar, capricious, abnormal, unpredictable, whimsical, changeable.

er·ra·tum (i·rā′təm, e·rä′-) n. pl. **·ra·ta** (-rä′tə, -rä′tə) An error, as in writing or printing. [L]

er·ro·ne·ous (ə·rō′nē·əs, e·rō′-) adj. Marked by error; incorrect; mistaken. —**er·ro′ne·ous·ly** adv. —**er·ro′ne·ous·ness** n.

er·ror (er′ər) n. 1 The condition of being incorrect, esp. in matters of opinion or belief. 2 Something done, said, or believed wrongly; inaccuracy; mistake. 3 Any misplay in baseball which prolongs the batter's time at bat or permits a base runner to make one or more bases. **4** A wrong-doing; transgression; sin. [< L < *errare* wander]

er·satz (er-zäts′) *n.* A substitute or replacement, usu. inferior to the original. —*adj.* Substitute. [< G *ersetzen* replace]

Erse (ûrs) *n.* **1** SCOTTISH GAELIC. **2** IRISH GAELIC. [< ME *Erisch* Irish]

erst (ûrst) *Archaic adv.* **1** Formerly; long ago; once. **2** In the beginnning. —*adj.* First. [< OE *ǣrest*]

erst·while (ûrst′ʰwīl′) *adj.* Former. —*adv. Archaic* Formerly.

e·ruct (i-rukt′) *v.t. & v.i.* BELCH. Also **e·ruc′tate.** [< L *e-* out + *ructare* belch] —**e·ruc′ta′tion** *n.*

er·u·dite (er′yōō-dīt) *adj.* Very learned; scholarly. [< L *erudire* instruct] —**er′u·dite·ly** *adv.* —**er′u·dite·ness** *n.*

er·u·di·tion (er′yōō-dish′ən) *n.* Extensive knowledge or learning.

e·rupt (i-rupt′) *v.i.* **1** To cast forth smoke, lava, etc., suddenly and with violence: The volcano *erupted.* **2** To burst forth: Steam is *erupting* from the volcano. **3** To break through a gum, as a tooth. **4** To become covered with a rash or pimples. —*v.t.* **5** To cause to burst forth. [< L *e-* out + *rumpere* burst]

e·rup·tion (i-rup′shən) *n.* **1** The act or process, or an instance, of erupting. **2** That which erupts, as lava from a volcano. **3** A breaking out, as in a rash. **4** Any sudden outbreak or outburst.

e·rup·tive (i-rup′tiv) or *adj.* Of, pertaining to, or formed by eruption. —**e·rup′tive·ly** *adv.* —**e·rup′tive·ness** *n.*

-ery *suffix of nouns* **1** A business, place of business, or place where something is done: *brewery.* **2** A place or residence for: *nunnery.* **3** A collection of goods, wares, etc.: *pottery.* **4** The qualities or practices of: *snobbery.* **5** An art, trade, or profession: *cookery.* **6** A state of being: *slavery.* [< OF *-ier*]

er·y·sip·e·las (er′ə-sip′ə-ləs, ir′ə-) *n.* An acute infectious disease of the skin, accompanied by inflammation and fever. [< Gk. *erysis* a reddening + *pella* skin]

e·ryth·ro·cyte (i-rith′rō-sīt) *n.* A red blood corpuscle, formed in bone marrow and containing hemoglobin, and serving to carry oxygen to body tissues. [< Gk. *erythros* red + -CYTE] —**e·ryth′ro·cyt′ic** (-sit′ik) *adj.*

-es[1] An inflectional ending used to form the plural of nouns ending in a sibilant *(glasses, fuses, fishes)* or an affricate *(witches, judges).* [< OE *-as*]

-es[2] An inflectional ending used to form the third person singular present indicative of verbs ending in a sibilant, affricate, or vowel: *kisses, poaches, goes.* [ME *-es*]

Es einsteinium.

E·sau (ē′sô) In the Bible, the elder son of Isaac and Rebecca, who sold his birthright to his brother Jacob.

es·ca·drille (es′kə-dril′) *n.* **1** A unit of a European air command; esp., in France, a squadron of six airplanes. **2** A squadron of naval vessels. [F < Sp. *escuadra* a squadron]

es·ca·lade (es′kə-lād′) *v.t.* **-lad·ed, -lad·ing** To scale (a wall, etc.) or enter (a fortress, etc.) by using ladders. —*n.* An attack by escalading. [< Sp. *escalar* to climb < L *scala* a ladder]

es·ca·late (es′kə-lāt) *v.t. & v.i.* **-lat·ed, -lat·ing 1** To increase or be increased: to *escalate* a war. **2** To ascend or carry up, as on an escalator. [Back formation from ESCALATOR] —**es′·ca·la′tion** *n.*

es·ca·la·tor (es′kə-lā′tər) *n.* A moving stairway, built on an endless loop of chain. [< *Escalator,* a trade name]

escalator clause A clause in a contract stipulating an increase or decrease in wages, prices, etc., under certain specified conditions.

es·cal·lop (e-skol′əp, -skal′-) *n. & v.* SCALLOP. Also **es·cal′op.**

es·ca·pade (es′kə-pād) *n.* **1** A reckless adventure or mischievous prank. **2** An escape from restraint. [< Sp. *escapar* to escape]

es·cape (ə-skāp′, e-skāp′) *v.* **es·caped, es·cap·ing** *v.t.* **1** To get away from; flee from, as guards or prison. **2** To avoid, as harm or evil. **3** To slip or come from involuntarily: No cry *escaped* him. **4** To slip away from or elude (notice or

recollection). —*v.i.* **5** To get free from or avoid arrest, custody, danger, etc. **6** To fade or slip away; disappear; vanish. **7** To come forth; emerge; leak: Gas is *escaping* from the stove. —*n.* **1** The act of escaping. **2** The fact or state of having escaped. **3** A means of escape. **4** Mental relief from monotony, anxiety, etc.: literature of *escape.* **5** Flow, as of a fluid; leakage. [< L *ex-* out + *cappa* a cloak] —**es·cap′·a·ble** *adj.* —**es·cap′er** *n.*

es·cape·ment (ə-skāp′mənt, e-skāp′-) *n.* **1** A device used in timepieces for regulating movement, consisting of an escape wheel and a detent or lock, through which periodic impulses are sent to the balance wheel. **2** A mechanism controlling the horizontal movement of a typewriter carriage.

escape velocity The minimum velocity at which a body has energy to escape from a gravitational field, as from that of the earth.

escape wheel A toothed wheel in an escapement.

es·cap·ism (ə-skā′piz·əm) *n.* A diversion of the mind from those realities of life which are unpleasant or monotonous, esp. by entertainment, daydreaming, etc. —**es·cap′ist** *adj., n.*

es·ca·role (es′kə-rōl) *n.* A variety of endive, used in salads.

es·carp·ment (es-kärp′mənt) *n.* **1** A precipitous artificial slope about a fortification or position. **2** A steep slope or cliff. [< Ital. *scarpa* a slope]

-esce *suffix* To become or grow; begin to be or do: *phosphoresce.* [< L *-escere,* suffix of inceptive verbs]

-escence *suffix* State or quality: *effervescence.* [< L *-escentia*]

-escent *suffix* Beginning to be, have, or do: *effervescent.* [< L *-escens,* suffix of pr.p. of inceptive verbs]

es·cheat (es-chēt′) *Law v.t. & v.i.* To revert, or cause to revert, to the state or crown. —*n.* **1** The reversion of property to the state in the U.S., or to the crown in England, when there are no legal heirs. **2** Property so reverted. [< OF *es-* out + *cheoir* fall] —**es·cheat′a·ble** *adj.* —**es·cheat′age** *n.*

es·chew (es-chōō′) *v.t.* To shun, as something unworthy or injurious. [< OF *eschiver*] —**es·chew′al** *n.*

es·cort (es-kôrt′) *v.t.* To accompany; go with, as from courtesy or to protect. —*n.* (es′kôrt) **1** One or more persons accompanying another person or persons, an object, etc., for protection or as a mark of respect. **2** One or more ships, planes, etc. accompanying another to furnish protection, guidance, etc. **3** A male who accompanies a woman on a date. [< Ital. *scorgere* lead]

es·cri·toire (es′kri·twär′) *n.* A writing desk. [< OF < L *scribere* write]

es·crow (es′krō, es·krō′) *n. Law* A deed, bond, piece of property, or money put in the custody of a third person until certain conditions are fulfilled. [< OF *escroe* a scroll]

es·cu·do (es·kōō′dō) *n. pl.* **-dos 1** The monetary unit of Portugal and Portuguese territories. **2** An obsolete silver or gold coin of the Hispanic countries. [< L *scutum* shield]

es·cu·lent (es′kyə·lənt) *adj.* Suitable for food; edible. —*n.* Anything suitable for food. [< L *esca* food]

es·cutch·eon (i-skuch′ən) *n. Her.* The surface, usu. shield-shaped, upon which armorial bearings are displayed; a heraldic shield. [< L *scutum* shield]

Escutcheon

Es·dras (ez′drəs) In the Douay Bible, the name for Ezra.

-ese *suffix* **1** A native or inhabitant of: *Milanese.* **2** The language or dialect of: *Chinese.* **3** Originating in; denoting the inhabitants or language of: *Tirolese.* **4** In the manner or style of: *journalese.* [< L *-ensis*]

ESE, E.S.E., ese, e.s.e. east southeast.

Es·ki·mo (es′kə·mō) *n. pl.* **-mos 1** A member of a Mongoloid people indigenous to the Arctic coasts of North America, Greenland, and NE Siberia. **2** The language of the Eskimos. —**Es′ki·mo′an** *adj.*

Eskimo dog One of a breed of large, sturdy, broad-chested dogs used by the Eskimos to pull sleds.

---

add, āce, câre, pălm; end, ēven; it, īce; odd, ōpen, ôrder; tŏŏk, pōōl; up, bûrn; ə = *a* in *above, u* in *focus;* yōō = *u* in *fuse;* oil; pout; check; go; ring; thin; ᵺis; zh, *vision.* < derived from; ? origin uncertain or unknown.

e·soph·a·gus (i·sof'ə·gəs) *n. pl.* **·gi** (-gī, -jī) The tube through which food passes from the mouth to the stomach; gullet. [< Gk. *oisophagos*] —**e·so·phag·e·al** (ē'sō·faj'ē·əl, i·sof'ə·jē'əl), **e·soph'a·gal** (-ə·gəl) *adj.* • See LIVER.

es·o·ter·ic (es'ə·ter'ik) *adj.* 1 Confined to a select circle; confidential. 2 Designed for or understood by an initiated and enlightened few; abstruse; profound. [< Gk. *esōterikos* inner] —**es'o·ter'i·cal·ly** *adv.*

ESP extrasensory perception.

esp., espec. especially.

es·pal·ier (es·pal'yər) *n.* 1 A trellis on which small trees, shrubs, etc., are trained to grow in flat patterns. 2 A tree or row of plants so trained. —*v.t.* To train on or furnish with an espalier. [F]

es·pe·cial (es·pesh'əl) *adj.* Exceptional; outstanding; special. [< OF, special] —**es·pe'cial·ly** *adv.*

Es·pe·ran·to (es'pə·rän'tō) *n.* An artificial language with a vocabulary based on words common to important European languages. [< Dr. *Esperanto*, pen name of L. L. Zamenhof, 1859–1917, Russ. scholar] —**Es'pe·ran'tism, Es'pe·ran'tist** *n.*

Espaliered tree

es·pi·al (es·pī'əl) *n.* 1 The act of spying or observing. 2 Discovery or notice.

es·pi·o·nage (es'pē·ə·näzh, -naj, -nij) *n.* 1 The practice of spying. 2 The employment and activities of spies and secret agents, esp. in time of war. [< F < *espier* espy]

es·pla·nade (es'plə·nād', -näd') *n.* A level open space, as before a fortress or along a waterside, for promenading, driving, etc. [F < L *ex* out + *planus* level]

es·pou·sal (es·pou'zəl) *adj.* Of or pertaining to a betrothal or marriage. —*n.* 1 Betrothal. 2 Marriage. 3 The act of taking up or supporting, as a cause or principle.

es·pouse (es·pouz') *v.t.* **·poused, ·pous·ing** 1 To take as a spouse; marry. 2 To take up or support, as a cause or doctrine. [< L *spondere* promise] —**es·pous'er** *n.*

es·pres·so (es·pres'sō) *n. pl.* **·sos** Coffee made from dark, roasted beans, usu. by an infusion of steam under pressure. [Ital. < *esprimere* to press out]

es·prit (es·prē') *n.* Spirit; wit. [F < L *spiritus*]

esprit de corps (də kôr') A feeling of pride in and devotion to the common goals of some group. [F, lit., spirit of a body]

es·py (es·pī') *v.t.* **es·pied, es·py·ing** To catch sight of; see. [< OF *espier* to look, spy]

Esq., Esqr. Esquire.

-esque *suffix* Like; in the manner or style of: *picturesque, arabesque.* [F < Ital. *-esco*]

Es·qui·mau (es'kə·mō) *n. pl.* **·mau** or **·maux** (mōz) ESKIMO.

es·quire (es'kwīr, es·kwīr') *n.* 1 *Usu. cap.* A title of courtesy, usu. abbreviated after a man's surname. 2 In England, a member of the gentry ranking next below a knight. 3 A candidate for knighthood serving as an attendant to a knight. [< LL *scutarius* shield-bearer]

-ess *suffix* Female: *goddess, lioness.* [< OF < LL *-issa*]

es·say (e·sā') *v.t.* To try to do or accomplish; attempt. —*n.* 1 (es'ā) A literary composition, esp. one dealing with a single subject from a personal point of view. 2 (e·sā') An endeavor; effort. [< OF *essai* a trial] —**es·say'er** *n.*

es·say·ist (es'ā·ist) *n.* A writer of essays.

es·sence (es'əns) *n.* 1 The intrinsic nature or characteristic quality of anything; that which makes a thing what it is. 2 Something that is; an existent being or entity. 3 A substance considered to have, in concentrated form, the special qualities (as flavor, scent, etc.) of the plant, food, drug, etc. from which it was taken. 4 An alcoholic solution of such a substance. 5 Perfume; scent. [< L *esse* be] —**Syn.** 1 substance, gist, quintessence, reality, kernel, pith, core.

es·sen·tial (ə·sen'shəl) *adj.* 1 Of or pertaining to the essence or intrinsic nature of anything; substantial; basic. 2 Indispensable, necessary, or highly important. —*n.* That which is fundamental, basic, or indispensable. —**es·sen'ti·al·i·ty** (-shē·al'ə·tē) *n.* —**es·sen'tial·ly** *adv.*

essential oil Any of a group of volatile oils which give to plants their characteristic odor and taste.

-est¹ *suffix* Most: used in the superlative degree of adjectives and adverbs: *hardest, latest.* [< OE *-ast, -est, -ost*]

-est² An archaic inflectional ending used in the second person singular present and past indicative, with *thou: eatest, walkest.* [< OE]

EST, E.S.T., e.s.t. eastern standard time.

es·tab·lish (es·tab'lish) *v.t.* 1 To settle or fix firmly; make stable or permanent. 2 To set up; found, as an institution or business. 3 To set up; install (oneself or someone else) in business, a position, etc. 4 To cause to be recognized or accepted. 5 To put into effect permanently; ordain, as laws. 6 To gain acceptance for; prove, as a theory or argument. 7 To appoint (a church) as a national institution. [< L *stabilire* to make firm or stable] —**es·tab'lish·er** *n.*

established church A church maintained by a nation and receiving financial support out of public funds.

es·tab·lish·ment (es·tab'lish·mənt) *n.* 1 The act of establishing. 2 The state of being established. 3 Anything established, as a place of business. —**the Establishment** Those collectively who occupy positions of influence and status in a society.

es·tate (es·tāt') *n.* 1 One's entire property, possessions, and wealth. 2 Landed property, esp. a large tract of land with an elaborate residence, etc. 3 Condition or state: man's *estate.* 4 A class or order of persons in a state. 5 *Law* The degree, nature, and amount of one's lawful interest in any property. [< L *status* state]

estate car *Brit.* STATION WAGON.

es·teem (es·tēm') *n.* Favorable opinion or estimation; respect; regard. —*v.t.* 1 To value highly. 2 To think to be; deem; consider: to *esteem* one fortunate. [< L *aestimare* to value]

es·ter (es'tər) *n. Chem.* Any of numerous organic compounds comparable to inorganic salts, formed by the reaction of an acid with an alcohol. [< G *Essigäther* vinegar ether]

Es·ther (es'tər) 1 In the Bible, the Jewish wife of a Persian king. 2 The Old Testament book that tells her story.

es·thete (es'thēt) *n.* AESTHETE.

es·thet·ic (es·thet'ik) *adj.* AESTHETIC.

es·thet·ics (es·thet'iks) *n.* AESTHETICS.

es·ti·ma·ble (es'tə·mə·bəl) *adj.* 1 Deserving of esteem. 2 That may be estimated or calculated. —**es'ti·ma·ble·ness** *n.* —**es'ti·ma·bly** *adv.*

es·ti·mate (es'tə·māt) *v.* **·mat·ed, ·mat·ing** *v.t.* 1 To form an approximate opinion of (size, amount, number, etc.); calculate roughly. 2 To form an opinion about; judge, as character. —*v.i.* 3 To make or submit an estimate. —*n.* (es'tə·mit) 1 A rough calculation. 2 A statement, as by a builder, in regard to the cost of certain work. 3 A judgment; opinion; evaluation. [< L *aestimare* to value] —**es'ti·ma·tive** *adj.* —**es'ti·ma·tor** *n.*

es·ti·ma·tion (es'tə·mā'shən) *n.* 1 The act of estimating. 2 Opinion; estimate. 3 Esteem; regard.

Es·to·ni·an (es·tō'nē·ən) *adj.* Of or pertaining to Estonia, its people, or their language. —*n.* 1 A native or citizen of Estonia. 2 The Finno-Ugric language of the Estonians.

es·top (es·top') *v.t.* **·topped, ·top·ping** To stop or prevent, esp. by estoppel. [< LL *stuppare* to stop up]

es·top·pel (es·top'əl) *n. Law* A legal impediment by which one is forbidden to contradict or deny one's own previous statement or act.

es·trange (es·trānj') *v.t.* **·tranged, ·trang·ing** 1 To make (someone previously friendly or affectionate) indifferent or hostile; alienate. 2 To remove or dissociate (oneself, etc.): to *estrange* oneself from society. [< L *extraneus* foreign] —**es·trange'ment** *n.*

es·tro·gen (es'trə·jən) *n.* Any of several hormones exercising a critical influence on the female sexual cycle. [< ESTRUS + -GEN] —**es'tro·gen'ic** *adj.*

es·trus (es'trəs, ēs'-) *n. Zool.* The peak of the sexual cycle in animals, culminating in ovulation; heat or rut, esp. in female mammals. [< Gk. *oistros* a gadfly] —**es'tru·al** *adj.*

es·tu·ar·y (es'chōō·er'ē) *n. pl.* **·ar·ies** 1 The wide mouth of a river where it is met by and mixes with the sea. 2 An arm or inlet of a sea. [< L *aestus* tide]

-et *suffix* Small; little: *islet.* [< OF < LL *-itus, -ita*]

e·ta (ā'tə, ē'-) *n.* The seventh letter of the Greek alphabet (H, η).

et al. and others (L *et alii*); and elsewhere (L *et alibi*).

etc. et cetera.

et cet·er·a (et set′ər·ə, set′rə) And other things; and the rest; and so forth. Also **et caet′er·a.** [L]

etch (ech) *v.t.* **1** To produce (a design, drawing, etc.) on glass, metal, etc. by the corrosive action of an acid. **2** To engrave (metal, glass, etc.) in this manner. **3** To impress deeply and clearly. —*v.i.* **4** To make etchings. [< G *ätzen*] —**etch′er** *n.*

etch·ing (ech′ing) *n.* **1** The act, art, or process of making designs on metal, glass, etc., by the corrosive action of acid. **2** A figure or design formed by etching. **3** An impression or print made from an etched plate.

e·ter·nal (i·tûr′nəl) *adj.* **1** Having neither beginning nor end of existence; infinite in duration. **2** Having no end; everlasting. **3** Continued without interruption; perpetual. **4** Independent of time or its conditions; timeless; unchangeable; immutable. **5** Of or pertaining to eternity. **6** Appearing interminable; incessant: Vaughn and his *eternal* jokes. —**the Eternal** God. [< L *aeternus*] —**e·ter′nal·ly** *adv.* —**e·ter′nal·ness** *n.*

Eternal City Rome.

e·ter·ni·ty (i·tûr′nə·tē) *n. pl.* **·ties 1** The fact, state, or quality of being eternal. **2** Infinite duration or existence. **3** A seemingly endless or limitless time. **4** Immortality.

e·ter·nize (i·tûr′nīz) *v.t.* **·nized, ·niz·ing 1** To make eternal. **2** To perpetuate the fame of; immortalize. *Brit. sp.* **e·ter′·nise.** —**e·ter′ni·za′tion** *n.*

-eth[1] An archaic inflectional ending used in the third person singular present indicative of some verbs: *eateth, drinketh.* [< OE *-ath, -eth, -oth*]

-eth[2] *suffix* Var. of **-TH**[2].

Eth. Ethiopia; Ethiopian; Ethiopic.

eth·ane (eth′ān) *n.* A colorless, odorless gas, of the paraffin series, contained in natural gas and illuminating gas. [< ETHYL]

eth·a·nol (eth′ə·nôl) *n.* ALCOHOL (def. 1).

e·ther (ē′thər) *n.* **1** *Chem* **a** A colorless, flammable, volatile, liquid organic compound, used as an anesthetic and solvent. **b** Any of a group of organic compounds in which an oxygen atom is joined with two organic radicals. **2** A perfectly elastic medium formerly assumed to pervade all of space. **3** The upper air. [< L *aether* sky]

e·the·re·al (i·thir′ē·əl) *adj.* **1** Having the nature of ether or air. **2** Light; airy; fine; subtle; exquisite. **3** Existing in or belonging to the ether or upper air; aerial; heavenly. **4** Of or pertaining to ether. —**e·the·re·al′i·ty, e·the′re·al·ness** *n.* —**e·the′re·al·ly** *adv.*

e·the·re·al·ize (i·thir′ē·əl·īz) *v.t.* & *v.i.* **·ized, ·iz·ing** To make or become ethereal. —**e·the′re·al·i·za′tion** *n.*

e·ther·ize (ē′thə·rīz) *v.t.* **·ized, ·iz·ing 1** To subject to the influence of ether; anesthetize. **2** To change into ether. —**e′ther·i·za′tion, e′ther·iz′er** *n.*

eth·ic (eth′ik) *adj.* Ethical; moral. —*n.* **1** The philosophy or a system of morals; ethics. **2** A single principle of a system of ethics. [< Gk. *ēthos* character, custom]

eth·i·cal (eth′i·kəl) *adj.* **1** Pertaining or relating to ethics. **2** Treating of morals. **3** In accordance with right principles, as defined by a given system of ethics or professional conduct. —**eth′i·cal′i·ty, eth′i·cal·ness** *n.* —**eth′i·cal·ly** *adv.* — **Syn. 3** moral, just, righteous, virtuous.

eth·ics (eth′iks) *n.pl.* (*construed as sing. in defs.* 1 & 3) **1** The study and philosophy of human conduct, with emphasis on the determination of right and wrong. **2** The basic principles of right action, esp. with reference to a particular person, profession, etc. **3** A work or treatise on morals.

E·thi·o·pi·a (ē′thē·ō′pē·ə) *n.* A constitutional monarchy in E Africa, 350,000 sq. mi., cap. Addis Ababa. —**E′thi·o′pi·an** *adj., n.* •See map at AFRICA.

eth·nic (eth′nik) *adj.* **1** Of, pertaining to, or belonging to groups of mankind who are of the same race or nationality and who share a common language, culture, etc. **2** Pertaining to peoples neither Jewish nor Christian. —*n. Informal* A member of a minority ethnic group, esp., in the U.S., a nonblack minority. Also **eth′ni·cal.** [< Gk. *ethnos* nation] —**eth′ni·cal·ly** *adv.* —**eth·nic·i·ty** (eth·nis′ə·te) *n.*

ethno- *combining form* Race, nation; peoples: *ethnography.* Also **ethn-.**

eth·nog·ra·phy (eth·nog′rə·fē) *n.* **1** The branch of anthropology that is concerned with the classification and description of particular, esp. primitive, human cultures. **2** Loosely, ethnology.

eth·nol·o·gy (eth·nol′ə·jē) *n.* The science of the subdivisions and families of men, their origins, characteristics, distribution, and physical and linguistic classification. —**eth·no·log·i·cal** (eth′nō·loj′i·kəl) or **eth′no·log′ic** *adj.* —**eth′·no·log′i·cal·ly** *adv.*

e·thol·o·gy (i·thol′e·jē) *n.* The science of animal behavior. [< Gk. *ēthos* character + -LOGY] —**e·tho·log·ic** (ē′thə·loj′ik) or **·i·cal** *adj.* —**e·thol′o·gist** *n.*

eth·yl (eth′il) *n. Chem.* The hydrocarbon radical of the paraffin series, present in numerous widely used compounds. [ETH(ER) + -YL] —**eth·yl′ic** *adj.*

ethyl alcohol ALCOHOL (def. 1).

eth·y·lene (eth′ə·lēn) *n. Chem.* A colorless, flammable, unsaturated hydrocarbon contained in coal gas.

e·ti·ol·o·gy (ē′tē·ol′ə·jē) *n.* **1** The science or branch of knowledge which deals with causes or origins. **2** That branch of medicine that treats of the causes of disease. **3** The causes or origin of a particular disease. [< Gk. *aitia* cause + -LOGY] —**e·ti·o·log·i·cal** (ē′tē·ə·loj′i·kəl) *adj.* — **e′ti·o·log′i·cal·ly** *adv.* —**e′ti·ol′o·gist** *n.*

et·i·quette (et′ə·ket, -kət) *n.* The rules and customs for polite social or professional behavior. [< OF *estiquette* routine, ticket]

Et·na (et′nə) *n.* A volcano in NE Sicily; 10,902 feet. —**Et·ne·an** (et·nē′ən) *adj.*

Eton jacket A short black jacket cut off square at the hips and worn open, usu. with a white, overlapping collar, the **Eton collar.** [< *Eton* College, British public school]

E·tru·ri·a (i·trŏŏr′ē·ə) *n.* An ancient country of W. CEN. Italy. —**E·tru′ri·an** *adj., n.*

E·trus·can (i·trus′kən) *adj.* Of or relating to ancient Etruria, its people, language, or culture. —*n.* **1** One of the ancient people of Etruria. **2** The extinct language of the Etruscans.

et. seq. and the following (L *et sequens*); and those that follow (L *et sequentes* or *et sequentia*).

-ette *suffix* **1** Little, small: *kitchenette.* **2** Resembling; like; imitating: *leatherette.* **3** Feminine: *farmerette.* [F]

é·tude (ā′tood) *n. Music* A composition designed to illustrate and develop some phase of technique, but often played as well for its artistic merit. [F, study]

et·y·mol·o·gy (et′ə·mol′ə·jē) *n. pl.* **·gies 1** The history of a word, prefix, suffix, etc., tracing it back to its earliest known form or root. **2** The branch of linguistics dealing with the origin and development of words, prefixes, etc. [< Gk. *etymon* original meaning + -LOGY]

eu- *prefix* Good; well: *euphony.* [< Gk. *eus* good]

Eu europium.

eu·ca·lyp·tus (yoo′kə·lip′təs) *n. pl.* **·lyp·tus·es** or **·lyp·ti** (-tī) Any of a genus of large, chiefly Australian evergreen trees of the myrtle family, widely used as timber and in the preparation of drugs, esp. the volatile, pungent, essential **oil of eucalyptus.** [< Gk. *eu-* well + *kalyptos* covered]

Eucalyptus branch

Eu·char·ist (yoo′kə·rist) *n.* **1** A Christian sacrament in which bread and wine are consecrated, distributed, and consumed in commemoration of the passion and death of Christ. **2** The consecrated bread and wine of this sacrament.[< Gk. *eu-* well + *charizesthai* give thanks] —**eu′cha·ris′tic** or **·ti·cal** *adj.*

eu·chre (yoo′kər) *n.* **1** A card game for two to four players, played with 32 cards. **2** An instance of euchring an opponent or of being euchred. —*v.t.* **eu·chred** (-kərd), **eu·chring 1** In the game of euchre, to prevent (an opponent) from taking three tricks. **2** *Informal* To outwit or defeat.

Eu·clid·e·an (yoo·klid′ē·ən) *adj.* Of or pertaining to Euclid, his geometry, or a geometry based on similar principles. Also **Eu·clid′i·an.**

---

add, āce, câre, pälm; end, ēven; it, īce; odd, ōpen, ôrder; took, pool; up, bûrn; ə = a in *above, u* in *focus;* yoo = u in *fuse;* oil; pout; check; go; ring; thin; this; zh, *vision.* < derived from; ? origin uncertain or unknown.

eu·gen·ic (yōō·jen'ik) *adj.* Relating to or fitted for the development and improvement of the race. Also **eu·gen'·i·cal.** [<Gk. *eugenēs* well-born] —**eu·gen'i·cal·ly** *adv.*

eu·gen·i·cist (yōō·jen'ə·sist) *n.* A student or advocate of eugenics. Also **eu·ge·nist** (yōō'jə·nist, yōō·jen'ist).

eu·gen·ics (yōō·jen'iks) *n. pl. (construed as sing.)* The science and art of improving a race or breed by mating individuals with desired characteristics.

eu·lo·gist (yōō'lə·jist) *n.* One who eulogizes.

eu·lo·gize (yōō'lə·jīz) *v.t.* **·gized, ·giz·ing** 1 To speak or write a eulogy about. 2 To praise highly. *Brit. sp.* **eu'lo·gise.** —**eu·lo·gis·tic** (yōō'lə·jis'tik) or **·ti·cal** *adj.* —**eu'lo·gis'ti·cal·ly** *adv.* **Meu'lo·giz'er** *n.* —**Syn.** 2 laud, extol, glorify.

eu·lo·gy (yōō'lə·jē) *n. pl.* **·gies** 1 A spoken or written composition in praise of a person's life or character. 2 High praise. Also **eu'lo·gism, eu·lo·gi·um** (yōō·lō'jē·əm). [<Gk. *eu-* well + *legein* speak] —**eu'lo·gist** *adj.*

Eu·men·i·des (yōō·men'ə·dēz) *Gk. Myth.* FURIES.

eu·nuch (yōō'nək) *n.* A castrated man, esp. one formerly employed as a harem attendant or an Oriental palace official. [<Gk. *eunouchos* chamber attendant]

eu·phe·mism (yōō'fə·miz'əm) *n.* 1 A mild or agreeable expression substituted for a realistic description of something disagreeable. 2 The use of such an expression. [< Gk. *euphemizein* to euphemize] —**eu'phe·mist** *n.* —**eu'phe·mis'tic** or **·ti·cal** *adj.* —**eu'phe·mis'ti·cal·ly** *adv.*

eu·phe·mize (yōō'fə·mīz) *v.t. & v.i.* **·mized, ·miz·ing** To say or write in euphemistic form. —**eu'phe·miz'er** *n.*

eu·phon·ic (yōō·fon'ik) *adj.* 1 Agreeable in sound; euphonious. 2 Of or pertaining to euphony.

eu·pho·ni·ous (yōō·fō'nē·əs) *adj.* Pleasant in sound, as a word; characterized by euphony. —**eu·pho'ni·ous·ly** *adv.* —**eu·pho'ni·ous·ness** *n.*

eu·pho·ni·um (yōō·fō'nē·əm) *n. Music* A type of small tuba, often used in bands. [<Gk. *euphōnos* euphonious]

eu·pho·ny (yōō'fə·nē) *n. pl.* **·nies** 1 Agreeableness of sound. 2 Pleasant-sounding combination or arrangement of words. [<Gk. *eu-* good + *phonē* sound]

eu·phor·bi·a (yōō·fôr'bē·ə) *n.* Any plant of a large and widely distributed genus of herbs, characterized by their milky juice and various medicinal properties [<*Euphorbos,* a Greek physician of the first century A.D.]

eu·pho·ri·a (yōō·fôr'ē·ə, -fō'rē·ə) *n.* 1 A sense of great well-being and joy. 2 *Psychol.* Exaggerated and usu. unfounded high spirits. [<Gk. *eupherein* be well] —**eu·phor·ic** (yōō·fôr'ik, -for'-) *adj.*

eu·phu·ism (yōō'fyōō·iz'əm) *n.* 1 An artificial, elegant style of speech or writing characterized by the excessive use of alliteration, antithesis, balance, etc. 2 An instance of such a style. 3 Affected elegance in language [<*Euphues,* character created by John Lyly, English writer, 1554?–1606] —**eu'phu·ist** *n.* —**eu'phu·is'tic** or **·ti·cal** *adj.* —**eu'phu·is'ti·cal·ly** *adv.*

Eur. Europe; European.

Eur·a·sian (yōō·rā'zhən, -shən) *adj.* 1 Pertaining to both Europe and Asia. 2 Of European and Asian descent. —*n.* A person of mixed European and Asian parentage.

eu·re·ka (yōō·rē'kə) *interj.* I have found (it): a triumphal exclamation. [<Gk. *heurēka*]

eu·rhyth·mics (yōō·rith'miks) *n.* EURYTHMICS.

Euro- *combining form* 1 Europe. 2 European. 3 Europe and. 4 European and. Also **Eur-.**

Eu·ro·crat (yōōr'ō·krat) *n.* A member of the administrative staff of the European Economic Community. [<EURO- + -CRAT, a pun on BUREAUCRAT]

Eu·ro·dol·lar (yōōr'ō·dol'ər) *n.* A U.S. dollar on deposit outside the U.S., esp. in one of the western European countries. [<EURO- + DOLLAR]

Eu·ro·pa (yōō·rō'pə) *Gk. Myth.* A Phoenician princess abducted to Crete by Zeus in the guise of a bull.

Eu·rope (yōōr'əp) *n.* A continent comprising the W part of the Eurasian land mass, between the Atlantic Ocean and Asia, about 3,800,000 square miles. —**Eu·ro·pe·an** (yōōr'ə·pē'ən) *adj., n.*

European Economic Community The official name of the Common Market, an economic association originally established in 1958 by France, Italy, West Germany, and the Benelux nations.

Eu·ro·pe·an·ize (yōōr'ə·pē'ən·īz) *v.t.* **·ized, ·iz·ing** To make European in characteristics, views, culture, etc. —**Eu'ro·pe'an·i·za'tion** *n.*

European plan The system of hotel-keeping by which lodging and service are charged for separately from meals.

eu·ro·pi·um (yōō·rō'pē·əm) *n.* A soft metallic element (symbol Eu) of the rare earth series. [<L *Europa* Europe]

Eu·ryd·i·ce (yōō·rid'ə·sē) *Gk. Myth.* The wife of Orpheus.

eu·ryth·mics (yōō·rith'miks) *n. pl. (construed as sing.)* The art of performing rhythmical bodily movement, usu. in interpretation of music. [<Gk. *eurythmia* harmony]

Eu·sta·chi·an tube (yōō·stā'shē·ən, -shən) A passage between the pharynx and the inner ear, serving to equalize air pressure on both sides of the eardrum. [<Bartolommeo *Eustachio,* Italian anatomist, died 1574.]

Eu·ter·pe (yōō·tûr'pē) *Gk. Myth.* The Muse of lyric song and music. —**Eu·ter'pe·an** *adj.*

eu·tha·na·si·a (yōō'thə·nā'zhē·ə, -zhə) *n.* 1 Painless, peaceful death. 2 The deliberate putting to death of a person suffering from a painful and incurable disease; mercy killing. [<Gk. *eu-* good + *thanatos* death]

eu·tha·nize (yōō'thə·nīz) *v.t.* **·nized, ·niz·ing** To put to death painlessly.

eu·then·ics (yōō·then'iks) *n. pl. (construed as sing.)* The science of improving the human race by the control of environmental factors. [<Gk. *euthenia* prosperity, welfare] —**eu'the·nist** *n.*

eu·troph·ic (yōō·trof'ik, -trō'fik) *adj. Ecol.* Of lakes and other bodies of water, enriched in nutrients resulting in luxurious organic growth and depletion of dissolved oxygen. —**eu·troph'i·ca'tion** *n.*

e·vac·u·ant (i·vak'yōō·ənt) *adj. Med.* Producing evacuation; cathartic, diuretic, or emetic.

e·vac·u·ate (i·vak'yōō·āt) *v.* **·at·ed, ·at·ing** *v.t.* 1 *Mil.* **a** To give up or abandon possession of; withdraw from, as a fortress or city. **b** To withdraw (troops, inhabitants, etc.) from a threatened area or place. 2 To depart from; vacate. 3 To produce a near vacuum in. 4 *Physiol.* To discharge or eject, as from the bowels. —*v.i.* 5 To withdraw, as from a threatened area or place. [<L<*e-* out + *vacuare* make empty] —**e·vac'u·a'tion** *n.* —**e·vac'u·a'tive** *adj.*

e·vac·u·ee (i·vak'yōō·ē') *n.* One who has been removed from or has abandoned his home.

e·vade (i·vād') *v.* **e·vad·ed, e·vad·ing** *v.t.* 1 To escape or get away from by tricks or cleverness. 2 To avoid or get out of. —*v.i.* 3 To avoid doing something by clever or deceitful means. [<L *e-* out + *vadere* go] —**e·vad'a·ble** *adj.* —**e·vad'er** *n.* —**Syn.** 1 elude. 2 dodge, neglect, foil, shun.

e·val·u·ate (i·val'yōō·āt) *v.t.* **·at·ed, ·at·ing** To find or determine the amount, worth, value, etc., of; appraise. [<OF *e-* out + *valu* value] —**e·val'u·a'tion** *n.* —**Syn.** assess, estimate, adjudge.

ev·a·nesce (ev'ə·nes') *v.t.* **·nesced, ·nesc·ing** To disappear by degrees; vanish. [<L *e-* out + *vanescere* vanish]

Europe

ev·a·nes·cent (ev′ə·nes′ənt) *adj.* Passing away, or liable to pass away, gradually or imperceptibly. —**ev′a·nes′·cence** *n.* —**ev′a·nes′cent·ly** *adv.*

e·van·gel[1] (i·van′jəl) *n.* **1** The Christian gospel. **2** *Usu. cap.* One of the four Gospels of the New Testament. **3** Any good news or glad tidings. [< Gk. *euangelion* good news]

e·van·gel[2] (i·van′jəl) *n.* EVANGELIST.

e·van·gel·i·cal (ē′van·jel′i·kəl, ev′ən-) *adj.* **1** In or agreeing with the four Gospels or the teachings of the New Testament. **2** Of, pertaining to, or believing in the authority of Scripture and salvation through Christ. **3** EVANGELISTIC. —*n.* A member of an evangelical church, or of an evangelical party within a church. Also **e′van·gel′ic.** —**e′van·gel′i·cal·ism, e′van·gel′i·cism** *n.* —**e′van·gel′i·cal·ly** *adv.*

e·van·gel·ism (i·van′jə·liz′əm) *n.* The zealous preaching or spreading of the gospel.

e·van·gel·ist (i·van′jə·list) *n.* **1** *Usu. cap.* One of the four writers of the New Testament Gospels; Matthew, Mark, Luke, or John. **2** An itinerant or missionary preacher; a revivalist.

e·van·gel·is·tic (i·van′jə·lis′tik) *adj.* **1** Of or pertaining to evangelism or an evangelist. **2** EVANGELICAL. **3** Zealous or missionary in character. —**e·van′gel·is′ti·cal·ly** *adv.*

e·van·gel·ize (i·van′jəl·īz) *v.* **·ized, ·iz·ing** *v.t.* **1** To preach the gospel to. **2** To convert to Christianity. —*v.i.* **3** To preach the gospel. —**e·van′gel·i·za′tion, e·van′gel·iz′er** *n.*

e·vap·o·rate (i·vap′ə·rāt) *v.* **·rat·ed, ·rat·ing** *v.t.* **1** To convert into vapor. **2** To remove moisture from. —*v.i.* **3** To become vapor. **4** To yield vapor. **5** To vanish; disappear. [< L *e-* out, away + *vapor* vapor] —**e·vap′o·ra′tive** *adj.* —**e·vap′o·ra′tion, e·vap′o·ra·tor** *n.*

evaporated milk Unsweetened milk with much of its water content removed.

e·va·sion (i·vā′zhən) *n.* **1** The act of evading. **2** A means or an instance of doing this; subterfuge.

e·va·sive (i·vā′siv) *adj.* **1** Not direct, open or straightforward: an *evasive* answer. **2** Tending to elude; elusive. —**e·va′sive·ly** *adv.* —**e·va′sive·ness** *n.*

eve (ēv) *n.* **1** EVENING. **2** The evening before some special day. **3** The time immediately preceding some event. [Var. of EVEN[2]]

Eve (ēv) In the Bible, the first woman, Adam's wife.

e·ven[1] (ē′vən) *adj.* **1** Flat; smooth; level: *even* surfaces. **2** Steady; unchanging; constant: to keep an *even* tempo. **3** The same, as in number or quantity. **4** Being on the same line or level: horses *even* in the stretch. **5** Not easily disturbed; calm; tranquil: an *even* disposition. **6** Owing nothing and being owed nothing. **7** Exact; precise: an *even* pint. **8** Exactly divisible by 2. **9** Fair; equitable. **10** Balanced. —**get even** To get revenge: retaliate. —*adv.* **1** Indeed; truly: to feel sad, *even* disconsolate. **2** Exactly; precisely: Do *even* as you are told. **3** Still, yet: an *even* better idea. **4** At the same time; while: It happened *even* as you spoke. **5** However unlikely it seems: *Even* I can understand the difficulties involved. —*v.t. & v.i.* To make or become even. [< OE *efen* level] —**e′ven·ly** *adv.* —**e′ven·ness** *n.* —**Syn. 2** regular, unvarying. **5** easy, serene, stable.

e·ven[2] (ē′vən) *n. Archaic* Evening. [< OE *æfen*]

e·ven·fall (ē′vən·fôl′) *n.* Early evening; dusk.

e·ven·hand·ed (ē′vən·han′did) *adj.* Treating all alike; impartial. —**e′ven·hand′ed·ly** *adv.* —**e′ven·hand′ed·ness** *n.*

eve·ning (ēv′ning) *n.* **1** The closing part of the day and beginning of the night. **2** The period, roughly, from after dinner until bedtime; also, this period spent in some specific activity, entertainment, etc. **3** A closing or declining part of any state or period: the *evening* of life. [< OE *æfen*]

evening dress Clothing worn on formal occasions in the evening. Also **evening clothes.**

evening primrose A biennial herb with conspicuous yellow flowers that open in the evening.

evening star A bright planet, as Venus, seen in the western sky just after sunset.

e·ven·song (ē′vən·sông′, -song′) *n.* **1** VESPERS. **2** In the Anglican Church, a service held in the evening. [< OE *æfensang*]

e·vent (i·vent′) *n.* **1** Anything that happens or comes to pass. **2** The result or outcome of any action. **3** One of the items making up a program of sports. [< L *e-* out + *venire* come] —**Syn. 1** occurrence, happening, episode, incident.

e·vent·ful (i·vent′fəl) *adj.* **1** Attended or characterized by important events. **2** MOMENTOUS. —**e·vent′ful·ly** *adv.* —**e·vent′ful·ness** *n.*

e·ven·tide (ē′vən·tīd′) *n.* Evening time.

e·ven·tu·al (i·ven′chōō·əl) *adj.* Taking place after a period of time or as a result of a succession of events; subsequent. [< EVENT] —**e·ven′tu·al·ly** *adv.*

e·ven·tu·al·i·ty (i·ven′chōō·al′ə·tē) *n. pl.* **·ties** A possible occurrence; possibility.

e·ven·tu·ate (i·ven′chōō·āt) *v.i.* **·at·ed, ·at·ing** To result finally. —**e·ven′tu·a′tion** *n.*

ev·er (ev′ər) *adv.* **1** At any time: Did you *ever* get there? **2** In any way: How can I *ever* repay you? **3** At all times; always: I shall be *ever* grateful. [< OE *æfre*]

ev·er·glade (ev′ər·glād) *n.* A tract of low swampy land covered with tall grass. —**the Everglades** A swampy subtropical region of southern Florida.

ev·er·green (ev′ər·grēn′) *adj.* Having leaves throughout the year. —*n.* **1** An evergreen tree or plant. **2** *pl.* Evergreen twigs and branches, used for decoration.

ev·er·last·ing (ev′ər·las′ting, -läs′-) *adj.* **1** Lasting forever; eternal. **2** Interminable; incessant. —*n.* **1** ETERNITY. **2** A plant, the flowers of which retain their form and color when dried. —**the Everlasting** God. —**ev′er·last′ing·ly** *adv.* —**ev′er·last′ing·ness** *n.*

ev·er·more (ev′ər·môr′, -mōr′) *adv.* Always.

e·ver·sion (i·vûr′zhən) *n.* **1** The act of everting. **2** The state of being everted.

e·vert (i·vûrt′) *v.t.* To turn inside out; turn outward. [< L *e-* out + *vertere* to turn]

eve·ry (ev′rē, ev′ər·ē) *adj.* **1** All taken one by one. **2** All possible; very great: Show him *every* consideration. **3** Each: *every* third man. [< OE *æfre* ever + *ælc* each]

eve·ry·bod·y (ev′rē·bod′ē, -bud′ē) *pron.* Every person; everyone.

eve·ry·day (ev′rē·dā′, -dā′) *adj.* **1** Suitable for every day. **2** Happening every day. **3** Common; usual; ordinary.

eve·ry·one (ev′rē·wun′, -wən) *pron.* All people in general; everybody.

every one Each individual person or thing out of a specific group or number: *Every one* of my front windows was broken.

eve·ry·thing (ev′rē·thing′) *pron.* **1** All things that exist. **2** All things that relate to a specific subject, circumstance, etc.: I have *everything* I need for the trip. —*n.* That which is of the highest importance: Money is *everything* to some people.

eve·ry·where (ev′rē·ʰwâr′) *adv.* At or in every place.

e·vict (i·vikt′) *v.t.* To expel (a tenant) by legal process; dispossess; put out. [< L *e-* out + *vincere* conquer] —**e·vic′tion, e·vic′tor** *n.*

ev·i·dence (ev′ə·dəns) *n.* **1** That which makes evident or clear; an outward sign or indication. **2** That which serves to prove. **3** *Law* That which is submitted to a court to establish the truth or falsehood of something alleged or presumed. **4** *Law* A witness. —**in evidence** In plain view; visible. —*v.t.* **·denced, ·denc·ing** **1** To make evident; show clearly; display. **2** To support by one's testimony; attest.

ev·i·dent (ev′ə·dənt) *adj.* Plain, manifest, or clear, as to the mind or the senses; obvious. [< L *e-* out + *videre* see] —**ev′i·dent·ly** *adv.*

ev·i·den·tial (ev′ə·den′shəl) *adj.* Being, pertaining to, or furnishing evidence. —**ev′i·den′tial·ly** *adv.*

e·vil (ē′vəl) *adj.* **1** Morally bad; wicked; sinful or depraved. **2** Injurious; unwholesome; harmful. **3** Causing or threatening misfortune; unlucky. **4** Arising from real or reputed immorality: an *evil* name. —*n.* **1** Wicked conduct or disposition; sinfulness; moral depravity. **2** Something that harms or hurts. [< OE *yfel*] —**e′vil·ly** *adv.* —**e′vil·ness** *n.*

e·vil·do·er (ē′vəl·dōō′ər) *n.* A wicked person. —**e′vil·do′ing** *n.*

evil eye In folklore, a look or stare having the power to harm anyone toward whom it is directed. —e′vil-eyed′ adj.

e·vil-mind·ed (ē′vəl·mīn′did) adj. Evil in thought or disposition. —e′vil-mind′ed·ly adv. —e′vil-mind′ed·ness n.

e·vince (i·vins′) v.t. e·vinced, e·vinc·ing To show plainly or certainly; make evident; display. [< L evincere to conquer] —e·vin′ci·ble adj. —e·vin′ci·bly adv.

e·vis·cer·ate (i·vis′ə·rāt) v.t. ·at·ed, ·at·ing 1 DISEMBOWEL. 2 To remove the essential or vital parts of (anything). [< L e- out + viscera entrails] —e·vis′cer·a′tion n.

e·voke (i·vōk′) v.t. e·voked, e·vok·ing 1 To call or summon forth; elicit, as an emotion or reply. 2 To summon up (spirits) by or as by spells. [< L e- out + vocare call] —ev·o·ca·ble (ev′ə·kə·bəl, i·vok′ə-) ev·o·ca·tive (i·vok′ə·tiv) adj. —ev·o·ca·tion (ev′ə·kā′shən, ē′vō-) n.

ev·o·lu·tion (ev′ə·lōō′shən, ēv′ə-) n. 1 The process of unfolding; development or growth. 2 Anything evolved. 3 Biol. a The theory that all forms of life originated by descent, with gradual or abrupt modifications, from preexisting forms which themselves trace backward in a continuing series to the most rudimentary organisms. b The series of changes by which a given type of organism has acquired the physiological and structural characteristics differentiating it from other types. 4 Math. The operation of extracting a root. 5 A move or maneuver, as of troops. 6 A movement forming one of a series of complex motions. 7 The emission or setting free, as of gas, energy, etc. [< L evolvere to evolve] —ev′o·lu′tion·al, ev·o·lu′tion·ar·y, adj. —ev′o·lu′tion·al·ly adv. —ev′o·lu′tion·ism n. —ev′o·lu′tion·ist n., adj.

e·volve (i·volv′) v. e·volved, e·volv·ing v.t. 1 To work out or develop gradually: to evolve a plan. 2 Biol. To develop, as by a differentiation of parts or functions, to a more highly organized condition. 3 To give or throw off (vapor, heat, etc.); emit. —v.i. 4 To undergo the process of evolution. 5 To open out; develop. [< L evolvere < e- out + volvere roll] —e·volv′a·ble adj. —e·volv′ent adj., n. —e·volve′ment n.

ewe (yōō, Regional yō) n. A female sheep. [< OE eowu]

ew·er (yōō′ər) n. A wide-mouthed pitcher, sometimes with a lid. [< OF evier]

ex¹ (eks) prep. 1 In finance, without the right to have or to participate in; excluding: ex bonus, ex dividend. 2 In commerce, free out of; not subject to charge until taken out of: ex elevator, ex ship, ex store. [L, out]

ex² (eks) n. pl. ex·es The letter X or x.

ex-¹ prefix 1 Out; out of: exit, exhale. 2 Remove from; free from: exonerate. 3 Thoroughly: exasperate. 4 Once; former: used with a hyphen: ex-president. [< L ex from, out of]

ex-² prefix Out of; from; forth: exodus. [< Gk. ex out]

Ex, Ex. Exodus.

ex. examined; example; exception.

ex·ac·er·bate (ig·zas′ər·bāt) v.t. ·bat·ed, ·bat·ing To make more intense or severe. [< L ex- completely + acerbus bitter, harsh] —ex·ac′er·ba′tion n.

ex·act (ig·zakt′) adj. 1 Clear and complete; definite; precise: exact instructions. 2 Absolutely accurate: exact answers. 3 Specified or required: an exact amount. 4 Rigorous; demanding; strict: an exact teacher. —v.t. 1 To compel the yielding or payment of; extort. 2 To demand; insist upon as a right. 3 To require; call for: The task will exact great effort. [< L exigere determine] —ex·act′a·ble adj. —ex·act′er, ex·ac′tor n.

ex·act·ing (ig·zak′ting) adj. 1 Strict and demanding: an exacting boss. 2 Requiring attention, patience, effort, etc.: an exacting task. —ex·act′ing·ly adv. —ex·act′ing·ness n.

ex·ac·tion (ig·zak′shən) n. 1 The act of exacting; extortion. 2 Something exacted, as a compulsory levy.

ex·act·ly (ig·zakt′lē) adv. 1 In an exact manner. 2 Yes indeed; quite so.

ex·act·ness (ig·zakt′nis) n. The condition or quality of being accurate and precise. Also ex·act′i·tude (-tyōōd).

ex·ag·ger·ate (ig·zaj′ə·rāt) v. ·at·ed, ·at·ing v.t. 1 To describe or think about as greater than is actually the case. 2 To increase or enlarge beyond what is normal or expected. —v.i. 3 To describe or think about something in

exaggerated terms. [< L ex- out + agger mound, heap] —ex·ag′ger·at′ed·ly, ex·ag′ger·at·ing·ly adv. —ex·ag′ger·a′tion, ex·ag′ger·a′tor n.

ex·alt (ig·zôlt′) v.t. 1 To raise high; lift up; elevate. 2 To raise in rank, character, honor, etc. 3 To glorify or praise; pay honor to. 4 To fill with delight, pride, etc. 5 To increase the force or intensity of, as colors. [< L ex- out + altus high] —ex·alt′er n.

ex·al·ta·tion (eg′zôl·tā′shən) n. 1 The act of exalting. 2 The state of being exalted. 3 An extreme or sometimes exaggerated sense of well-being, importance, or power.

ex·am (ig·zam′) n. Informal An examination.

ex·am·i·na·tion (ig·zam′ə·nā′shən) n. 1 The act or process of examining or the state of being examined. 2 A testing of knowledge, progress, skill, qualifications, etc.; also, the questions used in such testing. 3 Law A formal interrogation. —ex·am′i·na′tion·al adj.

ex·am·ine (ig·zam′in) v.t. ·ined, ·in·ing 1 To inspect or scrutinize with care; investigate critically. 2 To test as to knowledge, qualifications, physical fitness, etc. 3 To interrogate formally. [< L examen a testing] —ex·am′in·a·ble adj. —ex·am′i·nee′, ex·am′in·er n.

ex·am·ple (ig·zam′pəl, -zäm′-) n. 1 Something that belongs to and typifies a group of things, and that is singled out as a sample of the group. 2 A thing or person suitable to be used as a model. 3 A case serving or designed to serve as a warning. 4 A problem or exercise, as in mathematics, that is worked out or designed to be worked out to illustrate a method or principle. —v.t. ·pled, ·pling To exemplify: now used only in the passive. [< L exemplum something taken out]

ex·as·per·ate (ig·zas′pə·rāt) v.t. ·at·ed, ·at·ing 1 To irritate or annoy exceedingly; infuriate. 2 To make worse; intensify; inflame. [< L exasperare make rough] —ex·as′per·at′er, ex·as′per·a′tion n. —ex·as′per·at′ing adj. —ex·as′per·at′ing·ly adv.

Exc. Excellency.

Ex·cal·i·bur (eks·kal′ə·bər) n. In Arthurian legend, the sword of King Arthur.

ex ca·the·dra (eks kə·thē′drə, kath′i-) Officially; with authority: used esp. in certain papal pronouncements. [L, lit. from the chair]

ex·ca·vate (eks′kə·vāt) v.t. ·vat·ed, ·vat·ing 1 To make a hole or cavity in. 2 To form or make (a tunnel, etc.) by digging out or scooping. 3 To remove by digging or scooping out, as soil. 4 To uncover by digging, as ruins. [< L ex- out + cavus hollow] —ex′ca·va′tion, ex′ca·va′tor n.

ex·ceed (ik·sēd′) v.t. 1 To surpass, as in quantity, quality, measure, or value. 2 To go beyond the limit or extent of: to exceed one's income. —v.i. 3 To be superior; surpass others. [< L ex- out, beyond + cedere go]

ex·ceed·ing (ik·sē′ding) adj. Greater than usual; surpassing; extraordinary. —ex·ceed′ing·ly adv.

ex·cel (ik·sel′) v.t. & v.i. ·celled, ·cel·ling To go beyond or above; outdo; surpass (another or others). [< L excellere rise]

ex·cel·lence (ek′sə·ləns) n. 1 The state or quality of excelling; superiority. 2 That in which a person or thing excels or is superior. —ex′cel·len·cy.

Ex·cel·len·cy (ek′sə·lən·sē) n. pl. ·cies An honorary title of various high officials, as a governor, ambassador, foreign president, etc.: usu. preceded by His, Her, Your, etc.

ex·cel·lent (ek′sə·lənt) adj. Having good qualities in a high degree; superior in worth, value, etc. [< L excellere rise] —ex′cel·lent·ly adv. —Syn. admirable, capital, choice, fine, first-class.

ex·cel·si·or (ik·sel′sē·ər) n. A packing material composed of long, fine, wood shavings. [< Excelsior, a trade name]

ex·cept (ik·sept′) v.t. 1 To leave or take out; exclude; omit. —v.i. 2 To object; take exception; with to. —prep. With the exception of; save; but: Tell no one except me. —conj. 1 Informal But for the fact that; only: I'd go except I don't have time. 2 Archaic Unless. [< L ex- out + capere take]

ex·cept·ing (ik·sep′ting) prep. Except.

ex·cep·tion (ik·sep′shən) n. 1 The act of excepting or the condition of being excepted. 2 A person or thing different from or not conforming to a general rule, principle, class, etc. 3 An objection, complaint, or quibble. 4 Law A formal

Ewer

objection to the decision of a court during trial. —**take exception** To take offense, disagree, or object.

ex·cep·tion·a·ble (ik·sep′shən·ə·bəl) *adj.* Open to exception or objection. —**ex·cep′tion·a·bly** *adv.*

ex·cep·tion·al (ik·sep′shən·əl) *adj.* Unusual or uncommon, esp. in a superior way. —**ex·cep′tion·al·ly** *adv.*

ex·cerpt (ek′sûrpt) *n.* An extract from written or printed matter. —*v.t.* (ik·sûrpt′) To take out, as a passage or quotation; extract. [< L *ex-* out + *carpere* pluck, seize]

ex·cess (ik·ses′) *n.* 1 The condition of exceeding what is ordinary, reasonable, or required. 2 An amount greater than is necessary; overabundance. 3 The amount by which one thing is greater than another; surplus. 4 Overindulgence; intemperance. —**to excess** To an unnecessary or extreme degree or extent. —*adj.* (*also* ek′ses) Being above a stipulated amount; extra. [< L *excedere* go beyond]

ex·ces·sive (ik·ses′iv) *adj.* Being in, tending to, marked by excess; immoderate; extreme. —**ex·ces′sive·ly** *adv.* —**ex·ces′sive·ness** *n.*

excess profits Net profits beyond the normal average for a period of years.

exch. exchange; exchequer.

ex·change (iks·chānj′) *n.* 1 The act of giving or receiving one thing as an equivalent for another; bartering. 2 Interchange: an *exchange* of wit, remarks, etc. 3 A substituting of one thing for another. 4 Something given or substituted for another. 5 A place where merchants, brokers, etc., buy, sell, or trade: a stock *exchange.* 6 A central telephone office. 7 A system of paying debts without transfer of actual money but by means of credits, drafts, etc.; also, the fee charged for this. 8 BILL OF EXCHANGE. 9 The value of one currency in terms of another currency. 10 The difference in value between two currencies. 11 *pl.* Checks, drafts, etc., presented to a clearing-house for settlement. —*v.* ·changed, ·chang·ing 1 To give or part with for something regarded as of equal value, etc.: to *exchange* francs for dollars. 2 To give and receive in turn; reciprocate. 3 To replace by or give up for something else: to *exchange* poverty for wealth. —*v.i.* 4 To be given or taken in exchange. 5 To make an exchange. [< L *ex-* out + *cambiare* exchange] —**ex·change′a·bil′i·ty** *n.* —**ex·change′a·ble** *adj.* —**ex·change′a·bly** *adv.*

ex·cheq·uer (iks·chek′ər, eks′chek·ər) *n.* 1 The treasury, as of an organization or state. 2 *Informal* One's personal financial resources. [< OF *eschequier* counting table, chessboard]

Ex·cheq·uer (iks·chek′ər, eks′chek·ər) *n.* The administrative department of the British government having the management of the public revenue.

ex·cise[1] (ek′sīz, ek′sīs) *n.* 1 An indirect tax on commodities manufactured, produced, sold, used, or transported within a country. 2 A license fee for various sports, trades, or occupations. —*v.t.* ·cised, ·cis·ing To levy an excise upon. [< L *ad-* to + *census* a tax]

ex·cise[2] (ik·sīz′) *v.t.* ·cised, ·cis·ing To cut out or cut off, as in a surgical operation: to *excise* a cyst. [< L *ex-* out + *caedere* cut] —**ex·ci·sion** (ik·sizh′ən) *n.*

ex·cit·a·ble (ik·sī′tə·bəl) *adj.* 1 Easily excited; highstrung. 2 Susceptible to stimuli. —**ex·cit′a·bil′i·ty, ex·cit′a·ble·ness** *n.* —**ex·cit′a·bly** *adv.*

ex·ci·ta·tion (ek′sī·tā′shən) *n.* The act of exciting or the state of being excited.

ex·cite (ik·sīt′) *v.t.* ·cit·ed, ·cit·ing 1 To arouse (a feeling, interest, etc.) into being or activity; evoke. 2 To arouse feeling in; stimulate the emotions of. 3 To cause action in; stir to activity or motion. 4 To bring about; stir up: to *excite* a riot. 5 *Physics* To give increased energy to. [< L *ex-* out + *ciere* arouse, stir up] —**ex·cit′ed** *adj.* —**ex·cit′ed·ly** *adv.* —**ex·cit′er** *n.* —Syn. 1, 2, 3 awaken, stir, inspire, provoke, kindle, evoke. 4 foment, incite.

ex·cite·ment (ik·sīt′mənt) *n.* 1 The act of exciting or the state of being excited. 2 That which excites.

ex·cit·ing (ik·sī′ting) *adj.* Causing or full of excitement; stirring; rousing. —**ex·cit′ing·ly** *adv.*

ex·claim (iks·klām′) *v.t. & v.i.* To say or cry out abruptly,

as in surprise or anger. [< L *ex-* out + *clamare* cry] —**ex·claim′er** *n.*

ex·cla·ma·tion (eks′klə·mā′shən) *n.* 1 The act of exclaiming. 2 An abrupt or emphatic expression, outcry, etc. —**ex·clam·a·to·ry** (iks·klam′ə·tôr′ē, -tō′rē) *adj.*

exclamation mark A mark (!) placed after an interjection or exclamation to indicate its character. Also **exclamation point.**

ex·clude (iks·klood′) *v.t.* ·clud·ed, ·clud·ing 1 To keep from entering; shut out; bar. 2 To refuse to notice or consider. 3 To put out; eject. [< L *ex-* out + *claudere* close] —**ex·clud′a·ble** *adj.* —**ex·clud′er, ex·clu′sion** *n.*

ex·clu·sive (iks·kloo′siv) *adj.* 1 Intended for or possessed by a single group or individual; not shared: *exclusive* fishing rights. 2 Found, known, printed, etc., by only one person or source: an *exclusive* news item. 3 Regarded as totally incompatible, different, unrelated, etc.: mutually *exclusive* theories. 4 Restricting membership, admittance, etc.; reluctant to accept outsiders. 5 Expensive to frequent or patronize: an *exclusive* restaurant. 6 Complete; undivided: his *exclusive* attention to music. 7 Not including; not comprising: usu. followed by *of: exclusive* of fees. —*n.* Something exclusive, esp. an exclusive news item or story. —**ex·clu′sive·ly** *adv.* —**ex·clu′sive·ness** *n.*

ex·com·mu·ni·cate (eks′kə·myoo′nə·kāt) *v.t.* ·cat·ed, ·cat·ing 1 To punish by an ecclesiastical sentence of exclusion from the sacraments and communion of the church. 2 To expel in disgrace from any organization. —*adj.* Excommunicated. —*n.* An excommunicated person [< LL *excommunicare* to put out of the community] —**ex′com·mu′ni·ca′tion, ex′com·mu′ni·ca′tor** *n.*

ex·co·ri·ate (ik·skôr′ē·āt, -skō′rē-) *v.t.* ·at·ed, ·at·ing 1 To scratch or abrade the skin of. 2 To denounce scathingly. [< L *ex-* out, off + *corium* skin] —**ex·co′ri·a′tion** *n.*

ex·cre·ment (eks′krə·mənt) *n.* Refuse matter discharged from an animal body; feces. —**ex′cre·men′tal** *adj.*

ex·cres·cence (iks·kres′əns) *n.* 1 An unnatural or disfiguring outgrowth, as a wart. 2 Any unnatural addition or development. 3 A natural outgrowth, as hair. [< L *ex-* out + *crescere* grow] —**ex·cres′cent** *adj.*

ex·cre·ta (iks·krē′tə) *n. pl.* Waste matter, as urine, sweat, etc., eliminated from the bodily system. —**ex·cre′tal** *adj.*

ex·crete (iks·krēt′) *v.t.* ·cret·ed, ·cret·ing To eliminate, as waste matter, by normal discharge. [< L *excretus,* pp. of *excernere* separate out] —**ex·cre′tion** *n.* —**ex·cre′tive, ex′·cre·to′ry** *adj.*

ex·cru·ci·ate (iks·kroo′shē·āt) *v.t.* ·at·ed, ·at·ing To inflict extreme mental or physical pain upon. [< L *ex-* completely + *cruciare* torture] —**ex·cru′ci·a′tion** *n.*

ex·cru·ci·at·ing (iks·kroo′shē·āt·ing) *adj.* 1 Causing great physical or mental pain. 2 Extreme; intense. —**ex·cru′ci·at′ing·ly** *adv.*

ex·cul·pate (eks′kəl·pāt, ik·skul′-) *v.t.* ·pat·ed, ·pat·ing To declare free from blame; prove innocent. [< EX-[1] + L *culpare* blame. —**ex′cul·pa′tion** *n.* —**ex·cul′pa·to′ry** *adj.*

ex·cur·sion (ik·skûr′zhən, -shən) *n.* 1 A short journey, usu. for pleasure. 2 A boat or train trip at reduced rates, accommodating passengers in groups. 3 Such passengers collectively. 4 A digression; deviation. 5 *Physics* Half the amplitude of a vibration or oscillation. [< L *excursio* < *excurrere* to run out] —**ex·cur′sion·ist** *n.*

ex·cur·sive (ik·skûr′siv) *adj.* Digressive; rambling; wandering; desultory. —**ex·cur′sive·ly** *adv.* —**ex·cur′sive·ness** *n.*

ex·cuse (ik·skyooz′) *v.t.* ·cused, ·cus·ing 1 To pardon and overlook (a fault, offense, etc.). 2 To try to free (someone) from blame; seek to remove blame from. 3 To offer a reason or apology for (an error, fault, etc.); try to obtain pardon for or minimize. 4 To serve as a reason for; justify. 5 To release or dismiss, as from attendance. 6 To refrain from exacting or enforcing, as a demand or claim. —*n.* (ik·skyoos′) 1 A plea or reason given to justify an offense, neglect, failure, etc. 2 Something that excuses, as from attendance. 3 One who or that which is a bad or inferior example: a poor *excuse* for a statesman. [< L *ex-* out, away + *causa* charge, accusation] —**ex·cus′a·ble** *adj.* —**ex·cus′a·bly** *adv.* —**ex·cus′er** *n.*

exec. executive; executor.

ex·e·cra·ble (ek′sə·krə·bəl) *adj.* 1 Abominable; accursed. 2 Appallingly bad. —**ex′e·cra·bly** *adv.*

ex·e·crate (ek′sə·krāt) *v.* **·crat·ed, ·crat·ing** *v.t.* 1 To curse, or call down evil upon. 2 To detest; abhor. —*v.i.* 3 To utter curses. [< L *execrari* to curse] —**ex′e·cra′tion, ex′e·cra′tor** *n.* —**ex′e·cra′tive** *adj.*

ex·ec·u·tant (ig·zek′yə·tənt) *n.* 1 One who does or carries out something. 2 A performer, as of music.

ex·e·cute (ek′sə·kyōōt) *v.t.* **·cut·ed, ·cut·ing** 1 To do or carry out fully. 2 To put in force; administer, as a law. 3 To put to death by legal sentence. 4 *Law* To make (a will, deed, etc.) legal or valid. 5 To perform, as a maneuver or a musical work. 6 To produce or create. [< L *ex-* out + *sequi* follow] —**ex′e·cut′a·ble** *adj.* —**ex′e·cut′er** *n.* —**Syn.** 1 perform, fulfill, effect. 2 enforce.

ex·e·cu·tion (ek′sə·kyōō′shən) *n.* 1 The act of doing, putting into force, etc. 2 A putting to death, as by legal decree. 3 The manner, style, or skill with which something is done. 4 *Law* A judicial writ, as for the seizure of goods, etc.

ex·e·cu·tion·er (ek′sə·kyōō′shən·ər) *n.* One who executes a death sentence.

ex·ec·u·tive (ig·zek′yə·tiv) *adj.* 1 Having the function or skill of executing or performing. 2 Having ability or aptitude for directing or controlling. 3 Of or pertaining to direction or control; administrative, as distinguished from *judicial* and *legislative*. —*n.* 1 An official or body of officials charged with the administration of the laws and affairs of a nation or state. 2 A person or group having administrative control, as of a business or other organization.

Executive Mansion 1 The official residence of the president of the U.S. 2 The residence of the governor of a State.

ex·ec·u·tor (ig·zek′yə·tər) *n.* 1 *Law* A person nominated by the will of another to execute the will. 2 One who executes, in any sense. —**ex·ec·u·trix** (ig·zek′yə·triks) *n. Fem.* (*pl.* **·trix′es** or **ex·ec·u·tri′ces**) (-trī′sēz)

ex·e·ge·sis (ek′sə·jē′sis) *n. pl.* **·ses** (-sēz) Explanation of the language and thought of a literary work; esp. Biblical interpretation. [< Gk. *ēgeisthai* to lead the way] —**ex′e·get′ic** (-jet′ik) *adj.* —**ex′e·get′i·cal·ly** *adv.*

ex·em·plar (ig·zem′plər, -plär) *n.* 1 A model, pattern, or original, to be copied or imitated. 2 A typical example; archetype. [< L *exemplum* example]

ex·em·pla·ry (ig·zem′plər·ē) *adj.* 1 Serving as a model or example worthy of imitation; commendable. 2 Serving as a warning example: *exemplary* damages. 3 Serving to exemplify; illustrative. —**ex·em′pla·ri·ly** *adv.* —**ex·em′pla·ri·ness** *n.*

ex·em·pli·fy (ig·zem′plə·fī) *v.t.* **·fied, ·fy·ing** 1 To show by example; illustrate. 2 *Law* To make an authenticated transcript from, as a public record. [L *exemplum* example + *facere* make] —**ex·em′pli·fi·ca′tion** *n.* —**ex·em′pli·fi·ca′tive** *adj.*

ex·empt (ig·zempt′) *v.t.* To free or excuse from some obligation to which others are subject; grant immunity to. —*adj.* Free, clear, or excused, as from some duty. —*n.* A person who is exempted, as from military service. [< L *ex-* out + *emere* buy, take] —**ex·empt′i·ble** *adj.* —**ex·emp′tion** *n.* —**Syn.** *v.* release, remit, discharge, let off, spare.

ex·er·cise (ek′sər·sīz) *v.* **·cised, ·cis·ing** *v.t.* 1 To subject to drills, systematic movements, etc., so as to train or develop (troops, muscles, the mind, etc.). 2 To make use of; employ. 3 To perform or execute, as duties. 4 To wield; exert, as influence or authority. 5 To make a habit of: used reflexively or in the passive: to be *exercised* in good works. 6 To occupy the mind of; esp. to make anxious. —*v.i.* 7 To take exercise. 8 To undergo training. —*n.* 1 A putting into use or practice. 2 A specific bodily activity or movement for developing strength, agility, etc. 3 Something played or practiced to develop a specific skill or technique: a violin *exercise*. 4 A problem or lesson to be worked out. 5 *pl.* A program or ceremony: graduation *exercises*. [< L *exercere* to practice] —**ex′er·cis′a·ble** *adj.*

ex·er·cised (ek′sər·sīzd) *adj.* Harassed; agitated.

ex·er·cis·er (ek′sər·sī′zər) *n.* 1 One who exercises. 2 An apparatus for body exercise.

ex·ert (ig·zûrt′) *v.t.* To put forth or put in action, as

strength, force, or faculty; bring into strong or vigorous action. —**exert oneself** To put forth effort. [< L *exertus* < *exserere* thrust out] —**ex·er′tive** *adj.*

ex·er·tion (ig·zûr′shən) *n.* 1 The act of exerting some power, faculty, etc. 2 Vigorous action or effort.

ex·e·unt (ek′sē·ənt, -ōōnt) They go out: a stage direction. [L]

ex·fo·li·ate (eks·fō′lē·āt) *v.t. & v.i.* **·at·ed, ·at·ing** 1 To remove scales or splinters (from). 2 To peel off in thin flakes, as the bark of a tree. [< L *ex-* off + *folium* a leaf] —**ex·fo′li·a′tion** *n.* —**ex·fo′li·a·tive** *adj.*

ex·hale (eks·hāl′, ig·zāl′) *v.* **·haled, ·hal·ing** *v.i.* 1 To expel air or vapor; breathe out. 2 To pass off or rise as a vapor; evaporate. —*v.t.* 3 To breathe forth or give off. 4 To draw off; cause to evaporate. [< L *ex-* out + *halare* breathe] —**ex·hal′a·ble** *adj.* —**ex·ha·la·tion** (eks′hə·lā′shən, eg′zə-) *n.*

ex·haust (ig·zôst′) *v.t.* 1 To make tired; wear out completely. 2 To drain of resources, strength, etc.; use up. 3 To draw off, as gas, steam, etc., from or as from a container. 4 To empty (a container) or contents; drain. 5 To study, treat of, or develop thoroughly and completely: to *exhaust* a subject. —*v.i.* 6 To pass out as the exhaust: The steam *exhausts* from the pipe. —*n.* 1 **a** Waste gases or vapor discharged from an engine. **b** The system by which these are vented. 2 The discharge of any waste gas, as by a fan. [< L *ex-* out + *haurire* draw] —**ex·haust′er, ex·haust′i·bil′i·ty** *n.* —**ex·haust′i·ble** *adj.*

ex·haust·ed (ig·zôs′tid) *adj.* 1 Used up; consumed; spent. 2 Extremely tired or weak. —**ex·haust′ed·ly** *adv.*

ex·haust·ing (ig·zôs′ting) *adj.* Producing or tending to produce exhaustion; wearying.

ex·haus·tion (ig·zôs′chən) *n.* 1 Extreme fatigue or weakness. 2 The condition of being entirely used up or spent.

ex·haus·tive (ig·zôs′tiv) *adj.* 1 Having the effect or tendency to exhaust. 2 Complete and totally comprehensive: an *exhaustive* study. —**ex·haus′tive·ly** *adv.* —**ex·haus′tive·ness** *n.*

ex·hib·it (ig·zib′it) *v.t.* 1 To present to view; display. 2 To show or reveal. 3 To present for public inspection or entertainment. —*v.i.* 4 To place something on display. —*n.* 1 A public showing or display. 2 Any object or objects exhibited. 3 *Law* A document or object marked for use as evidence. [< L *ex-* out + *habere* hold, have] —**ex·hib′i·tive, ex·hib′i·to′ry** *adj.* —**ex·hib′i·tor, ex·hib′it·er** *n.*

ex·hi·bi·tion (ek′sə·bish′ən) *n.* 1 The act of exhibiting; display. 2 Anything exhibited. 3 A public showing, as of works of art, etc.

ex·hi·bi·tion·ism (ek′sə·bish′ən·iz′əm) *n.* 1 The tendency to display one's personal qualities in a manner that will attract attention. 2 A perversion characterized by a tendency to expose publicly a part of the body, as the genitals, for sexual pleasure. —**ex′hi·bi′tion·ist** *n.*

ex·hil·a·rate (ig·zil′ə·rāt) *v.t.* **·rat·ed, ·rat·ing** To induce a lively or enlivening feeling in; enliven; cheer; stimulate. [< L *ex-* completely + *hilaris* glad] —**ex·hil′a·ra′tion** *n.* —**Syn.** elate, exalt, animate, gladden, invigorate.

ex·hort (ig·zôrt′) *v.t.* To urge by earnest appeal or argument; advise or caution strongly. [< L *ex-* completely + *hortari* urge] —**ex·hor·ta·tion** (eg′zôr·tā′shən, ek′sər-), **ex·hort′er** *n.*

ex·hume (ig·zyōōm′, iks·hyōōm′) *v.t.* **·humed, ·hum·ing** 1 To dig out of the earth, as a dead body. 2 To disclose; reveal. [< L *ex-* out + *humus* ground] —**ex·hu·ma·tion** (eks′hyōō·mā′shən) *n.*

ex·i·gen·cy (ek′sə·jən·sē, ig·zij′ən-) *n. pl.* **·cies** 1 The state of being urgent or exigent. 2 A condition requiring immediate attention. 3 *Usu. pl.* Urgent needs or demands. Also **ex′i·gence.**

ex·i·gent (ek′sə·jənt) *adj.* 1 Urgent; pressing. 2 Very demanding or exacting. [< L *exigere* to demand]

ex·ig·u·ous (ig·zig′yōō·əs, ik·sig′-) *adj.* Scanty; meager. [< L *exiguus* scanty] —**ex·i·gu·i·ty** (ek′sə·gyōō′ə·tē), **ex·ig′u·ous·ness** *n.*

ex·ile (eg′zīl, ek′sīl) *n.* 1 Separation, either enforced or by choice, from one's home or native land. 2 One separated from his native country or home; an expatriate. —*v.t.* **ex·iled, ex·il·ing** To expel from and forbid to return to a native land or home; banish. [< L *exsilium*]

ex·ist (ig·zist′) *v.i.* 1 To have actual being or reality; be.

2 To continue to live or be. **3** To be present; occur. [< L *existere*] **—ex·is'tent** *adj.*

ex·is·tence (ig·zis'təns) *n.* **1** The state or fact of being or existing. **2** Possession or continuance of being; life. **3** A manner of being or existing. **4** Anything that exists; a being; entity.

ex·is·ten·tial (eg'zis·ten'shəl) *adj.* **1** Of, or pertaining to, or stating the fact of existence. **2** Of or pertaining to existentialism. **—ex'is·ten'tial·ly** *adv.*

ex·is·ten·tial·ism (eg'zis·ten'shəl·iz'əm) *n.* A philosophical doctrine holding that existence takes precedence over essence, and that man, being totally free in an indifferent and purposeless universe, is responsible only to himself for the actions he takes in the development of his self. **— ex'is·ten'tial·ist** *adj.*

ex·it (eg'zit, ek'sit) *n.* **1** A way or passage out; egress. **2** The departure of an actor from the stage. **3** Any departure. — *v.i.* To go out. [< L *exitus* < *exire* go out]

ex li·bris (eks li'bris, lē'-) **1** From the books (of): used as an inscription or label on a book. **2** BOOKPLATE. [L]

exo- *combining form* Out; outside; external: *exogamy.* Also, **ex-.** [< Gk. *exō* outside]

ex·o·bi·ol·o·gy (ek'sō·bī·ol'ə·jē) *n.* The science dealing with the search for and study of forms of life native to parts of the universe other than the earth. **—ex'o·bi'o·log'i·cal** *adj.* **—ex'o·bi·ol'o·gist** *n.*

Exod. Exodus.

ex·o·dus (ek'sə·dəs) *n.* A going forth, or departure. **—the Exodus** The departure of the Israelites from Egypt under the guidance of Moses, described in **Exodus,** the second book of the Old Testament. [< Gk. *ex-* out + *hodos* way]

ex of·fi·ci·o (eks ə·fish'ē·ō) By virtue of or because of office or position. [L]

ex·og·a·my (eks·og'ə·mē) *n.* The custom that dictates marrying outside one's own tribe or clan. **—ex·og'a·mous, ex·o·gam·ic** (ek'sō·gam'ik) *adj.*

ex·og·e·nous (eks·oj'ə·nəs) *adj.* **1** *Bot.* Growing by the addition of concentric rings under the surface and outside previous growth. **2** Originating from without. [< F *exogène* having additional layers] **—ex·og'e·nous·ly** *adv.*

ex·on·er·ate (ig·zon'ə·rāt) *v.t.* **·at·ed, ·at·ing 1** To free from accusation or blame; acquit. **2** To relieve or free from a responsibility. [< L *ex-* out, away + *onus, oneris* burden] **—ex·on·er·a'tion** *n.* **—ex·on'er·a'tive** *adj.*

ex·oph·thal·mic (ek'sof·thal'mik) *adj.* Pertaining to or accompanied by abnormal protrusion of the eyeballs. [< Gk. *ex-* out + *ophthalmos* eye] **—ex·oph·thal'mia, ex'oph·thal'mos** *n.*

ex·or·bi·tant (ig·zôr'bə·tənt) *adj.* Going beyond usual and proper limits; excessive; extravagant. [< LL *exorbitare* go astray] **—ex·or'bi·tance, ex·or'bi·tan·cy** *n.* **—ex·or'·bi·tant·ly** *adv.*

ex·or·cise (ek'sôr·sīz) *v.t.* **·cised, ·cis·ing 1** To cast out (an evil spirit) by prayers or incantations. **2** To free of an evil spirit. Also **ex'or·cize.** [< Gk. *exorkizein*] **—ex'or·cism', ex'·or·cist** *n.*

ex·or·di·um (ig·zôr'dē·əm, ik·sôr'-) *n. pl.* **·di·ums** or **·di·a** (-dē-ə) The introductory part, as of a discourse; a prelude. [< L *exordiri* begin] **—ex·or'di·al** *adj.*

ex·ot·ic (ig·zot'ik) *adj.* **1** Belonging by nature or origin to another part of the world; foreign. **2** Unusually strange or different; fascinating. **—***n.* Something exotic. [< Gk. *exōtikos* foreign < *exō* outside] **—ex·ot'i·cal·ly** *adv.* **—ex·ot'i·cism** *n.*

ex·pand (ik·spand') *v.t.* **1** To increase the range, scope, volume, size, etc., of. **2** To spread out by unfolding or extending; open. **3** To write or develop in full the details or form of. **—***v.i.* **4** To grow larger, wider, etc.; unfold; increase. [< L *ex-* out + *pandere* spread] **—ex·pand'er** *n.*

ex·panse (ik·spans') *n.* **1** A vast continuous area or stretch. **2** Expansion.

ex·pan·si·ble (ik·span'sə·bəl) *adj.* Capable of being expanded. **—ex·pan'si·bil'i·ty** *n.*

ex·pan·sion (ik·span'shən) *n.* **1** The act of expanding or the state of being expanded. **2** The amount of increase in size, scope, volume, etc. **3** That which is expanded.

ex·pan·sive (ik·span'siv) *adj.* **1** Able or tending to expand. **2** Characterized by expansion; broad; extensive; comprehensive. **3** Amiable and effusive; outgoing. **—ex·pan'sive·ly** *adv.* **—ex·pan'sive·ness** *n.*

ex·pa·ti·ate (ik·spā'shē·āt) *v.i.* **·at·ed, ·at·ing** To speak or write in a lengthy manner; elaborate: with *on* or *upon.* [< L *ex(s)patiari* to spread out] **—ex·pa'ti·a'tion, ex·pa'ti·a'tor** *n.* **—ex·pa'ti·a·to'ry** (-tôr'ē, -tō'rē) *adj.*

ex·pa·tri·ate (eks·pā'trē·āt) *v.t.* **·at·ed, ·at·ing 1** To exile; banish. **2** To withdraw (oneself) from one's native land. — *n.* (-it, -āt) An expatriated person. **—***adj.* Banished; exiled. [< L *ex-* out + *patria* native land] **—ex·pa'tri·a'tion** *n.*

ex·pect (ik·spekt') *v.t.* **1** To look forward to as certain or probable; anticipate in thought. **2** To look for as right, proper, or necessary; require. **3** *Informal* To presume; suppose. [< L *ex-* out + *spectare* look at] **—ex·pect'a·ble** *adj.*

ex·pec·tan·cy (ik·spek'tən·sē) *n. pl.* **·cies 1** The act or state of expecting; expectation. **2** An object of expectation. Also **ex·pec'tance.**

ex·pec·tant (ik·spek'tənt) *adj.* **1** Waiting or looking forward in expectation. **2** Awaiting the birth of a child. **—***n.* One who is expecting something. **—ex·pec'tant·ly** *adv.*

ex·pec·ta·tion (ek'spek·tā'shən) *n.* **1** The act of expecting something; also, the mental attitude of one who expects something. **2** *Often pl.* A prospect or hope of good to come. **3** Something expected.

ex·pect·ing (ik·spek'ting) *adj.* Pregnant; also, due to give birth.

ex·pec·to·rant (ik·spek'tər·ənt) *adj.* Relating to or promotive of the discharge of mucus from the respiratory tract. **—***n.* An expectorant medicine.

ex·pec·to·rate (ik·spek'tə·rāt) *v.t. & v.i.* **·rat·ed, ·rat·ing 1** To discharge, as mucus, by coughing up and spitting. **2** To spit. [< L *ex-* out + *pectus, -oris* breast] **—ex·pec'to·ra'·tion** *n.*

ex·pe·di·en·cy (ik·spē'dē·ən·sē) *n. pl.* **·cies 1** The state or quality of being expedient. **2** That which is expedient. **3** The doing of what is politic or advantageous, regardless of justice or right. Also **ex·pe'di·ence.**

ex·pe·di·ent (ik·spē'dē·ənt) *adj.* **1** Serving to promote a desired end; suitable; useful; advisable. **2** Pertaining to or based on utility or advantage rather than what is just or right. **—***n.* **1** That which furthers or promotes an end. **2** A device; shift. [< L *expedire* make ready] **—ex·pe'di·ent·ly** *adv.*

ex·pe·dite (ek'spə·dīt) *v.t.* **·dit·ed, ·dit·ing 1** To speed up the process or progress of; facilitate. **2** To do quickly. [< L *expedire* make ready] **—ex'pe·dit'er** *n.*

ex·pe·di·tion (ek'spə·dish'ən) *n.* **1** A journey, march or voyage for a definite purpose. **2** The body of persons engaged in such a journey, together with their equipment. **3** Speed; dispatch. [< L *expedire* make ready, extricate]

ex·pe·di·tion·ar·y (ek'spə·dish'ən·er'ē) *adj.* Of, like, or constituting an expedition.

ex·pe·di·tious (ek'spə·dish'əs) *adj.* Quick; speedy. **—ex'·pe·di'tious·ly** *adv.* **—ex'pe·di'tious·ness** *n.*

ex·pel (ik·spel') *v.t.* **·pelled, ·pel·ling 1** To drive out by force or authority; force out. **2** To dismiss, as a pupil from a school; eject. [< L *ex-* out + *pellere* drive, thrust] **—ex·pel'·la·ble** *adj.* **—Syn. 1** remove, dispel, evict, oust, banish, exile.

ex·pend (ik·spend') *v.t.* To pay out or spend; use up. [< L *ex-* out + *pendere* weigh]

ex·pend·a·ble (ik·spen'də·bəl) *adj.* **1** That may be expended. **2** Capable of being consumed, used, or sacrificed, as men and materiel in warfare.

ex·pen·di·ture (ik·spen'də·chər) *n.* **1** The act of expending; outlay. **2** That which is expended; expense.

ex·pense (ik·spens') *n.* **1** *pl.* **a** Costs or charges of something: the *expenses* of a trip. **b** Money to pay for such costs or charges. **2** Anything requiring the outlay of money: A boat is an *expense.* **3** Any cost, sacrifice, or loss: at the *expense* of his health.

ex·pen·sive (ik·spen'siv) *adj.* Causing or involving much expense; costly. **—ex·pen'sive·ly** *adv.* **—ex·pen'sive·ness** *n.*

ex·pe·ri·ence (ik·spir'ē·əns) *n.* **1** The act of undergoing or being involved in an event, situation, etc. **2** Something lived through or undergone: an amazing *experience*. **3** The sum total of one's knowledge, observations, perceptions, etc.: It is outside my *experience*. **4** The duration of one's involvement with a particular activity, occupation, etc. **5** The skill or knowledge acquired from such involvement. —*v.t.* **·enced, ·enc·ing** To undergo or be involved in personally. [< L *experiri* try out] —**Syn.** *v.* know, understand, feel, realize, have, apprehend.

ex·pe·ri·en·tial (ik·spir′ē·en′shǝl) *adj.* Pertaining to or acquired by experience; empirical. —**ex·pe′ri·en′tial·ly** *adv.*

ex·per·i·ment (ik·sper′ǝ·mǝnt) *n.* **1** A procedure or test meant to yield or illustrate a principle, effect, or fact. **2** The conducting of such procedures or tests. —*v.i.* (-ment) To make experiments. [< L *experimentum* < *experiri* try out] —**ex·per′i·ment′er** *n.*

ex·per·i·men·tal (ik·sper′ǝ·men′tǝl) *adj.* **1** Of, derived from, or known by experiment or experience. **2** Still in development: *experimental* aircraft. —**ex·per′i·men′tal·ism, ex·per′i·men′tal·ist** *n.* —**ex·per′i·men′tal·ly** *adv.*

ex·per·i·men·ta·tion (ik·sper′ǝ·mǝn·tā′shǝn, -men′-) *n.* The act or practice of experimenting.

ex·pert (ek′spûrt) *n.* One who has special skill or knowledge; a specialist. —*adj.* (*also* ik·spûrt′) **1** Skillful as the result of practice; dexterous. **2** Of or from an expert. [< L *expertus*, pp. of *experiri* try out] —**ex·pert′ly** *adv.* —**ex·pert′ness** *n.*

ex·per·tise (ek′spǝr·tēz′) *n.* The skill, knowledge, or experience of an expert. [F]

ex·pi·ate (ek′spē·āt) *v.t.* **·at·ed, ·at·ing** To atone for; make amends for. [< L *ex-* completely + *piare* appease] —**ex′pi·a′tion, ex′pi·a′tor** *n.* —**ex′pi·a·to′ry** *adj.*

ex·pi·ra·tion (ek′spǝ·rā′shǝn) *n.* **1** The natural termination of anything, as of a lease. **2** The act of breathing out, as air from the lungs. **3** That which is breathed out. **4** Death. —**ex·pir·a·to·ry** (ik·spī′rǝ·tôr′ē, -tō′rē) *adj.*

ex·pire (ik·spīr′) *v.* **·pired, ·pir·ing** *v.i.* **1** To exhale one's last breath; die. **2** To breathe out. **3** To die out, as embers. **4** To come to an end; terminate. —*v.t.* **5** To breathe out. [< L *ex-* out + *spirare* breathe] —**ex·pir′er** *n.*

ex·plain (ik·splān′) *v.t.* **1** To make plain or clear; make understandable. **2** To give a meaning to; interpret. **3** To give reasons for; state the cause or purpose of. —*v.i.* **4** To give an explanation. [< L *ex-* out + *planare* make level] —**ex·plain′a·ble** *adj.*

ex·pla·na·tion (ek′splǝ·nā′shǝn) *n.* **1** The act of explaining. **2** Something, as a statement, that explains. **3** Meaning; significance; sense.

ex·plan·a·to·ry (ik·splan′ǝ·tôr′ē, -tō′rē) *adj.* Serving or tending to explain. Also **ex·plan′a·tive.** —**ex·plan′a·to′ri·ly** *adv.*

ex·ple·tive (eks′plǝ·tiv) *n.* **1** An exclamation, often profane. **2** A word or syllable employed to fill out a sentence, complete a rhythmical pattern, etc. —*adj.* Added to fill out a sentence, etc.: also **ex′ple·to′ry** (-tôr′ē, -tō′rē). [< L *ex-* completely + *plere* fill]

ex·pli·ca·ble (eks′pli·kǝ·bǝl, iks·plik′ǝ·bǝl) *adj.* Capable of explanation.

ex·pli·cate (eks′plǝ·kāt) *v.t.* **·cat·ed, ·cat·ing** To clear from obscurity; explain. [< L *ex-* out + *plicare* fold] —**ex′pli·ca′tion, ex′pli·ca′tor** *n.* —**ex′pli·ca′tive** *adj.*

ex·plic·it (ik·splis′it) *adj.* **1** Plainly stated; clearly expressed. **2** Having no disguised meaning or reservation; definite; open. [< L *explicare* unfold, explicate. See EXPLICATE.] —**ex·plic′it·ly** *adv.* —**ex·plic′it·ness** *n.*

ex·plode (ik·splōd′) *v.* **·plod·ed, ·plod·ing** *v.t.* **1** To cause to expand violently or pass suddenly from a solid to a gaseous state. **2** To cause to burst or blow up violently and with noise. **3** To disprove utterly; refute. —*v.i.* **4** To be exploded or blow up. **5** To burst forth noisily or violently: to *explode* with laughter. **6** To become greater very quickly. [< L *explodere*, orig., drive off the stage, hiss < *ex-* out + *plaudere* clap] —**ex·plod′er** *n.*

ex·ploit (eks′ploit, ik·sploit′) *n.* A deed or act, esp. one marked by heroism, daring, skill, or brilliancy. —*v.t.* (ik·sploit′) **1** To use for one's own advantage; take advantage of. **2** To put to use; make use of. [< OF] —**ex·ploit′a·ble** *adj.* —**ex′ploi·ta′tion, ex·ploit′er** *n.*

ex·plore (ik·splôr′, -splōr′) *v.* **·plored, ·plor·ing** *v.* **1** To

search through or travel in or over, as new lands, for discovery. **2** To look into or examine carefully; scrutinize. —*v.i.* **3** To make explorations. [< L *explorare* investigate < *ex-* out + *plorare* cry out] —**ex′plo·ra′tion, ex·plor′er** *n.* —**ex·plor·a·to·ry** (ik·splôr′ǝ·tôr′ē), **ex·plor′a·tive** *adj.*

ex·plo·sion (ik·splō′zhǝn) *n.* **1** The act of exploding; rapid release of energy, usu. causing a loud noise. **2** A sudden and violent outbreak, as of physical or emotional forces. **3** A sudden and large increase.

ex·plo·sive (ik·splō′siv) *adj.* **1** Pertaining to or characterized by explosion. **2** Liable to explode, become violent, or cause turmoil: *explosive* news. —*n.* A material that can explode or cause an explosion. —**ex·plo′sive·ly** *adv.* —**ex·plo′sive·ness** *n.*

ex·po·nent (ik·spō′nǝnt) *n.* **1** One who explains or expounds. **2** *Math.* A number or symbol placed as a superscript to the right of a quantity to indicate a power, reciprocal, or root. **3** Any person or thing that symbolizes or exemplifies something. [< L *exponere* indicate] —**ex·po·nen·tial** (ek′spǝ·nen′shǝl) *adj.* —**ex′po·nen′tial·ly** *adv.*

ex·port (ik·spôrt′, -spôrt′, eks′pôrt, -pôrt) *v.t.* To carry or send, as goods or raw materials, to other countries for sale or trade. —*n.* (eks′pôrt, -pôrt) **1** The act of exporting; exportation. **2** That which is exported; esp. merchandise. —*adj.* (eks′pôrt, -pôrt) Of or pertaining to exports or exportation. [< L *ex-* out + *portare* carry] —**ex·port′a·ble** *adj.* —**ex′por·ta′tion, ex·port′er** *n.*

ex·pose (ik·spōz′) *v.t.* **·posed, ·pos·ing** **1** To lay open, as to harm, ridicule, etc. **2** To leave open to the action of a force or influence. **3** To present to view; show; display. **4** To cause to be known; make public, as a crime. **5** To lay open or make known the crimes, faults, etc., of (a person). **6** To abandon so as to cause the death of: to *expose* an unwanted child. **7** *Phot.* To admit light to (a sensitized film or plate). [< MF *exposer* < L *exponere*] —**ex·pos′er** *n.*

ex·po·sé (ek′spō·zā′) *n.* A disclosure or exposure of something corrupt, evil, etc. [F]

ex·po·si·tion (eks′pǝ·zish′ǝn) *n.* **1** A large, comprehensive, public exhibition, as a world's fair. **2** A detailed explanation or commentary. **3** Any detailed presentation of a topic, either written or oral. **4** The part of a play that tells something about the characters, what has happened before, etc. [< L *expositio* < *exponere* to expose] —**ex·pos′i·tor** *n.* —**ex·pos′i·to′ry** *adj.*

ex post fac·to (eks pōst fak′tō) Arising or done after the fact but having a retroactive effect. [L]

ex·pos·tu·late (ik·spos′chǝ·lāt) *v.i.* **·lat·ed, ·lat·ing** To reason earnestly with a person, against some action: usu. with *with*. [< L *ex-* out + *postulare* demand] —**ex·pos′tu·la′tion** *n.* —**ex·pos′tu·la′tive, ex·pos′tu·la·to′ry** *adj.*

ex·po·sure (ik·spō′zhǝr) *n.* **1** The act or process of exposing, or the state of being exposed in any sense. **2** Situation in relation to the sun, elements, or points of the compass: The house had a southern *exposure*. **3** *Phot.* **a** The act of subjecting a sensitized film or plate to light rays or other radiation. **b** The time necessary for this. **c** An amount of film necessary for one picture.

ex·pound (ik·spound′) *v.t.* **1** To set forth in detail; state, as a doctrine or theory. **2** To explain the meaning or significance of; interpret. [< L *exponere* to put forth, expose] —**ex·pound′er** *n.*

ex·press (ik·spres′) *v.t.* **1** To put (thought or opinion) into spoken or written words. **2** To make apparent; reveal. **3** To represent in symbols, as in art or mathematics. **4** To send by express. **5** To press out; squeeze out, as juice or moisture. **6** To force out by or as by pressure. —**express oneself** To make known one's thoughts, feelings, or creative impulses. —*adj.* **1** Set forth distinctly; explicit; direct. **2** Specially prepared; adapted to a specific purpose. **3** Traveling at high speeds. **4** Designed for fast driving. **5** Making few stops: an *express* elevator. **6** Exact: an *express* likeness. —*adv.* By fast delivery. —*n.* **1** A system of transporting goods rapidly. **2** The goods so sent. **3** A message, money, etc. sent with speed. **4** Any means of rapid transmission. **5** An express train, elevator, etc. [< L *ex-* out + *pressare* to press] —**ex·press′er** *n.* —**ex·press′i·ble** *adj.*

ex·press·age (ik·spres′ij) *n.* **1** The transportation of goods by express or special system. **2** Amount charged for this.

ex·pres·sion (ik·spresh′ǝn) *n.* **1** The act of representing or expressing something by using words, gestures, art, music, etc. **2** Any means by which some truth or idea is conveyed: the *expression* of pleasure. **3** The manner of expressing or doing something, esp. an effective or eloquent manner. **4** A phrase or saying. **5** A gesture, tone, facial aspect, etc., that conveys a thought or feeling. **6** A pressing out, as of juice. **7** *Math.* A meaningful group of characters, numbers, etc.

ex·pres·sion·ism (ik-spresh′ən·iz′əm) *n.* An early 20th-century movement in the arts, characterized by the use of distortion, abstraction, exaggeration, and symbolism to depict subjective experience rather than objective reality. —**ex·pres′sion·ist** *n., adj.* —**ex·pres′sion·is′tic** *adj.*

ex·pres·sive (ik-spres′iv) *adj.* **1** Of or characterized by expression. **2** Expressing or indicating: a look *expressive* of hate. **3** Meaningful; significant: an *expressive* glance. —**ex·pres′sive·ly** *adv.* —**ex·pres′sive·ness** *n.*

ex·press·ly (ik-spres′lē) *adv.* With definitely stated intent or application; exactly and unmistakably; in direct terms.

ex·press·way (ik-spres′wā′) *n.* A highway designed for rapid travel.

ex·pro·pri·ate (eks·prō′prē·āt) *v.t.* **·at·ed, ·at·ing 1** To take from the owner, esp. for public use. **2** To deprive of ownership or property. [< LL *ex-* out + *proprium* property] —**ex·pro′pri·a′tion, ex·pro′pri·a′tor** *n.*

ex·pul·sion (ik·spul′shən) *n.* **1** The act of expelling; forcible ejection. **2** The state of being expelled. —**ex·pul′sive** *adj.*

ex·punge (ik·spunj′) *v.t.* **·punged, ·pung·ing** To blot or scratch out, as from a record or list; obliterate. [< L *ex-* out + *pungere* prick] —**ex·pung′er** *n.*

ex·pur·gate (eks′pər·gāt) *v.t.* **·gat·ed, ·gat·ing** To remove from (a book, etc.) whatever is considered objectionable, immoral, etc. [< L *ex-* out + *purgare* cleanse] —**ex′pur·ga′tion, ex′pur·ga′tor** *n.* —**ex·pur·ga·to·ry** (ik·spûr′gə·tôr′ē, -tō′rē) *adj.*

ex·qui·site (eks′kwi·zit, ik·skwiz′it) *adj.* **1** Skillfully and delicately made or designed: an *exquisite* silk fan. **2** Delicately beautiful: an *exquisite* child. **3** Unusually refined and sensitive, as in perception or judgment: *exquisite* taste. **4** Extremely fine; consummate: an *exquisite* interpretation. **5** Intense; extreme: *exquisite* pain or pleasure. —*n.* One overly sensitive or fastidiously elegant in taste, manners, perceptions, etc. [< L *ex-* out + *quarere* seek] —**ex′qui·site·ly** *adv.* —**ex′qui·site·ness** *n.*

ext. extension; external; extinct; extra; extract.

ex·tant (ek′stənt, ik·stant′) *adj.* Still existing and known; not lost or extinct. [< L *ex-* out + *stare* stand]

ex·tem·po·ra·ne·ous (ik·stem′pə·rā′nē·əs) *adj.* **1** Done or made with no preparation; unpremeditated. **2** Somewhat prepared but not memorized, rehearsed, etc., as a speech. **3** Made with what is at hand; improvised. [< L *ex-* out + *tempus, temporis* time] —**ex·tem′po·ra′ne·ous·ly** *adv.* —**ex·tem′po·ra′ne·ous·ness** *n.*

ex·tem·po·rar·y (ik·stem′pə·rer′ē) *adj.* EXTEMPORANEOUS. —**ex·tem′po·rar′i·ly** *adv.* —**ex·tem′po·rar′i·ness** *n.*

ex·tem·po·re (ik·stem′pər·ē) *adj.* Extemporaneous; unstudied; offhand. —*adv.* Without special preparation; extemporaneously. [< L *ex tempore* out of the time]

ex·tem·po·rize (ik·stem′pə·rīz) *v.t. & v.i.* **·rized, ·riz·ing** To do, make, or compose without preparation; improvise. —**ex·tem′po·ri·za′tion, ex·tem′po·riz′er** *n.*

ex·tend (ik·stend′) *v.t.* **1** To open or stretch to full length. **2** To make longer. **3** To cause to last or continue until or for a specified time. **4** To widen or enlarge the range, scope, meaning, etc., of: to *extend* the duties of an office. **5** To hold out or put forth, as the hand. **6** To give or offer to give: to *extend* hospitality. **7** To straighten, as a leg or arm. —*v.i.* **8** To be extended; stretch. **9** To reach, as in a specified direction: This road *extends* west. —**extend oneself** To put forth great effort. [< L *ex-* out + *tendere* stretch] —**ex·tend′i·bil′i·ty** *n.* —**ex·tend′i·ble** *adj.*

ex·ten·si·ble (ik·sten′sə·bəl) *adj.* That may be extended. —**ex·ten′si·bil′i·ty, ex·ten′si·ble·ness** *n.*

ex·ten·sion (ik·sten′shən) *n.* **1** The act of extending or the condition of being extended. **2** Something extended or additional, as an annex to a building, a second telephone in a home, a branch of a school or university, an extended time limit for a debt, etc. **3** The straightening of a flexed limb. —*adj.* Capable of extending or being extended. —**ex·ten′sion·al** *adj.*

ex·ten·sive (ik·sten′siv) *adj.* **1** Great in area. **2** Broad or wide in scope, range, influence, etc. **3** Large in amount, extent, etc.; considerable: *extensive* damage. —**ex·ten′sive·ly** *adv.* —**ex·ten′sive·ness** *n.*

ex·ten·sor (ik·sten′sər, -sôr) *n.* A muscle that contracts to produce extension.

ex·tent (ik·stent′) *n.* **1** The dimension, amount, or degree to which anything is extended; reach; size. **2** Range, scope, or limits of something: the *extent* of his power. **3** A large area or space: an *extent* of pastureland.

Extensor muscle

ex·ten·u·ate (ik·sten′yoo·āt) *v.t.* **·at·ed, ·at·ing 1** To represent as less blameworthy; make excuses for. **2** To cause to seem less serious or blameworthy: *extenuating* circumstances. [< L *extenuare* weaken < *ex-* out + *tenuis* thin] —**ex·ten′u·a′tion, ex·ten′u·a′tor** *n.*

ex·te·ri·or (ik·stir′ē·ər) *adj.* **1** Of, on, or for the outside. **2** Acting or coming from outside. —*n.* **1** Something located outside; an outside part or surface. **2** External features or qualities. [< L compar. of *exterus* outside] —**ex·te′ri·or·ly** *adv.*

ex·ter·mi·nate (ik·stûr′mə·nāt) *v.t.* **·nat·ed, ·nat·ing** To destroy entirely; annihilate. [< L *exterminare* to drive out] —**ex·ter′min·a′tion** *n.* —**ex·ter′mi·na′tive, ex·ter′mi·na·to′ry** (-tôr′ē, -tō′rē) *adj.* —**Syn.** demolish, eradicate, remove, root out, abolish.

ex·ter·mi·na·tor (ik·stûr′mə·nā′tər) *n.* One who or that which exterminates; esp., one whose business is the elimination of rodents, insects, etc.

ex·ter·nal (ik·stûr′nəl) *adj.* **1** Of, pertaining to, or situated on the outside; exterior. **2** On, of, or for the outside of the body: an *external* medicine. **3** Visible from the outside. **4** Having existence separate from one's perceptions. **5** Coming or acting from outside. **6** Merely for outward appearance; superficial: *external* show. —*n.* **1** An exterior or outer part. **2** *Usu. pl.* Outward and often superficial appearances, circumstances, etc. [< L *externus* outer < *exterus* outside] —**ex′ter·nal′i·ty** *n.* —**ex·ter′nal·ly** *adv.*

ex·ter·nal·ize (ik·stûr′nəl·īz) *v.t.* **·ized, ·iz·ing 1** To give shape to; embody. **2** To make outwardly real. —**ex·ter′nal·i·za′tion** *n.*

ex·tinct (ik·stingkt′) *adj.* **1** No longer active or burning: an *extinct* volcano. **2** No longer existing: an *extinct* animal. **3** Void; lapsed: an *extinct* title. [< L *ex(s)tinguere* extinguish]

ex·tinc·tion (ik·stingk′shən) *n.* **1** The act of extinguishing, or the state of being extinguished; extinguishment. **2** A dying out or becoming extinct. **3** The act of destroying, or the state of being destroyed.

ex·tin·guish (ik·sting′gwish) *v.t.* **1** To put out; quench, as a fire. **2** To make extinct; wipe out. **3** To obscure or throw into the shade; eclipse. [< L *ex-* completely + *stinguere* quench] —**ex·tin′guish·a·ble** *adj.* —**ex·tin′guish·er, ex·tin′guish·ment** *n.*

ex·tir·pate (ek′stər·pāt) *v.t.* **·pat·ed, ·pat·ing** To root out or up; eradicate; destroy wholly. [< L *ex-* out + *stirps* stem, root] —**ex′tir·pa′tion** *n.* —**ex′tir·pa′tive** *adj.*

ex·tol (ik·stōl′) *v.t.* **·tolled, ·tol·ling** To praise in the highest terms; magnify. Also **ex·toll′**. [< L *ex-* out, up + *tollere* raise] —**ex·tol′ler, ex·tol′ment or ex·toll′ment** *n.*

ex·tort (ik·stôrt′) *v.t.* To obtain from a person by violence, threat, oppression, or abuse of authority; wring; wrest. [< L *ex-* out + *torquere* twist] —**ex·tort′er** *n.* —**ex·tor′tive** *adj.*

ex·tor·tion (ik·stôr′shən) *n.* **1** The act or practice of extorting. **2** The exacting of an excessively high price for something. **3** That which has been extorted. —**ex·tor′tion·ar′y, ex·tor′tion·ate** *adj.* —**ex·tor′tion·er or ·ist** *n.*

ex·tra (eks′trə) *adj.* **1** Being more, better, larger, etc., than what is required or expected. **2** Additional: an *extra* charge. —*n.* **1** An extra person or thing. **2** Something additional or special, often at an additional cost. **3** A copy or an edition of a newspaper issued for some special purpose, or at a special time. **4** An actor hired for a special scene, as a mob scene. —*adv.* Unusually; exceptionally. [Prob. short for EXTRAORDINARY]

extra- *prefix* Beyond or outside the scope, range, limits, etc., of. [L < *exter* on the outside] • *Adjectives* formed with the prefix *extra-* are usu. written solid, as in *extracurricular*. However, if the second element of the compound begins with an *a* or with a capital letter, the word is hyphenated, as in *extra-atmospheric*.

ex·tract (ik·strakt′) *v.t.* **1** To draw or pull out by force. **2** To obtain (pleasure, benefit, etc.) from some action, circumstance, or source. **3** To obtain by force, extortion, pressure, etc.: to *extract* money. **4** To obtain (a concentrate, juice, etc.) by pressing, chemical action, etc. **5** To copy out; select for quotation. **6** *Math.* To calculate (the root of a number). —*n.* (eks′trakt) Something extracted or drawn out, as: **a** A concentrate or essence of a food, flavoring, etc.: vanilla *extract*. **b** A selection or passage from written or spoken matter. [< L *ex-* out + *trahere* draw, pull] —**ex·tract′a·ble** or **ex·tract′i·ble** *adj.* —**ex·trac′tive** *adj., n.* —**ex·tract′or** *n.*

ex·trac·tion (ik·strak′shən) *n.* **1** The act of extracting, as a tooth. **2** That which is extracted. **3** Lineage; descent.

ex·tra·cur·ric·u·lar (eks′trə·kə·rik′yə·lər) *adj.* Of or pertaining to activities outside a school's regular curriculum, as clubs, school publications, etc.

ex·tra·dite (eks′trə·dīt) *v.t.* **·dit·ed, ·dit·ing** **1** To deliver up (an accused person, prisoner, etc.) as to another state or nation. **2** To obtain the extradition of. —**ex′tra·dit′a·ble** *adj.*

ex·tra·di·tion (eks′trə·dish′ən) *n.* The surrender of an accused person, prisoner, etc., by one government or state to another. [< L *ex-* out + *traditio* a surrender]

ex·tra·ne·ous (ik·strā′nē·əs) *adj.* Not intrinsic, relevant, or essential to matter under consideration. [< L *extraneus* foreign] —**ex·tra′ne·ous·ly** *adv.* —**ex·tra′ne·ous·ness** *n.*

ex·traor·di·nar·y (ik·strôr′də·ner′ē; *esp. for def. 3*, eks′·trə·ôr′də·ner′ē) *adj.* **1** Beyond or out of the common order, course, or method. **2** Exceeding the ordinary or usual; exceptional; remarkable. **3** Employed for a special purpose or occasion; special: an envoy *extraordinary*. —**ex·traor′di·nar′i·ly** *adv.* —**Syn.** **1,2** amazing, marvelous, uncommon, unusual, unprecedented, odd, rare.

ex·trap·o·late (ik·strap′ə·lāt) *v.t. & v.i.* **·lat·ed, ·lat·ing** **1** *Math.* To estimate (a function) beyond the range of known values. **2** To infer (a possibility) beyond the strict evidence of a series of facts, events, observations, etc. [< EXTRA- + (INTER)POLATE] —**ex·trap′o·la′tion** *n.*

ex·tra·sen·so·ry (eks′trə·sen′sər·ē) *adj.* Outside of or beyond normal sensory perception.

ex·tra·ter·res·tri·al (ek′trə·tə·res′trē·əl) *adj.* Being or from outside the earth or its atmosphere.

ex·tra·ter·ri·to·ri·al (eks′trə·ter′ə·tôr′ē·əl, -tō′rē-) *adj.* **1** Exempt from territorial jurisdiction; not subject to the laws of one's abode: the *extraterritorial* rights of an ambassador. **2** Beyond the national territory: *extraterritorial* possessions. —**ex′tra·ter′ri·to′ri·al′i·ty** (-al′ə·tē) *n.* —**ex′tra·ter′ri·to′ri·al·ly** *adv.*

ex·trav·a·gance (ik·strav′ə·gəns) *n.* **1** Excessive expenditure of money. **2** Exaggerated or unreasonable conduct or speech. **3** An instance of excessive or immoderate conduct, speech, or spending. Also **ex·trav′a·gan·cy.**

ex·trav·a·gant (ik·strav′ə·gənt) *adj.* **1** Excessively free or lavish in expenditure. **2** Immoderate; fantastic; unrestrained: *extravagant* behavior. **3** Unusually ornate or fanciful: an *extravagant* costume. **4** Exorbitant. [< L *extra-* outside + *vagari* wander] —**ex·trav′a·gant·ly** *adv.* —**ex·trav′a·gant·ness** *n.*

ex·trav·a·gan·za (ik·strav′ə·gan′zə) *n.* **1** A lavish or fantastic composition in literature, music, or the drama. **2** Any lavish and spectacular entertainment or show.

ex·treme (ik·strēm′) *adj.* **1** At or to the farthest limit or point; outermost. **2** In the utmost degree; very great: *extreme* joy. **3** Far from the normal, average, or usual. **4** Immoderate; radical; *extreme* opinions. **5** Drastic: *extreme* measures. **6** Last; final: *extreme* unction. —*n.* **1** The utmost or highest degree, limit, etc.: the *extreme* of cruelty. **2** Either of the two ends or limits of a series, range, etc.: *extremes* of temperature. **3** An act or condition that is extreme or drastic. —**go to extremes** To be excessive or immoderate in action, thought, etc. [< L *extremus*, superl. of *exterus* outside] —**ex·treme′ly** *adv.* —**ex·treme′ness** *n.*

extreme unction In the Roman Catholic Church, the rite of anointing those sick or injured who are in danger of death.

ex·trem·ist (ik·strē′mist) *n.* One who supports or advocates extreme measures or holds extreme views. —*adj.* Of or pertaining to extremists. —**ex·trem′ism** *n.*

ex·trem·i·ty (ik·strem′ə·tē) *n. pl.* **·ties** **1** The utmost or farthest point; termination, end, or edge. **2** The greatest degree. **3** Desperate distress or need. **4** *pl.* Extreme measures. **5** *Usu. pl.* The end part of a limb or appendage.

ex·tri·cate (eks′trə·kāt) *v.t.* **·cat·ed, ·cat·ing** To free from hindrance, difficulties, etc.; disentangle. [< L *ex-* out + *tricae* troubles] —**ex·tri·ca·ble** (eks′tri·kə·bəl) *adj.* —**ex′tri·ca·bly** *adv.* —**ex·tri·ca′tion** *n.*

ex·trin·sic (ek·strin′sik) *adj.* **1** Not belonging to the essential nature or makeup of something; not inherent. **2** Originating from the outside; extraneous. [< L *extrinsecus* outwardly < *exter* outside + *secus* besides] —**ex·trin′si·cal·ly** *adv.* —**ex·trin′si·cal·ness** *n.*

ex·tro·vert (eks′trō·vûrt) *n.* One whose attention and interest are directed chiefly towards other people and the external world rather than towards himself. [< EXTRA- + L *vertere* turn] —**ex′tro·ver′sion** *n.*

ex·trude (ik·strood′) *v.* **·trud·ed, ·trud·ing** *v.t.* **1** To force, thrust, or push out; expel, as through a small opening. —*v.i.* **2** To protrude. [< L *ex-* out + *trudere* thrust] —**ex·tru′·sion** *n.* —**ex·tru′sive** *adj.*

ex·u·ber·ance (ig·zoo′bər·əns) *n.* **1** The state or quality of being exuberant. **2** An instance of this. Also **ex·u′ber·an·cy.**

ex·u·ber·ant (ig·zoo′bər·ənt) *adj.* **1** Characterized by high spirits, enthusiasm, and vitality. **2** Effusive; overflowing; lavish. **3** Marked by plentifulness; producing copiously. [< L *ex-* completely + *uberare* be fruitful] —**ex·u′ber·ant·ly** *adv.*

ex·ude (ig·zood′, ik·sood′) *v.* **·ud·ed, ·ud·ing** —*v.i.* **1** To ooze or trickle forth, as sweat. —*v.t.* **2** To ooze or give off gradually. **3** To seem to possess; manifest: to *exude* hope. [< L *ex-* out + *sudare* sweat] —**ex·u·da·tion** (eks′yoo·dā′shən) *n.*

ex·ult (ig·zult′) *v.i.* To rejoice in or as in triumph; take great delight. [< L *ex-* out + *salire* leap] —**ex·ul·ta·tion** (ig′zul·tā′shən, ek′sul-) *n.* —**ex·ult′ing·ly** *adv.*

ex·ul·tant (ig·zul′tənt) *adj.* **1** Rejoicing triumphantly. **2** Denoting great joy. —**ex·ul′tant·ly** *adv.*

ex·ur·ban·ite (eks·ûr′bən·īt) *n.* One living outside a city in a residential area beyond the suburbs, who commutes to work in the city, and who is sometimes considered above a suburbanite in economic and social status. [< EX(TRA-) + (SUB)URBANITE]

ex·ur·bi·a (eks·ûr′bē·ə) *n.* A residential area outside a city, usu. beyond the suburbs; also, such areas collectively. [< EX- + L *urbs* city]

ex·u·vi·ate (ig·zoo′vē·āt, ik·soo′-) *v.t. & v.i.* **·at·ed, ·at·ing** To cast off or shed (skin, shell, etc.); molt. [< L *exuviae* parts cast off]

eye (ī) *n.* **1** Any organ of sight in animals. **2** Either of two balls of tissue set into the front of the vertebrate skull and consisting of specialized parts such as cornea, iris, lens, retina, optic nerve, and associated muscles, together with surrounding facial tissues, as eyelids, etc. **3** *Often pl.* The power to see; sight. **4** A glance; look. **5** Attentive observation. **6** A capacity for discerning, judging, appreciating, etc.: an *eye* for color. **7** *Often pl.* Judgment; estimation. **8** Anything that resembles the human eye in shape, function, place, etc.: the *eye* of a needle, the *eye* of

Human eye
a. retina. b. lens.
c. pupil. d. cornea.
e. iris. f. optic nerve.

a potato, etc. **9** *Meteorol.* The calm central area of a hurricane or cyclone. **—keep an eye out** or **peeled** To watch for; keep alert. **—lay** (or **set**) **eyes on** To see. **—see eye to eye** To share a common view; agree. **—with an eye to** Looking forward to; planning for; considering. **—v.t. eyed, ey·ing** or **eye·ing 1** To look at carefully; scrutinize. **2** To make a hole in. [< OE *ēage*]

eye·ball (ī′bôl′) *n.* The globe or ball of the eye. **—v.t. Slang** To look at in an intent way; stare at.

eye·brow (ī′brou′) *n.* **1** The bony arch over the eye. **2** Its covering, esp. the hairs.

eye·cup (ī′kup′) *n.* A small cup with rim curved to hold medicated or cleansing liquid against the eyeball.

eyed (īd) *adj.* **1** Having a specified kind or number of eyes: *blue-eyed.* **2** Having eyelike spots.

eye·drop·per *n.* DROPPER (def. 2)

eye·ful (ī′fŏŏl′) *n.* **1** An amount of something in the eye. **2** A full or complete look. **3** *Slang* A person or thing of striking or unusual appearance.

eye·glass (ī′glas′, ī′gläs′) *n.* **1** Any lens used to assist vision, as a monocle, loupe, etc. **2** *pl.* A pair of corrective lenses mounted in a supporting frame. **3** An eyecup.

eye·hole (ī′hōl′) *n.* **1** A round opening through which to pass a pin, hook, rope, or the like. **2** A peephole. **3** The eye's socket.

eye·lash (ī′lash′) *n.* One of the stiff curved hairs growing from the edge of the eyelids.

eye·less (ī′lis) *adj.* Lacking eyes; sightless.

eye·let (ī′lit) *n.* **1** A small hole or opening. **2** A hole made in canvas, leather, etc., and lined with metal. **3** A metal ring for such a hole. **4** In embroidery, a small hole with an edging of decorative stitches. **—v.t.** To make eyelets in.

eye·lid (ī′lid′) *n.* One of the folds of skin that sweep over and cover the eye.

eye·o·pen·er (ī′ō′pən·ər) *n.* **1** Anything startling or unusual. **2** *Informal* A drink of liquor, esp. one taken early in the morning.

eye·piece (ī′pēs′) *n.* The lens or system of lenses nearest the eye in an optical instrument.

eye shadow A cosmetic preparation, tinted blue, green, black, etc., applied to the eyelids to enhance the eyes.

eye·shot (ī′shot′) *n.* Range of vision.

eye·sight (ī′sīt′) *n.* **1** The power or sense of sight. **2** Extent of vision; view.

eye·sore (ī′sôr′, ī′sōr′) *n.* Anything that offends the sight.

eye·strain (ī′strān′) *n.* Fatigue of the eyes due to overuse or faulty focusing.

eye·tooth (ī′tōōth′) *n. pl.* **eye·teeth** One of the upper canine teeth.

eye·wash (ī′wosh′, ī′wôsh′) *n.* **1** A medicinal wash for the eyes. **2** *Slang* Nonsense; bunk.

eye·wit·ness (ī′wit′nis) *n.* One who has seen a thing or an occurrence with his own eyes and hence can give testimony about it.

ey·ry, ey·rie (âr′ē, ir′ē) *n.* AERIE.

F

F, f (ef) *n. pl.* **F's, f's, Fs, fs** (efs) *n.* **1** The sixth letter of the English alphabet. **2** Any spoken sound representing the letter *F* or *f.* **3** Something shaped like an F. **4** *Music* The fourth tone in the diatonic scale of C major. **5** In education, a grade meaning failure. **—adj.** Shaped like an F.

F Fahrenheit; farad; fluorine.

F. Fahrenheit; farad; February; Fellow; France; French; Friday.

f. farad; fathom; feminine; fluid; folio; following; *Music* forte; franc.

fa (fä) *n. Music* In solmization, the fourth tone of a diatonic scale. [< Ital.]

Fa·bi·an (fā′bē·ən) *adj.* Designating a policy of delay and caution. **—n.** A member of the Fabian Society. [< *Fabius,* Roman general who defeated Hannibal] **—Fa′bi·an·ism** *n.* **—Fa′bi·an·ist** *n., adj.*

Fabian Society An English association, formed in 1884, with the aim of achieving socialism by easy stages.

fa·ble (fā′bəl) *n.* **1** A brief story embodying a moral, often with animals as the characters. **2** A myth or legend. **3** A falsehood; lie. **—v.t. & v.i. fa·bled, fa·bling** To invent or tell (fables, lies, etc.). [< L *fabula* < *fari* say, speak]

fab·ric (fab′rik) *n.* **1** Any woven, felted, or knitted cloth. **2** Something that has been fabricated, constructed, or put together. **3** The manner of construction; workmanship. [< L *fabrica* a workshop]

fab·ri·cate (fab′rə·kāt) *v.t.* **·cat·ed, ·cat·ing 1** To make, assemble, or manufacture. **2** To invent, as lies or reasons; concoct. [< L *fabricare* to construct] **—fab′ri·ca′tion, fab′ri·ca′tor** *n.*

fab·u·list (fab′yə·list) *n.* **1** A composer of fables. **2** One who falsifies or fabricates.

fab·u·lous (fab′yə·ləs) *adj.* **1** Fictitious; mythical. **2** Unbelievable; incredible. [< L *fabula* FABLE] **—fab′u·lous·ly** *adv.* **—fab′u·lous·ness** *n.*

fa·cade (fə·säd′, fa-) *n.* **1** *Archit.* The front or chief face of a building. ● See ROMANESQUE. **2** A false or deceptive look or manner. [< L *facies* a face]

face (fās) *n.* **1** The front portion of the head. **2** The front or most important surface: the *face* of a clock; the *face* of

a playing card. **3** A side or surface of a solid. **4** The outward appearance, effect, or impression: to put on a bold *face.* **5** *Informal* Effrontery; audacity. **6** A grimace: to make a *face.* **7** *Printing* **a** The impression surface of type or of a printing plate. **b** The size or style of the type. **8** The value printed on a bond, paper money, etc. **—face to face 1** In one another's presence. **2** Confronting: with *with.* **—in the face of 1** In the presence of; confronting. **2** In opposition to; in defiance of **—lose face** To lose standing or reputation. **—save face** To protect one's dignity in the opinion of others. **—v. faced, fac·ing** *v.t.* **1** To bear or turn the face toward; front upon: The house *faces* the street. **2** To cause to turn in a given direction, as soldiers. **3** To meet face to face; confront: to *face* great odds. **4** To realize or be aware of: to *face* facts. **5** To cover with a layer or surface of another material. **6** To make smooth the surface of; dress: to *face* stone. **7** To turn face upward, as a playing card. **—v.i. 8** To be turned or placed with the face in a given direction: The house *faces* west. **9** To turn in a given direction: *Face* right. **—face down** To disconcert by a bold stare or manner. **—face the music** *Slang* To accept the consequences. **—face up to 1** To meet with courage; confront. **2** To realize; become aware of. [< L *facies*] **—face′·a·ble** *adj.*

face card A playing card bearing the picture of a king, queen, or jack.

face-lift·ing (fās′lif′ting) *n.* Cosmetic surgery that tightens sagging tissues and removes facial wrinkles.

fac·et (fas′it) *n.* **1** Any of the flat surfaces on a gem or similar object. **2** One side or aspect of a person's mind or character. **—v.t. fac·et·ed** or **·et·ted, fac·et·ing** or **·et·ting** To cut or work facets upon. [< F *facette,* lit., small face]

fa·ce·tious (fə·sē′shəs) *adj.* Indulging in or marked by wit or humor; jocular. [< L *facetia* wit + -OUS] **—fa·ce′tious·ly** *adv.* **—fa·ce′tious·ness** *n.* **—Syn.** clever, droll, funny, pungent, waggish.

Facets

face value 1 The value printed on paper money, coins, etc. 2 The apparent or seeming value; at *face value.*

fa·cial (fā′shəl) *adj.* Of, near, or affecting the face. —*n.* A massage or other treatment for the face. —**fa′cial·ly** *adv.*

fac·ile (fas′il) *adj.* 1 Easy to do or master. 2 Easily moved or persuaded; pliant. 3 Ready or quick in performance; dexterous. [< L *facilis* easy to do < *facere* do] —**fac′ile·ly** *adv.* —**fac′ile·ness** *n.* • *Facile* means *easy* but implies that little effort is expended and that the result is not worth much. A *facile* style of violin playing is superficial and lacking in depth. An *easy* style is relaxed but has both depth and precision.

fa·cil·i·tate (fə·sil′ə·tāt) *v.t.* **·tat·ed, ·tat·ing** To make easier or more convenient.

fa·cil·i·ty (fə·sil′ə·tē) *n. pl.* **·ties** 1 Ease or readiness in doing; dexterity. 2 Readiness of compliance; pliancy. 3 *Often pl.* Any means, aid, or convenience; dining *facilities.* 4 A place or office equipped to fulfill a special function: a government *facility.* [< L *facilitas* ability < *facere* do]

fac·ing (fā′sing) *n.* 1 The lining on the edge of a garment, as on the lapel of a coat or a hem. 2 A protective or decorative covering or layer. 3 A material used in facing.

fac·sim·i·le (fak·sim′ə·lē) *n.* 1 An exact copy or reproduction. 2 *Telecom.* A method of transmitting graphic information, as an electrical signal. —*adj.* Of or like a facsimile. [< L *fac simile* make like]

fact (fakt) *n.* 1 Anything that is done or happens. 2 Anything actually existent. 3 Any statement strictly true; truth; reality. [< L *factum* < *facere* do]

fac·tion (fak′shən) *n.* 1 A number of persons combined for a common purpose, esp. a dissenting group within a larger group; clique. 2 Violent opposition, as to a government; dissension. [< L *factio* < *facere* do.] —**fac′tion·al** *adj.* —**fac′tion·al·ism** *n.*

fac·tious (fak′shəs) *adj.* Given to, characterized by, or promoting faction; turbulent; partisan. —**fac′tious·ly** *adj.* —**fac′tious·ness** *n.*

fac·ti·tious (fak·tish′əs) *adj.* Artificial; affected; unnatural. [< L *factitius* < *facere* do] —**fac·ti′tious·ly** *adv.* —**fac·ti′tious·ness** *n.*

fac·toid (fak′toid′) *n.* Someone or something contrived to appear plausible or factual. [< FACT + -OID] —**fac′toid′al** *adj.*

fac·tor (fak′tər) *n.* 1 *Math.* One of two or more quantities that when multiplied make a given product. 2 One of several elements or causes that produce a result. 3 An agent who transacts business for another, usu. on commission. 4 *Biol.* A gene. —*v.t. Math.* To express as a product of factors. [< L *facere* make]

fac·to·ry (fak′tər·ē) *n. pl.* **·ries** A building or buildings used for manufacturing. [< L *factor* < *facere* make]

fac·to·tum (fak·tō′təm) *n.* An employee hired to do all kinds of work. [< L *facere* do + *totum* everything]

fac·tu·al (fak′chŏō·əl) *adj.* Pertaining to, containing, or consisting of facts; literal and exact. —**fac′tu·al·ly** *adv.*

fac·ul·ty (fak′əl·tē) *n. pl.* **·ties** 1 Any natural endowment or acquired power: the *faculty* of seeing, feeling, reasoning. 2 Any special skill or unusual ability; knack. 3 The members of any one of the learned professions, collectively. 4 The body of instructors in a school, university, or college. 5 A department of learning or instruction: the history *faculty.* [< L *facultas*]

fad (fad) *n.* A passing fancy or fashion. [?] —**fad′dish, fad′dy** *adj.* —**fad′dist** *n.*

fade (fād) *v.* **fad·ed, fad·ing** *v.i.* 1 To lose brightness or clearness; become indistinct. 2 To lose freshness, vigor, youth, etc. —*v.t.* 3 To cause to fade. —**fade in** In motion pictures, etc., to come into view gradually. —**fade out** In motion pictures, etc., to disappear gradually. [< OF *fade* pale, insipid] —**Syn.** 1 dim, pale. 2 age, decline, wane, wither.

fae·ces (fē′sēz) *n. pl.* FECES.

fa·er·ie (fā′ə·rē, fâr′ē) *n.* 1 Fairyland. 2 *Archaic* A fairy. —*adj. Archaic* Of or pertaining to fairies.

fag (fag) *v.* **fagged, fag·ging** *v.i.* 1 To weary oneself by working. 2 To work as a fag. —*v.t.* 3 To tire out by hard work. —*n.* 1 In an English public school, a boy who does menial tasks for an older boy. 2 A piece of drudgery. 3 *Slang* A cigarette. [?]

fag end 1 The frayed end, as of a rope. 2 A remnant or last part. 3 *Informal* The worse part of a bargain or similar arrangement. 4 The butt of a cigar or cigarette. [< ME *fagge* flap + END]

fag·ot (fag′ət) *n.* 1 A bundle of sticks or branches, as used for fuel. 2 Pieces of wrought iron or steel to be worked into bars. —*v.t.* 1 To make a fagot of. 2 To ornament by fagoting. [< OF] Also **fag′got.**

fag·ot·ing (fag′ət·ing) *n.* 1 Embroidery in which a number of threads of a material are drawn out and the cross-threads tied together in the middle. 2 Criss-cross hemstitching. Also **fag′got·ing.**

Fagoting *defs. 1 & 2*

Fahr·en·heit (far′ən·hīt) *adj.* Of, for, or designating a temperature scale in which the freezing point of water is 32° and the boiling point 212° at standard atmospheric pressure. [< G. D. *Fahrenheit*, 1686–1736, German physicist]

fail (fāl) *v.i.* 1 To be unsuccessful. 2 To be deficient or wanting, as in ability, faithfulness, etc. 3 To give out, break, or stop working. 4 To fade away; disappear. The light *failed* rapidly. 5 To weaken gradually, as in illness or death. 6 To go bankrupt. 7 To receive a failing grade. —*v.t.* 8 To prove to be inadequate or of no help to. 9 To leave undone or unfulfilled; neglect: He *failed* to carry out orders. 10 In education: **a** To receive a failing grade in. **b** To assign a failing grade to (a pupil). —*n.* Failure: now only in the phrase **without fail.** [< L *fallere* to deceive]

fail·ing (fā′ling) *n.* A minor fault; foible. —*adj.* 1 Characterized by failure. 2 Diminishing; weakening. —**fail′ing·ly** *adv.*

faille (fāl, fīl) *n.* An untwilled silk dress fabric having a light grain or cord. [F]

fail-safe (fāl′sāf′) *adj.* 1 Of or indicating a system that makes automatic adjustments for safety in case of failure. 2 *Mil.* Describing a system designed to prevent erroneous or unauthorized attacks.

fail·ure (fāl′yər) *n.* 1 The act of failing: *failure of sight.* 2 One who or that which fails. 3 A proving unsuccessful in business, etc. 4 Neglect or non-performance of a duty.

fain (fān) *adj. Archaic* 1 Reluctantly willing. 2 Glad; rejoiced. 3 Eager; desirous. —*adv.* Gladly: with *would.* [< OE *fægen*]

faint (fānt) *v.i.* To lose consciousness temporarily; swoon. —*adj.* 1 Lacking in purpose or courage; timid. 2 Ready to faint; weak. 3 Weak and feeble, as in effort. 4 Indistinct; dim. —*n.* A swoon: also **faint′ing.** [< OF *faindre* to feign] —**faint′ly** *adv.* —**faint′ness** *n.*

faint-heart·ed (fānt′här′tid) *adj.* Timid; cowardly. —**faint′-heart′ed·ly** *adv.* —**faint′-heart′ed·ness** *n.*

fair[1] (fâr) *adj.* 1 Free from clouds; sunny; clear. 2 Open; distinct. 3 Free from spot or blemish. 4 Just; upright; honest. 5 Having light color or hue: *fair* hair. 6 Pleasing to the eye; beautiful. 7 Moderately satisfactory or excellent; passably good or large: a *fair* crop. 8 Easily legible. 9 In games and sports, according to rule: a *fair* tackle. 10 In a favorable direction: *fair* wind. 11 Properly open to attack: He is *fair* game. —*adv.* 1 Justly; honestly: deal *fair* with me. 2 In clear view; squarely; distinctly. —**for fair** For sure. [< OE *fæger*] —**fair′ish** *adj.* —**fair′ness** *n.*

fair[2] (fâr) *n.* 1 An exhibit and sale of things, often for charity. 2 An exhibit of agricultural products, manufactures, or other articles of value or interest: a county *fair,* an industrial *fair.* 3 A regular gathering of buyers and sellers. [< L *feria* a holiday]

fair-and-square (fâr′ən·skwâr′) *adj.* Thoroughly fair-dealing and honest. —*adv.* In a straightforward way; honestly.

fair·ground (fâr′ground′) *n.* The ground or enclosure in which a fair is held.

fair-haired (fâr′hârd′) *adj.* 1 Flaxen-haired. 2 *Informal* Favorite.

fair·ly (fâr′lē) *adv.* 1 In a just manner; equitably. 2 Moderately; tolerably: a *fairly* tall building. 3 Positively; completely: The crowd *fairly* roared. 4 Clearly; distinctly.

fair-mind·ed (fâr′mīn′did) *adj.* Free from bias or bigotry; open to reason. —**fair′mind·ed·ly** *adv.* —**fair′mind·ed·ness** *n.*

fair shake *Slang* A fair chance or treatment.

fair·spo·ken (fâr′spō′kən) *adj.* Having grace of speech; pleasant; polite.

fair-trade (fâr′trād′) *v.t.* **-trad·ed, -trad·ing** To charge a price no less than the minimum price set by the manufacturer. —*adj.* Of or pertaining to such a price.

fair·way (fâr′wā′) *n.* 1 The proper course through a channel or harbor. 2 That part of a golf course on which the grass is short.

fair-weath·er (fâr′weth′ər) *adj.* 1 Suitable for fair weather. 2 Useful or dependable only in favorable circumstances: *fair-weather* friends.

fair·y (fâr′ē) *n. pl.* **fair·ies** 1 An imaginary being of small and graceful human form. 2 *Slang* A male homosexual. —*adj.* 1 Of or pertaining to fairies. 2 Like a fairy; dainty; graceful. [< OF *faerie* enchantment]

fair·y·land (fâr′ē·land′) *n.* The fancied abode of the fairies.

fairy tale 1 A tale about fairies; an imaginative story. 2 An incredible statement.

fait ac·com·pli (fā′tə·kôṅ·plē′, *Fr.* fe·tà-) *French* A thing done beyond recall or opposition.

faith (fāth) *n.* 1 Belief without evidence. 2 Confidence; trust. 3 Belief in God, the Bible, etc. 4 A specific religion. 5 Anything given adherence or credence: a man's political *faith.* 6 Allegiance; faithfulness. —**bad faith** Deceit; dishonesty. —**in faith** Indeed; truly. —**in good faith** Honestly.

faith·ful (fāth′fəl) *adj.* 1 True, trustworthy, or loyal: a *faithful* servant; *faithful* to one's agreement. 2 True; accurate; exact. 3 Worthy of belief or confidence. 4 Full of faith. —**the faithful** 1 Those who truly believe in a religion. 2 The devoted members of a group or organization. —**faith′ful·ly** *adv.* —**faith′ful·ness** *n.*

faith·less (fāth′lis) *adj.* 1 Not faithful; disloyal. 2 Deceptive and unreliable. 3 Lacking faith. —**faith′less·ly** *adv.* —**faith′less·ness** *n.* —**Syn.** 1 deceitful, false, perfidious, treacherous.

fake (fāk) *n. Informal* Anything or any person not genuine; a fraud. —*adj.* Spurious. —*v.* **faked, fak·ing** *v.t.* 1 To attempt to pass off as genuine. 2 To feign. —*v.i.* 3 To practice faking. [?] —**fak′er, fak′er·y** *n.*

fa·kir (fə·kir′, fā′kər) *n.* 1 A Muslim ascetic or religious mendicant. 2 Loosely, a Hindu Yogi. [< Ar. *faqīr* poor]

Fa·lange (fā′lanj, fə·lanj′) *n.* The official fascist party of Spain since 1939. [Sp., a phalanx] —**Fa·lan′gist** *n.*

fal·cate (fal′kāt) *adj.* Sickle- or scythe-shaped. [< L *falx* sickle]

fal·con (fal′kən, fô′-, fôl′-) *n.* 1 Any of various fast-flying birds of prey, having a large head and long tail. 2 Any of various hawks used in sport, esp. the peregrine falcon, with long, pointed wings. [< LL *falco*]

fal·con·ry (fal′kən·rē, fô′-, fôl′-) *n.* The training or using of falcons for sport. —**fal′con·er** *n.*

fal·de·ral (fäl′də·räl, fal′də·ral) *n.* 1 Any trifling ornament. 2 Nonsense. 3 A meaningless refrain in old songs.

fall (fôl) *v.* **fell, fall·en, fall·ing** *v.i.* 1 To drop by force of gravity from a higher to a lower place or position. 2 To drop from an erect position: He *fell* to his knees. 3 To collapse: The bridge *fell.* 4 To become less in measure, number, etc. 5 To descend or become less in rank, estimation, importance, etc. 6 To be wounded or slain, as in battle. 7 To be overthrown, as a government. 8 To be taken or captured: The fort *fell.* 9 To yield to temptation; sin. 10 To hit; land: The bombs *fell* short. 11 To slope downward. 12 To hang down; droop. 13 To begin and continue: Night *fell.* 14 To pass into a state or condition: to *fall* asleep. 15

Falcon *def. 2*

To experience or show dejection: His face *fell.* 16 To come or happen by chance: Suspicion *fell* on him. 17 To happen; occur: Hallowe'en *falls* on Tuesday. 18 To be directed: His glance *fell* on me. 19 To happen or come at a specific place: The accent *falls* on the last syllable. 20 To be classified or divided: with *into.* —**fall away** 1 To become lean or emaciated. 2 To die; decline. —**fall away from** To renounce allegiance to. —**fall back** To recede; retreat. —**fall back on** (or **upon**) 1 *Mil.* To retreat to. 2 To resort to; have recourse to. —**fall flat** To fail to produce the intended effect or result. —**fall for** *Informal* 1 To be deceived by. 2 To fall in love with. —**fall in with** 1 To meet and accompany. 2 To agree with; conform to. —**fall off** 1 To drop. 2 To become less. —**fall on** (or **upon**) 1 To attack; assail. 2 To find; discover. —**fall out** 1 To quarrel. 2 To happen; result. —**fall short** 1 To be inadequate. 2 To fail to reach something, as a target, goal, or standard. —**fall through** To come to nothing; fail. —*adj. Often cap.* 1 Of, for, or pertaining to autumn. 2 *Slang* Easily duped: a *fall* guy. — *n.* 1 The act, process, or result of falling. 2 *Usu. pl.* A waterfall; cascade. 3 That which falls or is caused to fall; also, the amount of descent. 4 *Often cap.* Autumn. 5 In wrestling, the throwing of an opponent, so that his back hits the floor. —**the Fall** The disobedience of Adam and Eve. [< OE *feallan*]

fal·la·cious (fə·lā′shəs) *adj.* Of, pertaining to, or involving a fallacy. —**fal·la′cious·ly** *adv.* —**fal·la′cious·ness** *n.* — **Syn.** deceptive, erroneous, illusory, misleading.

fal·la·cy (fal′ə·sē) *n. pl.* **·cies** 1 Something false or deceptive, as an idea or opinion. 2 The quality of being false or misleading. 3 Any reasoning, argument, etc., that contains an error of logic. [< L *fallere* deceive]

fall·en (fô′lən) *adj.* 1 Having come down by falling. 2 Overthrown; disgraced; ruined. 3 Dead.

fall guy *Slang* A dupe; gullible person.

fal·li·ble (fal′ə·bəl) *adj.* 1 Liable to error or mistake. 2 Liable to be erroneous or false. [< L *fallere* deceive] — **fal′li·bly** *adv.* —**fal′li·bil′i·ty, fal′li·ble·ness** *n.*

falling star METEOR.

Fal·lo·pi·an tube (fə·lō′pē·ən) One of a pair of slender ducts that carry the ovum from the ovary to the uterus. [< G. *Fallopio,* 16th c. Ital. anatomist] •See OVARY.

fall·out (fôl′out′) *n.* 1 The descent of minute particles of radioactive material resulting from a nuclear explosion. 2 The particles themselves. 3 Any incidental result; unplanned or unpredictable consequences. Also **fall′-out′.**

fal·low[1] (fal′ō) *adj.* Left unseeded after being plowed. — *n.* 1 Land left unseeded after plowing. 2 The act of plowing land and leaving unseeded. —*v.t. & v.i.* To make, keep, or become fallow. [< OE *fealga* fallow land] —**fal′low·ness** *n.*

fal·low[2] (fal′ō) *adj.* Pale yellow or pale red. [< OE *fealu* tawny]

fallow deer A fallow-colored, European deer about three feet high and spotted white in the summer.

false (fôls) *adj.* 1 Contrary to truth or fact. 2 Not real or genuine; artificial. 3 Added only for decoration, deception, etc.: a *false* door. 4 Lying; dishonest. 5 Faithless; treacherous. 6 Out of tune. 7 Not correctly named: *false* foxglove. [< L *falsus,* pp. of *fallere* deceive] —**false′ly** —**false′ness** *n.*

Fallow deer

false·hood (fôls′hood) *n.* 1 Lack of accord to fact or truth; untruthfulness. 2 An intentional untruth; a lie. 3 The act of lying. 4 An untrue belief.

false ribs The lower five pairs of ribs that in human beings do not unite directly with the sternum.

false step 1 A stumble. 2 An error or blunder.

fal·set·to (fôl·set′ō) *n. pl.* **·tos** The higher, less colorful register of a voice. —*adj.* Of, for, or singing in falsetto. — *adv.* In falsetto. [Ital., dim. of *falso* false]

fal·si·fy (fôl′sə·fī) *v.* **·fied, ·fy·ing** *v.t.* 1 To misrepresent; tell lies about. 2 To prove to be false; disprove. 3 To tamper fraudulently with, as a document. —*v.i.* 4 To tell false-hoods; lie. —**fal'si·fi·ca'tion, fal'si·fi'er** *n.*

fal·si·ty (fôl'sə·tē) *n. pl.* **·ties** 1 The quality of being false. 2 A false statement, thing, or appearance. 3 Deceitfulness; dishonesty.

fal·ter (fôl'tər) *v.i.* 1 To be hesitant or uncertain; waver. 2 To move unsteadily; stumble. 3 To speak haltingly; stammer. —*v.t.* 4 To utter haltingly. —*n.* A faltering. [ME *falteren*] —**fal'ter·er** *n.* —**fal'ter·ing·ly** *adv.*

fame (fām) *n.* 1 Public reputation, esp. when favorable. 2 Great renown. [< L *fama* report, reputation]

famed (fāmd) *adj.* Well-known; renowned; celebrated.

fa·mil·ial (fə·mil'yəl, -mil'ē·əl) *adj.* Of, pertaining to, or associated with the family.

fa·mil·iar (fə·mil'yər) *adj.* 1 Well acquainted; thoroughly versed; followed by *with.* 2 Intimate; close, as in friendship. 3 Informal: *familiar verse.* 4 Exercising undue intimacy; forward; bold. 5 Well known; common; frequent; customary. —*n.* 1 An intimate friend. 2 A spirit supposed to attend a witch or sorcerer. [< L *familia* family] —**fa·mil'iar·ly** *adv.*

fa·mil·i·ar·i·ty (fə·mil'ē·ar'ə·tē, -mil'yar'-) *n. pl.* **·ties** 1 The state or condition of being familiar. 2 Intimate knowledge, as of a subject. 3 Conduct implying familiar intimacy. 4 *Often pl.* Offensively familiar conduct.

fa·mil·iar·ize (fə·mil'yə·rīz) *v.t.* **·ized, ·iz·ing** 1 To make (oneself or someone) accustomed or familiar. 2 To cause to be well known or familiar. —**fa·mil'iar·i·za'tion** *n.*

fam·i·ly (fam'ə·lē, fam'lē) *n. pl.* **·lies** 1 A group of persons, consisting of parents and their children. 2 The children as distinguished from the parents. 3 A group of persons forming a household. 4 A succession of persons connected by blood, name, etc. 5 Distinguished or ancient lineage. 6 *Biol.* A taxonomic category higher than a genus. 7 Any class of like or related things, as a group of languages. —*adj.* Of, belonging to, or suitable for a family. [< L *familia* < *famulus* servant]

Family Allowance In Canada, a monthly allowance paid by the government to mothers for each child under the age of 16.

family name SURNAME.

family planning Control by means of contraceptive measures of the timing and number of births in a family.

family tree 1 A diagram of a family showing its ancestors and various branches of descendants. 2 The ancestors themselves.

fam·ine (fam'in) *n.* 1 A widespread scarcity of food. 2 A great scarcity of anything. 3 Starvation. [< L *fames* hunger]

fam·ish (fam'ish) *v.t. & v.i.* 1 To starve or cause to starve. 2 To have or cause to have great hunger.

fa·mous (fā'məs) *adj.* 1 Having fame or celebrity; renowned. 2 *Informal* Admirable, excellent. —**fa'mous·ly** *adv.* —**fa'mous·ness** *n.*

fan[1] (fan) *n.* 1 A wedge-shaped or circular device held in the hand and used for agitating the air, as for cooling or ventilation. 2 Any of various machines for producing currents of air. 3 Something shaped like a fan. —*v.* **fanned, fan·ning** *v.t.* 1 To move or stir (air) with or as with a fan. 2 To direct air upon, with or as with a fan. 3 To move or stir to action; excite. 4 To spread like a fan. 5 In baseball, to cause (a batter) to strike out. —*v.i.* 6 To spread out like a fan. 7 In baseball, to strike out. [< L *vannus* winnowing fan] —**fan'ner** *n.*

fan[2] (fan) *n.* An enthusiastic devotee or admirer, as of a sport, entertainment, performer, etc. [< FANATIC]

fa·nat·ic (fə·nat'ik) *adj.* Inordinately and unreasonably enthusiastic: also **fa·nat'i·cal.** —*n.* One who is fanatic about something. [< L *fanum* a temple] —**fa·nat'i·cal·ly** *adv.* —**fa·nat·i·cism** (fə·nat'ə·siz'əm) *n.* —**Syn.** *n.* enthusiast, monomaniac, zealot. *adj.* extreme, irrational, zealous.

fan·ci·er (fan'sē·ər) *n.* One having a taste for or knowledge about something: a bird *fancier.*

fan·ci·ful (fan'si·fəl) *adj.* 1 Proceeding from or produced by fancy; not real. 2 Imaginative. 3 Odd; curious. —**fan'ci·ful·ly** *adv.* —**fan'ci·ful·ness** *n.*

fan·cy (fan'sē) *n. pl.* **·cies** 1 Imagination, esp., if whimsical or odd. 2 Any imaginary notion, representation, or image. 3 A notion or whim. 4 A liking or fondness, resulting from

caprice. 5 A pet pursuit; hobby; fad. 6 Taste exhibited in artistic invention or design. —*adj.* **·ci·er, ·ci·est** 1 Ornamental; decorative; elaborate: *fancy* embroidery. 2 Evolved from the fancy; imaginary. 3 Capricious; whimsical. 4 In commerce, of higher grade than the average: *fancy* fruits. 5 Extravagant; exorbitant: *fancy* prices. 6 Selectively bred to a type, as an animal. 7 Performed with grace and skill: the *fancy* bowing of a violinist. —*v.t.* **·cied, ·cy·ing** 1 To imagine; picture. 2 To take a fancy to; like. 3 To believe without proof or conviction; suppose. [Short for FANTASY]

fan·cy·work (fan'sē·wûrk') *n.* Embroidery, tatting, crocheting, lacework, etc.

fan·dan·go (fan·dang'gō) *n. pl.* **·gos** 1 A Spanish dance in triple time. 2 The music for this dance. [Sp.]

fan·fare (fan'fâr') *n.* 1 A flourish, as of trumpets. 2 A noisy demonstration. [F]

fang (fang) *n.* 1 A long pointed tooth or tusk by which an animal seizes or tears its prey. 2 One of the long, curved, hollow or grooved teeth with which a serpent injects its poison into its victim. 3 Any of various pointed objects, organs, or devices. [< OE] —**fanged** (fangd) *adj.*

fan·light (fan'līt') *n.* A semicircular window, usu. over a door, with bars radiating from the middle of its base.

Fangs *def. 2*

fan mail Complimentary letters to public performers, as actors, musicians, etc.

fan·tail (fan'tāl') *n.* 1 A variety of domestic pigeon having fanlike tail feathers. 2 Any end or tail shaped like a fan. —**fan-tailed** (fan'tāld') *adj.*

fan·tan (fan'tan') *n.* 1 A Chinese gambling game. 2 A game of cards. [< Chinese *fan t'an* repeated divisions]

fan·ta·si·a (fan·tā'zē·ə, -zhə, fan'tə·zē'ə) *n. Music* A composition in a very free form. [Ital., lit., a fancy]

fan·ta·size (fan'tə·sīz) *v.* **·sized, ·siz·ing** *v.i.* 1 To imagine or daydream about fantastic events. —*v.t.* 2 To create in fantasy, as in daydreaming. —**fan'ta·sist** *n.*

fan·tasm (fan'taz·əm) *n.* PHANTASM.

fan·tas·ma·go·ri·a (fan·taz'mə·gôr'ē·ə, -gō'rē·ə) *n.* PHANTASMAGORIA.

fan·tas·tic (fan·tas'tik) *adj.* 1 Of an odd appearance; grotesque. 2 Capricious; whimsical: a *fantastic* imagination. 3 Unreal; fanciful; illusory. 4 Unbelievably good; incredible. —*n.* One who is fantastic in conduct or appearance. Also **fan·tas'ti·cal.** [< Gk. *phantazein* to present to the mind] —**fan·tas'ti·cal·ly** *adv.* —**fan·tas'ti·cal'i·ty** (-kal'ə·tē), **fan·tas'ti·cal·ness** *n.*

fan·ta·sy (fan'tə·sē, -zē) *n. pl.* **·sies** 1 Imagination; fancy. 2 A fantastic notion or mental image. 3 A sequence of mental images serving to fulfill a need. 4 *Music* FANTASIA. 5 An imaginative creative work, as a poem. [< Gk. *phantasia* appearance < *phainein* to show]

far (fär) *adj.* **far·ther** or **fur·ther, far·thest** or **fur·thest** 1 Very distant in space or time. 2 Extending widely or at great length. 3 Being the more distant of the two: the *far* end. —*adv.* 1 At a distant point or place. 2 To or from a great distance in space or time. 3 To a great degree; much: *far* wiser. —**by far** In a great degree; by much. —**far and away** By a great deal. —**far and wide** In every place; everywhere: also **far and near.** —**far out** FAR-OUT. [< OE *feor*] —**far'ness** *n.*

far·ad (far'əd, -ad) *n. Electr.* A unit equal to the measure of a capacitor that stores one coulomb per volt of impressed potential difference. [< Michael *Faraday,* 1791–1867, English scientist]

far·a·way (fär'ə·wā') *adj.* 1 Distant: a *faraway* town. 2 Absent-minded; abstracted: a *faraway* look.

farce (färs) *n.* 1 A short comedy with exaggerated effects and incidents. 2 A ridiculous proceeding; an absurd failure. —*v.t.* **farced, farc·ing** To fill out with witticisms, jibes, etc., as a play. [< L *farcire* to stuff] —**far·cial** (fär'shəl) *adj.*

far·ci·cal (fär'si·kəl) *adj.* Of, pertaining to, or of the nature of a farce; absurd. —**far'ci·cal·ly** *adv.* —**far'ci·cal·ness, far'ci·cal'i·ty** *n.* —**Syn.** comical, laughable, ludicrous, ridiculous.

fare (fâr) *v.i.* **fared, far·ing** 1 To be in a specified state; get

on. 2 To turn out; happen. 3 To eat; be supplied with food.
—*n.* 1 Money or its equivalent paid for transportation of
a passenger. 2 A passenger carried for hire. 3 Food and
drink. [< OE *faran* go, travel]

Far East The countries of E Asia, as China, Japan, Korea,
etc. —**Far Eastern**

fare·well (fâr'wel') *n.* —*interj.* 1 A parting salutation; a good-by.
2 The act of parting. —*interj.* (fâr'wel') May you fare well.
—*adj.* Parting; closing. [Earlier *fare well*]

far-fetched (fär'fecht') *adj.* Neither natural nor obvious; improbable.

far-flung (fär'flung') *adj.* Having great range; extending
over great distances.

fa·ri·na (fǝ-rē'nǝ) *n.* A meal or flour made from cereals,
nuts, potatoes, etc. and used as a breakfast food. [< L *far*
spelt]

far·i·na·ceous (far'ǝ-nā'shǝs) *adj.* 1 Containing or yielding starch. 2 Like meal; mealy.

farm (färm) *n.* 1 A tract of land forming a single property
and devoted to the cultivation of crops, the raising of
livestock, the production of dairy products, etc. 2 A tract
of water used for the cultivation of marine life: an oyster
farm. 3 In baseball, a minor-league club used for training
recruits. —*v.t.* 1 To cultivate (land). 2 To let out the services of (a person) for hire. 3 To arrange for (work) to be
performed by persons not in the main organization; subcontract: with *out.* 4 In baseball, to place (a player) with
a minor-league team for training: with *out.* —*v.i.* 5 To
practice farming; be a farmer. [< L *firmare* fix, settle <
firmus firm]

farm·er (färm·ǝr) *n.* A person whose occupation is farming land, raising livestock, producing dairy products, etc.;
esp., the owner, operator, or manager of a farm.

farm·hand (färm'hand') *n.* One who works for wages on
a farm. Also **farm laborer.**

farm·house (färm'hous') *n.* The main home on a farm,
occupied by the farmer's family.

farm·ing (fär'ming) *n.* 1 The act of one who farms. 2 The
management of or labor on a farm. —*adj.* Engaged in or
used for agriculture: a *farming* region.

farm·stead (färm'sted) *n.* A farm and the buildings on
it.

farm·yard (färm'yârd') *n.* A space surrounded or enclosed by farm buildings.

far·o (fâr'ō) *n.* A game of cards in which the players bet
as to the order in which certain cards will appear. [? <
Pharaoh]

far-off (fâr'ôf', -of') *adj.* Situated at a great distance;
remote.

far-out (fär'out') *adj.* **far·ther-out, far·thest-out** *Informal* 1
Far removed from the ordinary; unconventional; avant-
garde. 2 Highly theoretical; far from common experience;
abstruse. 3 Inspired; transported; wildly enthusiastic. 4
Far removed or very distant in space.

far-out·er (fär'out'ǝr) *n.* An unconventional person.

far·ra·go (fǝ-rā'gō, -rä'-) *n. pl.* **·goes** A confused mixture;
medley: a *farrago* of nonsense. [L, salad, mixture]

far-reach·ing (fä'rē'ching) *adj.* 1 Producing effects
that extend far: a *far-reaching* decision. 2 Reaching far
either in time or in space.

far·row (far'ō) *n.* A litter of pigs. —*v.t. & v.i.* To give birth
to (young): said of swine. [< OE *fearh* young pig]

far-see·ing (fär'sē'ing) *adj.* 1 Seeing afar. 2 Having foresight.

far·sight·ed (fär'sī'tid) *adj.* 1 Able to see things at a
distance more clearly than things near at hand. 2 Farsee-
ing. —**far'sight'ed·ly** *adv.* —**far'sight'ed·ness** *n.*

far·ther (fär'thǝr) Comparative of FAR. —*adj.* More distant in space; more advanced. —*adv.* 1 To or at a more
distant point in space. 2 More fully or completely.

far·ther·most (fär'thǝr·mōst') *adj.* Farthest.

far·thest (fär'thist) Superlative of FAR. —*adj. & adv.* 1
Most distant or advanced in space. 2 To the greatest degree or extent.

far·thing (fär'thing) *n.* 1 Formerly, one fourth of an English penny. 2 A small trifle. [< OE *feortha* a fourth]

far·thin·gale (fär'thing·gāl) *n.* A woman's hoop skirt of
the 16th and 17th centuries. [<
Sp. *verdugo* a rod, hoop]

fas·ces (fas'ēz) *n. pl.* In ancient
Rome, a bundle of rods enclosing
an ax, borne as a symbol of power.
[L]

fas·ci·a (fash'ē-ǝ) *n. pl.* **·ci·ae** (-ī-ē)
1 *Anat.* Connective tissue form-
ing sheets or layers. 2 Something
that binds together; a band. [L, a
band] —**fas'ci·al** *adj.*

fas·ci·cle (fas'i·kǝl) *n.* 1 A bundle or cluster, as of fibers in the
body. 2 A number of sheets of
printed work bound together. [<
L *fascia* a bundle]

Farthingale

fas·cic·u·late (fǝ-sik'yǝ-lit) *adj.*
Composed of or growing in bun-
dles. Also **fas'ci·cled, fas·cic'u·lar, fas·cic'u·lat'ed.**

fas·ci·nate (fas'ǝ-nāt) *v.* **·nat·ed, ·nat·ing** *v.t.* 1 To attract
irresistibly, as by beauty or other quality; captivate. 2 To
hold spellbound, as by terror. —*v.i.* 3 To be fascinating.
[< L *fascinare* to charm] —**fas'ci·nat'ing·ly** *adv.* —**fas'ci·
na'tor** *n.*

fas·ci·na·tion (fas'ǝ-nā'shǝn) *n.* 1 The act of fascinating.
2 The state of being fascinated. 3 Enchantment; charm.

fas·cism (fash'iz·ǝm) *n.* Any authoritarian system of government characterized by state economic control, milita-
ristic nationalism, propaganda, and the crushing of opposition. [< L *fascis* a bundle, group] —**fas·cis'tic** *adj.* —**fas·
cis'ti·cal·ly** *adv.* —**fas'cist** *n.*

Fas·cism (fash'iz·ǝm) *n.* The system of one-party government developed by the Fascisti in Italy. —**Fas'cist** *n.*

Fa·scis·ti (fǝ-shis'tē, *Ital.* fä-shē'stē) *n. pl.* of **Fa·scis'ta**
The members of a totalitarian society formed in Italy
under Benito Mussolini and in control of the government,
1922–43.

fash·ion (fash'ǝn) *n.* 1 The prevailing style or mode, esp.
in dress. 2 A manner of doing a thing; method; way. 3 The
make or shape of a thing. 4 Common practice or custom;
usage. 5 Something fashionable. —*v.t.* 1 To give shape or
form to. 2 To conform; accommodate; fit. [< L *facere* to
make] —**fash'ion·er** *n.*

fash·ion·a·ble (fash'ǝn·ǝ·bǝl) *adj.* 1 Conforming to fashion; stylish. 2 Of, pertaining to, or like persons of fashion.
—**fash'ion·a·bly** *adv.* —**fash'ion·a·ble·ness** *n.*

fash·ion·mon·ger (fash'ǝn·mung'gǝr, -mong'-) *n.* One
who follows or initiates fashions.

fashion plate One whose attire is perfect, according to
the current fashion.

fast[1] (fast, fäst) *adj.* 1 Firm in place; not easily moved. 2
Firmly secured or bound. 3 Constant; steadfast. 4 Not
subject to fading: said of colors. 5 Resistant: *acid-fast.* 6
Sound or deep, as sleep. 7 Acting or moving quickly; swift.
8 Performed quickly: *fast* work. 9 Suitable for quick movement: a *fast* track. 10 Requiring rapidity of action or motion: a *fast* schedule. 11 Indicating a time in advance of
the true time: The clock is *fast.* 12 Given to dissipation or
moral laxity: *fast* living. 13 *Phot.* Usable for short exposure, as a quick-moving shutter or a sensitive film. —*adv.*
1 Firmly; fixedly; securely. 2 Soundly: *fast* asleep. 3
Quickly; rapidly; swiftly. 4 Dissipatedly; recklessly: to live
fast. 5 *Archaic* Near: *fast* by. [< OE *fæst*]

fast[2] (fast, fäst) *v.i.* To go without food, wholly or in part,
as in observance of a religious duty. —*n.* 1 Abstinence
from food, partial or total. 2 A period prescribed for fasting. [< OE *fæstan*]

fast·back (fast'bak', fäst'-) *n.* 1 An automobile's continuous, downward-sloping roof from windshield to rear
bumper. 2 An automobile having such a design.

fast day A day set apart for religious fasting.

fast·en (fas'ǝn, fäs'-) *v.t.* 1 To attach or secure; connect.
2 To make fast; secure: to *fasten* a door. 3 To direct, as
attention or the eyes, steadily. 4 To cause to be attributed:
to *fasten* blame. —*v.i.* 5 To take fast hold; cling: usually

---

add, āce, câre, pălm; end, ēven; it, īce; odd, ōpen, ôrder; tŏŏk, pōōl; up, bûrn; ǝ = a in *above*; u in *focus*;
yŏŏ = u in *fuse*; oil; pout; check; go; ring; thin; this; zh, *vision.* < derived from; ? origin uncertain or unknown.

with *on*. **6** To become firm or attached. [< OE *fæst* fixed] —**fast′en·er** *n*.

fast·en·ing (fas′ən·ing, fäs′-) *n*. **1** The act of making fast. **2** That which fastens, as a bolt, hook, clasp, etc.

fas·tid·i·ous (fas·tid′ē·əs) *adj*. **1** Hard to please. **2** Overly delicate or sensitive; squeamish. [< L *fastidium* disgust] —**fas·tid′i·ous·ly** *adv*. —**fas·tid′i·ous·ness** *n*.

fast·ness (fast′nis, fäst′-) *n*. **1** A fortress; stronghold. **2** The state or quality of being fast.

fat (fat) *adj*. **fat·ter, fat·test 1** Having much or superfluous flesh; corpulent; obese. **2** Containing much oil, grease, etc. **3** Broad; thick: a *fat* book. **4** Stupid; dull. **5** Prosperous; thriving; flourishing. **6** Rich in products or in profits; rewarding: a *fat* office. **7** Well-filled: a *fat* larder. —*n*. **1** A greasy, soft or semisolid substance produced by animals and plants and having essential functions in vital processes. **2** An obese condition; corpulence. **3** The richest or most desirable part of anything: the *fat* of the land. **4** Any of various compounds of carbon, oxygen, and hydrogen which are glyceryl esters of certain acids. —*v.t.* & *v.i.* **fat·ted, fat·ting** FATTEN. [< OE *fætt*] —**fat′ly** *adv*. —**fat′ness** *n*.

fa·tal (fāt′l) *adj*. **1** Causing death. **2** Bringing ruin; destructive. **3** Portentous; ominous. **4** Determining fate or destiny; fateful. [< L *fatum* fate] —**fa′tal·ly** *adv*.

fa·tal·ism (fā′təl·iz′əm) *n*. **1** *Philos*. The doctrine that every event is predetermined by fate and inevitable. **2** A disposition to accept every event as preordained. —**fa′tal·is′tic** *adj*. —**fa′tal·is′ti·cal·ly** *adv*. —**fa′tal·ist** *n*.

fa·tal·i·ty (fā·tal′ə·tē, fə-) *n. pl.* **·ties 1** Destiny; a decree of fate. **2** A disastrous or fatal event. **3** A death resulting from a disastrous event; also, one who suffers such a death. **4** Liability to danger or disaster.

fate (fāt) *n*. **1** That power which is thought to determine one's future, success or failure, etc. **2** Destiny; fortune; lot. **3** Evil destiny; doom. **4** Outcome; final result. —*v.t.* **fat·ed, fat·ing** To predestine: obsolete except in passive: They were *fated* to meet again. [< L *fatum* < *fari* speak]

fat·ed (fā′tid) *adj*. Determined by fate; destined.

fate·ful (fāt′fəl) *adj*. **1** Full of a significance or meaning that can be understood only after the fact; prophetic. **2** Important; critical: a *fateful* decision. **3** Controlled by fate. —**fate′ful·ly** *adv*. —**fate′ful·ness** *n*.

Fates (fāts) *Gk. Myth*. The three goddesses who control human destiny.

fa·ther (fä′thər) *n*. **1** A man who has begotten a child. **2** A man fulfilling the role of father, as by adoption of a child. **3** STEPFATHER. **4** Any male ancestor; forefather. **5** An originator or founder of something. **6** A priest. **7** *Eccl*. Any one of the early historical or doctrinal writers of the Christian Church. **8** *pl*. The chiefs of a city or assembly. —*v.t.* **1** To beget as a father. **2** To found, create, or make. **3** To act as a father to. [< OE *fæder*] —**fa′ther·hood** *n*. —**fa′ther·less** *adj*.

Fa·ther (fä′thər) *n*. The Deity; God.

father confessor 1 A priest to whom one may confess. **2** Any one in whom one confides.

fa·ther-in-law (fä′thər·in·lô′) *n. pl.* **fa·thers-in-law** The father of one's husband or wife.

fa·ther·land (fä′thər·land′) *n*. The land of one's birth or the land where one's ancestors were born.

fa·ther·ly (fä′thər·lē) *adj*. **1** Of, pertaining to, or like a father. **2** Manifesting the affection of a father; paternal. —**fa′ther·li·ness** *n*.

Father's Day A memorial day observed in honor of fathers on the third Sunday in June.

fath·om (fath′əm) *n. pl.* **·oms** or **·om** A measure equal to six feet, used mainly for depths. —*v.t.* **1** To find the depth of; sound. **2** To get to the bottom of; understand; interpret. [< OE *fæthm* the span of two arms outstretched] —**fath′om·a·ble** *adj*. —**fath′om·less** *adj*.

fa·tigue (fə·tēg′) *n*. **1** Exhaustion of physical or mental strength. **2** *Metall*. The failure of metals under prolonged or repeated stress. **3** FATIGUE DUTY. **4** *pl*. Clothes worn on fatigue duty. —*v.t.* & *v.i.* **·tigued, ·ti·guing** To make or become weak or weary from physical or mental effort; tire out. [< L *fatigare*] —**fa·ti′guing·ly** *adv*.

fatigue duty Common labor done by soldiers.

fat·ling (fat′ling) *adj*. Fat; plump. —*n*. A young animal fattened for slaughter.

fat·ten (fat′n) *v.t.* & *v.i.* To make or become fat. —**fat′ten·er** *n*.

fat·tish (fat′ish) *adj*. Somewhat fat.

fat·ty (fat′ē) *adj*. **fat·ti·er, fat·ti·est 1** Containing fat. **2** Greasy. —**fat′ti·ly** *adv*. —**fat′ti·ness** *n*.

fatty acid Any of a series of organic acids which react with glycerol to form fats and with metallic bases to form soaps.

fa·tu·i·ty (fə·tyōō′ə·tē) *n. pl.* **·ties 1** Something idiotic or stupid. **2** Imbecility; idiocy. [< L *fatuus* foolish]

fat·u·ous (fach′ōō·əs) *adj*. Stubbornly or complacently stupid. [< L *fatuus* foolish] —**fat′u·ous·ly** *adv*. —**fat′u·ous·ness** *n*.

fau·ces (fô′sēz) *n. pl.* The passage between the back of the mouth and the pharynx. [L] —**fau′cal** (-kəl), **fau′cial** (-shəl) *adj*.

fau·cet (fô′sit) *n*. A spout fitted with a valve, for drawing liquids through a pipe. [< OF *fausser* break into, damage]

fault (fôlt) *n*. **1** A slight offense; misdeed. **2** Whatever impairs excellence; an imperfection or defect. **3** Responsibility for an error or misdeed. **4** *Geol*. A fracture in a rock formation that causes strata to shift along the line of fracture. **5** In tennis, etc., an error in serving. —**at fault 1** In the wrong. **2** Worthy of blame. —**to a fault** Exceedingly; excessively: generous *to a fault*. —*v.t.* **1** To find fault with; blame. **2** *Geol*. To cause a fault in. —*v.i.* **3** *Geol*. To fracture so as to produce a fault. [< L *fallere* deceive] —**fault′ful·ly** *adv*. —**fault′ful·ness** *n*.

Fault *def.* 4

fault·find·er (fôlt′fīnd′ər) *n*. A person given to finding fault. —**fault′find′ing** *adj., n*.

fault·less (fôlt′lis) *adj*. Without fault; flawless. —**fault′less·ly** *adv*. —**fault′less·ness** *n*.

fault·y (fôl′tē) *adj*. **fault·i·er, fault·i·est 1** Having faults or blemishes. **2** Characterized by faults of conduct. —**fault′i·ly** *adv*. —**fault′i·ness** *n*.

faun (fôn) *n. Rom. Myth*. A half-human deity with pointed ears and goat's feet. [< L]

fau·na (fô′nə) *n. pl.* **fau·nas** or **fau·nae** (-nē) Animals collectively, esp. those species represented in a given area or period. [< L *Fauna*, a rural goddess]

Faust (foust) In medieval legend, an old philosopher who sells his soul to the devil, Mephistopheles, for wisdom, power, and youth.

faux pas (fō pä′) *pl.* **faux pas** (fō päz′) A social error; a breach of tact or manners. [F, lit., false step]

Faun

fa·vor (fā′vər) *n*. **1** A kind or helpful act. **2** The state or condition of being approved. **3** Favoritism; bias; partiality. **4** Something given as a small gift or souvenir. —**in favor of 1** On the side of. **2** To the benefit of; payable to. —*v.t.* **1** To look upon with favor or kindness; like. **2** To treat with partiality. **3** To make easier; facilitate. **4** To be in favor of; support; help. **5** To do a favor for; oblige. **6** To use carefully; spare, as an injured foot. **7** *Informal* To resemble. *Brit. sp.* **fa′vour**. [< L *favere* to favor] —**fa′vor·er** *n*.

fa·vor·a·ble (fā′vər·ə·bəl) *adj*. **1** Advantageous: to obtain a loan on *favorable* terms. **2** Disposed to favor; approving. **3** Promising: a *favorable* outlook. —**fa′vor·a·ble·ness** *n*. —**fa′vor·a·bly** *adv*. —**Syn. 1** beneficial, convenient, helpful. **2** auspicious, propitious.

fa·vored (fā′vərd) *adj*. **1** Having a specific aspect or appearance: *ill-favored*. **2** Aided; privileged.

fa·vor·ite (fā′vər·it) *adj*. Regarded with special favor; preferred. —*n*. **1** A person or animal considered to have the best chance in a contest. **2** A person or thing particularly liked or favored.

fa·vor·it·ism (fā′vər-ə-tiz′əm) n. 1 A disposition to favor unfairly or unreasonably. 2 The state or condition of being a favorite.

fawn[1] (fôn) v.i. 1 To show cringing fondess, as a dog: often with on or upon. 2 To seek favor by or as by cringing. [<OE fægnian rejoice] —**fawn′er** n. —**fawn′ing·ly** adv.

fawn[2] (fôn) n. 1 A young deer in its first year. 2 Light yellowish brown. —adj. Having this color. [<L fetus offspring]

fax (faks) n. A facsimile (def. 2). —v.t. To send a facsimile electronically, as of a document over telephone lines.

faze (fāz) v.t. fazed, faz·ing Informal To worry; disturb; disconcert. [<OE fēsian frighten]

FBI, F.B.I. Federal Bureau of Investigation.

fcap., fcp. foolscap.

FCC, F.C.C. Federal Communications Commission.

F clef See CLEF.

FDA, F.D.A. Food and Drug Administration.

Fe iron (L ferrum)

Fawn

fe·al·ty (fē′əl-tē) n. pl. ·ties Fidelity, as of a vassal to his lord. [<L fidelitas fidelity]

fear (fir) n. 1 An emotion excited by danger, evil, or pain; apprehension; dread. 2 Uneasiness about a thing; anxiety. 3 That which causes fear. 4 Reverence or awe. —v.t. 1 To be afraid of; be fearful of. 2 To look upon with awe or reverence. 3 To be anxious about; be apprehensive about. —v.i. 4 To be afraid; feel fear. 5 To be anxious or doubtful. [<OE fǣr peril, sudden attack] —**fear′less** adj. —**fear′less·ly** adv. —**fear′less·ness** n.

fear·ful (fir′fəl) adj. 1 Experiencing fear; afraid. 2 Inspiring fear; terrible. 3 Caused by fear: fearful tremblings. 4 Informal Very bad, large, etc.: a fearful mistake. —**fear′ful·ly** adv. —**fear′ful·ness** n.

fear·some (fir′səm) adj. 1 Causing fear; alarming. 2 Timid; frightened. —**fear′some·ly** adv. —**fear′some·ness** n.

fea·si·ble (fē′zə·bəl) adj. 1 That may be done; practicable. 2 Capable of being successfully used. 3 Reasonable;probable. [<OF faisable <faire do] —**fea′si·bil′i·ty, fea′si·ble·ness** n. —**fea′si·bly** adv.

feast (fēst) n. 1 A sumptuous meal. 2 Anything affording great pleasure or enjoyment. 3 A festival. —v.t. 1 To give a feast for; entertain lavishly. 2 To delight; gratify: He feasted his eyes on her beauty. —v.i. 3 To partake of a feast. [<L festus joyful] —**feast′er** n.

feat (fēt) n. A notable act or performance, as one displaying skill, endurance, or daring. [<L factum a deed]

feath·er (feth′ər) n. 1 One of the elongated structures which cover the body and wings of a bird. 2 Something resembling a feather. 3 Kind; class or species: birds of a feather. 4 In rowing, the act of feathering. 5 pl. Plumage. 6 Dress or attire. —**a feather in one's cap** An achievement to be proud of. —v.t. 1 To fit with a feather, as an arrow. 2 To cover or adorn with feathers. 3 To join by a tongue and groove. 4 In rowing, to turn (the oar blade) horizontally as it comes from the water, thereby lessening resistance. 5 Aeron. To turn one edge of (a propeller blade) windward to cut drag. —v.i. 6 To grow or become covered with feathers. 7 To move, spread, or expand like feathers. —**feather one's nest** To provide well for one's future. [<OE fether] —**feath′ered** adj.

feath·er·bed (feth′ər·bed′) v.i. ·bed·ded, ·bed·ding To have unnecessary workmen or slow down production so as to reduce unemployment: said of labor unions.

feath·er·weight (feth′ər·wāt′) n. 1 A boxer or wrestler weighing from 118 to 126 pounds. 2 A person weighing very little. 3 An insignificant person or thing. —adj. 1 Of little weight. 2 Insignificant.

feath·er·y (feth′ər·ē) adj. 1 Covered with or resembling feathers. 2 Light, soft, or fluffy. —**feath′er·i·ness** n.

fea·ture (fē′chər) n. 1 Any part of the human face. 2 pl. The whole face. 3 A distinguishing part or characteristic; salient point. 4 A magazine or newspaper article or story

on a special subject. 5 A full-length motion picture. 6 Something or someone outstanding or special. —v.t. **fea·tured, fea·tur·ing** 1 To make a feature of, as in a newspaper story. 2 To be a feature of. 3 To portray or outline the features of. 4 Slang To imagine; fancy. [<L factura a making <facere do] —**fea′ture·less** adj.

fea·tured (fē′chərd) adj. 1 Having a particular kind of facial features: fine-featured. 2 Given special prominence.

Feb. February.

feb·ri·fuge (feb′rə·fyōōj) n. A medicine for reducing fever. [<L febris fever + fugere flee] —**fe·brif·u·gal** (fə·brif′yə·gəl) adj.

fe·brile (fē′brəl, feb′rəl) adj. 1 Pertaining to fever. 2 Caused by or indicating fever. [<L febris fever]

Feb·ru·ar·y (feb′rōō·er′ē) n. pl. ·ar·ies or ·ar·ys The second month of the year, having twenty-eight or, in leap years, twenty-nine days. [<L februa, a Roman purificatory festival, celebrated on Feb. 15]

fe·ces (fē′sēz) n. pl. Human or animal excrement. [<L faex sediment] —**fe·cal** (fē′kəl) adj.

feck·less (fek′lis) adj. 1 Feeble; helpless. 2 Futile; useless. [<Scot. feck vigor + -LESS] —**feck′less·ly** adv. —**feck′less·ness** n.

fe·cund (fē′kund, fek′und) adj. Fruitful, fertile. [<L fecundus] —**fe·cun·di·ty** (fi·kun′də·tē) n. —Syn. productive, prolific, rich, teeming.

fe·cun·date (fē′kən·dāt, fek′ən-) v.t. ·dat·ed, ·dat·ing To impregnate; fertilize. —**fe′cun·da′tion** n.

fed[1] (fed) p.t. & p.p. of FEED.

fed[2] (fed) n. Often cap. Slang A Federal agent. —**the Feds** The Federal Reserve Board.

fed. federal; federated; federation.

fed·er·al (fed′ər·əl, -rəl) adj. 1 Of or pertaining to a form of government in which each state agrees to grant control of common affairs to a central authority. 2 Of or pertaining to a government so established. —n. An advocate of federalism. [<L foedus a league] —**fed′er·al·ly** adv.

Fed·er·al (fed′ər·əl, -rəl) adj. 1 Of, pertaining to, or representing the United States. 2 Supporting the Union cause in the American Civil War. —n. One who favored or fought for the Union cause in the American Civil War.

Federal Bureau of Investigation A branch of the Department of Justice which investigates all violations of Federal laws other than those specifically assigned to other agencies.

fed·er·al·ism (fed′ər·əl·iz′əm, fed′rəl-) n. The doctrine of federal union in government.

Fed·er·al·ism (fed′ər·əl·iz′əm, fed′rəl-) n. The principles of the Federal Party.

fed·er·al·ist (fed′ər·əl·ist, fed′rəl-) n. An advocate of federalism. —**fed′er·al·is′tic** adj.

Fed·er·al·ist (fed′ər·əl·ist, fed′rəl-) n. One who supported the Federal Party.

fed·er·al·ize (fed′ər·əl·īz, fed′rəl-) v.t. ·ized, ·iz·ing To bring together under federal government. —**fed′er·al·i·za′tion** n.

Federal Party A political party (1787–1830) which advocated the adoption of the United States Constitution and the formation of a strong national government. Also **Federalist Party.**

fed·er·ate (fed′ə·rāt) v.t. & v.i. ·at·ed, ·at·ing To unite in a federation. —adj. United in a federation. [<L foedus a league]

fed·er·a·tion (fed′ə·rā′shən) n. 1 The act of uniting under a federal government or under a central authority. 2 A federated body; league. —**fed′er·a·tive** adj.

fe·do·ra (fə·dôr′ə, -dō′rə) n. A low hat, usu. of soft felt, with the crown creased lengthwise. [<Fédora, a play by V. Sardou, 1831–1908, French playwright]

fee (fē) n. 1 A payment, as for professional service. 2 A charge for a privilege, as a license, membership, etc. 3 A gratuity; tip. 4 Law An estate of inheritance in land. 5 In feudal law, a fief. [<OF fé, fief fief, property money]

fee·ble (fē′bəl) adj. **fee·bler, fee·blest** 1 Lacking muscular strength; weak; frail. 2 Lacking force or effectiveness; inadequate: a feeble argument. [<L flebilis tearful] —**fee′ble·ness** n. —**fee′bly** adv.

fee·ble-mind·ed (fē′bəl·mīn′did) *adj.* Mentally deficient. —**fee′ble-mind′ed·ly** *adv.* —**fee′ble-mind′ed·ness** *n.*

feed (fēd) *n.* 1 Food; esp. food for domestic animals; fodder. 2 The amount of fodder given at one time. 3 The motion that carries material into a machine. 4 The machinery supplying this motion. 5 The material supplied to a machine. 6 *Informal* A meal. —*v.* **fed, feed·ing** *v.t.* 1 To give food to; supply with food. 2 To give as food. 3 To furnish with what is necessary for the continuance, growth, or operation of: to *feed* a furnace; to *feed* steel to a factory. 4 To enlarge; increase: Compliments *feed* his vanity. —*v.i.* 5 To take food; eat: said of animals. 6 To subsist; depend: usu. with *on:* to *feed* on hopes. [< OE *fēdan*] —**feed′er** *n.*

feed·back (fēd′bak′) *n.* 1 The transfer of energy from the output of an electronic or other system to the input, usu. causing major changes in the system characteristics. 2 A process whereby the results of action serve continually to modify further action.

feed·stock (fēd′stok′) *n.* Any raw material supplied to a machine or factory that processes it into products.

feel (fēl) *v.* **felt, feel·ing** *v.t.* 1 To examine by touching. 2 To perceive by the senses: to *feel* pain. 3 To experience emotionally: to *feel* joy. 4 To be affected by: to *feel* a snub. 5 To be convinced of: to *feel* the need for reform. —*v.i.* 6 To seem; appear. The air *feels* humid. 7 To have a sensation of: to *feel* cold. 8 To have the emotions or opinions stirred: to *feel* strongly about something. 9 To have compassion for: to *feel* for a sick friend. 10 To be in a specific frame of mind: to *feel* scared. 11 To examine by touching; grope: to *feel* around a wall. —**feel like** *Informal* To have a desire or inclination for. —**feel out** 1 To examine the possibilities of (a situation). 2 To talk to (a person) so as to determine opinions, ideas, etc. —**feel up to** To feel able to do. —*n.* 1 The act of feeling. 2 The sense of touch. 3 A sensation: a *feel* of spring in the air. 4 The quality of a thing perceived by touch: Fur has a soft *feel.* [< OE *fēlan*]

feel·er (fē′lər) *n.* 1 One who or that which feels. 2 An organ of touch; an antenna; tentacle. 3 Something asked or proposed in order to ascertain another's viewpoint.

feel·ing (fē′ling) *n.* 1 The sense of touch. 2 A particular physical sensation: a *feeling* of cold. 3 A state of consciousness: a rested

Feelers

feeling, etc. 4 An emotion: a hostile *feeling.* 5 Often *pl.* Sensitivity; sensibility: to hurt one's *feelings.* 6 Pity; sympathy. 7 Presentiment; foreboding. 8 Opinion; conviction: my *feeling* on the matter. 9 The ability to express or portray emotion: to perform with great *feeling* —*adj.* Having warm sensibilities; sympathetic. —**feel′ing·ly** *adv.*

feet (fēt) *n.pl.* of FOOT.

feign (fān) *v.t.* 1 To simulate; pretend. 2 To invent deceptively, as excuses. 3 To make up or imagine, as stories. —*v.i.* 4 To pretend. [< L *fingere* to shape] —**feign′ing·ly** *adv.* —**feign′er** *n.*

feint (fānt) *n.* 1 A ruse or pretense. 2 In boxing, fencing, war, etc., an apparent or pretended blow or attack meant to divert an opponent's attention. —*v.i.* To make a feint. [< F *feindre* to feign]

feis·ty (fīs′tē) *adj.* **feis·ti·er, feis·ti·est** *Informal* 1 Lively or flamboyant in manner or appearance. 2 Spirited to the point of being challenging; spunky. —**feis′ti·ness** *n.*

feld·spar (feld′spär, fel′-) *n.* Any one of a group of crystalline minerals consisting of silicates of aluminum with potassium, sodium, or calcium. [< G *Feld* field + SPAR]

fe·lic·i·tate (fə·lis′ə·tāt) *v.t.* **·tat·ed, ·tat·ing** To wish joy or happiness to; congratulate. [< L *felix* happy] —**fe·lic′i·ta′tion** *n.*

fe·lic·i·tous (fə·lis′ə·təs) *adj.* 1 Marked by or producing felicity. 2 Appropriate; apt. —**fe·lic′i·tous·ly** *adv.*

fe·lic·i·ty (fə·lis′ə·tē) *n. pl.* **·ties** 1 Happiness, comfort, and content. 2 Something causing happiness. 3 A pleasing faculty for expression, as in art, writing, etc. 4 A clever or apt expression. [< L *felix* happy]

fe·line (fē′līn) *adj.* 1 Of or pertaining to cats or catlike animals. 2 Catlike; sly. —*n.* One of the cat family. [< L *felis* cats] —**fe′line·ly** *adv.* —**fe·lin·i·ty** (fə·lin′ə·tē) *n.*

fell¹ (fel) *v.t.* 1 To cause to fall: to *fell* a tree. 2 In sewing, to finish with a flat seam. —*n.* 1 A seam made by joining edges, folding them under, and stitching flat. 2 The timber cut down during one season. [< OE *fellan*] —**fell′a·ble** *adj.*

fell² (fel) *p.t.* of FALL.

fell³ (fel) *adj.* 1 Fierce; cruel; barbarous. 2 Hideous. [< OF *felon* felon]

fell⁴ (fel) *n.* A hide or pelt. [< OE, hide]

fel·lah (fel′ə) *n. pl.* **fel·lahs** or **fel·la·heen** or **·hin** (fel′ə·hēn′) A peasant; laborer, as in Egypt. [Ar. *fellāh*]

fel·la·ti·o (fə·lā′shē·ō, -lät′ē-) *n.* Oral contact with the penis. [< L *fellare* to suck]

fel·low (fel′ō) *n.* 1 A man; boy. 2 A person or individual. 3 A companion. 4 An equal. 5 One of a pair; mate. 6 A trustee in some educational institutions. 7 A member of a scholarly society. 8 A graduate student of a university holding a fellowship or stipend. 9 *Informal* A girl's beau. —*adj.* Joined or associated in some way: a *fellow* student. [< OE *fēolaga* business partner]

fel·low·ship (fel′ō·ship) *n.* 1 Association; companionship. 2 The condition of being sharers or partakers, as in some activity. 3 A body of persons having similar tastes, views, or interests. 4 A foundation, as in a college or university, the income of which is given to aid a student; also, the income so given. 5 Membership in a scholarly society.

fel·on¹ (fel′ən) *n.* One who has committed a felony. —*adj.* Wicked; criminal; treacherous. [< Med. L *fello*]

fel·on² (fel′ən) *n.* Inflammation of the tissue near the nail of a finger or toe. [< OF *feloun*]

fe·lo·ni·ous (fə·lō′nē·əs) *adj.* 1 Malicious; villainous. 2 Like or involving legal felony. —**fe·lo′ni·ous·ly** *adv.* —**fe·lo′ni·ous·ness** *n.* —Syn. 2 criminal, illegal, unlawful.

fel·o·ny (fel′ə·nē) *Law n. pl.* **·nies** One of the gravest of crimes, as treason, murder, rape, etc., and punishable by imprisonment or death.

felt¹ (felt) *p.t. & p.p.* of FEEL.

felt² (felt) *n.* 1 A fabric made by compacting wool, fur, or hair, by pressure, chemical action, moisture, and heat. 2 An article made of felt. —*adj.* Made of felt. —*v.t.* 1 To make into felt. 2 To overlay with felt. [< OE]

fe·luc·ca (fə·luk′ə, fe-) *n.* A small, swift Mediterranean vessel propelled by lateen-rigged sails and by oars. [< Ar. *falūkah*]

fem. female; feminine.

fe·male (fē′māl) *adj.* 1 Of or pertaining to the sex that brings forth young or produces ova. 2 Of, pertaining to, or like this sex; feminine. 3 Designating a plant or flower which has a pistil but no stamen. 4 *Mech.* Denoting a part having a hollow or bore into which a matching part fits. —*n.* A female person, animal, or plant. [< L *femina* woman] —**fe′male·ness** *n.*

fem·i·nine (fem′ə·nin) *adj.* 1 Of or pertaining to the female sex. 2 Belonging to or characteristic of womankind; womanly. 3 Lacking in manly qualities; effeminate. 4 *Gram.* Applicable to females only or to objects classified as female. —*n. Gram.* A word belonging to the feminine gender. [< L *femina* a woman] —**fem′i·nine·ly** *adv.* —**fem′i·nine·ness, fem·i·nin·i·ty** (fem′ə·nin′ə·tē) *n.*

feminine rhyme Rhyme in which the primary accent falls on the first syllable of a two- or three-syllable word, as *never, ever* or *laziness, craziness.*

fem·i·nism (fem′ə·niz′əm) *n.* 1 The doctrine which declares that social, political, and economic rights for women be the same as those for men. 2 A movement advocating this doctrine. —**fem′i·nist** *n.* —**fem′i·nis′tic** *adj.*

fem·i·nize (fem′ə·nīz) *v.t. & v.i.* **·nized, ·niz·ing** To make or become effeminate or feminine. —**fem′i·ni·za′tion** *n.*

femme (fàm) *n. French* A woman; wife.

fe·mur (fē′mər) *n. pl.* **fe·murs** or **fem·o·ra** (fem′ər·ə) *Anat.* The long bone that forms the chief support of the thigh; thighbone. [< L, thigh] —**fem·o·ral** (fem′ər·əl) *adj.*

fen (fen) *n.* A marsh; bog. [< OE *fenn*]

a. femur.
b. tibia.
c. fibula.

fence (fens) *n.* **1** An enclosing structure or barrier of rails, pickets, wires, or the like. **2** The art of fencing. **3** Skill in repartee or debate. **4** A receiver of stolen goods, or the place where such goods are received. —**on the fence** Undecided or noncommittal. —*v.* **fenced, fenc·ing** *v.t.* **1** To enclose with or as with a fence. **2** To separate with or as with a fence. —*v.i.* **3** To engage in the art of fencing. **4** To avoid giving direct answers; parry. **5** To deal in stolen goods. [Var. of DEFENSE] —**fenc'er** *n.*

fenc·ing (fen'sing) *n.* **1** The art of using a foil, sword, or other similar weapon. **2** Skillful parrying of prying questions. **3** Material for fences; also, fences collectively.

fend (fend) *v.t.* **1** To ward off; parry: usu. with *off.* —*v.i.* **2** To offer resistance; parry. **3** To provide or get along: with *for:* to *fend* for oneself. [Short for DEFEND]

fend·er (fen'dər) *n.* **1** One who or that which fends or wards off. **2** The part of a frame of a motor vehicle that covers each wheel. **3** A metal guard before an open fire. **4** A device at the front of a locomotive or streetcar, used to push aside objects on the tracks.

Fe·ni·an (fē'nē·ən, fēn'yən) *n.* A member of an Irish society formed in New York in the mid-19th century to seek independence for Ireland. —*adj.* Of the Fenians. [< Ir. *Fiann,* a legendary Irish warrior] —**Fe'ni·an·ism** *n.*

fen·nel (fen'əl) *n.* An edible herb of the parsley family, with yellow flowers and aromatic seeds.

feoff (fef, fēf) *v.t.* **feoffed, feoff·ing** To give or grant a fief to. —*n.* FIEF. [< OF *fief* FIEF] —**feof'fer, feoff'ment** *n.*

FEPC, F.E.P.C. Fair Employment Practices Committee.

-fer *combining form* One who or that which bears: *conifer.* [< L *ferre* bear]

fe·ral (fir'əl) *adj.* **1** Undomesticated; existing in a wild state. **2** Pertaining to or characteristic of the wild state; savage. [< L *ferus* wild]

fer-de-lance (fâr'də·läns') *n.* A venomous snake of tropical South America. [F, lit., iron head of a lance]

fer·ment (fər·ment') *v.t.* **1** To produce fermentation in. **2** To stir with anger; agitate. —*v.i.* **3** To undergo fermentation; work. **4** To be agitated, as by emotion. —*n.* (fûr'ment) **1** A substance productive of fermentation, as yeast. **2** FERMENTATION. **3** Excitement or agitation. [< L *fermentum* < *fervere* to boil] —**fer·ment'a·ble** or **·i·ble** *adj.* —**fer·ment'a·bil'i·ty** *n.*

fer·men·ta·tion (fûr'mən·tā'shən) *n.* **1** The decomposition of organic compounds by the action of enzymes. **2** Commotion, agitation, or excitement.

fer·mi·um (fer'mē·əm, fûr'-) *n.* An artificially produced radioactive element (symbol Fm). [< E. *Fermi,* 1901–54, Italian physicist]

fern (fûrn) *n.* Any of a widely distributed class of flowerless, seedless plants, having leaves (fronds) which carry the reproductive spores. [< OE *fearn*] —**fern'y** *adj.*

fern·er·y (fûr'nər·ē) *n. pl.* **·er·ies** A place in which ferns are grown.

fe·ro·cious (fə·rō'shəs) *adj.* **1** Savage; bloodthirsty; rapacious. **2** *Informal* Very great: *ferocious* heat. [< L *ferus* wild] —**fe·ro'cious·ly** *adv.* —**fe·ro'cious·ness** *n.*

fe·roc·i·ty (fə·ros'ə·tē) *n. pl.* **·ties** The state or quality of being ferocious. —**Syn.** savagery, cruelty, brutality.

-ferous *combining form* Bearing or producing: *coniferous.* [< L *ferre* to bear]

fer·ret (fer'it) *n.* A small weasel sometimes trained to hunt rodents. —*v.t.* **1** To search out by careful investigation: with *out.* **2** To drive out of hiding with a ferret. **3** To hunt with ferrets. —*v.i.* **4** To hunt by means of ferrets. **5** To search. [< L *fur* a thief] —**fer'ret·er** *n.*

fer·ric (fer'ik) *adj.* Pertaining to iron, esp. in the trivalent state. [< L *ferrum* iron + IC]

Ferret

Fer·ris wheel (fer'is) A giant, vertical, power-driven wheel that revolves on a stationary axle and bears swinging observation cars for passengers. [< G. W. G. *Ferris,* 1859–96, U.S. engineer]

fer·rite (fer'īt) *n.* Any of various ferromagnetic, nonmetallic substances composed of ferric oxide and other metallic oxides.

ferro- *combining form* **1** Derived from, containing, or alloyed with iron: *ferromagnetic.* **2** Containing ferrous iron. [< L *ferrum* iron]

fer·ro·con·crete (fer'ō·kon'krēt, -kon·krēt') *n.* Concrete reinforced with steel rods, bars, cables, etc.

fer·ro·mag·net·ic (fer'ō·mag·net'ik) *adj. Physics* Having magnetic properties similar to those of iron. —**fer'ro·mag'ne·tism** *n.*

fer·rous (fer'əs) *adj.* **1** *Chem.* Of or pertaining to bivalent iron. **2** Having or deriving from iron. [< L *ferrum* iron + -OUS]

fer·ru·gi·nous (fə·rōō'jə·nəs) *adj.* **1** Of or like iron. **2** Rust-colored. [< L *ferrum* iron]

fer·rule (fer'əl, -ōōl, -ōōl) *n.* **1** A metal ring or cap, as on the end of a cane. **2** A bushing or thimble. **3** FERULE. —*v.t.* **·ruled, ·rul·ing** To furnish with a ferrule. [< L *viriae* bracelets]

fer·ry (fer'ē) *v.* **fer·ried, fer·ry·ing** *v.t.* **1** To carry across a relatively narrow body of water in a boat. **2** To cross (a river, bay, etc.) in a boat. **3** To bring or take (an airplane or vehicle) to a point of delivery. —*v.i.* **4** To cross a body of water in a boat or by ferry. —*n. pl.* **·ries 1** FERRYBOAT. **2** The place of crossing a river, bay, or the like, by boat. **3** The legal right to operate a service that transports people or goods across waterways. [< OE *ferian* carry]

fer·ry·boat (fer'ē·bōt') *n.* A boat used to transport passengers, vehicles, goods, etc., across a river, bay, etc.

fer·ry·man (fer'ē·mən) *n. pl.* **·men** (-mən) One who has charge of or works on a ferry.

fer·tile (fûr'təl) *adj.* **1** Producing or capable of producing abundantly. **2** Reproducing or capable of reproducing. **3** Capable of growth or development; said of seeds or eggs. **4** Productive; prolific; inventive: a *fertile* imagination. [< L *fertilis* < *ferre* to bear] —**fer'tile·ly** *adv.* —**fer'tile·ness** *n.*

fer·til·i·ty (fər·til'ə·tē) *n.* The state or quality of being fertile.

fer·til·ize (fûr'təl·īz) *v.t.* **·ized, ·iz·ing 1** To render fertile or fruitful. **2** To render (an ovum) capable of growth, usu. by fusion with a male gamete. **3** To enrich, as soil. —**fer'til·iz'a·ble** *adj.* —**fer'til·i·za'tion** *n.*

fer·til·i·zer (fûr'təl·īz'ər) *n.* **1** One who or that which fertilizes. **2** A fertilizing material applied to soil, as guano, manure, etc.

fer·ule (fer'əl, -ōōl) *n.* A flat stick or ruler sometimes used for punishing children. —*v.t.* **fer·uled, fer·ul·ing** To punish with a ferule. [< L *ferula* giant fennel, rod]

fer·vent (fûr'vənt) *adj.* **1** Having or showing great emotional warmth, devotion, or enthusiasm; ardent; fervid. **2** Burning, or very hot. [< L *fervere* be hot] —**fer'ven·cy, fer'vent·ness** *n.* —**fer'vent·ly** *adv.*

fer·vid (fûr'vid) *adj.* **1** Fervent; zealous. **2** Hot; glowing; fiery. [< L *fervere* be hot] —**fer·vid'i·ty, fer'vid·ness** *n.* —**fer'vid·ly** *adv.*

fer·vor (fûr'vər) *n.* **1** Great intensity of feeling; ardor; zeal. **2** Heat; warmth. *Brit. sp.* **fer'vour.** [< L *fervere* be hot] —**Syn.** enthusiasm, passion, intenseness, gusto, zest.

fes·cue (fes'kyōō) *n.* A tough grass, valuable for pasturage. [< L *festuca* a stalk, straw]

fess (fes) *n. Her.* A horizontal band across the middle of the shield, having a breadth equal to one third of the field. Also **fesse.** [< L *fascia* band]

fes·tal (fes'təl) *adj.* Pertaining to a festival, feast, or holiday; festive. [< L *festum* a feast] —**fes'tal·ly** *adv.*

fes·ter (fes'tər) *v.i.* **1** To generate pus. **2** To become embittered; rankle. **3** To decay; rot. —*v.t.* **4** To cause to fester or rankle. —*n.* An ulcerous sore. [< L *fistula* ulcer]

fes·ti·val (fes'tə·vəl) *n.* **1** A period of feasting or celebration. **2** A season devoted periodically to some form of entertainment. **3** A series of performances, art exhibits, etc.: a jazz *festival.* —*adj.* FESTIVE. [< L *festivus* festive]

fes·tive (fes'tiv) *adj.* Pertaining or suited to a feast or festival; gay; joyful. [< L *festum* feast] —**fes'tive·ly** *adv.* —**fes'tive·ness** *n.*

fes·tiv·i·ty (fes·tiv′ə·tē) n. pl. **·ties 1** FESTIVAL (def. 1). **2** Gaiety; merrymaking. **3** A social activity or celebration.

fes·toon (fes·tōōn′) n. **1** A decorative garland hanging in a curve between two points. **2** An ornamental carving resembling such a garland. —v.t. **1** To decorate with festoons. **2** To fashion into festoons. **3** To link together by festoons. [< F < Ital. *festa* a feast] —**fes·toon′er·y** n.

fe·tal (fēt′l) adj. Of, pertaining to, or characteristic of a fetus: the *fetal* position.

fetch (fech) v.t. **1** To go after and bring back. **2** To draw forth; bring, as a reply. **3** To bring as a price. **4** *Informal* To captivate; charm. **5** *Naut.* To reach or arrive at. **6** *Informal* To strike or deliver, as a blow. —v.i. **7** To go after and bring things back. **8** *Naut.* To take a course. —n. The act of fetching. [< OE *feccan*] —**fetch′er** n.

fetch·ing (fech′ing) adj. *Informal* Most attractive; taking; fascinating. —**fetch′ing·ly** adv.

fete (fāt) n. A festival; holiday. —v.t. **fet·ed, fet·ing** To honor with festivities. Also **fête.** [F < OF *feste* feast]

fet·id (fet′id, fē′tid) adj. Emitting an offensive odor. [< L *fetere* stink] —**fet′id·ly** adv. —**fet′id·ness** n.

fet·ish (fet′ish, fē′tish) n. **1** A natural object believed to be endowed with magical powers. **2** Any object of excessive devotion. **3** *Psychiatry* An object, usu. nonsexual in nature, that arouses sexual feelings. Also **fet′ich.** [< Pg. *feitiço* a charm < L *factitius* artificial]

fet·ish·ism (fet′ish·iz′əm, fē′tish-) n. **1** The belief in or worship of fetishes. **2** *Psychiatry* Sexual pleasure or excitement derived from an object not normally associated with sex. Also **fet′ich·ism.** —**fet′ish·ist** n. —**fet′ish·is′tic** adj.

fet·lock (fet′lok′) n. **1** The tuft of hair above and behind a horse's hoof. **2** The joint at this place. [ME *fitlok, fetlak*] • See HORSE.

fet·ter (fet′ər) n. **1** A shackle for the ankles. **2** Anything that restricts or confines. —v.t. **1** To fasten fetters upon; shackle. **2** To prevent the activity of; restrain. [< OE *feter, fetor*]

fet·tle (fet′l) v.t. **fet·tled, fet·tling** *Regional* To put in good order; arrange. —n. State or condition, as of spirits: in fine *fettle.* [ME *fetlen* prepare < OE *fetel* a belt]

fe·tus (fē′təs) n. pl. **fe·tus·es** The young in the womb of animals, esp. in the later stages of development. [L]

feud[1] (fyōōd) n. **1** Vindictive strife or hostility between families or clans, often hereditary. **2** Any quarrel or conflict. —v.i. To engage in a feud; quarrel bitterly. [< OHG *fehida* hatred, revenge] —**feud′er, feud′ist** n.

feud[2] (fyōōd) n. In feudalism, a fief. [< Med. L *feudum*]

feu·dal (fyōō′dəl) adj. **1** Of, pertaining to, or like feudalism. **2** Relating to a fief. [< Med. L *feudum* feud[2]] —**feu′· dal·ly** adv.

feu·dal·ism (fyōō′dəl·iz′əm) n. The medieval European system of a vassal's holding land from a lord on condition of military aid and other services. Also **feudal system.** —**feu′dal·ist** n. —**feu′dal·is′tic** adj.

feu·dal·ize (fyōō′dəl·īz) v.t. **·ized, ·iz·ing** To bring under the feudal system; render feudal. —**feu′dal·i·za′tion** n.

feu·da·to·ry (fyōō′də·tôr′ē, -tō′rē) adj. Holding or held by feudal tenure. —n. pl. **·ries 1** A feud or fief. **2** A vassal.

fe·ver (fē′vər) n. **1** Body temperature above the normal. **2** A disorder or illness marked by high temperature. **3** Emotional excitement or enthusiasm. —v.t. To affect with fever. [< L *febris*]

fever blister COLD SORE. Also **fever sore.**

fe·ver·few (fē′vər·fyōō′) n. An erect bushy herb bearing white-rayed, composite flowers. [< L *febris* fever + *fugare* put to flight]

fe·ver·ish (fē′vər·ish) adj. **1** Affected with fever. **2** Causing a fever. **3** Very excited, eager, or impatient. —**fe′ver· ish·ly** adv. —**fe′ver·ish·ness** n.

fe·ver·ous (fē′vər·əs) adj. FEVERISH. —**fe′ver·ous·ly** adv.

fe·ver·wort (fē′vər·wûrt′) n. A perennial weedy herb of the honeysuckle family having a root sometimes used as a purgative and emetic. Also **fe′ver·root′** (-rōōt′, -rōot′).

few (fyōō) adj. Limited in number; not many. —n. & pron. A small number; some. —**quite a few** An appreciable number. —**the few** The minority. [< OE *fēawe*] —**few′· ness** n.

fey (fā) adj. Acting in an eccentric, somewhat whimsical, or otherworldly manner. [< F *féer* enchant]

fez (fez) n. pl. **fez·zes** A brimless, tapering, felt hat, usu. red with a black tassel, worn esp. by men in Egypt and elsewhere. [< Turkish *fes*, after *Fez*, a city in Morocco]

Fez

ff. folios; following; fortissimo.

FHA Federal Housing Authority.

fi·an·cé (fē·än·sā′, fē·än′sā) n. A man engaged to be married. [F < OF < *fier* to trust]

fi·an·cee (fē·än·sā′, fē·än′sā) n. A woman engaged to be married. [F < OF < *fier* to trust]

fi·as·co (fē·as′kō) n. pl. **·cos** or **·coes** A complete or humiliating failure. [Ital.]

fi·at (fē′at, -ət) n. An authoritative command that something be done; an order or decree. [L, let it be done]

fiat money Paper money made legal tender but not backed by gold or silver and usu. not redeemable into coin.

fib (fib) n. A petty falsehood. —v.i. **fibbed, fib·bing** To tell a fib. [?] —**fib′ber** n.

fi·ber (fī′bər) n. **1** A fine filament. **2** A threadlike component of a substance, as of wood, cotton, spun glass, etc. **3** A material composed of filaments. **4** The texture of anything. **5** Character; nature; make-up: a woman of strong *fiber.* Also **fi′bre.** [< L *fibra* fiber] —**fi′bered, fi′ber·less** adj.

fi·ber·board (fī′bər·bôrd′, -bōrd′) n. A tough, stiff material made of cellulose fibers compressed and rolled into sheets.

Fi·ber·glas (fī′bər·glas′, -gläs′) n. FIBERGLASS: a trade name.

fi·ber·glass (fī′bər·glas′, -gläs′) n. A flexible, nonflammable material of glass spun into filaments, used for textiles, insulators, etc. Also **fiber glass.**

fi·bril (fī′brəl) n. **1** A minute fiber. **2** *Bot.* ROOT HAIR. [< NL *fibrilla*, dim. of L *fibra* fiber] —**fi′bril·lar** adj.

fi·bril·late (fib′rə·lāt, fī′brə-) v.i. **·lat·ed, ·lat·ing** To undergo fibrillation.

fi·bril·la·tion (fib′rə·lā′shən, fī′brə-) n. Rapid, irregular, uncoordinated contractions of the muscle fibers of the heart.

fi·brin (fī′brin) n. An insoluble protein formed in and aiding the clotting of blood. [< L *fibra* fiber]

fi·broid (fī′broid) adj. Of the nature of fiber; fibrous: a *fibroid* tumor.

fi·bro·sis (fī·brō′sis) n. Increase of fibrous tissue due to disease; fibroid degeneration.

fi·brous (fī′brəs) adj. Composed of or having the character of fibers.

fib·u·la (fib′yōo·lə) n. pl. **·las** or **·lae** (-lē) The smaller of the two bones between the human knee and ankle or its counterpart in animals. [L, a clasp] —**fib′u·lar** adj. • See FEMUR.

-fic suffix Making; causing: *beatific.* [< L *facere* make]

-fication suffix The making, rendering, or causing to be of a certain character: *beatification.* [< L *facere* make]

fiche (fēsh) n. MICROFICHE.

fi·chu (fish′ōō) n. A triangular piece of light material worn about the neck. [F < *ficher* put on hastily]

fick·le (fik′əl) adj. Inconstant in feeling or purpose; capricious. [< OE *ficol* crafty] —**fick′le·ness** n. —Syn. changeable, unsteady, erratic, irresolute, mercurial.

fic·tion (fik′shən) n. **1** Literature made up of imaginary events and characters, as novels, short stories, plays, etc.; also, such works collectively. **2** The act of feigning or imagining that which does not exist or is not actual. **3** That which is feigned or imagined. [< L *fictio* < *fingere* to form] —**fic′· tion·al** adj. —**fic′tion·al·ly** adv. —**fic′tive** (fik′tiv) adj.

fic·ti·tious (fik·tish′əs) adj. **1** Of or like fiction; imaginary. **2** Not real; counterfeit; false: a *fictitious* name. —**fic·ti′tious·ly** adv. —**fic·ti′tious·ness** n.

fid (fid) n. *Naut.* **1** A supporting bar to hold a topmast in place. **2** A large tapering wooden pin used for opening ropes when splicing, etc. [?]

-fid combining form Divided into; split: *bifid.* [< L *findere* to split]

fid·dle (fid′l) n. **1** VIOLIN. **2** *Naut.* A rack or frame used at table on board ship in rough weather to keep the dishes

Fichu

in place. **—fit as a fiddle** In fine health and spirits. — **play second fiddle** To perform in a subordinate role. — *v.* **fid·dled, fid·dling** *v.i.* **1** *Informal* To play on a fiddle. **2** To toy or tinker nervously with an object. —*v.t.* **3** *Informal* To play (an air, tune, etc.) on a fiddle. **4** To trifle; fritter: to *fiddle* time away. [< OE *fithele*] —**fid′dler** *n.*

fiddler crab A small burrowing crab the male of which has one much enlarged claw.

fid·dle·stick (fid′l·stik′) *n.* **1** *Informal* A violin bow. **2** A trifling or absurd thing.

fid·dle·sticks (fid′l·stiks′) *interj.* Nonsense!

fi·del·i·ty (fə·del′ə·tē, fī-) *n. pl.* **·ties 1** Faithfulness in honoring an obligation, vow, duty, etc. **2** Strict adherence to truth or fact. **3** Exactness in the reproduction of something. **4** *Electronics* The accuracy with which an amplifier or other system reproduces the important characteristics of its input signal at the output. [< L *fides* faith] —**Syn. 1** constancy, loyalty, allegiance. **2** honesty, integrity.

fidg·et (fij′it) *v.i.* **1** To move about restlessly. **2** To toy with something nervously. —*v.t.* **3** To make restless. —*n.* **1** *Often pl.* Nervous restlessness: to have the *fidgets.* **2** A restless person; one who fidgets. [< obs. *fidge* move about] —**fidg′et·y** *adj.* (**·i·er, ·i·est**) —**fidg′et·i·ness** *n.*

fi·du·ci·ar·y (fi·dyōō′shē·er′ē, -shə·rē) *adj.* **1** Of or pertaining to a trustee or guardian. **2** Relying on the confidence of the public, as for paper currency or value. **3** Held in trust. —*n. pl.* **·ar·ies** *Law* A person who holds a thing in trust. [< L *fiducia* trust]

fie (fī) *interj.* An expression of impatience or disapproval. [< L *fi* an expression of disgust]

fief (fēf) *n.* A landed estate held under feudal tenure. [< Med. L *feudum* feud²]

field (fēld) *n.* **1** A relatively large area of open land. **2** A piece of cleared land set apart and enclosed for tillage or pasture. **3** A region of the countryside considered as yielding some natural product: a coal *field.* **4** Any wide or open expanse: an ice *field.* **5** An airport. **6** *Mil.* An area of action or operations. **7** In sports or contests: **a** The area on which the game is played. **b** An area usu. enclosed by a running track where contests in hurling, throwing, and leaping are held in track-and-field meets. **c** In baseball, the outfield. **d** The contestants, as in a race or other contest. **e** The players actually playing on a field. **8** A sphere or area of study, knowledge, or practice: the *field* of physics. **9** In business or research, an area of work away from the main office, laboratory, etc. **10** *Physics* A region of space throughout which a physical effect, as gravitational force, can be detected. **11** The background area of a painting, coin, flag, heraldic shield, etc. **12** *Optics* The space or apparent surface within which objects are seen in an optical instrument. —**play the field** *Informal* To be interested or active in all or many aspects of something. —**take** (or **leave**) **the field** To begin (or cease) an activity, military contest, etc. —*adj.* **1** Of, pertaining to, or found in the fields. **2** Used in, or for use in, the fields. **3** Played on a field. —*v.t.* **1** To catch and return (a ball in play), as in baseball. **2** To put (a player or team) on the field. —*v.i.* **3** In baseball, cricket, etc., to play as a fielder. [< OE *feld*]

field artillery Light or heavy artillery so mounted as to be freely movable.

field day 1 A day when troops are taken to the field for maneuvers. **2** A school holiday devoted to athletic sports. **3** Any day of display, excitement, or celebration.

field·er (fēl′dər) *n.* In baseball, cricket, etc., a player stationed in the field.

field glasses A small, portable telescope for binocular use. Also **field glass.**

field goal 1 In football, a goal scored from the field by means of a kick. **2** In basketball, a goal scored with the ball in active play.

field hand An agricultural laborer.

field hockey HOCKEY (def. 2).

field hospital A hospital established on or near a field of battle.

field marshal An officer of the highest rank in the armies of several European nations.

field officer An army major, lieutenant colonel, or colonel.

field of force *Physics* FIELD (def. 10).

field·stone (fēld′stōn′) *n.* Loose stone found naturally in fields, often used in building.

field trip A trip outside the classroom for purposes of first-hand observation and study.

field·work (fēld′wûrk′) *n.* A temporary fortification thrown up in the field.

field work Observations or performance in the field, as by scientists, surveyors, etc.

fiend (fēnd) *n.* **1** An evil spirit; a devil; demon. **2** An intensely malicious or wicked person. **3** *Informal* One exceptionally interested or skilled in a certain subject or activity. **4** *Informal* One addicted to some harmful habit. — **the Fiend** Satan; the devil. [< OE *fēond* devil]

fiend·ish (fēn′dish) *adj.* Of, pertaining to, or resembling a fiend; diabolical. —**fiend′ish·ly** *adv.* —**fiend′ish·ness** *n.*

fierce (firs) *adj.* **fierc·er, fierc·est 1** Having a violent and cruel nature or temper; savage; ferocious. **2** Violent in action; furious. **3** Vehement; passionate; extreme. **4** *Informal* Very bad, difficult, disagreeable, etc. [< L *ferus* wild] —**fierce′ly** *adv.* —**fierce′ness** *n.*

fier·y (fī′ər·ē, fīr′ē) *adj.* **fier·i·er, fier·i·est 1** Of, like, or containing fire. **2** Blazing; glowing. **3** Passionate; spirited; ardent. **4** Easily aroused, as to anger. **5** Inflamed, as a sore. —**fier′i·ly** *adv.* —**fier′i·ness** *n.*

fi·es·ta (fē·es′tä) *n.* **1** A religious festival. **2** Any celebration or holiday. [< Sp. < L *festa* feast]

fife (fīf) *n.* A small, shrill-toned, flutelike wind instrument. —*v.t. & v.i.* **fifed, fif·ing** To play on a fife. [< OHG *pfifa*, ult. < L *pipare* to peep, chirp] —**fif′er** *n.*

fif·teen (fif′tēn′) *n.* **1** The sum of 14 plus 1; 15; XV. **2** A set or group of 15 members. [< OE *fiftēne*] — **fif′teen** *adj., pron.*

fif·teenth (fif′tēnth′) *adj. & adv.* Next in order after the 14th. —*n.* **1** The element of an ordered set corresponding to the number 15. **2** One of fifteen equal parts.

Fife

fifth (fifth) *adj. & adv.* Next in order after the fourth. — *n.* **1** The element of an ordered set corresponding to the number 5. **2** One of five equal parts. **3** *Music* The interval between a tone and another tone four steps away in a diatonic scale. **4** One fifth of a U.S. gallon used as a measure of spirituous liquors. [< OE *fifta*]

fifth column A group, within a city or country, of civilian sympathizers with an enemy. —**fifth columnist**

fifth wheel A superfluous thing or person.

fif·ti·eth (fif′tē·ith) *adj. & adv.* Tenth in order after the 40th. —*n.* **1** The element of an ordered set that corresponds to the number 50. **2** One of 50 equal parts.

fif·ty (fif′tē) *n. pl.* **fif·ties 1** The product of five and ten; 50; L. **2** A set or group of 50 members. **3** The numbers, years, etc., between 50 and 60. [< OE *fiftig*] —**fif′ty** *adj., pron.*

fif·ty-fif·ty (fif′tē-fif′tē) *adj. Informal* Sharing equally, as benefits. —*adv. Informal* Equally.

fig (fig) *n.* **1** A small, sweet, many-seeded fruit, usu. marketed in dried, processed form. **2** The tree that bears this fruit. [< L *ficus*]

fig. figurative(ly); figure(s).

fig·eat·er (fig′ē′tər) *n.* A large beetle common in the s U.S. that eats ripe fruits.

Figs

fight (fīt) *v.* **fought, fight·ing** *v.t.* **1** To struggle against in battle or physical combat. **2** To box with in a boxing match. **3** To struggle against in any manner. **4** To carry on or engage in (a battle, duel, court action, etc.). **5** To make (one's way) by struggling. **6** To cause to fight, as dogs or gamecocks. —*v.i.* **7** To take part in battle or physical combat. **8** To box, esp. professionally. **9** To struggle in any manner. —**fight shy of** To avoid meeting or facing. —*n.* **1** Conflict or struggle between adversaries. **2** An effort to attain an object in spite of opposition. **3** Power or disposition to fight; pugnacity. [< OE *feohtan*]

fight·er (fī′tər) *n.* **1** One who fights. **2** A pugnacious or spirited person. **3** *Mil.* A fast, highly maneuverable airplane: also **fighter plane.**

fig·ment (fig′mənt) *n.* Something imagined or feigned; a fiction. [< L *figmentum* anything made < *fingere* to form]

fig·u·ra·tion (fig′yə·rā′shən) *n.* **1** The act of shaping something. **2** External form or shape. **3** Representation using figures. **4** *Music* Ornamentation or variation.

fig·u·ra·tive (fig′yər·ə·tiv) *adj.* **1** Of, using, or like a figure or figures of speech; not literal; metaphorical. **2** Of or pertaining to the representation of form or figure. **3** Representing by means of a form or figure; emblematic. —**fig′u·ra·tive·ly** *adv.* —**fig′u·ra·tive·ness** *n.*

fig·ure (fig′yər, *Brit.* fig′ər) *n.* **1** The visible form or outline of something. **2** The human form. **3** A person, esp. if active or prominent in some specific way: a *figure* in world affairs. **4** A representation or likeness of a person or thing. **5** The impression made by a person's appearance or conduct: a sorry *figure.* **6** An illustration, diagram, or drawing. **7** A pattern or design, as in a fabric. **8 a** A number or the numeral that represents it. **b** An amount represented by a number. **c** *pl.* Mathematical calculations: a head for *figures.* **9** In dancing or skating, a movement or pattern of movements. **10** *Geom.* A surface or space enclosed by lines or planes. **11** *Music* Any short succession of tones or chords that produces a single, complete impression. —*v.* **fig·ured, fig·ur·ing** *v.t.* **1** To make an image, picture, or other representation of; depict. **2** To form an idea or mental image of; imagine. **3** To ornament or mark with a design. **4** To compute numerically; calculate. **5** To express metaphorically; symbolize. **6** *Informal* To think; believe; predict. **7** *Music* To embellish; ornament —*v.i.* **8** To be conspicuous; appear prominently. **9** To make computations; do arithmetic. —**figure in** To include or add in. —**figure on** (or **upon**) **1** To think over; consider. **2** To plan; expect. —**figure out 1** To reckon; to ascertain. **2** To solve; understand. —**figure up** To total. [< L *figura* form < *fingere* to form] —**fig′ur·er** *n.*

fig·ured (fig′yərd) *adj.* **1** Adorned or marked with designs: *figured* cottons. **2** Represented by figures; pictured.

fig·ure·head (fig′yər·hed′) *n.* **1** A carved or ornamental figure on a prow of a vessel. **2** A person having nominal leadership but no real power.

figure of speech An expression, as a metaphor or simile, that uses words not in their usual or literal sense but to produce a fanciful or vivid impression.

fig·u·rine (fig′yə·rēn′) *n.* A small, ornamental figure made of porcelain, wood, ivory, etc.; a statuette.

Figurehead

fig·wort (fig′wûrt′) *n.* **1** A plant with small, dark-colored flowers, formerly supposed to cure scrofula. **2** Any plant of the figwort family.

Fi·ji (fē′jē) *n.* **1** A group of islands, a member of the Commonwealth of Nations, in the sw Pacific, 7,057 sq. mi., cap. Suva. **2** A native or citizen of Fiji. —**Fi′ji·an** *adj., n.*

fil·a·gree (fil′ə·grē) *n., adj., v.* FILIGREE.

fil·a·ment (fil′ə·mənt) *n.* **1** A fine thread or fiber. **2** Any threadlike structure or appendage. **3** *Bot.* The part of the stamen supporting the anther. • See STAMEN. **4** *Electr.* The slender wire in a lamp bulb that is heated to incandescence by an electric current. • See INCANDESCENT. [< LL *filare* spin < L *filum* a thread] —**fil·a·men·ta·ry** (fil′ə·men′tə·rē), **fil′a·men′tous** *adj.*

fi·lar·i·a (fi·lâr′ē·ə) *n. pl.* **·i·ae** (-i·ē) Any of various parasitic threadworms infecting man and other animals. [< L *filum* a thread] —**fi·lar′i·al, fi·lar′i·an** *adj.*

fil·bert (fil′bərt) *n.* The edible nut of various cultivated hazel trees; hazelnut. [< St. *Philibert,* near whose feast (Aug. 22) these nuts ripen]

filch (filch) *v.t.* To steal slyly and in small amounts; pilfer. [?] —**filch′er** *n.*

file[1] (fīl) *n.* **1** Any device to keep papers in order for reference. **2** A collection of papers, documents, or data ar-

ranged for reference. **3** Any orderly succession or line of men or things. —**on file** In or as in a file for reference. —*v.* **filed, fil·ing** *v.t.* **1** To put on file for reference. **2** To send (a news item or story) to a newspaper. **3** To submit (a job application, etc.) for consideration. **4** To institute (a legal action, divorce proceeding, etc.). —*v.i.* **5** To march in file, as soldiers. **6** To make an application, as for a job. [< L *filum* a thread] —**fil′er** *n.*

file[2] (fīl) *n.* **1** A hard steel tool with ridged faces for smoothing or abrading surfaces. **2** Anything used to abrade, smooth, or polish. —*v.t.* **filed, fil·ing 1** To cut, smooth, or sharpen with a file. **2** To remove with a file: with *away* or *off:* to *file* away rust. [< OE *fil*] —**fil′er** *n.*

file·fish *n. pl.* **·fish** or **·fish·es** Any of certain fish with prickly scales.

fi·let (fi·lā′, fil′ā) *n.* **1** Net lace having a square mesh. **2** FILLET (def. 2). [< L *filum* thread]

fi·let mi·gnon (fi·lā′ min·yon′, *Fr.* fē·le′ mē·nyôn′) *n. pl.* **fi·lets mi·gnons** A small, choice fillet of beef tenderloin. [F]

fil·i·al (fil′ē·əl, fil′yəl) *adj.* **1** Of, pertaining to, or befitting a son or daughter. **2** *Genetics* Pertaining to a generation following the parental. [< L *filius* a son] —**fil′i·al·ly** *adv.*

fil·i·bus·ter (fil′ə·bus′tər) *n.* **1** A member of a legislative body who attempts to obstruct legislation by prolonged speaking to consume time. **2** An instance of such prolonged speaking. **3** An adventurer who takes part in an unlawful military expedition into a foreign country. —*v.i.* **1** To obstruct legislation by long speeches. **2** To act as a freebooter or adventurer. —*v.t.* **3** To block passage of (legislation) by constant delay. [< Du. *vrijbuiter* freebooter] —**fil′i·bus′ter·er** *n.*

fil·i·gree (fil′ə·grē) *n.* **1** Delicate ornamental work formed of intertwisted gold or silver wire. **2** Anything fanciful and delicate, but purely ornate. —*adj.* Made of or adorned with filigree. —*v.t.* **·greed, ·gree·ing** To adorn with filigree. Also **fil′la·gree.** [< L *filum* thread + *granum* a grain]

fil·ing (fī′ling) *n.* **1** The act of using a file. **2** *Usu. pl.* A particle removed by a file.

Fil·i·pi·no (fil′ə·pē′nō) *n. pl.* **·nos** A native or citizen of the Philippines. —*adj.* Of or pertaining to the Philippines.

fill (fil) *v.t.* **1** To make full; put as much in as possible. **2** To occupy or be diffused through the whole of. **3** To abound in. **4** To stop up or plug: to *fill* a tooth. **5** To supply with what is necessary or ordered: to *fill* a prescription. **6** To occupy (an office or position). **7** To put someone into (an office or position). **8** To feed to fullness. **9** To build up or make full, as an embankment or a ravine, by adding fill. —*v.i.* **10** To become full. —**fill in 1** To fill completely, as an excavation. **2** To insert (something), as into a blank space. **3** To insert something into (a blank space). **4** To be a substitute. —**fill (someone) in on** *Informal* To bring (someone) up to date on additional details or facts. —**fill out 1** To become fuller or more rounded. **2** To make complete, as an application. —**fill the bill** *Informal* To do or be what is wanted or needed. —*n.* **1** That which fills or is sufficient to fill or satisfy: to have one's *fill* of adventure. **2** An embankment built up by filling in with stone, gravel, etc. **3** Something, as stone, gravel, etc., used to fill in a hole, depression, etc. [< OE *fyllan* fill]

fill·er (fil′ər) *n.* **1** One who or that which fills. **2** Any substance used for filling, as: **a** A substance used to add weight or bulk. **b** A composition for filling pores or holes in wood. **c** Tobacco used for the inside of cigars. **d** Paper for a loose-leaf notebook. **3** A brief piece of writing, used to fill space in a newspaper or magazine.

fil·let (fil′it) *n.* **1** A narrow band or ribbon for binding the hair. **2** (*usu.* fi·lā′, fil′ā) A strip of boneless meat or fish. **3** A thin band or strip of anything. —*v.t.* **1** To bind or adorn with a fillet or band. **2** (*usu.* fil′ā, fi·lā′) To bone and slice into fillets. [< L *filum*]

fill-in (fil′in′) *n.* **1** A person or thing included to fill a gap or omission. **2** *Informal* A summary of facts.

fill·ing (fil′ing) *n.* **1** The act of making or becoming full. **2** Something used to fill a cavity or vacant space. **3** In weaving, the weft or woof. **4** A food mixture used between slices of bread, layers of cake, etc.

filling station SERVICE STATION (def. 1).

fil·lip (fil′əp) *n.* **1** A quick snap or blow with the end of a

finger. **2** Anything which serves to stimulate or incite. —
v.t. **1** To strike or project by or as by a fillip. **2** To stimulate
or incite by a fillip. —*v.i.* **3** To make a fillip. [Var. of FLIP]

fil·ly (fil′ē) *n. pl.* **fil·lies** **1** A young mare. **2** *Informal* A
sprightly girl. [< ON *fylja*]

film (film) *n.* **1** A thin coating, layer, or membrane. **2** A
haze or blur. **3** A flexible roll or sheet of cellulose material
coated with light-sensitive emulsion, used for making
photographs. **4 a** A sequence of pictures, each slightly different from the last, photographed on a single strip of film
(def. 3) for projection on a screen, giving the optical illusion of continuous, ordered movement. **b** Such films, collectively; the movies. **c** The art of making such films. —*v.t.*
1 To cover or obscure by or as by a film. **2** To photograph,
esp. with a motion-picture camera. **3** To record on motion-
picture film, as a story or event. —*v.i.* **4** To become covered
or obscured by a film. **5** To take motion-picture films. [<
OE *filmen* membrane]

film·ic (fil′mik) *adj.* **1** Produced or represented in a motion-picture film. **2** Of, relating to, or suitable for films or
filmmaking.

film·mak·ing (film′māˈking, fil′-) *n.* The art or industry
of making motion-picture films. —**film′mak′er** *n.*

film·strip (film′strip′) *n.* A length of film containing
frames of still pictures projected on a screen, usu. as a
visual aid in lectures.

film·y (fil′mē) *adj.* **film·i·er, film·i·est** **1** Of or like a film. **2**
Covered with a film; hazy. —**film′i·ly** *adv.* —**film′i·ness** *n.*

fil·ter (fil′tər) *n.* **1** Any device used to strain solid particles
or remove impurities from a liquid, air, etc. **2** Any of
various devices that on the basis of frequency selectivity
block part of a flow of energy, as light, electricity, sound,
etc. —*v.t.* **1** To pass (liquids, air, etc.) through a filter. **2** To
separate (solid matter, impurities, etc.) from a liquid, air,
etc., by a filter. **3** To act as a filter for. —*v.i.* **4** To pass
through or as if through a filter. **5** To leak out, as news.
[< Med. L *filtrum*] —**fil′ter·er** *n.*

fil·ter·a·ble (fil′tər·ə·bəl) *adj.* **1** That can be separated by
filtering. **2** Capable of passing through a filter: *filterable
virus.* Also **fil·tra·ble** (fil′trə·bəl). —**fil′ter·a·bil′i·ty** *n.*

filth (filth) *n.* **1** Anything that soils or makes foul. **2** A foul
or dirty condition. **3** Moral defilement; obscenity. [< OE
fylth]

filth·y (fil′thē) *adj.* **filth·i·er, filth·i·est** **1** Of the nature of or
containing filth. **2** Obscene. **3** Morally foul. —**filth′i·ly** *adv.*
—**filth′i·ness** *n.*

fil·trate (fil′trāt) *v.t.* **·trat·ed, ·trat·ing** FILTER. —*n.* The liquid or other substance that has passed through a filter.
[< Med. L *filtrum* a filter] —**fil·tra′tion** *n.*

fin (fin) *n.* **1** A membranous extension from the body of a
fish or other aquatic animal, serving to propel, balance, or
steer it. **2** Any finlike or projecting part, appendage, or
attachment. **3** FLIPPER (def. 2). **4** *Slang* The hand. —*v.*
finned, fin·ning *v.t.* **1** To cut up or trim off the fins of (a fish).
—*v.i.* **2** To beat the water with the fins, as a whale when
dying. [< OE *finn*]

fin. finance; financial; finish.

fi·na·gle (fi·nāˈgəl) *v.* **·gled, ·gling** *Informal* **1** To get (something) by trickery or deceit. **2** To cheat or trick (someone).
—*v.i.* **3** To use trickery or deceit; be sly. **4** In card games,
to renege. [?] —**fi·na′gler** *n.*

fi·nal (fī′nəl) *adj.* **1** Being, pertaining to, or coming at the
end; ultimate; last. **2** Making further action or controversy unnecessary; conclusive. **3** Relating to or consisting
in the end or purpose aimed at: a *final* cause. —*n.* **1** Something that is terminal or last. **2** *Usu. pl.* The last match
in a series of games. **3** The last examination of a term in
a school or college. [< L *finis* end] —**fi′nal·ly** *adv.*

fi·na·le (fi·näˈlē, -nälˈē) *n.* The last part, as the final scene
of a theatrical presentation or the last movement in a
musical composition. [Ital., final]

fi·nal·ist (fī′nəl·ist) *n.* A contestant who takes part in the
final round of competition.

fi·nal·i·ty (fī·nalˈə·tē) *n. pl.* **·ties** **1** The state or quality of
being final. **2** A final, conclusive, or decisive act, determination, offer, etc.

fi·nal·ize (fī′nəl·īz) *v.t.* **·ized, ·iz·ing** To bring to a state of
completion. • *Finalize* was formed by the traditional pattern of conversion from adjective to verb that is apparent
in such words as *brutalize* and *fertilize.* Although it is
considered by some discriminating writers and speakers
as an example of bureaucratic jargon, *finalize* has had
wide acceptance in both American and British English.

fi·nance (fi·nansˈ, fī′nans) *n.* **1** The management or
science of monetary affairs. **2** *pl.* The monetary resources,
as of a country, business, or individual. —*v.t.* **·nanced,
·nanc·ing** **1** To manage the finances of. **2** To supply the
money for. [< OF *finer* settle < *fin* end]

fi·nan·cial (fi·nanˈshəl, fī-) *adj.* **1** Of or pertaining to finance; monetary. **2** Of or pertaining to those dealing
professionally with money and credit. —**fi·nan′cial·ly** *adv.*

fin·an·cier (finˈən·sirˈ) *n.* One skilled in or occupied with
financial affairs. —*v.i.* To manage financial operations,
esp. unscrupulously.

fin·back (fin′bakˈ) *n.* RORQUAL. Also **finback whale.**

finch (finch) *n.* A small, seed-eating bird, as a bullfinch,
goldfinch, or wild canary. [< OE
finc]

find (fīnd) *v.* **found, find·ing** *v.t.* **1**
To come upon unexpectedly. **2** To
perceive or discover, as by search,
experience, or examination. **3** To
recover (something lost). **4** To
reach; arrive at. **5** To give a judicial decision upon. **6** To gain or
recover the use of. **7** To consider or think: I *found* the play
a bore. —*v.i.* **8** To arrive at and express a judicial decision:
to *find* for the plaintiff. —**find oneself** To become aware
of one's special ability or vocation. —**find out** To detect
or discover. —**find out about** To learn the truth concerning. —*n.* A thing found or discovered. [< OE *findan*]

Finch

find·er (fīn′dər) *n.* **1** One who or that which finds. **2** An
optical viewer used to aim or focus a camera or large
telescope.

fin de siè·cle (fan də syeˈkl′) *French* The close of the
19th century, viewed as a period of transition in social and
moral values.

find·ing (fīn′ding) *n.* **1** The act of one who finds. **2** A discovery or conclusion.

fine[1] (fīn) *adj.* **fin·er, fin·est** **1** Excellent in quality; admirable; superior. **2** Enjoyable; pleasant. **3** Light and delicate,
as in texture, etc. **4** Made up of very small particles: *fine*
dirt. **5** Thin or narrow: *fine* wire. **6** Very small: *fine* print.
7 Very sharp: a *fine* cutting edge. **8** Cloudless; sunny: *fine*
weather. **9** Subtle; acute: a *fine* point. **10** Elegant; cultivated; polished. **11** Overly elegant; pretentious; showy.
12 Refined; pure, as syrup. **13** Containing a specified proportion of pure metal: said of gold or silver. —*adv. Informal* Very much; well. —*v.t. & v.i.* **fined, fin·ing** To make or
become fine or finer. [< L *finire* to complete < *finis* end] —
fine′ly *adv.* —**fine′ness** *n.*

fine[2] (fīn) *n.* An amount of money forfeited as a penalty.
—**in fine** Finally. —*v.t.* **fined, fin·ing** To exact a fine from.
[< OF *fin* settlement, end]

fine arts The arts of drawing, painting, and sculpture,
and often including music, literature, drama, dance, and
architecture.

fine-drawn (fīn′drônˈ) *adj.* **1** Drawn out finely. **2** Developed very subtly or too subtly.

fine-grained (fīn′grāndˈ) *adj.* Having a close, fine
grain, as some leathers and woods.

fin·er·y (fī′nər·ē) *n. pl.* **·er·ies** Elegant or showy clothes,
accessories, decorations, etc.

fines herbes (fēn ârb) *French* A mixture of herbs used
to season soups, stews, etc.

fine-spun (fīn′spunˈ) *adj.* **1** Drawn or spun out to an
extreme degree of fineness. **2** Subtle.

fi·nesse (fi·nesˈ) *n.* **1** Subtle skill or style, as in a performance. **2** Adroit and tactful handling of a situation or person. **3** A stratagem or artifice. **4** In bridge, an attempt to
take a trick with a lower card when one holds a higher
card, in the hope that the opposing hand yet to play will

not hold a taking card of intermediate value. —*v.* **finessed, fi·ness·ing** *v.t.* **1** To change or bring about by finesse. **2** In bridge, to play as a finesse. —*v.i.* **3** To use finesse. **4** In bridge, to make a finesse. [< F *fin* fine[1]]

fine-toothed comb (fīn′tōōtht′) A comb with fine teeth very close together. Also **fine′-tooth′ comb.** —**go over with a fine-toothed comb** To leave no part unsearched or unexamined.

fin·ger (fing′gər) *n.* **1** One of the digits of the hand, esp. excluding the thumb. **2** That part of a glove which covers a finger. **3** Any small projecting piece or part, like a finger. **4** A unit of measure, roughly equal to either the width of a finger or the length of the middle finger. —**burn one's fingers** To suffer the consequences of meddling or interfering. —**have a finger in the pie 1** To take part in some matter. **2** To meddle. —**have at one's finger tips** To have ready and available knowledge of or access to. —**put one's finger on** To identify or indicate correctly. —**put the finger on** *Slang* **1** To betray to the police. **2** To indicate (the victim) of a planned crime. —**twist around one's (little) finger** To be able to influence or manage with ease. —*v.t.* **1** To touch or handle with the fingers; toy with. **2** To steal; purloin. **3** *Music* **a** To play (an instrument) with the fingers. **b** To mark the notes of (music) showing which fingers are to be used. **4** *Slang* To betray. —*v.i.* **5** To touch or feel anything with the fingers. [< OE] —**fin′ger·er** *n.*

fin·ger·board (fing′gər-bôrd′, -bōrd′) *n. Music* The strip of wood upon which the strings are pressed by the fingers of the player of a stringed instrument.

fin·ger·bowl (fing′gər-bōl′) *n.* A bowl containing water for cleansing the fingers at the table after eating.

fin·gered (fing′gərd) *adj.* **1** Having fingers; digitate. **2** *Music* Having notations to mark the fingering.

fin·ger·ing (fing′gər·ing) *n.* **1** The act of touching or feeling with the fingers. **2** *Music* **a** The act or manner of using the fingers in playing an instrument. **b** The notation indicating what fingers are to be used.

fin·ger·ling (fing′gər·ling) *n.* A small or young fish, esp. a salmon or trout.

fin·ger·nail (fing′gər·nāl′) *n.* The horny plate at the end of a finger.

fin·ger·print (fing′gər·print′) *n.* An impression of the skin pattern on the inner surface of a finger tip, used for identification. —*v.t.* To take the fingerprints of.

fin·i·al (fin′ē·əl) *n. Archit.* An ornament at the apex of a spire, pinnacle, or the like. [< L *finis* end]

fin·i·cal (fin′i·kəl) *adj.* FINICKY [< FINE[1]] —**fin′i·cal·ly** *adv.* —**fin′i·cal′i·ty** (-kal′ə·tē) **fin′i·cal·ness** *n.*

fin·ick·ing (fin′i·king) *adj.* FINICKY.

fin·ick·y (fin′i·kē) *adj.* **·ick·i·er, ·ick·i·est** Overly fastidious, precise, or fussy. —**fin′ick·i·ness** *n.*

fi·nis (fin′is, fī′nis) *n. pl.* **fi·nis·es** The end. —**write finis to** To end. [L]

fin·ish (fin′ish) *v.t.* **1** To complete or bring to an end. **2** To come to or reach the end of: to *finish* a trip. **3** To use up entirely. **4** To kill or destroy. **5** To defeat; make powerless. **6** To bring the surface of (wood, leather, etc.) to a desired condition. —*v.i.* **7** To reach or come to an end; stop. —*n.* **1** The conclusion or last stage of anything. **2** Something that finishes or completes. **3** Completeness; perfection. **4** Refinement and poise in manners, speech, etc. **5** The surface quality or texture, as on wood, cloth, etc. **6** A material used to finish a surface, as wax, varnish, etc. **7** Downfall or defeat; also, the cause. [< L *finire* < *finis* end] —**fin′ish·er** *n.* —**Syn.** *v.* **1, 2** terminate, conclude, close. —*n.* **1** end, close, termination, cessation, completion.

fin·ished (fin′isht) *adj.* **1** Carried to a high degree of perfection; polished. **2** Ended; concluded. **3** Very accomplished. **4** Ruined; undone.

finishing school A school in which girls are taught various social graces.

fi·nite (fī′nīt) *adj.* **1** Having boundaries or limits; not infinite. **2** Subject to natural limitations: man's *finite* powers. **3** *Gram.* Limited by number, person, tense, and mood: said of verb forms that can serve as predicates in sentences. —

n. Finite things collectively, or that which is finite: usu. with *the.* [< L *finitus* limited, pp. of *finire* to end] —**fi′nite·ly** *adv.* —**fi′nite·ness** *n.*

fin·i·tude (fin′ə·t^yōōd, fī′nə-) *n.* The quality or condition of being finite.

fink (fingk) *n. Slang* **1** An unpleasant or obnoxious person. **2** A strikebreaker.

Fin·land (fin′lənd) *n.* A republic of N Europe, 117,913 sq. mi., cap. Helsinki.

Finn (fin) *n.* A native or citizen of Finland.

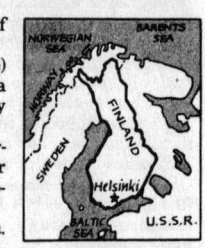

fin·nan had·die (fin′ən had′ē) Smoked haddock. [< *Findhorn*, a Scottish town where originally prepared]

Finn·ish (fin′ish) *adj.* Of or pertaining to Finland, its people, or their language. —*n.* The Finno-Ugric language of Finland.

Fin·no-U·gric (fin′ō·yōō′grik) *n.* A subfamily of the Uralic languages, including Finnish, Estonian, Lapp, Magyar, etc. Also **Fin′no-U′gri·an.**

fin·ny (fin′ē) *adj.* **1** Having fins. **2** Of or like a fish. **3** Abounding in fish.

fiord (fyôrd, fyōrd) *n.* A long, narrow inlet of the sea, with high rocky banks. [Norw.]

fir (fûr) *n.* **1** An evergreen tree of the pine family, conebearing and resinous. **2** Its wood. [< OE *fyrh*]

fire (fīr) *n.* **1** The state or form of combustion that is manifested in light, flame, and heat. **2** Something burning: the *fire* in the furnace. **3** A destructive burning: a brush *fire.* **4** Something resembling fire in its brilliance, heat, etc. **5** Intense feeling or enthusiasm; ardor. **6** An intense suffering, severe trial, or ordeal. **7** Torture or death by fire. **8** Vividness, as of imagination. **9** Fever. **10** A discharge of firearms. **11** Any rapid burst or volley: a *fire* of questions. —**between two fires** Exposed to attack, criticism, etc., from both sides. —**catch (on) fire** To ignite. —**hang fire 1** To fail or delay to discharge. **2** To be delayed, as a decision. —**miss fire 1** To fail to discharge. **2** To be ineffective; fail. —**on fire 1** Burning; ablaze. **2** Ardent; zealous. —**open fire 1** To begin to shoot. **2** To begin; commence. —**set on fire** or **set fire to 1** To ignite. **2** To excite, as passions. —**take fire 1** To begin to burn. **2** To begin to respond or be excited. —**under fire 1** Exposed to gunshot or artillery fire. **2** Exposed to critical or other attack. —*v.* **fired, fir·ing** *v.t.* **1** To set on fire. **2** To tend the fire of: to *fire* a furnace. **3** To bake or expose to heat. **4** To cause to glow or shine. **5** To inflame the emotions or passions of; excite. **6** To discharge, as a gun or bullet. **7** To hurl, as with force: to *fire* questions. **8** To discharge from employment. —*v.i.* **9** To become ignited. **10** To discharge firearms. **11** To discharge a missile. **12** To become inflamed or excited. **13** To tend a fire. —**fire away** To begin, esp. in asking questions. [< OE *fyr*] —**fir′er** *n.*

fire alarm 1 An alarm calling attention to a fire or its whereabouts. **2** An apparatus for giving an alarm of fire.

fire·arm (fīr′ärm′) *n.* Any weapon, esp. a rifle or pistol, from which a missile, as a bullet, is hurled by an explosive.

fire·ball (fīr′bôl′) *n.* **1** The cloud of intensely hot and glowing material at the center of a nuclear explosion. **2** A very bright meteor. **3** Ball-shaped lightning. **4** *Slang* An aggressive, energetic person.

fire boat A boat equipped to fight fires.

fire·bomb (fīr′bom′) *n.* A bomb designed to cause a fire, usu. on impact. —*v.t.* To attack with a firebomb. —**fire′bomb′er** *n.*

fire·box (fīr′boks′) *n.* The combustion chamber of a furnace, locomotive, etc.

fire·brand (fīr′brand′) *n.* **1** A burning or glowing piece of wood. **2** A person who causes trouble or dissension.

fire·break (fīr′brāk′) *n.* A strip of plowed or cleared land made to prevent the spread of fire in woods or on a prairie.

fire·brick (fīr′brik′) *n.* A heat-resistant brick, used for lining furnaces.

fire·bug (fīr′bug′) *n. Informal* A person who deliberately sets property on fire; a pyromaniac.

Finial

fire·clay (fīr′klā′) *n.* A heat-resistant clay.

fire·crack·er (fīr′krak′ər) *n.* A small paper cylinder charged with gunpowder, designed to explode with a loud noise.

fire·damp (fīr′damp′) *n.* 1 A flammable gas, esp. methane, found in coal mines. 2 An explosive mixture of this gas and air.

fire drill The drilling of persons to accustom them to proper action in case of fire.

fire·eat·er (fīr′ē′tər) *n.* 1 A performer who pretends to eat fire. 2 A hot-headed person eager to fight or quarrel.

fire engine A truck that carries personnel and equipment for fighting fires.

fire escape A means for escaping from a burning building, as a metal stairway or ladder, affixed to an outer wall.

fire extinguisher A portable fire-fighting apparatus containing certain chemicals that are ejected by pressure through a short hose.

fire·fly (fīr′flī′) *n. pl.* **·flies** Any of various luminescent, night-flying beetles.

fire·house (fīr′hous′) *n.* A building for the housing of fire-fighting equipment and personnel.

fire hydrant A hydrant for furnishing water in case of fire.

fire·light (fīr′līt′) *n.* The light from a fire.

fire·man (fīr′mən) *n. pl.* **·men** (-mən) 1 One trained or employed to extinguish fires. 2 One who tends a fire or furnace.

fire·place (fīr′plās′) *n.* A recess or structure built to contain a fire; esp., the part of a chimney that opens into a room.

fire·plug (fīr′plug′) *n.* FIRE HYDRANT.

fire·pow·er (fīr′pou′ər) *n. Mil.* 1 Capacity for delivering fire, as from the guns of a ship. 2 The total amount of fire delivered by a given weapon or unit.

fire·proof (fīr′prōōf′) *adj.* Resistant to fire; not easily burned. —*v.t.* To make resistant to fire.

fire sale A sale of goods damaged by fire.

fire·side (fīr′sīd′) *n.* 1 The hearth or space about the fireplace. 2 Home. 3 Family life.

fire station FIREHOUSE.

fire·storm (fīr′stôrm′) *n.* A violent, widespread fire, as one caused by a nuclear explosion.

fire·trap (fīr′trap′) *n.* A building in which the danger from fire is great.

fire·wall (fīr′wôl′) *n.* A fireproof wall designed to block the progress of a fire.

fire·wa·ter (fīr′wô′tər, -wot′ər) *n.* Strong liquor: a term first used by North American Indians.

fire·wood (fīr′wōōd′) *n.* Wood used as fuel.

fire·works (fīr′wûrks′) *n.pl.* 1 Any of various explosive or combustible devices that when ignited produce a brilliant or colored light display and usu. a loud noise. 2 An exhibition of or as of fireworks.

firing line 1 The line of active engagement in battle. 2 The troops within effective rifle range of the enemy. 3 The foremost position in any activity.

firing squad A group of military riflemen assigned to execute a death sentence.

fir·kin (fûr′kən) *n.* A wooden vessel for lard, etc. [< MDu. *vierdelkijn* little fourth]

firm[1] (fûrm) *adj.* 1 Not yielding readily to touch or pressure; solidly composed; compact. 2 Difficult to move; stable. 3 Enduring; steadfast; constant: a *firm* loyalty. 4 Having or showing strength, determination, etc.: a *firm* voice. 5 Not fluctuating widely, as prices. —*v.t. & v.i.* To make or become firm, solid, or compact. —*adv.* Solidly; resolutely; fixedly. [< L *firmus*] —**firm′ly** *adv.* —**firm′ness** *n.* — **Syn.** *adj.* 3 resolute, steady, immovable, true, stout.

firm[2] (fûrm) *n.* 1 A commercial, industrial, or financial partnership. 2 Any business organization. [< L *firmare* to confirm < *firmus* firm]

fir·ma·ment (fûr′mə·mənt) *n.* The expanse of the heavens; sky. [< L *firmamentum* a support] —**fir′ma·men′tal** *adj.*

first (fûrst) *adj.* 1 Preceding all others in the order of numbering. 2 Prior to all others in time; earliest. 3 Nearest or foremost in place from a given point. 4 Highest or foremost in character, rank, etc.; chief. 5 *Music* Of or designating the principal or highest part, voice, or instrument. — **in the first place** To start with. —*n.* 1 One who or that which is first in position, rank, time, etc. 2 The element of an ordered set that corresponds to the number one. 3 The beginning. 4 A winning position in a contest. 5 *Music* The principal or highest part, voice, or instrument. 6 In English universities, the highest rank in examinations for honors; also, one taking the highest rank. 7 *pl.* The best grade of certain commercial products. —**at first** (or **from the first**) At the beginning or origin. —*adv.* 1 Before all others in order, time, place, rank, etc. 2 Preferably; sooner. 3 For the first time. [< OE *fyrst*]

first aid Treatment given in any emergency while awaiting expert medical attention. —**first′-aid′** *adj.*

first base In baseball, the base first reached by the runner, at the right-hand angle of the infield.

first-born (fûrst′bôrn′) *adj.* First brought forth; eldest. —*n.* The child first born.

first-class (fûrst′klas′, -kläs′) *adj.* 1 Belonging to the highest rank or the best quality. 2 Of or designating a class of mail consisting of letters, post cards, or other matter sealed against inspection. 3 Of or using the most expensive accommodations. —*adv.* By first-class accommodations or mail.

first finger The finger next to the thumb; forefinger.

first·hand (fûrst′hand′) *adj. & adv.* Direct from the original source.

first lady The wife of the President of the U.S.

first lieutenant See GRADE.

first·ling (fûrst′ling) *n.* The first of anything.

first·ly (fûrst′lē) *adv.* In the first place; first.

first mortgage A mortgage having priority over all other liens.

first person 1 That form of a pronoun or verb that refers to the speaker or writer, as *I* (or *we*) *understand.* 2 A style of narrative writing in which the writer is or acts as the narrator of the story.

first-rate (fûrst′rāt′) *adj.* Of the finest class, quality, or character. —*adv.* Excellently.

first sergeant See GRADE.

first water 1 The finest quality and purest luster: said of gems. 2 The utmost excellence of anything.

firth (fûrth) *n.* An arm of the sea; estuary.

fis·cal (fis′kəl) *adj.* 1 Of or pertaining to the treasury or finances of a government. 2 Financial. [< L *fiscus* a purse]

fiscal year Any twelve-month period at the end of which financial accounts are balanced.

fish (fish) *n. pl.* **fish** or (with reference to different species) **fish·es** 1 A vertebrate, cold-blooded, aquatic animal with gills, usu. scales, and fins. 2 Loosely, any animal habitually living in the water. 3 The flesh of a fish used as food. —*adj.* Of, pertaining to, like, or made from, fish. —*v.t.* 1 To catch or try to catch fish in (a body of water). 2 To catch or try to catch (fish, eels, etc.). 3 To search or grope for and bring out: usu. with *up* or *out.* —*v.i.* 4 To catch or try to catch fish. 5 To try to get something in an artful or indirect manner: usu. with *for:* to *fish* for compliments. [< OE *fisc*] —**fish′a·ble** *adj.*

fish and chips *Brit.* Fish fillets fried in deep fat, and French fried potatoes.

fish bowl (fish′bōl′) *n.* A bowl, usu. glass, serving as a small aquarium for fish.

fish·er (fish′ər) *n.* 1 FISHERMAN. 2 A dark brown, forest-dwelling, weasel-like carnivore of N North America.

fish·er·man (fish′ər·mən) *n. pl.* **·men** (-mən) 1 One who fishes for sport or as an occupation. 2 A fishing boat.

fish·er·y (fish′ər·ē) *n. pl.* **·er·ies** 1 The fishing industry. 2 A place for fishing. 3 FISH HATCHERY.

Fishes *n.pl.* PISCES.

Fisher

---

add, āce, câre, pälm; end, ēven; it, īce; odd, ōpen, ôrder; tōōk, pōōl; up, bûrn; ə = a in above, u in focus; yōō = u in fuse; oil; pout; check; go; ring; thin; this; zh, vision. < derived from; ? origin uncertain or unknown.

fish hatchery A place designed for the propagation, hatching, and nurture of fish.

fish hawk OSPREY.

fish hook A hook, usu. barbed, for catching fish.

fishing tackle The equipment used for fishing, as rod, reel, line, hooks, etc.

fish·meal (fish′mēl′) n. Ground dried fish, used as fertilizer or animal food.

fish·mon·ger (fish′mung′gər, -mong′-) n. A dealer in fish.

fish story Informal An extravagant or incredible narrative.

fish·wife (fish′wīf′) n. pl. ·wives (-wīvz′) 1 A woman who sells fish. 2 A shrill-mouthed, abusive woman.

fish·y (fish′ē) adj. fish·i·er, fish·i·est 1 Of or like fish. 2 Abounding in fish. 3 Informal Questionable; improbable. 4 Vacant of expression; dull. —**fish′i·ly** adv. —**fish′i·ness** n.

fis·sile (fis′əl) adj. 1 Capable of being split or undergoing fission. 2 Tending to split. [< L fissilis < findere to split] —**fis·sil·i·ty** (fi-sil′ə-tē) n.

fis·sion (fish′ən) n. 1 The act of splitting or breaking apart. 2 Biol. The splitting of a unicellular organism into two daughter cells as a mode of asexual reproduction. 3 Physics The splitting of an atomic nucleus into particles and smaller nuclei with the release of energy. [< L fissus, pp. of findere to split] —**fis′sion·a·ble** adj.

fis·sure (fish′ər) n. 1 A narrow opening, cleft, or crevice. 2 A splitting apart or break; cleavage. —v.t. & v.i. fis·sured, fis·sur·ing To crack; split; cleave. [< L fissus, pp. of findere to split]

fist (fist) n. 1 The hand closed tightly, as for striking. 2 Informal a The hand. b Handwriting. 3 Printing An index mark (☞). —v.t. To strike with the fist. [< OE fȳst]

fist·ful (fist′fŏŏl′) n. pl. ·fuls A handful.

fist·ic (fis′tik) adj. Of or pertaining to boxing; pugilistic.

fist·i·cuffs (fis′ti·kufs) n.pl. A fight with the fists. [< FIST + cuff a blow]

fis·tu·la (fis′chŏŏ·lə) n. pl. ·las or ·lae (-lē) Pathol. An abnormal channel leading from a hollow organ or cavity to the outside or another part of the body. [< L, a pipe] —**fis′tu·lar, fis′tu·lous** adj.

fit¹ (fit) adj. fit·ter, fit·test 1 Adapted or suited to an end, purpose, situation, etc. 2 Proper; suitable; appropriate. 3 Informal Ready: fit to be tied. 4 In good physical condition. —v. fit·ted or fit, fit·ting v.t. 1 To be suitable for. 2 To be of the right size and shape for. 3 To make or alter to the proper size: to fit a suit. 4 To provide with what is suitable or necessary. 5 To put in place carefully or exactly. —v.i. 6 To be suitable or proper. 7 To be of the proper size, shape, etc. —n. 1 The condition or manner of fitting. 2 The act of fitting. 3 Something that fits. [ME] —**fit′ness, fit′ter** n. —Syn. adj. 1 apt, pertinent, applicable, relevant, germane, apropos. 2 meet, becoming.

fit² (fit) n. 1 A sudden onset of a disorder or symptom: a coughing fit. 2 Convulsions. 3 A sudden overmastering emotion or feeling: a fit of rage. 4 An impulsive or irregular action: a fit of industry. —**by fits** (or **by fits and starts**) Spasmodically; irregularly. [< OE fitt struggle]

fitch·ew (fich′ŏŏ) n. 1 POLECAT (def. 1). 2 The fur of this animal. Also **fitch** (fich). [< MDu. fisse, vitsche]

fit·ful (fit′fəl) adj. Occurring in or characterized by irregular or uneasy movements, phases, etc.; spasmodic. —**fit′ful·ly** adv. —**fit′ful·ness** n.

fit·ly (fit′lē) adv. In a fit manner or time; properly.

fit·ting (fit′ing) adj. Fit or suitable for the intended purpose. —n. 1 The act of adjusting, measuring, etc., for a proper fit. 2 A mechanical fixture or part. 3 pl. Furnishings or accessories for a house, boat, etc. —**fit′ting·ly** adv. —**fit′ting·ness** n.

five (fīv) n. 1 The sum of four plus one; 5; V. 2 A set or group of five members. [< OE fīf] —five adj., pron.

five-and-ten-cent store (fīv′ən·ten′sent′) A store selling miscellaneous, inexpensive articles. Also **five-and-dime** (fīv′ən·dīm′).

five·fold (fīv′fōld′) adj. 1 Made up of five. 2 Five times as much or as great. —adv. In a fivefold manner or degree.

Five Nations Five confederated tribes of Iroquois Indians in the NE U.S. and Canada, namely, Mohawks, Oneidas, Onondagas, Cayugas, and Senecas.

fiv·er (fī′vər) n. Informal A five-dollar bill or a five-pound note.

fix (fiks) v.t. 1 To make firm or secure; attach securely. 2 To set or direct (attention, gaze, etc.) steadily. 3 To look at steadily or piercingly: He fixed her with his eyes. 4 To attract and hold, as attention or regard. 5 To decide definitely; settle. 6 To decide or agree on; determine: We fixed a date. 7 To place firmly in the mind. 8 To lay, as blame or responsibility, on. 9 To repair, mend, tend to, heal, etc. 10 To arrange or put in order; adjust, as hair. 11 To make ready and cook (food or a meal). 12 Informal To arrange or influence the outcome, decision, etc., of (a race, game, jury, etc.) by bribery or collusion. 13 Informal To chastise or get even with. 14 To prepare (specimens) for microscopic study. 15 Chem. To cause to form a stable compound. 16 Phot. To bathe (exposed film) in chemicals which prevent further reaction to light. 17 To regulate or stabilize (wages, prices, etc.). —v.i. 18 To become firm or fixed. 19 Informal To intend or prepare: I'm fixing to go. —**fix on** (or **upon**) To decide upon; choose. —**fix up** Informal 1 To repair. 2 To arrange or put in order. 3 To supply the needs of. —n. 1 Informal A position of embarrassment; dilemma. 2 An observed or calculated position of a ship, aircraft, etc. 3 Slang A contest, decision, etc., that has been influenced by bribery or corruption. 4 Slang A single shot of an addictive drug. [< L fixus, pp. of figere fasten] —**fix′a·ble** adj. —**fix′er** n.

fix·a·tion (fik·sā′shən) n. 1 The act of fixing, or the state of being fixed. 2 An obsession. 3 Psychoanal. An early-occurring and excessive concentration of the libido on a particular object or person.

fix·a·tive (fik′sə·tiv) adj. Serving to render permanent. —n. A fixative substance, as a mordant or varnish.

fixed (fikst) adj. 1 Firmly attached; stable. 2 Established; unchanging. 3 Resolute; firm. 4 Keeping nearly the same relative position. 5 Equipped: all fixed for camp. 6 Informal Bribed: a fixed jury. 7 Informal Provided with money, possessions, etc.: He's well fixed. —**fix·ed·ly** (fik′sid·lē) adv. —**fix′ed·ness** n.

fix·ings (fik′singz) n. pl. Informal Accessories; trimmings: a dinner and all the fixings.

fix·i·ty (fik′sə·tē) n. pl. ·ties 1 The state or quality of being fixed; stability. 2 Anything fixed.

fix·ture (fiks′chər) n. 1 Anything fixed firmly in its place. 2 Any permanently attached device or apparatus in a house, store, etc.: a light fixture. 3 One so long associated with something as to be considered permanently fixed.

fizz (fiz) v.i. To make a hissing noise. —n. 1 A hissing noise. 2 An effervescing beverage. [Imit.] —**fizz′y** adj.

fiz·zle (fiz′əl) v.i. fiz·zled, fiz·zling 1 To make a hissing noise. 2 Informal To fail, esp. after a good start. —**fizzle out** Informal To become a failure. —n. 1 A spluttering; fizzing. 2 Informal A failure. [?]

fjord (fyôrd) n. FIORD.

FL Florida (P.O. abbr.).

fl. floor; florin(s); fluid.

Fla. Florida.

flab (flab) n. Flabby body tissue. [Back formation < FLABBY]

flab·ber·gast (flab′ər·gast) v.t. Informal To astound; confound; amaze.

flab·by (flab′ē) adj. ·bi·er, ·bi·est 1 Lacking muscle tone; flaccid. 2 Lacking vigor; feeble. [< FLAP] —**flab′bi·ness** n.

flac·cid (flak′sid) adj. 1 Lacking firmness or elasticity; flabby. [< L flaccidus < flaccus limp] —**flac′cid·ly** adv. —**flac·cid′i·ty, flac′cid·ness** n.

flack (flak) n. Slang PRESS AGENT. [?] —**flack′er·y** n.

fla·con (fla·kôn′) n. A stoppered bottle or flask. [F < Med. L flasco]

flag¹ (flag) n. 1 A piece of cloth commonly bearing a device or colors and used as a standard, symbol, or signal. 2 The bushy part of the tail of a dog, as that of a setter. 3 The tail of a deer. 4 pl. Ornithol. The long feathers on the leg of a hawk or other bird of prey. 5 Music Any of the flag-shaped lines extending from the stem of certain notes to indicate their value. —v.t. flagged, flag·ging 1 To mark out or adorn with flags. 2 To signal with a flag. —**flag down** To cause to stop, as a train, by signaling. [?] —**flag′ger** n.

flag² (flag) n. 1 Any of various plants having sword-shaped leaves and growing in moist places; iris. **2** The leaf of a flag. —*v.t.* **flagged, flag·ging** To calk the seams of (a cask) with flags or rushes. [ME *flagge*]

flag[3] (flag) *v.i.* **flagged, flag·ging 1** To become tired or weak. **2** To become limp. [?]

flag[4] (flag) *n.* Split stone for paving; a flagstone. —*v.t.* **flagged, flag·ging** To pave with flagstones. [< ON *flaga* slab of stone] —**flag′ger** *n.*

Flag Day June 14, a holiday commemorating the adoption of the official U.S. flag on June 14, 1777.

flag·el·lant (flaj′ə·lənt, flə·jel′ənt) *n.* A person given to whipping himself or being whipped, to secure pardon from sin or to excite himself sexually. Also **flag′el·la′tor**. [< L *flagellum* a whip]

flag·el·late (flaj′ə·lāt) *v.t.* **·lat·ed, ·lat·ing** To whip; scourge. —*n. Biol.* A protozoan having one or more whiplike processes. —*adj. Biol.* Having or resembling a flagellum: also **flag′el·lat′ed.** —**flag′el·la′tion** *n.*

fla·gel·lum (flə·jel′əm) *n. pl.* **·la** (-ə) **1** *Biol.* A lashlike appendage, as the mobile process of certain protozoa. **2** *Bot.* RUNNER (def. 5). **3** A whip. [L, whip]

flag·eo·let (flaj′ə·let′) *n.* A flute blown at the end instead of at the side. [F, dim. of OF *flageol*]

Flageolet

flag·ging[1] (flag′ing) *adj.* Growing weak; becoming languid or exhausted: *flagging* spirits.

flag·ging[2] (flag′ing) *n.* **1** A pavement of flagstones; also, flagstones collectively. **2** The act of paving with flagstones.

fla·gi·tious (flə·jish′əs) *adj.* Flagrantly wicked; atrocious; heinous. [< L *flagitium* disgraceful act] —**fla·gi′tious·ly** *adv.* —**fla·gi′tious·ness** *n.*

flag officer Any naval officer above the rank of captain who is entitled to fly the flag of his command.

flag·on (flag′ən) *n.* A vessel with a handle, spout, and lid, used to serve liquors. [< Med. L *flasco* < Gmc.]

flag·pole (flag′pōl′) *n.* A pole on which a flag is displayed. Also **flag′staff**′ (-staf′, -stäf′).

fla·grant (flā′grənt) *adj.* Openly scandalous; notorious. [< L *flagrare* to blaze, burn] —**fla′grance, fla′gran·cy** *n.* —**fla′grant·ly** *adv.* —**Syn.** glaring, outrageous, shocking.

flag·ship (flag′ship′) *n.* The ship in a naval formation that carries a flag officer and displays his flag.

flag·stone (flag′stōn′) *n.* A broad, flat stone suitable for pavements.

flail (flāl) *n.* An implement consisting of a wooden bar (the swingle) hinged or tied to a handle, for separating grain by beating. —*v.t.* & *v.i.* To beat with or as with a flail. [< L *flagellum* a whip]

flair (flâr) *n.* **1** Talent; aptitude. **2** Discernment; taste. **3** *Informal* A dashing style or quality. [< L *fragrare* to give off a smell]

flak (flak) *n.* **1** Anti-aircraft fire. **2** *Informal* Criticism: political *flak.* [G < *Fl(ieger)* aircraft + *A(bwehr)* defense + *K(anonen)* guns]

flake[1] (flāk) *n.* **1** A thin piece of anything; scale; fleck. **2** A small flat mass: a *flake* of snow. —*v.t.* & *v.i.* **flaked, flak·ing 1** To peel off in flakes. **2** To form into flakes. **3** To spot or become spotted with flakes. [< Scand.]

flake[2] (flāk) *v.i.* **flaked, flak·ing** *Slang v.i.* **1** To retire or go to sleep, as from exhaustion: usu. with *out.* —*v.t.* **2** To fatigue; exhaust: usu. with *out.*

flak·y (flā′kē) *adj.* **flak·i·er, flak·i·est 1** Resembling or consisting of flakes. **2** Easily separable into flakes. —**flak′i·ly** *adv.* —**flak′i·ness** *n.*

flam·beau (flam′bō) *n. pl.* **·beaux** (-bōz) A burning torch. [F< OF *flambe* flame]

flam·boy·ant (flam·boi′ənt) *adj.* **1** Characterized by extravagance; showy; bombastic. **2** Ornate. **3** Having a wavy edge, as of flame. [F< OF *flambe* flame] —**flam·boy′ance, flam·boy′an·cy** *n.* —**flam·boy′ant·ly** *adv.*

flamboyant architecture A highly florid style of French Gothic architecture.

flame (flām) *n.* **1** The burning, luminous gas of a fire; blaze. **2** A state of luminous burning. **3** Excitement or passion. **4** *Slang* A sweetheart. —*v.* **flamed, flam·ing** *v.i.* **1**

To give out flame; blaze; burn. **2** To light up or burn as if on fire; flash. **3** To become enraged or excited. —**flame up** To erupt in or as in flames. [< L *flamma*] —**flam′er** *n.* —**flam′ing·ly** *adv.*

fla·men·co (flə·meng′kō, -men′-, flä-) *n.* A style of singing and dancing practiced by the gypsies of Andalusia. [Sp., Flemish, because the gypsies were thought to be from Flanders]

flame·out (flām′out′) *n.* The sudden loss of the flame in a jet engine.

flame-throw·er (flām′thrō′ər) *n. Mil.* A weapon that throws a stream of burning fuel.

fla·min·go (flə·ming′gō) *n. pl.* **·gos** or **·goes** A long-necked bird of a pink or red color, having very long legs. [< Pg. *flamingo* or Sp. *flamenco*]

flam·ma·ble (flam′ə·bəl) *adj.* Easily set on fire and likely to burn rapidly; highly combustible. —**flam′ma·bil′i·ty** *n.*

flange (flanj) *n.* A projecting rim or edge, as on a car wheel, etc., used for guidance, strength, or attachment to another object. —*v.* **flanged, flang·ing** *v.t.* To supply with a flange. [?< OF *flangir* to bend]

Flamingo

flank (flangk) *n.* **1** The hind part of an animal's side, between the ribs and the hip. • See HORSE. **2** A cut of meat from this part. **3** The side of anything. **4** The side, right or left, of a military force or marching column. —*v.t.* **1** To be on one or both sides of. **2** *Mil.* **a** To get around and in back of (an enemy position or unit). **b** To attack the flank of. —*adj.* Of, on, or from the flank or side. [< OF *flanc*] —**flank′er** *n.*

flan·nel (flan′əl) *n.* **1** A loosely-woven, soft fabric of wool, or of cotton and wool. **2** *pl.* Clothing made of flannel, esp. heavy underwear. [?< Welsh *gwlân* wool] —**flan′nel·ly** *adj.*

flan·nel·et (flan′əl·et′) *n.* A cotton fabric similar to flannel. Also **flan′nel·ette′.**

flap (flap) *n.* **1** A broad, thin, and loosely hanging part or attachment. **2** The motion of such a part. **3** A movable control surface along the rear edge of a wing of an airplane. **4** *Slang* An agitated or tempestuous reaction. —*v.* **flapped, flap·ping** *v.t.* **1** To move by beating: to *flap* the wings. **2** To move with a flapping sound. **3** To strike with something flat and flexible. —*v.i.* **4** To move by beating the wings. **5** To move as if blown by the wind. **6** *Slang* To lose one's composure. [Imit.]

flap·jack (flap′jak′) *n.* A griddle cake or pancake.

flap·per (flap′ər) *n.* **1** One who or that which flaps. **2** *Informal* A young girl, esp. in the 1920's, given to exaggerated styles and to sophisticated conduct.

flare (flâr) *v.* **flared, flar·ing** *v.i.* **1** To blaze or burn with a brilliant, wavering light. **2** To break out in sudden emotion: often with *up* or *out.* **3** To open or spread outward. —*v.t.* **4** To cause to flare. —*n.* **1** A large, bright, but unsteady light. **2** A signaling device that makes a clear, bright flame. **3** A widening or spreading outward, as of the sides of a funnel; also, the part that widens or spreads out. [?] —**flar′ing·ly** *adv.* —**Syn.** *v.* **1**, *n.* **1** flash, flicker, glare, shine.

flare-up (flâr′up′) *n.* **1** A sudden outburst of flame or light. **2** A sudden outbreak of anger.

flash (flash) *v.i.* **1** To break forth with light or fire suddenly and briefly. **2** To gleam; glisten. **3** To move very quickly. **4** To be known or perceived in an instant. —*v.t.* **5** To send forth (fire, light, etc.) in brief flashes. **6** To send or communicate with great speed. **7** *Informal* To display briefly or ostentatiously: to *flash* a badge. —*n.* **1** A sudden gleam of light. **2** A sudden outburst, as of anger. **3** A moment; instant. **4** Display; esp., a vulgar, showy display. **5** A brief news dispatch. —*adj.* **1** Obtained by flashlight, as a photograph. **2** Flashy; smart; sporty. [ME *flaschen*] —**flash′er** *n.,* **flash′ing·ly** *adv.*

---

add, āce, câre, pälm; end, ēven; it, īce; odd, ōpen, ôrder; tŏŏk, pōōl; up, bûrn; ə = *a* in *above, u* in *focus;* yōō = *u* in *fuse;* oil; pout; check; go; ring; thin; this; zh, *vision.* < derived from; ? origin uncertain or unknown.

flash·back (flash′bak′) *n.* **1** In fiction, motion pictures, etc., a break in continuity made by the presentation of a scene or event occurring earlier. **2** Such a scene or event.

flash bulb An electric bulb that makes a short, bright flash, used in photography.

flash burn A severe burn produced by exposure to intense heat, esp. that of a nuclear explosion.

flash·cube (flash′kyoob′) *n.* A small, rotatable cube containing four flash bulbs for use with a camera.

flash flood A sudden, brief flood.

flash gun A device that holds a flashbulb and supplies electricity to trigger it.

flash·ing (flash′ing) *n.* **1** The act of one who or that which flashes. **2** A metal joint or flange used to keep a roof watertight. —*adj.* Emitting flashes. —**flash′ing·ly** *adv.*

flash lamp A lamp for taking flash photographs.

flash·light (flash′līt′) *n.* **1** A small, portable electric light powered by batteries. **2** A light, as in a lighthouse, shown only at regular intervals. **3** A brief and brilliant light for taking photographs.

flash·y (flash′ē) *adj.* **flash·i·er, flash·i·est 1** Pretentious and cheap; showy; tawdry. **2** Flashing or bright for a moment. —**flash′i·ly** *adv.* —**flash′i·ness** *n.*

flask (flask, fläsk) *n.* **1** Any of variously shaped receptacles, usu. of glass, used in laboratory work. **2** A small container, often of metal, for carrying liquids or liquor on the person. [< Med. L *flasco*]

flat¹ (flat) *adj.* **flat·ter, flat·test 1** Having a plane, usu. horizontal surface. **2** Broad, level, and thin: a *flat* board. **3** Having full contact with another surface. **4** Lying prone upon the ground; prostrate. **5** Positive; absolute: a *flat* refusal. **6** Having little flavor or sparkle: a *flat* drink. **7** Without air: a *flat* tire. **8** Having little activity; slow: a *flat* market. **9** Not varying; uniform: a *flat* rate. **10** *Music* a Below the true or right pitch. **b** Lowered by a semitone. **c** Having flats in the signature. **11** Without gloss, as a painted surface. **12** In painting: **a** Uniform in tint. **b** Lacking contrast and perspective: *flat* figures. —*adv.* **1** In a flat state or position. **2** In a flat manner. **3** *Music* Below the true pitch. **4** Exactly; precisely: It weighed ten pounds *flat.* —**flat out** *Informal* **1** With maximum effort; all-out. **2** Openly: to say *flat out* that he's a liar. —*n.* **1** A flat surface. **2** A strip of level land, esp. low meadowland over which the tide flows. **3** *Usu. pl.* Shoal. **4** Anything that is flat. **5** *Music* A tone a half step lower than a tone from which it is named, identified by the character ♭. **b** The character ♭. **6** A wooden frame covered with canvas, used as stage scenery. **7** A deflated pneumatic tire. **8** A shallow, earth-filled tray for seed germination. —*v.t. & v.i.* **flat·ted, flat·ting** To make or become flat. [< ON *flatr*] —**flat′tish** *adj.* —**flat′ly** *adv.* —**flat′ness** *n.*

flat² (flat) *n.* A set of rooms on one floor; apartment. [< OE *flet* floor]

flat·boat (flat′bōt′) *n.* A large boat with a flat bottom, for freighting merchandise.

flat-bot·tomed (flat′bot′əmd) *adj.* Having the bottom flat: usu. said of boats.

flat·car (flat′kär′) *n.* A railroad freight car, usu. without sides or covering.

flat·fish (flat′fish′) *n. pl.* **·fish** or **·fish·es** Any of various marine fishes having a compressed body and both eyes on one side, as the flounder, halibut, sole, etc.

flat·foot (flat′foot′) *n.* **1** An abnormal foot condition in which the entire sole touches the ground. **2** *Slang* A policeman.

flat-foot·ed (flat′foot′id) *adj.* **1** Having flat feet. **2** Uncompromising; resolute; positive. —**flat′·foot′ed·ly** *adv.*

flat·i·ron (flat′ī′ərn) *n.* An iron without a built-in heat source, used for pressing cloth.

flat silver Silver spoons, knives, forks, etc.

flat·ten (flat′n) *v.t. & v.i.* **1** To make or become flat or flatter. **2** To make or become prostrate. —**flat′ten·er** *n.*

flat·ter (flat′ər) *v.t.* **1** To praise unduly or insincerely. **2** To try to win over by flattery. **3** To please or gratify. **4** To represent too favorably: The picture *flatters* her. **5** To display to advantage. —*v.i.* **6** To use flattery. —**flatter oneself** To believe: I *flatter* myself that my gifts are acceptable. [< OF *flater* fawn, caress] —**flat′ter·er** *n.* —**flat′ter·ing·ly** *adv.*

flat·ter·y (flat′ər·ē) *n. pl.* **·ter·ies 1** The act of flattering. **2** Undue or insincere praise. —**Syn. 2** adulation, acclamation, compliments, plaudits.

flat·top (flat′top′) *n. Slang* **1** An aircraft carrier. **2** A crew cut.

flat·u·lence (flach′ə·ləns, -yoo-) *n.* **1** Gas in the stomach or intestines. **2** Pompousness; vanity. Also **flat′u·len·cy.** [< L *flatus* a blowing < *flare* to blow] —**flat′u·lent, flat′u·ous** *adj.* —**flat′u·lent·ly** *adv.*

flat·ware (flat′wâr′) *n.* **1** Dishes that are more or less flat. **2** Knives, forks, and spoons.

flat·worm (flat′wûrm′) *n.* Any of a large group of unsegmented, flat-bodied worms, often parasitic, as the tapeworm.

flaunt (flônt) *v.i.* **1** To make an ostentatious display. **2** To wave or flutter freely. —*v.t.* **3** To display in an ostentatious or impudent manner. —*n.* **1** The act of flaunting. **2** A boast; vaunt. [?< Scand.] —**flaunt′y** *adj.* (**·ier, ·i·est**) —**flaunt′ing·ly** *adv.* —**flaunt′er** *n.* • *Flaunt* and *flout* should not be confused. To *flaunt* is to wave or make an ostentatious display. To *flout* is to regard with contempt: to *flout* convention.

flau·tist (flô′tist) *n.* FLUTIST.

fla·vin (flā′vən) *n.* **1** Any of a group of natural yellow pigments, as riboflavin, etc. **2** A yellow dye derived from coal tar. Also **fla·vine** (flā′vēn). [< L *flavus* yellow + -IN]

fla·vor (flā′vər) *n.* **1** The quality of a thing that affects the sense of taste. **2** Odor; scent. **3** Distinctive quality. **4** Flavoring. —*v.t.* To give flavor or any distinguishing quality to. *Brit. sp.,* **fla·vour.** [< OF *flaor*] —**fla′vor·less, fla′vor·ous, fla′vor·y** *adj.*

fla·vor·ing (flā′vər·ing) *n.* A substance, as an essence or extract, for giving flavor.

flaw (flô) *n.* **1** An inherent defect, as in construction. **2** A crack; fissure. **3** A fault or error. —*v.t. & v.i.* To make or become defective or faulty. [< ON *flaga* slab of stone] —**flaw′less** *adj.* —**flaw′less·ly** *adv.* —**flaw′less·ness** *n.*

flax (flaks) *n.* **1** A plant with blue flowers, having a seed, called *flaxseed* or *linseed,* and a fibrous stem. **2** The soft fiber of the flax plant, used in the manufacture of linen. [< OE *fleax*] —**flax′y** *adj.* (**·i·er, ·i·est**)

flax·en (flak′sən) *adj.* **1** Of, pertaining to, or like flax. **2** Of a light golden color.

flax·seed (flaks′sēd′, flak′-) *n.* The seed of the flax plant; linseed.

flay (flā) *v.t.* **1** To strip off the skin from. **2** To attack with scathing criticism. **3** To pillage; rob. [< OE *flēan*] —**flay′er** *n.*

flea (flē) *n.* A jumping, wingless insect that feeds upon the blood of mammals or birds. [< OE *flēa*]

Flea

flea·bane (flē′bān′) *n.* Any of various plants supposed to repel fleas.

flea-bit·ten (flē′bit′n) *adj.* **1** Bitten by or swarming with fleas. **2** Squalid; shabby.

fleck (flek) *n.* **1** A dot or speck. **2** A particle; flake. —*v.t.* To mark with flecks. [? ON *flekkr* spot]

flec·tion (flek′shən) *n.* **1** The act of bending. **2** A curved or bent part. [< L *flectere* to bend] —**flec′tion·al** *adj.*

fled (fled) *p.t.* & *p.p.* of FLEE.

fledge (flej) *v.* **fledged, fledg·ing** *v.t.* **1** To furnish with feathers, as an arrow. **2** To bring up (a young bird) until ready for flight. —*v.i.* **3** To grow enough feathers for flight. [< OE -*flycge* feathered in *unflycge* not ready to fly]

fledg·ling (flej′ling) *n.* **1** A young bird just fledged. **2** A tyro; an inexperienced person. Also **fledge′ling.**

flee (flē) *v.* **fled, flee·ing** *v.i.* **1** To run away, as from danger. **2** To move away quickly; disappear. **3** To leave abruptly. —*v.t.* **4** To run away from. [< OE *flēon*] —**fle′er** *n.* —**Syn. 3** decamp, depart, escape, fly.

fleece (flēs) *n.* **1** The wool coat of a sheep. **2** The wool sheared from a sheep at one time. **3** Anything like fleece. **4** A textile fabric with a soft, silky pile. —*v.t.* **fleeced, fleec·ing 1** To shear the fleece from. **2** To defraud; cheat. [< OE *flēos*] —**fleec′er** *n.*

fleec·y (flē′sē) *adj.* **fleec·i·er, fleec·i·est** Pertaining to, like, or covered with a fleece. —**fleec′i·ly** *adv.* —**fleec′i·ness** *n.*

fleer (flir) *v.t.* **1** To jeer at. —*v.i.* **2** To sneer. —*n.* **1** Derision or scorn. **2** A leer. [< Scand.] —**fleer′ing·ly** *adv.*

fleet[1] (flēt) *adj.* Moving swiftly; rapid. —*v.i.* To move swiftly. [< OE *flēotan.* to float] —**fleet′ly** *adv.* —**fleet′ness** *n.*

fleet[2] (flēt) *n.* **1** A number of vessels under one command. **2** The entire number of vessels belonging to one government; a navy. **3** A number of vessels, aircraft, or vehicles engaged in the same activity: a fishing *fleet;* a *fleet* of trucks. [< OE *flēot* ship]

fleet·ing (flē′ting) *adj.* Passing quickly; transitory. —**fleet′ing·ly** *adv.* —**fleet′ing·ness** *n.*

Flem·ish (flem′ish) *adj.* Of or pertaining to Flanders, its people, or language. —*n.* **1** The people of Flanders. **2** The Low German language of Flanders.

flesh (flesh) *n.* **1** The soft tissues of a human or animal body, esp. the muscular portions. **2** Meat, esp. that of mammals. **3** The human body as opposed to the spirit. **4** Mankind. **5** All creatures. **6** The sensual side of human nature. **7** The color of a white person's skin. **8** The soft, edible parts of fruits and vegetables. —**in the flesh** **1** In person. **2** Alive. —**own flesh and blood** One's family; relatives. —*v.t.* **1** To initiate, as troops, in a first battle experience. **2** To incite, as hawks, for hunting by feeding with meat. **3** To make fat. —**flesh out** To give substance to: to *flesh out* an idea. [< OE *flæsc*] —**flesh′less** *adj.*

flesh-col·ored (flesh′kul′ərd) *adj.* Having the color of the skin of a white person.

flesh·ly (flesh′lē) *adj.* **·li·er, ·li·est** **1** Pertaining to the body; corporeal. **2** Sensual; carnal. **3** Fleshy; fat; plump. —*adv.* In a fleshly manner. —**flesh′li·ness** *n.*

flesh·pot (flesh′pot′) *n.* **1** A pot to cook meat in. **2** *pl.* Any form of indulgence; luxury.

flesh·y (flesh′ē) *adj.* **flesh·i·er, flesh·i·est** **1** Having much flesh; plump; fat. **2** Of, pertaining to, or like flesh. **3** Consisting of firm pulp; succulent, as a peach or an apple. —**flesh′i·ness** *n.*

fleur-de-lis (flœr′də·lē′, -lēs′) *n. pl.* **fleurs-de-lis** (-də·lēz′) **1** IRIS (defs. 2 & 3). **2** An ornament or heraldic device having the shape of an iris. Also **fleur′-de-lys′.** [F, flower of lily]

flew (flōō) *p.t.* of FLY[1].

flex (fleks) *v.t. & v.i.* **1** To bend. **2** To contract, as a muscle. —*n. Brit.* A pliant insulated electric cord. [< L *flexus,* pp. of *flectere* bend] —**flex·ion** (flek′shən) *n.*

flex·i·ble (flek′sə·bəl) *adj.* **1** Capable of being bent without breaking; pliant. **2** Tractable; yielding; compliant. Also **flex·ile** (flek′sil). —**flex′i·bil′i·ty, flex′i·ble·ness** *n.* —**flex′i·bly** *adv.*

Fleur-de-lis

flex·or (flek′sər) *n.* A muscle that contracts to bend a joint.

flex·time (fleks′tīm′) *n.* The system of allowing workers to arrange their own convenient working hours.

flex·u·ous (flek′shōō·əs) *adj.* **1** Winding or turning about. **2** Unsteady; wavering. [< L *flexus.* See FLEX.] —**flex·u·os·i·ty** (flek′shōō·os′ə·tē) *n.*

flex·ure (flek′shər) *n.* **1** The state of being bent or flexed. **2** A bent part; turn; curve.

flib·ber·ti·gib·bet (flib′ər·tē·jib′it) *n.* An impulsive, flighty, or gossipy person. Also **flib′ber·di·gib′bit, flib′ber·ty·gib′bet.** [Imit.]

flick[1] (flik) *v.t.* **1** To strike with a quick, light stroke, as with a whip. **2** To remove with such a motion: to *flick* dust. **3** To cause to snap, as a whip. —*v.i.* **4** To move in a quick, darting manner. **5** To flutter. —*n.* **1** A quick, light stroke, as with a whip. **2** The sound of such a stroke. **3** A streak or splash. [Imit.]

flick[2] (flik) *n. Slang* A movie. [Short for FLICKER[1]]

flick·er[1] (flik′ər) *v.i.* **1** To burn or shine with an unsteady light. **2** To move jerkily, as lightning. **3** To flutter the wings. —*v.t.* **4** To cause to flicker. —*n.* **1** A waving light. **2** A flickering or fluttering motion. [< OE *flicorian* move the wings] —**flick′er·ing·ly** *adv.* —**flick′er·y** *adj.* —**Syn.** *n.* 1, *v.* 1 flare, glimmer, sparkle, twinkle.

flick·er[2] (flik′ər) *n.* Any of several species of woodpecker. [Imit.]

Flicker

flied (flīd) *p.t. & p.p.* of FLY[1] (def. 7).

fli·er (flī′ər) *n.* **1** That which flies. **2** A pilot of an aircraft. **3** A printed handbill. **4** *Informal* A venture, as in the stock market.

flight (flīt) *n.* **1** The act, process, or power of flying. **2** The distance flown. **3** A group or flock flying through the air together. **4** A single trip of an airplane. **5** In the U.S. Air Force, a tactical unit of two or more aircraft. **6** A soaring and sustained effort or utterance. **7** A continuous series of stairs or steps. **8** The act of fleeing. —**put to flight** To cause to flee or run; rout. [< OE *flyht*] —**flight′less** *adj.*

flight·y (flī′tē) *adj.* **flight·i·er, flight·i·est** **1** Silly; capricious; frivolous. **2** Easily excited or confused; unstable. —**flight′i·ly** *adv.* —**flight′i·ness** *n.*

flim·sy (flim′zē) *adj.* **·si·er, ·si·est** **1** Not substantial or solid: a *flimsy* chair. **2** Ineffective; trivial: a *flimsy* reason. —*n. pl.* **flim·sies** A thin paper used for carbon copies. [? < FILM] —**flim′si·ly** *adv.* —**flim′si·ness** *n.*

flinch (flinch) *v.i.* To shrink back, as from pain or danger; wince. —*n.* Any act of flinching. [< OF *flenchir, flechier* to bend] —**flinch′er** *n.* —**flinch′ing·ly** *adv.*

fling (fling) *v.* **flung, fling·ing** *v.t.* **1** To throw with violence; hurl. **2** To cast off. **3** To put abruptly or violently. **4** To hurl (oneself) into something completely. **5** To overthrow, as in wrestling. **6** To emit, as a fragrance. —*v.i.* **7** To move or rush, as with anger. —*n.* **1** The act of flinging. **2** A try; attempt. **3** A time of lively action or indulgence. **4** A lively Scottish dance. [< Scand.] —**fling′er** *n.*

flint (flint) *n.* **1** A very hard, dull-colored variety of quartz which produces a spark when struck with steel. **2** A piece of material from which sparks are easily struck. **3** Anything very hard or cruel. [< OE]

flint glass A soft, lead-oxide glass, used esp. for lenses.

flint·lock (flint′lok′) *n.* **1** A gunlock in which a flint was used to ignite the powder in the pan. **2** A firearm equipped with such a gunlock.

flint·y (flin′tē) *adj.* **flint·i·er, flint·i·est** **1** Made of, containing, or resembling flint. **2** Hard; obdurate. —**flint′i·ly** *adv.* —**flint′i·ness** *n.*

Flintlock

flip[1] (flip) *v.* **flipped, flip·ping** *v.t.* **1** To throw or put in motion with a jerk; flick. **2** To toss, as a coin. —*v.i.* **3** To move with a jerk. **4** To strike lightly and quickly. **5** *Slang* To lose one's sanity or self-control, as from joy, anger, wonder, etc.: often with *out.* —*n.* A quick movement; flick. [?]

flip[2] (flip) *adj. Informal* Casual to the point of impudence; flippant. [Short for FLIPPANT]

flip-flop (flip′flop′) *n.* A somersault or handspring.

flip·pant (flip′ənt) *adj.* Marked by a lack of concern or respect; impertinent; disrespectful. [< FLIP[1]] —**flip′pan·cy, flip′pant·ness** *n.* —**flip′pant·ly** *adv.*

flip·per (flip′ər) *n.* **1** A flattened limb used in swimming, as by seals, etc. **2** A rubber shoe having a long, paddlelike piece, used by skin divers and other swimmers. **3** *Slang* The hand.

flirt (flûrt) *v.i.* **1** To play at courtship by trying to attract attention or admiration. **2** To trifle; toy: to *flirt* with danger. **3** To move with sudden jerk motions. —*v.t.* **4** To toss or throw with a jerk. —*n.* **1** A person who flirts. **2** A flirting motion; fling. [?] —**flir·ta′tion, flirt′er** *n.* —**flirt′y** *adj.*

flir·ta·tious (flər·tā′shəs) *adj.* Inclined to flirt. —**flir·ta′tious·ly** *adv.* —**flir·ta′tious·ness** *n.*

flit (flit) *v.* **flit·ted, flit·ting** *v.i.* **1** To move or pass rapidly and lightly. **2** To pass away, as time. —*n.* A flitting motion. [< ON *flytja* remove, move] —**flit′ter** *n.*

flitch (flich) *n.* A side of a hog salted and cured; side of bacon. —*v.t.* To cut into flitches. [< OE *flicce*]

flit·ter (flit′ər) *v.t. & v.i.* To flutter; flit. [Freq. of FLIT]

fliv·ver (fliv′ər) *n.* A cheap automobile. [?]

float (flōt) *v.i.* **1** To rest on the surface of a liquid. **2** To drift on the surface of a liquid, in air, etc. **3** To move or drift without purpose. **4** To hover; stay vaguely: The image *floated* in his mind. —*v.t.* **5** To cause to rest on the surface of a liquid. **6** To put in circulation; place on sale: to *float* a loan. **7** To irrigate; flood. —*n.* **1** An object that floats, as a cork on a bait line or a hollow ball in a tank. **2** A truck or wheeled platform, decorated for display in a pageant. [<OE *flotian* float] —**float′a·ble** *adj.*

float·a·tion (flō·tā′shən) *n.* FLOTATION.

float·er (flō′tər) *n.* **1** *Informal* A voter who votes fraudulently elsewhere than in his own district. **2** A vagrant.

float·ing (flō′ting) *adj.* **1** Buoyed up by a liquid or gas. **2** Not settled or attached; moving about. **3** Not in the normal position: a *floating* kidney. **4** Not funded: said of short-term debts. **5** Not invested permanently: said of capital. —*n.* The act of floating. —**float′ing·ly** *adv.*

floating ribs The two lowest pairs of ribs in a human being, attached to the vertebrae but not to the sternum or to the other ribs.

floc·cu·late (flok′yə·lāt) *v.t.* & *v.i.* **·lat·ed, ·lat·ing** To gather or be joined together in loose masses, as soil, clouds, etc. [<L *floccus* lock of wool] —**floc′cu·la′tion** *n.*

floc·cu·lent (flok′yə·lənt) *adj.* **1** Resembling wool; woolly; fluffy. **2** Covered with a soft, waxy secretion. **3** Coalescing in flakes. [<L *floccus* lock of wool]

flock[1] (flok) *n.* **1** A company or collection of animals, as sheep, goats, or birds. **2** The members of a church. **3** A company of persons; a crowd. —*v.i.* To assemble or go in flocks, crowds, etc.; congregate. [<OE *flocc*] —**Syn.** *n.* **1** bevy, drove, flock, herd.

flock[2] (flok) *n.* **1** A tuft of wool or the like. **2** Short refuse wool or cotton, used as stuffing and in upholstery. [Prob. < L *floccus* lock of wool]

floe (flō) *n.* A massive, flat sheet of floating ice; also, a broken piece of such ice floating freely. [?<ON *flo* a layer]

flog (flog, flôg) *v.t.* **flogged, flog·ging 1** To beat with a whip, rod, etc. **2** To work to a punishing degree: to *flog* one's memory. **3** *Brit. Informal* To sell, esp. fraudulently or illegally. [?<L *flagellare*] —**flog′ger** *n.*

flood (flud) *n.* **1** An unusually large overflow of water onto land. **2** The coming in of the tide. **3** A copious flow or stream, as of sunlight, lava, etc. **4** A stage light that throws a broad beam. —*v.t.* **1** To cover with a flood; deluge. **2** To fill or overwhelm as with a flood. —*v.i.* **3** To overflow. **4** To flow in a flood; gush. [<OE *flōd*] —**flood′er** *n.*

flood·gate (flud′gāt′) *n.* **1** A gate for regulating the flow of water. **2** Any free vent for an outpouring, as of tears.

flood·light (flud′līt′) *n.* **1** Artificial illumination of great brilliancy and broad beams. **2** A lighting unit for providing such illumination. —*v.t.* To illuminate with a floodlight.

flood tide 1 The rising tide. **2** The high point of anything.

floor (flôr, flōr) *n.* **1** The surface in a room upon which one walks. **2** A level of a building; story. **3** Any similar bottom surface: the *floor* of a bridge. **4** In any parliamentary body, the part of the hall occupied by its members. **5** The right to address an assembly: to have the *floor*. **6** The main business hall of an exchange. **7** The lowest price charged for a given thing. —*v.t.* **1** To cover or provide with a floor. **2** To throw down. **3** *Informal* To defeat. **4** *Informal* To baffle. [<OE *flōr*] —**floor′er** *n.*

floor·board (flôr′bôrd′, -bōrd′) *n.* **1** One of the boards of a floor. **2** The floor in an automobile.

floor·ing (flôr′ing, flō′ring) *n.* **1** Material for the making of a floor. **2** A floor or floors.

floor leader A legislative leader chosen by his own party and having charge of party organization and activities on the floor.

floor show Entertainment in a night club or cabaret.

floor·walk·er (flôr′wô′kər, flōr′-) *n.* In a retail store, one who oversees the employees on a floor, directs customers, etc.

flop (flop) *v.* **flopped, flop·ping** *v.i.* **1** To move or beat about with thuds. **2** To fall loosely and heavily. **3** *Informal* To fail. —*v.t.* **4** To cause to strike, slap, or drop with a thud. —*n.* **1** The sound or act of flopping. **2** *Informal* An utter failure. [Var. of FLAP] —**flop′pi·ly** *adv.* —**flop′pi·ness** *n.* —**flop′py** *adj.* (**·i·er, ·i·est**)

flop·house (flop′hous′) *n.* A cheap hotel

floppy disk A flexible computer disk.

flo·ra (flôr′ə, flō′rə) *n. pl.* **·ras** or **·rae** (-ē) Plants collectively, esp. the species respresented in a given area or period. [<L *Flora* < *flos, floris* flower]

Flo·ra (flôr′ə, flō′rə) *Rom. Myth.* The goddess of flowers.

flo·ral (flôr′əl, flō′rəl) *adj.* Of, like, or pertaining to flowers.

Flor·en·tine (flôr′ən·tēn, -tin, flor′-) *adj.* Of or pertaining to the city of Florence, Italy. —*n.* An inhabitant or native of Florence.

flo·res·cence (flô·res′əns, flō-) *n. Bot.* The state of being in blossom. [<L *florere* to bloom] —**flo·res′cent** *adj.*

flo·ret (flôr′it, flō′rit) *n.* **1** A little flower. **2** *Bot.* One of the small flowers that make up a head of a composite flower, as in sunflowers, dandelions, etc. [<L *flos, floris* flower]

flo·ri·cul·ture (flôr′ə·kul′chər, flō′rə-) *n.* The cultivation of flowers. —**flo′ri·cul′tur·al** *adj.* —**flo′ri·cul′tur·al·ly** *adv.* —**flo′ri·cul′tur·ist** *n.*

flor·id (flôr′id, flor′-) *adj.* **1** Having a lively reddish hue. **2** Extremely ornate. [<L *flos, floris* a flower] —**flo·rid·i·ty** (flə·rid′ə·tē), **flor′id·ness** *n.* —**flor′id·ly** *adv.* —**Syn. 1** rosy, rubicund, ruddy. **2** gaudy, ornate.

flor·in (flôr′in, flor′in) *n.* **1** A British coin, equal to two shillings. **2** GUILDER. [<Ital. *fiore* a flower; from the lily stamped on the old coins]

flo·rist (flôr′ist, flō′rist, flor′ist) *n.* A grower of or dealer in flowers. [<L *flos, floris* flower]

floss (flôs, flos) *n.* **1** FLOSS SILK. **2** The silk of some plants, as corn. **3** The stray silk on silkworm cocoons. **4** A flossy surface, fluff. [?<OF *flosche*]

floss silk Soft silk thread used in embroidery.

floss·y (flôs′ē, flos′ē) *adj.* **floss·i·er, floss·i·est 1** Like floss; light; silky. **2** *Informal* Ornate; frilly.

flo·ta·tion (flō·tā′shən) *n.* **1** The act or state of floating. **2** The act of floating or financing, as of an issue of bonds, etc., by bankers. **3** *Metall.* A method of separating pulverized ores by placing them in a froth of oils and chemicals to which they selectively adhere.

flo·til·la (flō·til′ə) *n.* **1** A small fleet. **2** In the U.S. Navy, an organized group of destroyers. [<Sp. *flota* a fleet]

flot·sam (flot′səm) *n.* **1** *Law* Goods cast or swept from a vessel into the sea and found floating. **2** Any worthless objects. **3** Vagrants or unattached persons. [<AF *floteson* <*floter* float]

flounce[1] (flouns) *n.* A gathered or plaited strip, as on a skirt. —*v.t.* **flounced, flounc·ing** To furnish with flounces. [<ME *frouncen* to curl]

flounce[2] (flouns) *v.i.* **flounced, flounc·ing 1** To move with exaggerated tosses of the body, as in anger or petulance. **2** To plunge; founder: said of animals. —*n.* The act of flouncing. [?]

floun·der[1] (floun′dər) *v.i.* **1** To struggle clumsily as if mired or injured. **2** To speak or act in a clumsy or confused manner. —*n.* A stumbling or struggling motion. [? Blend of FLOUNCE[2] and FOUNDER] —**floun′der·ing·ly** *adv.*

floun·der[2] (floun′dər) *n.* Any of certain species of flatfish, valued as food. [?<Scand.]

flour (flour) *n.* **1** The ground and bolted substance of wheat. **2** The finely ground particles of any cereal. **3** Any finely powdered substance. —*v.t.* **1** To make into flour. **2** To cover with flour. [Var. of FLOWER] —**flour′y** *adj.*

Flounder

flour·ish (flûr′ish) *v.i.* **1** To grow or fare well; thrive. **2** To be at the peak of success or development. **3** To move with sweeping motions. **4** To write with ornamental strokes.— *v.t.* **5** To brandish; wave. —*n.* **1** An ornamental mark or design, as in writing. **2** Anything done for display alone. **3** The act of brandishing or waving. **4** *Music* A short, elaborate passage; fanfare. [<L *florere* to bloom] —**flour′ish·er** *n.* —**flour′ish·ing·ly** *adv.*

flout (flout) *v.t.* To show contempt for; scoff at. —*v.i.* To mock; jeer. —*n.* A gibe; scoff. [?<ME *flouten* play the flute] —**flout′er** *n.* —**flout′ing·ly** *adv.* • See FLAUNT.

flow (flō) *v.i.* **1** To move along in a stream, as a liquid or gas. **2** To move like water. **3** To stream forth; proceed from a source. **4** To move with continuity and pleasing rhythm, as music. **5** To fall in waves, as garments or hair. **6** To be full or too full; abound. **7** To come in or rise, as the tide. —*v.t.* **8** To flood; inundate. —*n.* **1** The act of flowing. **2** That which flows; something flowing. **3** The incoming of the tide. **4** The quantity or rate of flow. [< OE *flōwan*]

flow chart A diagram showing the succession of steps in a process.

flow·er (flou′ər, flour) *n.* **1** *Bot.* The organ of reproduction in a plant; blossom. **2** A blooming plant. **3** The brightest, choicest part, period, or specimen of anything. **4** *pl. Chem.* A fine powder obtained by sublimation: *flowers* of sulfur. —*v.i.* **1** To put forth blossoms; bloom. **2** To come to full development. —*v.t.* **3** To decorate with flowers or a floral pattern. [< OF *flour, flor* < L *flos, floris* a flower] —**flow′·er·y** *adj.* (**·i·er, ·i·est**) —**flow′er·i·ly** *adv.* —**flow′er·i·ness** *n.*

flow·er·et (flou′ər·it) *n.* FLORET.

flow·er·pot (flou′ər·pot′, flour′-) *n.* A container, often of earthenware, for growing plants.

flown (flōn) *p.p.* of FLY[1].

fl. oz. fluid ounce(s).

flu (flōō) *n. Informal* Influenza.

flub (flub) *Informal v.t. & v.i.* **flubbed, flub·bing** To do or manage (something) badly; botch or bungle: to *flub* one's chance. —*n.* A blunder; failure. [?]

fluc·tu·ate (fluk′chōō·āt) *v.* **·at·ed, ·at·ing** *v.i.* **1** To change or vary often and in an irregular manner. **2** To move with successive rise and fall; undulate. —*v.t.* **3** To cause to fluctuate. [< L *fluctus* a wave] —**fluc′tu·ant** *adj.* —**fluc′tu·a′tion** *n.* —**Syn. 1** alternate, vacillate, waver, oscillate.

flue[1] (flōō) *n.* **1** A channel or passage for smoke, air, or gases, as in a chimney. **2** An air channel in a wind instrument. [?]

flue[2] (flōō) *n.* Lint; down; fluff. [< Flemish *vluwe* down]

flu·ent (flōō′ənt) *adj.* **1** Smooth and effortless, as in speaking or writing; facile. **2** Flowing freely and easily; smooth. [< L *fluere* to flow] —**flu′en·cy** (-sē) *n.* —**flu′ent·ly** *adv.*

fluff (fluf) *n.* **1** Nap or down. **2** Anything downy or fluffy. **3** *Informal* An error, esp. in reading or speaking lines. —*v.t.* **1** To shake (hair, etc.) so as to make soft and loose. **2** *Informal* To make an error, as in reading lines. —*v.i.* **3** To become fluffy. [? Blend of FLUE[2] + PUFF]

fluff·y (fluf′ē) *adj.* **fluff·i·er, fluff·i·est** **1** Downy; feathery. **2** Light and airy. —**fluff′i·ly** *adv.* —**fluff′i·ness** *n.*

flu·id (flōō′id) *adj.* **1** Capable of flowing, as a liquid or gas. **2** Of or pertaining to liquid. **3** Capable of changing; not fixed: a *fluid* policy. **4** Smooth: a *fluid* style. —*n.* A substance that flows, as a liquid or gas. [< L *fluere* to flow] — **flu·id·ic** (flōō·id′ik) *adj.* —**flu·id′i·ty, flu′id·ness** *n.* —**flu′id·ly** *adv.*

fluid dram A unit equal to 0.125 or ⅛ fluid ounce.

fluid ounce A unit of volume used for liquids, equal to ¹⁄₁₆ pint or 1.804 cubic inches.

fluke[1] (flōōk) *n.* **1** A pointed part of an anchor that holds to the ground. **2** One of the lobes of the tail of a whale. **3** A barb on a harpoon, arrow, etc. [?< FLUKE[2]]

fluke[2] (flōōk) *n.* **1** Any of several parasitic worms infesting sheep, etc. **2** A flatfish or flounder. [< OE *flōc*]

fluke[3] (flōōk) *n.* **1** A lucky stroke, as in pool. **2** Any lucky stroke. [?] —**fluk′ey** or **fluk′y,** (**·i·er, ·i·est**) *adj.*

flume (flōōm) *n.* **1** A chute or conduit with water flowing through, as for transporting logs. **2** A narrow passage through which a torrent passes. —*v.t.* **flumed, flum·ing** To move or transport, as logs, by means of a flume. [< L *flumen* river < *fluere* to flow]

flum·mer·y (flum′ər·ē) *n. pl.* **·mer·ies** **1** Any of several light, easily digested foods, as a kind of custard. **2** Empty talk; humbug. [< Welsh *llymru*]

flung (flung) *p.t. & p.p.* of FLING.

flunk (flungk) *Informal v.t.* **1** To fail in, as an examination. **2** To give a failing grade to. —*v.i.* **3** To fail, as in an examination. **4** To give up. —**flunk out** To leave or cause to leave a school because of failure in studies. —*n.* A complete failure. [?]

flunk·y (flung′kē) *n. pl.* **flunk·ies** **1** An obsequious or servile person. **2** An assistant assigned to do humble tasks. **3** A male servant in livery. Also **flunk′ey.** [?]

flu·or (flōō′ər, -ôr) *n.* FLUORITE. [< L, a flowing]

flu·o·resce (flōō′ə·res′) *v.i.* **·resced, ·resc·ing** To become fluorescent; exhibit fluorescence.

flu·o·res·cence (flōō′ə·res′əns) *n. Physics* **1** The property by which certain substances absorb radiation and emit light of a different, usu. longer wavelength. **2** The light so produced. [< FLUOR + -ESCENCE] —**flu′o·res′cent** *adj.*

fluorescent lamp A lamp, usu. tubular, containing a vapor that radiates on the passing of an electric current and energizes a fluorescent coating in the tube.

flu·or·i·date (flōō′ə·dāt, flōō′ə·ri·dāt) *v.t.* **·dat·ed, ·dat·ing** To add a fluoride to (drinking water), esp. as a means of preventing tooth decay. —**fluor′i·da′tion** *n.*

flu·o·ride (flōō′ə·rīd, -rid) *n. Chem.* A binary compound of fluorine and another element.

flu·o·rine (flōō′ə·rēn, -rin) *n.* An intensely reactive, normally gaseous element (symbol F) belonging to the halogen group.

flu·o·rite (flōō′ə·rīt) *n.* A variously colored mineral composed of calcium and fluorine, used in metallurgy.

fluoro- *combining form* **1** *Chem.* Indicating the presence of fluorine in a compound: *fluorite.* **2** Fluorescence: *fluoroscope.* Also **fluor-.**

fluor·o·scope (flōōr′ə·skōp, flōō′ər·ə-) *n.* A device for observing objects enclosed in media opaque to ordinary light, but transparent to X-rays. —**fluor′o·scop′ic** (-skop′ik) *adj.* —**fluor·os′co·py** (flōōr·os′kə·pē, flōō′ə·ros′-) *n.*

flu·or·spar (flōō′ôr·spär′, flōō′ər-) *n.* FLUORITE.

flur·ry (fûr′ē) *v.t.* **·ried, ·ry·ing** To bewilder or confuse. —*n. pl.* **flur·ries** **1** A light snowfall or rain. **2** A light gust of wind. **3** A sudden commotion or agitation. **4** A sudden spell of activity or movement, as in stock-market prices or in trading. **5** *Informal* Any sudden outburst: a *flurry* of base hits. [Blend of FLUTTER and HURRY]

flush[1] (flush) *v.i.* **1** To become red in the face; blush. **2** To flow suddenly; rush. **3** To be washed out or cleansed by a sudden flow of water. **4** To glow. **5** To rise from cover, as game birds. —*v.t.* **6** To cause to blush. **7** To encourage; excite: *flushed* with victory. **8** To wash out by a flow of water. **9** To startle (birds) from cover. **10** To make level or straight. —*n.* **1** A warm glow; blush. **2** Sudden elation or excitement. **3** A sudden growth; bloom: the first *flush* of manhood. **4** A sudden gush of water. **5** A sudden sensation of heat. —*adj.* **1** Full of life; vigorous. **2** Powerful and direct, as a blow. **3** Having the surfaces in the same plane; level. **4** Full; copious. **5** Well supplied with money. —*adv.* **1** So as to be level, straight, or even. **2** In a direct manner; squarely: a punch *flush* in the jaw. [ME *flusschen*] —**flush′er** *n.*

flush[2] (flush) *n.* In some card games, a hand of cards all of one color, esp., in poker, of one suit.

flus·ter (flus′tər) *v.t. & v.i.* To make or become confused, agitated, or befuddled. —*n.* Confusion of mind. [? < Scand.]

flute (flōōt) *n.* **1** A tubular wind instrument of small diameter with holes and usu. keys along the side and a mouthpiece on the side near one

Flute

end. **2** A groove, usu. semicircular, as in a column or drill. **3** A groovelike pleat in fabric. —*v.* **flut·ed, flut·ing** *v.i.* **1** To play on a flute. **2** To produce a high, clear sound. —*v.t.* **3** To sing or utter like a flute. **4** To make flutes in, as a column. [< OF *flaute*] —**flute′like′, flut′y** *adj.*

flut·ing (flōō′ting) *n.* Adornment with flutes or grooves.

flut·ist (flōō′tist) *n.* A flute player.

flut·ter (flut′ər) *v.i.* **1** To wave rapidly and irregularly, as in the wind. **2** To flap the wings rapidly. **3** To move or proceed with irregular motion. **4** To move about lightly and quickly; flit. **5** To be excited or nervous. —*v.t.* **6** To cause to flutter. **7** To excite; fluster. —*n.* **1** The act of fluttering. **2** Agitation or confusion. **3** A rapid, unwanted vibration in a device. [< OE *flotorian*] —**flut′ter·er** *n.* —**flut′ter·y** *adj.* —**Syn. v. 1** agitate flap, oscillate, vibrate.

flu·vi·al (flōō′vē·əl) *adj.* Of, found in, or formed by a river. [< L *fluvius* river]

flux (fluks) *n.* **1** A flowing; esp., the flowing in of the tide. **2** A constant changing; fluctuation. **3** An abnormal discharge of body fluids. **4** *Metall.* A substance that promotes the fusing of minerals or metals, as borax. **5** *Physics* The rate of flow of water, heat, electricity, etc., over a surface. —**bloody flux** DYSENTERY. —*v.t.* **1** To make fluid; melt; fuse. **2** To treat, as metal, with a flux. [< L *fluxus* < *fluere* to flow] —**flux·a'tion** *n.*

flux·ion (fluk'shən) *n.* **1** The act of flowing or melting. **2** Continuous change. **3** *Pathol.* An abnormal discharge of body fluids. —**flux'ion·al** *adj.* —**flux'ion·al·ly** *adv.*

fly[1] (flī) *v.* **flew** or **flied** (def. 7), **flown**, **fly·ing** *v.i.* **1** To move through the air by using wings, as a bird. **2** To travel by aircraft; also, to operate an aircraft. **3** To move through the air with speed, as an arrow or bullet. **4** To wave or move in the air, as a flag. **5** To pass swiftly: The years *flew* by. **6** To move swiftly. **7** In baseball, to bat a ball high into the air. **8** To flee. —*v.t.* **9** To cause to wave or float in the air. **10** To operate (an aircraft). **11** To pass over in an aircraft: to *fly* the Atlantic. **12** To transport by aircraft. **13** To flee from. —**fly at** To attack. —**fly in the face of** To defy openly. —*n. pl.* **flies 1** A strip on a garment to cover buttons, zippers, etc. **2** The flap at the entrance of a tent. **3** The length of an extended flag. **4** A baseball batted high into the air. **5** A light passenger carriage. **6** *pl.* In a theater, the space above the stage and behind the proscenium. —**on the fly 1** While flying. **2** *Informal* While in great haste. [< OE *flēogan*]

fly[2] (flī) *n. pl.* **flies 1** One of various small dipterous insects, esp. the common housefly. **2** Any of various other flying insects. **3** A fish hook concealed by feathers, etc., to resemble an insect. [< OE *flyge*]

fly·blown (flī'blōn') *adj.* Tainted or spoiled, as with fly eggs or larvae.

fly-by (flī'bī') *n. pl.* **-bys** The passage of a spacecraft relatively near a body in space.

fly-by-night (flī'bī·nīt') *adj.* Financially irresponsible. —*n.* One who is financially untrustworthy.

fly·catch·er (flī'kach'ər) *n.* Any of a large order of birds that feed upon insects while in flight.

fly·er (flī'ər) *n.* FLIER.

fly·fish (flī'fish') *v.i.* To fish with artificial flies as bait. —**fly'-fish'ing** *n.*

fly·ing (flī'ing) *adj.* **1** Intended or adapted for motion through the air. **2** Moving rapidly. **3** Floating or suspended: a *flying* banner. **4** Hasty; hurried: a *flying* trip. —*n.* The act of flight.

Flycatcher

flying buttress *Archit.* An arch extending from the wall of a building to a supporting abutment and serving to resist the outward thrust of the wall.

flying colors Victory or success.

flying fish A fish of warm seas, with large pectoral fins that enable it to glide through the air for short distances.

flying jib A small sail set beyond the jib.

Flying buttresses

flying saucer UFO.

fly·leaf (flī'lēf') *n. pl.* **·leaves** A blank leaf at the beginning or end of a book, pamphlet, etc.

fly·pa·per (flī'pā'pər) *n.* An adhesive paper, or one impregnated with poison, for catching or killing flies.

fly·speck (flī'spek') *n.* **1** The dot made by the excrement of a fly. **2** Any slight speck. —*v.t.* To mark with flyspecks.

fly·weight (flī'wāt') *n.* A boxer weighing 112 pounds or less, the lightest weight class.

fly·wheel (flī'hwēl') *n.* A heavy wheel that resists sudden changes of speed, thus securing uniform rotation in a machine.

FM frequency modulation.

Fm fermium.

F-num·ber (ef'num'bər) *n. Phot.* The ratio of the focal length of a lens to its effective diameter.

foal (fōl) *n.* The young of a horse, mule, etc. —*v.t. & v.i.* To give birth to (a foal). [< OE *fola*]

foam (fōm) *n.* **1** A collection of minute bubbles forming a frothy mass. **2** Frothy saliva or sweat. **3** The white crest of a breaking wave. —*v.i.* **1** To gather or form foam; froth. —*v.t.* To cause to foam. [< OE *fām*] —**foam'less** *adj.*

foam rubber Rubber having a porous structure due to incorporation of air bubbles prior to vulcanizing.

foam·y (fō'mē) *adj.* **foam·i·er, foam·i·est 1** Covered with or full of foam. **2** Like foam. —**foam'i·ly** *adv.* —**foam'i·ness** *n.*

fob[1] (fob) *n.* **1** A watch pocket in the waistband of trousers. **2** A chain or ribbon connected to a watch and hanging out of a watch pocket. **3** An ornament on a watch chain or ribbon. [?]

fob[2] (fob) *v.t.* **fobbed, fob·bing** *Archaic* To cheat; trick. —**fob off 1** To dispose of or palm off by craft or deceit: to *fob off* worthless stock. **2** To put off; attempt to placate, as with promises. [ME *fobben*]

F.O.B., f.o.b. free on board.

fo·cal (fō'kal) *adj.* Pertaining to, at, or limited to a certain point or focus. —**fo'cal·ly** *adv.*

fo·cal·ize (fō'kəl·īz) *v.t. & v.i.* **·ized, ·iz·ing** To adjust or come to a focus; focus. —**fo'cal·i·za'tion** *n.*

focal length *Optics* The distance from the surface of a lens or mirror to its focus. Also **focal distance**.

fo'c's'le (fōk'səl) *n.* FORECASTLE.

fo·cus (fō'kəs) *n. pl.* **·cus·es** or **·ci** (-sī) **1** *Optics* **a** The point

Foci

Refracted light rays of concave lens at left diverge, forming the virtual focus at a. Refracted rays of convex lens at right converge to focus at b.

where light rays converge after passage through a lens or after reflection from a mirror. **b** The point from which such rays appear to diverge. **2 a** Adjustment so as to form a clear image: to be out of *focus*. **b** The relative clarity of an image. **3** *Physics* The meeting point of any system of rays, beams, or waves. **4** Any central point of activity, attraction, etc.: the *focus* of an earthquake. —*v.t.* **fo·cused** or **fo·cussed, fo·cus·ing** or **fo·cus·sing 1** To adjust the focus of. **2** To bring to a focus. **3** To concentrate. —*v.i.* **4** To come to a focus. [L, hearth] —**fo'cus·er** *n.*

fod·der (fod'ər) *n.* Coarse feed, for horses, cattle, etc., as hay or straw. —*v.t.* To supply with fodder. [< OE *fōdor*]

foe (fō) *n.* An enemy; adversary. [Fusion of OE *fah* hostile and *gefāh* an enemy] —**Syn.** antagonist, competitor, opponent, rival.

foe·man (fō'mən) *n. pl.* **·men** (-mən) *Archaic* A foe.

foe·tus (fē'təs) *n.* FETUS. —**foe'tal** *adj.*

fog (fog, fôg) *n.* **1** Condensed water vapor suspended in the atmosphere at or near the earth's surface. **2** Any hazy condition of the atmosphere, or the material causing it. **3** Bewilderment; confusion. **4** A blur obscuring a developed photographic image. —*v.* **fogged, fog·ging** *v.t.* **1** To surround with or as with fog. **2** To confuse; bewilder. **3** *Phot.* To cloud with a fog. —*v.i.* **4** To become foggy. [? < Scand.]

fog bank A mass of fog.

fog·bound (fog'bound', fôg-) *adj.* **1** Covered with fog: the *fogbound* eastern states. **2** Unable to depart, as a ship or airplane, because of fog.

fog·gy (fog'ē, fôg'ē) *adj.* **fog·gi·er, fog·gi·est 1** Full of fog. **2** Indistinct; blurred. **3** Mentally confused. —**fog'gi·ly** *adv.* —**fog'gi·ness** *n.*

fog·horn (fog'hôrn', fôg'-) *n.* **1** A horn for sounding a warning to ships during a fog. **2** A powerful, harsh voice.

fo·gy (fō'gē) *n. pl.* **fo·gies** A person having old-fashioned notions: now usu. in the phrase **old fogy.** —*adj.* Old-fashioned; out-of-date. Also **fo'gey, fo'gie.** [?] —**fo'gy·ish** *adj.* —**fo'gy·ism** *n.*

foi·ble (foi'bəl) *n.* A slight fault or weakness in one's character. [< F < *faible* feeble]

foil[1] (foil) *v.t.* To prevent the success of; frustrate. [< OF *fouler, fuler* crush, trample down]

foil² (foil) n. 1 Metal in very thin sheets. 2 A leaf of bright metal placed beneath an inferior gem to heighten the color or luster. 3 A person or thing serving to set off by contrast something different. 4 The reflecting coating on the back of a mirror. 5 A leaflike, Gothic ornamentation, as in windows, etc. —v.t. 1 To apply foil to; cover with foil. 2 To set off by contrast. 3 To adorn, as windows, with foils. [< L *folium* leaf]

Foils *def. 5*

foil³ (foil) n. A long, flexible fencing sword having a protective button on the point. [?]

foist (foist) v.t. 1 To put in or introduce slyly. 2 To pass off (something spurious) as genuine. [? < dial. Du. *vuisten* hold in the hand]

fold¹ (fōld) v.t. 1 To turn back (something) upon itself one or more times. 2 To close; collapse: to *fold* an umbrella. 3 To place together and interlock: to *fold* one's hands. 4 To wrap up; enclose. 5 To embrace; enfold. —v.i. 6 To come together in folds. 7 *Slang* To fail; close: often with *up.* —n. 1 The act of folding. 2 Something folded. 3 The crease made by folding. 4 *Geol.* A smooth bend or flexure in a layer of rock. [< OE *fealdan*]

fold² (fōld) n. 1 A pen, as for sheep. 2 A flock of sheep. 3 Any group, as the congregation of a church. —v.t. To shut up in a fold, as sheep. [< OE *fald*]

-fold suffix 1 Having (a specified number of) parts: a *three-fold* blessing. 2 (A specified number of) times as great, or as much: to reward *tenfold.* [< OE *fealdan* fold]

fold·er (fōl′dər) n. 1 One who or that which folds. 2 A folded sheet of light cardboard for holding loose papers, as for storage in a file. 3 Any similar item used to hold papers, as a large envelope. 4 A timetable or other printed paper that may be readily folded.

fol·de·rol (fol′də·rol) n. FALDERAL.

fo·li·a·ceous (fō′lē·ā′shəs) adj. 1 Of the nature or form of a leaf. 2 Having leaves; foliate. [< L *folium* a leaf]

fo·li·age (fō′lē·ij) n. 1 Leaves collectively. 2 A representation of leaves, flowers, and branches, used in architectural ornamentation. [< F < L *folium* a leaf] —**fo′li·aged** adj.

fo·li·ate (fō′lē·āt, -it) adj. Having leaves. —v. **·at·ed, ·at·ing** v.t. 1 To beat into a thin plate, as gold. —v.i. 2 To split into leaves or laminae. 3 To put forth leaves. [< L *folium* a leaf]

fo·li·a·tion (fō′lē·ā′shən) n. 1 The process by which leaves are developed; growth and development into a leaf. 2 The act of beating a metal into a thin sheet or foil. 3 *Archit.* Decoration with leaflike shapes or tracery; also, one of such ornaments. 4 The numbering of the leaves of a book, etc.

fo·lic acid (fō′lik) A constituent of the vitamin-B complex, found in green leaves, etc. [< L *folium* leaf]

fo·li·o (fō′lē·ō, fōl′yō) n. pl. **·li·os** 1 A sheet of paper folded once, thereby forming two leaves or four pages of a book, etc. 2 A book of the largest size, usu. more than 11 inches high, composed of such sheets. 3 A page of a book with a number on one side only. 4 The number of a page. —adj. Consisting of a sheet or sheets folded once. —v.t. To number the pages of (a book or manuscript) consecutively. [< L *folium* a leaf]

folk (fōk) n. pl. **folk** or **folks** 1 A people; nation; race. 2 *Usu. pl.* People of a particular group or class: old *folks.* 3 pl. *Informal* People in general. 4 pl. *Informal* One's family. —adj. 1 Of, pertaining to, originating among, or characteristic of the common people of a district or country. 2 Of, pertaining to, or being music written by or characteristic of such common people, and handed down by them. 3 Of, pertaining to, or being music written in imitation of genuine folk music. [< OE *folc*]

Folk, in the adjectival use, may appear as the first element in two-word phrases; as in:

folk art	folk literature	folk song
folk custom	folk music	folk tale
folk dance	folk singer	folk tune

folk·lore (fōk′lôr′, -lōr′) n. 1 The traditions, beliefs, customs, sayings, stories, etc., preserved among the common people. 2 The study of folk cultures. —**folk′lor·ist** n.

folk·sy (fōk′sē) adj. **·si·er, ·si·est** *Informal* Friendly; sociable; unpretentious.

folk·ways (fōk′wāz′) n. pl. The traditional habits, customs, and behavior of a given group, tribe, or nation.

fol·li·cle (fol′i·kəl) n. 1 *Anat.* A small cavity or saclike structure: a hair *follicle.* 2 *Bot.* A dry seed vessel of one carpel. [< L *follis* bag] —**fol·lic·u·lar** (fə·lik′yə·lər) adj.

fol·low (fol′ō) v.t. 1 To go or come after. 2 To seek to overtake. 3 To accompany; attend. 4 To hold to the course of: to *follow* a path. 5 To conform to. 6 To be under the leadership of. 7 To work at as a livelihood. 8 To come after as a result. 9 To take as a model; imitate. 10 To watch or observe closely: to *follow* sports. 11 To understand the meaning of. —v.i. 12 To happen or come after something in time, sequence, or motion. 13 To understand. 14 To come after as a result. —**follow out** To carry out, as instructions. —**follow through** To perform fully; complete, as a stroke or action. —**follow up** To pursue closely. 2 To achieve more by acting upon what has already been done. —n. The act of following. [< OE *folgian*] —**Syn.** 2 chase, pursue. 11 comprehend, grasp, see.

fol·low·er (fol′ō·ər) n. 1 An imitator or disciple. 2 An attendant or servant.

fol·low·ing (fol′ō·ing) adj. Next in order; succeeding or ensuing. —n. A body of adherents, attendants, or disciples.

fol·low-through (fol′ō·thrōō′) n. 1 In some sports, the continuing of a motion, as the swing of a racket or bat, after contact with the ball. 2 Any continuing, as of an effort, to completion.

fol·low-up (fol′ō·up′) adj. Of or pertaining to a repeated or following action or thing; reinforcing; supplementary. —n. A supplementary action or thing that follows, reinforces, or expands upon an initial effort.

fol·ly (fol′ē) n. pl. **·lies** 1 The condition of being foolish or deficient in understanding. 2 Any foolish act, idea, or undertaking. 3 Immoral conduct. [< F *fol* fool]

fo·ment (fō·ment′) v.t. 1 To stir up or incite, as rebellion or discord. 2 To treat with warm water or medicated lotions. [< L *fomentum* a poultice] —**fo′men·ta′tion, fo·ment′·er** n.

fond (fond) adj. 1 Liking: with *of: fond* of music. 2 Cherished: *fond* hopes. 3 Loving or affectionate; devoted: a *fond* glance. 4 *Archaic* Silly. [< ME *fon* be foolish] —**fond′ly** adv. —**fond′ness** n.

fon·dant (fon′dənt) n. A soft, molded confection. [F < *fondre* melt]

fon·dle (fon′dəl) v. **·dled, ·dling** v.t. To handle lovingly; caress. [< FOND] —**fond′ler** n.

fon·due (fon·dōō′) n. A dish made of grated cheese with eggs, butter, etc. [F < *fondre* melt]

font¹ (font) n. 1 A receptacle for the water used in baptizing. 2 A receptacle for holy water. 3 A fountain. 4 Origin; source. [< L *fons, fontis* a fountain]

font² (font) n. A full assortment of printing type of a particular face and size. [< F *fondre* melt]

food (fōōd) n. 1 That which is taken in and absorbed for the growth and repair of organisms. 2 Solid as opposed to liquid nourishment. 3 That which increases, keeps active, or sustains. [< OE *fōda*] —**Syn.** 1 aliment, fare, nutriment, victuals.

food chain *Ecol.* The relationship of organisms considered as food sources or consumers or both.

food poisoning Illness caused by toxins present in food either naturally or as a result of bacterial spoilage.

food·stuff (fōōd′stuf′) n. Anything used as or made into food.

fool (fōōl) n. 1 A person lacking in understanding, judgment, or common sense. 2 A jester, formerly kept at court and in great households. 3 A dupe; butt. —v.i. 1 To act like a fool. —v.t. 2 To make a fool of; deceive. —**fool around** *Informal* 1 To waste time on trifles. 2 To hang about idly. —**fool away** *Informal* To spend foolishly; squander. —

fool with 1 To meddle with. **2** To joke with. **3** To play with. [< L *follis* a bellows; later, a windbag]

fool·er·y (fōō′lə·rē) *n. pl.* **·er·ies** Foolish conduct; anything foolish.

fool·har·dy (fōōl′här′dē) *adj.* Bold without judgment; reckless; rash. **—fool′har′di·ly** *adv.* **—fool′har′di·ness** *n.*

fool·ish (fōō′lish) *adj.* **1** Showing or resulting from folly or stupidity; unwise. **2** Ridiculous; absurd. **—fool′ish·ly** *adv.* **—fool′ish·ness** *n.*

fool·proof (fōōl′prōōf′) *adj.* **1** So simple as to be understood by anyone. **2** So constructed as to operate always smoothly and safely.

fools·cap (fōōlz′kap′) *n.* A size of writing paper about 13 by 16 inches or 13½ by 17 inches.

fool's gold PYRITE.

foot (fŏŏt) *n. pl.* **feet 1** The terminal part of the leg, upon which a person or animal stands or moves. **2** Anything corresponding to the foot: the *foot* of a chair; the *foot* of a stocking. **3** The lowest part; bottom: the *foot* of a ladder. **4** The part or end opposite the head: the *foot* of a bed. **5** A unit of length equal to 12 inches or 0.3048 meter. **6** A unit of poetic meter consisting of a fixed group of stressed and unstressed syllables. **7** *Brit.* Infantry. **—on foot 1** Walking. **2** Happening; going on. **—put one's foot down** To be decisive. **—put one's foot in it** To get into an embarrassing scrape. **—under foot 1** In the way. **2** On the ground. **—v.i. 1** To walk. **2** To dance. **—v.t. 3** To move on or through by walking or dancing. **4** To furnish with a foot, as a stocking. **5** To add, as a column of figures. **6** *Informal* To pay, as a bill. **—foot it** To walk, run, or dance. [< OE *fōt*]

Structure of the human foot
a. phalanges. b. metatarsal.
c. tibia.

foot·age (fŏŏt′ij) *n.* Length in feet.

foot-and-mouth disease (fŏŏt′ən·mouth′) An acute viral disease of domestic animals, esp. cattle, in which blisters form about the mouth and hoofs.

foot·ball (fŏŏt′bôl′) *n.* **1** A game played between two teams on a field with goals at each end, points being scored by running or passing an oval ball across the opponent's goal line, or kicking it between the goal posts. **2** The ball itself. **3** *Brit.* **a** Soccer. **b** Rugby.

foot·ball·er (fŏŏt′bôl′ər) *n.* A football player, esp., *Brit.,* a soccer player.

foot·board (fŏŏt′bôrd′, -bōrd′) *n.* **1** Something to rest the feet upon. **2** An upright piece at the foot of a bedstead.

foot·bridge (fŏŏt′brij′) *n.* A bridge for persons on foot.

foot·can·dle (fŏŏt′kan′dəl) *n.* A unit for measuring intensity of illumination, equal to one lumen per square foot.

foot·drag·ging (fŏŏt′drag′ing) *n.* Willful delay; reluctance to act. **—foot′drag′ger** *n.*

foot·ed (fŏŏt′id) *adj.* Having a specified kind or number of feet: used in combination: *four-footed; splayfooted.*

foot·er (fŏŏt′ər) *n.* A person or thing having a specified number of feet in height or length: used in combination: a *six-footer.*

foot·fall (fŏŏt′fôl′) *n.* The sound of a footstep; also, a footstep.

foot·hill (fŏŏt′hil′) *n.* A low hill near the base of a mountain.

foot·hold (fŏŏt′hōld′) *n.* **1** A support for the foot. **2** Established position.

foot·ing (fŏŏt′ing) *n.* **1** A place to stand or walk on, esp. with regard to its physical condition: insecure *footing.* **2** A foothold: to have a firm *footing.* **3** A secure, established position. **4** A basis for relationship: to be on a good *footing* with someone.

foot·lights (fŏŏt′līts′) *n. pl.* **1** Lights in a row near the front of a stage. **2** The profession of acting.

foot·loose (fŏŏt′lōōs′) *adj.* Not bound to any person or duty; unattached.

foot·man (fŏŏt′mən) *n. pl.* **·men** (-mən) A male servant who answers the door, waits at table, etc.

foot·note (fŏŏt′nōt′) *n.* A note of reference or explanation at the foot of a page.

foot·pad (fŏŏt′pad′) *n.* A robber on foot.

foot·path (fŏŏt′path′, -päth′) *n.* A path for persons on foot. Also **foot′way′** (-wā′).

foot·pound (fŏŏt′pound′) *n.* The work done in moving a body one foot against a force of one pound.

foot·print (fŏŏt′print′) *n.* An impression left by a foot. Also **foot′mark′** (-märk′). **—Syn.** spoor, trace, track.

foot·race (fŏŏt′rās′) *n.* A race among runners on foot. **—foot′rac′er, foot′rac′ing** *n.*

foot·rest (fŏŏt′rest′) *n.* A stool, chair extension, etc., for supporting the feet.

foot soldier A soldier who fights while on foot; infantryman.

foot·sore (fŏŏt′sôr′, -sōr′) *adj.* Having sore feet, as from excessive walking.

foot·step (fŏŏt′step′) *n.* **1** The action of or the distance covered by a foot in stepping. **2** The sound of a step. **3** FOOTPRINT. **4** A step for going up or down.

foot·stool (fŏŏt′stōōl′) *n.* A low stool for the feet of someone sitting.

foot·wear (fŏŏt′wâr′) *n.* Covering for the feet, as boots, shoes, socks, stockings.

foot·work (fŏŏt′wûrk′) *n.* Use or control of the feet, as in boxing or tennis.

fop (fop) *n.* A man affectedly fastidious in dress or deportment; a dandy. [ME] **—fop′pish** *adj.* **—fop′pish·ly** *adv.* **—fop′per·y, fop′pish·ness** *n.*

for (fôr, *unstressed* fər) *prep.* **1** To the extent of: a desert *for* miles. **2** Through the duration of: good *for* a week. **3** To the number or amount of: a check *for* six dollars. **4** At the price of: a hat *for* ten dollars. **5** On account of: He is respected *for* his ability. **6** In honor of: named *for* his grandfather. **7** Appropriate to: a time *for* work. **8** In place or instead of: using a book *for* a desk. **9** In favor of: a vote *for* peace. **10** In the interest of: Who speaks *for* me? **11** Tending toward, as with longing or desire: a passion *for* jewelry. **12** As affecting: good *for* your health. **13** Belonging, given, attributed, or assigned to: a package *for* you; the reason *for* going. **14** In proportion to: big *for* his age. **15** As the equivalent of: blow *for* blow. **16** In spite of: *for* all that. **17** In order to reach: He left *for* his office. **18** In order to become, find, keep, or obtain: looking *for* a job. **19** At (a particular time or occasion): We agreed to meet *for* lunch. **20** As being or supposed to be: We took him *for* an honest man. **—conj.** Owing to the fact that; because: He could not leave, *for* he was expecting a visitor. [< OE]

for- *prefix* **1** Away; off; past: *forget, forgo.* **2** Very; extremely: *forlorn.* [< OE *for-*]

for·age (fôr′ij, for′-) *n.* **1** Any food suitable for horses or cattle. **2** The act of seeking food. **—v. for·aged, for·ag·ing** *v.t.* **1** To search through for food or supplies. **2** To provide with forage. **3** To obtain by foraging. **—v.i. 4** To search for food or supplies. **5** To search: usu. with *about* or *for.* **6** To make a foray. [< OF *feurre* fodder] **—for′ag·er** *n.*

fo·ra·men (fō·rā′mən) *n. pl.* **·ram·i·na** (-ram′ə·nə) *Anat.* A natural aperture or passage, as in a bone, etc. [< L *forare* bore]

for·a·min·i·fer (fôr′ə·min′ə·fər, for′-) *n.* One of an order of tiny, unicellular marine animals, having a shell perforated by many holes. **—fo·ram·i·nif·e·ral** (fə·ram′ə·nif′ə·rəl), **fo·ram′i·nif′e·rous** *adj.* [< L *foramen* a hole + *ferre* to bear]

for·as·much as (fôr′əz·much′) Since; because. Also **for as much as.**

for·ay (fôr′ā, for′ā) *v.i.* **1** To venture out, as to raid or explore. **—v.t. 2** *Archaic* To pillage. **—n. 1** A raid, esp. on a military mission: a *foray* behind enemy lines. **2** A venturing out, as into unfamiliar surroundings. [< OF *feurre* forage] **—for′ay·er** *n.*

for·bade, for·bad (fər·bad′, fôr-) *p.t.* of FORBID.

for·bear¹ (fôr·bâr′) *v.* **·bore, ·borne, ·bear·ing** *v.t.* **1** To refrain from (an action) voluntarily. **—v.i. 2** To abstain or refrain. **3** To be patient or act patiently. [< OE *forberan*] **—for·bear′ing·ly** *adv.* **—for·bear′er** *n.*

for·bear² (fôr′bâr′) *n.* FOREBEAR.

for·bear·ance (fôr·bâr′əns, fər-) *n.* **1** The act of forbearing; the patient endurance of offenses. **2** A refraining from retaliation or retribution.

for·bid (fər·bid′, fôr-) v.t. **for·bade** or **for·bad**, **for·bid·den** or **for·bid**, **for·bid·ding** 1 To command not to do, use, enter, etc. 2 To prohibit the use or doing of. 3 To make impossible. [< OE forbēodan] —**for·bid′dance**, **for·bid′der** n.

for·bid·ding (fər·bid′ing, fôr-) adj. Such as to repel; frightening; repulsive. —**for·bid′ding·ly** adv.

force (fôrs, fōrs) n. 1 Power and energy, esp. when used to constrain or coerce. 2 Physics That which is capable of accelerating a body that has mass. 3 The capacity to convince or move. 4 Binding effect; efficacy: a rule still in force. 5 An organized body of individuals engaged in some activity: a police force. 6 A military or naval unit. 7 The total military power, as of a nation. 8 A person or group wielding power effectively. —v.t. **forced**, **forc·ing** 1 To compel to do something by or as by force. 2 To get or obtain by or as by force: to force an answer. 3 To bring forth by or as by effort: to force a smile. 4 To break open, as a door or lock. 5 To make, as a passage or way, by force. 6 To press or impose upon someone as by force. 7 To strain, as the voice. 8 To hasten the growth of, as plants in a hothouse. 9 In baseball: a To put out (a base runner) who has been compelled by another base runner to leave one base for the next. b To allow (a run) in such a manner when the bases are full. 11 In card games: a To compel (a player) to play a trump card. b To compel a player to play (a particular card). 12 To stimulate the growth of artificially, as plants in a hothouse. [< L fortis brave, strong] —**force′a·ble** adj. —**forc′er** n.

forced (fôrst, fōrst) adj. 1 Compelled; compulsory. 2 Strained; affected: forced gaiety. 3 Speeded up, with few or no pauses: a forced march.

force·ful (fôrs′fəl, fōrs′-) adj. Acting with or full of force; strong; effective. —**force′ful·ly** adv. —**force′ful·ness** n. —Syn. efficient, impressive, powerful, vigorous.

force·meat (fôrs′mēt′, fōrs′-) n. Finely chopped, seasoned meat served separately or used as stuffing. [< L farcire to stuff + MEAT]

for·ceps (fôr′səps) n. A two-bladed instrument for grasping and compressing or pulling, used by watchmakers, surgeons, dentists, etc. [L, pincers]

for·ci·ble (fôr′sə·bəl) adj. Accomplished by or having force. —**for′ci·ble·ness** n. —**for′ci·bly** adv.

ford (fôrd, fōrd) n. A place in a stream that can be crossed in a vehicle or by wading. —v.t. 1 To go across (a stream, river, etc.) at a ford. 2 To drive across a river or stream at a ford, as cattle, etc. [< OE] —**ford′a·ble** adj.

for·done (fôr·dun′) adj. Archaic Weary; exhausted.

fore (fôr, fōr) adj. 1 Preceding in place or time; antecedent; prior. 2 Situated at or toward the front. —n. The foremost part or place. —**to the fore** 1 To or at the front. 2 At hand; available. —adv. 1 Naut. At or toward the bow of a ship. 2 In front; forward. —interj. In golf, a warning to any person who stands in the way of the ball. [< OE]

fore- prefix 1 Prior in time, place, or rank, as in foreknow, foreman, etc. 2 In or at the front; front, as in forecastle, forefoot, etc. [< OE fore-, for- before]

fore-and-aft (fôr′ən·aft′, fōr′-) adj. Naut. Lying or going in the direction of the ship's length: fore-and-aft sails.

fore and aft Naut. 1 From the bow to the stern. 2 In, at, or toward both bow and stern.

fore·arm[1] (fôr·ärm′, fōr-) v.t. 1 To arm beforehand. 2 To prepare in advance.

fore·arm[2] (fôr′ärm′, fōr′-) n. The part of the arm between the elbow and the wrist.

fore·bear (fôr′bâr′, fōr′-) n. An ancestor. [Earlier fore-be-er, one who has existed formerly]

fore·bode (fôr·bōd′, fōr-) v.t. & v.i. **·bod·ed**, **·bod·ing** 1 To have a premonition of (evil or harm). 2 To portend; predict. [< FORE- + BODE] —**fore·bod′er** n.

fore·bod·ing (fôr·bōd′ing, fōr-) n. Apprehension of coming misfortune. —**fore·bod′ing·ly** adv.

fore·brain (fôr′brān′, fōr′-) n. The largest part of the brain in vertebrates, including the cerebral hemispheres, thalamus, etc.

fore·cast (fôr′kast′, -käst′, fōr′-) v.t. **·cast**, **·cast·ing** 1 To calculate or plan beforehand. 2 To predict; foresee. 3 To

foreshadow. —n. 1 Meteorol. A prediction of weather conditions on the basis of charted data. 2 A prophecy or prediction. —**fore′cast·er** n. —Syn. v. 2 augur, foretell, prophesy, prognosticate. n. 2 foresight, foreknowledge.

fore·cas·tle (fōk′səl, fôr′kas′əl, -käs′-, fōr′-) n. Naut. 1 The forward part of a ship. 2 In a merchant vessel, the forward compartment with living quarters for sailors.

fore·close (fôr·klōz′, fōr-) v. **·closed**, **·clos·ing** v.t. 1 Law a To deprive (a mortgager in default) of the right to redeem mortgaged property. b To take away the power to redeem (a mortgage or pledge). 2 To shut out; exclude. —v.i. 3 To foreclose a mortgage. [< OF for- outside + clore to close] —**fore·clos′a·ble** adj. —**fore·clo′sure** (-klō′zhər) n.

fore·fa·ther (fôr′fä′thər, fōr′-) n. An ancestor.

fore·fin·ger (fôr′fing′gər, fōr′-) n. The finger next to the thumb; index finger.

fore·foot (fôr′fŏŏt′, fōr′-) n. pl. **·feet** A front foot of a four-footed animal.

fore·front (fôr′frunt′, fōr′-) n. The front part or position, esp. with regard to rank, importance, etc.

fore·gath·er (fôr·gath′ər, fōr-) v. FORGATHER.

fore·go[1] (fôr·gō′, fōr-) v. FORGO.

fore·go[2] (fôr·gō′, fōr-) v.t. & v.i. **fore·went**, **fore·gone**, **fore·go·ing** To go before or precede in time, place, etc.

fore·go·ing (fôr·gō′ing, fōr-) adj. Occurring previously.

fore·gone (fôr′gôn′, -gon′, fōr′-) adj. 1 Determined already; previous. 2 Inevitable: a foregone conclusion.

fore·ground (fôr′ground′, fōr′-) n. 1 That part of a landscape or picture nearest the spectator. 2 Any prominent position.

fore·hand (fôr′hand′, fōr′-) adj. 1 Front. 2 Of or pertaining to a tennis stroke in which the palm of the racket hand faces forward in the direction of the stroke. —n. 1 Superiority; advantage. 2 A forehand tennis stroke.

fore·hand·ed (fôr′han′did, fōr′-) adj. 1 Done in good time; early. 2 Having money saved; thrifty. —**fore′hand′·ed·ness** n.

fore·head (fôr′id, for′-, -hed) n. 1 The part of the face above the eyes. 2 The front part of a thing.

for·eign (fôr′in, for′-) adj. 1 Situated outside one's own country or locale. 2 Belonging to, characteristic of, or derived from another country; not native. 3 Not usual or characteristic of: something foreign to one's nature. 4 Occurring where not normally found: a foreign object in the eye. 5 Not pertinent; irrelevant. [< LL forānus located on the outside] —**for′eign·ness** n.

foreign affairs International affairs in relation to the home government.

for·eign-born (fôr′in·bôrn′, for′-) adj. Born in another country; not native.

for·eign·er (fôr′in·ər, for′-) n. A native or citizen of a foreign country.

foreign office A department of a government in charge of foreign affairs.

fore·know (fôr·nō′, fōr-) v.t. **·knew**, **·known**, **·know·ing** To know beforehand. —**fore·knowl′edge** (fôr′nol′ij, fōr′-) n.

fore·leg (fôr′leg′, fōr′-) n. A front leg of a four-footed animal.

fore·lock (fôr′lok′, fōr′-) n. A lock of hair growing over the forehead.

fore·man (fôr′mən, fōr′-) n. pl. **·men** (-mən) 1 The overseer of a body of workers, as in a factory. 2 The spokesman of a jury. —**fore′man·ship** n.

fore·mast (fôr′mast′, -mäst′, -məst, fōr′-) n. The mast nearest a ship's bow.

fore·most (fôr′mōst, -məst, fōr′-) adj. First in place, time, rank, or importance. —adv. In the first place; first. [< OE formest, superl. of forma first]

fore·named (fôr′nāmd′, fōr′-) adj. Named before; mentioned previously.

fore·noon (fôr′nōōn′, fōr′-, fôr·nōōn′, fōr′-) n. That part of the day from sunrise to noon; the morning.

fo·ren·sic (fə·ren′sik) adj. 1 Of, pertaining to, or appropriate for courts of justice or public debate. 2 Argumentative; rhetorical. [< L forum market place, forum] —**fo·ren′si·cal·ly** adv.

---

fore·or·dain (fôr′ôr·dān′, fōr′-) *v.t.* To ordain beforehand; predestinate.

fore·paw (fôr′pô′, fōr′-) *n.* A front paw.

fore·quar·ter (fôr′kwôr′tər, fōr′-) *n.* The front portion of a side of beef, etc., including the leg and adjacent parts.

fore·run (fôr·run′, fōr′-) *v.t.* **·ran, ·run, ·run·ning** 1 To foreshadow; herald. 2 To run in advance of; precede. 3 To forestall.

fore·run·ner (fôr′run′ər, fōr′-) *n.* 1 A person sent before to give news, a warning, etc. 2 A sign or portent of something to come. 3 A predecessor; ancestor.

fore·sail (fôr′sāl′, -səl, fōr′-) *n. Naut.* 1 A square sail on the foremast of a square-rigged vessel. 2 The fore-and-aft sail on a schooner's foremast.

fore·see (fôr·sē′, fōr′-) *v.t.* **fore·saw, fore·seen, fore·see·ing** To know beforehand; anticipate. **—fore·see′a·ble** *adj.* **—fore·se′er** *n.*

fore·shad·ow (fôr·shad′ō, fōr′-) *v.t.* To suggest or indicate beforehand; prefigure. **—fore·shad′ow·er** *n.*

fore·sheet (fôr′shēt′, fōr′-) *n. Naut.* 1 A rope used to trim a foresail. 2 *pl.* The forward space in a boat.

fore·shore (fôr′shôr′, fōr′shōr′) *n.* That part of a shore uncovered at low tide.

fore·short·en (fôr·shôr′tən, fōr′-) *v.t.* In drawing, to shorten the lines of (an object) so as to create the illusion of depth and distance.

fore·show (fôr·shō′, fōr′-) *v.t.* **·showed, ·shown, ·show·ing** To show or indicate beforehand.

fore·side (fôr′sīd′, fōr′-) *n.* 1 The front. 2 Land along the shore.

fore·sight (fôr′sīt′, fōr′-) *n.* 1 Thoughtful care for the future. 2 The act or capacity of foreseeing. **—fore′sight′ed** *adj.* **—fore′sight′ed·ness** *n.*

fore·skin (fôr′skin′, fōr′-) *n.* The loose skin that covers the end of the penis; prepuce.

for·est (fôr′ist, for′-) *n.* 1 A large tract of land covered with trees and underbrush. 2 Such trees. **—adj.** Of or inhabiting a forest. **—v.t.** To plant with trees; make a forest of. [< Med. L (*silva*) *foresta* an unenclosed (wood)]

fore·stall (fôr·stôl′, fōr′-) *v.t.* 1 To prevent by taking prior measures. 2 To realize or prepare for beforehand; anticipate. [< OE *foresteall* an ambush] **—fore·stall′er** *n.* **—Syn.** 1 avert, deter, prohibit, ward off.

for·est·a·tion (fôr′is·tā′shən, for′-) *n.* The planting or conservation of forests.

fore·stay (fôr′stā′, fōr′-) *n. Naut.* A cable from the head of the foremast to the stem.

for·est·er (fôr′is·tər, for′-) *n.* 1 One in charge of a forest, its timber, or its game. 2 Any forest dweller.

for·est·ry (fôr′is·trē, for′-) *n.* The science of planting, developing, and managing forests.

fore·taste (fôr·tāst′, fōr′-) *v.t.* **·tast·ed, ·tast·ing** To have some experience or taste of beforehand. **—n.** (fôr′tāst′, fōr′-) A taste or brief experience beforehand. **—fore·tast′er** *n.*

fore·tell (fôr·tel′, fōr′-) *v.t. & v.i.* **·told, ·tell·ing** To tell or declare in advance; predict; prophesy. **—fore·tell′er** *n.*

fore·thought (fôr′thôt′, fōr′-) *n.* 1 Consideration or planning beforehand. 2 Prudent care for the future.

fore·to·ken (fôr·tō′kən, fōr′-) *v.t.* To foreshow or presage; foreshadow. **—n.** (fôr′tō′kən, fōr′-) A token in advance.

fore·top (fôr′top′, fōr′-) *n. Naut.* A platform at the head of the lower section of a foremast.

fore·top·gal·lant (fôr′top·gal′ənt, -tə-, fōr′-) *adj. Naut.* Of, pertaining to, or designating the mast, sail, yard, etc., immediately above the foretopmast.

fore·top·mast (fôr′top′mast′, -mäst′, -məst, fōr′-) *n. Naut.* The section of a mast above the foretop.

fore·top·sail (fôr′top′sāl′, -səl, fōr′-) *n.* The sail set on the foretopmast.

for·ev·er (fôr·ev′ər, fər-) *adv.* 1 To the end of time. 2 At all times; incessantly.

for·ev·er·more (fôr·ev′ər·môr′, -mōr′, fər-) *adv.* For all time and eternity; forever.

fore·warn (fôr·wôrn′, fōr′-) *v.t.* To caution beforehand. **—fore·warn′er** *n.*

fore·word (fôr′wûrd′, fōr′-) *n.* An introductory note or statement at the beginning of a publication; preface.

for·feit (fôr′fit) *v.t.* To incur the loss of through some

fault, omission, error, or offense. **—adj.** Lost by way of a penalty. **—n.** 1 A thing lost by way of penalty for some default. 2 **forfeiture.** [< OF *forfait* a misdeed < L *foris* outside + *factum* deed] **—for′feit·a·ble** *adj.* **—for′feit·er** *n.*

for·fei·ture (fôr′fi·chər) *n.* 1 The act of forfeiting. 2 That which is forfeited.

for·gath·er (fôr·gath′ər) *v.i.* 1 To meet or assemble. 2 To meet by chance. 3 To associate socially.

for·gave (fôr·gāv′, fər-) *p.t.* of **forgive.**

forge¹ (fôrj, fōrj) *n.* 1 A furnace for heating metal ready for hammering or shaping. 2 A shop or factory having such a furnace. 3 A place where metal is refined, as in producing wrought iron. **—v. forged, forg·ing** *v.t.* 1 To shape (metal) by heating and hammering. 2 To fashion or form in any way. 3 To make, alter, or imitate with intent to defraud. **—v.i.** 4 To commit forgery. 5 To work as a smith. [< OF, ult. < L *fabrica* smithy] **—forg′er** *n.*

forge² (fôrj, fōrj) *v.i.* **forged, forg·ing** 1 To move slowly forward, as in overcoming resistance. 2 To move suddenly with a spurt: to *forge* ahead into the lead. [? Alter. of FORCE]

for·ger·y (fôr′jər·ē, fōr′-) *n. pl.* **·ger·ies** 1 The illegal act of falsely making or altering something, as money, a signature, etc. 2 Anything forged.

for·get (fər·get′, fôr′-) *v.* **for·got, for·got·ten** or **for·got, for·get·ting** *v.t.* 1 To be unable to recall (something previously known) to the mind. 2 To fail (to do something) unintentionally; neglect. 3 To lose interest in or regard for: I will never *forget* you. **—v.i.** 4 To lose remembrance of something. **—forget oneself** 1 To be unselfish. 2 To act in an unbecoming manner. [< OE *forgietan*] **—for·get′ter** *n.*

for·get·ful (fər·get′fəl, fôr′-) *adj.* 1 Having little power to retain or recall. 2 Neglectful; careless. **—for·get′ful·ly** *adv.* **—for·get′ful·ness** *n.*

for·get-me-not (fər·get′mē·not′) *n.* An herb of the borage family, with blue or white flowers.

for·get·ta·ble (fər·get′ə·bəl, fôr′-) *adj.* That may be forgotten. Also **for·get′a·ble.**

for·give (fər·giv′, fôr′-) *v.* **for·gave, for·giv·en, for·giv·ing** *v.t.* 1 To grant pardon for or remission of (something). 2 To cease to blame or feel resentment against. 3 To remit, as a debt. **—v.i.** 4 To show forgiveness. [< OE *forgiefan*] **—for·giv′a·ble** *adj.* **—for·giv′er** *n.* **—Syn.** 1 absolve, exculpate, excuse, exonerate.

for·give·ness (fər·giv′nis, fôr′-) *n.* 1 The act of forgiving. 2 A disposition to forgive.

for·giv·ing (fər·giv′ing, fôr′-) *adj.* Disposed to forgive; merciful. **—for·giv′ing·ly** *adv.* **—for·giv′ing·ness** *n.*

for·go (fôr·gō′) *v.t.* **for·went, for·gone, for·go·ing** 1 To refrain from. 2 To give up; go without. [< OE *forgān* to pass over] **—for·go′er** *n.*

for·got (fər·got′, fôr′-) *p.t.* and alternative *p.p.* of **forget.**

for·got·ten (fər·got′n, fôr′-) *p.p.* of **forget.**

fork (fôrk) *n.* 1 An implement having a handle and two or more tines or prongs, used for handling food. 2 A pronged agricultural or mechanical implement: a *pitchfork.* 3 The point at which a road, stream, tree trunk, or bough branches off. 4 Each of the branches so formed. **—v.t.** 1 To make fork-shaped. 2 To pierce, pitch, or dig with a fork. **—v.i.** 3 To branch; bifurcate: The trail *forked.* **—fork out** (or **over** or **up**) *Slang* To pay or hand over. [< OE *forca* < L *furca*]

forked (fôrkt, fôr′kid) *adj.* 1 Having a fork, or shaped like a fork. 2 Diverging into two branches: *forked* lightning. **—fork′ed·ly** *adv.* **—fork′ed·ness** *n.*

for·lorn (fər·lôrn′, fôr′-) *adj.* 1 Left in distress; deserted. 2 Miserable; pitiable. 3 All but hopeless, as an effort. [< OE *forlēosan* lose, abandon] **—for·lorn′ly** *adv.* **—for·lorn′ness** *n.*

Forks def. 2
a. spading.
b. hay.
c. ensilage.

form (fôrm) *n.* 1 The outward or visible shape of a body as distinguished from its substance or color. 2 A body or figure of a living being. 3 A mold or frame for shaping. 4 A specific structure, condition, or appearance: carbon in the *form* of diamonds. 5 A specific type or species: democracy as a *form* of government. 6 Style, manner, and procedure, as opposed to content. 7 Behavior or conduct according to custom, ceremony, or decorum. **8** Manner or fashion of doing something. **9** Condition of body or mind: to be in good *form*. **10** A formula or draft used as a guide. **11** A document with spaces left for the insertion of information. **12** A long bench without a back. **13** *Brit.* A grade or class in a school. **14** *Printing* The body of type and cuts secured in a frame. **15** *Gram.* Any of the various shapes assumed by a word in a particular context, as *talk, talks, talked, talking.* —*v.t.* **1** To give shape to; mold; fashion. **2** To construct in the mind; devise. **3** To combine or organize into. **4** To develop; acquire, as a habit. **5** To go to make up; be an element of. **6** To shape by discipline or training. **7** *Gram.* To construct (a word) by adding or combining elements. —*v.i.* **8** To take shape; assume a specific form or arrangement. **9** To begin to exist. [< L *forma*] —**form′er** *n.*

-form *combining form* Like; in the shape of: *fusiform.* [< L *forma* form]

for·mal (fôr′məl) *adj.* **1** Of, pertaining to, made, or based on established forms, methods, rules, etc. **2** Marked by or demanding elaborate dress, ceremony, etc.: a *formal* banquet. **3** Correct for elaborate or ceremonious occasions: *formal* attire. **4** Regular or symmetrical in form, design, etc.: a *formal* garden. **5** Stiff; punctilious: a *formal* manner. **6** Made or done in accordance with social customs and etiquette: a *formal* invitation. **7** Of or pertaining to external appearance or form: the *formal* elements of a painting. **8** Of or designating language of a more elaborate vocabulary and construction than that of everyday speech or writing. **9** Of or pertaining to the characteristic composition of anything. —**for′mal·ly** *adv.* —**for′mal·ness** *n.*

for·mal·de·hyde (fôr·mal′də·hīd) *n.* A colorless pungent gas, used in solution as a preservative and disinfectant. [< FORM(IC) + ALDEHYDE]

for·mal·ism (fôr′məl·iz′əm) *n.* Scrupulous observance of prescribed forms, esp. in religious worship, social life, art, etc. —**for′mal·ist** *n.* —**for′mal·is′tic** *adj.*

for·mal·i·ty (fôr·mal′ə·tē) *n. pl.* ·**ties** **1** The state or character of being formal. **2** Adherence to standards and rules. **3** A proper order of procedure. **4** A formal act, method, or ceremony.

for·mal·ize (fôr′məl·īz) *v.t.* ·**ized**, ·**iz·ing** **1** To make official or binding. **2** To make formal. **3** To give form to. —**for′mal·i·za′tion, for′mal·iz′er** *n.*

for·mat (fôr′mat) *n.* **1** The form, size, typeface, and general style of a book or other publication. **2** Any plan or arrangement. [< L *formare* to form]

for·ma·tion (fôr·mā′shən) *n.* **1** The act or process of forming or developing. **2** Manner in which anything is shaped or composed; structure. **3** Anything that is formed. **4** The disposition of military troops, ships, persons, etc., as in a column, line, or square. **5** *Geol.* A series of associated rocks, having similar conditions of origin.

form·a·tive (fôr′mə·tiv) *adj.* **1** Serving to shape, develop, or form. **2** Pertaining to formation or development. **3** *Gram.* Serving to form words. —*n. Gram.* **1** An element, as a prefix or suffix, added to the root of a word to give it a new grammatical form. **2** A word formed in this way. —**form′a·tive·ly** *adv.* —**form′a·tive·ness** *n.*

for·mer (fôr′mər) *adj.* Going before in time; previously mentioned; preceding. —**the former** The first of two mentioned persons or things. [< OE *forma* first]

for·mer·ly (fôr′mər·lē) *adv.* In or at a past time.

for·mic (fôr′mik) *adj.* **1** Pertaining to ants. **2** Designating an organic acid found in ants, spiders, nettles, etc.

For·mi·ca (fôr·mī′kə, fər-) *n.* A plastic used in sheets as table tops, paneling, etc.: a trade name.

for·mi·da·ble (fôr′mi·də·bəl, fôr·mid′ə-) *adj.* **1** Exciting fear or awe; impressive. **2** Difficult to accomplish. [< L *formidare* to fear] —**for′mi·da·ble·ness** *n.* —**for′mi·da·bly** *adv.* —**Syn. 1** dire, dreadful, fearful, redoubtable. **2** insurmountable, overwhelming.

form·less (fôrm′lis) *adj.* Without form; shapeless. —**form′less·ly** *adv.* —**form′less·ness** *n.*

for·mu·la (fôr′myə·lə) *n. pl.* ·**las** or ·**lae** (-lē) **1** A fixed form of words, esp. a conventional expression or statement. **2** Any set method for doing something. **3** A medical pre-

scription. **4** A prescription for a baby's liquid food. **5** Any recipe. **6** *Math.* A rule or combination expressed in algebraic or symbolic form. **7** *Chem.* A symbolic representation of the composition and structure of a chemical compound. [L, dim. of *forma* form]

for·mu·lar·ize (fôr′myə·lə·rīz) *v.t.* ·**ized**, ·**iz·ing** FORMULATE.

for·mu·lar·y (fôr′myə·ler′ē) *n. pl.* ·**lar·ies** **1** A collection of forms, formulas, etc.: a *formulary* of drugs. **2** A church ritual. **3** A formula.

for·mu·late (fôr′myə·lāt) *v.t.* ·**lat·ed**, ·**lat·ing** **1** To express in a formula, or as a formula. **2** To put or state in exact, concise form. —**for′mu·la′tion, for′mu·la′tor** *n.*

for·mu·lize (fôr′myə·līz) *v.t.* ·**lized**, ·**liz·ing** FORMULATE (def. 1). —**for′mu·li′zer** *n.*

for·myl (fôr′mil) *n.* The univalent radical of formic acid. [< FORM(IC) + -YL]

for·ni·cate (fôr′nə·kāt) *v.i.* ·**cat·ed**, ·**cat·ing** To commit fornication. [< L *fornix* brothel, vault] —**for′ni·ca′tor** *n.*

for·ni·ca·tion (fôr′nə·kā′shən) *n.* Sexual intercourse between unmarried persons.

for·sake (fər·sāk′, fôr-) *v.t.* **for·sook** (-sŏŏk′), **for·sak·en** (-sā′kən), **for·sak·ing** **1** To give up; renounce. **2** To abandon; desert. [< OE *forsacan*]

for·sooth (fər·sŏŏth′, fôr-) *adv.* In truth; certainly: chiefly ironical. [< OE *forsōth*]

for·swear (fôr·swâr′) *v.* ·**swore**, ·**sworn**, ·**swear·ing** *v.t.* **1** To renounce seriously or upon oath. **2** To deny upon oath. —*v.i.* **3** To swear falsely; commit perjury. —**forswear oneself** To perjure oneself. [< OE *forswerian* swear falsely]

for·syth·i·a (fôr·sith′ē·ə, -sī′thē·ə, fər-) *n.* An early-blooming shrub having yellow flowers. [< William *Forsyth*, 1737–1804, Brit. botanist]

fort (fôrt, fōrt) *n.* A military enclosure armed and equipped against enemy attack; fortification. [< L *fortis* strong]

forte[1] (fôrt) *n.* That which one does most readily or excellently: Dancing is her *forte*. [< OF *fort* strong]

for·te[2] (fôr′tā, -tē) *Music n.* A musical chord or passage to be performed loudly. —*adj. & adv.* Loud. [< Ital. < L *fortis* strong]

forth (fôrth, fōrth) *adv.* **1** Forward in place, time, or order. **2** Outward, as from seclusion. —**and so forth** And so on; and the like: equivalent to *etc.* [< OE]

forth·com·ing (fôrth′kum′ing, fōrth′-) *adj.* **1** Ready or about to appear. **2** Available when expected or needed: Aid was not *forthcoming*. —*n.* A coming forth.

forth·right (fôrth′rīt′, fōrth′-) *adj.* Straightforward; direct. —*adv.* **1** Straightforwardly; with directness or frankness. **2** At once. —**Syn.** candid, blunt, open, honest.

forth·with (fôrth′with′, -with′, fōrth′-) *adv.* Without delay; immediately.

for·ti·eth (fôr′tē·ith) *adj. & adv.* Tenth in order after the 30th. —*n.* **1** The element of an ordered set that corresponds to the number 40. **2** One of 40 equal parts.

for·ti·fi·ca·tion (fôr′tə·fə·kā′shən) *n.* **1** A fortified structure or place, as a fort. **2** A strengthening or enriching. **3** The act or science of fortifying.

for·ti·fy (fôr′tə·fī) *v.* ·**fied**, ·**fy·ing** *v.t.* **1** To provide with defensive works against attack. **2** To confirm; corroborate. **3** To strengthen the structure of; reinforce. **4** To give physical or moral strength to. **5** To strengthen, as wine, by adding brandy. **6** To enrich (food) by adding minerals, vitamins, etc. —*v.i.* **7** To raise defensive works. [< L *fortis* strong + *facere* make] —**for′ti·fi′a·ble** *adj.* —**for′ti·fi′er** *n.*

for·tis·si·mo (fôr·tis′ə·mō, *Ital.* fôr·tēs′sē·mō) *adj. & adv. Music* Very loud. [Ital., superl. of *forte* strong]

for·ti·tude (fôr′tə·tyōōd) *n.* Patient and constant courage to endure pain, adversity, or peril. [< L *fortis* strong]

fort·night (fôrt′nīt′, -nit′) *n.* A period of two weeks; fourteen days. [< OE *fēowertēne* fourteen + *niht* night]

fort·night·ly (fôrt′nīt′lē) *adj.* Occurring, coming, or issued every fortnight. —*adv.* Once a fortnight.

for·tress (fôr′tris) *n.* A large permanent fort; a stronghold. —*v.t.* To furnish or strengthen with a fortress. [< L *fortis* strong]

for·tu·i·tous (fôr·tyoo'ə·təs) *adj.* 1 Occurring by chance; accidental: a *fortuitous* circumstance. 2 Fortunate; lucky. [< L *fortuitus* < *fors* chance] —**for·tu'i·tous·ly** *adv.* —**for·tu'i·tous·ness** *n.* • Although traditionally the use of *fortuitous* in the sense of fortunate has been deplored, such use is now widespread in all but the most formal written contexts.

for·tu·i·ty (fôr·tyoo'ə·tē) *n. pl.* **·ties** A chance occurrence.

for·tu·nate (fôr'chə·nit) *adj.* 1 Happening by a favorable chance; lucky. 2 Having good fortune. —**for'tu·nate·ly** *adv.* —**for'tu·nate·ness** *n.* • See FORTUITOUS.

for·tune (fôr'chən) *n.* 1 Chance or luck as the cause of good or bad in human affairs: often personified. 2 That which befalls one as his lot, whether good or bad. 3 Future destiny: to tell *fortunes.* 4 Good luck; success. 5 A large amount of money or possessions; wealth. [< L *fortuna* < *fors* chance]

fortune hunter One who seeks to obtain wealth by marriage.

for·tune·tell·er (fôr'chən·tel'ər) *n.* One who claims to foretell a person's future. —**for'tune·tell'ing** *adj., n.*

for·ty (fôr'tē) *n. pl.* **·ties** 1 The product of four and ten; 40; XL. 2 A set or group of 40 members. 3 *pl.* The numbers, years, etc., between 40 and 50. [< OE *fēowertig*] —**for'ty** *adj., pron.*

for·ty-nin·er (fôr'tē·nī'nər) *n.* An adventurer or pioneer who went to California in 1849, the year of the gold rush.

fo·rum (fôr'əm, fō'rəm) *n. pl.* **·rums** or **·ra** (-rə) 1 The public market place of an ancient Roman city, where most legal and political business was transacted. 2 A tribunal; a court. 3 An assembly for discussion of public affairs. [L]

for·ward (fôr'wərd) *adj.* 1 At, of, or toward the front. 2 For deferred delivery: a *forward* purchase. 3 Advanced toward maturity or completion; esp., precocious. 4 Bold; brash. 5 Advanced; progressive; also, extreme: *forward* in opinion. 6 Ready; eager. —*adv.* 1 Toward the future. 2 Toward the front; ahead; onward. 3 To a prominent position; into view: to come *forward.* —**forward of** In advance of. —*n.* A player who leads the attack and plays in the forward line of his team, as in basketball or hockey. —*v.i.* 1 To promote. 2 To send; transmit; esp. to send (mail) on to a new address. [< OE *foreweard*] —**for'ward·ly** *adv.* —**for'ward·er, for'ward·ness** *n.*

forward pass In football, a pass made toward the opponent's goal.

for·wards (fôr'wərdz) *adv.* FORWARD.

fos·sa (fôs'ə, fos'ə) *n. pl.* **fos·sae** (-ē) *Anat.* A shallow depression or trench. [L, ditch]

fosse (fôs, fos) *n.* Ditch; moat. Also **foss.** [F < L *fossa* ditch]

fos·sil (fos'əl, fôs'-) *n.* 1 A remnant or trace of an organism of a past geological age, preserved in the earth's crust. 2 *Informal* A person or thing that is behind the times, or out of date. —*adj.* 1 Dug out of the earth; petrified. 2 Of or like a fossil. 3 Outworn; antiquated. [< L *fossilis* dug up]

fos·sil·if·er·ous (fos'əl·if'ər·əs) *adj.* Containing fossils.

fos·sil·ize (fos'əl·īz) *v.* **·ized, ·iz·ing** *v.t.* 1 To change into a fossil; petrify. 2 To make antiquated or out of date. —*v.i.* 3 To become a fossil. —**fos'sil·i·za'tion** *n.*

Fossil fern

fos·ter (fôs'tər, fos'-) *v.t.* 1 To rear; bring up, as a child. 2 To promote the growth of; forward; help: to *foster* genius. 3 To keep; cherish; nurse: to *foster* a grudge. —*adj.* Having the relation of being a specific family member, but unrelated by blood: a *foster* child. [< OE *fōstrian* nourish]

fought (fôt) *p.t. & p.p.* of FIGHT.

foul (foul) *adj.* 1 Offensive or disgusting to the senses. 2 Dirty; filthy. 3 Clogged or choked with foreign matter: a *foul* pipe line. 4 Spoiled, as food. 5 Entangled; encumbered: a *foul* anchor. 6 Stormy or unpleasant: *foul* weather. 7 Obscene; profane: *foul* language. 8 Wicked; detestable. 9 Not according to justice or rule; unfair. 10 In baseball, of or pertaining to a foul ball or foul line. —*n.* 1 An act of fouling, colliding, or becoming entangled. 2 A breach of rule in various sports and games. 3 In baseball, a foul ball. —*v.t.* 1 To make foul or dirty. 2 To clog or

choke, as a drain. 3 To entangle; snarl, as a rope in a pulley. 4 *Naut.* To cover or encumber (a ship's bottom) with barnacles, seaweed, etc. 5 To collide with. 6 To dishonor; disgrace. 7 In sports, to commit a foul against. 8 In baseball, to bat (the ball) outside of the foul lines. —*v.i.* 9 To be or become foul or fouled. 10 In sports, to violate a rule. 11 In baseball: **a** To bat a foul ball. **b** To be retired by batting a foul ball which is caught before it strikes the ground: usually with *out.* —**foul up** *Slang* To bungle: make a mess (of). [< OE *fūl*] —**foul'ly** *adv.* —**foul'ness** *n.*

fou·lard (foo·lärd') *n.* A lightweight silk, cotton, or rayon fabric, usu. printed, used for dresses, ties, etc. [F]

foul ball In baseball, a ball batted so that it falls outside the foul lines.

foul line In baseball, a line drawn from home plate through first or third base to the limits of the field.

foul play 1 In games and sports, a violation of rule. 2 Any treacherous act, often with the implication of murder.

found[1] (found) *v.t.* To give origin to; establish: to *found* a college. —**found on** 1 To form and base one's opinion. 2 To rest as on a foundation. [< L *fundus* base, bottom] —**found'er** *n.*

found[2] (found) *v.t.* 1 To cast, as iron, by melting and pouring into a mold. 2 To make by casting molten metal. [< L *fundere* pour] —**found'er** *n.*

found[3] (found) *p.t. & p.p.* of FIND.

foun·da·tion (foun·dā'shən) *n.* 1 The act of founding or establishing. 2 That on which anything is founded; basis. 3 A fund or endowment for the permanent maintenance of an institution. 4 An endowed institution. 5 A base or supporting structure upon which a building, wall, machine, etc., is erected. 6 A cosmetic application underlying other makeup. —**foun·da'tion·al** *adj.*

foundation garment A girdle or corset.

foun·der (foun'dər) *v.i.* 1 *Naut.* To fill with water and sink. 2 To collapse; cave in; fail. 3 To stumble; go lame, as a horse. —*v.t.* 4 To cause to founder. [< OF *fondrer* to sink < L *fundus* bottom]

found·ling (found'ling) *n.* A deserted infant of unknown parentage. [< ME *founden*, pp. of *finden* find]

foun·dry (foun'drē) *n. pl.* **·dries** 1 A place in which articles are cast from metal. 2 The operation of founding. Also **foun'der·y** (-dər·ē).

fount[1] (fount) *n.* 1 FOUNTAIN. 2 Any source; wellspring.

fount[2] (fount) *n.* FONT[2].

foun·tain (foun'tən) *n.* 1 A spring or jet of water issuing from the earth. 2 The origin or source of anything. 3 An artificial jet or spray of water, as for drinking, cooling the air, or display. 4 A structure designed for such a jet to rise and fall in. 5 A container for holding oil, ink, etc. 6 SODA FOUNTAIN. [< L *fons, fontis*]

foun·tain·head (foun'tən·hed') *n.* 1 The source of a stream. 2 Any main source. —**Syn.** 2 beginning, fount, origin, wellspring.

four (fôr, fōr) *n.* 1 The sum of three plus one; 4; IV. 2 A set or group of four members. [< OE *fēower*] —**four** *adj., pron.*

four-flush (fôr'flush', fōr'-) *v.i.* 1 To bluff by betting on a hand containing four cards of one suit but lacking the fifth. 2 *Slang* To bluff. —**four'flush'er** *n.*

four·fold (fôr'fōld', fōr'-) *adj.* 1 Made up of four. 2 Being four times as great or as much. —*adv.* Four times as great or as much.

four-foot·ed (fôr'foot'id, fōr'-) *adj.* Having four feet.

Four Hundred The most exclusive social group of a place: with *the.*

four-in-hand (fôr'in·hand', fōr'-) *n.* 1 A four-horse team driven by one person; also, a vehicle drawn by four horses. 2 A necktie tied in a slipknot with the ends hanging vertically. —*adj.* Of or designating a four-in-hand.

four-let·ter word (fôr'let'ər, fōr'-) Any of various obscene or offensive words, typically of few letters and usu. having a sexual or scatological meaning.

four·pence (fôr'pəns, fōr'-) *n.* The sum of four English pennies; also, a former British silver coin of that value.

four-post·er (fôr'pōs'tər, fōr'-) *n.* A bedstead with four tall posts at the corners.

four·score (fôr'skôr', fōr'skōr') *adj. & n.* Four times twenty; eighty.

four·some (fôr′səm, fōr′-) *n.* **1** A game, esp. of golf, in which four players take part, two on each side; also, the players. **2** Any group of four.

four·square (fôr′skwâr′, fōr′-) *adj.* **1** Square. **2** Firm; solid. **3** Sincere; without guile. —*n.* A square.

four·teen (fôr′tēn′, fōr′-) *n.* **1** The sum of 13 plus 1; 14; XIV. **2** A set or group of 14 members. [< OE *fēowertēne*] —**four′teen′** *adj., pron.*

four·teenth (fôr′tēnth′, fōr′-) *adj. & adv.* Next in order after the 13th. —*n.* **1** The element of an ordered set corresponding to the number 14. **2** One of 14 equal parts.

fourth (fôrth, fōrth) *adj. & adv.* Next in order after the third. —*n.* **1** The element of a numbered set that corresponds to the number four. **2** One of four equal parts; a quarter. **3** *Music* The interval between a tone and another three steps away in a diatonic scale.

fourth dimension The temporal coordinate of a point in space-time.

fourth·ly (fôrth′lē, fōrth′-) *adv.* In the fourth place.

Fourth of July INDEPENDENCE DAY.

fowl (foul) *n. pl.* **fowl** or **fowls** **1** Any of the common domestic birds used as food, as the chicken, turkey, duck, etc. **2** The flesh of fowls. **3** Poultry in general. **4** Birds collectively: *wildfowl.* —*v.i.* To catch or hunt wildfowl. [< OE *fugol*] —**fowl′er** *n.*

fowl·ing-piece (fou′ling-pēs′) *n.* A light gun for bird-shooting.

fox (foks) *n.* **1** A wild, carnivorous animal of the dog family, having a pointed muzzle and long bushy tail, commonly reddish brown in color, noted for its cunning. **2** The fur of the fox. **3** A sly, crafty person. —*v.t.* **1** To trick; outwit. **2** To stain, as paper or timber, with a reddish color. —*v.i.* **3** To become reddish in color. [< OE]

Fox

fox·fire (foks′fīr′) *n.* The phosphorescent light emitted by certain fungi in rotted wood.

fox·glove (foks′gluv′) *n.* Any plant of a genus of the figwort family, esp. one that is a source of digitalis.

fox·hole (foks′hōl′) *n.* A shallow pit dug by a soldier as cover against enemy fire.

fox·hound (foks′hound′) *n.* A large, strong, very swift dog trained to hunt foxes.

fox·tail (foks′tāl′) *n.* **1** The tail of a fox. **2** Any of various species of grass bearing a dense spike of flowers.

fox terrier A small, wire- or smooth-haired terrier, formerly trained to drive out foxes from their lairs.

fox·trot (foks′trot′) *n.* **1** A pace between a trot and a walk: used of horses. **2** A ballroom dance in 2/4 or 4/4 time, having a variety of steps. Also **fox trot.** —*v.i.* **·trot·ted, ·trot·ting** To do a foxtrot.

fox·y (fok′sē) *adj.* **fox·i·er, fox·i·est 1** Of or like a fox; crafty. **2** Discolored; foxed. **3** Denoting a wild flavor found in wine made from some American grapes. —**fox′i·ness** *n.*

foy·er (foi′ər, -ā) *n.* **1** A public room or lobby, as in a theater or hotel. **2** An entrance room in a house. [F < L, hearth]

F.P., fp, f.p. footpound(s).

fp, fp., f.p. freezing point.

fps, f.p.s. feet per second; foot-pound-second (system).

Fr francium.

fr. fragment; franc; from.

Fra (frä) *n.* Brother: a friar's title. [Ital. < L *frater* brother]

fra·cas (frā′kəs) *n.* A noisy fight; brawl. [< Ital. *fracassare* shatter]

frac·tion (frak′shən) *n.* **1** A disconnected part; fragment. **2** A tiny bit. **3** *Math.* A number expressed as a quotient of two other numbers, esp. a pair of integers with the divisor greater than the dividend, as ⁷/₁₀. **4** *Chem.* A component separated from a mixture by crystallization, distillation, etc. —*v.t.* To separate into fractions. [< L *fractus,* pp. of *frangere* to break] —**frac′tion·al** *adj.* —**frac′tion·al·ly** *adv.*

frac·tious (frak′shəs) *adj.* **1** Disposed to rebel; unruly. **2** Peevish; cross. —**frac′tious·ly** *adv.* —**frac′tious·ness** *n.*

frac·ture (frak′chər) *n.* **1** The act of breaking, or the state of being broken. **2** A break or crack. **3** A break in a bone or cartilage. —*v.t. & v.i.* **·tured, ·tur·ing** To break or be broken; crack. [< L *fractus,* pp. of *frangere* to break] —**frac′·tur·al** *adj.*

frag (frag) *v.t.* **fragged, frag·ging** *Mil. Slang* To destroy or attempt to destroy with a grenade, as a superior officer or military property. [< *fragmentation bomb,* a type of grenade] —**frag′ging** *n.*

frag·ile (fraj′əl, -īl) *adj.* Easily broken; frail; delicate. [< L *frangere* to break] —**frag′ile·ly** *adv.* —**fra·gil·i·ty** (frə·jil′ə·tē), **frag′ile·ness** *n.*

frag·ment (frag′mənt) *n.* **1** A part broken off; a detached portion. **2** An unfinished or incomplete part: *fragments* of a novel. [< L *fragmentum*]

frag·men·tar·y (frag′mən·ter′ē) *adj.* Composed of fragments; broken; incomplete: also **frag·men′tal.** —**frag′men·tar′i·ly** *adv.* —**frag′men·tar′i·ness** *n.*

frag·men·ta·tion (frag′mən·tā′shən) *n.* The breaking up into fragments.

fra·grance (frā′grəns) *n.* The state or quality of being fragrant; a sweet odor. Also **fra′gran·cy.**

fra·grant (frā′grənt) *adj.* Having an agreeable or sweet smell. [< L *fragrare* smell sweet] —**fra′grant·ly** *adv.*

frail (frāl) *adj.* **1** Easily broken or destroyed. **2** Slender; delicate. **3** Easily tempted; liable to be led astray. [< L *fragilis* fragile] —**frail′ly** *adv.* —**frail′ness** *n.*

frail·ty (frāl′tē) *n. pl.* **·ties 1** The state of being frail. **2** A fault or moral weakness.

frame (frām) *v.* **framed, fram·ing** *v.t.* **1** To surround with or put in a frame. **2** To put together; build, as a house. **3** To put in words; utter: to *frame* a reply. **4** To draw up: to *frame* a law. **5** To think out; conceive, as a plan. **6** *Informal* To incriminate (an innocent person) by false charges. —*n.* **1** Something composed or constructed of parts united to one another in a system; a framework. **2** The general arrangement or constitution of a thing. **3** Structure or build, as of a person. **4** A machine characterized by a wooden framework or structure: a silk *frame.* **5** A case or border made to enclose or surround a thing, as a window, door, picture, etc. **6** A mental state or condition; mood. **7** In tenpins and bowling, a division of the game during which a player bowls at one setting of the pins. **8** The triangular rack in which the balls in a pool game are bunched ready for the break. **9** One of the individual exposures in a roll of motion-picture film. **10** In television, a single complete scanning of the field of view. [< OE *framian* to benefit] —**fram′er** *n.*

frame house A house built on a wooden framework covered by siding, boards, stucco, etc.

frame of reference 1 A preexisting body of circumstances, facts, or ideas that shape perception, thought, opinion, etc.; orientation. **2** *Physics* A set of orthogonal axes specifying position or motion.

frame-up (frām′up′) *n. Informal* **1** Anything deceitfully prearranged. **2** A conspiracy to convict a person on a false charge.

frame·work (frām′wûrk′) *n.* **1** A skeleton structure for supporting or enclosing something. **2** Any structure or arrangement; plan.

franc (frangk) *n.* **1** A French coin and the basic monetary unit of France. **2** The corresponding basic monetary unit of Belgium, Switzerland, etc. [< OF *Franc (orum rex)* king of the Franks, the motto on the first of these coins]

France (frans, fräns) *n.* A republic of w Europe, 212,974 sq. mi., cap. Paris.

fran·chise (fran′-

chīz) *n.* **1** A political or constitutional right reserved to or vested in the people, as the right of suffrage. **2** *Law* A right to do something, as run a railroad, a bus line, etc. **3** The territory or boundary of a special privilege or immunity. **4** Authorization granted by a manufacturer to sell his products. [< OF *franc, franche* free] —**fran′chised** *adj.* —**fran′chise-ment** *n.*

Fran·cis·can (fran-sis′kən) *n.* A member of the mendicant order founded in 1209 by St. Francis of Assisi. —*adj.* **1** Of or pertaining to St. Francis. **2** Of or pertaining to the religious order of Franciscans.

fran·ci·um (fran′sē-əm) *n.* A radioactive element (symbol Fr), isolated from actinium. [< FRANCE]

Franco- *combining form* French: *Franco-Prussian.* [< LL *Francus* a Frank]

Fran·co·phile (frang′kə-fīl) *n.* A non-French admirer of France, its people, customs, etc. —*adj.* Kindly disposed toward France.

Fran·co·phobe (frang′kə-fōb) *n.* A person who fears or dislikes France or French things. —*adj.* Fearful of France.

fran·gi·ble (fran′jə-bəl) *adj.* Easily broken; fragile. [< L *frangere* to break] —**fran′gi·bil′i·ty, fran′gi·ble·ness** *n.* —Syn. breakable, brittle, delicate, frail.

fran·gi·pan·i (fran′ji·pan′ē, -pä′nē) *n.* **1** A perfume derived from the West Indian red jasmine. **2** The plant. Also **fran′gi·pane** (-pān). [< *Marquis Frangipani,* 16th c. Roman nobleman, who created a perfume.]

frank¹ (frangk) *adj.* **1** Candid and open; honest. **2** Not concealed or disguised; evident. —*v.t.* **1** To mark, as a letter or package, so as to be sent free of charge. **2** To send, as a letter, free of charge. —*n.* **1** The right to send mail free. **2** The mail so sent. **3** The signature that authenticates it. [< OF *franc* frank, free] —**frank′ly** *adv.* —**frank′ness** *n.*

frank² (frangk) *n. Informal* FRANKFURTER.

Frank (frangk) *n.* **1** A member of one of the Germanic tribes settled on the Rhine early in the Christian era. **2** In the Near East, any European. [< LL *Francus* a Frank < Gmc.]

Frank·en·stein (frangk′ən-stīn) *n.* **1** The hero of Mary Wollstonecraft Shelley's *Frankenstein,* a medical student who creates a monster that finally slays him. **2** Frankenstein's monster. **3** Any created thing that gets beyond the control of the inventor.

frank·furt·er (frangk′fər-tər) *n.* A smoked sausage, as of beef or beef and pork. Also **frank′furt, frank′fort·er, frank-furt.** [< *Frankfurt,* Germany]

frank·in·cense (frangk′in-sens) *n.* An aromatic resin from various trees of Africa, Arabia, etc., used as incense. [< OF *franc* pure + *encens* incense]

Frank·ish (frang′kish) *adj.* Of or pertaining to the Franks. —*n.* The Germanic language of the Franks.

frank·lin (frangk′lin) *n.* In late medieval England, a free landholder not of noble birth, ranking below the gentry. [< Med. L *francus* free]

fran·tic (fran′tik) *adj.* Excessively excited by fear, worry, grief, etc.; frenzied. [< OF *frenetique* frenetic] —**fran′ti·cal·ly, fran′tic·ly** *adv.* —**fran′tic·ness** *n.*

frap·pé (fra-pā′) *adj.* Iced; chilled. —*n.* **1** A fruit juice frozen to a mush. **2** A liqueur or other beverage poured over shaved ice. [F, pp. of *frapper* to chill]

fra·ter·nal (frə-tûr′nəl) *adj.* **1** Of or befitting a brother; brotherly. **2** Of or pertaining to a fraternal order or association. **3** Derived from separately fertilized ova: said of twins who are not identical.[< L *frater* brother] —**fra·ter′nal·ism** *n.* —**fra·ter′nal·ly** *adv.*

fraternal society An organization, often secret, for fellowship and the attainment of some mutual benefit. Also **fraternal association, fraternal order.**

fra·ter·ni·ty (frə-tûr′nə-tē) *n. pl.* **·ties** **1** The condition or relation of brotherhood; brotherliness. **2** A social or service organization, usu. having Greek letter names, and consisting of men students of American colleges. **3** A group of men of the same profession, interests, etc.: the medical *fraternity.*

frat·er·nize (frat′ər·nīz) *v.* **·nized, ·niz·ing** *v.i.* **1** To be friendly or fraternal. **2** To be friendly with the enemy or with the people of an occupied or conquered territory. —**frat′er·ni·za′tion, frat′er·niz′er** *n.*

frat·ri·cide (frat′rə·sīd) *n.* **1** One who kills his brother or sister. **2** The killing of a brother or sister. [< L *frater* brother + -CIDE] —**frat′ri·ci′dal** *adj.*

Frau (frou) *n. pl.* **Frau·en** (-ən) *German* A married woman: as a title, the German equivalent of *Mrs.*

fraud (frôd) *n.* **1** Deception; trickery; guile. **2** *Law* Any artifice or deception practiced to cause one to surrender something of value or a legal right. **3** One who acts fraudulently; a cheat. **4** A deceptive or spurious thing. [< L *fraus, fraudis* deceit]

fraud·u·lent (frô′jə-lənt) *adj.* Proceeding from, characterized by, or practicing fraud. —**fraud′u·lence, fraud′u·len·cy** *n.* —**fraud′u·lent·ly** *adv.*

fraught (frôt) *adj.* Involving; full of: *fraught* with meaning. [< MDu. *vrachten* to load]

Fräu·lein (froi′līn) *n. German* An unmarried woman: as a title, the German equivalent of *Miss.*

fray¹ (frā) *n.* A fight; brawl. [Var. of AFFRAY]

fray² (frā) *v.t. & v.i.* To wear, rub, or become worn, as by friction; ravel. [< L *fricare* to rub]

fraz·zle (fraz′əl) *Informal v.t. & v.i.* **·zled, ·zling** **1** To fray or become frayed; fret or tatter. **2** To tire out; weary. **3** To be or cause to be nervous or worried. —*n.* The condition of being frazzled. [? Blend of FRAY² + obs. *fasel* ravel]

FRB, F.R.B. Federal Reserve Bank; Federal Reserve Board.

freak (frēk) *n.* **1** A sudden change of mind; a whim. **2** One who or that which is malformed or abnormal; monstrosity. **3** *Slang* One who is given to the use of drugs, esp. illegal drugs. **4** *Slang* One who is very unconventional by society's standards. **5** *Slang* One who is very interested in or enthusiastic about something: an opera *freak.* —*adj.* Very different; strange; abnormal. —**freak out** *Slang* **1** To experience, often in an unpleasant way, the effects of certain drugs, esp. psychedelic drugs. **2** To behave, without the use of such drugs, in ways similar to those of persons who do use them: to *freak out* over a rock concert.[?] —**freak′ish, freak′y** (·i·er, ·i·est) *adj.* —**freak′ish·ly** *adv.* —**freak′ish·ness** *n.*

freak-out (frēk′out′) *n. Slang* **1** The experience of freaking out. **2** One who freaks out; also, a gathering of such people. [?]

freck·le (frek′əl) *n.* A small mark on the skin produced by exposure to the sun. —*v.* **freck·led, freck·ling** *v.t.* **1** To mark with freckles. —*v.i.* **2** To become marked with freckles. [< ON *freknur* freckles]

free (frē) *adj.* **tre·er, free·est** **1** Having liberty of action or thought; independent. **2** Not confined, imprisoned, or enslaved. **3** Not subject to despotic or arbitrary rule. **4** Not subject to certain regulations or impositions: *free* trade. **5** Not encumbered or burdened: *free* from debt. **6** Without charge or cost: *free* samples. **7** Available to all; open: a *free* port. **8** Acquitted, as from a legal charge. **9** Not occupied or busy: I am *free* all day. **10** Not limited by strict rules or conventions: *free* verse. **11** Not literal or precise: a *free* translation. **12** Not formal or conventional. **13** Frank; candid. **14** Impertinent; forward. **15** Not constrained; easy. **16** Not attached or fixed: the *free* end of a rope. **17** Not combined chemically: *free* oxygen. **18** Unobstructed; open: a *free* road. **19** Generous; liberal. —**set free** To let go; release. —**make free with** To use freely. —*adv.* **1** Without cost or charge. **2** In a free manner. —*v.t.* **treed, free·ing** **1** To make free; release from bondage, obligation, worry, etc. **2** To clear or rid of obstruction. [< OE *frēo*] —**free′ly** *adv.* —**free′ness** *n.*

-free *combining form* Free of; devoid of: *carefree.*

free·bie (frē′bē) *n. Slang* Anything, as a ticket to a sports event, that is given free.

free·board (frē′bôrd′, -bōrd′) *n.* The side of a vessel between the water line and the main deck.

free·born (frē′bôrn′) *adj.* Not born in servitude.

free city A city having an independent government.

freed·man (frēd′mən) *n. pl.* **·men** (-mən) An emancipated slave.

free·dom (frē′dəm) *n.* **1** The condition or quality of being free. **2** Exemption from political restraint or autocratic control; independence. **3** Liberty of choice or action. **4** Exemption; immunity: *freedom* from want; *freedom* from arrest. **5** Exemption or release from obligations, ties, etc.

6 Ease; facility. **7** Frankness; candor. **8** A bold or excessive familiarity. **9** Unrestricted use: He had *freedom* of the library. [< OE *frēodōm*]

free enterprise An economic system based upon private ownership and operation of business with a minimum of government control.

free-for-all (frē'fə·rôl') *n.* A fight, game, or competition, open to all comers.

free-hand (frē'hand') *adj.* Drawn by hand without aid of measurements or instruments: a *freehand* drawing.

free hand Authority to act on one's own.

free-hand-ed (frē'han'did) *adj.* Generous.

free-hold (frē'hōld') *n.* **1** An estate in lands. **2** Land held for life without limitations or conditions. —**free'hold'er** *n.*

free-lance (frē'lans', -läns') *v.i.* **-lanced, -lanc-ing** To serve or work as a free lance. —*adj.* Working or acting as a free lance. —**free'-lanc'er** *n.*

free lance **1** A writer, performer, etc., who does not work exclusively for any one employer. **2** A medieval soldier who sold his services to any state or cause. **3** One who supports a cause independently.

free-man (frē'mən) *n. pl.* **-men** (-mən) **1** One not a slave or serf. **2** One having full political rights and privileges.

Free-ma-son (frē'mā'sən) *n.* A member of an extensive secret order dating from the Middle Ages, the members denoting themselves **Free and Accepted Masons.**

free-ma-son-ry (frē'mā'sən·rē) *n.* Sympathy or community of interests in general.

free on board Put on board a train, ship, or other carrier, without charge.

free-si-a (frē'zhē·ə, -sē·ə, -zhə) *n.* A South African plant of the iris family, having fragrant flowers. [< F.H.T. *Freese,* died 1876, German physician]

free silver The free and unlimited coinage of silver, particularly at a fixed ratio to gold.

Free-soil (frē'soil') *adj.* Of or pertaining to the Free-soil party, organized in the U.S. in 1848 to oppose the extension of slavery.

free-spo-ken (frē'spō'kən) *adj.* Unreserved or frank in speech; blunt; forthright. —**free'-spo'ken-ly** *adv.*

free-stone (frē'stōn') **1** Any stone, as sandstone or limestone, easily cut without splitting. **2** A peach or plum whose ripened pulp is easily freed from its pit. —*adj.* Having a pit from which the pulp is easily freed.

free-style (frē'stīl') *adj.* In competitive swimming, using or marked by the freedom to use whichever stroke the swimmer chooses. —*n.* Free-style swimming.

free-think-er (frē'thing'kər) *n.* An independent thinker; esp., one who forms his own religious beliefs without regard to church authority. —**free'think'ing** *adj., n.*

free trade Commerce between countries free from restrictions such as tariffs, customs duties, etc.

free verse Verse marked by the absence or irregularity of rhyme and by the use of irregular rhythms.

free-way (frē'wā') *n.* A multiple-lane road designed for high speeds.

free-will (frē'wil') *adj.* Made of one's own free choice.

free will The power of self-determination; the capacity to choose freely between alternatives.

freeze (frēz) *v.* **froze, fro-zen, freez-ing** *v.i.* **1** To become converted from a fluid to a solid state by loss of heat. **2** To become stiff or hard with cold, as wet clothes. **3** To be very cold: It's *freezing* in here! **4** To become covered or obstructed with ice. **5** To adhere by freezing. **6** To be damaged or killed by freezing or frost. **7** To become motionless, as if frozen, through fear, awe, etc. **8** To become formal or unyielding in manner. —*v.t.* **9** To change into ice. **10** To make stiff or hard by freezing the moisture of. **11** To cover or obstruct with ice. **12** To damage or kill by freezing or frost. **13** To make or hold motionless or in position, through fear, awe, etc. **14** To fix or stabilize (prices, stocks, wages, etc.) so as to prevent change, as by government order. —**freeze out** *Informal* To exclude or drive away, as by unfriendliness or severe competition. —*n.* **1** The act of freezing or the state of being frozen. **2** A spell of freezing weather. **3** The fixing of prices, labor, etc. [< OE *frēosan*]

freeze-dry (frēz'drī') *v.t.* **-dried, -dry-ing** To freeze (foods, bone tissue, etc.) and remove their water content in a near-vacuum.

freez-er (frē'zər) *n.* **1** A refrigerator for freezing foods or keeping frozen foods. **2** An apparatus for making ice-cream.

freez-ing (frē'zing) *n.* The freezing point of water: temperatures below *freezing.*

freezing point *Physics* The temperature at which a liquid passes into the solid state under given pressure.

freight (frāt) *n.* **1 a** The service of transporting commodities by land, air, or water. **b** The commodities so transported. **2** The price paid for the transportation of commodities. **3** FREIGHT TRAIN. —*v.t.* **1** To load with commodities for transportation. **2** To load; burden: a sentence *freighted* with adjectives. **3** To send or transport as or by freight. [< MDu. *vracht* a load]

freight-age (frā'tij) *n.* **1** A cargo. **2** The price charged for carrying goods. **3** The transportation of merchandise.

freight car A railway car for carrying freight.

freight-er (frā'tər) *n.* A ship for transporting freight.

freight train A railroad train comprised of freight cars.

French (french) *adj.* Of or pertaining to France, its people, or their language. —*n.* **1** The language of France. **2** The people of France: used with *the.*

French Canadian **1** A descendant of French settlers in Canada. **2** The language of the French Canadians. —**French'-Ca-na'di-an** *adj.*

French chalk A soft chalk for making lines on fabric or for removing grease stains.

French Community A political association comprising France and six of her former colonies, now the states of Chad, Central African Republic, Congo (Brazzaville), Gabon, Malagasy, and Senegal.

French cuff A cuff of a sleeve turned back and secured to itself with a link.

French doors A pair of adjoining doors, often set with glass panes, hinged to opposite door jambs and opening in the middle.

French dressing A salad dressing consisting of olive oil, spices, vinegar, salt, etc.

French fried Cooked by frying crisp in deep fat: said esp. of potatoes (**French fries**).

French horn A keyed, brass wind instrument with a long, coiled tube which ends in a widely flaring bell.

French-i-fy (fren'chə·fī') *v.t.* **-fied, -fy-ing** To make French in form or character.

French kiss A kiss with lips apart and tongues touching.

French leave An informal, unauthorized, or hurried departure.

French-man (french'mən) *n. pl.* **-men** (-mən) A native or citizen of France. —**French-wom-an** (french'wŏŏm'ən) *n. Fem.* (*pl.* **-wom-en**) (-wim'ən)

French horn

French Revolution The revolution in France against the monarchy, beginning in 1789 and ending in 1799 when Napoleon assumed power.

French toast Bread dipped in a batter of beaten eggs and milk, and fried in shallow fat.

French windows A pair of casement windows attached to opposite window jambs and opening in the middle.

fre-net-ic (frə·net'ik) *adj.* Frenzied; frantic. Also **fre-net'-i-cal.** [< Gk. *phrenitis* insanity] —**fre-net'i-cal-ly** *adv.* —*Syn.* distracted, distraught, maniacal, raving, wild.

fren-zy (fren'zē) *n. pl.* **-zies** **1** Violent agitation or action. **2** A brief madness or delirium. —*v.t.* **-zied, -zy-ing** To throw into frenzy; make frantic. [< Gk. *phrenitis* delirium < *phrēn* mind]

freq. frequency; frequently; frequentative.

fre-quen-cy (frē'kwən·sē) *n. pl.* **-cies** **1** Repeated or frequent occurrence. **2** *Physics* The number of occurrences of a periodic event, as a cycle of a wave, vibration, or oscillation, per unit of time. **3** *Stat.* The number of times a given case, value, or score occurs in a set of data. **4** *Ecol.* The relative number of plant and animal species in a given region. Also **fre′quence.**

frequency modulation *Telecom.* A system in which the modulation signal causes the carrier to vary in frequency.

fre·quent (frē′kwənt) *adj.* **1** Occurring or appearing often. **2** Habitual; persistent. —*v.t.* (*usu.* fri·kwent′) **1** To visit often. **2** To be in or at often or habitually. [< L *frequens, -entis* crowded] —**fre′quen·ta′tion, fre·quent′er** *n.* — **fre′quent·ly** *adv.*

fre·quen·ta·tive (fri·kwen′tə·tiv) *Gram. adj.* Denoting repeated or habitual action: a *frequentative* verb. —*n.* An iterative or frequentative verb.

fres·co (fres′kō) *n. pl.* **·coes** or **·cos 1** The art of painting on a surface of plaster, esp. while the plaster is still moist. **2** A picture so painted. —*v.t.* **fres·coed, fres·co·ing** To paint in fresco. [Ital., fresh] —**fres′co·er, fres′co·ist** *n.*

fresh[1] (fresh) *adj.* **1** Newly made, obtained, received, etc.: *fresh* coffee; *fresh* footprints. **2** Additional; further: *fresh* supplies. **3** Not salted, pickled, smoked, etc. **4** Not spoiled, stale, musty, etc. **5** Not faded, worn, etc.: *fresh* colors. **6** Not salt: *fresh* water. **7** Pure; refreshing: *fresh* air. **8** Appearing healthy or youthful. **9** Not fatigued; active. **10** Inexperienced; unsophisticated. **11** *Meteorol.* Moderately rapid and strong: a *fresh* breeze. **12** Having a renewed supply of milk: said of a cow that has recently calved. [< OF *freis* < Gmc.] —**fresh′ly** *adv.* —**fresh′ness** *n.*

fresh[2] (fresh) *adj. Slang* Flippant; impertinent. [< G *frech* impudent]

fresh·en (fresh′ən) *v.t. & v.i.* To make or become fresh. —**fresh′en·er** *n.*

fresh·et (fresh′it) *n.* **1** A sudden flood in a stream. **2** A fresh-water stream flowing into the sea.

fresh·man (fresh′mən) *n. pl.* **·men** (-mən) **1** A first-year student in a college, high school, etc. **2** A beginner; novice. —*adj.* Of or for a freshman.

fresh·wa·ter (fresh′wô′tər, -wot′ər) *adj.* **1** Pertaining to or living in fresh water. **2** Experienced in sailing on fresh water only. **3** Of no experience; untrained. **4** Not well known; somewhat provincial.

fret[1] (fret) *v.* **fret·ted, fret·ting** *v.t.* **1** To irritate; worry; annoy. **2** To wear or eat away, as by rubbing or gnawing. **3** To form by wearing away. **4** To make rough; agitate. —*v.i.* **5** To be angry, troubled, or irritated. **6** To be worn or eaten away. **7** To become rough or agitated. —*n.* **1** The act of fretting. **2** A worn spot. **3** A state of irritation, ill temper, or vexation. [< OE *fretan* devour]

fret[2] (fret) *n.* One of a series of ridges on the fingerboard of a musical instrument, as a guitar. —*v.t.* **fret·ted, fret·ting** To provide with frets, as of a stringed instrument. [?]

fret[3] (fret) *n.* Ornamental work or an ornament, usu. characterized by angular interlocked or interlacing lines. —*v.t.* **fret·ted, fret·ting** To ornament with fretwork. [< OF *frette* a lattice, trellis]

fret·ful (fret′fəl) *adj.* Inclined to fret; peevish. —**fret′ful·ly** *adv.* —**fret′ful·ness** *n.*

Frets[3]

fret·work (fret′wûrk′) *n.* **1** Interlaced ornamental work composed of frets. **2** Perforated ornamental work.

Freu·di·an (froi′dē·ən) *adj.* Pertaining or conforming to the teachings of Sigmund Freud. —*n.* One who upholds the psychoanalytic theories of Freud. —**Freu′di·an·ism** *n.*

Fri. Friday.

fri·a·ble (frī′ə·bəl) *adj.* Easily crumbled or pulverized. [< L *friare* crumble] —**fri′a·bil′i·ty, fri′a·ble·ness** *n.*

fri·ar (frī′ər) *n.* A member of one of the mendicant religious orders, as the Dominicans or Franciscans. [< L *frater* brother]

fri·ar·y (frī′ər·ē) *n. pl.* **·ar·ies 1** A monastery. **2** The institution of friars.

fric·as·see (frik′ə·sē′, frik′ə·sē′) *n.* A dish of meat cut small, stewed, and served with gravy. —*v.t.* **·seed, ·see·ing** To make into a fricassee. [< F *fricasser* sauté]

fric·a·tive (frik′ə·tiv) *Phonet. adj.* Describing those consonants produced by the forced escape and friction of the breath through a narrow aperture, as (f), (v), (th). —*n.* A consonant so produced. [< L *fricare* rub]

fric·tion (frik′shən) *n.* **1** The rubbing of one thing against

another. **2** The force that opposes relative motion of two surfaces in contact. **3** Lack of harmony; conflict. [< L *fricare* rub] —**fric′tion·al** *adj.* —**fric′tion·al·ly** *adv.* —**Syn.** abrasion, chafing, wearing. **3** disagreement, discord, dissent.

Fri·day (frī′dē, -dā) *n.* **1** The sixth day of the week. **2** The faithful servant of Robinson Crusoe. **3** Any loyal helper. [< OE *Frigedæg* day of the Norse goddess *Frigga,* wife of Odin]

fried (frīd) *p.t. & p.p.* of FRY.

fried cake A cruller or doughnut fried in fat.

friend (frend) *n.* **1** A person whom one knows well and cherishes. **2** An acquaintance. **3** A person who promotes or favors something: a *friend* of wildlife. **4** A person of the same nation or group as oneself; ally. [< OE *frēond*]

Friend (frend) *n.* A member of the Society of Friends; a Quaker. —**Friend′ly** *adj.*

friend·less (frend′lis) *adj.* Having no friends. —**friend′-less·ness** *n.*

friend·ly (frend′lē) *adj.* **·li·er, ·li·est 1** Pertaining to, befitting, or like a friend or friendship; amicable. **2** Not hostile. **3** Helpful; favorable. —*adv.* In a friendly manner. — **friend′li·ly** *adv.* —**friend′li·ness** *n.*

friend·ship (frend′ship) *n.* **1** The state or fact of being friends. **2** Mutual affection or regard.

fri·er (frī′ər) *n.* FRYER.

Frie·sian (frē′zhən) *n.* FRISIAN.

frieze[1] (frēz) *n. Archit.* **1** The horizontal band, either plain or elaborately sculptured, running between the cornice and architrave of an entablature. **2** Any ornamented horizontal band or strip, as around a building, wall, etc. [< Med. L *frisium* fringe]

a. cornice. b. frieze.
c. architrave.

frieze[2] (frēz) *n.* A coarse woolen cloth with shaggy nap. [< MF *frise*]

frig·ate (frig′it) *n.* A square-rigged war vessel in use up until the early 19th century. [< Ital. *fregata*]

frigate bird Either of two species of large, long-winged, tropical sea birds noted for their rapacity.

fright (frīt) *n.* **1** Sudden and violent alarm or fear. **2** *Informal* Anything ugly, ridiculous, or shocking in appearance. —*v.t.* FRIGHTEN. [< OE *fryhto*]

Frigate

fright·en (frīt′n) *v.t.* **1** To throw into a state of fear or fright; terrify; scare. **2** To drive by scaring: with *away* or *off.* —*v.i.* **3** To become frightened. —**fright′en·ing·ly** *adv.*

fright·ful (frīt′fəl) *adj.* **1** Causing fear or terror. **2** Shocking; repulsive. **3** *Informal* Fearfully bad or unpleasant: a *frightful* toothache. **4** *Informal* Great; extreme: a *frightful* gossip. —**fright′ful·ly** *adv.* —**fright′ful·ness** *n.*

frig·id (frij′id) *adj.* **1** Very cold. **2** Lacking in warmth of feeling; stiff. **3** Lacking in sexual feeling or response: said of women. [< L *frigere* be cold] —**frig′id·ly** *adv.* —**fri·gid′i·ty** (fra·jid′ə·tē), **frig′id·ness** *n.* —**Syn.** **1** bitter, freezing, glacial, icy. **2** distant, stuffy, remote, reserved.

frigid zone The areas within the Arctic or the Antarctic Circle. • See ZONE.

fri·jole (frē′hōl; *Sp.* frē·hō′lā) *n. pl.* **·joles** (-hōlz, *Sp.* -hō′-lās) A bean used as food by Latin-American peoples. Also **fri′jol.** [Sp.]

frill (fril) *n.* **1** An ornamental ruffle. **2** *pl.* Affected airs or manners. **3** Any unnecessary ornament or decoration. **4** *Zool.* A ruff of feathers, hair, or membrane on certain birds or animals. —*v.t.* **1** To make into a frill. **2** To put frills on. [?] —**frill′er** *n.* —**frill′y** *adj.* (**·i·er, ·i·est**).

fringe (frinj) *n.* **1** An ornamental border or trimming of hanging threads or tassels. **2** Any outer edge or margin. —*v.t.* **fringed, fring·ing 1** To ornament with a fringe. **2** To serve as a fringe or border for. [< L *fimbria* a fringe]

fringe benefit Any of various benefits received from an employer apart from salary, as insurance, pension, vacation, etc.

frip·per·y (frip′ər·ē) *n. pl.* **·per·ies 1** Showy or gaudy clothes. **2** Showy affectation in dress, manner, etc. [< OF *freperie*]

Fris·bee (friz′bē) *n.* A light plastic disk used in play by being tossed with a spin from person to person: a trade name. Also **fris′bee.**

fri·sé (fri·zā′) *n.* An upholstery or rug fabric having a thick pile of uncut loops or of cut and uncut loops in a design. [F < *friser* to curl]

Fris·ian (frizh′ən, -ē·ən) *adj.* Of or pertaining to the Dutch province of Friesland, its people, or their language. —*n.* **1** A native or inhabitant of Friesland. **2** The West Germanic language of the Frisians.

frisk (frisk) *v.t.* **1** To move briskly or playfully. **2** *Slang* To search (someone) for weapons, smuggled goods, etc., by running the hand rapidly over his clothing. **3** *Slang* To steal from in this way. —*v.i.* **4** To leap about playfully; frolic. —*n.* **1** A playful skipping about. **2** *Slang* A frisking. [< OF *frisque* lively] —**frisk′er** *n.*

frisk·y (fris′kē) *adj.* **frisk·i·er, frisk·i·est** Lively or playful. —**frisk′i·ly** *adv.* —**frisk′i·ness** *n.*

frit·il·lar·y (frit′ə·ler′ē) *n. pl.* **·lar·ies 1** A plant of the lily family with checkered flowers. **2** One of various butterflies having brown wings with black spots. [< L *fritillus* a dice box; with ref. to the spots on dice]

frit·ter[1] (frit′ər) *v.t.* **1** To waste (time, money, etc.) little by little: usu. with *away.* **2** To break or tear into small pieces. —*n.* A small piece or fragment: a shred. [?]

frit·ter[2] (frit′ər) *n.* A small fried cake, often containing corn, fruit, or pieces of meat. [< L *frigere* fry]

fri·vol·i·ty (fri·vol′ə·tē) *n. pl.* **·ties 1** The quality of being frivolous. **2** A frivolous act, thing, or practice.

friv·o·lous (friv′ə·ləs) *adj.* **1** Petty; trivial; unimportant. **2** Lacking seriousness, sense, or reverence; trifling; silly. [< L *frivolus* silly] —**friv′o·lous·ly** *adv.* —**friv′o·lous·ness** *n.*

frizz (friz) *v.t. & v.i.* **frizzed, frizz·ing 1** To form into tight, crisp curls, as the hair. **2** To form into small, tight tufts, as the nap of cloth. —*n.* That which is frizzed, as hair. Also **friz.** [< F *friser*] —**frizz′i·ly** *adv.* —**frizz′i·ness** *n.*

friz·zle[1] (friz′əl) *v.t. & v.i.* **friz·zled, friz·zling 1** To fry or cook with a sizzling noise. **2** To make or become curled or crisp, as by frying. [Blend of FRY and SIZZLE]

friz·zle[2] (friz′əl) *v.t. & v.i.* **friz·zled, friz·zling** To frizz hair. [?]

fro (frō) *adv.* Away from; back: used in the phrase *to-and-fro.* —*prep. Scot.* From. [< ON *frā* from]

frock (frok) *n.* **1** A dress. **2** A monk's robe. **3** FROCK COAT. —*v.t.* **1** To clothe in a frock. **2** To invest with ecclesiastic office. [< OF *froc*]

frock coat A coat for men's wear, usu. double-breasted, having knee-length skirts.

frog (frog, frôg) *n.* **1** One of various small, tailless, web-footed amphibians. **2** The triangular, horny pad in the sole of a horse's foot. **3** A section of a railway track where rails cross or join. **4** An ornamental fastening on a cloak or a coat. —**a frog in one's throat** A slight hoarseness. [< OE *frogga*]

Frog

frog·gy (frog′ē, frôg′ē) *adj.* **·gi·er, ·gi·est** Of, like, or abounding in frogs. —**frog′gi·ness** *n.*

frog·man (frog′mən, -man′, frôg′-) *n. pl.* **·men** (-mən, -men′) A swimmer or diver equipped for underwater work, as with a wet suit, flippers, and a breathing apparatus, used esp. for wartime demolition.

frol·ic (frol′ik) *n.* **1** A scene of gaiety. **2** A gay act; a prank. **3** A party. —*v.i.* **frol·icked, frol·ick·ing** To play merrily; gambol. —*adj.* Full of mirth or playfulness; merry. [< MDu. *vro* glad] —**frol′ick·er** *n.*

frol·ic·some (frol′ik·səm) *adj.* Full of frolic; playful: also **frol′ick·y.** —**Syn.** blithe, gleeful, lighthearted, merry.

from (frum, from; *unstressed* frəm) *prep.* **1** Starting at (a particular place or time): the plane *from* Chicago. **2** Out of: She drew a pistol *from* her purse. **3** Not near to or in contact with: We kept him *from* her. **4** Out of the control or authority of: released *from* custody. **5** Out of the totality of: six cigarettes *from* the pack. **6** As being other or another than: He couldn't tell me *from* my brother. **7** Outside or beyond the possibility of: We kept them *from* leaving. **8** Because of: Skill comes *from* practice. **9** With (some person, place, or thing) as the instrument, maker, or source: a note *from* your mother. [< OE *fram, from*]

frond (frond) *n. Bot.* **1** A leaflike expansion, as the so-called leaf of ferns and seaweeds. **2** The leaf of a palm. [L *frons, frondis* leaf]

front (frunt) *n.* **1** The forward part or surface of anything. **2** The position directly ahead or before a person or thing: the steps in *front* of the church. **3** A face of a building; usu. the face on the entrance side. **4** The line of contact of opposing armies; also, a battle zone. **5** Land facing a road, body of water, etc.; frontage. **6** A coalition of diverse forces working for a common aim: a labor *front.* **7** The forehead or face. **8** Bearing or demeanor, esp. in facing a problem. **9** Outward behavior contrasted with inner feelings: a bold *front.* **10** *Informal* An outward semblance of wealth or position. **11** A person chosen for his prestige to serve as an official of an organization; a figurehead. **12** A person, group, or business serving as a cover for underhanded activities. **13** A starched shirt front, worn by men with formal clothes. **14** In hotels, the bellhop first in line. **15** *Meteorol.* The boundary between masses of cold and warm air. —*adj.* **1** Of, pertaining to or viewed from the front. **2** Situated on, at, or in the front. **3** *Phonet.* Describing those vowels produced with the front of the tongue raised toward the hard palate, as (ē) in *feed.* —*v.t.* **1** To have the front opposite to; face. **2** CONFRONT. **3** To furnish with a front. **4** To serve as a front for. —*v.i.* **5** To face in a specific direction. **6** To be or serve as a front. [< L *frons, frontis* forehead]

front·age (frun′tij) *n.* **1** The front part of a building. **2** The land between a building and the street. **3** The length of something that fronts. **4** The fact or action of facing in a certain direction.

fron·tal (frun′təl) *adj.* **1** Of, pertaining to, on, or at the front. **2** Of or relating to the forehead. —**fron′tal·ly** *adv.*

fron·tier (frun·tir′) *n.* **1** The part of a nation's territory that borders on another country. **2** That portion of a country bordering on the wilderness, newly or thinly settled by pioneer settlers. **3** Any region of thought or knowledge not yet explored: a *frontier* of science. —*adj.* Of, from, inhabiting, or characteristic of a frontier. [< OF *front* front]

fron·tiers·man (frun·tirz′mən) *n. pl.* **·men** (-mən) One who lives on the frontier.

fron·tis·piece (frun′tis·pēs′, fron′-) *n.* **1** An illustration or picture facing the title page of a book. **2** An ornamental front; a façade. [< L *frons,* forehead + *specere* look at]

front-page (frunt′pāj′) *adj.* Of great significance or importance, meriting placement on the front page of a publication.

frost (frôst, frost) *n.* **1** Frozen water vapor or dew. **2** The action of freezing. **3** A temperature below the freezing point. **4** Coldness and austerity of manner. **5** *Slang* A failure. —*v.t.* **1** To cover with frost. **2** To damage or kill by frost. **3** To apply frosting to. [< OE] —**frost′less** *adj.*

frost·bite (frôst′bīt′, frost′-) *n.* The condition of having some part of the body partially frozen. —*v.t.* **·bit, ·bit·ten, ·bit·ing** To injure by partial freezing.

frost·ing (frôs′ting, fros′-) *n.* **1** A mixture of sugar, eggs, butter, etc., used to cover a cake. **2** The rough surface produced on metal, glass, etc., in imitation of frost.

frost·y (frôs′tē, fros′-) *adj.* **frost·i·er, frost·i·est 1** Attended with frost; freezing. **2** Covered with or as with frost; hoary. **3** Cold and distant in manner. —**frost′i·ly** *adv.* —**frost′i·ness** *n.*

froth (frôth, froth) *n.* **1** A mass of bubbles; foam. **2** Something trivial or frivolous. —*v.t.* (frôth, froth) **1** To cause

---

add, āce, câre, pälm; end, ēven; it, īce; odd, ōpen, ôrder; tŏŏk, pōōl; up, bûrn; ə = *a* in *above, u* in *focus;* yōō = *u* in *fuse;* oil; pout; check; go; ring; thin; this; zh, *vision.* < derived from; ? origin uncertain or unknown.

to foam. **2** To cover with froth. **3** To give forth in the form of foam. —*v.i.* **4** To form or give off froth; foam. [< ON *frodha*]

froth·y (frô'thē, -thē, froth'ē, froth'-) *adj.* froth·i·er, froth·l·est **1** Consisting of, covered with, or full of froth. **2** Frivolous; trivial. —**froth'i·ly** *adv.* —**froth'i·ness** *n.*

frou-frou (froo'froo') *n.* **1** A rustling, as of silk. **2** *Informal* Affected elegance; fanciness. [F]

fro·ward (frō'ərd, -wərd) *adj.* Disobedient; perverse. [< FRO + -WARD] —**fro'ward·ly** *adv.* —**fro'ward·ness** *n.*

frown (froun) *v.i.* **1** To contract the brow, as in displeasure or concentration; scowl. **2** To show one's displeasure or disapproval: with *on* or *upon.* —*v.t.* **3** To make known (one's displeasure, disgust, etc.) by contracting one' s brow. **4** To silence, rebuke, etc., by or as by a frown. —*n.* **1** A wrinkling of the brow, as in anger; a scowl. **2** Any manifestation of displeasure. [< OF *froigner*] —**frown'er** *n.* —**frown'ing·ly** *adv.*

frow·zled (frou'zəld) *adj.* Unkempt; disheveled.

frow·zy (frou'zē) *adj.* ·zi·er, ·zi·est Slovenly in appearance; unkempt; untidy. Also **frow'sy.** [?] —**frow'zi·ness** *n.*

froze (frōz) *p.t.* of FREEZE.

fro·zen (frō'zən) *p.p.* of FREEZE. —*adj.* **1** Having become ice or covered over with ice. **2** Killed or damaged by freezing. **3** Preserved by freezing. **4** Subject to extreme cold, as a climate or region. **5** Made motionless, as by fear. **6** Unfriendly; cold. **7** Not readily converted into cash: *frozen* assets. **8** Arbitrarily maintained at a given level: said of prices, wages, etc.

frozen custard A smooth-textured frozen dairy product, consisting of skim milk, sweetener, and flavoring, usu. served in an ice-cream cone; ice milk.

FRS Federal Reserve System.

F.R.S. Fellow of the Royal Society.

frt. freight.

fruc·ti·fy (fruk'tə·fī) *v.* ·fied, ·fy·ing *v.t.* **1** To make fruitful; fertilize. —*v.i.* **2** To bear fruit. [< L *fructus* fruit + *facere* do, make] —**fruc·tif'er·ous** *adj.* —**fruc'ti·fi·ca'tion** *n.*

fruc·tose (fruk'tōs) *n.* A simple sugar occurring in sweet fruit, honey, etc.

frug (froog) *n.* An energetic dance characterized by rhythmic twisting movements of the body. —*v.i.* **frugged, frug·ging** To perform this dance. [?] —**frug·ger** *n.*

fru·gal (froo'gəl) *adj.* **1** Exercising economy; saving; sparing. **2** Meager or inexpensive. [< L *frugalis*] —**fru·gal'i·ty** *n.* —**fru'gal·ly** *adv.* —Syn. **1** parsimonious, provident, thrifty, stinting. **2** mean, scanty.

fruit (froot) *n. pl.* **fruits** or, collectively, **fruit 1** The seed-bearing part of a plant. **2** An edible, usu. seed-bearing plant product, esp. a sweet and succulent one. **3** *Usu. pl.* Any natural product of value to man: the *fruits* of the earth. **4** Offspring; issue. **5** A consequence, outcome, or result; the *fruits* of labor. —*v.t. & v.i.* To bear or make bear fruit. [< OF < L *fructus*]

fruit·age (froo'tij) *n.* **1** Fruit collectively. **2** The state, process, or time of producing fruit. **3** Any result or effect of action.

fruit·er (froo'tər) *n.* **1** A vessel that carries fruit. **2** A fruit-bearing tree.

fruit·er·er (froo'tər·ər) *n. Chiefly Brit.* A dealer in fruits.

fruit fly Any of various flies whose larvae feed on fruit, esp. drosophila, a small fly used in genetic research.

fruit·ful (froot'fəl) *adj.* **1** Bearing fruit or offspring abundantly; prolific. **2** Producing results; productive. —**fruit'ful·ly** *adv.* —**fruit'ful·ness** *n.*

fru·i·tion (froo·ish'ən) *n.* **1** The bearing of fruit. **2** The yielding of natural or expected results; fulfillment. **3** Enjoyment. [< L < *frui* enjoy]

fruit·less (froot'lis) *adj.* **1** Yielding no fruit; barren. **2** Yielding no results; useless; vain. —**fruit'less·ly** *adv.* —**fruit'less·ness** *n.*

fruit sugar FRUCTOSE.

fruit·y (froo'tē) *adj.* **fruit·i·er, fruit·i·est 1** Like fruit in taste, flavor, etc. **2** Full of interest; intriguing. **3** Rich or sweet in tone or manner, often considered flusome. **4** *Slang* Odd; queer; crazy. —**fruit'i·ness** *n.*

frump (frump) *n.* A dowdily dressed, usu. unattractive woman. [? < MDu. *verrompelen* wrinkle] —**trump'ish,**

trump'y *adj.* (·i·er, ·i·est) —**frump'ish·ly, trump'i·ly** *adv.* —**frump'ish·ness, frump'i·ness** *n.*

frus·trate (frus'trāt) *v.t.* ·trat·ed, ·trat·ing **1** To keep (someone) from doing or achieving something; defeat the efforts or hopes of. **2** To keep, as plans or schemes, from being fulfilled; thwart. [< L *frustrari* disappoint] —Syn. **2** defeat, foil, balk, nullify.

frus·tra·tion (frus·trā'shən) *n.* **1** The act of frustrating or the state of being frustrated. **2** An instance of being frustrated. **3** Something that frustrates.

fry¹ (frī) *v.t. & v. i.* **fried, fry·ing** To cook or be cooked in hot fat, usu. over direct heat. —*n. pl.* **fries 1** A dish of anything fried. **2** A social occasion, usu. a picnic, at which foods are fried and eaten: a fish *fry.* [< L *frigere*]

fry² (frī) *n. pl.* **fry 1** Young fish. **2** Small adult fish, esp. in large numbers. **3** Young offspring. [? < OF *frier* spawn]

fry·er (frī'ər) *n.* **1** One who or that which fries. **2** A young chicken, suitable for frying.

frying pan A metal pan, usu. shallow and with a long handle, for frying foods. Also **fry pan.**

ft. feet; foot; fort.

FTC, F.T.C. Federal Trade Commission.

fth, fthm. fathom.

ft.-lb. foot-pound.

fuch·sia (fyoo'shə, -shē-ə) *n.* **1** A plant related to the evening primrose, having red, pink, white, or purple drooping flowers. **2** A bright bluish red. —*adj.* Bright bluish red. [< L. *Fuchs,* 1501–66, German botanist.]

fud·dle (fud'l) *v.* ·dled, ·dling *v. t.* To confuse or make stupid with drink. —*v.i.* To tipple. [?]

fud·dy-dud·dy (fud'ē-dud'ē) *n. pl.* ·dud·dies *Informal* **1** An old-fashioned person. **2** A faultfinding, fussy person. [?]

fudge (fuj) *n.* **1** A soft confection made of butter, sugar, chocolate, etc. **2** Humbug; nonsense. —*v.i.* **fudged, fudg·ing 1** To violate or ignore a rule or customary practice. **2** To fail to take a stand; equivocate; hedge. —*v.t.* **3** To make, adjust, or fit together in a clumsy or dishonest manner. **4** To fail to make clear or be decisive about. [?]

fu·el (fyoo'əl) *n.* **1** Combustible matter burned as a source of energy. **2** An element, as plutonium, used in a nuclear reaction to provide energy. **3** Whatever feeds or sustains any expenditure, outlay, passion, or excitement. —*v.t. & v.i.* **fu·eled** or **fu·elled, fu·el·ing** or **fu·el·ling** To supply with or take in fuel. [< OF *fouaille* ult. < L *focus* hearth] —**fu·el·er, fu·el·ler** *n.*

fu·gi·tive (fyoo'jə·tiv) *adj.* **1** Fleeing or having fled, as from pursuit, danger, arrest, etc. **2** Not fixed or lasting; transient. **3** Wandering; shifting. **4** Treating of subjects of passing interest; occasional. —*n.* One who or that which flees; a runaway or deserter. [< L *fugere* flee] —**fu'gi·tive·ly** *adv.* —**fu'gi·tive·ness** *n.*

fugue (fyoog) *n.* **1** *Music* A form or composition in polyphonic style based upon one, two, or more themes that are introduced by several voices or instruments in turn and are treated contrapuntally. **2** *Psychiatry* A period during which a patient suffers loss of memory, and, after recovery, recalls nothing of the amnesic period. [< F < Ital. *fuga* < L, flight]

Füh·rer (fyoor'ər, *Ger.* fü'rər) *German* Leader: a title applied to Adolf Hitler. Also **Fuehr'er.**

-ful *suffix* **1** Full of; characterized by: *joyful.* **2** Able to; tending to: *helpful.* **3** Having the character of: *manful.* **4** The quantity or number that will fill: *cupful.* [< OE < *full* full] • Nouns ending in *-ful* form the plural by adding *-s,* as in *cupfuls, spoonfuls.*

ful·crum (fool'krəm) *n. pl.* ·crums or ·cra (-krə) **1** The support on or against which a lever rests. **2** Any prop or support

ful·fill (fool·fil') *v.t.* **1** To perform, as a duty or command. **2** To bring into effect or to consummation. **3** To finish; come to the end of. **4** To fill the requirements of; satisfy, as the conditions of a contract. Also **ful·fil'** (·filled, ·fill·ing). [< OE

Fulcrum

fulfyllan] —**ful·fill'er** *n.* —**ful·fill'ment, ful·fil'ment** *n.*

ful·gent (ful'jənt) *adj.* Beaming or shining brightly radiant. [< L *fulgere* to gleam] —**ful′gen·cy** *n.* —**ful′gent·ly** *adv.*

full[1] (fo͞ol) *adj.* 1 Containing or holding all that is possible or usual; filled. 2 Complete; whole; entire: to charge the *full* price. 3 Total; absolute: a *full* stop. 4 Having many or abounding in: with *of*: *full* of errors. 5 Maximum in size, intensity, extent, degree, etc.: *full* speed. 6 Containing much information, detail, etc.: a *full* report. 7 Filled or satisfied, as with food or drink. 8 Having resonance, depth, and volume: a *full* tone. 9 Having the face wholly illuminated: said of the moon. • See MOON. 10 Having risen to its highest level: said of the tide. 11 Plump or rounded out: a *full* face. 12 Having ample, loose folds: a *full* skirt. 13 Engrossed in or affected by: *full* of ideas; *full* of fear. 14 Filled with emotion: My heart is *full*. —*n.* The maximum degree, extent, size, etc. —*adv.* 1 To the utmost degree or extent; completely. 2 Directly. —*v.t.* 1 To make full; gather, as a sleeve. —*v.i.* 2 To become full. [< OE *ful*]

full[2] (fo͞ol) *v.t. & v.i.* To make or become thicker and more compact, by shrinking: said of wool cloth. [Back formation < FULLER, *n.*]

full·back (fo͞ol′bak′) *n.* In American football, one of the backfield, traditionally the player farthest from the line of scrimmage.

full-blood·ed (fo͞ol′blud′id) *adj.* 1 Of pure or unmixed blood; thoroughbred: also **full′-blood′**. 2 Vigorous.

full-blown (fo͞ol′blōn′) *adj.* 1 Fully unfolded from the bud; in full bloom. 2 Completely developed.

full-dress (fo͞ol′dres′) *adj.* 1 Characterized by or requiring full dress: a *full-dress* dinner. 2 Complete and thorough.

full dress Formal day or evening clothes.

full·er (fo͞ol′ər) *n.* One who fulls and cleanses cloth. [< OE *fullere* < L *fullo*]

fuller's earth (fo͞ol′ərz) An absorbent clay used as a filter and in removing grease from wool.

full-fledged (fo͞ol′flejd′) *adj.* 1 Having grown feathers sufficient for flying. 2 Completely developed, trained, experienced, etc. 3 Of full rank.

full-grown (fo͞ol′grōn′) *adj.* Completely grown.

full moon 1 The moon when it shows its whole disk illuminated. 2 The time when this occurs.

full·ness (fo͞ol′nis) *n.* The state or quality of being full. Also **ful′ness.**

full-scale (fo͞ol′skāl′) *adj.* 1 Unreduced; scaled to actual size: a *full-scale* drawing. 2 All-out: a *full-scale* attack.

full stop A period ending a sentence.

full-time (fo͞ol′tīm′) *adj.* Working or involving full time: a *full-time* student.

full time The amount of time thought of as being equal to all of a person's normal or regular working hours: to go to school *full time*.

ful·ly (fo͞ol′ē) *adv.* 1 Completely; entirely. 2 Sufficiently. 3 At least: *fully* a hundred people.

ful·mi·nate (ful′mə-nāt) *v.* **·nat·ed, ·nat·ing** *v.i.* 1 To explode or detonate violently. 2 To shout accusations, threats, etc.; denounce. —*v.t.* 3 To cause to explode violently. 4 To shout (accusations, threats, etc.). —*n. Chem.* An explosively unstable compound. [< L *fulmen, fulminis* lightning] —**ful′mi·na′tion, ful′mi·na′tor** *n.* —**ful′mi·na·to·ry** (-tôr′ē, -tō′rē) *adj.*

ful·some (fo͞ol′səm, ful′-) *adj.* Offensive and distasteful because excessive: *fulsome* praise. [< FULL, *adj.* + -SOME] —**ful′some·ly** *adv.* —**ful′some·ness** *n.*

fum·ble (fum′bəl) *v.* **fum·bled, fum·bling** *v.i.* 1 To search for something blindly or clumsily; grope: with *for* or *after*. 2 To do something clumsily or nervously. 3 To handle or touch something nervously or awkwardly. 4 In sports, to fail to catch or hold the ball. —*v.t.* 5 To handle clumsily or awkwardly. 6 To do (something) badly or awkwardly; bungle. 7 To make (one's way) unsteadily. 8 In sports, to fumble (the ball). —*n.* The act or an instance of fumbling. [Prob. < Scand.] —**fum′bler** *n.*

fume (fyo͞om) *n.* 1 Any poisonous, irritating, or odorous smoke or vapor. 2 Furious anger. —*v.* **fumed, fum·ing** *v.i.*

1 To give off fumes. 2 To pass off in a mist or vapor. 3 To express or show anger, irritation, etc. —*v.t.* 4 To expose to fumes. [< L *fumus* smoke] —**fum′er** *n.*

fu·mi·gant (fyo͞o′mə·gənt) *n.* Any gaseous disinfectant or insecticide.

fu·mi·gate (fyo͞o′mə·gāt) *v.t.* **·gat·ed, ·gat·ing** To subject to smoke or fumes, as for killing vermin. [< L *fumus* smoke + *agere* to drive] —**fu′mi·ga′tion, fu′mi·ga′tor** *n.*

fun (fun) *n.* 1 Amusement; mirth; enjoyment. 2 One who or that which provides such amusement or enjoyment. 3 Playful, amusing activity. —*adj. Informal* Providing amusement or enjoyment. —*v.i.* **funned, fun·ning** *Informal* To indulge in fun; make sport; jest. [?< ME *fonne* a fool]

func·tion (fungk′shən) *n.* 1 The specific, natural, or proper action or activity of something. 2 One's appropriate or assigned duties or activities. 3 The normal action of any organ or set of organs: the respiratory *function.* 4 A public or official ceremony or entertainment. 5 *Math.* A variable whose value depends on the value of another variable. —*v.i.* 1 To perform as expected or required; operate properly. 2 To perform the role of something else. [< L *fungi* perform]

func·tion·al (fungk′shən·əl) *adj.* 1 Of or belonging to a function or functions. 2 Designed for or suited to a particular operation or use: *functional* architecture. 3 *Med.* Affecting performance only; not traceable to a physical cause. —**func′tion·al·ly** *adv.*

func·tion·ar·y (fungk′shən·er′ē) *n. pl.* **·ar·ies** A person who serves in a particular capacity, esp. one who works in a governmental or political position.

fund (fund) *n.* 1 A sum of money or stock of convertible wealth employed in, set aside for, or available for a business enterprise or other purpose. 2 *pl.* Money in general: out of *funds.* 3 A reserve store; an ample stock: a *fund* of humor. —*v.t.* 1 To convert into a more or less permanent debt bearing a fixed rate of interest. 2 To furnish a fund for. 3 To amass. [< L *fundus* bottom] —**fund′a·ble** *adj.*

fun·da·ment (fun′də·mənt) *n.* The buttocks; also, the anus. [< L *fundus* bottom, land]

fun·da·men·tal (fun′də·men′təl) *adj.* 1 Basic; indispensable; essential: *fundamental* principles. 2 Primary; chief: his *fundamental* error. 3 *Physics* Designating that component of a periodic oscillation that has the lowest frequency. —*n.* 1 Anything that serves as the foundation or basis of a system, as a truth, law, or principle. 2 *Music* The root of a chord. 3 *Physics* The fundamental component of a periodic oscillation. —**fun′da·men′tal·ly** *adv.*

fun·da·men·tal·ism (fun′də·men′təl·iz′əm) *n.* 1 *Often cap.* The belief that all statements made in the Bible are literally true. 2 *Often cap. U.S.* A movement among Protestants holding that such belief is essential to Christian faith. 3 Strict adherence to or observance of basic precepts. —**fun′da·men′tal·ist** *n.*

fu·ner·al (fyo͞o′nər·əl) *n.* 1 The rites and ceremonies preceding and accompanying burial; obsequies. 2 A gathering or procession of persons on the occasion of a burial. —*adj.* Pertaining to, suitable for, or used at a funeral. [< L *funus, funeris*]

funeral home A business establishment equipped to prepare the dead for burial or cremation, and often having facilities for funeral services. Also **funeral parlor.**

fu·ne·re·al (fyo͞o·nir′ē·əl) *adj.* 1 Pertaining to or suitable for a funeral. 2 Mournful; gloomy. —**fu·ne′re·al·ly** *adv.*

fun·gi·cide (fun′jə·sīd, fung′gə-) *n.* A compound that kills fungi or destroys their spores. —**fun′gi·ci′dal** *adj.*

fun·goid (fung′goid) *adj.* Resembling a mushroom or fungus. —*n.* A fungus.

fun·gous (fung′gəs) *adj.* Of, pertaining to, or like a fungus. Also **fun·gal.**

fun·gus (fung′gəs) *n. pl.* **fun·gus·es** or **fun·gi** (fun′jī, fung′-gī) 1 Any of a group of plants that reproduce by spores and have no stems, leaves, roots, or chlorophyll, comprising the mushrooms, puffballs, molds, smuts, etc. 2 Anything that springs up rapidly like a fungus. —*adj.* Fungous. [< L, a mushroom]

fu·nic·u·lar (fyo͞o·nik′yə·lər) *adj.* Pulled by a cable. —*n.*

A railway on which cars are pulled up or lowered by a cable. Also **funicular railway**. [< L *funiculus* small cord]

funk¹ (fungk) *n. Informal* **1** Cowardly fright; panic. **2** Low spirits; depression. —*v.t.* **1** To shrink from; be afraid of. **2** To frighten; scare. —*v.i.* **3** To shrink through fear or aversion; try to back out. [? < Flemish *fonck* fear]

funk² (fungk) *n. Slang* Jazz music that has an earthy, blues quality.

funk·y (fungk′ē) *adj.* **funk·i·er, funk·i·est 1** Having a foul odor; malodorous. **2** *Slang* **a** Having a quality expressive of jazz blues; soulful; earthy. **b** Earthily sensual. **c** Conspicuously individual; expressively idiosyncratic, as in dress.

fun·nel (fun′əl) *n.* **1** A wide-mouthed conical vessel, terminating in a tube, for filtering, decanting, etc. **2** A smoke pipe, chimney, or flue. **3** A smokestack on a steamship. **4** Any funnellike part or process. —*v.t. & v.i.* **·neled or ·nelled, ·nel·ing or ·nel·ling** To pass or move through or as through a funnel. [< L *infundibulum* < *in-* into + *fundere* pour]

Funnels

fun·ny (fun′ē) *adj.* **·ni·er, ·ni·est 1** Affording fun; comical; ludicrous; laughable. **2** *Informal* Puzzling; strange; unusual. —*n. pl.* **·nies** *Informal* **1** Something funny. **2** *pl.* A comic strip. —**fun′ni·ly** *adv.* —**fun′ni·ness** *n.* —**Syn.** *adj.* **1** amusing, humorous, droll, farcical, jolly, jovial.

funny bone A sensitive spot at the elbow where the ulnar nerve is near the surface.

fur (fûr) *n.* **1** The soft, fine, hairy coat covering the skin of many mammals. **2** The skin and hair of fur-bearing animals, esp. when prepared for use in making garments rugs, etc. **3** *Often pl.* Apparel made of such skins. **4** Any fuzzy covering, as coating on the tongue. —*v.* **furred, fur·ring** *v.t.* **1** To cover, line, trim or clothe with fur. **2** To apply furring to, as for lathing. —*v.i.* **3** To become coated, as the tongue. [< OF *forrer* line with fur < Gmc.]

fur·be·low (fûr′bə·lō) *n.* **1** A plaited flounce or ruffle. **2** Any showy ornament. —*v.t.* To decorate elaborately or fussily. [< F *falbala* fringe, flounce]

fur·bish (fûr′bish) *v.t.* **1** To make bright by rubbing; burnish. **2** To restore to brightness or beauty; renovate: often with *up.* [< OF *forbir*] —**fur′bish·er** *n.*

fur·cate (fûr′kāt) *v.i.* **·cat·ed, ·cat·ing** To separate into diverging parts; fork. —*adj.* Forked: also **fur′cat·ed.** [< L *furca* fork] —**fur′cate·ly** *adv.* —**fur·ca′tion** *n.*

Fu·ries (fyoor′ēz) *Gk. Myth.* The three goddesses who took vengeance on unpunished criminals.

fu·ri·ous (fyoor′ē·əs) *adj.* **1** Full of anger; raging. **2** Violent; fierce. **3** Very great; excessive. —**fu′ri·ous·ly** *adv.* —**fu′ri·ous·ness** *n.* —**Syn. 1** irate, fuming, angry, wrathful, boiling. **2** wild, vehement, turbulent, frenzied, frantic, stormy.

furl (fûrl) *v.t.* **1** To roll up and make secure, as a sail to a spar. —*v.i.* **2** To become furled. —*n.* **1** The act of furling. **2** Something furled. [< OF *fermlier* < *ferm* close + *lier* bind]

fur·long (fûr′lông, -long) *n.* A measure of length, one-eighth of a mile or 220 yards. [< OE *furh* furrow + *lang* long]

fur·lough (fûr′lō) *n.* An authorized leave of absence, esp. one granted to a person in the armed forces. —*v.t.* To grant a furlough to. [< Du. *verlof*]

fur·nace (fûr′nis) *n.* **1** A chamber for heating, fusing, hardening, etc., usu. by heat derived from burning a fuel. **2** A chamber in which fuel is burned to heat a building. [< L *fornax*]

fur·nish (fûr′nish) *v.t.* **1** To equip, or fit out, as with fittings or furniture. **2** To supply; provide. [< OF *furnir*] —**fur′nish·er** *n.*

fur·nish·ings (fûr′nish·ingz) *n. pl.* **1** Articles of clothing and accessories. **2** Furniture, carpets, etc., as for a home or office.

fur·ni·ture (fûr′nə·chər) *n.* **1** Movable household articles, such as chairs, tables, bureaus, beds, etc. **2** Necessary equipment, as for a ship, shop, etc. [< F *fourniture* < *fournir* furnish]

fu·ror (fyoor′ôr) *n.* **1** Fury. **2** Great excitement or enthusiasm. **3** An object of enthusiasm; a fad; a craze. [< L *furere* to rage]

furred (fûrd) *adj.* **1** Having fur. **2** Made, trimmed, or lined with fur. **3** Wearing fur. **4** Coated, as the tongue.

fur·ri·er (fûr′ē·ər, -yər) *n.* **1** A person who makes, sells, repairs, or stores fur garments. **2** A person who processes fur, as for garments.

fur·ring (fûr′ing) *n.* **1** Fur linings or trimmings. **2** Trimming or lining with fur. **3** A coating, as on the tongue. **4** The act of applying strips of wood or metal to create a level surface or air spaces. **5** The strips of wood or metal so used.

fur·row (fûr′ō) *n.* **1** A trench made in the earth by a plow. **2** One of the grooves in the face of a millstone. **3** Any groove or wrinkle. —*v.t.* **1** To make furrows in; plow. **2** To make wrinkles in, as the brow. —*v.i.* **3** To become wrinkled. [< OE *furh*] —**fur′row·er** *n.*

fur·ry (fûr′ē) *adj.* **fur·ri·er, fur·ri·est 1** Of or like fur. **2** Covered with or clad in fur. —**fur′ri·ness** *n.*

fur·ther (fûr′thər) Comparative of FAR. —*adv.* **1** At or to a more distant or remote point in space or time. **2** To a greater degree; more. **3** In addition; besides; also. —*adj.* **1** More distant or advanced in time or degree. **2** Wider or fuller; additional. **3** More distant in space; farther. —*v.t.* To help forward; promote. [< OE *furthra*] —**fur′ther·er** *n.*

fur·ther·ance (fûr′thər·əns) *n.* **1** The act of furthering; advancement. **2** That which furthers.

fur·ther·more (fûr′thər·môr′, -mōr′) *adv.* In addition; moreover.

fur·ther·most (fûr′thər·mōst′) *adj.* Furthest or most remote.

fur·thest (fûr′thist) Superlative of FAR. —*adv.* **1** At or to the most distant or remote point in space or time. **2** To the greatest degree. —*adj.* **1** Most distant, remote, or advanced in time or degree. **2** Most distant in space.

fur·tive (fûr′tiv) *adj.* **1** Done on the sly; secret; stealthy. **2** Not direct; evasive. [< F < L *fur* a thief] —**fur′tive·ly** *adv.* —**fur′tive·ness** *n.*

fu·ry (fyoor′ē) *n. pl.* **·ries 1** A state or fit of violent anger or rage. **2** Violent action or agitation; fierceness; frenzy. **3** A person of violent temper, esp. a woman. [< L *furere* rave]

furze (fûrz) *n.* A spiny evergreen leguminous shrub having yellow flowers. [< OE *fyrs*] —**furz′y** *adj.*

fuse¹ (fyooz) *n.* **1** A treated cord, ribbon, etc., used to carry fire to explosives. **2** FUZE. [< L *fusus* a spindle]

fuse² (fyooz) *v.t. & v.i.* **fused, fus·ing 1** To liquefy by heat; melt. **2** To join or cause to join as if by melting together. —*n. Electr.* An enclosed length of fusible metal set in a circuit to melt and open the circuit in case of an overload. [< L *fusus,* pp. of *fundere* pour]

fu·see (fyoo·zē′) *n.* **1** A wooden match not extinguishable by wind. **2** A flare used as a signal on a railroad, by truck drivers, etc. [< L *fusus* spindle]

fu·se·lage (fyoo′sə·läzh, -zə-) *n. Aeron.* The part of an airplane that accomodates the crew, passengers, etc., and to which the lifting and control surfaces are fastened. [F < L *fusus* a spindle] • See AIRPLANE.

fu·sel oil (fyoo′zəl, -səl) A volatile, poisonous liquid, consisting of a mixture of complex alcohols, produced in small amounts in the production of ethyl alcohol by fermentation. Also **fu′sel.** [< G *Fusel* inferior spirits]

fu·si·ble (fyoo′zə·bəl) *adj.* Capable of being fused or melted by heat. —**fu′si·bil′i·ty, fu′si·ble·ness** *n.* —**fu′si·bly** *adv.*

fu·si·form (fyoo′zə·fôrm) *adj.* Shaped like a spindle. [< L *fusus* spindle + -FORM]

fu·sil (fyoo′zəl) *n.* A flintlock musket. [< OF *foisil* a steel for striking sparks, ult. < L *focus* a hearth]

fu·si·lier (fyoo′zə·lir′) *n.* **1** A soldier armed with a fusil. **2** A title of certain British regiments whose soldiers formerly carried fusils. Also **fu′si·leers′.** [F]

fu·si·lade (fyoo′zə·lād′, -sə-, -läd′) *n.* **1** A simultaneous discharge of firearms. **2** Any rapid volley, as of questions. —*v.t.* **·lad·ed, ·lad·ing** To attack or kill by a fusillade. Also **fu′si·lade′** [< F *fusil* fusil]

fu·sion (fyoo′zhən) *n.* **1** The act of blending, or the state of being blended throughout. **2** The coalescing of two political parties, or the state of coalescence: often used attributively: a *fusion* ticket. **3** The act or process of changing from a solid into a liquid by the agency of heat;

melting. **4** *Physics* A nuclear reaction in which light nuclei fuse into those of a heavier element, with the release of great energy. [<L *fusus*, pp. of *fundere* pour]

fu·sion·ism (fyoo′zhən·iz′əm) *n.* The doctrine, advocacy, or practice of fusion in politics. —**fu′sion·ist** *n.*

fuss (fus) *n.* **1** Nervous agitation or excitement, esp. over trivial matters; bustle; ado. **2** A quarrel. **3** An excessive praising of something. **4** An objection or protest. —*v.i.* **1** To make a fuss. **2** To fret or fidget, as a baby. —*v.t.* **3** *Informal* To bother or perplex with trifles. [?] —**fuss′er** *n.*

fuss·budg·et (fus′buj′it) *n. Informal* One who is fussy or too particular.

fuss·y (fus′ē) *adj.* **fuss·i·er, fuss·i·est 1** Inclined to fuss; fidgety; fretful. **2** Troublesome to do or make. **3** Overly ornate or detailed. —**fuss′i·ly** *adv.* —**fuss′i·ness** *n.*

fus·tian (fus′chən) *n.* **1** Formerly, a kind of stout cloth made of cotton and flax; now, a coarse, twilled cotton fabric, such as corduroy or velveteen. **2** Pretentious verbiage; bombast. —*adj.* **1** Made of fustian. **2** Pompous; bombastic. [<Med. L]

fust·y (fus′tē) *adj.* **fust·i·er, fust·i·est 1** Musty; moldy; rank. **2** Old-fashioned; fogeyish. [<OF *fuste*, barrel odor] —**fust′i·ly** *adv.* —**fust′i·ness** *n.*

fu·tile (fyoo′təl, -til; *esp. Brit.* -tīl) *adj.* **1** Of no avail; done in vain; useless. **2** Frivolous; trivial: *futile* chatter. [<L *futilis* pouring out easily, useless] —**fu′tile·ly** *adv.* —**fu′tile·ness, fu·til′i·ty** *n.*

fu·ton (foo′ton) *n.* A tightly stuffed mat, used for sleeping directly on the floor. [<Jap.]

fu·ture (fyoo′chər) *n.* **1** The time yet to come. **2** That which will be or happen in time to come. **3** The condition, rank, status, etc., of a person or thing in time to come, esp. a condition of success or achievement: a business with a *future.* **4** *Usu. pl.* Any security sold or bought upon an agreement for future delivery. **5** *Gram.* **a** A verb tense denoting action that will take place at some time to come. **b** A verb in this tense. —*adj.* **1** Such as will or may be in time to come. **2** Pertaining to or expressing time to come. [<L *futurus*]

fu·tur·is·tic (fyoo′chər·is′tik) *adj.* Of or pertaining to the future. —**fu′tur·is′ti·cal·ly** *adv.*

fu·tu·ri·ty (fyoo·t′yoor′ə·tē) *n. pl.* **·ties 1** The future. **2** The state or quality of being future. **3** The people of the future. **4** A future possibility.

fuze (fyooz) *n.* **1** A mechanical or electrical device that fires the explosive charge of a shell, bomb, grenade, etc. **2** FUSE¹. [Var. of FUSE¹]

fu·zee (fyoo·zē′) *n.* FUSEE.

fuzz¹ (fuz) *n.* Fine particles of down, wool, vegetable fiber, etc. —*v.t. & v.i.* To cover or become covered with fuzz. [?]

fuzz² (fuz) *n. Slang* Police. [?]

fuzz·y (fuz′ē) *adj.* **fuzz·i·er, fuzz·i·est 1** Covered with fuzz. **2** Lacking clarity: *fuzzy* thinking; a *fuzzy* image. —**fuzz′i·ly** *adv.* —**fuzz′i·ness** *n.*

fwd. forward.

-fy *suffix of verbs* **1** Make; form into: *deify.* **2** Cause to be; become: *liquefy.* [<L *facere* do, make]

G

G, g (jē) *n. pl.* **G's, g's** or **Gs, gs, gees** (jēz) **1** The seventh letter of the English alphabet. **2** Any spoken sound representing the letter *G* or *g*. **3** *Music* The fifth tone in the diatonic scale of C major. **4** *Physics* The acceleration of a body due to gravity: written in lower case. **5** *Slang Usu. cap.* One thousand dollars; a grand. **6** Something shaped like a G. —*adj.* Shaped like a G.

G. German; (specific) gravity.

G., g. gauge; grain(s); gram(s); guinea(s); gulf.

g general intelligence; goalkeeper; (specific) gravity.

GA Georgia (P.O. abbr.).

G.A. General Agent; General Assembly.

G.A., G/a, g.a. general average.

Ga gallium.

Ga. Georgia.

gab (gab) *n. Informal* Idle talk; loquacity. —*v.i.* **gabbed, gab·bing** To talk much or idly; chatter. [?<ON *gabba* mock]

gab·ar·dine (gab′ər·dēn, gab′ər·dēn′) *n.* **1** A diagonally woven, twilled, worsted fabric, used for coats, suits, etc. **2** A similar, softer fabric of mercerized cotton. **3** GABERDINE (def. 1). [Var. of GABERDINE]

gab·ble (gab′əl) *v.* **·bled, ·bling** *v.i.* **1** To talk rapidly and incoherently; babble. **2** To utter rapid, cackling sounds, as geese. —*v.t.* **3** To utter rapidly and incoherently. —*n.* **1** Noisy and incoherent or foolish talk. **2** Cackling, as of geese. [? Freq. of GAB] —**gab′bler** *n.*

gab·by (gab′ē) *adj.* **·bi·er, ·bi·est** Given to talk; loquacious. —**gab′bi·ness** *n.*

gab·er·dine (gab′ər·dēn, gab′ər·dēn′) **1** A long, loose, coarse cloak worn by Jews in medieval times. **2** *Chiefly Brit.* GABARDINE. [<MF *gaverdine*]

ga·ble (gā′bəl) *n. Archit.* **1** The upper usu. triangular part of an end wall enclosed by the sloping ends of a ridged roof. **2** The entire end wall of a building, the upper section of which is a gable. —*v.t. & v.i.* **ga·bled, ga·bling** To

Gable

build or be built with gables. [Prob.<ON *gafl*] —**ga′· bled** *adj.*

gable roof A ridge roof terminating in a gable at each end.

Ga·bon (gà·bôn′) *n.* A republic of w Africa, 102,290 sq. mi., cap. Libreville. —**Ga·bon·ese** (gab·ə·nēz′) *adj., n.* • See map at AFRICA.

Ga·bri·el (gā′brē·əl) In the Bible, an archangel, appearing as the messenger of God.

gad¹ (gad) *v.i.* **gad·ded, gad·ding** To roam abroad idly; ramble; stray. —*n.* The act of gadding. [Back formation from obs. *gadling* vagabond] —**gad′der** *n.*

gad² (gad) *n.* **1** A pointed tool for breaking up ore or rock. **2** A goad (def. 1). —*v.t.* **gad·ded, gad·ding 1** To break up with a gad. **2** To use a gad or rod upon. [<ON *gaddr*]

Gad (gad) *interj. & n. Archaic* God: a variant form used euphemistically in oaths.

gad·a·bout (gad′ə·bout′) *n.* One who roams or strays habitually. —*adj.* Fond of gadding.

gad·fly (gad′flī′) *n. pl.* **·flies 1** A large fly that torments cattle and horses. **2** A person who annoys or pesters by criticizing, often constructively. [<GAD² + FLY]

gadg·et (gaj′it) *n.* Any small, usu. mechanical or electronic device or contrivance. [?] —**gadg′et·ry** *n.*

gad·o·lin·i·um (gad′ə·lin′ē·əm) *n.* A metallic element (symbol Gd) of the rare-earth series. [<J. *Gadolin*, 1760–1852, Finnish chemist]

Gael (gāl) *n.* One of the Celts of Ireland, the Scottish Highlands, and the Isle of Man.

Gael·ic (gā′lik) *adj.* Of or relating to the Gaels, or to their languages. —*n.* The languages of the Gaels.

gaff (gaf) *n.* **1** A sharp iron hook at the end of a pole, for landing a large fish. **2** *Naut.* A spar for extending the upper edge of a fore-and-aft sail. **3** A gamecock's steel spur. **4** *Slang* Loud or abusive talk. —*v.t.* To strike or land with a gaff. [<OF *gaffe*]

gaffe (gaf) *n.* A clumsy mistake; a blunder; faux pas. [F]

gaf·fer (gaf′ər) *n.* An old man. [Alter. of GODFATHER]

gag (gag) *n.* **1** Something placed in or across the mouth to prevent speech or crying out. **2** Any restraint on free speech or discussion. **3** An instrument for holding open the jaws during a dental operation. **4** A humorous remark or action interpolated by an actor in a play or the like. **5** A practical joke. —*v.* **gagged, gag·ging** *v.t.* **1** To keep from speaking or crying out by means of a gag. **2** To keep from speaking or discussing freely, as by force or authority. **3** To cause nausea in; cause to retch. **4** *Slang* To introduce one's own words or improvise actions into (a theatrical role): often with *up.* —*v.i.* **5** To heave with nausea; retch. **6** *Slang* To make jokes or actions of an improvised nature. [ME *gaggen;* prob. imit.] —**gag'ger** *n.*

gage[1] (gāj) *n., v.* **gaged, gag·ing** GAUGE.

gage[2] (gāj) *n.* **1** Something given as security for some act; a pledge. **2** Something, as a gauntlet, thrown down as a challenge. [< OF *gage* a pledge]

gag·gle (gag'əl) *v.i.* **gag·gled, gag·gling** To cackle; gabble. —*n.* **1** A flock of geese. **2** A group, as of talkative women. [Imit.]

gag·man (gag'man') *n. pl.* **·men** (-men') A person hired to write humorous material for comedians, etc.

gai·e·ty (gā'ə·tē) *n. pl.* **·ties 1** Merrymaking; fun. **2** A gay, merry manner. **3** Bright and showy finery.

gai·ly (gā'lē) *adv.* **1** Joyously; merrily. **2** Brightly; showily.

gain (gān) *v.t.* **1** To obtain by or as by effort; earn. **2** To get in competition; win. **3** To reach; arrive at. **4** To get or undergo as an increase, profit, addition, etc.: to *gain* interest or weight. —*v.i.* **5** To increase in weight or speed. **6** To make progress; increase; improve. **7** To draw nearer or farther away: He *gained* on me steadily. —*n.* **1** Often *pl.* An increase or profit, as in money. **2** An increase in size, weight, speed, etc. **3** An improvement or advantage. **4** *Electronics* The ratio of output signal power to input signal power. [< OF *gaaignier* < Gmc.] —**Syn.** *v.* **1** achieve, acquire, attain, get, master, realize, reap.

gain·er (gā'nər) *n.* **1** One who or that which gains. **2** A fancy dive, consisting of a back somersault from a forward facing takeoff.

gain·ful (gān'fəl) *adj.* Yielding profit; lucrative. —**gain'ful·ly** *adv.* —**gain'ful·ness** *n.*

gain·say (gān'sā') *v.t.* **gain·said, gain·say·ing 1** To deny. **2** To contradict. **3** To speak or act against; oppose. [< OE *gegn-* against + SAY] —**gain'say'er** *n.*

'gainst (genst) *prep.* Against.

gait (gāt) *n.* **1** The manner of walking or stepping. **2** Any of various movements of a horse's feet, as the canter, pace, trot, run, etc. —*v.t.* To train (a horse) to a particular gait. [< ON *gata* way]

gait·ed (gā'tid) *adj.* Having a (particular) gait.

gait·er (gā'tər) *n.* **1** A covering for the lower leg or ankle, as a legging or spat. **2** A shoe covering the ankle and having no opening in front and usu. elastic sides. **3** An overshoe with a cloth top. [< F *guêtre*]

Gal. Galatians.

gal. gallon(s).

ga·la (gā'lə, gal'ə, gä'lə) *n.* A festive celebration. —*adj.* Festive or appropriate for a festive occasion. [< MF *gale*]

Gaiter def. 1

ga·lac·tic (gə·lak'tik) *adj.* **1** *Astron.* Of or pertaining to a galaxy or to the Milky Way. **2** Relating to or obtained from milk. [< Gk. *galaktikos* milky]

Gal·a·had (gal'ə·had), **Sir** In Arthurian romance, the purest and noblest knight of the Round Table, son of Lancelot.

gal·an·tine (gal'ən·tēn) *n.* A cold preparation of boned, stuffed, and seasoned chicken, veal, etc., served in its own jelly. [F]

gal·ax·y (gal'ək·sē) *n. pl.* **·ax·ies 1** *Astron.* Any of the very large systems of stars, nebulae, and other celestial bodies, comparable with the Milky Way. **2** *Usu. cap.* MILKY WAY. **3** Any brilliant group, as of persons. [< L *galaxias* the Milky Way < Gk. *gala* milk]

gale[1] (gāl) *n.* **1** A strong wind, esp. one between 32 and 63 miles per hour. **2** An outburst: *gales* of merriment. [?]

gale[2] (gāl) *n.* A branching, sweet-smelling marsh shrub of the E U.S. [< OE *gagel*]

ga·le·na (gə·lē'nə) *n.* A mineral form of lead sulfide, an important ore of lead. Also **ga·le·nite** (gə·lē'nīt). [L, lead ore]

Gal·i·le·an (gal'ə·lē'ən) *adj.* Of or pertaining to Galileo.

Gal·i·lee (gal'ə·lē) *n.* A hill region of N Israel. —**Gal'i·le'an** *adj., n.*

gall[1] (gôl) *n.* **1** The bitter fluid secreted by the liver; bile. **2** Bitter feeling; rancor. **3** Something bitter. **4** *Slang* Cool impudence; effrontery. [< OE *gealla*]

gall[2] (gôl) *n.* **1** An abrasion or irritation produced by friction. **2** Irritation; annoyance. **3** A person or thing that irritates or annoys. —*v.t.* **1** To make sore by friction; chafe. **2** To vex or irritate. —*v.i.* **3** To be or become chafed or irritated. [Prob. < GALL³]

gall[3] (gôl) *n.* **1** An excrescence on plants, caused by various parasitic organisms. **2** A similar excrescence on animals. [< L *galla* the gallnut]

gal·lant (gal'ənt) *adj.* **1** Brave; daring; chivalrous. **2** Stately; imposing; noble. **3** Showy; gay, as in attire. **4** (gal·lant', -länt', gal'ənt) Polite and attentive to women; courteous. —*n.* (gə·lant', -länt', gal'ənt) **1** A brave and high-spirited man. **2** A man who is attentive to women; also, a man of fashion. [< OF *galer* rejoice] —**gal'lant·ly** *adv.* —**Syn.** *adj.* **1** courageous, fearless, valiant, bold. **4** mannerly, civil, gracious, cordial, affable.

gal·lant·ry (gal'ən·trē) *n. pl.* **·ries 1** Courage; heroism; chivalrousness. **2** Polite or showy attention to women. **3** A gallant act.

gall bladder A small, pear-shaped, muscular pouch situated beneath the liver in man and serving as a reservoir for bile. • See LIVER.

gal·le·on (gal'ē·ən) *n.* A sailing vessel of the 15th to 17th centuries, usu. armed and having three or four decks. [< Med. L. *galea* galley]

gal·ler·y (gal'ər·ē) *n. pl.* **·ler·ies 1** A long, narrow, usu. roofed balcony or other passage projecting from the inner or outer wall of a building. **2** *U.S.* In the South, a veranda. **3** A platform with seats which projects from the rear or side walls of a theater, legislative chamber, church, etc., out over the main floor; specifically, in a theater, the highest of such platforms, containing the cheapest seats. **4** The audience occupying the gallery seats; also, the spectators at a sporting event, etc. **5** The general public and its tastes. **6** A long, narrow room or corridor. **7** A room or building used for the display of works of art. **8** A collection of works of art. **9** A room suggestive of a gallery, used for business purposes: a shooting *gallery;* a photographer's *gallery.* **10** An underground passage, as in a mine. —*v.t.* **gal·ler·ied, gal·ler·y·ing** To furnish or adorn with a gallery or galleries. [< Med. L *galeria*]

gal·ley (gal'ē) *n. pl.* **·leys 1** A long, low vessel used in ancient and medieval times, propelled by oars and sails or by oars alone. **2** A large rowboat. **3** The kitchen of a ship. **4** *Printing* **a** A long tray, for holding composed type. **b** GALLEY PROOF. [< Med. L *galea*]

galley proof *Printing* Proof printed from composed type, used to correct errors or make changes before page composition.

gall·fly (gôl'flī') *n. pl.* **·flies** Any of various insects whose larvae promote the growth of galls on plants.

Gal·lic (gal'ik) *adj.* Of or pertaining to ancient Gaul or modern France.

gallic acid (gal'ik) A crystalline organic acid prepared from certain nutgalls and from tannin and used in the making of inks, dyestuffs, etc.

Gal·li·cism (gal'ə·siz'əm) *n.* A French idiom, as used in any other language.

Gal·li·cize (gal'ə·sīz) *v.t. & v.i.* **·cized, ·ciz·ing** To make or become French in character, language, etc.; Frenchify.

gal·li·na·ceous (gal'ə·nā'shəs) *adj.* Of or pertaining to an order of birds, including chickens, turkeys, partridges, etc. [< L *gallina* hen] —**gal'li·na'cean** *n.*

gall·ing (gô'ling) *adj.* Chafing; irritating; vexing. —**gall'ing·ly** *adv.*

gal·li·pot (gal'i·pot) *n.* A small earthen jar, used esp. by pharmacists for medicines. [? < GALLEY + POT]

gal·li·um (gal'ē·əm) *n.* A rare metallic element (symbol Ga), used in high-temperature thermometers, semiconductor devices, etc. [< L *gallus* a cock, trans. of *Lecoq* de Boisbaudran, 1838–1912, French chemist]

gal·li·vant (gal'ə·vant) *v.i.* To go about, esp. in search of fun and pleasure. [? Alter. of GALLANT]

gall·nut (gôl'nut') *n.* An excrescence on a plant, resembling a nut in form.

Gallo- *combining form* French; pertaining to the French or to France. [< L *Gallus* a Gaul]

gal·lon (gal'ən) *n.* 1 A unit of volume equal to 4 quarts. 2 A dry measure; one eighth of a bushel. [< OF]

gal·lop (gal'əp) *n.* 1 A fast, natural gait of a horse or other quadruped. 2 The act of riding, or a ride at a gallop. 3 Any speedy action. —*v.i.* 1 To ride at a gallop. 2 To go, run, or move very fast. —*v.t.* 3 To cause to run at a gallop. [< OF *galop* < Gmc.] —**gal'lop·er** *n.*

gal·lows (gal'ōz) *n. pl.* **·lows** or **·lows·es** A framework consisting of two or more uprights supporting a crossbeam, used for execution by hanging. Also **gallows tree.** [< OE *galga*]

gall·stone (gôl'stōn') *n.* A concretion found in the gall bladder or bile duct.

gal·op (gal'əp) *n.* 1 A lively dance in duple measure. 2 The music for such a dance. [F, a gallop]

ga·lore (gə·lôr', -lōr') *adj.* In abundance; in great numbers: refreshments *galore.* [< Irish *go leór*, enough]

ga·losh (gə·losh') *n. Usu. pl.* An overshoe reaching above the ankle and worn in stormy weather. Also **ga·loshe'.** [< OF *galoche*]

gal·van·ic (gal·van'ik) *adj.* 1 Pertaining to galvanism. 2 Resembling or pertaining to a physiological response to an electric current; spasmodic. Also **gal·van'i·cal.** —**gal·van'i·cal·ly** *adv.*

gal·va·nism (gal'və·niz'əm) *n.* 1 Electricity, esp. when produced by chemical action. 2 The therapeutic application of electric current. [< L. *Galvani,* 1737–98, Italian physiologist]

gal·va·nize (gal'və·nīz) *v.t.* **·nized, ·niz·ing** 1 To stimulate to muscular action by electricity. 2 To rouse to action; startle; excite. 3 To protect (iron or steel) from rust with a coating of zinc. —**gal'va·ni·za'tion** *n.*

galvanized iron Iron coated with zinc.

gal·va·nom·e·ter (gal'və·nom'ə·tər) *n.* An apparatus for measuring electric current. —**gal·va·no·met·ric** (gal'və·nō·met'rik, gal·van'ō-) or **·ri·cal** *adj.*

gam (gam) *n. Slang* A leg, esp. a shapely leg of a woman. [< OF *gambe*]

Gam·bi·a (gam'bē·ə) *n.* A republic in w Africa, 4,003 sq. mi., cap. Bathurst. Also **the Gambia.** —**Gam'bi·an** *adj., n.* • See map at AFRICA.

gam·bit (gam'bit) *n.* 1 One of various openings in chess, in which a pawn or piece is risked to obtain an advantage. 2 Any opening move or strategy. [< Ital. *gambetto* a tripping up]

gam·ble (gam'bəl) *v.* **gam·bled, gam·bling** *v.i.* 1 To risk or bet something of value on the outcome of an event, a game of chance, etc. 2 To take a risk to obtain a desired result. —*v.t.* 3 To wager or bet (something of value). 4 To lose or squander by gaming: usu. with *away.* —*n.* 1 Any risky or uncertain venture. 2 A gambling transaction. [< OE *gamenian* sport, play] —**gam'bler** *n.*

gam·bol (gam'bəl) *v.i.* **·boled** or **·bolled, ·bol·ing** or **·bol·ling** To skip or leap about in play; frolic. —*n.* A skipping about in sport. [< Ital. *gamba* leg]

gam·brel (gam'brəl) *n.* 1 The hock of an animal. 2 *Archit.* A roof having its slope broken by an obtuse angle: also **gambrel roof.** [< LL *gamba* leg]

game[1] (gām) *n.* 1 Any physical or mental contest, played according to rules, and depending on strength, skill, or luck to win. 2 A definite portion or division of such a contest. 3 The number of points required to win: *Game* is 100 points. 4 Success; victory: The *game* is ours. 5 Equipment used in certain games: to buy a *game.* 6 Manner or art of competitive playing. 7 Amusement; fun; sport; play: to make a *game* of cooking. 8 Something thought of as competitive, requiring skill, etc.: the *game* of politics. 9 A strategy; scheme; plan: What is your *game?* 10 Wild animals or birds pursued or caught for sport or profit; also their flesh.

Gambrel roof

11 Any object of pursuit or attack: They were fair *game* for ridicule. 12 *Slang* A business; vocation; esp. one involving risk. —*v.i.* **gamed, gam·ing** To gamble at cards, dice, etc., for money or other stakes. —*adj.* 1 Of or pertaining to hunted wild birds or animals or their flesh. 2 Plucky; spirited; intrepid. 3 Ready; willing. [< OE *gamen*]

game[2] (gām) *adj. Informal* Lame or hurt: a *game* leg. [?]

game bird Any bird commonly hunted as game, as pheasant, wild duck, or partridge.

game·cock (gām'kok') *n.* A rooster bred and trained for fighting. Also **game cock.**

game·keep·er (gām'kē'pər) *n.* A person having the care of game, as in a preserve or park.

game·ly (gām'lē) *adv.* In a game manner; pluckily. Also **gam'i·ly.**

game·ness (gām'nis) *n.* Pluck; bravery.

game·ster (gām'stər) *n.* One who gambles; gambler.

gam·ete (gam'ēt, gə·mēt') *n.* Either of two mature reproductive cells, an ovum or sperm, which in uniting produce a zygote. [< Gk. *gametē* wife, or *gametēs* husband] —**ga·met·ic** (gə·met'ik) *adj.* —**ga·met'i·cal·ly** *adv.*

game theory In games and conflicts, the mathematical analysis of various strategies in order to determine the specific strategy having maximum potential.

ga·me·to·phyte (gə·mē'tə·fīt) *n.* That phase or generation of a plant which produces gametes. —**gam·e·to·phyt·ic** (gam'ə·tō·fit'ik) *adj.*

gam·in (gam'in; *Fr.* gà·man') *n.* 1 A neglected boy of city streets. 2 A girl with elfin charm. [F]

gam·ing (gā'ming) *n.* The act or practice of gambling.

gam·ma (gam'ə) *n.* 1 The third letter in the Greek alphabet (Γ, γ). 2 The third in a series or group.

gamma globulin A component of blood serum which contains various antibodies.

gamma rays Electromagnetic waves having higher frequencies and energies than X-rays and, thus, greater penetrating power.

gam·mer (gam'ər) *n. Brit. Regional* An old woman; grandmother. [Alter. of GODMOTHER]

gam·mon[1] (gam'ən) *n.* In backgammon, a defeat in which the winner throws all his men before the loser throws off any. —*v.t.* To obtain a gammon over. [? ME *gamen* a game]

gam·mon[2] (gam'ən) *Brit. Informal n.* Deceitful nonsense or trickery. [?]

gam·mon[3] (gam'ən) *n.* 1 A cured ham. 2 The bottom end of a side of bacon. [< LL *gamba* leg]

-gamous *combining form* Pertaining to marriage or union for reproduction: *polygamous.* [< Gk. *gamos* marriage + -OUS]

gam·ut (gam'ət) *n.* 1 The entire range of musical tones. 2 The whole range of anything: the *gamut* of emotions. [< Med. L *gamma ut* < *gamma,* the first note of the early musical scale + *ut* (later, *do*); the names of the notes of the scale were taken from a medieval Latin hymn: *Ut* queant laxis *Re*sonare fibris, *Mi*ra gestorum *Fa*muli tuorum, *Sol*ve polluti *La*bii reatum, *Sancte Io*hannes]

gam·y (gā'mē) *adj.* **gam·i·er, gam·i·est** 1 Having the flavor of game, esp. when somewhat tainted. 2 Full of pluck; disposed to fight. 3 Risqué.

-gamy *combining form* Marriage or union for reproduction: *polygamy.* [< Gk. *gamos* marriage]

gan·der (gan'dər) *n.* 1 A male goose. 2 A dunce. 3 *Slang* A look; glance. [< OE *gandra*]

gang[1] (gang) *n.* 1 A group of persons acting or operating together: a *gang* of workers. 2 A group of criminals operating together as a unit. 3 A neighborhood group, usu. of young people, often engaged in antisocial behavior. 4 A group of friends. 5 A set of similar tools, etc. —*v.t.* 1 To unite into or as into a gang. 2 *Informal* To attack as a group. —*v.i.* 3 To come together as a gang; form a gang. [< OE *gangan* go]

gang·land (gang'land') *n.* Criminal gangs collectively.

gan·gling (gang'gling) *adj.* Awkwardly tall and loosely built. Also **gan'gly.** [< Regional *gangrel* wanderer < OE *gangan* go]

gan·gli·on (gang′glē·ən) *n. pl.* **·gli·ons** or **·gli·a** (glē·ə) **1** A nexus or center of nerve cells. **2** Any center of energy, activity, or strength. [< Gk., tumor] —**gan·gli·on·ic** (gang′glē·on′ik) *adj.*

gang·plank (gang′plangk′) *n.* A temporary passageway between a vessel and a wharf. [< obs. *gang* way, going + PLANK]

gang-rape (gang′rāp′) *n.* Rape committed successively by the individuals in a group. —*v.t.* **-raped, -rap·ing** To subject to gang-rape.

gan·grene (gang′grēn, gang·grēn′) *n.* Death and decay of tissue due to inadequate blood supply, injury, etc. —*v.t. & v.i.* **gan·grened, gan·gren·ing** To cause gangrene in or become affected by gangrene. [< Gk. *gangraina*] —**gan′gre·nous** (-grə·nəs) *adj.*

gang·ster (gang′stər) *n.* A member of a gang of criminals. —**gang′ster·ism** *n.*

gang·way (gang′wā′) *n.* **1** A passageway through, into, or out of any enclosure; esp. a temporary passageway made of planks. **2** GANGPLANK. —*interj.* Get out of the way! Stand aside! [< Obs. *gang* way, going + WAY]

gan·net (gan′it) *n.* Any of several large sea birds related to the pelicans. [< OE *ganot*]

gan·oid (gan′oid) *adj.* Of or pertaining to a large division of fishes, including sturgeons, bowfins, etc., having rows of hard, shiny scales or plates. —*n.* A ganoid fish. [< Gk. *ganos* brightness + -OID]

gant·let[1] (gônt′lit, gant′-) *n.* **1** GAUNTLET[1]. **2** GAUNTLET[2].

gan·try (gan′trē) *n. pl.* **·tries 1** A raised, horizontal framework for supporting a traveling crane, railway signals, etc. **2** A movable tower used in servicing or assembling rockets. **3** A frame to hold a barrel horizontally. [< OF *chantier* < L *cantherius* framework]

gaol (jāl) *n. Brit.* JAIL. [Var. of JAIL] —**gaol′er** *n.*

gap (gap) *n.* **1** An opening or parting in anything; aperture; breach; chasm. **2** A deep cleft in a mountain ridge. **3** A break in continuity; an interruption. **4** A difference, as between opinions. —*v.t. & v.i.* **gapped, gap·ping** To make or have a gap or opening in (something). [< ON, gap, abyss]

gape (gāp, gap) *v.i.* **gaped, gap·ing 1** To stare open-mouthed, as in awe or surprise. **2** To open the mouth wide, as in yawning. **3** To be or become open wide; present a wide opening. —*n.* **1** The act of gaping. **2** A gap. [< ON *gapa*] —**gap′er** *n.*

gar (gär) *n. pl.* **gars** or **gar** Any of several fishes having a spearlike snout. [< GARFISH]

G.A.R. Grand Army of the Republic.

ga·rage (gə·räzh′, -räj′, *Brit.* gar′ij) *n.* A building in which motor vehicles are parked, serviced, or repaired. —*v.t.* **ga·raged, ga·rag·ing** To put or keep in a garage. [< OF *garer* protect < Gmc.]

garb (gärb) *n.* **1** Clothes, esp. as characteristic of some office, rank, etc. **2** External appearance or manner. —*v.t.* To clothe; dress. [< MF *garbe* gracefulness]

gar·bage (gär′bij) *n.* **1** Refuse matter, as waste food, empty bottles, paper, etc. **2** Anything worthless or disgusting. [Prob. < AF]

gar·ble (gär′bəl) *v.t.* **gar·bled, gar·bling 1** To mix up or confuse; make incomprehensible: to *garble* a message. **2** To change the meaning of (a document, report, etc.) with intent to mislead or misrepresent. [< Ital. *garbellare* < Ar. *gharbala* sift]

gar·çon (gár·sôn′) *n. pl.* **·çons** (-sôn′) A waiter. [F, boy]

gar·den (gär′dən) *n.* **1** A place for the cultivation of flowers, vegetables, or small plants. **2** Any fertile or highly cultivated territory. **3** A piece of ground, commonly with ornamental plants or trees, used as a public park. —*adj.* **1** Of, for, used, or grown in a garden. **2** Ordinary; common. **3** Like a garden; ornamental: *garden* spot of the world. —*v.t.* **1** To cultivate as a garden. —*v.i.* **2** To till or work in a garden. [< AF *gardin*] —**gar′den·er** *n.*

gar·de·ni·a (gär·dēn′yə, -dē′nē·ə) *n.* **1** Any of a genus of mainly tropical evergreen shrubs or trees with fragrant yellow or white flowers. **2** The flower itself. [< A. *Garden,* 1730–91, Scottish naturalist]

gar·fish (gär′fish′) *n. pl.* **·fish** or **·fish·es** A fish with a spearlike snout; a gar. [< OE *gār* spear + FISH]

gar·gan·tu·an (gär·gan′chōō·ən) *adj. Often cap.* Huge; gigantic; prodigious. [< *Gargantua,* the peace-loving giant in Rabelais' satire *Gargantua and Pantagruel*]

gar·gle (gär′gəl) *v.* **gar·gled, gar·gling** *v.t.* **1** To rinse (the throat) with a liquid agitated by air from the windpipe. —*v.i.* **2** To use a gargle. **3** To make a sound as if gargling. —*n.* A liquid for gargling. [< OF *gargouille* throat]

gar·goyle (gär′goil) *n.* A waterspout, usu. carved in a grotesque human or animal figure, projecting from the gutter of a building. [< OF *gargouille* throat] —**gar′goyled** *adj.*

gar·ish (gâr′ish) *adj.* Bright and showy, esp. in a gaudy or vulgar manner. [< ME *gauren* to stare] —**gar′ish·ly** *adv.* —**gar′ish·ness** *n.* —**Syn.** flashy, ornate, tawdry, cheap, ostentatious.

Gargoyle

gar·land (gär′lənd) *n.* **1** A wreath of leaves, flowers, etc., as a token of victory, joy, or honor. **2** An anthology of short literary selections. —*v.t.* To deck with or as with a garland. [< OF *garlande*]

gar·lic (gär′lik) *n.* **1** A hardy bulbous perennial of the same genus as the onion. **2** Its pungent bulb, used in cooking. [< OE *gār* spear + *lēac* leek] —**gar′lick·y** *adj.*

gar·ment (gär′mənt) *n.* **1** An article of clothing. **2** *pl.* Clothes. **3** Any covering. —*v.t.* To clothe. [< OF *garnir* garnish]

gar·ner (gär′nər) *v.t.* To gather or store; collect. —*n.* **1** GRANARY. **2** Any storage place. [< L *granarium* a granary]

gar·net (gär′nit) *n.* **1** One of various glassy silicate minerals, used as abrasives and sometimes as gems. **2** Its usual color, a deep red. [< Med. L *granatum* a pomegranate]

gar·nish (gär′nish) *v.t.* **1** To decorate, as with ornaments; embellish. **2** In cookery, to decorate (food) for the table. **3** *Law* To give warning to (someone) to answer to an action; garnishee. —*n.* **1** Something placed around food for ornamentation or a relish. **2** Anything added as an ornament; embellishment. —**gar′nish·er** *n.* [< OF *garnir* prepare < Gmc.]

gar·nish·ee (gär·nish·ē′) *v.t.* **·eed, ·ee·ing** *Law* **1** To secure by garnishment (any debt or property, in the hands of a third person, which is due or belonging to the defendant in attachment). **2** To warn (a person) by garnishment. —*n. Law* A person warned not to pay or deliver money or effects to a defendant, pending a judgment of a court.

gar·nish·ment (gär′nish·mənt) *n.* **1** The act of garnishing. **2** That which garnishes; embellishment; ornament. **3** *Law* A warning or summons; specifically, a notice not to pay or deliver money or effects to a defendant, but to appear and answer the plaintiff's suit.

gar·ni·ture (gär′ni·chər) *n.* Anything used to garnish; embellishment.

gar·pike (gär′pīk′) *n. pl.* **·pike** or **·pikes** A freshwater gar.

gar·ret (gar′it) *n.* A space, room, or rooms directly under a roof. [< OF *garite* a watchtower]

gar·ri·son (gar′ə·sən) *n.* **1** The military force defending a fort, town, etc. **2** The place where such a force is stationed. —*v.t.* **1** To place troops in (a fort, town, etc.) for its defense. **2** To station (troops) in a fort, town, etc. **3** To be the garrison of. [< OF *garir* defend < Gmc.]

gar·rote (gə·rot′, -rōt′) *n.* **1** An iron collar tightened by a screw for strangling, formerly used as a means of capital punishment, esp. in Spain. **2** This method of punishment. **3** Any similar method of strangulation, as with a rope or wire. —*v.t.* **gar·rot·ed, gar·rot·ing 1** To execute with a garrote. **2** To throttle, esp. in order to rob. Also **ga·rote′, ga·rotte′, gar·rotte′.** [Sp. *garotte* a stick, cudgel] —**gar·rot′er, gar·rot′ter** *n.*

gar·ru·lous (gar′yə·ləs) *adj.* Given to continual and tedious talking. [< L *garrulus* talkative] —**gar′ru·lous·ly** *adv.* —**gar·ru·li·ty** (gə·rōō′lə·tē), gar′ru·lous·ness** *n.* —**Syn.** talkative, loquacious, verbose, effusive, long-winded.

gar·ter (gär′tər) *n.* An elastic band or fastening device used to hold a stocking in place. —*v.t.* To support or fasten with a garter. [< OF *garet* bend of the knee]

garter snake Any of a genus of small, harmless, viviparous, striped snakes.

gas (gas) *n.* **1** *Physics* That fluid form of matter which is compressible within limits, and which diffuses readily and is capable of indefinite expansion in all directions. **2** Any gas or vapor other than air: tear *gas*, fuel *gas*. **3** Flatulence. **4** *Informal* **a** Gasoline. **b** The accelerator of an automobile. **5** *Slang* Empty boasting. **6** *Slang* A person or thing that is fun, exciting, etc. —*v*. **gassed, gas·sing** *v.t.* **1** To overcome, affect, or kill by gas or gas fumes. **2** To treat or saturate with gas. **3** To supply with gas or gasoline. **4** *Slang* To provide fun, excitement, etc., for. —*v.i* **5** To give off gas. **6** *Slant* To boast. [Coined by J. B. van Helmont, 1577–1644, Belgian chemist]

gas chamber A chamber in which executions are performed by means of poison gas.

gas·e·ous (gas′ē·əs, -yəs) *adj.* **1** Having the nature or form of gas. **2** Unsubstantial.

gas fitter One who installs and repairs gas fixtures.

gash (gash) *v.t.* To make a long, deep cut in. —*n*. a long, deep cut or flesh wound. [< OF *garser* scratch]

gas·i·fy (gas′ə·fī) *v.t. & v.i.* **·fied, ·fy·ing** To convert into or become gas: to *gasify* coal. —**gas′i·fi·ca′tion, gas′i·fi′er** *n.*

gas jet **1** A burner or nozzle on a gas fixture. **2** The jet of flame on a gas burner.

gas·ket (gas′kit) *n.* **1** *Mech.* A ring, disk, or plate of packing used to seal a joint against leaks. **2** *Naut.* A rope or cord used to confine furled sails to the yard or boom. Also **gas′kin** (-kin), **gas′king** (-king). [?]

gas·light (gas′līt′) *n.* **1** Light from burning illuminating gas. **2** A lamp fueled by gas. —**gas′light′ing** *n.*

gas mask A covering for the nose, mouth, and eyes, equipped with a respirator and worn as protection against toxic or irritant gases.

gas·o·hol (gas′ə·hôl, -hol) *n.* A mixture of 90 percent gasoline and 10 percent alcohol, used as a fuel.

gas·o·line (gas′ə·lēn, gas′ə·lēn′) *n.* A volatile, flammable liquid hydrocarbon derived from petroleum and used as a fuel and solvent. Also **gas′o·lene.** [< GAS + -OL + -INE]

gas·om·e·ter (gas·om′ə·tər) *n.* **1** An apparatus for measuring gases. **2** A reservoir for storing gas.

gasp (gasp, gäsp) *v.i.* **1** To take in the breath suddenly and sharply; breathe convulsively, as from fear or exhaustion. —*v.t.* **2** To say or utter with gasps. —*n.* An act of gasping. [< ON *geispa*]

gas station SERVICE STATION (def. 1).

gas·sy (gas′ē) *adj.* **gas·si·er, gas·si·est** **1** Of, like, or containing gas. **2** Flatulent. **3** *Slang* Addicted to idle chatter or boastful talk. —**gas′si·ness** *n.*

gas·tight (gas′tīt′) *adj.* Not permitting the passage of gas.

gas·tric (gas′trik) *adj.* Of, pertaining to, in, or near the stomach.

gastric juice A thin, acid digestive fluid secreted by glands in the lining of the stomach.

gas·tri·tis (gas·trī′tis) *n*, Inflammation of the stomach. — **gas·trit·ic** (gas-trit′ik) *adj.*

gastro- *combining form* Stomach or stomach and: *gastrointestinal*. [< Gk. *gastēr* stomach]

gas·tro·in·tes·ti·nal (gas′trō·in·tes′tə·nəl) *adj.* Of or pertaining to the stomach and the intestines.

gas·tron·o·my (gas·tron′ə·mē) *n.* The art or science of good eating; epicurism. [< GASTRO- + Gk. *nomos* law] —**gas·tron′o·mer, gas·tro·nome** (gas′trə·nōm), **gas·tron′o·mist** *n.* — **gas′tro·mon′ic** or **·i·cal** *adj.*

gas·tro·pod (gas′trə·pod) *n.* One of a large class of mollusks, usu. having a spiral one-piece shell and a creeping organ, including the snails, slugs, limpets, etc., —*adj.* Of or like a gastropod. —**gas·trop′o·dan** (gas·trop′ə-dən) *adj.*

gas·tru·la (gas′trōō·lə) *n. pl.* **·lae** (-lē), **·las** An embryo at the stage after the blastula, consisting of two layers of tissue enfolding a central cavity with an opening to the outside. [< Gk. *gastēr* stomach] —**gas′tru·lar** *adj.*

gas·works (gas′wûrks′) *n. pl.* (*construed as sing.*) A factory where illuminating or fuel gas is prepared.

gat (gat) *n. Slang* A pistol. [Short for GATLING GUN]

gate (gāt) *n.* **1** A movable barrier, commonly swinging on hinges and usu. used as an entrance or exit through a fence or wall. **2** An opening or passageway, as in a barrier, fence, wall, or enclosure. **3** Any entrance, exit, or means of access. **4** A barrier that swings up or down, as at a railroad crossing. **5** A valve or structure controlling a flow of liquid or gas. • See VALVE. **6** The total paid admissions or total attendance, as at a sports event. **7** *Electronics* **a** Any of various circuits having several inputs and a single output whose state depends on the state of the inputs, used in computers. **b** A terminal of a semiconductor device that controls the flow of current through the device. —*v.t.* **gat·ed, gat·ing** *Electronics* To control (a current or voltage) by means of a gate. [< OE *geat* opening]

gate-crash (gāt′krash′) *v.t. Informal* To gain admittance to, as a party or other function, without invitation or without paying. —**gate′crash′er** *n.*

gate-leg table (gāt′leg′) A table with swinging legs which support drop leaves and fold back when the leaves are let down.

gate-post (gāt′pōst′) *n.* Either of two posts between which a gate swings.

gate·way (gāt′wā′) *n.* **1** An entrance that is or may be closed with a gate. **2** Any means of entrance or access.

gath·er (gath′ər) *v.t.* **1** To bring together in one place or group. **2** To bring together from various places, sources, etc. **3** To bring closer to oneself: to *gather* one's skirts. **4** To pick, harvest, or collect. **5** To collect or summon up, as one's energies. **6** To increase in amount or degree: The storm *gathered* force. **7** To clasp or enfold: to *gather* someone into one's arms. **8** To conclude or infer. **9** To draw (cloth) into folds or pleats. **10** To wrinkle (the brow). —*v.i.* **11** To come together. **12** To increase. **13** To wrinkle up, as the brow. **14** To come to a head, as a boil. —*n.* A pleat. [< OE *gadrian*] —**gath′er·a·ble** *adj.* —**gath′er·er** *n.*

gath·er·ing (gath′ər·ing) *n.* **1** The action of one who or that which gathers. **2** That which is gathered, as an assemblage of people. **3** A series of pleats. **4** An abcess or boil.

Gat·ling gun (gat′ling) An early machine gun having a rotating cluster of barrels. [< R. J. *Gatling*. 1818–1903, U.S. inventor]

GATT General Agreement on Tariffs and Trade.

gauche (gōsh) *adj.* Socially awkward or clumsy; boorish. [F, left]

gauche·rie (gōsh·rē′) *n.* **1** A gauche action or remark. **2** Clumsiness; tactlessness.

Gau·cho (gou′chō) *n. pl.* **·chos** A cowboy of the South American pampas. [Sp.]

gaud·y (gô′dē) *adj.* **gaud·i·er, gaud·i·est** Obtrusively brilliant in color: garish; flashy. —**gaud′i·ly** *adv.* —**gaud′i·ness** *n.*

gauge (gāj) *n.* **1** An instrument for measuring, indicating, or regulating quantity, dimension, capacity, etc. **2** A standard or system of measurement or comparison. **3** The measure of something as expressed by means of such a system or standard: the *gauge* of a shotgun bore. **4** The distance between rails of a railroad track or a pair of wheels on an axis. —*v.t.* **gauged, gaug·ing** **1** To measure or regulate with or as with a gauge. **2** To estimate, appraise, or judge. **3** To bring into conformity with a standard. [< OF, a measure] —**gauge′a·ble** *adj.* —**gaug′er** *n.*

Gaul (gôl) *n.* **1** An ancient name for what is, roughly, the area of modern France and Belgium. **2** A native of ancient Gaul. **3** A Frenchman.

Gaul·ish (gô′lish) *adj.* Of ancient Gaul, its people, or their Celtic language. —*n.* The extinct Celtic language of Gaul.

Gaull·ism (gôl′iz′əm) *n.* The policies or philosophy of Charles de Gaulle and his followers. —**Gaull′ist** *adj., n.*

gaunt (gônt) *adj.* **1.** Emaciated, as from lack of food; lank; lean; meager; thin. **2** Grim; desolate. [ME] —**gaunt′ly** *adv.*

gaunt·let[1] (gônt′lit, gänt′-) *n.* **1** In medieval armor, a leather glove covered with metal plates. **2** Any glove with a long, flaring extension over the wrist; also, the extension. [< OF *gant* glove] —**gaunt′let·ed** *adj.*

gaunt·let[2] (gônt′lit, gänt′-) *n.* **1** A punishment wherein the victim runs between two rows of men who strike him with clubs or switches as he passes. **2** A series of difficulties or unpleasant events. —**run the gauntlet** (or **gant-**

---

add, āce, câre, pälm; end, ēven; it, īce; odd, ōpen, ôrder; tŏŏk, pōōl; up, bûrn; ə = *a* in *above*, *u* in *focus*; yōō = *u* in *fuse*; oil; pout; check; go; ring; thin; ṯẖis; zh, *vision.* < derived from; ? origin uncertain or unknown.

let) To be exposed to a series of hostile attacks or unpleasant incidents. [< Sw. *gatlopp* a running down a lane]

gauss (gous) *n. pl.* **gauss** *Physics* A unit of magnetic induction, equal to 10⁴ webers per square meter. [< K. F. *Gauss*, 1777–1855, German mathematician]

gauze (gôz) *n.* 1 A light, loosely woven fabric. 2 Any thin open-woven material: wire *gauze*. 3 A mist. —*adj.* Resembling or made of gauze. [< MF *gaze*] —**gauz′i·ly** *adv.* — **gauz′i·ness** *n.* —**gauz·y** (·i·er, ·i·est) *adj.*

gave (gāv) *p.t.* of GIVE.

gav·el (gav′əl) *n.* A mallet used by a presiding officer to call for order or attention. [?]

ga·vi·al (gā′vē·əl) *n.* A large crocodile of s Asia, having long, slender jaws. [< Hind. *ghariyāl*]

ga·votte (gə·vot′) *n.* 1 A lively French dance, resembling the minuet. 2 Music for such a dance. [< Provençal *gavoto* Alpine dance]

G.A.W. guaranteed annual wage.

gawk (gôk) *v.i. Informal* To stare or behave awkwardly and stupidly. —*n.* An awkward, stupid fellow. [?]

gawk·y (gô′kē) *adj.* **gawk·i·er, gawk·i·est** Awkward and dull; clumsy. —**gawk′i·ly** *adv.* —**gawk′i·ness** *n.*

gay (gā) *adj.* 1 Joyous; light-spirited; merry. 2 Brilliant; showy: *gay* colors. 3 Loving or given to pleasure and amusement. 4 *Informal* HOMOSEXUAL. [< OF *gai*] —**gay′-ness** *n.* —**gay′some** *adj.* —**Syn.** 1 cheerful, happy, merry, vivacious, lively, sunny, blithe. 2 sparkling, bright, vivid, shiny.

gay·e·ty (gā′ə·tē) *n.* GAIETY.

gay·ly *adv.* GAILY.

Gay Nine·ties (nīn′tēz) The decade from 1890 to 1900.

gaz. gazette; gazetteer.

gaze (gāz) *v.i.* **gazed, gaz·ing** To look earnestly and steadily, as in scrutiny, admiration, or concern. —*n.* A continued or intense look. [< Scand.] —**gaz′er** *n.*

ga·ze·bo (gə·zē′bō, ·zä-) *n. pl.* **·bos** or **·boes** A small, open structure, as in a garden, and often commanding a wide view. [? < GAZE]

ga·zelle (gə·zel′) *n.* Any of various small antelopes with long necks and large, gentle eyes. [< Ar. *ghazāl* gazelle]

ga·zette (gə·zet′) *n.* 1 A newspaper. 2 *Brit.* Any official government journal announcing appointments, promotions, etc. —*v.t. Brit.* **ga·zet·ted, ga·zet·ting** To publish or announce in a gazette. [< dial. Ital. (Venetian) *gazeta* a coin, orig. the price of the paper]

Gazelle

gaz·et·teer (gaz′ə·tir′) *n.* 1 A dictionary or alphabetical list of geographical names. 2 A writer for a gazette.

gaz·pa·cho (gäz·pä′chō) *n. pl.* **·chos** A cold soup made with tomatoes and other ingredients, as olive oil, garlic, peppers, bread crumbs, and spices. [Sp.]

G.B. Great Britain.

GCT, G.C.T., G.c.t. Greenwich civil time.

Gd gadolinium.

gds. goods.

Ge germanium.

gear (gir) *n.* 1 *Mech.* **a** A set of moving parts that transmit motion, often changing its rate or direction. **b** One of several possible arrangements of such a set of parts: low *gear*. **c** A wheel with teeth around its edge, designed to engage a part with similar teeth and transmit motion; cogwheel. **d** Any group of parts performing a specific function: the steering *gear*. 2 Any equipment, tools, etc., for some specific task or purpose, as the rigging of a ship, a repairman's tools, etc. 3 Clothes, esp. for a specific purpose: a skier's *gear*. 4 Harmonious and effective action: out of *gear*. —*v.t.* 1 **a** To equip with gears. **b** To connect by means of gears. 2 To regulate so as to match or suit something else: to *gear* production to demand. 3 To put gear on; harness; dress. —*v.i.* 4 To come into or be in gear; mesh. [< ON *gervi* equipment]

Gears *def. 1c*

gear·box (gir′boks′) *n.* The transmission of an automobile, truck, bus, etc.

gear·ing (gir′ing) *n.* Gears or related parts that transmit mechanical power.

gear·shift (gir′shift′) *n.* A device for engaging or disengaging gears.

gear·wheel (gīr′ʰwēl′) *n.* COGWHEEL.

geck·o (gek′ō) *n. pl.* **geck·os** or **geck·oes** Any of a family of small lizards having toes with adhesive disks; wall lizard. [< Malay *gēkoq,* imit. of its cry]

gee¹ (jē) *v.t. & v.i.* To turn to the right. —*interj.* Turn to the right! a call in driving animals without reins. [?]

Gecko

gee² (jē) *interj. Informal* An exclamation of surprise, awe, etc. Also **gee whiz.** [Euphemistic contr. of JESUS]

geek (gēk) *n.* A carnival performer who publicly bites off the head of a live animal, as a chicken, as a sensational spectacle. [Prob. var. of Brit. dial. *geck* fool]

geese (gēs) *n. pl.* of GOOSE¹.

gee·zer (gē′zər) *n. Slang* An old, usu. eccentric man. [Var. of earlier *guiser* one in disguise < GUISE]

ge·fil·te fish (gə·fil′tə) Ground fish mixed with eggs, seasonings, bread crumbs, etc., made into balls or cakes and simmered in broth. Also **ge·fül′te.** [Yiddish, lit., filled]

Ge·hen·na (gi·hen′ə) *n.* 1 The valley of Hinnom near Jerusalem, where offal was thrown and fires kept burning to purify the air. 2 A place of torment. 3 In the New Testament, hell. [< Hebrew *ge- hinnom* valley of *Hinnom*]

Gei·ger counter (gī′gər) An electronic instrument for detecting and counting ionizing particles and rays, used to measure radioactivity. [< Hans *Geiger,* 1882–1945, German physicist]

gei·sha (gā′shə) *n. pl.* **·sha** or **·shas** A Japanese girl trained to entertain men by singing, dancing, etc.

gel (jel) *n.* A colloidal dispersion of a liquid in a solid, usu. forming a semisolid of jellylike consistency. —*v.i.* **gelled, gel·ling** To change into a gel; jellify. [Short for GELATIN]

gel·a·tin (jel′ə·tin) *n.* 1 A brittle, tasteless protein produced from animal tissues, which forms a gel with water. 2 A gel made usu. with gelatin and used as a base for desserts, aspics, etc. Also **gel′a·tine.** [< L *gelare* freeze]

ge·lat·i·nize (ji·lat′ə·nīz) *v.* **·nized, ·niz·ing** *v.t.* 1 To turn into or treat with gelatin. —*v.i.* 2 To be changed into gelatin or jelly. —**ge·lat′i·ni·za′tion** *n.*

ge·lat·i·nous (ji·lat′ə·nəs) *adj.* 1 Of the nature of gelatin. 2 Of or containing gelatin. —**ge·lat′i·nous·ly** *adv.* —**ge·lat′·i·nous·ness** *n.*

geld (geld) *v.t.* **geld·ed** or **gelt, geld·ing** To castrate, esp. a horse. [< ON *gelda*]

geld·ing (gel′ding) *n.* A castrated animal, esp. a horse.

gel·id (jel′id) *adj.* Very cold; icy; frozen. [< L *gelidus*] —**ge·lid′i·ty** *n.* —**gel′id·ly** *adv.*

gelt (gelt) *n. Slang* Money. [< G & Du. *geld* & Yiddish *gelt*]

gem (jem) *n.* 1 A precious or semiprecious stone, esp. when cut and polished; jewel. 2 Anything rare, delicate, and perfect, as a work of literature or art. 3 A light, muffinlike cake. —*v.t.* **gemmed, gem·ming** To adorn with or as with gems. [< L *gemma* jewel]

gem·i·nate (jem′ə·nāt) *v.t. & v.i.* **·nat·ed, ·nat·ing** To make or become double; pair. —*adj.* (-nit) *Bot.* Occurring in pairs, as leaves. [< L *geminus* a twin] —**gem′i·na′tion** *n.*

Gem·i·ni (jem′ə·nī) *n.* A constellation and the third sign of the zodiac; the Twins. • See ZODIAC.

gem·ma (jem′ə) *n. pl.* **·mae** (-ē) *Bot.* 1 A bud. 2 A budlike growth that becomes a new organism. [L]

gem·mate (jem′āt) *adj. Bot.* 1 Bearing buds. 2 Reproducing by buds. —**gem·ma′tion** *n.*

Gemsbok

gems·bok (gemz′bok) *n. pl.* **·bok** or **·boks** A South African antelope having long, sharp, nearly straight horns and a tufted tail. [< G *Gemse* chamois + *Bock* a buck]

ge·müt·lich·keit (gə·müt′likh·kīt) *n. Often cap.* Good feeling, geniality, and comfort..[G]

-gen *suffix of nouns* **1** That which produces: *oxygen.* **2** That which is produced: *antigen.* [< Gk. *-genēs* born]

Gen. General; Genesis; Geneva.

gen. gender; genera; general; generally; generator; genetic; genitive; genus.

gen·darme (zhän′därm; *Fr.* zhän·dárm′) *n. pl.* **-darmes** (-därmz; *Fr.* -dárm′) One of a corps of armed police, esp. in France. [F< *gens d'armes* men of arms]

gen·der (jen′dər) *n.* **1** *Gram.* In many languages, a grammatical designation of nouns and pronouns governing the form assumed by the words which modify or refer to them. **2** Any one of these designations, esp. masculine, feminine, or neuter. **3** *Informal* Sex. [< L *genus, -eris* kind]

gene (jēn) *n.* A unit occupying a distinct position on a chromosome and having a crucial function in the transmission of a specific characteristic from parent to offspring. [< G *Gen,* ult.< -GEN]

geneal. genealogical; genealogy.

ge·ne·al·o·gy (jē′nē·ol′ə·jē, -nē·al′-, jen′ē-) *n. pl.* **-gies 1** A record of descent from some ancestor; a list of ancestors and their descendants. **2** Descent in a direct line; pedigree. **3** The science that treats of pedigrees. [< Gk. *genea* race + -LOGY] —**ge·ne·a·log·i·cal** (jē′nē·ə·loj′i·kəl, jen′ē-) *adj.* —**ge′ne·a·log′i·cal·ly** *adv.* —**ge·ne·al′o·gist** *n.*

gen·er·a (jen′ər·ə) *n.pl. of* GENUS.

gen·er·al (jen′ər·əl, -rəl) *adj.* **1** Pertaining to, including, or affecting all or the whole; not local or particular: a *general* election. **2** Common to or current among the majority; prevalent: the *general* opinion. **3** Not restricted in application: a *general* principle. **4** Not limited to or dealing with a particular class; unspecialized: a *general* store; a *general* practitioner. **5** Not detailed or precise: a *general* idea. **6** Usual or customary: one's *general* habit. **7** Superior in rank: attorney *general.* —*n.* **1** See GRADE. **2** The chief of a religious order. **3** A general statement, fact, or principle. [< L *generalis* of a race or kind < *genus* kind]

General Assembly 1 The principal deliberative body of the United Nations in which every member nation is represented. **2** *U.S.* The legislature in some states.

gen·er·al·cy (jen′ər·əl·sē, -rəl-) *n. pl.* **-cies** Rank, authority, or tenure of office of a general.

general delivery 1 A post-office department in which mail is kept for the addressee until called for. **2** Mail so addressed.

general election 1 An election to choose from among previously nominated candidates. **2** An election in which all qualified voters participate.

gen·er·al·is·si·mo (jen′ər·əl·is′i·mō, -rəl-) *n. pl.* **-mos** In certain countries, the supreme commander of all the armed forces. [Ital.]

gen·er·al·ist (jen′ər·əl·ist, -rəl-) *n.* One who has a general knowledge of or background in several different fields, as distinguished from a specialist.

gen·er·al·i·ty (jen′ə·ral′ə·tē) *n. pl.* **-ties 1** The main part; majority. **2** Anything general or not specific; esp. a vague statement. **3** The state of being general or generalized.

gen·er·al·ize (jen′ər·əl·īz′, -rəl-) *v.* **-ized, -iz·ing** *v.t.* **1** To treat as having general or wide application. **2** To cause to be used or understood generally or widely; popularize. **3** To draw or frame (a general rule or principle) from particular evidence, facts, etc. **4** To draw or frame a general rule or principle from (particular evidence, facts, etc.). —*v.i.* **5** To talk in unspecific terms; be vague. **6** To draw general ideas or inferences from particulars. —**gen′er·al·i·za′tion** *n.*

gen·er·al·ly (jen′ər·əl·ē, -rəl-) *adv.* **1** For the most part; ordinarily; in most but not all cases. **2** Without going into particulars. **3** So as to include or apply to all.

gen·er·al·ship (jen′ər·əl·ship, -rəl-) *n.* **1** The rank, authority, or tenure of a general. **2** A general's military skill. **3** Management or leadership.

general staff A body of officers who assist a commander in military policy and strategy.

gen·er·ate (jen′ə·rāt) *v.t.* **-at·ed, -at·ing 1** To produce or cause to be; bring into being. **2** To beget as a parent; procreate. [< L *generare* < *genus* kind]

gen·er·a·tion (jen′ə·rā′shən) *n.* **1** The process of begetting or procreating. **2** Production or origination by any process; creation: the *generation* of electricity. **3** A step or degree in natural descent. **4** The average time elapsing between the birth of parent and offspring, and usu. estimated for humans at 30 years. **5** A body of persons existing at the same time or having common interests, characteristics, or outlooks.

gen·er·a·tive (jen′ə·rə·tiv, -rā′tiv) *adj.* **1** Of or relating to generation. **2** Having the power to generate.

gen·er·a·tor (jen′ə·rā′tər) *n.* **1** One who or that which generates or originates. **2** An apparatus in which the generation of a gas is effected. **3** A machine that changes heat or mechanical energy into electricity.

gen·er·ic (ji·ner′ik) *adj.* **1** Of or pertaining to a whole group or class; general. **2** Not having proprietary status: said esp. of names for drugs. **3** *Biol.* Of or like a genus. [< L *genus, generis* race, kind + -IC] —**gen·er′i·cal·ly** *adv.*

gen·er·os·i·ty (jen′ə·ros′ə·tē) *n. pl.* **-ties 1** The quality of being generous. **2** A generous act.

gen·er·ous (jen′ər·əs, -rəs) *adj.* **1** Giving or bestowing liberally; munificent. **2** Having noble qualities; honorable; high-minded: a *generous* nature. **3** Abundant; plentiful: a *generous* gift. **4** Full-flavored. [< L *generosus* of noble birth < *genus* kind] —**gen′er·ous·ly** *adv.* —**gen′er·ous·ness** *n.* —Syn. **1** bountiful, liberal, lavish, bounteous, prodigal. **2** magnanimous, humane, beneficent, benevolent.

gen·e·sis (jen′ə·sis) *n. pl.* **-ses** (-sēz) **1** The act or mode of originating; creation. **2** Origin; beginning. [< Gk. *genēsis* origin]

Gen·e·sis (jen′ə·sis) *n.* The first book of the Pentateuch in the Old Testament.

-genesis *combining form* Development; genesis; evolution: *parthenogenesis.*

gen·et[1] (jen′it, jə·net′) *n.* **1** Any of certain small carnivores related to the civets. **2** The fur of the genet. Also **ge·nette′.** [< Ar. *jarnait* genet]

gen·et[2] (jen′it) *n.* JENNET.

Genet

ge·net·ic (jə·net′ik) *adj.* **1** Of or pertaining to the origin of something. **2** Of or relating to genetics. Also **ge·net′i·cal.** —**ge·net′i·cal·ly** *adv.*

ge·net·ics (jə·net′iks) *n. pl.* (*construed as sing.*) **1** That branch of biology which deals with the interaction of the genes in producing the similarities and differences between individuals related by descent. **2** The inherited characteristics of an organism or group of organisms. —**ge·net′i·cist** *n.*

Geneva Convention An international agreement that set up certain principles concerning the treatment of prisoners, the wounded, and the dead in time of war, signed at Geneva, Switzerland in 1864.

gen·ial (jēn′yəl, jē′nē·əl) *adj.* **1** Kindly in disposition; cordial and pleasant in manner. **2** Imparting warmth, comfort, or life: a *genial* climate. [< L *genialis* of birth, pleasant] —**gen·i·al·i·ty** (jē′nē·al′ə·tē) *n.* —**ge′nial·ly** *adv.* —Syn. **1** affable, friendly, cheerful, blithe, sunny, light-hearted, warm, good-natured.

-genic *combining form* **1** Forming or producing. **2** Formed or produced by. **3** Suitable to. [< -GEN + -IC]

ge·nie (jē′nē) *n.* JINNI.

gen·i·tal (jen′ə·təl) *adj.* Of or pertaining to the reproductive organs, or to the process of generation. [< L *genitalis* of birth]

gen·i·ta·li·a (jen′ə·tā′lē·ə, -tāl′yə) *n. pl.* GENITALS.

gen·i·tals (jen′ə·təlz) *n. pl.* The external organs of generation; sexual organs.

gen·i·tive (jen′ə·tiv) *Gram. adj.* **1** Indicating source, origin, possession, or the like. **2** Pertaining to a case in Latin, Greek, etc., corresponding in part to the English possessive. —*n.* **1** The genitive case. **2** A word in this case. [< L *genitivus* of origin <*gignere* beget] —**gen·i·ti·val** (jen′ə·tī′·vəl) *adj.* —**gen′i·ti′val·ly** *adv.*

gen·ius (jēn′yəs) *n. pl.* **gen·ius·es**; *for def. 6* **ge·ni·i** (jē′·nē·ī). **1** Extraordinary intellectual or creative gifts. **2** Remarkable aptitude, talent, or capacity: a *genius* for oratory. **3** A person having such gifts or abilities. **4** The dominant nature or essential character of a nation, era, place, etc. **5** A representative type; embodiment. **6** In Roman antiquity: **a** A beneficient spirit or evil demon supposed to accompany one through life. **b** A guardian or tutelary spirit of a person or place. **7** A person having strong influence over another. [L, tutelary spirit]

gen·o·cide (jen′ə·sīd) *n.* The systematic extermination of a racial or national group. [<Gk. *genos* race + -CIDE]

gen·re (zhän′rə) *n.* A type or category, as of art, literature, etc. [F<L *genus, -eris* race, kind]

genre painting Painting that portrays everyday life.

gens (jenz) *n. pl.* **gen·tes** (jen′tēz) In Roman antiquity, a clan of descendants of a common male ancestor. [L]

gent (jent) *n. Slang* A gentleman.

gen·teel (jen·tēl′) *adj.* **1** Having or characterized by refinement, good taste, elegance, etc.: now used in a somewhat derogatory or humorous sense. **2** Artificially polite, refined, or elegant. [<MF *gentil* gentle] —**gen·teel′ly** *adv.*

gen·tian (jen′shən) *n.* **1** Any of a large genus of plants with flowers of various colors and usu. a tubular or bell-shaped corolla. **2** The root of the yellow gentian, having tonic properties. [<L *gentiana*]

gen·tile (jen′tīl) *n.* **1** *Often cap.* Any person not a Jew, esp. a Christian. **2** Formerly, among Christians, a pagan. **3** *Often cap.* Among Mormons, a non-Mormon. —*adj. Often cap.* Of, being, or relating to a gentile. [<L *gentilis* of a gens, foreign]

gen·til·i·ty (jen·til′ə·tē) *n. pl.* **·ties** **1** The quality of being genteel; refinement: now often used ironically. **2** The condition of being well-born. **3** Well-born persons collectively.

gen·tle (jen′təl) *adj.* **1** Mild and serene in nature or disposition. **2** Not harsh or rough; soft: a *gentle* touch. **3** Tame; docile: a *gentle* horse. **4** Not steep or abrupt: a *gentle* slope. **5** Of good birth; upper-class. **6** Refined; polite. —*v.t.* **gen·tled, gen·tling** **1** To tame, as a horse. **2** To soothe. [<L *gentilis* of good birth<*gens, gentis* race, clan] —**gen′tly** *adv.* —**gen′tle·ness** *n.*

gen·tle·folk (jen′təl·fōk′) *n. pl.* Persons of good family and good breeding. Also **gen′tle·folks′.**

gen·tle·man (jen′təl·mən) *n. pl.* **·men** (-mən) **1** A man who is considerate, courteous, and socially correct. **2** A man of good birth and social position. **3** Any man: in the plural, used as a form of address. —**gen′tle·man·ly, gen′tle·man·like′** *adj.*

gentleman farmer One who owns a farm, but hires others to work it.

gentleman's agreement An agreement, usu. less formal than a treaty or contract, guaranteed only by the honor of the parties involved.

gen·tle·wom·an (jen′təl·wŏŏm′ən) *n. pl.* **·wom·en** (-wim′in) **1** A woman of good birth and social position. **2** A considerate, gracious, well-mannered woman.

gen·tri·fi·ca·tion (jen′tri·fi·kā′shən) *n.* The rebuilding of older residential sections of a city for people able to pay for such improvements.

gen·try (jen′trē) *n.* **1** People of good position or birth; in England, the upper class exclusive of the nobility. **2** Any specified class or group of people. [<OF *gentil* gentle]

gen·u·flect (jen′yə·flekt) *v.i.* To bend the knee, as in worship. [<L *genu* knee + *flectere* to bend] —**gen·u·flec′tion** *n.*

gen·u·ine (jen′yōō·in) *adj.* **1** Of the original stock; purebred. **2** Not spurious, false, or counterfeit; real; authentic. **3** Not affected or hypocritical; frank; sincere; true. [<L *genuinus* innate] —**gen′u·ine·ly** *adv.* —**gen′u·ine·ness** *n.*

ge·nus (jē′nəs) *n. pl.* **gen·e·ra** (jen′ər·ə) **1** A biological category ranking below the family or subfamily and consisting of one or more species. **2** A kind; class. [L, race, kind]

geo- *combining form* Earth; ground: *geocentric.*

ge·o·cen·tric (jē′ō·sen′trik) *adj.* **1** Having or pertaining to the earth as center. **2** Measured from the earth or the earth's center. —**ge′o·cen′tri·cal** *adj.*

ge·ode (jē′ōd) *n. Geol.* A stone having a cavity lined with crystals. [<Gk. *geōdēs* earth] —**ge·od·ic** (jē·od′ik) *adj.*

geodesic dome An approximately hemispherical structure formed of straight elements that make up a network of rigid polygons.

ge·od·e·sy (jē·od′ə·sē) *n.* The study and measurement of the size and shape of the earth. [<Gk. *geodaisia* earth division] —**ge·o·des·ic** (jē′ə·des′ik, -dē′sik) *adj.* —**ge·od′e·sist** *n.*

ge·o·det·ic (jē′ə·det′ik) *adj.* Of, pertaining to, determined, or effected by geodesy. Also **ge·o·det′i·cal.** —**ge·o·det′i·cal·ly** *adv.*

geog. geographer; geographic; geography.

geographical mile NAUTICAL MILE.

ge·og·ra·phy (jē·og′rə·fē) *n. pl.* **·phies** **1** The science that describes the surface of the earth and its associated physical, biological, economic, political, and demographic characteristics. **2** The physical aspect, features, etc., of a place or area. [<GEO- + Gk. *graphein* write, describe] —**ge·og′ra·pher** *n.* —**ge′o·graph′ic** or **·i·cal** *adj.* —**ge′o·graph′i·cal·ly** *adv.*

geol. geologic; geological; geologist; geology.

ge·ol·o·gy (jē·ol′ə·jē) *n. pl.* **·gies** **1** The science that studies the origin, history, constitution, and structure of the earth. **2** The structure of a particular part of the earth. —**ge·o·log·ic** (jē′ə·loj′ik) or **·i·cal** *adj.* —**ge′o·log′i·cal·ly** *adv.* —**ge·ol′o·gist** *n.* • See GEOLOGICAL TIME SCALE, next page.

geom. geometer; geometric; geometrical; geometry.

ge·om·e·ter (jē·om′ət·ər) *n.* One who is expert in geometry. Also **ge·om·e·tri·cian** (jē·om·ə·trish′ən).

ge·o·met·ric (jē′ə·met′rik) *adj.* **1** Pertaining to or according to the rules and principles of geometry. **2** Of or characterized by straight lines, regular curves, and angles: a *geometric* design. Also **ge′o·met′ri·cal.** —**ge′o·met′ri·cal·ly** *adv.*

geometric progression *Math.* A sequence of terms in which each term except the first is a constant multiple of its predecessor, as 2, 4, 8, 16, 32, 64.

ge·om·e·try (jē·om′ə·trē) *n. pl.* **·tries** The branch of mathematics that deals with the properties, relations, and measurement of points, lines, angles, surfaces, and solids. [<GEO- + Gk. *metrein* measure]

ge·o·phys·ics (jē′ə·fiz′iks) *n. pl. (construed as sing.)* The science that investigates the physical forces, influences, and phenomena associated with the earth. —**ge′o·phys′i·cal** *adj.* —**ge′o·phys′i·cist** *n.*

ge·o·pol·i·tics (jē′ō·pol′ə·tiks) *n. pl. (construed as sing.)* The study of the interrelationship of geography, climate, etc., and politics. —**ge′o·po·lit′i·cal** *adj.* —**ge′o·po·lit′i·cal·ly** *adv.* —**ge′o·pol′i·ti′cian** *n.*

geor·gette (jôr·jet′) *n.* A sheer, lightly crinkled, silk or silklike fabric, used for blouses, gowns, etc. Also **georgette crepe.** [<*Georgette*, a trade name]

Geor·gian (jôr′jən) *adj.* **1** Of or pertaining to the reigns or period of the four Georges in England, 1714–1830, or of George V, 1910–36. **2** Of or pertaining to Georgia in the U.S.S.R., to the Georgians, or to their language. —*n.* **1** A native or citizen of the Georgian S.S.R. **2** The language of the Georgians.

ge·o·ther·mal (jē′ə·thûr′məl) *adj.* Of or pertaining to the earth's internal heat. [<GEO- + THERMAL]

geothermal energy Subterranean heat generated in vast quantities by natural radioactivity, utilized chiefly as steam and hot water from hot springs.

ge·ot·ro·pism (jē·ot′rə·piz′əm) *n.* A biological response to gravity, as the downward growth of the roots of a plant. —**ge·o·trop·ic** (jē′ə·trop′ik) *adj.* —**ge′o·trop′i·cal·ly** *adv.*

Ger. German; Germany.

ger. gerund.

ge·ra·ni·um (ji·rā′nē·əm) *n.* **1** Any of a large genus of plants with showy pink or purple flowers. **2** A cultivated plant with usu. scented leaves and red, pink, or white flowers in showy cymes. [<Gk. *geranion,* lit., little crane]

ger·bil (jûr′bil) *n.* A mouselike rodent with a long tail and long hind legs adapted for leaping, native to Africa and Asia. [<NL *gerboa* jerboa]

Gerbil

GEOLOGICAL TIME SCALE

This table defines the geological eras, time periods, and epochs listed in the first three columns. Each of these terms may be used as both a noun (e.g., *the Mesozoic, the Jurassic, the Pleistocene*) and as an adjective with the meaning: Of, pertaining to, or characteristic of that specific era, period, or epoch (e.g., the *Mesozoic* era, *Mesozoic* evolution, *Jurassic* reptiles, *Pleistocene* climate variation, etc.).

Read from bottom to top.

Eras	Time Periods Rock Systems	Time Epochs Rock Series	Approx. Duration Million Years	Approx. Percent Total Age	Life Forms
Cenozoic	Quaternary	Recent Pleistocene	1		Rise and dominance of man.
Cenozoic	Upper Tertiary	Pliocene Miocene	65	2	Modern animals and plants.
Cenozoic	Lower Tertiary	Oligocene Eocene Paleocene	65	2	Rapid development of modern mammals, insects, and plants.
Mesozoic	Upper Cretaceous		75		Primitive mammals; last dinosaurs; last ammonites.
Mesozoic	Lower Cretaceous		75	5	Rise of flowering plants.
Mesozoic	Jurassic		45	5	First birds, first mammals. Diversification of reptiles; climax of ammonites; coniferous trees.
Mesozoic	Triassic		45		Rise of dinosaurs; bony fishes.
Paleozoic	Permian		45		Rise of reptiles. Modern insects. Last of many plant and animal groups.
Paleozoic	Pennsylvanian } Carboniferous Mississippian		75		First reptiles. Amphibians; primitive insects; seed ferns; primitive conifers. Climax of shell–crushing sharks. Primitive ammonites.
Paleozoic	Devonian		50	9	First amphibians, first land snails. Primitive land plants. Climax of brachiopods.
Paleozoic	Silurian		20		First traces of land life. Scorpions. First lungfishes. Widespread coral reefs.
Paleozoic	Ordovician		70		First fish. Climax of trilobites. First appearance of many marine invertebrates.
Paleozoic	Cambrian		50		First marine invertebrates, including trilobites.
Proterozoic Archeozoic	Pre-Cambrian		About 3,000	84	First signs of life. Algae.

Age of oldest dated rocks: about 3,500,000,000 years.

ger·fal·con (jûr′fal′kən, -fôl′-, -fō′-) *n.* GYRFALCON.

ger·i·at·rics (jer′ē·at′riks) *n. pl. (construed as sing.)* The branch of medicine which deals with the diseases and physiological changes associated with aging and old people. [< Gk. *gēras* old age + *iatros* physician] —**ger·i·at·ric** *adj.*

ger·kin (gûr′kin) *n.* GHERKIN.

germ (jûrm) *n.* **1** Any rudimentary living substance that can develop into an organism. **2** A microorganism that causes disease; microbe. **3** The primary source from which something may be developed. [< L *germen* offshoot]

ger·man¹ (jûr′mən) *n.* **1** The cotillion, a dance. **2** A party at which it is the chief feature. [Short for *German cotillion*]

ger·man² (jûr′mən) *adj.* Having the same parents or grandparents: used after the noun: cousins *german*, brothers *german*. [< L *germanus* closely related]

Ger·man (jûr′mən) *adj.* Of, pertaining to, or characteristic of Germany, its people, or their language. —*n.* **1** A native or citizen of Germany. **2** The West Germanic language used throughout most of Germany and in parts of Switzerland and Austria: also **New High German.**

German cockroach A small, brownish, winged cockroach, a common household pest in urban buildings.

ger·man·der (jər·man′dər) *n.* **1** An herb of the mint family, with purple flowers. **2** A variety of speedwell. [<

OF < Med. L < Gk. < *chamai* on the ground + *drys* an oak]

ger·mane (jər·mān′) *adj.* **1** In close relationship; relevant; pertinent. **2** Akin; german. [See GERMAN²]

Ger·man·ic (jər·man′ik) *adj.* **1** GERMAN. **2** Of, relating to, or characteristic of any of the Germanic languages or of the people who speak or spoke them. —*n.* **1** A subfamily of the Indo-European family of languages, divided into the branches **East Germanic,** including Gothic (extinct); **North Germanic** or Scandinavian, including Norwegian, Swedish, Danish, Icelandic, and Faroese; and **West Germanic,** including all the High and Low German languages and dialects, among which are German, Dutch, Flemish, Frisian, English, Yiddish, Plattdeutsch, etc. **2** The prehistoric parent of these languages: called **Primitive Germanic, Pro′to-Germanic** (prō′tō-).

ger·ma·ni·um (jər·mā′nē·əm) *n.* A gray, brittle, metallic element (symbol Ge) used as a semiconductor, esp. in transistors. [< L *Germania* Germany]

Ger·man·ize (jûr′mən·īz) *v.t. & v.i.* **·ized, ·iz·ing** To make or become German in speech, customs, etc. —**Ger′man·i·za′tion** *n.*

German measles RUBELLA.

German shepherd A breed of dog with muscular body,

German shepherd dog

often trained as Seeing Eye dogs or as guard dogs. Also **German shepherd dog** or **German police dog**.

German silver NICKEL SILVER.

Ger·ma·ny (jûr′mə·nē) *n. pl.* **·ma·nys** A republic of CEN. EUROPE, 137,214 SQ. MI., CAP. BERLIN; DIVIDED 1945-1990 into the German Democratic Republic or East Germany, cap. Berlin, a Soviet ally, and the German Federal Republic or West Germany, cap. Bonn, a member of NATO.

germ cell A cell specialized for reproduction.

ger·mi·cide (jûr′mə·sīd) *n.* Any agent used to destroy pathogenic microorganisms. [< GERM + -CIDE] —**ger′mi·ci′dal** *adj.*

ger·mi·nal (jûr′mə·nəl) *adj.* 1 Pertaining to or constituting a germ. 2 Being in the first stage of development.

ger·mi·nant (jûr′mə·nənt) *adj.* That germinates or sprouts.

ger·mi·nate (jûr′mə·nāt) *v.* **·nat·ed, ·nat·ing** *v.i.* 1 To begin to grow or develop; sprout. —*v.t.* 2 To cause to sprout. [<L *germinare*] —**ger′mi·na′tion, ger′mi·na′tor** *n.* —**ger′mi·na′tive** *adj.*

germ plasm *Biol.* Reproductive cells, esp. the part which contains the genes.

ger·on·tol·o·gy (jer′ən·tol′ə·jē) *n.* The scientific study of the phenomena of aging. [<Gk. *gerōn, gerontos* old man + -LOGY] —**ger′on·tol′o·gist** *n.*

ger·ry·man·der (jer′i·man′dər, ger′-) *v.t.* To alter, as the shape of voting districts of a state or region, to the contrived advantage of a political party or other group. —*n.* A contrived or unfair redistricting of a state or region. [<E. *Gerry*, 1744–1814, + (SALA)MANDER; from the shape of a district formed in Massachusetts while Gerry was governor]

ger·und (jer′ənd) *n.* A verbal noun ending in -*ing*, functioning as a noun, but capable of taking objects and adverbial modifiers. Example: *Writing* poetry well is an art. [<L *gerundum* acting, doing] —**ge·run·di·al** (jə·run′dē·əl) *adj.*

ge·run·dive (jə·run′div) *adj.* Like, pertaining to, or having the nature of the gerund. —*n.* 1 In Latin, a verbal adjective having the gerund stem and used as future passive participle, expressing obligation, fitness, or necessity. 2 A similar verbal adjective in any language.

gest (jest) *n.* 1 *Archaic* A deed; exploit. 2 A tale of adventure, esp. one in verse. Also **geste**. [<L *gesta* deeds]

ge·stalt (gə·shtält′) *n. pl.* **ge·stalt·en** (-shtält′ən) or **ge·stalts** *Often cap.* An arrangement of elements comprising an entity having properties not to be found in its constituent parts. [<G, form]

Gestalt psychology A school of psychology which interprets biological and psychic processes in terms of closely integrated patterns that are different from the sums of their parts.

Ge·sta·po (gə·stä′pō) *n.* The secret police of Nazi Germany. [G *Ge(heime) Sta(ats)po(lizei)* Secret State Police]

ges·tate (jes′tāt) *v.t.* **·tat·ed, ·tat·ing** 1 To carry in the womb during pregnancy. 2 To form in the mind. [Back formation from GESTATION]

ges·ta·tion (jes·tā′shən) *n.* 1 Pregnancy, esp. the period of carrying a fetus in the womb. 2 The formation or period of development of an idea or program. [<L *gestare* carry young] —**ges·ta′tion·al** *adj.*

ges·tic·u·late (jes·tik′yə·lāt) *v.* **·lat·ed, ·lat·ing** *v.i.* 1 To make motions with the hands or arms, as in speaking. — *v.t.* 2 To express by gestures. [<L *gestus* bearing, gesture] —**ges·tic′u·la′tion** *n.* —**ges·tic′u·la′tive** *adj.*

ges·ture (jes′chər) *n.* 1 An expressive motion of the body

and esp. of the hand or hands, used for emphasis or to express some idea or emotion. 2 Something said or done for mere effect or as a concession to manners, courtesy, etc. —*v.* **·tured, ·tur·ing** *v.i.* 1 To make gestures. —*v.t.* 2 To express by gestures. [<L *gestus*, pp. of *gerere* carry on, do] —**ges′tur·er** *n.*

get (get) *v.* **got** or *Archaic* **gat, got** or *U.S.* **got·ten, get·ting** *v.t.* 1 To come into possession of; obtain. 2 To go for and bring back: to *get* one's hat. 3 To cause to come, go, move, etc.: We *got* him to talk; I can't *get* the window up. 4 To take; carry away: *Get* your things out of this house. 5 To prepare: to *get* breakfast. 6 To bring to a state or condition: to *get* the work done. 7 To find out or obtain by calculation, experiment, etc.: to *get* the range of a gun. 8 To communicate with; contact: We can't *get* them on the phone. 9 To receive as a reward, punishment, etc.: to *get* ten years in jail. 10 To obtain, receive, or earn: to *get* permission. 11 To capture; catch. 12 To learn or master: to *get* a lesson. 13 To become sick with. 14 To board; catch, as a train. 15 To beget: said chiefly of animals. 16 *Informal* To come to an understanding of; comprehend: I *get* the idea. 17 *Informal* To possess: with *have* or *has*: He has *got* quite a temper. 18 To square accounts with: I'll *get* you yet. 19 *Informal* To be obliged or forced to do: with *have* or *has*: I have *got* to go home. 20 *Informal* To make helpless or ineffective: Drink finally *got* him. 21 *Informal* To strike; hit: That shot *got* him in the arm. 22 *Slang* To puzzle; baffle. 23 *Slang* To cause irritation or pleasure to: His impudence *gets* me. 24 *Slang* To notice: *Get* that dress she's wearing. —*v.i.* 25 To arrive: When does the train *get* there? 26 To come or go: *Get* in here! 27 To board; enter: to *get* on a train. 28 To become: to *get* drunk. —**get across** 1 To make or be convincing or clear. 2 To be successful, as in projecting one's personality. —**get ahead** To succeed; prosper. —**get along** 1 To leave; go. 2 To be successful or fairly successful, as in business. 3 To be friendly. 4 To proceed. 5 To grow old or older. —**get around** 1 To become known. 2 To move about. 3 To avoid; circumvent. 4 To flatter, cajole, etc., so as to obtain the favor of. —**get at** 1 To reach; arrive at: to *get at* the truth. 2 To intend; mean: I don't see what you're *getting at*. 3 To apply oneself to: to *get at* a problem. —**get away** 1 To escape. 2 To leave; go. 3 To start. —**get away with** *Slang* To do (something) without discovery, criticism, or punishment. —**get back at** *Slang* To revenge oneself on. —**get by** 1 To pass: This *got by* the censor. 2 *Informal* To manage to survive. —**get in** 1 To arrive. 2 To interject effectively, as a remark. —**get lost** 1 To lose one's way. 2 *Slang* Go away! —**get off** 1 To descend from; dismount. 2 To leave; depart. 3 To be relieved, as of duty. 4 To be released without punishment; escape penalty. 5 To utter: to *get off* a joke. 6 To take off: *Get off* your wet clothes. —**get on** 1 To mount, as a horse. 2 To get along. —**get out** 1 To depart. 2 To escape. 3 To become known, as a secret. 4 To publish; issue. —**get over** 1 To recover from, as illness or surprise. 2 To get across. —**get through** 1 To finish. 2 To survive. —**get to** 1 To start or begin. 2 To succeed, as in reaching or making clear to: also **get through to.** —**get together** 1 To collect, as facts. 2 To meet; assemble. 3 *Informal* To come to an agreement. —**get up** 1 To rise, as from sleep. 2 To prepare and arrange; devise. 3 *Informal* To dress up. [<ON *geta*] —**get′ta·ble, get′a·ble** *adj.* —**get′ter** *n.* • See GOT and GOTTEN.

get·a·way (get′ə·wā′) *n.* 1 An escape. 2 The start, as of a race.

Geth·sem·a·ne (geth·sem′ə·nē) *n.* A garden outside Jerusalem, the scene of the agony, betrayal, and arrest of Jesus. *Matt.* 26:36.

get-to·geth·er (get′tə·geth′ər) *n.* An informal gathering.

get-up (get′up′) *n. Informal* 1 The general appearance or make-up of something. 2 Costume; dress.

gew·gaw (gyōō′gô) *adj.* Showy; gaudy. —*n.* A flashy trinket; bauble. [?]

gey·ser (gi′zər) *n.* A spring from which intermittent jets of steam, hot water, or mud are ejected. [<ON *geysa* gush]

Gha·na (gä′nə) *n.* A republic of the Commonwealth of Nations in w Africa, 92,100 sq. mi., cap. Accra. —**Gha′na·ian** (-nē·ən) *adj., n.* • See map at AFRICA.

ghast·ly (gast′lē, gäst′-) *adj.* **·li·er, ·li·est** 1 Having a haggard, deathlike appearance. 2 Terrifying or shocking. 3

Informal Very bad: a *ghastly* blunder. —*adv.* In a ghastly manner. [< OE *gāstlíc* ghostly] —**ghast′li·ness** *n.*

ghat (gôt) *n.* 1 In India, a stairway on a river bank, usu. leading to a temple. 2 In India, a mountain pass. Also **ghaut.** [< Hind. *ghāt*]

ghee (gē) *n.* In India, clarified butter, usu. made from milk of the water buffalo. Also **ghi.** [< Hind. *ghī*]

gher·kin (gûr′kin) *n.* 1 A small prickly cucumber used for pickles. 2 Any small, immature cucumber used for pickling. [< LGk. *angourion* cucumber]

ghet·to (get′ō) *n. pl.* **·tos** 1 In Europe, a part of a city in which Jews were formerly required to live. 2 A section of a city, often rundown or overcrowded, inhabited chiefly by a minority group. 3 Any community or group separated physically or culturally from the rest of society. [Ital.]

ghet·to·ize (get′ō·īz) *v.t.* **·ized, ·iz·ing** To make into a ghetto. —**ghet′to·iz·a′tion** *n.*

ghost (gōst) *n.* 1 A disembodied spirit, esp. of a dead person and supposedly able to manifest itself to the living in various ways. 2 The soul or spirit: now only in the phrase **give up the ghost,** to die. 3 A shadow or semblance; slight trace. 4 A false, secondary image produced in an optical instrument or on a television screen. 5 *Informal* A ghost writer. —*v.t. & v.i.* 1 To haunt as a ghost. 2 *Informal* To write as a ghost writer. [< OE *gāst* spirit] —**ghost′like′** *adj.*

ghost·ly (gōst′lē) *adj.* **·li·er, ·li·est** 1 Of, pertaining to, or like a ghost; spectral. 2 Spiritual. —**ghost′li·ness** *n.*

ghost town A deserted town.

ghost-write (gōst′rīt′) *v.i. & v.t.* **·wrote, ·writ·ten, ·writ·ing** To do literary work credited to another. —**ghost writer**

ghoul (gōōl) *n.* 1 In Oriental legend, an evil spirit supposed to prey on corpses. 2 A person who robs dead bodies. 3 One who delights in revolting things. [< Ar. *ghūl*] —**ghoul′ish** *adj.* —**ghoul′ish·ly** *adv.* —**ghoul′ish·ness** *n.*

GHQ General Headquarters.

GI (jē′ī) *n. pl.* **GI′s, GIs** *Informal* A soldier, esp. an enlisted man, in the U.S. Army. —*adj.* 1 Of, pertaining to, or issued by the government to U.S. military forces. 2 *Informal* Conforming to U.S. military regulations. Also **G.I.** [< G(overnment) I(ssue)]

G.I., g.i. gastrointestinal.

gi. gill².

gi·ant (jī′ənt) *n.* 1 Any imaginary person of gigantic size. 2 Any person or thing of great size, either physically, mentally, or figuratively. —*adj.* Gigantic. [< Gk. *gigas, gigantos*] —**gi′ant·ess** *n. Fem.*

gi·ant·ism (jī′ənt·iz′əm) *n.* GIGANTISM.

giant panda PANDA (def. 2).

giaour (jour) *n.* An unbeliever: a term of opprobrium applied by Muslims. [< Pers. *gaur*]

gib·ber (jib′ər, gib′-) *v.i.* To talk rapidly and incoherently; jabber. —*n.* Unintelligible talk; gibberish. [Imit.]

gib·ber·ish (jib′ər·ish, gib′-) *n.* 1 Incoherent or unintelligible talk. 2 Pretentiously difficult or obscure language. —**Syn.** 1 babble, gabble, double talk, gobbledygook.

gib·bet (jib′it) *n.* 1 An upright timber with a crosspiece projecting at right angles from its upper end, upon which criminals were formerly hanged. 2 GALLOWS. —*v.t.* **·bet·ed** or **·bet·ted, ·bet·ing** or **·bet·ting** 1 To execute by hanging. 2 To hang and expose on a gibbet. 3 To hold up to public contempt. [< OF *gibe* a staff]

gib·bon (gib′ən) *n.* A slender, long-armed arboreal ape of Asia. [F]

gib·bous (gib′əs, jib′-) *adj.* 1 Irregularly rounded; convex, as the moon when less than full and yet more than half full. 2 Humpbacked. Also **gib·bose** (gib′ōs, gi-bōs′). [< L *gibbus* a hump] —**gib′bous·ly** *adv.* —**gib′bous·ness** *n.* • See MOON.

Gibbon

gibe (jīb) *v.t. & v.i.* **gibed, gib·ing** To mock; sneer; scoff. —*n.* An expression of sarcasm and ridicule. [? < OF *giber* treat roughly in play] —**gib′er** *n.* —**Syn.** *v.* deride, taunt, scorn, ridicule.

gib·let (jib′lit, gib′-) *n.* One of the edible visceral parts of a fowl, as the gizzard, heart, or liver. [< OF *gibelet*]

gid·dy (gid′ē) *adj.* **·di·er, ·di·est** 1 Dizzy. 2 Causing dizziness. 3 Foolish; silly; frivolous. —*v.t. & v.i.* **gid·died, gid·dy·ing** To make or become giddy. [< OE *gydig* insane] —**gid′di·ly** *adv.* —**gid′di·ness** *n.*

gift (gift) *n.* 1 That which is given; a donation; present. 2 The act, right, or power of giving. 3 A natural endowment; aptitude; talent. —*v.t.* 1 To give as a present to. 2 To make a gift of. [< OE *gifan* give]

gift·ed (gif′tid) *adj.* Having unusual ability or talent: a *gifted* child. —**gift′ed·ly** *adv.* —**gift′ed·ness** *n.*

gig¹ (gig) *n.* 1 A light, two-wheeled vehicle drawn by one horse. 2 A long, light ship's boat; also, a speedy, light rowboat. —*v.* **gigged, gig·ging** *v.i.* To ride in a gig. [?]

gig² (gig) *n. Slang* 1 A demerit, as in the army. 2 A job or engagement, esp. as a musician or singer. [?]

giga- *prefix* One billion or 10⁹ (times a given unit). [< Gk. *gigas* giant]

gi·gan·tic (jī·gan′tik) *adj.* 1 Like a giant; colossal; huge. 2 Tremendous; extraordinary. [See GIANT.]

gi·gan·tism (jī·gan′tiz·əm) *n.* Excessive growth of the body due to disturbances in the pituitary gland.

gig·gle (gig′əl) *v.i.* **gig·gled, gig·gling** To laugh in a high-pitched, nervous manner; titter. —*n.* Such a laugh; titter. [Imit.] —**gig′gler** *n.* —**gig′gly** *adj.*

gig·o·lo (jig′ə·lō, zhig′-) *n. pl.* **·los** 1 A woman's paid dancing partner or escort. 2 A man supported by a woman as her lover. [F, prob. < *gigolette* a prostitute]

gig·ot (jig′ət, *Fr.* zhē·gō′) *n.* 1 A leg of lamb or mutton. 2 A sleeve having the shape of a leg of mutton. [F]

gigue (zhēg) *n.* A lively dance, often the final movement in a suite of dances. [F]

Gi·la monster (hē′lə) A large, poisonous lizard with a stout orange and black body, found in the sw U.S. [< *Gila* River in New Mexico and Arizona]

Gila monster

gild¹ (gild) *v.t.* **gild·ed** or **gilt, gild·ing** 1 To coat with or as with gold or gold leaf. 2 To give a pleasing or attractive appearance to; gloss over. [< OE *gyldan*] —**gild′er** *n.*

gild² (gild) *n.* GUILD.

gill¹ (gil) *n.* 1 A respiratory organ that absorbs dissolved oxygen from water circulating through it, as in fishes, mollusks, etc. • See OYSTER. 2 A flap of tissue at the side of the head or neck, as the wattle of a fowl. 3 One of the thin radial plates inside the cap of a mushroom. [< Scand.]

gill² (jil) *n.* A liquid measure, one fourth of a pint. [< OF *gelle* measure for wine]

gil·li·flow·er (jil′ē·flou′ər) *n.* Any of various plants having clove-scented flowers, esp. the carnation. Also **gil′ly·flow′er.** [< Gk. *karyophyllon* clove]

gilt¹ (gilt) A *p.t. & p.p.* of GILD. —*adj.* Gilded; yellow like gold. —*n.* The gold or goldlike material used in gilding.

gilt² (gilt) *n.* A young female pig. [< ON *gyltr*]

gilt-edge (gilt′ej′) *adj.* 1 Having the edges gilded: said of paper. 2 Of the best quality or highest price: said of bonds, securities, etc. Also **gilt′-edged′.**

gim·bals (gim′bəlz, jim′-) *n. pl.* (construed as sing.) A device for allowing a suspended object, as a ship's compass, to rotate freely on two axes 90° apart. [< L *gemellus*, dim. of *geminus* twin]

gim·crack (jim′krak) *n.* A useless trinket; bauble. —*adj.* Cheap and showy. [?] —**gim′crack·er·y** *n.*

Gimbals

gim·let (gim′lit) *n.* A small boring tool with a cross handle and a spiral point. —*v.t.* To make a hole in with a gimlet. [< OF *guimbelet*]

gim·mick (gim'ik) n. *Informal* 1 Something new or ingenious, as a gadget, scheme, stunt, etc., usu. devised to win publicity or make something more attractive. 2 A secret or surprising element; twist. 3 Any object whose name cannot be recalled. 4 A secret device for controlling the movements of a prize wheel. —v.t. *Slang* To add gimmicks to: often with *up*. [?] —**gim'mick·y** *adj.*

gim·mick·ry (gim'ik·rē) n. *Informal* 1 The use of gimmicks, esp. if indiscriminate. 2 Gimmicks. Also **gim'mick·e·ry** (-ə·rē).

gimp¹ (gimp) n. A narrow, flat, ornamental trimming, used for dresses, furniture, etc. [?]

gimp² (gimp) n. *Informal* 1 A lame or crippled person. 2 A limp. —v.i. To limp. [?] —**gimp'y** *adj.* (·i·er, ·i·est)

gin¹ (jin) n. 1 An alcoholic liquor distilled from various grains and flavored with juniper berries. 2 Such a liquor with other flavoring. [Short for Du. *jenever* juniper]

gin² (jin) v.t. & v.i. **gan, gin·ning** *Archaic* To begin.

gin³ (jin) n. 1 A machine for separating cotton fibers from the seeds. 2 A snare or trap. —v.t. **ginned, gin·ning** 1 To catch in a trap. 2 To remove the seeds from (cotton) in a gin. [Short for ME *engin* engine]

gin⁴ (jin) n. GIN RUMMY.

gin·ger (jin'jər) n. 1 The pungent, spicy rootstock of a tropical plant, used in medicine and cookery. 2 The plant itself. 3 *Informal* Liveliness; spunk. [< Gk. *zingiberis*]

ginger ale A carbonated soft drink flavored with ginger.

ginger beer A soft drink similar to ginger ale.

gin·ger·bread (jin'jər·bred') n. 1 A light sweet cake flavored with ginger. 2 Gaudy or unnecessary ornament. [Alter. of OF *gingebras* preserved ginger < LL]

gin·ger·ly (jin'jər·lē) *adj.* Cautious or careful. —*adv.* Cautiously; carefully. [?]

gin·ger·snap (jin'jər·snap') n. A flat, brittle cooky flavored with ginger and molasses.

ging·ham (ging'əm) n. A plain-weave cotton fabric, usu. in checks or stripes. [< Malay *ginggang*]

gin·gi·vi·tis (jin'jə·vī'tis) n. Inflammation of the gums. [< L *gingiva* gum]

gink (gingk) n. *Slang* An odd fellow; guy. [?]

gink·go (ging'kō) n. pl. **·goes** A hardy, widely cultivated deciduous tree native in China, having fanlike foliage. Also **ging'ko.** [Jap.]

gin·mill (jin'mil') n. *Slang* A saloon.

gin rummy A variety of rummy, a card game.

Ginkgo branch

gin·seng (jin'seng) n. 1 Either of two related herbs native in North America and China, having an aromatic root used medicinally. 2 The root, or a preparation made from it. [< Chin. *jen shen*]

gip (jip) n., v. **gipped, gip·ping** GYP.

Gip·sy (jip'sē) n. pl. **·sies** GYPSY.

gipsy moth GYPSY MOTH.

gi·raffe (jə·raf', -räf') n. pl. **·raffes** or **·raffe** A large spotted African ruminant, having a very long neck and limbs; the tallest of the quadrupeds. [< Ar. *zarāfah*]

gird (gûrd) v.t. **gird·ed** or **girt, gird·ing** 1 To surround with a belt or girdle. 2 To encircle; hem in. 3 To prepare (oneself) for action. 4 To clothe; equip. [< OE *gyrdan*]

gird·er (gûr'dər) n. A principal horizontal beam of a structure, receiving a vertical load.

gir·dle (gûr'dəl) n. 1 A belt, cord, or sash worn around the waist. 2 A woman's corsetlike, usu. elastic undergarment, reaching from the waist to below the hips. 3 Anything that encircles. 4 The edge of a cut gem. 5 An encircling cut through the bark of a branch or tree. —v.t. **gir·dled, gir·dling** 1 To fasten a girdle or belt around. 2 To encircle; encompass. 3 To make an encircling cut through the bark of (a branch or tree). [< OE *gyrdel*] —**gir'dler** n.

Giraffe

girl (gûrl) n. 1 A female child. 2 A young unmarried woman. 3 A female servant. 4 *Informal* A sweetheart. 5 *Informal* A woman of any age. [< ME *gurle*] —**girl'ish** *adj.* —**girl'ish·ly** *adv.* —**girl'ish·ness** n.

girl Friday A female office worker who performs a variety of tasks. [< GIRL + (MAN) FRIDAY]

girl friend *Informal* 1 A boy's or man's sweetheart, favorite female companion, etc. 2 A female friend.

girl·hood (gûrl'hŏŏd) n. The state or time of being a girl.

girl·ie (gûr'lē) *adj. Informal* Featuring nude or nearly nude women or pictures of them: a *girlie* magazine.

girl scout A member of an organization, **Girl Scouts of America**, formed in 1912.

girt¹ (gûrt) v.t. 1 To gird; girdle. 2 To fasten with a girth, strap, etc. [< GIRD]

girt² (gûrt) p.t. & p.p. of GIRD.

girth (gûrth) n. 1 A band or strap for fastening a pack or saddle to a horse's back. 2 A girdle. 3 The circumference of a person's waist, a tree, etc. —v.t. 1 To bind with a girth. 2 To encircle. 3 To find the girth of. [< ON *gjordh*]

gist (jist) n. The substance, point, or main idea. [< OF *giste* place of rest < *gesir* to lie] —**Syn.** heart, core, essence.

give (giv) v. **gave, giv·en, giv·ing** v.t. 1 To turn over to another without receiving anything in exchange. 2 To transfer to the possession or control of another for a price or equal value. 3 To hand over for safekeeping, delivery, etc. 4 To offer, esp. as entertainment: to *give* a play, toast, etc. 5 To be the cause or source of: The sun *gives* light. 6 To provide or furnish; impart: to *give* the news on TV. 7 To express by word or gesture. 8 To be the agent of transfer of, as a disease. 9 To grant: to *give* permission. 10 To impose, as a punishment. 11 To emit or show, as a movement, shout, etc. 12 To administer, as medicine. 13 To deal; inflict, as a blow. 14 To concede or yield: to *give* ground. 15 To devote or sacrifice: to *give* one's life. 16 To confer, as a title. —v.i. 17 To make gifts. 18 To yield, as from pressure, melting, or thawing; collapse. 19 To be springy or resilient; bend. —**give away** 1 To bestow as a gift. 2 To bestow (the bride) upon the bridegroom. 3 To reveal or disclose. —**give back** To return. —**give in** To yield. 2 To collapse, as under stress. —**give off** (or **forth**) To send forth; emit, as odors. —**give out** 1 To send forth; emit. 2 To distribute. 3 To make known; publish. 4 To become worn out, exhausted, etc. —**give rise to** To cause or result in. —**give up** 1 To surrender; cede; hand over. 2 To stop; cease. 3 To desist from as hopeless. 4 To lose all hope for. 5 To devote wholly. —n. The quality of being yielding; elasticity. [< OE *giefan*] —**giv'er** n.

give-and-take (giv'ən·tāk') n. 1 Fair exchange; equal compromise. 2 An exchange of ideas or wit.

give·a·way (giv'ə·wā') n. 1 A betrayal or revelation, often unintentional. —*adj.* Featuring awards of money or prizes, as a television show.

giv·en (giv'ən) *adj.* 1 Habitually inclined: with *to*. 2 Specified; stated. 3 Donated; presented. 4 Admitted as a fact or a premise. —n. A datum; premise.

given name One's first name, as distinguished from one's family name.

give-up (giv'up') n. The practice of splitting a stockbroker's commission with another broker at the direction of the customer.

giz·mo (giz'mō) n. pl. **·mos** *Informal* Any gadget. [?]

giz·zard (giz'ərd) n. 1 The second stomach of birds, in which the food is ground. 2 *Slang* The stomach. [< L *gigeria* cooked entrails of poultry]

Gk. Greek.

gla·brous (glā'brəs) *adj. Biol.* Without hair or down. [< L *glaber* bald, smooth]

gla·cé (gla·sā'; *Fr.* glå·sā') *adj.* 1 Iced; frozen. 2 Having a glossy surface resembling ice. 3 Covered with an icing or glaze, as certain candies. —v.t. **·céed, ·cé·ing** 1 To cover with icing. 2 To render smooth and glossy. [F < *glace* ice]

gla·cial (glā'shəl) *adj.* 1 Of, pertaining to, or caused by glaciers. 2 Of or pertaining to a glacial epoch. 3 Very cold or icy. 4 Cold in manner, appearance, etc.: a *glacial* look. [< L *glacies* ice] —**gla'cial·ly** *adv.*

glacial epoch Any portion of geological time in which glaciers covered much of the earth's surface.

gla·ci·ate (glā'shē·āt) v.t. **·at·ed, ·at·ing** 1 To cover with glacial ice. 2 To affect or change by glacial action. 3 To convert into ice. —**gla'ci·a'tion** n.

gla·cier (glā'shər) n. A field of ice which moves slowly downward over slopes or through valleys until it either melts or breaks off to form icebergs. [<L *glacies* ice]

glad (glad) adj. **glad·der, glad·dest 1** Happy; joyful. **2** Causing joy or happiness. **3** Most willing: She is *glad* to do it. **4** Bright; cheerful. [<OE *glæd* shining, glad] —**glad'ly** adv. —**glad'ness** n. —Syn. **1** pleased, contented, gay, merry, cheery, buoyant.

glad·den (glad'n) v.t. & v.i. To make or become glad.

glade (glād) n. **1** An open space in a wood. **2** An everglade. [Prob. akin to *glad* in obs. sense "sunny"]

glad hand Slang A hearty welcome.

glad·i·a·tor (glad'ē·ā'tər) n. **1** A man who fought with deadly weapons, as in the ancient Roman amphitheater, for popular amusement. **2** One who engages in any kind of fight or controversy. [<L *gladius* sword] —**glad·i·a·to·ri·al** (glad'ē·ə·tôr'ē·əl, -tōr'ē-) adj.

glad·i·o·lus (glad'ē·ō'ləs) n. pl. **·lus·es** or **·li** (-lī) A plant of the iris family with fleshy bulbs, sword-shaped leaves, and spikes of colored flowers. Also **glad·i·o·la** (glad'ē·ō'lə), **glad'i·ole** (-ōl). [<L *gladius* sword]

glad·some (glad'səm) adj. **1** Joyous; pleasing. **2** Cheerful. —**glad'some·ly** adv. —**glad'some·ness** n.

Glad·stone (glad'stōn, -stən) n. A suitcase hinged in the middle lengthwise so that it may open into halves: also **Gladstone bag.** [<W. E. *Gladstone*, 1809–98, English statesman]

glair (glâr) n. The white of eggs mixed with vinegar, used as a size in gilding, etc. **2** Anything slimy or sticky, as egg whites. —v.t. To treat with glair. Also **glaire.** [<OF *glaire*] —**glair'y** adj.

glam·or·ize (glam'ər·īz) v.t. **·rized, ·riz·ing** To make glamorous. —**glam'or·i·za'tion** n.

glam·or·ous (glam'ər·əs) adj. Radiating glamour; alluring. Also **glam'our·ous.** —**glam'or·ous·ly, glam'our·ous·ly** adv.

glam·our (glam'ər) n. **1** Alluring charm, fascination, or attraction. **2** Originally, a delusion caused by a magic spell. Also **glam'or.** [Scot., var. of GRAMMAR]

glance (glans, gläns) v. **glanced, glanc·ing** v.i. **1** To strike something at an angle and bounce off. **2** To look quickly or hurriedly. **3** To glint; flash. **4** To make passing reference; allude. —v.t. **5** To cause to strike something at an angle and bounce off. —n. **1** A quick look. **2** A momentary gleam. **3** A glancing movement or rebound. [<OF *glacier* to slip]

gland (gland) n. **1** Any of various tissues or organs that secrete substances essential to the body or for the elimination of waste products: salivary *glands;* endocrine *glands.* **2** A node of nonsecreting tissue: lymph *gland.* [<L *glandula,* dim. of *glans, glandis* acorn]

glan·ders (glan'dərz) n. pl. (construed as sing.) A contagious disease of horses, mules, etc., characterized by nasal discharges and fever. [<OF *glandre* a gland] —**glan'dered, glan'der·ous** adj.

glan·du·lar (glan'jə·lər) adj. Of, bearing, or like glands.

glans (glanz) n. pl. **glan·des** (-dēz) The rounded tip of the penis or clitoris. [L, lit., an acorn]

glare¹ (glâr) v. **glared, glar·ing** v.i. **1** To shine with great and dazzling intensity. **2** To gaze or stare fiercely. **3** To be conspicuous or ostentatious. —v.t. **4** To express with a glare. —n. **1** A dazzling light. **2** An intense, usu. hostile look or gaze. **3** Gaudiness. [<ME *glaren*]

glare² (glâr) n. A glassy, smooth surface, as of ice. —adj. Having a glassy, smooth surface. [? <GLARE¹]

glar·ing (glâr'ing) adj. **1** Looking or staring fixedly or hostilely. **2** Emitting an excessively brilliant light. **3** Plainly conspicuous: a *glaring* mistake. —**glar'ing·ly** adv.

glar·y (glâr'ē) adj. **glar·ier, glar·i·est** Dazzling; glaring.

glas·nost (glas'nost) n. An official policy of greater openness in governmental policymaking. [<Russ.]

glass (glas, gläs) n. **1** A hard, amorphous, brittle, usu. translucent substance of varying composition, usu. made y fusing sand with various oxides chosen according to the properties desired. **2** Any substance resembling glass.

3 An article made of glass, as a window pane, a goblet or tumbler, a mirror, telescope, barometer, etc. **4** pl. EYEGLASSES. **5** pl. BINOCULARS. **6** The amount of something contained in a drinking glass. **7** GLASSWARE. —v.t. **1** To enclose with glass. **2** To reflect; mirror. **3** To give a glazed surface to. —adj. Made of, relating to, or like glass. [<OE *glæs*]

glass·blow·ing (glas'blō'ing, gläs'-) n. The process of blowing air through a tube into molten glass to form a desired shape. —**glass'blow'er** n.

glass·ful (glas'fŏŏl, gläs'-) n. pl. **·fuls** As much as can be contained in a drinking glass.

glass snake A legless lizard of the southern U.S., having a very brittle tail.

glass·ware (glas'wâr', gläs'-) n. Articles made of glass.

glass wool A mass of fibers of spun glass used for filtration, insulation, etc.

glass·y (glas'ē, gläs'ē) adj. **glass·i·er, glass·i·est 1** Composed of or like glass. **2** Fixed, blank, and uncomprehending: a *glassy* stare. —**glass'i·ly** adv. —**glass'i·ness** n.

glau·co·ma (glou·kō'mə, glô-) n. A disease of the eye characterized by increased pressure within the eyeball and partial or total loss of vision. [<Gk. *glaukos* bluish gray] —**glau·com'a·tous** (-kom'ə·təs) adj.

glau·cous (glô'kəs) adj. **1** Having a yellowish green color. **2** Bot. Having a powdery, bluish white bloom, as grapes, blueberries, etc. [<Gk. *glaukos* bluish gray]

glaze (glāz) v. **glazed, glaz·ing** v.t. **1** To fit, as a window, with glass panes. **2** To provide (a building, etc.) with windows. **3** To coat, as pottery, with a glasslike surface applied by fusing. **4** To cover with a glaze, as meat or biscuits. **5** To make glossy, as by polishing. —v.i. **6** To become glassy; take on a glaze. —n. **1** A smooth, shining, transparent surface. **2** A substance used to produce it, as on pottery. **3** An icy surface. **4** Transparent stock or icing applied to the surface of meat, fish, vegetables, etc. [ME *glasen*<*glas* glass] —**glaz'er, glaz'i·ness** n. —**glaz'y** adj.

gla·zier (glā'zhər) n. **1** One who fits panes of glass. **2** One who applies glaze to pottery. —**gla'zier·y** n.

glaz·ing (glā'zing) n. **1** A glaze. **2** The act or art of applying glaze. **3** Window panes, collectively. **4** The act or art of setting glass.

gleam (glēm) n. **1** A glimmer or flash of light. **2** A small, faint light. **3** Something likened to a flash of light: a *gleam* of wit. —v.i. **1** To shine with a gleam. **2** To appear clearly and briefly, as a signal fire. —v.t. **3** To show with a gleam. [<OE *glǣm*] —**gleam'y** adj. —Syn. v. **1** flash, sparkle, glitter, glare, dazzle.

glean (glēn) v.t. & v.i. **1** To collect (information, facts, etc.) by patient effort. **2** To gather (the leavings) from a field after the crop has been reaped. **3** To gather the leavings from (a field, etc.). [<L *glenare*] —**glean'er** n.

glebe (glēb) n. **1** Land attached to an ecclesiastical benefice as part of its endowment. **2** Archaic Any field. [<L *gleba* lump of earth]

glee (glē) n. **1** Joy; gaiety; merriment. **2** A part song for three or more unaccompanied, usu. male voices. [<OE *glēo*] —**glee'some** (-səm) adj. —Syn. **1** mirth, exuberance, delight, hilarity, fun.

glee club A group organized to sing light choral music.

glee·ful (glē'fəl) adj. Feeling or exhibiting glee; joyous. —**glee'ful·ly** adv. —**glee'ful·ness** n.

glen (glen) n. A small, secluded valley. [Scot. Gael. *glenn*]

Glen·gar·ry (glen·gar'ē) n. A woolen Scottish cap for men, having a lengthwise crease along the top and short streamers in back. Also **Glengarry bonnet.** [<*Glengarry,* a valley in Scotland]

glib (glib) adj. **glib·ber, glib·best 1** Speaking or writing with smooth fluency. **2** More facile than sincere; superficial: a *glib* compliment. **3** Characterized by easiness or informality. [Prob.<MLG *glibberich* slippery] —**glib'ly** adv. —**glib'ness** n.

glide (glīd) v. **glid·ed, glid·ing** v.i. **1** To move, slip, or flow smoothly or easily. **2** To pass unnoticed, as time. **3** Aeron. To descend gradually and without power; also, to operate a glider. **4** Music & Phonet. To produce a glide. —v.t. **5** To cause to glide. —*n.* **1** The act of gliding; a gliding motion. **2** *Music* An unbroken passage from tone to tone. **3** *Phonet.* A transitional sound made in passing from the position of one speech sound to that of another. [< OE *glīdan*]

glid·er (glī′dər) *n.* **1** One who or that which glides. **2** An

Glider *def.* 2

aircraft similar to an airplane but without an engine, supported by currents of air. **3** A couch hung in a metal frame so as to glide back and forth.

glim·mer (glim′ər) *v.i.* **1** To shine with a faint, unsteady light; flicker. **2** To appear fitfully or faintly. —*n.* **1** A faint, unsteady light. **2** A momentary apprehension; glimpse: a *glimmer* of the truth. [Prob. < Scand.] —**glim′mer·ing** *n.*

glimpse (glimps) *n.* **1** A momentary view or look. **2** A glimmer; inkling. —*v.* **glimpsed, glimps·ing** *v.t.* **1** To see for an instant. —*v.i.* **2** To look for an instant. [< Gmc.]

glint (glint) *v.i.* To gleam; glitter. —*n.* A gleam. [< Scand.] —**Syn.** *v.* sparkle, flash, glimmer, shine.

glis·sade (gli·säd′, -säd′) *v.i.* **glis·sad·ed, ·sad·ing** To slide or glide. —*n.* **1** The act of gliding down a slope, as of ice or snow. **2** A sliding step in dancing. [< F *glisser* slip]

glis·san·do (gli·sän′dō) *n. pl.* **·di** (-dē) or **·dos** *Music* A rapid, gliding passage from tone to tone. [< GLISSADE]

glis·ten (glis′ən) *v.i.* To sparkle; shine; gleam. —*n.* A shining. [< OE *glisnian* shine] —**glis′ten·ing·ly** *adv.*

glis·ter (glis′tər) *Archaic v.i.* GLISTEN. —*n.* GLITTER. [< MDu. *glisteren*]

glitch (glich) *n. pl. Slang* **1** A malfunction or mishap. **2** A sudden shift from normal function, as in electric power. **3** A false signal. [Prob. < G *glitschen* to slide, slip]

glit·ter (glit′ər) *v.i.* **1** To sparkle with a gleaming light. **2** To be bright or colorful. —*n.* Sparkle; brilliancy. [< ON *glitra*] —**glit′ter·ing, glit′ter·y** *adj.*

gloam·ing (glō′ming) *n.* The twilight; dusk. [< OE *glōmung*]

gloat (glōt) *v.i.* **1** To look with cruel or triumphant satisfaction. **2** To think about something with exultation or avarice. [?]

glob·al (glō′bəl) *adj.* **1** Of or involving the world in its entirety: *global* war. **2** Spherical.

globe (glōb) *n.* **1** Something perfectly round; sphere. **2** The earth. **3** A spherical map of the earth or of the heavens. [< L *globus*]

globe·fish (glōb′fish′) *n. pl.* **·fish** or **·fish·es** A fish of tropical seas, covered with spines and able, when disturbed, to inflate its body into a globular form.

globe-trot·ter (glōb′trot′ər) *n.* One who travels all over the world. —**globe′-trot′ting** *n., adj.*

glo·bose (glō′bōs) *adj.* Spherical. Also **glo′bous** (-bəs). [< L *globus* ball] —**glo′bose·ly** *adv.* —**glo·bos·i·ty** (glō·bos′ə·tē) *n.*

glob·u·lar (glob′yə·lər) *adj.* **1** Spherical. **2** Formed of globules. **3** Worldwide.

glob·ule (glob′yōōl) *n.* A small globe or spherical particle. [< L < *globus* ball]

glock·en·spiel (glok′ən·spēl, -shpēl) *n.* A musical instrument consisting of a chromatic series of metal bars played by striking with hammers. [< G *Glocken* bells + *Spiel* play]

glom·er·ate (glom′ər·it) *adj.* Clustered compactly. [< L < *glomus, glomeris* a mass] —**glom′er·a′tion** (-ā′shən) *n.*

gloom (glōōm) *n.* **1** Depression of the mind or spirits; melancholy. **2** Partial or total darkness. **3** A dark or gloomy place. —*v.i.* **1** To look sullen or dejected. **2** To be or become dark or threatening. —*v.t.* **3** To make dark, sad, or sullen. [< ME *glom(b)en* look sad]

Glockenspiel

gloom·y (glōō′mē) *adj.* **gloom·i·er, gloom·i·est 1** Melancholy; morose. **2** Causing gloom or melancholy. **3** Dark; dismal; obscure. —**gloom′i·ly** *adv.* —**gloom′i·ness** *n.* —**Syn. 1** Sad, downcast, despondent, somber, sorrowful.

Glo·ri·a (glôr′ē·ə, glō′rē·ə) *n. pl.* **·ri·as 1** Any of several Christian doxologies sung in Latin and named for the opening phrase, as **Gloria in ex·cel·sis** (eks·chel′səs, ek·shel′-) (Glory to God in the highest) or **Gloria Pa·tri** (pä′trē) (Glory to the Father). **2** A musical setting for a Gloria. [L, glory]

glo·ri·fy (glôr′ə·fī, glō′rə-) *v.t.* **·fied, ·fy·ing 1** To honor or worship: to *glorify* God. **2** To make exalted or blessed. **3** To praise; extol. **4** To represent as better or finer than the facts warrant. [< L *gloria* glory + -FY] —**glo′ri·fi′er** *n.*

glo·ri·ous (glôr′ē·əs, glō′rē-) *adj.* **1** Full of glory. **2** Bestowing glory. **3** Deserving glory. **4** Extremely delightful; splendid: a *glorious* time. —**glo′ri·ous·ly** *adv.* —**glo′ri·ous·ness** *n.*

glo·ry (glôr′ē, glō′rē) *n. pl.* **·ries 1** Distinguished honor, praise, or renown. **2** Something that brings or deserves honor, praise, or renown. **3** Adoration; worshipful praise. **4** Splendor; magnificence. **5** The bliss of heaven. **6** A state of exaltation, well-being, prosperity, etc.: He was in his *glory*. **7** Radiance; brilliancy. **8** A nimbus; halo. —*v.i.* **glo·ried, glo·ry·ing** To rejoice proudly or triumphantly; exult: with *in*. [< L *gloria*]

gloss¹ (glôs, glos) *n.* **1** The brightness or sheen of a polished surface. **2** A deceptive or superficial appearance or show. —*v.t.* **1** To make smooth or lustrous, as by polishing. **2** To attempt to hide (errors, defects, etc.) by falsehood or equivocation: with *over*. —*v.i.* **3** To become shiny. [< Scand.] —**gloss′er** *n.*

gloss² (glôs, glos) *n.* **1** An explanatory note; esp. a marginal or interlinear note or translation. **2** A glossary. —*v.t.* **1** To write glosses for. **2** To excuse or change by false or superficial explanations: usu. with *over*. —*v.i.* **3** To make glosses. [< Gk. *glōssa* a foreign word, language] —**gloss′er** *n.*

glos·sa·ry (glos′ə·rē, glôs′-) *n. pl.* **·ries** An explanatory list of the difficult, technical, or foreign words used in a particular work or area of knowledge. [< L *glossa* gloss²] —**glos·sar·i·al** (glo·sâr′ē·əl, glô-) *adj.* —**glos·sar′i·al·ly** *adv.* —**glos′sa·rist** *n.*

gloss·y (glôs′ē, glos′ē) *adj.* **gloss·i·er, gloss·i·est 1** Having a bright or polished surface. **2** Outwardly or speciously attractive. —**gloss′i·ly** *adv.* —**gloss′i·ness** *n.*

glot·tal (glot′l) *adj.* Of, pertaining to, or articulated in the glottis.

glot·tis (glot′is) *n. pl.* **glot·tis·es** or **glot·ti·des** (-ə·dēz) The passage between the vocal folds at the upper opening of the larynx. [< Gk. *glōtta* tongue]

glove (gluv) *n.* **1** A covering for the hand, having a separate sheath for each finger. **2** A padded, leather mitt for catching a baseball. **3** BOXING GLOVE. —*v.t.* **gloved, glov·ing 1** To put gloves on. **2** To cover with or as with a glove. **3** To serve as a glove for. [< OE *glōf*]

glov·er (gluv′ər) *n.* A maker or seller of gloves.

glow (glō) *v.i.* **1** To give off light, with or without heat or flame. **2** To be bright or red, as with animation. **3** To be animated with strong emotion. **4** To be excessively hot; burn. —*n.* **1** Brightness or incandescence, as of a heated substance. **2** Bright color; ruddiness. **3** Strong emotion or enthusiasm. **4** Bodily warmth, as caused by exercise, etc. [< OE *glōwan*] —**glow′ing** *adj.* —**glow′ing·ly** *adv.*

glow·er (glou′ər) *v.i.* To stare with an angry frown; scowl sullenly. —*n.* A fierce or sullen stare. [? < Scand.] —**glow′er·ing·ly** *adv.*

glow·fly (glō′flī′) *n.* A firefly.

glow·worm (glō′wûrm′) *n.* **1** A European beetle, the larva and wingless female of which display bioluminescence. **2** The luminous larva of American fireflies.

glox·in·i·a (glok·sin′ē·ə) *n.* A plant having large bell-shaped spotted flowers. [< B. P. *Gloxin*, 18th-century German physician]

gloze (glōz) *v.t.* **glozed, gloz·ing** GLOSS² (def. 1). [< OF *gloser* explain, gloss²]

glu·cose (glōō′kōs) *n.* **1** A simple sugar, widely distributed in plants and animals and playing a key part in the storage and release of vital energy; dextrose. **2** A viscous, yellowish solution of various sugars obtained by incomplete hydrolysis of starch; corn syrup. [< Gk. *gleykys* sweet wine + -OSE] —**glu·cos′ic** (-kos′ik) *adj.*

glue (glōō) *n.* **1** A viscid cement or adhesive used to stick things together, derived from boiling animal skin, bones, and cartilage. 2 Any of a number of adhesive substances. —*v.t.* **glued, glu·ing** To stick together with or as with glue. [< LL *glus, glutis*] —**glue′y** *adj.*

glum (glum) *adj.* **glum·mer, glum·mest** Moody and silent; sullen. [Akin to GLOOM] —**glum′ly** *adv.* —**glum′ness** *n.*

glume (gloom) *n.* One of the chafflike bracts enclosing the flowers of grasses and sedges. [< L *gluma* husk]

glut (glut) *v.* **glut·ted, glut·ting** *v.t.* 1 To fill or supply to excess; satiate; gorge. 2 To furnish (the market) with an excessive quantity of goods so that supply exceeds demand. —*v.i.* 3 To eat gluttonously. —*n.* 1 An excessive supply; plethora. 2 The act of glutting, or the condition of being glutted. [< L *glutire* swallow]

glu·ten (gloot′n) *n.* A tough, sticky, nutritious protein substance found in wheat and other grain. [L, glue] —**glu′te·nous** *adj.*

glu·te·us (gloot′ē-əs, gloo·tē′əs) *n. pl.* **·te·i** (-tē·ī) Any of the three muscles that form each buttock. [< Gk. *gloutos* rump] —**glu′te·al** *adj.*

glu·ti·nous (gloo′tə-nəs) *adj.* Gummy; sticky. —**glu′ti·nous·ly** *adv.* —**glu′ti·nous·ness** *n.*

glut·ton[1] (glut′n) *n.* 1 An excessive eater. 2 One who has an excessive appetite for anything. [< L *gluto* a glutton] —**glut′ton·ous** *adj.* —**glut′ton·ous·ly** *adv.*

glut·ton[2] (glut′n) *n.* A wolverine, esp. of Europe. [Trans. of G *Vielfrass* great eater]

glut·ton·y (glut′ən·ē) *n. pl.* **·ton·ies** The act or habit of eating to excess.

glyc·er·in (glis′ər·in) *n.* GLYCEROL. Also **glyc′er·ine.**

glyc·er·ol (glis′ər·ōl, -ol) *n.* A sweet, oily, colorless alcohol formed by hydrolysis of fats. [< Gk. *glykeros* sweet + -OL]

gly·co·gen (glī′kə·jən) *n.* A complex carbohydrate formed in animal tissues, principally the liver, and readily convertible to glucose as needed. [< Gk. *glykys* sweet + -GEN] —**gly′co·gen′ic** (-jen′ik) *adj.*

gly·col (glī′kōl, -kol) *n.* 1 A colorless, viscid compound derived from ethylene and used as an antifreeze and solvent. 2 Any of a series of alcohols having two hydroxyl radicals. [< GLYC(ERIN) + -OL]

gm, gm. gram(s).

G-man (jē′man′) *n. pl.* **-men** (-men′) *Informal* An agent of the Federal Bureau of Investigation. [< G(OVERNMENT) MAN]

gnarl (närl) *n.* A hard protuberance or knot on a tree. —*v.t.* To make twisted or deformed. [Back formation from GNARLED]

gnarled (närld) *adj.* 1 Having gnarls; knotty. 2 Rough, weatherbeaten, and usu. bent: *gnarled* hands. Also **gnarl′y.** [Prob.< ME *knorre* a knot]

gnash (nash) *v.t.* 1 To grind (the teeth) together, as in rage or pain. 2 To bite with grinding teeth. —*v.i.* 3 To grind the teeth together. [< Scand.]

gnat (nat) *n.* Any of various small, usu. biting, two-winged flies. [< OE *gnæt*]

gnaw (nô) *v.* **gnawed, gnawed** or **gnawn** (nôn), **gnaw·ing** *v.t.* 1 To bite or eat away little by little. 2 To make by gnawing. 3 To bite on repeatedly. 4 To wear away; erode. 5 To torment or oppress with fear, pain, etc. —*v.i.* 6 To bite or chew, or corrode persistently. 7 To cause constant worry, pain, etc. [< OE *gnagan*] —**gnaw′er** *n.* —**gnaw′ing** *adj., n.* —**gnaw′ing·ly** *adv.*

gneiss (nīs) *n.* A coarse-grained, granitelike rock in which there is a distinctly layered arrangement of the components. [< G *Gneis*] —**gneiss′ic** *adj.*

gnome (nōm) *n.* In folklore, one of a race of dwarfs believed to live underground as guardians of treasure. [< NL *gnomus*] —**gnom′ish** *adj.*

gno·mic (nō′mik, nom′ik) *adj.* Of, like, or using maxims; aphoristic. Also **gno′mi·cal.** [< Gk. *gnōmē* thought, maxim]

gno·mon (nō′mon) *n.* The upright piece whose shadow points out the time of day on a sundial; also, anything, as a pillar, used for a similar purpose. [< Gk. *gnōmōn* an indicator]

gnos·tic (nos′tik) *adj.* Of or possessing knowledge. Also **gnos′ti·cal.** [< Gk. *gnōsis* knowledge.] —**gnos′ti·cal·ly** *adv.*

Gnos·tic (nos′tik) *adj.* Of or pertaining to the Gnostics or Gnosticism. —*n.* An adherent of Gnosticism.

Gnos·ti·cism (nos′tə·siz′əm) *n.* A philosophical and religious system (first to sixth century) teaching that knowledge rather than faith was the key to salvation.

GNP, G.N.P. gross national product.

gnu (nyoo) *n. pl.* **gnus** or **gnu** A South African antelope having an oxlike head with curved horns, a mane, and a long tail; a wildebeest. [< Kaffir *nqu*]

Gnu

go[1] (gō) *v.* **went, gone, go·ing** *v.i.* 1 To proceed or pass along; move. 2 To move from a place; leave; depart. 3 To pass away; disappear; end. 4 To be free or freed. 5 To be in motion or operation; work properly: The watch is *going* now. 6 To extend or reach: The pipe *goes* to the basement; a road *going* to Baltimore. 7 To be, continue, or appear in a specified state or condition: to *go* unpunished. 8 To be valid, accepted, etc.: Anything *goes.* 9 To pass into a state or condition; become: to *go* insane. 10 To proceed or end in a specified manner: The party *went* well. 11 To be suitable; fit: The music *goes* with these words. 12 To have a proper or specific place; belong: The towels *go* on top. 13 To be phrased, expressed, sung, etc.: The song *goes* like this. 14 To emit or produce a specified sound or signal. 15 To engage oneself in an activity or occupation: to *go* to sea; to *go* fishing. 16 To pass: said of time. 17 To be awarded, given, or applied: This *goes* toward canceling the debt. 18 To have recourse; resort: to *go* to court. 19 To be known: What name does she *go* by? 20 To be sold or bid for. 21 To help; tend: This *goes* to prove my argument. 22 To serve as a part; contribute: the talent and dedication that *go* to make an artist. 23 To be abolished or surrendered. 24 To collapse; fail: The walls *went* last in the fire. 25 To subject oneself: He *went* to great pains to do it. 26 To die. 27 To be about to do or act: They were *going* to protest. 28 *Informal* To use a toilet: said of children: Does he have to *go?* —*v.t.* 29 To tolerate; put up: to *go* bail. 30 To contribute; share: to *go* halves. 31 *Informal* To bet; wager. 32 *Informal* To put up with; tolerate. —**go about** 1 To be occupied or busy with. 2 *Naut.* To change to the other tack. —**go along** 1 To accompany. 2 To agree. —**go around** 1 To move about or circulate. 2 To be enough to furnish even shares. —**go at** 1 To attack. 2 To work at. —**go back on** 1 To forsake; be untrue to. 2 To fail to fulfill or abide by. —**go by** 1 To pass. 2 To conform to or be guided by: to *go by* the rules. —**go for** 1 To try to get: He *went for* his gun. 2 To attack. 3 *Informal* To be strongly attracted by. —**go in for** *Informal* 1 To strive for or advocate. 2 To have a liking for. —**go into** 1 To investigate. 2 To take up, as an occupation. 3 To be contained in. —**go off** 1 To explode or be discharged, as a gun. 2 *Informal* To happen; result. —**go on** 1 To act; behave. 2 To happen: What's *going on* here? —**go out** 1 To cease or be extinguished, as a light. 2 To be drawn forth in sympathy. 3 To strike. 4 To become obsolete. —**go over** 1 To turn on its side. 2 To rehearse; repeat. 3 To examine carefully. 4 *Informal* To succeed. —**go through** 1 To search thoroughly. 2 To experience; undergo. 3 To use up; exhaust. —**go through with** To undertake to finish. —**go under** 1 To be overwhelmed or conquered. 2 To fail, as a business. —**go up** To increase, as prices or values. —**go with** 1 To harmonize with. 2 *Informal* To keep company with. —**go without** To do or be without. —**let go of** 1 To release one's hold of. 2 To abandon one's interest or share in. —*n.* 1 The act of going. 2 *Informal* Energy; vigor. 3 *Informal* A try; attempt. 4 *Informal* A success. 5 *Informal* The fashion; mode: with *the.* 6 *Informal* A proceeding; turn of affairs. —**no go** *Informal* Useless; hopeless. —**on the go** *Informal* Busy; in constant motion. —*adj.* Operating or proceeding as planned: All systems are *go.* [< OE *gān*] —**go′er** *n.*

go[2] (gō) *n.* A Japanese game played with counters or stones on the intersections of lines on a board. [Jap.]

GO general orders.

goad (gōd) n. 1 A pointed stick for driving oxen. 2 Something that spurs or incites. —v.t. To urge or drive with or as with a goad. [< OE gād] —Syn. v. incite, spur, prick, urge.

go·a·head (gō'ə·hed') adj. 1 Giving permission to proceed: a go-ahead signal. 2 Energetic. —n. Permission to proceed: usu. with the.

goal (gōl) n. 1 A point, end, or place that one is striving to reach: the goal of a race; a goal in life. 2 In certain games, the area or object that a ball, puck, etc., must reach to score; also, the act of making such a score or the score so made. [ME gol]

goal·ie (gō'lē) n. A goalkeeper.

goal·keep·er (gōl'kē'pər) n. In certain games, as hockey, soccer, etc., a player stationed at the goal to prevent a score from being made. Also **goal'tend'er** (-ten'dər).

goat (gōt) n. 1 Any of various agile, bearded, hollow-horned mammals related to the sheep and including wild and domesticated forms. 2 A lecherous man. 3 Slang SCAPEGOAT. —get one's goat Slang To anger or annoy by teasing, tormenting, etc. [< OE gāt] —goat'ish adj. —goat'ish·ly adv. —goat'ish·ness n.

Goat n. CAPRICORN.

goat·ee (gō·tē') n. A small, pointed beard on a man's chin.

goat·herd (gōt'hûrd') n. One who tends goats.

goat·skin (gōt'skin') n. 1 The hide of a goat. 2 Leather made from it.

goat·suck·er (gōt'suk'ər) n. Any of numerous nocturnal, insectivorous birds with wide mouths, as the whippoorwill or nighthawk.

gob¹ (gob) n. A small piece, mass, or chunk. [< OF gobe mouthful, lump]

Goatee

gob² (gob) n. Slang A sailor. [?]

gob·bet (gob'it) n. 1 A piece or fragment, esp. of meat. 2 A chunk; lump. [< OF gobe lump]

gob·ble¹ (gob'əl) v. gob·bled, gob·bling v.t. 1 To swallow (food) greedily. 2 Slang To seize or acquire greedily. —v.i. 3 To eat greedily. [< ME gobben] —gob'bler n.

gob·ble² (gob'əl) n. The sound made by the male turkey. —v.i. gob·bled, gob·bling To utter a gobble. [Var. of GABBLE]

gob·ble·dy·gook (gob'əl·dē·gōōk') n. Informal Involved, pedantic, and pompous talk or writing. Also **gob'· ble·de·gook'**. • Gobbledygook usually refers to wordiness, the unnecessary use of long words, and a stuffy style often encountered in bureaucratic memoranda. "The writer is disposed to regard as contrary to efficient office procedure the utilization of government communications apparatus to conduct nongovernment business," for example, means "Don't use our phones to conduct your personal business."

gob·bler (gob'lər) n. A male turkey.

go·be·tween (gō'bə·twēn') n. An agent or mediator between other persons.

gob·let (gob'lit) n. A drinking glass with a stem, base, and no handle. [< OF gobel a drinking cup]

gob·lin (gob'lin) n. A supernatural, grotesque creature regarded as malicious or mischievous. [< OF gobelin]

go·by (gō'bē) n. pl. ·by or ·bies Any of various small, spiny-finned, chiefly marine fishes, usu. having ventral fins united to form a suction disk. [< Gk. kōbios, small fish]

go-by (gō'bī') n. pl. ·bys Informal An intended slight.

go·cart (gō'kärt') n. 1 STROLLER (def. 1). 2 A light carriage.

god (god) n. 1 A male being regarded as immortal and as possessing supernatural powers that control nature, man, or some aspect of life; deity. 2 An image or symbol of such a being; idol. 3 Any person or thing made an object of supreme or excessive devotion. [< OE] —god'ship n.

God (god) n. The Supreme Being, creator and ruler of the universe, conceived of as eternal, omniscient, good, and almighty.

god·child (god'chīld') n. pl. ·chil·dren (-chil'drən) A child for whom a person becomes sponsor at baptism.

god·daugh·ter (god'dô'tər) n. A female godchild.

god·dess (god'is) n. 1 A female being regarded as immortal and as possessing supernatural powers that con-

trol nature, man, or some aspect of life. 2 A surpassingly beautiful or beloved woman.

god·fa·ther (god'fä'thər) n. A man who becomes sponsor for a child at its baptism.

God-fear·ing (god'fir'ing) adj. Pious; devout.

God-giv·en (god'giv'ən) adj. 1 Given by God. 2 Fortunate; welcome.

god·head (god'hed') n. Godhood; divinity.

God·head (god'hed') n. God; the Deity.

god·hood (god'hōōd') n. The state or quality of being a god.

Go·di·va (gə·dī'və) An 11th-century noblewoman who, according to English legend, rode naked through Coventry as the condition of the removal of her husband's oppressive taxes.

god·less (god'lis) adj. 1 Not believing in God or a god; atheistic. 2 Wicked. —god'less·ly adv. —god'less·ness n.

god·like (god'līk') adj. Similar to or suited for God or a god.

god·ly (god'lē) adj. ·li·er, ·li·est Filled with love for God; pious. —god'li·ness n.

god·moth·er (god'muth'ər) n. A woman who becomes sponsor for a child at baptism.

god·par·ent (god'pâr'ənt) n. A godfather or godmother.

God's acre A cemetery.

god·send (god'send') n. A thing much needed or desired that comes unexpectedly at the opportune time, as if sent by God.

god·son (god'sun') n. A male godchild.

God·speed (god'spēd') n. God speed you: a wish for a safe journey or for success.

god·wit (god'wit) n. Any of various shore birds with long legs and a long, upturned bill. [?]

go-get·ter (gō'get'ər) n. Informal A hustling, energetic, aggressive person.

gog·gle (gog'əl) n. 1 A rolling or staring of the eyes. 2 pl. Large eyeglasses used as protection against strong light, wind, dust, etc. —adj. Prominent; staring. —v. gog·gled, gog·gling v.i. 1 To stare with bulging eyes. 2 To roll sidewise: said of the eyes. —v.t. 3 To roll (the eyes). [< ME gogelen look aside] —gog'gle-eyed' (-īd') adj.

go-go (gō'gō') adj. Slang 1 Of or describing discothèques, the usu. unrestrained, erotic dances performed there, or the dancers, typically young women, who entertain with such dances. 2 Lively, modern, glamorous, etc. [< F à gogo joyfully]

Goi·del·ic (goi·del'ik) n. A branch of the Celtic languages including Irish, the Gaelic of the Scottish Highlands, and Manx; Gaelic. —adj. Of or pertaining to the Gaels or their languages. Also **Goi·dhel'ic**. [< OIrish Gōidel a Gael]

go·ing (gō'ing) n. 1 The act of departing or moving; leaving. 2 The condition of the ground or roads with reference to ease of walking, riding, etc. 3 Progress or circumstances affecting it. —goings on Informal Behavior; conduct; actions. —adj. 1 Continuing to function: a going concern. 2 Moving; working. 3 In existence: available: the best bargain going. 4 Departing; leaving. —going on Informal Approaching (a particular age or time).

goi·ter (goi'tər) n. A chronic enlargement of the thyroid gland, often visible as a swelling on the front part of the neck. Also **goi'tre**. [< L guttur throat] —goi'trous adj.

go-kart (gō'kärt') n. KART. [< Go Kart, a trade name]

gold (gōld) n. 1 A precious metallic element (symbol Au) of yellow color; it is very heavy, ductile, and malleable, and occurs in nature uncombined with other elements. 2 A coin of gold. 3 Money; wealth. 4 The deep yellow color of gold. 5 Something likened to gold, as in worth or value. —adj. Of, like, or made of gold. [< OE]

gold·brick (gōld'brik') n. 1 Informal A worthless thing deceitfully sold or given as something valuable: also **gold brick**. 2 Slang A person who shirks or tries to shirk work: also **gold'brick'er**. —v.i. Slang 1 To shirk (work or duty). 2 To cheat.

gold digger Informal A woman who uses her personal relations with men to get money and gifts from them.

gold dust Gold in fine particles.

gold·en (gōl'dən) adj. 1 Made of or consisting of gold. 2 Having the color or luster of gold; bright yellow. 3 Unusually valuable or excellent. 4 Of great excellence or achievement: a *golden* age. **—gold'en·ly** *adv.* **—gold'en·ness** *n.*

Golden Fleece *Gk. Myth.* A fleece of gold guarded by a dragon and stolen by Jason with the aid of Medea.

gold·en·glow (gōl'dən·glō') *n.* A tall, flowering herb with showy composite heads of yellow-rayed flowers.

golden mean The avoidance of extremes; wise moderation.

gold·en·rod (gōl'dən·rod') *n.* A North American herb of the composite family, with erect stalks carrying clusters of small, yellow flowers in late summer.

golden rule The rule of life given in *Matt.* 7:12: "Whatsoever ye would that men should do to you, do ye even so to them."

golden wedding Fiftieth wedding anniversary.

gold-filled (gōld'fild') *adj.* Made of a base metal covered with gold.

gold·finch (gōld'finch') *n.* 1 A European finch having a yellow patch on the wings. 2 An American finch of which the male has a yellow body with a black tail.

gold·fish (gōld'fish') *n. pl.* **·fish** or **·fish·es** A small carp of golden color originally of China, now cultivated in many varieties.

gold leaf A very thin foil of gold. —**gold-leaf** (gōld'lēf') *adj.*

American goldfinches

gold·mine (gōld'mīn') *n.* 1 A place where gold is mined. 2 *Informal* A very productive or profitable source: A dictionary is a *goldmine* of information.

gold rush A mass movement of people to an area where gold has been discovered.

gold·smith (gōld'smith') *n.* One who makes objects of gold. —**gold·smith·ing** *n.*

gold standard A monetary system based on a specified weight of gold as the unit of value.

golf (gôlf, golf, gôf, gof) *n.* An outdoor game played on a large course with a small hard ball and a set of clubs, the object being to direct the ball into a series of holes in as few strokes as possible. —*v.i.* To play golf. [ME] —**golf'·er** *n.*

golf course The course over which a game of golf is played. Also **golf links.**

Gol·go·tha (gol'gə·thə) *n.* A place near Jerusalem where Jesus was crucified.

Golf clubs
a. driver. b. No. 6 iron.
c. No. 9 iron. d. putter.

Go·li·ath (gə·lī'əth) In the Bible, a Philistine giant, slain by David.

gol·ly (gol'ē) *interj.* An exclamation of surprise, awe, etc. [Euphemism for GOD]

go·losh (gə·losh') *n.* GALOSH.

Go·mor·rah (gə·môr'ə, -mor'ə) *n.* In the Bible, a city on the shore of the Dead Sea. Also **Go·mor'rha.** See SODOM.

-gon *combining form* Having (a certain number of) angles: *pentagon.* [< Gk. *gonia* an angle]

gon·ad (gō'nad) *n.* An organ in which reproductive cells develop; an ovary or testis. [< Gk. *gonos* seed] —**go·nad'al** *adj.*

gon·do·la (gon'də·lə) *n.* 1 A long, narrow, flat-bottomed boat, high-peaked at the ends, used in Venice on the canals. 2 A large flat-bottomed river boat of light build. 3 A long, shallow, open freight car. 4 *Aeron.* The car attached below a dirigible or balloon. 5 A small car suspended from a moving cable, as on a ski lift. [< Ital. *gondolar* to rock]

gon·do·lier (gon'də·lir') *n.* One who poles or rows a gondola.

Gondola *def. 1*

gone (gôn, gon) *p.p.* of GO. —*adj.* 1 Departed. 2 Ruined; lost. 3 Past. 4 Dead. 5 Faint; weak. 6 Finished; consumed.

7 *Slang* First-rate. —**far gone** 1 Exhausted. 2 Almost dead. 3 Absorbed; involved: *far gone* in reverie.

gon·er (gôn'ər, gon'-) *n. Informal* A person or thing that is ruined or beyond saving.

gon·fa·lon (gon'fə·lon', -lən) *n.* A flag or ensign fixed to a revolving frame or a crossyard, generally with streamers. [< Ital. *gonfalone* < Gmc.]

gong (gông, gong) *n.* 1 A metal percussion instrument shaped like a shallow dish. 2 A bell shaped like a saucer. [Malay]

gon·or·rhe·a (gon'ə·rē'ə) *n.* A venereal disease affecting the mucous membrane of the genital organs, usu. characterized by inflammation and a purulent discharge. Also **gon'or·rhoe'a.** [< Gk. *gonos* seed + *rheein* flow] —**gon'or·rhe'al, gon'or·rhoe'al** *adj.*

goo (gōō) *n. Informal* 1 Any sticky fluid. 2 Sentimentality; mawkishness. [?]

goo·ber (gōō'bər) *n. U.S.* A peanut. Also **goober pea.** [< Bantu *nguba*]

good (gōōd) *adj.* **bet·ter, best** 1 Satisfactory in quality or kind: *good* food; *good* eyes. 2 Striking in appearance: a *good* figure. 3 Morally excellent; virtuous; worthy. 4 Kind; benevolent. 5 Well-behaved. 6 Proper; desirable: *good* manners. 7 Pleasing; agreeable: *good* news. 8 Beneficial; salutary: *good* for business. 9 Favorable; approving: a *good* opinion. 10 Skillful; proficient: a *good* swimmer. 11 Orthodox; conforming: a *good* Democrat. 12 Reliable; dependable: a *good* investment. 13 Considerable: a *good* supply: a *good* while. 14 Full: a *good* two miles off. 15 Valid; sound: *good* money. —**as good as** Practically; virtually: It is *as good as* done. —**good and** *Informal* 1 Very: He's *good and* hungry. 2 Completely: when I'm *good and* ready. —**good for** *Informal* Able or likely to give, produce, etc.: *good for* ten dollars; *good for* a laugh. 2 Likely to continue or last: *good for* a week. —**hold good for** To apply: That *holds good for* everyone. —**make good** 1 To compensate for; replace. 2 To carry out; accomplish. 3 To prove. 4 To be successful. —*n.* 1 That which is good. 2 Benefit; profit; advantage: for the *good* of mankind. See also GOODS. —**for good (and all)** Finally; for the last time —**to the good** To one's profit, advantage, etc. —*interj.* An exclamation of satisfaction or assent. —*adv. Informal* Well. [< OE *gōd*]

Good Book The Bible: with *the.*

good-by (gōōd'bī') *adj., n. & interj. pl.* **-bys** (-bīz') Farewell. Also **good-bye.** [Contraction of *God be with you*]

good-for-noth·ing (gōōd'fər·nuth'ing) *n.* A worthless person. —*adj.* Useless.

Good Friday The Friday before Easter, a day commemorating the crucifixion of Jesus.

good-heart·ed (gōōd'här'tid) *adj.* Kind. —**good'heart'·ed·ly** *adv.* —**good'heart'ed·ness** *n.*

good humor A pleasant, cheerful mood or temper. —**good'-hu'mored** *adj.* —**good'hu'mored·ly** *adv.*

good·ies (gōōd'ēz) *n.pl.* of GOODY.

good·ish (gōōd'ish) *adj.* 1 Somewhat good; not bad. 2 Rather large; considerable.

good-look·ing (gōōd'lŏōk'ing) *adj.* Attractive; handsome. —**Syn.** beautiful, comely, becoming, fair, lovely.

good·ly (gōōd'lē) *adj.* **·li·er, ·li·est** 1 Comely; attractive. 2 Large; sizable. —**good'li·ness** *n.*

good·man (gōōd'mən) *n. pl.* **·men** (-mən) *Archaic* 1 Master; Mr.: a title for a man below the rank of gentleman. 2 A husband; head of a family.

good-na·tured (gōōd'nā'chərd) *adj.* Having a pleasant disposition; not easily provoked. —**good'na'tured·ly** *adv.* —**good'na'tured·ness** *n.*

good·ness (gōōd'nis) *n.* 1 The state or quality of being good. 2 Excellence. 3 Virtue. 4 Kindness. —*interj.* An exclamation of surprise, awe, etc.

goods (gōōdz) *n.pl.* 1 Merchandise. 2 Property, esp. personal property. 3 A fabric: linen *goods.* 4 *Brit.* Freight.

Good Samaritan A person who helps one in trouble.

Good Shepherd Jesus.

good-sized (gōōd'sīzd') *adj.* Fairly large.

good-tem·pered (gōōd'tem'pərd) *adj.* Of a good disposition. —**good'tem'pered·ly** *adv.*

good·wife (good'wīf') n. pl. ·wives (-wīvz') Archaic 1 Mrs. 2 The mistress of the house.

good will 1 A desire for the well-being of others. 2 Cheerful willingness or consent. 3 Prestige and friendly relations built up by a business or member of a profession. Also **good-will** (good'wil').

good·y¹ (good'ē) n. pl. **good·ies** Archaic A term of civility to women of humble station. [< GOODWIFE]

good·y² (good'ē) n. pl. **good·ies** Informal 1 Usu. pl. Anything coveted, considered attractive, or highly valued. 2 Usu. pl. Something good to eat. 3 A prissy or sanctimonious person: also **good'y-good'y**. —adj. Informal Mawkishly good or pious: also **good'y-good'y**. —interj. A childish exclamation of joy: also **good'y-good'y**.

goo·ey (goo'ē) adj. **goo·i·er, goo·i·est** Informal Like goo; sticky. 2 Sentimental; mawkish. —**goo'i·ness** n.

goof (goof) Slang n. 1 A stupid, foolish person. 2 A blunder. —v.i. & v.t. 1 To blunder; botch. 2 To waste time: usu. with off or around. [?] —**goof'y** adj. (·i·er, ·i·est) —**goof'i·ly** adv. —**goof'i·ness** n.

goof·ball (goof'bôl') n. Slang A barbiturate, as a sleeping pill, or an amphetamine, or a mixture of them.

goo·gol (goo'gol) n. 1 Math. The number 10 raised to the hundredth power (10¹⁰⁰) or 1 followed by 100 zeros. 2 Any enormous number. [Adopted by E. Kasner, 1878–1955, U.S. mathematician, from a child's word]

gook (gook) n. Slang A gummy or sticky substance or mixture. —**gook'y** adj. (·i·er, ·i·est)

goon (goon) n. Slang 1 A roughneck; thug; esp. one employed during a labor strike. 2 A stupid person. [< a character created by E. C. Segar, 1894–1938, U.S. cartoonist]

goose¹ (goos) n. pl. **geese** 1 One of a subfamily of wild or domesticated web-footed birds larger than ducks and smaller than swans. 2 The female of the goose: distinguished from gander. 3 pl. **goos·es** A tailor's heavy pressing iron, having a curved handle. 4 A silly creature; ninny. —**cook one's goose** Informal To spoil one's chances. [< OE gōs]

Blue goose

goose² (goos) Slang v.t. **goosed, goos·ing** 1 To prod or poke unexpectedly in the backside. 2 To accelerate an engine in irregular spurts. —n. pl. **goos·es** A sudden or unexpected prod or poke in the backside. [? Special use of GOOSE¹]

goose·ber·ry (goos'ber'ē, -bər·ē, gooz'-) n. pl. ·ries 1 The tart fruit of a spiny shrub. 2 This shrub. [? GOOSE¹ + BERRY]

goose·flesh (goos'flesh') n. A roughened condition of the skin produced by cold, fear, etc. Also **goose bumps, goose pimples**.

goose·neck (goos'nek') n. Any of various mechanical devices curved or able to bend like a goose's neck.

goose-step (goos'step') n. A marching step in some armies in which the legs are alternately lifted and held straight out. —v.i. To march in this manner.

G.O.P. Grand Old Party (Republican Party of the U.S.).

go·pher (gō'fər) n. 1 A burrowing North American rodent, esp. one with large cheek pouches. 2 One of various western North American ground squirrels. 3 A large, burrowing land tortoise of the s U.S. [?]

Gopher def. 1

Gor·di·an knot (gôr'dē·ən) 1 The intricate knot tied by Gordius, an ancient Phrygian king. The knot was incapable of being untied except by a future ruler of Asia, and it remained tied until Alexander the Great cut through it with his sword. 2 A difficulty that can be overcome only by the application of unusual or bold measures.

gore¹ (gôr, gōr) v.t. **gored, gor·ing** To pierce, as with a tusk or a horn. [< OE gar] —**gor'er** n.

gore² (gôr, gōr) n. 1 A triangular piece of cloth sewn into a garment, sail, etc., for greater fullness. —v.t. **gored, gor·ing** To shape into or furnish with a gore. [< OE gāra triangular piece of land]

gore³ (gôr, gōr) n. Blood after having been shed, esp. when clotted or dried. [< OE gor dirt, filth]

gorge (gôrj) n. 1 A deep, narrow ravine or passage. 2 A jam: an ice gorge. 3 The throat or gullet. 4 The act of gorging. 5 That which is gorged, as a full meal. 6 Anger, disgust, etc.: to make one's gorge rise. —v. **gorged, gorg·ing** v.t. 1 To stuff with food; glut. 2 To swallow gluttonously; gulp down. —v.i. 3 To stuff oneself with food. [< L gurges a whirlpool] —**gor'ger** n.

gor·geous (gôr'jəs) adj. 1 Resplendently beautiful, esp. as to color: a gorgeous sunset. 2 Informal Very pretty, delightful, amusing, etc. [< OF gorgias elegant] —**gor'geous·ly** adv. —**gor'geous·ness** n.

Gor·gon (gôr'gən) Gk. Myth. One of three sisters with serpents for hair, so hideous that they turned the beholder to stone.

Gor·gon·zo·la (gôr'gən·zō'lə) n. A soft, blue-veined Italian cheese, somewhat like Roquefort. [< Gorgonzola, a town in Italy]

go·ril·la (gə·ril'ə) n. 1 An African anthropoid ape about five and a half feet tall with a massive body and limbs, long arms, and tusklike canine teeth. 2 Slang A tough person, esp. a gangster. [< Gk. Gorillai, an African tribe]

Gorilla

gor·mand (gôr'mənd) n. GOURMAND.

gor·mand·ize (gôr'mən·dīz) v.t. & v.i. ·ized, ·iz·ing To eat voraciously or gluttonously. —**gor'·mand·iz'er** n.

gorse (gôrs) n. FURZE. [< OE gors(t)] —**gors'y** adj.

go·ry (gôr'ē, gō'rē) adj. ·ri·er, ·ri·est Bloody. —**gor'i·ly** adv. —**go'ri·ness** n.

gosh (gosh) interj. A mild oath. [Euphemistic var. of GOD]

gos·hawk (gos'hôk', gôs'-) n. A powerfully built, short-winged hawk formerly used in falconry. [< OE gōs goose + hafoc a hawk]

Go·shen (gō'shən) n. 1 In the Bible, the district in Egypt occupied by the Israelites. 2 A land of plenty.

gos·ling (goz'ling) n. A young goose.

gos·pel (gos'pəl) n. 1 Often cap. The teaching of the Christian Church, esp. the message of salvation preached by Jesus Christ and the apostles. 2 Any doctrine considered worthy of devoted or unquestioning support. 3 Anything regarded as absolutely true: also **gospel truth**. —adj. 1 Often cap. Of or relating to the gospel; evangelical. 2 Of, pertaining to, or being a type of religious music originally associated with evangelism, and combining elements of the spiritual, folk music, blues, and jazz. [< OE godspell good news]

Gos·pel (gos'pəl) n. Any of the first four books of the New Testament.

gos·sa·mer (gos'ə·mər) n. 1 A fine thread of spider's silk, usu. floating in the air. 2 A fine, transparent fabric. 3 Something fine and filmy, as gossamer. —adj. Thin and light as gauze; flimsy: also **gos'sa·mer·y**. [ME, Indian summer]

gos·sip (gos'əp) n. 1 Mischievous or idle talk, usu. about the affairs of others. 2 One who tattles or talks idly: also **gos'sip·er**. —v.i. To talk idly, usu. about the affairs of others. [< OE god sibb a godparent] —**gos'sip·y** adj.

got (got) p.t. & p.p. of GET. • **have** (or **has**) **got** In the sense of must, have or has got is in wide informal use to add emphasis: I have (or I've) got to leave. In the sense of possess, have or has got is still more common in informal speech: He has got plenty of money. This usage has long been challenged on the grounds (1) that have got properly means "have acquired," and (2) that got is superfluous, since have alone would convey the same meaning. However, since have is so much used as an auxiliary that it has lost much of its primary sense of "possess," got serves to restore and emphasize this meaning.

Goth (goth, gôth) n. 1 A member of an ancient East Germanic people that overran the Roman Empire in the third and fourth centuries. 2 A rude or uncivilized person.

Goth. Gothic; gothic.

goth·ic (goth'ik) adj. Often cap. 1 Medieval. 2 Barbaric; uncivilized. 3 Of or in a literary genre characterized by an atmosphere of mystery and gloom, violence, bizarre characters and happenings, etc. [< GOTH] —**goth'i·cal·ly** adv.

Goth·ic (goth'ik) adj. 1 Of the Goths or their language. 2 Of or like a style of architecture developed in w Europe from the 12th to 16th centuries and characterized by high steep roofs, pointed arches and vaulting, flying buttresses, and the use of large, stained-glass windows. —n. 1 The language of the Goths. 2 The Gothic style in architecture.

gothic type U.S. A type face having all the strokes of uniform width and without serifs.

got·ten (got'n) p.p. of GET. • Gotten, obsolete in British, is current in American English in the sense of "obtained": We have gotten the necessary funds. Gotten is also used in the sense of "become": He has gotten fat.

gouache (gwäsh) n. 1 A method of water-color painting with opaque colors mixed with water and gum. 2 A painting executed by this method. [< Ital. guazzo a spray]

Gou·da cheese (gou'də, gōō'-) A mild, yellow cheese, often coated with a red waxy rind. [< Gouda, a town in the Netherlands]

gouge (gouj) n. 1 A chisel having a curved, hollow blade, used for making grooves, etc. 2 A groove made, or as if made, by it. 3 Informal Stealing or cheating. —v.t. **gouged**, **goug·ing** 1 To cut or scoop out with or as with a gouge. 2 To scoop, force, or tear out. 3 Informal To cheat; also, to charge exorbitant prices to. [< LL gulbia] —**goug'er** n.

gou·lash (gōō'läsh, -lash) n. A stew made with beef or veal and vegetables, seasoned with paprika, etc. [< Hung. gulyas (hus) shepherd's (meat)]

gourd (gôrd, gōrd, gōōrd) n. 1 The fruit with a hard rind, as pumpkin or squash, of various trailing plants or vines. 2 The plant producing such fruit. 3 Any of various items made from the rinds of such fruit, as dippers, bowls, rattles, etc. [< L cucurbita]

gour·mand (gōōr'mənd; Fr. gōōr·mäń') n. A person who takes great pleasure in eating and drinking, but without the knowledge or discrimination of a gourmet. [< OF, a glutton]

gour·met (gōōr·mā'; Fr. gōōr·me') n. A person who has a considerable knowledge and appreciation of fine foods and wines. [F < OF, a winetaster]

Gourd def. 1

gout (gout) n. 1 A disease characterized by painful inflammation of a joint, as of the great toe, and an excess of uric acid in the blood. 2 A drop; clot. [< L gutta a drop]

gout·y (gou'tē) adj. **gout·i·er**, **gout·i·est** 1 Affected with gout. 2 Of or pertaining to gout. 3 Swollen. —**gout'i·ly** adv. —**gout'i·ness** n.

Gov. Governor.

gov., govt. government.

gov·ern (guv'ərn) v.t. 1 To rule or control by right or authority. 2 To control or influence morally or physically. 3 To serve as a rule or regulation for; determine: This decision governed the case. 4 To discipline or curb. —v.i. 5 To exercise authority. [< L gubernare to steer] —**gov'ern·a·ble** adj. —**gov'ern·ance** (-ər·nəns) n.

gov·ern·ess (guv'ər·nis) n. A woman employed in a private home to train and instruct children.

gov·ern·ment (guv'ərn·mənt, -ər-) n. 1 The authoritative direction and administration of the affairs of men in a nation, state, city, etc.; rule. 2 The governing body of a nation, state, city, etc. 3 A particular form of ruling or governing: democratic government. 4 A governed territory. 5 Management; control. —**gov'ern·men'tal** adj. —**gov'ern·men'tal·ly** adv.

Government House In British colonies, the official residence of a governor.

gov·er·nor (guv'ər·nər) n. 1 One who governs; esp. the chief executive of a state or colony. 2 A feedback controller, as for regulating the speed of a machine.

governor general pl. **governors general** or **governor generals** A high-ranking governor, esp. one who has deputy governors under him, as in the British Commonwealth. Brit. sp. **gov'er·nor-gen'er·al** n. pl. **gov'er·nors-gen'er·al**

gov·er·nor·ship (guv'ər·nər·ship) n. 1 The office of a governor. 2 A governor's term of office.

gown (goun) n. 1 A woman's dress, esp. when elegant or costly. 2 A long and loose outer robe worn as a distinctive or official habit, as by judges, clergymen, etc. 3 Any loose usu. long outer garment. 4 Those people associated administratively or educationally with a college or university in a town: town and gown. —v.t. & v.i. To dress in a gown. [< Med. L gunna a loose robe]

goy (goi) n. pl. **goy·im** (goi'im) or **goys** (goiz) A non-Jew; a Gentile. [Yiddish]

G.P. general paresis; general practitioner.

g.p.m. gallons per minute.

GPO, G.P.O. General Post Office; Government Printing Office.

g.p.s. gallons per second.

GQ, G.Q., g.q. general quarters.

Gr. Grecian; Greece; Greek.

gr. grade; grain(s); gram(s); grammar; gravity; great; gross; group.

Graaf·i·an follicle (gräf'ē·ən, gräf'-) Anat. Any of the small sacs in the ovary of a mammal that contain a developing ovum. [< Regnier de Graaf, 1641–73, Du. anatomist]

grab (grab) v. **grabbed**, **grab·bing** v.t. 1 To grasp or seize forcibly or suddenly. 2 To take possession of violently or dishonestly. —v.i. 3 To make a sudden grasp. 4 Slang To involve or hold emotionally; affect. —n. 1 The act of grabbing, or that which is grabbed. 2 An apparatus for grappling. —**up for grabs** Slang Available to anyone with the means or money. [< MDu. grabben] —**grab'ber** n.

grab bag 1 A bag or box filled with miscellaneous articles, from which one draws something unseen on payment of a price for each grab or draw. 2 Any miscellaneous collection.

grab·by (grab'ē) adj. **grab·bi·er**, **grab·bi·est** Informal Offensively acquisitive or pushy; grasping. —**grab'bi·ness** n.

grace (grās) n. 1 Beauty or harmony of form, movement, manner, mode of expression, etc. 2 Any attractive characteristic, quality, etc. 3 Social aptness or thoughtfulness. 4 An extension of time granted, as in the payment of a debt. 5 Theol. a The love of God toward mankind. b A state of mind or spirit that is pleasing to God. c A power coming from God that enables one to achieve such a state. d Any divine favor. 6 A short prayer before or after meals. 7 Good will; favor. 8 Music An ornament, as a trill or turn. —v.t. **graced**, **grac·ing** 1 To add grace and beauty to; adorn. 2 To dignify; honor. 3 Music To ornament with grace notes or other embellishments. [< L gratia favor]

grace·ful (grās'fəl) adj. Having or characterized by grace of form, movement, manner, etc. —**grace'ful·ly** adv. —**grace'ful·ness** n.

grace·less (grās'lis) adj. Lacking grace, charm, etc. —**grace'less·ly** adv. —**grace'less·ness** n.

grace note Music An ornamental, melodic note foreign to the harmony, esp. a short note on or just before the beat.

gra·cious (grā'shəs) adj. 1 Kind, courteous, and affable. 2 Compassionate; lenient. 3 Pleasantly luxurious and comfortable: gracious living. —**gra'cious·ly** adv. —**gra'cious·ness** n. —Syn. 1 polite, cordial, amiable. 2 benevolent, considerate, sympathetic.

grack·le (grak'əl) n. Any of several large North American blackbirds. [< L graculus a jackdaw]

grad (grad) n. Informal A graduate.

grad. graduate; graduated.

gra·date (grā'dāt) v.t. & v.i. **·dat·ed**, **·dat·ing** 1 To pass or cause to pass imperceptibly from one shade or degree of intensity to another, as colors. 2 To arrange or group, as to size, quality, etc.

gra·da·tion (grā·dā'shən) n. 1 Orderly or continuous change by steps or degrees from one size, quality, state, etc., to another. 2 A step, degree, rank, or relative position in a graded series. 3 The act or process of arranging in grades or stages. [< L gradatio a going by steps < gradus a step] —**gra·da'tion·al** adj. —**gra·da'tion·al·ly** adv.

---

add, āce, câre, pälm; end, ēven; it, īce; odd, ōpen, ôrder; tōōk, pōōl; up, bûrn; ə = a in above, u in focus; yōō = u in fuse; oil; pout; check; go; ring; thin; this; zh, vision. < derived from; ? origin uncertain or unknown.

COMPARATIVE GRADES IN THE UNITED STATES ARMED SERVICES

Army	Air Force	Marine Corps	Navy
General	General	General	Admiral
Lieutenant General	Lieutenant General	Lieutenant General	Vice Admiral
Major General	Major General	Major General	Rear Admiral (upper half)
Brigadier General	Brigadier General	Brigadier General	Rear Admiral (lower half)
Colonel	Colonel	Colonel	Captain
Lieutenant Colonel	Lieutenant Colonel	Lieutenant Colonel	Commander
Major	Major	Major	Lieutenant Commander
Captain	Captain	Captain	Lieutenant
1st Lieutenant	1st Lieutenant	1st Lieutenant	Lieutenant Junior Grade
2nd Lieutenant	2nd Lieutenant	2nd Lieutenant	Ensign
Chief Warrant Officer w-4			
Chief Warrant Officer w-3			
Chief Warrant Officer w-2	Same	Same	Same
Warrant Officer w-1			
Sergeant Major or Specialist 9	Chief Master Sergeant	Master Gunnery Sergeant or Sergeant Major	Master Chief Petty Officer
Master Sergeant, First Sergeant, or Specialist 8	Senior Master Sergeant	Master Sergeant or First Sergeant	Senior Chief Petty Officer
Sergeant First Class, Platoon Sergeant, or Specialist 7	Master Sergeant	Gunnery Sergeant	Chief Petty Officer
Staff Sergeant or Specialist 6	Technical Sergeant	Staff Sergeant	Petty Officer First Class
Sergeant or Specialist 5	Staff Sergeant	Sergeant	Petty Officer Second Class
Corporal or Specialist 4	Sergeant	Corporal	Petty Officer Third Class
Private First Class	Airman First Class	Lance Corporal	Seaman
Private e-2	Airman	Private First Class	Seaman Apprentice
Private e-1	Airman Basic	Private	Seaman Recruit

grade (grād) *n.* **1** A degree or step in any scale, as of quality, ability, dignity, etc. **2** A group of persons of the same rank or station. **3** A rank in the U.S. armed forces. **4** A class of things of the same quality or value: a high *grade* of wool. **5 a** One of the divisions of an elementary or secondary school, usu. covering a year of work. **b** The pupils in such a division. **6** *pl.* GRADE SCHOOL: with *the.* **7** A scholastic rating or mark on an examination or in a course. **8** The degree of inclination of the surface of a road or the like; also, the part of a road, etc., that slopes. —*v.* **grad·ed, grad·ing** *v.t.* **1** To arrange or classify by grades or degrees, according to size, quality, etc. **2** To assign a grade to. **3** To make level or properly inclined. —*v.i.* **4** To be of a specific rank, degree, or grade. [< L *gradus* step] —**grad′er** *n.*

-grade *combining form* Manner of moving or walking: *plantigrade*. [< L *gradi* walk]

grade crossing A place where a road and a railroad or two railroads cross on the same level.

grade school ELEMENTARY SCHOOL.

gra·di·ent (grā′dē·ənt) *adj.* Rising or descending gently or by degrees. —*n.* **1** A slope or grade. **2** The degree of inclination of such a slope. **3** *Physics* The maximum rate of change of a variable, as pressure, temperature, etc., with respect to position. [< L *gradi* to walk]

grad·u·al (graj′ōō·əl) *adj.* Moving, changing, developing, etc., slowly and by degrees. [< L *gradus* a step] —**grad′u·al·ly** *adv.* —**grad′u·al·ness** *n.*

grad·u·ate (graj′ōō·āt) *v.* **·at·ed, ·at·ing** *v.t.* **1** To grant a diploma or degree to. **2** To mark in units or degrees, as a thermometer scale; calibrate. **3** To arrange into grades or divisions, as according to size or quality. —*v.i.* **4** To receive a diploma or degree indicating completion of a course of study. **5** To change by degrees. —*n.* (graj′ōō·it) **1** One who has completed any academic or professional course. **2** A graduated vessel used in measuring liquids, etc. —*adj.* (graj′ōō·it) **1** Having a degree or diploma from a college, school, etc. **2** Designed for or pertaining to students working towards a degree beyond the bachelor's. [< L *gradus* step, degree] —**grad′u·a·tor** *n.*

grad·u·a·tion (graj′ōō·ā′shən) *n.* **1** The act of graduating, as a scale, or state of being graduated, as a series of colors. **2** An equal division or dividing line in a graduated scale. **3** In education: **a** A graduating or being graduated. **b** The ceremony marking this; commencement.

graf·fi·to (grə·fē′tō) *n. pl.* **·ti** (-tē) **1** Any design, or scribbled motto, etc., drawn on a wall or other exposed surface.

2 *Archeol.* A pictograph scratched on a wall or other surface. [< Ital. *graffio* a scratch, ult. < Gk. *graphein* write]

graft¹ (graft, gräft) *n.* **1** A piece of living plant or animal tissue excised and inserted in a new site in the same or a different organism. **2** The juncture between such a graft and the place where it is inserted. **3** A union resembling a graft. —*v.t.* **1** To implant (tissue) in a new site in a living organism. —*v.i.* **2** To insert grafts. **3** To be or become grafted. [< LL *graphium* stylus < Gk. *graphein* write] — **graft′age** (-ij), **graft′er** *n.*

graft² (graft, gräft) *n.* **1** The attainment of personal advantage or profit by dishonest or unfair means, esp. through one's political connections. **2** Anything thus gained. —*v.t.* **1** To obtain by graft. —*v.i.* **2** To practice graft. [?] —**graft′er** *n.*

gra·ham (grā′əm) *adj.* Made from unrefined wheat flour. [< S. *Graham*, 1794–1851, U.S. dietary reformer.]

Grail (grāl) *n.* In medieval legend, the cup or platter used by Jesus at the Last Supper. [< Med. L *gradalis*]

grain (grān) *n.* **1** A seed or kernel, as of wheat, corn, rice, etc. **2** Any of the common cereal plants, as wheat, oats, rye, barley, etc. **3** Any minute, hard particle, as of sugar or sand. **4** Any very small amount: a *grain* of sense. **5** The arrangement or direction of particles or fibers, as of wood, stone, leather, etc. **6** The patterns produced on a surface by such arrangements or directions. **7** The smallest unit used in the systems of weights of the U.S. and Great Britain. **8** The innate quality or character of a thing. **9** Natural disposition or nature. —*v.t.* **1** To form into grains; granulate. **2** To paint or stain in imitation of the grain of wood, marble, etc. —*v.i.* **3** To form grains. [< L *granum* a seed]

grain alcohol ETHYL ALCOHOL.

grain elevator A warehouse for the storage of grain.

grain·y (grā′nē) *adj.* **grain·i·er, grain·i·est** **1** Composed of grains or kernels; granular. **2** Having the patterns of grains, as the surface of wood. —**grain′i·ness** *n.*

gram (gram) *n.* A metric unit of mass or weight, equal to 10^{-3} (0.0001) kilogram, or about 0.035 ounce. [< Gk. *gramma* letter, small thing]

-gram¹ *combining form* Something written or drawn: *telegram*. [< Gk. *gramma* a letter]

-gram² *combining form* Gram: *kilogram*. [< GRAM]

gram. grammar; grammarian; grammatical.

gram calorie See CALORIE.

gram·mar (gram′ər) *n.* **1** The systematic analysis of the classes and structure of words (morphology) and of their arrangements and interrelationships in larger constructions (syntax). **2** A system of morphological and syntactical rules and principles for speaking and writing a given language. **3** A treatise or book dealing with such rules. **4** Speech or writing considered with regard to current standards of correctness. **5** The elements of any science or art, or a book or treatise dealing with them. [< Gk. *grammatikē (technē)* literary (art)]

gram·mar·i·an (grə-mâr′ē-ən) *n.* A specialist in grammar.

grammar school 1 ELEMENTARY SCHOOL. **2** *Brit.* SECONDARY SCHOOL.

gram·mat·i·cal (grə-mat′i-kəl) *adj.* **1** Conforming to the principles of standard speech or writing. **2** Of or pertaining to grammar. —**gram·mat′i·cal·ly** *adv.* —**gram·mat′i·cal·ness** *n.*

gram molecule MOLE⁴. Also **gram-mo·lec·u·lar weight** (gram′mə-lek′yoo-lər).

gram·o·phone (gram′ə-fōn) *n.* PHONOGRAPH. [< *Gramophone,* a trade name]

gram·pus (gram′pəs) *n. pl.* **·pus·es 1** A large dolphinlike cetacean of northern waters. **2** KILLER WHALE. [< L *crassus piscis* fat fish]

gran·a·ry (grā′nər-ē, gran′ər-) *n. pl. pl.* **·ries 1** A storehouse for grain. **2** A country or region where grain grows in abundance. [< L *granum* grain]

grand (grand) *adj.* **1** Of imposing character or aspect; magnificent, as in size, beauty, etc. **2** Main; principal: the *grand* hall. **3** Preeminent; noble, distinguished. **4** Highest in rank or order: a *grand* duke. **5** Pretentiously haughty or arrogant. **6** Lofty; exalted: a *grand* style. **7** Complete; overall: the *grand* total. **8** *Informal* Very good, excellent, etc.: We had a *grand* time. —*n.* **1** A grand piano. **2** *Slang* One thousand dollars. [< L *grandis*] —**grand′ly** *adv.* —**grand′ness** *n.* —**Syn. 1** great, mighty, impressive, sublime. **5** ostentatious, showy, pompous. **6** elevated, eloquent, sublime.

gran·dam (gran′dam, -dəm) *n. Archaic* **1** GRANDMOTHER. **2** An old woman. Also **gran′dame** (-dām, -dəm). [< AF *graund dame*]

Grand Army of the Republic An organization of Union veterans of the Civil War, organized in 1866.

grand·aunt (grand′ant′, -änt′) *n.* GREAT-AUNT.

grand·child (grand′child′) *n. pl.* **·chil·dren** A child of one's son or daughter.

grand·dad (gran′dad′) *n. Informal* Grandfather.

grand·daugh·ter (gran′dô′tər, grand′-) *n.* A daughter of one's son or daughter.

grand duchess 1 The wife or widow of a grand duke. **2** A woman holding sovereign rights over a grand duchy. **3** In czarist Russia, a daughter of a czar.

grand duchy The domain of a grand duke or grand duchess.

grand duke 1 A sovereign who rules over a grand duchy and ranks just below a king. **2** In czarist Russia, any brother, son, uncle, or nephew of a czar.

grande dame (gränd däm) A woman of great dignity or notable achievements. [F, lit., great lady]

gran·dee (gran-dē′) *n.* A Spanish or Portuguese nobleman of the highest rank. [< Sp. *grande* great]

gran·deur (gran′jər, -joor) *n.* The quality of being grand; magnificence; sublimity.

grand·fa·ther (grand′fä′thər) *n.* The father of one's father or mother. —**grand′fa′ther·ly** *adj.*

grand gui·gnol (grän gē-nyôl′) *Often cap.* A dramatic presentation of a sensationally gruesome or horrifying character. [< *Le Grand Guignol,* former theater in Paris featuring such dramas]

gran·dil·o·quent (gran-dil′ə-kwənt) *adj.* Speaking in or characterized by a pompous or bombastic style. [< L < *grandis* great + *loqui* speak] —**gran·dil′o·quence** *n.*

gran·di·ose (gran′dē-ōs) *adj.* **1** Having an imposing style; impressive. **2** Affecting grandeur; pompous, bombastic. [< L *grandis* great] —**gran′di·ose·ly** *adv.* —**gran·di·os·i·ty** (gran′dē-os′ə-tē) *n.*

grand jury A jury of 12 or more persons impaneled to evaluate accusations against a suspect and bring an indictment if there is enough evidence to merit a regular trial.

grand·ma (grand′mä′, gran′mä′, gram′mä) *n. Informal* Grandmother. Also **grand′ma·ma′** (-ma·ma′, -mä′mə).

grand mal (grän mäl′) An epileptic seizure characterized by severe convulsions followed by coma: distinguished from *petit mal.* [F, lit., great sickness]

grand·moth·er (grand′muth′ər) *n.* The mother of one's father or mother. —**grand′moth′er·ly** *adj.*

grand·neph·ew (grand′nef′yoo, -nev′-, gran′-) *n.* A son of one's nephew or niece.

grand·niece (grand′nēs′, gran′-) *n.* A daughter of one's nephew or niece.

Grand Old Party In U.S. politics, the Republican party.

grand opera An opera in which the entire text is sung.

grand·pa (grand′pä′, gram′pä′) *n. Informal* Grandfather. Also **grand′pa·pa′** (-pə-pä′, -pä′pə).

grand·par·ent (grand′pâr′ənt, gran′-) *n.* The parent of one's parent.

grand piano A piano in which the strings are placed horizontally in a curved frame.

grand·sire (grand′sīr′) *n. Archaic* **1** GRANDFATHER. **2** Any male ancestor preceding a father. **3** Any venerable man.

grand slam 1 In bridge, the winning of all 13 tricks in a round of play. **2** In baseball, a home run with all the bases loaded. **3** In certain sports, as golf, the winning of all major or specified contests in a season, on a tour, etc.

Grand piano

grand·son (grand′sun′, gran′-) *n.* A son of one's son or daughter.

grand·stand (grand′stand′, gran′-) *n.* The principal structure for spectators at any public spectacle or sports event. —*v.i. Informal* To show off in an attempt to win applause.

grand·un·cle (grand′ung′kəl) *n.* GREAT-UNCLE.

grange (grānj) *n. Brit.* A farm, with its dwelling house, barns, etc. [< L *granum* grain]

Grange (grānj) *n.* **1** The order of Patrons of Husbandry, a nation-wide association of U.S. farmers, founded in 1867. **2** One of the local lodges of the Patrons of Husbandry. —**Grang′er** *n.*

gran·ite (gran′it) *n.* **1** A hard, coarse-grained, igneous rock composed principally of quartz, feldspar, and mica. **2** Great strength, endurance, etc. [< Ital. *granire* make grainy] —**gra·nit·ic** (grə-nit′ik) or **·i·cal** *adj.*

gran·ite·ware (gran′it·wâr′) *n.* **1** A variety of ironware coated with hard enamel. **2** A variety of fine, hard pottery.

gran·ny (gran′ē) *n. pl.* **·nies** *Informal* **1** Grandmother. **2** An old woman. **3** An excessively fussy person. **4** GRANNY KNOT. Also **gran′nie**.

granny knot An incorrectly tied square knot. Also **granny's knot, granny's bend.**

gra·no·la (grə-nō′lə) *n.* A mixture of dry cereals, nuts, and raisins, chopped fine and marketed as a health food.

grant (grant, gränt) *v.t.* **1** To give or accord, as permission, a request, etc. **2** To confer or bestow, as a privilege, charter, favor, etc. **3** To admit as true, esp. something not proved, as for the sake of argument; concede. **4** To transfer (property), esp. by deed. —*n.* **1** The act of granting. **2** Something granted, as property, funds for a specific purpose, etc. [< AF *granter,* ult. < L *credere* believe] —**grant′a·ble** *adj.* —**grant′er,** *Law* **grant′or** *n.*

grant·ee (gran-tē′, grän-) *n.* One who receives a grant.

gran·u·lar (gran′yə-lər) *adj.* **1** Composed of, like, or containing grains or granules. **2** Having a grainy surface. Also **gran′u·lose** (-lōs). —**gran′u·lar′i·ty** (-lar′ə-tē) *n.*

gran·u·late (gran′yə-lāt) *v.t. & v.i.* **·lat·ed, ·lat·ing 1** To make or become granular; form into grains. **2** To become or cause to become rough on the surface by the formation of granules. —**gran′u·la′tion** *n.* —**gran′u·la′tive** *adj.*

gran·ule (gran′yool) *n.* A small grain or particle.

grape (grāp) n. 1 The smooth-skinned, edible, juicy, berrylike fruit of various species of the grapevine, from which most wines are made. 2 Any grapevine yielding this fruit. 3 Figuratively, wine. 4 A dark blue color with a slight reddish tint. |<OF, bunch of grapes, hook < Gmc.]

grape·fruit (grāp′frōōt′) n. A large, round, pale yellow citrus fruit.

grape·shot (grāp′shot′) n. A cluster of cast-iron shot to be discharged from a cannon.

grape sugar DEXTROSE.

grape·vine (grāp′vīn) n. 1 Any of a genus of woody, climbing plants characterized by profuse clusters of berrylike juicy fruit. 2 Informal Any secret or unofficial means by which information, rumors, etc., are circulated.

graph (graf, gräf) n. 1 A diagram indicating any sort of relationship between two or more things by means of a system of dots, curves, bars, or lines. 2 Math. A set of points drawn on a coordinate system so that each point satisfies a given function. —v.t. To represent in the form of a graph. [Short for graphic formula]

-graph combining form 1 That which writes or records: telegraph. 2 A writing or record: monograph. [<Gk. graphein write]

graph·ic (graf′ik) adj. 1 Vividly effective and detailed. 2 Of, like, or represented by graphs. 3 Of, pertaining to, or expressed in handwriting. 4 Written or expressed by means of signs, symbols, etc. 5 Of or pertaining to the graphic arts. Also **graph′i·cal.** [<Gk. graphein write] —**graph′i·cal·ly, graph′ic·ly** adv.

graphic arts 1 Loosely, any of the visual arts, as painting, drawing, photography, etc. 2 Those arts which involve impressions printed from blocks, screens, etc., as printing, lithography, etching, wood-engraving, etc.

graph·ics (graf′iks) 1 (n. pl., construed as singular) The art or science of drawing. 2 (n. pl.) Illustrations created by a computer.

graph·ite (graf′īt) n. A soft, black, chemically inert, crystalline form of carbon with a metallic luster and oily feel, used as a lubricant and in the making of lead pencils. [<Gk. graphein write] —**gra·phit·ic** (grə-fit′ik) adj.

graph·ol·o·gy (graf-ol′ə-jē) n. The analysis of handwriting, esp. to interpret character and personality. [<Gk. graphein write + -LOGY] —**graph·o·log·i·cal** (graf′ə-loj′i·kəl) adj. —**graph·ol′o·gist** n.

-graphy combining form A written description of: geography. [<Gk. graphein write]

grap·nel (grap′nəl) n. 1 A metal bar with hooks or claws at one end, used for grasping objects. 2 Naut. A boat's anchor with many flukes. [<OF grapin a hook]

grap·ple (grap′əl) v. **grap·pled, grap·pling** v.t. 1 To take hold of; grasp firmly. —v.i. 2 To use a grapnel. 3 To seize or come to grips with another, as in wrestling. 4 To deal or contend with with. —n. 1 A close hold, as in wrestling. 2 GRAPNEL (def. 1). [<OF grappil grapnel] —**grap′pler** n.

grappling iron (grap′ling) GRAPNEL (def. 1).

grasp (grasp, gräsp) v.t. 1 To lay hold of with or as with the hand; grip. 2 To seize greedily or eagerly; snatch. 3 To take hold of with the mind; understand. —v.i. 4 To make grasping motions. —**grasp at** 1 To try to seize. 2 To accept eagerly or desperately. —n. 1 The act of seizing or grasping. 2 The ability to seize and hold. 3 Power of comprehension; understanding. [ME graspen] —**grasp′er** n.

grasp·ing (gras′ping, gräs′-) adj. Greedy; avaricious.

grass (gras, gräs) n. 1 The vegetation typically forming a green carpet over the ground of lawns, pastures, etc. 2 Any of a large family of monocotyledons, as wheat, oats, sugar cane, bamboo, and various forage plants. 3 Ground covered with grass; lawn or pasture. 4 Any plants resembling the true grasses, as the sedges, the rushes, etc. 5 Slang MARIHUANA. —v.t. 1 To cover with grass or turf. 2 To feed with grass; pasture. —v.i. 3 To graze on grass. 4 To produce grass; become covered with grass. [<OE græs]

Grasshopper

grass·hop·per (gras′hop′ər, gräs′-) n. Any of several insects, including the locust and katydid, having powerful hind legs adapted for leaping.

grass·land (gras′land′, gräs′-) n. 1 Land reserved for pasturage or mowing. 2 Land in which grasses predominate.

grass roots 1 Ordinary people, esp. those apart from the centers of political power or influence. 2 The primary source or foundation. —**grass′roots′** adj.

grass widow A woman separated from her husband by causes other than death.

grass·y (gras′ē, gräs′ē) adj. **grass·i·er, grass·i·est** Abounding in, covered with, consisting of, or resembling grass. —**grass′i·ly** adv. —**grass′i·ness** n.

grate¹ (grāt) v. **grat·ed, grat·ing** v.t. 1 To reduce to small particles by rubbing against a rough surface. 2 To rub or grind so as to produce a harsh, scraping sound. 3 To annoy; irritate; to grate the nerves. —v.i. 4 To sound harshly, from or as from scraping or grinding; creak. 5 To have an irritating effect: with on or upon. [<OF grater < Gmc.] —**grat′er** n.

grate² (grāt) n. 1 A framework of bars to hold fuel in burning. 2 A similar framework used to prohibit entry through a window or other opening. 3 A fireplace. —v.t. **grat·ed, grat·ing** To fit with a grate or grates. [<L cratis a lattice]

grate·ful (grāt′fəl) adj. 1 Having or expressing gratitude; thankful. 2 Affording gratification; pleasurable; agreeable. [<L gratus pleasing + -FUL] —**grate′ful·ly** adv. —**grate′ful·ness** n. —Syn. 1 obliged, beholden, indebted to, under obligation.

grat·i·fi·ca·tion (grat′ə·fə·kā′shən) n. 1 The act of gratifying or the state of being gratified. 2 Something that gratifies.

grat·i·fy (grat′ə·fī) v.t. **·fied, ·fy·ing** 1 To give pleasure or satisfaction to. 2 To satisfy or indulge, as a desire or need. [<L gratus pleasing + -FY] —**grat′i·fi′er** n. —**grat′i·fy·ing** adj., —**grat′i·fy·ing·ly** adv.

grat·ing¹ (grā′ting) n. 1 GRATE² (def. 2). 2 Physics A series of fine grooves cut in a smooth surface, used to disperse light and produce spectra.

grat·ing² (grā′ting) adj. 1 Harsh in sound; rasping. 2 Annoying; irritating. —**grat′ing·ly** adv.

gra·tis (grat′is, grā′tis) adv. Without recompense; freely. —adj. Given free of charge. [<L gratia favor]

grat·i·tude (grat′ə·tⁿōōd) n. A feeling of thankfulness.

gra·tu·i·tous (grə·tⁿōō′ə·təs) adj. 1 Given freely without charge or conditions. 2 Without cause; uncalled for; unnecessary. [<L gratuitus given as a favor] —**gra·tu′i·tous·ly** adv. —**gra·tu′i·tous·ness** n.

gra·tu·i·ty (grə·tⁿōō′ə·tē) n. pl. **·ties** 1 A present. 2 Money given in return for service, etc.; a tip.

gra·va·men (grə·vā′men) n. pl. **·va·mens** or **·vam·i·na** (-vam′ə·nə) The essence of a charge or grievance; the burden of a complaint. [<L < gravis heavy]

grave¹ (grāv) adj. **grav·er, grav·est** 1 Of momentous import; weighty; important. 2 Severely dangerous; critical. 3 Serious; dignified; sedate, as in manner or speech. 4 Somber in color or fashion. 5 Low in tone or pitch. —n. (grāv, grāv) A mark (`) used in French to indicate the open quality of e or in English to indicate a falling inflection or the pronunciation of a final ed, as in preparèd: also **grave accent.** [<L gravis heavy] —**grave′ly** adv. —**grave′ness** n.

grave² (grāv) n. 1 A place for the burial of a dead body, usu. an excavation in the ground. 2 A tomb. —**the grave** Death. [<OE græf]

grave³ (grāv) v.t. **graved, grav·en, grav·ing** 1 To engrave; carve with a chisel. 2 To sculpture. 3 To impress deeply; on the memory. [<OE grafan dig]

grave·dig·ger (grāv′dig′ər) n. One who digs graves.

grav·el (grav′əl) n. 1 A mixture of small, usu. rounded, pebbles or stones. 2 Pathol. The formation in the kidneys of numerous granular concretions. —v.t. **grav·eled, grav·el·ing** or **grav·el·ling** 1 To cover or fill with gravel. 2 To bring up short, as in embarrassment or confusion. 3 Informal To irritate; annoy. [<OF grave sand] —**grav′el·ly, grav′el·y** adj.

grav·en (grā′vən) adj. Carved or cut.

graven image A carved or graven idol.

grave·stone (grāv′stōn′) n. A memorial stone, placed at a grave.

grave·yard (grāv′yärd′) *n.* A burial place; a cemetery.

graveyard shift *Informal* A work shift during the late night, usu. from midnight to eight in the morning.

grav·i·tate (grav′ə-tāt) *v.i.* ·tat·ed, ·tat·ing 1 To be attracted by force of gravity. 2 To move or be attracted as though drawn by a powerful force: with *to* or *toward*. 3 To sink or fall to the lowest level. —**grav′i·tat′er** *n.* —**grav′i·ta′tive** *adj.*

grav·i·ta·tion (grav′ə-tā′shən) *n.* 1 *Physics* The force whereby any two bodies attract each other in proportion to the product of their masses and inversely as the square of the distance between them. 2 The act or process of gravitating. —**grav′i·ta′tion·al** *adj.* —**grav′i·ta′tion·al·ly** *adv.*

grav·i·ty (grav′ə-tē) *n. pl.* ·ties 1 The force that attracts bodies toward the center of the earth. 2 A similar force exerted on other bodies by any object in space. 3 Weight. 4 Gravitation. 5 Extreme importance; seriousness. 6 Danger; peril: the *gravity* of their plight. 7 Dignified reserve; sedateness. —*adj.* Employing gravity; worked by gravity. [< L *gravis* heavy]

gra·vure (grə-vyŏor′) *n.* 1 A process of printing using etched plates, used esp. in photogravure. 2 A print made by such a process. [< F *graver* engrave]

gra·vy (grā′vē) *n. pl.* ·vies 1 The juice that exudes from meat being cooked. 2 A sauce made from these juices. 3 *Slang* Any added, easily acquired payment or income. [ME *gravey*]

gravy boat A boat-shaped dish in which gravy is served.

gray (grā) *adj.* 1 Of a color intermediate between black and white and lacking hue. 2 Having gray hair; hoary. 3 Old; aged. —*n.* 1 A color between black and white with no hue. 2 Something gray, esp. a gray animal. —*v.t. & v.i.* To make or become gray. [< OE *græg*] —**gray′ly** *adv.* —**gray′ness** *n.*

gray·beard (grā′bird′) *n.* An old man.

gray·ish (grā′ish) *adj.* Somewhat gray.

gray·ling (grā′ling) *n. pl.* ·ling or ·lings A freshwater, troutlike fish of N waters.

gray matter 1 The grayish substance of the brain, composed of nerve cell bodies and few fibers. 2 *Informal* Intelligence.

graze[1] (grāz) *v.* grazed, graz·ing *v.i.* 1 To feed upon growing grass or herbage. —*v.i.* 2 To put (cattle, etc.) to feed on growing grass or herbage. —*n.* The act of cropping or feeding upon growing grass or the like. [< OE *grasian* < *græs* grass] —**graz′er** *n.*

graze[2] (grāz) *v.* grazed, graz·ing *v.t.* 1 To touch or rub against lightly in passing. 2 To scrape or cut slightly in passing. —*v.i.* 3 To touch lightly in passing. 4 To scrape slightly. —*n.* 1 A light or passing touch. 2 A scrape or abrasion. [?] —**graz′er** *n.* —**graz′ing·ly** *adv.*

graz·ing (grā′zing) *n.* A pasture.

Gr.Br., Gr.Brit. Great Britain.

grease (grēs) *n.* 1 Animal fat, esp. when soft or melted. 2 A thick, oily substance derived from petroleum and used as a lubricant. —*v.t.* (grēs, grēz) greased, greas·ing 1 To apply grease to. 2 *Slang* To influence by gifts or bribes. [< L *crassus* fat] —**greas′er** *n.*

grease·paint (grēs′pānt′) *n.* A paste, with a grease base, used in theatrical make-up.

grease·wood (grēs′wŏod′) *n.* Any of various stunted, prickly shrubs of the w U.S. Also **grease′bush**′ (-bŏosh′).

greas·y (grē′sē, -zē) *adj.* greas·i·er, greas·i·est 1 Smeared or spotted with grease. 2 Containing much grease or fat: oily. 3 Resembling grease; smooth; unctuous. —**greas′i·ly** *adv.* —**greas′i·ness** *n.*

great (grāt) *adj.* 1 Very large in size, expanse, etc.; immense; vast. 2 Large in number, quantity, etc.: a *great* assembly. 3 Long in extent or time: a *great* distance; a *great* while. 4 Of very considerable degree, intensity, etc.: a *great* sorrow. 5 Unusually important, impressive, or remarkable: a *great* achievement. 6 Of unusual excellence; superior; eminent: a *great* dancer. 7 Noble and elevated, as in character, action, feeling, etc.: a *great* humanitarian. 8 Most important of its kind; chief; main: the *great* prize. 9 *Informal* Adept; skilled: usu. with *at*: *great* at sports. 10

Informal Excellent; first-rate: to have a *great* time. 11 More remote by a single generation than the relationship indicated: used in combination with a hyphen: *great*-uncle, *great*-grandson. —*adv. Informal* Very well. —*n. Usu. pl.* A person who is great, noble, distinguished, etc.: with *the:* one of the *greats.* [< OE *grēat*] —**great′ly** *adv.* —**great′ness** *n.*

great-aunt (grāt′ant′, -änt′) *n.* The aunt of either of one's parents; grandaunt.

Great Bear The constellation Ursa Major. • See Ursa Major.

Great Brit·ain (brit′n) The principal part of the United Kingdom of Great Britain and Northern Ireland, located on an island west of Europe and comprising England, Scotland, and Wales.

great calorie See CALORIE.

great circle *Geom.* A circle formed on the surface of a sphere by a plane which passes through the center of the sphere.

great·coat (grāt′kōt′) *n.* A heavy overcoat.

Great Dane One of a breed of short-haired dogs of large size and great strength.

great-grand·child (grāt′-grand′chīld′) *n.* A child of a grandchild.

great-grand·par·ent (grāt′-grand′pâr′ənt) *n.* The parent of a grandparent.

great-heart·ed (grāt′här′tid) *adj.* 1 Courageous; valorous. 2 Having a generous or noble nature; magnanimous.

Great Dane

Great Lakes A chain of five freshwater lakes on the Canada-United States border: Lakes Superior, Michigan, Huron, Erie, and Ontario.

great seal The chief seal of a government, used to authenticate important documents.

great-un·cle (grāt′-ung′kəl) *n.* The uncle of either of one's parents; granduncle.

greave (grēv) *n.* Armor to protect the leg from knee to ankle. [< OF *gieve*]

grebe (grēb) *n.* Any of a family of swimming and diving birds related to the loons. [F *grèbe*]

Gre·cian (grē′shən) *adj.* Greek. —*n.* 1 A Greek. 2 A scholar of Greek.

Greco- *combining form* Greek: *Greco-Roman.*

Gre·co-Ro·man (grē′kō-rō′mən) *adj.* Of or pertaining to Greece and Rome together: *Greco-Roman* art.

Greece (grēs) *n.* A republic of SE Europe, 50,547 sq. mi., cap. Athens.

greed (grēd) *n.* Eager and selfish desire for something. [Back formation < GREEDY]

greed·y (grē′dē) *adj.* greed·i·er, greed·i·est 1 Eager to obtain; covetous; grasping. 2 Having an excessive appetite for food or drink. [< OE *grǣdig*] —**greed′i·ly** *adv.* —**greed′i·ness** *n.*

Greek (grēk) *n.* 1 A native or citizen of Greece. 2 The language of ancient or modern Greece. —*adj.* 1 Of or pertaining to Greece, its people, or their language. 2 Of or pertaining to the Greek Orthodox Church.

Greek Catholic 1 A member of an Eastern Orthodox Church. 2 UNIATE.

Greek Orthodox Church 1 The established church of Greece, an autonomous branch of the Eastern Orthodox Church. **2** Loosely, the Eastern Orthodox Church. Also **Greek Church.**

green (grēn) *adj.* **1** Having the spectrum color between blue and yellow, the characteristic color of lawn grass. **2** Covered with grass, green plants or foliage: the *green* hills. **3** Not yet ripe. **4** Consisting of edible leaves and vegetables: a *green* salad. **5** Immature or unskilled; inexperienced. **6** Naive; gullible. **7** Not seasoned or ready for use: *green* wood. **8** Sickly pale; wan. **9** *Informal* Jealous. —*n.* **1** The color of the spectrum between blue and yellow, the characteristic color of lawn grass. **2** A green pigment or dye. **3** A level, grassy piece of land: the village *green.* **4** In golf: **a** The area of smooth, closely cropped turf surrounding the hole. **b** The entire course. **5** *pl.* The leaves and stems of certain plants, as lettuce, spinach, etc., used as food. **6** *pl.* Green leaves or branches, often used as decorations, etc. —*v.t. & v.i.* To become or cause to become green. [<OE *grēne*] —**green'ish** *adj.* —**green'ly** *adv.*

green·back (grēn'bak') *n.* Any piece of legal U.S. paper money printed in green on the back.

green bean A string bean.

green·bri·er (grēn'brī'ər) *n.* A species of smilax having woody stems with thorns and blue-black berries.

green·er·y (grē'nər-ē) *n. pl.* **·er·ies 1** A place where plants are grown. **2** A mass of green plants; verdure.

green·gage (grēn'gāj') *n.* A green-skinned variety of plum. [<GREEN + *gage* a plum]

green·horn (grēn'hôrn') *n. Informal* An inexperienced person. [<GREEN + HORN; with ref. to the horns of an immature animal]

green·house (grēn'hous') *n.* A building constructed mainly of glass, for the growing or protection of plants.

green·ing (grē'ning) *n.* One of several varieties of apples having a greenish yellow skin when ripe.

green light 1 A green signal used to indicate that traffic may proceed. **2** *Informal* Approval or authorization of an intended action, program, etc.

green onion A young onion having a long white bulb and green tubular leaves; scallion.

green pepper The unripe fruit of the red pepper, eaten as a vegetable.

green·room (grēn'rōōm', -rōōm') *n.* The common waiting room for performers in a theater when they are off stage.

green·sward (grēn'swôrd') *n.* Turf green with grass.

green tea Tea leaves withered and rolled but not allowed to undergo fermentation.

green thumb Success or skill in growing plants.

Green·wich time (gren'ich; *chiefly Brit.* gren'ij) The mean solar time at the meridian at Greenwich, England, used as a reference in determining standard time throughout most of the world.

green·wood (grēn'wōōd') *n.* A forest in leaf.

greet (grēt) *v.t.* **1** To address words of friendliness, courtesy, respect, etc., to, as in speaking or writing. **2** To receive or meet in a specified manner. **3** To come into the sight or awareness of: The sea *greeted* their eyes. [<OE *grētan*] —**greet'er** *n.*

greet·ing (grē'ting) *n.* **1** The act or words of one who greets. **2** *Often pl.* A message of welcome or regards.

greeting card A card sent to express sentiments in acknowledgment of an event, as a birthday; esp., such a card printed and illustrated and sold commercially.

gre·gar·i·ous (gri-gâr'ē-əs) *adj.* **1** Habitually living in flocks, herds, or companies. **2** Of or pertaining to a flock or herd. **3** Socially outgoing and affable. [<L *grex, gregis* a flock] —**gre·gar'i·ous·ly** *adv.* —**gre·gar'i·ous·ness** *n.*

Gre·go·ri·an calendar (grə·gôr'ē·ən') The calendar used now by most countries of the world and devised by Pope Gregory XIII in 1582 as a correction of the Julian calendar.

Gregorian chant The system of monodic plainsong used in the liturgy of the Roman Catholic and other churches, established during the reign of Gregory I.

grem·lin (grem'lin) *n.* **1** A mischievous, invisible imp said to ride airplanes and cause mechanical trouble. **2** Any unidentified source of trouble. [?]

gre·nade (gri·nād') *n.* **1** A small bomb designed to be thrown by hand or fired from a rifle or launching device. **2** A glass bottle containing a flammable mixture, tear gas, etc., that is ignited or dispersed when the bottle is broken. [F, a pomegranate]

gren·a·dier (gren'ə·dir') *n.* **1** Formerly, a soldier assigned to throw grenades. **2** A member of a specially constituted corps or regiment, as the British Grenadier Guards.

gren·a·dine¹ (gren'ə·dēn', gren'ə·dēn) *n.* A loosely woven silk, cotton, woolen, or rayon fabric. [F]

gren·a·dine² (gren'ə·dēn', gren'ə·dēn) *n.* A beverage syrup made from currants or pomegranates. [<F *grenade* a pomegranate]

grew (grōō) *p.t.* of GROW.

grew·some (grōō'səm) *adj.* GRUESOME.

grey (grā) *adj. Chiefly Brit.* GRAY.

grey·hound (grā'hound') *n.* One of a breed of tall, slender dogs with a long narrow head and smooth short coat, used for hunting and racing. [<OE *grīghund*]

Greyhound

grid (grid) *n.* **1** A grating of parallel bars; gridiron. **2** A system of parallel lines superimposed horizontally and vertically upon a map, chart, etc. **3** A metal bar or plate in an electric storage cell or battery. **4** *Electronics* An electrode mounted between the cathode and anode of an electron tube, used to control the flow of electrons. [Short for GRIDIRON]

grid·dle (grid'l) *n.* A shallow pan for baking or frying pancakes. —*v.t.* **grid·dled, grid·dling** To cook on a griddle. [<L *cratis* wickerwork]

grid·dle·cake (grid'l·kāk') *n.* A thin, flat batter cake baked on a griddle; pancake.

grid·i·ron (grid'ī'ərn) *n.* **1** A framework of metal bars for broiling or cooking foods. **2** Any object resembling a cooking gridiron. **3** A football field. [ME *gredire*]

grid·lock (grid'lok') *n.* A total stoppage of traffic, esp. when all cross traffic is blocked at intersections.

grief (grēf) *n.* **1** Intense sorrow or mental suffering resulting from loss, affliction, regret, etc. **2** A cause of such sorrow. [<OF *grever* grieve] —**Syn. 1** affliction, agony, distress, sadness, tribulation, trouble, woe.

grief-strick·en (grēf'strik'ən) *adj.* Overwhelmed by grief.

griev·ance (grē'vəns) *n.* **1** Something that annoys, causes resentment, etc. **2** A written or vocal complaint against a wrong suffered.

grieve (grēv) *v.* **grieved, griev·ing** *v.t.* **1** To cause great sorrow or grief to; make sad. —*v.i.* **2** To feel sorrow or grief; mourn; lament. [<L *gravis* heavy] —**griev'er** *n.* —**griev'ing** *adj.* —**griev'ing·ly** *adv.*

griev·ous (grē'vəs) *adj.* **1** Causing grief or sorrow. **2** Expressive of grief or distress: a *grievous* complaint. **3** Severe: a *grievous* pain or illness. **4** Atrocious; heinous: *grievous* sin. —**griev'ous·ly** *adv.* —**griev'ous·ness** *n.*

grif·fin (grif'ən) *n. Gk. Myth.* A creature with the head and wings of an eagle and the body of a lion. Also **grif'fon.** [<Gk. *gryps*]

grill (gril) *v.t.* **1** To cook on a gridiron; broil. **2** To torture with heat. **3** To cross-examine persistently and searchingly. —*v.i.* **4** To be cooked on a gridiron. —*n.* **1** A gridiron. **2** That which is broiled on a gridiron. **3** A grillroom. **4** A grille. [<OF *greil*]

Griffin

grille (gril) *n.* A grating or screen, esp. one of wrought metal for an open door or window. Also **grill.** [F, var. of *gril* grill]

grilled (grild) *adj.* **1** Having a grille. **2** Broiled.

grill·room (gril'rōōm', -rōōm') *n.* A restaurant or eating place specializing in grilled food.

grill·work (gril'wûrk') *n.* **1** A grille. **2** The design or structure of a grille.

grilse (grils) *n. pl.* **grilse** or **grils·es** A young salmon after its first return to fresh water. [?]

grim (grim) *adj.* **grim·mer, grim·mest 1** Stern and forbidding in aspect or nature. **2** Fierce; ferocious: a *grim* attack. **3** Unyielding; resolute: *grim* courage. **4** Unpleasant; repellent: the *grim* job of counting bodies. [< OE] **—grim′ly** *adv.* **—grim′ness** *n.*

gri·mace (grim′əs, gri·mās′) *n.* A distortion of the face, usu. occasioned by annoyance, disgust, contempt, etc.; a wry face. **—***v.i.* **·maced, ·mac·ing** To make grimaces. [< MF < Gmc.] **—gri′mac·er** *n.*

gri·mal·kin (gri·mal′kin, -môl′-) *n.* **1** A cat, esp. an old female cat. **2** A malevolent old woman. [< GRAY + dial. *malkin* hussy]

grime (grīm) *n.* Dirt or soot, esp. when rubbed into a surface. **—***v.t.* **grimed, grim·ing** To make dirty; begrime. [< MDu. *grīme*]

grim·y (grī′mē) *adj.* **grim·i·er, grim·i·est** Full of or covered with grime; dirty. **—grim′i·ly** *adv.* **—grim′i·ness** *n.*

grin (grin) *v.* **grinned, grin·ning** *v.i.* **1** To smile broadly. **2** To draw back the lips so as to show the teeth, as in pain, rage, etc. **—***n.* The act or facial look of grinning. [< OE *grennian*] **—grin′ner** *n.* **—grin′ning·ly** *adv.*

grind (grīnd) *v.* **ground, grind·ing** *v.t.* **1** To sharpen, polish, or shape by friction. **2** To reduce to fine particles, as by crushing or friction. **3** To rub or press gratingly or harshly: to *grind* one's teeth. **4** To oppress; harass cruelly. **5** To operate by turning a crank, as a coffee mill. **6** To produce by or as by grinding. **7** *Informal* To teach laboriously. **—***v.i.* **8** To perform the operation of grinding. **9** To undergo grinding. **10** To rub; grate. **11** *Informal* To study or work hard and steadily. **—***n.* **1** The act of grinding. **2** A degree of fineness obtained by grinding. **3** *Informal* Difficult, tedious work or study. **4** *Informal* A hard-working student. [< OE *grindan*] **—grind′ing** *adj., n.* **—grind′ing·ly** *adv.*

grind·er (grīn′dər) *n.* **1** One who or that which grinds, as a knife sharpener, coffee mill, etc. **2** A molar tooth.

grind·stone (grīnd′stōn′) *n.* **1** An abrasive wheel spun on its axis and used for shaping metal, sharpening tools, etc. **2** A millstone.

grin·go (gring′gō) *n. pl.* **·gos** In Latin America, a foreigner, particularly an American or Englishman: a contemptuous term. [Sp., gibberish]

grip (grip) *n.* **1** The act of grasping firmly or holding fast, as with the hands, teeth, etc. **2** The manner of doing this. **3** The power or strength to do this: He lost his *grip*. **4** Ability to understand mentally. **5** Self-control; mastery. **6** Control; power: in the *grip* of circumstances. **7** A valise; gripsack. **8** That part of a thing by which it is grasped. **9** One of various mechanical grasping devices. **10** *Slang* A stagehand; a scene-shifter. **—***v.* **gripped** or **gript, grip·ping** *v.t.* **1** To take firm hold of with or as with the hand; hold onto tightly. **2** To join or attach securely with a grip. **3** To seize or capture, as the mind or imagination of. **—***v.i.* **4** To take firm hold. **5** To take hold of the attention, imagination, etc. [< OE *gripe* < *gripan* seize] **—grip′per** *n.* **—grip′ping** *adj.* **—grip′ping·ly** *adv.*

gripe (grīp) *v.* **griped, grip·ing** *v.t.* **1** To cause pain in the bowels of. **2** *Slang* To vex; annoy. **—***v.i.* **3** *Informal* To grumble; complain. **4** To suffer pains in the bowels. **—***n.* **1** *pl.* Intermittent pains in the bowels. **2** *Slang* A complaint. [< OE *grīpan*] **—grip′er** *n.* **—grip′y** *adj.*

grippe (grip) *n.* INFLUENZA. [F < *gripper* seize] **—grip′py** *adj.*

grip·sack (grip′sak′) *n.* A traveling bag.

gris·ly (griz′lē) *adj.* **·li·er, ·li·est** Terrifying; horrible. [< OE *grislic*] **—gris′li·ness** *n.*

grist (grist) *n.* **1** A portion of grain to be ground. **2** Ground grain. **—grist for** (or **to**) **one's mill** Anything that one can use to advantage. [< OE *grist*]

gris·tle (gris′əl) *n.* Cartilage, esp. in meat. [< OE] **—gris′·tly** *adj.* **—gris′tli·ness** *n.*

grist·mill (grist′mil′) *n.* A mill for grinding grain.

grit (grit) *n.* **1** Rough, hard particles, as of sand or fine gravel. **2** A coarse compact sandstone adapted for grind-

stones. **3** Resolute courage; pluck. **—***v.* **grit·ted, grit·ting** *v.t.* **1** To grind or press (the teeth) together, as in anger or determination. **—***v.i.* **2** To give forth a grating sound. [< OE *grēot*]

Grit (grit) *Can. n.* A member of the Liberal Party. **—***adj.* Of or pertaining to the Liberal Party.

grits (grits) *n. pl.* Coarsely ground grain, esp. corn.

grit·ty (grit′ē) *adj.* **·ti·er, ·ti·est 1** Of, containing, or like grit. **2** Full of pluck. **—grit′ti·ly** *adv.* **—grit′ti·ness** *n.*

griz·zle (griz′əl) *v.t. & v.i.* **griz·zled, griz·zling** To become or cause to become gray. **—***n.* Gray. [< OF *gris* gray] **—griz′·zled** *adj.*

griz·zly (griz′lē) *adj.* **·zli·er, ·zli·est** Grayish. **—***n. pl.* **·zlies** GRIZZLY BEAR.

griz·zly bear A large, powerful, grayish bear of w North America.

gro. gross.

Grizzly bear

groan (grōn) *v.i.* **1** To utter a low, prolonged sound of or as of pain, sorrow, etc. **2** To be oppressed or overburdened. **—***v.t.* **3** To utter or express with groans. **—***n.* A low moaning sound uttered in anguish, distress, or derision. [< OE *grānian*] **—groan′er** *n.* **—groan′ing** *adj., n.* **—groan′ing·ly** *adv.*

groat (grōt) *n.* A former English silver coin of the 14th–17th centuries. [< MDu. *groot*]

groats (grōts) *n. pl.* Hulled and crushed oats or wheat. [< OE *grotan*]

gro·cer (grō′sər) *n.* A retail dealer in food supplies and other household articles. [< OF *grossier*, lit., one who trades in grosses]

gro·cer·y (grō′sər·ē, grōs′rē) *n. pl.* **·cer·ies 1** A grocer's store. **2** *pl.* Supplies sold by a grocer.

grog (grog) *n.* **1** A mixture of liquor, esp. rum, and water. **2** Any liquor. [< *Old Grog*, nickname of Admiral E. Vernon, 1684–1757, who first rationed it to English sailors]

grog·gy (grog′ē) *adj.* **·gi·er, ·gi·est 1** Dazed, as from weakness or exhaustion. **2** Drunk. [< GROG] **—grog′gi·ly** *adv.* **—grog′gi·ness** *n.*

grog·ram (grog′rəm) *n.* A rough-textured fabric of silk, silk and mohair, or silk and wool. [< F *gros grain* grosgrain]

grog·shop (grog′shop′) *n. Brit.* A barroom; saloon.

groin (groin) *n.* **1** The fleshy hollow where the thigh joins the abdomen. **2** *Archit.* The line of intersection of two vaults. • See VAULT. **—***v.t.* To build with or form into groins. [? < OE *grynde* abyss, hollow]

grom·met (grom′it) *n.* **1** *Naut.* A ring of rope, as on the peak of a sail. **2** A metallic eyelet, as for a mailbag. [< OF *gromette*]

groom (grōom, grŏŏm) *n.* **1** A person who cares for horses in the stable. **2** BRIDEGROOM. **—***v.t.* **1** To take care of; esp. to clean, curry, and brush (a horse). **2** To make neat, clean, and smart. **3** To prepare by training and developing, as for political or other service. [ME *grom*]

grooms·man (grōomz′mən, grŏŏmz′-) *n. pl.* **·men** (-mən) The best man at a wedding.

groove (grōov) *n.* **1** A furrow, channel, or long hollow, esp. one cut by a tool for something to fit into or work in. **2** A fixed routine in the affairs of life. **—***v.t.* **grooved, groov·ing 1** To form a groove in. **2** To fix in a groove. **3** *Slang* To take satisfaction or delight in; dig. **—***v.i.* **4** *Slang* To find satisfaction or delight. [< MDu. *groeve*] **—groov′er** *n.*

groov·y (grōo′vē) *adj.* **groov·i·er, groov·i·est** *Slang* Satisfying; delightful; great.

grope (grōp) *v.* **groped, grop·ing** *v.i.* To feel about with or as with the hands, as in the dark; feel one's way. **—***v.t.* To seek out or find by or as by groping. [< OE *grāpian.*] **—grop′er** *n.* **—grop′ing** *adj.*

gros·beak (grōs′bēk′) *n.* Any of various small birds allied to the finches and having a short stout beak. [F *gros* large + BEAK]

gros·grain (grō′grān) *n.* A closely woven, corded silk or rayon fabric, used for ribbons, etc. [F, large grain]

gross (grōs) *adj.* **1** Conspicuously bad; glaring; flagrant:

a *gross* lie or error. 2 Excessively or repulsively large and coarse. 3 Vulgar; obscene; indelicate. 4 Lacking in perception or feeling; dull; insensitive. 5 Coarse in texture or composition. 6 Dense; thick. 7 Undiminished by deductions; total; entire: *gross earnings.* —*n.* 1 *pl.* **gross** Twelve dozen, as a unit. 2 *pl.* **gross·es** The total or entire amount. —**in the gross** 1 In bulk; all together. 2 Wholesale: also **by the gross.** —*v.t. & v.i.* To make or earn (total profit) before deduction of expenses, taxes, etc. [< LL *grossus* thick] —**gross'ly** *adv.* —**gross'ness** *n.* —**Syn.** *adj.* 1 dreadful, deplorable, awful shocking, heinous. 2 lumpish, hulking, bulky. 3 improper, unseemly, coarse.

gross national product The total market value of a nation's goods and services before any deductions.

gross ton A unit of weight equal to 2,240 pounds.

gro·tesque (grō·tesk') *adj.* 1 Bizarre or extravagantly odd in shape, look, design, composition, etc. 2 Absurdly odd or eccentric; fantastically strange: *grotesque* behavior. —*n.* Something grotesque. [< Ital. *grotta* a grotto, excavation] —**gro·tesque'ly** *adv.* —**gro·tesque'ness** *n.*

grot·to (grot'ō) *n. pl.* **·toes** or **·tos** 1 A small cave. 2 An artificial cavelike structure. [< L *crypta* crypt]

grouch (grouch) *v.i.* To grumble; be surly or discontented. —*n.* 1 A discontented, grumbling person. 2 A grumbling, sulky mood. 3 A complaint. [< OF *groucher* murmur] —**grouch'i·ly** *adv.* —**grouch'i·ness** *n.* —**grouch'y** *adj.* (**·i·er, ·i·est**)

ground[1] (ground) *n.* 1 The firm, solid portion of the earth at or near the surface. 2 Soil; earth; dirt. 3 Any tract or portion of land, esp. one put to special use: a parade *ground.* 4 *Often pl.* Private land, esp. the lawns, gardens, etc., surrounding a home or estate. 5 A topic, discussion or subject, or any part thereof: to cover the same old *ground.* 6 *Often pl.* A sufficient cause; good reason; basis: *grounds* for divorce. 7 *Often pl.* A basic proposition or premise; foundation: *grounds* for an argument. 8 The background or main surface, as of a painting. 9 *pl.* The particles that settle at the bottom of a liquid; dregs. 10 a A point in an electric circuit considered to have zero potential and used as a reference for other voltages. b A point of this kind actually connected to the earth. —**cover ground** 1 To proceed rapidly or a certain distance. 2 To accomplish quickly and efficiently. —**from the ground up** In a detailed manner; thoroughly. —**gain ground** 1 To make progress. 2 To gain favor, popularity, power, etc. —**get off the ground** To get underway; develop. —**give ground** To concede; yield. —**hold (or stand) one's ground** To maintain one's position, opinions, etc. —**lose ground** 1 To slip backward; drop behind. 2 To lose in favor, popularity, power, etc. —**on home (or one's own) ground** 1 At home. 2 On a familiar topic, subject, etc. —*adj.* 1 Being on the ground or on a level with it. 2 Growing or living on or in the ground. 3 Fundamental. —*v.t.* 1 To put, place, or set on the ground. 2 To fix firmly on a basis; found; establish. 3 To train (someone) in first principles or elements. 4 To cause (an airplane or pilot) to stay on the ground. 5 *Naut.* To cause to run aground, as a ship. 6 To furnish (a surface) with a ground or background for painting, etc. 7 To connect (an electric circuit or device) to a ground. —*v.i.* 8 To come or fall to the ground. 9 In baseball: a To hit a grounder. b To be retired on a grounder: usu. with *out.* 10 *Naut.* To run aground. [< OE *grund*]

ground[2] (ground) *p.t. & p.p.* of GRIND.

ground bass *Music* A bass part repeated continually against varied melody and harmony in the other parts.

ground crew The crew required for the servicing, repairing, and maintenance of aircraft.

ground·er (groun'dər) *n.* In baseball, a batted ball that rolls or bounces along the ground. Also **ground ball.**

ground floor The floor of a building level or almost level with the ground.

ground·hog (ground'hôg', -häg) *n.* WOODCHUCK.

ground·less (ground'lis) *adj.* Without foundation, reason, or cause. —**ground'less·ly** *adv.* —**ground'less·ness** *n.*

ground·ling (ground'ling) *n.* 1 An animal that burrows in the ground. 2 A plant that grows close to the ground. 3 A fish that keeps to the bottom. 4 A person of unrefined tastes.

ground·nut (ground'nut') *n.* 1 Any of several plants having edible tubers attached to the roots, as the peanut. 2 The edible tuber of such a plant.

ground pine An evergreen, generally creeping plant.

ground plan 1 The plan of the ground floor of a building. 2 Any preliminary plan or outline.

ground rule 1 In sports, any of the rules applying to conditions peculiar to a particular playing field. 2 *pl.* The basic rules of operation in any activity.

ground·sel (ground'səl) *n.* 1 A common composite herb, having yellow flower heads without rays. 2 GROUNDSILL. [< OE *gundæswelgæ,* lit., that swallows pus]

ground·sill (ground'sil') *n.* The lowest horizontal timber in a frame building.

ground squirrel Any of various burrowing rodents related to the squirrels, as the chipmunk and gopher.

ground·swell (ground'swel') *n.* 1 A broad, deep swell or heaving of the sea caused by prolonged storms or earthquakes. 2 Any upsurge or wave of public sentiment, opinion, etc. Also **ground swell.**

ground water Water that collects beneath the surface of the earth.

ground·work (ground'wûrk') *n.* 1 Foundation; basis. 2 Preparation.

ground zero The point on the ground directly beneath or above the detonation of a nuclear bomb.

group (grōōp) *n.* 1 A number of closely placed or associated persons or things regarded as a unit. 2 A number of individuals classed together because of common characteristics, interests, etc. 3 Figures or objects forming a harmonious unit of design. 4 *Chem.* a A number of connected atoms constituting part of a molecule. b A set of elements having similar properties. 5 In the U.S. Air Force, a unit constituting a subdivision of a wing. 6 In the U.S. Army or Marine Corps, a tactical unit consisting of two or more battalions. —*v.t.* 1 To place or classify in a group or groups. —*v.i.* 2 To form a group or groups. [< Ital. *groppo* knot, lump < Gmc.]

group·er (grōō'pər) *n.* A large food fish of warm seas, related to the sea bass. [< Pg. *garupa*]

group·ie (grōō'pē) *n. Slang* A fan or supporter, esp. a young woman who follows a performer in a rock group on tour.

grouse[1] (grous) *n. pl.* **grouse** Any of a family of plump-bodied game birds having mottled plumage.

grouse[2] (grous) *v.i.* **groused,** **grous·ing** To grumble; complain. —*n.* A complaint; grievance. [?] —**grous'er** *n.*

Grouse

grove (grōv) *n.* A small wood or group of trees, esp. without underbrush. [< OE *grāf*]

grov·el (gruv'əl, grov'-) *v.i.* **grov·eled** or **grov·elled,** **grov·el·ing** or **grov·el·ling** 1 To crawl face downward or lie prostrate, as in servility or fear. 2 To act with abject humility. 3 To take pleasure in what is base or sensual. [Back formation < earlier *groveling,* prone < ON *ā grūfū* face down] —**grov'el·er** or **grov'el·ler** *n.*

grow (grō) *v.* **grew, grown, grow·ing** *v.i.* 1 To increase in size by assimilation of nourishment or a natural process. 2 To progress toward maturity. 3 To sprout and develop. 4 To flourish; thrive. 5 To increase in size, quantity, intensity, etc. 6 To become. 7 To come to be; develop. 8 To become fixed or attached by or as by growth. —*v.t.* 9 To cause to grow; raise by cultivation. 10 To produce or develop by a natural process. 11 To cover with a growth: used in the passive. —**grow on** To become gradually more pleasing or important to. —**grow up** To become an adult. [< OE *grōwan*] —**grow'er** *n.*

growl (groul) *n.* 1 A low, guttural sound, as that made by an angry animal. 2 A sound similar to this. —*v.i.* 1 To utter a growl. 2 To speak in a gruff, surly manner. 3 To rumble, as distant thunder. —*v.t.* 4 To express by growling. [ME *groulen* to rumble] —**growl'er** *n.*

grown (grōn) *p.p.* of GROW. —*adj.* Mature; fully developed.

grown-up (grōn'up') *n.* A mature person; adult: also **grown'up'.** —*adj.* 1 Adult. 2 Of, for, or typical of adults.

growth (grōth) n. 1 The process of growing. 2 A stage of development or maturity reached in growing. 3 An increase in size, number, etc. 4 Something produced by or in the process of growing. 5 An abnormal formation, as a wart, tumor, etc.

grub (grub) v. **grubbed, grub·bing** v.i. 1 To dig in the ground. 2 To drudge; toil. 3 To make careful or plodding search; rummage. —v.t. 4 To dig up; root out. 5 To clear (ground) of roots, stumps, etc. 6 Slang To get by begging; mooch. —n. 1 A fat, wormlike larva, as of beetles and some other insects. 2 DRUDGE. 3 Slang Food. [ME grubben] —grub'ber n.

grub·by (grub'ē) adj. ·bi·er, ·bi·est 1 Dirty; messy. 2 Full of grubs. —grub'bi·ly adv. —grub'bi·ness n. —Syn. 1 slovenly, sloppy, untidy, unkempt.

grub·stake (grub'stāk') n. Money, supplies, etc., provided, as to a mining prospector, on condition of receiving a share of his findings. —v.t. ·staked, ·stak·ing To supply with a grubstake.

grudge (gruj) v.t. grudged, grudg·ing 1 To envy the possessions or good fortunes of (another). 2 To give or allow unwillingly and resentfully; begrudge. —n. Ill will or resentment, as for some remembered wrong. [< OF groucher] —grudg'er n. —grudg'ing·ly adv.

gru·el (grōō'əl) n. A semiliquid food made by boiling meal in water or milk. —v.t. gru·eled or gru·elled, gru·el·ing or gru·el·ling To work, wear down, or exhaust by hard work, punishment, etc. [< OF, meal]

gru·el·ing (grōō'əl·ing) adj. Severely trying; exhausting. Also gru'el·ling.

grue·some (grōō'səm) adj. Inspiring horror and loathing; grisly. [? < MDu. gruwen to shudder + -SOME] —grue'some·ly adv. —grue'some·ness n.

gruff (gruf) adj. 1 Rough or brusque in manner. 2 Hoarse; harsh. [< Du. grof rough] —gruff'ly adv. —gruff'ness n.

grum·ble (grum'bəl) v. grum·bled, grum·bling v.i. 1 To complain in a surly manner; mutter discontentedly. 2 To make growling sounds in the throat. 3 To rumble, as thunder. —v.t. 4 To say with a grumble. —n. 1 A surly complaint; discontented muttering. 2 A rumble. [? < MDu. grommen to growl] —grum'bler n. —grum'bling·ly adv. —grum'bly adj.

grump·y (grum'pē) adj. grump·i·er, grump·i·est Ill-tempered; grouchy; cranky. [? Blend of GRUNT and DUMP] —grump'i·ly adv. —grump'i·ness n.

grun·ion (grun'yən) n. A small fish common on the coast of California, noted for the regularity of its inshore spawning activities at the time of a nearly full moon.

grunt (grunt) v.i. 1 To make a short, guttural sound typical of a hog. 2 To make a similar sound, as in annoyance, assent, effort, etc. —v.t. 3 To express by grunting. —n. 1 A short, guttural sound, as of a hog. 2 A chiefly tropical marine fish that makes grunting sounds. 3 Mil. Slang A U.S. infantryman. [< OE grunnettan] —grunt'er n.

Gru·yère (grē·yâr', grōō-; Fr. grü·yâr') n. A light yellow Swiss cheese, usu. without holes. [< Gruyère, a town in Switzerland]

gr. wt. gross weight.

gry·phon (grif'ən) n. GRIFFIN.

G.S. General Secretary; General Staff.

G.S.A. Girl Scouts of America.

G-string (jē'string') n. 1 A narrow loincloth. 2 A similar cloth, often gaudily ornamented, worn esp. by stripteasers. [?]

gt. great.

gtd. guaranteed.

GU, g.u. genitourinary.

gua·no (gwä'nō) n. pl. ·nos 1 The accumulated excrement of sea birds, found esp. on islands off the Peruvian coast and used as fertilizer. 2 A manufactured nitrogenous fertilizer resembling this. [< Quechua huanu dung]

guar. guaranteed.

guar·an·tee (gar'ən·tē') n. 1 A pledge or formal assurance that something will meet stated specifications or that a specified act will be performed. 2 Something given as security. 3 GUARANTOR. 4 Something that assures a certain outcome. —v.t. ·teed, ·tee·ing 1 To give a guarantee for; certify or vouch for. 2 To assume responsibility for. 3 To secure against loss or damage. 4 To give assurance of; promise. [Var. of GUARANTY]

guar·an·tor (gar'ən·tər, -tôr') n. One who guarantees or makes a guaranty.

guar·an·ty (gar'ən·tē) n. pl. ·ties 1 A pledge to assume responsibility in case of default for debts or obligations incurred by another. 2 A deposit, etc., made or held as security. 3 GUARANTOR. —v.t. ·tied, ·ty·ing To guarantee. [< OF guarantie < guarant a warrant < Gmc]

guard (gärd) v.t. 1 To keep protective watch over, as to shield or defend from harm or loss. 2 To maintain supervisory watch over, as to prevent escape. 3 To keep in check; control. —v.i. 4 To take precautions: with against. —n. 1 One who guards, as a sentry, prison employee, etc. 2 Watchful care or supervision. 3 Protection; defense. 4 A device that protects, shields, etc. 5 A posture or attitude of defense. 6 A person or body of persons providing protection, ceremonial escort, etc. 7 In football, either of two offensive line players whose position is next to the center. 8 In basketball, either of two players covering the rear of the court. —off (one's) guard Unprepared for defense, protection, etc. —on (one's) guard On the alert; vigilant. —stand guard 1 To act as sentry. 2 To keep careful watch. [< OF garder < Gmc.] —guard'er n. —Syn. v. 1 protect, safeguard, preserve.

guard·ed (gär'did) adj. Cautious; restrained: guarded comments. —guard'ed·ly adv. —guard'ed·ness n.

guard·house (gärd'hous') n. 1 Quarters for military guards. 2 A military jail for minor offenders.

guard·i·an (gär'dē·ən) n. 1 Law One who guards or has protective care. 2 One legally empowered to care for the person or property of another, esp. an infant or minor. —guard'i·an·ship n.

guard·rail (gärd'rāl') n. 1 A protective railing, as at the edge of a balcony or between opposing lanes of traffic. 2 A rail placed next to a main rail of a track to prevent trains from derailing.

guard·room (gärd'rōōm', -rōom') n. A room used by a military guard while on duty.

guards·man (gärdz'mən) n. pl. ·men (-mən) A member of certain military bodies, as the U.S. National Guard or the British royal household troops.

Gua·te·ma·la (gwä'tə·mä'lä) n. A republic of N Central America, 42,042 sq. mi., cap. Guatemala (also Guatemala City). —Gua'te·ma'lan adj., n. •See map at CENTRAL AMERICA.

gua·va (gwä'və) n. 1 A tropical American tree or shrub bearing sweet, yellow-skinned fruit. 2 Its fruit, used esp. for making jelly. [Sp. guayaba < S. Am.Ind.]

gua·yu·le (gwä·yōō'lā) n. 1 A woody composite plant of sw North America. 2 The resinous latex of this plant, yielding a natural rubber: also guayule rubber. [Sp. < Nah.]

gu·ber·na·to·ri·al (gyōō'bər·nə·tôr'ē·əl, -tō'rē) adj. Of or pertaining to a governor or the office of governor. [< L gubernare govern]

gudg·eon (guj'ən) n. 1 A small Old World freshwater fish. 2 A person easily duped. 3 Anything swallowed credulously. —v.t. To cheat; dupe. [< L gobio goby]

guer·don (gûr'dən) n. A reward; recompense. [< Med. L widerdonum]

Guern·sey (gûrn'zē) n. pl. ·seys One of a breed of dairy cattle originally from the island of Guernsey, Channel Islands.

guer·ril·la (gə·ril'ə) n. One of an irregular, independent band of partisan soldiers often harassing opposing troops. Also gue·ril'la. [< Sp. guerra a war] —adj. Of or carried on by guerrillas.

guess (ges) v.t. & v.i. 1 To form a judgment or opinion (of something) on uncertain or incomplete knowledge. 2 To judge or estimate correctly. 3 To believe; think. —n. 1 An opinion or conclusion reached by guessing. 2 The act of guessing. [Prob. < Scand.] —guess'er n.

guess·ti·mate (ges'tə·mit) n. Slang A prediction based in part on guesswork. [< GUESS + (ES)TIMATE]

---

add, āce, câre, pälm; end, ēven; it, īce; odd, ōpen, ôrder; tōōk, pōōl; up, bûrn; ə = a in above, u in focus; yōō = u in fuse; oil; pout; check; go; ring; thin; this; zh, vision. < derived from; ? origin uncertain or unknown.

guess·work (ges′wûrk′) *n.* The process or result of guessing.

guest (gest) *n.* **1** A person received or entertained by another as a visitor or recipient of hospitality. **2** One paying for lodging and services at a hotel, etc. **3** A visiting performer or participant in a program. [<ON *gestr*]

guff (guf) *n. Slang* Foolish or uncalled-for talk; nonsense. [Imit.]

guf·faw (gə-fô′) *n.* A burst of loud, boisterous laughter. —*v.i.* To utter such laughter. [Imit.]

gul·dance (gīd′ns) *n.* **1** The act, process, or result of guiding. **2** Advice; counseling. **3** Leadership; direction.

guide (gīd) *v.* **guid·ed, guid·ing** *v.t.* **1** To lead, accompany, direct, show the way, etc. **2** To direct the motion or action of, as a vehicle, tool, etc. **3** To lead or direct the affairs, standards, opinions, etc., of. —*v.i.* **4** To act as a guide. — *n.* **1** One who shows the way by accompanying or going in advance, as in conducting travelers, sightseers, etc. **2** One who or that which provides direction, inspiration, etc. **3** Something that guides or informs, as a book, sign, or set of instructions. **4** A device acting as an indicator or serving to restrict motion of a part. [<OF *guider*] —**guid′er** *n.*

guide·book (gīd′book′) *n.* A handbook for travelers or tourists, containing descriptions of places, routes, etc.

guided missile An unmanned missile whose course can be altered after launch.

guide·line (gīd′līn′) *n.* A statement, policy, etc. indicating the limits or scope of an undertaking.

guide·post (gīd′pōst′) *n.* A signpost giving directions to travelers.

gul·don (gīd′ən) *n.* A small flag carried by a military unit as an emblem. [<Ital. *guidone* <*guida* guide]

gul·gnol (gē-nyôl′) *n. Often cap.* GRAND GUIGNOL.

guild (gild) *n.* **1** In medieval times, an association of craftsmen or merchants. **2** An association of persons with kindred pursuits, interests, or aims. [<ON *gildi* payment] — **guilds′man** *n.* (*pl.* **·men**)

guil·der (gil′dər) *n.* The basic monetary unit of the Netherlands. [Alter. of Du. *gulden* gulden]

guild·hall (gild′hôl′) *n.* **1** The hall where a guild meets. **2** TOWN HALL.

guile (gīl) *n.* Deceitful slyness; duplicity. [<OF <Gmc.]

guile·ful (gīl′fəl) *adj.* Full of guile; slyly deceitful. — **guile′ful·ly** *adv.* —**guile′ful·ness** *n.*

guile·less (gīl′lis) *adj.* Free from guile; artless; ingenuous. —**guile′less·ly** *adv.* —**guile′less·ness** *n.*

guil·le·mot (gil′ə-mot′) *n.* Any of several narrow-billed diving birds of N latitudes. [<F *Guillaume* William]

guil·lo·tine (gil′ə-tēn, gē′ə-, gē-ə-tēn′) *n.* An instrument for beheading, consisting of a weighted knife dropped between two slotted uprights. —*v.t.* **·tined, ·tin·ing** To behead with the guillotine. [<Dr. J. I. *Guillotin*, 1738–1814, Fr. physician]

guilt (gilt) *n.* **1** The state or fact of having committed a crime, legal offense, or wrongdoing. **2** Responsibility for having committed a crime or wrong; culpability. **3** A feeling of blameworthiness for having committed a crime or wrong. [<OE *gylt*]

Guillotine

guilt·less (gilt′lis) *adj.* **1** Free from guilt; innocent; blameless. **2** Without experience or knowledge: with *of.* —**guilt′less·ly** *adv.* —**guilt′less·ness** *n.*

guilt·y (gil′tē) *adj.* **guilt·i·er, guilt·i·est** **1** Responsible for having committed a crime, offense, or wrongdoing. **2** Involving, expressing, feeling, or characterized by guilt. — **guilt′i·ly** *adv.* —**guilt′i·ness** *n.* —**Syn.** culpable, blameworthy.

guimpe (gamp, gimp) *n.* A blouse worn under a jumper or pinafore. [F]

guin·ea (gin′ē) *n.* **1** An amount or unit of British money equal to one pound and one shilling. **2** A former British gold coin equal to this amount. [<*Guinea*, Africa, orig. source of gold for the coin]

Guin·ea (gin′ē) *n.* **1** A republic of w Africa, 94,925 sq. mi.,

---

cap. Conakry. **2** Formerly, a coastal region of w Africa. • See map at AFRICA.

guinea fowl A domestic fowl of African origin, having dark gray plumage with white spots. Also **guinea hen.**

guinea pig **1** A domesticated rodent with short ears and no visible tail, used in biological and medical experiments. **2** Any subject of experimentation or research.

Guin·e·vere (gwin′ə-vir) In Arthurian legend, Arthur's queen and mistress of Lancelot. Also **Guin′e·ver** (-vər).

guise (gīz) *n.* **1** Outward appearance; aspect. **2** False appearance or assumed manner; pretense. **3** Garb; costume. [<OF <Gmc.]

gui·tar (gi-tär′) *n.* A musical instrument having a fretted fingerboard and usu. six strings, played by plucking. [<Gk. *kithara* lyre] —**gui·tar′ist** *n.*

Gu·lag (goo′läg) *n.* A Soviet labor camp. [<Russ.]

gulch (gulch) *n.* A narrow, steep-sided ravine.

gul·den (gool′dən) *n. pl.* **·dens** or **·den** GUILDER. [Du. and G, lit., golden]

gules (gyoolz) *n. Her.* The color red. [<OF *gueules* red-dyed ermine fur]

gulf (gulf) *n.* **1** A considerable area of marine water partly enclosed by an indentation of a coastline. **2** An abyss; chasm. **3** A wide separation or gap not easily bridged. —*v.t.* EN-GULF. [<Gk. *kolpos* a bay]

Guitar

Gulf States States bordering on the Gulf of Mexico: Alabama, Florida, Louisiana, Mississippi, and Texas.

gull[1] (gul) *n.* Any of various usu. gray and white aquatic birds with long wings, webbed feet, and a hooked bill. [ME]

gull[2] (gul) *v.t.* To trick; deceive; dupe. —*n.* One who is easily tricked or deceived; a dupe. [?]

Gul·lah (gul′ə) *n.* **1** One of a group of Negroes dwelling on a narrow coastal strip and outlying islands of South Carolina, Georgia, and NE Florida. **2** The language or dialect spoken by these people.

gul·let (gul′it) *n.* **1** The passage from the mouth to the stomach; esophagus. **2** The throat. [<L *gula* throat]

gul·li·ble (gul′ə-bəl) *adj.* Easily duped or deceived; credulous. [<GULL[2]] —**gul′li·bil′i·ty** *n.* —**gul′li·bly** *adv.*

gul·ly (gul′ē) *n. pl.* **·lies** A channel, ravine, etc., cut in the earth by running water, as after a rainfall. —*v.t.* **·lied, ·ly·ing** To cut or wear a gully in. [Var. of GULLET]

gulp (gulp) *v.t.* **1** To swallow avidly or in large amounts. **2** To keep back as if by swallowing. —*v.i.* **3** To swallow, gasp, or choke, as in nervousness or astonishment. —*n.* **1** The act of gulping. **2** An amount swallowed in gulping. [<MDu. *gulpen*] —**gulp′er** *n.* —**gulp′ing·ly** *adv.*

gum[1] (gum) *n.* **1** A sticky, colloidal substance exuded by various plants and forming on drying an amorphous, brittle mass. **2** A similar plant exudate, as resin, rubber, etc. **3** Any of various viscous, sticky, or adhesive substances. **4** CHEWING GUM. **5** Any of various trees that yield gum, as an eucalyptus, sweet gum, tupelo, etc.: also **gum tree.** — **gummed, gum·ming** *v.t.* **1** To smear, stiffen, or attach with gum. —*v.i.* **2** To exude or form gum. **3** To become sticky, clogged, etc., as with gum. —**gum up** *Slang* To bungle; ruin. [<Gk. *kommi*]

gum[2] (gum) *n. Often pl.* The fleshy tissue that surrounds the base of the teeth and the area of the jaws inside the mouth. —*v.t.* **gummed, gum·ming** To chew with the gums. [<OE *gōma* inside of mouth]

gum arabic The gum obtained from several species of acacia trees, and widely used as an emulsifier.

gum·bo (gum′bō) *n. pl.* **·bos** **1** The okra or its pods. **2** A soup or stew containing okra. **3** A fine soil of the North American plains that forms a very sticky mud. [<Bantu]

gum·boil (gum′boil′) *n.* A small boil or abscess formed on the gum.

gum·drop (gum′drop′) *n.* A chewy, sugar-coated candy usu. made with gum arabic or gelatin.

gum·my (gum′ē) *adj.* **·mi·er, ·mi·est** **1** Consisting of, containing, or resembling gum. **2** Covered with gum. **3** Sticky; viscous. —**gum′mi·ness** *n.*

gump·tion (gump′shən) *n. Informal* Initiative; enterprise; spirit. [?]

gum resin A mixture of gum and resin that exudes as a milky juice from certain plants and gradually hardens in the air.

gum·shoe (gum′shoo′) *n.* 1 *Slang* DETECTIVE. 2 *pl.* SNEAKERS. 3 A rubber shoe or overshoe. —*v.i.* **·shoed, ·shoe·ing** *Slang* To go stealthily and noiselessly; sneak.

gun (gun) *n.* 1 A piece of ordnance fixed in a mount, whose essential element is a metal tube from which a projectile is launched at high velocity, usu. in a fairly flat trajectory. 2 A portable firearm, as a pistol or rifle. 3 The firing of a large gun. 4 Any device resembling a gun in form or function. 5 The throttle of an engine. —**stick to one's guns** To persist in an opinion, course of action, etc. —*v.* **gunned, gun·ning** *v.i.* 1 To go hunting with a gun. —*v.t.* 2 To shoot with a gun: often with *down.* 3 To open the throttle of (an engine) so as to accelerate. —**gun for** 1 To seek with intent to harm, thwart, or kill. 2 To seek eagerly. [ME *gunne*]

gun·boat (gun′bōt′) *n.* A small, armed vessel used to patrol rivers and coastal waters.

gun·cot·ton (gun′kot′n) *n.* A highly explosive nitrocellulose.

gun·fire (gun′fīr′) *n.* The firing of a gun or guns.

gung-ho (gung′hō′) *adj. Slang* Irrepressibly or excessively enthusiastic. [< Chin., lit., work together]

gun·lock (gun′lok′) *n.* The mechanism of a gun by which the charge is exploded.

gun·man (gun′mən) *n. pl.* **·men** (-mən) A man armed with a gun, esp. a criminal or killer.

gun·met·al (gun′met′l) *n.* 1 A bronze alloy formerly used for making small cannon. 2 Any of various metals or alloys made to resemble this metal or used in making guns. 3 A dark gray: also **gunmetal gray.** —*adj.* Dark gray.

gun moll *Slang* A female associate of a gangster.

gun·nel[1] (gun′əl) *n.* GUNWALE.

gun·nel[2] (gun′əl) *n.* Any of several long-bodied fishes of N marine waters. [?]

gun·ner (gun′ər) *n.* 1 A soldier, sailor, or member of an aircraft crew who operates a gun. 2 See GRADE. 3 One who hunts with a gun.

gun·ner·y (gun′ər·ē) *n.* The science and techniques of making and using guns.

gun·ny (gun′ē) *n. pl.* **·nies** A coarse fabric of jute or hemp, used for making sacks. [< Hind. *gonī*]

gun·ny·sack (gun′ē·sak′) *n.* A sack made of gunny.

gun·pow·der (gun′pou′dər) *n.* An explosive mixture of potassium nitrate, charcoal, and sulfur.

gun·run·ner (gun′run′ər) *n.* One who smuggles or carries on illegal traffic in firearms and ammunition. —**gun′·run′ning** *n.*

gun·shot (gun′shot′) *n.* 1 The shooting of a gun. 2 Shot fired from a gun. 3 The range of a gun.

gun-shy (gun′shī′) *adj.* Afraid of the sound of gunfire.

gun·smith (gun′smith′) *n.* One who makes or repairs firearms.

gun·stock (gun′stok′) *n.* The wooden part of a firearm, holding the lock and barrel.

Gunstock

gun·wale (gun′əl) *n.* The upper edge of the side of a boat or ship. [< GUN + WALE (plank)]

gup·py (gup′ē) *n. pl.* **·pies** A small, colorful, tropical freshwater fish popular as an aquarium fish. [R. J. L. *Guppy,* early 20th c. naturalist of Trinidad]

gur·gle (gûr′gəl) *v.* **gur·gled, gur·gling** *v.i.* 1 To flow with a bubbling, liquid sound. 2 To make such a sound. —*v.t.* 3 To utter with a gurgling sound. —*n.* The act or sound of gurgling. [Var. of GARGLE] —**gur′gling·ly** *adv.*

gur·nard (gûr′nərd) *n. pl.* **·nards** or **·nard** A spiny-finned marine fish with winglike pectoral fins. [< F *grognard* grumbler]

gur·ney (gûr′nē) *n. pl.* **·neys** A stretcher mounted on wheels. [?]

gu·ru (goo′roo) *n. pl.* **·rus** 1 One who provides instruction or spiritual leadership in Hindu mysticism. 2 A teacher or leader regarded as having special knowledge, powers, etc. [< Hind.]

gush (gush) *v.i.* 1 To flow out suddenly and in volume. 2 To produce a sudden outflow. 3 To express oneself with exaggerated sentiment or enthusiasm. —*v.t.* 4 To pour forth (blood, tears, etc.). —*n.* 1 A sudden outpouring. 2 *Informal* An exaggerated display of sentiment. [Prob. < Scand.] —**gush′ing·ly** *adv.* —**Syn.** spurt, spout, jet.

gush·er (gush′ər) *n.* 1 One who or that which gushes. 2 A free-flowing oil well.

gush·y (gush′ē) *adj.* **gush·i·er, gush·i·est** Overly effusive or sentimental. —**gush′i·ly** *adv.* —**gush′i·ness** *n.*

gus·set (gus′it) *n.* A triangular piece of cloth fitted into a garment to give added strength or more room. —*v.t.* To furnish with a gusset. [< OF *gousse* a pod, shell]

gust (gust) *n.* 1 A sudden, strong blast of wind. 2 A sudden outburst of strong emotion. —*v.i.* To blow in gusts.

gus·ta·to·ry (gus′tə·tôr′ē, -tō′rē) *adj.* Of or relating to the sense of taste. [< L *gustus* taste]

gus·to (gus′tō) *n.* 1 Keen enjoyment; relish; zest. 2 Great vigor or fervor. [< L *gustus* taste]

gust·y (gus′tē) *adj.* **gust·i·er, gust·i·est** 1 Characterized by or blowing in gusts. 2 Bursting forth in or as in a gust. —**gust′i·ly** *adv.* —**gust′i·ness** *n.*

gut (gut) *n.* 1 The alimentary canal, esp. the intestine. 2 *Usu. pl.* The bowels. 3 CATGUT. 4 *pl. Slang* Stamina; courage; grit. —*v.t.* **gut·ted, gut·ting** 1 To take out the intestines of; eviscerate. 2 To destroy the interior or contents of. —*adj. Slang* 1 Central; basic; fundamental: *gut* issues. 2 Deeply felt, as though physically experienced: a *gut* conviction. [< OE *guttas* viscera]

gut·less (gut′lis) *adj. Slang* Lacking courage or spirit. —**gut′less·ly** *adv.* —**gut′less·ness** *n.*

gut·sy (gut′sē) *adj.* **gut·si·er, gut·si·est** *Slang* Courageous; dauntless; gritty. —**gut′si·ness** *n.*

gut·ta-per·cha (gut′ə·pûr′chə) *n.* A rubberlike substance obtained from the sap of various Malayan trees, used as an electrical insulator, a dental plastic, etc. [< Malay *getah* gum + *percha* gum tree]

gut·ter (gut′ər) *n.* 1 A trough or channel along the eaves of a house to carry off rainwater. 2 A waterway for carrying off surface water at the side of a road or street. 3 A groove, trench, or trough as on either side of a bowling alley. 4 A place or living condition characterized by great squalor, poverty, etc. —*v.t.* 1 To form gutters, channels, or grooves in. —*v.i.* 2 To flow in channels or streams. 3 To melt rapidly or flicker markedly, as a lighted candle. [< L *gutta* a drop]

gut·ter·snipe (gut′ər·snīp′) *n.* 1 A neglected child who roams the streets. 2 Anyone of a lowly and despised class or condition.

gut·tur·al (gut′ər·əl) *adj.* 1 Pertaining to the throat. 2 Produced or formed in the throat. 3 Hoarse; harsh; rasping. 4 *Phonet.* VELAR. —*n. Phonet.* A velar sound. [< L *guttur* throat] —**gut·tur·al·i·ty** (gut′ə·ral′ə·tē), **gut′tur·al·ness** *n.* —**gut′tur·al·ly** *adv.*

gut·ty (gut′ē) *adj.* **gut·ti·er, gut·ti·est** *Slang* Courageous; strong; plucky.

guy[1] (gī) *n.* A rope, cable, etc., that steadies or secures something, as a mast. —*v.t.* To secure with a guy. [?]

guy[2] (gī) *n.* 1 *Informal* A fellow; man. 2 *Brit.* A person of grotesque appearance. —*v.t.* To ridicule; make fun of. [< *Guy* Fawkes, 1570–1606, English conspirator]

Guy·a·na (gī·an′ə) *n.* A member of the Commonwealth of Nations in NE South America, 83,000 sq. mi., cap. Georgetown. • See map at BRAZIL.

guz·zle (guz′əl) *v.t.* & *v.i.* **·zled, ·zling** To drink greedily or immoderately. [? < OF *gosier* throat] —**guz′zler** *n.*

gym (jim) *n. Informal* 1 GYMNASIUM. 2 A course or class in physical training.

gym·na·si·um (jim·nā′zē·əm) *n. pl.* **·si·ums** or **·si·a** (-zē·ə) 1 A building or room containing equipment for physical education activities and sports. 2 (gim·nä′zē·ōōm) *Sometimes cap.* In Germany and some other European countries, a secondary school that prepares students for universities. [L < Gk. *gymnazein* exercise, train naked]

gym·nast (jim′nast, -nəst) n. One expert in gymnastics.
gym·nas·tic (jim·nas′tik) adj. Relating to gymnastics. — **gym·nas′ti·cal·ly** adv.
gym·nas·tics (jim·nas′tiks) n. pl. (construed as sing.) Exercises for the development of bodily strength and agility, often performed in a gymnasium with special equipment.
gym·no·sperm (jim′nə·spûrm′) n. One of a class of plants having ovules not enclosed in an ovary, as conifers, ginkgoes, etc. [< Gk. gymnos naked + SPERM] —**gym′no·sper′mous** adj.
gyn., gynecol. gynecology.
gy·ne·col·o·gy (gī′nə·kol′ə·jē, jī′nə-, jin′ə-) n. The branch of medicine dealing with the reproductive functions and diseases of women. [< Gk. gynē, gynaikos woman + -LOGY] —**gy′ne·co·log′i·cal** adj. —**gy′ne·col′o·gist** n.
gyp (jip) Informal v.t. & v.i. **gypped, gyp·ping** To cheat or swindle. —n. 1 An instance of gypping. 2 One who gyps. [< GYPSY]
gyp·sum (jip′səm) n. A mineral hydrous sulfate of lime, used in making plaster of Paris, fertilizers, etc. [< Gk. gypsos chalk]
gyp·sy (jip′sē) n. pl. **·sies** One who resembles or leads the wandering life of a Gypsy. —v.i. **·sied, sy·ing** To wander from place to place in the manner of the Gypsies.
Gyp·sy (jip′sē) n. pl. **·sies** 1 A member of a wandering people that migrated to Europe from India in the 15th century and now live in many parts of the world. 2 The language of these people; Romany. [Short for EGYPTIAN]

gypsy moth A small moth whose larvae feed on foliage and are highly destructive to trees.
gy·rate (jī′rāt) v.i. **·rat·ed, ·rat·ing** 1 To rotate or revolve. 2 To move in a spiral or circle. —adj. Convoluted; coiled. [< Gk. gyrus a circle] —**gy·ra′tion, gy′ra·tor** n. —**gy·ra·to·ry** (jī′rə·tôr·ē, -tō′rē) adj.
gyr·fal·con (jûr′fal′kən, -fôl′-, -fō′-) n. A large falcon of Arctic regions. [< OF < OHG Gir vulture + OF faucon falcon]
gy·ro (jī′rō) n. GYROSCOPE.
gyro- combining form Circle, ring, or spiral: gyroscope. [< Gk. gyros circle]
gy·ro·com·pass (jī′rō·kum′pəs, -kom′-) n. A compass that uses a gyroscope rather than the magnetic poles to maintain its reference direction.
gyro pilot AUTOMATIC PILOT.
gy·ro·plane (jī′rə·plān′) n. An airplane whose lift is obtained from rotation of airfoils about a nearly vertical axis.
gy·ro·scope (jī′rə·skōp) n. An instrument consisting of a rotating mass whose axis remains fixed in space unless it is subjected to external torque. —**gy′ro·scop′ic** (-skop′ik) adj.

Gyroscope

gyro stabilizer A device that uses a gyroscope as a reference in maintaining something in a stable position.
gyve (jīv) n. Usu. pl. A shackle, esp. for the leg. —v.t. **gyved, gyv·ing** To shackle. [ME]

H

H, h (āch) n. pl. **H's, h's, Hs, hs** (ā′chiz) 1 The eighth letter of the English alphabet. 2 Any spoken sound representing the letter H or h. 3 Something shaped like an H. —adj. Shaped like an H.
H hydrogen
h., h harbor; hardness; height; hit(s).
ha (hä) interj. An exclamation expressing surprise, triumph, laughter, etc.
ha hectare(s).
ha·be·as cor·pus (hā′bē·əs kôr′pəs) Law A writ commanding a person having another in custody to produce the detained person before a court. [L, you shall have the body]
hab·er·dash·er (hab′ər·dash′ər) n. 1 A dealer in men's furnishings, such as, shirts, socks, ties, etc. 2 Brit. A dealer in ribbons. trimmings, thread, needles, and other small wares. [< AF hapertas kind of fabric]
hab·er·dash·er·y (hab′ər·dash′ər·ē) n. pl. **·er·ies** 1 The goods sold by haberdashers. 2 A haberdasher's shop.
hab·er·geon (hab′ər·jən) n. A coat of mail for the breast and neck, shorter than a hauberk. [< OF hauberc hauberk]
ha·bil·i·ment (hə·bil′ə·mənt) n. 1 An article of clothing. 2 pl. Clothes; garb. [< OF habiller dress, make fit]
hab·it (hab′it) n. 1 A tendency toward an action or condition, which by repetition has become involuntary. 2 An action so induced. 3 Habitual condition, appearance, or temperament; physical or mental make-up. 4 Biol. A characteristic mode of growth or aspect of a plant or animal. 5 An outer garment or garments; esp., a woman's costume for horseback riding. 6 The distinctive garment of a religious order. —v.t. To furnish with a habit; clothe; dress. [< L habitus condition, dress < habere have] —Syn. n. 1 custom, practice, routine, rule, wont.
hab·it·a·ble (hab′it·ə·bəl) adj. Suitable to be lived in. [< L habitare inhabit] —**hab·it·a·bil·i·ty** (hab′it·ə·bil′ə·tē), **hab′it·a·ble·ness** n. —**hab′it·a·bly** adv.
hab·i·tant (hab′ə·tənt) n. 1 INHABITANT. 2 (hab′ə·tänt) In Canada, a farmer who is a French settler or a descendant of a French settler.
hab·i·tat (hab′ə·tat) n. The region where a species or individual naturally or usu. lives or is found. [L, it dwells]

hab·i·ta·tion (hab′ə·tā′shən) n. 1 A place of residence; home. 2 The act or state of inhabiting.
ha·bit·u·al (hə·bich′ōō·əl) adj. 1 Of, pertaining to, or constituting a habit. 2 Resulting from habit or repeated use; inveterate: a habitual liar. 3 Frequently seen, done, etc.; usual; inevitable: the habitual roar of city traffic. —**ha·bit′u·al·ly** adv. —**ha·bit′u·al·ness** n.
ha·bit·u·ate (hə·bich′ōō·āt) v.t. **·at·ed, ·at·ing** 1 To make familiar by repetition or use; accustom. 2 Informal To go to habitually; frequent. —**ha·bit′u·a′tion** n.
hab·i·tude (hab′ə·tyōōd) n. 1 Habitual method, character, constitution, or tendency; habit. 2 Customary relation or association.
ha·bit·u·é (hə·bich′ōō·ā′) n. A habitual visitor or frequenter of a place, such as a restaurant. [F < habituer accustom]
Habs·burg (haps′bûrg; Ger. häps′bŏŏrkh) n. HAPSBURG.
ha·ci·en·da (hä′sē·en′də) n. In Spanish America, a landed estate; a country house. [Sp. < L facienda things to be done]
hack¹ (hak) v.t. 1 To cut or chop crudely or irregularly. 2 To break up, as clods of earth. —v.i. 3 To make cuts or notches with heavy, crude blows. 4 To emit short, dry coughs. —**hack it** Slang To cope with it; do it. —n. 1 A gash, cut, or nick. 2 An ax or other tool for hacking. 3 A short, dry cough. [< OE haccian to cut] —**hack′er** n.
hack² (hak) n. 1 A horse for hire. 2 A horse used for work or for ordinary riding. 3 An old, worn-out horse. 4 A coach for hire. 5 TAXICAB. 6 A writer who hires himself out for any kind of writing jobs; a literary drudge. —v.t. 1 To let out for hire, as a horse. —v.i. 2 To ride a horse, as for recreation. 3 Informal To drive a taxicab. —adj. 1 Of or designated for a taxicab: a hack stand. 2 For hire for drudging work: a hack writer. 3 Done merely for pay: a hack job. [< HACKNEY]
hack·a·more (hak′ə·môr, -mōr) n. A rawhide halter or rope used for training colts. [< Sp. jaquima halter]
hack·ber·ry (hak′ber′ē, -bər·ē) n. pl. **·ries** 1 An American tree related to the elm and having cherrylike edible fruit. 2 The fruit or wood of this tree. [< ON heggr hedge + BERRY]
hack·le¹ (hak′əl) n. 1 One of the ruff feathers of a cock or

other bird. 2 An artificial fly made of a hackle feather, used as an angler's lure: also **hackle fly. 3** *pl.* The erectile hairs on the neck and back of a dog. —**get one's hackles up** To arouse one's anger; put one out of temper. —*v.t.* **hack·led, hack·ling** To furnish (a fly) with a hackle. [ME *hechele*] —**hack'ler** *n.*

hack·le² (hak'əl) *v.t. & v.i.* **hack·led, hack·ling** To cut or chop roughly or crudely; mangle; hack. [Freq. of HACK¹]

hack·ney (hak'nē) *n. pl.* **·neys 1** One of a breed of driving and saddle horses. 2 A horse kept for hire. 3 A coach for hire: also **hackney coach.** —*v.t.* **1** To make trite by constant use. 2 To let out or use as a hackney. —*adj.* Let out for hire. [ME *hakeney*]

hack·neyed (hak'nēd) *adj.* Made commonplace by too frequent use; trite.

hack·saw (hak'sô') *n.* A saw made up of a fine-toothed blade set in a frame, used for cutting metal.

had (had) *p.t. & p.p.* of HAVE.

had·dock (had'ək) *n. pl.* **·dock** or **·docks** A food fish of the North Atlantic, related to the cod. [ME]

Hacksaw

Ha·des (hā'dēz) *Gk. Myth.* **1** The god of the underworld; Pluto. 2 The kingdom over which Hades rules, the abode of the dead. —*n. Informal* Hell.

hadj (haj) *n.* The pilgrimage to Mecca required of every Muslim at least once in his life. [Ar. *hajj* pilgrimage]

hadj·i (haj'ē) *n.* A Muslim who has made the pilgrimage to Mecca. Also **hadj'ee.** [Ar. *ḥājjī* pilgrim]

had·n't (had'nt) Contraction of *had not.*

haem·or·rhoid (hem'ə·roid) *n.* HEMORRHOID.

haf·ni·um (haf'nē·əm) *n.* A metallic element (symbol Hf) occurring with and resembling zirconium. [< L *Hafnia* Copenhagen]

haft (haft, häft) *n.* A handle, esp. the handle of a cutting weapon. —*v.t.* To supply with or set in a haft or handle. [< OE *hæft*]

hag (hag) *n.* **1** An ugly, forbidding, malicious old woman. 2 A witch; sorceress. [< OE *hægtes* witch] —**hag'gish** *adj.* —Syn. 1 beldam, crone, granny.

Ha·gar (hā'gər) *n.* In the Bible, Abraham's concubine, mother of Ishmael.

hag·fish (hag'fish') *n. pl.* **·fish** or **·fish·es** A primitive eel-like marine fish with a circular, jawless mouth and horny teeth, parasitic on other fish.

Hag·ga·dah (hə·gä'də, *Hebrew* hä·gô'dô) *n. pl.* **·doth** (-dōth) **1** An anecdote or parable in the Talmud, used to clarify a point of law. 2 The ritual, including the story of the Exodus, read during the Seder on Passover. Also **Hag·ga'da.** [Heb.] —**hag·gad·ic** (hə·gad'ik, -gäd'-) *adj.* —**hag·ga·dist** (hə·gä'dist) *n.*

hag·gard (hag'ərd) *adj.* Worn and gaunt in appearance. [< OF *hagard* wild hawk] —**hag'gard·ly** *adv.* —**hag'gard·ness** *n.* —Syn. careworn, emaciated, exhausted, wan.

hag·gis (hag'is) *n.* A Scottish dish made of a sheep's heart and liver with onions and suet, mixed with oatmeal and boiled in a sheep's stomach. [ME *hagas*]

hag·gle (hag'əl) *v.* **hag·gled, hag·gling** *v.t.* **1** To cut unskillfully; mangle. —*v.i.* 2 To argue about price or terms. —*n.* The act of haggling. [< ON *höggva* to cut] —**hag'gler** *n.*

hag·i·og·ra·phy (hag'ē·og'rə·fē, hā'jē-) *n. pl.* **·phies 1** The writing or study of saints' lives. 2 A collection of biographies of saints. —**hag'i·og'ra·pher** *n.* —**hag'i·o·graph'ic** or **·i·cal** *adj.*

hag·i·ol·o·gy (hag'ē·ol'ə·jē, hā'jē-) *n. pl.* **·gies 1** A list of saints. 2 A treatise on saints' lives; sacred writings. [< Gk. *hagios* sacred + -LOGY] —**hag·i·o·log·ic** (hag'ē·ə·loj'ik, hā'jē-) *adj.* —**hag'i·ol'o·gist** *n.*

hag·rid·den (hag'rid'n) *adj.* Tormented or distressed, as by nightmares or painful thoughts.

hah (hä) *interj. & n.* HA.

hai·ku (hī'kōō) *n. pl.* **·ku** A Japanese verse form, consisting of three lines of five, seven, and five syllables respectively.

hail¹ (hāl) *n.* **1** Pellets of ice, sometimes fairly large, that often fall during thunderstorms. 2 Anything falling thickly and with violence: a *hail* of blows. —*v.i.* 1 To pour

down hail. —*v.t.* 2 To hurl or pour down like hail. [< OE *hægel*]

hail² (hāl) *v.t.* **1** To call loudly to in greeting; salute. 2 To call to so as to attract attention. 3 To name as; designate. —*v.i.* 4 To call out or signal so as to attract attention. —**hail from** To come from; have as one's original home. —*n.* 1 A call to attract attention; greeting. 2 The distance a shout can be heard: within *hail.* —*interj.* Salutations! [< ON *heill* whole, hale] —**hail'er** *n.*

hail·stone (hāl'stōn') *n.* A pellet of hail.

hail·storm (hāl'stôrm') *n.* A storm in which hail falls.

hair (hâr) *n.* **1** One of the filaments of modified epidermal tissue growing from the skin of people and animals. 2 Any mass of such filaments. 3 *Bot.* A threadlike outgrowth on plants. 4 An exceedingly minute space, degree, etc.: to escape by a *hair.* —*adj.* Like, made of, or for hair. —**let one's hair down** To drop one's reserve; relax. —**not turn a hair** To remain calm and unruffled. —**split hairs** To quibble; make petty distinctions. [< OE *hær*]

hair·breadth (hâr'bredth') *n.* An extremely small space or distance. —*adj.* Having only the breadth of a hair; very narrow. Also **hairs'-breadth', hair's-breadth'.**

hair·cloth (hâr'klôth', -kloth') *n.* A fabric containing horsehair, used chiefly in upholstering.

hair·cut (hâr'kut') *n.* The act of cutting the hair or the style in which it is cut. —**hair'cut'ter** *n.*

hair·do (hâr'dōō') *n.* A style of dressing the hair; coiffure.

hair·dress·er (hâr'dres'ər) *n.* One who arranges and cuts hair. —**hair'dress'ing** *n.*

hair·less (hâr'lis) *adj.* **1** Being without hair. 2 Having lost the hair; bald. —**hair'less·ness** *n.*

hair·line (hâr'līn') *n.* **1** A narrow stripe in textile fabrics. 2 The outline of hair on the head.

hair·pin (hâr'pin') *n.* A U-shaped pin made of wire, bone, plastic, etc., for keeping the hair in place. • See PIN.

hair-rais·ing (hâr'rā'zing) *adj.* Causing fright or shock. —**hair'-rais'er** *n.* —Syn. bloodcurdling, frightful, horrifying.

hair shirt A rough garment of haircloth worn for religious penance.

hair·split·ting (hâr'split'ing) *n.* Insistence upon minute or trivial distinctions. —*adj.* Drawing excessively nice distinctions. —**hair'-split'ter** *n.*

hair·spring (hâr'spring') *n.* The fine spring attached to the balance wheel of a watch or clock.

hair-trig·ger (hâr'trig'ər) *n.* A trigger, as of a firearm, actuated by a very small force. —*adj.* Set in operation by the slightest provocation.

hair·y (hâr'ē) *adj.* **hair·i·er, hair·i·est 1** Covered with, made of, or like hair. 2 *Slang* a Troublesome; difficult. b Dangerous; harrowing. —**hair'i·ness** *n.*

Hai·ti (hā'tē) *n.* A republic occupying the w part of Hispaniola in the Caribbean, 10,714 sq. mi., cap. Port-au-Prince. • See map at DOMINICAN REPUBLIC.

Hai·ti·an (hā'shən, -tē·ən) *n.* **1** A citizen or native of Haiti. 2 The dialect of French spoken in Haiti. —*adj.* Of or pertaining to Haiti, its people, or their dialect.

hake (hāk) *n. pl.* **hake** or **hakes** Any of various food fishes related to the cod. [ME]

ha·kim (hä·kēm') *n.* In Muslim countries, a governor; also, a judge or physician. Also **ha·keem', ha·kem'.** [Ar. wise, learned]

hal·berd (hal'bərd) *n.* A weapon in the form of a battle-ax and pike at the end of a long staff. Also **hal'bard, hal'bert** (-bərt). [< MHG < *helm* handle + *barte* broad-ax]

hal·ber·dier (hal'bər·dir') *n.* A soldier armed with a halberd.

hal·cy·on (hal'sē·ən) *n.* **1** A mythical bird, identified with the kingfisher, said to have calmed the sea at the time of the winter solstice. 2 Any kingfisher of Australasia. —*adj.* Calm; peaceful: the *halcyon* days of youth. [< Gk. *halkyōn* kingfisher]

hale¹ (hāl) *v.t.* **haled, hal·ing 1** To drag by force; haul; pull. 2 To compel to go. [< MLG *halen*] —**hal'er** *n.*

hale² (hāl) *adj.* Of sound and vigorous health. [< OE *hāl.*] —**hale'ly** *adv.* —**hale'ness** *n.* —Syn. bouncing, robust, strong, well.

---

add, āce, câre, pälm; end, ēven; it, īce; odd, ōpen, ôrder; tŏŏk, pōōl; up, bûrn; ə = a in *above*, u in *focus*; yōō = u in *fuse*; oil; pout; check; go; ring; thin; this; zh, *vision.* < derived from; ? origin uncertain or unknown.

half (haf, häf) *n. pl.* **halves** (havz, hävz) One of two equal parts or a quantity equal to such a part. —**by halves 1** Incompletely. **2** With little enthusiasm. —**go halves** To share in equal parts. —*adj.* **1** Being one of two equal parts of a thing. **2** Partial; approximately one half of, in amount or value. —*adv.* To the degree or extent of a half; partially. [< OE *hælf*]

half-and-half (haf′ən-haf′, häf′ən-häf′) *adj.* **1** *U.S.* A mixture of milk and cream in equal quantities. **2** *Brit.* A mixture of beer and stout, porter and ale, etc., in equal quantities. —*adv.* In two equal divisions; equally.

half-back (haf′bak′, häf′-) *n.* In American football, either of two players in the backfield, originally stationed halfway between the line and the fullback.

half-baked (haf′bākt′, häf′-) *adj.* **1** Baked on one side or not baked through; doughy. **2** *Informal* Imperfectly planned or conceived. **3** *Informal* Immature; unseasoned.

half-blood (haf′blud′) *n.* **1** A person having only one parent of a specified stock; a half-breed. **2** An animal, as a cow, sheep, etc., of crossed inferior and superior stock. —*adj.* Being half-blood or half-breed. Also **half′-blood′ed.**

half blood The relationship between persons who have one parent only in common.

half-breed (haf′brēd′, häf′-) *n.* One having parents of different racial origin. —*adj.* Half of one breed and half of another; coming of mixed stock: also **half′-bred′** (-bred′).

half brother A brother related through only one parent.

half-caste (haf′kast′, häf′kast′) *n.* One born of mixed European and Asian blood; also, any half-breed. —*adj.* Of mixed European and other blood.

half cock (haf′kok′, häf′-) The position of the hammer of a firearm when partly raised, but not releasable by the trigger. —**go off half-cocked** ,or **at half cock 1** To be discharged prematurely. **2** To act or speak hastily or without deliberation. —**half′-cocked′** *adj.*

half crown A British silver coin of the value of two shillings and sixpence.

half-dol·lar (haf′dol′ər, häf′-) *n.* A U.S. silver coin worth fifty cents.

half eagle A former gold coin of the U.S. having a value of five dollars.

half-heart·ed (haf′här′tid, häf′-) *adj.* Showing little interest or enthusiasm. —**half′heart′ed·ly** *adv.* —**half′heart′ed·ness** *n.*

half hitch A knot made by passing the end of a rope around itself once and then through the loop so formed.

half hour 1 A period of thirty minutes. **2** The point midway between the hours. —**half′-hour′ly** *adv.*

half-life (haf′līf′, häf′-) *n. Physics* The time taken for half the nuclei in a sample of a radioactive isotope to disintegrate. Also **half-life period.**

half-mast (haf′mast′, häf′mäst′) *n.* The position of a flag halfway up the staff, as in respect to the dead. —*v.t.* To put, as a flag, at half-mast.

half-moon (haf′mōōn′, häf′-) *n.* **1** The moon when half its disk is illuminated. **2** Something similar in shape to a half-moon. • See MOON.

half nel·son (nel′sən) A wrestling hold in which one arm is passed below the opponent's armpit and the hand is pressed against the back of his neck.

half note *Music* A note whose duration is half that of a whole note. • See NOTE.

half-pen·ny (hā′pən-ē, hāp′nē) *n. pl.* **half-pence** (hā′pəns) or **half-pen·nies** (hā′pən-ēz, hāp′nēz) A British coin equivalent to one half of a penny. —*adj.* **1** Worth a halfpenny. **2** Trifling in cost or value.

half pint 1 A measure of capacity equal to one half of a pint. **2** *Slang* A small person.

half sister A sister related through only one parent.

half-sole (haf′sōl′, häf′-) *v.t.* **-soled, -sol·ing** To repair by affixing a half sole.

half sole The sole of a shoe, boot, etc., extending from the shank to the toe.

half-staff (haf′staf′, häf′stäf′) *n. & v.* HALF-MAST.

half step 1 *Music* A semitone. **2** *Mil.* A step of 15 inches at quick time; in double time, one of 18 inches.

half-tim·bered (haf′tim′bərd, häf′-) *adj.* Built of heavy timbers, with the spaces between filled with masonry or plaster.

half-time (haf′tīm′, häf′-) *n.* An interval of suspended play between the halves of sports contests.

half·tone (haf′tōn′, häf′-) *n.* **1** An illustration obtained by photographing an original through a finely ruled glass screen, the lights and shadows appearing when printed as minute lines or dots. **2** *Music* A semitone. —*adj.* Of, pertaining to, using, or made by the halftone process.

half-track (haf′trak′, häf′-) *adj.* Designating a type of military vehicle propelled by endless tracks, but steered by a pair of wheels in front. —*n.* A half-track vehicle.

half·way (haf′wā′, häf′-) *adv.* At or to half the distance. —*adj.* **1** Midway between two points. **2** Partial; inadequate.

halfway house 1 A place to stop halfway through a journey. **2** A residence where people who have been withdrawn from society, as former drug addicts or prisoners, are prepared to return to an active life.

half-wit (haf′wit′, häf′) *n.* A stupid or foolish person; idiot. —**half′-wit′ted** *adj.* —Syn. dolt, imbecile, nitwit, simpleton.

hal·i·but (hal′ə-bət, hol′-) *n. pl.* **·but** or **·buts** Any of various large, edible flatfish of N seas. [< ME *haly* holy + *butte* fish]

hal·ide (hal′īd, -id, hā′līd, -lid) *n. Chem.* Any compound of a halogen with an element or radical, as a bromide, chloride, etc. —*adj.* Resembling a halide. Also **hal·id** (hal′id, hā′lid).

Halibut

hal·i·dom (hal′ə-dəm) *n. Archaic* **1** Holiness. **2** A holy relic. **3** A holy place; sanctuary. [< OE *halig* holy + -DOM]

hal·ite (hal′īt, hā′līt) *n.* Unrefined sodium chloride; rock salt. [< Gk. *hals* salt + -ITE]

hal·i·to·sis (hal′ə-tō′sis) *n.* Malodorous breath. [< L *halitus* breath + -OSIS]

hall (hôl) *n.* **1** A passage or corridor in a building. **2** A small room or enclosure at the entry of a house; a vestibule; lobby. **3** A building or room for public business, entertainments, meetings, etc. **4** In a school, university, or college, a building used as a dormitory, classroom building, laboratory, etc. **5** The meeting place or headquarters of an organization or society; also, the organization itself. **6** *Brit.* A college dining room. **7** The large main room of a castle or other great house. **8** The country residence of a baron, squire, etc. [< OE *heall*]

hal·le·lu·jah (hal′ə-lōō′yə) *interj.* Praise ye the Lord! —*n.* A musical composition whose principal theme is found in the word *hallelujah.* Also **hal′le·lu′iah.** [< Heb. *hallēlū* praise + *yāh* Jehovah]

hal·liard (hal′yərd) *n.* HALYARD.

hall·mark (hôl′märk′) *n.* **1** An official mark stamped on gold and silver articles in England to guarantee their purity. **2** Any mark or proof of genuineness. —*v.t.* To stamp with a hallmark. [< Goldsmiths' *Hall,* London, where the assaying and stamping were done + MARK]

hal·loo (hə-lōō′) *interj.* **1** An exclamation to attract attention, express surprise, etc. **2** A shout to incite hounds to the chase. —*n.* A cry of "halloo." —*v.i.* **1** To shout "halloo"; cry out. —*v.t.* **2** To incite or encourage with shouts. **3** To shout to; hail. **4** To shout (something). Also **hal·lo, hal·loa** (hə-lō). [< OF *halloer* pursue noisily]

hal·low (hal′ō) *v.t.* **1** To make holy; consecrate. **2** To look upon as holy; reverence. [< OE *halig* holy]

hal·lowed (hal′ōd; *in liturgical use, usu.* hal′ō·id) *adj.* **1** Sacred; holy. **2** Revered as sacred. —**hal′lowed·ness** *n.*

Hal·low·e·en (hal′ō-ēn′) *n.* The evening of Oct. 31, vigil of All Saints' Day, now popularly observed esp. by children by masquerading and playful solicitations for sweets, etc. [< *(All-)hallow(s) e(v)en*]

Hal·low·mass (hal′ō-məs) *n. Archaic* ALL SAINTS' DAY. Also **Hal′low·mas.** [< *(All-)hallow-mass*]

hal·lu·ci·nate (hə-lōō′sə-nāt) *v.i.* **·nat·ed, ·nat·ing 1** To have hallucinations. —*v.t.* **2** To envision or perceive as a hallucination. [< L *hallucinari* wander mentally]

hal·lu·ci·na·tion (hə-lōō′sə-nā′shən) *n.* **1** An apparent perception without any corresponding external stimulus. **2** A sense object perceived but not present in reality. —**hal·lu·ci·na·to·ry** (hə-lōō′sə-nə-tôr′ē, -tō′rē) *adj.*

hal·lu·ci·no·gen (hə-lōō′sin·ə-jən) *n.* Any substance capable of inducing hallucinations. —**hal·lu'ci·no·gen'ic** *adj.*

ha·lo (hā'lō) *n. pl.* **·los** or **·loes** 1 A luminous circle around the sun or the moon. 2 A radiance encircling the head in portrayals of sacred personages. 3 The splendor with which imagination surrounds an object of affection or esteem. —*v.* **·loed**, **·lo·ing** *v.t.* 1 To enclose in a halo. —*v.i.* 2 To form a halo. [< Gk. *halōs*]

hal·o·gen (hal'ə·jən) *n. Chem.* Any of a group of chemically similar elements comprising fluorine, chlorine, bromine, iodine, and astatine. [< Gk. *hals* sea, salt + -GEN] — **ha·log·e·nous** (hə·loj'ə·nəs) *adj.*

hal·oid (hal'oid, hā'loid) *adj.* 1 Resembling sea salt. 2 Pertaining to or derived from a halogen. —*n.* A haloid salt.

halt¹ (hôlt) *n.* A complete stop of progress, operation, etc. —**call a halt** To put a stop to. —*v.t. & v.i.* To stop; bring or come to a halt. [< OHG *halten* to stop] —**Syn.** *v.* cease, pause, rest, stay.

halt² (hôlt) *v.i.* 1 To be imperfect; proceed lamely. 2 To be in doubt; waver. 3 *Archaic* To walk with a limp. —*adj. Archaic* Crippled; limping in gait. —*n. Archaic* Lameness. —**the halt** Those who are crippled. [< OE *healt* lame] — **halt'ing·ly** *adv.* —**halt'ing·ness** *n.*

hal·ter (hôl'tər) *n.* 1 A strap or rope by which to hold or lead a horse or other animal. 2 A hangman's rope. 3 Execution by hanging. 4 A woman's blouse designed for exposing the back and arms to the sun, fastened around the neck and waist. —*v.t.* To secure with a halter. [< OE *hælftre*]

halve (hav, häv) *v.t.* **halved**, **halv·ing** 1 To divide into two equal parts; share equally. 2 To take away half of. 3 In golf, to play (a match or hole) in the same number of strokes as one's opponent. [< HALF]

halves (havz, hävz) *n.pl.* of HALF.

hal·yard (hal'yərd) *n. Naut.* A rope for hoisting or lowering a sail, a flag, etc. [< HALE¹]

ham (ham) *n.* 1 The thigh of a hog, smoked, salted, etc., for food. 2 *pl.* The buttocks. 3 The space or region behind the knee joint; the hock of quadrupeds. 4 *Slang* A performer who overacts. 5 An amateur radio operator. —*v.t.* **hammed**, **ham·ming** *Slang* To overact; use exaggerated speech and gestures: often in the expression **ham it up.** [< OE *hamm*] —**ham'my** *adj.* (**·i·er**, **·i·est**)

Ham (ham) In the Bible, the youngest son of Noah.

ham·a·dry·ad (ham'ə·drī'əd, -ad) *n. pl.* **·ads** or **·a·des** (-ə·dēz) *Gk. Myth.* A wood nymph whose life was connected with that of the tree she inhabited. [< Gk. *hama* together with + *drys* oak tree]

ham·burg (ham'bûrg) *n.* Hamburger. Also **hamburg steak.**

ham·burg·er (ham'bûr'gər) *n.* 1 Finely ground beef. 2 Such meat fried or broiled in the form of a patty. Also **hamburger steak.** 3 A sandwich consisting of such meat placed in a bun. [< *Hamburg*, Germany]

Ham·ite (ham'īt) *n.* 1 One alleged to be a descendant of Ham. 2 A member of the Caucasoid ethnic stock originating in NE Africa and the Canary Islands.

Ha·mit·ic (ha·mit'ik) *adj.* Of or pertaining to Ham, or the Hamites, or their languages. —*n.* A North African group of languages including ancient Egyptian, extinct Libyan, and the modern Berber dialects and the Cushitic languages of Ethiopia and Somaliland.

ham·let (ham'lit) *n.* A little village; a cluster of houses in the country. [< OF *hamelet*]

Ham·let (ham'lit) *n.* 1 One of Shakespeare's best-known tragedies. 2 The hero of this play.

ham·mer (ham'ər) *n.* 1 A hand tool with a head at right angles to the handle, used for driving nails, pounding, etc. 2 A machine or part of a machine performing functions similar to those of a heavy hand hammer. 3 That part of a gunlock which strikes the cap or cartridge. •See RE-VOLVER. 4 A padded piece that strikes the string of a piano. 5 An auctioneer's mallet. 6 *Anat.* The malleus of the middle ear. —**under the ham-**

Hammers
a. tack.
b. claw.

mer For sale at auction. —*v.t.* 1 To strike with or as with a hammer; drive, as a nail. 2 To shape or fasten with a hammer. 3 To form or force as if with hammer blows. — *v.i.* 4 To strike blows with or as with a hammer. [< OE *hamer*] —**ham'mer·er** *n.* —**Syn.** *v.* 1 bang, beat, pound, whack.

ham·mer·head (ham'ər·hed') *n.* A voracious shark of warm seas, having a transversely elongated head like that of a hammer with the eyes at each end.

ham·mer·lock (ham'ər·lok') *n.* A wrestling grip in which the arm is twisted behind the back and upwards.

ham·mock (ham'ək) *n.* A couch of canvas or netting, swung from supports at both ends. [Sp. *hamaca*]

ham·per¹ (ham'pər) *v.t.* To hinder the movements of: restrain. [ME *hampren*]

ham·per² (ham'pər) *n.* A large covered basket, as for food, laundry, etc. [< OF *hanapier*]

ham·ster (ham'stər) *n.* A small burrowing rodent often kept as a pet or for laboratory experiments. [< OHG *hamustro*]

ham·string (ham'string') *n.* A tendon at the back of the human knee or at the back of the hock of a quadruped. — *v.t.* **·strung**, **·string·ing** 1 To cut the hamstring of; cripple. 2 To make ineffective or helpless.

hand (hand) *n.* 1 The part of the human forelimb that is attached to the forearm below the wrist, used for holding and grasping. 2 The corresponding segment of a limb in apes, etc. 3 Side or direction: She sat at his right *hand.* 4 A role in doing something: They all had a *hand* in it. 5 *pl.* Possession; control: It is in your *hands* now. 6 Aid; assistance: to lend a *hand.* 7 A pledge of betrothal, or a giving in marriage. 8 A manual laborer. 9 A person as the performer of an action: a book written by many *hands.* 10 A person with reference to his ability: a good *hand* with children. 11 Skill; ability; touch. 12 A specified remove from a source: a story heard at second *hand.* 13 *pl.* The members of a group. 14 The cards held by a player at one deal; also, the player. 15 The playing of the cards at one deal. 16 Clapping of hands; applause. 17 Handwriting. 18 A person's signature. 19 The pointer of a clock or watch. 20 Four inches, the approximate width of the hand, used as a measure for the height of horses, etc. —**a great hand at** or **for** A person specially fond of or clever at. —**at first hand** At the source. —**at hand** Within reach; convenient. —**at the hand of** From the hand of; by the operation of. —**by hand** With the hands only: a dress made *by hand.* —**have one's hands full** To have all or more than one can do. —**in hand** 1 In one's possession. 2 In process of being done. 3 Entirely under control. —**off one's hands** Out of one's care or control. —**on hand** 1 In present or rightful possession. 2 In place; present. —**on one's hands** In one's care; under one's responsibility. —**on the other hand** Looking at the opposed point of view. —**out of hand** 1 Unruly; lawless. 2 Immediately; without delay. — **wash one's hands of** To dismiss from consideration. — *v.t.* 1 To give, pass, or deliver with or as with the hand. 2 To lead or help with the hand. —**hand down** 1 To transmit, as to one's successors. 2 To deliver, as the decision of a court. —**hand it to** *Slang* To acknowledge the abilities, success, etc., of. —**hand on** To pass on; transmit. —**hand out** To mete out; distribute. —**hand over** To give up possession of; surrender. [< OE]

hand·bag (hand'bag') *n.* 1 A bag or purse for personal articles, as a wallet, cosmetics, etc., carried by women. 2 A small suitcase.

hand·ball (hand'bôl') *n.* 1 A game in which a ball is struck with the hand and kept bounding against a wall. 2 The rubber ball used in this game.

hand·bar·row (hand'bar'ō) *n.* 1 A litter or stretcher, carried by two handles at each end. 2 A wheelbarrow.

hand·bill (hand'bil') *n.* A small advertising sheet or notice, usu. distributed by hand.

hand·book (hand'bŏŏk') *n.* A guidebook or reference manual of a size small enough to be carried about.

hand·breadth (hand'bredth') *n.* The breadth of the hand; a palm. Also **hand's'-breadth'** (handz'-).

hand cart A cart pushed by hand.

hand·clasp (hand'klasp', -kläsp') n. A clasping of a person's hand in greeting, agreement, farewell, etc.

hand·cuff (hand'kuf') n. One of two manacles connected by a chain, and designed to be locked around the wrists. —v.t. To put handcuffs on; manacle.

hand·ed (han'did) adj. 1 Having hands. 2 Having a specific type or number of hands: used in combination: *right-handed.*

Handcuffs

hand·ful (hand'fŏŏl) n. pl. **hand·fuls 1** As much as a hand can hold at once. **2** A small quantity. **3** *Informal* Something or someone hard to handle.

hand·gun (hand'gun') n. A firearm held and fired in one hand, as a pistol.

hand·i·cap (han'dē·kap') n. **1** A condition imposed to equalize the chances of competitors in a contest. **2** A race or contest in which such conditions are imposed. **3** A disadvantage or hindrance. —v.t. **·capped, ·cap·ping 1** To impose a handicap on. **2** To be a handicap to. [<*hand in cap,* a lottery game in which winners were penalized] —**hand'i·cap'per** n. —**Syn.** n. **3** burden, encumbrance, impediment, shortcoming.

hand·i·craft (han'dē·kraft', -kräft') n. **1** Skill and expertness in working with the hands. **2** A trade or craft calling for such skill. [<HAND + CRAFT]

hand·i·work (han'dē·wûrk') n. **1** Work done by the hands. **2** Work done by one's self. **3** The outcome of one's undertakings.

hand·ker·chief (hang'kər·chif) n. **1** A small, square piece of soft cloth for wiping the face or nose. **2** A neckerchief.

han·dle (han'dəl) v. **han·dled, han·dling** v.t. **1** To touch, feel, etc., with the hands. **2** To manage or use with the hands. **3** To manage or direct; control. **4** To deal with: to *handle* a disagreement. **5** To trade or deal in: to *handle* cotton. **6** To act toward; treat. —v.i. **7** To respond to handling. —n. That part of an object intended to be grasped with the hand. —**fly off the handle** To be suddenly and unreasonably angry. [<OE *handlian*]

han·dle·bar (han'dəl·bär') n. **1** A bent bar with grips on both ends, used in steering a bicycle, motorcycle, etc. **2** pl. *Informal* A long curved mustache.

han·dler (hand'lər) n. **1** One who or that which handles, esp. one who trains certain animals. **2** The trainer of a boxer, wrestler, etc.

hand·made (hand'mād') adj. Made by hand or by hand tools.

hand·maid (hand'mād') n. A female servant or attendant. Also **hand'maid'en.**

hand·me·down (hand'mē·doun') *Informal adj.* Passed on to another after use; secondhand. —n. A hand-me-down garment.

hand organ A device that produces music when a hand crank is turned.

hand·out (hand'out') n. *Informal* **1** Anything given to a beggar. **2** Anything given with little or no expectation of return. **3** A printed press release distributed to reporters.

hand·picked (hand'pikt') adj. Picked or selected with special care.

hand·rail (hand'rāl') n. A rail that can be grasped by the hand, as at the edge of a balcony or stairway.

hand·saw (hand'sô') n. A saw wielded with one hand.

hand·sel (hand'səl, han'-) n. **1** A gift as a token of good will or to secure good luck. **2** Money given as a gift at New Year's. —v.t. **·seled** or **·selled, ·sel·ing** or **·sel·ling** To give handsel to. [<ON *hand* hand + *sal* gift]

hand·set (hand'set') n. A telephone mouthpiece and receiver placed at opposite ends of a single unit.

hand·shake (hand'shāk') n. A clasping and shaking of a person's hand, as in greeting.

hand·some (han'səm) adj. **1** Agreeable to the eye or to good taste; of pleasing aspect. **2** Of liberal dimensions or proportions. **3** Marked by generosity or liberality. [<HAND + -SOME, orig. with sense "easy to handle"] —**hand'some·ly** adv. —**hand'some·ness** n.

hands-on (handz'on', -ôn') adj. Designating an action that requires active participation: *hands-on* techniques.

hand·spike (hand'spīk') n. A bar used as a lever.

hand·spring (hand'spring') n. A stunt in which the performer flips forward or backward from an upright position, landing first on the hands and then on the feet.

hand-to-hand (han'tə·hand') adj. At close quarters: a *hand-to-hand* fight.

hand-to-mouth (han'tə·mouth') adj. Being at or below the subsistence level, with nothing to spare: a *hand-to-mouth* existence.

hand·work (hand'wûrk') n. Work done by hand.

hand·writ·ing (hand'rī'ting) n. **1** The form of writing peculiar to a given person. **2** Penmanship. **3** Matter written by hand with a pencil, pen, etc.

hand·y (han'dē) adj. **hand·i·er, hand·i·est 1** Ready at hand or convenient for use; nearby. **2** Skillful with the hands. **3** Easy to handle: said of a ship or a tool. —**hand'i·ly** adv. —**hand'i·ness** n.

han·dy·man (han'dē·man') n. pl. **·men** (-mən) One good at odd jobs.

hang (hang) v. **hung** or (*esp. for v. defs. 3 & 9*) **hanged, hang·ing** v.t. **1** To fasten to something above; suspend. **2** To attach, so as to allow some motion. **3** To execute on a gallows. **4** To cover or furnish by something suspended. **5** To fasten in position or at the correct angle. **6** To cause a deadlock, as in a jury's vote. —v.i. **7** To be suspended; dangle. **8** To be suspended without visible support; float. **9** To be put to death on the gallows. **10** To project out; overhang. **11** To droop; incline downward. **12** To be imminent or impending. **13** To be dependent or contingent. **14** To be uncertain or in doubt. **15** To attend closely: to *hang* on someone's words. **16** To be or remain in deadlock, as a jury. —**hang around** (or **about**) **1** To linger or loiter. **2** To group around. —**hang back** To be reluctant. —**hang fire 1** To fail to fire promptly, as a firearm. **2** To be delayed. —**hang in** *Slang* To stay; persevere; hold on. —**hang out 1** To lean out. **2** To suspend out in the open. **3** *Slang* To reside or spend one's time: usu. with *at* or *in.* —**hang together 1** To stay together. **2** To be coherent or consistent. —**hang up 1** To place on hooks or hangers. **2** To end a telephone call by replacing the receiver. **3** To become caught or jammed, as a machine part. **4** To delay or suspend. —n. **1** The way a thing hangs. **2** *Informal* Familiar knowledge; knack. **3** A bit: I don't care a *hang.* —**get the hang of** *Informal* To come to understand or be able to do. [<OE *hangian* hang down and *hon* suspend and ON *hanga*] • *Hanged* and *hung* are the two past tenses and past participles of *hang,* and each has a distinct meaning. Criminals are *hanged.* Pictures, curtains, etc., are *hung.*

han·gar (hang'ər, -gär) n. A shelter or shed, esp. for aircraft. [F]

hang·dog (hang'dôg', -dog') adj. Of mean, sneaking, or abject appearance. —n. A skulking person; sneak.

hang·er (hang'ər) n. **1** One who hangs things. **2** A device on which something is hung. **3** A shaped frame on which a garment is suspended or draped.

hang·er-on (hang'ər·on') n. pl. **hang·ers-on** A self-attached dependent; parasite.

hang·ing (hang'ing) adj. **1** Suspended from something; dangling. **2** Involving death on the gallows. **3** Lying on a slope: a *hanging* garden. **4** Drooping and dejected. **5** Held in abeyance. —n. **1** The act of suspending. **2** Execution on the gallows. **3** Drapery, tapestry, etc., hung from a wall.

hang·man (hang'mən) n. pl. **·men** (-mən) A public executioner.

hang·nail (hang'nāl') n. Skin partially torn loose at the side or root of a fingernail. [Var. of earlier *agnail* <OE *ang-* painful + *nægl* NAIL]

hang·out (hang'out') n. *Slang* A habitual meeting place or resort.

hang·o·ver (hang'ō'vər) n. *Informal* **1** A person, thing, or idea surviving from the past. **2** The aftereffects from overindulgence in alcohol.

hang-up (hang'up') n. *Slang* **1** A psychological difficulty; esp., a neurotic obsession. **2** Anything blocking a natural or normal process.

hank (hangk) n. **1** A measure of yarn, varying for different materials. **2** A rope, string, coil, or tie. [<Scand.]

han·ker (hang'kər) v.i. To yearn; want greatly. [<Du. *hankeren* long for] —**han'ker·er** n.

han·ky-pan·ky (hang′kē-pang′kē) n. Slang Under-handed activity; deception.

Han·sard (han′sərd) n. The printed record of the proceed-ings of the British and Canadian Parliaments. [<Luke Hansard, 1752–1828, Brit. printer]

hanse (hans) n. 1 A guild of medieval merchants. 2 An en-trance fee; esp., one paid by merchants not members of a guild. —the Hanse HANSEATIC LEAGUE. [<OHG hansa band]

Han·se·at·ic League (han′sē-at′ic) A league of about 85 towns and cities in northern Germany and neighboring countries, called **Hanse towns,** which banded together in the Middle Ages for protection and trade.

han·sel (han′səl) n. & v. HANDSEL.

Han·sen's disease (han′sənz) LEPROSY.

han·som (han′səm) n. A low, two-wheeled, one-horse cab, with the driver mounted back of the top. Also **hansom cab.** [<J. A. Hansom, 1803–82, English ar-chitect]

Ha·nuk·kah (khä′-nŏŏ-kə) n. A Jewish festival occurring in early December, in memory of the rededi-cation of the temple at Jerusalem under the Maccabees in 164 B.C. Also **Ha′nu·kah** [<Heb., dedication]

Hansom

hap·haz·ard (hap′haz′ərd) adj. Accidental; happening by chance. —adv. By chance; at random. —n. Mere chance; hazard. [<HAP + HAZARD] —hap′haz′ard·ly adv. — hap′haz′ard·ness n.

hap·less (hap′lis) adj. Unfortunate; unlucky. —hap′-less·ly adv. —hap′less·ness n.

hap·pen (hap′ən) v.i. 1 To take place or occur. 2 To come about or occur by chance. 3 To chance; have the fortune. 4 To come by chance: to happen upon the answer. 5 To come or go by chance: with in, along, by, etc. —happen to 1 To befall. 2 To become of. [<HAP]

hap·pen·ing (hap′ən-ing) n. 1 Something that happens; an event. 2 A staged but usu. partly improvised event, often bizarre, intended to elicit a response.

hap·pen·stance (hap′ən-stans, -stəns) n. Informal A chance occurrence. [<HAPPEN + (CIRCUM)STANCE]

hap·py (hap′ē) adj. ·pi·er, ·pi·est 1 Enjoying, giving, or indi-cating pleasure; joyous; blessed. 2 Fortunately effective; opportune; felicitous. 3 Yielding or marked by great plea-sure. [<HAP] —hap′pi·ly adv. —hap′pi·ness n.

hap·py-go-luck·y (hap′ē-gō-luk′ē) adj. Trusting easily to luck; improvident; haphazard. —adv. As one pleases; anyhow; at will.

Haps·burg (haps′bûrg; Ger. häps′bŏŏrkh) n. A German family whose princes ruled over various parts of Europe from the Middle Ages to 1918. Also **House of Hapsburg.**

ha·ra·ki·ri (hä′rä·kē′rē) n. Ritual suicide by disembowel-ment, practiced by high-ranking Japanese when disgraced or in lieu of execution. Also **ha′ra·ka′ri** (-kä′rē). [<Jap. hara belly + kiri cut]

ha·rangue (hə-rang′) n. An oration; esp., a loud and ve-hement speech. —v. ·rangued, ·rangu·ing v.t. To address in a harangue. —v.i. To deliver a harangue. [<OF] —ha-rangu′er n.

har·ass (har′əs, hə-ras′) v.t. 1 To trouble or worry persist-ently. 2 Mil. To worry (an enemy) by repeated raids and small attacks. [<OF harer set dogs on] —har′ass·er, har′ass-ment n. —Syn. 1 annoy, bother, disturb, plague, torment.

har·bin·ger (här′bin·jər) n. A forerunner and announcer of something to come. —v.t. To act as a harbinger to; pres-age [<OF herbergeor provider of shelter]

har·bor (här′bər) n. 1 A port or haven that provides shel-ter for ships. 2 Any place of refuge or rest. —v.t. 1 To give refuge to; shelter; protect. 2 To entertain in the mind; cherish. —v.i. 3 To take shelter in a habor. Brit. sp. har′bour. [<OE here army + beorg refuge] —har′bor·er n.

har·bor·age (här′bər·ij) n. 1 A port or place of shelter for ships. 2 Any shelter or refuge.

har·bor·mas·ter (här′bər·mas′tər, -mäs′-) n. 1 An offi-cer who inspects vessels in harbor. 2 The chief of the har-bor police.

hard (härd) adj. 1 Solid and firm; not easily dented. 2 Ca-pable of endurance; hardy. 3 Difficult to accomplish or solve. 4 Unyielding; hardhearted. 5 Harsh or cruel: hard words. 6 Shrewd and obstinate. 7 Oppressive; difficult to endure. 8 Rigorous in terms: a hard bargain. 9 Persistent or energetic: a hard worker. 10 Harsh or unpleasant: a hard face. 11 Stormy; inclement: a hard winter. 12 Indis-putable; definite: hard facts. 13 Strictly factual: hard news. 14 Having mineral salts in solution that interfere with the action of soap: hard water. 15 Containing much alcohol: hard liquor. 16 Addictive: said of drugs. 17 Phonet. Denoting c or g when pronounced explosively, as in cod or god, rather than as a fricative or an affricate. —be hard on 1 To treat with severity. 2 To be burdensome or difficult for. —hard of hearing Deaf or partially deaf. —hard up Completely lacking in something, esp. money. —adv. 1 With great energy; vigorously. 2 Intently; earnestly. 3 Harshly or severely. 4 With effort or difficulty. 5 Securely; tightly. 6 So as to become hard: It was frozen hard. 7 In close proximity: We live hard by the church. [<OE heard] —hard′ness n.

hard-and-fast (härd′ən·fast′, -fäst′) adj. Absolutely binding: a hard-and-fast rule.

hard·back (härd′bak′) adj HARD-COVER. —n. A hard-cover book.

hard-bit·ten (härd′bit′n) adj. Tough; unyielding.

hard·board (härd′bôrd′, -bōrd′) n. A material composed of fibers from wood chips pressed into sheets.

hard-boiled (härd′boild′) adj. 1 Boiled until solidified: said of an egg. 2 Informal Hardened or unyielding in char-acter; tough.

hard cash Actual money as distinguished from debts or claims to be collected or settled.

hard coal ANTHRACITE.

hard-core (härd′kôr′) adj. 1 Thoroughly dedicated, de-termined, loyal, etc., to a cause or movement: hard-core radicals. 2 Extremely explicit: hard-core pornography. 3 Of or pertaining to the hard core.

hard core 1 The basic, central, or most important part; nucleus. 2 Unemployed or underemployed people not trained for any job.

hard-cov·er (hard′kuv′ər) adj. Designating a book bound in a rigid material. Also **hard′bound′.**

hard disk A nonflexible computer disk, capable of more information storage and faster read-write capability than a floppy disk.

hard·en (här′dən) v.t. 1 To make hard or harder; make solid. 2 To make unyielding, pitiless, or indifferent. 3 To strengthen or make firm in character, disposition, etc. 4 To make tough, strong, or hardy; inure. —v.i. 5 To become hard. 6 In commerce: a To become higher, as prices. b To become stable. —hard′en·er n.

hard-fist·ed (härd′fis′tid) adj. Avaricious or miserly; stingy. —hard′fist′ed·ly adv. —hard′fist′ed·ness n.

hard-hat (härd′hat′) Informal n. A construction worker. —adj. Having to do with construction work and workers.

hard hat Any of various helmets worn for protection, as by construction workers, motorcyclists, etc. • See HELMET.

hard-head·ed (härd′hed′id) adj. 1 Shrewd and practical. 2 Inclined to obstinacy; stubborn. —hard′head′ed·ly adv. — hard′head′ed·ness n.

hard-heart·ed (härd′här′tid) adj. Lacking pity or sym-pathy; unfeeling. —hard′heart′ed·ly adv. —hard′heart′ed-ness n.

har·di·hood (här′dē·hŏŏd) n. 1 Sturdy courage. 2 Bold-ness; effrontery.

hard line An unyielding position, as in negotiation. — **hard′-line′** adj. —**hard′-lin′er** n.

hard·ly (härd′lē) adv. 1 Scarcely; not quite or only just: He'd hardly arrived before we left. 2 With difficulty or great pains. **3** Not likely; not at all: Are you new on the job? *Hardly!* **4** Rigorously; harshly; severely.

hard-nosed (härd'nōzd') *adj. Slang* Hard-bitten, unyielding, or firmly businesslike.

hard palate The hard front portion of the roof of the mouth. • See MOUTH.

hard·pan (härd'pan') *n.* **1** Hard clay or soil under soft soil. **2** A firm foundation; solid basis.

hard sauce A creamed mixture of butter, sugar, and flavorings, used as a sauce with puddings, etc.

hard sell *Informal* The use of aggressive methods of salesmanship.

hard·shell (härd'shel') *adj.* **1** Having a hard shell, as a lobster or crab, previous to shedding the carapace. **2** Stubbornly devoted to one's principles; uncompromising.

hard·ship (härd'ship') *n.* **1** A difficult condition in life. **2** Anything hard to endure.

hard·tack (härd'tak') *n.* Large, unleavened biscuit used as army and navy rations. [< HARD + earlier *tack* food]

hard·top (härd'top') *adj.* Describing an automobile with the body design of a convertible, but with a rigid top. —*n.* Such a car.

hard·ware (härd'wâr') *n.* **1** Manufactured articles, esp. of metal, as machines, utensils, tools, weapons, etc. **2** The machines and equipment needed for a task or function, esp. in data processing, as distinct from personnel, plans, programs, etc. **3** *Informal* Weapons: military *hardware*.

hard·wood (härd'wood') *n.* **1** Wood of broad-leaved trees as distinguished from that of coniferous trees. **2** Any tough, heavy wood. **3** A tree yielding hardwood.

hard·working (härd'wûrk'ing, härd'wôrk'-) *adj.* Accustomed to working hard; industrious.

har·dy (här'dē) *adj.* **·di·er, ·di·est 1** Inured to hardship; robust. **2** Showing hardihood; bold; audacious; strenuous. **3** Able to survive cold weather without protection: said of plants. **4** Rigid; strong; durable. [< OF *hardir* embolden] —**har'di·ly** *adv.* —**har'di·ness** *n.*

hare (hâr) *n. pl.* **hares** or **hare** Any of various long-eared, herbivorous mammals closely related to rabbits, but larger and swifter. [< OE *hara*]

hare·bell (hâr'bel') *n.* A hardy, widely distributed species of campanula; bluebell. [ME *harebelle*]

hare·brained (hâr'brānd') *adj.* Foolish; flighty.

hare·lip (hâr'lip') *n.* A congenital fissure of the upper lip. —**hare'lipped'** *adj.*

har·em (hâr'əm, har'-) *n.* **1** The apartments of a Muslim household reserved for females. **2** The wives, concubines, etc., occupying the harem. Also **ha·reem** (hä·rēm'). [Ar. *harīm* something forbidden or sacred]

Hare

har·i·cot (har'ə·kō) *n.* **1** A stew of meat, esp. mutton. **2** The seeds or pods of edible beans; also, the kidney bean. [F]

ha·ri·ka·ri (hä'rē·kä'rē) *n.* HARA-KIRI.

hark (härk) *v.i.* To listen: usu. in the imperative. —**hark back** To return to some previous place or point. [ME *herkien*]

hark·en (här'kən) *v.* HEARKEN. —**hark'en·er** *n.*

har·le·quin (här'lə·kwin, -kin) *n.* A buffoon. —*adj.* **1** Comic; buffoonlike. **2** Many-colored, usu. in a diamond pattern. [< OF *Herlequin*]

Har·le·quin (här'lə·kwin, -kin) *n.* A traditional comic character in pantomime, dressed in many-colored tights, wearing a mask, and carrying a wooden sword.

har·lot (här'lət) *n.* A whore; prostitute. [< OF *herlot* fellow, rogue]

har·lot·ry (här'lət·rē) *n.* **1** The trade of a prostitute. **2** Prostitutes collectively.

harm (härm) *n.* **1** That which inflicts injury or loss. **2** The injury inflicted; hurt. **3** Offense against morality; wrong. —*v.t.* To damage; hurt. [< OE *hearm* insult] —**harm'er** *n.* —**Syn.** *n.* **1** blemish, detriment, impairment, abuse.

harm·ful (härm'fəl) *adj.* Able to injure; detrimental. —**harm'ful·ly** *adv.* —**harm'ful·ness** *n.*

harm·less (härm'lis) *adj.* **1** Not harmful; innocuous. **2** Without hurt, loss, or liability. —**harm'less·ly** *adv.* —**harm'less·ness** *n.*

har·mon·ic (här·mon'ik) *adj.* **1** Producing, characterized by, or pertaining to harmony; consonant. **2** *Music* Pertaining to harmony, as distinguished from melody or rhythm. **3** *Physics* Of or pertaining to a component of a periodic quantity whose frequency is an integral multiple of that of the periodic quantity. —*n.* **1** *Physics* **a** Any component of a periodic oscillation whose frequency is an integral multiple of the fundamental frequency. **b** A component of a complex tone having such a frequency. **2** *Music* An overtone, usu. with a harmonic frequency, sounded alone, as by lightly stopping a string. Also **har·mon'i·cal.** [< Gk. *harmonia* harmony] —**har·mon'i·cal·ly** *adv.*

har·mon·i·ca (här·mon'i·kə) *n.* **1** A musical instrument played by blowing through slots containing small metal reeds; a mouth organ. **2** An instrument composed of a series of hemispherical glasses, glass bowls or tubes, etc., played by rubbing the moistened rims with a finger. [< L *harmonicus* harmonic]

Harmonica

harmonic distortion A form of distortion, as in an amplifier, loudspeaker, etc., in which extraneous harmonics are added to the signal.

har·mo·ni·ous (här·mō'nē·əs) *adj.* **1** Characterized by harmony or agreement; in accord. **2** Having the parts pleasingly related; symmetrical, congruous. **3** Pleasing to the ear. —**har·mo'ni·ous·ly** *adv.* —**har·mo'ni·ous·ness** *n.*

har·mo·nist (här'mə·nist) *n.* A master of musical harmony.

har·mo·ni·um (här·mō'nē·əm) *n.* REED ORGAN. [< L *harmonia* harmony]

har·mo·nize (här'mə·nīz) *v.t. & v.i.* **·nized, ·niz·ing 1** To make or become harmonious or suitable. **2** To arrange or sing in musical harmony. *Brit. sp.* **har'mo·nise.** —**har'mo·ni·za'tion, har'mo·niz'er** *n.*

har·mo·ny (här'mə·nē) *n. pl.* **·nies 1** Accord or agreement in feeling, manner, or action. **2** A state of order, agreement, or completeness in the relations of parts of a whole to each other. **3** Pleasing sounds; music. **4** *Music* **a** Any agreeable combination of simultaneous tones. **b** The constitution and succession of groups of tones that sound simultaneously in music. [< Gk. *harmonia* < *harmos* joint]

har·ness (här'nis) *n.* **1** The combination of traces, straps, etc., forming the gear of a draft animal and used to attach it to a vehicle or plow. **2** *Archaic* The defensive armor of a soldier or of his horse. **3** Any similar apparatus or gear. —**in harness** Engaged in one's daily work. —*v.t.* **1** To put harness on, as a horse. **2** To make use of the power of: to *harness* a waterfall. [< OF *harneis*]

harp (härp) *n.* **1** A musical instrument consisting of a roughly triangular frame fitted with strings of graded lengths and played by plucking. **2** Something resembling a harp. —*v.i.* **1** To play on a harp. **2** To speak or write persistently; dwell tediously: with *on* or *upon.* [< OE *hearpe*] —**harp'er, harp'ist** *n.*

har·poon (här·pōōn') *n.* A barbed missile weapon, carrying a long cord, for catching whales or large fish. —*v.t.* To strike with a harpoon. [< OF *harpe* claw] —**har·poon'er, har·poon·eer'** (-ir') *n.*

harp·si·chord (härp'sə·kôrd') *n.* A keyboard instrument similar to a piano, but having the strings plucked by quills or leather points instead of being struck by felt-covered hammers. [< LL *harpa* harp + L *chorda* string] —**harp'si·chord·ist** *n.*

Harp

har·py (här'pē) *n. pl.* **·pies** A rapacious person; a plunderer. [< HARPY]

Har·py (här'pē) *n. pl.* **·pies** *Gk. Myth.* One of three winged monsters with the head of a woman and the legs and talons of a bird. [< Gk. *Harpyia*, lit., seizers]

har·que·bus (här′kwə-bəs) *n.* An ancient hand firearm, the predecessor of the musket. [< MDu. *hakebusse* hook-gun] —**har′que·bus·ier′** (-ir′) *n.*

Harquebus

har·ri·dan (har′ə-dən) *n.* A vixenish old woman; a hag. [< OF *haridelle* a worn-out horse]

har·ri·er¹ (har′ē-ər) *n.* 1 One who or that which harries. 2 Any of various hawks, esp. the marsh hawk.

har·ri·er² (har′ē-ər) *n.* 1 A small hound used for hunting hares. 2 A team runner in a cross-country race. [< HARE]

har·row (har′ō) *n.* A farm implement, commonly a frame set with spikes or vertical disks, for leveling plowed ground or breaking clods. —*v.t.* 1 To draw a harrow over. 2 To disturb the mind or feelings of painfully; distress. —*v.i.* 3 To undergo harrowing. [ME *harwe*] —**har′row·er** *n.* —**Syn.** *v.* 2 oppress, torment, worry. • See DISK HARROW.

har·row·ing (har′ō-ing) *adj.* Lacerating or tormenting to the feelings. —**har′row·ing·ly** *adv.*

har·ry (har′ē) *v.* **har·ried, har·ry·ing** *v.t.* 1 To lay waste; pillage; sack. 2 To harass. —*v.i.* 3 To make raids for plunder. [< OE *hergian* ravage]

harsh (härsh) *adj.* 1 Grating or rough to the senses; discordant; rasping. 2 Rigorous; severe; unfeeling: a *harsh* judge. 3 Bleak in appearance: a *harsh* landscape. [ME *harsk*] —**harsh′ly** *adv.* —**harsh′ness** *n.*

hart (härt) *n.* 1 The male of the European red deer, esp. after it has passed its fifth year. 2 A stag. [< OE *heort*]

harte·beest (härt′bēst′, här′tə-) *n. pl.* **·beests** or **·beest** A large antelope of Africa with long, backward-curving horns. Also **hart′beest.** [< Du. *hert* hart + *beest* beast]

harts·horn (härts′hôrn′) *n.* 1 Sal volatile, formerly obtained from deer horns. 2 The antler of a hart.

har·um-scar·um (hâr′əm·skâr′əm) *adj.* Reckless; irresponsible. —*adv.* In a reckless manner. —*n.* A reckless or thoughtless person. [< obs. *hare* frighten + SCARE]

har·vest (här′vist) *n.* 1 A crop, as of grain, vegetables, fruits, etc., ready for gathering. 2 The time or season of gathering. 3 The act of gathering in a crop. 4 The product of any toil or effort. —*v.t.* 1 To gather (a crop). 2 To gather the crop of (a field, etc.). 3 To achieve as a result of preparation and effort. —*v.i.* 4 To gather a crop. [< OE *hærfest*]

har·vest·er (här′vis·tər) *n.* 1 One who harvests. 2 A reaping machine.

har·vest·man (här′vist·mən) *n. pl.* **·men** (-mən) 1 One who labors in the harvest. 2 DADDY-LONGLEGS.

harvest moon The full moon closest to the autumnal equinox.

has (haz) Present indicative, third person sing. of HAVE.

has-been (haz′bin′) *n. Informal* A person or thing no longer popular or effective.

hash (hash) *n.* 1 A dish of chopped and cooked meat and vegetables, usu. fried. 2 A mess; jumble. 3 Any mixture. 4 *Slang* Hashish. —**make a hash of** *Informal* To bungle; spoil. —**settle (one's) hash** *Informal* To silence, finish off, or put down (a person). —*v.t.* To cut or chop into small pieces; mince. —**hash over** *Informal* To talk or think about carefully; mull. [< OF *hacher* to chop]

hash house *Slang* A cheap restaurant.

hash·ish (hāsh′ēsh, -ish) *n.* The extracted resin of the Indian hemp plant, chewed or smoked for its intoxicating effects. Also **hash′eesh.** [< Ar. *hashīsh* hemp]

Has·i·dim (khä·sē′dim) *n. pl.* of **Has·id** (khä′sid) CHASIDIM.

has·n't (haz′ənt) Contraction of *has not.*

hasp (hasp, häsp) *n.* A fastening for a door, box, etc., passing over a staple and secured usu. by a padlock. —*v.t.* To shut or fasten with a hasp. [< OE *hæpse*]

Hasp

has·sle (has′əl) *Slang n.* A quarrel; squabble. —*v.i.* **·sled, ·sling** 1 To argue. —*v.t.* 2 To annoy; harass. [? < HAGGLE + TUSSLE]

has·sock (has′ək) *n.* 1 An upholstered footstool. 2 A rank tuft of coarse or boggy grass. [< OE *hassuc* coarse grass]

hast (hast) Archaic second person singular, present tense, of HAVE.

haste (hāst) *n.* 1 Speed of movement or action; dispatch. 2 Necessity for speed; urgency. 3 Hurry; precipitancy. —**in haste** 1 Quickly. 2 Thoughtlessly; rashly. —**make haste** To hurry; rush. —*v.t. & v.i.* **hast·ed, hast·ing** *Archaic* To hasten. [< OF < Gmc.]

hast·en (hā′sən) *v.t.* To cause to hurry or move quickly; expedite. —*v.i.* To be quick; hurry. —**hast′en·er** *n.*

hast·y (hās′tē) *adj.* **hast·i·er, hast·i·est** 1 Acting or done with haste. 2 Acting or done impetuously; rash. 3 Quick-tempered; irascible. —**hast′i·ly** *adv.* —**hast′i·ness** *n.*

hasty pudding Pudding made of cereal, seasoning, and boiling water or milk.

hat (hat) *n.* A covering for the head, often with a crown and brim. —**pass the hat** To take up a collection. —**talk through one's hat** *Informal* To talk nonsense; also, to bluff. —**under one's hat** *Informal* Secret; private. —*v.t.* **hat·ted, hat·ting** To cover or supply with a hat. [< OE *hæt*]

hat·band (hat′band′) *n.* A ribbon or other band surrounding a hat above the brim.

hatch¹ (hach) *n.* 1 *Naut.* **a** An opening in the deck of a vessel affording passage to the hold. **b** The cover over a hatch. 2 Any similar opening in the floor or roof of a building. 3 The lid or cover for such an opening. [< OE *hæcc* grating]

hatch² (hach) *v.t.* 1 To bring forth (young) from the egg by incubation. 2 To bring forth young from (the egg). 3 To devise, as a plan. 4 To contrive secretly; plot. —*v.i.* 5 To emerge from the egg. 6 To produce young: said of eggs. —*n.* 1 The act of hatching. 2 The brood hatched at one time. [ME *hacchen*] —**hatch′er** *n.*

hatch³ (hach) *v.t.* To mark with hatchings. —*n.* A shade line in drawing or engraving. [< OF *hache* an ax]

hatch·back (hach′bak′) *n.* An automobile with a hatch that opens upward from the rear of the vehicle.

hatch·er·y (hach′ər·ē) *n. pl.* **·er·ies** A place where the eggs of poultry or fish are hatched in large quantities.

hatch·et (hach′it) *n.* A small short-handled ax, for use with one hand. —**bury the hatchet** To cease from hostilities; make peace. [< OF *hache* an ax]

hatch·ing (hach′ing) *n.* 1 In drawing and engraving, the marking with fine parallel lines for shading. 2 Such lines or shading.

hatch·ment (hach′mənt) *n. Her.* The armorial bearings of a dead person, usu. blazoned on a lozenge-shaped panel, as over a tomb. [Alter. of ACHIEVEMENT]

Hatchets

hatch·way (hach′wā′) *n.* HATCH¹.

hate (hāt) *v.* **hat·ed, hat·ing** *v.t.* 1 To regard with extreme aversion; detest. 2 To be unwilling; dislike. —*v.i.* 3 To feel hatred. —*n.* 1 Intense aversion; animosity. 2 A person or thing detested. [< OE *hatian*] —**hat′er** *n.*

hate·ful (hāt′fəl) *adj.* 1 Exciting strong aversion; odious. 2 Feeling or showing hatred. —**hate′ful·ly** *adv.*

hath (hath) Archaic third person singular, present tense, of HAVE.

ha·tred (hā′trid) *n.* Bitter dislike or aversion; antipathy; animosity. —**Syn.** abhorrence, detestation, enmity, hate, hostility.

hat·ter (hat′ər) *n.* One who makes or deals in hats.

hau·berk (hô′bûrk) *n.* A coat of chain mail. [< OF *hauberc*]

haugh·ty (hô′tē) *adj.* **·ti·er, ·ti·est** 1 Proud and disdainful; arrogant. 2 *Archaic* Lofty; exalted. [< OF *haut* high] —**haugh′ti·ly** *adv.* —**haugh′ti·ness** *n.*

haul (hôl) *v.t.* 1 To pull or draw with force; drag. 2 To transport as if by pulling. 3 *Naut.* To shift the course of (a ship) —*v.i.* 4 To drag or pull. 5 To shift in direction: said of the wind. 6 *Naut.* To change course, esp. so as to sail nearer the wind. —**haul off** 1 To draw back the arm so as to deliver a blow. 2 *Naut.* To change course so as to move

farther away from an object. **—haul up 1** To come to a stop. **2** *Naut.* To sail nearer the wind. **—n. 1** A pulling with force. **2** That which is obtained by hauling. **3** The drawing of a fish net. **4** The amount caught in, or as in, one pull of a net. **5** The distance over which anything is hauled. [< OF *haler* < Gmc.] **—haul′er** *n.*

haul·age (hô′lij) *n.* **1** The act of hauling. **2** The force used in hauling. **3** The charge made for hauling.

haunch (hônch, hänch) *n.* **1** The fleshy part of the hip, the buttock, and the upper thigh. **2** The combined loin and leg of an animal. [< OF *hanche* < Gmc.] **—haunched** *adj.*

haunt (hônt, hänt) *v.t.* **1** To visit frequently or customarily. **2** To appear to as a disembodied spirit. **3** To recur persistently to the mind or memory of. **4** To visit often; frequent, as a saloon. **—v.i. 5** To make ghostly appearances. **—n. 1** A place often visited. **2** *Regional* A ghost. [< OF *hanter* < Gmc.] **—haunt′er** *n.*

haunt·ed (hôn′tid, hän′-) *adj.* Frequently visited, esp. by ghosts or apparitions.

haunt·ing (hôn′ting, hän′-) *adj.* Difficult to forget; frequently occurring to memory. **—haunt′ing·ly** *adv.*

haut·boy (hō′boi, ō′-) *n.* OBOE. [< F *haut* high (in tone) + *bois* wood]

haute cou·ture (ōt kōō·tür′) High fashion, represented esp. by the leading designers of stylish apparel. [F, lit., high sewing]

haute cul·sine (ōt kwi·zēn′, *Fr.* ōt kwē·zēn′) An elaborate or elegant cuisine. [F, lit., high cooking]

hau·teur (hō·tûr′, *Fr.* ō·tœr′) *n.* Haughty manner or spirit; haughtiness. [F]

haut monde (ō mônd) *French* High society.

have (hav) *v.t.* Present indicative: I, you, we, they **have** (*Archaic* **thou hast**), he, she, it **has** (*Archaic* **hath**); past indicative **had** (*Archaic* **thou hadst**); present subjunctive **have**; past subjunctive **had**; *p.p.* **had**; *pr.p.* **hav·ing 1** To hold as a possession; own. **2** To possess as a characteristic, attribute, etc. **3** To receive; get: I *had* a letter today. **4** To entertain, as an opinion or doubt. **5** To manifest or exercise: *Have* patience! **6** To experience; undergo. **7** To be affected with. **8** To carry on; engage in. **9** To cause to be: *Have* him here at 9 o'clock. **10** To allow or tolerate: I will *have* no interference. **11** To possess a certain relation to: to *have* the wind at one's back. **12** To be in relationship or association with: to *have* three children. **13** To bring forth or beget (young). **14** To maintain or declare: so rumor *has* it. **15** *Informal* To baffle: He *had* me there. **16** *Informal* To trick; cheat: I've been *had!* **17** *Informal* To engage in sexual relations with. **—auxiliary** As an auxiliary *have* is used: **a** With past participles to express completed action: I *have* gone. **b** With the infinitive to express obligation: I *have* to go. **—have at** To attack. **—have done** To stop; desist. **—have it in for** *Informal* To hold a grudge against. **—have it out** To continue a fight or discussion to a final settlement. **—have on** To be clothed in. [< OE *habban*]

ha·ven (hā′vən) *n.* **1** An anchorage for ships; harbor; port. **2** A refuge; shelter. **—v.t.** To shelter (a vessel, etc.). [< OE *hæfen*] **—Syn.** *n.* **2** asylum, retreat, sanctuary.

have-not (hav′not′) *n.* A person or country lacking in resources and wealth.

have·n't (hav′ənt) Contraction of *have not.*

hav·er·sack (hav′ər·sak) *n.* A bag, slung from the shoulder, for a soldier's or a hiker's rations. [< G *Habersack* oat sack]

hav·oc (hav′ək) *n.* **1** General carnage or destruction; ruin. **2** Tumultuous disorder, confusion, or uproar. **—cry havoc** To give a signal for pillage and destruction. **—play havoc with** To bring to confusion; destroy; ruin. **—v.t.** **hav·ocked, hav·ock·ing** *Archaic* To lay waste; destroy. [< OF *havot* plunder < Gmc.] **—hav′ock·er** *n.*

haw¹ (hô) *n. & interj.* A sound used in hesitating speech. **—v.i.** To hesitate in speaking: to hem and *haw.*

haw² (hô) *n.* The fruit of the hawthorn. [< OE *haga*]

haw³ (hô) *n. & interj.* An order to turn to the left, given to a yoked team. **—v.t. & v.i.** To turn to the left. [?]

Ha·wai·ian (hə·wī′yən) *adj.* Of or pertaining to the Hawaiian Islands, their people, or their language. **—n.** **1** A native or citizen of the Hawaiian Islands. **2** The Polynesian language of the aboriginal Hawaiians.

Hawaiian Islands A group of islands in the N Pacific constituting the state of Hawaii.

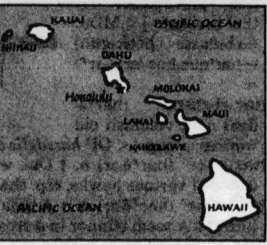

Hawaiian Islands

hawk¹ (hôk) *n.* **1** Any of various birds of prey related to eagles and kites, with relatively short rounded wings, a hooked beak, and strong claws. **2** One who favors militancy rather than conciliation and negotiation, as in a dispute. **—v.i. 1** To hunt game with trained hawks. **—v.t. 2** To hunt or catch in flight, as a hawk does. [< OE *hafoc, hafuc*] **—hawk′er** *n.* **—hawk′ish** *adj.*

hawk² (hôk) *v.t. & v.i.* To cry (goods) for sale in the streets or in public places; peddle. [Back formation < HAWKER]

hawk³ (hôk) *v.t.* **1** To cough up (phlegm). **—v.i. 2** To clear the throat with a coughing sound. **—n.** The sound of a forcible effort to raise phlegm from the throat. [Imit.]

hawk·er (hô′kər) *n.* One who cries goods for sale; a street peddler. [< MLG *hoker* a peddler, huckster]

hawk·eyed (hôk′īd′) *adj.* Having keen eyesight.

hawk moth Any of a family of stout-bodied moths having a long mouthpiece for sucking the nectar from flowers.

hawks·bill (hôks′bil′) A tropical sea turtle with a carapace of overlapping scales valued as tortoise shell. Also **hawk′bill, hawk′s-bill.**

hawse·hole (hôz′hōl′) *n. Naut.* A hole in the bow of a vessel for the passage of a hawser.

haw·ser (hô′zər) *n. Naut.* A large rope or cable used in mooring, towing, etc. [< OF *haucier* to lift]

haw·thorn (hô′thôrn) *n.* Any of various thorny, spring-flowering shrubs or small trees of the rose family with white or pink flowers and small applelike fruits. [< OE *haguthorn*]

hay (hā) *n.* Grass, clover, etc., cut and dried for fodder. **—v.t. 1** To plant (land) with hay. **—v.i. 2** To process grass, etc.; make hay. [< OE *hēg*]

hay·cock (hā′kok′) *n.* A dome-shaped pile of hay in a field.

hay fever An allergic reaction to pollen or other antigens characterized by sneezing and inflammation of the eyes and air passages.

hay·loft (hā′lôft′, -loft′) *n.* A loft in a barn or stable for storing hay.

hay·mak·er (hā′mā′kər) *n.* **1** One who makes hay. **2** *Slang* A powerful, swinging blow of the fist.

hay·mow (hā′mou′) *n.* **1** A mass of hay stored in a hayloft. **2** A hayloft.

hay·ride (hā′rīd′) *n.* A pleasure ride in a wagon partly filled with hay.

hay·seed (hā′sēd′) *n. Slang* A country person; yokel.

hay·stack (hā′stak′) *n.* A pile of hay. Also **hay·rick** (hā′rik′).

hay·wire (hā′wīr′) *n.* Wire for baling hay. **—adj.** *Slang* **1** Confused; mixed up. **2** Crazy: to go *haywire.* [Slang sense < loggers' term for poor or broken equipment mended with haywire]

haz·ard (haz′ərd) *n.* **1** Exposure to loss or injury; risk; peril. **2** A chance result or occurrence. **3** A gambling game played with dice. **4** An obstacle on a golf course, as a bunker or sand trap. **—v.t. 1** To expose to danger; imperil. **2** To risk; venture. [< OF *hasard*] **—Syn.** *n.* **1** danger, jeopardy. **2** gamble, risk, speculation.

haz·ard·ous (haz′ər·dəs) *adj.* Involving danger of risk or loss. **—haz′ard·ous·ly** *adv.* **—haz′ard·ous·ness** *n.*

haze¹ (hāz) *n.* **1** Very fine suspended particles in the air, as of smoke or dust. **2** A vague or muddled mental state. [Back formation < HAZY]

haze² (hāz) *v.t.* **hazed, haz·ing** To subject (new students, members, etc.) to humiliating horseplay or pointless harassment. [?] **—haz′er** *n.*

ha·zel (hā′zəl) *n.* **1** A bushy shrub or small tree of the birch family yielding a hard-shelled edible nut. **2** A yellowish brown. **—adj.** Of the color hazel. [< OE *hæsel*]

ha·zel·nut (hā′zəl·nut′) *n.* The nut of the hazel.

haz·y (hā′zē) *adj.* **haz·i·er, haz·i·est 1** Misty, smoky, etc. **2** Confused; obscure. [?] **—haz′i·ly** *adv.* **—haz′i·ness** *n.*

H-bomb (āch′bom′) *n.* HYDROGEN BOMB.

he (hē) *pron.* **1** The male person or being previously mentioned or understood, in the nominative case. **2** Anyone: *He* who hesitates is lost. **—***n. pl.* **hes** A male. [< OE]

He helium.

head (hed) *n.* **1** The part of the body of man and most animals that contains the brain and the ears, eyes, mouth, and nose. **2** An analogous part in other organisms. **3** A representation of a head, as in art. **4** Mind; intelligence: Use your *head.* **5** Mental aptitude: a good *head* for figures. **6** Mental poise; self-possession: He kept his *head.* **7** A person: learned *heads.* **8** (*pl.* **head**) An individual considered as a unit of counting: six *head* of cattle. **9** A part or end that has a shape, position, or relationship resembling or analogous to that of a head: the *head* of a bed. **10** The source, as of a river. **11** The fore or forward part: the *head* of a column of troops. **12** A headland; cape. **13** A leader, chief; director. **14** One having topmost rank: the *head* of one's profession. **15** The top or uppermost part: the *head* of the stairs. **16** A heading, headline, etc. **17** A division of a subject, discourse, etc.: He had little to say on that *head.* **18** Culmination; climax: to come to a *head.* **19** The maturated part of a boil or abscess before breaking. **20** Advance in the face of opposition: to make *head* against the storm. **21** A compact cluster of leaves, flowers, or seeds, as of cabbage, clover, or grain. **22** The foam that rises to the surface of beer, ale, etc. **23** The measure of stored-up force or capacity, as of steam. **24** The height of a column or body of fluid above a certain point, considered as causing pressure: a *head* of water driving a turbine. **25** The striking, holding, or pushing part, as of a club, hammer, pin, etc. **26** The obverse of a coin. **27** *Naut.* A toilet. **28** The membrane stretched over a drum or tambourine. **29** The active part of a tool or device: a cutting *head;* a recording *head.* **30** HEADMASTER. **31** *Slang* One who habitually uses a drug that distorts perception, as LSD or marihuana: an acid *head;* a *pothead.* **—go to one's head 1** To make intoxicated or lightheaded. **2** To cause to become conceited. **—out of** (or **off**) **one's head** Crazy; delirious. **—over one's head 1** Beyond one's ability to understand. **2** To someone of higher authority. **—turn one's head** To make vain or conceited. **—***v.t.* **1** To be first or foremost in or on: to *head* the list. **2** To be chief or leader of; command. **3** To turn or direct the course of: to *head* a vessel toward shore. **4** To furnish with a head. **5** To remove the head or top of, as a tree. **6** In soccer, to hit (the ball) with the head. **—***v.i.* **7** To move in a specified direction or toward a specified point. **8** To come to or form a head. **—head off** To intercept the course of: We'll *head* him *off* at the pass. **—head up** *Informal* To be in charge. **—***adj.* **1** Principal; chief. **2** Situated at the top or front. **3** Directed against the front: a *head* wind. [< OE *hēafod*]

head·ache (hed′āk′) *n.* **1** A pain in the head. **2** *Informal* A source of vexation or trouble. **—head′ach·y** (-ā′kē) *adj.*

head·board (hed′bôrd′, -bōrd′) *n.* A board at the head, as of a bed.

head·cheese (hed′chēz′) *n.* A pressed, jellied loaf made of small pieces of the head and feet of a hog or calf.

head·dress (hed′dres′) *n.* **1** A covering or ornament for the head. **2** A hair style; coiffure.

head·ed (hed′id) *adj.* **1** Furnished with a head or heading. **2** Formed or grown into a head. **3** Having a specified kind or number of heads: used in combination: *flat-headed, two-headed.*

head·er (hed′ər) *n.* **1** *Informal* A headlong fall or plunge. **2** A device for putting on the heads of nails, pins, etc. **3** A machine for removing the heads of grain.

head·first (hed′fûrst′) *adv.* **1** With the head leading or foremost. **2** Impetuously; precipitately. Also **head′fore′·most′** (-fôr′mōst′, -mōst, -fōr′-).

head·gear (hed′gir′) *n.* **1** A headdress or the like. **2** The parts of a harness fitted around the head.

head·hunt·ing (hed′hun′ting) *n.* Among certain primi-

tive peoples, the custom of decapitating slain enemies and preserving the heads as trophies. **—head′-hunt′er** *n.*

head·ing (hed′ing) *n.* **1** Something at the head or top part. **2** A title, caption, or the like at the top or beginning of a page, chapter, division, etc.

head·land (hed′land) A cliff or point of land projecting into a body of water.

head·less (hed′lis) *adj.* **1** Without a head. **2** Without a leader. **3** Stupid.

head·light (hed′līt′) *n.* A powerful front light, as of a vehicle.

head·line (hed′līn′) *n.* **1** An attention-getting word or words set in large type at the head of a newspaper column or news story. **2** A line at the head of a page, containing title, page number, etc. **—***v.t.* **·lined, ·lin·ing 1** To provide with a headline. **2** To be the headliner of (a show, etc.).

head·lin·er (hed′lī′nər) *n.* The main performer or act, as of a variety show.

head·lock (hed′lok′) *n.* A wrestling grip in which an adversary's head is held between one's arm and body.

head·long (hed′lông′, -long′) *adv.* **1** Headfirst. **2** Impetuously; rashly. **3** With unbridled speed or force. **—***adj.* **1** Done with the head leading: a *headlong* plunge. **2** Impetuous; rash. **3** Rapid and forceful.

head·man (hed′mən, -man′) *n. pl.* **·men** (mən) **1** A leader or person of authority. **2** A workman in charge of other workers; foreman; overseer.

head·mas·ter (hed′mas′tər, -mäs′-) *n.* The man in charge of a usu. private school. Also **head master.**

head·mis·tress (hed′mis′tris) *n.* The woman in charge of a usu. private school. Also **head mistress.**

head·most (hed′mōst′) *adj.* Most advanced; foremost.

head·on (hed′on′, -ôn′) *adj.* Front end to front end; a *head-on* collision. **—***adv.* **1** With the front ends meeting: to collide *head-on.* **2** Directly: to meet adversity *head-on.*

head·phone (hed′fōn′) *n.* A device for changing electric signals to sound, held to the ear by a band passing over the head.

head·piece (hed′pēs′) *n.* **1** A protective covering for the head. **2** Intelligence.

head·quar·ters (hed′kwôr′tərz) *n.pl.* (*often construed as sing.*) **1** The operating base of one in command, as of an army unit or police force. **2** Any center of operations.

head·set (hed′set′) *n.* **1** A pair of headphones. **2** A device for holding an earphone and a transmitter at one's head.

head·ship (hed′ship) *n.* The office or position of one having chief authority.

heads·man (hedz′mən) *n. pl.* **·men** (-mən) One who executes those condemned to be beheaded.

head·stall (hed′stôl′) *n.* The part of a bridle that fits over the horse's head.

head·stand (hed′stand′) *n.* The act of holding one's body upside-down in a vertical position.

head start An advance start or advantage, as in a race or comparable situation.

head·stock (hed′stok′) *n. Mech.* A device supporting the end or head of a part.

head·stone (hed′stōn′) *n.* A stone marking the head of a grave.

head·strong (hed′strông′, -strong′) *adj.* **1** Stubbornly bent on having one's own way; willfully obstinate. **2** Characterized by such obstinacy. **—head′strong′ness** *n.*

heads-up (hedz′up′) *adj. Slang* Smart or alert: used esp. of sports competition: a *heads-up* play.

head·wait·er (hed′wā′tər) *n.* In a restaurant, one who supervises the seating of guests, the activities of waiters, etc.

head·wa·ters (hed′wô′tərz, -wot′ərz) *n. pl.* The waters at or near the source of a river or stream.

head·way (hed′wā′) *n.* **1** Forward motion; progress. **2** The interval of time between scheduled vehicles. **3** Overhead clearance, as under an arch.

head wind A wind blowing directly opposite to the course of a ship, airplane, etc.

head·work (hed′wûrk′) *n.* Mental labor.

head·y (hed′ē) *adj.* **head·i·er, head·i·est 1** Tending to affect

---

the mind or senses; intoxicating. 2 Headstrong. —**head'i·ly** *adv.* —**head'i·ness** *n.*

heal (hēl) *v.t.* 1 To restore to health or soundness; make well again. 2 To cause the cure or recovery of (a wound, injury, etc.). 3 To smooth over or resolve (a breach, quarrel, etc.). 4 To free from grief, worry, etc. —*v.i.* 5 To become well or sound. 6 To perform a cure or cures. [< OE *hǣlan*] —**heal'a·ble** *adj.* —**heal'er** *n.*

health (helth) *n.* 1 Soundness of body or mind; well-being. 2 General condition of body or mind: poor *health.* 3 General well-being, as of a nation. 4 A toast wishing good health. [< OE *hǣlth*]

health·ful (helth'fəl) *adj.* 1 Promoting good health; wholesome. 2 Healthy. —**health'ful·ly** *adv.* —**health'ful·ness** *n.*

health·y (hel'thē) *adj.* **health·i·er, health·i·est** 1 Having good health. 2 Indicative or characteristic of sound health: a *healthy* complexion. 3 Conducive to health or well-being. 4 *Informal.* Hearty; big: a *healthy* shove. —**health'i·ly** *adv.* —**health'i·ness** *n.* —**Syn.** 1 healthful, well, sound, hardy, hale. 2 vigorous, strong, robust.

heap (hēp) *n.* 1 A collection of things piled up; a pile. 2 *Often pl. Informal* A large number; lot. —*v.t.* 1 To pile into a heap. 2 To fill or pile into or onto to an excessive degree. 3 To give or bestow in great quantities: to *heap* insults on someone. —*v.i.* 4 To form or rise in a heap. [< OE *hēap* a crowd]

hear (hir) *v.* **heard** (hûrd), **hear·ing** *v.t.* 1 To perceive (sound) by means of the ear. 2 To listen to. 3 To give heed to. 4 To learn or be informed of: I *hear* you are leaving town. 5 To listen to and review in an official capacity: to *hear* a case in court. 6 To respond to and grant: *Hear* our prayers! —*v.i.* 7 To perceive or be capable of perceiving sound by means of the ear. 8 To be informed or made aware. [< OE *hēran*] —**hear'er** *n.*

hear·ing (hir'ing) *n.* 1 The capacity to hear. 2 The sense by which sounds are perceived. 3 An opportunity to be heard. 4 The range within which sound may be heard. 5 A judicial examination, as of an accused person.

heark·en (här'kən) *v.i.* To pay attention; listen attentively. [< OE *heorcnian*]

hear·say (hir'sā') *n.* Information received indirectly, as through common talk; rumor.

hearse (hûrs) *n.* A vehicle used in a funeral for carrying a dead person to the cemetery. [ME *herse* a harrow, frame]

heart (härt) *n.* 1 A hollow muscular structure which maintains the circulation of the blood by alternate contraction and dilation. 2 Feeling, as compassion, earnest desire, or deep emotion, regarded as emanating from the heart. 3 Love; affection: to win her *heart.* 4 Mood; spirit: a heavy *heart.* 5 Courage; resolution: to lose *heart.* 6 A person, esp. one regarded with love or affection: many brave *hearts.* 7 Innermost part; core or center. 8 Essential part; gist: the *heart* of the matter. 9 A conventionalized representation of the heart. 10 a A playing card marked with this symbol. b *pl.* The suit of cards bearing this symbol. 11 *pl.* A card game in which one tries to win none or all of the hearts. [< OE *heorte*]

Heart
a. arteries to head and arms.
b. aorta. c. pulmonary artery.
d. pulmonary vein. e. left atrium.
f. left ventricle. g. aorta carries blood to abdomen and legs.
h. right ventricle. i. inferior vena cava. j. right atrium.
k. superior vena cava.

heart·ache (härt'āk') *n.* Deep mental anguish; grief; sorrow.

heart·beat (härt'bēt') *n.* One complete cycle of dilation and contraction of the heart.

heart·break (härt'brāk') *n.* Deep grief; overwhelming sorrow. —**heart'break'ing** *adj.* —**heart'break'ing·ly** *adv.*

heart·bro·ken (härt'brō'kən) *adj.* Overwhelmingly grieved.

heart·burn (härt'bûrn') *n.* A burning sensation in the esophagus, due to regurgitation of acid from the stomach.

heart·ed (här'tid) *adj.* Having a specified kind of heart: used in combination: *kindhearted.*

heart·en (här'tən) *v.t.* To give courage to.

heart·felt (härt'felt') *adj.* Deeply felt; most sincere.

hearth (härth) *n.* 1 The floor of a fireplace, furnace, etc. 2 The fireside; home. 3 In a blast furnace, the lowest part, through which the melted metal flows. [< OE *heorth*]

hearth·stone (härth'stōn') *n.* 1 A stone forming a hearth. 2 A fireside; home.

heart·i·ly (här'tə·lē) *adv.* 1 Sincerely or cordially. 2 Earnestly; enthusiastically. 3 Abundantly and with good appetite. 4 Completely; thoroughly.

heart·less (härt'lis) *adj.* Without sympathy or compassion; pitiless. —**heart'less·ly** *adv.* —**heart'less·ness** *n.*

heart·rend·ing (härt'ren'ding) *adj.* Causing great anguish or distress. —**heart'rend'ing·ly** *adv.*

heart·sick (härt'sik') *adj.* Deeply disappointed or despondent. Also **heart'sore'** (-sôr', -sōr').

heart·strick·en (härt'strik'ən) *adj.* Overwhelmed with grief or fear.

heart·strings (härt'stringz') *n.pl.* The strongest feelings or affections.

heart-to-heart (härt'tə-härt') *adj.* Frank, intimate, and sincere: a *heart-to-heart* talk.

heart·wood (härt'wŏŏd') *n.* The hard older wood at the central part of a tree trunk or woody stem.

heart·y (här'tē) *adj.* **heart·i·er, heart·i·est** 1 Cordial; genial: a *hearty* welcome. 2 Strongly felt; vigorous: a *hearty* dislike. 3 Healthy; robust. 4 Plentiful and satisfying: a *hearty* meal. —*n. pl.* **heart·ies** *Archaic* A fellow or comrade, esp. a sailor. —**heart'i·ness** *n.*

heat (hēt) *n.* 1 The condition or sensation of being hot. 2 Comparatively high temperature or degree of warmth. 3 Energy associated with and proportional to the random motions of the molecules of a substance or body. 4 The condition or process of maintaining a warm temperature, as in a home. 5 Hot weather or climate. 6 Intensity, as of feeling, excitement, or activity. 7 A time or instance of such activity or feeling: the *heat* of battle. 8 A recurring state of sexual activity in female mammals. 9 In sports: a A single bout or round. b A preliminary race to determine the finalists. —*v.t. & v.i.* 1 To make or become hot or warm. 2 To excite or become excited. [< OE *hǣtu*]

heat·ed (hē'tid) *adj.* Marked by aroused feelings, esp. anger: a *heated* debate. —**heat'ed·ly** *adv.*

heat·er (hē'tər) *n.* A device or apparatus designed to generate or transmit heat.

heath (hēth) *n.* 1 *Chiefly Brit.* An area of open land covered with heather or similar dense, low-growing, shrubby growth. 2 Heather or a similar plant. [< OE *hǣth*]

hea·then (hē'thən) *n. pl.* **·thens** or **·then** 1 One who does not worship the God of Judaism, Christianity, or Islam; a pagan. 2 Any irreligious or primitively ignorant person. —*adj.* Of or typical of a heathen or heathens; pagan. —**hea'then·dom** *n.* —**hea'then·ish** *adj.* [< OE *hǣthen*]

heath·er (heth'ər) *n.* Any of several low-growing evergreen shrubs with minute leaves and small, densely clustered pinkish-lavender flowers. [< ME *hadder?* < HEATH] —**heath'er·y** *adj.*

heat lightning Sporadic lightning without thunder, usu. seen near the horizon at the close of a hot day.

heat wave A prolonged period of hot weather.

heave (hēv) *v.* **heaved** or *chiefly Naut.* **hove, heav·ing** *v.t.* 1 To raise with effort. 2 To throw with effort or force. 3 To cause to swell, rise, or move up and down. 4 To emit with a deep breath, as a sigh. 5 *Naut.* a To raise, haul up, or pull on (an anchor, cable, etc.). b To cause (a ship) to move by or as by hauling on cables or ropes. —*v.i.* 6 To rise, swell up, or move up and down repeatedly. 7 To breathe with effort; gasp. 8 To vomit or retch. 9 *Naut.* a To move or proceed: said of ships. b To haul, pull, or push. —*n.* The action, effort, or result of heaving. [< OE *hebban*] —**heav'·er** *n.*

heav·en (hev'ən) *n.* **1** In Christian theology, the abode of God, the angels, and of deserving souls after death. **2** A similar state or concept in other religions. **3** A place or condition of supreme happiness. **4** *Often pl.* Divine providence. **5** *Usu. pl.* The region above and surrounding the earth; the sky. [< OE *heofon*] —**heav'·en·ward** *adj., adv.* —**heav'·en·wards** *adv.*

Heav·en (hev'ən) *n.* God; Providence.

heav·en·ly (hev'ən·lē) *adj.* **1** Of or belonging to the heaven of God or theology. **2** Of the sky or extraterrestrial universe: *heavenly* bodies. **3** Characterized by great happiness or beauty. —**heav'·en·li·ness** *n.*

heaves (hēvz) *n.pl. (construed as sing. or pl.)* A respiratory disease of horses resulting in quick, labored breathing, heaving of the flanks, and coughing.

Heav·i·side layer (hev'ē·sīd) A layer of the ionosphere which begins about 65 miles above the earth and reflects certain radio waves. [< O. *Heaviside*, d. 1925, English physicist]

heav·y (hev'ē) *adj.* **heav·i·er, heav·i·est** **1** Of great or considerable weight; hard to lift or carry. **2** Of relatively great weight in relation to volume: a *heavy* metal. **3** Of more than the usual weight, thickness, etc.: a *heavy* fabric. **4** Laden or as if laden or weighted: air *heavy* with moisture. **5** Of or involving a great amount, volume, etc.: *heavy* trading. **6** Forceful; powerful: a *heavy* blow. **7** Concentrated; intense: *heavy* gunfire. **8** Thick, broad, and massive: *heavy* features. **9** Pervasive and often oppressive: a *heavy* odor. **10** Hard to do: *heavy* work. **11** Hard to bear; oppressive: *heavy* taxes. **12** Sorrowful; despondent: a *heavy* heart. **13** Serious; grave: a *heavy* offense. **14** Dull; ponderous: a *heavy* prose style. **15** Lacking lightness, grace, etc.: a *heavy* tread. **16** Having a dense, doughy texture. **17** Not easily digested. **18** Using or consuming something in great amounts: a *heavy* eater. **19** Of a theatrical role, intensely dramatic. **20** Pregnant: *heavy* with child. **21** Producing on a large or massive scale: *heavy* industry. **22** *Mil.* **a** Of great size, weight, etc.: *heavy* artillery. **b** Armed with such equipment: *heavy* infantry. —*adv.* Heavily. —*n. pl.* **heav·ies** **1** A heavy, dramatic theatrical role, as that of a villain; also, one who plays such a role. **2** Something heavy. [< OE *hefig*] —**heav'·i·ly** *adv.* —**heav'·i·ness** *n.*

heav·y-dut·y (hev'ē·dyōō'tē) *adj.* Made so as to bear up under long wear, strain, or use.

heav·y-hand·ed (hev'ē·han'did) *adj.* **1** Lacking adroitness; clumsy. **2** Oppressive; overbearing. —**heav'·y-hand'ed·ly** *adv.* —**heav'·y-hand'ed·ness** *n.* —**Syn.** 1 bungling, awkward, unhandy. 2 inconsiderate, insensitive, thoughtless.

heav·y-heart·ed (hev'ē·här'tid) *adj.* Sad; despondent. —**heav'·y-heart'ed·ly** *adv.* —**heav'·y-heart'ed·ness** *n.*

heavy hydrogen DEUTERIUM.

heavy spar BARITE.

heavy water Water composed of oxygen and deuterium.

heav·y·weight (hev'ē·wāt') *n.* **1** One of more than average weight. **2** A boxer or wrestler over 175 pounds in weight. **3** *Informal* A person of considerable importance, influence, etc.

He·be (hē'bē) *Gk. Myth.* The goddess of youth and the cupbearer of the gods.

He·bra·ic (hi·brā'ik) *adj.* Relating to or characteristic of the Hebrew people, culture, language, etc. Also **He·bra'i·cal.** [< Gk. *Hebraios* Hebrew] —**He·bra'i·cal·ly** *adv.*

He·bra·ism (hē'brā·iz'əm, -brə-) *n.* **1** A distinctive characteristic of Hebrew culture, thought, etc. **2** A Hebrew idiom. **3** Judaism. —**He'bra·is'tic** or **·tic·al** *adj.*

He·bra·ist (hē'brā·ist, -brə-) *n.* One learned in Hebrew or having a scholarly knowledge of Hebraic thought and traditions.

He·brew (hē'brōō) *n.* **1** A member of one of the Semitic peoples claiming descent from Abraham; an Israelite. **2** The Semitic language of these people, used in the Old Testament and by Jews as a scholarly and religious language. **3** A modern form of this language, used esp. in Israel. —**Epistle to the Hebrews** A New Testament book

addressed to Hebrew Christians: also **Hebrews.** —*adj.* Of or relating to the Hebrews.

Hebrew calendar JEWISH CALENDAR.

Hec·a·te (hek'ə·tē) *Gk. Myth.* A goddess of the earth, moon, and underworld.

heck (hek) *interj. Slang* A euphemism for hell.

heck·le (hek'əl) *v.t.* **heck·led, heck·ling** To harass (a speaker) with taunts, annoying questions, etc. [< ME *hechele* a comb for flax] —**heck'ler** *n.*

hec·tare (hek'târ) *n.* A metric unit of area equal to 10,000 square meters, or 2.471 acres. [F < Gk. *hekaton* a hundred + F *are* ARE[2]]

hec·tic (hek'tik) *adj.* **1** Characterized by intense excitement, chaotic confusion, etc. **2** Characterized by the flushed, feverish, or wasted condition associated with certain diseases, as tuberculosis. [< Gk. *hektikos* consumptive] —**hec'ti·cal·ly** *adv.*

hec·to·graph (hek'tə·graf, -gräf) *n.* A duplicating device having a gelatin pad for making multiple copies of a writing or drawing. —*v.t.* To copy by hectograph. [< Gk. *hekaton* a hundred + -GRAPH] —**hec'to·graph'ic** *adj.*

hec·tor (hek'tər) *v.t. & v.i.* **1** To bully; badger. **2** To tease; torment. —*n.* A bully. [< HECTOR]

Hec·tor (hek'tər) *Gk. Myth.* A Trojan hero, son of Priam and Hecuba, killed by Achilles.

Hec·u·ba (hek'yōō·bə) *Gk. Myth.* The wife of Priam.

he'd (hēd) Contraction of *he had* or *he would.*

hedge (hej) *n.* **1** A fence or barrier formed by bushes set close together. **2** The act or an instance of hedging. —*v.* **hedged, hedg·ing** *v.t.* **1** To surround or border with a hedge. **2** To guard or hem in with or as with barriers: usu. with *in.* **3** To try to compensate for possible loss from (a bet, investment, etc.) by making offsetting bets or investments. —*v.i.* **4** To make offsetting bets, investments, etc. **5** To avoid definite statement or involvement; refuse to commit oneself. [< OE *hegg*] —**hedg'er** *n.*

hedge·hog (hej'hôg', -hog') *n.* **1** A small, nocturnal, insectivorous mammal of the Old World having the back and sides covered with stout spines. **2** The porcupine.

hedge·hop (hej'hop') *v.i.* **·hopped, ·hop·ping** To fly close to the ground in an airplane. —**hedge'hop'per** *n.*

hedge·row (hej'rō') *n.* A hedge formed by a row of shrubs or trees growing close together.

he·don·ism (hē'dən·iz'əm) *n.* **1** Devotion to or pursuit of pleasure; self-indulgence. **2** The ethical doctrine that the seeking of pleasure is the primary good. [< Gk. *hēdonē* pleasure] —**he'don·ist** *n.* —**he'don·is'tic** *adj.* —**he'don·is'ti·cal·ly** *adv.*

-hedral *combining form* Having a (specified) number of sides or surfaces: *octahedral.*

-hedron *combining form* A figure or crystal having a (specified) number of sides or surfaces: *octahedron.* [< Gk. *hedra* side, surface]

heed (hēd) *v.t.* To take special notice of; pay attention to. —*v.i.* To pay attention. —*n.* Careful attention or consideration. [< OE *hēdan*] —**heed'er** *n.*

heed·ful (hēd'fəl) *adj.* Attentive. —**heed'ful·ly** *adv.* —**heed'ful·ness** *n.*

heed·less (hēd'lis) *adj.* Not taking heed; inattentive or careless. —**heed'less·ly** *adv.* —**heed'less·ness** *n.*

hee-haw (hē'hô') *n.* **1** The bray of a donkey. **2** Loud laughter resembling this. —*v.i.* **1** To bray. **2** To guffaw. [Imit.]

heel[1] (hēl) *n.* **1** In man, the rounded posterior part of the foot. **2** A similar or corresponding part, as of the foot of an animal or the palm of the hand where it joins the wrist. **3** The part of a sock, shoe, etc., that covers the heel. **4** The supporting part of a shoe, boot, etc., attached to the sole beneath the heel. • See SHOE. **5** Something resembling or placed like a heel, as an end of a loaf of bread. **6** *Slang* A contemptible, treacherous fellow; a cad. —*v.t.* **1** To supply with a heel. **2** To follow or pursue closely. [< OE *hēla*] —**heel'less** *adj.*

heel[2] (hēl) *v.t. & v.i. Naut.* To lean or cause to lean to one side, as a ship. —*n.* The act of heeling; a list. [< OE *hieldan*]

---

add, āce, câre, pälm; end, ēven; it, īce; odd, ōpen, ôrder; tŏŏk, pōōl; up, bûrn; ə = *a* in *above, u* in *focus;* yōō = *u* in *fuse;* oil; pout; check; go; ring; thin; this; zh, *vision.* < derived from; ? origin uncertain or unknown.

heeled (hēld) *adj.* 1 Having heels, as shoes. 2 *Slang* a Supplied with money. b Armed, as with a gun.

heel·er (hē′lər) *n.* 1 *Informal* WARD HEELER. 2 One who heels shoes.

heft (heft) *v.t. Informal* 1 To test the weight of by lifting. 2 To lift up; heave. —*v.i.* 3 To weigh. —*n.* Heaviness; weight. [< HEAVE]

heft·y (hef′tē) *adj.* **heft·i·er, heft·i·est** *Informal* 1 Heavy; weighty. 2 Big and powerful; muscular. —**heft′i·ly** *adv.* —**heft′i·ness** *n.*

he·gem·o·ny (hi·jem′ə·nē, hi·gem′-, hej′ə·mō′nē) *n. pl.* **·nies** Dominance or influence, as of one state over others. [< Gk. *hēgemonia* < *hēgeesthai* lead] —**heg·e·mon·ic** (hej′ə·mon′ik) *adj.*

He·gi·ra (hi·jī′rə, hej′ə·rə) *n.* The flight of Mohammed from Mecca to Medina in 622, regarded as the beginning of the Mohammedan era. [< Ar. *hijrah* departure]

heif·er (hef′ər) *n.* A young cow, esp. one that has not borne a calf. [< OE *hēahfore*]

heigh (hā, hī) *interj.* An exclamation to attract attention, give encouragement, etc.

heigh-ho (hī′hō′, hā′-) *interj.* An exclamation of weariness, disappointment, surprise, etc.

height (hīt) *n.* 1 Measure or distance from the lowest part or level to the top or uppermost extent; altitude, elevation, or stature. 2 The condition of being high or tall. 3 The highest or uppermost part or point. 4 Something high; an eminence. 5 The greatest or most intense degree: the *height* of stupidity. [< OE *hīehtho*]

height·en (hīt′n) *v.t. & v.i.* 1 To make or become high or higher. 2 To make or become greater in degree, amount, etc.; intensify. —**height′en·er** *n.*

hei·nous (hā′nəs) *adj.* Extremely wicked; atrocious; hateful. [< OF *haine* hatred] —**hei′nous·ly** *adv.* —**hei′nous·ness** *n.*

heir (âr) *n.* 1 One who inherits or is legally entitled to inherit the property, title, or rank of another. 2 One who acquires a position, distinctive quality, etc., from a predecessor as if by inheritance. [< L *heres*] —**heir′dom, heir′·ship** *n.*

heir apparent *pl.* **heirs apparent** One who according to law becomes the heir if he survives his ancestor.

heir·ess (âr′is) *n.* A woman or girl who is an heir, esp. one of considerable wealth.

heir·loom (âr′lōōm) *n.* 1 Something, as a valued possession, that has been handed down within a family for generations. 2 *Law* A piece of personal property inherited by an heir. [< HEIR + obs. *loom* tool]

heir presumptive *pl.* **heirs presumptive** One who is at present heir to another but whose claims may become void by birth of a nearer relative.

heist (hīst) *Slang v.t.* To steal. —*n.* A robbery; theft. [Var. of HOIST]

He·ji·ra (hə·jī′rə, hej′ə·rə) *n.* HEGIRA.

Hek·a·te (hek′ə·tē) HECATE.

held (held) *p.t. & p.p.* of HOLD.

Hel·en of Troy (hel′ən) *Gk. Myth.* A beautiful woman who was the wife of Menelaus and whose elopement with Paris caused the Trojan War.

hel·i·cal (hel′i·kəl) *adj.* Of or shaped like a helix; spiral. —**hel′i·cal·ly** *adv.*

hel·i·ces (hel′ə·sēz) *n.pl.* of HELIX.

hel·i·cop·ter (hel′ə·kop′tər, hē′lə-) *n.* A type of aircraft whose lift is obtained from airfoils rotating on a vertical axis and which is capable of rising and descending vertically. [< Gk. *helix, -ikos* a spiral + *pteron* a wing]

he·li·o- *combining form* Sun; of the sun: *heliotropic.* [< Gk. *hēlios* the sun]

Four-passenger helicopter

he·li·o·cen·tric (hē′lē·ə·sen′trik) *adj.* Having or considering the sun as a center. Also **he′li·o·cen′tri·cal.** —**he′li·o·cen′tri·cal·ly** *adv.*

he·li·o·graph (hē′lē·ə·graf′, -gräf′) *n.* 1 An instrument for taking photographs of the sun. 2 A photograph taken by sunlight. 3 A mirror for signaling by flashes of light. —*v.t. & v.i.* To signal with a heliograph. —**he·li·og·ra·pher** (hē′lē·og′rə·fər), **he′li·og′ra·phy** *n.* —**he′li·o·graph′ic** *adj.*

He·li·os (hē′lē·os) *Gk. Myth.* The sun god.

he·li·o·trope (hē′lē·ə·trōp′, hēl′yə-) *n.* 1 Any of a genus of herbs with small white or purplish fragrant flowers. 2 Any of various plants which turn toward the sun. 3 The common valerian. 4 BLOODSTONE. 5 A pinkish purple. [< Gk. *hēlios* sun + *trepein* to turn]

he·li·ot·ro·pism (hē′lē·ot′rə·piz′əm) *n.* The tendency of certain organisms, esp. plants, to grow or move toward or away from the source of light. Also **he′li·ot′ro·py. —he·li·o·trop·ic** (hē′lē·ə·trop′ik, -trō′pik, hēl′yə-) *adj.* —**he′li·o·trop′i·cal·ly** *adv.*

hel·i·port (hel′ə·pôrt′, -pōrt′, hē′lə-) *n.* An airport for helicopters.

he·li·um (hē′lē·əm) *n.* An inert, odorless, nonflammable, gaseous element (symbol He), abundant on the sun and other stars. [NL < Gk. *hēlios* sun]

he·lix (hē′liks) *n. pl.* **he·lix·es** or **hel·i·ces** (hel′ə·sēz) 1 *Geom.* A curve lying on the surface of a cone or cylinder and cutting each element at a constant angle greater than 0° and less than 90°. 2 Any spiral. 3 *Anat.* The spiral cartilage of the external ear. 4 *Archit.* A small volute. [L < Gk., a spiral]

Helix

hell (hel) *n.* 1 *Sometimes cap.* a In Christianity and other religions, the abode of evil spirits after death, considered a place of eternal torment. b In certain ancient religions, the dwelling place of the spirits of the dead. 2 The powers of evil. 3 Any place, condition, or cause of extreme suffering, evil, etc. —*interj. Slang* An exclamation of anger, annoyance, disappointment, etc. —*v.i. Slang* To behave in an unrestrained or riotous manner: with *around.* [< OE *hel*]

he'll (hēl) Contraction of *he will* or *he shall.*

Hel·las (hel′əs) *n.* Greece.

hell·bend·er (hel′ben′dər) *n.* A large aquatic salamander of SE North America.

hell-bent (hel′bent′) *adj. Slang* Recklessly determined, directed, or eager: *hell-bent* for trouble.

hel·le·bore (hel′ə·bôr, -bōr) *n.* 1 A perennial herb related to the buttercup, having rhizomes that contain a toxic alkaloid with cathartic and stimulating properties. 2 Any of certain herbs of the lily family having rhizomes containing a similar toxic substance. [< Gk. *helleboros*]

Hel·lene (hel′ēn) *n.* A Greek. Also **Hel·le′ni·an.**

Hel·len·ic (he·len′ik, -lē′nik) *adj.* 1 Of or pertaining to the Hellenes; Greek. 2 Of or pertaining to the language and culture of ancient Greece. —*n.* The Greek language, including its ancient and modern forms.

Hel·len·ism (hel′ə·niz′əm) *n.* 1 Ancient Greek character, ideals, or civilization. 2 A characteristic Greek idiom or phrase. 3 Adoption of Greek speech, manners, and culture. —**Hel′len·ist** *n.*

Hel·len·is·tic (hel′ə·nis′tik) *adj.* 1 Of or pertaining to Greek culture, influence, or language, esp. when widespread following the conquests of Alexander the Great.

Hel·len·ize (hel′ə·nīz) *v.t. & v.i.* **·nized, ·niz·ing** To make or become Greek or Hellenic; adopt or imbue with Greek language or customs. —**Hel·len·i·za·tion** (hel′ə·nə·zā′shən, -nī·zā′-) *n.* —**Hel′len·iz′er** *n.*

hell·fire (hel′fīr′) *n.* The flames or torment of hell.

hell·ion (hel′yən) *n. Informal* A mischievous person given to wild and unpredictable actions. [?]

hell·ish (hel′ish) *adj.* 1 Of or like hell; diabolical. 2 *Informal* Extremely bad or unpleasant; horrible. —**hell′ish·ly** *adv.* —**hell′ish·ness** *n.*

hel·lo (hə·lō′) *interj.* 1 An exclamation used as a greeting or in answering the telephone. 2 An exclamation of surprise or to gain attention. —*n. pl.* **hel·loes** The greeting or calling of "hello." —*v.t. & v.i.* **·loed, ·lo·ing** To call "hello" to.

helm (helm) *n.* 1 *Naut.* The steering apparatus of a vessel, as the tiller or wheel. 2 A position of control, responsibility, or leadership. —*v.t.* To manage the helm of; steer; direct. [< OE *helma* rudder]

hel·met (hel′mit) *n.* **1** A protective covering for the head, used in ancient and modern warfare. **2** A protective head covering, as of leather or plastic, worn by athletes, firemen, motorcyclists, etc. **3** Something resembling a helmet. [< OF, dim. of *helme* < Gmc.] —**hel′met·ed** *adj.*

Helmets
a. construction.
b. football.

hel·minth (hel′minth) *n.* A worm, esp. a parasitic intestinal worm. [< Gk. *helmins* a worm]

helms·man (helmz′mən) *n. pl.* **·men** (-mən) One who steers a vessel by taking the helm.

hel·ot (hel′ət, hē′lət) *n.* **1** *Usu. cap.* A serf of ancient Sparta. **2** Any slave. [< Gk. *heilōs*]

help (help) *v.t.* **1** To give assistance to; aid. **2** To assist in some action, motion, etc.: with *on, into, out of, up, down,* etc. **3** To give support to; contribute to: to *help* a good cause. **4** To give relief to; ease: to *help* a cold. **5** To be responsible for: He can′t *help* his infirmities. **6** To refrain from: I couldn′t *help* giggling. **7** To serve, as with food. **8** To wait on, as a sales clerk. —*v.i.* **9** To give assistance. **10** To be useful or effective: Nothing seems to *help.* —**cannot help but** To be compelled to; must. —*n.* **1** Aid; assistance. **2** Support; comfort. **3** Remedy; relief. **4 a** A worker hired to help. **b** Such workers collectively. [< OE *helpan*] —**help′er** *n.* —**Syn.** *v.* 1 succor, assist. 4 benefit, improve.

help·ful (help′fəl) *adj.* Providing help; beneficial. —**help′·ful·ly** *adv.* —**help′ful·ness** *n.*

help·ing (hel′ping) *n.* A serving of food for one person.

help·less (help′lis) *adj.* **1** Unable to help oneself; feeble. **2** Incompetent; incapable. **3** Incapable of helping; powerless. —**help′less·ly** *adv.* —**help′less·ness** *n.*

help·mate (help′māt) *n.* A helper and partner, esp. a wife or husband. Also **help·meet** (help′mēt).

hel·ter-skel·ter (hel′tər-skel′tər) *adv.* In a hurried and confused manner. —*adj.* Hurried and confused. —*n.* Disorderly hurry or confusion. [?]

helve (helv) *n.* A handle, as of an ax. [< OE *helfe*]

hem¹ (hem) *n.* **1** A finished border on fabric, made by folding one edge over and sewing it down. **2** A comparable border or edge. —*v.t.* **hemmed, hem·ming 1** To make a hem on. **2** To border; edge. **3** To shut in; enclose; restrict: with *in, about,* etc. [< OE] —**hem′mer** *n.*

hem² (hem) *n. & interj.* A sound, as of clearing the throat. —*v.i.* **hemmed, hem·ming 1** To make the sound "hem." **2** To hesitate in speaking. [Imit.]

he-man (hē′man′) *n. pl.* **·men** (-men′) *Informal* A virile, muscular man.

hem·a·tite (hem′ə·tīt, hē′mə-) *n.* A red mineral form of iron oxide, one of the important ores of iron. [< Gk. *haima* blood] —**hem·a·tit·ic** (hem′ə·tit′ik, hē′mə-) *adj.*

hemato- *combining form* Blood: *hematology.* Also before vowels, **hemat-.** [< Gk. *haima, haimatos* blood]

he·ma·tol·o·gy (hē′mə·tol′ə·jē, hem′ə-) *n.* The study of the blood and its diseases. —**he′ma·tol′o·gist** *n.*

he·ma·to·ma (hē′mə·tō′mə, hem′ə-) *n. pl.* **·to·ma·ta** (-tō′·mə·tə) or **·to·mas** *Pathol.* A swelling containing a mass of effused blood.

hemi- *prefix* Half: *hemisphere.* [< Gk. *hēmi-* half]

hem·i·dem·i·sem·i·qua·ver (hem′ē-dem′ē-sem′ē-kwā′·vər) *n. Music Chiefly Brit.* A sixty-fourth note.

he·mip·ter·ous (hi·mip′tər·əs) *adj.* Pertaining to an order of insects having usu. suctorial mouth parts and four wings, including true bugs, crickets, etc. Also **he·mip′ter·al.** [< Gk. *hēmi-* half + *pteron* wing]

hem·i·sphere (hem′ə·sfir) *n.* **1** Half of a sphere. **2 a** A half of the terrestrial or celestial globe, esp. one of the halves of the earth, including the **Northern** and **Southern Hemispheres,** divided at the equator, and the **Eastern** and **Western Hemispheres,** divided at a meridian. The Eastern Hemisphere includes Europe, Asia, Africa, and Australia; the Western Hemisphere includes North and South America. **b** A map or projection of one of these. —**hem·i·spher·ic** (hem′ə·sfer′ik) or **·i·cal** *adj.*

hem·i·stich (hem′i·stik) *n.* **1** Half of a line of poetic verse.

2 A short or incomplete line of verse. [< Gk. *hēmi-* half + *stichos* a row, line of poetry]

hem·line (hem′līn′) *n.* The line formed by the lower edge of a garment, as a dress.

hem·lock (hem′lok) *n.* **1** Any evergreen tree of a genus of coniferous evergreen trees of North America and Asia. **2** The wood of this tree. **3** A large poisonous plant related to parsley: also **poison hemlock. 4** A poison made from this. [< OE *hymlice*]

Hemlock branch

hemo- *combining form* Blood: *hemoglobin.* [< Gk. *haima* blood]

he·mo·glo·bin (hē′mə·glō′bin, hem′ə-) *n.* The pigment in red blood corpuscles which readily forms unstable compounds with oxygen and carbon dioxide and thus transports these gases throughout the body.

he·mo·phil·i·a (hē′mə·fil′ē·ə, -fil′yə, hem′ə-) *n.* A sex-linked, hereditary disorder characterized by deficient clotting of the blood and profuse bleeding. [< Gk. *haima* blood + *philia* fondness] —**he·mo·phil·i·ac** (hē′mə·fil′ē·ak, hem′ə-) *n.* —**he·mo·phil·ic** (hē′mə-fil′ik, hem′ə-) *adj.*

hem·or·rhage (hem′ər·ij, hem′rij) *n.* Discharge of blood from a ruptured blood vessel. —*v.i.* **·rhaged, ·rhag·ing** To bleed copiously. [< Gk. *haima* blood + *rhēgnynai* burst] —**hem·or·rhag·ic** (hem′ə·raj′ik) *adj.*

hem·or·rhoid (hem′ə·roid) *n.* A varicose vein in the region of the anus. [< Gk. *haima* blood + *rheein* flow] —**hem·or·rhoi·dal** *adj.*

he·mo·stat (hē′mə·stat, hem′ə-) *n.* Any device or drug that checks bleeding.

hemp (hemp) *n.* **1** A tall, annual herb with small green flowers and fibrous stems. **2** The tough, strong fiber from this plant, used to make rope, cloth, etc. **3** Any similar fiber or plant. **4** A hallucinogenic drug prepared from the plant, as hashish. [< OE *henep*]

hemp·en (hem′pən) *adj.* Of hemp.

hem·stitch (hem′stich′) *n.* An ornamental openwork stitch made by pulling out a number of parallel threads and gathering the remaining cross threads in regularly spaced groups. —*v.t.* To sew or ornament with such stitches. —**hem′stitch′er** *n.*

hen (hen) *n.* A female bird, esp. the mature female of the common domestic fowl. [< OE *henn*]

hen·bane (hen′bān′) *n.* A poisonous plant related to belladonna and yielding a medicinal alkaloid.

hence (hens) *adv.* **1** Therefore; consequently. **2** From this time; from now: a month *hence.* **3** From this place; away. —*interj. Archaic* Depart; begone. [< OE *heonan* from here]

hence·forth (hens′fôrth′, -fôrth′, hens′fôrth′, -fôrth′) *adv.* From this time on. Also **hence′for′ward** (-fôr′wərd).

hench·man (hench′mən) *n. pl.* **·men** (-mən) **1** A faithful follower or retainer. **2** A subservient supporter of a powerful, often disreputable person. [< OE *hengst* horse + MAN]

hen·e·quen (hen′ə·kin) *n.* **1** A coarse, sisal-like plant fiber. **2** A tropical American agave yielding this fiber. Also **hen′e·quin.** [Sp. < Taino]

hen·na (hen′ə) *n.* **1** An Oriental shrub with lance-shaped leaves and fragrant flowers. **2** A reddish cosmetic dye made from the leaves of this plant. **3** A bright reddish brown. —*v.t.* **·naed, ·na·ing** To color with henna. [< Ar. *henna*]

hen·peck (hen′pek′) *v.t.* To domineer over or nag persistently at (one′s husband). —**hen′pecked** *adj.*

hen·ry (hen′rē) *n. pl.* **·ries** or **·rys** *Electr.* A unit of inductance equal to that of a circuit in which a change in current of one ampere per second induces an electromotive force of one volt. [< J. *Henry,* 1797–1878, U.S. physicist]

hep (hep) *adj. Slang* Knowledgeable; hip. [?]

he·pat·ic (hi·pat′ik) *adj.* **1** Of, pertaining to, or resembling the liver. **2** Affecting the liver. —*n.* A drug acting on the liver. [< Gk. *hēpar* the liver]

he·pat·i·ca (hi·pat′ə·kə) n. Any of several small perennial herbs related to butter-cups with three-lobed leaves and variously colored flowers. [< L *hepaticus* of the liver]

hep·a·ti·tis (hep′ə·tī′tis) n. Inflammation of the liver, usu. due to viral infection.

Hep·ple·white (hep′əl·hwīt) adj. Denoting an 18th-century English style of furniture characterized by graceful curves and light, slender woodwork. [< G. *Hepplewhite*, d. 1786, the designer]

Hepplewhite chair

hepta- combining form Seven: heptagon. Also, before vowels, **hept-**. [< Gk. *hepta* seven]

hep·ta·gon (hep′tə·gon) n. A polygon having seven sides and seven angles. —**hep·tag·o·nal** (hep·tag′ə·nəl) adj.

hep·tam·e·ter (hep·tam′ə·tər) n. A line of verse having seven metrical feet.

her (hûr) pron. The objective case of she. —pronominal adj. Of, belonging to, made or used by her: her garden; her style. [< OE *hire*]

Heptagon

Her·a·cles (her′ə·klēz) Gk. & Rom. Myth. HERCULES. Also **Her′a·kles**. —**Her′a·cle′an** adj.

her·ald (her′əld) n. 1 The bearer of significant news, an important message, etc. 2 A forerunner or portent of something to come; harbinger. 3 Brit. An official who traces and records genealogies, assigns heraldic arms, etc. —v.t. 1 To announce; proclaim. 2 To foretell the coming of. [< Gmc.] —**he·ral·dic** (hi·ral′dik) adj.

her·ald·ry (her′əl·drē) n. pl. ·ries 1 The art or occupation of establishing and devising coats of arms, tracing and recording genealogies, etc. 2 Coats of arms or similar heraldic bearings collectively. 3 Pomp or ceremony suggestive of heraldry.

herb (ûrb, hûrb) n. 1 A seed plant devoid of persistent woody tissue. 2 A plant used in medicine or for flavoring food. [< L *herba* grass, herbage]

her·ba·ceous (hûr·bā′shəs) adj. Of, pertaining to, or typical of herbs.

herb·age (ûr′bij, hûr′-) n. 1 Herbs or grass, esp. used as pasturage. 2 The succulent leaves, stems, etc., of herbaceous plants.

herb·al (hûr′bəl, ûr′-) adj. Of or pertaining to herbs. —n. A learned work on plants, esp. medicinal herbs.

herb·al·ist (hûr′bəl·ist, ûr′-) n. A dealer in or expert on herbs, esp. medicinal herbs.

her·bar·i·um (hûr·bâr′ē·əm) n. pl. ·bar·i·ums or ·bar·i·a (-bâr′ē·ə) 1 A collection of dried plants scientifically arranged. 2 A room or building containing such a collection.

her·bi·cide (hûr′bə·sīd) n. A substance used to kill plants, esp. weeds. —**her′bi·ci′dal** adj.

her·bi·vore (hûr′bə·vôr, -vōr) n. A herbivorous animal.

her·biv·o·rous (hûr·biv′ər·əs) adj. Feeding on plants or vegetable matter. [< L *herba* grass + *vorare* devour]

her·cu·le·an (hûr·kyōō′lē·ən, hûr′kyə·lē′ən) adj. 1 Having great physical strength. 2 Requiring great strength or endurance: a herculean task.

Her·cu·le·an (hûr·kyōō′lē·ən, hûr′kyə·lē′ən) adj. Of or pertaining to Hercules.

Her·cu·les (hûr′kyə·lēz) Gk. & Rom. Myth. A son of Zeus, renowned for his strength and endurance. —n. Any man of great size and strength.

herd[1] (hûrd) n. 1 A group of animals, as cattle or sheep, that stay or are kept together. 2 A large, often unthinking or easily led crowd. —v.t. & v.i. To bring or keep together in or as in a herd. [< OE *heord*] —**herd′er** n.

herd[2] (hûrd) n. A herdsman: used chiefly in combination: cowherd. —v.t. To care for or drive (sheep, cattle, etc.). [< OE *hirde* herdsman]

herds·man (hûrdz′mən) n. pl. ·men (-mən) One who tends a herd.

here (hir) adv. 1 In, at, or to this place: Come here. 2 At this point or stage: Here he gave up. 3 As indicated: often used for emphasis after a noun: these books here. 4 In this present life. —n. This point or stage: from here on. —interj. An exclamation used to answer a roll call, etc. [< OE *hēr*]• Here, as an adverb, is correctly used after a noun:

The people here need help. Although such use may appear somewhat adjectival in function, here is not an adjective, and it should not be used before a noun: These here people need help.

here·a·bout (hir′ə·bout′) adv. About this place; in this vicinity. Also **here′a·bouts′**.

here·af·ter (hir·af′tər, -äf′-) adv. 1 At some future time. 2 From this time forth. 3 In the state of life after death. —n. A future existence, esp. after death.

here·at (hir·at′) adv. 1 At this time or point. 2 Because of this.

here·by (hir·bī′) adv. By means of this.

he·red·i·ta·ble (hə·red′i·tə·bəl) adj. HERITABLE. —**he·red′i·ta·bil′i·ty** n. —**he·red′i·ta·bly** adv.

he·red·i·tar·y (hə·red′ə·ter′ē) adj. 1 a Inherited or capable of being inherited legally. b Having title or right through legal inheritance: hereditary ruler. 2 Transmitted by biological heredity from one's parents or ancestors. 3 Passed on by or as by one's forebears: hereditary rights. —**he·red′i·tar′i·ly** adv. —**he·red′i·tar′i·ness** n.

he·red·i·ty (hə·red′ə·tē) n. pl. ·ties 1 Transmission of characteristics from parents to offspring by a code embodied in the genes in the chromosomes. 2 The tendency of an organism to develop in the likeness of its progenitors because of such transmission. 3 The sum total of an individual's genetic inheritance.

Her·e·ford (her′ə·fərd) n. One of a breed of reddish cattle with white markings. [< *Hereford*, England]

here·in (hir·in′) adv. 1 In this; in this place or thing. 2 In this instance, circumstance, etc.

here·in·af·ter (hir′in·af′tər, -äf′-) adv. In a subsequent part of this (document, statement, text, etc.).

here·in·be·fore (hir′in·bi·fôr′, -fōr′) adv. In a preceding part of this (document, statement, text, etc.).

here·of (hir·uv′) adv. Of this; about this.

here·on (hir·on′, -ôn′) adv. On this: hereupon.

her·e·sy (her′ə·sē) n. pl. ·sies 1 A religious or doctrinal belief contrary to those of an established body or authority. 2 Any similar unorthodox or controversial belief. 3 Adherence to such beliefs. [< Gk. *hairesis* a sect]

her·e·tic (her′ə·tik) n. 1 One who maintains a heresy, esp. a religious heresy. 2 One whose views are unorthodox and controversial.

he·ret·i·cal (hə·ret′i·kəl) adj. Of, involving, or typical of heresy or heretics. —**he·ret′i·cal·ly** adv.

here·to (hir·tōō′) adv. To this thing, instance, etc.

here·to·fore (hir′tə·fôr′, -fōr′) adv. Previously; hitherto.

here·un·to (hir·un′tōō, -un·tōō′) adv. To this; hereto.

here·up·on (hir′ə·pon′, -pôn′, hir′ə·pon′, -pôn′) adv. Upon this; following immediately after this.

here·with (hir·with′, -with′) adv. 1 Along with this. 2 By this means; thus.

her·i·ta·ble (her′ə·tə·bəl) adj. 1 Capable of being inherited. 2 Capable of inheriting. [< OF *heriter* inherit] —**her′i·ta·bil′i·ty** n. —**her′i·ta·bly** adv.

her·i·tage (her′ə·tij) n. 1 Something that is or can be inherited. 2 Tradition, culture, rights, etc., transmitted from generation to generation. [< OF < *heriter* inherit]

her·maph·ro·dite (hûr·maf′rə·dīt) n. 1 A person or animal having both male and female sexual characteristics. 2 A single plant having both stamens and pistils. —adj. Of or like a hermaphrodite. [< Gk. *Hermaphroditos* son of Hermes and Aphrodite] —**her·maph′ro·dit′ic** (-dit′ik) adj. —**her·maph′ro·dit′i·cal·ly** adv. —**her·maph′ro·dit·ism**, **her·maph′ro·dism** n.

hermaphrodite brig A sailing vessel with a square-rigged foremast and a fore-and-aft rigged mainmast.

Her·mes (hûr′mēz) Gk. Myth. The messenger of the gods, and god of cunning, travelers, and commerce.

her·met·ic (hûr·met′ik) adj. Impervious to liquids or gases. Also **her·met′i·cal**. [< Gk. *Hermes (Trismegistus)*, god of alchemy] —**her·met′i·cal·ly** adv.

her·mit (hûr′mit) n. 1 A person who abandons society and lives alone, often for religious contemplation. 2 A spicy molasses cooky. [< Gk. *erēmos* solitary] —**her·mit′ic** or ·**i·cal** adj. —**her·mit′i·cal·ly** adv.

her·mit·age (hûr′mə·tij) n. 1 The dwelling place of a hermit. 2 A secluded dwelling; retreat.

hermit crab Any of a family of soft-bodied crabs that live in discarded shells of snails or other mollusks.

her·ni·a (hûr′nē·ə) *n.* Protrusion of an intestine or other organ through a barrier that normally holds it. [L] — **her′ni·al** *adj.*

he·ro (hir′ō) *n. pl.* **·roes 1** A person of great courage, spirit, etc., esp. one who has undergone great danger or difficulty. **2** Any admirable or highly regarded man. **3** The main male character in a fictional or dramatic work. **4** In classical mythology, a man of both mortal and divine parentage, noted for outstanding courage, fortitude, etc. **5** A sandwich made from a loaf of bread or large roll split lengthwise. [< Gk. *hērōs*]

he·ro·ic (hi·rō′ik) *adj.* **1** Of or typical of a hero. **2** Characterized by or requiring great daring, strength, etc.: a *heroic* attempt. **3** Describing or in a style befitting the deeds of heroes: *heroic* poetry. **4** Larger than life size, as a statue. Also **he·ro′i·cal.** —*n.* **1** *pl.* Melodramatic behavior intended to display one's bravery, prowess, etc. **2** *pl.* HEROIC VERSE. —**he·ro′i·cal·ly** *adv.*

heroic couplet An English verse form consisting of two rhyming lines of iambic pentameter.

heroic verse A verse form, as the heroic couplet or blank verse, used esp. in epic and dramatic poetry.

her·o·in (her′ō·in) *n.* A white, odorless, habit-forming narcotic derived from morphine. [< *Heroin*, a trade name]

her·o·ine (her′ō·in) *n.* **1** A girl or woman of heroic character. **2** The chief female character in a fictional or dramatic work.

her·o·ism (her′ō·iz′əm) *n.* Qualities or behavior of or befitting a hero or heroine.

her·on (her′ən) *n.* One of a family of long-necked and long-legged wading birds. [< OF *hairon* < Gmc.]

he·ro-wor·ship (hir′ō-wûr′-ship) *n.* Extravagant admiration for one regarded as a hero.

her·pes (hûr′pēz) *n.* Any of several acute viral diseases characterized by eruption of small blisters on the skin or mucous membrane. [< Gk. *herpein* to creep]

herpes zos·ter (zos′tər) SHINGLES.

Great blue heron

her·pe·tol·o·gy (hûr′pə·tol′ə·jē) *n.* The branch of zoology that treats of reptiles and amphibians. [< Gk. *herpeton* a reptile + -LOGY] —**her·pe·to·log·i·cal** (hûr′pə·tə·loj′i·kəl) *adj.* — **her′pe·tol′o·gist** *n.*

Herr (her) *n. pl.* **Her·ren** (her′ən) *German* A title of address, equivalent to the English *Mr.*

her·ring (her′ing) *n. pl.* **·rings** or **·ring** Any of various marine fishes, esp. a small, silvery, food fish of the North Atlantic. [< OE *hæring*]

her·ring·bone (her′ing·bōn′) *n.* **1** A pattern, as of a fabric, consisting of parallel rows of short, slanting lines arranged at opposing angles. **2** Something having or forming such a pattern. —*adj.* Having or forming such a pattern. —*v.t. & v.i.* **·boned, ·bon·ing** To form or mark with such a pattern.

hers (hûrz) *pron.* **1** Belonging or pertaining to her: the form of the possessive case of the pronoun *she* when used in predicative position, without a following noun, or after *of:* That book is *hers;* those eyes of *hers.* **2** The things or persons belonging to or relating to her; *Hers* is the best.

her·self (hər·self′) *pron.* **1** The reflexive form of *her:* She blamed *herself.* **2** The emphatic or intensive form of *she:* She *herself* called me. **3** Her normal or true self: She is not *herself* lately.

hertz (hûrts) *n. pl.* **hertz** or **hertz·es** *Physics* A unit of frequency, as of waves, equal to one cycle per second. [< H. *Hertz,* 1857–94, German physicist]

he's (hēz) Contraction of *he is* or *he has.*

hes·i·tan·cy (hez′ə·tən·sē) *n. pl.* **·cies** The act or condition of hesitating. Also **hes′i·tance.**

hes·i·tant (hez′ə·tənt) *adj.* Hesitating or tending to hesitate; faltering, indecisive, or uncertain. —**hes′i·tant·ly** *adv.* —Syn. irresolute, undecided, unsure, doubtful.

hes·i·tate (hez′ə·tāt) *v.i.* **·tat·ed, ·tat·ing 1** To delay doubtfully or irresolutely; pause uncertainly; waver. **2** To be unwilling; have qualms. **3** To pause or falter in speaking. [< L *haesitare,* freq. of *haerere* to stick] —**hes′i·tat′er** *n.* —**hes′i·tat′ing·ly** *adv.*

hes·i·ta·tion (hez′ə·tā′shən) *n.* **1** The act of hesitating. **2** A state of uncertainty or doubt. **3** A pause or faltering in speech. —**hes′i·ta′tive** *adj.* —**hes′i·ta′tive·ly** *adv.*

Hes·per·i·des (hes·per′ə·dēz) *Gk. Myth.* **1** The daughters of Atlas who guarded the golden apples later stolen by Hercules. **2** The garden where these apples grew. [< Gk. *hesperis* western]

Hes·pe·rus (hes′pər·əs) *n.* The evening star, esp. Venus. Also **Hes′per.** [< Gk. *Hesperos*]

Hes·sian (hesh′ən) *n.* **1** A native or inhabitant of Hesse. **2** A soldier from Hesse hired by the British to fight in the American Revolution. —*adj.* Of or from Hesse.

Hessian fly A small fly whose larva is very destructive to wheat.

he·tae·ra (hi·tir′ə) *n. pl.* **·tae·rae** (-tir′ē) or **·ras** In ancient Greece, an often educated or cultured courtesan or concubine. Also **he·tai·ra** (hi·tī′rə).

hetero- *combining form* Other; different: *heterogeneous.* Also, before vowels, **heter-.** [< Gk. *heteros* other]

het·er·o·dox (het′ər·ə·doks′) *adj.* At variance with an established or generally accepted doctrine or belief, esp. in religion; unorthodox. [< Gk. *hetero-* other + *doxa* opinion] —**het′er·o·dox′y** *n.*

het·er·o·dyne (het′ər·ə·dīn′) *adj. Telecom.* Describing a technique in which alternating currents of different frequencies are mixed so that they modulate each other and produce in the output components with frequencies equal to the sum and difference of the original frequencies. — *v.t.* **·dyned, ·dyn·ing** To cause such mixing and modulation of (electric signals).

het·er·o·ge·ne·ous (het′ər·ə·jē′nē·əs) *adj.* **1** Consisting of dissimilar elements or ingredients. **2** At variance; unlike; differing. [< Gk. *hetero-* other + *genos* kind] —**het·er·o·ge·ne·i·ty** (het′ər·ə·jə·nē′ə·tē), **het′er·o·ge′ne·ous·ness** *n.* —**het′er·o·ge′ne·ous·ly** *adv.*

het·er·o·nym (het′ər·ə·nim′) *n.* A word spelled like another, but having a different sound and meaning, as *bass* (a male voice) and *bass* (a fish). [< HETER(O)- + Gk. *onyma* name] —**het·er·on·y·mous** (het′ə·ron′ə·məs) *adj.*

het·er·o·sex·u·al (het′ər·ə·sek′shōō·əl) *adj.* **1** Of or characterized by sexual desire for members of the opposite sex. **2** *Biol.* Of or involving different sexes. —*n.* A heterosexual person. —**het′er·o·sex′u·al′i·ty** (-sek′shōō·al′ə·tē) *n.* —**het′er·o·sex′u·al·ly** *adv.*

heu·ris·tic (hyōō·ris′tik) *adj.* Guiding or stimulating to learn or make discoveries, as in education. [< Gk. *heuriskein* find out] —**heu·ris′ti·cal·ly** *adv.*

hew (hyōō) *v.* **hewed, hewn** or **hewed, hew·ing** *v.t.* **1** To make or shape with or as with blows of an ax. **2** To hack or chop with an ax, sword, etc. **3** To fell with or as with blows of an ax. —*v.i.* **4** To make repeated cutting blows, as with an ax. **5** To keep steadfastly. [< OE *hēawan*] —**hew′er** *n.*

hex (heks) *v.t. Informal* To cause bad luck to; jinx. —*n.* **1** An evil spell. **2** A persistent tendency to bad luck. [< G *Hexe* witch]

hexa- *combining form* Six: *hexagon.* Also, before vowels, **hex-.** [< Gk. *hex* six]

hex·a·chlo·ro·phene (hek′sə·klôr′ə·fēn′) *n.* An antibacterial agent used in some soaps.

hex·a·gon (hek′sə·gon) *n.* A polygon with six sides and six angles. [< HEXA- + Gk. *gonia* angle] —**hex·ag·o·nal** (hek·sag′ə·nəl) *adj.* —**hex·ag′o·nal·ly** *adv.*

hex·a·gram (hek′sə·gram) *n.* A figure formed by constructing exterior equilateral triangles on the sides of a regular hexagon.

Hexagon

hex·a·he·dron (hek′sə·hē′drən) *n. pl.*

·drons or ·dra (-drə) A polyhedron bounded by six plane faces. —hex'a·he'dral *adj.*

hex·am·e·ter (hek·sam'ə·tər) *n.* 1 A line of verse having six metrical feet. 2 Verse consisting of such lines. —hex·a·met·ric (hek'sə·met'rik), hex'a·met'ri·cal *adj.*

hex·a·pod (hek'sə·pod) *adj.* Having six legs. —*n.* INSECT (def. 1). —hex·ap·o·dous (hek·sap'ə·dəs) *adj.*

hey (hā) *interj.* An exclamation expressing surprise, calling for attention, etc.

hey·day (hā'dā') *n.* The time of greatest vitality, vigor, influence, etc. [?]

HF, h.f., h-f. high frequency.

Hf hafnium.

hf. half.

HG, H.G. High German.

Hg mercury (L *hydrargyrum*).

hg. hectogram(s); heliogram.

hgt. height.

H.H. His (or Her) Highness; His Holiness.

hhd. hogshead.

H-hour (āch'our') *n.* The hour appointed for a military operation to begin.

hi (hī) *interj. Informal* An exclamation of greeting.

HI Hawaii (P.O. abbr.).

hi·a·tus (hī·ā'təs) *n. pl.* ·tus·es or ·tus 1 A gap or break, with a part missing, as in a manuscript; lacuna. 2 Any interruption or break. 3 In pronunciation, a pause due to the concurrence of two separate vowels without an intervening consonant, as in *pre-eminent.* [L]

hi·ba·chi (hi·bä'chē) *n. pl.* ·chis A charcoal-burning brazier, used for cooking food, etc. [< Jap. *hi* fire + *bachi* bowl]

hi·ber·nal (hī·bûr'nəl) *adj.* Pertaining to winter; wintry. [< L *hibernus* wintry]

hi·ber·nate (hī'bər·nāt) *v.t.* ·nat·ed, ·nat·ing 1 To pass the winter, esp. in a torpid state, as certain animals. 2 To pass the time in seclusion or inactivity. [< L *hibernare*] —hi'ber·na'tion *n.*

Hi·ber·ni·a (hī·bûr'nē·ə) *n.* The Latin and poetic name for Ireland. —Hi·ber'ni·an *adj., n.*

hi·bis·cus (hī·bis'kəs, hi-) *n.* Any of a genus of usu. tropical plants with showy, variously colored flowers. [< Gk. *hibiskos* mallow]

hic·cup (hik'əp) *n.* A spasmodic contraction of the diaphragm accompanied by an involuntary sound. —*v.i.* ·cuped or ·cupped, ·cup·ing or ·cup·ping To have the hiccups; make a hiccup. Also hic·cough (hik'əp). [Imit.]

hic ja·cet (hik jā'set) Here lies: often inscribed on tombstones. [L]

hick (hik) *n. Informal* A person, usu. from rural areas, of unsophisticated manners, speech, dress, etc. [< RICHARD]

hick·o·ry (hik'ər·ē) *n. pl.* ·ries 1 Any of various North American trees of the walnut family, yielding an edible nut and having hard, tough, heavy wood. 2 Something made of this wood, as a switch. [< Amer. Ind.]

hid (hid) *p.t. & a p.p.* of HIDE[1].

hi·dal·go (hi·dal'gō; *Sp.* ē·thäl'gō) *n. pl.* ·gos (-gōz; *Sp.* -gōs) *Spanish* A Spanish nobleman of the lower rank. —hi·dal'ga (-gä) *n. Fem.*

hid·den (hid'n) *p.p.* of HIDE[1]. —*adj.* 1 Unseen; out of sight. 2 Not known or revealed.

hide[1] (hīd) *v.* hid, hid·den or hid, hid·ing *v.t.* 1 To put or keep out of sight; conceal. 2 To keep secret; withhold from knowledge: to *hide* one's fears. 3 To block or obstruct the sight of. —*v.i.* 4 To keep oneself out of sight; remain concealed. [< OE *hȳdan*] —hid'er *n.* —**Syn.** 1 secrete, cover, screen, bury. 2 cover up, cloak, mask, disguise, camouflage, veil, suppress.

hide[2] (hīd) *n.* 1 An animal skin, esp. as material for leather. 2 *Informal* The human skin. —*v.t.* hid·ed, hid·ing 1 To whip; flog severely. 2 To remove the hide from. [< OE *hȳd*]

hide·a·way (hīd'ə·wā') *n.* A place of seclusion or retreat.

hide·bound (hīd'bound') *adj.* 1 Obstinately fixed in opinion; narrow-minded. 2 Having the skin tight over the skeletal structure: said of animals.

hid·e·ous (hid'ē·əs) *adj.* Shocking or dreadful; ghastly; revolting. [< OF *hisde, hide* fright] —hid'e·ous·ly *adv.* —hid'e·ous·ness *n.*

hide-out (hīd'out') *n.* A place of concealment and safety; hiding place.

hid·ing[1] (hī'ding) *n.* 1 The act of one who hides. 2 The condition of being hidden.

hid·ing[2] (hī'ding) *n. Informal* A flogging.

hie (hī) *v.t. & v.i.* hied, hie·ing or hy·ing To hasten; hurry: often reflexive. [< OE *hīgian*]

hi·er·ar·chy (hī'ər·är'kē) *n. pl.* ·chies 1 A system of church government by ecclesiastics graded and empowered according to rank. 2 A body of ruling clergymen. 3 A group of things, people, ideas, etc., arranged in order of importance. [< Gk. *hieros* sacred + *archos* ruler] —hi'er·ar'chic, hi'er·ar'chi·cal, hi'er·ar'chal *adj.*

hi·er·at·ic (hī'ə·rat'ik) *adj.* 1 Of or used by priests; sacerdotal; consecrated. 2 Of or pertaining to a cursive form of ancient Egyptian hieroglyphs. Also hi'er·at'i·cal. [< Gk. *hieratikos* of a priest's office]

hi·er·o·glyph·ic (hī'ər·ə·glif'ik, hī'rə·glif'ik) *n.* 1 *Usu. pl.* Picture writing, esp. of the ancient Egyptians. 2 A character or symbol used in such writing. 3 A symbol, word, etc., difficult to understand. 4 *pl.* Illegible handwriting. Also hi·er·o·glyph (hī'ər·ə·glif', hī'rə·glif). —*adj.* Of, like, pertaining to, or written in hieroglyphics: also hi·er·o·glyphic (hī'ər·ə·glif', hī'rə·glif). [< Gk. *hieros* sacred + *glyphein* carve] —hi'er·o·glyph'i·cal·ly *adv.*

hi-fi (hī'fī') *adj.* Of or having high fidelity. —*n. pl.* -fis A sound-reproducing system, esp. one with high fidelity.

hig·gle (hig'əl) *v.i.* hig·gled, hig·gling To dispute about terms; haggle; chaffer. [Var. of HAGGLE] —hig'gler *n.*

hig·gle·dy-pig·gle·dy (hig'əl·dē·pig'əl·dē) *adj.* In a disordered state; jumbled; muddled. —*adv.* In a confused manner. [?]

high (hī) *adj.* 1 Having great or considerable height; lofty; tall. 2 Having a (specified) height: an inch *high.* 3 Located a considerable distance above the ground, street, etc. 4 Extending to or performed from a height: a *high* dive. 5 Of relatively great importance, influence, etc.: a *high* official. 6 Of relatively great force, measure, degree, etc.: *high* voltage. 7 Of superior quality, character, etc.: *high* art. 8 Advanced, well developed, or complex: usu. in the comparative degree: *higher* mathematics. 9 Most important; chief: a *high* priest. 10 Fully advanced or culminated: *high* noon. 11 Grave; serious: *high* treason. 12 Expensive; costly: Rent is *high.* 13 Luxurious: *high* living. 14 Strict or formal, as in doctrine, ceremony, etc. 15 Elated; merry: *high* spirits. 16 Far from the equator: *high* latitudes. 17 a Having a frequency of relatively great measure, as a tone. b Producing such tones: a *high* voice. 18 Of or indicating an arrangement of gears for producing the highest ratio of output speed to input speed. 19 Slightly tainted: said esp. of game meat. 20 *Informal* Feeling the effects of liquor or drugs. —*adv.* 1 To or at a high level, position, degree, etc. 2 In a high manner. 3 At a high pitch. —*n.* 1 A high level, position, etc. 2 *Meteorol.* A region of relatively high atmospheric pressure. 3 An arrangement of gears that produces the greatest ratio of output speed to input speed. 4 *Slang* The euphoria produced by drugs. [< OE *hēah*]

high and dry 1 Above the reach of water. 2 Stranded; helpless.

high and low Everywhere.

high and mighty Haughty; imperious.

high·ball[1] (hī'bôl') *n.* An alcoholic drink, usu. whiskey to which is added water or a carbonated beverage, served with ice. [?]

high·ball[2] (hī'bôl) *n.* A railroad signal meaning to go ahead. —*v.i. Slang* To go at great speed. [< a ball that could be raised or lowered, once used as a signal]

high·born (hī'bôrn') *adj.* Of noble birth.

high·boy (hī'boi') *n.* A tall chest of drawers usu. in two

Highboy

sections, with the upper section recessed, set upon legs.

high·bred (hī′bred′) *adj.* **1** Of a fine pedigree. **2** Characterized by fine manners or good breeding.

high·brow (hī′brou′) *Informal n.* A person of cultivated or intellectual tastes: sometimes a term of derision. —*adj.* Of or suitable for such a person.

high·chair (hī′châr′) *n.* A baby's chair having an eating tray and tall legs.

High Church The group in the Anglican Church that exalts the authority of the church and emphasizes the value of ritual. —**High′-Church′man** *n.*

high-class (hī′klas′, -kläs′) *adj.* Superior, as in quality, rank, etc.

high comedy Comedy presenting the world of polite society and relying chiefly on witty, sophisticated dialogue and situations.

high·er-up (hī′ər-up′) *n. Informal* A person of superior rank or position.

high·fa·lu·tin (hī′fə-lōōt′n) *adj. Informal* Excessively pompous or grand. Also **high′fa·lu′ting.** [?]

high fidelity The electronic processing of a signal without adding significant distortion. —**high′-fi·del′i·ty** *adj.*

high-flown (hī′flōn′) *adj.* **1** Pretentious. **2** Extravagant in style.

high·fly·ing (hī′flī′ing) *adj.* **1** Flying at a considerable height. **2** Having extravagant ideas or opinions, a lavish style of living, etc. —**high′fli′er, high′fly′er** *n.*

high frequency A wave frequency between 3 and 30 megahertz.

High German 1 The standard German language. **2** German as used in s Germany.

high-grade (hī′grād′) *adj.* Of superior quality.

high·hand·ed (hī′han′did) *adj.* Officious; overbearing. —**high′hand′ed·ly** *adv.* —**high′hand′ed·ness** *n.*

high-hat (hī′hat′) *Informal n.* A snob. —*adj.* Aristocratic; snobbish. —*v.t.* **-hat·ted, -hat·ting** To snub; treat snobbishly.

high hat A top hat.

high·jack (hī′jak′) *v. Informal* HIJACK. —**high′jack′er** *n.*

high jump An athletic event in which the contestants jump for height over a horizontal bar.

high·land (hī′lənd) *n.* An elevation of land, usu. mountainous in character. —**the Highlands** The mountainous part of N Scotland. —*adj.* Of or pertaining to a highland; mountaineer.

high·land·er (hī′lən-dər) *n.* An inhabitant of a highland.

High·land·er (hī′lən-dər) *n.* A native of the Scottish Highlands; a Gael.

Highland fling A lively Scottish dance.

high-lev·el language (hī′lev′əl) A computer programming language that uses plain English words or simple mathematical expressions.

high·light (hī′līt′) *n.* **1** *pl.* The bright spots in a photograph or picture. **2** A part or detail of special importance or vividness. —*v.t.* **1** *pl.* To give a highlight to. **2** To give special emphasis to; feature. **3** To be the highlight of.

high·ly (hī′lē) *adv.* **1** In a high rank or position. **2** Very much; extremely. **3** With much approval; favorably. **4** At a high price or rate.

High Mass In the Roman Catholic Church, a Mass that is sung and accompanied by full ceremony.

high-mind·ed (hī′mīn′did) *adj.* Having lofty ideals or feelings. —**high′-mind′ed·ly** *adv.* —**high′-mind′ed·ness** *n.*

high·ness (hī′nis) *n.* The quality or condition of being high.

High·ness (hī′nis) *n.* A title of honor belonging to persons of royal rank: with *His, Her,* or *Your.*

high-pitched (hī′picht′) *adj.* **1** High in pitch. **2** Having a steep slope: said of roofs.

high-pres·sure (hī′presh′ər) *adj.* **1** Having, withstanding, or using a high pressure. **2** Exerting vigorous, persuasive tactics: *high-pressure* salesmanship. —*v.t.* **-sured, -sur·ing** To persuade or influence by such methods.

high-rise (hī′rīz′) *adj.* Describing a relatively tall building or structure. —*n.* A tall building, as a many-storied apartment house: also **high rise.**

high school A secondary school, typically comprising grades 10, 11, and 12, and sometimes grade 9. —**high′-school′** *adj.* —**high′-school′er** *n.*

high seas The unenclosed waters of the ocean or sea, esp. those beyond the territorial jurisdiction of any one country or nation.

high-sound·ing (hī′soun′ding) *adj.* Ostentatious or imposing in sound or meaning.

high-spir·it·ed (hī′spir′ə·tid) *adj.* **1** Full of energy and courage. **2** Fun-loving; vivacious.

high-strung (hī′strung′) *adj.* Highly sensitive and nervous; excitable.

hight (hīt) *adj. Archaic* Called or named. [<OE *hātan* to call]

high-ten·sion (hī′ten′shən) *adj.* Of, for, at, or using a relatively high voltage.

high-test (hī′test′) *adj.* **1** Meeting difficult tests or requirements. **2** Denoting a very volatile gasoline with a high octane number.

high tide 1 The maximum tidal elevation of the water at any point; also, the time of its occurrence. **2** Any culminating point in a series of events.

high time 1 About time; not a moment too soon. **2** *Slang* An occasion of great fun and revelry: also **high old time.**

high-toned (hī′tōnd′) *adj.* **1** *Informal* Fashionable; swank. **2** Noble, lofty, and honorable. **3** High in pitch.

high treason Treason against the sovereign or state.

high-wa·ter mark (hī′wô′tər, -wot′ər) **1** The highest point reached by a body of water. **2** Any highest point, as of achievement.

high·way (hī′wā) *n.* **1** A public road, usu. a main road. **2** A way to some goal or objective.

high·way·man (hī′wā′mən) *n. pl.* **·men** (-mən) Formerly, one who practiced robbery on the highway.

H.I.H. His (or Her) Imperial Highness.

hi·jack (hī′jak′) *v.t. Informal* **1** To steal a shipment of (goods, bootleg liquor, etc.) by force. **2** To rob or steal (a truck, etc., carrying such goods). **3** To seize control of (an aircraft) while in flight by the threat or use of force and redirect it to a different destination; skyjack. **4** To rob, swindle, etc., by force or coercion. [?] —**hi′jack′er** *n.*

hi·jinks (hī′jingks′) *n. pl. Informal* Rough and often mischievous play; horseplay. [?]

hike (hīk) *v.* **hiked, hik·ing** *v.i.* **1** To go on foot, as for pleasure or on a military march; tramp. —*v.t.* **2** To increase, raise, or lift: usu. with *up.* —*n.* **1** A journey on foot; a long walk. **2** *Informal.* An increase: a price *hike.* [?]

hi·lar·i·ous (hi·lâr′ē·əs, -lar′-, hī-) *adj.* Boisterously funny and gay. —**hi·lar′i·ous·ly** *adv.* —**hi·lar′i·ous·ness** *n.*

hi·lar·i·ty (hi·lâr′ə·tē, -lar′-, hī-) *n. pl.* **·ties** Boisterous fun and gaiety. [<Gk. *hilaros* cheerful]

hill (hil) *n.* **1** A natural elevation rising above the earth's surface and smaller than a mountain. **2** A heap or pile: a *molehill.* **3** A small mound of earth placed over or around certain plants and tubers. **4** The plants and tubers so surrounded. —**the Hill** CAPITOL HILL. —*v.t.* **1** To surround or cover with hills, as potatoes. **2** To form a hill or heap of. [<OE *hyll*]

hill·bil·ly (hil′bil′ē) *n. pl.* **·lies** *Informal* A person from the mountains or a backwoods area, esp. of the s U.S.

hill·ock (hil′ək) *n.* A small hill; a mound. —**hill′ock·y** *adj.*

hill·side (hil′sīd′) *n.* The side of a hill.

hill·top (hil′top′) *n.* The summit of a hill.

hill·y (hil′ē) *adj.* **hill·i·er, hill·i·est 1** Full of hills. **2** Like a hill; steep. —**hill′i·ness** *n.*

hilt (hilt) *n.* The handle and guard of a sword or dagger. —*v.t.* To provide with a hilt. [<OE]

hi·lum (hī′ləm) *n. pl.* **·la** (-lə) The scar on a seed at its former point of attachment. Also **hi′lus** (-ləs). [<L, a trifle]

him (him) *pron.* The objective case of the pronoun *he.* [<OE]

H.I.M. His (or Her) Imperial Majesty.

him·self (him·self′) *pron.* **1** The emphatic or intensive form of the pronouns *he* or *him:* He *himself* told me. **2** The reflexive form of *him:* He asked *himself.* **3** His true or usual self or condition: He's not *himself* today.

---

add, āce, dâre, pälm; end, ēven; it, īce; odd, ōpen, ôrder; tōōk, pōōl; up; bûrn; ə = a in *above, u in focus;* yōō = u in *fuse;* oil; pout; check; go; ring; thin; this; zh, *vision.* < derived from; ? origin uncertain or unknown.

hind¹ (hīnd) *adj.* **hind·er, hind·most** or **hind·er·most** Rear; posterior. [< OE *hindan* behind]

hind² (hīnd) *n.* The female of the red deer, esp. when fully mature.

hind³ (hīnd) *n.* *Archaic* A farm laborer; also, a peasant. [< OE *hīwan* domestics]

Hind. Hindi; Hindu; Hindustan; Hindustani.

hind·brain (hīnd′brān′, hīn′-) *n.* The posterior part of the brain which includes the cerebellum and medulla oblongata.

hin·der¹ (hin′dər) *v.t.* **1** To keep back or delay; check. **2** To prevent; obstruct. —*v.i.* **3** To be an obstruction or obstacle. [< OE *hinder* behind] —**hin′der·er** *n.* —**Syn. 1** impede, stop, stay, halt, bar, block. **2** encumber, foil, frustrate.

hind·er² (hīn′dər) *adj.* Pertaining to or situated at the rear. [< OE]

Hin·di (hin′dē) *n.* The official language of India.

hind·most (hīnd′mōst′, hīn′-) *adj.* Closest to the rear. Also **hind′er·most′** (hīn′dər-).

Hin·doo (hin′dōō) *n.* HINDU.

Hin·doo·ism (hin′dōō·iz′əm) *n.* HINDUISM.

hind·quar·ter (hīnd′kwôr′tər, hīn′-) *n.* **1** One of the two back parts of a carcass of beef, veal, lamb, etc., including a hind leg. **2** *pl.* The posterior part of any quadruped.

hin·drance (hin′drəns) *n.* **1** The act of hindering. **2** A person or thing that hinders or obstructs.

hind·sight (hīnd′sīt′, hīn′-) *n.* **1** Insight into the nature and difficulties of a situation after the event. **2** The rear sight of a gun or rifle.

Hin·du (hin′dōō) *n.* **1** A person who professes Hinduism. **2** Loosely, a native of India. —*adj.* Of Hindus, their language, religion, etc.

Hin·du·ism (hin′dōō·iz′əm) *n.* The religion and social system of the Hindus, derived from Brahmanism, and influenced by Buddhism.

Hin·du·sta·ni (hin′dōō·stä′nē, -stan′ē) *n.* The principal dialect of Hindi. —*adj.* Of or pertaining to Hindustan, its people, or to Hindustani.

hinge (hinj) *n.* **1** A device allowing one part to turn upon another, esp. the hook or joint on which a door or shutter swings or turns. **2** A device consisting of two metal plates joined by a rod, used as to connect a lid to a box. **3** A natural joint, as in the shell of an oyster. **4** A pivotal point on which anything depends for its effect or course. —*v.* **hinged, hing·ing** *v.i.* **1** To have one's course determined by an action or eventuality; be dependent: with *on* or *upon.* —*v.t.* **2** To attach by or equip with hinges. [ME *hengen*]

Hinge

hin·ny (hin′ē) *n. pl.* **·nies** The offspring of a stallion and a female donkey. [< Gk. *ginnos*]

hint (hint) *n.* **1** An indirect suggestion or implication. **2** A small amount or part: a *hint* of rain. —*v.t.* **1** To suggest indirectly; imply. —*v.i.* **2** To make hints: often with *at.* [< OF *hentan* seize, grasp] —**hint′er** *n.* —**Syn.** *n.* **1** reminder, tip, prompting, innuendo, insinuation. —*v.* **1** allude to, insinuate, remind, prompt.

hin·ter·land (hin′tər·land′, -lənd) *n.* **1** The region lying behind the district along a seacoast or riverside. **2** The region remote from urban areas; the back country. [G]

hip¹ (hip) *n.* **1** The lateral part of the body between the brim of the pelvis and the free part of the thigh. **2** The joint between the thigh bone and the pelvis: also **hip joint. 3** *Archit.* The external angle in which adjacent roof slopes meet each other. —*v.t.* **hipped, hip·ping** *Archit.* To build with a hip or hips, as a roof. [< OE *hype*]

hip² (hip) *n.* The fruit of a rose. [< OE *hēope*]

hip³ (hip) *adj. Slang* Aware; informed: often followed by *to.* [?]

hip·bone (hip′bōn′) *n.* The innominate bone.

hipped¹ (hipt) *adj.* Having hips of a specified kind: used in combination: *heavy-hipped.*

hipped² (hipt) *adj.* **1** *Slang* Unduly interested or engrossed by something; obsessed: *hipped* on socialism. **2** *Brit.* Affected with hypochondria or depression.

hip·pie (hip′ē) *n.* One of a group of young people whose alienation from conventional society is expressed by informal and eccentric clothing, a preoccupation with drugs and mysticism, and an interest in communal living. [Var. of HIPSTER]

hip·po (hip′ō) *n. Informal* A hippopotamus.

Hip·po·crat·ic oath (hip′ə·krat′ik) An oath credited to Hippocrates, and detailing the ethical code of the medical profession, still administered to those entering the practice of medicine.

hip·po·drome (hip′ə·drōm) *n.* **1** An arena, stadium, or large structure for horse shows, circuses, etc. **2** In ancient Greece and Rome, a course or track for horse races and chariot races. [< Gk. *hippos* horse + *dromos* running]

hip·po·pot·a·mus (hip′ə·pot′ə·məs) *n. pl.* **·mus·es** or **·mi** (-mī) A massive, herbivorous, short-legged, thick-skinned African mammal. [< Gk. *hippos* horse + *potamos* river]

hip·ster (hip′stər) *n. Slang* One who is hip, as one versed in jazz. [< HIP³ + -STER]

Hippopotamus

hire (hīr) *v.t.* **hired, hir·ing 1** To obtain the services of (a person) or the use of (a thing) in exchange for payment; employ; rent: to *hire* a new plant manager; to *hire* a tuxedo for a formal dinner. **2** To grant the use of (a thing) or the services of (a person) for a fee; let: often with *out.* —*n.* **1** Compensation for labor, services, etc. **2** The act of hiring or the condition of being hired. [< OE *hȳran*] —**hir′a·ble, hire′a·ble** *adj.* —**hir′er** *n.*

hire·ling (hīr′ling) *n.* One who serves for hire, esp. such a one whose motives are primarily mercenary.

hir·sute (hûr′sōōt, hir′-, hûr·sōōt′, hir-) *adj.* Hairy. [< L *hirsutus* rough] —**hir′sute·ness** *n.*

his (hiz) *pron.* **1** Belonging or pertaining to him: the possessive case of the pronoun *he,* used predicatively or after *of:* This room is *his;* that laugh of *his.* **2** The things, persons, etc., belonging or pertaining to him: Her book is better than *his;* He protects himself and *his.* —*pronominal adj.* The possessive case of the pronoun *he,* used attributively: *his* book. [< OE]

His·pa·ni·a (his·pā′nē·ə, -nyə, -pä′-) *n.* The Latin name for what is now Spain and Portugal.

His·pan·ic (his·pan′ik) *adj.* Of or pertaining to the countries or people of Spain, Portugal, and Latin America, or to their languages, customs, or culture. —*n. U.S.* A native or inhabitant of Spanish America; Spanish American.

hiss (his) *n.* **1** The prolonged sound of *s,* as that made by escaping air. **2** Such a sound made to express disapproval, hatred, etc. —*v.i.* **1** To make or emit a hiss or hisses. **2** To express disapproval or hatred by hissing. —*v.t.* **3** To express disapproval or hatred of by hissing. **4** To express by means of a hiss or hisses. **5** To pursue, drive off, silence, etc., by hissing: usu. with *off, down,* etc. [< OE *hyscan* jeer at] —**hiss′er** *n.*

hist (hist) *interj.* An exclamation to attract attention, command silence, etc. [Imit.]

hist. histology; historian; historical; history.

his·ta·mine (his′tə·mēn, -min) *n.* A product of protein metabolism found in all organisms and released profusely in allergic reactions. [< Gk. *histion* tissue + AMINE]

his·tol·o·gy (his·tol′ə·jē) *n.* The branch of anatomy concerned with the microscopic structure of tissues. [< Gk. *histion* tissue + -LOGY] —**his·to·log·i·cal** (his′tə·loj′i·kəl) *adj.* —**his·tol′o·gist** *n.*

his·to·ri·an (his·tôr′ē·ən, -tō′rē-) *n.* **1** One who writes a history. **2** One versed in history.

his·tor·ic (his·tôr′ik, -tor′-) *adj.* **1** Celebrated in history; notable; memorable; outstanding: the *historic* ascent of Mt. Everest. **2** HISTORICAL. • Current usage favors *historic* (def. 1) rather than *historical* to describe any outstanding or memorable event or achievement.

his·tor·i·cal (his·tôr′i·kəl, -tor′-) *adj.* **1** Of or relating to history. **2** Serving as a record or as evidence of past events, etc.: a *historical* letter. **3** Dealing with past events, etc.: a *historical* novel. **4** Factually true or real. **5** HISTORIC (def. 1). —**his·tor′i·cal·ly** *adv.* —**his·tor′i·cal·ness** *n.* • See HISTORIC.

historical present *Gram.* The present tense used to narrate a past event.

his·to·ri·og·ra·pher (his·tôr′ē·og′rə·fər, -tō′rē-) *n.* A historian, esp. one hired to write an official history of an institution, etc. —**his·to′ri·og′ra·phy** *n.*

his·to·ry (his′tə·rē, his′trē) *n. pl.* ·**ries** 1 A recorded narrative of past events, esp. those concerning a particular period, nation, individual, etc. 2 The branch of knowledge dealing with the events and people of the past. 3 The aggregate of events concerning a given subject, object, etc.: the *history* of their marriage. 4 Past events in general: in the course of *history*. 5 A past worthy of notice. 6 Something in the past: This is all *history* now. 7 A drama, story, etc., of past events, whether real or imaginary. [< Gk. *historia* knowledge, narrative]

his·tri·on·ic (his′trē·on′ik) *adj.* 1 Of or pertaining to actors, acting, or to the stage. 2 Theatrical in manner, esp. if excessively so. [< L *histrio* actor] —**his′tri·on′i·cal·ly** *adv.*

his·tri·on·ics (his′trē·on′iks) *n.pl.* 1 (*construed as sing.*) The art of dramatic representation. 2 (*construed as pl.*) Excessive or artificial display of emotion.

hit (hit) *v.* **hit, hit·ting** *v.t.* 1 To come against or in contact with, usu. with impact or force. 2 To inflict (a blow, etc.). 3 To strike with a blow. 4 To cause to strike or come against with force: with *on, against,* etc.: I *hit* my leg on the door. 5 To strike with or as with a missile: He *hit* the robber in the leg. 6 To move or propel by striking: He *hit* the ball over the fence. 7 To reach, arrive at, or achieve: to *hit* a new low; to *hit* upon the solution. 8 To suit: The idea *hit* her fancy. 9 To affect adversely: His death *hit* her hard. 10 *Informal* To go at vigorously or to excess: to *hit* the bottle. 11 *Slang* To ask or demand of: with *for:* He *hit* me for a loan. 12 *Slang* To arrive at: We *hit* the city late. 13 In baseball, to make a (specified base) hit: to *hit* a triple. —*v.i.* 14 To deliver a blow or blows: often with *out.* 15 To strike with force; bump: often with *against.* —*n.* 1 A stroke, blow, shot, etc., that reaches its mark. 2 COLLISION. 3 A success: The play was a *hit.* 4 A piece of wit or sarcasm. 5 BASE HIT. [< ON *hitta* come upon] —**hit′ter** *n.*

hit-and-run (hit′ən·run′) *adj.* Designating or involving an automobile operator who hits a pedestrian or another vehicle and drives away without stopping.

hitch (hich) *n.* 1 A stop or sudden halt. 2 A hindrance or obstacle, as to an enterprise. 3 The act of catching or fastening, as by a rope, hook, etc.; also, a connection so made. 4 *Naut.* Any of various knots made with rope, rigging, etc. 5 A limp; hobble. 6 *Slang* A ride given in hitchhiking. 7 *Slang* A period of time spent in military service, prison, etc. —*v.t.* 1 To fasten or tie, esp. temporarily, with a knot, rope, strap, etc. 2 To secure to a vehicle: often with *up:* to *hitch* up a trailer to a car. 3 To move or shift with a jerk or jerks: He *hitched* himself around in his chair. 4 *Informal* To marry: usu. in the passive. 5 *Slang* To obtain (a ride) by hitchhiking. —*v.i.* 6 To move with jerks: to *hitch* forward. 7 To become caught or entangled. 8 *Slang* To travel by hitchhiking. [ME *hicchen*]

hitch·hike (hich′hīk′) *Informal v.i.* 1 To travel by signalling for rides from passing vehicles. —*v.t.* 2 To obtain (a ride) by this method. —**hitch′hik′er** *n.*

hith·er (hith′ər) *adv.* In this direction; toward this place. —*adj.* Nearer. [< OE *hider*]

hith·er·most (hith′ər·mōst′) *adj.* Nearest in this direction or to this place.

hith·er·to (hith′ər·tōō′, hith′ər·tōō′) *adv.* Up to this time; until now.

hith·er·ward (hith′ər·wərd) *adv.* HITHER. Also **hith′er·wards.**

hit-or-miss (hit′ər·mis′) *adj.* Heedless; haphazard. —*adv.* In a hit-or-miss way; haphazardly.

Hit·tite (hit′īt) *n.* 1 One of an ancient people who established a powerful empire in Asia Minor and N Syria about 2000–1200 B.C. 2 The language of the Hittites. —*adj.* Of the Hittites, their culture, or language.

Hitches *def. 4*
a. half. b. clove. c. rolling.

hive (hīv) *n.* 1 A structure in which bees may dwell. 2 A colony of bees. 3 A place full of activity. 4 A teeming crowd of people. —*v.* **hived, hiv·ing** *v.t.* 1 To cause (bees) to enter a hive. 2 To store (honey) in a hive. 3 To store (anything) for future use. —*v.i.* 4 To enter or dwell in or as in a hive. [< OE *hȳf*]

hives (hīvz) *n.* Any of various skin diseases characterized by wheals, itching, etc., esp. urticaria. [?]

H.J. here lies (L *hic jacet*).

H.L. House of Lords.

hl, hl. hectoliter(s).

H.M. His (or Her) Majesty.

hm, hm. hectometer(s).

H.M.S. His (or Her) Majesty's Service (or Ship, Steamer).

ho (hō) *interj.* 1 A call to excite attention. 2 An exclamation expressing surprise, pleasure, derision, etc. 3 An exclamation directing attention to some distant point: Land *ho!* Westward *ho!* Also **hoa.** [Imit.]

Ho holmium.

hoa·gie (hō′gē) *n.* HERO (def. 5). Also **hoa′gy** *n.* (*pl.* ·**gies**). [?]

hoar (hôr, hōr) *adj.* 1 White or gray with age; hoary. 2 White or grayish white in color. 3 Ancient. —*n.* 1 HOARFROST. 2 The condition of being white with age or frost; hoariness. [< OE *hār* gray-haired]

hoard (hôrd, hōrd) *n.* An accumulation of something put away for safeguarding or for future use. —*v.t.* 1 To gather and store away or hide for future use. —*v.i.* 2 To gather and store away food, money, etc. [< OE *hord* treasure] —**hoard′er** *n.*

hoar·frost (hôr′frôst′, -frost′, hōr′-) *n.* A white coating of frost on a surface.

hoar·hound (hôr′hound′, hōr′-) *n.* HOREHOUND.

hoarse (hôrs, hōrs) *adj.* **hoars·er, hoars·est** 1 Harsh and rough in sound. 2 Having the voice harsh and rough. [< OE *hā(r)s*] —**hoarse′ly** *adv.* —**hoarse′ness** *n.*

hoars·en (hôr′sən, hōr′-) *v.t. & v.i.* To make or become hoarse or harsh.

hoar·y (hôr′ē, hō′rē) *adj.* **hoar·i·er, hoar·i·est** 1 White or grayish white, as from age. 2 Ancient. —**hoar′i·ness** *n.*

hoax (hōks) *n.* A deception or fraud, usu. practiced as a joke. —*v.t.* To deceive with a hoax. [< HOCUS(-POCUS)] —**hoax′er** *n.*

hob¹ (hob) *n.* 1 A shelflike projection at the back or on the side of a fireplace, used as a warming place. 2 A steel mandrel for cutting screw threads. [?]

hob² (hob) *n.* A fairy; hobgoblin; elf. —**play hob with** To throw into confusion; upset; ruin. [Orig., a nickname for ROBERT]

hob·ble (hob′əl) *v.* **hob·bled, hob·bling** *v.i.* 1 To walk with or as with a limp. 2 To move or proceed in an irregular or clumsy manner. —*v.t.* 3 To hamper the free movement of (a horse, etc.), as by tying the legs together. 4 To cause to move lamely or awkwardly. —*n.* 1 A limping gait. 2 A rope, strap, etc., used to fetter the forelegs of an animal. [ME *hoppelen* hobble] —**hob′bler** *n.*

hob·ble·de·hoy (hob′əl·dē·hoi′) *n.* 1 An awkward youth. 2 An adolescent boy. Also **hob′be·de·hoy′** (hob′ə·dē-). [?]

hob·by (hob′ē) *n. pl.* ·**bies** A subject or activity pursued for pleasure rather than for payment. [< *Robin,* a personal name] —**hob′by·ist** *n.*

hob·by·horse (hob′ē·hôrs′) *n.* 1 ROCKING HORSE. 2 A toy consisting of a stick with a wooden horse's head attached.

hob·gob·lin (hob′gob′lin) *n.* 1 An imp or goblin. 2 An imaginary cause of fear or terror. [< HOB² + GOBLIN]

hob·nail (hob′nāl′) *n.* 1 A nail for studding the soles of heavy shoes. 2 Any of a series of ornamental knobs, as on glassware. —**hob′nailed** *adj.*

hob·nob (hob′nob) *v.i.* ·**nobbed,** ·**nob·bing** 1 To drink together familiarly and convivially. 2 To be on familiar terms. [< OE *habban* have + *nabban* have not]

ho·bo (hō′bō) *n. pl.* ·**boes** or ·**bos** 1 TRAMP. 2 A migratory, unskilled workman. [?] —**ho′bo·ism** *n.*

Hob·son's choice (hob′sənz) An apparent choice in which there is no real freedom to choose or in which the alternatives are equally unsatisfactory. [< T. Hobson, 1544–1631, English liveryman, who required his customers to take the horse nearest the door]

hock[1] (hok) *n.* The backward-projecting joint of the hind leg of the horse, ox, pig, etc., corresponding to the ankle in man. —*v.t.* To disable by cutting the tendons of the 'hock; hamstring. [< OE *hōh* heel] •See HORSE.

hock[2] (hok) *n.* Any white Rhine wine. [< *Hochheim*, a German town where it was first produced]

hock[3] (hok) *Informal v.t.* PAWN. —*n.* The state of being in pawn. —**in hock** *Informal* 1 In pawn. 2 In debt. 3 In prison. [< Du. *hok* prison, debt]

hock·ey (hok′ē) *n.* 1 A game played on ice by opposing players on skates who try to drive a puck into their opponent's goal with a hockey stick; ice hockey. 2 A game similar to this but played on foot on a turfed field, using a small ball instead of a puck; field hockey. [?]

hockey stick 1 A hooked stick used in ice hockey. 2 A curved stick used in field hockey.

hock·shop (hok′shop′) *n. Slang* PAWNSHOP.

ho·cus (hō′kəs) *v.t.* ·cused or ·cussed, ·cus·ing or ·cus·sing 1 To deceive by a trick. 2 To drug; dope. 3 To add drugs to, as a drink. [Abbreviation of HOCUS-POCUS]

ho·cus-po·cus (hō′kəs-pō′kəs) *n.* 1 A verbal formula used in conjuring. 2 A magician's trick. 3 Any trick or deception. —*v.t. & v.i.* ·cused or ·cussed, ·cus·ing or ·cus·sing *Informal* To cheat; trick. [A sham Latin phrase]

Hockey sticks
a. field. b. ice.

hod (hod) *n.* 1 A long-handled receptacle for holding bricks and mortar. 2 A coal scuttle. [< OF *hotte*]

hodge-podge (hoj′poj′) *n.* A jumbled mixture; conglomeration. [ME *hochepot*]

Hodg·kin's disease (hoj′kinz) A progressive disease marked by enlargement of the lymph nodes, lymphoid tissue, and spleen. [< Dr. T. *Hodgkin*, 1798–1866, English physician]

hoe (hō) *n.* A tool for digging, scraping, and tilling, having a flat, thin blade set nearly at a right angle to a long handle. — *v.t. & v.i.* hoed, hoe·ing To dig, scrape, or till with a hoe. [< OF *houe*] —ho′er *n.*

Hoes
a. garden. b. weeding.

hoe·cake (hō′kāk′) *n.* A thin cake of Indian meal, originally baked on a hoe.

hoe·down (hō′doun′) *n.* 1 A square dance. 2 A social occasion where hoedowns are danced. [?]

hog (hôg, hog) *n.* 1 A pig, esp. one that is full-grown. 2 An animal related to the pig, as the peccary. 3 *Informal* A filthy or gluttonous person. —*v.t.* hogged, hog·ging *Slang* To take more than one's share of; grab selfishly. [< OE *hogg*]

hog·gish (hôg′ish, hog′-) *adj.* 1 Of or like a hog. 2 Greedy, selfish, dirty, etc. —hog′gish·ly *adv.* —hog′gish·ness *n.*

hog·nose (hôg′nōz′, hog′-) *n.* A harmless North American snake with a flattened head and prominent snout.

hogs·head (hôgz′hed′, hogz′-) *n.* 1 A large cask. 2 Any of various liquid measures, esp., in the U.S., a unit equal to 63 gallons.

hog·tie (hôg′tī′, hog′-) *v.t.* ·tied, ·ty·ing or ·tie·ing 1 To tie all four feet or the hands and feet of. 2 *Informal* To keep from taking effective action.

hog·wash (hôg′wosh′, -wôsh′, hog′-) *n.* 1 Kitchen refuse, swill, etc., fed to hogs. 2 *Informal* Ridiculous speech or writing; nonsense.

hoi pol·loi (hoi′ pə·loi′) The common people; the masses: with *the:* usu. used contemptuously. [Gk., the many]

hoist (hoist) *v.t.* To raise to a higher position; lift or heave up, esp. by some mechanical means. —*n.* 1 A machine for hoisting; lift. 2 The act of hoisting; a boost. 3 *Naut.* The length of a sail between the boom and the peak or the jaws of the gaff. [?] —hoist′er *n.*

hol·ty-toi·ty (hoi′tē-toi′tē) *adj.* 1 Self-important; putting on airs. 2 Flighty; giddy. 3 Petulant; huffy. [Reduplication of obs. *hoit* to romp]

hoke (hōk) *Slang v.t.* hoked, hok·ing To make more intense, dramatic, spectacular, etc., by obvious or artificial means: usu. with *up.* —*n.* HOKUM. [< HOKUM]

ho·kum (hō′kəm) *n. Slang* 1 Obvious and contrived comic or sentimental devices or effects in a play, novel, movie, etc. 2 Nonsense; bunk. [Alter. of HOCUS]

hold[1] (hōld) *v.* held, held or *in legal use* hold·en, hold·ing *v.t.* 1 To take and keep in the hand, arms, etc.; grasp. 2 To prevent the movement or escape of: *Hold* the bus! 3 To restrain from acting or speaking: *Hold* your tongue! 4 To keep in a specified place, position, or state: to *hold* one's arm up. 5 To regard in a specified manner; consider: to *hold* someone dear. 6 To require to fulfill, as the conditions of a contract; obligate. 7 To support or keep in position: Ropes *held* the tower in position. 8 To be capable of enclosing or containing: The barrel *holds* ten gallons. 9 To maintain in the mind; believe: to *hold* an opinion. 10 To conduct or engage in; carry on: to *hold* court or services. 11 To have and retain ownership or control of; keep as one's own; occupy: to *hold* the position of chairman. 12 To get and retain possession or control of: to *hold* an enemy town; to *hold* one's attention. 13 To keep for later use, delivery, etc.: to *hold* a hotel room. 14 *Music* To prolong or sustain (a note or rest). —*v.i.* 15 To maintain a grip or grasp. 16 To remain firm or unbroken: if the rope *holds;* He *held* to his purpose. 17 To continue unchanged: The breeze *held* all day. 18 To be or remain true, valid, etc.: This decision *holds.* 19 To check or restrain oneself; forbear: usu. used in the imperative. —**hold down** 1 To suppress; keep under control. 2 *Informal* To occupy (a job, etc.) successfully. —**hold forth** To harangue; preach or speak at length. —**hold off** 1 To keep at a distance. 2 To refrain. —**hold on** 1 To maintain a grip or hold. 2 To persist; continue. 3 *Informal* To stop or wait: used in the imperative. —**hold one's own** To maintain one's position, as in a contest; lose no ground. —**hold out** 1 To stretch forth; offer. 2 To last to the end: Our supplies *held out.* 3 To continue resistance; endure; persist. 4 *U.S. Slang* To keep back part or all of (something). —**hold out for** *Informal* To insist upon as a condition of an agreement: He *held out for* a higher salary. —**hold up** 1 To support; prop. 2 To exhibit to view. 3 *Informal* To last; endure. 4 To delay; stop. 5 *Informal* To rob. —*n.* 1 The act or manner of holding, as with the hands. 2 In wrestling, a specific grip on an opponent. 3 A controlling force or influence. 4 A place to grasp. 5 A place of confinement. [< OE *haldan*]

hold[2] (hōld) *n. Naut.* The space below the decks of a vessel where cargo is stowed. [< HOLE]

hold·er (hōl′dər) *n.* 1 One who or that which holds. 2 An owner; possessor. 3 *Law* One who holds a check, promissory note, etc., for which he is entitled to receive payment.

hold·ing (hōl′ding) *n.* 1 The act of one who or that which holds. 2 A tenure or right of possession. 3 *Often pl.* Property held by legal right, esp. stocks or bonds.

holding company A company that holds stock in one or more companies for investment or operating purposes, or both.

hold·o·ver (hōld′ō′vər) *n.* 1 One who or that which remains from a previous time, engagement, or situation. 2 One who continues in office after his term has expired.

hold-up (hōld′up′) *n.* 1 Stoppage, delay, or obstruction of some activity. 2 A forcible stoppage to commit robbery, esp. of a traveler, a train, etc.

hole (hōl) *n.* 1 A cavity extending into a solid body, as a pit, cave, etc. 2 An opening or aperture in anything: a *hole* in a dress. 3 A deep place in a stream or creek. 4 An animal's burrow or den. 5 A small, dingy room, dwelling, etc. 6 A prison cell. 7 A fault or defect: the *holes* in his argument. 8 *Informal* A dilemma or predicament. 9 In golf: a A small sunken cup into which the ball must be hit. b Any of the 9 or 18 sections of a course, from the tee to the cup inclusive. 10 *Electronics* An empty electron energy state in a crystal, acting as a positive charge carrier' with the magnitude of an electron. —**in the hole** *Informal* In debt. —*v.* holed, hol·ing *v.t.* 1 To make a hole or holes in; perforate. 2 To drive or put into a hole, as in billiards or golf. **3** To dig (a shaft, tunnel, etc.). —*v.i.* **4** To make a hole or holes. —**hole up 1** To hibernate, as in a hole. **2** To take refuge in hiding. [< OE *hol*]

hol·i·day (hol'ə-dā) *n.* **1** A day appointed by law or custom for the suspension of general business, usu. in commemoration of some person or event. **2** Any day of rest. **3** *Often pl.* A period of festivity or leisure; a vacation. —*adj.* Suitable for a holiday; festive. —*v.i.* To vacation. [< OE *hālig dæg* holy day]

hol·i·day·mak·er (hol'ə-dā-mā'kər) *n. Brit.* One who is on vacation.

ho·li·ly (hō'lə-lē) *adv.* In a holy manner; piously; sacredly.

ho·li·ness (hō'lē-nis) *n.* The state or quality of being holy. —**His** (or **Your**) **Holiness** A title of the Pope.

hol·land (hol'ənd) *n.* Unbleached linen, glazed or unglazed. [< HOLLAND, where first made]

Hol·land (hol'ənd) *n.* NETHERLANDS.

hol·lan·daise sauce (hol'ən-dāz', hol'ən-dez') A creamy sauce made of butter, yolks of eggs, lemon juice or vinegar, and seasoning. [< F *hollandaise* of Holland]

hol·ler (hol'ər) *v.t. & v.i. Informal* To call out loudly; shout; yell. —*n.* A loud shout; yell. [Imit.]

hol·low (hol'ō) *adj.* **1** Having empty space or a cavity within; not solid: a *hollow* tree. **2** Sunken: *hollow* cheeks. **3** Depressed or sunk below the surface; concave. **4** Empty; vacant; insincere: *hollow* praise. **5** Muffled; dully reverberating: a *hollow* sound. **6** Hungry. —*n.* **1** Any depression in a body; a cavity. **2** A small valley. —*v.t. & v.i.* To make or become hollow. [< OE *holh*] —**hol'low·ly** *adv.* —**hol'low·ness** *n.*

hol·ly (hol'ē) *n. pl.* **·lies 1** Any of various trees and shrubs with glossy, sharp-pointed leaves and red berries, often used as Christmas ornaments. **2** The holm. [< OE *holen*]

hol·ly·hock (hol'ē-hok) *n.* A plant with hairy leaves and tall spikes of large flowers of numerous shades. [< ME *holi* holy + *hoc* mallow]

hol·mi·um (hōl'mē-əm) *n.* A metallic element (symbol Ho) of the rare-earth group. [< *Holmia*, Latinized name of Stockholm]

holo- *combining form* Whole; wholly: *holograph.* [< Gk. *holos* whole]

hol·o·caust (hol'ə-kôst) *n.* **1** A sacrifice wholly consumed by fire. **2** Wholesale destruction or loss of life by fire, war, etc. [< Gk. *holos* whole + *kaustos* burnt] —**hol'o·caus'tal, hol'o·caus'tic** *adj.*

Hol·o·cene (hol'ə-sēn) *adj. & n.* See GEOLOGY. [< HOLO- + Gk. *kainos* recent]

hol·o·gram (hol'ə-gram) *n.* An image on film of the interference pattern made by holography. [< HOLO- + GRAM[1]]

Hollyhocks
a. single.
b. double.

hol·o·graph (hol'ə-graf, -gräf) *n.* **1** A document wholly in the handwriting of the person whose signature it bears. **2** HOLOGRAM. [< HOLO- + Gk. *graphein* write] —**hol'o·graph'ic** or **·i·cal** *adj.*

ho·log·ra·phy (hə-log'rə-fē) *n.* A process in which light reflected by a laser-illuminated object interferes with a reference beam and forms on film a pattern containing all the information needed to project a three-dimensional image of the object. [< HOLO- + -GRAPHY]

Hol·stein (hōl'stīn, -stēn) *n.* One of a breed of black-and-white cattle bred for both beef and milk: also **Hol'stein-Frie'sian** (-frē'zhən). [< *Holstein*, a former Danish duchy, now part of Schleswig-Holstein]

hol·ster (hōl'stər) *n.* A pistol case. [< Du.]

ho·ly (hō'lē) *adj.* **·li·er, ·li·est 1** Devoted to religious or sacred use; consecrated; hallowed. **2** Of highest spiritual purity; saintly. **3** Evoking or worthy of veneration, awe, respect, etc. **4** Religious: a *holy* war. —*n. pl.* **ho·lies** A holy thing or place. [< OE *hālig*] —**Syn.** *adj.* **1** sanctified, sacred, sacrosanct. **2** godly, pure, angelic, righteous.

Holy City A city considered sacred by the believers in a religion, as Jerusalem or Mecca.

Holy Communion The Eucharist or Lord's Supper.

holy day A sacred day, as the Sabbath, or one set apart for religious uses.

Holy Father A title of the Pope.

Holy Ghost The third person of the Trinity. Also **Holy Spirit.**

Holy Grail GRAIL.

Holy Land PALESTINE.

Holy Mother VIRGIN MARY.

holy of holies The innermost and most sacred shrine of the Jewish tabernacle.

holy orders The state of being ordained to the ministry of a church: a term used chiefly in the Anglican, Eastern, and Roman Catholic churches.

Holy Roman Empire An empire in CEN. and W Europe, established in 962 and lasting until 1806, regarded as an extension of the Western Roman Empire.

Holy Saturday The Saturday before Easter.

Holy See The court, position, or authority of the Pope.

ho·ly·stone (hō'lē-stōn) *n.* A flat piece of soft sandstone used for cleaning the wood decks of a vessel. —*v.t.* **·stoned, ·ston·ing** To scrub with a holystone. [?]

Holy Synod The supreme governing body in any of the Eastern Orthodox churches.

Holy Week The week before Easter.

Holy Writ BIBLE.

hom·age (hom'ij, om'-) *n.* **1** Deep regard, honor, respect, or veneration, esp. as shown by some action. **2** In feudal law, formal acknowledgment of tenure by a tenant to his lord. [< LL *homo* vassal, client, man]

hom·bre (ôm'brā, om'brē) *n. Slang* A man. [Sp.]

hom·burg (hom'bûrg) *n.* A man's felt hat with slightly rolled-up brim and crown dented lengthwise. [< *Homburg*, Germany]

Homburg

home (hōm) *n.* **1** One's dwelling place or residence. **2** The country, state, city, etc., where one lives or was reared. **3** A family thought of as a unit: a happy *home.* **4** A place regarded as a home: She found a *home* in the convent. **5** The seat or habitat of something; the place of origin: New Orleans is the *home* of jazz. **6** An establishment for the shelter and care of the needy or infirm. **7** In some games, the goal that must be reached in order to win or score. —**at home 1** In one's own house, place, or country. **2** At ease, as if in familiar surroundings. **3** Prepared to receive callers. —*adj.* **1** Of or pertaining to one's home or country. **2** At the place regarded as the base of operations: the *home* office; a *home* game. **3** Going to the point; effective: a *home* thrust. —*adv.* **1** To, at, or in the direction of home. **2** To the place or point intended: to thrust the dagger *home.* **3** Deeply and intimately; to the heart: Her words struck *home.* —*v.* **homed, hom·ing** *v.t.* **1** To carry or send to a home. **2** To furnish with a home. —*v.i.* **3** To go to a home; fly home, as homing pigeons. **4** To have residence. —**home in on** To direct toward, seek, or find a destination, target, etc., esp. by radio or radar. [< OE *hām*]

home·bod·y (hōm'bod'ē) *n. pl.* **·bod·ies** A person who takes an interest in a home or who likes to stay at home.

home·bred (hōm'bred') *adj.* **1** Bred at home; native; domestic. **2** Uncultivated; crude.

home·brew (hōm'brōō') *n.* An alcoholic beverage distilled or brewed at home.

home·com·ing (hōm'kum'ing) *n.* **1** A return home. **2** In many American colleges and universities, an annual celebration for visiting alumni.

home economics The sciences and arts having practical application to domestic functions, including nutrition, cooking, child care, etc.

home-grown (hōm'grōn') *adj.* Grown at home, as fruits and vegetables.

home·land (hōm'land') *n.* The country of one's birth or allegiance.

home·less (hōm'lis) *adj.* Having no home. —**home'less·ness** *n.*

home·like (hōm′līk′) *adj.* Comfortable, pleasant, cozy, etc., as in a home.

home·ly (hōm′lē) *adj.* ·li·er, ·li·est 1 Having a familiar everyday character; unpretentious. 2 Having plain features; not good-looking. 3 Domestic. —**home′li·ness** *n.*

home·made (hōm′mād′) *adj.* 1 Made at home. 2 Simple; unpretentious; crude.

ho·me·op·a·thist (hō′mē·op′ə·thist, hom′ē-) *n.* One who advocates or practices homeopathy. Also **ho·me·o·path** (hō′mē·ə·path′, hom′ē-).

ho·me·op·a·thy (hō′mē·op′ə·thē, hom′ē-) *n.* A system of medicine that prescribes minute doses of such medicines as would produce in a healthy person the symptoms of the disease treated. [<Gk. *homoios* similar + -PATHY] —**ho·me·o·path·ic** (hō′mē·ə·path′ik, hom′ē-) *adj.*

home plate In baseball, the base at which the batter stands when batting and to which he must return to score.

hom·er (hō′mər) *n. Informal* HOME RUN.

Ho·mer·ic (hō·mer′ik) *adj.* Of or pertaining to Homer or his age or writings. Also **Ho·me·ri·an** (hō·mir′ē·ən), **Ho·mer′i·cal.**

home rule Self-government in local affairs.

home run In baseball, a base hit in which the ball is driven far enough to allow the batter to touch all bases and score a run.

home·sick (hōm′sik′) *adj.* Sad through longing for home; nostalgic. —**home′sick′ness** *n.*

home·spun (hōm′spun′) *n.* 1 Fabric woven at home. 2 A loose, rough fabric having the appearance of tweed. —*adj.* 1 Made at home. 2 Made of homespun. 3 Plain and simple; unpretentious.

home·stead (hōm′sted) *n.* 1 A home, together with subsidiary buildings and adjacent land. 2 A tract of land occupied by a settler under the Homestead Act (1862) or its revisions. —*v.i. U.S.* To become a settler on a homestead under the Homestead Act. —*v.t. U.S.* To settle on land under the Homestead Act. —**home′stead′er** *n.*

Homestead Act A Congressional enactment of 1862 which granted 160 acres of land to a settler to develop and later own.

home·stretch (hōm′strech′) *n.* 1 The last part of a racecourse before the winning post is reached. 2 The last part of any journey or endeavor.

home·ward (hōm′wərd) *adj., adv.* Toward home. Also **home′wards.**

home·work (hōm′wûrk′) *n.* 1 Lessons assigned to students to be done outside the classroom. 2 Work, esp. piecework, done for wages at home. 3 Preparatory work or research, as for a meeting.

home·y (hō′mē) *adj.* **hom·i·er, hom·i·est** *Informal* Simple, pleasant, comfortable, etc.; homelike. —**home′y·ness** or **hom′i·ness** *n.*

hom·i·cide (hom′ə·sīd, hō′mə-) *n.* 1 The killing of one human being by another. 2 A person who has killed another. [<L *homo* man + -CIDE] —**hom′i·ci′dal** *adj.* —**hom′i·ci′dal·ly** *adv.*

hom·i·let·ics (hom′ə·let′iks) *n. pl. (construed as sing.)* The branch of theology that treats of the composition and delivery of sermons. [<Gk. *homilētikos* sociable] —**hom′i·let′ic** or **·i·cal** *adj.* —**hom′i·let′i·cal·ly** *adv.* —**hom′i·list** *n.*

hom·i·ly (hom′ə·lē) *n. pl.* ·lies 1 A sermon, esp. one based on the Bible. 2 A lecture on morals or conduct. [<Gk. *homilia* <*homilos* assembly] —**hom′i·let′ic** or **·i·cal** *adj.*

hom·ing (hō′ming) *adj.* 1 Heading homeward. 2 Pertaining to methods and devices for directing an aircraft or missile to a given point.

homing pigeon A pigeon capable of finding its way home from great distances, used for conveying messages.

hom·i·nid (hom′ə·nid, hō′mə-) *n.* A member of a family of the primate order, now represented only by modern man. —*adj.* Of or pertaining to this group. [<L *homo, hominis* man]

hom·i·noid (hom′ə·noid, hō′mə-) *n.* Any of a superfamily of the primate order, including the large manlike apes and modern and prehistoric man. —*adj.* Of this superfamily. [<L *homo, hominis* man]

hom·i·ny (hom′ə·nē) *n.* Hulled dried corn (maize), coarsely ground and boiled for food. Also **hominy grits.**

[<Algonquian *rockahominie* parched corn]

ho·mo[1] (hō′mō) *n* Any of a genus of errect, large-brained primates, now represented only by modern man. [L]

ho·mo[2] (hō′mō) *n. pl* ·mos *Slang* HOMOSEXUAL.

homo- *combining form* Same; similar; equal: *homogeneous.* [<Gk. *homos* same]

ho·mo·ge·ne·ous (hō′mə·jē′nē·əs, hom′ə-) *adj.* 1 Of the same composition or character throughout. 2 Of the same kind, nature, etc., as another; similar. [<Gk. *homos* the same + *genos* race] —**ho′mo·ge′ne·ous·ly** *adv.* —**ho·mo·ge·ne·i·ty** (hō′mə·jə·nē′ə·tē, hom′ə-), **ho′mo·ge′ne·ous·ness** *n.*

ho·mog·en·ize (hə·moj′ə·nīz) *v.t.* ·ized, ·iz·ing 1 To render homogeneous. 2 a To distribute throughout a fluid, as tiny particles. b To make (milk) more uniform by emulsification of its butterfat. —**ho·mog′en·ized** *adj.* —**ho·mog′en·i·za′tion, ho·mog′en·iz′er** *n.*

hom·o·graph (hom′ə·graf, -gräf, hō′mə-) *n.* A word identical with another in spelling, but differing from it in origin and meaning, and sometimes in pronunciation, as *bass,* a fish, and *bass,* a male voice.

ho·mol·o·gize (hō·mol′ə·jīz) *v.* ·gized, ·giz·ing *v.t.* 1 To make homologous. 2 To demonstrate the homologies of. —*v.i.* 3 To be homologous; correspond in structure or value.

ho·mol·o·gous (hō·mol′ə·gəs) *adj.* 1 Having a similar structure, proportion, value, or position. 2 Identical in nature, relation, or the like. [<Gk. *homos* the same + *logos* speech]

ho·mol·o·gy (hō·mol′ə·jē) *n. pl.* ·gies The state or quality of being homologous; correspondence in structure and properties. [HOMO- + -LOGY]

hom·o·nym (hom′ə·nim, hō′mə-) *n.* 1 A word identical with another in pronunciation, but differing from it in meaning, origin, and usu. in spelling, as *fair* and *fare, read* and *reed.* 2 Loosely, a homograph. [<Gk. *homos* same + *onyma* name] —**hom·o·nym·ic** (hom′ə·nim′ik, hō′mə-) or **·i·cal** *adj.*

ho·mo·phile (hō′mō·fīl) *n.* A homosexual.

ho·mo·pho·bi·a (hō′mō·fō′bē·ə) *n.* Hatred or fear either of homosexuals or of homosexuality.

hom·o·phone (hom′ə·fōn, hō′mə-) *n.* HOMONYM (def.1).

hom·o·phon·ic (hom′ə·fon′ik, hō′mə-) *adj.* 1 Of, pertaining to, or having the same sound. 2 *Music* Having one predominant part carrying the melody, with other parts used for harmony. —**ho·moph·o·ny** (hō·mof′ə·nē) *n.*

ho·mop·ter·ous (hō·mop′tər·əs) *adj.* Of or pertaining to an order of insects having sucking mouth parts and two pairs of membranous wings of uniform thickness.

Homo sa·pi·ens (sā′pē·enz) The scientific term for the human race. [<HOMO + L *sapiēns* <*sapere* to have taste, be wise]

ho·mo·sex·u·al (hō′mə·sek′shoo·əl, hom′ə-) *adj.* Pertaining to or characterized by homosexuality. —*n.* A homosexual person.

ho·mo·sex·u·al·i·ty (hō′mə·sek′shoo·al′ə·tē, hom′ə-) *n.* 1 Sexual attraction toward a person of the same sex. 2 Sexual relations between persons of the same sex.

ho·mun·cu·lus (hō·mung′kyə·ləs) *n. pl.* ·li (-lī) An undersized man; dwarf. [L, dim. of *homo* man] —**ho·mun′cu·lar** *adj.*

Hon. Honorable.

hon. honorably; honorary.

Hond. Honduras.

Hon·du·ras (hon·d′yŏŏr′əs) A republic of NE Central America, 43,227 sq. mi., cap. Tegucigalpa. —**Hon·du′ran** *adj., n.* • See map at CENTRAL AMERICA.

hone (hōn) *n.* A block of fine compact stone for sharpening edged tools, razors, etc. —*v.t.* **honed, hon·ing** To sharpen, as a razor, on a hone. [<OE *hān* stone] —**hon′er** *n.*

hon·est (on′ist) *adj.* 1 Not given to lies, theft, cheating, etc. 2 Not false or misleading; true: an *honest* answer. 3 Free from fraud; fair; equitable: an *honest* test. 4 Earned or acquired in a just and fair manner: an *honest* living. 5 Frank; open; sincere: an *honest* face. [<L *honos* honor] —**hon′est·ly** *adv.* —Syn. 1 trustworthy, reliable, fair, honorable, upright. 2 frank, candid, straightforward, artless, forthright. 3 just, impartial, unbiased.

hon·es·ty (on′is·tē) *n.* The quality of being honest.

hon·ey (hun′ē) *n.* 1 A sweet food made by bees from the nectar of flowers. 2 Sweetness or lusciousness in general. 3 Darling; dear: a term of endearment. 4 *Informal* Something considered as an excellent example of its kind: a *honey* of a boat. —*v.* **hon·eyed** or **hon·ied, hon·ey·ing** —*v.t.* **1** To talk in an endearing or flattering manner to. **2** To sweeten. —*v.i.* **3** To talk fondly or in a coaxing manner. —*adj.* Honeylike; sweet. [< OE *hunig*]

hon·ey·bee (hun′ē·bē′) *n.* A bee that makes honey, esp. the common hive bee.

hon·ey·comb (hun′ē·kōm′) *n.* **1** A structure of close-packed, hexagonal cells with walls of wax, made by bees to contain their honey, eggs, etc. **2** Anything resembling a honeycomb. —*v.t.* **1** To fill with small holes or passages. **2** To pervade; corrupt. —*v.i.* **3** To become full of holes or passages. [< OE *hunigcamb*] —**hon′ey·combed′** *adj.*

Honeybee

hon·ey·dew (hun′ē·dyōō′) *n.* **1** A sweet secretion of certain plants and insects. **2** HONEYDEW MELON.

honeydew melon A greenish white melon with a smooth skin and sweet flesh.

hon·eyed (hun′ēd) *adj.* **1** Covered with or full of honey. **2** Sweetly flattering; soothing; agreeable.

honey locust A large, thorny North American tree with feathery foliage, bearing long pods with a sweet pulp between the seeds.

hon·ey·moon (hun′ē·mōōn) *n.* **1** A wedding trip. **2** A period of agreement or concord immediately after a marriage. **3** Any brief period of agreement or concord.

hon·ey·suck·le (hun′ē·suk′əl) *n.* **1** Any of a genus of ornamental shrubs having small, usu. fragrant tubular crimson flowers. **2** A plant resembling honeysuckle, as certain azaleas and columbines.

hon·ied (hun′ēd) *adj.* HONEYED.

honk (hôngk, hongk) *n.* The cry of a wild goose or a sound imitating it, as that of an automobile horn. —*v.i.* To utter or make a honk or honks. —*v.t.* To cause to emit a honk or honks, as an automobile horn. [Imit.]

honk·y-tonk (hông′kē·tôngk′, hong′kē·tongk′) *n. Slang* A noisy, disreputable barroom or night club. —*adj.* Describing a type of tinkling, ragtime piano playing or music. [Prob. imit.]

hon·or (on′ər) *n.* **1** High regard or respect. **2** Fame; renown; glory. **3** A cause of pride or esteem: an *honor* to be chosen. **4** A sense of what is right and just; integrity: to act with *honor*. **5** A reputation for being just, good, fair, etc.: a man of *honor*. **6** High rank or dignity: the *honor* of the office. **7** *Often pl.* An outward token or sign of respect or regard, as a decoration, ceremony, etc. **8** *pl.* **a** Recognition given to students for outstanding scholarship, etc. **b** Academic courses for advanced or exceptional students, usu. in addition to regular courses. **9** Privilege: May I have the *honor* of this dance? **10** In bridge, one of the five highest cards of any suit. **11** In golf, the privilege of playing first from the tee. —**do the honors** To act as host or hostess. —*v.t.* **1** To regard with honor or respect. **2** To treat with courtesy or respect. **3** To do or bestow something in honor of. **4** To accept or pay, as a check or draft. —*adj.* Of or showing honor or respect: an *honor* guard. *Brit. sp.* ·**our.** [< L] —**hon′or·er** *n.*

Hon·or (on′ər) *n.* A title or form of address for a judge, mayor, etc.: preceded by *Your, His,* or *Her.*

hon·or·a·ble (on′ər·ə·bəl) *adj.* **1** Worthy of honor. **2** Conferring honor. **3** Consistent with or acting in accordance with principles of honor; conforming to a code of honor. **4** Accompanied by marks or testimonials of honor. **5** Entitled to honor: formal title of respect prefixed to the names of persons holding important offices. *Brit. sp.* ·**our·a·ble.** —**hon′or·a·ble·ness** *n.* —**hon′or·a·bly** *adv.*

hon·o·rar·i·um (on′ə·râr′ē·əm) *n. pl.* ·**i·ums** or ·**i·a** A gratuity given for services rendered when law, custom, or propriety forbids a set fee. [< L *honorarium (donum)* honorary (gift)]

hon·or·ar·y (on′ə·rer′ē) *adj.* **1** Done, conferred, or held merely as an honor. **2** Designating an office or title bestowed as a sign of honor, without emoluments or without

powers or duties. **3** Depending solely on one's honor: said of a debt or other obligation not legally binding.

hon·or·if·ic (on′ə·rif′ik) *adj.* Conferring or implying honor or respect. —*n.* Any honorific title, word, phrase, etc. —**hon′or·if′i·cal·ly** *adv.*

honor system A system whereby work, school examinations, etc., are undertaken without supervision.

hooch[1] (hōōch) *n. Slang* Intoxicating liquor. [< *Hutsnuwu,* Alaskan Indian tribe that made liquor]

hooch[2] (hōōch) *Slang* **1** A thatched hut. **2** Any dwelling. [< Japanese *uchi* house]

hood[1] (hōōd) *n.* **1** A soft or flexible covering for the head and the back of the neck, often attached to a garment. **2** Anything of similar form or character, as a monk's cowl or an ornamental fold attached to the back of an academic gown. **3** In falconry, a cover for the entire head of a hawk. **4** A projecting cover to a hearth, ventilator, etc. **5** A movable cover, as of the engine of an automobile, etc. —*v.t.* To cover or furnish with or as with a hood. [< OE *hōd*]

hood[2] (hōōd) *n. Slang* A hoodlum.

-hood *suffix of nouns* **1** Condition of; state of being: *babyhood, falsehood.* **2** Class or totality of those having a certain character: *priesthood.* [< OE *-hād* state, condition]

hood·lum (hōōd′ləm, hōōd′-) *n.* **1** A rowdy or thug. **2** A criminal. [?] —**hood′lum·ism** *n.*

hoo·doo (hōō′dōō) *n.* **1** VOODOO. **2** *Informal* A person or thing that brings bad luck; a jinx. —*v.t. Informal* To bring bad luck to; bewitch. [Var. of VOODOO] —**hoo′doo·ism** *n.*

hood·wink (hōōd′wingk′) *v.t.* To deceive as if by blinding; dupe; delude. [< HOOD[1] + WINK] —**hood′wink′er** *n.*

hoo·ey (hōō′ē) *n. & interj. Slang.* Nonsense.

hoof (hōōf, hŏŏf) *n. pl.* **hoofs** or **hooves 1** The horny sheath encasing the ends of the foot in the horse, swine, ox, etc. **2** An animal with hoofs. —**on the hoof** Alive; not butchered: said of cattle. —*v.t. & v.i.* **1** To trample with the hoofs. **2** *Informal* To walk or dance: usu. with *it.* [< OE *hōf*] —**hoofed** (hōōft, hŏŏft) *adj.*

hoof-and-mouth disease (hōōf′ən·mouth′) FOOT-AND-MOUTH DISEASE.

hoof·er (hōōf′ər, hŏŏf′-) *n. Slang* A professional dancer, esp. a tap dancer.

hook (hŏŏk) *n.* **1** A curved or bent piece serving to catch or hold another object. **2** A fishhook. **3** A cutting tool having a curved blade, as a sickle. **4** A trap or snare. **5** Something shaped like a hook as: **a** A sharply curved organ of an animal or plant. **b** A bend in a river. **c** A curved point of land or a cape. **d** A hook-shaped written character. **6** In golf, a ball that curves to the left of a right-handed player or vice versa. **7** In baseball, a curve. **8** In boxing, a short blow delivered crosswise and with the elbow bent and rigid. —*v.t.* **1** To fasten, attach, or take hold of with or as with a hook. **2** To catch on a hook, as fish. **3** *Informal* To trick; take in: I've been *hooked.* **4** To make or bend in the shape of a hook; crook. **5** To catch on or toss with the horns, as a bull. **6** To make, as a rug, by looping thread, yarn, etc., through canvas or burlap with a hook. **7** *Slang* To steal; pilfer. **8** In baseball, to throw (a ball) with a hook. **9** In boxing, to strike with a hook. **10** In golf, to drive (the ball) in a hook. —*v.i.* **11** To curve like a hook; bend. **12** To be fastened with a hook. [< OE *hōc*]

hook·ah (hŏŏk′ə) *n.* A form of tobacco pipe by which the smoke is drawn through water; a narghile. Also **hook′a.** [< Ar. *huqqah*]

hooked (hŏŏkt) *adj.* **1** Curved like a hook. **2** Supplied with a hook. **3** Made with a hook. **4** *Slang* **a** Addicted, as to a narcotic: often with *on.* **b** Excessively enthusiastic or obsessed with a person or thing: often with *on.* **5** *Slang* Married.

hook·er[1] (hŏŏk′ər) *n.* A fishing boat used on the English and Irish coasts. [< Du. *hoek* hook]

hook·er[2] (hŏŏk′ər) *n. Slang* A drink, esp. an alcoholic one. [< HOOK, prob. with ref. to the bend of the arm in drinking]

hook·er[3] (hŏŏk′ər) *n. Slang* A prostitute. [< Corlears *Hook,* formerly a notorious waterfront district in Manhattan]

hook·up (hŏŏk′up′) n. 1 a An assembly of electronic parts, circuits, etc. b A diagram of such an assembly. 2 A mechanical connection, as of gas or water lines. 3 *Informal* An alliance or pact between governments, organizations, etc.

hook·worm (hŏŏk′wûrm′) n. 1 Any of various parasitic nematode worms infesting the intestines of man and several animals, such as sheep, dogs, cattle, etc. 2 Infestation with hookworms: also **hookworm disease.**

hook·y (hŏŏk′ē) n. *Informal* Truant: used only in the phrase **to play hooky.** [< HOOK in sense of "to escape"]

hoo·li·gan (hōō′lə-gən) n. A hoodlum; rowdy; ruffian. [< *Hooligan,* name of an Irish family in London] —**hoo′li·gan·ism** n.

hoop (hōōp, hŏŏp) n. 1 A circular band of metal, wood, etc., esp. one used to confine the staves of a barrel, cask, etc. 2 A child's toy in the shape of a large ring. 3 A framework made of rings of whalebone, steel, etc., used for expanding a woman's skirt. 4 The band of a finger ring. —v.t. 1 To surround or fasten with hoops. 2 To encircle. [< OE *hōp*]

hoop·la (hōōp′lä) n. *Slang* Excitement; fervor. [Orig., a coach driver's exclamation]

hoo·poe (hōō′pōō, -pō) n. A vividly colored European bird with an erectile crest and a long bill. [< L *upupa*]

hoop skirt A full skirt shaped over a structure of hoops.

hoo·ray (hŏŏ-rā′, hə-, hōō-) *interj.* n. & v. HURRAH.

hoose·gow (hōōs′gou) n. *Slang* Jail or prison. [< Sp. *juzgado* tribunal]

hoot (hōōt) v.i. 1 To jeer or call out, as in contempt or disapproval. 2 To utter the low, hollow cry of an owl. —v.t. 3 To jeer at or mock with hooting cries. 4 To drive off with shouts of contempt, disapproval, etc. 5 To express by hooting. —n. 1 A cry uttered in derision. 2 The cry of an owl. 3 *Slang* A whit: not worth a *hoot.* [Imit.]

Hoop skirt

hootch (hōōch) n. HOOCH².

hoot·en·an·ny (hōōt′n-an′ē) n. pl. **·nies** 1 A gathering of folk singers. 2 A gadget; thingamajig. [?]

hooves (hōōvz, hŏŏvz) A pl. of HOOF.

hop¹ (hop) v. **hopped, hop·ping** v.i. 1 To move in short leaps with one foot off the ground. 2 To jump about by raising both or all feet simultaneously, as a frog. 3 *Informal* To take a trip, esp. a brief one: with *up, down,* or *over.* —v.t. 4 To jump over, as a fence. 5 *Informal* To board or catch; get on: to *hop* a train. —n. 1 The act or result of hopping. 2 *Informal* A dance or dancing party. 3 *Informal* A short flight in an airplane. [< OE *hoppian*]

hop² (hop) n. 1 A climbing herb related to hemp with female flowers borne in small green cones. 2 pl. The dried multiple fruit of this plant: used to flavor beer and in medicine. [< MDu. *hoppe*]

hope (hōp) v. **hoped, hop·ing** v.t. 1 To desire with expectation of fulfilment. 2 To wish; want. —v.i 3 To have desire or expectation: usu. with *for:* to *hope* for the best. —n. 1 Desire accompanied by expectation. 2 The reason or cause of such desire. 3 The thing hoped for. 4 A person or thing about which one can be hopeful. [< OE *hopian*]

hope chest A box or chest used by young women to hold linen, clothing, etc., in anticipation of marriage.

hope·ful (hōp′fəl) adj. 1 Full of hope; promising. 2 Having qualities that excite hope. —n. A person who seems likely to succeed. —**hope′ful·ness** n.

hope·ful·ly (hōp′fə-lē) adv. 1 In a hopeful manner. 2 It is hoped; one hopes: *Hopefully,* a strike can be averted. • *Hopefully* (def. 2), considered by some a questionable usage, is current in formal as well as informal contexts. It modifies the entire clause that follows it (in the example above, *a strike can be averted*), not the verb only. It is thus analogous to *incidentally* (def. 2), and is hardly a grammatical anomaly.

hope·less (hōp′lis) adj. 1 Without hope; despairing. 2 Affording no ground for hope. —**hope′less·ly** adv. —**hope′less·ness** n.

Ho·pi (hō′pē) n. 1 One of a group of North American

Pueblo Indians of Shoshonean linguistic stock, now on a reservation in NE Arizona. 2 Their Shoshonean lauguage.

hopped·up (hopt′up′) adj. *Slang* 1 Stimulated by a narcotic drug. 2 Excited; exhilarated. 3 Modified for high speed, as an engine. [? < HOP²]

hop·per (hop′ər) n. 1 One who or that which hops. 2 A hopping insect. 3 A box, tank, or funnel-shaped container whose contents can be emptied by opening its bottom.

hop·scotch (hop′skoch′) n. A child's game in which the player hops on one foot over a diagram marked (scotched) on the ground to recover the block, pebble, etc., previously tossed into successive sections of the diagram.

hor. horizon; horizontal.

horde (hôrd, hōrd) n. 1 A multitude, pack, or swarm, as of men, animals, or insects. 2 A clan or tribe of Mongolian nomads. 3 Any nomadic group. —v.i **hord·ed, hord·ing** To gather in a horde. [< Turk. *ordū* camp]

hore·hound (hôr′hound′, hōr′-) n. 1 A whitish plant related to mint. 2 A bitter extract of this plant. 3 A candy flavored with horehound. [< OE *hārhūne*]

ho·ri·zon (hə-rī′zən) n. 1 The line of the apparent meeting of the sky with the earth or sea. 2 The plane passing through a position on the earth's surface at right angles to the line of gravity. 3 *Usu. pl.* The limits of one's knowledge, interests, experience, etc. [< Gk *horos* limit, bound] • See PERSPECTIVE.

hor·i·zon·tal (hôr′ə-zon′təl, hor′-) adj. 1 Parallel to the horizon; level. 2 In the plane of the horizon. 3 Of, on, or close to the horizon. 4 Equal and uniform: a *horizontal* tariff. 5 Made up of similar units; a *horizontal* trust. —n. A line or plane assumed to be parallel with the horizon. —**hor′i·zon′tal·ly** adv.

hor·mone (hôr′mōn) n. 1 An internal secretion released in minute amounts into the blood stream by a specific gland or other tissue and stimulating a specific physiological activity. 2 A similar substance in plants. [< Gk. *hormaein* excite] —**hor·mo·nal** (hôr-mō′nəl), **hor·mon·ic** (hôr·mon′ik) adj.

horn (hôrn) n. 1 A permanent bonelike growth projecting from the head of various hoofed animals, as oxen, sheep, etc.; also, the antler of a deer, shed annually. 2 Any natural growth that protrudes from an animal's head, as a feeler, antenna, tentacle, etc. 3 The substance of which animal horns are made. 4 A somewhat similar substance made synthetically. 5 An object formed from or shaped like a horn: a powder *horn.* 6 A wind instrument made of brass, esp. the French horn. 7 *Slang* A trumpet or other brass or wind instrument. 8 Any pointed or tapering projection. 9 One of the extremities of a crescent moon. 10 A cape or peninsula. 11 The pommel of a saddle. 12 The point of an anvil. 13 A flaring tube used to collect or project sound, as in some loudspeakers. 14 A device for sounding warning signals; an automobile *horn.* —**on the horns of a dilemma** Forced to choose between two painful alternatives. —adj. Of horn or horns. —v.t 1 To provide with horns. 2 To shape like a horn. To attack with the horns; gore. —**horn in** *Slang* To enter without invitation. [< OE] —**horned** adj.

horn·bill (hôrn′bil′) n. A large tropical bird having a large bill surmounted by a hornlike extension.

horn·blende (hôrn′blend) n. A common, greenish black, silicate mineral containing iron, magnesium, calcium, and aluminum.

horned toad A harmless, flat-bodied, spiny lizard with a very short tail and toadlike appearance.

horned viper A venomous African snake with a horny projection over each eye.

hor·net (hôr′nit) n. Any of various social wasps capable of inflicting a severe sting. [< OE *hyrnet*]

horn of plenty CORNUCOPIA.

horn·pipe (hôrn′pīp′) n. 1 A lively English country dance. 2 The music of such a dance. 3 An obsolete musical instrument resembling the clarinet.

horn·swog·gle (hôrn′swog′əl) v.t. **·gled, ·gling** *Slang* To deceive; bamboozle; cheat.

horn·y (hôr′nē) adj. **horn·i·er, horn·i·est** 1 Of or like horn. 2 Having horns. 3 Hard and calloused. 4 Translucent; semiopaque. —**horn′i·ness** n.

hor·o·loge (hôr′ə-lōj, hor′-) n. 1 A timepiece, as a clock, sundial, etc. **2** A clock tower. [< Gk. *hōra* time + *legein* tell]

ho·rol·o·ger (hô·rol′ə·jər, hō-) *n.* One skilled in horology. Also **ho·rol′o·gist.**

ho·rol·o·gy (hô·rol′ə·jē, hō-) *n.* The science of measuring time or building timepieces. **—hor·o·log·ic** (hôr′ə·loj′ik, hor′-) or **·i·cal** *adj.*

hor·o·scope (hôr′ə·skōp, hor′-) *n.* **1** In astrology, the aspect of the heavens, with special reference to the positions of the planets at any instant. **2** A figure or statement showing such aspect, from which astrologers profess to foretell the future of an individual, country, etc. [< Gk. < *hōra* hour + *skopeein* to watch]

hor·ren·dous (hô·ren′dəs, ho-) *adj.* Frightful; dreadful. [< L *horrere* to bristle] **—hor·ren′dous·ly** *adv.* **—hor·ren′· dous·ness** *n.*

hor·ri·ble (hôr′ə·bəl, hor′-) *adj.* **1** Arousing horror. **2** Very unpleasant or offensive. [< L *horrere* to bristle] **—hor′ri·ble·ness** *n.* **—hor′ri·bly** *adv.* **—Syn.** frightful, terrible, dreadful, hideous, ghastly.

hor·rid (hôr′id, hor′-) *adj.* **1** Causing horror or repugnance: dreadful. **2** Very unpleasant, obnoxious, etc. [< L *horrere* to bristle] **—hor′rid·ly** *adv.* **—hor′rid·ness** *n.*

hor·rif·ic (hô·rif′ik, ho-) *adj.* Causing horror.

hor·ri·fy (hôr′ə·fī, hor′-) *v.t.* **·fied, ·fy·ing** **1** To affect or fill with horror. **2** To shock; appall. **—hor′ri·fi·ca′tion** *n.*

hor·ror (hôr′ər, hor′-) *n.* **1** A strong feeling of fear, repugnance, terrified alarm, etc. **2** A quality, experience, etc., that arouses such feeling. **3** Intense dislike; aversion. **4** *Informal* Something very unpleasant, ugly, etc. [< L]

hors de com·bat (ôr də kôn·bá′) Out of combat; out of action. [F]

hors d'oeuvre (ôr dûrv′; *Fr.* ôr dœ′vr′) *pl.* **hors d'oeuvres** (-dûrvz′) or **hors d'oeuvre** An appetizer served usu. before a meal. [F]

horse (hôrs) *n.* **1** A large, hoofed mammal with a long mane and tail, used since early times for riding, pulling and carrying loads, etc. **2** The adult male of this animal, as distinguished from a mare. **3** Soldiers mounted on horses; cavalry. **4** A framelike, usu. four-legged device for supporting something. **5** A padded device used for gymnastic exercises such as vaulting. **—v. horsed, hors·ing** *v.t.* **1** To furnish with a horse or horses; mount. **—v.i. 2** *Informal* To engage in horseplay: usu. with *around.* **—adj.** Coarse or large for its kind: *horse* chestnut. [< OE *hors*]

Horse
a. shoulder. b. withers. c. loins. d. croup. e. hock. f. flank. g. pastern. h. fetlock.

horse·back (hôrs′bak′) *n.* A horse's back. **—adv.** On a horse's back.

horse car 1 A streetcar drawn by horses. **2** A car for transporting horses.

horse chestnut 1 A large ornamental tree having palmate compound leaves, clusters of white flowers, and glossy seeds in burs. **2** The seed of this tree.

horse·flesh (hôrs′flesh′) *n.* **1** HORSEMEAT. **2** Horses collectively, esp. racehorses or riding horses.

horse·fly (hôrs′flī′) *n. pl.* **·flies** A large fly, the female of which sucks the blood of horses and other mammals.

horse·hair (hôrs′hâr′) *n.* **1** The hair of a horse, esp. from the mane or tail. **2** Cloth made from such horse's hair.

Horse chestnut fruit, leaves, and flower

horse·hide (hôrs′hīd′) *n.* **1** The hide of a horse. **2** Leather made from a horse's hide.

horse latitudes The regions around 35° north or south latitude, characterized by calms and light variable winds.

horse·laugh (hôrs′laf′, -läf′) *n.* A loud, boisterous laugh.

horse·man (hôrs′mən) *n. pl.* **·men** (-mən) **1** A man who rides a horse. **2** A man who is skilled in riding or managing horses.

horse·man·ship (hôrs′mən·ship) *n.* Equestrian skill.

horse·meat (hôrs′mēt′) *n.* The flesh of a horse used for pet food and sometimes human food.

horse opera *Slang* A motion picture or television show about cowboys, ranch life, etc., in the w U.S.

horse·play (hôrs′plā′) *n.* Rough, boisterous play.

horse·pow·er (hôrs′pou′ər) *n.* A unit of power equal to 550 foot-pounds per second, or about 746 watts.

horse·rad·ish (hôrs′rad′ish) *n.* **1** A coarse plant with a large, pungent root. **2** A condiment made from this root.

horse sense *Informal* Common sense.

horse·shoe (hôr′shōō′, hôrs′-) *n.* **1** A U-shaped piece of metal nailed to the bottom of a horse's hoof for protection. **2** Something shaped like this. **3** *pl.* (construed as sing.) A game in which players toss horseshoes at a stake. **—v.t. ·shoed, ·shoe·ing** To equip with horseshoes.

horseshoe crab A large, marine arthropod with a carapace shaped like a horseshoe and a long, sharp tail.

horse·tail (hôrs′tāl′) *n.* Any of several nonflowering plants having hollow, jointed stems and reproducing by means of spores.

horse·whip (hôrs′hwip′) *n.* A whip for driving or managing horses. **—v.t. ·whipped, ·whip·ping** To thrash with a horsewhip.

horse·wom·an (hôrs′wōōm′ən) *n. pl.* **·wom·en** (-wim′in) A woman who is skilled in riding or managing horses.

hors·y (hôr′sē) *adj.* **hors·i·er, hors·i·est 1** Pertaining to or suggestive of horses. **2** Devoted to horses or horse racing. Also **hors′ey** (-i·er, -i·est). **—hors′i·ly** *adv.* **—hors′i·ness** *n.*

hort. horticultural; horticulture.

hor·ta·to·ry (hôr′tə·tôr′ē, -tō′rē) *adj.* Giving or expressing exhortation, encouragement, etc. Also **hor′ta·tive.** [< L *hortari* to urge]

hor·ti·cul·ture (hôr′tə·kul′chər) *n.* The art and science of growing vegetables, fruits, flowers, etc. [< L *hortus* garden + *cultura* cultivation] **—hor′ti·cul′tur·al** *adj.* **—hor′ti·cul′tur·al·ly** *adv.* **—hor′ti·cul′tur·ist** *n.*

Hos. Hosea.

ho·san·na (hō·zan′ə) *interj. & n.* An exclamation or cry of praise to God. [< Heb. *hōshī′āhnnā* save, I pray]

hose (hōz) *n. pl.* **hose** for defs. 1 & 2, **hos·es** for def. 3 **1** *pl.* Stockings or socks. **2** *Usu. pl.* A tight-fitting, trouserlike garment formerly worn by men. **3** A flexible tube or pipe for conveying water or other fluids. **—v.t. hosed, hos·ing** To water, wash, or douse with a hose. [< OE *hosa*]

Ho·se·a (hō·zē′ə, -zā′ə) *n.* **1** A Hebrew minor prophet of the eighth century B.C. **2** The book of the Old Testament bearing his name.

ho·sier·y (hō′zhər·ē) *n.* Stockings and socks collectively.

hosp. hospital.

hos·pice (hos′pis) *n.* A place of lodging or shelter, as one maintained by a monastic order. [< L *hospes* host, guest]

hos·pi·ta·ble (hos′pi·tə·bəl, hos·pit′ə·bəl) *adj.* **1** Welcoming and entertaining guests with generous kindness. **2** Characterized by hospitality. **3** Open-minded; receptive. [< L *hospitare* entertain] **—hos′pi·ta·ble·ness** *n.* **—hos′pi·ta·bly** *adv.*

hos·pi·tal (hos′pi·təl) *n.* An institution for the reception, care, and treatment of the sick or injured. [< L *hospes* guest]

hos·pi·tal·i·ty (hos′pə·tal′ə·tē) *n. pl.* **·ties** The spirit, practice, or act of being hospitable.

hos·pi·tal·ize (hos′pi·təl·īz′) *v.t.* **·ized, ·iz·ing** To put in a hospital for treatment. **—hos′pi·tal·i·za′tion** *n.*

host¹ (hōst) *n.* **1** One who entertains or receives guests. **2** An innkeeper. **3** A person who introduces and interviews guests, as on certain television or radio shows. **4** An organism that supports a parasite. **—v.t.** *Informal* To conduct

add, āce, câre, pälm; end, ēven; it, īce; odd, ōpen, ôrder; tōōk, pōōl; up, bûrn; ə = a in *above*, u in *focus*; yōō = u in *fuse*; oil; pout; check; go; ring; thin; this; zh, *vision*. < derived from; ? origin uncertain or unknown.

or entertain in the role of a host. [< L *hospes* guest, host]

host² (hōst) *n.* **1** A large number; a multitude. **2** An army. [< L *hostis* enemy]

host³ (hōst) *n. Often cap.* The bread or wafer of the Eucharist. [< L *hostia* sacrificial victim]

hos·tage (hos′tij) *n.* A person held as a pledge or prisoner until the terms of a stipulation are met. [< OF]

hos·tel (hos′tǝl) *n.* A lodging place, esp. one for young people while hiking or traveling. [< L *hospes* guest]

hos·tel·ry (hos′tǝl·rē) *n. pl.* **·ries** An inn, hotel, etc.

host·ess (hōs′tis) *n.* **1** A woman who acts as a host. **2** A woman employed to greet or be of service to customers, as at a restaurant, resort, etc.

hos·tile (hos′tǝl, *esp. Brit.* hos′tīl) *adj.* **1** Of or pertaining to an enemy. **2** Feeling, showing, or characterized by enmity, antagonism, etc. **3** Unfavorable or forbidding. [< L *hostilis*] **—hos′tile·ly** *adv.* **—Syn. 2** unfriendly, antagonistic, malicious, unsociable. **3** adverse, untoward, opposing, contrary.

hos·til·i·ty (hos·til′ǝ·tē) *n. pl.* **·ties 1** The state of being hostile. **2** *pl.* Warlike activities; warfare.

hos·tler (hos′lǝr, os′-) *n.* A stableman; groom. [< OF *hostelier* innkeeper]

hot (hot) *adj.* **hot·ter, hot·test 1** At or having a high or relatively high temperature. **2** Producing a burning or biting sensation to the taste or touch. **3** Marked by passion, zeal, or intensity. **4** Fiery; angry; wrathful. **5** Violent; raging: a *hot* battle. **6** *Informal* So new as not to have lost its freshness, excitement, etc.: a *hot* tip; a *hot* bulletin. **7** *Slang* Recently stolen or smuggled: *hot* goods. **8** *Music Slang* Characterized by rapid tempo, driving rhythm, and daring harmony, as some jazz. **9** Following very closely: in *hot* pursuit. **10** *Slang* Excellent; very good. **11** *Informal* Extremely controversial: a *hot* issue. **12** *Informal* Very popular: a *hot* new singer. **13** In hunting, distinct: said of a scent. **14** Energized with electricity: a *hot* wire. **15** Dangerously radioactive. **—adv.** In a hot manner. [< OE *hāt*] **—hot′ly** *adv.* **—hot′ness** *n.*

hot air *Slang* Empty or pretentious talk.

hot·bed (hot′bed′) *n.* **1** A bed of earth warmed by fermentation and usu. protected by glass, used for promoting rapid growth of plants. **2** A place or condition favoring rapid growth or activity, esp. of a kind to be deplored.

hot-blood·ed (hot′blud′id) *adj.* Excitable; passionate.

hot cake A pancake.

hotch·potch (hoch′poch) *n.* HODGEPODGE.

hot cross bun A bun marked with a cross of frosting, eaten esp. during Lent.

hot dog *Informal* A frankfurter, usu. served in a split roll.

ho·tel (hō·tel′) *n.* An establishment or building providing lodging, food, etc., for paying customers. [< OF *hostel* inn]

hot·foot (hot′fŏŏt′) *v.t. Informal* To hurry; go hastily. **—adv.** *Informal* Hurriedly; hastily. **—n. pl.** **·foots** The prank of furtively wedging a match between the upper and sole of someone's shoe and lighting it.

hot·head (hot′hed′) *n.* A hotheaded person.

hot·head·ed (hot′hed′id) *adj.* **1** Quick-tempered. **2** Impetuous; rash. **—hot′head′ed·ly** *adv.* **—hot′head′ed·ness** *n.*

hot·house (hot′hous′) *n.* A greenhouse heated artificially for the cultivation of certain plants.

hot line A direct means of communication, esp. a telephone line kept available for emergency use.

hot plate A small, portable, gas or electric stove, having one or two burners.

hot rod *Slang* An automobile modified for increased power and speed.

hot·shot (hot′shot) *n. Slang* One with great skill or expertise; a whiz.

Hot·ten·tot (hot′ǝn·tot) *n.* **1** A member of a people of s Africa believed to be related to the Bantus and Bushmen. **2** The language of these people.

hou·dah (hou′dǝ) *n.* HOWDAH.

hound (hound) *n.* **1** Any of various breeds of usu. short-haired, long-eared hunting dogs. **2** *Informal* A devotee; enthusiast. **—v.t. 1** To hunt or pursue persistently. **2** To nag persistently. [< OE *hund*]

hounds-tooth check (houndz′tŏŏth′) A textile pattern of broken checks. Also **hound's-tooth check.**

hour (our) *n.* **1** A unit of time equal to one twenty-fourth of a day; sixty minutes. **2** The point of time indicated by a chronometer, watch, or clock; the time of day. **3** A set, appointed, or definite time. **4** *pl.* Prayers to be repeated at stated times of the day. [< Gk. *hōra* time, period]

hour·glass (our′glas′, -gläs′) *n.* A glass vessel having two parts connected by a narrow neck, used for measuring time by the running of sand from the upper to the lower part.

hou·ri (hŏŏ′rē) *n.* **1** In Muslim belief, one of the beautiful virgins awaiting the faithful in Paradise. **2** Any sensually beautiful woman. [< Ar. *hūrīyah* black-eyed woman]

hour·ly (our′lē) *adj.* **1** Of, happening, done, etc., every hour. **2** Constant or frequent. **—adv. 1** At or during each or any hour. **2** Constantly; frequently.

Hourglass

house (hous) *n.* **1** A building intended for human habitation. **2** A household; family. **3** A building used for any purpose: a coffee *house.* **4** The abode of a fraternity, order, etc.: a sorority *house.* **5** A dormitory or residence hall in a college or university. **6** A legislative body; also, the chamber it occupies. **7** A place of business. **8** A business firm: the *house* of Morgan. **9** The management of a business, gambling establishment, etc. **10** A theater; also, the audience in a theater. **11** *Often cap.* A line of ancestors and descendants regarded as forming a single family: the *House* of Tudor. **12** In astrology, one of the twelve divisions of the heavens, each division having special significance in casting horoscopes. **—v.** (houz) **housed, hous·ing** *v.t.* **1** To take or put into a house. **2** To store in a house or building. **3** To fit into a mortise, joint, etc. **—v.i. 4** To take shelter or lodgings; dwell. [< OE *hūs*] **—house′ful** *n.*

house arrest Detention in one's own house, often under guard, instead of in prison.

house·boat (hous′bōt′) *n.* A boat or barge fitted out as a dwelling.

house·break·er (hous′brā′kǝr) *n.* One who breaks into a house to rob. **—house′break′ing** *n.*

house·bro·ken (hous′brō′kǝn) *adj.* Trained to live in a house by excreting only out-of-doors or in a specified place: said of animals.

house·coat (hous′kōt′) *n.* A long, loose-skirted garment designed for informal indoor wear.

house·fly (hous′flī′) *n. pl.* **·flies** The common fly found in nearly all parts of the world, an agent in transmitting certain diseases.

house guest A guest invited to stay one or more nights.

house·hold (hous′hōld) *n.* **1** A number of persons dwelling under the same roof. **2** The home and all the things pertaining to it. **—adj.** Domestic.

house·hold·er (hous′hōl′dǝr) *n.* **1** The head of a family. **2** One who owns or rents a home.

house·keep·er (hous′kē′pǝr) *n.* A woman who does or directs others to do the domestic work in a home. **—house′keep′ing** *n.*

house·maid (hous′mād′) *n.* A woman employed to do housework.

housemaid's knee A chronic inflammation of the bursa in front of the knee.

House of Commons The lower house of the British and Canadian Parliaments.

house of correction An institution for lesser criminals; reform school.

House of Lords The upper house of the British Parliament.

House of Representatives 1 The lower branch of the legislature of the U.S. and of many of its state legislative bodies. **2** A similar legislative body in certain other countries.

house organ A publication issued regularly by a business for its employees, affiliates, etc.

house party An entertaining of guests for several days, usu. in a country house or a college fraternity.

house physician A physician resident by appointment in a hospital, hotel, etc.

house sparrow A small brown and gray bird of European origin, now common in the U.S.

house·top (hous'top') n. The top or roof of a house. — **from the housetops** Publicly; for all to hear.

house·wife (hous'wīf') n. pl. ·wives (-wīvz') 1 A married woman who performs the domestic duties of a household as her principal occupation. 2 (usu. huz'if) A small sewing kit. —**house'wife'ly** adj., adv.

house·wife·ry (hous'wīf'rē) n. The work of a housewife.

house·work (hous'wûrk') n. The work of keeping house, as cleaning, cooking, laundering, etc.

hous·ing [1] (hou'zing) n. 1 The act of providing with a house or shelter. 2 A house or lodging: housing for the flood victims. 3 Houses, apartments, etc., provided or built for many people. 4 Something that shelters or covers. 5 Mech. A recess, enclosure, bracket, etc., in one part for holding or covering another part.

hous·ing [2] (hou'zing) n. 1 An ornamental covering for a horse. 2 pl. TRAPPINGS (def. 3). [< OF houce]

hove (hōv) A p.t. of HEAVE.

hov·el (huv'əl, hov'-) n. 1 A wretched dwelling; hut. 2 An open shed for sheltering animals, tools, etc. —v.t. ·eled or ·elled, ·el·ing or ·el·ling To shelter in a hovel. [?]

hov·er (huv'ər, hov'-) v.i. 1 To remain suspended in or near one place in the air. 2 To linger; be nearby, as if waiting or watching: with around, near, etc. 3 To remain in an uncertain or irresolute state: with between. —n. The act of hovering. [< obs. hove to float] —**hov'er·er** n.

Hov·er·craft (huv'ər·kraft', hov'-, -kräft') n. A vehicle traveling over ground or water on a cushion of air produced by fans directed downward: a trade name. Also **hov'er·craft'**.

how (hou) adv. 1 In what way or manner; by what means. 2 To what degree, extent, amount, etc. 3 In what state or condition. 4 For what reason or purpose. 5 For what price. 6 By what name or designation. 7 To what effect; with what meaning. 8 Informal What: How is that again? —n. Way of doing or becoming; method. [< OE hū]

how·be·it (hou·bē'it) adv. Archaic Be that as it may.

how·dah (hou'də) n. A seat on the back of an elephant. [< Hind. haudah]

how·dy (hou'dē) interj. Informal Hello; hi!

how·ev·er (hou·ev'ər) adv. 1 In whatever manner; by whatever means. 2 To whatever degree or extent. 3 How; in what manner: However did it happen? —conj. Notwithstanding; still; but: However, he arrived late.

how·it·zer (hou'it·sər) n. An artillery piece with a barrel longer than that of a mortar, and firing in a high trajectory with medium muzzle velocity. [< Czech houfnice catapult]

Howdah

howl (houl) v.i. 1 To utter the loud, mournful wail of a wolf or dog. 2 To utter such a cry in rage, grief, etc. 3 To make a similar sound. 4 To laugh loudly. —v.t. 5 To utter or express with a howl or howls. 6 To drive or effect with a howl or howls. —n. 1 The cry of a wolf or dog. 2 Any sound suggesting this, esp. a cry of grief or rage. 3 Informal Something considered hilariously funny. [Imit.]

howl·er (hou'lər) n. 1 One who or that which howls. 2 Informal An absurd mistake or blunder.

howl·ing (hou'ling) adj. 1 That howls. 2 Dismal; mournful. 3 Slang Prodigious; tremendous: a howling success.

how·so·ev·er (hou'sō·ev'ər) adv. 1 In whatever manner. 2 To whatever extent.

hoy·den (hoid'n) n. A romping, boisterous girl; tomboy. —adj. Rude or unseemly; bold. —v.i. To romp rudely or indecently. [?] —**hoy'den·ish** adj.

Hoyle (hoil) n. A book of rules for indoor games, esp. for card games. [< E. Hoyle, 1672–1769, English writer]

HP, H.P., hp, h.p. high pressure; horsepower.

HQ, H.Q., hq, h.q. headquarters.

H.R. Home Rule; House of Representatives.

hr, h.r. home run(s).

hr. hour(s).

H.R.H. His (or Her) Royal Highness.

H.S. High School.

ht. heat; height.

hub (hub) n. 1 The central part of a wheel. 2 Any center of activity, interest, etc. [? < HOB]

hub·bub (hub'ub) n. Tumult; uproar.

hu·bris (hyōō'bris) n. Overweening pride and insolence, often bringing about retribution. [Gk.]

huck·a·back (huk'ə·bak) n. A coarse, durable linen or cotton cloth used for towels. Also **huck, huck'a·buck** (-buk). [?]

huck·le·ber·ry (huk'əl·ber'ē) n. pl. ·ries 1 The edible berry of a species of heath often confused with the blueberry. 2 The shrub producing this berry. [?]

huck·ster (huk'stər) n. 1 A glib and aggressive salesman, esp. one having a flamboyant manner. 2 Any peddler or hawker of small wares. 3 Informal A producer or writer of advertising commercials, as on radio or television. —v.t. 1 To peddle. 2 To promote by showy or aggressive means. [< MDu. hoekster] —**huck'ster·ism** n.

HUD, H.U.D. Housing and Urban Development.

hud·dle (hud'l) v. hud·dled, hud·dling v.i. 1 To crowd closely together. 2 To draw or hunch oneself together, as from cold. 3 To come together for a conference or huddle. —v.t. 4 To bring together in a group. 5 To hunch (oneself) together. —n. 1 A confused crowd or collection of persons or things. 2 In football, the grouping of a team before each play, in which signals and instructions are given. 3 Any small, intimate conference. [?]

Hud·son seal (hud'sən) Muskrat fur dyed and trimmed to resemble sealskin. [< Hudson Bay in N Canada]

hue [1] (hyōō) n. 1 The particular shade or tint of a color. 2 The distinguishing attribute of a chromatic color, as red, green, blue, etc. 3 Color. [< OE hēow appearance]

hue [2] (hyōō) n. A vociferous cry; shouting. [< OF hu cry]

huff (huf) n. A feeling of anger and resentment. —v.t. 1 To offend; make angry. 2 To treat insolently or arrogantly. —v.i. 3 To be offended. 4 To puff; blow. [Imit.] —**huff'ish** adj. —**huff'ish·ly** adv. —**huff'ish·ness** n.

huff·y (huf'ē) adj. huff·i·er, huff·i·est 1 Easily offended. 2 Angry. —**huff'i·ly** adv. —**huff'i·ness** n.

hug (hug) v. hugged, hug·ging v.t. 1 To clasp tightly within the arms, as from affection. 2 To keep fondly in the mind; cherish, as a belief or opinion. 3 To keep close to, as a shore. —v.i. 4 To lie close; nestle. —n. A close embrace. [< Scand.]

huge (hyōōj) adj. Very large in size, degree, or extent. [< OF ahuge high] —**huge'ly** adv. —**huge'ness** n.

hug·ger·mug·ger (hug'ər·mug'ər) n. Confusion and disorder. —adj. 1 Confused; jumbled. 2 Secret; sly. [?]

huh (hu) interj. An exclamation of inquiry, surprise, contempt, etc.

hu·la (hōō'lə) n. A native Hawaiian dance that tells a story in pantomime. Also **hu'la-hu'la**. [< Hawaiian]

hulk (hulk) n. 1 The body of a ship, esp. of one that is old or wrecked. 2 A heavy, clumsy ship. 3 An abandoned wreck or shell. 4 A bulky or unwieldy object or person. —v.i. To rise or loom bulkily: usu. with up. [< Gk. holkas towed vessel]

hulk·ing (hul'king) adj. Bulky; unwieldy. Also **hulk'y**.

hull (hul) n. 1 An outer covering, as a husk of grain or a nutshell. 2 The calyx attached to a strawberry, tomato, etc. 3 Naut. The body of a ship, exclusive of the masts and rigging. 4 The outermost structures of a spacecraft, missile, etc. —v.t. To shell; free from the hull. [< OE hulu a covering] —**hull'er** n.

hul·la·ba·loo (hul'ə·bə·lōō') n. A loud and confused noise; uproar; tumult.

hum (hum) v. hummed, hum·ming v.i. 1 To make a low, continuous, buzzing sound, as a bee. 2 To sing with the lips closed. 3 To give forth a confused, indistinct sound, as of mingled voices. 4 Informal To be busily active. —v.t. 5 To sing, as a tune, with the lips closed. 6 To put into a specified state by humming: to hum someone to sleep. —n. A dull, low, continuous sound. [Imit.] —**hum'mer** n.

hu·man (hyōō'mən) adj. 1 Of, pertaining to, or like man

or mankind. **2** Created by or belonging to man or mankind: *human* problems. **3** Characterized by or exemplifying the strengths, weaknesses, emotions, struggles, etc., typical of man and mankind: a very *human* situation. — *n.* A human being. [< L *humanus*] —**hu'man·ness** *n.*

hu·mane (hyōō·mān') *adj.* **1** Having or showing kindness, tenderness, compassion, etc. **2** Tending to refine or make civilized. —**humane'ly** *adv.* —**hu·mane'ness** *n.* —**Syn. 1** charitable, merciful, sympathetic, benevolent, clement.

hu·man·ism (hyōō'mən·iz'əm) *n.* **1** The quality or condition of being human. **2** A humane concern for man and his welfare. **3** A philosophy in which man, his interests, and development are made central and dominant, tending to exalt the cultural and rational elements of man rather than the supernatural or speculative. **4** A devotion to the humanities. —**hu'man·ist** *n.* —**hu'man·is'tic** *adj.* —**hu'man·is'ti·cal·ly** *adv.*

Hu·man·ism (hyōō'mən·iz'əm) *n.* The intellectual and literary movement of the 14th to 16th centuries which exalted Greek and Roman culture. —**Hu'man·ist** *n.*

hu·man·i·tar·i·an (hyōō·man'ə·târ'ē·ən) *n.* One who seeks to promote the welfare of mankind; a philanthropist. —*adj.* **1** That aids others. **2** Of humanitarianism. —**hu·man'i·tar'i·an·ism** *n.*

hu·man·i·ty (hyōō·man'ə·tē) *n. pl.* **·ties 1** Mankind collectively. **2** Human nature. **3** The state or quality of being human. **4** The state or quality of being humane. —**the humanities** The branches of learning including literature, language, philosophy, fine arts, etc., as distinguished from the sciences.

hu·man·ize (hyōō'mən·īz) *v.t. & v.i.* **·ized, ·iz·ing** To make or become humane or human. —**hu'man·i·za'tion** *n.*

hu·man·kind (hyōō'mən·kīnd') *n.* Mankind.

hu·man·ly (hyōō'mən·lē) *adv.* **1** In accordance with man's nature or experience. **2** Within human power or knowledge. **3** Humanely.

hu·ma·noid (hyōō'me·noid) *adj.* Resembling a human being. —*n.* A creature resembling a human being.

hum·ble (hum'bəl) *adj.* **·bler, ·blest 1** Having or expressing a sense of selflessness, meekness, modesty, etc. **2** Lowly in condition, rank, etc.; unpretending. —*v.t.* **hum·bled, hum·bling 1** To reduce the pride of; humiliate. **2** To lower in rank or dignity; abase. [< L *humus* ground] —**hum'ble·ness, hum'bler** *n.* —**hum'bly** *adv.* —**Syn. adj. 1** modest, meek, selfless, unassuming, submissive.

humble pie A pie made of the edible entrails (**humbles**) of a deer, formerly served to servants at hunting feasts. —**eat humble pie** To be forced to admit one's mistakes and apologize.

hum·bug (hum'bug) *n.* **1** A deception; sham. **2** Foolish talk; nonsense. **3** An impostor. —*v.t.* **·bugged, ·bug·ging** To deceive. —*interj.* Nonsense! [?] —**hum'bug·ger, hum'bug·ger·y** *n.*

hum·ding·er (hum'ding'ər) *n. Slang* One who or that which excels. [?]

hum·drum (hum'drum') *adj.* Without interest; tedious. —*n.* Something humdrum. [< HUM + DRUM]

hu·mer·us (hyōō'mər·əs) *n. pl.* **·mer·i** (-mər·ī) The bone of the upper arm or forelimb. [L, shoulder] —**hu·mer·al** (hyōō'mər·əl) *adj.*

hu·mid (hyōō'mid) *adj.* Containing moisture; damp. [< L *humere* be moist] —**hu'mid·ly** *adv.*

hu·mid·i·fy (hyōō·mid'ə·fī) *v.t.* **·fied, ·fy·ing** To make moist or humid, as the atmosphere of a room. —**hu·mid'i·fi·ca'tion, hu·mid'i·fi'er** *n.*

hu·mid·i·ty (hyōō·mid'ə·tē) *n.* **1** Moisture; dampness, esp. of the atmosphere. **2** The measure of the water vapor in the air. • See RELATIVE HUMIDITY. Also **hu'mid·ness.**

hu·mi·dor (hyōō'mə·dôr) *n.* A place or container for storing cigars or tobacco so that moisture is retained.

a. humerus.
b. radius.
c. ulna.

hu·mil·i·ate (hyōō·mil'ē·āt) *v.t.* **·at·ed, ·at·ing** To lower or offend the pride or self-respect of; mortify; humble. [< L *humilis* lowly] —**hu·mil'i·a'tion** *n.*

hu·mil·i·ty (hyōō·mil'ə·tē) *n. pl.* **·ties** The state or quality of being humble. —**Syn.** modesty, meekness, unpretentiousness, docility, humbleness.

hum·ming·bird (hum'ing·bûrd') *n.* Any of a family of tiny, nectar-feeding birds with brilliant plumage, long, needle-like bills, and having very rapid wing motion.

hum·mock (hum'ək) *n.* **1** A small hill or knoll. **2** A pile or ridge of ice on an ice field. [?] —**hum'mock·y** *adj.*

Hummingbird

hu·mor (hyōō'mər) *n.* **1** A person's disposition, mood, or state of mind. **2** The quality of being amusing, comical, ludicrous, etc. **3** The capacity to perceive, appreciate, or give expression to what is amusing, comical, ludicrous, etc. **4** A sudden whim or caprice. **5** A fluid or fluidlike substance of the body. In medieval times the humors, consisting of blood, phlegm, yellow bile, and black bile, were supposed to give rise to the sanguine, phlegmatic, choleric, and melancholic temperaments, respectively. —**out of humor** Irritated; annoyed. —*v.t.* **1** To comply with the moods or caprices of. **2** To accommodate or adapt oneself to. *Brit. sp.* **hu'mour.** [L, liquid]

hu·mor·esque (hyōō'mə·resk') *n.* A lively or fanciful musical composition.

hu·mor·ist (hyōō'mər·ist) *n.* **1** A writer or entertainer who specializes in the narration of humorous stories or jokes. **2** A wag or joker.

hu·mor·ous (hyōō'mər·əs) *adj.* **1** Full of humor; amusing. **2** Having or able to express humor. —**hu'mor·ous·ly** *adv.* —**hu'mor·ous·ness** *n.* —**Syn.** comic, funny, witty, farcical, droll.

hump (hump) *n.* **1** A rounded protuberance, esp. one formed by a curved spine or by a fleshy growth on the back. **2** A mound. **3** *Slang* A fit of ill humor or gloominess. —**over the hump** Beyond the point where force or effort is needed. —*v.t.* **1** To bend or round (the back) in a hump; hunch. —*v.i.* **2** *Slang* **a** To put forth extra effort; go all-out. **b** To move fast. [?] —**hump'y** *adj.* (**·i·er, ·i·est**)

hump·back (hump'bak') *n.* **1** A back with a hump. **2** A hunchback. **3** A large whale with a low humplike dorsal Dfin. —**hump'backed'** *adj.*

humph (humf) *interj.* An exclamation of doubt or dissatisfaction.

hu·mus (hyōō'məs) *n.* The organic matter of the soil, as leaf mold and other decomposing materials. [L, ground]

Hun (hun) *n.* **1** One of a barbarous nomadic Asian people who invaded Europe in the fourth and fifth centuries. **2** Any barbarous or destructive person.

hunch (hunch) *n.* **1** A hump. **2** A lump or hunk. **3** A sudden shove. **4** *Informal* A premonition. —*v.t.* **1** To bend, as the back, so as to form a hump; arch. —*v.i.* **2** To move or thrust oneself forward. **3** To stand or sit with the body bent or crooked. [?]

hunch·back (hunch'bak') *n.* A person having a deformed back. —**hunch'backed'** *adj.*

hun·dred (hun'drid) *adj.* Being 10 more than 90. —*n.* The sum of 90 plus 10; 100; C. [< OE]

hun·dred·fold (hun'drid·fōld') *n.* An amount a hundred times as great as a given unit. —*adj.* Indicating a hundred times as much or as many. —*adv.* By a hundred: with *a* or (Brit.) *an.*

hun·dredth (hun'dridth) *n.* **1** The element of an ordered set that corresponds to the number 100. **2** One of a hundred equal parts. —*adj.* Being tenth in order after the ninetieth.

hun·dred·weight (hun'drid·wāt') *n.* **1** In the U.S., a weight of 100 pounds. **2** In Great Britain, a weight of 112 pounds.

hung (hung) *p.t. & p.p.* of HANG. • See HANG.

Hung. Hungarian; Hungary.

Hun·gar·i·an (hung·gâr'ē·ən) *adj.* Of or pertaining to Hungary, its people, or their language. —*n.* **1** A native or citizen of Hungary. **2** The Finno-Ugric language of the Hungarians; Magyar.

Hun·ga·ry (hung′gə·rē) A republic of CEN. Europe, 35,912 sq. mi., cap. Budapest.

hun·ger (hung′gər) n. 1 A need or craving for food. 2 The discomfort or physical debility caused by lack of food. 3 Any strong desire. —v.i. 1 To feel hunger. 2 To have a craving or desire: with *for* or *after:* to *hunger* for a chance to return to one's homeland. [< OE]

hunger strike A refusal to eat until certain demands are met.

hung over *Slang* Suffering from a hangover.

hun·gry (hung′grē) adj. **·gri·er, ·gri·est** 1 Having or feeling hunger. 2 Indicating hunger. 3 Eagerly desiring; craving. 4 Barren: said of land. **—hun′gri·ly** adv. **—hun′gri·ness** n.

hung up *Slang* 1 Delayed. 2 Preoccupied or obsessed. 3 Sidetracked or impeded: *hung up* on legal technicalities.

hunk (hungk) n. *Informal* A large piece; chunk. [?]

hun·ky-do·ry (hung′kē·dôr′ē, -dō′rē) adj. *Informal* OK; satisfactory. [< slang *hunky* safe, satisfactory]

hunt (hunt) v.t. 1 To pursue (game) for the purpose of killing or catching. 2 a To search (a region) for game. b To search (a place): to *hunt* a room. 3 To search for diligently; look for. 4 To use (hounds or horses) in hunting. 5 To chase; pursue. 6 To persecute; harass. —v.i. 7 To pursue game or other wild animals; follow the chase. 8 To make a search; seek. —n. 1 The act of hunting. 2 A search. 3 The participants in a hunt. 4 A district hunted over. [< OE *huntian*]

hunt·er (hun′tər) n. 1 A person who hunts. 2 A horse or dog used in hunting.

hunt·ing (hun′ting) n. The act of a person or animal that hunts.

hunt·ress (hun′tris) n. A woman who hunts.

hunts·man (hunts′mən) n. pl. **·men** (-mən) 1 One who hunts. 2 The attendant who has charge of the hounds in a hunt.

hur·dle (hûr′dəl) n. 1 In racing, a framework to be leaped over by horses or runners. 2 pl. A type of race in which this occurs: used with *the.* 3 Any obstacle or difficulty. —v. **·dled, ·dling** v.t. 1 To leap over, as an obstacle in a race. 2 To surmount (a difficulty, etc.). —v.i. 3 To leap over hurdles, obstacles, etc. [< OE *hyrdel*] **—hur′dler** n.

hur·dy-gur·dy (hûr′dē·gûr′dē) n. pl. **·dies** A hand or barrel organ. [?]

hurl (hûrl) v.t. 1 To throw with violence; fling. 2 To throw down; overthrow. 3 To utter with vehemence. —v.i. 4 To throw something. 5 To move or rush violently. —n. The act of throwing. [ME *hurlen*] **—hurl′er** n.

hur·ly-bur·ly (hûr′lē·bûr′lē) n. pl. **·lies** Tumult; uproar. [?]

Hu·ron (hyŏŏr′on) n. 1 A member of any one of four confederated tribes of North American Indians of Iroquoian stock. 2 The Iroquoian language of these tribes.

hur·rah (hŏŏ·rô′, hə·rä′) interj. An exclamation expressing triumph or joy. —n. A shout of "hurrah." —v.i. To shout a hurrah or hurrahs. [Imit.]

hur·ri·cane (hûr′ə·kān′) n. A tropical cyclone having winds moving at about 75 miles per hour or more, usu. originating in the West Indies. [< Cariban]

hurricane deck The upper deck of a passenger ship, esp. of a river steamer.

hur·ried (hûr′ēd) adj. 1 In haste; rushed. 2 Done in haste; hasty. **—hur′ried·ly** adv. **—hur′ried·ness** n.

hur·ry (hûr′ē) v. **hur·ried, hur·ry·ing** v.i. 1 To act or move rapidly or in haste; hasten. —v.t. 2 To cause or urge to act or move more rapidly. 3 To hasten the progress, completion, etc., of, often unduly: to *hurry* a decision. —n. pl. **hur·ries** 1 The act of hurrying. 2 Eager haste; precipitation. [?]

hur·ry-scur·ry (hûr′ē·skûr′ē) v.i. **·ried, ·ry·ing** To act hurriedly. —adj. Hurried; confused. —n. pl. **·ries** Bustling, confused haste. —adv. With disorderly haste; pell-mell.

hurt (hûrt) v. **hurt, hurt·ing** v.t. 1 To cause physical harm or suffering to; injure. 2 To harm or damage: to *hurt* one's reputation. 3 To cause mental or emotional suffering to; wound; offend. —v.i. 4 To be painful or sore: My feet *hurt.* 5 To cause damage, hurt, etc. —n. 1 An injury or wound. 2 Damage. 3 An injury to the feelings. [< OF *hurter* to hit] **—hurt′er** n.

hurt·ful (hûrt′fəl) adj. Causing hurt. **—hurt′ful·ly** adv. **—hurt′ful·ness** n.

hur·tle (hûr′təl) v. **hur·tled, hur·tling** v.i. 1 To crash violently: with *against* or *together.* 2 To move or rush swiftly and with force. —v.t. 3 To drive, shoot, or throw violently. [Freq. of ME *hurten* to hit, hurt]

hus·band (huz′bənd) n. A married man; man with a wife. —v.t. 1 To use or spend wisely; conserve. 2 *Archaic* To be a husband to; marry. 3 *Archaic* To till; cultivate. [< OE < *hūs* house + *bonda* freeholder]

hus·band·man (huz′bənd·mən) n. pl. **·men** (-mən) A farmer.

hus·band·ry (huz′bən·drē) n. 1 Farming. 2 Thrifty management.

hush (hush) v.t. 1 To make silent or quiet. 2 To soothe; allay, as fears. —v.i. 3 To be or become silent or still. — **hush up** 1 To make quiet. 2 To keep from becoming known. —n. Deep silence; stillness; quiet. —interj. Be still. [ME *hussht* quiet]

hush·a·by (hush′ə·bī) interj. An expression used to lull a child to sleep.

hush-hush (hush′hush′) adj. *Informal* Secret.

hush money A bribe to secure secrecy.

hush-pup·py (hush′pup′ē) n. pl. **·pies** In the s U.S., a fried ball of cornmeal dough. [< its use as dog food]

husk (husk) n. 1 The outer covering of certain fruits or seeds. 2 Any covering, esp. when comparatively worthless. —v.t. To remove the husk of. [ME *huske*] **—husk′er** n.

husk·y¹ (hus′kē) adj. **husk·i·er, husk·i·est** 1 Abounding in husks; like husks. 2 Somewhat hoarse: said of the voice. **—husk′i·ly** adv. **—husk′i·ness** n.

husk·y² (hus′kē) adj. **husk·i·er, husk·i·est** Strong; muscular. —n. pl. **husk·ies** A strong or powerfully built person. [with ref. to toughness of husks] **—husk′i·ness** n.

husk·y³ (hus′kē) n. pl. **husk·ies** *Often cap.* A strong, thick-furred dog, used to pull sleds in the Arctic. [? Alter. of ESKIMO]

hus·sar (hŏŏ·zär′) n. A member of any light-armed cavalry regiment in European armies, usu. with brilliant dress uniforms. [< Ital. *corsaro* corsair]

hus·sy (huz′ē, hus′ē) n. pl. **·sies** A saucy or forward girl: used in reproach or playfully. [Alter. of HOUSEWIFE]

hust·ings (hus′tingz) n.pl. (usu. construed as sing.) 1 A place where political speeches are made. 2 The proceedings at an election. 3 A political campaign. [< ON *hūs* house + *thing* assembly]

hus·tle (hus′əl) v. **hus·tled, hus·tling** v.t. 1 To push or knock about roughly; jostle. 2 To force or push roughly and hurriedly. 3 *Informal* To cause to be done or proceed rapidly. 4 *Slang* To sell or obtain in an aggressive, often underhanded manner. —v.i. 5 To push one's way; shove; elbow. 6 *Informal* To act or work with energy and speed. 7 *Slang* a To obtain money in an aggressive, usu. underhanded manner. b To be a prostitute. —n. 1 The act of hustling. 2 *Informal* Energetic activity; push. [MDu. *hutselen* shake, toss] **—hus′tler** n.

hut (hut) n. A small, crude cabin or shack. —v.t. & v.i. **hut·ted, hut·ting** To shelter or live in a hut. [< OHG *hutta*]

hutch (huch) n. 1 A box, chest, etc., for storage. 2 A low cupboard, as for china, with open shelves on top. 3 A coop or pen for rabbits, etc. 4 A hut. [< LL *hutica*]

huz·za (hə·zä′) n. & interj. Hurrah: a shout of joy. Also *huz·zah*, *huz·zay* (-zā).

H.V., hv, h.v. high voltage.

hwy. highway.

hy·a·cinth (hī′ə·sinth) n. 1 A plant related to the lily with a spike of small, fragrant flowers. 2 The bulb or flower of this plant. 3 A gem, a brownish, reddish, or orange zircon. [< L < Gk. *hyakinthos*] **—hy′a·cin′thine** (-thin, -thīn) adj.

hy·ae·na (hī·ē′nə) n. HYENA.

Hyacinth

hy·a·line (hī′ə-lin, -līn) *adj.* Resembling glass; transparent. —*n.* Something transparent or glassy. [< Gk. *hyalos* glass]

hy·brid (hī′brid) *n.* **1** An offspring of two animals or plants of different species, varieties, breeds, etc. **2** Anything of mixed origin or unlike parts. **3** *Ling.* A word composed of elements from more than one language. —*adj.* Of, pertaining to, or like a hybrid. [< L *hybrida*] —**hy′brid·ism** *n.*

hy·brid·ize (hī′brid·īz) *v.t. & v.i.* **·ized, ·iz·ing** To produce or cause to produce hybrids. —**hy·brid·i·za·tion** (hī′brid·ə·zā′shən, -ī·zā′-) *n.*

hy·dra (hī′drə) *n. pl.* **·dras** or **·drae** (-drē) **1** A freshwater polyp. **2** Any persistent evil. [< L *Hydra* < Gk.]

Hy·dra (hī′drə) *Gk. Myth.* The many-headed serpent that grew two heads for each one that was cut off.

hy·dran·ge·a (hī·drān′jē·ə, -jə) *n.* An ornamental shrub with opposite leaves and clusters of large, showy flowers. [< HYDR(O)- + Gk. *angeion* vessel]

hy·drant (hī′drənt) *n.* A large, upright street pipe from which water may be obtained from a water main for fighting fires, cleaning streets, etc. [< HYDR(O)- + -ANT]

hy·drate (hī′drāt) *n.* A compound formed by the union of molecules of water with other molecules or atoms. —*v.t.* **·drat·ed, ·drat·ing** To combine with water or its elements to form a hydrate. [< HYDR(O)- + -ATE] —**hy′drat·ed** *adj.* —**hy·dra·tion** (hī·drā′shən) *n.*

hy·drau·lic (hī·drô′lik) *adj.* **1** Of or involving the moving of water, or force exerted by water. **2** Denoting a machine or device operated by liquid under pressure. **3** Hardening under water: *hydraulic* cement. [< Gk. *hydraulos* water organ] —**hy·drau′li·cal·ly** *adv.*

hy·drau·lics (hī·drô′liks) *n.pl. (construed as sing.)* The science and technology dealing with or based on the mechanical behavior of liquids.

hy·dride (hī′drīd, -drid) *n.* A compound of hydrogen with another element or a radical. Also **hy′drid** (-drid).

hy·dro (hī′drō) *n. pl.* **·dros** *Can.* **1** Hydroelectric power. **2** A hydroelectric power plant.

hydro- *combining form* **1** Water; of, related to, or resembling water: *hydroelectric.* **2** *Chem.* Denoting a compound of hydrogen: *hydrochloric.* Also, before vowels, **hydr-**. [< Gk. *hydōr* water]

hy·dro·car·bon (hī′drə·kär′bən) *n.* A compound of hydrogen and carbon only, as methane, benzene, acetylene, etc.

hy·dro·ceph·a·lus (hī′drə·sef′ə·ləs) *n.* An abnormal, usu. congenital condition marked by an enlarged head and brain damage due to an accumulation of fluid within the cranium. [< HYDRO- + Gk. *kephalē* head] —**hy′dro·ceph′a·loid** (-loid), **hy′dro·ceph′a·lous** *adj.*

hy·dro·chlo·ric (hī′drə·klôr′ik, -klō′rik) *adj.* Pertaining to or designating a colorless, corrosive, gaseous compound of hydrogen and chlorine which forms a strong acid (**hydrochloric acid**) in aqueous solution.

hy·dro·cy·an·ic (hī′drō·sī·an′ik) *adj.* Of, pertaining to, or designating an unstable, volatile, colorless, and extremely poisonous compound of hydrogen, carbon, and nitrogen which forms a weak acid in aqueous solution.

hy·dro·dy·nam·ics (hī′drō·dī·nam′iks) *n.pl. (construed as sing.)* The branch of physics that deals with the dynamics of liquids.

hy·dro·e·lec·tric (hī′drō·i·lek′trik) *adj.* Of or pertaining to electricity developed from water power. —**hy·dro·e·lec·tric·i·ty** (hī′drō·i·lek·tris′ə·tē) *n.*

hy·dro·flu·or·ic (hī′drō·flōō′ər·ik) *adj.* Pertaining to or designating a volatile, colorless compound of hydrogen and fluorine which forms a corrosive acid in aqueous solution.

hy·dro·foil (hī′drə·foil) *n.* **1** One of a set of fins attached to a vessel to provide a reaction force with the water at high speeds and lift the hull from the water. **2** A vessel equipped with hydrofoils.

hy·dro·gen (hī′drə·jən) *n.* The lightest and most abundant element (symbol H) in the universe, on earth found mainly in combination with oxygen as water. [< Gk. *hydōr* water + *-genēs* born] —**hy·drog·e·nous** (hī·droj′ə·nəs) *adj.*

hy·dro·gen·ate (hī·droj′ə·nāt′, hī′drə·jə·nāt′) *v.t.* **·at·ed,**

·at·ing To treat with, expose to, or cause to combine with hydrogen. —**hy′dro·gen·a′tion** *n.*

hydrogen bomb An extremely powerful thermonuclear bomb based on the fusion of light nuclei, as of deuterium and lithium.

hydrogen ion The positively charged atom of hydrogen present in all acids.

hydrogen peroxide A very unstable compound that decomposes to form water and oxygen.

hydrogen sulfide A colorless, gaseous, poisonous compound of hydrogen and sulfur, having a characteristic odor of rotten eggs.

hy·drog·ra·phy (hī·drog′rə·fē) *n.* The scientific investigation and study of navigable waters, rivers, coasts, etc. —**hy·drog′ra·pher** *n.* —**hy′dro·graph′ic** or **·i·cal** *adj.*

hy·droid (hī′droid) *adj.* Of or pertaining to a class of mostly marine organisms including the hydra. —*n.* A hydra or polyp.

hy·drol·y·sis (hī·drol′ə·sis) *n.* A chemical reaction by which an aqueous solution of a neutral salt exhibits properties of a weak acid or a weak base or both. [< HYDRO- + -LYSIS] —**hy·dro·lyt·ic** (hī′drə·lit′ik) *adj.*

hy·dro·lyte (hī′drə·līt) *n.* Any substance capable of undergoing hydrolysis.

hy·dro·lyze (hī′drə·līz) *v.t. & v.i.* **·lyzed, ·lyz·ing** To undergo or cause to undergo hydrolysis. —**hy′dro·lyz′a·ble** *adj.* —**hy·dro·ly·za·tion** (hī′drə·lə·zā′shən, -lī·zā′-) *n.*

hy·drom·e·ter (hī·drom′ə·tər) *n.* An instrument for measuring the specific gravity of a liquid or solution. —**hy·dro·met·ric** (hī′drə·met′rik) or **·ri·cal** *adj.* —**hy·drom′e·try** *n.*

hy·drop·a·thy (hī·drop′ə·thē) *n.* A method of treating ailments of any kind by the use of water. —**hy·dro·path·ic** (hī′drə·path′ik) or **·i·cal** *adj.* —**hy·drop′a·thist** *n.*

hy·dro·pho·bi·a (hī′drə·fō′bē·ə) *n.* **1** RABIES. **2** Any morbid dread of water. —**hy′dro·pho′bic** *adj.*

hy·dro·phyte (hī′drə·fīt) *n.* Any plant living only in water or wet ground. —**hy·dro·phyt·ic** (hī′drə·fit′ik) *adj.*

hy·dro·plane (hī′drə·plān) *n.* **1** A seaplane. **2** A small motorboat designed so that its hull skims over the water at high speeds. **3** A hydrofoil. —*v.i.* **·planed, ·plan·ing 1** To operate or travel in a hydroplane. **2** To skim over the surface of water.

hy·dro·pon·ics (hī′drə·pon′iks) *n.pl. (construed as sing.)* The cultivation of plants without earth in tanks of nutrient solutions. [< HYDRO- + Gk. *ponos* labor] —**hy′dro·pon′ic** *adj.*

hy·dro·sphere (hī′drə·sfir) *n.* The total water of the earth.

hy·dro·stat (hī′drə·stat) *n.* A device that controls the level of liquid in a container. —**hy′dro·stat′ic** or **·i·cal** *adj.*

hy·dro·stat·ics (hī′drə·stat′iks) *n. pl. (construed as sing.)* The scientific study of the mechanical behavior of stationary liquids.

hy·dro·ther·a·peu·tics (hī′drō·ther′ə·pyōō′tiks) *n.pl. (construed as sing.)* Therapy involving the use of water. Also **hy′dro·ther′a·py** (-ther′ə·pē). —**hy′dro·ther′a·peu′tic** *adj.*

hy·drot·ro·pism (hī·drot′rə·piz′əm) *n.* The orientation of a plant or plant part in response to moisture. —**hy·dro·trop·ic** (hī′drə·trop′ik) *adj.*

hy·drous (hī′drəs) *adj.* Pertaining to or designating a hydrate.

hy·drox·ide (hī·drok′sīd) *n.* A compound containing hydroxyl.

hy·drox·yl (hī·drok′sil) *n.* The univalent radical consisting of one atom of oxygen and one of hydrogen. [< HYDR(O) + OX(YGEN) + -YL]

hy·dro·zo·an (hī′drə·zō′ən) *adj.* Of or pertaining to a class of coelenterates, mostly marine, including hydroids, medusas, etc. —*n.* A hydrozoan animal.

hy·e·na (hī·ē′nə) *n.* A wolflike carnivorous mammal of Africa and Asia, with very strong, large teeth, striped or spotted body, and a piercing cry. [< Gk. *hyaina* < *hys* pig]

Hyena

Hy·ge·ia (hī·jē′ə) *Gk. Myth.* The goddess of health.

hy·giene (hī′jēn, -ji·ēn) *n.* **1** The science and preservation of health. **2** Practices and conditions that promote good health. [< Gk. *hygienios* healthful]

hy·gi·en·ic (hī′jē·en′ik, hī·jē′nik, -jen′ik-) *adj.* **1** Of or pertaining to hygiene. **2** Sanitary; clean. **—hy′gi·en′i·cal·ly** *adv.*

hy·gi·en·ics (hī′jē·en′iks, hī·jē′niks) *n. pl. (construed as sing.)* The science of preserving and promoting health.

hy·gi·en·ist (hī′jē·ən·ist) *n.* One who studies or is versed in the principles of hygiene.

hygro- *combining form* Moisture; humidity: *hygroscope.* [< Gk. *hygros* wet]

hy·grom·e·ter (hī·grom′ə·tər) *n.* An instrument that measures humidity in the atmosphere. **—hy·gro·met·ric** (hī′grə·met′rik) *adj.*

hy·gro·scope (hī′grə·skōp) *n.* A device for estimating the humidity of the air.

hy·gro·scop·ic (hī′grə·skop′ik) *adj.* **1** Pertaining to the hygroscope. **2** Absorbing moisture from the atmosphere.

hy·la (hī′lə) *n.* Any of various species of tree frog. [< Gk. *hyle* wood]

hy·men (hī′mən) *n.* A thin membrane partially covering the entrance of the vagina of a virgin; maidenhead. [< Gk. *hymēn* membrane]

Hy·men (hī′mən) *Gk. Myth.* The god of marriage.

hy·me·ne·al (hī′mə·nē′əl) *adj.* Of marriage. **—n.** A wedding song.

hy·men·op·ter·an (hī′mən·op′tər·ən) *adj.* Of or pertaining to an order of insects typically living in colonies and, when winged, having four membranous wings: also **hy′men·op′ter·ous.** **—n.** An insect of this order, as a bee, wasp, ant, etc. [< Gk. *hymen* membrane + *pteron* a wing]

hymn (him) *n.* **1** A song of praise to God. **2** Any religious song. **3** A poem of praise. **—v. hymned, hymn·ing** *v.t.* **1** To express or praise in hymns. **—v.i.** **2** To sing hymns or praises. [< Gk. *hymnos* a song, ode] **—hym′nic** (-nik) *adj.* **—hym′nist** *n.*

hym·nal (him′nəl) *n.* A book of hymns: also **hymn book.** **—adj.** Of a hymn or hymns.

hym·nol·o·gy (him·nol′ə·jē) *n.* **1** The study of hymns, including their history, use, etc. **2** Hymns collectively.

hy·oid (hī′oid) *n.* A U-shaped bone at the base of the tongue. **—adj.** Of or pertaining to the hyoid. [< Gk. *u* the letter upsilon + *eidos* form]

hype (hīp) *Slang v.t.* **hyped, hyp·ing** **1** To deceive; fool. **2** To stimulate with or as with drugs: with *up.* **—n.** **1** A deception; fraud. **2** A promotional talk or message.

hyper- *prefix* Over; above; excessive: *hypertension.* [< Gk. *hyper* above]

hy·per·ac·id (hī′pər·as′id) *adj.* Excessively acid. **—hy′per·a·cid′i·ty** (-ə·sid′ə·tē) *n.*

hy·per·bar·ic (hī′pər·bar′ik) *adj.* Of, having, or using pressures in excess of the usual pressure of the atmosphere.

hy·per·bo·la (hī·pûr′bə·lə) *n. Math.* A curve formed by the set of points having the property that the difference of their distances from two fixed points is a constant. [< Gk. *hyperbolē* a throwing beyond, excess]

hy·per·bo·le (hī·pûr′bə·lē) *n.* Deliberate exaggeration in writing or speaking, used to create an effect, as in *He was as tall as a mountain.* [< Gk. *hyperbolē* excess]

hy·per·bol·ic (hī′pər·bol′ik) *adj.* **1** Of or containing hyperbole; exaggerating. **2** Of, pertaining to, or shaped like a hyperbola. Also **hy′per·bol′i·cal.** **—hy′per·bol′i·cal·ly** *adv.*

hy·per·bo·lize (hī·pûr′bə·līz) *v.t. & v.i.* **·lized, ·liz·ing** To express in or use hyperbole.

hy·per·bo·re·an (hī′pər·bôr′ē·ən, -bō′rē-) *adj.* Of the far north; arctic; frigid.

Hy·per·bo·re·an (hī′pər·bôr′ē·ən, -bō′rē-) *n. Gk. Myth.* One of a people supposed to dwell in a blessed land beyond the north wind. [< Gk. *hyper-* beyond + *Boreas* north wind]

hy·per·crit·i·cal (hī′pər·krit′i·kəl) *adj.* Excessively critical or fussy. **—hy′per·crit′i·cal·ly** *adv.*

hy·per·gol·ic (hī′pər·gol′ik) *adj.* Indicating a combina-

tion of rocket fuel and oxidizer that ignites spontaneously. [< HYP(ER)- + Gk. *ergon* work]

hy·per·me·tro·pi·a (hī′pər·mə·trō′pē·ə) *n.* A focusing defect of the eye in which distant objects are more distinct than those near at hand; far-sightedness. Also **hy′per·met′ro·py** (-met′rə·pē), **hy′per·o′pi·a** (-ō′pē·ə). [< Gk. *hypermetros* excessive + *ōps* eye] **—hy′per·me·trop′ic** (-mə·trop′·ik, -trō′pik) *adj.*

hy·per·son·ic (hī·pər·son′ik) *adj.* Of, at, or pertaining to speeds of mach 5 or greater.

hy·per·ten·sion (hī′pər·ten′shən) *n.* Excessively high arterial blood pressure. **—hy′per·ten′sive** *adj., n.*

hy·per·thy·roid·ism (hī′pər·thī′roid·iz′əm) *n.* **1** Excessive activity of the thyroid gland. **2** Any disorder caused by such activity. **—hy′per·thy′roid** *adj.*

hy·per·tro·phy (hī·pûr′trə·fē) *n.* The excessive development of an organ or tissue. **—v.i. ·phied, ·phy·ing** To grow excessively. **—hy·per·troph·ic** (hī′pər·trof′ik, -trō′fik) or **·i·cal** *adj.*

hy·phen (hī′fən) *n.* A mark (- or – or :) used to connect the elements of certain compound words, to show division of a word at the end of a line, and to indicate a unit modifier: a *hit-and-run* driver. [< Gk. *hypo-* under + *hen* one]

hy·phen·ate (hī′fən·āt) *v.t.* **·at·ed, ·at·ing** **1** To connect by a hyphen. **2** To write with a hyphen. **—hy′phen·a′tion** *n.*

hyp·no·sis (hip·nō′sis) *n.pl.* **·ses** (-sēz) A change in consciousness, sometimes induced in one person by another, that makes an individual highly receptive to suggestion. [< Gk. *hypnos* sleep]

hyp·not·ic (hip·not′ik) *adj.* **1** Of or producing hypnosis. **2** Tending to produce sleep. **3** Spellbinding; entrancing. **—n.** **1** An agent efficacious in producing sleep. **2** A hypnotized person. **—hyp·not′i·cal·ly** *adv.*

hyp·no·tism (hip′nə·tiz′əm) *n.* **1** The act, practice, or technique of inducing hypnosis. **2** The theory of hypnosis. **—hyp′no·tist** *n.*

hyp·no·tize (hip′nə·tīz) *v.t.* **·tized, ·tiz·ing** **1** To produce hypnosis in. **2** To fascinate; entrance. *Brit. sp.* **hyp′no·tise.** **—hyp′no·tiz′a·ble** *adj.* **—hyp′no·ti·za′tion** (-tə·zā′shən, -tī·zā′-), **hyp′no·tiz′er** *n.*

hy·po¹ (hī′pō) *n.* SODIUM THIOSULFATE.

hy·po² (hī′pō) *n. Informal* **1** A hypodermic syringe or injection. **2** A hypochondriac.

hypo- *prefix* **1** Under; beneath; less than: *hypodermic.* **2** *Chem.* Indicating the lowest degree of oxidation: *hypophosphate.* **3** *Med.* Denoting a lack of or deficiency in: *hypothyroidism.* [< Gk. *hypo* under]

hy·po·al·ler·gen·ic (hī′pō·al′ər·jen′ik) *adj.* Not likely to produce an allergic reaction.

hy·po·chlo·rite (hī′pə·klôr′īt, -klō′rīt) *n.* A salt of hypochlorous acid.

hy·po·chlo·rous (hī′pə·klôr′əs, -klō′rəs) *adj.* Denoting an unstable acid formed by the solution of chlorine in water, used as an oxidizing and bleaching agent.

hy·po·chon·dri·a (hī′pə·kon′drē·ə) *n.* Excessive anxiety about one's health or minor ailments, often accompanied by imagined symptoms of illness. Also **hy·po·chon·dri·a·sis** (hī′pō·kən·drī′ə·sis). [< HYPO- + Gk. *chondros* cartilage]

hy·po·chon·dri·ac (hī′pə·kon′drē·ak, hip′ə-) *adj.* **1** Pertaining to or affected by hypochondria. **2** Of, pertaining to, or situated in the hypochondrium. Also **hy·po·chon·dri·a·cal** (hī′pō·kən·drī′ə·kəl). **—n.** A person subject to hypochondria. **—hy′po·chon·dri′a·cal·ly** *adv.*

hy·po·chon·dri·um (hī′pə·kon′drē·əm, hip′ə-) *n. pl.* **·dri·a** (-drē·ə) The abdomen on either side just under the ribs. [< HYPO- + Gk. *chondros* cartilage]

hy·poc·ri·sy (hi·pok′rə·sē) *n. pl.* **·sies** A pretending to be what one is not; extreme insincerity; dissimulation. [< Gk. *hypokrisis* acting a part, feigning] **—Syn.** pretense, dissembling, affectation, sham, fakery.

hyp·o·crite (hip′ə·krit) *n.* One who pretends to have virtues, feelings, qualities, etc., that he does not possess. [< Gk. *hypokritēs* an actor.] **—hyp′o·crit′i·cal** *adj.* **—hyp′o·crit′i·cal·ly** *adv.* **—Syn.** deceiver, dissembler, pretender, cheat.

hy·po·der·mic (hī′pə·dûr′mik) *adj.* **1** Of or pertaining to the tissue just under the skin. 2 Of or pertaining to a hypodermic injection. —*n.* A hypodermic injection or syringe.

hypodermic injection An injection under the skin.

hypodermic syringe A syringe having a sharp, hollow needle for injection of a drug or medicine into the hypodermis.

hy·po·der·mis (hī′pə-dûr′məs) *n.* The tissue just under the skin.

hy·po·gas·tri·um (hī′pə-gas′trē-əm) *n. pl.* **·tri·a** (-trē-ə) *Anat.* The lower middle part of the abdomen. [<HYPO- + Gk. *gastēr* belly] —**hy′po·gas′tric** *adj.*

hy·po·gly·ce·mi·a (hī′pō-glī-sē′mē-ə) *n. Med.* A subnormal amount of blood sugar, usually caused by the presence of too much insulin. [<HYPO- + Gk. *glykys* sweet + -EMIA] —**hy′po·gly·ce′mic** *adj.*

hy·po·phos·phate (hī′pə-fos′fāt) *n.* A salt of hypophosphoric acid.

hy·po·phos·phite (hī′pə-fos′fīt) *n.* A salt of hypophosphorous acid.

hy·po·phos·phor·ic (hī′pō-fos-fôr′ik, -for′ik) *adj.* Denoting a crystalline acid formed from moist phosphorus by oxidation.

hy·po·phos·pho·rous (hī′pə-fos′fər-əs) *adj.* Denoting an acid composed of hydrogen, oxygen, and phosphorus, and having a powerful reducing action.

hy·po·sul·fite (hī′pō-sul′fīt) *n.* 1 SODIUM THIOSULFATE. 2 A salt of hyposulfurous acid.

hy·po·sul·fu·rous (hī′pō-sul-fyŏŏr′əs, hī′pə-sul′fər-əs) *adj.* Pertaining to or designating an unstable acid of strong reducing and bleaching properties.

hy·pot·e·nuse (hī-pot′ə-nŏŏs, hi-) *n. Geom.* The side of a right triangle opposite the right angle. Also **hy·poth′e·nuse** (-poth′-). [<Gk. *hypo-* under + *teinein* to stretch]

hy·po·thal·a·mus (hī′pə-thal′ə-məs) *n.* A region at the base of the brain that con-

Hypotenuse

trols temperature and various visceral activities. —**hy·po·tha·lam·ic** (hī′pə-thə-lam′ik) *adj.*

hy·poth·e·cate (hī-poth′ə-kāt, hi-) *v.t.* **·cat·ed, ·cat·ing** To give (personal property) in pledge as security for debt. [<LL *hypotheca* pledge] —**hy·poth′e·ca′tion, hy·poth′e·ca′tor** *n.*

hy·poth·e·sis (hī-poth′ə-sis, hi-) *n. pl.* **·ses** (-sēz) 1 A set of assumptions provisionally accepted as a basis of reasoning, experiment, or investigation. 2 An unsupported or ill-supported theory. [<Gk. *hypotithenai* put under]

hy·poth·e·size (hī-poth′ə-sīz, hi-) *v.* **·sized, ·siz·ing** *v.t.* To make a hypothesis of. —*v.i.* To conceive or suggest hypotheses.

hy·po·thet·i·cal (hī′pə-thet′i·kəl) *adj.* 1 Having the nature of or based on hypothesis; assumed conditionally or tentatively as a basis for argument or investigation. 2 Given to using hypotheses. Also **hy′po·thet′ic.** —**hy′po·thet′i·cal·ly** *adv.*

hy·po·thy·roid·ism (hī′pō-thī′roid·iz′əm) *n.* 1 Deficient production of thyroid hormone. 2 The resulting syndrome, including lethargy, obesity, etc. —**hy′po·thy′roid** *adj. & n.*

hy·son (hī′sən) *n.* A grade of green tea from China. [<Chin. *hsi-ch'un*, lit., blooming spring]

hys·sop (his′əp) *n.* 1 A bushy, medicinal herb of the mint family, with small clusters of blue flowers. 2 A plant furnishing the twigs used in certain Mosaic rites. [<Gk. *hyssōpos* <Heb. *ēzōb*]

hys·ter·ec·to·my (his′tə·rek′tə·mē) *n. pl.* **·mies** Removal of all or part of the uterus by surgery. [<Gk. *hystera* womb + *ek-* out + *tomē* a cutting]

hys·te·ri·a (his·tir′ē-ə, -ter′-) *n.* 1 A psychoneurotic condition characterized by symptons of organic disorders, as blindness, deafness, etc. 2 Uncontrollable emotional excitement. Also **hys·ter·ics** (his·ter′iks). [<Gk. *hystera* the womb, thought to be the source of such symptoms]

Hz hertz.

I

I, i (ī) *n. pl.* **I's, i's, Is, is** 1 The ninth letter of the English alphabet. 2 Any spoken sound representing the letter *I* or *i.* 3 In Roman notation, the symbol for one. 4 Something shaped like an I. —*adj.* Shaped like an I.

I (ī) *pron.* The first person singular pronoun in the nominative case, used to denote the person speaking or writing. —*n., pl.* **I's** The self; the ego. [<OE *ic*]

I iodine.

I. Island(s); Isle(s).

i. interest; intransitive; island.

IA Iowa (P.O. abbr.).

Ia. Iowa.

IAAF International Amateur Athletic Federation.

IAEA International Atomic Energy Agency (of the United Nations).

i·amb (ī′amb) *n.* In prosody, a metrical foot of two syllables, an unaccented one followed by an accented one. [<Gk. *iambos*]

i·am·bic (ī-am′bik) *adj.* Of, using, or like iambs. —*n.* 1 An iamb. 2 A verse of iambic feet.

i·am·bus (ī-am′bəs) *n. pl.* **·bus·es** or **·bi** (-bī) IAMB.

-iasis *suffix Med.* Denoting a disease or abnormal condition: *psoriasis.* [<Gk., suffix of action]

-iatrics *combining form* Denoting treatment of disease: *pediatrics.* [<Gk. *iatros* healer]

i·at·ro·gen·ic (ī-at′rə-jen′ik) *adj. Med.* Caused unintentionally by the physician or by the manner of treatment: said of disorders. [<Gk. *iatros* healer + -GENIC] —**i·at′ro·gen′i·cal·ly** *adv.*

-iatry *combining form* Medical or curative treatment: *psychiatry.* [<Gk. *iatreia* healing]

ib., ibid. ibidem.

I·be·ri·an (ī-bir′ē-ən) *adj.* Of or pertaining to Iberia, its people, or its dead language. —*n.* 1 A native or citizen of Iberia. 2 The language of the ancient Iberians. [<L *Iberus* <Gk.]

i·bex (ī′beks) *n.* **i·bex·es** or **i·bi·ces** (ī′bə·sēz, ib′ə-) One of various wild goats of Europe and Asia, with long, recurved horns. [L]

i·bi·dem (ib′ə-dem′, i·bī′dem) *adv. Latin* In the same place: used to refer to the same work, chapter, etc., just mentioned.

i·bis (ī′bis) *n. pl.* **i·bis·es** or **i·bis** A wading bird related to the heron, with a long bill curved downward. [<Gk. <Egypt. *hab*]

-ible *suffix* -ABLE.

-ic *suffix* (for forming adjectives with the following meanings) 1 Of or pertaining to: *volcanic.* 2 Like; resembling; characteristic of: *angelic.* 3 Consisting of; containing: *alcoholic.* 4 Produced by or in the manner of: *Homeric.* 5 Related to; connected with: *domestic.* 6 *Chem.* Having a higher valence than that indicated by *-ous*: said of elements in compounds: *cupric.* [<Gk. *-ikos*]

-ical *suffix* 1 Forming adjectives from nouns ending in *-ic* or *-ics*: *ethical, musical.* 2 Forming adjectives from adjectives ending in *-ic*, often parallel in meaning: *comic, comical,* but sometimes with extended or special meaning: *economic, economical.* [<-IC + -AL]

Ic·a·rus (ik′ə·rəs, ī′kə-) *Gk. Myth.* The son of Daedalus, who, escaping from Crete, flew too near the sun so that the wax that fastened his artificial wings melted and he fell into the sea. —**I·car·i·an** (i·kâr′ē-ən, ī-) *adj.*

ICBM Intercontinental Ballistic Missile.

ICC, I.C.C. Interstate Commerce Commission.

ice (īs) *n.* 1 The solid state of water, assumed at or below 32° F. or 0° C. 2 Something resembling ice. 3 A frozen dessert made without cream, as sherbet. 4 Icing for cake.

Ibex

5 *Slang* A diamond or diamonds. —**break the ice 1** To break through reserve or formality. **2** To make a start. —**on ice** *Slang* **1** Set aside for future action. **2** Sure; already determined. —**on thin ice** *Informal* In a difficult or dangerous situation. —*v.* **iced, ic·ing** *v.t.* **1** To cause to congeal into ice. **2** To cover with ice. **3** To chill with or as with ice. **4** To frost, as cake, with icing. **5** In ice hockey, to shoot (the puck) from one's own end of the rink past the opponent's goal line. **6** *Slang* To clinch victory in (a contest). —*v.i.* **7** To freeze. [< OE *īs*]

ice., Icel. Iceland; Icelandic.

ice age GLACIAL EPOCH.

ice·berg (īs′bûrg′) *n.* **1** A thick mass of floating ice that has separated from a glacier. **2** *Informal* A cold, unemotional person. [< Du. *ijsberg* ice mountain]

ice·boat (īs′bōt′) *n.* **1** A boatlike framework with runners and sails for sailing over ice. **2** ICEBREAKER.

ice·bound (īs′bound′) *adj.* Surrounded or obstructed by ice: an *icebound* ship or harbor.

ice·box (īs′boks′) *n.* REFRIGERATOR.

ice·break·er (īs′brā′kər) *n.* A ship having a strong prow and powerful engines, used to break up ice in icebound waters.

ice cap An extensive mass of ice permanently covering a tract of land and moving in all directions from a center.

ice cream A mixture of cream or butterfat, flavoring, sweetening, and often eggs, beaten to a uniform consistency and frozen. —**ice′-cream′** *adj.*

iced (īst) *adj.* **1** Coated or covered with ice. **2** Made cold with ice. **3** Covered with icing, as cake.

ice field A large field of floating ice. Also **ice floe.**

ice hockey HOCKEY (def. 1).

Ice·land (īs′lənd) *n.* A republic on an island in the North Atlantic, 39,758 sq. mi., cap. Reykjavik.

Ice·land·er (īs′lan′dər) *n.* A native or citizen of Iceland.

Ice·land·ic (īs·lan′dik) *adj.* Of or pertaining to Iceland, its people, or their language. —*n.* The language of Iceland.

ice·man (īs′man′, -mən) *n. pl.* **·men** (-men′, -mən) One who makes or delivers ice.

ice milk A sweet, smooth frozen food, like ice cream, made of skim milk.

ice pack 1 A large tract of floating ice cakes frozen together. **2** A container for cracked ice, used medically to relieve pain, reduce swelling, etc.

ice pick A sharp pointed tool for breaking ice into small pieces.

ice sheet A large continental glacier.

ice-skate (īs′skāt′) *v.i.* **-skat·ed, -skat·ing** To skate on ice. —**ice skater**

ice skate SKATE (defs. 1 & 2).

ich·neu·mon (ik-nyōō′mən) *n.* **1** MONGOOSE. **2** ICHNEUMON FLY. [< Gk. *ichneumōn*, lit., tracker]

ichneumon fly A hymenopterous insect the larvae of which feed upon other insects or insects. • See OVIPOSITOR.

i·chor (ī′kôr, ī′kər) *Gk. Myth.* An ethereal fluid supposed to flow in the veins of the gods. —*n.* A watery discharge from a sore. [< Gk. *ichōr*] —**i·chor·ous** (ī′kər·es) *adj.*

ichthyo- *combining form* Fish: *ichthyology.* [< Gk. *ichthys* fish]

ich·thy·ol·o·gy (ik′thē·ol′ə·jē) *n.* The branch of zoology that treats of fishes. —**ich·thy·o·log·ic** (ik′thē·ə·loj′ik), **ich′·thy·o·log′i·cal** *adj.* —**ich′thy·ol′o·gist** *n.*

ich·thy·o·sau·rus (ik′thē·ə·sôr′əs) *n. pl.* **·sau·ri** (-sôr′ī) Any of an order of extinct marine reptiles having a porpoiselike form with four paddlelike limbs. Also **ich′thy·o·saur′.** [< ICHTHYO- + Gk. *sauros* lizard]

-ician *suffix of nouns* One skilled in, or engaged in, the field of: *logician, mathematician.* [< F *-icien*]

i·ci·cle (ī′si·kəl) *n.* A hanging mass of ice formed by dripping water. [< OE *īs* ice + *gicel* piece of ice, icicle] —**i′ci·cled** *adj.*

i·ci·ly (ī′sə·lē) *adv.* In an icy manner.

ic·ing (ī′sing) *n.* A coating for cakes and pastry, usu. made of sugar and water, flavoring, egg whites, cream, butter, etc.; frosting.

ick·y (ik′ē) *adj.* **ick·i·er, ick·i·est** *Slang* Distasteful; repulsive. [Alter. of STICKY] —**ick′i·ness** *n.*

i·con (ī′kon) *n. pl.* **i·cons** or **i·con·es** (ī′kə·nēz) **1** In the Eastern Orthodox Church, a holy picture or mosaic of Jesus, Mary, etc. **2** An image or likeness. [< Gk. *eikon* image] —**i·con′ic, i·con′i·cal** *adj.*

icono- *combining form* Image; of or related to images: *iconoscope.* [< Gk. *eikōn* image]

i·con·o·clast (ī·kon′ə·klast) *n.* **1** One who destroys religious images. **2** One who attacks traditional beliefs or institutions. [< Gk. *eikōn* image + *-klastēs* breaker] —**i·con′o·clasm** *n.* —**i·con′o·clas′tic** *adj.* —**i·con′o·clas′ti·cal·ly** *adv.*

i·con·o·scope (ī·kon′ə·skōp) *n.* An electron tube used in television to convert an optical image to an electric signal, containing a photosensitive surface scanned by an electron beam.

-ics *suffix of nouns* **1** Art, science, or field of study of: *mathematics.* **2** Methods, practices, or activities of: *athletics.* [See -IC.] • Nouns ending in *-ics* are construed as singular when they strictly denote an art, science, or system (*Mathematics is difficult*). They are construed as plural if they denote personal attributes (*His mathematics are poor*), inherent qualities (*The acoustics are bad*), or specific activities (*Athletics are compulsory*).

ic·tus (ik′təs) *n. pl.* **·tus·es** or **·tus 1** A sudden attack or fit. **2** A metrical stress or accent. [L, pp. of *icere* to strike]

i·cy (ī′sē) *adj.* **i·ci·er, i·ci·est 1** Made of or covered with ice. **2** Extremely cold or slippery, like ice. **3** Resembling ice. **4** Unfriendly; cold: an *icy* stare. —**i′ci·ness,** *n.* Syn. **4** chilly, hostile, inimical, uncordial.

id (id) *n. Psychoanal.* The part of the psyche that is impelled towards fulfilling instinctual needs; the reservoir of libido. [< L *id* it]

I'd (īd) Contraction of *I would, I had,* or *I should.*

ID Idaho (P.O. abbr.).

I.D. identification; Infantry Division; Intelligence Department.

Id., Ida. Idaho.

id. the same (L *idem*).

-idae *suffix Zool.* Used to form the names of families of animals: *Canidae,* the dog family. [< Gk. *-idai* plural patronymic suffix]

-ide *suffix Chem.* **1** Denoting a binary compound: sodium *chloride.* **2** Used to form name of groups or series of related substances: *lanthanide* series. Also **-id.** [< L *-idus*]

i·de·a (ī·dē′ə) *n.* **1** A thought, concept, or image present in the mind. **2** A definitely formulated thought; belief; opinion. **3** A plan or project. **4** A vague thought or supposition: I had an *idea* you'd come. **5** *Informal* Meaning; aim: What's the *idea?* **6** In Platonic philosophy, the archetype or model of which all existing things are imperfect representations. [< Gk. < *ideein* see]

i·de·al (ī·dē′əl, ī·dēl′) *adj.* **1** Of, relating to, or existing in ideas, images, or concepts of the mind. **2** Existing only in imagination or notion as regards perfection, etc.; imaginary. **3** Supremely excellent or desirable; perfect: the *ideal* job. **4** In philosophy, existing as an archetypal idea or model. —*n.* **1** That which is taken as a standard of perfection, excellence, or beauty; model; type. **2** An ultimate aim or goal. **3** That which exists only in imagination. [< L *idealis*]

i·de·al·ism (ī·dē′əl·iz′əm) *n.* **1** The practice or habit of conceiving of things as ideal or as they should be rather than as they actually are. **2** The forming of and striving after ideals. **3** In art and literature, the treatment of persons or things according to an imaginative or preconceived idea of perfection instead of adhering strictly to facts. **4** In philosophy, any theory which holds that reality is essentially spiritual or mental and that there is no world of objects apart from a reacting mind or consciousness.

i·de·al·ist (ī·dē′əl·ist) *n.* **1** One who idealizes. **2** A visionary or a romantic. **3** An exponent of idealism in art, philosophy, or literature. —**i·de'al·is'tic** or **·ti·cal** *adj.* —**i·de'al·is'ti·cal·ly** *adv.*

i·de·al·ize (ī·dē'əl·īz) *v.* **·ized, ·iz·ing** *v.t.* To represent or think of (a person, thing, etc.) as conforming to some standard, usu. unattainable, of perfection or beauty; make ideal; exalt. —*v.i.* To form an ideal or ideals. —**i·de·al·i·za·tion** (ī·dē'əl·ə·zā'shən, -ī·zā'-), **i·de'al·iz'er** *n.*

i·de·al·ly (ī·dē'əl·ē) *adv.* **1** In an ideal manner; perfectly. **2** In imagination or theory.

i·de·ate (ī·dē'āt) *v.* **·at·ed, ·at·ing** *v.t.* To form an idea of; conceive. —*v.i.* To form ideas; think. —**i'de·a'tion** *n.* —**i'de·a'tion·al** *adj.*

i·dée fixe (ē·dā' fēks') *pl.* **i·dées fixes** (ē·dā' fēks') *French* A fixed idea; obsession.

i·dem (ī'dem, ē'-, id'em) *n. & adj. Latin* The same: often as referring to what was previously mentioned.

i·den·ti·cal (ī·den'ti·kəl) *adj.* **1** The very same. **2** Alike in all respects. [< L IDEM] —**i·den'ti·cal·ly** *adv.* —**i·den'ti·cal·ness** *n.*

identical twins Twins having the same genetic makeup, derived from a single fertilized ovum.

i·den·ti·fi·ca·tion (ī·den'tə·fə·kā'shən) *n.* **1** The act of identifying or the state of being identified. **2** Anything by which the identity of a person or thing can be established.

i·den·ti·fy (ī·den'tə·fī) *v.t.* **·fied, ·fy·ing 1** To determine as a particular person or thing. **2** To consider or treat as the same: He *identifies* money with happiness. **3** To serve as a means of identification of. **4** To join or associate in interest, action, etc.: usu. with *with.* **5** *Psychoanal.* To unconsciously incorporate (in one's self) the identity of someone else. [< LL *identitas* identity + -FY] —**i·den'ti·fi'a·ble** *adj.* —**i·den'ti·fi'er** *n.*

i·den·ti·ty (ī·den'tə·tē) *n. pl.* **·ties 1** The state of being identical. **2** The state of being exactly that which has been claimed, asserted, or described. **3** The distinctive character belonging to an individual; individuality. **4** A mathematical equation that is satisfied by all values of its variables for which the expressions involved have meaning. [< LL *identitas* < IDEM]

ideo- *combining form* Idea; of or pertaining to ideas: *ideograph.* [< Gk. *idea* a form, idea]

i·de·o·graph (ī'dē·ə·graf', -gräf, id'ē-) *n.* **1** A graphic symbol or sign of an object or idea but without representation of the actual word for the object or idea, as in Egyptian hieroglyphics. **2** A symbol, as +, =, ¶, $, etc. Also **i'de·o·gram'** (-gram'). —**i'de·o·graph'ic** or **·i·cal** *adj.* —**i'de·o·graph'·i·cal·ly** *adv.*

i·de·o·logue (ī'dē·ə·lôg, -log, id'ē-) *n.* One who is committed to an ideology. [F]

i·de·ol·o·gy (ī'dē·ol'ə·jē, id'ē-) *n. pl.* **·gies 1** The ideas, doctrines, or way of thinking characteristic of a political or economic theory or system. **2** The science that treats of the nature and evolution of ideas. **3** Visionary or impractical thinking. [IDEO- + -LOGY] —**i·de·o·log·ic** (ī'dē·ə·loj'ik, id'ē-) or **·i·cal** *adj.* —**i'de·ol'o·gist** *n.*

ides (īdz) *n.pl.* In the ancient Roman calendar, the 15th of March, May, July, and October, and the 13th of the other months. [< L *idus*]

id est (id est) *Latin* That is.

id·i·o·cy (id'ē·ə·sē) *n. pl.* **·cies 1** An extreme degree of congenital mental deficiency. **2** A foolish utterance or act.

id·i·om (id'ē·əm) *n.* **1** An expression not readily analyzable from its grammatical construction or from the meaning of its component parts, as *to put up with* (tolerate, endure). **2** The dialect or language characteristic of a certain group, class, trade, region, etc.: legal *idiom.* **3** The distinctive form or construction of a particular language. **4** Specific character, form, or style, as in art, literature, music, etc. [< Gk. *idiōma* peculiarity, property]

id·i·o·mat·ic (id'ē·ə·mat'ik) *adj.* **1** Using many idioms. **2** Of or like idioms. **3** Characteristic of a certain language or dialect. Also **id'i·o·mat'i·cal.** —**id'i·o·mat'i·cal·ly.** *adv.*

id·i·o·syn·cra·sy (id'ē·ə·sing'krə·sē) *n. pl.* **·sies 1** Any distinctive quality, characteristic, habit, etc. peculiar to an individual; quirk. **2** The physical and mental constitution unique to an individual or group. [< Gk. *idios* peculiar + *synkrasis* a mixing together] —**id'i·o·syn·crat'ic** (-sin·krat'ik) *adj.* —**id'i·o·syn·crat'i·cal·ly** *adv.*

id·i·ot (id'ē·ət) *n.* **1** A person having an extreme degree of congenital mental deficiency. **2** Any foolish or stupid person. [< Gk. *idiōtēs* private person]

id·i·ot·ic (id'ē·ot'ik) *adj.* **1** Of, like, or characteristic of an idiot. **2** Senseless; stupid. —**id'i·ot'i·cal·ly** *adv.*

i·dle (īd'l) *adj.* **1** Not occupied; doing nothing. **2** Not being used: *idle* factories. **3** Averse to labor; lazy. **4** Used for leisure. **5** Without effect; useless: *idle* talk. —*v.* **i·dled, i·dling** *v.i.* **1** To spend time in idleness. **2** To saunter or move idly. **3** To operate without a load, as an engine or motor. —*v.t.* **4** To pass in idleness; waste, as a day. **5** To cause to be idle, as a person or an industry. [< OE *idel* empty, useless] —**i'dle·ness, i'dler** *n.* —**i'dly** *adv.* —Syn. *adj.* **3** inactive, indolent, laggard, slothful. *v.* **1** dally, laze, loaf, lounge.

i·dol (īd'l) *n.* **1** An image of a god, esp. a heathen god, to which worship is offered. **2** In the Bible, a false god. **3** Any object of extreme or passionate devotion. **4** A source of error; a fallacy. [< Gk. *eidōlon* image, phantom]

i·dol·a·ter (ī·dol'ə·tər) *n.* **1** An adorer of images. **2** One who is inordinately fond of some person or thing. [< Gk. *eidōlon* an idol + *latreuein* worship] —**i·dol'a·tress** (-tris) *n. Fem.*

i·dol·a·trous (ī·dol'ə·trəs) *adj.* **1** Of or like idolatry. **2** Extravagant in admiration. —**i·dol'a·trous·ly** *adv.* —**i·dol'a·trous·ness** *n.*

i·dol·a·try (ī·dol'ə·trē) *n. pl.* **·tries 1** The worship of idols. **2** Excessive admiration or devotion.

i·dol·ize (ī'dəl·īz) *v.* **·ized, ·iz·ing** *v.t.* **1** To have inordinate love for; adore. **2** To worship as an idol. —*v.i.* **3** To worship idols. —**i'dol·i·za'tion, i'dol·iz'er** *n.*

i·dyll (īd'l) *n.* **1** A short poem or prose piece depicting simple scenes of pastoral life. **2** Any event or scene suitable for such a work. **3** A romantic episode. Also **i'dyl.** [< Gk. *eidos* form] —**i'dyl·list, i'dyl·ist** *n.*

i·dyl·lic (ī·dil'ik) *adj.* **1** Of or like an idyll. **2** Charmingly romantic or picturesque. —**i·dyl'li·cal·ly** *adv.*

-ie *suffix* Little; dear: *birdie:* often used in nicknames or affectionately, as in *Annie.* [Var. of -Y]

IE, I.E. Indo-European.

i.e. that is (L *id est*).

-ier *suffix of nouns* One who is concerned with or works with: *cashier.* Also **-yer:** *lawyer.* [< OF < L *-ārius*]

if (if) *conj.* **1** On the supposition or condition that: We'll go by plane *if* the weather permits. **2** Allowing that; although: *If* he was there, I didn't see him. **3** Whether: I am not sure *if* he is at home. —*n.* **1** A supposition. **2** A condition. [< OE *gif*]

if·fy (if'ē) *adj.* **if·fi·er, if·fi·est** *Informal* Uncertain or doubtful because dependent on unknown or chancy conditions: an *iffy* proposition. [< IF] —**if'fi·ness** *n.*

ig·loo (ig'lōō) *n. pl.* **·loos** An Eskimo house, dome-shaped and usu. built of blocks of packed snow. Also **ig'lu.** [< Eskimo *igdlu*]

ig·ne·ous (ig'nē·əs) *adj.* **1** Of or like fire. **2** *Geol.* Pertaining to the heat inside the earth: said esp. of rocks formed from molten magma. [< L *ignis* fire]

ig·nis fat·u·us (ig'nis fach'ōō·əs) *pl.* **ig·nes fat·u·i** (ig'nēz fach'ōō·ī) **1** An evanescent light seen in the air over marshy places; will-o'-the-wisp. **2** A deceptive goal or ambition; a delusion. [Med. L, lit., foolish fire]

ig·nite (ig·nīt') *v.* **ig·nit·ed, ig·nit·ing** *v.t.* **1** To set on fire; cause to burn. **2** To cause to glow with intense heat. **3** To excite. —*v.i.* **4** To start burning. [< L *ignire* set on fire] —**ig·nit'a·ble, ig·nit'i·ble** *adj.* —**ig·nit'a·bil'i·ty, ig·nit'i·bil'i·ty, ig·nit'er, ig·nit'or** (-ər) *n.*

ig·ni·tion (ig·nish'ən) *n.* **1** The act of igniting. **2** The explosion of the fuel mixture in the cylinder of an internal-combustion engine. **3** The electrical system that does this.

ig·no·ble (ig·nō'bəl) *adj.* Unworthy or degraded in character or quality. [< L *ignobilis* < IN-¹ + *nobilis* noble] —**ig·nob'ly** *adv.* —**ig'no·bil'i·ty, ig·no'ble·ness** *n.* —Syn. base, contemptible, despicable, low, mean.

ig·no·min·i·ous (ig'nə·min'ē·əs) *adj.* **1** Marked by or implying dishonor or disgrace. **2** Deserving ignominy; despicable. **3** Abasing; humiliating. —**ig'no·min'i·ous·ly** *adv.* —**ig'no·min'i·ous·ness** *n.*

ig·no·min·y (ig'nə·min'ē) *n. pl.* **·min·ies 1** Disgrace or dishonor. **2** That which causes disgrace. [< L *in-* not + *nomen* name, reputation]

ig·no·ra·mus (ig′nə·rā′məs, -ram′əs) *n. pl.* **·mus·es** An ignorant person. [< L, we do not know]

ig·no·rance (ig′nər·əns) *n.* The state or quality of being ignorant.

ig·no·rant (ig′nər·ənt) *adj.* **1** Lacking education or knowledge. **2** Lacking awareness: with *of.* **3** Not informed or experienced: with *in.* **4** Manifesting or caused by ignorance. [< L *ignorare* not to know] —**ig′no·rant·ly** *adv.*

ig·nore (ig·nôr′, -nōr′) *v.t.* **·nored, ·nor·ing** To refuse to notice or recognize; disregard intentionally. [< L *ignorare* not to know] —**ig·nor′er** *n.*

I·go·rot (ē′gə·rōt′, ig′ə-) *n. pl.* **·rot** or **·rots 1** One belonging to a group of Malay tribes living in northern Luzon, Philippines. **2** The Indonesian language of these tribes. Also **I·gor·ro·te** (ē′gôr·rō′tā).

i·gua·na (i·gwä′nə) *n.* Any of a family of large, harmless lizards of tropical America. [< Cariban]

IHS, ihs A monogram of the name Jesus, derived from the Greek IH(ΣΟΥ)Σ, Jesus.

i·kon (ī′kon) *n.* ICON.

IL Illinois (P.O. abbr.).

-ile *suffix* Of, like, pertaining to; capable of; suited to: *docile, mobile.* Also **-il,** as in *civil, fossil.* [< L *-ilis*]

Iguana

il·e·um (il′ē·əm) *n.* The last section of the small intestine, following the jejunum and leading to the large intestine. [L] —**il·e·ac** (il′ē·ak) *adj.*

i·lex (ī′leks) *n.* **1** A tree or shrub of the holly family. **2** The holm oak. [L, holm oak]

I.L.G.W.U. International Ladies' Garment Workers' Union.

Il·i·ad (il′ē·əd) *n.* An ancient Greek epic poem on the siege of Ilium (Troy), ascribed to Homer.

il·i·um (il′ē·əm) *n. pl.* **·i·a** (-ē·ə) *Anat.* The flat upper portion of the hipbone. [L, flank] —**il′i·ac** *adj.* •See PELVIS.

Il·i·um (il′ē·əm) TROY. Also **Il′i·on** (-on).

ilk (ilk) *adj. & n. Obs.* Same. —**of that ilk** Of that race, class, or kind. [< OE *ilka* the same]

ill (il) *adj.* **1** Not well; sick. **2** Evil; bad: *ill* repute. **3** Hostile; unfriendly: *ill* will. **4** Not favorable; dangerous: *ill* wind. **5** Of inferior quality; imperfect. —*n.* Anything that brings about misfortune, harm, sickness, evil, etc. —*adv.* **1** Not well; badly. **2** With difficulty; hardly. **3** Unfavorably; unkindly: to speak *ill* of someone. —**ill at ease** Uneasy; uncomfortable. [< ON *illr*]

I'll (īl) **1** I will. **2** I shall.

Ill. Illinois.

Ill., illus., illust. illustrated; illustration; illustrator.

ill-ad·vised (il′əd·vīzd′) *adj.* Acting or resulting from improper advice or deliberation; unwise. —**ill′-ad·vis′ed·ly** (-vīz′id·lē) *adv.*

ill-bred (il′bred′) *adj.* Badly taught, reared, or trained; rude. —**Syn.** boorish, discourteous, impolite, unmannerly.

ill breeding Bad manners.

ill-con·sid·ered (il′kən·sid′ərd) *adj.* Unwise.

ill-dis·posed (il′dis·pōzd′) *adj.* **1** Unfriendly. **2** Not willing or agreeable; averse.

il·le·gal (i·lē′gəl) *adj.* Contrary to the law; not legal. —**il·le·gal·i·ty** (il′ē·gal′ə·tē) *n.* (*pl.* **·ties**) —**il·le′gal·ly** *adv.*

il·leg·i·ble (i·lej′ə·bəl) *adj.* Not legible; undecipherable. —**il·leg′i·bly** *adv.* —**il·leg′i·bil′i·ty, il·leg′i·ble·ness** *n.*

il·le·git·i·mate (il′i·jit′ə·mit) *adj.* **1** Born out of wedlock. **2** Illogical; unsound. **3** Contrary to rule or proper procedure; irregular. —**il′le·git′i·mate·ly** *adv.* —**il′le·git′i·ma·cy** (-ə·mə·sē) *n.* (*pl.* **·cies**)

ill-fat·ed (il′fāt′id) *adj.* **1** Certain to end badly. **2** Unlucky.

ill-fa·vored (il′fā′vərd) *adj.* **1** Repulsive; ugly. **2** Objectionable.

ill-found·ed (il′foun′did) *adj.* Based on insufficient or faulty reasons or facts.

ill-got·ten (il′got′n) *adj.* Obtained dishonestly.

ill-hu·mor (il′hyōō′mər) *n.* A morose or disagreeable state of mind. —**ill′-hu′mored** *adj.*

il·lib·er·al (i·lib′ər·əl) *adj.* **1** Not generous; stingy. **2** Narrow-minded. **3** Lacking culture; vulgar. —**il·lib′er·al·ly** *adv.* —**il·lib′er·al·ism** (-iz′əm) *n.* —**il·lib′er·al′i·ty** (-al′ə·tē) *n.*

il·lic·it (i·lis′it) *adj.* Not permitted; unlawful. [< L *in-* not + *licitus* licit] —**il·lic′it·ly** *adv.* —**il·lic′it·ness** *n.*

il·lim·it·a·ble (i·lim′i·tə·bəl) *adj.* That cannot be limited; boundless; endless. —**il·lim′it·a·bly** *adv.* —**il·lim′it·a·bil′i·ty, il·lim′it·a·ble·ness** *n.*

Il·li·nois (il′ə·noi′, -noiz′) *n. pl.* **·nois** A North American Indian belonging to any one of the Algonquian tribes of Illinois.

illit. illiterate.

il·lit·er·a·cy (i·lit′ər·ə·sē) *n. pl.* **·cies 1** The state of being illiterate. **2** A mistake in speaking or writing, usu. resulting from a lack of education.

il·lit·er·ate (i·lit′ər·it) *adj.* **1** Unable to read or write. **2** Having or showing little or no education. —*n.* An illiterate person, esp. one who cannot read or write. [< L *in-* not + *literatus* literate] —**il·lit′er·ate·ly** *adv.* —**il·lit′er·ate·ness** *n.*

ill-man·nered (il′man′ərd) *adj.* Having bad manners; discourteous; rude.

ill nature Peevishness; surliness; sullenness. —**ill′-na′tured** *adj.* —**ill′-na′tured·ly** *adv.* —**ill′-na′tured·ness** *n.*

ill·ness (il′nis) *n.* **1** The state of being in poor health. **2** An ailment; sickness.

il·log·i·cal (i·loj′i·kəl) *adj.* Not logical or reasonable. —**il·log′i·cal′i·ty, il·log′i·cal·ness** *n.* —**il·log′i·cal·ly** *adv.*

ill-spent (il′spent′) *adj.* Unwisely wasted.

ill-starred (il′stärd′) *adj.* Unfortunate; unlucky, as if under an evil star.

ill-suit·ed (il′sōōt′əd) *adj.* Not well matched or suited.

ill temper A cross, irritable disposition. —**ill′-tem′pered** *adj.* —**ill′-tem′pered·ly** *adv.* —**ill′-tem′pered·ness** *n.*

ill-timed (il′tīmd′) *adj.* Inappropriate; not suitable.

ill-treat (il′trēt′) *v.t.* To treat badly; maltreat; abuse. —**ill′-treat′ment** *n.*

il·lu·mi·nant (i·lōō′mə·nənt) *adj.* Giving light; illuminating. —*n.* Any material used for illuminating.

il·lu·mi·nate (i·lōō′mə·nāt) *v.* **·nat·ed, ·nat·ing** *v.t.* **1** To give light to; light up. **2** To explain; make clear. **3** To enlighten, as the mind. **4** To make illustrious. **5** To decorate with lights. **6** To decorate (a manuscript, letter, etc.) with ornamental borders, figures, etc., of gold or other colors. —*v.i.* **7** To light up. [< L *in-* thoroughly + *luminare* to light] —**il·lu′mi·na′tive** *adj.* —**il·lu′mi·na′ting·ly** *adv.* —**il·lu′mi·na′tor** *n.*

il·lu·mi·na·tion (i·lōō′mə·nā′shən) *n.* **1** The act of illuminating or the state of being illuminated. **2** Decoration by lighting. **3** An amount of or the intensity of light. **4** Mental or spiritual enlightenment. **5** Embellishment of manuscript, with colors and gold, or a particular figure or design in such ornamentation.

il·lu·mine (i·lōō′min) *v.t. & v.i.* **·mined, ·min·ing** To illuminate or be illuminated. —**il·lu′mi·na·ble** *adj.*

ill-use (il′yōōz′) *v.t.* **·used, ·us·ing** To treat roughly, cruelly, or unjustly; abuse. —*n.* (-yōōs′) Bad treatment; misuse. —**ill′-us′age** (-yōō′sij, -yōō′zij) *n.*

il·lu·sion (i·lōō′zhən) *n.* **1** An unreal image or appearance. **2** A sensory impression which misrepresents the true character of the object perceived: an optical *illusion.* **3** A false or misleading idea or concept; delusion: the *illusions* of youth. **4** A thin material resembling tulle. [< L *illusio* mocking < *illudere* make sport of] —**il·lu′sion·al, il·lu′sion·ar·y** (-er·ē) *adj.*

Illusion
def. 2
Lines *a* and *b* are the same length, but *b* looks longer.

il·lu·so·ry (i·lōō′sər·ē, -zər-) *adj.* Misleading; deceptive; unreal. Also **il·lu′sive** (-siv). —**il·lu′so·ri·ly** *adv.* —**il·lu′so·ri·ness** *n.*

il·lus·trate (il′əs·trāt, i·lus′trāt) *v.t.* **·trat·ed, ·trat·ing 1** To explain or make clear by means of figures, examples, etc. **2** To furnish with drawings, pictures, etc., as a book or article. [< L *in-* thoroughly + *lustrare* illuminate] —**il′lus·tra′tor** *n.*

il·lus·tra·tion (il′əs·trā′shən) *n.* **1** That which illustrates, as an example, comparison, anecdote, etc. **2** A print, drawing, or picture inserted in written or printed text. **3** The act or art of illustrating.

il·lus·tra·tive (i·lus′trə·tiv, il′əs·trā′tiv) *adj.* Serving to illustrate or exemplify. —**il·lus′tra·tive·ly** *adv.*

il·lus·tri·ous (i·lus′trē·əs) *adj.* Very famous; celebrated; renowned. [< L *in-* in + *lustrum* light] —**il·lus′tri·ous·ly** *adv.* —**il·lus′tri·ous·ness** *n.*

ill will Enmity; hostility; hate. —**Syn.** animosity, antipathy, dislike, hatred.

il·ly (il′lē) *adv.* Badly; ill. • While *illy* is regularly formed from the adjective *ill*, discriminating writers prefer to use *ill* as the adverb as well.

Il·lyr·i·a (i·lir′ē·ə) *n.* An ancient country along the E coast of the Adriatic. —**Il·lyr·i·an** *adj.*, *n.*

I'm (īm) Contraction of *I am.*

im- *prefix* 1 EM-. 2 IN-.

im·age (im′ij) *n.* 1 A representation of a person or thing, as a statue, picture, idol, etc. 2 The picture or counterpart of an object produced by a lens, mirror, etc. 3 A natural resemblance; likeness; counterpart. 4 A mental picture, impression, or idea. 5 The way in which a person or thing is popularly perceived or regarded: a politician striving to improve his *image.* 6 A metaphor or a simile. 7 A symbol; embodiment; type. —*v.t.* **·aged, ·ag·ing** 1 To form a mental picture of; imagine. 2 To make a visible representation of; portray; delineate. 3 To mirror; reflect. 4 To describe vividly in speech or writing. 5 To symbolize. [< L *imago*]

im·age·ry (im′ij·rē, -ə·rē) *n. pl.* **·ries** 1 The act of making images. 2 Mental images. 3 Decorative images, esp. statues. 4 Figurative description in speech or writing.

im·ag·i·na·ble (i·maj′ə·nə·bəl) *adj.* That can be imagined. —**im·ag′i·na·bly** *adv.*

im·ag·i·nar·y (i·maj′ə·ner′ē) *adj.* 1 Existing only in imagination; unreal. 2 *Math.* Having a negative square, as $\sqrt{-1}$. —**im·ag′i·nar′i·ly** *adv.*

im·ag·i·na·tion (i·maj′ə·nā′shən) *n.* 1 The act or power of producing images in the mind of things not actually present to the senses. 2 The creative act or faculty of producing mental images and concepts that are or seem to be totally new and original. 3 That which is imagined, as a mental image or fantasy. 4 An irrational notion or belief. —**im·ag′i·na′tion·al** *adj.*

im·ag·i·na·tive (i·maj′ə·nə·tiv, -nā′tiv) *adj.* 1 Having a capacity for or given to imagining. 2 Characterized by or proceeding from imagination. —**im·ag′i·na·tive·ly** *adv.* —**im·ag′i·na·tive·ness** *n.*

im·ag·ine (i·maj′in) *v.* **·ined, ·in·ing** *v.t.* 1 To form a mental image of; conceive or create in the mind. 2 To suppose or conjecture. —*v.i.* 3 To use the imagination. 4 To make conjectures; suppose. [< L *imago* image]

im·a·gism (im′ə·jiz′əm) *n.* A movement in modern poetry characterized by the use of precise, concrete images and free verse. —**im′a·gist** (-jist) *n.* —**im′a·gis′tic** *adj.*

i·ma·go (i·mā′gō) *n. pl.* **i·ma·goes** or **i·mag·i·nes** (i·maj′ə·nēz) An insect in the reproductive phase following metamorphosis. [L, image]

im·bal·ance (im·bal′əns) *n.* A lack of proper equilibrium, proportion, functioning, etc.

im·be·cile (im′bə·sil) *adj.* 1 Mentally deficient. 2 Stupid; foolish. —*n.* 1 A person with a marked degree of congenital mental deficiency. 2 Any foolish or stupid person. [< L *imbecillus* weak]

im·be·cil·i·ty (im′bə·sil′ə·tē) *n. pl.* **·ties** 1 The condition or quality of being imbecile. 2 Foolishness or stupidity, as of action, speech, etc.

im·bibe (im·bīb′) *v.* **·bibed, ·bib·ing** *v.t.* 1 To drink in; drink. 2 To take in (moisture); absorb. 3 To receive into the mind or character. —*v.i.* 4 To drink. [< L *in-* in + *bibere* to drink] —**im·bib′er** *n.*

im·bri·cate (im′brə·kāt) *v.* **·cat·ed, ·cat·ing** *v.t.* 1 To lay so as to overlap, as tiles on a roof. —*v.i.* 2 To overlap. —*adj.* (-brə·kit) 1 Overlapping one another, as tiles, bird feathers, etc. 2 Decorated as with overlapping tiles: also **im′bri·cat′ed, im′bri·ca′tive.** [< L *imbricare* cover with tiles] —**im′·bri·ca′tion** *n.* —**im′bri·ca′tive·ly** *adv.*

im·bro·glio (im·brōl′yō) *n. pl.* **·glios** 1 A confused or troublesome misunderstanding; an entanglement. 2 Any confused situation. [Ital.]

im·brue (im·brōō′) *v.t.* **·brued, ·bru·ing** To stain or wet, esp. with blood. [< OF *embreuver*]

im·bue (im·byōō′) *v.t.* **·bued, ·bu·ing** 1 To wet thoroughly;

saturate. 2 To impregnate with color; dye. 3 To fill, as the mind, with emotions, principles, etc. [< L *imbuere* wet]

IMF International Monetary Fund.

imit. imitation; imitative.

im·i·tate (im′ə·tāt) *v.t.* **·tat·ed, ·tat·ing** 1 To try to be the same as. 2 To mimic. 3 To make a copy of; duplicate. 4 To assume the appearance of; look like. [< L *imitari* imitate] —**im′i·ta·ble** (im′ə·tə·bəl) *adj.* —**im′i·ta·bil′i·ty, im′i·ta′tor** *n.*

im·i·ta·tion (im′ə·tā′shən) *n.* 1 The act of imitating. 2 That which results from imitating; likeness; copy. —*adj.* Imitating something genuine or superior: *imitation* diamonds.

im·i·ta·tive (im′ə·tā′tiv) *adj.* 1 Given to or characterized by imitation. 2 Formed after a copy or model. 3 Fictitious; counterfeit. 4 *Ling.* Designating a word that approximates a natural sound, as *buzz, clink, swish.* —**im′i·ta′tive·ly** *adv.* —**im′i·ta′tive·ness** *n.*

im·mac·u·late (i·mak′yə·lit) *adj.* 1 Without spot or blemish; totally clean. 2 Without evil or sin; pure. 3 Faultless; flawless. [< L *in-* not + *maculatus* spotted] —**im·mac′u·late·ly** *adv.* —**im·mac′u·late·ness** *n.* —**Syn.** 1 impeccable, spotless, unsullied. 2 innocent, irreproachable, sinless.

Immaculate Conception In the Roman Catholic Church, the doctrine that the Virgin Mary was conceived in her mother's womb free from original sin.

im·ma·nence (im′ə·nəns) *n.* The condition or fact of being immanent. Also **im′ma·nen·cy.**

im·ma·nent (im′ə·nənt) *adj.* Remaining or operating within; inherent. [< L *in-* in + *manere* stay] —**im′ma·nent·ly** *adv.*

Im·man·u·el (i·man′yōō·əl) *n.* A name of the Messiah.

im·ma·te·ri·al (im′ə·tir′ē·əl) *adj.* 1 Not made of matter; incorporeal. 2 Unimportant. —**im′ma·te′ri·al·ly** *adv.* —**im′ma·te′ri·al·ness** *n.*

im·ma·ture (im′ə·choor′, -tyoor′) *adj.* 1 Not mature or ripe; not full-grown. 2 Not complete or perfected. —**im′ma·ture′ly** *adv.* —**im′ma·tur′i·ty** *n.*

im·meas·ur·a·ble (i·mezh′ər·ə·bəl) *adj.* Not capable of being measured; vast; boundless. —**im·meas′ur·a·bil′i·ty** *n.* —**im·meas′ur·a·bly** *adv.*

im·me·di·a·cy (i·mē′dē·ə·sē) *n.* The condition or quality of being immediate.

im·me·di·ate (i·mē′dē·it) *adj.* 1 Without anything intervening: the *immediate* cause of his death. 2 Not appreciably separated in space or time; closest; nearest: the *immediate* past. 3 Next or closest in rank, relationship, etc.: his *immediate* successor. 4 Present; current: our *immediate* problem. 5 Without delay; instant: his *immediate* reaction. [< Med. L *immediatus*] —**im·me′di·ate·ness** *n.*

im·me·di·ate·ly (i·mē′dē·it·lē) *adv.* 1 In an immediate manner. 2 Instantly; at once. 3 Without the intervention of anything; directly. —*conj.* As soon as.

im·me·mo·ri·al (im′ə·môr′ē·əl, -mō′rē-) *adj.* Reaching back beyond memory. —**im′me·mo′ri·al·ly** *adv.*

im·mense (i·mens′) *adj.* 1 Very great in degree or size; vast; huge. 2 *Informal* Very good; excellent. [< L *in-* not + *mensus*, pp. of *metiri* to measure] —**im·mense′ly** *adj.*

im·men·si·ty (i·men′sə·tē) *n. pl.* **·ties** 1 The state or quality of being immense; vastness. 2 Boundless space.

im·merge (i·mûrj′) *v.* **·merged, ·merg·ing** *v.t.* 1 To immerse. —*v.i.* 2 To plunge, as into a liquid; sink. [< L *in-* in + *mergere* dip] —**im·mer′gence** *n.*

im·merse (i·mûrs′) *v.t.* **·mersed, ·mers·ing** 1 To plunge or dip entirely in water or other fluid. 2 To involve deeply; engross: He *immersed* himself in study. 3 To baptize by submerging in water. [< L *immergere* dip] —**im·mer′sion** *n.*

im·mi·grant (im′ə·grənt) *n.* A person who immigrates. —*adj.* Immigrating.

im·mi·grate (im′ə·grāt) *v.* **·grat·ed, ·grat·ing** *v.i.* 1 To come into a new country or region for the purpose of settling there. —*v.t.* 2 To bring in as an immigrant or settler. [< L *in-* in + *migrare* migrate] —**im′mi·gra′tion** *n.* —**im′mi·gra·to′ry** (-tôr′ē, -tō′rē) *adj.*

im·mi·nence (im′ə·nəns) *n.* 1 The state of being imminent. 2 Something imminent, esp. impending evil. Also **im′mi·nen·cy.**

im·mi·nent (im′ə·nənt) *adj.* About to happen; impending: said esp. of danger or misfortune. [< L *imminere* lean over, impend] —**im′mi·nent·ly** *adv.*

immiscible

355

impede

im·mis·ci·ble (i·mis′ə·bəl) *adj.* Not capable of mixing, as oil and water. [< L *in-* not + *miscere* to mix] —im·mis′ci·bly *adv.* —im·mis′ci·bil′i·ty *n.*

im·mo·bile (i·mō′bəl, -bēl) *adj.* 1 Unmovable; stable. 2 Not moving; motionless. —im·mo·bil·i·ty (i′mō·bil′ə·tē) *n.*

im·mo·bi·lize (i·mō′bə·līz) *v.t.* -lized, -liz·ing 1 To make immovable; fix in place, as a limb. 2 To make unable to move or mobilize, as troops. 3 To withdraw (specie) from circulation and hold as security for banknotes. —im·mo′bi·li·za′tion (-lə·zā′shən, -lī·zā′-) *n.*

im·mod·er·ate (i·mod′ər·it) *adj.* Not moderate; excessive. —im·mod′er·ate·ly *adv.* —im·mod′er·ate·ness, im·mod′er·a′tion *n.*

im·mod·est (i·mod′ist) *adj.* 1 Wanting in modesty; indelicate or indecent. 2 Impudent; bold. —im·mod′est·ly *adv.* —im·mod′es·ty *n.*

im·mo·late (im′ə·lāt) *v.t.* -lat·ed, -lat·ing To sacrifice, esp. to kill as a sacrifice. [< L *immolare* sprinkle with sacrificial meal] —im′mo·la′tion, im′mo·la′tor *n.*

im·mor·al (i·môr′əl, i·mor′-) *adj.* 1 Contrary to moral principles; not right or good. 2 Impure; lewd; licentious. —im·mor′al·ly *adv.* • See UNMORAL.

im·mo·ral·i·ty (im′ə·ral′ə·tē) *n. pl.* -ties 1 The quality or condition of being immoral. 2 An immoral act.

im·mor·tal (i·môr′təl) *adj.* 1 Having unending existence; deathless. 2 Lasting or enduring forever. —*n.* 1 A person considered worthy of immortality. 2 In mythology, a god. —im·mor′tal·ly *adv.* —Syn *adj.* 1 deathless, imperishable, undying. 2 endless, infinite, permanent, perpetual.

im·mor·tal·i·ty (im′ôr·tal′ə·tē) *n.* 1 Exemption from death; eternal life. 2 Eternal fame.

im·mor·tal·ize (i·môr′təl·īz) *v.t.* -ized, -iz·ing To make immortal, as in fame or life.

im·mor·telle (im′ôr·tel′) *n.* Any of various xerophytic plants having usu. composite flowers that do not wilt. [F]

im·mov·a·ble (i·mōō′və·bəl) *adj.* 1 That cannot be moved or stirred from its place; fixed. 2 Motionless. 3 Steadfast; unchangeable. 4 Not having the feelings easily roused; impassive. —*n. Law* Any piece of land, together with trees, buildings, etc., that is considered not movable. —im·mov′a·bil′i·ty, im·mov′a·ble·ness *n.* —im·mov′a·bly *adv.*

im·mune (i·myōōn′) *adj.* 1 Exempt, as from a penalty, burden, duty, or taxation. 2 Protected from a communicable or allergic disease by the presence of antibodies in the blood. 3 Pertaining to immunity or immunization. [< L *in-* not + *munus* service, duty] —im·mu·ni·ty (i·myōō′nə·tē) *n.* (*pl.* -ties)

im·mu·nize (im′yə·nīz) *v.t.* -nized, -niz·ing To make immune, as by inoculation. —im·mu·ni·za·tion (im′yə·nə·zā′shən, -nī·zā′-) *n.*

immuno- *combining form* Immune; immunity: *immunology.* [< IMMUNE]

im·mu·nol·o·gy (im′yə·nol′ə·jē) *n.* The science which treats of the reactions of animal tissues against foreign proteins, as in viruses, allergens, tissue transplants, etc. [< IMMUNO- + -LOGY] —im·mu·no·log·ic (i·myōō′nə·loj′ik), im·mu·no·log′i·cal *adj.* —im′mu·nol′o·gist *n.*

im·mu·no·sup·pres·sive (im·yōō′nō·sə·pres′iv) *adj. Med.* Acting to suppress natural immune responses, as to foreign tissue in an organ transplant. —im·mu′no·su·pres′sion *n.*

im·mure (i·myōōr′) *v.t.* -mured, -mur·ing To shut up within or as within walls. [< L *in-* in + *muris* wall] —im·mure′ment *n.*

im·mu·ta·ble (i·myōō′tə·bəl) *adj.* Not changing or altering; unchangeable. [< L *immutabilis*] —im·mu·ta·bil′i·ty, im·mu′ta·ble·ness *n.* —im·mu′ta·bly *adv.*

imp (imp) *n.* 1 A small devil or demon. 2 A mischievous person, esp. a child. [< LL *impotus* a shoot]

imp. imperative; imperfect; imperial; impersonal; import; important; importer; imprimatur; improper.

im·pact (im·pakt′) *v.t.* To press firmly together; pack; wedge. —*n.* (im′pakt) 1 The act of striking; collision. 2 The forcible contact of a moving body with another. 3 A powerful influence: the *impact* of science on culture. [< L *impingere* to thrust against] —im·pac′tion *n.*

im·pact·ed (im·pak′tid) *adj.* 1 Packed firmly. 2 Denoting a tooth wedged between the jawbone and another tooth in such a way as to prevent its emergence through the gums.

im·pair (im·pâr′) *v.t.* To diminish in quality, strength, or value; injure; damage. [< LL *in-* thoroughly + *pejorare* make worse] —im·pair′er, im·pair′ment *n.*

im·pa·la (im·pä′lə) *n.* An African antelope with spreading horns in the male. [< native African name]

im·pale (im·pāl′) *v.t.* -paled, -pal·ing 1 To fix upon a pale or sharp stake. 2 To torture or put to death by thrusting a sharp stake through the body. 3 To make helpless: to *impale* someone with a glance. [< L *in-* in + *palus* a stake] —im·pale′ment *n.*

im·pal·pa·ble (im·pal′pə·bəl) *adj.* 1 Imperceptible to the touch. 2 Not easily grasped or discerned by the mind. —im·pal′pa·bil′i·ty *n.* —im·pal′pa·bly *adv.*

im·pan·el (im·pan′əl) *v.t.* -eled or -elled, -el·ing or -el·ling 1 To enroll upon a panel or list, as for jury duty. 2 To draw from such a list, as a jury. —im·pan′el·ment *n.*

im·part (im·pärt′) *v.t.* 1 To make known; tell; communicate. 2 To give a portion of; give. —*v.i.* 3 To give a part; share. [< L *in-* on + *partire* to share] —im·par·ta′tion, im·part′er *n.*

im·par·tial (im·pär′shəl) *adj.* Not partial; unbiased; just. —im·par′tial·ly *adv.* —im·par′tial·ness *n.*

im·par·ti·al·i·ty (im′pär·shē·al′ə·tē, im·pär′-) *n.* The quality or character of being impartial.

im·pass·a·ble (im·pas′ə·bəl, -päs′-) *adj.* Not capable of being traveled over or through. —im·pass′a·bly *adv.* —im·pass′a·bil′i·ty, im·pass′a·ble·ness *n.*

im·passe (im′pas, im·pas′) *n.* 1 A blind passage open only at one end; blind alley. 2 Any serious and insurmountable obstacle or problem. [F]

im·pas·si·ble (im·pas′ə·bəl) *adj.* 1 Incapable of suffering pain or injury. 2 Not easily aroused emotionally; apathetic. [< L *in-* not + *passibilis* suffering] —im·pas′si·bly *adv.* —im·pas′si·bil′i·ty, im·pas′si·ble·ness *n.*

im·pas·sion (im·pash′ən) *v.t.* To affect with passion; inflame.

im·pas·sioned (im·pash′ənd) *adj.* Fervent; passionate; ardent. —im·pas′sioned·ly *adv.*

im·pas·sive (im·pas′iv) *adj.* 1 Insensible to suffering or pain. 2 Unmoved by or not exhibiting feeling; calm. —im·pas′sive·ly *adv.* —im·pas′sive·ness, im·pas·siv·i·ty (im′pa·siv′ə·tē) *n.*

im·pa·tience (im·pā′shəns) *n.* 1 Lack of patience, esp. when faced with delay, opposition, etc. 2 A restless longing or eagerness.

im·pa·ti·ens (im·pā′shē·enz) *n.* Any of a genus of plants whose ripe seed vessels suddenly snap open when touched. [L]

im·pa·tient (im·pā′shənt) *adj.* 1 Not possessed of patience; disturbed by or intolerant of delay, pain, opposition, etc. 2 Exhibiting or expressing impatience. —im·pa′tient·ly *adv.* —im·pa′tient·ness *n.*

im·peach (im·pēch′) *v.t.* 1 To bring discredit upon; challenge: to *impeach* one's honesty. 2 To charge with crime or misdemeanor, esp. to arraign (a public official) before a competent tribunal on such a charge. [< LL *impedicare* entangle] —im·peach′a·bil′i·ty, im·peach′ment *n.* —im·peach′a·ble *adj.*

im·pec·ca·ble (im·pek′ə·bəl) *adj.* 1 Not liable to commit sin or wrong. 2 Without fault or error; flawless. [< L *in-* not + *peccare* to sin] —im·pec′ca·bil′i·ty *n.* —im·pec′ca·bly *adv.*

im·pe·cu·ni·ous (im′pə·kyōō′nē·əs) *adj.* Having no money; poor. [< L *in-* not + *pecunia* money] —im′pe·cu′ni·ous·ly *adv.* —im′pe·cu′ni·os′i·ty (-kyōō′nē·os′ə·tē), im′pe·cu′ni·ous·ness *n.*

im·pe·dance (im·pēd′ns) *n.* 1 The ratio of voltage to current in an alternating-current circuit, in general a complex number combining resistance and reactance. 2 Any analogous ratio, as in acoustics or mechanics.

impede (im·pēd′) *v.t.* -ped·ed, -ped·ing To retard or hinder in progress or action; obstruct. [L *impedire*, lit., shackle the feet] —im·ped′er *n.*

---

add, āce, câre, pälm; end, ēven; it, īce; odd, ōpen, ôrder; tōōk, pōōl; up, bûrn; ə = a in *above*, u in *focus*; yōō = u in *fuse*; oil; pout; check; go; ring; thin; ṭhis; zh, *vision*. < derived from; ? origin uncertain or unknown.

im·ped·i·ment (im·ped′ə·mənt) *n.* 1 That which hinders or impedes; an obstruction. 2 A speech defect, as a stammer. 3 *Law* Anything that prevents the contraction of a valid marriage. —**im·ped′i·men′tal, im·ped′i·men′ta·ry** *adj.* —Syn. 1 barrier, encumbrance, hindrance, obstacle.

im·ped·i·men·ta (im·ped′ə·men′tə) *n.pl.* Things that impede or burden, as baggage or supplies when traveling.

im·pel (im·pel′) *v.t.* **·pelled, ·pel·ling** 1 To drive or push (something) forward or onward. 2 To urge or force (someone) to an action, course, etc.; incite; compel. [< L *in-* on + *pellere* to drive] —**im·pel′lent** *adj., n.* —**im·pel′ler** *n.*

im·pend (im·pend′) *v.i.* 1 To be imminent; threaten, as something evil or destructive. 2 To be suspended; hang: with *over.* [< L *in-* on + *pendere* to hang] —**im·pen′dence, im·pen′den·cy** *n.*

im·pend·ing (im·pen′ding) *adj.* 1 About to happen; threatening; imminent. 2 Hanging over.

im·pen·e·tra·ble (im·pen′ə·trə·bəl) *adj.* 1 That cannot be penetrated or pierced. 2 That cannot be comprehended or solved: an *impenetrable* mystery. 3 Not to be affected or influenced: an *impenetrable* conscience. —**im·pen′e·tra·bil′i·ty, im·pen′e·tra·ble·ness** *n.* —**im·pen′e·tra·bly** *adv.*

im·pen·i·tent (im·pen′ə·tənt) *adj.* Not penitent; hardened. —**im·pen′i·tence, im·pen′i·ten·cy** *n.* —**im·pen′i·tent·ly** *adv.*

imper. imperative.

im·per·a·tive (im·per′ə·tiv) *adj.* 1 Expressive of positive command; authoritative. 2 *Gram.* Designating that mood of the verb which expresses command, entreaty, or exhortation. 3 Not to be evaded or avoided; obligatory. —*n.* 1 Something imperative, as a command, rule, duty, etc. 2 *Gram.* The imperative mood; also, a verb in this mood. [< L *imperare* to command] —**im·per′a·tive·ly** *adv.* —**im·per′a·tive·ness** *n.*

im·pe·ra·tor (im′pə·rā′tər, -tôr) *n.* The official designation of the Roman emperors. [L< *imperare* to command] —**im·per′a·to′ri·al** *adj.*

im·per·cep·ti·ble (im′pər·sep′tə·bəl) *adj.* That cannot easily be perceived by the senses or mind, as by reason of smallness, slowness, etc. —**im′per·cep′ti·ble·ness, im′per·cep′ti·bil′i·ty** *n.* —**im′per·cep′ti·bly** *adv.* —**im′per·cep′tive** *adj.*

imperf. imperfect; imperforate.

im·per·fect (im·pûr′fikt) *adj.* 1 Not perfect; defective. 2 Not complete; unfinished. 3 *Gram.* Pertaining to or of a tense of a verb that indicates past action as uncompleted, continuous, or synchronous with some other action. —*n.* *Gram.* The imperfect tense, or a verb expressing this tense. —**im·per′fect·ly** *adv.* —**im·per′fect·ness** *n.*

im·per·fec·tion (im′pər·fek′shən) *n.* 1 Lack of perfection: also **im·per′fect·ness.** 2 A defect; fault.

im·per·fo·ra·ble (im·pûr′fər·ə·bəl) *adj.* That cannot be perforated.

im·per·fo·rate (im·pûr′fər·it) *adj.* 1 Without perforations; not perforated. 2 Not separated by a line of perforations, as stamps. 3 *Med.* Lacking a normal opening. Also **im·per′fo·rat′ed** (-rā′tid). —*n.* An unperforated stamp. —**im·per′fo·ra′tion** *n.*

im·pe·ri·al (im·pir′ē·əl) *adj.* 1 Of or pertaining to an empire, or to an emperor or an empress. 2 Designating the legal weights and measures of the United Kingdom. 3 Of or pertaining to a country having control over colonies or the like. 4 Majestic; regal. 5 Superior in size or quality. —*n.* 1 A pointed tuft of hair on the chin. 2 Anything of more than usual size or excellence. 3 A size of paper, 23 in. × 31 in. [< L *imperium* rule] —**im·pe′ri·al·ly** *adv.*

imperial gallon The British gallon, equal to 277.42 cu. in.

im·pe·ri·al·ism (im·pir′ē·əl·iz′əm) *n.* 1 A policy that aims at creating, maintaining, or extending an empire comprising other nations, territories, etc., all controlled by a central government. 2 The development or exploitation of the economic resources of another country without necessarily assuming direct political control. 3 Imperial character, authority, or spirit. —**im·pe′ri·al·ist** *adj., n.* —**im·pe′ri·al·is′tic** *adj.* —**im·pe′ri·al·is′ti·cal·ly** *adv.*

im·per·il (im·per′il) *v.t.* **·iled** or **·illed, ·il·ing** or **·il·ling** To place in peril; endanger.

im·pe·ri·ous (im·pir′ē·əs) *adj.* 1 Domineering; overbear-

ing; arrogant. 2 Urgent; imperative. [< L *imperium* rule] —**im·pe′ri·ous·ly** *adv.* —**im·pe′ri·ous·ness** *n.*

im·per·ish·a·ble (im·per′ish·ə·bəl) *adj.* Not perishable or subject to decay; enduring; indestructible. —**im·per′ish·a·bil′i·ty, im·per′ish·a·ble·ness** *n.* —**im·per′ish·a·bly** *adv.*

im·per·ma·nent (im·pûr′mə·nənt) *adj.* Not permanent or lasting. —**im·per′ma·nence, im·per′ma·nen·cy** *n.* —**im·per′ma·nent·ly** *adv.*

im·per·me·a·ble (im·pûr′mē·ə·bəl) *adj.* Not permitting passage, esp. of fluids, moisture, etc. —**im·per′me·a·bil′i·ty** *n.* —**im·per′me·a·bly** *adv.*

impers. impersonal.

im·per·son·al (im·pûr′sən·əl) *adj.* 1 Not personal: an *impersonal* deity. 2 Not relating to a particular person or thing: an *impersonal* statement. 3 Unsympathetic; cold: an *impersonal* attitude. 4 *Gram.* Having or containing an intermediate subject: said esp. of verbs. In English the subject of an impersonal verb is usu. the pronoun *it.* —*n.* An impersonal verb. —**im·per′son·al′i·ty** (-al′ə·tē) *n.* —**im·per′son·al·ly** *adv.*

im·per·son·ate (im·pûr′sən·āt) *v.t.* **·at·ed, ·at·ing** 1 To mimic the appearance, mannerisms, etc., of. 2 To act or play the part of. 3 To represent in human form; personify: He *impersonates* the quality of virtue. —*adj.* (-it) Embodied in a person; personified. —**im·per′son·a′tion, im·per′son·a′tor** *n.*

im·per·ti·nence (im·pûr′tə·nəns) *n.* 1 The state or quality of being impertinent. 2 Insolence; rudeness. 3 Unfitness; irrelevancy. 4 An impertinent act. Also **im·per′ti·nen·cy.**

im·per·ti·nent (im·pûr′tə·nənt) *adj.* 1 Rude; impudent. 2 Irrelevant; not to the point. 3 Not suitable or fitting. —**im·per′ti·nent·ly** *adv.*

im·per·turb·a·ble (im′pər·tûr′bə·bəl) *adj.* Incapable of being agitated or perturbed; calm; impassive. —**im′per·turb′a·bil′i·ty, im′per·turb′a·ble·ness** *n.* —**im′per·turb′a·bly** *adv.*

im·per·vi·ous (im·pûr′vē·əs) *adj.* 1 Permitting no passage of fluids, light rays, etc.; impenetrable. 2 Not influenced or affected by. [< L *in-* not + *per-* through + *via* way, road] —**im·per′vi·ous·ly** *adv.* —**im·per′vi·ous·ness** *n.*

im·pe·ti·go (im′pə·tī′gō) *n.* A contagious bacterial skin infection characterized by blisters that break and form yellow encrusted sores. [L, an attack]

im·pet·u·ous (im·pech′ŏŏ·əs) *adj.* 1 Characterized by energy or violent force: *impetuous* haste. 2 Spontaneous; impulsive. [< L *impetuosus*] —**im·pet′u·os′i·ty** (-os′ə·tē), **im·pet′u·ous·ness** *n.* —**im·pet′u·ous·ly** *adv.*

im·pe·tus (im′pə·təs) *n.* 1 The energy or momentum of a moving body. 2 Any force that begins or sets in motion; incentive. [L< *impetere* rush upon]

impf. imperfect.

im·pi·e·ty (im·pī′ə·tē) *n. pl.* **·ties** 1 Lack of piety; irreverence. 2 An impious act. 3 Disrespect, as toward parents.

im·pinge (im·pinj′) *v.i.* **·pinged, ·ping·ing** 1 To strike; collide: with *on, upon,* or *against.* 2 To encroach; infringe: with *on* or *upon.* [< L *in-* against + *pangere* to strike] —**im·pinge′ment, im·ping′er** *n.*

im·pi·ous (im′pē·əs, im′pī′əs) *adj.* Not pious; lacking reverence, as toward God or one's parents. —**im′pi·ous·ly** *adv.* —**im′pi·ous·ness** *n.*

imp·ish (im′pish) *adj.* 1 Of or like an imp. 2 Mischievous. —**imp′ish·ly** *adv.* —**imp′ish·ness** *n.*

im·pla·ca·ble (im·plak′ə·bəl, -plā′kə-) *adj.* 1 That cannot be placated or appeased. 2 Unalterable; inexorable. —**im·pla′ca·bil′i·ty, im·pla′ca·ble·ness** *n.* —**im·pla′ca·bly** *adv.*

im·plant (im·plant′, -plänt′) *v.t.* 1 To insert or graft in or onto living tissue. 2 To instill, as principles. 3 To plant, as seeds. —*n.* (im′plant′, -plänt′) *Med.* Something implanted in the body, as a tissue graft or therapeutic device. —**im′plan·ta′tion, im·plant′er** *n.*

im·plau·si·ble (im·plô′zə·bəl) *adj.* Not plausible. —**im·plau′si·bly** *adv.*

im·ple·ment (im′plə·mənt) *n.* A thing used in work; a utensil; tool. —*v.t.* (-ment) 1 To fulfill; accomplish. 2 To provide what is needed for; supplement. 3 To furnish with implements. [< L *implementum* a filling up] —**im′ple·men′tal** *adj.* —**im′ple·men·ta′tion** *n.*

im·pli·cate (im′plə·kāt) *v.t.* **·cat·ed, ·cat·ing** 1 To show to be involved, as in a plot or crime. **2** To imply. **3** To fold or twist together; entangle. [< L *in-* in + *plicare* to fold] —**im·pli·ca′tive, im·pli·ca·to·ry** (im′pli·kə·tôr′ē, -tō′rē) *adj.*

im·pli·ca·tion (im′plə·kā′shən) *n.* **1** The act of implicating or the state of being implicated. **2** The act of implying. **3** Something implied, esp. so as to lead to a deduction.

im·plic·it (im·plis′it) *adj.* **1** Implied or to be understood, but not specifically stated. **2** Absolute; unquestioning: *implicit* trust. **3** Virtually contained or involved in, though not immediately apparent or stated; inherent. [< L *implicare* involve] —**im·plic′it·ly** *adv.* —**im·plic′it·ness** *n.*

im·plied (im·plīd′) *adj.* Contained, understood, or indicated, but not directly stated. —**im·pli·ed·ly** (im·plī′id·lē) *adv.*

im·plode (im·plōd′) *v.t. & v.i.* **·plod·ed, ·plod·ing** To burst inward, esp. forcibly. [< IN-² + (EX)PLODE]

im·plore (im·plôr′, -plōr′) *v.* **·plored, ·plor·ing** *v.t.* **1** To beseech; entreat. **2** To beg for urgently; pray for. —*v.i.* **3** To make urgent supplication. [< L *in-* thoroughly + *plorare* cry out] —**im·plor′er** *n.* —**im·plor′ing·ly** *adv.*

im·plo·sion (im·plō′zhən) *n.* An act or instance of imploding. —**im·plo′sive** (-siv) *adj.*

im·ply (im·plī′) *v.t.* **·plied, ·ply·ing** **1** To involve necessarily as a circumstance, condition, effect, etc.: An action *implies* an agent. **2** To indicate (a meaning not expressed); hint at; intimate. [< L *implicare* involve] • See INFER.

im·po·lite (im′pə·līt′) *adj.* Not polite; rude. —**im′po·lite′ly** *adv.* —**im′po·lite′ness** *n.*

im·pol·i·tic (im·pol′ə·tik) *adj.* Not politic; imprudent; injudicious. —**im′po·lit′i·cal·ly, im·pol′i·tic·ly** *adv.*

im·pon·der·a·ble (im·pon′dər·ə·bəl) *adj.* **1** Without weight. **2** Impossible to evaluate or foresee. —*n.* Anything imponderable. —**im·pon′der·a·bil′i·ty, im·pon′der·a·ble·ness** *n.* —**im·pon′der·a·bly** *adv.*

im·port (im·pôrt′, -pōrt′, im′pôrt, -pōrt) *v.t.* **1** To bring (goods) into one country from a foreign country in commerce. **2** To bring in; introduce. **3** To mean; signify. —*v.i.* **4** To be of importance or significance; matter. —*n.* (im′·pôrt, -pōrt) **1** Importation. **2** That which is imported. **3** Meaning; significance. **4** Importance. [< L *in-* in + *portare* carry] —**im·port′a·ble** *adj.*

im·por·tance (im·pôr′təns) *n.* The condition or quality of being important.

im·por·tant (im·pôr′tənt) *adj.* **1** Of great import, consequence, prominence, or value. **2** Pompous; pretentious. [< L *importare* bring in] —**im·por′tant·ly** *adv.* —**Syn. 1** momentous, serious, significant, weighty.

im·por·ta·tion (im′pôr·tā′shən, -pōr-) *n.* **1** The act of importing merchandise, etc. **2** That which is imported.

im·port·er (im·pôr′tər, -pōr′-) *n.* One who imports goods from a foreign country.

im·por·tu·nate (im·pôr′chə·nit) *adj.* Urgent in requesting or demanding; insistent; pertinacious. —**im·por′tu·nate·ly** *adv.* —**im·por′tu·nate·ness** *n.*

im·por·tune (im′pôr·t(y)ōon′, im·pôr′chən) *v.* **·tuned, ·tun·ing** *v.t.* **1** To annoy or trouble with persistent requests or demands. —*v.i.* **2** To make persistent requests or demands. [< L *importunus* having no access, vexatious] —**im′por·tun′er** *n.*

im·por·tu·ni·ty (im′pôr·t(y)ōo′nə·tē) *n. pl.* **·ties 1** The act of importuning. **2** The state of being importunate. **3** *pl.* Importunate demands.

im·pose (im·pōz′) *v.t.* **·posed, ·pos·ing** **1** To place or lay by authority: to *impose* a tax. **2** To place by or as by force: to *impose* opinions on another. **3** To force (oneself, one's presence, etc.) upon others. **4** To palm off (something) as true or genuine; foist. **5** *Printing* To arrange in a form, as pages of type. —**impose on** (or **upon**) **1** To take advantage of; presume. **2** To cheat or deceive by trickery. [< L *imponere* put in] —**im·pos′a·ble** *adj.* —**im·pos′er** *n.*

im·pos·ing (im·pō′zing) *adj.* Very impressive because of manner, appearance, size, etc. —**im·pos′ing·ly** *adv.* —**im·pos′ing·ness** *n.*

im·po·si·tion (im′pə·zish′ən) *n.* **1** The act of imposing. **2** A severe or unjust demand, requirement, duty, etc. **3** A deception; imposture. **4** A tax, toll, or duty.

im·pos·si·bil·i·ty (im·pos′ə·bil′ə·tē) *n. pl.* **·ties 1** The fact or state of being impossible. **2** That which is impossible.

im·pos·si·ble (im·pos′ə·bəl) *adj.* **1** Not capable of existing or occurring. **2** Hopelessly difficult to do or accomplish. **3** Utterly objectionable or intolerable. —**im·pos′si·bly** *adv.*

im·post (im′pōst) *n.* Something imposed, esp. a customs duty. —*v.t.* To classify (imported goods) so as to determine the customs duty. [< L *in-* on + *ponere* lay, place]

im·pos·tor (im·pos′tər) *n.* One who deceives, esp. one who goes under an assumed name or identity. [< L *imponere* lay on, impose]

im·pos·ture (im·pos′chər) *n.* Deception by means of false pretenses.

im·po·tence (im′pə·təns) *n.* The state or quality of being impotent. Also **im′po·ten·cy.**

im·po·tent (im′pə·tənt) *adj.* **1** Lacking in physical power; week; feeble. **2** Unable to have sexual intercourse: said of the male. **3** Powerless, defenseless, or ineffectual. —**im′po·tent·ly** *adv.*

im·pound (im·pound′) *v.t.* **1** To shut up in a pound, as a stray dog. **2** To place in legal custody. **3** To collect (water) in a reservoir, etc., as for irrigation. —**im·pound′age, im·pound′er** *n.*

im·pov·er·ish (im·pov′ər·ish) *v.t.* **1** To reduce to poverty. **2** To exhaust the fertility or quality of, as soil. [< OF *em-* thoroughly + *povre* poor] —**im·pov′er·ish·er, im·pov′er·ish·ment** *n.*

im·prac·ti·ca·ble (im·prak′ti·kə·bəl) *adj.* Impossible or unreasonably difficult to do or to use. —**im·prac′ti·ca·bil′i·ty, im·prac′ti·ca·ble·ness** *n.* —**im·prac′ti·ca·bly** *adv.*

im·prac·ti·cal (im·prak′ti·kəl) *adj.* Not practical. —**im·prac′ti·cal′i·ty** (-kal′ə·tē) *n.*

im·pre·cate (im′prə·kāt) *v.t.* **·cat·ed, ·cat·ing** To invoke, as a judgment, calamity, or curse. [< L *in-* on + *precari* pray] —**im′pre·ca·to′ry** (-kə·tôr′ē, -tō′rē) *adj.* —**im′pre·ca′tion, im′·pre·ca′tor** *n.*

im·preg·na·ble (im·preg′nə·bəl) *adj.* **1** Incapable of being taken by attack. **2** Unyielding; unassailable. [< L *in-* not + *prehendere* to take] —**im·preg′na·bil′i·ty** *n.* —**im·preg′·na·bly** *adv.*

im·preg·nate (im·preg′nāt) *v.t.* **·nat·ed, ·nat·ing** **1** To make pregnant. **2** To fertilize. **3** To saturate or permeate. **4** To fill or imbue with emotion, ideas, principles, etc. —*adj.* Made pregnant. —**im·preg′na·ble** (-nə·bəl) *adj.* —**im′preg·na′tion, im·preg′na·tor** *n.*

im·pre·sa·ri·o (im′prə·sä′rē·ō) *n. pl.* **·sa·ri·os** One who organizes or manages an opera or ballet company, concerts, etc. [Ital. < *impresa* undertaking]

im·pre·scrip·ti·ble (im′pri·skrip′tə·bəl) *adj.* Incapable of being taken away; inalienable: *imprescriptible* rights. [< F] —**im′pre·scrip′ti·bil′i·ty** *n.* —**im′pre·scrip′ti·bly** *adv.*

im·press¹ (im·pres′) *v.t.* **1** To produce a marked effect upon, as the mind; influence. **2** To fix firmly in the mind. **3** To form or make (an imprint or mark) by pressure; stamp. **4** To form or make an imprint or mark upon. **5** To press: to *impress* one's hand into the mud. —*n.* (im′pres) **1** The act of impressing. **2** A mark or seal produced by pressure. **3** A stamp. **4** An impression or effect made on the mind. [< L *in-* on + *premere* to press] —**im·press′er** *n.*

im·press² (im·pres′) *v.t.* **1** To compel to enter public service by force: to *impress* seamen. **2** To seize (property) for public use. [< *in-* in + PRESS¹] —**im·press′er, im·press′ment** *n.*

im·press·i·ble (im·pres′ə·bəl) *adj.* Capable of being impressed or of receiving an impression; susceptible. —**im·press′i·bil′i·ty, im·press′i·ble·ness** *n.* —**im·press′i·bly** *adv.*

im·pres·sion (im·presh′ən) *n.* **1** The act of impressing. **2** A stamp, mark, figure, etc. made by pressure. **3** An effect produced on the senses, the mind, or the feelings. **4** An effect or change: Our hard work made little *impression* on the lawn. **5** A vague or indistinct remembrance; a notion. **6** *Printing* **a** The imprint of type, illustrations, etc., on a page or sheet. **b** All the copies of a book, etc., printed at one time. **c** One copy of a book, engraving, etching, etc. —**im·pres′sion·al** *adj.*

im·pres·sion·a·ble (im·presh′ən·ə·bəl) *adj.* Sensitive to impressions; easily molded or influenced. —**im·pres′sion·a·bil′i·ty, im·pres′sion·a·ble·ness** *n.*

im·pres·sion·ism (im·presh′ən·iz′əm) *n* **1** A theory and school of art, developed in the 19th century, which attempted to produce, mainly by the vivid simulation of light, the immediate impressions made by the subject on the artist. **2** In literature, the presenting of the most immediate and arresting aspects of character, emotion, etc., without using explicit realistic detail. **3** *Music* A style of composition, developed by Debussy and Ravel, striving to create impressions, moods, etc., by the use of new tonal effects. —**im·pres′sion·ist** *adj., n.* —**im·pres′sion·is′tic** *adj.*

im·pres·sive (im·pres′iv) *adj.* Producing or tending to produce a strong impression on the mind, emotions, etc., esp. one of awe or admiration. —**im·pres′sive·ly** *adv.* —**im·pres′sive·ness** *n.*

im·pri·ma·tur (im′pri·mä′tər, -mā′-, im·prim′ə·t*y*ōōr) *n.* **1** An official license to print or publish a book or pamphlet. **2** Approval in general; sanction. [L, let it be printed]

im·print (im·print′) *v.t.* **1** To produce or reproduce (a figure, mark, etc.) by pressure: to *imprint* a design on wax. **2** To mark (something), as with a stamp or seal. **3** To fix firmly in the memory. —*n.* (im′print) **1** A mark or character made by imprinting. **2** An effect or impression, as on the mind or memory. **3** A publisher's or printer's name, place of publication, date, etc., printed in a book or other publication. [< L *in-* + *premere* to press]

im·pris·on (im·priz′ən) *v.t.* **1** To put into or keep in a prison. **2** To confine or restrain in any way. —**im·pris′on·ment** *n.* —**Syn.** 1 immure, incarcerate, jail. 2 constrain.

im·prob·a·ble (im·prob′ə·bəl) *adj.* Not likely to happen or to be true. —**im·prob·a·bil′i·ty** (im′prob·ə·bil′ə·tē, im·prob′-), **im·prob′a·ble·ness** *n.* —**im·prob′a·bly** *adv.*

im·promp·tu (im·promp′t*y*ōō) *adj.* Made, done, or uttered on the spur of the moment; extempore; offhand. —*n.* Anything impromptu. —*adv.* Without preparation. [F < L *in promptu* in readiness]

im·prop·er (im·prop′ər) *adj.* **1** Not fit or appropriate; unsuitable. **2** Contrary to accepted standards of taste, conduct, speech, etc. **3** Not true or correct. —**im·prop′er·ly** *adv.* —**im·prop′er·ness** *n.*

improper fraction A fraction in which the numerator is greater than or equal to the denominator, as ⁹/₅ or ³/₃.

im·pro·pri·e·ty (im′prə·prī′ə·tē) *n. pl.* **·ties 1** The state or quality of being improper. **2** Anything that is improper. **3** A violation of good usage in speech or writing.

im·prove (im·prōōv′) *v.* **·proved, ·prov·ing** *v.t.* **1** To make better the quality, condition, etc., of. **2** To use to good advantage; utilize. **3** To increase the value of, as land by cultivation. —*v.i.* **4** To become better. **5** To make improvements: with *on* or *upon.* [< OF *en-* into + *prou* profit] —**im·prov′a·bil′i·ty, im·prov′a·ble·ness, im·prov′er** *n.* —**im·prov′a·ble** *adj.* —**im·prov′a·bly** *adv.*

im·prove·ment (im·prōōv′mənt) *n.* **1** The act of improving. **2** An improved condition. **3** A person or thing that is better than its predecessors. **4** Anything that increases the value, excellence, etc., of something.

im·prov·i·dent (im·prov′ə·dənt) *adj.* Taking no thought for future needs; thriftless. —**im·prov′i·dence** *n.* —**im·prov′·i·dent·ly** *adv.*

im·pro·vise (im′prə·vīz) *v.t. & v.i.* **·vised, ·vis·ing 1** To compose, recite, sing, etc., without previous preparation; extemporize. **2** To make or devise from what is at hand. [< L *in-* not + *provisus* foreseen] —**im·pro′vi·sa′tion·al** *adj.* —**im·prov·i·sa·tion** (im·prov′ə·zā′shən, im′prə·vī·zā′shən), **im′pro·vis′er** *n.*

im·pru·dent (im·prōō′dənt) *adj.* Not prudent; lacking discretion. —**im·pru′dence** *n.* —**im·pru′dent·ly** *adv.*

im·pu·dence (im′py ə·dəns) *n.* **1** The quality of being impudent. **2** Impudent language or behavior. Also **im′pu·den·cy.**

im·pu·dent (im′pyə·dənt) *adj.* Offensively bold; insolent. [< L *in-* not + *pudens* modest] —**im′pu·dent·ly** *adv.*

im·pugn (im·pyōōn′) *v.t.* **1** To attack by words or arguments. **2** To challenge or oppose as false. [< L *in-* against + *pugnare* to fight] —**im·pugn′a·ble** *adj.* —**im·pug·na·tion** (im′pəg·nā′shən), **im·pugn′er, im·pugn′ment** *n.*

im·pulse (im′puls) *n.* **1** A force, esp. one that acts for a short time and produces motion. **2** The change in momentum produced by such a force. **3** A sudden mental urge to act, caused by the feelings or by some external stimulus. **4** Any natural, unreasoned tendency or propensity: a kind *impulse.* **5** *Physiol.* The propagation of a stimulus through nerve or muscle tissue. [< L *impulsus,* pp. of *impellere.* See IMPEL.]

im·pul·sion (im·pul′shən) *n.* **1** The act of impelling. **2** The state of being impelled. **3** That which impels, whether a force, tendency, or motive.

im·pul·sive (im·pul′siv) *adj.* **1** Acting on impulse: an *impulsive* child. **2** Resulting from impulse; unpremeditated: an *impulsive* act. **3** Having the power to impel or drive. —**im·pul′sive·ly** *adv.* —**im·pul′sive·ness** *n.*

im·pu·ni·ty (im·pyōō′nə·tē) *n. pl.* **·ties** Freedom from punishment or from injurious consequences. [< L *in-* not + *poena* punishment]

im·pure (im·pyōōr′) *adj.* **1** Containing something dirty; unclean. **2** Obscene; unchaste. **3** Containing idiomatic or grammatical faults. **4** Unfit for religious use; unhallowed. **5** Mixed with foreign matter; adulterated. **6** Not consistent in style, form, color, etc.; mixed. —**im·pure′ly** *adv.* —**im·pure′ness** *n.*

im·pu·ri·ty (im·pyōōr′ə·tē) *n. pl.* **·ties 1** The state of being impure. **2** Something impure.

im·pu·ta·tion (im′pyōō·tā′shən) *n.* **1** The act of imputing. **2** Something imputed, as an accusation or insinuation. —**im·pu·ta·tive** (im·pyōō′tə·tiv) *adj.* —**im·pu′ta·tive·ly** *adv.*

im·pute (im·pyōōt′) *v.t.* **·put·ed, ·put·ing** To attribute, as a fault or crime, to a person; ascribe. [< L *in-* in + *putare* reckon, think) —**im·put′a·bil′i·ty, im·put′er** *n.* —**im·put′a·ble** *adj.* —**im·put′a·bly** *adv.*

in (in) *prep.* **1** Contained or included within: six rooms *in* the house. **2** Amidst; surrounded by: *in* the rain. **3** Within the class or group of: a man *in* real estate. **4** Occupied or concerned with: *in* search of truth. **5** Wearing, decorated with, etc.: that girl *in* blue. **6** Made out of: This watch is *in* gold. **7** So as to form or constitute: arranged *in* a spiral. **8** Into: sinking *in* the mud. **9** As a part or function of; belonging to: We knew you had it *in* you. **10** According to or within the scope or range of: *in* my opinion; to come *in* hearing. **11** During the course of: a concert given *in* the evening. **12** At or before the end of: due *in* three days. **13** With regard or respect to: Students vary *in* talent. **14** Affected by; under the influence of: *in* doubt. **15** By means of; using: speaking *in* whispers. **16** For the purpose of: to run *in* pursuit. **17** By reason or as a result of: to run *in* fear. —*adv.* **1** To or toward the inside from the outside: Please come *in.* **2** Inside; indoors: to stay *in* all day. **3** So as to be part of, contained by, or included with: to join *in;* to stir *in* flour. **4** So as to be in a certain position, place, or condition: Pull *in* the net. —**all in** *Informal* Exhausted. —**be in for** *Informal* To have the certain expectation of receiving (usu. something unpleasant). —**have it in for** *Informal* To resent; bear ill will toward. —**in that** Because; since: *In that* you're here already, you might as well stay. —**in with** In association or friendship with. —*adj.* **1** Having control, success, or authority. **2** On the inside; inner. **3** Leading or going in: the *in* train. **4** *Informal* **a** Privileged in status. **b** Much publicized and often admired. **5** *Informal* Understandable only to a select few: *in* jokes. —*n.* **1** A member of a party in office or power, a team at bat, etc. **2** *Informal* Favored position or influence: an *in* with the boss. —**ins and outs** The full complexities, details, etc.: to know the *ins and outs* of a business. [< OE] • See INTO.

in-[1] *prefix* Not; without; un-; non-: *inactive.* Also **il-** (as in *illiterate*), **im-** (as in *imbalance*), **ir-** (as in *irregular*). [L] Following is a list of words beginning with this prefix.

inaffable	incompassionate	inconsumable
inauthentic	incompliance	incoordinate
incircumspect	incompliant	incoordination
incoercible	incomposite	indeciduous
incohesive	incomprehensive	indecorum
incommunicative	incomputable	indeficiency
incommutability	incondensable	indefinitive
incommutable	inconducive	indemonstrability
incompact	incongruent	indemonstrable

indetectable	ineloquent	inobservance
indetectible	inequable	inobtrusive
indevotion	ineradicable	inoppressive
indevout	inerasable	inopulent
indiscipline	inevident	inquietude
indiscoverable	inexcitable	insalubrious
indisposable	inexecution	insatiety
indistinction	inexertion	insubmissive
indistinctive	inexistence	insuppressible
individable	inexistent	intransferable
indivinity	inexplainable	intransformable
indivision	inexplicit	intransfusible
indocile	inexplosive	intransmissible
indocility	inextensible	intransmutable
inductile	inextension	intransparent
inductility	infeasible	inutilitarian
indurable	infecund	inveracity
inefficacious	infecundity	inverisimilitude
inefficacy	infrugal	invirile
ineffulgent	inhomogeneity	invirility
inelaborate	inhomogeneous	inviscid
ineloquence	inhumanitarian	invital

in-² *prefix* In; into; on; within; toward: *include*. Also used intensively, as in *inflame*. Also **il-, im-, ir-**. [Fusion of IN, *prep. & adv.* + L *in-*]

-in *suffix Chem.* Used generally to denote neutral compounds, as fats, proteins, and glycerides: *stearin*. [Var. of -INE²]

IN Indiana (P.O. abbr.).

In indium.

In. inch(es).

in·a·bil·i·ty (in′ə·bil′ə·tē) *n.* The state of being unable; lack of necessary power, ability, etc. —**Syn.** impotence, incapability, incapacity, incompetence.

in ab·sen·ti·a (in ab·sen′shē·ə, -shə) *Latin* In absence (of the person concerned).

in·ac·ces·si·ble (in′ak·ses′ə·bəl) *adj.* Not accessible; incapable of being reached, seen, obtained, etc. —**in′ac·ces′·si·bil′i·ty, in′ac·ces′i·ble·ness** *n.* —**in′ac·ces′si·bly** *adv.*

in·ac·cu·ra·cy (in·ak′yər·ə·sē) *n. pl.* **·cies** 1 The state or condition of being inaccurate. 2 Something which is inaccurate.

in·ac·cu·rate (in·ak′yər·it) *adj.* Not accurate, correct, or exact. —**in·ac′cu·rate·ly** *adv.* —**in·ac′cu·rate·ness** *n.*

in·ac·tion (in·ak′shən) *n.* Absence of action, activity, or motion; idleness.

in·ac·ti·vate (in·ak′tə·vāt) *v.t.* **·vat·ed, ·vat·ing** To make inactive. —**in·ac′ti·va′tion** *n.*

in·ac·tive (in·ak′tiv) *adj.* 1 Characterized by inaction; inert. 2 Marked by absence of effort or action; indolent. 3 *Mil.* Not engaged in military duty. —**in·ac′tive·ly** *adv.* —**in·ac·tiv′i·ty, in·ac′tive·ness** *n.*

in·ad·e·quate (in·ad′ə·kwit) *adj.* Not adequate; insufficient. —**in·ad′e·qua·cy, in·ad′e·quate·ness** *n.* —**in·ad′e·quate·ly** *adv.*

in·ad·mis·si·ble (in′əd·mis′ə·bəl) *adj.* Not allowed, approved, or to be admitted. —**in′ad·mis′i·bil′i·ty** *n.*

in·ad·ver·tence (in′əd·vûr′təns) *n.* 1 The quality of being inadvertent. 2 Something inadvertent, as an error or oversight. Also **in′ad·ver′ten·cy.**

in·ad·ver·tent (in′əd·vûr′tənt) *adj.* 1 Not careful or attentive; negligent. 2 Unintentional; not deliberate: an *inadvertent* omission of the translator's name. [< L *in-* not + *advertere* to turn toward] —**in′ad·ver′tent·ly** *adv.*

in·ad·vis·a·ble (in′əd·vī′zə·bəl) *adj.* Not advisable. —**in′·ad·vis′a·bil′i·ty** *n.* —**in′ad·vis′a·bly** *adv.*

in·al·ien·a·ble (in·āl′yən·ə·bəl) *adj.* Not transferable; that cannot be rightfully taken away. —**in·al′ien·a·bil′i·ty** *n.* —**in·al′ien·a·bly** *adv.*

in·am·o·ra·ta (in·am′ə·rä′tə, in′am-) *n.* A woman whom one loves; a fiancée or mistress. [Ital. < *in-* in + *amore* love] —**in·am′o·ra′to** (-tō) *n. Masc.*

in·ane (in·ān′) *adj.* 1 Lacking sense or significance; pointless; silly: an *inane* remark. 2 Empty; vapid. [< L *inanis* empty] —**in·ane′ly** *adv.*

in·an·i·mate (in·an′ə·mit) *adj.* 1 Without life; not animate. 2 Not lively; dull; torpid. —**in·an′i·mate·ly** *adv.* —**in·an′i·mate·ness** *n.*

in·a·ni·tion (in′ə·nish′ən) *n.* 1 The state of being empty. 2 Exhaustion from lack of nourishment. [< L *inanis* empty]

in·an·i·ty (in·an′ə·tē) *n. pl.* **·ties** 1 The condition of being inane. 2 A frivolous or silly act, remark, etc.

in·ap·pli·ca·ble (in·ap′lə·kə·bəl, in′ə·plik′ə·bəl) *adj.* 1 Not applicable. 2 Not suitable or fitting. —**in·ap′pli·ca·bil′i·ty, in·ap′pli·ca·ble·ness** *n.* —**in·ap′pli·ca·bly** *adv.*

in·ap·po·site (in·ap′ə·zit) *adj.* Not apposite; not pertinent. —**in·ap′po·site·ly** *adv.*

in·ap·pre·ci·a·ble (in′ə·prē′shē·ə·bəl, -shə·bəl) *adj.* So slight as to escape notice; negligible. —**in′ap·pre′ci·a·bly** *adv.*

in·ap·pro·pri·ate (in′ə·prō′prē·it) *adj.* Not appropriate; unsuitable. —**in′ap·pro′pri·ate·ly** *adv.* —**in′ap·pro′pri·ate·ness** *n.*

in·apt (in·apt′) *adj.* 1 Not apt; inappropriate. 2 Not skillful; clumsy. —**in·apt′ly** *adv.* —**in·apt′ness** *n.*

in·ap·ti·tude (in·ap′tə·t(y)ōōd) *n.* 1 Unsuitability. 2 Lack of aptitude; incapacity.

in·ar·tic·u·late (in′är·tik′yə·lit) *adj.* 1 Unintelligible; indistinct: an *inarticulate* howl. 2 Incapable of speech; dumb. 3 Unable to speak coherently or to express oneself fully. 4 *Zool.* Lacking joints or segments. —**in′ar·tic′u·late·ly** *adv.* —**in′ar·tic′u·late·ness** *n.*

in·ar·tis·tic (in′är·tis′tik) *adj.* Not artistic; devoid of good taste. —**in′ar·tis′ti·cal·ly** *adv.*

in·as·much as (in′əz·much′ az′) 1 Since; because; seeing that. 2 To the degree that.

in·at·ten·tion (in′ə·ten′shən) *n.* Lack of or failure to give attention; heedlessness.

in·at·ten·tive (in′ə·ten′tiv) *adj.* Failing to pay attention; not attentive. —**in′at·ten′tive·ly** *adv.* —**in′at·ten′tive·ness** *n.*

in·au·di·ble (in·ô′də·bəl) *adj.* That cannot be heard. —**in·au′di·bil′i·ty** *n.* —**in·au′di·bly** *adv.*

in·au·gu·ral (in·ô′gyə·rəl) *adj.* 1 Of or pertaining to an inauguration. 2 Being the first of a series; introducing. — *n.* 1 An inaugural speech. 2 INAUGURATION.

in·au·gu·rate (in·ô′gyə·rāt) *v.t.* **·rat·ed, ·rat·ing** 1 To induct into office with formal ceremony. 2 To begin or commence upon formally. 3 To celebrate the public opening or first use of. [< L *inaugurare* take omens, consecrate, install] — **in·au′gu·ra′tor** *n.*

in·au·gu·ra·tion (in·ô′gyə·rā′shən) *n.* The act of inaugurating; esp., a ceremony of induction into office.

in·aus·pi·cious (in′ô·spish′əs) *adj.* Not auspicious; unlucky. —**in′aus·pi′cious·ly** *adv.* —**in′aus·pi′cious·ness** *n.*

inbd. inboard.

in·board (in′bôrd′, -bōrd′) *adj. & adv.* 1 *Naut.* Inside the hull or bulwarks of a ship. 2 Near the fuselage of an airplane. 3 Mounted within the chassis of an automobile or other vehicle rather than on the wheels: *inboard* brakes.

in·born (in′bôrn′) *adj.* Present at birth; innate. —**Syn.** congenital, inbred, ingrained, inherent, intrinsic.

in·bound (in′bound′) *adj.* Bound inward; incoming: an *inbound* ship.

in·bred (in′bred′) *adj.* 1 Inborn; innate. 2 Bred from closely related parents.

in·breed (in′brēd′, in′brēd′) *v.t.* **·bred, ·breed·ing** 1 To develop within. 2 To breed by continual mating of closely related stock.

Inc. Incorporated.

inc. inclosure; including; inclusive; income; incorporated; increase.

In·ca (ing′kə) *n.* One of the native Quechuan Indians dominant in Peru at the time of the Spanish conquest. — **In′can** *adj., n.*

in·cal·cu·la·ble (in·kal′kyə·lə·bəl) *adj.* 1 That cannot be counted or calculated. 2 Uncertain; unpredictable. —**in·cal′cu·la·bil′i·ty** *n.* —**in·cal′cu·la·bly** *adv.*

in·can·desce (in′kən·des′) *v.t. & v.i.* **·desced, ·desc·ing** To be or cause to be incandescent. —**in′can·des′cence, in′can·des′cen·cy** *n.*

in·can·des·cent (in′kən·des′ənt) *adj.* 1 Made luminous or glowing with heat. 2 Extremely bright or brilliant. [<

L *in-* in + *candescere* to become hot] **—in′can·des′cent·ly** *adv.*

incandescent lamp An electric lamp whose filament is heated and made incandescent by an electric current.

in·can·ta·tion (in′kan·tā′shən) **1** The utterance of magical words for enchantment or exorcism. **2** The formula so used. [< L *incantare* make an incantation] **—in·can·ta·to·ry** (in·kan′tə·tôr′ē, -tō′rē) *adj.*

in·ca·pa·ble (in·kā′pə·bəl) *adj.* **1** Not capable; lacking power, capacity or ability: with *of.* **2** Without legal qualifications or eligibility. **—in·ca′pa·bil′i·ty, in·ca′pa·ble·ness** *n.* **—in·ca′pa·bly** *adv.*

in·ca·pac·i·tate (in′kə·pas′ə·tāt) *v.t.* **·tat·ed, ·tat·ing 1** To make incapable or unfit; disable. **2** *Law* To disqualify. **—in′ca·pac′i·ta′tion** *n.*

in·ca·pac·i·ty (in′kə·pas′ə·tē) *n. pl.* **·ties 1** Lack of capacity; incapability. **2** *Law* Want of competency.

in·car·cer·ate (in·kär′sər·āt) *v.t.* **·at·ed, ·at·ing 1** To imprison; put in jail. **2** To confine. [< L *in-* in + *carcer* jail] **—in·car′cer·a′tion, in·car′cer·a′tor** *n.*

in·car·na·dine (in·kär′nə·dīn, -din) *v.t.* **·dined, ·din·ing** To dye or stain red or flesh-colored. **—adj. 1** Flesh-colored. **2** Blood-red. [F < Ital. *incarnato* flesh-colored]

in·car·nate (in·kär′nāt) *v.t.* **·nat·ed, ·nat·ing 1** To give bodily form to. **2** To give concrete shape or form to; actualize. **3** To be the embodiment of; typify. **—adj.** (-nit) **1** Invested with flesh. **2** Embodied; personified: a fiend *incarnate.* **3** Flesh-colored. [< LL *incarnare* embody in flesh]

in·car·na·tion (in′kär·nā′shən) *n.* **1** The condition of being incarnate, esp. the embodiment of a god or spirit in human form, as an avatar. **2** *Often cap.* The assumption of human nature by Jesus Christ. **3** The embodiment of a quality, idea, principle, etc.

in·case (in·kās′) *v.t.* **·cased, ·cas·ing** ENCASE. **—in·case′·ment** *n.*

in·cau·tion (in·kô′shən) *n.* A lack of care or caution.

in·cau·tious (in·kô′shəs) *adj.* Not cautious or careful; rash. **—in·cau′tious·ly** *adv.* **—in·cau′tious·ness** *n.*

in·cen·di·ar·y (in·sen′dē·er′ē) *adj.* **1** Of, pertaining to, or involving a malicious setting on fire of property. **2** Generating intense heat so as to cause fire: an *incendiary* bomb. **3** Inciting riot, disturbance, etc. **—n. pl. ·ries 1** One who maliciously sets property on fire. **2** One who incites riots, quarrels, etc. **3** An incendiary bomb or substance. [< L *incendere* set on fire] **—in·cen′di·a·rism** (-ə·riz′əm) *n.*

in·cense¹ (in·sens′) *v.t.* **·censed, ·cens·ing** To inflame to anger; enrage. [< L *incendere* set on fire] **—in·cense′ment, in·cen′sor** *n.*

in·cense² (in′sens) *n.* **1** An aromatic substance that emits perfume during burning. **2** The odor or fumes from such a substance. **3** Any agreeable odor. **—v. ·censed, ·cens·ing** *v.t.* **1** To perfume with incense. **2** To burn incense to as an act of worship. **—v.i. 3** To burn incense. [< L *incendere* set on fire]

in·cen·tive (in·sen′tiv) *adj.* Encouraging or motivating action. **—n.** That which incites, or tends to incite, to action; motive; stimulus. [< L *incinere* set the tune] **—in·cen′tive·ly** *adv.*

in·cep·tion (in·sep′shən) *n.* A beginning or initial period; start. [< L *incipere* begin]

in·cep·tive (in·sep′tiv) *adj.* **1** Beginning; initial. **2** *Gram.* Denoting the commencement of an action. **—n.** *Gram.* An inceptive word. [< L *incipere* begin] **—in·cep′tive·ly** *adv.*

in·cer·ti·tude (in·sûr′tə·t(y)ood) *n.* The state of being uncertain; doubt.

in·ces·sant (in·ses′ənt) *adj.* Continued or repeated without cessation. [< L *in-* not + *cessare* cease] **—in·ces′san·cy** (-ən·sē) *n.* **—in·ces′sant·ly** *adv.* **—Syn.** ceaseless, constant, perpetual, unremitting, unending, persistent, continuous, unceasing.

in·cest (in′sest) *n.* Sexual intercourse between persons too closely related for legal marriage. [< L *in-* not + *castus* chaste]

in·ces·tu·ous (in·ses′choo·əs) *adj.* **1** Guilty of incest. **2** Of

the nature of incest. **—in·ces′tu·ous·ly** *adv.* **—in·ces′tu·ous·ness** *n.*

inch (inch) *n.* **1** A unit of length, equal to $\frac{1}{12}$ of a foot or 25.4 millimeters. **2** An exceedingly small amount, distance, degree, etc. **—by inches** (or **inch by inch**) Gradually; very slowly. **—v.t. & v.i.** To move by inches or small degrees. [< L *uncia* the twelfth part]

inch·meal (inch′mēl′) *adv.* Inch by inch; piecemeal. Also **by inchmeal.**

in·cho·ate (in·kō′it, in′kō·āt) *adj.* Only begun or entered upon; incipient. [< L *incohare* begin] **—in·cho′ate·ly** *adv.* **—in′cho·a′tion, in·cho′ate·ness** *n.*

in·cho·a·tive (in·kō′ə·tiv) *adj.* *Gram.* Inceptive. **—n.** An inceptive verb.

inch·worm (inch′wûrm′) *n.* MEASURING WORM.

in·ci·dence (in′sə·dəns) *n.* **1** A falling upon, or the direction or manner of falling upon or affecting. **2** ANGLE OF INCIDENCE. **3** The degree of occurrence or effect of something: a high *incidence* of typhus.

in·ci·dent (in′sə·dənt) *n.* **1** Anything that takes place; event; occurrence. **2** A subordinate or minor event or act. **—adj. 1** Falling or striking upon: *incident* rays. **2** Likely to occur in connection with: the discomfort *incident* to surgery. [< L *incidere* fall upon]

in·ci·den·tal (in′sə·den′təl) *adj.* **1** Occurring in the course of something else; contingent. **2** Happening without regularity or design; casual. **—n. 1** Something that is incidental. **2** *Usu. pl.* Minor expenses or items.

in·ci·den·tal·ly (in′sə·den′təl·ē; *for def. 2 usu.* -dent′lē) *adv.* **1** In an incidental manner. **2** By the way: *Incidentally,* I forgot to jot down her name.

in·cin·er·ate (in·sin′ər·āt) *v.t.* **·at·ed, ·at·ing** To consume with fire; reduce to ashes; cremate. [< L *in-* in + *cinis, cineris* ashes] **—in·cin′er·a′tion** *n.*

in·cin·er·a·tor (in·sin′ə·rā′tər) *n.* A furnace for reducing refuse, etc., to ashes.

in·cip·i·ent (in·sip′ē·ənt) *adj.* Just beginning; in the first stages. [< L *incipere* begin] **—in·cip′i·ence, in·cip′i·en·cy** *n.* **—in·cip′i·ent·ly** *adv.*

in·cise (in·sīz′) *v.t.* **·cised, ·cis·ing 1** To cut into with a sharp instrument. **2** To engrave. [< L *incidere* cut into]

in·ci·sion (in·sizh′ən) *n.* **1** The act of incising. **2** A cut; gash. **3** A slit or opening made with a cutting instrument, as in an operation. **4** Incisiveness; keenness.

in·ci·sive (in·sī′siv) *adj.* **1** Cutting; incising. **2** Acute; penetrating; sharp: *incisive* wit. **—in·ci′sive·ly** *adv.* **—in·ci′sive·ness** *n.*

in·ci·sor (in·sī′zər) *n.* A front or cutting tooth; in man, one of eight such teeth, four in each jaw. • See TOOTH.

in·ci·ta·tion (in′sī·tā′shən) *n.* **1** An act or inciting. **2** An incentive; stimulus.

in·cite (in·sīt′) *v.t.* **·cit·ed, ·cit·ing** To urge to action; instigate; stir up. [< L *in-* thoroughly + *citare* rouse] **—in·cite′ment, in·cit′er** *n.*

in·ci·vil·i·ty (in′sə·vil′ə·tē) *n. pl.* **·ties 1** The state or quality of being uncivil. **2** An uncivil or rude act.

incl. inclosure; including.

in·clem·ent (in·klem′ənt) *adj.* **1** Rough; stormy: *inclement* weather. **2** Merciless; harsh. [< L *in-* not + *clemens* clement] **—in·clem′en·cy** *n.* **—in·clem′ent·ly** *adv.*

in·cli·na·tion (in′klə·nā′shən) *n.* **1** Deviation or the degree of deviation from the vertical or horizontal; slant. **2** A slope. **3** A tendency; predilection. **—in′cli·na′tion·al** *adj.*

in·cline (in·klīn′) *v.* **·clined, ·clin·ing** *v.i.* **1** To slant; slope. **2** To have a tendency. **3** To tend in some quality or degree: purple *inclining* toward blue. **4** To bow or bend the head or body, as in courtesy. **—v.t. 5** To cause to bend, lean, or slope. **6** To influence. **7** To bow, as the head. **—incline one's ear** To hear with favor; heed. **—n.** (in′klīn) That which inclines from the horizontal; a gradient; slope. [< L *in-* on + *clinare* to lean] **—in·clin′a·ble** *adj.*

in·clined (in·klīnd′) *adj.* **1** Slanted; sloping. **2** Disposed; apt: *inclined* to be lazy.

Inclined plane

inclined plane A plane inclined to the horizontal, esp. a simple machine along which a body can be moved and lifted by a force smaller than its weight.

Incandescent lamp
a. filament.
b. glass bulb.
c. lead-in wires.

in·close (in·klōz′) *v.t.* ·closed, ·clos·ing ENCLOSE.

in·clude (in·klōōd′) *v.t.* ·clud·ed, ·clud·ing 1 To have as a component part; contain. 2 To place in a general category, aggregate, etc. 3 To enclose within; confine. [< L *in-* in + *claudere* to shut] —in·clud′a·ble, in·clud′i·ble *adj.*

in·clu·sion (in·klōō′zhən) *n.* 1 The act of including. 2 That which is included.

in·clu·sive (in·klōō′siv) *adj.* 1 Including the things, limits, or extremes mentioned: from A to Z *inclusive*. 2 Including or taking into account everything pertinent or applicable: an *inclusive* list of purchases. —in·clu′sive·ly *adv.* —in·clu′sive·ness *n.*

incog. incognito.

in·cog·ni·to (in·kog′nə·tō, in′kəg·nē′tō) *adj. & adv.* With one's true name or identity not revealed. —*n. pl.* ·tos (-tōz) 1 The state or disguise of being incognito. 2 One who lives, travels, etc., incognito. [< L *in-* not + *cognoscere* know]

in·co·her·ence (in′kō·hir′əns) *n.* 1 Want of coherence. 2 Something incoherent. Also in′co·her′en·cy.

in·co·her·ent (in′kō·hir′ənt) *adj.* 1 Without logical order or progression; disconnected. 2 Not clear; confused; muddled, as in speech or thought. 3 Without physical coherence of parts. —in′co·her′ent·ly *adv.*

in·com·bus·ti·ble (in·kəm·bus′tə·bəl) *adj.* Incapable of being burned. —*n.* An incombustible substance. —in·com·bus′ti·bil′i·ty, in′com·bus′ti·ble·ness *n.*

in·come (in′kum) *n.* Money, or other benefit, periodically received, as from one's labor, investments, etc. [ME, a coming in]

income tax A tax levied on the income or profits of individuals and of corporations.

in·com·ing (in′kum′ing) *adj.* Coming in or about to come in: *incoming* profits.

in·com·men·su·ra·ble (in′kə·men′shər·ə·bəl, -sər·ə-) *adj.* 1 Lacking a common measure or standard of comparison. 2 *Math.* Not expressible in terms of a common measure or unit: *incommensurable* numbers. —*n.* That which is incommensurable. —in′com·men′su·ra·bil′i·ty, in′com·men′su·ra·ble·ness *n.* —in′com·men′su·ra·bly *adv.*

in·com·men·su·rate (in′kə·men′shər·it) *adj.* 1 Incommensurable. 2 Inadequate; disproportionate. —in′com·men′su·rate·ly *adv.* —in′com·men′su·rate·ness *n.*

in·com·mode (in′kə·mōd′) *v.t.* ·mod·ed, ·mod·ing To cause inconvenience to; disturb. [< L *in-* not + *commodus* convenient] —Syn. annoy, bother, put out, trouble.

in·com·mo·di·ous (in′kə·mō′dē·əs) *adj.* 1 Not spacious or roomy. 2 Inconvenient. —in′com·mo′di·ous·ly *adv.* —in′com·mo′di·ous·ness, in′com·mod′i·ty (-mod′ə·tē) *n.*

in·com·mu·ni·ca·ble (in′kə·myōō′nə·kə·bəl) *adj.* 1 Not capable of being communicated or told. 2 Not communicative. —in′com·mu′ni·ca·bly *adv.* —in′com·mu′ni·ca·bil′i·ty *n.*

in·com·mu·ni·ca·do (in′kə·myōō′nə·kä′dō) *adj. & adv.* Confined without the opportunity to communicate, as a prisoner. [Sp.]

in·com·pa·ra·ble (in·kom′pər·ə·bəl) *adj.* 1 Not admitting of comparison, because of being so superior; matchless. 2 Unsuitable for comparison. —in·com′pa·ra·bil′i·ty, in·com′pa·ra·ble·ness *n.* —in·com′pa·ra·bly *adv.*

in·com·pat·i·ble (in′kəm·pat′ə·bəl) *adj.* 1 Incapable of living or acting together in agreement or harmony. 2 Incapable of being used in combination; mutually discordant or antagonistic. 3 In disagreement; contradictory. —*n. Usu. pl.* Incompatible persons or things. —in′com·pat′i·bil′·i·ty *n.* —in′com·pat′i·bly *adv.*

in·com·pe·tent (in·kom′pə·tənt) *adj.* 1 Not competent; unable to do what is required. 2 Not legally qualified. —*n.* An incompetent person. —in·com′pe·tence, in·com′pe·ten·cy *n.* —in·com′pe·tent·ly *adv.*

in·com·plete (in′kəm·plēt′) *adj.* 1 Not complete or finished. 2 Lacking in certain parts. 3 Imperfect. —in′com·plete′ly *adv.* —in′com·plete′ness, in′com·ple′tion *n.*

in·com·pre·hen·si·ble (in′kom·pri·hen′sə·bəl, in·kom′-) *adj.* 1 Not comprehensible; not understandable. 2 *Archaic* That cannot be included or confined within limits. —in·com′pre·hen·si·bil′i·ty, in·com′pre·hen′si·ble·ness *n.* —in·com′pre·hen′si·bly *adv.*

in·com·pre·hen·sion (in′kom·pri·hen′shən) *n.* Lack of comprehension or understanding.

in·com·press·i·ble (in′kəm·pres′ə·bəl) *adj.* Incapable of being pressed together or into a smaller space. —in′com·press′i·bil′i·ty *n.*

in·con·ceiv·a·ble (in′kən·sē′və·bəl) *adj.* That cannot be conceived, believed, imagined, etc. —in′con·ceiv′a·ble·ness, in′con·ceiv′a·bil′i·ty *n.* —in′con·ceiv′a·bly *adv.*

in·con·clu·sive (in′kən·klōō′siv) *adj.* 1 Not leading to an ultimate conclusion; indecisive. 2 Not achieving a definite result; ineffective. —in′con·clu′sive·ly *adv.* —in′con·clu′sive·ness *n.*

in·con·gru·i·ty (in′kən·grōō′ə·tē) *n. pl.* ·ties 1 The state or quality of being incongruous. 2 That which is incongruous.

in·con·gru·ous (in·kong′grōō·əs) *adj.* 1 Not harmonious or compatible. 2 Not fit or suitable. 3 Not consistent or corresponding; disagreeing. [< L *in-* not + *congruus* harmonious] —in·con′gru·ous·ly *adv.* —in·con′gru·ous·ness *n.*

in·con·se·quent (in·kon′sə·kwənt) *adj.* 1 Not following logically. 2 Irrelevant; inconsequential. 3 Not according to proper sequence. —in·con′se·quence *n.* —in·con′se·quent·ly *adv.*

in·con·se·quen·tial (in′kon·sə·kwen′shəl, in·kon′-) *adj.* 1 Of little consequence; trivial. 2 Illogical. —in·con′se·quen′ti·al′i·ty (-kwen′shē·al′ə·tē) *n.* —in·con′se·quen′tial·ly *adv.*

in·con·sid·er·a·ble (in′kən·sid′ər·ə·bəl) *adj.* Very small in amount or extent; trivial. —in′con·sid′er·a·ble·ness *n.* —in′con·sid′er·a·bly *adv.*

in·con·sid·er·ate (in′kən·sid′ər·it) *adj.* 1 Not considerate; thoughtless. 2 Lacking sufficient consideration. —in′·con·sid′er·ate·ly *adv.* —in′con·sid′er·ate·ness, in′con·sid′er·a′tion *n.*

in·con·sis·ten·cy (in′kən·sis′tən·sē) *n. pl.* ·cies 1 The state or quality of being inconsistent. 2 That which is inconsistent. Also in′con·sis′tence.

in·con·sis·tent (in′kən·sis′tənt) *adj.* 1 Not in agreement or compatible with other assertions, facts, etc. 2 Self-contradictory. 3 Changeable; erratic; capricious, as in thought or behavior. —in′con·sis′tent·ly *adv.*

in·con·sol·a·ble (in′kən·sōl′ə·bəl) *adj.* Not to be consoled or soothed. —in′con·sol′a·bil′i·ty, in′con·sol′a·ble·ness *n.* —in′con·sol′a·bly *adv.*

in·con·so·nant (in·kon′sə·nənt) *adj.* Not consonant; inharmonious. —in·con′so·nant·ly *adv.* —in·con′so·nance *n.*

in·con·spic·u·ous (in′kən·spik′yōō·əs) *adj.* Not conspicuous; not attracting attention. —in′con·spic′u·ous·ly *adv.* —in′con·spic′u·ous·ness *n.*

in·con·stant (in·kon′stənt) *adj.* Not constant; fickle; variable. —in·con′stan·cy *n.* —in·con′stant·ly *adv.*

in·con·test·a·ble (in′kən·tes′tə·bəl) *adj.* Not admitting of controversy. —in′con·test′a·bly *adv.*

in·con·ti·nent (in·kon′tə·nənt) *adj.* 1 Having no self-control, esp. in sexual matters. 2 Unable to hold back bodily discharges or evacuations. —in·con′ti·nence, in·con′ti·nen·cy *n.* —in·con′ti·nent·ly *adv.*

in·con·tro·vert·i·ble (in′kon·trə·vûr′tə·bəl) *adj.* Not admitting of dispute or controversy; undeniable. —in′con·tro·vert′i·bil′i·ty, in′con·tro·vert′i·ble·ness *n.* —in′con·tro·vert′i·bly *adv.*

in·con·ven·ience (in′kən·vēn′yəns) *n.* 1 The state or quality of being inconvenient. 2 Something inconvenient. —*v.t.* ·ienced, ·ienc·ing To cause inconvenience to; trouble.

in·con·ven·ient (in′kən·vēn′yənt) *adj.* Not convenient; causing difficulty or bother; troublesome. —in′con·ven′ient·ly *adv.*

in·con·vert·i·ble (in′kən·vûr′tə·bəl) *adj.* Not interchangeable, as paper money into specie. —in·con·vert′i·bil′i·ty, in′con·vert′i·ble·ness *n.* —in·con·vert′i·bly *adv.*

in·cor·po·rate (in·kôr′pə·rāt) *v.* ·rat·ed, ·rat·ing *v.t.* 1 To take into or include as part of a whole. 2 To form into a legal corporation. 3 To combine or unite into one body or whole; blend; mix. —*v.i.* 4 To become combined or united as one body or whole. 5 To form a legal corporation. —*adj.* (-pər·it) 1 Joined or combined into one. 2 Incorporated legally. [< LL *incorporare* embody] —**in·cor'po·ra'tive** *adj.* —**in·cor'po·ra'tor** *n.*

in·cor·po·rat·ed (in-kôr'pə-rā'tid) *adj.* 1 Constituting a legal corporation. 2 Combined.

in·cor·po·ra·tion (in-kôr'pə-rā'shən) *n.* 1 The act of incorporating. 2 A corporation.

in·cor·po·re·al (in'kôr-pôr'ē-əl, -pō'rē-) *adj.* 1 Not consisting of matter; immaterial; spiritual. 2 *Law* Having no material existence, but regarded as existing by the law; *incorporeal* rights. —**in'cor·po're·al·ly** *adv.*

in·cor·rect (in'kə-rekt') *adj.* 1 Inaccurate or untrue. 2 Not proper; unsuitable. 3 Erroneous; faulty. —**in'cor·rect'ly** *adv.* —**in'cor·rect'ness** *n.*

in·cor·ri·gi·ble (in-kôr'ə-jə-bəl, -kor'-) *adj.* That cannot be corrected, changed, or reformed: an *incorrigible* liar. — *n.* An incorrigible person. [< L *in-* not + *corrigere* to correct] —**in·cor'ri·gi·ble·ness, in·cor'ri·gi·bil'i·ty** *n.* —**in·cor'ri·gi·bly** *adv.*

in·cor·rupt (in'kə-rupt') *adj.* 1 Not morally corrupt. 2 Not spoiled or decayed; uncontaminated; pure. 3 Free from errors, changes, or alterations, as a text. Also **in'cor·rupt'ed.** —**in'cor·rupt'ly** *adv.* —**in'cor·rupt'ness** *n.*

in·cor·rupt·i·ble (in'kə-rup'tə-bəl) *adj.* Incapable of corruption; esp. not accessible to bribery. —**in'cor·rupt'i·bil'i·ty, in'cor·rupt'i·ble·ness** *n.* —**in'cor·rupt'i·bly** *adv.* —**Syn.** conscientious, honest, loyal, trustworthy.

incr. increased; increasing.

in·crease (in-krēs') *v.* ·creased, ·creas·ing *v.i.* 1 To become greater, as in amount, size, degree, etc.; grow. 2 To grow in numbers, esp. by reproduction. —*v.t.* 3 To make greater, as in amount, size, degree, etc.; augment; enlarge. —*n.* (in'krēs) 1 The act or process of increasing. 2 The result or amount of increasing. [< L *in-* in + *crescere* grow] —**in·creas'a·ble** *adj.* —**in·creas'ing·ly** *adv.*

in·cred·i·ble (in-kred'ə-bəl) *adj.* Seeming too far-fetched or extraordinary to be believed or possible. —**in·cred'i·bil'i·ty, in·cred'i·ble·ness** *n.* —**in·cred'i·bly** *adv.*

in·cre·du·li·ty (in'krə-dʸōō'lə·tē) *n.* Indisposition or refusal to believe. Also **in·cred·u·lous·ness** (in-krej'ə-ləs-nis).

in·cred·u·lous (in-krej'ə-ləs) *adj.* 1 Refusing belief; skeptical. 2 Caused by or showing doubt or disbelief. [< L *in-* not + *credulus* gullible] —**in·cred'u·lous·ly** *adv.*

in·cre·ment (in'krə-mənt) *n.* 1 The act of increasing; enlargement. 2 That which is added; increase. [< L *incre·scere*. See INCREASE] —**in'cre·men'tal** (-men'təl) *adj.*

in·crim·i·nate (in-krim'ə-nāt) *v.t.* ·nat·ed, ·nat·ing To charge with or involve in a crime or fault. [< L *in-* in + *criminare* accuse one of a crime] —**in·crim'i·na'tion, in·crim'i·na'tor** *n.* —**in·crim'i·na·to·ry** (-nə-tôr'ē, -tō'rē) *adj.*

in·crust (in-krust') *v.t.* ENCRUST.

in·cu·bate (in'kyə-bāt, ing'-) *v.* ·bat·ed, ·bat·ing *v.t.* 1 To sit upon (eggs) in order to hatch; brood. 2 To hatch (eggs) in this manner or by artificial heat. 3 To maintain under conditions favoring optimum growth or development, as bacterial cultures. —*v.i.* 4 To sit on eggs; brood. 5 To undergo incubation. [< L *in-* on + *cubare* to lie] —**in'cu·ba'tive** *adj.*

in·cu·ba·tion (in'kyə-bā'shən, ing'-) *n.* 1 The act of incubating or the condition of being incubated. 2 The period between exposure to an infectious disease and the appearance of symptoms.

in·cu·ba·tor (in'kyə-bā'tər, ing'-) *n.* Any of various enclosures kept at a stable temperature, as for incubating eggs or bacterial cultures, or nurturing a premature infant.

in·cu·bus (in'kyə-bəs, ing'-) *n. pl.* ·bus·es or ·bi (-bī) 1 Anything that tends to weigh down or discourage. 2 A nightmare. 3 A male demon supposed to have sexual intercourse with sleeping women. [< LL, nightmare]

in·cul·cate (in-kul'kāt, in'kul-) *v.t.* ·cat·ed, ·cat·ing To impress upon the mind by frequent and emphatic repetition; instill. [< L *inculcare* tread on] —**in·cul·ca·tion** (in'kul·kā'shən), **in'cul·ca'tor** *n.*

in·cul·pate (in-kul'pāt, in'kul-) *v.t.* ·pat·ed, ·pat·ing To incriminate. [< L *in-* in + *culpa* fault] —**in'cul·pa'tion** *n.* —**in·cul'pa·to·ry** (-pə-tôr'ē, -tō'rē) *adj.*

in·cum·ben·cy (in-kum'bən-sē) *n. pl.* ·cies 1 The state of being incumbent. 2 That which is incumbent. 3 The holding of an office or the period during which it is held.

in·cum·bent (in-kum'bənt) *adj.* 1 Resting upon one as a duty or moral obligation; obligatory. 2 Resting, leaning, or weighing wholly or partly upon something. —*n.* One who holds an office. [< L *incumbere* recline]

in·cum·ber *v.* ENCUMBER.

in·cu·nab·u·la (in'kyōō-nab'yə-lə) *n. pl. of* **in·cu·nab·u·lum** (-ləm) 1 The beginnings of anything. 2 Specimens of printing and block engraving that appeared before A.D. 1500. [< L *in-* in + *cunabula*, dim. pl. of *cunae* a cradle] —**in'cu·nab'u·lar** *adj.*

in·cur (in-kûr') *v.t.* ·curred, ·cur·ring To meet with or become subject to, as unpleasant consequences, esp. through one's own action; bring upon oneself. [< L *incurrere* run into]

in·cur·a·ble (in-kyŏŏr'ə-bəl) *adj.* Not able to be cured or remedied. —*n.* One having an incurable disease. —**in·cur'a·bil'i·ty, in·cur'a·ble·ness** *n.* —**in·cur'a·bly** *adv.*

in·cu·ri·ous (in-kyŏŏr'ē-əs) *adj.* Lacking curiosity; not interested. —**in·cu·ri·os·i·ty** (in·kyŏŏr·ē·os'ə·tē), **in·cu'ri·ous·ness** *n.* —**in·cu'ri·ous·ly** *adv.*

in·cur·sion (in-kûr'zhən, -shən) *n.* A hostile invasion; raid. [< L *incurrere* run into] —**in·cur'sive** *adj.*

in·curve (in-kûrv') *v.t. & v.i.* To curve inward. —*n.* (in'kûrv') In baseball, a pitched ball that curves inward toward the batter.

in·cus (ing'kəs) *n. pl.* **in·cu·des** (in-kyōō'dēz) *Anat.* The central one of three small bones in the middle ear; anvil. [L, anvil]

Ind. India; Indian; Indiana; Indies.

ind. independence; independent; index; indicated; indicative; indigo; indirect; industrial.

in·debt·ed (in-det'id) *adj.* 1 Having contracted a debt. 2 Owing gratitude; beholden.

in·debt·ed·ness (in-det'id-nis) *n.* 1 The state of being indebted. 2 The amount of one's debts.

in·de·cen·cy (in-dē'sən-sē) *n. pl.* ·cies 1 The quality of being indecent; offensiveness. 2 An indecent act, word, etc.

in·de·cent (in-dē'sənt) *adj.* 1 Offensive to decency or propriety; immodest; obscene. 2 Contrary to what is fit and proper. —**in·de'cent·ly** *adv.*

in·de·ci·pher·a·ble (in'di·sī'fər·ə·bəl) *adj.* Impossible to decipher or read; illegible. —**in'de·ci'pher·a·bil'i·ty** *n.*

in·de·ci·sive (in'də·sī'siv) *adj.* 1 Not decisive. 2 Hesitant; irresolute. —**in·de·ci·sion** (in'di·sizh'ən) *n.* —**in'de·ci'sive·ly** *adv.*

in·de·clin·a·ble (in'di·klīn'ə·bəl) *adj. Gram.* Not having any inflected forms indicating case, number, or gender. —**in'de·clin'a·bly** *adv.*

in·dec·o·rous (in·dek'ə·res, in'di·kôr'əs, -kō'rəs) *adj.* Not decorous or proper; unsuitable. —**in·dec'or·ous·ly** *adv.* —**in·dec'or·ous·ness** *n.*

in·deed (in-dēd') *adv.* Admittedly; truly; undeniably. —*interj.* An exclamation of surprise, irony, incredulity, etc. [< IN + DEED]

indef. indefinite.

in·de·fat·i·ga·ble (in'də·fat'ə·gə·bəl) *adj.* Not yielding readily to fatigue; tireless. [< L *in-* not + *defatigare* to tire out] —**in·de·fat'i·ga·bil'i·ty, in'de·fat'i·ga·ble·ness** *n.* —**in·de·fat'i·ga·bly** *adv.* —**Syn.** persevering, unfaltering, unflagging, untiring.

in·de·fea·si·ble (in'də·fē'zə·bəl) *adj.* Incapable of being annulled, set aside, or made void. —**in'de·fea'si·bil'i·ty** *n.* —**in'de·fea'si·bly** *adv.*

in·de·fen·si·ble (in'di·fen'sə·bəl) *adj.* 1 Incapable of being justified, excused, etc. 2 Incapable of being defended. —**in'de·fen'si·bil'i·ty, in'de·fen'si·ble·ness** *n.* —**in·de·fen'si·bly** *adv.*

in·de·fin·a·ble (in'di·fī'nə·bəl) *adj.* That cannot be defined or described; vague; subtle. —**in'de·fin'a·ble·ness** *n.* —**in'de·fin'a·bly** *adv.*

in·def·i·nite (in-def'ə-nit) *adj.* 1 Not definite or precise; uncertain; vague. 2 Without fixed boundaries or limits. 3 *Gram.* Not defining or determining, as the *indefinite* articles *a* and *an.* —**in·def'i·nite·ly** *adv.* —**in·def'i·nite·ness** *n.*

in·de·his·cent (in'də·his'ənt) *adj. Bot.* Not opening when ripe: said of certain grains and fruits. —**in'de·his'cence** *n.*

in·del·i·ble (in-del'ə-bəl) *adj.* 1 That cannot be removed, erased, etc. **2** Making indelible marks: an *indelible* pen. [< L *in-* not + *delibilis* perishable] —**in·del'i·bil'i·ty** *n.* —**in·del'i·bly** *adv.*

in·del·i·ca·cy (in·del'ə·kə·sē) *n. pl.* **·cies 1** The quality of being indelicate. **2** An indelicate act, word, etc., offensive to propriety or refined feeling.

in·del·i·cate (in·del'ə·kit) *adj.* **1** Offensive to propriety; immodest. **2** Unfeeling; tactless. —**in·del'i·cate·ly** *adv.*

in·dem·ni·fy (in·dem'nə·fī) *v.t.* **·fied, ·fy·ing 1** To compensate for loss or damage sustained. **2** To make good (a loss). **3** To give security against future loss or damage to. [< L *indemnis* unhurt + -FY] —**in·dem'ni·fi·ca'tion, in·dem'ni·fi'er** *n.*

in·dem·ni·ty (in·dem'nə·tē) *n. pl.* **·ties 1** That which is given as compensation for a loss or for damage. **2** An agreement to remunerate another for loss or to protect him against liability. **3** Exemption from penalties or liabilities incurred. [< L *indemnis* unhurt]

inden., indent. indention (printing).

indent¹ (in·dent') *v.t.* **1** To set, as the first line of a paragraph, in from the margin. **2** To cut or mark the edge of with toothlike notches; serrate. **3** To indenture, as an apprentice. —*v.i.* **4** To be notched or cut. **5** To set a line, etc., in from the margin. —*n.* (in'dent, in·dent') **1** A cut or notch in the edge of anything. **2** An indenture. **3** An indented line or paragraph. [< L *in-* in + *dens, dentis* tooth]

in·dent² (in·dent'; *n. also* in'dent) *v.t.* **1** To make a dent in. **2** To press inward so as to form a mark, hollow, etc. —*n.* A dent.

in·den·ta·tion (in·den·tā'shən) *n.* **1** The act of indenting. **2** A cut or notch in an edge or border. **3** An indention, as of a line or paragraph. **4** A dent.

in·den·tion (in·den'shən) *n.* **1** A dent. **2** *Printing* **a** The setting in of a line or body of type at the left side. **b** The space thus left blank.

in·den·ture (in·den'chər) *n.* **1** *Law* A contract in duplicate between parties. **2** *Often pl.* A legal instrument for binding an apprentice or a servant to his master. **3** The act of indenting, or the state of being indented. —*v.t.* **·tured, ·tur·ing 1** To bind by indenture, as an apprentice. **2** To indent.

in·de·pen·dence (in'di·pen'dəns) *n.* **1** The quality or condition of being independent, esp. freedom from dependence upon or control by others. **2** An income large enough to live on without being employed.

Independence Day July 4, a U.S. holiday, marking the adoption of the Declaration of Independence on July 4, 1776.

in·de·pen·den·cy (in'di·pen'dən·sē) *n. pl.* **·cies 1** Independence. **2** An independent state.

in·de·pen·dent (in'di·pen'dənt) *adj.* **1** Not under the control or rule of others; self-governing. **2** Not part of or connected to another group, etc.; separate: an *independent* merchant. **3** Not identified with any political party or faction. **4** Not under the influence or guidance of others; self-reliant. **5** Of, possessing, or indicating an income that permits one to live without labor or dependence on others. —*n.* **1** One who is independent. **2** *Often cap.* One who is not an adherent of any political party. —**in'de·pen'dent·ly** *adv.*

independent clause *Gram.* A clause that constitutes or is capable of constituting a sentence.

in-depth (in'depth') *adj.* Extensive and thorough; not superficial; penetrating: an *in-depth* opinion survey.

in·de·scrib·a·ble (in'di·skrīb'ə·bəl) *adj.* Impossible to describe; beyond description. —**in'de·scrib'a·bil'i·ty, in'de·scrib'a·ble·ness** *n.* —**in'de·scrib'a·bly** *adv.*

in·de·struct·i·ble (in'di·struk'tə·bəl) *adj.* Impossible to destroy; proof against damage or harm. —**in'de·struct'i·bil'i·ty, in'de·struct'i·ble·ness** *n.* —**in'de·struct'i·bly** *adv.*

in·de·ter·mi·na·ble (in'di·tûr'mi·nə·bəl) *adj.* **1** Not capable of exact determination or measurement. **2** Not capable of being clearly decided or established. —**in'de·ter'mi·na·ble·ness** *n.* —**in'de·ter'mi·na·bly** *adv.*

in·de·ter·mi·nate (in'di·tûr'mə·nit) *adj.* **1** Not definite in extent, amount, or nature. **2** Not clear or precise; vague; undefined. —**in'de·ter'mi·nate·ly** *adv.* —**in'de·ter'mi·na·cy** (-nə·sē), **in'de·ter'mi·nate·ness** *n.*

in·de·ter·mi·na·tion (in'di·tûr'mə·nā'shən) *n.* **1** Lack of determination. **2** The state of being indeterminate.

in·dex (in'deks) *n. pl.* **·dex·es** or **·di·ces** (-də·sēz) **1** Anything used to indicate, point out, or guide, as the hand of a clock, a pointer, etc. **2** Anything that manifests or denotes: an *index* of character. **3** An alphabetical list, usu. found at the back of a book or other publication, of the names and topics included in the work and the page numbers on which they can be found. **4** A descriptive list or catalogue: an *index* of paintings. **5** *Math.* **a** An exponent. **b** A number placed near a radical sign to indicate the order of the root. **c** A subscript or superscript indicating position, order, etc. **6** A number that is a function of and which represents a set of data: the air-pollution *index*. **7** A mark [☞] employed to direct attention. —*v.t.* **1** To provide with an index. **2** To enter in an index. **3** To indicate; mark. [L]

in·dex (in'deks) *n.* In the Roman Catholic Church, a list of books that cannot be read without special permission.

in·dex·a·tion (in'dek·sā'shən) *n.* The adjustment of income, prices, taxes, interest payments, etc. according to a rise or fall in the cost-of-living index.

index finger The forefinger: so called from its universal use as a pointer or indicator.

In·di·a (in'dē·ə) *n.* A republic of the Commonwealth of Nations located on a subcontinent of s Asia, 1,259,797 sq. mi., cap. New Delhi.

India ink 1 A black pigment composed of a mixture of lampblack with gelatin and water, used in drawing and printing. **2** A liquid ink made from this pigment.

In·di·a·man (in'dē·ə·mən) *n. pl.* **·men** (-mən) A large merchant ship formerly used in trade with India.

In·di·an (in'dē·ən) *n.* **1** A member of any of the aboriginal races of North America (**American Indians**), South America, and the West Indies. **2** A citizen or native of India. **3** A citizen or native of the East Indies. —*adj.* **1** Of or pertaining to the aboriginal races of North America, South America, or the West Indies, or any of their languages. **2** Of or pertaining to India, its peoples, or any of their languages, esp. Hindi. **3** Of or pertaining to the East Indies, its peoples, or any of their languages.

Indian club A bottle-shaped wooden club used in gymnastic exercises.

Indian corn CORN (defs. 1 & 2).

Indian file SINGLE FILE.

Indian giver *Informal* One who gives a present and then wants it back.

Indian meal CORNMEAL.

Indian pipe A saprophytic forest plant lacking leaves and chlorophyll, having a single flower on an unbranched stem.

Indian pudding A pudding made with cornmeal, milk, and molasses.

Indian summer A period of mild weather, usu. occurring after the first frosts in late autumn.

Indian tobacco An annual weedy plant with hairy leaves and small, pale-blue flowers.

India paper 1 A thin, yellowish, absorbent printing paper, used in taking the prints from engraved plates. **2** A thin, tough, and opaque printing paper, used for Bibles, etc.

India rubber Unvulcanized rubber derived from latex.

In·dic (in'dik) *adj.* Pertaining to India, its peoples, languages, and culture; Indian. —*n.* A branch of the Indo-Iranian subfamily of Indo-European languages, including Sanskrit, Hindi, Romany, etc.

in·di·cate (in'də·kāt) *v.t.* **·cat·ed, ·cat·ing 1** To be or give a sign of: Those clouds *indicate* rain. **2** To point out; direct attention to: to *indicate* the correct page. **3** To express or make known, esp. briefly or indirectly. **4** To show or suggest the need for. [< L *in-* in + *dicare* point out, proclaim] —in'di·ca·to'ry (-kə·tôr'ē, -tō'rē) *adj.* —Syn. **1** betoken, mean, signify. **2** designate. **3** imply.

in·di·ca·tion (in'də·kā'shən) *n.* **1** The act of indicating. **2** That which indicates. **3** A degree or reading as shown on an indicator.

in·dic·a·tive (in·dik'ə·tiv) *adj.* **1** Serving to indicate or signify. **2** *Gram.* Of or pertaining to a mood in which an act or condition is stated or questioned as an actual fact, rather than as a potentiality or an unrealized condition. —*n. Gram.* The indicative mood, or a verb in this mood. —in·dic'a·tive·ly *adv.*

in·di·ca·tor (in'də·kā'tər) *n.* **1** One who or that which indicates or points out. **2** Any device or apparatus that indicates the amount, condition, or position of something. **3** *Chem.* A substance that reveals states of acidity, oxidation, etc. by changing color under known conditions.

in·di·ces (in'də·sēz) *n.pl.* of INDEX.

in·dict (in·dīt') *v.t.* **1** *Law* To prefer an indictment against. **2** To charge with a crime. [< AF *enditer* make known, inform] —in·dict'a·ble *adj.* —indict'er, in·dict'or *n.*

in·dict·ment (in·dīt'mənt) *n.* **1** The act of indicting, or the state of being indicted. **2** A formal written charge of crime, presented by a grand jury on oath to a court.

in·dif·fer·ence (in·dif'ər·əns, -rəns) *n.* The state or quality of being indifferent.

in·dif·fer·ent (in·dif'ər·ənt, -rənt) *adj.* **1** Having no inclination, concern, or interest; apathetic. **2** Only average or ordinary in size, excellence, etc.; without distinction. **3** Without any preference; neutral. **4** Having little or no importance or value. [< L *indifferens* making no difference] —in·dif'fer·ent·ly *adv.*

in·dig·e·nous (in·dij'ə·nəs) *adj.* **1** Originating naturally in a (specified) place or country; native. **2** Innate; inherent. [< L *indigena* native] —in·dig'e·nous·ly *adv.* —in·dig'e·nous·ness *n.*

in·di·gent (in'də·jənt) *adj.* Needy; poor. [< L *indigere* to lack, want] —in'di·gence, in'di·gen·cy *n.* —in'di·gent·ly *adv.*

in·di·gest·i·ble (in'dī·jes'tə·bəl) *adj.* Not digestible; difficult to digest. —in'di·gest'i·bil'i·ty, in'di·gest'i·ble·ness *n.* —in'di·gest'i·bly *adv.*

in·di·ges·tion (in'dī·jes'chən) *n.* **1** Difficult or defective digestion of food. **2** An instance of indigestion.

in·dig·nant (in·dig'nənt) *adj.* Having or showing indignation. —in·dig'nant·ly *adv.*

in·dig·na·tion (in'dig·nā'shən) *n.* Anger, esp. at something unjust, mean, or base. [< L *indignari* think unworthy]

in·dig·ni·ty (in·dig'nə·tē) *n. pl.* ·ties Something that tends to degrade or mortify; an insult; affront.

in·di·go (in'di·gō) *n.* **1** A blue dye obtained from certain plants or synthetically produced. **2** A deep violet blue. Also **indigo blue. 3** A plant yielding indigo. —*adj.* Deep violet blue: also **in'di·go-blue'** (-blōō'). [< Gk. *Indikon (pharmakon)* Indian (dye)]

indigo bunting A North American finch, the male of indigo-blue color. Also **indigo bird.**

in·di·rect (in'də·rekt') *adj.* **1** Not straight or direct: an *indirect* route. **2** Not open, honest, or straightforward: an *indirect* answer to a question. **3** Not directly intended or related; secondary: an *indirect* result. **4** Not in the exact words of the speaker or source. —in'di·rect'ly *adv.* —in'di·rect'ness *n.*

indirect discourse *Gram.* Language reported or quoted but with changes made in person or tense, as in *He said he would go.*

in·di·rec·tion (in'də·rek'shən) *n.* **1** Indirect course, action, practice, or method. **2** Dishonest means; deceit.

indirect lighting Lighting that is reflected or diffused to give a minimum of glare and shadow.

indirect object *Gram.* The person or thing that receives the secondary or indirect action of the verb, as *him* in *She gave him the pie.*

indirect tax A tax paid for by one person, as an importer, but ultimately paid for by the consumer in the form of a higher market price.

in·dis·cern·i·ble (in'di·sûr'nə·bəl, -zûr'-) *adj.* Not able to be discerned; not easily perceived. —in'dis·cern'i·bly *adv.*

in·dis·creet (in'dis·krēt') *adj.* Lacking discretion; imprudent. —in'dis·creet'ly *adv.* —in'dis·creet'ness *n.* —Syn. tactless, undiplomatic, blunt.

in·dis·crete (in'dis·krēt') *adj.* Not discrete.

in·dis·cre·tion (in'dis·kresh'ən) *n.* **1** The state of being indiscreet. **2** An indiscreet act, word, etc.

in·dis·crim·i·nate (in'dis·krim'ə·nit) *adj.* **1** Showing no discrimination; careless, casual, or promiscuous: an *indiscriminate* collector of bric-à-brac. **2** Mingled in confusion; random. —in'dis·crim'i·nate·ly *adv.* —in'dis·crim'i·nat'ing *adj.* —in'dis·crim'i·na'tion *n.*

in·dis·pen·sa·ble (in'dis·pen'sə·bəl) *adj.* Not to be dispensed with; absolutely necessary. —*n.* An indispensable person or thing. —in'dis·pen'sa·bil'i·ty, in'dis·pen'sa·ble·ness *n.* —in'dis·pen'sa·bly *adv.*

in·dis·pose (in'dis·pōz') *v.t.* ·posed, ·pos·ing **1** To make unwilling or averse; disincline. **2** To make unfit; disqualify. **3** To make ill or ailing.

in·dis·posed (in'dis·pōzd') *adj.* **1** Ill; unwell. **2** Disinclined; unwilling. —in'dis·posed'ness (-pōzd'-, -pō'zid-) *n.*

in·dis·po·si·tion (in'dis·pə·zish'ən) *n.* **1** Slight illness. **2** Unwillingness; disinclination.

in·dis·put·a·ble (in'dis·pyōō'tə·bəl, in·dis'pyōō·tə·bəl) *adj.* Incapable of being disputed; unquestionable. —in'dis·put·a·bil'i·ty, in'dis·put·a·ble·ness *n.* —in'dis·put·a·bly *adv.*

in·dis·sol·u·ble (in'di·sol'yə·bəl) *adj.* **1** That cannot be dissolved, destroyed, or disintegrated. **2** Perpetually binding. —in'dis·sol'u·bil'i·ty, in'dis·sol'u·ble·ness *n.* —in'dis·sol'·u·bly *adv.*

in·dis·tinct (in'dis·tingkt') *adj.* **1** Not clearly distinguishable or separable by the senses; dim; vague. **2** Not well-defined or clear to the intellect; obscure; uncertain. —in'dis·tinct'ly *adv.* —in'dis·tinct'ness *n.* —Syn. **1** cloudy, faint, unclear, blurry, bleary. **2** abstruse, confused, undefined, vague.

in·dis·tin·guish·a·ble (in'dis·ting'gwish·ə·bəl) *adj.* **1** Not capable of being distinguished, as in size or appearance, from something else. **2** Not distinct; difficult to perceive clearly. —in'dis·tin·guish·a·bil'i·ty, in'dis·tin'guish·a·ble·ness *n.* —in'dis·tin'guish·a·bly *adv.*

in·dite (in·dīt') *v.t.* ·dit·ed, ·dit·ing To put into words or writing; write; compose. [< L *in-* in + *dictare* declare] —in·dite'ment, in·dit'er *n.*

in·di·um (in'dē·əm) *n.* A rare metallic element (symbol In), found mainly in zinc ores. [< NL *indicum* indigo]

in·di·vid·u·al (in'də·vij'ōō·əl) *adj.* **1** Existing as an entity; single; particular. **2** Designed or intended for a single person or thing. **3** Pertaining, belonging, or peculiar to one particular person or thing. **4** Having peculiar or distinctive characteristics: an *individual* style. —*n.* A single being or thing; esp., a particular human being. [< L in- not + *dividuus* divisible] • The use of *individual* as a noun to refer to one human being should be avoided except when a person is to be distinguished from others in a group: *Two individuals stepped forward to volunteer.* Even in such a context, *people* may be preferred as being less pretentious.

in·di·vid·u·al·ism (in'də·vij'ōō·əl·iz'əm) *n.* **1** The quality of being individual or separate. **2** Personal independence in action, character, or interest. **3** A personal peculiarity; idiosyncrasy. **4** A theory or doctrine in ethics and politics that stresses the supreme importance of the individual. **5** Egoism. —in'di·vid·u·al·ist *n.* —in'di·vid·u·al·is'tic *adj.*

in·di·vid·u·al·i·ty (in'də·vij'ōō·al'ə·tē) *n. pl.* ·ties **1** Something that distinguishes one person or thing from others. **2** Distinctive character or personality. **3** The quality or state of existing separately. **4** An individual.

in·di·vid·u·al·ize (in'də·vij'ōō·əl·īz') *v.t.* ·ized, ·iz·ing **1** To make individual; distinguish. **2** To treat, mention, or consider individually. —in'di·vid·u·al·i·za'tion (-ə·za'shən, -ī·zā'-) *n.*

in·di·vid·u·al·ly (in'də·vij'ōō·əl·ē) *adv.* **1** As a single person or thing; separately: to greet each guest *individually*; *individually* wrapped candies. **2** Having individual characteristics; distinctively.

in·di·vis·i·ble (in'də·viz'ə·bəl) *adj.* Not divisible; incapable of being divided. —in'di·vis'i·bil'i·ty *n.* —in'di·vis'i·bly *adv.*

In·do·chi·na (in'dō·chī'nə) n. 1 The SE peninsula of Asia,

Indochina

including Burma, Khmer Republic (Cambodia), Laos, Malaysia, Thailand, North Vietnam, and South Vietnam. 2 The E part of the peninsula, formerly under French domination, including Khmer Republic, Laos, North Vietnam, and South Vietnam.

In·do-Chi·nese (in'dō·chī·nēz', -nēs') n. pl. ·nese 1 A native or citizen of Indochina. 2 A member of the Mongoloid peoples living in Indochina. —adj. Of or pertaining to Indochina, its peoples, or their languages.

in·doc·tri·nate (in·dok'trə·nāt) v.t. ·nat·ed, ·nat·ing 1 To instruct in doctrines, principles, etc. 2 To instruct; teach. [< LL in- into + doctrinare teach] —in·doc'tri·na'tion, in·doc'tri·na'tor n.

In·do-Eu·ro·pe·an (in'dō·yŏŏr'ə·pē'ən) n. A very extensive family of languages comprising most of the languages of Europe and many of India and SW Asia. The principal subfamilies are Hellenic, Italic, Celtic, Germanic, Indo-Iranian, Armenian, Albanian, and Balto-Slavic. —adj. Of or pertaining to the Indo-European family of languages, or to the peoples speaking them.

In·do-Ger·man·ic (in'dō·jər·man'ik) n., adj. Indo-European: the German term.

in·do·lent (in'də·lənt) adj. Averse to exertion; habitually inactive or idle. [< L in- not + dolere feel pain] —in'do·lence n. —in'do·lent·ly adv.

in·dom·i·ta·ble (in·dom'i·tə·bəl) adj. Not easily subdued or disheartened; unconquerable. [< L in- not + domitus tamed] —in·dom'i·ta·ble·ness n. —in·dom'i·ta·bly adv.

In·do·ne·sia (in'dō·nē'zhə, -shə) n. A republic of SE Asia, comprising several large and numerous small islands, 735,268 sq. mi., cap. Djakarta.

In·do·ne·sian (in'dō·nē'zhən, -shən) n. 1 A native or citizen of Indonesia. 2 The language of Indonesia, officially named Ba·ha·sa Indonesia (bä·hä'sə), based on Malay. —adj. Of or pertaining to Indonesia, its peoples, or their languages.

in·door (in'dôr', -dōr') adj. 1 Being, living, done, etc., inside a building or house. 2 Of or pertaining to the inside of a building or house.

in·doors (in'dôrz', -dōrz') adv. In or toward the inside of a building or house.

in·dorse (in·dôrs') v.t. ·dorsed, ·dors·ing ENDORSE. —in·dorse'ment n.

In·dra (in'drə) In early Hindu mythology, the god of the firmament and of rain.

in·du·bi·ta·ble (in·dyŏŏ'bə·tə·bəl) adj. Not open to doubt; unquestionable; certain. [< L in- not + dubitare to doubt] —in·du'bi·ta·ble·ness n. —in·du'bi·ta·bly adv. —Syn. indisputable, manifest, sure, undeniable.

in·duce (in·dyŏŏs') v.t. ·duced, ·duc·ing 1 To lead on to a specific action, belief, etc.; persuade. 2 To bring on; cause: a sickness induced by fatigue. 3 Electr. To produce by a process of induction. 4 To reach as a conclusion by an inductive process of reasoning. [< L in- in + ducere to lead] —in·duc'er n. —in·duc'i·ble adj.

in·duce·ment (in·dyŏŏs'mənt) n. 1 An incentive; motive. 2 The act of inducing.

in·duct (in·dukt') v.t. 1 To install formally in an office, benefice, etc. 2 To introduce; initiate. 3 To bring into a military service. [< L inducere lead in]

in·duc·tance (in·duk'təns) n. 1 The property of an electric device or circuit whereby a changing current in itself or a circuit nearby produces a voltage in itself. 2 The measure of this property. 3 An ideal device whose only property is inductance.

in·duc·tee (in'duk·tē') n. One inducted into military service.

in·duc·tion (in·duk'shən) n. 1 The act or process of inducting or the state of being inducted; initiation; installation. 2 The process of arriving at a general conclusion from observation of particular facts; also, the conclusion so arrived at. 3 The bringing forward of separate facts as evidence in order to prove a general statement. 4 Electr. The production of magnetization or electrification in a body by the mere proximity of a magnetic field or electric charge, or of an electric current in a conductor by the variation of the magnetic field in its vicinity. —in·duc'tion·al adj.

induction coil Electr. A transformer in which pulses of direct current fed into the primary winding induce a high alternating voltage in the secondary, used in automotive ignition systems.

in·duc·tive (in·duk'tiv) adj. 1 Persuasive; inducing. 2 Of, using, or produced by logical induction. 3 Introductory. 4 Of or produced by electrical or magnetic induction. —in·duc'tive·ly adv. —in·duc'tive·ness n.

in·duc·tor (in·duk'tər) n. 1 One who or that which inducts. 2 Electr. Any device whose principal property is its inductance

in·due (in·dyŏŏ') v.t. ·dued, ·du·ing ENDUE.

in·dulge (in·dulj') v. ·dulged, ·dulg·ing v.t. 1 To gratify, as desires or whims. 2 To gratify the desires, whims, etc., of. —v.i. 3 To yield to or gratify one's desires; indulge oneself; with in. [< L indulgere be kind to, concede] —in·dulg'er n. —in·dulg·ing·ly adv.

in·dul·gence (in·dul'jəns) n. 1 The act of indulging or of being indulgent. 2 That which is indulged in. 3 A privilege or favor. 4 Permission to defer payment, as of a note. 5 In the Roman Catholic Church, remission of the temporal punishment still due to sin after sacramental absolution. Also in·dul'gen·cy.

in·dul·gent (in·dul'jənt) adj. Prone to indulge; lenient. —in·dul'gent·ly adv.

in·du·rate (in'dyŏŏ·rāt) v.t. & v.i. ·rat·ed, ·rat·ing 1 To make or become hard. 2 To make or become callous or unsympathetic; harden. —adj. (-rit) Hard or hardened: also in'du·rat'ed. [< L indurare make hard] —in'du·ra'tion n. —in'du·ra'tive adj.

in·dus·tri·al (in·dus'trē·əl) adj. 1 Of, like, or resulting from industry. 2 Engaged in industry. 3 Used specifically in industry. 4 Of or for workers in industry. —n. 1 One engaged in industry. 2 A stock or security issued by an established industry. —in·dus'tri·al·ly adv.

industrial arts The technical skills used in industry, esp. as subjects of study in schools.

in·dus·tri·al·ism (in·dus′trē·əl·iz′əm) *n.* A social or economic system that results from and is dominated by large-scale industries. —**in·dus′tri·al·ist** *adj., n.*

in·dus·tri·al·ize (in·dus′trē·əl·īz′) *v.t.* **-ized, -iz·ing** 1 To make industrial: to *industrialize* a village. 2 To make or organize into an industry. —**in·dus′tri·al·i·za′tion** (-ə·zā′·shən, -ī·zā′-) *n.*

industrial relations The relationships between employers and employees.

industrial union A labor union in which membership is open to all workers in a particular industry.

in·dus·tri·ous (in·dus′trē·əs) *adj.* Hard-working; diligent. —**in·dus′tri·ous·ly** *adv.* —**in·dus′tri·ous·ness** *n.* —Syn. assiduous, busy, occupied, persevering, sedulous.

in·dus·try (in′dəs·trē) *n. pl.* **·tries** 1 Diligent or constant application to work or business. 2 Any branch of productive work or manufacture; also, the capital or workers employed in it: the steel *industry;* the farming *industry.* 3 The business or the activities of manufacturing as a whole. [< L *industrius* diligent]

in·dwell (in′dwel′) *v.* **-dwelt, -dwel·ling** *v.t.* To dwell in; inhabit. —*v.i.* To dwell; abide: with *in.* —**in′dwell′er** *n.*

-ine¹ *suffix of adjectives* Like; pertaining to; of the nature of: *marine, canine.* [< L *-inus*, adj. suffix]

-ine² *suffix* 1 *Chem.* **a** Used in the names of halogens: *bromine, fluorine.* **b** Used to indicate an alkaloid or nitrogen base: *morphine, amine.* **c** Var. of -IN. 2 Used in names of commercial products: *gasoline.* [Special use of -INE¹]

-ine³ *suffix* Like; resembling: *crystalline.* [L -*inos*]

in·e·bri·ate (in·ē′brē·āt) *v.t.* **-at·ed, -at·ing** 1 To make drunk; intoxicate. 2 To exhilarate; excite. —*n.* (-it, -āt) A habitual drunkard. —*adj.* (-it, -āt) Intoxicated: also **in·e′·bri·at′ed.** [< L *in-* thoroughly + *ebriare* make drunk] —**in·e′·bri·a′tion** *n.*

in·e·bri·e·ty (in′ē·brī′ə·tē) *n.* Drunkenness.

in·ed·i·ble (in·ed′ə·bəl) *adj.* Not edible; not fit to eat. —**in·ed′i·bil′i·ty** *n.*

in·ef·fa·ble (in·ef′ə·bəl) *adj.* 1 Too overwhelming for expression in words; indescribable. 2 Too lofty or sacred to be spoken. [< L *in-* not + *effabilis* utterable] —**in·ef′fa·bil′i·ty** *n.* —**in·ef′fa·bly** *adv.*

in·ef·fec·tive (in′i·fek′tiv) *adj.* 1 Not effective. 2 Incompetent. —**in′ef·fec′tive·ly** *adv.* —**in′ef·fec′tive·ness** *n.*

in·ef·fec·tu·al (in′i·fek′chōō·əl) *adj.* Not effectual. 2 Unsuccessful; fruitless. —**in′ef·fec′tu·al′i·ty, in′ef·fec′tu·al·ness** *n.* —**in′ef·fec′tu·al·ly** *adv.*

in·ef·fi·cient (in′i·fish′ənt) *adj.* 1 Not efficient or productive as regards expenditure of time, energy, etc. 2 Not capable; incompetent. —**in′ef·fi′cien·cy** *n.* —**in′ef·fi′cient·ly** *adv.*

in·e·las·tic (in′i·las′tik) *adj.* Not elastic; inflexible; unyielding; unadaptable. —**in·e·las·tic·i·ty** (in′i·las′tis′ə·tē) *n.*

in·el·e·gant (in·el′ə·gənt) *adj.* 1 Not elegant; lacking in beauty, polish, grace, refinement, good taste, or the like. 2 Coarse; crude. —**in·el′e·gance, in·el′e·gan·cy** *n.* —**in·el′e·gant·ly** *adv.*

in·el·i·gi·ble (in·el′ə·jə·bəl) *adj.* Not eligible; disqualified; unsuitable. —*n.* An ineligible person. —**in·el′i·gi·bil′i·ty** *n.* —**in·el′i·gi·bly** *adv.*

in·e·luc·ta·ble (in′i·luk′tə·bəl) *adj.* Not to be escaped or avoided; inevitable. [< L *in-* not + *eluctabilis* surmountable] —**in′e·luc′ta·bil′i·ty** *n.* —**in·e·luc′ta·bly** *adv.*

in·ept (in·ept′) *adj.* 1 Not suitable or fit. 2 Absurd; foolish. 3 Clumsy; awkward. [< L *in-* not + *aptus* fit] —**in·ep′ti·tude, in·ept′ness** *n.* —**in·ept′ly** *adv.*

in·e·qual·i·ty (in′i·kwol′ə·tē) *n. pl.* **·ties** 1 The condition of being unequal; also, an instance of this. 2 Disparity in social position, opportunity, etc. 3 Lack of evenness or proportion, variableness: *inequalities* of surface. 4 *Math.* A statement indicating that two quantities are not equal, or esp. that one is greater than the other.

in·eq·ui·ta·ble (in·ek′wə·tə·bəl) *adj.* Not fair or just. —**in·eq′ui·ta·bly** *adv.*

in·eq·ui·ty (in·ek′wə·tē) *n. pl.* **·ties** 1 Want of equity; injustice. 2 An instance of injustice.

in·ert (in·ûrt′) *adj.* 1 Without any inherent power to move. 2 Very slow; sluggish. 3 Devoid of reactive properties: *inert* gas. [< L *iners*] —**in·ert′ly** *adv.* —**in·ert′ness** *n.*

in·er·tia (in·ûr′shə) *n.* 1 The state of being inert; sluggishness. 2 *Physics* The tendency of any material body to maintain its velocity indefinitely unless accelerated or decelerated by some force. [L, idleness] —**in·er′tial** *adj.*

in·es·cap·a·ble (in′ə·skā′pə·bəl) *adj.* Inevitable; unavoidable. —**in′es·cap′a·bly** *adv.*

in·es·sen·tial (in′ə·sen′shəl) *adj.* Not essential; unnecessary. —*n.* Something not essential.

in·es·ti·ma·ble (in·es′tə·mə·bəl) *adj.* That cannot be measured or estimated because of value, greatness, etc. —**in·es′ti·ma·bly** *adv.*

in·ev·i·ta·ble (in·ev′ə·tə·bəl) *adj.* 1 That cannot be prevented; unavoidable. 2 Customary; usual. [< L *in-* not + *evitare* avoid] —**in·ev′i·ta·bil′i·ty, in·ev′i·ta·ble·ness** *n.* —**in·ev′i·ta·bly** *adv.*

in·ex·act (in′ig·zakt′) *adj.* Not exact, accurate, or true. —**in′ex·act′i·tude, in′ex·act′ness** *n.* —**in′ex·act′ly** *adv.*

in·ex·cus·a·ble (in′ik·skyōō′zə·bəl) *adj.* Impossible to excuse or justify. —**in′ex·cus′a·bil′i·ty** *n.* —**in′ex·cus′a·bly** *adv.*

in·ex·haust·i·ble (in′ig·zôs′tə·bəl) *adj.* 1 Incapable of being exhausted or used up. 2 Incapable of fatigue; tireless. —**in′ex·haust′i·bil′i·ty, n.** —**in′ex·haust′i·bly** *adv.*

in·ex·o·ra·ble (in·ek′sər·ə·bəl) *adj.* Not to be moved by entreaty; unyielding. [< L *in-* not + *exorare* move by entreaty] —**in·ex′o·ra·bil′i·ty, in·ex′o·ra·ble·ness** *n.* —**in·ex′o·ra·bly** *adv.*

in·ex·pe·di·ent (in′ik·spē′dē·ənt) *adj.* Not expedient or suitable; impracticable. —**in′ex·pe′di·ence, in′ex·pe′di·en·cy** (*pl.* **·en·cies**) *n.* —**in′ex·pe′di·ent·ly** *adv.*

in·ex·pen·sive (in′ik·spen′siv) *adj.* Not expensive; costing little. —**in′ex·pen′sive·ly** *adv.* —**in′ex·pen′sive·ness** *n.*

in·ex·pe·ri·ence (in′ik·spir′ē·əns) *n.* Lack of the skill and knowledge derived from experience. —**in′ex·pe′ri·enced** *adj.*

in·ex·pert (in·ek′spərt, in′ik·spûrt′) *adj.* Not expert; not skilled. —**in·ex′pert·ly** *adv.* —**in·ex′pert·ness** *n.*

in·ex·pi·a·ble (in·ek′spē·ə·bəl) *adj.* That may not be expiated or made amends for. —**in·ex′pi·a·ble·ness** *n.* —**in·ex′·pi·a·bly** *adv.*

in·ex·plic·a·ble (in·eks′pli·kə·bəl, in′iks·plik′ə·bəl) *adj.* Not explicable; impossible to explain or understand. —**in′ex·pli·ca·bil′i·ty, in′ex·plic′a·ble·ness** *n.* —**in·ex′pli·ca·bly** *adv.*

in·ex·press·i·ble (in′iks·pres′ə·bəl) *adj.* Incapable of being expressed; unutterable. —**in′ex·press′i·bil′i·ty, in′ex·press′i·ble·ness** *n.* —**in′ex·press′i·bly** *adv.*

in·ex·pres·sive (in′ik·spres′iv) *adj.* Not expressive; conveying little meaning or expression. —**in′ex·press′ive·ly** *adv.* —**in′ex·press′ive·ness** *n.*

in ex·ten·so (in ik·sten′sō) *Latin* At full length.

in·ex·tin·guish·a·ble (in′ik·sting′gwish·ə·bəl) *adj.* Not to be extinguished or put out. —**in′ex·tin·guish·a·bly** *adv.*

in ex·tre·mis (in iks·trē′mis) *Latin* At the point of death.

in·ex·tri·ca·ble (in·eks′tri·kə·bəl) *adj.* 1 So involved that extrication is impossible. 2 That cannot be disentangled or undone. 3 Impossible to solve. —**in·ex′tri·ca·bil′i·ty, in·ex′tri·ca·ble·ness** *n.* —**in·ex′tri·ca·bly** *adv.*

inf. Infantry.

inf. below (L *infra*); inferior; infinitive; information.

in·fal·li·ble (in·fal′ə·bəl) *adj.* 1 Incapable of fallacy or error. 2 Not apt to fail; reliable; certain: an *infallible* cure. 3 In Roman Catholic theology, incapable of error in matters relating to faith and morals: said of the Pope speaking *ex cathedra.* —*n.* One who or that which is infallible. —**in·fal′li·bil′i·ty, in·fal′li·ble·ness** *n.* —**in·fal′li·bly** *adv.*

in·fa·mous (in′fə·məs) *adj.* 1 Having an odious reputation; notorious. 2 Involving or deserving infamy. [< L *in-* not + *fama* fame] —**in′fa·mous·ly** *adv.* —**in′fa·mous·ness** *n.*

in·fa·my (in′fə·mē) *n. pl.* **·mies** 1 Total lack of honor or reputation. 2 The state of being infamous. 3 An infamous act.

in·fan·cy (in′fən·sē) *n. pl.* **·cies** 1 The state of being an infant. 2 *Law* The years during which one is a minor. 3 The earliest period in the development of something.

in·fant (in′fənt) *n.* 1 A baby. 2 *Law* A minor; in most states of the U.S., a person under 21 years of age. —*adj.* 1 Of, for, or like infants or infancy. 2 In the earliest state. [< L *in-* not + *fans,* pr.p. of *fari* to talk]

in·fan·ta (in·fan′tə) n. 1 A daughter of a Spanish or Portuguese king. 2 The wife of an infante. [Sp., infant]

in·fan·te (in·fan′tā) n. A son, except the eldest, of a Spanish or Portuguese king. [Sp., infant]

in·fan·ti·cide (in·fan′tə·sīd) n. 1 The murder of a baby. 2 One who murders a baby.

in·fan·tile (in′fən·tīl, -til) adj. 1 Of, pertaining to, or characteristic of infants or infancy. 2 In the earliest period of development. Also **in′fan·tine** (-tīn, -tin).

infantile paralysis POLIOMYELITIS.

in·fan·til·ism (in′fən·təl·iz′əm) n. Abnormal persistence of infantile mental and physical qualities into adult life.

in·fan·try (in′fən·trē) n. pl. **·tries** Soldiers or units of an army that are trained and equipped to fight on foot. [< Ital. infante boy, page, foot soldier]

in·fan·try·man (in′fən·trē·mən) n. pl. **·men** (-mən) A foot soldier.

in·farc·tion (in·färk′shən) n. Death of tissue due to deprivation of blood caused by an obstruction, as in a heart attack. [< L in- in + farcire to stuff]

in·fat·u·ate (in·fach′ōō·āt) v.t. **·at·ed, ·at·ing** 1 To make foolish or fatuous. 2 To inspire with foolish passion. [< L in- very + fatuus foolish] —**in·fat′u·a′tion** n.

in·fect (in·fekt′) v.t. 1 To contaminate with disease-producing organisms. 2 To communicate disease to, as a person, etc. 3 To affect or influence, as with emotion, beliefs, etc., esp. harmfully; taint. [< L inficere dip into, stain] —**in·fect′er, in·fec′tor** n. —**Syn.** 3 corrupt, debauch, deprave, lead astray, pollute.

in·fec·tion (in·fek′shən) n. 1 The act of infecting, esp. the producing of a disease or harmful condition by entrance of disease-producing germs into an organism. 2 Any diseased condition so produced. 3 The communication of a quality, emotion, belief, etc., as by example. 4 That which infects.

in·fec·tious (in·fek′shəs) adj. 1 That may be communicated by infection. 2 Capable of causing infection. 3 Tending to spread from one to another: infectious laughter. —**in·fec′tious·ly** adv. —**in·fec′tious·ness** n.

in·fec·tive (in·fek′tiv) adj. Causing or capable of causing infection; infectious.

in·fe·lic·i·tous (in′fə·lis′ə·təs) adj. Not felicitous, happy, or suitable in application, condition, or result. —**in′fe·lic′i·tous·ly** adv. —**in′fe·lic′i·tous·ness** n.

in·fe·lic·i·ty (in′fə·lis′ə·tē) n. pl. **·ties** 1 The state of being infelicitous; unhappiness. 2 That which is infelicitous, as an inappropriate remark, act, etc.

in·fer (in·fûr′) v. **·ferred, ·fer·ring** v.t. 1 To conclude by reasoning from evidence or premises; deduce. 2 To involve or imply as a conclusion; give evidence of. 3 To suggest; hint. —v.i. 4 To draw inferences. [< L in- in + ferre carry] —**in·fer′a·ble, in·fer′ri·ble** adj. —**in·fer′rer** n. • **Infer, imply** To infer is to make a rational or logical conclusion based on evidence: I inferred from the absence of cutting teeth that the animal was herbivorous. Imply may refer to the drawing of a necessary conclusion, and in this sense it is interchangeable with infer: The possibility of life on other planets implies (or infers) the presence of amino acids. But more often imply means simply to suggest or hint, and in this sense the use of infer (def. 3) should be avoided because it is ambiguous. She implied that he was scared is clear, but She inferred . . . might mean that she concluded privately that he was scared because of his manner or appearance.

in·fer·ence (in′fər·əns) n. 1 The act of inferring. 2 That which is inferred, as a deduction.

in·fer·en·tial (in′fə·ren′shəl) adj. Of or deduced by inference. —**in′fer·en′tial·ly** adv.

in·fe·ri·or (in·fir′ē·ər) adj. 1 Poor or mediocre in quality: an inferior meal. 2 Lower in merit, importance, or rank. 3 Situated or placed lower, as certain parts of the body. 4 Astron. Between the earth and the sun: an inferior planet. —n. One who or that which is inferior. [< L inferus low]

in·fe·ri·or·i·ty (in·fir′ē·ôr′ə·tē, -or′-) n. The state or quality of being inferior.

inferiority complex An exaggerated sense of one's own limitations and incapacities, sometimes compensated for by aggressive behavior.

in·fer·nal (in·fûr′nəl) adj. 1 In mythology, of the world of the dead. 2 Of hell. 3 Hellish; diabolical. 4 Informal Damned; outrageous. [< L infernus situated below] —**in·fer′nal·ly** adv.

infernal machine A device maliciously contrived to destroy life or property by explosion.

in·fer·no (in·fûr′nō) n. pl. **·nos** 1 The infernal regions; hell. 2 Any place comparable to hell. [Ital.]

in·fer·tile (in·fûr′til) adj. Not fertile or productive; sterile; barren. —**in′fer·til′i·ty** n.

in·fest (in·fest′) v.t. To overrun or spread in large numbers so as to be unpleasant or unsafe. [< L infestus hostile] —**in′fes·ta′tion, in·fest′er** n.

in·fi·del (in′fi·dəl) n. 1 One who does not believe in a particular or the prevailing religion. 2 One who does not believe in any religion. 3 One who does not accept a particular theory, belief, etc. —adj. 1 That is an infidel. 2 Of infidels or unbelief. [< L in- not + fidelis faithful]

in·fi·del·i·ty (in′fi·del′ə·tē) n. pl. **·ties** 1 Lack of fidelity, esp. violation of the marriage vow by adultery. 2 Any disloyal act. 3 The state of being an infidel.

in·field (in′fēld′) n. 1 The space enclosed within the four base lines of a baseball field. 2 The infielders collectively.

in·field·er (in′fēl′dər) n. In baseball, the first, second, and third basemen, the shortstop, and, when fielding the ball, the pitcher and catcher.

in·fight·ing (in′fīt′ing) n. 1 Fighting or boxing at close range. 2 Bitter dissension or struggle, esp. between rivals within an organization: political infighting. —**in′fight′er** n.

in·fil·trate (in·fil′trāt; esp. for v. defs. 2, 3 in′fil·trāt) v. **·trat·ed, ·trat·ing** v.t. 1 To cause (a liquid or gas) to pass into or through something. 2 To pass through or into; permeate. 3 Mil. To pass through, as enemy lines. —v.i. 4 To pass into or through. —n. That which infiltrates or has infiltrated. —**in′fil·tra′tion** n. —**in·fil′tra·tive** adj.

in·fi·nite (in′fə·nit) adj. 1 So great as to be immeasurable and unbounded; limitless. 2 All-embracing; absolute: infinite love. 3 Very great, numerous, etc.: to take infinite pains. 4 Math. **a** Larger than any given number or value; arbitrarily large. **b** Capable of being arranged in a one-to-one correspondence with a proper subset of itself, as the set of natural numbers. —n. That which is infinite. —**the Infinite** God. [< L in- not + finitus finite] —**in′fi·nite·ly** adv. —**in′fi·nite·ness** n.

in·fin·i·tes·i·mal (in′fin·ə·tes′ə·məl) adj. 1 Too small to be measured or calculated. 2 Math. Arbitrarily close to zero in value. —n. An infinitesimal quantity. [< L infinitus infinite + -esimus (after centesimus hundredth)] —**in′fin·i·tes′i·mal·ly** adv.

in·fin·i·tive (in·fin′ə·tiv) Gram. adj. Of, pertaining to, or using the infinitive. —n. A verb form expressing action or condition without reference to person, tense, or number, as to run. In English, its sign to is omitted after most auxiliaries, as in "He should go now," but is retained when the infinitive functions as a noun, as in "To ride horses was his favorite sport." [< LL infinitivus unlimited]

in·fin·i·tude (in·fin′ə·tyōōd) n. 1 The quality of being infinite. 2 An infinite quantity.

in·fin·i·ty (in·fin′ə·tē) n. pl. **·ties** 1 The quality of being infinite. 2 Something, as space or time, regarded as boundless or endless. 3 Math. An infinite number or set. [< L infinitus infinite]

in·firm (in·fûrm′) adj. 1 Feeble or weak, as from age. 2 Lacking purpose or determination of mind. 3 Not legally secure. [< L in- not + firmus strong] —**in·firm′ly** adv. —**in·firm′ness** n. —**Syn.** 1 ailing, fragile, frail, ill, sickly.

in·fir·ma·ry (in·fûr′mər·ē) n. pl. **·ries** 1 A place for the treatment of the sick or injured, as in a school, factory, etc.; dispensary. 2 A small hospital.

in·fir·mi·ty (in·fûr′mə·tē) n. pl. **·ties** 1 A physical weakness or disability. 2 A defect of personality or character. 3 An infirm condition; feebleness.

in·fix (in·fiks′) v.t. 1 To fix or drive in, as by thrusting. 2

To instill; inculcate. **3** *Gram.* To insert (an infix) within a word. —*n.* (in′fiks) *Gram.* A modifying addition inserted in the body of a word. —**in·fix′ion** *n.*

infl. influence; influenced.

in·flame (in·flām′) *v.* ·**flamed**, ·**flam·ing** *v.t.* **1** To set on fire. **2** To excite to violent emotion or activity. **3** To excite or make more intense, as anger or lust. **4** To cause inflammation in; heat morbidly. —*v.i.* **5** To catch fire. **6** To become excited or aroused. **7** To become inflamed by infection, etc. [< L *in*- in + *flammare* to flame] —**in·flam′er** *n.*

in·flam·ma·ble (in·flam′ə·bəl) *adj.* **1** Readily set on fire; combustible; flammable. **2** Easily excited or roused to passion. —*n.* A combustible substance. —**in·flam′ma·bil′i·ty, in·flam′ma·ble·ness** *n.* —**in·flam′ma·bly** *adv.*

in·flam·ma·tion (in′flə·mā′shən) *n.* **1** *Pathol.* A localized reaction to infection, injury, etc., characterized by heat, redness, swelling, and pain. **2** The act of inflaming.

in·flam·ma·to·ry (in·flam′ə·tôr′ē, -tō′rē) *adj.* **1** Calculated to arouse passions, riot, violence, etc.; seditious. **2** Inducing or provoking inflammation.

in·flate (in·flāt′) *v.* ·**flat·ed**, ·**flat·ing** *v.t.* **1** To fill with gas or air so as to distend or expand; blow up. **2** To increase or puff up: to *inflate* one's pride. **3** To increase unduly, esp. so that the nominal value exceeds the real: to *inflate* currency or prices. —*v.i.* **4** To become inflated. [< L *in*- in + *flare* blow] —**in·fla′ta·ble** *adj.* —**in·fla′ter, in·fla′tor** *n.*

in·fla·tion (in·flā′shən) *n.* **1** The act of inflating, or the state of being inflated. **2** An increase of currency in circulation or an overissue of credit, resulting in a rise of price levels when or if demand for goods exceeds supply. **3** The resulting rise in price levels. —**in·fla′tion·ar′y** *adj.*

in·flect (in·flekt′) *v.t.* **1** *Gram.* To give the inflections of (a word); conjugate or decline. **2** To vary the pitch of (the voice); modulate. **3** To turn inward or aside; deflect; curve. [< L *in*- in + *flectere* to bend]

in·flec·tion (in·flek′shən) *n.* **1** A bending or bend; curvature; angle. **2** *Gram.* **a** A pattern of change undergone by words to express grammatical and syntactical relations, as of case, number, gender, person, tense, etc. **b** An inflectional element. **c** An inflected form. **3** A change in pitch or intensity in the voice. *Brit. sp.* **in·flex′ion.**

in·flec·tion·al (in·flek′shən·əl) *adj.* Of, having, relating to, or showing grammatical inflection. *Brit. sp.* **in·flex′ion·al.** —**in·flec′tion·al·ly** *adv.*

in·flex·i·ble (in·flek′sə·bəl) *adj.* **1** Unyielding; firm; stubborn. **2** Incapable of being physically bent; rigid. **3** That cannot be altered or varied: the *inflexible* laws of nature. —**in·flex′i·bil′i·ty, in·flex′i·ble·ness** *n.* —**in·flex′i·bly** *adv.* —Syn. **1** dogged, obstinate, steadfast. **2** stiff. **3** fixed, unalterable.

in·flict (in·flikt′) *v.t.* **1** To cause (pain, wounds, etc.), as with a blow. **2** To impose, as punishment. **3** To impose as if by force: to *inflict* one's views on the public. [< L *in*- on + *fligere* to strike] —**in·flict′er, in·flic′tor** *n.* —**in·flic′tive** *adj.*

in·flic·tion (in·flik′shən) *n.* **1** The act or process of inflicting. **2** That which is inflicted.

in·flo·res·cence (in′flə·res′əns) *n.* **1** The act of flowering. **2** The arrangement of flowers on a plant stem. **3** A single flower; also, flowers collectively. [< LL *inflorescere* come into flower] —**in′flo·res′cent** *adj.*

in·flow (in′flō′) *n.* The act of flowing in, or that which flows in.

in·flu·ence (in′flōō·əns) *n.* **1** The power of a person or thing to produce an effect upon others, often indirectly or intangibly. **2** The effect of such power. **3** Power arising from social, financial, moral, or similar authority. **4** A person or thing that has or exerts influence. —*v.t.* ·**enced**, ·**enc·ing** To have or exert influence on. [< L *in*- in + *fluere* to flow] —**in′flu·enc′er** *n.*

in·flu·en·tial (in′flōō·en′shəl) *adj.* Having or exercising great influence or power; effective. —**in′flu·en′tial·ly** *adv.*

in·flu·en·za (in′flōō·en′zə) *n.* An acute, sometimes epidemic, infectious disease of varying severity caused by a virus and characterized by inflammation of the air passages, fever, and nervous and muscular prostration. [< L *influere* flow in] —**in′flu·en′zal** *adj.*

in·flux (in′fluks′) *n.* **1** A continuous flowing or pouring in. **2** The mouth of a river. [< L *influere* flow in]

in·fold (in·fōld′) *v.t.* ENFOLD.

in·form (in·fôrm′) *v.t.* **1** To give (someone) facts or information; make something known to. **2** To give character to; animate. —*v.i.* **3** To give information, esp. to accuse or charge others, usu. for gain: with *on* or *against*. [< L *informare* give form to, describe.] —Syn. **1** advise, apprise, acquaint, notify.

in·for·mal (in·fôr′məl) *adj.* **1** Not in the usual or prescribed form; unofficial. **2** Without ceremony or formality; casual. **3** Not requiring formal clothes. **4** Describing a manner of speech or writing characteristic of familiar conversation. —**in·for′mal·ly** *adv.*

in·for·mal·i·ty (in′fôr·mal′ə·tē) *n. pl.* ·**ties 1** Absence of regular or official form. **2** An informal act or proceeding.

in·for·mant (in·fôr′mənt) *n.* **1** One who imparts information. **2** A native speaker of a language whose speech is used by linguists in recording and studying linguistic forms, sounds, etc.

in·for·ma·tion (in′fər·mā′shən) *n.* **1** Knowledge acquired or derived. **2** Timely or specific knowledge. **3** In computer science: **a** Anything that reduces uncertainty. **b** A numerical measure of the degree to which uncertainty is reduced. **c** Coded material fed to a computer or communications system. —**in′for·ma′tion·al** *adj.*

information retrieval The methods by which recorded and stored information, as that in a computer, may be retrieved and made use of when required. —**in′for·ma′tion·re·triev′al** *adj.*

in·form·a·tive (in·fôr′mə·tiv) *adj.* Instructive; affording information. Also **in·form′a·to′ry.**

in·form·er (in·fôr′mər) *n.* **1** One who makes a complaint or accusations against others, usu. for gain. **2** One who imparts information.

infra- *prefix* Below; beneath; on the lower part: *infrastructure.* [L *infra*]

in·frac·tion (in·frak′shən) *n.* The act of breaking or violating a rule, law, agreement, etc. [< L *infringere* destroy]

in·fran·gi·ble (in·fran′jə·bəl) *adj.* **1** Not breakable or capable of being broken into parts. **2** Not to be infringed or violated. [< L *in*- not + *frangere* to break] —**in·fran′gi·bil′i·ty, in·fran′gi·ble·ness** *n.* —**in·fran′gi·bly** *adv.*

in·fra·red (in′frə·red′) *adj.* Designating electromagnetic waves having wavelengths exceeding those of visible red light but shorter than those of radio waves.

in·fra·struc·ture (in′frə·struk′chər) *n.* The essential elements of a structure, system, plan of operations, etc.

in·fre·quent (in·frē′kwənt) *adj.* Occurring at widely separate intervals; uncommon. —**in·fre′quence, in·fre′quen·cy** *n.* —**in·fre′quent·ly** *adv.*

in·fringe (in·frinj′) *v.t.* ·**fringed**, ·**fring·ing** To break or disregard the terms or requirements of, as an oath or law; violate. —**infringe on** (or **upon**) To transgress or trespass on rights or privileges. [< L *in*- in + *frangere* to break] —**in·fringe′ment, in·fring′er** *n.*

in·fu·ri·ate (in·fyoor′ē·āt) *v.t.* ·**at·ed**, ·**at·ing** To make furious. —*adj.* (-it) Infuriated; enraged. [< L *in*- in + *furia* rage] —**in·fu′ri·ate·ly, in·fu′ri·at′ing·ly** *adv.* —**in·fu′ri·a′tion** *n.*

in·fuse (in·fyooz′) *v.t.* ·**fused**, ·**fus·ing 1** To instill or inculcate, as principles or qualities. **2** To inspire; imbue; with *with.* **3** To pour in or upon. **4** To steep or soak so as to make an extract: to *infuse* tea leaves. [< L *in*- in + *fundere* pour] —**in·fus′er** *n.*

in·fus·i·ble (in·fyoo′zə·bəl) *adj.* Incapable of or resisting fusion or melting. —**in·fus′i·bil′i·ty, in·fus′i·ble·ness** *n.*

in·fu·sion (in·fyoo′zhən) *n.* **1** The act of infusing, imbuing, or pouring in. **2** That which is infused. **3** The process of steeping or soaking any substance in a liquid to extract its properties without boiling. **4** The liquid extract so obtained.

in·fu·so·ri·an (in′fyoo·sô′rē·ən, -sō′rē-) *n.* Any of various aquatic protozoans found in infusions of decaying matter, that move by vibrating cilia. —*adj.* Of or pertaining to such protozoans.

-ing *suffix* **1** The act or art of doing the action expressed in the root verb: *hunting.* **2** The product or result of an action: a *painting.* **3** Material for: *flooring.* **4** That which performs the action of the root verb: a *covering.* [< OE *-ung, -ing*]

-ing² *suffix* Used in the present participle of verbs and in participial adjectives: He is *talking;* an *eating* apple. [< OE *-ende*]

in·gen·ious (in·jēn′yəs) *adj.* **1** Possessed of skill in making or inventing. **2** Cleverly conceived or made. [< L *ingenium* natural ability] —**in·gen′ious·ly** *adv.* —**in·gen′ious·ness** *n.* —Syn. **1** adroit, clever, creative, resourceful.

in·gé·nue (an′zhə·nōō′, än′-, -jə-; *Fr.* aṅ·zhā·nü′) *n. pl.* **·nues** (-nōōz′; *Fr.* -nü′) **1** A young woman or girl who is artless, ingenuous, or innocent. **2** In the theater, the role of such a person. **3** An actress who fills such a role. Also **in′ge·nue.** [< L *ingenuus* natural]

in·ge·nu·i·ty (in′jə·nyōō′ə·tē) *n.* **1** Cleverness in making or originating. **2** Originality of execution or design.

in·gen·u·ous (in·jen′yōō·əs) *adj.* **1** Free from dissimulation; frank. **2** Innocent; artless. [< L *ingenuus* inborn, natural, frank] —**in·gen′u·ous·ly** *adv.* —**in·gen′u·ous·ness** *n.*

in·gest (in·jest′) *v.t.* To swallow or absorb, as a food, poison, etc. [< L *in-* in + *gerere* carry] —**in·ges′tion** *n.* —**in·ges′tive** *adj.*

in·gle·nook (ing′gəl·nōōk′) *n.* A corner by the fireplace. [Scot.]

in·glo·ri·ous (in·glôr′ē·əs, -glō′rē-) *adj.* **1** Characterized by failure or disgrace. **2** Without glory; obscure. —**in·glo′ri·ous·ly** *adv.* —**in·glo′ri·ous·ness** *n.*

in·go·ing (in′gō′ing) *adj.* Entering; going in.

in·got (ing′gət) *n.* A mass of cast metal from the crucible, as a bar of gold. [< IN-² + OE *geoton* pour]

in·graft (in·graft′, -gräft′) *v.t.* ENGRAFT.

in·grain (in·grān′) *v.t.* To fix deeply; impress indelibly upon the mind or character.

in·grained (in·grānd′) *adj.* **1** Deeply rooted; firmly fixed. **2** Thorough; inveterate.

in·grate (in′grāt) *n.* One who is ungrateful. [< L *in-* not + *gratus* pleasing]

in·gra·ti·ate (in·grā′shē·āt) *v.t.* **·at·ed, ·at·ing** To bring (oneself) into the favor or confidence of others. —**in·gra′ti·at′ing·ly** *adv.* —**in·gra′ti·a′tion** *n.* —**in·gra′ti·a·to·ry** (-ə·tôr′ē, -tō′rē) *adj.* [< L *in gratiam* in favor]

in·grat·i·tude (in·grat′ə·t⁄ōōd) *n.* Lack of gratitude; thanklessness.

in·gre·di·ent (in·grē′dē·ənt) *n.* **1** Any of the things that enter into the composition of a mixture. **2** A component part of anything. [< L *in-* in + *gradi* to walk]

in·gress (in′gres) *n.* **1** The right of entrance. **2** A place of entrance. **3** The act of entering. [< L *ingredi* enter] —**in·gres′sion, in·gres′sive·ness** *n.* —**in·gres′sive** *adj.*

in-group (in′grōōp′) *n.* Any group, usu. with common interests and goals, considered by its members to have a certain exclusiveness.

in·grown (in′grōn′) *adj.* **1** Grown into the flesh, as a toenail. **2** Growing inward or within. —**in′grow′ing** *adj.*

in·gui·nal (ing′gwə·nəl) *adj.* Of, pertaining to, or near the groin: an *inguinal* hernia. [< L *inguen* groin]

in·gulf (in·gulf′) *v.t.* ENGULF. —**in·gulf′ment** *n.*

in·hab·it (in·hab′it) *v.t.* To live or dwell in (a specified region, house, etc.); occupy as a home. [< L *in-* in + *habitare* dwell] —**in·hab′it·a·bil′i·ty, in·hab′i·ta′tion, in·hab′i·ter** *n.* —**in·hab′it·a·ble** *adj.*

in·hab·i·tant (in·hab′ə·tənt) *n.* One making his home in a specified region, house, etc.; a resident.

in·ha·lant (in·hā′lənt) *adj.* Used for inhaling. —*n.* A medicine, etc., to be inhaled in vapor form.

in·hale (in·hāl′) *v.* **·haled, ·hal·ing** *v.t.* To draw into the lungs, as breath or fumes; breathe in. —*v.i.* To draw breath, fumes, etc., into the lungs. [< L *in-* in + *halare* breathe] —**in·ha·la′tion** (in′hə·lā′shən) *n.*

in·hal·er (in·hā′lər) *n.* **1** One who inhales. **2** A device for administering a medicinal vapor, oxygen, etc.: also **in·ha·la·tor** (in′hə·lā′tər).

in·har·mon·ic (in′här·mon′ik) *adj.* Not harmonic; harsh in sound: also **in·har·mon′i·cal.**

in·har·mo·ni·ous (in′här·mō′nē·əs) *adj.* Lacking in harmony or agreement; in conflict. —**in′har·mo′ni·ous·ly** *adv.* —**in′har·mo′ni·ous·ness** *n.*

in·here (in·hir′) *v.i.* **·hered, ·her·ing** To be a permanent or essential part: with *in.* [< L *in-* in + *haerere* to stick]

in·her·ent (in·hir′ənt, -her′-) *adj.* Naturally and inseparably associated with a person or thing; innate. —**in·her′ence, in·her′en·cy** (*pl.* **·cies**) *n.* —**in·her′ent·ly** *adv.* —Syn. essential, natural, characteristic, instinctual, native.

in·her·it (in·her′it) *v.t.* **1** To receive, as property or a title, by succession or will; fall heir to. **2** To receive (traits, qualities, etc.) by or as if by heredity: She *inherits* her mother's good looks. —*v.i.* **3** To come into or possess an inheritance. [< L *in-* in + *heres* heir] —**in·her′i·tor** *n.*

in·her·it·a·ble (in·her′ə·tə·bəl) *adj.* **1** Capable of being passed on to heirs or descendants. **2** Qualified to take by inheritance. [< AF *enheritable*] —**in·her′it·a·bil′i·ty, in·her′it·a·ble·ness** *n.* —**in·her′it·a·bly** *adv.*

in·her·i·tance (in·her′ə·təns) *n.* **1** Anything acquired by succession: legacy. **2** The act of inheriting. **3** The right to inherit. **4** Physical, mental, or cultural characteristics derived from one's ancestry.

inheritance tax A tax imposed on an inherited estate.

in·hib·it (in·hib′it) *v.t.* **1** To keep from happening or from acting; block or prevent the action of. **2** To keep from spontaneous activity, feeling, etc.; restrain. **3** To forbid or prohibit. —*v.i.* **4** To cause inhibition. [< L *in-* in + *habere* have, hold] —**in·hib′it·a·ble, in·hib′i·tive, in·hib′i·to′ry** *adj.* —**in·hib′i·tor or in·hib′i·ter** *n.*

in·hi·bi·tion (in′hi·bish′ən, in′i-) *n.* **1** The act of inhibiting or the state of being inhibited. **2** The repression of an impulse, as by a mental process. **3** The process by which an impulse is repressed.

in·hos·pi·ta·ble (in·hos′pi·tə·bəl, in′hos·pit′ə·bəl) *adj.* **1** Not hospitable. **2** Affording no shelter or subsistence; barren. —**in·hos′pi·ta·ble·ness, in·hos′pi·tal′i·ty** (-tal′ə·tē) *n.* —**in·hos′pi·ta·bly** *adv.*

in·hu·man (in·hyōō′mən) *adj.* Not being or acting in accordance with the nobler qualities of human beings; brutal or savage. —**in·hu′man·ly** *adv.* —**in·hu′man·ness** *n.*

in·hu·mane (in′hyōō·mān′) *adj.* Not humane; having no compassion for others. —**in′hu·mane′ly** *adv.*

in·hu·man·i·ty (in′hyōō·man′ə·tē) *n. pl.* **·ties 1** The state of lacking human or humane qualities; cruelty. **2** A cruel act.

in·im·i·cal (in·im′i·kəl) *adj.* **1** Like an enemy; unfriendly. **2** Tending to hurt; adverse: *inimical* to the public welfare. [< L *in-* not + *amicus* friend] —**in·im′i·cal′i·ty** (-kal′ə·tē) *n.* —**in·im′i·cal·ly** *adv.* —Syn. **1** antagonistic, hostile, alien. **2** contrary, disadvantageous.

in·im·i·ta·ble (in·im′ə·tə·bəl) *adj.* That cannot be imitated; matchless. —**in·im′i·ta·bil′i·ty, in·im′i·ta·ble·ness** *n.* —**in·im′i·ta·bly** *adv.*

in·iq·ui·tous (in·ik′wə·təs) *adj.* Wicked; unjust. —**in·iq′ui·tous·ly** *adv.* —**in·iq′ui·tous·ness** *n.*

in·iq·ui·ty (in·ik′wə·tē) *n. pl* **·ties 1** Deviation from right; wickedness. **2** A wrongful or unjust act. [< L *iniquus* unequal]

init. initial; in the beginning (L *initio*).

in·i·tial (in·ish′əl) *adj.* Having to do with or standing at the beginning; first. —*n.* The first letter of a word, esp. a name. —*v.t.* **·tialed** or **·tialled, ·tial·ing** or **·tial·ling** To mark or sign with initials. [< L *initium* beginning]

in·i·tial·ly (in·ish′ə·lē) *adv.* At first; at the beginning.

Initial Teaching Alphabet An alphabet of 43 characters representing the sounds of English, used in teaching children to read.

in·i·ti·ate (in·ish′ē·āt) *v.t.* **·at·ed, ·at·ing 1** To begin; originate. **2** To introduce, as into a club, usu. with ceremony. **3** To instruct in fundamentals or principles. —*adj.* (-it, -āt) Initiated. —*n.* (-it, -āt) **1** One who is being or has been newly initiated. **2** One who is learned in some special field. [< L *initium* beginning] —**in·i′ti·a′tor** *n.* —Syn. **1** start, commence, inaugurate, invent, create.

in·i·ti·a·tion (in·ish′ē·ā′shən) *n.* **1** The act of initiating. **2** Ceremonial admission, as into a society.

in·i·ti·a·tive (in·ish′ē·ə·tiv) *n.* **1** A first move. **2** The ability for original conception and independent action. **3** The process by which the electorate initiates or enacts legislation. **4** The process by which a group of citizens may propose by petition a legislative measure to the voters. —*adj.*

Pertaining to initiation; preliminary. —in·i'ti·a·tive·ly *adv.*

in·i·ti·a·to·ry (in·ish'ē·ə·tôr'ē, -tō'rē) *adj.* 1 Introductory. 2 Serving to initiate.

in·ject (in·jekt') *v.t.* 1 To force in (a fluid) under pressure. 2 To introduce a fluid into by means of a syringe or hypodermic needle. 3 To introduce (something new or lacking): with *into:* to *inject* life into a party. 4 To throw in, as a remark, usu. by way of interruption. [<L *in-* in + *jacere* to throw] —in·jec'tion, in·jec'tor *n.*

in·ju·di·cious (in'jōō·dish'əs) *adj.* Not judicious or wise; wanting in judgment. —in'ju·di'cious·ly *adv.* —in'ju·di'cious·ness *n.*

in·junc·tion (in·jungk'shən) *n.* 1 The act of enjoining; a command. 2 *Law* A judicial order requiring the party enjoined to take or, usu., to refrain from some specified action. [<L *injungere* join to, enjoin]

in·jure (in'jər) *v.t.* ·jured, ·jur·ing 1 To do harm or hurt to: 2 To do wrong to; treat with injustice. [<L *injuria* injury] —in'jur·er *n.*

in·ju·ri·ous (in·jŏŏr'ē·əs) *adj.* 1 Hurtful or harmful. 2 Offensive; insulting; abusive. —in·ju'ri·ous·ly *adv.* —in·ju'ri·ous·ness *n.*

in·ju·ry (in'jər·ē) *n. pl.* ·ries 1 Harm or damage, esp. to the body. 2 A wrong or injustice done to another. [<L *injurius* unjust]

in·jus·tice (in·jus'tis) *n.* 1 The violation or denial of justice. 2 An unjust act; a wrong.

ink (ingk) *n.* 1 A colored liquid or viscous substance, used in writing, printing, etc. 2 The dark fluid ejected by a cuttlefish, octopus, etc. —*v.t.* To spread ink upon; mark or color with ink. [<LL *encaustum* purple ink] —ink'er *n.*

ink·horn (ingk'hôrn') *n.* A small vessel made of horn, formerly used to hold ink.

ink·ling (ingk'ling) *n.* A slight intimation; a faint notion; hint. [ME *inkle* hint]

ink·stand (ingk'stand') *n.* A rack for holding pens and an inkwell.

ink·well (ingk'wel') *n.* A small container for ink.

ink·y (ingk'kē) *adj.* ink·i·er, ink·i·est 1 Consisting of, stained with, like, or containing ink. 2 Black. —ink'i·ness *n.*

in·laid (in·lād', in·lād') *adj.* 1 Inserted into a surface so as to form a decorative design. 2 Having a surface decorated in such a way.

Inlaid decoration

in·land (in'lənd) *adj.* 1 Remote from the sea. 2 Located in or limited to the interior of a country. 3 Not foreign; domestic. —*n.* (in'lənd, -land') The interior of a country. —*adv.* (in'lənd, -land') Toward the interior of a land.

in·law (in'lô') *n. Informal* A relative by marriage.

in·lay (in·lā', in'lā') *v.t.* in·laid, in·lay·ing 1 To set decorative patterns or designs of (ivory, gold, etc.) into the surface of an object. 2 To decorate by inserting such patterns or designs. —*n.* (in'lā) 1 That which is inlaid. 2 A pattern or design so produced. 3 A filling made to fit into a tooth cavity and then cemented in place. —in'lay'er *n.*

in·let (in'let) *n.* 1 A small body of water connected to a larger one. 2 An entrance, as to a culvert.

in loc. cit. in the place cited (L *in loco citato*).

in lo·co pa·ren·tis (in lō'kō pə·ren'tis) *Latin* In the place of a parent.

in·ly (in'lē) *adv.* 1 In the inner parts; inwardly. 2 Thoroughly.

in·mate (in'māt) *n.* 1 One who is kept or confined in an institution, hospital, prison, etc. 2 One who lives in a place with others. [?]

in me·di·as res (in mē'dē·əs rāz', rēz') *Latin* In the midst of things; into the heart of the matter.

in me·mo·ri·am (in mə·môr'ē·əm, -mō'rē-) *Latin* In memory (of); as a memorial (to).

in·most (in'mōst') *adj.* 1 Farthest from the exterior. 2 Most secret or most intimate.

inn (in) *n.* 1 A place providing lodging and meals for travelers; hotel. 2 A restaurant or tavern. [<OE <*inn* in]

in·nards (in'ərdz) *n. pl. Informal* Inner or interior parts or organs; the insides.

in·nate (i·nāt', in'āt) *adj.* Native to or original with the individual; inborn. [<L *in-* in + *nasci* be born] —in·nate'ly *adv.* —in·nate'ness *n.* —Syn. congenital, inherent, natural.

in·ner (in'ər) *adj.* 1 At a point farther in or inward; interior. 2 Of or pertaining to the mind or spirit. 3 Private or secret: *inner* feelings. —in'ner·ly *adv.* —in'ner·ness *n.*

inner city A central part of a large city, usu. characterized by poverty and often populated by minority groups. —in'ner·cit'y *adj.*

inner ear The innermost part of the ear, the essential organ of hearing, containing the cochlea, the auditory nerve, and the semicircular canals that govern equilibrium.

in·ner·most (in'ər·mōst') *adj.* Inmost; farthest within. —*n.* The inmost part, thing, or place.

inner tube A flexible, inflatable tube, used to hold the air in some tires.

in·ning (in'ing) *n.* 1 In baseball, the period in which one team is at bat, completed by three outs. 2 *Often pl.* The period during which a party or person is in power. [<OE *innung,* gerund of *innian* put in]

inn·keep·er (in'kē'pər) *n.* The proprietor of an inn.

in·no·cence (in'ə·səns) *n.* 1 The condition of being free from evil or guile. 2 Childlike simplicity. 3 Freedom from guilt, as for some specific crime or charge. Also in'no·cen·cy (*pl.* ·cies).

in·no·cent (in'ə·sənt) *adj.* 1 Free from evil, guile, or wrongdoing. 2 Free from the guilt of a specific crime or charge. 3 Free from qualities that can harm: *innocent* pastimes. 4 Not maliciously intended: an *innocent* remark. —*n.* One ignorant of evil, as a young child. [<L *in-* not + *nocere* to harm] —in'no·cent·ly *adv.*

in·noc·u·ous (i·nok'yōō·əs) *adj.* 1 Having no harmful qualities. 2 Not stimulating or controversial; banal, inoffensive, etc. [<L *in-* not + *nocuus* harmful] —in·noc'u·ous·ly *adv.* —in·noc'u·ous·ness *n.*

in·nom·i·nate bone (i·nom'ə·nit) The large, irregular bone, consisting of the ilium, ischium, and pubis, which in the adult grow together; the hipbone. [<LL *innominatus* without specific name]

in·no·vate (in'ō·vāt, in'ə-) *v.* ·vat·ed, ·vat·ing *v.i.* To make changes or alterations in; bring in new ideas, methods, etc. [<L *in-* in + *novare* make new] —in'no·va'tive *adj.* —in'no·va'tor *n.*

in·no·va·tion (in'ō·vā'shən, in'ə-) *n.* 1 The act of innovating. 2 Something new; a change or novelty.

in·nox·ious (i·nok'shəs) *adj.* Free from harmful qualities. [<L *in-* not + *noxius* noxious]

in·nu·en·do (in'yōō·en'dō) *n. pl.* ·dos or ·does An indirect suggestion, remark, etc., usu. disparaging; insinuation. [L, by nodding at, intimating]

in·nu·mer·a·ble (i·n'ⁿyōō'mər·ə·bəl) *adj.* Too numerous to be counted; myriad. —in·nu'mer·a·bil'i·ty, in·nu'mer·a·ble·ness *n.* —in·nu'mer·a·bly *adv.*

in·nu·mer·a·cy (in·n'ⁿyōō'mər·ə·sē) *n.* The state of being innumerate.

in·nu·mer·ate (in·n'ⁿyōō'mər·it) *adj.* Unable to understand the basic concepts of mathematics.

in·oc·u·late (in·ok'yə·lāt) *v.t.* ·lat·ed, ·lat·ing 1 To immunize (a person or animal) by administering a serum or vaccine to. 2 To introduce microorganisms into (a culture medium, soil, an animal or plant, etc.). 3 To implant ideas, opinions, etc., in the mind of. [<L *inoculare* engraft an eye or bud] —in·oc'u·la·ble, in·oc'u·la·tive *adj.* —in·oc'u·la'tion, in·oc'u·la'tor *n.*

in·of·fen·sive (in'ə·fen'siv) *adj.* Giving no offense; causing nothing displeasing or harmful. —in'of·fen'sive·ly *adv.* —in'of·fen'sive·ness *n.*

in·op·er·a·ble (in·op'ər·ə·bəl) *adj.* 1 Not suitable for surgical procedures. 2 Not practicable.

in·op·er·a·tive (in·op'ər·ə·tiv) *adj.* Having no effect or result; ineffectual. —in·op'er·a·tive·ness *n.*

in·op·por·tune (in·op'ər·t'ⁿyōōn') *adj.* Untimely, inappropriate, or inconvenient. —in·op'por·tune'ly *adv.* —in·op'por·tune'ness *n.*

in·or·di·nate (in·ôr'də·nit) *adj.* Not restrained by prescribed rules or bounds; immoderate. —in·or'di·na·cy (-nə·sē), in·or'di·nate·ness *n.* —in·or'di·nate·ly *adv.* —Syn. excessive, exorbitant, extravagant, unreasonable.

in·or·gan·ic (in'ôr·gan'ik) *adj.* 1 Devoid of organized vital structure; not being animal or vegetable. 2 Not the result of living or organic processes. —**in′or·gan′i·cal·ly** *adv.*

inorganic chemistry The branch of chemistry that treats of substances lacking carbon but includes the carbonates and cyanides.

in per·pet·u·um (in pər·pech′ōō·əm) *Latin* Forever; perpetually.

in·put (in′pŏŏt′) *n.* 1 Something put into a system or device, as energy into a machine, food into the body, data into a computer, or a signal into an electronic device. 2 A place or point of introduction, as of data into a computer. 3 An effect or influence resulting from contributing opinions, information, suggestions, etc.: The staff had real *input* in the directive.

in·quest (in′kwest) *n.* A judicial inquiry, aided by a jury, into a matter, esp. a death possibly resulting from a crime. [< L *inquisita (res)* (thing) inquired (into)]

in·quiet (in·kwī′ət) *adj.* Restless; uneasy. —**in·qui′e·tude** (·ə·t⁄ōōd′) *n.*

in·quire (in·kwīr′) *v.* ·quired, ·quir·ing *v.t.* 1 To seek information about. —*v.i.* 2 To ask questions; make inquiries. 3 To make investigation; search into carefully: with *into.* —**inquire after** To ask about the well-being of. [< L *into + quaerere* seek] —**in·quir′er** *n.* —**in·quir′ing·ly** *adv.*

in·quir·y (in·kwīr′ē, in′kwə·rē) *n. pl.* ·quir·ies 1 The act of inquiring. 2 Investigation; research. 3 A query.

in·qui·si·tion (in′kwə·zish′ən) *n.* 1 An investigation. 2 The proceedings and findings of a jury of inquest. 3 Any searching examination or questioning. [< L *inquisitio*] —**in′qui·si′tion·al** *adj.* —**in′qui·si′tion·al·ly** *adv.*

in·qui·si·tion (in′kwə·zish′ən) *n.* 1 A former tribunal of the Roman Catholic Church appointed to examine and punish heretics. 2 The activities of this tribunal.

in·quis·i·tive (in·kwiz′ə·tiv) *adj.* 1 Given to questioning, esp. to satisfy curiosity. 2 Inclined to the pursuit of knowledge. —**in·quis′i·tive·ly** *adv.* —**in·quis′i·tive·ness** *n.*

in·quis·i·tor (in·kwiz′ə·ter) *n.* 1 One who makes an official investigation. 2 *Often cap.* An official of the Inquisition.

in·quis·i·to·ri·al (in·kwiz′ə·tôr′ē·əl, -tō′rē-, in′kwiz-) *adj.* 1 After the manner of an inquisitor; disposed to ask searching questions. 2 Pertaining to a court of inquisition or to an inquisitor. —**in·quis′i·to′ri·al·ly** *adv.*

in re (in rē′) *Latin Law* In the case or matter of; concerning: *in re* Smith vs. Jones.

I.N.R.I. Jesus of Nazareth, King of the Jews (L *Iesus Nazarenus Rex Iudaeorum*).

in·road (in′rōd′) *n.* 1 A hostile entrance into a country or territory; a raid. 2 Any detrimental encroachment: *inroads* upon one's health.

in·rush (in′rush′) *n.* A sudden rushing in. —**in·rush·ing** *adj.*

ins. inches; inspector; insurance.

in·sane (in·sān′) *adj.* 1 Foolish, extravagant, or impractical. 2 Mentally ill; deranged. 3 Too mentally disturbed to be legally responsible. —**in·sane′ly** *adv.* —**in·sane′ness** *n.*

in·san·i·tar·y (in·san′ə·ter′ē) *adj.* Not clean; unhealthful. —**in·san′i·tar′i·ness, in·san′i·ta′tion** *n.*

in·san·i·ty (in·san′ə·tē) *n. pl.* ·ties 1 Irrationality; extreme folly. 2 Mental illness; derangement. 3 *Law* Mental unsoundness to the degree of being not responsible in various legally defined respects. • *Insanity* and *insane* are no longer scientific terms in medicine and psychiatry and have been replaced by more specific terms describing various states of mental illness. However, both words are still acceptable in legal parlance.

in·sa·tia·ble (in·sā′shə·bəl, -shē·ə·bəl) *adj.* Not to be sated or satisfied; unappeasable. Also **in·sa′ti·ate** (-it). —**in·sa′ti·a·bil′i·ty, in·sa′tia·ble·ness** *n.* —**in·sa′tia·bly** *adv.*

in·scribe (in·skrīb′) *v.t.* ·scribed, ·scrib·ing 1 To write or engrave (signs, words, names, etc.). 2 To mark the surface of with engraved or written characters. 3 To dedicate, as a book. 4 To enter the name of on a list. 5 *Geom.* To enclose (a figure) within another so that a particular subset of the points in one figure coincides with points in the other. [< L *in-* on, in + *scribere* write] —**in·scrib′er** *n.*

in·scrip·tion (in·skrip′shən) *n.* 1 The act of inscribing, or that which is inscribed. 2 Incised or relief lettering on a durable object. 3 An entry in a list, roll, etc. 4 A dedication written in a book or the like. —**in·scrip′tion·al, in·scrip′tive** *adj.*

in·scru·ta·ble (in·skrōō′tə·bəl) *adj.* That cannot be searched into; incomprehensible. [< L *in-* not + *scrutare* look at] —**in·scru′ta·bil′i·ty, in·scru′ta·ble·ness** *n.* —**in·scru′ta·bly** *adv.* —**Syn.** enigmatic, impenetrable, mysterious.

in·sect (in′sekt) *n.* 1 Any of a large class of arthropods having three distinct body segments, three pairs of legs, one pair of antennae, and usu. two pairs of wings. 2 Loosely, any small invertebrate resembling an insect, as spiders, centipedes, ticks, etc. [< L *(animal) insectum* (animal) notched] —**in·sec′te·an** (-sek′tē·ən) *adj.*

Insect (cicada killer)
a. abdomen. b. thorax.
c. head. d. antenna.

in·sec·ti·cide (in·sek′tə·sīd) *n.* Any substance that kills insects.

in·sec·ti·vore (in·sek′tə·vôr, -vōr) *n.* 1 Any of an order of insect-eating mammals, as shrews, moles, and hedgehogs. 2 Any animal or plant that feeds on insects. —**in·sec·tiv·o·rous** (in′sek·tiv′ər·əs) *adj.*

in·se·cure (in′sə·kyŏŏr′) *adj.* 1 Not secure or safe: *insecure* footing. 2 In danger of breaking or failing; not firm or stable. 3 Not confident; anxious; uncertain. —**in′se·cure′ly** *adv.* —**in′se·cure′ness, in·se·cu·ri·ty** (in′sə·kyŏŏr′ə·tē) *n.*

in·sem·i·nate (in·sem′ə·nāt) *v.t.* ·nat·ed, ·nat·ing 1 To impregnate by injecting semen. 2 To implant ideas in. 3 To sow seeds in, as soil. [< L *in-* in + *seminare* to sow] —**in·sem′i·na′tion** *n.*

in·sen·sate (in·sen′sāt, -sit) *adj.* 1 Showing a lack of sense or reason. 2 Hard-hearted; cruel. 3 Inanimate. —**in·sen′sate·ly** *adv.* —**in·sen′sate·ness** *n.*

in·sen·si·ble (in·sen′sə·bəl) *adj.* 1 Not capable of or deprived of perception or feeling. 2 Unconscious. 3 Indifferent, unaware, or apathetic. 4 Inanimate. 5 Imperceptible. —**in·sen′si·bil′i·ty, in·sen′si·ble·ness** *n.* —**in·sen′si·bly** *adv.*

in·sen·si·tive (in·sen′sə·tiv) *adj.* 1 Not sensitive to impressions. 2 Unresponsive to the feelings of others. —**in·sen′si·tive·ly** *adv.* —**in·sen′si·tive·ness, in·sen′si·tiv′i·ty** *n.*

in·sen·ti·ent (in·sen′shē·ənt, -shənt) *adj.* Inanimate. —**in·sen′ti·ence, in·sen′ti·en·cy** *n.*

in·sep·a·ra·ble (in·sep′ər·ə·bəl) *adj.* Incapable of being separated or disjoined: *inseparable* friends. —**in·sep′a·ra·ble·ness** *n.* —**in·sep′a·ra·bly** *adv.*

in·sert (in·sûrt′) *v.t.* 1 To put or place into something else. 2 To put between or among other things. —*n.* (in′sûrt) 1 That which is inserted. 2 A circular or the like placed within a newspaper or book for mailing. [< L *in-* in + *serere* place, join] —**in·sert′er** *n.*

in·ser·tion (in·sûr′shən) *n.* 1 The act of inserting, or the state of being inserted. 2 That which is inserted, as lace or embroidery placed between pieces of plain fabric. 3 Additional or explanatory material inserted in a written or printed page.

in·set (in·set′) *v.t.* To set in; implant. —*n.* (in′set′) 1 A leaf or leaves inserted, as in a book or newspaper. 2 Influx, as of the tide.

in·shore (in′shôr′, -shōr′, in′shôr′, -shōr′) *adj.* 1 Being or occurring near the shore. 2 Coming toward the shore. —*adv.* Toward the shore.

in·side (in′sīd′, -sīd′) *n.* 1 The side, surface, or part that is within. 2 That which is contained; contents. 3 Inner thoughts or feelings. 4 *pl. Informal* Inner organs; entrails. —*adj.* 1 Situated or occurring on or in the inside. 2 Suited for or pertaining to the inside. 3 For use indoors: *inside* paint. 4 Private; confidential: *inside* reports. —*adv.* (in′. sīd′) 1 In or into the interior. 2 Indoors. —**inside out** 1 Reversed so that the inside is exposed. 2 Thoroughly; completely. —*prep.* (in′sīd′) In or into the interior of; within. —**inside of** *Informal* Within the time or distance of.

in·sid·er (in·sī′dər) *n.* **1** One who is a member of a special group. **2** One who has special information or advantages.

in·sid·i·ous (in·sid′ē·əs) *adj.* **1** Designed to entrap; full of wiles. **2** Doing or contriving harm. **3** Awaiting a chance to harm. **4** Causing harm by stealthy, usu. imperceptible means: an *insidious* disease. [< L *insidere* sit in, lie in wait] —**in·sid′i·ous·ly** *adv.* —**in·sid′i·ous·ness** *n.*

in·sight (in′sīt′) *n.* **1** Intellectual discernment. **2** A perception of the inner nature of a thing; intuition.

in·sig·ni·a (in·sig′nē·ə) *n. sing. or pl.* **1** A badge, emblem, etc., used as a mark of office or distinction. **2** Something significant or indicative of a calling. [< L *in-* + *signum* sign, emblem] • In Latin and formerly in English, *insignia* was the plural form of **in·sig·ne** (in·sig′nē). Now, however, *insignia* has virtually replaced *insigne* in the singular. The plural form *insignias* is well established, although *insignia* is still sometimes used in its original plural sense.

in·sig·nif·i·cant (in′sig·nif′ə·kənt) *adj.* **1** Not significant; without importance. **2** Meaningless. **3** Without dignity; not imposing: an *insignificant* person. —**in′sig·nif′i·cance, in′sig·nif′i·can·cy** *n.* —**in′sig·nif′i·cant·ly** *adv.* —**Syn. 1** petty, trifling, trivial. **2** immaterial, irrelevant.

in·sin·cere (in′sin·sir′) *adj.* Not sincere, honest, or genuine; hypocritical. —**in′sin·cere′ly** *adv.*

in·sin·cer·i·ty (in′sin·ser′ə·tē) *n. pl.* **·ties 1** Lack of sincerity. **2** An insincere act, remark, etc.

in·sin·u·ate (in·sin′yōō·āt) *v.t.* **·at·ed, ·at·ing 1** To indicate slyly or deviously. **2** To infuse or instill gradually or subtly into the mind. **3** To introduce gradually, artfully, or stealthily: to *insinuate* oneself into an enviable position. [< L *insinuare* to curve] —**in·sin′u·a′ting·ly** *adv.* —**in·sin′u·a′tive** *adj.* —**in·sin′u·a′tor** *n.*

in·sin·u·a·tion (in·sin′yōō·ā′shən) **1** The act of insinuating. **2** An injurious suggestion or implication. **3** A subtly ingratiating act, remark, etc.

in·sip·id (in·sip′id) *adj.* **1** Without flavor; tasteless. **2** Unexciting; dull. [< L *in-* not + *sapidus* savory] —**in·sip′id·ly** *adv.* —**in·sip′id·ness** *n.*

in·si·pid·i·ty (in′si·pid′ə·tē) *n. pl.* **·ties 1** The quality of being insipid. **2** An insipid person or thing.

in·sist (in·sist′) *v.i.* **1** To make emphatic or repeated assertion, demand, or request: often with *on* or *upon* —*v.t.* **2** To state or demand emphatically: He *insisted* that he was right. [< L *in-* on + *sistere* to stand] —**in·sis′tence, in·sis′ten·cy** *n.*

in·sis·tent (in·sis′tənt) *adj.* **1** Emphatic; urgent. **2** Standing out prominently; conspicuous: *insistent* colors. —**in·sist′ence, in·sist′en·cy** *n.* (*pl.* **·cies**) —**in·sis′tent·ly** *adv.*

in si·tu (in sī′t′yōō, si′-) *Latin* In its original site or position.

in·snare (in·snâr′) *v.t.* **·snared, ·snar·ing** ENSNARE.

in·so·bri·e·ty (in′sə·brī′ə·tē) *n.* Lack of moderation, esp. in drinking.

in·so·far (in′sō·fär′) *adv.* To such extent: usu. with *as.*

in·sole (in′sōl′) *n.* **1** The fixed inner sole of a boot or shoe. **2** A removable inner sole used to improve the fit of a shoe.

in·so·lence (in′sə·ləns) *n.* The quality of being insolent; offensive impertinence.

in·so·lent (in′sə·lənt) *adj.* **1** Defiantly offensive in language or manner. **2** Grossly disrespectful. [< L *insolens* unusual, haughty] —**in′so·lent·ly** *adv.*

in·sol·u·ble (in·sol′yə·bəl) *adj.* **1** Not capable of being dissolved, as in a liquid; not soluble. **2** That cannot be explained or solved. —**in·sol′u·bil′i·ty, in·sol′u·ble·ness** *n.* —**in·sol′u·bly** *adv.*

in·solv·a·ble (in·sol′və·bəl) *adj.* Not able to be explained or solved; insoluble. —**in·sol′va·bly** *adv.*

in·sol·vent (in·sol′vənt) *adj.* **1** Unable to meet the claims of creditors; bankrupt. **2** Inadequate for the payment of debts. **3** Of or pertaining to bankrupts. —*n.* A bankrupt person. —**in·sol′ven·cy** *n.* (*pl.* **·cies**)

in·som·ni·a (in·som′nē·ə) *n.* Chronic inability to sleep. [< L *insomnis* sleepless] —**in·som′ni·ac′** (-nē·ak′) *n.*

in·so·much (in′sō·much′) *adv.* **1** To such a degree or extent: used with *that* or *as.* **2** Since: used with *as.*

in·sou·ci·ance (in·sōō′sē·əns; *Fr.* aṅ·sōō·syäns′) *n.* Carefree unconcern; heedlessness. [F]

in·sou·ci·ant (in·sōō′sē·ənt; *Fr.* aṅ·sōō·syäṅ′) *adj.* With-

out concern or care; carefree. [F< *in-* not + *souciant*, pr. p. of *soucier* to care] —**in·sou′ci·ant·ly** *adv.*

insp. inspected; inspector.

in·spect (in·spekt′) *v.t.* **1** To look at or examine carefully. **2** To examine or review officially, as troops. [< L *in-* into + *specere* to look] —**Syn. 1** investigate, scan, scrutinize.

in·spec·tion (in·spek′shən) *n.* **1** A critical viewing or investigation. **2** An official examination. —**in·spec′tion·al** *adj.*

in·spec·tor (in·spek′tər) *n.* **1** One who inspects. **2** An officer of the police usu. ranking next below the superintendent. —**in·spec′tor·al, in′spec·to′ri·al** (-tôr′ē·əl, -tō′rē-) *adj.* —**in·spec′tor·ship′** *n.*

in·spi·ra·tion (in′spə·rā′shən) *n.* **1** The infusion of an idea, an emotion, or mental influence. **2** That which is so infused. **3** A stimulus to creativity in thought or action. **4** The state or quality of being inspired. **5** Divine or supernatural influence. **6** A person or thing that inspires. **7** The act of drawing air into the lungs. —**in′spi·ra′tion·al** *adj.* —**in′spi·ra′tion·al·ly** *adv.*

in·spire (in·spīr′) *v.* **·spired, ·spir·ing** *v.t.* **1** To stir or affect by some mental or spiritual influence: stimulate. **2** To imbue with a specified idea or feeling: to *inspire* survivors with hope. **3** To give rise to: Fear *inspires* hatred. **4** To motivate or cause by supernatural influence. **5** To draw into the lungs; inhale. **6** To prompt the saying or writing of indirectly: This rumor was *inspired* by my enemies. — *v.i.* **7** To draw in breath; inhale. **8** To give or provide inspiration. [< L *inspirare* breathe into] —**in·spir′a·ble** *adj.* —**in·spir′er** *n.* —**in·spir′ing·ly** *adv.*

in·spir·it (in·spir′it) *v.t.* To fill with spirit or life; exhilarate. —**in·spir′it·ing·ly** *adv.*

in·spis·sate (in·spis′āt) *v.t. & v.i.* **·sat·ed, ·sat·ing** To thicken, as by evaporation; condense. —*adj.* Thickened; condensed. [< L *in-* thoroughly + *spissare* thicken] —**in·spis·sa·tion** (in′spi·sā′shən) **in′spis·sa′tor** *n.*

Inst. Institute; Institution.

inst. instant; instantaneous; instrument.

in·sta·bil·i·ty (in′stə·bil′ə·tē) *n. pl.* **·ties 1** Lack of stability or firmness. **2** Inconstancy; changeableness. **3** Flimsiness of construction.

in·sta·ble (in·stā′bəl) *adj.* UNSTABLE.

in·stall (in·stôl′) *v.t.* **1** To place in office, etc., with formal ceremony. **2** To establish in a place or position. **3** To place in position for service or use. [< Med. L *in-* in + *stallare* to seat] —**in·stal·la·tion** (in′stə·lā′shən), **in·stall′er** *n.*

in·stall·ment¹ (in·stôl′mənt) *n.* **1** A partial payment of a price due, made at regular intervals. **2** One of several parts of anything furnished at different times, as written material appearing serially in a magazine, newspaper, etc. Also **in·stal′ment.** [< obs. *estall* arrange payments < OF *estaler* stop, fix]

in·stall·ment² (in·stôl′mənt) *n.* The act of installing or the state of being installed. Also **in·stal′ment.**

installment plan The paying for goods or services by means of installments.

in·stance (in′stəns) *n.* **1** Something offered or occurring as an example; a case. **2** The act of suggesting or urging; a request. **3** A step in proceeding: in the first *instance.* — **for instance** For example. —*v.t.* **·stanced, ·stanc·ing 1** To refer to an illustration or example. **2** To serve as an example of; exemplify. [< L *instantia* a standing near]

in·stant (in′stənt) *adj.* **1** Immediately impending; imminent. **2** Of the current month. **3** Direct; immediate: an *instant* result. **4** Urgent: an *instant* need for help. **5** Available in premixed or soluble form for quick preparation, as pudding, coffee, etc. —*n.* **1** A particular point of time. **2** A very brief portion of time; moment. —**the instant** As soon as. [< OF < L *in-* upon + *stare* to stand]

in·stan·ta·ne·ous (in′stən·tā′nē·əs) *adj.* **1** Acting or done instantly. **2** Of or at a particular instant. —**in′stan·ta′ne·ous·ly** *adv.* —**in′stan·ta′ne·ous·ness** *n.*

in·stan·ter (in·stan′tər) *adv.* Without an instant of delay. [< L]

in·stant·ly (in′stənt·lē) *adv.* Immediately; at once.

in·state (in·stāt′) *v.t.* **·stat·ed, ·stat·ing** To establish in a certain office or rank; induct.

in·stead (in·sted′) *adv.* In one's or its stead or place: Give me that *instead.* —**instead of** In place of.

in·step (in′step′) *n.* 1 The upper part of the human foot from the toes to the ankle. 2 That part of a shoe, stocking, etc., that covers the instep.

in·sti·gate (in′stə-gāt) *v.t.* ·gat·ed, ·gat·ing 1 To bring about by inciting; foment. 2 To urge or incite to an action or course. [< L *instigare*] —**in′sti·ga′tion, in′sti·ga′tor** *n.* —**in′· sti·ga′tive** *adj.*

in·still (in·stil′) *v.t.* ·stilled, ·still·ing 1 To put into the mind gradually, as if drop by drop. 2 To pour in by drops. Also **in·stil′.** [< L *instillare* to drop, drip] —**in′stil·la′tion** (in′stə-lā′shən), **in·stil′ler, in·still′ment** or **in·stil′ment** *n.*

in·stinct (in′stingkt) *n.* 1 The innate ability of animals to perform functions peculiar to each species without training. 2 A natural aptitude. —*adj.* (in·stingkt′) Imbued or filled with: a picture *instinct* with life. [< L *instinguere* impel]

in·stinc·tive (in·stingk′tiv) *adj.* Of the nature of, or prompted by, instinct; innate: also **in·stinc′tu·al** (-chōō·əl). —**in·stinc′tive·ly** *adv.*

in·sti·tute (in′stə·tyōot′) *v.t.* ·tut·ed, ·tut·ing 1 To establish; found. 2 To set in operation; initiate. 3 To appoint to an office, position, etc. —*n.* 1 An established organization or society pledged to some special purpose and work. 2 The building occupied by such an organization. 3 An established principle, rule, or order. [< L *in-* in, on + *statuere* set up, stand] —**in′sti·tut′er, in′sti·tu′tor** *n.* —**Syn.** *v.* 1 erect, install, set up. 2 begin, commence, start.

in·sti·tu·tion (in′stə·tyōo′shən) *n.* 1 An established principle, law, or usage. 2 A corporate body or establishment organized for an educational, medical, charitable, or similar purpose. 3 The building occupied by such an establishment. 4 The act of instituting or establishing: the *institution* of an investigation. 5 *Informal* A well-known person or thing.

in·sti·tu·tion·al (in′stə·tyōo′shən·əl) *adj.* 1 Of, like, or pertaining to an institution. 2 Designating a form of advertising intended to promote good will and prestige, rather than to get immediate sales. —**in′sti·tu′tion·al·ly** *adv.*

in·sti·tu·tion·al·ize (in′stə·tyōo′shən·əl·īz) *v.t.* ·ized, ·iz·ing 1 To make institutional. 2 To turn into or regard as an institution. 3 *Informal* To put (someone) in an institution.

in·struct (in·strukt′) *v.t.* 1 To impart knowledge or skill to, esp. by systematic method. 2 To give specific orders or directions to. 3 To give information or explanation to; inform. [< L *in-* in + *struere* build]

in·struc·tion (in·struk′shən) *n.* 1 The act of instructing; teaching. 2 Imparted knowledge. 3 The act of giving specific directions or commands. 4 *pl.* The directions given. —**in·struc′tion·al** *adj.*

in·struc·tive (in·struk′tiv) *adj.* Serving to instruct; conveying knowledge; informative. —**in·struc′tive·ly** *adv.* —**in·struc′tive·ness** *n.*

in·struc·tor (in·struk′tər) *n.* 1 One who instructs; a teacher. 2 In the U.S., a college teacher of lower rank than the lowest professorial grade. —**in·struc′tor·ship** *n.*

in·stru·ment (in′strə·mənt) *n.* 1 A means by which work is done; an implement or tool. 2 A device for making measurements, records, etc. 3 Any means of accomplishment. 4 A device for the production of musical sounds. 5 A person doing the will of another. 6 *Law* A formal document, as a contract, deed, etc. [< L *instrumentum* < *instruere* fit out]

in·stru·men·tal (in′strə·men′təl) *adj.* 1 Serving as a means or instrument; serviceable. 2 For or produced by musical instruments. 3 Done by or pertaining to a mechanical instrument or a tool. —**in·stru·men′tal·ly** *adv.*

in·stru·men·tal·ist (in′strə·men′təl·ist) *n.* One who plays a musical instrument.

in·stru·men·tal·i·ty (in′strə·men·tal′ə·tē) *n.* *pl.* ·ties 1 The condition of being instrumental. 2 That which is instrumental; means.

in·stru·men·ta·tion (in′strə·men·tā′shən) *n.* 1 *Music* The arranging of compositions for performance by instruments. 2 The technique of using precision instruments.

instrument panel The panel containing the indicators

of performance in an automobile, airplane, or other apparatus. Also **instrument board.**

in·sub·or·di·nate (in′sə·bôr′də·nit) *adj.* Not obedient; not submitting to authority. —*n.* A disobedient person.

in·sub·or·di·na·tion (in′sə·bôr′də·nā′shən) *n.* An act of being disobedient to constituted authorities.

in·sub·stan·tial (in′səb·stan′shəl) *adj.* 1 Not substantial; flimsy. 2 Not material; unreal. —**in′sub·stan′ti·al′i·ty** (-shē·al′ə·tē) *n.*

in·suf·fer·a·ble (in·suf′ər·ə·bəl, -rə·bəl) *adj.* Not to be endured; intolerable. —**in·suf′fer·a·ble·ness** *n.* —**in·suf′fer·a·bly** *adv.*

in·suf·fi·cien·cy (in′sə·fish′ən·sē) *n.* *pl.* ·cies Lack of sufficiency; inadequacy in amount, power, etc.; deficiency.

in·suf·fi·cient (in′sə·fish′ənt) *adj.* Inadequate for some need, purpose, or use. —**in′suf·fi′cient·ly** *adv.*

in·su·lar (in′syə·lər) *adj.* 1 Of or pertaining to an island or its inhabitants. 2 Standing alone; isolated. 3 Not broad, liberal, or cosmopolitan: *insular* ideas. [< L *insula* island] —**in′su·lar·ism, in·su·lar·i·ty** (in′syə·lar′ə·tē) *n.*

in·su·late (in′sə·lāt) *v.t.* ·lat·ed, ·lat·ing 1 To place in a detached state or situation; isolate. 2 To apply (to walls, electric wiring, etc.) a nonconducting substance or device. 3 To prevent or slow the passage of heat, electricity, sound, or other energy to or from. [< L *insula* island]

in·su·la·tion (in′sə·lā′shən) *n.* 1 The act of insulating. 2 Any nonconducting material used in insulating.

in·su·la·tor (in′sə·lā′tər) *n.* 1 One who or that which insulates. 2 A nonconducting substance or device used to insulate.

in·su·lin (in′sə·lin) *n.* 1 A hormone essential for carbohydrate metabolism, secreted by island cells in the pancreas. 2 A preparation of this hormone made from animal pancreas and used to control diabetes. [< NL *insula* island]

in·sult (in·sult′) *v.t.* To treat with insolence, contempt, or rudeness. —*n.* (in′sult) Something offensive said or done; an indignity. [< L *insultare* leap at, insult] —**in·sult′er** *n.* —**in·sult′ing·ly** *adv.* —**Syn.** *v.* abuse, affront, hurt, offend.

in·su·per·a·ble (in·sōō′pər·ə·bəl) *adj.* That cannot be overcome; insurmountable. [< L *in-* not + *superare* overcome] —**in·su′per·a·bil′i·ty, in·su′per·a·ble·ness** *n.* —**in·su′per·a·bly** *adv.*

in·sup·port·a·ble (in′sə·pôr′tə·bəl, -pōr′-) *adj.* 1 Intolerable; insufferable. 2 Without grounds; unjustifiable. —**in′· sup·port′a·ble·ness** *n.* —**in′sup·port′a·bly** *adv.*

in·sur·ance (in·shōōr′əns) *n.* 1 The act of insuring. 2 Something that provides protection or security. 3 A system by which pecuniary indemnity is guaranteed by one party to another in certain contingencies, as death, accident, damage, etc. 4 A contract (**insurance policy**) made under such a system. 5 The consideration paid for insuring; premium. 6 The sum that the insurer has agreed to pay in case the specified contingency occurs.

in·sure (in·shōōr′) *v.* ·sured, ·sur·ing *v.t.* 1 To contract to pay or be paid an indemnity in the event of harm to or the loss or death of. 2 ENSURE (def. 1). 3 ENSURE (def. 2). —*v.i.* 4 To issue or take out a policy of insurance. [< OF *enseurer* make sure < *en-* in + *seur* sure] —**in·sur′a·bil′i·ty** *n.* —**in·sur′a·ble** *adj.*

in·sured (in·shōōrd′) *n.* A person who carries insurance against loss of life, damage to property, etc.

in·sur·er (in·shōōr′ər) *n.* A person or company that provides insurance against damage or loss.

in·sur·gence (in·sûr′jəns) *n.* The act of rising in revolt; uprising. —**in·sur′gen·cy** *n.* (*pl.* ·cies)

in·sur·gent (in·sur′jənt) *adj.* Rising in rebellion against an existing government. —*n.* One who takes part in active opposition to constituted authorities. [< L *in-* against + *surgere* to rise]

in·sur·mount·a·ble (in′sər·moun′tə·bəl) *adj.* That cannot be surmounted, passed over, or overcome. —**in′· sur·mount′a·bil′i·ty** *n.* —**in′sur·mount′a·bly** *adv.*

in·sur·rec·tion (in′sə·rek′shən) *n.* An organized resistance to established government. [< L *insurgere* rise up against] —**in′sur·rec′tion·al** *adj.* —**in′sur·rec′tion·ar′y** *adj., n.* —**in′sur·rec′tion·ism, in′sur·rec′tion·ist** *n.*

---

add, āce, câre, pălm; end, ēven; it, īce; odd, ōpen, ôrder; tŏŏk, pōōl; up, bûrn; ə = *a* in *above, u* in *focus;* yōō = *u* in *fuse;* oil; pout; check; go; ring; thin; this; zh, *vision.* < derived from; ? origin uncertain or unknown.

in·sus·cep·ti·ble (in′sə·sep′tə·bəl) *adj.* Not susceptible; incapable of being moved or impressed. —**in′sus·cep′ti·bil′i·ty** *n.* —**in′sus·cep′ti·bly** *adv.*

in·tact (in·takt′) *adj.* Left complete or unimpaired. [<L *intactus* untouched] —**in·tact′ness** *n.*

in·ta·glio (in·tal′yō, -tä′lyō) *n. pl.* **·glios** or **·gli** (-lyē) 1 A sunken design engraved into a surface. 2 The art of making such designs. 3 A work, esp. a gem, with such carving. —*v.t.* 1 To engrave with a sunken design. 2 To represent in intaglio. [<Ital. *in-* in + *tagliare* to cut]

in·take (in′tāk′) *n.* 1 That which is taken in. 2 The amount or substance taken in. 3 The point at which a fluid is taken into a channel or container.

in·tan·gi·ble (in·tan′jə·bəl) *adj.* 1 Not capable of being touched; impalpable. 2 Not directly perceivable or readily grasped. —*n.* Something intangible but often noteworthy or influential component. —**in·tan′gi·bil′i·ty, in·tan′gi·ble·ness** *n.* —**in·tan′gi·bly** *adv.*

in·te·ger (in′tə·jər) *n.* 1 Any member of the set [. . . −3, −2, −1, 0, 1, 2, 3, . . .]; a whole number. 2 A whole. [<L, whole]

in·te·gral (in′tə·grəl) *adj.* 1 Constituting a completed whole. 2 Constituting an essential part of a whole. 3 *Math.* Of or being an integer or integers. —*n.* An entire thing; a whole. —**in′te·gral·ly** *adv.* —**in′te·gral′i·ty** (-gral′ə·tē) *n.*

in·te·grate (in′tə·grāt) *v.* **·grat·ed, ·grat·ing** *v.t.* 1 To make or form into a whole; unify. 2 To combine (parts) into a whole. 3 *U.S.* **a** To make (schools, housing, public facilities, etc.) available to people of all races and ethnic groups on an equal basis. **b** To remove any barriers imposing segregation upon (religious, racial, or other groups). —*v.i.* 4 To become integrated. [<L *integer* whole, intact] —**in·te·gra·tion** (in′tə·grā′shən), **in′te·gra′tion·ist** (*esp. for def.* 3), **in′te·gra′tor** *n.* —**in′te·gra′tive** *adj.*

in·te·grat·ed cir·cuit (in′tə·gra′tid) A tiny electronic circuit and its connections fabricated on a chip, or slice, of a semiconductor made of silicon or gallium; chip.

in·teg·ri·ty (in·teg′rə·tē) *n.* 1 Uprightness of character; honesty. 2 Unimpaired state; soundness. 3 Undivided or unbroken state; completeness. [<L *integer* whole]

in·teg·u·ment (in·teg′yə·mənt) *n.* An outer covering or envelope, as the skin of an animal, coat of a seed, etc. [<L *integere* to cover] —**in·teg′u·men′ta·ry** *adj.*

in·tel·lect (in′tə·lekt) *n.* 1 The power to perceive, interpret, know, and understand. 2 Great and keen intelligence. 3 A person having such intelligence.

in·tel·lec·tu·al (in′tə·lek′chōo·əl) *adj.* 1 Of or pertaining to the intellect: *intellectual* ability. 2 Possessing or showing a high degree of intelligence and knowledge. 3 Requiring intelligence or study: *intellectual* pursuits. —*n.* A person of trained intelligence, or one whose work requires exercise of the intellect. [<L *intellectualis*] —**in′tel·lec′tu·al′i·ty, in′tel·lec′tu·al·ness** *n.* —**in′tel·lec′tu·al·ly** *adv.*

in·tel·lec·tu·al·ism (in′tə·lək′chōo·əl·iz′əm) *n.* Devotion to use of the intellect or to intellectual occupations.

in·tel·li·gence (in·tel′ə·jəns) *n.* 1 The ability to exercise mental functions. 2 The ability to grasp the significant factors of a complex problem or new situation. 3 Information acquired or communicated; news. 4 The gathering of secret information, esp. of a political or military nature. 5 A group of persons assigned to gather such secret information. 6 An intelligent being.

intelligence quotient A score obtained on any of various intelligence tests that are standardized to give an average score of 100 to the total population tested.

intelligence test Any test designed to measure the mental capacity of a person.

in·tel·li·gent (in·tel′ə·jənt) *adj.* 1 Learning easily; of active mind. 2 Showing intelligence: an *intelligent* reply. 3 Endowed with intellect; reasoning: Man is an *intelligent* animal. [<L *intelligere* understand, perceive] —**in·tel′li·gent·ly** *adv.* —Syn. 2 astute, bright, clever, discerning.

in·tel·li·gent·si·a (in·tel′ə·jent′sē·ə, -gent′-) *n. pl.* Those considered as, or considering themselves as, the enlightened, educated class of a country; intellectual people collectively. [<Russ. *intelligentsiya.*]

in·tel·li·gi·ble (in·tel′ə·jə·bəl) *adj.* Capable of being understood; clear. —**in·tel′li·gi·bil′i·ty, in·tel′li·gi·ble·ness** *n.* —**in·tel′li·gi·bly** *adv.*

in·tem·per·ance (in·tem′pər·əns) *n.* 1 Lack of moderation or due restraint. 2 Excessive use of alcohol.

in·tem·per·ate (in·tem′pər·it) *adj.* 1 Characterized by lack of moderation. 2 Given to excessive use of alcoholic liquors. 3 Stormy; inclement: *intemperate* weather. —**in·tem′per·ate·ly** *adv.* —**in·tem′per·ate·ness** *n.*

in·tend (in·tend′) *v.t.* 1 To have in mind to accomplish or do. 2 To make or destine for a purpose, use, etc.: a game *intended* for adults. 3 To mean: She *intended* nothing by the remark. [<L *intendere* stretch out (for)] —**in·tend′er** *n.*

in·ten·dant (in·ten′dənt) *n.* A supervisor or director, esp. a colonial or provincial administrative official serving under a French, Spanish, or Portuguese monarchy.

in·tend·ed (in·ten′did) *adj.* 1 Meant or planned; intentional. 2 Looking to the future; prospective. —*n. Informal* One's future wife or husband.

in·tense (in·tens′) *adj.* **·tens·er, ·tens·est** 1 Strained or exerted to a high degree; fervid: *intense* study. 2 Extreme in degree, concentration, or measure: *intense* light. 3 Putting forth strenuous effort. 4 Susceptible to or exhibiting strong emotions. [<L *intendere* stretch out (for)] —**in·tense′ly** *adv.* —**in·tense′ness** *n.*

in·ten·si·fy (in·ten′sə·fī) *v.t. & v.i.* **·fied, ·fy·ing** To make or become intense or more intense; increase in degree. —**in·ten′si·fi·ca′tion, in·ten′si·fi′er** *n.*

in·ten·si·ty (in·ten′sə·tē) *n. pl.* **·ties** 1 The state or quality of being intense. 2 Extreme depth or violence of feeling, activity, etc. 3 The measure of how intense a force, flow of energy, etc., is.

in·ten·sive (in·ten′siv) *adj.* 1 Increasing in force or degree. 2 Characterized by intensity and thoroughness: *intensive* research. 3 Characterized by a relatively heavy investment in (something specified) as compared with other factors: used in combination: a *labor-intensive* industry. 4 *Gram.* Adding emphasis or force, as the pronoun *myself* in "I myself did it." —*n.* 1 That which intensifies. 2 *Gram.* An intensive word, prefix, etc. —**in·ten′sive·ly** *adv.* —**in·ten′sive·ness** *n.*

in·tent (in·tent′) *adj.* 1 Having the mind fixed; earnest: *intent* on winning. 2 Firmly or constantly directed: an *intent* gaze. —*n.* 1 The meaning expressed by an act or words. 2 An aim or purpose. —**to all intents and purposes** In practically every aspect. [<L *intendere* stretch out (for)] —**in·tent′ly** *adv.* —**in·tent′ness** *n.*

in·ten·tion (in·ten′shən) *n.* 1 A settled plan for doing a certain thing. 2 That upon which the mind is set; purpose. 3 *pl. Informal* Purpose with respect to a proposal of marriage.

in·ten·tion·al (in·ten′shən·əl) *adj.* Done purposely or with intention. [Med. L *intentionalis*] —**in·ten′tion·al·ly** *adv.*

in·ter (in·tûr′) *v.t.* **·terred, ·ter·ring** To place in a grave or tomb; bury. [<L *in-* in + *terra* earth]

inter- *prefix* 1 With each other; together: *interact.* 2 Mutual; mutually: *intercommunion.* 3 Between (the units signified): *international.* 4 Occurring or situated between: *intercostal.* [<L *inter* between]

in·ter·act (in′tər·akt′) *v.i.* To act on each other. —**in′ter·ac′tion** *n.* —**in′ter·ac′tive** *adj.*

in·ter·breed (in′tər·brēd′) *v.* **·bred, ·breed·ing** *v.t.* 1 To breed (animals or plants) by uniting different varieties, etc. —*v.i.* 2 To be mated with another variety.

in·ter·ca·lar·y (in·tûr′kə·ler′ē) *adj.* Inserted into the calendar: said of a month, day, etc., such as February 29 in leap year. [<L *intercalarius*]

in·ter·ca·late (in·tûr′kə·lāt) *v.t.* **·lat·ed, ·lat·ing** 1 To insert or interpolate. 2 To insert, as an additional day or month, into the calendar. [<L *inter-* between + *calare* proclaim, call] —**in·ter·ca·la′tion** *n.*

in·ter·cede (in′tər·sēd′) *v.i.* **·ced·ed, ·ced·ing** 1 To plead in behalf of another. 2 To act as a mediator in order to resolve disagreements between or among others. [<L *inter-* between + *cedere* pass, go] —**in′ter·ced′er** *n.* —Syn. 2 arbitrate, intervene, moderate, referee.

in·ter·cel·lu·lar (in′tər·sel′yə·lər) *adj. Biol.* Situated between or among cells.

in·ter·cept (in′tər·sept′) *v.t.* 1 To seize or stop on the way to a destination: to *intercept* contraband; to *intercept* a pass. 2 To stop, interrupt, or prevent. 3 To cut off from connection, sight, etc. **4** *Math.* To contain or include, as between two points of a curve. —*v.i.* **5** In various sports, to intercept a pass intended for an opponent. —*n.* (in′.tər·sept) *Math.* A point in which a figure intersects an axis of a coordinate system. [< L *inter-* between + *capere* seize] —**in′ter·cep′tion** *n.* —**in′ter·cep′tive** *adj.*

in·ter·cep·tor (in′tər·sep′tər) *n.* **1** One who or that which intercepts. **2** A fast plane adapted to the pursuit and interception of enemy aircraft. Also **in′ter·cep′ter.**

in·ter·ces·sion (in′tər·sesh′ən) *n.* The act of interceding between persons; entreaty in behalf of others. —**in′ter·ces′sion·al, in′ter·ces′so·ry** (-ses′ə·rē) *adj.* —**in′ter·ces′sor** *n.*

in·ter·change (in′tər·chānj) *v.* ·**changed, ·chang·ing** *v.t.* **1** To put each of (two things) in the place of the other. **2** To give and receive in return, as gifts; exchange. **3** To alternate: to *interchange* work and rest. —*v.i.* **4** To make an interchange. —*n.* (in′.tər·chānj) **1** The act, process, or an instance of interchanging. **2** A system of roadways and ramps that allow traffic to pass between intersecting highways, expressways, etc. —**in′ter·chang′er** *n.*

Cloverleaf interchange

in·ter·change·a·ble (in′tər·chān′jə·bəl) *adj.* Capable of being interchanged or substituted one for the other. [OF *entrechangeable*] —**in′ter·change′a·bil′i·ty, in′ter·change′a·ble·ness** *n.* —**in′ter·change′a·bly** *adv.*

in·ter·col·le·giate (in′tər·kə·lē′jit, -jē·it) *adj.* Existing, representing, or conducted between colleges and universities: *intercollegiate* sports.

in·ter·com (in′tər·kom) *n. Informal* A system that enables voice communication between persons in different parts of a building, ship, airplane, etc.

in·ter·com·mu·ni·cate (in′tər·kə·myōō′nə·kāt) *v.t.* ·**cat·ed, ·cat·ing** To communicate mutually, as between individuals, rooms, different units of a factory, etc. —**in′ter·com·mu′ni·ca′tive** *adj.* —**in′ter·com·mu′ni·ca′tion** *n.*

in·ter·con·nect (in′tər·kə·nekt′) *v.t. & v.i.* To connect with one another. —**in′ter·con·nec′tion** *n.*

in·ter·con·ti·nen·tal (in′tər·kon′tə·nen′təl) *adj.* **1** Existing, extending, or carried on between or among continents. **2** Able to travel between or among continents: *intercontinental* ballistic missiles.

in·ter·cos·tal (in′tər·kos′təl) *adj.* Between the ribs. [< L *inter-* between + *costa* rib] —**in′ter·cos′tal·ly** *adv.*

in·ter·course (in′tər·kôrs, -kōrs) *n.* **1** Mutual exchange or communication. **2** The interchange of ideas. **3** SEXUAL INTERCOURSE. [< L *inter-* between + *currere* to run]

in·ter·de·nom·i·na·tion·al (in′tər·di·nom′ə·nā′shən·əl) *adj.* Carried on by or involving different religious denominations.

in·ter·de·pend·ence (in′tər·di·pen′dəns) *n.* Dependence on one another; mutual dependence. Also **in′ter·de·pend′en·cy** (-dən′sē). —**in′ter·de·pend′ent** *adj.* —**in′ter·de·pend′ent·ly** *adv.*

in·ter·dict (in′tər·dikt′) *v.t.* **1** To prohibit or restrain authoritatively. **2** In the Roman Catholic Church, to exclude from religious privileges. —*n.* **1** A prohibitive order; ban. **2** In the Roman Catholic Church, a ban excluding a person, parish, etc. from religious privileges. [< L *interdicere* forbid] —**in′ter·dic′tion, in′ter·dic′tor** *n.* —**in′ter·dic′tive, in′.ter·dic′to·ry** *adj.* —**in′ter·dic′tive·ly** *adv.*

in·ter·dis·ci·pli·nar·y (in′tər·dis′ə·plə·ner′ē) *adj.* Involving two or more disciplines: an *interdisciplinary* approach to the study of American history.

in·ter·est (in′tər·ist, -trist) *n.* **1** A feeling of attraction or curiosity about something. **2** The power to excite or hold such a feeling. **3** Something bringing about this feeling: a man of many *interests.* **4** *Often pl.* That which is of advan-

tage or profit. **5** Payment made for the use of money; also, the money so paid, usu. a percentage of the amount borrowed. **6** Something added in repaying: to return a blow with *interest.* **7** A right or share in something, esp. a business enterprise. **8** The persons involved in an industry, cause, etc.: the oil *interest.* **9** Importance: a story of little *interest.* **10** Power to procure favor or regard; influence. —**in the interest of** In behalf of; for. —*v.t.* (*also* in′tə·rest) **1** To excite or hold the curiosity or attention of. **2** To cause to have a share or interest in; induce to participate. [< L *interesse* lie between, be important]

in·ter·est·ed (in′tər·is·tid, -tris-, -təres′-) *adj.* **1** Having the attention attracted or the feelings engaged. **2** Biased; not impartial. **3** Being a part owner. —**in′ter·est·ed·ly** *adv.* —**in′ter·est·ed·ness** *n.*

in·ter·est·ing (in′tər·is·ting, -tris-, -tə·res′-) *adj.* Possessing or exciting interest. —**in′ter·est·ing·ly** *adv.* —**in′ter·est·ing·ness** *n.* —**Syn.** appealing, engaging, enthralling, fascinating.

in·ter·face (in′tər·fās′) *n.* **1** A surface common to two parts or bodies. **2** A stage or point at which separate things interact: the man-machine *interface.* —*v.* ·**faced, ·fac·ing** —*v.i.* **1** To act as an interface. —*v.t.* **2** To provide with an interface.

in·ter·fere (in′tər·fir′) *v.i.* ·**fered, ·fer·ing** **1** To come into conflict or opposition; clash. **2** To take part unasked in the concerns of others; meddle. **3** To intervene for a specific purpose. **4** *Physics* To act in opposition, as waves of light, sound, or electricity. **5** In sports, to obstruct the actions of an opponent in an illegal manner. —**interfere with** To thwart; hinder. [< L *inter-* between + *ferire* to strike] —**in′ter·fer′er** *n.* —**in′ter·fer′ing·ly** *adv.*

in·ter·fer·ence (in′tər·fir′əns) *n.* **1** The act of interfering; conflict; collision. **2** *Physics* The action of wave trains, as of light, sound, or electricity, that on meeting tend to cancel each other. **3** In sports, obstruction of the actions of an opponent in an illegal manner.

in·ter·fold (in′tər·fōld′) *v.t. & v.i.* To fold together or one within the other.

in·ter·fuse (in′tər·fyōoz′) *v.* ·**fused, ·fus·ing** *v.t.* **1** To cause to blend. **2** To cause to permeate. —*v.i.* **3** To blend; fuse. —**in′ter·fu′sion** *n.*

in·ter·im (in′tər·im) *n.* An intervening period of time; meantime. —*adj.* For or during an intervening period of time. [< L, meanwhile]

in·te·ri·or (in·tir′ē·ər) *adj.* **1** Existing, pertaining to, or occurring within something; internal. **2** Inland or far from the borders. **3** Of a private or confidential nature. —*n.* **1** The internal part; inside. **2** The inland or central region of a country. **3** The domestic affairs of a country. **4** Inner nature; basic character. [< L, compar. of *inter* within] —**in·te′ri·or′i·ty** (-ôr′ə·tē, -or′-) *n.* —**in·te′ri·or·ly** *adv.*

interior decorator One whose work is the furnishing and decorating of interiors of houses, offices, etc. —**interior decorating**

interj. interjection.

in·ter·ject (in′tər·jekt′) *v.t.* To throw between other things: introduce abruptly; interpose. [< L *inter-* between + *jacere* to throw]

in·ter·jec·tion (in′tər·jek′shən) *n.* **1** *Gram.* A word expressing emotion or simple exclamation, as *oh! alas! look!* **2** A sudden interposition or interruption. —**in′ter·jec′tion·al** *adj.* —**in′ter·jec′tion·al·ly** *adv.*

in·ter·lace (in′tər·lās′) *v.* ·**laced, ·lac·ing** *v.t.* **1** To pass over and under one another; weave. **2** To unite intricately. —*v.i.* **3** To pass over and under one another: *interlacing* branches. —**in′ter·lace′ment** *n.*

in·ter·lard (in′tər·lärd′) *v.t.* To scatter throughout with something different, as for variety. —**in′ter·lard′ment** *n.*

in·ter·lay (in′tər·lā′) *v.t.* ·**laid, ·lay·ing** **1** To lay between or among. **2** To decorate or diversify with something laid between.

in·ter·leaf (in′tər·lēf′) *n. pl.* ·**leaves** (-lēvz′) A blank leaf inserted or bound between others in a book, etc.

in·ter·leave (in′tər·lēv′) *v.t.* ·**leaved, ·leav·ing** To insert an interleaf or interleaves into (a book).

in·ter·line[1] (in'tər·līn') v.t. ·lined, ·lin·ing 1 To write or print between the lines of. 2 To insert between lines. —in'ter·lin'er n.

in·ter·line[2] (in'tər·līn') v.t. ·lined, ·lin·ing To put a lining between the usual lining and the outer fabric of a garment. [<L inter- between + ludus a game, play]

in·ter·lin·e·ar (in'tər·lin'ē·ər) adj. 1 Situated on or occurring between lines. 2 Having translations or glosses inserted between the lines, as in a text. Also **in'ter·lin'e·al** (-ē·əl).

in·ter·lin·ing (in'tər·lī'ning) n. 1 A lining between the usual lining and the outer fabric of a garment. 2 The material of which it is made.

in·ter·lock (in'tər·lok') v.t. & v.i. To join together; link with one another. —in'ter·lock'er n.

in·ter·loc·u·tor (in'tər·lok'yə·tər) n. 1 One who takes part in a conversation. 2 The center man in a minstrel troupe. [<L interloqui speak between, converse]

in·ter·loc·u·to·ry (in'tər·lok'yə·tôr'ē, -tō'rē) adj. 1 Consisting of or pertaining to dialogue; conversational. 2 Law Done during the progress of a lawsuit, but not final.

in·ter·lop·er (in'tər·lō'pər) n. One who thrusts himself into a place without right. [<INTER- + Du. loopen to run] —Syn. interposer, intruder, meddler, trespasser.

in·ter·lude (in'tər·lōōd) n. 1 An intervening time or space. 2 An independent performance, usu. light or humorous, introduced between the acts of a play or the parts of a performance. 3 A passage of music that forms a transition. [<L inter- between + ludus a game, play]

in·ter·mar·ry (in'tər·mar'ē) v.i. ·ried, ·ry·ing 1 To become connected by marriage: said of different races, religions, clans, families, etc. 2 To marry each other: said of members of the same clan, family, etc. —in'ter·mar'riage (-rij) n.

in·ter·med·dle (in'tər·med'l) v.i. ·dled, ·dling To interfere unduly in the affairs of others. —in'ter·med'dler n.

in·ter·me·di·ar·y (in'tər·mē'dē·er'ē) adj. 1 Situated, acting, or coming between. 2 Acting as a mediator. —n. pl. ·ies An agent or mediator.

in·ter·me·di·ate (in'tər·mē'dē·it) adj. Being or occurring in a middle place or degree. —n. 1 Something intermediate. 2 INTERMEDIARY. —v.i. (-āt) ·at·ed, ·at·ing To act as an intermediary; mediate. [<L intermedius middle] —in'ter·me'di·ate·ly adv. —in'ter·me'di·ate·ness n.

in·ter·ment (in'tər·mənt) n. The act of interring; burial.

in·ter·mez·zo (in'tər·met'sō, -med'zō) n. pl. ·zos or ·zi (-sē, -zē) 1 A song, chorus, or short ballet given between the acts of a play or opera. 2 A short movement connecting large divisions of a musical composition. 3 A short instrumental piece composed as if between larger movements. [Ital. <L intermedius intermediate]

in·ter·mi·na·ble (in·tûr'mə·nə·bəl) adj. Continuing, or seeming to continue, for a very long time; endless. —in·ter'mi·na·bly adv.

in·ter·min·gle (in'tər·ming'gəl) v.t. & v.i. ·gled, ·gling To mingle together; mix.

in·ter·mis·sion (in'tər·mish'ən) n. 1 Temporary cessation. 2 An interval, as between acts in the theater. [<L intermittere send between] —in'ter·mis'sive adj.

in·ter·mit (in'tər·mit') v.t. & v.i. ·mit·ted, ·mit·ting To stop temporarily or at intervals. [<L inter- between + mittere send, put] —in'ter·mit'tence n.

in·ter·mit·tent (in'tər·mit'ənt) adj. Alternately ceasing and beginning; not continuous. —in'ter·mit'tent·ly adv.

in·ter·mix (in'tər·miks') v.t. & v.i. To mix together; intermingle. —in'ter·mix'ture n.

in·ter·mod·u·la·tion distortion (in'tər·moj'ōō·lā'shən) Electronics A form of distortion produced when a flaw in an amplifier or other device causes signals of different frequencies that are present simultaneously to modulate each other.

in·tern[1] (in·tûrn') v.t. To confine within the limits of a country or area, as enemy aliens or prisoners of war. [<L internus internal] —in·tern'ment n.

in·tern[2] (in'tûrn) n. A medical doctor undergoing resident training in a hospital. —v.i. To serve as an intern in a hospital. [See INTERN[1].] —in'tern·ship n.

in·ter·nal (in·tûr'nəl) adj. 1 Situated in or applicable to the inside; interior. 2 Pertaining to or derived from the inside. 3 Pertaining to the inner self or the mind; subjective.

4 Pertaining to the domestic affairs of a country. —n. 1 pl. The internal bodily organs; entrails. 2 The essential quality of anything. [<L internus <in in] —in·ter'nal·ly adv.

in·ter·nal-com·bus·tion (in·tûr'nəl·kəm·bus'chən) adj. Denoting a type of engine in which the fuel is burned in the engine itself rather than in an external device.

internal medicine The branch of medicine concerned with diagnosis and nonsurgical treatment of internal diseases.

internal revenue Income accruing to a government from a variety of taxes.

in·ter·na·lize (in·tûr'nə·līz) v.t. ·ized, ·iz·ing To incorporate into one's own self the habits, beliefs, etc., of another or others. —in·ter'na·li·za'tion n.

in·ter·na·tion·al (in'tər·nash'ən·əl) adj. 1 Of or pertaining to the relations among nations: international law. 2 Carried on among nations: international trade. 3 Between two or more nations: an international treaty. —in'ter·na'tion·al'i·ty n. —in'ter·na'tion·al·ly adv.

in·ter·na·tion·al (in'tər·nash'ən·əl) n. Any of three consecutive international political organizations of socialists and communists.

International Date Line DATE LINE.

in·ter·na·tion·al·ism (in'tər·nash'ən·əl·iz'əm) n. The doctrine that political and economic cooperation among nations contributes to their common good. —in'ter·na'tion·al·ist adj., n.

in·ter·na·tion·al·ize (in'tər·nash'ən·əl·īz') v.t. ·ized, ·iz·ing To make international, as in character or administration. —in'ter·na'tion·al·i·za'tion n.

in·terne (in'tûrn) n. INTERN[2].

in·ter·ne·cine (in'tər·nē'sin, -nē'-, -sīn, in·tər'nə·sēn, -sən) adj. 1 Involving great slaughter to both sides. 2 Ruinous; deadly. [<L inter- among + necare to kill]

in·tern·ee (in·tûr·nē') n. A person detained as an enemy alien, prisoner of war, etc.

in·ter·nist (in·tûr'nist) n. A physician specializing in internal medicine.

in·ter·pel·late (in'tər·pel'āt, -pə·lāt') v.t. ·lat·ed, ·lat·ing To ask (a member of a government) for an official explanation of an action or a policy. [<L inter- between + pellere to drive] —in'ter·pel'lant adj., n. —in·ter·pel·la·tion (in'tər·pə·lā'shən, in·tûr'-) n.

in·ter·pen·e·trate (in'tər·pen'ə·trāt) v. ·trat·ed, ·trat·ing v.t. 1 To penetrate thoroughly; permeate. 2 To penetrate mutually. —v.i. 3 To penetrate each other. 4 To penetrate between or among parts or things. —in'ter·pen'e·tra'tion n.

in·ter·per·son·al (in'tər·pûr'sən·əl) adj. Existing between people: interpersonal relations.

in·ter·phone (in'tər·fōn') n. A system providing telephone communication within a building, office, ship, etc.

in·ter·plan·e·tar·y (in'tər·plan'ə·ter'ē) adj. Between or among planets.

in·ter·play (in'tər·plā') n. Mutual or reciprocal action or influence; interaction.

in·ter·po·late (in·tûr'pə·lāt) v. ·lat·ed, ·lat·ing v.t. 1 To alter, as a manuscript, by the insertion of new or unauthorized matter. 2 To insert (such matter). 3 Math. To estimate a value of (a function) between known values. —v.i. 4 To make interpolations. [<L inter- between + polire to polish] —in·ter'po·la'ter, in·ter'po·la'tion, in·ter'po·la'tor n. —in·ter'po·la'tive adj.

in·ter·pose (in'tər·pōz') v. ·posed, ·pos·ing v.t. 1 To place between other things; insert. 2 To introduce by way of intervention: He interposed his authority. 3 To inject, as a remark, into a conversation, argument, etc. —v.i. 4 To come between; intervene. 5 To put in a remark; interrupt. [<L inter- between + ponere put] —in'ter·pos'er, in·ter·po·si·tion (in·tər·pə·zish'ən) n. —in'ter·pos'ing·ly adv.

in·ter·pret (in·tûr'prit) v.t. 1 To give the meaning of; make clear. 2 To derive a particular understanding of; construe. 3 To bring out the meaning of by artistic representation or performance. 4 To translate. —v.i. 5 To act as interpreter. 6 To explain [<L interpres agent, interpreter] —in·ter'pret·a·bil'i·ty n. —in·ter'pret·a·ble adj. —Syn. 1 clarify, elucidate, explain, illuminate.

in·ter·pre·ta·tion (in·tûr'prə·tā'shən) n. 1 The act or result of interpreting. 2 The performance or representation of a work of art so as to reveal one's conception of it. [F] —in·ter'pre·ta'tion·al adj.

in·ter·pret·er (in·tûr′prit·ər) *n*. **1** One who interprets. **2** One who serves as translator between people speaking different languages.

in·ter·pre·tive (in·tûr′prə·tiv) *adj*. **1** Designed or fitted to interpret; explanatory: *interpretive* reporting. **2** Containing an interpretation; embodying ideas or facts. **3** Admitting of interpretation; constructive. Also **in·ter′pre·ta′tive** (-tā′tiv). —**in′ter′pre·tive·ly** *adv*.

in·ter·ra·cial (in′tər·rā′shəl) *adj*. Of, between, or for persons of different races. —**in′ter·ra′ci·al·ly** *adv*.

in·ter·reg·num (in′tər·reg′nəm) *n. pl.* **·nums** or **·na 1** The time during which a high executive office is vacant. **2** A suspension of executive authority through a change of government. **3** Any period of temporary suspension. [<L *inter-* between + *regnum* reign]

in·ter·re·late (in′tər·ri·lāt′) *v.t. & v.i.* **·lat·ed ·lat·ing** To bring or come into reciprocal relation. —**in′ter·re·la′tion**, **in′ter·re·la′tion·ship** *n*.

interrog. interrogative

in·ter·ro·gate (in·ter′ə·gāt) *v*. **·gat·ed, ·gat·ing** *v.t.* To put questions to; question. —*v.i.* To ask questions. [<L *inter-* between + *rogare* ask] —**in·ter′ro·ga′tor** *n*.

in·ter·ro·ga·tion (in·ter′ə·gā′shən) *n*. **1** The act of interrogating. **2** A question; query. **3** A formal or official questioning, as of a prisoner or witness. —**in·ter′ro·ga′tion·al** *adj*.

interrogation point QUESTION MARK. Also **interrogation mark.**

in·ter·rog·a·tive (in′tə·rog′ə·tiv) *adj*. Denoting inquiry; questioning. —*n. Gram.* A word, phrase, or sentence used to ask a question, as *Who is there?* —**in′ter·rog′a·tive·ly** *adv*.

in·ter·rog·a·to·ry (in′tə·rog′ə·tôr′ē, -tō′rē) *adj*. Pertaining to, expressing, or implying a question. —*n. pl.* **·to·ries** A question; interrogation. —**in′ter·rog′a·to′ri·ly** *adv*.

in·ter·rupt (in′tə·rupt′) *v.t.* **1** To cause a delay or break in: to *interrupt* service. **2** To break the continuity, course, or sameness of. **3** To break in on (someone) talking, working, etc. —*v.i.* **4** To break in upon an action or speech. [<L *inter-* between + *rumpere* to break] —**in′ter·rupt′er** *n*. —**in′ter·rup′tive** *adj*.

in·ter·rup·tion (in′tə·rup′shən) *n*. **1** The act of interrupting. **2** A break in continuity; an interval. **3** Obstruction caused by breaking in upon any course, progress, or motion.

in·ter·scho·las·tic (in′tər·skə·las′tik) *adj*. Between or among schools: *interscholastic* basketball.

in·ter·sect (in′tər·sekt′) *v.t.* **1** To pass across; cut through or into so as to divide. —*v.i.* **2** To cross each other. [<L *inter-* between + *secare* to cut]

in·ter·sec·tion (in′tər·sek′shən) *n*. **1** The act of intersecting. **2** The point or line of contact between two lines, planes, etc. **3** The area where two streets cross. —**in′ter·sec′tion·al** *adj*.

in·ter·sperse (in′tər·spûrs′) *v.t.* **·spersed, ·spers·ing 1** To scatter among other things; set here and there. **2** To diversify or adorn with other things scattered here and there. [<L *inter-* among + *spargere* scatter] —**in′ter·spers′ed·ly** *adv*. —**in′ter·sper′sion** (-spûr′zhən) *n*.

in·ter·state (in′tər·stāt′) *adj*. Between different states, as of the U.S.: *interstate* commerce.

in·ter·stel·lar (in′tər·stel′ər) *adj*. Situated or occurring among the stars.

in·ter·stice (in·tûr′stis) *n. pl.* **·stic·es** (-stə·sēz), **-stis·iz) 1** A narrow space betweeen adjoining parts or things. **2** A crack; crevice. [<L *inter-* between + *sistere* cause to stand] —**in·ter·stit·ial** (in′tər·stish′əl) *adj*. —**in′ter·stit′ial·ly** *adv*.

in·ter·twine (in′tər·twīn′) *v.t. & v.i.* **·twined, ·twin·ing** To unite by twisting or interlacing.

in·ter·twist (in′tər·twist′) *v.t. & v.i.* To twist together; interlace.

in·ter·ur·ban (in′tər·ûr′bən) *adj*. Between cities or towns. —*n*. A railroad connecting cities or towns.

in·ter·val (in′tər·vəl) *n*. **1** The time that intervenes between two events or periods. **2** An open space between two objects; distance between points. **3** *Music* **a** The difference in pitch between two tones. **b** A sound composed of two tones sounded simultaneously. —**at intervals 1** From time to time. **2** At a series of points with spaces between. [<L *inter-* between + *vallum* rampart] —Syn. **1** interim, interlude, intermission, pause.

in·ter·vene (in′tər·vēn′) *v.i.* **·vened, ·ven·ing 1** To come between by action or authority; interfere or mediate. **2** To occur, as something irrelevant or unexpected: I will come if nothing *intervenes*. **3** To be located between. **4** To take place between other events or times. [<L *inter-* between + *venire* come] —**in′ter·ven′er** *n*. —**in′ter·ven′ient** (-vēn′yənt) *adj., n*.

in·ter·ven·tion (in′tər·ven′shən) *n*. **1** The act of coming between. **2** Interference with the acts of others. **3** Interference in the affairs of one country by another. **4** An intervening time, event, or thing. —**in′ter·ven′tion·al** *adj*. —**in·ter·ven·tion·ist** (in′tər·ven′shən·ist) *adj., n*.

in·ter·view (in′tər·vyōō) *n*. **1** A meeting between two or more people, as to evaluate qualifications or consider for employment. **2** A meeting for soliciting views or opinions, as by reporters or investigators. **3** The report of such a meeting. —*v.t.* To have an interview with. [<L *inter-* between + *videre* see] —**in′ter·view′er** *n*.

in·ter·weave (in′tər·wēv′) *v.t. & v.i.* **·wove** or **·weaved, ·wo·ven, ·weav·ing** To weave together; intermingle or connect closely.

in·tes·tate (in·tes′tāt) *adj*. **1** Not having made a will. **2** Not legally devised or disposed of by will. —*n*. A person who dies intestate. [<L *in-* not + *testari* make a will] —**in·tes·ta·cy** (in·tes′tə·sē) *n*.

in·tes·tine (in·tes′tin) *n. Usu. pl.* The part of the alimentary canal between the stomach and the anus, consisting of the long **small intestine** and the shorter, wider **large intestine** including the colon and rectum. —*adj*. Internal with regard to state or community; domestic. [<L *intestinus* internal] —**in·tes′ti·nal** *adj*. —**in·tes′ti·nal·ly** *adv*.

in·thrall (in·thrôl′) *v*. ENTHRALL.

in·throne (in·thrōn′) *v*. **·throned, ·thron·ing** ENTHRONE.

Human intestines a. duodenum. b. small intestine. c. colon. d. vermiform appendix.

in·ti·fa·da (in′ti·fä′dä) *n. Arabic* Open rebellion.

in·ti·ma·cy (in′tə·mə·sē) *n. pl.* **·cies 1** Close or confidential friendship. **2** An intimate act. **3** Illicit sexual connection: a euphemism.

in·ti·mate¹ (in′tə·mit) *adj*. **1** Closely connected by friendship or association; personal; confidential. **2** Pertaining to the inmost being; innermost. **3** Adhering closely; close. **4** Proceeding from within; internal. **5** Having illicit sexual relations (with): a euphemism. —*n*. A close or confidential friend. [<L *intimus*, superl. of *intus* within] —**in′ti·mate·ly** *adv*.

in·ti·mate² (in′tə·māt) *v.t.* **·mat·ed, ·mat·ing 1** To make known without direct statement; hint; imply. **2** To make known formally; declare. [<L *intimare* announce] —**in′ti·ma′tor** *n*.

in·ti·ma·tion (in′tə·mā′shən) *n*. **1** Information communicated indirectly; a hint. **2** A declaration or notification.

in·tim·i·date (in·tim′ə·dāt) *v.t.* **·dat·ed, ·dat·ing 1** To make timid; cause fear in. **2** To force or restrain by threats or violence. [<L *in-* very + *timidus* afraid] —**in·tim′i·da′tion, in·tim′i·da′tor** *n*.

in·ti·tle (in·tīt′l) *v.t.* **·tled, ·tling** ENTITLE.

in·to (in′tōō) *prep*. **1** To or toward the inside of. **2** Extending within (a period of time). **3** In the direction of. **4** To the condition or form of: grew from a tadpole *into* a frog. **5** To the practice or study of: to go *into* medicine. **6** *Slang* Actively engaged or involved with, as an interest: He's *into* mysticism. [<OE] • *In, into, in to* all have different meanings. *In* shows presence or location: *She is in the office*. *Into* always implies motion: *She went into the office*. Confusion may arise if *in* and *into* are used interchangeably: *They walked into the water* means something quite different from *They walked in the water*. The phrase *in to* is

made up of the adverb *in* and the preposition *to: They went into the conference room,* but *They went in to the meeting.*

in·tol·er·a·ble (in·tol′ər·ə·bəl) *adj.* Not tolerable; insufferable. —**in·tol′er·a·bil′i·ty, in·tol′er·a·ble·ness** *n.* —**in·tol′er·a·bly** *adv.*

in·tol·er·ance (in·tol′ər·əns) *n.* **1** Refusal to tolerate opposing beliefs; bigotry. **2** Incapacity or unwillingness to bear or endure. Also **in·tol′er·an·cy.**

in·tol·er·ant (in·tol′ər·ənt) *adj.* **1** Not disposed to tolerate contrary beliefs or opinions; bigoted. **2** Unable or unwilling to bear or endure: with *of: intolerant* of opposition. —**in·tol′er·ant·ly** *adv.*

in·tomb (in·tōōm′) *v.t.* ENTOMB.

in·to·na·tion (in′tō·nā′shən, in′tə-) *n.* **1** The modulation of the voice in speaking. **2** The act of intoning, as of the church service by a priest. **3** *Music* Production of tones, as by the voice, esp. in regard to precision of pitch.

in·tone (in·tōn′) *v.* **·toned ·ton·ing** *v.t.* **1** To utter or recite in a musical monotone; chant. **2** To give particular tones or intonation to. —*v.i.* **3** To utter a musical monotone; chant. [< L *in-* in + *tonus* tone] —**in·ton′er** *n.*

in to·to (in tō′tō) *Latin* Entirely.

in·tox·i·cate (in·tok′sə·kāt) *v.t.* **·cat·ed, ·cat·ing 1** To make drunk; inebriate. **2** To elate or excite to a degree of frenzy. **3** To poison, as by toxins, drugs, etc. [< L *in-* in + *toxicum* poison] —**in·tox′i·cant** *adj., n.* —**in·tox′i·ca′tion** *n.* —**in·tox′i·ca′tive** *adj.*

intr. intransitive.

intra- *prefix* Within; inside of: *intramural.* [< L *intra* within]

in·trac·ta·ble (in·trak′tə·bəl) *adj.* **1** Not tractable; refractory. **2** Lacking plastic quality; difficult to treat or work. —**in·trac′ta·bil′i·ty, in·trac′ta·ble·ness** *n.* —**in·trac′ta·bly** *adv.* —**Syn. 1** obstinate, rebellious, stubborn.

in·tra·dos (in·trā′dos) *n.* The interior or lower surface of an arch or vault. [F < L *intra-* within + *dorsum* back]

in·tra·mu·ral in′trə·myŏŏr′əl) *adj.* **1** Situated or taking place within the walls or confines of a city, an educational institution, etc. **2** *Anat.* Situated or occurring within the substance of the walls of a bodily organ. [< INTRA- + L *murus* wall]

in·tra·mus·cu·lar (in′trə·mus′kyə·lər) *adj.* Situated or injected within a muscle or muscular tissue.

in·tran·si·gent (in·tran′sə·jənt) *adj.* Refusing to agree or compromise; irreconcilable. —*n.* One who is intransigent; a radical or revolutionary. [< L *in-* not + *transigere* agree] —**in·tran′si·gence, in·tran′si·gen·cy** (-jən·sē) *n.*

in·tran·si·tive (in·tran′sə·tiv) *Gram. adj.* **1** Not taking or requiring an object, as certain verbs. **2** Of or pertaining to such verbs. —*n.* An intransitive verb. —**in·tran′si·tive·ly** *adv.*

in·tra·state (in′trə·stāt′) *adj.* Confined within or pertaining to a single state, usu. of the U.S.

in·tra·u·ter·ine device (in′trə·yōō′tər·ən, -ēn) A contraceptive device consisting usu. of a plastic coil, spiral, or loop that is inserted and left within the uterus for as long as contraception is desired. Also **intrauterine contraceptive device.**

in·tra·ve·nous (in′trə·vē′nəs) *adj.* Injected into or situated within a vein. —**in′tra·ve′nous·ly** *adv.*

in·trench (in·trench′) *v.t. & v.i.* ENTRENCH.

in·trep·id (in·trep′id) *adj.* Unshaken in the presence of danger; dauntless. [< L *in-* not + *trepidus* agitated] —**in·tre·pid·i·ty** (in′trə·pid′ə·tē) *n.* —**in·trep′id·ly** *adv.*

in·tri·ca·cy (in′tri·kə·sē) *n. pl.* **·cies 1** The quality of being complicated or entangled. **2** A complication; complexity.

in·tri·cate (in′tri·kit) *adj.* **1** Exceedingly entangled, complicated, or involved. **2** Difficult to follow or understand. [< L *in-* in + *tricae* difficulties] —**in′tri·cate·ly** *adv.* —**in′tri·cate·ness** *n.*

in·trigue (in·trēg′, in′trēg) *n.* **1** The working for an end by secret or underhand means; a plot or scheme. **2** An illicit love affair; liaison. —*v.* **·trigued, ·tri·guing** *v.t.* **1** To arouse and hold the interest or curiosity of; beguile. **2** To plot for; bring on or get by secret or underhand means. —*v.i.* **3** The use secret or underhand means; make plots. **4** To carry on a secret or illicit love affair. [< L *in-* in + *tricae* difficulties] —**in·tri′guer** *n.*

in·trin·sic (in·trin′sik, -zik) *adj.* **1** Belonging to the na-

ture of a thing or person; inherent; essential. **2** Contained or being within. [< L *intrinsecus* internally] —**in·trin′si·cal·ly** *adv.*

introd. introduction; introductory.

in·tro·duce (in′trə·dʸōōs′) *v.t.* **·duced, ·duc·ing 1** To bring (someone) to acquaintance with another. **2** To present formally. **3** To bring (someone) to acquaintance with or knowledge of something: with *to.* **4** To bring into notice, use, or practice. **5** To bring or put into; insert. **6** To bring forward for consideration: to *introduce* a resolution. **7** To begin; start: to *introduce* a new line of questioning. [< L *intro-* in + *ducere* to lead] —**in′tro·duc′er** *n.* —**in′tro·duc′i·ble** *adj.*

in·tro·duc·tion (in′trə·duk′shən) *n.* **1** The act of introducing. **2** The means of introducing one person to another, as by letter, card, etc. **3** A preface by an author or speaker in explanation of the subject or design of his writing or discourse. **4** An elementary treatise: an *introduction* to chemistry. **5** *Music* A short opening passage or movement.

in·tro·duc·to·ry (in′trə·duk′tər·ē) *adj.* Serving as an introduction; preliminary. Also **in′tro·duc′tive.** —**in′tro·duc′to·ri·ly** *adv.*

in·tro·it (in·trō′it) *n.* **1** In the Roman Catholic Church, an antiphon said or chanted at the beginning of the Eucharist: also **Entrance Antiphon. 2** In the Anglican Church, an anthem or hymm sung at the beginning of a Communion service. [< L *intro-* in + *ire* go]

in·tro·spec·tion (in′trə·spek′shən) *n.* **1** The act of looking within. **2** The examination of one's own mental and emotional processes. [< L *intro-* within + *specere* to look] —**in′tro·spec′tive** *adj.* —**in′tro·spec′tive·ly** *adv.*

in·tro·ver·sion (in′trə·vûr′zhən, -shən, in′trə·vûr′zhən) *n.* **1** The act or process of introverting. **2** The condition of or tendency toward being an introvert. —**in′tro·ver′sive** (-vûr′siv) *adj.*

in·tro·vert (in′trə·vûrt) *n.* One whose attention and interest are primarily directed inwardly towards himself rather than towards other people or the external world. —*v.t.* To turn within; cause to take an inward direction. —*adj.* Characterized by or tending to introversion. [< L *intro-* within + *vertere* to turn]

in·trude (in·trōōd′) *v.* **·trud·ed, ·trud·ing** *v.t.* **1** To thrust or force in without leave or excuse. —*v.i.* **2** To come in without leave or invitation; thrust oneself in. **3** *Geol.* To enter by intrusion. [< L *in-* in + *trudere* to thrust] —**in·trud′er** *n.*

in·tru·sion (in·trōō′zhən) *n.* **1** The act of intruding; encroachment. **2** *Geol.* **a** The thrusting of molten rock into an earlier formation. **b** A rock thus formed within an earlier formation.

in·tru·sive (in·trōō′siv) *adj.* **1** Coming without warrant; intruding; obtrusive; prone to intrude. **2** *Geol.* Formed by intrusion, as certain igneous rocks. [See INTRUDE.] —**in·tru′sive·ly** *adv.* —**in·tru′sive·ness** *n.*

in·trust (in·trust′) *v.t.* ENTRUST.

in·tu·i·tion (in′tʸōō·ish′ən) *n.* **1** Quick perception of truth or knowledge without conscious attention or reasoning. **2** That which is perceived or known intuitively. [< L *intueri* look upon] —**in′tu·i′tion·al** *adj.* —**in′tu·i′tion·al·ly** *adv.*

in·tu·i·tive (in·tʸōō′ə·tiv) *adj.* **1** Perceived by the mind without rigorous logic or analysis. **2** Discovering truth or reaching a just conclusion without resort to the powers of reason. —**in·tu′i·tive·ly** *adv.* —**in·tu′i·tive·ness** *n.*

In·u·it (in′ōō·wit) *n.* **1** One of a Mongoloid people indigenous to the Arctic coasts of North America, Greenland, and NE Siberia. **2** The language of the Inuit, belonging to the Eskimo-Aleut family. [<Eskimo *inuit* people, men]

in·un·date (in′ən·dāt) *v.t.* **·dat·ed, ·dat·ing** To cover or fill by overflowing. [< L *in-* in + *undare* overflow] —**in′un·da′tion, in′un·da′tor** *n.* —**Syn.** deluge, drown, flood, overwhelm.

in·ure (in·yōōr′) *v.* **·ured, ·ur·ing** *v.t.* **1** To harden or toughen; habituate. —*v.t.* **2** To have or take effect; be applied. [< OF *en-* (causative) + *euvre* work, use] —**in·ure′ment** *n.*

in u·te·ro (in yōō′tər·ō) *Latin* In the uterus; prior to birth.

inv. invented; invention; inventor; invoice.

in·vade (in·vād′) *v.* **·vad·ed, ·vad·ing** *v.t.* **1** To enter with hostile intent, as for conquering. **2** To encroach upon; trespass on. **3** To spread over or penetrate injuriously: Disease *invaded* the lungs. —*v.i.* **4** To make an invasion. [< L *in-* in + *vadere* go] —**in·vad′er** *n.*

in·va·lid¹ (in′və·lid) *n.* A sickly person, or one disabled, as by wounds, disease, etc. —*adj.* **1** Enfeebled by ill health. **2** Pertaining to or for the use of sick persons. —*v.t.* **1** To cause to become invalid; disable. **2** To release (a soldier, sailor, etc.) from active service because of injury or illness. [< F < L *invalidus* not strong] —**in′va·lid·ism** *n.*

in·val·id² (in·val′id) *adj.* Without force, weight, or cogency; void. [< L *invalidus*] —**in·va·lid·i·ty** (in′və·lid′ə·tē) *n.* —**in·val′id·ly** *adv.*

in·val·i·date (in·val′ə·dāt) *v.t.* **·dat·ed, ·dat·ing** To weaken or destroy the force or validity of; annul. —**in·val′i·da′tion,** **in·val′i·da′tor** *n.*

in·val·u·a·ble (in·val′yōo·ə·bəl, -yōo·bəl) *adj.* Of a value beyond estimation; very precious. —**in·val′u·a·ble·ness** *n.* —**in·val′u·a·bly** *adv.*

in·var·i·a·ble (in·vâr′ē·ə·bəl) *adj.* That does not or cannot vary or be varied; always uniform. —**in·var′i·a·bil′i·ty, in·var′i·a·ble·ness** *n.* —**in·var′i·a·bly** *adv.*

in·var·i·ant (in·vâr′ē·ənt) *adj.* Constant or unchanged, esp. with respect to a mathematical operation. —*n.* An invariant quantity. —**in·var′i·ance** *n.*

in·va·sion (in·vā′zhən) *n.* **1** The act of invading; a military incursion for conquest, reconquest, or plunder. **2** Any attack with harmful intent or result. **3** Encroachment, as by an act of intrusion or trespass. —**in·va·sive** (in·vā′siv) *adj.*

in·vec·tive (in·vek′tiv) *n.* Violent, verbal denunciation or accusation; vituperation. —*adj.* Using or characterized by harsh words of abuse. [< L *invectus,* p.p. of *invehere.* See INVEIGH.] —**in·vec′tive·ly** *adv.* —**in·vec′tive·ness** *n.*

in·veigh (in·vā′) *v.i.* To utter vehement censure or invective: with *against.* [< L *in-* into + *vehere* carry] —**in·veigh′er** *n.*

in·vei·gle (in·vā′gəl, -vē′-) *v.t.* **·gled, ·gling 1** To lead on, as by trickery or flattery; draw; entice. **2** To win over or seduce; captivate. [< OF *aveugle* blind] —**in·vei′gle·ment, in·vei′gler** *n.*

in·vent (in·vent′) *v.t.* **1** To create the idea, form, or existence of by original thought or effort; devise. **2** To make up, as something untrue or contrary to fact. [< L *invenire* come upon, discover] —**in·vent′i·ble** *adj.*

in·ven·tion (in·ven′shən) *n.* **1** The act or process of inventing (something new). **2** That which is invented. **3** Skill or ingenuity in contriving. **4** A fabrication; falsehood.

in·ven·tive (in·ven′tiv) *adj.* **1** Skillful at inventing; ingenious. **2** Of or having to do with invention. —**in·ven′tive·ly** *adv.* —**in·ven′tive·ness** *n.*

in·ven·tor (in·ven′tər) *n.* One who invents; esp., the originator of some method, process, or device.

in·ven·to·ry (in′vən·tôr′ē, -tō′rē) *n. pl.* **·ries 1** An itemized list of articles, with the number and value of each. **2** The items so listed or to be listed, as the stock of goods of a business. —*v.t.* **·ried, ·ry·ing 1** To make an inventory of; to list in detail. **2** To list in an inventory. [< L *invenire* come upon, find out] —**in′ven·to′ri·al** (-tôr′ē·əl, -tō′rē-) *adj.* —**in′·ven·to′ri·al·ly** *adv.*

in·ver·ness (in′vər·nes′) *n.* A long coat with a wide, usu. removable, cape. Also **Inverness cape.** [< *Inverness,* Scotland]

in·verse (in·vûrs′, in′vûrs) *adj.* Opposite in order or effect; inverted. —*n.* That which is inverted. —*v.t.* **·versed, ·vers·ing** To invert. —**in·verse′ly** *adv.*

in·ver·sion (in·vûr′zhən, -shən) *n.* **1** The act of inverting. **2** The state of being inverted. **3 a** A change in the order of a set of things. **b** That which results from such a change. **4** In rhetoric or grammar, a reversal of the natural order of words in a phrase or sentence. **5** *Meteorol.* A condition in which atmospheric temperature increases with increasing altitude, often trapping pollutants near the ground. —**in·ver′sive** *adj.*

in·vert (in·vûrt′) *v.t.* **1** To turn upside down or inside out. **2** To reverse the position, order, or sequence of. **3** To change to the opposite. **4** *Music* To interchange the tones or parts of. —*v.i.* **5** To undergo inversion. —*n.* (in′vûrt) **1** One who or that which is inverted. **2** HOMOSEXUAL. [< L *in-* in + *vertere* to turn] —**in·vert′i·ble** *adj.* —**in·ver′tor** *n.*

in·ver·te·brate (in·vûr′tə·brit, -brāt) *adj.* Lacking a backbone; not vertebrate. —*n.* Any animal having no backbone. —**in·ver′te·bra·cy** (-brə·sē), **in·ver′te·brate·ness** *n.*

in·vest (in·vest′) *v.t.* **1** To use (money or capital) for the purchase of property, stocks, securities, etc., with the expectation of profit or income. **2** To spend (money, time, effort, etc.) in hopes of a return. **3** To place in office formally; install. **4** To give power, authority, or rank to. **5** To cover or surround as if with a garment: Mystery *invested* the whole affair. **6** To surround or hem in; lay siege to. —*v.i.* **7** To make an investment or investments. [< L *in-* on + *vestire* clothe] —**in·ves′tor** *n.*

in·ves·ti·gate (in·ves′tə·gāt) *v.* **·gat·ed, ·gat·ing** *v.t.* **1** To search or inquire into; examine into. —*v.i.* **2** To make an investigation. [< L *in-* in + *vestigare* to track, trace] —**in·ves′ti·ga·ble** (-tə·gə·bəl), **in·ves′ti·ga′tive** *adj.* —**in·ves′ti·ga′tor** *n.* —**Syn.** explore, inspect, review, scrutinize, study.

in·ves·ti·ga·tion (in·ves′tə·gā′shən) *n.* **1** The act of investigating; careful inquiry or research. **2** An inquiry by authority, as by a legislative committee, into certain facts. **3** A systematic examination of some scientific question.

in·ves·ti·ture (in·ves′tə·chər) *n.* **1** The act or ceremony of investing (a person) with power, rank, or authority. **2** That which invests, clothes, or covers.

in·vest·ment (in·vest′mənt) *n.* **1** The placing of money, capital, or other resources to gain a profit, as in interest. **2** That which is invested. **3** That in which one invests. **4** INVESTITURE (def. 1). **5** *Mil.* The surrounding of a fort or town by an enemy force to create a state of siege; a blockade.

in·vet·er·ate (in·vet′ər·it) *adj.* **1** Firmly established by long continuance; deep-rooted. **2** Confirmed in a particular character or habit. [< L *inveterare* make old] —**in·vet′·er·a·cy** (*pl.* **·cies**), **in·vet′er·ate·ness** *n.* —**in·vet′er·ate·ly** *adv.*

in·vid·i·ous (in·vid′ē·əs) *adj.* **1** Expressing, prompted by, or provoking envy or ill will. **2** Unjustly discriminating. [< L *invidia* envy] —**in·vid′i·ous·ly** *adv.* —**in·vid′i·ous·ness** *n.*

in·vig·or·ate (in·vig′ər·āt) *v.t.* **·at·ed, ·at·ing** To give energy to; animate. [< L *in-* in + *vigor* vigor + -ATE²] —**in·vig′or·at′ing·ly** *adv.* —**in·vig′or·a′tion** *n.*

in·vin·ci·ble (in·vin′sə·bəl) *adj.* Not to be overcome; unconquerable. [< L *invincibilis*] —**in·vin′ci·bil′i·ty, in·vin′ci·ble·ness** *n.* —**in·vin′ci·bly** *adv.*

in·vi·o·la·ble (in·vī′ə·lə·bəl) *adj.* That must not or cannot be violated: an *inviolable* agreement. —**in·vi′o·la·bil′i·ty, in·vi′o·la·ble·ness** *n.* —**in·vi′o·la·bly** *adv.*

in·vi·o·late (in·vī′ə·lit) *adj.* Not violated or profaned; unbroken. —**in·vi′o·late·ly** *adv.* —**in·vi′o·la·cy** (-ə·lə·sē), **in·vi′o·late·ness** *n.*

in·vis·i·ble (in·viz′ə·bəl) *adj.* **1** Not visible; not capable of being seen. **2** Not in sight; concealed. **3** Referring to resources or reserves that do not appear in regular processes or in financial statements. —*n.* One who or that which is invisible. —**the Invisible 1** God. **2** The spiritual world. —**in·vis′i·bil′i·ty, in·vis′i·ble·ness** *n.* —**in·vis′i·bly** *adv.*

in·vi·ta·tion (in′və·tā′shən) *n.* **1** The act of inviting. **2** A means of inviting: a written *invitation.* **3** An act of alluring or encouraging; inducement: The unlocked door was an *invitation* to burglary.

in·vite (in·vīt′) *v.* **·vit·ed, ·vit·ing** *v.t.* **1** To ask (someone) politely to be present in some place or to perform some action. **2** To make formal or polite request for: to *invite* suggestions. **3** To present inducement for: The situation *invites* criticism. **4** To tempt; entice. —*n.* (in′vīt) *Slang* An invitation. [< L *invitare* entertain] —**in·vit′er** *n.*

in·vit·ing (in·vī′ting) *adj.* That invites or allures. —**in·vit′·ing·ly** *adv.* —**in·vit′ing·ness** *n.*

in·vo·ca·tion (in′və·kā′shən) *n.* **1** The act of invoking. **2** An opening prayer in a church service. **3** The act of conjuring an evil spirit. **4** The formula or incantation thus used. —**in·voc·a·to·ry** (in·vok′ə·tôr′ē, -tō′rē) *adj.*

in·voice (in′vois) *n.* A list of goods sent to a purchaser, etc., containing prices and charges for shipping. —*v.t.* **·voiced, ·voic·ing** To itemize; make an invoice of. [< F *envoyer* send]

in·voke (in·vōk′) *v.t.* **·voked, ·vok·ing 1** To call on for aid, protection, etc.; address, as in prayer. **2** To call for, as in supplication. **3** To summon or conjure by incantation, as evil spirits. [< L *in-* on + *vocare* to call] —**in·vok′er** *n.*

in·vo·lu·cre (in′və·lōō′kər) *n. Bot.* A ring of bracts surrounding the base of a flower, flower cluster, or fruit. [< L *involucrum* covering] —**in′vo·lu′cral** *adj.*

in·vol·un·tar·y (in·vol′ən·ter′ē) *adj.* **1** Contrary to one's will or wish. **2** Unintentional. **3** Independent of conscious control: *involuntary* muscles. —**in′vol′un·tar′i·ly** *adv.* —**in′vol′un·tar′i·ness** *n.*

Involucre of thistle

in·vo·lute (in′və·lōōt) *adj.* **1** Complicated; not straightforward. **2** *Bot.* Having the edges rolled inward, as a leaf. **3** *Zool.* Coiled in a close spiral, as a shell. Also **in′vo·lut′ed**. [< L *involutus* involved]

in·vo·lu·tion (in′və·lōō′shən) *n.* **1** The act of involving or the state of being involved; complication. **2** Something involved, rolled up, or entangled. **3** *Math.* The raising of a number or quantity to a power.

in·volve (in·volv′) *v.t.* **·volved**, **·volv·ing** **1** To have as a necessary circumstance, condition, or outcome; entail: The study of medicine *involves* hard work. **2** To affect: The collision *involved* four cars. **3** To commit (oneself); engage, as in a productive effort: usu. in p.p.: to want to feel *involved*. **4** To draw into entanglement, trouble, etc.; implicate. **5** To make intricate or difficult; complicate. **6** To hold the attention of; engross. **7** To wrap up or conceal; envelop. **8** To wind in spirals or curves; coil. [< L *involvere* roll into or up] —**in·volve′ment** *n.*

in·vul·ner·a·ble (in·vul′nər·ə·bəl) *adj.* Not capable of being wounded; having no weak point. —**in·vul′ner·a·bil′i·ty, in·vul′ner·a·ble·ness** *n.* —**in·vul′ner·a·bly** *adv.* —**Syn.** indomitable, invincible, inviolable, unassailable.

in·ward (in′wərd) *adv.* **1** Toward the inside, center, or interior. **2** Into the spirit or mind. Also **in′wards**. —*adj.* **1** Situated within, esp. with reference to the body; inner. **2** Pertaining to the mind or spirit. **3** Proceeding toward the inside. **4** Inland. —*n. pl.* (in′ərdz) The internal organs; entrails. [< OE *inweard*]

in·ward·ly (in′wərd·lē) *adv.* **1** In an inward manner; esp., in one's thoughts and feelings; secretly. **2** Within. **3** Toward the center or interior; inward.

in·ward·ness (in′wərd·nis) *n.* **1** The inner quality or meaning. **2** The state of being inward or internal, mentally or physically.

in·weave (in·wēv′) *v.t.* **·wove** or **·weaved**, **·wov·en**, **·weav·ing** To weave in or together.

in·wrap (in·rap′) *v.t.* **·wrapped**, **·wrap·ping** ENWRAP.

in·wreathe (in·rēth′) *v.t.* **·wreathed**, **·wreath·ing** ENWREATHE.

in·wrought (in·rôt′) *adj.* Worked into, as a fabric or metalwork, so as to form part of it.

I·o (ī′ō) *Gk. Myth.* A maiden loved by Zeus and changed by him into a heifer to escape the jealous wrath of Hera.

i·o·dide (ī′ə·dīd) *n.* A compound of iodine with another element or radical.

i·o·dine (ī′ə·dīn, -din, -dēn) *n.* **1** A grayish black crystalline element (symbol I) of the halogen group, having a metallic luster and yielding violet-colored fumes when heated. **2** An antiseptic solution (**tincture of iodine**) of iodine in alcohol. Also **i′o·din**. [< Gk. *iōdēs* violetlike]

i·o·dize (ī′ə·dīz) *v.t.* **·dized**, **·diz·ing** To treat with an iodide or iodine. —**i′o·diz′er, i′o·di·za′tion** *n.*

i·o·do·form (ī·ō′də·fôrm′) *n.* A yellow, crystalline compound of iodine, used as an antiseptic. [< IODINE + FORM(YL)]

i·on (ī′ən, ī′on) *n.* An atom or connected group of atoms that has an excess or deficiency of electrons and is, hence, electrically charged. [< Gk. *iōn*, p.p. of *ienai* go]

-ion *suffix* **1** Action or process of: *communion*. **2** Condition or state of being: *union*. **3** Result of: *opinion*. [< L *-io, -ionis*]

I·on·ic (ī·on′ik) *adj.* Of, pertaining to, or composed of ions.

I·on·ic (ī·on′ik) *adj. Archit.* Of or pertaining to an order of Greek architecture characterized by decorative scrolls on the capitals of the columns. • See CAPITAL.

i·on·ize (ī′ən·īz) *v.t.* **·ized**, **·iz·ing** To convert, totally or in part, into ions. —**i′on·iz′a·ble** *adj.* —**i′on·i·za′tion, i′on·iz′er** *n.*

i·on·o·sphere (ī·on′ə·sfir) *n.* A layer of the earth's atmosphere extending from about 30 miles to over 250 miles above the surface, consisting of partially ionized gases. [< ION + SPHERE]

i·o·ta (ī·ō′tə) *n.* **1** The ninth letter and fourth vowel in the Greek alphabet (I,ι): corresponding to English I,i. **2** A small or insignificant mark or part. —**Syn.** **2** jot, particle, shred, speck, whit.

I O U **1** I owe you. **2** A paper having on it these letters followed by a named sum of indebtedness and the borrower's signature. Also **I.O.U.**

i.p. in passing (chess).

IPA, I.P.A. International Phonetic Alphabet; International Phonetic Association.

ip·e·cac (ip′ə·kak) *n.* **1** A South American plant related to madder. **2** The dried roots of this plant. **3** An extract of the root of this plant, used to induce vomiting. Also **ip·e·cac·u·an·ha** (ip′ə·kak′yōō·ä′nə). [< Tupian *ipe* little + *kaa* tree, herb + *guéne* causing sickness]

Iph·i·ge·ni·a (if′ə·jə·nī′ə) *Gk. Myth.* The daughter of Agamemnon, sacrificed by her father to Artemis, who rescued her and made her a priestess.

ip·se dix·it (ip′sē dik′sit) *Latin* A dogmatic assertion; dictum: lit., he himself has said.

ip·so fac·to (ip′sō fak′tō) By the fact itself; in and by the very fact or act. [L]

IQ, I.Q. intelligence quotient.

Ir iridium.

Ir. Ireland; Irish.

I.R.A. Irish Republican Army.

I·ran (i·ran′, ē·rän′) *n.* A constitutional monarchy in sw Asia, 630,000 sq. mi., cap. Teheran. —**I·ra·ni·an** (ī·rā′nē·ən) *adj., n.*

I·raq (i·rak′, ē·räk′) *n.* A republic of sw Asia, 171,599 sq. mi., cap. Baghdad. Also **I·rak′**.

I·ra·qi (ē·rä′kē) *n. pl.* **·qi** or **·qis** A citizen or native of Iraq. —*adj.* Of or pertaining to Iraq or its people.

Iran and Iraq

i·ras·ci·ble (i·ras′ə·bəl, ī-) *adj.* **1** Easily angered; irritable. **2** Caused by anger. [< L *irasci* be angry.] —**i·ras′ci·bil′i·ty, i·ras′ci·ble·ness** *n.* —**i·ras′ci·bly** *adv.*

i·rate (ī·rāt′, ī′rāt) *adj.* Moved to anger; wrathful. [< L *ira* anger] —**i·rate′ly** *adv.* —**i·rate′ness** *n.*

IRBM intermediate range ballistic missile.

ire (īr) *n.* Strong resentment; anger. [< L *ira* anger] —**ire′ful** (-fəl) *adj.* —**ire′ful·ly** *adv.* —**ire′ful·ness** *n.*

Ire. Ireland.

Ire·land (īr′lənd) *n.* A republic occupying most of the island Ireland, 26,260 sq. mi., cap. Dublin.

ir·i·des·cence (ir′ə·des′əns) *n.* The rainbowlike appearance shown by various bodies, as oil films, mother-of-pearl, etc., when they reflect light. [< Gk. *iris, iridos* rainbow + -ESCENCE] —**ir′i·des′cent** *adj.* —**ir′i·des′cent·ly** *adv.*

ir·id·i·um (i·rid′ē·əm, ī-) *n.* A brittle, silver-gray, metallic element (symbol Ir) of extreme hardness, used in certain alloys for penpoints, jewelry, etc. [< Gk. *iris, iridis* rainbow + -IUM]

i·ris (ī′ris) *n. pl.* **i·ris·es** or **ir·i·des** (ir′ə·dēz, ī′rə-) **1** The colored muscular membrane that surrounds the pupil of the eye. • See EYE. **2** Any of a genus of plants with sword-shaped leaves and large flowers. **3** The flower itself, having three upright petals and three drooping sepals. **4** A rainbow. [< Gk. *iris* rainbow]

I·ris (ī′ris) *Gk. Myth.* The goddess of the rainbow.

Bearded iris

I·rish (ī′rish) *n.* **1** The people of Ireland: used with *the.* **2** People of Irish parentage, collectively. **3** The Celtic language used in Ireland. —*adj.* Of or pertaining to Ireland, its people, or their language.

Irish Gaelic IRISH (def. 3).

I·rish·man (ī′rish·mən) *n. pl.* **·men** (-mən) **1** A citizen or native of Ireland. **2** A person of Irish descent. —**I′rish·wom′an** (*pl.* **·wom·en**) *n. Fem.*

Irish potato The common or white potato.

Irish setter A large long-haired hunting dog with a silky, red-brown coat.

Irish stew A stew usu. made with mutton, potatoes, and onions.

Irish terrier A small dog with a wiry reddish or golden brown coat.

Irish wolfhound A large, powerful hunting dog.

irk (ûrk) v.t. To annoy or weary; irritate. [ME *irken*]

irk·some (ûrk′səm) adj. Troublesome or tiresome. —**irk′·some·ly** adv. —**irk′some·ness** n. —Syn. annoying, tedious, vexing, wearisome.

i·ron (ī′ərn) n. 1 A tough, abundant, malleable, ductile, and strongly magnetic metallic element (symbol Fe) essential to animal and plant life, used in a wide range of alloys essential to industry. 2 A tool, weapon, utensil, etc., made of iron. 3 pl. Fetters, esp. for the feet. 4 A golf club having a metal head. • See GOLF. 5 A device with a smooth, flat surface that is heated and used to press wrinkles out of cloth. 6 A preparation of iron used as a medicine. —**in irons** Fettered or in chains. —adj. 1 Made of iron. 2 Resembling iron in hardness, firmness, etc.: an *iron* constitution. —v.t. 1 To smooth or press (cloth) with an iron. 2 To fetter. 3 To furnish or arm with iron. —v.i. 4 To smooth or press cloth, clothing, etc. with an iron. —**iron out** To eliminate, as difficulties. [< OE *īren*] —**i′ron·er** n.

Iron Age The last and most advanced of the three prehistoric stages of human technology, preceded by the Stone Age and Bronze Age.

i·ron·bound (ī′ərn·bound′) adj. 1 Bound with iron. 2 Faced or surrounded with rocks; rugged. 3 Hard to change; unyielding.

i·ron·clad (ī′ərn·klad′) adj. 1 Protected by iron or steel. 2 Inflexible: an *ironclad* contract. 3 Strong. —n. A former type of warship sheathed with armor.

iron curtain An impenetrable barrier of secrecy and censorship, originally used to describe the dividing line between w Europe and the Soviet Union's sphere of influence.

iron hand Severe and rigorous control; despotism. —**i′ron-hand′ed** adj.

i·ron·ic (ī·ron′ik) adj. 1 Conveying a meaning that contradicts the literal sense of the words used. 2 Being the reverse of what was expected. 3 Of the nature of or given to the use of irony. Also **i·ron′i·cal.** —**i·ron′i·cal·ly** adv. —**i·ron′i·cal·ness** n.

i·ron·ing board (ī′ərn·ing) A board, usu. on legs, covered with smooth material and used for ironing clothes, etc.

iron lung An apparatus used to maintain artificial respiration in a person enclosed in it from the neck down.

i·ron·mon·ger (ī′ərn·mung′gər, -mong′-) n. *Chiefly Brit.* A dealer in iron articles and hardware. —**i·ron·mon·ger·y** (ī′ərn·mung′gər·ē, -mong′-) n.

iron pyrites PYRITE.

i·ron·side (ī′ərn·sīd′) n. 1 A person or thing of tremendous strength or endurance. 2 pl. (construed as sing.) An ironclad vessel.

i·ron·ware (ī′ərn·wâr′) n. Iron utensils, tools, ornaments, etc.; hardware.

i·ron·weed (ī′ərn·wēd′) n. Any of a genus of weedy plants with hard stems and heads of tubular purple flowers.

i·ron·wood (ī′ərn·wood′) n. 1 Any of various trees of unusually hard, heavy, or strong wood. 2 The wood itself.

i·ron·work (ī′ərn·wûrk′) n. Anything made of iron, as parts of a building. —**i′ron·work′er** n.

i·ron·works (ī′ərn·wûrks′) n. sing. & pl. An establishment for the manufacture of iron or of heavy ironwork.

i·ro·ny (ī′rə·nē) n. pl. **·nies** 1 The use of words to signify the opposite of what they usu. express, as: "When he lost his wallet, he said, 'This is my lucky day.'" 2 A condition of affairs or events exactly the reverse of what was expected or hoped for. [< Gk. *eirōneia* affected ignorance, pretense]

Ir·o·quoi·an (ir′ə·kwoi′ən) n. 1 A large North American Indian linguistic stock including the confederacy of the Five Nations and certain other tribes. 2 A member of any of the Iroquoian tribes. —adj. Of or pertaining to the Iroquois Indians, or to any of their languages.

Ir·o·quois (ir′ə·kwoi, -kwoiz) n. pl. **·quois** A member of any of the North American Indian tribes formerly living in New York State, comprising the confederacy of the Five Nations.

ir·ra·di·ate (i·rā′dē·āt) v. **·at·ed, ·at·ing** v.t. 1 To expose to or treat with light or other radiant energy. 2 To make clear or understandable; enlighten. 3 To send forth in or as in rays of light; radiate. —v.i. 4 To emit rays; shine. 5 To become radiant. [< L *in-* thoroughly + *radiare* to shine] —**ir·ra′di·ance, ir·ra′di·a′tion, ir·ra′di·a′tor** n. —**ir·ra′di·ant, ir·ra′di·a′tive** adj.

ir·ra·tion·al (i·rash′ən·əl) adj. 1 Not possessed of or not exercising reasoning powers. 2 *Math.* Not expressible as an integer or a quotient of integers, as $\sqrt{3}$. 3 Contrary to reason; absurd. —**ir·ra′tion·al′i·ty, ir·ra′tion·al·ness** n. —**ir·ra′tion·al·ly** adv.

ir·re·claim·a·ble (ir′i·klā′mə·bəl) adj. That cannot be reclaimed or redeemed. —**ir′re·claim′a·bil′i·ty, ir′re·claim′a·ble·ness** n. —**ir′re·claim′a·bly** adv.

ir·re·con·cil·a·ble (i·rek′ən·sī′lə·bəl, i·rek′ən·sī′lə·bəl) adj. That cannot be reconciled. —n. One who will not agree or become reconciled. —**ir·rec′on·cil′a·bil′i·ty, ir·rec′on·cil′a·ble·ness** n. —**ir·rec′on·cil′a·bly** adv.

ir·re·cov·er·a·ble (ir′i·kuv′er·ə·bəl) adj. That cannot be recovered or regained; lost beyond recall. —**ir′re·cov′er·a·bil′i·ty** n. —**ir′re·cov′er·a·bly** adv.

ir·re·deem·a·ble (ir′i·dē′mə·bəl) adj. 1 Not to be redeemed or replaced by an equivalent. 2 That cannot be changed or corrected. 3 Not to be redeemed in coin: said of certain types of paper money. —**ir′re·deem′a·bly** adv.

ir·re·den·tist (ir′i·den′tist) n. Any member of a political party, esp. one established in Italy in 1878, that advocates the reunion with the "mother country" of a separated national group or region. [< Ital. (*Italia*) *irredenta* unredeemed (Italy)] —**ir′re·den′tism** n.

ir·re·duc·i·ble (ir′i·dyōō′sə·bəl) adj. Not reducible. —**ir′re·duc′i·bil′i·ty, ir′re·duc′i·ble·ness** n. —**ir′re·duc′i·bly** adv.

ir·re·fra·ga·ble (i·ref′rə·gə·bəl, ir′i·frag′ə·bəl) adj. That cannot be refuted or disproved. [< L *in-* not + *refragari* oppose] —**ir·ref′ra·ga·bil′i·ty, ir·ref′ra·ga·ble·ness** n. —**ir·ref′ra·ga·bly** adv.

ir·re·fu·ta·ble (i·ref′yə·tə·bəl, ir′i·fyōō′tə·bəl) adj. Not refutable; that cannot be disproved. —**ir·ref′u·ta·bil′i·ty** n. —**ir·ref′u·ta·bly** adv.

irreg. irregular; irregularly.

ir·re·gard·less (ir′i·gärd′lis) adj. & adv. *Nonstand.* Regardless.

ir·reg·u·lar (i·reg′yə·lər) adj. 1 Not regular; departing from the usual or accepted state of things: an *irregular* heartbeat. 2 Not symmetrical or even: *irregular* features. 3 Not conforming in action or character to rule, duty, discipline, etc.: *irregular* habits. 4 Not belonging to a regular military force. 5 *Gram.* Not inflected or conjugated according to the most prevalent pattern: *irregular* verbs. 6 Not according to rule; not complying with legal formalities. —n. An irregular person or thing. —**ir·reg′u·lar·ly** adv. —Syn. 1 abnormal, erratic. 2 asymmetrical, uneven. 3 lawless, uncontrolled.

ir·reg·u·lar·i·ty (i·reg′yə·lar′ə·tē) n. pl. **·ties** 1 The condition of being irregular; an aberration, inconsistency, etc. 2 Something in an irregular state or condition.

ir·rel·e·vant (i·rel′ə·vənt) adj. Not relevant or pertinent. —**ir·rel′e·vance, ir·rel′e·van·cy** (pl. **·cies**) n. —**ir·rel′e·vant·ly** adv.

ir·re·li·gion (ir′i·lij′ən) n. The state of being without or opposed to religion; unbelief. —**ir·re·lig′ion·ist** n.

ir·re·li·gious (ir′i·lij′əs) adj. 1 Not religious; indifferent or opposed to religion. 2 Not in accordance with religious practices; profane. —**ir′re·lig′ious·ly** adv. —**ir′re·lig′ious·ness** n.

ir·re·me·di·a·ble (ir′i·mē′dē·ə·bəl) adj. Not to be remedied; irreparable. —**ir′re·me′di·a·ble·ness** n. —**ir′re·me′di·a·bly** adv.

ir·re·mis·si·ble (ir′ə·mis′ə·bəl) adj. Impossible to forgive or pardon; not remissible. —**ir're·mis'si·bil'i·ty, ir're·mis'si·ble·ness** n. —**ir're·mis'si·bly** adv.

ir·re·mov·a·ble (ir'i·mōō'və·bəl) adj. Not removable; permanent. —**ir're·mov·a·bil'i·ty** n. —**ir're·mov'a·bly** adv.

ir·rep·a·ra·ble (i·rep'ər·ə·bəl) adj. That cannot be repaired, rectified, or made amends for. —**ir·rep'a·ra·bil'i·ty, ir·rep'a·ra·ble·ness** n. —**ir·rep'a·ra·bly** adv.

ir·re·place·a·ble (ir'i·plā'sə·bəl) adj. Not capable of being replaced by another.

ir·re·pres·si·ble (ir'i·pres'ə·bəl) adj. Not repressible; that cannot be restrained. —**ir're·pres'si·bil'i·ty, ir're·pres'si·ble·ness** n. —**ir're·pres'si·bly** adv.

ir·re·proach·a·ble (ir'i·prō'chə·bəl) adj. Not reproachable; blameless. [< F *irréprochable*] —**ir're·proach'a·bil'i·ty, ir're·proach'a·ble·ness** n. —**ir're·proach'a·bly** adv.

ir·re·sis·ti·ble (ir'i·zis'tə·bəl) adj. Not resistible; too urgent, inviting, etc., to be withstood —**ir're·sis'ti·bil'i·ty, ir're·sis'ti·ble·ness** n. —**ir're·sis'ti·bly** adv.

ir·res·o·lute (i·rez'ə·lōōt) adj. Wanting in firmness of purpose; wavering. —**ir·res'o·lute'ly** adv. —**ir·res'o·lute'ness, ir·res'o·lu'tion** n.

ir·re·spec·tive (ir'i·spek'tiv) adj. Regardless: with of. —**ir're·spec'tive·ly** adv.

ir·re·spon·si·ble (ir'i·spon'sə·bəl) adj. 1 Not responsible or sober in action; careless in heeding responsibilities. 2 Not responsible for one's actions; not accountable, as because of age or mental illness. —n. A person who is irresponsible. —**ir're·spon'si·bil'i·ty, ir're·spon'si·ble·ness** n. —**ir're·spon'si·bly** adv.

ir·re·spon·sive (ir'i·spon'siv) adj. Giving no response. —**ir're·spon'sive·ness** n.

ir·re·triev·a·ble (ir'i·trē'və·bəl) adj. Not retrievable; irreparable. —**ir're·triev·a·bil'i·ty, ir're·triev'a·ble·ness** n. —**ir're·triev'a·bly** adv.

ir·rev·er·ence (i·rev'ər·əns) n. 1 The quality or condition of being irreverent. 2 An irreverent act or remark.

ir·rev·er·ent (i·rev'ər·ənt) adj. Lacking in proper reverence; without respect. —**ir·rev'er·ent·ly** adv.

ir·re·vers·i·ble (ir'i·vûr'sə·bəl) adj. That cannot be reversed, repealed, or annulled. —**ir're·vers'i·bil'i·ty, ir're·vers'i·ble·ness** n. —**ir're·vers'i·bly** adv.

ir·rev·o·ca·ble (i·rev'ə·kə·bəl) adj. Incapable of being revoked; unalterable. —**ir·rev'o·ca·bil'i·ty, ir·rev'o·ca·ble·ness** n. —**ir·rev'o·ca·bly** adv.

ir·ri·gate (ir'ə·gāt) v.t. **·gat·ed, ·gat·ing** 1 To supply (land) with water by means of ditches or other artificial channels. 2 Med. To wash out (a wound, body cavity, etc.) with water or other fluid. [< L *irrigare* bring water to] —**ir'ri·ga·ble** (ir'ə·gə·bəl) adj. —**ir'ri·ga'tion, ir'ri·ga'tor** n.

ir·ri·ta·ble (ir'ə·tə·bəl) adj. 1 Showing impatience or ill temper on little provocation; irascible. 2 Responsive to stimuli. 3 Pathol. Abnormally sensitive. [< L *irritare* irritate] —**ir'ri·ta·bil'i·ty, ir'ri·ta·ble·ness** n. —**ir'ri·ta·bly** adv.

ir·ri·tant (ir'ə·tənt) adj. Causing irritation. —n. 1 An agent of inflammation, pain, etc. 2 A provocation; spur. —**ir'ri·tan·cy** n.

ir·ri·tate (ir'ə·tāt) v.t. **·tat·ed, ·tat·ing** 1 To excite ill temper or impatience in; exasperate. 2 To make sore or inflamed. 3 Biol. To excite, as organic tissue, to a characteristic reaction. [< L *irritare* irritate] —**ir'ri·tat'ing·ly** adv. —**ir'ri·ta'tive** adj. —**ir'ri·ta'tor** n.

ir·ri·ta·tion (ir'ə·tā'shən) n. 1 The act of irritating. 2 The state of being irritated. 3 A person or thing that irritates.

ir·rup·tion (i·rup'shən) n. 1 A breaking or rushing in. 2 A violent incursion. [< L *irruptus*, pp. of *irrumpere* burst in] —**ir·rup'tive** adj.

IRS Internal Revenue Service.

is (iz) Present tense, third person singular of BE. [< OE]

Is, Is., Isa. Isaiah.

is. island(s); isle(s).

I·saac (ī'zək) In the Bible, the son of Abraham and Sarah, and father of Esau and Jacob.

i·sa·go·ge (ī'sə·gō'jē) n. An introduction, as to a work of scholarship. [< Gk. *eisagein* introduce] —**i'sa·gog'ic** (-goj'ik) adj.

I·sa·iah (ī·zā'ə, ī·zī'ə) A major Hebrew prophet of the eighth century B.C. —n. A book of the Old Testament attributed wholly or in part to him. Also **I·sai·as** (-əs). —**I·sa'ian** adj.

Is·car·i·ot (is·kar'ē·ət) JUDAS ISCARIOT.

is·che·mi·a (is·kē'mē·ə) n. Inadequate blood circulation in an organ or tissue. Also **is·chae'mi·a.** [< Gk. *ischein* to hold, check + *haima* blood] —**is·che'mic** adj.

is·chi·um (is'kē·əm) n. pl. **·chi·a** (-kē-ə) The posterior part of the hipbone. Also **is·chi·on** (is'kē·ən). [< Gk. *ischion* hip, hip joint] —**is'chi·al** (-əl) adj. • See PELVIS.

-ise Chiefly Brit. -IZE.

-ish suffix 1 Of or belonging to (a national group): Danish. 2 Of the nature of; like: clownish. 3 Verging toward the character of: bookish. 4 Somewhat; rather: tallish. 5 Informal Approximately: fiftyish. [< OE -isc]

Ish·ma·el (ish'mā·əl) In the Bible, the son of Abraham and Hagar, exiled with the latter. —n. An outcast.

Ish·ma·el·ite (ish'mē·əl·īt') n. 1 A traditional descendant of Ishmael. Gen. 21: 9–21. 2 Any wanderer; outcast. —**Ish·ma·el·it'ish** (-ī'tish) adj.

Ish·tar (ish'tär) In Babylonian and Assyrian mythology, the wife of Tammuz and goddess of love and fertility.

i·sin·glass (ī'zing·glas, ī'zən-, -gläs) n. 1 A preparation of gelatin made from fish bladders. 2 Mica, esp. in thin, translucent sheets. [< MDu. *huysenblas* sturgeon bladder]

I·sis (ī'sis) In Egyptian mythology, the goddess of fertility, sister and wife of Osiris.

isl. island(s).

Is·lam (is'ləm, iz'-, is·läm') n. 1 The religion of the Muslims, which maintains that there is but one God, Allah, and that Mohammed is his prophet. 2 The body of Muslim believers, their culture, and the countries they inhabit. —**Is·lam'ic** adj. —**Is'lam·ism, Is'lam·ite** n.

Is·lam·ize (is'ləm·īz, iz'-) v.t. & v.i. **·ized, ·iz·ing** To convert or conform to Islam.

is·land (ī'lənd) n. 1 A land mass, usu. of moderate size, surrounded by water. 2 Anything isolated or like an island. 3 A raised safety area in the middle of a wide street or at a crossing. 4 Anat. A group of cells differing from the surrounding tissue. —v.t. To make into an island or islands; insulate. [< OE *igland*, lit., island land]

is·land·er (ī'lən·dər) n. An inhabitant of an island.

isle (īl) n. A small island. —v. **isled, isl·ing** v.t. To make into an isle. [< L *insula* island]

is·let (ī'lit) n. A little island. • See ATOLL.

ism (iz'əm) n. A doctrine or system: often applied satirically or disparagingly. [< -ISM]

-ism suffix of nouns 1 The act, process, or result of: ostracism. 2 The condition of being: skepticism. 3 The characteristic action or behavior of: heroism. 4 The beliefs, teachings, or system of: Calvinism. 5 Devotion to; adherence to the teachings of: nationalism. 6 A characteristic or peculiarity of: said of language or idiom: Americanism. 7 Med. An abnormal condition: alcoholism. [< Gk. -ismos]

is·n't (iz'ənt) Contraction of is not.

iso- combining form Equal; the same; identical: isobar. Also **is-.** [< Gk. *isos* equal]

i·so·bar (ī'sə·bär) n. 1 Meteorol. A line, as on a weather map, composed of points having identical barometric pressure. 2 Physics Any of several nuclei of different elements that have the same mass number. [< ISO- + Gk. *baros* weight] —**i'so·bar'ic** (-bar'ik) adj.

i·soch·ro·nal (ī·sok'rə·nəl) adj. Of or characterized by equal intervals of time. Also **i·so·chron·ic** (ī'sə·kron'ik), **i·soch'ro·nous.** [< ISO- + Gk. *chronos* time] —**i·soch'ro·nous·ly** adv.

i·so·cline (ī'sə·klīn) n. Geol. A rock fold in which the strata are so closely pressed that they are parallel. [< ISO- + Gk. *klinein* to bend] —**i·so·cli·nal** (ī'sə·klī'nəl), **i'so·clin'ic** (-klin'ik) adj.

i·so·gon·ic (ī'sə·gon'ik) adj. 1 Having equal angles. 2 Denoting a line composed of points on the earth having identical magnetic declination. Also **i·sog·o·nal** (ī·sog'ə·nəl). —n. An isogonic line. [< ISO- + Gk. *gōnia* angle]

i·so·late (ī'sə·lāt, is'ə-) v.t. **·lat·ed, ·lat·ing** 1 To place in a detached or separate situation; set apart. 2 Electr. To insulate. 3 Chem. To obtain in a pure form, as an element or compound. 4 Med. To set apart from others, as a person with a communicable disease. 5 Bacteriol. To obtain a pure culture of (a specified virus or bacterium). —n. A unit or group that is set apart. [< Ital. *isolare* isolate <

isola island < L *insula* island] —**i·so·la′tion, i′so·la′tor** *n.* —
Syn. *v.* **1** banish, seclude, segregate. **4** quarantine.

i·so·la·tion·ism (ī′sə·lā′shən·iz′əm) *n.* The advocacy of
national self-sufficiency and freedom from foreign political and economic alliances. —**i′so·la′tion·ist** *adj., n.* —**i′so·**
la′tion·is′tic *adj.*

i·so·mer (ī′sə·mər) *n.* Any of two or more compounds having the same molecular formula but with a different arrangement of the atoms in a molecule. [< ISO- + Gk. *meros*
part] —**i′so·mer′ic** (-mer′ik) *adj.* —**i·som·er·ism** (ī·som′ər·
iz′əm) *n.*

i·som·er·ous (ī·som′ər·əs) *adj.* Equal in number, as the
members of the successive whorls of a flower.

i·so·met·ric (ī′sō·met′rik) *adj.* **1** Having equal measures.
2 Having a constant measure. Also **i′so·met′ri·cal.** [< ISO-
+ Gk. *metron* measure] —**i′so·met′ri·cal·ly** *adv.*

isometric exercises A means of strengthening muscles by forcefully contracting them against immovable
resistance. Also **i′so·met′rics.**

i·so·morph (ī′sə·môrf) *n.* An organism or crystal superficially like another morphologically. [< ISO- + Gk. *morphē*
form] —**i′so·mor′phism** *n.*

i·so·mor·phic (ī′sə·môr′fik) *adj.* **1** Of or denoting an iso-
morph. **2** *Math.* Exhibiting a one-to-one correspondence
between elements and analogy between the operations
performed on those elements, as two sets.

i·sos·ce·les (ī·sos′ə·lēz) *adj. Geom.* Having two sides of
equal length, as a triangle. [< Gk. *isos-*
kelēs equal-legged]

i·so·therm (ī′sə·thûrm) *n.* A line, as on a
weather map, composed of points that
have the same temperature. [< ISO- + Gk.
thermē heat]

Isosceles
triangle
(ac = bc)

i·so·ther·mal (ī′sə·thûr′məl) *adj.* Having
a constant or uniform temperature. —*n.* ISOTHERM. —**i′so·**
ther′mal·ly *adv.*

i·so·ton·ic (ī′sə·ton′ik) *adj.* **1** Having the same tension.
2 *Physiol.* Exerting the same osmotic pressure, as blood or
other specified fluid. **3** *Music* Pertaining to, characterized
by, or having equal tones. [< ISO- + Gk. *tonos* accent, tone]
—**i·so·ton·ic·i·ty** (ī′sə·tō·nis′ə·tē) *n.*

i·so·tope (ī′sə·tōp) *n.* Any of two or more forms of an
element having the same atomic number and similar
chemical properties but differing in atomic weight. [< ISO-
+ Gk. *topos* place] —**i·so·top·ic** (ī′sə·top′ik, -tō′pik) *adj.* —
i·sot·o·py (ī·sot′ə·pē) *n.*

i·so·trop·ic (ī′sə·trop′ik, -trō′pik) *adj. Physics* Exhibiting the same physical properties in every direction. Also
i′so·trope, i·sot·ro·pous (ī·sot′rə·pəs). [< ISO- + Gk. *tropos* a
turn]

Is·ra·el (iz′rē·əl) *n.* **1** A republic at the E end of the Mediterranean, 7,993 sq. mi., cap. Jerusalem. •See map at
JORDAN. **2** The Jewish people, traditionally regarded as
descended from Israel (Jacob). **3** The kingdom in the
northern part of ancient Palestine. **4** The name bestowed
upon Jacob after he had wrestled with the angel. *Gen.*
32:28.

Is·rae·li (iz·rā′lē) *n. pl.* **·lis** or **·li** A citizen or native of modern Israel. —*adj.* Of or pertaining to modern Israel or its
people.

Is·ra·el·ite (iz′rē·əl·īt′) *n.* Any of the people of ancient
Israel or their descendants; a Hebrew; a Jew. —*adj.* Of or
pertaining to ancient Israel or the Israelites. —**Is′ra·el·it′·**
ish (-ī′tish), **Is′ra·el·it′ic** (-it′ik) *adj.*

is·su·ance (ish′yōō·əns) *n.* The act of putting, sending, or
giving out; distribution. —**is′su·ant** *adj.*

is·sue (ish′yōō) *v.* **·sued, ·su·ing** *v.t.* **1** To give out or deliver
in a public or official manner: to *issue* a magazine. **2** To
deal out or distribute: to *issue* ammunition. **3** To send
forth; let out. —*v.i.* **4** To come forth or flow out; emerge.
5 To come as a result or consequence; proceed. **6** To be
given out or published; appear. **7** To come as profit or
revenue; accrue: with *out of.* —*n.* **1** A subject of discussion
or interest; the matter at hand. **2** Result; outcome; upshot.
3 The action of giving out or supplying officially or publicly. **4** An item or amount which is issued. **5** Offspring;

progeny. **6** Profits; proceeds. **7** The act of going out; outflow. **8** A place or way of egress. **9** *Law* The point in question between parties to an action. [< L *ex-* out of + *ire* go]
—**at issue** Under dispute; in question. —**take issue** To
disagree. —**is′su·er** *n.* —**Syn.** *v.* **1** print, publish. **2** allot,
dispense. **3** discharge, emit.

-ist *suffix* **1** One who or that which does or has to do with:
catechist. **2** One whose profession is: *pharmacist.* **3** A student or devotee of: *genealogist.* **4** One who advocates or
adheres to: *socialist.* [< Gk. *-istēs*]

isth·mi·an (is′mē·ən) *adj.* Of or pertaining to an isthmus.
—*n.* An inhabitant of an isthmus.

isth·mus (is′məs) *n. pl.* **·mus·es** or **·mi** (-mī) A narrow body
of land connecting two larger bodies. —**the Isthmus** The
Isthmus of Panama. [< Gk. *isthmos* narrow passage]

is·tle (ist′lē) *n.* A fiber derived from various tropical
American plants, used for carpets, cordage, etc. [< Nahuatl *ichtli*]

it (it) *pron.* The neuter pronoun, nominative and objective
of the third person singular, used: **1** As a substitute for
things or for infants and animals when the sex is unspecified. **2** As the subject of an impersonal verb: *It* rained. **3**
As the subject or object of a clause regarding a general
condition or state of affairs: *It* was warm. **4** As the subject
or predicate nominative of a verb whose logical subject is
anticipated: Who was *it*? *It* was John. **5** As the indefinite
subject of a verb introducing a clause or phrase: *It* seems
that he knew. **6** *Informal* As the indefinite object after
certain verbs in idiomatic expressions: to lord *it* over; to
face *it*. —*n.* In certain children's games, the player required to perform some specified act. [< OE *hit*]

It., Ital. Italian; Italy.

it., ital. italic; italics.

I.T.A., i/t/a Initial Teaching Alphabet.

I·tal·ian (i·tal′yən) *n.* **1** A native or citizen of Italy. **2** A
person of Italian parentage. **3** The language of Italy. —
adj. Of or pertaining to Italy, its people, or their language.

i·tal·ic (i·tal′ik) *Printing n.* A style of type in which the
letters slope, as *these:* also **i·tal′ics.** —*adj.* Designating, or
printed in, italic.

I·tal·ic (i·tal′ik) *adj.* Relating to any of the peoples of ancient Italy. —*n.* A subfamily of the Indo-European languages.

i·tal·i·cize (i·tal′ə·sīz) *v.t. & v.i.* **·cized, ·ciz·ing** **1** To print
in italics. **2** To underscore (written words or phrases) with
a single line to indicate italics. *Brit. sp.* **·cise.**

It·a·ly (it′ə·lē) *n.* A republic of s Europe, 116,286 sq. mi.,
cap. Rome.

itch (ich) *v.i.* **1** To feel
a peculiar irritation of
the skin which in-
clines one to scratch
the part affected. **2** To
have a desire or long-
ing; crave. —*n.* **1** SCA-
BIES. **2** An itching of
the skin. **3** A restless
desire or yearning. [<
OE *giccan*] —**itch′i·**
ness *n.* —**itch′y** *adj.*

-ite [1] *suffix of nouns* **1**
A native of: *Brook-*
lynite. **2** An adherent
of: *Darwinite.* **3** A descendant of: *Israelite.*
4 *Mineral.* A rock or
mineral: *graphite.* **5**
Zool. A part of the body or of an organ: *somite.* **6** *Paleontol.*
A fossil: *ammonite.* **7** Like; resembling; related to: often
used in the names of commercial products: *dynamite.* [<
Gk. *-itēs*]

-ite [2] *suffix* A salt or ester of an acid whose name ends in
-ous: sulfite. [< F *-ite*]

i·tem (ī′təm) *n.* **1** A separate article or entry in an account,
etc. **2** A newspaper paragraph. —*v.t.* To set down by items.
—*adv.* Likewise. [L, likewise]

i·tem·ize (ī'təm·īz) v.t. **-ized, -iz·ing** To set down or specify by items. —**i'tem·i·za'tion, i'tem·iz'er** n.

it·er·ate (it'ə·rāt) v.t. **-at·ed, -at·ing** To utter or do again. [< L *iterum* again] —**it'er·a·ble** (it'ər·ə·bəl) adj. —**it'er·ance, it'er·a'tion** n.

it·er·a·tive (it'ə·rā'tiv, it'ər·ə·tiv) adj. Characterized by repetition; repetitious.

i·tin·er·an·cy (ī·tin'ə·rən·sē, i·tin'-) n. A passing from place to place in circuit. Also **i·tin'er·a·cy.**

i·tin·er·ant (ī·tin'ər·ənt, i·tin'-) adj. Going from place to place. —n. One who travels from place to place. [< L *iter, itineris* journey] —**i·tin'er·ant·ly** adv. —**Syn.** adj. nomadic, peripatetic, wandering, wayfaring.

i·tin·er·ar·y (ī·tin'ə·rer'ē, i·tin'-) n. pl. **·ar·ies 1** A detailed account or diary of a journey. **2** A plan of a proposed tour. **3** A route pursued in traveling. **4** A guidebook. —adj. **1** Pertaining to or done on a journey. **2** ITINERANT. [< L *iter, itineris* journey, route]

i·tin·er·ate (ī·tin'ər·āt, i·tin'-) v.i. **-at·ed, -at·ing** To journey from place to place in or on circuit. —**i·tin'er·a'tion** n.

-itis suffix Inflammation of: *laryngitis.* [< Gk.]

it'll (it'l) Contraction of *it will* and *it shall.*

its (its) pronominal adj. (possessive case of the pronoun *it*) Belonging or pertaining to it: *its* color.

it's (its) Contraction of *it is* and *it has.*

it·self (it·self') pron. It: an intensive or reflexive use.

IU, I.U. international unit(s).

IUD, IUCD intrauterine (contraceptive) device.

I've (īv) Contraction of *I have.*

-ive suffix of adjectives **1** Having a tendency or predisposition to: *disruptive.* **2** Having the nature, character, or quality of: *massive.* [< L *-ivus*]

i·vied (ī'vēd) adj. Overgrown with ivy.

i·vo·ry (ī'vər·ē) n. pl. **·ries 1** The hard, creamy-white dentine that forms the tusks of the elephant, walrus, etc. **2** Any ivorylike substance. **3** pl. Things made of or similar to ivory; esp. in slang use, the teeth, dice, keys of a piano, etc. **4** The color of ivory. —adj. Made of or resembling ivory. [< L *ebur* ivory]

Ivory Coast A republic of w Africa, 128,364 sq. mi., cap. Abidjan. •See map at AFRICA.

ivory nut The hard, ivorylike seed of a South American palm, used for small carvings, buttons, etc.

ivory tower A retreat from reality and action to the world of dreams and ideals.

i·vy (ī'vē) n. pl. **i·vies 1** Any of a genus of woody climbing plants with glossy, trilobate, evergreen leaves. **2** Any of various climbing or creeping plants, as poison ivy, Virginia creeper, etc. [< OE *ifig*]

Ivy League An association of colleges and universities in the NE U.S., regarded as high in scholastic and social distinction.

IWW, I.W.W. Industrial Workers of the World.

-ize suffix of verbs **1** To make; cause to become or resemble: *Christianize.* **2** Subject to the action of; affect with: *oxidize.* **3** Change into; become: *mineralize.* **4** To act in the manner of; to practice: *sympathize.* Brit. sp., often **-ise.** [< Gk. *-izein*]

J

J, j (jā) n. pl. **J's, j's, Js, js** (jāz) **1** The tenth letter of the English alphabet. **2** Any spoken sound representing the letter *J* or *j.* **3** Something shaped like a J, as a bolt or hook. —adj. Shaped like a J.

J joule.

J. Judge; Justice.

JA, J.A. Joint Account; Judge Advocate.

jab (jab) v.t. & v.i. **jabbed, jab·bing 1** To poke or thrust sharply. **2** To punch or strike with sharp blows. —n. A sharp thrust or poke: punch. [ME *jobben*]

jab·ber (jab'ər) v.t. & v.i. To speak rapidly or unintelligibly; chatter. —n. Rapid or unintelligible talk. [Imit.]

ja·bot (zha·bō', jab'ō; Fr. zhà·bō') n. pl. **·bots** (-bōz'; Fr. -bō') A frill, as of lace, worn down the front of a woman's blouse or, formerly, on a man's shirt. [F]

ja·cinth (jā'sinth, jas'inth) n. **1** HYACINTH. **2** A reddish orange color. [< L *hyacinthus* hyacinth]

jack (jak) n. **1** Mech. **a** One of various machines or devices used to replace a human worker: often used in combination: *bootjack.* **b** Any of various devices using the principle of a lever, screw, etc., placed under or against a load and used to lift or move it. **2** A man or boy. **3** A manual laborer: often used in combination: *lumberjack.* **4** Often cap. A sailor. **5** A male donkey; jackass. **6** JACK RABBIT. **7** Any of various birds, as a jackdaw. **8** Electr. A socket equipped with a spring clip for holding a plug to make a connection. **9** A playing card with a young man's picture on it; knave. **10** One of the small, pronged metal pieces used in the game of jacks; a jackstone. **11** A ship's flag showing its nationality; union jack. **12** Slang Money. —v.t. **1** To raise or lift with or as with a jack. **2** Informal To advance, as a price or charge: often with *up.* [< *Jack*, a personal name]

jack·al (jak'əl, -ôl) n. **1** Any of various wild dogs of Africa and Asia, usu. yellowish gray in color. **2** One who does base or menial work for another. [< Pers. *shaghal*]

jack·a·napes (jak'ə·nāps) n. An impertinent fellow; an upstart. [< *Jack Napes*, nickname of William de la Pole, 15th c. Duke of Suffolk]

jack·ass (jak'as') n. **1** The male ass. **2** A stupid person; fool.

jack·boot (jak'bōōt') n. A heavy boot reaching above the knee.

jack·daw (jak'dô') n. A small, black bird of Europe, related to the crow.

jack·et (jak'it) n. **1** A short coat, usu. not extending below the hips. **2** A close-fitting outer covering, as the paper cover for a bound book, a paper or cardboard cover for a phonograph record, the skin of a potato, the casing of a bullet, an open envelope or folder for filing letters, documents, etc. —v.t. To cover with or put into a jacket. [< OF *jaque* a coat] —**jack'et·ed** adj.

Jack Frost Wintry or frosty weather personified.

jack-in-the-box (jak'in·thə·boks') n. pl. **-box·es** A toy consisting of a grotesque figure in a box, springing up when the lid is unfastened. Also **jack'-in-a-box'.**

jack-in-the-pul·pit (jak'in·thə·pŏŏl'pit) n. pl. **·pits** A small woodland plant of the arum family, with flowers on a spadix enclosed in a greenish purple spathe.

jack·knife (jak'nīf') n. pl. **·knives** (-nīvz) **1** A large pocket knife with recessed handle into which the blade is folded. **2** A dive during which the body is doubled from the hips with the hands touching the ankles, and then straightened before entering the water. —v.t. & v.i. **-knifed, -knif·ing** To fold or double up, as a jackknife.

jack-of-all-trades (jak'əv·ôl'trādz') n. One who is able to do many kinds of work.

jack-o'-lan·tern (jak'ə·lan'tərn) n. **1** IGNIS FATUUS (def. 1). **2** A lantern made of a pumpkin carved into a face.

Jack-in-the-pulpit Fruit and flower

jack·pot (jak'pot')n. **1** In poker, a pot that must accumulate till one of the players gets a pair of jacks or cards of higher value on the deal. **2** Any prize or stakes in which winnings or contributions accumulate. —**hit the jackpot** Informal To win the biggest possible prize; to achieve a major success.

jack rabbit One of a genus of large American hares with strong hind legs and long ears.

Jabot

jacks (jaks) *n. pl. (construed as sing.)* A children's game in which small, pronged pieces of metal are picked up in a certain sequence while bouncing a ball.

jack·stone (jak′stōn′) *n.* **1** JACK (def. 10). **2** *pl. (construed as sing.)* JACKS.

jack·straw (jak′strô′) *n.* **1** A straw effigy. **2** One of a set of straws or thin strips of wood used in playing a child's game (**jackstraws**).

Ja·cob (jā′kəb) In the Bible, a Hebrew patriarch, son of Isaac and father of the founders of the twelve tribes of Israel.

Jac·o·be·an (jak′ə·bē′ən) *adj.* Of or pertaining to the time of James I of England and sometimes of James II. — *n.* A Jacobean writer or politician. [< LL *Jacobus* James]

Jac·o·bin (jak′ə·bin) *n.* **1** A member of a French revolutionary society that inaugurated the Reign of Terror, 1793. **2** An extreme revolutionist. [< LL *Jacobus* James; with ref. to the church of St. James, in Paris, where the society met]

Jac·o·bite (jak′ə·bīt) *n.* An adherent of James II of England after his abdication in 1688, or of his royal line. — *adj.* Of the Jacobites: also **Jac·o·bit·ic** (jak′ə·bit′ik) or **·i·cal.**

Jacob's ladder 1 A ladder from earth to heaven that Jacob saw in a dream. *Gen.* 28:12. **2** *Naut.* A rope ladder, often with wooden steps.

jade¹ (jād) *n.* **1** A tough, hard, silicate mineral, usu. green or white, used for making jewelry. **2** The color of green jade. [< Sp. *(piedra de) ijada* (stone for) colic]

jade² (jād) *n.* **1** An old, worn-out horse. **2** A flirtatious or disreputable girl or woman. — *v.t. & v.i.* **jad·ed, jad·ing** To weary or become weary by hard service. [?]

jad·ed (jā′did) *adj.* **1** Worn-out; exhausted. **2** Bored or indifferent, as from overindulgence or too much experience. —**jad′ed·ly** *adv.* —**jad′ed·ness** *n.*

jae·ger (yā′gər, *also* jā′gər *for def.* 1) *n.* **1** A sea bird that pursues and robs smaller birds of their prey. **2** A huntsman or hunting attendant. [< OHG *jagon* to hunt]

jag¹ (jag) *n.* A projecting point; notch; tooth. — *v.t.* **jagged, jag·ging 1** To cut notches or jags in. **2** To cut unevenly or with slashing strokes, as a garment. [ME *jagge*]

jag² (jag) *n. Slang* A spree or fit: a crying *jag.* —**have a jag on** *Slang* To be intoxicated, as on liquor or drugs. [?]

jag·ged (jag′id) *adj.* Having jags or notches. —**jag′ged·ly** *adv.* —**jag′ged·ness** *n.*

jag·uar (jag′wär, jag′yŏŏ·är) *n.* A large, tawny, spotted cat of tropical America. [< Tupian *jaguara*]

Jah·veh (yä′ve) YAHWEH. Also **Jah′we.**

jai a·lai (hī′lī′, hī′ə·lī′) A Latin-American game, similar to handball, in which players wear a long curved basket attached to one arm. [< Basque, jolly festival]

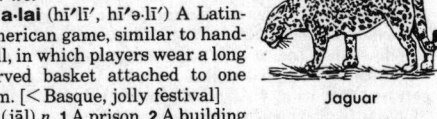
Jaguar

jail (jāl) *n.* **1** A prison. **2** A building used to confine persons awaiting trial or those guilty of minor offenses. — *v.t.* To put or hold in jail. [< OF *jaiole*]

jail·bird (jāl′bûrd′) *n. Informal* A prisoner, esp. one often confined to prison.

jail·er (jā′lər) *n.* The officer in charge of a jail. Also **jail′or.**

Jain (jīn) *n.* An adherent of Jainism. Also **Jai·na** (jī′nə). [< Hind. *Jaina* < *jina* victorious]

Jain·ism (jī′niz·əm) *n.* A religion of India founded in the sixth century B.C. and marked by asceticism and belief in the transmigration of the soul.

jal·ap (jal′əp) *n.* **1** The dried root of any of several Mexican plants related to the morning glory. **2** A purgative drug obtained from this root. [< Sp. *(purga de) Jalapa* (medicine from) Jalapa] —**ja·lap·ic** (jə·lap′ik) *adj.*

ja·lop·y (jə·lop′ē) *n. pl.* **·lop·ies** *Informal* A decrepit automobile. [?]

ja·lou·sie (jal′ŏŏ·sē, zhal′ŏŏ·zē′) *n.* A blind, window, shutter, or door having adjustable horizontal slats, as of metal or glass, for regulating the passage of light and air. [< F, lit., jealousy]

jam¹ (jam) *v.* **jammed, jam·ming** *v.t.* **1** To press or force into a tight place or position; wedge or squeeze in. **2** To fill and block up by crowding. **3** To bruise or crush by violent pressure. **4** To cause (a machine, part, etc.) to become wedged or stuck fast so that it cannot work. **5** To transmit signals designed to block reception of (a radio broadcast, station, etc.). — *v.i.* **6** To become wedged; stick fast. **7** To press or wedge; push. **8** In jazz music, to take part in a jam session. — *n.* **1** A jamming or being jammed. **2** A number of people or objects closely crowded together. **3** *Informal* A predicament. — *adv.* Completely: *jam* full. [?]

jam² (jam) *n.* A pulpy conserve of fruit boiled with sugar. [? < JAM¹, *v.*]

Jam. Jamaica.

Ja·mai·ca (jə·mā′kə) *n.* An independent member of the Commonwealth of Nations, located on an island in the Caribbean, 4,411 sq. mi., cap. Kingston. —**Ja·mai′can** *adj., n.* • See map at CUBA.

jamb (jam) *n.* A side post or side of a doorway, window, etc. [< OF *jambe* leg, support]

jam·bo·ree (jam′bə·rē′) *n.* **1** *Informal* A boisterous frolic or spree. **2** A large, esp. international, assembly of Boy Scouts. [?]

jam session An informal gathering of jazz musicians performing improvisations.

Jan., Jan. January

jan·gle (jang′gəl) *v.* **·gled, ·gling** *v.i.* **1** To make harsh, annoying sounds. **2** To quarrel or bicker. — *v.t.* **3** To cause to make harsh, annoying sounds. — *n.* **1** Discordant sound. **2** Quarreling. [< OF *jangler*] —**jan′gler** *n.*

jan·i·tor (jan′i·tər) *n.* One who has the care of a building, offices, etc. [< L < *janua* door]

jan·i·zar·y (jan′ə·zer′ē) *n. pl.* **·zar·ies** *Often cap.* **1** A soldier in a corps of Turkish troops, established in the 14th century and abolished in 1826. **2** A loyal or submissive supporter. Also **jan′i·sar·y, jan′is·sar·y.**

Jan·u·ar·y (jan′yŏŏ·er′ē) *n. pl.* **·ar·ies** or **·ar·ys** The first month of the year, containing 31 days. [< JANUS]

Ja·nus (jā′nəs) *Rom. Myth.* The god of portals and beginnings, having two faces, one in front, one in back of his head.

Ja·nus-faced (jā′nəs·fāst′) *adj.* Deceitful; two-faced.

Jap. Japan; Japanese.

ja·pan (jə·pan′) *n.* **1** Any of various lacquers or varnishes having a hard glossy finish. **2** Objects decorated or lacquered in the Japanese manner. **3** A varnish used as a drier for pigments. — *v.t.* **·panned, ·pan·ning** To varnish or lacquer with or as with japan. [< JAPAN]

Ja·pan (jə·pan′) *n.* A constitutional monarchy of E Asia, located on a group of islands, 142,720 sq. mi., cap. Tokyo.

Jap·a·nese (jap′ə·nēz′, -nēs′) *adj.* Of or pertaining to Japan, its people, or their language. — *n.* **1** A native or citizen of Japan. **2** The language of Japan.

Japanese beetle A lustrous green and brown beetle that feeds on grasses, leaves, and fruits.

jape (jāp) *v.i.* **japed, jap·ing** To joke; make jests. — *n.* A joke or trick. [ME *jappen*] —**jap′er, jap′er·y** *n.*

ja·pon·i·ca (jə·pon′i·kə) *n.* Any of various ornamental flowering shrubs native to Japan, as the camellia, etc. [< NL, Japanese]

jar¹ (jär) *n.* **1** A deep, wide-mouthed vessel, as of glass. **2** The quantity a jar contains: also **jar′ful′.** [< Ar. *jarrah*]

jar² (jär) *v.* **jarred, jar·ring** *v.i.* **1** To shake or rattle, as from a shock or blow. **2** To make a harsh, discordant sound. **3** To have an unpleasant or painful effect: with *on* or *upon.* **4** To disagree or conflict; clash. — *v.t.* **5** To cause to shake or rattle, as by a shock or blow. **6** To affect unpleasantly or painfully; shock. **7** To cause to make a harsh, noisy sound. —*n.* **1** A jolting or shaking, as from a sudden shock. **2** A noisy, harsh sound. **3** Discord; strife. [Imit.]

jar·di·nière (jär'də·nir'; *Fr.* zhàr·dē·nyâr') *n.* An ornamental pot or stand for flowers or plants. [F]

jar·gon (jär'gən) *n.* **1** Unintelligible speech; gibberish. **2** Any language thought to be meaningless or excessively confused. **3** The technical or specialized language of a particular profession, group, etc. **4** A mixture of two or more dissimilar languages; pidgin. —*v.i.* to talk in jargon; gabble. [< OF]

jas·mine (jas'min, jaz'-) *n.* **1** An ornamental shrub related to the olive, with fragrant flowers used in scented tea and in making perfume. **2** Any of various similar plants. [< Per. *yāsmin*]

Ja·son (jā'sən) *Gk. Myth.* The prince who led the Argonauts in search of the Golden Fleece.

jas·per (jas'pər) *n.* An opaque, usu. red, brown, or yellow variety of quartz, used for vases and other articles. Also **jas'per·ite.** [< Gk. *jaspis*]

jaun·dice (jôn'dis, jän'-) *n.* **1** Abnormal yellowness of the skin, eyeballs, etc., due to bile pigments in the blood. **2** A hostile or resentful state of mind, as that caused by prejudice, envy, etc. —*v.t.* **·diced, ·dic·ing 1** To affect with jaundice. **2** To affect with prejudice, envy, etc. [< L *galbinus* yellowish]

jaunt (jônt, jänt) *n.* A short journey; pleasure trip; excursion. —*v.i.* To make such a trip. [?]

jaunt·y (jôn'tē, jän'-) *adj.* **jaunt·i·er, jaunt·i·est** Sprightly; lively. [< F *gentil* elegant] —**jaunt'i·ly** *adv.* —**jaunt'i·ness** *n.*

Ja·va (jä'və, jav'ə) *n. Sometimes cap. Slang* Coffee.

Ja·va (jä'və, jav'ə) *n.* **1** A type of coffee. **2** A domestic fowl. [< *Java,* where first grown]

Java man An extinct species of man identified with bone fragments found in Java.

Jav·a·nese (jav'ə·nēz', -nēs') *adj.* Of or pertaining to Java, its language, or its people. —*n. pl.* **·nese 1** A native or citizen of Java. **2** The Indonesian language of central Java, closely related to Malay.

jave·lin (jav'lin, jav'ə·lin) *n.* **1** A short, light spear. **2** A long spear with wooden shaft, thrown for distance in an athletic contest. [< MF]

jaw (jô) *n.* **1** One of the two bony structures forming the framework of the mouth; a maxilla or a mandible. **2** The mouth. **3** Anything like or suggesting a jaw, as one of the gripping parts of a vise. **4** *Slang* Needless talk; scolding; abuse. —*v.i. Slang* **1** To talk; jabber. **2** To scold. —*v.t.* **3** *Slang* To scold. [ME *jawe*] • See TOOTH.

jaw·bone (jô'bōn') *n.* One of the bones of the jaw, esp. of the lower jaw. —*v.t.* **·boned, ·bon·ing** *Slang* **1** To urge vigorously; esp., to urge to abide voluntarily by price or wage guidelines fixed by government. —*v.i.* **2** To argue vigorously. —*adj. Slang* Based on voluntary compliance: *jawbone* controls.

jaw·break·er (jô'brā'kər) *n. Informal* **1** Very hard candy. **2** A word hard to pronounce.

jay (jā) *n.* **1** Any of various medium-sized birds related to crows, usu. having a raucous voice and striking coloring. **2** The bluejay. **3** *Slang* A newcomer; greenhorn. [< OF]

jay·walk (jā'wôk') *v.i. Informal* To cross a street without observing the traffic regulations. [< JAY (def. 3) + WALK] —**jay'walk'er** *n.*

jazz (jaz) *n.* **1** A kind of music achieving its effects by syncopated rhythms, dissonances, solo and ensemble improvisation, and, in the newer styles, by sophisticated harmonic patterns. **2** Popular dance music. **3** *Slang* Nonsense; claptrap. —*adj.* Of or pertaining to jazz. —*v.t.* **1** To play or arrange (music) as jazz. —*v.i.* **2** To dance to or play jazz. —**jazz up** *Slang* To make exciting or more exciting. [?]

jazz·y (jaz'ē) *adj.* **jazz·i·er, jazz·i·est 1** Resembling or characteristic of jazz. **2** *Slang* **a** Showy or loud, as clothes. **b** Lively or swinging. —**jazz'i·ly** *adv.* —**jazz'i·ness** *n.*

J.C. Jesus Christ; Julius Caesar.

J.C.D. Doctor of Canon Law (L *Juris Canonici Doctor*); Doctor of Civil Law (L *Juris Civilis Doctor*).

jct., jctn. junction.

JD juvenile delinquent (or delinquency).

J.D. Doctor of Laws (L *Jurum Doctor*).

Je, Je. June.

jeal·ous (jel'əs) *adj.* **1** Suspicious and resentful of a rival or of rivalry in general. **2** Hostile or envious over the advantages, good fortune, etc., of others. **3** Earnestly vigilant in guarding or keeping something: *jealous* of our freedoms. **4** Resulting from or showing such feelings: a *jealous* rage. [< Gk. *zēlos* zeal] —**jeal'ous·ly** *adv.* —**jeal'ous·ness** *n.*

jeal·ous·y (jel'əs·ē) *n. pl.* **·ous·ies** The state or quality of being jealous in any sense.

jean (jēn) *n.* **1** A sturdy, twilled cotton cloth, used esp. in work clothes or for casual wear. **2** *pl.* Trousers made of this fabric. **3** *pl. Informal* Trousers. [< ME *Jene, Gene* Genoa, where it was made]

jeep (jēp) *n.* A small, sturdy motor vehicle with four-wheel drive and a load capacity of one quarter of a ton. [Alter. of *G.P.,* for General Purpose (Vehicle), its military designation]

Jeep

jeer (jir) *v.i.* **1** To speak or shout in a derisive, mocking manner; scoff. —*v.t.* **2** To treat with derision or mockery; scoff at. —*n.* A derisive or taunting sound or word. [?] —**jeer'er** *n.* —**jeer'ing·ly** *adv.*

Je·ho·vah (ji·hō'və) God. [< Heb. *YHWH,* used as a symbol for the name of God, which is never spoken]

Jehovah's Witnesses A Christian sect strongly opposed to war, firmly believing in a literal interpretation of the Bible and in the imminence of the Last Judgment.

je·june (jə·jōōn') *adj.* **1** Lifeless; dry; dull. **2** Wanting in substance; barren. **3** Not mature; puerile; childish. [< L *jejunus* hungry] —**je·june'ly** *adv.* —**je·june'ness** *n.*

je·ju·num (jə·jōō'nəm) *n. pl.* **·na** (-nə) The part of the small intestine between the duodenum and the ileum. [< L *jejunus* hungry, empty]

jell (jel) *v.i. & v.t.* **1** To jelly; congeal. **2** To assume or cause to assume definite form. [< JELLY]

jel·li·fy (jel'ə·fī) *v.t. & v.i.* **·fied, ·fy·ing** To make or turn into jelly. —**jel'li·fi·ca'tion** *n.*

Jel·lo (jel'ō) *n.* A fruit-flavored gelatin dessert. [< *Jell-O,* a trade name]

jel·ly (jel'ē) *n. pl.* **·lies 1** A semisolid gelatinous food product, as fruit juice boiled with sugar or meat juice boiled down. **2** Any substance having the consistency of jelly. —*v.t. & v.i.* **·lied, ·ly·ing** To bring or turn to jelly. [< L *gelare* freeze]

jel·ly·bean (jel'ē·bēn') *n.* A bean-shaped candy with a glazed outer coating.

jel·ly·fish (jel'ē·fish') *n. pl.* **·fish** or **·fish·es 1** Any of a class of marine coelenterates having transparent and usu. umbrella-shaped bodies with stinging tentacles. **2** *Informal* A person with a weak will.

jen·net (jen'it) *n.* **1** A small Spanish horse. **2** A female donkey. [< Sp. *jinete* a light horseman]

jen·ny (jen'ē) *n. pl.* **·nies 1** SPINNING JENNY. **2** The female of certain birds and animals: *jenny* wren, *jenny* ass. [< *Jenny,* a personal name]

jeop·ard·ize (jep'ər·dīz) *v.t.* **·ized, ·iz·ing** To put in jeopardy; expose to loss or injury; imperil. Also **jeop'ard.**

jeop·ard·y (jep'ər·dē) *n. pl.* **·ard·ies 1** Exposure to death, loss, or injury; danger; peril. **2** The peril in which a defendant is put when placed on trial for a crime. [< OF *jeu parti* even chance]

Jer, Jer. Jeremiah.

jer·bo·a (jər·bō'ə) *n.* Any of various small nocturnal rodents with the long hind legs adapted for jumping. [< Ar. *yarbu'*]

jer·e·mi·ad (jer'ə·mī'ad) *n.* A lament; tale of woe. [< F *Jérémie* Jeremiah]

Jer·e·mi·ah (jer'ə·mī'ə) A major Hebrew prophet who flourished in the seventh century B.C. —*n.* An Old Testament book containing his prophecies. Also **Jer'e·mi'as.**

Jerboa

jerk[1] (jûrk) *v.t.* **1** To give a sharp, sudden pull or twist to. **2** To throw or move with a sharp, suddenly arrested motion. **3** To utter in broken or abrupt manner. —*v.i.* **4** To give a jerk or jerks. **5** To move with sharp, sudden motions; twitch. —*n.* **1** A short, sharp pull, twitch, or fling. **2** An involuntary muscular spasm. **3** *Slang* A stupid or unsophisticated person. [?] —**jerk′i·ly** *adv.* —**jerk′i·ness** *n.* —**jerk′y** *adj.* (**·i·er, ·i·est**)

jerk² (jûrk) *v.t.* To cure (meat) by cutting into strips and drying. —*n.* Jerked meat: also **jerk′y.** [< Sp. *charquear*]

jer·kin (jûr′kin) *n.* A sleeveless, close-fitting jacket. [?]

jerk·wa·ter (jûrk′wô′tər, -wot′ər) *adj. Informal* Insignificant; small: a *jerkwater* college. —*n.* A train serving a branch line. [< JERK¹, *v.* + WATER]

jer·ry·build (jer′ē·bild′) *v.t.* **·built, ·build·ing** To build flimsily and of inferior materials. [?] —**jer′ry·built′** *adj.*

jer·sey (jûr′zē) *n. pl.* **·seys 1** A plain-knitted, elastic, ribbed fabric of wool, cotton, etc. **2** Any close-fitting, pullover, upper garment, as those worn by athletes, sailors, etc. —*adj.* Made of jersey.

Jer·sey (jûr′zē) *n.* One of a breed of fawn-colored cattle, originating in the island of Jersey and noted for milk rich in butterfat.

Je·ru·sa·lem artichoke (ji·rōō′sə·ləm, -lem) **1** A tall sunflower having an edible tuber. **2** Its potatolike tuber. [Alter. of Ital. *girasole* sunflower + ARTICHOKE]

jess (jes) *n.* A short strap fastened to the leg of a hawk, used in falconry. [< L *jactus* a throw] —**jessed** *adj.*

jes·sa·mine (jes′ə·min) *n.* JASMINE.

jest (jest) *n.* **1** Something said or done as a joke, prank, witticism, etc. **2** A mood of frivolity or fun: said in *jest.* **3** An object of laughter or raillery; a laughingstock. —*v.i.* **1** To speak or act in a playful or trifling manner. **2** To scoff; jeer. —*v.t.* **3** To scoff at; ridicule. [< L *gesta* deeds]

jest·er (jes′tər) *n.* **1** One who jests. **2** A medieval court fool.

Je·su (jē′zōō, -sōō, jā′-) Jesus.

Jes·u·it (jezh′ōō·it, jez′yōō-) *n.* **1** A member of the Society of Jesus, a religious order founded in 1534 by Ignatius Loyola. **2** A crafty or scheming person. —**Jes′u·it′ic** or **·i·cal** *adj.* —**Jes′u·it′i·cal·ly** *adv.*

Je·sus (jē′zəs) The founder of Christianity, probably living from about 6 B.C. to A.D. 29 or 30, revered as the Christ or Messiah. Also **Jesus Christ, Jesus of Nazareth.** See CHRIST.

jet¹ (jet) *n.* **1** A rich black variety of hard coal, used, when highly polished, for beads, etc. **2** A deep, glossy black. —*adj.* Made of or resembling jet. [< Gk. *gagatēs*]

jet² (jet) *n.* **1** A flow or gush, as of gas or liquid, coming from a narrow orifice. **2** A spout or nozzle. **3** JET AIRPLANE. **4** JET ENGINE. —*v.t. & v.i.* **jet·ted, jet·ting 1** To spurt forth or emit in a stream; spout. **2** To travel or send by jet airplane. [< F *jeter* to throw]

jet airplane A jet-propelled airplane. Also **jet aircraft.**

jet-black (jet′blak′) *adj. & n.* Deep, glossy black.

jet engine An engine that develops thrust by ejecting a fluid to the rear, esp. gases and heated air.

jet lag A disruption of the body's accustomed rhythms of sleep, hunger, etc., owing to the change of time zones when traveling long distances by jet aircraft.

jet·lin·er (jet′lī′nər) *n.* A large, commercial jet aircraft.

jet·port (jet′pôrt′, -pōrt′) *n.* An airport designed to accommodate jet aircraft.

jet-pro·pelled (jet′prə·peld′) *adj.* Driven by jet propulsion.

jet propulsion 1 Propulsion by means of a jet of gas or other fluid. **2** *Aeron.* Aircraft propulsion by means of jet engines. —**jet′-pro·pul′sion** *adj.*

jet·sam (jet′səm) *n.* **1** Discarded cargo, equipment, etc., which is thrown overboard from a ship in peril and which either sinks or is washed ashore. **2** Any discarded objects. [< JETTISON]

jet set A group of wealthy, international celebrities who frequently travel long distances, as by jet aircraft, for vacations, social events, etc. —**jet-set·ter** (jet′set′ər) *n.*

jet stream 1 The exhaust gas or fluid expelled from a jet engine, rocket motor, etc. **2** *Meteorol.* A high-velocity, usu. westerly wind circulating near the base of the stratosphere.

jet·ti·son (jet′ə·sən) *v.t.* **1** To eject, drop, throw, etc., as from a ship, airplane, or spacecraft. **2** To discard or aban-

don (an impediment). —*n.* **1** The act of ejecting fuel, cargo, etc. **2** Jetsam. [< L *jactatio*]

jet·ty (jet′ē) *n. pl.* **·ties 1** A wall-like structure in a body of water serving to control or divert a current, protect a harbor, etc. **2** A wharf or pier. [< OF < *jeter* to throw]

Jew (jōō) *n.* **1** A member or descendant of the Hebrew people. **2** Any person professing Judaism. —**Jew·ess** (jōō′is) *n. Fem. (sometimes considered disparaging)*

jew·el (jōō′əl) *n.* **1** A precious stone; gem. **2** A pin, ring, etc., usu. made of precious metals set with gems, etc. **3** Any person or thing of rare excellence. **4** A bit of precious stone, crystal, or glass used as a bearing in a watch. —*v.t.* **·eled** or **·elled, ·el·ing** or **·el·ling** To adorn with or as with jewels. [< L *jocus* a game, joke]

jew·el·er (jōō′əl·ər) *n.* A dealer in or maker of jewelry. Also **jew′el·ler.**

jew·el·ry (jōō′əl·rē) *n.* Jewels collectively. *Brit. sp.* **jew·el·ler·y.**

jew·fish (jōō′fish′) *n. pl.* **·fish** or **·fish·es** Any of various large fish of American waters, as the giant sea bass found off California or the grouper found off Florida.

Jew·ish (jōō′ish) *adj.* Of or having to do with the Jews or Judaism. —*n. Informal* YIDDISH. —**Jew′ish·ness** *n.*

JEWISH CALENDAR

Months correspond approximately to those in parentheses. The civil year begins with Tishri, the ecclesiastical year with Nisan.

Name of month	Number of days
Tishri (September–October)	30
Heshvan (October–November)	29
in some years	30
Kislev (November–December)	29
in some years	30
Tebet (December–January)	29
Shebat (January–February)	30
Adar * (February–March)	29
in leap year	30
Nisan (March–April)	30
Iyar (April–May)	29
Sivan (May–June)	30
Tammuz (June–July)	29
Av (July–August)	30
Elul (August–September)	29

* Adar is followed in leap year by the intercalary month Veadar, or Adar Sheni, having 29 days.

Jew·ry (jōō′rē) *n. pl.* **·ries** Jewish people collectively.

jew's-harp (jōōz′härp′) *n.* A small musical instrument with a lyre-shaped metal frame held between the teeth, and played by plucking a free and flexible strip of metal.

Jez·e·bel (jez′ə·bel) In the Bible, the wife of Ahab, notorious for her evil life. —*n.* A bold, shameless, or wicked woman.

jg, j.g. junior grade.

jib¹ (jib) *n. Naut.* A triangular sail extending from the foretopmast to the jib boom or the bowsprit. —*Informal* **cut of one's jib** One's appearance. —*v.t. & v.i.* **jibbed, jib·bing** *Naut.* To shift or swing; jibe. Also **jibb.** [?]

jib² (jib) *v.i.* **jibbed, jib·bing 1** To move restively sidewise or backward; refuse to go forward, as a horse. **2** To refuse to do something; balk. —*n.* A horse that jibs: also **jib′ber.** [?]

jib boom *Naut.* A spar forming a continuation of the bowsprit.

jibe¹ (jīb) *v.* **jibed, jib·ing** *v.i.* **1** *Naut.* To swing from one side of a vessel to the other: said of a sail or its boom. **2** To change course so that the sails shift in this manner. —*v.t.* **3** To cause to swing from one side of a vessel to the other. [< Du. *gijben*]

jibe² (jīb) *n. & v.* **jibed, jib·ing** GIBE.

jibe³ (jīb) *v.i.* **jibed, jib·ing** To agree; be in accordance. [?]

jif·fy (jif′ē) *n. pl.* **·fies** *Informal* An instant; moment. Also **jiff.** [?]

jig (jig) *n.* **1** A rapid, gay dance or the music for it, usu. in triple time. **2** *Mech.* A tool or fixture used to guide cutting tools.

a. drill jig.
b. matter to be drilled.
c. support block.

---

3 A fish hook that is jiggled up and down or drawn through the water. **4** A wire sieve or system of sieves used in separating ore by vibration. —*v.* **jig·ged, jig·ging** *v.i.* **1** To dance or play a jig. **2** To move with quick, jerky motions. **3** To fish with a jig. **4** To use a jig. —*v.t.* **5** To jerk up and down or to and fro. **6** To catch (fish) with a jig. **7** To hold, produce, etc., with a jig. [?]

jig·ger[1] (jig′ər) *n.* **1** One who or that which jigs. **2** A small glass or cup for measuring liquor, usu. holding 1½ fluid ounces; also, the amount of liquor so measured. **3** *Naut.* **a** Any of several small sails. **b** JIGGERMAST. **4** Any of various mechanical devices having a jolting movement. **5** An unidentified gadget.

jig·ger[2] (jig′ər) *n.* CHIGGER.

jig·ger·mast (jig′ər·mast′, -mäst′) *n. Naut.* The aftermast in a yawl or a four-masted vessel.

jig·gle (jig′əl) *v.t. & v.i.* **·gled, ·gling** To move with slight, quick jerks. —*n.* A jiggling movement. [Freq. of JIG] —**jig·gly** *adj.*

jig·saw (jig′sô′) *n.* A fine, narrow saw, often power-operated, capable of cutting intricate curves.

jigsaw puzzle A puzzle, the object of which is to reassemble a mounted picture or design which has been cut into interlocking pieces.

jilt (jilt) *v.t.* To cast off (a previously favored lover or sweetheart). —*n.* One who capriciously discards a lover. [?] —**jilt′er** *n.*

jim crow (jim′krō′) Segregation of or discrimination against Negroes. Also **Jim Crow.** [< a Negro character in an old minstrel song] —**jim′-crow′** *adj.* —**jim′-crow′ism** *n.*

jim·my (jim′ē) *n. pl.* **·mies** A short crowbar, often used by burglars. —*v.t.* **·mied, ·my·ing** To break or pry open with a jimmy. [< *Jimmy,* dim. of *James.*]

jim·son·weed (jim′sən·wēd′) *n.* A tall, coarse, evil-smelling, very poisonous annual weed of the nightshade family, with white and purple flowers. Also **jimp·son weed** (jimp′sən). [< *Jamestown,* Va., where first observed.]

jin·gle (jing′gəl) *v.* **·gled, ·gling** *v.i.* **1** To make light, ringing sounds, as keys striking together. **2** To sound rhythmically or pleasingly on the ear. —*v.t.* **3** To cause to jingle. —*n.* **1** A tinkling or clinking sound. **2** A light, rhythmical verse; also, a short song using such verse: She is a composer of TV *jingles.* [Imit.] —**jin′gly** *adj.*

jin·go (jing′gō) *n. pl.* **·goes** One who boasts of his patriotism and favors an aggressive foreign policy. —*adj.* Of or like jingoes. [?] —**jin′go·ism, jin′go·ist** *n.* —**jin′go·is′tic** *adj.*

jin·ni (ji·nē′, jin′ē) *n. pl.* **jinn** *Muslim Myth.* A supernatural being able to assume animal or human form, and often called upon to serve men. Also **jin·nee′.** [< Ar. *jinnī*]

jin·rik·sha (jin·rik′shô) *n.* A small, two-wheeled passenger carriage drawn by one man. Also **jin·rick′sha, jin·rik′i·sha.** [< Jap. *jin* man + *riki* power + *sha* carriage]

jinx (jingks) *n.* A person or thing supposed to bring bad luck; a hoodoo. —*v.t.* To bring bad luck to. [< Gk. *iynx* the wryneck (a bird used in witchcraft)]

Jinriksha

jit·ney (jit′nē) *n. pl.* **·neys** A motor vehicle that carries passengers for a small fare. [?]

jit·ter (jit′ər) *v.i. Informal* To talk or act nervously. —**the jitters** *Informal* Nervousness and anxiety. [?] —**jit′ter·y** *adj.* —**jit′ter·i·ness** *n.*

jit·ter·bug (jit′ər·bug′) *n.* **1** A person who dances energetically to swing or jazz music. **2** A fast, energetic dance performed to such music. —*v.i.* **·bugged, ·bug·ging** To dance energetically to swing or jazz music.

jiu·jit·su, jiu·jut·su (jōō·jit′sōō) *n.* JUJITSU.

jive (jīv) *n. Slang* **1** The jargon of jazz music and its enthusiasts. **2** Jazz music. **3** Misleading or nonsensical talk; bull. —*v.* **jived, jiv·ing** *v.t.* **1** To talk to nonsensically or misleadingly. —*v.i.* **2** To talk to someone nonsensically or misleadingly. **3** To play or dance to jive. [?]

Jl July.

job (job) *n.* **1** A piece of work of a definite extent or character done for a set fee. **2** A specific duty, chore, or task. **3** A position of employment; situation. **4** An object or the material being worked on. **5** The act or result of working

on something: That was a bad *job.* **6** *Informal* An illegal or criminal act, as a robbery. **7** *Informal* Any affair, circumstance, happening, etc.: to make the best of a bad *job.* **8** *Informal* A difficult task. —*v.* **jobbed, job·bing** *v.i.* **1** To work by the job or piece. **2** To be a jobber. —*v.t.* **3** To buy in bulk and resell in lots to dealers. **4** To sublet (work) among separate contractors. —*adj.* Of or pertaining to a job. [?]

Job (jōb) A Biblical character who suffered many afflictions as a test of his faith. —*n.* The book of the Old Testament recounting his story.

job·ber (job′ər) *n.* **1** One who buys goods in bulk from the manufacturer or importer and sells to the retailer. **2** One who works by the job, or on small jobs.

job·less (job′lis) *adj.* **1** Without a job. **2** Of or pertaining to those without a job. —**job′less·ness** *n.*

job lot A collection of miscellaneous goods sold as a lot.

Jo·cas·ta (jō·kas′tə) *Gk. Myth.* The queen of Thebes who unwittingly married her own son Oedipus.

jock[1] (jok) *n.* **1** *Informal* JOCKSTRAP. **2** *Slang* An athlete. [< JOCK(STRAP)]

jock[2] (jok) *n. Informal* **1** JOCKEY. **2** DISC JOCKEY.

jock·ey (jok′ē) *n. pl.* **·eys** One employed to ride horses in races. —*v.* **·eyed, ·ey·ing** *v.i.* **1** To maneuver for an advantage. **2** To be tricky; cheat. **3** To ride as a jockey. —*v.t.* **4** To maneuver or guide by skillful handling or control. **5** To trick; cheat. **6** To ride (a horse) in a race. [Dim. of *Jock,* a nickname for *John*]

jock·strap (jok′strap′) *n.* An elastic support for the male genitals, as of athletes. [Slang *jock* the male genitals + STRAP]

jo·cose (jō·kōs′) *adj.* Humorous; funny. [< L *jocus* joke] —**jo·cose′ly** *adv.* —**jo·cose′ness, jo·cos·i·ty** (jō·kos′ə·tē) *n.* — Syn. droll, facetious, jocular, merry.

joc·u·lar (jok′yə·lər) *adj.* **1** Humorous; joking. **2** Intended as a joke. [< L *jocus* a joke] —**joc·u·lar′i·ty** (-lar′ə·tē) *n.* — **joc′u·lar·ly** *adv.*

joc·und (jok′ənd, jō′kənd) *adj.* Cheerful; gay; jovial. [< L *jucundus* pleasant] —**jo·cun·di·ty** (jō·kun′də·tē) *n.* (*pl.* **·ties**). —**joc′und·ly** *adv.*

jodh·pur (jod′pər) *n.* **1** A riding shoe that ends just above the ankle, buckled on the side. **2** *pl.* Wide riding breeches, close-fitting from knee to ankle. [< *Jodhpur,* India]

jog (jog) *v.* **jogged, jog·ging** *v.t.* **1** To push or touch with a slight jar; shake. **2** To nudge. **3** To stimulate (one's memory). —*v.i.* **4** To move with a slow, steady pace. **5** To proceed slowly or monotonously: with *on* or *along.* —*n.* **1** A slight push or nudge. **2** A slow steady motion or pace. [?] —**jog′ger** *n.*

jog·gle[1] (jog′əl) *v.t. & v.i.* **·gled, ·gling** To shake slightly; jolt. —*n.* A slight shake; jolt. [Freq. of JOG]

Jodhpurs
def. 2

jog·gle[2] (jog′əl) *n.* **1** A joint created by making a projection in one surface that will fit into a notch made in another. **2** DOWEL. —*v.t.* **·gled, ·gling** To put together with joggles. [?]

jog trot **1** A slow, easy trot. **2** A humdrum or unhurried routine.

john (jon) *n. Slang* A toilet.

John (jon) One of the twelve apostles, reputed author of the fourth Gospel, three Epistles, and the Book of Revelation: also **Saint John.** —*n.* The Gospel or one of the three Epistles credited to him.

John Bull The personification of England or of an Englishman.

John Doe (dō) **1** In a legal action or document, a name given to someone whose real name is unknown. **2** An average man.

John Han·cock (han′kok′) *Informal* A person's autograph. [< *John Hancock,* first signer of the Declaration of Independence]

john·ny·cake (jon′ē·kāk′) *n.* A kind of bread made with cornmeal.

john·ny-jump-up (jon′ē·jump′up′) *n.* **1** A naturalized, wild variety of pansy. **2** Any of various violets.

joie de vi·vre (zhwá də vēv′r′) Zest for life. [F, lit., joy of living]

join (join) *v.t.* **1** To set or bring together; connect. **2** To come to a junction with; become part of. **3** To become a member of, as a club. **4** To unite in act or purpose: to *join* forces. **5** To come to as a companion or participant: When will you *join* us? **6** To unite in marriage. **7** To engage in (battle. etc.). **8** *Informal* To adjoin. —*v.i.* **9** To come together; connect; unite. **10** To enter into association or agreement. **11** To take part: usu. with *in*. —*n.* A place of joining; joint. [< L *jungere*]

join·er (joi'nər) **1** One who or that which joins. **2** An artisan who finishes woodwork in houses. **3** *Informal* One who becomes a member of many organizations, clubs, etc.

join·er·y (joi'nər-ē) *n.* **1** The art or work of a joiner. **2** The articles constructed by a joiner.

joint (joint) *n.* **1** The place, point, or line where two or more things are joined together. **2** The manner in which two things are joined together: a tight *joint*. **3** One of the components of an articulated whole. **4** *Anat.* A place of union of two bones; an articulation. **5** One of the large pieces into which a carcass is divided by a butcher. **6** *Slang* A marihuana cigarette. **7** *Slang* A somewhat disreputable bar, nightclub, etc. **8** *Slang* Any place of dwelling or gathering. —**out of joint 1** Not fitted at the joint; dislocated. **2** Disordered; disorganized. —*adj.* **1** Produced by combined action. **2** Shared by two or more. **3** Participated in or used by two or more. —*v.t.* **1** To fasten by means of a joint or joints. **2** To form or shape into a joint or joints, as a board. **3** To separate into joints, as meat. [< L *junctus* joined]

joint account A bank account in the name of two or more persons, each of whom may deposit and withdraw funds.

joint committee A committee made up of members from both houses of a bicameral legislature.

joint·ed (join'tid) *adj.* Having joints.

joint·ly (joint'lē) *adv.* In a joint manner.

joint return A single income tax return in which the incomes of a husband and wife are combined.

joint-stock company (joint'stok') A business company whose capital is divided into shares owned by each of the members in the form of transferable stocks.

join·ture (join'chər) *n. Law* **1** A settlement, as of land, made to a wife by her husband to be used by her after his death. **2** The property so settled. [< L *jungere* join]

joist (joist) *n.* A horizontal timber supporting a floor or ceiling. —*v.t.* To furnish with joists. [< L *jacere* to lie down]

a. joists. b. floor boards.

joke (jōk) *n.* **1** Something said or done to cause amusement, esp. a brief, comic story. **2** A person or thing that causes laughter, ridicule, etc. **3** Something said or done in fun or to tease. —*v.* **joked, jok·ing** *v.t.* **1** To tease; kid. —*v.i.* **2** To make jokes; jest. [< L *jocus*] —**jok'ing·ly** *adv.* —**Syn.** *n.* 1 jest, witticism, gag, crack, wisecrack, quip.

jok·er (jō'kər) *n.* **1** One who jokes. **2** In a deck of cards, an extra card to be used in certain games. **3** *U.S.* A concealed provision in a legislative bill to render it ineffectual or to undermine its original purpose. **4** Any hidden ruse or difficulty.

jol·li·fy (jol'ə·fī) *v.t.* & *v.i.* **·fied, ·fy·ing** *Informal* To be or cause to be merry or jolly. —**jol·li·fi·ca·tion** (jol'ə·fə·kā'shən) *n.*

jol·ly (jol'ē) *adj.* **·li·er, ·li·est** Full of life and mirth; gay; merry. —*adv. Brit. Informal* Extremely; very: a *jolly* good time. —*v.t.* **·lied, ·ly·ing** *Informal* **1** To attempt to put in good humor by flattery or coaxing: often with *along* or *up*. **2** To make fun of. [< OF *joli*] —**jol'li·ly** *adv.* —**jol'li·ness, jol·li·ty** (jol'ə·tē) *n.* —**Syn.** *adj.* joyful, gleeful, jovial, joyous.

jol·ly·boat (jol'ē·bōt') *n.* A small boat belonging to a ship. [< Dan. *jolle* yawl + BOAT]

Jolly Roger A black flag bearing a white skull and crossbones; a pirate flag.

jolt (jōlt) *v.t.* **1** To strike or shake about, as with a blow. **2** To surprise or stun. —*v.i.* **3** To move with jolts or bumps,

as over a rough road. —*n.* **1** A sudden bump or jerk. **2** A surprise or shock. [?] —**jolt'er** *n.* —**jolt'y** *adj.*

Jo·nah (jō'nə) In the Bible, a Hebrew prophet of the eighth or ninth century B.C., who was thrown overboard and swallowed by a large fish, but three days later was cast upon shore alive. —*n.* **1** The book of the Old Testament telling his story. **2** Any person or thing regarded as bringing bad luck. Also **Jo·nas** (jō'nəs).

Jon·a·than (jon'ə·thən) In the Bible, the son of Saul and close friend of David. —*n.* A variety of late autumn apple.

jon·gleur (jong'glər; *Fr.* zhôn·glœr') *n.* A medieval minstrel; also, later, a storyteller or buffoon. [< OF]

jon·quil (jon'kwil, jong'-) *n.* A species of narcissus having short-crowned yellow or white flowers. [< L *juncus* a rush]

Jor·dan (jôr'dən) *n.* A constitutional monarchy of w Asia, 37,000 sq. mi., cap. Amman. —**Jor·da·ni·an** (jôr·dā'nē·ən) *adj., n.*

Jordan, Syria, and Israel

Jordan almond 1 A large Spanish almond. **2** A candy-coated almond. [< OF *jardin* garden + ALMOND]

Jos. Joseph.

Jo·seph (jō'zəf, -səf) In the Bible: **1** A Hebrew patriarch, son of Jacob and Rachel, sold into slavery in Egypt by his brothers. **2** Husband of Mary, the mother of Jesus.

josh (josh) *Slang v.t.* & *v.i.* To tease (someone) good-humoredly. —*n.* A good-natured joke. [? Blend of JOKE and BOSH] —**josh'er** *n.*

Josh. Joshua.

Josh·u·a (josh'ōō·ə) In the Bible, the successor of Moses as leader of the Israelites. —*n.* The book of the Old Testament ascribed to him.

Joshua tree A tall, treelike desert plant with branches that end in a cluster of leaves.

joss (jos) *n.* A statue or idol of a Chinese god. [Pidgin English < Pg. *deos* God]

joss house A Chinese temple.

joss stick A stick of perfumed paste burned by the Chinese as incense.

jos·tle (jos'əl) *v.t.* & *v.i.* **·tled, ·tling** To push or crowd; elbow; hustle; bump. —*n.* A collision, bumping against, or slight shaking. [Freq. of JOUST] —**jos'tler** *n.*

jot (jot) *v.t.* **jot·ted, jot·ting** To make a hasty note of: usu. with *down*. —*n.* The least bit; an iota. [< IOTA]

jot·ting (jot'ing) *n.* A brief note.

joule (joul, jōol) *n. Physics* A unit of work or energy equal to one watt acting for one second. [< James Prescott *Joule*, 1818–89, English physicist]

jounce (jouns) *v.t.* & *v.i.* **jounced, jounc·ing** To shake or bounce; jolt. —*n.* A shake; a bump. [?]

jour. journal; journalist; journeyman.

jour·nal (jûr'nəl) *n.* **1** A record of daily occurrences, as a diary. **2** A record of the proceedings of a legislature, club, etc. **3** A daily newspaper. **4** Any periodical or magazine. **5** *Naut.* A logbook. **6** In bookkeeping: **a** DAYBOOK. **b** In double entry, a book in which transactions of the day are entered in systematic form in order to facilitate later posting in the ledger. **7** *Mech.* The part of a shaft or axle which is held by a bearing. [< L *diurnus* daily]

journal box *Mech.* The box or bearing for a rotating axle or shaft.

jour·nal·ese (jûr'nəl·ēz', -ēs') *n.* A style of writing supposedly characteristic of newspapers, magazines, etc.

jour·nal·ism (jûr'nəl·iz'əm) *n.* **1** The gathering, writing, editing, or publishing of news, as for a newspaper, magazine, radio, or television. **2** Newspapers and magazines collectively.

jour·nal·ist (jûr′nəl·ist) n. One whose occupation is journalism. —**jour′nal·is′tic** adj. —**jour′nal·is′ti·cal·ly** adv.

jour·ney (jûr′nē) n. 1 Travel from one place to another; a trip. 2 Something that suggests such travel: one's journey through life. —v.i. To travel; go on a journey. [<OF journee a day's travel] —**jour′ney·er** n. —**Syn.** n. 1 excursion, tour, voyage, cruise, expedition.

jour·ney·man (jûr′nē·mən) n. pl. ·men (-mən) 1 A craftsman who has finished his apprenticeship and is employed by another. 2 Any ordinary, competent, but not exceptional worker, craftsman, etc.

joust (joust, just, jōost) n. A match with lances between mounted knights. —v.i. To engage in a joust. [<LL juxtare to approach] —**joust′er** n.

Jove (jōv) JUPITER. —**by Jove!** An exclamation expressing surprise, emphasis, etc. —**Jo·vi·an** (jō′vē·ən) adj.

jo·vi·al (jō′vē·əl) adj. Possessing or expressive of good-natured mirth or gaiety; jolly. [<LL Jovialis (born under the influence) of Jupiter] —**jo·vi·al·i·ty** (jō′vē·al′ə·tē) n. —**jo′vi·al·ly** adv.

jowl[1] (joul, jōl) n. 1 The fleshy part of the lower jaw, esp. when pendulous. 2 The wattle of fowls. 3 The dewlap of cattle. [ME cholle] —**jowl′y** adj.

jowl[2] (joul, jōl) n. The cheek or jaw. [<OE ceafl] —**jowled** adj.

joy (joi) n. 1 A lively emotion of happiness, delight, and pleasure. 2 Anything causing such emotion. 3 The expression of such emotion. —v.i. To be glad; rejoice. [<L gaudium] —**Syn.** n. 1 gladness, glee, cheerfulness, gaiety.

joy·ful (joi′fəl) adj. Full of, expressing, or causing joy. —**joy′ful·ly** adv. —**joy′ful·ness** n.

joy·less (joi′lis) adj. Destitute of joy. —**joy′less·ly** adv.

joy·ous (joi′əs) adj. Happy; merry; gay. —**joy′ous·ly** adv.

joy·ride (joi′rīd′) n. Informal A ride taken exclusively for pleasure, esp. in a stolen car or other vehicle and often operated recklessly. —**joy′rid′er** n. —**joy′rid′ing** n.

joy·stick (joi′stik′) n. A hand-operated, upright, tiltable electronic device used in playing computer and video games.

J.P. Justice of the Peace.

Jr., jr. junior.

ju·bi·lant (jōo′bə·lənt) adj. Filled with or showing great joy or triumph. [<L jubilare exult] —**ju′bi·lance** n. —**ju′bi·lant·ly** adv. —**Syn.** overjoyed, rapturous, elated, exultant, triumphant.

ju·bi·late (jōo′bə·lāt) v.t. & v.i. ·lat·ed, ·lat·ing To rejoice; exult. [<L jubilare] —**ju′bi·la′tion** n.

ju·bi·lee (jōo′bə·lē′, jōo′bə·lē′) n. 1 A special anniversary of an event, as the 50th; also, the celebration of this. 2 Any time or season of rejoicing; a commemoration or festivity. [LL<Heb. yōbēl ram's horn, trumpet]

Ju·dah (jōo′də) In the Bible, the fourth son of Jacob and Leah, or the tribe descended from him. —n. The kingdom of ancient Palestine, comprising the tribes of Judah and Benjamin.

Ju·da·ic (jōo·dā′ik) adj. Of the Jews or Judaism; Jewish. Also **Ju·da′i·cal.** —**Ju·da′i·cal·ly** adv.

Ju·da·ism (jōo′dē·iz′əm) n. 1 The religion of the Jews, comprising a belief in and worship of one God only, with doctrines based on ancient Hebrew Scripture, the Talmud, and rabbinical tradition. 2 The culture, traditions, ceremonies, practices, etc., of the Jews. 3 Jews collectively. —**Ju′da·ist** n. —**Ju′da·is′tic** adj.

Ju·das (jōo′dəs) In the Bible, the disciple of Jesus who betrayed him: also **Judas Is·car·i·ot** (is·kar′ē·ət). —n. One who betrays another under the guise of friendship.

Judas tree A leguminous tree having profuse reddish purple flowers. [From a tradition that Judas hanged himself from such a tree]

Ju·de·a (jōo·dē′ə) The southern part of ancient Palestine under the Roman Empire. —**Ju·de′an** adj., n.

judge (juj) n. 1 An official, elected or appointed, invested with authority to administer legal justice. 2 In contests, controversies, etc., one who selects the winner, evaluates the merits of contestants, etc. 3 One qualified to have opinions on the worth or value of something: a good judge of wines. 4 In Jewish history, one of the rulers of the Israelites from the death of Joshua to the anointing of Saul. —v. **judged, judg·ing** v.t. 1 To hear and decide in an official capacity the merits of (a case) or the guilt of (a person); try. 2 To select the winner of (a contest). 3 To settle (a controversy). 4 To appraise or evaluate: to judge a painting. 5 To estimate: to judge a distance. 6 To consider; think: We judged it improper. 7 To censure; criticize: Judge her not. —v.i. 8 To act as a judge; sit in judgment. 9 To form a judgment or estimate. 10 To make a decision. [<L judex] —**judg′er** n.

judge advocate pl. **judge advocates** Mil. A legal officer of the U.S. Army, esp. the prosecutor at a court-martial.

Judg·es (juj′iz) n. pl. (construed as sing.) The seventh book of the Old Testament.

judge·ship (juj′ship) n. The office, duties, or period in office of a judge.

judg·ment (juj′mənt) n. 1 The act of judging. 2 The result or outcome of judging; as: **a** A legal decision, order, or sentence. **b** An obligation or debt resulting from a court decision. **c** A record of such a decision. **d** Any decision or opinion. **e** An evaluation or estimation. **f** Censure; criticism. 3 An ability to make decisions or evaluations that are wise, reasonable, and valid. 4 A disaster or affliction regarded as inflicted by God. Also **judge′ment.** —**judg′men′tal** adj.

Judgment Day Theol. The day or time of the Last Judgment.

ju·di·ca·to·ry (jōo′də·kə·tôr′ē, -tō′rē) adj. Pertaining to the administration of justice. —n. pl. ·ries 1 A court of law; also, such courts collectively. 2 Any system of administering justice. [<L judicare to judge]

ju·di·ca·ture (jōo′də·kə·chōor′) n. 1 The action of administering justice. 2 The right or power to administer justice; jurisdiction. 3 A court of justice. 4 Judges collectively.

ju·di·cial (jōo·dish′əl) adj. 1 Of, pertaining to, or resulting from the administration of justice. 2 Of, pertaining to, or connected with a court or judge. 3 Discriminating; unbiased; impartial. [<L judex a judge] —**ju·di′cial·ly** adv.

ju·di·ci·ar·y (jōo·dish′ē·er′ē, -dish′ə·rē) adj. Of or pertaining to courts of justice, judges, or their duties. —n. pl. ·ar·ies 1 That department of government which administers the law. 2 A system of legal courts. 3 Judges collectively.

ju·di·cious (jōo·dish′əs) adj. Having, acting on, or resulting from sound judgment: wise; prudent. [<L judicium a judgment] —**ju·di′cious·ly** adv. —**ju·di′cious·ness** n.

Ju·dith (jōo′dith) A Jewish woman who rescued her countrymen by slaying the Assyrian general Holofernes. —n. A book in the Apocrypha relating her story.

ju·do (jōo′dō) n. A type of jujitsu. [<Jap. ju gentle, pliant + do way of life]

jug (jug) n. 1 A narrow-necked, stout vessel, usu. with a handle and a cork, for keeping or carrying liquids. 2 Slang A jail. —v.t. **jugged, jug·ging** 1 To put into a jug. 2 To stew (meat, esp. hare) in an earthenware pot. 3 Slang To imprison. [<Jug, a nickname for Joan]

jug·ger·naut (jug′ər·nôt) n. A massive force that destroys whatever resists it. [<JUGGERNAUT]

Jug·ger·naut (jug′ər·nôt) An incarnation of the Hindu deity Vishnu whose idol was drawn on a heavy car under the wheels of which devotees were said to have thrown themselves to be crushed. [<Hind. jagannāth lord of the universe]

jug·gle (jug′əl) v. ·gled, ·gling v.t. 1 To toss (balls, plates, etc.) into the air, keeping them in continuous motion by successively catching and tossing them up again. 2 To hold or catch (a ball, etc.) awkwardly or precariously. 3 To manipulate in order to deceive. —v.i. 4 To perform as a juggler. 5 To practice deception or trickery. —n. 1 A feat of juggling. 2 A trick or deception. [<L joculari to jest] —**jug′gler** n.

jug·gler·y (jug′lər·ē) n. pl. ·gler·ies 1 The art of a juggler. 2 Deception; trickery.

jug·u·lar (jug′yə·lər, jōo′gyə-) adj. Anat. Pertaining to the throat or neck. —n. One of the large veins on either side of the neck that returns blood from the head to the heart. Also **jugular vein.** [<L jugulum a collar bone]

juice (jōos) n. 1 The watery matter in fruits, plants, and vegetables. 2 Usu. pl. The fluids of the body. 3 The essence of anything. 4 Slang **a** Electric current. **b** Any liquid fuel. 5 Informal Vital energy. [<L jus]

juic·er (jōō'sər) *n.* A device for extracting juice from fruits or vegetables.

juic·y (jōō'sē) *adj.* **juic·i·er, juic·i·est 1** Abounding with juice; moist. **2** *Informal* Full of interest; colorful; spicy. **3** *Informal* Financially profitable; lucrative. —**juic'i·ly** *adv.* — **juic'i·ness** *n.*

ju·jit·su (jōō·jit'sōō) *n.* A Japanese system of unarmed self-defense in which the strength and weight of one's opponent are used to one's own advantage. Also **ju·jut·su** (jōō·jit'sōō, -jōōt'-). [< Jap. *ju* soft + *jitsu* art]

ju·jube (jōō'jōōb) *n.* **1** Any of several trees or shrubs related to the buckthorn. **2** Its edible fruit. **3** (*often* jōō'·jōō·bē') A gelatinous candy lozenge. [< Gk. *zizyphon*]

juke·box (jōōk'boks') *n.* A large automatic phonograph, usu. coin-operated and permitting selection of the records to be played. Also **juke box.** [< Gullah *juke*, orig. a brothel (of west African origin) + BOX¹]

Jul, Jul. July.

ju·lep (jōō'lip) *n.* A drink made of brandy or whisky, sugar, cracked ice, and flavored with fresh green mint. Also **mint julep.** [< Pers. *gulāb* rose water]

Jul·ian (jōōl'yən) *adj.* Of, pertaining to, or named after Julius Caesar.

Julian calendar The calendar introduced by Julius Caesar in 46 B.C., having each year divided into 12 months and 365 days with every fourth year containing 366 days.

ju·li·enne (jōō'lē·en') *n.* A clear meat soup containing vegetables chopped or cut into thin strips. —*adj.* Cut into thin strips: *julienne* potatoes. [< F *Julienne,* a personal name]

Ju·li·et (jōō'lē·et, jōōl'yit) The heroine of Shakespeare's *Romeo and Juliet.*

Ju·ly (jōō·lī', jōō-) *n. pl.* **Ju·lies** or **·lys** The seventh month of the calendar year, having 31 days. [< L (*mensis*) *Julius* (month) of Julius Caesar]

jum·ble (jum'bəl) *v.* **·bled, ·bling** *v.t.* **1** To mix in a confused mass; put or throw together without order. **2** To confuse in the mind. —*v.i.* **3** To meet or unite confusedly. —*n.* A confused mixture. [?]

jum·bo (jum'bō) *n. pl.* **·bos** A very large person, animal, or thing. —*adj.* Larger than usual. [< *Jumbo,* an elephant exhibited by P. T. Barnum]

jump (jump) *v.i.* **1** To spring from the ground, floor, etc., by the action of the muscles of the feet and legs. **2** To move abruptly or with jerks. **3** To leap off or from something, esp. from an airplane when using a parachute. **4** To pass abruptly from one thing or subject to another. **5** To rise abruptly, as prices. **6** *Slang* To be full of noisy activity. **7** In bridge, to make a jump bid. **8** In checkers, to capture an opponent's piece by passing over it to a vacant square beyond. —*v.t.* **9** To leap over. **10** To cause to rise, as prices. **11** To pass over; leave out; skip. **12** To leave or move from abruptly: to *jump* the track. **13** *Informal* To get on or off (a train, etc.) by or as by jumping. **15** *Informal* To assault; attack. **16** *Slang* To leave or quit abruptly or secretly: to *jump* town. **17** *Informal* To respond to before the proper time: to *jump* a traffic light. **18** In checkers, to capture (an opponent's piece). **19** In bridge, to raise (the bid) by making a jump bid. —**jump at 1** To accept quickly or eagerly. **2** To reach (a conclusion) hastily and illogically. —*n.* **1** The act of jumping; a leap. **2** The length or height of a leap. **3** That which is jumped over. **4** An athletic contest to determine skill in jumping. **5** An abrupt rise or increase: a *jump* in prices. **6** *Informal* A head start; advantage. **7** An involuntary movement, as when startled. **8** A short trip. **9** In checkers, the capture of another's piece. [?]

jump bid In bridge, a bid higher than needed to beat or raise a previous declaration.

jump·er¹ (jum'pər) *n.* **1** One who or that which jumps. **2** *Electr.* A short length of connecting wire, esp. one used temporarily.

jump·er² (jum'pər) *n.* **1** A one-piece, sleeveless dress worn over a blouse or sweater. **2** *pl.* ROMPERS. **3** A loose outer jacket worn over or instead of other clothes. [< OF *juppe* a jacket]

jumping bean The seed of certain Mexican plants which rolls or jerks about owing to the movements of the larva of a small moth inside.

jumping jack A toy figure of a man, whose jointed limbs are moved by strings.

jump·ing-off place (jum'ping-ôf', -of') **1** A very remote or deserted place. **2** The beginning of a venture or enterprise.

jump seat An extra seat that folds up, as in the rear of a limousine or taxi.

jump shot In basketball, a shot attempted at the height of a leap.

jump suit 1 A one-piece garment consisting of pants with a blouse or shirt attached. **2** A kind of coverall worn by parachutists, mechanics, etc.

jump·y (jum'pē) *adj.* **jump·i·er, jump·i·est 1** Subject to sudden changes; fluctuating. **2** Nervous; apprehensive. —**jump'i·ness** *n.*

Jun, Jun. June.

Jun., jun. junior.

junc., junct. junction.'

jun·co (jung'kō) *n. pl.* **·cos** Any of various sparrowlike birds having white underparts. [< Sp., a rush]

junc·tion (jungk'shən) *n.* **1** The act of joining, or condition of being joined. **2** A place of union or meeting, as of railroads. [< L *jungere* join] —**junc'tion·al** *adj.*

junc·ture (jungk'chər) *n.* **1** An act of joining; junction. **2** A point or line of joining. **3** A point in time. **4** A crisis; exigency. **5** *Ling.* A significant manner of transition between consecutive speech sounds.

June (jōōn) *n.* The sixth month of the calendar year, having 30 days. [< L (*mensis*) *Junius* (month) of the Junii, a Roman gens]

June bug A large, brightly colored beetle that appears in May or early June. Also **June beetle.**

jun·gle (jung'gəl) *n.* **1** Land, usu. in tropical regions, covered with trees and a dense thicket of high grass, vines, brush, etc. **2** Any similar tangled mass. **3** *Slang* A camp for hoboes. **4** *Slang* A place or circumstance of fierce competition for survival, success, etc. [< Skt. *jangala* dry, desert]

jun·ior (jōōn'yər) *adj.* **1** Younger in years or lower in rank. **2** Denoting the younger of two, and distinguishing a father from a son, usu. abbreviated *Jr.* **3** Belonging to youth or earlier life. **4** Later in date. **5** Pertaining to a junior or juniors in a high school or college. —*n.* **1** The younger of two. **2** One later or lower in service or rank. **3** A third-year student in a high school or college. [< L comp. of *juvenis* young]

junior college A college offering only two years of study after high school.

junior high school The school that is attended between elementary school and senior high school, usu. comprising grades 7, 8, and 9.

ju·ni·per (jōō'nə·pər) *n.* Any of a genus of evergreen shrubs and trees having scalelike leaves and aromatic, berrylike cones. [< L *juniperus*]

junk¹ (jungk) *n.* **1** Castoff materials, as metal, glass, paper etc. **2** Anything of little value or importance. **3** *Slang* A narcotic, esp. heroin. —*v.t.* To scrap, demolish, or cast aside. [< L *juncus* rush] — **junk'y** *adj.* (**·i·er, ·i·est**)

Juniper branch

junk² (jungk) *n.* A large Chinese vessel with high poop, prominent stem, full stern and lugsails. [< Malay *djong* a ship]

Jun·ker (yŏŏng'kər) *n.* A member of the landowning Prussian aristocracy. [< G *jung* young + *Herr* master]

jun·ket (jung'kit) *n.* **1** A feast or picnic. **2** A pleasure trip. **3** A trip taken with all expenses paid by a government, company, etc. **4** A dessert made of milk and rennet. —*v.i.* To go on a junket. [< AF *jonquette* rush basket]

junk·ie (jung'kē) *n. Slang* One addicted to narcotic drugs, esp. to heroin. Also **junk·y** (*pl.* **·ies**).

---

add, āce, câre, pälm; end, ēven; it, īce; odd, ōpen, ôrder; tŏŏk, pōōl; up, bûrn; ə = *a* in *above, u* in *focus;* yōō = *u* in *fuse;* oil; pout; check; go; ring; thin; this; zh, *vision.* < derived from; ? origin uncertain or unknown.

junk·man (jungk'man') *n. pl.* **·men** (-men') One who purchases, collects, and sells junk.

junk·yard (jungk'yärd') *n.* A place where junk is thrown or collected.

Ju·no (jōō'nō) *Rom. Myth.* The wife of Jupiter, queen of the gods and goddess of marriage.

Ju·no·esque (jōō'nō·esk') *adj.* Resembling the stately beauty of Juno.

jun·ta (hŏōn'tə, jun'-) *n.* 1 A Central or South American legislative council. 2 A group of people, often military leaders, who exercise control over a government, esp. following a coup d'état. Also **jun'to** (-tō). [< L *juncta* joined]

Ju·pi·ter (jōō'pə·tər) *Rom. Myth.* The god ruling over all the other gods and all men. —*n.* The planet of the solar system fifth in distance from the sun. See PLANET.

Ju·ras·sic (jōō·ras'ik) *adj., n.* See GEOLOGY. [< the *Jura* mountain range in E France and w Switzerland]

ju·rid·i·cal (jōō·rid'i·kəl) *adj.* Relating to law and judicial proceedings. Also **ju·rid'ic.** [< L *jus, juris* law + *dicere* declare] —**ju·rid'i·cal·ly** *adv.*

ju·ris·dic·tion (jŏŏr'is·dik'shən) *n.* 1 Lawful right to exercise official authority. 2 The range or scope of such authority. 3 A court, or series of courts, of justice. 4 Power, authority, or control. [< L *jus, juris* law + *dicere* declare] —**ju'ris·dic'tion·al** *adj.* —**ju'ris·dic'tion·al·ly** *adv.*

ju·ris·pru·dence (jŏŏr'is·prŏŏd'ns) *n.* 1 The philosophy or science of law. 2 A particular system or division of law: medical *jurisprudence.* [< L *jus, juris* law + *prudentia* knowledge]

ju·ris·pru·dent (jŏŏr'is·prŏŏd'nt) *adj.* Skilled in jurisprudence.—*n.* A person learned in the law. —**ju'ris·pru·den'·tial** (-prŏŏ·den'shəl) *adj.*

ju·rist (jŏŏr'ist) *n.* 1 One versed in the science of laws. 2 A judge. [< L *jus, juris* law]

ju·ris·tic (jŏō·ris'tik) *adj.* Of a jurist or the law. Also **ju·ris'·ti·cal.** —**ju·ris'ti·cal·ly** *adv.*

ju·ror (jŏŏr'ər, -ôr) *n.* One who serves on a jury or is sworn in for jury duty.

ju·ry¹ (jŏŏr'ē) *n. pl.* **·ries** 1 A body of persons (usu. twelve) sworn to hear evidence in a legal proceeding and to arrive at an unprejudiced verdict on the basis of the facts as presented. 2 A committee to decide the winner or winners in a competition. [< L *jurare* swear < *jus, juris* law]

ju·ry² (jŏŏr'ē) *adj. Naut.* Rigged up temporarily: a *jury* mast. [?]

just (just) *adj.* 1 Upright; honest. 2 Fair; impartial: a *just* trial. 3 Merited; deserved: a *just* tribute. 4 Correct; accurate. 5 Valid; legitimate: a *just* complaint. 6 Righteous. —*adv.* 1 To the exact point, instant, or degree; precisely. 2

But now; this moment or time: He is *just* beginning. 3 A moment ago: He has *just* left. 4 By very little; barely: *just* missed. 5 Only: *just* an amateur. 6 *Informal* Simply; positively: That gift is *just* wonderful. —**just about** Almost; nearly. [< L *justus* < *jus* law] —**just'ly** *adv.* —**just'ness** *n.*

jus·tice (jus'tis) *n.* 1 The quality of being just, fair, or impartial; evenhandedness. 2 Adherence to truth or fact; validity; correctness. 3 The rendering of what is due or merited; also, that which is due or merited; just deserts. 4 Conformity to right principles; honesty; integrity. 5 A judge. 6 JUSTICE OF THE PEACE. 7 The administration of law. —**do justice to** 1 To deal with adequately. 2 To enjoy or appreciate fully. —**do oneself justice** 1 To be fair to oneself. 2 To do the best of which one is capable. [< L *justus* < *jus* law]

justice of the peace A magistrate elected or appointed within a county or township, to punish minor offenses against the law, commit cases to a higher court, perform marriages, etc.

jus·ti·fi·a·ble (jus'tə·fī'ə·bəl, jus'tə·fī'-) *adj.* Capable of being justified. —**jus'ti·fi·a·bil'i·ty** *n.* —**jus'ti·fi'a·bly** *adv.*

jus·ti·fi·ca·tion (jus'tə·fə·kā'shən) *n.* 1 The act of justifying or the state of being justified. 2 The grounds of justifying; that which justifies. —**jus'ti·fi·ca'tive** *adj.*

jus·ti·fy (jus'tə·fī) *v.* **·fied, ·fy·ing** *v.t.* 1 To show to be just, right, or proper. 2 To declare or prove guiltless or blameless. 3 To show sufficient reason for (something done). 4 *Printing* To adjust (lines) to the proper length by spacing. —*v.i.* 5 *Law* a To show sufficient reason for something done. b To qualify as a bondsman. 6 *Printing* To be properly spaced. [< L *justus* just + *facere* make] —**jus'ti·fi'er** *n.*

jut (jut) *v.i.* **jut·ted, jut·ting** To extend beyond the main portion; project: often with *out.* —*n.* Anything that juts; a projection. [Var. of JET²]

jute (jōōt) *n.* 1 Either of two Asian plants cultivated for the strong fibers in the stem. 2 The fiber of this plant, used for bags, cordage, etc. [< Skt. *jūta* a braid of hair]

Jute (jōōt) *n.* A member of a Germanic tribe that invaded Britain in the fifth century.

ju·ve·nile (jōō'və·nīl, -nəl) *adj.* 1 Characteristic of youth; young. 2 Adapted to or suitable for youth. —*n.* 1 A young person; child. 2 An actor who interprets youthful roles. 3 A book for children. [< L *juvenis* young]

juvenile court A law court in which cases involving children under a specified age are heard.

jux·ta·pose (juks'tə·pōz') *v.t.* **·posed, ·pos·ing** To place close together; put side by side. [< L *juxta* near + POSE]

jux·ta·po·si·tion (juks'tə·pə·zish'ən) *n.* A placing close together or side by side; contiguity.

K

K, k (kā) *n. pl.* **K's, k's, Ks, ks** (kāz) 1 The 11th letter of the English alphabet. 2 Any spoken sound representing the letter *K* or *k.* 3 Something shaped like a K. —*adj.* Shaped like a K.

K potassium (L *kalium*); Kelvin.

K., k. karat (carat); kilogram; king; knight; knot *(naut.)*; kopec; calends (L *kalendae*).

KA Kansas (P.O. abbr.).

Ka·a·ba (kä'ə·bə, kä'bə) *n.* The Muslim shrine at Mecca enclosing a sacred black stone, supposedly given to Abraham by the angel Gabriel.

kab·a·la (kab'ə·lə, kə·bä'lə) *n.* CABALA.

ka·bu·ki (kä·bŏō'kē, kə-) *n.* A form of Japanese drama based on popular themes and employing elaborate costume, stylized gesture, music, and dancing. [Jap.]

kad·dish (kä'dish) *n. Often cap.* In Judaism, a daily prayer recited in the synagogue service, in one form used by mourners. [< Aramaic *qaddīsh* holy]

kaf·fee·klatsch (kôf'ē·klach', -kläch', kof'-) *n.* A social gathering for conversation while coffee is served. [G, lit., coffee + gossip]

kaf·fir (kaf'ər) *n.* A variety of sorghum grown in dry regions as a grain and forage plant. Also **kaf'ir, kafir corn, kaffir corn.**

Kaf·fir (kaf'ər) *n.* 1 A member of a group of South African Bantu tribes. 2 The language of these tribes. Also **Kaf'ir.**

Kaf·ka·esque (käf'kə·esk') *adj.* Characteristic of the novels of Franz Kafka; esp., bizarre or absurd, and often marked by the ineffectuality of the individual: made helpless by the *Kafkaesque* turn of events.

kaf·tan (kaf'tən, käf·tän') *n.* CAFTAN.

kai·ak (kī'ak) *n.* KAYAK.

kai·ser (kī'zər) *n.* 1 Emperor. 2 *Usu. cap.* The title designating the rulers of the Holy Roman Empire (962–1806), of Austria (1804–1918), and of Germany (1871–1918). [G < L *Caesar* Caesar]

kale (kāl) *n.* 1 A variety of headless cabbage yielding curled leaves. 2 *Slang* Money. [Var. of COLE]

ka·lei·do·scope (kə·lī'də·skōp) *n.* 1 A device consisting of a tube that contains mirrors and a hole for viewing, capable of producing symmetrical patterns by reflection of an image, often the image of small bits of material contained within. 2 A rapidly changing series of scenes, events, patterns, etc. [< Gk. *kalos* beautiful + *eidos* form

+ -SCOPE) —**ka·lei·do·scop·ic** (kə·lī′də·skop′ik), **ka·lei·do·scop′i·cal** adj. —**ka·lei′do·scop′i·cal·ly** adv.

kal·ends (kal′əndz) n.pl. CALENDS.

Ka·le·va·la (kä′lə·vä′lä) n. The national epic of Finland.

ka·lif (kā′lif, kal′if) n. CALIPH.

kal·mi·a (kal′mē·ə) n. Any of several North American evergreen shrubs with clusters of rose, purple, or white flowers. [< Peter *Kalm*, 1716–79, Swedish botanist]

Kal·muck (kal′muk) n. 1 A member of one of the Mongol tribes extending from western China to the valley of the Volga river. 2 The language of these tribes. Also **Kal′muk**.

kal·so·mine (kal′sə·mīn) n. CALCIMINE.

ka·mi·ka·ze (kä′mi·kä′zē) n. In World War II, a Japanese pilot pledged to die by crashing his bomb-laden plane against a target. [< Jap. *kami* a god + *kaze* the wind]

Kan., Kans., Kas. Kansas.

Ka·nak·a (kə·nak′ə, kan′ə·kə) n. 1 A native of Hawaii. 2 Any South Sea Islander.

kan·ga·roo (kang′gə·rōō′) n. pl. **·roos** Any of a large family of leaping herbivorous marsupials of the Australian region, having short forelimbs, strong hind limbs, and a long, tapering tail. [native Australian name]

Kangaroo

kangaroo court An unofficial court in which the law is disregarded or willfully misinterpreted or misapplied.

kangaroo rat Any of various hopping, mouselike rodents of the sw U.S. and Mexico.

ka·o·lin (kā′ə·lin) n. A pure, white clay used in making porcelain. Also **ka′o·line**. [< Chin. *Kao Ling* High Ridge, a mountain where first mined]

ka·pok (kā′pok) n. A cottonlike fiber covering the seeds of a tropical tree, used for stuffing mattresses, etc. [< Malay *kāpoq*]

kap·pa (kap′ə) n. The tenth letter in the Greek alphabet (Κ, κ).

ka·put (kä·pŏŏt′, kə-) adj. Slang. Ruined; done for. [G]

kar·a·kul (kar′ə·kəl) n. 1 A breed of sheep of central Asia. 2 The curly, lustrous fur of newborn karakul lambs. [< *Kara Kul*, lake in central Siberia]

kar·at (kar′ət) n. A measure used to express the percentage of gold in an alloy on a scale from 0 to 24; for example, 18-karat gold is 75% pure. [Var. of CARAT]

ka·ra·te (kə·rä′tē) n. An Oriental style of self-defense using sudden forceful blows with the side of the hand. [Jap., lit., empty-handed]

kar·ma (kär′mə, kûr′-) n. The law of cause and effect regulating one's future life; inevitable retribution, a concept developed by the Buddhists. [Skt., action]

kart (kärt) n. A small, low, motorized vehicle for one person, used esp. in racing. [Var. of CART] —**kart′ing** n.

karyo- combining form Biol. Nucleus: *karyotype*. [< Gk. *karyon* a nut]

kar·y·o·tin (kar′ē·ō′tin) n. CHROMATIN. [< KARYO- + (CHROMA)TIN]

kar·y·o·type (kar′ē·ə·tīp′) n. The complete array of somatic chromosomes characteristic of any given species, type, or strain of organism.

ka·sher (kä′shər) adj., n., v. KOSHER.

kata- prefix CATA-.

ka·ty·did (kā′tē·did) n. Any of several large, arboreal, green insects related to grasshoppers and crickets. [Imit. of its sound]

kau·ri (kou′rē) n. 1 A tall, coniferous, evergreen tree of New Zealand. 2 The wood of this tree. 3 KAURI GUM. Also **kau′ry**. [< Maori]

kauri gum A fresh or fossil resinous exudation of the kauri tree, used in varnishes, etc. Also **kauri copal, kauri resin**.

kay·ak (kī′ak) n. A hunting canoe of arctic America, made of sealskins stretched over a point-

Kayak

ed frame, leaving a hole amidships where the navigator sits. [< Eskimo]

kay·o (kā′ō) Slang v.t. **kay·oed, kay·o·ing** In boxing, to knock out. —n. A knockout. [< *k(nock) o(ut)*]

ka·zoo (kə·zōō′) n. pl. **·zoos** A toy musical instrument, a tube to which is attached a membrane which vibrates when the player hums into the tube. [?]

K.C. King's Counsel; Knights of Columbus.

kc, kc. kilocycle(s).

ke·a (kā′ə, kē′ə) n. A large, green New Zealand parrot. [Maori]

kedge (kej) Naut. n. A light anchor used in warping, to free a vessel from shoals, etc. Also **kedge anchor**. —v. **kedged, kedg·ing** v.i. 1 To move a vessel by hauling up to a kedge anchor placed at a distance. 2 To be moved in this way. —v.t. 3 To move (a vessel) in this way. [? < ME *caggen* to tie]

keel (kēl) n. 1 Naut. The lowest lengthwise member of the framework of a vessel, serving to give it stability. 2 Figuratively, a ship. 3 Anything suggesting a keel in shape or function. —**on an even keel** 1 In a level position. 2 Steady. —v.t. 1 To provide with a keel. 2 To upset (a vessel). —v.i. 3 To roll over. —**keel over** 1 To turn bottom up; capsize. 2 To fall over or be felled unexpectedly. 3 Informal To faint. [< ON *kjölr*]

keel·haul (kēl′hôl′) v.t. 1 Naut. To haul (a man) under a ship from one side to the other or from stem to stern, a former punishment. 2 To reprove severely.

keel·son (kēl′sən) n. Naut. A beam running lengthwise above the keel of a ship. [< LG *kielswīn*, lit., keel timber]

keen[1] (kēn) adj. 1 Very sharp, as a knife. 2 Cutting; piercing, as wit. 3 Vivid; pungent. 4 Having or exhibiting sharpness or penetration. 5 Acute: keen sight. 6 Exceptionally intelligent. 7 Characterized by intensity: a *keen* appetite. 8 Informal Impatient; eager: *keen* to be off. [< OE *cēne*] —**keen′ly** adv. —**keen′ness** n. —Syn. 2 acute, sharp. 6 brilliant, penetrating.

keen[2] (kēn) n. A wailing cry; dirge. —v.i. To wail loudly over the dead. [< Irish *caoinim* I wail] —**keen′er** n.

keep (kēp) v. **kept, keep·ing** v.t. 1 To have and retain possession or control of; hold. 2 To withhold knowledge of, as a secret. 3 To manage or conduct: to *keep* a shop. 4 To guard or defend from harm: May God *keep* you. 5 To be faithful to the conditions of: *keep* a promise. 6 To maintain by action or conduct: to *keep* silence. 7 To preserve unchanged: *Keep* the home fires burning. 8 To make regular entries in: to *keep* a diary. 9 To maintain a written record of: to *keep* accounts. 10 To have regularly for sale: to *keep* groceries. 11 To have in one's employ. 12 To celebrate or observe, as a holiday. 13 To conduct, as a meeting. 14 To detain or restrain; prevent: What *kept* you? 15 To hold prisoner; confine. 16 To remain; hold to: *Keep* your present course. 17 To hold or maintain in the same position or state as before: *Keep* your seat. —v.i. 18 To continue in a condition, place, or action: They *kept* firing. 19 To remain; stay: often with *up, down, in, out, off, away,* etc. 20 To remain sound, fresh, etc. 21 Informal To be in session: School *keeps* till three o'clock. —**keep back** 1 To restrain. 2 To withhold. —**keep in with** Informal To remain in the good graces of. —**keep on** To continue; persist. —**keep time** 1 To indicate time correctly, as a clock. 2 To count or observe rhythmic accents. —**keep to oneself** 1 To refrain from revealing. 2 To be solitary. —**keep track of** (or **tabs on**) To continue to be informed about. —**keep up** 1 To keep pace with; not fall behind. 2 To maintain in good condition or repair. 3 To cause to stay awake. —n. 1 Means of subsistence; livelihood. 2 A medieval castle or fortress. 3 That in which something is kept. —**for keeps** Informal For permanent keeping; for ever. [< OE *cēpan* observe]

keep·er (kē′pər) n. 1 An overseer, guard, or guardian. 2 One who observes or obeys: a *keeper* of promises.

keep·ing (kē′ping) n. 1 Custody, charge, or possession. 2 Maintenance; support. 3 Observance: the *keeping* of Christmas. 4 Preservation for the future. —**in keeping with** In accord with.

---

add, āce, câre, pälm; end, ēven; it, īce; odd, ōpen, ôrder; tŏŏk, pōōl; up, bûrn; ə = a in above, u in focus; yōō = u in fuse; oil; pout; check; go; ring; thin; this; zh, vision. < derived from; ? origin uncertain or unknown.

keep·sake (kēp'sāk') *n.* Anything kept, or given to be kept; a memento.

kef (kĕf, kāf), *n.* 1 A voluptuous, dreamy condition. 2 Indian hemp, smoked to produce this condition. [<Ar. *kaif* good humor]

keg (keg) *n.* 1 A small, strong barrel, usu. of 5- to 10-gallon capacity. 2 One hundred pounds of nails. [<ON *kaggi*]

keg·ler (keg'lər) *n. Informal* One who bowls; a bowler. [G *Kegel* ninepin]

kelp (kelp) *n.* 1 Any of various large, brown, coarse seaweeds. 2 The ashes of seaweed, used as a source of iodine.

Kel·vin scale (kel'vin) The absolute scale of temperature, having zero equal to about −273°C or −459.4°F. [<Lord *Kelvin*, 1824–1907, British physicist]

ken (ken) *v.t.* **kenned** or **kent, ken·ning** *Scot.* To know; have knowledge of —*n.* Reach of sight or knowledge; cognizance. [<OE *cennan* make known]

Ken. Kentucky.

ken·nel (Kən'əl) *n.* 1 A house for a dog or for a pack of hounds. 2 A pack of hounds. 3 *pl.* A professional establishment where dogs are bred, raised, boarded, trained, etc. —*v.* ·neled or ·nelled, ·nel·ing or ·nel·ling *v.t.* 1 To keep or confine in a kennel. —*v.i.* 2 To take shelter in a kennel. [<L *canis* a dog]

ke·no (kē'nō) *n.* A game of chance resembling lotto.

Kenya (kĕn'yə, kēn'-) *n.* An independent member of the Commonwealth of Nations in E Africa, 224,960 sq. mi., cap. Nairobi. —**Kenyan** *adj., n.* • See map at AFRICA.

kep·i (kep'ē) *n. pl.* **kep·is** A military cap with a flat crown and a visor. [<G *Kappe* a cap]

kept (kept) *p.t. & p.p.* of KEEP.

ker·a·tin (ker'ə·tin) *n.* A tough, insoluble protein that forms the main ingredient of hair, horns, nails, etc. [<Gk. *keras, keratos* horn] —**ke·rat·i·nous** (kə·rat'ə·nəs) *adj.*

kerb (kûrb) *n. Brit.* The curb of a pavement.

ker·chief (kûr'chif) *n.* 1 A square of linen, silk, or other fabric used to cover the head or neck. 2 A handkerchief. [<OF *covrir* to cover + *chef* head] —**ker'chiefed** *adj.*

kerf (kûrf) *n.* 1 The cut made by a saw, ax, etc. 2 A piece cut off. [<OE *cyrf* a cutting]

ker·mes (kûr'mēz) *n.* 1 The dried bodies of a species of scale insect. 2 A red dye made from these bodies. 3 A small oak tree of the Mediterranean area on which the insects are found: also **kermes oak.** [<Ar. *qirmiz*]

ker·mess (kûr'mis) *n.* 1 In Belgium and the Netherlands, a carnival or outdoor festival. 2 Any similar festival, usu. to raise funds for charity. Also **ker'mis.** [<Du. *kerk misse* church mass]

kern (kûrn) *n. Printing* That part of a type which overhangs the shaft or shank, as of an italic *f.* —*v.t.* To make (type) with a kern. [<F *carne* projecting angle]

ker·nel (kûr'nəl) *n.* 1 A grain or seed, as of corn or other cereal. 2 The inner, fleshy part of a nut or fruit stone. 3 The central part of anything; —*v.i.* To envelop as a kernel. [<OE *cyrnel*, dim. of *corn* a seed]

ker·o·sene (ker'ə·sēn, kar'-, ker·ə·sēn', kar-) *n.* A liquid mixture of hydrocarbons, derived from petroleum and used as fuel. [<Gk. *kēros* wax + -ENE]

ker·sey (kûr'zē) *n. pl.* **·seys** A lightweight, ribbed woolen cloth. [<*Kersey*, village in England]

kes·trel (kes'trəl) *n.* A European falcon noted for its ability to hover in the air against the wind. [<OF *cresserelle*]

ketch (kech) *n.* A fore-and-aft rigged, two-masted vessel having the jigger mast forward of the rudder post and aft of the mainmast. [ME *cache*]

ketch·up (kech'əp) *n.* A condiment of the consistency of a thick purée, made of tomatoes, onions, and various spices. [<Chin. *ketsiap* brine of pickled fish]

Ketch

ke·tone (kē'tōn) *n.* Any of a series of organic compounds composed of two hydrocarbon radicals and a single bivalent group containing an atom of carbon bonded to an atom of oxygen. [<F *acétone* acetone] —**ke·ton·ic** (kē·ton'ik) *adj.*

ket·tle (ket'l) *n.* 1 A metallic vessel for stewing or boiling. 2 TEAKETTLE. [<ON *ketill*] —**kettle of fish** A troublesome situation.

ket·tle·drum (ket'l·drum') *n.* A drum having a brass shell and tunable parchment head.

key¹ (kē) *n.* 1 A device for turning the catch or bolt of a lock in order to lock or unlock something. 2 An instrument for turning a bolt, etc., as in winding a clock. 3 Anything serving to explain or solve something: the *key* to a mystery. 4 Any one of the finger levers used to operate typewriters, typesetting machines, a telegraph sending apparatus, etc. 5 *Music* **a** A lever to be pressed by a finger in playing an instrument. **b** A set of associated tones forming a diatonic scale and all related to one principal tone, the tonic. 6 The tone or pitch of the voice. 7 Tone or style of expression. 8 *Archit.* KEYSTONE. —*v.t.* 1 To fasten with or as with a key. 2 To wedge tightly or support firmly with a key, wedge, etc. 3 To complete (an arch) by adding the keystone. —**key up** 1 to raise the pitch of. 2 To cause excitement, anticipation, etc., in. —*adj.* Of chief or decisive importance: a *key* position. [<OE *cæg*]

key² (kē) *n.* A low island, esp. one of coral, along a coast. [<Sp. *cayo*]

key·board (kē'bôrd', -bōrd') *n.* 1 A row of keys as in a piano or typewriter. 2 A set of keys or buttons for entering information into a computer.

keyed (kēd) *adj.* 1 Having keys: said of musical instruments, etc. 2 Pitched in a specific key. 3 Secured by a keystone.

key·hole (kē'hōl') *n.* A hole for a key, as in a door or lock.

key·note (kē'nōt') *n.* 1 *Music* The tonic of a key: also **key tone.** 2 A basic idea, fact, principle, or sentiment. —*v.t.* ·not·ed, ·not·ing 1 To sound the keynote of. 2 To give the essential points of, as a political platform.

keynote speech A speech, as at a political convention, presenting the primary issues of interest. Also **keynote address.**

key·pad (kē'pad') *n.* A set of keys, like those on a typewriter keyboard, used to insert sets of numbers into a computer.

key·punch (kē'punch') *n.* A machine with a keyboard, used to record information on punch cards or tapes by punching patterns of holes thereon.

key signature *Music* The sharps or flats following the clef at the beginning of each staff, to indicate the key.

key·stone (kē'stōn') *n.* 1 *Archit.* The uppermost and last-set stone of an arch, which locks its members together. 2 The fundamental element, as of a science or doctrine.

Keystone

kg, kg. kilogram(s); keg(s).

khak·i (kak'ē, kä'kē) *adj.* Having a tannish brown or olive-drab color. —*n. pl.* **khak·is** 1 A tannish brown or olive-drab color. 2 A cloth of this color, used esp. for ·military uniforms. 3 *Usu. pl.* Trousers or a uniform of this cloth. [<Hind. *khākī* dusty]

khan¹ (kän, kan) *n.* An Oriental inn surrounding a courtyard. [<Ar. *khān* an inn]

khan² (kän, kan) *n.* 1 In various Oriental countries during the Middle Ages, a ruler or chief. 2 A title of respect for any of various dignitaries in Iran, India, Afghanistan, etc. [<Pers. *khān* prince]

khe·dive (kə·dēv') *n.* The title of the Turkish viceroys of Egypt from 1867 to 1914.

Khmer Republic (kmer) A country of SW Indochina, 69,844 sq. mi., cap. Pnompenh. • See map at INDOCHINA.

kHz kilohertz.

kib·butz (ki·boots') *n. pl.* **kib·butz·im** (-boot·sēm') A collective farming settlement in Israel. [<Heb. *qibbūs*]

kib·itz (kib'its) *v.i. Informal* To act as a kibitzer.

kib·itz·er (kib'it·sər) *n. Informal* One who observes other persons' affairs, esp. someone who watches and offers gratuitous advice to a player or players in a card game. [Yiddish]

ki·bosh (ki'bosh) *n. Slang* Nonsense or humbug. —**put the kibosh on** To put a stop to; quash. [?]

kick (kik) *v.i.* 1 To strike out with the foot or feet; give a blow with the foot. 2 To strike out with the foot habitually; this horse *kicks*. 3 To recoil, as a firearm. 4 *Informal* To object; complain. —*v.t.* 5 To strike with the foot. 6 To drive or impel by striking with the foot. 7 To strike in recoiling. 8 In football, to score (a goal) by a kick. 9 *Slang* To rid oneself of (a habit, esp. a drug habit). —**kick about** (or **around**) 1 To abuse; neglect. 2 *Informal* To roam from place to place. 3 *Informal* To give thought or consideration to; discuss. —**kick back** 1 To recoil violently or unexpectedly, as a gun. 2 *Informal* To pay (part of a commission, salary, etc.) to someone in a position to grant privileges. —**kick in** 1 *Informal* To contribute or participate by contributing. 2 *Slang* To die. —**kick off** 1 In football, to put the ball in play. 2 *Slang* To die. —**kick oneself** To have remorse or regret. —**kick out** *Informal* To eject violently, as with a kick. —**kick the bucket** *Slang* To die. —**kick up** *Slang* To make or stir up (trouble, confusion, etc.). —**kick upstairs** To give an apparent promotion to (someone) in order to remove from a position of actual power. —*n.* 1 A blow with the foot. 2 The recoil of a firearm. 3 In football, one who kicks. 4 *Slang* An act of violent opposition or objection. 5 Something that excites, as the alcoholic content of drink. 6 Effective action or power. 7 *Often pl. Slang* Stimulation; pleasure: to do something for *kicks.* —**on a kick** *Slang* Intensely but often temporarily interested in a subject or activity. [ME *kiken*]

kick·back (kik′bak′) *n.* 1 A recoil; repercussion. 2 Money comprising part of a commission, fee, etc., returned by prior agreement or coercion, often illegal or unethical.

kick·er (kik′ər) *n.* 1 One who or that which kicks. 2 *Slang* A surprising element or turn of events.

kick·off (kik′ôf′, -of′) *n.* 1 In football, the kick with which a game or half is begun. 2 Any beginning.

kick·shaw (kik′shô) *n.* 1 Something fantastic or trifling. 2 Any fancy or unrecognizable dish of food. Also **kick′·shaws.** [< F *quelque chose* something]

kick·y (kik′ē) *adj.* **kick·i·er, kick·i·est** *Slang* Stimulating; exciting. —**kick′i·ness** *n.*

kid (kid) *n.* 1 A young goat. 2 Leather made from the skin of young goats, esp. as used in gloves, shoes, etc. 3 The meat of a young goat. 4 *Informal* A child or infant. —*adj.* 1 Made of kidskin. 2 *Informal* Younger: my *kid* brother. —*v.t. & v.i.* **kid·ded, kid·ding** 1 To give birth to (young): said of goats. 2 *Slang* To tease jokingly. 3 *Slang* To deceive or try to deceive (someone). [< ON *kidh*] —**kid′der** *n.*

kid·dy (kid′ē) *n. pl.* **kid·dies** *Informal* A small child. Also **kid′die.**

kid glove A glove made of kidskin or similar material. —**handle with kid gloves** To treat in a tactful or gingerly manner.

kid·nap (kid′nap) *v.t.* **·naped** or **·napped, ·nap·ing** or **·nap·ping** 1 To seize and carry off (someone) by force or fraud, usu. followed by a demand for ransom. 2 To steal (a child). [< KID + *nap,* dial. var. of NAB] —**kid′nap·er, kid′nap·per** *n.*

kid·ney (kid′nē) *n. pl.* **·neys** 1 One of a pair of organs at the back of the abdominal cavity in vertebrates. They regulate the volume, acidity, and composition of body fluids by filtering the blood and excreting waste products as urine. 2 This organ of a slaughtered animal, used as food. 3 Temperament; disposition. 4 Type or kind. [?]

kidney bean The kidney-shaped seed of a plant of the bean family, cultivated for food.

kidney stone Any calculus occurring in the kidney or urinary passages.

kid·skin (kid′skin′) *n.* Leather from the skin of a young goat, used for gloves, shoes, etc.

kif (kēf) *n.* KEF.

Ki·ku·yu (kē·kōō′yōō) *n. pl.* **·yu** or **·yus** 1 A member of one of the main Negro tribes of Kenya. 2 The Bantu language of this tribe.

kill[1] (kil) *v.t.* 1 To deprive of life; slay. 2 To slaughter for food; butcher. 3 To put an end to. 4 To destroy the active qualities of; neutralize: to *kill* lye. 5 To spoil the effect of; offset, as a color. 6 To cancel; cross out: to *kill* a

paragraph. 7 To stop (an engine, electric current, etc.). 8 To pass (time) aimlessly. 9 *Informal* To overwhelm with strong emotion, laughter, etc. —*v.i.* 10 To slay or murder. 11 To suffer or undergo death; die: These plants *kill* easily. —*n.* 1 An animal killed as prey. 2 The act of killing, esp. in hunting. —**in at the kill** Present at the climax of a chase or other undertaking. [ME *killen*] —**Syn.** *v.* 1 assassinate, execute, murder, slaughter.

kill[2] (kil) *n.* A creek, stream, or channel. [< Du. *kil*]

kill·deer (kil′dir) *n. pl.* **·deers** or **·deer** A small North American plover marked with two black bands at the breast. Also **kill′dee** (-dē). [Imit. of its cry]

kill·er (kil′ər) *n.* 1 A destroyer of life; a slayer. 2 A murderer or an assassin.

killer whale Any of various small predaceous whales, as the grampus, etc.

kill·ing (kil′ing) *n.* 1 The act of taking life. 2 *Informal* A phenomenal profit resulting from bold financial speculation. —*adj.* 1 Lethal; destructive. 2 Very tiring: a *killing* pace. 3 *Slang* Very amusing.

Killer whale (grampus)

kill·joy (kil′joi′) *n.* One who dampens the enthusiasm or pleasure of others.

kiln (kil, kiln) *n.* An oven or furnace for baking, burning, or drying various products, as bricks, lime, enamel, pottery, etc. [< L *culina* kitchen]

kiln-dry (kil′drī′, kiln′-) *v.t.* **·dried, ·dry·ing** To dry in a kiln.

kil·o (kil′ō, kē′lō) *n. pl.* **kil·os** 1 KILOGRAM. 2 KILOMETER.

kilo- *prefix* One thousand (times a given unit): used chiefly in the metric system of weights and measures: *kilogram.* [< Gk. *chilioi* a thousand]

kil·o·cal·o·rie (kil′ə·kal′ə·rē) *n.* A great calorie: equal to 1,000 calories.

kil·o·cy·cle (kil′ə·sī′kəl) *n.* 1 One thousand cycles. 2 KILO-HERTZ.

kil·o·gram (kil′ə·gram) *n.* 1 The basic metric unit of mass and weight, equal to the mass of a prototype kept in Sèvres, France, and equal to approximately 2.2 pounds. 2 The weight of a one-kilogram mass at the surface of the earth. Also **kil′o·gramme.**

kilogram calorie See CALORIE.

kil·o·hertz (kil′ə·hûrts′) *n. pl.* **·hertz, hertz·es** A unit of frequency equal to 1,000 cycles per second. [< KILO- + HERTZ]

kil·o·me·ter (ki·lom′ə·tər, kil′ə·mē′tər) *n.* A metric unit of length equal to 1,000 meters or about ⅝ mile. Also **kil′o·me′tre.**

kil·o·ton (kil′ə·tun) *n.* 1 A thousand tons. 2 A unit equivalent to the explosive power of 1,000 tons of TNT: used in expressing the energy of nuclear weapons.

kil·o·watt (kil′ə·wät) *n.* One thousand watts.

kil·o·watt-hour (kil′ə·wät·our′) *n.* The work done or the energy released by one kilowatt acting for one hour.

kilt (kilt) *n.* 1 A short pleated skirt worn by Scottish Highland men. 2 A girl's or woman's skirt resembling a kilt. —*v.t.* 1 To pleat. 2 To furnish with a kilt. [Prob.< Scand.]

kil·ter (kil′tər) *n. Informal* Proper or working order: My radio is out of *kilter. Brit.* sp. **kel′ter.** [?]

ki·mo·no (kə·mō′nə, ki·mō′nō) *n. pl.* **·nos** 1 A Japanese loose robe fastened with a sash. 2 A woman's dressing gown.

kin (kin) *n.* 1 Relationship; consanguinity. 2 Collectively, relatives by blood. —*adj.* Of the same blood or ancestry. [< OE *cyn*] —**Syn.** *n.* 1 blood, descent, family, stock.

-kin *suffix* Little; small: *lambkin.* [< MDu. *-kijn*]

kin·aes·the·sia (kin′is·thē′zhə, -zhē-ə), *n.* KINESTHESIA.

kind[1] (kīnd) *adj.* 1 Friendly and helpful: a *kind* act. 2 Gentle: *kind* to children. 3 Characterized by friendliness and

a. plaid.
b. kilt.
c. sporran.

gentleness: a *kind* remark. [< OE *gecynde*] —**Syn. 1** charitable, generous, good, good-hearted. **2** humane, kindly.

kind² (kīnd) *n.* **1** Variety; sort. **2** Basic nature; essence. **3** A number of persons or things of the same character; a class. **4** A modification of a given sort of thing; a species. —**in kind** With something of the same sort: to repay a blow *in kind.* —**kind of** *Informal* Rather; somewhat. —**of a kind 1** Of the same sort or variety. **2** Of imperfect quality: poetry *of a kind.* [< OE *cynd*]

kin·der·gar·ten (kin′dər-gär′tən) *n.* A school for children, usu. five or six years of age, to encourage socialization by group play and readiness for first-grade skills. [< G < *Kinder* children + *Garten* garden]

kin·der·gart·ner (kin′dər-gärt′nər) *n.* **1** A kindergarten teacher. **2** A kindergarten pupil.

kind·heart·ed (kīnd′här′tid) *adj.* Having a kind and sympathetic nature. —**kind′heart′ed·ly** *adv.*

kin·dle (kin′dəl) *v.* **·dled, ·dling** *v.t.* **1** To cause (a flame, fire, etc.) to burn; light. **2** To set fire to; ignite. **3** To excite or inflame, as the feelings. **4** To make bright or glowing. —*v.i.* **5** To start burning. **6** To become excited. **7** To become bright or glowing. [< ON *kynda*] —**kin′dler** *n.*

kin·dling (kind′ling) *n.* Small sticks of wood and other inflammable material with which a fire is kindled.

kind·ly (kīnd′lē) *adj.* **·li·er, ·li·est 1** Having or manifesting kindness; sympathetic. **2** Having a favorable or grateful effect; beneficial. —*adv.* In a kind manner or spirit; good-naturedly. —**kind′li·ness** *n.*

kind·ness (kīnd′nəs) *n.* **1** The quality of being kind; good will. **2** A kind act; a favor. **3** A kindly feeling.

kin·dred (kin′drəd) *adj.* **1** Of the same family. **2** Of a like nature or character; congenial. —*n.* **1** Relationship; consanguinity. **2** Relatives by blood. **3** Affinity. [< OE *cyn* family + *ræden* condition, state]

kine (kīn) *n. Archaic* Cattle; plural of cow¹.

kin·e·mat·ics (kin′ə-mat′iks) *n.pl. (construed as sing.)* The branch of mechanics dealing with motion without reference to forces. [< Gk. *kineein* to move] —**kin′e·mat′ic** or **·i·cal** *adj.* —**kin′e·mat′i·cal·ly** *adv.*

kin·e·scope (kin′ə-skōp) *n.* **1** A cathode-ray tube on which a television picture is displayed. **2** A film record of a television program. [KINE(TIC) + -SCOPE]

ki·ne·sics (ki-nē′siks) *n.* The study of the nonverbal part of language, esp. gestures and body language, as part of overall communication. [< Gk. *kinesis* motion + -ICS]

kin·es·the·si·a (kin′əs-thē′zhə, -zhē-ə) *n.* The sensation of muscular movement, bodily position, etc. Also **kin′es·the′sis** (-thē′sis). [< Gk. *kineein* to move + *aisthēsis* perception] —**kin′es·thet′ic** (-thet′ik) *adj.*

ki·net·ic (ki-net′ik) *adj.* **1** Producing motion; motor. **2** Consisting in or depending upon motion: *kinetic* energy. [< Gk. *kineein* to move]

kinetic energy Energy in motion, as in electric currents, waterfalls, burning fuel, etc.

ki·net·ics (ki-net′iks) *n.pl. (construed as sing.)* The branch of mechanics that deals with the dynamics of material bodies.

kin·folk (kin′fōk′) *n. pl.* Relatives collectively; kin. Also **kin′folks.**

king (king) *n.* **1** The sovereign male ruler of a kingdom. **2** A person or thing of great importance, position, or power: a *king* of finance. **3** A playing card bearing the semblance of a king. **4** In chess, the principal piece. **5** In checkers, a piece that has reached the adversary's king row. —*adj.* Great, as in size or importance: often in combination: *kingbolt, king* cobra. [< OE *cyng*]

king·bird (king′bûrd′) *n.* Any of various aggressive American flycatchers.

king·bolt (king′bōlt′) *n.* A vertical bolt attaching the body of a vehicle to the front axle and serving as a pivot in turning.

king cobra A large, poisonous snake found in India.

king crab 1 HORSESHOE CRAB. **2** Any of several very large edible crabs, esp. a variety found in Alaska.

king·dom (king′dəm) *n.* **1** The territory, people, state, or realm ruled by a king or a queen; a monarchy. **2** Any field of independent authority, action, or influence; sphere. **3** One of the three divisions of the natural world, known as the *animal, vegetable,* and *mineral kingdoms.*

king·fish (king′fish′) *n. pl.* **·fish** or **·fish·es 1** One of various American food fishes common in N Atlantic coastal waters. **2** *Informal* An uncontested leader in a local government, legislative body, etc.

king·fish·er (king′fish′ər) *n.* Any of several brightly colored birds, usu. crested, which feed on fish.

King James Version The Authorized Version, an English translation of the Bible published in 1611 under the auspices of James I, still used by English-speaking Protestants.

king·let (king′lit) *n.* **1** A little or unimportant king. **2** Any of several small birds resembling the warblers.

king·ly (king′lē) *adj.* **·li·er, ·li·est** Pertaining to or worthy of a king; regal. —*adv.* In a regal or kingly way. —**king′li·ness** *n.*

Kingfisher

king·pin (king′pin′) *n.* **1** KINGBOLT. **2** In tenpins, the foremost pin of a set. **3** In ninepins, the center pin. **4** *Slang* A person of first importance.

king post In carpentry, a single vertical strut supporting the apex of a triangular truss and resting on a crossbeam.

king row In checkers, the row of squares nearest to either of the players.

Kings (kingz) *n.pl. (construed as sing.)* **1** Either of two books of the Old Testament, I and II Kings. **2** In the Douay Bible, four books including I and II Kings and I and II Samuel.

King's English A style of English considered as standard. Also **Queen's English.**

king's evil Scrofula: once supposed to be curable by a monarch's touch.

king·ship (king′ship) *n.* **1** Royal state; kinghood **2** Government by a king. **3** The person of a king.

king-size (king′sīz′) *adj. Informal* Larger or longer than normal. Also **king′-sized′.**

king snake A large harmless snake of the s U.S. that feeds largely on rats, mice, and other snakes.

king's ransom A very large amount of money.

kink (kingk) *n.* **1** An abrupt bend, twist, or tangle, as in a wire or rope. **2** A tightly twisted curl, as in hair or wool. **3** A mental quirk or prejudice. **4** A hindrance, obstruction, or difficulty. **5** A crick; cramp. —*v.t. & v.i.* To form or cause to form a kink or kinks. [Du., twist, curl]

kink·a·jou (king′kə-jōō) *n.* A nocturnal, arboreal carnivore of South and Central America, having large eyes and a prehensile tail. [< F *quincajou*]

kink·y (kingk′ē) *adj.* **kink·i·er, kink·i·est 1** Having many kinks: *kinky* hair. **2** *Slang* Odd, eccentric, or zany: *kinky* sexuality. —**kink′i·ness** *n.*

kins·folk (kinz′fōk′) *n.pl.* KINFOLK.

kin·ship (kin′ship) *n.* **1** Family relationship. **2** Close relationship.

kins·man (kinz′mən) *n. pl.* **·men** (-mən) A blood relation. —**kins′wom′an** (-woom′ən) (*pl.* **·wom·en**) *n. Fem.*

ki·osk (kē′osk, kē-osk′) *n.* **1** An open ornamental summerhouse in Turkey. **2** A similar, smaller structure made to serve as a booth, newsstand, bandstand, or the like. [< Turk. *köshk* < Pers. *kūshk*]

kip (kip) *n.* The untanned skin of a calf or other young or small animal. Also **kip′skin′** (-skin′) [?]

kip·per (kip′ər) *n.* **1** A salmon, herring, or other food fish cured by kippering. **2** The male salmon during the spawning season. —*v.t.* To cure by drying or smoking. [< OE *cypera* spawning salmon]

Kiosk *def.* 2

Kir·ghiz (kir-gēz′) *n. pl.* **·ghiz** or **·ghiz·es 1** One of a Turkic people of the Mongoloid race, largely nomadic, dwelling in central Asia. **2** The Turkic language of the Kirghiz.

kirk (kûrk) *n. Scot.* A church. —**the Kirk** The established Presbyterian Church of Scotland.

kir·mess (kûr′mis) *n.* KERMESS.

kir·tle (kûrt′l) *n.* A garment with a skirt; a frock or mantle. [< OE *crytel*] —**kir′tled** *adj.*

kis·met (kiz'met, kis'-) *n.* Appointed lot; fate. [Turk. < Ar. *qisma* < *qasama* divide]

kiss (kis) *n.* 1 A caress with the lips. 2 A gentle touch. 3 Any of various forms of candy. —*v.t. & v.i.* 1 To touch with the lips, as in greeting or love. 2 To touch slightly. [< OE *cyssan* to kiss] —**kiss'a·ble** *adj.*

kit (kit) *n.* 1 A container, as a box or a knapsack, in which to pack belongings. 2 A small pail. 3 A collection of articles and appliances for any special purpose: a tool *kit.* 4 A set of parts for assembly, esp. by the consumer. —**the whole kit and caboodle** The whole collection of persons or things. [< MDu. *kitte* jug]

kitch·en (kich'ən) *n.* 1 A room set apart for cooking food. 2 A culinary department; cuisine. [< L *coquina*]

kitch·en·ette (kich'ən·et') *n.* A small kitchen.

kitchen garden A garden in which vegetables and fruits are grown for home use.

kitchen police *Mil.* 1 Enlisted men detailed to perform kitchen chores. 2 These chores.

kitch·en·ware (kich'ən·wâr') *n.* Kitchen utensils.

kite (kīt) *n.* 1 Any of certain birds of prey of the hawk family, having long, pointed wings and a forked tail. 2 A light frame, usu. of wood, covered with paper or light fabric, to be flown in the air at the end of a long string. 3 Any of several light sails for use in a very light wind. 4 In commerce: a Any negotiable paper not representing a genuine transaction but so employed as to obtain money. b A bank check drawn with insufficient funds on deposit to secure the advantage of the time period prior to collection. —*v.* **kit·ed, kit·ing** *v.i.* 1 *Informal* To soar or fly like a kite. 2 In commerce, to obtain money by the use of kites. —*v.t.* 3 In commerce, to issue as a kite. [< OE *cyta*]

kith and kin (kith) Friends and relatives. [< OE *cyth* acquaintance]

kitsch (kich) *n.* Art or literary works, etc., having broad popular appeal and little aesthetic merit. [G]

kit·ten (kit'n) *n.* A young cat or other feline animal. [< OF *chitoun*]

kit·ten·ish (kit'ən·ish) *adj.* Playfully coy. —**kit'ten·ish·ly** *adv.* —**kit'ten·ish·ness** *n.*

kit·ti·wake (kit'ē·wāk) *n.* A gull of northern seas having the hind toe rudimentary.

kit·ty[1] (kit'ē) *n. pl.* **·ties** 1 In certain card games, the pool to which each player contributes a percentage of his winnings. 2 Money pooled or set aside for any specific purpose. [< KIT]

kit·ty[2] (kit'ē) *n. pl.* **·ties** 1 A kitten. 2 A pet name for a cat.

kit·ty-cor·nered (kit'ē·kôr'nərd) *adj.* CATERCORNERED.

ki·wi (kē'wē) *n. pl.* **·wis** A flightless bird of New Zealand, having a long bill. [Maori; imit. of its cry]

KKK, K.K.K. Ku Klux Klan.

kl, kl. kiloliter(s).

Klan (klan) *n.* KU KLUX KLAN.

Klans·man (klanz'mən) *n. pl.* **·men** (-mən) A member of the Ku Klux Klan.

Kleen·ex (klē'neks) *n.* A soft, paper tissue, used as a handkerchief: a trade name.

klep·to·ma·ni·a (klep'tə·mā'nē·ə) *n.* An uncontrollable, abnormal propensity to steal. [< Gk. *kleptein* to steal + -MANIA] —**klep'to·ma'ni·ac** (-mā'nē·ak) *n.*

klieg light (klēg) A powerful arc light used while making motion pictures. [< A. *Kliegl*, 1872–1927, and his brother John, 1869–1959, U.S. stage-lighting pioneers.]

klutz (klutz) *n. Slang* A clumsy or inept person; oaf. [< G *Klotz* block of wood, lout] —**klutz'y** *adj.* (**·i·er, ·i·est**)

km, km. kilometer(s).

knack (nak) *n.* 1 The trick of doing a thing readily and well. 2 Cleverness; adroitness. 3 A clever device. [ME, a sharp blow] —**Syn.** 2 aptitude, dexterity, facility.

knack·wurst (näk'wûrst) *n.* A short, thick sausage, usu. highly seasoned. [G < *knacken* sputter + *Wurst* sausage]

knap·sack (nap'sak) *n.* A bag of leather or canvas worn across the shoulders, for carrying clothing, supplies, etc. [< Du. *knappen* to bite + *zak* a sack]

knave (nāv) *n.* 1 A dishonest person; rogue. 2 A playing card, the jack. [< OE *cnafa* servant]

knav·er·y (nā'vər·ē) *n. pl.* **·er·ies** 1 Deceitfulness; trickery. 2 An instance of deceitful action or behavior.

knav·ish (nā'vish) *adj.* Of, pertaining to, or characteristic of a knave. —**knav'ish·ly** *adv.* —**knav'ish·ness** *n.*

knead (nēd) *v.t.* 1 To mix and work, as dough or clay, into a uniform mass, usu. by pressing, turning, etc., with the hands. 2 To work upon with the hands; massage. 3 To make by or as by kneading. [< OE *cnedan*] —**knead'er** *n.*

knee (nē) *n.* 1 The joint of the human leg midway between the hip and the ankle. 2 A joint in the foreleg of various animals corresponding to the knee. 3 Anything like or suggesting a bent knee. 4 The part of a stocking or garment covering the knee. —**bring to one's knees** To cause to surrender. —*v.t.* To touch or strike with the knee. [< OE *cnēow*]

knee·cap (nē'kap') *n.* 1 PATELLA: also **knee'pan'.** 2 A protective covering or padding for the knee: also **knee'pad'.**

knee-deep (nē'dēp') *adj.* 1 Up to the knees. 2 Sunk to the knee.

knee·hole (nē'hōl') *n.* A recess for the knees, as in a desk. —*adj.* Having such a recess.

knee-jerk (nē'jûrk') *adj. Informal* Acting in a way that displays unthinking acceptance of preconceived ideas or stereotypes: *knee-jerk* liberals.

knee jerk A reflex action of the lower leg caused by a tapping of the tendon just below the kneecap.

kneel (nēl) *v.i.* **knelt** or **kneeled, kneel·ing** To fall or rest on the bent knee or knees. [< OE *cnēowlian*] —**kneel'er** *n.*

knell (nel) *n.* 1 The tolling of a bell, as in announcing a death. 2 An omen of death, failure, etc. —*v.i.* 1 To sound a knell; toll. 2 To give a sad or warning sound. —*v.t.* 3 To proclaim or announce by a knell. [< OE *cnyllan* knock]

knelt (nelt) *p.t. & p.p.* of KNEEL.

knew (nyōō) *p.t.* of KNOW.

Knick·er·bock·er (nik'ər·bok'ər) *n.* 1 A descendant of one of the early Dutch settlers in New York State. 2 A New Yorker. [< Diedrich *Knickerbocker*, fictitious author of Washington Irving's *History of New York* (1809)]

knick·er·bock·ers (nik'ər·bok'ərz) *n. pl.* Wide short breeches gathered below the knee.

knick·ers (nik'ərz) *n. pl.* 1 KNICKERBOCKERS. 2 Formerly, a woman's undergarment, similar to bloomers.

knick·knack (nik'nak') *n.* A trifling article; trinket; trifle. [Reduplication of KNACK]

knife (nīf) *n. pl.* **knives** (nīvz) 1 A cutting instrument consisting of a sharp single-edged or double-edged blade, commonly set in a handle. 2 An edged blade forming a part of an implement or machine. 3 A weapon such as a cutlass or sword. —**go under the knife** *Informal* To undergo a surgical operation. —*v.t.* **knifed, knif·ing** 1 To stab or cut with a knife. 2 *Slang* To work against with underhand methods. —**knife in the back** *Informal* To undermine the reputation, position, etc., of. [< OE *cnīf*]

knight (nīt) *n.* 1 In medieval times, a gentleman admitted with special ceremonies to honorable military rank. 2 *Brit.* The holder of an honorary, nonhereditary rank next below that of baronet, giving him the title of *Sir.* 3 A champion or devoted follower, as of a cause, principle, or woman. 4 A member of any society in which the official title of knight obtains. 5 A chessman bearing a horse's head. —*v.t.* To make (someone) a knight. [< OE *cniht* boy, servant]

knight-er·rant (nīt'er'ənt) *pl.* **knights-er·rant** A medieval knight who went forth to redress wrongs or seek adventures.

knight-er·rant·ry (nīt'er'ən·trē) *n. pl.* **·ries** 1 The customs and practices of the knights-errant. 2 Quixotic behavior or action.

knight·hood (nīt'hŏŏd) *n.* 1 The character, dignity, rank, or vocation of a knight. 2 Knights collectively. 3 CHIVALRY.

knight·ly (nīt′lē) *adj.* 1 Pertaining to a knight; chivalrous. 2 Composed of knights: a *knightly* order. —**knight′li·ness** *n.*

Knights of Columbus A fraternal society of Roman Catholic men.

Knight Templar *pl.* **Knights Templars** *for def. 1;* **Knights Templar** *for def. 2* 1 A member of a great military order founded in 1119 for the protection of pilgrims in Jerusalem; also **Templar.** 2 A member of a certain Masonic order in the U.S.

knish (kə·nish′) *n.* A small square or round of dough filled with potatoes, meat, kasha, etc., and baked or fried. [Yiddish]

knit (nit) *v.* **knit** or **knit·ted, knit·ting** *v.i.* 1 To form (a fabric or garment) by interlocking loops of a single yarn or thread by means of needles. 2 To make into fabric by interlocking loops of thread, as on a machine, instead of by weaving. 3 To fasten or unite closely and firmly. 4 To contract (the brows). —*v.i.* 5 To make a fabric by interweaving a yarn or thread. 6 To grow together firmly, as a broken bone. —*n.* A knitted garment or fabric. [< OE *cnyttan*] —**knit′ter** *n.*

knit·ting (nit′ing) *n.* 1 The act of one who or that which knits. 2 The fabric or garment thus produced.

knitting needle A straight, slender rod, pointed at one or both ends, used in sets of two or more for hand knitting.

knives (nīvz) *n.pl.* of KNIFE.

knob (nob) *n.* 1 A rounded protuberance. 2 A rounded handle, as of a door. 3 A rounded mountain; knoll. [< MLG *knobbe.*] —**knobbed** (nobd) *adj.*

knob·by (nob′ē) *adj.* **·bi·er, ·bi·est** Shaped like a knob: *knobby* knees. 2 Full of knobs. —**knob′bi·ness** *n.*

knock (nok) *v.t.* 1 To give a heavy blow to; hit. 2 To strike (one thing) against another; bring into collision. 3 To drive or impel by striking: to *knock* a ball over a fence. 4 To make or cause by striking: to *knock* a hole in a wall. 5 *Slang* To find fault with; carp. at. —*v.i.* 6 To strike a blow or blows, as with the fist or a club. 7 To come into collision; bump. 8 To make a pounding noise: to *knock* on a door. 9 *Slang* To find fault; carp. —**knock about** (or **around**) 1 To strike repeatedly; hit from side to side. 2 To wander from place to place. 3 To treat neglectfully; abuse. —**knock down** 1 To take apart for convenience in shipping or storing. 2 In auctions, to sell to the highest bidder. —**knock off** 1 To leave off; stop, as work, talking, etc. 2 To deduct. 3 To do or make quickly or easily. 4 *Slang* To kill or defeat. —**knock out** 1 In boxing, to defeat (an opponent) by striking him to the ground. 2 To render unconscious or exhausted. —**knock together** To build or make roughly or hurriedly. —**knock up** 1 *Brit.* To rouse, as by knocking on the door. 2 *Brit. Informal* To tire out; exhaust. —*n.* 1 A sharp blow; a rap; also, a knocking. 2 *Mech.* A sharp noise indicating some malfunction, as badly timed combustion in an engine. 3 *Informal* Hostile criticism. [< OE *cnocian*] —**Syn.** *v.* 1 bang, punch, smack, smite, strike, pat, smash, clobber, rap, hammer, hit, pound, thrash, wallop.

knock·a·bout (nok′ə·bout′) *adj.* 1 Characterized by noisiness or roughness. 2 Adapted for any kind of rough use. —*n.* 1 *Naut.* A small, partially decked yacht, carrying a mainsail and jib rigged fore-and-aft. 2 Something fit for knockabout use.

knock·down (nok′doun′) *adj.* 1 Having sufficient force to fell or overthrow. 2 Constructed so as to be easily taken apart. —*n.* 1 A blow that fells. 2 Any unassembled, prefabricated article.

knock·er (nok′ər) *n.* 1 One who knocks. 2 A hinged metal hammer fastened to a door as a means of signaling for admittance.

knock·knee (nok′nē′) *n.* An inward curvature of the legs that causes the knees to touch in walking. —**knock′-kneed**′ *adj.*

knock·out (nok′out′) *adj.* Rendering insensible; overpowering. —*n.* 1 A knockout blow. 2 *Slang* An overwhelmingly attractive person or thing.

knockout drops Drops of a powerful drug put into a drink to produce unconsciousness.

knock·wurst (näk′wûrst) *n.* KNACKWURST.

knoll (nōl) *n.* A small hill; mound. [< OE *cnoll* hill]

knot (not) *n.* 1 A fastening made by tightly intertwining one or more ropes, cords, etc. 2 A lump formed of hard tangles in a string, cord, etc. 3 An ornamental bow of silk, lace, etc. 4 A hard, gnarled portion of the trunk of a tree where a branch grows out. 5 *Bot.* A node or joint in a stem. 6 A cluster or group, as of persons. 7 *Naut.* a A division of a log line used to determine the rate of a ship's motion. b A speed of one nautical mile per hour. c One nautical mile. 8 A knob. 9 A bond or union. 10 A hard lump resembling a knot: a *knot* of muscle. 11 An intricate or complex difficulty; problem. 12 A state of being drawn taut, as from nervous tension: a stomach in *knots*. —*v.* **knot·ted, knot·ting** *v.t.* 1 To tie in a knot; form a knot or knots in. 2 To secure or fasten by a knot. 3 To form knobs, bosses, etc., in. —*v.i.* 4 To form a knot or knots. 5 To tie knots for fringe. [< OE *cnotta*]

Knots
a. square or reef. b. single bowknot.

knot·grass (not′gras′, -gräs′) *n.* A widely distributed weed related to buckwheat, with jointed stems. Also **knot′weed.**

knot·hole (not′hōl′) *n.* A hole, as in a plank, left by the falling out of a knot.

knot·ted (not′əd) *adj.* 1 Tied with a knot or into knots. 2 Having knots; knotty. 3 Ornamented with knots. 4 KNOTTY (def. 2).

knot·ter (not′ər) *n.* 1 A person or machine employed for removing knots. 2 One who or that which knots.

knot·ty (not′ē) *adj.* **·ti·er, ·ti·est** 1 Having, full of, or tied in knots. 2 Difficult; intricate. —**knot′ti·ness** *n.*

knout (nout) *n.* A whip or scourge used formerly in Russia to inflict punishment. —*v.t.* To flog with the knout. [< Russ. *knut*]

know (nō) *v.* **knew, known, know·ing** *v.t.* 1 To perceive or understand clearly or with certainty: to *know* the truth. 2 To have information about: to *know* their plans. 3 To have experience of or familiarity with. 4 To distinguish between: to *know* peas from beans. 5 To have securely in the mind or memory: to *know* historical facts. 6 To have practical skill in or knowledge of: often with *how.* —*v.i.* 7 To have knowledge: often with *of.* 8 To be or become aware or cognizant. —*n.* The fact or condition of knowing; knowledge. —**in the know** *Informal* Having full or privileged information. [< OE *cnāwan*] —**know′a·ble** *adj.* —**know′er** *n.* —**Syn.** *v.* 1 apprehend, comprehend, discern, perceive.

know-how (nō′hou′) *n. Informal* Knowledge of how to perform a complicated procedure; technical skill.

know·ing (nō′ing) *adj.* 1 Perceptive; astute. 2 Possessing sly or secret knowledge. 3 Conscious; intentional. 4 Having knowledge or information. —**know′ing·ly** *adv.* —**know′ing·ness** *n.* —**Syn.** 1 acute, clever, discerning, keen, shrewd.

knowl·edge (nol′ij) *n.* 1 Information or understanding acquired through experience. 2 Information acquired through study. 3 The act, fact, or state of knowing. 4 The accumulated body of facts concerning a specified field of study. 5 Everything that has been learned, discovered, or perceived. —**to the best of one's knowledge** As far as one can determine. [< OE *cnawan* know]

knowl·edge·a·ble (nol′ij·ə·bəl) *adj. Informal* Having knowledge or intelligence.

known (nōn) *p.p.* of KNOW.

know·noth·ing (nō′nuth′ing) *n.* An uneducated person; an ignoramus.

Know-Noth·ing (nō′nuth′ing) *n.* A member of a party in U.S. politics (1853–56), which aimed at excluding foreign-born persons from the government.

knuck·le (nuk′əl) *n.* 1 One of the joints of the fingers, esp. one connecting the fingers to the rest of the hand. 2 The knee or ankle joint of certain animals, used as food. 3 *pl.* A device of metal, fitting over the knuckles, used as a weapon. —*v.i.* **knuck·led, knuck·ling** To hold the knuckles on the ground in shooting a marble. —**knuckle down** To apply oneself seriously and assiduously. —**knuckle under** To give in; yield. [< MLG *knökel*]

knurl (nûrl) *n.* 1 A protuberance; knot. 2 One of a series of small ridges on the edge of a thumbscrew or coin. —*v.t.* To produce a series of knurls on. [?] —**knurl′y** *adj.*

KO, K.O., k.o. knockout.

ko·a·la (kō·ä′lə) *n.* An arboreal marsupial of Australia having thick gray fur, large hairy ears, and sharp claws. [< native Australian name]

Ko·di·ak bear (kō′dē·ak) A very large brown bear found along the coast of Alaska. [< *Kodiak* Island, Alaska]

Koh·i·nor (kō′i·nôr′) *n.* A very large diamond, one of the British crown jewels since 1849. Also **Koh′i·noor′, Koh′i·nur′.** [< Pers. *kōhinūr* mountain of light]

Koalas

kohl·ra·bi (kōl·rä′bē, kōl′rä-) *n. pl.* **·bies** A vegetable related to cabbage, having a bulbous edible stem. [< Ital. *cavolo* cabbage + *rapa* turnip]

ko·la (kō′lə) *n.* COLA.

kola nut The seed of the cola, bitter in taste and containing caffeine. Also **cola nut.**

ko·lin·sky (kə·lin′skē, kō-) *n. pl.* **·skies** 1 Any of several minks of northern China and Russia. 2 The fur of any of these. [< Russ. *kolinski* of Kola, a Russian peninsula]

ko·mat·ik (kō·mad′ik) *n. Can.* An Eskimo sled. [< Eskimo]

koo·doo (kōō′dōō) *n.* KUDU.

kook (kōōk) *n. Slang* An unconventional, eccentric, or unbalanced person [? < CUCKOO]

kook·y (kō′kē) *adj.* **kook·i·er, kook·i·est** *Slang* Of or characteristic of a kook. Also **kook′ie.** **—kook′i·ness** *n.*

kop (kop) *n.* In South Africa, a hill; headland. [< Du., a head]

ko·peck (kō′pek) *n.* A monetary unit and small copper or bronze coin of Russia; one one-hundredth of a ruble.

Ko·ran (kō·rän′, -rän′) *n.* The Muslims' sacred scripture, accepted by them as the revelations of Allah (God) to Mohammed.

Ko·re·a (kō·rē′ə, kō-) *n.* A former country located on a peninsula of E Asia, divided into the **Democratic People's Republic of Korea,** a republic on the N part of the peninsula, 46,812 sq. mi., cap. Pyongyang: also **North Korea;** and the **Republic of Korea,** a republic on the S part of the peninsula, 38,542 sq. mi., cap. Seoul: also **South Korea. —Ko·re′an** *adj., n.*

ko·ru·na (kô·rōō′nä) *n.* The basic monetary unit of Czechoslovakia.

ko·sher (kō′shər) *adj.* 1 Permitted by the Jewish ceremonial law; clean: said usu. of food. 2 Dealing in kosher food. 3 *Slang* All right; legitimate. **—***n.* A shop selling kosher food; also the food sold there. **—***v.t.* (kosh′ər) To make kosher. [< Heb. *kā-shēr* fit, proper]

kou·miss (kōō′mis) *n.* KUMISS.

kow·tow (lou′tou′) *n.* Formerly, a Chinese form of obeisance in which one knelt and touched the forehead to the ground before a superior. **—***v.i.* 1 To make such obeisance. 2 To act in an obsequious or servile manner. [< Chin. *k'o-t'ou*, lit., knock the head] **—kow′tow′er** *n.*

KP, K.P. kitchen police.

Kr krypton.

kraal (kräl) *n.* 1 A village or group of native huts in S Africa, usu. surrounded by a stockade. 2 The social unit such a community represents. 3 An enclosure for cattle. [Afrikaans]

krait (krīt) *n.* Any of several very venomous snakes of S Asia. [< Hind. *karait*]

K-ra·tion (kā′rash′ən, -rä′shən) *n.* An emergency ration for soldiers of the U.S. Armed Forces in World War II.

krem·lin (krem′lin) *n.* The citadel of a Russian town. [< Russ. *kreml′* citadel]

Krem·lin (krem′lin) 1 The citadel of Moscow, enclosing

the former palace of the Czar. 2 The government of the U.S.S.R.

Krem·lin·ol·o·gist (krem′lin·ol′ə·jist) *n.* A political analyst of the operation, policies, etc., of the government of the U.S.S.R. **—Krem′lin·ol′o·gy** *n.*

kreu·zer (kroit′sər) *n.* Any of several former small silver or copper coins of Austria and Germany. Also **kreut′zer.**

krill (kril) *n.* Tiny crustaceans, the chief food of antarctic whales and other marine animals. [< Norw. *kril* the young of fish]

krim·mer (krim′ər) *n.* A fur resembling Persian lamb prepared from skins of Crimean lambs. [< G *Krim* Crimea]

kris (krēs) *n.* A dagger with a wavy blade used in Malaysia. [< Malay]

Krish·na (krish′nə) *n.* A celebrated Hindu deity, an incarnation of Vishnu. **—Krish′na·ism** *n.*

Kriss Krin·gle (kris kring′gəl) St. Nicholas; Santa Claus. [< G *Christkindl* Christ child]

Kris with sheath

kro·na (krō′nə; *Sw.* krōō′nä) *n. pl.* **kro·nor** (krō′nôr) The basic monetary unit of Sweden.

kro·ne (krō′nə) *n.* 1 *pl.* **kro·ner** (krō′nər) A gold coin, the basic monetary unit of Norway and Denmark. 2 *pl.* **kro·nen** (krō′nən) Any of several former European gold coins.

kryp·ton (krip′ton) *n.* A colorless, inert, gaseous element (symbol Kr) present in minute amounts in the atmosphere. [< Gk. *kryptos* hidden]

KS Kansas (P.O. abbr.).

kt. karat.

ku·chen (kōō′khən) *n.* A yeast dough coffee cake. [G]

ku·dos (kyōō′dos) *n.* Glory, credit, or acclaim because of achievement. [< Gk. *kydos* glory] • *Kudos* is sometimes mistakenly assumed to be the plural of "*kudo.*"

ku·du (kōō′dōō) *n.* A large striped African antelope, having long, spiraling horns in the male. [< native African name]

Ku Klux·er (kyōō′kluk′sər) A member of the Ku Klux Klan

Ku Klux Klan (kyōō′kluks′ klan′) 1 A secret society in the S U.S. after the Civil War, aiming to prevent Negro ascendancy. 2 A modern secret society, founded in 1915 at Atlanta, Ga., aiming at arbitrary regulation of life by white Protestants. [< Gk. *kyklos* a circle + CLAN]

Kudu

ku·lak (kyōō′lak, kyōō·lak′) *n.* A well-to-do Russian peasant who exploited poorer peasants and opposed Soviet collectivization of the land. [Russ., lit., fist]

ku·miss (kōō′mis) *n.* Fermented mare's milk, used by the Tatar tribes of CEN Asia. Also **ku′mys.** [< Russ. *kumys*]

kum·mel (kim′əl; *Ger.* kü′mal) *n.* A German or Russian liqueur flavored with aniseed, cumin, or caraway. [< L *cuminum* cumin]

kum·quat (kum′kwot) *n.* 1 A small orange-colored citrus fruit having a sweet rind and sour pulp. 2 The small tree bearing this fruit. [< Chin. *chin-chü*, lit., golden orange]

Kuo·min·tang (kwō′min′tang′) *n.* The nationalist party of China, founded in 1911 by Sun Yat-sen and led after 1927 by Chiang Kai-shek.

Kurd (kûrd, kŏŏrd) *n.* One of a Muslin people dwelling chiefly in Kurdistan.

Kurd·ish (kûr′dish, kŏŏr′-) *adj.* Of or pertaining to the Kurds, their language, etc. **—***n.* The Iranian language of the Kurds.

Ku·wait (kōō·wāt′) *n.* A Shiekdom of NE Arabia, 5,000 sq. mi. cap. Kuwait. • See map at SAUDI ARABIA.

kw, kw. kilowatt(s).

kwash·i·or·kor (kwäsh′ē·ôr′kôr) *n.* A disease produced in children by prolonged lack of protein in the diet and characterized by potbelly, edema, and permanently impaired development. [< native African name]

K.W.H., kw-h, kw.-hr., kw-hr kilowatt-hour(s).

KY Kentucky (P.O. abbr.).

Ky. Kentucky.

---

add, āce, câre, pälm; end, ēven; it, īce; odd, ōpen, ôrder; tōŏk, pōōl; up, bûrn; ə = *a* in *above, u* in *focus;* yōō = *u* in *fuse;* oil; pout; check; go; ring; thin; this; zh, *vision.* < derived from; ? origin uncertain or unknown.

L

L, l (el) *n. pl.* **L's, l's, Ls, ls** (elz) **1** The 12th letter of the English alphabet. **2** Any spoken sound representing the letter *L* or *l.* **3** In Roman notation, the symbol for 50. **4** Something shaped like an L. —*adj.* Shaped like an L.

L Latin; length; longitude; Linnaeus.

L., l. lake; latitude; law; leaf; league; left; length; line; link; lira; lire; low; pound (L *libra*).

l, l. liter(s).

la¹ (lä) *n. Music* In solmization, the sixth tone of a diatonic scale. [< Med. L. See GAMUT.]

la² (lä, lô) *interj.* Look! O!: an exclamation expressing surprise, emphasis, etc.

LA Louisiana (P.O. abbr.)

L.A. (el′ā′) *Informal* Los Angeles.

La lanthanum.

La. Louisiana.

lab (lab) *n. Informal* A laboratory.

lab. laboratory.

la·bel (lā′bəl) *n.* **1** A slip, as of paper, affixed to something to indicate its character, ownership, destination, etc. **2** A brief, descriptive, written or spoken phrase designating certain characteristics of a person or group. —*v.t.* **·beled** or **·belled, ·bel·ing** or **·bel·ling 1** To mark with a label; attach a label to. **2** To classify; designate. [< OF, a ribbon]—**la′bel·er** or **la′bel·ler** *n.*

la·bi·a (lā′bē·ə) *n.pl.* of LABIUM.

la·bi·al (lā′bē·əl) *adj.* **1** Of or pertaining to the lips. **2** *Phonet.* Formed, articulated, or modified by the lips. —*n. Phonet.* A labial sound, as *b, p, m.* [< L *labium* a lip] —**la′bi·al·ly** *adv.*

la·bi·ate (lā′bē·āt, -it) *adj.* Having lips or liplike parts. Also **la′bi·at′ed.** [< L *labium* a lip]

la·bile (lā′bīl, -bil) *adj.* Prone to undergo change; unstable. [< L *labi* to slip, fall] —**la·bil′i·ty** *n.*

la·bi·o·den·tal (lā′bē·ō·den′təl) *adj. Phonet.* Formed with the lower lip and the upper front teeth, as *f* and *v* in English. —*n.* A sound so formed. [< Latin *labium* lip + *dens* tooth]

la·bi·um (lā′bē·əm) *n. pl.* **·bi·a** (-bē·ə) **1** A lip or liplike organ or part. **2** *pl.* The folds of skin and of mucous membrane of the vulva. [L, a lip]

la·bor (lā′bər) *n.* **1** Hard and exhausting physical or mental exertion. **2** That which requires exertion or effort; a task. **3** Wage earners collectively. **4** Workers who engage in manual work. **5** Work done by workers as a group. **6** The process of giving birth. —*v.i.* **1** To do work; toil. **2** To move with difficulty or painful exertion. **3** To be in the process of giving birth. —*v.t.* **4** To develop in too minute detail: to *labor* a point. —**labor under** To be hindered or troubled by: to *labor under* a misapprehension. *Brit. sp.* **la′bour.** [< L, toil, distress] —**la′bor·ing·ly** *adv.*

lab·o·ra·to·ry (lab′rə·tôr′ē, -tō′rē; *Brit.* lə·bor′ə·trē) *n. pl.* **·ries 1** A place adapted to conducting scientific experiments, analyses, etc. **2** A department, as in a factory, for research, testing, etc. —*adj.* Pertaining to or performed in a laboratory. [< L *laborare* to labor]

Labor Day In the U.S. and Canada, the first Monday in September, set aside as a legal holiday in honor of labor.

la·bored (lā′bərd) *adj.* Performed laboriously; strained: a *labored* joke. *Brit. sp.* **la′boured.**

la·bor·er (lā′bər·ər) *n.* One who performs physical or manual work, esp. if unskilled. *Brit. sp.* **la′bour·er.**

la·bo·ri·ous (lə·bôr′ē·əs, -bō′rē-) *adj.* **1** Requiring much labor; toilsome. **2** Diligent; industrious. **3** Strained; labored. *Brit. sp.* **la·bo′ri·ous.** —**la·bo′ri·ous·ly** *adv.* —**la·bo′ri·ous·ness** *n.* —**Syn. 1** arduous, difficult, onerous. **2** assiduous; persevering.

la·bor·ite (lā′bər·īt) *n.* One who supports labor interests, esp. in politics. *Brit. sp.* **la′bour·ite.**

la·bor-sav·ing (lā′bər·sā′ving) *adj.* Doing away with, or lessening the need for, manual work.

labor union An association of working men and women organized to protect and promote their common interests, esp. in negotiations with management with regard to wages, hours, working conditions, etc.; a trade union.

Labour Party In Great Britain, a political party drawing its chief support from the working class and committed to socialistic reform. —**La·bour·ite** (lā′bər·īt) *n.*

la·bur·num (lə·bûr′nəm) *n.* Any of a genus of leguminous shrubs or trees having pendulous yellow flowers and poisonous seeds. [L]

lab·y·rinth (lab′ə·rinth) *n.* **1** A confusing, winding network of passages or paths; a maze. **2** Any perplexing combination or condition. **3** *Anat.* The winding passages of the inner ear. —**lab′y·rin′thine** (-thin, -thēn) or **·thi·an** or **·thic** or **·thi·cal** *adj.* —**lab′y·rin′thi·cal·ly** *adv.*

Labyrinth

Lab·y·rinth (lab′ə·rinth) *n. Gk. Myth.* The maze used to confine the Minotaur, constructed by Daedalus for Minos of Crete. [< Gk. *labyrinthos*]

lac¹ (lak) *n.* A resinous substance exuded by a s Asian scale insect and used in making varnishes, etc.

lac² (lak) *n.* LAKH.

lace (lās) *n.* **1** A cord or string for fastening together the parts of a shoe, a corset, etc. **2** A delicate network of threads of linen, silk, cotton, etc., arranged in figures or patterns. **3** A dash of spirits, as in tea or coffee. —*v.* **laced, lac·ing** *v.t.* **1** To draw together by tying the lace or laces of. **2** To pass (a cord or string) through hooks, eyelets, etc., as a lace. **3** To trim with or as with lace. **4** To compress the waist of (a person) by tightening laces, as of a corset. **5** To intertwine or interlace. **6** To streak, as with color. **7** To add a dash of spirits to. **8** *Informal* To beat; thrash. —*v.i.* **9** To be fastened by means of a lace. —**lace into 1** To attack. **2** To scold. [< L *laqueus* a noose, trap]

lac·er·ate (las′ər·āt) *v.t.* **·at·ed, ·at·ing 1** To tear raggedly, as the flesh. **2** To hurt; injure, as the feelings. —*adj.* Jagged; torn. [< L *lacer* mangled] —**lac′er·a·ble, lac′er·a′tive** *adj.* —**lac′er·a′tion** *n.* —**Syn. v. 1** rend, rip, rupture, split, sunder.

lace·wing (lās′wing′) *n.* Any of certain insects having four lacy wings, including species that destroy insect pests.

lace·work (lās′wûrk′) *n.* **1** Lace. **2** Any openwork resembling lace.

lach·es (lach′iz) *n. Law* Inexcusable delay in asserting a right. [< L *laxus* lax]

Adult lacewing

lach·ry·mal (lak′rə·məl) *adj.* **1** Of or pertaining to tears. **2** Pertaining to tear-producing glands. —*n. pl.* The glands that secrete tears. Also **lac′ri·mal.** [< L *lacrima* a tear]

lach·ry·ma·to·ry (lak′rə·mə·tôr′ē, -tō·rē) *n. pl.* **·ries** A small, narrow-necked bottle found in ancient tombs, used to contain the tears of mourners. —*adj.* **1** Producing tears. **2** Containing tears. Also **lac′ri·ma·to′ry.**

lach·ry·mose (lak′rə·mōs′) *adj.* **1** Shedding tears; tearful. **2** Causing sadness; mournful. Also **lac′ri·mose.** —**lach′·ry·mose·ly** *adv.*

lac·ing (lā′sing) *n.* **1** The act of fastening, as with a lace. **2** Lace. **3** A connecting or strengthening member; crosspiece. **4** *Informal* A thrashing. **5** Any ornamental braid, as of gold or silver.

lack (lak) *v.t.* **1** To be without; have none or too little of. **2** To be short by; require: It *lacks* two months till summer. —*v.i.* **3** To be wanting or deficient; be missing. —*n.* **1** The state of being needy or without something. **2** Want; deficiency. **3** That which is needed. [ME *lac*]

lack·a·dai·si·cal (lak′ə-dā′zi-kəl) *adj.* Languishing; listless; apathetic. —**lack′a·dai′si·cal·ly** *adv.* —**lack′a·dai′si·cal·ness** *n.*

lack·ey (lak′ē) *n. pl.* **·eys** 1 A male servant. 2 Any servile attendant or follower. —*v.t. & v.i.* To attend or act as a lackey. Also **lac′quey.** [< OF *laquay*]

lack·lus·ter (lak′lus′tər) *adj.* 1 Wanting luster; dull, as hair. 2 Lacking spirit or liveliness; dull or perfunctory: a *lackluster* performance. —*n.* A lack of luster; dullness. *Brit. sp.* **·lus·tre.**

La·co·ni·a (lə-kō′nē-ə) *n.* A region and ancient country in the SE Peloponnesus, Greece, of which Sparta was the capital. —**La·co′ni·an** *adj., n.*

la·con·ic (lə-kon′ik) *adj.* Using or consisting of few words; short and forceful. Also **la·con′i·cal.** [< Gk. *Lakōn* a Spartan, with ref. to the habitual terseness of Spartan speech]

lac·quer (lak′ər) *n.* 1 A quick-drying varnish made from resin, nitrocellulose, and sometimes a pigment, dissolved in a volatile solvent. 2 A varnish yielding a high polish made from the resin of a tree of SE Asia. 3 Objects coated with such varnish: also **lac′quer·work.** —*v.t.* To coat or varnish with lacquer. Also **lack′er.** [< Pg. *lacré* sealing wax]

la·crosse (lə-krôs′, -kros′) *n.* A field sport played with a ball and long-handled, netted rackets in which two teams of ten players each try to send the ball between the opponents' goal posts. [< F *la crosse* hooked stick]

lac·tate (lak′tāt) *v.i.* **·tat·ed, ·tat·ing** To form or secrete milk. —*n.* A salt or ester of lactic acid. [< L *lac, lactis* milk] —**lac·ta′tion** *n.*

lac·te·al (lak′tē·əl) *adj.* Pertaining to or like milk; conveying a milklike fluid. Also **lac′te·an, lac′te·ous.** —*n.* One of the lymphatic vessels that take up chyle from the small intestine. [< *lac, lactis* milk]

lac·tic (lak′tik) *adj.* Of or derived from milk.

lactic acid A bitter, syrupy acid contained in sour milk and produced by the fermentation of lactose.

lac·to·fla·vin (lak′tō-flā′vin) *n.* RIBOFLAVIN.

lac·tose (lak′tōs) *n.* A white crystalline sugar present in milk.

la·cu·na (lə-kyōō′nə) *n. pl.* **·nas** or **·nae** (-nē) 1 A space from which something has been omitted; gap. 2 A minute cavity in bone or tissue. Also **la·cune′** (-kyōōn′). [L, a hole, pool] —**la·cu′nal** (-nəl), **la·cu′nar** (-nər) *adj.*

lac·y (lā′sē) *adj.* **lac·i·er, lac·i·est** Having an open design or pattern like lace. 2 Of lace. —**lac′i·ly** *adv.* —**lac′i·ness** *n.*

lad (lad) *n.* A boy or youth. Also **lad′die.** [ME *ladde*]

lad·der (lad′ər) *n.* 1 A device of wood, metal, etc., for climbing up and down that consists of two vertical side pieces connected by horizontal pieces. 2 A means of raising one's status or position by stages. [< OE *hlædder*]

lade (lād) *v.* **lad·ed, lad·ed** or **lad·en, lad·ing** *v.t.* 1 To load with a burden or cargo. 2 To weight down; burden. 3 To dip or lift (a liquid) in or out with a ladle or dipper. —*v.i.* 4 To receive cargo. 5 To dip or lift a liquid. [< OE *hladan* to load]

lad·en (lād′n) A *p.p.* of LADE. —*adj.* Burdened: *laden* with care.

lad·ing (lā′ding) *n.* 1 The act of loading. 2 A load or cargo.

la·dle (lād′l) *n.* 1 A cup-shaped utensil, with a long handle, for dipping out or conveying liquids. 2 A device like this in form or function. —*v.t.* **·dled, ·dling** To dip up and carry in a ladle. [< OE *hladan* lade] —**la′dler** *n.*

la·dy (lā′dē) *n. pl.* **·dies** 1 A refined and well-bred woman. 2 A woman of good family and recognized social standing. 3 Any woman: in the plural, used as a form of address. 4 A woman who is at the head of a household: the *lady* of the house. 5 A sweetheart or wife. 6 In Great Britain: **a** A marchioness, countess, viscountess, or baroness. **b** A title given by courtesy to a daughter of a duke, marquis, or earl, or to the wife of a baronet or knight or one having the courtesy title of *Lord.* —*adj.* 1 Of, like or becoming to a lady. 2 Female: a *lady* carpenter. [< OE *hlæfdige*, lit., bread-kneader] • In modern usage, *lady* in the sense of any woman is considered to be either falsely genteel or old-fashioned. Terms such as *saleslady, cleaning lady, lady doctor,* etc., are to be avoided. *Woman* is the more appropriate term for any adult female human being as well as for female persons in various occupations: a *woman* doctor, a *saleswoman,* a cleaning *woman.*

La·dy (lā′dē) *n. pl.* **·dies** 1 The Virgin Mary: usu. with *Our.* 2 In Great Britain, a title of honor or nobility.

la·dy·bug (lā′dē-bug′) *n.* A small, roundish, spotted, usu. brightly colored beetle that feeds on aphids and other insect pests. Also **lady beetle, la′dy·bird′** (-burd′)

Lady Day March 25, the feast of the Annunciation, observed in honor of the Virgin Mary.

la·dy·fin·ger (lā′dē-fing′gər) *n.* A small sponge cake; so called from its shape.

Ladybug

la·dy-in-wait·ing (lā′dē-in-wā′ting) *n. pl.* **la·dies-in-wait·ing** A lady of a royal household in attendance at court upon a queen or princess.

la·dy-kill·er (lā′dē-kil′ər) *n. Informal* A man supposed to be peculiarly fascinating to women. —**la′dy-kill′ing** *adj., n.*

la·dy·like (lā′dē-līk) *adv.* Like or suitable to a lady; refined.

la·dy·ship (lā′dē-ship) *n.* 1 The rank or condition of a lady. 2 *Often cap.* The term used in speaking to or of a woman having the title of *Lady:* with *her* or *your.*

la·dy-slip·per (lā′dē-slip′ər) *n.* Any of a genus of wild orchids having flowers with pouchlike petals resembling a slipper. Also **la′dy's-slip′per.**

lag (lag) *v.i.* **lagged, lag·ging** To stay or fall behind. —*n.* 1 The act of lagging; retardation of motion, development, etc. 2 The amount of such retardation. [?] —**Syn.** *v.* dawdle, drag, linger, loiter, retard.

la·ger (lä′gər) *n.* Beer that has been aged for several months before use. Also **lager beer.** [< G *Lagerbier,* lit., storehouse beer]

lag·gard (lag′ərd) *n.* One who lags; a loiterer. —*adj.* Falling behind; slow. —**lag′gard·ly** *adv.* —**lag′gard·ness** *n.*

la·gniappe (lan·yap′, lan′yap) *n.* A small present given to the purchaser of an article by a storekeeper; a gratuity. Also **la·gnappe′.** [< Amer. Sp. *la* the + *ñapa* lagniappe]

la·goon (lə-gōōn′) *n.* 1 A shallow body of salt water separated from but connecting with the sea, esp. one within an atoll. • See ATOLL 2 A shallow body of fresh water usu. connecting with a river or lake. [< L *lacuna* hole, pond]

la·ic (lā′ik) *adj.* Pertaining to the laity; secular or non-professional. Also **la′i·cal.** —*n.* A layman. [< Gk. *laos* the people] —**la′i·cal·ly** *adv.*

laid (lād) *p.t. & p.p.* of LAY[1]. —**laid up** 1 Injured or sick. 2 Out of service, as a dismantled ship. 3 Stored or put away for future use.

laid-back (lād′bak′) *adj. Slang.* Relaxed; not uptight.

laid paper Paper covered with close, parallel, watermarked lines.

lain (lān) *p.p.* of LIE[1].

lair (lâr) *n.* The resting place or den of a wild animal. [< OE *leger* bed]

laird (lârd) *n. Scot.* A lord; also, the proprietor of a landed estate. —**laird′ly** *adj.* —**laird′ship** *n.*

lais·sez faire (les′ā fâr′) 1 The principle of permitting industrial and commercial competition without government control. 2 Noninterference in any undertaking. Also **lais′ser faire.** [F, lit., let do] —**lais′sez-faire′** *adj.*

la·i·ty (lā′ə·tē) *n. pl.* **·ties** 1 People who are not members of the clergy. 2 Those outside any specified profession. [< LAY[2]]

lake[1] (lāk) *n.* 1 A sizable inland body of water, usu. fresh. 2 A pond formed by the widening of a river or stream. 3 A pool of any liquid: a *lake* of asphalt. [< L *lacus*]

lake[2] (lāk) *n.* 1 A red pigment made by combining a dye, as cochineal, with a metallic oxide. 2 Any insoluble pigment fixed within the fibers of a fabric by the interaction of mordant and dye. [Var. of LAC[1]]

lake dwelling A prehistoric dwelling erected on piles over the waters of a lake. —**lake dweller**

lake trout Any of various freshwater trout and salmon, esp. a large game trout of N North America. Also **lake salmon.**

lakh (lak) *n.* In India and Pakistan: **1** The amount 100,000: said esp. of rupees. **2** Any very large number or amount. [< Skt. *lākshā* mark]

lam[1] (lam) *v.t.* **lammed, lam·ming** *Slang* To beat; thrash; punish. [?]

lam[2] (lam) *Slang v.i.* **lammed, lam·ming** To run away; flee hastily. —*n.* Sudden flight. —**on the lam** In flight; fleeing. —**take it on the lam** To flee hastily; run away. [?]

Lam, Lam. Lamentations.

la·ma (lä′mə) *n.* **1** A priest or monk of Lamaism ranking high in the hierarchy. **2** A title of courtesy given to all monks of Lamaism. [< Tibetan *blama*]

La·ma·ism (lä′mə·iz′əm) *n.* The religious system of Tibet and Mongolia, a variety of Buddhism, introduced into Tibet in the 7th century. —**La′ma·ist** *n.* —**La′ma·is′tic** *adj.*

la·ma·ser·y (lä′mə·ser′ē) *n. pl.* **·ser·ies** A Buddhist monastery of Tibet or Mongolia. [< F *lama* a lama]

lamb (lam) *n.* **1** A young sheep. **2** Its flesh consumed as food. **3** Any gentle or innocent person. **4** An unsophisticated person; simpleton. —**like a lamb 1** Mildly; very gently. **2** Unsuspicious; easily misled. —*v.i.* To give birth: said of sheep. [< OE]

lam·baste (lam·bāst′) *v.t.* **·bast·ed, ·bast·ing** *Slang* **1** To beat or thrash. **2** To scold; castigate. [?]

lamb·da (lam′də) *n.* The 11th letter of the Greek alphabet (Λ, λ).

lam·bent (lam′bənt) *adj.* **1** Playing with a soft, undulatory movement; gliding. **2** Softly radiant. **3** Touching lightly but brilliantly: *lambent* wit. —**lam′bent·ly** *adv.* [< L *lambere* to lick] —**lam′ben·cy, lam′bent·ness** *n.* —**Syn. 1** dancing, flickering, licking, wavering. **2** glistening, lustrous, refulgent.

lamb·kin (lam′kin) *n.* **1** A little lamb. **2** Figuratively, a cherished child. Also **lamb′ie.**

Lamb of God Christ.

lam·bre·quin (lam′bər·kin, -brə-) *n.* **1** A draped strip, as of cloth or leather, hanging from the casing above a window, doorway, etc. **2** An ornamental covering for a helmet. [< Du. *lamperkin*]

lamb·skin (lam′skin′) *n.* **1** A lamb's skin, esp. with the wool preserved. **2** Leather or parchment made from the pelt of a lamb.

lame (lām) *adj.* **1** Crippled or disabled, esp. in the legs. **2** Poor; halting: a *lame* apology. **3** Sore; painful: a *lame* back. —*v.t.* **lamed, lam·ing** To make lame; cripple. [< OE *lama*] —**lame′ly** *adv.* —**lame′ness** *n.*

la·mé (la·mā′) *n.* A fabric woven of flat gold or silver thread, sometimes mixed with silk or other fiber. [< F *lamer* laminate]

lame duck *Informal* **1** A helpless or disabled person. **2** An elected government official whose term continues some time after his defeat for reelection.

la·mel·la (lə·mel′ə) *n. pl.* **·lae** (-ē) *Biol.* A thin plate or lamina, as the gills of a bivalve, the radial plates on the underside of a mushroom cap, etc. [< L, dim. of *lamina* lamina] —**lam·el·lar** (lə·mel′ər, lam′ə·lər), **lam·el·late** (lam′·ə·lāt, lə·mel′āt) *adj.*

la·mel·li·branch (lə·mel′i·brangk) *n.* One of a class of bivalve mollusks, having platelike gills and a compressed body, as clams, mussels, and oysters. —*adj.* Of or pertaining to this class. [< L *lamella* lamella + Gk. *branchia* gills] —**la·mel′li·bran′chi·ate** (-brang′kē·āt, -it) *adj., n.*

la·ment (lə·ment′) *v.t.* **1** To feel or express sorrow for. —*v.i.* **2** To feel or express sorrow; mourn. —*n.* **1** The expression of grief; lamentation. **2** A plaintive song or melody. [< L *lamentum* a wailing, weeping] —**la·ment′er** *n.*

lam·en·ta·ble (lam′ən·tə·bəl, lə·men′-) *adj.* **1** Expressing sorrow; mournful. **2** Exciting regret or dissatisfaction: a *lamentable* failure. —**lam′en·ta·bly** *adv.*

lam·en·ta·tion (lam′ən·tā′shən) *n.* **1** The act of lamenting or bewailing. **2** An utterance of profound regret or grief.

Lam·en·ta·tions (lam′ən·tā′shəns) *n. pl.* (*construed as sing.*) A lyrical poetic book of the Old Testament, attributed to Jeremiah.

lam·i·na (lam′ə·nə) *n. pl.* **·nae** (-nē) or **·nas 1** A thin scale, sheet, or layer. **2** *Bot.* The flat expanded portion of a leaf. [L] —**lam′i·nal, lam′i·nar** *adj.*

lam·i·nate (lam′ə·nāt) *v.* **·nat·ed, ·nat·ing** *v.t.* **1** To beat,

roll, or press, as metal, into thin sheets. **2** To cut or separate into thin sheets. **3** To make, as plastic materials or plywood, of layers joined together. **4** To cover with thin sheets. —*v.i.* **5** To become separated into sheets or laminae. —*adj.* Consisting of or disposed in laminae. [< L *lamina* a leaf] —**lam′i·na′tion** *n.*

lamp (lamp) *n.* **1** A device used to produce light artificially, as from electricity or burning fuel. **2** A similar device for producing therapeutic heat or light. **3** Something that holds such a device. —*v.t. Slang* To look at. [< Gk. *lampein* to shine]

lamp·black (lamp′blak′) *n.* Fine carbon deposited from smoke, used as a pigment in printer's ink, etc.

lam·poon (lam·pōōn′) *n.* A written satire designed to bring a person into ridicule or contempt. —*v.t.* To abuse or satirize in a lampoon. [< MF *lampons* let's drink] —**lam·poon′er** or **lam·poon′ist, lam·poon′er·y** *n.* —**Syn.** *v.* deride, mock, ridicule.

lamp·post (lamp′pōst′) *n.* A post supporting a lamp in a street, park, etc.

lam·prey (lam′prē) *n.* An eel-like, parasitic, jawless fish, having a circular suctorial mouth and rasping teeth. Also **lam′per eel, lamprey eel.** [< L *lambere* to lick + *petra* rock]

lance (lans, läns) *n.* **1** A long shaft with a spearhead, used as a thrusting weapon. **2** A lancet. **3** A thrust with a lance or lancet. **4** One who uses a lance; lancer. —*v.t.* **lanced, lanc·ing 1** To pierce with a lance. **2** To cut or open with a lancet. [< L *lancea* a light spear]

lance corporal In the British army, a private serving as corporal, but not receiving extra pay.

lance·let (lans′lit, läns′-) *n.* Any of several small, fish-like, invertebrate sea animals having some vertebrate characteristics.

Lan·ce·lot (lan′sə·lot, län′-) In Arthurian romance, the bravest of the knights of the Round Table, lover of Guinevere.

lan·ce·o·late (lan′sē·ə·lit, -lāt) *adj.* Shaped like the head of a lance or spear, as some leaves. Also **lan′ce·o·lar** (-lər), **lan′ce·o·lat′ed.** [< L *lanceola* a small lance] • See LEAF.

lanc·er (lan′sər, län′-) *n.* A cavalry soldier armed with a lance.

lance sergeant In the British army, a corporal assigned the duties of a sergeant without additional pay.

lan·cet (lan′sit, län′-) *n.* **1** A surgeon's small, pointed knife, usu. two-edged. **2** *Archit.* **a** A lancet-shaped or sharply pointed window: also **lancet window. b** A sharply pointed arch: also **lancet arch. 3** A small lance. [< F *lancette,* dim. of *lance*]

lance·wood (lans′wōōd′, läns′-) *n.* **1** A tough, elastic wood used for fishing rods, billiard cues, etc. **2** Any of various tropical trees yielding this wood.

land (land) *n.* **1** The solid part of the earth, esp. where not covered by water. **2** Ground or soil: fertile *land.* **3** A nation or country; also its people. **4** Ground held as property; real estate. **5** Rural or farming regions: to return to the *land.* **6** In economics, natural resources. —*v.t.* **1** To transfer from a vessel to the shore. **2** To bring to rest on land or water: He *landed* the plane at Washington. **3** To bring to some point, condition, or state: His words *landed* him in trouble. **4** In fishing, to bring (a fish) from the water or into a net, boat, etc. **5** *Informal* To obtain or win: to *land* a job. **6** *Informal* To deliver, as a blow. —*v.i.* **7** To go or come ashore, as from a boat. **8** To touch at a port: said of ships. **9** To descend and come to rest, as after flight. **10** To come to some place, condition, or state: to *land* in jail. [< OE]

lan·dau (lan′dô, -dou) *n.* **1** A type of closed automobile body the rear top of which may be raised or lowered. **2** A four-wheeled covered carriage with a double top that can be folded back. [< *Landau,* a German city where it was first made]

Lancet windows

Landau *def. 2*

land bank A bank taking mortgages on real estate.

land·ed (lan'did) *adj.* 1 Having an estate in land. 2 Consisting of land: *landed* holdings.

landed immigrant *Can.* A person who has been admitted to Canada as a potential citizen.

land·fall (land'fôl') *n.* 1 A sighting of or coming to land from the air or sea. 2 The land so sighted.

land·fill (land'fil') *n.* 1 The disposal of garbage, trash, excavated earth, etc., by depositing in a site, often used to build up swampy or shoreline areas. 2 Materials so used. 3 A site where such deposits are made.

land·form (land'fôrm') *n.* A physical feature of the earth's surface, as a plateau, cape, or mountain.

land grant Governmental land granted to a railroad, state educational institution, etc. —**land'-grant'** *adj.*

land·hold·er (land'hōl'dər) *n.* A person who owns or occupies land. —**land'hold'ing** *adj., n.*

land·ing (lan'ding) *n.* 1 The act of going or placing ashore. 2 The act of coming to earth, as after flying, falling, etc. 3 The place where a ship or boat docks to take on or discharge cargo or passengers; pier. 4 The place at the head of a staircase, or a platform interrupting a flight of stairs.

landing craft One of several types of military vessels esp. designed for the landing of men and material upon a hostile shore.

landing field A tract of ground properly surfaced for the landing and take-off of aircraft.

landing gear The structure under an aircraft designed to support it when on land or water.

landing strip A narrow, surfaced runway for the landing and takeoff of aircraft.

land·la·dy (land'lā'dē) *n. pl.* **·dies** 1 A woman who owns and lets real estate to others. 2 A woman who keeps an inn, hotel, boarding house, etc.

land·less (land'lis) *adj.* Owning no land.

land·locked (land'lokt') *adj.* 1 Surrounded, or almost surrounded, by land, as a bay. 2 Living in or confined to fresh instead of sea water: *landlocked* salmon.

land·lord (land'lôrd') *n.* 1 An owner of land, buildings, etc., that are leased or let to others. 2 A person who keeps an inn, hotel, boarding house, etc.

land·lub·ber (land'lub'ər) *n.* An awkward or inexperienced person on board a ship.

land·mark (land'märk') *n.* 1 A fixed object serving as a boundary mark to a tract of land. 2 A prominent or memorable object in the landscape, serving as a guide. 3 A distinguishing fact, event, etc., of a period. 4 A historic or architecturally important building, site, etc., preserved by law for posterity.

land mine An explosive weapon hidden on or just under the surface of the ground.

land office A U.S. government office of the Department of the Interior for the transaction of business pertaining to public lands.

land-office business (land'ô'fis, -of'is) *Informal* A flourishing business conducted at a rapid pace.

land·own·er (land'ō'nər) *n.* One who owns real estate.

land·scape (land'skāp) *n.* 1 A stretch of country as seen from a single point. 2 A picture representing natural scenery. —*v.* **·scaped**, **·scap·ing** *v.t.* 1 To improve or change the natural features or appearance of, as a park or garden. —*v.i.* 2 To be a landscape gardener. [<Du. *land* land + *-schap* -ship] —**land'scap·er** *n.*

landscape architecture The art of converting a given area of land into a unified ornamental development. —**landscape architect.**

landscape gardening The art of improving the appearance of a plot of ground by planting trees, lawns, flower beds, etc. —**landscape gardener.**

land·scap·ist (land'skā·pist) *n.* A painter of landscapes.

land·slide (land'slīd') *n.* 1 The slipping of a mass of earth from a higher to a lower level. 2 The mass that has slipped down. 3 *Informal* An overwhelming plurality of votes for one political party or candidate in an election.

lands·man (landz'mən) *n. pl.* **·men** (-men) 1 One who

lives on the land. 2 An inexperienced sailor.

land·ward (land'wərd) *adv.* Being or going toward the land. Also **land'wards.** —*adj.* Facing the land.

lane (lān) *n.* 1 A narrow way or path, confined between fences, walls, hedges, or similar boundaries. 2 Any prescribed route or passage to avoid collisions, as for vehicles on a highway or for airplanes and ships. [<OE *lanu* lane]

lang·syne (lang'sīn', -zīn') *Scot. adv.* Long since; long ago. —*n.* The past; old times. Also **lang syne.**

lan·guage (lang'gwij) *n.* 1 The expression and communication of emotions or ideas between human beings by means of speech, either written or spoken. 2 The vocal sounds or their written symbol used in such expression and communication. 3 The means of communication among members of a single nation or group; tongue: the French *language.* 4 Transmission of emotions or ideas between any living creatures by any means. 5 The vocabulary or technical expressions used in a specific business, science, etc.; jargon. 6 One's characteristic manner of expression or use of speech. 7 The study of a language or languages. [<L *lingua* tongue, language]

lan·guid (lang'gwid) *adj.* 1 Indisposed to physical exertion; affected by weakness. 2 Wanting in interest or animation. 3 Lacking in force or quickness of movement. [<*languere* languish] —**lan'guid·ly** *adv.* —**lan'guid·ness** *n.* —**Syn.** 1 drooping, fatigued, languorous, listless, weary.

lan·guish (lang'gwish) *v.i.* 1 To grow faint or listless. 2 To live or be in wretched circumstances: to *languish* in a dungeon. 3 To affect a look of sentimental longing or melancholy. 4 To pine with love or desire. [<L *languere* languish] —**lan'guish·er, lan'guish·ment** *n.*

lan·guis·ing (lang'gwish·ing) *adj.* 1 Lacking interest or force. 2 Sentimentally pensive. 3 Becoming weak or listless. —**lan'guish·ing·ly** *adv.*

lan·guor (lang'gər) *n.* 1 Lassitude of body or depression of mind. 2 Amorous dreaminess. 3 The absence of activity: dullness. [<L *languere* languish] —**lan'guor·ous** *adj.* —**lan'guor·ous·ly** *adv.* —**lan'guor·ous·ness** *n.*

lan·gur (läng-gyoor') *n.* Any of various agile, long-tailed Asian monkeys. [<Skt. *längülin,* lit., having a tail]

lan·iard (lan'yərd) *n.* LANYARD.

lank (langk) *adj.* 1 Long and lean. 2 Long, straight, and thin: *lank* hair. [<OE *hlanc* flexible] —**lank'ly** *adv.* —**lank'ness** *n.*

lank·y (lang'kē) *adj.* **lank·i·er, lank·i·est** Tall and thin in an ungainly way. —**lank'i·ly** *adv.* —**lank'i·ness** *n.*

lan·o·lin (lan'ə·lin) *n.* A fatty substance obtained from the wool of sheep, used as an ingredient in cosmetics. Also **lan'o·line** (-lin, -lēn). [<L *lan(a)* wool + *ol(eum)* oil + -IN]

lan·tern (lan'tərn) *n.* 1 A case with transparent sides, as on a lamppost or of portable character, for enclosing and protecting a light. 2 *Archit.* A glassed-in or open structure on a roof or tower, open below and admitting light and air. 3 The chamber at the top of a lighthouse housing the light. 4 MAGIC LANTERN. [<Gk. *lamptēr*]

Lantern

lantern jaws Long, thin jaws, giving the cheeks a hollow appearance. —**lan'tern-jawed'** (-jôd') *adj.*

lan·tha·nide (lan'thə·nīd) *n.* Any of a series of elements beginning with lanthanum and ending with lutetium in the periodic table and having almost identical chemical properties. • See PERIODIC TABLE OF ELEMENTS. [<LANTHAN(UM)]

lan·tha·num (lan'thə·nəm) *n.* A soft, silvery metallic element (symbol La) of the lanthanide series. [NL <Gk. *lanthanein* lie concealed]

lan·yard (lan'yərd) *n.* 1 *Naut.* A short, thick rope used on a ship, esp. for setting up riggings. 2 A cord used in firing certain kinds of cannon. 3 A stout cord worn around the neck by sailors for attaching a knife. [<OF *lasniere* a thong]

Lao (lou) *adj., n. pl.* **Lao** or **Laos** LAOTIAN.

La·oc·o·on (lā·ok'ə·won, -ō·won) *Gk. Myth.* A priest of

Apollo who warned the Trojans against the wooden horse of the Greeks, and was destroyed with his two sons by two serpents.

La·os (la'os, lä'ōs) *n.* A republic in NW Indochina, 91,428 sq. mi., cap. Vientiane. • See map at INDOCHINA.

La·o·tian (lā·ō'shən, lou'-) *adj.* Of or pertaining to Laos, its people, or their language. —*n.* 1 A native or citizen of Laos. 2 The language of these people.

lap[1] (lap) *n.* 1 The upper and front surface of the thighs and knees when one is seated. 2 The part of the clothing that covers the front of the thighs when one sits down. 3 A place for supporting or fostering: fortune's *lap.* 4 A loose fold or flap of a garment. 5 That part of a thing that extends over another thing: the *lap* of a shingle. 6 One course around a race track. —*v.* **lapped, lap·ping** *v.t.* 1 To fold and wrap around something. 2 To lay (one thing) partly over or beyond another. 3 To reach or extend partly over or beyond; overlap. 4 To surround with love, care, etc.: *lapped* in luxury. 5 To get one or more laps ahead of (an opponent) in a race. —*v.i.* 6 To be folded. 7 To lie partly upon or beside something else; overlap. [<OE *lappa* a fold or hanging part of a garment] —**lap'per** *n.*

lap[2] (lap) *v.t.* & *v.i.* **lapped, lap·ping** 1 To scoop up (a liquid) into the mouth with the tongue: said usu. of animals. 2 To wash against (the shore, etc.) with a slight, rippling sound: said of water. —**lap up** 1 To scoop up (a liquid) with the tongue. 2 *Informal* To accept eagerly: to *lap up* praise. —*n.* 1 The act of lapping; a lick. 2 The sound of lapping. [<OE *lapian*] —**lap'per** *n.*

lap·a·ro·scope (lap'ə·rə·skōp) *n.* A narrow, cylindrical optical instrument used for examination of abdominal organs. —**lap·a·ros·co·py** (lap'ə·ros'kə·pē) *n.*

lap dog A very small pet dog.

la·pel (lə·pel') *n.* One of the parts of the front of a coat that is attached to the collar and is folded back. [Dim. of LAP[1]]

lap·i·dar·y (lap'ə·der'ē) *adj.* Of the art of working in precious stones. —*n. pl.* **·dar·ies** One who cuts, engraves, and sets precious stones. [<L *lapis, lapidis* stone]

lap·is laz·u·li (lap'is laz'yoo·lē) 1 A rich blue semiprecious stone. 2 The color of this stone. [<L *lapis* a stone + Med. L *lazulus* azure]

Lapp (lap) *n.* 1 One of a Mongoloid people of short stature inhabiting Lapland: also **lap'land'er.** 2 The Finno-Ugric language of the Lapps: also **Lapp'ish** (-pish).

lap·pet (lap'it) *n.* 1 A small lap or flap for ornamenting a garment, etc. 2 A hanging, fleshy process, as a bird's wattle, an ear lobe, etc.

lap robe A heavy blanket used to keep the lap and lower limbs warm, as while sitting in a wheelchair, riding in an open vehicle, or watching outdoor sports.

lapse (laps) *v.i.* **lapsed, laps·ing** 1 To pass slowly or by degrees; slip: to *lapse* into a coma. 2 To deviate from virtue or truth. 3 To pass, as time. 4 To become void, usu. by disuse or neglect: The agreement *lapsed.* 5 *Law* To be forfeited to another because of the negligence, failure, or death of the holder. —*n.* 1 A gradual slipping or passing away, as of time. 2 A minor fault or mistake. 3 A fall to a lower form or state. 4 A deviation from what is right, proper, or just: a *lapse* in conduct. 5 *Law* The defeat of a right or privilege through fault, failure, or neglect. [<L *lapsus* a slip <*labi* glide, slip] —**laps'a·ble, laps'i·ble** *adj.* —**laps'er** *n.* —**Syn.** *v.* 1 fall, sink. 2 err, stray. 3 elapse, slip by. *n.* 2 blunder, error.

lap·wing (lap'wing') *n.* A plover like, crested bird of the Old World, having an unsteady flight and shrill cry. [<OE *hlēapwince*]

lar·board (lä'bərd, -bôrd', -bōrd') *adj.* & *adv. Naut.* Being on the left, or port, side of a ship as one faces the bow. —*n.* The left, or port, side of a ship. [ME *laddebord*]

lar·ce·nist (lär'sə·nist) *n.* A thief; one who commmits larceny. Also **lar'ce·ner** (-nər).

lar·ce·ny (lär'sə·nē) *n. pl.* **·nies** *Law* The taking, without claim

Lapwing

of right or without permission, of the personal goods of another; theft. [<L *latrocinari* rob] —**lar'ce·nous** *adj.* —**lar'ce·nous·ly** *adv.* • The distinction between **grand larceny** (more than a specified amount) and **petty** (or **petit**) **larceny** (less than such an amount) has been dropped in many parts of the U.S.

larch (lärch) *n.* 1 Any of several cone-bearing deciduous trees. 2 The strong, durable wood of this tree. [<L *larix*]

lard (lärd) *n.* The semisolid oil of hog's fat after rendering. —*v.t.* 1 To prepare (meat or poultry) for cooking by covering with or inserting something, as strips of fat. 2 To cover or smear with grease. 3 To mix with something so as to enrich or improve. [<L *lardum*] —**lard'y** *adj.*

lar·der (lär'dər) *n.* 1 A room where the provisions of a household are kept. 2 Provisions. [<L *lardum* lard]

lar·es and pe·na·tes (lâr'ēz; lā'rēz; pə·nā'tēz) 1 *Usu. cap.* The household gods of ancient Rome. 2 The cherished belongings of a household.

large (lärj) *adj.* **larg·er, larg·est** 1 Absolutely or relatively big as regards size, dimensions, quantity, range, etc. 2 Having unusual breadth or scope: *large* ideas. 3 Extensive in operation: a *large* car dealer. —*n.* Liberty: now used only in the phrase **at large** 1 To the fullest extent; in full. 2 Free or unrestrained in movement; at liberty. 3 Not included within particular limitations: in general. 4 Elected from a state as a whole rather than from a particular district: a congressman *at large*. [<L *largus* abundant] —**large'ness** *n.* —**Syn.** 1 ample, colossal, enormous, huge, vast, great.

large calorie See CALORIE.

large·ly (lärj'lē) *adv.* 1 In a large quantity. 2 To a great extent; generally.

large-scale (lärj'skāl') *adj.* Of large size or scope.

lar·gess (lär·jes', -zhes', lär'jəs) *n.* 1 A gift, gratuity. 2 Liberality; bounty. Also **lar·gesse'.** [<L *largus* abundant]

lar·ghet·to (lär·get'ō) *Music adj.* & *adv.* Slow, in a time not quite so slow as *largo.* —*n. pl.* **·tos** A larghetto movement or section. [Ital. <*largo* largo]

larg·ish (lär'jish) *adj.* Somewhat large.

lar·go (lär'gō) *Music adj.* & *adv.* Slow; stately. —*n. pl.* **·gos** A largo movement. [Ital. <L *largus* abundant]

lar·i·at (lâr'ē·ət) *n.* 1 A rope, esp. of horsehair, for tethering animals. 2 LASSO. —*v.t.* To fasten or catch with a lariat. [<Sp. *la* the + *reata* rope]

lark[1] (lärk) *n.* 1 Any of a large family of small songbirds, as the European skylark. 2 Any of various similar birds, as the meadowlark, etc. [<OE *lāferce*]

lark[2] (lärk) *n. Informal* A hilarious time; humorous adventure. —*v.t.* 1 To make fun of; tease. —*v.i.* 2 To play pranks; frolic. [<ON *leika* to leap] —**lark'er** *n.* —**lark'some, lark'y** *adj.* (**·i·er, ·i·est**)

lark·spur (lärk'spûr') *n.* DELPHINIUM.

lar·ri·gan (lar'ə·gən) *n. Can.* A moccasin made of prepared oiled leather, used chiefly by lumbermen. [?]

lar·ri·kin (lar'ə·kin) *n. Chiefly Austral.* A rough, disorderly fellow; rowdy. [?]

lar·rup (lar'əp) *Informal v.t.* **·ruped, ·rup·ing** To beat; thrash. —*n.* A blow. [?] —**lar'rup·er** *n.*

lar·va (lär'və) *n. pl.* **·vae** (·vē) or **·vas** An early, immature form of an animal that is structurally unlike the adult, as the first stage of an insect after leaving the egg, the tadpole of a frog, etc. [L, a ghost, a mask] —**lar'val** *adj.*

la·ryn·ge·al (lə·rin'je·əl, -jəl) *adj.* 1 Of, pertaining to, or near the larynx: also **la·ryn'ge·an.** 2 Used for treating the larynx, as an instrument.

lar·yn·gi·tis (lar'ən·jī'tis) *n.* Inflammation of the larynx —**lar·yn·git'ic** (-jit'ik) *adj.*

laryngo- *combining form.* The larynx; pertaining to the larynx: *laryngoscope.*

la·ryn·go·scope (lə·ring'gə·skōp, ·rin'jə·) *n.* An instrument for inspecting the larynx. —**la·ryn'go·scop'ic** (·skop'ik) *adj.* —**lar·yn·gos·co·py** (la'ring·gos'kə·pē) *n.*

lar·ynx (lar'ingks) *n. pl.* **la·ryn·ges** (lə·rin'jēz) or **lar·ynx·es** 1 The human organ of voice, consisting of a structure of carti-

Larynx

lage and muscle in the upper trachea, and containing the vocal cords whose vibrations produce sound. **2** A similar structure in most vertebrates. [<Gk. *larynx*]

las·car (las'kər) *n.* An East Indian native, serving as a sailor. [<Ar. *al-askar* the army]

las·civ·i·ous (lə·siv'ē·əs) *adj.* **1** Having wanton desires; lustful; lewd. **2** Producing sensual desires. [<L *lascivus* wanton, lustful] —**las·civ'i·ous·ly** *adv.* —**las·civ'i·ous·ness** *n.*

la·ser (lā'zər) *n.* A device in which energy supplied to an atomic or molecular system is released as a narrow beam of coherent light whose wavelength depends on the energy transitions of the atoms or molecules. [<l(ight) a(m-plification by) s(timulated) e(mission of) r(adiation)]

lash (lash) *n.* **1** A thong on a whip handle; a whip. **2** A stroke with or as with a whip. **3** A sharp, sarcastic remark. **4** An eyelash. **5** Any heavy blow, as of waves beating the shore. —*v.t.* **1** To strike or urge forward with or as with a whip. **2** To throw or move quickly or suddenly, as from side to side: to *lash* the tail. **3** To beat or dash against with force or violence: The waves *lashed* the pier. **4** To attack or criticize severely. **5** To arouse the emotions of, as with words. **6** To bind or tie with or as with a lashing. —*v.i.* **7** To move quickly or violently; dash. —**lash out 1** To strike out violently or wildly. **2** To break into angry or vehement speech. [ME *lashe*] —**Syn.** *v.* **1** beat, flog, hit, thrash, whip. **4** berate, scold, upbraid.

lash·ing (lash'ing) *n.* **1** A fastening made by passing a rope, cord, or the like, around two or more objects. **2** The rope used to do this. **3** A whipping. **4** A severe scolding.

lass (las) *n.* A young woman; girl. [<Scand.]

las·sie (las'ē) *n.* A little girl; a lass.

las·si·tude (las'ə·tʸo͞od) *n.* A feeling of languor; weariness. [<L *lassus* faint]

las·so (las'ō, las·ō') *n. pl.* **·sos** or **·soes** A long rope or leather thong, with a running noose, for catching horses and cattle. —*v.t.* To catch with a lasso. [<L *laqueus* a snare] —**las'so·er** *n.*

last¹ (last, läst) *adj.* **1** Having no successor; final. **2** Next before the present; most recent. **3** Least fit or likely; most remote. **4** Beyond or above all others; utmost. **5** Beneath all others. —*adv.* **1** After all others in time or order. **2** At a time next preceding the present: He was *last* seen heading west. **3** In conclusion. —*n.* **1** The end: a rebel to the *last*. **2** The final appearance, experience, or mention. **3** The element of an ordered set that has no successor. —**at last** Finally. —**at long last** Finally. —**breathe one's last** To die. —**see the last of** Never to see again. [<OE *latost*] —**last'ly** *adv.*

last² (last, läst) *v.i.* **1** To remain in existence; endure. **2** To continue unchanged or unaltered; persevere. **3** To be as much as or more than needed; hold out: Will our supplies *last?* [<OE *læsten* follow a track] —**last'er** *n.*

last³ (last, läst) *n.* A shaped form, usu. of wood, on which to make a boot or shoe. —*v.t.* To fit to or form on a last. —**stick to one's last** to attend to one's own business or work. [<OE *læst* a boot] —**last'er** *n.*

last·ing (las'ting, läs'-) *adj.* Continuing, durable, or permanent: a *lasting* sorrow. —*n.* Endurance; continuance. —**last'ing·ly** *adv.* —**last'ing·ness** *n.*

Last Judgment The final judgment of mankind to be rendered by God at the end of the world.

last straw The final element in a series of trying situations that results in loss of patience, etc.

Last Supper The last meal of Jesus with his disciples before the Crucifixion.

last word 1 The final say, as in a dispute. **2** *Informal* Something considered not capable of being improved. **3** *Informal* The latest or most modern fashion, style, advancement, etc.

Lat. Latin; Latvia.

lat. latitude.

latch (lach) *n.* A catch for fastening a door, lid, shutter, etc. —*v.t. & v.i.* To fasten by means of a latch; close. —**latch on to** *Slang* **1** To fasten (oneself) **2** To obtain; get. [<OE *læccan* seize]

latch·key (lach'kē') *n.* A key for releasing a latch, esp. on an outside or front door.

latchkey child A child who comes home after school to an empty house, the parents or guardians being still at work.

latch·string (lach'string') *n.* A string for lifting a latch, passing through a hole above it to the outside.

late (lāt) *adj.* **lat·er** or **lat·ter**, **lat·est** or **last 1** Coming after the appointed time; tardy. **2** Far advanced toward the end or close. **3** Recent or comparatively recent. **4** Deceased, esp. recently deceased. —*adv.* **lat·er**, **lat·est** or **last 1** After or beyond the usual proper or appointed time. **2** Not long ago; recently. **3** After a while; in course of time. —**of late** In time not long past; recently. [<OE *læt* late, slow] —**late'ness** *n.*

la·teen (la·tēn') *adj. Naut.* **1** Designating a rig common in the Mediterranean, having a triangular sail (**lateen sail**) suspended from a long yard set obliquely to the mast. **2** Equipped with such a sail. —*n.* A craft equipped with a lateen sail. [<F *(voile) latine* Latin (sail)]

Late Greek The Greek language from about A.D. 200 to 600.

Late Latin the Latin language from about A.D. 200 to 700.

late·ly (lāt'lē) *adv.* Not long ago; recently.

Lateen sail

la·tent (lā'tənt) *adj.* Not visible or apparent; dormant. [<L *latere* be hidden] —**la'ten·cy** *n.* —**la'tent·ly** *adv.*

lat·er (lā'tər) Comparative of LATE. —**later on** Subsequently.

lat·er·al (lat'ər·əl) *adj.* Pertaining to, proceeding from, or directed toward the side. —*n.* **1** A lateral protuberance or outgrowth. **2** LATERAL PASS. [<L *latus, lateris* a side] —**lat'er·al·ly** *adv.*

lateral pass In football, a pass thrown parallel to the line of scrimmage or toward one's own goal.

lat·est (lā'tist) A superlative of LATE. —**at the latest** No later than (a particular time). —**the latest** *Informal* **1** The newest, most fashionable style, trend, etc. **2** The most recent news or development.

la·tex (lā'teks) *n. pl.* **lat·i·ces** (lat'ə·sēz) or **la·tex·es 1** The viscid, milky emulsion secreted by certain plants, as the milkweed, rubber tree, etc. **2** A watery emulsion of rubber or synthetic plastic, used in making adhesives, paint, etc. [L, a liquid]

lath (lath, läth) *n.* **1** One of a number of strips of wood or metal serving to support plaster, shingles, slates, etc. **2** Any building material of similar use. Lathing. —*v.t.* To cover or line with laths. [<OE *lætt*] —**lath'er** *n.*

lathe (lāth) *n.* A machine for shaping articles on which an object is mounted and rotated, while a cutting tool is thrust against it. —*v.t.* **lathed, lath·ing** To form or shape on a lathe. [?]

lath·er (lath'ər) *n.* **1** Foam or froth of soapsuds. **2** Foam of profuse sweating, as of a horse. —**in a lather** *Informal* In a state of intense excitement or agitation. —*v.t.* **1** To cover with lather. **2** *Informal* To flog; thrash. —*v.i.* **3** To become covered with lather. **4** To form lather. [<OE *lēathor* washing soda] —**lath'er·y** *adj.* —**lath'er·er** *n.*

lath·ing (lath'ing, läth'-) *n.* **1** The act or process of covering with laths. **2** The foundation of laths on which plaster may be laid. **3** Any work with laths or like material. Also **lath·work** (-wûrk')

Lat·in (lat'n) *adj.* **1** Pertaining to ancient Latium or its inhabitants. **2** Pertaining to or denoting the peoples or countries, as France, Italy, Spain, Portugal, Rumania, etc., whose languages are derived from that of ancient Rome. —*n.* **1** One of the people of ancient Latium. **2** A member of any of the modern Latin peoples. **3** The Indo-European Italic language of ancient Latium and Rome. —**La·tin·ic** (lə·tin'ik) *adj.*

Latin America Those countries of the Western Hemisphere s of the U.S. in which the languages spoken, Spanish, Portuguese, and French, are derived from Latin. —**Lat'in-A·mer'i·can** *adj*

Latin American A native or inhabitant of Latin America.

Lat·in·ate (lat′ən·āt) *adj.* Resembling or derived from Latin.

Latin Church That part of the Catholic Church which accepts the pope as supreme authority on earth; Roman Catholic Church.

Lat·in·ism (lat′ən·iz′əm) *n.* An idiom peculiar to or imitating Latin. —**Lat′in·is′tic** *adj.*

Lat·in·ist (lat′ən·ist) *n.* A scholar versed in Latin.

Lat·in·ize (lat′ən·īz) *v.* ·**ized**, ·**iz·ing** *v.t.* 1 To translate into Latin. 2 To give Latin characteristics to. —*v.i.* 3 To use Latin words, forms, etc. —**Lat′in·i·za′tion, Lat′in·iz′er** *n.*

la·ti·no (la·tē′nō) *n. pl.* ·**nos** *Often cap.* A Latin American. [Am. Sp. < Sp., Latin]

lat·ish (lā′tish) *adj.* Rather late.

lat·i·tude (lat′ə·t▽ood) *n.* 1 *Geog.* Distance on the earth's surface toward or away from the equator expressed as an arc of a meridian. 2 A region or place with reference to its distance north or south of the equator: warm *latitudes.* 3 Freedom from restrictions, as in action or thought. 4 Range or scope. [< L *latus* broad] —**lat′i·tu′di·nal** *adj.*

lat·i·tu·di·nar·i·an (lat′ə·t▽oo′də·nâr′ē·ən) *adj.* Broad, tolerant, or lax, esp. in religious principles. —*n.* One who is extremely tolerant; a freethinker. [< L *latitudo* latitude] —**lat′i·tu′di·nar′i·an·ism** *n.*

La·ti·um (lā′shē·əm) *n.* A region and ancient country in CEN. Italy, original home of the Latins.

la·trine (lə·trēn′) *n.* A toilet, esp. in a camp, barracks, etc. [< L *latrina* a bath]

lat·ter (lat′ər) A comparative of LATE. —*adj.* 1 Of, relating to, or nearer the end. 2 Recent or more recent; later. —**the latter** The second of two mentioned persons or things. [< OE *lætra*] —**lat′ter·ly** *adv.*

lat·ter-day (lat′ər·dā′) *adj.* Belonging to the present; modern. —**Syn.** contemporary, current, recent, up-to-date.

Latter-Day Saint MORMON.

lat·tice (lat′is) *n.* 1 Openwork of metal or wood, formed by crossing or interlacing strips or bars. 2 Anything made of such work, as a window, a blind, or a screen. 3 *Physics* An arrangement consisting of a module periodically repeated throughout a region or space. —*v.t.* **lat·ticed, lat·tic·ing** 1 To furnish or enclose with a lattice. 2 To arrange or interlace like latticework. [< OF *latte* a lath]

lat·tice·work (lat′is·wûrk′) *n.* 1 A lattice. 2 In embroidery, stitching in an outline resembling a lattice.

Lattice

Lat·vi·an (lat′vē·ən) *adj.* Of or pertaining to Latvia, its people, or their language. —*n.* 1 A native or citizen of Latvia. 2 The language of the Latvians.

laud (lôd) *n.* 1 Praise or commendation. 2 A song or hymn of praise or honor. 3 *pl.* In the Roman Catholic Church, a morning service consisting of the psalms, immediately following matins, and constituting with the latter the first of the seven canonical hours: also **Lauds.** —*v.t.* To praise; extol. [< L *laus, laudis* praise] —**laud′er** *n.*

laud·a·ble (lô′də·bəl) *adj.* Worthy of approval; praiseworthy. —**laud′a·bil′i·ty, laud′a·ble·ness** *n.* —**laud′a·bly** *adv.*

lau·da·num (lô′də·nəm) *n.* 1 Tincture of opium. 2 Formerly, any preparation of opium. [< L *ladanum* a resinous juice]

lau·da·tion (lô·dā′shən) *n.* The act of praising; praise.

laud·a·to·ry (lô′də·tôr′ē, -tō′rē) *adj.* Eulogizing; praising. Also **laud′a·tive.** [< L *laudare* praise, celebrate]

laugh (laf, läf) *v.i.* 1 To show amusement, hilarity, derision, etc., by expressions of the face and by a series of explosive sounds made in the chest and throat. 2 To be or appear gay or lively. 3 To express by laughter. 4 To move or influence by laughter or ridicule: He *laughed* himself out of his worries. —**laugh at** 1 To express amusement concerning. 2 To make light of; belittle —**laugh off** To dismiss or reject lightly or scornfully. —*n.* 1 The act or sound of laughter. 2 *Informal* Anything producing laughter. —**have the last laugh** To triumph after apparent defeat. [< OE *hlæhhan*] —**laugh′er** *n.*

laugh·a·ble (laf′ə·bəl, läf′-) *adj.* Ridiculous; exciting laughter. —**laugh′a·ble·ness** *n.* —**laugh′a·bly** *adv.*

laugh·ing (laf′ing, läf′-) *adj.* 1 Expressing amusement, etc., by laughing: a *laughing* child. 2 Seeming to laugh: a *laughing* hyena. —**no laughing matter** A very serious matter. —*n.* LAUGHTER. —**laugh′ing·ly** *adv.*

laughing gas Nitrous oxide used as an anesthetic, sometimes with exhilarating effect.

laugh·ing·stock (laf′ing·stok′, läf′-) *n.* A butt for ridicule.

laugh·ter (laf′tər, läf′-) *n.* 1 The sound or action of laughing. 2 Any exclamation or expression indicating merriment or derision.

launch[1] (lônch, länch) *v.t.* 1 To cause to move into water for the first time, as a newly built ship. 2 To set afloat, as a boat or log. 3 To make a beginning of: to *launch* an enterprise. 4 To start (someone) on a career, course, etc. 5 To give a start to the flight or course of, as a rocket, torpedo, or airplane. —*v.i.* 6 To put or go to sea: usu. with *out* or *forth.* 7 To start on a career, course, etc. 8 To begin something with vehemence or urgency. He *launched* into an argument. —**launch out** To start; commence, esp. something new. —*n.* 1 The act of launching. 2 The process of being launched. [< OF *lance* lance] —**launch′er** *n.*

launch[2] (lônch, länch) *n.* 1 The largest of the boats carried by a warship. 2 A large, open boat, propelled by steam or electricity, and used as a pleasure craft. [< Pg. *lancha*]

launching pad The platform from which a rocket or spacecraft is launched.

laun·der (lôn′dər, län′-) *v.t.* 1 To wash, or wash and iron, as clothing. 2 To cleanse or purify. 3 *Slang* To conceal the original source of (funds). —*v.i.* 4 To wash or wash and iron laundry. [< OF *lavendier* a washerwoman] —**laun′der·er** *n.* —**laun′dress** (-dris) *n. Fem.*

laun·dro·mat (lôn′drə·mat, län′-) *n.* An establishment, usu. self-service, where the customer brings laundry to be washed and dried in coin-operated machines. [< *Laundromat,* a trade name]

laun·dry (lôn′drē, län′-) *n. pl.* ·**dries** 1 A room or building for laundering clothes. 2 Articles to be washed. [< OF *lavendier*] —**laun′dry·man** (-mən) *n.*

lau·re·ate (lô′rē·it) *adj.* 1 Crowned or decked with laurel, as an honor. 2 Deserving of distinction; preeminent, esp. as a poet. —*n.* 1 A person honored for achievement, as in an art or science. 2 POET LAUREATE. [< L *laurus* laurel] —**lau′re·ate·ship′** *n.*

lau·rel (lôr′əl, lor′-) *n.* 1 An evergreen shrub of the Mediterranean area, with aromatic, lance-shaped leaves. 2 The leaves of this shrub. 3 Any of various similar shrubs, as the mountain laurel. 4 *pl.* A crown or wreath of laurel, indicating honor or high merit. —**rest on one's laurels** To be content with what one has already achieved. —*v.t.* ·**reled** or ·**relled,** ·**rel·ing** or ·**rel·ling** 1 To wreathe or crown with laurel. 2 To honor. [< L *laurus*]

laus De·o (lôs dē′ō, dā′ō) *Latin* Praise be to God.

la·va (lä′və, lav′ə) *n.* 1 Melted rock, issuing from a volcanic crater or a fissure in the earth's surface. 2 Such rock when solidified. [< Ital., orig., a stream of rain]

lav·a·liere (lav′ə·lir′) *n.* A piece of jewelry, consisting of a necklace and pendant. Also **lav·a·lier′.** [< F < Louise de La Vallière, 1644–1710, mistress of Louis XIV]

lav·a·to·ry (lav′ə·tôr′ē, -tō′rē) *n. pl.* ·**ries** 1 A room in a public or semipublic place, as in a school or hotel, provided with appliances for washing, usu. toilets, and sometimes urinals. 2 Any bathroom. 3 A basin to wash in. [< L *lavare* to wash]

lave (lāv) *v.t. & v.i.* **laved, lav·ing** 1 To wash; bathe. 2 To flow along or against as if washing. [< L *lavare* to wash]

lav·en·der (lav′ən·dər) *n.* 1 A plant of the mint family yielding a fragrant oil (**oil of lavender**). 2 The dried flowers and leaves of this plant, used to scent linens, etc. 3 The color of lavender flowers, a pale purple. —*adj.* Of, pertaining to, or like lavender. —*v.t.* To scent with lavender. [< Med. L *lavendula*]

Spike lavender

lav·ish (lav′ish) *adj.* 1 Bestowed, expended, or existing in profusion: *lavish* gifts. 2 Spending extravagantly; prodigal. 3 Exaggerated; unrestrained: *lavish* compliments. —*v.t.* To give or bestow profusely or generously.

[< OF *lavache* a downpour of rain] —**lav′ish·er, lav′ish·ness** *n.* —**lav′ish·ly** *adv.* —**Syn.** *adj.* 1 abundant, bountiful, copious, generous. *v.* indulge with, heap upon.

law (lô) *n.* 1 A custom or rule of conduct which a community, state, etc., considers binding upon its members, and which is enforced by compelling authority or legislation. 2 A body of such rules. 3 The condition of society when such rules are observed: to establish *law* and order. 4 The body of rules related to a specified subject: criminal *law.* 5 Statute and common law, as opposed to equity. 6 An enactment of a legislature, as opposed to a constitution. 7 The system of courts administering remedial justice: to resort to the *law.* 8 The branch of knowledge concerned with jurisprudence: to study *law.* 9 The vocation of an attorney, solicitor, etc.: to practice *law.* 10 The legal profession as a whole. 11 A rule of conduct having divine origin. 12 An imperative rule or command: His word is *law.* 13 Any rule of conduct or procedure: the *laws* of hospitality. 14 In science, a statement of the manner or order in which a defined group of natural phenomena occur under certain conditions. 15 *Math.* A rule or formula governing a function or the performance of an operation. 16 The police, personifying legal force: preceded by *the.* [< OE *lagu*] —**go to law** To take a case or complaint to court to be settled. —**lay down the law** 1 To scold thoroughly. 2 To give firm orders. —**read law** To study for a legal degree. —**the Law** 1 The first five books of the Old Testament, containing the Mosaic law. 2 The Old Testament.

law·a·bid·ing (lô′ə-bī′ding) *adj.* Obedient to or abiding by the law.

law-break·er (lô′brā′kər) *n.* One who violates the law. —**law′-break′ing** *n., adj.*

law court A court where trials or hearings are held and justice under the law is administered.

law·ful (lô′fəl) *adj.* 1 Permitted by law; legitimate: *lawful* acts. 2 Enforceable at law: *lawful* claims. 3 Valid, or regarded as valid: said of a marriage. —**law′ful·ly** *adv.* —**law′ful·ness** *n.*

law·giv·er (lô′giv′ər) *n.* One who makes or enacts a law or laws; a legislator. —**law′giv′ing** *adj., n.*

law·less (lô′lis) *adj.* 1 Not subject or obedient to law of any sort. 2 Without the sanction or authority of law. 3 Without the protection of law: a *lawless* fugitive. 4 Uncontrollable; unbridled. —**law′less·ly** *adv.* —**law′less·ness** *n.*

law·mak·ing (lô′mā′king) *n.* The enacting of laws; legislation. —**law′mak′er** *n.*

lawn¹ (lôn) *n.* A piece of ground, esp. around a home, with grass kept closely mown. [< OF *launde*] —**lawn′y** *adv.*

lawn² (lôn) *n.* Fine thin linen or cotton fabric. [ME < *Laon,* France, where it was formerly made]

lawn mower A machine for clipping the grass of lawns, either power-driven or propelled by hand.

lawn tennis Tennis played outdoors on a clay or grass-covered court.

Law of Moses The Pentateuch; the Mosaic law.

law·ren·ci·um (lô-ren′sē·əm) *n.* An artificially produced radioactive element (symbol Lr). [< E. O. *Lawrence,* 1901–58, U.S. physicist]

law·suit (lô′sōōt′) *n.* A proceeding in a court of law for redress of wrongs.

law·yer (lô′yər) *n.* One who practices law and represents clients in lawsuits or gives legal advice.

lax (laks) *adj.* 1 Lacking tenseness or firmness; yielding. 2 Not stringent or energetic. 3 Wanting exactness of meaning or application. [< L *laxus* loose] —**lax′i·ty, lax′ness** *n.* —**lax′ly** *adv.*

lax·a·tive (lak′sə·tiv) *n.* A substance that has the power to loosen the bowels, as milk of magnesia. —*adj.* Tending to loosen the bowels or subside, as dust, a storm, etc. [< L *laxatus,* p.p. of *laxare* relax]

lay¹ (lā) *v.* **laid, lay·ing** *v.t.* 1 To cause to lie. 2 To put or place; *Lay* the book on the table. 3 To strike or beat down; overthrow. 4 To cause to settle or subside, as dust, a storm, etc. 5 To calm or allay, as doubts. 6 To place in regular order or proper position: to *lay* tile. 7 To think out; devise:

to *lay* plans. 8 To attribute or ascribe: to *lay* blame. 9 To give importance to. 10 To bring forward; advance, as a claim. 11 To bring forth from and deposit, as an egg. 12 To construct; build, as a foundation. 13 To make (a table) ready for a meal. 14 To bury; inter. 15 To impose, as taxes, punishment, etc. 16 To spread over a surface: to *lay* a fixative. 17 To strike with or apply, as in punishment. 18 To locate: The scene is *laid* in the boudoir. 19 To set or prepare, as a trap. 20 To place as a wager or bet: He *laid* twenty dollars on the favorite. —*v.i.* 21 To bring forth and deposit eggs. 22 To place a bet or bets. 23 To lie; recline: an incorrect use. —**lay aside** (or **by**) To store up; save. —**lay away** 1 To store up; save. 2 To bury. —**lay before** To put forward or present, as a report. —**lay down** 1 To give up (one's life). 2 To state or proclaim: to *lay down* the law. 3 To bet. —**lay for** *Informal* To wait to attack or harm. —**lay hold of** To seize or grasp. —**lay in** To procure and store. —**lay into** *Informal* To attack vigorously. —**lay it on** *Informal* To be extravagant or exorbitant, as in praise or demands. —**lay off** 1 To take off and put aside, as clothes. 2 To survey; mark off. 3 To dismiss (a worker) from a job, usu. temporarily. 4 *Informal* To take a rest; stop working. 5 *Slang* To stop annoying, teasing, etc. —**lay on** 1 To put on; apply, as color. 2 To beat or strike; attack. —**lay out** 1 To spend. 2 To prepare for burial. 3 *Slang* To stretch prostrate or unconscious. 4 To set forth, as a plan. —**lay over** To stop, as for a rest on a journey. —**lay siege to** To besiege. —**lay up** 1 To make a store of. 2 To confine, as by illness or injury. —*n.* 1 The manner in which something lies or is placed; relative arrangement: the *lay* of the land. 2 *Whaling* A share in the profits. [< OE *lecgan*] • **lay, lie** Educated speaking and writing require a careful distinction between these two related verbs. *Lay (laid, laying),* meaning to place or put, takes an object: *He lays his briefcase on the desk. Lie (lay, lain, lying),* meaning to rest, recline, or be situated, does not take an object: *The dog lies on the rug.* The confusion occurs because the present tense of *lay* is identical with the past tense of *lie: Lay your coat over that chair; Yesterday he lay on the couch for two hours.*

lay² (lā) *adj.* Pertaining to the laity; nonprofessional; inexperienced. [< Gk. *laos* the people]

lay³ (lā) *p.t.* of LIE¹.

lay⁴ (lā) *n.* A song, ballad, or narrative poem. [< OF *lai.*]

lay·a·bout (lā′ə·bout′) *n. Chiefly Brit.* A lazy, idle person; a good-for-nothing.

lay·a·way (lā′ə·wā′) *n.* An agreement to make a series of payments to buy merchandise that is delivered when fully paid for. Also **layaway plan.**

lay-by (lā′bī′) *n. pl.* **-bys** *Brit.* A roadside area where vehicles may turn off, as for repairs or parking.

lay·er (lā′ər) *n.* 1 One who or that which lays. 2 A single horizontal thickness, as a stratum or lamina. 3 *Bot.* A shoot or twig bent into the ground to take root without being detached from the parent plant. —*v.t. Bot.* To propagate (a plant) by means of a layer. —**lay′er·ing** *n.*

Layer *def. 3*

layer cake A cake of two or more layers separated by a sweetened filling or icing and usu. frosted.

lay·ette (lā·et′) *n.* A full equipment of clothes, bedding, etc., for a newly born child. [< MDu. *lade* a chest, trunk]

lay figure 1 A jointed model of the human body that can be arranged in various positions and used by artists as a model. 2 A mere puppet; a tool of the interests of others.

lay·man (lā′mən) *n. pl.* **-men** (-mən) A man not belonging to the clergy or other profession or body of experts.

lay·off (lā′ôf′, -of′) *n.* 1 The act of discharging or firing workmen or employees, esp. temporarily. 2 A period of discontinuance of work.

lay·out (lā′out′) *n.* 1 That which is laid out; a set of articles set out or provided. 2 A laying out or planning, as of a piece of work, a campaign, etc. 3 The make-up of a book, magazine, etc. Also **lay′out.**

lay·o·ver (lā′ō′vər) *n.* STOPOVER.

lay-up (lā′up′) *n.* In basketball, a shot taken close to the basket and usu. bounced off the backboard.

la·zar (la′zər, lăz′ər) *n.* A diseased beggar, esp. a leper. [< LAZARUS]

laz·a·ret·to (laz′ə·ret′ō) *n. pl.* **·tos** 1 A hospital for people with contagious diseases, esp. leprosy. 2 A ship or building used for quarantine. 3 In certain ships, a storeroom near the stern. Also **laz′a·ret′, laz′a·rette′.** [< Ital.]

Laz·a·rus (laz′ə·rəs) In the Bible: **a** A brother of Martha and Mary, raised from the dead by Jesus. **b** A sick beggar described in a parable as being rewarded after death, while a rich man was punished in hell. *Luke* 16:19–31.

laze (lāz) *v.* **lazed, laz·ing** *v.i.* 1 To be lazy; loaf. —*v.t.* 2 To pass (time) in idleness. —*n.* Idleness; laziness.

la·zy (lā′zē) *adj.* **·zi·er, ·zi·est** 1 Indisposed to exertion; indolent. 2 Moving or acting slowly or heavily. [?] —**la′zi·ly** *adv.* —**la′zi·ness** *n.* —Syn. 1 idle, inactive, slothful, sluggish.

la·zy·bones (lā′zē·bōnz′) *n. Informal* A lazy person.

lb. pound (L *libra*).

lbs. pounds.

L.C. Library of Congress.

L/C, l/c letter of credit; lower case.

lc. left center; lower case (printing); in the place cited (L *loco citato*).

LD, L.D. Low Dutch.

ldg. landing; loading.

lea (lē) *n.* A grassy field or plain. [< OE *lēah*]

lea. league; leather; leave.

leach (lēch) *v.t.* 1 To run a liquid through (ashes, etc.) so as to remove the soluble portions. 2 To remove (soluble portions) by passing a liquid through them. —*v.i.* 3 To lose soluble matter by percolating. 4 To be removed by percolating. —*n.* 1 The process of leaching. 2 The solution obtained by leaching. [< OE *leccan* wet, irrigate] —**leach′er** *n.*

lead[1] (lēd) *v.* **led, lead·ing** *v.t.* 1 To go with or ahead of so as to show the way; guide. 2 To guide by or as by pulling: to *lead* a person by the hand. 3 To serve as a direction or route for: The path *led* them to a valley. 4 To cause to go in a certain direction, as wire, water, etc. 5 To direct the affairs, actions, etc., of: to *lead* an army. 6 To have the first or foremost place among: He *led* the field. 7 To influence or control the opinions, thoughts, actions, etc., of. 8 To live or experience; pass: to *lead* a happy life. 9 To begin or open: to *lead* a discussion. 10 In card games, to begin a round of play with: He *led* the ace. —*v.i.* 11 To act as guide; conduct. 12 To have leadership or command; be in control. 13 To submit to being guided: The horse *leads* easily. 14 To be first or in advance. 15 To afford a way or passage: The road *led* into a swamp. 16 In card games, to make the first play. 17 In boxing, to strike at an opponent: to *lead* with a left. —**lead off** To make a beginning; start. —**lead on** To entice or tempt. —**lead to** To result in; cause: His carelessness *led to* his downfall. —*n.* 1 Position in advance or at the head; priority. 2 The distance, time, etc., by which anything precedes. 3 Leadership; guidance. 4 A clue or hint: Have you any *leads?* 5 In cards, etc., the right to play first or the card or suit played first. 6 In drama, the principal part or the actor who performs in such a part. 7 *Electr.* A wire that joins to a circuit device. 8 In baseball, the distance from base of a runner ready to run to the next base. 9 A leash for leading a dog. 10 In journalism, the opening paragraph of a news story. —*adj.* Acting as leader: the *lead* dog. [< OE *lǣden* cause to go] —Syn. *v.* 1 conduct, direct, escort. 7 induce, persuade.

lead[2] (led) *n.* 1 A soft, heavy, gray metallic element (symbol Pb) forming many technologically useful alloys and compounds. 2 Any one of various articles made of lead or its alloys. 3 *Printing* A thin strip of type metal used to separate lines of type. 4 *Naut.* A weight of lead used in sounding at sea. 5 A thin rod of graphite, used in pencils. 6 WHITE LEAD. 7 Bullets. —*v.t.* 1 To cover, weight, fasten, line, or fill with lead. 2 *Printing* To separate (lines of type) with leads. —*v.i.* 3 To become filled or clogged with lead. [< OE *lēad*] —**lead′y** *adj.*

lead·en (led′n) *adj.* 1 Made of lead. 2 Of a dull gray color. 3 Heavy. 4 Dull or sluggish. 5 Depressed; sad. —**lead′en·ly** *adv.* —**lead′en·ness** *n.*

lead·er (lē′dər) *n.* 1 One who leads or commands. 2 One who has the ability to lead. 3 That which leads, as the foremost horse of a team. 4 *Music* **a** A conductor of an orchestra, band, etc. **b** A principal musician or vocalist. 5 In journalism, the chief editorial or article of a newspaper. 6 An article of merchandise offered at a special price to attract customers. 7 *Printing pl.* Dots, dashes, etc., printed in rows and used to guide the eye from one side of a page to the other. 8 In fishing, a short line of gut, nylon, etc., attaching the hook or lure to the line. 9 A pipe to carry water, as from a roof.

lead·er·ship (lē′dər·ship) *n.* 1 The office or position of a leader. 2 Ability to lead. 3 Leaders as a group.

lead-in (lēd′in′) *n.* 1 A wire connecting an antenna to a transmitter or receiver. 2 Anything that introduces something.

lead·ing[1] (lē′ding) *adj.* 1 First or most prominent; foremost. 2 That guides, directs, or influences: a *leading* question. 3 Situated at the head or front. —*n.* A directing or guiding. —**lead′ing·ly** *adv.*

lead·ing[2] (led′ing) *n.* 1 The act of covering or separating with lead. 2 Sheets or strips of lead.

lead-off (lēd′ôf′, -of′) *n.* 1 A beginning. 2 The opening movement in any of various games. 3 The player who leads off.

lead pencil (led) A pencil of graphite encased in wood, etc.

lead poisoning (led) Poisoning due to cumulative absorption of small amounts of lead into the body.

lead time (lēd) The time required to put into effect a plan or program, as to manufacture a commercial product or a military weapon.

leaf (lēf) *n. pl.* **leaves** (lēvz) 1 A photosynthetic, lateral outgrowth from the stem of a plant, commonly broad, flat, thin, and green. 2 Leaves collectively; leafage. 3 Loosely, a petal. 4 A single sheet of paper, as in a book, on each side of which is a page. 5 A hinged, folding, sliding, or removable part or section, as of a table, gate, screen, or folding door. 6 A very thin sheet of metal: gold *leaf.* —**turn over a new leaf** To change one's ways or conduct for the better. —*v.i.* 1 To put forth or produce leaves. —*v.t.* 2 To turn or run through the pages of a book: often with *through.* [< OE *lēaf*]

Types of tree leaves
a. linear. b. lanceolate. c. acuminate. d. acute. e. obtuse. f. ovate. g. serrate. h. sagittate. i. binate. j. digitate. k. compound.

leaf·age (lē′fij) *n.* FOLIAGE.

leaf bud A bud that develops into a leaf or a branch.

leaf·less (lēf′lis) *adj.* Having or bearing no leaves. —**leaf′less·ness** *n.*

leaf·let (lēf′lit) *n.* 1 A little leaf or leaflike part. 2 *Bot.* One of the separate divisions of a compound leaf. 3 A small printed sheet (or sheets) of printed matter, often folded but left unstitched.

leaf·stalk (lēf′stôk′) *n.* PETIOLE.

leaf·y (lē′fē) *adj.* **leaf·i·er, leaf·i·est** 1 Having or full of leaves. 2 Producing broad leaves. 3 Like a leaf or leaves. —**leaf′i·ness** *n.*

league[1] (lēg) *n.* A measure of distance, varying from about 2.42 to 4.6 statute miles. [< LL *leuga, leuca*]

league[2] (lēg) *n.* 1 An alliance of persons or states for mutual support in a common cause. 2 In sports, an association of ball teams that play among themselves. —*v.t. & v.i.* **leagued, lea·guing** To join in a league; combine. [< Ital. < *legare* to bind] —**lea·guer** (lē′gər) *n.*

League of Nations An international organization

(1920–1946) established primarily for the preservation of peace.

Le·ah (lē′ə) In the Bible, one of Jacob's wives.

leak (lēk) *n.* **1** An opening that permits the unintended entrance or escape of something. **2** Anything which permits the transmission, loss, or escape of something: *a leak in the espionage system.* **3** Leakage. —*v.i.* **1** To let a liquid, etc., enter or escape undesignedly, as through a hole or crack. **2** To pass in or out accidentally: often with *in* or *out.* **3** To become known despite efforts at secrecy: usu. with *out.* —*v.t.* **4** To let (a liquid, etc.) enter or escape undesignedly. **5** To disclose (privileged information) with or without authorization. [< ON *leka* to drip] —**leak′i·ness** *n.* —**leak′y** *adj.* (·i·er, ·i·est)

leak·age (lē′kij) *n.* **1** The act of leaking. **2** Something that leaks. **3** The quantity that leaks.

lean¹ (lēn) *v.* **leaned** or **leant** (lent), **lean·ing** *v.i.* **1** To incline from an erect position. **2** To incline against or rest on something for support. **3** To depend or rely: with *on* or *upon:* to *lean* on friendship. **4** To have a mental inclination: to *lean* toward an opinion. —*v.t.* **5** To cause to incline from an erect position. **6** To place (one thing) against another for support. —*n.* A leaning; inclination. [< OE *hleonian*]

lean² (lēn) *adj.* **1** Not fat or stout; thin. **2** With little or no fat: *lean* meat. **3** Lacking in richness, productiveness, etc.: *a lean* harvest. —*n.* Meat with little or no fat. [< OE *hlæne* thin] —**lean′ly** *adv.* —**lean′ness** *n.*

Le·an·der (lē·an′dər) *Gk. Myth.* The lover of Hero. [Gk., lion man]

lean·ing (lē′ning) *n.* **1** The act of one who or that which leans. **2** An inclination; tendency.

lean-to (lēn′tōō′) *n. pl.* **-tos** (·tōōz′) **1** A building having a single-sloping roof with its apex against an adjoining wall. **2** A rude shelter of branches or planks which slope from a crossbar to the ground.

leap (lēp) *v.* **leaped** or **leapt** (lēpt or lept), **leap·ing** *v.i.* **1** To jump with the feet in the air; spring. **2** To move suddenly by or as by jumping. —*v.t.* **3** To clear by jumping over. **4** To cause to leap: to *leap* a horse. —*n.* **1** The act of leaping. **2** A place to leap from or over. **3** The space passed over in leaping. **4** A sudden change or transition. [< OE *hlēapan*] —**leap′er** *n.*

leap·frog (lēp′frôg′, -frog′) *n.* A game in which one player puts his hands on the bent back of another and leaps over him. —*v.* **·frogged**, **·frog·ging** *v.i.* **1** To jump over as in the game of leapfrog. **2** To move ahead of by turns or stages. —*v.i.* **3** To jump as in the game of leapfrog.

leap year A year of 366 days, an additional day being added to February. Every year exactly divisible by four, or, in century years, by 400, is a leap year.

learn (lûrn) *v.* **learned** or **learnt**, **learn·ing** *v.t.* **1** To acquire knowledge of or skill in by observation, study, instruction, etc. **2** To find out; ascertain: to *learn* the facts. **3** To memorize. **4** To acquire by or as by practice: to *learn* good habits. —*v.i.* **5** To gain knowledge; acquire skill. **6** To be informed; hear. [< OE *leornian*] —**learn′er** *n.*

learn·ed (lûr′nid) *adj.* **1** Having extensive learning or knowledge. **2** Characterized by or demanding extensive study or scholarship. —**learn′ed·ly** *adv.* —**learn′ed·ness** *n.*

learn·ing (lûr′ning) *n.* **1** The act of acquiring knowledge or skill. **2** The knowledge or skill thus acquired.

lease (lēs) *v.t.* **leased**, **leas·ing** **1** To grant the temporary possession and profits of, as lands, buildings, etc., usu. for a specified rent; let. **2** To hold under a lease. —*n.* **1** A contract for leasing land, buildings, etc. **2** The duration of such leasing. [< L *laxare* loosen] —**leas′a·ble** *adj.*

leash (lēsh) *n.* A line or thong, as for holding in check a dog, etc. —*v.t.* To hold or restrain by or as by a leash. [< L *laxus* loose]

least (lēst) *adj.* Smallest in size, value, etc. —*n.* That which is least. —**at least** **1** By the lowest estimate. **2** At any rate. —**not in the least** Not in any degree; not at all. —*adv.* In the smallest degree. [< OE *læssa* less]

least·wise (lēst′wīz′) *adv. Informal* At least; at any rate. Also **least′ways** (-wāz′).

leath·er (leth′ər) *n.* **1** The skin or hide of an animal, when tanned or dressed for use. **2** Something made of leather. —*v.t.* **1** To cover or furnish with leather. **2** *Informal* To beat with or as with a leather strap. [< OE *lether*] —**leath′er·y** *adj.* —**leath′er·i·ness** *n.*

leath·ern (leth′ərn) *adj.* Made of leather.

leath·er·neck (leth′ər·nek′) *n. Slang* A member of the U.S. Marine Corps.

leave¹ (lēv) *v.* **left**, **leav·ing** *v.t.* **1** To go or depart from; quit. **2** To allow to remain behind: to *leave* a plow in a field. **3** To place or deposit so as to cause to remain behind: to *leave* word. **4** To cause to remain after departure, cessation, healing, etc.: The war *left* its mark. **5** To allow to continue or be as specified: *Leave* the light on. **6** To refer or entrust to another for doing, deciding, etc.: I *leave* the matter to you. **7** To terminate connection, employment, etc., with: to *leave* a job. **8** To have as a remainder: Three minus two *leaves* one. **9** To have remaining after death: to *leave* a large family. **10** To bequeath. —*v.i.* **11** To depart or go away. —**leave off** To cease. —**leave out 1** To omit from consideration. **2** To fail to include. [< OE *læfan*, lit., let remain] —**leav′er** *n.* —**Syn. 2** abandon, desert, forsake, relinquish. **11** withdraw, flee, set out. • The use of *leave* as a synonym for *let* in the sense of refraining from disturbing, bothering, etc., is only acceptable when *leave* is followed by a noun or pronoun and also by the word "alone." Thus, *Leave your little brother alone* may be substituted for *Let your little brother alone*. However, such a substitution can result in ambiguity since *leave alone*, in this context, may be interpreted to mean that the little brother is to be left by himself.

leave² (lēv) *n.* **1** Permission to do something. **2** Permission to be absent from duty or the period when such permission is effective: also **leave of absence.** —**take leave 1** To depart; go away. **2** To abandon; quit: with *of:* He *took leave* of his senses. [< OE *lēaf* permission]

leave³ (lēv) *v.i.* **leaved**, **leav·ing** To put forth leaves.

leaved (lēvd) *adj.* **1** Having leaves. **2** Having a certain number or kind of leaves.

leav·en (lev′ən) *n.* **1** An agent that lightens baked goods by forming gas bubbles in it, as yeast or baking powder. **2** A piece of yeasty dough; sourdough. **3** Any influence or addition that causes general change of the whole. —*v.t.* **1** To add a leaven to; make light. **2** To affect in character; imbue. [< L *levare* raise] —**leav′en·ing** *n.*

leaves (lēvz) *n. pl.* of LEAF.

leave-tak·ing (lēv′tā′king) *n.* A taking leave; a farewell.

leav·ing (lē′ving) *n.* **1** The act of departure. **2** *pl.* Things left; scraps. **3** *pl.* Refuse; offal.

Leb·a·nese (leb′ə·nēz′, -nēs′) *n.* A citizen or native of Lebanon. —*adj.* Of or pertaining to Lebanon or its people.

Leb·a·non (leb′ə·nən) *n.* A republic of sw Asia, 3,400 sq. mi., cap. Beirut. • See map at JORDAN.

Le·bens·raum (lā′bəns·roum) *n. German* Territory into which a nation claims it must expand to fulfill its economic needs; literally, space for living.

lech·er (lech′ər) *n.* A habitually lewd or excessively sensual man. [< OHG *leccôn* lick]

lech·er·ous (lech′ər·əs) *adj.* Given to or characterized by lewdness or lust. —**lech′er·ous·ly** *adv.* —**lech′er·ous·ness** *n.*

lech·er·y (lech′ər·ē) *n.* Free indulgence in lust; gross sensuality.

lec·i·thin (les′ə·thin) *n.* A complex ester containing phosphorus and nitrogen, an essential constituent of plant and animal cells, esp. abundant in nerve tissue, egg yolk, semen, etc. [< Gk. *lekithos* an egg's yolk + -IN]

lect. lecture; lecturer.

lec·tern (lek′tərn) *n.* A reading desk, esp. one in a church, from which parts of the service are read. [< L *lectus*, pp. of *legere* read]

lec·ture (lek′chər) *n.* **1** A talk delivered aloud for instruction or entertainment. **2** A lengthy reprimand. —*v.* **·tured**, **·tur·ing** *v.t.* **1** To deliver lectures to; instruct by lecturing. **2** To rebuke authoritatively or at length. —*v.i.* **3** To give a lecture. [< L *lectura* an act of reading] —**lec′tur·er, lec′ture·ship** *n.* —**Syn. 1** address, discourse, oration, speech.

---

add, āce, câre, pälm; end, ēven; it, īce; odd, ōpen, ôrder; tŏŏk, pōōl; up, bûrn; ə = a in *above*, u in *focus;* yŏŏ = u in *fuse;* oil; pout; check; go; ring; thin; ṭhis; zh, *vision.* < derived from; ? origin uncertain or unknown.

led (led) *p.t. & p.p.* of LEAD[1].

Le·da (lē′də) *Gk. Myth.* The mother of Clytemnestra, of Helen of Troy, and of Castor and Pollux.

ledge (lej) *n.* 1 A shelf. 2 Something resembling a shelf, as a ridge of rock or a projection from a building. 3 A lode or vein. [ME *legge*] —**ledg′y** *adj.*

ledg·er (lej′ər) *n.* The principal book of accounts of a business establishment, in which all transactions are entered to show the debits and credits of each account. [ME *legger*]

ledger line *Music* A short line added above or below a staff for notes too high or too low to be written on the staff.

lee (lē) *n.* 1 The direction opposite that from which the wind comes. 2 The side, as of a ship, that is sheltered from the wind. 3 Any shelter or protection. —*adj.* Pertaining to the side opposite to that from which the wind comes: a *lee* shore. [< OE *hlēo* a shelter]

leech[1] (lēch) *n.* 1 Any of various segmented, bloodsucking worms living in water or damp ground; esp. one formerly used in medicine for drawing blood. 2 One who clings to another in order to gain something. 3 *Archaic* A physician. —*v.t.* To bleed with leeches. [< OE *læce*, orig., a physician] —**leech′er** *n.*

leech[2] (lēch) *n. Naut.* 1 Either of the vertical edges of a square sail. 2 The after edge of a fore-and-aft sail. [ME *lich*]

leek (lēk) *n.* An edible plant of the lily family, closely allied to the onion. [< OE *lēac*]

leer (lir) *n.* A sly look or glance expressing lust, malicious intent, etc. —*v.i.* To look with a leer. [< OE *hlēor* a cheek, face] —**leer′ing·ly** *adv.*

leer·y (lir′ē) *adj.* **leer·i·er, leer·i·est** *Informal* Suspicious; wary. —**leer′i·ness** *n.*

lees (lēz) *n. pl.* Sediment, esp. of wine, dregs. [< OF *lie*]

lee·ward (lē′wərd, *Naut.* lōo′ərd) *adj. Naut.* Of or toward the direction in which the wind blows: opposed to *windward.* —*n.* The lee side or direction. —*adv.* Toward the lee; also **lee′ward·ly.**

lee·way (lē′wā) *n.* 1 The leeward drift of a vessel or aircraft. 2 Something, as extra time, space, or money, that provides for greater freedom of action; margin.

left[1] (left) *p.t. & p.p.* of LEAVE[1].

left[2] (left) *adj.* 1 Of, designating, for, or on that side of the body which is toward the north when one faces the rising sun. 2 Situated closer to the left hand of an observer than to his right: the *left* fork of a road. 3 Designating that side or bank of a river which is on the left when the observer faces downstream. —*n.* 1 The left side. 2 Anything on, toward, or for the left side. 3 *Often cap.* In politics, a liberal, socialistic, or radical position, or a party or group advocating such a position, so designated because of the views of the party occupying seats on the left side of the presiding officer in certain European legislative bodies: used with *the.* 4 In boxing, the left hand or a blow with the left hand. [< OE *lyft*]

left-hand (left′hand′) *adj.* 1 Of, for, or located on the left side or hand. 2 Turning, opening, or swinging to the left.

left-hand·ed (left′han′did) *adj.* 1 Having a tendency to use the left hand or arm more than the right. 2 Done with the left hand. 3 Adapted for use by the left hand, as a tool. 4 Clumsy; awkward. 5 Without sincerity; indirect: a *left-handed* compliment. 6 Turning or moving from right to left; counterclockwise. —**left′hand′ed·ly** *adv.* —**left′hand′ed·ness** *n.*

left·ist (lef′tist) *n.* In politics, one who is a member of or sympathetic to the left. —*adj.* Liberal or radical.

left-o·ver (left′ō′vər) *n.* A part not used or consumed. —*adj.* Remaining unconsumed.

left wing That part of any group advocating leftist policies. —**left′-wing′** *adj.* —**left′-wing′er** *n.*

left·y (lef′tē) *n. pl.* **·ies** *Slang* A left-handed person.

leg (leg) *n.* 1 One of the limbs of man or an animal used for supporting the body and for walking. 2 Something that resembles a leg or gives support: the *leg* of a table. 3 That portion of a garment or stocking which covers the leg. 4 *Naut.* The distance run by a vessel on one tack. 5 Any appreciable section of a journey. 6 *Geom.* Any side of a triangle except its base or hypotenuse. —**have not a leg to stand on** To have no valid excuse, argument, etc. —**on one's last legs** On the verge of failure, death, or collapse.

—**pull one's leg** *Slang* To fool or make fun of someone. —**shake a leg** *Slang* To make haste; hurry. —*v.i.* **legged, leg·ging** *Informal* To walk; run: often with *it.* [< ON *leggr*]

leg. legal; legate; legato; legislation.

leg·a·cy (leg′ə·sē) *n. pl.* **·cies** 1 Something left by will; a bequest. 2 Something handed down or derived from an ancestor or earlier time. [< L *legare* bequeath]

le·gal (lē′gəl) *adj.* 1 Created or permitted by law. 2 Of, pertaining to, or connected with law. 3 Capable of being remedied by a resort to statute law rather than to equity. 4 Of or suitable for lawyers: a *legal* approach. [< L *lex, legis* law] —**le′gal·ly** *adv.*

le·gal·ese (lē′gə·lēz′, -lēs′) *n.* A style of writing characteristic of members of the legal profession.

le·gal·ism (lē′gəl·iz′əm) *n.* A too strict or literal interpretation of or adherence to a law or code. —**le′gal·is′tic** *adj.* —**le′gal·ist** *n.*

le·gal·i·ty (li·gal′ə·tē) *n. pl.* **·ties** 1 The condition or quality of being legal. 2 Something legal, as a law.

le·gal·ize (lē′gəl·īz) *v.t.* **·ized, ·iz·ing** To make legal; sanction. *Brit. sp.* **·ise.** —**le′gal·i·za′tion** (-ə·zā′shən, -ī·zā′-) *n.*

legal tender Money that may not be legally refused by a creditor.

leg·ate (leg′it) *n.* 1 An official envoy or emissary. 2 A representative of the pope in various functions. [< L *legare* send as a deputy, bequeath] —**leg′ate·ship** *n.*

leg·a·tee (leg′ə·tē′) *n.* The recipient of a legacy.

le·ga·tion (li·gā′shən) *n.* 1 A diplomatic mission sent to a foreign country; also, those persons composing it. 2 The official residence or place of business of such a diplomatic mission, usu. ranking below an embassy.

le·ga·to (li·gä′tō) *adj. & adv. Music* In a smooth, connected manner. [< Ital. *legare* to bind]

leg·end (lej′ənd) *n.* 1 An unauthenticated story from early times, preserved by tradition and popularly thought to have a basis in fact. 2 Such stories, collectively. 3 An unusually famous or notable person, thing, or event. 4 An inscription or motto on a coin or monument. 5 A key to a map or chart. 6 A title, brief explanation, etc., accompanying an illustration. [< L *legere* read]

leg·en·dar·y (lej′ən·der′ē) *adj.* 1 Of, based on, or known from legends. 2 Traditional.

leg·er·de·main (lej′ər·də·mān′) *n.* 1 Sleight of hand. 2 Any artful trick or deception. [< F *léger de main*, lit., light of hand] —**leg′er·de·main′ist** *n.*

leg·ged (leg′id, legd) *adj.* Having a specified kind or number of legs: used in combination: *two-legged.*

leg·ging (leg′ing) *n. Usu. pl.* A warm or protective covering for the leg.

leg·gy (leg′ē) *adj.* **·gi·er, ·gi·est** 1 Having disproportionately long legs. 2 Having shapely legs: said of women.

leg·horn (leg′ərn, -hôrn) *n.* 1 A fine plaiting of wheat straw. 2 A bonnet or hat made of this plaiting. 3 *Often cap.* One of a breed of small, hardy, domestic fowls. [< *Leghorn,* a port in NW Italy]

leg·i·ble (lej′ə·bəl) *adj.* Capable of being deciphered or read with ease. [< L *legere* to read] —**leg′i·bil′i·ty, leg′i·ble·ness** *n.* —**leg′i·bly** *adv.*

le·gion (lē′jen) *n.* 1 A division of the ancient Roman army, comprising between 4,200 and 6,000 men. 2 *Usu. pl.* A large military force. 3 A great number; multitude. [< L *legere* choose, levy an army]

le·gion·ar·y (lē′jən·er′ē) *adj.* Of pertaining to, or being a legion. —*n. pl.* **·ar·ies** A soldier of a legion.

le·gion·naire (lē′jən·âr′) *n.* A member of a legion.

legis. legislation; legislative.

leg·is·late (lej′is·lāt) *v.* **·lat·ed, ·lat·ing** *v.i.* 1 To make a law or laws. —*v.t.* 2 To bring about or effect by legislation.

leg·is·la·tion (lej′is·lā′shən) *n.* 1 The making of a law or laws. 2 The law or laws made by a legislative power. [< L *lex, legis* a law + *latus* carried]

leg·is·la·tive (lej′is·lā′tiv) *adj.* 1 Having the power to make or enact laws. 2 Of, pertaining to, or suitable to legislation. 3 Of or pertaining to a legislature. 4 Created or enforced by legislation. —*n.* LEGISLATURE.

leg·is·la·tor (lej′is·lā′tər) *n.* A member of a legislature.

leg·is·la·ture (lej′is·lā′chər) *n.* A body of persons empowered to make laws for a country or state.

le·git (lə·jit′) *Slang n.* The legitimate theater. —*adj.* Legitimate.

le·git·i·mate (lə·jit′ē·mit) *adj.* 1 Having the sanction of law, lawful. 2 Born in wedlock. 3 Genuine; valid. 4 Logically correct; reasonable. 5 Based on or resulting from strict hereditary rights: a *legitimate* heir to the throne. 6 In the theater, designating or of plays or musicals produced live on a stage, as distinguished from motion pictures, etc. —*v.t.* (lə·jit′ə·māt) ·mat·ed, ·mat·ing 1 To make legitimate. 2 To justify. [< L *legitimus* lawful] —**le·git′i·ma·cy, le·git′i·mate·ness** *n.* —**le·git′i·mate·ly** *adv.* —**Syn.** 1 legal, licit, rightful. 3 authentic, bona fide, real.

le·git·i·mist (lə·jit′ə·mist) *n.* One who supports legitimate authority or supports a person having a legitimate claim to a throne. Also **le·git′i·ma·tist.** —**le·git′i·mism** *n.* —**le·git′i·mis′tic** *adj.*

le·git·i·mize (lə·jit′ə·mīz) *v.t.* ·mized, ·miz·ing 1 To make legitimate. 2 To make acceptable or tolerable: to assert that some TV programs *legitimize* violence. Also **le·git′i·ma·tize** (-mə·tīz). —**le·git′i·mi·za′tion** *n.*

leg-of-mut·ton (leg′ə·mut′n) *adj.* Being full at one end and tapering at the other, as a leg of mutton: a *leg-of-mutton* sleeve or sail.

leg·ume (leg′yŏŏm, lə·gyŏŏm′) *n.* 1 The fruit of a leguminous plant, a pod splitting open along two sutures, as a bean pod. 2 Any leguminous plant. [< L *legumen*, lit., a gatherable thing]

le·gu·mi·nous (lə·gyŏŏ′mə·nəs) *adj.* 1 Of or pertaining to legumes. 2 Belonging to the group of plants bearing fruit in a pod and usu. having compound leaves.

leg·work (leg′wûrk′) *n. Informal* The physical activity incidental to doing research.

lei (lā, lā′ē) *n. pl.* **leis** In Hawaii, a garland or wreath of flowers and leaves, usu. worn around the neck. [< Hawaiian]

lei·sure (lē′zhər, lezh′ər) *n.* Time during which one is free from the demands of work or duty. —**at leisure** 1 Free from work or duties. 2 Not employed. —**at one's leisure** When it is convenient or easy. —*adj.* 1 Free or unoccupied: *leisure* time. 2 Having leisure: the *leisure* class. [< L *licere* be permitted]

lei·sure·ly (lē′zhər·lē, lezh′ər-) *adj.* Without hurry; deliberate; slow: also **lei′sured** (-zhərd) —*adv.* In a leisurely manner. —**lei′sure·li·ness** *n.*

leit·mo·tif (līt′mō·tēf′) *n.* 1 *Music* A recurring theme used to indicate a certain person, attribute, or idea, as in an opera. 2 Something recurring like a musical theme. Also **leit′mo·tiv′.** [< G *Leitmotiv* leading motif]

LEM (lem) lunar excursion module.

lem·an (lem′ən, lē′mən) *n. Archaic* A lover; esp., a mistress. [< OE *lēof* beloved + *mann* a man]

lem·ming (lem′ing) *n.* Any of several small, mouselike, arctic rodents with a short tail and furry feet. [Norw.]

lem·on (lem′ən) *n.* 1 A citrus fruit with a yellow rind and very acid pulp and juice. 2 The tree that produces this fruit. 3 A bright yellow. 4 *Slang* Something or someone disappointing or unpleasant. —*adj.* 1 Flavored with or containing lemon. 2 Bright yellow. [< Pers. *līmūn*]

lem·on·ade (lem′ən·ād′) *n.* A drink made of lemon juice, water, and sugar.

le·mur (lē′mər) *n.* A small, mostly nocturnal mammal related to the monkeys, with fox-like face and soft fur, found chiefly in Madagascar. [< L *lemures* ghosts]

lend (lend) *v.* **lent, lend·ing** *v.t.* 1 To grant the temporary use of. 2 To grant the use of (money) at interest. 3 To impart; furnish. 4 To accommodate (oneself or itself): The statement *lends* itself to misinterpretation. —*v.i.* 5 To make a loan or loans. [< OE *lǣnan*] —**lend′er** *n.*

Ring-tailed lemur

lend-lease (lend′lēs′) *n.* In World War II, the furnishing of goods and services to any

country whose defense was deemed vital to the defense of the U.S.

length (lengkth) *n.* 1 Linear extension from end to end, usu. the greatest dimension of a surface or body. 2 The state or quality of being long. 3 Duration in time. 4 Distance in space. 5 A long expanse. 6 A piece or section of something: a *length* of rope. 7 The linear extent of something specified or understood, used as a unit of measure: an arm's *length.* —**at length** 1 Finally; at last. 2 In full. —**go to great lengths** (or **any length**) To do everything that is needed. [< OE *lengthu* < *lang* long]

length·en (lengk′thən) *v.t. & v.i.* To make or become longer. —**Syn.** elongate, expand, extend, stretch.

length·wise (lengkth′wīz′) *adj. & adv.* In the direction of the length. Also **length′ways** (-wāz′).

length·y (lengk′thē) *adj.* **length·i·er, length·i·est** Long, esp. unduly long. —**length′i·ly** *adv.* —**length′i·ness** *n.*

le·ni·en·cy (lē′nē·ən·sē, lēn′yən-) *n. pl.* **·cies** 1 The quality of being lenient; mercifulness. 2 A lenient act. Also **le′ni·ence.**

le·ni·ent (lē′nē·ənt, lēn′yənt) *adj.* Not exacting full retribution; merciful or mild. [< L *lenis* soft, mild] —**le′ni·ent·ly** *adv.*

Len·in·ism (len′in·iz′əm) *n.* The social and political doctrines based upon the teachings of Lenin. —**Len′in·ist, Len′in·ite** *n., adj.*

len·i·tive (len′ə·tiv) *adj.* Soothing; mitigating. —*n.* That which soothes or mitigates. [< L *lenire* soothe]

len·i·ty (len′ə·tē) *n.* The state or quality of being lenient. [< L *lenitas* softness]

lens (lenz) *n.* 1 A piece of glass or other transparent substance, having one surface curved and the other plane, or both curved, by which rays of light may be made to converge or to diverge. 2 Two or more lenses used in combination. 3 Any device for concentrating or dispersing radiation. 4 A biconvex transparent body, whose function is to focus light rays upon the retina. [< L *lens* a lentil; so called from the similarity in form] •See EYE.

Lenses
a. biconvex.
b. biconcave.

lent (lent) *p.t. & p.p.* of LEND.

Lent (lent) *n. Eccl.* A period of forty days (excluding Sundays), observed in Christian churches from Ash Wednesday to Easter as a season of penitence and self-denial. [< OE *lengten* the spring]

Lent·en (len′tən) *adj.* 1 Of or suitable for Lent. 2 Plain; meager. Also **lent′en.**

len·til (len′təl) *n.* 1 A leguminous plant with small, lens-like, edible seeds. 2 The seed itself. [< L *lens, lentis* a lentil]

len·to (len′tō) *adj. & adv. Music* Slow; slowly. [Ital.< L *lentus*]

l'en·voi (len′voi; *Fr.* län·vwá′) *n.* A postscript to or the closing stanza of certain poems. Also **l'en′voy.**

Le·o (lē′ō) *n.* A constellation and the fifth sign of the zodiac; the Lion. [L, a lion] •See ZODIAC.

Le·o·nid (lē′ə·nid) *n.* One of the meteors that form a shower about November 14. [< LEO, whence they appear to radiate]

le·o·nine (lē′ə·nīn) *adj.* Of, pertaining to, or like a lion. [< L *leo, leonis* a lion]

leop·ard (lep′ərd) *n.* 1 A ferocious mammal of the cat family of Asia and Africa, having a fawn, dark-spotted coat. 2 The jaguar. [< Gk. *leōn* a lion + *pardos* a panther]

le·o·tard (lē′ə·tärd) *n. Often pl.* A closefitting garment, usu. with long sleeves and legs, worn as practice clothes by dancers, acrobats, etc. [< J. *Léotard*, 19th c. French aerialist]

Leopard *def. 1*

lep·er (lep′ər) *n.* One afflicted with leprosy. [< Gk. *lepros* scaly]

lep·i·dop·ter·ous (lep′ə·dop′tər·əs) *adj.* Of or pertaining to an order of insects, the butterflies and moths, having four wings covered with minute scales. Also **lep'i-dop'ter-al.** [< Gk. *lepis, lepidos* scale + *pteron* wing] **—lep'i-dop'ter-an** *n., adj.*

lep·re·chaun (lep'rə-kôn) *n.* In Irish folklore, a fairy cobbler who, if caught and held, must reveal the location of treasure. [< O Irish *lu* little + *corpán*, dim. of *corp* body]

lep·ro·sy (lep'rə-sē) *n.* A chronic, bacterial disease characterized by skin lesions, nerve paralysis, and physical mutilation. [< L *lepra* leper]

lep·rous (lep'rəs) *adj.* 1 Having leprosy. 2 Of or like leprosy. Also **lep'er·ous** (-ər-əs). **—lep'rous·ly** *adv.* **—lep'rous·ness** *n.*

-lepsy *combining form* Seizure; attack: *catalepsy.* Also **-lepsia.**

les·bi·an (lez'bē-ən) *Often cap.* *n.* A homosexual woman. **—adj.** Of or pertaining to lesbians. [< *Lesbos*, the home of Sappho, reputed to have been homosexual]

les·bi·an·ism (lez'bē-ən-iz'əm) *n.* *Often cap.* Homosexuality among women.

lese-maj·es·ty (lēz'maj'is-tē) *n.* An offense against the sovereign power; treason. Also *Fr.* **lèse-ma·jes·té** (lez'ma·zhes·tā') [< L *laedere* injure + *majestas* majesty]

le·sion (lē'zhən) *n.* 1 A hurt; injury. 2 Any abnormal or injurious change in an organ or tissue. [< L *laedere* injure]

Le·so·tho (le·sō'tō) *n.* An independent member of the Commonwealth of Nations in s Africa, 11,716 sq. mi., cap. Maseru. • See map at AFRICA.

less (les) Comparative of LITTLE. **—adj.** 1 Not as large or great in size, quantity, or degree. 2 Inferior in rank, importance, etc. **—n.** A smaller part or amount. **—adv.** To an inferior or smaller degree or extent; not so much. **—prep.** Minus: nine *less* six. [< OE *læssa*]

-less *suffix* 1 Deprived of; without: *motherless.* 2 That does not or is not: *harmless.* 3 Beyond the range of (the action of the main element): *countless.* [< OE *lēas* free from]

les·see (les·ē') *n.* One holding property under a lease. [< OF *lesser, laissier* let, leave]

less·en (les'ən) *v.t.* 1 To make less; decrease. 2 To make little of; disparage. **—v.i.** 3 To become less. **—less'en·er** *n.* **—less'en·ing** *adj., n.* **—Syn.** 1 abate, diminish, dwindle, shrink, wane. 2 belittle, depreciate.

less·er (les'ər) *adj.* Less; smaller; inferior.

Lesser Bear The constellation Ursa Minor.

les·son (les'ən) *n.* 1 A specific assignment or division in a course of instruction. 2 *pl.* A course of instruction: painting *lessons.* 3 Knowledge gained by experience. 4 A portion of the Bible read or appointed to be read in divine service. 5 A reprimand. [< L *lectio* a reading]

les·sor (les'ôr, les-ôr') *n.* One who grants a lease.

lest (lest) *conj.* 1 For fear that: We hid it *lest* he should see it. 2 That: following expressions indicating alarm or anxiety: We were worried *lest* the money run out. [< OE *(thy) læs the* (by the) less that]

let[1] (let) *v.* **let, let·ting** *v.t.* 1 To allow; permit. 2 To allow to go, come, or pass: They would not *let* us on board. 3 To cause; make: She *let* him know the truth. 4 To cause to escape or be released: to *let* blood. 5 To rent (a room, house, etc.). 6 To assign, as a contract, esp. after bidding. 7 As an auxiliary verb, *let* is used to express command, suggestion, or acquiescence: *Let* it pour!; *Let* Bonnie play the lead. **—v.i.** 8 To be rented or leased. **—let alone** 1 To refrain from disturbing, bothering, etc. 2 To say nothing of; not to mention: He can't float, *let alone* swim. **—let be** 1 To leave alone. 2 To stop; cease. **—let down** 1 To lower. 2 To reduce effort or concentration. 3 To disappoint. **—let off** 1 To discharge or reduce, as pressure. 2 To excuse from an engagement, duty, or penalty; dismiss. **—let on** *Informal* 1 To pretend. 2 To reveal; allow to be known. **—let out** 1 To release. 2 To reveal; divulge. 3 To make (a garment) larger by releasing a part. 4 To rent or lease. 5 *Informal* To dismiss or be dismissed, as a school. **—let up** *Informal* To cease applying pressure or harsh measures to. [< OE *lætan*] • See LEAVE.

let[2] (let) *n.* 1 Anything that obstructs or hinders. 2 In tennis or other racket games, a stroke or point that does not count and must be played over. **—without let or hindrance** With no hindrance or obstruction. **—v.t.** *Archaic* **let** or **let·ted, let·ting** To hinder or impede; obstruct. [< OE *lettan* hinder]

-let *suffix of nouns* 1 Small; little: *kinglet.* 2 A band or small article for (a specific part of the body): *wristlet.* [< OF]

let·down (let'doun') *n.* 1 Decrease, as of speed or energy. 2 *Informal* Disillusionment; disappointment.

le·thal (lē'thəl) *adj.* 1 Causing death; fatal. 2 Pertaining to death. [< L *lethum, letum* death] **—le'thal·ly** *adv.*

le·thar·gic (li·thär'jik) *adj.* Affected by lethargy. Also **le·thar'gi·cal.** **—le·thar'gi·cal·ly** *adv.*

leth·ar·gize (leth'ər·jīz) *v.t.* **·gized, ·giz·ing** To make lethargic.

leth·ar·gy (leth'ər·jē) *n.* *pl.* **·gies** 1 A state of abnormal drowsiness or prolonged sleep. 2 Great indifference; apathy. [< Gk. *lēthē* oblivion] **—Syn.** 1 coma, stupor. 2 inactivity, sluggishness.

Le·the (lē'thē) *Gk. Myth.* The river of forgetfulness, one of the five rivers surrounding Hades. **—n.** Oblivion; forgetfulness. **—Le·the·an** (lē'thē·ən, li·thē'-) *adj.*

let's (lets) Contraction of *let us.*

Lett (let) *n.* 1 A native or inhabitant of Latvia and adjacent Baltic regions. 2 LETTISH.

let·ter (let'ər) *n.* 1 A mark or character used to represent a speech sound and usu. part of an alphabet. 2 A written or printed communication, usu, sent by mail. 3 A document granting authority, right, privilege, or the like. 4 Literal or exact meaning. 5 *pl.* Literary knowledge or erudition; also, literature in general: the domain of *letters.* 6 An emblem given in schools to athletes, etc., usu. in the form of the initial letter of the school. **—v.t.** 1 To write with letters. 2 To mark with letters. [< L *littera* a letter of the alphabet, in pl., an epistle] **—let'ter·er** *n.*

letter carrier A person whose work is to deliver mail.

let·tered (let'ərd) *adj.* 1 Able to read and write; literate. 2 Having literary learning. 3 Inscribed with letters.

let·ter·head (let'ər·hed') *n.* 1 A printed heading, usu. a name and address, at the top of a sheet of letter paper. 2 A sheet of paper with such a heading.

let·ter·ing (let'ər·ing) *n.* 1 The act of drawing letters or of marking or stamping with letters. 2 Letters so drawn, marked, or stamped.

letter of credit A letter issued by a bank authorizing the bearer to draw money up to a certain amount from other banks.

let·ter-per·fect (let'ər·pûr'fikt) *adj.* 1 Perfectly memorized, as a speech, dramatic role, etc. 2 Correct in every detail.

let·ter·press (let'ər·pres') *n.* 1 Letters and words printed, as distinguished from illustrations. 2 Printing made from type or plates with a raised surface.

letters of marque A governmental document licensing an individual to arm a vessel and prey upon enemy merchant shipping.

letters patent An open document, under seal of the government, granting some special right, authority, privilege, or property.

Let·tish (let'ish) *adj.* Of or pertaining to the Letts or their language. **—n.** The Baltic language of the Letts.

let·tuce (let'is) *n.* 1 A garden plant of several varieties whose crisp, edible leaves are used for salad. 2 *Slang* Paper money. [< L *lac, lactis* milk; with ref. to its milky juice]

let-up (let'up') *n.* *Informal* 1 A stopping; cessation. 2 A brief pause or lull.

le·u (le'oo) *n.* *pl.* **lei** (lā) A silver coin, the basic monetary unit of Rumania. Also **ley.**

leu·co·cyte (loo'kə·sīt') *n.* LEUKOCYTE.

leu·ke·mi·a (loo·kē'mē·ə) *n.* Any of various diseases of the bloodmaking tissues, characterized by a marked increase in the number of leukocytes, usu. accompanied by anemia and swelling of lymph nodes, spleen, etc. **—leu·ke'mic** *adj.*

leu·ko·cyte (loo'kə·sīt) *n.* Any of various colorless cells formed in the bone marrow and lymph nodes and found in the blood and various tissues, where they constitute an important agent against infection. [< Gk. *leukos* white + -CYTE]

Lev, Lev., Levit. Leviticus.

le·vant (lə·vant') *n.* A morocco leather having a somewhat irregular grain. Also **Levant morocco.** [< the LEVANT]

Le·vant (lə·vant') *n.* The regions on the E Mediterranean, from w Greece to w Egypt: with *the*. —**Le·van·tine** (lə·van′tin, lev′ən·tīn, -tēn) *adj., n.*

le·va·tor (lə·vā′tər) *n. pl.* **le·va·to·res** (lev′ə·tôr′ēz, -tō′rēz) or **le·va·tors** *Anat.* A muscle that raises an organ or part. [< L *levare* to raise]

lev·ee[1] (lev′ē) *n.* **1** An embankment built beside a river to prevent overflow. **2** A steep natural bank. —*v.t.* To furnish with a levee or levees. [< L *levare* to raise]

lev·ee[2] (lev′ē, lə·vē′) *n.* A morning reception or assembly at the house of a sovereign or great personage. [< L *levare* to raise]

lev·el (lev′əl) *adj.* **1** Having a flat and even surface without any variations in height. **2** Conforming to a horizontal plane; not sloping. **3** Having the same height as or being in the same plane with something else. **4** Equal to something or someone in importance, development, rank, etc. **5** Calm; sensible; well-balanced. **6** Even or steady in tone, color, etc. —**one's level best** *Informal* One's very best. — *n.* **1** A horizontal line, surface, plane, or position. **2** A horizontal or flat area of land, etc. **3** The condition of being horizontal: Water seeks its own *level*. **4** Height or altitude. **5** A device for determining a horizontal line or plane; also, a measuring of variations in height by using such a device. **6** Rank or position in any scale of values. —**on the level** *Informal* Honest; fair. —*v.* **lev·eled** or **lev·elled**, **lev·el·ing** or **lev·el·ling** *v.t.* **1** To give a flat or horizontal surface to: often with *off*. **2** To reduce to the ground: to *level* a building. **3** To bring to a common condition, state, etc. **4** To knock down. **5** To aim or direct, as a rifle, the eyes, etc. —*v.i.* **6** To aim a weapon directly at a mark or target. **7** To bring persons or things to a common state or condition. **8** *Informal* To be honest: Let me *level* with you. —**level off** To fly a plane parallel with the ground. —*adv.* In or on a level line. [< L *libella*, dim. of *libra* balance] —**lev′el·ly** *adv.* —**lev′el·er, lev′el·ler, lev′el·ness** *n.* —**Syn.** *adj.* **1** horizontal, plane, smooth. *v.* **1** smooth. **2** demolish, raze.

lev·el-head·ed (lev′əl·hed′id) *adj.* Having sound common sense; not impulsive. —**lev′el-head′ed·ness** *n.*

lev·er (lev′ər, lē′vər) *n.* **1** A device consisting of a rigid structure, often a straight bar, turning freely on a fixed point (the fulcrum). A force applied at one point of the rigid structure does work at another with a mechanical advantage equal to the ratio of the distances of the points from the fulcrum. **2** Any one of various tools used for prying, as a crowbar. **3** Any means of exerting effective power. —*v.t. & v.i.* To move with or use a lever. [< L *levare* to raise]

Lever
a. force. b. fulcrum.
c. weight.

lev·er·age (lev′ər·ij, lē′vər-) *n.* **1** The action of a lever. **2** The mechanical advantage of a lever. **3** Increased power or advantage.

lev·er·et (lev′ər·it) *n.* A hare less than a year old. [< L *lepus* a hare]

Le·vi (lē′vī) In the Bible: **1** The third son of Jacob. **2** The tribe descended from him.

le·vi·a·than (lə·vī′ə·thən) *n.* **1** A large aquatic but unidentified animal mentioned in the Bible. **2** Anything colossal in size of its kind. [< Heb. *liwyāthān*]

Le·vis (lē′vīz) *n. pl.* Tight-fitting, heavy denim trousers, with rivets inserted at points of greatest strain: a trade name. Also **le′vis**. [< *Levi* Strauss, U.S. manufacturer]

lev·i·tate (lev′ə·tāt) *v.i. & v.t.* **·tat·ed**, **·tat·ing** To rise or cause to rise and float in the air. [L *levis* light, on analogy with *gravitate*] —**lev′i·ta′tor** *n.*

lev·i·ta·tion (lev′ə·tā′shən) *n.* **1** The act of levitating or the state of being levitated. **2** The illusion of suspending heavy objects or the human body in the air without support.

Le·vite (lē′vīt) *n.* One of the tribe or family of Levi, acting as assistant to the priests of the tribe.

Le·vit·i·cal (lə·vit′i·kəl) *adj.* Of the Levites, the book of Leviticus, or its laws.

Le·vit·i·cus (lə·vit′i·kəs) *n.* The third book of the Old Testament, containing ceremonial laws.

lev·i·ty (lev′ə·tē) *n. pl.* **·ties** **1** Lightness or humor; lack of gravity in mood, character, or behavior. **2** Fickleness. [< L *levis* light]

lev·u·lose (lev′yə·lōs) *n.* FRUCTOSE. [< L *laevus* left + -UL(E) + -OSE[2]]

lev·y (lev′ē) *v.* **lev·ied, lev·y·ing** *v.t.* **1** To impose (a tax, fine, etc.). **2** To enlist or call up (troops, etc.) for military service. **3** To prepare for or wage (war). —*v.i.* **4** To make a levy. **5** *Law* To seize property in order to fulfill a judgment: usu. with *on*. —*n. pl.* **lev·ies** **1** The act of levying (a tax, troops, etc.). **2** Something levied. [< L *levare* to raise] —**lev′i·er** *n.*

lewd (lood) *adj.* **1** Characterized by lust; lascivious. **2** Obscene; bawdy. [< OE *læwede* lay, unlearned] —**lewd′ly** *adv.* —**lewd′ness** *n.* —**Syn.** **1** carnal, lecherous, licentious, lustful. **2** indecent.

lew·is·ite (loo′is·īt) *n.* An organic compound containing arsenic, prepared as a blister-producing poison gas. [< W. L. *Lewis*, 1878–1943, U.S. chemist]

lex (leks) *n. pl.* **le·ges** (lē′jēz) Law. [L]

lex. lexicon.

lexicog. lexicographer; lexicography.

lex·i·cog·ra·phy (lek′sə·kog′rə·fē) *n.* The act, business, or principles of writing or compiling a dictionary. [< Gk. *lexikon* lexicon + *graphein* write] —**lex′i·cog′ra·pher** *n.* —**lex′i·co·graph′ic** (-kō·graf′ik) or **·i·cal** *adj.* —**lex′i·co·graph′i·cal·ly** *adv.*

lex·i·con (lek′sə·kon) *n.* **1** A word list or vocabulary pertaining to a specific subject, field, author, etc. **2** DICTIONARY. [< Gk. *lexikos* pertaining to words]

Ley·den jar (lī′dən) *Electr.* A condenser for static electricity, consisting of a glass jar coated inside and out with metal foil and with a conducting rod passing through the stopper and connected to the inner coating. [< *Leyden*, Netherlands]

LF, L.F., l.f., l-f. low frequency.

LG, LG., L.G. Low German.

lg. lge. large.

LGk. Late Greek.

lgth. length.

LH, L.H., l.h. left hand.

L.I. Long Island.

Li lithium.

Leyden jar
a. brass rod and ball.
b. metal foil.
c. discharging wire.

li·a·bil·i·ty (lī′ə·bil′ə·tē) *n. pl.* **·ties** **1** The state of being liable. **2** That for which one is liable. **3** *pl.* Debts or financial obligations. **4** Any drawback or obstacle.

li·a·ble (lī′ə·bəl) *adj.* **1** Justly or legally responsible, as for payment. **2** Inclined to get or have; subject to: *liable* to headaches. **3** Likely; apt: I am *liable* to see them. **4** Undesirably likely: *liable* to lose his money. [< L *ligare* to bind]

li·aise (lē·āz′) *v.i.* **·aised, ·ais·ing** *Chiefly Brit. Informal* To act as an agent or intermediary; communicate. [Back formation < LIAISON]

li·ai·son (lē′ə·zon, lē·ā′zon; *Fr.* lē·ā·zôn′) *n.* **1** A bond or close relationship; union. **2** An illicit sexual relationship. **3** Any form of intercommunication, as between military units, etc. **4** In cookery, a thickening agent. **5** In speaking French, the carrying over of a final consonant to a succeeding word beginning with a vowel or silent *h*. —*adj.* Of, bringing about, or involved in a liaison. [< L *ligare* to bind]

li·an·a (lē·an′ə, -ä′nə) *n.* A twining or climbing plant of tropical forests, with ropelike, woody stems. Also **li·ane** (lē·än′). [< F *liane*]

li·ar (lī′ər) *n.* One who tells lies.

lib (lib) *n. Slang* LIBERATION (def. 2). —**lib′ber** *n.*

Lib. Liberal; Liberia.

lib. book (L *liber*); librarian; library.

li·ba·tion (lī·bā′shən) *n.* **1** The act of pouring out liquid, as in honor of a deity. **2** The liquid poured out. **3** Humorously, a drink. [< L *libare* pour out (as an offering)]

li·bel (lī′bəl) *n. Law* **1** Anything written, drawn, etc., esp. if published or publicly circulated, that tends to damage a person's reputation. **2** The act or crime of publishing or circulating such libel. —*v.t.* **·beled** or **·belled, ·bel·ing** or **·bel·ling 1** To publish or circulate a libel concerning. **2** To defame or disparage in any way. [< L *libellus,* dim. of *liber* book] —**li'bel·er, li'bel·ler** *n.* • See SLANDER.

li·bel·ous (lī'bəl·əs) *adj.* **1** Containing that which defames or libels. **2** Given to uttering libels. Also **li'bel·lous. —li'bel·ous·ly, li'bel·lous·ly** *adv.*

lib·er·al (lib'ər·əl, lib'rəl) *adj.* **1** Generous in giving; bounteous. **2** Abundant; lavish: a *liberal* reward. **3** Of or based on the liberal arts: a *liberal* education. **4** Characterized by or favoring policies of reform and progress and generally opposing conservatism or reaction. **5** Not bigoted or prejudiced; broad-minded. **6** Not restricted to the literal meaning: a *liberal* interpretation of a rule. —*n.* One favoring liberal policies or doctrines, as in politics, religion, etc. Also **lib'er·al·ist.** [< L *liber* free] —**lib'er·al·is'tic** *adj.* —**lib'er·al·ly** *adv.*

Lib·er·al (lib'ər·əl, lib'rəl) *adj.* Of or pertaining to any of various political parties, esp. the Liberal Party of Great Britain or of Canada. —*n.* A member of such a party.

liberal arts The course of study that includes literature, philosophy, languages, history, etc., as distinguished from purely scientific or technical subjects; the humanities.

lib·er·al·ism (lib'ər·əl·iz'əm, -rəl-) *n.* **1** Liberal beliefs or principles, as in politics, religion, etc. **2** The quality or condition of being liberal.

lib·er·al·i·ty (lib'ə·ral'ə·tē) *n. pl.* **·ties 1** The quality of being liberal. **2** Generosity. **3** Broad-mindedness. **4** A gift; donation.

lib·er·al·ize (lib'ər·əl·īz') *v.t. & v.i.* **·ized, ·iz·ing** To make or become liberal. —**lib'er·al·i·za'tion** (lib'ər·əl·ə·zā'shən, -ī·zā'-, lib'rəl-), **lib'er·al·iz'er** *n.*

Liberal Party 1 In Great Britain, a political party formed about 1832, but whose power, since 1918, has declined with the rise of the Labour Party. **2** One of the principal political parties of Canada.

lib·er·ate (lib'ə·rāt) *v.t.* **·at·ed, ·at·ing 1** To set free, as from bondage, foreign occupation, etc. **2** *Informal* To free from oppression or from conventions considered oppressive. **3** To release from chemical combination. [< L *liber* free] —**lib'er·a'tor** *n.*

lib·er·a·tion (lib'ər·ā'shən) *n.* **1** The act of liberating, or the state of being liberated. **2** A political and social movement formed to promote the interests of a group regarded as the object of unfair discrimination or bias: women's *liberation.* —**lib'er·a'tion·ist** *n.*

Li·be·ri·a (lī·bir'ē·ə) *n.* A republic of W Africa, 43,000 sq. mi., cap. Monrovia. —**Li·ber'i·an** *adj., n.* • See map at AFRICA.

lib·er·tine (lib'ər·tēn) *n.* One who does not restrain his desires or appetites; a debauchee. —*adj.* Dissolute; licentious. [< L *liber* free] —**lib'er·tin·ism** *n.*

lib·er·ty (lib'ər·tē) *n. pl.* **·ties 1** The state of being free in action or thought from the domination of others or from restricting circumstances; freedom. **2** The possession and exercise of the right of self-government. **3** A particular permission, right, or privilege. **4** In the U.S. Navy, permission to be absent from one's ship or station, usu. for less than 48 hours. **5** *Often pl.* Unusual or undue freedom or familiarity. —**at liberty 1** Free; unconfined. **2** Having permission to do something. **3** Not in use. **4** Unemployed. [< L *libertas* < *liber* free] —**Syn. 1** emancipation, independence, liberation, self-determination.

Liberty Bell The bell in Independence Hall, Philadelphia, rung July 4, 1776, when the Declaration of Independence was adopted.

Liberty Ship A U.S. merchant ship of about 10,000 tons displacement and built in large numbers during World War II.

li·bid·i·nous (li·bid'ə·nəs) *adj.* Lustful; lewd. [< L *libido* lust] —**li·bid'i·nous·ly** *adv.* —**li·bid'i·nous·ness** *n.*

li·bi·do (li·bē'dō, -bī'-) *n.* **1** *Psychoanal.* The instinctual craving or drive behind all human activities. **2** Sexual desire or instinct. [L, lust] —**li·bid'i·nal** (-bid'ə·nəl) *adj.*

Li·bra (lī'brə, lē'-) *n.* A constellation and the seventh sign of the zodiac; the Scales. [L, a balance] • See ZODIAC.

li·brar·i·an (lī'brâr'ē·ən) *n.* **1** A person in charge of a library. **2** A person qualified by training for library service.

li·brar·y (lī'brer·ē, -brə·rē) *n. pl.* **·brar·ies 1** A collection of books, pamphlets, computer programs, etc., esp. one arranged for easy location of desired material. **2** A building, room, etc., containing such a collection. [< L *liber* book]

li·bret·tist (li·bret'ist) *n.* A writer of librettos.

li·bret·to (li·bret'ō) *n. pl.* **·tos** or **·ti** (-ē) **1** The words of an opera, oratorio, etc. **2** A book containing these words. [Ital. < L *liber* book]

Lib·y·a (lib'ē·ə) *n.* A republic of N Africa, 679,358 sq. mi., caps. Tripoli and Benghazi. —**Lib'y·an** *adj., n.* • See map at AFRICA.

lice (līs) *n.pl.* of LOUSE.

li·cense (lī'səns) *n.* **1** A legal permit to do something. **2** A written or printed certificate of a legal permit. **3** Unrestrained liberty of action; disregard of propriety. **4** Allowable deviation from an established rule, form, or standard: poetic *license.* —*v.t.* **·censed, ·cens·ing** To grant a license to or for; authorize. Also **li'cence. —li'cens·a·ble** *adj.* —**li'cens·er, li'cenc·er** *n.*

li·cen·see (lī'sən·sē') *n.* One to whom a license is granted. Also **li'cen·cee'.**

li·cen·ti·ate (lī·sen'shē·it, -āt) *n.* **1** A person licensed to practice a certain profession: a *licentiate* in dental surgery. **2** In some Continental universities, a person holding a degree intermediate between bachelor and doctor.

li·cen·tious (lī·sen'shəs) *adj.* Morally or sexually unrestrained; wanton; lewd. [< L *licentia* freedom] —**li·cen'tious·ly** *adv.* —**li·cen'tious·ness** *n.*

li·chee (lē'chē) *n.* LITCHI.

li·chen (lī'kən) *n.* Any of numerous low-growing plants composed of an alga and a fungus growing symbiotically, usu. on surfaces inhospitable to higher plants, as bare rock. —*v.t.* To cover with lichens. [< Gk. *leichēn,* lit., licker] —**li'chen·ous** *adj.*

lic·it (lis'it) *adj.* Lawful; permitted. [< L *licere* be allowed] —**lic'it·ly** *adv.*

lick (lik) *v.t.* **1** To pass the tongue over the surface of. **2** To bring to a specified condition by passing the tongue over: to *lick* a surface clean. **3** To take in by the tongue. **4** To move or pass lightly over: The waves *licked* the shore. **5** *Informal* **a** To defeat. **b** To thrash; beat. —*v.i.* **6** To move quickly or lightly. —**lick into shape** *Informal* To put in proper form or condition. —**lick up** To consume or devour entirely. —*n.* **1** A stroke of the tongue in licking. **2** A small amount: a *lick* of paint. **3** SALT LICK. **4** *Informal* A blow or whack. **5** *Usu. pl. Informal* An opportunity or turn: to get in one's *licks.* **6** *Informal* A stroke: Not a *lick* of work was done. [< OE *liccian* to lick] —**lick'er** *n.*

lick·er·ish (lik'ə·rish) *adj.* **1** Eager to taste or enjoy. **2** Lustful. [Var. of LECHEROUS] —**lick'er·ish·ly** *adv.* —**lick'er·ish·ness** *n.*

lick·e·ty-split (lik'ə·tē·split') *adv. Slang* At full speed.

lick·spit·tle (lik'spit'l) *n.* A servile flatterer.

lic·o·rice (lik'ə·rish, -ris) *n.* **1** A perennial plant of the pea family. **2** Its root or a flavoring agent made from it. **3** A usu. black candy having this flavor. [< Gk. *glycyrrhiza* sweet root]

lic·tor (lik'tər) *n.* In ancient Rome, one of the officers or guards attending the chief Roman magistrates and bearing the fasces as a symbol of office. [L]

lid (lid) *n.* **1** A movable cover for putting on top of a pan, box, or other receptacle. **2** An eyelid. **3** *Slang* A hat. [< OE *hlid*] —**lid'ded** *adj.*

lie¹ (lī) *v.i.* **lay, lain, ly·ing 1** To be or place oneself in a horizontal position, as on a bed: often with *down.* **2** To be on or rest against a usu. horizontal surface: The book is *lying* on the shelf. **3** To be or continue in a specified condition or position: to *lie* in ambush. **4** To be situated: Rome *lies* in a plain. **5** To extend in some direction: Our route *lies* northward. **6** To have source or cause; exist: usu. with *in:* His trouble *lies* in his carelessness. **7** To be buried. —**lie** (or **lay**) **down on the job** *Informal* To do less than one's best. —**lie in wait (for)** To wait in ambush (for). —**lie low** *Slang* To go into hiding or remain inactive so as to conceal one's motives, plans, etc. —**lie over** To wait for attention, etc., until a later

Lictor

time. —*n.* The position or arrangement in which a thing lies; manner of lying; lay. [OE *licgan*] • See LAY[1].

lie[2] (lī) *n.* **1** An untrue statement intended to deceive; falsehood. **2** Anything that deceives or creates a false impression. —**give the lie to 1** To accuse of lying. **2** To expose as false. —*v.* **lied, ly·ing** *v.i.* **1** To make untrue statements knowingly, esp. with intent to deceive. **2** To give an erroneous or misleading impression: Figures do not *lie.* —*v.t.* **3** To obtain by lying: He *lied* his way out of trouble. [< OE *licgan*] —**Syn.** *n.* **1** fabrication, falsification, fib, untruth.

Liech·ten·stein (lik′ten·stīn; *Ger.* lēkh′ten·shtīn) *n.* A principality of CEN. Europe, 61 sq. mi., cap. Vaduz.

lied (lēd; *Ger.* lēt) *n. pl.* **lied·er** (lē′dər) *German* A lyric poem or ballad set to music.

Lie·der·kranz (lē′dər·kränts) *n.* A soft cheese with a strong flavor and odor: a trade name.

lie detector A polygraph for recording variations in the pulse, rate of respiration, electrical resistance of the skin, etc., that occur while responding to questions, interpretable as evidence of lying.

lief (lēf) *adv.* Willingly; freely: now only in the phrase **would** (or **had**) **as lief.** [< OE *lēof* dear]

liege (lēj) *adj.* **1** In feudal law: **a** Bound in vassalage to a lord. **b** Having the right to the allegiance of a vassal. **2** Faithful; loyal. —*n.* In feudal law: **1** A vassal; also, a citizen. **2** A lord. [< Med. L *laeticus* free]

lien (lēn, lē′ən) *n.* A legal claim on property, as security for a debt. [< L *ligare* to tie]

lieu (lōō) *n.* Place; stead: now only in the phrase **in lieu of.** [< L *locus*]

Lieut. Lieutenant.

lieu·ten·ant (lōō·ten′ənt, *Brit.* lef·ten′ənt) *n.* **1** See GRADE. **2** A person who fills the place of a superior, as during his absence. [< F *lieu* place + *tenant*, pr.p. of *tenir* hold] —**lieu·ten′an·cy** *n.*

lieutenant colonel See GRADE.

lieutenant commander See GRADE.

lieutenant general See GRADE.

lieutenant governor 1 An officer authorized to perform the duties of a governor in case of his absence, disability, or death. **2** In Canada, the official head of the government of a province, appointed by the governor general. —**lieu·ten′ant-gov′er·nor·ship′** *n.*

life (līf) *n. pl.* **lives** (līvz) **1** That state in which animals and plants exist which distinguishes them from inorganic substances and is characterized by metabolism, growth, and reproduction. **2** That vital state, the loss of which means death: to give one's *life.* **3** The period of animate existence from birth until death, or a part or specific aspect of it. **4** Any conscious and intelligent existence: *life* after death. **5** Energy and animation; spirit; to put *life* into an enterprise. **6** A source of liveliness, animation, etc.: to be the *life* of the party. **7** A vital property, principle, or essence of something: Rhythm is the *life* of jazz. **8** A living being; a person: Many *lives* were lost. **9** Living things in the aggregate: plant *life.* **10** Human existence or affairs: daily *life* in the city. **11** A certain manner or way of living: the *life* of a recluse. **12** A biography. **13** The duration of efficiency, usefulness, popularity, etc., of anything: the *life* of a machine. **14** In art, the form or shape of something that actually exists: to paint from *life.* —**for dear life** with great urgency or intensity. —**for life 1** For the remainder of one's existence. **2** To save one's life. —**take life** To kill. —**take one's own life** To kill oneself. —*adj.* **1** Lasting from a given point until death: a *life* sentence. **2** In art, studying from a living model: a *life* class. [< OE *līf*]

life belt A life preserver in the form of a belt.

life·blood (līf′blud′) *n.* **1** The blood necessary to life; vital blood. **2** The essence or vital principle of something.

life·boat (līf′bōt′) *n.* A strong, buoyant boat used in rescuing shipwrecked or drowning persons; esp., one of such boats carried on a ship.

life buoy A life preserver, usu. in the shape of a ring.

life expectancy The statistically probable length of life of a person.

life·guard (līf′gärd′) *n.* An expert swimmer hired by a

bathing resort, pool, etc., to protect the safety of bathers.

life insurance 1 Insurance in which a specified sum is paid to the beneficiary or beneficiaries after the death of the insured. **2** Insurance paid to the insured upon reaching a certain age. Also **life assurance.**

life jacket A life preserver in the form of a jacket.

life·less (līf′lis) *adj.* **1** Dead. **2** Inanimate: *lifeless* stone. **3** Wanting in energy, power, vigor, or spirit; dull. **4** Uninhabited by living things. —**life′less·ly** *adv.* —**life′less·ness** *n.* —**Syn.** **1** deceased, defunct. **2** inert. **3** listless, spiritless, torpid.

life·like (līf′līk′) *adj.* Resembling something living; true to life. —**life′like′ness** *n.*

Life jacket

life line 1 Any rope or line used, grasped by, or attached to persons in dangerous situations. **2** Any route for transporting vital supplies, rescuing persons, etc.

life·long (līf′lông′, -long′) *adj.* Lasting or continuing throughout one's life: a *lifelong* handicap.

life preserver A buoyant device, often inflatable, in the form of a belt, jacket, ring, etc., used to keep a person afloat in water.

lif·er (lī′fər) *n. Slang* One serving a prison sentence for life.

life·sav·er (līf′sā′vər) *n.* **1** One who or that which saves drowning persons. **2** *Informal* One who or that which aids a person in need, distress, etc. —**life′sav′ing** *n.*

life-size (līf′sīz′) *adj.* Of natural size; of the size of the object portrayed. Also **life′-sized′.**

life style A person's typical mode of conduct or behavior; a way of living.

life·time (līf′tīm′) *n.* The whole period of one's life. —*adj.* Lasting for the duration of one's life: a *lifetime* job.

life·work (līf′wûrk′) *n.* The work to which one devotes his entire working life.

lift (lift) *v.t.* **1** To raise to a higher position or place; hoist. **2** To hold up or support in the air. **3** To raise to a higher degree or condition; exalt. **4** To make clearly audible; shout: to *lift* a cry. **5** To subject (the face) to plastic surgery, so as to restore an appearance of youth. **6** *Informal* To take surreptitiously; steal; also, to plagiarize. **7** To pay off, as a mortgage. —*v.i.* **8** To put forth effort in order to raise something: All together now; *lift!* **9** To yield to upward pressure; rise. **10** To rise or disperse; dissipate: The fog *lifted.* —*n.* **1** The act or an instance of lifting or rising. **2** The distance through which something rises or is raised. **3** The amount lifted. **4** A machine or device for lifting. **5** A stimulation of the mind or feelings. **6** A rise in condition; promotion. **7** Elevated carriage or position: the *lift* of her chin. **8** Any assistance. **9** A ride in a vehicle offered to a pedestrian. **10** *Brit.* An elevator. **11** A slight rise in the ground. **12** In shoemaking, any layer of material forming the heel. **13** *Aeron.* The vertical component of the aerodynamic force on an aircraft. [< ON *lypta* raise in the air] —**lift′er** *n.*

lift-off (lift′ôf′, -of′) *n.* The vertical ascent of a rocket or spacecraft.

lig·a·ment (lig′ə·mənt) *n.* **1** A band of tough tissue binding together bones, etc., or holding organs in place. **2** A bond or connecting tie. [< L *ligare* to bind] —**lig′a·men′tal, lig′a·men′ta·ry, lig′a·men′tous** *adj.*

li·gate (lī′gāt, lī·gāt′) *v.t.* **·gat·ed, ·gat·ing** To tie with a ligature. —**li·ga′tion** *n.*

lig·a·ture (lig′ə·chər) *n.* **1** The act of tying, binding, or constricting. **2** Something used for this, esp. a thread or wire used in surgery. **3** *Printing* Two or more connected letters, as fi, ffi, œ. **4** *Music* A slur or the notes joined by a slur. —*v.t.* **·tured, ·tur·ing** LIGATE. [< L *ligare* to bind]

light[1] (līt) *n.* **1** *Physics* **a** The form of electromagnetic radiation that stimulates the organs of sight, having wavelengths between about 3,900 and 7,700 angstroms. **b** Ultraviolet or infrared light radiation. **2** The natural condition that permits vision; luminosity. **3** The sensation produced by exciting the organs of vision and visual centers of the brain. **4** A source of light, as the sun, a lamp, beacon, etc. **5** That which admits light, as a window. **6** Daylight; dawn. **7** A point of view; aspect; to see things in a new *light*. **8** A flame to kindle something. **9** A traffic signal. **10** A noteworthy or eminent person. **11** In art, the representation of light. **12** A particular expression on the face or in the eyes: a *light* of recognition. —**according to one's lights** In accord with one's principles, abilities, etc. — **come to light** To be exposed or revealed. —**in the light of** In view of; considering —**see the light (of day) 1** To be born or to begin. **2** To comprehend; become enlightened. **3** To come into public knowledge. —**shed light on** To make plain or clear. —*adj.* **1** Full of light; not dark; bright. **2** Giving off light. **3** Of a faint or pale color. —*v.* **light·ed** or **lit, light·ing** *v.t.* **1** To set burning; ignite; kindle. **2** To illuminate or cause to be illuminated: to *light* a lamp. **3** To brighten or animate. **4** To guide or conduct with light: The fires *lighted* him home. —*v.i.* **5** To take fire; start burning. **6** To become bright or luminous; usu. with *up*. [<OE *lēoht*] —**light′er** *n.* —**light′less** *adj.*

light² (līt) *adj.* **1** Having little weight; not heavy. **2** Not heavy in relation to size, bulk, etc.: a *light* car. **3** Below the proper or usual weight: a *light* coin. **4** Having little force: a *light* blow. **5** Not clumsy or heavy in appearance or construction: a *light* building. **6** Less than normal or usual in amount: a *light* snowfall. **7** Easy to digest: a *light* dessert. **8** Well leavened; not coarse: *light* bread. **9** Low in alcoholic content: a *light* wine. **10** Not long or loud: *light* applause. **11** Soft and clear, as a sound or voice. **12** Loose or porous: *light* soil. **13** Easy to do, bear, handle, etc.: a *light* task. **14** Not important or serious: *light* party chatter. **15** Gay; cheerful: a *light* mood. **16** Flighty; giddy: *light* in the head. **17** Loose in morals. **18** Easy; nimble: *light* on one's feet. **19** Meant primarily for entertainment: *light* reading. **20** Easily awakened: a *light* sleeper. **21** Not heavily armed: *light* troops. **22** *Meteorol.* Designating a breeze moving from 4 to 7 miles an hour. —**make light of** To treat or consider as trifling. —*v.i.* **light·ed** or **lit, light·ing 1** To descend and settle down after flight, as a bird; land. **2** To happen or come, as by chance: with *on* or *upon*. **3** To get down, as from a horse; dismount. **4** To fall; strike, as a blow. —**light into** *Slang* To attack. **2** To scold. —**light out** *Slang* To depart in haste. —*adv.* Lightly. [<OE *lēoht, līht*] —**Syn.** *adj.* **4** soft, weak. **6,10** mild, moderate. **15** happy, airy, carefree. **light-armed** (līt′ärmd′) *adj.* Carrying light weapons. **light·en¹** (līt′n) *v.t.* **1** To illuminate. **2** To make light or more light, as a color. —*v.i.* **3** To become light or more light. **4** To flash or shine. **5** To flash lightning. **light·en²** (līt′n) *v.t.* **1** To make less heavy. **2** To reduce the load of: to *lighten* ship. **3** To make less burdensome or oppressive. **4** To relieve from distress; gladden. —*v.i.* **5** To become less heavy. —**Syn. 3** alleviate, lessen, reduce. **4** cheer, encourage, enliven. **light·er¹** (līt′ər) *n.* One who or that which lights something, esp. a device for lighting a cigarette, cigar, or pipe. **light·er²** (līt′ər) *n.* A bargelike vessel used in loading or unloading ships lying offshore. —*v.t. & v.i.* To transport (goods) by lighter. [<Du. *lichten* make light, unload]

light·er·age (līt′ər·ij) *n.* **1** The price for unloading a ship by lighters. **2** The removal or conveying of a cargo by lighters. **light·face** (līt′fās′) *n. Printing* Type having light, thin lines. — **light′faced′** *adj.*

light-fin·gered (līt′fing′gərd) *adj.* Skilled at petty theft, esp. at picking pockets. **light-foot·ed** (līt′fŏŏt′id) *adj.* Nimble or swift in running or dancing. —**light′-foot′ed·ly** *adv.* —**light′-foot′ed·ness** *n.* **light-head·ed** (līt′hed′id) *adj.* **1** Silly; frivolous. **2** Dizzy; delirious. —**light′-head′ed·ly** *adv.* —**light′-head′ed·ness** *n.* **light-heart·ed** (līt′här′tid) *adj.* Free from care; gay. — **light′heart′ed·ly** *adv.* —**light′heart′ed·ness** *n.* **light heavyweight** A boxer or wrestler weighing between 161 and 175 pounds.

Lighter

light·house (līt′hous′) *n.* A tower equipped with high-power lamps, for guiding ships at night.

light·ing (līt′ing) *n.* **1** Illumination. **2** A distribution of light, as in a picture. **3** An arrangement of lights, esp. on a stage; also, the devices providing such light. **light·ly** (līt′lē) *adv.* **1** With little weight, force, or pressure. **2** In a slight degree or amount. **3** Gaily; cheerily. **4** With no difficulty; easily. **5** With a light or swift step or motion. **6** Carelessly; heedlessly. **7** Wantonly; irreverently. **8** For slight reasons. **light-mind·ed** (līt′mīn′did) *adj.* Lacking seriousness; frivolous; silly. —**light′-mind′ed·ly** *adv.* —**light′-mind′ed·ness** *n.* **light·ness¹** (līt′nis) *n.* **1** The state or quality of being bright or illuminated. **2** Paleness, as of a color.

Lighthouse

light·ness² (līt′nis) *n.* **1** The state or quality of having little weight. **2** Cheerfulness. **3** Lack of seriousness; levity. **4** Nimbleness or grace. **5** Lack of severity or harshness. **light·ning** (līt′ning) *n.* **1** A sudden discharge of electricity between clouds or between a cloud and the earth. **2** The flash made by this. —*adj.* Fast; rapid: a *lightning* movement. [<ME *lighten* to flash] **lightning bug** FIREFLY. **lightning rod** A sharp-pointed, grounded metallic conductor used to protect buildings from lightning. Also **lightning conductor**. **light opera** OPERETTA. **light pen** A pen-shaped electronic device used to generate graphics by drawing with it on a computer screen. **light·ship** (līt′ship′) *n.* A vessel, having warning lights, signals, etc., moored in dangerous waters as a guide to ships. **light·some** (līt′səm) *adj.* **1** Lighthearted. **2** Nimble. **3** Frivolous. —**light′some·ly** *adv.* —**light′some·ness** *n.* **light·weight** (līt′wāt′) *n.* **1** A boxer or wrestler weighing between 127 and 135 pounds. **2** *Slang* An unimportant, incompetent, or stupid person. —*adj.* **1** Having little weight. **2** Of or pertaining to lightweights. **3** Trivial. **light-year** (līt′yir′) *n.* The distance that light travels in one year, 5.878 trillion miles: used as a unit of astronomical distance.

lig·ne·ous (lig′nē·əs) *adj.* Composed of or like wood; woody. [<L *lignum* wood] **lig·nite** (lig′nīt) *n.* A brownish coal, often retaining the original woody texture, and intermediate between peat and true coal. [<L *lignum* wood] —**lig·nit′ic** (-nit′ik) *adj.* **lig·num vi·tae** (lig′nəm vī′tē) *n.* **1** A small tropical American tree. **2** Its greenish brown, hard, heavy wood. [L, lit., wood of life] **like¹** (līk) *v.* **liked, lik·ing** *v.t.* **1** To take pleasure in; enjoy. **2** To have affection or kindly feeling for. **3** To wish; prefer: He would *like* us to do it. —*v.i.* **4** To feel inclined; choose: Do as you *like!* —*n. Usu. pl.* Preference; inclination: one's *likes* and dislikes. [<OE *līcian*] —**lik′a·ble, like′a·ble** *adj.* — **lik′a·ble·ness, like′a·ble·ness, lik′er** *n.* —**Syn.** *v.* **1** appreciate, relish, savor. **2** care for, fancy, love. **like²** (līk) *adj.* **1** Similar in qualities, appearance, etc. **2** Identical or nearly identical; equal: Take a *like* amount of plaster. **3** *Regional:* Likely or about to; expected: I am *like* to cry. —**like . . . , like . . .** As the one is, so the other will be: *like* father, *like* son. —*adv.* **1** In the manner of; as if: To run *like* mad. **2** *Informal* Likely: *Like* as not we'll meet again. **3** *Slang* To a certain extent; somewhat: he was fat, *like*. **4** *Slang* Approximately; about: We had *like* two weeks to get ready. **5** *Slang* The point is; you must understand that: modifying a whole clause: *Like*, he had nowhere to go. —*prep.* **1** Similar to; resembling: you look *like* your father. **2** Characteristic of: That's just *like* him! **3** In the mood or frame of mind for: to feel *like* sleeping. **4** So as to indicate, promise, or presage: to look *like* rain. **5** Such as: furs *like* beaver. —**like anything** (or **blazes, the devil,** etc.) *Informal* With great speed, force, violence, etc. —*n.* That which is similar to equivalent to, or of the same nature as, something else. —**the like** (or **likes**) **of** *Informal* Any thing or person like. —*v.i. Regional* To

come near: He *liked* (or *had liked*) to have died. —*conj.*
1 *Informal* As; in the manner that: It all happened *like*
you said. **2** *Informal* As if: It looks *like* he's going to fall.
[< OE *gelīc*] • **like, as** *Like* is nonstandard as a conjunction at the formal level of writing, where clauses being
compared are related by *as: He entertained us with great
charm, as we knew he would.* At the informal level, because *like* signals a coming comparison more strongly
than *as, like* is in widespread use. Moreover, *like* is well
accepted informally when it serves to complete a linking
verb with the sense of *as if: It sounds like a train's coming; It looks like we're in for trouble.*

-like *suffix of adjectives* Resembling or similar to: *childlike, wavelike, shell-like.*
like·li·hood (līk′lē·hŏŏd) *n.* Probability: In all *likelihood,*
he will be late.
like·ly (līk′lē) *adj.* **-li·er, -li·est 1** Apparently true or real;
probable. **2** Reasonably to be expected; liable. **3** Apt to
please; promising. **4** Suitable: a *likely* place to swim. —
adv. Probably.
like-mind·ed (līk′mīn′did) *adj.* Similar in opinions,
tastes, etc.
lik·en (lī′kən) *v.t.* To represent as similar; compare.
like·ness (līk′nis) *n.* **1** The state or quality of being like;
a resemblance. **2** A copy, picture, or representation. **3**
Form; guise: to appear in the *likeness* of an eagle.
like·wise (līk′wīz′) *adv.* **1** In like manner. **2** Also; moreover.
lik·ing (lī′king) *n.* **1** Fondness. **2** Taste; preference.
li·lac (lī′lak, -lək, -lok) *n.* **1** An ornamental shrub having
clusters of small, fragrant, usu. purplish flowers. **2** The
flower. **3** A light purple color, like that of a lilac. —*adj.* Of
a light purple color. [< Pers. *līlak* bluish]
lil·i·a·ceous (lil′ē·ā′shəs) *adj.* Of or pertaining to lilies or
plants of the lily family, as onions, hyacinths, etc.
Lil·li·put (lil′i·put, -pət) In Swift's *Gulliver's Travels,* a
country inhabited by tiny people.
Lil·li·pu·tian (lil′i·pyōō′shən) *adj.* **1** Of Lilliput or its inhabitants. **2** Very small. —*n.* **1** An inhabitant of Lilliput.
2 A very small person.
lilt (lilt) *n.* **1** A brisk, merry song. **2** Rhythmic movement,
swing, or flow. —*v.t. & v.i.* To sing or speak in a light,
rhythmic manner. [ME *lulte*]
lil·y (lil′ē) *n. pl* **lil·ies 1** Any of a large genus of bulbous
plants having showy, usu. trumpetlike flowers. **2** The
flower of these plants. **3** Any of
numerous plants resembling the
true lilies: *waterlily.* **4** The heraldic fleur-de-lis. —*adj.* Like a
white lily; pure and delicate. [< L
lilium]
lil·y-liv·ered (lil′ē·liv′ərd) *adj.*
Cowardly.
lily of the valley A low liliaceous plant with two leaves and a
raceme of white, fragrant, cup-
shaped flowers.

Tiger lily

lil·y-white (lil′ē-hwīt′) *adj.* **1** White as a lily. **2** Pure; unsullied: often used ironically. **3** Composed of or admitting
white people only: a *lily-white* college.
li·ma bean (lī′mə) **1** A common cultivated bean with
broad pods. **2** Its large flat edible seed. Also **Li′ma bean.** [<
Lima, Peru]
limb[1] (lim) *n.* **1** A leg, arm, or wing. **2** A large, major
branch of a tree. **3** A person or thing forming a part,
branch, or extension of something else. —**out on a limb**
Informal In a risky position or situation. —*v.t.* To dis-
member. [< OE *lim*]
limb[2] (lim) *n.* An edge, as of a disk; esp. the edge of the disk
of the moon or other heavenly body. [< L *limbus* edge]
limbed (limd) *adj.* Having a specified number or kind of
limbs: used in combination: *strong-limbed, four-limbed.*
lim·ber[1] (lim′bər) *adj.* **1** Easily bent; flexible. **2** Lithe and
agile; supple. —*v.t. & v.i.* To make or become limber: often
with *up.* [?] —**lim′ber·ly** *adv.* —**lim′ber·ness** *n.* —**Syn.** *adj.* **1**
elastic, pliable, pliant. **2** lissom, nimble.

lim·ber[2] (lim′bər) *n.* A two-wheeled, detachable vehicle at
the forepart of a gun carriage. —*v.t. & v.i.* To attach a
limber. [?]
lim·bo (lim′bō) *n.* **1** *Often cap. Theol.* A region on the edge
of hell to which are consigned the souls of the righteous
who died before the coming of Jesus and the souls of
infants who died before baptism. **2** A place of neglect or
oblivion for unwanted persons or things. [< L *limbus* bor-
der]
Lim·burg·er cheese (lim′bûr′gər) A soft, white cheese
with a strong odor. Also **Lim′burg cheese.** [< *Limburg,* Bel-
gium]
lime[1] (līm) *n.* Calcium oxide in either its dry state (**quick-
lime**) or combined with water (**slaked lime**), used in mortar, cement, and as a conditioner for acid soil. —*v.t.* **limed,
lim·ing** To treat or mix with lime. [< OE *līm*]
lime[2] (līm) *n.* **1** A small, acid, citrus fruit with a green rind.
2 The small, semitropical tree bearing this fruit. [< Ar.
limah]
lime[3] (līm) *n.* LINDEN. [< OE *lind* linden]
lime·kiln (līm′kil′, -kiln′) *n.* A kiln for burning limestone,
seashells, etc., to produce lime.
lime·light (līm′līt′) *n.* **1** A powerful light produced by
burning lime, originally used in the theatre as a spotlight.
2 A position of prominence or notoriety.
lim·er·ick (lim′ər·ik) *n.* A humorous verse of five anapes-
tic lines. [< *Limerick,* a county in Ireland]
lime·stone (līm′stōn′) *n.* A rock composed wholly or in
part of calcium carbonate.
lime·wa·ter (līm′wô′tər, -wot′ər) *n.* A saturated solution
of lime in water, used as an antacid.
lim·ey (lī′mē) *n. Slang* **1** A British sailor: from the former
practice of averting scurvy on long voyages by eating
limes. **2** Any Englishman.
lim·it (lim′it) *n.* **1** A boundary enclosing a specified area.
2 *pl.* An area near or enclosed by a boundary: city *limits.*
3 The utmost point, degree, or extent beyond which something no longer functions, avails, etc.: to reach the *limit*
of one's patience. **4** The maximum amount permitted: a
limit of two cans per person. **5** *Math.* A number such that
the difference between it and the final term of a sequence
of numbers becomes arbitrarily small as the sequence is
made arbitrarily long. —**off limits** Forbidden to military
personnel except on official business. —**the limit** *Slang*
One who or that which is considered intolerable, exasperating, etc. —*v.t.* To keep within a limit; restrict. [< L
limes, limites] —**lim′it·a·ble, lim·i·ta·tive** (lim′ə·tā′tiv) *adj.* —
lim′it·er *n.* —**Syn.** *v.* check, circumscribe, restrain, restrict.
lim·i·ta·tion (lim′ə·tā′shən) *n.* **1** The act of limiting or the
condition of being limited. **2** Something that limits; restriction. **3** *Law* A period of time fixed by law within which
certain acts are to be performed to render them valid.
lim·it·ed (lim′it·id) *adj.* **1** Having or confined to certain
limits; restricted. **2** Held in check by law or or a constitution, as a government, monarchy, etc. **3** Making only a few
specific stops or carrying only a certain number of passengers, as a train. **4** *Brit. & Can.* Restricted in liability to the
amount invested in stock of a business: a *limited* company. —*n.* A limited train, bus, etc. —**lim′i·ted·ly** *adv.* —
lim′i·ted·ness *n.*
lim·it·ing (lim′it·ing) *adj. Gram.* Designating adjectives
that limit or specify rather that describe, as *several, this,
two,* etc.
lim·it·less (lim′it·lis) *adj.* Without limits; infinite; boundless.
limn (lim) *v.t.* **1** To draw or paint. **2** To describe in words.
[< L *lumen* light] —**lim·ner** (lim′ər, -nər) *n.*
Li·moges ware (lē·mōzh′; *Fr.* lē·môzh′) A type of fine
porcelain manufactured at Limoges, France.
lim·ou·sine (lim′ə·zēn′, lim′ə·zēn) *n.* **1** A large automobile, originally with a closed compartment for passengers,
and a roof projecting over the driver's open seat. **2** Any
large, luxurious automobile. [< *Limousin,* France]
limp[1] (limp) *v.i.* **1** To walk with a halting or irregular gait.
2 To proceed in a defective or irregular manner: His logic
limps. —*n.* The step of a lame person. [?] —**limp′er** *n.*

limp² (limp) *adj.* **1** Lacking stiffness; flaccid. **2** Not positive, firm, or vigorous. [?] —**limp′ly** *adv.* —**limp′ness** *n.*

lim·pet (lim′pit) *n.* Any of several usu. marine gastropods with a small conical shell, that clings to underwater plants, rocks, etc. [< LL *lampreda* lamprey]

lim·pid (lim′pid) *adj.* **1** Characterized by liquid clearness; transparent. **2** Clear and intelligible; lucid: a *limpid* style. [< L *limpidus* clear] —**lim·pid·i·ty** (lim·pid′ə·tē), **lim′pid·ness** *n.* —**lim′pid·ly** *adv.*

lim·y (lī′mē) *adj.* **lim·i·er**, **lim·i·est** **1** Containing or covered with lime or birdlime. **2** Resembling lime.

lin. lineal; linear.

lin·age (lī′nij) *n.* **1** The number of lines of printed or written matter. **2** Payment based on lines written.

linch·pin (linch′pin′) *n.* A pin through that part of an axle outside the wheel, to keep a wheel in place. [< OE *lynis* linchpin + PIN]

lin·den (lin′dən) *n.* Any of a genus of trees with heart-shaped leaves and usu. fragrant, cream-colored flowers. [< OE *lind* linden, lime tree]

line¹ (līn) *n.* **1** A string, rope, or cord, as used for hanging clothes, fishing, measuring, etc. **2** A pipe, wire, cable, etc., for conveying electricity, gas, oil, etc. **3** In a telephone or telegraph system: **a** A wire or cable conducting communication signals between two stations. **b** The system as a whole. **c** A connection in such a system. **4** Any slender mark or stroke, as drawn with a pen, pencil, tool, etc. **5** Something resembling this, as a band or strip. **6** A furrow or wrinkle on the face or hands. **7** In art, a mark or stroke used to represent a form or forms, as distinguished from shading or color. **8** *Music* One of the parallel horizontal strokes that form a musical staff. **9** A boundary or border: the Mason-Dixon *line.* **10** Contour; outline: the shore *line.* **11** *Geog.* **a** The equator. **b** Any circle, arc, or boundary used to plot the earth's surface: the date *line.* **12** *Math.* A set of points, straight or curved, conceived of as having length without breadth or thickness. **13** A row of persons or things. **14** A row of printed or written words bounded by the margins of a page or column. **15** A single row of words forming a verse of poetry. **16** A short letter; note. **17** *pl.* The words of a play or of an actor's part. **18** Alignment. **19** Agreement; conformity: Bring him into *line.* **20** A division or demarcation between contrasting qualities, classes, etc. **21** A course of action, thought, procedure, etc.: a *line* of argument. **22** A course of movement; route: the *line* of march. **23** General plan, concept, or construction: a novel on heroic *lines.* **24** One's business, vocation, or branch of activity. **25** Extent or scope of one's talent, ability, etc.: Comedy is not in his *line.* **26** Merchandise of a particular type or quality: the cheap *line.* **27** A series of persons or things connected chronologically: the *line* of senators from Ohio. **28** Lineage; ancestry. **29** A railroad track or roadbed. **30** Any system of public transportation. **31** *Mil.* **a** A series of fortifications presenting an extended front. **b** A trench or rampart. **c** An arrangement or disposition of troops: the front *line.* **d** Combat forces, as distinguished from the staff, special services, etc. **32** In football: **a** The linemen collectively. **b** LINE OF SCRIMMAGE. **33** *Informal* **a** A glib manner of speech. **b** The words spoken in this manner, intended to sway or influence —**draw the (a) line** To establish a limit. —**get a line on** *Informal* To get information about. —**hold the line 1** To stand firm. **2** To prevent others from advancing. —**in line for** Next in succession for. —**toe the line** To obey; behave. —*v.* **lined**, **lin·ing** *v.t.* **1** To mark with lines. **2** To place in a line; bring into alignment or conformity: often with *up.* **3** To form a line along: Police *lined* the side of the road. **4** To place something in a line along: to *line* a wall with archers. **5** In baseball, to bat (the ball) in a line drive. —*v.i.* **6** To form a line: usu. with *up.* —**line out** In baseball, to be retired by batting a line drive to a fielder. —**line up 1** To form a line. **2** To bring into alignment. **3** To organize for or against some activity, issue, etc. [< L *linea* linen thread]

line² (līn) *v.t.* **lined**, **lin·ing** **1** To apply a covering or layer to the inside surface of. **2** To serve as a covering or surface for: Paintings *lined* the wall. **3** To fill or supply: to *line* one's pockets with candy. [< OE *līn* flax]

lin·e·age (lin′ē·ij) *n.* **1** Direct descent from a progenitor. **2** Ancestry; family. [< L *linea* line]

line·age² (lī′nij) *n.* LINAGE.

lin·e·al (lin′ē·əl) *adj.* **1** Of or being in a direct line of descent. **2** Based upon or derived from ancestors; hereditary. **3** Made of lines; linear. —**lin′e·al·ly** *adv.*

lin·e·a·ment (lin′ē·ə·mənt) *n.* **1** An outline or contour, esp. of the face. **2** A distinguishing feature of the face.

lin·e·ar (lin′ē·ər) *adj.* **1** Pertaining to or composed of lines. **2** Very narrow and long: a *linear* leaf. • See LEAF. **3** Denoting a measurement in one dimension.

linear measure 1 Measurement by length. **2** A unit or system of units for measuring length.

line·back·er (līn′bak′ər) *n.* In football, a defensive player whose normal position is just behind the line of scrimmage. —**line′back′ing** *n.*

line drive In baseball, a ball batted with such force as to travel almost parallel to the ground.

line·man (līn′mən) *n. pl.* **·men** (-mən) **1** In surveying, a man who holds the tape, line, or chain. **2** A man who installs or repairs lines, as for electricity, telephones, etc. **3** A man who inspects railroad tracks. **4** In football, one of the players making up the line, which includes the center, two guards, two tackles and two ends.

lin·en (lin′in) *n.* **1** A thread or fabric spun or woven from the fibers of flax. **2** Articles made of linen but now often of cotton: bed *linen,* table *linen.* —*adj.* Made of linen. [< OE *līn* flax]

line of force *Physics* A line in a field of force tangent to the direction of the force at each of its points.

line of scrimmage In football, the imaginary line, parallel to the goal lines, on which the ball rests and along which the opposing linemen take position at the start of play.

lin·er¹ (lī′nər) *n.* **1** A ship, aircraft, etc., operated commercially by a specific line. **2** One who or that which marks or traces lines. **3** In baseball, a line drive.

lin·er² (lī′nər) *n.* **1** One who makes linings. **2** A lining, or a piece used in forming a lining.

lines·man (līnz′mən) *n. pl.* **·men** (-mən) **1** In tennis, the official watching the lines of the court for faults. **2** In football, the official marking the distances gained or lost in each play. **3** LINEMAN.

line·up (līn′up′) *n.* **1** In football, basketball, etc.: **a** The arrangement of players when drawn up for action. **b** Those players who are going to start in the game. **2** Suspects in crime lined up for identification and questioning. **3** An array of people united by some common aim or purpose. Also **line′-up′.**

ling¹ (ling) *n.* **1** A codlike food fish of the North Atlantic. **2** BURBOT. [ME *leng*]

ling² (ling) *n.* HEATHER. [< ON *lyng*]

-ling *suffix of nouns:* **1** Little; young; *duckling.* **2** A person or thing related to or characterized by: *worldling.* [< OE]

lin·ger (ling′gər) *v.i.* **1** To stay on as if reluctant to leave. **2** To move slowly; saunter: to *linger* on the way. **3** To delay or be slow: often with *over:* to *linger* over a meal. **4** To continue in life —*v.t.* **5** To pass (time) slowly or idly: with *away* or *out.* [< OE *lengen* to delay] —**lin′ger·er** *n.* —**Syn.** **1** dawdle, delay. **2** hang back, lag, loiter.

lin·ge·rie (län′zhə·rē) *n.* Women's underwear. [< F *linge* linen]

lin·go (ling′gō) *n. pl.* **lin·goes 1** Language, esp. if strange or unintelligible. **2** The specialized vocabulary and idiom of a profession, class, etc.: medical *lingo.* [< L *lingua* tongue]

lin·gua fran·ca (ling′gwə frang′kə) **1** A mixture of French, Spanish, Italian, Greek, and Arabic, spoken in the Mediterranean ports. **2** Any mixed jargon used as a commercial or trade language, such as pidgin English. [Ital., lit., language of the Franks]

lin·gual (ling′gwəl) *adj.* **1** Pertaining to the tongue. **2** Pertaining to the use of the tongue in utterance. —*n.* *Phonet.* A sound pronounced chiefly with the tongue, as (t), (d), and (l). [< L *lingua* the tongue]

lin·guist (ling′gwist) *n.* **1** One who knows many languages. **2** An authority in linguistics. [< L *lingua* the tongue + -IST]

lin·guis·tic (ling·gwis′tik) *adj.* Of or pertaining to language or to linguistics. Also **lin·guis′ti·cal.** —**lin·guis′ti·cal·y** *adv.*

lin·guis·tics (ling·gwis′tiks) *n. pl.* (*Construed as singular*) The science of language, its origin, structure, modifications, etc., including phonetics, phonemics, morphology, syntax, and semantics.

lin·i·ment (lin′ə·mənt) *n.* A medicated liquid used externally to soothe sprains, muscular soreness, etc. [<L *linire* anoint]

lin·ing (lī′ning) *n.* Material used to line something, often by being attached: the *lining* of a skirt.

link¹ (lingk) *n.* **1** One of the loops or rings of which a chain is made. **2** Something which connects separate things; a tie: a *link* with the past. **3** A single part or element in a whole: the weak *link* in his story. **4** A section of a chain of sausages. **5** A measure equal to 7.92 inches, used in surveying. **6** *Chem.* BOND. —*v.t. & v.i.* To connect by or as by links; unite. [<Scand.] —**Syn.** *v.* attach, combine, fuse, join.

link² (lingk) *n.* A torch. [?]

link·age (ling′kij) *n.* **1** The act of linking, or the state of being linked. **2** A series or system of links.

linking verb A verb that merely connects the subject and the predicate complement of a sentence without asserting action, as the verbs *be, appear, become, feel,* etc.

links (lingks) *n. pl.* GOLF COURSE. [<OE *hlic* slope]

link·up (lingk′up′) *n.* **1** A linking together; contact: the *linkup* of space vehicles. **2** A pooling or combining, as of resources or efforts.

lin·net (lin′it) *n.* Any of various small, Old World songbirds related to finches. [<L *linum* flax; from its feeding on flax seeds]

lino. linotype.

li·no·le·um (li·nō′lē·əm) *n.* A floor covering with a smooth, washable surface, made of oxidized linseed oil, ground cork, pigments, etc., pressed into a flat sheet. [<L *linum* flax + *oleum* oil]

Li·no·type (lī′nə·tīp) *n.* A typesetting machine, operated by a keyboard, which casts a complete line of type on a single metal bar: a trade name. Also **li·no·type.** —**li′no·typ′er, li′no·typ′ist** *n.*

lin·seed (lin′sēd′) *n.* FLAXSEED. [<OE *līn* flax + SEED]

linseed oil An oil made from flaxseed, used in oil paints, linoleum, etc.

lin·sey-wool·sey (lin′zē·wŏŏlzē) *n. pl.* —**wool·seys** A cloth made of linen and wool or cotton and wool mixed. [ME *lynsy-wolsye*]

lint (lint) *n.* **1** The soft down of raveled or scraped linen. **2** Fuzzy bits of thread, cloth, etc. [<L *linum* flax] —**lint′y** *adj.* (**·i·er, ·i·est**)

lin·tel (lin′təl) *n.* horizontal top piece, as over a doorway or window opening. [<L *limes, limites* limit]

lint·ers (lin′tərz) *n. pl.* Cotton fuzz and fibers left behind on a cotton gin, used as batting, for stuffing upholstery, etc.

li·on (lī′ən) *n.* **1** A large, tawny carnivore of the cat family, native to Africa and Asia, the adult male having a long mane. **2** An animal resembling the lion, as the cougar. **3** A person of great courage, strength, etc. **4** A prominent or notable person. [<Gk. *leōn*]

Lion

Li·on (lī′ən) *n.* LEO.

li·on·ess (lī′ən·is) *n.* A female lion.

li·on·heart·ed (lī′ən·härt′tid) *adj.* Brave; courageous.

li·on·ize (lī′ən·īz) *v.t.* **·ized, ·iz·ing** To treat or regard as a celebrity. —**li′on·i·za′tion** *n.*

lip (lip) *n.* **1** One of the two folds of flesh that cover the mouth. **2** Something resembling a lip, as the edge of a wound. **3** Any edge or rim of a cavity or something hollow. **4** A projecting or flared edge, as on a bell, pitcher, spout, etc. **5** EMBOUCHURE. **6** *Slang* Impertinent speech; sass. **7** *Anat.* LABIUM. **8** *Bot.* Any liplike structure, as the lower petal of an orchid. —**bite one's lips** To refrain from showing anger, annoyance, etc. —**hang on (someone's) lips** To listen with great attention. —**keep a stiff upper lip** To keep up one's courage; be stoical. —*v.t.* **lipped, lip·ping** To touch with the lips; esp., to kiss. —*adj.* **1** Of,

formed by, or applied to the lips. **2** Superficial; insincere: *lip* service. [<OE *lippa*]

lip·oid (lip′oid) *adj.* Of or like fat. [<Gk. *lipos* fat + -OID]

lip·o·suc·tion (lip′ō·suk′shən) *n.* The surgical removal of fat cells from bodily tissue by vacuum suction.

lipped (lipt) *adj.* Having a lip or lips: used in combination: *tight-lipped.*

lip-read (lip′rēd) *v.t. & v.i.* **-read, -read·ing** To interpret (speech) by lip reading.

lip reading Interpretation of speech by watching the position of the lips and mouth of the speaker, practiced esp. by the deaf. —**lip reader**

lip·stick (lip′stik′) *n.* A small, colored cosmetic stick of creamy texture, used to tint lips.

lip-sync (lip′singk) *v.t. & v.i.* To synchronize movements of the lips and mouth with sound recorded earlier, esp. a singer's voice.

liq. liquid; liquor.

liq·ue·fac·tion (lik′wə·fak′shən) *n.* The process of liquefying or the state of being liquefied.

liq·ue·fy (lik′wə·fī) *v.t. & v.i.* **·fied, ·fy·ing** To convert into or become liquid. [<L *liquere* be liquid + *facere* make]

li·ques·cent (li·kwes′ənt) *adj.* Being or having a tendency to become liquid. —**li·ques′cence, li·ques′cen·cy** *n.*

li·queur (li·kûr′) *n.* A strong alcoholic beverage, usu. sweet and having various flavorings; a cordial. [<OF *licur* liquor]

liq·uid (lik′wid) *adj.* **1** Flowing or capable of flowing. **2** *Physics* Composed of molecules having free movement among themselves, but without a tendency to expand indefinitely like a gas. **3** Limpid; clear. **4** Smooth and flowing, as movements or sounds. **5** *Phonet.* Vowellike in production, as the consonants (l) and (r). **6** Easily converted into cash: *liquid* assets. —*n.* **1** A liquid substance. **2** *Phonet.* The consonants (l) and (r). [<L *liquere* be liquid] —**liq·uid·i·ty** (li·kwid′ə·tē), **liq′uid·ness** *n.* —**liq′uid·ly** *adv.*

liq·ui·date (lik′wə·dāt) *v.* **·dat·ed, ·dat·ing** *v.t.* **1** To determine and settle the liabilities of (an estate, firm, etc.) and apportion the assets. **2** To determine and settle the amount of, as indebtedness or damages. **3** To pay, as a debt. **4** To convert into cash. **5** To do away with, esp. to murder. —*v.t.* **6** To settle one's debts. [<Med. L *liquidare* make liquid or clear] —**liq′ui·da′tor** *n.*

liq·ui·da·tion (lik′wə·dā′shən) *n.* The act of liquidating or the state of being liquidated. —**go into liquidation** To cease from transacting business and gather in assets, settle debts, and divide surpluses, if any.

liquid measure A unit or system of units for measuring liquids. • See MEASURE.

liq·uor (lik′ər) *n.* **1** Any alcoholic drink, esp. one that is distilled. **2** A liquid, as broth, milk, etc. —*v.t.* **1** *Slang* To ply with alcoholic liquor: often with *up.* —*v.i.* **2** *Slang* To drink alcoholic liquor, esp. in quantity: usu. with *up.* [<L *liquor*]

liq·uo·rice (lik′ə·ris, -rish) *n.* LICORICE.

li·ra (lir′ə; *Ital.* lē′rä) *n. pl.* **li·re** (lir′ə; *Ital.* lē′rā) **1** A small coin and the basic monetary unit of Italy. **2** The Turkish pound, the basic monetary unit of Turkey. **3** *pl.* **lir·oth** or **lir·ot** The Israeli pound, the basic monetary unit of Israel.

lisle (līl) *n.* A fine, strong, twisted cotton thread, used in knitting stockings, etc. [<*Lisle*, now Lille, France]

lisp (lisp) *n.* **1** A speech defect or affectation in which the sibilants (s) and (z) are pronounced like (th) in *thank* and (th) in *this.* **2** The act or habit of speaking with a lisp. **3** The sound of a lisp. —*v.t. & v.i.* **1** To pronounce or speak with a lisp. **2** To speak imperfectly or in a childlike manner. [<OE *wlispian*] —**lisp′er** *n.*

lis·some (lis′əm) *adj.* **1** Flexible; lithe. **2** Nimble; agile. Also **lis′som.** [Alter. of LITHESOME] —**lis′some·ly** *adv.*

list¹ (list) *n.* A series of words, numbers, names, etc.; a roll or catalogue. —*v.t.* To place on or in a list or catalogue, esp. in alphabetical or numerical order. [<OF *liste*]

list² (list) *n.* **1** The selvage or edge of a woven textile fabric. **2** A strip of fabric, wood, etc. **3** A colored stripe. —*adj.* Made of list. —*v.t.* **1** To edge with lists of cloth. **2** To sew or arrange in strips or stripes. [<OE *līste*]

list³ (list) v.t. & v.i. To lean or incline to one side, as a ship. —n. A leaning or inclination to one side. [< OE *lystan* please]

list⁴ (list) v.t. & v.i. Archaic To listen to or listen. [< OE *hlyst* hearing]

lis·ten (lis′ən) v.i. 1 To make an effort to hear; give ear. 2 To pay attention, as to warning or advice. —**listen in** 1 To overhear others talking, esp. on a telephone. 2 To hear a radio program. —n. The act of listening. [< OE *hlysnan*] —**lis′ten·er** n. —Syn. v. 1 attend, hearken. 2 heed.

list·er (lis′tər) n. Agric. A plow having a double moldboard for throwing up ridges on both sides of the furrow.

list·ing (lis′ting) n. 1 LIST¹. 2 A place or item in a list. 3 The act of including an item in a list or of compiling a list.

list·less (list′lis) adj. Inattentive or indifferent, as from lack of energy or spirit; languid. [< OE *lust* desire + -LESS] —**list′less·ly** adv. —**list′less·ness** n.

list price The price of goods as published in price lists or catalogues.

lists (lists) n. pl. 1 A jousting field or the barriers surrounding it. 2 A jousting tournament. 3 Any area of combat. —**enter the lists** To accept a challenge; enter combat. [< OF *liste* border]

lit (lit) A p.t. & p.p. of LIGHT¹ and LIGHT².

lit. liter; literal; literally; literature.

lit·a·ny (lit′ə·nē) n. pl. ·nies 1 A form of prayer, consisting of a series of supplications said by the clergy, to which the choir or people repeat the same response. 2 Any repetitive listing or dreary account. [< Gk. *litaneuein* pray]

li·tchi (lē′chē) n. 1 A Chinese evergreen tree of the soapberry family, producing small, thin-shelled, edible fruits called, when dried, **litchi nuts.** 2 The fruit of this tree. [< Chin. *li-chih*]

-lite combining form Mineral. Stone; stonelike: *cryolite.* [< Gk. *lithos* stone]

li·ter (lē′tər) n. The basic metric unit of volume or capacity, equal to the volume of one kilogram of water at 4°C and 760 mm. atmospheric pressure; 10⁻³ (0.001) cubic meter or about 1.06 liquid quarts. [< Gk. *litra* pound]

lit·er·a·cy (lit′ər·ə·sē) n. The state of being literate.

lit·er·al (lit′ər·əl) adj. 1 Strictly based on the exact, standard meanings of the words or expressions: a *literal* interpretation of the Bible. 2 Following the exact words or construction of the original: a *literal* translation. 3 Matter-of-fact; unimaginative: a *literal* person. 4 Exact as to fact or detail; not exaggerated. [< L *littera* letter] —**lit′er·al·i·ty, lit′er·al·ness** n.

lit·er·al·ism (lit′ər·əl·iz′əm) n. 1 Close adherence to the exact word or sense. 2 REALISM (def. 2). —**lit′er·al·ist** n.

lit·er·al·ly (lit′ər·ə·lē) adv. 1 In a literal manner. 2 *Informal* In a manner of speaking; figuratively: used for emphasis: He was *literally* green with envy.

lit·er·ar·y (lit′ə·rer′ē) adj. 1 Of, pertaining to, or used in literature. 2 Versed in or devoted to literature. 3 Engaged or occupied in the field of literature: a *literary* man. —**lit′·er·ar′i·ly** adv. —**lit′er·ar′i·ness** n.

lit·er·ate (lit′ər·it) adj. 1 Able to read and write. 2 Educated; well-read. 3 LITERARY (def. 2). 4 Clear; lucid. —n. A literate person. [< L *littera* letter]

lit·e·ra·ti (lit′ə·rä′tē) n. pl. Educated, cultured, or literary people collectively.

lit·e·ra·tim (lit′ə·rā′tim, -rä′-) adv. Letter for letter; with exact literalness; literally. [L]

lit·er·a·ture (lit′ər·ə·chŏŏr, lit′rə·chər) n. 1 Written or printed works collectively, esp. those works characterized by creativeness and imagination, as poetry, fiction, essays, etc. 2 The writings that pertain to a particular epoch, country, language, or branch of learning: French *literature.* 3 The act or occupation of producing literary works. 4 Music The total number of compositions for a particular instrument or ensemble. 5 Any printed matter: campaign *literature.* [< L *littera* letter]

-lith combining form Stone; rock: *monolith.* [< Gk. *lithos* a stone]

Lith. Lithuania; Lithuanian.

lith., litho., lithog. lithograph; lithography.

lith·arge (lith′ärj, li·thärj′) n. A yellow or red oxide of lead used in glassmaking, storage batteries, etc. [< Gk. *lithos* stone + *argyros* silver]

lithe (līth) adj. Bending easily; limber. [< OE *lithe*] —**lithe′ly** adv. —**lithe′ness** n.

lithe·some (līth′səm) adj. Lithe; nimble.

lith·i·a (lith′ē·ə) n. A white, alkaline compound of lithium and oxygen. [< Gk. *lithos* stone]

-lithic combining form Pertaining to a (specified) stage in the use of stone: *neolithic.*

lith·i·um (lith′ē·əm) n. A very light, soft metallic element (symbol Li) having properties similar to sodium. [< Gk. *lithos* stone]

litho- combining form Stone; related to stone. [< Gk. *lithos* stone]

lith·o·graph (lith′ə·graf, -gräf) v.t. To produce or reproduce by lithography. —n. A lithographic print. [LITHO- + -GRAPH] —**li·thog·ra·pher** (li·thog′rə·fər) n. —**lith′o·graph′·ic** or **·i·cal** adj. —**lith′o·graph′i·cal·ly** adv.

li·thog·ra·phy (li·thog′rə·fē) n. The art of producing printed matter from a stone or metal plate on which the design or matter to be printed consists of a material that accepts ink, the other parts being ink-repellent.

lith·o·sphere (lith′ə·sfir) n. The crust of the earth.

li·thot·o·my (li·thot′ə·mē) n. pl. ·mies A surgical operation to remove a stone from the bladder. [< Gk. *lithos* stone + *temnein* to cut] —**lith·o·tom·ic** (lith′ə·tom′ik) or **·i·cal** adj.

Lith·u·a·ni·an (lith′ŏŏ·ā′nē·ən) adj. Of or pertaining to Lithuania, its people, or their language. —n. 1 A native or citizen of Lithuania. 2 The Balto-Slavic language of the Lithuanians.

lit·i·gant (lit′ə·gənt) adj. Engaged in litigation. —n. A party to a lawsuit.

lit·i·gate (lit′ə·gāt) v. ·gat·ed, ·gat·ing v.t. 1 To bring before a court of law. —v.i. 2 To carry on a lawsuit. [< L *lis, litis* lawsuit + *agere* do, act] —**lit′i·ga·ble** (-gə·bəl) adj. —**lit′i·ga′tor** n.

lit·i·ga·tion (lit′ə·gā′shən) n. 1 The act of litigating. 2 A lawsuit.

li·ti·gious (li·tij′əs) adj. 1 Inclined to carry on litigations. 2 Subject to litigation. 3 Of or pertaining to litigation. —**li·tig′ious·ly** adv. —**li·tig′ious·ness** n.

lit·mus (lit′məs) n. A dyestuff made from various lichens which turns red in an acid and blue in a basic medium. [< ON *litr* color + *mosi* moss]

litmus paper An acid and alkali indicator made of paper colored with litmus.

li·tre (lē′tər) n. LITER.

lit·ter (lit′ər) n. 1 The offspring borne at one time by a cat, dog, or other multiparous animal. 2 A stretcher used for conveying sick or wounded. 3 A couch carried on shafts protruding at each end, and used to carry one person. 4 Straw, hay, or other similar material, used as bedding for horses, cattle, etc.

Litter *def.* 3

5 Things scattered about in disorder. 6 Discarded trash scattered about, as in a public park or street. —v.t. 1 To bring forth young: said of animals. 2 To furnish, as cattle, with litter. 3 To cover or strew with or as with litter. 4 To throw or spread about carelessly. —v.i. 5 To give birth to a litter of young. 6 To strew trash, garbage, etc., about. [< L *lectus* bed] —**lit′ter·y** adj.

lit·té·ra·teur (lit′ər·ə·tûr′) n. A professional literary man, esp. a writer. Also **lit′ter·a·teur′.** [F]

lit·ter·bug (lit′ər·bug′) n. Informal A person who litters sidewalks, parks, and other public places.

lit·tle (lit′l) adj. **less** or **lit·tler, least** or **lit·tlest** 1 Small or comparatively small in size: a *little* car. 2 Small or smaller than is usual in amount, degree, or scope: a *little* talent. 3 Being in the early years of life: when I was *little.* 4 Below the normal distance or time; brief. 5 Insignificant; trivial: a *little* quarrel. 6 Narrow-minded; mean: a *little* nature. 7 Lacking effectiveness, force, intensity, etc.: *little* perseverance. —n. A small quantity, space, time, degree, etc. —**little by little** By small degrees or amounts; gradually.

—make little of To treat as unimportant. **—think little of 1** To regard as unimportant or trivial. **2** To have no hesitation or reluctance about. **—adv. less, least 1** In a small degree; slightly. **2** Not at all: used before a verb: *She little knows how much I care.* [<OE *lytel*] **—lit′tle·ness** *n.*

Little Bear URSA MINOR.

Little Dipper A group of stars, somewhat dipper-shaped; Ursa Minor. • See URSA MINOR.

little magazine A usu. noncommercial magazine that publishes new or experimental writing and art work.

little slam In bridge, the winning of 12 tricks in one round of play.

little theater 1 A theater primarily for the production of low-cost or experimental drama. **2** The drama produced in these theaters.

lit·to·ral (lit′ər·əl) *n.* A shore and the country contiguous to it. **—adj.** Of or on the shore. [<L *litus, litoris* seashore]

li·tur·gi·cal (li·tûr′ji·kəl) *adj.* Of, pertaining to, or used in liturgies. Also **li·tur′gic. —li·tur′gi·cal·ly** *adv.*

lit·ur·gy (lit′ər·jē) *n. pl.* **·gies 1** A collection of prescribed forms for public worship. **2** The Eucharistic rite. [<Gk. *leitourgia* public duty]

liv·a·ble (liv′ə·bəl) *adj.* **1** Agreeable or fit for living in or with. **2** Endurable. Also **live′a·ble. —liv′a·ble·ness, live′a·ble·ness** *n.*

live[1] (liv) *v.* **lived, liv·ing** *v.i.* **1** To be alive; have life. **2** To continue in life. **3** To endure or persist; last: *This day will live in infamy.* **4** To maintain life; subsist: *to live on a pittance.* **5** To depend for food; feed: with *on* or *upon*: *to live on carrion.* **6** To dwell; abide. **7** To conduct or pass one's life in a specified manner: *to live frugally.* **8** To enjoy a varied and active life. **—v.t. 9** To pass: *to live the life of a saint.* **10** To practice in one's life: *to live a lie.* **—live down** To live in such a manner as to expiate or erase the memory of (a crime, error, shame, etc.). **—live high** To live luxuriously. **—live in** To reside, as a domestic, at one's place of employment. **—live through** To have experience of and survive. **—live up to** To fulfill the hopes, terms, or character of. [<OE *lifian* live]

live[2] (līv) *adj.* **1** Possessing life; living; alive. **2** Of or pertaining to life or living beings. **3** Burning or glowing: a *live coal.* **4** Of present interest and importance; vital: a *live topic.* **5** Possessing liveliness; energetic. **6** In television, radio, etc., transmitted directly to audiences at the time of performance rather than being filmed or recorded. **7** In records, tapes, etc., performed and recorded before an audience. **8** Unexploded: a *live shell.* **9** Carrying an electrical current: a *live wire.* **10** Ready for printing: *live type;* also, ready for typecasting: *live copy.* **11** Swarming with living creatures. **12** Pure; vivid: *live color.* **13** In mechanics, having ability to impart motion or force. **14** In sports, being in play: a *live ball.* [Short for ALIVE]

-lived *combining form* Having a (specified kind of) life or life span or (a given number of) lives: *long-lived, nine-lived.* [<LIFE] • Having been formed from *life, -lived* is properly pronounced (līvd). The pronunciation (livd) is based on the mistaken assumption that the verb *live* is the source of *-lived.*

live-in (liv′in′) *adj.* Living at the home or other place where one works: a *live-in* housekeeper.

live·li·hood (līv′lē·hŏŏd) *n.* Means of maintaining life: subsistence. [<ME <OE *līf* life + *lād* way]

live·long (liv′lông′, -long′) *adj.* Whole; entire: the *livelong* day. [ME *lefe longe*]

live·ly (līv′lē) *adj.* **·li·er, ·li·est 1** Full of energy or motion: a *lively* child. **2** Filled with activity or incident: a *lively* party. **3** Intensely active or alive, as in the mind: a *lively* wit. **4** Joyful; gay: a *lively* song. **5** Vivid; bright: *lively* colors. **6** Brisk: a *lively* wind. **7** Responsive to impact; resilient: a *lively* ball. **—adv.** In a lively manner. [<OE *līflīce*] **—live′li·ly** *adv.* **—live′li·ness** *n.* **—Syn.** *adj.* **1** active, bouncy, energetic, vivacious.

liv·en (lī′vən) *v.t. & v.i.* To make or become lively or cheerful: often with *up.*

live oak 1 Any of several species of evergreen oak trees. **2** Its hard, durable wood.

liv·er[1] (liv′ər) *n.* **1** The largest glandular organ of vertebrates, having many vital functions, as storing vitamins and nutrients, purifying the blood, producing bile, etc. **2** A digestive gland in invertebrates. **3** The liver of certain animals, used as food. [<OE *lifer*]

liv·er[2] (liv′ər) *n.* **1** One who lives, esp. in a specified way: a high *liver.* **2** A dweller; resident.

liv·er·ied (liv′ər·ēd) *adj.* Dressed in livery.

liv·er·ish (liv′ər·ish) *adj.* **1** Having a liver disorder; bilious. **2** Out of sorts; peevish.

liv·er·wort (liv′ər·wûrt′) *n.* **1** Any of a class of primitive, nonvascular plants related to mosses. **2** HEPATICA.

a. liver. b. stomach.
c. gall bladder.
d. esophagus.

liv·er·wurst (liv′ər·wûrst′) *n.* A sausage containing ground liver. [<G *Leberwurst*]

liv·er·y (liv′ər·ē) *n. pl.* **·er·ies 1** A particular dress or uniform worn by servants. **2** The distinguishing dress of any association or organization. **3** Any characteristic covering or outward appearance. **4** The stabling and care of horses for compensation. **5** A livery stable. [<L *liber* free]

liv·er·y·man (liv′ər·ē·mən) *n. pl.* **·men** (-mən) A man who keeps a livery stable.

livery stable A stable where horses are boarded for a fee and horses and vehicles are kept for hire.

lives (līvz) *n.pl.* of LIFE.

live·stock (līv′stok′) *n.* Domestic animals kept for farm purposes, sale, or profit.

live wire 1 A wire carrying an electric current. **2** *Informal* An energetic person.

liv·id (liv′id) *adj.* **1** Black-and-blue, as bruised flesh. **2** Ashy-pale; pallid. **3** Very angry; furious. [<L *livere* be livid] **—li·vid·i·ty** (li·vid′ə·tē), **liv′id·ness** *n.* **—liv′id·ly** *adv.*

liv·ing (liv′ing) *adj.* **1** Having life; live. **2** Of or suitable for life or its sustenance: *living* conditions. **3** Enough to sustain life or live on: a *living* wage. **4** Still operating, functioning, or in use: a *living* language. **5** True to life: lifelike: a *living* image. **6** Involving persons still alive. **—n. b** The condition of being alive. **2** Means of supporting life; livelihood. **3** Manner of life. **—the living** Those who are alive.

living death A painful, wretched existence.

living room A room designed for the general occupancy of a family and entertainment of guests.

liz·ard (liz′ərd) *n.* **1** Any of a large group of reptiles having an elongate, scaly body, a long tail, and usu. four legs, as the chameleon, iguana, gecko, etc. **2** Leather made from the skin of a lizard. [<L *lacerta*]

LL, L.L. Late Latin; Legal Latin; Low Latin.

ll. leaves; lines.

lla·ma (lä′mə) *n.* A south American wooly-haired, humpless animal related to the camel, used in the Andes as a beast of burden and as a source of wool and milk. [<Quechua]

lla·no (lä′nō; *Sp.* lyä′nō) *n. pl.* **·nos** A flat, grassy plain, as those of N South America. [<L *planus* plain, flat]

LL.D. Doctor of Laws (L *Legum Doctor*).

LM (lem) lunar module.

lo (lō) *interj.* Look! observe! [<OE *lā*]

Llama

loach (lōch) *n.* Any of various small, freshwater, Old World fishes having barbels at the mouth. [<OF *loche*]

load (lōd) *n.* **1** That which is laid upon or put into anything for conveyance. **2** A quantity carried or conveyed at one time: often used in combination: a *busload.* **3** The weight supported by a structure. **4** Something carried or borne with difficulty, esp. a grievous mental burden. **5** A charge for a firearm. **6** An amount of work expected from an employee. **7** *pl. Informal* A great amount; abundance: *loads* of time. **8** *Mech.* The resistance met by a motor or engine in driving its machinery. **9** *Electr.* **a** The power delivered by a generator or circuit. **b** The device to which the power is delivered. —**get a load of** *Slang* To listen to or look at. —*v.t.* **1** To put something on or into to be carried. **2** To place in or on a carrier: to *load* wood. **3** To supply with something excessively or in abundance: to *load* one with honors. **4** To weigh down or oppress: burden. **5** To charge (a firearm) with ammunition. **6** To put film into (a camera). **7** To make heavy on one side or end: to *load* dice. **8** To add a substance to for the purpose of falsifying; adulterate. —*v.i.* **9** To take on or put on a load or cargo. **10** To charge a firearm with ammunition. [< OE *lād* way, journey, act of carrying goods] —**load'er** *n.*

load·ed (lō'did) *adj. Slang* **1** Having a great deal of money. **2** Drunk.

load·star (lōd'stär) *n.* LODESTAR.

load·stone (lōd'stōn') *n.* LODESTONE.

loaf[1] (lōf) *v.i.* **1** To spend time lazily or aimlessly. **2** To neglect one's work. —*v.t.* **3** To spend (time) idly: with *away.* [Back formation < LOAFER]

loaf[2] (lōf) *n. pl.* **loaves** (lōvz) **1** A shaped mass of bread. **2** Any mass of food having a somewhat rectangular shape. [< OE *hlāf* bread]

loaf·er (lō'fər) *n.* **1** One who loafs; an idler. **2** A casual shoe resembling a moccasin. [? < G *Landläufer* an idler]

loam (lōm) *n.* A rich soil of sand and clay, containing organic matter. —*v.t.* To cover or fill with loam. [< OE *lām*] —**loam'y** (-i·er, -i·est) *adj.*

loan (lōn) *n.* **1** Something lent, esp. a sum of money lent at interest. **2** The act of lending. —*v.t. & v.i.* To lend. [< OE *lān*]

loan shark *Informal* One who lends money at extremely high or illegal rates of interest.

loan word A word adopted from another language and naturalized, as the English word *chauffeur,* taken from the French.

loath (lōth, lōth) *adj.* Strongly disinclined; averse: often with *to.* —**nothing loath 1** Willing. **2** Willingly. [< OE *lāth* hateful]

loathe (lōth) *v.t.* **loathed, loath·ing** To feel great hatred or disgust for; abhor; detest. [< OE *lāthian* be hateful] —**loath'er** *n.*

loath·ing (lō'thing) *n.* Extreme dislike or disgust; aversion; abhorrence.

loath·ly[1] (lōth'lē) *adj.* Loathsome; repulsive.

loath·ly[2] (lōth'lē) *adv.* Not willingly.

loath·some (lōth'səm) *adj.* Causing loathing. —**loath'some·ly** *adv.* —**loath'some·ness** *n.*

loaves (lōvz) *n.pl.* of LOAF.

lob (lob) *v.* **lobbed, lob·bing** *v.t.* **1** To pitch or strike (a ball, etc.) in a high, arching curve. —*v.i.* **2** To move clumsily or heavily. **3** To lob a ball. —*n.* **1** In tennis, a stroke that sends the ball high into the air. **2** In cricket, a slow, underhand ball. [?] —**lob'ber** *n.*

lo·bate (lō'bāt) *adj.* **1** Composed of or having lobes. **2** Lobelike. Also **lo'bat·ed.** —**lo'bate·ly** *adv.*

lo·ba·tion (lō·bā'shən) *n.* **1** A lobate structure. **2** LOBE.

lob·by (lob'ē) *n. pl.* **·bies 1** A hall, vestibule, or foyer on the main floor of a theater, hotel, etc. **2** The persons or groups of persons who lobby in the interest of a special group, industry, etc. —*v.* **bied, ·by·ing** *v.i.* **1** To attempt to influence a legislator or legislators. —*v.t.* **2** To attempt to obtain passage or defeat of (a bill, etc.) by such means. [Med. L *lobia* porch] —**lob'by·er** *n.* —**Syn. 1** entrance hall, lounge, waiting room.

lob·by·ist (lob'ē·ist) *n.* One who engages in the practice of lobbying. —**lob'by·ism** *n.*

lobe (lōb) *n.* **1** A rounded projecting part, as of a body organ, leaf, etc. **2** The soft lower extension of the external ear. [< Gk. *lobos*] —**lo'bar, lobed** *adj.*

lo·be·li·a (lō·bē'lē·ə, -bēl'yə) *n.* Any of a large genus of plants with showy flowers, usu. borne in racemes. [< Matthias de *Lobel,* 1538–1616, Flemish botanist]

lob·lol·ly (lob'lol·ē) *n. pl.* **·lies 1** A pine of the s U.S., having a scaly bark. **2** The wood of this tree. Also **loblolly pine.** [< dial. E *lob* bubble + *lolly* broth]

lo·bo (lō'bō) *n. pl.* **·bos** TIMBER WOLF. [Sp., wolf]

lob·ster (lob'stər) *n.* **1** Any of numerous edible marine crustaceans having five pairs of legs, the first pair forming claws, and compound eyes. **2** One of various similar crustaceans. **3** The flesh of these crustaceans, used as food. [< L *locusta* lobster, locust]

Lobster

lob·ule (lob'yōōl) *n.* A small lobe, or a subdivision of a lobe. —**lob'u·lar, lob'u·late** (-lit, -lāt) *adj.*

loc. local; location.

lo·cal (lō'kəl) *adj.* **1** Of, pertaining to, or characteristic of a particular place or a limited portion of space. **2** Pertaining to place in general. **3** Not broad or universal: *local* customs. **4** Relating to or affecting a specific part of the body. **5** Making every stop on its run: a *local* train. —*n.* **1** A local subway, bus, or train. **2** A local branch of a trade union or fraternal organization. **3** An item of local interest in a newspaper. [< L *locus* place] —**lo'cal·ly** *adv.*

local color In literature and art, the presentation of the characteristic manners, speech, dress, scenery, etc., of a certain period or region so as to achieve a sense of realism.

lo·cale (lō·kal', -käl') *n.* Locality, esp. with reference to events or features associated with it. [F]

lo·cal·ism (lō'kəl·iz'əm) *n.* **1** A local custom or idiom. **2** A word, meaning, pronunciation, etc., peculiar to a locality. **3** Fondness for a particular place or locality.

lo·cal·i·ty (lō·kal'ə·tē) *n. pl.* **·ties 1** A definite place, location, or position. **2** The condition of having a location.

lo·cal·ize (lō'kəl·īz) *v.t.* **·ized, ·iz·ing 1** To limit or assign to a specific area or locality. **2** To determine the place of origin of. —**lo'cal·i·za'tion** *n.*

local option The right of a county, town, etc., to determine by vote whether something, as the sale of liquor, shall be permitted within its limits.

lo·cate (lō'kāt, lō·kāt') *v.* **·cat·ed, ·cat·ing** *v.t.* **1** To discover the position or source of; find. **2** To assign place or locality to: to *locate* a scene in a valley. **3** To establish in a place; situate: My office is *located* in Portland. **4** To designate the site of, as a mining claim. —*v.i.* **5** *Informal* To establish oneself or take up residence; settle. [< L *locare* < *locus* place] —**lo'ca·tor** *n.*

lo·ca·tion (lō·kā'shən) *n.* **1** The act of locating, or the state of being located. **2** A place, position, or site. **3** A plot of ground used or to be used for a special purpose. **4** A site, away from a studio, selected for filming scenes in a motion picture.

loc·a·tive (lok'ə·tiv) *adj. Gram.* In Latin, Greek, Sanskrit, etc., designating the case of the noun denoting place where or at which. —*n.* **1** The locative case. **2** A word in this case. [< L *locare* locate]

loc. cit. in the place cited (L *loco citato*).

loch (lokh, lok) *n. Scot.* **1** A lake. **2** A bay, or arm of the sea.

lo·ci (lō'sī, -kī, -kē) *n.pl.* of LOCUS.

lock[1] (lok) *n.* **1** A device to secure a door, drawer, etc., operated by a special key or combination. **2** Any of various mechanical devices used to fix something in place, prevent something from working, etc. **3** A spring mechanism for exploding the charge of a firearm. **4** A section of a canal, etc., enclosed by gates at either end, within which the water level may be varied to raise or lower vessels from one level to another. **5** An interlocking or fastening together. **6** Any of various holds in wrestling. —**lock, stock, and barrel** *Informal* Totally; completely. —*v.t.* **1** To secure or fasten by means of a lock. **2** To shut, confine, or exclude by means of a lock: with *in, up,* or *out.* **3** To join or unite; link: to *lock* arms. **4** To embrace closely. **5** To make immovable, as by jamming or by a lock. **6** To move (a ship) by means of locks. —*v.i.* **7** To become locked or fastened. **8** To become joined or linked. —**lock out** To subject (workers) to a lockout. —**lock up 1** To fasten the doors of by locking. **2** To put in jail. **3** To make sure that (something specified) will turn out the way one wants it to: enough backing to *lock up* the nomination. [< OE *loc* fastening, enclosure] —**Syn.** *n.* **1** bolt, catch, fastening, latch.

lock² (lok) *n.* **1** A tuft of hair; tress. **2** *pl.* A head of hair. **3** A small quantity of hay, wool, etc. [< OE *locc*]

lock·er (lok′ər) *n.* **1** One who or that which locks. **2** A closet, cabinet, chest, etc., usu. having a lock, and used for personal belongings. **3** A refrigerated cabinet for frozen foods.

locker room A room equipped with lockers.

lock·et (lok′it) *n.* A small, hinged case suspended on a necklace or chain, often holding a portrait. [< OF *loc* latch]

lock·jaw (lok′jô′) *n.* **1** TETANUS. **2** Abnormal muscular contraction causing the jaws to clench.

lock·out (lok′out′) *n.* The closing of a place of business to force workers to accept the employer's terms.

lock·smith (lok′smith′) *n.* A maker or repairer of locks.

lock step A marching step in which each marcher follows as closely as possible the one ahead.

lock·up (lok′up′) *n.* **1** The act of locking up or the state of being locked up. **2** A jail.

lo·co (lō′kō) *n.* **1** LOCOWEED. **2** LOCO DISEASE. —*adj. Slang* Crazy; insane. [Sp., insane]

lo·co ci·ta·to (lō′kō sī·tā′tō) *Latin* In the place cited.

loco disease An ailment affecting the nervous system of livestock that have eaten locoweed. Also **lo·co·ism** (lō′-kō·iz′əm).

lo·co·mo·tion (lō′kə·mō′shən) *n.* The act or power of moving from one place to another. [< L *loco* from a place + *motio* movement]

lo·co·mo·tive (lō′kə·mō′tiv) *adj.* **1** Pertaining to locomotion. **2** Moving or able to move from one place to another. **3** Self-propelling: said of machines. —*n.* A self-propelling electric, diesel, or steam engine on wheels, esp. one for use on a railway.

lo·co·mo·tor (lō′kə·mō′tər) *adj.* Of or pertaining to locomotion. —*n.* One who or that which has the power of locomotion.

locomotor ataxia A chronic disease of the spinal cord, usu. caused by syphilis and characterized by lack of muscular coordination and loss of reflexes.

lo·co·weed (lō′kō·wēd′) *n.* Any of several leguminous plants of w U.S., often poisonous to livestock.

lo·cus (lō′kəs) *n. pl.* **·ci** (-sī, -kī, kē) **1** A place; locality. **2** *Math.* A set containing those points and only those points that satisfy a given set of conditions. [L]

lo·cust (lō′kəst) *n.* **1** Any of various large grasshoppers, esp. those moving in swarms and destructive of vegetation. **2** A cicada. **3** Any of various leguminous North American trees and shrubs having compound leaves and drooping racemes of flowers. **4** The hard, durable wood of certain of these trees. **5** Any of various other trees, esp. the honey locust. [< L *locusta*]

lo·cu·tion (lō·kyōō′shən) *n.* **1** A manner of speech. **2** A verbal idiom or phrase. [< L *loqui* speak]

lode (lōd) *n.* **1** A mineral-bearing vein filling a fissure in rock. **2** A deposit of ore between definite boundaries of associated rock. [< OE *lād* way, journey]

lode·star (lōd′stär′) *n.* **1** A guiding star, esp. the North Star. **2** Any guiding principle or ideal.

lode·stone (lōd′stōn′) *n.* **1** A magnetically polarized piece of magnetite. **2** Anything that has magnetic or magneticlike attraction.

lodge (loj) *v.* **lodged, lodg·ing** *v.t.* **1** To furnish with temporary living quarters; house. **2** To rent a room or rooms to. **3** To serve as a shelter or dwelling for. **4** To deposit for safekeeping or storage. **5** To place or implant, as by throwing, thrusting, etc. **6** To place (a complaint, information, etc.) before proper authority. **7** To confer or invest (power, etc.). —*v.i.* **8** To take temporary shelter or quarters. **9** To live in a rented room or rooms. **10** To become fixed in some place or position. —*n.* **1** A small house, hut, or cabin. **2** A small dwelling on an estate. **3** The lair of a wild animal, esp. of beavers. **4** A local chapter of a secret or fraternal society, or its meeting place. **5** A small hut or tepee of

American Indians; also, its inhabitants. [< Med. L *lobia, laubia* porch, gallery]

lodg·er (loj′ər) *n.* One who lodges; esp. one who rents a room or rooms in the house of another.

lodg·ing (loj′ing) *n.* **1** A place of temporary abode. **2** *pl.* A room or rooms hired as a place of residence in the house of another.

lodging house A house other than a hotel where lodgings are let.

lodg·ment (loj′mənt) *n.* **1** The act of lodging or the state of being lodged. **2** LODGINGS. **3** Accumulated material left by deposit. Also **lodge′ment.**

loess (lō′is, lœs) *n. Geol.* A powdery, yellowish brown loam found widely in North America, Europe, and Asia, believed to have been chiefly deposited by the wind. [< G *lösen* pour, dissolve]

loft (lôft, loft) *n.* **1** A low space or attic directly under a roof. **2** A large, unpartitioned storeroom on an upper floor of a warehouse, etc. **3** An elevated gallery, as in a church. **4** HAYLOFT. **5** A backward slope on the face of a golf club; also, a stroke with such a club which lifts the ball high in the air. **6** A place for keeping pigeons. —*v.t.* **1** To keep or house in a loft. **2** In sports, to strike (a ball) so that it rises or travels in a high arc. —*v.i.* **3** To strike a ball so that it rises in a high arc. [< ON, upper room, air, sky]

loft·y (lôf′tē, lof′-) *adj.* **loft·i·er, loft·i·est** **1** Very high. **2** Exalted or elevated in character, language, etc. **3** Haughty; arrogant. —**loft′i·ly** *adv.* —**loft′i·ness** *n.* —**Syn.** **1** tall. **2** grand, majestic, sublime. **3** disdainful.

log¹ (lôg, log) *n.* **1** A bulky piece or length of timber cut down and cleared of branches. **2** *Naut.* **a** A device for showing the speed of a vessel. **b** A record of the daily speed and progress of a vessel. **3** Any of various records of performance, progress, etc. —*v.* **logged, log·ging** *v.t.* **1** To cut (trees) into logs. **2** To cut down the trees of (a region) for timber. **3** *Naut. & Aeron.* **a** To enter in a logbook. **b** To travel (a specified distance) as shown by a log. **c** To travel at (a specified speed). —*v.i.* **4** To cut down trees and transport logs for sawing into lumber. [? < Scand.]

log² (lôg, log) *n.* LOGARITHM.

lo·gan·ber·ry (lō′gən·ber′ē) *n. pl.* **·ries** **1** A hybrid shrub obtained by crossing the red raspberry with the blackberry. **2** The edible fruit of this shrub. [< J. H. *Logan,* 1841–1928, of California, the originator]

log·a·rithm (lôg′ə·rith′əm, log′-) *n. Math.* The exponent showing the power to which a constant, called the base, must be raised in order to produce a given number. [< Gk. *logos* word, ratio + *arithmos* number] —**log′a·rith′mic** or **·mi·cal** *adj.* —**log′a·rith′mi·cal·ly** *adv.*

log·book (lôg′book′, log′-) *n.* The book in which the official record of a ship, aircraft, etc., is entered. Also **log book.**

loge (lōzh) *n.* A box in a theater; stall. [< OF]

log·ger (lôg′ər, log′-) *n.* **1** A person engaged in logging; a lumberjack. **2** A machine used for loading logs.

log·ger·head (lôg′ər·hed′, log′-) *n.* **1** A blockhead; fool. **2** A large sea turtle of tropical Atlantic waters: also **loggerhead turtle.** —**at loggerheads** Engaged in a quarrel. [< regional E *logger* log tied to a horse's leg + HEAD]

log·gi·a (loj′ē·ə, lō′jə; *Ital.* lôd′jä) *n.* A roofed, open gallery, attached to the side, or sides, of a building and having a colonnade on one or more sides. [< OF *loge*]

log·ging (lôg′ing, log′-) *n.* The occupation of felling timber and transporting logs to a mill or market.

Loggia

log·ic (loj′ik) *n.* **1** The science which investigates the principles of valid reasoning and correct inference. **2** The basic principles of reasoning applicable to any field of knowledge: the *logic* of science. **3** Reasoning or argumentation in general, esp. when relevant or effective: The *logic* of his answer was unassailable. **4** The connection or interrelation of facts, events, etc., esp. when viewed as inevitable. [< Gk. *logos* word, speech, thought]

log·i·cal (lŏj′i·kəl) *adj.* 1 Relating to or of the nature of logic. 2 Conforming to the laws of logic. 3 Capable of or characterized by clear reasoning. —**log′i·cal′i·ty** (-kal′ə·tē), **log′i·cal·ness** *n.* —**log′i·cal·ly** *adv.*

-logical *combining form* Of or related to a (specified) science or study: *biological.* Also **-logic.** [< -LOG(Y)]

logic circuit Any of various circuits used in computers and electronic control systems, having several inputs and an output that is on or off, depending on the condition of the inputs; a gate.

lo·gi·cian (lō·jish′ən) *n.* One versed in logic.

lo·gis·tics (lō·jis′tiks) *n. pl.* (construed as singular) The branch of military science concerned with procurement, equipment, maintenance, and transportation, as of personnel, facilities, and materiel. [< Gk. *logistēs* calculator] —**lo·gis′tic, lo·gis′ti·cal** *adj.*

log·o (lôg′ō, log′ō) *n. pl.* **log·os** LOGOTYPE (def. 2).

Lo·gos (lō′gos, -gōs, log′os) *n.* 1 In classical Greek philosophy, reason, thought of as the controlling principle of the universe. 2 In Christian theology, the creative and sustaining spirit of divine wisdom, esp. as made manifest in the second person of the Trinity, Jesus Christ.

log·o·type (lôg′ə·tīp, log′-) *n.* 1 *Printing* A type bearing a syllable or word. 2 A distinctively styled representation of a company name, trademark, etc.

log·roll (lôg′rōl′, log′-) *v.t.* 1 To obtain passage of (a bill) by logrolling. —*v.i.* 2 To engage in logrolling.

log·roll·ing (lôg′rō′ling, log′-) *n.* 1 Handling and removing of logs, as in clearing land. 2 A trading of votes among politicians for mutual assistance on their separate projects. 3 BIRLING. —**log′roll′er** *n.*

-logue *combining form* Speech; recitation; discourse: *monologue.* Also **-log.** [< Gk. *logos* word, speech]

log·wood (lôg′wŏŏd′, log′-) *n.* 1 A Central American tree. 2 Its heavy, reddish wood. 3 A dye obtained from this wood.

lo·gy (lō′gē) *adj.* **·gi·er, ·gi·est** *Informal* Dull; lethargic. [? < Du. *log* dull]

-logy *combining form* 1 The science or study of: *biology.* 2 Speech; discourse. [< Gk. *logos* word, study]

Lo·hen·grin (lō′ən·grin) In German medieval legend, son of Parsifal and a knight of the Holy Grail.

loin (loin) *n.* 1 The part of the body of a human being or quadruped between the lower ribs and hip bone. 2 *pl.* Loosely, the hips, thighs, and the genital region. 3 The forepart of the hindquarters of beef, lamb, veal, etc., with the flank removed. [< L *lumbus*] • See HORSE. —**gird up one's loins** To prepare for action.

loin·cloth (loin′klôth′, -kloth′) *n.* A piece or strip of cloth worn about the loins.

loi·ter (loi′tər) *v.i.* 1 To pass time idly or aimlessly; loaf. 2 To linger on the way; dawdle. —*v.t.* 3 To pass (time) idly: with *away.* [ME *loyteren*] —**loi′ter·er** *n.* —**loi′ter·ing·ly** *adv.* —Syn. 1 laze. 2 delay, lag, procrastinate, tarry.

Lo·ki (lō′kē) In Norse mythology, a god who created disorder and mischief.

loll (lol) *v.i.* 1 To lie or lean in a relaxed or languid manner. 2 To hang loosely; droop. —*v.t.* 3 To permit to droop or hang, as the tongue. —*n.* The act of lolling. [ME *lollen*] —**loll′er** *n.*

Lol·lard (lol′ərd) *n.* One of a sect of religious and political reformers in England in the 14th and 15th centuries, followers of John Wyclif. [< MDu. *lollaerd,* lit., grumbler, mumbler (of prayers)]

lol·li·pop (lol′ē·pop) *n.* A lump or piece of hard candy attached to the end of a stick. Also **lol′ly·pop.** [? < dial. E *lolly* tongue + POP[1]]

lol·ly (lol′ē) *n. pl.* **·lies** *Brit.* 1 A piece of candy, esp. hard candy. 2 *Informal* Ice cream, flavored ices, etc., frozen on a stick. 3 *Slang* Money. [Short for LOLLIPOP]

Lom·bard (lom′bərd, -bärd, lum′-) *n.* 1 One of a Germanic tribe that established a kingdom in northern Italy, 568–774. 2 A native or citizen of Lombardy. —**Lom·bar′dic** *adj.*

lone (lōn) *adj.* 1 Standing by itself; isolated. 2 Unaccompanied; solitary. 3 Unmarried or widowed. 4 Lonesome. [Var. of ALONE] —**lone′ness** *n.*

lone·ly (lōn′lē) *adj.* **·li·er, ·li·est** 1 Deserted or unfrequented by human beings. 2 Solitary or isolated. 3 Sad from being alone. 4 Producing such sadness: a *lonely* melody. —**lone′li·ly** *adv.* —**lone′li·ness** *n.*

lo·ner (lō′nər) *n. Informal* One who keeps away from other people.

lone·some (lōn′səm) *adj.* 1 Depressed or sad because of loneliness. 2 Producing a feeling of loneliness. 3 Deserted; secluded. —**lone′some·ly** *adv.* —**lone′some·ness** *n.*

long[1] (lông, long) *adj.* 1 Having relatively great linear extension; not short. 2 Having relatively great extension in time; prolonged. 3 Extended either in space or time to a specified degree: an hour *long,* a foot *long.* 4 Of relatively great distance: a *long* trip. 5 In excess of the usual or standard duration, quantity, extent, etc.: a *long* five minutes; a *long* movie. 6 Retentive: a *long* memory. 7 Having many items or units: a *long* list. 8 Extending into the future or beyond present considerations: to take a *long* look at a problem. 9 Slow; tedious. 10 Great in risk: a *long* chance. 11 In finance, holding stocks, securities, etc., in anticipation of a rise in prices. 12 *Phonet.* Indicating the sounds of *a, e, i, o, u* as they are pronounced in *mate, scene, nice, dote, fuse.* 13 In English prosody, accented. —*n.* Something long, as a garment, vowel, syllable, etc. —**the long and (the) short of** The entire story of; gist. —*adv.* 1 For or during a long time or period: I can't stay *long.* 2 For a (specified) length of time: How *long* did the play run? 3 Through the whole extent or duration. 4 At a point of duration far distant: *long* before or after. —**as** (or **so**) **long as** 1 During the time that. 2 Under condition that; since. —**before long** Soon. —**for long** For a long time. [< OE *lang, long*]

long[2] (lông, long) *v.i.* To have a strong or yearning wish: with *for.* [< OE *langian*] —Syn. covet, crave, desire, hanker, pine.

long. longitude.

long·boat (lông′bōt′, long′-) *n. Naut.* The largest boat carried on a sailing vessel.

long·bow (lông′bō′, long′-) *n.* A wooden bow, often six feet long, drawn by hand.

long-dis·tance (lông′dis′təns, long′-) *adj.* 1 To or from a distant place. 2 Of or relating to long distances: a *long-distance* runner. —*adv.* By long-distance telephone.

long distance The telephone exchange or operator dealing with long-distance calls.

long division Arithmetical division involving numbers whose numerals have several digits and showing each step of the process.

long-drawn (lông′drôn′, long′-) *adj.* Prolonged. Also **long′-drawn′-out′** (-out′).

lon·gev·i·ty (lon·jev′ə·tē) *n.* 1 Great age or length of life. 2 The tendency to live long. [< L *longus* long + *aevum* age]

long face An expression indicating sadness. —**long-faced** (lông′fāst′, long′-) *adj.*

long green *Slang* Paper money.

long·hair (lông′hâr′, long′-) *n. Slang* 1 A person having intellectual interests or tastes, esp. for classical music. 2 A man or boy with long hair, esp. a hippie. —**long′hair′, long′haired′** *adj.*

long·hand (lông′hand′, long′-) *n.* Ordinary handwriting with the words spelled in full.

long·head·ed (lông′hed′id, long′-) *adj.* 1 DOLICHOCE-PHALIC. 2 *Informal* Shrewd; foresighted. Also **long′-head′-ed.** —**long′head′ed·ly** *adv.* —**long′head′ed·ness** *n.*

long·horn (lông′hôrn′, long′-) *n.* One of a breed of domestic cattle with long horns: also **Texas longhorn.**

long·ing (lông′ing, long′-) *n.* A strong, eager craving. —*adj.* Having or showing such a craving. —**long′ing·ly** *adv.*

Longhorn

lon·gi·tude (lon′jə·tood) *n.* 1 *Geog.* Distance east or west on the earth measured by the angle which the meridian through a specific place makes as it intersects with some standard meridian, as that of Greenwich, England. 2 *Astron.* The angular distance from the vernal equinox to the great circle passing through a point on the celestial sphere. [< L *longus* long]

lon·gi·tu·di·nal (lon'ji·t$\overline{oo}$'də·nəl) *adj.* **1** Of or pertaining to longitude or length. **2** Running lengthwise. —**lon'gi·tu'·di·nal·ly** *adv.*

long-lived (lông'līvd', -livd', long'-) *adj.* Existing or living for an unusually long time. —**long'-lived'ness** *n.*

long-play·ing (lông'plā'ing, long'-) *adj.* Designating a phonograph record with microgrooves, played at 33⅓ revolutions per minute.

long-range (lông'rānj', long'-) *adj.* **1** Designed to shoot or move over distances: a *long-range* projectile. **2** Taking account of, or extending over, a long span of future time.

long·shore·man (lông'shôr'mən, -shōr'-, long'-) *n. pl.* **·men** (-mən) A person whose occupation is loading and unloading ships.

long shot *Informal* **1** A bet made with little chance of winning and hence carrying great odds. **2** Something backed at great odds, as a horse. —**not by a long shot** Decidedly not.

long·sight·ed (lông'sī'tid, long'-) *adj.* **1** Having or showing foresight; sagacious. **2** Farsighted. —**long'sight'ed·ness** *n.*

long·stand·ing (lông'stan'ding, long'-) *adj.* Having existed for a long time.

long·suf·fer·ing (lông'suf'ər·ing, long'-) *adj.* Patiently enduring trouble, misfortune, etc., for a long time. —*n.* Patient endurance of injuries or offense: also **long'suf'fer·ance.**

long-term (lông'tûrm', long'-) *adj.* Active or valid for a relatively long time: a *long-term* lease.

long·time (lông'tīm', long'-) *adj.* For a long time.

long ton 2,240 pounds avoirdupois.

long-wind·ed (lông'win'did, long'-) *adj.* **1** Not losing one's breath easily. **2** Speaking or writing in a tedious, overlong manner. —**long'-wind'ed·ly** *adv.* —**long'-wind'ed·ness** *n.*

long·wise (lông'wīz', long'-) *adv.* LENGTHWISE. Also **long'ways'** (-wāz')

loo[1] (l$\overline{oo}$) *n.* **1** An old card game. **2** A pool of forfeits used in loo. [< F *lanturelu*]

loo[2] (l$\overline{oo}$) *n. Brit. Informal* Toilet. [? < F *lieux (d'aisances)* public convenience, toilets]

look (l$\overline{oo}$k) *v.i.* **1** To direct the eyes toward something in order to see. **2** To direct one's attention or consideration. **3** To make examination or inquiry: to *look* through a desk. **4** To appear to be; seem. **5** To face in a specified direction; front. **6** To expect: with an infinitive. —*v.t.* **7** To direct the eyes upon: He *looked* her up and down. **8** To express by looks: to *look* one's hatred. **9** To give the appearance of being (a specified age). **10** To influence by looks: to *look* someone into silence. —**look after** To take care of. —**look down on** To regard condescendingly or contemptuously. —**look for 1** To search for. **2** To expect. —**look forward to** To anticipate pleasurably. —**look in** (or **in on**) To make a short visit to. —**look into** To examine; make inquiry. —**look like 1** To resemble. **2** To indicate the probability of: It *looks like* rain. —**look on 1** To be a spectator. **2** To consider; regard. —**look oneself** To seem to be in good health, good spirits, etc. —**look out** To be on the watch; take care. —**look over** To examine; scrutinize. —**look to 1** To attend to. **2** To turn to, as for help, advice, etc. —**look up 1** To search for and find, as in a file, dictionary, etc. **2** *Informal* To discover the whereabouts of. **3** *Informal* To improve; become better. —**look up to** To have respect for. —*n.* **1** The act of looking or seeing. **2** Aspect or expression: a fiendish *look.* **3** *Usu. pl. Informal* Personal appearance, esp. when attractive. **4** Appearance in general: I do not like the *look* of the thing. [< OE *lōcian*] —**Syn.** *v.* **1** gaze, glance, regard. **3** search. **6** anticipate.

look-a·like (l$\overline{oo}$k'ə·līk') *n. Informal* One of two or more that are alike in appearance; a double.

look·er (l$\overline{oo}$k'ər) *n.* **1** One who looks or watches. **2** *Slang* A handsome or good-looking person.

look·er-on (l$\overline{oo}$k'ər·on') *n. pl.* **look·ers-on** A spectator; onlooker.

look·ing-glass (l$\overline{oo}$k'ing·glas', -gläs') *n.* A mirror.

look·out (l$\overline{oo}$k'out') *n.* **1** Careful or alert watchfulness. **2** An elevated place for observation. **3** A person or group engaged in keeping watch. **4** *Informal* Concern; care: It's your own *look-out.*

loom[1] (l$\overline{oo}$m) *v.i.* **1** To appear or come into view indistinctly, esp. so as to seem large or ominous. **2** To appear to the mind as threatening or portentous. [?]

loom[2] (l$\overline{oo}$m) *n.* A machine in which yarn or thread is woven into a fabric. [< OE *gelōma* tool]

loon[1] (l$\overline{oo}$n) *n.* Any of several diving, fish-eating waterfowl, having a distinctive cry. [< ON *lomr*]

loon[2] (l$\overline{oo}$n) *n.* A crazy or stupid person. [ME *loun*]

loon·y (l$\overline{oo}$'nē) *Slang. adj.* **loon·i·er, loon·i·est 1** Lunatic or demented. **2** Foolish; erratic. —*n. pl.* **loon·ies** A demented or crazy person.

Loon

loop (l$\overline{oo}$p) *n.* **1** The more or less oval-shaped bend that is created when a string, rope, etc., is crossed over on itself. **2** Something shaped like a loop, as certain ornamental fastenings. **3** A complete, vertical, circular turn made by an airplane in flight. **4** *Electr.* A closed path in an electric circuit. **5** Any of several types of intrauterine contraceptive devices. —**loop the loop** To make a vertical, circular turn, as an airplane in flight. —*v.t.* **1** To form a loop or loops in or of. **2** To fasten, connect, or encircle by means of a loop or loops. **3** To fly (an aircraft) in a loop or loops. —*v.i.* **4** To make a loop or loops. **5** To move by forming loops, as a measuring worm. [ME *loupe*]

looped (l$\overline{oo}$pt) *adj. Slang* Drunk.

loop·hole (l$\overline{oo}$p'hōl') *n.* **1** A narrow opening, as in a wall, through which small arms are fired. **2** A means of escaping or evading something disagreeable.

loose (l$\overline{oo}$s) *adj.* **loos·er, loos·est 1** Not fastened or confined; unattached. **2** Not tightly stretched; slack. **3** Not tight, as a garment. **4** Not firmly fastened or secured: a *loose* bolt. **5** Not bundled, tied, or fastened together. **6** Not dense or compact: *loose* soil. **7** Not in individual packages or containers: *loose* sugar. **8 a** Not constricted: a *loose* cough. **b** Moving freely or too often: *loose* bowels. **9** Free from confinement, restraint, etc. **10** Not controlled or restrained: a *loose* tongue. **11** Not chaste; lewd. **12** Not precise or exact: a *loose* translation. **13** Free and relaxed: a *loose* walk. —**on the loose 1** Unconfined; at large. **2** *Informal* Free and unrestrained in behavior. —*adv.* **1** In a loose manner. **2** So as to become loose: The dog broke *loose.* —*v.* **loosed, loos·ing** *v.t.* **1** To set free, as from bondage, penalty, etc. **2** To untie or undo. **3** To loosen; slacken. **4** To make less strict or rigid. **5** To let fly; shoot, as arrows. —*v.i.* **6** To become loose. **7** To loose something. [< ON *lauss*] —**loose'ly** *adv.* —**loose'ness** *n.*

loose-joint·ed (l$\overline{oo}$s'join'tid) *adj.* **1** Having joints not tightly articulated. **2** Limber.

loose-leaf (l$\overline{oo}$s'lēf') *adj.* Designed for the easy insertion and removal of pages.

loos·en (l$\overline{oo}$'sən) *v.t.* **1** To untie or undo, as bonds. **2** To set free; release. **3** To make less tight, firm, or compact. **4** To relax the strictness of, as discipline. —*v.i.* **5** To become loose or looser. —**loos'en·er** *n.*

loot (l$\overline{oo}$t) *v.t. & v.i.* To plunder. —*n.* **1** Goods taken as spoils by an enemy during war. **2** Anything unlawfully taken. **3** *Slang* Money. [< Hind. *lūt*] —**loot'er** *n.*

lop[1] (lop) *v.t.* **lopped, lop·ping 1** To trim the branches, twigs, etc., from, as a tree. **2** To cut off, as branches, twigs, etc. —*n.* Something lopped off. [?] —**lop'per** *n.*

lop[2] (lop) *v.* **lopped, lop·ping** *v.i.* **1** To droop or hang down. **2** To move about in an awkward manner. —*v.t.* **3** To permit to droop or hang down. —*adj.* Drooping. [?]

lope (lōp) *v.t. & v.i.* **loped, lop·ing** To run or cause to run with a steady, swinging stride. —*n.* A slow, easy stride. [< ON *hlaupa* to leap, run] —**lop'er** *n.*

lop-eared (lop'ird') *adj.* Having drooping ears.

lop-sid·ed (lop'sī'did) *adj.* **1** Heavy or hanging down on one side. **2** Lacking in symmetry or balance. —**lop'-sid'ed·ly** *adv.* —**lop'-sid'ed·ness** *n.*

loq. he (or she, or it) speaks (L *loquitur*).

lo·qua·cious (lō·kwā′shəs) *adj.* Given to continual talking. [< L *loqui* to talk] —**lo·qua′cious·ly** *adv.* —**lo·qua′cious·ness, lo·quac·i·ty** (lō·kwas′ə·tē) *n.* —**Syn.** chattering, garrulous, talkative, verbose, vociferous.

lo·ran (lôr′an, lō′ran) *n.* A navigation system by which a ship or an aircraft may determine its position from radio signals transmitted by fixed stations. [< *lo(ng-)ra(nge) n(avigation)*]

lord (lôrd) *n.* 1 One possessing supreme power and authority; a ruler. 2 In feudal law, the owner of a manor under grant from the crown. 3 In Great Britain: a Any nobleman (**lord temporal**) holding the title of marquis, earl, viscount, or baron and having a seat in the House of Lords. b An archbishop or bishop (**lord spiritual**) who is a member of the House of Lords. —**the Lords** The House of Lords. —*v.t.* To invest with the title of lord. —**lord it** (**over**) To act in a domineering or arrogant manner (toward). [< OE *hlǣford*, lit., bread-keeper]

Lord (lôrd) *n.* 1 God. 2 Jesus. 3 In Great Britain, a title of honor or nobility.

Lord Chancellor The highest British officer of state, presiding officer of the House of Lords. Also **Lord High Chancellor**.

lord·ly (lôrd′lē) *adj.* **·li·er, ·li·est** 1 Of, pertaining to, or befitting a lord. 2 Lofty; noble. 3 Haughty; insolent. —*adv.* In a lordly manner. —**lord′li·ness** *n.*

lor·do·sis (lôr·dō′sis) *n.* Inward curvature of the spine. [< Gk. *lordos* bent backward] —**lor·dot·ic** (-dot′ik) *adj.*

Lord's Day Sunday.

lord·ship (lôrd′ship) *n.* 1 The dominion, power, or authority of a lord. 2 Sovereignty in general. 3 *Often cap.* The title by which noblemen (excluding dukes), bishops, and judges in England are addressed: preceded by *Your* or *His*.

Lord's Prayer The prayer taught by Jesus to his disciples. *Matt.* 6: 9–13.

Lord's Supper *Eccl.* 1 The Eucharist; the Holy Communion. 2 The Last Supper.

lore (lôr, lōr) *n.* 1 The body of traditional, popular, often anecdotal knowledge about a particular subject. 2 Learning or erudition. [< OE *lār*]

Lo·re·lei (lôr′ə·lī; *Ger.* lō′rə·lī) In German folklore, a siren on a rock in the Rhine, who lured boatmen to shipwreck by her singing.

lor·gnette (lôr·nyet′) *n.* A pair of eyeglasses or opera glasses with a handle. [< F *lorgner* to spy, peer]

lorn (lôrn) *adj. Archaic* 1 Without kindred or friends; forlorn. 2 Lost. [< OE *loren*, p.p. of *lēosan* lose]

lor·ry (lôr′ē, lor′ē) *n. pl.* **·ries** 1 A low, four-wheeled wagon without sides. 2 *Brit.* A motor truck. [?]

lo·ry (lō′rē, lôr′ē) *n. pl.* **·ries** Any of certain parrots of Australia and neighboring islands. [Malay *lūrī*]

lose (lōōz) *v.* **lost, los·ing** *v.t.* 1 To be unable to find; mislay. 2 To fail to keep, control, or maintain: to *lose* one's footing. 3 To suffer or undergo the loss of, as by accident, death, removal, etc. 4 To fail to gain or win. 5 To fail to utilize or take advantage of; miss: to *lose* a chance. 6 To fail to see or hear: I *lost* not a word of the speech. 7 To fail to keep in sight, memory, etc. 8 To cease to have: to *lose* one's sense of duty. 9 To squander; waste, as time. 10 To wander from so as to be unable to find: to *lose* the path. 11 To outdistance or elude. 12 To cause the loss of: His rashness *lost* him his opportunity. 13 To bring to destruction or ruin: All hands were *lost*. —*v.i.* 14 To suffer loss. 15 To be defeated. —**lose oneself** 1 To lose one's way. 2 To disappear or hide. 3 To become engrossed. —**lose out** *Informal* To fail or be defeated. [< OE *lōsian* be lost] —**los′er** *n.*

los·ing (lōō′zing) *n.* 1 The act of one who or that which loses. 2 *pl.* Money lost, esp. in gambling. —*adj.* 1 That incurs loss: a *losing* business. 2 Not winning; defeated: the *losing* team.

loss (lôs, los) *n.* 1 The act of losing or the state of being lost. 2 One who or that which is lost. 3 The harm, privation, etc., caused by losing someone or something. 4 *pl.* Soldiers killed, wounded, or captured in battle. 5 In insurance, the amount owed to the insured by the insurer because of death, property damage, theft, etc. 6 *Physics* Any part of the energy of a system that cannot be made to do useful work. —**at a loss** 1 At so low a price as to result in a loss. 2 In confusion or doubt. [< OE *los*]

loss leader An item in a store sold at a reduced price or below cost to bring in customers.

lost (lôst, lost) *adj.* 1 Not to be found or recovered; missing. 2 No longer seen, enjoyed, etc.: *lost* friends. 3 Not won or gained: a *lost* cause. 4 Having wandered from the way. 5 Helpless. 6 Ruined physically or morally. 7 Wasted; squandered: a *lost* opportunity. 8 Abstracted; rapt: *lost* in thought. 9 Bewildered; perplexed. 10 No longer known or used: a *lost* art. —**be lost to** 1 To belong to no longer. 2 To be insensible or hardened to. 3 To be unavailable to. —**be lost upon** (or **on**) To have no effect upon (a person). —**Syn.** 1 mislaid, misplaced. 4 astray. 9 confused, dazed.

lot (lot) *n.* 1 Anything, as dice or a piece of paper, used in determining something by chance. 2 The act or the result of deciding something in this manner. 3 The share that comes to one as the result of drawing lots. 4 The part in life that comes to one without his planning; chance; fate. 5 A number of persons or things considered as a group. 6 A parcel or quantity of land. 7 *Informal* A certain kind of person: he is a bad *lot*. 8 *Often pl. Informal* A great quantity or amount: a *lot* of money, *lots* of trouble. 9 A motion-picture studio and the adjacent area. —**the lot** The entire amount or quantity. —**throw** (or **cast**) **in one's lot with** To share the fortunes of. —*adv.* Very much: a *lot* worse. —*v.* **lot·ted, lot·ting** *v.t.* 1 To divide, as land, into lots. 2 To apportion by lots; allot. —*v.i.* 3 To cast lots. [< OE *hlot*]
• **lots, lots of** These words, meaning "a great deal" or "many," are common and unobjectionable in informal speech and writing: *She is lots cleverer than I; They make lots of complaints*. They should be avoided, however, in formal contexts.

Lot (lot) In the Bible, a nephew of Abraham who was permitted to escape the destruction of Sodom. Lot's wife, disobeying a warning, looked back at the city and was turned into a pillar of salt.

loth (lōth) *adj.* LOATH.

Lo·thar·i·o (lō·thâr′ē·ō) *n. pl.* **·os** A seducer; libertine. [< *Lothario*, a rake in Nicholas Rowe's play *The Fair Penitent*, 1703]

lo·tion (lō′shən) *n.* A cosmetic or medicinal liquid preparation for external use. [< L *lotio* washing]

lot·ter·y (lot′ər·ē) *n. pl.* **·ter·ies** 1 A method of awarding prizes involving numbered chances, the winning numbers being selected by drawing lots. 2 Any chance disposition of any matter. [< Ital. *lotto* lottery, lot]

lot·to (lot′ō) *n.* A game of chance played with numbered cards and disks. [Ital., lot, lottery]

lo·tus (lō′təs) *n.* 1 One of various tropical waterlilies with large floating leaves and showy flowers; esp. the **white** and **blue lotuses** of the Nile and the **sacred lotus** of India. 2 Any of a genus of leguminous herbs or shrubs. 3 *Archit.* A representation or conventionalization of the lotus flower, bud, or leaves. Also **lo′tos**. [< Gk. *lōtos*]

Lotus. a. bud and leaf. b. blossom and leaf.

lo·tus-eat·er (lō′təs-ē′tər) *n.* 1 In the *Odyssey*, one who lives in irresponsible enjoyment from eating the fruit of a certain unidentified plant. 2 Any indolent or irresponsible person.

loud (loud) *adj.* 1 Having great volume or intensity of sound. 2 Making a great sound or noise: a *loud* engine. 3 Pressing or urgent; clamorous: a *loud* demand. 4 *Informal* Very showy: a *loud* tie. 5 *Informal* Offensively noisy and talkative: a *loud* boor. —*adv.* With loudness; loudly. [< OE *hlūd*] —**loud′ly** *adv.* —**loud′ness** *n.*

loud·ish (loud′ish) *adj.* Somewhat loud.

loud-mouthed (loud′mouthd′, -moutht′) *adj.* Possessed of a loud voice; offensively clamorous or talkative.

loud·speak·er (loud′spē′kər) *n.* A device for converting electrical energy to sound.

lou·is (lōō′ē) *n.* LOUIS D'OR.

lou·is d'or (lōō′ē dôr) 1 A French gold coin worth twenty francs. 2 An old French gold coin not issued after the Revolution.

lounge (lounj) *v.* **lounged, loung·ing** *v.i.* 1 To lie, lean, move, etc., in an idle or lazy manner. **2** To pass time indolently. —*v.t.* **3** To spend or pass indolently, as time. —*n.* **1** The act of lounging. **2** A room in a hotel, club, etc., for lounging. **3** A couch or sofa. —**loung'er** *n.* [?]

loupe (lo͞op) *n.* A small magnifying glass held in the eye, used esp. by jewelers. [F]

lour (lour) *v.* LOWER².

louse (lous) *n. pl.* **lice** (līs) **1** Any of various small, wingless, parasitic insects that suck blood and inhabit the hair, fur, or feathers of the host animal. **2** Any of various insects or arthropods externally parasitic on various animals. **3** An aphid (**plant louse**). **4** *Slang pl.* **lous·es** A contemptible person. —*v.t.* & *v.i. Slang* To ruin; bungle: with *up*. [< OE *lūs*]

lous·y (lou'zē) *adj.* **lous·i·er, lous·i·est 1** Infested with lice. **2** *Slang* Dirty. **3** *Slang* Contemptible; mean. **4** *Slang* Inferior; poor. **5** *Slang* Having plenty (of): usu. with *with: lousy* with money.

lout (lout) *n.* An awkward, stupid fellow; boor. [? < ON *lutr* bent, stooped] —**lout'ish** *adj.* —**lout'ish·ly** *adv.* —**lout'-ish·ness** *n.*

lou·ver (lo͞o'vər) *n.* **1** A window or other opening designed for ventilation and having slats (**louver boards**) sloped to keep out the rain while admitting light and air. **2** A slat in such an opening. **3** Any of several narrow openings used for ventilation. [< OF *lover*]

Louver
a. detail. *b.* installed.

lov·a·ble (luv'ə-bəl) *adj.* Worthy of love; amiable; also, inspiring love. Also **love'a·ble.** —**lov'a·bly** *adv.* —**lov'a·bil'i·ty, lov'a·ble·ness** *n.*

love (luv) *n.* **1** A strong tender affection; deep devotion, as to one's child, parent, etc. **2** The affection felt by two persons who are sexually attracted to one another. **3** A person who is the object of another's affection. **4** A very great interest or fondness: *love* of learning. **5** *Often cap.* A god of love, as Cupid or Eros. **6** In tennis, a score of nothing. —**fall in love** To begin feeling affection and passionate interest. —**for the love of** For the sake of. —**in love** Experiencing love; enamored. —**make love 1** To have sexual intercourse. **2** To embrace; kiss. —*v.* **loved, lov·ing** *v.t.* **1** To feel love or affection for. **2** To take pleasure or delight in; like very much. **3** To caress. —*v.i.* **4** To feel love, esp. for one of the opposite sex; be in love. [< OE *lufu*] —**Syn.** *n.* **1** attachment, fondness.

love apple TOMATO.

love·bird (luv'bûrd') *n.* Any of several small parrots that appear to show great affection for their mates.

love knot A knot tied in pledge of love and constancy; also, a representation of it, as in jewelry.

love·less (luv'lis) *adj.* **1** Unloving. **2** Unloved. —**love'less·ly** *adv.* —**love'less·ness** *n.*

love-lies-bleed·ing (luv'līz'blē'ding) *n.* A species of amaranth with drooping spikes of red flowers.

love·lorn (luv'lôrn) *adj.* Forsaken by or pining for a lover.

love·ly (luv'lē) *adj.* **·li·er, ·li·est 1** Possessing mental or physical qualities that inspire admiration or love. **2** Beautiful. **3** *Informal* Enjoyable; pleasing: a *lovely* visit. [< OE *luflic*] —**love'li·ness** *n.*

love potion A magic drink designed to arouse love toward a certain person in the drinker.

lov·er (luv'ər) *n.* **1** One who loves. **2** One who is in love; specifically, a paramour: said esp. of a man. **3** *pl.* A couple who are in love with each other. **4** One who enjoys or is strongly attracted by some object or diversion. —**lov'er·ly** *adj., adv.*

love seat A small sofa for two persons.

love·sick (luv'sik') *adj.* **1** Languishing with love. **2** Indicating or expressing such a condition: a *lovesick* serenade. —**love'sick'ness** *n.*

lov·ing (luv'ing) *adj.* **1** Feeling love. **2** Expressing love. — **lov'ing·ly** *adv.* —**lov'ing·ness** *n.*

loving cup 1 A drinking cup, usu. with two or more handles, formerly passed from hand to hand around a circle of friends. **2** A cup like this, given as a trophy.

lov·ing-kind·ness (luv'ing-kīnd'nis) *n.* Kindness that comes from or expresses love.

low¹ (lō) *adj.* **1** Not high or tall. **2** Near the horizon: a *low* moon. **3** Situated below a recognized level: a *low* marsh. **4** Having less than the normal or regular height or depth: The river is *low.* **5** Cut so as to expose the shoulders, back, or neck. **6** Having depth of pitch; deep. **7** Having little volume or strength; soft. **8** Being little in degree, number, amount, etc. **9** Below standard quality: a *low* grade of beef. **10** Dead; prostrate: He lies *low.* **11** Deep, as a bow. **12** Depressed or melancholy. **13** Humble, as in rank or position. **14** Not refined; coarse; vulgar. **15** Not favorable; poor: a *low* opinion of oneself. **16** Relatively recent: a *low* date. **17** Not well provided with: *low* on supplies. **18** *Phonet.* Pronounced with the tongue low and flat; open: said of vowels. **19** Little advanced in structure, complexity, function, etc.: a *low* form of plant life. **20** Lacking in vigor. **21** *Mech.* Giving the greatest force and the least speed: *low* gear. **22** *Geog.* Pertaining to latitudes near the equator. — *adv.* **1** In a low way. **2** In or to a low position. **3** At a low price; cheap. **4** In a humble rank or degraded condition. **5** Softly. **6** At a low pitch. **7** Near the equator or the horizon. —**lie low 1** To be or remain in hiding. **2** To hold one's tongue till the proper moment; wait. —*n.* **1** A low level, degree, etc. **2** An arrangement of gears in a motor vehicle, etc., providing the greatest force or torque and the lowest speed. [< ON *lāgr*] —**low'ness** *n.*

low² (lō) *n.* The moo or bellow of cattle: also **low'ing.** —*v.i.* **1** To bellow, as cattle; moo. —*v.t.* **2** To utter by lowing. [< OE *hlōwan*]

low-born (lō'bôrn') *adj.* Of humble birth.

low·boy (lō'boi') *n.* A short-legged dressing table, with drawers.

low-bred (lō'bred') *adj.* Vulgar; ill-bred.

low·brow (lō'brou') *Informal n.* A person of uncultivated tastes; a nonintellectual. —*adj.* Of or suitable for such a person: also **low'browed'.** —**low'brow'ism** *n.*

Low Church A group in the Anglican Church that stresses evangelical doctrine and attaches little importance to ritual, church authority, and the sacraments. — **Low'-Church'** *adj.* —**Low-Church·man** (lō'chûrch'mən) *n.*

low comedy Comedy characterized by slapstick and lively physical action rather than by witty dialogue.

Low Countries The Netherlands, Belgium, and Luxembourg.

low-down¹ (lō'doun') *n. Slang* Inside or secret information; the truth of a matter.

low-down² (lō'doun') *adj. Informal* Degraded; mean.

low·er¹ (lō'ər) Comparative of LOW. —*adj.* **1** Inferior in position, value, rank, etc. **2** *Geol.* Older; designating strata normally beneath the newer (and upper) rock formations. —*n.* That which is beneath something above; esp., a lower berth. —*v.t.* **1** To bring to a lower position or level; let down, as a window. **2** To reduce in degree, quality, amount, etc.: to *lower* prices. **3** To bring down in estimation, rank, etc.; humble or degrade. **4** To weaken or undermine. **5** To change, as a sound, to a lower pitch or volume. —*v.i.* **6** To become lower; sink. —**Syn.** *v.* **2** decrease, diminish, lessen. **3** abase, debase. **6** fall.

low·er² (lou'ər) *v.i.* **1** To look angry or sullen; scowl. **2** To appear dark and threatening, as the weather. —*n.* A scowl; a gloomy aspect. [ME *louren*]

low·er-case (lō'ər-kās') *adj. Printing* Of, in, or describing lower case. —*v.t.* **-cased, -cas·ing** To set as or change to lower-case letters.

lower case *Printing* The small letters of a font of type, distinguished from capital letters.

low·er-class·man (lō'ər-klas'mən, -kläs'-) *n. pl.* **-men** (-mən) A freshman or a sophomore.

Lower House In a legislature having two branches, the more representative and, usu., larger branch; in the U.S., the House of Representatives; in Great Britain and Canada, the House of Commons.

---

low·er·ing (lou′ər·ing) adj. 1 Overcast with clouds; threatening. 2 Frowning or sullen. —**low′er·ing·ly** adv. —**low′er·ing·ness** n.

low·er·most (lō′ər·mōst′) adj. Lowest.

lower world 1 The abode of the dead; hell; Hades: also **lower regions.** 2 The earth.

Low German 1 The collective languages of the Low Countries, including Dutch, Flemish, and Frisian, and of the N lowlands of Germany (Plattdeutsch). 2 That division of the Germanic languages which includes Dutch, Flemish, Frisian, English, etc.

low-key (lō′kē′) adj. Having a low degree of intensity; understated. Also **low-keyed** (lō′kēd′).

low·land (lō′lənd) adj. Pertaining to or characteristic of a low or level country. —n. (also lō′land′) Usu. pl. Land lower than the adjacent country; level land. —**the Lowlands** The less elevated districts lying in the south and east of Scotland. —**Low′land·er** n.

Low Latin The Latin language of any period after the classical, esp. of the Middle Ages.

low·ly (lō′lē) adj. ·li·er, ·li·est 1 Low, as in position, rank, etc. 2 Meek, modest, or humble. —adv. 1 In a low position, manner, etc. 2 Meekly, modestly, or humbly. —**low′li·ness** n.

low mass A mass without music celebrated by one priest, usu. assisted by an altar boy.

low-mind·ed (lō′mīn′did) adj. Having low, mean, or vulgar thoughts, sentiments, or motives.

low-pitched (lō′picht′) adj. Low in tone, key, or range of tone, as a voice.

low-pres·sure (lō′presh′ər) adj. Requiring or having a low degree of pressure.

low-rise (lō′rīz′) adj. Describing a relatively low building or structure. —n. A building having no more than a few stories and usu. not having an elevator: also **low rise.**

low-spir·it·ed (lō′spir′it·id) adj. Lacking spirit or animation; despondent. —**low′-spir′it·ed·ly** adv. —**low′-spir′it·ed·ness** n.

low tide 1 The lowest stage of an ebb tide. 2 The time when this stage occurs.

low water 1 The lowest level of the water, as in a lake or river. 2 Low tide.

lox[1] (loks) n. Smoked salmon. [<G lachs salmon]

lox[2] (loks) n. Liquid oxygen. [<l(iquid) ox(ygen)]

loy·al (loi′əl) adj. 1 Constant and faithful in any relationship implying trust or confidence. 2 Unswerving in allegiance to constituted authority, as one's country or sovereign. 3 Characterized by or showing loyalty. [<L legalis legal] —**loy′al·ism** n. —**loy′al·ly** adv. —Syn. 1 devoted, steadfast, true, trustworthy.

loy·al·ist (loi′əl·ist) n. One who adheres to and defends his sovereign or state.

Loy·al·ist (loi′əl·ist) n. 1 One who was loyal to the British crown during the American Revolution. 2 One who was loyal to the Republic during the Spanish Civil War.

loy·al·ty (loi′əl·tē) n. pl. ·ties The state, quality, or an instance of being loyal; allegiance; fidelity.

loz·enge (loz′inj) n. A small medicated or sweetened tablet. [<OF losenge]

LP (el′pē′) adj. Designating a phonograph record with fine grooves, played at 33⅓ revolutions per minute. —n. An LP record: a trade name. [<L(ONG)-P(LAYING)]

Lr lawrencium.

l.s.c. in the place cited above (L loco supra citato)

LSD (el′es′dē′) n. A drug that produces states similar to those of schizophrenia, used illicitly as a hallucinogen. [< l(y)s(ergic acid) d(iethylamide)]

£.s.d. pounds, shillings, pence (Brit.).

Lt. Lieutenant.

l.t., l.tn. long ton.

Ltd., ltd. limited.

Lu lutetium.

lub·ber (lub′ər) n. 1 An awkward, ungainly fellow. 2 LANDLUBBER. [?] —**lub′ber·ly** adj., adv. —**lub′ber·li·ness** n.

lu·bri·cant (lōō′brə·kənt) adj. Lubricating. —n. A substance, as grease or oil, used to coat parts that move against each other, to make them work easily and to reduce friction.

lu·bri·cate (lōō′brə·kāt) v.t. ·cat·ed, ·cat·ing 1 To apply grease, oil, or other lubricant to so as to reduce friction and wear. 2 To make slippery or smooth. [<L lubricus slippery] —**lu′bri·ca′tive** adj. —**lu′bri·ca′tion, lu′bri·ca′tor** n.

lu·bric·i·ty (lōō·bris′ə·tē) n. 1 Smoothness; slipperiness. 2 Shiftiness; trickiness. 3 Lewdness. —**lu·bri·cous** (lōō′brə·kəs), lu·bri·cious (lōō·brish′əs) adj. [<L lubricus slippery]

lu·cent (lōō′sənt) adj. 1 Giving off light; shining; luminous. 2 Clear or translucent.

lu·cerne (lōō·sûrn′) n. Chiefly Brit. ALFALFA. Also **lu·cern′.**

lu·cid (lōō′sid) adj. 1 Easily understood; clear. 2 Mentally sound; rational. 3 Giving forth light; shining. 4 Translucent. [<L lucere to shine] —**lu·cid·i·ty** (lōō·sid′ə·tē), **lu′cid·ness** n. —**lu′cid·ly** adv.

lu·ci·fer (lōō′sə·fər) n. A match that ignites by friction. [<Lucifer]

Lu·ci·fer (lōō′sə·fər) n. 1 The planet Venus when it is the morning star. 2 Satan, esp. as the leader of the revolt of the angels before his fall from heaven. [<L lux, lucis light + ferre to bear] —**Lu·ci·fer·ous** (lōō·sif′ər·əs) adj.

Lu·cite (lōō′sīt) n. A thermoplastic transparent plastic: a trade name.

luck (luk) n. 1 That which happens by chance; fortune or lot. 2 Happy chance; good fortune; success. —**be down on one's luck** To be unlucky. —**be in luck** To be lucky. —**be out of luck** To be unlucky. —**try one's luck** To try to do something without certainty of success. —v.i. Informal 1 To be fortunate; succeed through good luck: with out. 2 To happen upon something by good luck: with in, on, onto, etc.

luck·less (luk′lis) adj. Unlucky. —**luck′less·ly** adv.

luck·y (luk′ē) adj. luck·i·er, luck·i·est 1 Favored by fortune; fortunate. 2 Bringing or resulting in good luck. 3 Thought to bring good luck. —**luck′i·ly** adv. —**luck′i·ness** n. —Syn. 1 blessed, happy, successful. 2 auspicious, propitious.

lu·cra·tive (lōō′krə·tiv) adj. Productive of wealth; profitable. [<L lucrum wealth] —**lu′cra·tive·ly** adv.

lu·cre (lōō′kər) n. Money or riches: now chiefly in the phrase **filthy lucre**, usu. used humorously. [<L lucrum gain]

lu·cu·brate (lōō′kyōō·brāt) v.i. ·brat·ed, ·brat·ing 1 To study or write laboriously, esp. at night. 2 To write in a learned manner. [<L lucubrare to work by candlelight]

lu·cu·bra·tion (lōō′kyōō·brā′shən) n. 1 Close and earnest meditation or study. 2 The product of such study; esp., a pedantic or overelaborated work. 3 Often pl. Any literary work. —**lu′cu·bra·to·ry** (-brə·tôr′ē, -tō′rē) adj.

lu·di·crous (lōō′də·krəs) adj. Exciting laughter because absurd, incongruous, ridiculous, etc. [<L ludere to play] —**lu′di·crous·ly** adv. —**lu′di·crous·ness** n.

luff (luf) n. Naut. 1 The sailing of a ship close to the wind. 2 The foremost edge of a fore-and-aft sail. —v.i. Naut. To bring the bow of a vessel toward the wind; sail near the wind. [<OF lof]

Luft·waf·fe (lōōft′väf′ə) n. German The German air force in World War II.

lug[1] (lug) n. 1 A projection for carrying or supporting something. 2 Slang A clumsy or stupid fellow. [?]

lug[2] (lug) v.t. & v.i. lugged, lug·ging To carry or pull with effort; drag. —n. LUGSAIL. [Prob.<Scand.]

lug[3] (lug) n. LUGWORM.[?]

luge (lōōzh) n. A specially designed, streamlined sled for racing. —v.i. luged, lug·ing, luge·ing To race using a luge.

lug·gage (lug′ij) n. Suitcases, valises, etc., used by a traveler; baggage. [<LUG[2]]

lug·ger (lug′ər) n. A small boat with lugsails.

lug·sail (lug′səl, -sāl′) n. A four-cornered sail, hung from a yard that slants across the mast. [<LUG[2]]

lu·gu·bri·ous (lōō·g′yōō′brē·əs) adj. Sad, mournful, or dismal, esp. in a ludicrous way. [<L lugere mourn] —**lu·gu′bri·ous·ly** adv. —**lu·gu′bri·ous·ness** n.

lug·worm (lug′wûrm′) n. An annelid worm with bristles on the back, found along seashores.

Luke (lōōk) The evangelist and reputed author of the third Gos-

Lugsails

pel and the Acts of the Apostles: also **Saint Luke.** —*n.* The third Gospel.

luke·warm (lo͞ok′wôrm′) *adj.* **1** Moderately warm; tepid. **2** Without conviction, warmth, or indifference. [Prob.< OE *hlēow* warm + WARM] —**luke′warm′ly** *adv.* —**luke′warm′ness** *n.*

lull (lul) *v.t.* **1** To soothe to sleep. **2** To calm; allay, as suspicions. —*v.i.* **3** To become calm. —*n.* An interval of calm, quiet, or diminishing activity. [ME *lullen*] —**Syn.** *v.* **1** hush, pacify, quiet, tranquilize. **2** alleviate, mitigate.

lull·a·by (lul′ə·bī) *n. pl.* **·bies** A song to lull a child to sleep. —*v.t.* **·bied, ·by·ing** To soothe with or as with a lullaby.

lu·lu¹ (lo͞o′lo͞o′) *n. Slang* Anything exceptional or remarkable, as a difficult examination, a beautiful person, etc. [Prob. < *Lulu,* formed from *Louise*]

lu·lu² (lo͞o′lo͞o′) *n. Slang* A sum of money paid to legislators for expenses. [< in *lieu* of (itemized accounting of expenses)]

lum·ba·go (lum·bā′gō) *n.* Pain in the lower part of the back. [< L *lumbus* loin]

lum·bar (lum′bər, -bär) *adj.* Pertaining to or situated near the loins. [< L *lumbus* loin]

lum·ber¹ (lum′bər) *n.* **1** Timber sawed into boards, planks, etc. **2** Disused articles, as household furniture, that take up room or are stored away. —*v.t.* **1** To cut down (timber). **2** To fill or obstruct with useless articles. —*v.i.* **3** To cut down or saw timber for marketing. [? var. of *Lombard* in obs. sense of "money-lender, pawnshop"; hence, stored articles] —**lum′ber·er** *n.*

lum·ber² (lum′bər) *v.i.* **1** To move or proceed in a heavy or awkward manner. **2** To move with a rumbling noise. —*n.* A rumbling noise. [ME *lomeren*] —**lum′ber·ing·ly** *adv.* —**lum′ber·ing·ness** *n.*

lum·ber·jack (lum′bər·jak) *n.* A person whose occupation is felling trees, cutting them into logs, and transporting the logs to a sawmill.

lum·ber·man (lum′bər·mən) *n. pl.* **·men** (-mən) **1** LUMBERJACK. **2** One who deals in lumber.

lum·ber·yard (lum′bər·yärd′) *n.* A yard for the storage or sale of lumber.

lu·men (lo͞o′mən) *n. pl.* **·mens** or **·mi·na** (-mə·nə) *Physics* A unit for measuring luminous flux, equal to the light emitted in a unit solid angle by a uniform point source of one candela. [L, light]

lu·mi·nar·y (lo͞o′mə·ner′ē) *n. pl.* **·nar·ies** **1** Any body that gives light, as the sun or moon. **2** One who has achieved great fame. [< L *lumen* light]

lu·mi·nesce (lo͞o′mə·nes′) *v.i.* **·nesced, ·nesc·ing** To exhibit luminescence.

lu·mi·nes·cence (lo͞o′mə·nes′əns) *n.* An emission of light, as fluorescence, not directly attributable to the heat which produces incandescence. [< L *lumen* light + -ESCENCE] —**lu′mi·nes′cent** *adj.*

lu·mi·nif·er·ous (lo͞o′mə·nif′ər·əs) *adj.* Producing or conveying light. [< L *lumen* light + -FEROUS]

lu·mi·nous (lo͞o′mə·nəs) *adj.* **1** Giving or emitting light; shining. **2** Full of light; well lighted; bright. **3** Easily understood; clear. [< L *lumen* light] —**lu′mi·nous·ly** *adj.* —**lu·mi·nos·i·ty** (lo͞o′mə·nos′ə·tē), **lu′mi·nous·ness** *n.*

lum·mox (lum′əks) *n. Informal* A heavy, clumsy, usu. stupid person. [?]

lump¹ (lump) *n.* **1** A shapeless mass. **2** A mass of things thrown together. **3** A protuberance; swelling. **4** A heavy, ungainly person, esp., one who is stupid. —**in a** (or **the**) **lump** All together; with no distinction. —*v.t.* **1** To put together in one mass, group, etc. **2** To consider or treat collectively: to *lump* facts. **3** To make lumps in or on. —*v.i.* **4** To become lumpy. [Prob. < Scand.]

lump² (lump) *v.t. Informal* To put up with (something disagreeable): Like it or *lump* it. [?]

lump·ish (lum′pish) *adj.* **1** Like a lump. **2** Stupid; dull. **3** Clumsy; heavy. —**lump′ish·ly** *adv.* —**lump′ish·ness** *n.*

lump sum An entire amount paid at one time.

lump·y (lum′pē) *adj.* **lump·i·er, lump·i·est** **1** Full of or covered with lumps. **2** Lumpish or gross. **3** Rough: a *lumpy* sea. —**lump′i·ly** *adv.* —**lump′i·ness** *n.*

Lu·na (lo͞o′nə) *Rom. Myth.* The goddess of the moon. —*n.* The moon.

lu·na·cy (lo͞o′nə·sē) *n. pl.* **·cies** **1** Insanity. **2** Wild foolishness; senseless conduct. [< LUNATIC]

luna moth A large North American moth having light green wings with long tails. Also **Luna moth.** [< L *luna* moon; from the crescent-shaped spots on its wings]

Luna moth

lu·nar (lo͞o′nər) *adj.* **1** Of or pertaining to the moon. **2** Round or shaped like a crescent. **3** Measured by revolutions of the moon. [< L *luna* the moon]

lunar module *Aerospace* A part of a space vehicle designed to land astronauts on the moon and lift them off to link up with the command module. Also **lunar excursion module.**

lunar month The interval between two new moons.

lunar year Twelve lunar months.

lu·nate (lo͞o′nāt) *adj.* Crescent-shaped. Also **lu′nat·ed.** [< L *luna* the moon]

lu·na·tic (lo͞o′nə·tik) *adj.* **1** Insane. **2** Of, pertaining to, or for the insane. **3** Irrational; wildly foolish. Also **lu·nat·i·cal** (lo͞o·nat′i·kəl). —*n.* **1** An insane person. **2** A very foolish person. [< L *luna* the moon] —**Syn.** *adj.* **1** demented, deranged, mad, unbalanced. **3** foolhardy, rash.

lunch (lunch) *n.* **1** A light meal, esp. the one between breakfast and dinner. **2** Food provided for a lunch. —*v.i.* **1** To eat lunch. —*v.t.* **2** To furnish lunch for. [?] —**lunch′er** *n.*

lunch·eon (lun′chən) *n.* A lunch, esp. one taken with others.

lunch·eon·ette (lun′chən·et′) *n.* A restaurant where light lunches can be obtained.

lunch·room (lunch′ro͞om′, -ro͝om′) *n.* **1** A room, as in a school, where lunches may be eaten and sometimes where food may be obtained. **2** LUNCHEONETTE.

lung (lung) *n.* Either of the two porous organs of respiration in the thorax of vertebrates, having the function of absorbing oxygen and discharging carbon dioxide. [< OE *lungen*]

lunge (lunj) *n.* **1** A sudden pass or thrust, as with a sword or a bayonet. **2** A sudden forward lurch; plunge. —*v.* **lunged, lung·ing** —*v.i.* **1** To make a lunge or pass; thrust. **2** To move with a lunge. —*v.t.* **3** To thrust with or as with a lunge. [< F *allonger* prolong < L *ad* to + *longus* long] —**lung′er** *n.*

lung·fish (lung′fish′) *n. pl.* **·fish** or **·fish·es** Any of various fishes having both lungs and gills.

lung·wort (lung′wûrt′) *n.* Any of various herbs related to borage, having spotted leaves and bluish flowers.

Lu·per·ca·li·a (lo͞o′pər·kā′lē·ə, -kāl′yə) *n.* An ancient Roman fertility festival celebrated on February 15. Also **Lu′per·cal** (-kal). —**Lu′per·ca′li·an** *adj.*

lu·pine¹ (lo͞o′pīn) *adj.* Of, pertaining to, or like a wolf; wolfish. [< L *lupus* wolf]

lu·pine² (lo͞o′pin) *n.* Any of a genus of leguminous plants bearing flowers in long racemes, used for forage. [< L *lupinus* wolflike]

lu·pus (lo͞o′pəs) *n.* Any of various diseases affecting the skin, esp. **lupus vul·ga·ris** (vul·gar′is) or tuberculosis of the skin. [L, wolf]

lurch¹ (lûrch) *v.i.* **1** To roll suddenly to one side, as a ship at sea. **2** To move unsteadily; stagger. —*n.* A lurching or unsteady movement. [?]

lurch² (lûrch) *n.* A specified defeat in cribbage. —**leave in the lurch** To leave in an embarrassing or difficult position. [< F *lourche,* name of a game]

lure (lo͞or) *n.* **1** A feathered device resembling a bird, sometimes baited with food and fastened to a falconer's wrist to recall the hawk. **2** In angling, an artificial bait; also, a decoy for animals. **3** Anything that invites by the prospect of advantage or pleasure. —*v.t.* **lured, lur·ing** **1** To attract or entice.

Lures *def.* 2

2 To recall (a hawk) with a lure. [<OF *leurre* bait] —**lur′er** *n.* —*Syn. v.* **1** allure, draw, inveigle, invite, tempt.

lu·rid (loor′id) *adj.* **1** Violent; terrible; sensational: a *lurid* crime. **2** Shining or suffused with a red glow, as of flames seen through smoke or clouds. **3** Pale; sallow. [<L *luridus* sallow] —**lu′rid·ly** *adv.* —**lu′rid·ness** *n.*

lurk (lûrk) *v.i.* **1** To lie hidden, as in ambush. **2** To exist unnoticed or unsuspected. **3** To move secretly or furtively; slink. [ME *lurken*] —**lurk′er** *n.* —**lurk′ing·ly** *adv.*

lus·cious (lush′əs) *adj.* **1** Very pleasant to taste and smell; delicious. **2** Appealing to any of the senses. **3** Too sweet; cloying. [? Blend of LUSH and DELICIOUS] —**lus′cious·ly** *adv.* —**lus′cious·ness** *n.*

lush¹ (lush) *adj.* **1** Full of juice or succulence; fresh and tender. **2** Of or characterized by abundant growth. **3** Elaborate, extravagant, or ornate. [? <L *laxus* loose] —**lush′ly** *adv.* —**lush′ness** *n.*

lush² (lush) *Slang n.* **1** A drunkard; sot: also **lush′er.** **2** Strong or intoxicating liquor. —*v.t. & v.i. Slang* To drink (alcoholic liquor). [?]

lust (lust) *n.* **1** A very strong craving or desire. **2** An intense sexual appetite. —*v.i.* To have an intense desire, esp. sexual desire. [<OE, pleasure]

lus·ter (lus′tər) *n.* **1** Sheen; gloss. **2** Radiance; brightness. **3** Brilliance or splendor, as of beauty, character, or achievement. **4** The glossy look given to certain pottery by glazing. **5** A glossy fabric of wool and cotton. —*v.* **·tered** or **·tred, ·ter·ing** or **·tring** *v.t.* **1** To give a luster or gloss to. —*v.i.* **2** To be or become lustrous. Also **lus′tre.** [<L *lustrum* purification]

lus·ter·ware (lus′tər·wâr′) *n.* Pottery given an irridescent look by the application of metallic compounds to the glaze.

lust·ful (lust′fəl) *adj.* Characterized or motivated by lust. —**lust′ful·ly** *adv.* —**lust′ful·ness** *n.*

lus·trate (lus′trāt) *v.t.* **·trat·ed, ·trat·ing** To make pure by ceremony. [<L *lustrum* purification] —**lus·tra′tion** *n.* —**lus′tra′tive** (-trə-tiv) *adj.*

lus·trous (lus′trəs) *adj.* Having luster. —**lus′trous·ly** *adv.* —**lus′trous·ness** *n.* —*Syn.* bright, burnished, effulgent, luminous.

lus·trum (lus′trəm) *n.* **1** The solemn ceremony of purification of the ancient Roman people, made every five years. **2** A period of five years. [L]

lust·y (lus′tē) *adj.* **lust·i·er, lust·i·est** Full of vigor and health; robust. —**lust′i·ly** *adv.* —**lust′i·ness** *n.*

lu·ta·nist (loo′tə·nist) *n.* One who plays the lute. Also **lu′te·nist.**

lute¹ (loot) *n.* A stringed musical instrument having a large, pear-shaped body, played by plucking the strings with the fingers. [<Ar. *al′ūd* the piece of wood]

lute² (loot) *n.* A cementlike composition used to exclude air, as around pipe joints. —*v.t.* **lut·ed, lut·ing** To seal with lute. [<L *lutum* mud] —**lu·ta′tion** *n.*

Lute

lu·te·tium (loo·tē′shəm) *n.* A metallic element (symbol Lu) of the lanthanide series. [< *Lutetia*, ancient name for Paris]

Lu·ther·an (loo′thər·ən) *n.* A member of a Protestant sect (**Lutheran Church**) founded by Martin Luther in the 16th century. —*adj.* Pertaining to or devoted to the Lutheran Church or its doctrines. —**Lu′ther·an·ism** *n.*

lux (luks) *n. pl.* **lux·es** or **lu·ces** (loo′sēz) *Physics* A unit of illumination equivalent to one lumen per square meter of surface. [L, light]

Lux. Luxembourg.

Lux·em·bourg (luk′səm·bûrg) *n.* A constitutional monarchy of N Europe, 998 sq. mi., cap. Luxembourg. Also **Lux′em·burg.** • See map at BELGIUM.

lux·u·ri·ance (lug·zhoor′ē·əns, luk·shoor′-) *n.* The quality or state of being luxuriant. Also **lux·u′ri·an·cy.**

lux·u·ri·ant (lug·zhoor′ē·ənt, luk·shoor′-) *adj.* **1** Exhibiting or characterized by vigor and abundance in growth. **2** Rich in nature, form, or content; extravagant, ornate, or abundant. **3** LUXURIOUS. —**lux·u′ri·ant·ly** *adv.*

lux·u·ri·ate (lug·zhoor′ē·āt, luk·shoor′-) *v.i.* **·at·ed, ·at·ing** **1** To take great pleasure; indulge oneself fully. **2** To live sumptuously. **3** To grow profusely. [<L *luxuria* luxury] —**lux·u′ri·a′tion** *n.*

lux·u·ri·ous (lug·zhoor′ē·əs, luk·shoor′-) *adj.* **1** Loving or indulging in luxury. **2** Characterized by or providing luxury. —**lux·u′ri·ous·ly** *adv.* —**lux·u′ri·ous·ness** *n.*

lux·u·ry (luk′shər·ē, lug′zhər·ē) *n. pl.* **·ries** **1** A way of life characterized by great comfort or pleasure. **2** Anything that contributes to comfort or pleasure but is not necessary to life, health, subsistence, etc. [<L *luxus* extravagance]

lv. leave(s).

-ly¹ *suffix of adjectives* **1** Like; characteristic of; pertaining to: *manly.* **2** Occurring every (specified interval): *weekly, daily.* [<OE *-lic*]

-ly² *suffix of adverbs* **1** In a (specified) manner: used to form adverbs from adjectives: *busily.* **2** Occurring every (specified interval): *yearly.* [<OE *-lice* <-*lic* -LY¹] • In cases where an adjective already ends in *-ly*, the forms of the adverb and the adjective are often identical: a *kindly* smile; to speak *kindly.* Occasionally *-ly* is added to *-ly* (which then becomes *-li*), as in *surlily*, an awkward word to pronounce.

ly·cée (lē·sā′) *n. French* A public secondary school in France qualifying its students for a university. [<L *Lyceum* Lyceum]

ly·ce·um (lī·sē′əm) *n. pl.* **·ce·ums** or **·ce·a** (-sē′ə) **1** An organization providing popular instruction by lectures, debates, concerts, etc. **2** A public hall, as for lectures, discussions, etc. [<LYCEUM]

Ly·ce·um (lī·sē′əm) *n.* A grove near Athens in which Aristotle taught. [<Gk. *lykeios*, epithet of Apollo]

lyd·dite (lid′īt) *n.* A high explosive composed mainly of picric acid. [<*Lydd*, England]

lye (lī) *n.* **1** A solution leached from wood ashes, used in making soap. **2** Any strong alkali. [<OE *lēah*]

ly·ing¹ (lī′ing) *n.* The practice of telling lies; untruthfulness. —*adj.* Addicted to, conveying, or constituting falsehood. —*v.t.* **ly′ing·ly** *adv.* —*Syn. n.* deceit, deception, fabrication, prevarication. *adj.* false, mendacious.

ly·ing² (lī′ing) *pr. p.* of LIE¹.

ly·ing-in (lī′ing·in′) *n.* The confinement of women during childbirth. —*adj.* Of, for, or pertaining to childbirth: a *lying-in* hospital.

Lyme disease (līm) A tick-borne disease first marked by a rash, subsequently by arthritis and cardiac damage.

lymph (limf) *n.* A colorless fluid resembling plasma and containing white blood corpuscles, which moves in the lymph vessels of vertebrates and merges with the blood through certain veins. [<L *limpa* water]

lym·phat·ic (lim·fat′ik) *adj.* **1** Pertaining to, containing, or conveying lymph. **2** Without energy; listless. —*n.* A vessel that conveys lymph.

lymph node Any of the nodular bodies of spongy tissue found in the system of lymphatic vessels. Also **lymph gland.**

lympho- *combining form* Lymph; of or pertaining to lymph or the lymphatic system: *lymphocyte.*

lym·pho·cyte (lim′fə·sīt) *n.* A variety of leukocyte arising in the lymphatic system.

lym·phoid (lim′foid) *adj.* Of, pertaining to, or resembling lymph or a lymph node.

lynch (linch) *v.t.* To kill by mob action without legal sanction. [<LYNCH LAW] —**lynch′er, lynch′ing** *n.*

lynch law The practice of administering punishment by lynching. [<Capt. Wm. *Lynch*, 1742–1820, Virginia magistrate]

lynx (lingks) *n.* Any of several wildcats of Europe and North America, with a short tail, tufted ears, and long limbs. [<Gk. *lynx*]

lynx-eyed (lingks′īd′) *adj.* Having acute sight.

ly·on·naise (lī′ə·nāz′) *adj.* Made with finely sliced onions: *lyonnaise* potatoes. [<F *lyonnais* of Lyon]

Ly·ra (lī′rə) *n.* A northern constellation containing the star Vega. [Gk., lyre]

ly·rate (lī′rāt) *adj.* Resembling or suggesting the shape of a lyre. Also **ly′rat·ed.** —**ly′rate·ly** *adv.*

lyre (līr) *n.* A harplike stringed instrument, used by the ancient Greeks to accompany song and poetry. [<Gk.]

Lyre

lyre·bird (līr′bûrd′) *n.* An Australian bird distinguished in the male by tail feathers which resemble a lyre when spread.

lyr·ic (lir′ik) *adj.* **1** Of poetry, expressing the poet's personal emotions. **2** Of, pertaining to, or having written such poetry. **3** Musical; singing or meant to be sung. **4** Having or suitable for a relatively light, flexible vocal quality: a *lyric* tenor; a *lyric* aria. Also **lyr′i·cal.** —*n.* **1** A lyric poem. **2** *Usu. pl.* The words of a song, esp. as distinguished from the music. [<Gk. *lyra* a lyre] —**lyr′i·cal·ly** *adv.*

lyr·i·cist (lir′ə·sist) *n.* **1** One who writes the words of a song or the lyrics for a musical play. **2** A lyric poet.

ly·ser·gic acid (lī·sûr′jik) A toxic substance derived from ergot and forming the base of **lysergic acid di·eth-**

yl·am·ide (dī′eth·əl·am′id), or LSD. [<Gk. *lusis* a loosening + ERG(OT) + -IC]

ly·sin (lī′sin) *n.* An antibody capable of destroying bacteria, blood corpuscles, etc. [See LYSIS]

ly·sis (lī′sis) *n.* **1** The process of cell destruction brought about by a lysin. **2** The gradual disappearing of a disease. [<Gk. *lyein* loose]

-lysis *combining form* A loosing, dissolving, etc.: *paralysis.* [<Gk., *loosening*]

-lyte[1] *combining form* A substance decomposed by a (specified) process: *electrolyte.* [<Gk. *lytos* dissolved]

-lyte[2] *combining form* -LITE.

-lytic *combining form* Loosing; dissolving: *paralytic.* [<Gk. *lysis* a loosening]

M

M, m (em) *n. pl.* **M's, m's, Ms, ms** (emz) **1** The 13th letter of the English alphabet. **2** Any spoken sound representing the letter *M* or *m.* **3** Something shaped like an M. **4** In Roman notation, the symbol for 1,000. **5** *Printing* EM. —*adj.* Shaped like an M.

M. Medieval; Monday; Monsieur.

M., m. male; married; masculine; medium; meridian; noon (L *meridies*).

m meter.

ma (mä, mô) *n.* Mama; mother. [Short for MAMA]

MA Massachusetts (P.O. abbr.).

M.A. Master of Arts (L *Magister Artium*); mental age.

ma'am (mam, mäm, məm) *n.* Madam.

ma·ca·bre (mə·kä′brə, -bər) *adj.* Grim; gruesome. Also **ma·ca′ber.** [<F *(danse) macabre* (dance) of death]

mac·ad·am (mə·kad′əm) *n.* **1** Small, broken stones for macadamizing a road. **2** A macadamized road. [<John L. McAdam, 1756–1836, British engineer]

mac·ad·am·ize (mə·kad′ə·mīz) *v.t.* **·ized, ·iz·ing** To make or finish (a road) with small broken stones, often with a tar or asphalt binder. —**mac·ad′am·i·za′tion** *n.*

ma·caque (mə·käk′) *n.* Any of a group of monkeys from Africa, Asia, and the East Indies. [<Pg. *macaco*]

mac·a·ro·ni (mak′ə·rō′nē) *n. pl.* **·nis** or **·nies 1** An edible paste of wheat flour made into short tubes. **2** An English dandy of the 18th century. Also **mac′ca·ro′ni.** [<Ital. *macherone*]

mac·a·roon (mak′ə·rōon′) *n.* A small cooky of ground almonds or coconut, white of egg, and sugar. [<Ital. *macherone* macaroni]

ma·caw (mə·kô′) *n.* A tropical American parrot with a long tail, harsh voice, and brilliant plumage. [<Pg. *macao*]

Mac·beth (mək·beth′) A king of Scotland, died 1057; hero of Shakespeare's tragedy of the same name.

Mac·ca·bees (mak′ə·bēz) A family of Jewish patriots who led a successful revolt against Syrian religious oppression. —*n. pl. (construed as sing.)* Two books of the Old Testament Apocrypha describing this revolt.

mace[1] (mās) *n.* **1** A club-shaped staff representing authority or an office. **2** A medieval steel war club, often with spiked metal head, for use against armor. [<OF *masse, mace*]

mace[2] (mās) *n.* An aromatic spice made from the covering of nutmeg seed. [<Gk. *makir* a spicy bark from India]

Mace (mās) *n.* A chemical solution that temporarily blinds or incapacitates one when sprayed in the face, used as a weapon. —*v.t.* **Maced, Mac·ing** To spray with Mace. [<Chemical *Mace,* a trade name]

Mac·e·do·ni·a (mas′ə·dō′nē·ə) *n.* The ancient Greek kingdom of **Mac·e·don** (mas′ə·don), a leading world power under Alexander the Great. —**Mac′e·do′ni·an** *adj., n.*

mac·er·ate (mas′ə·rāt) *v.* **·at·ed, ·at·ing** *v.t.* **1 a** To reduce to a soft mass by soaking. **b** To separate the soft parts of by soaking; digest. **2** To make thin; emaciate. —*v.i.* **3** To undergo maceration. [<L *macerare* make soft, knead]

mach., machin. machine; machinery; machinist.

ma·chet·e (mə·shet′ē, mə·shet′) *n.* A heavy knife used both as an implement and as a weapon in tropical America. [<L *marcus* a hammer]

Mach·i·a·vel·li·an (mak′ē·ə·vel′ē·ən) *adj.* Of or pertaining to Machiavelli, or to the unscrupulous doctrines of political opportunism associated with his name. —*n.* A follower of Machiavelli. Also **Mach′i·a·vel′i·an.** —**Mach′i·a·vel′li·an·ism′** *n.*

ma·chic·o·late (mə·chik′ə·lāt) *v.t.* **·lat·ed, ·lat·ing** To furnish with machicolations. [<Med. L *machicolare*]

ma·chic·o·la·tion (mə·chik′ə·lā′shən) *n. Archit.* An opening between a wall and a parapet, on a roof over an entrance, etc., to permit the dropping of missiles or boiling liquids on an enemy.

mach·i·nate (mak′ə·nāt) *v.t. & v.i.* **·nat·ed, ·nat·ing** To scheme, esp. with evil intent. [<L *machinari* contrive]

mach·i·na·tion (mak′ə·nā′shən) *n.* **1** The act of contriving a secret or hostile plan. **2** Such a plan or plot. —**mach′i·na′tor** *n.*

ma·chine (mə·shēn′) *n.* **1** Any combination of parts for utilizing, modifying, applying, or transmitting energy, performing a specific function, etc. **2** An automobile or other vehicle, as a bicycle, airplane, etc. **3** One who acts in a mechanical manner; a robot. **4** The organization of the powers of any complex body: the *machine* of government. **5** An organization within a political party, controlled by politicians chiefly by the use of patronage. —*adj.* **1** Of, for, or produced by a machine or machinery. **2** Mechanical; stereotyped. —*v.t.* **·chined, ·chin·ing** To shape, make, etc., by machinery. [<L *machina* contrivance]

ma·chine-gun (mə·shēn′gun′) *v.t.* **·gunned, ·gun·ning** To fire at or shoot with a machine gun.

machine gun An automatic gun that discharges small-arms ammunition in a rapid sequence.

machine language A language for programming a computer, written solely in binary digits (0, 1).

ma·chine-read·a·ble (mə·shēn′rē′də·bəl) *adj.* Being in a form that can be detected automatically for use by a computer: *machine-readable* numbers on a check.

ma·chin·er·y (mə·shē′nər·ē) *n. pl.* **·er·ies 1** The parts of a machine, or a number of machines collectively. **2** Any combination of means working together to achieve a specific action or result: the *machinery* of elections.

machine shop A workshop for making or repairing machines.

machine tool A power-driven tool, esp. one designed for use on metals.

ma·chine-wash·a·ble (mə-shēn'wash'ə-bəl, -wôsh'-) *adj.* Capable of being washed in a washing machine without damage to color or fabric and without excessive shrinkage: said of garments, etc.

ma·chin·ist (mə-shē'nist) *n.* **1** One skilled in the use of machine tools. **2** A maker or repairer of machines.

ma·chis·mo (mä-chēz'mō, -chiz'-) *n.* Maleness or masculinity, esp. when associated with strong or exaggerated pride in or a conspicuous display of the qualities, attitudes, etc., considered characteristically masculine. [Sp. < *macho* male]

mach number (mak, mäk) The ratio of the speed of an object in a fluid medium to the speed of sound in the same medium. [< Ernst *Mach*, 1838–1916, Austrian physicist]

ma·cho (mä'chō) *n. pl.* **·chos** (-chōs) A virile man, esp. one who takes excessive pride in his virility. —*adj.* Of or characteristic of a macho. [Sp., male]

mack·er·el (mak'ər-əl) *n.* An Atlantic food fish, steel-blue above with blackish bars, and silvery beneath. [< OF *makerel*]

mackerel sky A high cloud formation resembling the markings on a mackerel's back.

mack·i·naw (mak'ə-nô) *n.* A short, double-breasted, outdoor coat, usu. made of heavy wool with a plaid pattern. Also **Mack'i·naw coat.** [< *Mackinac* Island, Michigan]

mack·in·tosh (mak'ən·tosh) *n.* **1** A raincoat. **2** A lightweight, waterproof fabric, originally rubber-coated. Also **mac'in·tosh.** [< Charles *Macintosh*, 1766–1843, Scottish chemist, inventor of the cloth]

mac·ra·mé (mak'rə-mā) *n.* **1** A fringe, lace, wall hanging, etc., made of coarsely knotted thread or cord. **2** The technique of making such items. [< Ar. *miqramah* a veil]

macro- *combining form* Large or long in size or duration: *macrocephaly.* Also **macr-.** [< Gk. *makros* large]

mac·ro·bi·ot·ics (mak'rō-bī-ot'iks) *n. pl. (construed as sing.)* A dietetic regimen advocating the use of whole-grain cereals, the avoidance of meat, etc. [< MACRO- + -BIOTIC] —**mac'ro·bi·ot'ic** *adj.* —**mac'ro·bi·ot'ic·al·ly** *adv.*

mac·ro·ceph·a·ly (mak'rō·sef'ə-lē) *n.* Excessive size of the head. [< MACRO- + Gk. *kephalē* head] —**mac'ro·ce·phal'ic** (-sə-fal'ik) *adj., n.* —**mac'ro·ceph'a·lous** *adj.*

mac·ro·cosm (mak'rə-koz'əm) *n.* **1** The great world; the universe. **2** Any large, multifaceted totality. [< MACRO- + Gk. *kosmos* world] —**mac'ro·cos'mic** *adj.*

ma·cron (mā'krən, -kron) *n.* A straight line (⁻) over a vowel to show that it represents a long sound, as the ā in *day.* [< Gk. *makron* long, neut. of *makros* long]

mac·u·la (mak'yə-lə) *n. pl.* **·lae** (-lē) **1** A spot, as of color on the skin. **2** *Astron.* A dark spot on the sun's surface. [L]

mad (mad) *adj.* **mad·der, mad·dest** **1** Mentally deranged; insane. **2** Overpowered by strong emotion: *mad* with grief. **3** Foolish; reckless; unwise: a *mad* plan. **4** Wildly enthusiastic or fond of: *mad* about jazz. **5** Hilariously amusing or entertaining: a *mad* farce. **6** Angry; furious. **7** Having rabies. [< OE *gemād* insane] —**mad'ly** *adv.* —**mad'ness** *n.* —**Syn. 1** crazy, demented. **2** frantic, frenzied, wild, distracted, overwrought. **4** wild, crazy. **6** raging, fuming, infuriated, angered, wrathful.

mad·am (mad'əm) *n. pl.* **mes·dames** (mā-däm', *Fr.* dåm') *for def. 1,* **mad·ams** (mad'əmz) *for def. 2* **1** My lady; mistress: a respectful or polite term of address. **2** A woman in charge of a brothel. [< OF *ma* my + *dame* lady]

mad·ame (mad'əm, *Fr.* má·dàm') *n. pl.* **mes·dames** (mā-däm', *Fr.* mā·dàm') The French title of courtesy for a married woman, equivalent to *Mrs.:* abbreviated *Mme.* [F]

mad·cap (mad'kap') *adj.* Wild; rattle-brained. —*n.* One who acts wildly or rashly.

mad·den (mad'n) *v.t. & v.i.* **1** To make or become mad or wild. **2** To inflame with anger; enrage. —**mad'den·ing** *adj.* —**mad'den·ing·ly** *adv.*

mad·der[1] (mad'ər) Comparative of MAD.

mad·der[2] (mad'ər) *n.* **1** Any of various shrubby, perennial hairy plants, esp. a vine with small, yellow flowers and a red, fleshy root. **2** A brilliant red dye formerly made from the madder root. [< OE *mædere*]

mad·ding (mad'ing) *adj.* Being or growing mad; delirious; raging.

made (mād) *p.t. & p.p.* of MAKE. —*adj.* **1** Put together; constructed: a badly *made* house. **2** Produced, esp. artificially. **3** Assured of success. —**have it made** *Slang* To be certain to succeed.

Ma·dei·ra (mə-dir'ə) *n.* A fortified wine made in the Madeira islands.

mad·e·moi·selle (mad'ə-mə-zel', *Fr.* mád·mwá·zel') *n. pl.* **mad·e·moi·selles,** *Fr.* **mes·de·moi·selles** (mād-mwá·zel') **1** The French title of courtesy for unmarried women, equivalent to *Miss:* abbreviated *Mlle.* **2** A French nurse or governess. [F < *ma* my + *demoiselle* young lady]

made-to-or·der (mād'tə·ôr'dər) *adj.* **1** Made to specific measurements or for specific requirements. **2** Absolutely right or suitable.

made-up (mād'up') *adj.* **1** Artificial; fictitious. **2** Complete; finished. **3** With make-up or cosmetics applied.

mad·house (mad'hous') *n.* **1** A lunatic asylum. **2** A place of confusion, turmoil, and uproar.

mad·man (mad'man', -mən) *n. pl.* **·men** (-men', -mən) A lunatic; maniac. —**mad'wom'an** (-wōōm'ən) *n. Fem.*

Ma·don·na (mə-don'ə) *n.* **1** Mary, mother of Jesus. **2** A painting or statue of her. [Ital.< *ma* my + *donna* lady]

ma·dras (mə-dras', -dräs', mad'rəs) *n.* **1** A cotton cloth, usu. of several colors woven in various designs, esp. a plaid design. **2** A cotton or rayon fabric for curtains or draperies. **3** A large, brightly colored kerchief. [< *Madras,* India]

mad·re·pore (mad'rə·pôr, -pōr) *n.* Any of various corals that build reefs. [< Ital. *madrepora,* lit., mother stone] —**mad're·por'ic** (-pôr'ik, -por'ik) *adj.*

mad·ri·gal (mad'rə-gal) *n.* **1** A short lyric poem, usu. dealing with a pastoral or amatory subject. **2** A musical setting for such a poem, esp. a part song. **3** Any part song. [< LL *matricale* original, chief < L *matrix* womb]

mael·strom (māl'strəm) *n.* **1** A powerful, dangerous whirlpool. **2** Any violent, irresistible influence, emotion, etc. [< MDu. *malen* grind + *stroom* a stream]

mae·nad (mē'nad) *n.* **1** A priestess of Dionysus; a bacchante. **2** Any woman beside herself with frenzy or excitement. [< Gk. *mainas* frenzied] —**mae·nad'ic** *adj.*

ma·es·to·so (mä'es·tō'sō) *adj. & adv. Music* With majesty; stately. [Ital.]

ma·es·tro (mä·es'trō, mī'strō) *n.* A master in any art, esp. in music. [Ital]

Ma·fi·a (mä'fē·ä, maf'ē·ə) *n.* **1** In Sicily, a secret society, characterized by hostility to and deliberate flouting of the law. **2** A similar, criminal organization believed to exist in other countries. Also **Maf'fi·a.** [< Ital. *maffia*]

ma·fi·o·so (mäf'ē·ō'sō, -zō, maf'-) *n. pl. ·si* (-sē, -zē) *Sometimes cap.* A member of the Mafia. [Ital. < MAFIA]

mag. magazine; magnet; magnetism; magnitude.

mag·a·zine (mag'ə·zēn', mag'ə-zēn) *n.* **1** A periodical publication containing sketches, stories, essays, etc. **2** A depot, warehouse, etc., for storage, esp. for storage of explosives, ammunition, etc. **3** A chamber in a repeating firearm which holds the supply of reserve cartridges. **4** A supply chamber in a battery, camera, or the like. [< Ar. *makhzan* a storehouse]

Magazine of a rifle

mag·da·len (mag'də-lin) *n.* A reformed prostitute. Also **mag'da·lene** (-lēn). [< Mary *Magdalene*]

Ma·gel·lan·ic cloud (maj'ə-lan'ik) *Astron.* Either of two galaxies near the south pole of the heavens, looking like detached fragments of the Milky Way. [< F. *Magellan,* 1480–1521, Portuguese navigator]

ma·gen·ta (mə·jen'tə) *n.* **1** A red dyestuff derived from aniline. **2** A strong, purplish red. —*adj.* Purplish red. [< *Magenta,* Italy, where first discovered]

mag·got (mag'ət) *n.* A wormlike insect larva; a grub. [ME *maddock, mathek*] —**mag'got·y** *adj.*

Ma·gi (mā'jī) *n. pl.* of **Ma·gus** (mā'gəs) **1** The priestly caste of the Medes and Persians. **2** The three "wise men" who came "from the east" to Bethlehem to pay homage to the infant Jesus. [< Pers. *magu* priest, magician]

mag·ic (maj'ik) *n.* **1** Any supernatural power or control over natural laws or the forces of nature, esp. by the use of charms, etc. **2** The theatrical art of performing tricks

and illusions by sleight of hand, mechanical devices, etc.
3 Any mysterious or spellbinding power or enchantment: the *magic* of her voice. —*adj.* **1** Of, used in, or produced by magic. **2** Bringing forth unusual results, as if by magic. • See MAGICAL. [< Gk. *magikos* of the Magi]

mag·i·cal (maj′i·kəl) *adj.* Magic. • The adjective *magic* is applied more commonly to the powers, influences, or practices, while *magical* is more frequently used of the effects of magic: *magic* arts, a *magic* wand, but a *magical* evening, a *magical* solution. —**mag′i·cal·ly** *adv.*

ma·gi·cian (mə·jish′ən) *n.* **1** An expert in magic arts. **2** Any person of unusual abilities.

magic lantern A device formerly used for projecting transparencies on a screen.

mag·is·te·ri·al (maj′is·tir′ē·əl) *adj.* **1** Of a magistrate, his duties, etc. **2** Like or befitting a master; commanding; authoritative. **3** Domineering; pompous. —**mag′is·te′ri·al·ly** *adv.*

mag·is·tra·cy (maj′is·trə·sē) *n. pl.* **·cies 1** The office or dignity of a magistrate. **2** The district under a magistrate's jurisdiction. **3** Magistrates collectively.

mag·is·trate (maj′is·trāt, -trit) *n.* **1** One clothed with public civil authority; an executive or judicial officer. **2** A minor public official, as a justice of the peace. [< L *magister* a master]

mag·ma (mag′mə) *n.* The molten mass within the earth from which igneous rocks are formed. [< Gk.] —**mag·mat·ic** (mag·mat′ik) *adj.*

Mag·na Car·ta (mag′nə kär′tə) **1** The Great Charter of English liberties, delivered June 19, 1215, by King John, at Runnymede, on the demand of the English barons. **2** Any fundamental constitution that secures personal liberty and civil rights. Also **Mag′na Char′ta**. [Med. L, lit., Great Charter]

mag·na cum lau·de (mag′nə kum lô′dē, mäg′nä koōm lou′də) With high honors: to be graduated *magna cum laude*. [L]

mag·na·nim·i·ty (mag′nə·nim′ə·tē) *n. pl.* **·ties 1** The quality or condition of being magnanimous. **2** A magnanimous deed.

mag·nan·i·mous (mag·nan′ə·məs) *adj.* Noble and generous; not petty, mean, or selfish. [< L *magnus* great + *animus* mind, soul] —**mag·nan′i·mous·ly** *adv.* —**mag·nan′i·mous·ness** *n.*

mag·nate (mag′nāt, -nit) *n.* A person of rank, power, or importance in any sphere. [< L *magnus* great]

mag·ne·sia (mag·nē′zhə, -shə, -zē·ə) *n.* The oxide of magnesium, used in medicine, glassmaking, etc. [< Gk. *Magnēsia (lithos)* (stone) of Magnesia] —**mag·ne′sian, mag·ne′sic** *adj.*

mag·ne·si·um (mag·nē′zē·əm, -zhəm) *n.* A light, malleable, ductile, metallic element (symbol Mg), used in structural alloys and in incendiary and photographic flash powders. [NL, magnesia]

mag·net (mag′nit) *n.* **1** Any mass of material capable of attracting bodies that are magnetized or capable of being magnetized. **2** A person or thing exercising a strong attraction. [< Gk. *Magnēs (lithos)* Magnesian (stone)]

mag·net·ic (mag·net′ik) *adj.* **1** Of, pertaining to, or caused or operated by a magnet or magnetism. **2** Capable of being magnetized. **3** Of the earth's magnetism. **4** Fascinatingly attractive or dynamic: a *magnetic* personality. —**mag·net′i·cal·ly** *adv.*

magnetic field That region in the neighborhood of a magnet or electric current in which magnetic effects are observable.

magnetic head A device for recording and playback by which magnetized particles on a moving tape are impressed with a pattern analogous to that of incident sound waves.

magnetic needle A freely movable, needle-shaped bar of

Magnetic needle
a. magnetic north.
b. true north.

magnetized material which tends to align with an external magnetic field.

magnetic north The direction toward the magnetic pole of the earth that is closest to the North Pole.

magnetic pickup A phonograph pickup in which the movements of the stylus cause relative motion between a coil and a magnetic field and induce an electrical signal. Also **magnetic cartridge.**

magnetic pole 1 Either of the points of a magnet, usu. occurring in pairs of opposite polarity, at which the magnetic field is most intense. **2** Either of the earth's magnetic poles, called the **North (or South) Magnetic Pole**. These slowly change position and do not coincide with the geographical poles.

magnetic recording The process or the product of storing sound, TV programs, and other data in the form of ordered patterns of magnetized particles on tape which can be played back in the original form.

magnetic tape A thin ribbon coated with magnetized particles, usu. wound on a reel and used to preserve magnetic recordings.

mag·net·ism (mag′nə·tiz′əm) *n.* **1** The specific properties of a magnet, produced by the alignments of certain atoms and the movements of their electrons. **2** The science that studies magnetic phenomena. **3** The measure of the force of a magnetic field. **4** The sympathetic personal quality that attracts or interests.

mag·net·ite (mag′nə·tīt) *n.* A black, magnetic form of iron oxide; lodestone. [< MAGNET] —**mag′net·it′ic** (-tit′ik) *adj.*

mag·net·ize (mag′nə·tīz) *v.* **ized, ·iz·ing** *v.t.* **1** To produce magnetic properties in. **2** To attract by strong personal influence; captivate. —*v.i.* **3** To become magnetic. —**mag′·net·iz′a·ble** *adj.* —**mag′net·i·za′tion, mag′net·iz′er** *n.*

mag·ne·to (mag·nē′to) *n. pl.* **·tos** An electric alternator using a field produced by permanent magnets, sometimes used in ignition systems of internal-combustion engines.

mag·ne·tom·e·ter (mag′nə·tom′ə·tər) *n.* An instrument for measuring the intensity and direction of magnetic forces. —**mag′ne·tom′e·try** *n.*

Mag·nif·i·cat (mag·nif′ə·kat) *n.* The hymn or canticle of the Virgin Mary, beginning with the word *Magnificat* in the Latin version. *Luke* 1:46–55. [L, it magnifies]

mag·nif·i·cence (mag·nif′ə·səns) *n.* The state or quality of being magnificent.

mag·nif·i·cent (mag·nif′ə·sənt) *adj.* **1** Grandly imposing or beautiful: a *magnificent* ruin. **2** Sublime; exalted: *magnificent* prose. **3** Lavish; sumptuous: a *magnificent* banquet. **4** Exceptionally fine; excellent: a *magnificent* physique. [< L *magnus* great + *facere* make] —**mag·nif′i·cent·ly** *adv.*

mag·nif·i·co (mag·nif′ə·kō) *n. pl.* **·coes** A lordly personage. [Ital., magnificent]

mag·ni·fy (mag′nə·fī) *v.t.* **·fied, ·fy·ing 1** To increase the apparent size of, as with an optical instrument. **2** To increase the size of; enlarge. **3** To cause to seem greater; intensify. **4** To exaggerate. **5** *Archaic* To extol; exalt. [< L *magnus* great + *facere* make] —**mag′ni·fi′a·ble** *adj.* —**mag′·ni·fi·ca′tion, mag′ni·fi′er** *n.*

mag·nil·o·quent (mag·nil′ə·kwənt) *adj.* Characterized by a pompous or high-flown style or manner. [< L *magnus* great + *loqui* speak] —**mag·nil′o·quence** *n.* —**mag·nil′o·quent·ly** *adv.*

mag·ni·tude (mag′nə·t^yoōd) *n.* **1** Great size or extent. **2** Great importance or significance. **3** *Math.* **a** Any of the numbers associated with individual elements of a set and by which they can be compared. **b** That which is measurable. **4** *Astron.* A logarithmic measure of the relative or absolute brightness of stars, with lower numbers denoting greater brightness. [< L *magnus* large]

mag·no·li·a (mag·nō′lē·ə, -nōl′-

Magnolia blossom

y·ə) n. 1 Any of a genus of trees or shrubs with large, fragrant flowers. 2 The flower. [<Pierre *Magnol*, 1638–1715, French botanist]

mag·num (mag′nəm) n. A wine bottle of twice the ordinary size, holding about two quarts. [<L *magnus* great]

magnum o·pus (ō′pəs) The chief or most important work of an artist, writer, composer, etc. [L]

mag·pie (mag′pī) n. 1 Any of a genus of birds related to jays, having black and white plumage and a long tail. 2 A chatterbox; a garrulous gossip. [<*Mag*, dim. of *Margaret*, a personal name + PIE²]

mag·uey (mə·gā′, mag′wā) n. 1 Any of various Mexican agave plants including species yielding fiber or potable juice. 2 The fiber of certain of these plants. [<Taino]

Mag·yar (mag′yär, *Hungarian* mud′yär) n. 1 One of a people who invaded and conquered Hungary at the end of the ninth century; a Hungarian. 2 The Finno-Ugric language of Hungary. —adj. Of or pertaining to the Magyars or their language.

ma·ha·ra·ja (mä′hə·rä′jə) n. A Hindu prince; the title of some native rulers. Also **ma·ha·ra′jah**. [<Skt. *maha* great + *rājā* a king]

ma·ha·ra·ni (mä′hə·rä′nē) n. 1 A sovereign Hindu princess. 2 The wife of a maharaja. Also **ma·ha·ra′nee**. [<Skt. *maha* great + *rānī* a queen]

ma·hat·ma (mə·hat′mə, -hät′-) n. A great spiritual leader; a sage: a title of respect. [<Skt. *maha* great + *ātman* soul] —**ma·hat′ma·ism** n.

Ma·hi·can (mə·hē′kən) n. One of a tribe of Algonquian Indians formerly occupying the upper Hudson River valley. —adj. Of this tribe. [<Algonquian, lit., a wolf]

mah jong (mä′jong′, jông′) A game of Chinese origin, usu. for four persons, played with 144 marked tiles. Also **mah jongg**. [<dial. Chin. < Chin. *ma ch'iao*, lit., a house sparrow; from the design on one of the titles]

ma·hog·a·ny (mə·hog′ə·nē) n. 1 A large tropical American tree, with fine-grained, hard, reddish wood much used for cabinet work. 2 The wood itself. 3 Any of various shades of reddish brown. —adj. 1 Of mahogany. 2 Reddish brown. [?]

Ma·hom·e·tan (mə·hom′ə·tən) adj., n. MOHAMMEDAN.

ma·hout (mə·hout′) n. The keeper and driver of an elephant. [<Skt. *mahāmātra*, lit., great in measure]

maid (mād) n. 1 An unmarried woman or young girl. 2 A virgin. 3 A female servant. [Short for MAIDEN]

maid·en (mād′n) n. 1 An unmarried woman. 2 A young girl. 3 A virgin. 4 A race horse that has never won an event. —adj. 1 Of or for a maiden. 2 Virgin. 3 Unmarried. 4 First; initiatory: a *maiden* voyage. [<OE *mægden*] — **maid′en·li·ness** n. —**maid′en·ly** adj., adv.

maid·en·hair (mād′n·hâr′) n. A delicate and graceful fern with an erect black stem. Also **maidenhair fern**.

maid·en·head (mād′n·hed′) n. HYMEN.

maid·en·hood (mād′n·hŏŏd) n. The state of being a maiden. Also **maid′hood**.

maiden name A woman's surname before marriage.

maid of honor 1 An unmarried lady, usu. of noble birth, attendant upon a queen or princess. 2 An unmarried woman serving as the chief attendant of a bride at a wedding ceremony.

maid·ser·vant (mād′sûr′vənt) n. A female servant.

mail¹ (māl) n. 1 The governmental system for handling letters, etc., by post. 2 Letters, magazines, parcels, etc., sent from place to place by the post office. 3 The collection or delivery of postal matter. 4 A conveyance, as a train, plane, etc., for carrying postal matter. —adj. Pertaining to or used in handling mail. —v.t. To send by mail; post. [<OHG *malha* a pouch] — **mail′a·ble** adj.

mail² (māl) n. 1 Armor of chains, rings, or scales. 2 Any strong covering or defense, as the shell of a turtle. —v.t. To cover with or as with mail. [<L *macula* spot, mesh of a net]

Chain mail armor

mail·box (māl′boks′) n. 1 A box in which letters, etc., are posted for collection. 2 A box into which private mail is put when delivered. Also **mail box**.

mail·gram (māl′gram′) n. *U.S.* A telegram, the message of which is usu. first telephoned to the receiver, then converted to written form and delivered in the next scheduled distribution of mail. [<MAIL + (TELE)GRAM]

mail·man (māl′man′, -mən) n. pl. **·men** (-men′, -mən) A man whose work is to deliver mail; postman.

mail order An order for goods, sent and filled by mail. —**mail′-or′der** adj.

maim (mām) v.t. To deprive of the use of a bodily part; mutilate; disable. [<OF *mahaigner*] —**maim′er** n.

main (mān) n. 1 A chief conduit or conductor, as for gas, water, or electricity. 2 The ocean. 3 Violent effort; strength: chiefly in the phrase **with might and main**. 4 The chief part; the most important point. —**in the main** On the whole; mostly. —adj. 1 First or chief in size, rank, importance, etc.; principal; chief; leading. 2 *Naut.* Near or connected with the mainsail or mainmast. —**by main force** (or **strength**) By sheer, undivided force or strength. [<OE *mægen*] —**main′ly** adv.

main drag *Slang* The principal street or section of a city.

main·frame (mān′frām′) n. The main part of a computer, or central processing unit, without the attached peripherals.

main·land (mān′land′, -lənd) n. A principal body of land; a continent, or part of a continent, as distinguished from an island. —**main′land·er** n.

main·line (mān′līn′) n. A main road, railroad line, etc. —v.t. & v.i. **·lined**, **·lin·ing** *Slang* To inject (a narcotic drug, esp. heroin) directly into a vein. —**main′li′ner** n.

main·mast (mān′məst, -mast′) n. *Naut.* The principal mast of a vessel, usu. the second mast from the bow.

main·sail (mān′səl, -sāl′) n. *Naut.* A sail carried on the mainmast.

main·sheet (mān′shēt′) n. *Naut.* The sheet, or rope, by which the mainsail is trimmed and set.

main·spring (mān′spring′) n. 1 The principal spring of a mechanism, as of a watch. 2 The most important cause or motive.

main·stay (mān′stā′) n. 1 *Naut.* The supporting rope that extends forward from the mainmast. 2 A chief support.

Main Street 1 The principal business street of a small town. 2 The typically provincial customs, ways of thinking, etc., of a small town.

main·street·ing (mān′strēt′ing) n. *Can.* The practice of walking on the main streets of a town, esp. by a politician wishing to greet potential supporters.

main·tain (mān·tān′) v.t. 1 To carry on or continue; engage in, as a correspondence. 2 To keep unimpaired or in proper condition: to *maintain* roads. 3 To supply with food or livelihood; support; pay for. 4 To uphold; claim to be true. 5 To assert or state; affirm. 6 To hold or defend, as against attack. [<L *manu tenere*, lit., hold in one's hand] —**main·tain′a·ble** adj. —**main·tain′er** n.

main·te·nance (mān′tə·nəns) n. 1 The act of maintaining or the state of being maintained. 2 Means of support.

main·top (mān′top′) n. *Naut.* A platform at the head of the lower section of the mainmast.

main·top·mast (mān′top′məst) n. *Naut.* The mast next above the mainmast.

main yard *Naut.* The lower yard on the mainmast.

maî·tre d' (mā′trə dē′) pl. **maître d's** (dēz′) HEADWAITER. [F < MAÎTRE D'HÔTEL]

maî·tre d'hô·tel (mā′trə dō·tel′; *Fr.* me′tr′) pl. **maîtres d'hôtel** (mā′trə; *Fr.* me′tr′) 1 MAJORDOMO. 2 HEADWAITER. [F, lit. master of the house]

maize (māz) n. 1 CORN (defs. 1 & 2). 2 The yellow color of ripe corn. [<Taino *mahiz*]

Maj. Major.

maj. majority.

ma·jes·tic (mə·jes′tik) adj. Having or exhibiting majesty; stately; dignified. Also **ma·jes′ti·cal**. —**ma·jes′ti·cal·ly** adv. —**ma·jes′ti·cal·ness** n. —Syn. grand, impressive, awesome, grandiose, magnificent.

maj·es·ty (maj′is·tē) n. pl. **·ties** 1 Exalted dignity; stateliness; grandeur. 2 Sovereign power: the *majesty* of the law. [<L *majestas* greatness]

Maj·es·ty (maj′is·tē) n. pl. **·ties** A title or form of address for a sovereign: preceded by *His, Her, Your,* etc.

Maj. Gen. Major General.

ma·jol·i·ca (mə·jol′i·kə, -yol′-) *n.* A kind of Italian pottery, glazed and decorated, usu. in rich colors and Renaissance designs. [< Ital. *Majolica,* early name of *Majorca,* Spain]

ma·jor (mā′jər) *adj.* 1 Greater in number, quantity, or extent. 2 Greater in dignity, rank, or importance; principal; leading. 3 Considerable in extent, degree, etc.: a *major* repair. 4 Serious; grave: a *major* illness. 5 In education, of or designating the specific field of study specialized in by a candidate for a degree. 6 *Music* Of or characteristic of the tone successions or chords of a major scale, esp. the triad built on the tonic. 7 *Law* Being of legal age. —*n.* 1 See GRADE. 2 *Law* One who is of legal age. 3 *Music* A major key, chord, or interval. 4 In education: a A major subject or field of study. b A student who follows a (specified) course of study: an English *major.* —*v.i.* To pursue a definite field of study: with *in*: to *major* in history. [L, greater]

ma·jor·do·mo (mā′jər·dō′mō) *n. pl.* **-mos** 1 The chief steward of a royal or great household. 2 A butler. [< L *major* an elder + *domus* a house]

major general *pl.* **major generals** See GRADE.

ma·jor·i·ty (mə·jôr′ə·tē, -jor′-) *n. pl.* **-ties** 1 More than half of a given number or group; the greater part. 2 The amount or number by which one group of things exceeds another group; excess. 3 The age at which a person becomes legally responsible. 4 The rank or commission of a major. 5 In U.S. politics, the number of votes cast for a candidate over and above the number cast for his nearest opponent; a plurality. 6 The party having the most power in a legislature. [< L *major* greater]

major key *Music* A key based on the tones of a major scale.

major league 1 In baseball, either of the two main groups of professional teams in the U.S. 2 Any principal league in a professional sport. —**ma′jor-league′** *adj.*

major scale *Music* A diatonic scale with half steps after the third and seventh tones.

major suit In bridge, the suit of spades or of hearts.

make (māk) *v.* **made, mak·ing** *v.t.* 1 To bring about the existence of by the shaping or combining of materials; produce; build; construct; fashion. 2 To bring about; cause: Don't *make* trouble. 3 To bring to some state or condition; cause to be: The wind *made* him cold. 4 To appoint or assign; elect: They *made* him captain. 5 To form or create in the mind, as a plan. 6 To compose or create, as a poem or piece of music. 7 To understand or infer to be the meaning or significance: with *of*: What do you *make* of it? 8 To put forward; advance: to *make* an offer. 9 To utter or express: to *make* a declaration. 10 To obtain for oneself; earn; accumulate. 11 To add up to: Four quarts *make* a gallon. 12 To bring the total to: That *makes* five attempts. 13 To develop into; become: He *made* a good soldier. 14 To accomplish; effect or form: to *make* an agreement. 15 To estimate to be; reckon. 16 To induce or force; compel: He *made* me do it! 17 To draw up, enact, or frame, as laws, testaments, etc. 18 To prepare for use, as a bed. 19 To afford or provide: This brandy *makes* good drinking. 20 To be the essential element or determinant of: Stone walls do not a prison *make.* 21 To cause the success of: His speech *made* him politically. 22 To traverse; cover: to *make* fifty miles before noon. 23 To travel at the rate of: to *make* fifty miles per hour. 24 To arrive at; reach: to *make* Boston. 25 To board before departure: to *make* a train. 26 To earn so as to count on a score: to *make* a touchdown. 27 *Electr.* To complete (a circuit). 28 *Informal* To win a place on: to *make* the team. 29 In bridge, to win (a bid). 30 *Slang* To seduce. —*v.i.* 31 To cause something to assume a specified condition: to *make* fast. 32 To act in a certain manner: to *make* merry. 33 To start: They *made* to go. 34 To go or extend in some direction: with *to* or *toward.* 35 To flow, as the tide; rise, as water. —**make believe** To pretend, as in play. —**make do** To get along with what is available, esp. with an inferior substitute. —**make for** 1 To go toward. 2 To attack; assail. 3 To have effect on; contribute to. —**make it** *Informal* To do or achieve something; succeed. —**make off** To run away. —**make off with** To carry away;

filch; purloin. —**make out** 1 To see; discern. 2 To comprehend; understand. 3 To try to prove or imply to be: They *made* us *out* criminals. 4 To fill out, as a printed form. 5 To succeed; manage. 6 *Slang* a To neck. b To have sexual intercourse. —**make over** 1 To renovate. 2 To transfer title or possession of. —**make up** 1 To compose; compound, as a prescription. 2 To be the parts of; comprise. 3 To settle differences: to kiss and *make up.* 4 To devise; invent: to *make up* an answer. 5 To supply what is lacking in. 6 To compensate for; atone for. 7 To settle; decide: to *make up* one's mind. 8 *Printing* To arrange, as lines, into columns or pages. 9 To put cosmetics on. —**make up to** *Informal* To make a show of friendliness and affection toward. —*n.* 1 The manner in which something is constructed. 2 Brand: a new *make* of automobile. 3 The act of making or producing. 4 The amount produced; yield. 5 The physical or mental qualities of a person. 6 The closing or completion of an electrical circuit. —**on the make** *Informal* 1 Greedy for profit, success, etc. 2 Eager for amorous conquest. [< OE *macian*]

make-be·lieve (māk′bi·lēv′) *adj.* Pretended; unreal. —*n.* A mere pretense; sham. —**Syn.** *adj.* false, sham, counterfeit, spurious, specious, fake.

mak·er (mā′kər) *n.* 1 One who or that which makes. 2 *Law* One who signs a promissory note.

Mak·er (mā′kər) *n.* God.

make·shift (māk′shift′) *adj.* Being a temporary substitute. —*n.* A temporary substitute in any emergency.

make·up (māk′up′) *n.* 1 The arrangement or manner in which the parts of anything are put together. 2 Mental or physical constitution or disposition. 3 *Printing* The arrangement of composed type in pages, columns, or forms. 4 The costumes, wigs, cosmetics, etc., used to assume a theatrical role; also, the art of applying or assuming them. 5 Cosmetics in general.

mak·ing (mā′king) *n.* 1 The act or process of causing, doing, forming, or constructing. 2 That which contributes to improvement or success. 3 A quantity of anything made at one time; batch. 4 *Often pl.* The necessary materials or qualities.

mal- *prefix* 1 Bad; ill; not: *maladjusted.* 2 Wrong(ly); defective(ly): *malformation; malformed.* [< L *malus* bad]

Mal, Mal. Malachi; Malay; Malayan.

Ma·lac·ca cane (mə·lak′ə) A walking stick made of rattan. [< *Malacca,* Malaya]

mal·a·chite (mal′ə·kīt) *n.* A green mineral carbonate of copper, used as an ore. [< Gk. *malachē* mallow; so called because resembling mallow leaves in color]

mal·ad·just·ed (mal′ə·jus′tid) *adj.* Poorly adjusted, as to the circumstances of one's life. —**mal′ad·just′ment** *n.*

mal·ad·min·is·ter (mal′əd·min′is·tər) *v.t.* To administer badly or dishonestly. —**mal′ad·min′is·tra′tion** *n.*

mal·a·droit (mal′ə·droit′) *adj.* Clumsy or blundering. [< MAL- + F *adroit* clever] —**mal′a·droit′ly** *adv.* —**mal′a·droit′ness** *n.*

mal·a·dy (mal′ə·dē) *n. pl.* **-dies** 1 A disease; illness. 2 Any disordered condition. [< LL *male habitus,* lit., ill kept]

Mal·a·ga (mal′ə·gə) *n.* 1 A sweet white wine made originally in Málaga, Spain. 2 A variety of large, white grape.

Mal·a·gas·y (mal′ə·gas′ē) *n.* 1 A citizen or native of the Malagasy Republic. 2 The language of the Malagasy Republic. —*adj.* Of or pertaining to the Malagasy Republic, its people, or their language.

Malagasy Republic A republic comprising Madagascar and nearby islands, 228,000 sq. mi., cap. Tananarive. • See map at AFRICA.

mal·aise (mal·āz′, ma·lez′) *n.* 1 A feeling of uneasiness or discontent. 2 A physical feeling of weakness or languor. [F < *mal* ill + *aise* ease]

ma·la·mute (mä′lə·myoōt, mal′ə-) *n.* A large, thick-coated sled dog of Alaska. [< *Malemute,* an Alaskan tribe]

mal·a·prop (mal′ə·prop) *n.* MALAPROPISM. —*adj.* Using or marked by malapropisms: also **mal·a·prop·i·an** (mal′ə·prop′ē·ən). [< Mrs. *Malaprop.* a character in Sheridan's play, *The Rivals,* who absurdly misuses words]

---

mal·a·prop·ism (mal′ə·prop·iz′əm) n. 1 An absurd misuse of words that sound somewhat alike. 2 An example of this, as *Measles is highly contiguous* (instead of *contagious*). [< Mrs. *Malaprop*. See MALAPROP.]

mal·ap·ro·pos (mal′ap·rə·pō′) adj. Out of place; not appropriate. [< F *mal à propos* not to the point]

ma·lar·i·a (mə·lâr′ē·ə) n. 1 An infectious disease caused by a protozoan transmitted by infected anopheles mosquitoes, and resulting in intermittent chills and fever. 2 Any foul or unwholesome air; miasma. [< Ital. *mal′ aria*, lit., bad air] —**ma·lar′i·al, ma·lar′i·an, ma·lar′i·ous** adj.

ma·lar·ky (mə·lär′kē) n. Slang Insincere or senseless talk; bunk. Also **ma·lar′key.** [?]

Ma·la·wi (mä′lä·wē) n. An independent member of the Commonwealth of Nations in SE Africa, 49,177 sq. mi., cap. Zomba. • See map at AFRICA.

Ma·lay (mā′lā, mə·lā′) n. 1 A member of the dominant race in Malaysia; a Malayan. 2 The Indonesian language spoken on the Malay Peninsula. —adj. Of or pertaining to Malaya or Malaysia.

Ma·lay·a (mə·lā′ə) n. A former federation of eleven states in the Commonwealth of Nations, now incorporated in Malaysia.

Mal·a·ya·lam (mal′ə·yä′ləm) n. The Dravidian language of the Malabar coast, India, related to Tamil.

Ma·lay·an (mə·lā′ən) adj. 1 MALAY. 2 INDONESIAN. —n. 1 MALAY (def. 1). 2 MALAY (def. 2). 3 INDONESIAN.

Ma·lay·o·Pol·y·ne·sian (mə·lā′ō·pol′ə·nē′zhən, -shən) adj. & n. AUSTRONESIAN.

Ma·lay·sia (mə·lā′zhə, -shə) n. An independent member

Malaysia

of the Commonwealth of Nations in SE Asia, 127,344 sq. mi., cap. Kuala Lumpur. —**Ma·lay′sian** adj., n.

mal·con·tent (mal′kən·tent, mal′kən·tent′) adj. Discontented or dissatisfied, esp. with a government or economic system. —n. A discontented person, esp. one rebellious against authority.

mal de mer (mal də mâr′) SEASICKNESS. [F]

Mal·dive Islands (mal′dīv, -dēv) A republic located on an island group SW of Sri Lanka, 115 sq. mi., cap. Malé. —**Mal·div′e·an** (mal·div′ē·ən) adj., n.

male (māl) adj. 1 Of or pertaining to the sex that begets young. 2 Masculine. 3 Made up of men or boys. 4 Bot. Having stamens, but no pistil; also, adapted to fertilize, but not to produce fruit, as stamens. 5 Denoting a tool or object which fits into a corresponding hollow part. —n. A male person, animal, or plant. [< L *masculus*]

mal·e·dic·tion (mal′ə·dik′shən) n. 1 An invocation of evil; a curse. 2 Slander. [< L *male* ill + *dicere* speak] — **mal′e·dic′to·ry** adj.

mal·e·fac·tor (mal′ə·fak′tər) n. One who commits a crime. [< L *male* ill + *facere* do] —**mal′e·fac′tion** n.

ma·lef·i·cent (mə·lef′ə·sənt) adj. Causing or doing evil or mischief; harmful. [< L *male* ill + *facere* do]

ma·lev·o·lent (mə·lev′ə·lənt) adj. Wishing evil toward others; malicious. [< L *male* ill + *volens* wishing] —**ma·lev′o·lence** n. —**ma·lev′o·lent·ly** adv.

mal·fea·sance (mal·fē′zəns) n. Law The performance of an unlawful or wrongful act, esp. by a public official. [< OF *mal* ill + *faire* do] —**mal·fea′sant** adj., n.

mal·for·ma·tion (mal′fôr·mā′shən) n. Any irregularity or deformation in the structure of an organism.

mal·formed (mal·fôrmd′) adj. Badly formed or made; deformed.

mal·func·tion (mal·fungk′shən) n. Impairment or dis-

turbance of proper functioning. —v.i. To function incorrectly.

Ma·li (mä′lē) n. A republic of W Africa, 464,872 sq. mi., cap. Bamako. • See map at AFRICA.

mal·ic (mal′ik, mā′lik) adj. 1 Of, pertaining to, or obtained from apples. 2 Pertaining to or designating an acid contained in apples and other fruits. [< L *malum* apple]

mal·ice (mal′is) n. 1 A disposition to injure another; spite; ill will. 2 Law A willfully formed design to do another an injury: also **malice aforethought.** [< L *malus* bad]

ma·li·cious (mə·lish′əs) adj. Harboring or resulting from malice, ill will, or enmity; spiteful. —**ma·li′cious·ly** adv. — **ma·li′cious·ness** n. —Syn. hostile, malevolent, hateful, harmful, treacherous, invidious.

ma·lign (mə·līn′) v.t. To speak slander of. —adj. 1 Having an evil disposition toward others; ill-disposed; malevolent. 2 Tending to injure; pernicious. [< L *malignare* contrive maliciously] —**ma·lign′er** n. —**ma·lign′ly** adv. —Syn. v. slur, vilify, defame, depreciate, discredit, belittle, disparage.

ma·lig·nant (mə·lig′nənt) adj. 1 Having or manifesting extreme malevolence or enmity. 2 Evil in nature, or tending to do great harm. 3 Pathol. Tending to grow progressively worse. —**ma·lig′nance, ma·lig′nan·cy** n. —**ma·lig′nant·ly** adv.

ma·lig·ni·ty (mə·lig′nə·tē) n. pl. **·ties** 1 The state or quality of being malign; violent animosity. 2 Destructive tendency; virulence. 3 Often pl. An evil thing or event.

ma·lin·ger (mə·ling′gər) v.i. To feign sickness or incapacity, so as to avoid work. [< F *malingre* sickly] —**ma·lin′ger·er** n.

mall[1] (môl, mal) n., v. MAUL.

mall[2] (môl, mal) n. 1 A shaded, public promenade. 2 A large, often completely enclosed complex of shops and stores, usu. grouped around a central plaza or promenade and closed to motor vehicles. 3 A median strip between highways. [Short for *Pall-Mall*, a street in London]

mal·lard (mal′ərd) n. The common wild duck, closely related to domesticated ducks. [< OF *malart*] • See DUCK.

mal·le·a·ble (mal′ē·ə·bəl) adj. 1 Capable of being shaped by hammering, rolling, pressure, etc. 2 Capable of being disciplined, trained, changed, etc. [< L *malleus* hammer] —**mal′le·a·bil′i·ty, mal′le·a·ble·ness** n. —**mal′le·a·bly** adv.

mal·let (mal′it) n. 1 A wooden hammer or light maul. 2 A long-handled, hammerlike implement used to strike the ball in croquet or polo. 3 A light hammer with a round, usu. felt-covered head, for playing the vibraphone, etc. [< L *malleus* hammer]

mal·le·us (mal′ē·əs) n. pl. **·le·i** (-lē·ī) Anat. The outermost of the three small bones of the middle ear. [L, a hammer]

Mallet *def. 1*

mal·low (mal′ō) n. Any of a family of plants, including the hollyhock and marsh mallow, with lobed leaves and showy flowers. [< L *malva*]

malm·sey (mäm′zē) n. A rich sweet wine made in the Canary Islands, Madeira, Spain, and Greece. [< Gk. *Monembasia* Monemvasia, Greece]

mal·nu·tri·tion (mal′nyōō·trish′ən) n. Faulty or inadequate nutrition.

mal·oc·clu·sion (mal′ə·klōō′zhən) n. Faulty closure of the upper and lower teeth. [< MAL- + OCCLUSION]

mal·o·dor·ous (mal·ō′dər·əs) adj. Having a disagreeable smell. —**mal·o′dor·ous·ly** adv. —**mal·o′dor·ous·ness** n.

mal·prac·tice (mal·prak′tis) n. 1 Improper or illegal practice, as in medicine or law. 2 Improper or immoral conduct. —**mal·prac·ti·tion·er** (mal′prak·tish′ən·ər) n.

malt (môlt) n. 1 Grain, usu. barley, germinated and dried, used in brewing and as a nutrient. 2 Malt liquor; beer or ale. —v.t. 1 To cause (grain) to germinate and become malt. 2 To treat with malt, or extract of malt. —v.i. 3 To be changed into or become malt: said of grain. 4 To convert grain into malt. [< OE *mealt*] —**malt′y** adj. (**·i·er, ·i·est**)

Mal·ta (môl′tə) n. An independent member of the Commonwealth of Nations, an island in the CEN. Mediterranean, 122 sq. mi., cap. Valletta.

malted milk 1 A powder made of dehydrated milk and malted cereals, soluble in milk or water. 2 The beverage made with this powder.

Mal·tese (môl·tēz′, -tēs′) adj. Of or pertaining to Malta, its inhabitants, or their language. —*n. pl.* ·**tese 1** A citizen or native of Malta. **2** The language of Malta. **3** MALTESE CAT.

Maltese cat A breed of domestic cat with long bluish gray hair.

Maltese cross A cross in the shape of four inward-pointing arrowheads meeting at the center. • See CROSS.

Mal·thu·si·an (mal·thoo′zē·ən, -zhən) *adj.* Pertaining to the theory of Thomas R. Malthus that population increases faster than food supplies and is restricted only by famine, disease, and war. —*n.* A believer in the theories of Malthus. [< Thomas R. *Malthus*, 1766–1834, English economist] —**Mal·thu′si·an·ism** *n.*

malt·ose (môl′tōs) *n.* A sweet, white, crystalline carbohydrate formed by the action of amylase on starch. Also **malt sugar.** [< MALT]

mal·treat (mal·trēt′) *v.t.* To treat badly or maliciously; abuse. —**mal·treat′ment** *n.*

mam·bo (mäm′bō) *n. pl.* ·**bos 1** A rhumbalike ballroom dance. **2** The music for this dance. —*v.i.* To dance the mambo.

mam·ma[1] (mam′ə) *n. pl.* ·**mae** (-ē) The milk-secreting organ of a mammal; a breast, udder, or bag. [L, breast]

mam·ma[2] (mä′mə, mə·mä′) *n.* Mother. Also **ma′ma.** [< L *mamma* breast, ult. < baby talk]

mam·mal (mam′əl) *n.* Any of a class of vertebrate animals, including man, whose female suckles its young. [< L *mamma* breast]

mam·ma·ry (mam′ər·ē) *adj.* Of, pertaining to, or of the nature of the mammae or breasts.

mam·mog·ra·phy (ma·mog′rə·fē) *n.* X-ray examination of the breast or breasts. [< L *mamma* breast]

mam·mon (mam′ən) *n. Often cap.* Riches; wealth, esp. as a source of corruption. [< Aramaic *māmōnā* riches]

mam·moth (mam′əth) *n.* Any of a genus of extinct elephants with coarse hair and enormous upward-curving tusks. —*adj.* Huge; colossal. [< Russ. *mammot*]

Woolly mammoth

mam·my (mam′ē) *n. pl.* ·**mies 1** Mother; mamma. **2** A Negro nurse of white children, esp. formerly in the s U.S. [Dim. of MAMMA]

man (man) *n. pl.* **men** (men) **1** A human being, specifically the most highly developed of the primates, differing from other animals in having erect posture, extraordinary development of the brain, and the power of articulate speech. **2** The human race. **3** An adult male of the human kind. **4** The male part of the race collectively. **5** A male person who is manly; also, manhood. **6** An adult male servant, member of a team, employee, etc. **7** A piece used in playing certain games, as chess or checkers. **8** A ship or vessel: used in composition: a *man-of-war.* **9** A husband; lover: *man* and wife; Her *man* is dead. **10** *Slang* Fellow: used in direct address: Hey, *man,* look at this! —**the Man** *Slang* A white man regarded as an agent of power. —*v.t.* **manned, man·ning 1** To supply with men. **2** To take stations at, on, or in for work, defense, etc.: *Man* the pumps! —*adj.* Male. [< OE *mann*]

Man. Manila paper; Manitoba.

man. manual.

man·a·cle (man′ə·kəl) *n.* **1** *Usu. pl.* One of a connected pair of metallic instruments for confining or restraining the hands; a handcuff. **2** Anything that constrains or fetters. —*v.t.* ·**cled, ·cling 1** To put manacles on. **2** To hamper; constrain. [< OF < L, dim. of *manus* hand]

man·age (man′ij) *v.,* ·**aged, ·ag·ing** *v.t.* **1** To direct or conduct the affairs or interests of. **2** To control the direction, operation, etc., of, as a machine. **3** To cause to do one's bidding; handle; manipulate. **4** To bring about or contrive: He always *manages* to win. **5** To handle or wield, as a weapon or implement. —*v.i.* **6** To carry on or conduct busi-

ness or affairs. **7** To contrive to get along: I'll *manage.* [< L *manus* a hand]

man·age·a·ble (man′ij·ə·bəl) *adj.* Capable of being managed; tractable; docile. —**man′age·a·bil′i·ty, man′age·a·ble·ness** *n.* —**man′age·a·bly** *adv.*

man·age·ment (man′ij·mənt) *n.* **1** The act, art, or manner of managing, controlling, or conducting. **2** The skillful use of means to accomplish a purpose. **3** Managers or directors collectively.

man·ag·er (man′ij·ər) *n.* **1** One who manages; esp. one who has the control of a business. **2** One who directs or oversees the affairs of a household, athletic team, etc. **3** An adroit schemer; intriguer. —**man′ag·er·ship** *n.*

man·a·ge·ri·al (man′ə·jir′ē·əl) *adj.* Of, pertaining to, or characteristic of a manager or management.

ma·ña·na (mä·nyä′nä) *n. & adv. Spanish* Tomorrow.

man-at-arms (man′ət·ärmz′) *n. pl.* **men-at-arms** (men′-) A soldier; esp. a heavily armed soldier of medieval times.

man·a·tee (man′ə·tē′) *n.* A large, aquatic mammal of tropical Atlantic shores. [< Cariban *manattoui*]

Man·chu (man·choo′, man′choo) *n.* **1** One of a Mongoloid people that conquered China in 1643 and established the dynasty overthrown in 1912. **2** The language of this people. —*adj.* Of or pertaining to Manchuria, its people, or their language. —**Man·chu′ri·an** (-choor′ē·ən) *adj., n.*

-mancy *combining form* Divining, foretelling, or discovering by means of: *necromancy.* [< Gk. *manteia* power of divination]

man·da·mus (man·dā′məs) *n. Law* A writ issued by a higher court to a subordinate court, city, business, etc., commanding it to do something. [L, we command]

man·da·rin (man′də·rin) *n.* **1** A high official of the former Chinese Empire, either civil or military. **2** A distinguished, influential, usu. elderly person, esp. one of literary or intellectual attainment. **3** MANDARIN ORANGE. **4** A reddish orange color. —*adj.* **1** Of a mandarin. **2** Complex and ornate, as a literary style. [< Skt. *mantra* counsel]

Man·da·rin (man′də·rin) *n.* The Chinese language of N China, in the Peking dialect now the official language of the country.

mandarin orange Any of several sweet, loose-skinned oranges, as the tangerine.

man·da·tar·y (man′də·ter′ē) *n. pl.* ·**tar·ies** One to whom a mandate is given.

man·date (man′dāt, -dit) *n.* **1** An authoritative command or order. **2** A charge given to a nation by a congress or league of nations to develop and administer a conquered territory; also, the territory itself. **3** A judicial command from a higher court to a subordinate court or court officer. **4** An order from an electorate to the legislative body, or its representative, to follow a certain course of action. —*v.t.* (-dāt) ·**dat·ed, ·dat·ing** To assign (a territory) to a specific nation under a mandate. [< L *mandare* to command]

man·da·to·ry (man′də·tôr′ē, -tō′rē) *adj.* **1** Of, containing, or having received a mandate. **2** Positively required; obligatory. —*n. pl.* ·**ries 1** MANDATARY. **2** MANDATE.

man·di·ble (man′də·bəl) *n.* **1** The lower jaw. **2** Either part of the beak of a bird. **3** One of a pair of biting jaws in an insect. [< L *mandere* chew] —**man·dib·u·lar** (man·dib′yə·lər), **man·dib′u·late** (-lit, -lāt) *adj., n.*

man·do·lin (man′də·lin, man′də·lin′) *n.* A stringed musical instrument related to the lute, having five pairs of strings. [< Ital. *mandolino* < L *pandura* a kind of lute] —**man′do·lin′ist** *n.*

man·drake (man′drāk) *n.* **1** A poisonous Old World plant of the nightshade family. **2** Its fleshy roots. **3** The May apple. Also **man·drag·o·ra** (man·drag′ə·rə). [< Gk. *mandragoras*]

man·drel (man′drəl) *n. Mech.* **1** A shaft on which an object or tool may be fixed for rotation. **2** A core about which wire may be coiled or metal or glass forged. Also **man′·dril.** [< F *mandrin* a lathe]

man·drill (man′dril) *n.* A large, ferocious w African baboon, hav-

Mandrill

ing cheeks and rump colored blue and scarlet. [< MAN + *drill,* a native African name]

mane (mān) *n.* **1** The long hair growing on and about the neck of some animals, as the horse, lion, etc. **2** Long human hair. [< OE *manu*] —**maned** (mānd) *adj.*

man·eat·er (man'ē'tər) *n.* **1** A cannibal. **2** An animal that devours or is supposed to devour human flesh, as a tiger, shark, etc.

ma·nège (ma·nezh') *n.* **1** The art of training and riding horses. **2** A school of horsemanship; riding school. **3** The style and movements of a trained horse. Also **ma·nege'.** [F < Ital. *maneggiare* manage]

ma·neu·ver (ma·nōō'vər) *n.* **1 a** An extensive, planned movement of troops, warships, aircraft, etc. **b** *Often pl.* Such movements used in training or practice. **2** Any physically adroit movement or skill. **3** A controlled change in the flight path of an aircraft or spacecraft. **4** A skillful or cunning action to gain some specific end or object, often involving trickery. —*v.t.* **1** To put through a maneuver or maneuvers. **2** To put, bring, make, etc., by a maneuver or maneuvers. **3** To manipulate; conduct adroitly. —*v.i.* **1** To perform a maneuver or maneuvers. **5** To use tricks or stratagems; manage adroitly. [< L *manu operari* work with the hand] —**ma·neu'ver·a·bil'i·ty, ma·neu'ver·er** *n.* —**ma·neu'ver·a·ble** *adj.*

man Friday A person who devotedly serves another, like Robinson Crusoe's servant of that name; a factotum.

man·ful (man'fəl) *adj.* Having courage, strength, determination, etc. —**man'ful·ly** *adv.* —**man'ful·ness** *n.*

man·ga·nese (mang'gə·nēs, -nēz) *n.* A hard, brittle, metallic element (symbol Mn), used mainly in alloys. [< Med. L *magnesia* magnesia]

mange (mānj) *n.* A skin disease of domestic animals, caused by various burrowing mites and marked by itching and loss of hair. [< OF *manjue* an itch, eating]

man·ger (mān'jər) *n.* A trough or box for feeding horses or cattle. [< L *manducare* chew]

man·gle¹ (mang'gəl) *v.t.* **·gled, ·gling** **1** To disfigure or mutilate, as by cutting, bruising, or crushing; lacerate. **2** To mar or ruin; spoil. [< AF *mangler*] —**man'gler** *n.*

man·gle² (mang'gəl) *n.* A machine for smoothing fabrics by pressing them between rollers. —*v.t.* **·gled, ·gling** To smooth with a mangle. [< Gk. *manganon* a pulley, a war machine]

man·go (mang'gō) *n. pl.* **·goes** or **·gos** **1** The edible, fleshy fruit of a tropical evergreen tree. **2** The tree producing the fruit. [< Tamil *mān* a mango tree + *kāy* a fruit]

man·grove (mang'grōv, man'·) *n.* A tropical tree having branches that take root, forming dense thickets. [< Taino *mangle*]

man·gy (mān'jē) *adj.* **·gi·er, ·gi·est** **1** Affected with the mange. **2** Shabby; threadbare. —**man'gi·ly** *adv.* —**man'gi·ness** *n.*

man·han·dle (man'han'dəl) *v.t.* **·dled, ·dling** To handle roughly, as in anger.

man·hat·tan (mən·hat'ən, man·) *n. Often cap.* A cocktail made of whisky and vermouth, often with a dash of bitters and a cherry. [< *Manhattan,* borough of New York City]

man·hole (man'hōl') *n.* An opening through which one may enter a boiler, conduit, sewer, etc., for making repairs.

man·hood (man'hood) *n.* **1** The state or time of being an adult male. **2** The state of being human. **3** Manly qualities, as courage, strength, etc. **4** Adult males collectively; men.

man·hour (man'our') *n.* A unit equal to the average amount of work that can be done by one person in one hour.

ma·ni·a (mā'nē·ə, mān'yə) *n.* **1** A psychotic state characterized by an exaggerated sense of well-being, accompanied by excessive mental and physical activity. **2** A strong, ungovernable desire; a craze. [< Gk., madness]

-mania *combining form* A persistent or irrational preoccupation with: *nymphomania.*

ma·ni·ac (mā'nē·ak) *adj.* Having a mania; raving. —*n.* A person wildly or violently insane; a madman. —**ma·ni·a·cal** (mə·nī'ə·kəl) *adj.* —**ma·ni'a·cal·ly** *adv.*

man·ic (man'ik, mā'nik) *adj.* Pertaining to, like, or affected by mania.

man·ic-de·pres·sive (man'ik·di·pres'iv) *adj.* Denoting a mental disorder characterized by alternating depression and mania. —*n.* One who suffers from this disorder.

man·i·cure (man'ə·kyŏŏr') *n.* The care or treatment of the hands and fingernails. —*v.t. & v.i.* **·cured, ·cur·ing** To take care of or treat (the hands and nails). [< L *manus* hand + *cura* care] —**man'i·cur'ist** *n.*

man·i·fest (man'ə·fest') *adj.* Clearly apparent to the understanding or the senses; palpable; obvious. —*v.t.* **1** To make plain to sight or understanding; reveal; display. **2** To prove; be evidence of. —*v.i.* **3** To appear or become evident; reveal itself. —*n.* A detailed listing of the cargo of a ship or plane for customs inspection. [< L *manifestus* evident, lit., struck by the hand] —**man'i·fest'ly** *adv.*

man·i·fes·ta·tion (man'ə·fə·stā'shən, -fes-) *n.* **1** The act of manifesting or the state of being manifested. **2** Something that manifests or reveals. **3** A public demonstration, as by a government or party, to display its power or special views. —**man'i·fes'tant** *n.*

man·i·fes·to (man'ə·fes'tō) *n. pl.* **·toes** An official declaration by an organized group or government body of intentions, motives, or principles of action. [< L *manifestus* manifest]

man·i·fold (man'ə·fōld) *adj.* **1** Of great variety; numerous. **2** Manifested in many ways, or including many acts or elements; complex. **3** Existing in great abundance. —*v.t.* To make more than one copy of at once, as with carbon paper on a typewriter. —*n.* **1** A copy made by manifolding. **2** A tube or pipe with several inlets or outlets. [< OE *manigfeald* varied, numerous] —**man'i·fold·ly** *adv* —**man'·i·fold·ness** *n.*

man·i·kin (man'ə·kin) *n.* **1** A model of the human body. **2** A little man; dwarf. **3** MANNEQUIN. [< Du. *manneken,* dim. of *man* man]

ma·nil·a (mə·nil'ə) *n.* The fiber of the abaca. Also **Manila hemp, ma·nil'la.**

Ma·nil·a paper (mə·nil'ə) A heavy, light brown paper originally made of Manila hemp, now made of various fibers, used for wrapping, etc.

man·i·oc (man'ē·ok, mā'nē-) *n.* CASSAVA. [< Tupian *mandioca*]

ma·nip·u·la·ble (mə·nip'yə·lə·bəl) *adj.* Capable of being manipulated. Also **ma·nip'u·lat'a·ble.** —**ma·nip'u·la·bil'i·ty** *n.*

Manikin
def. 1

ma·nip·u·late (mə·nip'yə·lāt) *v.t.* **·lat·ed, ·lat·ing** **1** To handle, operate, or use with or as with the hands, esp. with skill. **2** To influence or control artfully or deceptively. **3** To change or alter (figures, accounts, etc.), usu. fraudulently. [< L *manipulus* a handful] —**ma·nip'u·la'tion, ma·nip'u·la'tor** *n.* —**ma·nip'u·la'tive** *adj.*

man·kind (man'kīnd', man'kīnd') *n. (construed as sing. or pl.)* **1** The whole human species. **2** (man'kīnd') Men collectively as distinguished from women.

man·ly (man'lē) *adj.* **·li·er, ·li·est** **1** Possessing the qualities thought characteristic of or desirable in a man, as courage, strength, determination, etc. **2** Suitable to a man: the *manly* art of boxing. —**man'li·ly** *adv.* —**man'li·ness** *n.*

man·na (man'ə) *n.* **1** The miraculously supplied food on which the Israelites subsisted in the wilderness. *Exodus* 16:14–36. **2** Anything pleasant or rewarding that comes as a surprise. **3** A sweetish juice extracted from the stems of the European ash and used as a mild laxative. [< Aramaic *mannā*]

man·ne·quin (man'ə·kin) *n.* **1** A woman who models new clothes for display to potential customers. **2** A figure of the human body used by fashion designers, tailors, and display artists. [< Du. *manneken,* dim. of *man* man]

man·ner (man'ər) *n.* **1** The way in which something is done or takes place. **2** The demeanor, bearing, or behavior peculiar to a person; also, a distinguished air or bearing. **3** *pl.* General modes of life or conduct; esp., social behavior. **4** *pl.* Polite, civil, or well-bred behavior. **5** A characteristic style in art, literature, music, etc. **6** Sort or kind. **7** Character; guise. —**in a manner of speaking** In one way of describing; in a sense: She was, *in a manner of speaking,* a hard-nosed negotiator. [< L *manuarius* of the hand]

man·nered (man'ərd) *adj.* **1** Having a (specified) manner or manners: *ill-mannered.* **2** Affected; stilted; artificial.

man·ner·ism (man'ər·iz'əm) n. 1 An action, way of behaving, speech pattern, etc., that is characteristic of a particular person. 2 An artificial or affected manner or style. —**man'ner·ist** n. —**man'ner·is'tic** adj.

man·ner·ly (man'ər·lē) adj. Well-behaved; polite. —adv. With good manners; politely. —**man'ner·li·ness** n.

man·ni·kin (man'ə·kin) n. MANIKIN.

man·nish (man'ish) adj. 1 Resembling or characteristic of men, as in appearance, attitudes, etc.: said of a woman. 2 Suggesting that of a man: her mannish suit. —**man'nish·ly** adv. —**man'nish·ness** n.

ma·noeu·vre (mə·nyōō'vər) n., v. Chiefly Brit. MANEUVER.

man-of-war (man'əv·wôr', man'ə-) n. pl. **men-of-war** (men'-) A naval vessel armed for active hostilities.

man-of-war bird FRIGATE BIRD.

ma·nom·e·ter (mə·nom'ə·tər) n. An instrument for measuring pressure of a fluid. [< Gk. manos thin, rare + -METER] —**man·o·met·ric** (man'ə·met'rik) or ·ri·cal adj.

man·or (man'ər) n. 1 Brit. A nobleman's or gentleman's landed estate. 2 In feudal England, a tract of land granted by the king to one as lord, with authority to exercise jurisdiction over it. 3 In colonial America, a tract of land originally granted as a manor and let by the proprietor to tenants. 4 A mansion, esp. one on an estate. [< L manere stay, remain] —**ma·no·ri·al** (mə·nôr'ē·əl, ·nō'rē-) adj.

manor house The residence of the lord of a manor.

man·pow·er (man'pou'ər) n. 1 Power supplied by human physical effort: also **man power.** 2 The number of persons available for any specific service, as for military duty or for industrial work.

man·qué (män·kā') adj. That has failed in or fallen short of one's ambitions or aspirations: a painter manqué. [F, pp. of manquer to fail]

man·sard (man'särd) n. A roof with a double slope or pitch on all sides. Also **mansard roof.** [< F. Mansard, 1598–1666, French architect]

manse (mans) n. A clergyman's house. esp. a Presbyterian minister's house. [< Med. L mansa, mansus. See MANSION.]

Mansard roof

man·ser·vant (man'sûr'vənt) n. An adult male servant.

man·sion (man'shən) n. A large, imposing house. [< L < mansus, pp. of manere remain, dwell]

man·slaugh·ter (man'slô'tər) n. Law The unlawful killing of a person by another person but without malice.

man·tel (man'təl) n. The facing about a fireplace, including the shelf above it; also, the shelf. [< L mantellum cloak]

man·tel·et (man'təl·et, mant'lit) n. 1 A small mantle or short cloak. 2 A protective screen or shelter.

man·tel·piece (man'təl·pēs') n. A mantel shelf.

man·til·la (man·til'ə, man·tē'yə) n. 1 A woman's light scarf or head covering of lace, as worn in Spain, Mexico, Italy, etc. 2 Any short mantle. [Sp.]

Mantel

man·tis (man'tis) n. pl. ·tis·es or ·tes (-tēz) n. PRAYING MANTIS [< Gk. mantis, a prophet, also a kind of insect]

man·tis·sa (man·tis'ə) n. Math. The decimal or fractional part of a logarithm. [< L, a trifling addition ? < Etruscan]

man·tle (man'təl) n. 1 A loose cloak, usu. without sleeves, worn over other garments, often thought of figuratively as a symbol of authority, greatness, etc. 2 Anything that covers, envelops, or conceals. 3 Zool. A membranous flap or fold in the body wall of a mollusk. • See OYSTER. 4 A mesh supporting certain salts, used to enclose a flame and produce light when heated. 5 The layer of the earth beneath the crust and outside the core. 6 MANTEL. —v. ·tled, ·tling v.t. 1 To cover with or as with a mantle; conceal. —v.i. 2 To overspread or cover the surface of something.

3 To be or become covered, overspread, or suffused. [< L mantellum, a cloak, towel]

man·tra (man'trə) n. In Hinduism, a sacred word or phrase chanted repeatedly and used as an aid in meditation or in the attainment of psychic states. [Skt.]

man·u·al (man'yōō·əl) adj. 1 Of or involving the hands. 2 Done or operated by hand. 3 Involving or using physical strength or dexterity: manual labor. —n. 1 A compact handbook of instruction or directions. 2 A keyboard, as of an organ. 3 A systematic exercise in the handling of some military weapon. [< L manus hand] —**man'u·al·ly** adv.

manual training The training of pupils in carpentry, woodworking, etc.

manuf., manufac. manufacture; manufactured; manufacturer.

man·u·fac·to·ry (man'yə·fak'tər·ē) n. pl. ·ries A factory.

man·u·fac·ture (man'yə·fak'chər) v.t. ·tured, ·tur·ing 1 To make or fashion by hand or machinery, esp. in large quantities. 2 To work into useful form, as wool or steel. 3 To invent (evidence, testimony, etc.) falsely; concoct. 4 To produce in a mechanical way, as art, poetry, etc. —n. 1 The production of goods by hand or by industrial processes. 2 Anything made by industrial art or processes; manufactured articles collectively. 3 The making or contriving of anything. [< L manus hand + factura a making] —**man'u·fac'tur·er** n. —**man'u·fac'tur·ing** adj., n.

man·u·mit (man'yə·mit') v.t. ·mit·ted, ·mit·ting To free from bondage, as a slave; emancipate; liberate. [< L manu emittere, lit., send forth from one's hand] —**man'u·mis'sion** (-mish'ən) n.

ma·nure (mə·nyōōr') n. Any substance, as dung, decaying animal or vegetable matter, or certain minerals, applied to fertilize soil. —v.t. ·nured, ·nur·ing To apply manure or other fertilizer to, as soil. [< AF maynoverer work with the hands] —**ma·nur'er** n.

man·u·script (man'yə·skript) n. 1 A piece of writing, either written or typewritten, as distinguished from printed matter; esp., an author's copy of a work to be considered for publication. 2 Matter written by hand. —adj. Written by hand or typed. [< L manus hand + scriptus written]

Manx (mangks) adj. Pertaining to the Isle of Man, its people, or their language. —n. 1 The people of the Isle of Man collectively: with the. 2 The Gaelic language of the Manx, virtually extinct.

Manx cat (mangks) A variety of domestic cat having no tail.

man·y (men'ē) adj. more, most Constituting a large number; numerous. —n. 1 A large number. 2 The masses; crowd; multitude: with the. —pron. A large number of persons or things. [< OE manig]
• Many followed by a, an, or another indicates a great number thought of singly: Many a man has had to find this out for himself. The phrase a great many is idiomatic; it resembles a collective noun, but takes only a plural verb: A great many are involved.

Manx cat

Ma·o·ri (mä'ō·rē, mou'rē) n. pl. ·ris or ·ri 1 One of an aboriginal, light brown people of New Zealand, chiefly Polynesian, mixed somewhat with Melanesian. 2 The Polynesian language of these people. —adj. Of or pertaining to the Maoris or their language.

map (map) n. 1 A representation, esp. on a flat surface, of any region or part of the earth or sky. 2 Any maplike delineation. 3 Slang The face. —v.t. mapped, map·ping 1 To make a map of. 2 To plan in detail: often with out. [< L, cloth, napkin] —**map'per** n.

ma·ple (mā'pəl) n. 1 Any of a large genus of deciduous trees of the north temperate zone, with opposite leaves and a two-winged fruit. 2 Its fine-grained, hard wood. 3 The amber-yellow color of the finished wood. 4 The flavor of maple sugar. [< OE mapel(trēow) maple (tree)]

maple sugar A brown, crystalline sugar obtained from maple syrup.

---

maple syrup The boiled, condensed sap of certain maple trees.

ma·quis (mä·kē′) *n.* **1** A zone of shrubby, mostly ever-green plants in the Mediterranean region, known as cover for game or bandits. **2** *pl.* **·quis** *Often cap.* A member of the French underground in World War II. [< Ital. *macchia* a thicket, orig., a spot]

mar (mär) *v.t.* **marred, mar·ring 1** To do harm to; impair or ruin. **2** To deface; disfigure. —*n.* A disfiguring mark; blem-ish; injury. [< OE *merran* injure] —**mar′rer** *n.*

Mar, Mar. March.

mar. marine; maritime; married.

mar·a·bou (mar′ə·bōō) *n.* **1** Any of various large storks, esp. the **African marabou**, whose soft, white, lower tail and wing feathers are used in milli-nery. **2** A plume from the mara-bou. Also **mar′a·bout** (-bōōt). [F]

mar·a·ca (mə·rä′kə) *n.* A percus-sion instrument made of a gourd or gourd-shaped rattle with beans or beads inside it. [< Tupian]

mar·a·schi·no (mar′ə·skē′nō, -shē′-) *n.* A cordial distilled from the fermented juice of a wild cherry. [Ital. < *marasca* a wild cherry]

maraschino cherry A cherry preserved in maraschino-flavored syrup or an imitation of it.

Marabou

mar·a·thon (mar′ə·thon) *n.* **1** A footrace of 26 miles, 385 yards: so called from a messen-ger's legendary run from Marathon to Athens to an-nounce the Athenian victory over the Persians, 490 B.C. **2** Any endurance contest. [< *Marathon*, a plain in Greece]

ma·raud (mə·rôd′) *v.i.* **1** To rove in search of booty. —*v.t.* **2** To invade for plunder; raid. —*n.* A foray. [< F *maraud* a rogue] —**ma·raud′er** *n.* —**Syn.** *v.t.* despoil, loot, pillage, ransack, ravage.

mar·ble (mär′bəl) *n.* **1** A compact, partly crystallized, var-iously colored limestone, used for building or ornaments. **2** A sculptured or inscribed piece of this stone. **3** A small ball made of this stone, or of baked clay, glass, or por-celain. **4** *pl.* A game played with such balls. —*v.t.* **·bled, ·bling** To color or vein in imitation of marble. —*adj.* **1** Made of or like marble. **2** Without feeling; cold. [< Gk. *marmaros*, lit., sparkling stone] —**mar′bly** *adj.*

marble cake A cake made of light and dark batter mixed to give a marblelike appearance.

mar·ble·ize (mär′bəl·īz) *v.t.* **·ized, ·iz·ing** To streak or grain in imitation of marble.

mar·cel (mär·sel′) *n.* A style of dressing the hair in even, continuous waves by means of special irons. Also **marcel wave.** —*v.t.* **·celled, ·cel·ling** To dress (the hair) in such a style. [< *Marcel* Grateau, d.1936, French hairdresser]

march[1] (märch) *n.* **1** Movement together on foot and in time, as of soldiers. **2** A movement, as of soldiers, from one stopping place to another. **3** The distance thus passed over. **4** Onward progress. **5** A piece of music for setting a marching tempo. —*v.i.* **1** To move with measured steps. **2** To walk in a solemn or dignified manner. **3** To proceed steadily; advance. —*v.t.* **4** To cause to march. [< MF *marcher* to walk, trample] —**march′er** *n.*

march[2] (märch) *n.* A region or district lying along a boundary line; frontier. [< OF *marche* < Gmc.]

March (märch) *n.* The third month of the year, having 31 days. [< L *Martius (mensis)* (month) of Mars]

March hare A hare in the breeding season, regarded as a symbol of madness.

mar·chion·ess (mär′shən·is) *n.* **1** The wife or widow of a marquis. **2** A woman having the rank corresponding to that of a marquis. [< Med. L *marchio, -onis* a captain of the marches]

march·pane (märch′pān) *n.* MARZIPAN.

Mar·di gras (mär′dē grä′) Shrove Tuesday; last day before Lent: celebrated as a carnival in certain cities. [F., lit., fat Tuesday]

mare[1] (mâr) *n.* The female of the horse and other equine animals. [< OE *mēre*]

mar·e[2] (mâr′ē) *n. pl.* **mar·i·a** (mâr′ē·ə) Any of the dark, seemingly flat areas of the moon. [L, sea]

mare's nest (mârz) *n.* **1** A seemingly important discov-ery that proves to be a fraud. **2** A chaotic or disorderly condition.

mar·ga·rine (mär′jə·rin, -rēn) *n.* A blend of hydro-genated vegetable oils resembling butter: also **mar′ga·rin** (-jə·rin). [F]

marge[1] (märj) *n. Archaic* A margin; border.

marge[2] (märj) *n. Brit. Informal* Margarine.

mar·gin (mär′jin) *n.* **1** A bounding line; border. **2** An al-lowance or reservation for contingencies or changes, as of time or money. **3** Range or scope; provision for increase or progress. **4** A sum of money deposited with a broker to protect him against loss in contracts undertaken for a buyer or seller of stocks, etc. **5** The difference between selling price and cost of production: profit *margin.* **6** The blank parts of a page that surround the printed or written text. —*v.t.* **1** To furnish with a margin; border. **2** In com-merce, to deposit a margin upon. [< L *margo* edge] —**Syn.** *n.* **1** boundary, brink, edge, verge.

mar·gi·nal (mär′jə·nəl) *adj.* **1** Of or constituting a mar-gin. **2** Written, printed, or placed on the margin. **3** *Econ.* Operating or furnishing goods at a rate barely meeting the costs of production. **4** Of a nature that barely qualifies as useful, productive, or necessary. —**mar′gi·nal·ly** *adv.*

mar·gi·nate (mär′jə·nāt) *v.t.* **·nat·ed, ·nat·ing** To provide with a margin or margins. —*adj.* Having a margin: also **mar′gi·nat′ed.** —**mar′gi·na′tion** *n.*

mar·grave (mär′grāv) *n.* **1** A hereditary title of certain German princes. **2** Formerly, the governor of a German border province. [< MHG *mark* a march[2] + *graf* a count]

mar·gue·rite (mär′gə·rēt′) *n.* **1** A daisy. **2** A cultivated chrysanthemum with single flowers. [F]

ma·ri·a·chi (mär·ē·ä′chē) *n.* **1** A wandering band of Mexi-can street musicians. **2** The mu-sicians, usu. made up of singers and guitarists. **3** The music they play. [Mex. Sp.]

mar·i·gold (mar′ə·gōld) *n.* Any of various composite plants hav-ing yellow, orange, or red flowers. [< MARY, prob. with ref. to the Virgin Mary + GOLD]

mar·i·hua·na (mar′ə·hwä′nə, mär′-) *n.* **1** The hemp plant. **2** Its dried leaves and flower tops which when smoked in cigarettes or otherwise ingested can produce distorted perception and other hallucinogenic effects. Also **ma′ri·jua′na.** [Am. Sp.]

Marihuana plant

ma·rim·ba (mə·rim′-bə) *n.* A form of xylo-phone having resona-tors. [< Bantu *marim-ba*]

ma·ri·na (mə·rē′nə) *n.* A basin or safe an-chorage for small ves-sels, esp. one at which

Marimba

supplies, etc., may be obtained. [< L *marinus* of the sea]

mar·i·nade (mar′ə·nād′) *n.* **1** Any liquid, usu. spiced, in which meat, salad, etc., is steeped to modify flavor. **2** A dish so prepared. [< Sp. *marinar* pickle in brine < *marino* marine]

mar·i·nate (mar′ə·nāt) *v.t.* **·nat·ed, ·nat·ing** To soak in marinade preparatory to cooking or serving.

ma·rine (mə·rēn′) *adj.* **1** Of, native to, or produced by the sea. **2** Having to do with shipping. **3** Naval. **4** Intended for use at sea or in navigation. **5** Trained for service on ship-board. —*n.* **1** A soldier trained for service at sea and on land, esp. a member of the U.S. Marine Corps: also **Marine.** **2** Shipping, or shipping interests generally: the merchant *marine.* **3** A picture of the sea. [< L *marinus* < *mare* sea]

mar·i·ner (mar′ə·nər) *n.* A sailor. [< L *marinus* marine]

mar·i·o·nette (mar′ē·ə·net′) *n.* A jointed puppet moved by strings.

Ma·ri·po·sa lily (mar′ə·pō′zə) A plant of the lily family, with showy, tulip-shaped flowers, growing in California and Mexico. Also **Mariposa tulip.** [< Sp. *mariposa* butterfly]

mar·i·tal (mar'ə-təl) *adj.* 1 Of or pertaining to marriage. 2 Of or pertaining to a husband. [< L *maritus* a husband] —**mar'i·tal·ly** *adv.*

mar·i·time (mar'ə-tīm) *adj.* 1 Situated on or near the sea: a *maritime* region. 2 Living on the borders of the sea: a *maritime* people. 3 Pertaining to the sea or matters connected with the sea. [< L *mare* sea]

Maritime Provinces The provinces of New Brunswick, Nova Scotia, and Prince Edward Island on the Atlantic seaboard of E Canada.

mar·jo·ram (mär'jər-əm) *n.* Any of several perennial herbs related to mint, esp. **sweet marjoram** and **wild marjoram** (oregano) both used for seasoning in cookery. [< Med. L *majorana*]

mark¹ (märk) *n.* 1 A visible impression or sign produced or left on any substance by another. 2 A line, scratch, dot, scar, stain, or blemish. 3 TRADEMARK. 4 A cross made instead of a signature by one who cannot write. 5 A letter of the alphabet, number, or character by which quality is registered, as on a student's paper or record. 6 A symbol, written or printed: a punctuation *mark.* 7 An object serving to guide, direct, or point out, as a boundary, a place in a book, etc. 8 That which indicates the presence of something; a characteristic or symptom. 9 That which is aimed at, or toward which effort is directed; goal. 10 A proper bound or limit; standard. 11 A person easily duped: an easy *mark.* 12 An observing or noting; heed. —**make one's mark** To succeed. —**of mark** Famous; influential. —**up to the mark** Up to standard; in good health or condition, etc. —**wide of** (or **beside**) **the mark** Pointless. —*v.t.* 1 To make a mark or marks on. 2 To trace the boundaries of; limit. 3 To indicate by a mark or sign. 4 To make or produce by writing, drawing, etc. 5 To be a characteristic of; typify. 6 To destine: He was *marked* for fame. 7 To pay attention to; notice. 8 To make known; manifest. 9 To apply a price, identification, etc., to. 10 To give marks or grades to; grade. —*v.i.* 11 To take notice; pay attention. 12 To keep score or count. 13 To make a mark or marks. —**mark down** 1 To note down; record. 2 To put a lower price on, as for a sale. —**mark time** 1 To keep time by moving the feet but not advancing. 2 To pause in action. —**mark up** 1 To make marks on; deface. 2 To increase the price of. [< OE *mearc* boundary mark] —**mark'er** *n.*

mark² (märk) *n.* The former basic monetary unit of Germany, superseded in 1924 by the **reichs·mark** (rīkhs'märk) and, after World War II, by the **deut·sche·mark** (doi'chə·märk') in West Germany and the **ost·mark** (ôst'märk') in East Germany. [< MHG *marke*]

Mark (märk) 1 The evangelist and reputed author of the second Gospel: also **Saint Mark.** 2 The second Gospel.

marked (märkt) *adj.* Brought prominently to notice; prominent. —**mark·ed·ly** (mär'kid·lē) *adv.* —**mark'ed·ness** *n.*

mar·ket (mär'kit) *n.* 1 An open space or large building where merchandise, esp. produce, is displayed for sale: also **market place.** 2 A private store for the sale of provisions: a meat *market.* 3 The state of trade in goods, stocks, etc.; traffic: a brisk *market.* 4 A locality or country where anything can be bought or sold: the South American *markets.* 5 A gathering of people for selling and buying, esp. of a particular commodity: the wheat *market.* 6 Demand for commercial products or services. —**be in the market for** To be looking for an opportunity to buy. —**be on the market** To be for sale. —**play the market** To speculate in stocks, bonds, etc. —*v.t.* 1 To take or send to market for sale; sell. —*v.i.* 2 To deal in a market; sell or buy. 3 To buy food. [< L *merx, mercis* merchandise] —**mar'ket·a·bil'i·ty, mar'ket·er** *n.* —**mar'ket·a·ble** *adj.*

market price The current price.

market value The price which may be expected for a given commodity, security, or service under the conditions of a given market.

mark·ing (mär'king) *n.* 1 A distinctive mark or an arrangement of marks, as on an animal's coat: the zebra's *markings.* 2 The act of making a mark.

mark·ka (märk'kä) *n.* The basic monetary unit of Finland.

marks·man (märks'mən) *n. pl.* **·men** (-mən) One skilled in hitting the mark, as with a rifle or other weapon. —**marks'man·ship** *n.* —**marks'wom'an** (-wŏŏm'ən) *n. Fem.*

mark-up (märk'up') *n.* 1 A raising in the price of anything. 2 The difference between the wholesale cost price and the retail selling price.

marl (märl) *n.* A soil containing lime, clay, and sand, used as fertilizer. —*v.t.* To fertilize or spread with marl. [< LL *marga*] —**marl'y** *adj.* (**·i·er, ·i·est**)

mar·lin (mär'lin) *n.* Any of various deep-sea game fishes having the upper jaw protruding like a spike. [< MARLINE-(SPIKE); because of the shape of its snout]

mar·line (mär'lin) *n. Naut.* A small rope used for winding around the ends of larger ropes to prevent raveling. Also **mar'ling** (-ling). [< MDu. *marren* to tie + *lijn* a line]

mar·line·spike (mär'lin·spīk') *n. Naut.* A sharp-pointed iron pin used in splicing ropes. Also **mar'lin·spike', mar'ling·spike'** (-ling-).

mar·ma·lade (mär'mə·lād) *n.* A preserve made in part with the rind of fruits, esp. citrus fruits. [< Gk. *melimēlon,* lit., honey apple]

mar·mo·set (mär'mə·set, -zet) *n.* A small Central and South American monkey with soft, woolly hair and a long tail. [< OF *marmouset* a grotesque figure]

mar·mot (mär'mət) *n.* Any of various small, stout, short-tailed, burrowing rodents with coarse fur, as the woodchuck. [< L *mus, muris* a mouse + *mons, montis* a mountain]

Marmoset

ma·roon¹ (mə·rōōn') *v.t.* 1 To put ashore and abandon on a desolate island or coast. 2 To abandon; leave helpless. —*n.* 1 In the West Indies and Dutch Guiana, formerly a fugitive Negro slave. 2 One of the descendants of these slaves. [< Sp. *cimarrón* wild]

ma·roon² (mə·rōōn') *n. & adj.* Dull, dark red. [< F *marron* a chestnut]

mar·plot (mär'plot') *n.* One who, by meddling, mars or frustrates a design or plan.

marque (märk) *n.* A license of reprisal upon an enemy, as at sea in wartime. [F, mark, imprint]

mar·quee (mär·kē') *n.* 1 An awning or rooflike structure over the entrance to a hotel, theater, etc. 2 A large field tent, esp. one used at lawn entertainments. [< F *marquise* a canopy]

Mar·que·san (mär·kā'sən) *adj.* Of the Marquesas Islands, their inhabitants, or their language. —*n.* 1 A native of the Marquesas Islands. 2 The Polynesian language spoken there.

mar·quess (mär'kwis) *n.* MARQUIS.

mar·que·try (mär'kə·trē) *n.* Inlaid work of wood, stones, ivory, etc., used to decorate furniture and floors. Also **mar'que·te·rie.** [< MF *marque* a mark]

mar·quis (mär'kwis, *Fr.* mar·kē') *n.* The title of a nobleman next in rank below a duke. [< OF *marche* boundary, a march²]

mar·quise (mär·kēz') *n.* 1 The wife or widow of a marquis. 2 A woman who has a rank equal to that of a marquis.

mar·qui·sette (mär'ki·zet', ·kwi-) *n.* A sheer, lightweight, open-mesh fabric, used esp. for curtains. [F, dim. of *marquise* a canopy]

mar·riage (mar'ij) *n.* 1 The act of marrying, or the state of being married; wedlock. 2 A wedding. 3 Any close union. [< L *maritus* a husband]

mar·riage·a·ble (mar'ij·ə·bəl) *adj.* Fitted by age, physical condition, etc., for marriage. —**mar'riage·a·bil'i·ty, mar'riage·a·ble·ness** *n.*

mar·ried (mar'ēd) *adj.* 1 Pertaining to marriage. 2 Having a spouse; wedded. —*n. Usu. pl. Informal* A married person. —Syn. 1 conjugal, connubial, hymeneal, matrimonial, nuptial.

mar·row (mar′ō) *n.* 1 A soft vascular tissue found in the central cavities of most bones. 2 The interior substance of anything; essence. [< OE *mearg*] —**mar′row·y** *adj.*

mar·row·bone (mar′ō·bōn′) *n.* 1 A bone containing marrow: also **marrow bone.** 2 *pl.* One's knees.

mar·row·fat (mar′ō·fat′) *n.* A variety of large, rich pea. Also **marrow pea, marrowfat pea.**

mar·ry (mar′ē) *v.* **·ried, ·ry·ing** *v.t.* 1 To join as husband and wife in marriage. 2 To take in marriage. 3 To give in marriage: usu. with *off.* 4 To unite closely. —*v.i.* 5 To take a husband or wife. [< L *maritus* a husband, married] —**mar′ri·er** *n.*

Mars (märz) *Rom. Myth.* The god of war. —*n.* The planet of the solar system fourth distant from the sun. • See PLANET.

Mar·sa·la (mär·sä′lä) *n.* A light, sweet white wine originally made in Marsala, Sicily.

Mar·seil·laise (mär′sə·lāz′, *Fr.* mär·sā·yez′) *n.* The national anthem of the French Republic, written in 1792 by Rouget de Lisle. [F < *Marseille*]

mar·seille (mär·sāl′) *n.* A thick cotton fabric having a raised weave, similar to piqué. Also **mar·seilles** (mär·sālz′). [< *Marseille*, France]

marsh (märsh) *n.* A tract of low, wet land; swamp. [< OE *mersc*] —**marsh′i·ness** *n.* —**marsh′y** *adj.* **(·i·er, ·i·est)**

mar·shal (mär′shəl) *n.* 1 An officer authorized to regulate ceremonies, processions, etc. 2 A U.S. federal official appointed to a judicial district and having functions similar to those of a sheriff. 3 The head of the police force or fire department in some cities. 4 In some European countries, a military officer of high rank. —*v.t.* **·shaled** or **·shalled, ·shal·ing** or **·shal·ling** 1 To arrange or dispose in order, as facts. 2 To array or draw up, as troops for battle. 3 To lead; usher. [< OHG *marah* a horse + *scalh* a servant] —**mar′· shal·cy** (-sē), **mar′shal·ship** *n.*

marsh gas METHANE.

marsh hawk An American hawk that nests on the ground in fields and marshes.

marsh·mal·low (marsh′mal′ō, -mel′ō) *n.* A soft, spongy confection made of syrup and gelatin.

marsh mallow A marsh plant with showy pink flowers.

marsh marigold A showy swamp plant related to the buttercup, having bright yellow flowers.

mar·su·pi·al (mär·sōō′pē·əl) *n.* Any of an order of mammals lacking a placenta and carrying their young in a marsupium, as the kangaroo, opossum, etc. —*adj.* 1 Having a marsupium. 2 Pertaining to or like a marsupium or pouch.

mar·su·pi·um (mär·sōō′pē·əm) *n. pl.* **·pi·a** (-pē·ə) A pouch-like fold, as on the abdomen of female marsupials, in which the young are carried. [L, a pouch, purse]

mart (märt) *n.* A market. [< L *mercatus* market]

mar·ten (mär′tən) *n.* 1 Any of a genus of weasellike, fur-bearing carnivorous mammals. 2 The valuable fur of the marten. [< OF *martre*]

Mar·tha (mär′thə) In the Bible, a friend of Jesus and sister of Lazarus and Mary.

mar·tial (mär′shəl) *adj.* 1 Pertaining to war or military life: court *martial.* 2 Suitable for war: *martial* music. 3 Fond of war; brave. [< L *Martialis* pertaining to Mars] —**mar′tial·ly** *adv.*

Marten

martial law Military jurisdiction exercised by a government temporarily over the population of a locality during war or an emergency.

Mar·tian (mär′shən) *adj.* Pertaining to the planet Mars. —*n.* One of the supposed inhabitants of Mars.

mar·tin (mär′tən) *n.* Any of certain short-beaked birds of the swallow family, as the **purple martin,** the **sand martin,** and the **house martin.** [ME]

mar·ti·net (mär′tə·net′) *n.* An overly strict disciplinarian, esp. military or naval. [< General *Martinet,* 17th c. French drillmaster]

mar·tin·gale (mär′tən·gāl) *n.* 1 A forked strap for holding down a horse's head by connecting the head gear with the bellyband. 2 *Naut.* A vertical spar under the bowsprit used in guying the stays. Also **mar′tin·gal** (-gal). [F]

mar·ti·ni (mär·tē′nē) *n. pl.* **·nis** A cocktail made of gin or vodka and dry vermouth, usu. served with a green olive or a twist of lemon peel. [? < *Martini* and Rossi, a company making vermouth]

mar·tyr (mär′tər) *n.* 1 One who submits to death rather than forswear his faith. 2 One who dies or suffers for principles, or sacrifices all for a cause. 3 One who suffers much or long, as from ill health or misfortune. —*v.t.* 1 To put to death as a martyr. 2 To torture; persecute. [< Gk. *martyr* a witness] —**mar′tyr·dom** *n.*

mar·tyr·ize (mär′tər·īz) *v.* **·ized, ·iz·ing** *v.t.* 1 To make a martyr of. —*v.i.* 2 To become a martyr. —**mar′tyr·i·za′tion** *n.*

mar·vel (mär′vəl) *v.* **·veled** or **·velled, ·vel·ing** or **·vel·ling** *v.i.* 1 To be filled with wonder, surprise, etc. —*v.t.* 2 To wonder at or about: with a clause as object. —*n.* 1 That which excites wonder; a prodigy. 2 A miracle. [< L *mirari* wonder at]

mar·vel·ous (mär′vəl·əs) *adj.* 1 Provoking astonishment or wonder; remarkable. 2 Supernatural; miraculous. 3 *Informal* Splendid; extraordinarily good. Also **mar′vel·lous.** —**mar′vel·ous·ly** *adv.* —**mar′vel·ous·ness** *n.* —**Syn.** 1 amazing, extraordinary, prodigious, wonderful, singular.

Marx·ism (märk′siz·əm) *n.* The body of doctrine formulated by Karl Marx and Friedrich Engels which formed the foundations of socialism and communism. —**Marx′i·an** (-ē·ən) *adj.* —**Marx′ist** *adj., n.*

Marx·ism-Len·in·ism (märk′siz·əm·len′in·iz′əm) *n.* The philosophy of history and politics based upon the works of Marx and Lenin. —**Marx′ist-Len′in·ist** *n.*

Mar·y (mâr′ē) In the Bible: 1 The mother of Jesus. 2 The sister of Lazarus and Martha.

Mary Jane (jān) 1 A low-heeled, usu. patent-leather slipper with an ankle strap, worn esp. by young girls 2 *Slang* MARIHUANA.

Mary Mag·da·lene (mag′də·lēn, -lin) 1 The woman out of whom Jesus cast seven devils. 2 The penitent sinner whom Jesus forgave. Also **Mary Mag′da·len.**

mar·zi·pan (mär′zə·pan) *n.* A confection of grated almonds, sugar, and white of eggs, usu. made into a paste and molded into various shapes. [< Ital. *marzapane,* orig. a small box, a dry measure, a weight]

mas., masc. masculine.

mas·car·a (mas·kar′ə) *n.* A cosmetic used to darken the eyelashes. [< Sp. *máscara* a mask]

mas·con (mas′kon, mäs-) *n.* Any of various areas on the moon where increased gravitational forces cause deviations in the course of orbiting spacecraft. [< MAS(S) + CON-(CENTRATION)]

mas·cot (mas′kot, -kət) *n.* A person, animal, or thing thought to bring good luck by its presence. [< Provençal *masco* a sorcerer]

mas·cu·line (mas′kyə·lin) *adj.* 1 Having the distinguishing qualities of the male sex. 2 Of, pertaining to, or suitable for males; manly. 3 *Gram.* Being of the male gender. —*n.* *Gram.* The masculine gender or a word of this gender. [< L *masculus* male] —**mas′cu·line·ly** *adv.* —**mas′cu·lin′i·ty** *n.*

ma·ser (mā′zər) *n. Physics* A device similar to a laser that operates with microwaves. [< m(icrowave) a(mplification by) s(timulated) e(mission of) r(adiation)]

mash (mash) *n.* 1 A pulpy mass. 2 A mixture of meal, bran, etc., and water, fed to cattle. 3 Crushed or ground grain or malt, infused in hot water to produce wort. 4 In wine-making, the crushed grapes before fermentation. —*v.t.* 1 To crush or beat into a mash. 2 To convert into mash, as malt or grain, by infusing in hot water. [< OE *māsc*]

mash·er (mash′ər) *n.* 1 One who or that which mashes. 2 *Slang* A man who persistently makes overtures to women unacquainted with him.

mash·ie (mash′ē) *n.* An iron golf club with a deep, short blade and much loft. Also **mash′y.** [?]

mask (mask, mäsk) *n.* 1 A cover or disguise for the features. 2 A protective appliance for the face

Masks
a. Greek tragedy.
b. Greek comedy.
c. domino.

or head: a gas *mask*. **3** Anything used to disguise or dissimilate; subterfuge. **4** A likeness of a face cast in plaster, clay, etc. **5** An elaborate dramatic presentation with music, fanciful costumes, etc., and actors masked as allegorical or mythological subjects; also, the text or music for it. **6** MASQUERADE. **7** An artistic covering for the face, used esp. by Greek and Roman actors. —*v.t.* **1** To cover, shield, or protect with or as with a mask. **2** To hide or conceal with or as with a mask; disguise. —*v.i.* **3** To put on a mask; assume a disguise. [< Ar. *maskharah* a buffoon] —**mask'er** *n.*

masking tape An adhesive tape used to protect those parts of a surface not to be painted, sprayed, or otherwise treated.

mas·o·chism (mas'ə·kiz'əm) *n.* The obtaining of pleasure, esp. sexual gratification, by submitting to physical or mental cruelty. [< Leopold von Sacher-*Masoch*, 1835–95, Austrian writer] —**mas'o·chist** *n.* —**mas'o·chis'tic** *adj.* —**mas'och·is'ti·cal·ly** *adv.*

ma·son (mā'sən) *n.* One who lays brick and stone in building; also, a stonecutter. [< Med. L *macio*]

Ma·son (mā'sən) *n.* A member of the order of Freemasons.

Ma·son-Dix·on line (mā'sən·dik'sən) The boundary between Pennsylvania and Maryland, regarded as dividing the North and the South. Also **Mason and Dixon's line.**

Ma·son·ic (mə·son'ik) *adj.* Of or pertaining to Freemasons or Freemasonry. Also **ma·son'ic.**

Ma·son·ite (mā'sən·īt) *n.* A tough, dense fiberboard used as a building and construction material: a trade name.

ma·son·ry (mā'sən·rē) *n. pl.* **·ries** **1** The art or work of building with brick or stone. **2** That which is built by masons or of materials which masons use.

masque (mask, mäsk), *n.* **1** MASK (def. 5). **2** MASQUERADE.

mas·quer·ade (mas'kə·rād', mäs'-) *n.* **1** A party attended by persons masked and costumed. **2** The costumes and disguises worn on such an occasion. **3** A false show or disguise. —*v.i.* **·ad·ed, ·ad·ing** **1** To take part in a masquerade. **2** To wear a mask or disguise. **3** To disguise one's true character; assume a false appearance. [< Sp. *máscara* a mask] —**mas'quer·ad'er** *n.*

mass (mas, mäs) *n.* **1** An assemblage of things that collectively make one quantity. **2** A body of matter; a lump. **3** The principal part of anything. **4** Extent of volume: bulk. **5** *Physics* The measure of the degree to which a body resists acceleration by a force, used also as a measure of the matter contained in the body. —**the masses** The common people. —*adj.* **1** Of, for, or consisting of the public in general. **2** Done on a large scale: *mass* production. —*v.t. & v.i.* To form into a mass; assemble. [< Gk. *maza* barley cake, lump] —**Syn.** *n.* **1** accumulation, aggregate, heap, collection, pile, group. *v.* accumulate, amass, gather, collect, pile up.

Mass (mas, mäs) *n. Eccl.* **1** The eucharistic liturgy in the Roman Catholic and some Anglican churches. **2** A celebration of this. **3** A musical setting for the fixed portions of this liturgy. Also **mass.** [< OE *mæsse*]

Mass. Massachusetts.

mas·sa·cre (mas'ə·kər) *n.* The indiscriminate, ruthless killing of human beings or animals; slaughter. —*v.t.* **·cred** (-kərd), **·cring** To kill indiscriminately or in great numbers. [< OF *maçacre* < *mache-col* butcher] —**mas'sa·crer** (-kə·rər, -krər) *n.*

mas·sage (mə·säzh') *n.* A remedial treatment of kneading, rubbing, and otherwise manipulating a part or the whole of the body. —*v.t.* **·saged, ·sag·ing** To treat by massage. [< F *masser* to massage] —**mas·sag'er, mas·sag'ist** *n.*

mass·cult (mas'kult') *n.* Someone or something having immense popularity and considered as an expression of popular culture: often used attributively. [< MASS + CULT(URE)]

mas·sé (ma·sā') *n.* In billiards, a stroke with a cue held perpendicularly, causing the cue ball to return in a straight line or to describe a curve. Also **mas·sé' shot.** [< F *masse* billiard cue, a mace]

mas·seur (má·sûr', *Fr.* má·sœr') *n.* A man whose work

is giving massages. [F] —**mas·seuse** (ma·sōōz', -sōōs'; *Fr.* má·sœz') *n. Fem.*

mas·sive (mas'iv) *adj.* **1** Constituting a large mass; ponderous. **2** Belonging to the total mass of anything. **3** Without definite form, as a mineral; amorphous. **4** Imposing in scope or degree; having considerable magnitude. —**mas'·sive·ly** *adv.* —**mas'sive·ness** *n.* —**Syn.** **1** ample, broad, capacious, extensive, spacious.

mass media Newspapers, magazines, radio, television, and motion pictures, considered as means of reaching a very wide public audience.

mass meeting A large public gathering for the discussion or promotion of some topic or cause, usu. political.

mass number *Physics* The number of protons and neutrons in an atom.

mass-pro·duce (mas'prə·d^yōōs') *v.t.* **·duced, ·duc·ing** To manufacture or produce by machinery (goods or articles) in great numbers or quantities. —**mass production**

mass·y (mas'ē) *adj.* **mass·i·er, mass·i·est** Massive; bulky. —**mass'i·ness** *n.*

mast¹ (mast, mäst) *n.* **1** *Naut.* A pole or spar, as of round timber or tubular metal, set upright in a sailing vessel to sustain the yards, sails, etc. **2** The upright pole of a derrick. **3** Any large, upright pole. —**before the mast** Serving as a common sailor. —*v.t.* To furnish with a mast or masts. [< OE *mæst*]

mast² (mast, mäst) *n.* The fruit of the oak, beech, and other trees; acorns, etc. [< OE *mæst*]

mas·ta·ba (mas'tə·bə) *n.* In ancient Egypt, an oblong, slope-sided building used as a mortuary chapel and place of offerings. Also **mas'ta·bah.** [< Ar. *maṣṭabah* bench]

mas·tec·to·my (mas·tek'tə·mē) *n. pl.* **·mies** The surgical removal of the breast. [< Gk. *mastos* breast + -ECTOMY]

Mastabas

mas·ter (mas'tər, mäs'-) *n.* **1** One who has authority over others, as the principal of a school, an employer, the head of a household, the owner of a domestic animal, etc. **2** One who has control of something; an owner. **3** In the U.S. merchant marine, the captain of a vessel. **4** One who is highly skilled; esp., an expert craftsman. **5** An artist of the first rank. **6** An original or a copy made from an original, as of a phonograph record, tape recording, or film, used as a source of making usu. numerous copies, as for commercial distribution. **7** A master key, switch, or other device. **8** *Chiefly Brit.* A male schoolteacher. **9** A title of respect for a young boy: *Master* Wilson. **10** An officer of the court who assists the judges. **11** One who has disciples or followers, esp. a religious leader. **12** One who gains the victory; a victor. —**the** (or **our**) **Master** Jesus. —*v.t.* **1** To overcome or subdue. **2** To become expert in: to *master* Greek. **3** To control or govern. —*adj.* **1** Being a master; being in control; chief. **2** Being an acknowledged expert: a *master* tactician. **3** Being a master from which others are duplicated. **4** Being a device that controls or can function in place of other mechanisms or that serves as a standard: a *master* key or switch. [< L *magister* greater] —**mas'ter·dom** *n.*

master builder **1** A contractor who employs men to build. **2** Formerly, an architect.

mas·ter·ful (mas'tər·fəl, mäs'-) *adj.* **1** Having the characteristics of a master; domineering. **2** Showing mastery, as of an art, situation, etc. —**mas'ter·ful·ly** *adv.* —**mas'ter·ful·ness** *n.*

mas·ter·ly (mas'tər·lē, mäs'-) *adj.* Characteristic of a master; befitting a master. —*adv.* In a masterly manner. —**mas'ter·li·ness** *n.*

mas·ter·mind (mas'tər·mīnd', mäs'-) *n.* A person of great intelligence and executive ability. —*v.t.* To plan and direct (a project) skillfully.

Master of Arts 1 A degree conferred by an institution of higher learning for the completion of a prescribed course of graduate study. 2 A person who has received this degree.

master of ceremonies A person presiding over an entertainment or dinner and introducing the performers or speakers.

mas·ter·piece (mas′tər·pēs′, mäs′-) n. An artistic work done with consummate skill.

master sergeant See GRADE.

mas·ter·ship (mas′tər·ship, mäs′-) n. 1 The state, personality, or character of a master; also, mastery. 2 Masterly skill; preeminence.

master stroke A masterly or decisive action or achievement.

mas·ter·y (mas′tər·ē, mäs′-) n. 1 The condition of having power and control. 2 Great knowledge or skill. 3 Superiority in a contest; victory. —Syn. 1 command, dominion, sway. 2 expertness. 3 triumph.

mast·head (mast′hed′, mäst′-) n. 1 Naut. The top of a lower mast. 2 That part of a newspaper or magazine listing the ownership, publishers, editors, etc. —v.t. To raise to or display at the masthead, as a flag.

mas·tic (mas′tik) n. 1 A resin obtained from a small Mediterranean tree, used in varnish and as a styptic. 2 The tree: also **mastic tree**. 3 Any of various quick-drying adhesive pastes. [< Gk. mastichē]

mas·ti·cate (mas′tə·kāt) v.t. ·cat·ed, ·cat·ing 1 To crush or grind (food) for swallowing; chew. 2 To reduce, as rubber, to a pulp by crushing or kneading. [< Gk. mastichaein gnash the teeth] —**mas′ti·ca′tion, mas′ti·ca′tor** n.

mas·ti·ca·to·ry (mas′tə·kə·tôr′ē, -tō′rē) adj. 1 Of, pertaining to, or used in mastication. 2 Adapted for chewing. —n. pl. ·ries A substance chewed to increase the secretion of saliva.

mas·tiff (mas′tif, mäs′-) n. One of an English breed of large hunting dogs, with a heavy body and broad skull. [< OF mastin]

mas·to·don (mas′tə·don) n. Any of various extinct elephantlike mammals distinguished from mammoths chiefly by their molar teeth. [< Gk. mastos breast + odous, odontos tooth; from the nipple-shaped projections on its teeth]

Mastodon

mas·toid (mas′toid) adj. 1 Designating or pertaining to a process of the temporal bone behind the ear. 2 Nipplelike; breastlike. —n. 1 The mastoid process. 2 MASTOIDITIS. [< Gk. mastos breast + eidos form] • See SKULL.

mas·toid·i·tis (mas′toid·ī′tis) n. Inflammation of the mastoid process.

mas·tur·bate (mas′tər·bāt) v. ·bat·ed, ·bat·ing v.i. 1 To excite one's genitals, as by contact, for sexual pleasure, usu. inducing orgasm. —v.t. 2 To induce orgasm in (another) by exciting the genitals without having sexual intercourse. [< L masturbari] —**mas′tur·ba′tion, mas′tur·ba′tor** n. —**mas′tur·ba·to′ry** (-bə·tôr′ē, -tō′rē) adj.

mat¹ (mat) n. 1 A flat article, woven or plaited, or made of a thick, sturdy material, to be laid on a floor and used to wipe one's feet. 2 Any flat piece of straw, plastic, etc., used as a floor covering, table protection, ornament, etc. 3 A thick, mattresslike pad used in a gymnasium for wrestling, acrobatics, etc. 4 Any twisted growth, as of hair or rushes. —v. **mat·ted, mat·ting** v.t. 1 To cover with or as with mats. 2 To knot or entangle into a mat. —v.i. 3 To become knotted or entangled. [< LL matta]

mat² (mat) n. 1 MATTE. 2 Printing MATRIX. 3 A border of cardboard, serving as the frame, or part of the frame, of a picture. —v.t. **mat·ted, mat·ting** 1 To produce a dull surface on, as metal or glass. 2 To provide (a picture) with a border of cardboard. —adj. MATTE. [< OF, dull]

mat·a·dor (mat′ə·dôr) n. A bullfighter who kills the bull with a thrust of a sword. [< Sp., matar to slay]

match¹ (mach) n. 1 A person or thing equal to another. 2 Two or more persons or things that harmonize or are alike. 3 A contest of skill, strength, etc.: a tennis match. 4 A marriage or an agreement to marry. 5 A person considered as a future husband or wife. —v.t. 1 To be similar to or in accord with in quality, degree, etc.: His looks match his mood. 2 To make or select as equals or as suitable for one another: to match pearls. 3 To marry. 4 To adapt: Match your efforts to your strength. 5 To compare so as to decide superiority; test: to match wits. 6 To set (equal opponents) in opposition: to match boxers. 7 To equal: No one could match him. —v.i. 8 To be equal, similar, or corresponding; suit. 9 To get married. —**match coins** To flip or reveal coins to make a decision. [< OE gemæcca companion] —**match′a·ble** adj. —**match′er** n.

match² (mach) n. 1 A splinter of soft wood or a piece of cardboard with a combustible tip that ignites by friction. 2 Formerly, a fuse of cotton wicking prepared to burn quickly or slowly, and used for firing cannon. [< Gk. myxa wick of a candle]

match·book (mach′book′) n. A folder enclosing and usu. stapled to a set of cardboard matches.

match·less (mach′lis) adj. That cannot be matched or equaled; peerless. —**match′less·ly** adv. —**match′less·ness** n. —Syn. incomparable, unequaled, unparalleled, unrivaled.

match·lock (mach′lok′) n. 1 An old type of musket fired by placing a lighted match against the powder in the pan. 2 The gunlock on such a musket.

match·mak·er (mach′mā′kər) n. 1 One who plans or schemes to bring about marriages for others. 2 One who arranges games or contests. —**match′mak′ing** adj., n.

match play In golf, a form of play in which the score is computed by totaling the number of holes won or lost by each side.

mate¹ (māt) n. 1 An associate; comrade. 2 One that is paired with another, as in matrimony; also, an animal paired for propagation. 3 An equal in a contest; a match. 4 An officer of a merchant vessel, ranking next below the captain. 5 Nav. A petty officer. —v. **mat·ed, mat·ing** v.t. 1 To join as mates; marry. 2 To pair for breeding, as animals. 3 To associate; couple. —v.i. 4 To match; marry. 5 To pair. 6 To consort; associate. [< MLG gemate]

mate² (māt) v.t. **mat·ed, mat·ing** 1 In chess, to checkmate. 2 To defeat or confound. —n. A checkmate. —interj. Checkmate. [< CHECKMATE]

ma·té (mä′tā, mat′ā) n. 1 A beverage made by steeping the leaves of a Brazilian holly. 2 The plant or its dried leaves. [< Quechua]

ma·ter (mā′tər, mä′-) n. Latin Mother.

ma·te·ri·al (mə·tir′ē·əl) n. 1 That of which anything is composed or may be constructed. 2 Collected facts, impressions, ideas, etc., for use in completing a creative endeavor. 3 The tools, instruments, articles, etc., for doing something. 4 A cloth or fabric. —adj. 1 Pertaining to anything having a physical existence. 2 Of or pertaining to the body or the appetites. 3 More interested in worldly things than in spiritual ones. 4 Important; significant: It makes no material difference to me. 5 Pertaining to matter as opposed to form. [< L materia matter]

ma·te·ri·al·ism (mə·tir′ē·əl·iz′əm) n. 1 The doctrine that the facts of experience are all to be explained by reference to the reality and laws of physical or material substance. 2 Undue regard for material and worldly rather than spiritual matters. —**ma·te′ri·al·ist** adj., n. —**ma·te′ri·al·is′tic** adj. —**ma·te′ri·al·is′ti·cal·ly** adv.

ma·te·ri·al·ize (mə·tir′ē·əl·īz′) v. **·ized, ·iz·ing** v.t. 1 To give material or actual form to; represent as material. 2 To cause (a spirit, etc.) to appear in visible form. —v.i. 3 To assume material or visible form; appear. 4 To take form or shape; be realized: Our plans never materialized. —**ma·te′ri·al·i·za′tion, ma·te′ri·al·iz′er** n.

ma·te·ri·al·ly (mə·tir′ē·əl·ē) adv. 1 In a material and important manner. 2 In essence or substance. 3 From a physical point of view.

ma·te·ri·a med·i·ca (mə·tir′ē·ə med′i·kə) Med. 1 The science that deals with medicinal substances, their nature, uses, effects, etc. 2 The substances employed as remedial agents. [< L materia matter + medicus medical]

ma·te·ri·el (mə·tir′ē·el′) n. Materials and equipment required for some purpose; esp., in an army, material things, as distinguished from personnel. Also **ma·té·ri·el'**. [< F]

ma·ter·nal (mə·tûr'nəl) *adj.* **1** Pertaining to a mother; motherly. **2** Connected with or inherited from one's mother. [< L *mater* a mother] —**ma·ter'nal·ly** *adv.*

ma·ter·ni·ty (mə·tûr'nə·tē) *n. pl.* **·ties 1** The condition of being a mother. **2** The qualities of a mother; motherliness. —*adj.* Pertaining to pregnancy or childbirth: *maternity* dress; *maternity* hospital.

math (math) *n. Informal* Mathematics.

math. mathematical; mathematician; mathematics.

math·e·mat·i·cal (math'ə·mat'i·kəl) *adj.* **1** Pertaining to or of the nature of mathematics. **2** Rigidly exact or precise. Also **math'e·mat'ic**. [< Gk. < *mathēma* learning] — **math'e·mat'i·cal·ly** *adv.*

math·e·ma·ti·cian (math'ə·mə·tish'ən) *n.* One skilled or trained in mathematics.

math·e·mat·ics (math'ə·mat'iks) *n.pl. (construed as sing.)* **1** The logical study of quantity, form, arrangement, and magnitude; esp., the methods for disclosing, by the use of rigorously defined concepts and symbols, the properties of quantities and relations. **2** A particular application or use of mathematics.

mat·in (mat'in) *n.* **1** *pl. Eccl.* The first of the canonical hours, usu. said at midnight. **2** *pl.* In the Anglican Church, the order for public worship in the morning. —*adj.* Of or belonging to the morning: also **mat'in·al**. [< OF *matin* early]

mat·i·née (mat'ə·nā') *n.* An entertainment or reception held in the daytime; esp. a theatrical or cinematic performance given in the afternoon. Also **mat'i·nee'**. [F< *matin* morning]

matri- *combining form* Mother: *matricide*. [< L *mater*, *matris* mother]

ma·tri·arch (mā'trē·ärk) *n.* A woman who rules in her family or tribe. [< MATRI- + Gk. *archos* ruler] —**ma'tri·ar'·chal** *adj.* —**ma'tri·ar'chy** *n.*

mat·ri·cide (mat'rə·sīd, mā'trə-) *n.* **1** The killing of one's mother. **2** One who kills his or her mother. [< MATRI- + -CIDE] —**mat'ri·ci'dal** *adj.*

ma·tric·u·late (mə·trik'yə·lāt) *v.t. & v.i.* **·lat·ed, ·lat·ing 1** To enroll, esp. in a college or university as a candidate for a degree. **2** *Can.* To pass final high-school examinations. —*n.* A candidate for a college or university degree. [< Med. L. *matrix* womb, origin, public roll] —**ma·tric'u·lant, ma·tric'u·la'tion, ma·tric'u·la'tor** *n.*

mat·ri·mo·ny (mat'rə·mō'nē) *n. pl.* **·nies 1** The union of a man and a woman in marriage; wedlock. **2** The state of being married. [< L *matrimonium*] —**mat'ri·mo'ni·al** *adj.* —**mat'ri·mo'ni·al·ly** *adv.*

ma·trix (mā'triks) *n. pl.* **ma·tri·ces** (mā'trə·sēz, mat'rə-) or **ma·trix·es 1** That which contains and gives shape or form to anything. **2** A mold in which anything is cast or shaped. **3** *Printing* A papier-mâché, plaster, or other impression of a form, from which a plate for printing may be made. [L, womb, breeding animal]

ma·tron (mā'trən) *n.* **1** A married woman. **2** A woman of established age and dignity. **3** A housekeeper, or a female superintendent, as of an institution. [< L *mater* mother] —**ma'tron·al, ma'tron·ly** *adj.* —**ma'tron·li·ness** *n.*

matron of honor A married woman acting as chief attendant to a bride at her wedding.

Matt. Matthew.

matte (mat) *n.* A lusterless, dull, or roughened surface. —*adj.* Presenting a lusterless surface. Also **matt** (mat). [< OF, dull]

mat·ted (mat'id) *adj.* **1** Covered with mats or matting. **2** Clustered into a dense, tangled mass. —**mat'ted·ly** *adv.* —**mat'ted·ness** *n.*

mat·ter (mat'ər) *n.* **1** That which makes up the substance of anything; material. **2** *Physics* That which occupies space, is reciprocally convertible with energy, and from which all physical objects are made. **3** A specific substance: inorganic *matter*. **4** Importance: It's of no *matter*. **5** That which is actually stated or written, as contrasted with style or form. **6** A subject or thing: a family *matter*. **7** A subject for discussion or feeling. **8** A condition of affairs, esp. if unpleasant or unfortunate: What's the *matter*? **9** Pus. **10** Written or printed documents sent by mail. **11** Amount: a *matter* of a few dollars. —**as a matter of fact** Actually; in fact. —**for that matter** As far as that is concerned. —*v.i.* To be of concern or importance. [< L *materia* stuff]

matter of course That which is naturally and logically expected. —**mat·ter-of-course** (mat'ər·əv·kôrs', -kōrs') *adj.*

mat·ter-of-fact (mat'ər·əv·fakt') *adj.* Closely adhering to facts; straightforward.

mat·ter-of-fact·ly (mat'ər·əv·fakt'lē) *adv.* In a matter-of-fact manner; straightforwardly. —**mat'ter-of-fact'ness** *n.*

Mat·thew (math'yōō) One of the twelve apostles, reputed author of the first Gospel. Also **Saint Matthew.** —*n.* The first Gospel.

mat·ting (mat'ing) *n.* **1** A woven fabric of fiber, straw, etc., used as a floor covering, etc. **2** The act or process of making mats. **3** A dull, flat surface effect.

mat·tock (mat'ək) *n.* A tool for digging and grubbing, resembling a pickax but having blades instead of points. [< OE *mattuc*]

mat·tress (mat'rəs) *n.* A casing of ticking or other strong fabric filled with hair, cotton, foam rubber, etc., and used on or as a bed. [< Ar. *matrah* place where something is thrown]

Mattock

mat·u·rate (mach'ŏŏ·rāt, mat'yŏŏ-) *v.i.* **·rat·ed, ·rat·ing 1** To ripen or mature. **2** To suppurate; form pus. [< L *maturare* ripen] —**mat'u·ra'tion** *n.* —**mat·u·ra·tive** (mach'ŏŏ·rā'tiv, mə·chŏŏr'ə·tiv) *adj.*

ma·ture (mə·chŏŏr', -tyŏŏr') *adj.* **1** Completely developed; full-grown. **2** Fully developed in character and powers. **3** Highly developed; complete in detail: a *mature* scheme. **4** Due and payable, having reached its time limit: a *mature* bond. —*v.* **·tured, ·tur·ing** *v.t.* **1** To cause to ripen or come to maturity. **2** To perfect; complete. —*v.i.* **3** To come to maturity or full development; ripen. **4** To become due, as a note. [< L *maturus* of full age] —**ma·ture'ly** *adv.* —**ma·ture'ness** *n.* —**Syn.** *adj.* **1** adult, grown, grown-up, ripe.

ma·tur·i·ty (mə·chŏŏr'ə·tē, -tyŏŏr'-) *n.* **1** The state or condition of being mature. **2** Full development, as of the body. **3** The time at which a thing matures: a note payable at *maturity*.

ma·tu·ti·nal (mə·t/yŏŏ'tə·nəl) *adj.* Pertaining to morning; early. [< L *matutinus* early in the morning < *Matuta*, goddess of morning] —**ma·tu'ti·nal·ly** *adv.*

mat·zo (mät'sə, -sō) *n. pl.* **mat·zoth** (mät'sōth, -sōs) or **mat·zos** (-səs, -səz) Wafers of unleavened bread. [< Heb. *matstsāh* unleavened]

maud·lin (môd'lin) *adj.* **1** Foolishly and tearfully sentimental. **2** Made foolish from drinking too much alcoholic liquor. [< OF *Maudelene*, (Mary) Magdalen, who was often depicted with eyes swollen from weeping]

mau·gre (mô'gər) *prep. Archaic* In spite of. Also **mau'ger.** [< OF]

maul (môl) *n.* A heavy mallet for driving wedges, piles, etc. —*v.t.* **1** To beat and bruise; batter. **2** To handle roughly; abuse. [< L *malleus* hammer] —**maul'er** *n.*

maun·der (môn'dər) *v.i.* **1** To talk in a wandering or incoherent manner. **2** To move dreamily or idly. [?] —**maun'der·er** *n.*

Maun·dy Thursday (môn'dē) The day before Good Friday, commemorating the Last Supper of Jesus with his disciples. [< L *mandatum* command + THURSDAY]

Mau·ri·ta·ni·a (môr'ə·tā'nē·ə) *n.* A republic of w Africa, 419,229 sq. mi., cap. Nouakchott. —**Mau'ri·ta'ni·an** *adj., n.* • See map at AFRICA.

Mau·ri·ti·us (mô·rish'ē·əs) *n.* An independent member of the Commonwealth of Nations on an island in the Indian Ocean, 804 sq. mi., cap. Port Louis. —**Mau·ri'ti·an** *adj., n.*

mau·so·le·um (mô'sə·lē'əm) *n. pl.* **·le·ums** or **·le·a** (-lē'ə) A large, stately tomb. [< Gk. *Mausōleion* tomb of King

Mausolus, erected at Halicarnassus about 350 B.C.] — **mau′so·le′an** *adj.*

mauve (mōv, môv) *n.* Any of various pale purple shades of color. —*adj.* Of any of these shades. [< L *malva* mallow]

mav·en (mā′vən) *n.* An experienced person in some field. [< Yiddish]

mav·er·ick (mav′ər·ik) *n.* **1** An unbranded or orphaned animal, esp. a calf. **2** A person characterized by independence or nonconformity in relation to a group with which he is affiliated, as a political party. [< S. A. *Maverick,* 1803–70, Texas lawyer, who did not brand his cattle]

ma·vis (mā′vis) *n.* The European song thrush. [< OF *mauvis*]

ma·vour·neen (ma·vŏŏr′nēn, -vôr′-) *n. Irish* My darling. Also **ma·vour′nin.** [< Irish *mo muirnín*]

maw (mô) *n.* **1** The gullet, jaws, or mouth of a voracious animal. **2** Anything that swallows up or consumes. **3** The stomach. **4** The craw of a bird. [< OE *maga* stomach]

mawk·ish (mô′kish) *adj.* **1** Characterized by false or feeble sentimentality. **2** Provoking disgust; sickening. [< obs. *mawk* a maggot] —**mawk′ish·ly** *adv.* —**mawk′ish·ness** *n.*

max. maximum.

max·i (maks′ē) *n. pl.* **max·is** A long skirt or coat, usu. reaching to the ankle.

maxi- *combining form* **1** Very long. **2** Very great.

max·il·la (mak·sil′ə) *n. pl.* **·lae** (-ē) **1** The upper jawbone in vertebrates. **2** One of the pair or pairs of mouth parts behind the mandibles of an insect, crab, etc. [L, jaw] — **max·il·lar·y** (mak′sə·ler′ē, mak·sil′ər·ē) *adj., n. (pl.* **·lar·ies).**

max·im (mak′sim) *n.* A brief statement of a practical principle or proposition; a saying. [< L *maxima (propositio)* greatest (premise)] —**Syn.** adage, aphorism, epigram, motto, proverb.

max·i·mal (mak′sə·məl) *adj.* Greatest; highest possible.

max·i·mize (mak′sə·mīz) *v.t.* **·mized,** **·miz·ing** To make as great as possible. —**max′i·mi·za′tion** *n.*

max·i·mum (mak′sə·məm) *n. pl.* **·mums** or **·ma** (-mə) The greatest quantity, amount, degree, or magnitude that is possible. —*adj.* **1** As large or great as possible. **2** Pertaining to or setting a maximum: *maximum* weight. [< L *maximus* greatest]

may (mā) *v., present* **may,** *past* **might** A verb now used only as an auxiliary followed by the infinitive without *to,* to express: **1** Permission or allowance: *May* I go? You *may.* **2** Desire or wish: *May* your tribe increase! **3** Contingency, esp. in clauses of result, concession, purpose, etc.: He died that we *might* live. **4** Possibility: You *may* be right. **5** *Law* Obligation or duty: the equivalent of *must* or *shall.* [< OE *mæg*] • See CAN¹.

May (mā) *n.* The fifth month of the year, containing 31 days. [< L *Maia,* goddess of growth]

Ma·ya (mä′yə) *n.* **1** A member of a tribe of Central American Indians, of Yucatán, N Guatemala, and British Honduras. **2** The language of the Mayas. —**Ma′yan** *adj., n.*

May apple 1 The oblong, yellowish fruit of a North American plant. **2** The plant itself.

may·be (mā′bē) *adv.* Perhaps; possibly.

May·day (mā′dā′) *n.* An international radiotelephone signal of distress. [< F *m'aider* help me]

May Day 1 May 1, sometimes celebrated as a spring festival by crowning a May Queen, dancing around a Maypole, etc. **2** In some countries, an international labor holiday, observed with parades, rallies, etc.

may·flow·er (mā′flou′ər) *n.* Any of various plants that bloom in the spring, as the trailing arbutus, the hawthorn of Britain, etc.

Mayflower The ship on which the Pilgrims came to American in 1620.

may·fly (mā′flī′) *n.* An insect with gauzy wings, which has a very brief life span in the adult phase.

may·hap (mā′hap) *adv. Archaic* It may happen; perhaps.

may·hem (mā′hem) *n.* **1** *Law* The offense of depriving a person by violence of any limb, member, or organ, or causing any mutilation of the body. **2** Egregious disorder or damage. [< OF *mahaigner* maim]

may·n't (mā′ənt, mānt) Contraction of *may not.*

may·on·naise (mā′ə·nāz′, mā′ə·nāz′) *n.* A sauce or dressing made by beating together raw egg yolk, olive oil, lemon juice or vinegar, and condiments. [F]

may·or (mā′ər, mâr) *n.* The chief magistrate of a city, borough or municipal corporation. [< L *major* greater] — **may′or·al** *adj.*

may·or·al·ty (mā′ər·əl·tē, mâr′əl-) *n. pl.* **·ties** The office or term of a mayor. [< OF *mairalté*]

May·pole (mā′pōl′) *n.* A pole decorated with flowers and ribbons, around which dancing takes place on May Day.

May Queen A young girl crowned with flowers in May Day festivities.

mayst (mā′ist, māst) Archaic second person singular, present tense, of MAY. Also **may′est.**

May·time (mā′tīm′) *n.* The month of May. Also **May′tide′** (-tīd′)

maze (māz) *n.* **1** An intricate network of paths or passages; a labyrinth. **2** Uncertainty; perplexity. [< AMAZE] — **maz′i·ly** *adv.* —**maz′i·ness** *n.* —**maz′y** (I·er, I·est) *adj.*

ma·zur·ka (mə·zûr′kə, -zoor′-) *n.* **1** A lively Polish dance resembling the polka. **2** The music for such a dance. Also **ma·zour′ka.** [Polish, woman from Mazovia, a Polish province]

M.C. Maritime Commission; Master of Ceremonies; Medical Corps; Member of Congress.

Mc·Car·thy·ism (mə·kär′thē·iz′əm) *n.* The practice of making public and sensational accusations of disloyalty or corruption, usu. with doubtful evidence, ostensibly to expose pro-Communist activity. [< Joseph *McCarthy,* 1909–1957, U.S. Senator]

Mc·Coy (mə·koi′), *Slang* The authentic person or thing: used with *the.* Also **the real McCoy.** [? < Kid *McCoy,* 1873–1940, U.S. boxer]

Mc·In·tosh (mak′ən·tosh) *n.* A variety of apple. [< J. *McIntosh,* 18th c. fruit grower of Ontario, Canada]

MD 1 Maryland (P.O. abbr.) **2** muscular dystrophy.

M.D. Doctor of Medicine (L *Medicinae Doctor*); Medical Department; mentally deficient.

Md mendelevium.

Md. Maryland.

M-Day (em′dā′) *n. Mil.* Mobilization day; the day a department of defense orders mobilization for war.

mdse. merchandise.

me (mē) *pron.* The objective case of *I.* [< OE *mē*] • **It's me, It's him, It's us,** etc. Anyone who answers the question "Who's there?" by saying "It's me" is using acceptable informal idiom. Here *It is I* would seem stilted, although at the formal level of writing it is expected: *They have warned me that it is I, and not he, who will have to bear the brunt of the criticism.*

ME Maine (P.O. abbr.).

Me, Me., M.E. Middle English.

Me methyl.

Me. Maine.

mead¹ (mēd) *n.* A alcoholic liquor of fermented honey and water to which malt, yeast, and spices are added. [< OE *meodu*]

mead² (mēd) *n. Archaic* A meadow. [< OE *mæd*]

mead·ow (med′ō) *n.* A tract of low or level grassland, esp. one producing grass for hay. [< OE *mædwe < mæd* mead] —**mead′ow·y** *adj.*

mead·ow·lark (med′ō·lärk′) *n.* Any of a genus of North American songbirds related to the orioles.

mea·ger (mē′gər) *adj.* **1** Deficient in quantity or quality; scanty. **2** Scantily supplied with fertility, strength, or richness. **3** Wanting in flesh; thin. Also **mea′gre.** —**mea′ger·ly** *adv.* —**mea′ger·ness** *n.* —**Syn. 1** inadequate, sparse, paltry, slight, exiguous. **3** emaciated, gaunt, skinny, spare.

Meadowlark

meal¹ (mēl) *n.* **1** Comparatively coarsely ground and unbolted grain. **2** Any powder produced by grinding. [< OE *melu*]

meal² (mēl) *n.* **1** The food taken at one time; a repast. **2** Its occasion or time. [< OE *mæl* measure, time, meal]

meal·ie (mē′lē) *n.* In South Africa: **a** An ear of maize, **b** *pl.* Maize; Indian corn. [< Afrikaans *milje < Pg. milho* millet]

meal·time (mēl'tīm') *n.* The habitual time for eating a meal.

meal·y (mē'lē) *adj.* **meal·i·er, meal·i·est** 1 Resembling meal; powdery. 2 Consisting of or containing meal. 3 Pale; wan. —**meal'i·ness** *n.*

meal·y-mouthed (mē'lē-moutht', -mouthd') *adj.* Unwilling to express adverse opinions plainly; insincere.

mean¹ (mēn) *v.* **meant, mean·ing** *v.t.* 1 To have in mind as a purpose or intent: I *meant* to visit him. 2 To intend or design for some purpose, destination, etc.: Was that remark *meant* for me? 3 To denote: The Latin word "vir" *means* "man." 4 To portend: Those clouds *mean* rain. —*v.i.* 5 To be disposed: He *means* well. 6 To be of specified importance or influence: Her beauty *means* everything to her. [< OE *mænan* tell, wish, intend]

mean² (mēn) *adj.* 1 Poor in quality; low in grade. 2 Of humble antecedents; lowly. 3 Having little value or importance. 4 Shabby, as in appearance. 5 Unkind or selfish. 6 *Informal* Ashamed; guilty: to feel *mean* about something. 7 Stingy; miserly. 8 *Informal* Sick or irritable: He feels *mean* in the morning. 9 *Slang* Excellent; skillful: to play a *mean* game of chess. 10 Ill-tempered; unmanageable: said of animals: a *mean* dog. [< OE (ge)*mæne*, common, ordinary] —**mean'ly** *adv.* —**mean'ness** *n.* —Syn. 1 inferior. 2 common, ordinary, plebeian. 5 base, contemptible, ignoble.

mean³ (mēn) *n.* 1 The middle state between two extremes; moderation. 2 *Math.* An average, often an arithmetic mean. 3 *pl.* (often construed as *sing.*) The medium through which anything is done: a *means* to an end. 4 *pl.* Money or property; wealth. —**by all means** Without hesitation; certainly. —**by any means** In any manner possible; somehow. —**by means of** By the help or use of; through. —**by no means** Most certainly not. —*adj.* 1 Intermediate as to position between extremes. 2 Intermediate as to size, degree, or quality; average. 3 Of or indicating an average: the *mean* distance covered daily. [< L *medius* middle]

me·an·der (mē·an'dər) *v.i.* 1 To wind and turn in a course. 2 To wander aimlessly. —*n.* 1 A tortuous or winding course. 2 An aimless wandering. [< Gk. *Maiandros* a river known for its winding course] —**me·an'der·er** *n.*

mean·ie (mē'nē) *n. Informal* A mean or disagreeable person. Also **mean'y.**

mean·ing (mē'ning) *n.* 1 That which is intended to be conveyed or understood; the object or aim of an effort or expression. 2 That which is conveyed or understood; sense; significance. —*adj.* Having purpose or intention: usu. in combination: *well-meaning.* —**mean'ing·ful** *adj.* —**mean'ing·ful·ly, mean'ing·ly** *adv.*

mean·ing·less (mē'ning·lis) *adj.* Without meaning or significance. —**mean'ing·less·ly** *adv.* —**mean'ing·less·ness** *n.*

mean sun *Astron.* A fictitious sun considered to be moving uniformly with respect to the equator, a concept used to facilitate the computation of time.

meant (ment) *p.t. & p.p.* of MEAN¹.

mean·time (mēn'tīm') *n.* Intervening time or occasion. —*adv.* MEANWHILE.

mean time Time reckoned on the motion of the mean sun. Also **mean solar time.**

mean·while (mēn'hwīl') *adv.* In or during the intervening time. —*n.* MEANTIME.

meas. measure; measurable.

mea·sles (mē'zəlz) *n.* Either of two distinct, contagious viral diseases characterized by small red skin eruptions: **a** RUBEOLA. **b** RUBELLA, or German measles. [ME *masel* a blister]

mea·sly (mēz'lē) *adj.* **·sli·er, ·sli·est** 1 Affected with measles. 2 *Slang* So skimpy or paltry as to be beneath contempt.

meas·ur·a·ble (mezh'ər ə·bəl) *adj.* 1 Capable of being measured or computed. 2 Limited; moderate. —**meas'ur·a·bil'i·ty, meas'ur·a·ble·ness** *n.* —**meas'ur·a·bly** *adv.*

meas·ure (mezh'ər) *n.* 1 The extent or dimensions of anything. 2 A standard or unit of measurement. 3 A system of measurements. • See pp. 448–449 for tables of MEASURES AND WEIGHTS for metric and U.S. systems. 4 An

---

instrument or utensil used in measurement. 5 The act of measuring. 6 A quantity measured. 7 Reasonable limits; moderation: reward beyond *measure.* 8 A certain proportion; relative extent. 9 *Often pl.* A

Two measures of music

specific act or course: to take drastic *measures.* 10 A legislative bill. 11 That which makes up a total. 12 Any quantity regarded as a unit and standard of comparison with other quantities. 13 *Music* **a** The division of time by which melody and rhythm are regulated. **b** The portion of music contained between two bar lines; bar. 14 In prosody, meter. 15 A slow and stately dance or dance movement. —**in a measure** Somewhat; partly. —**take one's measure** To estimate one's character. —*v.* **·ured, ·ur·ing** *v.t.* 1 To take or ascertain the dimensions, quantity, capacity, etc., of, esp. by means of a measure. 2 To set apart, mark off, etc., by measuring: often with *off* or *out.* 3 To estimate by comparison; judge; weigh. 4 To serve as the measure of. 5 To bring into competition or comparison. 6 To traverse as if measuring; travel over. 7 To adjust; regulate. 8 To appraise or observe carefully with the eyes: She *measured* him up and down before replying. —*v.i.* 9 To make or take measurements. 10 To yield a specified measurement: The table *measures* six by four feet. 11 To admit of measurement. —**measure one's length** To fall prostrate at full length. —**measure out** To distribute or allot by measure. —**measure up** To fulfill, as expectations: often with *to.* [< L *metiri* to measure] —**meas'ur·er** *n.*

meas·ured (mezh'ərd) *adj.* 1 Ascertained, adjusted, or proportioned by rule. 2 Slow and stately. 3 Deliberate. 4 Rhythmical. 5 Restrained. —**meas'ured·ly** *adv.* —**meas'ured·ness** *n.*

meas·ure·less (mezh'ər·lis) *adj.* Incapable of measurement; unlimited; immense.

meas·ure·ment (mezh'ər·mənt) *n.* 1 The process or result of measuring anything; mensuration. 2 The amount or extent determined by measuring. 3 A system of measuring units.

measuring worm A caterpillar larva of a moth that assumes the shape of a loop when in motion by alternately moving up the rear and forward parts of its body.

meat (mēt) *n.* 1 The flesh of animals used as food: sometimes excluding fish and fowl. 2 Anything eaten for nourishment; victuals: *meat* and drink. 3 The edible part of anything. 4 The essence, gist, or pith: the *meat* of an essay. 5 *Slang* Anything one likes very much or does with special ease. [< OE *mete*] —**meat'less** *adj.*

meat·ball (mēt'bôl) *n.* 1 Ground or chopped meat shaped into a ball and cooked in various ways, usu. served in a sauce. 2 *Slang* A dull or stupid person.

me·a·tus (mē·ā'təs) *n. pl.* **·tus** or **·tus·es** *Anat.* A passage or canal, esp. its external opening. [L, a passage]

meat·y (mē'tē) *adj.* **meat·i·er, meat·i·est** 1 Full of or resembling meat. 2 Full of genuine insight or significance; stimulating to the intellect. —**meat'i·ness** *n.*

mec·ca (mek'ə) *n.* 1 A place visited by many people; any attraction. 2 The object of one's aspiration, yearning, or effort. [< *Mecca*, Saudi Arabia, holy city of Islam]

mech., mechan. mechanical; mechanics; mechanism.

me·chan·ic (mə·kan'ik) *n.* One engaged in mechanical employment, esp. in making, using, or repairing machines or tools. —*adj.* 1 Pertaining to mechanics; mechanical. 2 Involving manual labor or skill. [< Gk. *mēchanē* a machine]

me·chan·i·cal (mə·kan'i·kəl) *adj.* 1 Of or pertaining to mechanics or the laws of mechanics. 2 Produced by a machine. 3 Operated by mechanism. 4 Operating as if by a machine or machinery. 5 Doing or done by mere force of habit. 6 Lifeless; expressionless: a *mechanical* recitation. 7 Skilled in the use of tools and mechanisms. 8 Having to do with certain physical skills or techniques: the *mechanical* aspects of singing. —**me·chan'i·cal·ly** *adv.* —**me·chan'i·cal·ness** *n.*

MEASURES AND WEIGHTS
Metric System

LENGTH

Unit	Equivalent in Meters	U.S. Equivalent
millimeter (mm)	0.001	0.03937 inch
centimeter (cm) = 10 millimeters	0.01	0.3937 inch
decimeter (dm) = 10 centimeters	0.1	3.937 inches
meter (m) = 10 decimeters or 100 centimeters or 1,000 millimeters	1	39.37 inches or 3.28 feet or 1.09 yards
decameter (dkm) = 10 meters	10	32.81 feet or 10.93 yards
hectometer (hm) = 10 decameters	100	328.08 feet or 109.36 yards
kilometer (km) = 10 hectometers	1,000	0.6214 mile or 1,093.6 yards or 3,280.8 feet

AREA

Unit	Equivalent in Square Meters	U.S. Equivalent
square millimeter (sq mm, mm²)	0.000001	0.00155 square inch
square centimeter (sq cm, cm²) = 100 square millimeters	0.0001	0.155 square inch
square decimeter (sq dm, dm²) = 100 square centimeters	0.01	15.5 square inches
square meter (sq m, m²) or **centare (ca)** = 100 square decimeters or 10,000 square centimeters or 1,000,000 square millimeters	1	10.76 square feet or 1.196 square yards
square decameter (sq dkm, dkm²) or **are (a)** = 100 centares	100	119.60 square yards or 0.0247 acre
square hectometer (sq hm, hm²) or **hectare (ha)** = 100 ares	10,000	2.47 acres
square kilometer (sq km, km²) = 100 hectares	1,000,000	0.386 square mile or 247.105 acres

VOLUME (LIQUID MEASURE)

Unit	Equivalent in Liters	U.S. Equivalent
milliliter (ml)	0.001	0.034 fluid ounce
centiliter (cl) = 10 milliliters	0.01	0.338 fluid ounce
deciliter (dl) = 10 centiliters	0.1	3.38 fluid ounces
liter (l) = 10 deciliters or 100 centiliters or 1,000 milliliters	1	1.05 liquid quarts or 33.814 fluid ounces or 0.908 dry quart
decaliter (dkl) = 10 liters	10	2.64 gallons or 0.284 bushel
hectoliter (hl) = 10 decaliters	100	26.418 gallons or 2.838 bushels
kiloliter (kl) = 10 hectoliters	1,000	264.18 gallons

CUBIC MEASURE

Unit	Equivalent in Cubic Meters	U.S. Equivalent
cubic centimeter (cc, cu cm, cm³) = 1,000 cubic millimeters	0.000001	0.061 cubic inch
cubic decimeter (cu dm, dm³) = 1,000 cubic centimeters	0.001	61.023 cubic inches
decistere (ds)	0.1	3.53 cubic feet
cubic meter or **stere (s)** = 1,000 cubic decimeters or 1,000,000 cubic centimeters	1	1.308 cubic yards
decastere (dks)	10	13.1 cubic yards

MASS OR WEIGHT

Unit	Equivalent in Grams	U.S. Equivalent in Avoirdupois Weight
milligram (mg)	0.001	0.0154 grain
centigram (cg) = 10 milligrams	0.01	0.1543 grain
decigram (dg) = 10 centigrams	0.1	1.543 grains
gram (g) = 10 decigrams or 100 centigrams or 1,000 milligrams	1	15.43 grains or 0.03527 ounce
decagram (dkg) = 10 grams	10	0.3527 ounce
hectogram (hg) = 10 decagrams	100	3.527 ounces
kilogram (kg) = 10 hectograms	1,000	2.2046 pounds
quintal (q) = 100 kilograms	100,000	220.46 pounds
metric ton (t or MT) = 10 quintals or 1,000 kilograms	1,000,000	1.1 tons or 2,204.6 pounds

A metric carat (car.) (used in weighing gems) = 200 milligrams or 3.086 grains avoirdupois.

Other metric prefixes occasionally used are: micro- (one-millionth of), myria- (10,000 times), mega- (1,000,000 times) (a unit).

SYMBOLS

t	10^{12} times (a unit); tera-	c	10^{-2} times (a unit); centi-
g	10^{9} times (a unit); giga-	m	10^{-3} times (a unit); milli-
m	10^{6} times (a unit); mega-	μ	10^{-6} times (a unit); micro-
k	10^{3} times (a unit); kilo-	n	10^{-9} times (a unit); nano-
h	10^{2} times (a unit); hecto-	p or $\mu\mu$	10^{-12} times (a unit); pico- or micromicro-
dk	10 times (a unit); deka-	Å, λ	Angstrom unit
		$\mu\mu$	micromicron
d	10^{-1} times (a unit); deci-	μ	micron

mechanical advantage The ratio of the output force of a mechanism performing useful work to the input force.

mechanical energy The energy manifested in the motion of material bodies, as in the global motions of the winds and tides or in the release of a coiled spring.

me·chan·ics (mə·kan′iks) n. (construed as sing. defs. 1, 2; usu. construed as pl. def. 3) 1 The branch of physics that deals with the phenomena caused by the action of forces on material bodies. 2 The science and technology of machinery. 3 The mechanical or technical aspects of anything.

mech·a·nism (mek′ə·niz′əm) n. 1 The parts of a machine collectively. 2 The action or operation of a machine or a mechanical device. 3 Something similar to a machine in the arrangement and working of its parts, as the human body. 4 A process by which a given result is achieved: the mechanisms of heredity. 5 Technique; mechanical execution or action. 6 The philosophical doctrine that physical and chemical agencies alone are sufficient to explain all phenomena, including life. —mech′a·nist n. —mech′a·nis′· tic adj. —mech′a·nis′ti·cal·ly adv.

mech·a·nize (mek′ə·nīz) v.t. ·nized, ·niz·ing 1 To make mechanical. 2 To convert (an industry, etc.) to machine pro-

MEASURES AND WEIGHTS
U.S. System

LENGTH

Unit	Metric Equivalent
inch (in.)	2.54 centimeters
foot (ft.) = 12 inches	30.48 centimeters or 0.3048 meter
yard (yd.) = 3 feet or 36 inches	0.9144 meter
rod (rd.) = 5.5 yards or 16.5 feet	5.0292 meters
furlong = 220 yards or 40 rods or ⅛ mile	201.168 meters
mile (mi.) = 5,280 feet or 1,760 yards or 8 furlongs	1.6093 kilometers

AREA

Unit	Metric Equivalent
square inch (sq. in.)	6.452 square centimeters
square foot (sq. ft.) = 144 square inches	0.093 square meter or 929.03 square centimeters
square yard (sq. yd.) = 9 square feet	0.836 square meter
square rod (sq. rd.) = 30.25 square yards	25.293 square meters
acre (A.) = 160 square rods or 4,840 square yards or 43,560 square feet	0.4047 hectare or 4,047 square meters
square mile (sq. mi.) = 640 acres	259.00 hectares or 2.590 square kilometers

LIQUID MEASURE

Unit	U.S. Equivalent in Cubic Inches	Metric Equivalent
gill (gi.) = 4 fluid ounces	7.219	0.118 liter
pint (pt.) = 4 gills	28.875	0.473 liter
quart (qt.) = 2 pints	57.75	0.946 liter
gallon (gal.) = 4 quarts	231	3.785 liters

The British imperial gallon (4 imperial quarts) = 4.546 liters or 277.42 cubic inches. The U.S. gallon is approximately ⅚ of the British imperial gallon.

APOTHECARIES' FLUID MEASURE

Unit	U.S. Equivalent in Cubic Inches	Metric Equivalent
minim (min.)	0.0038	0.0616 milliliter
fluid dram (fl. dr.) = 60 minims	0.225	3.697 milliliters
fluid ounce (fl. oz.) = 8 fluid drams	1.805	29.573 milliliters
pint (pt.) = 16 fluid ounces	28.875	0.473 liter

DRY MEASURE

Unit	U.S. Equivalent in Cubic Inches	Metric Equivalent
pint (pt.)	33.600	0.551 liter
quart (qt.) = 2 pints	67.200	1.101 liters
peck (pk.) = 8 quarts	537.605	8.810 liters
bushel (bu.) = 4 pecks	2,150.42	35.239 liters

CUBIC MEASURE

Unit	Metric Equivalent
cubic inch (cu. in.)	16.387 cubic centimeters
cubic foot (cu. ft.) = 1,728 cubic inches	0.028 cubic meter
cubic yard (cu. yd.) = 27 cubic feet	0.765 cubic meter
cord (cd.) (for cordwood) = 128 cubic feet	3.625 cubic meters

AVOIRDUPOIS WEIGHT

Unit	Metric Equivalent
grain (gr.)	0.0648 gram
dram (dr.) = 27.34 grains	1.772 grams
ounce (oz.) = 16 drams or 437.5 grains	28.349 grams
pound (lb.) = 16 ounces or 7,000 grains	453.59 grams or 0.453 kilograms
hundredweight (cwt.) = 100 pounds	45.36 kilograms
ton = 2,000 pounds	0.907 metric ton or 907.18 kilograms

TROY WEIGHT

Unit	Metric Equivalent
grain (gr.)	0.0648 gram
pennyweight (dwt.) = 24 grains	1.555 grams
ounce (oz. t.) = 20 pennyweight or 480 grains	31.103 grams
pound (lb. t.) = 12 ounces or 240 pennyweight or 5,760 grains	373.24 grams or 0.373 kilogram

APOTHECARIES' WEIGHT

Unit	Metric Equivalent
grain (gr.)	0.0648 gram
scruple (s.) = 20 grains	1.296 grams
dram (dr.) = 3 scruples or 60 grains	3.888 grams
ounce (oz.) = 8 drams or 480 grains	31.103 grams
pound (lb.) = 12 ounces or 5,760 grains	373.24 grams or 0.373 kilogram

SYMBOLS

#	pound(s)
'	foot, feet
"	inch(es)

Apothecaries' Measure

℔	pound(s)	℥	ounce(s)
ʒ	dram(s)	℈	scruple(s)
		♏, ♏, ♏	minim

---

duction. 3 *Mil.* To equip with tanks, trucks, etc. —**mech'a·ni·za'tion** *n.*

mech·a·no·ther·a·py (mek'ə·nō·ther'ə·pē) *n.* The treatment of disease with mechanical appliances of any kind. —**mech'a·no·ther'a·pist** *n.*

med. medical; medicine; medieval; medium.

med·al (med'l) *n.* A small piece of metal, bearing a device, usu. commemorative of some event or deed of bravery, scientific research, etc. —*v.t.* ·aled or ·alled, ·al·ing or ·al·ling To confer a medal upon. [< L *metallum* metal] —**me·dal·lic** (mə·dal'ik) *adj.*

med·al·ist (med'l·ist) *n.* 1 A collector, engraver, or designer of medals. 2 The recipient of a medal awarded for services or merit. 3 In golf, the winner at medal play. Also **med'al·list.**

me·dal·lion (mə·dal'yən) *n.* 1 A large medal. 2 A decorative element, as of fabrics, shaped like a large medal.

medal play In golf, competition in which the score is based on the total number of strokes taken.

med·dle (med'l) *v.i.* ·dled, ·dling To take part in or concern oneself with something that is not one's proper business; interefere: often with *in* or *with.* [< OF *medler, mesdler*] —**med·dler** (med'lər) *n.*

med·dle·some (med'l·səm) *adj.* Given to meddling or interfering. —**med'dle·some·ly** *adv.* —**med'dle·some·ness** *n.* —**Syn.** intrusive, obtrusive, officious.

Mede (mēd) *n.* One of an ancient Asiatic people who flourished in sw Asia.

Me·de·a (mə·dē'ə) *Gk. Myth.* A sorceress who helped Jason to obtain the Golden Fleece, and, when deserted by him, killed their children.

med·e·vac (med'ə·vak') *n.* The evacuation of the wounded, as from battle sites, usu. by helicopter. [< *med(ical) evac(uation)*]

Med. Gk. Medieval Greek.

me·di·a (mē'dē·ə) *n. pl. of* **me·di·um** 1 Means of disseminating information, entertainment, etc., such as books, newspapers, radio, television, motion pictures, and magazines.

---

add, āce, câre, pälm; end, ěven; it, īce; odd, ōpen, ôrder; tŏŏk, pōōl; up, bûrn; ə = *a* in *above, u* in *focus;* yōō = *u* in *fuse;* oil; pout; check; go; ring; thin; ᵺis; zh, *vision.* < derived from; ? origin uncertain or unknown.

2 In advertising, all means of communication that carry advertisements.
me·di·ae·val (mē′dē·ē′vəl, med′ē-, mid′-, mē·dē′vəl) *adj.* MEDIEVAL.
me·di·al (mē′dē·əl) *adj.* **1** Of or pertaining to the middle, in position or character or in calculation. **2** Ordinary; average. [< L *medius* middle] —**me′di·al·ly** *adv.*
me·di·an (mē′dē·ən) *n.* **1** *Geom.* A line that extends from a vertex of a triangle to the midpoint of the opposite side. **2** *Stat.* Of or designating a number *x* in a set of data such that if the data is divided into equal subsets *A* and *B*, every number in *A* is greater than or equal to *x* and every number in *B* is less than or equal to *x*. —*adj.* Of, being, or pertaining to a median or to the middle. —**me′di·an·ly** *adv.*
me·di·ate (mē′dē·āt) *v.* ·**at·ed**, ·**at·ing** *v.t.* **1** To settle or reconcile by mediation, as differences. **2** To bring about or effect by mediation. **3** To serve as the medium for effecting (a result) or conveying (an object, information, etc.). —*v.i.* **4** To act between disputing parties in order to bring about a settlement, compromise, etc. **5** To occur or be in an intermediate relation or position. —*adj.* (-it) **1** Acting as an intervening agency; indirect. **2** Occurring or effected as a result of indirect or median agency. **3** Intermediate. [< L *mediare* stand between] —**me′di·ate·ly** *adv.* —**me′di·a′tive** *adj.* —**me′di·a′tor** *n.*
me·di·a·tion (mē′dē·ā′shən) *n.* **1** The act of mediating; intercession; interposition. **2** A friendly intervention in the disputes of others, with their consent, for the purpose of adjusting differences.
med·ic[1] (med′ik) *n.* Any of several cloverlike forage plants, esp. alfalfa. [< Gk. *Mēdikē (poa)* Median (grass) < *Mēdos* a Mede]
med·ic[2] (med′ik) *n. Informal* **1** A doctor, physician, or intern. **2** A medical aide or corpsman.
med·i·ca·ble (med′ə·kə·bəl) *adj.* Capable of relief by medicine; curable.
Med·i·caid (med′i·kād′) *n.* In the U.S., a tax-supported health insurance program for low-income people.
med·i·cal (med′i·kəl) *adj.* **1** Pertaining to medicine or its practice. **2** Having curative properties. [< L *medicus* a physician] —**med′i·cal·ly** *adv.*
med·i·ca·ment (med′ə·kə·mənt, mə·dik′ə-) *n.* Any substance used for the alleviation of disease or wounds. [< L *medicare* to heal]
Med·i·care (med′i·kâr′) *n.* In the U.S., a health insurance program supported in part by government funds, serving esp. the aged.
med·i·cate (med′ə·kāt) *v.t.* ·**cat·ed**, ·**cat·ing** **1** To treat with a drug or other substance. **2** To tincture or impregnate with medicine. [< L *medicus* a physician] —**med′i·ca′tive**, **med′i·ca·to′ry** (-kə·tôr′ē, -tō′rē) *adj.*
med·i·ca·tion (med′ə·kā′shən) *n.* **1** Any substance used to treat disease, heal wounds, etc.; a medicine. **2** The act or process of medicating.
me·dic·i·nal (mə·dis′ə·nəl) *adj.* Adapted to cure or mitigate disease. —**me·dic′i·nal·ly** *adv.*
med·i·cine (med′ə·sin) *n.* **1** A substance used to treat disease, as a drug. **2** The science of preserving health and treating disease. **3** This science exclusive of surgery or obstetrics. **4** Among North American Indians, any agent or rite, as a **medicine dance**, **medicine song**, etc., used to invoke supernatural aid in health or disease. —**take one's medicine** To endure deserved or necessary hardship. —*v.t.* ·**cined**, ·**cin·ing** To treat with medicine. [< L *medicus* physician]
medicine ball A large, heavy, leather-covered ball, thrown and caught for physical exercise.
medicine man Among North American Indians, one professing supernatural powers of healing and of invoking the spirits; a shaman.
med·i·co (med′ə·kō) *n. pl.* ·**cos** *Informal* A doctor or a medical student.
me·di·e·val (mē′dē·ē′vəl, med′ē-, mid′-, mē·dē′vəl) *adj.* Belonging to or descriptive or characteristic of the Middle Ages. [< L *medius* middle + *aevum* age] —**me′di·e′val·ly** *adv.*
Medieval Greek The Greek language used from about 600 to 1500.

me·di·e·val·ism (mē′dē·ē′vəl·iz′əm, med′ē-, mid′-, mē·dē′vəl-) *n.* **1** The spirit or practices of the Middle Ages; general tone of medieval life. **2** Devotion to the institutions, ideas, or traits of the Middle Ages. **3** A custom, idea, etc., of the Middle Ages. —**me′di·e′val·ist** *n.*
Medieval Latin The Latin language used from about 600 to 1500.
me·di·o·cre (mē′dē·ō′kər, mē′dē·ō′kər) *adj.* Of only middle quality; ordinary; commonplace. [< L *medius* middle]
me·di·oc·ri·ty (mē′dē·ok′rə·tē) *n. pl.* ·**ties 1** The condition of being mediocre. **2** Commonplace ability. **3** A commonplace person.
Medit. Mediterranean.
med·i·tate (med′ə·tāt) *v.* ·**tat·ed**, ·**tat·ing** *v.i.* **1** To engage in contemplative thought. —*v.t.* **2** To think about; consider. **3** To think about doing; intend: to *meditate* mischief. [< L *meditari* muse, ponder] —**med′i·ta′tive** *adj.* —**med′i·ta′tive·ly** *adv.* —**med′i·ta′tor** *n.* —**Syn. 1** contemplate, muse, reflect, ponder, consider, weigh.
med·i·ta·tion (med′ə·tā′shən) *n.* The act of meditating; deep, deliberate thought; contemplation.
Med·i·ter·ra·ne·an (med′ə·tə·rā′nē·ən) *n.* **1** The Mediterranean Sea or the regions surrounding it. **2** One who lives on or near the Mediterranean Sea. —*adj.* Of, pertaining to, or dwelling near the Mediterranean Sea.
me·di·um (mē′dē·əm) *n. pl.* ·**di·ums** or **me·di·a** (-dē·ə) **1** An intermediate quality, degree, or condition; mean. **2** A surrounding or enveloping element; environment. **3** Any substance, as air, through or in which something may move or an effect be produced. **4** (*pl., usu.* **me·di·a**) An intermediate means or agency; instrument; esp., a means of communication that includes advertising: the mass *media*; Radio is the best *medium* to reach motorists. **5** (*pl.* **me·di·ums**) A person believed to be in communication with the spirits of the dead. **6** In painting, a liquid which gives fluency to the pigment. **7** Any nutritive substance adapted to the development of bacteria, viruses, and other microorganisms: also **culture medium**. —*adj.* Intermediate in quantity, quality, position, size, or degree; middle. [< L *medius* middle]
Med. L. Medieval Latin.
med·lar (med′lər) *n.* **1** A small tree related to the apple. **2** Its hard, bitter fruit, edible when it begins to decay. [< Gk. *mespilē*]
med·ley (med′lē) *n.* **1** A mingled and confused mass of ingredients, usu. incongruous; jumble. **2** A composition of different songs or parts of songs arranged to run as a continuous whole. —*adj.* Composed of parts that are not alike; mixed. [< OF *medlee*]
me·dul·la (mə·dul′ə) *n. pl.* ·**las** or ·**lae** (-ē) **1** The inner portion of an organ or part. • See KIDNEY. **2** The marrow of long bones. **3** MEDULLA OBLONGATA. [< L *medius* middle] —**me·dul′lar**, **med·ul·lar·y** (med′ə·ler′ē, mi·dul′ər·ē) *adj.*
medulla ob·lon·ga·ta (ob′lông·gä′tə) The part of the brain next to the spinal cord. [L, oblong medulla]
me·du·sa (mə·dyōō′sə, -zə) *n. pl.* ·**sas** or ·**sae** (-sē, -zē) A jellyfish. —**me·du′san** *adj.*, *n.* —**me·du′soid** *adj.*
Me·du·sa (mə·dyōō′sə, -zə) *Gk. Myth.* One of the three Gorgons killed by Perseus, who gave her head to Athena.
meed (mēd) *n. Archaic* A well-deserved reward; recompense. [< OE *mēd*]
meek (mēk) *adj.* **1** Of gentle and long-suffering disposition. **2** Submissive; compliant. **3** Humble; lowly. —*adv.* In a meek manner. [< ON *miukr* gentle, soft] —**meek′ly** *adv.* —**meek′ness** *n.*
meer·schaum (mir′shəm, -shôm, -shoum) *n.* **1** A soft, light, heat-resistant magnesium silicate mineral used for tobacco pipes, cigar holders, etc. **2** A pipe made from this material. [< G *Meer* sea + *Schaum* foam]
meet[1] (mēt) *v.* **met**, **meet·ing** *v.t.* **1** To come upon; encounter. **2** To make the acquaintance of. **3** To be at the place of arrival of: We *met* him at the station. **4** To come into contact or intersection with: where the path *meets* the road. **5** To keep an appointment with. **6** To come into the view, hearing, etc., of: A ghastly sight *met* our eyes. **7** To experience; undergo: to *meet* bad weather. **8** To oppose in battle; fight with. **9** To face or counter: to *meet* a blow with a blow. **10** To deal with; refute: to *meet* an accusation. **11** To comply with; act or result in conformity with, as expec-

tations or wishes. **12** To pay, as a bill. —*v.i.* **13** To come together, as from different directions. **14** To come together in contact, conjunction, or intersection; join. **15** To assemble. **16** To make acquaintance or be introduced. **17** To come together in conflict or opposition; contend. **18** To agree. —**meet with 1** To come upon; encounter. **2** To deal or confer with. **3** To experience. —*n.* A meeting or assembly for some specific activity, esp. for an athletic contest. [< OE *mētan*]

meet² (mēt) *adj.* Suitable; appropriate; fit. [< OE *gemæte*] —**meet′ly** *adv.* —**meet′ness** *n.*

meet·ing (mē′ting) *n.* **1** A coming together. **2** An assembly of persons for some specific purpose. **3** A permanent group or unit of worshipers in the Society of Friends; also, their meeting house.

meeting house 1 A house used for public meetings of any kind. **2** A place of worship used by the Society of Friends.

meg. megacycle.

mega- *combining form* **1** Great; large; powerful: *megaphone.* **2** In the metric system, electricity, etc., a million, or a million times (a specific unit): *megahertz.* [< Gk. *megas* large]

meg·a·cy·cle (meg′ə·sī′kəl) *n.* **1** A million cycles. **2** MEGAHERTZ.

meg·a·death (meg′ə·deth) *n.* The death of one million persons: a term used in reference to nuclear warfare. [< MEGA- + DEATH]

meg·a·hertz (meg′ə·hûrtz′) *n.* A unit of frequency equal to one million cycles per second.

megalo- *combining form* Big; indicating excessive or abnormal size: *megalomania.* [< Gk. *megas, megalou* big]

meg·a·lo·ceph·a·ly (meg′ə·lō·sef′ə·lē) *n.* Unusual largeness of the head. Also **meg′a·lo·ce·pha′li·a** (-sə·fā′lē·ə). [< MEGALO- + Gk. *kephalē* head] —**meg′a·lo·ce·phal′ic** (-sə·fal′ik), **meg′a·lo·ceph′a·lous** *adj.*

meg·a·lo·ma·ni·a (meg′ə·lō·mā′nē·ə, -mān′yə) *n.* A mental disorder in which the subject thinks himself great or exalted. —**meg′a·lo·ma′ni·ac** *adj., n.*

meg·a·lop·o·lis (meg′ə·lop′ə·lis) *n.* A densely populated urban area, usu. including one or more major cities. [< MEGALO- + Gk. *polis* city] —**meg·a·lo·pol·i·tan** (meg′ə·lō·pol′ə·tən) *adj., n.*

meg·a·phone (meg′ə·fōn) *n.* A funnel-shaped device for projecting or directing sound. —*v.t. & v.i.* **·phoned, ·phon·ing** To address or speak through a megaphone.

Megaphone

meg·a·ton (meg′ə·tun′) *n.* A unit of nuclear explosive power equivalent to one million tons of TNT.

me·grim (mē′grim) *n.* **1** MIGRAINE. **2** *pl.* Dullness; depression of spirits. **3** A whim or fad. [< OF *migraine*]

mei·o·sis (mī·ō′sis) *n.* The process of cell division that gives rise to reproductive cells containing half the number of chromosomes normally present in the somatic cells of the organism. [< Gk. *meiōsis* lessening] —**mei·ot′ic** (-ot′ik) *adj.*

Meis·ter·sing·er (mīs′tər·sing′ər, *Ger.* mīs′tər·zing′ər) *n. pl.* **·sing·er** A member of any of various guilds of Germany, from the 14th to 16th centuries, who were devoted to the promotion of music and poetry. [G, master singer]

mel·an·cho·li·a (mel′ən·kō′lē·ə) *n.* A mental disorder characterized by apathy and depression of spirits. —**mel′an·cho′li·ac** *adj., n.*

mel·an·chol·y (mel′ən·kol′ē) *adj.* **1** Gloomy; sad. **2** Causing sadness or dejection. **3** Pensive. —*n.* **1** Low spirits; depression. **2** Pensive or sober reflection. [< Gk. *melas* black + *cholē* bile] —**mel′an·chol′ic** *adj., n.* —**mel′an·chol′i·cal·ly** *adv.* —**Syn.** *adj.* **1** dejected, depressed, downcast. *n.* **1** dejection, despondency, sadness.

Mel·a·ne·sian (mel′ə·nē′zhən, -shən) *n.* **1** One of the native people of Melanesia, having dark skins and thick, kinky hair. **2** A branch of the Austronesian family of

languages spoken in Melanesia. —*adj.* Of or pertaining to Melanesia, its native inhabitants, or their languages.

mé·lange (mā·länzh′, -länj) *n.* A mixture or medley; miscellany. [F]

mel·a·nin (mel′ə·nin) *n.* The brownish black animal pigment contained in skin, hair, and other tissues. [< Gk. *melas* black]

Mel·ba toast (mel′bə) Thinly sliced bread toasted until brown and crisp. [< Nellie *Melba*, 1861–1931, Australian soprano]

meld¹ (meld) *v.t. & v.i.* In pinochle and other card games, to announce or declare (a combination of cards in the hand), for inclusion in one's total score. —*n.* A group of cards to be declared, or the act of declaring them. [< G *melden* announce]

meld² (meld) *v.t. & v.i.* To merge or blend. [Blend of MELT and WELD] —**meld′er** *n.*

me·lee (mā′lā, mā·lā′) *n.* A disorganized hand-to-hand fight involving a number of people; a brawl. Also *Fr.* **mê·lée** (me·lā′). [< OF *medlee* medley]

mel·io·rate (mēl′yə·rāt) *v.t. & v.i.* **·rat·ed, ·rat·ing** To improve, as in quality or condition; ameliorate. [< L *melior* better] —**mel′io·ra·ble, mel′io·ra′tive** *adj.* —**mel′io·ra′tion, mel′io·ra′tor** *n.* —**Syn.** **1** amend, better, mend, promote.

mel·lif·er·ous (mə·lif′ər·əs) *adj.* Producing or bearing honey. Also **mel·lif′ic.** [< L *mel* honey + *ferre* bear]

mel·lif·lu·ent (mə·lif′lōō·ənt) *adj.* Mellifluous. —**mel·lif′·lu·ence** *n.* —**mel·lif′lu·ent·ly** *adv.*

mel·lif·lu·ous (mə·lif′lōō·əs) *adj.* Sweetly or smoothly flowing; dulcet: a *mellifluous* voice. [< L *mel* honey + *fluere* flow] —**mel·lif′lu·ous·ly** *adv.* —**mel·lif′lu·ous·ness** *n.*

mel·low (mel′ō) *adj.* **1** Soft and sweet because of ripeness: *mellow* fruit. **2** Well-matured, as wines. **3** Full and rich; not harsh or strident: the *mellow* tones of a cello. **4** Gentle and understanding, as from age or experience. **5** Happy and relaxed, as from liquor. **6** Soft and friable, as soil. —*v.t. & v.i.* To make or become mellow. [ME *melwe*] —**mel′low·ly** *adv.* —**mel′low·ness** *n.*

me·lo·de·on (mə·lō′dē·ən) *n.* A small reed organ; harmonium. [< Gk. *melōdia* melody]

me·lod·ic (mə·lod′ik) *adj.* **1** Of or containing melody. **2** Melodious.

me·lo·di·ous (mə·lō′dē·əs) *adj.* **1** Producing or characterized by melody; tuneful. **2** Pleasant to hear. —**me·lo′di·ous·ly** *adv.* —**me·lo′di·ous·ness** *n.*

mel·o·dra·ma (mel′ə·drä′mə, -dram′ə) *n.* **1** Originally, a drama with a romantic story or plot, sensational incidents, and usu. including some music and song. **2** Any sensational and emotional drama, usu. having a happy ending. **3** Excessively dramatic or emotional behavior or language. [< Gk. *melos* song + *drama* drama]

mel·o·dra·mat·ic (mel′ə·drə·mat′ik) *adj.* Of, pertaining to, or like melodrama; sensational. —**mel′o·dra·mat′i·cal·ly** *adv.*

mel·o·dra·mat·ics (mel′ə·drə·mat′iks) *n.pl.* Melodramatic behavior.

mel·o·dy (mel′ə·dē) *n. pl.* **·dies 1** Pleasing sounds or an agreeable arrangement of such sounds. **2** *Music* **a** A succession of tones constituting, in combination, a whole. **b** The chief part or voice in a composition; the air. [< Gk. *melos* song + *aoidos* singer]

mel·on (mel′ən) *n.* **1** Any of various trailing plants of the gourd family bearing large, many-seeded fruits with a thick rind and sweet, pulpy flesh. **2** The fruit of any of these plants, as the watermelon, cantaloupe, etc. —**cut a** (or **the**) **melon** *Slang* To divide surplus profits, as among stockholders. [< Gk. *mēlopepōn* apple-shaped melon]

Mel·pom·e·ne (mel·pom′ə·nē) *Gk. Myth.* The Muse of tragedy.

Melons

melt (melt) *v.t. & v.i.* **melt·ed, melt·ed** (*Archaic* **mol·ten**), **melt·ing 1** To reduce or change from a solid to a liquid state by heat. **2** To dissolve, as in water.

---

add, āce, câre, pälm; end, ēven; it, īce; odd, ōpen, ôrder; tŏŏk, pōōl; up, bûrn; ə = *a* in *above, u* in *focus;* yōō = *u* in *fuse;* oil; pout; check; go; ring; thin; ᵺis; zh, *vision.* < derived from; ? origin uncertain or unknown.

3 To disappear or cause to disappear; dissipate: often with *away*. **4** To blend by imperceptible degrees; merge: often with *into*. **5** To make or become softened in feeling or attitude. —*n*. **1** Something melted. **2** A single operation of melting. **3** The amount melted in such an operation. [<OE *meltan*] —**melt′a·ble** *adj*. —**melt′er** *n*. —**Syn.** *v*. **1** fuse, liquefy. **5** appease, mollify, pacify.

melt·down (melt′doun′) *n*. An overheating and eventual melting of radioactive nuclear fuel through its protective insulation, because of a malfunctioning cooling system in a nuclear reactor.

melting point The temperature at which a specified solid substance becomes liquid.

melting pot 1 A vessel in which things are melted; crucible. **2** A country, city, or region in which immigrants of various racial and cultural backgrounds are assimilated.

mel·ton (mel′tən) *n*. A heavy woolen cloth with a short nap, used for overcoats. [<*Melton* Mowbray, England]

mem·ber (mem′bər) *n*. **1** A person belonging to an incorporated or organized body, society, etc.: a *member* of a club. **2** A limb or other functional organ of an animal body or plant. **3** A part or element of a structural or composite whole. **4** *Math.* **a** The expression on one side or the other of an equation. **b** An element contained in a set. [<L *membrum* limb]

mem·ber·ship (mem′bər·ship) *n*. **1** The state of being a member. **2** The members of an organization, collectively. **3** The number of members.

mem·brane (mem′brān) *n*. A thin, pliable sheet of material, esp. animal or vegetable tissue serving as a cover, connection, or lining. [<L *membrana*, lit., limb coating]

me·men·to (mə·men′tō) *n. pl.* **·toes** or **·tos** A hint or reminder to awaken memory, esp. a souvenir. [<L *meminisse* remember]

memento mo·ri (môr′ī) *Latin* An emblem or reminder of death, as a skull, etc.: lit., remember that you must die.

mem·o (mem′ō) *n. pl.* **mem·os** *Informal* A memorandum.

mem·oir (mem′wär) *n.* **1** *pl*. A written account of a person's experiences, reminiscences, etc.; an autobiography. **2** A biography. **3** A monograph or report. [F <L *memoria* memory] —**mem′oir·ist** *n*.

mem·o·ra·bil·i·a (mem′ə·rə·bil′ē·ə) *n.pl.* Things worthy of remembrance, or an account of them. [<L *memorabilis* memorable]

mem·o·ra·ble (mem′ər·ə·bəl) *adj*. Worthy to be remembered; noteworthy. —**mem′o·ra·bil′i·ty, mem′o·ra·ble·ness** *n*.

mem·o·ran·dum (mem′ə·ran′dəm) *n. pl.* **·dums** or **·da** (-də) **1** A brief note of a thing or things to be remembered. **2** An informal note or letter, usu. sent from on person to another in an office. **3** *Law* A brief written outline of the terms of a transaction. **4** A statement of goods sent from a consignor to a consignee. [L, a thing to be remembered]

me·mo·ri·al (mə·môr′əl, -mō′rē-) *adj*. Commemorating the memory of a deceased person or of any event. —*n*. **1** Something designed to keep in remembrance a person, event, etc. **2** A presentation of facts made to a government or an official, and usu. accompanies by a petition. [<L *memorialis*]

Memorial Day The last Monday in May, a day set apart to honor the dead of any U.S. war, formerly celebrated May 30.

me·mo·ri·al·ize (mə·môr′ē·əl·īz′, -mō′rē-) *v.t.* **·ized, ·iz·ing 1** To commemorate. **2** To present a memorial to; petition.

mem·o·rize (mem′ə·rīz) *v.t.* **·rized, ·riz·ing** To commit to memory. —**mem′o·ri·za′tion, mem′o·riz′er** *n*.

mem·o·ry (mem′ər·ē, mem′rē) *n. pl.* **·ries 1** The act, faculty, or capacity of remembering something that is past. **2** Everything that one can remember. **3** A specific act, event, person, or thing remembered. **4** The period of time covered by the faculty of remembrance: beyond the *memory* of man. **5** The state of being remembered. **6** Commemoration or remembrance: in *memory* of her parents. **7** The information storage unit of a computer. [<L *memor* mindful] —**Syn.** 1 recollection, remembrance, reminiscence.

mem·sah·ib (mem′sä·ib) *n. Anglo-Indian* A European lady: a name used by servants. [<MA′AM + Ar. *sāhib* master]

men (men) *n. pl.* of MAN.

men·ace (men′is) *v.* **·aced, ·ac·ing** *v.t.* **1** To threaten with evil or harm. —*v.i.* **2** To make threats; appear threatening. —*n*. **1** A threat. **2** A person or thing that is troublesome or dangerous. [<L *minari* threaten] —**men′ac·ing·ly** *adv*.

me·nad (mē′nad) *n*. MAENAD.

me·nage (mā·näzh′; *Fr.* mā·nazh′) *n*. **1** The persons of a household, collectively. **2** Household management. Also **me·nage′**. [<L *mansio* house]

me·nag·er·ie (mə·naj′ər·ē) *n*. **1** A collection of wild animals kept for exhibition. **2** The enclosure in which they are kept. [<F]

mend (mend) *v.t.* **1** To make sound or seviceable again by repairing. **2** To correct errors or faults in; reform: *Mend* your ways. **3** To correct (some defect). —*v.i.* **4** To become better, as in health. **5** To heal. **6** To improve, as conditions. —*n*. **1** The act of repairing or patching. **2** A mended portion of a garment. —**on the mend** Recovering health; recuperating. [Var. of AMEND] —**mend′a·ble** *adj*. —**mend′er** *n*. —**Syn.** *v*. **1** patch, repair, restore, fix, overhaul. **2** better, improve, rectify.

men·da·cious (men·dā′shəs) *adj*. **1** Addicted to lying; deceitful. **2** Untrue; false. [<L *mendax* lying] —**men·da′cious·ly** *adv*. —**men·da′cious·ness, men·dac·i·ty** (men·das′ə·tē) *n*.

men·de·le·vi·um (men′de·lē′vē·əm) *n*. A man-made radioactive element (symbol Md). [<D. I. *Mendeleyev*, 1834–1907, Russ. chemist]

Men·de·li·an (men·dē′lē·ən, -del′yen) *adj*. Of or pertaining to the principles of heredity discovered and set forth by Gregor Mendel. —**Men·de′li·an·ism, Men′del·ism** *n*.

men·di·cant (men′də·kənt) *adj*. **1** Depending on alms for a living; begging. **2** Pertaining to or like a beggar. —*n*. **1** A beggar. **2** A begging friar. [<L *mendicus* needy]

Men·e·la·us (men′ə·lā′əs) *Gk. Myth.* King of Sparta, a brother of Agamemnon and the husband of Helen of Troy.

men·ha·den (men·hād′n) *n*. A herringlike fish found along the N Atlantic coast, used as bait and as a source of oil and fertilizer. [Alter. of Algonquian *munnawhat* fertilizer]

me·ni·al (mē′nē·əl, mēn′yəl) *adj*. **1** Pertaining or appropriate to servants. **2** Servile; base. **3** Low; humble; esp., marked by low prestige or tedious routine: a *menial* job; *menial* tasks. —*n*. **1** A domestic servant. **2** A person of low or servile nature. [<L *mansio* house] —**me′ni·al·ly** *adv*.

me·nin·ges (mə·nin′jez) *n. pl.* of **me·ninx** (mē′ningks) The thin membranes enveloping the brain and spinal cord. [<Gk. *mēninx* membrane] —**me·nin′ge·al** *adj*.

men·in·gi·tis (men′ən·jī′tis) *n*. Inflammation of the meninges, often caused by infection. —**men′in·git′ic** (-jit′ik) *adj*.

me·nis·cus (mə·nis′kəs) *n. pl.* **·nis·cus·es** or **·nis·ci** (-nis′ī) **1** Any crescent-shaped body. **2** A lens convex on one side and concave on the other. **3** *Physics* The surface of a liquid column in a container, made convex or concave by capillarity. [<Gk. *mēniskos* crescent, dim. of *mēnē* the moon]

Men·non·ite (men′ən·īt) *n*. A member of a Protestant sect characterized by simplicity in life and dress and opposed to the taking of oaths, the holding of public office, and military service. [<*Menno* Simons, 1492–1559, a leader of the sect in the Netherlands]

Meniscus lenses

me·no (mā′nō) *adv. Music* Less. [<L *minus*]

men·o·pause (men′ə·pôz) *n*. Final cessation of menstruation; change of life. [<Gk. *mēn* month + PAUSE]

mensch (mensh) *n. pl.* **men·schen** *Colloq.* A genuine, respected, or honored person. [<Yiddish <G, person]

men·ses (men′sēz) *n. pl.* MENSTRUATION. [L, pl. of *mensis* month]

Men·she·vik (men′shə·vik) *n. pl.* **·vi·ki** (-vē′kē) or **·viks** A member of the conservative element in the Russian Social Democratic Party. Also **Men′she·vist**. [Russ. <*menshe* smaller, minority] —**Men′she·vism** *n*.

men·stru·al (men′strōō·əl) *adj*. **1** Of or pertaining to menstruation. **2** Monthly. Also **men′stru·ous**.

men·stru·ate (men′strōō·āt) *v.i.* **·at·ed, ·at·ing** To undergo menstruation. [<L *mensis* month]

men·stru·a·tion (men′strōō·ā′shən) *n*. A bloody flow from the uterus, resulting when an ovum is not fertilized and occurring in women at about monthly intervals.

men·stru·um (men'strōō-əm) *n. pl.* **-stru·ums** or **-stru·a** (-strōō-ə) The medium in which a substance is dissolved; solvent. [Med. L, solvent, menstrual blood]

men·su·ra·ble (men'shər-ə-bəl) *adj.* That can be measured. [<L *mensurare* to measure] **—men'su·ra·bil'i·ty** *n.*

men·su·ra·tion (men'shə-rā'shən) *n.* 1 The act, art, or process of measuring. 2 The mathematics of measurement.

-ment *suffix of nouns* 1 The product or result of: *achievement.* 2 The instrument or means of: *atonement.* 3 The process or action of: *government.* 4 The quality, condition, or state of being: *astonishment.* [<L *-mentum*]

men·tal (men'təl) *adj.* 1 Of or pertaining to the mind. 2 Done by or occurring in the mind, esp. without the aid of written symbols: *mental* arithmetic. 3 Affected by a disorder of the mind: a *mental* patient. 4 Psychiatric: a *mental* hospital. [<L *mens, mentis* mind] **—men'tal·ly** *adv.*

men·tal·i·ty (men-tal'ə-tē) *n. pl.* **-ties** 1 Mental power, capacity, or activity. 2 A characteristic way of thinking; pattern of thought: a criminal *mentality.*

mental retardation *Psychol.* A failure in mental development that is severe enough to prevent normal participation in ordinary life; feeble-mindedness. Also **mental deficiency.**

men·thol (men'thôl, -thōl, -thol) *n.* A white, waxy, pungent organic compound used in medicines, cigarettes, etc. [<L *mentha* mint + -OL[1]] **—men·tho·lat·ed** (men'thə·lā'tid) *adj.*

men·tion (men'shən) *v.t.* 1 To speak of incidentally, briefly, or in passing. 2 To cite, as for achievement. *—n.* 1 A brief or casual reference or notice. 2 A citing, as for achievement. [<L *mens, mentis* mind] **—men'tion·a·ble** *adj.* **—men'tion·er** *n.*

men·tor (men'tər, -tôr) *n.* A wise and trusted teacher, guide, and friend. [<*Mentor,* the wise guardian of Telemachus in the Odyssey.]

men·u (men'yōō, mān'-) *n. pl.* **men·us** 1 A list of various dishes that are available at a restaurant or that comprise a specific meal. 2 The dishes themselves. 3 A list of options or functions that enable a computer user to make choices. [<L *minutus* small, detailed]

me·ow (mē·ou', myou) *n.* The plaintive cry of a cat. *—v.i.* To make this sound. [Imit.]

Meph·is·toph·e·les (mef'is·tof'ə·lēz) In medieval legend, a devil to whom Faust sold his soul for wisdom and power. *—n.* A diabolical person. Also **Me·phis·to** (mə·fis'tō). **—Me·phis·to·phe·le·an** (mə·fis'tə·fē'lē·ən), **Me·phis·to·phe·li·an** *adj.*

me·phit·ic (mə·fit'ik) *adj.* 1 Poisonous; foul. 2 Foul-smelling. Also **me·phit'i·cal.** [<L *mephitis* noxious odor]

mer. meridian; meridional.

merc. mercantile; mercurial; mercury.

mer·can·tile (mûr'kən·til, -tīl) *adj.* 1 Of, pertaining to, or characteristic of merchants. 2 Of or like mercantilism. [<Ital. *mercante* merchant]

mer·can·til·ism (mûr'kən·til·iz'əm) *n.* A theory in political economy which states that the well-being of a country consists of a favorable balance of trade, an accumulation of bullion, and the development of agriculture and industry, all of which are to be regulated by the government. Also **mercantile system. —mer'can·til·ist** *adj., n.*

Mer·ca·tor projection (mər·kā'tər) A system of making maps in which the meridians form parallel straight lines, and the parallels of latitude (running perpendicular to the meridians) are increasingly further apart as they reach the poles, causing a corresponding distortion in areas and distances. [<G. *Mercator,* 1512–94, Flemish cartographer] • See map, next column.

mer·ce·nar·y (mûr'sə·ner'ē) *adj.* 1 Influenced by desire for gain or reward; greedy. 2 Serving in a foreign army for pay or profit; hired: *mercenary* soldiers. *—n. pl.* **-nar·ies** 1 A mercenary soldier. 2 Any hireling. [<L *merces* reward, pay] **—mer'ce·nar'i·ly** *adv.* **—mer'ce·nar'i·ness** *n.*

mer·cer (mûr'sər) *n. Brit.* A dealer in cloth. [<L *merx, mercis* wares]

mer·cer·ize (mûr'sə·rīz) *v.t.* **-ized, -iz·ing** To treat (cotton fabrics) with caustic soda so as to increase strength and

color-absorbing qualities and impart a silky gloss. [<J. *Mercer,* 1791–1866, English inventor] **—mer'cer·i·za'tion** *n.*

mer·chan·dise (mûr'chən·dīz, -dīs) *n.* Anything bought and sold for profit; wares. *—v.t. & v.i.* (-dīz) **-dised, -dis·ing** 1 To buy and sell. 2 To promote the sale of (an article) through advertising, etc. Also **mer'chan·dize.** [See MERCHANT.] **—mer'chan·dis'er** *n.*

mer·chant (mûr'chənt) *n.* 1 A person who buys and sells commodities as a business or for profit. 2 A storekeeper. *—adj.* 1 Of or pertaining to merchants or merchandise. 2 Of the merchant marine. [<L *mercari* to traffic, buy <*merx* wares] **—Syn.** *n.* 1 businessman, trader, bourgeois. 2 dealer, shopkeeper, tradesman.

mer·chant·a·ble (mûr'chən·tə·bəl) *adj.* That can be bought or sold.

mer·chant·man (mûr'chənt·mən) *n. pl.* **-men** (-mən) A trading or merchant vessel.

merchant marine 1 All the vessels of a nation that are engaged in commerce and trade. 2 The officers and men employed on these vessels.

mer·ci (mer·sē') *interj. French* Thank you.

Mer·ci·a (mûr'shē·ə, -shə) *n.* An ancient Anglo-Saxon kingdom of central England. **—Mer'ci·an** *adj., n.*

mer·ci beau·coup (mer·sē' bō·kōō') *French* Thank (you) very much.

mer·ci·ful (mûr'sə·fəl) *adj.* 1 Full of mercy; compassionate. 2 Characterized by or showing mercy. **—mer'ci·ful·ly** *adv.* **—mer'ci·ful·ness** *n.*

mer·ci·less (mûr'sə·lis) *adj.* Having or showing no mercy; pitiless. **—mer'ci·less·ly** *adv.* **—mer'ci·less·ness** *n.*

mer·cu·ri·al (mər·kyōōr'ē·əl) *adj.* 1 Apt to change moods abruptly and with little cause; volatile. 2 Suggestive of the qualities associated with the god Mercury; lively, quick, and ingenious: a *mercurial* wit. 3 Of, containing, or caused by the element mercury. *—n.* A preparation containing mercury. **—mer·cu'ri·al·ly** *adv.* **—mer·cu'ri·al·ness** *n.*

mer·cu·ri·al·ism (mər·kyōōr'ē·əl·iz'əm) *n.* Mercury poisoning.

mer·cu·ric (mər·kyōōr'ik) *adj.* Of or containing bivalent mercury.

mercuric chloride A white, crystalline, poisonous compound, used in photography and as a disinfectant. Also **mercury bichloride.**

Mercator projection

Mer·cu·ro·chrome (mər·kyōōr'ə·krōm) *n.* An aqueous solution of an organic dye containing mercury and bromine, used as a local antiseptic: a trade name.

mer·cu·rous (mər·kyōōr'əs) *adj.* Of or containing monovalent mercury.

mer·cu·ry (mûr'kyə·rē) *n. pl.* **-ries** 1 A heavy, silver-white metallic element (symbol Hg), liquid at ordinary temperatures; quicksilver. 2 The calibrated column of mercury in a thermometer or barometer. [<MERCURY]

Mer·cu·ry (mûr′kyə·rē) *Rom. Myth.* The herald and messenger of the gods, god of commerce, eloquence, and skill. —*n.* The planet of the solar system nearest the sun. • See PLANET. —**Mer·cur·i·al** (mər·kyŏŏr′ē·əl) *adj.*

mer·cy (mûr′sē) *n. pl.* **·cies** 1 Kind or compassionate behavior shown to an enemy, offender, etc., who is in one's power. 2 Compassion or kindness towards others, esp. those in distress. 3 The power to show clemency or forgiveness. 4 A fortunate happening or circumstance. —**at the mercy of** Wholly in the power of. [< L *merces* hire, payment, reward] —**Syn.** 1 benevolence, compassion, forbearance, leniency.

mere[1] (mir) *adj.* **mer·est** (*superl.*) Being no more or less than; nothing but: a *mere* child. [< L *merus* unmixed, bare]

mere[2] (mir) *n.* A pond; pool. [< OE *mere*]

mere·ly (mir′lē) *adv.* Nothing more than; only.

mer·e·tri·cious (mer′ə·trish′əs) *adj.* Deceitfully or artificially attractive; tawdry. [< L *meretrix* prostitute] —**mer′e·tri′cious·ly** *adv.* —**mer′e·tri′cious·ness** *n.*

mer·gan·ser (mər·gan′sər) *n.* Any of various fish-eating ducks, having long, saw-toothed bills and crested heads. [< L *mergere* to plunge + *anser* goose]

merge (mûrj) *v.t. & v.i.* **merged, merg·ing** To combine or be combined so as to lose separate identity; blend. [< L *mergere* dip, immerse]

merg·er (mûr′jər) *n.* 1 The act of merging. 2 A combination of two or more commercial interests or companies into one.

me·rid·i·an (mə·rid′ē·ən) *n.* 1 *Astron.* A great circle passing through the poles of the celestial sphere. 2 *Geog.* **a** A great circle of the earth, passing through both poles. **b** Either half of such a great circle, extending from one pole to the other. 3 The highest or culminating point of anything; the zenith. 4 In acupuncture, a pathway beneath the skin through which energy is believed to flow and along which specific acupuncture points are located.

Meridians *def. 2*

—*adj.* 1 Of or pertaining to noon. 2 Of or at the highest or culminating point. 3 Of or pertaining to a meridian. [< L *meridies* noon, south]

me·ringue (mə·rang′) *n.* 1 The beaten white of eggs, sweetened and usu. baked as a topping for pies or other pastry. 2 A small baked shell of meringue. [F]

me·ri·no (mə·rē′nō) *n. pl.* **·nos** 1 A breed of sheep having very fine, silky wool. 2 This wool. 3 A soft fabric, originally made of merino wool. 4 A kind of fine yarn, used for hosiery, underwear, etc. —*adj.* Made of merino. [Sp.]

mer·it (mer′it) *n.* 1 The quality or fact of deserving praise, reward, etc. 2 Worth, value, or excellence; quality. 3 That which deserves esteem, praise, or reward. 4 *pl.* The actual rights or wrongs of a matter: to decide a case on its *merits.* —*v.t.* To deserve. [< L *meritus,* pp. of *merere* deserve]

mer·i·toc·ra·cy (mer′ə·tok′rə·sē) *n. pl.* **·ra·cies** 1 A system or society in which talent, intellectual achievements, and excellence of performance are considered worthier of reward than race, sex, social status, or wealth. 2 The leaders produced by such a system or society. —**mer·i·to·crat** (mer′ə·tə·krat′) *n.* —**mer·i·to·crat·ic** (mer′ə·tə·krat′ik) *adj.*

mer·i·to·ri·ous (mer′ə·tôr′ē·əs, -tō′rē-) *adj.* Deserving of reward, praise, etc. —**mer′i·to′ri·ous·ly** *adv.* —**mer′i·to′ri·ous·ness** *n.*

merit system A system in the civil service whereby appointments and promotions are made on the basis of merit, ascertained through qualifying examinations.

merle (mûrl) *n.* A European thrush. Also **merl.** [< L *merula* blackbird]

Mer·lin (mûr′lin) In medieval legends, a magician and prophet who aided King Arthur.

mer·maid (mûr′mād′) *n.* A legendary sea creature having the head and body of a woman and the tail of a fish. Also **mer′maid′en** (-mād′n). [< MERE[2] + MAID]

Mer·o·vin·gi·an (mer′ə·vin′jē·ən, -jən) *adj.* Of or pertaining to the first Frankish dynasty, founded by Clovis I in 486, and lasting until 751. —*n.* A member of this dynasty.

mer·ri·ment (mer′i·mənt) *n.* Gaiety; mirth.

mer·ry (mer′ē) *adj.* **·ri·er, ·ri·est** 1 Given to mirth and laughter. 2 Marked by cheerfulness and gay spirits. —**make merry** To be in high spirits. [< OE *myrige* pleasant] —**mer′ri·ly** *adv.* —**mer′ri·ness** *n.* —**Syn.** 1 blithe, frolicsome, gleeful, light-hearted.

mer·ry-an·drew (mer′ē·an′drōō) *n.* A clown.

mer·ry-go-round (mer′ē·gō·round′, mer′i-) *n.* 1 A revolving platform fitted with wooden horses, seats, etc., on which people ride for amusement; a carousel. 2 A whirl, as of pleasure.

mer·ry·mak·ing (mer′ē·mā′king) *n.* Festivity; gaiety. —**mer′ry·mak′er** *n.*

me·sa (mā′sə) *n.* A high, broad plateau with sharp, usu. rocky, slopes. [Sp. < L *mensa* table]

mé·sal·li·ance (mā·zal′ē·əns, *Fr.* mā·zȧ·lyäns′) *n.* A marriage with one of inferior social position. [F]

mes·cal (mes·kal′) *n.* 1 A spineless cactus of the sw U.S. and N Mexico, whose tops, **mescal buttons,** contain a hallucinogen. 2 An intoxicating liquor distilled from certain species of agave. [< Nahuatl *mexcalli*]

mes·ca·line (mes′kə·lēn, -lin) *n.* A white, crystalline alkaloid with hallucinogenic properties, extracted from mescal buttons.

mes·dames (mā·däm′, *Fr.* mā·dȧm′) *n.pl.* of MADAME.

mes·de·moi·selles (mād·mwȧ·zel′) *n.pl.* of MADEMOISELLE.

me·seems (mē·sēmz′) *v.* **me·seemed** *impersonal Archaic* It seems to me.

mes·en·ter·y (mes′ən·ter′ē) *n. pl.* **·ter·ies** A supporting membrane, esp. one that holds an intestine to the abdominal wall. [< Gk. *mesos* middle + *enteron* intestine] —**mes′·en·ter′ic** *adj.*

mesh (mesh) *n.* 1 One of the open spaces in a net, screen, sieve, etc. 2 *pl.* The cords or wires that form such open spaces. 3 A net or network. 4 Anything that entangles or involves. 5 *Mech.* The engagement of gear teeth. —*v.t. & v.i.* 1 To make or become entangled, as in a net. 2 To make or become engaged, as gear teeth. [< MDu. *maesche*]

mesh·work (mesh′wûrk′) *n.* Meshes; network.

mes·mer·ism (mes′mə·riz′əm, mez′-) *n.* HYPNOTISM. [< F. A. *Mesmer,* 1734–1815, German physician] —**mes·mer·ic** (mes·mer′ik, mez-), **mes·mer′i·cal** *adj.* —**mes·mer′i·cal·ly** *adv.* —**mes′mer·ist** *n.*

mes·mer·ize (mes′mə·rīz, mez′-) *v.t.* **·ized, ·iz·ing** 1 HYPNOTIZE. 2 To fascinate as if hypnotized. —**mes′mer·i·za′tion, mes′mer·iz′er** *n.*

meso- *combining form* 1 Situated in the middle: *mesocarp.* 2 Intermediate; between: *Mesolithic.* [< Gk. *mesos* middle]

mes·o·blast (mes′ə·blast, mē′sə-) *n.* The middle layer of cells of the embryo. [< MESO- + Gk. *blastos* sprout] —**mes′·o·blas′tic** *adj.*

mes·o·carp (mes′ə·kärp, mē′sə-) *n.* The middle layer of a mature fruit, as the flesh of a peach.

mes·o·derm (mes′ə·dûrm, mē′sə-) *n.* The mesoblast or tissues developed from it. —**mes′o·der′mal, ·der′mic** *adj.*

Mes·o·lith·ic (mes′ə·lith′ik, mē′sə-) *adj. Anthropol.* Pertaining to or describing the period of human culture following the Paleolithic, characterized by small, delicately worked stone artifacts and an economy transitional between food gathering and a settled agriculture. [< MESO- + Gk. *lithos* stone]

mes·on (mes′on, mē′son) *n. Physics* Any of a group of short-lived particles having a mass intermediate between that of the electron and the proton. [< Gk. *mesos* middle]

Mes·o·po·ta·mi·a (mes′ə·pə·tā′mē·ə) *n.* An ancient country of sw Asia between the Tigris and the lower Euphrates rivers, included in modern Iraq. [< Gk. < *mesos* middle + *potamos* river] —**Mes′o·po·ta′mi·an** *n., adj.*

Mes·o·zo·ic (mes′ə·zō′ik, mē′sə-) *adj. & n.* See GEOLOGY. [< MESO- + Gk. *zōion* animal]

mes·quite (mes·kēt′, mes′kēt) *n.* A spiny, deep-rooted shrub or small tree of the pea family, found from sw U.S. to Peru, having sweet pods used as fodder: also **mes·quit′.** [< Nahuatl *mizquitl*]

mess (mes) *n.* 1 A state of disorder, confusion, or untidiness. 2 A confusing, troublesome, or embarrassing situation. 3 A quantity of food sufficient for one meal or for a dish. **4** A portion of soft, partly liquid food, as porridge. **5** A number of persons who habitually take their meals together, as in military units; also, a meal taken by them. **6 MESS HALL. 7** Unpleasant or unclean food. —*v.i.* **1** To make a mess: often with *up.* **2** To eat with a mess (def. **5**). —*v.t.* **3** To make a mess of; muddle: often with *up.* **4** To make dirty; befoul: often with *up.* **5** To provide meals for. —**mess around** (or **about**) To busy oneself; dabble. [< L *missus* course at a meal]

mes·sage (mes′ij) *n.* **1** A communication sent in any way. **2** A formal communication, as from a chief executive to a legislative body. **3** A communication embodying a truth, principle, or advice. **4** The carrying out of a mission; errand. **5** A television or radio commercial. [< L *missus*, pp. of *mittere*]

mes·sa·line (mes′ə·lēn′, mes′ə·lēn) *n.* A lightweight, lustrous, twilled silk fabric. [F]

mes·sen·ger (mes′ən·jər) *n.* **1** One sent with a message or on an errand of any kind. **2** A forerunner; herald.

mess hall A building or room where meals are regularly eaten, as by a military group.

Mes·si·ah (mə·sī′ə) *n.* **1** In Judaism, the name for the promised deliverer of the Hebrews. **2** In Christianity, Jesus. **3** Any long-awaited liberator. [< Hebrew *māshīah* anointed] —**Mes·si·an·ic** (mes′ē·an′ik) *adj.*

mes·sieurs (mes′ərz, *Fr.* mā·syœ′) *n. pl.* of MONSIEUR.

mess jacket A man's short, tailored jacket terminating at the waistline, worn by waiters, etc.

mess kit A small, compactly arranged unit containing cooking and eating utensils, used by soldiers and campers.

mess·mate (mes′māt′) *n.* A person with whom one eats at a mess, as in the army.

Messrs. (mes′ərz) *n.pl.* Messieurs: now used in English as the plural of *Mr.*

mes·sy (mes′ē) *adj.* **mess·si·er, mess·si·est** In or causing a mess. —**mess′i·ly** *adv.* —**mess′i·ness** *n.*

mes·ti·zo (mes·tē′zō) *n. pl.* ·**zos** or ·**zoes** Any one of mixed blood, esp. in Mexico and the w U.S., a person of Spanish and Indian blood. [Sp., lit., mixed] —**mes·ti′za** (-zə) *n. Fem.*

met (met) *p.t.* & *p.p.* of MEET[1].

meta- *prefix* **1** Changed in place or form; altered: *metamorphosis.* **2** *Anat.* & *Zool.* Behind; after; on the farther side of; later: *metacarpus.* **3** With; alongside. **4** Beyond; over; transcending: *metaphysics.* **5** *Chem.* **a** A modification of. **b** A derivative of. [< Gk. *meta* after, beside, with]

met·a·bol·ic (met′ə·bol′ik) *adj.* Of, pertaining to, or exhibiting metabolism.

me·tab·o·lism (mə·tab′ə·liz′əm) *n.* The aggregate of physical and chemical processes by which a living organism converts assimilated materials into living tissue, energy, and waste. [< Gk. *meta-* beyond + *ballein* throw]

me·tab·o·lize (mə·tab′ə·līz) *v.t.* & *v.i.* ·**lized, ·liz·ing** To change by metabolism.

met·a·car·pus (met′ə·kär′pəs) *n.* **1** The five bones of the hand between the wrist and finger bones. **2** The corresponding bones in the forelimb of land vertebrates. [< Gk. *meta-* beyond + *karpos* wrist] —**met′a·car′pal** *adj., n.*

met·al (met′l) *n.* **1** Any of the elements that tend to lose electrons and form positive ions in chemical reactions, form bases in combination with hydroxyl groups and are usu. lustrous, malleable, ductile, and good conductors of heat and electricity. **2** A combination of such elements; an alloy. **3** Molten glass. **4** *Printing* Type metal; also, composed type. **5** The essential quality or substance of a person or thing. —*adj.* Of, like, or consisting of metal. —*v.t.* ·**aled** or ·**alled,** ·**al·ing** or ·**al·ling** To furnish or cover with metal. [< L *metallum* mine, metal]

metal., metall. metallurgy.

me·tal·lic (mə·tal′ik) *adj.* **1** Made of, containing, or being a metal. **2** Yielding or producing metal. **3** Like or suggesting a metal: a *metallic* luster. **4** Hard; harsh: a *metallic* voice. —**me·tal′li·cal·ly** *adv.*

met·al·lif·er·ous (met′ə·lif′ər·əs) *adj.* Yielding or containing metal.

met·al·lur·gy (met′ə·lûr′jē) *n.* The technology of extracting metals from ores and producing alloys with desired properties. [< Gk.< *metallon* metal + *-ergos* working] —**met′al·lur′gic** or ·**gi·cal** *adj.* —**met′al·lur′gist** *n.*

met·al·work (met′l·wûrk′) *n.* **1** Articles made of metal. **2** The making of such articles: also **met′al·work′ing.** —**met′al·work′er** *n.*

met·a·mor·phic (met′ə·môr′fik) *adj.* **1** Of or pertaining to metamorphosis. **2** *Geol.* Of, producing, or caused by metamorphism. Also **met′a·mor′phous.**

met·a·mor·phism (met′ə·môr′fiz·əm) *n.* **1** *Geol.* The changes in the composition and texture of rocks caused by heat, pressure, moisture, etc. **2** METAMORPHOSIS.

met·a·mor·phose (met′ə·môr′fōz) *v.* ·**phosed, ·phos·ing** *v.t.* **1** To change the form of. —*v.i.* **2** To undergo metamorphism or metamorphosis.

met·a·mor·pho·sis (met′ə·môr′fə·sis) *n.pl.* ·**pho·ses** (-fə·sēz) **1** A passing from one form or shape into another, esp. by means of sorcery, etc. **2** Complete transformation of character, purpose, circumstances, etc. **3** A person or thing metamorphosed. **4** *Biol.* A developmental change in form, structure, or function in an organism, esp. after leaving the egg and before attaining sexual maturity. [< Gk. *meta-* beyond + *morphē* form]

met·a·phor (met′ə·fôr, -fər) *n.* A figure of speech in which one object is likened to another by speaking of it as if it were that other, as in *The sun was a chariot of fire.* [< Gk. *meta-* beyond, over + *pherein* to carry] —**met′a·phor′ic** (-fôr′ik, -for′ik) or ·**i·cal** *adj.* —**met′a·phor′i·cal·ly** *adv.* • *Metaphors* and *similes* both make comparisons, but the metaphor is distinguished from the simile by the omission of an introductory word such as "like" or "as." For example, *The moon is a silver coin* is a metaphor; *The moon is like a silver coin* is a simile.

met·a·phys·i·cal (met′ə·fiz′i·kəl) *adj.* **1** Of, pertaining to, or like metaphysics. **2** Very abstract or abstruse. **3** Designating certain poets of the 17th century whose verses were characterized by complex, intellectualized imagery. —**met′a·phys′i·cal·ly** *adv.*

met·a·phys·ics (met′ə·fiz′iks) *n.pl.* (construed as sing.) **1** The branch of philosophy that deals with the first principles of being and knowledge and with the essential nature of reality. **2** All speculative philosophy. [< Med. Gk. *ta meta ta physika* (the works) after the physics; in ref. to Aristotle's *Physics*] —**met′a·phy·si′cian** *n.*

me·tas·ta·sis (mə·tas′tə·sis) *n. pl.* ·**ses** (-sēz) The transfer of a disease or its manifestations, as the cells of a malignant tumor, from one part of the body to another. [< Gk. *meta-* after + *histanai* to place] —**met′a·stat′ic** (-stat′ik) *adj.* —**met′a·stat′i·cal·ly** *adv.*

me·tas·ta·size (mə·tas′tə·sīz) *v.i.* ·**sized, ·siz·ing** To spread by metastasis.

met·a·tar·sus (met′ə·tär′səs) *n. pl.* ·**si** (-sī) **1** In human beings, the five bones between the ankle and the toes. **2** The corresponding part of the hind limb in land vertebrates. [< META- + TARSUS] —**met′a·tar′sal** *adj., n.*

me·tath·e·sis (mə·tath′ə·sis) *n. pl.* ·**ses** (-sēz) **1** The transposition of letters, syllables, or sounds in a word. **2** Any change or reversal. [< Gk. *meta-* over + *tithenai* to place] —**met′a·thet·ic** (met′ə·thet′ik) or ·**i·cal** *adj.*

met·a·zo·an (met′ə·zō′ən) *n.* Any of a primary division of animals that develop from a single cell into a multicellular system of distinct tissues and organs: also **met′a·zo′on.** —*adj.* Of the metazoans: also **met′a·zo′ic.** [< META- + Gk. *zōion* animal]

Metatarsus

mete[1] (mēt) *v.t.* **met·ed, met·ing** To distribute by measure; apportion: usu. with *out.* [< OE *metan* to measure] —**Syn.** allot, dispense, dole, parcel.

mete[2] (mēt) *n.* A boundary, usu. in the phrase **metes and bounds.** [< L *meta*]

me·tem·psy·cho·sis (mə·temp′sə·kō′sis, met′əm·sī-) *n. pl.* ·**ses** Transmigration of souls. [< Gk. *meta-* over + *empsychoein* to animate]

me·te·or (mē′tē·ər, -ôr) *n. Astron.* A brief light produced by a small piece of matter from space which enters the earth's atmosphere with great velocity and is disintegrated by heat. [<Gk. *meteōros* high in the air]

meteor., meteorol. meteorological; meteorology.

me·te·or·ic (mē'tē·ôr'ik, -or'ik) *adj.* **1** Of or pertaining to meteors. **2** Pertaining to atmospheric phenomena; meteorological. **3** Like a meteor in brilliance or swiftness: a *meteoric* career. —me'te·or'i·cal·ly *adv.*

me·te·or·ite (mē'tē·ə·rīt') *n.* **1** A solid mass that has fallen to the earth from space. **2** METEOROID. —me'te·or·it'ic (-ə·rit'ik) *adj.*

me·te·or·oid (mē'tē·ə·roid) *n. Astron.* One of innumerable small particles of matter moving through space.

me·te·or·ol·o·gy (mē'tē·ə·rol'ə·jē) *n.* The science that deals with atmospheric pheneomena, esp. those that relate to weather. [<Gk. *meteōros* high in the air + -LOGY] —me'te·or'o·log'i·cal (-ôr'ə·loj'ə·kəl) or ·log'ic (·ik) or ·me'te·or'o·log'i·cal·ly *adv.* —me'te·or·ol'o·gist *n.*

me·ter¹ (mē'tər) *n.* An instrument for measuring and recording something. —*v.t.* To measure or test by means of a meter. [<METE¹]

me·ter² (mē'tər) *n.* **1** The basic unit of length in the metric system, defined as equal to 1,650,763.73 wavelengths, in a vacuum, of the orange-red radiation of krypton 86, equal to about 39.37 inches. **2** A measured verbal rhythm, having, in verse, a definite arrangement of groups of accented and unaccented syllables in a line; also, a specific arrangement or pattern of such syllables. **3** *Music* The character of a composition as being divisible into measures equal in duration and similar in rhythmic construction. [<Gk. *metron* a measure]

-meter *combining form* **1** An instrument by which a thing is measured: *calorimeter.* **2** (A specified number of) units or meters: *kilometer.* **3** Containing (a specified number of) metrical feet: *hexameter.*

Meth. Methodist.

meth·a·done (meth'ə·dōn) *n.* A synthetic opiate used as an analgesic and experimentally as a substitute for heroin in the treatment of addicts. Also **meth'a·don** (-don). [<(*di)meth(yl)a(mino) d(iphenylheptan)one*]

meth·a·qua·lone (meth'ə·kwä'lon) *n.* An addictive drug used as a sedative; QUAALUDE.

meth·am·phet·a·mine (meth'am·fet'ə·mēn, - min) *n.* A chemical compound that allays hunger and stimulates the central nervous system. [<*meth(yl)* + AMPHETAMINE]

meth·ane (meth'ān) *n.* A colorless, flammable gas composed of one atom of carbon and four of hydrogen and forming the main constituent of natural gas. [<METH(YL) + -ANE]

methane series A series of saturated hydrocarbons in which the carbon atoms are linked in progressively longer chains.

meth·a·nol (meth'ə·nōl, -nol) *n.* A colorless, volatile, flammable, and highly toxic alcohol widely used in industry. [<METHAN(E) + -OL¹]

Meth·e·drine (meth'ə·drēn) *n.* METHAMPHETAMINE: a trade name.

me·thinks (mē·thingks') *v.* **me·thought** *impersonal Archaic* It seems to me; I think. [<OE *me* me + *thyncan* seem]

meth·od (meth'əd) *n.* **1** A systematic, established, or orderly procedure or way of doing anthing. **2** System, order, or regularity in general. **3** The disciplines and techniques used in any field of knowledge, creativity, etc.: the Renaissance *methods* of painting. **4** Orderly and systematic arrangement, as of ideas and topics, etc. [<Gk. *meta-* after + *hodos* way]

me·thod·i·cal (mə·thod'i·kəl) *adj.* **1** Characterized by or performed with method and order. **2** Orderly; systematic: a *methodical* worker. Also **me·thod'ic.** —me·thod'i·cal·ly *adv.* —me·thod'i·cal·ness *n.*

Meth·od·ist (meth'əd·ist) *n.* A member of any one of the Protestant churches that have grown out of the religious movement begun by John and Charles Wesley in England during the first half of the 18th century. —*adj.* Pertaining to or typical of methodists or Methodism. [<METHOD] —Meth'od·ism *n.* —Meth'od·is'tic or ·ti·cal *adj.*

meth·od·ize (meth'əd·īz) *v.t.* **·ized, ·iz·ing** To subject to method; systematize. —meth'od·i·za'tion *n.*

meth·od·ol·o·gy (meth'ə·dol'ə·jē) *n. pl.* **·gies** **1** The science of methodical, systematic thinking, procedure, arrangement, etc. **2** The methods or procedures used in a particular field or discipline.

Me·thu·se·lah (mə·thōō'zə·lə) In the Bible, a Hebrew patriarch reputed to have lived 969 years. —*n.* Any very old man.

meth·yl (meth'əl) *n.* A univalent hydrocarbon radical having a single carbon atom. [<Gk. *methy* wine + *hylē* wood] —meth·thyl·ic (mə·thil'ik) *adj.*

methyl alcohol METHANOL.

meth·yl·ate (meth'əl·āt) *v.t.* **·at·ed, ·at·ing** **1** To mix methanol into, as ethanol, esp. to make unfit to drink. **2** To introduce a methyl radical into. —meth'yl·a'tion *n.*

me·tic·u·lous (mə·tik'yə·ləs) *adj.* Extremely or excessively careful about details; finical. [<L *meticolosus* fearful] —me·tic'u·los'i·ty (-los'ə·tē) *n.* —me·tic'u·lous·ly *adv.* —Syn. exacting, fastidious, finicky, particular, punctilious.

mé·tier (mā·tyā') *n.* **1** Trade; profession. **2** Activity or work in which one is an expert. [F]

mé·tis (mā·tē') *n. pl.* **mé·tis** (-tē', -tēs) A person of mixed American Indian and European, esp. French, ancestry. [F, lit., mixed]

me·ton·y·my (mə·ton'ə·mē) *n.* **·mies** A figure of speech that employs an associated or closely connected word rather than the word itself, as "the crown prefers" for "the king prefers." [<Gk. *meta-* altered + *onyma* name] —met·o·nym·ic (met'ə·nim'ik), met'o·nym'i·cal *adj.* —met'o·nym'i·cal·ly *adv.*

me·too·ism (mē'tōō'iz'əm) *n.* The practice of representing as one's own the popular or successful policies of another, esp. a political rival. —me'-too'er *n.*

Met·ra·zol (met'rə·zōl, -zol) *n.* A synthetic drug used as a heart and central nervous system stimulant: a trade name.

me·tre (mē'tər) *n. Chiefly Brit.* METER².

met·ric (met'rik) *adj.* **1** Of or pertaining to the metric system. **2** METRICAL (def. 1).

met·ri·cal (met'ri·kəl) *adj.* **1** Of, relating to, or composed in poetic meter. **2** Of, pertaining to, or used in measurement. —met'ri·cal·ly *adv.*

metric system A decimal system of weights and measures. • See MEASURE.

met·ri·fi·ca·tion (met'rə·fə·kā'shən) *n.* The adoption of the metric system or the conversion to metric units from those of another system. Also *Brit.* **met·ri·ca·tion** (met'rə·kā'shən). —met·ri·fy (met'rə·fī) *v.t. & v.i.* (·fied, ·fy·ing)

met·ro- *combining form* Measure: *metronome.* [<Gk. *metron* measure]

met·ro·nome (met'rə·nōm) *n.* An instrument for indicating tempo in music, consisting of a mechanical or electronic oscillator producing pulses at a fixed, controllable rate. [<METRO- + Gk. *nomos* law] —met'ro·nom'ic (-nom'ik) *adj.*

me·trop·o·lis (mə·trop'ə·lis) *n.* **1** The capital or the largest or most important city of a state or country. **2** Any large city that is the center of some activity. **3** The seat of a metropolitan bishop. [<Gk. *mētēr* mother + *polis* city]

met·ro·pol·i·tan (met'rə·pol'ə·tən) *adj.* **1** Of, like, or constituting a metropolis (defs. 1 & 2). **2** Of or designating a metropolitan or his province. —*n.* **1** An archbishop who has authority over the bishops of his ecclesiastical province. **2** One who lives in a metropolis or has the manners and customs of a metropolis.

-metry *combining form* The process, science, or art of measuring: *geometry.* [<Gk. *metron* a measure]

met·tle (met'l) *n.* **1** Inherent quality of character. **2** Courage; spirit. —**on one's mettle** Aroused to one's best efforts. [Var. of METAL] —met'tled *adj.*

met·tle·some (met'l·səm) *adj.* Having courage or spirit; ardent; fiery.

mew¹ (myōō) *n.* **1** A cage for molting hawks. **2** Any hiding place. **a** *pl. Chiefly Brit.* A stable, usu. on an inner court or alley. **b** A narrow back street or alley. —*v.t.* To confine in or as in a cage: often with *up.* [<L *mutare* to change]

mew² (myōō) *n. & v.* MEOW.

mew³ (myōō) *n.* A European sea gull. Also **mew gull.** [<OE *mæw*]

mewl (myōōl) *v.i.* To cry, as an infant. —*n.* An infant's cry or crying. [Imit.]

Mex. Mexican; Mexico.

Mex·i·can (mek'sə·kən) *n.* A citizen or native of Mexico. —*adj.* Of or pertaining to Mexico or its people.

Mexican War A war between the U.S. and Mexico (1846–48).

Mex·i·co (mek'sə·kō) *n.* A republic of s North America, 760,373 sq. mi., cap. Mexico (also Mexico City).

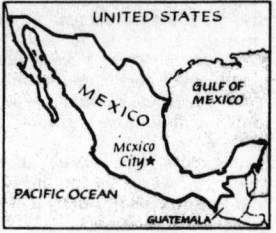

mez·za·nine (mez'ə·nēn, mez·ə·nēn') *n.* 1 A low-ceilinged story or long, inner balcony between two main stories. Also **mezzanine floor, mezzanine story.** 2 In a theater, the first balcony or the front rows of the first balcony. [<Ital. *mezzano* middle]

mez·zo (met'sō, med'zō, mez'ō) *adj.* Half; medium; moderate. —*adv. Music* Moderately: *mezzo* forte. [<L *medius* middle]

mez·zo-so·pran·o (met'sō·sə·pran'ō, -prän'ō, med'zō-, mez'ō) *n.* 1 A voice lower than a soprano and higher than a contralto. 2 A person possessing, or a part written for, such a voice.

mez·zo·tint (met'sō·tint', med'zō-, mez'ō-) *n.* 1 A method of engraving on copper or steel by scraping or polishing those roughened parts of the plate where light and shadow are desired. 2 An impression so produced. —*v.t.* To engrave in or represent by mezzotint. [<Ital. *mezzo* middle + *tinto* tint] —**mez'zo·tint'er** *n.*

MF, MF. Middle French.

mfg. manufacturing.

mfr. manufacture; manufacturer.

Mg magnesium.

mg, mg., mgm milligram(s).

mgt. management.

MHG, MHG., M.H.G. Middle High German.

mi (mē) *n. Music* In solmization, the third tone of a diatonic scale. [Ital. See GAMUT.]

MI Michigan (P.O. abbr.).

mi, mi. mile(s).

mi·aou, mi·aow (mē·ou') *n. & v.* MEOW.

mi·as·ma (mī·az'mə, mē-) *n. pl.* **·mas** or **·ma·ta** (-mə·tə) 1 The poisonous effluvium once supposed to rise from putrid matter, swamps, etc. 2 Any unwholesome influence or atmosphere. [<Gk., pollution] —**mi·as'mal, mi·as·mat·ic** (mī'az·mat'ik), **mi·as'mic** *adj.*

mica (mī'kə) *n.* Any of a class of silicate minerals that readily separate into thin, tough sheets. [<L, crumb] —**mi·ca·ceous** (mī·kā'shəs) *adj.*

mice (mīs) *n. pl.* of MOUSE.

Mich. Michigan.

Mi·chael (mī'kəl) One of the archangels, conqueror of Lucifer. Also **Saint Michael.**

Mich·ael·mas (mik'əl·məs) *n.* September 29, the feast of St. Michael. Also **Michaelmas Day.**

mick·ey finn (mik'ē fin') *Slang* A drugged, usu. alcoholic drink. Also **mick'ey, Mick'ey Finn.** [?]

Mic·mac (mik'mak) *n. pl.* **·mac** or **·macs** One of a tribe of Algonquian Indians of Nova Scotia, New Brunswick, and Newfoundland.

micro- *combining form* 1 Very small; minute: *microfilm, microgroove.* 2 Known or seen only by microscopic examination: *microorganism.* 3 In the sciences, using, requiring, or involved in microscopy: *microbiology.* 4 Enlarging or increasing in size or volume: *microscope.* 5 In systems of measurement, the one-millionth part of (the specified unit) (symbol µ): *microgram, microwatt.* Also **micr-.** [<Gk. *mikros* small]

mi·cro·bar (mī'krō·bär) *n.* A unit of pressure equal to 1.458×10^{-5} (0.00001458) pound per square inch.

mi·crobe (mī'krōb) *n.* A microscopic organism, esp. a disease-producing bacterium. [<Gk. *mikro-* small + *bios* life] —**mi·cro'bi·al, mi·cro'bi·an, mi·cro'bic** *adj.*

mi·cro·bi·ol·o·gy (mī'krō·bī·ol'ə·jē) *n.* The branch of biology that deals with microorganisms. —**mi'cro· bi'o·log'i·cal** *adj.* —**mi'cro·bi·ol'o·gist** *n.*

mi·cro·ceph·a·ly (mī'krō·sef'ə·lē) *n.* Abnormal smallness of the head or cranium. [<MICRO- + Gk. *kephalē* head] —**mi'cro·ce·phal'ic** (-sə·fal'ik), **mi'cro·ceph'a·lous** *adj.*

mi·cro·chem·is·try (mī'krō·kem'is·trē) *n.* The investigation of chemical reactions using minute quantities of substances. —**mi'cro·chem'i·cal** *adj.* —**mi'cro·chem'i·cal·ly** *adv.* —**mi'cro·chem'ist** *n.*

mi·cro·chip (mī'krō·chip') *n.* A chip (def. 8).

mi·cro·com·put·er (mī'krō·kəm·pyōō'tər) *n.* A very small electronic computer.

mi·cro·cop·y (mī'krō·kop'ē) *n. pl.* **cop·ies** A reduced photographic copy, as of a letter, manuscript, etc.

mi·cro·cosm (mī'krə·koz'əm) *n.* 1 A little world; esp., a community or environment regarded as a small-scale version or example of the universe or of a much larger entity. 2 Man seen as the epitome of the universe. Also **mi'cro·cos'mos** (-koz'məs). [<Gk. *mikros kosmos*, lit., little world]

mi·cro·fiche (mī'krō·fēsh') *n.* A sheet of microfilm. [F <MICRO- + *fiche* card, slip of paper]

mi·cro·film (mī'krə·film) *n.* A film on which is a photographic reproduction of a printed page, document, or other object, highly reduced for ease in transmission and storage, and capable of reenlargement. —*v.t. & v.i.* To reproduce on microfilm.

mi·cro·form (mī'krō·fôrm') *n.* A method of reproducing images greatly reduced in size, as on microfilm.

mi·cro·gram (mī'krə·gram) *n.* One millionth of a gram (symbol µg). Also **mi'cro·gramme.**

mi·cro·groove (mī'krə·grōōv) *n.* A very fine groove cut in the surface of a long-playing phonograph record.

mi·crom·e·ter (mī·krom'ə·tər) *n.* 1 An instrument for measuring very small distances or dimensions as used on a microscope or telescope. 2 MICROMETER CALIPER.

micrometer caliper A caliper or gauge having a micrometer screw.

micrometer screw A screw with finely cut threads and a circular, graduated head, which shows the position of the screw.

mi·crom·e·try (mī·krom'ə·trē) *n.* Measurement with a micrometer. —**mi·cro·met·ric** (mī'krō·met'rik) or **·ri·cal** *adj.* —**mi'cro·met'ri·cal·ly** *adv.*

Micrometer

mi·cron (mī'kron) *n.* The one-millionth part of a meter (symbol µ). [<Gk. *mikros* small]

Mi·cro·ne·sian (mī'krə·nē'zhən, -shən) *n.* 1 A native of Micronesia. 2 A group of Austronesian languages spoken in Micronesia. —*adj.* Of or pertaining to Micronesia, its people, or their languages.

mi·cro·or·gan·ism (mī'krō·ôr'gən·iz'əm) *n.* An organism visible only in an optical or electron microscope, as a bacterium, protozoan, or virus. Also **mi'cro·or'gan·ism.**

mi·cro·phone (mī'krə·fōn) *n.* A device for changing sound waves into corresponding electric signals.

mi·cro·pho·to·graph (mī'krō·fō'tə·graf, -gräf) *n.* 1 A very small or microscopic photograph, usu. magnified for viewing. 2 PHOTOMICROGRAPH. —**mi'cro·pho'to·graph'ic** *adj.* —**mi'cro·pho·tog'ra·phy** (-fə·tog'rə·fē) *n.*

mi·cro·print (mī'krə·print) *n.* A microphotograph examined only by means of a magnifying device.

mi·cro·proc·es·sor (mī'krō·pros'es·ər) *n.* An electronic computer contained on a single chip.

mi·cro·scope (mī'krə·skōp) *n.* Any of various instruments for magnifying objects too small to be seen or clearly observed by the naked eye. [<MICRO- + -SCOPE]

mi·cro·scop·ic (mī'krə·skop'ik) *adj.* 1 So small as to be visible only with the aid of a microscope. 2 Exceedingly small or minute. 3 Of, relating to, or done with a microscope or microscopy. 4 Resembling a microscope. Also **mi'cro·scop'i·cal.** —**mi'cro·scop'i·cal·ly** *adv.*

mi·cros·co·py (mī·kros'kə·pē, mī'krə·skō'pē) *n.* 1 The technique of using a microscope. 2 Investigation with a microscope. —**mi·cros'co·pist** *n.*

---

add, āce, câre, pälm; end, ēven; it, īce; odd, ōpen, ôrder; tŏŏk, pōōl; up, bûrn; ə = a in *above*, u in *focus*; yōō = u in *fuse*; oil; pout; check; go; ring; thin; **th**is; zh, *vision*. < derived from; ? origin uncertain or unknown.

mi·cro·wave (mī′krə·wāv) *n.* An electromagnetic wave having a wavelength in the range longer than red light and shorter than radio waves.

mic·tu·rate (mik′chə·rāt) *v.i.* **·rat·ed, ·rat·ing** To urinate. [< L *micturire* desire to urinate] **—mic′tu·ri′tion** (-rish′ən) *n.*

mid[1] (mid) *adj.* Being in the middle. [< OE *midd*]

mid[2] (mid) *prep.* Amid; among. Also **'mid.**

mid- *combining form* **1** Being the middle point or part of: *mid-April, midmorning.* **2** In a middle or central position: *midpoint, midrib.*

mid. middle; midshipman.

Mi·das (mī′dəs) *Gk. Myth.* A king of Phrygia who had the power of turning whatever he touched into gold.

mid·brain (mid′brān′) *n.* The middle division of the brain.

mid·channel (mid′chan′əl) *n.* The middle part of a channel.

mid·day (mid′dā′) *n.* The middle part of the day; noon. **—adj.** Of or at midday.

mid·dle (mid′l) *adj.* **1** Equally distant from the extremes of place, position, time, etc.; central. **2** Being in neither the one nor the other extreme; intermediate. **3** *Often cap.* Designating a language midway in development between an earlier (Old) and later (Modern) form. **—n.** **1** The part or point equally distant from the extremes of place, position, time, etc. **2** Something that is intermediate. **3** The middle part of the body; waist. **—v.t. ·dled, ·dling** To place in the middle. [< OE *middel*] **Syn.** *adj.* **1** median, mid, moderate. *n.* **1** midway, center.

middle age The time of life between youth and old age, commonly between 40 and 60. **—mid′dle-aged′** (-ājd′) *adj.*

Middle Ages The period in European history between classical antiquity and the Renaissance, usu. regarded as extending from the downfall of Rome, in 476, to about 1450.

mid·dle·brow (mid′l·brou′) *n.* A person who has conventional or middle-class tastes, interests, opinions, etc.

middle C *Music* The note written on the first ledger line above the bass staff and the first ledger line below the treble staff; also, the corresponding tone or key.

middle class The class of a society that occupies a position between the laboring class and the very wealthy or the nobility. **—mid′dle-class′** *adj.*

middle ear The part of the ear between the eardrum and the inner ear, including the tympanum and the ossicles (hammer, anvil, and stirrup). • See EAR.

Middle East The region usu. thought of as including Egypt and the countries of sw Asia west of India.

Middle English English as written and spoken from about 1100 to 1500.

Middle French French as written and spoken from the 14th to the 16th century.

Middle High German High German as written and spoken from about 1050 to 1450.

Middle Latin MEDIEVAL LATIN.

Middle Low German Low German as written and spoken from about 1100 to 1500.

mid·dle·man (mid′l·man′) *n. pl.* **·men** (-men′) **1** One who acts as an agent or go-between; intermediary. **2** One who buys in bulk from producers and sells to retailers or directly to consumers.

mid·dle·most (mid′l·mōst′) *adj.* MIDMOST.

mid·dle-of-the-road (mid′l·əv·thə·rōd′) *adj.* Tending toward neither side or extreme; moderate, esp. in politics. **—mid′dle-of-the-road′er** *n.*

mid·dle·weight (mid′l·wāt′) *n.* A boxer or wrestler weighing between 147 and 160 pounds. **—adj.** Of middleweights.

Middle West That section of the U.S. between the Rocky Mountains and the eastern border of Ohio and north of the Ohio River and the southern borders of Kansas and Missouri. Also **middle west. —Middle Western —Middle Westerner**

mid·dling (mid′ling) *adj.* **1** Of middle rank, condition, size, or quality. **2** *Informal* In fair health. **—adv.** *Informal* Moderately; somewhat. **—n.** **1** Any of various products of medium size, quality, etc. **2** *pl.* The coarser part of ground wheat.

mid·dy (mid′ē) *n. pl.* **·dies** **1** *Informal* A midshipman. **2** MIDDY BLOUSE.

middy blouse A loosely fitting blouse having a wide sailor collar, worn by women and children.

midge (mij) *n.* **1** A gnat or small fly. **2** A small person. [< OE *mycge*]

midg·et (mij′it) *n.* **1** An abnormally small person. **2** Anything very small of its kind. **—adj.** Small; diminutive. [Dim. of MIDGE]

Middy blouse

mid·i (mid′ē) *n. pl.* **mid·is** A skirt, dress, or coat with a hemline at mid-calf. [< MIDDLE]

Mid·i·an·ite (mid′ē·ən·īt′) *n.* One of an ancient nomadic tribe of NW Arabia.

mid·i·ron (mid′ī′ərn) *n.* A golf club having a metal head and a medium loft.

mid·land (mid′lənd) *n.* The interior of a country or region. **—adj.** Of or located in the central part of a country or region.

Mid·land (mid′lənd) *n.* The dialect of Middle English spoken in London and the midland counties of England; esp. **East Midland,** the branch of Midland that is the direct predecessor of Modern English.

mid·most (mid′mōst′) *adj.* **1** Situated exactly in the middle. **2** Very intimate. **—adv.** In the midst or middle.

mid·night (mid′nīt′) *n.* The middle of the night; twelve o'clock at night. **—adj.** **1** Of or at midnight. **2** Like midnight in darkness, etc.

midnight sun The sun visible at midnight during the arctic and the antarctic summer.

mid·rib (mid′rib′) *n.* The central vein of a leaf.

mid·riff (mid′rif) *n.* **1** The diaphragm. **2** The part of the body between the chest and the abdomen. [< OE *midd* mid + *hrif* belly]

mid·ship (mid′ship′) *adj. Naut.* At or pertaining to the middle of a vessel's hull.

mid·ship·man (mid′ship·mən, mid·ship′-) *n. pl.* **·men** (-mən) **1** A student training to be a naval officer, esp. at the U.S. Naval Academy in Annapolis. **2** A British naval officer ranking between a naval cadet and the lowest commissioned officer. [< *amidshipman;* so called from being amidships when on duty]

mid·ships (mid′ships) *adv. Naut.* AMIDSHIPS.

midst (midst) *n.* The central part; middle: usu. in the phrase **in the midst of. —in our (your or their) midst** Among us (you, or them). **—prep.** Amidst. [< OE *midd* mid] **—Syn.** *n.* center, hub. *prep.* amid, among.

mid·stream (mid′strēm′) *n.* The middle of a stream.

mid·sum·mer (mid′sum′ər) *n.* **1** The middle of summer. **2** The time of the summer solstice, about June 21. **—adj.** Of, in, or like midsummer.

mid·term (mid′tûrm′) *adj. & adv.* In the middle of the term. **—n.** **1** The middle of the term. **2** *Informal* A midterm examination.

mid·Vic·to·ri·an (mid′vik·tôr′ē·ən, -tō′rē-) *adj.* **1** Of or characteristic of the middle period of Queen Victoria's reign in England, approximately 1850–80. **2** Outwardly strict in morals, manners, etc.; prudish. **—n.** **1** A person living in this era. **2** A person of Victorian ideas or tastes.

mid·way (mid′wā′, -wā′) *adj.* Being in the middle of the way or distance. **—adv.** Halfway. **—n.** (mid′wā′) At a fair, exposition, etc., the area where various amusements and sideshows are located.

mid·week (mid′wēk′) *n.* The middle of the week. **—adj.** In the middle of the week. **—mid′week′ly** *adj., adv.*

Mid·west (mid′west′) *n.* MIDDLE WEST. **—Mid′west′ern** *adj.*

mid·wife (mid′wīf′) *n. pl.* **·wives** (-wīvz′) A woman who assists women in childbirth. [< OE *mid* with + *wīf* wife]

mid·wife·ry (mid′wī′fər·ē, -wīf′rē) *n.* The act or skill of assisting women in childbirth.

mid·win·ter (mid′win′tər) *n.* **1** The middle of winter. **2** The winter solstice, about Dec. 21. **—adj.** Of, like, or in midwinter.

mid·year (mid′yir′) *n.* **1** The middle of the year. **2** An examination given in the middle of a school year.

mien (mēn) *n.* The bearing, demeanor, or expression of a person. [< DEMEAN]

miff (mif) *Informal v.t. & v.i.* To be or cause to be irritated or offended. —*n.* A huff. [?]

Mig (mig) *n.* A type of jet fighter plane of the Soviet air force. [< *Mi(koyan)* and *G(urevich)*, Soviet aircraft designers] Also **MIG.**

might[1] (mīt) *p.t.* of MAY[1].

might[2] (mīt) *n.* **1** Physical strength. **2** Great power, ability, or resources of any kind. —**with might and main** With one's whole strength. [< OE *meaht, miht*] —**Syn. 1** force, potency, puissance, vigor, power.

might·y (mī′tē) *adj.* **might·i·er, might·i·est 1** Possessed of might; powerful; strong. **2** Of unusual size, consequence, etc. —*adv. Informal* Very; exceedingly. —**might′i·ly** *adv.* —**might′i·ness** *n.*

mi·gnon·ette (min′yən·et′) *n.* A small plant having racemes of greenish, fragrant flowers. [F]

mi·graine (mī′grān) *n.* A recurrent, severe form of headache, temporarily disabling, usu. affecting one side of the head and often accompanied by nausea, dizziness, and sensitivity to light. [< Gk. *hēmi* half + *kranion* skull]

mi·grant (mī′grənt) *adj.* Migratory. —*n.* **1** A person or animal that migrates. **2** A worker who moves from place to place to find employment, esp. in harvesting crops: also **migrant worker.**

mi·grate (mī′grāt) *v.i.* **·grat·ed, ·grat·ing 1** To move, as from one place, region, etc., to another. **2** To move periodically from one region or climate to another, as birds or fish. [< L *migrare* roam, wander] —**mi′gra·tor** *n.*

mi·gra·tion (mī·grā′shən) *n.* **1** The act of migrating. **2** The totality of persons or animals migrating at one time. **3** *Chem.* The shifting of one or more atoms from one position in the molecule to another. **4** *Physics* The drift or movement of ions due to the effect of an electric field. —**mi·gra′tion·al** *adj.* —**mi·gra′tion·ist** *n.*

mi·gra·to·ry (mī′grə·tôr′ē, -tō′rē) *adj.* **1** Of or pertaining to migration. **2** Given to migrating. **3** Roving; nomadic.

mi·ka·do (mi·kä′dō) *n. pl.* **·dos** An emperor of Japan.

mike (mīk) *n. Informal* A microphone.

mil (mil) *n.* **1** A unit of length equal to .001 inch. **2** *Mil.* A unit of angular measure equal to 1/6400 of a circle, or about 0.0560 degree. [< L *millesimus* thousandth]

mil. mileage; military; militia; million.

mi·la·dy (mi·lā′dē) *n. pl.* **·dies** An English noblewoman or gentlewoman. [< *my lady*]

Mil·an·ese (mil′ən·ēz′, -ēs′) *adj.* Of or pertaining to Milan or its people. —*n. pl.* **·ese** A citizen or inhabitant of Milan.

milch (milch) *adj.* Giving milk, as a cow. [< OE *-milce*]

mild (mīld) *adj.* **1** Gentle in nature or disposition. **2** Moderate; temperate: a *mild* winter. **3** Not harsh or strong, as in flavor. [< OE *milde*] —**mild′ly** *adv.* —**mild′ness** *n.*

mil·dew (mil′dʸo͞o) *n.* **1** Any of various fungi that form a spotty coating on damp surfaces, as plant leaves, clothing, leather, etc. **2** Any of various plant diseases due to these fungi. —*v.t. & v.i.* To affect or be affected with mildew. [< OE *mildēaw* honeydew] —**mil′dew·y** *adj.*

mile (mīl) *n.* **1** A unit of length equal to 5,280 feet or 1.609 kilometers: also **statute mile. 2** NAUTICAL MILE. **3** AIR MILE. [< L *mille* thousand]

mile·age (mī′lij) *n.* **1** Length or distance as measured in miles. **2** An allowance for expenses while traveling, reckoned at so much per mile. **3** Length of service, quality of performance, etc.; usefulness; advantage. Also **mil′age.**

mile·post (mīl′pōst′) *n.* A signpost indicating the distance in miles to or from a specified place.

mil·er (mī′lər) *n.* A person or animal who competes in a mile race.

mile·stone (mīl′stōn′) *n.* **1** A post, pillar, or stone set up to indicate distance in miles to or from a specified place. **2** An important event or turning point.

Milestone

mi·lieu (mēl·yō͞o′; *Fr.* mē·lyœ′) *n.* Surroundings; environment. [F< OF *mi* middle + *lieu* place]

mil·i·tant (mil′ə·tənt) *adj.* **1** Actively engaged in war; fighting. **2** Aggressive or combative, esp. in support of a cause. —*n.* A militant person. [< L *militare* be a soldier] —**mil′i·tan·cy** *n.* —**mil′i·tant·ly** *adv.*

mil·i·ta·rism (mil′ə·tə·riz′əm) *n.* A policy or system emphasizing and exalting the military spirit and stressing the need of constant preparation for war. —**mil′i·ta·rist** *n.* —**mil′i·ta·ris′tic** *adj.* —**mil′i·ta·ris′ti·cal·ly** *adv.*

mil·i·ta·rize (mil′ə·tə·rīz′) *v.t.* **·rized, ·riz·ing 1** To imbue with militarism. **2** To prepare for war. —**mil′i·ta·ri·za′tion** *n.*

mil·i·tar·y (mil′ə·ter′ē) *adj.* **1** Of or relating to soldiers or to the army. **2** Made, performed, or supported by soldiers or the army. —*n.* **1** Armed forces; army: with *the.* **2** Army officials or officers: with *the.* [< L *miles, militis* soldier] —**mil′i·tar′i·ly** *adv.*

military attaché An army officer attached to his country's embassy or legation in a foreign country.

military intelligence 1 Information that is of military value to a country. **2** The branch of a government engaged in obtaining and interpreting such information.

military police A body of soldiers charged with police duties among troops.

mil·i·tate (mil′ə·tāt) *v.i.* **·tat·ed, ·tat·ing** To have influence: usu. with *against.* [< L *militare* be a soldier]

mi·li·tia (mə·lish′ə) *n.* An organized body of citizens, as the National Guard, drilled and equipped as soldiers but called to active service only in emergencies. —**mi·li′tia·man** (-mən) (*pl.* **·men**) [L, military service]

milk (milk) *n.* **1** The whitish emulsion secreted by the mammary glands of female mammals for the nourishment of their young, esp. cow's milk. **2** A liquid resembling milk, as coconut milk, latex, etc. —*v.t.* **1** To draw milk from the teats of (a female mammal). **2** To draw off as if by milking; extract: to *milk* sap from a tree. **3** To draw or extract something from: to *milk* someone of information. **4** To exploit; take advantage of. —*v.i.* **5** To milk a cow, etc. **6** To yield milk. [< OE *meolc, milc*]

milk-and-wa·ter (milk′ən·wô′tər, -wot′ər) *adj.* Weak and vacillating; namby-pamby.

milk leg A form of phlebitis sometimes affecting one or both legs of a woman after childbirth.

milk·maid (milk′mād′) *n.* DAIRYMAID.

milk·man (milk′man′) *n. pl.* **·men** (-men′) A man who sells or delivers milk.

milk of magnesia A white, aqueous suspension of hydroxide of magnesium, used as a laxative and antacid.

milk·shake (milk′shāk′) *n.* A drink made of chilled, flavored milk, and sometimes ice cream, mixed until frothy.

milk snake A small constrictor snake of North America having varying coloration in different areas. Also **milk adder.**

milk·sop (milk′sop′) *n.* A timid or unaggressive man.

milk sugar Lactose, the natural sugar in milk.

milk tooth Any of the first, temporary set of teeth in children and other young mammals.

milk·weed (milk′wēd′) *n.* Any of various plants having a milky juice.

milk·y (mil′kē) *adj.* **milk·i·er, milk·i·est 1** Containing or yielding milk. **2** Like milk, as in color. **3** Very mild or timid; spiritless. —**milk′i·ly** *adv.* —**milk′i·ness** *n.*

Milky Way *Astron.* A luminous band seen across the sky at night and composed of the aggregation of stars that contains the solar system; the Galaxy.

mill[1] (mil) *n.* **1** A machine for grinding grain into flour; also, the building in which this is done. **2** A machine for grinding or crushing hard substances of any kind: a pepper *mill.* **3** Any of various machines that by cutting, shaping, rolling, etc., treat or process raw material; usu. in combination: *sawmill.* **4** A factory. **5** Anything, as an agency or institution, that turns out products quickly and mechanically: a propaganda *mill.* **6** A difficult or painful experience: used chiefly in the phrase **through the mill.** —*v.t.* **1** To grind, shape, polish, roll, etc., in or with a mill.

2 To raise and ridge or corrugate the edge of (a coin). —*v.i.*
3 To undergo a milling process. **4** To move in a circular motion, as cattle: usu. with *about.* [<L *mola* millstone]

mill² (mil) *n.* The tenth part of a cent. [<L *millisimus* thousandth]

mill·dam (mil'dam') *n.* A dam built across a watercourse to raise its level sufficiently to turn a millwheel.

mil·len·ni·um (mi·len'ē·əm) *n. pl.* ·ni·a (-ē·ə) or ·ums **1** A period of a thousand years. **2** The thousand years during which Christ is to establish his kingdom on earth. *Rev.* 20:1–5. **3** Any period of happiness, peace, etc. [<L *mille* thousand + *annus* year] —**mil·len'ni·al** *adj.*

mil·le·pede (mil'ə·pēd) *n.* MILLIPEDE.

mil·le·pore (mil'ə·pôr, -pōr) *n.* Any of various reef-building corals forming massive concretions with numerous perforations. [<F *mille* thousand + *pore* pore]

mill·er (mil'ər) *n.* **1** One who keeps or tends a mill, esp. a flour mill. **2** A milling machine. **3** Any of various moths with scales forming a fine powder on their wings.

miller's thumb Any of various small, freshwater sculpins.

mil·let (mil'it) *n.* Any of various small-seeded cereal grasses cultivated for forage and as a cereal. [<L *milium*]

milli- *combining form* **1** The thousandth part of (a specified unit): *millimeter.* **2** A thousand: *millipede.* [<L *mille* a thousand]

mil·liard (mil'yərd, -yärd) *n. & adj.* See NUMBER. [<OF *milion* million]

mil·li·gram (mil'ə·gram) *n.* A metric unit of mass or weight equal to 10^{-6} (one millionth) kilogram or one thousandth of a gram. *Chiefly Brit. sp.* **mil'li·gramme.**

mil·li·li·ter (mil'ə·lē'tər) *n.* A metric unit of volume, equal to 10^{-3} (0.001) liter, or about 0.034 fluid ounce. *Chiefly Brit. sp.* **mil'li·li'tre.**

mil·li·me·ter (mil'ə·mē'tər) *n.* A metric unit of length equal to 10^{-3} (0.001) meter, or about 0.04 inch. *Chiefly Brit. sp.* **mil'li·me'ter.**

mil·li·ner (mil'ə·nər) *n.* A person who makes, trims, or sells women's hats. [<*Milaner* a man from Milan, Italy, who imported silks, etc.]

mil·li·ner·y (mil'ə·ner'ē, -nər·ē) *n.* **1** Women's hats. **2** The business of a milliner.

mil·lion (mil'yən) *n. & adj.* **1** See NUMBER. **2** An indefinitely great number. —*adj.* **1** Being a million. **2** Very many. [<Ital. *milione,* aug. of *mille* thousand]

mil·lion·aire (mil'yən·âr', mil'yən·âr') *n.* One whose wealth is valued at a million or more, as of dollars, pounds, etc.: also **mil'lion·naire'.**

mil·li·pede (mil'ə·pēd) *n.* Any of various arthropods having a cylindrical body marked by numerous segments bearing two pairs of walking legs. Also **mil'li·ped** (-ped). [<MILLI- + L *pes, pedis* foot]

mil·li·rem (mil'ə·rem') *n.* The thousandth part of a rem, the unit of absorbed radiation. [<MILLI- + rem]

mill·pond (mil'pond') *n.* A body of water dammed up to run a mill.

mill·race (mil'rās') *n.* The sluice through which the water runs to turn a millwheel.

mill·stone (mil'stōn') *n.* **1** One of a pair of thick, heavy, stone disks for grinding something, as grain. **2** That which grinds or pulverizes. **3** A heavy burden. —*Syn.* **3** encumbrance, hindrance, onus, weight.

mill·wheel (mil'hwēl') *n.* The waterwheel that drives a mill.

mill·wright (mil'rīt') *n.* One who plans, builds, or installs machinery in a mill.

mi·lord (mi·lôrd') *n.* An English nobleman or gentleman. [<*my lord*]

milque·toast (milk'tōst') *n.* Any timid or excessively apologetic person. [<Caspar *Milquetoast,* a character created by H. T. Webster, 1885–1952, U.S. cartoonist]

mil·reis (mil'rās) *n.* **1** A former Brazilian monetary unit. **2** A former Portuguese monetary unit. [Pg., lit., a thousand reis]

milt (milt) *n.* **1** The sperm of a fish. **2** The reproductive organs of a male fish when filled with seminal fluid. —*v.t.* To impregnate (fish roe) with milt. [<OE *milte*]

mime (mīm) *n.* **1** The art or technique of portraying character or of narration by the use of body movement and without words. **2** A performer who practices this art; pantomimist. **3** In ancient Greece and Rome, a comedy or farce representing real persons or events. **4** An actor in such a mime. —*v.t. & v.i.* mimed, mim·ing To play (a part) using body movement only, without words. [<Gk. *mimos*] —**mim'er** *n.*

mim·e·o·graph (mim'ē·ə·graf', -gräf') *n.* An apparatus for reproducing copies of written or typewritten matter by means of a stencil. —*v.t.* To reproduce by means of a mimeograph. [<*Mimeograph,* a trade name]

mi·met·ic (mi·met'ik, mī-) *adj.* **1** Imitative. **2** Of, relating to, or exhibiting mimicry. [<Gk. *mimēsis* imitation] —**mi·met'i·cal·ly** *adv.*

mim·ic (mim'ik) *v.t.* ·icked, ·ick·ing **1** To imitate the speech or actions of. **2** To copy closely; ape. **3** To have or assume the color, shape, etc., of. —*n.* One who or that which mimics. —*adj.* **1** Of the nature of mimicry. **2** Imitative. **3** Copying the real; simulated; mock: a *mimic* court. [<Gk. *mimos* mime] —**mim'i·cal** *adj.* —**mim'ick·er** *n.*

mim·ic·ry (mim'ik·rē) *n. pl.* ·ries **1** The act or art of mimicking or imitating. **2** *Biol.* A superficial resemblance of one organism to another or to its environment, resulting in concealment or protection. —*Syn.* **1** imitation, parody, burlesque, take off.

mi·mo·sa (mi·mō'sə, -zə) *n.* Any of a genus of leguminous tropical herbs, shrubs, or trees, with feathery foliage and clusters of small flowers. [<L *mimus* mime; from its supposed mimicry of animal life]

min. mineralogy; minim(s); minimum; mining; minor; minute(s).

mi·na (mī'nə) *n.* MYNA. Also **mi'nah.**

min·a·ret (min'ə·ret') *n.* A high, slender tower attached to a Muslim mosque and surrounded by balconies, from which the summons to prayer is called by a muezzin. [<Ar. *manārah* lamp, lighthouse]

min·a·to·ry (min'ə·tôr'ē, -tō'rē) *adj.* Threatening. Also **min'a·to'ri·al.** [<L *minari* threaten] —**min'a·to'ri·al·ly, min'a·to'ri·ly** *adv.*

Minaret

mince (mins) *v.* minced, minc·ing *v.t.* **1** To cut or chop into small bits, as meat. **2** To subdivide minutely. **3** To diminish the force or strength of; moderate: He didn't *mince* words with her. **4** To do or express with affected primness or elegance. —*v.i.* **5** To walk with short steps or affected daintiness. **6** To speak or behave with affected primness. —*n.* MINCEMEAT. [<L *minuere* lessen, make smaller] —**minc'er** *n.* —**minc'ing·ly** *adv.*

mince·meat (mins'mēt') *n.* A mixture of chopped apples, raisins, spices, etc., usu. without meat, used in mince pie. —**make mincemeat of** To destroy or defeat completely.

mince pie A pie made of mincemeat.

mind (mīnd) *n.* **1** The aggregate of all conscious and unconscious processes originating in and associated with the brain. **2** Memory: to bear in *mind.* **3** Opinion: to change one's *mind.* **4** Desire; inclination: to have a *mind* to leave. **5** Mental disposition, character, or temper: a cheerful *mind.* **6** Intellectual power or capacity: He has a fine *mind.* **7** An extremely intelligent person: She is one of the great *minds* of our time. **8** Sanity; reason: to lose one's *mind.* **9** Attention; concentration: to let one's *mind* wander. —**a piece of one's mind** An opinion, criticism, or rebuke very frankly or bluntly expressed. —**on one's mind** Occupying one's thoughts. —**out of one's mind 1** Insane. **2** Deeply agitated; frantic. —**take one's mind off** To turn one's thoughts from. —*v.t.* **1** To pay attention to. **2** To be careful concerning: *Mind* your step. **3** To obey. **4** To care for; tend. **5** To object to; dislike: Do you *mind* the noise? **6** *Regional* To notice; perceive. **7** *Regional* To remember. —*v.i.* **8** To pay attention; take notice. **9** To be obedient. **10** To be concerned; care: I don't *mind.* **11** To be careful. [<OE *gemynd*] —**mind'er** *n.*

mind·ed (mīn'did) *adj.* **1** Having a specified kind of mind: *evil-minded.* **2** Inclined; disposed: usu. with *to.* **3** Keeping in mind; concerned about: *conservation-minded.*

mind·ful (mīnd′fəl) *adj.* Keeping in mind; heeding; aware. —**mind′ful·ly** *adv.* —**mind′ful·ness** *n.*

mind·less (mīnd′lis) *adj.* 1 Devoid of intelligence. 2 Not giving heed or attention; careless. —**mind′less·ly** *adv.*

mind reader One who claims to be able to know another person's thoughts. —**mind reading**

mine¹ (mīn) *n.* 1 An excavation in the earth for the extraction of coal, ore, precious stones, etc. 2 Any deposit of such material suitable for extraction. 3 *Mil.* **a** An underground tunnel dug beneath an enemy's fortifications. **b** A case of explosive material buried in the earth, or floating on or beneath the surface of water. 4 Any source of supply: a *mine* of ideas. —*v.* **mined, min·ing** *v.t.* 1 To dig (coal, ores, etc.) from the earth. 2 To dig into (the earth, etc.) for coal, ores, etc. 3 To make by digging, as a tunnel. 4 To obtain information, ideas, etc., from 5 UNDERMINE. 6 To place an explosive mine or mines in or under. —*v.i.* 7 To dig in a mine for coal, ores, etc. 8 To make a tunnel, etc., by digging 9 To place explosive mines. [<OF] —**min′er** *n.*

mine² (mīn) *pron.* 1 The possessive case of *I*, used predicatively: That book is *mine*. 2 The things of persons belonging or pertaining to me: His work is better than *mine*. —**of mine** Belonging or relating to me; my. —*pronominal adj. Archaic* My: *mine* eyes. [<OE *mīn*]

mine detector An instrument for locating explosive mines.

mine field An area in water or on land systematically planted with explosive mines.

mine layer A naval vessel provided with special equipment for the laying of mines.

min·er·al (min′ər·əl) *n.* 1 A naturally occurring substance obtained from the earth by mining, as ore, coal, granite, etc. 2 Any of certain elements essential to life and usu. having special physiological functions, as iron, calcium, iodine, etc. 3 Any substance that is neither animal nor vegetable. —*adj.* 1 Pertaining to, consisting of, or resembling minerals. 2 Impregnated with mineral constituents. [<L *minera* a mine]

min·er·al·ize (min′ər·əl·īz′) *v.t.* **ized, ·iz·ing** 1 To convert from a metal to a mineral, as iron to rust. 2 To convert to a mineral substance; petrify. 3 To impregnate with minerals or other inorganic substances.

min·er·al·o·gy (min′ə·ral′ə·jē, -räl′-) *n.* The science that deals with minerals. —**min′er·al′o·gist** *n.*

mineral oil 1 Any oil obtained from underground deposits, as petroleum. 2 A colorless, tasteless oil deprived from petroleum, used as a laxative.

mineral water Any water naturally or artificially impregnated with mineral salts or gases.

Mi·ner·va (mi·nûr′və) *Rom. Myth.* The goddess of wisdom, invention, and technical dexterity.

min·e·stro·ne (min′ə·strō′nē) *n.* A thick vegetable soup containing vermicelli, barley, etc., in a meat broth. [Ital.]

mine sweeper A ship equipped for the detection, destruction, and removal of marine mines.

Ming (ming) *n.* A Chinese dynasty (1368–1644), noted for its scholarship and artistic works, as porcelains.

min·gle (ming′gəl) *v.* **min·gled, min·gling** *v.t.* 1 To mix or unite together; blend. 2 To make or concoct by mixing. —*v.i.* 3 To be or become mixed, united, or closely joined. 4 To enter into company; mix or associate, as with a crowd. [<OE *mengan* to mix] —**min′gler** *n.*

min·i (min′ē) *n. pl.* **min·is** 1 MINISKIRT. 2 *Informal* Anything smaller or shorter than others of its class. —*adj.* **·i·er, ·i·est** *Informal* Very small or miniaturized. [<MINI-]

mini- *combining form* Small; tiny; miniskirt. [<L *minimus* least, smallest]

min·i·a·ture (min′ē·ə·chər, min′ə·chər) *n.* 1 A portrait or painting of very small dimensions and delicate workmanship. 2 The art of painting such pictures. 3 A portrayal or copy of anything on a small scale. 4 Reduced scale, dimensions, or extent. —*adj.* Being or done on a small scale. [<L *miniare* paint red]

min·i·a·tur·ize (min′ē·ə·chər·īz, min′ə·chər·īz′) *v.t.* **ized, ·iz·ing** To reduce the size of, as the parts of an instrument or machine. —**min′i·a·tur′i·za′tion** *n.*

min·i·bike (min′ē·bīk′) *n.* A small motorcycle with one seat.

min·i·cam (min′ə·kam) *n.* A small portable camera, usually one using 35-mm. film.

min·i·com·put·er (min′ē·kəm·pyōō′tər) *n.* A computer intermediate in size between a mainframe and a microcomputer.

min·im (min′im) *n.* 1 An apothecaries' measure, equal to ¹⁄₆₀ of a fluid dram, or about one drop. 2 *Music Brit.* A half note. 3 Something extremely small. —*adj.* Smallest. [<L *minimus* least, smallest]

min·i·mal (min′ə·məl) *adj.* Being or pertaining to a minimum; least; smallest. —**min′i·mal·ly** *adv.*

min·i·mize (min′ə·mīz) *v.t.* **mized, ·miz·ing** 1 To reduce to the smallest possible amount or degree. 2 To regard or represent as having the least possible importance, value, etc.

min·i·mum (min′ə·məm) *n. pl.* **·mums** or **·ma** (-mə) 1 The least possible quantity, amount, or degree. 2 The lowest degree, variation, etc., reached or recorded. —*adj.* Of, relating to, or being a minimum. [<L *minimus* smallest]

minimum wage A wage fixed by law or agreement as the smallest amount an employer may offer an employee in a specific group.

min·ing (mī′ning) *n.* The act, process, or business of extracting coal, ores, etc., from mines.

min·ion (min′yən) *n.* A servile favorite or follower: a term of contempt. [<F *mignon* darling]

min·i·scule (min′əs·kyōōl) *adj.* MINUSCULE.

min·i·ser·ies (min′ē·sir′ēz) *n.* A single program shown as a series over a sequence of several days.

min·i·skirt (min′i·skûrt′) *n.* A short skirt worn by women with the hemline well above the knee. [<MINI- + SKIRT]

min·is·ter (min′is·tər) *n.* 1 One who is authorized to preach, administer the sacraments, etc. in a church; clergyman. 2 The chief of a department of a government. 3 One commissioned to represent his government in diplomatic relations with another government, esp. one ranking next below an ambassador. 4 An agent of someone or something. —*v.i.* 1 To provide for the wants or needs of someone. 2 To be conductive; contribute. —*v.t.* 3 To administer or apply (a sacrament, aid, etc.) [<L, an attendant]

min·is·te·ri·al (min′is·tir′ē·əl) *adj.* 1 Of or pertaining to a minister or the ministry. 2 Pertaining to an administrative act performed on the basis of legal authority and not on the initiative of the agent. 3 Instrumental; causative.

min·is·trant (min′is·trənt) *adj.* Ministering.

min·is·tra·tion (min′is·trā′shən) *n.* 1 The act of serving as a minister. 2 Help; aid. —**min′is·tra′tive** *adj.*

min·is·try (min′is·trē) *n. pl.* **·tries** 1 The clergy. 2 The office or duties of a minister of religion. 3 *Govt.* **a** Ministers collectively. **b** The office or duties of a minister; also, the building where his work is conducted. **c** A department presided over by a minister. 4 Ministration; service.

min·i·ver (min′ə·vər) *n.* A white fur, esp. such fur used in the Middle Ages for trimming. [<OF *menu vair*, lit., little spotted (fur)]

mink (mingk) *n.* 1 A small, semiaquatic, carnivorous mammal, related to the weasel and valued for its soft, thick, usu. brown fur. 2 The fur of this mammal. [<Scand.]

Minn. Minnesota.

min·ne·sing·er (min′ə·sing′ər) *n.* A lyric poet and singer of medieval Germany. [G<*Minne* love + *Singer* singer]

Mink

min·now (min′ō) *n.* 1 Any of various small cyprinoid fishes, often used as bait. 2 Any very small fish. Also **min′nie** (-nē). [<OE *myne* small fish]

Mi·no·an (mi·nō′ən) *adj.* Of or pertaining to an advanced Bronze Age civilization that flourished in Crete from about 3000 to 1100 B.C.

mi·nor (mī′nər) *adj.* 1 Less in number, quantity, or extent. 2 Of secondary importance or consideration. 3 Not yet of legal age. 4 In education, of or designating a course of study requiring fewer hours in class than a major field of study. 5 *Music* **a** Smaller than the corresponding major interval by a semitone. **b** Characterized by minor intervals, scales, or tones. **c** In a minor key. —*n.* **1** One not yet of legal age. **2** In education, a minor course of study. **3** *Music* A minor key, interval, etc. —*v.i.* In education, to study as a minor subject: with *in:* to *minor* in art. [L, less]

mi·nor·i·ty (mə·nôr′ə·tē, -nor′-, mī-) *n. pl.* **·ties 1** The smaller in number of two parts or parties. **2** The state or period of being under legal age. **3** MINORITY GROUP.

minority group A group comprising less than half of a population and differing from the others and esp. from a larger predominant group, as in race, religion, political affiliation, etc.

minor key *Music* A key or mode containing a minor third, characterized usu. by numerous chromatic tones.

minor league Any professional sports league not having the standing of a major league. —**mi′nor-league′** *adj.* —**mi′nor-lea′guer** *n.*

minor scale *Music* A scale, either diatonic or with various chromatic tones, containing a minor third.

minor suit In bridge, diamonds or clubs.

Mi·nos (mī′nəs, -nos) *Gk. Myth.* A king of Crete who became a judge of the lower world after his death.

Min·o·taur (min′ə·tôr) *Gk. Myth.* A monster, half man and half bull, who was confined in the Labyrinth where it was annually fed human flesh until killed by Theseus. [< Gk. *Minōs* Minos + *tauros* bull]

min·ster (min′stər) *n.* **1** A monastery church. **2** Any large church or cathedral. [< OE *mynster*]

min·strel (min′strəl) *n.* **1** In the Middle Ages, a wandering musician and poet, esp. one who composed and sang his own songs. **2** A performer in a minstrel show. **3** A poet; singer; musician. [< LL *ministerialis* servant, jester]

minstrel show A comic variety show of songs, dances, jokes, etc., given by a company of performers in blackface.

min·strel·sy (min′strəl·sē) *n. pl.* **·sies 1** The art of a minstrel. **2** Ballads or lyrics. **3** A troupe of minstrels.

mint¹ (mint) *n.* **1** A place where the coin of a country is manufactured. **2** A large sum or amount. **3** The source of a fabrication or invention. —*v.t.* **1** To make (money) by stamping; coin. **2** To invent or fabricate, as a word. —*adj.* Unused; in original condition: a *mint* stamp. [< L *Moneta* epithet of Juno, whose temple at Rome was used as a mint] —**mint′er** *n.*

mint² (mint) *n.* **1** Any of several aromatic herbs, esp. spearmint and peppermint. **2** A mint-flavored candy. [< Gk. *mintha*]

mint·age (min′tij) *n.* **1** The act of minting. **2** The coins so minted. **3** The duty paid for coining. **4** The impression placed upon a coin.

mint julep A drink made of bourbon or brandy mixed with crushed ice and sugar and flavored with fresh mint.

min·u·end (min′yōō·end) *n.* The number from which another is to be subtracted. [< L *minuere* lessen]

min·u·et (min′yōō·et′) *n.* **1** A stately dance for couples, introduced in France in the 17th century. **2** Music for or using the rhythm of this dance. [< L *minutus* small]

mi·nus (mī′nəs) *prep.* **1** Lessened by; less: 10 *minus* 5. **2** *Informal* Deprived of; lacking: *minus* a hat. —*adj.* **1** Of or used in subtraction. **2** Negative: a *minus* quantity. **3** Less than in quantity or quality: a B *minus*. —*n.* **1** MINUS SIGN. **2** A negative quantity. **3** A defect; drawback. [L, neut. of *minor* less]

min·us·cule (min′əs·kyool, mi·nus′kyool) *n.* **1** A small, cursive script used in the Middle Ages. **2** A letter in this script. **3** Any lower-case letter. —*adj.* **1** Of, like, or composed of minuscules. **2** Very small; miniature. [< L *minusculus*, dim. of *minor* less] • The spelling *miniscule*, often used in the sense of adj., def. 2, is apparently based on the erroneous assumption that the word is formed with the popular combining form *mini-*, meaning small.

minus sign A sign (–) denoting subtraction or a negative quantity.

min·ute¹ (min′it) *n.* **1** The 60th part of an hour; 60 seconds. **2** Any short period of time; moment. **3** The 60th part of a degree, indicated by the sign ('). **4** A memorandum. **5** *pl.* The official record of the proceedings of a meeting. — **up to the minute** In or having the latest style, equipment, etc. —*v.t.* **·ut·ed, ·ut·ing** To make a brief note of; record. [< L *minutus* small]

mi·nute² (mī·nyoot′, mi-) *adj.* **1** Exceedingly small. **2** Unimportant; trifling. **3** Marked by exact, careful attention to details. [< L *minutus* small] —**mi·nute′ly** *adv.* —**mi·nute′ness** *n.* —**Syn. 1** infinitesimal, imperceptible, diminutive. **2** insignificant, inconsequential.

minute hand (min′it) The long hand of a timepiece that marks the minutes.

min·ute·man (min′it·man′) *n. pl.* **·men** (-men′) In the American Revolution, an armed citizen pledged to be ready for service at a minute's notice.

minute steak (min′it) A small, thin piece of beefsteak that can be cooked quickly.

mi·nu·ti·ae (mi·nyoo′shi·ē) *n.pl. of* **mi·nu′ti·a** (-shē-ə, -shə) Small or unimportant details. [L]

minx (mingks) *n.* A saucy, pert, or bold girl. [Prob. < LG *minsk* impudent woman]

Mi·o·cene (mī′ə·sēn) *adj. & n.* See GEOLOGY. [< Gk. *meiōn* less + *kainos* recent]

MIr. Middle Irish.

mir·a·cle (mir′ə·kəl) *n.* **1** An act or event that seems to transcend or contradict all known natural or scientific laws and is usu. thought to be supernatural in origin. **2** Any wonderful or amazing thing, fact, or event; a wonder. [< L *mirus* wonderful]

miracle play A medieval dramatic representation of the lives of the saints and their miracles.

mi·rac·u·lous (mi·rak′yə·ləs) *adj.* **1** Of the nature of a miracle; supernatural. **2** Surpassingly strange; wonderful. **3** Possessing the power to work miracles. —**mi·rac′u·lous·ly** *adv.* —**mi·rac′u·lous·ness** *n.*

mi·rage (mi·räzh′) *n.* **1** An optical illusion, as of an oasis in the desert or ships seen inverted in the air, that occurs when light rays from these usu. distant objects are refracted through layers of the atmosphere having different densities. **2** Anything that appears to be real or attainable but is not. [< L *mirari* wonder at]

mire (mīr) *n.* **1** Wet, swampy ground. **2** Deep mud or slush. —*v.* **mired, mir·ing** *v.t.* **1** To cause to sink or become stuck in mire. **2** To defile or soil with mud. **3** To entrap or involve. —*v.i.* **4** To sink in mire; bog down. [< ON *mȳrr*]

mirk (mûrk) *adj. & n.* MURK.

mir·ror (mir′ər) *n.* **1** Any of various reflecting surfaces, esp. glass when backed with a silver or aluminum coating. **2** Whatever reflects or clearly represents. **3** An exemplar; model. —*v.t.* To reflect or show an image of, as in a mirror. [< L *mirari* wonder at, admire]

mirth (mûrth) *n.* Gaiety of spirits; merriment; jollity. [< OE *myrig* pleasant, merry] —**mirth′ful** *adj.* —**mirth′ful·ly** *adv.* —**mirth′ful·ness** *n.*

MIRV multiple independently targeted reentry vehicle.

mir·y (mīr′ē) *adj.* **·i·er, ·i·est 1** Muddy; swampy. **2** Dirty. — **mir′i·ness** *n.*

mis- *prefix* Bad; badly; wrongly; unfavorably; dishonestly: *misdeed, misjudge*. [< OE *mis-* wrong]

mis·ad·ven·ture (mis′əd·ven′chər) *n.* An unlucky happening; misfortune. [< OF *mesaventure*]

mis·ad·vise (mis′əd·vīz′) *v.t.* **·vised, ·vis·ing** To advise wrongly or badly.

mis·al·li·ance (mis′ə·lī′əns) *n.* An undesirable alliance, esp. an unsuitable marriage.

mis·an·thrope (mis′ən·thrōp, miz′-) *n.* One who hates or distrusts his fellow men. Also **mis·an·thro·pist** (mis·an′thrə·pist). [< Gk. *misein* hate + *anthrōpos* a man] —**mis′an·throp′ic** (-throp′ik) or **·i·cal** *adj.* —**mis′an·throp′i·cal·ly** *adv.*

mis·an·thro·py (mis·an′thrə·pē) *n.* Hatred or distrust of mankind.

mis·ap·ply (mis′ə·plī′) *v.t.* **·plied, ·ply·ing** To use or apply incorrectly or dishonestly.

mis·ap·pre·hend (mis′ap·ri·hend′) *v.t.* To apprehend or understand wrongly.

mis·ap·pro·pri·ate (mis′ə·prō′prē·āt) *v.t.* **·at·ed, ·at·ing** To use or take improperly or dishonestly; misapply. — **mis′ap·pro′pri·a′tion** *n.*

mis·be·come (mis′bi·kum′) *v.t.* **·came, ·come, ·com·ing** To be unbecoming or not befitting to.

mis·be·got·ten (mis′bi·got′n) *adj.* Begotten unlawfully; illegitimate. Also **mis′be·got′.**

mis·be·have (mis′bi·hāv′) *v.i.* To behave badly. —**mis′· be·hav′ior** (-hāv′yər) *n.*

mis·be·lief (mis′bi·lēf′) *n.* A wrong or false belief.

mis·be·lieve (mis′bi·lēv′) *v.i.* ·lieved, ·liev·ing To hold a false or unorthodox belief. —**mis′be·liev′er** *n.*

misc. miscellaneous; miscellany.

mis·cal·cu·late (mis·kal′kyə·lāt) *v.t. & v.i.* ·lat·ed, ·lat·ing To calculate wrongly. —**mis′cal·cu·la′tion** *n.*

mis·call (mis·kôl′) *v.t.* To call by a wrong name.

mis·car·riage (mis·kar′ij) *n.* 1 *Med.* A premature delivery of a nonviable fetus; abortion. 2 Failure to reach a proper or just conclusion. 3 Failure to reach an expected destination.

mis·car·ry (mis·kar′ē) *v.i.* ·ried, ·ry·ing 1 To fail; go wrong. 2 To bring forth a fetus prematurely. 3 To fail to reach an expected destination, as mail.

mis·ce·ge·na·tion (mis′i·jə·nā′shən, mi·sej′ə-) *n.* Intermarriage or interbreeding between different races. [< L *miscere* mix + *genus* race] —**mis′ce·ge·net′ic** (-jə·net′ik) *adj.*

mis·cel·la·ne·ous (mis′ə·lā′nē·əs) *adj.* 1 Consisting of various things or types; varied; mixed. 2 Having various qualities, interests, or capabilities. [< L *miscellus* mixed] —**mis′cel·la·ne·ous·ly** *adv.* —**mis′cel·la·ne·ous·ness** *n.*

mis·cel·la·ny (mis′ə·lā′nē) *n. pl.* ·nies 1 Often *pl.* A collection of literary compositions on various subjects. 2 Any miscellaneous collection.

mis·chance (mis·chans′, -chäns′) *n.* An instance of bad luck; a mishap.

mis·chief (mis′chif) *n.* 1 Action or conduct, often playful in intent, that annoys or vexes. 2 A disposition to tease or annoy. 3 Damage, harm, or trouble. 4 A person or thing that causes harm, annoyance, etc. [< OF *meschever* come to grief]

mis·chie·vous (mis′chi·vəs) *adj.* 1 Inclined to tease, play pranks, annoy, etc. 2 Causing harm, injury, or damage. 3 Annoying; troublesome. —**mis′chie·vous·ly** *adv.* —**mis′chie·vous·ness** *n.*

mis·ci·ble (mis′i·bəl) *adj.* Capable of being mixed. [< L *miscere* mix] —**mis′ci·bil′i·ty** *n.*

mis·con·ceive (mis′kən·sēv′) *v.t. & v.i.* ·ceived, ·ceiv·ing To conceive wrongly; misunderstand. —**mis′con·ceiv′er, mis′con·cep′tion** (-sep′shən) *n.*

mis·con·duct (mis·kən·dukt′) *v.t.* 1 To behave (oneself) improperly. 2 To mismanage. —*n.* (mis·kon′dukt) 1 Improper conduct, esp. adultery. 2 Unlawful conduct. 3 Mismanagement, esp. if dishonest.

mis·con·strue (mis′kən·strōō′) *v.t.* ·strued, ·stru·ing To interpret erroneously; misunderstand. —**mis′con·struc′tion** (-struk′shən) *n.*

mis·count (mis·kount′) *v.t. & v.i.* To count incorrectly. —*n.* (mis′kount′) An incorrect count.

mis·cre·ant (mis′krē·ənt) *n.* 1 One who does evil. 2 *Archaic* An unbeliever. —*adj.* 1 Villainous; evil. 2 *Archaic* Unbelieving. [< OF *mescreant* unbelieving]

mis·cue (mis·kyōō′) *n.* 1 In billiards, a stroke spoiled by a slipping of the cue. 2 *Informal* A mistake; slip. —*v.i.* ·cued, ·cu·ing 1 To make a miscue. 2 In the theater, to miss one's cue to or to answer another's cue.

mis·deal (mis·dēl′) *v.t. & v.i.* ·dealt (-delt′), ·deal·ing In card games, to deal incorrectly. —*n.* An incorrect deal.

mis·deed (mis·dēd′) *n.* A wrong or improper act. —**Syn.** offense, sin, transgression, violation.

mis·de·mean·or (mis′di·mē′nər) *n. Law* Any offense less serious than a felony.

mis·di·rect (mis′di·rekt′, -dī·rekt′) *v.t.* To direct or send wrongly. —**mis′di·rec′tion** *n.*

mis·do (mis·dōō′) *v.t. & v.i.* ·did, ·done, ·do·ing To do wrongly; bungle. —**mis·do′er** *n.* —**mis·do′ing** *n.*

mis·em·ploy (mis′im·ploi′) *v.t.* To use wrongly or improperly. —**mis′em·ploy′ment** *n.*

mi·ser (mī′zər) *n.* Any stingy, grasping person, esp. one who hoards money avariciously. [< L *miser* wretched]

mis·er·a·ble (miz′ər·ə·bəl, miz′rə-) *adj.* 1 Wretchedly poor or unhappy. 2 Causing misery, discomfort, or unhappiness: a *miserable* cold. 3 Proceeding from or exhibiting misery: a bare, *miserable* room. 4 Of bad quality; inferior; worthless. 5 Pitiable; sorry. 6 Shameful; disgraceful. [< L

miserari to pity] —**mis′er·a·ble·ness** *n.* —**mis′er·a·bly** *adv.* —**Syn.** 4 unsatisfactory, shoddy, second-rate.

Mis·e·re·re (miz′ə·râr′ē, -rir′ē) *n.* 1 The 51st Psalm (the 50th in the Vulgate or Douay versions). 2 A musical setting of this psalm. [< L *miserere* have mercy]

mi·ser·ly (mī′zər·lē) *adj.* Of or like a miser; grasping; stingy. —**mi′ser·li·ness** *n.*

mis·er·y (miz′ər·ē) *n. pl.* ·er·ies 1 Extreme distress or suffering, esp. as a result of poverty, physical or mental pain, etc. 2 A cause of such distress or suffering. [< L *miser* wretched]

mis·fea·sance (mis·fē′zəns) *n. Law* The performance of a lawful act in an unlawful or culpably negligent manner. [< OF *mes-* mis- + *faire* do] —**mis·fea′sor** *n.*

mis·fire (mis·fīr′) *v.i.* ·fired, ·fir·ing 1 To fail to explode, fire, or become properly ignited, as a gun or engine. 2 To miss the desired or proper effect. —*n.* An act or instance of misfiring.

mis·fit (mis·fit′) *v.t. & v.i.* ·fit·ted, ·fit·ting To fail to fit or make fit. —*n.* (mis′fit′, mis·fit′) 1 Something that fits badly. 2 (mis′fit′) A person who does not adjust well to his surroundings. 3 The act or condition of fitting badly.

mis·for·tune (mis·fôr′chən) *n.* 1 Bad luck; trouble; adversity. 2 An unlucky occurrence; calamity.

mis·give (mis·giv′) *v.* ·gave, ·giv·ing *v.t.* 1 To make fearful, suspicious, or doubtful: My heart *misgives* me. —*v.i.* 2 To be apprehensive.

mis·giv·ing (mis·giv′ing) *n.* A feeling of doubt, premonition, or apprehension.

mis·gov·ern (mis·guv′ərn) *v.t.* To govern or administer badly. —**mis·gov′ern·ment** *n.*

mis·guide (mis·gīd′) *v.t.* ·guid·ed, ·guid·ing To guide wrongly in action or thought; mislead: *misguided* confidence. —**mis·guid′ance, mis·guid′er** *n.*

mis·han·dle (mis·han′dəl) *v.t.* ·dled, ·dling 1 To handle or treat roughly. 2 To manage badly.

mis·hap (mis′hap, mis·hap′) *n.* An unfortunate accident.

mish·mash (mish′mash′, -mosh′) *n.* A hodge-podge; jumble. Also **mish′-mash′.** [Reduplication of MASH]

mis·in·form (mis′in·fôrm′) *v.t.* To give false or erroneous information to. —**mis′in·form′ant, mis′in·for·ma′tion, mis′in·form′er** *n.*

mis·in·ter·pret (mis′in·tûr′prit) *v.t.* To interpret wrongly. —**mis′in·ter·pre·ta′tion, mis′in·ter′pret·er** *n.* —**Syn.** misunderstand, misconstrue, mistake, confuse.

mis·judge (mis·juj′) *v.t. & v.i.* To judge wrongly or unfairly. —**mis·judg′ment, mis·judge′ment** *n.*

mis·lay (mis·lā′) *v.t.* ·laid, ·lay·ing 1 To lay in a place not remembered; misplace. 2 To put down incorrectly: to *mislay* a carpet. —**mis·lay′er** *n.*

mis·lead (mis·lēd′) *v.t.* ·led (-led′), ·lead·ing 1 To direct wrongly. 2 To lead astray or into error. —**mis·lead′er** *n.* —**mis·lead′ing** *adj.* —**mis·lead′ing·ly** *adv.*

mis·like (mis·līk′) *v.t.* 1 To dislike. 2 To displease. —*n.* Dislike; disapproval.

mis·man·age (mis·man′ij) *v.t. & v.i.* ·aged, ·ag·ing To manage badly or improperly. —**mis·man′age·ment, mis·man′ag·er** *n.*

mis·match (mis·mach′) *v.t.* To match badly or unsuitably. —*n.* (mis′mach′) A bad or unsuitable match.

mis·mate (mis·māt′) *v.t. & v.i.* ·mated, ·mat·ing To mate badly or inappropriately.

mis·name (mis·nām′) *v.t.* ·named, ·nam·ing To call by a wrong name.

mis·no·mer (mis·nō′mər) *n.* 1 A name wrongly applied. 2 The giving of a wrong name to a person in a legal document. [< OF *mes-* wrongly + *nomer* name]

miso- *combining form* Hating; hatred: *misogynist.* [< Gk. *misein* hate]

mis·og·a·my (mis·og′ə·mē) *n.* Hatred of marriage. [< MISO- + -GAMY] —**mis·og′a·mist** *n.*

mis·og·y·ny (mis·oj′ə·nē) *n.* Hatred of women. [< MISO- + Gk. *gynē* woman] —**mis·og′y·nist** *n.* —**mis·og′y·nous** *adj.*

mis·place (mis·plās′) *v.t.* ·placed, ·plac·ing 1 To put in a wrong place. 2 To put in a place not remembered. 3 To give (trust, confidence, affection, etc.) unwisely.

mis·play (mis·plā′; *for n. also* mis′plā′) *v.t. & v.i.* In games, to play incorrectly or unskillfully. —*n.* A wrong play or move.

mis·print (mis·print′; *for n. also* mis′print′) *v.t.* To print incorrectly. —*n.* An error in printing.

mis·pri·sion (mis·prizh′ən) *n.* 1 *Law* Concealment of a crime, esp. of treason or felony. 2 Misconduct or neglect of duty by a public official. [< OF < *mes-* wrong + *prendre* take]

mis·prize (mis·prīz′) *v.t.* **prized**, **·priz·ing** To undervalue the worth of; despise.

mis·pro·nounce (mis′prə·nouns′) *v.t. & v.i.* **·nounced**, **·nounc·ing** To pronounce incorrectly or in a nonstandard way. —**mis′pro·nun′ci·a′tion** (-nun′sē·ā′shən) *n.*

mis·quote (mis·kwōt′) *v.t. & v.i.* **·quoted**, **·quot·ing** To quote incorrectly. —**mis′quo·ta′tion** *n.*

mis·read (mis·rēd′) *v.t. & v.i.* **·read** (-red′), **·read·ing** (-rē′ding) 1 To read incorrectly. 2 To misinterpret in or as if in reading.

mis·rep·re·sent (mis′rep·ri·zent′) *v.t.* 1 To give an incorrect or false representation of. 2 To represent (a client, constituent, etc.) badly. —**mis′rep·re·sen·ta′tion** *n.* —**mis′·rep·re·sen′ta·tive** *adj., n.*

mis·rule (mis·rōōl′) *v.t.* **·ruled**, **·rul·ing** To rule unwisely or unjustly. —*n.* 1 Bad rule or government. 2 Disorder or riot.

miss[1] (mis) *n.* 1 A young girl: chiefly informal or in trade use: clothing for *misses*. 2 *Often cap.* A title used in speaking to an unmarried woman or girl: used without the name. See also MISS. [Contraction of MISTRESS]

miss[2] (mis) *v.t.* 1 To fail to hit or strike. 2 To fail to meet, catch, obtain, accomplish, see, hear, perceive, etc.: to *miss* the point. 3 To fail to attend, keep, perform, etc.: to *miss* church. 4 To overlook or fail to take advantage of, as an opportunity. 5 To discover or feel the loss or absence of. 6 To escape; avoid: He just *missed* being wounded. —*v.i.* 7 To fail to hit; strike wide of the mark. 8 To be unsuccessful; fail. —*n.* A failure to hit, find, attain, succeed, etc. [< OE *missan*]

Miss (mis) *n.* A title of address used with the name of a girl or an unmarried woman.

Miss. Mississippi.

mis·sal (mis′əl) *n.* The book containing all the prayers, lessons, etc., for the celebration of mass throughout the year. [< Med. L. *missalis (liber)* mass (book)]

mis·shape (mis·shāp′, mish·shāp′) *v.t.* **·shaped**, **·shaped** or **·shap·en**, **·shap·ing** To shape badly; deform. —**mis·shap′·en** *adj.*

mis·sile (mis′əl, *chiefly Brit.* mis′īl) *n.* 1 Any object, esp. a weapon, intended to be thrown or discharged, as a spear, bullet, arrow, etc. 2 GUIDED MISSILE. [< L *missus*, pp. of *mittere* send]

mis·sile·ry (mis′əl·rē) *n.* The science and technology of designing, building, and launching missiles, esp. guided missiles. Also **mis′sil·ry.**

miss·ing (mis′ing) *adj.* 1 Absent; lost; gone. 2 *Mil.* Absent: said of soldiers after combat whose fate has not been definitely ascertained.

missing link 1 Something lacking to complete a series. 2 A hypothetical creature assumed to be intermediate in development between man and the anthropoid ape.

mis·sion (mish′ən) *n.* 1 Any group of people delegated or sent to perform some specific task, business, or service. 2 The specific business, task, or service any person or group is sent or authorized to accomplish. 3 A group authorized by its government to conduct diplomatic, business, or political negotiations in a foreign country. 4 The foreign embassy or legation of an ambassador or envoy. 5 A group of missionaries authorized by a church to convert, teach, or aid the people of a foreign country or region. 6 The headquarters used or the specific region served by such a group of missionaries. 7 *pl.* The organized work of such missionaries. 8 A special series of religious services designed to convert people to or stimulate their faith in Christianity or another religion. 9 An educational, religious, or welfare center for the underprivileged. 10 That goal or task which one is or feels destined to accomplish in life. 11 *Mil.* A definite task assigned to an individual or unit, esp. a flight operation of a single aircraft or forma-

tion. —*adj.* Pertaining or belonging to a mission. —*v.t.* 1 To send on a mission. 2 To establish a mission in. [< L *missus*, pp. of *mittere* send] —**mis′sion·er** *n.*

mis·sion·ar·y (mish′ən·er′ē) *n. pl.* **·ar·ies** 1 A person sent to propagate religion or to do educational or charitable work, esp. in some foreign country or region. 2 One who spreads any new system or doctrine. —*adj.* Of, pertaining to, or like missions or missionaries.

Mis·sis·sip·pi·an (mis′ə·sip′ē·ən) *adj.* 1 Of or pertaining to the Mississippi River. 2 See GEOLOGY. —*n.* See GEOLOGY.

mis·sive (mis′iv) *n.* A letter or written message. [< L *missus*, pp. of *mittere* send]

mis·speak (mis·spēk′) *v.t. & v.i.* **·spoke**, **·speak·ing** To speak or say incorrectly.

mis·spell (mis·spel′) *v.t. & v.i.* **·spelled** or **·spelt**, **·spell·ing** To spell incorrectly.

mis·spell·ing (mis·spel′ing) *n.* An incorrect spelling.

mis·spend (mis·spend′) *v.t.* **·spent**, **·spend·ing** To spend wastefully or wrongly.

mis·state (mis·stāt′) *v.t.* **·stat·ed**, **·stat·ing** To state wrongly or falsely. —**mis·state′ment** *n.*

mis·step (mis·step′) *n.* 1 A false or wrong step. 2 An error in conduct; blunder.

mis·sus (mis′əz) *n. Informal* Wife: used with *the*. Also **mis′sis.** [Alter. of MISTRESS]

mist (mist) *n.* 1 An aggregation of fine drops of water in the atmosphere, similar to but less dense than fog. 2 Any suspension or cloud of small particles, as of dust. 3 Anything that dims or obscures, esp. a watery film before one's eyes. —*v.i.* 1 To be or become dim or misty; blur. 2 To rain in very fine drops. —*v.t.* 3 To make dim or misty; blur. [< OE]

mis·tak·a·ble (mis·tāk′ə·bəl) *adj.* Capable of being misunderstood or mistaken. —**mis·tak′a·bly** *adv.*

mis·take (mis·tāk′) *n.* An error in action, judgment, perception, impression, etc. —*v. ·took, ·tak·en, ·tak·ing v.t.* 1 To understand wrongly; misinterpret. 2 To take (a person or thing) to be another. —*v.i.* 3 To make a mistake. [< ON *mis-* wrongly + *taka* take]

mis·tak·en (mis·tā′kən) *adj.* 1 Incorrect; wrong; erroneous: a *mistaken* idea. 2 Wrong in opinion, judgment, understanding, etc.: You are *mistaken.* —**mis·tak′en·ly** *adv.*

mis·ter (mis′tər) *n. Informal* Sir: used without the name. [Var. of MASTER]

Mis·ter (mis′tər) *n.* Master: a title of address prefixed to the name and to some official titles of a man: commonly written *Mr.: Mr.* Darwin; *Mr.* Chairman.

mis·tle·toe (mis′əl·tō) *n.* 1 An evergreen shrub with yellowish green leaves and poisonous white berries, parasitic on various trees. 2 A sprig of this hung as a Christmas decoration. [< OE *misteltān* mistletoe twig]

mis·took (mis·tōōk′) *p.t.* of MISTAKE.

mis·tral (mis′trəl, *Fr.* mēs·tràl′) *n.* A cold, dry, and violent NW wind blowing mostly through the s provinces of France. [F, lit., master (wind)]

Mistletoe

mis·treat (mis·trēt′) *v.t.* To treat badly or unkindly; abuse. —**mis·treat′ment** *n.*

mis·tress (mis′tris) *n.* 1 A woman in authority or control, as: **a** The head of a household, institution, or estate. **b** An employer or supervisor of servants. **c** An animal owner. 2 *Chiefly Brit.* A female schoolteacher. 3 A woman with whom a man has an unlawful but usu. a long-lasting sexual relationship. 4 *Often cap.* Something having supremacy or power and personified as feminine. 5 A woman who is well skilled in or has mastered anything. [< OF *maistre* master]

Mis·tress (mis′tris) *n.* A title of address formerly applied to women, now generally supplanted by *Mrs.* or *Miss.*

mis·tri·al (mis·trī′əl) *n. Law* A trial that is void because of legal errors or because the jury cannot agree on a verdict.

mis·trust (mis·trust′) *n.* Lack of trust or confidence. —*v.t. & v.i.* To regard (someone or something) with suspicion or doubt. —**mis·trust′ful** *adj.* —**mis·trust′ful·ly** *adv.* —**mis·trust′·ful·ness** *n.* —**Syn.** *v.* distrust, suspect, doubt, disbelieve.

mist·y (mis'tē) *adj.* **mist·i·er, mist·i·est** 1 Containing, characterized by, or like mist. 2 Dimmed or obscured by or as by mist. 3 Lacking clarity; indistinct; vague. —**mist'i·ly** *adv.* —**mist'i·ness** *n.*

mis·un·der·stand (mis'un·dər·stand', mis·un'-) *v.t. & v.i.* **·stood, ·stand·ing** To understand wrongly; misinterpret.

mis·un·der·stand·ing (mis'un·dər·stan'ding, mis·un'-) *n.* 1 A mistake as to meaning or motive. 2 A quarrel; disagreement.

mis·un·der·stood (mis'un·dər·stood', mis·un'-) *adj.* 1 Wrongly understood or interpreted. 2 Not appreciated at true worth.

mis·us·age (mis·yōō'sij, -zij) *n.* 1 Wrong or improper use, as of a word. 2 Ill-treatment; abuse.

mis·use (mis·yōōs') *n.* 1 Wrong or improper use; misapplication. 2 Ill-treatment; abuse. —*v.t.* (mis·yōōz') **·used, ·us·ing** 1 To use or apply wrongly or improperly. 2 To abuse; maltreat. —**mis·us'er** *n.*

mis·val·ue (mis·val'yōō) *v.t.* **·ued, ·u·ing** To value wrongly.

mite[1] (mīt) *n.* Any of various minute arachnids including forms that are parasitic on man or on specific animals or plants. [< OE *mīte*] — **mit'y** *adj.*

mite[2] (mīt) *n.* 1 Any very small amount, particle, or creature. 2 Any very small coin or sum of money. [< MDu. *mīte*]

mi·ter (mī'tər) *n.* 1 A tall, ornamental headdress terminating in two peaks, worn by popes, archbishops, bishops, and abbots. 2 The office or rank of a bishop. 3 **MITER JOINT.** 4 Either of the two beveled angles forming a miter joint. —*v.t.* 1 To confer a miter upon; raise to the rank of bishop. 2 To make or join with a miter joint. [< Gk. *mitra* belt, turban] —**mi'ter·er** *n.*

Mite

miter joint A joint made by the joining together of two pieces of material beveled at angles, as at the corner of a picture frame.

mit·i·gate (mit'ə·gāt) *v.t. & v.i.* **·gat·ed, ·gat·ing** To make or become milder or less severe; moderate. [< L *mitis* mild + *agere* do, drive] —**mit'i·ga'tion, mit'i·ga'tor** *n.* — **mit'i·ga·tive, mit'i·ga·to·ry** (-gə·tôr'ē, -tō'rē) *adj.*

mi·to·sis (mī·tō'sis) *n.* The type of cell division occurring in somatic cells, in which the chromosomes duplicate themselves longitudinally and then separate, so that each daughter cell has the same number and kind of chromosomes as the original cell. [< Gk. *mitos* thread + -OSIS] — **mi·tot·ic** (mī·tot'ik) *adj.* —**mi·tot'i·cal·ly** *adv.*

Miter *def. 1*

mi·tral (mī'trəl) *adj.* 1 Pertaining to or like a miter. 2 Of or pertaining to the mitral valve.

mitral valve *Anat.* A membranous valve between the left atrium and the left ventricle of the heart that functions to prevent the backflow of blood into the atrium.

mi·tre (mī'tər) *n. & v.* **·tred, ·tring** MITER.

mitt (mit) *n.* 1 A woman's glove that does not extend over the fingers. 2 In baseball, a padded glove used by the catcher and the first baseman. 3 MITTEN (def. 1). 4 *pl. Slang* The hands. 5 *Slang* A boxing glove.

mit·ten (mit'n) *n.* 1 A covering for the hand, encasing the four fingers together and the thumb separately. 2 MITT (def. 1). [< MF *mitaine*]

mix (miks) *v.* **mixed** or **mixt, mix·ing** *v.t.* 1 To put together in one mass or composite; blend. 2 To make by combining ingredients: to *mix* dough. 3 To combine or join: to *mix* business with pleasure. 4 To cause to associate or mingle: to *mix* social classes together. 5 HYBRIDIZE. —*v.i.* 6 To be mixed or blended. 7 To associate; get along. 8 To take part; become involved. —**mix up** 1 To blend thoroughly. 2 To confuse. 3 To implicate or involve. —*n.* 1 The act of mixing. 2 A mixture, esp. a commercial mixture of prepared ingredients: a cake *mix*. 3 A beverage, as soda or ginger ale, used in mixed drinks. 4 *Telecom.* The correct blending of two or more input signals into a composite signal. 5 A proportion, as of things that make up a mixture: evaluating the *mix* of black and white students in the city schools. 6 A combination of various elements; mixture: a movie providing a heady *mix* of violence, sex, and glamour. [< L *mixtus,* pp. of *miscere* mix]

mixed (mikst) *adj.* 1 Mingled or blended in a single mass. 2 Made up of different or incongruous elements, races, religions, qualities, etc. 3 Containing persons of both sexes: a *mixed* foursome.

mixed bag A mixture or assortment of miscellaneous elements.

mixed marriage Marriage between persons of different religions or races.

mixed number A number, as 3½, which is the sum of an integer and a fraction.

mixed-up (mikst'up') *adj.* Confused or disordered.

mix·er (mik'sər) *n.* 1 One who or that which mixes. 2 *Informal* A person with reference to his ability to get along well in various groups. 3 *Informal* A party for getting acquainted with others.

mix·ture (miks'chər) *n.* 1 The act of mixing or the condition of being mixed. 2 Anything made or resulting from mixing things of different qualities, kinds, or types: a tea *mixture.* 3 *Chem.* A substance containing in variable proportions two or more ingredients which retain their individual properties and which may be separated without chemical change.

mix-up (miks'up') *n.* 1 A confusion; muddle. 2 *Informal* A fight.

miz·zen (miz'ən) *n. Naut.* 1 MIZZENMAST. 2 A triangular sail set on the mizzenmast. —*adj.* Of or pertaining to the mizzenmast. Also **miz'en.** [< Ital. *mezzano* middle]

miz·zen·mast (miz'ən·məst, -mast', -mäst') *n. Naut.* 1 The mast aft or next aft of the mainmast. 2 The shorter of the two masts of a ketch or yawl.

mks, m.k.s., M.K.S. meter-kilogram-second (system).

mkt. market.

ML, ML., M.L. Medieval (or Middle) Latin.

ml, ml. milliliter(s).

MLG, MLG., M.L.G. Middle Low German.

Mlle, Mlle. Mademoiselle.

Mlles, Mlles. Mesdemoiselles.

MM. Messieurs.

mm, mm. millimeter(s).

Mme, Mme. Madame.

Mmes, Mmes. Mesdames.

MN Minnesota (P.O. abbr.).

Mn manganese.

mne·mon·ic (ni·mon'ik) *adj.* Pertaining to, aiding, or designed to aid the memory. Also **mne·mon'i·cal.** [< Gk. *mnēmōn* mindful]

mne·mon·ics (ni·mon'iks) *n. pl. (construed as sing.)* The science of or the techniques used in memory improvement.

-mo *suffix Printing* Folded into a (specified) number of leaves: said of a sheet of paper: 12*mo* or *duodecimo.* [L]

MO Missouri (P.O. abbr.).

M.O. mail order; Medical Officer; money order.

Mo molybdenum.

Mo. Missouri; Monday.

mo. month(s); monthly.

mo·a (mō'ə) *n.* Any of various extinct, ostrichlike birds of New Zealand. [< native name]

Mo·ab (mō'ab) *n.* An ancient country in the upland area east of the Dead Sea. —**Mo·ab·ite** (mō'əb·īt) *adj., n.*

moan (mōn) *n.* 1 A low mournful sound indicative of grief or pain. 2 A similar sound. —*v.i.* 1 To utter moans of grief or pain. 2 To make a low, mournful sound, as wind in trees. —*v.t.* 3 To lament; bewail. 4 To say with a moan. [ME *mone*]

moat (mōt) *n.* A deep, broad ditch, usu. filled with water, at the outside base of a fortress wall or castle. —*v.t.* To surround with or as with a moat. [< OF *mote* embankment]

mob (mob) *n.* 1 A disorderly or lawless crowd. 2 Any large crowd. 3 The lowest class of people; the masses; populace. 4 *Slang* A gang, as of criminals. —*v.t.* mobbed, mob·bing 1 To attack in a mob. 2 To crowd around and annoy. 3 To crowd into, as a hall. [<L *mobile (vulgus)* movable (crowd)] — mob′ber *n.* —mob′bish *adj.* —mob′bish·ly *adv.*

mo·bile (mō′bəl, -bēl) *adj.* 1 Characterized by freedom of movement; movable. 2 Flowing freely. 3 Changing easily or quickly, as in expression, mood, etc. 4 Easily adaptable; versatile: a *mobile* intelligence. 5 Having or permitting movement or change in social status: a *mobile* society. 6 Designating a mobile. —*n.* (mō′bēl) A form of sculpture having freely moving parts, usu. suspended from rods, wires, etc. [<L *mobilis* movable] —mo·bil·i·ty (mō·bil′ə·tē) *n.*

mobile home *U.S.* A movable living unit, originally conceived of as a trailer but now designed more like a ranch house, which can be connected to utilities and is often put on a foundation as a permanent dwelling.

mo·bi·lize (mō′bə·līz) *v.* ·lized, ·liz·ing *v.t.* 1 To make ready for war, as an army, industry, etc. 2 To assemble for use; organize. 3 To put into circulation, movement, or use. —*v.i.* 4 To undergo mobilization. *Brit. sp.* mo′bi·lise. —mo′· bi·li·za′tion (-lə·zā′shən, -lī·zā′-) *n.*

mob·ster (mob′stər) *n. Slang* A gangster.

moc·ca·sin (mok′ə·sin) *n.* 1 A heelless foot covering made of soft leather or buckskin, formerly worn by North American Indians. 2 A shoe or slipper somewhat like a moccasin. 3 COTTONMOUTH. [<Algon.]

moccasin flower LADYSLIPPER.

mo·cha (mō′kə) *n.* 1 Any choice coffee, esp. one originally grown in Mocha, Arabia. 2 A coffee or coffee and chocolate flavoring. 3 A fine sheepskin leather used for making gloves.

mock (mok) *v.t.* 1 To treat or address scornfully or derisively; hold up to ridicule. 2 To ridicule by imitation; mimic derisively. 3 To deceive; delude. 4 To defy; make futile. 5 To imitate; counterfeit. —*v.i.* 6 To express or show ridicule, scorn, or contempt; scoff. —*adj.* Imitation; sham. —*n.* 1 An act of mocking; a jeer. 2 One who or that which is mocked. 3 An imitation; counterfeit. [<OF *mocquer*] — mock′er *n.* —mock′ing·ly *adv.*

mock·er·y (mok′ər·ē) *n. pl.* ·er·ies 1 Derisive or contemptuous action or speech. 2 A person or thing laughed at or derided. 3 A deceitful or contemptible imitation: a *mockery* of justice. 4 Something ridiculously inappropriate or inadequate.

mock-he·ro·ic (mok′hi·rō′ik) *adj.* Imitating or satirizing the heroic manner, style, attitude, or character.

mock·ing·bird (mok′ing·bûrd′) *n.* A long-tailed, gray songbird common in the SE U.S., noted for imitating the songs of other birds.

mock orange Any of a genus of hardy, deciduous shrubs with fragrant white flowers resembling orange blossoms.

mock-tur·tle soup (mok′tûr′· təl) Soup prepared from calf's head or other meat, and flavored to resemble green turtle soup.

mock·up (mok′up′) *n.* A model, usu. full-scale, as of a structure, machine, or apparatus, for purposes of study, testing, etc.

Mockingbird

mod (mod) *adj.* Bold, flamboyant, and unconventional, as in dress or behavior. —*n. Sometimes cap.* One who dresses or behaves in a flamboyant or unconventional manner. [<MODERN]

mod. moderate; moderato; modern.

mo·dal (mōd′l) *adj.* Of or denoting a mode, esp. a mode of grammar, a mode in music, or a statistical mode. — mo·dal′i·ty (-dal′ə·tē) *n.* —mo′dal·ly *adv.*

modal auxiliary An auxiliary verb used with and indicating the mood of a principal verb. Modal auxiliaries are *may, might, must, can, would,* and *should.*

mode (mōd) *n.* 1 Manner, way, or method of acting, being, doing, etc. 2 Prevailing style or fashion of dress, behavior, etc. 3 *Gram.* MOOD. 4 *Music* Any of the seven possible permutations of the tones of a major scale in which the

original order is preserved. 5 *Stat.* That value, magnitude, or score which occurs the greatest number of times in a given series of observations; norm. [<L *modus* measure, manner]

mod·el (mod′l) *n.* 1 An object, usu. in miniature, representing accurately something already existing, or something to be made or tested. 2 One who or that which serves as an example or pattern of excellence. 3 A person who poses for painters, sculptors, etc. 4 A person employed to wear articles of clothing to display them. 5 A type, style, or design. 6 An analogue or analogy: a mathematical *model* of an atom. —*v.* ·eled or ·elled, ·el·ing or ·el·ling *v.t.* 1 To plan or fashion after a model or pattern. 2 To make a model of. 3 To fashion; make. 4 To display by wearing, as an article of clothing. —*v.i.* 5 To make a model or models. 6 To pose or serve as a model (defs. 3 and 4). 7 To assume the appearance of natural form. —*adj.* 1 Serving or used as a model. 2 Worthy or suitable to be used as a model. [<L *modus* measure, manner] —mod′el·er, mod′el·ler *n.*

mo·dem (mō′dem) *n.* An electronic device that converts computer digital signals to analog form, and vice versa, so that information can be sent and received by telephone.

mod·er·ate (mod′ər·it) *adj.* 1 Keeping or kept within reasonable limits; not extreme. 2 Not strongly partisan, radical, or excessive: said of political, social, or religious beliefs or those holding such beliefs. 3 Mild; temperate: a *moderate* climate. 4 Medium or average, as in quality, extent, effect, etc. —*n.* A person of moderate views, opinions, or practices. —*v.* (mod′ə·rāt) ·at·ed, ·at·ing *v.t.* 1 To reduce the violence, severity, etc., of; make less extreme; restrain. 2 To preside over. —*v.i.* 3 To become less intense or violent; abate. 4 To act as moderator. [<L *moderare* regulate] — mod′er·ate·ly *adv.* —mod′er·ate·ness *n.*

mod·er·a·tion (mod′ə·rā′shən) *n.* 1 The quality or state of being moderate. 2 The act of moderating. —in moderation Within reasonable limits.

mod·e·ra·to (mod′ə·rä′tō) *adj. & adv. Music* In moderate time; moderately. [Ital.]

mod·er·a·tor (mod′ə·rā′tər) *n.* 1 One who or that which moderates. 2 One who presides over a meeting, debate, etc. 3 *Physics* A substance, as heavy water or graphite, that slows down neutrons in a nuclear reactor.

mod·ern (mod′ərn) *adj.* 1 Of, pertaining to, or characteristic of the present or most recent past; contemporary. 2 *Usu. cap.* Of, pertaining to, or characteristic of the present or most recent development of a language: *Modern* English. 3 Up-to-date: the most *modern* equipment. —*n.* 1 A person living in modern times or having modern views, characteristics, etc. 2 *Printing* A style of typeface characterized by contrasting heavy downstrokes and thin crossstrokes. [<LL *modernus* recent <L *modo* just now]

Modern English The English language after 1500.

Modern Greek The language of Greece since 1500.

mod·ern·ism (mod′ərn·iz′əm) *n.* 1 A practice, idiom, thought or behavior pattern, art form, etc., characteristic of modern times. 2 *Often cap.* The tendency in religious thought to reinterpret certain theological beliefs and teachings so as to be consistent with new scientific and philosophical learning. —mod′ern·ist *adj., n.* —mod′ern·is′·tic *adj.* —mod′ern·is′ti·cal·ly *adv.*

mo·der·ni·ty (mə·dûr′nə·tē) *n. pl.* ·ties 1 The quality or condition of being modern. 2 Something modern.

mod·ern·ize (mod′ərn·īz) *v.t. & v.i.* ·ized, ·iz·ing To make or become modern in ideas, standards, methods, etc. — mod′ern·i·za′tion, mod′ern·iz′er *n.*

mod·est (mod′ist) *adj.* 1 Having a moderate or unpretentious opinion of one's worth, ability, etc. 2 Characterized by reserve, propriety, or purity in dress, actions, speech, etc. 3 Not excessive; moderate; limited: a *modest* income. [<L *modestus* moderate] —mod′est·ly *adv.*

mod·es·ty (mod′is·tē) *n.* 1 Freedom from vanity. 2 Propriety and decorum, as in dress or behavior. 3 Moderation.

mod·i·cum (mod′i·kəm) *n. pl.* ·cums or ·ca (-kə) A moderate or small amount. [<L *modus* measure] —Syn. bit, little, minimum, smidgen.

mod·i·fi·ca·tion (mod′ə·fə·kā′shən) *n.* 1 The act of modifying, or the state of being modified. 2 A qualification, as in meaning. 3 A slight change or improvement, as in form or function. 4 A reduction or moderation.

mod·i·fi·er (mod′ə·fī′ər) *n.* 1 One who or that which modifies. 2 *Gram.* A word, phrase, or clause that modifies another word or group of words.

mod·i·fy (mod′ə·fī) *v.* **·fied, ·fy·ing** *v.t.* 1 To make somewhat different in form, character, etc.; vary. 2 To reduce in degree or extent; moderate. 3 *Gram.* To qualify the meaning of; restrict; limit. —*v.i.* 4 To be or become modified; change. [< L *modus* measure + *facere* make]

mod·ish (mō′dish) *adj.* In the current mode or style. —**mod′ish·ly** *adv.* —**mod′ish·ness** *n.* —Syn. fashionable, stylish, à la mode.

mo·diste (mō·dēst′) *n.* A woman who makes or deals in fashionable women's clothing. [F]

Mod. L. Modern Latin.

mod·u·late (moj′ŏŏ·lāt) *v.* **·lat·ed, ·lat·ing** *v.t.* 1 To vary the tone, inflection, or pitch of. 2 To regulate or adjust. 3 *Music* To change or cause to change to a different key. 4 To intone or sing. 5 *Electronics* To vary a parameter, as frequency or amplitude of (a carrier wave). —*v.i.* 6 *Electronics* To alter a parameter of a carrier wave. 7 *Music* To make a transition from one key to another. [< L *modulari* regulate] —**mod·u·la·to·ry** (-lə·tôr′ē, -tō′rē) *adj.*

mod·u·la·tion (moj′ŏŏ·lā′shən) *n.* 1 The act of modulating, or the state of being modulated. 2 A change in pitch or stress in the voice. 3 *Music* A transition from one key to another. 4 *Telecom.* **a** The changing of one or more of the parameters of a carrier wave. **b** The information transmitted by the carrier wave as a result of this.

mod·u·la·tor (moj′ŏŏ·lā′tər) *n.* One who or that which modulates.

mod·ule (moj′ŏŏl) *n.* 1 A standard or unit of measurement. 2 *Archit.* A unit of measure, usu. the size of a single part of a construction, by which the proportions of the whole are determined. 3 A standard structural component repeatedly used, as in a building, computer, etc.: cubic *modules* used in the design of a table. 4 A preassembled, self-contained unit, usu. a component or subassembly of a larger structure: a housing *module;* a lunar *module.* [< L *modulus* < *modus* measure] —**mod′u·lar** *adj.*

mo·dus op·er·an·di (mō′dəs op′ə·ran′dē, -dī) A manner of operation or procedure. [L]

modus vi·ven·di (vi·ven′dē, -dī) 1 A manner of living. 2 A temporary arrangement pending a final settlement. [L]

mo·gul (mō′gul, mō·gul′) *n.* Any great or pretentious personage. —Syn. magnate, bigwig, big wheel, personage.

Mo·gul (mō′gul, mō·gul′) *n.* A Mongol; Mongolian; esp. one of the Mongol conquerors of Hindustan. Also **Mo·ghul′.**

mo·hair (mō′hâr) *n.* 1 The hair of the Angora goat. 2 A fabric made of mohair pile with a cotton or wool backing. [< Ar. *mukhayyar*]

Mo·ham·me·dan (mō·ham′ə·dən) *adj.* Of or pertaining to Mohammed or to his religion and institutions. —*n.* A follower of Mohammed or believer in Islam; a Muslim.

Mo·ham·me·dan·ism (mō·ham′ə·dən·iz′əm) *n.* The religion founded by Mohammed; Islam.

Mo·ha·ve (mō·hä′vē) *n.* A member of a tribe of North American Indians formerly living along the Colorado River. —*adj.* Of or pertaining to this tribe.

Mo·hawk (mō′hôk) *n.* 1 One of a tribe of North American Indians of Iroquoian stock, formerly ranging from the Mohawk River to the St. Lawrence. 2 The Iroquoian language of this tribe.

Mo·he·gan (mō·hē′gən) *n.* 1 One of a tribe of North American Indians of Algonquian linguistic stock, formerly living in Connecticut. 2 MAHICAN.

Mo·hi·can (mō·hē′kən) *n.* MAHICAN.

moi·dore (moi′dôr, -dōr) *n.* A former Portuguese or Brazilian gold coin.

moi·e·ty (moi′ə·tē) *n. pl.* **·ties** 1 A half. 2 An indefinite portion. [< L *medius* half]

moil (moil) *v.i.* To work hard; toil; drudge. —*n.* 1 Confusion; trouble. 2 Toil; drudgery. [< L *mollis* soft] —**moil′er** *n.* —**moil′ing·ly** *adv.*

moi·ré (mwä·rā′) *adj.* Having a wavelike or watered appearance, as certain fabrics. —*n.* 1 A fabric, as silk or rayon, having a wavy or watered pattern produced by engraved cylinders: also **moire** (mwär). 2 The wavy pattern. [F]

moist (moist) *adj.* 1 Having slight wetness; damp. 2 Tearful: *moist* eyes. [< OF *moiste*] —**moist′ly** *adv.* —**moist′ness** *n.*

mois·ten (mois′ən) *v.t. & v.i.* To make or become moist. —**mois′ten·er** *n.*

mois·ture (mois′chər) *n.* A small amount of liquid exuding from, diffused through, or resting on a substance; dampness. —**mois′tur·ize** *v.t.* (**·ized, ·iz·ing**)

mol (mōl) *n.* MOLE⁴.

mo·lar (mō′lər) *n.* A grinding tooth with flattened crown, situated behind the canine and incisor teeth. —*adj.* 1 Grinding, or adapted for grinding. 2 Pertaining to a molar. [< L *mola* mill] • See TOOTH.

mo·las·ses (mə·las′iz) *n.* A thick, dark-colored syrup drained from raw sugar during the refining process. [< L *mellaceus* honeylike]

mold¹ (mōld) *n.* 1 A hollow form or matrix for shaping anything that is in a fluid or plastic condition. 2 A frame on or around which something is made or shaped. 3 That which is made or shaped in or on a mold. 4 The form or shape given by a mold. 5 General form or shape. 6 Distinctive character or type. —*v.t.* 1 To work into a particular shape or form; model. 2 To shape or cast in, as in, or on a mold. 3 To influence or direct: to *mold* another's opinions. 4 In founding, to form a mold of or from. 5 To ornament with molding. [< L *modulus,* dim. of *modus* measure, limit] —**mold′er** *n.*

mold² (mōld) *n.* 1 Any of various fungous growths usu. forming a furry coating on decaying food or in moist, warm places. 2 Any fungus producing such growths. —*v.t. & v.i.* To become or cause to become moldy. [Prob. < Scand.]

mold³ (mōld) *n.* Earth that is fine and soft, and rich in organic matter. —*v.t.* To cover with mold. [< OE *molde* earth]

mold·board (mōld′bôrd′, -bōrd′) *n.* The curved metal plate of a plow, by which the earth is turned over and pulverized. [< MOLD³ + BOARD]

mold·er (mōl′dər) *v.i.* To decay gradually and turn to dust. [Prob. < Scand.]

mold·ing (mōl′ding) *n.* 1 The act of shaping with or as with a mold. 2 Anything molded. 3 *Archit.* **a** A more or less ornamental strip, as around doors, windows, ceilings, etc. **b** A cornice or other projecting decorative member on a surface or angle of any part of a building.

mold·y (mōl′dē) *adj.* **mold·i·er, mold·i·est** 1 Covered with mold. 2 Musty, as from age, neglect, etc. —**mold′i·ness** *n.*

mole¹ (mōl) *n.* A small permanent spot on the skin, usu. elevated slightly and pigmented. [< OE *māl*]

mole² (mōl) *n.* Any of a family of small, insectivorous mammals with velvety fur, tiny eyes, and broad forefeet adapted for tunneling underground. [< MLG *molle*]

mole³ (mōl) *n.* A jetty or breakwater partially enclosing an anchorage or harbor. [< L *moles* great mass]

Mole

mole⁴ (mōl) *n.* That number of grams of a substance that is equal to its molecular weight; a gram molecule. [Short for MOLECULAR WEIGHT.]

Mo·lech (mō′lek) MOLOCH.

mo·lec·u·lar (mə·lek′yə·lər) *adj.* Of, effected by, or consisting of molecules.

molecular weight The sum of the atomic weights of all the constituent atoms of a molecule.

mol·e·cule (mol′ə·kyōōl) *n.* 1 The smallest particle of an element or compound having all the properties of the element or compound. 2 Any small particle. [< NL *molecula,* dim. of L *moles* mass]

mole·hill (mōl′hil′) *n.* A small heap or ridge of earth raised by a burrowing mole.

mole·skin (mōl′skin′) n. 1 The soft skin of a mole, used as fur. 2 A heavy, twill fabric, usu. cotton, having a thick, soft nap on one side. 3 *Usu. pl.* Garments made of this fabric.

mo·lest (mə·lest′) v.t. 1 To annoy or disturb. 2 To accost or interfere with sexually. [<L *molestus* troublesome] — **mo·les·ta·tion** (mō′les·tā′shən, mol′es-), **mo·lest′er** n.

moll (mol) n. *Slang* 1 A gangster's girl friend. 2 A prostitute. [<*Molly*, dim. of *Mary*]

mol·li·fy (mol′ə·fī) v.t. **·fied**, **·fy·ing** 1 To make less angry. 2 To reduce the violence or intensity of. [<L *mollis* soft + *facere* make] —**mol′li·fi·ca′tion, mol′li·fi′er** n. —**mol′li·fy′ing·ly** adv. —**Syn.** 1 soothe, pacify, appease, conciliate. 2 mitigate, ease, temper, allay.

mol·lusk (mol′əsk) n. Any of a large phylum of unsegmented, soft-bodied invertebrates, usu. having gills and a mantle which secretes a calcareous shell, and including snails, oysters, cuttlefish, slugs, octopuses, etc. Also **mol′·lusc.** [<L *molluscus (nux)* soft, thin-shelled (nut)]

mol·ly·cod·dle (mol′ē·kod′l) n. 1 Any excessively pampered or protected person. 2 An effeminate man or body. — v.t. **·dled**, **·dling** To pamper; coddle. [<*Molly*, dim. of *Mary* + CODDLE] —**mol′ly·cod′dler** n.

Mo·loch (mō′lok) In the Bible, a god of the Ammonites and Phoenicians to whom human sacrifices were offered. —n. Any system or principle involving merciless sacrifice.

molt (mōlt) v.t. & v.i. to cast off or shed (feathers, horns, outer skin, etc.) in preparation for replacement by new growth. —n. 1 The molting process or season. 2 That which is molted. [<L *mutare* to change] —**molt′er** n.

mol·ten (mōl′tən) *Archaic p.p.* of MELT. —adj. 1 Reduced to fluid by heat; melted. 2 Made by being melted and then cast in a mold.

mol·to (mōl′tō) adv. *Music* Much; very: *molto adagio*. [Ital. <L *multum* much]

mo·lyb·de·num (mə·lib′də·nəm) n. A hard, heavy, silver-white, metallic element (symbol Mo) having properties similar to tungsten, used in electrical equipment and hard steel alloys. [<Gk. *molybdos* lead]

mom (mom) n. *Informal* Mother.

mo·ment (mō′mənt) n. 1 A very short period of time; an instant. 2 A definite point in time, esp. the present time. 3 Consequence or importance: something of little *moment*. 4 A time of excellence, accomplishment, enjoyment, etc.: She has her *moments*. 5 *Physics* a The product of a quantity and its distance to some significant related point: *moment* of inertia. b The measure of a force about a given point or axis; torque. [<L *momentum* movement]

mo·men·tar·i·ly (mō′mən·ter′ə·lē) adv. 1 For a moment. 2 From moment to moment. 3 At any moment.

mo·men·tar·y (mō′mən·ter′ē) adj. Lasting but a moment. —**mo′men·tar′i·ness** n.

mo·men·tous (mō·men′təs) adj. Of great importance. — **mo·men′tous·ly** adv. —**mo·men′tous·ness** n. —**Syn.** weighty, serious, outstanding, memorable.

mo·men·tum (mō·men′təm) n. pl. **·ta** (-tə) or **·tums** 1 *Physics* a The quantity of motion in a body as measured by the product of its mass and velocity. b A similar quantity defined with respect to angular motion. 2 Any forward or ongoing motion; impetus. [L, movement]

Mon. Monday; Monseigneur.

Mon·a·co (mon′ə·kō, mə·nä′kō) n. An independent principality on the SE coast of France, 368 acres.

mon·ad (mon′ad, mō′nad) n. 1 An indestructible unit. 2 *Biol.* Any single-celled organism. 3 *Chem.* A univalent atom, radical, or element. —adj. Of, pertaining to, or consisting of a monad. [<Gk. *monas* a unit]

mon·arch (mon′ärk) n. 1 A hereditary constitutional sovereign, as a king, queen, etc. 2 One who or that which surpasses others of the same kind. 3 A large butterfly with orange-brown, black-veined wings whose larvae feed on milkweed. [<Gk. *monos* alone + *archein* rule] —**mo·nar′chal** (mə·när′kəl) adj. —**mo·nar′chal·ly** adv.

mo·nar·chi·cal (mə·när′ki·kəl) adj. Pertaining to, governed by, or favoring a monarch or monarchy. Also **mo·nar′chic, mo·nar′chic.** —**mo·nar′chi·cal·ly** adv.

mon·arch·ism (mon′ärk·iz′əm) n. 1 The government or principles of a monarchy. 2 The advocacy of a monarchy. —**mon′arch·ist** adj., n. —**mon′arch·is′tic** adj.

mon·ar·chy (mon′ər·kē) n. pl. **·chies** 1 Government by a monarch; sovereign control. 2 A government or territory ruled by a monarch.

mon·as·ter·y (mon′əs·ter′ē) n. pl. **·ter·ies** 1 A dwelling place occupied by monks, living under religious vows. 2 The monks living in such a place. [<Gk. *monastēs* a monk <*monazein* be alone]

mo·nas·tic (mə·nas′tik) adj. 1 Of, pertaining to, or like a monastery or the people who live there. 2 Ascetic. Also **mon·as·te·ri·al** (mon′əs·tir′ē·əl), **mo·nas′ti·cal.** —n. A monk or other religious recluse. —**mo·nas′ti·cal·ly** adv.

mo·nas·ti·cism (mə·nas′tə·siz′əm) n. 1 The monastic life or system. 2 Asceticism.

mon·a·tom·ic (mon′ə·tom′ik) adj. *Chem.* 1 Consisting of a single atom, as the molecules of certain elements. 2 Containing one replaceable or reactive atom. 3 UNIVALENT.

mon·au·ral (män·ôr′əl) adj. 1 Pertaining to the perception of sound by one ear only. 2 Designating the transmission or reproduction of sound through a single channel. [<MON(O)- + AURAL]

Mon·day (mun′dē, -dā) n. The second day of the week. [<OE *mōnandæg* day of the moon]

monde (mônd) n. *French* The world; society.

mo·ne·cious (mə·nē′shəs, mō-) adj. MONOECIOUS.

Mo·nel metal (mō·nel′) A corrosion-resistant alloy of nickel, copper, and iron: a trade name.

mo·ner·an (mə·nir′ən) n. A living organism of the kingdom *Monera*, lacking a cell nucleus, including bacteria and some forms of algae. [<Gk. *monos* alone]

mon·e·tar·y (mon′ə·ter′ē, mun′-) adj. 1 Of or pertaining to currency or coinage. 2 Of or pertaining to money. [<L *moneta* mint] —**mon′e·tar′i·ly** adv.

mon·e·tize (mon′ə·tīz, mun′-) v.t. **·tized**, **·tiz·ing** 1 To legalize as money. 2 To coin into money. [<L *moneta* mint, money] —**mon′e·ti·za′tion** n.

mon·ey (mun′ē) n. pl. **mon·eys** or **mon·ies** 1 Anything that serves as a common medium of exchange, a measure of value, or as a means for the payment of debts or services rendered, esp. coins and paper currency officially issued by a government. 2 A specific form or denomination of coin or paper currency. 3 MONEY OF ACCOUNT. 4 Assets having monetary value. 5 Profit or pecuniary gain: to make *money*. 6 Wealth: That town has *money*. [<L *moneta* money, mint]

mon·ey·bag (mun′ē·bag′) n. 1 A bag for holding money. 2 pl. *Slang* A rich person; also, wealth.

mon·ey·chang·er (mun′ē·chān′jər) n. 1 A person who exchanges different kinds or denominations of money at a prescribed rate. 2 A device for holding and dispensing coins.

mon·eyed (mun′ēd) adj. 1 Possessed of money. 2 Consisting of or representing money: *moneyed* interests. —**Syn.** 1 wealthy, well-off, well-to-do, flush.

mon·ey-mak·ing (mun′ē·mā′king) adj. Likely to bring in money; profitable. —n. The acquisition of money or wealth. —**mon′ey-mak′er** n.

money of account A monetary denomination used in keeping accounts, but usu. not represented by a coin, as the mill.

money order An order for the payment of a specified sum of money, esp. such an order issued at a post office, bank, or telegraph office and payable at another.

mon·ger (mung′gər, mong′-) n. 1 A dealer or trader: chiefly in combination: *fishmonger*. 2 One who engages in or promotes discreditable practices: *scandalmonger; warmonger*. [<OE *mangian* to traffic]

Mon·gol (mong′gəl, -gol, -gōl) n. 1 A member of any of the Mongoloid peoples of Mongolia. 2 The Mongolian language of any of these peoples. 3 Any member of the Mongoloid ethnic group. —adj. 1 MONGOLIAN (def. 1) 2 MONGOLOID (def. 1).

Mon·go·li·an (mong·gō′lē·ən, -gōl′yən, mon-) —adj. 1 Of or pertaining to Mongolia or the Mongolian People's Republic. 2 MONGOLOID (def. 1). —n. 1 A native or citizen of the Mongolian People's Republic. 2 Any one of a group of related languages used in Mongolia or the Mongolian People's Republic. 3 MONGOLOID.

Mongolian People's Republic A republic of CEN.

Asia, 590,966 sq. mi., cap. Ulan Bator. ● See map at CHINA.

Mon·gol·ism (mong′gəl·iz′əm) *n.* DOWN'S SYNDROME.

Mon·go·loid (mong′gə·loid) *adj.* 1 Of or pertaining to one of the major racial groups of mankind, including most of the peoples of N and E Asia, the Eskimos, Malaysians, and some American Indians. 2 Resembling a Mongol or a Mongolian. 3 Of or afflicted with Down's syndrome or Mongolism. —*n.* A member of this racial group.

mon·goose (mong′gōōs, mung′-) *n. pl.* **-goos·es** A small, ferretlike, Old World mammal valued as a predator of rats and snakes, including venomous snakes. [<Marathi (an Indic language) *mangūs*]

mon·grel (mong′grəl, mung′-) *n.* 1 A plant or animal resulting from interbreeding different types or varieties; esp., a dog of mixed breed. 2 Any incongruous mixture. —*adj.* Of mixed breed, origin, character, etc. [<OE *gemang* mixture]

mon·i·ker (mon′ə·kər) *n. Slang* A name, signature, or mark of identification. Also **mon′ick·er.** [?]

mo·nism (mō′niz·əm, mon′iz·əm) *n. Philos.* The doctrine that only one ultimate substance or principle is responsible for the phenomena of the universe. [<Gk. *monos* single + -ISM] —**mo′nist** *n.* —**mo·nis′tic** or **-ti·cal** *adj.* —**mo·nis′ti·cal·ly** *adv.*

mo·ni·tion (mō·nish′ən) *n.* 1 A warning or admonition. 2 A legal or official notice or summons. [<L *monitus,* p.p. of *monere* warn]

mon·i·tor (mon′ə·tər) *n.* 1 A student selected to assist a teacher in various tasks. 2 One who advises or cautions. 3 Something that warns or advises. 4 Formerly, an iron-clad vessel having a low, flat deck with one or more turrets carrying heavy guns. 5 Any of several large carnivorous lizards of Australia, Africa and Asia. 6 *Telecom.* **a** A high-fidelity loudspeaker in the control room of a sound studio, used to check fidelity of reproduction. **b** A receiver for checking the quality of a station's broadcasts. 7 A computer screen; cathode-ray tube; video-display terminal. — *v.t.* 1 *Telecom.* To check (a station, broadcast, etc.) with or as with a monitor. 2 To assist or have charge of (a person or group) as a monitor (def. 1). 3 To keep watch over or check as a means of control: to *monitor* tax returns. [<L *monere* warn] —**mon′i·to′ri·al** *adj.*

mon·i·to·ry (mon′ə·tôr′ē, -tō′rē) *adj.* Conveying a warning; admonitory.

monk (mungk) *n.* 1 A man who is a member of a monastic order and is usu. vowed to poverty, chastity, and obedience. 2 Formerly, a religious hermit. [<Gk. *monos* alone]

mon·key (mung′kē) *n. pl.* **-keys** 1 Any of the primates except lemurs, anthropod apes, and man, as marmosets, baboons, etc. 2 A person likened to a monkey, as a mischievous child. —*v.i. Informal* To play or trifle; meddle: often with *with* or *around with.* [?<MLG *Moneke,* name of an ape in a medieval epic]

monkey business *Slang* Foolish tricks; deceitful or mischievous behavior.

mon·key·shines (mung′kē·shīnz′) *n. pl. Slang* Frolicsome tricks or pranks.

monkey wrench A type of adjustable wrench

Monkey wrench

monks·hood (mungks′hōōd′) *n.* Any of several species of aconite having usu. purple flowers with the upper sepal arched like a hood.

mon·o (mon′ō) *adj.* MONOPHONIC (def. 1) —*n.* MONONUCLEOSIS.

mono- *combining form* Single; one: *monobasic.* Also, before vowels, **mon-.** [<Gk. *monos* single]

mon·o·ba·sic (mon′ə·bā′sik) *adj. Chem.* Possessing a single hydrogen atom replaceable by a metal or positive radical: applied to acids.

mon·o·chro·mat·ic (mon′ə·krō·mat′ik) *adj.* Of a single color or different shades of a single color. — **mon′o·chro·mat′i·cal·ly** *adv.*

mon·o·chrome (mon′ə·krōm) *n.* A painting or drawing in a single color, or different shades of a single color. —*adj.* MONOCHROMATIC. —**mon′o·chro′mic** or **-mi·cal** *adj.*

mon·o·cle (mon′ə·kəl) *n.* An eyeglass for one eye. [<MONO- + L *oculus* eye] —**mon′o·cled** *adj.*

mon·o·cli·nal (mon′ə·klī′nəl) *adj. Geol.* Having an inclination in only one direction, or composed of rock strata so inclined. —**mon·o·cli′nal·ly** *adv.*

mon·o·cline (mon′ə·klīn) *n. Geol.* A stratum or fold of rocks inclined in only one direction. [<MONO- + Gk. *klinein* incline]

mon·o·cli·nous (mon′ə·klī′nəs) *adj. Bot.* Having both stamens and pistils in the same flower. [<MONO- + Gk. *klinē* bed, couch]

mon·o·cot·y·le·don (mon′ə·kot′ə·lēd′n) *n.* Any of a large class of flowering plants having only one cotyledon in the seed, no endosperm, and usu. parallel-veined leaves, as grasses, lilies, etc. Also **mon′o·cot.** —**mon′o·cot′yle′·do·nous** *adj.*

mon·o·dy (mon′ə·dē) *n. pl.* **-dies** 1 An elegy or dirge, esp. a poem on the death of a friend. 2 In Greek tragedy, an ode sung by one voice. 3 *Music* **a** A style in which one vocal part predominates. **b** A composition or passage in such a style. [<Gk. *monos* alone + *aedein* sing] —**mo·nod′ic** (mə·nod′ik), **mo·nod′i·cal** *adj.* —**mo·nod′i·cal·ly** *adv.* — **mon′o·dist** *n.*

mo·noe·cious (mə·nē′shəs) *adj.* Having stamens and pistils in separate blossoms on the same plant. [<MON(o)- + Gk. *oikos* house]

mo·nog·a·my (mə·nog′ə·mē) *n.* 1 The principle or practice of marriage with but one person at a time. 2 *Zool.* The habit of having but one mate. [<Gk. *monos* single + *gamos* marriage] —**mo·nog′a·mous** *adj.* —**mo·nog′a·mist** *n.*

mon·o·gram (mon′ə·gram) *n.* Two or more letters interwoven into one, as the initials of one's name. —*v.t.* **-grammed, -gram·ming** To mark with a monogram. [<Gk. *monos* single + *gramma* letter] —**mon′o·gram·mat′ic** (-grə·mat′ik) *adj.*

mon·o·graph (mon′ə·graf, -gräf) *n.* A book, paper, or treatise written about a single topic, usu. in great detail. —**mo·nog·ra·pher** (mə·nog′rə·fər) *n.* —**mon′o·graph′ic** *adj.*

mon·o·lith (mon′ə·lith) *n.* 1 A single, usu. very large piece or block of stone, often in the shape of an obelisk. 2 Something like a monolith, as in size, structure, aspect, or quality.

mon·o·lith·ic (mon′ə·lith′ik) *adj.* 1 Of or resembling a monolith. 2 Single in character, as a political movement or ideology; marked by uniformity.

mon·o·logue (mon′ə·lôg, -log) *n.* 1 A story or drama told or performed by one person. 2 A lengthy speech by one person, occurring in conversation. 3 A literary composition, or a poem, written as a soliloquy. Also **mon′o·log.** [<Gk. *monos* alone + *logos* discourse] —**mon′o·logu·ist**, **mo·nol·o·gist** (mə·nol′ə·jist) *n.*

mon·o·ma·ni·a (mon′ə·mā′nē·ə, -mān′yə) *n.* 1 A mental disorder characterized by obsession with one idea or subject. 2 An unreasonable interest in or pursuit of something; craze. —**mon′o·ma′ni·ac** *n.*

mon·o·met·al·ism (mon′ō·met′l·iz′əm) *n.* The theory or system of a single metallic standard in coinage. Also **mon′o·met′al·ism.** —**mon′o·met′al·lic** (-ə·tal′ik) *adj.*

mo·no·mi·al (mə·nō′mē·əl) *adj.* Consisting of a single term: a *monomial* expression. —*n. Math.* An expression consisting of a single term. [<MONO- + -*nomial,* as in *binomial*]

mon·o·nu·cle·o·sis (mon′ō·n′yōō′klē·ō′sis) *n.* A disease in which the blood contains an abnormal number of leukocytes with a single nucleus. Also **infectious mononucleosis.** [<MONO- + NUCLE(US) + -OSIS]

mon·o·phon·ic (mon′ə·fon′ik) *adj.* 1 Of, pertaining to, or functioning in the reproduction of sound through a single channel: a *monophonic* recording. 2 *Music* Consisting of a single unaccompanied melody.

mon·o·plane (mon′ə·plān) *n.* An airplane with only one wing on either side of the fuselage.

mo·nop·o·lize (mə·nop′ə·līz) *v.t.* **-lized, -liz·ing** 1 To obtain or exercise a monopoly of. 2 To assume exclusive possession or control of. *Brit. sp.* **mo·nop′o·lise.** —**mo·nop′o·li·za′·tion, mo·nop′o·liz′er** *n.*

mo·nop·o·ly (mə·nop′ə·lē) n. pl. **·lies 1** The exclusive ownership or control of a specific commodity or service. **2** A person, company, etc. having a monopoly. **3** Exclusive possession or control of anything. **4** The commodity or service under the control of a monopoly. **5** *Law* An exclusive license from the government for buying, selling, making, or using anything. [< Gk. *monos* alone + *pōlein* sell] —**mo·nop′o·lism** n. —**mo·nop′o·list** adj., n. —**mo·nop′o·lis′tic** adj.

mon·o·rail (mon′ō·rāl) n. **1** A single rail serving as a track for railway cars. **2** A railway using such a track.

mon·o·so·di·um glu·ta·mate (mon′ə·sōd′ē·əm glōō′tə·māt) A white salt obtained from various vegetable sources and having the property of intensifying the sensation of taste.

mon·o·syl·lab·ic (mon′ə·si·lab′ik) adj. **1** Having only one syllable. **2** Using or speaking in monosyllables. **3** Very brief; terse, as in replying. —**mon′o·syl·lab′i·cal·ly** adv.

Monorail

mon·o·syl·la·ble (mon′ə·sil′ə·bəl, mon′ə·sil′-) n. A word of one syllable.

mon·o·the·ism (mon′ə·thē·iz′əm) n. The doctrine that there is but one God. [< MONO- + Gk. *theos* god + -ISM] —**mon′o·the′ist** n. —**mon′o·the·is′tic** or **·ti·cal** adj. —**mon′o·the·is′ti·cal·ly** adv.

mon·o·tone (mon′ə·tōn) n. **1** Speech that does not vary in tone, pitch, or stress. **2** A sameness or monotony, as in style, color, etc. **3** A single musical tone unvaried in pitch; also, a chant in such a tone.

mo·not·o·nous (mə·not′ə·nəs) adj. **1** Tiresomely uniform or repetitious. **2** Not varied in inflection, cadence, or pitch. [< Gk. *monotonos* having a single tone] —**mo·not′o·nous·ly** adv. —**mo·not′o·nous·ness** n. —**Syn. 1** tedious, dull, dreary.

mo·not·o·ny (mə·not′ə·nē) n. **1** A tiresome or tedious uniformity. **2** Sameness of tone or sound.

mon·o·treme (mon′ə·trēm) n. Any of an order of primitive, egg-laying mammals, including only duckbills and echidnas. [< MONO- + Gk. *trēma* hole] —**mon′o·trem′a·tous** (-trem′ə·təs) adj.

mon·o·type (mon′ə·tīp) n. **1** *Biol.* A unique member of a taxonomic group, as a single species in a genus. **2** *Printing* A print from a metal plate on which a design, painting, etc., has been made. —**mon·o·typ·ic** (mon′ə·tip′ik) adj.

Mon·o·type (mon′ə·tīp) n. *Printing* A machine which casts and sets type in single characters or units: a trade name.

mon·o·va·lent (mon′ə·vā′lənt) adj. *Chem.* UNIVALENT. —**mon′o·va′lence, mon′o·va′len·cy** n.

mon·ox·ide (mon·ok′sīd, mon·ok′-) n. An oxide with a single atom of oxygen per molecule.

Mon·roe Doctrine (mən·rō′) The doctrine, essentially formulated by President James Monroe, that any attempt by European powers to interfere in the affairs of the American countries or to acquire territory on the American continents would be regarded by the U.S. as an unfriendly act.

Mon·sei·gneur (mon·sēn′yər; *Fr.* môn′se·nyœr′) n. pl. **Mes·sei·gneurs** (me·se·nyœr′) **1** My lord: a French title given to princes of the church and formerly to the higher nobility. **2** One having this title. [< F *mon* my + *seigneur* lord]

mon·sieur (mə·syûr′, *Fr.* mə·syœ′) n. pl. **mes·sieurs** (mes′ərz, *Fr.* me·syœ′) The French title of courtesy for men, equivalent to *Mr.* and *sir:* abbreviated M. [< F *mon* + *sieur,* short for *seigneur* lord]

Mon·si·gnor (mon·sēn′yər, *Ital.* môn′sē·nyôr′) n. pl. **·gnors** or *Ital.* **·gno·ri** (-nyô′rē) A title of honor of certain prelates and Roman Catholic officials. Also **Mon·si·gno·re** (môn′sē·nyô′rā). [< F *monseigneur*]

mon·soon (mon·sōōn′) n. *Meteorol.* **1** A wind that blows along the Asiatic coast of the Pacific and from the Indian Ocean, in winter from the NE (**dry monsoon**), in summer from the SW (**wet monsoon**). **2** The rainy season of the summer monsoon. [< Ar. *mausim* season]

mon·ster (mon′stər) n. **1** Any plant or animal of markedly abnormal structure and appearance. **2** A person or thing that is abhorred because of its ugliness, cruelty, wickedness, etc. **3** An abnormally huge person, animal, or thing. **4** An imaginary animal of huge or hideous form. —adj. Enormous; huge. [< L *monstrum* divine omen]

mon·strance (mon′strəns) n. In Roman Catholic ritual, a sacred vessel in which the consecrated Host is exposed for adoration. [< L *monstrare* to show]

mon·stros·i·ty (mon·stros′ə·tē) n. pl. **·ties 1** Anything unnaturally huge, malformed, or distorted. **2** The character or condition of being monstrous.

mon·strous (mon′strəs) adj. **1** Deviating greatly from the natural or normal. **2** Of extraordinary size; huge. **3** Hateful; hideous; intolerable. **4** Incredible; absurd. **5** Like an imaginary monster. —**mon′strous·ly** adv. —**mon′strous·ness** n.

mon·tage (mon·täzh′) n. **1** A composite picture made by superimposing several different pictures on one another. **2** In films or television, a swiftly run sequence of images or pictures illustrating a group of associated ideas. **3** A similar technique used in writing. [F, lit., a mounting]

month (munth) n. **1** One of the 12 parts into which the calendar year is divided, called a **calendar month. 2** Loosely, thirty days or four weeks. **3** The twelfth part of a solar year, called a **solar month. 4** The time during which the moon makes one revolution, equal on the average to 29.53 days, called a **lunar month.** [< OE *mōnath*]

month·ly (munth′lē) adj. **1** Continuing a month. **2** Payable, done, or happening once a month. —adv. Once a month. —n. pl. **·lies 1** A periodical published once a month. **2** pl. *Informal* A menstrual period.

mon·u·ment (mon′yə·mənt) n. **1** Something, as a statue, building, plaque, etc., erected to perpetuate the memory of a person or of an event. **2** A notable work of art, heroic deed, scholarly production, etc., thought of as having enduring significance. **3** A stone boundary marker. **4** A tomb. [< L *monere* remind]

mon·u·men·tal (mon′yə·men′təl) adj. **1** Of, like, or serving as a monument. **2** Massive; impressive; enduring. **3** Outstanding; significant. **4** Very great: a *monumental* fraud. —**mon′u·men′tal·ly** adv.

moo (mōō) v.i. To make the low, mournful sound of a cow; low. —n. pl. **moos** This sound. [Imit.]

mooch (mōōch) *Slang* v.t. **1** To obtain without paying; beg. **2** To steal. —v.i. **3** To loiter about; skulk; sneak. [< OF *muchier* hide, skulk] —**mooch′er** n.

mood¹ (mōōd) n. **1** A particular, usu. temporary state of mind; humor; disposition. **2** pl. Fits of morose or sullen behavior. [< OE *mōd*]

mood² (mōōd) n. *Gram.* The form or forms of a verb which indicate that the speaker regards what he is saying as either a fact (indicative mood), a possibility, desire, etc. (subjunctive mood), or a command (imperative mood). [Var. of MODE]

mood·y (mōō′dē) adj. **mood·i·er, mood·i·est 1** Given to petulant, sullen, or melancholy moods. **2** Expressive of such moods. —**mood′i·ly** adv. —**mood′i·ness** n.

moon (mōōn) n. **1** A body that orbits the earth from west

Phases of the moon
E. earth. S. sun. The outer circle represents views of the moon as seen from earth. a. new. b, b¹. crescent. c. 1st quarter. d, d¹. gibbous. e. full. f. 3rd quarter.

to east in 29.53 days. The moon has a mean diameter of 2,160 miles and a mean distance from the earth of 238,900 miles. 2 A particular phase of the moon: full *moon.* 3 A satellite revolving about any planet. 4 A month, esp. a lunar month. 5 Something resembling a moon or crescent. 6 Moonlight. —*v.i.* 1 To stare or wander about in an abstracted or listless manner. —*v.i.* 2 To pass (time) thus. [< OE *mōna*]

moon·beam (mōōn′bēm′) *n.* A ray of moonlight.

moon·calf (mōōn′kaf′, -käf′) *n.* 1 A stupid person; idiot. 2 A deformed person. [With ref. to the supposed bad influence of the moon]

moon·craft (mōōn′kraft′, -kräft′) *n.* A spacecraft designed to travel to the moon.

moon·light (mōōn′līt′) *n.* The light of the moon. —*adj.* Pertaining to or illuminated or done by moonlight. —*v.i. Informal* To work at a job in addition to one's regular job. —**moon′light·er, moon′light·ing** *n.*

moon·lit (mōōn′lit′) *adj.* Lighted by the moon.

moon·quake (mōōn′kwāk′) *n.* A trembling or shaking of the moon's surface analogous to an earthquake.

moon·scape (mōōn′skāp′) *n.* 1 The moon's surface or a view of it. 2 Any barren or bleak terrain or site.

moon·shine (mōōn′shīn′) *n.* 1 Moonlight. 2 Foolish talk; nonsense. 3 *Informal* Smuggled or illicitly distilled liquor.

moon·shin·er (mōōn′shī′nər) *n. Informal* A person who makes liquor illegally.

moon·stone (mōōn′stōn′) *n.* A whitish, cloudy feldspar, valued as a gem.

moon·struck (mōōn′struk′) *adj.* 1 Lunatic; deranged. 2 Sentimentally romantic. Also **moon′strick′en** (-strik′ən).

moon·y (mōō′nē) *adj.* **moon·i·er, moon·i·est** 1 MOONSTRUCK. 2 Absent-minded.

moor¹ (mōōr) *v.t.* 1 To secure (a ship, etc.) in one place by means of cables attached to shore, anchors, etc. 2 To secure in place; fix. —*v.i.* 3 To secure a ship in position; anchor. 4 To be secured by chains or cables. [< MDu. *māren* to fasten]

moor² (mōōr) *n.* 1 A tract of often elevated, rolling wasteland sometimes covered with heath. 2 A marshy area often abounding in peat. [< OE *mōr*]

Moor (mōōr) *n.* 1 A person of mixed Berber and Arab blood, inhabiting Morocco and the s Mediterranean coast. 2 Any of the Muslim people who invaded Spain in the 8th century. —**Moor′ish** *adj.*

moor·cock (mōōr′kok′) *n.* The male moorfowl.

moor·fowl (mōōr′foul′) *n.* A ptarmigan of the British Isles having reddish brown plumage throughout the year.

moor·hen (mōōr′hen′) *n.* The female moorfowl.

moor·ing (mōōr′ing) *n. Chiefly pl.* 1 The place where a vessel is moored. 2 Anything by which an object is fastened.

moose (mōōs) *n. pl.* **moose** A very large deer of N North America having huge, palmate antlers in the male. 2 A large Old World elk. [< Algon.]

moot (mōōt) *adj.* 1 Still open to discussion; debatable: a *moot* point. 2 Altogether academic; having no practical significance. —*n.* 1 Discussion or argument. 2 In Anglo-Saxon times, a meeting of freemen for the discussion of local affairs. —*v.t.* 1 To debate; discuss. 2 To argue (a case) in a moot court. [< OE *mōt* assembly]

Moose

moot court A court for the trial of a fictitious suit by law students.

mop¹ (mop) *n.* 1 A bundle or mass of absorbent fabric, a sponge, or the like, attached to a handle, used for cleaning floors. 2 Any loosely tangled bunch or mass, as of hair. —*v.t.* **mopped, mop·ping** To rub or wipe with or as with a mop. [? < L *mappa* napkin]

mop² (mop) *n.* A grimace. —*v.i.* To make a wry face; grimace. [?]

mope (mōp) *v.i.* **moped, mop·ing** To be gloomy, listless, or dispirited. —*n.* 1 One who mopes. 2 *pl.* Dejection; depression. [Prob.< Scand.]—**mop′er** *n.*—**mop′ey** *adj.* (·i·er, ·i·est).

mop·pet (mop′it) *n.* A child; youngster. [Dim. of ME *moppe* rag doll]

mo·raine (mə-rān′, mō-) *n. Geol.* A ridge or heap of earth, stones, etc., carried and deposited by a glacier. [F] —**mo·rain′al, mo·rain′ic** *adj.*

mor·al (môr′əl, mor′-) *adj.* 1 Of or pertaining to character and behavior from the point of view of right and wrong. 2 Good and virtuous in behavior, character, etc.; esp., sexually virtuous. 3 Concerned with the principles of right and wrong; ethical: *moral* values. 4 Capable of understanding the difference between right and wrong: a *moral* agent. 5 Coming from a sense of duty or one's conscience: a *moral* obligation. 6 Arising from one's sympathies or sense of justice but without overt action: *moral* support. 7 Probable but not yet proven objectively: a *moral* certainty. —*n.* 1 The moral point or lesson made by a story, action, etc. 2 *pl.* Conduct or behavior from the point of view of right and wrong, esp. sexual conduct. 3 A maxim. [< L *mos, moris* custom; in the pl., manners, morals] —**mor′al·ly** *adv.* • **moral, morale** *Moral,* with the stress on the first syllable, is both an adjective (meaning virtuous or ethical) and a noun (meaning a moral point or lesson): *It took moral courage to admit she was wrong; The moral is, "The weed of crime bears bitter fruit." Morale,* with the stress on the second syllable, is a noun only, and refers to a feeling of confidence or spirit, esp. within a group: *When the pay raise was canceled, morale fell sharply.*

mo·rale (mə-ral′, -räl′, mô-) *n.* State of mind with reference to confidence, courage, hope, etc. [< F *moral,* moral] • See MORAL.

mor·al·ist (môr′əl·ist, mor′-) *n.* 1 A teacher of morals. 2 One who leads a virtuous life. —**mor′al·is′tic** *adj.*

mo·ral·i·ty (mə-ral′ə-tē, mô-) *n. pl.* **·ties** 1 A doctrine or system of moral principles or conduct: Victorian *morality.* 2 Moral conduct; virtue. 3 The quality or condition of being morally right or wrong. 4 A moral lesson. 5 MORALITY PLAY.

morality play A form of allegorical drama of the 15th and 16th centuries in which the characters were personified virtues, vices, mental attributes, etc.

mor·al·ize (môr′əl·īz, mor′-) *v.* **·ized, ·iz·ing** *v.i.* 1 To make moral reflections; talk about morality. —*v.t.* 2 To explain in a moral sense; derive a moral from. 3 To improve the morals of. *Brit. sp.* **·ise.**—**mor′al·i·za′tion, mor′al·iz′er** *n.*

mo·rass (mə·ras′, mô-, mō-) *n.* 1 A tract of low-lying, soft, wet ground; marsh. 2 Anything that impedes or creates difficulties. [< OF *maresc*]

mor·a·to·ri·um (môr′ə·tôr′ē·əm, -tō′rē-, mor′-) *n. pl.* **·ri·ums** or **·ri·a** (-ē·ə) 1 A legal act authorizing a debtor or bank to suspend payments for a given period; also, the period during which it is in force. 2 Any authorized suspension of an activity. [< L *morari* to delay]

Mo·ra·vi·an (mô·rā′vē·ən, mō-) *adj.* Of or pertaining to Moravia or the Moravians. —*n.* 1 A native of Moravia. 2 One of a Christian sect founded in the 15th century by disciples of John Huss in Moravia.

mo·ray (môr′ā, mō·rā′) *n.* A brightly colored, voracious eel inhabiting tropical and subtropical waters, esp. among coral reefs. Also **moray eel.** [< L *muraena*]

mor·bid (môr′bid) *adj.* 1 Of, caused by, or having a disease. 2 Abnormally intrigued by the gruesome or unwholesome. 3 Grisly; gruesome: a *morbid* story. [< L *morbus* disease] —**mor·bid′i·ty, mor′bid·ness** *n.*—**mor′bid·ly** *adv.*

mor·dant (môr′dənt) *adj.* 1 Biting; pungent; sarcastic: *mordant* wit. 2 Acting to fix colors in dyeing. —*n.* 1 A substance that serves to fix a dye in a fabric, etc. 2 A corrosive substance used in etching lines on a metal plate. —*v.t.* To treat or imbue with a mordant. [< OF *mordre* to bite] —**mor′dan·cy** *n.*—**mor′dant·ly** *adv.*

more (môr, mōr) *adj. superlative* **most** 1 Greater in amount, extent, or number: comparative of *much* and *many.* 2 Additional; extra: *More* champagne, please. —*n.* 1 A greater or additional quantity, amount, degree, etc. 2 Something that exceeds something else. —*adv.* 1 In or to a greater extent or degree. 2 In addition; further. —**more or less** 1 Somewhat. 2 Approximately. [< OE *māra*]

more·o·ver (môr·ō′vər, mōr-) *adv.* Beyond what has been said; further; besides; likewise.

mo·res (môr′ēz, mō′rēz) *n.pl.* Established, traditional customs regarded as having the force of law. [L, pl. of *mos, moris* custom]

mor·ga·nat·ic (môr′gə·nat′ik) *adj.* Of or designating a legitimate marriage between a member of certain royal or noble families of Europe and a person of inferior rank, in which the titles and estates are not shared by the offspring or the inferior parent. [< OHG *morgen(geba)* morning (gift) (in lieu of a share in the estate)] —**mor′ga·nat′i·cal·ly** *adv.*

morgue (môrg) *n.* 1 A place where cadavers are kept awaiting identification or determination of cause of death. 2 The department of a newspaper or other periodical where reference material, back issues, etc., are filed. [F]

mor·i·bund (môr′ə·bund, -bənd, mor′-) *adj.* Dying; at the point of death. [< L *mori* die] —**mor′i·bun′di·ty** *n.*

mo·ri·on (môr′ē·on, mō′rē-) *n.* A crested helmet without visor worn by men in the 16th and 17th centuries. [< Sp. *morra* crown of the head]

Mo·ris·co (mə·ris′kō) *adj.* Moorish. —*n.* pl. ·**cos** or ·**coes** A Moor, esp. a Spanish Moor.

Mor·mon (môr′mən) *n.* 1 A member of a religious sect officially called *The Church of Jesus Christ of Latter-Day Saints,* founded in the U.S. by Joseph Smith in 1830. 2 In Mormon belief, a prophet of the fourth century A.D. who wrote the **Book of Mormon,** a history of an early American people. —**Mor′mon·ism** *n.*

morn (môrn) *n.* 1 DAWN. 2 MORNING. [< OE *morgen*]

morn·ing (môr′ning) *n.* 1 The time from midnight to noon, or from sunrise to noon. 2 The first or early stage of anything. —*adj.* Pertaining to or occurring in the morning. [< MORN, by analogy with EVENING]

morn·ing-glo·ry (môr′ning·glôr′ē, -glō′rē) *n.* pl. ·**ries** Any of various twining vines having funnel-shaped flowers of various colors.

morning sickness Nausea and vomiting experienced by some pregnant women in the morning hours, esp. in early pregnancy.

morning star Any of the planets, esp. Venus, when rising in the E sky shortly before the sun.

Morning-glories

Mo·ro (môr′ō, mō′rō) *n.* pl. ·**ros** 1 A member of one of the Muslim tribes of the s Philippines. 2 The Indonesian language of the Moros.

mo·roc·co (mə·rok′ō) *n.* A fine leather made from goatskin tanned with sumac. Also **morocco leather.**

Mo·roc·co (mə·rok′ō) *n.* A constitutional monarchy of NW Africa, 160,000 sq. mi., cap. Rabat. —**Mo·roc′can** *adj., n.* ● See map at AFRICA.

mo·ron (môr′on, mō′ron) *n.* A person with a mild degree of mental retardation. [< Gk. *mōros* dull, sluggish] —**mo·ron·ic** (mô·ron′ik, mō-) *adj.* —**mo·ron′i·cal·ly** *adv.* —**mo′ron·ism, mo·ron′i·ty** *n.*

mo·rose (mə·rōs′) *adj.* Sullen; gloomy. [< L *mos, moris* manner, habit] —**mo·rose′ly** *adv.* —**mo·rose′ness** *n.* —**Syn.** sad, melancholy, surly, ill-tempered.

-morph *combining form* Having a (specified) form or shape. [< Gk. *morphē* form]

mor·pheme (môr′fēm) *n. Ling.* The smallest meaningful unit of a language, as a word, root, affix, or inflectional ending. *Man, run, pro-, -ess, -ing,* etc., are morphemes. [< Gk. *morphē* form]

Mor·phe·us (môr′fē·əs, -fyōōs) *Gk. Myth.* The god of dreams. —**Mor′phe·an** *adj.*

-morphic *combining form* Having the form or shape of: *anthropomorphic.* [< Gk. *morphē* form]

mor·phine (môr′fēn) *n.* A bitter, white, crystalline alkaloid derived from opium, used in medicine to allay pain. Also **mor′phi·a** (-fē·ə). [F < MORPHEUS]

mor·phin·ism (môr′fin·iz′əm) *n.* Addiction to morphine.

mor·phol·o·gy (môr·fol′ə·jē) *n.* 1 The branch of biology that deals with the form and structure of plants and animals. 2 The branch of linguistics that deals with the ar-

rangement, composition, and inflection of the morphemes of a language. [< Gk. *morphē* form + -LOGY] —**mor·pho·log·ic** (môr′fə·loj′ik) or ·**i·cal** *adj.* —**mor′pho·log′i·cal·ly** *adv.* —**mor·phol′o·gist** *n.*

mor·ris (môr′is, mor′-) *n.* An old English folk dance. [Earlier *morys* Moorish]

Mor·ris chair (môr′is, mor′-) A large armchair with an adjustable back. Also **morris chair.** [< William *Morris,* 1834–96, English poet, artist, and craftsman]

mor·row (môr′ō, mor′ō) *n.* 1 The first day after the present or after a specified day or event. 2 *Archaic* Morning: good *morrow.* [< OE *morgen* morning]

Morse code A system of telegraphic signals used in transmitting messages composed of dots and dashes or short and long flashes representing the letters of the alphabet, numerals, etc. [< Samuel F. B. *Morse,* 1791–1872, U.S. inventor]

mor·sel (môr′səl) *n.* 1 A bit of food; bite. 2 A small piece of anything. [< OF, dim. of *mors* bite]

mor·tal (môr′təl) *adj.* 1 Subject to death. 2 Causing death; fatal. 3 Of or connected with death: *mortal* agony. 4 Deadly and unrelenting: a *mortal* foe. 5 Human: *mortal* desires. 6 Very great; extreme: a *mortal* fright. 7 Very long and tedious. 8 *Theol.* Incurring eternal death unless repented of: said of grave sins. 9 *Informal* Conceivable: every *mortal* reason for not going. —*n.* A human being. —*adv. Regional* Very; exceedingly: *mortal* tired. [< L *mors, mortis* death] —**mor′tal·ly** *adv.*

mor·tal·i·ty (môr·tal′ə·tē) *n.* 1 The quality of being mortal. 2 Death, esp. of large numbers of people. 3 The number of deaths in a population during a specified time. 4 Humanity; mankind.

mor·tar¹ (môr′tər) *n.* 1 A strong bowllike vessel in which substances are crushed or pounded with a pestle. 2 *Mil.* A muzzle-loading cannon for firing heavy shells at low muzzle velocity and great angles of elevation. [< L *mortarium*]

mor·tar² (môr′tər) *n.* A mixture of lime, cement, etc., with sand and water, used in masonry, plastering, etc. —*v.t.* To plaster or join with mortar. [< L *mortarium*]

Mortar and pestle

mor·tar·board (môr′tər·bôrd′, -bōrd′) *n.* 1 A square board with a handle, on which a mason holds mortar. 2 An academic cap having a square, flat top and tassel.

mort·gage (môr′gij) *n. Law* 1 A transfer of ownership of property to a creditor as security for a loan or debt. 2 The contract effecting such a transfer. —*v.t.* ·**gaged,** ·**gag·ing** 1 To make over or pledge (property) by mortgage. 2 To pledge. [< OF, lit., dead pledge]

mort·ga·gee (môr′gi·jē′) *n.* The person to whom property is mortgaged.

mort·ga·gor (môr′gi·jər) *n.* A person who mortgages his property. Also **mort′gag·er.**

mor·ti·cian (môr·tish′ən) *n.* A funeral director; undertaker. [< L *mors, mortis* death + -ICIAN]

mor·ti·fi·ca·tion (môr′tə·fə·kā′shən) *n.* 1 Shame or humiliation caused by a loss of self-esteem or wounded pride. 2 The cause of such humiliation or shame. 3 Necrosis; gangrene. 4 In religion, the act of subduing the passions and appetites by fasting, penance, etc.

mor·ti·fy (môr′tə·fī) *v.* ·**fied,** ·**fy·ing** *v.t.* 1 To humiliate. 2 To discipline or punish (the body, passions, etc.) by fasting or other ascetic practices. 3 To cause (a part of the body) to become gangrenous. —*v.i.* 4 To practice ascetic self-discipline. 5 To become gangrenous. [< L *mors, mortis* death + *facere* make] —**mor′ti·fi′er** *n.* —**mor′ti·fy′ing·ly** *adv.*

mor·tise (môr′tis) *n.* A space hollowed out, as in a piece of wood, to receive a tenon or other projecting part. —*v.t.* ·**tised,** ·**tis·ing** 1 To cut or make a mortise in. 2 To join by a tenon and mortise. [< OF *mortaise*]

a. mortise.
b. tenon.

mort·main (môrt′mān) *n. Law* The perpetual and untransferable ownership of property, as by a religious or other corporation. [< Med. L *mortua manus* dead hand]

mor·tu·ar·y (môr′chōō·er′ē) *n.* pl. ·**ar·ies** A place for the temporary reception of the dead before burial, esp. a funeral home. —*adj.* **1** Of or pertaining to the burial of the dead. **2** Of death or the dead. [< L *mortuarius* belonging to the dead]

mos. months.

mo·sa·ic (mō·zā′ik) *n.* **1** Inlaid work composed of bits of stone, glass, etc., forming a pattern or picture. **2** The art or process of making a mosaic. **3** Anything resembling a mosaic. —*adj.* Of, pertaining to, or resembling mosaic. —*v.t.* **·icked, ·ick·ing 1** To make by or as if by combining in a mosaic. **2** To decorate with mosaic. [< Gk. *mouseios* of the Muses, artistic] —**mo·sa·i·cist** (mō·zā′ə·sist) *n.*

Mo·sa·ic (mō·zā′ik) *adj.* Of or pertaining to Moses or his laws. Also **Mo·sa′i·cal.**

Mo·ses (mō′ziz) In the Bible, the leader who led the Israelites out of Egypt into the Promised Land and received the Ten Commandments from God.

mo·sey (mō′zē) *v.i. Slang* **1** To saunter, or stroll. **2** To go away. [?]

Mos·lem (moz′ləm, mos′-) *n. pl.* **·lems** or **·lem** MUSLIM. —*adj.* MUSLIM. —**Mos′lem·ism** *n.*

mosque (mosk) *n.* A Muslim temple of worship. [< Ar. *masjid*]

mos·qui·to (məs·kē′tō) *n. pl.* **·toes** or **·tos** Any of a family of small, dipterous insects having in the female mouth parts that puncture the skin of animals and suck their blood. [< Sp. *mosca* fly] —**mos·qui′tal** *adj.*

Mosquito

mosquito boat A patrol torpedo boat.
mosquito net A fine netting or gauze **(mosquito netting)** placed over beds, etc., to keep out mosquitoes.

moss (môs, mos) *n.* **1** Any of a large class of widespread, primitive, small plants having leaves and rootlike and stemlike parts, and reproducing by spores. **2** Any of several similar plants, as certain lichens. —*v.t.* To cover with moss. [< OE *mos*] —**moss′y** *adj.* (**·i·er, ·i·est**) —**moss′i·ness** *n.*

moss·back (môs′bak′, mos′-) *n.* An extremely conservative or reactionary person.

moss rose A cultivated variety of rose with a rough, mosslike calyx and flower stem.

most (mōst) *adj.* **1** Consisting of the greatest number: superlative of *many.* **2** Consisting of the greatest amount or degree: superlative of *much.* **3** In the majority of instances: *Most dogs are friendly.* —**for the most part** Generally; usually. —*n.* **1** The greater number; the larger part: the *most* of my belongings. **2** The greatest amount, quantity, or degree. —**at (the) most** Not more than; at the utmost extreme. —**make the most of** To take the utmost advantage of. —*adv.* **1** In or to the greatest or highest degree, quantity, or extent: used with adjectives and adverbs to form the superlative degree. **2** Very. **3** *Informal* Almost; nearly. [< OE *mǽst*]

-most *suffix* Most: added to form superlatives: *hindmost.* [< OE *-mest*]

most·ly (mōst′lē) *adv.* For the most part; principally.

mot (mō) *n.* A witty remark. [F, word]

mote (mōt) *n.* A minute particle or speck, as of dust. [< OE *mot*]

mo·tel (mō·tel′) *n.* A hotel for motorists, usu. comprising cabins or rooms directly accessible from parking areas. [< MO(TOR) + (HO)TEL]

mo·tet (mō·tet′) *n. Music* A polyphonic song of a sacred nature, usu. unaccompanied. [< OF, dim. of *mot* word]

moth (môth, moth) *n. pl.* **moths** (môthz, môths, mothz, moths) Any of various, usu. nocturnal, lepidopterous insects distinguished from butterflies by their featherlike antennae and wings that fold flat over the abdomen. [< OE *moththe*]

moth·ball (môth′bôl′, moth′-) *n.* A ball of naphthalene, camphor, or other substance whose fumes repel moths that destroy woolen fabrics. —*adj.* In protective storage or in reserve: a *mothball* fleet. —*v.t.* To put in protective storage or reserve.

moth-eat·en (môth′ēt′n, moth′-) *adj.* **1** Eaten by the larvae of moths. **2** Worn out. **3** Old-fashioned.

moth·er¹ (muth′ər) *n.* **1** A woman who has borne a child. **2** A woman fulfilling the role of mother, as by adoption of a child. **3** STEPMOTHER. **4** The source or origin of anything. **5** An abbess or other nun of rank or dignity. **6** An elderly woman. —*v.t.* **1** To care for as a mother. **2** To bring forth as a mother; produce. **3** To admit or claim parentage, authorship, etc., of. —*adj.* **1** Native: *mother* tongue. **2** Of or characteristic of a mother: *mother* love. **3** Holding a maternal relation. [< OE *mōdor*] —**moth′er·less** *adj.*

moth·er² (muth′ər) *n.* A ropy, jellylike mass of bacteria that forms in vinegar and other fermenting liquids, used to start new batches. Also **mother of vinegar.** [Special use of MOTHER¹]

Mother Car·ey's chicken (kâr′ēz) The petrel; esp., the storm petrel. [?]

Mother Goose 1 The imaginary narrator of a volume of folk tales, compiled in French by Charles Perrault in 1697. **2** The imaginary compiler of a collection of English nursery rhymes published in London about 1760 by John Newbery.

moth·er·hood (muth′ər·hood) *n.* **1** The state of being or the qualities characteristic of a mother. **2** Mothers collectively.

Mother Hub·bard (hub′ard) **1** The main character in an old nursery rhyme. **2** A woman's loose, flowing gown.

moth·er-in-law (muth′ər·in·lô′) *n. pl.* **moth·ers-in-law** The mother of one's spouse.

moth·er·land (muth′ər·land) *n.* **1** The country of one's birth. **2** The land of one's ancestors.

mother lode Any principal or rich vein of ore in a mine.

moth·er·ly (muth′ər·lē) *adj.* Of, resembling, or befitting a mother. —*adv.* In the manner of a mother. —**moth′er·li·ness** *n.*

moth·er-of-pearl (muth′ər·əv·pûrl′) *n.* The hard, iridescent lining of certain mollusk shells; nacre. —*adj.* Made of or ornamented with mother-of-pearl.

Mother's Day A day observed in honor of mothers, on the second Sunday in May.

mother tongue 1 One's native language. **2** A language from which another language has developed.

mother wit Natural or native intelligence; common sense.

moth·y (môth′ē, moth′ē) *adj.* **moth·i·er, moth·i·est 1** Motheaten. **2** Full of moths.

mo·tif (mō·tēf′) *n.* **1** The main idea or central theme of a literary, musical, or artistic work. **2** In the decorative arts, a distinctive element of design. **3** The shortest fragment of a musical theme in which structure is evident. [F]

mo·tile (mō′til) *adj. Biol.* Having the power of or exhibiting spontaneous motion. [< L *motus,* p.p. of *movere* move] —**mo·til′i·ty** *n.*

mo·tion (mō′shən) *n.* **1** Any physical movement or spatial change in position or place. **2** A formal proposition in a deliberative assembly. **3** *Law* An application to a court to obtain an order, ruling, or direction. **4** A mental impulse or inclination. —*v.i.* **1** To make a gesture of direction or intent, as with the hand. —*v.t.* **2** To direct or guide by a gesture. [< L *motus,* p.p. of *movere* move] —**mo′tion·al, mo′tion·less** *adj.* —**mo′tion·less·ly** *adv.* —**mo′tion·less·ness** *n.* —**Syn.** *n.* **1** action, passage, transit.

motion picture 1 A sequence of filmed pictures giving the illusion of continuous movement; film (def. 4). **2** A story, drama, etc., adapted for and photographed as a motion picture. —**mo′tion-pic′ture** *adj.*

motion sickness Nausea and sometimes vomiting caused by the effect of certain movements on the inner ear, typically experienced in a moving vehicle, ship, or airplane.

mo·ti·vate (mō′tə·vāt) *v.t.* **·vat·ed, ·vat·ing** To provide with a motive; instigate; induce. —**mo′ti·va′tion** *n.* —**mo′ti·va′tion·al** *adj.*

mo·tive (mō′tiv) *n.* **1** Something, as a need or desire, that impels or incites a person to a certain course of action or behavior. **2** MOTIF. —*adj.* **1** Causing motion. **2** Relating to a motive or motives. —*v.t.* **·tived, ·tiv·ing** MOTIVATE. [< L *motus,* p.p. of *movere* move]

mot·ley (mot'lē) *adj.* 1 Composed of many different elements or types. 2 Variegated in color.—*n.* 1 A garment of various colors, such as was formerly worn by court jesters. 2 A many-colored, woolen fabric. 3 An incongruous mixture. [ME *motteley*]

mo·to·cross (mō'tō·kros', -krôs') *n.* A motorcycle race operated on a cross-country ski run or other trail, rather than on a paved surface.

mo·tor (mōtər) *n.* 1 A machine that converts electric energy into mechanical power. 2 An internal-combustion engine. 3 Anything that produces motion. 4 AUTOMOBILE. —*adj.* 1 Causing, producing, or imparting motion. 2 Driven or operated by a motor. 3 Of, pertaining to, or for vehicles operated by a motor. 4 Transmitting impulses from the nerve centers to the muscles. 5 Of or involving muscular movement. —*v.i.* To travel or ride in an automobile. [<L *motus*, p.p. of *movere*]

mo·tor·bike (mō'tər·bīk') *n. Informal* 1 A bicycle driven by a motor. 2 A lightweight motorcycle.

mo·tor·boat (mō'tər·bōt') *n.* A boat propelled by a motor.

mo·tor·bus (mō'tər·bus') *n. pl.* **·bus·es** or **·bus·ses** A passenger bus. Also **motor coach.**

mo·tor·cade (mō'tər·kād) *n.* A procession of automobiles.

mo·tor·car (mō'tər·kär') *n.* AUTOMOBILE.

motor court MOTEL. Also **motor hotel, inn, lodge.**

mo·tor·cy·cle (mō'tər·sī'kəl) *n.* A two-wheeled vehicle propelled by an internal-combustion engine. —*v.i.* **·cled, ·cling** To travel or ride on a motorcycle. —**mo'tor·cy'clist** *n.*

motor home *U.S.* An automotive vehicle equipped with living accommodations and resembling a trailer but built on a single chassis.

Motorcycle

mo·tor·ist (mō'tər·ist) *n.* One who drives an automobile or travels by automobile.

mo·tor·ize (mō'tər·īz) *v.t.* **ized, ·iz·ing** To equip with a motor or motors or with motor-propelled vehicles.

mo·tor·man (mō'tər·mən) *n. pl.* **·men** (-mən) One who operates a passenger vehicle that is drawn by an electric motor, as a streetcar or subway.

motor pool A group of motor vehicles owned by a governmental or military agency for use by its personnel.

motor scooter A two- or three-wheeled vehicle having a floorboard for the feet, and a driver's seat, and propelled by an internal-combustion engine.

motor vehicle Any of various motor-driven vehicles that do not run on rails or tracks.

mot·tle (mot'l) *v.t.* **·tled ·tling** To mark with spots or streaks of different colors or shades. —*n.* 1 A spotted, blotched, or variegated appearance. 2 A spot or blotch. [<MOTLEY]

mot·tled (mot'ld) *adj.* Marked with spots of different colors or shades; variegated.

mot·to (mot'ō) *n. pl.* **·toes** or **·tos** 1 A word or phrase expressing a guiding principle or rule of conduct. 2 A phrase inscribed on something as being indicative of its qualities or uses. [Ital., word]

mou·jik (mōō·zhēk') *n.* MUZHIK.

mould (mōld) *n. & v. Brit.* MOLD.

moult (mōlt) *v. Brit.* MOLT.

mound (mound) *n.* 1 A heap or pile of earth, stones, etc., either natural or artificial. 2 A small hill or knoll. 3 In baseball, the slightly raised ground from which the pitcher pitches the ball. —*v.t.* 1 To fortify or enclose with a mound. 2 To heap up in a mound. [?]

Mound Builder One of the prehistoric Indians who built the burial mounds and fortifications found in the Mississippi basin and adjoining regions.

mount¹ (mount) *v.t.* 1 To ascend by climbing; go up, as stairs. 2 To climb or get up upon: to *mount* a horse. 3 To put on horseback. 4 To furnish with a horse. 5 To set or place in an elevated position: to *mount* a plaque on a wall. 6 To place or fix in or on a support, frame, slide, etc., as for exhibition, examination, etc.: to *mount* a photograph, to *mount* a butterfly. 7 To furnish, as a play, with scenery,

costumes, etc. 8 To copulate with a female: said of a male animal. 9 *Mil.* a To place in position for use, as a cannon. b To stand or post (guard). c To prepare for and begin: to *mount* an offensive. —*v.i.* 10 To rise or ascend; to up. 11 To increase. 12 To get up on or on top of something. —*n.* 1 Anything, as a support, frame, jewel setting, etc., on or in which something is mounted. 2 Something which one mounts and rides, as a horse, bicycle, etc. 3 The act or manner of mounting or riding a horse, etc. [<L *mons, montis* mountain] —**mount'er** *n.*

mount² (mount) *n.* A mountain or hill: often used as part of a proper name: *Mount* Washington. [<L *mons, montis* mountain]

moun·tain (moun'tən) 1 A natural elevation of the earth's surface, higher than a hill and rising more or less steeply to a small summit area. 2 A large number or amount. 3 Something of great size. —*adj.* 1 Of, pertaining to, or like a mountain. 2 Living, growing, or located on a mountain. [<L *mons, montis* mountain]

mountain ash Any of various small trees and shrubs having compound leaves, dense clusters of white flowers, and vivid red fruit.

moun·tain·eer (moun'tən·ir') *n.* 1 An inhabitant of a mountainous district. 2 One who climbs mountains. —*v.i.* To climb mountains.

mountain goat A goatlike antelope of mountainous regions of w North America.

mountain laurel An evergreen shrub of e North America, having poisonous, shiny leaves and white or pink flowers.

mountain lion A large, tawny, unspotted wild cat of North and South America.

moun·tain·ous (moun'tən·əs) *adj.* 1 Full of mountains. 2 Huge. —**moun'tain·ous·ly** *adv.*

mountain sheep 1 BIGHORN. 2 Any wild sheep of mountainous regions.

Mountain Standard Time See STANDARD TIME.

moun·te·bank (moun'tə·bangk) *n.* 1 A vendor of quack medicines at fairs. 2 Any charlatan. [<Ital. *montare* to mount + *in* on + *banco* bench]

mount·ed (moun'tid) *adj.* 1 Seated on a horse. 2 Equipped with horses: *mounted* police. 3 Fitted or positioned for use or display.

Moun·tie (moun'tē) *n. Informal* A member of the Royal Canadian Mounted Police. Also **Mount'y.**

mount·ing (moun'ting) *n.* A frame, support, or setting for something.

mourn (môrn, mōrn) *v.i.* 1 To feel or express grief or sorrow, esp. for the dead. —*v.t.* 2 To grieve or sorrow for (someone dead). 3 To grieve over or lament (misfortune, failure, etc.). [<OE *murnan*] —**mourn'er** *n.*

mourner's bench *U.S.* At revival meetings, a bench near the preacher reserved for penitents.

mourn·ful (môrn'fəl, mōrn'-) *adj.* 1 Indicating or expressing grief. 2 Oppressed with grief. 3 Causing sorrow. —**mourn'ful·ly** *adv.* —**mourn'ful·ness** *n.* —Syn. 2 sorrowful, rueful, disconsolate, grief-stricken.

mourn·ing (môr'ning, mōr'-) *n.* 1 The act of sorrowing or expressing grief, esp. for the dead. 2 The outward manifestations of such grief, as the use of black clothes, half-masting of flags, etc. 3 The period during which one mourns.

mourning dove A wild dove of North America having gray plumage and a long, pointed, white-edged tail: so called for its plaintive call.

mouse (mous) *n. pl.* **mice** (mīs) 1 Any of numerous small rodents found throughout the world, esp. the common **house mouse,** which frequents human habitations. 2 *Informal* A timid person. 3 *Slang* A black eye. 4 A small, hand-held electronic device, used to control a cursor, or point to commands on a menu, instead of typing commands via the computer keyboard. —*v.* (mouz) **moused, mous·ing** *v.i.* 1 To hunt or catch mice. 2 To hunt for something cautiously and softly; prowl. [<OE *mūs*]

mous·er (mou'zər) *n.* A cat, dog, etc., that catches mice.

mousse (mōōs) *n.* 1 .A light, frozen dessert made of whipped cream, white of egg, sugar, flavoring, etc. 2 A similar dish made with meat, fish, or vegatables: lobster *mousse.* [F]

mous·tache (məs·tash', mus'tash) *n.* MUSTACHE.

mous·y (mou'sē, -zē) *adj.* **mous·i·er, mous·i·est** 1 Infested with mice. **2** Of or like a mouse. **3** Quiet and timid. Also **mous′ey.**

mouth (mouth) *n. pl.* **mouths** (mouthz) **1** The opening at which food is taken into the body; also, the cavity between the lips and throat. **2** The human mouth thought of in terms of eating and speaking: *Shut your mouth; mouths to feed.* **3** An opening or entrance that can be likened to a mouth: as **a** That part of a stream where its waters are discharged into a river, lake, etc. **b** The entrance to a harbor. **c** The entrance or opening into a mine or cave. **d** The opening of a jar or similar container. —**down in** (or

Human mouth
a. hard palate. b. soft palate. c. uvula. d. epiglottis. e. esophagus. f. trachea. g. tongue.

at) the mouth Disconsolate; dejected. —*v.t.* (mouth) **1** To utter in a forced or affected manner; declaim. **2** To seize or take in the mouth. **3** To repeat mechanically and without understanding. **4** To form (words) as if speaking but without sound. —*v.i.* **5** To speak in a forced or affected manner. [< OE *mūth*] —**mouth′er** (mou′thər) *n.*

mouthed (mouthd, moutht) *adj.* Having a (specified kind of) mouth: used in combination: *loudmouthed.*

mouth·ful (mouth′fŏŏl′) *n. pl.* **·fuls** (-fŏŏlz) **1** As much as can be or is usually put into the mouth at one time. **2** A small quantity. **3** *Slang* A meaningful remark, usu. in the phrase **say a mouthful.**

mouth organ HARMONICA.

mouth·piece (mouth′pēs′) *n.* **1** Something that forms a mouth. **2** That part of any musical instrument, sports equipment, telephone, etc., that is used in or near the mouth. **3** One who speaks for others. **4** *Slang* A criminal lawyer.

mouth-to-mouth (mouth′tə-mouth′) *adj.* Of or describing a form of artificial respiration in which the rescuer places his mouth over the victim's mouth and breathes rhythmically and forcefully to inflate the victim's lungs and start respiration: *mouth-to-mouth resuscitation.*

mouth·wash (mouth′wash, -wôsh) *n.* A flavored solution, often antiseptic, used for cleansing the mouth or teeth, or for gargling.

mouth·y (mou′thē, -thē) *adj.* **mouth·i·er, mouth·i·est** Very talkative; garrulous. —**mouth′i·ly** *adv.* —**mouth′i·ness** *n.*

mou·ton (mōō′ton) *n.* Processed sheepskin dyed and cut to resemble beaver or seal. [F, sheep]

mov·a·ble (mōō′və-bəl) *adj.* **1** Capable of being moved. **2** Changing in date from year to year: *movable holidays.* —*n.* **1** Anything that can be moved. **2** *Usu. pl. Law* Personal property, as distinguished from real or fixed property. Also **move′a·ble.** —**mov′a·ble·ness, mov·a·bil′i·ty** *n.* —**mov′·a·bly** *adv.*

move (mōōv) *v.* **moved, mov·ing** *v.i.* **1** To change place or position; go: to go from one place to another. **2** To change one's residence. **3** To make progress; advance. **4** To live or associate; be active: *to move in cultivated circles.* **5** To operate or revolve; work: said of machines, etc. **6** To take action; begin to act. **7** To be disposed of by sale. **8** To make an application, appeal, or proposal: *to move for adjournment.* **9** To evacuate: said of the bowels. **10** In chess, checkers, etc., to change the position of a piece. **11** *Informal* To go or depart rapidly. —*v.t.* **12** To change the place or position of. **13** To set or keep in motion. **14** To rouse, influence, or urge to some action. **15** To affect with passion, sympathy, etc.; stir; excite. **16** To propose for consideration, action, etc. **17** To cause (the bowels) to evacuate. —*n.* **1** The act of moving; movement. **2** A purposeful act or maneuver in the carrying out of a plan. **3** In chess, checkers, etc., the act of moving a piece; also, one's turn to move. **4** A change of residence. —**on the move 1** Moving about from place to place. **2** Making progress. [< L *movere*]

move·ment (mōōv′mənt) *n.* **1** The act of changing place or position or of moving in any way. **2** A particular instance, technique, or manner of moving. **3** A series of actions, plans, etc., tending toward some goal or objective;

also, the people so involved. **4** A trend or inclination. **5** *Mech.* A particular arrangement of related parts that produces a definite motion. **6** *Mil.* A maneuver. **7** *Music* One of the sections of a larger work, as of a symphony. **8** In art or literature, a quality that suggests motion or action. **9** In prosody, rhythmic flow; cadence. **10** An emptying of the bowels, or the matter so emptied.

mov·er (mōō′vər) *n.* One who or that which moves; esp., one engaged in the business of moving household goods.

mov·ie (mōō′vē) *n.* **1** A motion-picture film. **2** A motion-picture theater. **3** *pl.* A showing of films. **4** *pl.* The film industry. —*adj.* Of, in, or for movies. [Contraction of *moving picture*]

mov·ing (mōō′ving) *adj.* **1** Capable of or exhibiting movement. **2** Causing or producing motion or action. **3** Exciting or arousing the feelings or passions. —**mov′ing·ly** *adv.* —**mov′ing·ness** *n.* —Syn. **3** touching, affecting, stirring.

moving picture MOTION PICTURE.

moving staircase ESCALATOR.

mow[1] (mō) *v.* **mowed, mowed** or **mown, mow·ing** *v.t.* **1** To cut down (grain, grass, etc.) with a scythe or machine. **2** To cut the grain or grass of (a lawn, field, etc.). **3** To cut down or kill rapidly or indiscriminately: with *down.* —*v.i.* **4** To cut down grass or grain. [< OE *māwan*] —**mow′er** *n.*

mow[2] (mou) *n.* Hay or grain stored in a barn; also, the place of storage. —*v.t.* To store in a mow. [< OE *mūga*]

moz·za·rel·la (mot′sə-rel′ə) *n.* A soft, white, mild Italian cheese, used mainly in cooking. [Ital.]

MP, M.P. Member of Parliament; Military Police.

M.P., mp, m.p. melting point.

mp moderately soft (It. *mezzo piano*).

MPH, mph, m.p.h. miles per hour.

Mr. (mis′tər) *n. pl.* **Messrs.** (mes′ərz) A title prefixed to the name of a man. [Contraction of MISTER]

Mrs. (mis′iz) *n. pl.* **Mmes.** (mā-däm′) A title prefixed to the name of a married woman. [Contraction of MISTRESS]

Ms. (miz) *n. pl.* **Ms.'s** (miz′əz) A title prefixed to the name of a woman without specifying marital status. [Contraction of MISTRESS]

MS Mississippi (P.O. abbr.); multiple sclerosis.

MS, MS., ms, ms. (*pl.* **MSS, MSS., mss, mss.**) manuscript.

M.S., M.Sc. Master of Science (L *Magister Scientiae*).

MSG monosodium glutamate.

Msgr. Monsignor.

M.Sgt., M/Sgt Master Sergeant.

MST, M.S.T., m.s.t. Mountain Standard Time.

MT Montana (P.O. abbr.).

mt. (*pl.* **mts.**) mount; mountain.

m.t. mean time; metric ton; mountain time.

mtg. meeting; mortgage.

mtn. mountain.

Mt. Rev. Most Reverend.

mu (myōō) *n.* **1** The 12th letter in the Greek alphabet (M, μ), equivalent to *m.* **2** MICRON.

much (much) *adj.* **more, most** Great in quantity, amount, degree, etc. —*n.* **1** A great quantity, amount, degree, etc. **2** Something remarkable, important, or extensive. —**make much of** To treat or think of as of great importance. —*adv.* **1** To a great degree or extent. **2** For the most part; approximately. [< OE *mycel*] —**much′ness** *n.*

mu·ci·lage (myōō′sə-lij) *n.* **1** An aqueous solution of vegetable gum or similar substance, used as an adhesive. **2** Any of various gummy or gelatinous substances obtained from certain plants. [< LL *mucilago*] —**mu·ci·lag·i·nous** (myōō′si·laj′ə·nes) *adj.* —**mu′ci·lag′i·nous·ness** *n.*

muck (muk) *n.* **1** Any moist dirt or filth, esp. mud. **2** Moist manure. **3** Dark soil consisting largely of decaying organic matter. **4** Something, as writings, that defames or injures. —*v.t.* **1** To fertilize with manure. **2** *Informal* To make dirty; pollute. **3** To remove muck from. [< ON *mykr*] —**muck′y** *adj.* (**·i·er, ·i·est**)

muck·rake (muk′rāk) *v.i.* **·raked, ·rak·ing** To search for or expose real or alleged corruption on the part of political officials, businessmen, etc. [< obs. *muckrake* a rake for dung] —**muck′rak′er** *n.*

mu·cous (myōō′kəs) *adj.* **1** Secreting mucus. **2** Pertaining

to or resembling mucus; slimy. Also **mu′coid** (-koid). — **mu·cos′i·ty** (-kos′ə·tē) n.

mucous membrane The soft, smooth, moist tissue that lines the passages and cavities inside the body.

mu·cus (myoō′kəs) n. A viscid secretion of mucous membrane, serving as a lubricant.

mud (mud) n. 1 Wet and sticky earth; mire. 2 Informal Slanderous or malicious abuse. —v.t. **mud·ded, mud·ding** To soil or cover with mud. [?]

mud·dle (mud′l) v. **·dled, ·dling** v.t. 1 To mix in confusion; jumble. 2 To confuse mentally; bewilder. 3 To make muddy or turbid; roil. 4 To make a mess of; bungle. —v.i. 5 To act or think in a confused or ineffective manner. —n. A mixed or confused condition, as of the mind; a mess. [? < MUD]

mud·dle-head·ed (mud′l·hed′id) adj. Mentally confused.

mud·dler (mud′lər) n. 1 A stick for stirring liquids, esp. drinks. 2 One who muddles.

mud·dy (mud′ē) adj. **·di·er, ·di·est** 1 Spattered or filled with mud. 2 Unclear; cloudy, as a color. 3 Confused or muddled in thought, meaning, etc. —v.t. & v.i. **·died, ·dy·ing** To become or cause to become muddy. —**mud′di·ly** adv. —**mud′di·ness** n.

mud·guard (mud′gärd′) n. A guard over the wheel of a vehicle to protect from splashing mud.

mud·pup·py (mud′pup′ē) n. pl. **·pies** A salamander with four limbs and external, feathery gills, often found in muddy or stagnant water.

mud·sling·ing (mud′sling′ing) n. The practice of casting malicious slurs at an opponent, esp. in a political campaign. —**mud′sling′er** n.

mud turtle Any of various small turtles inhabiting muddy or brackish water.

mu·ez·zin (myoō·ez′in) n. In Muslim countries, a crier who calls the faithful to prayer, usu. from a minaret. Also **mu·ed′din** (-ed′in). [< Ar. mu'adhdhin]

muff[1] (muf) v.t. & v.i. 1 To perform (some act) clumsily; blunder. 2 In baseball, to fail to hold (the ball) in attempting a catch. —n. A bungling action. [?]

muff[2] (muf) n. A covering of fur or cloth, usu. cylindrical, into which the hands are thrust from opposite ends to keep them warm. [< F moufle]

muf·fin (muf′in) n. 1 A light, quick bread, baked in small cup-shaped tins. 2 ENGLISH MUFFIN. [?]

muf·fle (muf′əl) v.t. **·fled, ·fling** 1 To wrap up in a blanket, scarf, etc., as for warmth or concealment. 2 To prevent from seeing, hearing, or speaking by wrapping the head. 3 To deaden the sound of by or as by wrapping. 4 To deaden (a sound). 5 To stifle; suppress. —n. Something used for muffling. [< OF moufle heavy mitten]

muf·fler (muf′lər) n. 1 A heavy scarf worn about the neck. 2 A device to reduce noise, as from the exhaust of an internal-combustion engine. 3 Anything used for muffling.

Muffler def. 2
a. assembled.
b. cross section.

muf·ti[1] (muf′tē) n. In Muslim countries, an expounder of religious law. [Ar.]

muf·ti[2] (muf′tē) n. Civilian dress; plain clothes, esp. when worn by one who normally wears a uniform. [< MUFTI[1]]

mug (mug) n. 1 A large drinking cup with a handle. 2 Slang The human face or mouth. 3 Slang A photograph of the face of a suspect: also **mug shot.** 4 Slang A criminal. —v. mugged, mug·ging Slang v.t. 1 To assault, usu. with the intent to rob. 2 To photograph (someone), esp. for official purposes. —v.i. 3 To make faces; grimace exaggeratedly. [?]

mug·ger (mug′ər) n. One who assaults another, often by surprise and in a public place or apartment house, usu. in order to rob. —**mug′ging** n.

mug·gy (mug′ē) adj. **·gi·er, ·gi·est** Warm, humid, and close. [< ON mugga drizzle] —**mug′gi·ness** n.

mug·wump (mug′wump) n. U.S. An independent, esp. in politics. [< Algon.] —**mug′wump·er·y, mug′wump·ism** n.

Mu·ham·mad·an (moō·ham′ə·dən) n. MOHAMMEDAN. —**Mu·ham′mad·an·ism** n.

mu·jik (moō·zhēk′, moō′zhik) n. MUZHIK.

mu·lat·to (mə·lat′ō, myoō-, -lä′tō) n. pl. **·toes** 1 A person having one white and one Negro parent. 2 Anyone having mixed white and Negro ancestry. —adj. Of a light brown color. [< Sp. mulato of mixed breed < mulo mule]

mul·ber·ry (mul′ber′ē, -bər·ē) n. pl. **·ries** 1 Any of various trees whose leaves are valued for silkworm culture. 2 The edible, blackberrylike fruit of a mulberry. 3 A deep purplish red color. [< L morum mulberry + OE berie a berry]

mulch (mulch) n. Any covering, as straw, compost, etc., placed on the ground around plants to protect their roots, as from frost or drying. —v.t. To cover with mulch. [ME molsh]

mulct (mulkt) v.t. 1 To punish by a fine. 2 To deprive (a person) of something fraudulently; cheat. —n. A fine or similar penalty. [< L mulcta, multa a fine]

mule[1] (myoōl) n. 1 A hybrid bred of the ass and horse, esp. a jackass and a mare. 2 A spinning machine that draws, stretches, and twists at one operation. 3 Informal A stubborn person. [< L mulus]

mule[2] (myoōl) n. A backless lounging slipper. [< L muleus red slipper]

mule deer A deer of the w U.S., having long ears.

mule-skin·ner (myoōl′skin′ər) n. Informal A mule-driver.

mu·le·teer (myoō′lə·tir′) n. A mule-driver.

mul·ish (myoōl′ish) adj. Stubborn; recalcitrant. —**mul′ish·ly** adv. —**mul′ish·ness** n.

mull[1] (mul) v.t. To heat and spice, as wine or beer. [?]

mull[2] (mul) v.t. To ponder; cogitate: usu. with over. [< obs. mull grind < ME mul dust]

mul·lah (mul′ə, moōl′ə) n. A Muslim trained in Islamic religious law and doctrine. Also **Mul′la.** [< Ar. mawlā master, sir]

mul·lein (mul′ən) n. Any of various tall, usu. hairy plants of the figwort family. Also **mul′len.** [< L mollis soft]

mul·let (mul′it) n. pl. **·lets** or **·let** Any of various marine and freshwater food fish, as the gray mullet and the red mullet. [< L mullus red mullet]

mul·li·gan (mul′i·gən) n. 1 A stew, originally made by tramps, composed of odds and ends of meat, vegetables, etc. Also **mulligan stew.** 2 In golf, an extra shot, esp. a tee shot, after an inept first shot. [< Mulligan, Irish surname]

mul·li·ga·taw·ny (mul′i·gə·tô′nē) n. An East Indian soup of meat and curry. [< Tamil milagu-tannīr pepper water]

mul·lion (mul′yən) n. A vertical dividing piece between lights or panels of windows, doors, etc. —v.t. To furnish with mullions. [? Var. of earlier monial]

Mullions

multi- combining form 1 Much; many; consisting of many; as in:

multiangular	multifaced	multinational
multicellular	multifaceted	multipointed
multicolored	multihued	multipurpose
multidenominational	multilevel	multiracial
multidimensional	multilingual	multistoried
multidirectional	multimillion	multisyllable
multidisciplinary	multimolecular	multivoiced
multiethnic	multination	multivolume

2 Having more than two (or sometimes, more than one), as in **multicylinder, multiengine.** 3 Many times over: **mul·timillionaire.** Also **mult-.** [< L multus much]

mul·ti·far·i·ous (mul′tə·fâr′ē·əs) adj. Having great diversity or variety. [< L multifarius] —**mul′ti·far′i·ous·ly** adv. —**mul′ti·far′i·ous·ness** n.

mul·ti·fold (mul′tə·fōld) adj. Many times doubled.

mul·ti·form (mul′tə·fôrm) adj. Having many forms, shapes, or appearances. —**mul′ti·form′i·ty** n.

mul·ti·lat·er·al (mul′ti·lat′ər·əl) adj. 1 Having many sides. 2 Involving more than two nations, states, or parties.

mul·ti·me·di·a (mul′ti·mē′dē·ə) adj. Relating to or using two or more media, esp. a combination apprehended by different senses, as sight and hearing.

mul·ti·mil·lion·aire (mul′ti·mil′yən·âr′, -mil′yən·âr′, mul′tī-) n. A person having a fortune of many millions.

mul·tip·a·rous (mul·tip′ə·rəs) *adj.* 1 Having borne more than one child. 2 *Zool.* Giving birth to many at one time. [< MULTI- + *parere* give birth to]

mul·ti·par·tite (mul′ti·pär′tīt) *adj.* 1 Divided into many parts. 2 MULTILATERAL (def. 2).

mul·ti·ple (mul′tə·pəl) *adj.* 1 Containing or consisting of more than one part, element, characteristic, etc.; manifold. 2 Shared by or involving many. 3 *Electr.* Of or being a circuit having two or more conductors connected in parallel. —*n.* The product of a given number and another factor. [< LL *multiplus* manifold]

multiple myeloma A malignant tumor of the bone marrow occurring at numerous sites.

multiple sclerosis A chronic disease of the nervous system in which hard patches develop in the brain and spinal cord.

mul·ti·plex (mul′tə·pleks) *adj.* 1 Multiple; manifold. 2 *Telecom.* Designating a system for the simultaneous transmission of two or more messages or signals over the same channel.

mul·ti·pli·cand (mul′tə·plə·kand′) *n.* A number multiplied, or to be multiplied, by another. [< L *multiplicandus* to be multiplied]

mul·ti·pli·ca·tion (mul′tə·plə·kā′shən) *n.* 1 The process of multiplying. 2 The process of finding the sum (the *product*) of a number (the *multiplicand*) repeated a given number of times (the *multiplier*).

mul·ti·plic·i·ty (mul′tə·plis′ə·tē) *n.* 1 The condition of being manifold or various. 2 A large number.

mul·ti·pli·er (mul′tə·plī′ər) *n.* 1 One who or that which multiplies or causes multiplication. 2 The number by which a second number is multiplied.

mul·ti·ply (mul′tə·plī) *v.* **·plied**, **·ply·ing** *v.t.* 1 To increase the quantity, amount, or degree of. 2 To perform the operation of multiplication upon. —*v.i.* 3 To become more in number, amount, or degree; increase. 4 To perform multiplication. [< L *multiplex* manifold] —Syn. 3 grow, enlarge, proliferate, expand.

mul·ti·stage (mul′tə·stāj) *adj.* 1 Having or characterized by stages in the completion of a process. 2 *Aerospace* Having several sections, as a rocket, each of which fulfills a given task.

mul·ti·tude (mul′tə·t 00 d) *n.* 1 A large crowd or gathering. 2 A great number. 3 The condition of being many. [< L *multus* much, many]

mul·ti·tu·di·nous (mul′tə·t 00 ′də·nəs) *adj.* 1 Consisting of a vast number; numerous. 2 Having many elements, parts, aspects, etc. —**mul′ti·tu′di·nous·ly** *adv.* —**mul′ti·tu′di·nous·ness** *n.*

mul·ti·va·lent (mul′ti·vā′lənt) *adj. Chem.* Having three or more valences. —**mul′ti·va′lence** *n.*

mul·ti·ver·si·ty (mul′ti·vûr′sə·tē) *n. pl.* **·ties** A very large university with a student enrollment of many thousands, offering instruction and graduate study in many fields and often on a number of campuses. [< MULTI- + (UNI)VERSITY]

mum[1] (mum) *adj.* Silent; saying nothing. —*interj.* Hush! Be quiet! —**mum's the word** Say nothing.

mum[2] (mum) *v.i.* **mummed**, **mum·ming** To play or act in a mask, as at Christmas; be a mummer. [< OF *momer*]

mum[3] (mum) *n. Informal* A chrysanthemum.

mum·ble (mum′bəl) *v.t. & v.i.* **·bled**, **·bling** To speak or utter in low, indistinct tones; mutter. —*n.* A low, mumbling speech; mutter. [ME *momelen*] —**mum′bler** *n.*

mum·ble·ty·peg (mum′bəl·tē·peg′) *n.* A game played with a jackknife, which is tossed and flipped in various ways so as to stick into the ground. Also **mum·ble·the·peg** (mum′bəl·thə·peg′).

mum·bo jum·bo (mum′bō jum′bō) 1 Any meaningless, usu. elaborate ritual or incantation. 2 Anything overly complicated or involved. [< *Mumbo Jumbo,* a village god of certain African tribes]

mum·mer (mum′ər) *n.* 1 One who wears a mask or disguise, as for certain festivals. 2 An actor, esp. one in a pantomime.

mum·mer·y (mum′ər·ē) *n. pl.* **·mer·ies** 1 A performance by mummers. 2 Any hypocritical or pretentious ceremony or performance.

mum·mi·fy (mum′ə·fī) *v.* **·fied**, **·fy·ing** *v.t.* 1 To make a mummy; preserve by drying. —*v.i.* 2 To dry up; shrivel. —**mum′mi·fi·ca′tion** *n.*

mum·my (mum′ē) *n. pl.* **·mies** 1 A body embalmed in the ancient Egyptian manner. 2 Any dead body which is very well preserved. 3 A person or thing that is dried up and withered. —*v.t. & v.i.* **·mied**, **·my·ing** MUMMIFY. [< Pers. *mūm* wax]

mumps (mumps) *n.pl. (construed as singular)* An acute, contagious, febrile disease of viral origin, characterized by swelling of the salivary glands. [pl. of obs. *mump* grimace]

munch (munch) *v.t. & v.i.* To chew with a crunching sound. [ME *monchen, manchen*] —**munch′er** *n.*

Mummy and case

mun·dane (mun·dān′, mun′dān) *adj.* 1 Characterized by being ordinary, practical, and everyday. 2 Of or pertaining to the world. [< L *mundus* world] —**mun·dane′ly** *adv.* —**mun·dane′ness** *n.*

mu·nic·i·pal (myoo·nis′ə·pəl) *adj.* 1 Of or pertaining to a town or city or its government. 2 Having local self-government. [< L *municeps* free citizen] —**mu·nic′i·pal·ly** *adv.*

mu·nic·i·pal·i·ty (myoo·nis′ə·pal′ə·tē) *n. pl.* **·ties** An incorporated borough, town, or city.

mu·nic·i·pal·ize (myoo·nis′ə·pəl·īz) *v.t.* **·ized**, **·iz·ing** To place under municipal authority or transfer to municipal ownership. —**mu·nic′i·pal·i·za′tion** *n.*

mu·nif·i·cent (myoo·nif′ə·sənt) *adj.* Extraordinarily generous or bountiful; liberal. [< L *munus* gift + *facere* to make] —**mu·nif′i·cence** *n.* —**mu·nif′i·cent·ly** *adv.*

mu·ni·tion (myoo·nish′ən) *n. Usu. pl.* Ammunition and all necessary war materiel. —*v.t.* To furnish with munitions. [< L *munire* fortify]

mu·ral (myoor′əl) *n.* A painting or decoration on a wall. —*adj.* 1 Executed on or applied to a wall. 2 Of, pertaining to, or like a wall. [< L *murus* wall] —**mu′ral·ist** *n.*

mur·der (mûr′dər) *v.t.* 1 To kill (a human being) with premeditated malice. 2 To kill in a barbarous or inhuman manner; slaughter. 3 *Informal* To spoil by bad performance, etc.; mangle; butcher. —*v.i.* 4 To commit murder. —*n.* 1 The unlawful and intentional killing of one human being by another; homicide. 2 *Informal* Something very difficult, unpleasant, or dangerous. [Fusion of OE *morthor* + OF *murdre*] —**mur′der·er** *n.* —**mur′der·ess** *n. Fem.*

mur·der·ous (mûr′dər·əs) *adj.* 1 Of, pertaining to, or causing murder. 2 Capable of or plotting murder. 3 Violently hostile; menacing: a *murderous* look. 4 *Informal* Very difficult, unpleasant, or dangerous. —**mur′der·ous·ly** *adv.* —**mur′der·ous·ness** *n.*

mu·ri·at·ic acid (myoor′ē·at′ik) HYDROCHLORIC ACID. [< L *muria* brine]

murk (mûrk) *n.* Darkness; gloom. [ME *mirke*]

murk·y (mûr′kē) *adj.* **murk·i·er**, **murk·i·est** 1 Dark; obscure. 2 Hazy; misty, as with fog. 3 Lacking in clarity; confused or ambiguous. —**murk′i·ly** *adv.* —**murk′i·ness** *n.*

mur·mur (mûr′mər) *n.* 1 A low sound continually repeated. 2 A complaint uttered in a low, indistinct voice. 3 An abnormal sound heard in some region of the body during auscultation: a heart *murmur.* —*v.i.* 1 To make a murmur. 2 To complain in a low tone. —*v.t.* 3 To utter in a low tone. [< L] —**mur′mur·er** *n.* —**mur′mur·ous** *adj.*

mur·rain (mûr′in) *n.* Any of various infectious diseases of domestic animals. [< L *mori* to die]

mus. museum; music.

mus·ca·dine (mus′kə·din, -dīn) *n.* A species of grape with a tough skin and musky flavor, grown in the s U.S. [< Prov. *muscat* muscat]

mus·cat (mus′kat, -kət) *n.* 1 A variety of sweet European grape used in making wine and raisins. 2 MUSCATEL. [< LL *muscus* musk]

mus·ca·tel (mus′kə·tel′) *n.* **1** A rich, sweet wine made from the muscat grape. **2** The muscat grape. Also **mus′ca·del′** (-del′).

mus·cle (mus′əl) *n.* **1** Any of the organs, composed of bundles of fibers, by whose contraction all bodily motion is effected. **2** The fibrous, elastic tissue of these organs. **3** Muscular strength. **4** *Informal* Power; force: a law with *muscle.* —*v.i.* ·cled, ·cling *Informal* To push in or ahead by sheer physical strength. [< L *musculus*, lit., little mouse] —**mus′cled** *adj.*

mus·cle-bound (mus′əl·bound′) *adj.* Having enlarged, inelastic muscles, as from excessive exercise.

Mus·co·vite (mus′kə·vīt) *n.* **1** A native or inhabitant of Muscovy or of Moscow. **2** A Russian. —*adj.* Of or pertaining to Muscovy or to Russia.

Mus·co·vy (mus′kə·vē) *n.* Ancient Russia.

mus·cu·lar (mus′kyə·lər) *adj.* **1** Of, pertaining to, or accomplished by muscles. **2** Possessing strong muscles; powerful. —**mus′cu·lar′i·ty** (-lar′ə·tē) *n.* —**mus′cu·lar·ly** *adv.*

muscular dystrophy Any of various chronic diseases of undetermined cause, characterized by wasting away of muscles.

mus·cu·la·ture (mus′kyə·lə·chŏŏr′) *n.* **1** The disposition or arrangement of muscles in a part or organ. **2** The muscle system as a whole.

muse¹ (myōōz) *n.* A source of inspiration for artists, poets, etc. [< MUSE]

muse² (myōōz) *v.t. & v.i.* **mused, mus·ing** To consider thoughtfully or at length; ponder; meditate. —*n.* The state of musing; reverie. [< OF *muser* reflect] —**mus′er** *n.* —**Syn.** *v.* reflect, deliberate, dream, meditate.

Muse (myōōz) *Gk. Myth.* Any of the nine goddesses presiding over poetry, the arts, and the sciences.

mu·se·um (myōō·zē′əm) *n.* A building or place preserving and exhibiting works of nature, art, curiosities, etc.; also, any collection of such objects. [< Gk. *mouseion* temple of the Muses]

mush¹ (mush) *n.* **1** Thick porridge, made by boiling cornmeal in water or milk. **2** Anything soft and pulpy. **3** *Informal* Sentimentality. [Var. of MASH] —**mush′y** *adj.* (·i·er, ·i·est)

mush² (mush) *v.i.* In Alaska and N Canada, to travel on foot, esp. over snow with a dog sled. —*interj.* Get along! a call of the drivers of a dog team. [? < F (Canadian) *marchons,* the cry of trappers to their dogs]

mush·room (mush′rōōm, ·rŏŏm) *n.* **1** The fleshy, spore-bearing body of any of an order of fungi, consisting of an erect stalk and a caplike expansion. **2** Any nonpoisonous mushroom used as food, esp. the **field mushroom.** —*v.i.* **1** To grow or spread rapidly. **2** To expand into a mushroomlike shape. —*adj.* **1** Pertaining to or made of mushrooms. **2** Like a mushroom in shape or rapid growth. [< OF *mouscheron*]

Agaric mushrooms

mu·sic (myōō′zik) *n.* **1** The art of organizing tones, esp. with respect to time, to form an aesthetic whole. **2** A composition, or mass of compositions: contemporary *music.* **3** Any pleasing succession or combination of sounds. —**face the music** To accept the consequences or punishment for one's actions. [< Gk. *mousikē (technē)* (art) of the Muses]

mu·si·cal (myōō′zi·kəl) *adj.* **1** Of, pertaining to, or characteristic of music. **2** Talented in or appreciative of music. **3** Set to music. —*n.* A theatrical or film production that tells a story by means of dialogue interspersed with music, songs, and dancing in a more or less popular idiom: also **musical comedy, musical play.** —**mu′si·cal·ly** *adv.* —**mu′si·cal′i·ty** (-kal′ə·tē), **mu′si·cal·ness** *n.*

mu·si·cale (myōō′zə·kal′) *n.* An informal concert or private recital, often held in a home. [F]

music box A case containing a mechanism that reproduces melodies.

music hall 1 A public building devoted to musical entertainments. **2** *Brit.* A vaudeville house.

mu·si·cian (myōō·zish′ən) *n.* One skilled in music, esp. a professional performer or composer. —**mu·si′cian·ly** *adj.* —**mu·si′cian·ship** *n.*

mu·si·col·o·gy (myōō′zə·kol′ə·jē) *n.* The scientific and historical study of music. —**mu·si·col′o·gist** *n.*

mus·ing (myōō′zing) *adj.* Thoughtful; meditative. —*n.* The act of one who muses. —**mus′ing·ly** *adv.*

musk (musk) *n.* **1** A substance having a penetrating odor, obtained from a sac (**musk bag**) on the abdomen of the male musk deer. **2** A similar substance from certain other animals. **3** This substance, or a synthetic substitute, used to make perfumes. [< Pers. *mushk*]

musk deer A small hornless deer of CEN. and E Asia, of which the male has a musk-secreting gland.

mus·kel·lunge (mus′kə·lunj) *n. pl.* ·**lunge** *n.* A large North American pike valued as a game fish. Also **mus′kal·lunge, mus′kie** (-kē). [< Algon.]

mus·ket (mus′kit) *n.* A large, long-barreled shoulder firearm, used esp. by soldiers on foot until superseded by the rifle. [< L *musca* fly]

mus·ket·eer (mus′kə·tir′) *n.* Formerly, a soldier armed with a musket.

mus·ket·ry (mus′kit·rē) *n.* **1** Muskets collectively. **2** The technique of operating small arms.

Mus·kho·ge·an (mus·kō′gē·ən, mus′kō·gē′ən) *n.* One of the principal North American Indian linguistic stocks, formerly inhabiting the SE U.S. Also **Mus·ko′gi·an.**

musk·mel·on (musk′mel′ən) *n.* Any of various melons having a pronounced aroma, esp. the cantaloupe.

musk ox A shaggy, horned ruminant of Greenland and North America, emitting a strong odor of musk.

musk·rat (musk′rat′) *n. pl.* ·**rats** or ·**rat 1** A North American aquatic rodent yielding a valuable, glossy, dark brown fur and secreting a substance with a musky odor. **2** Its fur.

musk·y (mus′kē) *adj.* **musk·i·er, musk·i·est** Like or smelling of musk. —**musk′i·ly** *adv.* —**musk′i·ness** *n.*

Mus·lim (muz′ləm, mŏŏz′-, mōōs′-) *n. pl.* ·**lims** or ·**lim** A believer in Islam; Mohammedan. —*adj.* Of or pertaining to Islam or the Muslims. Also **Mus′lem.** —**Mus′lim·ism** *n.*

mus·lin (muz′lin) *n.* Any of several varieties of plain-weave cotton cloth ranging in texture from fine to heavy. [< F < Ital. *Mussolo* Mosul, city in Iraq where made]

muss (mus) *v.t. Informal* To make messy or untidy; rumple; often with *up.* —*n. Informal* **1** A state of disorder; mess. **2** A squabble. [Alter. of MESS]

mus·sel (mus′əl) *n.* **1** Any of various bivalve marine mollusks, esp. the common edible mussel. **2** Any of several freshwater mollusks, including species with bivalve shells yielding commercial mother-of-pearl. [< L *musculus,* dim. of *mus* mouse]

Mus·sul·man (mus′əl·mən) *n. pl.* ·**mans** (-mənz) or ·**men** (-mən) MUSLIM.

muss·y (mus′ē) *adj. Informal* **muss·i·er, muss·i·est** Disarranged; rumpled. —**muss′i·ly** *adv.* —**muss′i·ness** *n.*

must¹ (must) *v.* An auxiliary verb expressing: **1** Obligation or compulsion: *Must* you go? **2** Requirement: You *must* be healthy to be accepted. **3** Probability or supposition: You *must* be tired. **4** Conviction or certainty: War *must* follow. —*n. Informal* Something that ought to be done, required, seen, enjoyed, etc. —*adj. Informal* Important and essential: a *must* book. [< OE *mōste,* p.t. of *mōtan* may]

must² (must) *n.* Mustiness; mold. [Back formation < MUSTY]

must³ (must) *n.* Unfermented juice pressed from the grape or other fruit. [< L *mustum (vinum)* new wine]

mus·tache (mus′tash, məs·tash′) *n.* **1** The growth of hair on the upper lip. **2** The hair or bristles growing near the mouth of an animal. Also **mus·ta′chio** (-tä′shō). [< Gk. *mystax* upper lip]

mus·tang (mus′tang) *n.* The wild horse of the American plains. [< Sp. *mesteño* wild animal]

mus·tard (mus′tərd)·*n.* **1** Any of various plants related to cabbage, having yellow flowers and pods of round seeds. **2** The pungent seed of certain kinds of mustard, crushed for use as a condiment. **3** A strong, dark yellow color. [< OF *moustarde*]

mustard gas A synthetic organic sulfide, having a pungent odor and disabling effects, developed as a poison gas for military use.

mustard plaster A paste made of powdered mustard for use as a poultice.

mus·ter (mus′tər) *v.t.* **1** To summon or assemble (troops, etc.), as for service, review, or roll call. **2** To collect or summon: often with *up*: to *muster* up courage. —*v.i.* **3** To come together or assemble, as troops. —**muster in** (or **out**) To enlist in (or discharge from) military service. —*n.* **1** An assembling or an assemblage, esp. of troops for parade or review. **2** An official list of officers and men in a military troop or a ship's crew: also **muster roll**. **3** A specimen; pattern; sample. —**pass muster 1** To pass inspection. **2** To be acceptable or accepted. [< L *monstrare* to show]

must·y (mus′tē) *adj.* **must·i·er, must·i·est 1** Having a moldy, stale odor or taste. **2** Not original; trite; stale. **3** Dull; lifeless. [? Alter. of earlier *moisty* < MOIST] —**must′i·ly** *adv.* —**must′i·ness** *n.*

mu·ta·ble (myōō′tə·bəl) *adj.* **1** Capable of or liable to change. **2** Fickle; unstable. [< *mutare* to change] —**mu′ta·ble·ness, mu·ta·bil′i·ty** *n.* —**mu′ta·bly** *adv.*

mu·tant (myōō′tənt) *n.* A plant or animal showing a mutation.

mu·tate (myōō′tāt) *v.t. & v.i.* **·tat·ed, ·tat·ing** To undergo or subject to mutation.

mu·ta·tion (myōō·tā′shən) *n.* **1** The act or process of change; alteration. **2** A change or modification in form, function, etc. **3** *Biol.* A heritable characteristic not inherited from forebears but due to an alteration in a gene or genes in a germ cell. [< L *mutare* to change] —**mu·ta′tion·al, mu·ta·tive** (myōō′tə·tiv) *adj.*

mute (myōōt) *adj.* **1** Uttering no word or sound; silent. **2** Lacking the power of speech; dumb. **3** Expressed without speech or sound: a *mute* refusal. **4** *Law* Refusing to plead upon arraignment. **5** *Phonet.* Not pronounced, as the *e* in *house.* —*n.* **1** One who refuses or is unable to speak. **2** *Music* A device to soften or muffle the tone of an instrument. **3** *Phonet.* A stop consonant. —*v.t.* **mut·ed, mut·ing** To soften or muffle the sound of (a musical instrument). [< L *mutus* dumb] —**mute′ly** *adv.* —**mute′ness** *n.*

mu·ti·late (myōō′tə·lāt) *v.t.* **·lat·ed, ·lat·ing 1** To deprive (a person, animal, etc.) of a limb or essential part; maim. **2** To damage or injure by the removal of an important part or parts: to *mutilate* a speech. [< L *mutilare* maim] —**mu′ti·la′tion, mu′ti·la′tor** *n.* —**mu′ti·la′tive** *adj.*

mu·ti·neer (myōō′tə·nir′) *n.* or One who takes part in mutiny. —*v.i.* To mutiny.

mu·ti·nous (myōō′tə·nəs) *adj.* **1** Disposed to or engaged in mutiny. **2** Characteristic of, relating to, or constituting mutiny. **3** Rebellious; unruly. —**mu′ti·nous·ly** *adv.* —**mu′ti·nous·ness** *n.*

mu·ti·ny (myōō′tə·nē) *n. pl.* **·nies** Rebellion against constituted authority; esp., a revolt of soldiers or sailors against their officers or commander. —*v.i.* **·nied, ·ny·ing** To take part in a mutiny. [< OF *mutin* riotous]

mutt (mut) *n. Slang* **1** A cur; mongrel dog. **2** A stupid person; blockhead. [< earlier *muttonhead* a stupid person]

mut·ter (mut′ər) *v.i.* **1** To speak in a low, indistinct tone. **2** To complain; grumble. **3** To make a low, rumbling sound. —*v.t.* **4** To say in a low, indistinct tone. —*n.* A low, indistinct utterance. [ME *muteren*] —**mut′ter·er** *n.* —**Syn. 1** mumble, murmur, whisper.

mut·ton (mut′n) *n.* The flesh of mature sheep as food. [< OF *moton* ram] —**mut′ton·y** *adj.*

mut·ton·chops (mut′n·chops′) *n. pl.* Side whiskers that are narrow at the temples and become broader at the cheeks.

mu·tu·al (myōō′chōō·əl) *adj.* **1** Shared, felt, received, etc., by each of two or more; reciprocal: *mutual* trust. **2** Having similar feelings each for the other or others: *mutual* enemies. **3** Possessed in common. [< L *mutuus* lent, exchanged, mutual] —**mu′tu·al′i·ty** *n.* —**mu′tu·al·ly** *adv.*

muttonchops

muu·muu (mōō′mōō′) *n.* A long, loose gown for women, originally worn in Hawaii.

Mu·zak (myōō′zak′) *n.* Unobtrusive popular recorded mu-sic played as background music, as in restaurants, shops, offices, etc.; also, the system for transmitting such music: a trade name.

mu·zhik (mōō·zhēk′, mōō′zhēk) *n.* A Russian peasant in Czarist times. Also **mu·zjik′.**

muz·zle (muz′əl) *n.* **1** The projecting jaws and nose of an animal. **2** A guard or covering for an animal's snout. **3** The discharging end of a firearm. —*v.t.* **·zled, ·zling 1** To put a muzzle on. **2** To restrain from speaking, expressing opinions, etc. [< LL *musus* snout] —**muz′zler** *n.*

Muzzle def. 2

muz·zle·load·er (muz′əl·lō′dər) *n.* A firearm loaded through the muzzle. —**muz·zle·load′ing** *adj.*

m.v. softly (It. *mezzo voce*).

my (mī) *pronominal adj.* **1** The possessive case of the pronoun *I* employed attributively. **2** An adjective used in certain forms of address: *my* lord. —*interj.* An exclamation of surprise: oh *my!* [< OE *mīn*]

my·ce·li·um (mī·sē′lē·əm) *n. pl.* **·li·a** (·lē·ə) The network of fine hyphae that makes up the main plant body of certain fungi, as mushrooms and molds. [< MYC(o) · + Gk. *hēlos* nail] —**my·ce′li·al, my·ce′li·an, my·ce′li·oid, my·ce·loid** (mī′sə·loid) *adj.*

My·ce·nae (mī·sē′nē) *n.* An ancient city in NE Peloponnesus, Greece. —**My′ce·nae′an** *adj., n.*

myco- *combining form* Fungus: *mycology.* Also **myc-.** [< Gk. *mykēs* fungus]

my·col·o·gy (mī·kol′ə·jē) *n.* The branch of botany dealing with fungi. [< MYCO- + -LOGY] —**my·co·log·ic** (mī′kə·loj′ik) or **·i·cal** *adj.* —**my·col′o·gist** *n.*

my·co·sis (mī·kō′sis) *n. pl.* **·ses** (·sēz) **1** A parasitic fungous growth. **2** A disease caused by a parasitic fungus, as ringworm. [< MYC(o)· + -OSIS] —**my·cot′ic** (-kot′ik) *adj.*

my·e·li·tis (mī′ə·lī′tis) *n.* Inflammation of the spinal cord or of the bone marrow. [< Gk. *myelos* marrow + -ITIS]

my·na (mī′nə) *n.* One of various Asian, starlinglike birds often tamed and taught to mimic speech. Also **my′nah.** [< Hind. *mainā*]

Myn·heer (mīn·hâr′, ·hir′) *n.* Sir; Mr.: a Dutch title of address. [< Du. *mijn heer*, lit., my lord]

my·o·car·di·um (mī′ō·kär′dē·əm) *n.* The muscular tissue forming the heart. [< Gk. *mys* muscle + *kardia* heart] —**my′o·car′di·al** *adj.*

my·o·pi·a (mī·ō′pē·ə) *n.* **1** A defect in vision in which objects can be seen distinctly only when very near the eye; nearsightedness. **2** Lack of insight or good judgment. [< Gk. *myein* to close + *ōps* eye] —**my·op′ic** (-op′ik) *adj.*

myr·i·ad (mir′ē·əd) *adj.* Multitudinous; innumerable. —*n.* **1** A vast indefinite number. **2** Ten thousand. [< Gk. *myrios* numberless]

myr·i·a·pod (mir′ē·ə·pod) *n.* An arthropod having an elongated, segmented body bearing many pairs of appendages, a centipede or a millipede. [< Gk. *myrios* numberless + *pous, podos* foot]

myr·mi·don (mûr′mə·don, -dən) *n.* A faithful, obedient follower. [< MYRMIDON]

Myr·mi·don (mûr′mə′·don, -dən) *Gk. Myth.* One of a warlike people of Thessaly, followers of Achilles in the Trojan War.

myrrh (mûr) *n.* **1** An aromatic gum resin that exudes from several trees or shrubs of Arabia and E Africa, used in perfumes, incense, etc. **2** Any shrub or tree that yields this gum. [< L < Gk. *myrrha* < Ar. *myrr*]

myr·tle (mûr′təl) *n.* **1** An evergreen shrub with dense, glossy leaves that are fragrant when crushed, white or pink flowers, and black berries. **2** One of various other plants, as the periwinkle. [< Gk. *myrtos*]

my·self (mī·self′) *pron.* A form of the first person singular pronoun, used: **1** As a reflexive: I hurt *myself.* **2** As an intensive: I *myself* will see to it. **3** Informally as a compound object of a verb: She invited Helen, Jeff, and *myself.* **4** As a designation of one's normal or usual state: I haven't been *myself* lately.

mys·te·ri·ous (mis·tir′ē·əs) *adj.* **1** Of, implying, or characterized by mystery. **2** Unexplained; baffling. —**mys·te′ri·**

ous·ly adv. —**mys·te′ri·ous·ness** n. —**Syn. 1** mystical, occult, secret, deep. **2** enigmatic, inexplicable, inscrutable, puzzling, perplexing.

mys·ter·y (mis′tər-ē) n. pl. ·ter·ies **1** Something that cannot be explained or comprehended. **2** Any action, affair, or event so obscure or concealed as to arouse suspense, curiosity, or fear. **3** A story, play, film, etc. dealing with such actions or affairs. **4** Secrecy or obscurity: an event wrapped in *mystery*. **5** *Theol.* A truth known only through faith or revelation and incomprehensible to human reason. **6** *Eccl.* A sacrament, esp. the Eucharist. **7** *Usu. pl.* Secret rites or practices. **8** MYSTERY PLAY. [<Gk. *mystērion* secret worship, secret thing]

mystery play A medieval dramatic representation based on Biblical events or characters.

mys·tic (mis′tik) adj. **1** Of or pertaining to mystics or mysticism. **2** Of or designating an occult or esoteric rite, practice, belief, etc. **3** Mysterious; enigmatic. —n. One who practices mysticism or has mystical experiences. [<Gk. *mystikos* pertaining to secret rites]

mys·ti·cal (mis′ti·kəl) adj. **1** Characteristic of, relating to, or involving mysticism or mystics. **2** Believing in or practicing mysticism. **3** Inscrutable; inexplicable.

mys·ti·cism (mis′tə·siz′əm) n. **1** Any of various disciplines, usu. involving meditation and asceticism, by which one can supposedly attain intuitive knowledge of or direct union with God or some ultimate reality. **2** The experience of such knowledge or union. **3** Any theory or belief which states that it is possible to have immediate, intuitive experience of realities beyond man's senses or rational faculties. **4** Vague or obscure thinking.

mys·ti·fy (mis′tə·fī) v.t. ·fied, ·fy·ing **1** To confuse or perplex, esp. deliberately. **2** To make obscure or mysterious. [<L *mysterium* mystery] —**mys′ti·fi·ca′tion, mys′ti·fi′er** n.

mys·tique (mis·tēk′) n. A kind of legendary or superhuman quality or aura with which certain persons, things, or occupations are invested, making them objects of awe, curiosity, or veneration: the *mystique* of de Gaulle. [F]

myth (mith) n. **1** A traditional story, presented as historical, often purporting to explain some natural phenomenon, as the creation of life, and expressive of the character of a people, their gods, culture, heroes, religious beliefs, etc. **2** Any real or imaginary story, theme, or character that excites the interest or imagination of a people. **3** Myths collectively. **4** Any imaginary person or thing. **5** A false belief or opinion. [<Gk. *mythos* word, speech, story]

myth., mythol. mythology; mythological.

myth·i·cal (mith′i·kəl) adj. **1** Of or like a myth. **2** Existing only in a myth. **3** Imaginary; fictitious. Also **myth′ic.**

my·thol·o·gize (mi·thol′ə·jīz) v.t. ·gized, ·giz·ing To make into a myth; glorify. [<F *mythologiser*]

my·thol·o·gy (mi·thol′ə·jē) n. pl. ·gies **1** A collection of myths of a people, person, thing, event, etc. **2** The scientific collection and study of myths. —**myth·o·log·i·cal** (mith′ə·loj′i·kəl), **myth′o·log′ic** adj. —**myth′o·log′i·cal·ly** adv. —**my·thol′o·gist** n.

N

N, n (en) n. pl. **N's, n's, Ns, ns** (enz) **1** The 14th letter of the English alphabet. **2** Any spoken sound representing the letter N or n. **3** *Printing* EN. **4** *Math.* An indefinite number. **5** Something shaped like an N. —adj. Shaped like an N.

N nitrogen; knight (chess).

N, N., n. north; northern.

N. Navy; Norse; November.

n neutron.

n. name; net; neuter; noon; note; noun; number; born (L *natus*); our (L *noster*).

N.A. North America.

Na sodium (L *natrium*).

NAACP, N.A.A.C.P. National Association for the Advancement of Colored People.

nab (nab) v.t. **nabbed, nab·bing** *Informal* **1** To catch or arrest, as a criminal. **2** To seize suddenly. [? <Scand.]

na·bob (nā′bob) n. **1** A native governor in India under the Mogul empire. **2** A very rich and prominent man. [<Ar. *nuwwab*] —**na′bob·er·y, na′bob·ism** n. —**na′bob·ish** adj.

na·celle (nə·sel′) n. *Aeron.* An enclosure for the cargo or power plant and sometimes the personnel of an airplane. [F, lit., small boat]

na·cho (nä′chō) n. pl. ·chos A tortilla chip baked with a covering of beans, cheese, and peppers. [<Sp.]

na·cre (nā′kər) n. MOTHER-OF-PEARL. [F] —**na·cre·ous** (nā′krē·əs) adj.

na·dir (nā′dər, -dir) n. **1** The point of the celestial sphere intersected by a diameter extending from the zenith. **2** The lowest possible point. [<Ar. *nadir (es-semt)* opposite (the zenith)]

nag¹ (nag) v. **nagged, nag·ging** v.t. To torment with constant faultfinding, scolding, and urging. —v.t. To scold, find fault, or urge continually. —n. One who nags, esp. a woman. [Scand.] —**nag′ger** n. —**nag′ging·ly** adv. —**Syn.** v. berate, carp, harp, henpeck.

nag² (nag) n. **1** A pony or small horse. **2** An old or inferior horse. [ME *nagge*]

Na·hua·tl (nä′wät′l) n. The Uto-Aztecan language of the Aztecs and other Mexican and Central American Indian tribes. —adj. Designating or pertaining to this language.

nai·ad (nā′ad, nī′-) n. pl. ·ads or ·a·des (-ə·dēz) *Gk. & Rom. Myth.* One of the nymphs believed to dwell in and preside over watery sites.

na·if (nä·ēf′) adj. NAIVE. Also **na·ïf′.** [F]

nail (nāl) n. **1** A thin, horny plate on the end of a finger or toe. **2** Claw, talon, or hoof. **3** A slender piece of metal having a point and a head, driven through or into wood, etc., as a fastener. —**hit the nail on the head 1** To express something aptly. **2** To perform correctly. —**on the nail** *Informal* **1** Right away; immediately. **2** At the exact spot or moment. —v.t. **1** To fasten or fix in place with a nail or nails. **2** To close up or shut in by means of nails. **3** To secure by prompt action: to *nail* a contract. **4** To fix firmly or immovably: Terror *nailed* him to the spot. **5** To succeed in hitting or striking. **6** *Informal* To catch; intercept. **7** *Informal* To detect and expose, as a lie or liar. [<OE *nægel*] —**nail′er** n.

Nails *def. 3*
a, b. common. c. fiberboard. d. finishing.
e. roofing. f. flooring.
a. masonry.

nail·brush (nāl′brush′) n. A brush with stiff bristles, used for cleaning the hands and fingernails.

nail file A fine, flat file used for smoothing and shaping the tips of the fingernails.

nain·sook (nān′sŏŏk) n. A soft, lightweight cotton fabric. [<Hind. *nainsukh* pleasure of the eye]

na·ive (nä·ēv′) adj. **1** Simple and without affectation or sophistication. **2** Not consciously logical; uncritical. Also **na·ïve′.** [<F <L *nativus* natural, native] —**na·ive′ly** adv. —**na·ive′ness** n. —**Syn. 1** artless, candid, open, unaffected, ingenuous.

na·ive·té (nä·ēv·tā′, nä·ēv′tā) n. The state or quality of being naive. Also **na·ive·té′, na·ive·ty** (nä·ēv′tē, -ē′və·tē).

na·ked (nā′kid) adj. **1** Having no clothes or garments on. **2** Having no covering, as an unsheathed sword. **3** Having no defense or protection; exposed. **4** Being without concealment or excuse. [<OE *nacod*] —**na′ked·ly** adv. —**na′ked·ness** n.

naked eye The eye unaided by optical instruments.

N.A.M. National Association of Manufacturers.

N. Am. North American.

nam·ay·cush (nam′ə·kush, -ā-) n. The great lake trout of North America. Also **nay′ma·cush.** [<Algon. (Cree) *namekus* trout]

nam·by-pam·by (nam′bē-pam′bē) *adj.* Weakly sentimental or insipid. —*n. pl.* **-pam·bies 1** Namby-pamby talk, action, etc. **2** A person given to such talk or action. [<satirical name for Ambrose Philips, 1671–1749, Eng. poet]

name (nām) *n.* **1** The distinctive appellation by which a person or thing is known. **2** A descriptive designation; title. **3** General reputation. **4** An abusive appellation. **5** A memorable person, character, or thing: great *names* in music. —**by the name of** Named. —**call names** To insult by using uncomplimentary terms. —**in the name of** In behalf of. —**to one's name** Belonging to one: not a cent *to her name.* —*v.t.* **named, nam·ing 1** To give a name to. **2** To mention or refer to by name; cite. **3** To designate for some particular purpose or office; nominate. **4** To give the name of: *Name* the capital of Peru. **5** To set or specify, as a price or requirement. [<OE *nama*] —**nam′er** *n.*

name·less (nām′lis) *adj.* **1** Having no name; unnamed. **2** Having no fame or reputation. **3** Not suitable or fit to be spoken of. **4** Not to be named; inexpressible. **5** Illegitimate. —**name′less·ly** *adv.* —**name′less·ness** *n.*

name·ly (nām′lē) *adv.* That is to say; to wit.

name·plate (nām′plāt′) *n.* A piece of wood, metal, or plastic with a name inscribed on it, as on a door or desk.

name·sake (nām′sāk′) *n.* One who is named after or has the same name as another.

nan·a (nan′ə, nä′nä) *n.* Grandmother.

nan·keen (nan·kēn′) *n.* **1** A buff-colored Chinese cotton fabric. **2** *pl.* Clothes made of nankeen. Also **nan·kin′** [<*Nanking,* where originally made]

nan·ny (nan′ē) *n. pl.* **·nies** *Informal* **1** A female goat: also **nanny goat. 2** *Brit.* A child's nurse. [<*Nanny,* dim. of Ann]

nan·o·gram (nan′ə-gram) *n.* One billionth of a gram.

nan·o·me·ter (nan′ə-mē′tər) *n.* One billionth of a meter.

Na·o·mi (nā-ō′mē) In the Bible, the mother-in-law of Ruth.

nap¹ (nap) *n.* A short sleep; doze. —*v.i.* **napped, nap·ping** To take a nap; doze. —**be caught napping** To be caught unprepared or off guard. [<OE *hnappian* doze] —**nap′per** *n.*

nap² (nap) *n.* The short fibers on the surface of certain fabrics. —*v.t.* **napped, nap·ping** To raise a nap on. [<MDu. *noppe*] —**napped** *adj.*

na·palm (nā′päm) *n.* A jellied incendiary mixture based on gasoline. —*v.t. & v.i.* To attack or burn with napalm. [<NA(PHTHA) + *palm(itic) acid,* a fatty acid]

nape (nāp) *n.* The back of the neck. [ME]

na·per·y (nā′pər-ē) *n. pl.* **·per·ies** Household linen, as napkins, tablecloths, etc. [<OF *nape*]

naph·tha (naf′thə, nap′-) *n.* **1** A volatile, flammable mixture of hydrocarbons obtained by distilling petroleum, wood, etc. **2** Petroleum. [<Gk.]

naph·tha·lene (naf′thə-lēn, nap′-) *n.* A white, solid, volatile hydrocarbon, obtained from coal tar, used as a moth repellent and in making dyestuffs. Also **naph′tha·line** (-lēn, -lin), **naph′tha·lin.**

nap·kin (nap′kin) *n.* **1** A small cloth or piece of paper used during eating to wipe the mouth and hands and to protect the clothing. **2** *Brit.* A diaper. [<L *mappa* a cloth]

na·po·le·on (nə-pō′lē-ən, -pōl′yən) *n.* **1** A former French gold coin, equivalent to 20 francs. **2** A pastry composed of layers of puff paste filled with cream or custard. [<*Napoleon* Bonaparte, 1769–1821, Fr. emperor]

nap·py¹ (nap′ē) *adj.* **·pi·er, ·pi·est 1** Having or covered with nap. **2** Resembling nap. —**nap′pi·ness** *n.*

nap·py² (nap′ē) *n. pl.* **·pies** *Brit. Informal* A diaper.

nar·cis·sism (när′sə-siz′əm) *n.* Excessive interest in or admiration for oneself; self-love. Also **nar·cism** (när′siz·əm). [<NARCISSUS] —**nar′cis·sist** *n.* —**nar′cis·sis′tic** *adj.*

nar·cis·sus (när·sis′əs) *n. pl.* **·cis·sus·es, ·cis·si** (-sis′ē) Any of a genus of bulbous plants having straplike leaves and flowers with a central, tubular crown, as the daffodil and jonquil. [<Gk. *narkissos*]

Nar·cis·sus (när·sis′əs) *Gk. Myth.* A youth who died for love of his own image in a pool, and was changed into a narcissus.

nar·co·sis (när·kō′sis) *n.* **·ses** (sēz) Stupor or unconsciousness produced by a narcotic drug. [<Gk.]

nar·co·syn·the·sis (när′kō·sin′thə·sis) *n.* Psychiatric treatment involving the use of certain drugs to encourage a patient to talk freely about himself.

nar·cot·ic (när·kot′ik) *n.* **1** Any of various drugs, as opium and its derivatives, that induce sleep and relieve pain, and are usu. addictive when used repeatedly. **2** Anything that serves to soothe, calm, or make drowsy. —*adj.* **1** Causing narcosis or stupor. **2** Pertaining to addiction to drugs or to persons addicted. **3** Causing drowsiness or dullness. [<Gk. *narkē* torpor] —**nar·cot′i·cal·ly** *adv.*

nar·co·tism (när′kə·tiz′əm) *n.* **1** NARCOSIS. **2** Addiction to narcotic drugs.

nar·co·tize (när′kə·tīz) *v.t.* **·tized, ·tiz·ing** To bring under the influence of a narcotic; stupefy. **nar′co·ti·za′tion** *n.*

nard (närd) *n.* SPIKENARD.

nar·es (nâr′ēz) *n. pl. of* **nar·is** (nâr′is) The nostrils or nasal passages. [L, nostrils]

nar·ghi·le (när′gə·li) *n.* HOOKAH. Also **nar′gi·le, nar′gi·leh.** [<Pers. *nārgīl* a coconut]

nark (närk) *n. Slang* A police undercover agent concerned with the detection of traffic in illegal drugs. Also **narc.** [?<NARC(OTIC AGENT)]

nar·rate (nar′āt, na·rāt′) *v.t.* **·rat·ed, ·rat·ing** To tell or relate as a story; give an account of. [<L *narrare* relate] —**nar′ra·tor, nar′rat·er** *n.*

nar·ra·tion (na·rā′shən) *n.* **1** The act of narrating the particulars of an event or series of events. **2** That which is narrated; narrative.

nar·ra·tive (nar′ə·tiv) *n.* **1** An orderly, continuous account of an event or series of events. **2** The act or art of narrating. —*adj.* Pertaining to narration. —**nar′ra·tive·ly** *adv.* —**Syn.** 1 anecdote, report, story, tale.

nar·row (nar′ō) *adj.* **1** Having comparatively little distance from side to side. **2** Limited in extent or duration; circumscribed. **3** Illiberal; bigoted. **4** Limited in means or resources. **5** Niggardly; parsimonious. **6** Barely accomplished or sufficient: a *narrow* escape. **7** Scrutinizing closely: a *narrow* gaze. —*v.t. & v.i.* To make or become narrower, as in width or scope. —*n. Usu. pl.* A narrow strait or similar passage. [<OE *nearu*] —**nar′row·ly** *adv.* —**nar′row·ness** *n.*

narrow gauge 1 A width between railway tracks of less than 56.5 inches. **2** A railroad having narrow-gauge track. Also **narrow gage.** —**nar′row-gauge′, nar′row-gage′** *adj.*

nar·row-mind·ed (nar′ō·mīn′did) *adj.* **1** Having limited interests. **2** Prejudiced or bigoted. —**nar′row-mind′ed·ly** *adv.* —**nar′row-mind′ed·ness** *n.*

nar·whal (när′hwəl) *n.* An arctic cetacean having in the male a long, straight, spiraled tusk. Also **nar′wal, nar′whale′.** [<Dan. or Norw. *narhval*]

Narwhal

nar·y (nâr′ē) *adj. Regional* Never a; not one: with *a* or *an: nary* a cent. [<*ne'er a* never a]

NASA (nas′ə) National Aeronautics and Space Administration.

na·sal (nā′zəl) *adj.* **1** Of or pertaining to the nose. **2** *Phonet.* Pronounced with the voiced breath passing through the nose, as in (m), (n) and (ng). —*n. Phonet.* A nasal sound. [<L *nasus* the nose] —**na·sal·i·ty** (nā·zal′ə·tē) *n.* —**na′sal·ly** *adv.*

na·sal·ize (nā′zəl·īz) *v.* **·ized, ·iz·ing** *v.t.* **1** To give a nasal sound to. —*v.i.* **2** To pronounce oral sounds in the manner of nasals; talk through the nose. —**na′sal·i·za′tion** *n.*

nas·cent (nas′ənt, nā′sənt) *adj.* Beginning to exist or develop. [<L *nasci* be born] —**nas′cence, nas′cen·cy** *n.*

nascent state *Chem.* The condition of an atom or radical at the moment it is set free from a compound and ready to enter into combination with some other atom or radical. Also **nascent condition.**

na·stur·tium (na·stûr′shəm) *n.* **1** A common garden plant having spurred flowers of varying colors and rounded leaves with a cresslike taste. **2** The flower. [L]

nas·ty (nas′tē) *adj.* **·ti·er, ·ti·est 1** Filthy or offensively dirty. **2** Morally objectionable; indecent. **3** Difficult to handle or deal with: a *nasty* turn of events. **4** Painful; bad: a *nasty* cut. **5** Ill-natured; mean. [ME] —**nas′ti·ly** *adv.* —**nas′ti·ness** *n.*

---

add, āce, câre, pälm; end, ēven; it, īce; odd, ōpen, ôrder; tŏŏk, pōōl; up, bûrn; ə = a in *above,* u in *focus;* yōō = u in *fuse;* oil; pout; check; go; ring; thin; this; zh, *vision.* < derived from; ? origin uncertain or unknown.

na·tal (nāt′l) *adj.* Pertaining to one's birth; dating from birth. [< L *natus*, pp. of *nasci* be born]

na·tant (nā′tənt) *adj.* Floating on or swimming in water. [< L *natare* to swim]

na·ta·to·ri·al (nā′tə·tôr′ē·əl, -tō′rē-) *adj.* Swimming, or adapted for swimming. Also **na′ta·to′ry.**

na·ta·to·ri·um (nā′tə·tôr′ē·əm, -tō′rē-) *n. pl.* **·to·ri·ums** or **·to·ri·a** (-tôr′ē·ə, -tō′rē·ə) A swimming pool.

nathe·less (nāth′lis, nath′-) *adv. Archaic* Nevertheless. Also **nath·less** (nath′lis).

na·tion (nā′shən) *n.* **1** A people as an organized body politic, usu. associated with a particular territory and possessing a distinctive language and way of life. **2** A race or tribe having the same ancestry, history, language, etc.; a people. [< L *natio* breed, race]

na·tion·al (nash′ən·əl) *adj.* **1** Belonging to a nation as a whole. **2** Of, pertaining to, or characteristic of a specified nation. —*n.* One who is a member of a nation. —**na′tion·al·ly** *adv.*

national bank **1** A bank associated with and controlling the finances of a national government. **2** *U.S.* A bank chartered and supervised by the federal government.

National Guard The militia of each state of the U.S., supported in part by the federal government and subject to federal service in times of national emergency.

na·tion·al·ism (nash′ən·əl·iz′əm) *n.* **1** Devotion to the nation as a whole; patriotism. **2** A system demanding national ownership and control of all industries. **3** A demand for national independence. —**na′tion·al·ist** *adj., n.* —**na′tion·al·is′tic** *adj.* —**na′tion·al·is′ti·cal·ly** *adv.*

na·tion·al·i·ty (nash′ən·al′ə·tē) *n. pl* **·ties 1** The condition of being national; national character. **2** A nation. **3** The condition of being a member of a specific nation by birth or citizenship.

na·tion·al·ize (nash′ən·əl·īz) *v.t.* **·ized, ·iz·ing 1** To place under the control or ownership of a national government. **2** To give a national character to. **3** To make into a nation. *Brit. sp.* **·ise.** —**na′tion·al·i·za′tion, na′tion·al·iz′er** *n.*

na·tion·wide (nā′shən·wīd′) *adj.* Throughout the entire nation.

na·tive (nā′tiv) *adj.* **1** Born or produced in a region or country in which one lives; indigenous. **2** Of or pertaining to one's birth or to its place or circumstances. **3** Natural rather than acquired; inborn. **4** Of or pertaining to original inhabitants: usu. applied to non-European peoples. **5** Natural to any one or any thing. **6** Plain or simple; untouched by art. **7** Occurring in nature as a free element: *native* copper. —*n.* **1** One born in, or any product of, a given country or place. **2** Plants or animals common to a country or region. [< L *natus*, pp. of *nasci* be born.] —**na′tive·ly** *adv.* —**na′tive·ness** *n.* —**Syn.** *adj.* **3** innate, inherent.

na·tive-born (nā′tiv·bôrn′) *adj.* Born in the region or country specified.

na·tiv·i·ty (nā·tiv′ə·tē, nə-) *n. pl.* **·ties 1** The coming into life or the world; birth. **2** A horoscope. **3** The condition of being a native. —**the Nativity 1** The birth of Jesus. **2** Christmas Day.

Natl. national.

NATO (nā′tō) North Atlantic Treaty Organization.

nat·ty (nat′ē) *adj.* **·ti·er, ·ti·est** Smart; spruce; tidy: a *natty* dresser. [?] —**nat′ti·ly** *adv.* —**nat′ti·ness** *n.*

nat·u·ral (nach′ər·əl, -rəl) *adj.* **1** Of or pertaining to one's nature or constitution; inborn. **2** Of or pertaining to nature: *natural* history. **3** Of or pertaining to the existing order of things: *natural* law. **4** Coming within common experience: a *natural* result. **5** Not forced or artificial. **6** Without affectation. **7** Produced by nature: a *natural* bridge. **8** Connected by ties of consanguinity; being such by birth: a *natural* brother. **9** Born out of wedlock; illegitimate. **10** *Music* Neither sharped nor flatted: G *natural.* —*n.* **1** *Music* **a** A note on a line or a space that is affected by neither a sharp nor a flat. **b** A character (♮) which cancels the effect of an earlier flat or sharp: also **natural sign. 2** In keyboard musical instruments, a white key. **3** One lacking powers of reason or understanding; idiot. **4** *Informal* A person or thing admirably suited for some purpose or obviously destined for success. [< L *natura* nature] —**nat′u·ral·ness** *n.*

natural childbirth Childbirth regarded as a natural and relatively painless function in which the prospective mother is encouraged to participate consciously.

natural foods Foods processed minimally, although not necessarily organically grown.

natural gas A mixture of gaseous hydrocarbons, chiefly methane, generated naturally in petroleum deposits, used as a fuel.

natural history The observation and study, often not technical, of animals, plants, minerals, etc.

nat·u·ral·ism (nach′ər·əl·iz′əm, -rəl-) *n.* **1** Action or thought derived from or identified with exclusively natural desires and instincts. **2** In literature, art, etc., literal and unidealized representation of life and nature. **3** *Philos.* The doctrine that phenomena are derived from natural causes and can be explained by scientific laws.

nat·u·ral·ist (nach′ər·əl·ist, -rəl-) *n.* **1** One versed in natural sciences, as a zoologist or botanist. **2** An adherent of naturalism.

nat·u·ral·is·tic (nach′ər·əl·is′tik, -rəl-) *adj.* **1** In accordance with nature; not conventional or ideal. **2** According to the doctrines of naturalism. **3** Pertaining to naturalists.

nat·u·ral·ize (nach′ər·əl·īz, -rəl-) *v.* **·ized, ·iz·ing** *v.t.* **1** To confer the rights and privileges of citizenship upon, as an alien. **2** To adopt (a foreign word, custom, etc.) into the common use of a country or area. **3** To adapt (a foreign plant, animal, etc.) to the environment of a country or area. **4** To make natural; free from conventionality. —*v.i.* **5** To become as if native; adapt. *Brit. sp.* **·ise.** —**nat′u·ral·i·za′tion, nat′u·ral·iz′er** *n.*

nat·u·ral·ly (nach′ər·əl·ē, -rəl-) *adv.* **1** Without effort; spontaneously. **2** Without affectation or exaggeration. **3** As might have been expected; of course.

natural numbers The set of numbers (1, 2, 3, 4, . . .); the positive integers.

natural philosophy 1 NATURAL HISTORY. **2** PHYSICAL SCIENCES.

natural resource Any resource provided by nature, as soil, forests, minerals, water supply, and wild game.

natural sciences The sciences dealing with the physical universe.

natural selection *Biol.* The process whereby individual variations of advantage in a certain environment tend to become perpetuated in the race.

na·ture (nā′chər) *n.* **1** The qualities or essential traits of anything; essence. **2** General type or kind; behavior of a questionable *nature.* **3** The entire physical universe and its phenomena. **4** *Often cap.* The force that supposedly controls these. **5** The inherited or habitual condition and tendencies of a person; also, a specified cast of character: a gentle *nature.* **6** Man in a natural state; also, a simplified way of life resembling this state. **7** Natural scenery or the open spaces. [< L *natus*, pp. of *nasci* be born] —**Syn. 1** substance. **2** class, sort. **3** cosmos. **5** disposition, temperament.

naught (nôt) *n.* **1** Not anything; nothing. **2** A cipher; zero; the character 0. —*adj.* Of no value or account. —*adv.* Not in the least. [< OE *nā* not + *wiht* thing]

naugh·ty (nô′tē) *adj.* **·ti·er, ·ti·est** Perverse and disobedient; wayward. [< NAUGHT] —**naugh′ti·ly** *adv.* —**naugh′ti·ness** *n.*

nau·sea (nô′zhə, -zē·ə, -shə, -sē·ə) *n.* **1** A disagreeable sensation accompanied by an impulse to vomit. **2** A feeling of loathing. [< Gk. *nausia* seasickness < *naus* ship]

nau·se·ate (nô′zhē·āt, -zē, -shē-, -sē-) *v.t. & v.i.* **·at·ed, ·at·ing** To affect with nausea or disgust. —**nau′se·a′tion** *n.*

nau·seous (nô′zhəs, -shəs) *adj.* **1** Nauseating; disgusting. **2** *Informal* Affected with nausea; queasy. —**nau′seous·ly** *adv.* —**nau′seous·ness** *n.* —**Syn. 1** offensive, repulsive, revolting, sickening. • *Nauseous* means provoking nausea or disgust: *a nauseous display of sentimentality. Nauseated* means affected with nausea or disgust: *nauseated during a boat ride; nauseated at political corruption. Nauseous* is widely used to mean *nauseated,* but especially in formal usage the distinction is observed.

naut. nautical.

nautch (nôch) *n.* In India, an entertainment featuring dancing girls (**nautch girls**). [< Hind. *nāch* dance]

nau·ti·cal (nô′ti·kəl) *adj.* Pertaining to ships, seamen, or navigation. [< Gk. *naus* ship] —**nau′ti·cal·ly** *adv.*

nautical mile A measure of distance equal to 1,852

meters or about 6,076 feet, used in sea and air navigation.

nau·ti·lus (nô'tə·ləs) *n. pl.* **·lus·es** or **·li** (-lī) A mollusk of southern seas, having a spiral shell with chambers lined with mother-of-pearl, esp. the **chambered** or **pearly nautilus**. [< Gk. *nautilos* sailor]

nav. naval; navigation.

Nav·a·ho (nav'ə·hō) *n. pl.* **·hos** or **·hoes** One of a tribe of North American Indians now living on reservations in Arizona, New Mexico, and Utah. Also **Nav'a·jo**.

Chambered nautilus

na·val (nā'vəl) *adj.* **1** Pertaining to ships and a navy. **2** Having a navy: a *naval* power. [< L *navis* ship]

nave (nāv) *n. Archit.* The main body of a cruciform church, between the side aisles. [< L *navis* ship]

na·vel (nā'vəl) *n.* **1** The depression on the abdomen where the umbilical cord was attached. **2** A central part or point. [< OE *nafela*]

navel orange An orange, usu. seedless, having a small secondary fruit at the apex.

nav·i·cert (nav'ə·sûrt) *n. Brit.* A safe-conduct document authorizing a merchant vessel of a friendly or neutral nation to pass through a blockade. [< L *navis* ship + CERT(IFICATE)]

navig. navigation; navigator.

nav·i·ga·ble (nav'ə·gə·bəl) *adj.* **1** Capable of being traveled over by boats and ships: a *navigable* river. **2** Capable of being steered or directed: a *navigable* glider. **3** In condition for sailing. —**nav'i·ga·bly** *adv.* —**nav'i·ga·bil'i·ty, nav'i·ga·ble·ness** *n.*

nav·i·gate (nav'ə·gāt) *v.* **·gat·ed, ·gat·ing** *v.t.* **1** To travel over, across, or on by ship or aircraft. **2** To steer; direct the course of. —*v.i.* **3** To travel by means of ship or aircraft. **4** To steer or manage a ship or aircraft. **5** To plot a course for a ship or aircraft. [< L *navis* a boat + *agere* to drive]

nav·i·ga·tion (nav'ə·gā'shən) *n.* **1** The act of navigating. **2** The art of directing the course of vessels at sea or of aircraft in flight. —**nav'i·ga'tion·al** *adj.*

nav·i·ga·tor (nav'ə·gā'tər) *n.* **1** One who navigates, or directs the course of a ship, aircraft, etc. **2** A person skilled in navigation.

nav·vy (nav'ē) *n. pl.* **·vies** *Brit.* A laborer on canals, railways, etc.

na·vy (nā'vē) *n. pl.* **·vies 1** The marine military force of a country, under the control of a government department. **2** The entire shipping of a country engaged in trade and commerce; the merchant marine. **3** A fleet of ships.

navy bean The common small, dried, white bean.

navy blue Any of various shades of dark blue. Also **navy**.

navy yard A dockyard for the construction, repair, equipment, or care of warships.

na·wab (nə·wôb') *n.* NABOB (def. 1). Also **na·wob'** [< Hind. *nawwāb* nabob]

nay (nā) *adv.* **1** No. **2** Not only so, but also: He is a good, *nay*, an excellent man. —*n.* **1** A negative vote or voter. **2** A negative; denial. [< ON *ne* not + *ei* ever]

Naz·a·rene (naz'ə·rēn) *n.* **1** An inhabitant of Nazareth. **2** A member of a group of early Christians. —the Nazarene Jesus. —*adj.* Of or pertaining to Nazareth or the Nazarenes. Also **Naz'a·re'an** (-rē'ən).

Naz·a·rite (naz'ə·rīt) *n.* A member of an ancient Hebrew sect who assumed certain vows, including abstaining from wine. Also **Naz'i·rite**. [< Heb. *nāzar* abstain] —**Naz'a·rit'ic** (-rit'ik), **Naz'i·rit'ic** *adj.*

Na·zi (nä'tsē, nat'sē, na'zē) *n.* A member of the National Socialist German Workers' Party, founded in 1919 and dominant from 1933 to 1945 in Germany under Hitler. —*adj.* Of or pertaining to the Nazis or their party. [G, short for *Nationalsozialistische (Partei)*]

Na·zi·fy (nä'tsə·fī, nat'sə-) *v.t.* **·fied, ·fy·ing** To subject to Nazi influence or control. —**Na'zi·fi·ca'tion** *n.*

Na·zism (nä'tsiz·əm, nat'siz-) *n.* The doctrines or practices of the Nazi party. Also **Na·zi·ism** (nä'tsē·iz'əm, nat'sē-).

N.B. New Brunswick.

N.B., n.b. note well (L *nota bene*).

Nb niobium.

NC North Carolina (P.O. abbr.).

N.C., N. Car. North Carolina.

NCO, N.C.O., n.c.o. noncommissioned officer.

ND North Dakota (P.O. abbr.).

N.D., n.d. no date.

N.D., N. Dak. North Dakota.

Nd neodymium.

NE Nebraska (P.O. abbr.).

NE, N.E., Ne, ne, n.e. northeast; northeastern.

N.E. New England.

Ne neon.

Ne·an·der·thal (nē·an'dər·täl, -thôl, -thol) *adj.* **1** Pertaining to a primitive, extinct form of man represented by various Old World fossils. **2** Uncouth; brutish. [< *Neanderthal*, a valley in w Germany]

Ne·a·pol·i·tan (nē'ə·pol'ə·tən) *adj.* Of or pertaining to Naples. —*n.* A citizen or resident of Naples.

Neanderthal skull

neap tide (nēp) A tide having the lowest difference between high and low water levels and occurring at the first and third quarters of the moon. [< OE *nēp-* in *nēpflod* low tide]

near (nir) *adj.* **1** Not distant in place, time, or degree. **2** Closely related by blood or affection; familiar. **3** Closely touching one's interests. **4** In riding or driving, placed on the left. **5** Following or imitating closely; literal; a *near* copy. **6** Resembling or substituted for: *near* beer. **7** Avoiding by a narrow margin: a *near* escape. —**near at hand** **1** Close by. **2** In the immediate future. —*adv.* **1** At little distance: Don't come *near*. **2** *Informal* Nearly; approximately. **3** In a close relation. —*v.t. & v.i.* To come or draw near (to); approach. —*prep.* Close by or to. [< OE *nēar*, comp. of *nēah* nigh] —**near'ness** *n.*

near·by (nir'bī') *adj. & adv.* Close at hand; adjacent.

near·ly (nir'lē) *adv.* **1** Almost: *nearly* asleep. **2** At no great distance; closely.

near·sight·ed (nir'sī'tid) *adj.* Able to see distinctly at short distances only; myopic. —**near'sight'ed·ly** *adv.* —**near'sight'ed·ness** *n.*

neat¹ (nēt) *adj.* **1** Characterized by strict order and cleanliness. **2** Well-proportioned; shapely. **3** Clever; adroit: a *neat* move. **4** Clear of extraneous matter; undiluted. **5** Remaining after every deduction; net. [< OF *net* < L *nitidus* shining] —**neat'ly** *adv.* —**neat'ness** *n.* —**Syn. 1** orderly, spruce, tidy, trig, trim. **3** deft.

neat² (nēt) *n. Archaic* **1** Bovine cattle. **2** A single bovine animal. —*adj.* Of bovine animals. [< OE *nēat*]

neath (nēth) *prep. Regional* BENEATH. Also **'neath**.

neat's-foot oil (nēts'fŏŏt') An oil obtained by boiling the feet of cattle, used to dress leather.

neb (neb) *n.* **1** The beak or bill, as of a bird. **2** The tip end of a thing; nib, as of a pen. [< OE *nebb*]

Neb., Nebr. Nebraska.

neb·bish (neb'ish) *n.* A timid, weak, unaggressive person. [< Yiddish *nebach, nebech* poor thing]

neb·u·la (neb'yə·lə) *n. pl.* **·lae** (-lē) or **·las** *Astron.* A rarified, luminous or nonluminous mass of interstellar gas or dust. [L, vapor, mist] —**neb'u·lar** *adj.*

nebular hypothesis In astronomy, a hypothesis that the solar system existed originally in the form of a nebula.

neb·u·los·i·ty (neb'yə·los'ə·tē) *n. pl.* **·ties 1** NEBULA. **2** A misty or nebulous appearance.

neb·u·lous (neb'yə·ləs) *adj.* **1** Having its parts confused or mixed; indistinct: a *nebulous* idea. **2** Like a nebula. —**neb'u·lous·ly** *adv.* —**neb'u·lous·ness** *n.*

nec·es·sar·i·ly (nes'ə·ser'ə·lē) *adv.* **1** Inevitably; unavoidably. **2** Through necessity.

nec·es·sar·y (nes′ə·ser′ē) *adj.* **1** Being such in its nature that it must exist, occur, or be true; inevitable. **2** Absolutely needed to accomplish a desired result. —*n. pl.* **·sar·ies** That which is indispensable: usu. in the plural: the *necessaries* of life. [< L *necessarius*]

ne·ces·si·tate (nə·ses′ə·tāt) *v.t.* **·tat·ed, ·tat·ing 1** To make necessary, unavoidable, or certain. **2** To compel. —**ne·ces′si·ta′tion** *n.* —**ne·ces′si·ta′tive** *adj.*

ne·ces·si·tous (nə·ses′ə·təs) *adj.* **1** Needy; poverty-stricken. **2** Urgent. **3** Essential. —**ne·ces′si·tous·ly** *adv.* —**ne·ces′si·tous·ness** *n.*

ne·ces·si·ty (nə·ses′ə·tē) *n. pl.* **·ties 1** The quality of being necessary: the *necessity* for sleep. **2** That which is indispensable. **3** *Often pl.* That which is indispensable to a desired end. **4** The condition of being in want; poverty. —**of necessity** Necessarily; unavoidably. [< L *necessitas*] —**Syn. 1** exigency. **2** essential, requisite, requirement.

neck (nek) *n.* **1** The part of a person or animal that connects the head with the trunk. **2** Something likened to a neck, in position, shape, etc. **3** The part of a violin, or other stringed instrument, between the end and the body. **4** The narrow part of a bottle, flask, etc. **5** A narrow passage of water connecting two larger bodies. **6** A peninsula, isthmus, or cape. **7** That part of a garment that fits about the neck. —**break one's neck** *Slang* To make a tremendous effort. —**get it in the neck** *Slang* To suffer criticism or punishment. —**neck and neck** Keeping abreast. —*v.i. Slang* To kiss and caress in making love. —*v.t. Slang* To kiss and caress in such a manner. [< OE *hnecca*]

neck·band (nek′band′) *n.* **1** The part of a garment that fits around the neck, esp. the strip on the inside of a collar. **2** A band around the neck.

neck·cloth (nek′klôth′) *n.* A folded cloth worn around the neck and collar; a cravat.

neck·er·chief (nek′ər·chif) *n.* A kerchief or scarf for the neck.

neck·lace (nek′lis) *n.* A string of precious stones, precious metal, beads, or the like, worn around the neck.

neck·line (nek′līn′) *n.* The line formed by the upper edge of a garment around or near the neck.

neck of the woods *Informal* A region or neighborhood.

neck·piece (nek′pēs′) *n.* A scarf, usu. of fur.

neck·tie (nek′tī′) *n.* A band or scarf passing round the neck or collar and tying in front.

neck·wear (nek′wâr′) *n.* **1** Any article worn around the throat. **2** Ties, cravats, mufflers, etc., collectively.

necro- *combining form* **1** Death. **2** Corpse: *necropolis.* [< Gk. *nekros* a corpse]

ne·crol·o·gy (ne·krol′ə·jē) *n. pl.* **·gies 1** A list of persons who have died in a certain place or time. **2** A treatise on or an account of the dead. [NECRO- + -LOGY] —**nec·ro·log·ic** (nek′rə·loj′ik), **nec′ro·log′i·cal** *adj.* —**nec′ro·log′i·cal·ly** *adv.* —**ne·crol′o·gist** *n.*

nec·ro·man·cy (nek′rə·man′sē) *n.* **1** Divination by means of communication with the dead. **2** Black magic; sorcery. [< L *niger* black + Gk. *mantis* prophet] —**nec′ro·man′cer** *n.* —**nec′ro·man′tic** *adj.*

ne·crop·o·lis (ne·krop′ə·lis) *n.* A cemetery, esp. one belonging to an ancient city. [< NECRO- + Gk. *polis* city]

ne·cro·sis (ne·krō′sis) *n. pl.* **·ses** (-sēz) Localized death of tissue in a plant or animal. [< Gk. *nekrōsis* deadness] —**ne·crot′ic** (-krot′ik) *adj.*

nec·tar (nek′tar) *n.* **1** *Gk. Myth.* The drink of the gods. **2** Any sweet, delicious drink. **3** A sweet liquid secreted by cells at the base of some flowers. [< Gk. *nektar*] —**nec·tar·e·an** (nek·târ′ē·ən), **nec·tar′e·ous** *adj.*

nec·tar·ine (nek′tə·rēn′, nek′tə·rēn) *n.* A variety of peach having a smooth, waxy skin. [< NECTAR]

née (nā) *adj.* Born: noting the maiden name of a married woman: Mrs. Jones, *née* Burney. Also **nee.** [F, p.p. of *naître* be born]

need (nēd) *v.t.* **1** To have want of; require. —*v.i.* **2** To be in want. **3** To be necessary: It *needs* not. **4** To be obliged or compelled: He *need* not go. —*n.* **1** A lack of something requisite or desirable. **2** A situation of want or peril: to be a friend in *need.* **3** The thing needed: His *need* is education. —**have need to** Must; should. —**if need be** If necessary. [< OE *nīed, nēd*] —**need′er** *n.*

need·ful (nēd′fəl) *adj.* **1** Needed; necessary. **2** Needy. —**need′ful·ly** *adv.* —**need′ful·ness** *n.*

nee·dle (nēd′l) *n.* **1** A small, slender, pointed instrument containing an eye at the head, or, in sewing machines, at the point, to carry thread through a fabric in sewing. **2** The straight rod used in knitting. **3** The hooked rod used in crocheting. **4** Any instrument or object shaped like a needle, as a pinnacle or rock, or a leaf, such as that of the pine. **5** A thin pointer, such as a magnetic needle. **6** The sharp-pointed end of a hypodermic syringe. **7** *Informal* A hypodermic syringe. **8** An obelisk. **9** A phonograph stylus. —*v.* **·dled, ·dling** *v.t.* **1** To sew or pierce with a needle. **2** *Informal* To heckle or goad. —*v.i.* **3** To sew or work with a needle. [OE *nǣdl*]

nee·dle·craft (nēd′l·kraft′, -kräft′) *n.* **1** The art of doing needlework, esp. embroidery. **2** NEEDLEWORK.

nee·dle·point (nēd′l·point′) *n.* **1** Embroidery similar to tapestry, made on a stiff mesh material or canvas and used to cover chair seats, etc. **2** The stitch used in needlepoint. **3** Lace made entirely with a sewing needle rather than bobbins.

need·less (nēd′lis) *adj.* Useless; not required. —**need′less·ly** *adv.* —**need′less·ness** *n.*

needle valve A valve having an opening closed by a thin, needlelike rod.

nee·dle·wom·an (nēd′l·wŏŏm′ən) *n. pl.* **·wom·en** (-wim′in) **1** A woman skilled in needlework. **2** A seamstress.

nee·dle·work (nēd′l·wûrk′) *n.* Work done with a needle; sewing and embroidery. —**nee′dle·work′er** *n.*

needs (nēdz) *adv.* Necessarily; indispensably: often with *must.*

need·y (nē′dē) *adj.* **need·i·er, need·i·est** Being in need, want, or poverty. —**need′i·ly** *adv.* —**need′i·ness** *n.*

ne'er (nâr) *adv.* Contraction of *never.*

ne'er-do-well (nâr′dŏŏ·wel′) *n.* A useless, unreliable person. —*adj.* Useless; good-for-nothing.

ne·far·i·ous (ni·fâr′ē·əs) *adj.* Wicked in the extreme; heinous. [< L *nefas* a crime] —**ne·far′i·ous·ly** *adv.* —**ne·far′i·ous·ness** *n.* —**Syn.** atrocious, flagrant, infamous, villainous.

neg. negative; negatively.

ne·gate (ni·gāt′) *v.t.* **·gat·ed, ·gat·ing 1** To make ineffective; nullify. **2** To deny the existence of. [< L *negare* deny]

ne·ga·tion (ni·gā′shən) *n.* **1** The act of denying. **2** Absence of anything affirmative; nullity.

neg·a·tive (neg′ə·tiv) *adj.* **1** Containing contradiction or expressing negation. **2** Characterized by denial or refusal: a *negative* reply. **3** Exhibiting the absence of positive or affirmative character. **4** *Phot.* Showing dark for light and light for dark: a *negative* plate or film. **5** *Math.* Less than zero. **6** *Electr.* Denoting a charge like that carried by an electron. **7** *Biol.* In a direction

a. negative *def.* 4
b. positive.

away from a stimulus: a *negative* response. **8** *Med.* Not showing evidence of a suspected condition: a *negative* biopsy. —*n.* **1** A proposition, word, or act expressing refusal or denial. **2** The side in an argument that denies or is against the affirmative. **3** The right to veto. **4** A photograph having the lights and shades reversed, used for printing positives. **5** *Gram.* A word or particle, such as *non-* or *not*, employing or expressing denial. **6** *Math.* A negative number or sign. —**in the negative 1** Being on the side against the affirmative. **2** Denying or refusing. —*v.t.* **·tived, ·tiv·ing 1** To deny; contradict. **2** To refuse to sanction or enact; veto. **3** To prove to be false; disprove. [< L *negare* deny] —**neg′a·tive·ly** *adv.* —**neg′a·tive·ness, neg′a·tiv′i·ty** *n.*

negative income tax Payment by the government to those whose incomes fall below a specified level, regarded as a means of replacing or supplementing welfare payments.

neg·a·tiv·ism (neg′ə·tiv·iz′əm) *n.* The tendency to reject or ignore what others suggest or order. —**neg′a·tiv·ist** *n.* —**neg′a·tiv·is′tic** *adj.*

neg·lect (ni·glekt′) *v.t.* **1** To disregard; ignore. **2** To fail to give proper attention to or take proper care of. **3** To fail to do or perform. —*n.* **1** The act of neglecting, or the state of being neglected. **2** Habitual want of attention or care. [< L *nec-* not + *legere* gather, pick up] **—neg·lect′er** *n.* — **Syn.** *v.* **1** slight. **3** overlook. *n.* **2** carelessness, heedlessness, oversight, slackness.

neg·lect·ful (ni·glekt′fəl) *adj.* Exhibiting or indicating neglect. **—neg·lect′ful·ly, neg·lect′ing·ly** *adv.*

neg·li·gée (neg′li·zhā′, neg′li·zhā) *n.* **1** A woman's soft, flowing dressing gown. **2** Any informal, careless, or incomplete attire. **—adj.** Careless or informal in dress. Also **neg′li·gé′.** [< F *négliger* to neglect]

neg·li·gence (neg′lə·jəns) *n.* **1** The act of neglecting or failing to pay proper heed to. **2** Carelessness; lack of interest.

neg·li·gent (neg′lə·jənt) *adj.* **1** Apt to omit what ought to be done; neglectful. **2** Inattentive; careless. [< L *negligere* neglect] **—neg′li·gent·ly** *adv.*

neg·li·gi·ble (neg′lə·jə·bəl) *adj.* That can be disregarded; inconsiderable. **—neg′li·gi·bil′i·ty, neg′li·gi·ble·ness** *n.* — **neg′li·gi·bly** *adv.*

ne·go·ti·a·ble (ni·gō′shē·ə·bəl, -shə·bəl) *adj.* **1** That can be negotiated. **2** *Law* Transferable to a third person, as for the payment of debts. **3** That can be managed or successfully dealt with. **—ne·go′ti·a·bil′i·ty** *n.* **—ne·go′ti·a·bly** *adv.*

ne·go·ti·ate (ni·gō′shē·āt) *v.* **·at·ed, ·at·ing** *v.i.* **1** To treat or bargain with others in order to reach an agreement. — *v.t.* **2** To procure, arrange, or conclude by mutual discussion: to *negotiate* an agreement. **3** To transfer for a value received; assign, as a note or bond. **4** To surmount, cross, or cope with (some obstacle). [< L *negotium* business] **—ne·go′ti·a′tion, ne·go′ti·a′tor** *n.* **—ne·go′ti·a·to′ry** *adj.*

Ne·gress (nē′gris) *n.* A Negro woman or girl: sometimes considered disparaging.

Ne·gri·to (ni·grē′tō) *n. pl.* **·tos** or **·toes** *Anthropol.* One belonging to any of the small Negroid peoples of s Africa, SE Asia, Malaya, and the Philippine Islands. [< Sp. *negro* black] **—Ne·grit′ic** (-grit′ik) *adj.*

Ne·gro (nē′grō) *n. pl.* **·groes** **1** A member of the Negroid racial division of mankind, esp. one belonging to the tribes inhabiting CEN. and s Africa. **2** One who is, in whole or in part, descended from the African and other Negroid peoples. **—adj.** Of, pertaining to, or being, a Negro. [< L *niger* black]

Ne·groid (nē′groid) *adj.* **1** Of or pertaining to the so-called black race, including the peoples originally inhabiting CEN. and s Africa, parts of SE Asia, Malaya, the Philippine Islands, and Melanesia, characterized by skin color varying from light brown to almost black. **2** Resembling, related to, or characteristic of Negroes. **—n.** A member of this racial group.

neigh (nā) *v.i.* To utter the cry of a horse; whinny. **—n.** A whinny. [< OE *hnægan*]

neigh·bor (nā′bər) *n.* **1** One who lives near another. **2** One who is near another. **—adj.** Close at hand; adjacent. **—v.t.** **1** To live or be near to or next to; adjoin. **—v.i.** **2** To be in proximity; lie close. *Brit. sp.* **neigh′bour.** [< OE *nēah* near + *gebūr* farmer]

neigh·bor·hood (nā′bər·hood) *n.* **1** The region near where one is or resides; vicinity. **2** The people collectively who dwell in the vicinity. **3** Nearness. **4** A district considered with reference to a given characteristic. **—in the neighborhood of** *Informal* About; near. *Brit. sp.* **neigh′bour·hood.**

nei·ther (nē′thər, nī-) *adj.* Not either. **—pron.** Not the one nor the other. **—conj.** **1** Not one nor the other: followed by correlative *nor:* He will *neither* eat nor drink. **2** Nor yet. [< OE *nā* no + *hwæther*]

nem·a·tode (nem′ə·tōd) *n.* Any of a phylum of unsegmented worms, some of which are parasites in man and other animals. [< Gk. *nēma, -atos* a thread]

nem·e·sis (nem′ə·sis) *n.* Retributive justice; retribution. [< Gk. *nemein* distribute]

Nem·e·sis (nem′ə·sis) *Gk. Myth.* The goddess of retributive justice or vengeance.

neo- *combining form* **1** New; recent: *neologism.* **2** A modern or modified form of: *neoclassicism.* [< Gk. *neos* new]

ne·o·clas·si·cism (nē′ō·klas′ə·siz′əm) *n.* A revival of classical style in literature art, etc., esp. the revival in the later 17th and the 18th centuries. **—ne·o·clas·sic** (nē′ō·klas′ik), **ne′o·clas′si·cal** *adj.* **—ne′o·clas′si·cist** *n.*

ne·o·dym·i·um (nē′ō·dim′ē·əm) *n.* A metallic rare-earth element (symbol Nd). [< NEO- + Gk. *didymos* twin]

Ne·o·lith·ic (nē′ə·lith′ik) *adj. Anthropol.* Of or pertaining to the late Stone Age, in which man made polished stone implements and introduced a settled agriculture. [< NEO- + Gk. *lithos* stone]

ne·ol·o·gism (nē·ol′ə·jiz′əm) *n.* **1** A new word or phrase. **2** The use of new words or new meanings for old words. Also **ne·ol′o·gy** (*pl.* **·gies**). [< NEO- + Gk. *logos* word] **—ne·ol′o·gist** *n.* **—ne·ol′o·gis′tic, ne·ol′o·gis′ti·cal** *adj.*

ne·o·my·cin (nē′ə·mī′sin) *n.* An antibiotic obtained from a soil mold, used to treat certain skin and eye infections.

ne·on (nē′on) *n.* A colorless, odorless, gaseous element (symbol Ne) of very low chemical activity, used in neon lamps. [< Gk. *neos* new]

ne·o·nate (nē′ō·nāt) *n.* A newborn infant. [< NEO- + L *natus* born] **—ne′o·na′tal** *adj.*

neon lamp A glass tube containing neon in which an electric discharge produces a red or orange glow.

ne·o·phyte (nē′ə·fīt) *n.* **1** A recent convert. **2** Any novice or beginner. [< Gk. *neophytos* novice]

ne·o·plasm (nē′ə·plaz′əm) *n.* An abnormal growth of tissue; a tumor.

ne·o·prene (nē′ə·prēn) *n.* A synthetic rubber made from chlorinated hydrocarbons.

Ne·pal (ni·pôl′) *n.* A constitutional monarchy located between India and Tibet, 54,362 sq. mi., cap. Katmandu. **—Nep·al·ese** (nep′ə·lēz′, -lēs′) *adj., n.* • See map at INDIA.

ne·pen·the (ni·pen′thē) *n.* **1** A drug or potion used by the ancient Greeks to banish pain and sorrow. **2** Any agent causing oblivion. [< Gk. *nē-* not + *penthos* sorrow] **—ne·pen′the·an, ne·pen′thic** *adj.*

neph·ew (nef′yōō, *esp. Brit.* nev′yōō) *n.* **1** The son of one's sister or brother. **2** The son of one's sister-in-law or brother-in-law. [< L *nepos*]

ne·phrit·ic (ni·frit′ik) *adj.* **1** Pertaining to the kidneys. **2** Pertaining to or affected with nephritis.

ne·phri·tis (ni·frī′tis) *n.* Any of variously caused acute or chronic inflammations of the kidneys. [< Gk. *nephros* kidney + -ITIS]

ne plus ul·tra (nē′ plus ul′trə) Perfection. [L, lit., nothing more beyond]

nep·o·tism (nep′ə·tiz′əm) *n.* Favoritism by those in power extended toward relatives, esp. by appointing them to desirable positions. [< L *nepos* a grandson, nephew] **—ne·pot·ic** (ni·pot′ik) *adj.* **—nep′o·tist** *n.*

Nep·tune (nep′tōōn) *Rom. Myth.* The god of the sea, identified with the Greek Poseidon. **—n.** The planet of the solar system eighth in distance from the sun. • See PLANET. **—Nep·tu′ni·an** *adj.*

nep·tu·ni·um (nep·tōō′nē·əm) *n.* An artificially produced radioactive element (symbol Np).

Ne·re·id (nir′ē·id) *pl.* **Ne·re·i·des** (ni·rē′ə·dēz) or **Ne·re·ids** *Gk. Myth.* One of the sea nymphs who attend Poseidon.

ner·va·tion (nûr·vā′shən) *n.* The arrangement of veins, as in a leaf or an insect's wing.

nerve (nûrv) *n.* **1** A cordlike structure, composed of delicate filaments by which impulses are transmitted between different parts and organs of the body and the central nervous system. **2** Anything likened to a nerve, as a rib or vein of a leaf or of an insect's wing. **3** *Slang* Offensive boldness; effrontery. **4** Fearlessness; intrepidity. **5** *pl.* Nervous excitability; a nervous attack. **—get on one's nerves** To try the patience of; exasperate. **—v.t. nerved, nerv·ing** To give strength, vigor, or courage to. [< L *nervus* sinew]

nerve block The injection of an anesthetic into a nerve leading to a definite area, thus producing local anesthesia.

nerve cell A neuron.

nerve center A group of nerve cells having a specific function, as hearing, respiration, etc.

nerve·less (nûrv′lis) *adj.* **1** Without vigor; weak. **2** Showing no stress; self-controlled. **—nerve′less·ly** *adv.*

ădd, āce, cåre, pälm; end, ēven; It, īce; odd, ōpen, ôrder; tŏŏk, pōōl; up, bûrn; ə = *a* in *above, u* in *focus*; yōō = *u* in *fuse;* oil; pout; check; go; ring; thin; **this**; zh, *vision.* < derived from; ? origin uncertain or unknown.

nerve-rack·ing (nûrv′rak′ing) *adj.* Extremely irritating or exasperating. Also **nerve′-wrack′ing.**

ner·vous (nûr′vəs) *adj.* **1** Of or pertaining to the nerves or the nervous system. **2** Having or made up of nerves. **3** Strong; forceful, as literary style: *nervous prose.* **4** Easily disturbed or agitated. **5** Fearful; timid. —**ner′vous·ly** *adv.* —**ner′vous·ness** *n.* —**Syn. 4** excitable, high-strung, tense. **5** anxious, apprehensive.

nervous prostration NEURASTHENIA.

nervous system The organized network of all the nerve cells in an organism, in vertebrates branching out from the **central nervous system,** which comprises the spinal cord and brain.

ner·vure (nûr′vyŏŏr) *n.* A vein, as on a leaf or an insect's wing. [<L *nervus* sinew]

nerv·y (nûr′vē) *adj.* **nerv·i·er, nerv·i·est 1** Exhibiting force or strength; sinewy. **2** Full of nerve or courage. **3** *Slang* Displaying brazen assurance. **4** *Brit.* Nervous; excitable. —**nerv′i·ness** *n.*

nes·cience (nesh′əns, nēsh′-, -ē·əns) *n.* The state of not knowing; ignorance. [<L *ne-* not + *scire* know] —**nes′cient** *adj.*

-ness *suffix of nouns* **1** State or quality of being: *darkness.* **2** An example of this state or quality: to do someone a *kindness.* [<OE *-nis(s), -nes(s)*]

nest (nest) *n.* **1** The habitation prepared by a bird for the hatching of its eggs and the rearing of its young. **2** The bed or home of certain fish, insects, turtles, mice, etc. **3** Any cozy place or abode; a retreat. **4** A haunt, usu. for evil activities; also, those frequenting it: a *nest* of pirates. **5** A series or set of similar things of graduated sizes, fitting one inside another: a *nest* of bowls. —*v.t.* **1** To place in or as in a nest. **2** To pack or place one inside another. —*v.i.* **3** To build or occupy a nest. **4** To fit compactly inside another. [<OE]

Nests
a. hornet.
b. tailorbird.

nest egg 1 A natural or artificial egg placed in a nest to stimulate a hen to lay eggs there. **2** Something laid by, as a sum of money, for emergencies.

nes·tle (nes′əl) *v.* **·tled, ·tling** *v.i.* **1** To lie closely or snugly; cuddle. **2** To settle down in comfort. **3** To lie as if sheltered; be half-hidden: a lake *nestled* in the valley. —*v.t.* **4** To place or press lovingly or fondly. **5** To shelter in or as in a nest. [<OE *nestlian*] —**nes′tler** *n.*

nest·ling (nest′ling, nes′-) *n.* **1** A bird too young to leave the nest. **2** A young child.

Nes·tor (nes′tər) *Gk. Myth.* The oldest and wisest Greek chief in the Trojan War. —*n.* Any wise old man.

net¹ (net) *n.* **1** An open fabric, woven or tied with meshes, for the capture of fishes, birds, etc. **2** An openwork fabric, as lace. **3** Something constructed with meshes, as a tennis net. —*v.t.* **net·ted, net·ting 1** To catch in or as in a net; ensnare. **2** To make into a net. **3** To cover or enclose with a net. —*adj.* Made of or resembling netting. [<OE]

net² (net) *adj.* **1** Free from everything extraneous; obtained after deducting all expenses. **2** Not subject to any discount or deduction. —*n.* A net profit, amount, weight, etc. —*v.t.* **net·ted, net·ting** To earn or yield as clear profit. [<OF, neat]

Neth. Netherlands.

neth·er (neth′ər) *adj.* Situated at the lowest part. [<OE *neothera* under]

Neth·er·lands (neth′ər·ləndz) *n.* A constitutional monarchy of NW Europe, 15,780 sq. mi., official cap. Amsterdam, de facto cap. The Hague. —**Neth′er·land′er** *n.* —**Neth′er·land·ish** *adj.*

neth·er·most (neth′ər·mōst′) *adj.* Lowest.

nether world The world of the dead, esp. that of punishment after death; hell.

net·ting (net′ing) *n.* **1** A fabric of openwork; a net. **2** The act or operation of making net.

net·tle (net′l) *n.* Any of various plants having stinging hairs or bristles, usu. borne on the leaves. —*v.t.* **·tled, ·tling 1** To sting as the nettle does. **2** To annoy or irritate. [<OE *netle*] —**net′tler** *n.* —**Syn. v. 2** chafe, exasperate, irk, vex.

net·work (net′wûrk′) *n.* **1** NETTING. **2** A system of interlacing lines, tracks, or channels. **3** An interconnection of electric devices. **4** *Telecom.* A chain of broadcasting stations.

neu·ral (nyŏŏr′əl) *adj.* Of or pertaining to the nerves or nervous system. [<Gk. *neuron* nerve]

neu·ral·gi·a (nyŏŏ·ral′jē·ə, -jə) *n.* Severe pain along the course of a nerve. [<NEUR(O)- + Gk. *algos* pain] —**neu·ral′gic** *adj.*

neu·ras·the·ni·a (nyŏŏr′əs·thē′nē·ə, -thēn′yə) *n.* A kind of neurosis marked by headaches, digestive disturbances, depression, etc. [<NEUR(O)- + Gk. *asthenia* weakness] —**neu′ras·then′ic** (-then′ik) *adj., n.*

neu·ri·tis (nyŏŏ·rī′tis) *n.* Inflammation of a nerve. —**neu·rit′ic** (-rit′ik) *adj.*

neuro- *combining form* Nerve; pertaining to a nerve or system of nerves: *neurology.* [<Gk. *neuron* sinew, nerve]

neu·ro·chem·is·try (nŏŏr′ō·kem′ə·strē) *n.* That branch of chemistry that has to do with chemicals, esp. the neurotransmitters, that affect the nervous system.

neu·rol·o·gy (nyŏŏ·rol′ə·jē) *n.* The branch of medicine concerned with the nervous system. —**neu·ro·log·i·cal** (nyŏŏr′ə·loj′i·kəl) *adj.* —**neu·rol′o·gist** *n.*

neu·ron (nyŏŏr′on) *n.* A nerve cell, consisting of a nucleated central body and two long processes. Also **neu′rone** (-ōn). [<Gk. *neuron* nerve] —**neu·ron·ic** (nyŏŏ·ron′ik), **neu′ron·al** (-rən·əl) *adj.*

neu·ro·path (nyŏŏr′ə·path) *n.* One suffering from or subject to neuroses. —**neu′ro·path′ic, neu′ro·path′i·cal** *adj.* —**neu′ro·path′i·cal·ly** *adv.*

neu·ro·psy·chi·a·try (nyŏŏr′ō·sī·kī′ə·trē) *n.* The study and treatment of diseases involving both neurological and mental factors. —**neu′ro·psy′chi·at′ric** (-sī′kē·at′rik) *adj.* —**neu′ro·psy·chi′a·trist** (-sī·kī′ə·trist) *n.*

neu·rop·ter·ous (nyŏŏ·rop′tər·əs) *adj.* Of or pertaining to an order of insects having four fine-veined wings and biting mouth parts. [<NEUR(O)- + Gk. *pteron* wing]

neu·ro·sis (nyŏŏ·rō′sis) *n. pl.* **·ses** (-sēz) Any of several functional mental disorders usu. characterized by anxiety, depression, etc. [<Gk. *neuron* nerve]

neu·rot·ic (nyŏŏ·rot′ik) *adj.* **1** Of, being, or suffering from neurosis. **2** Having a morbid nature or tendency. —*n.* A person afflicted with neurosis. —**neu·rot′i·cal·ly** *adv.* —**neu·rot′i·cism** *n.*

neut. neuter; neutral.

neu·ter (nyŏŏ′tər) *adj.* **1** *Gram.* Neither masculine nor feminine in gender. **2** *Biol.* Having functionless or imperfectly developed sex organs. **3** Taking the part of neither side; neutral. —*n.* **1** An animal of no apparent sex, as a worker bee. **2** A eunuch. **3** A castrated animal. **4** *Gram.* a The neuter gender. b A word in this gender. **5** A neutral in warfare or other conflict. —*v.t. Informal* To castrate or spay, esp. cats; alter. [<L *ne-* not + *uter* either]

neu·tral (nyŏŏ′trəl) *adj.* **1** Refraining from taking the part of either side in a quarrel, contest, or war. **2** Having no decided character; indefinite. **3** Having no decided color; predominantly brownish or grayish. **4** *Biol.* Neuter. **5** *Bot.* Lacking pistils or stamens. **6** *Chem.* Being neither acid nor alkaline. **7** *Electr.* Neither positive nor negative. —*n.* One who or that which is neutral. [<L *neuter* neuter] —**neu′tral·ly** *adv.*

neu·tral·ism (nyŏŏ′trəl·iz′əm) *n.* A political doctrine holding that neutrality in international relations serves a country's best interests. —**neu′tral·ist** *adj., n.* —**neu′tral·is′tic** *adj.*

neu·tral·i·ty (nyŏŏ·tral′ə·tē) *n. pl.* **·ties 1** The state of being a neutral nation during a war. **2** The state of being neutral.

neu·tral·ize (nyŏŏ′trəl·īz) *v.t.* **·ized, ·iz·ing 1** To counteract or destroy by an opposite force or influence; counterbalance. **2** To declare (a nation, area, etc.) to be neutral and not involved in hostilities. **3** *Chem.* To make neutral by adding either acid or base. **4** *Mil.* To render incapable of effective action. *Brit. sp.* **neu′tral·ise.** —**neu·tral·i·za·tion** (nyŏŏ′trəl·ə·zā′shən), **neu′tral·iz′er** *n.*

neu·tri·no (nyŏŏ·trē′nō) *n. pl.* **·nos** *Physics* Either of two stable subatomic particles having no electric charge and a theoretical mass of zero when at rest.

neu·tron (nyŏŏ′tron) *n. Physics* An electrically neutral particle of the atom, having a mass approximately equal to that of the proton. [<NEUTRAL]

neutron star One of a class of objects, identified by some astrophysicists with pulsars, that are produced when fairly massive stars undergo gravitational collapse and form matter so dense that all the electrons and protons are in effect forced together to form neutrons.

Nev. Nevada.

nev·er (nev′ər) *adv.* **1** Not at any time. **2** Not at all; positively not: *Never fear.* [< OE *ne* not + *æfre* ever]

nev·er·more (nev′ər·môr′, -mōr′) *adv.* Never again.

nev·er·the·less (nev′ər·thə·les′) *conj. & adv.* None the less; however; yet.

ne·vus (nē′vəs) *n. pl.* **·vi** (-vī) A birthmark or congenital mole. Also **nae·vus.** [< L *naevus* blemish] —**ne′void, nae′· void** (-void) *adj.*

new (nyoo͞) *adj.* **1** Lately made: a *new* car. **2** Lately discovered or become well known: a *new* invention. **3** Beginning or recurring afresh: the *new* moon. **4** Changed in essence, constitution, etc.: I feel a *new* man. **5** Different from that heretofore known or used; unfamiliar: This game is *new* to me. **6** Up-to-date: *new* styles in clothing. **7** Unaccustomed: a horse *new* to the saddle. **8** Named for another: used to distinguish a place from its namesake: *New* Orleans. **9** Having reached a specified rank, position, etc.: a *new* governor. **10** More; additional: *new* data. —*adv.* Newly; recently. —*n.* Something new: off with the old and on with the *new*. [< OE *nēowe*] —**new′ness** *n.* —**Syn.** *adj.* **2** fresh, novel. **4** better. **6** latest, modern. **10** further.

new·born (nyoo͞′bôrn′) *adj.* **1** Newly born. **2** About to start a new life; reborn. —*n.* A newborn infant or animal.

new·com·er (nyoo͞′kum′ər) *n.* One who has recently arrived.

New Deal The policies and principles of the U.S. administration under President Franklin D. Roosevelt, embracing various social, economic, and political innovations. —**New Dealer**

new·el (nyoo͞′əl) *n.* **1** The pillar from which the steps of a spiral staircase radiate. **2** A post supporting the end of a stair rail. Also **newel post.** [< OF *nouel* stone of a fruit]

new·fan·gled (nyoo͞′fang′gəld) *adj.* **1** Of new fashion: generally in depreciation: *new-fangled* notions. **2** Fond of novelty. —**new′·fan′gled·ness** *n.* [< NEW + OE *fangen* seized]

New·found·land (nyoo͞′fənd·lənd, nyoo͞·found′-) *n.* A large dog characterized by a broad head, square muzzle, and usu. black coat, originally bred in Newfoundland.

Newel *def. 2*

New France The region settled by the French in North America from 1534 to 1763.

New·gate (nyoo͞′git, -gāt) *n.* A prison in London, destroyed 1902.

New Jerusalem Heaven. *Rev.* 21:2.

New Latin The Latin in use since about 1500, esp. in scientific nomenclature.

New Left An activist movement in the 1960s made up largely of students and youthful extremist groups, which advocated sweeping political, social, and educational reforms.

new·ly (nyoo͞′lē) *adv.* **1** In a new or recent manner; lately. **2** In a different way; so as to be or appear new; afresh.

new·ly·wed (nyoo͞′lē·wed′) *n.* A person recently married.

new moon 1 The phase of the moon when it is between the earth and the sun, and is nearly invisible. **2** The crescent moon. • See MOON.

new-mown (nyoo͞′mōn′) *adj.* Recently cut or mown, as hay.

news (nyoo͞z) *n. pl. (construed as sing.)* **1** Fresh information concerning something that has recently taken place. **2** Information about anything new or strange. —**break the news** To make known; tell about. —**Syn. 1** information, intelligence, report, tidings.

news·boy (nyoo͞z′boi′) *n.* A boy who sells or delivers newspapers.

news·cast (nyoo͞z′kast′, -käst′) *n.* A radio or television news program. —*v.t. & v.i.* To broadcast (news). —**news′· cast′er** *n.*

news·mag·a·zine (nyoo͞z′mag′ə·zēn) *n.* A periodical, esp. a weekly, that summarizes the news and reports current events of general interest.

news·man (nyoo͞z′man′, -mən) *n. pl.* **·men** (-men′, -mən) A newspaper reporter. —**news′wom′an** (-woo͞m′ən) *n. Fem.*

news·pa·per (nyoo͞z′pā′pər) *n.* A publication issued for general circulation at frequent, usu. regular, intervals.

news·pa·per·man (nyoo͞z′pā′pər·man′) *n. pl.* **·men** (-men′, -mən) **1** One who publishes a newspaper. **2** One who writes or edits news for a newspaper. —**news′pa′per·wom′· an** *n. Fem.*

news·print (nyoo͞z′print′) *n.* The thin, unsized paper on which the ordinary daily or weekly newspaper is printed.

news·reel (nyoo͞z′rēl′) *n.* A motion picture, usually of short duration, showing events of current interest.

news·stand (nyoo͞z′stand′) *n.* A stand or stall at which newspapers and periodicals are offered for sale.

news·worth·y (nyoo͞z′wûr′the) *adj.* Important enough to be written up in a newspaper; considered to be of current interest. —**news′wor′thi·ness** *n.*

news·y (nyoo͞z′zē) *adj.* **new·si·er, new·si·est** *Informal* Full of news, usu. of a gossipy nature. —*n. Informal* A newsboy.

newt (nyoot) *n.* A small, amphibious salamander. [< ME *an ewt,* taken as *a newt*]

New Testament The portion of the Bible containing the life and teachings of Jesus and his followers.

Newt

new·ton (nyoo͞′tən) *n. Physics* A unit of force equal to that which will accelerate a mass of 1 kilogram by 1 meter per second per second. [< Isaac *Newton,* 1642–1727, English mathematician]

new town A planned, new community, often under government auspices or with government support, consisting of various types of housing, schools, parks, and sometimes local industries.

New World The Western Hemisphere, including North and South America.

new year The year just begun or just about to begin.

New Year January 1, the first day of the year, widely observed as a legal holiday. Also **New Year's Day.**

New Year's Eve The evening of December 31, the day before New Year's Day.

next (nekst) *adj.* Being nearest to, in time, space, order, rank, etc.; immediately succeeding or preceding. —**next door to** In the next building, dwelling, etc. —**next to 1** Closest to. **2** Almost: *next to* impossible. —*adv.* In the nearest time, place, or rank, esp. immediately succeeding: when *next* I met her. —*prep.* Nearest to. [< OE *nēahst,* superl. of *nēah* nigh]

next door In or to the next building, dwelling, etc. —**next door to** Next to. —**next′-door′** *adj.*

next of kin The living person or persons most closely related to one.

nex·us (nek′səs) *n. pl.* **·us·es** or **·us** A bond or tie between the several members of a group or series; link. [< L, pp. of *nectere* to tie]

Nez Per·cé (nez′ pûrs′, *Fr.* nā per·sā′) One of a tribe of North American Indians formerly dwelling in Idaho, Oregon, and Washington. [F, pierced nose]

NF Norman French.

N.F. National Formulary; Newfoundland.

N.G., n.g. no good.

NGk, N.Gk. New Greek.

NH New Hampshire (P.O. abbr.).

N.H. New Hampshire.

N.I., N.Ire. Northern Ireland.

Ni nickel.

ni·a·cin (nī′ə·sin) *n.* The antipellagra factor in the vitamin B complex. [< NI(COTINIC) AC(ID) + -IN]

nib (nib) *n.* **1** A projecting, pointed part. **2** A beak of a bird; neb. **3** The point of a pen. —*v.t.* **nibbed, nib·bing** To furnish with a nib. [Var. of NEB]

nib·ble (nib′əl) *v.* **·bled, ·bling** *v.t.* **1** To eat (food) with small, quick bites. **2** To bite gently or cautiously, as bait. —*v.i.* **3** To bite off or eat little bits. **4** To take gentle or cautious bites: usu. with *at.* —*n.* A little bite. [? < LG *nibbelen*] —**nib′bler** *n.*

nib·lick (nib′lik) *n.* A golf club with a slanted iron head for lifting the ball out of bunkers, long grass, etc. [?]

Nic·a·ra·gua (nik′ə·rä′gwə) *n.* A republic of Central America, 57,100 sq. mi., cap. Managua. —**Nic′a·ra′guan** *adj., n.* • See map at CENTRAL AMERICA.

nice (nīs) *adj.* **nic·er, nic·est 1** Agreeable or pleasant: *nice* weather. **2** Warm; kindly: a *nice* person. **3** Requiring careful consideration; subtle: a *nice* point. **4** Exact; accurate: a *nice* eye for color. **5** Refined in tastes or habits; fastidious. **6** Suitable: That dress will be *nice* for the party. **7** Scrupulous; honest. **8** Refined or cultivated: *nice* manners. **9** Needing tact, care, etc.: a *nice* situation. **10** Well performed: a *nice* throw. [< L *nescius* ignorant] —**nice′ly** *adv.* —**nice′ness** *n.* —**Syn. 1** enjoyable. **2** friendly. **5** exacting; particular. **6** fitting; proper.

Ni·cene Creed (nī′sēn, nī·sēn′) *Eccl.* A Christian confession of faith, adopted by the first Council of Nicaea in 325 A.D., and now generally accepted by most Christian sects. [< *Nicaea*, ancient town in Asia Minor]

ni·ce·ty (nī′sə·tē) *n. pl.* **·ties 1** The quality of being nice. **2** A delicate point or distinction; subtlety. **3** A rare or delicious thing; delicacy. **4** Fastidiousness.

niche (nich) *n.* **1** A recessed space or hollow, esp. one in a wall for a statue, etc. **2** Any position specially adapted to its occupant. —*v.t.* **niched, nich·ing** To put in a niche. [< L *nidus* a nest]

nick (nik) *n.* A slight cut, chip, or indentation in the surface or edge of anything. — **in the nick of time** At the last moment possible to be effective. —*v.t.* **1** To make a nick or nicks in; notch. **2** To cut through or into. **3** *Slang* To cheat or trick. [ME *nyke*] —**nick′er** *n.*

Niche

nick·el (nik′əl) *n.* **1** A hard, silver-white metallic element (symbol Ni) widely used in steel and other alloys. **2** A five-cent coin of the U.S. or of Canada. —*v.t.* To plate with nickel. [< G (*Kupfer*)*nickel,* lit., copper demon; because its ore looks like an ore of copper but contains none]

nick·el·o·de·on (nik′əl·ō′dē·ən) *n.* **1** A former type of motion-picture theater charging an admission fee of five cents. **2** A juke box.

nick·el-plate (nik′əl·plāt′) *v.t.* **-plat·ed, -plat·ing** To cover with a thin layer of nickel.

nickel plate A thin layer of nickel on a surface.

nickel silver A hard, silvery alloy of nickel, copper, and zinc that resists corrosion.

nick·er (nik′ər) *v.i.* To neigh or whinny. —*n.* The sound of nickering. [Imit.]

nick-nack (nik′nak′) *n.* KNICK-KNACK.

nick·name (nik′nām′) *n.* **1** A diminutive, as Tom for Thomas. **2** A descriptive or facetious name given to a person, place, or thing in derision or affection. —*v.t.* **·named, ·nam·ing 1** To give a nickname to. **2** To misname. [ME *an ekename* an additional name, taken as *a nickname*]

nic·o·tine (nik′ə·tēn, -tin) *n.* A poisonous alkaloid contained in the leaves of tobacco. [< J. *Nicot,* 1530–1604, French courtier, who introduced tobacco into France] — **nic·o·tin·ic** (nik′ə·tin′ik) *adj.*

nicotinic acid NIACIN.

nic·ti·tate (nik′tə·tāt) *v.i.* **·tat·ed, ·tat·ing** To blink. Also **nic′tate.** [< L *nictare* to wink] —**nic′ti·ta′tion, nic·ta′tion** *n.*

nictitating membrane A transparent third eyelid found in certain animals. Also **nic·ta′ting membrane.**

niece (nēs) *n.* **1** The daughter of one's brother or sister. **2** The daughter of one's brother-in-law or sister-in-law. [< L *neptis* niece]

nif·ty (nif′tē) *adj.* **·ti·er, ·ti·est** *Slang* Stylish; pleasing. [?]

Ni·ger (nī′jər, -gər) *n.* A republic of CEN. Africa, 458,976 sq. mi., cap. Niamey. • See map at AFRICA.

Ni·ge·ri·a (nī·jir′ē·ə) *n.* An independent member of the Commonwealth of Nations in w Africa, 339,169 sq. mi., cap. Lagos. —**Ni·ge′ri·an** *adj., n.* • See map at AFRICA.

nig·gard (nig′ərd) *n.* A parsimonious person. —*adj.* Niggardly. [< Scand.]

nig·gard·ly (nig′ərd·lē) *adj.* **1** Avaricious; stingy. **2** Scanty or measly: a *niggardly* portion. —*adv.* Stingily. — **nig′gard·li·ness** *n.* —**Syn. adj. 1** miserly, parsimonious, tight-fisted.

nig·gle (nig′əl) *v.i.* **·gled, ·gling** To occupy oneself with trifles; be too precise. [Prob. < Scand.] —**nig′gler** *n.*

nigh (nī) *adj.* **nigh·er, nigh·est** or, formerly, **next** Being close by; near in time or place. —*adv.* **1** Not remote in time or place. **2** Almost; nearly. —*prep.* Close to; near. [< OE *nēah*]

night (nīt) *n.* **1** The period during which the sun is below the horizon from sunset to sunrise. **2** The dark. **3** A condition of gloom or misfortune. **4** Death. —**night and day** Continuously. —**nights** *Informal* At night. [< OE *niht*]

night blindness Impaired vision in dim light due to vitamin A deficiency.

night-bloom·ing ce·re·us (nīt′blōō′ming sir′ē·əs) Any of several cactuses having fragrant flowers that open at night.

night·cap (nīt′kap′) *n.* **1** A headcovering to be worn in bed. **2** *Informal* A drink of liquor taken just before going to bed.

night·clothes (nīt′klōz′, -klōthz′) *n.pl.* Clothes to be worn in bed, as pajamas and nightgowns.

night·club (nīt′klub′) *n.* A restaurant open only at night, providing entertainment, food, and drink.

night·fall (nīt′fôl′) *n.* The close of day.

night·gown (nīt′goun′) *n.* A long, loose gown worn in bed. Also **night′dress′.**

night·hawk (nīt′hôk′) *n.* A bird of nocturnal habits, related to the whippoorwill.

night·in·gale (nī′tən·gāl, nī′ting-) *n.* A small, Old World thrush noted for the melodious song of the male. [< OE *nihtegale,* lit., night-singer]

night letter A telegram transmitted at night, usu. at a reduced rate.

night·long (nīt′lông′, -long′) *adj.* Lasting through the night.

night·ly (nīt′lē) *adj.* Occurring at night or every night. —*adv.* By night; every night.

Nighthawk

night·mare (nīt′mâr) *n.* **1** A terrifying dream. **2** Any oppressive or terrifying experience. [< NIGHT + OE *mare* goblin] —**night′mar·ish** *adj.*

night owl *Informal* A person who customarily stays up until late at night.

night school A school that holds classes during the evening.

night·shade (nīt′shād) *n.* Any of various plants related to the tomato and potato; esp., the **common** or **black nightshade,** a poisonous weed with white flowers and black berries; or **deadly nightshade** (belladonna); or **woody nightshade** (bittersweet).

night·shirt (nīt′shûrt′) *n.* A loose, shirtlike garment worn in bed, esp. formerly by men or boys.

night spot *Informal* A night club.

night·stick (nīt′stik′) *n.* A long, stout club carried by policemen.

night·time (nīt′tīm′) *n.* The time from sunset to sunrise, or from dark to dawn.

night·walk·er (nīt′wô′kər) *n.* **1** One who frequents the streets at night. **2** A large earthworm that emerges at night: also **night crawler.**

night watchman A person hired to keep watch and be on guard at night.

ni·hil·ism (nī′əl·iz′əm, nī′hil-) *n.* **1** *Philos.* The doctrine that nothing exists or can be known. **2** The rejection of religious and moral creeds. **3** A political doctrine holding that the existing structure of society should be destroyed. [< L *nihil* nothing + -ISM] —**ni′hil·ist** *n.* —**ni′hil·is·tic** *adj.*

-nik *suffix* One associated, concerned, or connected with: *peacenik.* [< Russ., noun suffix]

Ni·ke (nī′kē) *Gk. Myth.* The winged goddess of victory.

nil (nil) *n.* Nothing. [L, contraction of *nihil* nothing]

Nile green (nīl) Any of several light green tints.

nil·gai (nil′gī) *n. pl.* **·gais** or **·gai** A large, short-maned an-

telope of India. Also **nil'ghai.** [< Pers. *nīl* blue + *gāu* cow]
nim·ble (nim'bəl) *adj.* **·bler, ·blest** 1 Light and quick in motion or action; agile. 2 Intellectually alert or acute. [< OE *numel* quick at learning & *nǣmel* receptive] —**nim'·ble·ness** *n.* —**nim'bly** *adv.* —**Syn.** 1 lively, sprightly, spry.
nim·bo·stra·tus (nim'bō·strā'təs, -strat'əs) *n.* A gray cloud at a low altitude, often giving off precipitation.
nim·bus (nim'bəs) *n. pl.* **·bus·es** or **·bi** (-bī) 1 A halo or bright disk encircling the head, as of Jesus, saints, etc., in pictures, on medallions, etc. 2 A cloud of glory about a god, a person, or thing. 3 Any atmosphere or aura of fame, glamour, etc. 4 Formerly, a nimbostratus. [L, rain cloud]
Nim·rod (nim'rod) In the Bible, the grandson of Ham; a mighty hunter. —*n.* A hunter.
nin·com·poop (nin'kəm·poōp) *n.* A foolish or silly person; simpleton. [?]
nine (nīn) *n.* 1 The sum of eight plus one; 9; IX. 2 A set or group of nine members. [< OE *nigon*] —**nine** *adj., pron.*
nine·fold (nīn'fōld') *adj. & adv.* Nine times as many or as great.
nine·pins (nīn'pinz') *n.pl. (construed as sing.)* A game similar to tenpins, in which nine large wooden pins are set up to be knocked down by a ball.
nine·teen (nīn'tēn') *n.* 1 The sum of 18 plus 1; 19; XIX. 2 A set or group of nineteen members. —**nine'teen'** *adj., pron.*
nine·teenth (nīn'tēnth') *adj. & adv.* Next in order after the 18th. —*n.* The element of an ordered set that corresponds to the number 19. 2 One of 19 equal parts.
nine·ti·eth (nīn'tē·ith) *adj. & adv.* Tenth in order after the 80th. —*n.* The element of an ordered set that corresponds to the number 90. 2 One of 90 equal parts.
nine·ty (nīn'tē) *n. pl.* **·ties** 1 The product of nine and ten; 90; XC. 2 A set or group of 90 members. 3 *pl.* The numbers, years, etc., between 90 and 100. —**nine'ty** *adj., pron.*
Nin·e·veh (nin'ə·və) *n.* An ancient city, capital of Assyria.
nin·ny (nin'ē) *n. pl.* **·nies** A simpleton. [? Short for *an innocent*]
ninth (nīnth) *adj. & adv.* Next in order after the eighth. —*n.* 1 The element of an ordered set that corresponds to the number nine. 2 One of nine equal parts.
Ni·o·be (nī'ə·bē) *Gk. Myth.* The mother whose children were killed by the gods because she kept boasting about them; later turned by Zeus into a stone fountain from which her tears continued to flow.
ni·o·bi·um (nī·ō'bē·əm) *n.* A steel-gray, metallic element (symbol Nb), valuable as an alloy metal. [< NIOBE]
nip¹ (nip) *v.t.* **nipped, nip·ping** 1 To compress tightly between two surfaces or points; bite. 2 To remove by pinching or clipping. 3 To check or destroy the development of. 4 To benumb: said of cold. —**nip in the bud** To put a stop to at the beginning. —*n.* 1 The act of compressing sharply. 2 A biting, pinching, or clipping off. 3 A sudden blight, as by frost. —**nip and tuck** *Informal* With the outcome undecided; neck and neck. [ME *nippen*] —**nip'ping·ly** *adv.*
nip² (nip) *n.* A small dram, esp. of alcoholic liquor. —*v.t. & v.i.* To drink (liquor) in sips. [< earlier *nipperkin* half-pint measure]
nip·per (nip'ər) *n.* 1 One who nips. 2 One of various pincers for nipping. 3 A great claw, as of a crab. 4 *Brit.* A small boy.
nip·ple (nip'əl) *n.* 1 The pigmented cone-shaped process of the breast in humans and other mammals containing the milk duct; teat. 2 A perforated cap on a nursing bottle through which a baby sucks milk. 3 Any nipple-shaped projection. [Earlier *neble*, ? dim. of NEB]

Nipper def. 2

nip·py (nip'ē) *adj.* **·pi·er, ·pi·est** 1 Biting; sharp. 2 Chilly; frosty. —**nip'pi·ly** *adv.* —**nip'pi·ness** *n.*
nir·va·na (nir·vä'nə, nər·van'ə) *n.* 1 In Buddhism, the ideal and goal of all religious effort, absorption of the individual into the supreme spirit: also **Nirvana.** 2 A place or condition of sublime happiness or fulfillment. [< Skt. *nirvāna* a blowing out]

Ni·sei (nē·sā) *n. pl.* **·sei** or **·seis** An American citizen of immigrant Japanese parentage who was born in the U.S.
nit (nit) *n.* 1 The egg of a louse or similar insect. 2 The immature insect itself. [< OE *hnitu*] —**nit'ty** *adj.*
nite (nīt) *n. Nonstand.* NIGHT.
ni·ter (nī'tər) *n.* Potassium or sodium nitrate. Also **ni'tre.** [< Gk. *nitron*, a sodium mineral]
nit·e·ry (nīt'ə·rē) *n. pl.* **·ries** *Slang* A nightclub.
ni·ton (nī'ton) *n.* A former name for radon. [< L *nitere* to shine]
nit-pick·ing (nit'pik·ing) *n. Informal* A fussing over trivial details, usu. with the aim of finding fault. —**nit'·pick'** *v.i.* —**nit'·pick·er** *n.* [< NIT + PICKING]
ni·trate (nī'trāt) *v.t.* **·trat·ed, ·trat·ing** To treat with nitric acid; to change into a nitrate. —*n.* 1 A salt or ester of nitric acid: silver *nitrate*. 2 A fertilizer consisting of sodium or potassium nitrate. [< L *nitrum*, a native sodium salt] —**ni·tra'tion** *n.*
ni·tric (nī'trik) *adj.* 1 Of, pertaining to, or obtained from nitrogen. 2 Containing nitrogen in the higher state of valence.
nitric acid A heavy, volatile, unstable, corrosive liquid having strong acid properties in aqueous solution.
ni·tri·fy (nī'trə·fī) *v.t.* **·fied, ·fy·ing** 1 To combine with nitrogen. 2 To oxidize, as atmospheric nitrogen, ammonia, etc., into nitric or nitrous acid or into nitrates or nitrites. 3 To treat or impregnate (soil, etc.) with nitrates. —**ni·tri·fi·ca·tion** (nī'trə·fə·kā'shən), **ni'tra·fi'er** *n.* —**ni'tri·fi'a·ble** *adj.*
ni·trite (nī'trīt) *n.* A salt of nitrous acid.
nitro- *combining form Chem.* Containing the univalent nitrous radical: *nitrobenzene*. Also **nitri-.** [< L *nitrum,* a native sodium salt]
ni·tro·ben·zene (nī'trō·ben'zēn, -ben·zēn') *n.* A yellow, poisonous liquid formed by nitrating benzene, used in making dyes.
ni·tro·cel·lu·lose (nī'trō·sel'yə·lōs) *n.* Any of various compounds obtained by treating cellulose with nitric and sulfuric acids, used to make plastics, explosives, etc.
ni·tro·gen (nī'trə·jən) *n.* An odorless, colorless, gaseous element (symbol N) forming 78 percent of the atmosphere and forming essential compounds in all living organisms. [< NITRO- + -GEN] —**ni·trog'e·nous** (-ə·nəs) *adj.*
nitrogen fixation The conversion of atmospheric nitrogen into useful nitrogen compounds, either by certain soil bacteria or by various industrial processes. —**ni'tro·gen·fix'ing** *adj.*
ni·trog·en·ize (nī·troj'ən·īz, nī'trə·jən·īz') *v.t.* **·ized, ·iz·ing** To treat or combine with nitrogen.
ni·tro·glyc·er·in (nī'trō·glis'ər·in) *n.* A pale yellow, oily, explosively unstable liquid, made by nitrating glycerol, used to form dynamite and in medicine. Also **ni'tro·glyc'·er·ine.**
ni·trous (nī'trəs) *adj.* 1 Of, pertaining to, or containing niter. 2 Denoting compounds of nitrogen containing less oxygen than the corresponding nitric compounds.
nitrous acid An unstable compound occurring only in solution.
nitrous oxide An unstable, gaseous compound of nitrogen and oxygen, used as an anesthetic in dentistry.
nit·ty-grit·ty (nit'ē-grit'ē) *Slang. n.* The basic question or details; the heart of the matter. —*adj.* Down-to-earth; basic. [?]
nit·wit (nit'wit') *n.* A silly or stupid person. [Prob. < NIT + WIT]
nix¹ (niks) *n.* In Teutonic mythology, a water spirit. [G] —**nix'ie** *n. Fem.*
nix² (niks) *Slang n.* 1 Nothing. 2 No. —*adv.* No. —*interj.* Stop! Watch out!. —*v.t.* To forbid or disagree with. [< G *nichts* nothing]
ni·zam (ni·zäm', -zam', nī-) *n. pl.* **·zam** 1 Formerly, a Turkish regular soldier. 2 *Often cap.* The former title of the native ruler of Hyderabad, India. [< Ar. *naẓāma* govern]
NJ New Jersey (P.O. abbr.).
N.J. New Jersey.
NL, NL., N.L. New Latin.
NLRB National Labor Relations Board.

---

add, āce, câre, pälm; end, ēven; it, īce; odd, ōpen, ôrder; tŏŏk, pōōl; up, bûrn; ə = *a* in *above*, *u* in *focus*; yōō = *u* in *fuse*; oil; pout; check; go; ring; thin; this; zh, *vision.* < derived from; ? origin uncertain or unknown.

NM New Mexico (P.O. abbr.).

NNW, N.N.W., nnw, n.n.w. north-northwest.

no¹ (nō) *adv.* **1** Nay; not so. **2** Not at all; not in any way. **3** Not: used to express an alternative after *or:* whether or *no.* —*adj.* Not any; not one. —*n. pl.* **noes 1** A negative reply; a denial. **2** A negative vote or voter: The *noes* have it. [< OE *ne* not + *ā* ever]

no² (nō) *n.* The classical drama of Japan, traditionally tragic or noble in theme. Also **Noh.**

No nobelium.

No·ah (nō'ə) In the Bible, a patriarch who, at the command of God, built an ark to save his family and two of every sort of living thing from the Flood.

nob (nob) *n.* **1** *Slang* The head. **2** A knob or protuberance. [Var. of KNOB]

nob·by (nob'ē) *adj.* **·bi·er, ·bi·est** *Brit. Slang* Flashy; showy; stylish. [?]

no·bel·i·um (nō·bel'ē·əm) *n.* An artificially produced radioactive element (symbol No). [< *Nobel* Institute, Stockholm]

No·bel Prizes (nō·bel') Six prizes usu. awarded annually to those whose work in physics, chemistry, medicine, literature, economics, and world peace is thought of most benefit to humanity. [< Alfred *Nobel*, 1833–96, Swedish philanthropist]

no·bil·i·ty (nō·bil'ə·tē) *n. pl.* **·ties 1** The state of being noble, as in character or rank. **2** A class composed of nobles. **3** In Great Britain, the peerage. **4** High-mindedness; magnanimity. **5** Great moral excellence. **6** Noble lineage.

no·ble (nō'bəl) *adj.* **·bler, ·blest 1** Of or pertaining to an aristocracy; of lofty lineage. **2** Characterized by or indicative of virtue or magnanimity; high-minded. **3** Imposing in appearance; grand: a *noble* face. —*n.* A person having hereditary title, rank, and privileges; in Great Britain, a peer. [< L *nobilis* noble, well-known] —**no'ble·ness** *n.* —**no'bly** *adv.* —**Syn.** *adj.* **2** excellent, honorable, worthy, righteous, fine. **3** impressive, magnificent, splendid.

no·ble·man (nō'bəl·mən) *n. pl.* **·men** (-mən) A man of noble rank; in England, a peer. —**no'ble·wom'an** (-wŏŏm'ən) *n. Fem.*

no·blesse o·blige (nō·bles' ō·blēzh') The duty of persons of noble birth or high rank to behave courageously, honorably, and generously toward others. [F, lit., nobility obliges]

no·bod·y (nō'bod'ē, -bəd·ē) *pron.* Not anybody. —*n. pl.* **·bod·ies** A person of no importance or influence.

nock (nok) *n.* **1** The notch on the butt end of an arrow. **2** The notch on the horn of a bow for securing the bowstring. —*v.t.* To fit (an arrow) to the bowstring. [ME *nocke*]

noc·tu·id (nok'chōō·id) *n.* Any of a large family of medium-sized moths that usu. fly at night, including many with destructive larvae, as the army worm and the cutworm. —*adj.* Pertaining to these moths. [< L *noctua* night owl]

noc·tur·nal (nok·tûr'nəl) *adj.* **1** Pertaining to night. **2** Occurring or active at night. **3** Seeking food by night, as animals. **4** Having blossoms that open by night. [< L *nocturnus* < *nox* night] —**noc·tur'nal·ly** *adv.*

noc·turne (nok'tûrn) *n.* **1** In painting, a night scene. **2** *Music* A composition evocative of night. [< L *nocturnus* nightly]

nod (nod) *n.* A forward and downward motion of the head, more or less quick or jerky. —*v.* **nod·ded, nod·ding** *v.i.* **1** To make a brief forward and downward movement of the head, as in agreement, invitation, etc. **2** To let the head fall forward involuntarily, as when drowsy. **3** To be inattentive or careless. **4** To incline the top or upper part as if nodding: said of trees, flowers, etc. —*v.t.* **5** To bend (the head) forward and downward briefly. **6** To express or signify by nodding: to *nod* approval. [ME *nodden*] —**nod'der** *n.*

Nod (nod) *n.* **1** The land east of Eden in which Cain settled after killing Abel. *Gen.* 4:16. **2** Sleep. Also **Land of Nod.**

nod·dle (nod'l) *n. Informal* The head: a humorous use. [< NOD]

nod·dy (nod'ē) *n. pl.* **·dies 1** A dunce; a fool. **2** Any of several terns of warm seas noted for their exceptional tameness. [< NOD]

node (nōd) *n.* **1** A knot or knob; swelling. **2** *Bot.* The joint or knob on the stem of a plant, from which leaves grow. **3** *Astron.* Either of the two points at which the intersection of the planes of two orbits touches the celestial sphere. **4** *Physics* A point, line, or plane in a vibrating body where the amplitude is virtually zero. [< L *nodus* knot] —**no·dal** (nōd'l) *adj.*

nod·ule (noj'ōōl) *n.* **1** A little knot, lump, or node. **2** *Bot.* A tubercle. —**nod·u·lar** (noj'-ə·lər) *adj.*

Nodes *def. 2*

No·ël (nō·el') *n.* **1** Christmas. **2** A Christmas carol: also **no·el'.** [< L *natalis* birth]

nog (nog) *n.* **1** A strong ale. **2** Eggnog. Also **nogg.** [?]

nog·gin (nog'in) *n.* **1** A small mug, or its contents. **2** A liquid measure equal to about a gill. **3** *Informal* A person's head. [?]

no·how (nō'hou') *adv. Informal* In no way; not by any means.

noise (noiz) *n.* **1** Any annoying or undesired sound, esp. one that is random. **2** A similar electrical signal. **3** Clamor caused by raised voices and restless moving about. **4** Any sound. —*v.* **noised, nois·ing** *v.t.* **1** To spread by rumor or report; often with *about* or *abroad.* —*v.i.* **2** To make a noise. **3** To talk in a loud manner. [< OF *noyse*]

noise·less (noiz'lis) *adj.* Causing or making little or no noise. —**noise'less·ly** *adv.* —**noise'less·ness** *n.*

noi·some (noi'səm) *adj.* **1** Very offensive, particularly to the sense of smell. **2** Injurious; harmful. [< *noy*, var. of ANNOY + -SOME] —**noi'some·ly** *adv.* —**noi'some·ness** *n.* —**Syn. 1** fetid, foul, mephitic, stinking. **2** destructive, detrimental, hurtful, noxious.

nois·y (noi'zē) *adj.* **nois·i·er, nois·i·est 1** Making a loud noise. **2** Characterized by much noise. —**nois'i·ly** *adv.* —**nois'i·ness** *n.*

nol·le pros·e·qui (nol'ē pros'ə·kwī) *Law* An entry of record to signify that the plaintiff or prosecutor will not press a case. [L, to be unwilling to prosecute]

no·lo con·ten·de·re (nō'lō kən·ten'də·rē) *Law* A plea by a defendant in a criminal action, which, while not an admission of guilt, states that he will make no defense. [L, I am unwilling to contend]

nol·pros (nol'pros') *v.t.* **-prossed, -pros·sing** *Law* To subject to a nolle prosequi.

nol. pros. nolle prosequi.

nom. nomenclature; nominal; nominative.

no·mad (nō'mad, nom'ad) *adj.* Nomadic. —*n.* A rover; one of an unsettled, wandering people, tribe, or race. [< Gk. *nomein* to pasture, feed] —**no'mad·ism** *n.*

no·mad·ic (nō·mad'ik) *adj.* **1** Of or pertaining to nomads. **2** Wandering from one place to another; unsettled. Also **no·mad'i·cal.** —**no·mad'i·cal·ly** *adv.*

no man's land 1 Waste or unowned land. **2** In warfare, the part of a battlefield between the opposing armies.

nom de guerre (nôn də gâr') An assumed name. [F, lit., war name]

nom de plume (nom' də plōōm', *Fr.* nôn də plüm') A pen name; a writer's assumed name. [F]

no·men·cla·ture (nō'mən·klā'chər) *n.* A system of names used in any art, science, or other specialized field. [L *nomenclatura* list of names]

nom·i·nal (nom'ə·nəl) *adj.* **1** Of or pertaining to a name or names. **2** Existing in name only; not actual: a *nominal* peace. **3** So slight as to be hardly worth naming: a *nominal* sum. [< L *nomen* name] —**nom'i·nal·ly** *adv.*

nom·i·nate (nom'ə·nāt) *v.t.* **·nat·ed, ·nat·ing 1** To name as a candidate for elective office. **2** To appoint to some office or duty. —*adj.* Nominated. [< L < *nomen, nominis* a name] —**nom·i·na'tion, nom'i·na'tor** *n.*

nom·i·na·tive (nom'ə·nə·tiv, nom'ə·nā'-) *adj.* **1** *Gram.* Designating the case of the subject of a finite verb, or of a word agreeing with, or in apposition to, the subject. **2** Appointed by nomination; nominated. —*n. Gram.* **1** The nominative case. **2** A word in this case.

nom·i·nee (nom'ə·nē') *n.* A person who receives a nomination, esp. for an election.

-nomy *combining form* The science or systematic study of: *astronomy.* [< Gk. *nomos* law]

non- *prefix* Not. [< L *non* not] • **Non-** is the Latin negative adverb adopted as a prefix in English. It denotes in general simple negation or absence of, as in *nonaggression.* Words beginning with *non-* are now usu. written without a hyphen except when one element is a capitalized word: *non-American.* Even words with the initial letter *n* are now often combined with the prefix *non-* to form a solid word: *nonnative.* Following is a list of words beginning with this prefix.

nonabsolute	nonconflict	nonfictive
nonabsorbable	nonconfrontation	nonfinancial
nonabsorbent	non-Congressional	nonfinite
nonabstract	nonconnotative	nonfiscal
nonacceptance	nonconscious	nonflammable
nonachievement	nonconsciousness	nonfood
nonachiever	nonconsensual	nonfraternization
nonacquaintance	nonconsent	nonfreedom
nonacquisition	nonconsideration	nonfreeman
nonaction	nonconsumption	non-Freudian
nonactive	noncontagious	nonfunctioning
nonactivist	noncontest	nonhazardous
nonactor	noncontingent	non-Hellenic
nonactress	noncontrolling	nonhero
nonadherence	noncontroversial	nonholiday
nonadherent	nonconversion	nonhuman
nonadjacent	noncriminal	nonidentity
nonadmirer	noncritical	nonideological
nonadmission	noncrystallized	nonimperial
nonadoption	noncurrency	nonimprovement
nonadult	nondefense	noninductive
nonadversary	nondeliquescent	noninflammable
nonaesthetic	nondelivery	nonintellectual
nonaffluent	nondepartmental	noninterference
nonagreement	nondevelopment	noninvolved
nonalcoholic	nondifferentiated	noninvolvement
nonaligned	nondirective	nonionized
nonallegiance	nondiscrimination	nonirritating
non-American	nondissemination	non-Jewish
nonanswer	nondistinctive	nonjusticiable
nonantagonistic	nondistribution	nonlethal
nonapproved	nondivisible	nonlinear
nonarranged	nondoctrinal	nonliterary
nonarrival	nondrinker	nonluminous
nonart	nondurable	nonmagnetic
nonassociative	noneconomic	nonmanagement
nonathlete	noneducational	nonmaterial
nonatomic	noneffective	nonmateriality
nonattached	nonefficient	nonmeaning
nonattendance	nonego	nonmechanical
nonattention	nonelastic	nonmember
nonautomatic	nonelectoral	nonmembership
nonbeing	nonelectric	nonmilitancy
nonbelieving	nonelectronic	nonmilitant
nonbelligerent	nonemergency	nonmodulated
nonbinding	nonempirical	nonmonetary
nonbiodegradable	nonenforceable	nonmotile
nonblack	nonentry	nonmusical
nonbook	nonequation	nonnarcotic
nonbudding	nonerotic	nonnative
noncancelable	noneternal	nonnatural
noncancerous	noneternity	nonnegotiable
noncandidacy	non-Euclidean	nonnuclear
noncanonical	non-European	nonnucleated
noncareer	nonexclusive	nonnutritive
non-Catholic	nonexcusable	nonobservance
noncentral	nonexecution	nonofficial
noncharacter	nonexempt	nonofficially
non-Christian	nonexercise	nonoperative
noncitizen	nonexistence	nonorthodox
noncoercive	nonexistent	nonowner
noncollapsible	nonexisting	nonoxidating
noncollege	nonexpendable	nonparallel
noncollegiate	nonexpert	nonparasitic
noncolonial	nonexplosive	nonparticipant
noncombustible	nonexpressive	nonparticipating
noncommercial	nonextant	nonpaying
noncommunicant	nonextension	nonpayment
non-Communist	nonextremist	nonperformance
noncompetitive	nonfactual	nonpermanent
nonconception	nonfamous	nonperson
nonconcur	nonfarm	nonphysical
nonconducive	nonfatal	nonpigmented
nonconfiguration	nonferrous	nonpoisonous

nonpolemical	nonresisting	nonsubscribing
nonpolitical	nonresonant	nonsupporter
nonpolluting	nonrestraint	nonsupporting
nonpossessor	nonrestricted	nonsyllabic
nonpractical	nonreturnable	nonsympathizer
nonprofessional	nonrevolutionary	nonsympathy
nonproliferation	nonrigid	nontax
nonproperty	nonsalaried	nonteaching
nonpropulsive	nonscientific	nontechnical
nonprotection	nonselective	nontenured
non-Protestant	nonsensitive	nonterminating
nonproven	nonsentient	nontoxic
nonpublic	nonsequential	nontruth
nonpublication	nonserious	nonunionization
nonpunishment	nonsexual	nonunionized
nonracial	nonsexually	nonuser
nonreader	nonsignificant	nonvariable
nonrechargeable	nonsmoker	nonvenomous
nonrecognition	nonsociety	nonviability
nonrecurring	nonsolid	nonviable
nonreigning	nonspecialist	nonvolatile
nonrelative	nonspecific	nonvolition
nonrelevant	nonstick	nonvoluntary
nonrenewable	nonstriated	nonwar
nonreproductive	nonstudent	nonworker
nonreserved	nonsubscriber	nonworking

non·age (non′ij, nō′nij) *n.* **1** The period of legal minority. **2** An immature or early stage. [< OF *non-* not + *age* age]

non·a·ge·nar·i·an (non′ə·jə·nâr′ē·ən, nō′nə-) *adj.* Pertaining to the nineties in age. —*n.* One between the ages of ninety and a hundred. [< L *nonagenarius* of ninety]

non·ag·gres·sion (non′ə·gresh′ən) *n.* A lack of or abstention from aggression. —**non′ag·gres′sive** *adj.*

non·a·gon (non′ə·gon) *n.* A nine-sided polygon. [< L *nonus* ninth + Gk. *gōnia* angle]

non·ap·pear·ance (non′ə·pir′əns) *n.* Failure to appear, esp. in court in answer to a summons.

nonce (nons) *n.* Present time or occasion. —**for the nonce** For the present time or occasion. [ME *for then ones* for the one (occasion), misread as *for the nones*]

Nonagon

nonce word A word coined for one occasion and usu. not remaining in general use.

non·cha·lance (non′shə·läns′, non′shə·ləns) *n.* Jaunty indifference or unconcern.

non·cha·lant (non′shə·länt′, non′shə·lənt) *adj.* Without concern; casual; indifferent. [< L *non* not + *calere* be warm] —**non′cha·lant·ly** *adv.*

non·com (non′kom′) *Informal adj.* Noncommissioned. —*n.* A noncommissioned officer.

non·com·bat·ant (non′kəm·bat′ənt, -kom′bə·tənt, -kum′-) *n.* **1** One attached to a military force who is not required to fight, as a chaplain or medical officer. **2** Anyone not connected with the military service in time of war; a civilian. —*adj.* Of or pertaining to noncombatants.

non·com·mis·sioned (non′kə·mish′ənd) *adj.* Not holding a military commission, as a corporal or sergeant.

non·com·mit·tal (non′kə·mit′l) *adj.* Not having or expressing a decided opinion. —**non′com·mit′tal·ly** *adv.*

non·com·pli·ance (non′kəm·plī′əns) *n.* Failure, neglect, or refusal to comply. —**non′com·pli′ant** *adj., n.*

non com·pos men·tis (non kom′pəs men′tis) *Latin* Not of sound mind: often shortened to **non compos.**

non·con·duc·tor (non′kən·duk′tər) *n.* A substance or material that offers resistance to the passage of some form of energy.

non·con·form·ist (non′kən·fôr′mist) *n.* One who does not conform to established beliefs and procedures, esp. in religious matters. —**non′con·form′ance** (-məns), **non′con·for′mi·ty** (-fôr′mə·tē) *n.*

non·co·op·er·a·tion (non′kō·op′ə·rā′shən) *n.* Refusal to cooperate; esp. civil resistance to a government. —**non′co·op′er·a·tive** (-kō·op′ə·rə·tiv, -ə·rā′tiv) *adj.* —**non′co·op′er·a·tor** *n.*

non·de·script (non′di·skript) *adj.* Not distinctive enough to be described; difficult to classify. —*n.* A nondescript person or thing. [< NON- + L *descriptus*]

none (nun) *pron.* **1** Not one; no one. **2** No or not one specifically named person or thing. **3** Not any: That is *none* of her business. **4** *(construed as pl.)* Not any (of the persons or things specified). *None* of the apples are rotten. —*adv.* In no respect; not at all: *none* the worse for wear. [< OE *ne* not + *ān* one]

non·en·ti·ty (non·en′tə·tē) *n. pl.* ·ties **1** A person or thing of small significance. **2** The negation of being; nonexistence.

nones (nōnz) *n.pl.* **1** The ninth day before the ides in the Roman calendar. **2** The fifth of the seven daily canonical hours; also, the service for it. [< L *nonus* ninth]

non·es·sen·tial (non′ə·sen′shəl) *adj.* Not really needed. —*n.* An unneeded person or thing.

none·such (nun′such′) *n.* A person or thing having no equal.

none·the·less (nun′thə·les′) *adv.* In spite of that; however; nevertheless.

non·e·vent (non′i·vent′) *n.* A hoped-for event that either never occurs or fails to come up to expectations.

non·fea·sance (non·fē′zəns) *n. Law* The nonperformance of some act which one is bound by legal or official duty to perform. [< NON- not + OF *faisance* doing] —**non·fea′sor** *n.*

non·fic·tion (non·fik′shən) *n.* **1** A literary work, such as a biography, history, etc., based on actual rather than imaginary persons and events. **2** Such works collectively. —**non·fic′tion·al** *adj.*

non·ful·fill·ment (non′ful·fil′mənt) *n.* **1** Failure to satisfy. **2** Failure to be satisfied. Also **non′ful·fil′ment.**

no·nil·lion (nō·nil′yən) *n. & adj.* See NUMBER. —**no·nil′. lionth** (-yənth) *adj., n.*

non·in·ter·ven·tion (non′in·tər·ven′shən) *n.* **1** A refusal to intervene or interfere. **2** The policy of a nation to avoid interference in the affairs of other nations. —**non′in·ter·ven′tion·ist** *adj., n.*

non·ju·ror (non·jŏŏr′ər) *n.* One who refuses to swear allegiance to a leader or to take any oath.

non·met·al (non·met′l) *n.* Any element, as oxygen, nitrogen, carbon, or sulfur, etc., which forms acids, combines with metals to form salts, and gains, borrows, or shares electrons during chemical reactions.

non·me·tal·lic (non′mə·tal′ik) *adj.* **1** Not metallic. **2** Pertaining to a nonmetal.

non·mor·al (non·môr′əl, -mor′-) *adj.* Having no relation to ethical ideals; neither moral nor immoral.

no-no (nō′nō′) *n. pl.* **-nos** *Informal* Something forbidden or very undesirable.

non·ob·jec·tive (non′əb·jek′tiv) *adj.* **1** Not objective. **2** NONREPRESENTATIONAL.

non·pa·reil (non′pə·rel′) *adj.* Of unequaled excellence. —*n.* **1** Something of unequaled excellence. **2** *Printing* A name for 6-point type. [< OF *non* not + *pareil* equal]

non·par·ti·san (non·pär′tə·zən, -sən) *adj.* **1** Not partisan. **2** Not pertaining or adhering to any established political party. —*n.* A nonpartisan person or group.

non·plus (non·plus′, non′plus) *v.t.* **·plused** or **·plussed,** **·plus·ing** or **·plus·sing** To baffle; perplex. —*n.* A mental standstill; perplexity. [< L *non plus* no further] —**Syn.** *v.* confound, embarrass, mystify, puzzle.

non·pro·duc·tive (non′prə·duk′tiv) *adj.* **1** Not producing. **2** Pertaining to those workers not directly involved with production, as clerical help, etc. —**non′pro·duc′tive·ly** *adv.* —**non′pro·duc′tive·ness** *n.*

non·prof·it (non·prof′it) *adj.* **1** Receiving no profit. **2** Established for purposes other than profit: a *nonprofit* organization.

non·pros (non·pros′) *v.t.* **-prossed, -pros·sing** *Law* To enter judgment against (a plaintiff who fails to prosecute).

non pro·seq·ui·tur (non prō·sek′wi·tər) *Law* A judgment entered at common law against a plaintiff who fails to prosecute. [L, he does not prosecute]

non·rep·re·sen·ta·tion·al (non′rep′ri·zen·tā′shən·əl) *adj.* Denoting a form of art that does not attempt to represent the form of objects as they appear in nature; abstract.

non·res·i·dent (non·rez′ə·dənt) *adj.* Not residing in a specified location, esp. where one works, goes to school, etc. —*n.* A nonresident person. —**non·res′i·dence** *n.*

non·re·sis·tant (non′ri·zis′tənt) *adj.* Willing to cooperate; obedient. —*n.* One who believes that authority should not be opposed by force and violence. —**non′re·sis′tance** *n.*

non·re·stric·tive (non′ri·strik′tiv) *adj. Gram.* Denoting a modifier that merely adds descriptive detail and is not essential to the meaning. • See RESTRICTIVE.

non·sched·uled (non·skej′ŏŏld, -əld) *adj.* Not operating in accordance with a formal or regular schedule.

non·sec·tar·i·an (non′sek·târ′ē·ən) *n.* Not allied formally with or restricted to any religious denomination.

non·sense (non′sens, -səns) *n.* **1** That which is without good sense; meaningless or ridiculous language. **2** Things of no importance. **3** Absurd or affected behavior. —*adj.* Consisting of a grouping of letters or sounds that are not intelligible but often formed on a pattern of standard words: "Glip" is a *nonsense* word. —*interj.* How absurd! —**non·sen′si·cal** *adj.* —**non·sen′si·cal·ly** *adv.*

non seq·ui·tur (non sek′wə·tər, -wə·tŏŏr) The fallacy of irrelevant conclusion; an inference that does not follow from the premises. [L, it does not follow]

non·sked (non′sked′) *Informal adj.* Nonscheduled: applied esp. to passenger airplane service. —*n.* Something not operating on or holding to a schedule.

non·skid (non′skid′) *adj.* Having the surface treaded to reduce skidding: said of tires, shoe soles, etc.

nonstand. nonstandard.

non·stand·ard (non·stan′dərd) *adj.* **1** Not standard. **2** Not in accordance with the usage, pronunciation, spelling, grammatical construction, etc., generally accepted by educated speakers and writers of a language.

non·stop (non′stop′) *adj.* Making, having made, or scheduled to make no stops.

non·such (nun′such′) *n.* NONESUCH.

non·suit (non′sōōt′) *Law v.t.* To order the dismissal of the suit of. —*n.* A judgment dismissing a suit when the plaintiff abandons it or fails to establish a cause of action.

non·sup·port (non′sə·pôrt′, -pōrt′) *n.* Failure to provide for the support of dependents.

non·un·ion (non·yōōn′yən) *adj.* **1** Not belonging to a trade union. **2** Not employing or recognizing any trade union or its members. —**non·un′ion·ism,** **non·un′ion·ist** *n.*

non·vi·o·lent (non′vī′ə·lənt) *adj.* **1** Free from violence: a *nonviolent* demonstration. **2** Not given to or believing in violence. —**non′vi′o·lence** *n.* —**non·vi′o·lent·ly** *adv.*

non·vot·er (non·vōt′ər) *n.* One who does not or may not vote. —**non·vot′ing** *adj.*

non·white (non·ʰwīt′) *adj.* **1** Not white. **2** Being other than Caucasian. —*n.* A nonwhite person, as a Negro.

noo·dle¹ (nōōd′l) *n. Slang* **1** A stupid person: also **noo′. dle·head.** **2** The head. [?]

noo·dle² (nōōd′l) *n.* A thin, flat strip of dried dough, usu. made with egg, used in soup, etc. [< G *Nudel*]

nook (nŏŏk) *n.* **1** A corner or recess, esp. in a room. **2** Any small, cozy or sheltered place. [ME *noke* corner]

noon (nōōn) *n.* **1** That time of day when the sun is on the meridian; the middle of the day. **2** The highest point of any period or career. —*adj.* Of or taking place at noon: the *noon* meal. [< L *nona (hora)* ninth (hour)]

noon·day (nōōn′dā′) *n.* The middle of the day. —*adj.* Pertaining to midday.

no one Not anyone; no person.

noon·time (nōōn′tīm′) *n.* The time of midday; noon. —*adj.* Of or occurring at noon. Also **noon′tide′** (-tīd′).

noose (nōōs) *n.* **1** A loop furnished with a running knot, as in a hangman's halter or a snare. **2** Anything that restricts one's freedom. —*v.t.* **noosed, noos·ing 1** To capture or secure with a noose. **2** To make a noose in (a rope). [< L *nodus* a knot]

no-par (nō′pär′) *adj.* Having no par, or face, value, as a share of stock.

nope (nōp) *adv. Slang* No.

nor (nôr) *conj.* And not; likewise not: used chiefly as a correlative of a preceding negative, usu. *neither* or *not.* [Contraction of ME *nother* neither]

nor′ (nôr) *adj., adv. & n.* North: often used in combination: *nor′easter.* Also **nor.**

Nor. Norman; Norway; Norwegian.

Nor., nor. north; northern.

Noose

Nor·dic (nôr'dik) *adj.* Pertaining or belonging to a typically blond, tall, long-headed physical type inhabiting N Europe. —*n.* A person of this type. [< F *nord* north]

Nor'·east·er (nôr-ēs'tər) *n.* NORTHEASTER.

Nor·folk jacket (nôr'fək) A loose-fitting jacket with side pockets, belt, and two box pleats. [< *Norfolk,* England]

no·ri·a (nō'rē-ə) *n.* In Spain and the Orient, an undershot water wheel having buckets on its rim to raise water. [< Ar. *nā'ūrah*]

norm (nôrm) *n.* 1 A model, type, pattern, or value considered as representative of a specified group. 2 *Psychol.* The average or median of performance in a given function or test. [< L *norma* rule]

nor·mal (nôr'məl) *adj.* 1 Conforming to a type or standard; regular. 2 Constituting a standard; model. 3 *Math.* Perpendicular. 4 Average; mean. 5 *Chem.* Denoting a salt having no replaceable hydrogen. 6 *Psychol.* Of average intelligence or mental health. 7 In good physical health. —*n.* 1 A common or natural condition. 2 A usual or accepted rule or process. 3 The average or mean value of observed quantities. 4 *Math.* A straight line perpendicular to a curve or surface at a point. [< L *norma* rule] —**nor'mal·cy** (-sē), **nor·mal·i·ty** (nôr-mal'ə-tē), **nor'mal·ness** *n.* —**nor'mal·ly** *adv.* —**Syn.** 1 common, everyday, ordinary, typical, usual.

nor·mal·ize (nôr'məl-īz) *v.t.* **·ized, ·iz·ing** To make normal. —**nor'mal·i·za'tion, nor'mal·iz'er** *n.*

normal school A school for the training of elementary-school teachers.

Nor·man (nôr'mən) *adj.* Pertaining to Normandy or to the Normans. —*n.* 1 One of a people of Scandinavian heritage who settled in Normandy, France, in the 10th century. 2 A native or inhabitant of Normandy, France. 3 One of the Norman or French invaders who conquered England in 1066 (the **Norman Conquest**). 4 NORMAN FRENCH.

Norman French The dialect of French spoken by the Norman conquerors in England.

Norse (nôrs) *adj.* 1 Scandinavian. 2 West Scandinavian, i.e., Norwegian, Icelandic, and Faroese. —*n.* 1 The Scandinavians or West Scandinavians collectively: with *the.* 2 The Scandinavian or North Germanic group of the Germanic languages; esp., the language of Norway. 3 The West Scandinavian languages.

Norse·man (nôrs'mən) *n. pl.* **·men** (-mən) A Scandinavian of Viking times.

north (nôrth) *n.* 1 The general direction to the left of sunrise. 2 The point of the compass at 0° or 360°, directly opposite south. 3 Any region north of a given point. 4 *Sometimes cap.* The northern part of any region, country, etc. —**the North** 1 The states in the part of the U.S. north of Maryland, Missouri, and the Ohio river. 2 The states that opposed the Confederacy. —*adj.* 1 Lying toward or in the north. 2 Issuing from or inhabiting the north. 3 Facing or proceeding toward the north. 4 *Usu. cap.* Denoting the northern part of a country, continent, hemisphere, etc.: *North* America. —*adv.* Toward the north. [< OE]

North America The northern continent in the Western Hemisphere, 9,390,000 sq. mi. —**North American**

north·bound (nôrth'bound') *adj.* Going northward: also **north'bound'.**

north·east (north'ēst', *in nautical usage* nôr·ēst') *n.* 1 That point on the compass midway between north and east. 2 Any region lying toward that point on the horizon. —**the Northeast** The NE part of the U.S., including New England and New York, and sometimes New Jersey and Pennsylvania. —*adj.* From the northeast. —*adv.* Toward the northeast. —**north'east'er·ly** *adj., adv.* —**north'east'ern** *adj.*

north·east·er (north'ēs'tər, *in nautical usage* nôr·ēs'tər) *n.* A gale from the northeast.

north·east·ward (north'ēst'wərd) *adv.* Toward the northeast: also **north'east'wards.** —*adj.* Northeast; toward the northeast. —*n.* Northeast. —**north'east'ward·ly** *adj., adv.*

north·er (nôr'thər) *n.* A cold windstorm from the north.

nor·ther·ly (nôr'thər·lē) *adj. & adv.* 1 Toward the north. 2 From the north. —**north'er·li·ness** *n.*

north·ern (nôr'thərn) *adj.* Pertaining to the north or the North. —*n.* 1 A northerner. 2 A north wind. [< OE *northerne*] —**north'ern·most** *adj.*

north·ern·er (nôr'thər·nər) *n.* One born or residing in the north.

North·ern·er (nôr'thər·nər) *n.* One from the northern part of the U.S., as distinguished from a Southerner.

Northern Hemisphere See HEMISPHERE.

northern lights The aurora borealis.

Northern Spy A large, yellow-and-red variety of apple.

North Korea See KOREA.

north·land (nôrth'lənd) *n.* A land in the north. —*adj.* Of or pertaining to a northern land or lands. —**north'land·er** *n.*

North·man (nôrth'mən) *n. pl.* **·men** (-mən) A Scandinavian; esp. a Scandinavian of the Viking period.

North Pole The northern extremity of the earth's axis.

North Star POLARIS.

North·um·bri·a (nôr·thum'brē-ə) *n.* An ancient Anglo-Saxon kingdom of Great Britain.

North·um·bri·an (nôr·thum'brē-ən) *adj.* Of the ancient English kingdom of Northumbria, its people, or their dialect. —*n.* 1 A native or inhabitant of Northumbria. 2 The Old English dialect of these people.

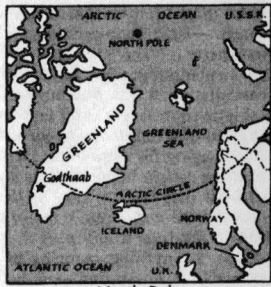

North Pole

North Vietnam See VIETNAM.

north·ward (nôrth'wərd) *adv.* Toward the north. Also **north'wards.** —*adj.* Directed or lying toward the north. —*n.* The northward direction or point of the compass. —**north'ward·ly** *adj., adv.*

north·west (north'west', *in nautical usage* nôr'west') *n.* 1 The direction midway between north and west. 2 Any region situated toward that direction. —**the Northwest** 1 The NW part of the U.S., esp. the states of Washington, Oregon, and Idaho. 2 The NW part of Canada. —*adj.* From the northwest. —*adv.* Toward the northwest. —**north'west'er·ly** *adj., adv.* —**north'west'ern** *adj.*

north·west·er (north'wes'tər, *in nautical usage* nôr'wes'tər) *n.* A gale which blows from the northwest.

Northwest Passage A water route from the Atlantic to the Pacific along the northern coast of America.

north·west·ward (north'west'wərd) *adv.* Toward the northwest; also **north'west'wards.** —*adj.* Northwest; toward the northwest. —*n.* Northwest. —**north'west'ward·ly** *adj., adv.*

Norw. Norway; Norwegian.

Nor·way (nôr'wā) *n.* A constitutional monarchy of N Europe, 119,240 sq. mi., cap. Oslo. • See map at SWEDEN.

Nor·we·gian (nôr·wē'jən) *n.* 1 A citizen or native of Norway. —*adj.* Of or pertaining to Norway, its people, or their language.

nor'·west·er (nôr·wes'tər) *n.* An oilskin coat worn by mariners in stormy weather.

Nos., nos. numbers.

nose (nōz) *n.* 1 The part of the face just above the mouth, containing the nostrils and the organ of smell. 2 The power or sense of smelling. 3 Anything resembling a nose, as a ship's prow. 4 The ability to discover: a *nose* for the facts. —**lead by the nose** To control absolutely. —**look down one's nose at** *Informal* To show contempt for. —**pay through the nose** To pay an exorbitant price. —**turn up one's nose at** To reject scornfully. —**under one's (very) nose** In plain sight; obvious. —*v.* nosed, nos·ing *v.t.* 1 To perceive or discover by or as by the sense of smell. 2 To examine or touch with the nose. —*v.i.* 3 To smell; sniff. **4** To pry; meddle. **5** To push (one's way) slowly and carefully. **—nose out** To defeat by a small margin. [< OE *nosu*]

nose bag A canvas bag that hangs over a horse's nose and contains feed.

nose·band (nōz′band′) *n.* That part of a bridle passing over the nose of a horse and attached to the cheek pieces.

nose·bleed (nōz′blēd′) *n.* Bleeding from the nose.

nose cone The conical and separable forward section of a missile or rocket.

nose-dive (nōz′dīv′) *n.* **1** A steep downward plunge of an airplane. **2** Any sudden descent or crash. *—v.i.* **·dived, ·div·ing** To plunge downward.

nose·gay (nōz′gā′) *n.* A small bouquet. [< NOSE + GAY, in obs. sense "a bright object"]

nose-piece (nōz′pēs′) *n.* **1** Any protective covering for the nose. **2** The band fitting across the nose in a pair of spectacles.

nosh (näsh) *Informal n.* A snack; tidbit. *—v.i.* **1** To eat a snack. *—v.t.* **2** To munch on. [< Yiddish] **—nosh′er** *n.*

no-show (nō′shō′) *n.* **1** One who makes a reservation for an airplane flight but fails to claim the seat or make a cancellation. **2** One who buys a ticket for a performance, athletic contest, etc., and fails to attend.

nos·tal·gi·a (nos·tal′jē·ə, -jə) *n.* **1** Severe homesickness. **2** Any longing for something far away or long ago. [< Gk. *nostos* a return home + *algos* a pain] **—nos·tal′gic** *adj.*

nos·tril (nos′trəl) *n.* One of the outer openings in the nose. [< OE *nosu* nose + *thyrel* a hole]

nos·trum (nos′trəm) *n.* **1** A patent medicine; quack recipe. **2** Anything savoring of quackery: political *nostrums.* [< L *noster* our own; because prepared by those selling it]

nos·y (nō′zē) *adj.* **nos·i·er, nos·i·est** *Informal* Prying; snooping; inquisitive. Also **nos′ey.** **—nos′i·ness** *n.*

not (not) *adv.* In no manner, or to no extent or degree. [ME, contraction of NAUGHT]

no·ta be·ne (nō′tä bē′nē) Note well; take notice. [L]

no·ta·ble (nō′tə·bəl) *adj.* Worthy of note; distinguished. *—n.* One who is worthy of note; a distinguished person. [< L *nota* a mark] **—no·ta·bil·i·ty** (nō′tə·bil′ə·tē), **no′ta·ble·ness** *n.* **—no′ta·bly** *adv.*

no·ta·rize (nō′tə·rīz′) *v.t.* **·rized, ·riz·ing** To attest to or authenticate as a notary. **—no′ta·ri·za′tion** *n.*

no·ta·ry (nō′tə·rē) *n. pl.* **·ries** An officer empowered to authenticate contracts, administer oaths, take depositions, etc. Also **notary public.** [< L *notarius* a clerk < *notare* to note] **—no·tar·i·al** (nō·târ′ē·əl) *adj.*

no·ta·tion (nō·tā′shən) *n.* **1** The process of designating by figures, etc. **2** Any system of signs, figures, or abbreviations used for convenience in a science or art. **3** A brief note; annotation. **—no·ta′tion·al** *adj.*

notch (noch) *n.* **1** A hollow cut or mark made in anything; a nick. **2** A narrow pass between hills or mountains. **3** *Informal* A degree: He is a *notch* above the others. *—v.t.* **1** To make a notch or notches in. **2** To record by means of notches; tally. [< OF *oschier* to notch] **—notch′er** *n.*

note (nōt) *n.* **1** A brief written record kept as a reminder. **2** *Often pl.* A written summary of a meeting, conversation, etc., to serve as a record for future reference: students taking copious *notes.* **3** A comparatively short letter. **4** An official communication in writing from one government to another. **5** A brief comment in a margin, at the bottom of a page, or at the end of a text. **6** A guarantee in writing to pay a specified sum at a certain time. **7** A government or bank certificate, usu. payable in cash upon pres-

Musical notes

a. whole. b. half. c. quarter. d. eighth. e. sixteenth.
f. thirty-second. g. sixty-fourth.

entation. **8** An account or bill. **9** *Music* **a** A written character used to indicate the pitch and length of a tone. **b** Any musical sound. **c** A key of a keyboard instrument. **10** A bird's song. **11** The general tone or quality

of something: a *note* of anxiety. **12** High importance or repute: people of *note.* **13** Special notice or attention: He took *note* of the situation. **—compare notes** To exchange opinions; talk over. *—v.t.* **not·ed, not·ing 1** To take notice or note of; observe. **2** To set down, as in writing; make a note of. **3** To mention specially or separately in the course of writing. **4** To set down in musical notation. [< L *nota* a mark, orig. pp. fem. of *noscere* know] **—not′er** *n.*

note·book (nōt′bŏŏk′) *n.* A book in which to enter memoranda or other notes.

not·ed (nō′tid) *adj.* Well known by reputation or report. **—not′ed·ly** *adv.*

note·pa·per (nōt′pā′pər) *n.* Paper for writing notes or letters.

note·wor·thy (nōt′wûr′thē) *adj.* **·wor·thi·er, ·worth·i·est** Worthy of note; significant. **—note′wor′thi·ly** *adv.* **—note′·wor′thi·ness** *n.*

noth·ing (nuth′ing) *n.* **1** Not any being or any particular thing. **2** A state of nonexistence. **3** A person or thing of slight significance, consideration, or value. **4** Zero; naught. **—make nothing of 1** To be unable to comprehend. **2** To treat as insignificant or worthless. **3** To neglect to use or do. **—think nothing of** To think of as easy to do. *—adv.* In no degree; not at all.

noth·ing·ness (nuth′ing·nis) *n.* **1** A state of nonexistence. **2** Worthlessness. **3** Unconsciousness.

no·tice (nō′tis) *v.t.* **·ticed, ·tic·ing 1** To pay attention to or take cognizance of. **2** To treat courteously or with favor. **3** To mention or comment on. **4** To serve with a notice; notify. *—n.* **1** The act of noticing or observing. **2** Announcement; warning. **3** Respectful treatment; civility. **4** A formal written or printed notification, instruction, or warning, as of the termination or intended termination of an agreement. **5** A public communication openly displayed. **6** A critique or review: The play closed because of bad *notices.* [< L *notus* known] **—no′tice·a·ble** *adj.* **—no′·tice·a·bly** *adv.*

no·ti·fi·ca·tion (nō′tə·fə·kā′shən) *n.* **1** The act of notifying. **2** Notice given. **3** Written matter that gives information.

no·ti·fy (nō′tə·fī′) *v.t.* **·fied, ·fy·ing 1** To give notice to; inform. **2** To make known. [< L *notus* known + *facere* to make] **—no′ti·fi′er** *n.*

no·tion (nō′shən) *n.* **1** A thought; idea. **2** A hastily formed theory. **3** Intention; inclination. **4** *pl.* Miscellaneous small articles, such as ribbons, thread, pins, needles, etc. [< L *notus,* pp. of *noscere* know]

no·tion·al (nō′shən·əl) *adj.* **1** Pertaining to, expressing, or consisting of notions or concepts. **2** Existing in imagination only. **3** Given to pet ideas or fancies. **—no′tion·al·ly** *adv.*

no·to·ri·e·ty (nō′tə·rī′ə·tē) *n. pl.* **·ties 1** The character of being notorious. **2** Common knowledge or talk. **3** One who or that which is notorious.

no·to·ri·ous (nō·tôr′ē·əs, -tō′rē-) *adj.* **1** Being publicly and unfavorably known and discussed. **2** Well-known. [< L *notus* known, orig. pp. of *noscere* know] **—no·to′ri·ous·ly** *adv.* **—no·to′ri·ous·ness** *n.* **—Syn. 1** egregious, flagrant, outrageous, unsavory.

not·with·stand·ing (not′with·stan′ding, -with-) *adv.* All the same; nevertheless: Though imprisoned, he escaped *notwithstanding.* *—prep.* In spite of: He left *notwithstanding* your orders. *—conj.* In spite of the fact that.

nou·gat (nōō′gət, -gä) *n.* A confection consisting usu. of a honey or sugar paste with chopped almonds, pistachios, etc. [< L *nux, nucis* a nut]

nought (nôt) *n., adj., adv.* NAUGHT.

noun (noun) *Gram. n.* A word used as the name of a thing, quality, or action existing or conceived by the mind; a substantive. *—adj.* Of or used as a noun or nouns: also **noun·al** (noun′əl). [< L *nomen* name]

nour·ish (nûr′ish) *v.t.* **1** To furnish material to sustain the life and promote the growth of (a living organism). **2** To support; maintain: to *nourish* illusions. [< L *nutrire* nourish] **—nour′ish·er** *n.*

nour·ish·ment (nûr′ish·mənt) *n.* **1** Nutriment; food. **2** The act of nourishing or the state of being nourished. **3** Anything that promotes growth and sustains life.

nou·veau riche (nōō′vō′ rēsh′) *pl.* **nou·veaux riches** (nōō′vō′ rēsh′) One recently become rich, esp. one given to vulgar ostentation. [F, lit., new rich]

Nov, Nov. November.

no·va (nō′və) *n. pl.* **·vas** or **·vae** (-vē) A star which suddenly increases in brightness, then fades to its former magnitude after a time. [< L *novus* new]

nov·el (nov′əl) *n.* A fictional prose narrative of considerable length with a plot and characters. —*adj.* New in a striking or unusual way. [Fusion of Ital. *novella* a novel and OF *novel* new] —**Syn.** *adj.* fresh, unfamiliar, unusual. *n.* 1 romance, story, tale.

nov·el·ette (nov′əl·et′) *n.* A short novel.

nov·el·ist (nov′əl·ist) *n.* A writer of novels.

nov·el·is·tic (nov′əl·is′tik) *adj.* Of, pertaining to, characteristic of, or found in novels. —**nov′el·is′ti·cal·ly** *adv.*

no·vel·la (nō·vel′ə) *n. pl.* **·las** or **·le** (-lā) 1 A short tale or narrative, often satirical. 2 A short novel. [Ital.]

nov·el·ty (nov′əl·tē) *n. pl.* **·ties** 1 The quality of being novel. 2 *pl.* Small manufactured articles or trinkets. 3 An innovation.

No·vem·ber (nō·vem′bər) *n.* The 11th month of the year, containing 30 days. [< L *November* ninth month of the Roman calendar]

no·ve·na (nō·vē′nə) *n.* In the Roman Catholic Church, a devotion consisting of a prayer said on nine successive days, asking for some special blessing. [< L *novem* nine]

nov·ice (nov′is) *n.* 1 A beginner in any business or occupation; tyro. 2 *Eccl.* One who enters a religious house or community on probation. [< L *novus* new] —**nov′ice·hood** (-hŏŏd) *n.*

no·vi·ti·ate (nō·vish′ē·it, -āt) *n.* 1 The state of being a novice. 2 *Eccl.* The period of probation of a novice in a religious order. 3 A novice.

No·vo·cain (nō′və·kān) *n.* A local anesthetic containing procaine: a trade name.

now (nou) *adv.* 1 At once. 2 At or during the present time. 3 Nowadays. 4 In the immediate past: He said so just *now*. 5 In the immediate future: He is going just *now*. 6 Things being as they are. 7 At this point in the proceedings, narrative, etc. —*conj.* Since; seeing that. —*n.* The present time or occasion: the here and *now*. —*adj. Informal* 1 Of the present time. 2 Excitingly novel: *now* movies. 3 Practicing and conscious of what is new: the *now* generation. [< OE *nū*]

now·a·days (nou′ə·dāz′) *adv.* In the present time or age.

no·way (nō′wā′) *adv.* In no way, manner, or degree. Also **no′ways′**.

no·where (nō′ʰwâr′) *adv.* In no place; not anywhere. — *n.* No place. Also *Regional* **no′wheres′**.

no·wise (nō′wīz′) *adv.* In no manner or degree.

nox·ious (nok′shəs) *adj.* Causing, or tending to cause, injury to health or morals; poisonous. [< L *nocere* to hurt] —**nox′ious·ly** *adv.* —**nox′ious·ness** *n.* —**Syn.** deadly, hurtful, pernicious.

noz·zle (noz′əl) *n.* A projecting spout from which something, esp. a fluid, issues. 2 An inlet or outlet pipe. [Dim. of NOSE]

N.P. Notary Public.

Np neptunium.

N.S. New Style; Nova Scotia.

NT., N.T. New Testament.

Nozzle of a hose

nth (enth) *adj.* 1 Of or indicating the element of an ordered set corresponding to a number *n*. 2 Arbitrarily large. —**to the nth degree** To the utmost. —*n.* 1 The *n*th element of an ordered set. 2 One of *n* equal parts.

nt. wt. net weight.

nu (nyōō) *n.* The 13th letter in the Greek alphabet (N, ν).

nu·ance (nyōō′äns, nyōō·äns′) *n.* 1 A shade of difference in tone or color. 2 A slight degree of difference in anything perceptible to the mind. [< OF *nuer* to shade]

nub (nub) *n.* 1 A protuberance; knob. 2 The core of a matter: the *nub* of the story. [< MLG *knobbe* knob]

nub·bin (nub′in) *n.* 1 An imperfectly developed ear of corn. 2 Anything small and stunted. [< NUB]

nu·bile (nyōō′bil, -bīl) *adj.* Of suitable age and physical development to marry: said of young women. [< L *nubere* to wed] —**nu·bil′i·ty** *n.*

nu·cle·ar (nyōō′klē·ər) *adj.* 1 Of, pertaining to, forming, of the nature of, or depending upon a nucleus or nuclei: also **nu′cle·al.** 2 Of or using energy of atomic nuclei.

nuclear energy ATOMIC ENERGY.

nuclear family A family consisting of parents and child or children considered as a discrete group.

nuclear fission FISSION (def. 3).

nuclear physics The branch of physics that studies atomic nuclei.

nuclear reaction REACTION (def. 5).

nuclear reactor REACTOR (def. 2).

nu·cle·ate (nyōō′klē·āt) *adj.* Having a nucleus. Also **nu′cle·at′ed.** —*v.t.* & *v.i.* **·at·ed, ·at·ing** To form or gather into a nucleus. —**nu′cle·a′tion** *n.*

nu·cle·o·lus (nyōō·klē′ə·ləs) *n. pl.* **·li** (-lī) *Biol.* A well-defined particle found within the nucleus of most cells. Also **nu′cle·ole** (-ōl). [< LL, dim. of *nucleus*] —**nu·cle′o·lar** *adj.*

nu·cle·on (nyōō′klē·on) *n. Physics* Any particle that occurs in an atomic nucleus.

nu·cle·on·ics (nyōō′klē·on′iks) *n. pl.* (construed as sing.) The technology based on nuclear energy. —**nu′cle·on′ic** *adj.*

nu·cle·us (nyōō′klē·əs) *n. pl.* **·cle·i** (-klē·ī) 1 A central mass; kernel. 2 *Biol.* A complex, spheroidal body found in plant and animal cells and essential in the vital activities of the cell, as growth, reproduction, etc. 3 *Astron.* A bright central point as in the head of a comet or at the center of a nebula. 4 *Physics & Chem.* The central core of an atom, having a positive charge, composed mainly of protons and neutrons, and containing most of the atomic mass. [L, a kernel, dim. of *nux, nucis* a nut]

a. cell wall. b. nucleus. c. cell body.

nude (nyōōd) *adj.* Without clothing or covering; naked. —*n.* 1 A nude figure, as in painting or sculpture. 2 The state of being nude: to appear in the *nude*. [< L *nudus* naked] —**nude′ly** *adv.* —**nude′ness** *n.*

nudge (nuj) *v.* **nudged, nudg·ing** *v.t.* 1 To touch or push gently, in order to attract attention. —*v.i.* 2 To give a nudge. —*n.* The act of nudging, as with the elbow. [?]

nud·ism (nyōō′diz·əm) *n.* The practice of living in the state of nudity for hygienic reasons. —**nud′ist** *adj., n.*

nu·di·ty (nyōō′də·tē) *n. pl.* **·ties** 1 The state of being nude. 2 Something that is naked.

nu·ga·to·ry (nyōō′gə·tô′rē, -tō′rē) *adj.* 1 Having no power; inoperative. 2 Having no worth or meaning. [< L *nugae* trifles] —**nu′ga·to′ri·ly** *adv.* —**nu′ga·to′ri·ness** *n.*

nug·get (nug′it) *n.* 1 A lump. 2 A lump of precious metal, as gold. 3 A small amount of anything of value: a *nugget* of good sense. [?]

nui·sance (nyōō′səns) *n.* A person or thing that annoys, vexes, or harms. [< OF *nuire* to harm]

nuisance tax A small tax paid by the consumer and considered a nuisance by both the collector and the payer.

null (nul) *adj.* 1 Of no legal force or effect. 2 Having no existence. 3 Lacking distinction or individuality. 4 Zero. —**null and void** Having no force or effect; invalid. [< L *nullus* no, none]

nul·li·fy (nul′ə·fī) *v.t.* **·fied, ·fy·ing** 1 To bring to nothing; render ineffective or valueless. 2 To deprive of legal force or effect; make void. [< L *nullus* none + *facere* make] —**nul·li·fi·ca·tion** (nul′ə·fə·kā′shən), **nul′li·fi′er** *n.*

nul·li·ty (nul′ə·tē) *n. pl.* **·ties** 1 The state of being null. 2 A nonentity. 3 *Law* A void act or instrument.

Num, Num., Numb. Numbers.

num. number(s); numeral(s).

numb (num) *adj.* Wholly or partially without the power of sensation or of motion. —*v.t.* To make numb. [< ME *nomen* taken, seized] —**numb′ly** *adv.* —**numb′ness** *n.* —**Syn.** *adj.* benumbed, deadened, frozen, insensible.

---

add, āce, câre, pälm; end, ēven; it, īce; odd, ōpen, ôrder; tŏŏk, pōōl; up, bûrn; ə = *a* in *above, u* in *focus;* yōō = *u* in *fuse;* oil; pout; check; go; ring; thin; this; zh, *vision.* < derived from; ? origin uncertain or unknown.

num·ber (num′bər) *n.* **1** An element of one of various mathematical sets, defined, often by axioms, as having certain properties, esp. with respect to certain operations, as integers, real numbers, imaginary numbers, etc. **2** A collection of units or individuals, whether large or small: a *number* of facts; large *numbers* of people. **3** *pl.* Arithmetic. **4** The character or quality of being numerous: Reliance is placed more on spirit than on *number*. **5** An element of an ordered set. **6** One of the divisions or movements of a piece of music. **7** A series of digits used for identification: a serial *number*. **8** *Often pl.* Poetic measure; rhythm. **9** *Gram.* The form of inflection of a noun, pronoun, adjective, or verb, that indicates whether one thing or more is meant. **10** *Informal* An article of merchandise: our most popular *number*. **11** A single issue, as of a periodical. **12** *Informal* A person or thing set apart: That blouse is a stylish *number*. **—a number of** More than two or three; many. **—get** (or **have**) **someone's number** *Informal* To have insight into a person's motives, character, etc. **—the numbers** NUMBERS POOL. **—**v.t. **1** To determine the total number of; count. **2** To assign a number to. **3** To include as one of a collection or group. **4** To amount to; total: We *number* fifty men. **5** To set or limit the number of: Your days are *numbered*. **—**v.i. **6** To make a count; total. **7** To be included, as in a group: He was *numbered* among the civilians. [< L *numerus*] **—num′ber·er** *n.*

TABLE OF NUMBERS

The comparative values of denominations between one million and one decillion in the U.S. and British systems of numeration are indicated below. In the U.S. system, each denomination above one million is 1,000 times greater than the one preceding. In the British system, each denomination above one billion (equal to one U.S. trillion) is 1,000,000 times greater than the one before.

U.S. System	Number of Zeros	Value as Power of 10	British System
million	6	10^6	million
billion	9	10^9	milliard
trillion	12	10^{12}	billion
quadrillion	15	10^{15}	(1,000 billions)
quintillion	18	10^{18}	trillion
sextillion	21	10^{21}	(1,000 trillions)
septillion	24	10^{24}	quadrillion
octillion	27	10^{27}	(1,000 quadrillions)
nonillion	30	10^{30}	quintillion
decillion	33	10^{33}	(1,000 quintillions)
	36	10^{36}	sextillion
	42	10^{42}	septillion
	48	10^{48}	octillion
	54	10^{54}	nonillion
	60	10^{60}	decillion

num·ber·less (num′bər·lis) *adj.* **1** Very numerous; innumerable. **2** Having no number. **—Syn. 1** countless, endless, illimitable, measureless, unbounded.

Num·bers (num′bərz) *n.* The fourth book of the Old Testament, giving the two censuses of Israel.

numbers pool A lottery in which wagers are laid on the appearance of some particular, unpredictable number. Also **numbers game, numbers racket.**

nu·mer·a·ble (nyōō′mər·ə·bəl) *adj.* That can be numbered or counted.

nu·mer·a·cy (nyōō′mə·rə·sē) *n.* The acquired ability to reason quantitatively and to apply scientific principles.

nu·mer·al (nyōō′mər·əl) *n.* A symbol, character, letter, or word, used to express a number: Arabic *numerals*. **—**adj. **1** Used in expressing a number. **2** Denoting a number. [< L *numerus* number] **—nu′mer·al·ly** *adv.*

nu·mer·ate (nyōō′mə·rāt) *v.t.* **·at·ed, ·at·ing** **1** To enumerate; count. **2** To read, as a numerical expression. [< L *numerus* number] **—nu·mer·a′tion** *n.*

nu·mer·a·tor (nyōō′mə·rā′tər) *n.* **1** *Math.* In a common fraction, the term which stands above or to the left of the line. **2** A person or thing that numbers.

nu·mer·i·cal (nyōō·mer′i·kəl) *adj.* **1** Of, pertaining to or denoting number. **2** Capable of being numbered; numerable. **3** Represented by numbers or figures, as in arithmetic, and not by letters. [< L *numerus* number] **—nu·mer′i·cal·ly** *adv.*

nu·mer·ol·o·gy (nyōō′mə·rol′ə·jē) *n.* A system that pur-

ports to explain the occult influence of numbers, as that of the day of one's birth, etc. **—nu′mer·o·log′i·cal** *adj.*

nu·mer·ous (nyōō′mə·rəs) *adj.* Consisting of a great number of units; being many. **—nu′mer·ous·ness** *n.*

Nu·mid·i·a (nyōō·mid′ē·ə) *n.* An ancient kingdom and Roman province in N Africa. **—Nu·mid′i·an** *adj., n.*

nu·mis·mat·ics (nyōō′miz·mat′iks, -mis-) *n.pl. (construed as sing.)* The science of coins and medals. [< L *numisma* a coin] **—nu′mis·mat′ic, nu′mis·mat′i·cal** *adj.* **—nu·mis′ma·tist, nu·mis′ma·tol′o·gist** *n.*

num·skull (num′skul) *n.* A blockhead; a stupid person. Also **numb′skull.**

nun (nun) *n.* A woman devoted to a religious life, and living under vows of poverty, chastity, and obedience, often in a convent. [< Med. L *nonna*] **—nun′nish** *adj.*

nun·ci·o (nun′shē·ō) *n. pl.* **·ci·os** **1** An ordinary ambassador of the pope to a foreign court. **2** Any messenger. Also **nun′ci·us** (-shē·əs). [< L *nuntius* messenger]

nun·ner·y (nun′ər·ē) *n. pl.* **·ner·ies** A convent for nuns.

nup·tial (nup′shəl) *adj.* Pertaining to marriage or the marriage ceremony. **—**n.pl. A wedding; marriage ceremony. [< L *nuptus*, pp. of *nubere* marry] **—nup′tial·ly** *adv.*

nurse (nûrs) *n.* **1** A person who cares for the sick, esp. professionally. **2** A female servant who takes care of young children. **3** A person who fosters, protects, or promotes. **—**v. **nursed, nurs·ing** *v.t.* **1** To take care of, as in sickness or infirmity. **2** To feed (an infant) at the breast; suckle. **3** To feed and care for in infancy. **4** To promote the growth and development of. **5** To preserve from injury or undue strain: to *nurse* a weak wrist. **6** To try to cure, as a cold, by taking care of oneself. **7** To clasp or hold carefully or caressingly; fondle. **8** To keep in mind, as a grievance. **9** To use or consume slowly: to *nurse* a drink. **—**v.i. **10** To act or serve as a nurse. **11** To take milk from the breast. **12** To suckle an infant. [< L *nutrix* < *nutrire* nourish, foster] **—nurs′er** *n.*

nurse·maid (nûrs′mād′) *n.* A girl or woman employed to care for children.

nurs·er·y (nûr′sər·ē) *n. pl.* **·er·ies** **1** A room set apart for the use of children and babies. **2** A place where trees, shrubs, etc., are raised for sale or transplanting. **3** The place where anything is fostered, bred, or developed.

nurs·er·y·man (nûr′sər·ē·mən) *n. pl.* **·men** (-mən) One who owns or manages a nursery for the cultivation of trees and shrubs.

nursery rhyme A simple story presented in rhymed verse or jingle for children.

nursery school A school for children too young to enter kindergarten.

nursing home A usu. private institution for the care of convalescents, the chronically ill, or the aged who are unable to care for themselves.

nurs·ling (nûrs′ling) *n.* An infant, esp. one that is breastfed. Also **nurse′ling.**

nur·ture (nûr′chər) *v.t.* **·tured, ·tur·ing** **1** To feed; nourish. **2** To bring up or train; educate. **—**n. **1** The act of rearing or bringing up. **2** Nourishment. [< L *nutrire* nourish] **—nur′tur·er** *n.* **—Syn.** *v.* **2** cherish, foster, raise, rear.

nut (nut) *n.* **1** A fruit consisting of a usu. edible kernel or seed enclosed in a woody shell. **2** The kernel of such fruit. **3** *Mech.* A small block of metal having an internal screw thread so that it may be fitted upon a bolt, screw, etc. **4** *Slang* The head. **5** *Slang* A crazy or irresponsible person. **6** *Slang* The whole amount of money. **—**v.i. **nut·ted, nut·ting** To seek or gather nuts. [< OE *hnutu*] **—nut′ter** *n.*

Mechanical nuts. **a.** lock. **b.** wing. **c.** square, plain.

nut·crack·er (nut′krak′ər) *n.* **1** Any of various devices for cracking nuts. **2** One of several crowlike birds that eat nuts.

nut·gall (nut′gôl′) *n.* A nut-shaped gall, as on an oak tree.

nut·hatch (nut′hach′) *n.* Any of various small, short-tailed birds related to the titmouse, having a thin, sharp bill and feeding on nuts and insects.

nut·meg (nut′meg) *n.* **1** The aromatic kernel of the fruit of the nutmeg tree of the Molucca Islands. **2** The tree itself. [< NUT + OF *mugue* musk]

nu·tri·a (nyōō′trē·ə) *n.* **1** A water-inhabiting rodent somewhat like a beaver, of South American origin. **2** Its soft, brown fur. [Sp., an otter < L *lutra*]

nu·tri·ent (nʸo̅o̅′trē·ənt) *adj.* **1** Giving nourishment. **2** Conveying nutrition. —*n.* Something that nourishes. [< L *nutrire* nourish]

nu·tri·ment (nʸo̅o̅′trə·mənt) *n.* **1** That which nourishes. **2** That which promotes development. [< L *nutrire* nourish] —**nu′tri·men′tal** *adj.* —**Syn. 1** food, meat, nourishment, sustenance.

nu·tri·tion (nʸoo·trish′ən) *n.* **1** The aggregate of all the processes by which food is assimilated in living organisms. **2** Food. —**nu·tri′tion·al** *adj.* —**nu·tri′tion·al·ly** *adv.*

nu·tri·tion·ist (nʸoo·trish′ən·ist) *n.* One who specializes in the processes and problems of nutrition.

nu·tri·tious (nʸoo·trish′əs) *adv.* Nourishing; promoting nutrition. —**nu·tri′tious·ly** *adv.* —**nu·tri′tious·ness** *n.*

nu·tri·tive (nʸoo′trə·tiv) *adj.* **1** Having nutritious properties. **2** Of or relating to nutrition. —**nu′tri·tive·ly** *adv.* —**nu′tri·tive·ness** *n.*

nuts (nuts) *Slang adj.* **1** Crazy; demented. **2** Madly in love: with *about.* **3** Extremely enthusiastic: with *about:* He's *nuts* about baseball. —*interj.* An exclamation of scorn, disapproval, etc. [< NUT]

nut·shell (nut′shel′) *n.* The shell of a nut. —**in a nutshell** In brief and concise statement.

nut·ty (nut′ē) *adj.* ·ti·er, ·ti·est **1** Abounding in nuts. **2** Having the flavor of nuts. **3** *Slang* Crazy. —**nut′ti·ly** *adv.* —**nut′ti·ness** *n.*

nux vom·i·ca (nuks′ vom′i·kə) **1** The seed of an Indian tree containing strychnine and other poisonous alkaloids. **2** The tree producing this fruit. **3** A drug prepared from the seed, sometimes used as a stimulant. [< L *nux* a nut + *vomere* to vomit]

nuz·zle (nuz′əl) *v.* ·zled, ·zling *v.i.* **1** To rub with the nose. **2** To nestle or snuggle; lie close. —*v.t.* **3** To rub with the nose. [< NOSE] —**nuz′zler** *n.*

NV Nevada (P.O. abbr.).

NW, N.W., nw, n.w. northwest; northwestern.

NWT Northwest Territories.

NY New York (P.O. abbr.).

N.Y. New York.

N.Y.C. New York City.

ny·lon (nī′lon) *n.* **1** A synthetic substance that may be formed into fibers, bristles, sheets, etc., and characterized by extreme toughness, elasticity, and strength. **2** *pl.* Stockings made of nylon thread. [< *Nylon*, a tradename]

nymph (nimf) *Gk. & Rom. Myth.* A beautiful maiden inhabiting groves, forests, fountains, springs, mountains, etc. —*n.* **1** Any lovely young woman. **2** The young of certain insects which undergo incomplete metamorphosis. [< Gk. *nymphē* nymph, bride] —**nymph′al, nym·phe·an** (nim·fē′ən), **nymph′ic, nymph′i·cal** *adj.*

nym·pho·ma·ni·a (nim′fə·mā′nē·ə, -mān′yə) *n.* Abnormal and ungovernable sexual desire in women. [< Gk. *nymphē* nymph + -MANIA] —**nym′pho·ma·ni′ac** *adj., n.*

N.Z., N. Zeal. New Zealand.

O

O, o (ō) *n. pl.* **O's, o's, Os, os** (ōz) **1** The 15th letter of the English alphabet. **2** Any spoken sound representing the letter *O* or *o.* **3** Something shaped like an O. —*adj.* Shaped like an O.

O (ō) *interj.* Oh!

O oxygen.

O. Ocean; October; Ohio; Ontario.

O., o. octavo; old; order.

o ohm.

o' *prep.* Of: one *o'*clock, man-*o'*-war.

oaf (ōf) *n.* A stupid, vulgar person, esp. a man. [< ON *alfr* elf] —**oaf′ish** *adj.* —**oaf′ish·ly** *adv.* —**oaf′ish·ness** *n.*

oak (ōk) *n.* **1** Any of various hardwood, acorn-bearing trees and shrubs of the beech family. **2** The hard, durable wood or timber of the oak. **3** Any of various other plants having a resemblance or relation to the oak: poison *oak.* [< OE *āc*]

oak apple A gall produced on an oak by an insect; a nutgall. Also **oak gall.**

Oak leaves and acorns

oak·en (ō′kən) *adj.* Made of oak.

oak·um (ō′kəm) *n.* Hemp fiber, sometimes treated with preservative or tar: used in caulking, etc. [< OE *ā-* off + *cemban* to comb]

oar (ôr, ōr) *n.* **1** An implement for propelling or, occasionally, for steering a boat, consisting of a long shaft with a blade at one end. **2** An oarsman. —*v.t.* **1** To propel with or as with oars; row. **2** To make (one's way) or traverse (water) with or as with oars. —*v.i.* **3** To proceed by or as by rowing.

oar·lock (ôr′lok′, ōr′-) *n.* A device on the side of a boat for keeping an oar in place.

oars·man (ôrz′mən, ōrz′-) *n. pl.* ·men (-mən) One who rows, esp. expertly. —**oars′man·ship,** *n.*

OAS Organization of American States.

o·a·sis (ō·ā′sis) *n. pl.* ·ses (-sēz) **1** An area in a waste or desert made fertile by ground water or by surface irrigation. **2** Any place providing relief or refreshment; refuge:

a small city park that provided an *oasis* of quiet amidst the street noises. [< Gk., fertile spot]

oat (ōt) *n. Usu. pl.* A cereal grass extensively cultivated for its edible grain. [< OE *āte*] —**oat′en** *adj.*

oat·cake (ōt′kāk′) *n.* A thin cake of oatmeal, usu. baked hard. Also **oat cake.**

oath (ōth) *n. pl.* **oaths** (ōt͟hz, ōths) **1** A solemn confirmation of a promise, course of action, etc., made by appealing to God or to some person or thing regarded as high and holy. **2** The course of action, promise, etc., so supported, or the form of words used in supporting it. **3** An irreverent or profane use of the name of the Deity or of any sacred name or object. **4** A swearword; curse. [< OE *āth*] —**Syn. 3** blasphemy, curse, imprecation, profanity.

oat·meal (ōt′mēl′) *n.* **1** The meal of oats. **2** Porridge made of it. Also **oat meal.**

ob- *prefix* **1** Toward; to; facing: *obverse.* **2** Against; in opposition to: *obstruct.* **3** Over; upon: *obliterate.* **4** Completely: *obdurate.* [< L *ob* toward, for, against]

Ob, Ob., Obad. Obadiah.

ob. obstetrics; he (or she) died (L *obiit*); in passing (L *obiter*)

ob·bli·ga·to (ob′lə·gä′tō, *Ital.* ôb′blē·gä′tō) *adj. Music* Referring to accompaniments, usu. by a single instrument, that are to be played as written and are not to be omitted. —*n. pl.* ·tos or ·ti (-tē) An obbligato accompaniment. [< Ital. *obbligare* obligate]

ob·du·rate (ob′dʸə·rit) *adj.* **1** Unmoved by feelings of humanity or pity; hard. **2** Perversely impenitent. **3** Unyielding; stubborn. [< L *ob-* completely + *durare* harden] —**ob′du·ra·cy** (-rə·sē), **ob′du·rate·ness** *n.* —**ob′du·rate·ly** *adv.*

o·be·di·ence (ō·bē′dē·əns, ə·bē′-) *n.* **1** The state of being obedient; willingness to obey. **2** The act of obeying, or an instance of it.

o·be·di·ent (ō·bē′dē·ənt, ə·bē′-) *adj.* Complying with or submitting to a command, prohibition, law, or duty. [< L *obedire* obey] —**o·be′di·ent·ly** *adv.*

o·bei·sance (ō·bā′səns, ō·bē′-) *n.* **1** An act of courtesy or deference, as a bow or curtsy. **2** Reverent courtesy; deference. [< OF *obeir* obey] —**o·bei′sant** *adj.* —**o·bei′sant·ly** *adv.*

ob·e·lisk (ob′ə·lisk, ō′bə-) *n.* **1** A usu. monumental structure with a square, tapered shaft and a pyramidal top. **2** *Printing* The dagger sign (†) used as a mark of reference: also **ob·e·lus** (ob′ə·ləs). [< Gk. *obeliskos*, dim. of *obelos* a spit, pointed pillar]

O·ber·on (ō′bə·ron) In medieval folklore, the king of the fairies.

o·bese (ō·bēs′) *adj.* Very fat; corpulent. [< L *ob-* completely + *edere* eat] —**o·be·si·ty** (ō·bē′sə·tē) *n.*

o·bey (ō·bā′, ə·bā′) *v.t.* **1** To do the bidding of; be obedient to. **2** To carry into effect; execute, as a command. **3** To act in accordance with; be guided by: to *obey* the law. —*v.i.* **4** To be obedient. [< L *obedire*] —**o·bey′· er** *n.*

ob·fus·cate (ob′fəs·kāt, ob·fus′-) *v.t.* **·cat·ed, ·cat·ing 1** To obscure the clarity or meaning of; muddle. **2** To confuse or bewilder. **3** To darken or obscure. [< L *ob-* completely + *fuscare* darken] —**ob·fus·ca′tion** *n.* —**ob·fus·ca·tor·y** (ob·fus′kə·tôr′ē, -tō′rē) *adj.*

o·bi (ō′bē) *n.* A broad sash with a bow in the back, worn with a Japanese kimono. [Japanese]

o·bit (ō′bit, ob′it) *n.* OBITUARY.

o·bi·ter dic·tum (ob′ə·tər dik′təm, ō′bə-) *pl.* **ob·i·ter dic·ta** (dik′tə) **1** A remark made in passing by a judge. **2** An incidental remark. [L]

o·bit·u·ar·y (ō·bich′oo̅·er′ē) *n. pl.* **·ar·ies** A published notice of a person's death, often including a biographical sketch. —*adj.* Of or pertaining to a death. [< L *obitus*, pp. of *obire*, die, go down]

obj. object; objective.

ob·ject¹ (əb·jekt′) *v.i.* **1** To offer arguments or opposition; dissent. **2** To feel or state disapproval or dissent. —*v.t.* **3** To offer as opposition or criticism; charge. [< L *ob-* towards, against + *jacere* to throw] —**ob·jec′tor** *n.*

ob·ject² (ob′jikt, -jekt) *n.* **1** Anything that lies within the cognizance of the senses; esp. anything tangible or visible; any material thing. **2** Something to which feeling or action is directed: an *object* of affection. **3** A purpose or goal; aim. **4** *Gram.* A noun or pronoun that receives the action of a verb or is governed by a preposition. [< Med. L *objectum* something thrown in the way]

ob·jec·ti·fy (əb·jek′tə·fī) *v.t.* **·fied, ·fy·ing** To present from an external viewpoint; make objective. —**ob·jec′ti·fi·ca′tion** *n.*

ob·jec·tion (əb·jek′shən) *n.* **1** The act of objecting. **2** An argument, fact, etc., used in dissent or disapproval. **3** A feeling of disapproval or disinclination.

ob·jec·tion·a·ble (əb·jek′shən·ə·bəl) *adj.* Deserving of disapproval; offensive. —**ob·jec′tion·a·bil′i·ty, ob·jec′tion·a·ble·ness** *n.* —**ob·jec′tion·a·bly** *adv.*

ob·jec·tive (əb·jek′tiv) *adj.* **1** Of or belonging to an object; having the nature of an object; esp., being that which is external to the mind or perceived by the senses and subject to verification. **2** Treating of or representing facts or reality without reference to feelings or opinions: an *objective* report or test. **3** Not prejudiced; unbiased. **4** *Gram.* Denoting the case of an object of a transitive verb or preposition. —*n.* **1** A goal or purpose, as of a mission or assignment. **2** Something that is objective. **3** *Gram.* **a** The objective case. **b** A word in this case. **4** The lens or lenses of an optical instrument closest to the object observed. — **ob·jec′tive·ly** *adv.* —**ob·jec·tiv·i·ty** (ob′jek·tiv′ə·tē), **ob·jec′· tive·ness** *n.* —**Syn.** *adj.* **2** impersonal. **3** detached, disinterested, fair-minded.

ob·ject lesson (ob′jikt, -jekt) A practical representation or exemplification of a principle or moral.

ob·jet d'art (ôb·zhā där′, ob′-) *pl.* **ob·jets d'art** (ôb·zhā′, ob′- där′) An article, such as a vase, statuette, etc. of artistic value. [F, lit., object of art]

ob·jur·gate (ob′jər·gāt) *v.t.* **·gat·ed, ·gat·ing** To rebuke severely; scold sharply. [< L *ob-* completely + *jurgare* scold] —**ob′jur·ga′tion, ob′jur·ga′tor** *n.* —**ob·jur′ga·to·ry** *adj.*

obl. oblique; oblong.

ob·late (ob′lāt, ob·lāt′) *adj.* Flattened at the poles. [< L *ob-* against + *-latus* carried] —**ob′late·ly** *adv.* —**ob′late·ness** *n.*

ob·la·tion (ob·lā′shən) *n.* **1** Anything offered in worship, esp. the elements of the Eucharist. **2** Any grateful and solemn offering. [< L *oblatus*, carried toward, offered] — **ob·la′tion·al, ob·la·to·ry** (ob′lə·tôr′ē, -tō′rē) *adj.*

ob·li·gate (ob′lə·gāt) *v.t.* **·gat·ed, ·gat·ing** To bind or compel, as by contract, conscience, promise, etc. —*adj.* (ob′lə·git, -gāt) Bound or restricted. [< L *obligare* oblige]

ob·li·ga·tion (ob′lə·gā′shən) *n.* **1** The act of obligating, or state of being obligated. **2** A duty, promise, etc., by which one is bound; responsibility. **3** The constraining power of conscience or law. **4** A requirement imposed by the customs of society or the laws of propriety; what one owes in return for a service, kindness, or favor. **5** A binding legal agreement bearing a penalty. **6** The condition of being indebted for an act of kindness, a service received, etc. — **ob′li·ga′tor** *n.*

ob·lig·a·to·ry (ə·blig′ə·tôr′ē, -tō′rē, ob′lə·gə-) *adj.* **1** In civil or moral law, binding. **2** Of the nature of or constituting a duty or obligation; imperative.

o·blige (ə·blīj′) *v.t.* **·bliged, ·blig·ing 1** To obligate; constrain. **2** To place under an obligation, as for a favor or kindness. **3** To do a favor or service for. [< L *ob-* towards + *ligare* to bind] —**o·blig′er** *n.*

o·blig·ing (ə·blī′jing) *adj.* Disposed to do favors; accommodating; kind. —**o·blig′ing·ly** *adv.* —**o·blig′ing·ness** *n.*

ob·lique (ō·blēk′, ə-, *in military usage* ə·blīk′) *adj.* **1** Neither perpendicular nor horizontal; slanting. **2** Acute or obtuse, as an angle. **3** Indirect or allusive rather than straightforward: an *oblique* reference to his uncertain paternity. —*v.i.* **·liqued, ·li·quing 1** To deviate from the perpendicular; slant. **2** *Mil.* To march or advance in an oblique direction. [< L *ob-* against, completely + *liquis* slanting, awry] —**ob·lique′ly** *adv.* —**ob·lique′ness** *n.*

ob·liq·ui·ty (ə·blik′wə·tē) *n. pl.* **·ties 1** Oblique quality or state. **2** Inclination from a vertical or horizontal line or plane; also, the amount or the angle of such inclination.

ob·lit·er·ate (ə·blit′ə·rāt) *v.t.* **·at·ed, ·at·ing 1** To destroy utterly; leave no trace of. **2** To blot or wipe out; erase, as writing. [< L *obliterare* blot out] —**ob·lit′er·a′tion, ob·lit′er·a′tor** *n.* —**ob·lit′er·a′tive** *adj.*

ob·liv·i·on (ə·bliv′ē·ən) *n.* **1** The state or fact of being utterly forgotten. **2** The act or fact of forgetting completely; forgetfulness. [< L *oblivisci* forget]

ob·liv·i·ous (ə·bliv′ē·əs) *adj.* **1** Taking no notice, as though unaware or indifferent: usu. with *of* or *to*: *oblivious* of the noise. **2** Distracted; forgetful: usu. with *of.* —**ob· liv′i·ous·ly** *adv.* —**ob·liv′i·ous·ness** *n.*

ob·long (ob′lông, -long) *adj.* Longer in one dimension than in another; esp., elongated along the horizontal axis. —*n.* An oblong figure, as a rectangle. [< L *oblongus* somewhat long]

ob·lo·quy (ob′lə·kwē) *n. pl.* **·quies 1** An expression of severe censure or denunciation. **2** The state of one who is so censured; disgrace. —**Syn. 1** reprobation, vilification, defamation, calumny, opprobrium. **2** ignominy. [< L *ob-* against + *loqui* speak]

ob·nox·ious (əb·nok′shəs) *adj.* Strongly offensive; disgusting; repulsive; odious. [< L *ob-* towards + *noxa* injury] —**ob·nox′ious·ly** *adv.* —**ob·nox′ious·ness** *n.*

o·boe (ō′bō) *n.* A double-reed wind instrument with a high, penetrating tone. [Ital.] —**o′bo·ist** *n.*

obs. obsolete.

ob·scene (ob·sēn′, əb-) *adj.* **1** Offensive to one's sense of modesty or propriety. **2** Intended to provoke lust; licentious; lewd. **3** Disgusting; foul. [< L *obs-*, var of *ob-* towards + *caenum* filth] —**ob·scene′ly** *adv.*

ob·scen·i·ty (ob·sen′ə·tē, -sē′nə-, əb-) *n. pl.* **·ties 1** The state or quality of being obscene. **2** An obscene remark, act, representation, etc. Also **ob·scene′ness.**

ob·scur·ant·ism (ob·skyoor′ənt·iz′əm, əb-) *n.* **1** Opposition to education or popular enlightenment. **2** The practice of being deliberately obscure. —**ob· scur′ant·ist** *adj., n.* [< L *obscurans, obscurare* darken]

ob·scure (ob·skyoor′, əb-) *adj.* **·scur·er, ·scur·est 1** Lacking in light; dim; dark; dusky. **2** Not clear to the mind; vague; abstruse. **3** Faintly marked; hard to discern; undefined. **4** Remote or apart; hidden from view or notice. **5** Little

Oboe

Obelisk

known; unnoticed: an *obscure* hamlet. —*v.t.* **·scured, ·scur·ing 1** To darken or cloud; dim. **2** To hide from view; conceal. **3** To make unintelligible; confuse. [< L *obscurus*, lit., covered over] —**ob·scure′ly** *adv.* —**ob·scu′ri·ty** (-skyŏŏr′ə·tē), **ob·scure′ness** *n.*

ob·se·qui·ous (ob·sē′kwē·əs, əb-) *adj.* Too eager to please; fawning; servile. [< L *ob-* towards + *sequi* follow] —**ob·se′qui·ous·ly** *adv.* —**ob·se′qui·ous·ness** *n.*

ob·se·quy (ob′sə·kwē) *n. pl.* **·quies** *Usu. pl.* A funeral service. [< L *obsequium* dutiful service]

ob·serv·a·ble (əb·zûr′və·bəl) *adj.* **1** That can be observed; manifest. **2** Deserving of notice. **3** Customary; demanding observance. —**ob·serv′a·ble·ness** *n.* —**ob·serv′a·bly** *adv.*

ob·ser·vance (əb·zûr′vəns) *n.* **1** The act of observing, as a custom or ceremony; compliance, as with law or duty. **2** Any common custom, form, rite, etc. **3** Heedful attention; observation. **4** *Eccl.* The rule or constitution of a religious order.

ob·ser·vant (əb·zûr′vənt) *adj.* **1** Carefully attentive; alert or watchful. **2** Having the habit of keen perception. **3** Strict in observing; heedful: usu. with *of: observant* of protocol. —**ob·ser′vant·ly** *adv.*

ob·ser·va·tion (ob′zər·vā′shən) *n.* **1** The act, faculty, or habit of observing. **2** The fact of being observed. **3** The practice of observing and recording, as for scientific study, certain data, events, etc.; also, the record so obtained, or an item within the record. **4** A remark apparently based upon things observed. —**ob′ser·va′tion·al** *adj.*

ob·ser·va·to·ry (əb·zûr′və·tôr′ē, -tō′rē) *n. pl.* **·ries 1** A building designed and equipped for the systematic observation of astronomical or other natural phenomena. **2** A tower built for obtaining a panoramic view.

ob·serve (əb·zûrv′) *v.* **·served, ·serv·ing** *v.t.* **1** To notice by the sense of sight; see. **2** To watch attentively; keep under surveillance. **3** To make methodical observation of, as for scientific purposes. **4** To abide by or conform to: to *observe* the law. **5** To celebrate or solemnize (an occasion), as with appropriate ritual. **6** To say as a comment or opinion; mention. —*v.i.* **7** To make a remark; comment: often with *on* or *upon*. **8** To take notice. **9** To act as an observer. [< L *ob-* towards + *servare* keep, watch] —**ob·serv′er** *n.* —**ob·serv′ing·ly** *adv.*

ob·sess (əb·ses′) *v.t.* To occupy or trouble the mind of to an excessive degree; preoccupy; harass; haunt. [< L *ob-* towards, against + *sedere* sit]

ob·ses·sion (əb·sesh′ən) *n.* **1** The state of being obsessed with an idea or emotion. **2** An idea or emotion that obsesses one. —**ob·ses′sion·al** *adj.* —**ob·ses′sion·al·ly** *adv.*

ob·ses·sive (əb·ses′iv, ob-) *adj.* **1** Characteristic or of the nature of an obsession. **2** Of or causing an obsession. —**ob·ses′sive·ly** *adv.* —**ob·ses′sive·ness** *n.*

ob·sid·i·an (əb·sid′ē·ən, ob-) *n.* A glassy, usu. black volcanic rock. [< L *Obsius*, a Roman said by Pliny to be its discoverer]

ob·so·les·cent (ob′sə·les′ənt) *adj.* Becoming obsolete. —**ob′so·les′cence** *n.* —**ob′so·les′cent·ly** *adv.*

ob·so·lete (ob′sə·lēt) *adj.* Being out of use or out of fashion, as a word or style. [< L *obsolescere* grow old] —**ob′so·lete′ly** *adv.* —**ob′so·lete′ness** *n.*

ob·sta·cle (ob′stə·kəl) *n.* Something that stands in the way; a hindrance or obstruction. [< L *ob-* before, against + *stare* stand]

ob·ste·tri·cian (ob′stə·trish′ən) *n.* A physician specializing in obstetrics.

ob·stet·rics (əb·stet′riks) *n.pl.* *(construed as sing.)* The branch of medical science relating to pregnancy and childbirth. [< L *obstetrix* a midwife] —**ob·stet′ri·cal, ob·stet′ric** *adj.* —**ob·stet′ri·cal·ly** *adv.*

ob·sti·nate (ob′stə·nit) *adj.* **1** Persistently and unreasonably resolved in a purpose or opinion; stubborn. **2** Hard to control or cure, as a disease. [< L *obstinare* persist] —**ob′sti·na·cy** (-nə·sē), **ob′sti·nate·ness** *n.* —**ob′sti·nate·ly** *adv.* —Syn. **1** dogged, willful, headstrong, obdurate, unyielding.

ob·strep·er·ous (əb·strep′ər·əs, ob-) *adj.* **1** Making a great disturbance; clamorous; boisterous. **2** Unmanage-

able; unruly. [< L *ob-* against + *strepere* to roar] —**ob·strep′er·ous·ly** *adv.* —**ob·strep′er·ous·ness** *n.*

ob·struct (əb·strukt′) *v.t.* **1** To stop or impede movement through (a way or passage) by obstacles or barriers; choke; clog. **2** To block or retard the progress or way of. **3** To obscure from sight: to *obstruct* a view. [< L *ob-* against + *struere* pile, build] —**ob·struct′er, ob·struc′tor, ob·struc′tive·ness** *n.* —**ob·struc′tive** *adj.* —**ob·struc′tive·ly** *adv.*

ob·struc·tion (əb·struk′shən) *n.* **1** Anything that obstructs; hindrance; obstacle. **2** The act of obstructing, or the state of being obstructed.

ob·struc·tion·ist (əb·struk′shən·ist) *n.* One who obstructs; esp. one who delays the progress of business, as in a legislature. —**ob·struc′tion·ism** *n.* —**ob·struc′tion·is′tic** *adj.*

ob·tain (əb·tān′) *v.t.* **1** To gain possession of, esp. by effort; acquire; get. —*v.i.* **2** To be established or prevail; exist: When the play was made into a film, a different impression *obtained.* [< L *ob-* against + *tenere* hold, keep] —**ob·tain′a·ble** *adj.* —**ob·tain′er, ob·tain′ment** *n.*

ob·trude (əb·trōōd′) *v.* **ob·trud·ed, ob·trud·ing** *v.t.* **1** To thrust or force (oneself, an opinion, etc.) upon others without request or warrant. **2** To push forward or out; eject. —*v.i.* **3** To intrude oneself. [< L *ob-* towards, against + *trudere* to thrust] —**ob·trud′er, ob·tru′sion** *n.*

ob·tru·sive (əb·trōō′siv) *adj.* **1** Forcing itself to the attention; too conspicuous: *obtrusive* colors. **2** Bold or meddlesome in manner; pushing. **3** Tending to obtrude. —**ob·tru′sive·ly** *adv.* —**ob·tru′sive·ness** *n.*

ob·tuse (əb·tōōs′) *adj.* **1** Blunt or rounded. **2** Lacking alertness or sensitivity; intellectually sluggish or slow. **3** Heavy, dull, and indistinct, as a sound. **4** Having a measure between 90° and 180°: an *obtuse* angle. • See ANGLE. [< L *obtusus* blunt] —**ob·tuse′ly** *adv.* —**ob·tuse′ness** *n.*

ob·verse (ob·vûrs′, ob′vûrs) *adj.* **1** Turned toward or facing one. **2** Narrower at the base than at the apex. **3** Corresponding to something else as its counterpart. —*n.* (ob′-vûrs) **1** The side of a coin or medal bearing the face or main device. **2** The side of any object that is meant to be seen; the front as opposed to the back. **3** A counterpart of a truth or fact. [< L *ob-* towards, against + *vertere* to turn] —**ob·verse′ly** *adv.*

ob·vi·ate (ob′vē·āt) *v.t.* **·at·ed, ·at·ing** To meet or provide for, as an objection or difficulty, by effective measures; make unnecessary: The burglar alarm system *obviated* the need for a guard. [< L *obviare* meet, withstand] —**ob′·vi·a′tion, ob′vi·a′tor** *n.*

ob·vi·ous (ob′vē·əs) *adj.* Immediately evident; easily perceived; manifest. [< L *obvius* in the way, obvious] —**ob′vi·ous·ly** *adv.* —**ob′vi·ous·ness** *n.* —Syn. clear, apparent, plain.

Oc., oc. ocean.

o/c overcharge.

oc·a·ri·na (ok′ə·rē′nə) *n.* A small musical wind instrument with a rounded body, a mouthpiece, and holes stopped by the fingers. [Ital., a goose]

oc·ca·sion (ə·kā′zhən) *n.* **1** A particular event or juncture of events. **2** An important event or celebration. **3** A time at which an event occurs. **4** A circumstance that presents some reason, opportunity, or cause for action: no *occasion* for haste. **5** A circumstance that precipitates an event or condition: His confusion was the *occasion* of much merriment. **6** A need or exigency. —**on occasion** Now and then; occasionally. —*v.t.* To cause or bring about; cause accidentally or incidentally. [< L *occasio*, a falling towards, an opportunity]

oc·ca·sion·al (ə·kā′zhən·əl) *adj.* **1** Occurring at irregular intervals. **2** Belonging or suitable to some special occasion. **3** Happening casually or incidentally.

oc·ca·sion·al·ly (ə·kā′zhən·əl·ē) *adv.* Now and then; once in a while.

oc·ci·dent (ok′sə·dənt) *n.* The west. [< OF < L *occidens, -entis* sunset, the west, orig. pr.p. of *occidere* to fall]

Oc·ci·dent (ok′sə·dənt) The countries west of Asia, esp. Europe and the Americas; the West.

oc·ci·den·tal (ok′sə·den′təl) *adj.* Of or belonging to the west, or the countries constituting the Occident. —*n.* One born or living in a western country. Also **Oc'ci·den'tal.** — **oc'ci·den'tal·ly** *adv.*

oc·cip·i·tal (ok·sip′ə·təl) *adj.* Pertaining to the occiput or the occipital bone. —*n.* OCCIPITAL BONE.

occipital bone *Anat.* The bone that forms the back of the skull. • See PARIETAL BONE.

oc·ci·put (ok′sə·pət) *n. pl.* **·ci·puts** or **·cip·i·ta** (-sip′ə·tə) The lower back part of the skull. [< L *oc-* against + *caput* head]

oc·clude (ə·klōōd′) *v.* **·clud·ed, ·clud·ing** *v.t.* **1** To shut up or block off: to *occlude* an artery. **2** *Chem.* To absorb or adsorb. —*v.i.* **3** *Dent.* To fit together: said of the upper and lower teeth. [< L *ob-* against, upon + *claudere* to close] — **oc·clu′dent, oc·clu′sive** *adj.* —**oc·clu·sion** (ə·klōō′zhən) *n.*

oc·cult (ə·kult′, ok′ult) *adj.* **1** Of or designating those mystic arts involving magic, astrology, alchemy etc. **2** Not divulged; secret. **3** Beyond human understanding; mysterious. —*n.* Occult arts or sciences. —*v.t.* **1** To hide or conceal from view. **2** *Astron.* To block the light from or view of. —*v.i.* **3** To become hidden or concealed from view. [< L *occulere* cover over, hide] —**oc·cult′ism, oc·cult′ist, oc·cult′ness** *n.* —**oc·cult′ly** *adv.*

oc·cul·ta·tion (ok′ul·tā′shən) *n.* **1** The act of occulting, or the state of being occulted. **2** *Astron.* Concealment of one celestial body by another.

oc·cu·pan·cy (ok′yə·pən·sē) *n. pl.* **·cies** **1** The act of occupying; a taking possession. **2** The state of being occupied. **3** The time during which anything is occupied.

oc·cu·pant (ok′yə·pənt) *n.* **1** One who occupies, as an office or position. **2** A resident of a house, building, etc.

oc·cu·pa·tion (ok′yə·pā′shən) *n.* **1** One's regular, principal, or immediate business. **2** The state of being busy. **3** The possession and holding of land by military force. — **oc′cu·pa′tion·al** *adj.* —**oc′cu·pa′tion·al·ly** *adv.*

occupational therapy The treatment of mental or physical disabilities by activities designed to favor recovery. —**occupational therapist**

oc·cu·py (ok′yə·pī) *v.t.* **·pied, ·py·ing** **1** To take and hold possession of, as by conquest. **2** To fill or take up (space or time). **3** To inhabit; dwell in. **4** To hold; fill, as an office or position. **5** To busy; employ: to *occupy* oneself with a hobby. [< L *ob-* against + *capere* take] —**oc′cu·pi′er** *n.*

oc·cur (ə·kûr′) *v.i.* **·curred, ·cur·ring** **1** To happen; come about. **2** To be found or met with; appear. **3** To present itself; come to mind. [< L *ob-* towards, against + *currere* run]

oc·cur·rence (ə·kûr′əns) *n.* **1** The act or fact of occurring. **2** An event or incident that occurs; happening.

o·cean (ō′shən) *n.* **1** The great body of salt water that covers over two thirds of the earth's surface. **2** Any one of its five main divisions: the Atlantic, Pacific, Indian, Arctic, or Antarctic Ocean. **3** Any unbounded expanse or quantity. [< Gk. *ōkeanos*] —**o·ce·an·ic** (ō′shē·an′ik) *adj.* — **o′ce·an′i·cal·ly** *adv.*

o·cean·og·ra·phy (ō′shən·og′rə·fē) *n.* The branch of physical geography that deals with oceanic life and phenomena. —**o′ce·an·og′ra·pher** *n.* —**o′ce·an·o·graph′ic** (-ə·graf′ik) or **-i·cal** *adj.* —**o′ce·an·o·graph′i·cal·ly** *adv.*

o·cel·lus (ō·sel′əs) *n. pl.* **·li** (-ī) **1** A minute simple eye, as of many invertebrates. **2** An eyelike spot of color, as in the tail of a peacock. [L, dim. of *oculus* eye] —**o·cel′lar** *adj.*

o·ce·lot (os′ə·lot, ō′sə-) *n.* A large, spotted wildcat of the New World. [< Nahuatl *ocelotl* a jaguar]

o·cher (ō′kər) *n.* **1** A yellow or rust-colored clay containing iron oxides, used as a pigment. **2** The dark yellow color of ocher. Also **o′chre.** [< Gk. *ōchros* yellow] — **o′cher·ous, o·chre·ous** (ō′krē·əs) *adj.*

Ocelot

o′clock (ə·klok′) *adv.* **1** Of, according to, or by the clock. **2** According to the positions of the numbers on a clock face with the number 12 directly ahead or above: aircraft approaching at 3 *o'clock.*

OCS Officer Candidate School.

Oct, Oct. October.

oct. octavo.

oc·ta·gon (ok′tə·gon) *n.* A polygon with eight sides and

eight angles. [< Gk. *okta-* eight + *gōnia* an angle] —**oc·tag′o·nal** (ok·tag′ə·nəl) *adj.* —**oc·tag′o·nal·ly** *adv.*

oc·ta·he·dron (ok′tə·hē′drən) *n. pl.* **·drons** or **·dra** (-drə) A solid figure bounded by eight plane faces. [< Gk. *okta-* eight + *hedra* a seat] —**oc·ta·he′dral** *adj.*

oc·tane (ok′tān) *n.* A hydrocarbon containing a chain of eight carbon atoms per molecule. [< OCTO- + -ANE]

octane number A measure of the antiknock properties of a gasoline. Also **octane rating.**

oc·tave (ok′tiv, -tāv) *n.* **1** *Music* The interval between any tone and another having twice or half its frequency. **2** The eighth day from a feast day; also, the lengthening of a festival to include eight days. **3** Any group or series of eight. **4** In prosody, the first eight lines in an Italian sonnet, or a stanza of eight lines. —*adj.* **1** Composed of eight. **2** In prosody, composed of eight lines. Also **oc·ta·val** (ok·tā′vəl, ok′tə-) *adj.* [< L *octo* eight]

oc·ta·vo (ok·tā′vō, -tä′-) *n. pl.* **·vos** The page size (6 × 9½ inches) of a book made up of printer's sheets folded into eight leaves; also, a book consisting of pages of this size; often written *8vo* or *8°.* —*adj.* In octavo; consisting of pages of this size. [< L, an eighth]

oc·tet (ok·tet′) *n.* **1** A musical composition for eight parts. **2** A group of eight musical performers. **3** Any group of eight; esp., OCTAVE (def. 4). Also **oc·tette′.** [< L *octo* eight]

oc·til·lion (ok·til′yən) *n. & adj.* See NUMBER. [< MF < L *octo* eight; on analogy with *million*] —**oc·til′lionth** (-yənth) *adj., n.*

octo- *combining form* Eight: *octopus.* Also **oct-, octa-.** [< L *octo* and Gk. *oktō* eight]

Oc·to·ber (ok·tō′bər) *n.* The tenth month of the year, containing 31 days. [L, the eighth (month) of the Roman calendar]

oc·to·ge·nar·i·an (ok′tə·jə·nâr′ē·ən) *adj.* Being eighty or from eighty to ninety years of age: also **oc·tog·e·nar·y** (ok·toj′ə·ner′ē). —*n.* A person between eighty and ninety years of age. [< L *octoginta* eighty]

oc·to·pus (ok′tə·pəs) *n. pl.* **·pus·es** or **·pi** (-pī) **1** Any of a genus of cephalopods having a saclike body with a mouth on the under surface and eight tentacles covered with suckers. **2** Any organized power with far-reaching influence. [< Gk. *okta-* eight + *pous* a foot]

Octopus

oc·to·roon (ok′tə·rōōn′) *n.* A person who is the offspring of a white person and a quadroon. [< OCTO- + (QUAD)ROON]

oc·tu·ple (ok′tyōō·pəl, ok·tyōō′pəl) *adj.* **1** Consisting of eight parts or copies. **2** Multiplied by eight. —*v.t.* **·pled, ·pling** To multiply by eight. —*n.* A number or sum eight times as great as another. [< L *octuplus* eightfold] —**oc′.tu·ply** *adv.*

oc·u·lar (ok′yə·lər) *adj.* Pertaining to, like, derived from, or connected with the eye; visual. —*n.* The eyepiece of an optical instrument. [< L *oculus* eye] —**oc′u·lar·ly** *adv.*

oc·u·list (ok′yə·list) *n.* OPHTHALMOLOGIST. [< L *oculus* eye]

O.D. Doctor of Optometry; Officer of the Day; overdraft; overdrawn.

o.d. olive drab; on demand; outside diameter; overdose.

o·da·lisk (ō′də·lisk) *n.* A female slave or concubine in a harem. Also **o′da·lisque.** [< Turk. *ōdaliq* chambermaid]

ODan. Old Danish.

odd (od) *adj.* **1** Not even; leaving a remainder when divided by two. **2** Marked with an odd number. **3** Left over after a division. **4** Plus an additional number: 200-*odd* miles. **5** Occasional; casual: to work at *odd* jobs. **6** Peculiar; singular; queer; eccentric. **7** Single: an *odd* slipper. [< ON *oddi* a point of land, triangle] —**odd′ly** *adv.* —**odd′ness** *n.* —**Syn. 6** bizarre, extraordinary, fantastic, strange.

odd·ball (od′bôl′) *n. Slang* An odd or eccentric person. — *adj.* Habitually odd or eccentric.

odd·i·ty (od′ə·tē) *n. pl.* **·ties** **1** The state or quality of being odd. **2** A person or thing that is odd or peculiar.

odd·ment (od′mənt) *n.* **1** Something left over; a scrap. **2** *pl.* Small belongings; odds and ends.

odds (odz) *n.pl. (sometimes construed as singular)* **1** A difference to the advantage of one side over another: The *odds* are in my favor. **2** The amount of difference in advantage between competing sides: to fight against overwhelming *odds*. **3** The probability or ratio of probabilities that something will happen or be found to be the case. **4** An equalizing allowance based on the apparent chances of success of an opponent or contestant: to give *odds*. **—at odds** At variance; disagreeing. **—by all odds** Far and away; beyond doubt.

odds and ends Fragments; scraps.

odds-on (odz′on′) *adj.* Considered as having the best chance of winning.

ode (ōd) *n.* A lyric poem, originally intended to be sung or chanted, typically marked by lofty tone, dignified theme, and often in the form of an address. [< Gk. *ōidē* a song] **—od·ic** (ō′dik) *adj.*

-ode *combining form* Way; path: *anode, cathode.* [< Gk. *hodos* a way]

O·din (ō′din) In Norse mythology, the supreme deity, god of war and founder of culture.

o·di·ous (ō′dē·əs) *adj.* **1** Exciting hate, repugnance, or disgust. **2** Regarded with aversion or disgust. [< L *odium* hatred] **—o′di·ous·ly** *adv.* **—o′di·ous·ness** *n.*

o·di·um (ō′dē·əm) *n.* **1** The state of being odious; offensiveness; opprobrium. **2** A feeling of extreme repugnance, disgust, or hate. [L, hatred < *odisse* to hate]

o·dom·e·ter (ō·dom′ə·tər) *n.* A device for measuring distance traveled, as by an automobile. [< Gk. *hodos* a way, a road + -METER]

o·don·tol·o·gy (ō′don·tol′ə·jē) *n.* The science that relates to the structure, health, and growth of the teeth. [< Gk. *odous, odontos* tooth + -LOGY]

o·dor (ō′dər) *n.* **1** That quality of a substance that renders it perceptible to the sense of smell. **2** A smell or scent. **3** A quality detected by the mind or feelings; air: an *odor* of righteousness. **4** Regard or estimation: to be in bad *odor*. *Brit. sp.* **o′dour.** [L] **—o′dored** *adj.*

o·dor·if·er·ous (ō′də·rif′ər·əs) *adj.* Diffusing an odor. **—o′dor·if′er·ous·ly** *adv.* **—o′dor·if′er·ous·ness** *n.*

o·dor·less (ō′dər·lis) *adj.* Having no odor. **—o′dor·less·ly** *adv.* **—o′dor·less·ness** *n.*

o·dor·ous (ō′dər·əs) *adj.* Having an odor; fragrant. **—o′dor·ous·ly** *adv.* **—o′dor·ous·ness** *n.*

O·dys·seus (ō·dis′yōōs, -ē·əs) *Gk. Myth.* The king of Ithaca, one of the Greek leaders in the Trojan War; Ulysses.

od·ys·sey (od′ə·sē) *n. pl.* **·seys** *Sometimes cap.* A long, wandering journey or quest. [< ODYSSEY]

Od·ys·sey (od′ə·sē) *n.* An ancient Greek epic poem attributed to Homer, describing the wanderings of Odysseus during the ten years after the fall of Troy.

oe- See also words beginning E-.

OE, OE., O.E. Old English.

oec·u·men·i·cal (ek′yōō·men′i·kəl, *Brit.* ē′kyoo·men′i·kəl) *adj.* ECUMENICAL.

oed·i·pal (ed′ə·pəl, ē′də-) *adj. Often cap.* Of or pertaining to the Oedipus complex.

Oed·i·pus (ed′ə·pəs, ē′də-) *Gk. Myth.* The son of Laius and Jocasta, who unwittingly killed his father, and married his mother, and became king of Thebes.

Oedipus complex A strong, usu. unconscious attachment of a child to the parent of the opposite sex, with antagonism toward the other parent.

o′er (ôr, ōr) *prep. & adv.* Over.

oe·soph·a·gus (i·sof′ə·gəs) *n.* ESOPHAGUS.

oes·trus (es′trəs, ēs′-) *n.* ESTRUS.

oeu·vre (œ′vr′) *n. pl.* **oeu·vres** (œ′vr′) *French* **1** A work, as of art or literature. **2** The totality of works, as of an author.

of (uv, ov; *unstressed* əv) *prep.* **1** Coming from; originating at or from. **2** Associated with; included among: Is he *of* your party? **3** Located at. **4** Away or at a distance from: within six miles *of* home. **5** Named; specified as: the city *of* Athens; a fall *of* ten feet. **6** Characterized by: a man *of* strength. **7** With regard to: a leader *of* men. **8** About; concerning: What do you say *of* that? **9** Because of: dying

of pneumonia. **10** Possessing: a man *of* means. **11** Belonging to: the lid *of* a box. **12** Pertaining to: the majesty *of* the law. **13** Composed of; made of: a ship *of* steel. **14** Containing: a glass *of* water. **15** Taken from; from the number or class of: one *of* three people. **16** So as to be without: relieved *of* anxiety. **17** Proceeding from; produced by: the plays *of* Shakespeare. **18** Directed toward; exerted upon: a love *of* opera. **19** During or at a specified time or occasion: *of* recent years. **20** Set aside for or devoted to: a program *of* songs. **21** Before; until: used in telling time: ten minutes *of* ten. **22** *Archaic* By: loved *of* all men. [< OE]

OF, OF., O.F. Old French.

off (ôf, of) *adj.* **1** Farther or more distant; remote. **2** In a (specified) circumstance or situation: to be well *off*. **3** Not accurate; wrong: Your figures are *off*. **4** Not up to standard, as in activity or quality: an *off* season. **5** Not in existence; no longer effective: The deal is *off*. **6** Away from work; not on duty: *off* hours. **7** Gone away: *off* to the office. **8** Not in a position to operate; also, not operating. **9** Odd; eccentric. **10** *Naut.* Seaward; farther from the coast. **—adv.** **1** To a distance; so as to be away: My dog ran *off*. **2** To or at a (specified) future time or distance: a week *off*; a mile *off*. **3** So as to be no longer in place, connection, etc.: Take *off* your hat. **4** So as to be no longer functioning, continuing, or in operation: Turn the lights *off*. **5** So as to be away from one's work, duties, etc.: to take the day *off*. **6** So as to be completed, exhausted, etc.: to finish *off* an assignment. **—prep.** **1** So as to be separated, detached, distant, or removed from (a position, source, etc.): Take your feet *off* the table. **2** Not engaged in or occupied with; relieved from: *off* duty. **3** Below standard in: *off* one's game. **4** On or from the substance using: living *off* nuts and berries. **5** *Informal* No longer using, engaging in, or advocating: to be *off* drinking. **6** *Naut.* Opposite to and seaward of. **—n.** The state or condition of being off. [ME, orig. stressed var. of OF]

off. office; officer; official.

of·fal (ô′fəl) *n.* **1** Those parts of a butchered animal that are rejected as worthless. **2** Rubbish or refuse of any kind. [< OFF + FALL]

off·beat (ôf′bēt′, of′-) *n. Music* Any weak beat. **—adj.** (ôf′bēt′, of′-) *Slang* Unconventional; unusual.

off-col·or (ôf′kul′ər, of′-) *adj.* **1** Of doubtful or offensive taste; indelicate or indecent. **2** Unsatisfactory in color, as a gem. **3** *Brit.* Slightly ill; under the weather. *Brit. sp.* **-col·our.**

of·fend (ə·fend′) *v.t.* **1** To give displeasure or offense to; displease; anger. **2** To affect (the senses or sensibilities) in a way that causes displeasure, outrage, etc. **—v.i.** **3** To give displeasure or offense; be offensive. **4** To commit an offense, sin, or crime. [< L *ob-* against + *fendere* to hit, thrust] **—of·fend′er** *n.*

of·fense (ə·fens′) *n.* **1** The act of offending; a fault, sin, or crime. **2** The act of injuring another's feelings, of causing displeasure, etc. **3** That which injures the feelings, causes displeasure, etc. **4** That which affects the senses or sensibilities with displeasure, outrage, etc. **5** The state of being offended. **6** Assault or attack. **7** In sports, the team or team members attempting to score. *Brit. sp.* **of·fence.**

of·fen·sive (ə·fen′siv) *adj.* **1** Giving offense; disagreeable; displeasing, outrageous, etc. **2** Pertaining to or marked by attack; aggressive. **—n.** **1** Aggressive methods, operations, or attitudes: often with *the*. **2** An attack. **—of·fen′sive·ly** *adv.* **—of·fen′sive·ness** *n.*

of·fer (ô′fər, of′ər) *v.t.* **1** To present for acceptance or rejection. **2** To suggest for consideration or action; propose. **3** To present with solemnity or in worship. **4** To show readiness to do or attempt. **5** To attempt or to begin to do or inflict. **6** To suggest as payment; bid. **7** To present for sale. **—v.i.** **8** To present itself; appear. **9** To make an offering in worship or sacrifice. **—n.** **1** The act of offering. **2** Something offered, as a bid, proposal, etc. **3** An attempt or endeavor to do something. [< L *ob-* before + *ferre* bring] **—of′fer·er, of′fer·or** *n.*

of·fer·ing (ô′fər·ing, of′ər-) *n.* **1** The act of making an offer. **2** That which is offered, as the sacrifice presented in an act of religious worship. **3** A gift, esp. a contribution at a religious service.

of·fer·to·ry (ô′fər·tôr′ē, -tō′rē, of′ər-) *n. pl.* **·ries** *Eccl.* **1** *Usu. cap.* A section of the eucharistic liturgy, during which the bread and wine to be consecrated are offered to God. **2** A collection taken during a religious service; also, the part of a service when it is taken. **3** The prayer said or the music played or sung during the offertory.

off·hand (ôf′hand′, of′-) *adv.* Without preparation; extemporaneously. —*adj.* Done, said, or made extemporaneously. Also **off′hand′ed.** —**off′hand′ed·ly** *adv.*

of·fice (ô′fis, of′is) *n.* **1** A particular duty, charge, or trust, esp. a part of one's work. **2** A post or position held officially, esp. a position of trust or authority under a government. **3** That which is performed, assigned, or intended to be done by a particular person or thing. **4** *U.S.* A branch of the federal government, ranking next below the departments. **5** A room or building in which the affairs of a business, profession, or governmental branch are conducted; also, the people employed there. **6** *Eccl.* A prescribed religious or devotional service, esp. that for the canonical hours. **7** Any religious or social ceremony; rite. **8** *pl.* A proffered action of any kind; esp. a service: reinstated through the good *offices* of a friend. [< L *officium* a service]

office boy A boy hired to run errands or do odd jobs in an office.

of·fice-hold·er (ô′fis·hōl′dər, of′-) *n.* One who holds an office under a government.

of·fi·cer (ô′fə·sər, of′ə-) *n.* **1** One elected or appointed to office, as in a business, a society, etc. **2** One appointed to a certain military or naval rank and authority, specifically by commission. **3** On a nonnaval ship, the captain or any of the mates. **4** A policeman. —*v.t.* **1** To furnish with officers. **2** To command; direct; manage.

officer of the day An officer, in a military post or camp, responsible for a 24-hour period for the safety of the command, its property, maintenance of order, etc.

of·fi·cial (ə·fish′əl) *adj.* **1** Of, pertaining to, or holding an office or public trust. **2** Derived from the proper office or officer; authoritative. **3** Formal; studied; ceremonious. — *n.* One holding an office or performing duties of a public nature. —**of·fi′cial·dom, of·fi′cial·ism** *n.* —**of·fi′cial·ly** *adv.*

of·fi·ci·ate (ə·fish′ē·āt) *v.i.* **·at·ed, ·at·ing 1** To perform the duties or functions of an office. **2** To serve as a priest or minister; conduct a service. [< L *officium* service] —**of·fi′ci·a′tion, of·fi′ci·a′tor** *n.*

of·fic·i·nal (ə·fis′ə·nəl) *adj.* Prepared and on hand in drug stores: *officinal* medicines. —*n.* Any drug or medicine kept ready for sale. [< L *officina* a workshop]

of·fi·cious (ə·fish′əs) *adj.* Volunteering unwanted service or advice, esp. in an unduly forward manner. [< L *officium* service] —**of·fi′cious·ly** *adv.* —**of·fi′cious·ness** *n.* — **Syn.** meddlesome, interfering, obtrusive, nosy.

off·ing (ô′fing, of′ing) *n. Naut.* **1** The distant part of the open sea visible from the shore. **2** A position some distance offshore. —**in the offing** Soon to happen, arrive, etc.

off·ish (ô′fish, of′ish) *adj.* Inclined to be distant in manner; aloof. —**off′ish·ly** *adv.* —**off′ish·ness** *n.*

off-put·ting (ôf′pŏŏt′ing) *adj.* Putting one off; causing hostility, indifference, etc.

off-scour·ing (ôf′skour′ing, of′-) *n.* **1** That which is scoured off; something vile; refuse. **2** An outcast; pariah.

off·set (ôf′set′, of′-) *n.* **1** Anything which counterbalances or compensates for something else. **2** An extension, branch, spur, or offshoot. **3** A ledge in a wall formed by a reduction in its thickness above. **4** A bend in a pipe, bar, etc. that allows it to pass an obstruction. **5** OFFSET PRINTING. **6** An impression made by the offset printing method. —*v.* (ôf′set′, of′-) **·set, ·set·ting** *v.t.* **1** To compensate for; counterbalance. **2** To print by offset printing. **3** *Archit.* To make an offset in. —*v.i.* **4** To make an offset, as in printing. **5** To branch off; project as an offset.

offset printing A method of printing from a lithographic surface to a rubber-surfaced cylinder, and thence onto the paper.

off·shoot (ôf′shoot′, of′-) *n.* **1** *Bot.* A side shoot or branch from the main stem of a plant. **2** Anything that branches off from a main source.

off·shore (ôf′shôr′, -shōr′, of′-) *adj.* **1** Moving or directed away from the shore. **2** Situated or occurring at some distance from the shore. —*adv.* From or away from the shore.

off·side (ôf′sīd′, of′-) *adv. & adj.* In football, illegally ahead of the ball during a scrimmage.

off·spring (ôf′spring′, of′-) *n.* **1** The progeny of any person, animal, or plant. **2** A result; product. [< OE *of* off + *springan* to spring]

off-stage (ôf′stāj′, of′-) *n.* The area behind or to the side of a stage, out of view of the audience. —*adj.* In or from this area. —*adv.* To this area.

oft (ôft, oft) *adv. Archaic* Often. [< OE]

oft·en (ôf′ən, of′-) *adv.* On frequent or numerous occasions; repeatedly. [ME *ofte* oft]

oft·en·times (ôf′ən·tīmz′, of′-) *adv.* Frequently; often. Also *Archaic* **oft·times** (ôf′tīmz′, of′-).

o·gee (ō′jē, ō·jē′) *n. Archit.* **1** A molding having an S-shaped profile. **2** Such a curve used in any construction. **3** An arch with two such curves meeting at the apex: also **ogee arch.** [< OF *ogive* a kind of arch]

o·give (ō′jīv, ō·jīv′) *n.* **1** A diagonal rib of a vaulted arch or bay. **2** A pointed arch. [MF] —**o·gi′val** *adj.*

o·gle (ō′gəl) *v.* **o·gled, o·gling** *v.t.* **1** To look at with amorous or impertinent glances. —*v.i.* **2** To look or stare in an amorous or impertinent manner. —*n.* An amorous or coquettish look. [Prob. < LG *oegelen* oege an eye] —**o′gler** *n.*

Ogive arch

o·gre (ō′gər) *n.* **1** In fairy tales, a man-eating giant or monster. **2** A dreadful, monstrous, or cruel person. [F] — **o′gre·ish, o′grish** *adj.* —**o·gress** (ō′gris) *n. Fem.*

oh (ō) *interj.* **1** An exclamation expressing surprise, emotion, etc. **2** A word used in direct address: *Oh,* waiter! Would you please bring some water?

OH Ohio (P.O. abbr.)

OHG, OHG. O.H.G. Old High German.

ohm (ōm) *n.* The unit of electrical resistance, equal to the resistance of a conductor in which a current of one ampere is produced by a potential difference of one volt. [< G. S. *Ohm,* 1787–1854, German physicist] —**ohm′ic** *adj.*

ohm·me·ter (ōm′mē′tər) *n.* A meter for measuring the resistance of a conductor.

-oid *suffix* Like; resembling; having the form of: *ovoid.* [< Gk. *eidos* form]

oil (oil) *n.* **1** A slippery, combustible liquid of vegetable, animal, or mineral origin, insoluble in water but soluble in ether. **2** PETROLEUM. **3** An oil paint; also, an oil painting. **4** Anything of an oily consistency. **5** Fawning or flattering speech. —*v.t.* **1** To smear, lubricate, or supply with oil. **2** To bribe; flatter. —*adj.* Of, like, relating to, yielding, or producing oil. [< L *oleum* oil] —**oil′er** *n.*

oil·cake (oil′kāk′) *n.* A mass of compressed seeds of cotton, flax, etc., from which oil has been expressed.

oil·cloth (oil′klôth′, -kloth′) *n.* A cotton fabric waterproofed with an oil or paint preparation, used for table, shelf, or floor coverings, etc.

oil color A pigment ground in linseed or other oil.

oil of vitriol SULFURIC ACID.

oil paint A paint in which the vehicle is an oil, as linseed oil, that forms a tough elastic substance on exposure in thin films to air.

oil painting 1 The art of painting in oil colors. **2** A painting done in pigments mixed in oil.

oil·paper (oil′pā′pər) *n.* Paper treated with oil for transparency and moisture resistance.

oil·skin (oil′skin′) *n.* **1** Cloth made waterproof with oil. **2** *Often pl.* A garment of such material.

oil·stone (oil′stōn′) *n.* A whetstone treated with oil, used for sharpening tools, etc.

oil well A boring into an underground store of petroleum. • See DERRICK.

oil·y (oi′lē) *adj.* **oil·i·er, oil·i·est 1** Pertaining to or containing oil. **2** Smeared, soaked, or coated with oil. **3** Too smooth; unctuous. —**oil′i·ly** *adv.* —**oil′i·ness** *n.*

oint·ment (oint′mənt) *n.* A medicated fat or oil used to soothe, heal, or protect the skin. [< L *unguentum* an unguent]

O.Ir. Old Irish.

O·jib·wa (ō·jib′wä) *n. pl.* **·wa** or **·was 1** One of a tribe of North American Indians of Algonquian linguistic stock, formerly inhabiting the regions around Lake Superior. **2** The Algonquian language of this tribe. Also **O·jib′way.**

OK (ō′kā′) *interj., adj., & adv.* All correct; all right: expressing approval, agreement, etc. —*n. pl.* **OK's** An endorsement; approval. —*v.t.* (ō·kā′) **OK'd, OK'ing** To endorse; approve, as by signing with an OK. Also **O.K., o′kay′, o′keh′.** [Prob. < *o(ll) k(orrect),* humorous misspelling of *all correct;* but possibly < The Democratic *O.K.* Club, organized in 1840 to support President Martin Van Buren, nicknamed *Old Kinderhook,* from *Kinderhook,* N.Y., his birthplace]

OK Oklahoma (P.O. abbr.).

o·ka·pi (ō·kä′pē) *n. pl.* **·pi** or **·pis** A small African ruminant related to the giraffe, but with a shorter neck. [< native African name]

O·kie (ō′kē) *n.* A migrant farm-worker, esp. one from Oklahoma, forced to leave his land during the 1930's.

Okla. Oklahoma.

o·kra (ō′krə) *n.* **1** A tall annual herb cultivated for its edible, mucilaginous pods. **2** Its green pods, used in soups and as a vegetable. [< native African name]

Okapi

-ol¹ *suffix Chem.* Denoting an alcohol or phenol: *methanol.* [< (ALCOH)OL]

-ol² *suffix Chem.* Var. of -OLE.

OL, O.L. Old Latin.

old (ōld) *adj.* **old·er** or **eld·er, old·est** or **eld·est 1** Having lived or existed for a long time; aged; mature. **2** Of, like, or pertaining to an aged or mature person; exhibiting discretion, judgment, etc. **3** Having some specific age: a child two months *old.* **4** Having been made some time ago; used, or known for a long time; not new. **5** *Sometimes cap.* Belonging to an early or remote period; ancient; antique: the *old* Greeks, *Old* English. **6** Preceding the present; previous; former. **7** *Often cap.* Belonging to the former of two or the earliest of several things: the *Old* Testament. **8** Worthless on account of age; shabby; worn-out: an *old* coat. **9** Stale; trite: an *old* joke. **10** Continued, known, or used for a long time; familiar: an *old* comrade. **11** Having had long experience or practice: an *old* hand at farming. **12** Dear; familiar, through long acquaintance: *old* boy. **13** *Informal* Excellent; great; wonderful: a great *old* time. — *n.* **1** Past time: days of *old.* **2** A long time; long standing: my friend of *old.* **3** A person having some specified age: a two-year-*old.* —**the old** Old persons. [< OE *ald*] —**old′·ness** *n.*

old country The native land of any emigrant.

old·en (ōl′dən) *adj.* Old; ancient.

Old English 1 The English language from about 450 to 1050; Anglo-Saxon. **2** BLACK LETTER.

old-fash·ioned (ōld′fash′ənd) *adj.* Having the characteristics or customs of former times. —Syn. dated, obsolete, antiquated, passé.

old fo·gy (fō′gē) A person of extremely conservative or old-fashioned ideas. Also **old fo′gey.** [< Scot., an old soldier] —**old-fo′gy·ish, old-fo′gey·ish** *adj.*

Old French The French language from the 9th to the 16th century, esp. from the 9th to the 13th century.

Old Glory The flag of the United States.

old guard The conservative element in a community, political party, etc. [< trans. of F *Vieille Garde,* the imperial guard formed by Napoleon I in 1804]

Old High German High German as used from about 800 to 1100.

Old Irish The Irish Gaelic language from its origins to about 1100.

old lady *Slang* **1** One's wife. **2** One's mother.

Old Latin The Latin language before the first century B.C.

old-line (ōld′līn′) *adj.* **1** Having a well-established reputation or history. **2** Traditional; conservative.

old maid 1 An elderly single woman; spinster. **2** A fussy, prim, or prudish person. —**old′-maid′ish** *adj.*

old man *Slang* **1** One's father. **2** One's husband. **3** Any man in a position of authority, as the captain of a vessel.

Old Nick The devil.

Old Norse The language of Norway, Denmark, and Iceland before 1400.

Old Persian The Persian language in its oldest form, in use from 700 to 400 B.C.

old rose A grayish or purplish red.

Old Saxon An early form of the West Germanic language, in use during the ninth and tenth centuries.

Old South The South before the Civil War.

old·ster (ōld′stər) *n. Informal* A person of advanced years; an old or elderly person.

old style (ōld′stīl′) *n. Printing* A typeface characterized by slanted serifs and by down-strokes and cross-strokes of nearly the same thickness.

Old Style The old method of reckoning time by the Julian Calendar.

Old Testament The first of the two main divisions of the Bible, containing the early history and the laws and customs of the Jews and including the books of the prophets.

old-time (ōld′tīm′) *adj.* **1** Of or relating to past times. **2** Of long standing.

old-tim·er (ōld′tī′mər) *n. Informal* **1** One who has been a long-time member, resident, or job-holder. **2** An old-fashioned person.

old-world (ōld′wûrld′) *adj.* **1** Of or pertaining to the Old World or Eastern Hemisphere. **2** Charming; picturesque; quaint.

Old World The Eastern Hemisphere, including Europe, Asia, Africa, and Australia. • *Old World* is often used with reference to Europe in particular: *Old World charm.*

-ole *suffix Chem.* Denoting various organic compounds having a ring structure comprising five members. [< L *oleum* oil]

o·le·ag·i·nous (ō′lē·aj′ə·nəs) *adj.* **1** Of or pertaining to oil. **2** Unctuous; oily. [< L *oleaginus* pertaining to the olive] —**o′le·ag′i·nous·ly** *adv.* —**o′le·ag′i·nous·ness** *n.*

o·le·an·der (ō′lē·an′dər) *n.* A poisonous shrub with leathery evergreen leaves and clusters of fragrant flowers. [< Med. L]

o·le·ate (ō′lē·āt) *n.* A salt or ester of oleic acid.

o·le·ic acid (ō·lē′ik, ō·lā′-) An oily compound contained as an ester in most animal and vegetable oils and fats. [< L *oleum* oil]

o·le·in (ō′lē·in) *n.* The colorless, liquid ester of glycerol and oleic acid. Also **o·le·ine** (ō′lē·in, ō′li·ēn). [< L *oleum* oil]

Oleander blossoms

o·le·o (ō′lē·ō) *n.* MARGARINE. [< OLEO(MARGARINE)]

oleo- *combining form* **1** Oil; of oil: *oleoresin.* **2** Olein; oleic: *oleomargarine.* [< L *oleum* oil]

o·le·o·mar·ga·rine (ō′lē·ō·mär′jə·rin, -rēn) *n.* MARGARINE. Also **o′le·o·mar′ga·rin.**

o·le·o·res·in (ō′lē·ō·rez′in) *n.* A compound, either natural or prepared, of an essential oil and a resin.

ol·fac·tion (ol·fak′shən) *n.* **1** The sense of smell. **2** The process of smelling. [< L *olfacere* to smell]

ol·fac·to·ry (ol·fak′tər·ē, -trē) *adj.* Pertaining to the sense of smell. Also **ol·fac′tive.** —*n. pl.* **·ries 1** *Usu. pl.* The organ of smell. **2** The capacity to smell. [< L *olere* have a smell + *facere* make]

ol·i·garch (ol′ə·gärk) *n.* A ruler in an oligarchy.

ol·i·gar·chy (ol′ə·gär′kē) *n. pl.* **·chies 1** A form of government in which supreme power is restricted to a few persons. **2** The persons who exercise such power. **3** A state governed by an oligarchy. [< Gk. *oligos* few + *archein* to rule] —**ol′i·gar′chic, ol′i·gar′chal, ol′i·gar′chi·cal** *adj.*

add, āce, câre, pälm; end, ēven; it, īce; odd, ōpen, ôrder; tŏŏk, pōōl; up, bûrn; ə = *a* in *above, u* in *focus;* yōō = *u* in *fuse;* oil; pout; check; go; ring; thin; this; zh, *vision.* < derived from; ? origin uncertain or unknown.

oligo- *combining form* Small; few; scanty: *oligopoly*. [< Gk. *oligos* few]

Ol·i·go·cene (ol′ə·gō·sēn′) *adj., n.* See GEOLOGY.

ol·i·gop·o·ly (ol′ə·gop′ə·lē) *n. pl.* **·lies** A market situation in which the effective control of a market is exercised by a limited number of competitive sellers. [<OLIGO- + (MONO)POLY] —**ol′i·gop′o·list** *n.* —**ol′i·gop′o·lis′tic** *adj.*

o·li·o (ō′lē·ō) *n. pl.* **o·li·os** 1 A medley, as of musical pieces. 2 A highly seasoned meat and vegetable stew. [<Sp. *olla* olla]

ol·ive (ol′iv) *n.* 1 An evergreen tree with leathery leaves. hard yellow wood, and an oily fruit. 2 The fruit of the olive tree. 3 A medium yellowish green color: also **olive green.** 4 An olive branch. —*adj.* 1 Of or pertaining to the olive. 2 Having a dull yellowish green color. [<L *oliva*]

olive branch 1 A branch of the olive tree, as an emblem of peace. 2 An conciliatory proposal.

olive drab 1 A shade of greenish brown. 2 A woolen material of this color, used for uniforms by the U.S. Army. 3 *Often pl.* A uniform of this material. —**ol′ive-drab′** (-drab′) *adj.*

Olive

olive oil A pale yellow, edible oil obtained from ripe olives.

ol·la (ol′ə; *Sp.* ô′lyä, ô′yä) *n.* 1 A wide-mouthed pot or jar, usu. of earthenware. 2 A highly spiced stew. [<L, a pot]

ol·o·gy (ol′ə·jē) *n. pl.* **·gies** *Informal* A science or branch of learning: a humorous term. [<-LOGY]

O·lym·pi·ad (ō·lim′pē·ad) *n.* 1 In ancient Greece, the interval of four years between two successive celebrations of the Olympic games. 2 The modern Olympic games.

O·lym·pi·an (ō·lim′pē·ən) *adj.* 1 *Gk. Myth.* Pertaining to Mount Olympus or to the gods who dwelt there. 2 Pertaining to Olympia, a plain in ancient Greece, or to the Olympic games: also **O·lym′pic.** 3 Lofty; majestic. —*n.* 1 *Gk. Myth.* One of the twelve higher gods who dwelt on Olympus. 2 A contestant in the Olympic games.

Olympic games 1 Contests of sports, literature, and music held ·at the chief ancient Pan-Hellenic festival, which was celebrated every four years at Olympia in honor of Zeus. 2 A modern international athletic competition, held every four years at some city chosen for this event. Also **Olympian games, Olympics.**

O·man (ō·män′, ō·man′) *n.* An independent sultanate of SE Arabia, 82,000 sq. mi., cap. Muscat. • See map at SAUDI ARABIA.

o·ma·sum (ō·mā′səm) *n. pl.* **·sa** (-sə) The third division of the stomach of a ruminant. [L, bullock's tripe, paunch]

om·buds·man (om′bŏŏdz·mən, -budz-, om·bŏŏdz′mən) *n. pl.* **·men** (-mən) A government official appointed to receive and report grievances against the government. [Norw.]

o·me·ga (ō·mē′gə, ō·mā′gə, ō·meg′ə) *n.* 1 The 24th and last letter in the Greek alphabet (Ω, ω). 2 The end.

om·e·let (om′ə·lit, om′lit) *n.* A dish of eggs, beaten together, cooked and then folded, often around a filling, as of cheese, jelly, etc. Also **om′e·lette.** [<OF *alemette*, lit., a thin plate]

o·men (ō′mən) *n.* A phenomenon or incident believed to foretell some future event. —*v.t.* To foretell as or by an omen. [L] —*Syn. n.* portent, sign, indication, augury, *v.* indicate, presage, augur, portend.

om·i·cron (om′ə·kron, ō′mə-) *n.* The 15th letter of the Greek alphabet (O, o). Also **om′i·kron.**

om·i·nous (om′ə·nəs) *adj.* Like or marked by an evil omen; sinister; threatening. [<L *omen, ominis* an omen] —**om′i·nous·ly** *adv.* —**om′i·nous·ness** *n.*

o·mis·si·ble (ō·mis′ə·bəl) *adj.* That can be omitted.

o·mis·sion (ō·mish′ən) *n.* 1 The act of omitting or state of being omitted or neglected. 2 Anything omitted or neglected.

o·mit (ō·mit′) *v.t.* **o·mit·ted, o·mit·ting** 1 To leave out; fail to include. 2 To fail to use or do; neglect. [<L *ob-* down, away + *mittere* send]

omni- *combining form* All; totally: *omnipotent*. [<L *omnis* all]

om·ni·bus (om′nə·bəs, -bus) *n.* 1 BUS 2 A printed an-

thology, either of works by a single author or of works of the same general type. —*adj.* Of, pertaining to, or including many things, classes, situations, etc. [<L, for all]

om·ni·far·i·ous (om′nə·fâr′ē·əs) *adj.* Of all varieties or kinds. [<L *omni-* all + *fari* speak]

om·nip·o·tence (om·nip′ə·təns) *n.* 1 Unlimited and universal power. 2 *Usu. cap.* An omnipotent force, esp. God.

om·nip·o·tent (om·nip′ə·tənt) *adj.* Unlimited in authority or power. —**the Omnipotent** God. —**om·nip′o·tent·ly** *adv.* —*Syn.* mighty, almighty, powerful, authoritative.

om·ni·pres·ence (om′nə·prez′əns) *n.* The quality of being everywhere present at the same time; ubiquity. —**om′ni·pres′ent** *adj.*

om·ni·scient (om·nish′ənt) *adj.* Having infinite knowledge; knowing everything. —**the Omniscient** God. [<L *omni-* all + *sciens* knowing] —**om·ni·science** (om·nish′əns) *n.* —**om·ni′scient·ly** *adv.*

om·ni·um-gath·er·um (om′nē·əm·gath′ər·əm) *n. pl.* **·ums** A miscellaneous collection; a medley. [<L *omnium* of all + GATHER]

om·niv·o·rous (om·niv′ər·əs) *adj.* 1 Eating both animal and vegetable food. 2 Taking in everything; consuming or devouring, as with the mind. [<L *omni-* all + *vorare* devour] —**om·niv′o·rous·ly** *adv.* —**om·niv′o·rous·ness** *n.*

on (on, ôn) *prep.* 1 In contact with the upper surface of; above and supported by. 2 In contact with any surface or part of. 3 So as to be suspended from: a puppet *on* a string. 4 Directed or moving along the course of: Be *on* your way. 5 Near; adjacent to: the store *on* your right. 6 Within the duration of: He arrived *on* my birthday. 7 At the moment or occasion of: *on* the hour. 8 In a state or condition of: *on* fire. 9 By means of: with the support of: *on* wheels. 10 Using as a means of sustenance, activity, etc.: living *on* fruit. 11 In the interest or favor of: betting *on* a horse. 12 Concerning; about: a work *on* economics. 13 Engaged in; occupied or connected with: *on* the job. 14 As a consequence or result of: making a profit *on* tips. 15 In accordance with or relation to: to do something *on* purpose. 16 Directed, tending, or moving toward or against: war *on* the enemy. 17 Following after: disease *on* the heels of famine. 18 *Informal* With; accompanying, as about one's person: Do you have five dollars *on* you? 19 *Informal* At the expense of; paid by: The joke is *on* them. —**have something on** *Informal* To have knowledge, possess evidence, etc., against (a person). —*adv.* 1 In or into a position or condition of contact, adherence, covering, etc.: He put his hat *on.* 2 In the direction of something: He looked *on* while they played. 3 Ahead; forward: They moved *on.* 4 Continuously or in succession: The music went *on.* 5 In or into operation, performance, or existence: to turn the electricity *on.* —**and so on** And like what has gone before; et cetera. —**be on to** *Slang* To be aware of or informed about (someone, something, etc.); understand. —**on and on** Without interruption; continuously. —*adj.* In operation, progress, or application: The radio is *on.* —*n.* The state or fact of being on. [<OE *on, an*] • See UPON.

ON, ON., O.N., Old Norse.

o·nan·ism (ō′nən·iz′əm) *n.* 1 Withdrawal in sexual intercourse before orgasm; incomplete coitus. 2 MASTURBATION. [<*Onān*, son of Judah, + -ISM] —**o′nan·ist** *n.*

once (wuns) *adv.* 1 One time, without repetition. 2 During some past time. 3 At any time; ever; also, at some future time. 4 By one degree or grade of relationship. —*adj.* Former; formerly existing. —*conj.* As soon as; whenever. —*n.* One time. —**all at once** 1 Suddenly. 2 All at the same time. —**at once** 1 Simultaneously. 2 Immediately. —**once (and) for all** Finally. —**once in a while** Occasionally. —**this once** On this occasion only. [<OE *anes*, genitive of *an* one]

once-o·ver (wuns′ō′vər) *n. Slang.* A quick, esp. comprehensive and appraising glance or survey.

on·co·gene (ong′kə·jēn′) *n.* A gene common to all body cells that can cause normal cells to become malignant. [<Gk. *onkos* mass + *-genēs* born]

on·com·ing (on′kum′ing) *adj.* Approaching. —*n.* An approach.

one (wun) *adj.* 1 Being a single person or thing. 2 Being uniquely or preeminently the person or thing indicated. 3 Being a person or thing thought of as indefinite or unspecified. **4** Designating a person, thing, or group as contrasted with another; this; that. **5** Single in kind; the same. **6** Marked by unity; united. —n. **1** The number of a set, as of the natural numbers, that when multiplied by any other number of the set give a product equal to that other number; unity. **2** A single person or thing. —pron. **1** Someone or something. **2** Anyone or anything. **3** One of certain persons or things already mentioned. —**at one** In harmony; the same. **one another** Each other: said of an action or relation involving two or more persons or things reciprocally: They love one another. [<OE ān]

-one suffix Chem. Denoting a ketone: acetone. [<Gk. -ōnē, fem. patronymic]

one-horse (wun′hôrs′) adj. **1** Drawn or worked by one horse. **2** Informal Of small size, importance, etc.

O·nei·da (ō·nī′də) n. pl. **·da** or **·das** A member of a tribe of North American Indians of Iroquoian stock.

one-lin·er (wun′lī′nər) n. Informal A brief remark, meant to be humorous, clever, critical, etc., often used by a comedian in a performance.

one·ness (wun′nis) n. **1** Singleness or unity. **2** Agreement; concord. **3** Sameness; identity.

one-night stand (wun′nīt′) U.S. **1** A performance, lecture, etc., given one time only in a particular locality. **2** The place where such a performance, lecture, etc., is given.

on·er·ous (on′ər-əs) adj. Imposing or characterized by difficulty, labor, responsibility, etc. [<L onus, oneris a burden] —**on′er·ous·ly** adv. —**on′er·ous·ness** n. —Syn. arduous, burdensome, exacting, oppressive.

one·self (wun′self′, wunz′-) pron. One's own self; himself or herself. Also **one's self**. —**be oneself 1** To function in a normal manner. **2** To behave naturally.

one-sid·ed (wun′sī′did) adj. **1** On or having one side only. **2** Partial; unfair. **3** Marked by the clear dominance of one side; unequal: a one-sided game. **4** Unilateral. **5** Unequal-sided, as elm leaves. —**one′sid·ed·ly** adv. —**one′sid·ed·ness** n.

one-step (wun′step′) n. **1** A dance consisting of quick, walking steps in two-four time. **2** The music for this dance.

one-time (wun′tīm′) adj. Former.

one-track (wun′trak′) adj. Informal Limited to a single idea or pursuit; undiversified.

one-up (wun′up′) v. **-upped, -up·ping** Informal To try to gain an advantage over.

one-up·man·ship (wun′up′mən-ship′) n. Informal The practice or technique of trying to gain an advantage over another.

one-way (wun′wā′) adj. Moving or permitting movement in one direction only.

on·go·ing (on′gō′ing) adj. Going on, continuing, or progressing.

on·ion (un′yən) n. **1** A plant of the lily family with a pungent, edible bulb. **2** The bulb. [<L unio unity, an onion]

on·ion·skin (un′yən-skin′) n. A thin, strong, translucent paper with a glossy surface.

on-line (on′līn′, ôn′līn) adj. Directly connected to a computer.

on·look·er (on′look′ər, ôn′-) n. One who looks on; a spectator. —**on′look·ing** adj., n.

on·ly (ōn′lē) adv. **1** Solely, merely, or exclusively. **2** As recently as: only yesterday. **3** Nevertheless in the end: to defeat one contestant, only to face a stronger one. —adj. **1** Alone in its class; having no fellow or mate; sole; single. **2** Standing alone by reason of excellence. —conj. Except that; but. [<OE ān. one + -lic-ly]

Onion

on·o·mat·o·poe·ia (on′ə·mat′ə·pē′ə) n. **1** The formation of words in imitation of natural sounds, as crack, splash, or bow-wow. **2** The use of such words, as in poetry. [<Gk. onoma name + poieein make] —**on′o·mat′o·poe′ic** or **-i·cal, on′o·mat′o·poet′ic** (-pō·et′ik) adj. —**on′o·mat′o·poet′i·cal·ly** adv.

On·on·da·ga (on′ən·dä′gə) n. One of a tribe of North American Indians of Iroquoian stock formerly living in New York and Ontario. —**On′on·da′gan** adj.

on·rush (on′rush′, ôn′-) n. An onward rush or flow. —**on′rush·ing** adj.

on·set (on′set′, ôn′-) n. **1** An attack; assault, as of troops. **2** A setting out; start; beginning.

on·shore (on′shôr′, -shōr′, ôn′-) adv. & adj. To, toward, or on the shore.

on·side (on′sīd′, ôn′-) adv. & adj. In a legal position, according to the rules of a game; not offside.

on·slaught (on′slôt′, ôn′-) n. A violent hostile assault. [<Du. annslag a striking at] —Syn. attack, incursion.

on-the-job (on′thə·job′, ôn′-) adj. Pertaining to skills acquired, esp. under guidance, while actually doing the job, as distinguished from formal preparation before employment: on-the-job training.

on·to (on′tōō, ôn′-) prep. To a position on; to and upon: The cat jumped onto the table.

onto- combining form **1** Being; existence; ontology. **2** Organism: ontogeny. Also **ont-**. [<Gk. < ōn, ontos < einai be]

on·tog·e·ny (on·toj′ə·nē) n. Biol. The development of an organism from egg cell to maturity. Also **on·to·gen·e·sis** (on′tō·jen′ə·sis). —**on·to·ge·net·ic** (on′tō·jə·net′ik), **on′to·gen′ic** (-jen′ik) adj. —**on·tog′e·nist** n.

on·tol·o·gy (on·tol′ə·jē) n. pl. **·gies 1** The branch of metaphysics that deals with the nature of being and reality. **2** A particular theory about being and reality. —**on′to·log′i·cal** adj. —**on′to·log′i·cal·ly** adv.

o·nus (ō′nəs) n. **1** A burden or obligation; duty. **2** Responsibility or blame. [L]

on·ward (on′wərd, ôn′-) adv. Toward or at a point that is ahead in space or time; forward. Also **on′wards**. —adj. Moving or directed onward.

on·yx (on′iks) n. A variety of quartz consisting of layers of different colors. [Gk, a nail or claw, onyx]

oo·dles (ōōd′lz) n. pl. Informal A great deal; many; more than plenty. [? var. of HUDDLE, n.]

o·ol·o·gy (ō·ol′ə·jē) n. The branch of ornithology that treats of birds' eggs. [<Gk. ōon egg + -LOGY] —**o·o·log·ic** (ō′ə·loj′ik), **o′o·log′i·cal** adj. —**o·ol′o·gist** n.

oo·long (ōō′lông) n. A variety of dark tea that is partly fermented before being dried. [<Chin. wu black + lung a dragon]

oo·mi·ak (ōō′mē·ak) n. UMIAK. Also **oo′mi·ac**.

ooze[1] (ōōz) v. **oozed, ooz·ing** v.i. **1** To flow or leak out slowly or gradually, as through pores or small holes. **2** To exude moisture. **3** To escape or disappear: His courage oozed away. —v.t. **4** To emit, give off, or exude. —n. **1** A slow, gradual leak; gentle flow. **2** That which oozes. [<OE wōs sap, juice] —**ooz′i·ness** n. —**ooz′y** adj.

ooze[2] (ōōz) n. **1** Slimy mud or moist, spongy soil, esp. a deposit of sediment found on the bottom of the ocean, a lake, etc. **2** A place of muddy or marshy ground; bog; fen. [<OE wāse] —**ooz′i·ly** adv. —**ooz′i·ness** n. —**ooz′y** adj.

op. opera; operation; opposite; opus.

o·pac·i·ty (ō·pas′ə·tē) n. pl. **·ties 1** The condition, quality, or degree of being opaque. **2** That which is opaque.

o·pal (ō′pəl) n. A colored, translucent silica, softer and less dense than quartz, valued as a gemstone. [<Skt. upala a precious stone]

o·pal·esce (ō′pəl·es′) v.i. **esced, ·esc·ing** To exhibit an iridescent play of colors, as in an opal. —**o′pal·es′cence** n. —**o′pal·es′cent** adj.

o·paque (ō·pāk′) adj. **1** Impervious to light or other radiation. **2** Loosely, imperfectly transparent. **3** Impervious to reason; unintelligent. **4** Having no luster; dull. **5** Unintelligible; obscure: an opaque style. —n. Something opaque. [<L opacus shaded, darkened] —**o·paque′ly** adv. —**o·paque′ness** n.

op art (op) A style of art of the 1960's characterized by complex geometric patterns designed to create optical distortions, illusions, etc. [<optical art]

op. cit. in the work cited (L opere citato).

ope (ōp) v.t. & v.i. **oped, op·ing** Archaic To open.

o·pen (ō′pən) adj. **1** Affording approach, view, passage, or access: unobstructed: an *open* door. 2 Public; accessible to all: the *open* market. 3 Unconcealed; overt; *open* hostility. 4 Expanded; unfolded: an *open* flower. 5 Exposed; uncovered: an *open* car. 6 Ready for business, appointment, etc.: an *open* day in the schedule. 7 Not settled or decided; pending: an *open* question. 8 Available: The job is still *open*. 9 Unbiased; receptive: an *open* mind. 10 Generous; liberal: He gives with an *open* hand. 11 *Phonet.* a Pronounced with a wide opening above the tongue; low: said of vowels, as the *a* in *father*. b Ending in a vowel or diphthong: said of a syllable. 12 Frank; ingenuous: *open* and aboveboard. 13 Eager or willing to receive: with *open* arms. 14 In hunting or fishing, without prohibition: *open* season. 15 Liable to attack, robbery, temptation, etc. 16 Having openings, or perforations, as woven goods or needlework. 17 Free from ice: *open* water. 18 *Music* a Not stopped by a finger, as a string or hole. b Having no string or hole stopped. c Produced by an open string or instrument. d Closed at neither end, as an organ pipe. 19 Unrestricted by union regulations in the employment of labor: an *open* shop. 20 *Informal* Not under control in the sale of intoxicants, gambling, or vice: an *open* town. 21 Out of doors. 22 In elementary education, characterized by an environment designed to encourage self-motivation by giving children freedom of movement within the class or school area: *open* classrooms. 23 *U.S.* Designating a policy of admitting students for matriculation without regard to academic preparedness: *open* admissions. 24 *Mil.* Designating a city that, during a war, is unfortified but safe from enemy attack under international law. —*v.t.* 1 To set open or ajar, as a door. 2 To make passable; free from obstacles. 3 To make or force (a hole, passage, etc.). 4 To remove the covering, lid, etc., of. 5 To expand, as for viewing; unfold, as a map. 6 To make an opening or openings into: to *open* an abscess. 7 To make or declare ready for commerce, use, etc.: to *open* a store. 8 To make or declare public or free of access, as a park. 9 To make less compact; expand: to *open* ranks. 10 To make more receptive to ideas or sentiments; enlighten: to *open* the mind. 11 To bare the secrets of; reveal: to *open* one's heart. 12 To begin; commence, as negotiations. —*v.i.* 13 To become open. 14 To come apart or break open; rupture. 15 To spread out; unroll. 16 To afford access or view: The door *opened* on a courtyard. 17 To become receptive or enlightened. 18 To begin; be started. 19 In the theater, to begin a run, season, etc. —*n.* An open space. —**the open** 1 A large, unobstructed clearing. 2 The outdoors. 3 Public view. [< OE] —**o′pen·ly** *adv.* —**o′pen·ness** *n.*

open air The out-of-doors. —**o′pen-air′** *adj.*

o·pen-and-shut (ō′pən·ənd·shut′) *adj.* Simple; easily determinable.

open chain *Chem.* A molecular structure in which atoms, esp. carbon atoms, are linked in a straight or branched chain. —**o′pen-chain′** *adj.*

open door 1 The policy of giving equal and unrestricted opportunities to all nations, esp. for trade. 2 Admission to all without charge. —**o′pen-door′** *adj.*

o·pen-eyed (ō′pən·īd′) *adj.* 1 Having the eyes open; watchful. 2 Amazed: in *open-eyed* wonder.

o·pen-faced (ō′pən·fāst′) *adj.* 1 Possessing a countenance suggestive of frankness and honesty. 2 Denoting a sandwich without a slice of bread on top.

o·pen-hand·ed (ō′pən·han′did) *adj.* Giving freely; generous. —**o′pen-hand′ed·ly** *adv.* —**o′pen-hand′ed·ness** *n.*

o·pen-heart·ed (ō′pən·här′tid) *adj.* Unreserved; candid. —**o′pen-heart′ed·ly** *adj.* —**o′pen-heart′ed·ness** *n.*

o·pen-hearth (ō′pən·härth′) *adj. Metall.* Designating a type of reverberatory furnace with a shallow hearth, used in making steel.

open house 1 An informal party in which hospitality is extended to all comers. 2 An occasion when a school, clubhouse, etc., is open to visitors.

o·pen·ing (ō′pən·ing) *n.* 1 The act of becoming open or of causing to be open. 2 A hole, passage, or gap. 3 A clearing in a forest. 4 An aperture in a wall. 5 A formal beginning; prelude. 6 In chess, checkers, etc., the series of initial moves. 7 An opportunity for action, esp. in business.

o·pen-mind·ed (ō′pən·mīn′did) *adj.* Receptive to new ideas; amenable to reason. —**o′pen-mind′ed·ly** *adv.*

o·pen-mouthed (ō′pən·mouthd′, -moutht′) *adj.* 1 Having the mouth open; gaping, as in wonder or surprise. 2 Noisy; clamorous.

open question A matter as yet undecided.

open sesame An unfailing means or formula for gaining entrance or success. [< the magic words spoken in the story of *Ali Baba and the Forty Thieves*]

open shop An establishment in which union labor and nonunion labor are employed.

o·pen·work (ō′pən·wûrk′) *n.* Numerous small openings decoratively worked in fabric, silver, etc.

op·er·a[1] (op′ər·ə, op′rə) *n.* 1 A musical drama made up of arias, recitatives, choruses, etc., with orchestral accompaniment, scenery, acting, and sometimes dance. 2 A particular musical drama or its music or libretto; also, its performance. 3 The theater in which operas are given: also **opera house**. [< L *opus, operis* work] —**op·er·at·ic** (op′ə·rat′ik) *adj.* —**op′er·at′i·cal·ly** *adv.*

op·er·a[2] (op′ə·re) *n.pl.* of OPUS.

op·er·a·ble (op′ər·ə·bəl) *adj.* 1 Capable of treatment by surgical operation. 2 Feasible. —**op′er·a·bil′i·ty** (-bil′ə·tē) *n.* —**op′er·a·ble·ness** *n.* —**op′er·a·bly** *adv.*

opera glasses A binocular telescope of small size, suitable for use at the theater. Also **opera glass**.

opera hat A man's tall hat with a collapsible crown.

op·er·ant (op′ər·ənt) *adj.* 1 Producing a specified effect. 2 *Psychol.* Designating conditioning by which desired behavior is elicited by rewards that reinforce appropriate responses.

Opera glasses

op·er·ate (op′ə·rāt) *v.* **·at·ed, ·at·ing** *v.i.* 1 To act or function; work. 2 To bring about or produce the proper effect. 3 To perform a surgical operation. 4 To carry on a military or naval operation: usu. with *against*. —*v.t.* 5 To control the working or function of, as a machine. 6 To conduct the affairs of: to *operate* a business. 7 To bring about or cause. [< L *operari* to work, have an effect < *opus, operis* a work]

op·er·a·tion (op′ə·rā′shən) *n.* 1 The act or process of operating. 2 A method of exercising or applying force. 3 A single specific act or transaction. 4 A series of acts to effect a certain purpose; process. 5 The state of being in action. 6 *Surg.* A manipulation performed on the body to remedy a defect or disorder. 7 *Math.* A process or procedure that associates elements of a set, as numbers, with elements of the same or a different set. 8 A military or naval campaign.

op·er·a·tion·al (op′ə·rā′shən·əl) *adj.* 1 Pertaining to an operation. 2 Organized to carry out assigned tasks. 3 Fit or ready for some specified use. 4 In actual service.

op·er·a·tive (op′ər·ə·tiv, -ə·rā′tiv) *adj.* 1 Exerting force or influence. 2 Moving or working efficiently; effective. 3 Connected with surgical operations: *operative* technique. 4 Concerned with practical work. 5 Engaged in practical activity. —*n.* 1 A person employed as a skilled worker. 2 *Informal* A detective; one who works secretly. —**op′er·a′tive·ly** *adv.* —**op′er·a·tive′ness** *n.*

op·er·a·tor (op′ə·rā′tər) *n.* 1 One who operates; specifically, a worker at a telephone switchboard, a telegraph, etc. 2 The director of a large industrial organization. 3 *Slang* An aggressive, shrewd person who manages to get what he wants, often by unscrupulous means. 4 *Math.* A symbol that indicates an operation.

o·per·cu·lum (ō·pûr′kyōō·ləm) *n. pl.* **·la** (-lə) or **·lums** *Biol.* A lid, cover, or lidlike part in plants or animals, as a gill cover in fishes, etc. [< L *operire* to cover] —**o·per′cu·lar, o·per′cu·late, o·per′cu·lat′ed** *adj.*

op·e·ret·ta (op′ə·ret′ə) *n.* A musical dramatic work with a light or romantic plot, spoken dialogue, many songs, and dancing. [Ital.]

oph·thal·mi·a (of·thal′mē·ə) *n.* Inflammation of the eye or the lining of the eyelids. [< Gk. *ophthalmos* an eye]

oph·thal·mic (of·thal′mik) *adj.* Of, for, or pertaining to the eye: an *ophthalmic* ointment.

ophthalmo- *combining form* Eye; pertaining to the eyes: *ophthalmology*. [< Gk. *ophthalmos* the eye]

oph·thal·mol·o·gy (of′thal·mol′ə·jē) *n.* The study of the structure, functions, and diseases of the eye. —**oph·thal′mo·log′ic** (-mə·loj′ik) or ·**i·cal** adj. —**oph′thal·mol′o·gist** n.

oph·thal·mo·scope (of·thal′mə·skōp) n. An optical instrument for illuminating and viewing the inside of the eye. —**oph·thal′mo·scop′ic** (-skop′ik) or ·**i·cal** adj. —**oph·thal·mos·co·py** (of′thal·mos′kə·pē) n.

o·pi·ate (ō′pē·it, -āt) n. 1 A preparation of opium or any derivative; a narcotic. 2 Something inducing sleep or relaxation. —adj. 1 Consisting of opium. 2 Inducing sleep or relaxation.

o·pine (ō·pīn′) v.t. & v.i. o·pined, o·pin·ing To think; conjecture: now usu. humorous. [< L opinari think] —o·pin′er n.

o·pin·ion (ə·pin′yən) n. 1 A conclusion or judgment held with confidence, but falling short of positive knowledge. 2 An estimate, judgment, or evaluation. 3 A judgment by an expert: a medical opinion. 4 Law The formal announcement of the conclusions of a court in a case before it. [< L opinari think]

o·pin·ion·at·ed (ə·pin′yən·ā′tid) adj. Unwarrantably attached to one's own opinion; obstinate. —o·pin′ion·at′ed·ly adv. —o·pin′ion·at′ed·ness n.

o·pin·ion·a·tive (ə·pin′yən·ā′tiv) adj. Opinionated. —o·pin′ion·a′tive·ly adv. —o·pin′ion·a′tive·ness n.

o·pi·um (ō′pē·əm) n. A powerful, addictive narcotic obtained from the seed capsules of the opium poppy, the source of a number of substances, including morphine, used in medicine. [< Gk. opion]

o·pos·sum (ə·pos′əm, pos′əm) n. A tree-dwelling, American marsupial of nocturnal habits. [< Algon.]

opp. oppose; opposed; opposite.

op·po·nent (ə·pō′nənt) n. One who opposes another, as in battle or debate; antagonist. —adj. 1 Acting against something or someone; opposing. 2 Opposite. [< L ob- against + ponere to place]

op·por·tune (op′ər·t(y)ōōn′) adj. Meeting some requirement, esp. at the right time; timely. [< L opportunus suitable, lit., at the port.] —op′por·tune′ly adv. —op′por·tune′ness n. —Syn. auspicious, convenient, favorable, fortunate, well-chosen.

op·por·tun·ism (op′ər·t(y)ōōn′iz·əm) n. The governing of one's course of action by opportunities or circumstances rather than by regard for principles. —op′por·tun′ist n. —op′por·tu·nis′tic adj.

op·por·tu·ni·ty (op′ər·t(y)ōō′nə·tē) n. pl. ·ties A fit or convenient time; favorable occasion.

op·pos·a·ble (ə·pō′zə·bəl) adj. 1 Capable of being placed opposite: said esp. of the thumb in relation to the other fingers. 2 That can be opposed. —op·pos′a·bil′i·ty n. —op·pos′a·bly adv.

op·pose (ə·pōz′) v. ·posed, ·pos·ing v.t. 1 To act or be in opposition to; resist. 2 To set in opposition or contrast. 3 To place before or in front. —v.i. 4 To act or be in opposition. [< L oppositus opposite] —op·pos′er n. —op·pos′ing·ly adv.

op·po·site (op′ə·zit) adj. 1 Situated or placed on the other side, or on each side, of an intervening space or thing. 2 Facing or moving the other way; contrary. 3 Contrary in tendency or character: opposite opinions. 4 Bot. Arranged (as similar parts or organs) in pairs, but separated by a stem. —n. 1 Something or someone that is opposite, opposed, or contrary. 2 An antonym. —adv. In an opposite or complementary direction or position. —prep. 1 Across from; facing. 2 Complementary to, as in theatrical roles: He played opposite her. [< L oppositus, pp. of opponere to place against] —op′po·site·ly adv. —op′po·site·ness n.

op·po·si·tion (op′ə·zish′ən) n. 1 The act of opposing or resisting; antagonism. 2 The state of being opposite or opposed; antithesis. 3 An obstacle to some result: The stream flows without opposition. 4 Often cap. The political party opposed to the party in power. 5 Astron. The relative position of two bodies 180° apart in longitude. —op′po·si′tion·al adj. —op′po·si′tion·ist n.

op·press (ə·pres′) v.t. 1 To burden or subjugate by use of force or authority. 2 To lie heavy upon physically or mentally; weigh down. [< L ob- against + premere to press] —

op·pres′sor n. —Syn. 1 persecute, tyrannize. 2 crush, depress.

op·pres·sion (ə·presh′ən) n. 1 The act of oppressing. 2 Subjection to unjust hardships; tyranny. 3 Weariness or dullness of spirits. 4 Hardship; cruelty.

op·pres·sive (ə·pres′iv) adj. 1 Characterized by oppression; burdensome; tyrannical. 2 Producing a sense of depression, physical or mental. —op·pres′sive·ly adv. —op·pres′sive·ness n.

op·pro·bri·ous (ə·prō′brē·əs) adj. 1 Contemptuously abusive; imputing disgrace: opprobrious names. 2 Shameful; disgraceful. —op·pro′bri·ous·ly adv. —op·pro′bri·ous·ness n.

op·pro·bri·um (ə·prō′brē·əm) n. 1 Infamy; public disgrace. 2 A cause of disgrace; shame. [< L ob- against + probum infamy]

opt (opt) v.i. To choose; decide. —opt out (of) To decide to withdraw from or discontinue (an organization, activity, etc.) [< L optare choose, wish]

op·ta·tive (op′tə·tiv) adj. 1 Expressing or indicative of desire or choice. 2 Gram. Denoting that mood in Greek and certain other languages which expresses wish or desire. —n. Gram. The optative mood, or a verb in this mood. [< L optare to wish] —op′ta·tive·ly adv.

op·tic (op′tik) adj. 1 Pertaining to the eye or to vision. 2 Optical. —n. Informal An eye. [< Gk optos seen]

op·ti·cal (op′ti·kəl) adj. 1 Pertaining to optics. 2 Of or pertaining to eyesight. 3 Designed to assist or improve vision. —op′ti·cal·ly adv.

optical art OP ART.

op·ti·cian (op·tish′ən) n. One who makes or sells eyeglasses and other optical equipment.

op·tics (op′tiks) n.pl. (construed as sing.) The science that deals with the phenomena of light and vision. [< OPTIC]

op·ti·mal (op′tə·məl) adj. Most favorable. —op′ti·mal·ly adv.

op·ti·mism (op′tə·miz′əm) n. 1 A disposition to regard with cheerful confidence the course of events and the resolution of present uncertainties or conditions. 2 The philosophical doctrine that everything is ordered for the best. [< L optimus best] —op′ti·mist n. —op′ti·mis′tic adj. —op′ti·mis′ti·cal·ly adv.

op·ti·mum (op′tə·məm) n. pl. ·ma (-mə) or ·mums 1 The condition or degree producing the best result. 2 The most favorable degree, conditions, etc. —adj. Producing or conducive to the best results. [L, neut. of optimus best]

op·tion (op′shən) n. 1 The right, power, or liberty of choosing; the exercise of choice. 2 The purchased privilege of buying or selling something at a specified price within a specified time. 3 A thing that is or can be chosen. [< L optare choose]

op·tion·al (op′shən·əl) adj. Depending on choice; elective. —op′tion·al·ly adv.

op·tom·e·trist (op·tom′ə·trist) n. One who is skilled in optometry.

op·tom·e·try (op·tom′ə·trē) n. The profession of measuring the power of vision and prescribing corrective lenses. [< OPT(IC) + -METER] —op·to·met·ric (op′tə·met′rik), op′to·met′ri·cal adj.

op·u·lence (op′yə·ləns) n. 1 Wealth; affluence. 2 Luxuriance. Also op′u·len·cy.

op·u·lent (op′yə·lənt) adj. 1 Possessing great wealth. 2 Exuberant; profuse. [< L ops, opis power, wealth] —op′u·lent·ly adv.

o·pus (ō′pəs) n. pl. op·er·a (op′ər·ə, op′rə) or opus·es A literary or musical work or composition. [L, a work]

or[1] (ôr, unstressed ər) conj. 1 Introducing an alternative: stop or go. 2 Offering a choice of a series: Will you take milk or coffee or chocolate? 3 Introducing an equivalent: the culinary art or art of cookery. 4 Indicating uncertainty: He lives in Chicago or thereabouts. 5 Introducing the second alternative of a choice limited to two: with either or whether: It must be either black or white. 6 Either; whether: or in the heart or in the head. [< OE oththe or]

or[2] (ôr) n. Her. Gold. [< L aurum gold]

-or[1] *suffix* The person or thing performing the action expressed in the root verb: *competitor.* [< L]

-or[2] *suffix* The quality, state, or condition of: *demeanor. Brit. sp., often -our.* [< L]

OR Oregon (P.O. abbr.).

OR, O.R. operating room.

or·a·cle (ôr′ə·kəl, or′-) *n.* **1** The seat of some ancient divinity, as of Apollo at Delphi, where prophecies were given out by the priests. **2** A prophecy thus given. **3** The deity whose prophecies were given. **4** A person of unquestioned wisdom or knowledge; an infallible authority. [< L *orare* speak, pray]

o·rac·u·lar (ô·rak′yə·lər, ō-) *adj.* **1** Pertaining to an oracle. **2** Prophetic. —**o·rac·u·lar·i·ty** (ô·rak′yə·lar′ə·tē), **o·rac′u·lar·ness** *n.* —**o·rac′u·lar·ly** *adv.*

o·ral (ôr′əl, ō′rəl) *adj.* **1** Uttered through the mouth; spoken. **2** Pertaining to or situated at or near the mouth. **3** Of, pertaining to, or using speech. —*n.* An oral examination, as in a college. [< L *os, oris* mouth] —**o′ral·ly** *adv.* —**o′ral·ness** *n.* • **oral, verbal** Both of these words are commonly used with the sense of "spoken": *an oral* (or *verbal*) *agreement. Verbal,* however, can also mean "composed of or relating to words, as distinguished from ideas or things": *verbal skills. Oral,* derived from the Latin word for *mouth,* suggests the source of expression, whereas *verbal,* from the Latin word for *word,* suggests the form of expression.

or·ange (ôr′inj, or′-) *n.* **1** An edible, round, juicy citrus fruit with a reddish yellow rind. **2** Any of the evergreen trees or related shrubs yielding this fruit. **3** A reddish yellow color. —*adj.* **1** Reddish yellow. **2** Of or pertaining to an orange. [< Pers. *nārang*]

or·ange·ade (ôr′inj·ād′) *n.* A beverage made of orange juice, sugar, and water.

orange pekoe A fine grade of black tea of India, Ceylon, and Java.

or·ange·wood (ôr′inj·wŏŏd′, or′-) *n.* The fine-grained, yellowish wood of the orange tree. —*adj.* Of orangewood.

o·rang·u·tan (ō·rang′ə·tan′) *n. pl.* **·tans** or **·tan** A large anthropoid ape of Borneo and Sumatra, having brownish red hair, small ears, a hairless face, and very long arms. Also **o·rang′, o·rang′u·tan′, o·rang′ou·tan′, o·rang′u·tang′** (-ə·tang′). [< Malay *oran* a man + *utan* a forest]

o·rate (ô·rāt′, ō·rāt′) *v.i.* **o·rat·ed, o·rat·ing** To deliver an oration; speechify: chiefly humorous. [< L *orare* to speak]

o·ra·tion (ô·rā′shən, ō·rā′-) *n.* A formal public speech delivered on a ceremonial occasion. —**Syn.** address, discourse, talk.

Orang-utan

or·a·tor (ôr′ə·tər, or′-) *n.* One who delivers an oration; an eloquent public speaker.

or·a·tor·i·cal (ôr′ə·tôr′ə·kəl, -tō′rə-, or′-) *adj.* Of, like, or characteristic of oratory or an orator. —**or′a·tor′i·cal·ly** *adv.*

or·a·to·ri·o (ôr′ə·tôr′ē·ō, -tō′rē·ō, or′-) *n. pl.* **·os** A narrative musical composition, usu. on a sacred theme, for solo voices, chorus, and orchestra. [Ital., lit., a small chapel]

or·a·to·ry (ôr′ə·tôr′ē, -tō′rē, or′-) *n. pl.* **·ries 1** The art of public speaking; eloquence. **2** Eloquent language. **3** A place for prayer; a private chapel. [< L *orator* one who speaks]

orb (ôrb) *n.* **1** A sphere or globe. **2** A celestial body, as the sun, moon, etc. **3** A sphere topped by a cross: symbolic of royal power. **4** Eyeball; eye. —*v.t.* To shape into a sphere or circle. [< L *orbis* a circle]

or·bic·u·lar (ôr·bik′yə·lər) *adj.* **1** Having the form of an orb or orbit. **2** Well-rounded. **3** *Bot.* Circular, as a leaf or petal. Also **or·bic′u·late** (-lit, -lāt), **or·bic′u·lat′ed.** [< L *orbiculus,* dim. of *orbis* a circle] —**or·bic′u·lar′i·ty** (-lar′ə·tē) *n.* —**or·bic′u·lar·ly** *adv.*

or·bit (ôr′bit) *n.* **1** *Astron.* The path in space along which a celestial body moves. **2** *Anat.* One of the two sockets of the eyes. **3** *Physics* The path of a body subject to a field of force, esp. that of an electron around the atomic nucleus.

4 A range of influence or action: the *orbit* of imperialism. —*v.t.* **1** To cause to move in an orbit, as an artificial satellite. —*v.i.* **2** To move in an orbit. [< L *orbis* a wheel, a circle] —**or′bi·tal** *adj.*

orch. orchestra; orchestral.

or·chard (ôr′chərd) *n.* A plantation of trees grown for their products, as fruit, nuts, oils, etc.; also, the enclosure or ground containing them. [< Med. L *ortus* a garden + OE *geard* a yard, enclosure]

or·ches·tra (ôr′kis·trə) *n.* **1** A fairly large group of musicians playing together, esp. a symphony orchestra. **2** The instruments on which they play. **3** In theaters, the place immediately before the stage, occupied by the musicians: also **orchestra pit. 4** In the U.S., the main floor of a theater. [< Gk. *orchēstra,* lit., a dancing space] —**or·ches·tral** (ôr·kes′trəl) *adj.* —**or·ches′tral·ly** *adv.*

or·ches·trate (ôr′kis·trāt) *v.t. & v.i.* **·trat·ed, ·trat·ing 1** To compose or arrange (music) for an orchestra. **2** To arrange or bring about, as by manipulation or careful planning, esp. so as to create a desired effect: a well-*orchestrated* attack on the press. —**or′ches·tra′tion** *n.*

or·chid (ôr′kid) *n.* **1** Any of a widely distributed family of plants having bulbous roots and often very showy flowers. **2** The flower of any of these plants. **3** A delicate, rosy purple color. [< Gk. *orchis* a testicle: so called from the shape of its tubers]

or·chis (ôr′kis) *n.* An orchid, esp. one having dense spikes of small flowers. [< L, ORCHID]

Orchid flower

ord. ordained; order; ordinal; ordinary; ordnance.

or·dain (ôr·dān′) *v.t.* **1** To order or decree; establish. **2** To predestine; destine: said of God, fate, etc. **3** To invest with ministerial or priestly functions. [< L *ordo* an order] —**or·dain′er** *n.*

or·deal (ôr·dēl′, -dē′əl, ôr′dēl) *n.* **1** Any trying or painful experience. **2** An old method of trial in which the accused underwent physical ordeals, as carrying or walking over burning coals, which, if he were innocent, would supposedly leave him unharmed. [< OE *ordāl*]

or·der (ôr′dər) *n.* **1** Methodical and harmonious arrangement, as of successive things in a formation. **2** Proper or working condition. **3** A command or authoritative regulation. **4** *Law* Any direction of a court made to be entered of record in a cause, and not included in the final judgment. **5** A commission or instruction to supply, purchase, or sell something. **6** Established use or customary procedure. **7** Established or existing state of things. **8** *Sometimes cap.* A group of persons united by some common bond: the *Order* of Odd Fellows. **9** A group of persons upon whom a government has conferred an honor and who are thus entitled to affix to their names designated initials and to wear specific insignia; also, the insignia worn. **10** Social rank. **11** A class, kind, or degree: a chef of the first *order.* **12** *Usu. pl.* Any of the various grades or degrees of the Christian ministry: also **holy orders, sacred orders. 13** *Archit.* The general character of a column and its parts as distinguishing a style of architecture: the Ionic *order.* **14** *Biol.* A taxonomic category ranking below the class and above the family. **15** *Math.* A number indicating how many times an operation is performed or implied. **16** *Gram.* The sequence of words in a sentence or construction. **17** The position of the rifle as a result of the command **order arms. 18** Any one of the ancient nine grades of angels. —**call to order** To ask to be quiet in order to start, as a meeting. —**in order 1** In accordance with rule. **2** Neat; tidy. —**in order that** So that; to the end that. —**in order to** For the purpose of; to the end that. —**in short order** Quickly; without delay. —**on order** Ordered but not yet delivered. —**on the order of** Similar to. —**take orders 1** To enter the ministry. **2** To obey. —**to order** As specified by the buyer. —*v.t.* **1** To give a command or direction to. **2** To command to go, come, etc. **3** To give an order that (something) be done; prescribe. **4** To give an order for: to *order* a new suit. **5** To put in systematic arrangement. **6** To ordain: He was *ordered* deacon. —*v.i.* **7** To give an order or orders. [< L *ordo* a row, series, an order] —**or′der·er** *n.*

ordered set *Math.* A set in which each element has a unique correspondence with a natural number, beginning with one and proceeding on.

or·der·ly (ôr′dər·lē) *adj.* 1 Neat; systematic. 2 Peaceful and law-abiding: an *orderly* demonstration. 3 Characterized by order. —*n. pl.* **·lies** 1 A soldier or noncommissioned officer detailed to carry orders for superior officers. 2 A male hospital attendant. —**or′der·li·ness** *n.* —**Syn.** *adj.* 1 clean, methodical, tidy. 2 peaceful, quiet.

or·di·nal (ôr′də·nəl) *adj.* 1 Denoting position in an order or succession. 2 Pertaining to an order, as of plants, animals, etc. —*n.* 1 ORDINAL NUMBER. 2 *Sometimes cap.* A book of forms for special church services. [< L *ordo, ordinis* an order]

ordinal number A number that shows the order of a unit in a given series, as *first, second, third,* etc.

or·di·nance (ôr′də·nəns) *n.* 1 An authoritative rule; decree. 2 A religious rite or ceremony. 3 A municipal statute. [< L *ordinans* ordained]

or·di·nar·i·ly (ôr′də·ner′ə·lē, ôr′də·nâr′ə·lē) *adv.* In ordinary cases; commonly; usually.

or·di·nar·y (ôr′də·ner′ē) *adj.* 1 Of common or everyday occurrence; usual. 2 According to an established order; regular. 3 Mediocre; commonplace. —*n. pl.* **·nar·ies** 1 That which is usual or common. 2 *Brit.* A meal provided regularly at a fixed price. 3 *Brit.* An eating place. 4 One who exercises jurisdiction in his own right, esp. a church official. 5 A rule or book prescribing the form for saying mass. —**in ordinary** In actual and constant service. —**out of the ordinary** Very unusual. [< L *ordinarius* < *ordo* an order] —**or′di·nar′i·ness** *n.*

or·di·nate (ôr′də·nit) *n. Math.* The coordinate that indicates the distance from a point to the *x*-axis, parallel to the *y*-axis; the *y* coordinate. [< L *ordinare* ordain]

or·di·na·tion (ôr′də·nā′shən) *n.* 1 The rite of consecration to the ministry. 2 The state of being ordained.

ord·nance (ôrd′nəns) *n. Mil.* 1 All military weapons. 2 Cannon or artillery. [Contraction of ORDINANCE]

    Ordinate
AC: axis of ordinates.
AB: axis of abscissas.
Ad or ef: ordinate of point f.

Or·do·vi·cian (ôr′də·vish′ən) *adj. & n.* See GEOLOGY. [< L *Ordovices,* an ancient Celtic tribe]

or·dure (ôr′jər, -dyŏŏr) *n.* Excrement; feces. [< L *horridus* HORRID]

ore (ôr, ōr) *n.* A mineral or similar material from which a valuable substance, esp. a metal, can be extracted at reasonable cost. [< OE *ār* brass, copper]

Ore., Oreg. Oregon.

o·reg·a·no (ə·reg′ə·nō) *n.* A species of marjoram having pungent leaves used for seasoning. [< L *origanum*]

O·res·tes (ō·res′tēz, ō-) *Gk. Myth.* The son of Agamemnon and Clytemnestra who, having killed his mother to avenge his father's murder, was pursued by the Furies.

org. organic; organism; organized.

or·gan (ôr′gən) *n.* 1 Any of various keyboard musical instruments capable of sustained tones, esp. a collection of pipes made to sound by means of compressed air; a pipe organ. 2 A musical instrument resembling the pipe organ: a barrel *organ.* 3 A structure of specialized tissue in a plant or animal performing some definite function. 4 A means of making public the opinions and ideas of a person or group, as a periodical. [< Gk. *organon* a tool, a musical instrument]

or·gan·dy (ôr′gən·dē) *n. pl.* **·dies** A thin, crisp, transparent, cotton muslin, used for dresses, collars, etc. Also **or′gan·die.** [< F *organdi*]

or·gan·elle (ôr′gə·nəl′) *n.* Any of various distinctive submicroscopic structures having specialized functions within a living cell. [Dim. of ORGAN]

or·gan-grind·er (ôr′gən·grīn′dər) *n.* A street musician who plays a hand organ.

or·gan·ic (ôr·gan′ik) *adj.* 1 Of, pertaining to, or of the nature of animals and plants. 2 Having a physical basis in a bodily organ. 3 Serving the purpose of an organ. 4 *Chem.* Of or pertaining to carbon compounds. 5 Inherent in or pertaining to the organization or fundamental structure; structural. 6 Of or characterized by systematic coordination of parts; organized. 7 *Law* Designating the basic laws or principles of a government. 8 Pertaining to foodstuffs grown with only natural fertilizers of animal or plant origin. Also **or·gan′i·cal.** —**or·gan′i·cal·ly** *adv.*

organic chemistry The branch of chemistry that relates to carbon compounds.

organic disease *Pathol.* A disease accompanied by a physical change in an organ or tissue.

or·gan·ism (ôr′gən·iz′əm) *n.* 1 An animal or plant internally organized to maintain vital activities. 2 Anything analogous in structure and function to a living thing. —**or′gan·is′mal** *adj.*

or·gan·ist (ôr′gən·ist) *n.* One who plays the organ.

or·gan·i·za·tion (ôr′gən·ə·zā′shən, -ī·zā′-) *n.* 1 The act of organizing, or the state of being organized. 2 A number of individuals systematically united for some end or work, as a business enterprise, a political party, club, church, etc. 3 The way in which something is organized. —**or′gan·i·za′tion·al** *adj.* —**or′gan·i·za′tion·al·ly** *adv.*

organization man A member of an organization, party, company, etc., who is fully committed to its aims and methods of operation.

or·gan·ize (ôr′gən·īz) *v.* **·ized, ·iz·ing** *v.t.* 1 To arrange systematically; order. 2 To furnish with organic structure. 3 To enlist (workers) in a trade union. 4 To unionize the workers of (a factory, etc.). —*v.i.* 5 To form or join an organization. *Brit sp.* **or′gan·ise.** —**or′gan·iz′er** *n.*

or·gasm (ôr′gaz·əm) *n.* The climax of excitement at the culmination of a sexual act, accompanied in the male by ejaculation of semen and in both sexes followed by relaxation of erectile organs. [< Gk. *orgasmos* a swelling] —**or·gas′mic** *adj.*

or·gy (ôr′jē) *n. pl.* **·gies** 1 Wild and drunken revelry; debauch. 2 Any immoderate indulgence in something: an *orgy* of reading. 3 *pl.* In ancient Greece and Rome, the rites honoring certain gods, as Dionysus, marked by frenzied songs and dances. [< Gk. *orgia* secret rites.] —**or′gi·as′tic** (-as′tik) *adj.* —**or′gi·as′ti·cal·ly** *adv.*

o·ri·el (ôr′ē·əl, ō′rē-) *n. Archit.* A bay window, esp. one built out from a wall and resting on a support. [< OF *oriol* a porch, gallery]

o·ri·ent (ôr′ē·ənt, ō′rē-) *n.* 1 The east. 2 The eastern sky. 3 The iridescent luster of a pearl. —*v.t.* 1 To cause to face or turn to the east. 2 To place or adjust, as a map, in exact relation to the points of the compass. 3 To adjust the physical position of. 4 To adjust or adapt according to first principles or recognized facts. —*adj.* 1 Resembling sunrise; bright. 2 Ascending. [< L *oriens* rising sun, east]

Oriel

O·ri·ent (ôr′ē·ənt, ō′rē-) *n.* Asia, esp. E Asia; the East.

o·ri·en·tal (ôr′ē·en′təl, ō′rē-) *adj.* Eastern. —**o′ri·en′tal·ly** *adv.*

O·ri·en·tal (ôr′ē·en′təl, ō′rē-) *adj.* Of or pertaining to the Orient or to its people. —*n.* An inhabitant of Asia; an Asian.

O·ri·en·tal·ism (ôr′ē·en′təl·iz′əm, ō′rē-) *n.* 1 A quality or character attributed to Orientals. 2 Knowledge or study of Oriental languages, culture, etc. Also **o′ri·en′tal·ism.** —**O′ri·en′tal·ist** *n.*

Oriental rug 1 A one-piece rug, usu. having colorful, intricate designs, woven or knotted by hand in the Orient. 2 Any rug similar in appearance. Also **Oriental carpet.**

o·ri·en·tate (ôr′ē·en·tāt′, ō′rē-) *v.* **·tat·ed, ·tat·ing** *v.t.* 1 To orient. —*v.i.* 2 To face or turn eastward.

o·ri·en·ta·tion (ôr′ē·en·tā′shən, ō′rē-) *n.* 1 The act of orienting, or the state of being oriented. 2 The determination or adjustment of one's position with reference to circumstances, ideals, etc.

o·ri·en·ted (ôr′ē·en·tid, ō′rē-, -ən·tid) *adj.* **1** Directed toward; interested in: *oriented* to the arts. **2** Directed or centered: used in combination: a *child-oriented* family.

or·i·fice (ôr′ə·fis, or′-) *n.* A small opening into a cavity; an aperture. [< L *os, oris* mouth + *facere* make]

or·i·flamme (ôr′ə·flam, or′-) *n.* **1** The ancient banner of the kings of France, red silk split at one end to form flamelike streamers. **2** Any flag or standard. [< L *aurum* gold + *flamma* a flame]

orig. original; originally.

or·i·ga·mi (ôr′i·gä′mē) *n.* The ancient Japanese art of folding paper into animal and other forms. [Jap.]

or·i·gin (ôr′ə·jin, or′-) *n.* **1** The commencement of the existence of anything; primary source. **2** Parentage; ancestry. **3** *Math.* The point at which the axes of a Cartesian coordinate system intersect [< L *origo* a rise < *oriri* to rise]

o·rig·i·nal (ə·rij′ə·nəl) *adj.* **1** Of or belonging to the beginning. **2** Immediately produced by one's own mind; not copied. **3** Able to produce new creations; inventive. **4** Fresh; new: What an *original* idea! —*n.* **1** The first form of anything from which copies, imitations, translations, etc., are made. **2** The language in which a book is first written. **3** A person of unique character or genius; also, an eccentric. **4** Origin. —**o·rig′i·nal·ly** *adv.*

o·rig·i·nal·i·ty (ə·rij′ə·nal′ə·tē) *n. pl.* **·ties** **1** The power of originating; inventiveness. **2** The quality of being original or novel.

original sin *Theol.* The corruption and depravity inherent in mankind as a consequence of Adam's first disobedience.

o·rig·i·nate (ə·rij′ə·nāt) *v.* **·nat·ed, ·nat·ing** *v.t.* **1** To bring into existence; create; initiate. —*v.i.* **2** To come into existence; have origin; arise. —**o·rig′i·na′tion, o·rig′i·na′tor** *n.* —**o·rig′i·na′tive** *adj.* —**o·rig′i·na′tive·ly** *adv.*

o·ri·ole (ôr′ē·ōl, ō′rē-) *n.* **1** Any of a family of black-and-yellow birds related to the crows. **2** One of various American birds building a hanging nest and having yellow or orange and black plumage. [< L *aureus* golden] • See **BALTIMORE ORIOLE.**

O·ri·on (ō·rī′ən) *Gk. & Rom. Myth.* A giant huntsman who pursued the Pleiades and was killed by Diana. —*n.* An equatorial constellation.

o·ri·son (ôr′i·sən, or′-, -zən) *n. Usu. pl.* A devotional prayer. [< L *oratio* a prayer]

Or·lon (ôr′lon) *n.* A synthetic textile fiber with a high resistance to heat, light, and chemicals: a trade name.

or·mo·lu (ôr′mə·lōō) *n.* An imitation gold made of an alloy of copper and tin, used in decorating clocks, etc. [< F *or moulu*, lit., ground gold]

or·na·ment (ôr′nə·mənt) *n.* **1** Something that contributes to the beauty or elegance of a thing. **2** Any thing or person considered as a source of honor or credit. **3** *Music* A decorative melodic tone or tones independent of the harmony. —*v.t.* (ôr′nə·ment) To adorn with ornaments. [< L *ornare* adorn] —**or′na·ment′er** *n.* —**Syn.** *v.* beautify, decorate, embellish.

or·na·men·tal (ôr′nə·men′təl) *adj.* Serving to adorn. — *n.* An ornamental object. —**or′na·men′tal·ly** *adv.*

or·na·men·ta·tion (ôr′nə·men·tā′shən, -mən-) *n.* **1** The act of adorning, or the state of being adorned. **2** Ornamental things collectively.

or·nate (ôr·nāt′) *adj.* Ornamented or decorated to a marked degree. [< L *ornatus* adorned] —**or·nate′ly** *adv.* — **or·nate′ness** *n.*

or·ner·y (ôr′nər·ē, ôrn′rē) *adj. Regional* **1** Mean; low. **2** Unruly; stubborn. **3** Common; ordinary. [Alter. of ORDINARY] —**or′ner·i·ness** *n.*

or·ni·thol·o·gy (ôr′nə·thol′ə·jē) *n.* The branch of zoology that deals with the study of birds. [< Gk. *ornis, ornithos* bird + -LOGY] —**or′ni·tho·log′ic** (-thə·loj′ik) or **·i·cal** *adj.* — **or′ni·tho·log′i·cal·ly** *adv.* —**or′ni·thol′o·gist** *n.*

o·rog·e·ny (ô·roj′ə·nē, ō-) *n.* The process of mountain formation. [< Gk. *oros* mountain + -GENY] —**or·o·gen·ic** (ôr′ə·jen′ik, or′-) *adj.*

o·ro·tund (ôr′ə·tund, ō′rə-) *adj.* **1** Full, clear, rounded, and resonant: said of the voice. **2** Pompous; inflated, as a manner of speech. [< L *os, oris* mouth + *rotundus* round] —**o′ro·tun′di·ty** *n.*

or·phan (ôr′fən) *n.* A child whose parents are dead. —*adj.* **1** Having lost one or both parents: said of a child. **2** Pertaining to a child so bereaved. —*v.t.* To bereave of parents or of a parent. [< Gk. *orphanos* bereaved] —**or′phan·hood** (-hŏŏd) *n.*

or·phan·age (ôr′fən·ij) *n.* **1** The state of being an orphan. **2** An institution for orphans.

Or·phe·us (ôr′fē·əs) *Gk. Myth.* A singer and lyre player with magical powers. When his wife Eurydice died he was permitted to lead her back from Hades provided he did not look at her, but she disappeared when he glimpsed her. —**Or′phe·an** *adj.*

Or·phic (ôr′fik) *adj.* **1** Belonging, relating, or similar to Orpheus or his music. **2** Oracular; mysterious.

or·pine (ôr′pin) *n.* Any of various small, fleshy-leaved plants with yellow, white or purple flowers, often cultivated in rock gardens. Also **or′pin.** [< OF *orpin*]

Or·ping·ton (ôr′ping·tən) *n.* A variety of domestic fowl. [< *Orpington*, a village in Kent, England]

or·ris (ôr′is, or′-) *n.* Any of the several species of iris having a scented root. [Var. of IRIS]

or·ris·root (ôr′is·rōōt′, -rŏŏt′) *n.* The dried rootstock of a species of orris, used in cosmetics, perfumes, etc.

ortho- *combining form* **1** Straight; upright; in line: *orthopteran.* **2** At right angles: *orthogonal.* **3** Correct; proper; *orthography.* **4** *Med.* The correction of irregularities or deformities of: *orthodontia.* [< Gk. *orthos* straight]

or·tho·clase (ôr′thō·klās, -klāz) *n.* A brittle, glassy potassium-aluminum silicate related to feldspar. [< ORTHO- + Gk. *klasis* a fracture] —**or′tho·clas′tic** *adj.*

or·tho·don·tics (ôr′thə·don′tiks) *n.pl.* (construed as *sing.*) The branch of dentistry which is concerned with preventing and correcting faulty positions of the teeth. Also **or·tho·don′tia** (-shə, -shē·ə). [< ORTHO- + Gk. *odous, odontos* a tooth] —**or′tho·don′tic** (-don′tik) *adj.* —**or′tho·don′tist** *n.*

or·tho·dox (ôr′thə·doks) *adj.* **1** Correct or sound in doctrine. **2** Holding the commonly accepted faith, esp. in religion. **3** Approved; accepted. [< Gk. *orthos* right + *doxa* opinion] —**or′tho·dox′ly** *adv.* —**Syn. 3** acknowledged, conventional, established, fixed, traditional.

Orthodox *adj.* Designating any church in the Eastern Orthodox Church.

or·tho·dox·y (ôr′thə·dok′sē) *n. pl.* **·dox·ies** **1** Belief in established religious doctrine. **2** Agreement with established or accepted doctrines, ideas, etc. —**or′tho·dox′i·cal** *adj.*

or·tho·e·py (ôr·thō′ə·pē, ôr′thō·ep′ē) **1** The art of correct pronunciation. **2** Pronunciation in general. [< Gk. *orthos* right + *epos* a word] —**or·tho·ep·ic** (ôr′thō·ep′ik) or **·i·cal** *adj.* —**or′tho′e·pist** *n.*

or·thog·o·nal (ôr·thog′ə·nəl) *adj.* Having, meeting at, or determined by right angles. [< Gk. *orthos* right + *gōnia* an angle] —**or·thog′o·nal·ly** *adv.*

or·thog·ra·phy (ôr·thog′rə·fē) *n. pl.* **·phies** **1** A mode or system of spelling, spelling correctly or according to usage. **2** The study of spelling. —**or·thog′ra·pher** *n.* —**or·tho·graph·ic** (ôr′thə·graf′ik), **or′tho·graph′i·cal** *adj.*

or·tho·pe·dics (ôr′thə·pē′diks) *n.pl.* (construed as *sing.*) The branch of surgery concerned with treating chronic disorders of the joints, spine, bones, and muscles used in movement. Also **or′tho·pae′dics.** [< Gk. *orthos* right + *paideia* training of children] —**or′tho·pe′dic** or **·di·cal** *adj.* —**or′tho·pe′dist** *n.*

or·thop·ter·an (ôr·thop′tər·ən) *n.* Any of an order of insects with membranous hind wings and hard, narrow forewings, as locusts, crickets, grasshoppers, cockroaches, etc. —*adj.* Of or pertaining to this order. [< ORTHO- + Gk. *pteron* a wing] —**or·thop′ter·al, or·thop′ter·ous** *adj.*

or·to·lan (ôr′tə·lən) *n.* **1** A European bunting esteemed as a table delicacy. **2** Any of several birds of the U.S., as the sora and bobolink. [< Ital. *ortolano* a gardener]

Or·well·i·an (ôr·wel′ē·ən) *adj.* Of, relating to, or typical of the writings of George Orwell (1903–50), British novelist and political satirist.

-ory[1] *suffix* A place or instrument for (performing the action of the main element): *dormitory.* [< L *-orium*]

-ory[2] *suffix* Related to; resembling: *laudatory.* [< L *-orius*]

o·ryx (ôr′iks, or′-, ō′riks) *n. pl.* **o·ryx** or **o·ryx·es** Any of a genus of Asian and African antelopes with long, straight horns, as the gemsbok. [<Gk., a pickax, a kind of antelope; so called from its pointed horns] • See GEMSBOK.

os¹ (os) *n. pl.* o·ra (ôr′ə, ō′rə) *Anat.* A mouth or opening into the interior of an organ. [L]

os² (os) *n. pl.* os·sa (os′ə) *Anat.* A bone. [L]

OS, Os, O.S. Old Saxon.

Os osmium

O·sage orange (ō′sāj) **1** A small, thorny N. American tree related to the mulberry, having glossy leaves and a large, inedible fruit. **2** The fruit of this tree. [<the *Osage,* a tribe of N. American Indians]

Os·car (os′kər) *n.* A gold statuette awarded annually by the Academy of Motion Picture Arts and Sciences for outstanding performances, productions, photography, etc., in motion pictures. [?]

os·cil·late (os′ə-lāt) *v.* ·lat·ed, ·lat·ing *v.i.* **1** To go periodically through an orderly series or cycle of changes, as a pendulum or other physical system. **2** To vary undecidedly; waver. —*v.t.* **3** To cause to oscillate. [<L *oscillum* a swing] —os′cil·la′tor *n.* —os′cil·la·to′ry (-lə-tôr′ē, -tō′rē) *adj.*

os·cil·la·tion (os′ə-lā′shən) *n.* **1** The act or state of oscillating. **2** *Physics* A single cycle of an oscillating system.

os·cil·lo·scope (ə-sil′ə-skōp′) *n.* An electronic instrument that displays waveforms corresponding to external signals on the screen of a cathode ray tube.

os·cine (os′īn) *adj.* Of or belonging to a group of perching birds, as thrushes, finches, etc., with very highly developed vocal ability. —*n.* An oscine bird. [<NL <L *obtowards + canere* to sing]

os·cu·late (os′kyə-lāt) *v.t. & v.i.* ·lat·ed, ·lat·ing **1** To kiss. **2** To bring or come into close contact or union. **3** *Biol.* To have (characteristics) in common. [<L *osculari* to kiss] —os′cu·la′tion *n.* —os′cu·la·to′ry (-lə-tôr′ē, -tō′rē) *adj.*

-ose¹ *suffix* Full of or abounding in: *verbose.* **2** Like; resembling (the main element): *grandiose.* [<L *-osus*]

-ose² *suffix Chem.* A carbohydrate: *cellulose.* [<(GLUC)OSE]

o·sier (ō′zhər) *n.* Any of several willows producing long, flexible shoots used in wickerwork. —*adj.* Consisting of shoots of willow, etc. [<Med. L *osaria* a bed of willows]

O·si·ris (ō-sī′ris) *Egyptian Myth.* The god of the underworld and lord of the dead.

-osis *suffix* **1** The condition, process, or state of: *metamorphosis.* **2** *Med.* **a** A diseased or abnormal condition of: *melanosis.* **b** A formation of: *sclerosis.* [<Gk. *-ōsis*]

-osity *suffix* Forming nouns corresponding to adjectives in *-ose: verbosity, grandiosity.* [<L *-ositas*]

os·mi·um (oz′mē-əm, os′-) *n.* A hard, heavy, metallic element (symbol Os) of the platinum group. [<Gk. *osmē* an odor]

os·mose (oz′mōs, os′-) *v.t. & v.i.* ·mosed, ·mos·ing To subject to or to undergo the process of osmosis. [<OSMOSIS]

os·mo·sis (oz·mō′sis, os-) *n.* **1** The diffusion of a solvent through a semipermeable membrane in such a manner as to equalize the solution concentration on both sides of the membrane. **2** *Informal* A process resembling diffusion and marked esp. by the absence of effort: Living in Paris, he learned French by *osmosis.* [<Gk. *ōsmos* a thrust, push] —os·mot·ic (oz-mot′ik, os-) *adj.* —os·mot′i·cal·ly *adv.*

O Sp. Old Spanish.

os·prey (os′prē) *n.* A large hawk that dives and feeds exclusively on fish. [ME *ospray*]

OSS, O.S.S. Office of Strategic Services.

os·se·ous (os′ē-əs) *adj.* Pertaining to, of the nature of, or containing bone. [<L *os, ossis* a bone] —os′se·ous·ly *adv.*

os·si·fy (os′ə-fī) *v.t. & v.i.* ·fied, ·fy·ing **1** To convert or be converted into bone. **2** To make or become set, conventional, etc. [<L *os, ossis* a bone + -FY] —os·sif·ic (o-sif′ik) *adj.* —os′si·fi·ca′tion *n.*

os·ten·si·ble (os·ten′sə-bəl) *adj.* Offered as real or having the character represented; seeming; professed or pretended. [<L *ostendere* to show] —os·ten′si·bly *adv.*

Osprey

os·ten·sive (os·ten′siv) *adj.* **1** Exhibiting; showing; revealing. **2** OSTENSIBLE. —os·ten′sive·ly *adv.*

os·ten·ta·tion (os′tən·tā′shən) *n.* Elaborate or pretentious display; showiness. [<L *ostendere* to show]

os·ten·ta·tious (os′tən·tā′shəs) *adj.* Marked by a showy or pretentious display. —os′ten·ta′tious·ly *adv.* —os′ten·ta′tious·ness *n.*

osteo- *combining form* Bone: *osteology.* Also oste-. [<Gk. *osteon* a bone]

os·te·ol·o·gy (os′tē-ol′ə-jē) *n.* The study of the functions and structure of bones. —os′te·o·log′i·cal (-ə-loj′i·kəl) *adj.* —os′te·o·log′i·cal·ly *adv.* —os′te·ol′o·gist *n.*

os·te·o·ma (os′tē-ō′mə) *n. pl.* ·ma·ta (-mə-tə) A tumor consisting of bony substance. [<OSTE(O)- + NL *-oma* tumor]

os·te·o·my·e·li·tis (os′tē-ō-mī′ə-lī′tis) *n.* Inflammation of the bone marrow.

os·te·op·a·thy (os′tē-op′ə-thē) *n.* Therapy based on a theory that most disorders are due to structural abnormalities that may be corrected by manipulation. —os′te·o·path′, os′te·op′a·thist *n.* —os′te·o·path·ic *adj.*

os·te·o·po·ro·sis (os′tē-ō-pə-rō′sis) *n. Med.* A disease marked by loss of calcium from the bones, causing them to weaken.

os·tler (os′lər) *n.* HOSTLER.

Ost·mark (ôst′märk′) *n.* MARK².

os·tra·cism (os′trə-siz′əm) *n.* **1** Exclusion, as from society or common privileges, by general consent. **2** In ancient Greece, banishment by popular vote.

os·tra·cize (os′trə-sīz) *v.t.* ·cized, ·ciz·ing To exclude, banish, etc., by ostracism. [<Gk. *ostrakon* a potsherd, shell, voting tablet] —**Syn.** reject, expatriate, expel, oust.

os·trich (ôs′trich, os′-) *n.* **1** A large, two-toed bird of Africa and Arabia, with aborted wings and long, powerful legs. **2** RHEA. [<L *avis* a bird + LL *struthio* an ostrich]

Os·tro·goth (os′trə-goth) *n.* A member of the eastern branch of the Goths. —Os′tro·goth′ic *adj.*

O.T. Old Testament; overtime.

oth·er (uth′ər) *adj.* **1** Being the remaining one, as of two or more persons or things. **2** Distinct or different from the one or more persons or things first mentioned. **3** Different, as in nature or quality. **4** Additional; further. **5** Former. **6** Second or alternate. —**the other day** (**night,** etc.) Recently. —*pron.* **1** A different or additional person or thing. **2** The second of two; the other one. —*adv.* Otherwise: with *than.* —*n.* **1** The remaining one or ones of two or more persons or things. **2** A different or additional person or thing. [<OE *ōther*] —oth′er·ness *n.*

Ostrich

oth·er·wise (uth′ər·wīz′) *adv.* **1** In another or different manner. **2** In other circumstances or conditions. **3** In all other respects: an *otherwise* sensible writer. —*adj.* Different: How could such notions be *otherwise* than useless?

other world A world after death.

oth·er·world·ly (uth′ər·wûrld′lē) *adj.* **1** Of, pertaining to, or characteristic of a future or ideal world. **2** Concerned with the hereafter or with imaginative or imaginative interests. —oth′er·world′li·ness *n.*

-otic *suffix* **1** *Med.* Of, related to, or affected by: *psychotic.* **2** Causing or producing: *narcotic.* [<Gk. *-ōtikos*]

o·ti·ose (ō′shē-ōs, -tē-) *adj.* **1** Being at rest or ease; idle. **2** Futile or useless. [<L *otium* leisure] —o′ti·ose·ly *adv.* —o′ti·os′i·ty (-os′ə-tē) *n.*

o·ti·tis (ō-tī′tis) *n.* Inflammation of the ear. [<OT(O)- + -ITIS]

oto- *combining form* Ear; pertaining to the ear: *otology.* [<Gk. *ōtos* the ear]

o·tol·o·gy (ō-tol′ə-jē) *n.* The science of the ear and its disorders. —o·to·log·i·cal (ō′tə-loj′i·kəl) *adj.* —o·tol′o·gist *n.*

OTS, O.T.S. Officer Training School.

ot·ter (ot′ər) **1** A weasel-like, carnivorous, swimming mammal with webbed feet and a flattened, oarlike tail. **2** Its valuable, dark-brown fur. [<OE *oter*]

Otter

ot·to·man (ot′ə-mən) *n. pl.* **-mans 1** An upholstered, often cushioned, backless and armless seat or sofa. **2** A cushioned footstool. [< OTTOMAN]

Ot·to·man (ot′ə-mən) *n. pl.* **-mans** A Turk. —*adj.* Of or pertaining to the Turks or Turkey; Turkish.

Ottoman Empire A former empire (1300–1919) of the Turks in Asia Minor, NE Africa, and SE Europe, cap. Constantinople.

ouch (ouch) *interj.* An exclamation indicating sudden pain.

ought[1] (ôt) *v.* An auxiliary verb used with an infinitive to express: **1** Obligation or moral duty: He *ought* to keep his promises. **2** Advisability or expedience: You *ought* to be careful. **3** Probability or expectation: He *ought* to be here tomorrow. [< OE *āhte*, p.t. of *āgan* owe, possess]

ought[2] (ôt) *n. & adv.* AUGHT.

oui (wē) *adv.* French Yes.

Oui·ja (wē′jə, -jē) *n.* A board inscribed with the alphabet and other characters, and a small, usu. triangular board resting on two casters and a pencil, which is thought to spell out spiritualistic or telepathic communications: a trade name. Also **oui′ja.**

ounce[1] (ouns) *n.* **1 a** A unit of weight equal to .0625 pound avoirdupois. **b** A unit of weight equal to .0833 pound troy. **2** FLUID OUNCE. **3** A small quantity. [< L *uncia* twelfth part (of a pound or foot)]

ounce[2] (ouns) *n.* A large cat of CEN. Asia, having long, whitish fur with dark spots. [< OF *l'once*, var. of *lonce* the lynx]

our (our) *pronominal adj.* The possessive case of the pronoun *we*, employed attributively. [< OE *ūre*]

ours (ourz) *pron.* **1** The possessive case of *we* used predicatively: That dog is *ours*. **2** The things or persons belonging or pertaining to us: their country and *ours*. —**of ours** Belonging or relating to us; our.

our·self (our-self′) *pron.* Myself: only in formal or regal usage.

our·selves (our-selvz′) *pron. pl.* A form of the first person plural pronoun, used: **1** As a reflexive: We only hurt *ourselves*. **2** As an intensive: We *ourselves* will do it. **3** As the designation of a normal or usual state: We're not *ourselves* today.

-ous *suffix of adjectives* **1** Full of; having; characterized by: *glorious*. **2** *Chem.* Having a lower valence than that indicated by the suffix *-ic: nitrous*. [< L *-osus*]

ou·sel (ōō′zəl) *n.* OUZEL.

oust (oust) *v.t.* To force from possession or occupancy; eject. [< L *ob-* against + *stare* stand] —**Syn** dispossess, evict, expel, turn out.

oust·er (ous′tər) *n.* **1** The act of putting one out of possession or occupancy; dispossession. **2** One who or that which ousts.

out (out) *adv.* **1** Away from the inside or center: to branch *out*. **2** Away from a specified or usual place: to set *out*. **3** From a source: to pour *out* wine. **4** So as to free of: to thresh *out* grain. **5** From among others: to pick *out* a dress. **6** Into the charge or care of others: to deal *out* cards. **7** So as to project or be extended: to stretch *out*. **8** Into extinction or inactivity: The flame went *out*. **9** To a result or conclusion: to find *out*. **10** Completely; fully: tired *out*. **11** Into existence or manifestation: An epidemic broke *out*; The sun came *out*. **12** Into blossom or leaf. **13** Into public notice or circulation: to bring *out* a new edition. **14** Aloud: to call *out*. **15** Into disagreement; at odds: to be put *out* over trifles. **16** *Informal* Into unconsciousness: to pass *out*. **17** In baseball, so as to be retired from active play. —*adj.* **1** External; exterior; outer. **2** Away from a place regarded as a base: *out* of school. **3** Away at a distance: *out* in the hills. **4** Exposed or bare: *out* at the knees. **5** Manifest; apparent: The stars are *out*. **6** In blossom or leaf. **7** Mistaken; in error. **8** Extinguished; exhausted: The fire is *out*. **9** Finished; at an end: before the week is *out*. **10** At a financial loss: to be *out* five dollars. **11** Not in effective operation. **12** *Informal* Unconscious. **13** In baseball, no longer in active play. **14** *Informal* No longer in fashion. **15** *Informal* Not to be considered; out of the question. —*prep.* From within; outside: *out* the door. —**out of 1** From or beyond the inside of. **2** Beyond the limits, reach, scope, or proper position of: *out* of view. **3** Without: *out* of breath.

4 Influenced or caused by: *out of* respect. —*n.* **1** Something that is out. **2** An escape; a way to dodge involvement: He had an *out*. **3** *Often pl.* A person not in office or position of power. **4** In baseball, retirement of a batter or base runner. —**on the outs** At odds; in disagreement. —*v.t.* **1** To drive out; expel. —*v.i.* **2** To come or go out; be revealed. —*interj.* Go out! away! begone! [< OE *ūt*]

out- *combining form* **1** Living or situated outside; external; away from the center: *outlying, outpatient.* **2** Going forth: issuing; outward: *outbound, outstretch.* **3** Used to denote the time, place, or result of the action expressed by the root verb: *outcome, outcry.* **4** Excessive; surpassing; more; beyond: *outdo.*

out·age (out′ij) *n.* An interruption or suspension, as in the supply of electric current.

out-and-out (out′ənd-out′) *adj.* Thoroughgoing; blatant: an *out-and-out* lie.

out·back (out′bak′) *n.* Rural country remote from settled areas, esp. in Australia.

out·bid (out-bid′) *v.t.* **-bid, -bid·den** or **-bid, -bid·ding** To bid more than.

out·board (out′bôrd′, -bōrd′) *adj.* Situated on the outside of a vessel, as a motor for temporary attachment to the stern of a small boat. —*adv.* Away from the center. —*n.* An outboard motor.

out·bound (out′bound′) *adj.* Outward bound.

out·break (out′brāk′) *n.* **1** A sudden breaking forth, as of disease or violence. **2** An insurrection. — **Syn. 1** eruption, outburst. **2** disturbance, uprising.

Outboard motor

out·build·ing (out′bil′ding) *n.* A smaller building near a main building, as a woodshed.

out·burst (out′bûrst′) *n.* A bursting out; a violent manifestation, as of feeling.

out·cast (out′kast′, -käst′) *n.* One who is cast out from home or country. —*adj.* Rejected as unworthy or useless.

out·class (out-klas′, -kläs′) *v.t.* To exceed decisively in skill, quality, or powers.

out·come (out′kum′) *n.* A consequence or result.

out·crop (out′krop′) *n.* **1** The exposure of rock at or above the surface of the ground. **2** The rock so exposed. —*v.i.* **-cropped, -crop·ping 1** To crop up or out. **2** To appear above the ground, as rocks.

out·cry (out′krī′) *n. pl.* **-cries 1** A loud cry, as of distress or alarm. **2** A strong protest by several or many sources.

out·dat·ed (out-dā′tid) *adj.* No longer fashionable or popular; old-fashioned. —**out·dat′ed·ness** *n.*

out·dis·tance (out-dis′təns) *v.t.* **-tanced, -tanc·ing 1** To outrun; outstrip. **2** To surpass completely; outdo.

out·do (out-dōō′) *v.t.* **-did, -done, -do·ing** To exceed in performance; surpass.

out·door (out′dôr′, -dōr′) *adj.* Being or done in the open air; belonging or occurring outside the house: *outdoor* sports.

out·doors (out-dôrz′, -dōrz′) *adv.* Outside of the doors; out of the house; in the open air. —*n.* **1** The world beyond the house. **2** The open air.

out·door·sy (out′dôr′zē, -dōr′-) *adj.* **-si·er, -si·est** *Informal* **1** Of or suitable for the outdoors. **2** Fond of engaging in outdoor activities.

out·er (ou′tər) *adj.* **1** Being on the exterior side; external. **2** Farther from a center or the inside.

Outer Mon·go·li·a (mong-gō′lē-ə, mon-) MONGOLIAN PEOPLE'S REPUBLIC.

out·er·most (ou′tər-mōst′) *adj.* Farthest out.

outer space Space beyond the earth's atmosphere.

out·face (out-fās′) *v.t.* **-faced, -fac·ing 1** To weaken the confidence of or overcome by or as by an exchange of looks. **2** To defy or confront fearlessly.

out·field (out′fēld′) *n.* In baseball, cricket, etc., the players who take their positions in the outer part of the field, or the field occupied by them. —**out′field′er** *n.*

out·fit (out′fit′) *n.* **1** A set of garments or equipment for a particular purpose, as for a camping trip. **2** A set of clothes worn together and regarded as harmonious. **3** A group of people engaged in a common undertaking: a military *outfit.* —*v.t.* & *v.i.* **.fit·ted, .fit·ting** To provide with or acquire an outfit. —**out′fit′ter** *n.*

out·flank (out-flangk′) *v.t.* 1 To get around and in back of the flank of (an opposing force or army); turn the flank of. 2 To outwit; circumvent.

out·flow (out′flō′) *n.* 1 That which flows out, or the process of flowing out. 2 An outlet.

out·fox (out-foks′) *v.t. Informal* To outwit.

out·gen·er·al (out-jen′ər-əl, -jen′rəl) *v.t.* **.aled** or **.alled, .al·ing** or **.al·ling** To surpass in generalship; outmaneuver.

out·go (out-gō′) *v.t.* **.went, .gone, .go·ing** To go farther than; exceed or outstrip. —*n.* (out′gō′) *pl.* **.goes** 1 That which goes out; esp., cost or expenditure. 2 A going out.

out·go·ing (out′gō′ing) *adj.* 1 Going out; leaving. 2 Retiring, as from an office: the *outgoing* chairman. 3 Friendly; sociable; approachable. —*n.* 1 The act of going out; departure. 2 That which goes out.

out·grow (out-grō′) *v.t.* **.grew, .grown, .grow·ing** 1 To surpass in growth. 2 To grow too large for. 3 To lose or get rid of in the course of time or growth: to *outgrow* a habit.

out·growth (out′grōth′) *n.* 1 That which grows out of something else; an excrescence. 2 A consequence or offshoot; development.

out·guess (out-ges′) *v.t.* To anticipate the actions of; outwit.

out·house (out′hous′) *n. pl.* **.hous·es** A small outbuilding containing a toilet, typically built over a deep pit and without plumbing.

out·ing (ou′ting) *n.* An excursion; short pleasure trip.

out·land (out′land′) *n.* Land lying beyond the limits of occupation or cultivation. —**out′land′er** *n.*

out·land·ish (out-lan′dish) *adj.* 1 Strange, as in appearance or behavior; bizarre; freakish. 2 Situated in an unfamiliar spot; remote. 3 *Archaic* Foreign. [< OE *ūtlandisc* of the outland] —**out·land′ish·ly** *adv.* —**out·land′ish·ness** *n.*

out·last (out-last′, -läst′) *v.t.* To last longer than.

out·law (out′lô′) *n.* 1 A person deprived of the benefit of the law, as for having committed a crime. 2 One who habitually breaks or defies the law. —*v.t.* 1 To declare an outlaw; proscribe. 2 To prohibit; ban. 3 To deprive of legal force or protection, as contracts or debts. [< ON *ūtlagi*] —**out′law·ry** *n.*

out·lay (out′lā′) *n.* 1 The act of laying out or disbursing, as money or effort. 2 That which is laid out; expenditure. —*v.t.* (out·lā′) **.laid, .lay·ing** To expend (money).

out·let (out′let, -lit) *n.* 1 A passage or vent for escape or discharge. 2 A means of expressing needs or desires: an *outlet* for aggression. 3 In trade or commerce, a retail or wholesale market. 4 A point in an electrical wiring system at which an appliance can be connected.

out·line (out′līn′) *n.* 1 A bordering line that defines a figure. 2 A sketch made of such lines without shading. 3 *Often pl.* A preliminary sketch showing the principal features of a thing; general plan. —*v.t.* **.lined, .lin·ing** 1 To draw the outline of; sketch. 2 To describe in general terms; give the main points of.

out·live (out-liv′) *v.t.* **.lived, .liv·ing** 1 To live longer than. 2 To survive.

out·look (out′lŏok′) *n.* 1 A view from a particular place. 2 A place having a view. 3 A predicted or probable course; prospect: the *outlook* for the nation's economy. 4 A mental view or position.

out·ly·ing (out′lī′ing) *adj.* Situated away from the main part or center.

out·man (out-man′) *v.t.* **.manned, .man·ning** To surpass in number of men.

out·mo·ded (out-mō′did) *adj.* Out of fashion; obsolete.

out·most (out′mōst′) *adj.* OUTERMOST.

out-of-bounds (out′əv-boundz′) *adv.* Outside the playing area of a ball field. —*adj.* 1 Being outside the proper bounds. 2 Beyond normal or proper limits, as of taste or behavior; uncalled-for.

out of commission Out of order; not working.

out-of-date (out′əv-dāt′) *adj.* Old-fashioned.

out-of-door (out′əv-dôr′, -dōr′) *adj.* OUTDOOR.

out-of-doors (out′əv-dôrz′, -dōrz′) *adv., n.* OUTDOORS.

out-of-the-way (out′əv-thə-wā′) *adj.* 1 Remotely situated; difficult to reach; secluded. 2 Different from what is common.

out·pa·tient (out′pā′shənt) *n.* A patient, not an inmate, treated at a hospital or dispensary.

out·place·ment (out′plās′mənt) *n.* The help in finding other work given to a terminated employee by the former employer.

out·play (out-plā′) *v.t.* To play better than.

out·point (out-point′) *v.t.* 1 To score more points than. 2 *Naut.* To sail closer to the wind than.

out·post (out′pōst′) *n.* 1 A detachment of troops stationed at a distance from the main body as a guard against surprise. 2 The station occupied by them. 3 A settlement in an outlying or frontier area.

out·pour (out-pôr′, -pōr′) *v.t.* & *v.i.* To pour out. —*n.* (out′pôr′, -pōr′) A free outflow; a pouring out. —**out′pour′er, out′pour′ing** *n.*

out·put (out′pŏot′) *n.* 1 The quantity put out or produced in a specified time; amount or rate of production. 2 a The useful energy delivered by a machine, system, etc. b The point at which this energy is available. 3 The information derived by a computer from processing a given input.

out·rage (out′rāj′) *n.* 1 An act of shocking violence, cruelty, immorality, or viciousness. 2 A gross insult. 3 Vehement anger or resentment. —*v.t.* **.raged, .rag·ing** 1 To commit outrage upon; wrong or abuse grossly; violate; offend. 2 To make violently angry. 3 To rape. [< OF *ultrage* < L *ultra* beyond]

out·ra·geous (out-rā′jəs) *adj.* 1 Of the nature of an outrage; atrocious. 2 Indifferent to or contemptuous of reasonable authority or decency; violating the limits of tolerable behavior; shocking. 3 Unrestrained; flagrant: an *outrageous* practical joker. —**out·ra′geous·ly** *adv.* —**out·ra′geous·ness** *n.*

ou·tré (ōō-trā′) *adj.* Deviating from conventional usage; strikingly odd or exaggerated. [F]

out·reach (out-rēch′) *v.t.* 1 To reach or go beyond; surpass. 2 To reach out; extend. —*v.i.* 3 To reach out. —*n.* (out′rēch′) 1 The act of reaching out. 2 The outermost extent.

out·ride (out-rīd′) *v.t.* **.rode, .rid·den, .rid·ing** To ride faster, farther, or better than.

out·rid·er (out′rī′dər) *n.* A mounted servant who rides in advance of or beside a carriage.

out·rig·ger (out′rig′ər) *n.* 1 A part built or arranged to project beyond a natural outline, as of a vessel or machine. 2 A projecting contrivance braced to the side of a canoe to prevent capsizing. 3 *Naut.* Any construction that extends beyond the rail of a ship, as a spar for extending a sail or rope, a boom, etc.

Outrigger canoe

out·right (out′rīt′) *adj.* 1 Free from reserve or restraint; downright. 2 Complete; entire. —*adv.* (out′rīt′) 1 Without reservation or limitation; utterly; openly. 2 Without delay; straightaway.

out·sell (out-sel′) *v.t.* **.sold, .sell·ing** 1 To sell more readily; surpass in selling. 2 To sell more goods than.

out·set (out′set′) *n.* A beginning; start; opening. —**Syn.** commencement, inception, origin, initiation.

out·shine (out-shīn′) *v.* **.shone, .shin·ing** *v.t.* 1 To shine brighter than. 2 To surpass, as in excellence. —*v.i.* 3 To shine forth.

out·side (out′sīd′) *n.* 1 The external part of a thing. 2 The part or side that is seen. 3 Superficial appearance. 4 The space beyond a bounding line or surface; outer region. —**at the outside** At the farthest, longest, or most, as in an estimate. —*adj.* 1 Pertaining to, located on, or restricted to the outside; exterior. 2 Originating or situated beyond designated limits; foreign. 3 Reaching the limit; extreme: an *outside* estimate. 4 Slight; inconsequential: an *outside* possibility. —*adv.* 1 On or to the outside; externally. 2 Beyond the outside limits of. 3 In the open air; outdoors. —*prep* (out′sīd′) 1 On or to the exterior of: *outside* the box. **2** Beyond the limit of: Don't tell it *outside* the club. **3** *Informal* Except: No one knows *outside* yourself. **—outside of 1** *Informal* Except; besides. **2** OUTSIDE (prep.).

out·sid·er (out′sī′dər) *n.* **1** One who is outside; esp., one who is regarded as alien or unfamiliar by the members of a group. **2** A contestant, as in a race, considered to have only a slight chance.

out·size (out′sīz′) *n.* A size, as of clothing, that is larger than the regular sizes. **—adj.** Of unusual size: also **out′sized′.**

out·skirt (out′skûrt′) *n.* *Usu. pl.* A place far from the center; an outlying area.

out·smart (out·smärt′) *v.t.* *Informal* To outwit; fool.

out·spo·ken (out·spō′kən) *adj.* **1** Bold or free of speech; frank. **2** Spoken boldly or frankly. **—out·spo′ken·ly** *adv.* **— out·spo′ken·ness** *n.*

out·spread (out·spred′) *v.t. & v.i.* **·spread, ·spread·ing** To spread out; extend.

out·stand·ing (out·stan′ding) *adj.* **1** Standing prominently forth; preeminent. **2** Standing out; conspicuous. **3** Unsettled; continuing. **4** Still standing, as an unpaid debt.

out·stretch (out·strech′) *v.t.* **1** To stretch out; expand; extend. **2** To extend beyond.

out·strip (out·strip′) *v.t.* **·stripped, ·strip·ping 1** To leave behind; outrun, as in a race. **2** To excel; surpass.

out·take (out′tāk′) *n.* Something taken out, esp. film deleted in the editing process.

out·ward (out′wərd) *adj.* **1** Of or pertaining to the exterior of an object; outer; external. **2** Tending or directed to the outside. **3** Not inherent; extraneous; superficial. **4** Relating to the physical or bodily as distinguished from the mental. **—adv.** **1** To or in the direction of the outside; away from an inner place. **2** On the surface; superficially. **3** Away from port or home. Also **out′wards. —out′ward·ly** *adv.* **—out′ward·ness** *n.*

out·wear (out·wâr′) *v.t.* **·wore, ·worn, ·wear·ing 1** To wear or stand use better than; outlast. **2** To wear out, as by constant use.

out·weigh (out·wā′) *v.t.* **1** To weigh more than. **2** To exceed in importance, value, etc.

out·wit (out·wit′) *v.t.* **·wit·ted, ·wit·ting** To defeat by superior ingenuity or cunning.

out·work¹ (out·wûrk′) *v.t.* **·worked** or **·wrought, ·work·ing** To work faster or better than; excel in working.

out·work² (out′wûrk′) *n.* *Mil.* Any minor defensive structure built or dug out beyond the main fortifications.

out·worn (out·wôrn′) *p.p.* of OUTWEAR. **—adj.** OUTMODED.

ou·zel (ōō′zəl) *n.* **1** Any of a genus of European thrushes, as the **ring ouzel. 2** Any of various related aquatic or diving birds, as the water ouzel. [< OE *ōsle*]

o·va (ō′və) *n.pl.* of OVUM.

o·val (ō′vəl) *adj.* **1** Having the shape of an egg. **2** Elliptical. **—n.** A figure or body of such form or outline. [< L *ovum* egg] **—o′val·ly** *adv.* **—o′val·ness** *n.*

o·va·ry (ō′və·rē) *n. pl.* **·ries 1** *Biol.* The genital organ of female animals in which are produced the eggs and usu. certain sex hormones. **2** *Bot.* In flowering plants, the enlarged portion of the pistil in which the seed develops. [< L *ovum* an egg] **—o·var′i·al, o·var′i·an** *adj.*

Ovaries

A. human genital tract. a. ovary. b. Fallopian tube. c. uterus. B. floret of dandelion. a. ovary. b. pappus. c. stamen. d. pistil.

o·vate (ō′vāt) *adj.* *Bot.* Oval: said of leaves. [< L *ovum* egg] **—o′vate·ly** *adv.* • See LEAF.

o·va·tion (ō·vā′shən) *n.* A spontaneous acclamation, as of applause, cheers, etc. [< L *ovare* rejoice, exult] **—o·va′tion·al** *adj.*

ov·en (uv′ən) *n.* An enclosed chamber in which substances are heated, cooked, dried, etc. [< OE *ofen*]

ov·en·bird (uv′ən·bûrd′) *n.* **1** Any of several South American birds having dome-shaped nests. **2** An American warbler that builds a domed nest on the ground.

o·ver (ō′vər) *prep.* **1** In or to a place or position above: the sky *over* our heads. **2** So as to pass or extend across: walking *over* the bridge. **3** On the other side of: lying *over* the ocean. **4** Upon the surface or exterior of: Oil was smeared *over* the axle. **5** Here and there upon or within; throughout all parts of: traveling *over* land and sea. **6** So as to rise above, cover, or submerge: The mud is now *over* my boots. **7** So as to close or cover: a cloth tied *over* the mouth of the jar. **8** During; through: a diary kept *over* the years. **9** Up to the end of and beyond: Stay with us *over* the holidays. **10** More than; in excess of, as in amount, degree, number, extent, etc.: *over* a million dollars in assets. **11** In preference to: chosen *over* all other contenders. **12** Above in rank, authority, power, etc.: They want a strong man *over* them. **13** Upon, as an effect: His influence *over* her is profound. **14** Concerning; with regard to: time wasted *over* trifles. **15** While engaged in or partaking of: a bargain made *over* a bottle of wine. **16** So as to be concerned about the well-being of: a dog watching *over* her puppies. **—adv.** **1** Above; overhead: A plane just flew *over*. **2** So as to close, cover, or be covered: The pond froze *over*. **3** Across an intervening space, brim, or edge: Come on *over* to this side of the room. **4** At or on the other side; at a distance in a specified direction or place: *over* in Europe. **5** From one side, opinion, etc. to another: to be won *over* to a point of view. **6** From one person, condition, or custody to another: to make property *over* to someone. **7** From beginning to end; all through; completely: I'll think the matter *over*. **8** From an upright position, esp. so as to invert, reverse, or transpose: to turn one's hand *over;* to topple *over*. **9** Again: He added his figures *over*. **10** So as to overflow: The cup ran *over*. **11** So as to constitute a surplus; in excess; beyond: enough to have some left *over*. **12** Beyond a stated time; until later: Plan to stay *over*. **—all over 1** Everywhere. **2** Finished. **—adj.** **1** Finished; complete: The match is *over*. **2** On the other side; having got across: Is the boat *over* yet? **3** Outer, superior, upper, or excessive: usu. in combination: *over*hastiness. **4** In excess or addition; extra: We are three dollars *over*. **—n.** Something remaining or in addition. [< OE *ofer*]

over- *combining form* **1** Above; on top of; superior: *over*lord. **2** Passing above; going beyond the top or limit of: *over*flow. **3** Moving or causing to move downward, as from above: *over*throw. **4** Excessive or excessively; too or too much. • Following is a list of compounds formed with *over-* in the sense of def. 4.

overabound	overcapitalize	overcorrect
overabundance	overcaptious	overcorrupt
overabundant	overcareful	overcostly
overaccentuate	overcasual	overcount
overaccumulation	overcaution	overcourteous
overachiever	overcautious	overcredit
overactive	overcautiously	overcredulous
overactivity	overcentralization	overcriticize
overadvantaged	overcentralize	overcrop
overambitious	overcharitable	overcrowd
overanalyze	overcheap	overcrowded
overanxiety	overcivil	overcultivate
overanxious	overcivilized	overcultivation
overapplication	overclever	overcured
overapprehensive	overcold	overcurious
overassertive	overcommercial	overcuriousness
overassess	overcommitment	overdainty
overassessment	overcompetitive	overdecorate
overattentive	overcomplacency	overdecorative
overbake	overcomplacent	overdeliberate
overbanked	overcomplex	overdeliberation
overbitter	overcompliant	overdelicate
overblame	overcondense	overdelicately
overboastful	overconfidence	overdemand
overbold	overconfident	overdemocratic
overbooking	overconscientious	overdepress
overbright	overconscious	overdepressive
overbrilliant	overconsciousness	overdesign
overbrush	overconservatism	overdesirous
overbuilding	overconservative	overdestructive
overburden	overconsiderate	overdestructiveness
overburdensome	overconsume	overdetermined
overbusy	overconsumption	overdevoted
overbuoy	overcontribute	overdevotion
overcall	overcontrol	overdiffuse
overcapacity	overcook	overdignified

overdiligence
overdiligent
overdilute
overdirected
overdiscipline
overdistant
overdiversification
overdiversify
overdogmatic
overdominate
overdramatic
overdry
overdye
overeager
overearnest
overeasily
overeasy
overeat
overeducate
overelaborate
overelaboration
overelegant
overembellish
overemotional
overemphasis
overemphasize
overemphatic
overenthusiastic
overesteem
overestimate
overestimation
overexcitable
overexcite
overexcitement
overexercise
overexert
overexertion
overexpand
overexpansion
overexpectant
overexpenditure
overexplicit
overexpose
overextended
overexuberant
overfaithful
overfamiliar
overfanciful
overfast
overfastidious
overfastidiousness
overfat
overfatigue
overfatten
overfearful
overfed
overfeed
overfond
overfondness
overfrank
overfree
overfreedom
overfreely
overfrequency
overfrequent
overfull
overfullness
overfunctioning
overfunding
overfurnish
overfussy
overgenerous
overgenial
overgentle
overgracious
overgrasping
overgrateful
overgratify
overgraze
overgreediness
overgreedy
overgrieve
overhandle
overharden

overharsh
overhasty
overhaughty
overhelpful
overhot
overhotly
overidealistic
overillustrate
overimaginative
overimitate
overimitative
overimpress
overinclined
overindividualistic
overindulge
overindulgence
overindulgent
overindustrialization
overindustrialize
overinflate
overinflation
overinfluential
overink
overinsistent
overinsure
overintellectual
overintense
overinterest
overinventoried
overinvest
overirrigate
overirrigation
overissue
overjoyful
overjoyous
overjudicious
overlate
overlavish
overlax
overlaxness
overliberal
overliberality
overlighted
overlinger
overliteral
overliterary
overliveliness
overlively
overlofty
overlogical
overloud
overloyal
overluscious
overlustiness
overlusty
overluxuriant
overluxurious
overmagnify
overmanage
overmeasure
overmechanize
overmelt
overmerciful
overmerry
overmighty
overmild
overminutely
overmix
overmodest
overmoist
overmortgage
overmournful
overmultiply
overmystical
overnarrow
overneat
overneglect
overnegligence
overnegligent
overnervous
overnervousness
overnourish
overnumerous
overobedient

overoblige
overobvious
overoccupied
overoptimism
overoptimistic
overoptimistically
overorganized
overornamented
overpamper
overpartial
overpartiality
overparticular
overpassionate
overpatient
overpatriotic
overpay
overpensive
overpersonal
overpessimism
overpessimistic
overpessimistically
overplentiful
overplenty
overplotted
overplowed
overplump
overpolish
overpopular
overpopulate
overpopulation
overpopulous
overpositive
overpowerful
overpraise
overprecise
overpreciseness
overprecision
overpreoccupation
overprescribe
overpressure
overpretty
overprivileged
overprize
overproductive
overprogramed
overpromise
overproportion
overprotect
overproud
overprovide
overprovision
overpublicity
overpublicize
overpunctuate
overpunish
overpunishment
overqualified
overreadiness
overready
overrealistic
overrefinement
overreflection
overreflective
overregimented
overrelax
overreliant
overreligious
overrepresent
overrepresentation
overreserved
overresolute
overreward
overrighteous
overrighteousness
overrigid
overrigorous
overripe
overroast
overrough
oversalt
oversalty
oversanguine
oversaturate
oversaturation

overschematic
overscrupulous
overseason
overseasoned
oversecure
oversensitive
oversensitivity
oversentimental
overserious
oversevere
overseverely
overseverity
oversharp
overshort
overshorten
overshrink
oversilent
oversimple
oversimplicity
oversimplification
oversimplify
overskeptical
oversoak
oversoft
oversoftness
oversolemn
oversolicitous
oversophisticated
oversophistication
overspacious
overspecialization

overspecialize
overspecific
overspeculate
overspeculation
overspeculative
overspeed
overspeedily
overspend
overstaffed
oversteady
oversteer
overstimulate
overstimulation
overstrain
overstress
overstretch
overstrict
overstriving
overstudious
overstudiousness
oversubtle
oversubtlety
oversuperstitious
oversusceptible
oversuspicious
oversweet
oversystematic
oversystematize
overtalkative
overtalkativeness
overtechnical

overtender
overtenderness
overtense
overtension
overthick
overthin
overthoughtful
overthrifty
overtight
overtimid
overtimorous
overtire
overtrade
overtrain
overurbanization
overurge
overuse
overutilize
overvaluation
overvalue
overvehement
overventilate
overvoltage
overwary
overwealthy
overweary
overwet
overwilling
overwithholding
overzealous
overzealousness

o·ver·act (ō'vər·akt') v.t. & v.i. To act in an exaggerated or flamboyant manner.

o·ver·age¹ (ō'vər·ij) n. A surplus or excess.

o·ver·age² (ō'vər·āj') adj. 1 Past some specified age. 2 Too old to be of service: overage guns.

o·ver·all (ō'vər·ôl') adj. 1 From one end to the other. 2 Including everything. —adv. Generally.

o·ver·alls (ō'vər·ôlz') n.pl. Loose, coarse trousers, often with suspenders and a piece extending over the breast, worn over the clothing as protection from soiling.

o·ver·awe (ō'vər·ô') v.t. ·awed, ·aw·ing To subdue or restrain by awe.

o·ver·bal·ance (ō'vər·bal'əns) v. ·anced, ·anc·ing v.t. 1 To exceed in weight, importance, etc. 2 To cause to lose balance. —n. Excess of weight or value.

o·ver·bear (ō'vər·bâr') v. ·bore, ·borne, ·bear·ing v.t. 1 To crush or bear down by physical weight or force. 2 To prevail over; dominate. —v.i. 3 To be too fruitful.

o·ver·bear·ing (ō'vər·bâr'ing) adj. 1 Arrogant; dictatorial. 2 Of greatest importance; dominant. 3 Overwhelming. —o'ver·bear'ing·ly adv. —o'ver·bear'ing·ness n. —Syn. 1 haughty, arbitrary, domineering, presumptuous, dogmatic, imperious.

o·ver·bid (ō'vər·bid') v.t. & v.i. ·bid, ·bid·den or ·bid, ·bid·ding 1 To outbid (someone). 2 To bid more than the fair value of (something). —n. A bid that is excessive or higher than one previously made.

o·ver·blown (ō'vər·blōn') adj. 1 Swollen or blown up. 2 Exaggerated. 3 Pretentious; flamboyant.

o·ver·board (ō'vər·bôrd', ·bōrd') adv. Over the side of or out of a boat or ship. —go overboard Informal To be extremely or excessively enthusiastic. —throw overboard To get rid of.

o·ver·cast (ō'vər·kast', ·käst', ō'vər·kast', ·käst') v.t. ·cast, ·cast·ing 1 To overcloud; darken. 2 To sew, as the edge of a fabric, so as to prevent raveling. —adj. 1 Clouded; dark; gloomy. 2 Sewn with long wrapping stitches. —n. A covering, esp. of clouds over the sky.

o·ver·charge (ō'vər·chärj') v.t. ·charged, ·charg·ing 1 To charge (someone) too high a price. 2 To load or fill to excess; overburden. 3 To exaggerate. —n. An excessive charge.

o·ver·cloud (ō'vər·kloud') v.t. 1 To cover with clouds. 2 To darken or make gloomy.

o·ver·coat (ō'vər·kōt') n. A warm outdoor coat worn over a suit or other clothing.

o·ver·come (ō'vər·kum') v.t. 1 To get the better of; defeat; conquer. 2 To prevail over or surmount, as difficulties, obstacles, etc. **3** To make helpless, as by emotion, sickness, etc. —*v.i.* **4** To win. [< OE *ofercuman*] **—o'ver·com'er** *n.*

o·ver·com·pen·sate (ō'vər·kom'pən·sāt) *v.* **·sat·ed, ·sat·ing** *v.i.* *Psychol.* To engage in exaggerated or excessive forms of behavior or attitudes in order to compensate for the fact or feeling of inferiority. —*v.t.* **2** To make too great a compensation for. **—o'ver·com'pen·sa'tion** *n.* **—o'ver·com·pen'sa·to·ry** (-kəm·pen'sə·tôr'ē, -tō'rē) *adj.*

o·ver·de·vel·op (ō'vər·di·vel'əp) *v.t.* To develop excessively, esp. to subject (an exposed plate or film) to chemicals to too great a degree. **—o'ver·de·vel'op·ment** *n.*

o·ver·do (ō'vər·do͞o') *v.* **·did, ·done, ·do·ing** *v.t.* **1** To do excessively; carry too far. **2** To overtax; exhaust. **3** To cook too much, as meat. **4** To exaggerate. —*v.i.* **5** To do too much.

o·ver·dose (ō'vər·dōs') *v.t.* **·dosed, ·dos·ing** To dose to excess. —*n.* (ō'vər·dōs') An excessive dose.

o·ver·draft (ō'vər·draft', -dräft') *n.* **1** The act of overdrawing an account, as at a bank. **2** The amount by which a check or draft exceeds the sum against which it is drawn. Also **o'ver·draught'** (-draft', -dräft') *n.*

o·ver·draw (ō'vər·drô') *v.t.* **·drew, ·drawn, ·draw·ing** **1** To draw against (an account) beyond one's credit. **2** To exaggerate.

o·ver·drive (ō'vər·drīv') *n.* *Mech.* A gear which causes the driving shaft of a machine to turn at a speed greater than that of the engine.

o·ver·due (ō'vər·dyo͞o') *adj.* **1** Remaining unpaid after becoming due. **2** Past due: an *overdue* plane or train.

o·ver·flight (ō'vər·flīt') *n.* The flight of an aircraft over or beyond a place or area; esp., such a flight made for reconnaissance or espionage purposes.

o·ver·flow (ō'vər·flō') *v.* **·flowed, ·flown, ·flow·ing** *v.i.* **1** To flow or run over the brim or bank, as water, rivers, etc. **2** To be filled beyond capacity; spill over. **3** To be extremely full. —*v.t.* **4** To flow over the brim or bank of. **5** To flow or spread over; cover. **6** To fill beyond capacity; cause to overflow. —*n.* (ō'vər·flō') **1** The act of overflowing. **2** That which flows over; excess; surplus. **3** A passage or outlet for liquid. **—o'ver·flow'ing** *adj.* **—o'ver·flow'ing·ly** *adv.*

o·ver·grow (ō'vər·grō') *v.* **·grew, ·grown, ·grow·ing** *v.t.* **1** To grow over; cover with growth. **2** To grow too big for; outgrow. —*v.i.* **3** To grow or increase excessively; grow too large. **—o'ver·grown'** *adj.*

o·ver·growth (ō'vər·grōth') *n.* **1** Luxuriant or excessive growth. **2** A growth upon or over something.

o·ver·hand (ō'vər·hand') *adj.* **1** Done with the hand above the level of the elbow or shoulder. **2** In sewing, done by carrying the thread over two edges to sew them together. **3** With the hand above the object which it holds, seizes, or throws. —*adv.* In an overhand manner. —*v.t.* To sew overhand. —*n.* An overhand stroke.

o·ver·hang (ō'vər·hang') *v.* **·hung, ·hang·ing** *v.t.* **1** To hang or project over (something); jut over. **2** To impend over; threaten. —*v.i.* **3** To hang or jut over something. —*n.* Something that projects over another thing; also, the amount or degree of such projection.

o·ver·haul (ō'vər·hôl') *v.t.* **1** To examine carefully, as for needed repairs; also, to make such repairs. **2** To catch up with; gain on. —*n.* (ō'vər·hôl') A thorough inspection and repair. Also **o'ver·haul'ing.**

o·ver·head (ō'vər·hed') *adj.* **1** Situated, working, or passing above or over the head. **2** Of or pertaining to the overhead of a business. —*n.* General expenditure applicable to all departments of a business, as light, heat, taxes, etc. —*adv.* (ō'vər·hed') Above one's head; aloft.

o·ver·hear (ō'vər·hir') *v.t.* **·heard, ·hear·ing** To hear (something said or someone speaking) without the knowledge or intention of the speaker. **—o'ver·hear'er** *n.*

o·ver·heat (ō'vər·hēt') *v.t.* **1** To heat to excess. —*v.i.* **2** To become too hot.

o·ver·joy (ō'vər·joi') *v.t.* To delight or please greatly.

o·ver·kill (ō'vər·kil') *n.* **1** The capacity of a nation's nuclear weapons which is considered in excess of the number needed to demolish all key enemy targets. **2** *Informal* Any action regarded as excessive or extreme.

o·ver·land (ō'vər·land') *adj.* Journeying or accomplished by or principally by land. —*adv.* Across, over, or via land.

o·ver·lap (ō'vər·lap') *v.t.* & *v.i.* **·lapped, ·lap·ping** **1** To lie or extend partly over or upon (another or one another). **2** To extend in time over or into (another period of time, activity, etc.). —*n.* (ō'vər·lap') The state, extent, or place of overlapping; also, the part that overlaps.

o·ver·lay (ō'vər·lā') *n.* **1** Anything that overlies, covers, or partly covers something. **2** Something used to overlay something else, as ornamental work on wood. —*v.t.* (ō'vər·lā') **·laid, ·lay·ing** **1** To cover, as with a decorative pattern or layer. **2** To lay or place over or upon something else.

o·ver·leap (ō'vər·lēp') *v.t.* **1** To leap over or across. **2** To omit; overlook. **3** To leap farther than; outleap. **—overleap oneself** To miss one's purpose by going too far.

o·ver·lie (ō'vər·lī') *v.t.* **·lay, ·lain, ·ly·ing** To lie over or upon.

o·ver·load (ō'vər·lōd') *v.t.* To load excessively. —*n.* (ō'vər·lōd') An excessive load.

o·ver·look (ō'vər·lo͞ok') *v.t.* **1** To fail to see or notice; miss. **2** To disregard purposely or indulgently; ignore. **3** To look over or see from a higher place. **4** To afford a view of: The castle *overlooks* the harbor. **5** To supervise; oversee. —*n.* (ō'vər·lo͞ok') **1** An elevated place from which one may view the surroundings; also, the view from such a place. **2** Oversight; neglect.

o·ver·lord (ō'vər·lôrd') *n.* **1** A superior lord or chief. **2** One who holds supremacy over another. **—o'ver·lord'ship** *n.*

o·ver·ly (ō'vər·lē) *adv.* To an excessive degree; too much; too.

o·ver·man (ō'vər·man') *v.t.* **·manned, ·man·ning** To provide with more men than necessary: The ship was *overmanned.*

o·ver·mas·ter (ō'vər·mas'tər, -mäs'-) *v.t.* To overcome; overpower. **—o'ver·mas'ter·ing** *adj.*

o·ver·match (ō'vər·mach') *v.t.* To be more than a match for; surpass.

o·ver·much (ō'vər·much') *adj.* Too much. —*adv.* In too great a degree. —*n.* An excess; too much.

o·ver·night (ō'vər·nīt') *adj.* **1** Of, pertaining to, or caused by the previous evening: *overnight* euphoria that vanished at dawn. **2** Lasting or staying one night: an *overnight* flight; an *overnight* guest. **3** Used for a brief visit: an *overnight* bag. **4** Occurring or appearing quickly or suddenly: *overnight* fame. —*adv.* (ō'vər·nīt') **1** During or through the night: to stay *overnight.* **2** On or during the previous evening: remembering a joke he'd heard *overnight.* **3** Quickly or suddenly: to achieve success *overnight.*

o·ver·pass (ō'vər·pas', -päs') *v.t.* **1** To pass across, over, or through; cross. **2** To surpass or exceed. **3** To overlook; disregard. **4** To transgress. —*n.* (ō'vər·pas', -päs') An elevated section of highway or a pedestrian bridge crossing other lines of travel.

o·ver·play (ō'vər·plā') *v.t.* To play or act (a part or role) to excess; overdo; exaggerate. **—overplay one's hand** To exaggerate one's value, importance, strength, etc., and suffer a defeat as a result.

o·ver·pow·er (ō'vər·pou'ər) *v.t.* **1** To gain supremacy over; subdue; overcome. **2** To supply with more power than necessary. **—o'ver·pow'er·ing** *adj.* **—o'ver·pow'er·ing·ly** *adv.*

o·ver·print (ō'vər·print') *v.t.* To print additional material on (matter already printed). —*n.* (ō'vər·print') Anything printed over another impression, as a word, symbol, etc., printed on a stamp.

o·ver·pro·duce (ō'vər·prə·dyo͞os') *v.t.* **·duced, ·duc·ing** To produce too much of or so as to exceed demand.

o·ver·pro·duc·tion (ō'vər·prə·duk'shən) *n.* Production in excess of demand, or of the possibility of profitable sale.

o·ver·rate (ō'vər·rāt') *v.t.* **·rat·ed, ·rat·ing** To rate or value too highly.

o·ver·reach (ō'vər·rēch') *v.t.* **1** To reach over or beyond. **2** To spread over; cover. **3** To defeat (oneself), as by trying too hard or being too clever. **4** To get the advantage of, as by cheating; outwit. —*v.i.* **5** To reach too far. **—o'ver·reach'er** *n.*

o·ver·re·act (ō'vər·rē·akt') *v.i.* To react to a person, situation, etc., in an excessively emotional or uncontrolled manner. **—o'ver·re·ac'tion** *n.*

o·ver·ride (ō'vər·rīd') *v.t.* **·rode, ·rid·den, ·rid·ing** **1** To ride over or across. **2** To trample down. **3** To prevail over;

conquer; dominate. **4** To disregard summarily; overrule. **5** To ride (a horse) to exhaustion.

o·ver·rid·ing (ō′vər·rī′ding, ō′vər·rī′-) *adj.* Chief; primary; principal: an *overriding* concern.

o·ver·rule (ō′vər·rōōl′) *v.t.* **·ruled, ·rul·ing 1** To decide or rule against; nullify by superior authority; set aside; invalidate. **2** To prevail over.

o·ver·run (ō′vər·run′) *v.* **·ran, ·run, ·run·ning** *v.t.* **1** To spread or swarm over, esp. harmfully, as vermin or invaders do. **2** To run or flow over so as to cover. **3** To spread rapidly across or throughout: said of fads, ideas, etc. **4** To run or extend beyond; pass the limit of. —*v.i.* **5** To run over; overflow. **6** To pass the usual or desired limit. —*n.* (ō′vər·run′) **1** The act or an instance of overrunning. **2** The amount or extent of overrunning.

o·ver·seas (ō′vər·sēz′) *adv.* Beyond the sea; abroad. —*adj.* With, for, from, or to countries beyond or across the sea: an *overseas* phone call; *overseas* commerce; *overseas* friends.

o·ver·see (ō′vər·sē′) *v.t.* **·saw, ·seen, ·see·ing 1** To direct or supervise. **2** To survey; watch.

o·ver·se·er (ō′vər·sē′ər) *n.* A person who oversees; esp. one who directs the work of others.

o·ver·sell (ō′vər·sel′) *v.t.* **·sold, ·sell·ing 1** To sell more than one can deliver. **2** To make exaggerated claims for (a person or thing). **3** To persuade by exaggerated claims.

o·ver·set (ō′vər·set′) *v.* **·set, ·set·ting** *v.t.* **1** To upset mentally or physically. **2** To cause to overturn. —*v.i.* **3** To overturn. —*n.* (ō′vər·set′) A turning over; upset.

o·ver·shad·ow (ō′vər·shad′ō) *v.t.* **1** To render unimportant or insignificant by comparison; loom above; dominate. **2** To throw a shadow over; dim; obscure. —**Syn.** **1** prevail over, master, domineer, control.

o·ver·shoe (ō′vər·shōō′) *n.* A shoe, as of rubber, worn for protection over another.

o·ver·shoot (ō′vər·shōōt′) *v.* **·shot, ·shoot·ing** *v.t.* **1** To shoot, pass, fly, etc. over or beyond. **2** To go beyond; exceed, as a limit. —*v.i.* **3** To shoot or go too far or beyond a mark.

o·ver·shot (ō′vər·shot′) *adj.* **1** Projecting, as the upper jaw beyond the lower jaw. **2** Driven by water flowing over from above: an *overshot* wheel.

o·ver·sight (ō′vər·sīt′) *n.* **1** An error due to inattention; an inadvertent mistake or omission. **2** Watchful supervision.

Overshot wheel

o·ver·size (ō′vər·sīz′) *adj.* Too large or larger than regular. —*n.* A size that is larger than regular sizes. —**o′ver·sized′** *adj.*

o·ver·skirt (ō′vər·skûrt′) *n.* A skirt worn over another skirt.

o·ver·sleep (ō′vər·slēp′) *v.i.* **·slept, ·sleep·ing** To sleep beyond an intended time for waking.

o·ver·spread (ō′vər·spred′) *v.t.* **·spread, ·spread·ing** To spread or extend over.

o·ver·state (ō′vər·stāt′) *v.t.* **·stat·ed, ·stat·ing** To state in too strong terms; exaggerate. —**o′ver·state′ment** *n.*

o·ver·stay (ō′vər·stā′) *v.t.* To stay beyond the proper limits or duration of.

o·ver·step (ō′vər·step′) *v.t.* **·stepped, ·step·ping** To step over or go beyond; exceed (some limit or restriction).

o·ver·stock (ō′vər·stok′) *v.t.* To stock more than is required or can be handled. —*n.* (ō′vər·stok′) An excessive stock.

o·ver·strung (ō′vər·strung′) *adj.* Too sensitive or highly strung.

o·ver·stuff (ō′vər·stuf′) *v.t.* **1** To stuff excessively. **2** To cover, as a chair or sofa, with deeply stuffed upholstery.

o·ver·sub·scribe (ō′vər·səb·skrīb′) *v.t.* **·scribed, ·scrib·ing** To subscribe for more than is offered or available.

o·ver·sup·ply (ō′vər·sə·plī′) *n. pl.* **·plies** An excessive supply. —*v.t.* (ō′vər·sə·plī′) **·plied, ·ply·ing** To supply in excess.

o·vert (ō′vûrt, ō·vûrt′) *adj.* Open to view; outwardly manifest. [< OF, pp. of *ovrir* to open] —**o·vert′ly** *adv.* —**Syn.** apparent, evident, obvious, clear, patent.

o·ver·take (ō′vər·tāk′) *v.t.* **·took, ·tak·en, ·tak·ing 1** To catch up with. **2** To catch up with and go past; leave behind. **3** To come upon suddenly.

o·ver·tax (ō′vər·taks′) *v.t.* **1** To tax too much. **2** To put too heavy a strain on. —**o′ver·tax·a′tion** (-tak·sā′shən) *n.*

o·ver-the-count·er (ō′vər·thə·koun′tər) *adj.* **1** Not sold on the floor of a stock exchange: said of certain stocks and bonds. **2** Sold lawfully without a prescription, as drugs.

o·ver·throw (ō′vər·thrō′) *v.t.* **·threw, ·thrown, ·throw·ing 1** To throw over or down; upset. **2** To bring down or remove from power by force; defeat; ruin. —*n.* (ō′vər·thrō′) **1** The act of overthrowing. **2** The condition of being overthrown.

o·ver·time (ō′vər·tīm′) *v.t.* **·timed, ·tim·ing** *Phot.* To expose too long, as a plate or film. —*n.* (ō′vər·tīm′) **1** Time spent beyond some specified limit. **2** Wages paid for work done during such time. —*adj.* Of, during, or for extra working time: *overtime* pay. —*adv.* Beyond the stipulated time.

o·ver·tone (ō′vər·tōn′) *n.* **1** *Music* A higher tone heard with and above the fundamental tone produced by a musical instrument or the human voice. **2** The color of the light reflected, as by a painted surface. **3** An association, connotation, implication, etc., as of language, thoughts, etc.

o·ver·top (ō′vər·top′) *v.t.* **·topped, ·top·ping 1** To rise above the top of; tower over. **2** To surpass; excel.

o·ver·ture (ō′vər·chər) *n.* **1** *Music* An instrumental prelude, as to an opera or other large work. **2** An introductory proposal or offer; approach. [< L *apertura* an opening]

o·ver·turn (ō′vər·tûrn′) *v.t.* **1** To turn or throw over; capsize; upset. **2** To destroy the power of; overthrow; defeat. —*v.i.* **3** To turn over; capsize; upset. —*n.* (ō′vər·tûrn′) The act of overturning or the state of being overturned.

o·ver·view (ō′vər·vyōō′) *n.* A broad survey or review of a subject, field of activity, etc.

o·ver·ween·ing (ō′vər·wē′ning) *adj.* Presumptuous; arrogant. [< OE *ofer* over + *wēnan* think] —**o′ver·ween′ing·ly** *adv.* —**o′ver·ween′ing·ness** *n.* —**Syn.** haughty, overbearing, patronizing, pompous.

o·ver·weigh (ō′vər·wā′) *v.t.* **1** To outweigh. **2** To oppress; burden.

o·ver·weight (ō′vər·wāt′) *n.* **1** Excess of weight, as beyond the legal or customary amount. **2** More than normal weight; too much or burdensome weight. —*adj.* Being more than the normal or permitted weight. —*v.t.* (ō′vər·wāt′) To weigh down; burden.

o·ver·whelm (ō′vər·ʰwelm′) *v.t.* **1** To bury or submerge completely, as with a wave or flood. **2** To overcome or defeat by or as by irresistible force or numbers; crush. —**o′ver·whelm′ing** *adj.* —**o′ver·whelm′ing·ly** *adv.*

o·ver·work (ō′vər·wûrk′) *v.t.* **·worked** or **·wrought, ·work·ing 1** To cause to work too hard. **2** To work on or use excessively: to *overwork* an argument. —*v.i.* **3** To work too hard or too long. —*n.* (ō′vər·wûrk′) Excessive work.

o·ver·write (ō′vər·rīt′) *v.t. & v.i.* **·wrote, ·writ·ten, ·writ·ing 1** To write over (other writing). **2** To write too much or in too elaborate or labored a style about (a subject).

o·ver·wrought (ō′vər·rôt′) *adj.* **1** Worked up or excited excessively; strained. **2** Having the surface adorned. **3** Too elaborate; overdone.

ovi- *combining form* Egg; of or pertaining to eggs: *oviparous.* [< L *ovum* an egg]

o·vi·duct (ō′vi·dukt) *n.* The passage through which ova are conveyed from an ovary.

o·vi·form (ō′vi·fôrm) *adj.* Egg-shaped.

o·vip·a·rous (ō·vip′ər·əs) *adj.* Reproducing by means of eggs that are hatched outside the body. [< ovi- + L *parere* give birth to] —**o·vip′a·rous·ly** *adv.* —**o·vip′a·rous·ness** *n.*

o·vi·pos·i·tor (ō′vi·poz′ə·tər) *n.* A special organ in certain female insects, by which the eggs are deposited.

o·void (ō′void) *adj.* Egg-shaped: also **o·voi′dal.** —*n.* An egg-shaped body.

o·vu·late (ov′yə·lāt, ōv′-) *v.i.* **·lat·**

Ovipositor of ichneumon fly

---

ed, ·lat·ing To produce and discharge ova from an ovary. —
o'vu·la'tion n.

o·vule (ov'yōōl, ōv'-) n. 1 Bot. The rudimentary body
within the ovary which, upon fertilization, becomes the
seed. 2 A small egg. [< L ovum an egg] —o'vu·lar, o·vu·
lar·y (ō'vyə·ler'ē) adj.

o·vum (ō'vəm) n. pl. o·va (ō'və) Biol. 1 A female reproductive cell; an egg. 2 OVULE. [L]

owe (ō) v. owed, ow·ing v.t. 1 To be indebted to (a person).
2 To be obligated to pay or repay the sum of. 3 To be
obligated to render or offer: to owe an apology. 4 To have
or possess by virtue of gift, labor, etc.: with to: He owes his
success to his own efforts. 5 To cherish (a certain feeling)
toward another: to owe a grudge. —v.i. 6 To be in debt.
[< OE āgan]

OWI, O.W.I. Office of War Information.

ow·ing (ō'ing) adj. Due; yet to be paid: six dollars owing.
—owing to On account of; because of.

owl (oul) n. 1 Any of a large order of predatory nocturnal
birds having large forward-looking eyes, a short, sharply
hooked bill, long powerful claws, and a circular facial disk
of radiating feathers. 2 A person having a solemn,
thoughtful appearance, nocturnal habits, etc. [< OE ūle]
—owl'ish adj. —owl'ish·ly adv. —owl'ish·ness n.

owl·et (ou'lit) n. 1 A small owl. 2 A young owl.

own (ōn) adj. Belonging or relating to oneself or itself: my
own idea; under its own momentum. —n. That which belongs to oneself or itself: The success was her own. —
come into one's own 1 To obtain possession of one's
property. 2 To receive one's reward, as recognition or
praise. —**hold one's own** To maintain one's place, position, condition, etc. —**on one's own** Entirely dependent
on one's self for support or success. —v.t. 1 To have or hold
as one's own; possess. 2 To admit or acknowledge. —v.i. 3
To confess: with to. —**own up (to)** To confess (to). [< OE
āgen, orig. pp. of āgan owe, possess] —own'a·ble adj. —
own'er n.

own·er·ship (ō'nər·ship) n. 1 The state of being an
owner. 2 Legal title to something.

ox (oks) n. pl. ox·en (ok'sən) 1 An adult castrated bull, used
as a draft animal or for food. 2 Any bovine mammal. [<
OE oxa]

ox·al·ic acid (ok·sal'ik) A poisonous organic acid found
in wood sorrel and other plants and made synthetically,
used in bleaching and dyeing.

ox·a·lis (ok·sal'is) n. WOOD SORREL. [< Gk. < oxys sharp,
acid]

ox·blood (oks'blud') n. A deep red color.

ox·bow (oks'bō') n. 1 A U-shaped piece of wood in an ox
yoke, that forms a collar for the ox. 2 A bend in a river
shaped like this.

ox·eye (oks'ī') n. 1 Any of various plants having composite flowers with yellow rays and a dark center. 2 The
common N. American daisy: also **oxeye daisy.**

ox·eyed (oks'īd') adj. Having large, calm eyes like an ox.

ox·ford (oks'fərd) n. 1 A kind of low-cut shoe laced over
the instep: also **oxford shoe.** 2 A cloth made in a basketlike
weave, used for men's shirts, etc.: also **oxford cloth.** [<
Oxford, England]

oxford gray A very dark gray.

ox·heart (oks'härt') n. A variety of sweet cherry.

ox·i·da·tion (ok'sə·dā'shən) n. Chem. 1 The union of a
substance with oxygen. 2 The process by which atoms,
ions, or radicals lose electrons and gain in positive electric
charge. —ox'i·da'tive adj.

ox·ide (ok'sīd) n. Any binary compound of oxygen either

with an element or with an organic radical. [< F ox(ygène)
oxygen + (ac)ide acid]

ox·i·dize (ok'sə·dīz) v. ·dized, ·diz·ing v.t. 1 To cause the
oxidation of. —v.i. 2 To undergo oxidation. Brit. sp. ·dise.
—ox'i·diz'a·ble adj. —ox'i·diz'er n.

ox·lip (oks'lip') n. A species of primrose having yellow
flowers. [< OE oxanslippe, lit., ox dung]

Oxon. of Oxford (Univ.) (L Oxoniensis)

Ox·o·ni·an (ok·sō'nē·ən) adj. Of or pertaining to Oxford,
England, or to its university. —n. 1 A student or graduate
of Oxford University. 2 A native or inhabitant of Oxford,
England.

ox·tail (oks'tāl') n. The tail of an ox, esp. when skinned
for use in soup.

oxy-¹ combining form 1 Sharp; keen: oxymoron. 2 Acid:
oxygen. [< Gk. oxys sharp, keen]

oxy-² combining form Chem. Of or containing oxygen:
oxyacetylene. [< OXYGEN]

ox·y·a·cet·y·lene (ok'sē·ə·set'ə·lēn) adj. Designating or
pertaining to a mixture of acetylene and oxygen, used as
a high-temperature fuel in welding torches.

ox·y·gen (ok'sə·jin) n. A highly reactive element (symbol
O) essential to life, occurring as an odorless gas in the
atmosphere and in chemical combination in water and
rocks, and comprising about 50 percent of the material in
and above the earth's crust. [< oxy-¹ + -gen]

ox·y·gen·ate (ok'sə·jən·āt') v.t. ·at·ed, ·at·ing To treat,
combine, or mix with oxygen. —ox'y·gen·a'tion n.

ox·y·gen·ize (ok'sə·jən·īz') v.t. ·ized, ·iz·ing 1 OXIDIZE. 2
OXYGENATE.

oxygen mask A device worn over the nose and mouth
to deliver oxygen from a container when atmospheric oxygen is inadequate or absent.

oxygen tent A tentlike chamber placed over a patient's
bed and supplied with oxygen as an aid to breathing.

ox·y·hy·dro·gen (ok'si·hī'drə·jən) adj. Of, pertaining
to, or using a mixture of oxygen and hydrogen, esp. to
produce high temperatures.

ox·y·mo·ron (ok'si·môr'on, -mō'ron) n. pl. ·mo·ra
(-môr'ə, -mō'rə) A figure of speech in which contradictory
or incongruous terms are brought together, as in "solemn
jests." [< Gk. oxys keen + mōros foolish]

o·yez (ō'yez, ō'yā) interj. Hear! hear ye! an introductory
word to call attention to a proclamation, as by a court
crier: usu. repeated three times. Also **o'yes** (ō'yes). [< OF
oyez, imperative of oir hear]

oys·ter (ois'tər) n. Any of a family of irregularly shaped
marine bivalves, including various edible species. [< Gk.
ostreon]

oyster bed An area on the
ocean floor where oysters are cultivated.

oyster crab Any of various
minute crabs that live in the gill
cavities of oysters, clams, etc.

oyster plant SALSIFY.

oz. (pl. ozs.) ounce.

o·zone (ō'zōn) n. 1 An acrid, unstable, allotropic form of oxygen
having three atoms per molecule,
formed by electric discharge in
air and by high-energy solar
radiation in the upper atmos-
phere. 2 Informal Air that is pure and refreshing. [< Gk.
ozein to smell] —o·zon·ic (ō·zon'ik, ō·zō'nik), o·zo·nous
(ō'zə·nəs) adj.

Oyster
a. shell. b. hinge.
c. mantle. d. gills.

P

P, p (pē) *n. pl.* **P's, p's** or **Ps, ps** (pēz) **1** The 16th letter of the English alphabet. **2** Any spoken sound representing the letter *P* or *p*. **3** Something shaped like a P. —*adj.* Shaped like a P.

P pawn (chess); phosphorus.

P. president.

p. page; part; participle; past; penny; pint; pitcher; softly (Ital. *piano*).

pa (pä) *n. Informal* Papa.

PA Pennsylvania (P.O. abbr.); public address (system).

P.A., P/A power of attorney.

Pa protactinium.

Pa. Pennsylvania.

p.a. participial adjective; per annum.

pab·u·lum (pab′yə·ləm) *n.* Food. [< L *pabulum* fodder]

Pac. Pacific.

pace¹ (pās) *n.* **1** A step in walking. **2** A conventional measure of length approximating the average length of stride in walking, usu. estimated at from 30 to 40 inches. **3** The manner of movement in going on the legs; gait, esp. of a horse. **4** Rate of speed in moving on the legs: a fast *pace*. **5** Rate of movement or work, or of any process or activity. **6** A gait of a horse, etc. in which both feet on the same side are lifted and moved forward at once. —*v.* **paced, pac·ing** *v.t.* **1** To walk back and forth across. **2** To measure by paces. **3** To set or make the pace for. **4** To train to a certain gait or pace. —*v.i.* **5** To walk with slow or regular steps. **6** To move at a pace. [< L *passus* step] —**pac′er** *n.*

pa·ce² (pā′sē) *prep.* With the permission of: used to express courteous disagreement. [L, ablative of *pax, pacis* peace, pardon]

pace·mak·er (pās′mā′kər) *n.* **1** One who makes or sets the pace for another in a race. **2** A node of muscle fibers in the heart that regulates the heartbeat. **3** Any of various devices, usu. electronic, used to regulate the heartbeat. —**pace′mak′ing** *adj., n.*

pach·y·derm (pak′ə·dûrm) *n.* Any of certain thick-skinned, hoofed mammals, as an elephant, hippopotamus, or rhinoceros. [< Gk. *pachys* thick + *derma* skin] —**pach′y·der′ma·tous, pach′y·der′mous** *adj.*

pa·cif·ic (pə·sif′ik) *adj.* **1** Pertaining to the making of peace; leading to peace. **2** Peaceable; calm. [< L < *pax, pacis* peace + *facere* make] —**pa·cif′i·cal·ly** *adv.*

Pa·cif·ic (pə·sif′ik) *adj.* **1** Of, near, in, on, or pertaining to the Pacific Ocean. **2** Of, near, on, or pertaining to the w coast of the U.S. —*n.* The Pacific Ocean.

pac·i·fi·ca·tion (pas′ə·fə·kā′shən) *n.* The act of pacifying, or the state of being pacified. —**pa·cif′i·ca·tor** *n.* —**pa·cif′i·ca·to·ry** (-kə·tôr′ē, -tō′rē) *adj.*

Pacific Standard Time See STANDARD TIME.

pac·i·fi·er (pas′ə·fi′ər) *n.* **1** One who or that which pacifies; a peacemaker. **2** A rubber nipple or ring for a baby to suck.

pac·i·fism (pas′ə·fiz′əm) *n.* Opposition to violence, esp. war, for any purpose, often accompanied by the refusal to bear arms by reason of conscience or religious conviction. —**pac′i·fist** *adj., n.* —**pac′i·fis′tic** *adj.*

pac·i·fy (pas′ə·fī) *v.t.* **·fied, ·fy·ing 1** To bring peace to; end war or strife in. **2** To allay the anger or agitation of. [< L *pax, pacis* peace + *facere* make] —**Syn. 2** appease, calm, allay, tranquilize.

pack¹ (pak) *n.* **1** A bundle or large package, esp. one to be carried on the back of a man or animal. **2** A full set of like or associated things handled or considered as a unit: a *pack* of cards; a *pack* of lies. **3** A group of animals, as dogs or wolves. **4** Any gang or band. **5** A large area of floating broken ice: also **ice pack. 6** A cosmetic paste spread on the skin and allowed to dry. **7** A wrapping about a patient: a wet or cold *pack.* —*v.t.* **1** To make a pack or bundle of. **2** To place compactly in a trunk, box, etc. **3** To fill compactly, as for storing or carrying. **4** To compress tightly; crowd together. **5** To fill to overflowing; cram. **6** To cover, fill, or surround so as to prevent leakage, damage, etc. **7** To load with a pack; burden. **8** To carry or transport, as on pack animals. **9** To carry habitually: to *pack* a gun. **10** To send or dispatch summarily: with *off* or *away.* **11** To treat (a patient) with a pack. **12** *Slang* To be able to inflict: He *packs* a wallop. —*v.i.* **13** To place one's clothing and belongings in trunks, boxes, etc., for storing or carrying. **14** To crowd together. **15** To settle in a hard, firm mass. **16** To leave in haste: often with *off* or *away.* —**send packing** To send away or dismiss abruptly. [ME *pakke*] —**pack′er** *n.*

pack² (pak) *v.t.* To arrange, select, or manipulate to one's own advantage: to *pack* a jury.

pack·age (pak′ij) *n.* **1** Something wrapped up or bound together; a parcel. **2** A receptacle in which something is contained or packed. **3** A combination of items considered as a unit: a salary increase and fringe benefits all in one *package.* —*v.t.* **·aged, ·ag·ing 1** To bind or make into a package or bundle. **2** To offer as a package. —**pack′ag·er** *n.*

package store *U.S.* A store that sells liquor by the bottle only, for consumption elsewhere.

pack animal An animal, as a horse or mule, used to carry packs or burdens.

pack·et (pak′it) *n.* **1** A small package; parcel. **2** A boat carrying passengers, freight, and mail, esp. along a coast: also **packet boat.**

pack·ing (pak′ing) *n.* **1** The act or process of packing. **2** The canning or putting up of meat, fish, fruit, etc., for market. **3** Material used to protect or insulate something.

packing plant *U.S.* A factory where meats and meat products are processed and packed; also, a similar establishment where other foodstuffs are processed and packed. Also **packing house.**

pack rat 1 Any of various North American rats that collect and store small objects in their nests. **2** *Slang* A person addicted to collecting and saving various, often useless, objects.

pack·sack (pak′sak′) *n.* A canvas or leather sack strapped across the shoulders for those traveling on foot.

pack·sad·dle (pak′sad′l) *n.* A saddle for a pack animal, to which the packs are fastened so as to balance evenly.

pack·thread (pak′thred′) *n.* Strong thread or twine used for binding packages.

pact (pakt) *n.* An agreement, esp. between nations; compact. [< L *pactum* agreement]

pad¹ (pad) *n.* **1** Anything stuffed and soft enough to protect from jarring, friction, etc.; cushion. **2** A launching pad. **3** A soft saddle. **4** A number of sheets of paper gummed together at the edge. **5** A floating leaf of an aquatic plant: a lily *pad.* **6 a** A soft cushion of flesh under the toes of an animal. **b** An animal's footprint. **7** *Slang* A room or apartment; lodgings. —*v.t.* **pad·ded, pad·ding 1** To stuff, line, or protect with pads or padding. **2** To lengthen (speech or writing) by inserting unnecessary matter. **3** To expand (an expense account) by recording nonexistent expenditures.

pad² (pad) *v.i.* **pad·ded, pad·ding 1** To travel by walking; tramp. **2** To move with soft, almost noiseless footsteps. —*n.* A dull, padded sound.

pad³ (pad) *n.* An easy-paced road horse. Also **pad horse.** [< LG *pad* path]

pad·ding (pad′ing) *n.* **1** The act of stuffing or forming a pad. **2** Any material used to make a pad. **3** Matter used in writing to fill space.

pad·dle (pad′l) *n.* **1** An implement resembling a short oar with a broad blade at one or both ends, used to propel a canoe or small boat. **2** A similarly shaped implement for inflicting bodily punishment. —v. **·dled, ·dling** v.i. **1** To move a canoe, etc., on or through water by means of a paddle. **2** To row gently or lightly. **3** To swim with short, downward strokes. —v.t. **4** To propel by means of a paddle or paddles. **5** To beat with a paddle. [ME *padell* small spade] —**pad′dler** n.

pad·dle·ball (pad′l·bôl′) n. A game resembling squash in which paddles are used to hit a ball in a walled court.

pad·dle·fish (pad′l·fish′) n. pl. **·fish** or **·fish·es** A large fish of the sturgeon family, having a flattened snout.

paddle wheel A wheel having projecting boards for propelling a boat.

pad·dock (pad′ək) n.
1 A pasture lot or enclosure for exercising horses. **2** A grassed enclosure at a racecourse where horses are walked about and saddled before a race. —v.t. To confine, as horses, in a paddock. [< OE *pearruc* enclosure]

Paddle wheel on a steamboat

pad·dy (pad′ē) n. pl. **·dies 1** Rice in the husk, whether gathered or growing. **2** A field in which rice is grown: also **rice paddy**. [< Malay *pādī*]

paddy wagon Slang PATROL WAGON. [< *Paddy,* a nickname for Patrick]

pad·lock (pad′lok′) n. A detachable lock with a shackle hinged at one end, and devised so as to pass through a staple or chain and lock at the other end. —v.t. To fasten with or as with a padlock. [ME *padlocke*]

pa·dre (pä′drā) n. **1** Father: a title used in Italy, Spain, and Spanish America in addressing or speaking of priests. **2** An army or navy chaplain. [Sp. & Pg. & Ital.< L *pater* father]

pae·an (pē′ən) n. A song of praise, joy, thanksgiving, or exultation. [< Gk. *paian* a hymn addressed to Paian, the god Apollo]

pa·el·la (pī·el′ə, pī·el′ə, Sp. pī·ā′yə, pī·ā′lyə) n. A Spanish dish of rice flavored with saffron, shellfish, chicken and other meats, and vegetables. [Catalan, lit., pot]

pa·gan (pā′gən) n. **1** One who is neither a Christian, a Jew, nor a Muslim; a heathen. **2** An irreligious person. —adj. Pertaining to pagans; heathenish. [< L *paganus* a rural villager] —**pa′gan·dom, pa′gan·ism** n.

pa·gan·ize (pā′gən·īz) v.t. & v.i. **·ized, ·iz·ing** To make or become pagan. —**pa′gan·iz′er** n.

page¹ (pāj) n. **1** A male attendant; esp. in chivalry, a lad or young man in training for knighthood. **2** A young person attending legislators while in session, as by delivering messages and doing errands. **3** A man employed in a hotel, club, theater, etc., to perform light duties. —v.t. **paged, pag·ing** To seek or summon (a person) by calling his name, as a hotel page does. [< Ital. < Gk. *paidion,* dim. of *pais, paidos* child]

page² (pāj) n. **1** One side of a leaf of a book, letter, manuscript, etc. **2** The written or printed matter on such a leaf. **3** An entire leaf of a book, magazine, etc.: to tear out a *page.* **4** Something that marks a stage, esp. a memorable one, in a process or sequence: a *page* from one's experience. **5** Any source or record of knowledge. —v.t. **paged, pag·ing** To mark the pages of with numbers. [< L *pagina*]

pag·eant (paj′ənt) n. **1** A public exhibition, parade, or spectacle, as of floats or other elaborate display. **2** Empty and elaborate display; ostentation. [< Med. L *pagina* a framework]

pag·eant·ry (paj′ən·trē) n. pl. **·ries 1** Pageants collectively. **2** Elaborate and colorful display; splendor. **3** Empty, ostentatious display.

pag·i·nate (paj′ə·nāt) v.t. **·nat·ed, ·nat·ing** To number the pages of (a book) consecutively. [< L *pagina* page]

pag·i·na·tion (paj′ə·nā′shən) n. **1** The numbering of the pages, as of a book. **2** The figures used in paging. **3** The arrangement and number of pages.

pa·go·da (pə·gō′də) n. In the countries of the Far East, a tower having several stories, each of which has a roof that curves upward, built as a temple or memorial. [Pg. *pagode*]

paid (pād) p.t. & p.p. of PAY.

pail (pāl) n. **1** A usu. cylindrical container for carrying liquids, etc. **2** The amount carried in this vessel: also **pail′ful′**. [< L *patella* a small pan]

pain (pān) n. **1** A feeling of distress resulting from the stimulation of certain nerve endings by some physical injury or disorder. **2** Mental suffering, as anxiety, grief, etc. **3** pl. Care or exertion expended on anything. **4** pl. The pangs of childbirth. **5** Slang A person or thing that irritates or annoys; nuisance. —**on** (or **upon** or **under) pain of** With the penalty of (some specified punishment). —v.t. **1** To cause pain to; hurt or grieve; disquiet. —v.i. **2** To cause pain. [< Gk. *poinē* a penalty] —**Syn.** n. **1** ache, discomfort. **2** anguish, distress, misery, wretchedness.

Pagoda

pain·ful (pān′fəl) adj. **1** Giving or attended with pain; distressing. **2** Requiring labor, effort, or care; arduous. **3** Affected with pain: a *painful* toe. —**pain′ful·ly** adv. —**pain′ful·ness** n.

pain-kill·er (pān′kil′ər) n. Informal A medicine that relieves pain; analgesic.

pain·less (pān′lis) adj. Free from pain; causing no pain. —**pain′less·ly** adv. —**pain′less·ness** n.

pains·tak·ing (pānz′tā′king) adj. Taking pains; careful; assiduous. —n. Diligent and careful endeavor. —**pains′-tak′ing·ly** adv.

paint (pānt) n. **1** A color or pigment, either dry or mixed with oil, water, etc. **2** A cosmetic, as rouge. —v.t. **1** To make a representation of in paints or colors. **2** To make, as a picture, by applying paints or colors. **3** To cover or coat with or as with paint. **4** To describe vividly in words. **5** To apply cosmetics to. **6** To apply (medicine, etc.), as with a swab. —v.i. **7** To cover or coat something with paint. **8** To practice the art of painting. **9** To apply cosmetics to the face, etc. [< L *pingere* to paint]

paint·brush (pānt′brush′) n. A brush for applying paint.

paint·er¹ (pān′tər) n. **1** One whose occupation is painting surfaces with a coat of paint. **2** One who paints pictures; an artist.

paint·er² (pān′tər) n. Naut. A rope with which to fasten a boat by its bow. [< OF *pentoir* a rope for hanging things]

paint·er³ (pān′tər) n. Regional PUMA. [Var. of PANTHER]

paint·ing (pān′ting) n. **1** The act or employment of laying on paints with a brush. **2** The art of applying paint to produce pictures. **3** A painted picture.

pair (pâr) n. **1** Two things of a kind that are joined, complementary, or otherwise related, and are used together: a *pair* of socks. **2** Something consisting of two like parts: a *pair* of eyeglasses. **3** Any two persons, animals, or things considered to share certain characteristics or circumstances, as a married couple or mated animals. **4** In legislative bodies, two opposed members who agree to abstain from voting, and so offset each other. —v.t. **1** To bring together or arrange in a pair or pairs; match; couple; mate. —v.i. **2** To come together as a couple or pair. **3** To marry or mate. —**pair off 1** To separate into couples. **2** To arrange by pairs. [< L *paria,* neut. plural of *par* equal]

pais·ley (pāz′lē) adj. Often cap. **1** Made of or resembling a woolen fabric patterned with colorful, curved shapes. **2** Of or resembling this pattern. —n. A paisley fabric or garment, esp. a shawl or necktie. [< *Paisley,* Scotland]

pa·ja·mas (pə·jä′məz, -jam′əz) n.pl. **1** Loose trousers with jackets or blouses to match, used as nightwear. **2** Loose trousers worn by both men and women in the Orient. Brit. sp. **py·ja·mas.** [< Pers. *pāi* a leg + *jāmah* a garment] —**pa·ja′ma** adj.

Pa·ki·stan (pä′ki·stän′, pak′i·stan′) n. A republic of the Commonwealth in s Asia, 310, 403 sq. mi., cap. Islamabad. —**Pa′ki·stan′i** adj., n. • See map at AFGHANISTAN.

pal (pal) n. Informal A close friend; chum. [< Romany *phral* brother < Skt. *bharātr*]

pal·ace (pal′is) n. **1** A royal residence, or the official residence of some high dignitary. 2 Any splendid residence or stately building. 3 A spacious and often showy place of public entertainment. [< L *palatium*, orig., the Palatine Hill at Rome, on which stood the palace of the Caesars]

pal·a·din (pal′ə-din) *n.* 1 A paragon of knighthood. 2 Any distinguished champion of a cause. [< L *palatinus* of the palace]

pal·an·quin (pal′ən-kēn′) *n.* A type of covered litter borne by poles on the shoulders of two or more men. [< Skt. *palyaṅka* bed]

pal·at·a·ble (pal′it-ə-bəl) *adj.* 1 Agreeable to the taste or palate; savory. 2 Acceptable. —**pal′at·a·bly** *adv.*

pal·a·tal (pal′ə-təl) *adv.* 1 Pertaining to the palate. 2 *Phonet.* Produced by placing the front (not the tip) of the tongue near or against the hard palate, as *y* in English *yoke.* —*n. Phonet.* A palatal sound. —**pal′a·tal·ly** *adv.*

pal·a·tal·ize (pal′ə-təl-īz′) *v.t. & v.i.* **·ized, ·iz·ing** *Phonet.* To change to a palatal sound, as (t) to (ch) in *nature.*

pal·ate (pal′it) *n.* 1 The roof of the mouth, comprising the anterior bony hard palate and the posterior fleshy soft palate. •See MOUTH. 2 The sense of taste; relish: the gourmet's sensitive *palate.* 3 Intellectual taste or preference. [< L *palatum*]

pa·la·tial (pə-lā′shəl) *adj.* Of, like, or befitting a palace; magnificent. —**pa·la′tial·ly** *adv.*

pa·lat·i·nate (pə-lat′ə-nāt, -nit) *n.* The political division ruled over by a prince possessing certain prerogatives of royalty within his own domain. [< ML *palatinus* palatine]

pal·a·tine (pal′ə-tīn, -tin) *adj.* 1 Pertaining to a royal palace or its officials. 2 Possessing royal prerogatives within a certain domain. —*n.* The ruler of a palatinate. [< L *palatinus* of the palace]

pa·lav·er (pə-lav′ər) *n.* 1 A discussion or talk; conference. 2 Originally, a lengthy conference between European explorers and native Africans. —*v.i.* 1 To talk idly and at length. 2 To meet in conference. —*v.t.* 3 To flatter; cajole. [< Pg. *palavra* word, speech < LL *parabola* a story, word]

pale[1] (pāl) *n.* 1 A pointed stick of wood; a fence picket. 2 A territory within established bounds. 3 A defined or delimited area: beyond the *pale* of the law. 4 A boundary; limit. [< L *palus* a stake]

pale[2] (pāl) *adj.* 1 Of a whitish or ashen appearance. 2 Of any color containing a large proportion of white; lacking in saturation. —*v.t. & v.i.* **paled, pal·ing** To make or turn pale; blanch. [< L *pallidus*] —**pale′ly** *adv.* —**pale′ness** *n.* —Syn. 1 pallid, wan, ashy, bloodless.

pale·face (pāl′fās) *n.* A white person: a term allegedly originated by North Amercian Indians.

paleo- *combining form* 1 Ancient; old: *paleography.* 2 Primitive: *Paleolithic.* [< Gk. *palaios* old, ancient]

Pa·le·o·cene (pā′lē-ə-sēn′) *adj. & n.* See GEOLOGY.

pa·le·og·ra·phy (pā′lē-og′rə-fē) *n.* 1 An ancient mode of writing, or ancient writing collectively. 2 The science of describing or deciphering ancient writings. —**pa′le·og′ra·pher** *n.* —**pa′le·o·graph′ic** or **·i·cal** *adj.*

Pa·le·o·lith·ic (pā′lē-ō-lith′ik) *adj. Anthropol.* Of, pertaining to, or associated with a period of human culture characterized by increasingly refined stone implements.

pa·le·on·tol·o·gy (pā′lē-on-tol′ə-jē) *n.* The science dealing with fossil organisms. —**pa′le·on′to·log′i·cal, pa′le·on′to·log′ic** *adj.* —**pa′le·on·tol′o·gist** *n.*

Pa·le·o·zo·ic (pā′lē-ō-zō′ik) *adv. & n.* See GEOLOGY. [< PALEO- + Gk. *zōē* life]

Pal·es·tine (pal′is-tīn) *n.* 1 In biblical times, a territory on the E coast of the Mediterranean, the country of the Jew. 2 A former British mandate west of the Jordan River, from 1923 to 1948 when the state of Israel was established. —**Pal′es·tin′i·an** (-tin′ē-ən) *adj., n.*

pal·ette (pal′it) *n.* 1 A thin tablet providing a surface for the mixing of colors by an artist, usu. designed to be held in the hand. 2 The colors used by an artist in his work as a whole or in a particular work. [F, dim. of *pale* shovel]

palette knife A thin, flat knife with a flexible blade for mixing and applying an artist's colors.

pal·frey (pôl′frē) *n.* A saddle horse, esp. a woman's saddle horse. [< Gk. *para* beside + LL *veredus* post horse]

Pa·li (pä′lē) *n.* The sacred language of the early Buddhist writings, comprising various Indic dialects. [< Skt. *pāli*]

pal·i·mo·ny (pal′ə-mō·nē) *n. Slang* Alimony paid to a person for having lived for a time with another, without being legally married.

pal·imp·sest (pal′imp·sest) *n.* A parchment, tablet, etc. written upon two or three times, the earlier writing having been wholly or partially erased to make room for the next. [< Gk. *palimpsēstos*, lit., scraped again]

pal·in·drome (pal′in·drōm) *n.* A word or phrase that reads the same forward or backward, as "radar." [< Gk. *palindromos* a running back again]

pal·ing (pā′ling) *n.* 1 One of a series of upright pales forming a fence; also, pales collectively. 2 A fence of pales.

pal·i·sade (pal′ə·sād′) *n.* 1 A fence made of strong stakes set in the ground 2 *pl.* A sheer cliff, usu. along a river. —*v.t.* **·sad·ed, ·sad·ing** To enclose or fortify with a palisade. [< MF *palisser* enclose with pales]

pall[1] (pôl) *n.* 1 A heavy cloth fabric, often black, used to cover a coffin. 2 Anything that darkens or dispirits: a *pall* of smoke; The war cast a *pall* over the festivities. 3 *Eccl.* A chalice cover. —*v.t.* To cover with or as with a pall. [< L *pallium* a cover]

pall[2] (pôl) *v.i.* 1 To become insipid or uninteresting. 2 To have a dulling or displeasing effect: with *on.* —*v.t.* 3 To satiate. [< APPALL]

pal·la·di·um[1] (pə·lā′dē·əm) *n. pl.* **·di·a** (-dē·ə) Any object considered essential to the safety of something; a safeguard. [< GK. *palladios* of Pallas (Athena), whose statue in Troy was believed to protect the city]

pal·la·di·um[2] (pə·lā′dē·əm) *n.* A rare, white, tarnishresistant metallic element (symbol Pd) related to platinum. [< *Pallas*, an asteroid]

Pal·las (pal′əs) *Gk. Myth.* ATHENA. Also **Pallas Athena.**

pall·bear·er (pôl′bâr′ər) *n.* One who escorts or bears a coffin at a funeral.

pal·let[1] (pal′it) *n.* 1 A wooden implement with a flat blade, used for mixing and shaping clay. 2 A movable platform for the storage or transportation of goods. 3 A machine part that changes reciprocating motion to rotary motion or vice versa. [Var. of PALETTE]

pal·let[2] (pal′it) *n.* A humble or makeshift bed, as a straw mattress or a blanket laid on the floor. [< L *palea* chaff]

pal·li·ate (pal′ē·āt) *v.t.* **·at·ed, ·at·ing** 1 To cause (a crime, fault, etc.) to appear less serious or offensive. 2 To relieve the symptoms of without curing, as a disease. [< LL *palliare* to cloak] —**pal′li·a′tion, pal′li·a′tor** *n.* —Syn. 1 extenuate, excuse. 2 alleviate, mitigate.

pal·li·a·tive (pal′ē·ā′tiv, -ə·tiv) *adj.* Having a tendency to palliate. —*n.* That which serves to palliate.

pal·lid (pal′id) *adj.* 1 Of a pale or wan appearance. 2 Lacking in color or spirit: a *pallid* version of the original show. [< L *pallere* be pale] —**pal′lid·ly** *adv.* —**pal′lid·ness** *n.*

pal·lor (pal′ər) *n.* The state of being pale or pallid.

palm[1] (päm) *n.* 1 The inner surface of the hand between the wrist and the base of the fingers. 2 The breadth (three or four inches) of the hand used as a rough measure. 3 That which covers the palm, as part of a glove. 4 The flattened portion of an antler, as of a moose. 5 The flat expanding end of any armlike projection, as the blade of an oar. —*v.i.* 1 To hide (cards, dice, etc.) in or about the hand, as in sleight of hand. 2 To handle or touch with the palm. —**palm off** To pass off or impose fraudulently. [< L *palma* a hand] —**palm′ar** (pal′mər) *adj.*

palm[2] (päm) *n.* 1 Any of a large and varied family of tropical trees or shrubs usu. having a branchless trunk topped by large palmate or pinnate leaves. 2 A leaf or branch of the palm, used as a symbol of victory or joy. 3 Supremacy; triumph. [< L *palma*] —**pal·ma·ceous** (pal·mā′shəs) *adj.*

pal·mate (pal′māt) *adj.* 1 Resembling an open hand with fingers spread. 2 Branching out radially from a common center. 3 *Zool.* Webbed, as a bird's foot. Also **pal′mat·ed.** [< L *palma* a hand] —**pal′mate·ly** *adv.*

Palm tree

palm·er (pä′mər) n. A medieval pilgrim who had visited Palestine and brought back a palm branch as a sign.

pal·met·to (pal·met′ō) n. pl. **·tos** or **·toes** Any of various palms with fanlike leaves, esp. the cabbage palm of the s U.S.

palm·is·try (pä′mis·trē) n. The art of reading the past life or future of a person by the lines and marks in the palm of the hand. [< OF *paulme* palm + *maistrie* mastery] — **palm′ist** n.

palm oil A yellow or reddish fat obtained from the fruit of various palms, used in making soap, candles, etc.

Palm Sunday The Sunday before Easter, commemorating Christ's triumphal entry into Jerusalem.

palm·y (pä′mē) adj. **palm·i·er, palm·i·est** 1 Marked by prosperity; flourishing. 2 Abounding in or resembling palms.

pal·my·ra (pal·mī′rə) n. A tall, tropical palm yielding wood, edible fruit, and sap. [< Pg. *palmeira* palm tree]

pal·o·mi·no (pal′ə·mē′nō) n. pl. **·nos** A golden brown horse, usu. having a mane and tail of paler color. [< Sp. *paloma* a dove]

palp (palp) n. PALPUS.

pal·pa·ble (pal′pə·bəl) adj. 1 That may be touched or felt. 2 Readily perceived; apparent. 3 Obvious to the mind; manifest. [< L *palpare* to touch] —**pal′pa·bil′i·ty, pal′pa·ble·ness** n. —**pal′pa·bly** adv.

pal·pate (pal′pāt) v.t. **·pat·ed, ·pat·ing** To examine by touch, esp. for medical diagnosis. —**pal·pa′tion** n.

pal·pi·tate (pal′pə·tāt) v.i. **·tat·ed, ·tat·ing** 1 To quiver; tremble. 2 To throb, usu. at increased speed: said of the heart. [< L *palpitare* to tremble, freq. of *palpare* to touch] —**pal′pi·ta′tion** n.

pal·pus (pal′pəs) n. pl. **·pi** (-pī) Zool. A feeler, esp. one appended to the oral region of certain insects, lobsters, worms, etc. [< L *palpus* a feeler]

pal·sy (pôl′zē) n. Paralysis or trembling due to impairment of nerves controlling voluntary movement. —v.t. **·sied, ·sy·ing** To affect with or as if with palsy. [< L *paralysis* paralysis] —**pal′sied** adj.

pal·ter (pôl′tər) v.i. 1 To speak or act insincerely. 2 To treat something lightly; trifle. 3 To haggle or quibble. [?] —**pal′ter·er** n.

pal·try (pôl′trē) adj. **·tri·er, ·tri·est** Having little or no worth or value; trifling; trivial [< regional E *palt* a piece of coarse or dirty cloth] —**pal′tri·ly** adv. —**pal′tri·ness** n.

pam., pamph. pamphlet.

pam·pas (pam′pəz) n.pl. The great treeless plains of South America. —adj. Pertaining to or growing on the pampas. [< Quechua] —**pam·pe·an** (pam′pē·ən, pam·pē′ən) adj.

pam·per (pam′pər) v.t. To treat too indulgently; gratify the whims of; coddle. [ME *pamperen*] —**pam′per·er** n.

pam·phlet (pam′flit) n. A printed publication having relatively few pages and unbound, stapled, or stitched. [< L *Pamphilus seu de Amore,* popular 12th c. love poem]

pam·phlet·eer (pam′flə·tir′) n. One who writes pamphlets, esp. on politically controversial subjects. —v.i. To write and issue pamphlets.

pan¹ (pan) n. 1 A wide, shallow vessel for holding liquids or for cooking. 2 A circular sheet-iron dish with sloping sides, in which gold is separated. 3 The powder cavity of a flintlock. 4 HARDPAN (def. 1). 5 Either of the two receptacles on a pair of scales. 6 Informal A severe criticism. — v. **panned, pan·ning** v.t. 1 To separate (gold) by washing gold-bearing earth in a pan. 2 To wash (earth, gravel, etc.) for this purpose. 3 Informal To criticize severely. —v.i. 4 To search for gold by washing earth, gravel, etc., in a pan. —**pan out** Informal To result or turn out; transpire. [< L *patina* a pan or dish]

pan² (pan) v.t. **panned, pan·ning** To move (a motion-picture or television camera) across a scene in order to secure a panoramic effect.

Pan (pan) Gk. Myth. A horned, goat-footed, pipe-playing god of forests, flocks, and shepherds.

pan- combining form 1 All; every; the whole; *panchromatic.* 2 Comprising, including, or applying to all: *Pan-American.* [< Gk., neut. of *pas* all]

pan·a·ce·a (pan′ə·sē′ə) n. A remedy for all diseases or ills; a cure-all. [< Gk. *panakeia* a universal remedy] —**pan′a·ce′an** adj.

pa·nache (pə·nash′, -näsh′) n. 1 A plume or bunch of feathers, esp. as an ornament on a helmet. 2 Dash; spirit; liveliness. [< Ital. *pennacchio* < *penna* feather]

Pan·a·ma (pan′ə·mä, -mô, Sp. pä′nä·mä′) n. A republic of Central America, 28,575 sq. mi., cap. Panama (also Panama City). —**Pan′a·ma′ni·an** (-mä′nē·ən) adj., n. • See map at CENTRAL AMERICA.

Panama hat A hat woven of fine, pale straw obtained from a palmlike plant of Central and South America.

Pan-A·mer·i·can (pan′ə·mer′ə·kən) adj. Of or pertaining to the countries of both North and South America. — **Pan′-A·mer′i·can·ism** n.

pan·cake (pan′kāk′) n. A thin flat batter cake fried in a pan or baked on a griddle; griddlecake.

pan·chro·mat·ic (pan′krō·mat′ik) adj. Phot. Sensitive to all the colors in proportion to their brightness, as a film or plate. —**pan·chro′ma·tism** (-krō′mə·tiz′əm) n.

pan·cre·as (pan′krē·əs, pang′-) n. A large gland situated behind the stomach and manufacturing fat-digesting enzymes and the hormone insulin. [< Gk. *pankreas* sweetbread] —**pan′cre·at′ic** (-at′ik) adj.

pan·da (pan′də) n. pl. **·das** or **·da** 1 A small raccoonlike carnivore of the SE Himalayas with reddish fur and ringed tail: also **lesser panda.** 2 A large, bearlike, herbivorous mammal of Tibet and China, having a black and white coat: also **giant panda.** [?]

pan·dem·ic (pan·dem′ik) adj. Widely epidemic, as a disease. —n. An epidemic occurring over a very large area or worldwide. [< Gk. *pan,* neut. of *pas* all + *dēmos* people]

pan·de·mo·ni·um (pan′də·mō′nē·əm) n. A tumultuous uproar; wild disorder. —**Syn.** riot, chaos, tumult. [< Gk. *pan,* neut. of *pas* all + *daimōn* an evil spirit]

pan·der (pan′dər) v.i. To seek to satisfy another's immoral, vulgar, or uninformed tastes or desires: to *pander* to the mob. —n. One who panders; esp., a go-between in sexual intrigues; procurer; pimp. [< *Pandarus,* a character in the Iliad] —**pan′der·er** n.

P. and L., P. & L. profit and loss.

Pan·do·ra (pan·dôr′ə, -dō′rə) Gk. Myth. The first mortal woman, whose curiosity led her to open a box (**Pandora's box**) from which all human ills escaped.

pan·dow·dy (pan·dou′dē) n. pl. **·dies** A deep-dish pie or pudding made of baked sliced apples. Also **apple pandowdy.** [?]

pane (pān) n. 1 A piece of window glass filling one opening in a frame. 2 A piece or compartment, esp. if flat and rectangular. 3 A flat surface or side. [< L *pannus* a piece of cloth] —**paned** adj.

pan·e·gyr·ic (pan′ə·jir′ik) n. A formal public eulogy, either written or spoken; encomium. [< Gk. < *panēgyris* an assembly] —**pan′e·gyr′i·cal** adj. —**pan′e·gyr′i·cal·ly** adv. — **pan′e·gyr′ist** n.

pan·el (pan′əl) n. 1 A rectangular section, as part of a fence or wall, often set in a frame and sometimes raised above or depressed below the surrounding surface. 2 A vertical section of a woman's skirt of a distinctive fabric or color. 3 A tablet of wood used as the surface for a painting; also, a painting on such a surface. 4 A set of instruments and controls displayed in an aircraft, automobile, or other complex system. 5 Law a The official list of persons called for jury duty; also, the persons so called. b The persons composing a jury. 6 A group of people selected to act cooperatively for some purpose, as to conduct a public investigation, judge a contest, participate in a discussion, etc. —v.t. **·eled or ·elled, ·el·ing or ·el·ling** 1 To fit, furnish, or adorn with panels. 2 To divide into panels. [< L *pannus* rag]

panel discussion A public discussion by a group of people, usu. selected because they represent divergent points of view or are experts.

pan·el·ing (pan′əl·ing) n. Panels collectively, as a series of panels in a wall. Also **pan′el·ling.**

pan·el·ist (pan′əl·ist) n. One of a group of people serving on a panel, as to judge a contest or discuss an issue.

pan fish Any little fish that can be fried whole.

pan-fry (pan′frī′) v.t. **-fried, -fry·ing** To fry in a frying pan.

pang (pang) n. 1 A sudden, brief, penetrating pain. 2 A sudden feeling of keen mental anguish. [?] —**Syn.** 1 stab, ache. 2 throe.

pan·go·lin (pang′gə·lin, pan·gō′lin) *n.* Any of various long-tailed, scale-covered, toothless mammals of Asia and Africa that feed on ants. [< Malay *peng-goling*]

pan·han·dle[1] (pan′han′dəl) *v.i.* **·dled**, **·dling** *Informal* To beg, esp. on the street. **—pan′han′dler** *n.*

pan·han·dle[2] (pan′han′dəl) *n.* A narrow strip of land projecting from a larger region: from its resemblance to the handle of a pan.

Pan·hel·len·ic (pan′hə·len′ik) *adj.* **1** Of or pertaining to all Greek people. **2** Of or pertaining to fraternities or sororities bearing Greek names.

pan·ic (pan′ik) *n.* **1** A sudden, overpowering fear often affecting many simultaneously and compelling immediate, unreasoning action, esp. flight. **2** Any sudden fear or alarm that provokes unreasonable action, as a sudden loss of confidence in the soundness of the financial system. **3** *Slang* Something extremely funny. **—adj.** **1** Of, like, or caused by panic. **2** Of or caused by the god Pan, believed to inspire fear. **—v.** **·icked**, **·ick·ing** *v.t.* **1** To affect with panic. **2** *Slang* To cause to laugh or otherwise express pleasure without restraint. **—v.i.** **3** To become affected with panic. [< Gk. *panikos* of or for the god Pan] **—pan′·ick·y** *adj.*

pan·i·cle (pan′i·kəl) *n.* *Bot.* A loose, irregularly branched flower cluster. [< L *panus* a swelling] **—pan′i·cled, pa·nic·u·late**, (pə·nik′yə·lāt, -lit), **pa·nic′u·lat′ed** *adj.*

pan·ic-strick·en (pan′ik·strik′ən) *adj.* Overcome by panic. Also **pan′ic-struck′.**

pan·jan·drum (pan·jan′drəm) *n.* A character of exaggerated importance; a pompous personage in a small place. [< a character in a play by Samuel Foote, 1720–1770, English dramatist]

pan·nier (pan′yər) *n.* **1** One of a pair of baskets adapted to be slung on both sides of a beast of burden. **2** A basket for carrying a load on the back. **3** A framework or hoop for extending a woman's dress at the hips. **4** A skirt extended at the hips. [< L *panis* bread]

pa·no·cha (pə·nō′chə) *n.* **1** A coarse Mexican sugar. **2** PENUCHE. [< L *panis* bread]

pan·o·ply (pan′ə·plē) *n.* *pl.* **·plies 1** The complete equipment of a warrior. **2** Any complete covering that protects or magnificently arrays. [< Gk. *panoplia* full armor] **—pan′o·plied** *adj.*

pan·o·ram·a (pan′ə·ram′ə, -rä′mə) *n.* **1** A complete view in every direction. **2** A complete or comprehensive view of a subject or of constantly passing events. **3** A picture unrolled before the spectator and representing a continuous scene. **4** CYCLORAMA. [< PAN- + Gk. *horama* sight] **—pan′o·ram′ic** *adj.* **—pan′o·ram′i·cal·ly** *adv.*

pan·pipes (pan′pīps′) *n.pl.* A primitive multiple flute made of reeds bound together.

pan·sy (pan′zē) *n.* *pl.* **·sies 1** A species of garden violet having velvety blossoms of varied colors. **2** *Slang* An effeminate or homosexual boy or man: used contemptuously. [< MF *pensée* thought]

pant (pant) *v.i.* **1** To breathe rapidly or spasmodically; gasp for breath. **2** To emit smoke, steam, etc., in loud puffs. **3** To have a strong desire; yearn: with *for* or *after*. **4** To beat or pulsate rapidly; throb, as the heart. **—v.t.** **5** To breathe out or utter gaspingly. **—n.** **1** A short or labored breath. **2** A quick or violent heaving, as of the breast. [< OF *pantoisier* to gasp] **—pant′er** *n.*

pan·ta·lets (pan′tə·lets′) *n.* *pl.* Long ruffled drawers, formerly worn by women and children. Also **pan′ta·lettes′.** [< PANTALOONS]

pan·ta·loon (pan′tə·lōōn′) *n.* **1** In pantomimes, an absurd old man on whom the clown plays tricks. **2** *pl.* Trousers; esp., tight-fitting trousers worn in the 19th century. [< Ital. *pantalone* a clown]

Pantalets

Pan·ta·loon (pan′tə·lōōn′)*n.* In early Italian comedies, an old dotard wearing tight-fitting trousers.

pan·the·ism (pan′thē·iz′əm) *n.* The doctrine that identifies the universe as a whole and the laws that govern it as God. **2** The worship of all gods. **—pan′the·ist** *n.* **—pan′the·is′tic** or **pan′the·is′ti·cal** *adj.* **—pan′the·is′ti·cal·ly** *adv.*

pan·the·on (pan′thē·on) *n.* **1** All the gods of a people. **2** A mausoleum or temple commemorating the great. [< L *pantheon* < Gk. *pan,* neut. of *pas* all + *theos* a god]

Pan·the·on (pan′thē·on) *n.* A circular temple at Rome, dedicated to all the gods, built about 27 B.C.

pan·ther (pan′thər) *n.* **1** A leopard, esp. one having black fur. **2** MOUNTAIN LION. **3** JAGUAR. [< Gk. *panthēr*]

pant·ies (pan′tēz) *n.pl.* A woman's or child's underpants. Also **pant′ie.**

pan·to·graph (pan′tə·graf, -gräf) *n.* An instrument for copying a drawing, diagram, or map, on the same or an altered scale. [< PAN- + -GRAPH] **—pan′to·graph′ic** or **·i·cal** *adj.* **—pan·tog′ra·phy** (pan·tog′rə·fē) *n.*

pan·to·mime (pan′tə·mīm) *n.* **1** A series of gestures and postures, used without words to express ideas or convey information. **2** Any play in which the actors express themselves without speaking. **3** An ancient, classical play or part of a play in which the actors used gestures or movement only. **—v.t. & v.i.** **·mimed, ·mim·ing** To act or express in pantomime. [< Gk. *pantomimos* an imitator of all] **—pan′to·mim′ic** (-mim′ik) or **·i·cal** *adj.* **—pan′to·mi′mist** (-mī′mist) *n.*

pan·try (pan′trē) *n.* *pl.* **·tries** A room or closet for keeping provisions, dishes, table linen, etc. [< L *panis* bread]

pants (pants) *n.pl.* **1** A garment extending from the waist to the ankles or knees and divided so as to cover each leg separately; trousers. **2** Drawers or panties.

pant·suit (pant′sōōt′) *n.* A woman's two-piece garment consisting of a jacket and matching pants. Also **pants suit.**

pan·ty·hose (pan′tē·hōz′) *n.pl.* A woman's undergarment combining panties and stockings. Also **panty hose.**

pan·ty·waist (pan′tē·wāst′) *n.* **1** A child's waist with buttons on which to fasten short pants. **2** *Slang* A weak or cowardly youth; sissy.

pan·zer (pan′zər, *Ger.* pän′tsər) *adj.* **1** Armored. **2** Using armored tanks or mechanized troops. [G]

pap (pap) *n.* Any soft food for babies or sick people. [ME *pape*]

pa·pa (pä′pə, pə·pä′) *n.* Father. [< Gk. *papas,* a child's word]

pa·pa·cy (pā′pə·sē) *n.* *pl.* **·cies 1** The dignity, office, or jurisdiction of the pope of Rome. **2** The succession of popes in the Roman Catholic Church. **3** The tenure of office of the pope. [< L *papa* pope]

Pa·pa·cy (pā′pə·sē) *n.* The Roman Catholic system of church government.

pa·pal (pā′pəl) *adj.* **1** Of or pertaining to the papacy or the pope. **2** Of or pertaining to the Roman Catholic Church.

pa·paw (pə·pô′, pô′pô) *n.* **1** A small, deciduous, North American tree bearing small, pulpy, edible fruit. **2** The fruit of this tree. **3** PAPAYA. [< Sp. *papaya* papaya]

pa·pa·ya (pä·pä′yä, pə·pä′yə) *n.* **1** A tropical American palmlike tree bearing a large, melonlike fruit. **2** Its edible fruit. [Sp.]

pa·per (pā′pər) *n.* **1** A substance typically prepared in thin, flat sheets, made from chemically treated fibrous cellulose, usu. from wood, rags, etc., and used as a writing and printing surface, in packaging, etc. **2** A sheet of paper. **3** A printed or written document. **4** NEWSPAPER. **5** A written essay, report, or examination, as for a school assignment. **6** A scholarly study or treatise read aloud or published in a journal. **7** Written or printed pledges or promises to pay which are negotiable, as bills of exchange, notes, etc.: also **commercial paper. 8** WALLPAPER. **9** *pl.* Personal or business documents, as of identification, permission, agreement, credit, etc. **10** Free tickets, as to a theater; also, the audience so admitted. **—on paper 1** In writing or print. **2** Based upon theoretical sources or superficial evidence. **—adj.** **1** Of, made of, or like paper. **2** Theoretical rather than actual: *paper* profits. **—v.t.** **1** To put paper on; cover with wallpaper. **2** To fold or enclose in paper. **3** To issue free tickets of admission to (a place of amusement). [< L *papyrus*] **—pa′per·er** *n.* **—pa′per·y** *adj.*

pa·per·back (pā′pər·bak′) *n.* A book having a paper cover or binding. —*adj.* Being or relating to such a book.

paper boy A boy or man who delivers newspapers.

paper gold SPECIAL DRAWING RIGHTS.

pa·per·hang·er (pā′pər·hang′ər) *n.* One who covers walls, etc., with wallpaper. —**pa′per·hang·ing** *n.*

paper money Currency consisting of paper on which certain fixed values are printed, as banknotes.

paper nautilus A cephalopod named for its thin, paper-like shell.

paper profit A potential profit, as in the stock market, that can be realized only by the sale of an appreciated holding.

paper tiger Something that seems mighty or threatening but is actually ineffectual or trivial.

pa·per·weight (pā′pər·wāt′) *n.* A small, heavy object set on loose papers to hold them in place.

pa·per·work (pā′pər·wûrk′) *n.* Work involving the preparation or handling of reports, letters, etc.

pa·pier-mâ·ché (pā′pər·mə·shā′, *Fr.* pá·pyä′mä·shā′) *n.* A tough material molded from paper pulp and a binding material. [F, lit., chewed paper]

pa·pil·la (pə·pil′ə) *n. pl.* **·lae** (-ē) **1** *Anat.* **a** The nipple of a mammary gland. **b** Any small nipplelike process, as on the tongue. **2** *Bot.* A small, nipple-shaped protuberance on a flower or leaf. [L, dim. of *papula* a swelling, pimple] —**pap·il·lar·y** (pap′ə·ler′ē), **pap·il·lose** (pap′ə·lōs) *adj.*

pap·il·lo·ma (pap′ə·lō′mə) *n. pl.* **·mas** or **·ma·ta** (-mə·tə) A small benign tumor on skin or mucous membrane.

pa·pist (pā′pist) *n. & adj.* Roman Catholic: a disparaging usage. [< L *papa* pope] —**pa′pis·try** *n.*

pa·poose (pa·pōōs′) *n.* A North American Indian infant. Also **pap·poose′**. [< Algonquian (Narraganset) *papoos* child]

pap·pus (pap′əs) *n. pl.* **pap·pi** (pap′ī, -ē) *Bot.* A tuft or cluster of hairs, scales, bristles, etc., on the calyx of a floret of the composite family, functioning to disperse the fruit. [< Gk. *pappos* grandfather] —**pap′pose** (-ōs), **pap′·pous** (-əs) *adj.*

pa·pri·ka (pa·prē′kə, pap′ri·kə) *n.* A condiment made from the fruit of a mild red pepper. [< Gk. *peperi* pepper]

Pap smear A method of early detection of cervical cancer, consisting of removal of cervical cell samples, which are stained and examined. Also **Pap test**. [after George Papanicolaou, 1883–1962, U.S. scientist]

a. pappus.
b. fruit.

pa·py·rus (pə·pī′rəs) *n.pl.* **·ruses** or **·ri** (-rē, -rī) **1** A perennial rushlike sedge having stems six to ten feet high. **2** The writing paper of the ancient Egyptians, made from this plant. **3** A manuscript written on this material. [< Gk. *papyros*]

par (pär) *n.* **1** The established value of a national monetary unit defined in monetary units of another country. **2** The value printed on a negotiable document, as a stock certificate or bond. **3** An accepted standard with which to compare variation: not feeling up to *par.* **4** Equivalent level, status, value, etc.; equal basis: on a *par.* **5** In golf, the number of strokes allotted to a round or hole on the basis of faultless play. —*adj.* Equal to par. [L, equal]

par. paragraph; parallel; parenthesis.

para-[1] *prefix* **1** Beside; near by; along with: *paradigm.* **2** Beyond; aside from; amiss: *paradox.* **3** *Med.* **a** Diseased or abnormal: *paranoia.* **b** Similar to: *paratyphoid.* Also **par-.** [< Gk. *para* beside]

para-[2] *combining form* Shelter or protection against: *parachute.* [< Ital. *parare* defend]

par·a·ble (par′ə·bəl) *n.* A short, simple tale based on familiar things, meant to convey a moral or religious lesson. [< Gk. *parabolē* a placing side by side, a comparison]

pa·rab·o·la (pə·rab′ə·lə) *n. Math.* A curve composed of a set of points in a plane having their distances from a fixed point and a fixed straight line equal. [< Gk. *parabolē* a comparison]

par·a·bol·ic (par′ə·bol′ik) *adj.* **1** Pertaining to or having the form of a parabola. **2** Pertaining to a parable.

par·a·chute (par′ə·shōōt) *n.* An apparatus of lightweight fabric that when unfurled assumes the shape of a large umbrella and acts to retard the speed of a body moving or descending through air. —*v.* **·chut·ed**, **·chut·ing** *v.t.* **1** To land (troops, materiel, etc.) by means of parachutes. —*v.i.* **2** To descend by parachute. [< F < PARA- + *chute* fall] —**par′a·chut·ist** *n.*

pa·rade (pə·rād′) *n.* **1** A marshaling and maneuvering of troops for display or official inspection. **2** A ceremonious, public procession. **3** A promenade or public walk. **4** Pompous show; ostentation. —*v.* **·rad·ed**, **·rad·ing** *v.t.* **1** To walk or march through or about. **2** To display or show off ostentatiously; flaunt. **3** To cause to assemble for military parade or review. —*v.i.* **4** To march formally or with display. **5** To walk in public for the purpose of showing oneself. **6** To assemble in military order for inspection or review. [< LL *parare* adorn, prepare] —**pa·rad′er** *n.*

par·a·digm (par′ə·dim, -dīm) *n.* **1** A pattern or example. **2** *Gram.* A list of the inflected forms of a word, as of a declension or conjugation. [< Gk. *paradeigma* a pattern] —**par′a·dig·mat′ic** (-dig·mat′ik) *adj.*

par·a·dise (par′ə·dīs) *n.* **1** The intermediate place or state where the souls of the saved await the resurrection. **2** Heaven. **3** Any region or state of surpassing delight. [< OPers. *pairidaēza* an enclosure, park] —**par′a·di·sa′ic** (-di·sā′ik) or **·i·cal**, **par′a·dis′al**, **par′a·dis′i·ac** (-dis′ē·ak) or **par·a·di·si·a·cal** (par′ə·di·sī′ə·kəl) *adj.*

Par·a·dise (par′ə·dīs) *n.* The garden of Eden.

par·a·dox (par′ə·doks) *n.* **1** A statement that seems to contradict common belief but may nevertheless be true. **2** A self-contradictory statement or proposition. **3** A person or thing that seems to possess contradictory qualities and is thus inexplicable or inscrutable; enigma. [< Gk. *para-* contrary to + *doxa* opinion] —**par′a·dox′i·cal** *adj.* —**par′a·dox′i·cal·ly** *adv.* —**par′a·dox′i·cal·ness.** *n.*

par·af·fin (par′ə·fin) *n.* **1** A white, water-repellent, waxy mixture of hydrocarbons, usu. derived from petroleum, used for making candles, matches, etc.: also **paraffin wax**. **2** Any of a series of saturated, open-chain hydrocarbons analogous to methane in molecular structure. **3** *Brit.* Kerosene. —*v.t.* To treat or impregnate with paraffin. Also **par′af·fine** (-fin, -fēn). [< L *parum* too little + *affinis* related to, because it has little affinity for other bodies]

par·a·gon (par′ə·gon) *n.* **1** A model of excellence: a *paragon* of virtue. **2** A round pearl of exceptional size. [< Gk. *para-* beside + *akonē* whetstone]

par·a·graph (par′ə·graf, -gräf) *n.* **1** A passage in a written work begun on a new and usu. indented line and usu. signaling a distinct thought, statement, or expression. **2** A short article, complete and unified. **3** A mark (¶) used to indicate where a paragraph is to start. —*v.t.* **1** To arrange in or into paragraphs. **2** To comment on or express in a paragraph. [< Gk. *para-* beside + *graphein* write] —**par′a·graph′er, par′a·graph′ist** *n.*

Par·a·guay (par′ə·gwā, -gwī; *Sp.* pä·rä·gwī′) *n.* A republic of CEN. South America, 157,047 sq. mi., cap. Asunción. —**Par′a·guay′an** *adj., n.* • See map at BRAZIL.

Paraguay tea MATÉ.

par·a·keet (par′ə·kēt) *n.* Any of certain small parrots having a long, slender tail. [< Ital. *parrochetto*, dim of *parroco* parson]

par·a·le·gal (par′ə·lē′gəl) *adj.* Of or pertaining to the legal profession at the paraprofessional level. —*n.* A legal paraprofessional.

par·al·lax (par′ə·laks) *n.* **1** The difference in the apparent position of an object, esp. of a celestial body, as would appear if viewed from two points. **2** Any apparent displacement of an object due to an observer's position. [< Gk. *para-* beside + *allassein* change] —**par′al·lac′tic** (-lak′tik) or **·ti·cal** *adj.*

par·al·lel (par′ə·lel) *adj.* **1** Extending in the same direction and being equidistant at all points: *parallel* rows of seats. **2** *Geom.* Not intersecting, however far extended: said of planes or straight lines in the same plane. **3** Having parallel sides or parts. **4** Of the same kind or form;

Parabola

x = any point on parabola. F = focus. xC and x^1C^1 are perpendicular to AB. $Fx = xC$, $Fx^1 = x^1C^1$, etc.

functioning in like ways: *parallel* clauses. **5** Displaying the same pattern or course: *parallel* development; *parallel* careers. —*n.* **1** Something essentially similar to another; counterpart. **2** Essential likeness; correspondence. **3** A comparison tracing similarity: to draw a *parallel* between two presidents. **4** *Geom.* A line parallel to another line or to a plane. **5** An imaginary circle parallel to the equator and having all of its points the same latitude. **6** The state of being parallel. —*v.t.* **·leled,** or **·lelled, ·lel·ing** or **·lel·ling 1** To be, go, or extend parallel to. **2** To furnish with a parallel; equal. **3** To be a parallel to; correspond. **4** To compare; liken. **5** To make parallel. [< Gk. *para-* beside + *allēlos* one another]

par·al·lel bars A gymnastic apparatus consisting of two parallel, horizontal bars supported on posts a few feet from the ground.

par·al·lel·e·pi·ped (par′ə·lel′ə·pī′pid, -pip′id) *n.* A prism with six faces, each of which is a parallelogram. Also **par·al·lel·e·pip·e·don** (-pip′ə·don, -pī′pə-). [< Gk. *parallēlos* parallel + *epipedon* a plane surface]

par·al·lel·ism (par′ə·lel·iz′əm) *n.* **1** The state of being parallel. **2** Essential likeness; similarity; correspondence.

par·al·lel·o·gram (par′ə·lel′ə·gram) *n.* A four-sided plane figure whose opposite sides are parallel and equal.

pa·ral·y·sis (pə·ral′ə·sis) *n. pl.* **·ses** (-sēz) **1** Partial or complete loss of sensation and the power of voluntary motion. **2** Inability to act or respond effectively. [< Gk. < *paralyein* disable]

Parallelograms
a. square. b. rhomboid.
c. rectangle. d. rhombus.

par·a·lyt·ic (par′ə·lit′ik) *adj.* **1** Of, causing, or affected with paralysis. **2** Subject to paralysis. — *n.* A person subject to or suffering from paralysis.

par·a·lyze (par′ə·līz) *v.t.* **·lyzed, ·lyz·ing 1** To bring about paralysis in. **2** To render powerless, ineffective, or inactive. —**par′a·ly·za′tion, par·a·lyz′er** *n.*

par·a·me·ci·um (par′ə·mē′shē·əm, -sē·əm) *n. pl.* **·ci·a** (-shē·ə, -sē·ə) Any of a genus of slipper-shaped protozoans moving by means of cilia. [< Gk. *paramēkēs* oblong, oval]

par·a·med·ic (par′ə·med′ik) *n.* One trained to assist a physician.

par·a·med·i·cal (par′ə·med′ə·kəl) *adj.* Designating or pertaining to medical personnel trained to assist physicians, as by conducting routine tests, or to attend patients. —**par′a·med′i·cal·ly** *adv.*

pa·ram·e·ter (pə·ram′ə·tər) *n.* **1** *Math.* A variable or constant whose values determine the form of an expression, function, etc. **2** A number expressing some aspect of the behavior of a physical system. **3** A fixed limit or guideline. [< Gk. *para-* beside + *metron* a measure] —**par·a·met·ric** (par′ə·met′rik) *adj.*

par·a·mil·i·tar·y (par′ə·mil′ə·ter′ē) *adj.* Having a military structure and capable of supplementing or becoming a military force; quasi-military.

par·a·mount (par′ə·mount) *adj.* Having the highest title or rank; superior to all others. —*n.* A supreme lord. [< L *per* by + *ad montem* to the hill] —**par′a·mount·ly** *adv.* — **par′a·mount·cy** *n.* —**Syn.** *adj.* chief, foremost, preeminent, supreme.

par·a·mour (par′ə·mŏŏr) *n.* A lover, esp. one who unlawfully takes the place of a husband or wife. [< L *per* through + *amor* love]

par·a·noi·a (par′ə·noi′ə) *n. Psychiatry* A mental disorder characterized by delusions, as of persecution or grandeur. [< Gk. *paranoos* distraught]

par·a·noid (par′ə·noid) *adj.* **1** Of, like, or suffering from paranoia: also **par′a·noi′dal.** **2** Exhibiting symptoms suggestive of paranoia; esp., suspicious without cause. — *n.* A paranoid person. Also **par′a·noi′ac** (-noi′ak, -ək).

par·a·pet (par′ə·pit, -pet) *n.* **1** A barrier or wall used to shield soldiers from attack; breastwork. **2** A low wall about the edge of a roof, terrace, etc. [< Ital. *parapetto*] — **par′a·pet·ed** *adj.*

par·a·pher·na·li·a (par′ə·fər·nā′lē·ə, -nāl′yə, -fə-) *n.pl.* (*construed as sing. or pl.*) **1** Personal belongings. **2** Articles or accessories of equipment or adornment; furnishings; trappings. [< Gk. *para-* beside + *phernē* dower]

par·a·phrase (par′ə·frāz) *n.* A restatement of the meaning of a passage, work, etc. —*v.t. & v.i.* **·phrased, ·phras·ing** To express in or make a paraphrase. [< Gk. < *paraphrazein* tell the same thing in other words] —**par′a·phras′er** *n.* —**par·a·phras′tic** (-fras′tik) *adj.* —**par′a·phras′ti·cal·ly** *adv.*

par·a·ple·gi·a (par′ə·plē′jē·ə, -jə) *n.* Paralysis of the lower half of the body. [< Gk. *paraplēgia,* a stroke on one side] —**par·a·ple·gic** (par′ə·plē′jik, -plej′ik) *adj., n.*

par·a·pro·fes·sion·al (par′ə·prə·fesh′ə·nəl) *n.* One who assists professionals, as teachers or physicians, by performing tasks not requiring professional skills.

par·a·psy·chol·o·gy (par′ə·sī·kol′ə·jē) *n.* The investigation of psychic phenomena, as extrasensory perception, telepathy, etc.

Pa·ra rubber (pä·rä′) Crude rubber obtained from certain tropical American trees. [< *Pará*, Brazil]

par·a·site (par′ə·sīt) *n.* **1** *Biol.* An animal or plant that lives on or in another living organism from which it takes nourishment, usu. with harm to the host. **2** A person or thing that lives or survives by dependence on and at the expense of another. [< Gk. *parasitos*, lit., one who eats at another's table] —**par·a·sit′ic** (-sit′ik) or **·i·cal** *adj.* —**par·a·sit′i·cal·ly** *adv.* —**par·a·sit·ism** (par′ə·sī′tiz·əm, -sə·tiz′əm) *n.*

par·a·sol (par′ə·sôl, -sol) *n.* A small, light umbrella used as a sunshade, esp. by women. [< Ital. *parasole*]

par·a·sym·pa·thet·ic nervous system (par′ə·sim′·pə·thet′ik) The part of the autonomic nervous system that controls such involuntary actions as the constriction of pupils, dilation of blood vessels, and slowing of heartbeat.

par·a·thi·on (par′ə·thī′on, -ən) *n.* An extremely poisonous synthetic organic compound, used as an agricultural insecticide. [< PARA-¹ + Gk. *theion* sulfur]

par·a·thy·roid (par′ə·thī′roid) *adj.* Pertaining to any of several small endocrine glands on or near the thyroid glands, which produce hormones that regulate calcium and phosphorus metabolism. —*n.* A parathyroid gland.

par·a·troops (par′ə·trōōps) *n.pl.* A military force trained to parachute into hostile territory from an airplane. — **par′a·troop** *adj.* —**par′a·troop′er** *n.*

par·a·ty·phoid (par′ə·tī′foid) *adj.* Resembling typhoid fever but due to infection by distinct bacteria. —*n.* Paratyphoid fever.

par·boil (pär′boil′) *v.t.* **1** To boil partially. **2** To make uncomfortable with heat. [< LL *per-* through + *bullire* to bubble]

par·cel (pär′səl) *n.* **1** Anything wrapped up; a package; bundle. **2** An integral part: part and *parcel*. **3** A group or lot of merchandise offered for sale. **4** A group or assortment, as of people or things: a *parcel* of misfits. **5** A distinct portion of land. **6** A separated part of anything. —*v.t.* **·celed** or **·celled, ·cel·ing** or **·cel·ling 1** To divide or distribute in parts or shares: usu. with *out.* **2** To make up into a parcel. [< L *particula*, dim. of *pars, partis* part]

parcel post A postal service for the carrying and delivery of parcels.

parch (pärch) *v.t.* **1** To make extremely dry; shrivel with heat. **2** To dry (corn, peas, etc.) by exposing to great heat; roast slightly. —*v.i.* **3** To become extremely dry; shrivel with heat. [< L *per-* thoroughly + *siccare* dry]

Par·chee·si (pär·chē′zē) *n.* A board game in which moves are regulated by a throw of the dice: a trade name. Also **par·che′si, par·chi′si.**

parch·ment (pärch′mənt) *n.* **1** Animal skin, as of sheep, goats, etc., prepared for writing. **2** A paper resembling this. **3** A college graduation diploma. [< Gk. *Pergamon*, the ancient city of Pergamum, Asia Minor]

pard (pärd) *n. Regional* PARDNER.

pard·ner (pärd′nər) *n. Regional* Chum; friend; mate. [Alter. of PARTNER]

par·don (pär′dən) *v.t.* **1** To remit the penalty of (a crime, insult, etc.). **2** To release from punishment; forgive for an offense. **3** To allow for; forgive. —n. **1** The act of pardoning. **2** A waiving of the execution of the penalties of a violated law. **3** Courteous forbearance: used in making polite excuses. **4** An indulgence. [< L per- through + donare give] —**par′don·a·ble** adj. —**par′don·a·bly** adv.

par·don·er (pär′dən·ər) n. **1** One who pardons. **2** In the Middle Ages, a layman commissioned to collect offerings for promised indulgences.

pare (pâr) v.t. **pared, par·ing 1** To cut off the covering layer or part of. **2** To cut off or trim away (a covering layer or part): often with off or away. **3** To reduce or diminish, esp. gradually. [< L parare prepare] —**par′er** n.

par·e·gor·ic (par′ə·gôr′ik, -gör′ik) n. A soothing preparation, esp. a camphorated tincture of opium. [< Gk. parēgorikos soothing]

paren. (pl. **parens.**) parenthesis.

pa·ren·chy·ma (pə·reng′ki·mə) n. **1** Biol. The distinctive, functioning tissue in a gland or other organ. **2** Bot. A thin-walled, soft, undifferentiated tissue forming the bulk of leaves, fruit pulp, etc. [< Gk. para- beside + enchyma infusion] —**par·en·chym·a·tous** (par′eng·kim′ə·təs) adj.

par·ent (pâr′ənt) n. **1** A father or a mother. **2** Any organism that generates another. **3** A source or wellspring; basis; cause. [< L parens parent, orig. pr.p. of parere beget] —**pa·ren·tal** (pə·ren′təl) adj. —**pa·ren′tal·ly** adv.

par·ent·age (pâr′ən·tij) n. **1** The relation of a parent; parenthood. **2** Descent or derivation from parents.

pa·ren·the·sis (pə·ren′thə·sis) n. pl. **·ses** (-sēz) **1** A word, phrase, or clause inserted in a sentence that is grammatically complete without it, separated usually by commas, dashes, or upright curves. **2** Either or both of the upright curves ( ) so used. **3** Any intervening episode or incident. [< Gk. < parentithenai put in beside]

pa·ren·the·size (pə·ren′thə·sīz) v.t. **·sized, ·siz·ing 1** To insert as a parenthesis. **2** To insert parentheses in.

par·en·thet·i·cal (par′ən·thet′i·kəl) adj. **1** Of or pertaining to a parenthesis. **2** Used within parentheses. **3** Employing parentheses. **4** Added or inserted as a parenthesis; interjected. **5** Employing or including parentheses. Also **par·en·thet′ic.** —**par·en·thet′i·cal·ly** adv.

par·ent·hood (pâr′ənt·hŏŏd) n. The condition or relation of a parent.

pa·re·sis (pə·rē′sis, par′ə·sis) n. pl. **·ses** (-sēz) **1** Weakness or partial paralysis. **2** A brain disease marked by dementia, paralysis, etc., and due to advanced syphilis: also **general paresis.** [< Gk., a letting go < parienai let go] —**pa·ret·ic** (pə·ret′ik, -rē′tik) adj., n. —**pa·ret′i·cal·ly** adv.

par ex·cel·lence (pär ek′sə·läns, Fr. pár ek·se·läns′) Of the highest excellence; beyond comparison. [F, lit., by way of excellence]

par·fait (pär·fā′) n. **1** A dessert made with eggs, sugar, whipped cream, brandy or other flavoring, or fruit, frozen in a tall, thin glass called a **parfait glass. 2** A dessert composed of layers of ice cream and syrup served in a parfait glass. [F, lit., perfect]

pa·ri·ah (pə·rī′ə) n. **1** One of a people of low caste in s India and Burma. **2** A social outcast. [< Tamil paraiyar drummer, because drummers at festivals came from this caste]

pa·ri·e·tal (pə·rī′ə·təl) adj. Of, pertaining to, or forming the walls of any cavity in the body. —n. **PARIETAL BONE.** [< L paries wall]

parietal bone Either of two bones forming a part of the top and sides of the cranium.

par·i·mu·tu·el (par′i·myŏŏ′chŏŏ·əl) n. **1** A system of betting at races in which the winners share in the total amount wagered: also **par′i·mu′tu·el. 2** A machine for recording bets under this system. [F, a stake or mutual wager]

Par·is (par′is) Gk. Myth. A son of Priam who carried off Helen, thus causing the Trojan War.

Paris green A poisonous, emerald-green compound containing arsenic, used largely as an insecticide.

par·ish (par′ish) n. **1** Eccl. In cer-

tain churches, a district in charge of a priest or other clergyman. **2** U.S. **a** A religious congregation, comprising all those who worship at the same church. **b** The district in which they live. **3** In Louisiana, a civil district corresponding to a county. **4** Can. In Quebec and New Brunswick, a political division resembling a township. [< Gk. paroikia, orig., a neighborhood]

pa·rish·ion·er (pə·rish′ən·ər) n. A member of a parish.

par·i·ty (par′ə·tē) n. pl. **·ties 1** The state or quality of being like or equal, as in rank, value, or position; equivalence. **2** The equivalence of value of currency between two countries, or of the prices of commodities as expressed in a currency. **3** In the U.S., a level for farm prices which gives to the farmer the same purchasing power averaged during a base period. [< L pars equal]

park (pärk) n. **1** A tract of land for public use in or near a city, usu. laid out with walks, drives, and recreation grounds. **2** An open square or plaza in a city, usu. containing shade trees. **3** A large area of country containing natural scenery, plants, and wildlife, reserved by the government for public enjoyment: a national park. **4** A wooded expanse forming part of a country estate. **5** In the w U.S., a plateaulike valley between mountain ranges. **6** Mil. An enclosure where munitions, vehicles, etc., are stored. — v.t. **1** To place or leave (an automobile, etc.) standing for a time, as on the street. **2** Informal To place; set: Park your hat on the table. **3** To assemble or mass together. —v.i. **4** To park an automobile, etc. [< OF parc a game preserve] —**park′er** n.

par·ka (pär′kə) n. **1** An outer fur garment with a hood, worn in arctic regions. **2** A similar hooded garment, often lined with pile, for sports and casual wear.

parking lot An area designed for the parking of motor vehicles.

parking meter A device into which a coin is inserted as a fee for parking a vehicle, the time allowed being shown on a scale.

Parka def. 2

Par·kin·son's disease (pär′kin·sənz) A chronic, progressive nervous disease characterized by muscle tremor when at rest, stiffness, and a rigid facial expression. Also **par′kin·son·ism.** [< James Parkinson, 1755–1824, English physician]

park·land (pärk′land′) n. Often pl. **1** Land used or designated for use as a park. **2** Grassland with trees, suitable for use as a park.

park·way (pärk′wā′) n. A landscaped expressway or large highway.

Parl. Parliament; Parliamentary.

par·lance (pär′ləns) n. Manner of speech; language: legal parlance. [< OF < parler speak]

par·lay (pär·lā′, pär′lē) v.t. **1** To place (an original bet and its winnings) on a later race, contest, etc. **2** To increase or exploit (any asset or advantage) successfully. —n. **1** The act of parlaying. **2** A bet and its winnings parlayed. [F < Ital., a grand cast at dice < paro equal < L par]

par·ley (pär′lē) n. An oral conference or discussion, as with an enemy. —v.i. To hold a conference, esp. with an enemy. [< OF parler speak]

par·lia·ment (pär′lə·mənt) n. A meeting or assembly for consultation and deliberation; esp., a national legislative body. [< OF parler speak]

Par·lia·ment (pär′lə·mənt) n. **1** The supreme legislature of Great Britain and Northern Ireland. **2** Any of various other legislatures resembling it.

par·lia·men·ta·ry (pär′lə·men′tər·ē, -men′trē) adj. **1** Pertaining to, characterized by, or enacted by a parliament. **2** According to the rules of Parliament. **3** Admissible in a deliberative assembly. —**par·lia·men·tar′i·an** (-men·târ′ē·ən) adj., n.

par·lor (pär′lər) n. **1** A room for reception of callers or entertainment of guests. **2** A room in an inn, hotel, etc., for private conversation, appointments, etc. **3** A place of business equipped to perform specialized personal services: a beauty parlor. Brit. sp. **·lour.** [< LL parabolare speak]

parlor car A railway car fitted with individual chairs.

par·lous (pär′ləs) adj. Archaic Dangerous or exciting;

a. parietal bones.
b. occipital bone.

perilous. —*adv.* Exceedingly; very. [Var. of PERILOUS] —
par'lous·ly *adv.*

Par·me·san cheese (pär'mə·zon, -zən, -zan) A hard,
dry cheese, usu. grated and served on soups, spaghetti,
etc. [after *Parma*, Italy, where originally made]

Par·nas·si·an (pär·nas'ē·ən) *adj.* 1 Belonging or relating
to the mountain Parnassus. 2 Of or pertaining to a school
of French poetry of the 19th century.

pa·ro·chi·al (pə·rō'kē·əl) *adj.* 1 Pertaining to, supported
by, or confined to a parish. 2 Restricted in scope; narrow;
provincial. [< LL *parochialis*]—**pa·ro'chi·al·ism** *n.* —**pa·ro'·
chi·al·ly** *adv.* —**Syn.** 2 limited, uniformed, unenlightened.

parochial school A school supported and directed by
a church.

par·o·dy (par'ə·dē) *n. pl.* ·**dies** 1 A literary composition
imitating and ridiculing some serious work. 2 Any burlesque imitation of something serious. 3 A poor imitation.
—*v.t.* ·**died**, ·**dy·ing** To make a parody of; travesty. [< Gk.
parōidia a burlesque poem or song] —**pa·rod·ic** (pə·rod'ik)
or ·**i·cal** *adj.* —**par'o·dist** *n.*

pa·role (pə·rōl') *n.* 1 The conditional release of a prisoner
from jail prior to the expiration of his term. 2 A pledge of
honor by a prisoner of war in return for his release, as
that he will not serve against his captors. —*v.t.* ·**roled**, ·**rol·
ing** To release on parole. [F *parole (d'honneur)* word (of
honor)]

pa·rot·id (pə·rot'id) *adj. Anat.* Situated near the ear. —*n.*
PAROTID GLAND. [< Gk. *para-* beside + *ous, ōtos* ear]

parotid gland Either of two large salivary glands
located below and in front of the ear.

-parous *suffix* Giving birth to; bearing; producing: *oviparous.* [< L *parere* beget]

par·ox·ysm (par'ək·siz'əm) *n.* 1 A sudden attack or wors-
ening of a disease; a fit. 2 A sudden and violent outburst,
as of anger or laughter. [< Gk. *para-* beside + *oxynein* to
goad] —**par·ox·ys·mal** (par'ək·siz'məl) *adj.*

par·quet (pär·kā') *n.* 1 The main-floor space of a theater;
orchestra. 2 Flooring of inlaid woodwork; parquetry. —*v.t.*
·**queted** (-kād'), ·**quet·ing** (-kā'ing) To make of or ornament
with parquetry. Also **par·quette** (pär·ket'). [< OF *parchet*
a small compartment, dim. of *parc* park]

parquet circle The section of theater seats at the rear
of the parquet and under the balcony.

par·quet·ry (pär'kit·rē) *n.* Inlaid woodwork forming geometric patterns, used esp. for floor surfaces.

parr (pär) *n.* A young salmon before its first migration
seaward. [?]

par·ra·keet (par'ə·kēt) *n.* PARAKEET.

par·ri·cide (par'ə·sīd) *n.* 1 The murder of a parent, or of
a close relative. 2 One who commits such a crime. [< L
paricidium a killing of a relative] —**par'ri·ci'dal** *adj.*

par·rot (par'ət) *n.* 1 Any of certain birds of warm regions
having a hooked bill, usu. brilliant plumage, and, in some,
an ability to simulate human speech. 2 A person who
repeats or imitates without understanding. —*v.t.* To repeat or imitate without understanding. [? < F *Pierrot*,
dim. of *Pierre* Peter, a personal name] —**par'rot·er** *n.*

parrot fever PSITTACOSIS.

parrot fish Any of many small, vividly colored fishes
inhabiting warm seas, having beaklike jaws.

par·ry (par'ē) *v.* ·**ried**, ·**ry·ing** *v.t.* 1 To ward off, as a blow
or a thrust in fencing. 2 To avoid, esp. by a deft evasion:
to *parry* a question. —*v.i.* 3 To make a parry. 4 To avoid
something, as by skillful maneuvers. —*n. pl.* ·**ries** 1 A defensive movement, as in fencing. 2 An evasion or diversion. [< Ital. *parare* defend] —**Syn.** *v.* 2 evade, dodge, side-
step, duck.

parse (pärs) *v.t.* **parsed**, **pars·ing** 1 To describe (a sentence)
grammatically by giving the form, function, etc., of each
of its components. 2 To describe (a word) as to its part of
speech, form, and relation to the other sentence elements.
[< L *pars, partis* part] —**pars'er** *n.*

Par·see (pär'sē, pär·sē') *n.* A Zoroastrian, esp. one whose
ancestors fled to India about the eighth century. Also
Par'si. —**Par'see·ism, Par'si·ism, Par'sism** *n.*

par·si·mo·ni·ous (pär'sə·mō'nē·əs) *adj.* Stingy; nig-

gardly; miserly. —**par'si·mo'ni·ous·ly** *adv.* —**par'si·mo'ni·
ous·ness** *n.*

par·si·mo·ny (pär'sə·mō'nē) *n.* Undue reluctance to
spend money; stinginess. [< L *parcere* spare]

pars·ley (pärs'lē) *n.* A cultivated edible herb with aromatic, finely divided leaves, used as a garnish and for
flavoring. [< Gk. *petra* rock + *selinon* parsley]

pars·nip (pärs'nip) *n.* 1 A cultivated plant related to
parsley, with a pale, edible root. 2 The root, used as a
vegetable. [< L *pastinaca*]

par·son (pär'sən) *n.* 1 The clergyman of a parish or congregation. 2 Any minister. [< Med. L *persona* a rector]

par·son·age (pär'sən·ij) *n.* A clergyman's residence provided by his church.

part (pärt) *n.* 1 A certain portion or amount of anything;
a piece. 2 One of a number of separable elements that
together constitute a whole: the *parts* of a motor. 3 An
essential portion of a body or an organism; a member. 4
Usu. pl. A portion of territory; region: in foreign *parts.* 5
An individual share, as of duty, business, or performance:
to do one's *part.* 6 A side, cause, or party opposed to another. 7 The role or lines assigned to an actor. 8 *Usu. pl.*
A quality of mind or character; talent: a man of *parts.* 9
Music **a** The series of sounds to be made by a single voice
or instrument in a concerted piece. **b** The notated version
of this. 10 A line formed by dividing the hair. —**for my
part** As far as I am concerned. —**for the most part** On
the whole; generally. —**in part** Partly. —**on the part of**
So far as regards. —**part and parcel** An essential part.
—**take part** To participate: usu. with *in.* —**take someone's part** To support someone's position, as in a dispute.
—*v.t.* 1 To divide or break (something) into parts. 2 To
sever or discontinue (a relationship or connection): to *part*
company. 3 To separate by being or coming between. 4 To
comb (the hair) so as to leave a dividing line. —*v.i.* 5 To
become divided or broken into parts; come apart; divide.
6 To go away from each other; separate. 7 To depart; leave.
—**part from** To separate from; leave. —**part with** 1 To
give up; relinquish. 2 To part from. —*adj.* Of or concerning only a part; partial. —*adv.* In some degree; to some
extent; partly. [< L *pars, partis* part] —**Syn.** *n.* 1 segment,
section, fraction. 2 component, constituent, ingredient,
module.

part. participle.

par·take (pär·tāk') *v.* ·**took**, ·**tak·en**, ·**tak·ing** *v.i.* 1 To take
part or have a share: with *in.* 2 To receive or take a por-
tion: with *of:* to *partake* of food and drink. 3 To have
something of the quality or character: with *of.* —*v.t.* 4 To
take or have a part in; share. [< *part taker*] —**par·tak'er** *n.*

part·ed (pär'tid) *adj.* Situated or placed apart; separated;
cloven.

par·terre (pär·târ') *n.* 1 A flower garden having beds arranged in a pattern. 2 PARQUET CIRCLE. [< MF *par terre* on
(the) ground]

par·the·no·gen·e·sis (pär'thə·nō·jen'ə·sis) *n.* Reproduction by means of unfertilized eggs, seeds, or spores, as
in certain insects, algae, etc. [< Gk. *parthenos* virgin +
GENESIS] —**par'the·no·ge·net'ic** (-jə·net'ik), **par'the·no·gen'ic**
adj. —**par'the·no·ge·net'i·cal·ly** *adv.*

Par·the·non (pär'thə·non) *n.* The Doric temple of
Athena on the Acropolis at Athens, built in the fifth century B.C.

par·tial (pär'shəl) *adj.*
1 Pertaining to, con-
stituting, or involving
a part only; not com-
plete or total. 2 Favor-
ing one side; prejud-
iced; biased. 3 Having
a special liking: with
to. —**par'tial·ly** *adv.*

par·ti·al·i·ty (pär'shē·
al'ə·tē) *n.* 1 The state
of being partial. 2 Unfairness; bias. 3 A particular fondness. Also **par'tial·ness.**

partial tone *Music* A fundamental tone or overtone.

The Parthenon

par·tic·i·pant (pär·tis′ə·pənt) *n.* One who participates. —*adj.* Participating.

par·tic·i·pate (pär·tis′ə·pāt) *v.i.* ·pat·ed, ·pat·ing To take part or have a share in common with others: with *in.* [< L *pars, partis* a part + *capere* take] —**par·tic′i·pa′tion, par·tic′i·pance, par·tic′i·pa·tor** *n.* —**par·tic′i·pa·to·ry** (-pə·tôr′ē, -tō′rē) *adj.*

par·ti·cip·i·al (pär′tə·sip′ē·əl) *adj. Gram.* Having the nature, form, or use of a participle. —**par′ti·cip′i·al·ly** *adv.*

par·ti·ci·ple (pär′tə·sip′əl) *n. Gram.* A word derived from a verb and functioning as both a verb and an adjective. [< L *participium* a sharing, partaking] • **A dangling participle** is a participle that appears to modify the wrong word and therefore makes no sense, as in *Hopping aboard the train, the whistle blew* (instead of *I heard the whistle blow*). But the meaning of sentences including participles like *concerning* or *considering,* when functioning as prepositions, is perfectly clear, and such usage is well established: *Concerning the debt, you may have a month's extension; Considering everything, he did well.*

par·ti·cle (pär′ti·kəl) *n.* 1 A minute part, piece, or portion. 2 Any very small amount or slight degree: without a *particle* of truth. 3 *Physics* Any of the minute components of matter; esp., an **elementary particle,** one of the elementary constituents of an atom, thought to be irreducible, as an electron, neutron, proton, etc. 4 *Gram.* **a** A short, uninflected part of speech, as a conjunction. **b** A prefix or suffix. [< L *particula,* dim. of *pars, partis* a part]

par·ti-col·ored (pär′tē·kul′ərd) *adj.* Having various colors. [< F *partir* divide + COLORED]

par·tic·u·lar (pər·tik′yə·lər) *adj.* 1 Of, being, or pertaining to a single or separate thing. 2 Having a special character; distinctive: a *particular* way of doing things. 3 More than usual; especial: no *particular* hurry. 4 Comprising all details or circumstances: a *particular* description. 5 Characterized by careful attention to detail; requiring high standards of performance; exacting; fastidious. —**in particular** Especially. —*n.* 1 A specific fact or detail, as distinguished from a generalization. 2 A separate or single instance; item. —**Syn.** *adj.* 1 definite, specific. 2 individual, peculiar. [< L *particularis* concerning a part]

par·tic·u·lar·i·ty (pər·tik′yə·lar′ə·tē) *n. pl.* ·ties 1 The state or quality of being particular as distinguished from general. 2 Careful attention to detail; fastidiousness. 3 Something that is particular, as a circumstance or detail.

par·tic·u·lar·ize (pər·tik′yə·lə·rīz′) *v.* ·ized, ·iz·ing *v.t.* 1 To speak of or treat individually or in detail. —*v.i.* 2 To give particulars; be specific. —**par·tic′u·lar·i·za′tion** *n.*

par·tic·u·lar·ly (pər·tik′yə·lər·lē) *adv.* 1 With specific reference. 2 In an unusually great degree: *particularly* difficult. 3 Part by part; in detail.

part·ing (pär′ting) *n.* 1 The act of separating or dividing. 2 A place, line, or point of division. 3 A leave-taking. —*adj.* Occurring while taking leave: a *parting* glance.

par·ti·san (pär′tə·zən, -sən) *n.* 1 One who supports or endorses a party or cause with great devotion or zeal; esp., an overzealous or fanatical devotee. 2 A member of a body of irregular troops; a guerrilla. —*adj.* Pertaining to or characteristic of a partisan. Also **par′ti·zan.** [< Ital. *parte* a part] —**par′ti·san·ship** *n.*

par·tite (pär′tīt) *adj.* Divided into or composed of parts: usu. used in combination: *bipartite, tripartite.* [< L *partire* divide]

par·ti·tion (pär·tish′ən) *n.* 1 The act of parting, or the state of being parted; division; separation. 2 A wall or other barrier dividing an area, esp. an interior space. —*v.t.* 1 To divide into parts, segments, etc. 2 To separate by a partition: with *off.* 3 To divide, as property, into shares or portions. [< L *partire* divide] —**par·ti′tion·er** *n.*

par·ti·tive (pär′tə·tiv) *adj.* 1 Separating into integral parts. 2 *Gram.* Denoting a part as distinct from the whole: *partitive* genitive. —*n. Gram.* A partitive word or case. [< L *partitus,* p.p. of *partire* divide] —**par′ti·tive·ly** *adv.*

part·ly (pärt′lē) *adv.* In some part; in some degree; somewhat.

part·ner (pärt′nər) *n.* 1 One who takes part or is associated with another or others in a business or other enterprise. 2 A husband or wife. 3 Either of two people dancing together. 4 One of two or more people comprising a side or team in a competitive game or sport. [< L *partitio* a share]

part·ner·ship (pärt′nər·ship) *n.* 1 The state of being a partner or partners. 2 Joint interests or ownership. 3 An association founded on a contract between two or more persons to share the profits, expenses, and losses of a business enterprise; also, the contract itself. 4 The group of persons so associated.

part of speech One of the eight traditional classes of words in English, namely: noun, pronoun, verb, adjective, adverb, conjunction, preposition, and interjection.

par·took (pär·tŏŏk′) *p.t.* of PARTAKE.

par·tridge (pär′trij) *n.* Any of various chickenlike game birds, as the ruffed grouse, bobwhite, etc. [< Gk. *perdix* a partridge]

part song A song for two or more voices, esp. without accompaniment.

part-time (pärt′tīm′) *adj.* Working or occupied with an activity for only a part of the time customarily devoted to that activity. —*adv.* On a part-time schedule or basis. —**part′-tim′er** *n.*

Gray partridge

par·tu·ri·ent (pär·t′ŏŏr′ē·ənt) *adj.* 1 Bringing forth or about to bring forth young. 2 Pertaining to childbirth.

par·tu·ri·tion (pär′tyŏŏ·rish′ən, -chŏŏ-) *n.* The act or process of bringing forth young; childbirth. [< L *parturire* be in labor]

par·ty (pär′tē) *n. pl.* ·ties 1 A body of persons united for some common purpose, as a political organization. 2 One who participates in or is involved with an action, proceeding, inquiry, etc.: a *party* to the investigation. 3 *Law* One of the persons named on the record in an action. 4 A social gathering: a dinner *party.* 5 A detachment of soldiers. 6 *Informal* A person. —*adj.* 1 Of or pertaining to a political party. 2 Suitable for a social party: a *party* dress. —*v.i.* ·tied, ·ty·ing *Informal* To attend or give social parties. [< L *pars, partis* a part]

party line 1 A telephone line or circuit serving two or more subscribers: also **party wire.** 2 A boundary line between the properties of two or more owners. 3 A belief or principle of a political party, esp. the Communist party, regarded as an essential conviction of every loyal member. —**par′ty-lin′er** *n.*

par·ve·nu (pär′və·nyŏŏ) *n.* One who has suddenly attained wealth or power but lacks the social status commensurate with it; an upstart. —*adj.* 1 Being a parvenu. 2 Like or characteristic of a parvenu. [< L *pervenire* to come through]

par·vo·vi·rus (pär′vō·vī·rəs) *n.* A tiny virus, containing DNA, occurring in various animals, esp. canines. [< L *parvus* small + VIRUS]

pas (pä) *n.* 1 A step. 2 A dance. [F, a step]

pas·chal (pas′kəl) 1 Of or pertaining to the Jewish Passover. 2 Of or pertaining to Easter. [< L *pascha* Passover]

pa·sha (pə·shä′, pash′ə, pä′shə) *n.* 1 A Turkish honorary title placed after the name. 2 A title given a high-ranking official in Turkey.

pasque·flow·er (pask′flou′ər) *n.* Any of several anemones, esp. an early-blooming, crocuslike wildflower of North America with purplish flowers and hairy leaves. Also **pasch′flow′er.** [< OF <*passer* excel + *fleur* flower]

pass (pas, päs) *v.t.* 1 To go by or move past and leave behind. 2 To go across, around, over, or through. 3 To permit to go unnoticed or unmentioned. 4 To undergo; experience: to *pass* a bad night. 5 To meet the requirements of. 6 To go beyond; surpass: It *passes* comprehension. 7 To cause to go or move: to *pass* one's eyes over a book. 8 To cause to go or move past: to *pass* troops in review. 9 To cause or allow to advance or proceed. 10 To spend: to *pass* the night at an inn. 11 To give approval to. 12 To enact, as a law. 13 To be approved by: The bill *passed* the senate. 14 To omit paying (a dividend). 15 To put in circulation: *Pass* the word. 16 To pronounce, esp. judicially, as judgment or sentence. 17 To discharge from the body. 18 To pledge, as one's word. 19 To perform a pass (*n.* def. 6) on or over. 20 In sports, to transfer (the ball, etc.)

to another player on the same side. **21** *Law* To transfer or assign ownership of to another by will, deed, etc. —*v.i.* **22** To go or proceed; move. **23** To have course or direction; extend: The road *passed* under a bridge. **24** To go away; depart. **25** To come to an end; disappear. **26** To elapse or go by; be spent: The day *passed* slowly. **27** To die. **28** To go by; move past in or as in review. **29** To go from person to person; circulate. **30** To be mutually given and received, as greetings. **31** To go or change from one condition, circumstance, etc., to another. **32** To take place; happen. **33** To go unheeded or unpunished. **34** To undergo a test, examination, etc., successfully. **35** To be approved, ratified, enacted, etc. **36** To obtain or force passage. **37** To be excreted or voided. **38** *Law* To give or pronounce judgment, sentence, etc.: with *on* or *upon.* **b** To be transferred or assigned to another by will, deed, etc. **39** In sports, to transfer the ball, etc., to another player on the same side. **40** In fencing, to make a thrust; lunge. **41** In card games, to decline to make a play, bid, etc. —**bring to pass** To cause to happen or to be realized. —**come to pass** To happen; come about. —**pass away 1** To come to an end. **2** To die. **3** To allow (time) to elapse. —**pass for** To be accepted as, usu. fraudulently. —**pass off 1** To come to an end. **2** To give out or circulate as genuine; palm off. —**pass out 1** To distribute. **2** *Informal* To faint. —**pass over** To fail to notice or consider. —**pass up** *Informal* To fail to take advantage of, as an offer. —*n.* **1** The act of passing. **2** A way or opening that affords a passage, as a gap in a mountain range. **3** Permission or a permit to proceed. **4** A state of affairs; crisis. **5** The successful undergoing of an examination, test, or inspection. **6** A sleight-of-hand movement of a hand, wand, etc. **7** A movement made in attempting to stab or strike. **8** In sports, the action of passing the ball, puck, etc., in the course of play. **9** *Slang* **a** An attempt to caress. **b** Any aggressive action intended to lead to sexual familiarity. —**a pretty pass** *Informal* An unpleasant or difficult situation. [< L *passus* a step] —**pass′er** *n.* • **passed, past** *Passed* is the past tense of the verb *to pass*, but unlike many participles, its use as an adjective is restricted to a very few expressions in which the sense is that of an object physically moving by, as in the baseball term *passed ball*. *Past*, on the other hand, is commonly used as an adjective *(past time)*, adverb *(a bird flew past)*, noun *(in the past)*, or preposition *(ten minutes past the hour)*, and is found only in archaic contexts as the past participle of *pass.*

pass·a·ble (pas′ə·bəl, päs′-) *adj.* **1** Capable of being penetrated or traversed. **2** Fairly good or acceptable. **3** Fit for general circulation. —**pass′a·ble·ness** *n.* —**pass′a·bly** *adv.* —Syn. **2** mediocre, moderate, tolerable, unobjectionable.

pas·sage (pas′ij) *n.* **1** A corridor, hall, or gallery affording access from one part, as of a building, to another. **2** A way through or over. **3** Free entrance, exit, or transit. **4** A passing: the *passage* of the days. **5** A portion of a discourse, writing, etc.: a *passage* from Shakespeare. **6** A journey, as by ship. **7** A navigable route. **8** The enactment of a legislative measure. **9** A personal encounter: a *passage* with swords. **10** Migration, esp. of birds. **11** In music, any short portion of a composition.

pas·sage·way (pas′ij·wā′) *n.* A way affording passage between rooms, areas, etc.

pass·book (pas′bŏŏk′, päs′-) *n.* A bankbook.

pas·sé (pa·sā′, pas′ā) *adj.* **1** Past the prime; faded. **2** Old-fashioned. [F, orig., pp. of *passer*]

passed ball In baseball, a pitch that passes by the catcher and enables a runner to advance a base.

pas·sen·ger (pas′ən·jər) *n.* A person who travels in a car, train, bus, etc. [< OF *passager* < *passage*]

passenger pigeon The wild migratory pigeon of North America, now extinct.

pas·ser-by (pas′ər·bī′, päs′-, pas′ər·bī) *n. pl.* **pas·sers-by** A person who passes by, usu. casually.

pas·ser·ine (pas′ər·in) *adj.* Pertaining to a very large order of birds having feet adapted to perching and young that are naked and blind when hatched. —*n.* Any of these birds. [< L *passer* sparrow + -INE]

pas·sim (pas′im) *adv.* Here and there; in various passages: used as a bibliographic reference. [L]

pass·ing (pas′ing, päs′-) *adj.* **1** Going by or away. **2** Transitory; fleeting. **3** Happening or occurring; current. **4** Done, said, found, used, or given in or as in passing. **5** Indicating fulfillment of requirements for advancement. —*n.* **1** A going away. **2** Dying. **3** An act of passing or passage. —**in passing** Incidentally; in the course of discussion. —*adv. Archaic* In a surpassing degree; exceedingly.

pas·sion (pash′ən) *n.* **1** Fervent devotion. **2** Ardent sexual feelings and desire; love. **3** The object of such feelings. **4** A fit of intense anger; rage. **5** Any transport of excited feeling. **6** *Archaic* Suffering; agony. [< L *passus*, pp. of *pati* suffer] —**pas′sion·less** *adj.* —**pas′sion·less·ly** *adv.*

Pas·sion (pash′ən) *n.* The sufferings of Christ, esp. in the agony of the garden and on the cross.

pas·sion·ate (pash′ən·it) *adj.* **1** Susceptible to strong emotion; excitable. **2** Easily moved to anger. **3** Expressing or displaying some intense feeling. **4** Ardent in expressing sexual desire. [< L *passio* suffering] —**pas′sion·ate·ly** *adv.* —**pas′sion·ate·ness** *n.*

pas·sion·flow·er (pash′ən·flou′ər) *n.* Any of various tendril-climbing vines or shrubs of tropical America, with showy flowers and sometimes edible fruit.

passion fruit The melonlike fruit of certain cultivated passionflowers.

Passion play A drama representing the Passion of Christ.

pas·sive (pas′iv) *adj.* **1** Acted upon or receiving impressions from external agents or causes. **2** In a state of rest or quiescence; unresponsive. **3** Unresisting; submissive. **4** *Chem.* Inert; inactive. **5** *Gram.* Designating a voice of a verb which indicates that the subject is being acted upon, as *Caesar was killed by Brutus.* —*n. Gram.* **1** The passive voice. **2** A verb or construction in this voice. [< L *passus*, pp. of *pati* suffer] —**pas′sive·ly** *adv.* —**pas′sive·ness, pas·siv·i·ty** (pa·siv′ə·tē)

passive resistance Opposition to constituted authority expressed typically in voluntary fasting, refusal to obey laws, etc.

pass·key (pas′kē′, päs′-) *n.* A skeleton key or master key.

Pass·o·ver (pas′ō′vər, päs′-) *n.* An annual Jewish feast celebrated in the spring, commemorating the night when the Lord, smiting the firstborn of the Egyptians, "passed over" the houses of the children of Israel. *Ex.* 12.

pass·port (pas′pôrt′, -pōrt′, päs′-) *n.* **1** An official warrant certifying the citizenship of the bearer when traveling abroad. **2** Anything that gives the privilege or right to enter into some place or sphere of action. [< F *passer* pass + *port* harbor]

pass-through (pas′thrōō′, päs′-) *n.* A wall opening, often with a shelf, as between a kitchen and a dining area, for passing dishes, food, etc.

pass·word (pas′wûrd′, päs′-) *n.* A word identifying one as entitled to pass; a watchword.

past (past, päst) *adj.* **1** Belonging to time gone by. **2** Recently gone by: the *past* week. **3** *Gram.* Denoting a tense or construction which refers to time or action belonging to the past. —*n.* **1** The past life of a person, people, etc. **2** One's record, esp. if disreputable or kept secret. **3** *Gram.* **a** The past tense. **b** A verb or construction in this tense. —**the past** Time gone by; former days collectively. —*adv.* In such manner as to go by and beyond. —*prep.* **1** Beyond in time: It is now *past* noon. **2** Beyond in place or position: walking *past* the house. **3** Beyond the reach or influence of. **4** Beyond in amount or degree: He couldn't count *past* ten. [Orig. pp. of PASS] • See PASS.

pas·ta (päs′tə) *n.* Any of a number of foods made of flour pastes or doughs, as spaghetti, macaroni, etc. [< LL, dough]

paste (pāst) *n.* **1** An adhesive mixture used for joining or affixing paper articles and the like. **2** A mixture of flour and water, often with other materials, for cooking purposes; dough. **3** Any doughy or moist plastic substance: *toothpaste;* almond *paste.* **4** A vitreous composition for making imitation gems. —*v.t.* **past·ed, past·ing 1** To stick or fasten with paste or the like. **2** *Slang* To strike, as with the fist. [< Gk. *pastē* barley porridge]

paste·board (pāst′bôrd′, -bōrd′) *n.* **1** Paper pulp compressed, or paper pasted together to form a stiff sheet. **2** *Slang* Something made of pasteboard, as a playing card. —*adj.* **1** Made of or resembling pasteboard. **2** Thin and flimsy.

pas·tel (pas·tel′) *n.* **1** A picture drawn with colored crayons. **2** The art of drawing such pictures. **3** A hard crayon made of pipe clay and a pigment, mixed with gum and water. **4** A soft, delicate shade of a color. —*adj.* **1** Of or pertaining to a pastel. **2** Having a delicate, soft tint. [< Ital. *pastello*] —**pas·tel′ist** or **pas·tel′list** *n.*

past·er (pās′tər) *n.* **1** One who pastes. **2** A strip of gummed paper to paste over something.

pas·tern (pas′tərn) *n.* The part of a horse's foot between the fetlock and the hoof. [< OF *pasture* a tether for a grazing animal]

paste-up (pāst′up′) *n.* **1** In printing, a layout of a page or pages of columns set in type, illustrations, etc., pasted on a stiff paper backing. **2** A collage.

pas·teur·i·za·tion (pas′tər·ə·zā′shən, -chər-) *n.* A process of controlled heating of milk, beer, etc., to destroy bacteria and arrest spoilage without affecting flavor. *Brit. sp.* **pas′teur·i·sa′tion.** [< Louis *Pasteur,* 1822–95, French chemist] —**pas·teur·ize** (-pas′tə·rīz, -chə·rīz) *v.t.* (**·ized, ·iz·ing**)

Pastern

pas·tille (pas·tēl′, -til′) *n.* **1** A medicated, flavored lozenge. **2** A pellet of combustible aromatic substances for deodorizing or fumigation. Also **pas·til** (pas′til). [F< L *pastillus* a little loaf]

pas·time (pas′tīm′, päs′-) *n.* Something that serves to make time pass agreeably; recreation. [< PASS, *v.* + TIME]

past master 1 One who has held the office of master in certain benevolent organizations. **2** One who has thorough experience in something; an adept.

pas·tor (pas′tər, päs′-) *n.* A Christian minister who has a church or congregation under his official charge. [< L *pastor* a shepherd, lit., a feeder]

pas·tor·al (pas′tər·əl, päs′-) *adj.* **1** Pertaining to shepherds and their work. **2** Describing the conventionalized life of shepherds and rustics: a *pastoral* poem. **3** Having the peaceful simplicity of country life; natural. **4** Pertaining to a pastor and his work. —*n.* **1** A poem, play, etc., set in rustic surroundings. **2** A picture illustrating rural scenes. **3** *Eccl.* A letter from a pastor to his congregation. —**Syn.** *adj.* **3** bucolic, rustic.

pas·tor·ate (pas′tər·it, päs′-) *n.* **1** The office or jurisdiction of a pastor. **2** The duration of a pastoral charge. **3** Pastors collectively.

past participle A verb form used to indicate a time or action completed in the past, as *cooked* in *She has cooked dinner.*

past perfect *Gram.* **1** Denoting the tense of a verb indicating an action completed prior to a specified past time, as *had finished* in *He had finished before the bell rang.* **2** The past perfect tense, or a verb in this tense.

pas·tra·mi (pə·strä′mē) *n.* Smoked beef, heavily seasoned and unu. cut from the shoulder. [< Magyar]

pas·try (pās′trē) *n. pl.* **·tries 1** Articles of food made with a crust of shortened dough, as pies. **2** Any of various sweet baked goods, as cakes, buns, etc. [< PASTE + -RY]

pas·tur·age (pas′chər·ij, päs′-) *n.* **1** Grass and herbage for cattle. **2** Ground used or suitable for grazing. **3** The business or right of grazing cattle.

pas·ture (pas′chər, päs′-) *n.* **1** Ground for the grazing of domestic animals. **2** Grass or herbage that grazing domestic animals eat. —*v.* **·tured, ·tur·ing** *v.t.* **1** To lead to or put in a pasture to graze. **2** To graze on (grass, land, etc.). —*v.i.* **3** To graze. [< L *pastus,* pp. of *pascere* to feed] —**pas′tur·er** *n.*

past·y¹ (pās′tē) *adj.* **past·i·er, past·i·est 1** Like paste in consistency. **2** Sickly and pale: a *pasty* complexion. —**past′i·ness** *n.*

past·y² (pās′tē, *Brit.* pas′tē, päs′tē) *n. pl.* **past·ies** A meat pie. [< LL *pasta* dough]

pat¹ (pat) *v.* **pat·ted, pat·ting** *v.t.* **1** To touch or tap lightly with the hand. **2** To shape or mold by a pat or pats. **3** To strike with lightly sounding steps, as in running. —*v.i.* **4** To tap or strike gently. **5** To run or walk with light steps. —*n.* **1** A light, caressing stroke. **2** The sound of patting or pattering. **3** A small, molded mass, as of butter. [ME *patte*] —**pat′ter** *n.*

pat² (pat) *adj.* **1** Suitable, as a response; fitting. **2** Formulated in a customary way without much thought; facile. —*adv.* In a fit manner. —**stand pat** *Informal* To refuse to reconsider or change, as an opinion, decision, etc. —**pat′ly** *adv.* —**pat′ness** *n.*

pat. patent; patented; patrol; pattern.

patch (pach) *n.* **1** A small piece of material, used to repair a hole, tear, or worn place. **2** A piece of adhesive tape or the like, applied to the skin to hide a blemish or protect a small wound. **3 a** A small piece of ground. **b** The plants growing on it: a *patch* of corn. **4** A piece of cloth or other material worn over an injured eye. **5** A small piece of cloth sewed on a garment, esp. a uniform, as an emblem or insignia of rank. **6** A shred or scrap. —*v.t.* **1** To put a patch or patches on. **2** To repair or put together hurriedly or crudely: often with *up* or *together.* **3** To make of patches, as a quilt. —**patch (things) up** To resolve or settle, as a quarrel. [ME *pacehe*] —**patch′er** *n.*

patch·ou·li (pach′ōō·lē, pə·chōō′lē) *n.* **1** An East Indian herb of the mint family. **2** A fragrant oil or perfume obtained from it. Also **patch′ou·ly.** [< Tamil *paccu* green + *ilai* a leaf]

patch test A skin test for determining hypersensitivity by applying small pads of possibly allergy-producing substances to the skin's surface.

patch·work (pach′wûrk′) *n.* **1** A fabric made of patches of cloth, as for quilts, etc. **2** Work done hastily or carelessly; a jumble.

patch·y (pach′ē) *adj.* **patch·i·er, patch·i·est 1** Of, containing, or consisting of patches. **2** Occurring here and there rather than uniformly: *patchy* fog. —**patch′i·ly** *adv.* —**patch′i·ness** *n.*

patd. patented.

pate (pāt) *n.* **1** The top of the head, esp. a human head. **2** Brains; intellect: usu. humorous. [ME]

pâté de foie gras (pä·tā′ də fwa grä′) *French* A paste made from the livers of fattened geese.

pa·tel·la (pə·tel′ə) *n. pl.* **·las** or **·tel·lae** (-tel′ē) The flat, movable, oval bone at the front of the human knee joint. [L, dim. of *patina* a pan] —**pa·tel′lar, pa·tel·late** (pə·tel′āt, -it) *adj.*

pat·en (pat′n) *n.* **1** A plate for the eucharistic bread. **2** A thin, metallic plate. [< L *patena* a pan]

pa·ten·cy (pāt′n·sē) *n.* **1** The condition of being evident. **2** The state of being without obstruction.

pat·ent (pat′nt, *Brit.* pāt′nt; *for adj. defs. 2 & 3, usu.* pāt′nt) *n.* **1** A government protection to an inventor, securing to him for a specific time exclusive rights to his invention. **2** The rights so granted. **3** Any official document securing a right. —*v.t.* To obtain a patent on (an invention). —*adj.* **1** Protected or conferred by a patent. **2** Manifest or apparent to everybody. **3** Open; unobstructed, as a duct in the body. [< L *patens* pr.p. of *patere* lie open]

Patella

patent leather (pat′nt) Leather finished with a glossy, varnishlike coat: so called from the formerly patented process.

pa·tent·ly (pāt′nt·lē, pat′nt-) *adv.* Manifestly; clearly.

pa·ter (pā′tər) *n. Brit. Informal* Father. [L]

pa·ter·fa·mil·i·as (pā′tər·fə·mil′ē·əs) *n. pl.* **pa·tres·fa·mil·i·as** (pā′trēz-) The father of a family or master of a house. [< L *pater* father + *familia* family]

pa·ter·nal (pə·tûr′nəl) *adj.* **1** Pertaining to a father; fatherly. **2** Derived from one's father; hereditary. **3** Related through one's father: a *paternal* aunt. [< L *pater* a father] —**pa·ter′nal·ly** *adv.*

pa·ter·nal·ism (pə·tûr′nəl·iz′əm) *n.* The control of a country, community, or group in a manner suggestive of a father looking after his children. —**pa·ter′nal·is′tic** *adj.* —**pa·ter′nal·is′ti·cal·ly** *adv.*

pa·ter·ni·ty (pə·tûr′nə·tē) *n.* **1** The condition of being a father. **2** Parentage on the male side. **3** Origin in general.

pa·ter·nos·ter (pā′tər·nos′tər) *n.* **1** The Lord's Prayer, esp. in Latin: also **Pater Noster. 2** A bead of the rosary representing one recitation of the Lord's Prayer. [< L *pater noster* our father]

path (path, päth) *n. pl.* **paths** (pathz, päthz, paths, päths) **1** A walk or way, as one beaten by the foot, used by men or animals. **2** Any road, track, or course. **3** A way of life or course of action. [< OE *pæth*]

path., pathol. pathology.

Pa·than (pə·tän′, pä′thən) *n.* One of a people of Afghanistan of Indo-Iranian stock and Muslim religion.

pa·thet·ic (pə·thet′ik) *adj.* Inspiring pity; arousing compassion. Also **pa·thet′i·cal.** [< Gk. *pathētikos* sensitive] — **pa·thet′i·cal·ly** *adv.*

pathetic fallacy The attribution of human feelings and emotions to inanimate nature, as in *The November sky wept.*

path·find·er (path′fīn′dər, päth′-) *n.* One skilled in leading or finding a way into unknown regions or in new fields of endeavor.

patho- *combining form* Suffering; disease: *pathogenesis.* [< Gk. *pathos* suffering]

path·o·gen (path′ə·jən) *n.* A disease-producing organism, as a fungus, virus, etc. Also **path′o·gene** (-jēn). — **path′o·gen′ic** *adj.*

path·o·gen·e·sis (path′ə·jen′ə·sis) *n.* The cause or development of a disease. Also **pa·thog·e·ny** (pə·thoj′ə·nē).

pa·thol·o·gist (pə·thol′ə·jist) *n.* A physician or other expert specializing in pathology.

pa·thol·o·gy (pə·thol′ə·jē) *n. pl.* **·gies 1** The branch of medical science dealing with the causes, nature, and effects of diseases, esp. disease-induced changes in organs, tissues, and body chemistry. **2** A diseased or abnormal condition. —**path·o·log·i·cal** (path′ə·loj′i·kəl) or **path′o·log′ic** *adj.* —**path·o·log′i·cal·ly** *adv.*

pa·thos (pā′thos) *n.* The quality, attribute, or element, in events, speech, or art, that rouses the tender emotions, as compassion or sympathy. [Gk., suffering]

path·way (path′wā′, päth′-) *n.* PATH.

-pathy *combining form* **1** Feeling; emotion: *sympathy.* **2** Disease: *psychopathy.* **3** The treatment of disease: *hydropathy.* [< Gk. *pathos* suffering]

pa·tience (pā′shəns) *n.* **1** The quality of enduring without complaint. **2** The exercise of sustained perseverance. **3** Forbearance toward the faults or infirmities of others. **4** *Brit.* Any solitaire card game. —**Syn. 1** endurance, fortitude, resignation. **2** steadiness. **3** leniency, tolerance.

pa·tient (pā′shənt) *adj.* **1** Possessing quiet, uncomplaining endurance under distress. **2** Tolerant and forbearing. **3** Capable of tranquilly awaiting events. **4** Persevering. — *n.* A person undergoing medical care. [< L *patiens,* pr.p. of *pati* suffer] —**pa′tient·ly** *adv.*

pat·i·na (pat′ə·nə, pə·tē′nə) *n.* **1** A green coating on copper and its alloys, usu. formed by prolonged weathering. **2** Any surface of antique appearance. [< L *patina* a plate]

pa·ti·o (pä′tē·ō, pat′ē·ō) *n. pl.* **·ti·os 1** An open inner court of a Spanish dwelling. **2** An outdoor terrace next to a house, used for relaxation, dining, etc. [Sp.]

pat·ois (pat′wä, *Fr.* pá·twá′) *n. pl.* **pat·ois** (pat′wäz, *Fr.* pá·twá′) **1** A dialect, esp. one that is provincial and nonstandard. **2** The distinctive language of an occupational group; jargon. [< OF]

pat. pend. patent pending.

patri- *combining form* Father: *patricide.* [< L *pater, -tris* father]

pa·tri·arch (pā′trē·ärk) *n.* **1** The leader of a family or tribe who rules by paternal right. **2** One of the earliest fathers of the human race, as Adam or Noah. **3** One of the fathers of the Hebrew race, Abraham, Isaac, or Jacob. **4** A venerable man; esp. the founder of a religion. **5** A prelate in the early Roman Catholic church or in the modern Greek Church. [< Gk. *patria* family, clan + *archein* to rule] —**pa′tri·ar′chal, pa′tri·ar′chic** *adj.* —**pa′tri·ar′chal·ly** *adv.*

pa·tri·ar·chate (pā′trē·är′kit) *n.* **1** The office, dominion, or residence of a patriarch. **2** A patriarchal system of government.

pa·tri·ar·chy (pā′trē·är′kē) *n. pl.* **·chies** A social system in which the father rules the family or clan, and in which descent is traced through the male line.

pa·tri·cian (pə·trish′ən) *n.* **1** A member of a nobility; aristocrat. **2** A member of the aristocracy of ancient Rome. — *adj.* **1** Of or pertaining to an aristocracy. **2** Aristocratic; having high rank. **3** Belonging to or suitable for an aristocrat. [< L *pater, -tris* a senator, lit., a father]

pat·ri·cide (pat′rə·sīd) *n.* **1** The killing of a father. **2** One who slays a father; a parricide. —**pat′ri·ci′dal** *adj.*

pat·ri·mo·ny (pat′rə·mō′nē) *n. pl.* **·nies 1** An inheritance from a father or an ancestor. **2** An endowment of property to a church. **3** Any heritage. [< L *pater* a father] —**pat′ri·mo′ni·al** *adj.* —**pat′ri·mo′ni·al·ly** *adv.*

pa·tri·ot (pā′trē·ət, -ot) *n.* One who loves his country and zealously guards its welfare. [< Gk. *patris* fatherland] — **pa′tri·ot′ic** (-ot′ik) *adj.* —**pa′tri·ot′i·cal·ly** *adv.*

pa·tri·ot·ism (pā′trē·ə·tiz′əm) *n.* Devotion to one's country.

pa·tris·tic (pə·tris′tik) *adj.* Of or pertaining to the early fathers of the Christian church or to their writings. Also **pa·tris′ti·cal.** [< L *pater* father] —**pa·tris′ti·cal·ly** *adv.*

pa·trol (pə·trōl′) *v.t. & v.i.* **·trolled, ·trol·ling** To walk or go through or around (an area, town, etc.) for the purpose of guarding or inspecting. — *n.* **1** One or more soldiers, policemen, etc., patrolling a district. **2** A reconnaissance group of ships, planes, vehicles, or men on foot sent out to observe the enemy. **3** The act of patrolling. **4** A small unit of Boy Scouts. [< MF *patouiller,* orig., paddle in mud] —**pa·trol′ler** *n.*

pa·trol·man (pə·trōl′mən) *n. pl.* **·men** (-mən) A policeman patrolling a specific area.

patrol wagon A police wagon or truck for the conveyance of prisoners.

pa·tron (pā′trən) *n.* **1** One who protects, fosters, or supports some person or thing; benefactor. **2** A regular customer. **3** A saint regarded as one's personal guardian. **4** One who sponsors a charitable entertainment or a cause. [< L *patronus* protector] —**pa′tron·al** *adj.* —**pa′tron·ess** *n. Fem.*

pa·tron·age (pā′trən·ij, pat′rən-) *n.* **1** Encouragement and support given by a patron. **2** Favor or support given with a condescending manner. **3** The power to make appointments to certain positions or offices in public service. **4** Such positions or offices. **5** The financial support given by customers to commercial enterprises.

pa·tron·ize (pā′trən·īz, pat′rən-) *v.t.* **·ized, ·iz·ing 1** To give support or protection to. **2** To treat in a condescending manner. **3** To trade with as a regular customer. —**pa′tron·iz′er** *n.* —**pa′tron·iz′ing·ly** *adv.*

pat·ro·nym·ic (pat′rə·nim′ik) *n.* A name derived from a father or an ancestor; a family name. Also **pat′ro·nym.** [< Gk. *patēr* father + *onyma* name] —**pat′ro·nym′i·cal·ly** *adv.*

pa·troon (pə·trōōn′) *n.* Under old Dutch law, a holder of entailed estates, chiefly in New York and New Jersey. [< L *patronus* patron]

pat·ten (pat′n) *n.* A shoe having a thick, wooden sole; a clog. [< OF *patte* a paw, foot]

pat·ter¹ (pat′ər) *v.i.* **1** To make a succession of light, sharp sounds. **2** To move with light, quick steps. — *v.t.* **3** To cause to patter. — *n.* Pattering, or the sound of pattering. [Freq. of PAT¹]

pat·ter² (pat′ər) *v.t. & v.i.* To speak or say glibly or rapidly. — *n.* **1** Glib and rapid talk, as used by comedians, etc. **2** Patois or dialect. [Short for PATERNOSTER; from the rapid repetition of the prayer] —**pat′ter·er** *n.*

pat·tern (pat′ərn) *n.* **1** An original or model proposed for or worthy of imitation. **2** Anything shaped or designed to serve as a model or guide in making something else. **3** Any decorative design or figure worked on something: a vase with a geometrical *pattern.* **4** Arrangement of natural or accidental markings. **5** The stylistic composition or design of a work of art. **6** A complex of integrated parts functioning as a whole: *patterns* of American culture. —*v.t.* 1 To make after a model or pattern: with *on, upon,* or *after.* 2 To decorate or furnish with a pattern. [<L *patronus* patron]

pat·ty (pat′ē) *n. pl.* **·ties** 1 A small pastry shell in which to serve creamed chicken, fish, etc.: also **patty shell.** 2 A flat round cake of food or candy. [Alter. of F *pâté*]

pau·ci·ty (pô′sə·tē) *n.* 1 Smallness of number or quantity. 2 Scarcity; insufficiency. [<L *paucus* few]

Paul Bun·yan (bun′yən) In American folklore, a lumberjack of superhuman size and strength, credited with amazing feats.

Paul·ine (pô′lēn, -līn) *adj.* Of or relating to Saint Paul, his teachings, and his writings.

paunch (pônch) *n.* 1 The abdomen. 2 A protruding abdomen; potbelly. 3 RUMEN. [<L *pantex* belly, bowels] — **paunch′i·ness** *n.* —**paunch′y** *adj.* (·i·er, ·i·est)

pau·per (pô′pər) *n.* 1 Any very poor person. 2 A destitute person who receives public charity. [L, poor]

pau·per·ism (pô′pə·riz′əm) *n.* 1 Poverty. 2 Paupers collectively. —Syn. 1 beggary, destitution, indigence, penury.

pau·per·ize (pô′pər·īz) *v.t.* ·ized, ·iz·ing To make a pauper of.

pause (pôz) *v.i.* paused, paus·ing 1 To cease action or utterance temporarily. 2 To dwell or linger: with *on* or *upon:* to *pause* on a word. —*n.* 1 A ceasing of action. 2 A holding back because of doubt or irresolution. 3 A momentary cessation in speaking or music for emphasis. 4 A character or sign indicating such cessation. —**give (one) pause** To cause (one) to hesitate or be uncertain, as from trepidation. [<L *pausa* a stop] —**paus′er** *n.*

pave (pāv) *v.t.* paved, pav·ing To cover or surface with concrete, macadam, etc., as a road. —**pave the way (for)** To make preparation (for); lead up to. [<L *pavire* ram down]

pave·ment (pāv′mənt) *n.* 1 A hard, solid surface for a road or sidewalk, usu. resting immediately on the ground. 2 A paved road or sidewalk. 3 The material with which a surface is paved.

pa·vil·ion (pə·vil′yən) *n.* 1 A movable or open structure for temporary shelter. 2 A related or connected part of a principal building: the dancing *pavilion.* 3 A canopy or tent. 4 A detached building for patients, as at a hospital. —*v.t.* 1 To provide with a pavilion or pavilions. 2 To shelter by a pavilion. [<L *papilio* a butterfly, tent]

pav·ing (pā′ving) *n.* 1 The laying of a pavement. 2 The material used for pavement.

paw (pô) *n.* 1 The foot of an animal having nails or claws. 2 *Informal* A clumsy human hand. —*v.t. & v.i.* 1 To strike or scrape with the feet or paws: to *paw* at the ground. 2 *Informal* To handle rudely or with too great familiarity; maul. [<OF *powe*] —**paw′er** *n.*

pawl (pôl) *n. Mech.* A hinged or pivoted part shaped to engage with ratchet teeth.[?<L *palus* a stake]

pawn¹ (pôn) *n.* 1 Any of the 16 chessmen of lowest rank. 2 Any insignificant person used at another's will. [<OF *peon, pedon* a foot soldier]

pawn² (pôn) *n.* 1 Something, as personal property, pledged to secure a loan. 2 The condition of being held as a pledge for money loaned. —*v.t.* 1 To give (personal property) as security for a loan. 2 To risk or stake; pledge. [<L *pannus* a cloth]

Double pawl

pawn·brok·er (pôn′brō′kər) *n.* One engaged in the business of lending money on pledged personal property. — **pawn′brok′ing** *n.*

Paw·nee (pô·nē′) *n. pl.* ·nee or ·nees 1 A member of one of four tribes of North American Indians formerly of Nebraska, now living in Oklahoma. 2 Their language.

pawn·shop (pôn′shop′) *n.* The place of business of a pawnbroker.

pawn ticket A certificate for goods pawned.

paw·paw (pô′pô) *n.* PAPAW.

pay (pā) *v.* paid, pay·ing *v.t.* 1 To give to (someone) what is due for a debt, purchase, etc. 2 To give (money, etc.) for a purchase, service rendered, etc. 3 To discharge, as a debt, bill, etc. 4 To yield as return or recompense. 5 To afford

profit or benefit to. 6 To defray, as expenses. 7 To answer in kind; requite, as for a favor or an insult. 8 To render or give, as a compliment, attention, etc. 9 To make (a call or visit). —*v.i.* 10 To make recompense or payment. 11 To afford compensation or profit: It *pays* to be honest. —**pay back** To repay. —**pay off** 1 To pay the entire amount of. 2 To pay the wages of and discharge. 3 To gain revenge upon or for. 4 *Informal* To afford full return. 5 *Slang* To bribe. 6 *Naut.* To turn or cause to turn to leeward. —**pay out** 1 To disburse or expend. 2 *Naut.* To let out by slackening, as a rope or cable. —**pay up** To make full payment of. —*n.* 1 That which is given as a recompense or to discharge a debt. 2 That act of paying or the state of being paid. 3 Whatever compensates for labor or loss. —**in the pay of** Employed by: sometimes derogatory. —*adj.* 1 Of or pertaining to payments, persons who pay, or services paid for: *pay* day. 2 Yielding enough metal to be worth mining: *pay* dirt. [<L *pacare* appease<*pax* peace]

pay·a·ble (pā′ə·bəl) *adj.* 1 Due to be paid; owed. 2 That may be paid: *payable* on demand. —**pay′a·bly** *adv.*

pay-as-you-go (pā′əz·yoo·gō′) *adj.* Of or pertaining to a policy of meeting expenses as they occur or become due instead of deferring payment.

pay dirt 1 Soil containing enough metal, esp. gold, to be profitable to mine. 2 *Informal* Anything promising to yield rich rewards.

pay·ee (pā·ē′) *n.* One to whom payment is made.

pay·load (pā′lōd) *n.* 1 That part of a cargo producing revenue. 2 The explosive material in the warhead of a missile. 3 The persons, instruments, etc., carried in a spacecraft that are directly related to the objective of the flight rather than to the operation of the craft.

pay·mas·ter (pā′mas′tər, -mäs′-) *n.* One who has charge of the paying of employees.

pay·ment (pā′mənt) *n.* 1 The act of paying. 2 Something that is paid. 3 Something done in requital.

pay·off (pā′ôf′, -of′) *n.* 1 Payment, as of wages or profits. 2 *Informal* Any reward or punishment. 3 *Informal* The climax of an incident or narrative. 4 *Informal* Anything serving to explain or resolve an issue in dispute or doubt. 5 *Slang* A bribe.

pay·roll (pā′rōl′) *n.* 1 A list of those entitled to receive pay, with the amounts due them. 2 The total sum of money needed to make the payments.

payt. payment.

Pb lead (L *plumbum*)

PBX, P.B.X. private branch (telephone) exchange.

PC (pē′sē) *n.* Personal computer, a microcomputer for use at a table or desk, designed for routine personal or business matters.

pc. piece; price.

pct. percent; precinct.

P.D. Police Department.

P.D., p.d. by the day (L *per diem*).

Pd palladium.

pd. paid.

pea (pē) *n.* 1 A tendril-climbing annual leguminous herb widely cultivated for food and fodder. 2 Its edible seed or green pod. 3 Any of various other plants of the same family or their pods or seeds, as the cowpea. [<L *pisum* pea]

peace (pēs) *n.* 1 The absence or cessation of war. 2 General order and tranquillity. 3 A state of reconciliation after strife or enmity. 4 Freedom from mental agitation or anxiety. —**hold (or keep) one's peace** To be silent. [< L *pax, pacis*] —Syn. 1 amity, concord. 3 agreement, reconciliation. 4 content, relaxation, repose.

peace·a·ble (pē′sə·bəl) *adj.* 1 Inclined to peace; accommodating; not combative. 2 Peaceful; tranquil. —**peace′a·ble·ness** *n.* —**peace′a·bly** *adv.*

Peace Corps A U.S. agency that recruits and trains volunteers who live and work in underdeveloped countries for a period of time.

peace·ful (pēs′fəl) *adj.* 1 Free from war, commotion, or other disturbance. 2 Inclined to be accommodating; not combative or pugnacious: a *peaceful* disposition. 3 Of or characteristic of peace or of a time of peace. 4 Serene; still: a *peaceful* scene. 5 Inclined to or used in peace. —**peace′·ful·ly** *adv.* —**peace′ful·ness** *n.*

peace·mak·er (pēs′mā′kər) n. One who effects, or seeks to effect, a reconciliation between unfriendly parties. — **peace′mak′ing** adj., n.

peace·nik (pēs′nik) n. Informal A person who demonstrates against war or a particular war: a derogatory term. [< PEACE + -NIK]

peace officer A sheriff, constable, or policeman.

peace pipe CALUMET.

peach[1] (pēch) n. 1 The fleshy, juicy, edible fruit of the peach tree. 2 The tree, widely cultivated in many varieties. 3 The orange-yellow color of the fruit. 4 Slang Any person or thing particularly beautiful or excellent. [< L persicum (malum) Persian (apple)]

peach[2] (pēch) v.i. Slang To turn informer. [Alter. of IMPEACH]

peach·y (pē′chē) adj. peach·i·er, peach·i·est 1 Resembling a peach. 2 Slang Delightfully pleasant. —**peach′i·ness** n.

pea·cock (pē′kok) n. 1 A male peafowl, having a crested head, long erectile tail feathers marked with eyelike spots, and iridescent greenish blue neck and breast. 2 A person of excessive vanity. [< OE pēa, pāwa a peacock + COCK] —**pea′cock·ish** adj.

pea·fowl (pē′foul) n. 1 A peacock or peahen. 2 A large pheasant of s Asia. [< OE pēa peacock + FOWL]

pea green Any of several shades of light yellowish green. — **pea′-green′** adj.

pea·hen (pē′hen) n. A female peafowl.

Peacock

pea·jack·et (pē′jak·it) n. A short coat of thick woolen cloth, worn by seamen. [Prob. < MDu. pie a kind of wool + JACKET]

peak (pēk) n. 1 A projecting point or edge; an end terminating in a point: the peak of a roof. 2 a A mountain with a pointed summit. b The summit itself. 3 The highest point in a pattern of change or development: at the peak of his career. 4 A point formed on the forehead by the growth or cut of the hair. —v.i. 1 To reach a peak; climax. —v.t. 2 To raise to or almost to a vertical position. [?]

peaked (pēkt, pē′kid) adj. Having a summit or peak.

peak·ed[2] (pē′kid) adj. Having a wan or sickly appearance. [?]

peal (pēl) n. 1 A prolonged, sonorous sound, as of a bell, trumpet, or thunder. 2 A set of large bells attuned to the major scale. 3 A change rung on a chime. —v.t. & v.i. To sound with a peal or peals. [< OF apeler call, appeal]

pe·an (pē′ən) n. PAEAN.

pea·nut (pē′nut′) n. 1 An annual, leguminous vine that bears underground pods containing one or more oily, edible seeds. 2 The seeds of this plant, with or without the brittle pod. 3 A small or insignificant person.

peanut butter A food product made from ground, roasted peanuts.

pear (pâr) n. 1 Any of numerous varieties of a juicy, edible fruit, usu. having a globular shape which narrows into a neck at the stem end. 2 Any of a species of trees of the rose family bearing this fruit. [< L pirum]

pearl (pûrl) n. 1 A lustrous calcareous concretion found in the shells of various mollusks, and valued as a gem. 2 Something like or likened to such a jewel in form, luster, etc. 3 Nacre or mother-of-pearl. 4 A delicate gray color: also **pearl gray**. 5 Printing A size of type, smaller than agate, 5 points. —adj. 1 Pertaining to or made of pearl or mother-of-pearl: a pearl button. 2 Shaped like a pearl. — v.i. 1 To seek or fish for pearls. 2 To form beads like pearls. [< OF perle] —**pearl′i·ness** n. —**pearl′y** adj. (·i·er, ·i·est)

pearl diver A person occupied in diving for pearl-bearing mollusks. Also **pearl fisher**.

peart (pirt, pûrt) adj. Regional In good health and spirits; active; lively. [Var. of PERT] —**peart′ly** adv. —**peart′ness** n.

peas·ant (pez′ənt) n. In Europe and Asia, a small farmer or farm laborer. [< OF païs country]

peas·ant·ry (pez′ən·trē) n. The peasant class; a body of peasants.

peas·cod (pēz′kod) n. Archaic A pea pod. Also **pease′·cod**. [< PEAS(E) + E cod pod, husk]

pease (pēz) n.pl. Archaic Peas. [< OE pise]

peat (pēt) n. 1 An accumulation of partly decomposed vegetable material, found usu. in bogs. 2 A block of this substance, pressed and dried for fuel. [< Med. L peta] — **peat′y** adj. (·i·er, ·i·est)

peat moss SPHAGNUM.

pea·vy (pē′vē) n. pl. ·vies An iron-pointed lever fitted with a movable hook and used for handling logs. Also **pea′vey**. [< Joseph Peavey, 19th c. American blacksmith]

peb·ble (peb′əl) n. 1 A small, rounded fragment of rock, its form being due to the action of water, ice, etc. 2 Leather that has been pebbled. —v.t. ·bled, ·bling 1 To impart a rough grain to (leather). 2 To pave, cover, or pelt with pebbles. [< OE pabol(stān) a pebble(stone)] —**peb′bly** adj.

pe·can (pi·kan′, -kän′, pē′kan) n. 1 A species of hickory with olive-shaped, thin-shelled nuts. 2 The nut borne by this tree. [< Algon.]

pec·ca·dil·lo (pek′ə·dil′ō) n. pl. ·los or ·loes A slight or trifling sin; a fault. [< L peccare to sin]

pec·cant (pek′ənt) adj. 1 Guilty of sin. 2 Violating some rule or principle. [< L peccare to sin] —**pec′can·cy** n. — **pec′cant·ly** adv.

pec·ca·ry (pek′ər·ē) n. pl. ·ries Either of two species of tropical American animals resembling and related to pigs. [< Cariban pakira]

peck[1] (pek) v.t. 1 To strike with the beak, as a bird does, or with something pointed. 2 To make by striking thus: to peck a hole in a wall. 3 To pick up, as food, with the beak. 4 Informal To kiss lightly. —v.i. 5 To make strokes with the beak. —**peck at** Informal 1 To eat by taking small and infrequent bites. 2 To nag; carp at. —n. 1 A quick, sharp blow, as with a beak or something pointed. 2 A mark, dent, or hole made by such a blow. [ME pecken] —**peck′er** n.

Peccary

peck[2] (pek) n. 1 A measure equal to 0.25 bushel, or eight quarts. 2 A vessel for measuring a peck. 3 Informal A great quantity. [< OF pek, a measure of oats for horses]

pec·tin (pek′tin) n. A gummy, water-soluble carbohydrate present in many fruits and used as the basis of fruit jellies. [< Gk. pēktos congealed] —**pec·tic** (pek′tik) adj.

pec·to·ral (pek′tər·əl) adj. 1 Of or pertaining to the breast or chest. 2 Used to treat diseases of the lungs or chest. —n. 1 A pectoral fin or muscle. 2 A pectoral medicine. [< L pectus, -oris the breast] —**pec′tor·al·ly** adv.

pectoral fin Either of the pair of fins located just behind the head of a fish.

pec·u·late (pek′yə·lāt) v.t. & v.i. ·lat·ed, ·lat·ing To appropriate wrongfully (funds, esp. public funds) entrusted to one's care; embezzle. [< L peculari embezzle] —**pec′u·la′· tion, pec′u·la′tor** n.

pe·cu·liar (pi·kyōōl′yər) adj. 1 Odd or strange; queer; singular. 2 Having a character exclusively its own. 3 Select or special. 4 Belonging exclusively to one: a talent peculiar to him. [< L peculiaris < peculium private property] —**pe·cu′liar·ly** adv.

pe·cu·li·ar·i·ty (pi·kyōō′lē·ar′ə·tē, -kyōōl′yar′-) n. pl. ·ties 1 The quality of being peculiar. 2 Something that is odd or peculiar, as a trait. 3 A distinguishing trait: The thumb is a peculiarity of primates. —**Syn.** 2 eccentricity, idiosyncrasy, oddity. 3 attribute, characteristic.

pe·cu·ni·ar·y (pi·kyōō′nē·er′ē) adj. Consisting of or relating to money; monetary. [< L pecunia money < pecus cattle] —**pe·cu′ni·ar′i·ly** adv.

-ped Var. of -PEDE: quadruped.

ped·a·gog·ic (ped′ə·goj′ik, -gō′jik) adj. Of or pertaining to teachers and the art of teaching. Also **ped′a·gog′i·cal**. — **ped′a·gog′i·cal·ly** adv.

ped·a·gogue (ped′ə·gog, -gôg) n. A school teacher, esp.

a pedantic, narrow-minded one. Also **ped′a·gog**. [<Gk. *pais* child + *agōgos* leader]

ped·a·go·gy (ped′ə·gō′jē, -goj′ē) *n.* **1** The science or profession of teaching. **2** The theory or the teaching of how to teach.

ped·al (ped′l) *adj.* Of or relating to a foot, feet, or a foot-like part. —*n.* A lever operated by the foot, as that used to control the tone of a piano, organ, etc., or to govern the rate of movement of an automobile, bicycle, or a mechanical part. —*v.t.* & *v.i.* ·**aled** or ·**alled**, ·**al·ing** or ·**al·ling** To move or operate by working pedals. [<L *pes, pedis* the foot]

pedal pushers Women's and girls' trousers reaching to the calf, originally used for bicycling.

ped·ant (ped′ənt) *n.* **1** A scholar who makes needless display of his learning, esp. in trifling points of scholarship. **2** A dull, narrow-minded teacher. [<Ital. *pedante*] —**pe·dan·tic** (pi·dan′tik) *adj.* —**pe·dan′ti·cal·ly** *adv.*

ped·ant·ry (ped′ən·trē) *n. pl.* ·**ries** **1** Ostentatious display of knowledge. **2** Undue and slavish adherence to forms or rules.

ped·dle (ped′l) *v.* ·**dled**, ·**dling** *v.i.* **1** To travel about selling small wares. —*v.t.* **2** To carry about and offer for sale. **3** *Informal* To put forth or issue as if seeking to sell: to *peddle* an idea. [Back-formation from ME *pedlere* peddler] —**ped′dler, ped′lar** *n.*

-pede *combining form* Footed: *centipede*. [<L *pes, pedis* foot]

ped·er·ast (ped′ə·rast, pē′də-) *n.* One who practices pederasty.

ped·er·as·ty (ped′ə·ras′tē, pē′də-) *n.* Sodomy, esp. as practiced between men and boys. [<Gk. *paiderastēs* a lover of boys] —**ped′er·as′tic** *adj.* —**ped′er·as′ti·cal·ly** *adv.*

ped·es·tal (ped′is·təl) *n.* **1** A base or support for a column, statue, or vase. **2** Any foundation, base, or support, either material or immaterial. —**put on a pedestal** To hold in high estimation; idolize. [<Ital. *piè, pied* foot + *di* of + *stallo* a stall, standing place]

pe·des·tri·an (pə·des′trē·ən) *adj.* **1** Moving on foot. **2** Commonplace, prosaic, or dull. —*n.* One who journeys or moves from place to place on foot; a walker. [<L *pedester* on foot] —**pe·des′tri·an·ism** *n.*

pe·di·at·rics (pē′dē·at′riks, ped′ē-) *n. pl.* (*construed as sing.*) The branch of medicine dealing with the care and treatment of children and their diseases. [<Gk. *pais, paidos* a child + *iatros* healer] —**pe′di·at′ric** *adj.* —**pe·di·a·tri·cian** (-trish′ən), **pe′di·at′rist** *n.*

ped·i·cel (ped′ə·səl) *n. Biol.* A slender supporting structure, as a stalk supporting a single flower. Also **ped′i·cle** (-kəl). [<L *pediculus*, dim. of *pes, pedis* a foot] —**ped′i·cel′lar** (-sel′ər) *adj.*

ped·i·cure (ped′i·kyŏŏr) *n.* **1** Care of the feet, as by trimming toenails, corns, bunions, etc. **2** PODIATRIST. [<L *pes, pedis* a foot + *cura* care] —**ped′i·cur′ist** *n.*

ped·i·gree (ped′ə·grē) *n.* **1** A line of ancestors; lineage. **2** A genealogical register, esp. of an animal of pure breed. [<MF *pié de grue* a crane's foot; from a mark denoting succession in pedigrees] —**ped′i·greed** *adj.*

ped·i·ment (ped′ə·mənt) *n. Archit.* A broad triangular part above a portico or door. [Earlier *periment*, prob. alter. of PYRAMID] —**ped′i·men′tal** (-men′təl) *adj.*

pe·dom·e·ter (pi·dom′ə·tər) *n.* An instrument that measures distance traveled by recording the number of steps taken by the person who wears it. [<L *pes, pedis* foot + Gk. *metron* measure]

pe·dun·cle (pi·dung′kəl) *n.* **1** *Bot.* The main supporting stalk of an inflorescence. **2** *Anat.* A stalk or stem, as for the attachment of an organ. [<NL *pedunculus* a foot-stalk, dim. of *pes, pedis* a foot] —**pe·dun′cled, pe·dun′cu·lar, pe·dun′cu·late, pe·dun′cu·lat·ed** *adj.*

peek (pēk) *v.i.* To look furtively, slyly, or quickly. —*n.* A peep; glance. [ME *piken*]

peel¹ (pēl) *n.* The skin of certain fruits, as oranges, etc. — *v.t.* **1** To strip off the bark, skin, etc., of. **2** To strip off; remove. —*v.i.* **3** To lose bark, skin, etc. **4** To come off: said of bark, skin, etc. **5** *Slang* To undress. —**keep one's eye peeled** *Informal* To keep watch; be alert. —**peel off** *Aeron.* To veer off from a flight formation. [<OF *peler* to strip off skin]

peel² (pēl) *n.* A broad, thin, long-handled, shovel-like im-

plement used by bakers in moving bread, etc., about an oven. [<L *pala* a spade]

peel·ing (pē′ling) *n.* Something peeled off, as a strip of rind, skin, or outer layer.

peen (pēn) *n.* The end of a hammer head opposite the face, usu. shaped for indenting, chipping, etc. — *v.t.* To beat, bend, or shape with the peen. [?]

Peens
a. straight.
b. ball.

peep¹ (pēp) *v.i.* **1** To utter a small, sharp cry; chirp; cheep. **2** To speak in a weak, small voice. —*n.* The cry of a small bird or of certain frogs; chirp. [ME *pepen*] —**peep′er** *n.*

peep² (pēp) *v.i.* **1** To peek furtively or quickly; peek. **2** To begin to appear; be just visible. —*n.* **1** A furtive look. **2** A glimpse or glance. **3** The earliest appearance: the *peep* of day. [ME *pepen*] —**peep′er** *n.*

peep·hole (pēp′hōl) *n.* An aperture, as a hole or small window, through which one may peep.

peeping Tom (tom) One who seeks to look at others clandestinely or from concealment, usu. for sexual pleasure. [<*Peeping Tom*, a tailor in English legend, struck blind because he peeped at the naked Lady Godiva]

peer¹ (pir) *v.i.* **1** To look searchingly, as in an effort to see clearly. **2** To come partially into view. [Var. of APPEAR]

peer² (pir) *n.* **1** An equal, as in natural gifts or in social rank. **2** An equal before the law. **3** A noble, as a duke, marquis, earl, viscount, or baron. —**peer of the realm** Any British peer entitled to serve in the House of Lords. [<L *par* equal]

peer·age (pir′ij) *n.* **1** The office or rank of a peer. **2** Peers collectively; the nobility. **3** A book containing a genealogical list of the nobility.

peer·ess (pir′is) *n.* A woman who holds a title of nobility, either in her own right or by marriage with a peer.

peer·less (pir′lis) *adj.* Of unequaled excellence. —**peer′less·ly** *adv.* —**peer′less·ness** *n.*

peeve (pēv) *v.t.* & *v.i.* **peeved, peev·ing** *Informal* To make or become peevish or irritable. —*n.* *Informal* A complaint; grievance. [Back formation <PEEVISH]

pee·vish (pē′vish) *adj.* **1** Irritable or fretful; cross. **2** Showing petulant discontent and vexation. [ME *pevische*] —**pee′vish·ly** *adv.* —**pee′vish·ness** *n.*

pee·wee (pē′wē) *n. Informal* A person or thing esp. small or diminutive. —*adj.* Tiny; insignificant.

peg (peg) *n.* **1** A wooden pin used for fastening articles together. **2** A projecting wooden pin upon which something may be fastened or hung, or which may serve to mark a boundary. **3** A reason or excuse for an action: a *peg* to hang an argument upon. **4** A degree or step, as in rank or estimation. **5** *Brit.* A drink of liquor. **6** *Informal* A leg, often one of wood. —**take (one) down a peg** To lower the conceit of (a person), as by humiliating. —*v.* **pegged, peg·ging** *v.t.* **1** To drive or force a peg into; fasten with pegs. **2** To mark or designate with pegs. **3** To strike or pierce with a peg or sharp instrument. —*v.i.* **4** To work or strive hard and perseveringly: usu. with *away*. [ME *pegge*]

Peg·a·sus (peg′ə·səs) *Gk. Myth.* A winged horse, the symbol of poetic inspiration. —*n. Astron.* A northern constellation.

peg leg *Informal* **1** An artificial leg. **2** A person with such a leg.

peg top **1** A child's spinning top, pear-shaped with a metal tip. **2** *pl.* Trousers that are wide at the hips and taper in at the ankles. —**peg′-top′** *adj.*

pei·gnoir (pān·wär′, pān′wär) *n.* A loose dressing robe worn by women; a negligée. [F< *peigner* to comb]

pe·jo·ra·tion (pē′jə·rā′shən, pej′ə-) *n.* **1** A deterioration. **2** *Ling.* A degeneration in the meaning of a word, as in *silly* (formerly "blessed"). [<L *pejorare* make worse]

pe·jo·ra·tive (pi·jôr′ə·tiv, -jor′-, pej′ər-, pej′ər·ā′tiv, pē′jər-) *adj.* **1** Tending to disparage; derogatory: the *pejorative* connotations of "huckster." **2** *Ling.* Of or relating to the process of pejoration. —*n.* A pejorative word. —**pe·jo′ra·tive·ly** *adv.*

Pe·kin·ese (pē′kə·nēz′) *n. pl.* ·**ese** A small dog with long silky hair, a snub nose, and short legs. Also **Pe′king·ese′** (-king·ēz′).

pe·koe (pē′kō, *Brit.* pek′ō) *n.* A superior kind of black tea, made from the downy tips of the young white buds of the tea plant. [< Chinese *pek* white + *ho* down]

pe·lag·ic (pə·laj′ik) *adj.* Of, pertaining to, or inhabiting the open sea. [< Gk. *pelagos* the sea]

pelf (pelf) *n.* Money; wealth: often implying ill-gotten gains. [< OF *pelfre* spoil] —**Syn.** affluence, fortune, funds, opulence, riches.

pel·i·can (pel′i·kən) *n.* Any of a genus of large, fish-eating, web-footed birds, having a distensible, membranous pouch on the lower bill for scooping up and holding fish. [< Gk. *pelekan*]

pe·lisse (pə·lēs′) *n.* A long outer garment or cloak, esp. one of fur or lined with fur. [< L *pellis* skin]

pel·la·gra (pə·lā′grə, -lag′rə) *n.* A chronic disease due to deficiency of niacin in the diet, marked by gastric disturbance, skin eruptions, and mental derangement. [Ital.] —**pel·la′grous** *adj.*

White pelican

pel·let (pel′it) *n.* **1** A small round ball, as of wax, paper, bread, etc. **2** A small shot. **3** A very small pill. **4** A bullet. —*v.t.* **1** To make into pellets. **2** To strike with pellets. [< Med. L *pelota, pilota* ball.]

pell-mell (pel′mel′) *adv.* **1** In a confused or disorderly manner. **2** With a headlong rush. —*adj.* Devoid of order or method. —*n.* Confusion; disorder. Also **pell′mell′**. [< OF *pesle-mesle*]

pel·lu·cid (pə·lōō′sid) *adj.* **1** Permitting the passage of light; translucent or transparent. **2** Clear; understandable. [< L *perlucere* shine through] —**pel·lu′cid·ly** *adv.* —**pel·lu′cid·ness, pel·lu·cid·i·ty** (pel′ōō·sid′ə·tē) *n.*

Pel·o·pon·ne·sian (pel′ə·pə·nē′shən, -zhən) *adj.* Of or pertaining to the Peloponnesus, a peninsula of Greece. —*n.* An inhabitant of the Peloponnesus.

pelt[1] (pelt) *n.* **1** An undressed fur skin; raw hide. **2** *Slang* The human skin. [Prob. back formation < PELTRY]

pelt[2] (pelt) *v.t.* **1** To strike repeatedly with or as with missiles or blows. **2** To throw or hurl (missiles). —*v.i.* **3** To beat or descend with violence. **4** To move rapidly; hurry. —*n.* **1** A blow, as one given by something thrown. **2** Speed, esp. in the phrase **at full pelt**. [ME *pelten*] —**pelt′er** *n.* —**Syn.** *v.* **1** assail, attack, beat. **4** rush, speed.

pel·tate (pel′tāt) *adj. Bot.* Forming a shield, as a leaf attached to the stalk near the center of the lower surface. Also **pel′tat·ed**. [< Gk. *peltē* a shield] —**pel′tate·ly** *adv.*

pelt·ry (pel′trē) *n. pl.* **·ries** **1** Pelts collectively. **2** A pelt. [< L *pellis* a skin]

pel·vis (pel′vis) *n. pl.* **·vis·es** or **·ves** (-vēz) **1** A basinlike or funnel-shaped structure. **2** The part of the skeleton that forms a bony girdle joining the lower or hind limbs to the body: also **pelvic arch, pelvic girdle**. [L, basin] —**pel′vic** *adj.*

pem·mi·can (pem′ə·kən) *n.* Venison cut into strips, dried, and pounded into paste with melted fat. Also **pem′i·can**. [< Algon.]

Human pelvis
a. ilium. b. coccyx.
c. ischium. d. sacrum.
e. lumbar vertebrae.

pen[1] (pen) *n.* **1** Any of various instruments for writing with a fluid ink. **2** The profession of writing. **3** Literary style. —*v.t.* **penned, pen·ning** To write. [< L *penna* a feather] —**pen′ner** *n.*

pen[2] (pen) *n.* **1** A small enclosure, as for animals. **2** The animals contained in a pen collectively. **3** Any small place of confinement. —*v.t.* **penned** or **pent, pen·ning** To enclose in or as in a pen; confine. [< OE *penn*]

pen[3] (pen) *n. Slang* A penitentiary.

pen. peninsula.

pe·nal (pē′nəl) *adj.* **1** Of, relating to, or prescribing punishment: a *penal* code; a *penal* institution. **2** Liable, or rendering liable, to punishment. [< L *poena* a penalty]

pe·nal·ize (pē′nəl·īz, pen′əl-) *v.t.* **·ized, ·iz·ing** **1** To subject to a penalty, as for a violation. **2** To declare subject to a penalty. *Brit. sp.* **pe·nal·ise**. —**pe′nal·i·za′tion** *n.*

pen·al·ty (pen′əl·tē) *n. pl.* **·ties** **1** The consequences that follow the breaking of any law, rule, or custom. **2** Judicial punishment for crime or violation of the law. **3** A handicap imposed for a violation of rules of a game. **4** Any unpleasant consequence: the *penalties* of a misspent life. [< L *poenalis* penal]

pen·ance (pen′əns) *n.* **1** *Eccl.* A sacramental rite involving contrition, confession to a priest, the acceptance of penalties, and absolution. **2** A feeling of sorrow for sin or fault, evinced by some outward act; repentance. —**do penance** To perform an act or acts of penance. [< L *paenitens* penitent]

Pe·na·tes (pə·nā′tēz) *n.pl.* In the ancient Roman religion, the household gods, associated with the Lares.

pence (pens) *Brit. n.pl.* of PENNY.

pen·chant (pen′chənt) *n.* A strong leaning or inclination: a *penchant* for jotting down ideas on scraps of paper. [F < L *pendere* hang]

pen·cil (pen′səl) *n.* **1** A long, pointed strip of graphite, colored chalk, slate, etc., often encased in wood, used for writing or drawing. **2** Any slender instrument used for similar purposes. **3** A set of rays diverging from or converging to a point. **4** A small stick of any substance having caustic or styptic properties. —*v.t.* **·ciled** or **·cilled, ·cil·ing** or **·cil·ling** To mark, write, or draw with or as with a pencil. [< L *penicillum* a paint brush] —**pen′cil·er** or **pen′cil·ler** *n.*

pend (pend) *v.i.* To await or be in process of adjustment or settlement. [< L *pendere* hang]

pen·dant (pen′dənt) *n.* **1** Any hanging ornament, as an earring or locket. **2** A suspended chandelier. **3** An ornament hanging from a ceiling or roof. —*adj.* PENDENT. [< OF *pendre* hang]

pen·dent (pen′dənt) *adj.* **1** Hanging loosely; drooping downward. **2** Projecting or overhanging. **3** Undetermined; pending. —*n.* PENDANT. [< OF *pendre* hang] —**pen′den·cy** *n.* —**pen′dent·ly** *adv.*

pend·ing (pen′ding) *adj.* Remaining unfinished or undecided. —*prep.* **1** During. **2** Awaiting; until: The court adjourned *pending* the jury's verdict. —**Syn.** *adj.* imminent, impending, unsettled.

pen·drag·on (pen·drag′ən) *n.* In ancient Britain, a title used for a supreme ruler or chief, esp. in wartime. [< Welsh]

pen·du·lous (pen′jōō·ləs) *adj.* Hanging, esp. so as to swing. [< L *pendere* hang] —**pen′du·lous·ly** *adv.* —**pen′du·lous·ness** *n.*

pen·du·lum (pen′jōō·ləm, pen′də-) *n.* **1** A body suspended from a fixed point, and free to swing to and fro. **2** Such a device serving to regulate the rate of a clock. [< L *pendulus* hanging]

Pe·nel·o·pe (pə·nel′ə·pē) In the *Odyssey*, the faithful wife of Odysseus, who, during her husband's absence, kept her many suitors in check for twenty years.

pen·e·trate (pen′ə·trāt) *v.* **·trat·ed, ·trat·ing** *v.t.* **1** To force a way into or through; pierce. **2** To spread or diffuse itself throughout; permeate. **3** To perceive the meaning of; understand. **4** To affect profoundly. —*v.i.* **5** To enter or pass through something. **6** To have effect on the mind or emotions. [< L *penetrare* put within] —**pen′e·tra′tive** *adj.* —**pen′e·tra′tive·ly** *adv.*

pen·e·trat·ing (pen′ə·trā′ting) *adj.* **1** Tending or having power to penetrate; intrusive: a *penetrating* noise or smell. **2** Marked by keen discernment or insight, or having the capacity of such discernment: a *penetrating* analysis; a *penetrating* mind. **3** Deep, as a wound. —**pen′e·trat′ing·ly** *adv.* —**pen′e·trat′ing·ness** *n.* —**Syn.** **1** piercing. **2** incisive, shrewd, profound, deep, acute.

pen·e·tra·tion (pen′ə·trā′shən) *n.* **1** The act or power of penetrating physically. **2** Ability to penetrate mentally; acuteness.

pen·e·tra·tive (pen′ə·trā′tiv) *adj.* Tending or having power to penetrate, physically or mentally; a *penetrative* odor; *penetrative* wisdom. —**pen′e·tra′tive·ly** *adv.* —**pen′e·tra′tive·ness** *n.*

pen·guin (pen′gwin, peng′-) *n.* Any of various web-footed, flightless, aquatic birds of the southern hemisphere, with flipperlike wings.

pen·hold·er (pen′hōl′dər) *n.* 1 A handle with a device for inserting a metallic pen point. 2 A rack for pens.

pen·i·cil·lin (pen′ə·sil′in) *n.* An antibiotic found in a species of penicillium.

pen·i·cil·li·um (pen′ə·sil′ē·əm) *n. pl.* **·li·a** (-ē·ə) Any of a genus of fungi often seen as blue-green mold on bread, cheese, etc. [< L *penicillus* a brush; from the resemblance of its tufts to small paint brushes]

pen·in·su·la (pə·nin′sə·lə, -syə-) *n.* An area of land almost surrounded by water, and connected with the mainland by an isthmus. [< L *paene* almost + *insula* an island] **—pen·in′·su·lar** *adj.* **—pen·in·su·lar·i·ty** (pən·in′sə·lar′ə·tē, -syə-) *n.*

Emperor penguin

pe·nis (pē′nis) *n. pl.* **·nis·es** or **·nes** (-nēz) The male organ of sexual intercourse and the excretion of urine. [L, tail, penis]

pen·i·tence (pen′ə·təns) *n.* Sorrow for sin, with desire to amend and atone. [< L *paenitare* repent]

pen·i·tent (pen′ə·tənt) *adj.* Affected by sorrow because of one's own guilt. **—n.** 1 One who is penitent. 2 One who confesses his sins to a priest and submits himself to the penance prescribed. **—pen′i·tent·ly** *adv.* **—Syn.** *adj.* contrite, remorseful, repentant, regretful.

pen·i·ten·tial (pen′ə·ten′shəl) *adj.* 1 Pertaining to or expressing penitence. 2 Pertaining to penance or punishment. **—n.** 1 *Eccl.* A book of rules relating to penance. 2 A penitent. **—pen′i·ten′tial·ly** *adv.*

pen·i·ten·tia·ry (pen′ə·ten′shər·ē) *n. pl.* **·ries** A prison, esp. a state or federal prison for those convicted of serious crimes. **—adj.** 1 Pertaining to penance. 2 Relating to or used for the punishment and discipline of criminals. 3 Rendering the offender liable to imprisonment in a penitentiary. [< L *paenitentia*]

pen·knife (pen′nīf′) *n. pl.* **·knives** (-nīvz′) A small pocket knife. [< former use in sharpening quill pens]

pen·man (pen′mən) *n. pl.* **·men** (-mən) 1 A person considered with regard to the high quality of his handwriting. 2 A writer.

pen·man·ship (pen′mən·ship) *n.* 1 The art of writing by hand. 2 Handwriting; calligraphy.

Penn., Penna. Pennsylvania.

pen name An author's assumed name; pseudonym.

pen·nant (pen′ənt) *n.* 1 A long, narrow flag displayed on ships or used as a signal. 2 A flag symbolizing a championship in certain sports competitions, as baseball. [< PENNON; infl. by PENDANT]

pen·ni·less (pen′i·lis) *adj.* 1 Being without even a penny. 2 Very poor. **—pen′ni·less·ly** *adv.* **—pen′ni·less·ness** *n.*

pen·non (pen′ən) *n.* 1 A small, pointed or swallow-tailed flag, borne by medieval knights on their lances. 2 A wing. 3 A banner or flag of any sort. [< L *penna* a feather]

Penn·syl·va·ni·a Dutch (pen′sil·vā′nyə, -nē·ə) 1 Descendants of immigrants from sw Germany and Switzerland who settled in Pennsylvania in the 17th and 18th centuries. 2 The language spoken by these people. Also **Pennsylvania German. —Penn′syl·va′ni·a-Dutch′** *adj.*

Penn·syl·va·ni·an (pen′sil·vā′nyən, -nē·ən) *adj. & n.* See GEOLOGY.

pen·ny (pen′ē) *n. pl.* **pen·nies** or *Brit.* **pence** (pens) 1 In the U.S. and Canada, a cent. 2 A coin of Great Britain, Ireland, and various members of the Commonwealth. 3 In the United Kingdom, a coin equal in value to 1/100 pound. 4 A piece of money. [< OE *penning, penig*] **—a pretty penny** *Informal* A large sum of money.

pen·ny·roy·al (pen′ē·roi′əl) *n.* 1 Any of various strong-scented herbs of the mint family. 2 An aromatic oil obtained from this plant. [< L *pulegium* fleabane + AF *real* royal]

pen·ny·weight (pen′ē·wāt′) *n.* A unit equal to 1/20 troy ounce.

pen·ny·wise (pen′ē·wīz′) *adj.* Unduly economical in small matters. **—penny-wise and pound-foolish** Economical in small matters, but wasteful in large ones.

pen·ny·worth (pen′ē·wûrth′) *n.* 1 As much as can be bought for a penny. 2 A bargain. 3 A small amount; trifle.

pe·nol·o·gy (pē·nol′ə·jē) *n.* The study dealing with the punishment of crime, the rehabilitation of criminals, and the management of prisons. [< L *poena* a penalty + -LOGY] **—pe·no·log·i·cal** (pē′nə·loj′i·kəl) *adj.* **—pe·nol′o·gist** *n.*

pen·sile (pen′sīl) *adj.* 1 Hanging loosely. 2 Constructing pensile nests: said of birds. [< L *pensus,* pp. of *pendere* hang]

pen·sion¹ (pen′shən) *n.* A periodical and continuing allowance to an individual because of long service, special merit, or injury while serving. **—v.t.** 1 To grant a pension to. 2 To dismiss with a pension: with *off.* [< L *pensio* payment < *pendere* weigh, pay] **—pen·sion·ar·y** (pen′shən·er′ē) *adj., n.*

pen·sion² (pän·syôn′) *n. French* 1 Room and board. 2 A boarding house. Also *Ital.* **pen·si·o·ne** (pen·sē·ō′nä).

pen·sion·er (pen′shən·ər) *n.* 1 One who receives a pension. 2 A boarder, as in a convent or school.

pen·sive (pen′siv) *adj.* 1 Engaged in or accustomed to serious or quiet reflection. 2 Expressive of, suggesting, or causing sad thoughtfulness. [< OF *penser* think] **—pen′·sive·ly** *adv.* **—pen′sive·ness** *n.* **—Syn.** 1 meditative, reflective. 2 grave, melancholy, sad, sober.

pent (pent) *p.p. & p.t.* of PENT².

penta- *combining form* Five: *pentagon.* [< Gk. *pente* five]

pen·ta·cle (pen′tə·kəl) *n.* A figure composed of five straight lines connecting the vertices of a pentagon and used as a magical symbol. [< Gk. *pente* five]

pen·ta·gon (pen′tə·gon) *n.* A figure with five angles and five sides. **—the Pentagon** 1 The military establishment of the U.S. 2 A five-sided building in Arlington, Va., housing the offices of the Department of Defense and the U.S. Armed Forces. [< Gk. *pentagōnon*] **—pen·tag·o·nal** (pen·tag′ə·nəl) *adj.* **—pen·tag′o·nal·ly** *adv.*

Pentacle

pen·ta·he·dron (pen′tə·hē′drən) *n. pl.* **·dra** (-drə) A solid bounded by five plane faces. **—pen′ta·he′dral** *adj.*

pen·tam·e·ter (pen·tam′ə·tər) *n.* 1 A line of verse of five metrical feet. 2 Verse composed of pentameters; heroic verse. **—adj.** Consisting of five metrical feet.

Pen·ta·teuch (pen′tə·tⁿook) *n.* The first five books of the Bible taken collectively. [< Gk. *pente* five + *teuchos* a book, implement] **—Pen′ta·teuch′al** *adj.*

pen·tath·lon (pen·tath′lən) *n.* An athletic contest consisting of five different events in all of which each contestant participates. [< Gk. *pente* five + *athlon* a contest]

Pen·te·cost (pen′tə·kôst, -kost) *n.* 1 A Jewish festival occurring fifty days after the Passover. 2 The feast of Whitsunday, commemorating the descent of the Holy Ghost upon the apostles. *Acts* 2. [< Gk. *pentēkostē (hēmera)* the fiftieth (day)]

Pen·te·cos·tal (pen′tə·kôs′təl, -kos′-) *adj.* 1 Of or pertaining to Pentecost. 2 Of or designating any of various Christian groups typically holding revivalist services where vocal and often emotional expression is given to religious devotion.

pent·house (pent′hous′) *n.* An apartment or dwelling on the roof of a building. [< OF *apentis*]

pent-up (pent′up′) *adj.* Confined; repressed: *pent-up emotions.*

pe·nu·che (pə·nⁿoo′chē) *n.* A kind of fudge made from brown sugar, milk or cream, butter, and nuts.

pe·nult (pē′nult, pi·nult′) *n.* The syllable next to the last in a word. Also **pe·nul·ti·ma** (pi·nul′tə·mə). [< L *paene* almost + *ultimus* last] **—pe·nul·ti·mate** (pi·nul′tə·mit) *adj., n.*

pe·num·bra (pi·num′brə) *n. pl.* **·brae** (-brē) or **·bras** 1 *Astron.* The partial shadow between the umbra, or region of total eclipse, and the region of unobstructed light. 2 The dark fringe around the central part of a sunspot. [< L *paene* almost + *umbra* a shadow] **—pe·num′bral, pe·num′·brous** (-brəs) *adj.*

pe·nu·ri·ous (pə·nⁿoor′ē·əs) *adj.* Excessively sparing or saving in the use of money. **—pe·nu′ri·ous·ly** *adv.* **—pe·nu′·ri·ous·ness** *n.* **—Syn.** frugal, miserly, stingy, tight-fisted.

pen·u·ry (pen′yə·rē) *n.* Extreme poverty or want. [< L *penuria* want]

pe·on (pē′ən) *n.* 1 In Latin America, a laborer. 2 In the sw U.S., a person kept in virtual servitude until he has worked out a debt. [< LL *pedo, -onis* a foot soldier]

pe·on·age (pē'ən·ij) *n.* The condition of a peon, or the system of employing this form of labor. Also **pe'on·ism.**

pe·o·ny (pē'ə·nē) *n. pl.* **·nies 1** Any of a genus of perennial plants having large, usu. double, flowers. **2** Its flower. [< Gk. *paiōnia*]

peo·ple (pē'pəl) *n. pl.* **·ple** or *(for defs. 1 and 2)* **·ples 1** The aggregate of human beings living under the same government: the *people* of England. **2** A body of human beings belonging to the same linguistic stock and having the same culture. **3** The whole body of persons composing a common class or profession. **4** Persons collectively: Who cares what *people* say? **5** The populace; public. **6** Subjects: A ruler cares for his *people.* **7** Family; relatives: Her *people* are from Ohio. **8** Human beings in general: Most *people* are friendly. —*v.t.* **·pled, ·pling** To fill with inhabitants; populate. [< L *populus* the populace] —**peo'pler** *n.*

pep (pep) *Slang n.* Vim; energy; sprightliness. —*v.t.* **pepped, pep·ping** To inspire with energy or pep: usu. with *up.* [Short for PEPPER]

pep·lum (pep'ləm) *n. pl.* **·lums** A short ruffle or flounce attached to a blouse or coat at the waist, and extending down over the hips. [< Gk. *peplos* a kind of shawl]

pep·per (pep'ər) *n.* **1** A spice made from the black, dried berries of an East Indian climbing shrub. **2** CAYENNE PEPPER. **3** GREEN PEPPER. **4** Any plant yielding pepper. **5** *Informal* Spiciness; pungency; raciness. —*v.t.* **1** To sprinkle or season with pepper. **2** To sprinkle like pepper. **3** To shower, as with missiles; spatter. —*v.i.* **4** To discharge missiles at something. [< Gk. *peperi*]

Peplum

pep·per-and-salt (pep'ər·ən·sôlt') *adj.* Mixed white and black, intermingled as to present a speckled grayish appearance.

pep·per·corn (pep'ər·kôrn') *n.* A dried berry of pepper.

pep·per·grass (pep'ər·gras', -gräs') *n.* Any of various small plants of the mustard family with pungent, edible leaves. Also **pep'per·wort** (-wûrt).

pep·per·mint (pep'ər·mint') *n.* **1** An aromatic herb used in medicine and confectionery. **2** A pungent oil obtained from peppermint. **3** A confection flavored with peppermint.

pep·per·pot (pep'ər·pot') *n.* Any of several highly seasoned stews or soups.

pep·per·y (pep'ər·ē) *adj.* **1** Pertaining to or like pepper; pungent. **2** Quick-tempered; hasty. —**pep'per·i·ness** *n.*

pep pill *Slang* Any of various pills or tablets that stimulate the central nervous system.

pep·py (pep'ē) *adj.* **·pi·er ·pi·est** *Slang* Full of pep; lively. —**pep'pi·ness** *n.* —Syn. active, energetic, spry, vigorous.

pep·sin (pep'sin) *n.* **1** A digestive enzyme that acts on proteins in the stomach. **2** A preparation obtained from the stomachs of pigs, calves, etc., used to aid digestion. Also **pep'sine.** [< Gk. *pepsis* digestion]

pep·tic (pep'tik) *adj.* **1** Of, pertaining to, or promotive of digestion. **2** Of, pertaining to, or producing pepsin. **3** Pertaining to or connected with the action of digestive secretions: *peptic* ulcer. —*n.* An agent that promotes digestion. [< Gk. *peptein* to digest]

peptic ulcer An ulcer of the mucous membrane of the stomach (**gastric ulcer**) or of the small intestine (**duodenal ulcer**) aggravated by acid digestive juices.

pep·tone (pep'tōn) *n.* Any of various soluble protein compounds resulting from the action of pepsin on complex proteins. [< Gk. *peptein* to digest] —**pep·ton·ic** (pep·ton'ik) *adj.*

Pe·quot (pē'kwot) *n.* A member of a tribe of North American Indians of Algonquian stock. Also **Pe'quod** (-kwod).

per (pûr) *prep.* **1** By; by means of; through. **2** For each: ten cents *per* yard. **3** *Informal* According to: *per* your memo. [L, through, by]

per- *prefix* **1** Through; throughout: *pervade.* **2** Thoroughly; completely; very: *perturb.* **3** Away: *pervert.* **4** *Chem.* Denot-

ing an element or radical in a high or the highest valence: *peroxide.* [< L *per* through, by means of]

per. period; person.

per·ad·ven·ture (pûr'ad·ven'chər) *adv. Archaic* Possibly; perhaps. —*n. Archaic* Chance; uncertainty; doubt. [< OF *par aventure* by chance]

per·am·bu·late (pə·ram'byə·lāt) *v.* **·lat·ed, ·lat·ing** *v.t.* **1** To walk through or over; traverse. **2** To walk through or around so as to inspect (a boundary) —*v.i.* **3** To walk about; stroll. [< L *per-* through + *ambulare* to walk] —**per·am'bu·la'tion** *n.* —**per·am'bu·la·to'ry** *adj.*

per·am·bu·la·tor (pə·ram'byə·lā'tər) *n.* **1** One who perambulates. **2** *Chiefly Brit.* A baby carriage.

per an·num (pûr an'əm) *Latin* By the year; annually.

per·cale (pər·kāl', -kal') *n.* A closely woven cotton fabric used for sheets, etc. [< Pers. *pergālah* a rag]

per cap·i·ta (pûr kap'ə·tə) For each person. [L, lit., by heads]

per·ceive (pər·sēv') *v.t. & v.i.* **·ceived, ·ceiv·ing 1** To become aware of (something) through the senses. **2** To come to understand; apprehend with the mind. [< L *per-* thoroughly + *capere* take] —**per·ceiv'a·bly** *adv.* —**per·ceiv'er** *n.*

per·cent (pər·sent') *adj. & adv.* For, in, or to every hundred. —*n. pl.* **·cent** or **·cents 1** A one-hundreth part. **2** *Informal* PERCENTAGE. **3** *pl.* Securities bearing a certain percentage of interest. Also **per cent, per cent** [Short for L *per centum* by the hundred]

per·cent·age (pər·sen'tij) *n.* **1** A part considered in its quantitative relation to the whole, expressed in hundredths. **2** A proportion; part. **3** A share or portion, as an allowance, commission, duty, interest, etc., that varies in proportion to some larger sum. **4** *Informal* Advantage; profit.

per·cen·tile (pər·sen'tīl, -til) *n. Stat.* A number indicating the relative position of an individual score per 100 scores ranged in a graded series. —*adj.* Of or pertaining to a percentile.

per·cept (pûr'sept) *n.* A mental event resulting from a sensory stimulus. [< L *percipere* perceive]

per·cep·ti·ble (pər·sep'tə·bəl) *adj.* Capable of being perceived. —**per·cep'ti·bil'i·ty, per·cep'ti·ble·ness** *n.* —**per·cep'ti·bly** *adv.* —Syn. evident, apparent, obvious, visible.

per·cep·tion (pər·sep'shən) *n.* **1** The act, power, process, or product of perceiving. **2** Cognition of fact or truth; appreciation. **3 a** Knowledge acquired through the senses. **b** The process of acquiring such knowledge. **c** The mental product so obtained; percept. **4** Insight or intuitive judgment. [< L *percipere* perceive] —**per·cep'tion·al** *adj.*

per·cep·tive (pər·sep'tiv) *adj.* **1** Perceiving, or having the power of perception. **2** Of or pertaining to perception. —**per·cep'tive·ly** *adv.* —**per·cep'tive·ness, per·cep·tiv·i·ty** (pûr'sep·tiv'ə·tē) *n.*

perch¹ (pûrch) *n.* **1** A pole, slat, or wire, etc., used as a roost by birds. **2** An elevated seat or situation. **3** *Chiefly Brit.* **a** A measure of length: one rod (5½ yds.) **b** A measure of area: a sq. rod (30¼ sq. yards.) **c** Any of several units of measure used in stonework. —*v.i.* **1** To alight or sit on or as on a perch; roost. —*v.t.* **2** To set on or as on a perch. [< L *pertica* pole] —**perch'er** *n.*

perch² (pûrch) *n.* **1** A small freshwater food fish with spiny fins. **2** Any of various other similar, usu. marine fishes. [< Gk. *perkē*]

per·chance (pər·chans', -chäns') *adv.* Possibly; perhaps. **2** *Obs.* By chance. [< AF *par chance* by chance]

Yellow perch

Per·che·ron (pûr'chə·ron, -shə-) *n.* Any of a breed of large, usu. dapple-gray or black draft horses. [< *Perche*, a region of NW France]

per·cip·i·ent (pər·sip'ē·ənt) *adj.* Having the power to perceive, esp. rapidly or keenly. —*n.* One who perceives. [< L *percipere* perceive] —**per·cip'i·ence** or **·en·cy** *n.*

per·co·late (pûr'kə·lāt) *v.t. & v.i.* **·lat·ed, ·lat·ing 1** To pass or cause to pass through fine pores or openings; filter. **2** To

add, āce, câre, pälm; end, ēven; it, īce; odd, ōpen, ôrder; tŏŏk, pōōl; up, bûrn; ə = a in above, u in focus; yōō = u in fuse; oil; pout; check; go; ring; thin; this; zh, vision. < derived from; ? origin uncertain or unknown.

brew (coffee) in a percolator. —*n.* That which has percolated; a filtered liquid. [< L *per-* through + *colare* to strain] —**per'co·la'tion** *n.*

per·co·la·tor (pûr'kə·lā'tər) *n.* **1** One who or that which percolates, as a filter. **2** A coffee pot in which boiling water rises through a tube and repeatedly filters back down through ground coffee contained in a perforated basket.

per·cus·sion (pər·kush'ən) *n.* **1** The impact of one body against another, as that of the hammer against the percussion cap in a firearm. **2** The impression of sound upon the ear. **3** *Med.* A tapping on the back, chest, etc., for diagnosing the condition of the organ beneath. **4** Those musical instruments, collectively, whose tone is produced by striking or hitting, as the timpani, piano, etc. [< L *per-* thoroughly + *quatere* to shake] —**per·cus'sive** (-kus'iv) *adj.* —**per·cus'sive·ly** *adv.* —**per·cus'sive·ness** *n.*

percussion cap CAP (*n.*, def. 4).

percussion instruments Musical instruments played by striking, as cymbals, drums, etc.

per di·em (pər dē'əm, dī'əm) **1** By or for the day. **2** An allowance (of money) for expenses each day. [L]

per·di·tion (pər·dish'ən) *n.* **1** *Theol.* Future misery or eternal death as the condition of the wicked; hell. **2** *Archaic* Utter destruction or ruin. [< L *perdere* destroy, lose]

père (pâr) *n. French* Father: used after a surname to distinguish father from son.

per·e·gri·nate (per'ə·gri·nāt') **·nat·ed**, **·nat·ing** *v.i.* **1** To travel from place to place. —*v.t.* **2** To travel through or along. [< L *peregrinari* travel abroad] —**per'e·gri·na'tion** *n.*

per·e·grine (per'ə·grin) *n.* A large, very swift falcon. Also **peregrine falcon.** [< L *pereger* traveling]

per·emp·to·ry (pə·remp'tər·ē) *adj.* **1** *Law* Precluding or putting an end to debate or discussion; final. **2** Not admitting of debate or appeal; decisive; absolute. **3** Opinionated; dogmatic. [< L *peremptorius* destructive] —**per·emp'to·ri·ly** *adv.* —**per·emp'to·ri·ness** *n.*

per·en·ni·al (pə·ren'ē·əl) *adj.* **1** Continuing or enduring through the year. **2** Enduring, unceasing, or recurrent. **3** *Bot.* Lasting more than two years. —*n.* A perennial plant. [< L *per-* through + *annus* a year] —**per·en'ni·al·ly** *adv.*

perf. perfect; perforated.

per·fect (pûr'fikt) *adj.* **1** Having all the qualities or elements requisite to its nature or kind; complete. **2** Thoroughly qualified or informed; skilled: a *perfect* teacher. **3** Correct, exact, or accurate: a *perfect* replica. **4** Meeting all requirements; lacking no essential: a *perfect* antidote. **5** *Informal* Excessive in degree; very great: She has a *perfect* horror of spiders. **6** Total; utter: a *perfect* idiot. **7** *Gram.* Denoting the tense of a verb expressing action completed at the time of speaking or in the past. In English, the perfect tenses include a *present perfect, past perfect* (or *pluperfect*), and a *future perfect* tense. **8** *Music* Denoting a fifth containing seven semitones or a fourth containing five semitones. —*n. Gram.* The perfect tense, or a verb in this tense. —*v.t.* (pər·fekt') **1** To bring to perfection; complete; finish. **2** To make thoroughly skilled or accomplished: to *perfect* oneself in art. [< L *per-* thoroughly + *facere* do, make] —**per·fect'i·bil'i·ty** *n.* —**per·fect'i·ble** *adj.* —**per'fect·ly** *adv.*

per·fec·tion (pər·fek'shən) *n.* **1** The state or condition of being perfect; also, an embodiment of this. **2** The act or process of perfecting.

per·fec·tion·ist (pər·fek'shən·ist) *n.* One who demands perfect or flawless results or performance of himself or others. —**per·fec'tion·ism** *n.*

per·fec·tive (pər·fek'tiv) *adj.* Tending to make perfect. —**per·fec'tive·ly** *adv.* —**per·fec'tive·ness** *n.*

per·fec·to (pər·fek'tō) *n.* A cigar shaped to taper at both ends. [Sp. See PERFECT.]

per·fer·vid (pər·fûr'vid) *adj.* Excessively fervid. [< L *per-* thoroughly + *fervidus* glowing]

per·fid·i·ous (pər·fid'ē·əs) *adj.* Of or characterized by perfidy. —**per·fid'i·ous·ly** *adv.* —**per·fid'i·ous·ness** *n.*

per·fi·dy (pûr'fə·dē) *n. pl.* **·dies** The deliberate violation of faith or trust. [< L *perfidia*] —**Syn.** treachery, disloyalty, betrayal, faithlessness.

per·fo·li·ate (pər·fō'lē·it, -āt) *adj. Bot.* Growing so that the stem seems to pass through it: said of a leaf. [< L *per-* through + *folium* a leaf] —**per·fo'li·a'tion** *n.*

per·fo·rate (pûr'fə·rāt) *v.t.* **·rat·ed**, **·rat·ing** **1** To make a hole or holes through, by or as by stamping or drilling. **2** To pierce with holes in rows or patterns, as sheets of stamps, etc. —*adj.* (-rit) Pierced with a hole or a series of holes. [< L *per-* through + *forare* to bore] —**per'fo·rat·ed** *adj.* —**per'fo·ra'tor** *n.*

per·fo·ra·tion (pûr'fə·rā'shən) *n.* **1** A perforating or state of being perforated. **2** A hole or series of holes drilled in or stamped through something.

per·force (pər·fôrs', -fōrs') *adv.* By force; by or of necessity; necessarily. [< OF *par force*]

per·form (pər·fôrm') *v.t.* **1** To execute; do: to *perform* an operation. **2** To act in accord with the requirements or obligations of; fulfill; discharge, as a duty or promise. **3** To act (a part) or give a performance of (a play, piece of music, etc.). —*v.i.* **4** To carry through to completion. **5** To give an exhibition or performance. [< OF *par-* thoroughly + *fournir* accomplish, furnish] —**per·form'er** *n.*

per·form·ance (pər·fôr'məns) *n.* **1** The act of performing. **2** Something performed; deed, feat, etc. **3** The ability to perform; also, the effectiveness of performance. **4** A presentation before spectators; any entertainment: two *performances* daily.

per·fume (pûr'fyōōm, pər·fyōōm') *n.* **1** A pleasant odor, as from flowers; fragrance. **2** A fragrant substance, usu. a volatile liquid, prepared to emit a pleasant odor; scent. —*v.t.* (pər·fyōōm') **·fumed**, **·fum·ing** To give a fragrant odor to; scent. [< Ital. *perfumare*, lit., impregnate with smoke]

per·fum·er (pər·fyōō'mər) *n.* **1** One who makes or deals in perfumes. **2** One who or that which perfumes.

per·fum·er·y (pər·fyōō'mər·ē) *n. pl.* **·er·ies** **1** The art or business of making perfume. **2** Perfumes in general, or a specific perfume. **3** A place where perfumes are manufactured.

per·func·to·ry (pər·fungk'tər·ē) *adj.* **1** Done mechanically or routinely; superficial. **2** Without interest or concern; apathetic. [< L *per-* through + *fungi* perform] —**per·func'to·ri·ly** *adv.* —**per·func'to·ri·ness** *n.*

per·go·la (pûr'gə·lə) *n.* An arbor, esp. one with a roof of trelliswork that is supported by columns or posts on which climbing plants are grown. [< L *pergula* a projecting roof, arbor]

per·haps (pər·haps', -aps') *adv.* Maybe; possibly. [< PER + *haps*, pl. of HAP[1]]

pe·ri (pir'ē) *n. Persian Myth.* A fairy or elf.

peri- *prefix* **1** Around; encircling: *periphery.* **2** Situated near; adjoining: *perihelion.* [< Gk. *peri* around]

per·i·anth (per'ē·anth) *n.* The calyx and corolla of a flower. [< Gk. *peri-* around + *anthos* a flower] —**per'i·an'the·ous** *adj.*

per·i·car·di·um (per'ə·kär'dē·əm) *n. pl.* **·di·a** (-dē·ə) A thin membrane enclosing the heart. [< Gk. *peri-* around + *kardia* heart] —**per'i·car'di·al, per'i·car'di·ac** *adj.*

per·i·carp (per'ə·kärp) *n. Bot.* The wall of a mature ovary. [NL < Gk. *peri-* around + *karpos* fruit] —**per'i·car'pi·al** *adj.*

per·i·cra·ni·um (per'ə·krā'nē·əm) *n. pl.* **·ni·a** (-nē·ə) A tough membrane covering the skull. [< Gk. *peri-* around + *kranion* skull] —**per'i·cra'ni·al** *adj.*

per·i·gee (per'ə·jē) *n. Astron.* The point in the orbit of the moon or of an artificial earth satellite where it is nearest the earth. [< Gk. *peri-* around + *gē* earth] —**per'i·ge'al, per'i·ge'an** *adj.*

p. perigee.
a. apogee.

per·i·he·li·on (per'ə·hē'lē·ən) *n. pl.* **·li·a** (-lē·ə) *Astron.* The point in the orbit of a planet or comet where it is nearest the sun. [< PERI- + Gk. *helios* the sun]

per·il (per'əl) *n.* Exposure to the chance of injury, loss, or destruction. —*v.t.* **·iled** or **·illed**, **·il·ing** or **·il·ling** To expose to danger. [< L *periculum* trial, danger] —**Syn.** *n.* danger, jeopardy, risk, insecurity. *v.* imperil, endanger, jeopardize, risk.

per·il·ous (per'əl·əs) *adj.* Full of, involving, or attended with peril. —**per'il·ous·ly** *adv.* —**per'il·ous·ness** *n.*

pe·rim·e·ter (pə·rim'ə·tər) *n.* **1** *Math.* The bounding line or curve of a plane area. **2** *Math.* The measure of this line

PERIODIC TABLE OF THE ELEMENTS

1a																	0
1 H	2a											3a	4a	5a	6a	7a	2 He
3 Li	4 Be											5 B	6 C	7 N	8 O	9 F	10 Ne
11 Na	12 Mg	3b	4b	5b	6b	7b	—8—		1b	2b		13 Al	14 Si	15 P	16 S	17 Cl	18 Ar
19 K	20 Ca	21 Sc	22 Ti	23 V	24 Cr	25 Mn	26 Fe	27 Co	28 Ni	29 Cu	30 Zn	31 Ga	32 Ge	33 As	34 Se	35 Br	36 Kr
37 Rb	38 Sr	39 Y	40 Zr	41 Nb	42 Mo	43 Tc	44 Ru	45 Rh	46 Pd	47 Ag	48 Cd	49 In	50 Sn	51 Sb	52 Te	53 I	54 Xe
55 Cs	56 Ba	57* La	72 Hf	73 Ta	74 W	75 Re	76 Os	77 Ir	78 Pt	79 Au	80 Hg	81 Tl	82 Pb	83 Bi	84 Po	85 At	86 Rn
87 Fr	88 Ra	89** Ac															

*Lanthanides	58 Ce	59 Pr	60 Nd	61 Pm	62 Sm	63 Eu	64 Gd	65 Tb	66 Dy	67 Ho	68 Er	69 Tm	70 Yb	71 Lu
**Actinides	90 Th	91 Pa	92 U	93 Np	94 Pu	95 Am	96 Cm	97 Bk	98 Cf	99 Es	100 Fm	101 Md	102 No	103 Lr

The properties of the elements are related to the configuration of electrons surrounding the atomic nucleus, and they show a repetitive, cyclic variation when arranged in order of increasing atomic number. They fall into horizontal rows, or *periods,* which usually begin on the left with metals, shade into nonmetals on the right, and end with the group of virtually inert rare gases. The vertical columns comprise *groups* of elements with similar properties. The subgroups, indicated by the letter **b,** comprise elements that resemble each other more closely than they resemble elements in the main groups, marked by the letter **a.** The lanthanide series and the actinide series both consist of elements with almost identical chemical properties. Each box contains an atomic number and the corresponding chemical symbol. See also the table of *Chemical Elements* at ELEMENT.

or curve. **3** A strip or boundary defining or protecting an area. [<Gk. *peri-* around + *metron* a measure] **—per·i·met'ric** (per'ə·met'rik) or **-ri·cal** *adj.* **—per'i·met'ri·cal·ly** *adv.*

per·i·ne·um (per'ə·nē'əm) *n. pl.* **-ne·a** (-nē'ə) *Anat.* The region of the body at the lower end of the trunk, between the genital organs and the rectum. Also **per'i·nae'um.** [< Gk. *perinaion*] **—per'i·ne'al** *adj.*

pe·ri·od (pir'ē·əd) *n.* **1** A portion of time marked and defined by certain events or phenomena, or by the existence of a specific culture. **2** A portion of time between successive occurrences of some astronomical event. **3** A portion of time between certain events: the *period* between the two World Wars. **4** A conclusion or end, as of any sequence of years, events, acts, or phenomena. **5** A portion of time marking one of the divisions of a game, academic day, etc. **6** *Med.* The course of a disease or one of its phases. **7** MENSES. **8** *Gram.* A sentence, esp. a well-constructed complex sentence. **9** The full pause in speaking at the end of a sentence. **10** A dot (.) used in writing as a mark of punctuation after every complete declarative sentence and after most abbreviations. **11** *Geol.* A division of geologic time that may contain two or more epochs. **12** *Physics* The time between two successive similar phases of a wave or oscillation. [<Gk. *periodos* a going around.]

pe·ri·od·ic (pir'ē·od'ik) *adj.* **1** Of, pertaining to, or of the nature of a period. **2** Happening or recurring at regular intervals. **3** Happening now and then; intermittent. **4** Repeating exactly after a given interval, as a mathematical function, physical variable, etc. **5** Of, expressed in, or characterized by periodic sentences.

pe·ri·od·i·cal (pir'ē·od'i·kəl) *adj.* **1** PERIODIC (def. 2). **2** Pertaining to publications, as magazines, professional journals, etc., that are published at fixed intervals of more than one day. **3** Published at such intervals. **—n.** A publication, usu. a magazine, appearing at such fixed intervals. **—pe'ri·od'i·cal·ly** *adv.*

pe·ri·o·dic·i·ty (pir'ē·ə·dis'ə·tē) *n.* The quality or property of being periodic.

periodic law *Chem.* The statement that the properties of the elements are related to their atomic numbers and recur periodically when the elements are arranged in the order of these numbers.

periodic sentence A sentence that leaves the completion of its main clause to the end.

periodic table *Chem.* A chart of elements arranged in rows in order of their atomic numbers, and falling into columns or groups of elements having similar properties.

per·i·o·don·tics (per'ē·ə·don'tiks) *n. pl. (construed as sing.)* The branch of dentistry dealing with the diagnosis and treatment of gum diseases. Also, **per'i·o·don'ti·a** (-shə, -shē·ə) [<PERI- + Gk. *odous* tooth]—**per'i·o·don'tist** *n.*

per·i·os·te·um (per'ē·os'tē·əm) *n.* A tough, fibrous membrane covering the bones. [<Gk. *peri-* around + *osteon* a bone] **—per'i·os'te·al, per'i·os'te·ous** *adj.*

per·i·pa·tet·ic (per'i·pə·tet'ik) *adj.* Walking about; moving from place to place. **—n.** One given to walking about. [<Gk. *peri-* around + *pateein* to walk]

Per·i·pa·tet·ic (per'i·pə·tet'ik) *adj.* Pertaining to the philosophy of Aristotle, who lectured to his disciples while walking in the Lyceum at Athens. **—n.** A disciple of Aristotle.

pe·ripn·er·al (pə·rif'ər·əl) *adj.* **1** Of, pertaining to or forming a periphery. **2** Away from the center; external. **3** Of, pertaining to, at, or near the surface of the body. **—n.** Any device not part of the main computing unit, such as a printer, keyboard, modem, etc. **—periph'er·al·ly** *adv.*

pe·riph·er·y (pə·rif'ər·ē) *n. pl.* **·er·ies** **1** The outer bounds of any surface or area. **2** The surface of the body. **3** PERIMETER (def. 1). **4** A surrounding region, country, or area. [<Gk. *periphereia* circumference]

pe·riph·ra·sis (pə·rif'rə·sis) *n. pl.* **·ses** (-sēz) **1** The use of more words than are needed; circumlocution. **2** An instance of this. [<Gk. *peri-* around + *phrazein* speak]

per·i·phras·tic (per'ə·fras'tik) *adj.* **1** Of, pertaining to, or involving periphrasis. **2** *Gram.* Denoting a construction in which a particle or auxiliary verb is substituted for an inflected form of similar function, as, *the hat of John* for *John's hat.* Also **per′i·phras′ti·cal.** —**per′i·phras′ti·cal·ly** *adv.*

per·i·scope (per′ə·skōp) *n.* An instrument capable of reflecting an image down a vertical tube. [< PERI- + -SCOPE] —**per′i·scop′ic** or **·i·cal** (-skop′i·kəl) *adj.*

per·ish (per′ish) *v.i.* **1** To die, esp. to suffer a violent or untimely death. **2** To be destroyed; pass from existence. [< L *per-* away + *ire* go]

per·ish·a·ble (per′ish·ə·bəl) *adj.* **1** Liable to perish. **2** Liable to speedy decay, as fruit in transportation. —*n.pl.* Goods liable to rapid decay: used chiefly of foods in transit. —**per′ish·a·bil′i·ty, per′ish·a·ble·ness** *n.* —**per′ish·a·bly** *adv.*

Periscope

per·i·stal·sis (per′ə·stôl′sis, -stal′-) *n. pl.* **·ses** (-sēz) *Physiol.* A rhythmic muscular contraction of any hollow organ of the body, as of the intestines, which propels the contents toward the point of expulsion. [< Gk. *peristellein* surround] —**per′i·stal′tic** *adj.*

per·i·style (per′ə·stīl) *n. Archit.* **1** A system of columns about a building or an internal court. **2** An area or space so enclosed. [< Gk. *peri-* around + *stylos* a pillar] —**per′i·sty′lar** *adj.*

per·i·to·ne·um (per′ə·tə·nē′əm) *n. pl.* **·ne·a** (-nē′ə) The membrane that lines the abdominal cavity and covers the viscera. Also **per′i·to·nae′um.** [< Gk. *peritonos* stretched round] —**per′i·to·ne′al** or **·nae′al** *adj.*

per·i·to·ni·tis (per′ə·tə·nī′tis) *n.* Inflammation of the peritoneum.

per·i·wig (per′ə·wig) *n.* A wig. [< MF *perruque* peruke]

per·i·win·kle[1] (per′ə·wing′kəl) *n.* **1** Any of several small marine snails having a thick, conical shell. **2** The shell of these snails. [< OE *pinewincle*]

per·i·win·kle[2] (per′ə·wing′kəl) *n.* Any of several trailing plants with shining, evergreen leaves and usu. blue flowers. [< L *pervinca*]

per·jure (pûr′jər) *v.t.* **·jured, ·jur·ing** To make (oneself) guilty of perjury. [< L *per-* through, badly + *jurare* swear] —**per′jur·er** *n.*

per·jured (pûr′jərd) *adj.* Guilty of or marked by perjury.

per·ju·ry (pûr′jə·rē) *n. pl.* **·ries 1** *Law* The willful giving of false testimony while under lawfully administered oath. **2** The breaking of any oath, vow, or promise.

perk[1] (pûrk) *v.i.* **1** To recover one's spirits or vigor: with *up.* **2** To carry oneself or lift one's head jauntily. —*v.t.* **3** To raise quickly or smartly, as the ears: often with *up.* **4** To make (oneself) trim and smart in appearance: often with *up* or *out.* [ME *perken*]

perk[2] (pûrk) *v.i. Informal* To percolate.

perk[3] (pûrk) *n. Usu. pl. Chiefly Brit. Slang* PERQUISITE.

perk·y (pûr′kē) *adj.* **·i·er, ·i·est** Brisk, jaunty, spirited, or aggressive. —**perk′i·ly** *adv.* —**perk′i·ness** *n.*

perm. permanent.

per·ma·frost (pûr′mə·frôst, -frost) *n.* A permanently frozen layer of subsoil occurring in frigid climates. [< PERMA(NENT) + FROST]

per·ma·nence (pûr′mə·nəns) *n.* The state of being permanent; durability; fixity.

per·ma·nen·cy (pûr′mə·nən·sē) *n. pl.* **·cies 1** PERMANENCE. **2** Something permanent.

per·ma·nent (pûr′mə·nənt) *adj.* Continuing or intended to continue in the same state or without essential change. —*n.* PERMANENT WAVE. [< L *per-* through + *manere* remain] —**per′ma·nent·ly** *adv.* —**Syn.** durable, stable, fixed, lasting.

permanent wave A persistent curl produced by heat or chemicals in growing hair.

per·man·ga·nate (pər·mang′gə·nāt) *n.* A dark purple salt of permanganic acid.

per·man·gan·ic acid (pûr′man·gan′ik) An unstable acid containing manganese and oxygen.

per·me·a·ble (pûr′mē·ə·bəl) *adj.* Allowing passage, esp. of fluids. —**per·me·a·bil′i·ty** (pûr′mē·ə·bil′ə·tē) *n.* —**per′me·a·bly** *adv.*

per·me·ate (pûr′mē·āt) *v.* **·at·ed, ·at·ing** *v.t.* **1** To spread thoroughly through; pervade. **2** To pass through the pores or interstices of. —*v.i.* **3** To spread itself through some-

thing. [< L *per-* through + *meare* to pass] —**per′me·a′tion** *n.* —**per′me·a′tive** *adj.*

Per·mi·an (pûr′mē·ən) *adj. & n.* See GEOLOGY. [< *Perm,* a former E Russian province]

per·mis·si·ble (pər·mis′ə·bəl) *adj.* That can be permitted; allowable. —**per·mis·si·bil′i·ty** *n.* —**per·mis′si·bly** *adv.*

per·mis·sion (pər·mish′ən) *n.* The act of permitting or allowing; formal authorization; consent.

per·mis·sive (pər·mis′iv) *adj.* **1** That permits; granting permission. **2** That is permitted; optional. **3** Tolerant; lenient; indulgent: *permissive* parents. —**per·mis′sive·ly** *adv.* —**per·mis′sive·ness** *n.*

per·mit (pər·mit′) *v.* **·mit·ted, ·mit·ting** *v.t.* **1** To allow the doing of; consent to. **2** To give (someone) leave or consent; authorize. **3** To afford opportunity for: His answer *permits* no misinterpretation. —*v.i.* **4** To afford possibility or opportunity. —*n.* (pûr′mit) **1** Permission or warrant. **2** A formal, written authorization to do something. [< L *per-* through + *mittere* send, let go] —**per·mit′ter** *n.*

per·mu·ta·tion (pûr′myōō·tā′shən) *n.* **1** The act of permuting; transformation. **2** *Math.* **a** Change in the order of the elements of a set. **b** Any one of the set of arrangements that can be produced in this way.

per·mute (pər·myōōt′) *v.t.* **·mut·ed, ·mut·ing 1** To alter; change the order of. **2** *Math.* To subject to permutation. [< L *per-* thoroughly + *mutare* to change]

per·ni·cious (pər·nish′əs) *adj.* **1** Destructive; deadly. **2** *Archaic* Malicious; wicked. [< L *per-* thoroughly + *nex, necis* death] —**per·ni′cious·ly** *adv.* —**per·ni′cious·ness** *n.*

pernicious anemia A severe, progressive anemia of middle age and later, now controllable by administering certain vitamins.

per·nick·e·ty (pər·nik′ə·tē) *adj.* PERSNICKETY.

Pe·ron·ist (pə·rōn′ist) *n.* A follower of Juan Perón or of his policies. Also **Pe·ron·is·ta** (per′ə·nēs′tə).

per·o·rate (per′ə·rāt) *v.i.* **·rat·ed, ·rat·ing 1** To speak at length; harangue. **2** To sum up or conclude a speech. [< L *per-* thoroughly + *orare* speak]

per·o·ra·tion (per′ə·rā′shən) *n.* The concluding portion of an oration; the recapitulation of an argument.

per·ox·ide (pə·rok′sīd) *n.* **1** HYDROGEN PEROXIDE. **2** Any oxide yielding hydrogen peroxide when treated with an acid. —*v.t.* **·id·ed, ·id·ing** To bleach, as hair, with hydrogen peroxide.

per·pen·dic·u·lar (pûr′pən·dik′yə·lər) *adj.* **1** Being at right angles to the plane of the horizon; upright or vertical. **2** *Math.* Meeting a given line or plane at right angles. —*n.* **1** A perpendicular line. **2** A device used to indicate the vertical line from any point. **3** A vertical line or vertical face. **4** Perpendicular position. [< L *perpendiculum* a plumb line] —**per′pen·dic′u·lar′i·ty** (-lar′ə·tē) *n.* —**per′pen·dic′u·lar·ly** *adv.*

C

A —— B
D

CD is perpendicular to AB

per·pe·trate (pûr′pə·trāt) *v.t.* **·trat·ed, ·trat·ing** To perform or commit (a crime, etc.). [< L *perpetrare* carry through] —**per′pe·tra′tion, per′pe·tra′tor** *n.*

per·pet·u·al (pər·pech′ōō·əl) *adj.* **1** Continuing for all time. **2** Happening continually; repeated ceaselessly. [< L *per-* through + *petere* seek] —**per·pet′u·al·ly** *adv.* —**per·pet′u·al·ness** *n.*

per·pet·u·ate (pər·pech′ōō·āt) *v.t.* **·at·ed, ·at·ing** To make perpetual or enduring. —**per·pet′u·a′tion, per·pet′u·a′tor** *n.*

per·pe·tu·i·ty (pûr′pə·t′ōō′ə·tē) *n. pl.* **·ties 1** The quality or state of being perpetual. **2** Something that has perpetual existence or worth, as an annuity that is to be paid for life. **3** Unending or unlimited time.

per·plex (pər·pleks′) *v.t.* **1** To cause to hesitate, as from doubt; confuse; puzzle. **2** To make complicated, intricate, or confusing. [< L *per-* thoroughly + *plectere* to twist] —**per·plexed′** *adj.* —**per·plex′ed·ly** (-plek′sid·lē) *adv.*

per·plex·i·ty (pər·plek′sə·tē) *n. pl.* **·ties 1** The state of being perplexed; bewilderment; confusion, etc. **2** That which perplexes; also, an instance of bewilderment.

per·qui·site (pûr′kwə·zit) *n.* **1** Any incidental profit from service beyond salary or wages. **2** A privilege or benefit claimed as due. [< L *perquisitum* a thing diligently sought]

Pers. Persia; Persian.

pers. person; personal.

per se (pûr sā′, sē′) By, in, or of itself, oneself, or themselves; intrinsically. [L]

per·se·cute (pûr′sə·kyōōt) v.t. **·cut·ed, ·cut·ing 1** To harass with cruel or oppressive treatment, esp. because of race, religion, or opinions. **2** To annoy or harass persistently. [< L *per-* thoroughly + *sequi* follow] **—per′se·cu′tion, per′·se·cu′tor** n. **—per′se·cu′tion·al, per′se·cu′tive** adj.

Per·seph·o·ne (pər·sef′ə·nē) Gk. Myth. The daughter of Zeus and Demeter, abducted by Pluto and made queen of the kingdom of the dead.

Per·seus (pûr′syōōs, -sē·əs) Gk. Myth. The son of Zeus, slayer of Medusa and savior and husband of Andromeda. —n. A northern constellation.

per·se·ver·ance (pûr′sə·vir′əns) n. **1** The act or habit of persevering. **2** Steadfastness; tenacity.

per·se·vere (pûr′sə·vir′) v.i. **·vered, ·ver·ing** To persist in any purpose or enterprise; continue striving in spite of opposition, difficulty, etc. [< L *per-* thoroughly + *severus* strict] **—per′se·ver′ing·ly** adv. **—Syn.** endure, carry on, strive, hold out.

Per·sia (pûr′zhə, -shə) n. The former name for IRAN.

Per·sian (pûr′zhən, -shən) adj. Of or pertaining to ancient Persia or modern Iran, its people, or its language. —n. **1** A native or citizen of Persia or Iran. **2** The Iranian language of the Persians.

Persian Empire An ancient empire of sw Asia, extending from the Indus to the Mediterranean: founded by Cyrus the Great (sixth century B.C.) and destroyed by Alexander the Great (331 B.C.).

Persian lamb 1 The young of certain sheep, esp. the karakul. **2** Its skin, used as a fur; astrakhan.

per·si·flage (pûr′sə·fläzh′) n. **1** A light, flippant style of talking or writing. **2** Talking or writing of this kind. [< F *persifler* to banter]

per·sim·mon (pər·sim′ən) n. **1** A tree related to ebony with astringent, plumlike fruit. **2** The fruit of this tree. [< Algon.]

per·sist (pər·sist′, -zist′) v.i. **1** To continue firmly in some course, state, etc., esp. despite opposition or difficulties. **2** To be insistent, as in repeating a statement. **3** To continue to exist; endure. [< L *per-* thoroughly + *sistere* to stand]

per·sis·tence (pər·sis′təns, -zis′-) n. **1** The act of persisting. **2** The quality of being persistent; perseverance. **3** The continuance of an effect longer than the cause that first produced it.

per·sis·tent (pər·sis′tənt, -zis′-) adj. **1** Firm and persevering in a course or resolve. **2** Continuing to exist; enduring; permanent. **3** Constantly repeated; continual. **—per·sis′tent·ly** adv.

per·snick·e·ty (pər·snik′ə·tē) adj. Informal **1** Unduly fastidious; fussy; overprecise. **2** Demanding or displaying great care or precision. [< dial. alter. of PARTICULAR] **—per·snick′e·ti·ness** n.

per·son (pûr′sən) n. **1** A human being; an individual. **2** The body of a human being or its characteristic appearance and condition. **3** The personality of a human being; self. **4** Law Any human being, corporation, or other legal entity having legal rights and responsibilities. **5** Gram. **a** A modification of the pronoun and verb that distinguishes the speaker (**first person**), the person or thing spoken to (**second person**), and the person or thing spoken of (**third person**). **b** Any of the forms or inflections indicating this, as *I* or *we, you, he, she, it.* **—in person** Present in the flesh; in bodily presence. [< L *persona* mask for actors]

per·so·na (pər·sō′nə) n. **1** pl. **·nae** (-nē) A character in a drama, novel, etc.: dramatis *personae.* **2** pl. **·nas** Psych. The public role adopted by an individual. [L]

per·son·a·ble (pûr′sən·ə·bəl) adj. Pleasing in appearance and personality. **—per′son·a·bly** adv.

per·son·age (pûr′sən·ij) n. **1** A person of importance or rank. **2** Any person. **3** A character in fiction, history, etc. [< L *persona* a person]

per·so·na gra·ta (pər·sō′nə grä′tə, grā′tə) An acceptable person; one who is welcome. [L]

per·son·al (pûr′sən·əl) adj. **1** Of, pertaining to, characteristic of, or affecting a person. **2** Performed by or done to the person directly concerned. **3** Carried on directly by the persons concerned. **4** Of or pertaining to the body or appearance: *personal* beauty. **5** Directly relating to a person's character, conduct, personal affairs or habits, etc. **6** Making or tending to make personal remarks or to ask personal questions, esp. of a derogatory nature. **7** Law Of, pertaining to, or constituting personal property. **8** Gram. Denoting or indicating grammatical person. —n. A news item or advertisement that is personal in nature.

per·son·al·ism (pûr′sən·əl·iz′əm) n. A doctrine or movement stressing the uniqueness, significance and rights of the individual. **—per·son·al·ist** adj., n. **—per·son·al·is·tic** adj.

per·son·al·i·ty (pûr′sən·al′ə·tē) n. pl. **·ties 1** The state or quality of being a person, esp. a particular person. **2** Those special characteristics that distinguish a person, a group, or a nation. **3** The sum of such characteristics as they impress or tend to impress others. **4** Excellent or distinctive traits of character, sociability, etc. **5** A person having such traits. **6** A person who is famous or notorious. **7** Usu. pl. A remark, esp. one that is personally disparaging.

per·son·al·ize (pûr′sən·əl·īz′) v.t. **·ized, ·iz·ing 1** To make personal. **2** To personify. **3** To have engraved, monogrammed, etc. with one's name or initials, as stationery. Brit. sp. **per′son·al·ise′**.

per·son·al·ly (pûr′sən·əl·ē) adv. **1** In person; not through an agent. **2** As a person: I like her *personally.* **3** With reference to one's own opinion: *Personally,* I prefer the theater to the ballet. **4** As if directed at oneself: to take a comment *personally.*

per·son·al·ty (pûr′sən·əl·tē) n. pl. **·ties** Personal property.

per·so·na non gra·ta (pər·sō′nə non grä′tə, grā′tə) A person not acceptable. [L]

per·son·ate (pûr′sən·āt) v.t. **·at·ed, ·at·ing 1** To act the part of, as a character in a play. **2** To personify, as in poetry, art, etc. **3** Law To impersonate with intent to deceive. **—per′son·a′tion, per′son·a′tor** n. **—per′son·a·tive** adj.

per·son·i·fi·ca·tion (pər·son′ə·fə·kā′shən) n. **1** The endowment of inanimate objects or qualities with human attributes. **2** Striking or typical exemplification of a quality in one's person; embodiment: She was the *personification* of joy. **3** The representation of an abstract quality or idea by a human figure.

per·son·i·fy (pər·son′ə·fī) v.t. **·fied, ·fy·ing 1** To think of or represent as having life or human qualities. **2** To represent (an abstraction or inanimate object) as a person; symbolize. **3** To be the embodiment of; typify. [< L *persona* a mask, person + *facere* make] **—per·son′i·fi′er** n.

per·son·nel (pûr′sə·nel′) n. **1** Persons collectively. **2** The persons employed in a business or in military service. • *Personnel,* when it is construed as a unit, takes a singular verb: *The company's personnel has been cut.* When the term refers to the individuals that make up a unit, it takes a plural verb: *All personnel were requested to donate blood.*

per·spec·tive (pər·spek′tiv) n. **1** The art or theory of representing, by a drawing made on a flat or curved surface, solid objects or surfaces conceived of as not lying in that surface. **2** The art of conveying the impression of depth and distance by means of correct drawing, shading, etc. **3** The effect of distance upon the appearance of objects, by means of which the eye judges spatial relations. **4** The relative importance of facts or matters from any special point of view; also, the ability to discern this relative importance **5** A distant

Perspective
ab. horizon. c. vanishing point.
dc. line of sight. ef. ground line.

view; vista; prospect. —*adj.* **1** Of or pertaining to perspective. **2** Drawn in perspective. [< L *per-* through + *specere* look] —**per·spec'tive·ly** *adv.*

per·spi·ca·cious (pûr'spə·kā'shəs) *adj.* Keenly discerning or understanding. [< L *perspicax* sharp-sighted] —**per'spi·ca'cious·ly** *adv.* —**per'spi·ca'cious·ness, per'spi·cac'i·ty** (-kas'ə·tē) *n.*

per·spi·cu·i·ty (pûr'spə·kyōō'ə·tē) *n.* Clearness of expression or style; lucidity.

per·spic·u·ous (pər·spik'yōō·əs) *adj.* Having the quality of perspicuity; clear; lucid. [< L *perspicuus* clear, transparent] —**per·spic'u·ous·ly** *adv.* —**per·spic'ous·ness** *n.*

per·spi·ra·tion (pûr'spə·rā'shən) *n.* **1** The exuding of the saline fluid secreted by the sweat glands of the skin. **2** The saline fluid excreted; sweat. —**per·spir·a·to·ry** (pər·spī'rə·tôr'ē, -tō'rē, per'spə-) *adj.*

per·spire (pər·spīr') *v.* **·spired**, **·spir·ing** *v.i.* **1** To give off perspiration through the pores of the skin; sweat. —*v.t.* **2** To give off through pores; exude. [< L *per-* through + *spirare* breathe] —**per·spir'a·ble** *adj.*

per·suade (pər·swād') *v.t.* **·suad·ed**, **·suad·ing** **1** To move (a person, etc.) to do something by arguments, inducements, pleas, etc. **2** To induce to a belief; convince. [< L *per-* thoroughly + *suadere* advise] —**per·suad'a·ble** *adj.* —**per·suad'er** *n.*

per·sua·sion (pər·swā'zhən) *n.* **1** The act of persuading. **2** The state of being persuaded; conviction. **3** The power to persuade; persuasiveness. **4** A particular sect, denomination, etc. **5** *Informal* Sort; kind: the male *persuasion.*

per·sua·sive (pər·swā'siv) *adj.* Having the power or tendency to persuade. —**per·sua'sive·ly** *adv.* —**per·sua'sive·ness** *n.* —Syn. convincing, influential, assuring, cogent.

pert (pûrt) *adj.* **1** Disrespectfully forward or free; impudent. **2** Of fine appearance; comely; sprightly. [< L *apertus* open] —**pert'ly** *adv.* —**pert'ness** *n.*

pert. pertaining.

per·tain (pər·tān') *v.i.* **1** To have reference; relate. **2** To belong as an adjunct, function, quality, etc. **3** To be fitting or appropriate. [< L *pertinere* extend]

per·ti·na·cious (pûr'tə·nā'shəs) *adj.* **1** Marked by a dogged or even perverse firmness, as of purpose. **2** Stubbornly tenacious; hard to get rid of. [< L *per-* thoroughly, very + *tenax* tenacious] —**per'ti·na'cious·ly** *adv.* —**per'ti·na'cious·ness, per'ti·nac'i·ty** (-nas'ə·tē) *n.*

per·ti·nent (pûr'tə·nənt) *adj.* Related to or properly bearing upon the matter in hand; relevant. [< OF *partenir* pertain] —**per'ti·nence, per'ti·nen·cy** *n.* —**per'ti·nent·ly** *adv.*

per·turb (pər·tûrb') *v.t.* **1** To disquiet or disturb greatly; alarm; agitate. **2** To cause confusion or disorder in. [< L *per-* thoroughly + *turbare* disturb] —**per'tur·ba'tion** *n.*

Pe·ru (pə·rōō') *n.* A republic of w South America, 533,916 sq. mi., cap. Lima.

pe·ruke (pə·rōōk') *n.* A wig. [< Ital. *perruca*]

pe·ruse (pə·rōōz') *v.t.* **·rused**, **·rus·ing** **1** To read carefully or attentively. **2** To read. **3** To examine; scrutinize. [< PER- + USE, *v.*] —**pe·rus'a·ble** *adj.* —**pe·ru'sal, pe·rus'er** *n.*

Pe·ru·vi·an (pə·rōō'vē·ən) *adj.* Of or pertaining to Peru, its people, or their culture. —*n.* A native or citizen of Peru.

Peruvian bark CINCHONA.

per·vade (pər·vād') *v.t.* **·vad·ed**, **·vad·ing** To pass or spread through every part of; be diffused throughout; permeate. [< L *per-* through + *vadere* go] —**per·va'sion** (-zhən) *n.*

per·va·sive (pər·vā'siv) *adj.* Broadly or thoroughly penetrating; widespread. —**per·va'sive·ly** *adv.* —**per·va'sive·ness** *n.*

per·verse (pər·vûrs') *adj.* **1** Different or varying from the correct or normal. **2** Wicked; corrupt. **3** Obstinate and unreasonable in resisting what is reasonable, accepted, etc. **4** Petulant; peevish. [< L *pervertere* turn the wrong way] —**per·verse'ly** *adv.* —**per·verse'ness, per·ver'si·ty** *n.* —**per·ver'sive** *adj.*

per·ver·sion (pər·vûr'zhən, -shən) *n.* **1** The act of perverting, or the state of being perverted. **2** Something per-

verted. **3** A deviation from the normal, esp. in sexual desires or activities.

per·vert (pər·vûrt') *v.t.* **1** To turn to an improper use or purpose; misapply. **2** To distort the meaning of; misconstrue. **3** To turn from approved opinions or conduct; lead astray; corrupt. —*n.* (pûr'vûrt) A person who is perverted, esp. one affected with or addicted to sexual perversion. [< L *per-* away + *vertere* turn] —**per·vert'er** *n.* —**per·vert'i·ble** *adj.*

per·vert·ed (pər·vûr'tid) *adj.* Of, pertaining to, caused by, or characterized by perversion. —**per·vert'ed·ly** *adv.*

per·vi·ous (pûr'vē·əs) *adj.* **1** Capable of being penetrated; permeable. **2** Having a mind open to argument, suggestion, etc. [< L *per-* through + *via* way] —**per'vi·ous·ly** *adv.* —**per'vi·ous·ness** *n.*

Pe·sach (pä'säkh) *n.* PASSOVER. Also **Pe'sah.**

pe·se·ta (pə·sā'tə, *Sp.* pā·sā'tä) *n.* A silver coin, the basic monetary unit of Spain.

pes·ky (pes'kē) *adj.* **·ki·er, ·ki·est** *Informal* Annoying; troublesome; irksome. [Prob. < PEST] —**pes'ki·ly** *adv.* —**pes'ki·ness** *n.*

pe·so (pā'sō) *n. pl.* **·sos** The basic monetary unit of Argentina, Colombia, Cuba, the Dominican Republic, Mexico, the Philippines, and Uruguay. [Sp.]

pes·sa·ry (pes'ə·rē) *n. pl.* **·ries** Any device worn inside the vagina, as a contraceptive or a support to correct uterine prolapse. [< Gk. *pessos* an oval stone]

pes·si·mism (pes'ə·miz'əm) *n.* **1** A disposition to expect the worst possible conclusion of the course of events or of the resolution of present uncertainties or conditions. **2** The philosophical doctrine that the world as it exists is basically evil. **3** The belief that the evils in life outweigh the good and the happiness. [< L *pessimus* worst + -ISM] —**pes'si·mist** *n.* —**pes'si·mis'tic** *adj.* —**pes'si·mis'ti·cal·ly** *adv.*

pest (pest) *n.* **1** An annoying or harmful person or thing, esp. a destructive or injurious insect. **2** A virulent epidemic; pestilence. [< L *pestis* a plague]

pes·ter (pes'tər) *v.t.* To harass with petty annoyances. [< OF *empestrer* hobble a grazing horse] —**pes'ter·er** *n.*

pest·hole (pest'hōl') *n.* A breeding place for disease.

pest·house (pest'hous') *n. Archaic* A hospital for patients with infectious diseases.

pes·ti·cide (pes'tə·sīd) *n.* A chemical used to destroy weeds or vermin. —**pes'ti·ci'dal** *adj.*

pes·tif·er·ous (pes·tif'ər·əs) *adj.* **1** Carrying pestilence. **2** Threatening or bringing danger or evil. **3** *Informal* Annoying; disagreeable. [< L *pestis* a plague + *ferre* bear] —**pes·tif'er·ous·ly** *adv.* —**pes·tif'er·ous·ness** *n.*

pes·ti·lence (pes'tə·ləns) *n.* **1** Any widespread infectious malady. **2** A dangerous or harmful infection, influence, etc. [< L *pestis* a plague] —**pes'ti·lent, pes'ti·len'tial** (-shəl) *adj.* —**pes'ti·lent·ly, pes'ti·len'tial·ly** *adv.*

pes·tle (pes'əl) *n.* **1** An implement used for crushing or mixing substances, as in a mortar. **2** A vertical moving bar employed in pounding, as in a stamp mill, etc. —*v.t. & v.i.* **·tled, ·tling** To pound, grind, or mix with or as with a pestle. [< L *pistillum*]

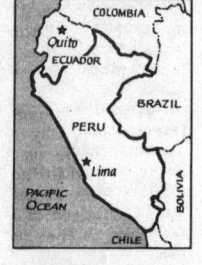
Pestle

pet¹ (pet) *n.* **1** A tamed or domesticated animal that is treated with affection. **2** Any person who is treated with affection or to whom great attention is paid. —*adj.* **1** Being or treated like a pet. **2** Regarded as a favorite; cherished: my *pet* hobby. —*v.* **pet·ted, pet·ting** —*v.t.* **1** To pamper; indulge. **2** To stroke or caress. —*v.i.* **3** *Informal* To kiss and caress or fondle in making love. [?]

pet² (pet) *n.* A fit of pique or ill temper; peevish mood. [?]

pet·al (pet'l) *n. Bot.* A division of a corolla. [< Gk. *petalon* a thin plate, leaf] —**pet'aled** or **pet'alled** *adj.*

pe·tard (pi·tärd') *n.* An explosive device formerly used for making breaches, etc., as in walls. —**hoist with** (or **by**) **one's own petard** To undo (one who plots the ruin of others) by ensnaring in his own machinations. [< MF *péter* break wind]

pet·cock (pet'kok') *n. Mech.* A small tap or valve, as for draining a steam cylinder or pump. [? < obs. *pet* a fart + COCK¹ a valve]

pe·ter (pē'tər) *v.i. Informal* To diminish gradually and then cease or disappear; become exhausted: with *out*. [Orig. U.S. mining slang]

pet·i·ole (pet′ē·ōl) *n.* **1** *Bot.* The stalk supporting the blade of a leaf. **2** *Zool.* A stalk or peduncle. [< L *petiolus* a stem, dim. of *pes, pedis* a foot] —**pet′i·o·lar, pet′i·o·late′, pet′i·o·lat′ed** *adj.*

pet·it (pet′ē) *adj.* Small; lesser; minor; trivial: used in legal phrases. [< OF, small]

pe·tite (pə·tēt′) *adj.* Diminutive; little: said of women. [F]

pet·it four (pet′ē fôr′, fōr; *Fr.* pə·tē′ fōōr′) *n. pl.* **pet·its fours** (pet′ē fôrz′, fōrz′; *Fr.* pə·tē′ fōōr′) A small cake, often elaborately frosted. [F, lit., little oven]

pe·ti·tion (pə·tish′ən) *n.* **1** A request, supplication, or prayer; a solemn or formal supplication. **2** A formal request, written or printed, setting forth such a request, addressed to a person or persons in authority and often signed by a group of petitioners. **3** *Law* A formal application in writing made to a court, requesting judicial action concerning some matter therein set forth. **4** That which is requested or asked for. —*v.t.* **1** To make a petition to; entreat. **2** To ask for. —*v.i.* **3** To make a petition. [< L < *petere* seek] —**pe·ti′tion·ar′y** *adj.* —**pe·ti′tion·er** *n.*

petit jury A jury of 12 persons selected to weigh the evidence in and decide upon the facts at issue in a trial in court.

pe·tit mal (pə·tē′ mal′, mäl′) *Pathol.* A minor epileptic seizure characterized by a momentary loss of consciousness. [F, lit., small illness]

pet·rel (pet′rəl) *n.* Any of various small sea birds that fly low over the water with feet hanging. [?]

pet·ri·fy (pet′rə·fī) *v.* **·fied, ·fy·ing** *v.t.* **1** To replace (organic material) with stony minerals. **2** To make fixed and unyielding; harden. **3** To immobilize with fear, surprise, etc. —*v.i.* **4** To become stone or a stony substance. [< L *petra* rock + *facere* make] —**pet′ri·fac′tion** (-fak′shən), **pet′ri·fi·ca′tion** *n.* —**pet′ri·fac′tive** *adj.*

petro- *combining form* Rock; stone: *petrography*. [Gk. *petros* a stone]

pet·ro·chem·i·cal (pet′rō·kem′i·kəl) *n.* Any compound derived from petroleum or natural gas. —*adj.* Pertaining to petrochemicals. —**pet·ro·chem·is·try** (-is·trē) *n.*

pet·ro·dol·lars (pet′rō·dol′ərz) *n. pl.* Dollars accumulated by oil-producing countries from oil sales, and usually invested in industrial countries.

pe·trog·ra·phy (pə·trog′rə·fē) *n.* The systematic description and classification of rocks. —**pe·trog′ra·pher** *n.* —**pet·ro·graph·ic** (pet′rə·graf′ik) or **·i·cal** *adj.*

pet·rol (pet′rəl) *n. Brit.* GASOLINE. [< F *pétrole*]

pet·ro·la·tum (pet′rə·lā′təm) *n.* A greasy semisolid mixture of hydrocarbons obtained from petroleum, used as a lubricant and in medicinal salves. Also **petroleum jelly.** [< PETROLEUM]

pe·tro·le·um (pə·trō′lē·əm) *n.* An oily, liquid mixture of hydrocarbons found in scattered subterranean deposits, and used as a source of fuels, as gasoline, kerosene, etc. and as raw material for many synthetic products. [< L *petra* rock + *oleum* oil]

pe·trol·o·gy (pə·trol′ə·jē) *n.* The study of the origin and characteristics of rocks. —**pet·ro·log·ic** (pet′rə·loj′ik) or **·i·cal** *adj.* —**pet′ro·log′i·cal·ly** *adv.* —**pe·trol′o·gist** *n.*

pet·ti·coat (pet′ē·kōt) *n.* **1** A skirt, esp. an underskirt worn by young girls and women. **2** *Informal* A girl or woman. —*adj.* Of, pertaining to, or influenced by, women: *petticoat* politics. [< PETTY + COAT]

pet·ti·fog (pet′i·fog, -fôg) *v.i.* **·fogged, ·fog·ging** To be a pettifogger. [Back formation < PETTIFOGGER]

pet·ti·fog·ger (pet′i·fog′ər, -fôg′ər) *n.* **1** A disreputable lawyer, esp. one chiefly employed on mean or petty cases, or resorting to small or tricky methods. **2** A person who quibbles over unimportant details. [< PETTY + obs. *fogger* a trickster for gain] —**pet′ti·fog′ger·y** *n.*

pet·tish (pet′ish) *adj.* Capriciously ill-tempered; petulant. [Prob. < PET²] —**pet′tish·ly** *adv.*

pet·ty (pet′ē) *adj.* **·ti·er, ·ti·est** **1** Having little worth, importance, position, or rank. **2** Having little generosity; small-minded; mean; spiteful. [< OF *petit* small] —**pet′ti·ly** *adv.* —**pet′ti·ness** *n.*

petty cash Money for small incidental expenses.

petty jury PETIT JURY.

petty officer See GRADE.

pet·u·lant (pech·ōō·lənt) *adj.* Displaying or characterized by bad humor, esp. over a minor irritation. [< L *petulans* forward] —**pet′u·lance, pet′u·lan·cy** *n.* —**pet′u·lant·ly** *adv.* — **Syn.** fretful, peevish, grumpy, complaining.

pe·tu·ni·a (pə·tyōō′nē·ə) *n.* A plant of the nightshade family, with funnel-shaped, fragrant flowers in various shades of red, purple, and white. [< F *petun* tobacco; from its close relation to tobacco]

pew (pyōō) *n.* **1** A bench with a back for seating people in church. **2** A boxlike enclosure with seats, for seating a family or other group in a church. [< L *podium* balcony]

pe·wee (pē′wē) *n.* Any of several small flycatchers, including the phoebe. [Imit.]

pe·wit (pē′wit, pyōō′it) *n.* **1** PEWEE. **2** LAPWING.

pew·ter (pyōō′tər) *n.* **1** An alloy of tin with lead and other meals. **2** Tableware, etc., made of pewter. —*adj.* Made of pewter. [< OF *peutre*]

pe·yo·te (pā·ō′tē; *Sp.* pā·yō′tā) *n.* **1** The mescal cactus. **2** The hallucinogen obtained from this cactus. Also **pe·yo′tl** (-yōt′l). [< Nah. *peyotl*, lit., a caterpillar; from the down at its center]

pf. pfennig, preferred.

Pfc, Pfc. private first class.

pfd. preferred.

pfen·nig (fen′ig; *Ger.* pfen′ikh) *n. pl.* **·nigs** or **pfen·ni·ge** (pfen′i·ge) A unit of German currency, equivalent to 1/100 of a Deutsche mark or of a mark or Ostmark.

Pg. Portugal; Portuguese.

pH *Chem.* The symbol used in expressing acidity and alkalinity on a numerical scale such that a pH of 1 represents a strongly acid condition, 7 represents neutrality, and pH values 7 to about 14 indicate increasing alkalinity. [< P(OTENTIAL OF) H(YDROGEN)]

Phae·dra (fē′drə) *Gk. Myth.* The wife of Theseus: she fell in love with her stepson Hippolytus and killed herself because he spurned her.

Pha·e·thon (fē′ə·thon) *Gk. Myth.* The son of Helios, who borrowed his father's chariot of the sun, and would have set heaven and earth on fire if Zeus had not slain him with a thunderbolt.

pha·e·ton (fā′ə·tən; *esp. Brit.* fā′tən) *n.* **1** A light four-wheeled horse-drawn carriage. **2** An early type of open two-seated automobile; usu. with a folding top. [< Phaethon]

phago- *combining form* Consuming: *phagocyte*. Also **phag-.** [< Gk. *phagein* eat]

phag·o·cyte (fag′ə·sīt) *n.* A leukocyte that engulfs and destroys foreign particles, as bacteria, etc. [< Gk. *phagein* eat + -CYTE] —**phag′o·cyt′ic** (-sit′ik) or **·i·cal** *adj.*

Phaeton *def.* 1

pha·lan·ger (fə·lan′jər) *n.* any of various small arboreal marsupials of Australia and New Guinea. [< NL *phalanx* phalanx (def. 3); in ref. to the peculiar construction of its hind feet]

pha·lanx (fā′langks, *esp. Brit.* fal′angks) *n. pl.* **pha·lanx·es** or **pha·lan·ges** (fə·lan′jēz) **1** In ancient Greece, a dense formation of heavy infantry. **2** Any massed or compact body or corps. **3** *pl* **pha·lan·ges** *Anat.* Any of the bones of the fingers or toes. [Gk., a line of battle] • See FOOT.

phal·li·cism (fal′ə·siz′əm) *n.* Worship of the generative power in nature as symbolized by the phallus.

phal·lus (fal′əs) *n. pl.* **·lus·es** or **·li** (-ī) **1** A figure of the penis as a symbol of male generative power, used in many systems of religion. **2** The penis. [< Gk. *phallos* penis] —**phal′lic** or **phal′li·cal** *adj.*

phan·tasm (fan′taz·əm) *n.* **1** A figment of the imagination, as a ghost or specter. **2** A deceptive likeness or appearance. —**phan·tas′mal, phan·tas′mic,** *adj.*

---

add, āce, câre, pälm; end, ēven; it, īce; odd, ōpen, ôrder; tōōk, pōōl; up, bûrn; ə = *a* in *above, u* in *focus;* yōō = *u* in *fuse;* oil; pout; check; go; ring; thin; this; zh, *vision.* < derived from; ? origin uncertain or unknown.

phan·tas·ma·go·ri·a (fan·taz′mə·gôr′ē·ə, -gō′rē·ə) *n.* A fantastic, rapidly changing series of things, actually seen or imagined.

phan·ta·sy (fan′tə·sē, -zē) *n. pl.* **phan·ta·sies** FANTASY.

phan·tom (fan′təm) *n.* **1** Something that exists only in appearance; illusion. **2** An apparition; specter. **3** Something dreaded or feared. **4** The visible representative of an abstract state or incorporeal person. —*adj.* Of, like, or being a phantom. [< Gk. *phantasma* an appearance]

Phar·aoh (fâr′ō, fā′rō) *n.* Any one of the monarchs of ancient Egypt. [< Egypt. *pr-ʿōh* the great house] —**Phar′a·on′ic** (-ā·on′ik) or **·i·cal** *adj.*

phar·i·sa·ic (far′ə·sā′ik) *adj.* Observing the form rather than the spirit of religion; self-righteous; hypocritical. Also **phar′i·sa′i·cal.** —**phar′i·sa′i·cal·ly** *adv.* —**phar′i·sa′i·cal·ness** *n.*

Phar·i·sa·ic (far′ə·sā′ik) *adj.* Of or pertaining to the Pharisees.

phar·i·sa·ism (far′ə·sā·iz′əm) *n.* Formality, self-righteousness, censoriousness, or hypocrisy. Also **phar′i·see·ism** (-sē·iz′əm).

Phar·i·sa·ism (far′ə·sā·iz′əm) *n.* The principles and practices of the Pharisees.

phar·i·see (far′ə·sē) *n.* A formal, sanctimonious, hypocritical person.

Phar·i·see (far′ə·sē) *n.* One of an ancient, exclusive Jewish sect that paid excessive regard to tradition and ceremonies, and in so doing separated themselves from the other Jews. [< Heb. *pārūsh* separated]

pharm. pharmaceutical; pharmacist; pharmacy.

phar·ma·ceu·ti·cal (fär′mə·sōō′ti·kəl) *adj.* Pertaining to, using, or relating to pharmacy or pharmacists. —*n.* A drug. Also **phar′ma·ceu′tic.** [< Gk. *pharmakon* a drug] —**phar′ma·ceu′ti·cal·ly** *adv.* —**phar′ma·ceu′tist** *n.*

phar·ma·ceu·tics (fär′mə·sōō′tiks) *n. pl.* (construed as *sing.*) The science of pharmacy.

phar·ma·cist (fär′mə·sist) *n.* A qualified druggist; pharmaceutist.

phar·ma·col·o·gy (fär′mə·kol′ə·jē) *n.* The science of the action of drugs, their nature, preparation, administration, and effects. —**phar′ma·co·log′ic** (-kə·loj′ik) or **·i·cal** *adj.* —**phar′ma·co·log′i·cal·ly** *adv.* —**phar′ma·col′o·gist** *n.*

phar·ma·co·poe·ia (fär′mə·kə·pē′ə) *n.* **1** A reference book on drugs. **2** A stock or collection of drugs. [< Gk. *pharmakon* a drug + *poieein* make] —**phar′ma·co·poe′ial** *adj.* —**phar′ma·co·poe′ist** *n.*

phar·ma·cy (fär′mə·sē) *n. pl.* **·cies** **1** The art or business of compounding and dispensing medicines. **2** A drugstore. [< Gk. *pharmakon* a drug]

pha·ryn·ge·al (fə·rin′jē·əl, far′in·jē′əl) *adj.* Of or pertaining to the pharynx. Also **pha·ryn′gal** (-gəl).

phar·yn·gi·tis (far′in·jī′tis) *n.* Inflammation of the pharynx.

phar·ynx (far′ingks) *n. pl.* **pha·ryn·ges** (fə·rin′jēz) or **phar·ynx·es** The tract between the palate and the esophagus, serving as a passage for air and food. [Gk., throat]

Pharynx

phase (fāz) *n.* **1** Any one of the aspects, parts, etc., that are a distinguishable part of a cycle, development, etc. **2** *Astron.* One of the appearances or forms presented periodically by the moon and planets. **3** *Physics* **a** A stage in a periodic process or phenomenon, as an oscillation, wave, etc. **b** Any homogeneous form of a given substance that may occur alone, or exist independently as a component of a heterogeneous system, as ice in water, etc. **4** *Biol.* Any distinct stage in the reproduction, growth, development, or life pattern of a cell or organism. —**in phase** Having the same phase at a given time and place, as two waves. —*v.t.* **phased, phas·ing** To accomplish in planned phases. —**phase down** To reduce or lessen in planned phases. —**phase in** To introduce in planned phases. —**phase out** To terminate work on, production of, etc., step by step, according to plan. [< Gk. *phasis* an appearance] —**pha·sic** (fā′zik) *adj.*

phase·out (fāz′out′) *n.* A termination, closing down, withdrawal, etc., in planned phases.

Ph.D. Doctor of Philosophy (L *Philosophiae Doctor*).

pheas·ant (fez′ənt) *n.* **1** A long-tailed chickenlike bird noted for the gorgeous plumage of the male. **2** One of various other birds, as the ruffed grouse. [< Gk. *Phasianos (ornis)* (bird) of Phasis, a river in the Caucasus]

phe·nac·e·tin (fə·nas′ə·tin) *n.* A white, synthetic compound used to reduce fever and relieve pain. [< PHEN(O)- + ACET(O)- + -IN]

phe·nix (fē′niks) *n.* PHOENIX.

pheno- *combining form Chem.* Related to or derived from benzene: *phenobarbital.* [< Gk. *phainen* to show, shine]

phe·no·bar·bi·tal (fē′nō·bär′bə·tôl) *n.* A white, odorless powder, used as a sedative.

phe·nol (fē′nōl, -nol) *n.* A derivative of benzene containing a hydroxyl radical; carbolic acid. [< PHEN(O)- + -OL¹] —**phe·nol′ic** (-nol′ik, -nō′lik) *adj.*

phe·nol·phthal·ein (fē′nōl·thal′ēn, fē′nolf·thal′ē·in) *n.* A whitish crystalline compound that turns red in alkaline solutions, used as an acid-base indicator and in medicine as a laxative.

phe·nom·e·nal (fi·nom′ə·nəl) *adj.* **1** Of, pertaining to, or being a phenomenon. **2** Extraordinary or marvelous. —**phe·nom′e·nal·ly** *adv.*

phe·nom·e·non (fi·nom′ə·non) *n. pl.* **·na** (-nə) or, *for defs. 3 and 4,* **·nons** **1** A fact, event, etc., that can be explained on the basis of scientific principles, as a lunar eclipse. **2** Any fact, appearance, etc., as it is apprehended by the senses, in contrast with or in opposition to the thing in itself. **3** Any unusual fact, thing, occurrence, etc. **4** An unusual, exceptional, or extraordinary person; prodigy. [< Gk. *phainomenon* an appearance]

phen·yl (fen′əl, fē′nəl) *n.* A univalent hydrocarbon radical containing six carbon atoms in a ring linkage, forming the basis of numerous derivatives. [< PHEN(O)- + -YL]

phen·yl·ke·to·nu·ri·a (fen′əl·kēt′n·yŏŏr′ē·ə, fē′nəl·) *n. Pathol.* A rare, inherited metabolic disorder that can cause permanent mental impairment if untreated within a few weeks after birth. [< PHENYL + KETON(E) + Gk. *ouron* urine]

pher·o·mone (fer′ə·mōn′) *n.* An external animal secretion having a taste, smell, or other characteristic that stimulates a behavioral or physiological response in members of the species that produces it. [< Gk. *pherein* carry + (HOR)MONE] —**pher′o·mon′al, ·mon′ic,** *adj.*

phew (fyōō) *interj.* An exclamation of relief, surprise, disgust, etc.

phi (fī, fē) *n.* The 21st letter in the Greek alphabet (Φ,φ).

phi·al (fī′əl) *n.* VIAL.

Phi Be·ta Kap·pa (fī bā′tə kap′ə) **1** An American honorary society composed of college students and graduates of high academic standing. **2** A member of this society.

Phil. Philippians; Philippine.

Philadelphia lawyer *Informal* An unusually clever lawyer, esp. one who is unscrupulous in the application of legal technicalities.

phi·lan·der (fi·lan′dər) *v.i.* To make love casually or without serious intentions. [< Gk. *philein* to love + *andros* man] —**phi·lan′der·er** *n.*

phi·lan·thro·py (fi·lan′thrə·pē) *n. pl.* **·pies** **1** The disposition or effort to promote the well-being of mankind, as by making donations to charities, working for the improvement of social conditions, etc. **2** A charitable donation, work for the improvement of social conditions, etc. **3** An organization devoted to charity, social improvement, etc. [< Gk. *philein* love + *anthropos* man] —**phil·an·throp·ic** (fil′ən·throp′ik) or **·i·cal** *adj.* —**phil′an·throp′i·cal·ly** *adv.* —**phi·lan′thro·pist** *n.* —**Syn. 1** benevolence, charity, generosity, munificence.

phi·lat·e·ly (fi·lat′ə·lē) *n.* The study and collection of postage stamps, stamped envelopes, wrappers, etc.; stamp collecting. [< Gk. *philos* loving + *ateleia* exemption from tax; with ref. to prepaid postage] —**phil·a·tel·ic** (fil′ə·tel′ik) or **·i·cal** *adj.* —**phil′a·tel′i·cal·ly** *adv.* —**phi·lat′e·list** *n.*

-phile *combining form* One who supports or is fond of; one devoted to: *bibliophile.* [< Gk. *phileein* to love]

Phi·le·mon (fi·lē′mən) A Greek converted to Christianity by Paul. —*n.* The epistle addressed by Paul to Philemon, forming a book of the New Testament.

phil·har·mon·ic (fil′här·mon′ik, -ər·mon′-) *adj.* **1** Fond of harmony or music. **2** *Often cap.* Pertaining to a particular musical society or orchestra. —*n. Often cap.* An association sponsoring a symphony orchestra, or the orchestra itself. [< Gk. *philos* loving + *harmonikos* harmony]

-philia *combining form* **1** A tendency toward: *hemophilia.* **2** Abnormal fondness for. [< Gk. *phileein* to love]

Phi·lip·pi·ans (fi·lip′ē·ənz) *n.pl. (construed as sing.)* In the New Testament, an epistle of St. Paul to the Christians at Philippi, an ancient town in N Macedonia.

phi·lip·pic (fi·lip′ik) *n.* An impassioned speech characterized by invective. —**the Philippics** A series of twelve speeches in which Demosthenes denounced Philip of Macedon.

Phil·ip·pines (fil′ə·pēnz′, fil′ə·pēnz′) *n.* A republic located on an island group in the Pacific, SE of China, 115,707 sq. mi., cap. Quezon City, administrative center Manila. Also **Republic of the Philippines.** —**Phil′ip·pine′** *adj.*

Phi·lis·ti·a (fi·lis′tē·ə) *n.* A region on the Mediterranean, in ancient SW Palestine.

phi·lis·tine (fil′ə·stin, -stēn, fə·lis′tən, -tēn′) *Sometimes cap. n.* An ignorant, narrow-minded person, devoid of culture and indifferent to art. —*adj.* Smugly indifferent to culture and art. —**phi·lis·tin·ism** (fil′ə·stin·iz′əm, -stēn′-) *n.*

Phi·lis·tine (fil′ə·stin, -stēn, fə·lis′tən, tēn′) *n.* One of a warlike race of ancient Philistia. —*adj.* Of or pertaining to the ancient Philistines.

philo- *combining form* Loving; fond of: *philogyny.* [< Gk. *phileein* to love]

phil·o·den·dron (fil′ə·den′drən) *n.* Any of several tropical American climbing plants, with glossy, evergreen leaves, cultivated as an ornamental house plant. [< Gk. *philodendros* fond of trees]

phi·log·y·ny (fi·loj′ə·nē) *n.* Fondness for or devotion to women. [< Gk *philos* fond + *gynē* a woman] —**phi·log′y·nist** *n.* —**phi·log′y·nous** *adj.*

phi·lol·o·gy (fi·lol′ə·jē) *n.* **1** The scientific study of written records, esp. literary works, to determine their meaning, authenticity, etc. **2** LINGUISTICS. **3** Literary scholarship. [< Gk. *philos* fond + *logos* a word] —**phil·o·log·ic** (fil′ə·loj′ik) or **·i·cal** *adj.* —**phil′o·log′i·cal·ly** *adv.* —**phi·lol′o·gist** *n.*

Phil·o·mel (fil′ə·mel) *n.* In poetic usage, the nightingale. Also **Phil·o·me·la** (fil′ə·mē′lə). [< *Philomela,* Greek mythological princess changed into a nightingale]

phi·los·o·pher (fi·los′ə·fər) *n.* **1** A student of or a specialist in philosophy. **2** The creator of a system of philosophy. **3** A person who is reasonable, calm, patient, etc., under all circumstances.

philosopher's stone An imaginary stone thought to have the power of transmuting the baser metals into gold.

phil·o·soph·i·cal (fil′ə·sof′i·kəl) *adj.* **1** Of, pertaining to, or founded on the principles of philosophy or of a philosopher. **2** Learned in or devoted to philosophy. **3** Reasonable, calm, patient, thoughtful, etc. Also **phil′o·soph′ic.** —**phil′o·soph′i·cal·ly** *adv.*

phi·los·o·phize (fi·los′ə·fīz) *v.i.* **·phized, ·phiz·ing** To speculate like a philosopher; seek ultimate causes and principles. —**phi·los′o·phiz′er** *n.*

phi·los·o·phy (fi·los′ə·fē) *n. pl.* **·phies 1** The search for knowledge of general principles; the study of the elements, powers, or causes and laws that explain facts and existences. **2** A philosophical system or treatise based on such a search or study. **3** The general laws that furnish the rational explanation of anything: the *philosophy* of banking. **4** The system of values adopted by an individual, group, etc. **5** Calm judgment and equable temper; practical wisdom; fortitude. **6** A study of human behavior, ethics, morals, character, etc. [< Gk. *philos* loving + *sophos* wise]

phil·ter (fil′tər) *n.* **1** A charmed draft supposed to have power to excite sexual love. **2** Any magic potion. —*v.t.* To charm with a philter. Also **phil′tre.** [< Gk. *philtron* a love potion]

phle·bi·tis (fli·bī′tis) *n.* Inflammation of a vein. [< Gk. *phleps* vein + -ITIS] —**phle·bit′ic** (-bit′ik) *adj.*

phle·bot·o·mize (fli·bot′ə·mīz) *v.t.* **·mized, ·miz·ing** To treat by phlebotomy.

phle·bot·o·my (fli·bot′ə·mē) *n.* The practice of bloodletting as a remedial measure. [< Gk. *phleps* vein + -TOMY] —**phleb·o·tom·ic** (fleb′ə·tom′ik) or **·i·cal** *adj.* —**phle·bot′o·mist** *n.*

phlegm (flem) *n.* **1** A viscid, stringy mucus secreted in the air passages. **2** Apathy; cold, undemonstrative temper; self-possession. **3** One of the four natural humors in ancient physiology. [< Gk. *phlegma* inflammation]

phleg·mat·ic (fleg·mat′ik) *adj.* Having a sluggish or stolid temperament; not easily moved or excited. Also **phleg·mat′i·cal.** —**phleg·mat′i·cal·ly** *adv.* —**Syn.** indifferent, calm, dull, undemonstrative.

phlo·em (flō′em) *n. Bot.* The food-conducting tissue in the leaves, roots and stems of ferns and seed plants. [< Gk. *phloos* bark]

phlo·gis·ton (flō·jis′tən) *n.* The principle formerly assumed to inhere in combustible bodies, and to be given up by them in burning. [< Gk. *phlogistos* inflammable] —**phlo·gis′tic** *adj.*

phlox (floks) *n.* A plant or flower of a genus of herbs with opposite leaves and clusters of showy flowers. [< Gk. *phlox* wallflower, flame]

pho·bi·a (fō′bē·ə) *n.* A compulsive and persistent fear of any specified object or situation. [< Gk. *phobos* fear] —**pho′bic** (-bik) *adj.*

-phobia *combining form* Aversion to; fear of: *claustrophobia.* [< Gk. *phobos* fear]

phoe·be (fē′bē) *n.* Any of a genus of American flycatchers with slightly crested head. [Imit. of its cry]

Phoe·be (fē′bē) *Gk. Myth.* A name for Artemis as goddess of the moon. —*n.* The moon. Also **Phœ′be.**

Perennial phlox

Phoe·bus (fē′bəs) *Gk. Myth.* Apollo as god of the sun. —*n.* The sun. Also **Phœ′bus.**

Phoe·ni·cia (fə·nē′shə, -nish′ə) *n.* An ancient country of the Mediterranean in the region of modern Syria and Lebanon.

Phoe·ni·cian (fə·nē′shən, -nish′ən) *adj.* Of or pertaining to ancient Phoenicia, its people, or its language. —*n.* **1** One of the people of ancient Phoenicia or any of its colonies. **2** The Semitic language of these people.

phoe·nix (fē′niks) *n.* In Egyptian mythology, a bird which was supposed to live for 500 to 600 years, consume itself by fire, and rise again from its ashes young and beautiful to live through another cycle: a symbol of immortality. Also **phe′nix.** [< Gk. *phoinix*]

pho·nate (fō′nāt) *v.t.* **·nat·ed, ·nat·ing** To make articulate sounds; vocalize. [< Gk. *phōnē* sound + -ATE¹] —**pho·na′tion** *n.*

phone¹ (fōn) *n. & v. Informal* Telephone.

phone² (fōn) *n.* A single sound used in human speech. [< Gk. *phōne* a sound]

-phone *combining form* Voice; sound: often used in names of musical instruments and other sound-transmitting devices: *saxophone, microphone.* [< Gk. *phōnē* voice]

pho·neme (fō′nēm) *n. Ling.* A speech sound or a group of phonetically similar speech sounds comprising one member of a set of the sounds in any language that differentiate between utterances, as /s/ in *sun* and /f/ in *fun.* •The *t* sounds in *tip, stop,* and *pit,* which are not phonetically identical, are members of the phoneme /t/. [< Gk. *phōnē* a voice, sound] —**pho·ne·mic** (fə·nē′mik) *adj.* —**pho·ne′mi·cal·ly** *adv.*

pho·ne·mics (fə·nē′miks) *n.pl. (construed as sing.)* The study of the phonemic system of a language.

pho·net·ic (fə·net′ik) *adj.* **1** Of or pertaining to phonetics, or to speech sounds and their production. **2** Representing speech or speech sounds by characters that refer to specific properties, such as place or manner of articulation. Also **pho·net′i·cal**. [< Gk. *phōnē* sound] —**pho·net′i·cal·ly** *adv.*

pho·ne·ti·cian (fō′nə·tish′ən) *n.* An authority on phonetics.

pho·net·ics (fə·net′iks) *n.pl. (construed as sing.)* **1** The branch of linguistics which deals with the analysis, description, and classification of the sounds of speech. **2** The system of sounds of a language or group of languages: the *phonetics* of American English.

pho·ney (fō′nē) *adj. & n.* PHONY.

phon·ic (fon′ik, fō′nik) *adj.* **1** Of, pertaining to, or producing sound or the sounds of speech. **2** Of or pertaining to phonics.

phon·ics (fon′iks, fō′niks) *n.pl. (construed as sing.)* A method of teaching spelling, pronunciation, and reading by the use of elementary phonetics.

phono- *combining form* Sound; speech; voice: *phonograph.* [< Gk. *phōnē* sound, voice]

pho·no·gram (fō′nə·gram) *n.* A graphic character symbolizing an articulate sound, word, syllable, etc., as in shorthand. —**pho′no·gram′ic** or **·gram′mic** *adj.* —**pho′no·gram′i·cal·ly** or **·gram′mi·cal·ly** *adv.*

pho·no·graph (fō′nə·graf, -gräf) *n.* An apparatus for recording and reproducing sounds on and from plastic disks. —**pho′no·graph′ic** *adj.* —**pho′no·graph′i·cal·ly** *adv.*

pho·nog·ra·phy (fə·nog′rə·fē) *n.* **1** Phonetic spelling or writing. **2** Any of the systems of shorthand based on phonetic transcription of speech. —**pho·nog′ra·pher, pho·nog′ra·phist** *n.*

pho·nol·o·gy (fə·nol′ə·jē) *n.* **1** Phonetics or phonemics, or both considered together. **2** The historical study of speech sounds, esp. of the sound changes that have taken place in a particular language. —**pho·no·log·i·cal** (fō′nə·loj′i·kəl) **pho′no·log′ic** *adj.* —**pho′no·log′i·cal·ly** *adv.* —**pho·nol′o·gist** *n.*

pho·ny (fō′nē) *Slang adj.* **·ni·er, ·ni·est** Fake; false; spurious; counterfeit. —*n.* **1** Something fake or not genuine. **2** One who pretends to be something he is not. [?] —**pho′ni·ness** *n.*

-phony *combining form* A (specified) type of sound or sounds: *cacophony.* [< Gk. *phōnē* sound, voice]

phos·gene (fos′jēn) *n.* A colorless, highly toxic, volatile liquid, used as a poison gas and in making synthetic chemicals. [< Gk. *phōs* light + -GEN]

phos·phate (fos′fāt) *n.* **1** A salt or ester of phosphoric acid. **2** A fertilizer containing phosphate. **3** A beverage containing small amounts of phosphoric acid. [< PHOS-PHORUS] —**phos·phat′ic** (fos·fat′ik) *adj.*

phos·phide (fos′fīd, -fid) *n.* A binary compound of phosphorus with a more positive element: calcium *phosphide.* Also **phos′phid** (-fid).

phos·phite (fos′fīt) *n.* A salt of phosphorous acid.

phos·phor (fos′fər) *n.* A substance that reflects incident radiation as light.

phos·phor·esce (fos′fə·res′) *v.i.* **·esced, ·esc·ing** To glow with a faint light while producing negligible heat. [Back formation < PHOSPHORESCENT]

phos·phor·es·cence (for′fə·res′əns) *n.* **1** The emission of light with negligible heat. **2** The light so emitted. [< PHOSPHOR(US) + -ESCENCE] —**phos′phor·es′cent,** *adj.*

phos·phor·et·ed (fos′fə·ret′id) *adj.* Combined or treated with phosphorus. Also **phos′phor·et′ted.**

phos·phor·ic (fos·fôr′ik, -for′-) *adj.* Of, pertaining to or derived from phosphorus, esp. in its highest valence.

phosphoric acid An acid of phosphorus used widely in industrial chemical manufacturing.

phos·pho·rous (fos′fər·əs, fos·fôr′əs, -fō′rəs) *adj.* Of, pertaining to, resembling, containing, or derived from phosphorus, esp. in its lower valence.

phos·pho·rus (fos′fər·əs) *n.* **1** A soft nonmetallic element (symbol P) having three allotropic forms and taking part in various biochemical reactions essential to life. **2** Any phosphorescent substance. [< Gk. *phōs* a light + *phoros* bearing]

pho·to (fō′tō) *n. pl.* **·tos** *Informal* A photograph.

photo- *combining form* **1** Light; of, pertaining to, or pro-

duced by light: *photometer.* **2** Photograph; photographic: *photoengrave.* [< Gk. *phōs, phōtos* light]

pho·to·chem·is·try (fō′tō·kem′is·trē) *n.* The branch of chemistry dealing with reactions produced or influenced by light. —**pho′to·chem′i·cal** *adj.*

pho·to·com·po·si·tion (fō′tō·kom′pə·zish′ən) *n.* The composing of printed matter directly on film or photosensitive paper for reproduction.

pho·to·cop·y (fō′tō·kop′ē) *n. pl.* **·cop·ies** A photographic reproduction of printed or other graphic material. —*v.* **·cop·ied, ·cop·y·ing** *v.t.* **1** To make a photocopy of. —*v.i.* **2** To make a photocopy. —**pho′to·cop′i·er** *n.*

pho·to·e·lec·tric (fō′tō·i·lek′trik) *adj.* Of, pertaining to, or indicating the electric effects due to the action of light. Also **pho′to·e·lec′tri·cal.**

photoelectric cell A device in which a flow of light produces or controls a flow of electricity.

pho·to·en·grave (fō′tō·in·grāv′) *v.t.* **·graved, ·grav·ing** To reproduce by photoengraving. —**pho′to·en·grav′er** *n.*

pho·to·en·grav·ing (fō′tō·in·grā′ving) *n.* **1** The act or process of producing by the aid of photography a relief plate for printing. **2** A plate so produced. **3** A print produced from such a plate.

photo finish 1 The finish of a race in which the leaders are so close that only a photograph taken as they cross the finish line can determine the winner. **2** A close finish.

pho·to·flash bulb (fō′tō·flash′) FLASH BULB.

pho·to·flood lamp (fō′tō·flud′) An electric lamp that produces a powerful light for taking photographs and motion pictures.

pho·to·gen·ic (fō′tō·jen′ik) *adj.* **1** Generating or producing light; phosphorescent, as fireflies. **2** Having visually interesting qualities suitable for being photographed: said esp. of a person. —**pho′to·gen′i·cal·ly** *adv.*

pho·to·graph (fō′tə·graf, -gräf) *n.* A picture or image taken by photography. —*v.t.* **1** To take a photograph of. —*v.i.* **2** To practice photography. **3** To undergo photographing. —**pho·tog·ra·pher** (fə·tog′rə·fər) *n.*

pho·to·graph·ic (fō′tə·graf′ik) *adj.* **1** Pertaining to, used in, or produced by photography. **2** Like a photograph; vividly depicted. **3** Capable of precise retention or recall. —**pho′to·graph′i·cal·ly** *adv.*

pho·tog·ra·phy (fə·tog′rə·fē) *n.* The art or process of forming and fixing images by the chemical action of light and other forms of radiant energy on sensitive surfaces.

pho·to·gra·vure (fō′tō·grə·vyŏŏr′) *n.* **1** The process of producing prints from an intaglio printing plate or cylinder. **2** A print so produced.

pho·to·lith·o·graph (fō′tō·lith′ə·graf, -gräf) *v.t.* To reproduce by photolithography. —*n.* A picture produced by photolithography.

pho·to·li·thog·ra·phy (fō′tō·li·thog′rə·fē) *n.* Lithography in which the plate for printing is made photographically. —**pho′to·lith′o·graph′ic** (-lith′ə·graf′ik) *adj.*

pho·tol·y·sis (fō·tol′ə·sis) *n.* Decomposition due to the action of light. [< PHOTO- + Gk. *lysis* a loosening] —**pho·to·lyt·ic** (fō′tə·lit′ik) *adj.*

pho·tom·e·ter (fō·tom′ə·tər) *n.* An instrument for measuring the intensity of light.

pho·tom·e·try (fō·tom′ə·trē) *n.* Measurement of the energy, intensity, etc., of light. —**pho·to·met·ric** (fō′tə·met′rik) *adj.* —**pho·tom′e·trist** *n.*

pho·to·mi·cro·graph (fō′tō·mī′krə·graf, -gräf) *n.* A photograph of an object taken through a microscope. —**pho·to·mi·crog·ra·phy** (fō′tō·mī·krog′rə·fē) *n.*

pho·to·mon·tage (fō′tō·mon·täzh′, -môn-) *n.* **1** The process of montage with photographs. **2** A picture produced by this process.

pho·to·mu·ral (fō′tō·myŏŏr′əl) *n.* A photograph enlarged to a size suitable for wall decoration.

pho·ton (fō′ton) *n. Physics* A quantum of light or other electromagnetic radiation. [< PHOT(O) + (ELECTR)ON] —**pho·ton′ic** *adj.*

pho·to·off·set (fō′tō·ôf′set, -of′-) *n.* Offset printing from a metal surface on which the text or design has been imprinted by photography.

pho·to·play (fō′tō·plā′) *n.* MOTION PICTURE (def. 2).

pho·to·print (fō′tō·print) *n. Phot.* A print produced on photographic paper.

pho·to·sen·si·tive (fō′tō·sen′sə·tiv) *adj.* Sensitive to light. —**pho′to·sen′si·tiv′i·ty** *n.*

pho·to·stat (fō′tə·stat) *v.t.* & *v.i.* **·stat·ed** or **·stat·ted, ·stat·ing** or **·stat·ting** To make a reproduction (of) with a Photostat. —*n.* The reproduction so produced. —**pho′to·stat′ic** *adj.*

Pho·to·stat (fō′tə·stat) *n.* A device designed to reproduce documents, drawings, etc., directly as positives on special paper: a trade name.

pho·to·syn·the·sis (fō′tō·sin′thə·sis) *n.* The formation of carbohydrates from carbon dioxide and water through the agency of sunlight acting upon chlorophyll. —**pho′to·syn·thet′ic** (-sin·thet′ik) *adj.* —**pho′to·syn·thet′i·cal·ly** *adv.*

pho·tot·ro·pism (fō·tot′rə·piz′əm) *n.* The orientation or movement of an organism in response to light. —**pho·to·trop·ic** (fō′tə·trop′ik) *adj.* —**pho′to·trop′i·cal·ly** *adv.*

pho·to·type·set·ting (fō′tə·tīp′set′ing) *n.* PHOTOCOMPOSITION.

phrase (frāz) *n.* **1** A manner or style of expression; phraseology. **2** *Gram.* A group of words denoting a single idea or forming a separate part of a sentence, but not containing a subject and predicate. **3** A concise, forceful, or colorful expression. **4** *Music* A section of a melody or composition, several measures long. —*v.t.* & *v.i.* **phrased, phras·ing** **1** To express or be expressed in words or phrases, esp. in a certain way: He *phrased* his objections tactfully. **2** *Music* To execute or divide (music) in or into phrases. [< Gk. *phrazein* point out, tell] —**phras′al** *adj.*

phrase-mak·er (frāz′mā′kər) *n.* **1** A person who coins phrases that are pointed, vivid, incisive, witty, etc. **2** A person who coins phrases that sound pointed, witty, etc., but that often lack meaning or significance. —**phrase′mak′ing** *n.*

phra·se·ol·o·gy (frā′zē·ol′ə·jē) *n.* The choice and arrangement of words and phrases to express ideas in speech or writing; diction; style. —**phra′se·o·log′i·cal** (-ə·loj′i·kəl) *adj.* —**phra′se·ol′o·gist** *n.*

phre·net·ic (frə·net′ik) *adj.* FRENETIC. Also **phre·net′i·cal.**

phre·nol·o·gy (fri·nol′ə·jē) *n.* The estimation of character and intelligence by the conformation of the skull. [< Gk. *phrēn* mind + -LOGY] —**phren·o·log·ic** (fren′ə·loj′ik) or **·i·cal** *adj.* —**phren′o·log′i·cal·ly** *adv.* —**phre·nol′o·gist** *n.*

Phryg·i·a (frij′ē·ə) *n.* An ancient country in Asia Minor. —**Phryg′i·an** *adj., n.*

PHS Public Health Service.

phthi·sis (thī′sis, tī′-, thi′-, ti′-) *n.* **1** Tuberculosis of the lungs. **2** Progressive emaciation; any continuous destruction of tissue. [< Gk., a wasting away] —**phthis·ic** (tiz′ik) *n., adj.* —**phthis′i·cal. phthis′ick·y** *adj.*

phy·co·my·cete (fī′kō·mī′sēt, -mī·sēt′) *n.* Any of a class of fungi resembling algae, but lacking chlorophyll. [< Gk. *phykos* seaweed + *mykēs* a mushroom] —**phy′co·my·ce′tous** *adj.*

phy·lac·ter·y (fi·lak′tər·ē) *n. pl.* **·ter·ies** **1** A charm or amulet. **2** A small leather case containing slips inscribed with passages of Scripture, one of which is worn on the forehead and another on the left arm by orthodox Jewish men during morning weekday prayers. **3** A reminder. [< Gk. *phylaktēr* a guard]

-phyll *combining form* Leaf: *chlorophyll.*

phyllo- *combining form* Leaf: *phyllotaxy.* [< Gk. *phyllon* a leaf]

phyl·lo·tax·y (fil′ə·tak′sē) *n. Bot.* **1** The arrangement of leaves on a stem. **2** The laws governing this arrangement. Also **phyl′lo·tax′is.** [< PHYLLO- + Gk. *taxis* arrangement] —**phyl′lo·tac′tic** (-tak′tik) *adj.*

phyl·lox·e·ra (fil′ək·sir′ə, fi·lok′sər·ə) *n.* Any of various plant lice, esp. a species of minute aphis or plant louse destructive to grape vines. [< PHYLLO- + Gk. *xēros* dry]

phy·log·e·ny (fī·loj′ə·nē) *n. Biol.* The history of the evolution of a genetically related group of plants or animals. Also **phy·lo·gen·e·sis** (fī′lə·jen′ə·sis). [< Gk. *phylon* a race + *-geneia* birth, origin] —**phy′lo·ge·net′ic** (-jə·net′ik), **phy′·lo·gen′ic** (-jen′ik) *adj.* —**phy′lo·ge·net′i·cal·ly** *adv.*

phy·lum (fī′ləm) *n. pl.* **·la** (-lə) Any of the main divisions of the animal and plant kingdoms. [< Gk. *phylon* a race]

phys. physical; physician; physicist; physics.

phys·ic (fiz′ik) *n.* **1** A cathartic; a purge. **2** *Archaic* The art or practice of medicine —*v.t.* **phys·icked, phys·ick·ing** **1** To treat with medicine, esp. a cathartic; purge. **2** To cure or relieve. [< Gk. *physikē (epistēmē)* (the knowledge) of nature]

phys·i·cal (fiz′i·kəl) *adj.* **1** Of or relating to the material universe, the natural sciences, or to physics. **2** Of, relating to, or concerned with the human body. [< Gk. *physis* nature] —**phys′i·cal·ly** *adv.*

physical chemistry The branch of chemistry that deals with the physical properties of substances, esp. in relation to energy transformations and chemical change.

physical education Training and development of the human body by athletics and other exercises; also, education in hygiene.

physical geography Geography dealing with the natural, exterior features of the earth, as vegetation, land forms, ocean currents, etc.

phys·i·cal·i·ty (fiz′ə·kal′ə·tē) *n.* **1** The state of being physical, as distinguished from spiritual. **2** Excessive concern with physical sensations or with the body.

physical sciences The sciences that deal with the structure, properties, and energy relations of matter.

physical therapy The treatment of disability or disease by external physical means, as heat, massage, exercise, etc.

phy·si·cian (fi·zish′ən) *n.* **1** A doctor authorized to practice medicine. **2** One engaged in the general practice of medicine as distinguished from a surgeon. **3** Any healer. [< L *physica* natural medicine]

phys·i·cist (fiz′ə·sist) *n.* A scientist whose specialty is physics.

phys·ics (fiz′iks) *n. pl. (construed as sing.)* The science of matter and energy and their mutual interactions.

physio- *combining form* **1** Nature or natural: *physiography.* **2** Physical: *physiotherapy.* Also **phys-.** [< Gk. *physis* nature]

phys·i·og·no·my (fiz′ē·og′nə·mē) *n. pl.* **·mies** **1** The face or features as revealing character or disposition. **2** Outward appearance; external features. **3** The art or practice of reading character by the features of the face or form of the body. [< Gk. *physiognōmonia* the judging of a man's nature (by his features)] —**phys′i·og·nom′ic** (-og·nom′ik) or **·i·cal** *adj.* —**phys′i·og·nom′i·cal·ly** *adv.* —**phys′i·og·no·mist** *n.*

phys·i·og·ra·phy (fiz′ē·og′rə·fē) *n.* **1** A description of nature. **2** PHYSICAL GEOGRAPHY. —**phys′i·og′ra·pher** *n.* —**phys′i·o·graph′ic** (-ə·graf′ik) or **·i·cal** *adj.* —**phys′i·o·graph′i·cal·ly** *adv.*

physiol. physiological; physiology.

phys·i·ol·o·gy (fiz′ē·ol′ə·jē) *n.* **1** The branch of biology that deals with the functions of living organisms or their parts; the science of the vital processes of animals or plants. **2** The aggregate of organic processes of an organism or a part of it: the *physiology* of the frog. [< Gk. *physis* nature + *logos* a word] —**phys′i·ol′o·gist** *n.* —**phys′i·o·log·i·cal** (fiz′ē·ə·loj′i·kəl), **phys′i·o·log′ic** *adj.* —**phys′i·o·log′i·cal·ly** *adv.*

phys·i·o·ther·a·py (fiz′ē·ō·ther′ə·pē) *n.* PHYSICAL THERAPY.

phy·sique (fi·zēk′) *n.* The physical structure, organization, appearance, strength, etc., of a person's body.

pi¹ (pī) *n.* **1** The 16th letter in the Greek alphabet (Π,π). **2** The symbol (π) used to designate the ratio of the circumference of a circle to its diameter, 3.14159+ ; also, this ratio.

pi² (pī) *n.* **1** *Printing* Type that has been thrown into disorder. **2** Any jumble or disorder. —*v.t.* **pied, pie·ing** To jumble or disorder, as type. [Var. of PIE¹]

pi·a ma·ter (pī′ə mā′tər, pē′ə mä′tər) The inner vascular membrane that envelops the brain and spinal cord. [Med. L, tender mother]

pi·a·nis·si·mo (pē′ə·nis′i·mō, *Ital.* pyä·nēs′sē·mō) *adj.* & *adv. Music* Very soft or softly. —*n. pl.* **·mi** (-mē) or **·mos** A section or passage of music rendered pianissimo. [Ital. See PIANO²]

pi·an·ist (pē·an'ist, pē'ə·nist) *n.* One who plays the piano; esp. an expert or a professional performer.

pi·an·o·¹ (pē·an'ō) *n. pl.* **·an·os** A musical instrument having felt-covered hammers, operated from a manual keyboard, which strike steel wires to produce the tones. [Ital., short for PIANOFORTE]

pi·a·no² (pē·ä'nō, *Ital.* pyä'nō) *adj. & adv.* Soft or softly. —*n.* A section or passage of music rendered softly. [Ital. < L *planus* flat, soft (of sound)]

pi·an·o·for·te (pē·an'ə·fôr'tē, -fôr'-, -fôrt', -fôrt') *n.* A piano. [Ital. < *piano e forte* soft and loud]

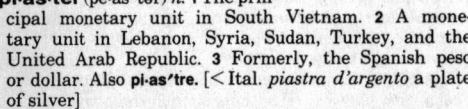
Grand piano

pi·as·ter (pē·as'tər) *n.* **1** The principal monetary unit in South Vietnam. **2** A monetary unit in Lebanon, Syria, Sudan, Turkey, and the United Arab Republic. **3** Formerly, the Spanish peso or dollar. Also **pi·as'tre**. [< Ital. *piastra d'argento* a plate of silver]

pi·az·za (pē·az'ə, *Ital.* pē·ät'tsä) *n.* **1** A veranda or porch. **2** In Europe, esp. in Italy, an open square. **3** A covered outer walk or gallery. [Ital. < L *platea* a broad street]

pi·broch (pē'brokh) *n.* A martial or dirgelike air played on the bagpipe. [< Scot. Gaelic *piobair* a piper]

pi·ca¹ (pī'kə) *n.* **1** A size of type, 12-point or about ⅙ inch. **2** A size of typewriter type equivalent to 12-point, with 10 characters to the inch. [Med. L, church book]

pi·ca² (pī'kə) *n.* An appetite for substances unfit to eat, as clay, chalk, ashes, etc. [< L *pica* a magpie, with ref. to the bird's omnivorousness] —**pi'cal** *adj.*

pic·a·dor (pik'ə·dôr, *Sp.* pē'kä·thôr') *n.* In bullfighting, a horseman armed with a lance, whose function it is to prick and thereby weaken the bull's neck muscles. [< Sp. *picar* prick, pierce]

pic·a·resque (pik'ə·resk') *adj.* **1** Of or pertaining to adventurers or clever rogues. **2** Designating a type of fiction of Spanish origin consisting of loosely connected episodes involving rogues and vagabonds. [< Sp. *pícaro* a rogue]

pic·a·yune (pik'i·yōōn') *adj.* **1** Little; worthless. **2** Concerned with unimportant or petty matters. —*n.* **1** A former small Spanish-American coin; a half-real. **2** *U.S.* A person or thing of trifling value. [< Prov. *picaioun*, dim. of *picalo* money] —**pic'a·yun'ish** *adj.* —**Syn.** *adj.* **1** paltry, worthless, measly. **2** trivial, mean, narrow-minded.

pic·ca·lil·li (pik'ə·lil'ē) *n.* A highly seasoned relish of chopped vegetables. [? < PICKLE]

pic·co·lo (pik'ə·lō) *n. pl.* **·los** A small flute with tones an octave higher than those of the ordinary flute. [Ital., small]

pick¹ (pik) *v.t.* **1** To select; cull, as from a group. **2** To detach; pluck: to *pick* a flower. **3** To harvest: to *pick* cotton. **4** To prepare by removing the feathers, hulls, etc.: to *pick* a chicken. **5** To remove extraneous matter from: to *pick* the teeth. **6** To pull apart, as rags. **7** To penetrate with or as with a pointed instrument. **8** To form or make in this manner: to *pick* a hole. **9** To point out too critically: to *pick* flaws. **10** To bring on purposely; provoke: to *pick* a quarrel. **11** To remove the contents of by stealth: to *pick* a pocket. **12** To open (a lock) by a piece of wire, etc. **13 a** To pluck (the strings) of a musical instrument. **b** To play (an instrument) in this way. —*v.i.* **14** To eat daintily; nibble. —**pick at 1** To touch or irritate with the finger. **2** To eat without appetite. **3** *Informal* To nag at. —**pick off 1** To remove by picking. **2** To shoot one at a time. —**pick on** *Informal* To tease; annoy. —**pick out 1** To choose or select. **2** To distinguish (something) from its surroundings. **3** To grasp (the meaning). —**pick over** To examine one by one. —**pick up 1** To take up, as with the hand. **2** To take up or receive into a vehicle, etc. **3** To acquire by chance. **4** To gain speed. **5** To recover spirits, health, etc. **6** *Informal* To make the acquaintance of, casually or informally. **7** To make orderly; tidy. —*n.* **1** Selection; choice. **2** The choicest part or thing. **3** The quantity of a crop picked at one time. **4** The act of picking. **5** A plectrum for a stringed instrument. [ME *piken*] —**pick'er** *n.* —**Syn.** *v.* **1** choose. **3** collect, gather. **7** pierce.

pick² (pik) *n.* **1** A double-headed, pointed metal tool, used for breaking ground, etc.; pickax. **2** Any of various sharp-pointed implements, as an ice pick, toothpick, etc. [ME *pik*]

pick-a-back (pik'ə·bak') *adj., adv., n.* PIGGYBACK.

pick·ax (pik'aks') *n.* A tool with one end of the head edged like a chisel and the other pointed, used to break rocks, dirt, etc.: also **pick'axe'**. [< OF *picois*]

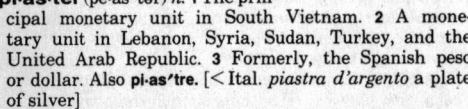
Pickax

picked (pikt) *adj.* **1** Carefully selected. **2** Cleaned by picking out feathers, hulls, etc.

pick·er·el (pik'ər·əl) *n.* **1** Any of various North American pikes, esp. one of the smaller species. **2** A young pike. [Dim. of PIKE²]

pick·er·el·weed (pik'ər·əl·wēd') *n.* Any of several water plants with a spike of blue flowers and long arrow-shaped leaves.

pick·et (pik'it) *n.* **1** A pointed stick, tent peg, bar, fence paling, or stake. **2** *Mil.* A soldier or detachment of soldiers posted to guard a camp, army, etc. **3** A person stationed by a labor union outside a place affected by a strike to attempt to keep out employees or customers. —*v.t.* **1** To fence or fortify with pickets or pointed stakes. **2** *Mil.* **a** To guard by means of a picket. **b** To post as a picket. **3** To station pickets outside of. **4** To tie to a picket, as a horse. —*v.i.* **5** To act as a picket (def. 3). [< OF *piquer* pierce] —**pick'et·er** *n.*

picket fence A fence made of upright pickets.

picket line A line or group of people acting as pickets.

pick·ings (pik'ingz) *n. pl.* **1** An amount picked. **2** That which is left to be picked up or gleaned. **3** Something taken by questionable means; spoils.

pick·le (pik'əl) *n.* **1** A liquid, as brine or vinegar, usu. spiced, for preserving meat, fish, vegetables. etc. **2** A vegetable, esp. a cucumber, preserved in a pickling solution. **3** Diluted acid used in cleaning metal castings, etc. **4** *Informal* An embarrassing condition or position. —*v.t.* **·led**, **·ling** To preserve or clean in a pickling solution. [MDu. *pekel*] —**pick'ler** *n.*

pick-me-up (pik'mē'up') *n.* *Informal* Something taken to renew one's energy or spirits.

pick·pock·et (pik'pok'it) *n.* One who steals from people's pockets or purses.

pick·up (pik'up') *n.* **1** Acceleration, as in the speed of an automobile, engine, etc. **2** A device, as that coupled to the stylus of a phonograph, that changes mechanical motion to an electric signal. **3** *Telecom.* **a** In radio, the location of microphones in relation to program elements. **b** The system for broadcasting material gathered outside the studio. **4** *Informal* Gain; improvement: *a pickup in the stock market.* **5** *Slang* A stranger with whom a casual acquaintance is made, as for sexual purposes. **6** One of a group casually enlisted or assembled, as for a sport or game. **7** A small, usu. open, truck for light loads. **8** The act of calling for, as a parcel. **9** *Informal* Something taken to renew energy or spirits; a pick-me-up.

Pick·wick·i·an (pik·wik'ē·ən) *adj.* **1** Having or characterized by the qualities associated with Samuel Pickwick, a character in Dickens' novel *Pickwick Papers;* esp., kind, simple, and generous. **2** Having an esoteric or unusual sense: said of a word or expression.

pick·y (pik'ē) *adj.* **pick·i·er, pick·i·est** *Informal* Choosy; fussy. —**pick'i·ness** *n.*

pic·nic (pik'nik) *n.* **1** An outdoor party, during which a meal is eaten. **2** *Slang* An easy or pleasant time or experience. —*v.i.* **·nicked, ·nick·ing** To have or attend a picnic. Also **pick'nick**. [< F *pique-nique*] —**pic'nick·er** *n.*

pico- *combining form* One trillionth (10⁻¹²) times a unit. [? < Ital. *piccolo* small]

pi·cot (pē'kō) *n.* Any of the small loops of an ornamental edging on ribbon, lace, etc. —*v.t. & v.i.* To trim with this edging. [< OF *pic* a point]

pic·ric acid (pik'rik) A yellow, crystalline, organic compound used to make dyes and explosives. [< Gk. *pikros* bitter]

Pict (pikt) *n.* One of an ancient people who inhabited Britain and the Scottish Highlands, conquered in 846 by the Scots. —**Pict'ish** *adj., n.*

pic·to·graph (pik′tə·graf, -gräf) n. 1 A picture representing an idea. 2 Writing done in pictographs; picture writing. [< L *pictus* painted + -GRAPH] —**pic′to·graph′ic** adj. — **pic′to·graph′i·cal·ly** adv. —**pic·tog·ra·phy** (pik·tog′rə·fē) n.

pic·to·ri·al (pik·tôr′ē·əl, -tō′rē-) adj. 1 Pertaining to or concerned with pictures. 2 Representing in or as if in pictures; graphic. 3 Containing or illustrated by pictures. —n. An illustrated publication. [< L *pictor* painter] —**pic·to′ri·al·ly** adv.

pic·ture (pik′chər) n. 1 A surface representation of an object or scene or a design, as by a painting, drawing, engraving, or photograph. 2 A mental image. 3 A vivid or graphic description. 4 A striking resemblance: She is the *picture* of her mother. 5 TABLEAU. 6 A visual image or scene. 7 MOTION PICTURE. 8 Something beautiful or striking. 9 The sum of significant facts in an event. —v.t. **·tured**, **·tur·ing** 1 To give visible representation to; draw, paint, etc. 2 To describe graphically. 3 To form a mental image of. [< L *pictus*, p.p. of *pingere* to paint]

Pic·ture·phone (pik′chər·fōn′) n. A telephone equipped with a television screen: a trade name.

pic·tur·esque (pik′chə·resk′) adj. 1 Having pictorial quality; like or suitable for a picture. 2 Having quaintness or charm. 3 Abounding in striking or original expression or imagery; richly graphic. [< L *pictor* painter] —**pic′tur·esque′ly** adv. —**pic′tur·esque′ness** n.

picture window A large window, usu. in a living room, designed to give a wide view of the outside.

picture writing 1 The use of pictures or pictorial symbols in writing 2 PICTOGRAPH.

pid·dle (pid′l) v. **·died**, **·dling** v.t. & v.i. To trifle; dawdle. [?] —**pid′dler** n. —**pid′dling** adj.

pidg·in English (pij′in) A jargon composed of English and local native elements, used by English-speaking traders in Melanesia, Northern Australia, w Africa, and formerly in China. Also **pidg′in.** [< pronunciation in this jargon of *business English*]

pie¹ (pī) n. 1 A baked food consisting of one or two layers of pastry with a filling, as of fruit, meat, etc. 2 *Slang* Anything very good or very easy.

pie² (pī) n. A magpie, or a related bird. [< L *pica*]

pie³ (pī) n. & v.t. **pied, pie·ing** *Printing* PI².

pie·bald (pī′bôld′) adj. Having spots, esp. of white and black. —n. A spotted animal, esp. a horse. [< PIE² + BALD; because like a magpie's plumage]

piece (pēs) n. 1 A portion considered as a distinct part of a whole. 2 A thing existing as an individual entity: a *piece* of paper; a *piece* of music. 3 A single object forming one of a group: a *piece* of furniture. 4 A definite quantity or length in which an article is manufactured or sold. 5 An instance: a *piece* of luck. 6 A firearm. 7 A coin: a fifty-cent *piece*. 8 A single artistic creation, as a literary, dramatic, or musical composition; also, a painting or sculpture. 9 *Regional* A short time, space, or distance: to walk a *piece*. 10 A figure, disk, or counter used in such games as chess, checkers, backgammon, etc. —**a piece of one's mind** Criticism or censure frankly expressed. —**go to pieces** 1 To fall apart. 2 To lose self-control. —**in one piece** Unharmed; intact. —**of a piece** Of the same sort or class. — adj. Of, made of, or by the piece. —v.t. **pieced, piec·ing** 1 To add or attach a piece or pieces to. 2 To unite or reunite the pieces of. 3 To find meaning or coherence in by linking elements: often with *together*: to *piece* together a sequence of events from the testimony of eyewitnesses. [< OF *pece*] —**piec′er** n.

pièce de ré·sis·tance (pē·es′ də rā·zē′stäns′) pl. **pièces** (pē·es′) **de ré·sis·tance** 1 The most substantial dish of a dinner. 2 The principal work in a collection, as of art, etc. [F, lit., piece of resistance]

piece goods Dry goods; fabrics, usu. sold by the piece.

piece·meal (pēs′mēl′) adj. Made up of pieces or done one piece at a time. —adv. 1 Piece by piece; gradually. 2 Into pieces. [< PIECE + OE *mæl* a measure]

piece of eight pl. **pieces of eight** An old Spanish silver dollar.

piece·work (pēs′wûrk′) n. Work paid for by the piece or

quantity completed, rather than by the hour, week, etc. —**piece′work′er** n.

pied (pīd) adj. Spotted; piebald. [< PIE²]

pied·mont (pēd′mont) adj. At the foot of a mountain or mountain range: a *piedmont* plain. —n. A piedmont region or area. [< *Piedmont*, Italy]

pie·plant (pī′plant′) n. The rhubarb, much used for pies.

pier (pir) n. 1 A plain, detached mass of masonry, usu. serving as a support: the *pier* of a bridge. 2 An upright projecting portion of a wall. 3 A jetty; projecting wharf. 4 A solid portion of a wall between window openings, etc. [< AF *pere*]

Pier *def. 3*

pierce (pirs) v.t. **pierced, pierc·ing** 1 To pass into or through; penetrate, as with a pointed object. 2 To make an opening or hole in, into, or through. 3 To force a way into or through: to *pierce* the wilderness. 4 To affect sharply or deeply, as with emotion, pain, etc. 5 To sound suddenly and sharply, as a scream. 6 To penetrate as if seeing; understand: to *pierce* a mystery. [< OF *percer*] —**pierc′er** n. —**pierc′ing·ly** adv. —Syn. 1 perforate, puncture.

pier glass A large, high mirror originally intended to fill the space between two openings in the wall.

Pi·e·ri·an (pī·ir′ē·ən) adj. Of or pertaining to the Muses, learning, or the arts. [< *Pieria*, region of ancient Macedon where the Muses were worshipped]

Pi·er·rot (pē′ə·rō′) n. A comic character wearing white pantaloons and loose white jacket with big buttons, originally a stock figure in French pantomime. Also **pi′er·rot′.** [F, dim. of *Pierre* Peter]

pi·e·tism (pī′ə·tiz′əm) n. 1 Piety or godliness; devotion, as distinguished from ritualism. 2 Affected or exaggerated piety. —**pi′e·tist** n. —**pi′e·tis′tic** adj.

pi·e·ty (pī′ə·tē) n. pl. **·ties** 1 Religious reverence; devoutness. 2 Filial honor and obedience as due to parents or country, etc. 3 A pious action or belief. [< L < *pius* dutiful]

pi·e·zo·e·lec·tric·i·ty (pē·ā′zō·i·lek′tris′ə·tē) n. Electricity or electric phenomena resulting from pressure upon certain bodies, esp. crystals. [< Gk. *piezein* to press + ELECTRICITY] —**pi·e′zo·e·lec′tric** or **·tri·cal** adj.

pif·fle (pif′əl) *Informal* v.i. **·fled, ·fling** To talk nonsensically; babble. —n. Nonsense. [?]

pig (pig) n. 1 A hog or hoglike animal, esp. when small or young. 2 Pork. 3 An oblong mass of metal just run from the smelter and cast in a rough mold. 4 *Informal* A person regarded as like a pig, esp. one who is filthy, gluttonous, or grasping. [ME *pigge*]

pig·eon (pij′ən) n. 1 Any of a widely distributed family of birds with small heads; a dove. 2 *Slang* One easily swindled. [< LL *pipio* a young chirping bird]

pigeon breast A deformity associated with rickets in which the breastbone projects forward and outward. — **pig′eon-breast′ed** adj.

pigeon hawk A medium-sized American falcon.

pig·eon·hole (pij′ən·hōl′) n. 1 A hole for pigeons to nest in, esp. in a compartmented pigeon house. 2 A small compartment, as in a desk, for filing papers. —v.t. **·holed, ·hol·ing** 1 To place in a pigeonhole; file. 2 To file away and ignore. 3 To place in categories; classify mentally.

pig·eon-toed (pij′ən·tōd′) adj. Having the feet turned inward, esp. in walking.

pig·ger·y (pig′ər·ē) n. pl. **·ger·ies** PIGPEN (def. 1).

pig·gish (pig′ish) adj. Like a pig; greedy, dirty, or selfish. —**pig′gish·ly** adv. —**pig′gish·ness** n.

pig·gy (pig′ē) adj. **·gi·er, ·gi·est** Greedy or dirty.

pig·gy·back (pig′ē·bak′) adv. 1 On the back or shoulders. 2 On a railroad flatcar, as a loaded truck body. —n. 1 The act of carrying piggyback. 2 The transporting of loaded truck bodies on railroad flatcars. —adj. 1 Done up on the back or shoulders: a *piggyback* ride. **2** Of or pertaining to the transporting of loaded truck bodies on railroad flatcars. —*v.t. & v.i.* **1** To carry or be carried on the back or shoulders. **2** To transport or be transported on railroad flat cars. Also **pig′gy·back′.**

pig-head·ed (pig′hed′id) *adj.* Stupidly obstinate. —**pig′-head′ed·ly** *adv.* —**pig′-head′ed·ness** *n.* —**Syn.** headstrong, obdurate, stubborn, unyielding.

pig iron Crude iron obtained by treating ore in a blast furnace.

pig·ment (pig′mənt) *n.* **1** Any of a class of finely powdered, insoluble coloring matters suitable for making paints, enamels, oil colors, etc. **2** Any substance that imparts color to animal or vegetable tissues. [< L *pingere* to paint] —**pig′men·tar′y** *adj.*

pig·men·ta·tion (pig′mən·tā′shən) *n.* **1** Coloration by pigment of plant or animal tissue. **2** *Biol.* Deposition of pigment by cells.

pig·my (pig′mē) *adj. & n.* PYGMY.

Pig·my (pig′mē) *adj. & n. pl.* **·mies** PYGMY.

pig·nut (pig′nut′) *n.* **1** The astringent nut of several species of hickory. **2** Any of these trees.

pig·pen (pig′pen′) *n.* **1** A place for keeping or raising pigs; sty. **2** Any dirty, untidy place.

pig·skin (pig′skin′) *n.* **1** The skin of a pig. **2** Something made of this skin, as a saddle or football.

pig-stick·ing (pig′stik′ing) *n.* The hunting of wild boars with spears.

pig·sty (pig′stī′) *n. pl.* **·sties** PIGPEN.

pig·tail (pig′tāl′) *n.* **1** The tail of a pig. **2** *Informal* A plait of hair. **3** A twist of tobacco. —**pig′tailed′** *adj.*

pike[1] (pīk) *n.* A long pole having a metal spearhead, used by foot soldiers in medieval warfare. —*v.t.* **piked, pik·ing** To run through or kill with a pike. [< MF *piquer* pierce] —**pike′man** (*pl.* **·men**) *n.*

pike[2] (pīk) *n.* Any of a family of large, carnivorous, freshwater food fishes with a long snout, long cylindrical body, and forked tail. [? < PIKE[1]]

pike[3] (pīk) *n.* TURNPIKE.

pike[4] (pīk) *n.* A spike or sharp point, as the central spike in a buckler. [< OE *pīc*]

Pike heads

pik·er (pī′kər) *n. Slang* A person who does things in a small, stingy way; cheapskate. [? < *Pike County, Missouri*]

pike·staff (pīk′staf′, -stäf′) *n. pl.* **·staves** (-stāvz′) The wooden handle of a pike. [< PIKE[4] + STAFF[1]]

pi·las·ter (pi·las′tər) *n. Archit.* A rectangular column, with capital and base, projecting from a wall. [< L *pila* a column]

pi·lau (pi·lou′, -lô′) *n.* An Oriental dish of boiled rice, spices, and meat or fish. Also **pi·laf** (pi·läf′), **pi·laff′, pi·law** (pi·lô′). [< Pers. *pilāw*]

pil·chard (pil′chərd) *n.* A small herringlike marine food fish; the commercial sardine. [?]

pile[1] (pīl) *n.* **1** A quantity of anything gathered up together; a heap. **2** A funeral pyre. **3** A large accumulation or number of something. **4** A massive building or group of buildings. **5** *Informal* A great quantity of money. **6** *Physics* A nuclear fission reactor. —**make one's pile** To amass a fortune. —*v.* **piled, pil·ing** *v.t.* **1** To make a heap of: often with *up*. **2** To load with a pile or piles: to *pile* a plate with food. —*v.i.* **3** To form a heap. **4** To proceed or go in a confused mass: to *pile* off a bus. —**pile up 1** To accumulate; collect, as in a heap: The bills kept *piling up.* **2** *Informal* To reduce or become reduced to a pile or wreck. [< L *pila* a pillar]

pile[2] (pīl) *n.* A heavy timber pointed at one end, forced into the earth to form a foundation —*v.t.* **piled, pil·ing 1** To drive piles into. **2** To furnish or strengthen with piles. [< L *pilum* a heavy javelin]

pile[3] (pīl) *n.* **1** Soft hair, fur, down, etc. **2** The cut or uncut loops which make the surface of certain fabrics, as velvets, corduroys, carpets, etc. [< L *pilus* hair] —**piled** *adj.*

pi·le·at·ed (pī′lē·ā′tid, pil′ē-) *adj.* Having a crest from

Pilaster

the bill to the nape, as some birds. Also **pi′le·ate.** [< L *pileus* a felt cap]

pileated woodpecker A large black and white woodpecker with a red crest.

pile driver A machine for driving piles, usu. a heavy weight raised and released so as to fall, or be driven down, as by steam, to strike the head of the pile.

pi·le·ous (pī′lē·əs) *adj.* PILOSE.

piles (pīlz) *n.pl.* HEMORRHOIDS. [< L *pila* a ball]

pi·le·um (pī′lē·əm, pil′ē-) *n. pl.* **·le·a** (-lē·ə) The top of the head of a bird from bill to nape. [< L *pileus* a felt cap]

pile-up (pīl′up′) *n.* **1** An accumulation: a garbage *pile-up.* **2** A collision involving several or many motor vehicles, usu. causing injury and damage; also, the damaged vehicles. **3** Any group, as of people, piled up after colliding: a *pile-up* on the 40-yard line.

pi·le·us (pī′lē·əs, pil′ē-) *n. pl.* **·le·i** (-lē·ī) The cap of a mushroom. [L, a felt cap]

pil·fer (pil′fər) *v.t. & v.i.* To steal in small quantities. [< OF *pelfre* plunder] —**pil′fer·age** (-ij), **pil′fer·er** *n.*

pil·grim (pil′grim) *n.* **1** One who journeys to some sacred place from religious motives. **2** Any wanderer or wayfarer. [< L *peregrinus* foreigner]

Pil·grim (pil′grim) *n.* One of the English Puritans who founded Plymouth Colony in 1620.

pil·grim·age (pil′grə·mij) *n.* **1** A journey made to a sacred place. **2** Any long journey.

Pilgrim Fathers The Pilgrims.

Pilgrim's Progress A religious allegory in two parts by John Bunyan (1678, 1684).

pil·ing (pī′ling) *n.* **1** Heavy timbers, or piles, driven into the ground. **2** A structure formed of such timbers.

pill (pil) *n.* **1** A medicine in pellet form convenient for swallowing whole. **2** A disagreeable necessity. **3** *Slang* An unpleasant or tiresome person. **4** *Informal* A baseball or golf ball. —**the pill** or **the Pill** Any of various oral contraceptives. —*v.t.* **1** To form into pills. **2** To dose with pills. [< L *pila* a ball]

pil·lage (pil′ij) *n.* **1** The act of pillaging; open robbery, as in war. **2** Spoil; booty. —*v.* **·laged, ·lag·ing** *v.t.* **1** To strip of money or property by violence, esp. in war; loot. **2** To take as loot. —*v.i.* **3** To take plunder. [< OF *piller* to plunder] —**pil′lag·er** *n.*

pil·lar (pil′ər) *n.* **1** A firm, slender, upright column, used to support a roof, etc. **2** A single column designed as a monument. **3** One who or that which strongly supports a work or cause. —**from pillar to post** From one thing to another; hither and thither. —**pillar of society** A person holding an important position. [< L *pila*] —**pil′lared** *adj.*

pill·box (pil′boks′) *n.* **1** A small box for pills. **2** A small concrete emplacement for a machine gun, antitank gun, etc.

pil·lion (pil′yən) *n.* A pad on a horse's back, behind the saddle, on which a second person may ride, esp. a woman. [< L *pellis* a skin]

pil·lo·ry (pil′ər·ē) *n. pl.* **·ries 1** Formerly, a framework in which an offender was fastened by the neck and wrists and exposed to public scorn. **2** Any public ridicule or disgrace. —*v.t.* **·ried, ·ry·ing 1** To set in the pillory. **2** To hold up to public scorn or ridicule. [< OF *pellori*]

Pillory

pil·low (pil′ō) *n.* **1** A case stuffed with feathers, batting, etc., or inflated with air, used as a support for the head, as in sleeping. **2** Any cushion. —*v.t.* **1** To rest on or as on a pillow. **2** To act as a pillow for. —*v.i.* **3** To recline as on a pillow. [< L *pulvinus* a cushion] —**pil′low·y** *adj.*

pil·low-case (pil′ō·kās′) A covering drawn over a pillow. Also **pil′low-slip′** (-slip′).

pillow lace Lace made with bobbins.

pi·lose (pī′lōs) *adj.* Covered with hair, esp. with fine and soft hair; hairy. Also **pi′lous.** [< L *pilus* hair] —**pi·los·i·ty** (pī·los′ə·tē) *n.*

pi·lot (pī′lət) *n.* **1** A helmsman, esp. one qualified by training and licensed by law to conduct a ship into and out of port. **2** Any guide. **3** One who operates an aircraft or spacecraft. **4** A device for guiding the action of a part of a machine, etc. —*v.t.* **1** To act as the pilot of; steer. **2** To guide. **3** To serve as pilot on, over, or in. [< Ital. *pilota*] — **Syn.** *v.* **2** conduct, direct, lead.

pi·lot·age (pī′lət-ij) *n.* **1** The act of piloting a vessel or aircraft. **2** The fee for such service.

pilot balloon A small balloon sent up to show the direction and velocity of the wind.

pilot bread HARDTACK. Also **pilot biscuit.**

pilot fish A small fish often seen in company with sharks.

pi·lot·house *n.* (pī′lət-hous′) *n.* An enclosed structure, usu. in the forward part of a vessel, containing the steering wheel and compass.

pilot lamp A small electric light used to indicate when a circuit is energized.

pilot light A minute jet of gas kept burning beside a main burner to ignite it when the gas is turned on.

pilot plant An experimental factory, power station, etc.

Pilt·down man (pilt′doun′) A spurious example of prehistoric man based on bone fragments found in gravel beds at Piltdown, Sussex, England in 1911, and exposed as a hoax in 1953.

pi·men·to (pi·men′to) *n. pl.* **-tos 1** The red fruit of a mild variety of capsicum, used as a garnish: also **pi·mien·to** (pi·myen′to). **2** ALLSPICE. [< Sp. *pimienta* pepper]

pimp (pimp) *n.* A man who finds clients for prostitutes and usu. lives on their earnings. —*v.i.* To act as a pimp. [?]

pim·per·nel (pim′pər-nel) *n.* Any of a genus of plants of the primrose family, as the **scarlet pimpernel,** having usu. red flowers that close in bad weather. [< OF *pimprenele*]

pim·ple (pim′pəl) *n.* A small, usu. inflamed swelling on the skin. [ME *pimplis* pimples] —**pim′pled, pim′ply** *adj.* (·pli·er, ·pli·est)

pin (pin) *n.* **1** A short stiff piece of wire, with a sharp point and a round head, used in fastening things together. **2** An ornamental device mounted on a clasp to fasten to a garment; also, a badge. **3** A rigid peg or bar of wood used for a fastening or support. **4** Anything like a pin, as a hairpin, clothespin, rolling pin, belaying pin, etc. **5** *Usu. pl.* A wooden club turned in long, oval, or cylindrical shape, set up as a target in bowling games. **6** *pl.* Legs. **7** The merest trifle. **8** A peg holding the string of a violin, guitar, or other stringed instrument. **9** A peg to keep an oar in place. —**on pins and needles** Anxious; worried. —*v.t.* **pinned, pin·ning 1** To fasten with a pin or pins. **2** To transfix with a pin, spear, etc. **3** To seize and hold firmly: to *pin* an opponent against a wall. **4** To force (someone) to make a definite statement, abide by a promise, etc.: usu. with *down.* [< OE *pinn* a peg]

Pins
a. straight. b. safety.
c. hairpins.

pin·a·fore (pin′ə-fôr, -fōr) *n.* A sleeveless garment worn as an apron or as a light dress. [< PIN, *v.* + AFORE]

pin·ball (pin′bôl) *n.* A game in which a ball, spring-propelled to the top of an inclined board, contacts in its descent any of various numbered pins, holes, etc.

pince·nez (pans′nā′, pins′-, *Fr.* pãns·nā′) *n. pl.* **pince·nez** Eyeglasses held upon the nose by a spring. [< F *pincer* to pinch + *nez* nose]

pin·cers (pin′sərz, -chərz) *n.pl.* (*sometimes construed as sing.*) **1** An instrument having two handles and a pair of jaws working on a pivot, used for holding objects. **2** *Zool.* A grasping organ, as the chela of a lobster. [< OF *pincier* to pinch]

pinch (pinch) *v.t.* **1** To squeeze between two hard edges, or between a finger and thumb. **2** To bind or compress painfully. **3** To affect with pain or distress. **4** To contract or make thin, as from cold or hunger. **5** To limit, as for

lack of something: *pinched* for time. **6** *Informal* To distress financially: usu. in the passive. **7** *Slang* To capture or arrest. **8** *Slang* To steal. —*v.i.* **9** To squeeze; hurt. **10** To be stingy. **11** To become narrow or constricted. —**pinch pennies** To be economical or stingy. —*n.* **1** The act of pinching. **2** Painful pressure of any kind. **3** A case of emergency. **4** So much of a loose substance as can be taken between the finger and thumb. **5** *Slang* A theft. **6** *Slang* An arrest or raid. [< OF *pincier*] —**pinch′er** *n.*

pinch·beck (pinch′bek) *n.* **1** An alloy of copper and zinc that resembles gold. **2** Anything spurious or pretentious. —*adj.* **1** Made of pinchbeck. **2** Spurious; false. [< Christopher *Pinchbeck,* 1670?–1732, English inventor]

pinch·ers (pin′chərz) *n.pl.* PINCERS.

pinch-hit (pinch′hit′) *v.i.* **-hit, -hit·ting 1** In baseball, to go to bat in place of a regular player, as when a hit is needed. **2** *Informal* To substitute for another in an emergency. [< PINCH an emergency + HIT] —**pinch hitter**

pin·cush·ion (pin′koŏsh′ən) *n.* A small cushion into which pins and needles are stuck when not in use.

Pin·dar·ic (pin·dar′ik) *adj.* Of or pertaining to an ode written in the complex style of Pindar, Greek lyric poet.

pind·ling (pind′ling) *adj. Informal* **1** Sickly; puny. **2** Trifling; small. [Var. of PIDDLING]

pine¹ (pīn) *n.* **1** Any of several cone-bearing trees having needle-shaped evergreen leaves growing in clusters. **2** The wood of a pine tree. [< L *pinus*]

pine² (pīn) *v.i.* **pined, pin·ing 1** To grow thin or weak with longing, grief, etc.; languish. **2** To have great desire: with *for.* [< OE *pīnian* to torment] —**Syn. 2** crave, long, yearn.

pin·e·al body (pin′ē·əl) *Anat.* A small, conical, glandlike structure of unknown function found in the brain of vertebrates. Also **pineal gland.** [< L *pinea* pine cone]

pine·ap·ple (pīn′ap′əl) *n.* **1** A tropical plant having spiny leaves and a large cone-shaped fruit. **2** The edible fruit of this plant. **3** *Slang* A bomb or hand grenade. [< OE *pīn* a pine + *æppel* apple]

pine cone The cone-shaped fruit of the pine tree.

pine needle The needle-shaped leaf of a pine tree.

pine tar A dark, viscous tar obtained from the wood of pine trees: used in medicines, disinfectants, etc.

pine·y (pī′nē) *adj.* **pin·i·er, pin·i·est** PINY.

Pineapple

pin·feath·er (pin′feth′ər) *n.* A rudimentary feather just beginning to grow through the skin.

pin·fold (pin′fōld′) *n.* A pound for stray animals; esp. a cattle pound. —*v.t.* To shut in a pinfold; confine. [< OE *pund-* POUND + *fald* FOLD²]

ping (ping) *n.* A sharp, metallic, ringing sound. —*v.i.* To make this sound. [Imit.]

Ping-Pong (ping′pong′, -pông′) *n.* TABLE TENNIS: a trade name.

pin·head (pin′hed′) *n.* **1** The head of a pin. **2** *Slang* A brainless or stupid person; a fool. **3** Something insignificant or small. —**pin′head′ed** *adj.*

pin·hole (pin′hōl′) *n.* A minute puncture made by or as by a pin.

pin·ion¹ (pin′yən) *n.* **1** The wing of a bird. **2** A wing feather. **3** The outer segment of a bird's wing, bearing the flight feathers. —*v.t.* **1** To cut off one pinion or bind the wings of (a bird) so as to prevent flight. **2** To bind or hold the arms of. [< L *pinna* feather]

pin·ion² (pin′yən) *n. Mech.* A toothed wheel meshing with a larger cogwheel. [< OF *peigne* a comb] • See RACK.

pink¹ (pingk) *n.* **1** A pale hue of red. **2** Any of a genus of garden plants having pink, red, or white flowers with a clovelike scent. **3** The flower of the pink. **4** A type of excellence or perfection. **5** *Often cap.* A person who holds somewhat radical opinions: a derogatory term. —**in the pink** *Informal* In the best of health and spirits. —*adj.* **1** Pale red in color; rose. **2** Somewhat radical in opinion. [?]

pink² (pingk) *v.t.* **1** To cut or finish the edges of (cloth) with a notched pattern. **2** To decorate, as cloth or leather, with a pattern of holes. **3** To prick or stab. [ME *pynken*] —**pink′er** *n.*

pink·eye (pingk′ī′) *n.* An acute, contagious inflammation of the conjunctiva.

pink·ie (pingk′ē) *n. pl.* **·ies** The fifth, or little, finger. Also **pink′y.**

pinking shears Shears with serrated blades for scalloping the edges of fabrics.   Pinked seam

pink·o (pingk′ō) *n. pl.* **·os** PINK¹ (def. 5).

pin money Any trifling sum of money set aside for incidentals.

pin·na (pin′ə) *n. pl.* **pin·nae** (pin′ē) **1** *Bot.* A leaflet of a pinnate leaf. **2** *Anat.* The external ear. **3** *Zool.* A wing, fin, etc. [< L *pinna* feather] —**pin′nal** *adj.*

pin·nace (pin′is) *n. Naut.* **1** A ship's boat. **2** Formerly, a small schooner-rigged vessel. [< Ital. *pinaccia*]

pin·na·cle (pin′ə·kəl) *n.* **1** The topmost point; acme. **2** A small turret or tall ornament, as on a parapet. **3** A mountain peak. —*v.t.* **·cled, ·cling** **1** To place on or as on a pinnacle. **2** To furnish with a pinnacle; crown. [< L *pinna* wing, pinnacle] —**Syn.** *n.* **1** apex, zenith. **3** summit.

pin·nate (pin′āt, -it) *adj.* **1** Resembling a feather. **2** *Bot.* Having leaflets arranged on each side of a common axis: said of compound leaves. Also **pin′nat·ed.** [< L *pinna* a feather, wing] —**pin′nate·ly** *adv.* —**pin·na′tion** *n.*

pi·noch·le (pē·nuk′əl, -nok′-) *n.* A card game resembling bezique, played with a double pack of 48 cards, ranking as follows: ace, ten, king, queen, jack, and nine. Also **pi′noc·le.** [?]

pi·ñon (pin′yən, pēn′yōn) *n.* **1** The edible seed of various pines of the Pacific coast. **2** Any of these trees. [Sp., a pine nut]

pin·point (pin′point′) *n.* **1** The point of a pin. **2** Something extremely small. —*v.t.* To locate or define precisely. —*adj.* Located or aimed very precisely.

pint (pīnt) *n.* A unit of volume, liquid or dry, equal to ½ quart. [< OF *pinte*]

pin·tail (pin′tāl′) *n.* **1** A variety of duck, the male of which has a long, sharp tail. **2** A sharp-tailed grouse.

pin·tle (pin′təl) *n.* A pin upon which anything pivots, as in a hinge, etc. [< OE *pintel* penis]

pin·to (pin′tō) *adj. Regional* Piebald; pied, as an animal. —*n. pl.* **·tos** **1** A pied animal: said esp. of a horse. **2** A kind of spotted bean of the sw U.S.: also **pinto bean.** [< Sp., lit., painted]

pin-up (pin′up′) *n. Informal* **1** A picture of an attractive girl hung on a wall or board for display. **2** A lamp fastened on a wall. —*adj.* Designating a photograph or lighting device so affixed.

pin·wheel (pin′ʰwēl′) *n.* **1** A firework that forms a rotating wheel of fire when ignited. **2** A child's plastic or paper toy resembling a windmill revolving on a pin attached to a stick.

pin·worm (pin′wûrm′) *n.* A small nematode worm parasitic in the lower intestines and rectum of humans.

pin·y (pī′nē) *adj.* **·i·er, ·i·est** Pertaining to, like, or covered with pines.

pi·o·neer (pī′ə·nir′) *n.* **1** One of the first explorers, settlers, or colonists of a new region. **2** One of the first investigators or developers in a new field of research, enterprise, etc. **3** *Mil.* An engineer who goes before the main body building roads, bridges, etc. —*v.t.* **1** To prepare (a way, etc.). **2** To prepare the way for. **3** To be a pioneer of. —*v.i.* **4** To act as a pioneer. [< OF *paonier* a foot soldier]

pi·ous (pī′əs) *adj.* **1** Actuated by religious reverence; godly. **2** Dutiful, respectful, or sanctimonious. **3** Practiced in the name of religion. [< L *pius* dutiful, devout] —**pi′ous·ly** *adv.* —**pi′ous·ness** *n.*

pip¹ (pip) *n.* **1** The seed of an apple, orange, etc. **2** *Slang* A person or thing unusual of its kind. [Short for PIPPIN]

pip² (pip) *n.* A spot, as on a playing card, domino, or die. [?]

pip³ (pip) *v.* **pipped, pip·ping** *v.t.* To break through (the shell), as a chick in the egg. —*v.i.* To peep; chirp. [Prob. var. of PEEP¹]

pip⁴ (pip) *n.* **1** A contagious disease of fowls in which mucus forms in the throat or a scale on the tongue. **2**

Slang Any mild human ailment. [< L *pituita* mucus, the pip]

pipe (pīp) *n.* **1** An apparatus, usu. a small bowl with a hollow stem, for smoking tobacco, opium, etc. **2** Enough tobacco to fill the bowl of a pipe. **3** A duct of metal, etc., for conveying a fluid. **4** A single section of such a duct. **5** Any hollow or tubular part in an animal or plant body. **6** *Music* **a** A wind instrument consisting of a tube or tubes. **b** Any of the tubular tone-producing parts used in an organ. **c** *pl.* The bagpipe. **7** A high-pitched voice; also, a bird's call. **8** A large cask for wine. **9** A boatswain's whistle. —*v.* **piped, pip·ing** *v.i.* **1** To play on a pipe. **2** To make a shrill sound. **3** *Naut.* To signal the crew by means of a pipe. —*v.t.* **4** To convey by or as by means of pipes, esp. to transmit (television programs) by coaxial cables or wire instead of by airwaves. **5** To provide with pipes. **6** To play, as a tune, on a pipe. **7** To utter shrilly or in a high key. **8** *Naut.* To call to order by means of a boatswain's pipe. **9** To lead, entice, or bring by piping. **10** To trim, as a dress, with piping. —**pipe down** *Slang* To become silent; stop making noise. —**pipe up** **1** To start playing or singing. **2** To speak out, esp. in a shrill voice. [< L *pipare* to cheep]

pipe clay A white clay used for making clay pipes and, formerly, for whitening and cleaning leather.

pipe dream *Informal* Any groundless hope or impractical idea; a daydream.

pipe·line (pīp′līn′) *n.* **1** A line of pipe, as for the transmission of water, oil, etc. **2** A channel for the transmission of information.

pipe organ ORGAN (def. 1).

pip·er (pī′pər) *n.* **1** A person who plays a pipe or pipes. **2** A person who makes, installs, or repairs piping (def. 4).

pipe·stem (pīp′stem′) *n.* **1** The stem of a tobacco pipe. **2** *pl.* Things of similar shape, as long, thin legs. —*adj.* Shaped like a pipestem; thin.

pi·pette (pī·pet′, pi-) *n.* A slender tube for transferring or measuring small portions of a fluid. Also **pi·pet′.** [F, dim. of *pipe* pipe]

pip·ing (pī′ping) *adj.* **1** Playing on the pipe. **2** Hissing or sizzling: *piping* hot. **3** Having a shrill sound. —*n.* **1** The act of one who pipes. **2** The music of pipes. **3** A wailing or whistling sound. **4** A system of pipes, as in plumbing. **5** A narrow fold of cloth for trimming seams.

pip·it (pip′it) *n.* One of various larklike birds of open country that sing in flight and walk with tail bobbing. [Imit.]

pip·kin (pip′kin) *n.* A small earthenware jar. [? Dim. of PIPE]

pip·pin (pip′in) *n.* Any of several varieties of apple. [< OE *pepin* seed of a fruit]

American pipit

pip·sis·se·wa (pip·sis′ə·wə) *n.* A low-growing plant related to wintergreen, having jagged, evergreen leaves and white or pink flowers. [< Algon.]

pip-squeak (pip′skwēk′) *n.* A petty and contemptible person or thing.

pi·quant (pē′kənt, -känt′) *adj.* **1** Having an agreeably pungent or tart taste. **2** Interesting; tart; racy; also, charmingly lively. [< F *piquer* sting] —**pi′quan·cy** *n.* —**pi′quant·ly** *adv.*

pique (pēk) *n.* A feeling of irritation or resentment. —*v.t.* **piqued, pi·quing** **1** To excite resentment in. **2** To stimulate or arouse; provoke. [< MF *piquer* to sting, prick] —**Syn.** *v.* **1** anger, displeasure. *v.* **1** irritate, nettle, offend.

pi·qué (pē·kā′) *n.* A fabric, usu. of cotton, with raised cord or welts running lengthwise. [F, lit., quilted]

pi·quet (pē·ket′, pē·kā′) *n.* A two-handed game of cards using 32 cards. [F]

pi·ra·cy (pī′rə·sē) *n. pl.* **·cies** **1** Robbery on the high seas. **2** The unauthorized publication, reproduction, or use of another's invention, idea, or literary creation. [< Gk. *peiratēs* a pirate]

pi·ra·nha (pi·rä′nyə) *n.* A small, carnivorous, freshwater fish of South America that, in schools, attacks and severely wounds large animals and man. Also **pi·ra′ya** (-rä′yä). [Tupian, toothed fish]

pi·rate (pī′rit) *n.* **1** A rover and robber on the high seas. **2** A vessel engaged in piracy. **3** A person who appropriates without right the work of another. —*v.t.* & *v.i.* **·rat·ed, ·rat·ing 1** To practice or commit piracy (upon). **2** To publish or appropriate (the work, ideas, etc., of another) illegally; plagiarize. [< Gk. *peiraein* to attach] —**pi·rat·ic** (pī·rat′ik) or **·i·cal** *adj.* —**pi·rat′i·cal·ly** *adv.*

pi·rogue (pi·rōg′) *n.* A flat-bottomed two-masted boat. [< Cariban *piragua*]

pir·ou·ette (pir′ōō·et′) *n.* A rapid whirling upon the toes in dancing. —*vi.* **·et·ted, ·et·ting** To make a pirouette. [F, a spinning top] —**pir′ou·et′ter** *n.*

pis·ca·to·ri·al (pis′kə·tôr′ē·əl, -tō′rē-) *adj.* Pertaining to fishes, fishermen, or fishing. Also **pis′ca·to′ry.** [< L *piscator* a fisherman] —**pis′ca·to′ri·al·ly** *adv.*

Pis·ces (pī′sēz, pis′ēz) *n. pl.* (*construed as sing*) A constellation and the twelfth sign of the zodiac; the Fishes. [< L *piscis* a fish] • See ZODIAC.

pis·ci·cul·ture (pis′i·kul′chər) *n.* The science or business of hatching and rearing fish. [< L *piscis,* fish + CULTURE] —**pis′ci·cul′tur·al** *adj.* —**pis′ci·cul′tur·ist** *n.*

Pis·gah (piz′gə), **Mount** A mountain of ancient Palestine, now Jordan, NE of the Dead Sea: in the Old Testament, the peak from which Moses beheld the Promised Land: highest peak, Mount Nebo.

pis·mire (pis′mīr) *n.* An ant. [< ME *pisse* urine + *myre* an ant; with ref. to odor of formic acid]

pis·ta·chi·o (pis·tä′shē·ō, -tash′ē·ō) *n. pl.* **·chi·os 1** A small tree of w Asia and the Levant. **2** Its pale green, edible seed: also **pistachio nut. 3** The flavor of the pistachio nut. **4** A delicate shade of green. [< Gk. *pistakion*]

pis·til (pis′til) *n.* The seed-bearing organ of flowering plants, composed of the ovary, the stigma, and usu. a style. [< L *pistillum* a pestle] • See OVARY.

pis·til·late (pis′tə·lit, -lāt) *adj.* **1** Having a pistil. **2** having pistils and no stamens. Also **pis′til·lar′y** (-ler′ē).

pis·tol (pis′təl) *n.* A small firearm held and fired by one hand. —*v.t.* **·toled** or **·tolled, ·tol·ing** or **·tol·ling** To shoot with a piston. [< F *pistole*]

pis·tole (pis·tōl′) *n.* An obsolete gold coin of varying value, formerly current in Europe. [F]

pis·ton (pis′tən) *n.* **1** *Mech.* A disk fitted to slide in a cylinder and connected with a rod for receiving the pressure of or exerting pressure upon a fluid in the cylinder. **2** A valve in a wind instrument for altering the pitch of tones. [< Ital. *pistane*]

piston ring *Mech.* An open ring fitted on a piston body to prevent leakage between the piston and the cylinder wall.

Steam-engine piston
a. piston. b. piston rod.

pit¹ (pit) *n.* **1** A cavity in the ground. **2** A pitfall for animals; snare. **3** A deep abyss. **4** Hell. **5** In Great Britain, the portion of the main floor of the auditorium of a theater under the first balcony. **6** The space just in front of and below the stage, usu. occupied by the orchestra. **7** An enclosed space in which animals engage in fighting: a *cockpit.* **8** Any natural cavity or depression in the body: the *armpit.* **9** A scar like that made by a healed smallpox pustule. **10** That part of the floor of an exchange where a special line of trading is done: the wheat *pit.* **11** A mining excavation. —*v.* **pit·ted, pit·ting** *v.t.* **1** To mark with dents or hollows. **2** To match as antagonists. —*v.i.* **3** To become marked with pits. [< OE *pytt*]

pit² (pit) *n.* A hard, single seed of certain fruits, as the plum. —*v.t.* **pit·ted, pit·ting** To remove pits from, as fruits. [< MDu. *pitte* kernel]

pitch¹ (pich) *n.* **1** A sticky nonvolatile residue obtained from the distillation of petroleum, coal tar, etc. **2** Asphalt. **3** A resin exuded by certain conifers. —*v.t.* To caulk, waterproof, cover, or treat with pitch. [< L *pix, picis* pitch]

pitch² (pich) *v.t.* **1** To erect or set up (a tent, camp, etc.). **2** To throw or hurl. **3** To set the level, angle degree, etc., of. **4** To put in a definite place or position. **5** In baseball, to deliver (the ball) to the batter. **6** *Music* To set the pitch or key of. —*v.i.* **7** To fall or plunge forward or headlong. **8** to lurch. **9** To rise and fall alternately at the front and back. **10** To incline downward; slope. **11** To encamp. **12** In baseball, to deliver the ball to the batter. —**pitch in** *Informan* To start vigorously. —**pitch into** To attack, assail. —*n* **1** Point or degree of elevation or depression. **2** The degree of descent or inclination of a slope. **3** *Mech.* **a** The amount of advance of a screw thread in a single turn. **b** The distance between two corresponding points on the teeth of a gearwheel. **4** *Music* The subjective characteristic of a tone that correlates essentially with frequency. **5** In games, the act of pitching; a throw. **6** Something pitched. **7** The act of dipping or plunging downward. **8** An attempt to sell or persuade: to make a *pitch.* [ME *picchen*] —**Syn.** *v.* **2** cast, fling, heave, toss.

pitch-black (pich′blak′) *adj.* Intensely black.

pitch-blende (pich′blend′) *n.* A black or brown mineral form of uranium oxide: an ore of uranium and radium. [< G *Pech* pitch¹ + *Blende* blende]

pitch-dark (pich′därk′) *adj.* Very dark.

pitched battle A fierce battle in which the antagonists fight in close contact.

pitch·er¹ (pich′ər) *n.* On who pitches, esp., in baseball, the player who delivers the ball to the batter.

pitch·er² (pich′ər) *n.* A vessel with a spout and a handle, used for holding liquids to be poured out. [< Gk. *bikos* a wine jar]

pitcher plant Any of several plants having leaves that form pitcherlike vessels in which insects are trapped and digested.

pitch·fork (pich′fôrk′) *n.* A large fork, often having a long handle for moving about hay, straw, etc. —*v.t.* To lift and throw with a pitchfork. [< PITCH² + FORK]

pitch·man (pich′mən) *n. pl.* **·men** (mən) *Slang* One who sells small articles from a temporary stand, as at a fair, etc.

pitch pine Any of several pines that yield turpentine and pitch.

pitch·y (pich′ē) *adj.* **pitch·i·er, pitch·i·est 1** Resembling pitch; intensely dark. **2** Full of or daubed with pitch. **3** Sticky. —**pitch′i·ly** *adv.* —**pitch′i·ness** *n.*

pit·e·ous (pit′ē·əs) *adj.* Exciting great pity or sympathy. —**pit′e·ous·ly** *adv.* —**pit′e·ous·ness** *n.* • **piteous, pitiable, pitiful**

Pitchforks

These words all mean "causing or deserving pity," but they have different shades of meaning. *Piteous* is the strongest, connoting a heart-rending anguish that is keenly felt by the observer: *the piteous cry of a wounded animal.* A *pitiable* thing gives rise to milder compassion mixed with understanding: *his pitiable attempts to appear respectable.* A *pitiful* thing tends to inspire stronger feeling than does a *pitiable* one: *a pitiful account of an unhappy childhood.* The pity suggested by *pitiable* and *pitiful* may be mixed with contempt or condescension.

pit·fall (pit′fôl) *n.* **1** A pit contrived for entrapping beasts or men. **2** Any hidden danger. [< PIT¹ + OE *fealle* a trap]

pith (pith) *n.* **1** The soft, spongy tissue in the center of the stems and branches of certain plants. **2** Any soft central part, as the marrow of bones. **3** Concentrated force; substance. **4** The essential part; quintessence. —*v.t.* To remove the pith from, as a plant stem. [< OE *pitha*]

Pith·e·can·thro·pus (pith′ə·kan′thrə·pəs, -kan·thrō′·pəs) *n. pl.* **·pi** (-pī) The generic name formerly given to Java man as a supposed transitional form between ape and man. [< Gk. *pithēkos* an ape + *anthropos* a man] —**pith′e·can′thro·pine** (-pēn, -pin), **pith′e·can′thro·poid** *adj.*

pith·y (pith′ē) *adj.* **pith·i·er, pith·i·est 1** Consisting of or like pith. **2** Forcible; effective. —**pith′i·ly** *adv.* —**pith′i·ness** *n.*

pit·i·a·ble (pit′ē·ə·bəl) *adj.* **1** Arousing or meriting pity or compassion; pathetic. **2** Insignificant; contemptible. —**pit′·i·a·ble·ness** *n.* —**pit′i·a·bly** *adv.* • See PITEOUS.

pit·i·ful (pit′i·fəl) *adj.* **1** Arousing pity or compassion. **2** Arousing contempt or scorn. **3** *Archaic* Full of pity; compassionate. —**pit′i·ful·ly** *adv.* —**pit′i·ful·ness** *n.* —**Syn. 1** lamentable, miserable, pathetic, touching. **2** abject, contemptible, paltry. • See PITEOUS.

pit·i·less (pit′i·lis) *adj.* Having no pity or mercy; ruthless. —**pit′i·less·ly** *adv.* **pit′i·less·ness** *n.*

pit·man (pit′mən) *n. pl.* **·men** (-mən) One who works in a pit, esp., in mining, the man in charge of the underground machinery.

pit·tance (pit′əns) *n.* **1** A small allowance of money. **2** Any meager income or remuneration. [<OF *pitance*, orig. a monk's food allotment, pity]

pit·ter-pat·ter (pit′ər-pat′ər) *n.* A rapid series of light sounds or taps. —*adv.* With a pitter-patter. [Imit.]

pi·tu·i·tar·y (pi·t^yōō′ə·ter′ē) *adj.* Of or pertaining to the pituitary gland. —*n. pl.* **·tar·ies 1** The pituitary gland. **2** Any of various preparations made from extracts of the pituitary gland. [<L *pituita* phlegm]

pituitary gland *Anat.* A small, bilobate, endocrine gland at the base of the brain in vertebrates which secretes various hormones having specific effects on other glands in the body and on growth, metabolism, etc. Also **pituitary body.**

pit·y (pit′ē) *n. pl.* **pit·ies 1** The feeling of grief or pain awakened by the misfortunes of others; compassion. **2** A cause for compassion or regret: It's a *pity* that their house burned down. —*v.t. & v.i.* **pit·ied, pit·y·ing** To feel compassion or pity (for). [<LL *pietas*] —**pit′i·er** *n.* —**pit′y·ing·ly** *adv.*

più (pyōō) *adv. Music* More: *più* allegro: faster. [Ital. < L *plus*]

piv·ot (piv′ət) *n.* **1** *Mech.* Something upon which a related part oscillates or rotates. **2** Something on which an important matter hinges or turns; a turning point. **3** *Mil.* In wheeling troops, the soldier, officer, or point upon which the line turns. —*v.t.* **1** To place on, attach by, or provide with a pivot or pivots. —*v.i.* **2** To turn on a pivot; swing. [F] —**piv′ot·al** *adj.* —**piv′ot·al·ly** *adv.*

pix·el (pik′səl) *n.* A picture element, one of the tiny dots that make up a character or a graphic on a cathode-ray tube.

pix·i·lat·ed (pik′sə·lā′tid) *adj.* **1** Somewhat crazy or erratic. **2** Whimsical; droll.

pix·y (pik′sē) *n. pl.* **pix·ies** A fairy or elf. Also **pix′ie.** [< Scand.]

piz·za (pēt′sə) *n.* A doughy crust overlaid and baked with a mixture of cheese, tomatoes, spices, etc. [Ital.]

piz·zazz (pə·zaz′) *n. Slang* A quality of irresistible and exciting charm. Also **piz·zazz′.**

piz·ze·ri·a (pēt′sə·rē′ə) *n.* A place where pizzas are prepared, sold, and eaten.

piz·zi·ca·to (pit′sə·kä′tō) *Music adj. & adv.* Plucked or in a plucked manner: used to indicate that the strings of a normally bowed instrument are to be plucked. —*n. pl.* **·ti** (-tē) A pizzicato note, phrase, passage, etc. [<Ital. *pizzicare* to pluck, pinch]

pk. pack; park; peak; peck.

pkg. package(s).

PKU phenylketonuria.

pl. place; plate; plural.

pla·ca·ble (plak′ə·bəl, plā′kə-) *adj.* Appeasable; yielding. [<L *placare* appease] —**pla′ca·bil′i·ty, pla′ca·ble·ness** *n.*

plac·ard (plak′ərd, plak′ärd) *n.* A printed or written notice to be publicly displayed. —*v.t.* (*usu.* plak′ärd) **1** To announce by means of placards. **2** To post placards on or in. **3** To display as a placard. [<OF *plackart*]

pla·cate (plā′kāt, plak′āt) *v.t.* **·cat·ed, ·cat·ing** To appease the anger of; pacify. [<L *placare* appease] —**pla′cat·er, pla·ca′tion** *n.* —**pla′ca·tive, pla′ca·to·ry** (-tō′rē, -tō′rē) *adj.*

place (plās) *n.* **1** A particular point or portion of space; a definite locality or location. **2** An occupied situation or building; space regarded as abode or quarters. **3** An open space or square in a city; also, a court or street. **4** Position in relative order. **5** Station in life; degree; rank. **6** An office, appointment, or employment; also, rank, position, or station. **7** Room; stead: One thing gives *place* to another. **8** A particular passage, as in a book. **9** The second position among the first three competitors in a horse race. **10** *Math* The position of a digit, and hence its weight, in relation to other digits of a numeral. —**in place 1** In its natural position; also, in a suitable place, position, job, etc. **2** IN SITU. —**in place of** Instead of. —**out of place 1** Not in the appropriate place, order, or relation. **2** Inappropriate; ill-timed. —**take place** To happen; occur. —*v.*

placed, plac·ing *v.t.* **1** To put in a particular place or position. **2** To put or arrange in a particular relation or sequence. **3** To find a situation, home, etc., for. **4** To appoint to a post or office. **5** To identify; classify: Historians *place* him in the time of Nero. **6** To arrange for: to *place* an order. **7** To bestow or entrust: I *place* my life in your hands. **8** To invest, as funds. **9** To adjust the tones of (the voice) consciously, as in singing. —*v.i.* **10** In racing, to finish among the first three contestants; esp., to finish second. [< L *platea* a wide street] —**Syn.** *v.* **1** lay, locate, set, situate.

pla·ce·bo (plə·sē′bō) *n. pl.* **·bos** or **·boes** Any inactive substance given out as medication either to humor a patient or as a control in testing the effects of other medicines. [<L *placebo* I shall please]

place kick In football, a kick for a goal in which the ball is placed on the ground for kicking. —**place′-kick′** *v.i.*

place·ment (plās′mənt) *n.* **1** The act of placing or the state of being placed. **2** The finding of a suitable situation or job for a person. **3** In football, the putting of the ball in position for a place kick from the field.

pla·cen·ta (plə·sen′tə) *n. pl.* **·tas** or **·tae** (-tē) In higher mammals, the vascular organ of interlocking fetal and maternal tissue by which the fetus is nourished in the uterus. [<NL *placenta* (*uterina*) (uterine) cake] —**pla·cen′tal, pla·cen′tate** *adj.*

plac·er (plas′ər) *n. Mining* **1** A deposit of sand, gravel, etc., containing gold or other mineral in particles that can be isolated by washing. **2** Any place where deposits are washed for valuable minerals. [<Am. Sp. *placer* a deposit]

plac·id (plas′id) *adj.* Quiet; calm. [<L *placere* to please] —**pla·cid′i·ty** (plə·sid′ə·tē), **plac′id·ness** *n.* —**plac′id·ly** *adv.* —**Syn.** pacific, peaceful, tranquil, unruffled.

plack·et (plak′it) *n.* The opening or slit in the upper part of a skirt, usu. closed by a zipper. Also **placket hole.** [?]

pla·gia·rism (plā′jə·riz′əm, -jē·ə-) *n.* The act of plagiarizing, or something plagiarized. —**pla′gia·rist** *n.* —**pla′gia·ris′tic** *adj.*

pla·gia·rize (plā′jə·rīz, -jē·ə-) *v.* **·rized, ·riz·ing** *v.t.* **1** To appropriate as one's own the writings, ideas, etc., of another). **2** To appropriate and use passages, ideas, etc., from. —*v.i.* **3** To commit plagiarism. *Brit. sp.* **pla′gia·rise.** —**pla′gia·riz′er** *n.*

pla·gia·ry (plā′jər·ē, -jē·ər·ē) *n. pl.* **·ries 1** PLAGIARISM. **2** *Archaic* A plagiarist. [<Gk. *plagios* oblique, treacherous]

plague (plāg) *n.* **1** A pestilence or epidemic disease of man or animals, usu. very deadly and contagious: bubonic *plague.* **2** A person or thing that is troublesome and harassing. —*v.t.* **plagued, pla·guing 1** To harass or torment; annoy. **2** To afflict with plague or disaster. [<LL *plaga* pestilence]

pla·guy (plā′gē) *Informal adj.* Characterized by vexation or annoyance; troublesome. —*adv.* Vexatiously; intolerably. Also **pla·guey.** —**pla′gui·ly** *adv.*

plaice (plās) *n.* Any of various flatfishes of the coasts of Europe and North America. [<Gk. *platys* broad]

plaid (plad) *adj.* Having a tartan pattern; checkered. —*n.* **1** An oblong woolen scarf of tartan or checkered pattern, worn in the Scottish Highlands as a cloak fastened over one shoulder. **2** Any fabric of this pattern. [< Scot. Gaelic *plaide* a blanket]

plain (plān) *adj.* **1** Presenting few difficulties; easy. **2** Clear; understandable: *plain* English. **3** Lowly in station; humble. **4** Having no conspicuous ornamentation; unadorned. **5** Not figured or twilled: said of textiles. **6** Flat; smooth. **7** Homely. **8** Not rich, as food. —*n.* An expanse of level, treeless land; a prairie. [< L *planus* flat] —**plain′ly** *adv.* —**plain′ness** *n.*

plain·clothes man (plān′klōz′, -klōthz′) A police detective wearing civilian clothes while on duty. Also **plain·clothes·man** (plān'klōz'mən, -klōthz'-) (*pl.* **·men**).

plains·man (plānz'mən) *n. pl.* **·men** (-mən) A dweller on the plains.

plain·song (plān'sông', -song') *n.* Ecclesiastical music of the early Christian church, sung in unison, as the Gregorian chant. Also **plain·chant** (plān'chant', -chänt').

plain-spo·ken (plān'spō'kən) *adj.* Plainly or frankly speaking or spoken.

plaint (plānt) *n.* 1 COMPLAINT. 2 *Archaic* A lamentation. [< L *plangere* to lament]

plain·tiff (plān'tif) *n.* The person that begins an action at law. [< OF *plaintif* plaintive]

plain·tive (plān'tiv) *adj.* Expressing a subdued sadness; mournful. [< OF *plaintif*] —**plain'tive·ly** *adv.* —**plain'tive·ness** *n.*

plait (plāt, plat) *v.t.* 1 BRAID. 2 PLEAT. 3 To make by pleating or braiding. —*n.* 1 A braid of hair. 2 PLEAT. [< L *plicitum* a folded thing] —**plait'er** *n.*

plan (plan) *n.* 1 A means for the attainment of some object; a scheme. 2 A drawing showing the proportion and relation of parts, as of a building. 3 A mode of action. —*v.t.* **planned, plan·ning** 1 To form a scheme or method for doing, achieving, etc. 2 To make a plan of, as a building; design. 3 To have as an intention or purpose. [< OF, a plane (surface), a ground plan] —**plan'ner** *n.* —**Syn.** *n.* 1 design, method, arrangement, program. *v.* 1 contrive, devise, invent, organize.

plane[1] (plān) *n.* 1 *Geom.* A surface such that a straight line joining any two of its points lies wholly within the surface. 2 Any flat or uncurved surface. 3 A grade of development; stage; level, as of thought, knowledge, rank, etc. 4 *Aeron.* A lifting surface of an airplane; airfoil. 5 An airplane. —*adj.* 1 Of or lying in a plane. 2 Having a flat surface. —*v.i.* **planed, plan·ing** 1 To glide; soar. 2 To rise partly out of the water, as a power boat at high speed. [< L *planus* flat]

plane[2] (plān) *n.* A tool used for smoothing boards or other surfaces of wood. —*v.t.* **planed, plan·ing** 1 To make smooth or even with a plane. 2 To remove with a plane. [< L *planus* flat]

plane[3] (plān) *n.* Any of a genus of large, deciduous trees with maplelike leaves and bark that is shed in patches. Also **plane tree**. [< Gk. *platys* broad; because of its broad leaves]

Plane

plan·er (plā'nər) *n.* A machine for making smooth surfaces on wood or metal. [< PLANE[2]]

plan·et (plan'it) *n.* 1 *Astron.* One of the large bodies that orbit the sun and shine by reflected sunlight. The major solar planets are Mercury, Venus, Earth, Mars, Jupiter, Saturn, Uranus, Neptune, and Pluto. 2 A similar body revolving around another star. 3 In ancient astronomy, one of the seven heavenly bodies (the Sun, Moon, Mercury, Venus, Mars, Jupiter, and Saturn) that have an apparent motion among the fixed stars. 4 In astrology, one

2 A building containing such an apparatus. [< LL *planetarius* planetary]

plan·e·tar·y (plan'ə·ter'ē) *adj.* 1 Of or pertaining to a planet or planets. 2 Mundane; terrestrial. 3 Wandering; erratic: a *planetary* career. 4 *Mech.* Of or denoting a gear in which one or more small wheels mesh with the toothed circumference of a larger wheel, around which they revolve as they rotate. 5 *Physics* Orbiting in the manner of a planet: a *planetary* electron.

plan·e·toid (plan'ə·toid) *n.* ASTEROID. —**plan'e·toi'dal** *adj.*

plan·ish (plan'ish) *v.t.* To condense, smooth, toughen, or polish, as metal, by hammering, rolling, etc. [< L *planus* flat] —**plan'ish·er** *n.*

plank (plangk) *n.* 1 A broad piece of sawed timber, thicker than a board. 2 One of the principles of a political platform. —**walk the plank** To walk off a plank projecting from the side of a ship: a method used by pirates for executing prisoners. —*v.t.* 1 To cover, furnish, or lay with planks. 2 To broil or bake and serve on a plank, as fish. 3 *Informal* To put down emphatically. [< LL *planca* board]

plank·ing (plangk'ing) *n.* 1 The act of laying planks. 2 Planks collectively.

plank·ton (plangk'tən) *n.* The floating or drifting, usu. microscopic, plants and animals living near the surface of bodies of water. [< Gk. *planktos* drifting] —**plank·ton·ic** (plangk·ton'ik) *adj.*

plant (plant, plänt) *n.* 1 Any member of one of the two great kingdoms of organisms, usu. distinguishable from animals by various criteria, as the ability to carry on photosynthesis, the presence of cellulose cell walls, a fixed position, etc. 2 One of the smaller forms of vegetable life, as distinct from shrubs and trees. 3 A set of machines, tools, apparatus, etc., comprising a manufacturing enterprise or other business. 4 A building or buildings used for a manufacturing or industrial process: a packing *plant*. 5 The buildings and equipment needed for any institution, as a college. 6 A sapling; a slip or cutting from a tree or bush. 7 *Slang* A trick; swindle. —*v.t.* 1 To set in the ground for growing. 2 To furnish with plants or seed: to *plant* a field. 3 To place firmly; put in position. 4 To found; establish. 5 To introduce into the mind. 6 To deposit (fish or spawn) in a body of water. 7 *Slang* To deliver, as a blow. 8 *Slang* To place (a person or thing) for purposes of deception. [< L *planta* a sprout]

Plan·tag·e·net (plan·taj'i·net) *n.* A member of the English royal family from Henry II (1154) to the accession of the House of Tudor (1485).

Plantain[1]

plan·tain[1] (plan'tin) *n.* Any of a genus of low-growing, weedy plants of temperate regions. [< L *plantago*]

plan·tain[2] (plan'tin) *n.* 1 A tropical tree having coarse, bananalike fruit. 2 Its fruit, usu. eaten cooked. [< Sp. *plátano*]

PLANETS

Name	Symbol	Distance from sun: miles	Mean diameter: miles	Period of sidereal revolution	Period of rotation	Number of satellites	Mass: earth considered as 1.
Mercury	☿	36,000,000	3,000	88 days	88 days?	0	0.0543
Venus	♀	67,000,000	7,600	225 days	20–30 days	0	0.8136
Earth	⊕	93,000,000	7,918	365.25 days	23 hr. 56 min.	1	1.0000
Mars	♂	142,000,000	4,200	687 days	24 hr. 37 min.	2	0.1069
Jupiter	♃	483,000,000	87,000	12 years	9 hr. 50 min.	12	318.35
Saturn	♄	886,000,000	72,000	29.5 years	10 hr. 14 min.	9	95.3
Uranus	♅	1,780,000,000	29,600	84 years	10 hr. 45 min.	5	14.58
Neptune	♆	2,790,000,000	27,700	165 years	15 hr. 48 min.	2	17.26
Pluto	♇	3,670,000,000	4,000	248 years	?	0	.1?

of these bodies in relation to its supposed influence on human beings and their affairs. [< Gk. *planētes* wanderer]

plan·e·tar·i·um (plan'ə·târ'ē·əm) *n. pl.* **·tar·i·ums** or **·tar·i·a** 1 An apparatus for exhibiting the features of the heavens as they exist at any time and for any place on earth.

plan·tar (plan'tər) *adj.* Pertaining to the sole of the foot. [< L *planta* sole of the foot]

plan·ta·tion (plan·tā'shən) *n.* 1 A farm or estate of many acres, esp. in the s U.S., planted in cotton, tobacco, rice, or sugar cane. 2 A newly settled region; a settlement;

colony. **3** A grove cultivated to provide a certain product. [<L *plantare* to plant]

plant·er (plan'tər) *n.* **1** A person or machine that plants. **2** An owner of a plantation. **3** A decorative container for growing shrubs and flowers, esp. indoors.

plan·ti·grade (plan'tə·grād) *adj.* Walking on the whole sole of the foot, as men, bears, etc. —*n.* A plantigrade animal. [<L *planta* the sole of the foot + *gradi* to walk]

plant louse An aphid or similar insect.

plaque (plak) *n.* **1** A plate, disk, or slab of metal, porcelain, etc., ornamented, as for wall decoration. **2** A brooch. **3** A hardened deposit of microorganisms and mucus on teeth. [<MDu. *placke* flat disk]

plash (plash) *n.* A slight splash. —*v.t.* & *v.i.* To splash lightly. [Prob. imit.] —**plash'y** *adj.*

-plasm *combining form Biol.* The viscous, basic material of organic cells: *protoplasm.* [<Gk. *plasma* a form]

plas·ma (plaz'mə) *n.* **1** The liquid portion of blood, lymph, milk, or similar fluids containing suspended solids. **2** PROTOPLASM. **3** *Physics* An intensely ionized, electrically neutral gas. [<Gk. *plassein* to mold, form] —**plas·mat·ic** (plaz·mat'ik), **plas'mic** *adj.*

plas·ter (plas'tər, pläs'-) *n.* **1** A composition of lime, sand, and water for coating walls and partitions. **2** Plaster of Paris. **3** A viscid substance spread on cloth and applied to the body for healing purposes. —*v.t.* **1** To cover or overlay with plaster. **2** To apply a plaster to, as a part of the body. **3** To apply like plaster: to *plaster* posters on a fence. **4** To cause to adhere or lie flat like plaster. [<Gk. *emplastron*]

plas·ter·board (plas'tər·bôrd', pläs'-, -bōrd') *n.* A laminated wallboard of paper and gypsum.

plas·tered (plas'tərd, pläs'-) *adj. Slang* Drunk.

plaster of Paris Calcined gypsum that solidifies readily after mixture with water and is useful in making molds, splints, statuary, etc.

plas·tic (plas'tik) *adj.* **1** Giving form or fashion to matter. **2** Capable of being molded; pliable. **3** Pertaining to modeling or molding; sculptural. **4** Made of plastic. **5** *Slang* Not genuine; sham: *plastic* moral values. —*n.* Any of a class of synthetically produced organic compounds capable of being molded and hardened into any form required by commercial use. [<Gk. *plastos* formed<*plassein* to form, mold] —**plas'ti·cal·ly** *adv.*

Plas·ti·cine (plas'tə·sēn) *n.* A claylike substance with an oil base, used for modeling: a trade name.

plas·tic·i·ty (plas·tis'ə·tē) *n.* The property or quality of being plastic or malleable.

plastic surgery Surgery that deals with structural remodeling or restoration of lost, injured, or deformed parts of the body. —**plastic surgeon**

plastic wood A synthetic paste which when dried resembles wood, used to fill cracks, holes, etc., in wooden articles.

plas·tron (plas'trən) *n.* **1** The under part of the shell of a turtle. **2** An iron breastplate. [<OF] —**plas'tral** *adj.*

plat (plat) *n.* **1** A small piece of ground; a plot. **2** A plotted map, chart, or plan. —*v.t.* **plat·ted, plat·ting** To make a plot or plan of. [<OF]

plat. plateau; platform; platoon.

plate (plāt) *n.* **1** A shallow, usu. round dish upon which food is served. **2** A portion of food; plateful. **3** Service, dishes, food, etc., for one person: a fund-raising dinner at $25 a *plate.* **4** Household utensils covered or lined with a thin coating of silver or gold. **5** Metal in sheets. **6** A cup or other article of silver or gold offered as a prize in a contest. **7** A piece of flat metal bearing an engraved design or inscription. **8** An electrotype or stereotype, esp. a full-page illustration printed on special paper. **9** A horizontal timber for supporting a framework. **10** *Dent.* A device fitted to the mouth and holding one or more artificial teeth. **11** Armor made from metal plates. **12** A thin part of the brisket of beef. **13** A sensitized sheet of glass, metal, or the like, for taking photographs. **14** In baseball, the home base. **15** *Biol.* A platelike structure; a lamina or a lamella. **16** *Geol.* A section of the earth's crust that floats on the surface of the mantle. **17** A dish used in taking up collections, as in churches; also, such a collection. **18** A hinge. **19** The principal anode in an electron tube. —*v.t.* **plat·ed, plat·ing 1** To coat with a thin layer of gold, silver,

etc. **2** To cover or sheathe with metal plates for protection. **3** *Printing* To make an electrotype or stereotype plate from. [<Gk. *platys* broad, flat]

pla·teau (pla·tō') *n. pl.* **·teaus** or **·teaux** (-tōz') **1** A stretch of elevated and comparatively level land; tableland. **2** A period of relatively little change in circumstance. **3** A comparatively horizontal area of a graph indicating an unchanging variable. [<OF *platel* a flat piece of metal or wood]

plat·ed (plā'tid) *adj.* **1** Provided with plates of metal, as for defense. **2** Coated with a layer of silver, gold, etc.

plate·ful (plāt'fool') *n. pl.* **·fuls** The quantity that fills a plate.

plate glass Glass fabricated in heavy sheets.

plate·let (plāt'lit) *n.* **1** A small disk or flake. **2** Any of the minute, colorless disk-shaped particles found in blood and essential to clot formation. [Dim. of PLATE]

plat·en (plat'n) *n.* The part of a printing press or typewriter on which the paper is supported to receive the impression. [<OF *platine* a flat piece, metal plate]

plat·er (plā'tər) *n.* **1** One who plates articles with a layer of gold, silver, etc. **2** An inferior race horse.

plat·form (plat'fôrm) *n.* **1** Any floor or flat surface raised above the adjacent level, as a stage for public speaking. **2** An enclosed space at the end of a railroad car, etc. **3** A raised walk, usu. of wood, built parallel to the tracks at a railroad station. **4** A statement of principles or objectives put forth by a political party, etc. [<MF *plate* flat + *forme* form]

plat·ing (plā'ting) *n.* **1** A coating of metal of varying thickness: silver *plating.* **2** A sheathing of metal plates, or plate armor for protection. **3** The act or process of sheathing or coating something with plates or metal.

plat·i·nize (plat'ə·nīz) *v.t.* **·nized, ·niz·ing** To coat or combine with platinum.

plat·i·num (plat'ə·nəm) *n.* A heavy, whitish metallic element (symbol Pt) that is highly resistant to corrosion and fusion, and is widely used as a catalyst, for jewelry, etc. [<Sp. *plata* silver]

platinum blonde 1 A very light, almost white blonde hair color, esp. of a woman. **2** A woman whose hair is of this color.

plat·i·tude (plat'ə·tʸood) *n.* **1** A dull or commonplace statement; an obvious truism. **2** Dullness; triteness. [F, flatness] —**plat'i·tu'di·nous** *adj.* —**plat'i·tu'di·nous·ly** *adv.* — Syn. **2** banality, flatness, staleness.

plat·i·tu·di·nize (plat'ə·tʸood'ə·nīz) *v.i.* **·nized, ·niz·ing** To utter platitudes.

Pla·ton·ic (plə·ton'ik) *adj.* **1** Of, pertaining to Plato or Platonism. **2** Designating love (**Platonic love**) that is spiritual rather than sensual. Also **pla·ton'ic.** —**Pla·ton'i·cal·ly, pla·ton'i·cal·ly** *adv.*

Pla·to·nism (plā'tə·niz'əm) *n.* **1** The philosophy of Plato and his followers. **2** The doctrine or practice of Platonic love. —**Pla'to·nist** *n.*

pla·toon (plə·tōōn') *n.* **1** A subdivision of a company, troop, or other military unit consisting of two or more squads and commanded by a lieutenant. **2** Any similar company of people. **3** In football, a group of players specializing in either defense or offense and put into or taken from the game as a unit. —*v.t.* In baseball, etc., to use (one player) alternately with another at the same position. [< F *peloton* ball, group of men]

Platt·deutsch (plät'doich') *n.* The Low German vernacular of N Germany. [G]

plat·ter (plat'ər) *n.* **1** An oblong shallow dish for serving meat or fish. **2** *Informal* A phonograph record. [<AF *plat* dish]

plat·y·pus (plat'ə·pəs) *n. pl.* **·pus·es, ·pi** (-pī) A small, aquatic, egg-laying monotreme of Australia, with a ducklike bill and webbed forepaws. [<Gk. *platys* flat + *pous* foot]

plau·dit (plô'dit) *n. Usu. pl.* An expression of applause or praise. [<L *plaudere* applaud]

Platypus

plau·si·ble (plô'zə·bəl) *adj.* **1** Seeming likely to be true, but open to doubt. **2** Superficially endeavoring or calculated to gain trust: a *plausible* witness. [< L *plausibilis* deserving applause] —**plau·si·bil'·i·ty, plau·si·ble·ness** *n.* —**plau'si·bly** *adv.*

play (plā) *v.i.* 1 To engage in sport or diversion; amuse oneself. 2 To take part in a game or game of skill or chance; gamble. 3 To act in a way which is not to be taken seriously. 4 To act in a specified manner: to *play* false. 5 To deal carelessly or insincerely: with *with.* 6 To make love sportively. 7 To move quickly or irregularly: lights *playing* along a wall. 8 To discharge or be discharged freely or continuously: a fountain *playing* in the square. 9 To perform on a musical instrument. 10 To give forth musical sounds; sound. 11 To be performed: *Hamlet* is *playing* tonight. 12 To act on a stage; perform. —*v.t.* 13 To engage in (a game, etc.). 14 To imitate in play: to *play* cowboys. 15 To perform sportively: to *play* a trick. 16 To oppose in a game or contest. 17 To move or employ (a piece, card, etc.) in a game. 18 To employ (someone) in a game as a player. 19 To cause; bring about: to *play* hob. 20 To perform upon (a musical instrument). 21 To perform or produce, as a piece of music, a drama, etc. 22 To act the part of: to *play* the fool. 23 To perform in: to *play* Chicago. 24 To cause to move quickly or irregularly: to *play* lights over a surface. 25 To put into or maintain in action; ply. 26 In games of chance: **a** To bet. **b** To bet on. —**play at** 1 To take part in. 2 To do half-heartedly. —**play by ear** To play (a musical instrument or composition) without memorization of or reference to written music. —**play down** To minimize. —**play into the hands of** To act to the advantage of (a rival or opponent). —**play it by ear** *Informal* To handle a situation with no prior planning; improvise. —**play it cool** *Slang* To act unconcerned or nonchalant. —**play off** 1 To oppose against one another. 2 To decide (a tie) by playing one more game. —**play on** (or **upon**) 1 To exploit (another's hopes, emotions, etc.). 2 To continue: The band *played on.* —**play up** *Informal* To emphasize. —**play up to** *Informal* To curry favor. —*n.* 1 Activity for diversion, recreation, or sport. 2 A move or turn in a game. 3 The carrying on of a game or sport. 4 The manner of contending in a game: rough *play.* 5 Joking; humor; jest. 6 A dramatic composition; also, a dramatic performance. 7 Action: sword *play.* 8 Light, quick, fitful movement. 9 Freedom of movement. 10 Free motion of a machine part. 11 Active operation. 12 Gambling. —**make a play for** *Informal* To attempt to win or gain by artful means. [< OE *plegan*]

play·back (plā'bak') *n.* The reproduction of sound or pictures or both from a disk, tape, or film recording.

play·bill (plā'bil') *n.* 1 A poster advertising a play. 2 A program giving the cast, etc., of a play.

play·boy (plā'boi') *n. Informal* A man, usu. wealthy, whose main interest is the pursuit of pleasure.

play·er (plā'ər) *n.* 1 A participant or a specialist in a game or sport. 2 An actor or actress. 3 A performer on a musical instrument. 4 A gambler. 5 A mechanical device for playing a musical instrument, esp. a piano.

player piano A piano operated by machinery.

play·fel·low (plā'fel'ō) *n.* A playmate.

play·ful (plā'fəl) *adj.* 1 Lively and frolicsome. 2 Humorous; joking. —**play'ful·ly** *adv.* —**play'ful·ness** *n.*

play·go·er (plā'gō'ər) *n.* A frequenter of the theater.

play·ground (plā'ground') *n.* An outdoor place used esp. by children for play and often equipped for certain activities, as climbing, ball playing, etc.

play·house (plā'hous') *n.* 1 A theater. 2 A small house for children to play in.

playing card One of any of various decks of cards used in playing a number of games, esp. the pack divided into four suits (spades, hearts, diamonds, clubs) of 13 cards each.

play·mate (plā'māt') *n.* A companion in sports, games, or recreation.

play-off (plā'ôf', -of') *n.* In sports, a decisive game or contest, esp. after a tie.

play·thing (plā'thing') *n.* A thing to play with.

play·time (plā'tīm') *n.* Time allowed for or given up to play or amusement.

play·wright (plā'rīt') *n.* A writer of plays.

pla·za (plä'zə, plaz'ə) *n.* An open square or market place, esp. in a town. [Sp.]

plea (plē) *n.* 1 An act of pleading, or that which is pleaded; an appeal; entreaty. 2 An excuse; pretext or justification. 3 *Law* **a** An allegation made by either party in a cause. **b** In common-law practice, a defendant's answer of fact to the plaintiff's declaration. [< L *placere* seem right, please]

plea-bar·gain·ing (plē'bär'gən·ing) *n.* A process in which a defendant in a law case arranges, as with a district attorney, to plead guilty to a lesser charge in order to avoid standing trial for a more serious one and the risk of severer punishment.

plead (plēd) *v.* **plead·ed** (*Informal* or *Regional* **pled**), **plead·ing** *v.i.* 1 To make earnest entreaty; implore. 2 *Law* To advocate a case in court. **b** To file a pleading. —*v.t.* 3 To allege as an excuse or defense: to *plead* insanity. 4 *Law* To discuss or maintain (a case) by argument. [< OF *plaider*] —**plead'er** *n.* —**plead'ing·ly** *adv.* —**Syn.** 1 ask, beg, beseech, entreat, supplicate.

plead·ings (plē'dingz) *n.pl.* The formal written statements of the parties to a legal action, in which are set forth the allegations of the plaintiff and the answer of the defendant.

pleas·ant (plez'ənt) *adj.* 1 Giving or promoting pleasure; pleasing; agreeable. 2 Conducive to merriment; gay. [< L *placere* please] —**pleas'ant·ly** *adv.* —**pleas'ant·ness** *n.*

pleas·ant·ry (plez'ən·trē) *n. pl.* **·tries** 1 The spirit of playfulness in conversation. 2 A playful or good-natured remark; joke.

please (plēz) *v.* **pleased, pleas·ing** *v.t.* 1 To give pleasure to; gratify. 2 To be the wish or will of: May it *please* you. —*v.i.* 3 To give satisfaction or pleasure. 4 To have the will or preference; wish: Go when you *please.* [< L *placere* please]

pleas·ing (plē'zing) *adj.* Affording pleasure or satisfaction. —**pleas'ing·ly** *adv.* —**pleas'ing·ness** *n.*

pleas·ur·a·ble (plezh'ər·ə·bəl) *adj.* Affording gratification; pleasant. —**pleas'ur·a·ble·ness** *n.* —**pleas'ur·a·bly** *adv.*

pleas·ure (plezh'ər) *n.* 1 An agreeable sensation or emotion; enjoyment. 2 Sensual gratification. 3 Amusement in general; diversion. 4 One's preference; choice. [< OF *plaisir* please]

pleat (plēt) *n.* A fold of cloth doubled on itself and pressed or sewn in place. —*v.t.* To make a pleat or pleats in. [Var. of PLAIT] —**pleat'er** *n.*

plebe (plēb) *n.* A member of the lowest class in the U.S. Military Academy at West Point, the Naval Academy at Annapolis, or the Air Force Academy at Colorado Springs. [Short for PLEBEIAN]

ple·be·ian (pli·bē'ən) *n.* 1 One of the common people of ancient Rome. 2 One of the common people. 3 A vulgar, crude person —*adj.* 1 Pertaining to the common people. 2 Vulgar; crude. [< L] —**ple·be'ian·ism** *n.*

Pleated skirt

pleb·i·scite (pleb'ə·sīt, -sit) *n.* An expression of the popular will by means of a vote by the whole people, usu. resorted to in important changes, as those dealing with the constitution, sovereignty, etc. [< L *plebs* people + *scitum* decree] —**ple·bis·ci·tar·y** (plə·bis'ə·ter'ē), **pleb'i·scit'ic** *adj.*

plec·trum (plek'trəm) *n. pl.* **·trums** or **·tra** (-trə) A small implement with which the player of a guitar, banjo, etc. plucks the strings; pick. Also **plec'tron** (-tron). [< Gk. *plektron* spur]

pled (pled) *Informal or Regional p.t. & p.p.* of PLEAD.

pledge (plej) *v.t.* **pledged, pledg·ing** 1 To give or deposit as security for a loan, etc.; pawn. 2 To bind by or as by a pledge. 3 To promise solemnly, as assistance. 4 To offer (one's word, life, etc.) as a guaranty or forfeit. 5 To drink a toast to. 6 To promise to join (a fraternity). —*n.* 1 A guaranty for the performance of an act, contract or duty. 2 A solemn promise. 3 The drinking of a health or to good cheer. 4 A pawn of personal property. 5 One who has promised to join a fraternity 6 A token. —**take the**

add, āce, câre, pälm; end, ēven; it, īce; odd, ōpen, ôrder; tŏŏk, pōōl; up, bûrn; ə = *a* in *above*, *u* in *focus*; yŏŏ = *u* in *fuse*; oil; pout; check; go; ring; thin; this; zh, *vision*. < derived from; ? origin uncertain or unknown.

pledge To make a vow to abstain from alcoholic liquor. [< OF *plege* security] —**pledg′ee, pledg′er** *n.*

pledg·or (plej′ər) *n. Law* A person who formally deposits something as a pledge. Also **pledge′or.**

Plei·a·des (plē′ə·dēz, plī′-) *Gk. Myth.* The seven daughters of Atlas, who were set by Zeus among the stars. —*n. Astron.* A cluster of hundreds of stars in the constellation Taurus, six of which are visible to unaided sight.

Plei·o·cene (plī′ə·sēn) *adj. &* PLIOCENE. See GEOLOGY.

Pleis·to·cene (plīs′tə·sēn) *adj. & n.* See GEOLOGY. [< Gk. *pleistos* most + -CENE]

ple·na·ry (plē′nə·rē, plen′ə-) *adj.* 1 Full in all respects or requisites. 2 Fully attended by its qualified members: said of an assembly. [< L *plenus* full] —**ple′na·ri·ly** *adv.* —**ple′na·ri·ness** *n.*

plen·i·po·ten·ti·ar·y (plen′i·pə·ten′shē·er′ē, -shə·rē) *adj.* Possessing or conferring full powers. —*n. pl.* ·**ar·ies** A person, as an ambassador, minister, or envoy, invested with full powers by a government. [< L *plenus* full + *potens* powerful]

plen·i·tude (plen′ə·t^yōōd) *n.* The state of being full, complete, or abounding. [< L *plenus* full] —**plen·i·tud·i·nous** (plen′ə·t^yōō′də·nəs) *adj.*

plen·te·ous (plen′tē·əs) *adj.* 1 Characterized by plenty; amply sufficient. 2 Yielding an abundance. —**plen′te·ous·ly** *adv.* —**plen′te·ous·ness** *n.*

plen·ti·ful (plen′ti·fəl) *adj.* Existing in great quantity; abundant. —**plen′ti·ful·ly** *adv.* —**plen′ti·ful·ness** *n.* —**Syn.** abounding, ample, bounteous, copious, lavish, plenteous.

plen·ty (plen′tē) *n. pl.* ·**ties** 1 The state of having an abundance. 2 As much as can be required: *plenty* of water. —*adj.* Existing in abundance: plentiful. —*adv. Informal* In a sufficient degree: The house is *plenty* large. [< L *plenus* full]

ple·num (plē′nəm) *n. pl.* ·**nums** or ·**na** (-nə) 1 Space completely filled with matter. 2 A completely attended meeting, as of both houses of a legislature. [< L *plenus* full]

ple·o·nasm (plē′ə·naz′əm) *n.* 1 The use ˘of needless works; redundancy. 2 An unneeded word or phrase. [< Gk. *pleōn* more] —**ple′o·nast** *n.* —**ple′o·nas′tic** (-nas′tik) *adj.* —**ple′o·nas′ti·cal·ly** *adv.*

pleth·o·ra (pleth′ər·ə) *n.* A state of excessive fullness; superabundance. [< Gk. *plēthein* be full] —**ple·thor·ic** (ple·thôr′ik, -thor′-, pleth′ə·rik) *adj.*

pleu·ra (ploor′ə) *n. pl.* **pleu·rae** (ploor′ē) or ·**ras** A thin, slippery, double membrane that covers each lung and lines the chest cavity. [< Gk. *pleura* side] —**pleu′ral** *adj.*

pleu·ri·sy (ploor′ə·sē) *n.* Inflammation of the pleura, commonly attended with fever, pain in the chest, difficult breathing, etc. [< Gk. *pleura* side] —**pleu·rit·ic** (ploor·rit′ik) *adj.*

Plex·i·glas (plek′si·glas, -gläs) *n.* A thermoplastic synthetic resin used to make transparent objects: a trade name.

plex·us (plek′səs) *n. pl.* ·**us·es** or ·**us** 1 A network. 2 *Anat.* An interlacement of cordlike structures, as blood vessels or nerves. [L, braid]

pli·a·ble (plī′ə·bəl) *adj.* 1 Easily bent or twisted; flexible. 2 Easily persuaded or controlled. —**pli′a·bil′i·ty, pli′a·ble·ness** *n.* —**pli′a·bly** *adv.*

pli·ant (plī′ənt) *adj.* 1 Capable of being bent or twisted with ease. 2 Easily yielding to influence; tractable. [< OF *plier* to fold] —**pli′an·cy, pli′ant·ness** *n.* —**pli′ant·ly** *adv.* —**Syn.** 1 limber, lithe, pliable, supple. 2 adaptable, compliant.

pli·cate (plī′kāt) *adj.* Plaited; folded in plaits like a fan, as a leaf. Also **pli′cat·ed.** —**pli′cate·ly** *adv.* —**pli·ca′tion, plic·a·ture** (plik′ə·chŏŏr) *n.*

pli·ers (plī′ərz) *n.pl. (often construed as sing.)* Small pincers for bending, holding, or cutting. Also **pair of pliers.**

plight¹ (plīt) *n.* A condition, state, or case, usu. distressed or complicated. [< OF *pleit* a fold]

plight² (plīt) *n.* A solemn pledge or promise. —*v.t.* 1 To pledge (one's word, faith, etc.). 2 To promise, as in marriage;

betroth. —**plight one's troth** 1 To pledge one's solemn word. 2 To promise oneself in marriage. [< OE *pliht* peril] —**plight′er** *n.*

Plim·soll line (plim′sol) A mark painted on the outside of a British vessel's hull to show how deeply she may be loaded; load line. Also **Plimsoll mark.** [< Samuel *Plimsoll,* 1824–98, English legislator]

plinth (plinth) *n. Archit.* The slab, block, or stone on which a column, pedestal, or statue rests. [< Gk. *plinthos* a brick]

Pli·o·cene (plī′ə·sēn) *adj. & n.* See GEOLOGY. [< Gk. *pleiōn* more + -CENE]

plod (plod) *v.* **plod·ded, plod·ding** *v.i.* 1 To walk heavily; trudge. 2 To work in a steady, laborious manner; drudge. —*v.t.* 3 To walk along heavily or laboriously. —*n.* 1 The act of plodding. 2 A heavy step. 3 The sound of a heavy step, as of a horse. [Imit.] —**plod′der** *n.* —**plod′ding·ly** *adv.*

plonk (plonk) *n. & v.* PLUNK.

plop (plop) *v.t. & v.i.* **plopped, plop·ping** To drop with a sound like that of an object striking the water. —*n.* The act or sound of plopping. —*adv.* With the sound of plop. [Imit.]

plo·sive (plō′siv) *Phonet. adj.* Designating a speech sound produced by a total blockage of the breath stream followed by an explosive release, as (p) and (t) before vowels. —*n.* A consonant so produced. [< L *explodere* explode]

plot (plot) *n.* 1 A piece or patch of ground set apart. 2 **a** A chart or diagram, as of a building. **b** A surveyor's map. 3 A secret plan; conspiracy. 4 The series of incidents forming the plan of action of a novel, play, etc. —*v.* **plot·ted, plot·ting** *v.t.* 1 To make a map, chart, or plan of. 2 To plan for secretly; conspire. 3 To arrange the plot of (a novel, etc.). 4 To represent or position (something), as on a chart, map, or graph. —*v.i.* 5 To form a plot; conspire. [< OE] —**plot′ter** *n.*

plough (plou) *n. & v.* PLOW.

plov·er (pluv′ər, plō′vər) *n.* Any of various plump, round-headed shore birds with pigeonlike bills and pointed wings. [< AF]

plow (plou) *n.* 1 An implement for cutting, turning over, stirring, or breaking up the soil. 2 Any implement that operates like a plow: a *snowplow.* —*v.t.* 1 To turn up the surface of (land) with a plow. 2 To make or form (a furrow, ridge, etc.) by means of a plow. 3 To furrow or score the surface of. 4 To dig out or remove with a plow: with *up* or *out.* 5 To move or cut through (water): to *plow* the waves. —*v.i.* 6 To turn up soil with a plow. 7 To undergo plowing, as land. 8 To advance laboriously; plod. —**plow into** 1 To start work energetically. 2 To collide with. [< OE *plōh*] —**plow′er** *n.*

plow·man (plou′mən) *n. pl.* ·**men** (-mən) 1 One who plows. 2 A farm worker. Also **plough′man.**

plow·share (plou′shâr′) *n.* The cutting blade of a plow. Also **plough′share′.**

ploy (ploi) *n.* A stratagem, as an action or remark, intended to upset or to gain an advantage over someone. [< EMPLOY]

pluck (pluk) *v.t.* 1 To pull out or off; pick: to *pluck* a flower. 2 To pull with force; snatch: with *off, away,* etc. 3 To pull out the feathers, hair, etc., of. 4 To pull and release suddenly. 5 To cause the strings of (a musical instrument) to sound by such action. 6 *Slang* To rob; swindle. —*v.i.* 7 To give a sudden pull; tug: with *at.* —**pluck up** To rouse or summon (one's courage). —*n.* 1 Confidence and spirit in the face of difficulty or danger. 2 A sudden pull; twitch. 3 The act of plucking or state of being plucked. [< OE *pluccian*] —**pluck′er** *n.*

pluck·y (pluk′ē) *adj.* **pluck·i·er, pluck·i·est** Showing bravery; courageous. —**pluck′i·ly** *adv.* —**pluck′i·ness** *n.* —**Syn.** brave, fearless, undaunted, valiant.

plug (plug) *n.* 1 Anything, as a piece of wood or a cork, used to stop a hole. 2 A spark plug. 3 A fireplug. 4 *Electr.* A device for inserting in an outlet, etc., so as to complete a circuit or make contact. 5 A flat cake of pressed or twisted tobacco. 6 Any worn-out or useless thing, esp. an old horse. 7 *Slang* A man's high silk hat: also **plug hat.** 8 *Informal* Mention of a product, song, etc., as on a radio or television program; an advertisement. —*v.* **plugged, plug·ging** *v.t.* 1 To stop or close, as a hole, by inserting a plug:

Pliers
a. round-nose.
b. flat-nose.

often with *up*. 2 To insert as a plug. 3 *Slang* To shoot a bullet into. 4 *Slang* To advertise frequently or insistently. —*v.i.* 5 *Informal* To work doggedly; persevere. 6 To become stopped or closed: with *up*. —**plug in** To insert the plug of (a lamp, etc.) in an electric outlet. [< MDu. *plugge*]

plug·ug·ly (plug′ug′lē) *n. pl.* **-lies** *Slang* A ruffian.

plum (plum) *n.* 1 The edible, juicy, smooth-skinned fruit of any one of various trees. 2 The tree. 3 A raisin when used in cooking. 4 A choice piece or portion. 5 A desirable post or appointment. 6 A dividend higher than expected. 7 Any of various shades of dull reddish purple or purplish red. —*adj.* Dull reddish purple. [< LL *pruna*]

plum·age (plōō′mij) *n.* The feathers that cover a bird. [< F *plume* feather]

plumb (plum) *n.* 1 A weight hung on a line used to find the exact perpendicular: also **plumb bob**. 2 A nautical sounding lead, a sinker on a fishing line, etc. —**off** (or **out of**) **plumb** Not exactly vertical. —*adj.* 1 Vertical or perpendicular. 2 *Informal* Sheer; complete. —*adv.* 1 In a line perpendicular to the plane of the horizon. 2 *Informal* With exactness; correctly. —*v.t.* 1 To test with a plumb. 2 To make vertical; straighten. 3 To learn the facts about; solve. [< L *plumbum* lead]

Plumb

plumb·er (plum′ər) *n.* One whose work is plumbing.

plumb·ing (plum′ing) *n.* 1 The art or trade of installing and maintaining tanks, pipes, etc., as for water, gas and sewage. 2 A system of pipes, ducts, etc. 3 The act of sounding for depth, etc., with a plumb line.

plumb line A cord by which a plumb is suspended.

plume (plōōm) *n.* 1 A feather, esp. when long and ornamental. 2 A large feather, tuft of feathers, or flowing tuft of hair, worn as an ornament, esp. on a helmet. 3 Something that resembles this: a *plume* of smoke. 4 A prize. —*v.t.* **plumed**, **plum·ing** 1 To adorn, dress, or furnish with or as with plumes. 2 To smooth or dress (itself or its feathers); preen. —**plume oneself on** (or **upon**) To congratulate oneself on; be proud of. [< L *pluma* small soft feather]

plum·met (plum′it) *n.* PLUMB (def. 1). —*v.i.* To drop straight down; plunge. [< OF *plommet*, dim. of *plom* lead]

plu·mose (plōō′mōs) *adj.* Bearing or resembling feathers. [< L *pluma* feather] —**plu·mos·i·ty** (plōō·mos′ə·tē) *n.*

plump[1] (plump) *adj.* 1 Swelled out or enlarged. 2 Somewhat fat; pudgy. —*v.t.* & *v.i.* To make or become plump: often with *up* or *out*. [< MDu. *plomp*] —**plump′ness** *n.*

plump[2] (plump) *v.i.* 1 To fall suddenly or heavily. —*v.t.* 2 To drop or throw down heavily or all at once. —**plump for** 1 To give one's complete support to. 2 To vote for. —*n.* 1 The act of plumping or falling. 2 The sound made by the impact of a falling object. —*adj.* Blunt; downright. —*adv.* 1 With a sudden impact. 2 Straight down. 3 Directly; bluntly. [< MDu. *plompen*] —**plump′er** *n.* —**plump′ly** *adv.*

plum·y (plōō′mē) *adj.* **plum·i·er**, **plum·i·est** 1 Covered with feathers. 2 Adorned with plumes. 3 Feathery.

plun·der (plun′dər) *v.t.* 1 To rob of goods or property by open violence, as in war. 2 To despoil by robbery or fraud. 3 To take as plunder. —*v.i.* 4 To take plunder; steal. —*n.* 1 That which is taken by plundering; booty. 2 The act of plundering or robbing. 3 *Informal* Personal belongings or goods. 4 Political booty. [< G *plündern*] —**plun′der·age**, **plun′der·er** *n.* —**plun′der·ous** *adj.*

plunge (plunj) *v.* **plunged**, **plung·ing** *v.t.* 1 To thrust or force suddenly into a penetrable substance. 2 To force into some condition or state: to *plunge* a nation into debt. —*v.i.* 3 To dive, jump, or fall into a fluid, chasm, etc. 4 To move suddenly or with a rush. 5 To move violently forward and downward, as a horse or ship. 6 To descend abruptly or steeply. 7 *Informal* To gamble or speculate heavily and recklessly. —*n.* 1 The act of plunging. 2 A sudden and violent motion, as of a breaking wave. 3 An exceptionally heavy bet or speculation. —**take the** (**a**) **plunge** To begin an uncertain endeavor or enterprise. [< L *plumbum* lead]

plung·er (plun′jər) *n.* 1 One who or that which plunges.

2 A heavy or reckless speculator. 3 *Mech.* A part that has a plunging motion. 4 A cuplike device made of rubber and attached to a stick, used to open clogged drains.

plunk (plungk) *Informal v.t.* 1 To pluck, as a banjo or its strings; strum. 2 To place or throw heavily and suddenly: with *down*. —*v.i.* 3 To emit a twanging sound. 4 To fall heavily or suddenly; plump. —*n.* A heavy blow. [Imit.]

plu·per·fect (plōō·pûr′fikt) *adj.* & *n.* PAST PERFECT. [Short for L *plus quam perfectum* more than perfect]

plu·ral (plōōr′əl) *adj.* 1 Containing, consisting of, or designating more than one. 2 *Gram.* Denoting words or forms that indicate more than one. —*n. Gram.* 1 The plural number. 2 A plural form of a word. [< L *pluralis*, < *plus* more] —**plu′ral·ly** *adv.*

plu·ral·ism (plōōr′əl·iz·əm) *n.* 1 *Philos.* The doctrine that there is a plurality of ultimate substances, as spirit and matter. 2 The existence within a society of diverse groups, as in religion, race, or ethnic origin, which contribute to the cultural matrix of the society while retaining their distinctive characters; also, a doctrine advocating this. —**plu′ral·ist** *adj., n.* —**plu·ral·is·tic** (plōōr′əl·is′tik) *adj.*

plu·ral·i·ty (plōō·ral′ə·tē) *n. pl.* **-ties** 1 The state of being plural. 2 The greater number; majority. 3 In politics: **a** The excess of the highest number of votes cast for any one candidate over the next highest number. **b** In an election involving more than two candidates, the number of votes cast for any one that exceeds that for any of the others, but does not exceed half of the total number of votes cast.

plu·ral·ize (plōōr′əl·īz) *v.t.* **-ized**, **-iz·ing** 1 To make plural. 2 To express in the plural.

plus (plus) *prep.* 1 Added to or to be added to: Three *plus* two equals five. 2 Increased by: salary *plus* commission. —*adj.* 1 Being or indicating more than zero; positive. 2 Extra; supplemental: *plus* value. 3 *Informal* Denoting a value higher than ordinary in a specified grade: B *plus*. —*n. pl.* **plus·es** 1 The plus sign. 2 An addition; an extra quantity. 3 A positive quantity. 4 *Informal* Something considered advantageous or desirable. [L, more]

plus fours Knickers, cut very full and four inches longer below the knees than ordinary knickers.

plush (plush) *n.* A fabric having a pile deeper than that of velvet. —*adj.* 1 Of or made of plush. 2 *Slang* Luxurious: a *plush* apartment house. [< L *pilus* hair] —**plush′i·ness** *n.* —**plush′y** *adj.* (**·i·er**, **·i·est**)

plus sign The symbol (+) signifying addition or a positive quantity.

Plu·to (plōō′tō) *Gk. & Rom. Myth.* The god of the dead. —*n.* The planet of the solar system furthest from the sun. • See PLANET. —**Plu·to·ni·an** (plōō·tō′nē·ən), **Plu·ton′ic** *adj.*

plu·toc·ra·cy (plōō·tok′rə·sē) *n. pl.* **·cies** 1 A class that controls the government by its wealth. 2 Government by the wealthy. 3 A state or nation so governed. [< Gk *ploutos* wealth + *kratein* rule]

plu·to·crat (plōō′tə·krat) *n.* 1 One who exercises power by virtue of his wealth. 2 Any very wealthy person. —**plu′to·crat′ic** or **·i·cal** *adj.* —**plu′to·crat′i·cal·ly** *adv.*

plu·ton·ic (plōō·ton′ik) *adj. Geol.* Deeply subterranean in position or origin. [< PLUTO]

plu·to·ni·um (plōō·tō′nē·əm) *n.* A radioactive metallic element (symbol Pu), used as a nuclear fuel. [< PLUTO (the planet)]

plu·vi·al (plōō′vē·əl) *adj.* 1 Pertaining to rain; rainy. 2 Arising from the action of rain. [< L *pluvia* rain]

ply[1] (plī) *v.* **plied**, **ply·ing** *v.t.* To bend, mold, or shape. —*n. pl.* **plies** 1 A web, layer, fold, or thickness, as in a cloth, etc. 2 A strand, turn, or twist of rope, yarn, thread, etc. 3 A bent or bias; inclination. —*adj.* Having a specified number (of) strands, etc.: used in combination: *two-ply*. [< L *plicare* to fold]

ply[2] (plī) *v.* **plied**, **ply·ing** *v.t.* 1 To use in working, fighting, etc. 2 To work at: to *ply* a trade. 3 To work steadily, as with a tool. 4 To keep furnishing: to *ply* a child with sweets. 5 To ask urgently; importune: to *ply* a witness with questions. 6 To strike persistently. 7 To traverse regularly: ferryboats that *ply* the river. —*v.i.* 8 To work steadily; be occupied. **9** To make regular trips: usu. with *between*. [< APPLY] —**ply′er** *n.* —**Syn. 1** employ, wield. **2** follow, practice. **5** urge.

Plym·outh Rock (plim′əth) **1** The rock at Plymouth, Massachusetts, on which the Pilgrim Fathers are said to have landed in 1620. **2** One of a breed of large domestic fowls.

ply·wood (plī′wŏŏd′) *n.* A material composed of a number of thin sheets of wood glued together with the grains of adjacent sheets at right angles.

PM, P.M. Postmaster; Provost Marshal.

P.M. Pacific Mail; Past Master; Paymaster; Police Magistrate; Prime Minister.

P.M., p.m. afternoon (L *post meridiem*); after death (L *post mortem*).

Pm prometheum.

pneu·mat·ic (nyŏŏ·mat′ik) *adj.* **1** Describing machines that make use of compressed air. **2** Containing air or gas. **3** Pertaining to pneumatics. Also **pneu·mat′i·cal.** —*n.* A tire containing air. [< Gk. *pneuma* breath] —**pneu·mat′i·cal·ly** *adv.*

pneu·ma·tics (nyŏŏ·mat′iks) *n.pl.* (*construed as sing.*) The branch of physics that deals with the properties, such as pressure, elasticity, and density, of air and other gases.

pneumo- *combining form* Lung; relating to the lungs: *pneumothorax.* Also **pneum-.** [< Gk. *pneumon* lung]

pneu·mo·coc·cus (nyŏŏ′mə·kok′əs) *n. pl.* **·coc·ci** (-kok′sī) Any of a group of bacteria that cause a common type of pneumonia and some other diseases. [< Gk. *pneuma* breath + COCCUS] —**pneu′mo·coc′cal, pneu′mo·coc′cic** (-kok′sik) **pneu′mo·coc′cous** *adj.*

pneu·mo·con·i·o·sis (nyŏŏ′mō·kon′ē·ō′sis) *n.* Any of various lung disorders, such as silicosis or black lung disease, resulting from the inhalation of dust or other minute particles. Also **pneu′mo·no·con′i·o·sis** (nyŏŏ′mə·nō-). [< Gk. *pneuma* breath + *konia* dust + -OSIS]

pneu·mon·ia (nyŏŏ·mōn′yə) *n.* Acute inflammation of the lungs characterized by accumulation of fluid in the alveoli and difficult breathing. [< Gk. *pneumōn* lung] —**pneu·mon·ic** (nyŏŏ·mon′ik) *adj.*

pneu·mo·tho·rax (nyŏŏ′mō·thôr′aks, -thō′raks) *n.* An accumulation of air or gas within the pleural cavity, causing the lung to collapse, as from injury or disease, or by injection (**artificial pneumothorax**) in the treatment of tuberculosis. [< PNEUMO- + THORAX]

P.O., p.o. personnel officer; petty officer; postal order; post office.

Po polonium.

poach[1] (pōch) *v.t.* To cook (eggs without their shells, fish, etc.) in boiling water, milk, or other liquid. [< OF *pochier* put in a pocket]

poach[2] (pōch) *v.i.* **1** To trespass on another's property, etc., esp. for the purpose of taking game or fish. **2** To take game or fish unlawfully. **3** To become soft and muddy by being trampled: said of land. —*v.t.* **4** To trespass on. **5** To take (game or fish) unlawfully. **6** To make muddy by trampling. [< OF *pochier* thrust one's fingers into] —**poach′er** *n.*

pock (pok) *n.* **1** A pustule in an eruptive disease, as in smallpox. **2** A pockmark. [< OE *poc*]

pock·et (pok′it) *n.* **1** A small bag or pouch; esp. one stitched to a garment. **2** A cavity, opening, or receptacle. **3** *Mining* **a** A cavity containing gold or other ore. **b** A small deposit of ore in one spot. **4** One of the pouches in a billiard or pool table. **5** An air pocket. —**in one's pocket** Under one's influence or control. —**line one's pockets** To acquire a lot of money. —*adj.* **1** Small enough to fit into a pocket. **2** Pertaining to, for, or carried in a pocket. —*v.t.* **1** To put into or confine in a pocket. **2** To appropriate as one's own, esp. dishonestly. **3** To enclose as if in a pocket. **4** To accept or endure, as an insult. **5** To conceal or suppress: *Pocket* your pride. [< OF *poque, poche* bag, pouch] —**pock′et·er** *n.* —**Syn.** *v.* **2** embezzle, purloin, steal, take. **5** hide, swallow.

pock·et·book (pok′it·bŏŏk′) *n.* **1** A woman's purse or handbag. **2** A notebook for the pocket. **3** One's financial resources.

pock·et·ful (pok′it·fŏŏl′) *n. pl.* **·fuls** As much as a pocket will hold.

pock·et·knife (pok′it·nīf′) *n. pl.* **·knives** (-nīvz) A knife having one or more blades, tools, etc., which fold into the handle.

pocket money Money for small expenses.

pocket veto In the U.S., the act of a chief executive who does not sign a bill passed by Congress within ten days of the latter's adjournment and thus simply retains ("pockets") it and achieves an indirect veto.

Pocketknife

pock·mark (pok′märk′) *n.* A pit or scar left on the skin by smallpox or similar diseases. —**pock′marked′** *adj.*

po·co (pō′kō) *adv. Music* Slightly. [Ital.]

pod (pod) *n.* **1** A dehiscent seed vessel containing one or more seeds. **2** A housing for an aircraft part that is mounted outboard. —*v.i.* **pod·ded, pod·ding 1** To fill out like a pod. **2** To produce pods. [?]

podg·y (poj′ē) *adj.* **podg·i·er, podg·i·est** Dumpy and fat. [Var. of PUDGY] —**podg′i·ness** *n.*

po·di·a·try (pə·dī′ə·trē, pō-) *n.* The branch of medicine concerned with disorders of the feet. [< Gk. *pous, podos* foot + *iatros* healer] —**po·di′a·trist** *n.*

po·di·um (pō′dē·əm) *n. pl.* **·di·ums** or **·di·a** (-dē-ə) **1** A raised platform, esp. one for the conductor of an orchestra. **2** *Zool.* A foot, or any footlike structure. [< Gk. *podion,* dim. of *pous, podos* foot]

Po·dunk (pō′dungk) *n. Informal* Any small town regarded as dull and nonprogressive. [?< *Podunk,* Massachusetts]

po·em (pō′əm) *n.* **1** A composition in verse, either in meter or in free verse, characterized by the imaginative treatment of experience, usu. by the use of language more intensive than ordinary speech, and typically presented with the initial letter of each line capitalized. **2** Any composition in verse. **3** Any composition characterized by beauty of language or thought: a prose *poem.* **4** Any beautiful object or experience. [< Gk. *poiēma,* lit., anything made]

po·e·sy (pō′ə·sē, -zē) *n. pl.* **·sies 1** *Archaic* Poetry taken collectively. **2** *Obs.* A poem. [< Gk. *poiēsis* a making]

po·et (pō′it) *n.* **1** One who writes poems. **2** One esp. endowed with imagination and creativity. [< Gk. *poiētēs*]

po·et·as·ter (pō′it·as′tər) *n.* An inferior poet. [< POET + -ASTER]

po·et·ic (pō·et′ik) *adj.* **1** Of or pertaining to poets or poems. **2** Characteristic of or suitable for poetry: *poetic* language. **3** Highly imaginative: a *poetic* nature. **4** Made up of poems. Also **po·et′i·cal.** —**po·et′i·cal·ly** *adv.*

poetic justice An outcome in which a person receives what he deserves in a way that is often ironically appropriate.

po·et·ics (pō·et′iks) *n.pl.* (*construed as sing.*) **1** The principles and nature of poetry. **2** A treatise on poetry.

poet laureate *pl.* **poets laureate 1** The poet officially invested with the title of laureate by the crown of England. **2** A poet acclaimed as the most eminent of a group, in a locality, etc.

po·et·ry (pō′ə·trē, pō′it·rē) *n.* **1** The writings of a poet; poems. **2** The art of writing poems. **3** Anything resembling poetry in spirit or feeling: Dancing is the *poetry* of motion. **4** Poetic works in general.

po·gey (pō′gē) *n. Can. Slang* **1** Money, food, clothing, and other forms of relief given by the government to people in need. **2** An office providing such relief. —**on the pogey** On relief. Also **po′gy.** [?]

po·go stick (pō′gō) A stiltlike toy with a spring at the base, used to propel oneself in a series of hops.

po·grom (pō′grəm, pō·grom′) *n.* An officially instigated massacre, esp. one directed against Jews. [Russ., destruction]

poi (poi, pō′ē) *n.* A native Hawaiian food made from the ground root of the taro.

poign·ant (poin′yənt, poi′nənt) *adj.* **1** Severely painful or acute to the feelings: *poignant* grief. **2** Keenly piercing: *poignant wit.* **3** Sharp or stimulating to the taste; pungent. [< L *pungere* to prick] —**poign′an·cy** *n.* —**poign′ant·ly** *adv.* —**Syn. 1** agonizing, excruciating, piercing, sharp.

poi·lu (pwa·lü′) *adj.* Hairy; bearded. —*n.* In World War I, a French soldier. [F]

poin·ci·a·na (poin′sē·ā′nə, -an′ə) *n.* A tropical tree with bright orange and scarlet flowers and large flat pods. [< M. de *Poinci*, a 17th c. governor of French West Indies]

poin·set·ti·a (poin·set′ē·ə) *n.* A shrub of varying size with small yellow flowers surrounded by large vermilion bracts. [< J. R. *Poinsett*, 1779–1851, U.S. diplomat]

Poinsettia

point (point) *n.* **1** The sharp end of a thing, esp. of anything that tapers. **2** A tool or instrument having a sharp, tapering end. **3** A tapering tract of land extending into water. **4** A distinguishing attribute: Her smile is her best *point*. **5** A physical attribute of an animal, used in judging. **6** The main idea under consideration: the *point* of a story. **7** A particular place or position. **8** A position considered as one of a series: to gain a *point*. **9** A precise degree or grade attained, as in a game. **10** A particular juncture in the course of events: at one *point* during the day. **11** A detail or step: Let us go over this *point* by *point*. **12** Purpose; object: There's no *point* in waiting. **13** For students, a unit of credit. **14** The moment when something is about to take place: He is on the *point* of leaving. **15** NEEDLEPOINT (def. 3). **16** A punctuation mark, esp. a period. **17** *Phonet.* A diacritical mark used to indicate a vowel in a Semitic language. **18** A decimal point. **19** A geometric entity having position as its only inherent property. **20** The attitude assumed by a hunting dog when it finds game. **21** In fencing, a thrust. **22** *Printing* A unit measure for type, about 1/72 in.: 8-*point* type. **23** One of the 32 divisions of a compass card. **24** A unit of variation in the price of shares, stocks, etc. **25** A fixed place from which distance is reckoned. **26** *Electr.* Any of a set of contacts controlling current flow in a circuit. **27** *Brit.* (*Usu. pl.*) A tapering section of a railroad track switch. —**at** (or **on**) **the point of** On the verge of. —**beside the point** Irrelevant. —**in point** Pertinent. —**in point of** In the matter of; as regards. —**make a point of** To treat as vital or essential. —**see the point** To understand the meaning of a story, joke, etc. —**to the point** Relevant. —*v.t.* **1** To direct or aim, as a finger or weapon. **2** To give force or point to, as a meaning or remark. **3** To shape or sharpen to a point. **4** To punctuate. **5** To mark with points, as decimal fractions: with *off.* **6** In hunting, to indicate the presence of (game) by standing rigid: said of dogs. —*v.i.* **7** To call attention or indicate direction by extending the finger: usu. with *at* or *to*. **8** To have a specified direction: with *to* or *toward*. **9** To point game. —**point out** To call attention to. [< L *punctus*, pp. of *pungere* to prick]

point-blank (point′blangk′) *adj.* **1** Aimed directly at the mark. **2** Direct; plain: a *pointblank* question. —*n.* A shot with direct aim. —*adv.* **1** In a horizontal line. **2** Directly; plainly: to object *pointblank*.

point·ed (poin′tid) *adj.* **1** Having or coming to a point. **2** Being to the point; apt; acute. **3** Intended for a particular person or group: a *pointed* remark. —**point′ed·ly** *adv.* —**point′ed·ness** *n.*

point·er (poin′tər) *n.* **1** One who or that which points. **2** An index or hand, as on a clock or scale. **3** A long tapering rod used in classrooms to point out things on wall maps, etc. **4** One of a breed of dogs trained to scent and point out game. **5** A useful suggestion or bit of information.

point lace Lace made entirely with a needle.

point·less (point′lis) *adj.* **1** Without a point; blunt. **2** Having no significance or force: a *pointless* remark. —**point′less·ly** *adv.* —**point′less·ness** *n.* —**Syn.** **1** dull. **2** inane, insipid, silly, stupid.

point of honor Something that vitally affects one's honor.

point of order In parliamentary language, a question of procedure under the rules.

point of view **1** The position from which something is evaluated, considered, etc. **2** An attitude or opinion.

poise (poiz) *v.* **poised**, **pois·ing** *v.t.* **1** To bring into or hold

in balance. **2** To hold; support, as in readiness. —*v.i.* **3** To be balanced or suspended; hover. —*n.* **1** Balance; equilibrium. **2** Equanimity and dignity of manner; composure. **3** Suspense; indecision. [< L *pensare*, intens. of *pendere* weigh]

poi·son (poi′zən) *n.* **1** A substance that produces illness or death if swallowed, inhaled, or otherwise introduced into a living organism. **2** Anything that tends to destroy or corrupt. —*v.t.* **1** To kill or injure with poison. **2** To put poison into or on. **3** To affect harmfully. —*adj.* Killing; venomous. [< L *potio* a drink, poisonous draft] —**poi′son·er** *n.*

poison ivy A small shrub or vine of North America having three leaflets and small, green flowers and causing a skin rash on contact.

poison oak **1** A low, nonclimbing shrub related to poison ivy and having similar effects. **2** POISON IVY.

poi·son·ous (poi′zən·əs) *adj.* **1** Containing a poison. **2** Having the effect of a poison; toxic. —**poi′son·ous·ly** *adv.* —**poi′son·ous·ness** *n.*

poison sumac A tall shrub of E North America, related to poison ivy and poisonous to taste or touch.

poke[1] (pōk) *v.* **poked**, **pok·ing** *v.t.* **1** To push or prod. **2** To make by thrusting: to *poke* a hole. **3** To thrust in, out, through, from, etc.: to *poke* one's head from a window. **4** To stir (a fire, etc.) —*v.i.* **5** To make thrusts. **6** To intrude or meddle. **7** To look curiously; pry. **8** To proceed slowly; dawdle; putter. —**poke one's nose into** To meddle in. —**poke fun at** To ridicule. —*n.* **1** A push; prod. **2** One who dawdles. **3** *Informal* A punch. [ME *poken*]

poke[2] (pōk) *n. Regional* **1** A pocket. **2** A small bag or sack. [< OF *poche* pocket]

poke[3] (pōk) *n.* A large bonnet with projecting front. Also **poke bonnet**. [< POKE[1]]

poke·ber·ry (pōk′ber′ē) *n. pl.* **·ries** **1** A berry of the pokeweed. **2** The plant. [< Algon.]

pok·er[1] (pō′kər) *n.* **1** One who or that which pokes. **2** An iron rod for poking a fire.

pok·er[2] (pō′kər) *n.* Any of several games of cards in which the players bet on the value of the cards dealt to them. [?]

poker face *Informal* A face that reveals no thoughts or feelings. [From the inscrutable face maintained by poker players] —**po·ker-faced** (pō′kər·fāst′) *adj.*

poke·weed (pōk′wēd′) *n.* A stout perennial herb of North America having dark purple berries and poisonous roots. Also **poke**, **poke′root′** (-rŏŏt′, -rŏŏt′). [< Algon.]

pok·y (pō′kē) *adj.* **pok·i·er**, **pok·i·est** **1** Lacking spirit. **2** Shabby. **3** Cramped; stuffy. Also **poke′y**.

pol (pol) *n. Slang* A politician.

Pol. Poland; Polish.

Po·land (pō′lənd) *n.* A republic of CEN. Europe, 120,359 square miles, cap. Warsaw.

po·lar (pō′lər) *adj.* **1** Of, pertaining to, coming from or found near the North or South Pole. **2** Of, pertaining to, or proceeding from a pole or poles, as of a sphere, magnet, etc. **3** Exhibiting polarity. **4** Opposite, as in character, direction, etc. [< L *polus* pole]

polar bear A large, white bear of Arctic coasts and ice floes.

Po·lar·is (pō·lar′is) *n.* **1** The star in the northern sky that is in line with the earth's axis and hence appears to maintain a fixed position as the earth rotates. **2** A U.S. missile designed to be launched from a submerged submarine. [L]

po·lar·i·ty (pō·lar′ə·tē) *n.* **1** The quality or property of having paired but opposed tendencies, as positive and negative. **2** Either of such an opposed pair: a negative *polarity*. **3** *Physics* The property of a body that exhibits a preferred alignment with respect to a field of force.

---

add, āce, câre, pälm; end, ēven; it, īce; odd, ōpen, ôrder; tŏŏk, pōōl; up, bûrn; ə = a in *above*, u in *focus*; yŏŏ = u in *fuse*; oil; pout; check; go; ring; thin; this; zh, *vision*. < derived from; ? origin uncertain or unknown.

po·lar·i·za·tion (pō′lər·ə·zā′shən, -ī·zā′-) *n.* 1 The act of polarizing or the property of being polarized. 2 *Physics* A condition of radiation, esp. light or other electromagnetic radiation, in which the direction of any field or disturbance associated with the radiation and transverse to its direction of propagation is not random. 3 *Electr.* A change in the potential of the electrode of a cell due to the accumulation of reaction products. 4 A separation into opposing factions.

po·lar·ize (pō′lə·rīz) *v.* ·ized, ·iz·ing *v.t.* 1 To cause to acquire polarization or polarity. 2 To separate into opposing factions. —*v.i.* 3 To become polarized. *Brit. sp.* **po′lar·ise.** —**po′lar·iz′er** *n.*

pole[1] (pōl) *n.* 1 Either of the points in which a diameter of a sphere intersects the surface. 2 One of two points where the axis of rotation, as of the earth, meets the surface. 3 *Physics* One of the two points at which opposite physical qualities are concentrated; esp. a point of maximum electric or magnetic force. 4 Either of the ends of any axis. [< Gk. *polos* pivot, pole]

pole[2] (pōl) *n.* 1 A long slender piece of wood or metal: a *flagpole.* 2 In linear and surface measure, a rod or a square rod. —*v.* **poled, pol·ing** *v.t.* To propel, as a boat, with a pole. [< L *palus* stake]

Pole (pōl) *n.* A citizen or native of Poland.

pole·ax (pōl′aks′) *n.* A medieval battleaxe. —*v.t.* To strike or fell with a poleax. Also **pole′axe′.** [< ME *pol* head + AX]

pole·cat (pōl′kat′) *n.* 1 A small, weasellike European carnivore. 2 A skunk. [< F *poule* pullet + CAT]

po·lem·ic (pō·lem′ik) *adj.* Pertaining to controversy. Also **po·lem′i·cal.** —*n.* 1 A controversy. 2 One who engages in controversy. [< Gk. *polemos* war] —**Syn.** *adj.* disputatious. *n.* 1 argument, debate, dispute.

po·lem·ics (pō·lem′iks) *n.pl. (construed as sing.)* 1 The use of aggressive argument to refute errors of doctrine, esp. in theology. 2 A controversy.

pole·star (pōl′stär) *n.* 1 POLARIS. 2 That which governs, guides, or directs.

pole vault A vault for height in which a long, flexible pole is used to help propel one over a crossbar, often a competitive field event. —**pole′-vault′** *v.t. & v.i.* —**pole′-vault′er** *n.*

po·lice (pə·lēs′) *n.* 1 A body of persons organized to maintain order and enforce law. 2 The whole system of the department of government that maintains and enforces law and order. 3 The regulation of safety, conduct, and public order in a community. 4 The keeping clean of a camp or garrison. —*v.t.* ·liced, ·lic·ing 1 To protect, regulate, or maintain order with or as with police. 2 To make clean or orderly, as a military camp. [< Gk. *politeia* polity]

police dog 1 GERMAN SHEPHERD. 2 Any dog trained to assist policemen.

po·lice·man (pə·lēs′mən) *n. pl.* ·men (-mən) A member of a police force. —**po·lice′wom·an** (*pl.* ·wom·en) *n. Fem.*

police state A country rigidly supervised by a national police, often working secretly.

pol·i·cy[1] (pol′ə·sē) *n. pl.* ·cies 1 Prudence or sagacity in the conduct of affairs. 2 A course of administrative action. 3 Any system of management. [< Gk. *politeia*]

pol·i·cy[2] (pol′ə·sē) *n. pl.* ·cies A written contract of insurance. [< Ital. *polizza*]

policy game NUMBERS POOL. Also **policy racket.**

pol·i·cy·hol·der (pol′ə·sē·hōl′dər) *n.* One who holds a policy of insurance.

pol·i·cy·mak·er (pol′ə·sē·mā′kər) *n.* A person who makes decisions and controls policy at a high level, esp. in a government. —**pol′i·cy·mak′ing** *n.*

po·li·o (pō′lē·ō) *n. Informal* POLIOMYELITIS.

pol·i·o·my·e·li·tis (pol′ē·ō·mī′ə·lī′tis, pō′lē-) *n.* An acute viral disease affecting the central nervous system and often followed by paralysis and atrophy of muscles. [< Gk. *polios* gray + *myelos* marrow + -ITIS]

pol·ish (pol′ish) *n.* 1 Smoothness or glossiness of surface. 2 A substance used to produce such a surface. 3 Refinement of manner or style. 4 The process of polishing. —*v.t.* 1 To make smooth or lustrous. 2 To make refined or elegant. —*v.i.* 3 To take a gloss; shine. 4 To become elegant

or refined. —**polish off** *Informal* 1 To do or finish quickly. 2 To dispose of. —**polish up** *Informal* To improve. [< L *polire* make smooth] —**pol′ish·er** *n.*

Po·lish (pō′lish) *n.* The language of Poland. —*adj.* Of or pertaining to Poland, its people, or their language.

Po·lit·bu·ro (po′lit·byoor′ō) *n.* The leading policy-forming committee of the Communist party in the U.S.S.R. until 1952, when it was replaced by the Presidium.

po·lite (pə·līt′) *adj.* 1 Exhibiting in manner or speech a considerate regard for others; courteous. 2 Elegant; refined: *polite* society. [< L *politus,* pp. of *polire* to polish] —**po·lite′ly** *adv.* —**po·lite′ness** *n.* —**Syn.** 1 civil, courtly, gracious, well-mannered. 2 cultivated, genteel, polished.

po·li·tesse (pô·lē·tes′) *n.* Politeness; civility. [F]

pol·i·tic (pol′ə·tik) *adj.* 1 Sagacious and wary in planning; artful. 2 Wisely expedient. 3 Pertaining to the state or its government; political. [< Gk. *politikos* civic] —**pol′i·tic·ly** *adv.*

po·lit·i·cal (pə·lit′i·kəl) *adj.* 1 Concerned in the administration of government. 2 Belonging to the science of government. 3 Having an organized system of government. 4 Pertaining to or connected with a party or parties seeking to control government. —**po·lit′i·cal·ly** *adv.*

political science The science of the form and principles of government.

pol·i·ti·cian (pol′ə·tish′ən) *n.* 1 One engaged in politics. 2 One who engages in politics for personal or partisan aims. 3 *Brit.* One skilled in the science of government; a statesman. 4 One holding a political position.

po·lit·i·cize (pə·lit′ə·sīz′) *v.t.* ·cized, ·ciz·ing 1 To make politically active or aware. 2 To make into a political issue. Also **po·lit′i·cal·ize** (-kəl·īz′). —**po·lit′i·ci·za′tion** *n.*

pol·i·tick·ing (pol′ə·tik·ing) *n.* Involvement in political activity. —**pol′i·tick·er** *n.*

po·lit·i·co (pə·lit′i·kō) *n. pl.* ·cos A politician. [< Sp. *político*]

pol·i·tics (pol′ə·tiks) *n. (construed as sing. or pl.)* 1 The science of government. 2 The administration of political affairs. 3 Political sentiments or beliefs. 4 Political methods or procedures. 5 Participation in political affairs. —**play politics** To scheme for an advantage.

pol·i·ty (pol′ə·tē) *n. pl.* ·ties 1 The form or method of government of a nation, state, etc. 2 Any community living under some definite form of government. [< OF *politie*]

pol·ka (pōl′kə, pō′-) *n.* 1 A lively round dance. 2 Music for such a dance. —*v.i.* ·kaed, ·ka·ing To dance the polka. [< Czech *pulka* half (step)]

polka dot 1 One of a series of spots of various sizes and spacing on a textile fabric. 2 A pattern made up of such spots. —**pol′ka-dot′, -dot′ted** *adj.*

poll (pōl) *n.* 1 The head, esp. the top or back of the head. 2 A list of persons, esp. voters. 3 The voting at an election. 4 The number of votes thus cast. 5 *pl.* The place where voting is done and votes are counted. 6 A survey of public opinion on a given subject. —*v.t.* 1 To receive (a specified number of votes). 2 To register for taxation or voting. 3 To cast at the polls. 4 To interview in a poll. 5 To cut off or trim, as hair, horns, etc. —*v.i.* 6 To vote at the polls. [< MDu. *polle* top of the head] —**poll′er** *n.*

pol·len (pol′ən) *n.* The fine yellowish powder borne by the anthers of a flower and consisting of male sex cells. [< L, fine flour]

pol·li·nate (pol′ə·nāt) *v.t.* ·nat·ed, ·nat·ing To transfer pollen from an anther to a stigma of (a flower). Also **pol′len·ate.** —**pol′li·na′tion** *n.*

pol·li·wog (pol′ē·wog) *n.* TADPOLE. Also **pol′ly·wog.** [ME *polwygle*]

poll·ster (pōl′stər) *n.* One who takes public opinion polls. Also **poll′ist.**

poll tax A tax on a person, as distinguished from that on property, esp. as a prerequisite for voting.

pol·lut·ant (pə·loo′tənt) *n.* Something that pollutes, esp. a harmful chemical or waste substance introduced into the air, water, or soil.

pol·lute (pə·loot′) *v.t.* ·lut·ed, ·lut·ing 1 To make unclean or impure, as by introducing wastes: fumes *polluting* the air. 2 To desecrate; profane. [< L *polluere* make unclean] —**pol·lut′ed·ly** *adv.* —**pol·lut′ed·ness, pol·lut′er, pol·lu′tion** *n.* —**Syn.** 1 contaminate, foul, befoul. 2 defile.

Pol·lux (pol′əks) *Gk. Myth.* One of the twin sons of Zeus and Leda. —*n. Astron.* One of the two brightest stars in the constellation Gemini.

Pol·ly·an·na (pol′ē·an′ə) *n.* An overly zealous optimist. [< *Polyanna*, heroine of a novel, *Polyanna*, by Eleanor H. Porter, 1868–1920]

po·lo (pō′lō) *n.* A game played on horseback, usu. with a light wooden ball and long-handled mallets. [< Tibetan *pulu* ball] —**po′lo·ist** *n.*

pol·o·naise (pol′ə·nāz′, pō′lə-) *n.* 1 A stately, marchlike Polish dance. 2 The music for this dance. [F]

po·lo·ni·um (pə·lō′nē·əm) *n.* A radioactive element (symbol Po), present in uranium minerals as a disintegration product of radium. [< Med. L *Polonia* Poland]

pol·troon (pol·trōōn′) *n.* A mean-spirited coward. [< Ital. *poltrone* cowardly] —**pol·troon′er·y** *n.*

poly- *combining form* 1 Many; several: *polygamy*. 2 Polymerized, or a polymer of: *polyester*. [< Gk. *polys* much, many]

pol·y·an·dry (pol′ē·an′drē) *n.* The condition of having more than one husband at the same time. [< POLY- + Gk. *anēr, andros* a man] —**pol′y·an′drous** *adj.*

pol·y·an·thus (pol′ē·an′thəs) *n. pl.* **·an·thus·es** or **·an·thi** (-an′thī) 1 A hybrid variety of primrose. 2 A narcissus with clusters of small, fragrant flowers. [< POLY- + Gk. *anthos* flower]

pol·y·clin·ic (pol′i·klin′ik) *n.* A hospital or clinic for treating diverse diseases.

pol·y·es·ter (pol′ē·es′tər) *n.* Any of various polymerized esters of high tensile strength, used esp. in making **polyester fiber** for synthetic fabrics.

pol·y·eth·y·lene (pol′ē·eth′ə·lēn) *n.* A thermoplastic resin made by polymerizing ethylene, used widely to make moisture-proof film, containers, insulators, etc.

po·lyg·a·my (pə·lig′ə·mē) *n.* The condition of having more than one wife or husband at the same time. [< POLY- + Gk. *gamos* marriage] —**po·lyg′a·mist** *n.* —**po·lyg′a·mous** *adj.* —**po·lyg′a·mous·ly** *adv.*

pol·y·glot (pol′i·glot) *adj.* 1 Expressed in several tongues. 2 Speaking several languages. —*n.* A person or book that is polyglot. [< Gk. *polyglōttos*] —**pol·y·glot′tal, pol·y·glot′tic** *adj.*

pol·y·gon (pol′i·gon) *n.* A closed plane figure bounded by straight lines. —**po·lyg·o·nal** (pə·lig′ə·nəl), **po·lyg′o·nous** *adj.* —**po·lyg′o·nal·ly** *adv.*

pol·y·graph (pol′i·graf, -gräf) *n.* An instrument for the simultaneous recording of various physiological reactions that are influenced by emotion, as pulse, breathing, perspiration, etc. —**pol′y·graph′ic** or **·i·cal** *adj.*

Polygon

po·lyg·y·ny (pə·lij′ə·nē) *n.* The marriage or cohabitation of one male with more than one female. [< POLY- + Gk. *gynē* woman]

pol·y·he·dron (pol′i·hē′drən) *n. pl.* **·dra** (-drə) or **·drons** *Geom.* A solid bounded by plane faces. —**pol′y·he′dral** *adj.*

Pol·y·hym·ni·a (pol′i·him′nē·ə) *Gk. Myth.* The Muse of sacred song. Also **Po·lym·ni·a** (pə·lim′nē·ə).

pol·y·math (pol′i·math) *n.* One who is learned in many different fields or disciplines. [< POLY- + Gk. *mathanein* learn] —**pol′y·math′ic** *adj.*

pol·y·mer (pol′i·mər) *n.* 1 Any compound formed by polymerization. 2 Any of a pair or group of polymeric compounds. [< POLY- + Gk. *meros* part]

pol·y·mer·ic (pol′i·mer′ik) *adj.* Having the same percentage composition but different molecular weights and different properties: said of two or more chemical compounds. —**po·lym′er·ism** *n.*

po·lym·er·i·za·tion (pə·lim′ər·ə·zā′shən, pol′i·mər·ə-) *n.* The combination of unit molecules to form large complex molecules that are polymeric with the original molecules. —**po·lym·er·ize** (·īzed, ·iz·ing) *v.*

pol·y·mor·phous (pol′i·môr′fəs) *adj.* Occurring in or having several forms. Also **pol′y·mor′phic** (-fik). [< POLY- + Gk. *morphē* form] —**pol′y·mor′phism** (-fiz·əm) *n.*

Pol·y·ne·sian (pol′i·nē′zhən, -shən) *n.* 1 One of the na-tive brown-skinned people of Polynesia. 2 The languages spoken by these people. —*adj.* Of or pertaining to Polynesia, its people, or their languages.

pol·y·no·mi·al (pol′i·nō′mē·əl) *adj.* Of, pertaining to, or consisting of many terms. —*n. Math.* An expression written as a sum of terms. [< POLY- + (BI)NOMIAL]

pol·yp (pol′ip) *n.* 1 Any of various coelenterates having a fringe of tentacles at the end of a cylindrical body, as a hydra, sea anemone, etc. 2 An outgrowth arising from mucous membrane, as of the nose, bladder, uterus, or rectum. [< Gk. *poly-* many + *pous* a foot]

pol·y·phon·ic (pol′i·fon′ik) *adj.* 1 *Phonet.* Representing more than one sound or combination of sounds, as some written characters. 2 Consisting of many sounds or voices. 3 *Music* **a** Designating or involving the simultaneous combination of two or more independent parts or melodies. **b** Denoting an instrument, as a piano, by which two or more tones can be sounded at once. Also **po·lyph·o·nous** (pə·lif′ə·nəs) [< Gk. *polyphōnos* having many tones]

po·lyph·o·ny (pə·lif′ə·nē) *n.* 1 Multiplicity of sounds, as in an echo. 2 Polyphonic music; counterpoint.

pol·y·syl·la·ble (pol′i·sil′ə·bəl) *n.* A word of several syllables, esp. of more than three. —**pol′y·syl·lab′ic** (-si·lab′ik) or **·i·cal** *adj.* —**pol′y·syl′la·bism** or **·syl·lab′i·cism** (pol′i·si·lab′ə·siz′əm) *n.*

pol·y·tech·nic (pol′i·tek′nik) *adj.* Embracing many sciences and technical fields. Also **pol′y·tech′ni·cal.** —*n.* A school of applied science and the industrial arts. [< POLY- + Gk. *technē* an art]

pol·y·the·ism (pol′i·thē·iz′əm) *n.* The belief in and worship of more gods than one. —**pol′y·the′ist** *n.* —**pol′y·the·is′tic** or **·is′ti·cal** *adj.*

pol·y·un·sat·u·rat·ed (pol′ə·un·sach′ə·rā′tid) *adj.* Having many double or triple bonds uniting adjacent carbon atoms and forming potential sites for adding hydrogen or various radicals: used esp. of edible oils and fats.

pol·y·u·re·thane (pol′ē·yŏŏr′ə·thān′) *n.* Any of a group of synthetic, nitrogen-containing polymers with diverse properties, widely used in the manufacture of rigid or flexible solid foams for insulation and upholstery, resins for waterproofing, etc.

pol·y·va·lent (pol′i·vā′lənt) *adj.* 1 *Bacteriol.* Designating a vaccine effective against two or more different strains of one species of microorganism. 2 *Chem.* Multivalent. —**pol′y·va′lence** *n.*

pom·ace (pum′is) *n.* 1 The pulp remaining after the removal of juice from apples or like fruit. 2 The cake left after the expression of oil from nuts, seeds, etc. [< L *pomum* an apple]

po·made (pō·mād′, -mäd′) *n.* A perfumed dressing for the hair. —*v.t.* **·mad·ed, ·mad·ing** To anoint with pomade. [< Ital. *pomo* an apple]

pome (pōm) *n.* A fleshy, many-celled fruit with a core, as an apple, pear, etc. [< L *pomum* apple] —**po·ma·ceous** (pō·mā′shəs) *adj.*

pome·gran·ate (pom′gran·it, pum′-) *n.* 1 A fruit with a leathery rind containing many seeds surrounded with juicy, edible pulp. 2 The tropical shrub bearing this fruit. [< L *pomum* apple + *granum*, a grain, seed]

Pom·er·a·ni·an (pom′ə·rā′nē·ən) *n.* A small dog with a bushy tail turned over the back and a long, straight, silky coat. [< *Pomerania*, a region of N CEN. Europe]

Pomeranian

pom·mel (pum′əl, pom′-) *v.t.* **·meled** or **·melled, ·mel·ing** or **·mel·ling** To beat with or as if with the fists. —*n.* 1 A knob at the front of a saddle. 2 A knob on the hilt of a sword. [< OF *pomel* a rounded knob] • See SADDLE.

po·mol·o·gy (pō·mol′ə·jē) *n.* The science of fruit culture. [< L *pomum* apple + -LOGY] —**po·mo·log·i·cal** (pō′mə·loj′i·kəl) *adj.* —**po·mo·log′i·cal·ly** *adv.* —**po·mol′o·gist** *n.*

pomp (pomp) *n.* 1 Magnificent and majestic display: royal *pomp.* 2 Ostentatious display. [< Gk. *pompē* a parade] — **Syn.** 1 flourish, grandeur, magnificence, splendor. 2 showiness.

pom·pa·dour (pom′pə·dôr, -dŏŏr, -dōr) *n.* A style of arranging the hair by brushing it up high over the forehead. [< Marquise de *Pompadour*, 1721–64, French courtesan]

pom·pa·no (pom′pə·nō) *n. pl.* **·nos** Any of various spiny-finned food fishes of Caribbean and neighboring coastal waters. [< Sp. *pámpano*]

pom-pom (pom′pom′) *n.* A rapid-fire, automatic cannon used as an antiaircraft weapon. [Imit.]

pom·pon (pom′pon) *n.* 1 A tuft or ball, as of feathers or ribbon, worn on a hat, shoes, etc. 2 A variety of chrysanthemum or dahlia having compact, globular flower heads: also **pom′-pom.** [< OF *pompe* pomp]

pom·pous (pom′pəs) *adj.* 1 Marked by assumed stateliness; overbearing. 2 Magnificent; ceremonious or impressive. **—pom·pos·i·ty** (pom·pos′ə·tē), **pom′pous·ness** *n.* **—pom′pous·ly** *adv.*

pon·cho (pon′chō) *n. pl.* **·chos** A garment shaped like a blanket with a hole in the middle for the head, and often waterproofed. [Sp.]

pond (pond) *n.* A body of still water, smaller than a lake. [ME *ponde*]

pon·der (pon′dər) *v.t.* 1 To weigh in the mind; consider carefully. **—v.i.** 2 To meditate. [< L *pondus* a weight] — **pon′der·er** *n.* **—Syn.** 1 deliberate, examine. 2 muse, reflect.

pon·der·o·sa pine (pon′də·rō′sə) 1 A tall tree of NW U.S. with long, dark green needles. 2 Its strong reddish wood. Also **pon′der·o′sa.** [< L *ponderōsus* ponderous]

pon·der·ous (pon′dər·əs) *adj.* 1 Having great weight; bulky. 2 Dull; lumbering. [< L *pondus* a weight] **—pon′der·os′i·ty** (-də·ros′ə·tē), **pon′der·ous·ness** *n.* **—pon′der·ous·ly** *adv.*

pond·weed (pond′wēd′) *n.* Any of a widely distributed genus of usu. submerged aquatic plants having straplike leaves.

pone (pōn) *n. Regional* 1 Bread made of cornmeal. 2 A small cake or patty of cornbread. [< Algon.]

pon·gee (pon·jē′, pon′jē) *n.* A thin, natural, unbleached silk with a knotty, rough weave.

pon·iard (pon′yərd) *n.* A small dagger. [< L *pugnus* fist]

pon·tiff (pon′tif) *n.* 1 The pope. 2 A bishop. [< L *pontifex* a high priest of ancient Rome.] **—pon·tif′ic** *adj.*

pon·tif·i·cal (pon·tif′i·kəl) *adj.* 1 Of, pertaining to or appropriate for a pontiff. 2 Having the pomp or dogmatism sometimes ascribed to a pontiff. **—n. Usu. pl.** The vestments, insignia, etc., used by pontiffs on certain ceremonious occasions. — **pon·tif′i·cal·ly** *adv.*

pon·tif·i·cate (pon·tif′ə·kit, -kāt) *n.* 1 The office of a pontiff. **—v.i.** (-kāt) **·cat·ed, ·cat·ing** To act or speak pompously or dogmatically. —

pon·toon (pon·tōōn′) *n.* 1 A flat-bottomed boat, airtight cylinder, etc., used in the construction of temporary floating bridges. 2 Either of two floats on the landing gear of a seaplane. [< L *ponto* < *pons* a bridge]

pontoon bridge A bridge supported on pontoons.

Poniards

Pontoons supporting bridge

po·ny (pō′nē) *n. pl.* **·nies** 1 A horse of any of several small breeds. 2 Anything small of its kind. 3 *Slang* A translation used in the preparation of foreign language lessons. 4 *Informal* A very small glass for alcoholic liquor. **—v.t. & v.i.** **·nied, ·ny·ing** *Slang* 1 To translate (lessons) with the aid of a pony. 2 To pay (money) that is due: with *up.* [< L *pullus* a young animal]

pony express In 1860–61, a postal system by which mail was relayed from Missouri to California by riders mounted on swift ponies.

po·ny·tail (pō′nē·tāl′) *n.* 1 A style of arranging long hair by gathering it tightly at the back of the head and letting it hang down like a pony's tail. 2 Hair worn in this way.

pooch (pōōch) *n. Slang* A dog, esp. a small mongrel. [?]

poo·dle (pōōd′l) *n.* One of a breed of dogs with long, curly hair, usu. clipped short in a conventional pattern. [G *pudel*]

pooh (pōō) *interj.* Bah!: an exclamation of disdain or impatience.

pooh-pooh (pōō′pōō′) *v.t.* To reject or speak of disdainfully. **—pooh′-pooh′er** *n.*

pool¹ (pōōl) *n.* 1 A small body of water. 2 A deep place in a stream. 3 Any small, isolated body of liquid. [< OE *pōl*]

pool² (pōōl) *n.* 1 A collective stake in a gambling game. 2 A combination whereby companies or corporations agree to fix rates or prices and divide the collective profits pro rata. 3 Any of various games played on a six-pocket billiard table. 4 A combining of efforts or resources for mutual benefit. 5 The persons forming such a combination. **—v.t.** 1 To combine in a mutual fund or pool. **—v.i.** 2 To form a pool. [< F *poule* a stake, a hen]

pool·room (pōōl′rōōm′, -rŏŏm′) *n.* A place for playing pool, billiards, etc. or for betting on races.

poop¹ (pōōp) *Naut. n.* 1 A short deck built over the after part of the regular deck of a sailing vessel: also **poop deck.** 2 The stern of a ship. **—v.t.** To break over the stern or poop of: said of a wave. [< L *puppis*]

poop² (pōōp) *Slang v.t.* To bring to exhaustion: usu. used passively. [?]

poor (pŏŏr) *adj.* 1 Lacking means of comfortable subsistence; needy. 2 Lacking in good qualities. 3 Wanting in strength or spirit; cowardly. 4 Devoid of elegance or refinements. 5 Deserving of pity: the *poor dog.* 6 Devoid of merit; unsatisfactory. [< L *pauper*] **—poor′ly** *adj., adv.* **—poor′ness** *n.* **—Syn.** 1 indigent, penniless, poverty-stricken. 2 deficient. 4 squalid. 5 pitiable, wretched.

poor·house (pŏŏr′hous′) *n.* A public establishment maintained as a dwelling for paupers.

poor-mouth (pŏŏr′mouth′) *v.i. Informal* To exaggerate one's financial difficulties. **—poor mouth**

pop¹ (pop) *v.* **popped, pop·ping** *v.i.* 1 To make a sharp, explosive sound. 2 To burst open with such a sound. 3 To move or go suddenly or quickly: with *in, out,* etc. 4 To protrude; bulge. **—v.t.** 5 To cause to burst or explode, as corn by heating. 6 To thrust or put suddenly: with *in, out,* etc. 7 To fire (a gun, etc.). 8 *Slang* To take (habit-forming or harmful drugs) by mouth or injection: to *pop* pills. — **pop the question** *Informal* To make a proposal of marriage. **—n.** 1 A sharp explosive noise, as of a firearm. 2 A nonintoxicating, variously flavored drink, usu. carbonated. 3 A shot, as in basketball. **—adv.** Like, or with the sound of a pop. [Imit.]

pop² (pop) *n. Slang* Papa. [Short for *poppa*]

pop³ (pop) *Informal adj.* 1 Of or pertaining to a pervasive mass culture: esp. that of young persons. 2 Of or pertaining to the music favored by this group. 3 Of or pertaining to pop art. [Short for POPULAR]

pop. popular; population.

pop art A style of painting, the subjects and manner of which resemble those of comic strips and advertising posters. **—pop artist**

pop·corn (pop′kôrn′) *n.* 1 A variety of maize, the kernels of which explode when heated. 2 The fluffy white mass thus formed.

Pope (pōp) *n.* The bishop of Rome, the supreme head of the Roman Catholic Church. Also **pope.** [< Gk. *pappas* father]

pop·eyed (pop′īd′) *adj.* 1 Having bulging or protruding eyes. 2 Amazed.

pop·gun (pop′gun′) *n.* A tube with a piston that expels a pellet with a pop.

pop·in·jay (pop′in·jā) *n.* A silly, vain fellow. [< Ar. *babhagā* a parrot]

pop·ish (pō′pish) *adj.* Pertaining to popes or the Roman Catholic Church; a contemptuous term. **—pop′ish·ly** *adv.* **—pop′ish·ness** *n.*

pop·lar (pop′lər) *n.* 1 Any of a genus of trees and bushes of the willow family. 2 The soft, light wood of any of these trees. [< L *populus*]

pop·lin (pop′lin) n. A durable ribbed silk, cotton, or wool fabric. [< F *popeline*]

pop·o·ver (pop′ō′vər) n. A very light, hollow muffin that pops up as it bakes.

pop·per (pop′ər) n. 1 Anything that makes an explosive noise. 2 A container or device for popping corn.

pop·py (pop′ē) n. pl. **·pies** 1 Any of a large genus of plants having a milky juice, showy flowers of various colors, and a capsule containing many small seeds. 2 The flower of any poppy plant. 3 An extract, as opium, from the juice of certain species of poppy. 4 The yellowish-red color of certain poppy blossoms: also **poppy red**. [< L *papaver*]

pop·py·cock (pop′ē·kok) n. & interj. Informal Nonsense.

Pop·si·cle (pop′sik·əl) n. A slab of frozen colored and flavored water at the end of two flat sticks: a trade name. Also **pop′si·cle**.

pop·u·lace (pop′yə·lis) n. The mass of common people. [< L *populus* people]

pop·u·lar (pop′yə·lər) adj. 1 Of or carried on by the people at large. 2 Possessing many friends. 3 Widely approved or admired. 4 Suitable for the common people. 5 Prevalent among the people. 6 Suited to the means of the people: *popular* prices. 7 Of folk origin: the *popular* ballad. [< L *populus* the people] —**pop′u·lar·ly** adv. —Syn. 2 well-liked. 5 common, universal, widespread.

pop·u·lar·i·ty (pop′yə·lar′ə·tē) n. The condition of possessing the confidence and favor of others.

pop·u·lar·ize (pop′yə·lə·rīz′) v.t. **·ized, ·iz·ing** To make popular. Brit. sp. **·ise′**. —**pop′u·lar·i·za′tion, pop′u·lar·iz′er** n.

pop·u·late (pop′yə·lāt) v.t. **·lat·ed, ·lat·ing** 1 To furnish with inhabitants; people. 2 To inhabit. [< L *populus* the people]

pop·u·la·tion (pop′yə·lā′shən) n. 1 The total group of people or animals of a specified kind in a given area. 2 The number of individuals in such a group. 3 The act or process of populating. 4 The stated experimental base of a statistical study. [< L *populus* the people]

Pop·u·lism (pop′yə·lizm) n. The platform of a U.S. political party (**People's party**) founded in 1891, that advocated free coinage of silver, public control of railways, an income tax, and limitation of ownership of land. —**Pop′u·list** adj., n. —**Pop′u·lis′tic** adj.

pop·u·list (pop′yə·list) n. A politician who represents or claims to represent the grass roots. —**pop′u·lism** n.

pop·u·lous (pop′yə·ləs) adj. Having many inhabitants; thickly settled. —**pop′u·lous·ly** adv. —**pop′u·lous·ness** n.

porce·lain (pôrs′lin, pōrs′-, pôr′sə-, pōr′-) n. A white, hard, translucent ceramic ware, usu. glazed, existing in many varieties. [< Ital. *porcellana*, orig. a cowry]

porch (pôrch, pōrch) n. 1 A covered structure forming an entrance to a building. 2 A veranda. [< L *porta* a gate]

por·cine (pôr′sīn, -sin) adj. Pertaining to, like, or characteristic of pigs or hogs. [< L *porcus* a hog]

por·cu·pine (pôr′kyə·pīn) n. Any of various rodents having the back and tail covered with long, sharp, defensive spines. [< OF *porc* a hog + *espin* a thorn]

pore¹ (pôr, pōr) v.i. **pored, por·ing** 1 To study or read with care and application: with *over*. 2 To meditate; ponder. [ME *pouren*]

pore² (pôr, pōr) n. 1 A small natural opening, as a stoma on a leaf or the open end of a sweat gland. 2 A minute hole in any material. [< Gk. *poros*]

Canada porcupine

por·gy (pôr′gē) n. pl. **·gies** Any of various deep-bodied, saltwater food fishes. [?]

pork (pôrk, pōrk) n. 1 The flesh of pigs and hogs, used as food. 2 Slang Government money, favors, etc., obtained by political patronage. [< L *porcus* a hog]

pork barrel Informal A government appropriation for some local enterprise made to win favor with a representative's constituents.

pork·er (pôr′kər, pōr′-) n. A young hog fattened to be butchered.

pork·pie (pôrk′pī, pōrk′-) n. 1 A thick-crusted pie with pork filling. 2 A man's hat with a low, flat crown.

pork·y (pôr′kē, pōr′-) adj. **pork·i·er, pork·i·est** 1 Of or like pork. 2 Obese; fat.

porn (pôrn) Slang adj. Pornographic. —n. Pornography. Also **por·no** (pôr′nō).

por·no·graph·ic (pôr′nə·graf′ik) adj. Of or having the nature of pornography. —**por′no·graph′i·cal·ly** adv.

por·nog·ra·phy (pôr·nog′rə·fē) n. 1 Depictions of sexual acts or behavior, as in writing, photographs, motion pictures, etc., to stimulate erotic feelings. 2 The material containing such descriptions. [< Gk. *pornē* a harlot + *graphein* write] —**por·nog′ra·pher** n.

po·ros·i·ty (pō·ros′ə·tē, pō-) n. 1 The property of being porous; porousness. 2 A porous part or structure.

po·rous (pôr′əs, pō′rəs) adj. 1 Having pores. 2 Having many tiny holes. —**po′rous·ly** adv. —**po′rous·ness** n.

por·phy·ry (pôr′fə·rē) n. pl. **·ries** An igneous rock that encloses crystals of feldspar or quartz. [< Gk. *porphyros* purple]

por·poise (pôr′pəs) n. pl. **·poises** or **·poise** 1 Any of various small, usu. gregarious, toothed whales with a blunt snout. 2 A dolphin. [< L *porcus* a hog + *piscis* fish]

Porpoise

por·ridge (pôr′ij, por′-) n. A soft food made by boiling oatmeal or other cereal in water or milk. [Alter. of POTTAGE]

por·rin·ger (pôr′in·jər, por′-) n. A small, shallow dish, in which soft foods can be served.

port¹ (pôrt, pōrt) n. 1 A harbor or haven. 2 A harbor at which ships take on or unload cargo. 2 PORT OF ENTRY. [< L *portus* a harbor]

port² (pôrt, pōrt) n. 1 An opening in the side of a ship, as for a gun, or for the passage of cargo. 2 PORTHOLE. 3 A passageway into or out of a machine or device. [< L *porta* gate]

port³ (pôrt, pōrt) n. 1 The way in which one bears or carries himself. 2 The position of a rifle when ported. —v.t. 1 Mil. To carry, as a weapon, diagonally across the body and sloping to the left shoulder. 2 To carry. [< L *portare* carry]

port⁴ (pôrt, pōrt) Naut. n. The left side of a vessel as one looks from stern to bow. —v.t. & v.i. To put or turn (the helm) to the port side. —adj. Left. [Prob. < PORT¹]

port⁵ (pôrt, pōrt) n. A fortified sweet wine, usu. of a dark red color. [< *Oporto*, Portugal]

Port. Portugal; Portuguese.

port·a·ble (pôr′tə·bəl, pōr′-) adj. That can be readily carried or moved. [< L *portare* carry] —**port′a·ble·ness, port′a·bil′i·ty** n. —**port′a·bly** adv.

port·age (pôr′tij, pōr′-) n. 1 The act of transporting canoes, boats, and goods over land from one navigable water to another. 2 The route over which such transportation is made. 3 The charge for transportation. [< L *portare* carry]

por·tal (pôr′təl, pōr′-) n. A passage for gaining entrance; door, esp. one that is grand and imposing. [< L *porta* a gate]

por·tal-to-por·tal pay (pôr′təl·tə·pôr′təl, pōr′-) A wage paid to cover the time a worker spends going to his work location from the entrance to a mine, factory, etc., plus that spent in going back after work.

port·cul·lis (pôrt·kul′is, pōrt-) n. A grating made of strong bars of wood or iron that can be let down suddenly to close the portal of a fortified place. [< OF *porte* a gate + *coleis* sliding]

Porte (pôrt, pōrt) n. The Turkish government prior to 1923.

porte-co·chère (pôrt′kō·shâr′, pōrt′-) n. A porch at the door of a building for sheltering persons entering or leaving vehicles. [F, lit., coach door]

por·tend (pôr·tend′, pōr-) v.t. To warn of as an omen; presage. [< L *portendere* < *pro-* forth + *tendere* to stretch]

por·tent (pôr'tent, pōr'-) *n.* 1 Anything that warns of a future event; omen. 2 Ominous significance.

por·ten·tous (pôr·ten'təs, pōr-) *adj.* 1 Full of portents of ill; ominous. 2 Amazing; extraordinary. 3 Pretentiously solemn. —**por·ten'tous·ly** *adv.* —**por·ten'tous·ness** *n.*

por·ter[1] (pôr'tər, pōr'-) *n.* 1 One who carries things, esp. a man hired to carry travelers' luggage, etc. 2 An attendant in a railway parlor car or sleeper. 3 A man who works as a janitor in a hospital, bank, etc. [< L *portare* carry]

por·ter[2] (pôr'tər, pōr'-) *n.* A keeper of a door or gate. [< L *porta* a gate, a door]

por·ter[3] (pôr'tər, pōr'-) *n.* A dark brown, heavy, English malt liquor. [Short for *porter's ale;* formerly drunk chiefly by porters]

por·ter·house (pôr'tər·hous', pōr'-) *n.* 1 Formerly, a place where porter, ale, etc., were sold. 2 A choice cut of beefsteak including a part of the tenderloin: also **porterhouse steak.**

port·fo·li·o (pôrt·fō'lē·ō, pōrt-) *n. pl.* **·li·os** 1 A portable case for holding documents, etc. 2 The position or office of a minister of state or member of a government. 3 A list of investments. [< L *portare* carry + *folium* leaf]

port·hole (pôrt'hōl', pōrt'-) *n.* A small round opening in a ship's side to admit air and light.

por·ti·co (pôr'ti·kō, pōr'-) *n. pl.* **·coes** or **·cos** An open porch or place for walking with a roof upheld by columns. [< L *porticus*] —**por'ti·coed** *adj.*

por·tière (pôr·tyâr', pōr-) *n.* A curtain for a doorway. Also **por·tiere'.** [< F *porte* a door]

por·tion (pôr'shən, pōr'-) *n.* 1 A part of a whole. 2 An allotment; share. 3 The quantity of food served to one person. 4 The part of an estate coming to an heir. 5 A dowry. 6 One's fortune or destiny. —*v.t.* 1 To divide into shares for distribution: often with *out.* 2 To give a dowry to. [< L *portio*] —**por'tion·er** *n.* —**por'tion·less** *adj.* —**Syn.** *n.* 1 division, piece. 3 serving. 4 inheritance. 6 fate, lot.

Portland cement A calcined powder of clay and limestone that hardens when combined with water.

port·ly (pôrt'lē, pōrt'-) *adj.* **·li·er, ·li·est** 1 Rather stout or heavy. 2 Of a stately appearance and carriage. [< PORT[3]] —**port'li·ness** *n.*

port·man·teau (pôrt·man'tō, pōrt-) *n. pl.* **·teaus** or **·teaux** (-tōz) An oblong leather suitcase, hinged at the back, and having two compartments. [< MF *porter* carry + *manteau* coat]

portmanteau word A word blended from two distinct words, as *chortle,* from *chuckle* and *snort.*

port of entry A place, whether on the coast or inland, where customs officials check the entry of foreign persons or goods into a country.

por·trait (pôr'trit, pōr'-, -trāt) *n.* 1 A likeness of a person, esp. of the face. 2 A vivid description of something or someone. [< OF *pourtraire* portray] —**por'trait·ist** *n.*

por·trai·ture (pôr'tri·chər, pōr'-) *n.* 1 A portrait. 2 The art or practice of making portraits.

por·tray (pôr·trā', pōr-) *v.t.* 1 To represent by drawing, painting, etc. 2 To describe in words. 3 To represent, as in a play. [< L *protrahere* draw forth] —**por·tray'al, por·tray'er** *n.* —**Syn.** 1 delineate. 2 depict, picture, show. 3 act, perform.

Por·tu·gal (pôr'chə·gəl, pōr'-) *n.* A republic of sw Europe, 35,419 sq. mi., cap. Lisbon. • See map at SPAIN.

Por·tu·guese (pôr'chə·gēz', -gēs', pōr'-) *n.* 1 A citizen or native of Portugal. 2 The language of Portugal. —*adj.* Of or pertaining to Portugal, its people, or their language.

Portuguese man-of-war A colony of organisms of warm seas, having long, stinging tentacles hanging from a central bladderlike float.

Portuguese West Africa ANGOLA.

por·tu·lac·a (pôr'chə·lak'ə, pōr'-) *n.* Any of a genus of low, fleshy-leaved plants related to purslane, with flowers of many colors. [L, purslane]

pos., posit. position; positive.

pose (pōz) *n.* 1 A position of the whole or part of the body, esp. one held for an artist, photographer, etc. 2 A mental attitude assumed for effect. —*v.* **posed, pos·ing** *v.i.* 1 To assume or hold a position, as for a portrait. 2 To affect attitudes. 3 To represent oneself: to *pose* as an expert. —*v.t.* 4 To cause to assume a position, as for a portrait. 5 To

put forward for consideration or discussion: to *pose* a difficult question. [< OF *poser* to pose]

Po·sei·don (pō·sī'dən) *Gk. Myth.* The god of the sea: identified with the Roman Neptune.

pos·er[1] (pō'zər) *n.* One who poses.

pos·er[2] (pō'zər) *n.* A baffling question or problem.

po·seur (pō·zœr') *n.* One who affects a particular attitude to make an impression on others. [F]

posh (posh) *adj. Brit. Slang* Very luxurious or elegant. [?] —**posh'ly** *adv.* —**posh'ness** *n.*

pos·it (poz'it) *v.t.* To lay down or assume as a fact; postulate. [< L *positus,* pp. of *ponere* to place]

po·si·tion (pə·zish'ən) *n.* 1 The manner in which a thing is placed. 2 The place in which a thing is located. 3 An advantageous location: to jockey for *position.* 4 Disposition of the parts of the body; posture. 5 The manner of being placed: an awkward *position.* 6 Social standing, esp. if high. 7 A job; employment. 8 Point of view; stand. —*v.t.* To place in a particular or appropriate position. [< L *positus,* pp. of *ponere* to place] —**po·si'tion·al** *adj.*

position paper A report from a person or group setting forth a set of principles, a description of policy, or recommendations for action on a specific issue.

pos·i·tive (poz'ə·tiv) *adj.* 1 That is or may be directly affirmed; sure. 2 Inherent in a thing by and of itself, regardless of its relations to other things; absolute. 3 Openly and plainly expressed; emphatic: a *positive* denial. 4 Confident; self-possessed: a *positive* person. 5 Overly confident; arrogant: a *positive* manner. 6 Incontestable: *positive* proof. 7 Helpful; constructive: *positive* suggestions. 8 Noting one of two opposite directions, qualities, properties, etc., which is taken as primary, or as indicating increase or progression. 9 *Math.* Greater than zero. 10 *Electr.* Having a charge or potential capable of attracting electrons. 11 ELECTROPOSITIVE. 12 Tending to move toward a stimulus: a *positive* tropism. 13 Indicating the presence of a specified condition, disease, or microorganism. 14 Having the lights and shades in their natural relation, as in a photograph. 15 *Gram.* Denoting the simple, uncompared degree of the adjective or adverb. —*n.* 1 That which is positive, as a photograph print, a battery terminal, a quality, a degree, a quantity, etc. 2 *Gram.* a The positive degree of an adjective or adverb. b A word in this degree. [< L *positivus* < *positus* placed] —**pos'i·tive·ly** *adv.* —**pos'i·tive·ness** *n.* —**Syn.** *adj.* 1 actual, existing, real. 3 explicit. 6 indisputable.

a. positive *def. 14.*
b. negative.

pos·i·tiv·ism (poz'ə·tiv·iz'əm) *n.* 1 A system of philosophy holding that man can have no knowledge of anything but actual phenomena and facts. 2 Certitude; dogmatism. —**pos'i·tiv·ist** *adj., n.* —**pos'i·tiv·is'tic** *adj.*

pos·i·tron (poz'ə·tron) *n. Physics* A positively charged particle with a mass equal to that of the electron. [< POSI(TIVE) + (ELEC)TRON]

poss. possession; possessive; possible; possibly.

pos·se (pos'ē) *n.* A force of men gathered together by a sheriff or other law-enforcement officer to help quell a riot, pursue criminal suspects, etc. [L, be able]

pos·sess (pə·zes') *v.t.* 1 To have as property; own. 2 To have as a quality, attribute, etc. 3 To exert control over; dominate: his fear *possessed* him. 4 *Archaic* To seize; gain. [< L *possessus,* pp. of *possidere* possess] —**pos·ses'sor** *n.*

pos·sessed (pə·zest') *adj.* 1 Calm; cool. 2 Controlled by or as if by evil spirits; frenzied. —**possessed of** Having; owning.

pos·ses·sion (pə·zesh'ən) *n.* 1 The act or state of possessing or being possessed; ownership or occupancy. 2 A thing possessed or owned. 3 *pl.* Property; belongings. 4 The state of being dominated by an idea, emotion, evil spirit, etc. 5 Self-possession. 6 A territory under the control of a foreign country.

pos·ses·sive (pə·zes'iv) *adj.* 1 Pertaining to possession or ownership. 2 Overly desirous of owning or controlling. 3 *Gram.* Designating a case of a noun or pronoun indicating possession. —*n. Gram.* 1 The possessive case. 2 A possessive form or construction. —**pos·ses'sive·ly** *adv.* —

pos·ses'sive·ness n. • In English the *possessive* is formed in nouns by adding *'s* to the singular and irregular plurals: *Larry's* hammer; *men's* minds, and a simple apostrophe to the regular plural and sometimes to singulars and proper names ending in a sibilant: *boys'* games; *Dickens'* (or *Dickens's*) novels. Pronouns have special possessive forms: *my, mine, your, yours, his, her, hers, our, ours, their, theirs, whose.*

pos·set (pos'it) n. A drink of hot milk with liquor, sweetened and spiced. [ME *possot*]

pos·si·bil·i·ty (pos'ə·bil'ə·tē) n. pl. ·ties 1 The fact of being possible. 2 A possible thing.

pos·si·ble (pos'ə·bəl) adj. 1 That may be or may become true. 2 That may come about or be done. 3 That may be suitable: a *possible* site for a camp. [< L *posse* be able] —**pos'si·bly** adv.

pos·sum (pos'əm) n. *Informal* An opossum. —**play possum** To feign sleep, illness, death, etc.

post¹ (pōst) n. 1 An upright piece of timber or other material used as a support. 2 A line serving to mark the starting or finishing point of a racecourse. —v.t. 1 To put up (a poster, etc.) in some public place. 2 To fasten posters upon. 3 To announce by or as by a poster. 4 To publish the name of on a list. 5 To forbid trespassing on (land, etc.) by posting signs. [< L *postis* a door post]

post² (pōst) n. 1 Any fixed place where a soldier or policeman is stationed. 2 A place where troops are garrisoned. 3 The troops occupying a military installation. 4 A local unit of a veterans' organization. 5 An office or employment; position. 6 A trading post, esp. in an undeveloped region. —v.t. To assign to a particular position or post. [< L *positum*, pp. neut. of *ponere* to place]

post³ (pōst) n. 1 An established system for transporting and delivering letters, packages, and other mail matter. 2 The mail delivered and carried at one time. 3 Formerly, a courier who traveled over a fixed route carrying letters and dispatches. 4 Formerly, any of the series of stations on such a route, furnishing relays of men and horses, and carriages for travelers. —v.t. 1 To place in a mailbox; mail. 2 To inform: He *posted* us on the latest news. 3 In bookkeeping, to transfer (items or accounts) to the ledger. —v.i. 4 To travel with post horses. 5 To travel with speed; hasten. 6 In horseback riding, to rise from the saddle in rhythm with a horse's trot. —adv. Speedily; rapidly. [< L *posita*, pp. fem. of *ponere* to place]

post- prefix After in time or order; following: *postdate, postwar.* [< L *post* behind, after]

post·age (pōs'tij) n. The charge levied on mail matter.

postage stamp A small, printed label issued and sold by a government to be affixed to letters, parcels, etc., in payment of postage.

pos·tal (pōs'təl) adj. Pertaining to the mails or to mail service. —n. A postal card.

postal card A card, issued officially, for carrying a written or printed message through the mails under government stamp.

post·bel·lum (pōst'bel'əm) adj. Coming or occurring after the war, esp. the American Civil War. [< L *post* after + *bellum* war]

post box MAILBOX.

post card 1 POSTAL CARD. 2 A card, usu. with a picture on one side, transmissible through the mails on prepayment of the same postage as for a postal card.

post chaise A closed, horse-drawn carriage.

post·date (pōst'dāt') v.t. ·dat·ed, ·dat·ing 1 To assign or affix a future date to (a check, document, etc.). 2 To follow in time.

post·er (pōs'tər) n. A printed sheet for advertising, public information, etc., to be posted on a wall or other surface. —**Syn.** bill, notice, placard, sign.

poster color An opaque water paint, usu. sold in jars, used for making posters, etc.

pos·te·ri·or (pos·tir'ē·ər) adj. 1 Situated behind or toward the hinder part. 2 Coming after another in a series. —n. Often pl. The buttocks. [< L *posterus* following] —**pos·te·ri·or·i·ty** (pos·tir'ē·ôr'ə·tē, -or'ə-) n. —**pos·te'ri·or·ly** adv.

pos·ter·i·ty (pos·ter'ə·tē) n. 1 A person's descendants. 2 Succeeding generations, collectively. [< L *posterus* following]

pos·tern (pōs'tərn, pos'-) n. A back gate or door; a private entrance. —adj. Situated at the back; private: a *postern* gate. [< L *posterus* following]

post exchange Often cap. An establishment for the sale of merchandise and services to military personnel.

post·gla·cial (pōst'glā'shəl) adj. *Geol.* Existing or occurring later than the glacial epoch.

post·grad·u·ate (pōst'graj'ōō·it, -āt) adj. Of or pertaining to studies pursued after receiving a first degree; graduate. —n. One who pursues or has completed a postgraduate course.

post·haste (pōst'hāst') n. Great haste or speed. —adv. With utmost speed; hurriedly. [?< *Haste, post, haste,* an old direction written on letters]

post horse A horse kept for hire to travelers.

post·hu·mous (pos'chōō·məs) adj. 1 Born after the father's death: said of a child. 2 Published after the author's death, as a book. 3 Arising after a person's death: a *posthumous* reputation. [< L *postumus* latest, last] —**post'hu·mous·ly** adv.

pos·til·ion (pōs·til'yən, pos-) n. A rider of the left-hand horse of a team drawing a vehicle. Also **pos·til'lion.** [< Ital. *posta* a post, station]

post·lude (pōst'lōōd) n. An organ solo concluding a church service. [< POST- + (PRE)LUDE]

post·man (pōst'mən) n. pl. ·men (-mən) A man who picks up and delivers letters, parcels, etc.

post·mark (pōst'märk') n. The mark of a post office on mail handled there, serving to cancel stamps, and usu. giving the date and place of mailing. —v.t. To stamp with a postmark.

post·mas·ter (pōst'mas'tər, -mäs'-) n. An official having charge of a post office. —**post'mis'tress** (-mis'tris) n. Fem.

postmaster general pl. **postmasters general** The executive head of the postal service of a government.

post·me·rid·i·an (pōst'mə·rid'ē·ən) adj. Pertaining to the afternoon.

post me·rid·i·em (pōst mə·rid'ē·əm) After midday.

post·mor·tem (pōst·môr'təm) adj. Occurring, done, or made soon after death. —n. AUTOPSY. [L]

post·na·tal (pōst·nāt'l) adj. Occurring in or pertaining to the period immediately after birth.

post office 1 A branch or agency of a government charged with carrying and delivering the mails. 2 An office for the receipt, transmission, and delivery of mails. 3 A kissing game. —**post·of·fice** (pōst'ôf'is, -of'-) adj.

post·paid (pōst'pād') adj. Having postage prepaid.

post·par·tum (pōst'pär'təm) adj. Med. Existing or occurring after childbirth: a *postpartum* fever. [< POST- + L *partus* childbirth < *parere* to bear]

post·pone (pōst·pōn') v.t. ·poned, ·pon·ing To put off to a future time. [< L *post-* after + *ponere* put] —**post·pone'·ment, post·pon'er** n. —**Syn.** defer, delay, procrastinate.

post·pran·di·al (pōst·pran'dē·əl) adj. After-dinner. [< POST- + L *prandium* lunch]

post·rid·er (pōst'rī'dər) n. A person who journeys by relays of horses.

post road A road built and maintained for the transportation of mail, formerly having stations at specified distances.

post·script (pōst'skript') n. 1 A supplemental addition to a written or printed document. 2 Something added to a letter after the writer's signature. [< L *postscribere* write after]

pos·tu·late (pos'chə·lit) n. 1 A basis of argument laid down as well known or too plain to require proof. 2 A proposition assumed as true; an axiom. —v.t. (pos'chə·lāt) ·lat·ed, ·lat·ing 1 To claim; demand. 2 To set forth as self-evident or already known. 3 To assume the truth or reality of. [< L *postulare* to demand] —**pos'tu·la'tion, pos'tu·la'tor** n.

pos·ture (pos'chər) n. 1 The way in which the body is held; bearing. 2 Situation or condition at a given time;

circumstances: the military *posture* of a nation. **3** Frame of mind; attitude. —*v.* ·**tured,** ·**tur·ing** *v.t.* **1** To place in a specific posture; pose. —*v.i.* **2** To assume a specific posture. **3** To pose for effect; attitudinize. [< L *positus*, p.p. of *ponere* to place] —**pos′tur·al** *adj.* —**pos′tur·er, pos′tur·ist** *n.*

post·war (pōst′wôr′) *adj.* After a war.

po·sy (pō′zē) *n. pl.* ·**sies 1** A flower. **2** A bunch of flowers. [Contraction of POESY]

pot (pot) *n.* **1** A round earthen, metal, or glass vessel used in cooking. **2** A metal drinking cup; mug. **3** A mug of liquor. **4** The contents of a pot; potful. **5** POTBELLY. **6** The amount of stakes wagered or played for, as in poker. **7** *Informal* A large sum of money. **8** A basketlike trap for catching lobsters, eels, fish, etc. **9** *Slang* Marihuana. —**go to pot** *Informal* To go to ruin; deteriorate. —*v.* **pot·ted, pot·ting** *v.t.* **1** To put into a pot. **2** To preserve in pots or jars. **3** To cook in a pot; stew. **4** To shoot or kill with a pot shot. —*v.i.* **5** To take a pot shot. [< OE *pott*] —**pot′ful** *adj.*

pot. potential.

po·ta·ble (pō′tə·bəl) *adj.* Suitable for drinking. —*n. Usu. pl.* Anything drinkable. [< L *potare* to drink] —**po′ta·bil′i·ty** *n.*

po·tage (pō·täzh′) *n.* A thick soup. [F]

pot·ash (pot′ash′) *n.* **1** POTASSIUM CARBONATE. **2** POTASSIUM HYDROXIDE. **3** The crude mixture of potassium salts obtained by leaching the ashes of plants. [< *pot ashes*]

po·tas·si·um (pə·tas′ē·əm) *n.* A soft, highly reactive metallic element (symbol K) essential to life. [< POTASH]

potassium carbonate A white, alkaline compound found in wood ashes, used in making soap, glass, etc.

potassium chlorate A colorless crystalline salt used in making matches, explosives, etc.

potassium chloride A colorless crystalline salt occurring naturally in mineral deposits and in certain giant kelps of the Pacific coast.

potassium cyanide An intensely poisonous, white, crystalline compound used chiefly in metallurgy.

potassium hydroxide A white, deliquescent, caustic alkali that absorbs carbon dioxide from air.

potassium nitrate A white, crystalline compound used in fertilizers, gunpowder, meat preservatives, etc.

potassium permanganate A purple crystalline salt used as an oxidizing agent, antiseptic, etc.

po·ta·tion (pō·tā′shən) *n.* **1** The act of drinking; a drink. **2** A drinking bout. [< L *potare* to drink]

po·ta·to (pə·tā′tō) *n. pl.* ·**toes 1** A starchy, edible tuber of a plant of the nightshade family. **2** The plant. **3** SWEET POTATO. [< Sp. *patata*]

potato beetle A destructive yellowish beetle with black stripes that feeds on the potato, tomato, and other plants. Also **potato bug.**

potato chip A very thin slice of potato fried crisp and salted.

pot·bel·ly (pot′bel′ē) *n. pl.* ·**lies** A protuberant belly. —**pot′bel′lied** *adj.*

Potato beetle

pot·boil·er (pot′boi′lər) *n. Informal* A literary or artistic work, often of poor quality, produced simply to earn money. —**pot′boil′ing** *n.*

po·tent (pōt′nt) *adj.* **1** Producing marked effects: a *potent* drug. **2** Convincing: a *potent* argument. **3** Having great authority. **4** Able to perform sexual intercourse: said of males. [< L *potens* prp. of *posse* able, have power] — **po′ten·cy** (*pl.* ·**cies**), **po′tence** *n.* —**po′tent·ly** *adv.*

po·ten·tate (pōt′n·tāt) *n.* One having great power or sway; a sovereign.

po·ten·tial (pə·ten′shəl) *adj.* **1** Possible but not actual. **2** Having capacity for existence, but not yet existing. **3** *Physics* Existing by virtue of position: said of energy. **4** *Gram.* Indicating possibility or capability by the use of *can, could, may,* etc. **5** Having force or power. —*n.* **1** Anything that may be possible. **2** *Gram.* The potential mood. **3** *Physics* The work required to move a body from a point infinitely distant to a given point in a field of force. **4** *Electr.* A difference of electric potential; voltage. [< L *potens* potent] —**po·ten·ti·al·i·ty** (pə·ten′shē·al′ə·tē) (*pl.* ·**ties**) *n.* —**po·ten′tial·ly** *adv.*

potential energy Energy stored in any of numerous forms, as chemical energy in coal, mechanical energy in a coiled spring, etc.

pot·head (pot′hed′) *n. Slang* A person who habitually smokes marihuana.

poth·er (poth′ər) *n.* Excitement mingled with confusion. —*v.t. & v.i.* To worry; bother. [?] —**Syn.** *n.* ado, bother, bustle, disturbance, fuss.

pot·herb (pot′ûrb′, -hûrb′) *n.* Any plant having leaves or stems used in cookery.

pot·hold·er (pot′hōl′dər) *n.* A padded cloth or mitten used for handling hot cooking pots and pans.

pot·hook (pot′hōok′) *n.* **1** A curved piece of iron for lifting or hanging pots. **2** A curved mark used in teaching penmanship.

pot·house (pot′hous′) *n. Brit.* An alehouse; saloon.

po·tion (pō′shən) *n.* A draft, as of a liquid having medicinal, poisonous, or supposed magical properties. [< L *potare* to drink]

pot luck Whatever happens to be available and ready for a meal: usu. in the phrase **take pot luck.**

pot·pie (pot′pī′) *n.* **1** A pie, baked in a deep dish, containing meat and vegetables. **2** Meat stewed with dumplings.

pot·pour·ri (pō·pōō·rē′) *n.* **1** A mixture of dried sweet-smelling flower petals used to perfume a room. **2** A collection of various things; miscellany. [F, lit., rotten pot]

pot roast Meat braised and cooked in a pot until tender, often with vegetables.

pot·sherd (pot′shûrd) *n.* A bit of broken pottery. Also **pot′shard** (-shärd). [< POT + SHARD]

pot shot 1 A shot fired within easy range. **2** A random shot. **3** *Informal* A sarcastic or critical remark.

pot·tage (pot′ij) *n.* A thick broth or stew. [< F *pot* pot]

pot·ted (pot′id) *adj.* **1** Placed in a pot. **2** Preserved in a pot or can. **3** *Slang* Drunk.

pot·ter¹ (pot′ər) *v. Chiefly Brit.* PUTTER². —**pot′ter·er** *n.* — **pot′ter·ing·ly** *adv.*

pot·ter² (pot′ər) *n.* One who makes earthenware or porcelain. [< OE *potere*]

potter's field A piece of ground appropriated as a burial ground for the destitute or unidentified. [< the Biblical ref. (*Matt.* 27:7) of a potter's field for the burial of strangers]

potter's wheel A usu. horizontal rotating disk used by potters for shaping clay.

pot·ter·y (pot′ər·ē) *n. pl.* ·**ter·ies 1** A factory where potters' ware is made. **2** The manufacture of earthenware or porcelain. **3** Clay ware molded and hardened.

pot·ty (pot′ē) ·**i·er, ·i·est** *adj. Brit. Informal* **1** Insignificant; trivial. **2** Slightly crazy. [Prob.< POT, in the phrase *go to pot* deteriorate]

pouch (pouch) *n.* **1** A small bag or sack. **2** *Zool.* **a** A saclike part for containing or carrying food. **b** MARSUPIUM. —*v.t.* **1** To put in or, as in a pouch; pocket. **2** To fashion or arrange in pouchlike form. —*v.i.* **3** To take on a pouchlike shape. [< OF *poche*] —**pouch′y** *adj.* (·**i·er, ·i·est**)

Potter's wheel
a. clay. b. rotating
wheel. c. treadle.

poul·ter·er (pōl′tər·ər) *n. Chiefly Brit.* A dealer in poultry.

poul·tice (pōl′tis) *n.* A warm, pulpy mass applied externally to relieve pain and inflammation. —*v.t.* ·**ticed,** ·**tic·ing** To cover with a poultice. [< L *puls* porridge]

poul·try (pōl′trē) *n.* Domestic fowls, as chickens, ducks, turkeys, and geese. [< OF *poulet* fowl]

pounce (pouns) *v.i.* **pounced, pounc·ing** To swoop, as in seizing prey: with *on, upon,* or *at.* —*n.* The act of pouncing. [?] —**Syn.** *n.,v.* jump, leap, spring. —**pounc′er** *n.*

pound¹ (pound) *n.* **1 a** A unit of avoirdupois weight equal to 0.45359 kilogram or 16 avoirdupois ounces. **b** A unit of troy weight equal to 0.37324 kilogram or 12 troy ounces. **2** The basic monetary unit of the United Kingdom, formerly equal to 20 shillings, but after 1971 equal to 100 pence: also **pound sterling. 3** The basic monetary unit of various other countries, as Cyprus, Gambia, Ireland, Israel, Lebanon, Libya, Malawi, Malta, Nigeria, Rhodesia, Sudan, Syria, Turkey, and Egypt. [< L *pondus* weight]

pound² (pound) *n.* **1** A place, enclosed by authority, in which stray animals are kept. **2** An enclosed shelter for cattle or sheep. **3** A trap for wild animals. —*v.t.* To confine in or as in a pound. [< OE *pund*]

pound³ (pound) *v.t.* **1** To strike heavily and repeatedly. **2** To reduce to a pulp or powder by beating. **3** To teach or impress by constant repetition: to *pound* facts into someone's head. —*v.i.* **4** To strike heavy, repeated blows: with *on, at,* etc. **5** To move or proceed heavily. **6** To throb heavily or resoundingly. —*n.* **1** A heavy blow. **2** The act of pounding. **3** The sound produced by pounding; thump. [< OE *punian*] —**pound'er** *n.*

pound·age (poun'dij) *n.* A tax, rate, etc., of so much per pound sterling or per pound of weight.

pound cake A rich cake having ingredients equal in weight, as a pound each of flour, butter, and sugar, with eggs added.

pound-fool·ish (pound'fōō'lish) *adj.* Extravagant with large sums of money.

pour (pôr, pōr) *v.t.* **1** To cause to flow by gravity in a continuous stream, as water, sand, etc. **2** To emit or utter continuously. —*v.i.* **3** To flow in a continuous stream; gush. **4** To rain heavily. **5** To serve as a hostess at a social tea. **6** To move in great numbers; swarm. —*n.* A pouring or downfall. [ME *pouren*] —**pour'er** *n.* —**pour'ing·ly** *adv.*

pour·boire (pŏŏr·bwàr') *n.* A gift of money as a tip. [F, lit., for drink]

pout¹ (pout) *v.i.* **1** To thrust out the lips, esp. in ill humor. **2** To be sullen. **3** To swell out; protrude. —*v.t.* **4** To utter with a pout. —*n.* **1** A pushing out of the lips as in petulance. **2** Ill humor; sullenness. [ME *pouten*] —**pout'er** *n.*

pout² (pout) *n.* One of various freshwater catfishes having a pouting appearance. [< OE *pūte*]

pout·er (pou'tər) *n.* A breed of pigeon that habitually puffs out the crop. Also **pouter pigeon.**

pov·er·ty (pov'ər·tē) *n.* **1** The state of being poor; need. **2** Scarcity of something needed. **3** Meagerness; inadequacy: *poverty* of language. [< L *pauper* poor]

pov·er·ty-strick·en (pov'ər·tē·strik'ən) *adj.* Suffering from poverty; destitute.

POW, P.O.W. Prisoner of War.

pow·der (pou'dər) *n.* **1** A mass of fine, free particles of a solid substance. **2** A cosmetic preparation. **3** A medicine in the form of powder. **4** GUNPOWDER. —**take a powder** *Slang* To run off; disappear suddenly. —*v.t.* **1** To pulverize. **2** To sprinkle or cover with or as with powder. —*v.i.* **3** To be reduced to powder. **4** To use powder as a cosmetic. [< L *pulvis, pulveris* dust] —**pow'der·er** *n.* —**pow'der·y** *adj.*

powder blue A soft medium blue.

powder horn The hollow horn of an ox or cow, fitted with a cover and formerly used by hunters or soldiers for holding gunpowder.

powder puff A soft pad used to apply powder to the skin.

pow·er (pou'ər) *n.* **1** Ability to act; potency. **2** Potential capacity. **3** Strength or force. **4** The right, ability, or capacity to exercise control. **5** Any agent that exercises control or dominion: naval *power.* **6** Great or telling force or effect. **7** Any form of energy that can perform work: water *power.* **8** *Physics* The time rate at which energy is transferred, or work is done. **9** *Math.* **a** The product of a number taken a given number of times as a factor. **b** An exponent. **10** *Optics* Magnifying capacity, as of a lens. —**in power** **1** In office. **2** In control. —**the powers that be** Those in control. —*v.t.* **1** To provide with means of propulsion. **2** To force or push, esp. when overcoming resistance: He *powered* his way through for a touchdown. —*v.i.* **3** To force one's way: The truck *powered* through the mud. —*adj.* Operated by a motor or by electricity: *power* tool. [< OF *poeir* be able] —**Syn.** *n.* **1** capacity, efficacy. **3** energy, might. **4** authority, command.

pow·er·boat (pou'ər·bōt') *n.* A motorboat.

pow·er·ful (pou'ər·fəl) *adj.* **1** Possessing great force. **2** Having great intensity or energy. **3** Exercising great authority. **4** Having great effect on the mind; convincing. —*adv. Informal* Very; exceedingly. —**pow'er·ful·ly** *adv.*

pow·er·house (pou'ər·hous') *n.* **1** A station where electricity is generated. **2** *Slang* A person or thing of great might or force.

pow·er·less (pou'ər·lis) *adj.* **1** Completely lacking power; helpless or weak. **2** Without authority. —**pow'er·less·ly** *adv.* —**pow'er·less·ness** *n.*

power of attorney *Law* **1** The power to act for another conferred upon an agent. **2** The document by which such authority is conferred.

power play In politics, business, diplomacy, military operations, etc., a maneuver made by the use or threatened use of superior power.

power politics The use or threatened use by nations of superior military or economic force to exact international concessions.

power structure **1** The group of persons who control a political or business organization. **2** The chain of command existing among the members of such a group.

pow·wow (pou'wou') *n.* **1** A North American Indian ceremony of a medicine man involving a dance, feast, or other demonstration, to cure the sick or effect success in hunting, war, etc. **2** An Indian council. **3** *Informal* Any meeting or conference. —*v.i.* To hold a deliberative council. [< Algon.]

pox (poks) *n.* **1** Any disease characterized by skin eruptions: chicken *pox.* **2** Syphilis. [Var. of *pocks,* pl. of POCK]

P.P., p.p. parcel post; parish priest; postpaid.

pp pianissimo.

p.p., pp., past participle.

pp. pages; privately printed.

ppd. postpaid; prepaid.

pph. pamphlet.

ppl. participle.

ppr., p.pr. present participle.

P.P.S., p.p.s. additional postscript (L *post postscriptum*).

P.Q. Province of Quebec.

PR Puerto Rico (P.O. abbr.)

PR, P.R., p.r. Public Relations.

P.R. Puerto Rico; proportional representation.

Pr praseodymium.

pr. pair; pairs; paper; power; present; price; priest; prince; printing; pronoun.

prac·ti·ca·ble (prak'tə·kə·bəl) *adj.* **1** That can be put into practice; feasible. **2** Usable. —**prac'ti·ca·bil'i·ty, prac'ti·ca·ble·ness** *n.* —**prac'ti·ca·bly** *adv.*

prac·ti·cal (prak'ti·kəl) *adj.* **1** Pertaining to actual use and experience rather than theory. **2** Trained by practice or experience. **3** Useful. **4** Manifested in practice. [< Gk. *praktikos* fit for doing] —**prac'ti·cal'i·ty** (-kal'ə·tē), **prac'ti·cal·ness** *n.*

practical joke A joke involving action instead of wit or words; a trick.

prac·ti·cal·ly (prak'tik·lē) *adv.* **1** In a practical manner. **2** To all intents and purposes.

practical nurse A nurse with practical experience in the care of the sick, but who is not a registered nurse.

prac·tice (prak'tis) *v.* **·ticed, ·tic·ing** *v.t.* **1** To make use of habitually: to *practice* economy. **2** To apply in action: *Practice* what you preach. **3** To work at as a profession: to *practice* law. **4** To do or perform repeatedly in order to acquire skill. —*v.i.* **5** To repeat or rehearse something in order to acquire proficiency. **6** To work at or pursue a profession. —*n.* **1** Any customary action; habit. **2** An established custom or usage. **3** The act or process of executing or accomplishing. **4** The pursuit of a profession; the *practice* of medicine. **5** Frequent and repeated exercise in order to gain skill. **6** The skill so gained: The violinist was out of *practice.* **7** The rules by which legal proceedings are governed. Also **prac'tise.** [< LL *practicus* practical] —**prac'tic·er** *n.* —**Syn.** *v.* **4** drill, exercise, rehearse. • In Britain, *practice* is almost invariably the spelling used for the noun, *practise* for the verb. In the U.S., the noun form is more commonly *practice,* although *practise* is also used; both spellings are widely used as verbs.

prac·ticed (prak'tist) *adj.* **1** Expert by use or habit; experienced. **2** Acquired by practice. Also **prac'tised.**

---

add, āce, câre, pälm; end, ēven; it, īce; odd, ōpen, ôrder; tŏŏk, pōōl; up, bûrn; ə = a in *above, u* in *focus;* yŏŏ = u in *fuse;* oil; pout; check; go; ring; thin; this; zh, *vision.* < derived from; ? origin uncertain or unknown.

prac·ti·tion·er (prak·tish'ən·ər) *n.* 1 One who practices an art or profession. 2 A Christian Science healer.

prae·no·men (prē·nō'mən) *n. pl.* **·no·mens** or **·nom·i·na** (-nom'ə·nə) The name prefixed to an ancient Roman family name to mark the individual. [< L *prae* before + *nomen* name]

prae·tor (prē'tər) *n.* A magistrate or judge in ancient Rome, ranking just below a consul. [L] —**prae·to·ri·al** (prē·tôr'ē·əl, -tō'rē-) *adj.* —**prae·tor'i·an** *adj., n.*

prag·mat·ic (prag·mat'ik) *adj.* 1 Practical; dealing with facts. 2 Active rather than thoughtful. 3 Of or pertaining to pragmatism. 4 Officious; interfering. 5 Opinionated. Also **prag·mat'i·cal**, esp. for defs. 1, 2, 4, 5. [< Gk. *pragma* a thing done] —**prag·mat'i·cal·ly** *adv.* —**prag·mat'i·cal·ness** *n.*

prag·ma·tism (prag'mə·tiz'əm) *n. Philos.* The doctrine that ideas have value only in terms of their practical consequences. —**prag'ma·tist** *n.*

prai·rie (prâr'ē) *n.* A level or rolling tract of treeless land covered with coarse grass and generally of rich soil. [< L *pratum* meadow]

prairie chicken A large, henlike grouse of North American grasslands. Also **prairie hen.**

prairie dog A burrowing rodent of the plains of North America, that lives in large communities.

prairie schooner COVERED WAGON.

prairie wolf COYOTE.

praise (prāz) *v.t.* **praised, prais·ing** 1 To express approval of; applaud. 2 To express adoration of; glorify (God, etc.). —*n.* The act of praising or the state of being praised; commendation or adoration. —**sing (one's) praises** To praise highly. [< L *pretium* price] —**prais'er** *n.* —**Syn.** *v.* 1 commend, eulogize, extol, laud. *n.* acclaim, applause, eulogy, plaudit.

praise·wor·thy (prāz'wûr'thē) *adj.* Worthy of praise; commendable. —**praise'wor'thi·ly** *adv.* —**praise'wor'thi·ness** *n.*

pra·line (prä'lēn, prā'-) *n.* A crisp confection made of pecans or other nuts browned in boiling sugar. [< Count Duplessis-*Praslin*, 1598–1675, French soldier]

pram (pram) *n. Brit. Informal* A baby carriage. [Short for PERAMBULATOR]

prance (prans, präns) *v.* **pranced, pranc·ing** *v.i.* 1 To move with high steps, esp. by springing from the hind legs, as a spirited horse. 2 To ride on a prancing horse. 3 To move in an arrogant manner; swagger. 4 To gambol; caper. — *v.t.* 5 To cause to prance. —*n.* The act of prancing. [< Scand.] —**pranc'er** *n.* —**pranc'ing·ly** *adv.*

prank[1] (prangk) *n.* A mischievous act; joke. —*v.i.* To play pranks or tricks. [?] —**prank'ish** *adj.* —**prank'ish·ly** *adv.* —**prank'ish·ness, prank'ster** *n.*

prank[2] (prangk) *v.t.* 1 To decorate gaudily. —*v.i.* 2 To make an ostentatious show. [?]

pra·se·o·dym·i·um (prā'zē·ō·dim'ē·əm, prā'sē-) *n.* A soft, silvery, rare-earth element (symbol Pr). [< Gk. *prasios* light green + (DI)DYMIUM]

prate (prāt) *v.* **prat·ed, prat·ing** *v.i.* 1 To talk idly; chatter. —*v.t.* 2 To utter idly or emptily. —*n.* Idle talk; prattle. [ME *praten*] —**prat'er** *n.* —**prat'ing·ly** *adv.*

prat·fall (prat'fôl') *n. Slang* A fall on the buttocks, esp. viewed as comical. [< earlier *prat* buttocks + FALL]

prat·tle (prat'l) *v.* **·tled, ·tling** *v.i.* 1 To talk like a child; prate. —*v.t.* 2 To utter in a foolish way: to *prattle* secrets. —*n.* 1 Childish speech; babble. 2 Idle or foolish talk. [Freq. of PRATE] —**prat'tler** *n.* —**prat'tling·ly** *adv.*

prawn (prôn) *n.* Any of various edible, shrimplike shellfish. [ME *prane*]

pray (prā) *v.i.* 1 To address prayers to a deity. 2 To make entreaty; beg. —*v.t.* 3 To ask (someone) earnestly; entreat. 4 To ask for by prayers or entreaty. 5 To effect by prayer. [< L *precari* ask, pray]

prayer (prâr) *n.* 1 The act of offering reverent petitions to a deity. 2 Any earnest request. 3 *Often pl.* A religious service made up largely of prayer. 4 Something prayed for. 5 A form of words appropriate to prayer. [< L *precari*

pray] —**prayer'ful** *adj.* —**prayer'ful·ly** *adv.* —**prayer'ful·ness** *n.*

prayer book A book of ritual prescribed for conducting a church service.

praying mantis Any of various predatory, long-bodied insects which grasp their prey with forelegs folded as if in prayer.

Praying mantis

pre- *prefix* 1 Before in time or order; prior to; preceding: *precancel.* 2 Preliminary to; preparing for: *preschool.* [< L *prae* before]

preach (prēch) *v.i.* 1 To deliver a sermon. 2 To give advice or urge a course of action, esp. in a meddlesome or tedious way. —*v.t.* 3 To advocate or recommend urgently: to *preach* peace. 4 To proclaim; expound upon. 5 To deliver (a sermon, etc.). [< L *prae-* before + *dicare* make known]

preach·er (prē'chər) *n.* One who preaches; specifically, a clergyman.

preach·i·fy (prē'chə·fī) *v.i.* **·fied, ·fy·ing** *Informal* To preach or discourse tediously. —**preach'i·fi·ca'tion** *n.*

preach·ment (prēch'mənt) *n.* A moral lecture, esp. a wearisome one.

preach·y (prē'chē) *adj. Informal* **preach·i·er, preach·i·est** Marked by sanctimony or cant. —**preach'i·ness** *n.*

pre·am·ble (prē'am·bəl) *n.* 1 A statement introductory to and explanatory of what follows, as in a constitution or a contract. 2 A preliminary event or action. [< L *prae* before + *ambulare* to walk] —**pre·am'bu·lar'y** *adj.*

pre·ar·range (prē'ə·rānj') **·ranged, ·rang·ing** *v.t.* To plan or arrange ahead of time. —**pre·ar·range'ment** *n.*

preb·end (preb'ənd) *n.* 1 A stipend allotted to a clergyman from the revenues of a cathedral or church. 2 A clergyman who receives a prebend: also **preb·en·dar·y** (preb'ən·der'ē). [< L *prae-* in front of, before + *habere* have] —**preb·en'dal** *adj.*

prec. preceding.

Pre-Cam·bri·an (prē·kam'brē·ən) *adj. & n.* See GEOLOGY. Also **Pre·cam'bri·an.**

pre·can·cel (prē·kan'səl) *v.t.* **·celed** or **·celled, ·cel·ing** or **·cel·ling** To cancel (stamps) before use on mail. —*n.* A stamp so canceled.

pre·car·i·ous (pri·kâr'ē·əs) *adj.* 1 Subject to uncertainty. 2 Subject to or leading to danger; hazardous. [< L *precarius* obtained by prayer] —**pre·car'i·ous·ly** *adv.* —**pre·car'i·ous·ness** *n.* —**Syn.** 1 doubtful. 2 insecure, perilous, risky.

pre·cau·tion (pri·kô'shən) *n.* 1 Care taken in advance against danger, etc. 2 A provision made for some emergency. [< L *prae-* before + *cavere* take care] —**pre·cau'tion·al, pre·cau·tion·ar·y** (pri·kô'shən·er'ē) *adj.*

pre·cede (pri·sēd') *v.t. & v.i.* **·ced·ed, ·ced·ing** To go before in order, place, rank, time, etc. [< L *prae-* before + *cedere* go]

pre·ce·dence (pri·sēd'ns, pres'ə·dəns) *n.* 1 The act or right of preceding in place, time, or rank. 2 Higher or superior rank. Also **pre·ce'den·cy.**

prec·e·dent (pres'ə·dənt) *n.* A case that may serve as an example or model for a future action, procedure, etc. —*adj.* (pri·sēd'nt) Previous; preceding. —**prec·e·den'tial** (pres'ə·den'shəl) *adj.* —**prec'e·dent·ly** *adv.*

pre·ced·ing (pri·sē'ding) *adj.* Going before, as in time, place, or rank; foregoing.

pre·cen·tor (pri·sen'tər) *n.* The leader of the musical part of a church service. [< L *prae-* before + *canere* to sing] —**pre·cen·to·ri·al** (prē'sen·tôr'ē·əl, -tō'rē-) *adj.*

pre·cept (prē'sept) *n.* A prescribed rule of conduct or action. [< L *prae-* before + *capere* receive, take]

pre·cep·tor (pri·sep'tər) *n.* A teacher. [< L *praeceptor* teacher] —**pre·cep·to·ri·al** (prē'sep·tôr'ē·əl, -tō'rē-) *adj.*

pre·ces·sion (pri·sesh'ən) *n.* 1 The act of preceding or coming first. 2 The complex motion of a rotating body whose axis is displaced by a torque. —**pre·ces'sion·al** *adj.*

pre·cinct (prē'singkt) *n.* 1 A place definitely marked off by fixed lines. 2 A minor territorial or jurisdictional district. 3 An election district. 4 A police subdivision of a city or town. [< LL *praecingere* gird about]

pre·ci·os·i·ty (presh'ē·os'ə·tē) *n.* Extreme fastidiousness, as in speech, style, or taste. [< L *pretiosus* precious]

precious 571 prefabricate

pre·cious (presh′əs) *adj.* 1 Highly priced or prized, as for rarity or other value. 2 Beloved; cherished. 3 *Informal* Very considerable. 4 Too refined; fastidious: a *precious* writer. [< L *pretiosus* < *pretium* price] —**pre′cious·ly** *adv.* —**pre′cious·ness** *n.* —**Syn.** 1 costly, priceless, valuable.

prec·i·pice (pres′i·pis) *n.* A high, steep place; the brink of a cliff. [< L *praeceps* headlong < *prae-* before + *caput* head]

pre·cip·i·tant (pri·sip′ə·tənt) *adj.* 1 Rushing onward quickly and heedlessly: *precipitant* speed. 2 Rash in thought or action. —*n. Chem.* A substance that causes a precipitate to form. —**pre·cip′i·tance, pre·cip′i·tan·cy** *n.* —**pre·cip′i·tant·ly** *adv.*

pre·cip·i·tate (pri·sip′ə·tit) *adj.* 1 Rushing down headlong. 2 Lacking due deliberation; hasty. 3 Sudden and brief. —*v.* (pri·sip′ə·tāt) **·tat·ed, ·tat·ing** *v.t.* 1 To hasten the occurrence of. 2 To hurl from or as from a height. 3 *Meteorol.* To cause (water vapor) to condense and fall as a liquid or solid. 4 *Chem.* To separate (a constituent) in solid form, as from a solution. —*v.i.* 5 *Meteorol.* To fall as water or ice. 6 *Chem.* To separate out of solution as a solid. 7 To fall headlong; rush. —*n.* (pri·sip′ə·tit, -tāt) *Chem.* A solid precipitated from a solution. [< L *praeceps* headlong] —**pre·cip′i·tate·ly** *adv.* —**pre·cip′i·tate·ness, pre·cip′i·ta′tor** *n.* —**pre·cip′i·ta′tive** *adj.*

pre·cip·i·ta·tion (pri·sip′ə·tā′shən) *n.* 1 The state of being thrown downward. 2 Headlong or rash haste. 3 A falling, flowing, or rushing down with violence or rapidity. 4 *Chem.* a The process of precipitating any of the constituents of a solution. b PRECIPITATE. 5 *Meteorol.* The depositing of moisture or ice from the atmosphere upon the surface of the earth. 6 Rain, snow, sleet, etc.

pre·cip·i·tous (pri·sip′ə·təs) *adj.* 1 Very steep. 2 Headlong and downward in motion. 3 Headlong in disposition. [< L *praeceps* headlong] —**pre·cip′i·tous·ly** *adv.* —**pre·cip′i·tous·ness** *n.*

pré·cis (prā·sē′, prā′sē) *n. pl.* **·cis** (-sēz′, -sēz) A concise summary. [F, lit., precise]

pre·cise (pri·sīs′) *adj.* 1 Sharply or clearly determined; accurate. 2 No more and no less than. 3 Scrupulously observant of rule; punctilious. [< L *praecisus,* p.p. of *praecidere* cut off short] —**pre·cise′ness** *n.*

pre·cise·ly (pri·sīs′lē) *adv.* In a precise manner. —*interj.* Yes, indeed; quite so.

pre·ci·sion (pri·sizh′ən) *n.* The quality of being precise; accuracy. —**pre·ci′sion·ist** *n.*

pre·clude (pri·klood′) *v.t.* **·clud·ed, ·clud·ing** To render impossible or ineffectual by antecedent action; prevent. [< L *prae-* before + *cludere* to shut] —**pre·clu′sion** (-kloo′zhən) *n.* —**pre·clu′sive** (-kloo′siv) *adj.* —**pre·clu′sive·ly** *adv.*

pre·co·cious (pri·kō′shəs) *adj.* 1 Developing before the natural season. 2 Unusually forward or advanced, as a child. [< L *praecox*] —**pre·co′cious·ly** *adv.* —**pre·co′cious·ness, pre·coc′i·ty** (-kos′ə·tē) *n.*

pre·con·ceive (prē′kən·sēv′) *v.t.* **·ceived, ·ceiv·ing** To form an idea or opinion of beforehand. —**pre·con·cep·tion** (prē′kən·sep′shən) *n.*

pre·con·cert (prē′kən·sûrt′) *v.t.* To arrange in advance, as by agreement. —**pre′con·cert′ed·ly** *adv.*

pre·con·di·tion (prē′kən·dish′ən) *n.* Something that is required for something that follows; prerequisite.

pre·cur·sor (pri·kûr′sər) *n.* One who or that which precedes; forerunner. [< L *prae-* before + *currere* to run]

pre·cur·so·ry (pri·kûr′sə·rē) *adj.* 1 Being a precursor. 2 Preliminary; introductory.

pred. predicate; predication; prediction.

pre·da·cious (pri·dā′shəs) *adj.* PREDATORY. Also **pre·da′ceous.** [< L *praeda* prey] —**pre·da′cious·ness, pre·dac′i·ty** (-das′ə·tē) *n.*

pred·a·to·ry (pred′ə·tôr′ē, -tō′rē) *adj.* 1 Living by preying upon other animals: a *predatory* animal. 2 Characterized by plundering or stealing. [< L *praeda* prey] —**pred′a·tor, pred′a·to′ri·ness** *n.* —**pred′a·to′ri·ly** *adv.*

pre·de·cease (prē′di·sēs′) *v.t.* **·ceased, ·ceas·ing** To die before, as another person.

pred·e·ces·sor (pred′ə·ses′ər) *n.* 1 One who goes or has

gone before another in a position, office, etc. 2 A thing that has preceded another. 3 An ancestor. [< L *prae-* before + *decedere* retire]

pre·des·ti·nate (prē·des′tə·nit, -nāt) *adj.* Foreordained by divine decree. —*v.t.* **·nat·ed, ·nat·ing** (-nāt) To foreordain by divine decree or purpose. [< L *prae-* before + *destinare* destine]

pre·des·ti·na·tion (prē·des′tə·nā′shən) *n.* 1 The act of predestinating; fate. 2 *Theol.* The foreordination of all things by God.

pre·des·tine (prē·des′tin) *v.t.* **·tined, ·tin·ing** 1 To decree or destine beforehand. 2 PREDESTINATE.

pre·de·ter·mine (prē′di·tûr′min) *v.t.* **·mined, ·min·ing** To determine beforehand; decide in advance. —**pre′de·ter′mi·nate** (-mə·nit) *adj.* —**pre′de·ter′mi·na′tion** *n.*

pred·i·ca·ble (pred′i·kə·bəl) *adj.* That may be predicated or affirmed. —**pred′i·ca·bil′i·ty, pred′i·ca·ble·ness** *n.* —**pred′i·ca·bly** *adv.*

pre·dic·a·ment (pri·dik′ə·mənt) *n.* 1 A trying, embarrassing, or puzzling situation. 2 A specific state, position, or situation. [< LL *praedicamentum* that which is predicated] —**Syn.** 1 dilemma, fix, plight, strait.

pred·i·cate (pred′i·kāt) *v.* **·cat·ed, ·cat·ing** *v.t.* 1 To declare; affirm. 2 To affirm concerning the subject of a proposition. 3 To found or base (an argument, proposition, etc.): with *on* or *upon.* —*v.i.* 4 To make a statement or affirmation. —*adj.* 1 Predicated. 2 *Gram.* Belonging to the predicate. In "Trees are leafy," *leafy* is a **predicate adjective;** in "He was king," *king* is a **predicate noun.** —*n.* (pred′i·kit) *Gram.* The word or words in a sentence that express what is affirmed or denied of a subject. In the sentence, "Life is short," "is short" is the predicate. [< L *praedicare* make known] —**pred′i·ca′tion** *n.* —**pred′i·ca′tive** *adj.* —**pred′i·ca′tive·ly** *adv.*

pre·dict (pri·dikt′) *v.t.* 1 To make known beforehand. 2 To assert on the basis of theory, data, or experience but in advance of proof. —*v.i.* 3 To make a prediction. [< L *prae-* before + *dicere* say] —**pre·dict′a·ble** *adj.* —**pre·dict′a·bly** *adv.* —**pre·dic′tor** *n.*

pre·dic·tion (pri·dik′shən) *n.* 1 The act of predicting. 2 The thing predicted; forecast. —**pre·dic′tive** *adj.* —**pre·dic′tive·ly** *adv.*

pre·di·gest (prē′di·jest′, -dī-) *v.t.* To treat (food), as with digestive enzymes, before introduction into the stomach. —**pre′di·ges′tion** *n.*

pre·di·lec·tion (pred′ə·lek′shən, prē′də-) *n.* A preference or liking: with *for.* [< L *prae-* before + *diligere* love, choose]

pre·dis·pose (prē′dis·pōz′) *v.t.* **·posed, ·pos·ing** To give a tendency to; make susceptible: Exhaustion *predisposes* one to sickness. —**pre′dis·po·si·tion** (prē′dis·pə·zish′ən) *n.*

pre·dom·i·nant (pri·dom′ə·nənt) *adj.* Superior in power, influence, number, or degree. —**pre·dom′in·ance, pre·dom′in·an·cy** *n.* —**pre·dom′i·nant·ly** *adv.*

pre·dom·i·nate (pri·dom′ə·nāt) *v.i.* **·nat·ed, ·nat·ing** 1 To have influence or control: with *over.* 2 To be superior to all others, as in power, height, number, etc. —**pre·dom′i·nat′ing·ly** *adv.* —**pre·dom′i·na′tion** *n.*

pre·em·i·nent (prē·em′ə·nənt) *adj.* Supremely eminent; distinguished above all others. —**pre·em′i·nent·ly** *adv.* —**pre·em′i·nence** *n.*

pre·empt (prē·empt′) *v.t.* 1 To seize or appropriate beforehand. 2 To occupy (public land) so as to acquire by preemption. —**pre·emp′tor** *n.*

pre·emp·tion (prē·emp′shən) *n.* 1 The right or act of purchasing before others. 2 Public land obtained by exercising this right. [< L *prae-* before + *emptus,* pp. of *emere* buy] —**pre·emp′tive, pre·emp′to·ry** (-tər·ē) *adj.*

preen (prēn) *v.t.* 1 To trim with the beak, as birds their feathers. 2 To dress or adorn (oneself) carefully. —*v.i.* 3 To primp; prink. [ME *preinen*] —**preen′er** *n.*

pref. preface; prefatory; preference; preferred; prefix.

pre·fab (prē′fab′) *Informal n.* A prefabricated structure. —*adj.* Prefabricated. —*v.t.* **·fabbed, ·fab·bing** PREFABRICATE.

pre·fab·ri·cate (prē·fab′rə·kāt) *v.t.* **·cat·ed, ·cat·ing** 1 To

add, āce, câre, pälm; end, ēven; it, īce; odd, ōpen, ôrder; tōōk, pōōl; up, bûrn; ə = a in above, u in focus; yōō = u in fuse; oil; pout; check; go; ring; thin; this; zh, vision. < derived from; ? origin uncertain or unknown.

fabricate beforehand. **2** To manufacture in sections that can be rapidly assembled, as a building. —**pre·fab′ri·ca′tion** *n.*

pref·ace (pref′is) *n.* **1** A brief explanation to the reader at the beginning of a publication. **2** Any introductory speech, writing, etc. —*v.t.* ·**aced,** ·**ac·ing 1** To introduce or furnish with a preface. **2** To be or serve as a preface for. [< L *prae-* before + *fari* speak]

pref·a·to·ry (pref′ə·tôr′ē, -tō′rē) *adj.* Of the nature of a preface; introductory. Also **pref′a·to′ri·al.** —**pref′a·to′ri·ly** *adv.*

pre·fect (prē′fekt) *n.* **1** In ancient Rome, any of various civil and military officials. **2** In France, the chief administrator of a department. [< L *prae-* before + *facere* make, do]

pre·fec·ture (prē′fek·chər) *n.* The office, district, or authority of a prefect. —**pre·fec′tur·al** *adj.*

pre·fer (pri·fûr′) *v.t.* ·**ferred,** ·**fer·ring 1** To hold in higher regard or esteem; like better. **2** To give priority to. **3** To advance or promote. **4** To offer, as a suit or charge, for consideration or decision before a court. [< L *prae-* before + *ferre* to bear] —**pre·fer′rer** *n.*

pref·er·a·ble (pref′ər·ə·bəl) *adj.* To be preferred; more desirable. —**pref′er·a·bil′i·ty, pref′er·a·ble·ness** *n.* —**pref′er·a·bly** *adv.*

pref·er·ence (pref′ər·əns) *n.* **1** The choice of one thing or person over another. **2** The state of being preferred. **3** An object of favor or choice. **4** The giving of priority to one person over others; favoritism. **5** The right to a prior choice or claim.

pref·er·en·tial (pref′ə·ren′shəl) *adj.* **1** Indicating or arising from partiality. **2** Possessing or giving priority. —**pref′er·en′tial·ism** *n.* —**pref′er·en′tial·ly** *adv.*

preferential shop A shop that gives precedence to union members when hiring, granting promotions, etc.

pre·fer·ment (pri·fûr′mənt) *n.* **1** The act of promoting or appointing to higher office. **2** A superior post or dignity: said esp. of ecclesiastical rank.

pre·ferred (pri·fûrd′) *adj.* **1** Having the first claim: *preferred* bonds or stock. **2** Having gained promotion. **3** Chosen by or as if by preference.

preferred stock The stock of a corporation that assures the holder of dividends before any are paid on common stock.

pre·fig·ure (prē·fig′yər) *v.t.* ·**ured,** ·**ur·ing 1** To represent in advance; foreshadow. **2** To imagine or picture to oneself beforehand. —**pre·fig′u·ra′tion** *n.* —**pre·fig·ur·a·tive** (prē·fig′yər·ə·tiv) *adj.*

pre·fix (prē′fiks) *n.* **1** *Gram.* A syllable affixed to the beginning of a word to modify or alter the meaning, as *non-* in *nonessential* or *post-* in *postwar.* **2** Something placed before, as a title before a name. —*v.t.* (prē·fiks′) To put before or at the beginning. [< L< *prae-* before + *figere* to fix] —**pre′fix·al** *adj.* —**pre·fix·ion** (prē·fik′shən) *n.*

preg·na·ble (preg′nə·bəl) *adj.* Weak enough to be conquered. [< L *prehendere* seize] —**preg′na·bil′i·ty** *n.*

preg·nan·cy (preg′nən·sē) *n. pl.* ·**cies** The condition or a time of being pregnant.

preg·nant (preg′nənt) *adj.* **1** Carrying developing offspring in the uterus. **2** Carrying great weight or significance. **3** Fruitful; teeming with ideas. **4** Implying more than is expressed. [< L *praegnans*] —**preg′nant·ly** *adv.*

pre·hen·sile (pri·hen′sil) *adj.* Adapted for grasping or holding, as the tail of a monkey. [< L *prehendere* seize] —**pre·hen·sil·i·ty** (prē′hen·sil′ə·tē) *n.*

pre·his·tor·ic (prē′his·tôr′ik, -tor′-, prē·is-) *adj.* Of or belonging to a time before that covered by written history. Also **pre′his·tor′i·cal.** —**pre′his·tor′i·cal·ly** *adv.* —**pre′his·to·ry** *n.*

pre·judge (prē·juj′) *v.t.* ·**judged,** ·**judg·ing** To judge before or without proper inquiry. —**pre·judg′er, pre·judg′ment, pre·judge′ment** *n.*

prej·u·dice (prej′oo·dis) *n.* **1** A judgment or opinion formed without due examination of facts, etc. **2** An unreasonable judgment held despite facts to the contrary. **3** Fear and hatred for other races, religions, etc. **4** Detriment arising from a hasty and unfair judgment. —*v.t.* ·**diced,** ·**dic·ing 1** To affect or influence with a prejudice; bias. **2** To affect detrimentally by some action or opinion.

[< L *prae-* before + *judicium* judgment] —**Syn.** *n.* **1** bias, preconception. **3** bigotry, intolerance, racism.

prej·u·di·cial (prej′oo·dish′əl) *adj.* Having power or tendency to injure. —**prej′u·di′cial·ly** *adv.*

prel·a·cy (prel′ə·sē) *n. pl.* ·**cies 1** The system of church government by prelates. **2** The function of a prelate. **3** Prelates collectively.

prel·ate (prel′it) *n.* A member of a higher order of clergy, as a bishop. [< L *praelatus* set over] —**prel′ate·ship** *n.*

prelim. preliminary.

pre·lim·i·nar·y (pri·lim′ə·ner′ē) *adj.* Antecedent or introductory to the main discourse, proceedings, or business; prefatory; preparatory. —*n. pl.* ·**ries 1** A preparatory step or procedure. **2** A preliminary examination. [< PRE- + L *limen, liminis* threshold] —**pre·lim′i·nar′i·ly** *adv.*

prel·ude (prel′yōōd, prāl-, prā′lōōd, prē′-) *n.* **1** *Music* **a** An independent instrumental composition of moderate length. **b** An opening piece at the start of a church service. **c** The overture of an opera. **d** An opening section or movement for a composition. **2** Any introductory or opening performance or event. —*v.* ·**ud·ed,** ·**ud·ing** *v.t.* **1** To introduce with a prelude. **2** To serve as a prelude to. —*v.i.* **3** To serve as a prelude. **4** To provide or play a prelude. [< L *prae-* before + *ludere* to play]

prem. premium.

pre·mar·i·tal (prē·mar′ə·təl) *adj.* Occurring or existing before marriage. —**pre·mar′i·tal·ly** *adv.*

pre·ma·ture (prē′mə·chōōr′, -tyōōr′) *adj.* Existing, arriving, or done before the proper time; untimely. [< L < *prae-* before + *maturus* ripe] —**pre′ma·ture′ly** *adv.* —**pre′ma·tu′ri·ty, pre′ma·ture′ness** *n.*

pre·med·i·cal (prē·med′i·kəl) *adj.* Pertaining to studies required for admission to medical school.

pre·med·i·tate (prē·med′ə·tāt) *v.t. & v.i.* ·**tat·ed,** ·**tat·ing** To plan or consider beforehand. —**pre·med′i·tat′ed·ly** *adv.* —**pre·med′i·ta′tive** *adj.* —**pre·med′i·ta′tor** *n.*

pre·med·i·ta·tion (prē·med′ə·tā′shən) *n.* The deliberate intention to do a certain thing, esp. to commit a crime.

pre·mi·er (pri·mir′, -myir′, prē′mē·ər, *esp. Brit.* prem′yər) *adj.* **1** First in rank or position; principal. **2** First in order of occurrence; earliest. —*n.* **1** The head of government, esp. a prime minister. **2** In Canada, the prime minister of a province. [F< L *primus* first] —**pre′mi·er·ship** *n.*

pre·miere (pri·myâr′, -mir′, -mē·âr′) *adj.* **1** First. **2** Leading; chief: *premiere* ballerina. —*n.* The formal opening of a play, opera, film, ballet, etc. —*v.* ·**miered,** ·**mier·ing** *v.t.* **1** To present publicly for the first time, as a play. —*v.i.* **2** To make one's first public performance. **3** To present a play, opera, etc., publicly for the first time. Also **pre·mière.** [< F *première*]

prem·ise (prem′is) *n.* **1** A proposition laid down that serves as a ground for argument or for a conclusion. **2** *Logic* Either of the two propositions in a syllogism from which the conclusion necessarily follows. **3** *pl.* A distinct portion of real estate; land with its appurtenances, as buildings. —*v.* (prem′is, pri·mīz′) ·**ised,** ·**is·ing** *v.t.* **1** To state beforehand, as by way of introduction or explanation. —*v.i.* **2** To make a premise. [< L *praemissus,* pp. of *praemittere* send before]

pre·mi·um (prē′mē·əm) *n.* **1** A reward or prize. **2** A sum offered or given to secure a loan. **3** The rate at which stocks, shares, or money are valued in excess of their nominal value. **4** The amount paid for insurance. **5** An object offered free or at low cost as an inducement to purchasers of certain goods or services. —**at a premium** Above par; valuable and in demand. [< L *prae-* before + *emere* to buy]

pre·mo·lar (prē·mō′lər) *adj.* Situated in front of a molar tooth. —*n.* A premolar tooth.

pre·mo·ni·tion (prē′mə·nish′ən, prem′ə-) *n.* **1** A warning of something yet to occur. **2** An instinctive foreboding; presentiment. [< L *prae-* before + *monere* warn] —**pre·mon·i·to·ry** (pri·mon′ə·tôr′ē, -tō′rē) *adj.* —**pre·mon′i·to′ri·ly** *adv.*

pre·na·tal (prē·nāt′l) *adj.* Happening, done, or made before birth: *prenatal* care. —**pre·na′tal·ly** *adv.*

pre·oc·cu·py (prē·ok′yə·pī) *v.t.* ·**pied,** ·**py·ing 1** To engage fully; engross, as the mind. **2** To take possession of in advance of another or others. —**pre·oc′cu·pan·cy** (-pən·sē), **pre·oc·cu·pa·tion** (prē·ok′yə·pā′shən) *n.*

pre·or·dain (prē'ôr·dān') v.t. To decide or decree beforehand; foreordain. —**pre·or·di·na·tion** (prē'ôr·də·nā'shən) n.

prep (prep) adj. *Informal* Preparatory: a *prep* school.

prep. preparation; preparatory; prepare; preposition.

pre·pack·age (prē·pak'ij) v.t. **·aged, ·a·ging** To package manufactured articles, food, etc., before placing on sale for consumers.

prep·a·ra·tion (prep'ə·rā'shən) n. 1 The act, process, or operation of preparing. 2 The fact or state of being prepared; readiness. 3 Something made or prepared, as a compound for a specific purpose; medicinal *preparations*. 4 Preliminary study, as for college or business.

pre·par·a·to·ry (pri·par'ə·tôr'ē, -tō'rē) adj. 1 Serving as a preparation; introductory. 2 Occupied in preparation, esp. for higher learning. —**pre·par'a·tor'i·ly** adv.

preparatory school A school in which students are prepared for admission to a college or university.

pre·pare (pri·pâr') v. **·pared, ·par·ing** v.t. 1 To make ready, fit, or qualified. 2 To provide with what is needed; outfit. 3 To bring to a state of completeness. —v.i. 4 To make preparations; get ready. [< L *prae-* before + *parare* make ready] —**pre·par·ed·ly** (pri·pâr'id·lē) adv. —**pre·par'er** n.

pre·par·ed·ness (pri·pâr'id·nis, -par'-) n. 1 Readiness. 2 Military readiness for war.

pre·pay (prē·pā') v.t. **·paid, ·pay·ing** To pay or pay for in advance. —**pre·pay'ment** n.

pre·pon·der·ant (pri·pon'dər·ənt) adj. Having superior force, weight, importance, number, etc. —**pre·pon'der·ance, pre·pon'der·an·cy** (-ən·sē) n. —**pre·pon'der·ant·ly** adv.

pre·pon·der·ate (pri·pon'də·rāt) v.i. **·at·ed, ·at·ing** 1 To be of greater weight. 2 To be of greater power, importance, quantity, etc.; predominate. [< L *prae-* before + *ponderare* weigh] —**pre·pon'der·a'tion** n.

prep·o·si·tion (prep'ə·zish'ən) n. *Gram.* 1 A word such as *for, from, in, to, with*, etc., functioning to indicate certain relations between other words. A preposition is usually placed before its object (whence its name), and together they constitute a prepositional phrase: He sat *beside* the fire; sick *at* heart; a man *of* honor. 2 Any word or construction that functions in a similar manner: He telephoned *in reference to* (equals *about*) your letter. [< L *prae-* before + *ponere* to place] —**prep·o·si'tion·al** adj. —**prep·o·si'tion·al·ly** adv.

pre·pos·sess (prē'pə·zes') v.t. 1 To preoccupy to the exclusion of other ideas, beliefs, etc. 2 To impress or influence beforehand favorably. 3 To prejudice. —**pre'pos·ses'sion** n.

pre·pos·sess·ing (prē'pə·zes'ing) adj. Inspiring a favorable opinion from the start. —**pre'pos·sess'ing·ly** adv.

pre·pos·ter·ous (pri·pos'tər·əs) adj. Contrary to nature, reason, or common sense; ridiculous. [< L *praeposterus* the last first, inverted] —**pre·pos'ter·ous·ly** adv. —**pre·pos'ter·ous·ness** n. —Syn. absurd, foolish, idiotic, irrational, silly.

pre·puce (prē'pyōōs) n. FORESKIN. [< L *praeputium*]

pre·quel (prē'kwəl) n. A story in the form of a book, movie, or television program that predates the events of an earlier story. [< PRE- + (SE)QUEL]

pre·req·ui·site (prē·rek'wə·zit) adj. Required as necessary to something that follows. —n. Something that is prerequisite.

pre·rog·a·tive (pri·rog'ə·tiv) n. 1 An unquestionable right, esp. a hereditary or official right: the royal *prerogative*. 2 Any generally recognized privilege. —adj. Of or holding a prerogative. [< L *praerogativa* right of voting first]

Pres. President.

pres. present; presidency.

pres·age (pres'ij) n. 1 An indication of something to come. 2 A presentiment; foreboding. 3 Prophetic meaning or import; prediction. —v. (pri·sāj') **·saged, ·sag·ing** v.t. 1 To give a portent of. 2 To have a presentiment of. 3 To predict; foretell. —v.i. 4 To make a prediction. [< L *prae-* before + *sagire* be aware of] —**pre·sag'er** n. —**pre·sag'ing·ly** adv.

pres·by·ter (prez'bə·tər, pres'-) n. 1 In the early church,

one of the elders. 2 In the Presbyterian church, an ordained clergyman or a layman who is a member of the governing body of a congregation. [< Gk. *presbyteros* an elder] —**pres'by·te'ri·al** (-bə·tir'ē·əl), **pres·byt'er·al** (-bit'ər·əl) adj.

Pres·by·te·ri·an (prez'bə·tir'ē·ən, pres'-) n. 1 One who believes in the government of the church by presbyters. 2 A member of the Presbyterian church. —adj. Of or pertaining to the Presbyterian church. —**Pres'by·te'ri·an·ism** n.

pres·by·ter·y (prez'bə·ter'ē, pres'-) n. pl. **·ter·ies** 1 In the Presbyterian church, a court having the ecclesiastical rule of a given district. 2 The district so represented. 3 The part of a church set apart for the officiating clergy.

pre·school (prē'skōōl') adj. For or designating a child past infancy but under school age. —n. (prē'skōōl') A nursery school.

pre·school·er (prē'skōōl'ər) n. 1 A child under school age. 2 A child attending a nursery school.

pre·sci·ence (presh'ē·əns, presh'ē·əns) n. Knowledge of events before they take place. [< L *prae-* before + *scire* know] —**pre'sci·ent** adj. —**pre'sci·ent·ly** adv.

pre·scribe (pri·skrīb') v. **·scribed, ·scrib·ing** v.t. 1 To set down as a direction or rule to be followed. 2 To order (a medicine or treatment) as a remedy. —v.i. 3 To lay down laws or rules. 4 To order medical treatment. [< L *prae-* before + *scribere* write] —**pre·scrib'er** n. —Syn. 1 command, designate, enjoin, ordain.

pre·script (prē'skript) n. A prescription or direction, as a rule of conduct. —adj. (pri·skript', prē'skript) Prescribed.

pre·scrip·tion (pri·skrip'shən) n. 1 The act of prescribing, directing, or dictating. 2 That which is prescribed. 3 a A physician's order for a medicine. b The remedy so ordered. —**pre·scrip'tive** adj. —**pre·scrip'tive·ly** adv.

pres·ence (prez'əns) n. 1 The state or fact of being present. 2 Vicinity within view or access: He said that in my *presence*. 3 Something invisible, but sensed, as a ghost. 4 Personal appearance; bearing. 5 Personal qualities collectively. 6 A person of high rank: a royal *presence*.

presence of mind Alertness and readiness of thinking in a situation of sudden danger, embarrassment, etc.

pres·ent[1] (prez'ənt) adj. 1 Being in a place or company referred to; being at hand. 2 Now going on; current. 3 *Gram.* Relating to or signifying what is going on at the time being: the *present* tense. —n. 1 Present time; now. 2 *Gram.* a The present tense. b A verb in this tense. —**at present** Now. —**by these presents** *Law* By this document. —**for the present** For the time being. [< L *praesens* being in front of or at hand]

pre·sent[2] (pri·zent') v.t. 1 To bring into the presence or acquaintance of another. 2 To display. 3 To suggest to the mind: This *presents* a problem. 4 To put forward for consideration or action, as a petition. 5 To make a gift to. 6 To offer formally: to *present* a diploma. 7 To exhibit before the public: to *present* a play. 8 To give or send: to *present* a bill. —**present arms** 1 To hold a gun vertically in front of and close to the body in salute. 2 This salute. 3 The command for a soldier to salute in this way. —n. (prez'ənt) That which is presented or given. [< L *praesentare* set before < *praesens* present] —**pre·sent'er** n.

pre·sent·a·ble (pri·zen'tə·bəl) adj. 1 Fit to be offered or bestowed. 2 In suitable condition or attire for company. 3 Fit to be shown or seen. —**pre·sent'a·bil'i·ty, pre·sent'a·ble·ness** n. —**pre·sent'a·bly** adv.

pres·en·ta·tion (prez'ən·tā'shən, prē'zən-) n. 1 The offering of a gift. 2 That which is bestowed; a present. 3 A formal introduction, esp. to a superior: *presentation* at court. 4 The bringing before the public, as a play. 5 A submitting for consideration: the *presentation* of a plan.

pres·ent-day (prez'ənt·dā') adj. Of the present time; current.

pre·sen·ti·ment (pri·zen'tə·mənt) n. A prophetic sense of something to come; a foreboding. [< L *prae-* before + *sentire* feel]

pres·ent·ly (prez'ənt·lē) adv. After a little time; shortly.

---

add, āce, câre, pälm; end, ēven; it, īce; odd, ōpen, ôrder; tŏŏk, pōōl; up, bûrn; ə = a in *above*, u in *focus*; yŏŏ = u in *fuse*; oil; pout; check; go; ring; thin; ᵺis; zh, *vision*. < derived from; ? origin uncertain or unknown.

pre·sent·ment (pri·zent′mənt) *n.* 1 The act of presenting. 2 A stage representation or a portrait.

present participle *Gram.* A participle expressing present action: *falling* snow.

present perfect *Gram.* The verb tense expressing an action completed by the present time: By now he *has finished* the task.

present tense *Gram.* The tense marking present time: I *go, do go, am going.*

pre·ser·va·tive (pri·zûr′və·tiv) *adj.* Serving or tending to preserve. —*n.* A substance that prevents deterioration or spoilage.

pre·serve (pri·zûrv′) *v.* **·served, ·serv·ing** *v.t.* 1 To keep in safety; guard. 2 To keep intact or unimpaired. 3 To prepare (food) for future consumption, as by drying, salting, pickling, canning, etc. 4 To keep from decomposition: to *preserve* a specimen in alcohol. 5 To keep for one's private use. —*v.i.* 6 To make preserves, as of fruit. —*n.* 1 *Usu. pl.* Fruit which has been cooked, usu. with sugar, to prevent its fermenting. 2 A place set apart for one's own private use. 3 An area set aside for the protection of wildlife. [< L *prae-* before + *servare* keep] —**pre·serv′a·bil′i·ty, pres·er·va·tion** (prez′ər·vā′shən), **pre·serv′er** *n.* —**Syn.** *v.* 1 defend, protect, secure, shield. 2 maintain, uphold.

pre·side (pri·zīd′) *v.i.* **·sid·ed, ·sid·ing** 1 To be in charge of an assembly, government, etc. 2 To exercise control. [< L *praesidere* sit in front of, protect, guard] —**pre·sid′er** *n.*

pres·i·den·cy (prez′ə·dən·sē) *n. pl.* **·cies** 1 The office, function, or term of office of a president. 2 *Often cap.* The office of president of the United States.

pres·i·dent (prez′ə·dənt) *n.* 1 One who is chosen to preside over an organized body, as a corporation, society, college, etc. 2 *Usu. cap.* The chief executive of a republic, as of the United States. —**pres·i·den·tial** (prez′ə·den′shəl) *adj.*

pre·sid·i·um (pri·sid′ē·əm, -zid′-) *n.* Any of several permanent executive committees in the U.S.S.R.

Pre·sid·i·um (pri·sid′ē·əm, -zid′-) *n.* The supreme policy-making committee of the Communist party of the U.S.S.R.

press[1] (pres) *v.t.* 1 To act upon by weight or pressure. 2 To compress so as to extract the juice. 3 To extract by pressure, as juice. 4 To exert pressure upon so as to smooth or shape. 5 To smooth or shape by heat and pressure, as clothes; iron. 6 To embrace closely; hug. 7 To force or impel; drive. 8 To distress or harass: I am *pressed* for time. 9 To urge persistently; importune. 10 To advocate persistently. 11 To put forward insistently: to *press* a gift on a friend. 12 To urge onward; hasten. —*v.i.* 13 To exert pressure; bear heavily. 14 To advance forcibly or with speed: *Press* on! 15 To press clothes, etc. 16 To crowd; cram. 17 To be urgent or importunate. —*n.* 1 A dense throng. 2 The act of crowding together or of straining forward. 3 Hurry or pressure of affairs. 4 An upright closet for clothes, etc.: a linen *press.* 5 An apparatus or machine by which pressure is applied, as for making wine, cider, etc. 6 Newspapers or periodical literature collectively. 7 The body of persons writing for such publications. 8 The art, process, or business of printing. 9 The place of business in which a printing press is set up. 10 Criticism, comments, news, etc., in newspapers and periodicals. [< L *pressare,* freq. of *premere* to press] —**press′er** *n.*

Press *def.5*

press[2] (pres) *v.t.* 1 To force into military or naval service. 2 To put to use in a manner not intended or desired.

press agent A person employed to advance the interests of his client by advertisements and other notices; a publicity agent. —**press·a·gen·try** (pres′ā′jən·trē) *n.*

press conference An interview granted by a celebrity, government official, etc., to a number of journalists at the same time.

press·ing (pres′ing) *adj.* Demanding immediate attention; urgent. —**press′ing·ly** *adv.* —**Syn.** exigent, imperative, important, necessary.

press·man (pres′mən) *n. pl.* **·men** (-mən) A man who operates or manages a printing press.

press release 1 A bulletin prepared by a news service.

2 A statement by a press agent, public relations department, etc., released to the press.

pres·sure (presh′ər) *n.* 1 The act of pressing, or the state of being pressed. 2 *Physics* A force distributed over a surface, expressed as units of force per unit area. 3 Pressure of a fluid exceeding atmospheric pressure: a hose under *pressure.* 4 An impelling or constraining influence: the *pressure* to conform socially. 5 Exigent demand on one's time or energy: to be under daily *pressure.* —*v.t.* **·sured, ·sur·ing** *Informal* To compel, as by forceful persuasion or influence. —**pres′sur·al** *adj.*

pressure cooker A vessel for cooking food at high temperature by means of steam under pressure.

pressure group An organized group which seeks to influence legislators and public opinion in behalf of its own special interests.

pres·sur·ize (presh′ə·rīz) *v.t.* **·ized, ·iz·ing** 1 To maintain near-normal atmospheric pressure in (an aircraft, space vehicle, or other enclosure in a low-pressure environment). 2 To maintain air pressure inside (an underwater vehicle, caisson, etc.) equal to the ambient water pressure. 3 To design (a bathysphere, etc.) to withstand high external pressure. 4 To increase pressure on or in. —**pres′sur·i·za′tion** *n.*

press·work (pres′wûrk′) *n.* 1 The operating or management of a printing press. 2 The work done by the press.

pres·ti·dig·i·ta·tion (pres′tə·dij′ə·tā′shən) *n.* The art of sleight of hand. [< LL *praestus* nimble + *digitus* finger] —**pres′ti·dig′i·ta′tor** *n.*

pres·tige (pres·tēzh′, -tēj′) *n.* Authority or importance based on past achievements or reputation. [< L *praestigium* illusion]

pres·ti·gious (pres·tij′əs, -tē′jəs) *adj.* Having or bestowing prestige or renown. —**pres·ti′gious·ly** *adv.* —**pres·ti′gious·ness** *n.*

pres·tis·si·mo (pres·tis′i·mō, *Ital.* pres·tēs′sē·mō) *adj. & adv. Music* As fast as possible. —*n.* A prestissimo passage, section, or movement. [Ital., superlative of *presto*]

pres·to (pres′tō) *adv. & adj.* 1 *Music* Very fast. 2 At once; speedily. —*n.* A presto passage or movement. [Ital.]

pre·stressed concrete (prē′strest′) Concrete cast over taut steel cables, etc., to increase its tensile strength.

pre·sume (pri·zōōm′) *v.* **·sumed, ·sum·ing** *v.t.* 1 To take upon oneself without permission. 2 To assume to be true until disproved: I *presume* you are right. —*v.i.* 3 To make excessive demands: with *on* or *upon:* He *presumes* on my good nature. [< L *praesumere* take first] —**pre·sum′a·ble** *adj.* —**pre·sum′a·bly, pre·sum·ed·ly** (pri·zōō′mid·lē) *adv.* —**pre·sum′er** *n.*

pre·sump·tion (pri·zump′shən) *n.* 1 The act of presuming. 2 Something taken for granted. 3 A reason for presuming; probability. 4 Overweening self-assertion; arrogance.

pre·sump·tive (pri·zump′tiv) *adj.* 1 Affording reasonable grounds for belief; probable. 2 Based on presumption or probability: an heir *presumptive.* —**pre·sump′tive·ly** *adv.*

pre·sump·tu·ous (pri·zump′chōō·əs) *adj.* Unduly confident or bold; forward. —**pre·sump′tu·ous·ly** *adv.* —**pre·sump′tu·ous·ness** *n.*

pre·sup·pose (prē′sə·pōz′) *v.t.* **·posed, ·pos·ing** 1 To imply or involve as a necessary antecedent condition. 2 To take for granted. —**pre·sup·po·si·tion** (prē′sup·ə·zish′ən) *n.*

pret. preterit.

pre·tend (pri·tend′) *v.t.* 1 To assume or display a false appearance of. 2 To claim or assert falsely. 3 To feign in play; make believe. —*v.i.* 4 To make believe, as in play or for the purpose of deception. 5 To put forward a claim: with *to.* [< L *prae-* before + *tendere* spread out]

pre·tend·er (pri·ten′dər) *n.* 1 One who pretends. 2 One who advances a dubious claim, esp. to a throne.

pre·tense (prē′tens, pri·tens′) *n.* 1 The act of pretending, as in play; a making believe. 2 Something pretended; ruse. 3 The false assumption of a character or condition. 4 A claim to a right or title. 5 A false claim. *Brit. sp.* **pre·tence.** —**Syn.** 2 pretext, wile. 3 affectation, dissimulation, show.

pre·ten·sion (pri·ten′shən) *n.* 1 A claim put forward, as to a right, title, etc. 2 The making of such a claim. 3 Affectation; display. 4 A bold or presumptuous assertion.

pre·ten·tious (pri·ten′shəs) *adj.* 1 Making unwarranted or exaggerated claims to greatness or importance: a *pretentious* person. 2 Showy or ostentatious: a *pretentious* style of living. —**pre·ten′tious·ly** *adv.* —**pre·ten′tious·ness** *n.*

pret·er·it (pret′ər·it) *Gram. adj.* Signifying past time. — *n.* 1 The past tense. 2 A verb form expressing this tense. *Came* is the preterit of *come* and *called* of *call.* Also **pret′·er·ite.** [< L *praeteritus* past]

pre·ter·nat·u·ral (prē′tər·nach′ər·əl, -rəl) *adj.* 1 Diverging from or exceeding the common order of nature; extraordinary. 2 Supernatural. —**pre′ter·nat′u·ral·ism** *n.* —**pre′ter·nat′u·ral·ly** *adv.*

pre·text (prē′tekst) *n.* A fictitious reason given to conceal a real one; a specious excuse or explanation. [< L *prae-* before + *texere* to weave]

pret·ti·fy (prit′i·fī) *v.t.* **·fied, ·fy·ing** To make pretty, esp. in a fussy way. —**pret′ti·fi·ca′tion** *n.*

pret·ty (prit′ē) *adj.* **·ti·er, ·ti·est** 1 Characterized by delicacy or gracefulness; attractive. 2 Good; nice: often used ironically: A *pretty* mess you've made of it! 3 *Informal* Considerable. —*adv.* 1 Moderately; to a fair extent: He looked *pretty* well. 2 Very; quite: He's grown *pretty* fast. —**sitting pretty** *Informal* In good circumstances. — *n. pl.* **·ties** A pretty thing or person. [< OE *prættig* tricky, cunning] —**pret′ti·ly** *adv.* —**pret′ti·ness** *n.*

pret·zel (pret′səl) *n.* A glazed salted biscuit in the form of a loose knot. [< G *Brezel*]

pre·vail (pri·vāl′) *v.i.* 1 To gain mastery: with *over* or *against.* 2 To be effective; succeed. 3 To be prevalent. 4 To have general or widespread use or acceptance. —**prevail on (upon or with)** To persuade; influence. [< L *prae-* before + *valere* be strong]

pre·vail·ing (pri·vā′ling) *adj.* 1 Current; prevalent. 2 Having effective power or influence. —**pre·vail′ing·ly** *adv.* —**pre·vail′ing·ness** *n.*

prev·a·lent (prev′ə·lənt) *adj.* 1 Predominant. 2 Of wide extent or frequent occurrence. [< L *praevalere* prevail] —**prev′a·lence** *n.* —**prev′a·lent·ly** *adv.*

pre·var·i·cate (pri·var′ə·kāt) *v.i.* **·cat·ed, ·cat·ing** To speak or act in a deceptive manner; lie. [< L *praevaricare* walk crookedly] —**pre·var′i·ca′tion, pre·var′i·ca′tor** *n.*

pre·vent (pri·vent′) *v.t.* 1 To keep from happening, as by previous measures: to *prevent* accidents. 2 To keep from doing something; hinder. [< L *prae-* before + *venire* come] —**pre·vent′a·ble** or **·i·ble** *adj.* —**pre·vent′a·bil′i·ty** or **·i·bil′i·ty, pre·vent′er** *n.*

pre·ven·tion (pri·ven′shən) *n.* 1 The act of preventing. 2 A hindrance; obstruction.

pre·ven·tive (pri·ven′tiv) *adj.* Intended or serving to prevent, esp. to ward off a disease. —*n.* That which prevents or hinders, esp. a method of warding off disease. Also **pre·vent·a·tive** (pri·ven′tə·tiv). —**pre·ven′tive·ly** *adv.* —**pre·ven′tive·ness** *n.*

pre·view (prē′vyoo) *n.* 1 A showing to the public, as of a motion picture, etc., before its formal opening. 2 The showing of scenes from a motion picture or television show in advance of its scheduled presentation as a means of advertisement. —*v.t.* (prē·vyoo′) To view in advance.

pre·vi·ous (prē′vē·əs) *adj.* 1 Being or taking place before something else in time or order. 2 *Informal* Acting, occurring, or speaking too soon. —**previous to** Before. [< L *praevius* going before] —**pre′vi·ous·ly** *adv.* —**pre′vi·ous·ness** *n.* —*Syn.* 1 antecedent, former, preceding, prior.

pre·vi·sion (prē·vizh′ən) *n.* 1 Foresight; prescience. 2 A prediction.

pre·vue (prē·vyoo′) *n.* PREVIEW (def. 2). [< F *prévoir* foresee]

pre·war (prē′wôr′) *adj.* Of, pertaining to, or happening in a time before a war.

prey (prā) *n.* 1 Any animal seized by another for food. 2 Booty; pillage. 3 A person or thing made a victim: a *prey* to swindlers. 4 The act of hunting other animals for food: a bird of *prey.* —*v.i.* 1 To seek or take prey for food. 2 To make a victim of someone, as by cheating. 3 To exert a wearing or harmful influence: to *prey* upon impressionable children. [< L *praeda* booty] —**prey′er** *n.*

Pri·am (prī′əm) *Gk. Myth.* The king of Troy during the Trojan War.

price (prīs) *n.* 1 The amount of money or goods given or asked in exchange for something. 2 Anything given or done to obtain something. 3 Worth; cost. 4 A reward for the capture or death of. —**beyond price** 1 So valuable that no adequate price can be set. 2 Not able to be bribed. —**set a price on one's head** To offer a reward for the capture of a person, dead or alive. —*v.t.* **priced, pric·ing** 1 To ask the price of. 2 To set a price on. —**price out of the market** To charge such high prices for goods that no one will buy them. [< L *pretium*] —*Syn. n.* 1 charge, cost, outlay. 3 value.

price·less (prīs′lis) *adj.* 1 Beyond price or valuation; invaluable. 2 *Informal* Wonderfully amusing or absurd. —**price′less·ness** *n.*

prick (prik) *v.t.* 1 To pierce slightly, as with a sharp point; puncture. 2 To affect with sharp mental pain. 3 To outline or indicate by punctures. 4 To cause to stick up: often with *up.* 5 To urge on; goad. —*v.i.* 6 To have or cause a stinging or piercing sensation. 7 To stick up; point, as a dog's ears. —*n.* 1 A mark or puncture made by pricking. 2 A stinging or prickling sensation. 3 Something sharply pointed, as a thorn. 4 A mental sting or spur: the *prick* of conscience. [< OE *prica* sharp point] —**prick′er** *n.*

prick·le (prik′əl) *n.* 1 A small, sharp point, as a thorn. 2 A tingling or stinging sensation. —*v.* **·led, ·ling** *v.t.* 1 To prick; pierce. 2 To cause a tingling or stinging sensation in. —*v.i.* 3 To have a tingling sensation. [< OE *pricel*]

prick·ly (prik′lē) *adj.* **·li·er, ·li·est** 1 Furnished with prickles. 2 Stinging; tingling. —**prick′li·ness** *n.*

prickly heat A rash due to inflammation of the sweat glands.

prickly pear 1 Any of a genus of flat-stemmed cactus plants bearing a pear-shaped fruit. 2 The edible fruit.

pride (prīd) *n.* 1 An undue sense of one's own superiority; arrogance; conceit. 2 A proper sense or feeling of personal dignity and worth. 3 That of which one is justly proud. 4 The best part of a group, nation, etc. 5 The best or prime period: in the *pride* of youth. 6 A group or family of lions. —*v.t.* **prid·ed, prid·ing** To take pride in (oneself) for something: with *on* or *upon.* [< OE *prūt* proud] —**pride′ful** *adj.* —**pride′ful·ly** *adv.* —**pride′ful·ness** *n.*

prie-dieu (prē·dyœ′) *n.* A small desk to support a book and with an extension on which to kneel for prayers. [F, pray God]

pri·er (prī′ər) *n.* One who pries.

priest (prēst) *n.* 1 One consecrated to the service of a divinity, and serving as mediator between the divinity and his worshipers. 2 In the Anglican, Greek, and Roman Catholic churches, a clergyman ranking next below a bishop, and having authority to administer the sacraments. [< L *presbyter* elder] —**priest′hood** *n.*

Prie-dieu

priest·ess (prēs′tis) *n.* A woman or girl who performs sacred rites.

priest·ly (prēst′lē) *adj.* Of, like, or concerning a priest or the priesthood. —**priest′li·ness** *n.*

prig (prig) *n.* A formal and narrow-minded person who assumes superior virtue, wisdom, or learning; pedant. [?] —**prig′gish** *adj.* —**prig′gish·ly** *adv.* —**prig′gish·ness** *n.*

prim (prim) *adj.* Affectedly precise and formal; stiffly proper and neat. —*v.t.* **primmed, prim·ming** To fix in a precise or prim manner. [Prob.< OF *prim* first, prime] —**prim′ly** *adv.* —**prim′ness** *n.*

prim. primary; primitive.

pri·ma·cy (prī′mə·sē) *n. pl.* **·cies** 1 The state of being first, as in rank or excellence. 2 The rank, office, or province of a primate. [< LL *primas, primatis* one of the first]

pri·ma don·na (prē′mə don′ə, prim′ə) *pl.* **pri·ma don·nas** 1 A leading female singer, as in an opera company. 2 *Informal* A temperamental or vain person. [Ital., lit., first lady]

---

add, āce, câre, pälm; end, ēven; it, īce; odd, ōpen, ôrder; took, pōōl; up, bûrn; ə = a in *above, u* in *focus*; yōō = u in *fuse*; oil; pout; check; go; ring; thin; this; zh, *vision.* < derived from; ? origin uncertain or unknown.

pri·ma fa·ci·e (prī′mə fā′shi·ē, fā′shē) At first view; so far as at first appears. [L]

pri·mal (prī′məl) *adj.* 1 First; original. 2 Most important; chief. [< L *primus* first]

pri·ma·quine (prī′mə·kwīn) *n.* A synthetic chemical used to cure malaria. [< PRIM(E) + A(MINO)- + QUIN(IN)E]

pri·ma·ri·ly (prī·mâr′ə·lē, prī·mâr′-) *adv.* 1 In the first place; originally. 2 Mainly; essentially.

pri·ma·ry (prī′mer·ē, -mər·ē) *adj.* 1 First in time or origin; primitive; original. 2 First in a series or sequence. 3 First in degree, rank, or importance; chief. 4 Constituting the fundamental or original elements of which a whole is comprised; basic; elemental: the *primary* forces of life. 5 Of the first stage of development; elementary: *primary* school. 6 *Electr.* Of or designating the input or input circuit of a transformer or similar device. —*n. pl.* **·ries** 1 That which is first in rank, dignity, quality, importance, etc. 2 Any of the primary colors. 3 In the U.S. a A meeting in which voters belonging to one political party in an election district nominate candidates for office, choose delegates for a party convention, etc. b DIRECT PRIMARY. [< L *primus* first]

primary accent See ACCENT.

primary cell *Electr.* A cell for generating electricity which cannot be efficiently recharged after use owing to an irreversible electrochemical reaction.

primary colors Those colors considered basic to the formation of all other colors; loosely, red, blue, and yellow to which black and white may be added.

pri·mate (prī′māt, -mit) *n.* 1 The prelate highest in rank in a nation or province. 2 Any of an order of mammals having five digits with nails on hands and feet, binocular vision, a large brainpan, etc., and including man, apes, monkeys and several monkeylike forms. [< L *primus* first] —**pri·ma·tial** (prī·mā′shəl) *adj.*

prime[1] (prīm) *adj.* 1 First in rank, dignity, or importance; chief. 2 First in value or excellence; first-rate. 3 First in time or order; original; primitive; primeval. 4 *Math.* Having no integral factors other than itself and unity, as certain integers. 5 Not derived from anything else; original; first. —*n.* 1 The period succeeding youth and preceding age. 2 The period of full perfection or vigor in anything. 3 The beginning of anything. 4 The best part of anything; a *prime* grade. 5 A mark or accent (′) written above and to the right of a letter or figure to indicate feet, minutes of time, minutes of angle, etc. 6 *Music* The interval of unison. —*v.* primed, prim·ing *v.t.* 1 To prepare; make ready for some purpose. 2 To put a primer into (a gun, mine, etc.) preparatory to firing. 3 To pour water into (a pump) so as to displace air and promote suction. 4 To cover (a surface) with sizing, a first coat of paint, etc. 5 To supply beforehand with facts, information, etc.: to *prime* a witness. —*v.i.* 6 To carry water along with the steam into the cylinder: said of a steam boiler or engine. 7 To make a person or thing ready or prepared for something. [< L *primus* first] —**prime′ly** *adv.* —**prime′ness** *n.* —**Syn.** *adj.* 1 main, leading, premiere, head, principal, top.

prime[2] (prīm) *n. Often cap.* 1 The first canonical hour of the day. 2 The office recited at this time. [< LL *prima (hora)* first (hour)]

prime meridian The meridian that passes through Greenwich, England and from which longitude is reckoned east and west.

prime minister The principal minister of a sovereign, or, in parliamentary governments, the chief executive.

prim·er[1] (prim′ər) *n.* 1 An elementary reading and spelling book. 2 A beginner's textbook in any subject. [< Med. L *primarius* basic]

prim·er[2] (prī′mər) *n.* 1 Any device, as a cap, tube, etc., used to detonate the charge of a gun, mine, etc. 2 A first coat of paint or sizing.

prime time In radio and television, the hours which consistently attract the largest audience, usu. the evening hours.

pri·me·val (prī·mē′vəl) *adj.* Of or pertaining to the first ages; primordial. [< L *primus* first + *aevum* age] —**pri·me′val·ly** *adv.*

prim·ing (prī′ming) *n.* 1 The act of one who or that which primes. 2 A substance, as paint or sizing, used as a first

coat. 3 A device or substance used to fire an explosive charge.

prim·i·tive (prim′ə·tiv) *adj.* 1 Of or belonging to the earliest ages. 2 Of, like, or belonging to an early period or stage of development: *primitive* Christianity. 3 Characteristic of the earliest ages of man, as in style, manner of living, etc.: a *primitive* tribe of Indians in Brazil. 4 Rough, simple, plain, undeveloped, etc.: *primitive* vacation facilities. 5 Basic; primary. —*n.* 1 A primitive person or thing. 2 A work of art created during the very early, often prehistoric, ages of man; also, a work of art imitative of this. 3 A work of art characterized by a naive, childlike simplicity; also, the artist, often untrained, of such a work. 4 A simple, unsophisticated person. [< L *primitivus* < *primus* first] —**prim′i·tive·ly** *adv.* —**prim′i·tive·ness** *n.*

prim·i·tiv·ism (prim′ə·tiv·iz′əm) *n.* Belief in or adherence to primitive forms and customs.

pri·mo·gen·i·tor (prī′mə·jen′ə·tər) *n.* An earliest ancestor; a forefather. [< L *primus* first + *genitor* a father]

pri·mo·gen·i·ture (prī′mə·jen′ə·chər) *n.* 1 The state of being the first-born of the same parents. 2 The right of inheritance of the eldest son to the exclusion of all other children. [< L *primus* first + *genitura* birth]

pri·mor·di·al (prī·môr′dē·əl) *adj.* 1 First in time; primitive; primeval. 2 Original; fundamental. [< L *primus* first + *ordiri* begin a web] —**pri·mor′di·al·ism′** *n.* —**pri·mor′di·al·ly** *adv.*

primp (primp) *v.t. & v.i.* To groom oneself or dress up, esp. with superfluous attention to detail. [Akin to PRIM] —**primp′er** *n.*

prim·rose (prim′rōz) *n.* 1 Any of a genus of early-blossoming perennials having variously colored, tubular flowers. 2 The flower. 3 A pale yellow color. —*adj.* 1 Pertaining to a primrose. 2 Pale yellow. [< Med. L *primula*, fem. dim. of L *primus* first]

prin. principal; principally; principle.

prince (prins) *n.* 1 A nonreigning male member of a royal family, esp. the son of a sovereign. 2 A male ruler of a state or principality. 3 One of a high order of nobility. 4 One of the highest rank of the class to which he belongs: a merchant *prince*. [< L *princeps* first, principal]

Primrose

Prince Albert A long, double-breasted frock coat. [< *Albert*, Prince of Wales, later Edward VII, 1841–1910]

prince consort The husband of a reigning female sovereign.

prince·ling (prins′ling) *n.* 1 A young prince. 2 A subordinate prince.

prince·ly (prins′lē) *adj.* **·li·er, ·li·est** 1 Of, suitable for, or belonging to a prince. 2 Noble; regal; distinguished: a *princely* bearing. 3 Generous; liberal; kind. 4 Sumptuous; magnificent. —*adv.* In a princely manner. —**prince′li·ness** *n.*

Prince of Darkness SATAN.

Prince of Peace JESUS CHRIST.

Prince of Wales The eldest son or male heir apparent of the British sovereign: a title conferred by the sovereign.

prin·cess (prin′sis, prin·ses′) *n.* 1 A nonreigning female member of a royal family, esp. the daughter of a sovereign or of a son of a sovereign. 2 The wife of a prince. 3 A female sovereign. 4 A woman or girl having the traditional beauty, grace, etc., of a princess.

prin·cesse (prin·ses′, prin′sis) *adj.* Of or designating a woman's close-fitting garment cut in a single piece from shoulder to flared hem. Also **prin′cess**. [F, princess]

prin·ci·pal (prin′sə·pəl) *adj.* First in rank, character, or importance; chief. —*n.* 1 One who takes a leading part in some action. 2 *Law* a The actor in a crime, or one present aiding and abetting. b The employer of one who acts as an agent. c One primarily liable for whom another has become surety. d The capital or body of an estate. 3 The head officer or teacher of a school. 4 The leading actor or performer. 5 Any person in authority. 6 The amount of money owed or invested, minus the interest charged or accumulated. 7 The face value: the *principal* of a stock. 8 Any of the chief rafters of a roof. [< L *princeps* chief] —**prin′ci·pal·ly** *adv.* —**prin′ci·pal·ship′** *n.* —**Syn.** *adj.* 1 main, central, foremost, leading.

prin·ci·pal·i·ty (prin'sə·pal'ə·tē) n. pl. **·ties 1** The office or dignity of a prince. **2** A territory ruled by a prince, or one that gives title to a prince.

principal parts The principal inflected forms of a verb from which all other inflected forms may be derived. In English, the principal parts of a verb are the infinitive, the past tense, and the past participle (walk, walked, walked; go, went, gone). The present participle (-ing added to the infinitive) is sometimes considered a fourth principal part, as walking, going.

prin·ci·ple (prin'sə·pəl) n. **1** A basic truth, law, force, etc., on which others can be founded: the principle of self-government. **2** An essential character or quality of something. **3** A fundamental origin or cause of something. **4** Moral standards or rules of conduct, esp. superior standards or rules: a man of principle. **5** In natural phenomena, an established law or mode of action: the principle of gravity. **6** The essential mode of operation of something: the principle of a digital computer. [<L principium a beginning]

prin·ci·pled (prin'sə·pəld) adj. Having principles, esp. moral principles.

print (print) n. **1** An impression or mark made upon a surface by pressure; imprint. **2** Something having such a mark on it. **3** A device for making such a mark. **4** An impression made by type or plates that have been inked. **5** Type used in printing. **6** Printed matter, as a newspaper. **7** The state of being printed. **8** A photographic reproduction of a work of art. **9** An original picture or design made from an engraved plate, stone, woodblock, etc. **10** A fabric stamped with a design; also, a garment made from such fabric. **11** A positive photographic copy made from a negative. **—in print** Still available at the publisher. **—out of print** No longer available at the publisher, the edition being exhausted. **—v.t. 1** To mark, as with inked type, a stamp, die, etc. **2** To stamp or impress (a mark, seal, etc.) on or into a surface. **3** To fix as if by impressing: The scene is printed on my memory. **4** To produce (a book, newspaper, etc.) by the application of inked type, plates, etc., to paper or similar material. **5** To cause to be put in print; publish: The newspaper printed the story. **6** To write in letters similar to those used in print. **7** Phot. To produce (a positive picture) by transmitting light through a negative onto a sensitized surface. **—v.i. 8** To be a printer. **9** To take or give an impression in printing. **10** To form letters similar to printed ones. **—print out** To deliver (information) automatically in printed form, as a computer. [<L premere to press]

print·a·ble (print'ə·bəl) adj. **1** Capable of being printed. **2** Fit to print or publish.

print·er (prin'tər) n. **1** A person who prints or sets type. **2** A mechanism attached to a computer that produces printed information.

printer's devil A printer's apprentice.

print·ing (prin'ting) n. **1** The act of one who or that which prints. **2** That which is printed. **3** The art or occupation of a printer. **4** All of the printed copies, as of a book, made at one time or from a single type setting.

printing press A mechanism for printing from inked type, plates, etc.

print·out (print'out') n. Material printed automatically, as by a computer.

pri·or (prī'ər) adj. Preceding in time, order, or importance. **—prior to** Before in time. **—n. 1** In an abbey, a monastic officer next in rank below an abbot. **2** The man in charge of a priory. [L, earlier, superior]

pri·or·ess (prī'ər·is) n. **1** In an abbey of nuns, a monastic officer next in rank below an abbess. **2** A woman in charge of a priory.

pri·or·i·tize (prī·ôr'ə·tīz) v.t. **-tized, -tiz·ing** Colloq. To arrange in order of priority.

pri·or·i·ty (prī·ôr'ə·tē, -or'-) n. pl. **·ties 1** The condition of being prior; precedence. **2** A preferential rating or right to do, buy, or use something. **3** A certificate giving this right. **4** Something that takes precedence over another thing or things.

pri·or·y (prī'ər·ē) n. pl. **·or·ies** A monastic house presided over by a prior or prioress.

prism (priz'əm) n. **1** Geom. A solid whose bases or ends are equal and parallel plane figures, and whose lateral faces are parallelograms. **2** Optics An instrument consisting of such a solid, usu. having triangular ends and made of glass or other transparent material. [<Gk. prisma something sawed]

Prism
Beam of white light (a) undergoes refraction in prism and produces its spectrum (b).

pris·mat·ic (priz·mat'ik) adj. **1** Refracted or formed by a prism. **2** Exhibiting the colored bands of the spectrum. **3** Pertaining to or shaped like a prism. **4** Variously and brilliantly colored. **—pris·mat'i·cal·ly** adv.

pris·on (priz'ən) n. **1** A public building for the safekeeping of persons in legal custody, as in punishment for having committed a crime; a penitentiary. **2** Any place of confinement. **3** Imprisonment. **—v.t.** IMPRISON. [<L praehensio seizure]

pris·on·er (priz'ənər, -nər) n. **1** One who is confined in a prison. **2** Any person whose liberty is forcibly restrained. **3** A person whose freedom is restricted by some cause or condition: a prisoner of ignorance.

pris·sy (pris'ē) adj. **·si·er, ·si·est** Very precise; prim; fussy. [Blend of PRIM + SISSY] **—priss'i·ly** adv. **—priss'i·ness** n.

pris·tine (pris'tēn, -tin, pris·tēn') adj. **1** Of or pertaining to the earliest state or time; primitive. **2** Uncontaminated; pure. [<L. pristinus primitive] **—pris'tine·ly** adv.

pri·va·cy (prī'və·sē; Brit., also priv'ə·sē) n. pl. **·cies 1** The condition of being private; seclusion. **2** Personal matters that are or should be private. **3** Secrecy.

pri·vate (prī'vit) adj. **1** Removed from public view; secluded. **2** Confidential; secret. **3** That is one's own; personal: a private sorrow. **4** Not for the public at large: private schools. **5** Not in the public or governmental employ: a private citizen. **6** Working or conducted independently of other groups, organizations, etc.: a private detective; a private practice. **—n.** See GRADE. **—in private** In secret; privately. [<L privus single, one's own] **—pri'vate·ly** adv. **—pri'vate·ness** n.

private enterprise FREE ENTERPRISE.

pri·va·teer (prī'və·tir') n. **1** A vessel privately owned and manned but carrying on maritime war under letters of marque. **2** The commander or one of the crew of privateer: also **pri'va·teers'man.** **—v.i.** To cruise in or as a privateer. **—pri'va·teer'ing** n.

private first class See GRADE.

private parts The genitals.

pri·va·tion (prī·vā'shən) n. **1** The state of lacking something necessary or desirable. **2** Want of the common comforts or necessities of life. [<L privare deprive]

priv·a·tive (priv'ə·tiv) adj. **1** Causing privation; depriving. **2** Gram. Expressing negation or absence of something. **—n.** Gram. A prefix or suffix indicating negation or absence, as a-, in-, -less. **—priv'a·tive·ly** adv.

priv·et (priv'it) n. **1** An ornamental, bushy shrub with white flowers and black berries, used for hedges. **2** Any of various related shrubs and trees. [?]

priv·i·lege (priv'ə·lij, priv'lij) n. **1** A special or peculiar benefit, advantage, right or immunity. **2** A fundamental civil right: the privilege of voting. **—v.t. ·leged, ·leg·ing** To grant a privilege to. [<L privus one's own + lex, legis law]

priv·i·leged (priv'ə·lijd) adj. **1** Having or invested with a privilege or with advantages: a privileged class. **2** Exempt from the usual conditions or rules: privileged information.

priv·y (priv'ē) adj. **1** Participating with another or others in the knowledge of a secret transaction: with to: privy to the plot. **2** Archaic Secret. **—n.** pl. **priv·ies** A toilet or outhouse. [<L privatus private] **—priv'i·ly** adv.

privy council A body of confidential advisers, as to a sovereign, executive, etc. **—privy councilor**

prix fixe (prē fēks′) In certain restaurants, a set price for a meal no matter which courses or entrées are chosen. [F, lit., fixed price]

prize¹ (prīz) n. 1 That which is offered or won as an honor and reward for superiority. 2 Anything offered or won in a contest, game of chance, etc. 3 Something desirable, either acquired or to be striven for. —adj. 1 Offered or awarded as a prize. 2 Having received a prize. 3 Highly valued or esteemed. —v.t. prized, priz·ing 1 To value highly. 2 To appraise. [Var. of PRICE]

prize² (prīz) n. 1 In international law, property, as a vessel and cargo, lawfully captured by a belligerent at sea. 2 The act of capturing; also, the person or thing captured. —v.t. prized, priz·ing To seize as a prize, as a ship. [< L praehendere seize]

prize·fight (prīz′fīt′) n. A boxing match between professional boxers. —prize′fight′er, prize′fight′ing n.

pro¹ (prō) n. pl. pros 1 An argument or vote in favor of something. 2 One who votes for or favors something. —adv. In favor of; for. [L, for]

pro² (prō) n. pl. pros PROFESSIONAL. —adj. PROFESSIONAL.

pro-¹ prefix 1 Forward; forth: project. 2 In place of; substituted for: procaine. 3 In favor of: pro-Russian. [< L pro before, in front]

pro-² prefix 1 Prior: prognosis. 2 Situated in front; forward; before: prognathous. [< Gk. pro before, in front]

PRO, P.R.O. public relations officer.

pro·a (prō′ə) n. A swift Malaysian vessel having a single outrigger and a lateen sail. [< Malay prāu]

prob. probable; probably; problem.

prob·a·bil·i·ty (prob′ə·bil′ə·tē) n. pl. ·ties 1 The state or quality of being probable; likelihood. 2 Something probable. 3 Stat. The ratio of the chances favoring an event to the total number of chances for and against it.

prob·a·ble (prob′ə·bəl) adj. 1 Likely to be true or to happen, but leaving room for doubt. 2 That renders something worthy of belief, but fails to prove: probable evidence. [< L probare prove, test] —prob′a·bly adv.

pro·bate (prō′bāt) n. 1 The act or legal process of proving the genuineness of a document, as a will. 2 The final determination of the genuineness of a will. 3 The authentic copy of a probated will. —adj. Of probate or probate court. —v.t. ·bat·ed, ·bat·ing To secure probate of, as a will. [< L probare prove]

probate court A court having jurisdiction over probating wills, the settlement of estates, and the guardianship of minors or incompetents.

pro·ba·tion (prō·bā′shən) n. 1 A trial or period of testing of a person's character, qualifications, etc. 2 A legal procedure allowing a person convicted of an offense to go at large under suspension of sentence, but usu. under the supervision of a probation officer. 3 The status or condition of one undergoing probation; also, the period of probation. —pro·ba′tion·al, pro·ba′tion·ar′y adj.

pro·ba·tion·er (prō·bā′shən·ər) n. One on probation or trial.

probation officer A person delegated to supervise an offender on probation.

probe (prōb) v. probed, prob·ing v.t. 1 To explore with a probe. 2 To investigate or examine thoroughly. —v.i. 3 To investigate; search. —n. 1 Med. An instrument for exploring wounds, etc. 2 The act of probing. 3 An examination or exploratory search, esp. an investigation or inquiry into crime, malpractice, etc. 4 A spacecraft designed to explore and collect and transmit data to earth about the upper atmosphere, celestial bodies, or outer space. [< L probare prove] —prob′er n.

pro·bi·ty (prō′bə·tē) n. Virtue or integrity tested and confirmed; strict honesty. [< L probus good, honest]

prob·lem (prob′ləm) n. 1 A perplexing question presented for solution. 2 A puzzling or difficult circumstance, situation, person, etc. 3 Math. Something to be worked out or solved, as by a series of operations. —adj. 1 Presenting and dealing with a problem. 2 Being a problem: a problem child. [< Gk. problēma something thrown forward (for discussion)]

prob·lem·at·ic (prob′lem·at′ik) adj. 1 Constituting or involving a problem. 2 Uncertain; questionable; contingent. Also prob′lem·at′i·cal. —prob′lem·at′i·cal·ly adv.

pro·bos·cis (prō·bos′is) n. pl. ·bos·cis·es or ·bos·ci·des (-bos′ə·dēz) 1 An elephant's trunk, or any long flexible snout. 2 A tubular structure used for sucking, sensing, etc., as of certain insects, worms, and mollusks. 3 A human nose: a humorous use. [< Gk. pro- before + boskein to feed]

Proboscis of elephant

pro·caine (prō·kān′, prō′kān) n. A common local anesthetic in dentistry and medicine. [< PRO-¹ + (CO)CAINE]

pro·ce·dure (prə·sē′jər, prō-) n. 1 A manner of proceeding or acting. 2 A special course of action. 3 The established methods or forms for the conduct of various proceedings, as in business, legal courts, etc. —pro·ce′du·ral adj.

pro·ceed (prə·sēd′, prō-) v.i. 1 To go on or forward. 2 To begin and carry on an action or process. 3 To issue or come, as from some cause, source, or origin: with from. 4 Law To institute and carry on legal proceedings. [< L pro- forward + cedere go]

pro·ceed·ing (prə·sē′ding, prō-) n. 1 An act or course of action; a transaction or procedure. 2 The action of issuing forth; emanation. 3 pl. The records or minutes of the meetings of a society, etc. 4 Law a Any action instituted in a court. b Any of the various steps taken in a cause by either party.

pro·ceeds (prō′sēdz) n. pl. The amount derived from the disposal of goods, a commercial undertaking, etc; return.

proc·ess (pros′es, pros′əs, esp. Brit. prō′ses) n. pl. proc·ess·es (pros′ə·siz, pros′es·əz, pros′ə·sēz′) 1 A course or method of operations in the production of something: a metallurgical process. 2 A forward movement or continuous development, as of time, growth, etc. 3 Law a Any judicial writ or order. b A writ issued to bring a defendant into court. c The whole course of proceedings in a cause. 4 Biol. An accessory outgrowth of an organism. —adj. Produced by a special method: process cheese. —v.t. 1 To treat or prepare by a special method. 2 Law a To issue or serve a process on. b To proceed against. [< L processus pp. of procedere proceed]

pro·ces·sion (prə·sesh′ən, prō-) n. 1 A line, as of persons or vehicles, moving in a formal manner; a parade. 2 A continuous course: the procession of the stars. 3 The act of proceeding or issuing forth.

pro·ces·sion·al (prə·sesh′ən·əl, prō-) adj. Of or pertaining to or moving in a procession. —n. 1 A book containing the services in a religious procession. 2 A hymn sung during a religious procession. —pro·ces′sion·al·ly adv.

process printing Color printing from halftone plates each of which carries one of the primary colors, red, yellow, and blue, with sometimes a fourth plate for black.

pro·claim (prō·klām′, prə-) v.t. 1 To announce or make known publicly or officially; declare. 2 To make plain; manifest. 3 To praise; laud. [< L pro- before + clamare to call] —pro·claim′er n.

proc·la·ma·tion (prok′lə·mā′shən) n. 1 The act of proclaiming. 2 That which is proclaimed.

pro·cliv·i·ty (prō·kliv′ə·tē) n. pl. ·ties Natural disposition or tendency, esp. toward something not desirable. [< L proclivus downward]

pro·con·sul (prō·kon′səl) n. 1 In ancient Rome, an official who exercised authority over a province or an army. 2 An administrator of a dependency or colony. [< L] —pro·con′su·lar (-sə·lər) adj. —pro·con′su·late (-sə·lit), pro·con′sul·ship n.

pro·cras·ti·nate (prō·kras′tə·nāt) v. ·nat·ed, ·nat·ing v.i. To put off taking action until a future time; be dilatory. —v.t. 2 To defer or postpone. [< L pro- forward + cras tomorrow] —pro·cras′ti·na′tion, pro·cras′ti·na′tor n.

pro·cre·ate (prō′krē·āt) v.t. & v.i. ·at·ed, ·at·ing 1 To engender or beget (offspring). 2 To bring or come into existence; originate. [< L pro- before + creare create] —pro′cre·a′tion, pro′cre·a′tor n. —pro′cre·a′tive, pro′cre·ant adj.

Pro·crus·te·an (prō·krus′tē·ən) adj. 1 Of Procrustes. 2 Ruthlessly or violently forcing to conform.

Pro·crus·tes (prō·krus′tēz) *Gk. Myth.* A giant who tied travelers to an iron bed and amputated or stretched their limbs until they fitted it.

proc·tol·o·gy (prok·tol′ə·jē) *n.* The branch of medicine which deals with diseases of the lower colon, rectum, and anus. [< Gk. *proktos* anus + -LOGY] —**proc·to·log·i·cal** (prok′tə·loj′i·kəl) *adj.* —**proc·tol′o·gist** *n.*

proc·tor (prok′tər) *n.* 1 An agent acting for another; proxy. 2 A university or college official charged with maintaining order, supervising examinations, etc. —*v.t. & v.i.* To supervise (an examination). [< PROCURATOR] —**proc·to·ri·al** (prok·tôr′ē·əl, -tō′rē-) *adj.*

proc·to·scope (prok′tə·skōp) *n.* A surgical instrument for examining the interior of the rectum. —**proc·tos·co·py** (prok·tos′kə·pē) *n.*

pro·cum·bent (prō·kum′bənt) *adj.* 1 *Bot.* Lying on the ground; trailing. 2 Lying face down; prone. [< L *pro-* forward + *cubare* lie down]

proc·u·ra·tor (prok′yə·rā′tər) *n.* 1 A person authorized to manage the affairs of another. 2 In ancient Rome, one in charge of imperial revenues, esp. in a province. —**proc′u·ra·to′ri·al** (-rə·tôr′ē·əl, -tō′rē-) *adj.*

pro·cure (prō·kyŏŏr′) *v.* **·cured, ·cur·ing** *v.t.* 1 To obtain by some effort or means; acquire. 2 To bring about; cause. 3 To obtain for the sexual gratification of others. —*v.i.* 4 To obtain women for prostitution. [< L *procurare* look after] —**pro·cur′a·ble** *adj.* —**pro·cure′ment, pro·cur′er** *n.*

Pro·cy·on (prō′sē·on) *n.* The most conspicuous star in the constellation Canis Minor. [< Gk. *pro-* before + *kyōn* dog]

prod (prod) *v.t.* **prod·ded, prod·ding** 1 To punch or poke with or as with a pointed instrument. 2 To arouse mentally; urge; goad. —*n.* 1 Any pointed instrument used for prodding. 2 Something that incites one to action. [?] —**prod′der** *n.*

prod. produce; produced; product.

prod·i·gal (prod′ə·gəl) *adj.* 1 Wastefully extravagant, as of money, time, etc. 2 Yielding in profusion; bountiful. 3 Lavish; profuse. —*n.* One who is wastefully extravagant; a spendthrift. [< L *prodigus* wasteful] —**prod′i·gal′i·ty** (-gal′ə·tē) *n.* —**prod′i·gal·ly** *adv.*

pro·di·gious (prə·dij′əs, prō-) *adj.* 1 Enormous or extraordinary in size, quantity, or degree. 2 Marvelous; amazing. —**pro·dig′ious·ly** *adv.* —**pro·dig′ious·ness** *n.*

prod·i·gy (prod′ə·jē) *n. pl.* **·gies** 1 Something extraordinary or awe-inspiring. 2 An exceptionally gifted child. 3 A monstrosity of nature. [< L *prodigium*]

pro·duce (prə·d(y)ōōs′) *v.* **·duced, ·duc·ing** *v.t.* 1 To bring forth or bear; yield. 2 To bring forth by mental effort; compose, write, etc. 3 To cause to happen or be: His words *produced* a violent reaction. 4 To bring to view; exhibit; show: to *produce* evidence. 5 To manufacture; make. 6 To bring to performance before the public, as a play. 7 To extend or lengthen, as a line. 8 *Econ.* To create (anything with exchangeable value). —*v.i.* 9 To yield or generate an appropriate product or result. —*n.* (prod′yōōs, prō′d(y)ōōs) That which is produced, esp. farm products collectively. [< L *pro-* forward + *ducere* to lead] —**pro·duc′i·ble** *adj.*

pro·duc·er (prə·d(y)ōō′sər) *n.* 1 One who or that which produces. 2 One who makes things for sale and use. 3 One in charge of the production of a public presentation, as of a play, motion picture, etc.

prod·uct (prod′əkt, -ukt) *n.* 1 Anything produced or obtained as a result of some operation or work. 2 *Math.* The result obtained by multiplication. 3 *Chem.* Any substance resulting from chemical change.

pro·duc·tion (prə·duk′shən) *n.* 1 The act or process of producing. 2 The amount produced. 3 Something produced, esp. an artistic work, as a play, motion picture, etc. 4 In political economy, a producing of goods or services.

pro·duc·tive (prə·duk′tiv) *adj.* 1 Producing easily or abundantly. 2 Characterized by fruitful work and accomplishment: a *productive* meeting. 3 Causing; resulting in: with *of.* —**pro·duc′tive·ly** *adv.* —**pro·duc·tiv·i·ty** (prō′duk·tiv′ə·tē), **pro·duc′tive·ness** *n.*

pro·em (prō′əm) *n.* A preface; prelude. [< Gk. *pro-* before + *oimē* song] —**pro·e·mi·al** (prō·ē′mē·əl) *adj.*

prof (prof) *n. Informal* PROFESSOR.

Prof. Professor. • See PROFESSOR.

prof·a·na·tion (prof′ə·nā′shən, prō·fə-) *n.* The act of profaning or the condition of being profaned.

pro·fane (prō·fān′, prə-) *v.t.* **·faned, ·fan·ing** 1 To treat (something sacred) with irreverence or abuse; desecrate. 2 To put to an unworthy or degrading use; debase. —*adj.* 1 Manifesting irreverence or disrespect toward sacred things. 2 Not sacred or religious in theme, content, use, etc.; secular. 3 Not esoteric; ordinary. 4 Vulgar. [< L *pro-* before + *fanum* temple] —**pro·fan·a·to·ry** (prō·fan′ə·tôr′ē, -tō′rē, prə-) *adj.* —**pro·fane′ly** *adv.* —**pro·fan′er** *n.*

pro·fan·i·ty (prō·fan′ə·tē, prə-) *n. pl.* **·ties** 1 The state of being profane. 2 Profane speech or action. Also **pro·fane′ness** (-fān′nis).

pro·fess (prə·fes′, prō-) *v.t.* 1 To declare openly; avow; affirm. 2 To assert, usu. insincerely; make a pretense of: to *profess* remorse. 3 To declare or affirm faith in. 4 To have as one's profession: to *profess* the law. 5 To receive into a religious order. —*v.i.* 6 To make open declaration; avow; offer public affirmation. 7 To take the vows of a religious order. [< L *professus,* pp. of *profiteri* avow, confess] —**pro·fessed′** *adj.* —**pro·fess′ed·ly** (-fes′id·lē) *adv.*

pro·fes·sion (prə·fesh′ən) *n.* 1 An occupation that involves a higher education or its equivalent, and mental rather than manual labor, as law, medicine, teaching, etc. 2 The collective body of those following such an occupation. 3 Any calling or occupation requiring special skills, talents, etc.: the acting *profession.* 4 Any occupation. 5 The act of professing or declaring: *professions* of good will. 6 That which is avowed or professed.

pro·fes·sion·al (prə·fesh′ən·əl) *adj.* 1 Connected with, preparing for, engaged in, appropriate, or conforming to a profession: *professional* courtesy; *professional* skill. 2 Performing or doing for pay an activity often engaged in only for pleasure or recreation: a *professional* golfer. 3 Engaged in by performers, players, etc., who are paid: *professional* hockey. 4 Single-minded and zealous, often excessively so: a *professional* do-gooder. —*n.* 1 One who practices any profession or engages in any activity for pay. 2 One who is exceptionally skilled in some activity. —**pro·fes′sion·al·ism′** *n.* —**pro·fes′sion·al·ly** *adv.*

pro·fes·sion·al·ize (prə·fesh′ən·əl·īz′) *v.t.* **·ized, ·iz·ing** To make professional in character or quality: to *professionalize* tourism. —**pro·fes′sion·al·i·za′tion** *n.*

pro·fes·sor (prə·fes′ər) *n.* 1 A teacher of the highest grade in a university or college. 2 One who professes skill and offers instruction in some sport or art: a *professor* of gymnastics. 3 One who makes open declaration of his opinions, religious faith, etc. —**pro·fes·so·ri·al** (prō′fə·sôr′ē·əl, -sō′rē-, prof′ə-) *adj.* —**pro′fes·so′ri·al·ly** *adv.* —**pro′fes·so′ri·ate** (-it), **pro·fes′sor·ship** *n.* • In writing to a college or university professor, one may use either *Professor* or *Prof.* if the name is written in full or if the initials are used with the last name: *Professor Alfred Kern; Prof. C. E. Young.* If only the last name is used, *Professor* is spelled out.

prof·fer (prof′ər) *v.t.* To offer for acceptance. —*n.* The act of proffering, or that which is proffered. [< L *pro-* in behalf of + *offerre* to offer] —**prof′fer·er** *n.*

pro·fi·cien·cy (prə·fish′ən·sē) *n. pl.* **·cies** The fact or quality of being proficient; skill; competence; expertness.

pro·fi·cient (prə·fish′ənt) *adj.* Thoroughly competent; skilled; expert. —*n.* An expert. [< L *proficere* make progress, go forward] —**pro·fi′cient·ly** *adv.*

pro·file (prō′fīl, *esp. Brit.* prō′fēl) *n.* 1 A human head or face, as viewed from the side; also, a drawing of such a side view. 2 A drawing or view of something in outline or contour. 3 A somewhat brief biographical sketch. 4 Degree of exposure to public attention; public image: The army generals who seized control maintained a very low *profile.* 5 A vertical section of stratified soil or rock. —*v.t.* **filed, fil·ing** 1 To draw a profile of; outline. 2 To write a profile of. [< Ital. *profilare* draw in outline]

Profile *def. 1*

prof·it (prof′it) n. 1 Any benefit, advantage, or return. 2 *Often pl.* Excess of returns over outlay or expenditure. 3 *Often pl.* The gain obtained from invested capital; also, the ratio of gain to the amount of capital invested. 4 Income gained from property, stocks, etc. —*v.i.* 1 To be of advantage or benefit. 2 To derive gain or benefit. —*v.t.* 3 To be of profit or advantage to. [< L *profectus*, p.p. of *proficere* go forward] —**prof′it·less** *adj.*

prof·it·a·ble (prof′it·ə·bəl) *adj.* Bringing profit or gain. —**prof·it·a·bil·i·ty** (prof′ə·tə·bil′ə·tē), **prof′it·a·ble·ness** n. —**prof′it·a·bly** *adv.* —**Syn.** advantageous, beneficial, desirable, expedient, gainful, lucrative, productive, useful, worthwhile.

prof·i·teer (prof′ə·tir′) *v.i.* To seek or obtain excessive profits. —n. One who makes excessive profits, esp. to the detriment of others. —**prof′i·teer′ing** n.

profit sharing A system by which employees are given a percentage of the net profits of a business.

prof·li·ga·cy (prof′lə·gə·sē) n. The condition or quality of being profligate.

prof·li·gate (prof′lə·git, -gāt) *adj.* 1 Extremely immoral or dissipated; dissolute. 2 Recklessly extravagant. —n. A profligate person. [< L *profligare* strike to the ground, destroy] —**prof′li·gate·ly** *adv.*

pro·found (prə·found′, prō-) *adj.* 1 Intellectually deep or exhaustive: *profound* learning. 2 Reaching to, arising from, or affecting the depth of one's being: a *profound* look; *profound* respect. 3 Reaching far below the surface; deep: a *profound* chasm. 4 Complete; total: a *profound* revision of the book. [< L *pro-* very + *fundus* deep] —**pro·found′ly** *adv.* —**pro·found′ness** n.

pro·fun·di·ty (prə·fun′də·tē, prō-) n. pl. ·ties 1 The state or quality of being profound. 2 A deep place. 3 A profound statement, theory, etc.

pro·fuse (prə·fyōōs′, prō-) *adj.* 1 Giving or given forth lavishly; extravagantly generous. 2 Copious; abundant: *profuse* vegetation. [< L *profusus*, pp. of *profundere* pour forth] —**pro·fuse′ly** *adv.* —**pro·fuse′ness** n.

pro·fu·sion (prə·fyōō′zhən, prō-) n. 1 A lavish supply or condition: a *profusion* of ornaments. 2 The act of pouring forth or supplying in great abundance; prodigality.

prog. progress; progressive.

pro·gen·i·tor (prō·jen′ə·tər) n. 1 A forefather or parent. 2 The originator or source of something. [< L *progignere* beget] —**pro·gen′i·tor·ship′** n.

prog·e·ny (proj′ə·nē) n. pl. ·nies Offspring; descendants. [< L *progignere* beget]

pro·ges·ter·one (prō·jes′tə·rōn) n. An ovarian hormone active in preparing the uterus for reception of the fertilized ovum. Also **pro·ges′tin** (-tin). [< PRO-¹ + GE(STATION) + STER(OL) + -ONE]

prog·na·thous (prog′nə·thəs, prog·nā′-) *adj.* Having projecting jaws. Also **prog·nath·ic** (prog·nath′ik). [< PRO-² + Gk. *gnathos* jaw] —**prog·na·thism** (prog′nə·thiz′əm) n.

prog·no·sis (prog·nō′sis) n. pl. ·ses (-sēz) A prediction or forecast, esp. as to the future course of a disease. [< Gk. *pro-* before + *gignōskein* know]

prog·nos·tic (prog·nos′tik) *adj.* 1 Predictive. 2 Of or useful in a prognosis. —n. 1 A sign of some future occurrence. 2 A basis for a prognosis.

prog·nos·ti·cate (prog·nos′tə·kāt) *v.t.* ·cat·ed, ·cat·ing 1 To foretell by present indcations. 2 To indicate beforehand; foreshadow. —**prog·nos′ti·ca′tion, prog·nos′ti·ca′tor** n. —**prog·nos′ti·ca′tive** (-kā′tiv) *adj.*

pro·gram (prō′gram, -grəm) n. 1 A printed list giving in order the items, selections, etc., making up an entertainment; also, the selections, etc., collectively. 2 A printed list of the cast of characters, the performers, the acts or scenes, etc., in a play, opera, or the like. 3 A radio or television show. 4 Any prearranged plan or course of proceedings. 5 A sequence of instructions to be executed by a computer in solving a problem, usu. with means for automatically modifying the sequence depending on conditions that arise. *Brit. sp.* ·gramme. —*v.t.* ·gramed or ·grammed, ·gram·ing or ·gram·ming 1 To arrange a program of or for: to *program* one's day. 2 To schedule (an act, performer, etc.) for a program. 3 To furnish a program for (a computer). 4 To feed (information, instructions, etc.) into a computer. [< LL *programma* public announcement]

—**pro·gram·mat·ic** (prō′grə·mat′ik) *adj.* —**pro′gram·er, pro′·gram·mer** n.

programed instruction Instruction in which the learner responds to a prearranged series of questions, items, or statements, using various printed texts, audiovisual means, or a teaching machine. Also **programmed instruction.**

program music Music intended to suggest moods, scenes, or incidents.

prog·ress (prog′res, *esp. Brit.* prō′gres) n. 1 A moving forward in space, as toward a destination. 2 Advancement toward something better; improvement. —*v.i.* (prə·gres′) 1 To move forward or onward. 2 To advance toward completion or improvement. [< L *progressus*, pp. of *progredi* go forward]

pro·gres·sion (prə·gresh′ən) n. 1 The act of progressing. 2 A successive series of events, happenings, etc. 3 *Math.* A sequence of numbers or elements each of which is derived from the preceding by rule. 4 *Music* a An advance from one tone or chord to another. b A sequence or succession of tones or chords. 5 Course or lapse of time; passage. —**pro·gres′sion·al** *adj.* —**pro·gres′sion·ism** n.

pro·gres·sive (prə·gres′iv) *adj.* 1 Moving forward in space; advancing. 2 Increasing by successive stages: a *progressive* deterioration. 3 Aiming at or characterized by progress toward something better: a *progressive* country. 4 Favoring or characterized by reform, new techniques, etc.: a *progressive* party, jazz, etc. 5 Increasing in severity: said of a disease. 6 *Gram.* Designating an aspect of the verb which expresses continuing action: formed with any tense of the auxiliary *be* and the present participle; as, He *is speaking*; he *had been speaking*. —n. One who favors or promotes reforms or changes, as in politics. —**pro·gres′sive·ly** *adv.* —**pro·gres′sive·ness** n.

pro·hib·it (prō·hib′it, prə-) *v.t.* 1 To forbid, esp. by authority or law; interdict. 2 To prevent or hinder. [< L *prohibere*] —**pro·hib′it·er** n. —**Syn.** 1 disallow, ban, deny, bar, debar. 2 impede, restrict, constrain, check, block, obstruct.

pro·hi·bi·tion (prō′ə·bish′ən) n. 1 A prohibiting or being prohibited. 2 A decree or order forbidding anything. 3 *Often cap.* The forbidding of the manufacture, transportation, and sale of alcoholic liquors as beverages. —**pro′hi·bi′tion·ist** n.

pro·hib·i·tive (prō·hib′ə·tiv, prə-) *adj.* Prohibiting or tending to prohibit. Also **pro·hib′i·to·ry** (-tôr′ē, -tō′rē). —**pro·hib′i·tive·ly** *adv.*

proj·ect (proj′ekt) n. 1 A course of action; a plan. 2 An organized, usu. rather extensive undertaking: a research *project*. 3 A group of single dwellings or of apartment houses forming a residential complex. —*v.t.* (prə·jekt′) 1 To cause to extend forward or out. 2 To throw forth or forward, as missiles. 3 To cause (an image, shadow, etc.) to fall on a surface. 4 To plan or estimate something in the future: to *project* living expenses. 5 To create or invent in the mind: to *project* an image of one's destiny. 6 To cause (one's voice) to be heard at a distance. 7 To have the ability to communicate (a dramatic role, one's personality, ideas, etc.) effectively, as to an audience. 8 *Psychol.* To ascribe or impute (one's own ideas, feelings, etc.) to another person, group, or object. 9 To make a projection (def. 4) of. —*v.i.* 10 To extend out; protrude. 11 To cause one's voice to be heard at a distance. 12 To communicate effectively, as to an audience. 13 *Psychol.* To impute one's own ideas, feelings, etc., to another person, group, or object. [< L *pro-* before + *jacere* throw]

pro·jec·tile (prə·jek′təl, -tīl) *adj.* 1 Projecting, or impelling forward. 2 Capable of being or intended to be projected or shot forth. —n. 1 A body projected or thrown forth by force. 2 A missile for discharge from a gun, cannon, etc.

pro·jec·tion (prə·jek′shən) n. 1 The act of projecting. 2 That which projects. 3 A prediction or estimation of something in the future based on current information, data, etc. 4 A system of lines drawn on a gíven fixed plane, as on a map, which represents, point for point, a given terrestrial or celestial surface. 5 *Psychol.* The process or an instance of projecting. 6 The exhibiting of pictures upon a screen. —**pro·jec′tive** *adj.* —**pro·jec′tive·ly** *adv.*

pro·jec·tion·ist (prə·jek′shən·ist) *n.* The operator of a motion-picture or slide projector.

pro·jec·tor (prə·jek′tər) *n.* One who or that which projects, esp. an apparatus for throwing images on a screen: a motion-picture *projector.*

pro·lapse (prō·laps′) *v.i.* **·lapsed, ·laps·ing** *Med.* To fall out of place, as an organ or part. —*n. Med.* (*also* prō′laps) Displacement of a part, esp. toward a natural orifice. [< L *pro-* forward + *labi* glide, fall]

pro·late (prō′lāt) *adj.* **1** Extended lengthwise. **2** Lengthened toward the poles. [< L *prolatus*]

prole (prōl) *n. & adj. Informal* PROLETARIAN.

pro·le·tar·i·an (prō′lə·târ′ē·ən) *adj.* Of the proletariat. — *n.* A member of the proletariat. [< L *proletarius* a Roman citizen of a class that, lacking property, served the state only by having children < *proles* offspring] —**pro′le·tar′i·an·ism** *n.*

pro·le·tar·i·at (prō′lə·târ′ē·ət) *n.* **1** Formerly, the lower classes. **2** The laboring class, esp. industrial wage earners.

pro·lif·er·ate (prō·lif′ə·rāt, prə-) *v.t. & v.i.* **·at·ed, ·at·ing** To create or reproduce in rapid succession. [< L *proles* offspring + *ferre* bear] —**pro·lif′er·a′tion** *n.* —**pro·lif′er·a′tive, pro·lif′er·ous** *adj.*

pro·lif·ic (prō·lif′ik, prə-) *adj.* **1** Producing abundantly, as offspring or fruit. **2** Producing creative or intellectual products abundantly: a *prolific* writer. [< L *proles* offspring + *facere* make] —**pro·lif′i·ca·cy** (-i·kə·sē), **pro·lif′ic·ness** *n.* —**pro·lif′i·cal·ly** *adv.*

pro·lix (prō′liks, prō·liks′) *adj.* **1** Unduly long and wordy. **2** Indulging in long and wordy discourse. [< L *prolixus* extended] —**pro·lix·i·ty** (prō·lik′sə·tē), **pro′lix·ness** *n.* —**pro′lix·ly** *adv.*

pro·logue (prō′lôg, -log) *n.* **1** A preface, esp. an introduction, often in verse, spoken or sung by an actor before a play or opera. **2** Any anticipatory act or event. —*v.t.* To introduce with a prologue or preface. Also **pro′log.** [< Gk. *pro-* before + *logos* discourse]

pro·long (prə·lông′, -long′) *v.t.* To extend in time or space; continue; lengthen. Also **pro·lon′gate** (-lông′gāt, -long′-). [< L *pro-* forth + *longus* long] —**pro′lon·ga′tion, pro·long′ment, pro·long′er** *n.*

prom (prom) *n. Informal* A formal college or school dance or ball. [Short for PROMENADE]

prom. promenade; promontory.

prom·e·nade (prom′ə·nād′, -näd′) *n.* **1** A leisurely walk taken for pleasure. **2** A place for promenading. **3** A concert or ball opened with a formal march. —*v.* **·nad·ed, ·nad·ing** *v.i.* **1** To take a promenade. —*v.t.* **2** To take a promenade through or along. **3** To take or exhibit on or as on a promenade; parade. [< L *prominare* drive forward] —**prom′e·nad′er** *n.*

Pro·me·theus (prə·mē′thē·əs) *Gk. Myth.* A Titan who stole fire from heaven for mankind and as a punishment was chained to a rock, where an eagle daily devoured his liver. —**Pro·me′the·an** *adj.*

pro·me·thi·um (prə·mē′thē·əm) *n.* A radioactive element (symbol Pm) produced by uranium fission and belonging to the lanthanide series. [< PROMETHEUS]

prom·i·nence (prom′ə·nəns) *n.* **1** The state of being prominent; conspicuousness. **2** Something that extends forth or protrudes. **3** *Astron.* One of the great luminous clouds arising from the sun's surface, seen during total eclipses: also **solar prominence.** Also **prom′i·nen·cy.**

prom·i·nent (prom′ə·nənt) *adj.* **1** Jutting out; projecting; protuberant. **2** Conspicuous. **3** Very well known; eminent: a *prominent* lawyer. [< L *prominere* to project] —**prom′i·nent·ly** *adv.* —**Syn. 3** famous, noted, renowned, celebrated, popular, honored, outstanding.

prom·is·cu·i·ty (prom′is·kyōō′ə·tē, prō′mis-) *n. pl.* **·ties** The state, quality, or an instance of being promiscuous, esp. in sexual relations.

pro·mis·cu·ous (prə·mis′kyōō·əs) *adj.* **1** Composed of persons or things confusedly mingled. **2** Indiscriminate; esp., having sexual relations indiscriminately or casually with various persons. **3** Casual; irregular. [< L *promiscuus* mixed] —**pro·mis′cu·ous·ly** *adv.* —**pro·mis′cu·ous·ness** *n.*

prom·ise (prom′is) *n.* **1** An assurance given that a specified action will or will not be taken. **2** Reasonable ground for hope or expectation of future excellence, satisfaction, etc. **3** Something promised. —*v.* **·ised, ·is·ing** *v.t.* **1** To engage or pledge by a promise: He *promised* to do it. **2** To make a promise of (something) to someone. **3** To give reason for expecting. **4** *Informal* To assure (someone). —*v.i.* **5** To make a promise. **6** To give reason for expectation: often with *well* or *fair.* [< L *promissum,* pp. of *promittere* send forward] —**prom′is·er** *n.*

Promised Land 1 Canaan, promised to Abraham by God. *Gen.* 15:18. **2** Any longed-for place of happiness or improvement.

prom·is·ing (prom′is·ing) *adj.* Giving promise of good results or development. —**prom′is·ing·ly** *adv.*

prom·is·so·ry (prom′ə·sôr′ē, -sō′rē) *adj.* Containing or of the nature of a promise.

promissory note A written promise by one person to pay another unconditionally a certain sum of money at a specified time.

pro·mo (prō′mō) *Slang n.* PROMOTION (def. 3). —*adj.* Of, for, or relating to promotion (def. 3); promotional.

prom·on·to·ry (prom′ən·tôr′ē, -tō′rē) *n. pl.* **·ries** A high point of land extending into a body of water; headland. [< L *promunturium*]

pro·mote (prə·mōt′) *v.t.* **·mot·ed, ·mot·ing 1** To contribute to the progress, development, or growth of; further; encourage. **2** To advance to a higher position, grade, or rank. **3** To advocate actively. **4** To publicize (a person, product, event, etc.), as by advertising, public appearances, etc. [< L *pro-* forward + *movere* to move] —**pro·mot′a·ble** *adj.*

pro·mot·er (prə·mō′tər) *n.* One who or that which promotes, esp. one who assists, by securing capital, etc., in promoting some enterprise, as a sports event, commercial venture, etc.

pro·mo·tion (prə·mō′shən) *n.* **1** Advancement in dignity, rank, grade, etc. **2** Furtherance or development, as of a cause. **3** Anything, as advertising, public appearances, etc., done to publicize a person, product, event, etc. —**pro·mo′tion·al** *adj.*

pro·mo·tive (prə·mō′tiv) *adj.* Tending to promote.

prompt (prompt) *v.t.* **1** To incite to action; instigate. **2** To suggest or inspire (an act, thought, etc.). **3** To remind of what has been forgotten or of what comes next; give a cue to. —*v.i.* **4** To give help or suggestions. —*adj.* **1** Quick to act, respond, etc.; ready. **2** Taking place at the appointed time; punctual. [< L *promptus* brought forth, hence, at hand] —**promp′ti·tude, prompt′ness** *n.* —**prompt′ly** *adv.*

prompt·er (promp′tər) **1** In a theater, one who follows the lines and prompts the actors. **2** One who or that which prompts.

prom·ul·gate (prom′əl·gāt, prō·mul′gāt) *v.t.* **·gat·ed, ·gat·ing 1** To make known or announce officially, as a law, dogma, etc. **2** To make known or effective over a wide area or extent. [< L *promulgare* make known] —**prom·ul·ga·tion** (prom′əl·gā′shən, prō′mul-), **prom′ul·gat·or** *n.*

pron. pronoun; pronounced; pronunciation.

prone (prōn) *adj.* **1** Lying flat, esp. with the face, front, or palm downward; prostrate. **2** Leaning forward or downward. **3** Mentally inclined or predisposed: with *to.* [< L *pronus*] —**prone′ly** *adv.* —**prone′ness** *n.*

prong (prông, prong) *n.* **1** A pointed end of a fork. **2** Any pointed and projecting part, as the end of an antler, etc. —*v.t.* To prick or stab with a prong. [ME *pronge*] —**pronged** *adj.*

prong·horn (prông′hôrn′, prong′-) *n. pl.* **·horns** or **·horn** A small, deerlike mammal of w North America.

pro·nom·i·nal (prō·nom′ə·nəl) *adj.* Of, pertaining to, like, or having the nature of a pronoun. —**pro·nom′i·nal·ly** *adv.*

pro·noun (prō′noun) *n.* A word used as a substitute for a noun, as *he, she, that.* [< L *pro-* in place of + *nomen* name, noun]

pro·nounce (prə·nouns′) *v.*

Pronghorn

·nounced, ·nounc·ing *v.t.* **1** To utter or deliver officially or solemnly; proclaim. **2** To assert; declare, esp. as one's judgment: The judge *pronounced* her guilty. **3** To give utterance to; articulate (words, etc.). **4** To articulate in a prescribed manner: hard to *pronounce* his name. **5** To indicate the sound of (a word) by phonetic symbols. —*v.i.* **6** To make a pronouncement or assertion. **7** To articulate words; speak. [< L *pronuntiare* proclaim < *pro-* forth + *nuntiare* announce] —**pro·nounce′a·ble** *adj.* —**pro·nounc′er** *n.*

pro·nounced (prə·nounst′) *adj.* Clearly noticeable; decided. —**pro·nounc·ed·ly** (prə·noun′sid·lē) *adv.*

pro·nounce·ment (prə·nouns′mənt) *n.* **1** The act of pronouncing. **2** A formal declaration or announcement.

pron·to (pron′tō) *adv. Slang* Quickly; promptly; instantly. [< L *promptus*]

pro·nun·ci·a·men·to (prə·nun′sē·ə·men′tō) *n. pl.* **·tos** A public announcement; proclamation; manifesto. [< L *pronuntiare* pronounce]

pro·nun·ci·a·tion (prə·nun′sē·ā′shən) *n.* The act or manner of pronouncing words.

proof (proof) *n.* **1** The act or process of proving; esp., the establishment of a fact by evidence or a truth by other truths. **2** A trial of strength, truth, fact, or excellence, etc.; a test. **3** Evidence and argument sufficient to induce belief. **4** *Law* Anything that serves to convince the mind of the truth or falsity of a fact or proposition. **5** The state or quality of having successfully undergone a proof or test. **6** The standard of strength of alcoholic liquors: see PROOF SPIRIT. **7** *Printing* A printed trial sheet showing the contents or condition of matter in type. **8** In engraving and etching, a trial impression taken from an engraved plate, stone, or block. **9** *Phot.* A trial print from a negative. **10** *Math.* A procedure that shows that a proposition is true. **11** Anything proved true; experience. **12** In philately, an experimental printing of a stamp. —*adj.* **1** Employed in or connected with proving or correcting. **2** Capable of resisting successfully; firm: with *against: proof* against bribes. **3** Of standard alcoholic strength, as liquors. —*v.t.* **1** To make a test or proof of. **2** To protect or make impervious: to *proof* a garment against stains. **3** PROOFREAD. [< L *probare* PROVE]

-proof *combining form* **1** Impervious to; not damaged by: *waterproof.* **2** Protected against: *mothproof.* **3** As strong as: *armorproof.* **4** Resisting; showing no effects of: *panic-proof.*

proof·read (proof′rēd′) *v.t. & v.i.* **·read** (-red′), **·read·ing** (-rē′ding) To read and correct (printers' proofs). —**proof′read·er** *n.*

prop¹ (prop) *v.t.* **propped, prop·ping 1** To support or keep from falling by or as by means of a prop. **2** To lean or place: usu. with *against.* **3** To support; sustain. —*n.* A support. [< MDu. *proppe* a vine prop]

prop² (prop) *n.* PROPERTY (def. 5).

prop³ (prop) *n. Informal* PROPELLER.

prop. proper; properly; property; proposition; proprietor.

prop·a·gan·da (prop′ə·gan′də) *n.* **1** Any widespread scheme or effort to spread or promote an idea, opinion, or course of action in order to help or do damage to a cause, person, etc. **2** The ideas, opinions, etc., so spread or promoted: now often used disparagingly because of the deceitful or distorted character of much propaganda. [< NL *(congregatio de) propaganda (fide)* (the congregation for) propagating (the faith)]

prop·a·gan·dism (prop′ə·gan′diz·əm) *n.* The art, practice, or system of using propaganda. —**prop′a·gan·dist** *adj., n.* —**prop′a·gan·dis′tic** *adj.* —**prop′a·gan·dis′ti·cal·ly** *adv.*

prop·a·gan·dize (prop′ə·gan′dīz) *v.* **·dized, ·diz·ing** *v.t.* **1** To subject to propaganda. **2** To spread by means of propaganda. —*v.i.* **3** To carry on or spread propaganda.

prop·a·gate (prop′ə·gāt) *v.* **·gat·ed, ·gat·ing** *v.t.* **1** To cause (animals, plants, etc.) to multiply by natural reproduction; breed. **2** To reproduce (itself). **3** To spread abroad or from person to person; disseminate. **4** *Physics* To transmit (a form of energy) through space. —*v.i.* **5** To multiply by natural reproduction; breed. **6** *Physics* To pass or spread through space, as waves, heat, etc. [< L *propago* a slip for transplanting] —**prop′a·ga′tion, prop′a·ga′tor** *n.* —**prop′a·ga′tive** *adj.*

pro·pane (prō′pān) *n.* A gaseous hydrocarbon of the paraffin series. [< PROP(YL) + (METH)ANE]

pro·pel (prə·pel′) *v.t.* **·pelled, ·pel·ling** To cause to move forward or ahead; drive or urge forward. [< L *pro-* forward + *pellere* drive]

pro·pel·lant (prə·pel′ənt) *n.* That which propels, esp. an explosive or fuel that propels a projectile, rocket, etc.

pro·pel·lent (prə·pel′ənt) *adj.* Propelling; able to propel.

pro·pel·ler (prə·pel′ər) *n.* **1** One who or that which propels. **2** Any device for propelling a craft through water or air; esp., a set of rotating vanes operating like a screw. Also **pro·pel′lor.**

Propeller

pro·pen·si·ty (prə·pen′sə·tē) *n.* *pl.* **·ties** Natural disposition to or for; tendency. [< L *pro-* forward + *pendere* hang]

PROOFREADER'S MARKS

Symbols in the column headed Margin are used only in the outer margins of the proof; the symbols used within the body of the text are given in the Text column.

Margin		Text
l.c.	Set in lower-case type	circled or /
cap.	Set in capitals	underscored
s.c.	Set in small capitals	underscored
c.+s.c.	Set in caps and small caps	
l.f.	Set in lightface type	circled
b.f.	Set in boldface type	underscored
Rom.	Set in roman type	circled
T.ital	Set in italic type	underscored
⊙	Insert period	∧
∧ ∧	Insert colon; semicolon	∧ ∧
⋏	Insert comma	∧
∨	Insert apostrophe	∧
/?/	Insert question mark	∧
/!/	Insert exclamation mark	∧
/=/	Insert hyphen	∧
∜	Insert quotation marks	∧
∨	Insert superior figure or letter.	∧
∧	Insert inferior figure or letter.	∧
𝟷/𝚖	Insert one em-dash	∧
𝟥	Take out (delete matter marked)	/
wf.	Wrong font	circled or /

Margin		Text
×	Broken letter: examine	circled
tr.	Transpose matter marked	⌐⌐
eq.♯	Equalize spacing	⋀⋀⋀
Γ	Move to left to point marked	Γ
⌐	Move to right to point marked	⌐
⌐⌐	Raise to point marked	⌐⌐
⌐⌐	Lower to point marked	⌐⌐
∪	Push down space	/
⌒	Close up	⌒
⁋	Begin new paragraph	⌒⌐
no ⁋	Run on, not a paragraph	~~
=	Align type	∥∥
stet	Retain words crossed out	······
⟨	Take out and close up	⟨
∥	Line up matter	∥
Out	Omission here; see copy	∧
⊏	Move this to left	
⊐	Move this to right	
Qu.?	Query: is this right?	∧
sp.	Spell out	circled
#	Insert space	∧

---

proof spirit An alcoholic liquor of a standard strength, in the U.S., containing ethyl alcohol in the amount of 50 percent of its volume, equal to 100 proof.

prop·er (prop′ər) *adj.* **1** Having special fitness; specially suited; appropriate. **2** Conforming to a standard; correct: the *proper* pronunciation. **3** Seemly; right; fitting: the *proper* outfit. **4** Genteel and respectable, often excessively so. **5** Understood in the most correct or strict sense: usu. following the noun modified: Boston *proper*. **6** Naturally belonging to a person or thing: with *to*: Snow is *proper* to winter. —*n. Often cap.* That portion of the breviary or missal containing the prayers and collects suitable to special occasions. [< L *proprius* one's own] —**prop′er·ly** *adv.* — **prop′er·ness** *n.*

proper fraction A fraction in which the denominator exceeds the numerator.

proper noun A noun designating a specific person, place, or thing, always capitalized in English, as *John, Mount Everest, Apollo II.*

proper subset Any subset not identical with the entire set.

prop·er·tied (prop′ər·tēd) *adj.* Owning property.

prop·er·ty (prop′ər·tē) *n. pl.* **·ties 1** Any object that a person may lawfully acquire and own; any possession, esp. land or real estate. **2** A specific piece of land or real estate. **3** The legal right to the possession, use, and disposal of a thing. **4** An inherent quality or characteristic. **5** In the theater, movies, television, ballet, etc., any portable article, except scenery and costumes, used by the performers while performing. [< L *proprius* one's own]

proph·e·cy (prof′ə·sē) *n. pl.* **·cies 1** A prediction made under divine influence. **2** Any prediction. [< Gk. *pro-* before + *phanai* speak]

proph·e·sy (prof′ə·sī) *v.* **·sied, ·sy·ing** *v.t.* **1** To utter or foretell with or as with divine inspiration. **2** To predict (a future event). **3** To point out beforehand. —*v.i.* **4** To speak by divine influence. **5** To foretell the future. [< PROPHECY] —**proph′e·si′er** *n.*

proph·et (prof′it) *n.* **1** One who delivers divine messages or interprets the divine will. **2** One who foretells the future. **3** A religious leader. **4** An interpreter or spokesman for any cause. —**the Prophet** According to Islam, Mohammed. —**the Prophets** The Old Testament books written by the prophets. [< Gk. *pro-* before + *phanai* speak] — **proph′et·ess** *n. Fem.* —**proph′et·hood** (-hŏŏd) *n.*

pro·phet·ic (prə·fet′ik) *adj.* **1** Of or pertaining to a prophet or prophecy. **2** Predicting or foreshadowing a future event. Also **pro·phet′i·cal.** —**pro·phet′i·cal·ly** *adv.*

pro·phy·lac·tic (prō′fə·lak′tik, prof′ə-) *adj.* Pertaining to prophylaxis. —*n.* **1** A prophylactic medicine or appliance. **2** A condom.

pro·phy·lax·is (prō′fə·lak′sis, prof′ə-) *n.* Preventive treatment for disease. [< Gk. *pro-* before + *phylaxis* a guarding]

pro·pin·qui·ty (prō·ping′kwə·tē) *n.* **1** Nearness in place or time. **2** Kinship. [< L *propinquus* near]

pro·pi·ti·ate (prō·pish′ē·āt) *v.t.* **·at·ed, ·at·ing** To cause to be favorably disposed; appease; conciliate. [< L *propitiare* render favorable, appease] —**pro·pi·ti·a·ble** (prō·pish′ē·ə·bəl), **pro·pi′ti·a′tive, pro·pi′ti·a·to′ry** *adj.* —**pro·pi·ti·a·tion** (prō·pish′ē·ā′shən), **pro·pi′ti·a′tor** *n.* —**Syn.** pacify, placate, mollify, reconcile.

pro·pi·tious (prō·pish′əs) *adj.* **1** Kindly disposed; gracious. **2** Attended by favorable circumstances; auspicious. [< L *propitius* favorable] —**pro·pi′tious·ly** *adv.* —**pro·pi′· tious·ness** *n.* —**Syn. 2** timely, fortunate, lucky, providential, happy, felicitous.

pro·po·nent (prə·pō′nənt) *n.* **1** One who makes a proposal or puts forward a proposition. **2** *Law* One who presents a will for probate. **3** One who advocates or supports a cause or doctrine. [< L *pro-* forth + *ponere* put]

pro·por·tion (prə·pôr′shən, -pōr′-) *n.* **1** Relative magnitude, number, or degree, as existing between parts, a part and a whole, or different things. **2** Balance and harmony; symmetry. **3** A proportionate or proper share. **4** *pl.* Size; dimensions. **5** An equality or identity between ratios. **6** *Math.* An identity or equation involving a pair of fractions, in the general form $\frac{4}{2} = \frac{8}{4}$. —*v.t.* **1** To adjust properly as to relative magnitude, amount, or degree. **2** To form with a harmonious relation of parts. [< L *pro-* before + *portio* a share] —**pro·por′tion·a·ble** *adj.* —**pro·por′tion·a·bly** *adv.* —**pro·por′tion·er** *n.*

pro·por·tion·al (prə·pôr′shən·əl, -pōr′-) *adj.* **1** Of, pertaining to, or being in proportion. **2** *Math.* Being the product of a given function or variable and a constant: The area of a circle is *proportional* to the square of the radius. —**pro·por′tion·al·ly** *adv.* —**pro·por′tion·al′i·ty** (-al′ə·tē) *n.*

pro·por·tion·ate (prə·pôr′shən·it, -pōr′-) *adj.* Being in due proportion; proportional. —*v.t.* (-āt) **·at·ed, ·at·ing** To make proportionate. —**pro·por′tion·ate·ly** *adv.* —**pro·por′· tion·ate·ness** *n.*

pro·po·sal (prə·pō′zəl) *n.* **1** An offer proposing something to be accepted or adopted. **2** An offer of marriage. **3** Something proposed.

pro·pose (prə·pōz′) *v.* **·posed, ·pos·ing** *v.t.* **1** To put forward for acceptance or consideration. **2** To nominate, as for admission or appointment. **3** To intend; purpose. **4** To suggest the drinking of (a toast or health). —*v.i.* **5** To form or announce a plan or design. **6** To make an offer, as of marriage. [< OF *pro-* forth + *poser* put] —**pro·pos′er** *n.*

prop·o·si·tion (prop′ə·zish′ən) *n.* **1** A scheme or proposal offered for consideration or acceptance. **2** *Informal* Any matter or person to be dealt with: a tough *proposition.* **3** *Informal* A proposal for illicit sexual intercourse. **4** A subject or statement presented for discussion. **5** *Logic* A statement in which the subject is affirmed or denied by the predicate. **6** *Math.* A statement whose truth is assumed or demonstrated. —*v.t. Informal* To make a proposal to (someone) to have illicit sexual intercourse. —**prop′o·si′· tion·al** *adj.* —**prop′o·si′tion·al·ly** *adv.*

pro·pound (prə·pound′) *v.t.* To put forward for consideration, solution, etc. [< L *proponere* set forth] —**pro·pound′· er** *n.*

pro·pri·e·tar·y (prə·prī′ə·ter′ē) *adj.* **1** Pertaining to a proprietor. **2** Protected as to name, composition, or process of manufacture by copyright, patent, etc. —*n. pl.* **·tar· ies 1** A proprietor or proprietors collectively. **2** Proprietorship. [< LL *proprietas* property]

pro·pri·e·tor (prə·prī′ə·tər) *n.* A person having the exclusive title to anything; owner. —**pro·pri′e·tor·ship′** *n.* —**pro· pri′e·tress** *n. Fem.*

pro·pri·e·ty (prə·prī′ə·tē) *n. pl.* **·ties** The character or quality of being proper; esp., accordance with recognized usage, custom, or principles. —**the proprieties** The standards of good social behavior. [< L *proprius* one's own]

pro·pul·sion (prə·pul′shən) *n.* **1** A propelling or being propelled. **2** Something that propels. [< L *propulsus*, pp. of *propellere* propel] —**pro·pul′sive** (-siv) *adj.*

pro·pyl (prō′pil) *n.* The univalent radical derived from propane.

pro ra·ta (prō rā′tə, rat′ə, rä′tə) Proportionate or proportionately: The loss was shared *pro rata.* [< L *pro rata (parte)* according to the calculated (share)]

pro·rate (prō·rāt′, prō′rāt′) *v.t. & v.i.* **·rat·ed, ·rat·ing** To distribute or divide proportionally. [< PRO RATA] —**pro· rat′a·ble** *adj.* —**pro·ra′tion** *n.*

pro·rogue (prō·rōg′) *v.t.* **·rogued, ·ro·guing** To discontinue a session of (an assembly, esp. the British Parliament). [< L *pro-* forth + *rogare* ask] —**pro·ro·ga·tion** (prō′rō·gā′shən) *n.*

pro·sa·ic (prō·zā′ik) *adj.* **1** Unimaginative; commonplace; dull. **2** Of or like prose. [< L *prosa* prose] —**pro·sa′i· cal·ly** *adv.* —**pro·sa′ic·ness** *n.*

pro·sce·ni·um (prō·sē′nē·əm) *n. pl.* **·ni·ums** or **·ni·a** (-nē·ə) **1** In a modern theater, that part of the stage between the curtain and the orchestra, sometimes including the curtain and its arch (**proscenium arch**). **2** In the ancient Greek or Roman theater, the stage. [< Gk. *proskēnion* < *pro-* before + *skēnē* a stage, orig. a tent]

pro·sciut·to (prō·shōō′tō) *n. pl.* **·ti** (-tē) or **·tos** A spicy, dry-cured ham, usu. sliced very thin. [Ital.]

pro·scribe (prō·skrīb′) *v.t.* **·scribed, ·scrib·ing 1** To denounce or condemn; prohibit; interdict. **2** To outlaw or banish. **3** In ancient Rome, to publish the name of (one condemned or exiled). [< L *pro-* before + *scribere* write] — **pro·scrib′er, pro·scrip′tion** (-skrip′shən) *n.* —**pro·scrip′tive** *adj.* —**pro·scrip′tive·ly** *adv.*

---

prose (prōz) *n.* 1 Speech or writing as found in ordinary conversation, letters, newspapers, etc. 2 Writing, esp. in literature, distinguished from poetry by the lack of conscious rhyme and usu. by rhythms suggesting ordinary speech or by a presentation in the form of a series of sentences with the initial letters capitalized. 3 Commonplace or tedious talk, style, quality, etc. —*adj.* 1 Of or in prose. 2 Tedious. —*v.t. & v.i.* **prosed, pros·ing** To write or speak in prose. [<L *prosa (oratio)* straight-forward (discourse)]

pros·e·cute (pros′ə·kyōōt) *v.* **·cut·ed, ·cut·ing** *v.t.* 1 To go on with so as to complete; pursue to the end: to *prosecute* an inquiry. 2 To carry on or engage in, as a trade. 3 *Law* a To bring suit against for redress of wrong or punishment of crime. b To seek to enforce or obtain, as a claim or right, by legal process. —*v.i.* 4 To begin and carry on a legal proceeding. [<L *prosequi* pursue]

prosecuting attorney The attorney empowered to act in behalf of the government, whether state, county, or national, in prosecuting for penal offenses.

pros·e·cu·tion (pros′ə·kyōō′shən) *n.* 1 The act or process of prosecuting. 2 *Law* a The instituting and carrying forward of a judicial or criminal proceeding. b The party instituting and conducting it.

pros·e·cu·tor (pros′ə·kyōō′tər) *n.* 1 One who prosecutes. 2 *Law* a One who institutes and carries on a suit, esp. a criminal suit. b PROSECUTING ATTORNEY.

pros·e·lyte (pros′ə·līt) *n.* One who has been converted to any opinion, belief, sect, or party. —*v.t. & v.i.* **·lyt·ed, ·lyt·ing** PROSELYTIZE. [<Gk. *prosélytos* a convert to Judaism] —**pros′e·lyt·ism** (-līt′iz·əm, -lə·tiz′əm), **pros′e·lyt·ist** *n.*

pros·e·lyt·ize (pros′ə·lə·tīz′) *v.t. & v.i.* **·ized, ·iz·ing** To convert or try to convert (a person) to one's religion, opinions, party, etc. —**pros′e·ly·tiz′er** *n.*

pro·sit (prō′sit) *interj.* A toast used in drinking health. [L, lit., may it benefit (you)]

pros·o·dy (pros′ə·dē, proz′-) *n.* The study of poetical forms, including meter, rhyme schemes, structural analysis, etc. [<Gk. *prosōidia* a song sung to music] —**pro·sod·ic** (prə·sod′ik, -zod′-) or **·i·cal** *adj.* —**pros′o·dist** *n.*

pros·pect (pros′pekt) *n.* 1 A future probability or something anticipated. 2 *Usu. pl.* Chances, as for success. 3 A scene; an extended view. 4 The direction in which anything faces; an exposure; outlook. 5 A potential buyer, candidate, etc. 6 The act of observing or examining; survey. 7 *Mining* a A place having signs of the presence of mineral ore. b The sample of mineral obtained by washing a small portion of ore or dirt. —*v.t. & v.i.* To explore (a region) for gold, oil, etc. [<L *pro-* forward + *specere* look]

pro·spec·tive (prə·spek′tiv) *adj.* 1 Anticipated; expected. 2 Looking toward the future; anticipatory. —**pro·spec′tive·ly** *adv.*

pros·pec·tor (pros′pek·tər) *n.* One who prospects for mineral deposits, oil, etc.

pro·spec·tus (prə·spek′təs) *n.* 1 A paper containing information of a proposed literary or business undertaking. 2 A summary; outline. [L, a look-out, prospect]

pros·per (pros′pər) *v.i.* 1 To thrive; flourish. —*v.t.* 2 To render prosperous. [<OF<L favorable]

pros·per·i·ty (pros·per′ə·tē) *n.* The state of being prosperous; esp., wealth or success.

pros·per·ous (pros′pər·əs) *adj.* 1 Successful; flourishing. 2 Wealthy; well-to-do. 3 Promising; favorable [<L *prosper* favorable] —**pros′per·ous·ly** *adv.* —**pros′per·ous·ness** *n.*

pros·ta·gland·in (pros′tə·glan′din) *n.* A fatty acid, found in many body tissues, including the prostate gland, that regulates many bodily functions.

pros·tate (pros′tāt) *adj.* Of the prostate gland. —*n.* PROSTATE GLAND. [<Gk. *prostatēs* one who stands before]

prostate gland A partly muscular gland at the base of the bladder around the urethra in male mammals.

pros·the·sis (pros·thē′sis, pros′thə-) *n. pl.* **·the·ses** (-thē′sēz) 1 Replacement of a missing part of the body with an artificial substitute. 2 A device used in prosthesis, as an artificial leg, eye, etc. [<Gk. *pros-* toward, besides + *tithenai* place, put] —**pros·thet·ic** (pros·thet′ik) *adj.*

pros·ti·tute (pros′tə·tyōōt) *n.* 1 A woman who engages in sexual intercourse for money. 2 A person who engages in

sexual acts for money: a male *prostitute*. 3 A person who uses his talents or gifts for unworthy or corrupt purposes. —*v.t.* **·tut·ed, ·tut·ing** 1 To put to base or unworthy purposes. 2 To offer (oneself or another) for lewd purposes, esp. for hire. [<L *prostituere* expose publicly, prostitute] —**pros′ti·tu′tion, pros′ti·tu′tor** *n.*

pros·trate (pros′trāt) *adj.* 1 Lying prone, or with the face to the ground. 2 Brought low in mind or body, as from grief, exhaustion, etc. 3 Lying at the mercy of another; defenseless. 4 *Bot.* Trailing along the ground. —*v.t.* **·trat·ed, ·trat·ing** 1 To bow or cast (oneself) down, as in adoration or pleading. 2 To throw flat; lay on the ground. 3 To overthrow or overcome; reduce to helplessness. [<L *prostratus,* pp. of *prosternere* lay flat] —**pros·tra′tion** *n.*

pros·y (prō′zē) *aaj.* **pros·i·er, pros·i·est** 1 Like prose. 2 Dull; commonplace. —**pros′i·ly** *adv.* —**pros′i·ness** *n.*

Prot. Protestant.

pro·tac·tin·i·um (prō′tak·tin′ē·əm) *n.* A radioactive element (symbol Pa) occurring in small amounts in uranium ores. [<PROT(O)· + ACTINIUM]

pro·tag·o·nist (prō·tag′ə·nist) *n.* 1 The actor who played the chief part in a Greek drama. 2 A leader in any enterprise or contest. [<Gk. *prōtos* first + *agōnistēs* a contestant, an actor]

pro·te·an (prō′tē·ən, prō·tē′ən) *adj.* Readily assuming different forms or aspects; changeable. [<PROTEUS]

pro·tect (prə·tekt′) *v.t.* 1 To shield or defend from attack, harm, or injury; guard; defend. 2 *Econ.* To assist (domestic industry) by protective tariffs. 3 In commerce, to provide funds to guarantee payment of (a draft, etc.). [<L *pro-* before + *tegere* to cover] —**pro·tec′tive** *adj.* —**pro·tec′tive·ly** *adv.* —**pro·tec′tive·ness, pro·tec′tor** *n.*

pro·tec·tion (prə·tek′shən) *n.* 1 The act of protecting or the state of being protected. 2 That which protects: Our dog is a great *protection.* 3 A system aiming to protect the industries of a country, as by imposing duties. 4 A safeconduct pass. 5 *Slang* Security purchased under threat of violence from racketeers; also, the money so paid.

pro·tec·tion·ism (prə·tek′shən·iz′əm) *n.* The economic doctrine or system of protection. —**pro·tec′tion·ist** *adj., n.*

protective coloration Any natural coloration of a plant or animal that tends to disguise or conceal it from its enemies.

protective tariff A tariff that is intended to insure protection of domestic industries against foreign competition.

pro·tec·tor·ate (prə·tek′tər·it) *n.* 1 A relation of protection and partial control by a strong nation over a weaker power. 2 A country or region so protected.

pro·té·gé (prō′tə·zhā, prō·tə·zhā′) *n.* One aided, esp. in promoting a career, by another who is older or more powerful. [F, pp. of *protéger* protect] —**pro′té·gée** *n. Fem.*

pro·tein (prō′tēn, -tē·in) *n.* Any of a class of complex nitrogenous compounds found in all living matter and forming an essential part of the diet of animals. —*adj.* Composed of protein.

pro tem·po·re (prō tem′pə·rē) For the time being; temporary: usu. shortened to **pro tem.** [L]

Prot·er·o·zo·ic (prot′ər·ə·zō′ik, prō′tər-) *adj., n.* • See GEOLOGY. [<Gk. *proteros* former + *zōion* animal]

pro·test (prō′test) *n.* 1 An objection, complaint, or declaration of disapproval. 2 A public expression of dissent, esp. if organized. 3 A formal certificate attesting the fact that a note or bill of exchange has not been paid. —*adj.* Of or relating to public protest: *protest* demonstrations. —*v.* (prə·test′) *v.t.* 1 To assert earnestly or positively; state formally, esp. against opposition or doubt. 2 To make a protest against; object to. 3 To declare formally that payment of (a promissory note, etc.) has been duly submitted and refused. —*v.i.* 4 To make solemn affirmation. 5 To make a protest; object. [<L *pro-* forth + *testari* affirm] —**pro·test′er, pro·test′or** *n.*

Prot·es·tant (prot′is·tənt) *n.* Any Christian who is not a member of the Roman Catholic or Eastern Orthodox Churches. —*adj.* Pertaining to Protestants or Protestantism. —**Prot′es·tant·ism** *n.*

Protestant Episcopal Church A religious body in the U.S. which is descended from the Church of England.

prot·es·ta·tion (prot′is·tā′shən, prō′tes-) *n.* 1 The act of protesting, **2** That which is protested. **3** Any protest or objection.

Pro·te·us (prō′tē·əs, -tyōōs) *Gk. Myth.* A sea god who had the power of assuming different forms. **—Pro′te·an** *adj.*

proto- *combining form* **1** First in rank or time; chief; typical: *protozoan.* **2** Primitive; original: *prototype.* Also **prot-.** [< Gk. *prōtos* first]

pro·to·col (prō′tə·kol) *n.* **1** The preliminary draft of an official document, as a treaty. **2** The preliminary draft or report of the negotiations and conclusions arrived at by a diplomatic conference, having the force of a treaty when ratified. **3** The rules of diplomatic and state etiquette and ceremony. **—***v.i.* To write or form protocols. [< LGk. *prōtokollon* the first glued sheet of a papyrus roll]

pro·ton (prō′ton) *n.* A stable, positively charged subatomic particle found typically in atomic nuclei, having a charge equal in magnitude to that of an electron and a mass of about 1.672×10^{-24} gram. [< Gk. *prōtos* first]

pro·to·plasm (prō′tə·plaz′əm) *n.* The basic living substance of plant and animal cells. [< Gk. *prōtos* first + PLASMA] **—pro′to·plas′mic** *adj.*

pro·to·type (prō′tə·tīp) *n.* A first or original model; an archetype. **—pro′to·typ′al** (-tī′pəl), **pro′to·typ′ic** (-tip′ik), **pro′to·typ′i·cal** *adj.*

pro·to·zo·an (prō′tə·zō′ən) *n.* *pl.* **·zo·a** (-zō′ə) Any of a phylum of single-celled animals, including free-living, aquatic forms and pathogenic parasites. Also **pro′to·zo′on.** **—***adj.* Pertaining or belonging to the phylum of protozoans: also **pro′to·zo′ic.** [< PROTO- + Gk. *zōion* animal]

pro·tract (prō·trakt′, prə-) *v.t.* **1** To extend in time; prolong. **2** In surveying, to draw or map by means of a scale and protractor; plot. **3** *Zool.* To protrude or extend. [< L *protractus,* pp. of *protrahere* extend] **—pro·trac′tion** *n.* **—pro·tract′i·ble, pro·trac′tive** *adj.*

pro·tract·ed (prō·trak′tid, prə-) *adj.* Unduly or unusually extended or prolonged. **—pro·tract′ed·ly** *adv.* **—pro·tract′ed·ness** *n.*

pro·trac·tile (prō·trak′til) *adj.* Capable of being protracted or protruded; protrusile.

pro·trac·tor (prō·trak′tər) *n.* **1** An instrument for measuring and laying off angles. **2** One who or that which protracts.

pro·trude (prō·trōōd′, prə-) *v.t.* & *v.i.* **·trud·ed, ·trud·ing** To push or thrust out; project outward. [< L *pro-* forward + *trudere* thrust] **—pro·tru′dent** *adj.* **—pro·tru′sion** (-trōō′zhən) *n.*

pro·tru·sile (prō·trōō′sil) *adj.* Adapted to being thrust out, as a tentacle, etc. Also **pro·tru′si·ble.**

pro·tru·sive (prō·trōō′siv) *adj.* **1** Tending to protrude. **2** Pushing or driving forward. **—pro·tru′sive·ly** *adv.* **—pro·tru′sive·ness** *n.*

pro·tu·ber·ance (prō·t‵ōō′bər·əns) *n.* **1** Something that protrudes; a knob; prominence. **2** The state of being protuberant. Also **pro·tu′ber·an·cy.** [< LL *protuberare* bulge out] **—pro·tu′ber·ant** *adj.* **—pro·tu′ber·ant·ly** *adv.*

proud (proud) *adj.* **1** Moved by, having, or exhibiting a due sense of pride; self-respecting. **2** Characterized by excessive or immoderate pride. **3** Being a cause of honorable pride: a *proud* occasion. **4** Appreciative of an honor; glad: *proud* of his heritage. **5** High-mettled, as a horse; spirited. [< OE *prūd*] **—proud′ly** *adv.* **—Syn. 2** arrogant, haughty, supercilious, disdainful.

proud flesh An excessive growth of tissue at a healing wound or ulcer.

Prov., Prov. Proverbs.

prov. province; provincial; provisional; provost.

prove (prōōv) *v.* **proved, proved** or **prov·en** (prōō′vən), **prov·ing** *v.t.* **1** To show to be true or genuine, as by evidence or argument. **2** To determine the quality or genuineness of; test. **3** To establish the authenticity or validity of, as a will. **4** *Math.* To verify the accuracy of by an independent process. **5** *Printing* To take a proof of or from. **6** *Archaic* To learn by experience. **—***v.i.* **7** To turn out to be: His hopes *proved* vain. [< L *probare* to test, try] **—prov′a·ble** *adj.* **—prov′er** *n.*

prov·e·nance (prov′ə·nəns) *n.* Origin or source, as of an

archeological find or an object of art. [F< *provenant,* pr.p. of *provenir* come forth]

Pro·ven·çal (prō′vən·säl′, *Fr.* prō·väN·sȧl′) *n.* **1** The Romance language of Provence, France. **2** A native or resident of Provence. **—***adj.* Of or pertaining to Provence, its inhabitants, or their language.

prov·en·der (prov′ən·dər) *n.* **1** Dry food for cattle, as hay. **2** Provisions. [< OF *provende* an allowance of food]

pro·ve·ni·ence (prō·vē′nē·əns, -vēn′yəns) *n.* PROVENANCE.

prov·erb (prov′ərb) *n.* **1** A terse expression of a popularly accepted piece of wisdom. **2** Something proverbial; a typical example; byword. [< L *pro-* before + *verbum* a word] **—Syn. 1** adage, aphorism, maxim, motto, saying, truism.

pro·ver·bi·al (prə·vûr′bē·əl) *adj.* **1** Of the nature of or pertaining to a proverb. **2** Generally known or remarked. **—pro·ver′bi·al·ly** *adv.*

Prov·erbs (prov′ərbz) *n.pl. (construed as sing.)* A book of the Old Testament consisting of moral sayings.

pro·vide (prə·vīd′) *v.* **·vid·ed, ·vid·ing** *v.t.* **1** To acquire for or supply; furnish. **2** To afford; yield: to *provide* pleasure. **3** To set down as a condition; stipulate. **—***v.i.* **4** To take measures in advance: with *for* or *against.* **5** To furnish means of subsistence: usu. with *for.* **6** To make a stipulation. [< L *providere* foresee] **—pro·vid′er** *n.*

pro·vid·ed (prə·vī′did) *conj.* On condition that.

prov·i·dence (prov′ə·dəns) *n.* **1** *Often cap.* The care exercised by nature or God's will over the universe. **2** Care exercised for the future; foresight. [< L *providentia* < *providens,* pr.p. of *providere* foresee]

Prov·i·dence (prov′ə·dəns) *n.* God; the Deity.

prov·i·dent (prov′ə·dənt) *adj.* **1** Anticipating and preparing for future wants or emergencies; exercising foresight. **2** Economical; thrifty. **—prov′i·dent·ly** *adv.*

prov·i·den·tial (prov′ə·den′shəl) *adj.* **1** Resulting from or revealing the action of God's providence. **2** As if caused by divine intervention; wonderful. **—prov′i·den′tial·ly** *adv.*

pro·vid·ing (prə·vī′ding) *conj.* Provided; in case that.

prov·ince (prov′ins) *n.* **1** An administrative division within a country: the *provinces* of Canada. **2** A region or country ruled by the Roman Empire. **3** *pl.* Those regions that lie at a distance from the capital or major cities. **4** A sphere of knowledge or activity: the *province* of chemistry. **5** Proper concern or compass, as of responsibilities or duties: The *province* of the judge is to apply the laws. [< L *provincia* an official duty or charge, a province]

pro·vin·cial (prə·vin′shəl) *adj.* **1** Of or characteristic of a province. **2** Confined to a province; rustic. **3** Narrow; unsophisticated; uninformed. **—***n.* **1** A native or inhabitant of a province. **2** One who is provincial. **—pro·vin′ci·al′i·ty** (-shē·al′ə·tē) *n.* **—pro·vin′cial·ly** *adv.*

pro·vin·cial·ism (prə·vin′shəl·iz′əm) *n.* **1** The quality of being provincial. **2** Provincial peculiarity, esp. of speech.

pro·vi·sion (prə·vizh′ən) *n.* **1** A measure taken in advance, as against future need. **2** *pl.* Food or a supply of food; victuals. **3** Something provided or prepared in anticipation of need. **4** A stipulation or requirement. **—***v.t.* To provide with food or provisions. [< L *provisus,* p.p. of *providere* foresee] **—pro·vi′sion·er** *n.*

pro·vi·sion·al (prə·vizh′ən·əl) *adj.* Provided for a present service or temporary necessity: a *provisional* army. Also **pro·vi′sion·ar′y** (-er′ē). **—pro·vi′sion·al·ly** *adv.*

pro·vi·so (prə·vī′zō) *n.* *pl.* **·sos** or **·soes** **1** A conditional stipulation. **2** A clause, as in a contract or statute, limiting, modifying, or rendering conditional its operation. [< Med. L *proviso (quod)* it being provided (that)]

pro·vi·so·ry (prə·vī′zər·ē) *adj.* **1** Conditional. **2** Provisional. **—pro·vi′so·ri·ly** *adv.*

pro·vo (prō′vō) *n.* *pl.* **·vos** A youthful member of any of various groups committed to violent political action. [Du. < F *provocateur*]

prov·o·ca·tion (prov′ə·kā′shən) *n.* **1** The act of provoking. **2** Something that provokes or incites; esp., something that provokes anger or annoyance.

pro·voc·a·tive (prə·vok′ə·tiv) *adj.* Serving to provoke or excite; stimulating: a *provocative* theory. **—***n.* That which provokes or tends to provoke. **—pro·voc'a·tive·ly** *adv.* — **pro·voc'a·tive·ness** *n.*

pro·voke (prə-vōk') *v.t.* **·voked, ·vok·ing 1** To stir to anger or resentment; irritate; vex. **2** To arouse or stimulate to some action. **3** To stir up or bring about: to *provoke* a quarrel. [< L *pro-* forth + *vocare* to call]

prov·ost (prō'vōst, prō'vəst, prov'əst) *n.* **1** A person having charge or authority over others. **2** The chief magistrate of a Scottish burgh. **3** An administrative official in some English and American colleges. **4** *Eccl.* The head of a collegiate chapter or a cathedral; a dean. [< L *praepositus* a prefect] **—prov'ost·ship** *n.*

pro·vost marshal (prō'vō) A military officer commanding a company of military police (**provost guard**).

prow (prou) *n.* **1** The forward part of a ship; the bow. **2** Any pointed projection, as of an airplane. [< Gk. *prōira*]

prow·ess (prou'is) *n.* **1** Strength, skill, and courage, esp. in battle. **2** Formidable skill; expertise. [< OF *prou* brave]

prowl (proul) *v.t. & v.i.* To roam about stealthily, as in search of prey or plunder. **—n.** The act of prowling. [ME *prollen*] **—prowl'er** *n.*

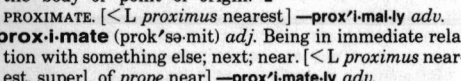

Prow of a ship

prowl car SQUAD CAR.

prox·i·mal (prok'sə·məl) *adj.* **1** Relatively nearer the center of the body or point of origin. **2** PROXIMATE. [< L *proximus* nearest] **—prox'i·mal·ly** *adv.*

prox·i·mate (prok'sə·mit) *adj.* Being in immediate relation with something else; next; near. [< L *proximus* nearest, superl. of *prope* near] **—prox'i·mate·ly** *adv.*

prox·im·i·ty (prok·sim'ə·tē) *n.* The state or fact of being near; nearness. [< L *proximus* nearest]

prox·i·mo (prok'sə·mō) *adv.* In or of the next or coming month. [< L *proximo* (*mense*) in the next (month)]

prox·y (prok'sē) *n. pl.* **prox·ies 1** A person empowered by another to act for him. **2** The means or agency of one so empowered: to vote by *proxy*. **3** The office or right to act for another. **4** A document conferring the authority to act for another. [< L *procurare* procure]

pr.p. present participle.

prude (prōōd) *n.* One who displays an exaggerated devotion to modesty and propriety, esp. in sexual matters. [F < *prudefemme* an excellent woman] **—prud'ish** *adj.* — **prud'ish·ly** *adv.* **—prud'ish·ness** *n.*

pru·dence (prōōd'ns) *n.* **1** The exercise of thoughtful care, sound judgment, or discretion; cautious wisdom. **2** Economy; thrift. **—pru·den·tial** (prōō·den'shəl) *adj.*

pru·dent (prōōd'nt) *adj.* **1** Habitually careful to avoid errors and to follow the most reasonable or practical course; politic. **2** Exercising sound judgment; wise; judicious. **3** Characterized by discretion; cautious in manner. **4** Frugal; provident. [< L *prudens* knowing, skilled] **—pru'dent·ly** *adv.* **—Syn. 1** shrewd. **2** sensible, sagacious, thoughtful. **3** circumspect.

prud·er·y (prōō'dər·ē) *n. pl.* **·er·ies 1** Exaggerated devotion to modesty and propriety, esp. in sexual matters. **2** An action characteristic of a prude.

prune[1] (prōōn) *n.* **1** The dried fruit of any of several varieties of plum. **2** *Slang* A stupid or disagreeable person. [< Gk. *prounon* a plum]

prune[2] (prōōn) *v.t. & v.i.* **pruned, prun·ing 1** To trim or cut superfluous branches or parts (from). **2** To cut off (superfluous branches or parts). [< OF *proignier*] **—prun'er** *n.*

pru·ri·ent (prōōr'ē·ənt) *adj.* **1** Tending to excite lustful thoughts or desires; lewd. **2** Characterized by or having lustful thoughts or desires: *prurient* interest. [< L *prurire* itch, long for] **—pru'ri·ence, pru'ri·en·cy** *n.* **—pru'ri·ent·ly** *adv.*

Prussian blue 1 A dark blue pigment or dye composed of various cyanogen compounds of iron. **2** A strong, blue color.

prussic acid HYDROCYANIC ACID.

pry[1] (prī) *v.i.* **pried, pry·ing** To look or peer carefully, curiously, or slyly; snoop. [ME *prien*]

pry[2] (prī) *v.t.* **pried, pry·ing 1** To raise, move, or open by

means of a lever. **2** To obtain by effort. **—n. 1** A lever, as a bar, stick, or beam. **2** Leverage. [< PRIZE[2]]

pry·er (prī'ər) *n.* PRIER.

P.S. public school.

P.S., p.s. postscript.

Ps, Ps., Psa. Psalms.

psalm (säm) *n.* A sacred song or lyric, esp. one contained in the Old Testament Book of Psalms; a hymn. [< Gk. *psalmos* a song sung to the harp]

psalm·ist (sä'mist) *n.* A composer of psalms. **—the Psalmist** King David, the traditional author of many of the Scriptural psalms.

psalm·o·dy (sä'mə·dē, sal'-) *n. pl.* **·dies 1** The singing of psalms in divine worship. **2** A collection of psalms. [< Gk. *psalmos* a psalm + *ōidē* a song] **—psalm'o·dist** *n.*

Psalms (sämz) *n.pl.* (*construed as sing.*) A lyrical book of the Old Testament, containing 150 hymns. Also **Book of Psalms.**

psal·ter (sôl'tər) *n.* A version of the Book of Psalms used in religious services. [< L *psalterium* a psaltery]

Psal·ter (sôl'tər) *n.* The Book of Psalms. Also **Psal'ter·y.**

psal·ter·y (sôl'tər·ē) *n. pl.* **·ter·ies** An ancient stringed musical instrument played by plucking. [< Gk. *psaltērion* < *psallein* to twitch, twang]

Psaltery

pseud. pseudonym.

pseu·do (sōō'dō) *adj.* Pretended; sham; false.

pseudo- *combining form* **1** False; pretended: *pseudonym.* **2** Closely resembling; serving or functioning as: *pseudopodium.* Also **pseud-.** [< Gk. *pseudēs* false]

pseu·do·nym (sōō'də·nim) *n.* A fictitious name; pen name. [< Gk. *pseudēs* false + *onyma* a name] **—pseu·don·y·mous** (sōō·don'ə·məs) *adj.* **—pseu·don'y·mous·ly** *adv.* — **pseu·don'y·mous·ness, pseu·do·nym·i·ty** (sōō'də·nim'ə·tē) *n.*

pseu·do·po·di·um (sōō'də·pō'dē·əm) *n. pl.* **·di·a** (-dē·ə) A temporary extension of the protoplasm of a cell or unicellular organism, serving for taking in food, locomotion, etc. Also **pseu'do·pod** (-pod). [< PSEUDO- + Gk. *podion* little foot] **—pseu'do·po'di·al, pseu·do·pod·al** (sōō·dop'ə·dəl) *adj.*

psf, p.s.f. pounds per square foot.

pshaw (shô) *interj. & n.* An exclamation of annoyance, disgust, or impatience.

psi (sī, psī, psē) *n.* The twenty-third letter of the Greek alphabet (Ψ, ψ).

psi, p.s.i. pounds per square inch.

psi·lo·cy·bin (sī'lə·sī'bin) *n.* A hallucinogenic drug derived from a Mexican mushroom. [< *Psilocybe,* generic name of the mushroom + -IN]

psit·ta·co·sis (sit'ə·kō'sis) *n.* A viral infection affecting parrots, pigeons, etc., and sometimes humans, in whom it causes pneumonia, fever, etc. [< Gk. *psittakos* a parrot + -OSIS]

pso·ri·a·sis (sə·rī'ə·sis) *n.* A chronic skin condition characterized by reddish patches and white scales. [< Gk. *psōra* an itch] **—pso·ri·at·ic** (sôr'ē·at'ik, sō'rē-) *adj.*

PST, P.S.T., P.s.t. Pacific standard time.

psych (sīk) *v.t.* **psyched, psych·ing** *Slang* **1** To make mentally ready, as by inducing alertness or tension; key up: often with *up.* **2** To cause to lose self-assurance, esp. in order to place at a competitive disadvantage; demoralize: often with *out:* to *psych* rivals. **3** To manipulate by the use of psychology; esp., to outwit: often with *out: psyched* him into giving me a loan. **4** To understand: with *out:* couldn't *psych* it out. Also **psyche. —Syn. 2** intimidate, distress, put off, disconcert, discountenance.

psych., psychol. psychologist; psychology.

psy·che (sī'kē) *n.* **1** The human soul. **2** The mind. [< Gk. *psychē* the soul < *psychein* breathe, blow]

Psy·che (sī'kē) *Gk. & Rom. Myth.* A maiden beloved by Cupid and regarded as a personification of the soul.

psy·che·de·li·a (sī'kə·dē'lē·ə, -dēl'yə) *n.* Psychedelic drugs and accessories, or things associated with them.

psy·che·del·ic (sī'kə·del'ik) *adj.* Causing or having to do with abnormal alterations of consciousness or perception: *psychedelic* drugs. [< Gk. *psychē* soul + *del(os)* manifest + -IC] **—psy'che·del'i·cal·ly** *adv.*

psy·chi·a·trist (sĭ·kī′ə·trist) *n.* A medical doctor specializing in the practice of psychiatry.

psy·chi·a·try (sĭ·kī′ə·trē) *n.* The branch of medicine concerned with mental and emotional disorders. [< PSYCH(O)- + Gk. *iatros* healer] —**psy·chi·at·ric** (sī′kē·at′rik) or ·**ri·cal** *adj.* —**psy′chi·at′ri·cal·ly** *adv.*

psy·chic (sī′kik) *adj.* **1** Of or pertaining to the psyche or mind. **2** Inexplicable with reference to present knowledge or scientific theory: *psychic* phenomena. **3** Sensitive or responsive to phenomena apparently independent of normal sensory stimuli: a *psychic* person. Also **psy′chi·cal.** — *n.* **1** A psychic person. **2** A spiritualistic medium. [< Gk. *psychē* soul] —**psy′chi·cal·ly** *adv.*

psy·cho (sī′kō) *n. pl.* ·**chos** *Slang* A mentally disturbed person; a neurotic or psychopath. —*adj.* **1** Psychologically disturbed. **2** Psychological or psychiatric. [< PSYCHO(NEU·ROTIC)]

psycho- *combining form* Mind; soul; spirit: *psychosomatic.* Also **psych-.** [< Gk. *psychē* spirit, soul]

psy·cho·ac·tive (sī′kō·ak′tiv) *adj.* Having an effect on the mind or on behavior.

psy·cho·a·nal·y·sis (sī′kō·ə·nal′ə·sis) *n.* **1** A method of psychotherapeutic treatment developed by Sigmund Freud and others, which seeks to alleviate certain mental and emotional disorders. **2** The theory or practice of such treatment. —**psy′cho·an′a·lyt′ic** (-an′ə·lit′ik) or ·**i·cal** *adj.* —**psy′cho·an′a·lyt′i·cal·ly** *adv.*

psy·cho·an·a·lyst (sī′kō·an′ə·list) *n.* One who practices psychoanalysis.

psy·cho·an·a·lyze (sī′kō·an′ə·līz) *v.t.* ·**lyzed,** ·**lyz·ing** To treat by psychoanalysis. *Brit. sp.* ·**lyse.**

psy·cho·dra·ma (sī′kō·drä′mə, -dram′ə) *n.* A form of psychotherapy in which the patient acts out, occasionally before an audience, situations involving his problems. —**psy′cho·dra·mat′ic** *adj.*

psy·cho·gen·ic (sī′kō·jen′ik) *adj.* Originating in the mind; caused by a mental or emotional condition. —**psy′·cho·gen′i·cal·ly** *adv.*

psy·cho·log·i·cal (sī′kə·loj′i·kəl) *adj.* **1** Of or pertaining to psychology. **2** Of or in the mind. **3** Suitable for affecting the mind: the *psychological* moment. Also **psy′cho·log′ic.** —**psy′cho·log′i·cal·ly** *adv.*

psy·chol·o·gist (sī·kol′ə·jist) *n.* A specialist in psychology.

psy·chol·o·gize (sī·kol′ə·jīz) *v.* ·**gized,** ·**giz·ing** *v.i.* **1** To theorize psychologically. —*v.t.* **2** To interpret psychologically.

psy·chol·o·gy (sī·kol′ə·jē) *n.* **1** The science of the mind in any of its aspects. **2** The systematic investigation of human or animal learning, behavior, etc. **3** The pattern of mental processes characteristic of an individual or type.

psy·cho·neu·ro·sis (sī′kō·n°oo·rō′sis) *n. pl.* ·**ses** (-sēz) NEUROSIS. —**psy′cho·neu·rot′ic** (-rot′ik) *adj., n.*

psy·cho·path (sī′kō·path) *n.* One exhibiting severely deranged behavior. —**psy′cho·path′ic** *adj.*

psy·cho·pa·thol·o·gy (sī′kō·pə·thol′ə·jē) *n.* The pathology of the mind. —**psy′cho·path′o·log′i·cal** (-path′ə·loj′i·kəl) *adj.* —**psy′cho·pa·thol′o·gist** *n.*

psy·chop·a·thy (sī·kop′ə·thē) *n.* Mental disorder.

psy·cho·sis (sī·kō′sis) *n. pl.* ·**ses** (-sēz) A severe mental disorder marked by disorganization of the personality. [< Gk. *psychōsis* a giving of life]

psy·cho·so·mat·ic (sī′kō·sō·mat′ik) *adj.* **1** Of or pertaining to the interrelationships of mind and body, esp. with reference to disease. **2** Designating a physical ailment caused or influenced by emotional stress. [< PSYCHO- + SOMATIC]

psy·cho·sur·ger·y (sī′kō·sûr′jər·ē) *n.* Brain surgery performed to treat a mental disorder or alter behavior. —**psy′cho·sur′geon** (-sûr′jən) *n.* —**psy′cho·sur′gi·cal** *adj.*

psy·cho·ther·a·py (sī′kō·ther′ə·pē) *n.* The treatment of certain nervous and mental disorders by psychological techniques such as counseling, psychoanalysis, etc. Also **psy′cho·ther′a·peu′tics** (-ther′ə·py°oo′tiks). —**psy′cho·ther′·a·peu′tic** *adj.* —**psy′cho·ther′a·pist** *n.*

psy·chot·ic (sī·kot′ik) *n.* One suffering from a psychosis. —*adj.* Of psychosis or a psychotic. —**psy·chot′i·cal·ly** *adv.*

Pt platinum.

pt. (*pl.* **pts.**) part; payment; pint; point; port; preterit.

p.t. past tense; for the time being (L *pro tempore*).

PTA, P.T.A. Parent-Teacher Association.

ptar·mi·gan (tär′mə·gən) *n. pl.* ·**gans** or ·**gan** Any of various species of grouse of northern regions, usu. having white winter plumage. [< Scot. Gaelic *tarmachan*]

PT boat (pē′tē′) A high-speed, easily maneuverable motorboat equipped with torpedoes and, usu. machine guns and depth charges. [< *p(atrol) t(orpedo)*]

pter·i·do·phyte (ter′i·dō·fīt′) *n.* Any of a division of flowerless plants comprising the ferns, horsetails, and related plants with vascular stems, roots, and leaves. [< Gk. *pteris, pteridos* a fern + *phyton* a plant] —**pter′i·do·phyt′ic** (-fit′ik), **pter′i·doph′y·tous** (-dof′ə·təs) *adj.*

ptero- *combining form* Wing; feather; plume; resembling wings: *pterodactyl.* Also **pter-.** [< Gk. *pteron* wing]

pter·o·dac·tyl (ter′ə·dak′til) *n.* PTEROSAUR. [< Gk. *pteron* a wing + *daktylos* a finger]

pter·o·saur (ter′ə·sôr′) *n.* Any of various fossil reptiles having batlike wings. [< Gk. *pteros* wing + *sauros* lizard] —**pter′o·saur′i·an** *adj.*

-pterous *combining form* Having a specified number or kind of wings: *dipterous.* [< Gk. *pteron* wing]

ptg. printing.

Ptol·e·ma·ic (tol′ə·mā′ik) *adj.* Of or pertaining to Ptolemy, the astronomer who lived in the second century A.D., or to the Ptolemies who ruled Egypt.

Ptolemaic system The astronomical system of Ptolemy, which assumed that the earth was the central body around which the sun, planets, stars, etc., moved.

pto·maine (tō′mān, tō·mān′) *n.* Any of a class of usu. nontoxic compounds derived from decomposing protein. Also **pto′main.** [< Gk. *ptōma* a corpse]

ptomaine poisoning FOOD POISONING. • The term is based upon the erroneous idea that ptomaines usually cause food poisoning.

pty. proprietary.

pty·a·lin (tī′ə·lin) *n.* A digestive enzyme converting starch into dextrin and maltose. [< Gk. *ptyalon* saliva + -IN]

Pu plutonium.

pub (pub) *n. Brit.* A tavern or bar. [< PUB(LIC) (HOUSE)]

pub. public; publication; published; publisher.

pu·ber·ty (py°oo′bər·tē) *n.* **1** The state in an individual's development when he or she is physically capable of sexual reproduction. **2** The age at which puberty begins, usu. fixed legally at 14 years in boys and 12 in girls. [< L *pubes, puberis* an adult]

pu·bes (py°oo′bēz) *n.* **1** The hair that appears on the body at puberty. **2** The genital area that is covered with hair in the adult. [L, pubic hair]

pu·bes·cent (py°oo·bes′ənt) *adj.* **1** Arriving or having arrived at puberty. **2** *Biol.* Covered with fine hair or down, as leaves, etc. [< L *pubescere* attain puberty] —**pu·bes′·cence** *n.*

pu·bic (py°oo′bik) *adj.* Of or pertaining to the region in the lower part of the abdomen.

pu·bis (py°oo′bis) *n. pl.* ·**bes** (-bēz) Either of the two bones which join to form the front arch of the pelvis. [< L *(os) pubis* pubic (bone)]

publ. publication; published; publisher.

pub·lic (pub′lik) *adj.* **1** Of, pertaining to, or affecting the people at large. **2** Of or relating to the community as distinguished from private or personal matters. **3** For the use of or open to all; maintained by or for the community: *public* parks. **4** Well-known; open: a *public* scandal. **5** Occupying an official position. **6** Acting before or for the community: a *public* speaker. —*n.* **1** The people collectively. **2** A group of people sharing some attribute or purpose: the church-going *public.* [< L *publicus*] —**pub′lic·ly** *adv.* —**pub′lic·ness** *n.*

pub·li·can (pub′lə·kən) *n.* **1** In England, the keeper of a public house. **2** In ancient Rome, one who collected the public revenues. [< L *publicanus* a tax gatherer]

pub·li·ca·tion (pub′lə·kā′shən) n. 1 The act of publishing. 2 That which is published; any printed work placed on sale or otherwise distributed.

public domain 1 Lands owned by a government. 2 The condition of being freely available for unrestricted use and not protected by copyright or patent.

public house 1 An inn, tavern, or hotel. 2 Brit. A saloon or bar.

pub·li·cist (pub′lə·sist) n. 1 One who publicizes, as an activity, a person, etc. 2 A writer on international law.

pub·lic·i·ty (pub·lis′ə·tē) n. 1 The state of being public. 2 Information, news, or promotional material intended to elicit public interest in some person, product, cause, etc.; also the work or business of preparing and releasing such material. 3 The attention or interest of the public.

pub·li·cize (pub′lə·sīz) v.t. ·cized, ·ciz·ing To give publicity to; promote. Brit. sp. **pub′li·cise.**

public opinion The prevailing ideas, beliefs, or attitudes of a community.

public relations The business of representing and promoting the interests or reputation of a person or an organization in its relations with the public.

public school 1 A school maintained by public funds for the free education of the children of the community, usu. covering elementary and secondary grades. 2 In England, a private, endowed boarding school preparing students for the universities.

public servant A government official.

pub·lic-spir·it·ed (pub′lik-spir′it·id) adj. Showing an enlightened interest in the welfare of the community.

public utility A business organization which performs some public service, as the supplying of water or electric power, and is subject to governmental regulations.

public works Works built with public money, as post offices, roads, etc.

pub·lish (pub′lish) v.t. 1 To print and issue (a book, magazine, etc.) to the public. 2 To make known or announce publicly. 3 To print and issue the work of. —v.i. 4 To engage in the business of publishing books, magazines, newspapers, etc. 5 To have one's work printed and issued. [< L publicare make public] —**pub′lish·a·ble** adj. —Syn. 2 promulgate, proclaim, declare, advertise.

pub·lish·er (pub′lish·ər) n. One who makes a business of publishing books, periodicals, etc.

puce (pyōōs) n. Dark purplish brown. —adj. Of this color. [F, lit., flea < L pulex]

puck[1] (puk) n. A mischievous sprite or hobgoblin. [< OE pūca a goblin] —**puck′ish** adj. —**puck′ish·ly** adv. —**puck′ish·ness** n.

puck[2] (puk) n. A hard rubber disk used in playing hockey. [? var. of POKE[1]]

puck·a (puk′ə) adj. PUKKA.

puck·er (puk′ər) v.t. & v.i. To gather or draw up into small folds or wrinkles. —n. A wrinkle. [?< POKE[2]]

pud·ding (pŏŏd′ing) n. 1 A sweetened and flavored dessert of soft food. 2 A sausage stuffed with seasoned, minced meat, blood, etc. [ME poding]

pud·dle (pud′l) n. 1 A small pool of water or other liquid. 2 A pasty mixture of clay and water. —v.t. ·dled, ·dling 1 To convert (molten pig iron) into wrought iron by melting and stirring in the presence of oxidizing agents. 2 To mix (clay, etc.) with water to obtain a watertight paste. 3 To line, as canal banks, with such a mixture. 4 To make muddy; stir up. [ME < OE pudd a ditch] —**pud′dler** n.

pud·dling (pud′ling) n. The operation of making wrought iron from pig iron by agitation in a molten state with oxidizing agents present.

pu·den·dum (pyōō·den′dəm) n. pl. ·da (-də) 1 The vulva. 2 pl. The external genitals of either sex. [L, neut. of pudendus (something) to be ashamed of] —**pu·den′·dal** adj.

pudg·y (puj′ē) adj. **pudg·i·er, pudg·i·est** Short and thick; fat. [< Scot. pud belly] — **pudg′i·ly** adv. —**pudg′i·ness** n.

pueb·lo (pweb′lō for

Hopi Indian pueblo

def. 1, pwä′blō for def. 2) n. pl. ·los 1 A communal adobe or stone building or group of buildings of the Indians of the sw U.S. 2 A town or village of Indians or Spanish Americans, as in Mexico. [Sp., a town, people < L populus]

Pueb·lo (pweb′lō) n. A member of one of the Indian tribes of Mexico and the sw U.S.

pu·er·ile (pyōō′ər·il, pwer′il, -īl) adj. Childish; immature; silly. [< L puer boy] —**pu′er·ile·ly** adv. —**pu′er·il′i·ty, pu′er·ile·ness** n.

pu·er·per·al (pyōō·ûr′pər·əl) adj. Pertaining to or resulting from childbirth. [< L puer boy + parere bring forth]

Puerto Ri·co (pwer·tə rē′kō, pôr-) An island commonwealth of the West Indies, a part of the U.S., 3,423 sq. mi., cap. San Juan. •See map at DOMINICAN REPUBLIC. — **Puer′to Ri′can** adj., n.

puff (puf) n. 1 A short, mild explosive force or emission, as a gust of air or expelled breath. 2 The sound of such a force. 3 The air, breath, etc., so felt or emitted: a small puff of smoke. 4 The act of sucking in and exhaling in the course of smoking a cigarette, etc. 5 A light, air-filled piece of pastry. 6 A pad for dusting powder on the skin. 7 A small protuberance or swelling. 8 A loose roll of hair. 9 A quilted bed coverlet. 10 A part of a fabric gathered at the edges. 11 A public expression of fulsome praise. —v.i. 1 To blow in puffs, as the wind. 2 To breathe hard, as after violent exertion. 3 To emit smoke, steam, etc., in puffs. 4 To smoke a cigarette, etc., with puffs. 5 To move, act, or exert oneself while emitting puffs: with away, up, etc. 6 To swell, as with air or pride; dilate: often with up. —v.t. 7 To send forth or emit with short puffs or breaths. 8 To move, impel, or stir up with or in puffs. 9 To smoke, as a cigarette or pipe, with puffs. 10 To swell or distend. 11 To praise fulsomely. 12 To arrange (the hair) in a puff. [< OE pyffan] —**puff′i·ly** adv. —**puff′i·ness** n. —**puff′y** adj. (·i·er, ·i·est)

puff adder 1 A large African viper that puffs and hisses when disturbed. 2 HOGNOSE.

puff·ball (puf′bôl′) n. A globular fungus that puffs out dustlike spores if broken open when ripe.

puff·er (puf′ər) n. 1 One who puffs. 2 Any of various fishes that can inflate themselves with air or water.

puff·er·y (puf′ər·ē) n. Excessive praise, esp. to obtain publicity.

puf·fin (puf′in) n. Any of various northern sea birds with a chunky body and a large, triangular bill. [ME poffin]

pug[1] (pug) v.t. pugged, pug·ging 1 To work (clay) with water in molding pottery or making bricks. 2 To fill in or cover with mortar, clay, felt, etc., to deaden sound. —n. A mixture of clay worked with water for brick-making, etc. [< dial. E]

pug[2] (pug) n. 1 A short-haired dog with a square body, upturned nose and curled tail. 2 PUG NOSE. [?]

Puffin

pug[3] (pug) n. Slang A professional prizefighter. [Short for PUGILIST]

pu·gi·lism (pyōō′jə·liz′əm) n. BOXING. [< L pugil a boxer] —**pu′gi·list** n. —**pu′gi·lis′tic** adj. —**pu′gi·lis′ti·cal·ly** adv.

pug·na·cious (pug·nā′shəs) adj. Disposed or inclined to fight; quarrelsome. [< L pugnus fist] —**pug·na′cious·ly** adv. —**pug·nac′i·ty** (-nas′ə·tē), **pug·na′cious·ness** n.

pug nose A thick, short, upturned nose. [< PUG[2] + NOSE] —**pug′-nosed′** adj.

pu·is·sant (pyōō′ə·sənt, pyōō·is′ənt, pwis′ənt) adj. Powerful; mighty. [< L posse be able] —**pu′is·sance** n. —**pu′is·sant·ly** adv.

puke (pyōōk) v.t. & v.i. puked, puk·ing, n. Informal VOMIT. [?]

puk·ka (puk′ə) adj. Genuine; sound. [< Hind. pakkā cooked; ripe]

pul·chri·tude (pul′krə·tyōōd) n. Beauty; grace. [< L pulcher beautiful] —**pul·chri·tu·di·nous** (-tyōō′də·nəs) adj.

pule (pyōōl) v.i. puled, pul·ing To cry plaintively, as a child; whimper; whine. [< MF pioler chirp] —**pul′er** n.

Pul·it·zer Prize (pōōl′it·sər, pyōō′lit-) Any of several annual awards for outstanding work in American journalism, literature, drama, and music, established by Joseph Pulitzer, 1847–1911, U.S. journalist.

pull (pōōl) *v.t.* **1** To apply force to so as to cause motion toward or after the person or thing exerting force; drag; tug. **2** To draw or remove from a natural or fixed place: to *pull* a tooth or plug. **3** To give a pull or tug to. **4** To pluck, as a fowl. **5** To draw asunder; tear; rend: with *to pieces, apart,* etc. **6** To strain so as to cause injury: to *pull* a ligament. **7** In sports, to strike (the ball) so as to cause it to curve obliquely from the direction in which the striker faces. **8** *Informal* To put into effect; carry out: to *pull* off a robbery. **9** *Informal* To make a raid on; arrest. **10** *Informal* To draw out so as to use: to *pull* a knife. **11** To make or obtain by impression from type: to *pull* a proof. **12** In boxing, to deliver (a punch, etc.) with less than full strength. **13** In horse-racing, to restrain (a horse) so as to prevent its winning. **14** To operate (an oar) by drawing toward one. —*v.i.* **15** To use force in hauling, dragging, moving, etc. **16** To move: with *out, in, away, ahead,* etc. **17** To drink or inhale deeply. **18** *Informal* To attract attention or customers: an ad that *pulls.* **19** To row. —**pull for 1** To strive in behalf of. **2** *Informal* To declare one's allegiance to. —**pull oneself together** To regain one's composure. —**pull through** To survive in spite of illness, etc. —**pull up** To come to a halt. —*n.* **1** The act or process of pulling. **2** Something that is pulled, as a handle. **3** A long swallow or a deep puff. **4** The drawing of an oar in rowing. **5** A steady, continuous effort, as in climbing: a long *pull* to the top. **6** *Informal* Influence, esp. with those in power: political *pull.* **7** An attractive force: the *pull* of gravity. [< OE *pullian* pluck] —**pull′er** *n.*

pull·back (pōōl′bak′) *n.* A withdrawal, as of troops.

pul·let (pōōl′it) *n.* A young hen, usu. less than a year old. [< L *pullus* chicken]

pul·ley (pōōl′ē) *n.* **1** A wheel or wheels grooved to receive a rope, usu. mounted in a block, used singly to reverse the direction of force applied, as in lifting a weight, and in various combinations to increase force at the expense of distance. **2** A flat or flanged wheel driving, carrying, or being driven by a flat belt, used to transmit power. [< Gk. *polos* a pivot, axis]

Pull·man (pōōl′mən) *n.* A railroad car with compartments for sleeping or other special accommodations. Also **Pullman car.** [< George M. *Pullman,* 1831–97, U.S. inventor]

pull·out (pōōl′out′) *n.* **1** A withdrawal or removal, as of troops. **2** Something to be pulled out, as an oversize leaf folded into a magazine.

pull·o·ver (pōōl′ō′vər) *adj.* Put on by being drawn over the head. —*n.* A garment put on in such a way, as a sweater.

pul·mo·nar·y (pōōl′mə·ner′ē, pul′-) *adj.* **1** Pertaining to or affecting the lungs. **2** Having lunglike organs. **3** Designating the blood vessels carrying blood between the lungs and heart. Also **pul·mon·ic** (pōōl·mon′ik, pul-). [< L *pulmo, pulmonis* lung] • See HEART.

Pul·mo·tor (pōōl′mō′tər, pul′-) *n.* A machine for applying artificial respiration: a trade name.

pulp (pulp) *n.* **1** A moist, soft, slightly cohering mass, as the soft, succulent part of fruit. **2** A mixture of wood fibers or rags, made semifluid and forming the basis from which paper is made. **3** *pl.* Magazines printed on rough, unglazed, wood-pulp paper, and usu. having contents of a sensational nature. **4** Powdered ore mixed with water. **5** The soft tissue of vessels and nerves that fills the central part of a tooth. • See TOOTH. —*v.t.* **1** To reduce to pulp. **2** To remove the pulp from. —*v.i.* **3** To be or become pulp. [< L *pulpa* flesh, pulp] —**pulp′i·ness** *n.* —**pulp′y** *adj.*

pul·pit (pōōl′pit, pul′-) *n.* **1** An elevated stand or desk for preaching in a church. **2** The office or work of preaching. **3** The clergy. [< L *pulpitum* platform]

pulp·wood (pulp′wŏŏd′) *n.* Soft wood used in the manufacture of paper.

pul·que (pul′kē, pōōl′-; *Sp.* pōōl′kā) *n.* A fermented Mexican drink made from agave. [Sp.]

pul·sar (pul′sär) *n.* An astronomical object that emits radio waves in pulses whose repetition rate is extremely stable. [< *puls(ating)* + *(st)ar*]

pul·sate (pul′sāt) *v.i.* **·sat·ed, ·sat·ing 1** To move or throb with rhythmical impulses, as the pulse or heart. **2** To vibrate; quiver. [< L *pulsare,* freq. of *pellere* beat] —**pul·sa′tion, pul′sa·tor** *n.* —**pul′sa·tive** (-sə-tiv), **pul′sa·to·ry** *adj.*

pulse¹ (puls) *n.* **1** The rhythmic pressure in the arteries due to the beating of the heart. **2** Any short, regular throbbing; pulsation. **3** A brief surge of energy, esp. electrical or electromagnetic energy. **4** Feelings and attitudes sensitively perceived as belonging to a group or community; also, an indication of such feelings. —*v.i.* **pulsed, puls·ing** To manifest a pulse; pulsate; throb. [< L *pulsus* p.p. of *pellere* beat]

pulse² (puls) *n.* Leguminous plants collectively, as peas, beans, etc., or their edible seeds. [< L *puls* pottage]

pulse·jet (puls′jet′) *n.* A jet engine that operates intermittently and produces power in rapid bursts.

pul·ver·ize (pul′və·rīz) *v.* **·ized, ·iz·ing** *v.t.* **1** To reduce to powder or dust, as by grinding or crushing. **2** To demolish; annihilate. —*v.i.* **3** To become reduced to powder or dust. *Brit. sp.* ·**ise.** [< L *pulvis, pulveris* a powder, dust] —**pul′ver·iz′a·ble, pul′ver·a·ble** (pul′və·rə·bəl) *adj.* —**pul′ver·i·za′tion, pul′ver·iz′er** *n.*

pu·ma (pyōō′mə) *n.* MOUNTAIN LION. [< Quechua]

pum·ice (pum′is) *n.* Porous volcanic lava, used as an abrasive and polisher, esp. when powdered. Also **pumice stone.** —*v.t.* **·iced, ·ic·ing** To smooth, polish, or clean with pumice. [< L *pumex*] —**pu·mi·ceous** (pyōō·mish′əs) *adj.*

pum·mel (pum′əl) *v.t.* **·meled** or **·melled, ·mel·ing** or **·mel·ling** POMMEL.

pump¹ (pump) *n.* A device using suction or pressure to raise, circulate, exhaust, or compress a liquid or gas. —*v.t.* **1** To raise (a liquid) with a pump. **2** To remove the water, etc., from. **3** To inflate with air by means of a pump. **4** To propel, discharge, force, etc., from or as if from a pump. **5** To cause to operate in the manner of a pump. **6** To question persistently or subtly. **7** To obtain (information) in such a manner. —*v.i.* **8** To work a pump. **9** To raise water or other liquid with a pump. **10** To move up and down like a pump or pump handle. [< MDu. *pompe*] —**pump′er** *n.*

pump² (pump) *n.* A low-cut shoe without a fastening, worn esp. by women. [?]

pum·per·nick·el (pum′pər·nik′əl) *n.* A coarse, dark bread made with rye flour. [G]

pump·kin (pump′kin, pum′-, pung′-) *n.* **1** A coarse trailing vine with gourdlike fruit. **2** Its large, edible, orange-yellow fruit. [< Gk. *pepōn* a melon]

pun (pun) *n.* The humorous use of two words having the same or similar sounds but different meanings, or of a word having two more or less incongruous meanings. —*v.i.* **punned, pun·ning** To make a pun or puns. [? < Ital. *puntiglio* quibble]

punch¹ (punch) *n.* **1** A tool for perforating or indenting, or for driving an object into a hole. **2** A machine for impressing a design or stamping a die. —*v.t.* To perforate, shape, indent, etc., with a punch. [ME *punchon* puncheon]

punch² (punch) *v.t.* **1** To strike sharply, esp. with the fist. **2** To poke with a stick; prod. **3** To drive (cattle). —*n.* **1** A swift blow with the fist. **2** A thrust or nudge. **3** *Informal* Vitality; effectiveness; force. — **punch in** (or **out**) To activate a time clock and record the hour at the start (or completion) of a period of work. [ME *punchen*] —**punch′er** *n.* —**Syn. 1** hit, pound, pommel, box.

a b c d
Punches
a. square.
b. revolving.
c. stamping.

punch³ (punch) *n.* A hot or cold beverage made with fruit

Pulleys
a. single
fixed. b.
fixed and
runner.

juices, spices, and other ingredients, as tea or soda water, and often mixed with alcoholic spirits. [< Skt. *pañchan* five; from the five original ingredients]

Punch (punch) *n.* The quarrelsome, grotesque hero of a comic puppet show, **Punch and Judy.** —**pleased as Punch** Extremely pleased; highly gratified. [Short for PUNCHINELLO]

punch card In data processing, a card having an arrangement of positions into which holes may be punched for the storage of information. Also **punched card.**

pun·cheon (pun′chən) *n.* **1** An upright supporting timber. **2** A punch or perforating tool. **3** A broad, heavy piece of roughly dressed timber, having one flat, hewed side. **4** A liquor cask of variable capacity, from 72 to 120 gallons. **5** The amount held by such a cask. [< OF *poinçon, poinchon* a punch]

pun·chi·nel·lo (pun′chə·nel′ō) *n. pl.* **·los** or **·loes 1** *Usu. cap.* A character in an Italian puppet show, the original of the English Punch. **2** A grotesque character; buffoon. [< dial. Ital. *Polcenella*]

punching bag An inflated or stuffed ball, usu. suspended, that is punched for exercise.

punch press A machine equipped with dies for cutting or forming metal.

punch·y (pun′chē) *adj.* **punch·i·er, punch·i·est** *Informal* **1** Dazed or confused, as from having been struck on the head: also **punch-drunk** (punch′drungk′). **2** Lively; snappy. —**punch′i·ly** *adv.* —**punch′i·ness** *n.*

punc·til·i·o (pungk·til′ē·ō) *n. pl.* **·til·i·os 1** A fine point of etiquette. **2** Preciseness in the observance of etiquette. [< L *punctum* a point]

punc·til·i·ous (pungk·til′ē·əs) *adj.* Very exacting in observing rules or conventions. [< Ital. *puntiglio* small point] —**punc·til′i·ous·ly** *adv.* —**punc·til′i·ous·ness** *n.*

punc·tu·al (pungk′chōō·əl) *adj.* **1** Arriving on time; prompt. **2** Habitually exact as to appointed time. **3** Consisting of or confined to a point. [< L *punctus* a point] —**punc′tu·al′i·ty** *n.* —**punc′tu·al·ly** *adv.*

punc·tu·ate (pungk′chōō·āt) *v.* **·at·ed, ·at·ing** *v.t.* **1** To divide or mark with punctuation. **2** To interrupt at intervals. **3** To emphasize. —*v.i.* **4** To use punctuation. [< L *punctus* a point] —**punc′tu·a′tor** *n.*

punc·tu·a·tion (pungk′chōō·ā′shən) *n.* **1** The use of points or marks in written or printed matter to aid in the better comprehension of the meaning and grammatical relation of the words. **2** The marks so used.

punctuation mark Any of the marks used in punctuating, as the period or comma.

punc·ture (pungk′chər) *v.* **·tured, ·tur·ing** *v.t.* **1** To pierce with a sharp point. **2** To make by pricking, as a hole. **3** To cause to collapse: to *puncture* a cherished illusion. —*v.i.* **4** To be pierced or punctured. —*n.* **1** A small hole, as one made by piercing. **2** The act of puncturing. [< L *punctus,* p.p. of *pungere* prick]

pun·dit (pun′dit) *n.* **1** One who is or assumes the part of an expert in making pronouncements, criticisms, predictions, etc. **2** In India, a Brahmin versed in Sanskrit lore, Hindu religion, etc. [< Skt. *paṇḍita* learned] —**pun′dit·ry** (-rē) *n.*

pun·gent (pun′jənt) *adj.* **1** Causing a sharp pricking, stinging, piercing, or acrid sensation. **2** Affecting the mind or feelings so as to cause pain; piercing; sharp. **3** Caustic; keen; cutting: *pungent* sarcasm. **4** Telling; pointed. [< L *pungere* prick] —**pun′gen·cy** *n.* —**pun′gent·ly** *adv.*

Pu·nic (pyōō′nik) *adj.* Of or pertaining to ancient Carthage or the Carthaginians.

pun·ish (pun′ish) *v.t.* **1** To subject (a person) to pain, confinement, or other penalty for a crime or fault. **2** To subject the perpetrator of (an offense) to a penalty. **3** To treat roughly; injure; hurt. [< L *punire*] —**pun′ish·a·ble** *adj.* —**pun′ish·a·bil′i·ty, pun′ish·er** *n.*

pun·ish·ing (pun′ish·ing) *adj.* Requiring exhausting effort; taxing; demanding: a *punishing* schedule.

pun·ish·ment (pun′ish·mənt) *n.* **1** Penalty imposed, as for a violation of law. **2** Any pain or loss inflicted in response to wrongdoing. **3** The act of punishing. **4** Physical damage or abuse.

pu·ni·tive (pyōō′nə·tiv) *adj.* Pertaining to or inflicting punishment. —**pu′ni·tive·ly** *adv.* —**pu′ni·tive·ness** *n.*

punk¹ (pungk) *n.* **1** Decayed wood, used as tinder. **2** Any substance that smolders when ignited. [< Algon.]

punk² (pungk) *Slang n.* **1** Rubbish; nonsense; anything worthless. **2** A petty hoodlum. **3** An inexperienced youth, esp. a young man: usu. contemptuous. —*adj.* Worthless; useless. [?]

pun·ky (pung′kē) *n. pl.* **·kies** Any of various tiny, bloodsucking insects. Also **pun′kie, pun′kie.** [< PUNK¹]

pun·ster (pun′stər) *n.* One who enjoys making puns. Also **pun′ner.**

punt¹ (punt) *n.* A flat-bottomed, square-ended boat for use in shallow waters, and propelled with a pole. —*v.t.* **1** To propel (a boat) by pushing with a pole against the bottom of a shallow stream, lake, etc. **2** To convey in a punt. —*v.i.* **3** To go or hunt in a punt. [< L *ponto*] —**punt′er** *n.*

Punt

punt² (punt) *v.i.* To gamble or bet in certain card games, esp. against the banker. [< L *punctum* a point]

punt³ (punt) *n.* In football, a kick made by dropping the ball from the hands and kicking it before it strikes the ground. —*v.t.* **1** To propel (a football) with a punt. —*v.i.* **2** In football, to make a punt. [?] —**punt′er** *n.*

pu·ny (pyōō′nē) *adj.* **·ni·er, ·ni·est** Small or inferior, as in power, significance, etc. [< OF *puisne* born afterward] —**pu′ni·ly** *adv.* —**pu′ni·ness** *n.* —**Syn.** slight, minor, unimportant, frail.

pup (pup) *n.* The young of certain animals, as a dog, wolf, fox, seal, whale, etc. —*v.i.* **pupped, pup·ping** To bring forth pups. [Short for PUPPY]

pu·pa (pyōō′pə) *n. pl.* **·pae** (-pē) or **·pas** A quiescent stage between larva and adult in the metamorphosis of certain insects. [L, a girl, puppet] —**pu′pal** *adj.*

pu·pate (pyōō′pāt) *v.i.* **·pat·ed, ·pat·ing** To enter upon or undergo the pupal condition. —**pu·pa′tion** *n.*

pu·pil¹ (pyōō′pəl) *n.* A person under the care of a teacher, as in a school. [< L *pupillus* and *pupilla,* dim. of *pupus* boy and *pupa* girl] —**pu′pil·age, pu′pil·lage** *n.* —**Syn.** student, disciple, scholar, learner.

Pupa of a butterfly

pu·pil² (pyōō′pəl) *n.* The circular opening in the iris of the eye, through which light reaches the retina. [< L *pupilla* pupil of the eye] • See EYE.

pup·pet (pup′it) *n.* **1** A small figure, as of a person or animal, manipulated usu. by the hands, or by pulling strings or wires attached to its jointed parts. **2** A person controlled by the will or whim of another. **3** A doll. —*adj.* **1** Of puppets. **2** Performing the will of an unseen power; not autonomous: a *puppet* state or government. [< L *pupa* a girl, doll, puppet] —**pup′pet·ry** (-rē) *n.*

pup·pet·eer (pup′i·tir′) *n.* One who manipulates puppets.

pup·py (pup′ē) *n. pl.* **·pies** A young dog. [< L *pupa* a girl, doll]

puppy love Temporary affection or love that a boy and girl feel for each other.

pup tent A small tent providing shelter for one or two people.

pur (pûr) *n. & v.* PURR.

pur·blind (pûr′blīnd′) *adj.* **1** Partly blind. **2** Having little or no insight. **3** *Obs.* Totally blind. [< ME *pur* totally + *blind* blind] —**pur′blind′ly** *adv.* —**pur′blind′ness** *n.*

pur·chase (pûr′chəs) *v.t.* **·chased, ·chas·ing 1** To acquire by paying money or its equivalent; buy. **2** To obtain by exertion, sacrifice, flattery, etc. **3** To move, hoist, or hold by a mechanical purchase. —*n.* **1** The act of purchasing. **2** That which is purchased. **3** A mechanical hold or grip. **4** A device that gives a mechanical advantage, as a tackle or lever. [OF *porchacier* seek for] —**pur′chas·er** *n.* —**Syn. 1,** **2** get, obtain, procure, secure.

pur·dah (pûr′də) *n.* **1** A curtain or screen used to seclude Muslim and Hindu women, esp. in India. **2** The state of seclusion so secured. [< Pers. *pardah* a veil]

pure (pyŏŏr) *adj.* **pur·er, pur·est 1** Free from mixture or contact with that which weakens, impairs, or pollutes. **2** Free from adulteration; clear; clean: *pure* water. **3** Faultless; righteous: *pure* motives. **4** Chaste; innocent. **5** Concerned with fundamental research, as distinguished from practical application: *pure* science. **6** Bred from stock having no admixture for many generations. **7** Nothing but; sheer: *pure* luck. [< L *purus* clean, pure] —**pure'ness** *n.*

pu·rée (pyŏŏ·rā', pyŏŏr'ā) *n.* **1** A thick pulp, usu. of vegetables, boiled and strained. **2** A thick soup so prepared. —*v.t.* **·reed, ·ree·ing** To put (cooked or soft food) through a sieve, blender, etc. Also **pu·ree'**. [F< OF *purer* strain< L *purus* pure]

pure·ly (pyŏŏr'lē) *adv.* **1** So as to be free from admixture, taint, or any harmful substance. **2** Chastely; innocently. **3** Merely; only: *purely* as a hobby. **4** Completely: *purely* up to him.

pur·ga·tive (pûr'gə·tiv) *adj.* Purging; cathartic. —*n.* A medication used in purging; cathartic.

pur·ga·to·ry (pûr'gə·tôr'ē, -tō'rē) *n. pl.* **·ries 1** In Roman Catholic theology, a state or place where the souls of those who have died penitent are made fit for paradise by expiating venial sins. **2** Any place or state of temporary banishment, suffering, or punishment. [< AF < L *purgare* cleanse] —**pur'ga·to'ri·al** *adj.*

purge (pûrj) *v.* **purged, purg·ing** *v.t.* **1** To cleanse of what is impure or extraneous; purify. **2** To remove (impurities, etc.) in cleansing: with *away, off,* or *out.* **3** To rid (a group, nation, etc.) of individuals regarded as undesirable. **4** To remove or kill such individuals. **5** To cleanse or rid of sin, fault, or defilement. **6** *Med.* **a** To cause evacuation of (the bowels, etc.). **b** To induce evacuation of the bowels of. —*v.i.* **7** To become clean or pure. **8** *Med.* To have or induce evacuation of the bowels. —*n.* **1** The action of an organization, esp. a government, in removing from office or positions of power individuals regarded as undesirable. **2** The act of purging. **3** That which purges; a cathartic. [< L *purgare* cleanse] —**pur·ga·tion** (pûr·gā'shən), **purg'er** *n.*

pu·ri·fy (pyŏŏr'ə·fī) *v.* **·fied, ·fy·ing** *v.t.* **1** To make pure or clean; rid of extraneous or noxious matter. **2** To free from sin or defilement. **3** To free of debasing elements. —*v.i.* **4** To become pure or clean. [< L *purus* pure + *facere* make] —**pu·ri·fi·ca·to·ry** (pyŏŏ·rif'ə·kə·tôr'ē, -tō'rē) *adj.* —**pu·ri·fi·ca·tion** (pyŏŏr'ə·fə·kā'shən), **pu'ri·fi'er** *n.*

Pu·rim (pyŏŏr'im; *Hebrew* pŏŏ·rēm') *n.* A Jewish festival commemorating the defeat of Haman's plot to massacre the Jews. *Esth.* 9:26.

pur·ism (pyŏŏr'iz·əm) *n.* **1** Strong endorsement of a strict compliance with standards, rules, or conventions considered correct or pure, as in language. **2** Strict compliance with rules of correctness. **3** An instance of such compliance. —**pur'ist** *n.* —**pu·ris'tic, pu·ris'ti·cal** *adj.* —**pu·ris'ti·cal·ly** *adv.*

pu·ri·tan (pyŏŏr'ə·tən) *n.* One who is unusually or excessively strict regarding adherence to morality or religious practice. —*adj.* Of or characteristic of puritans. [< LL *puritas* purity] —**pu'ri·tan'ic** or **·i·cal** *adj.* —**pu'ri·tan'i·cal·ly** *adv.* —**pu'ri·tan·ism, pu'ri·tan·ism** *n.*

Pu·ri·tan (pyŏŏr'ə·tən) *n.* One of a group of English Protestants of the 16th and 17th centuries, many of whom emigrated to the American colonies, who advocated simpler forms of creed and ritual in the Church of England. —*adj.* Of or relating to the Puritans. —**Pu'ri·tan'ic** or **·i·cal** *adj.* —**Pu'ri·tan·ism** *n.*

pu·ri·ty (pyŏŏr'ə·tē) *n.* **1** The character or state of being pure. **2** Absence of admixture or adulteration. **3** Innocence; blamelessness. **4** Degree of absence of white; saturation: said of a color.

purl[1] (pûrl) *v.i.* **1** To whirl; turn. **2** To flow with a bubbling sound. **3** To move in eddies. —*n.* **1** A circling movement of water; an eddy. **2** A gentle murmur, as of a rippling stream. [< Norw. *purla*]

purl[2] (pûrl) *v.t.* **1** To decorate, as with a border. **2** In knitting, to make (a stitch) backward. **3** To edge with lace, embroidery, etc. —*v.i.* **4** To do edging with lace, etc. —*n.* **1** An edge of lace, embroidery, etc. **2** In lacework, a spiral of gold or silver wire. **3** In knitting, the inversion of the knit stitch. [Earlier *pyrle*]

pur·lieu (pûr'lōō) *n.* **1** *pl.* Outlying districts; outskirts. **2**

A place habitually visited; a haunt. **3** *pl.* Bounds. [< OF *puraler* go through]

pur·lin (pûr'lin) *n.* One of several horizontal timbers supporting rafters. Also **pur'line** (-lin). [ME *purlyn*]

pur·loin (pûr·loin') *v.t. & v.i.* To steal; filch. [< AF *purloignier* remove, put far off] —**pur·loin'er** *n.*

pur·ple (pûr'pəl) *n.* **1** A color of mingled red and blue, between crimson and violet. **2** Cloth or a garment of this color, an emblem of royalty. **3** Royal power or dignity. **4** Preeminence in rank. —*adj.* **1** Of the color of purple. **2** Imperial; regal. **3** Conspicuously fanciful or ornate: *purple* prose. —*v.t. & v.i.* **·pled, ·pling** To make or become purple. [< Gk. *porphyra* purple dye] —**pur'plish** *adj.*

Purple Heart A U.S. military decoration of honor awarded to members of the armed forces wounded in action.

pur·port (pər·pôrt', -pōrt', pûr'pôrt, -pōrt) *v.t.* **1** To have or bear as its meaning; signify; imply. **2** To claim or profess (to be), esp. falsely. —*n.* (pûr'pôrt, -pōrt) **1** That which is conveyed or suggested as the meaning. **2** The substance of a statement, etc., given in other than the exact words. [< L < *pro-* forth + *portare* carry] —**Syn.** *n.* **1** import, significance. **2** gist, meaning. —**pur·port'ed·ly** *adv.*

pur·pose (pûr'pəs) *n.* **1** An end of effort or action; something to be attained; plan; design; aim. **2** Settled resolution; determination. —**on purpose** Intentionally. —*v.t. & v.i.* **·posed, ·pos·ing** To intend to do or accomplish; aim. [< OF *porposer*] —**pur'pose·less** *adj.* —**pur'pose·less·ly** *adv.* —**pur'pose·less·ness** *n.*

pur·pose·ful (pûr'pəs·fəl) *adj.* Having, or marked by, purpose; intentional. —**pur'pose·ful·ly** *adv.* —**pur'pose·ful·ness** *n.*

pur·pose·ly (pûr'pəs·lē) *adv.* Intentionally; deliberately; on purpose.

purr (pûr) *n.* An intermittent murmuring sound, such as a cat makes when pleased. —*v.i.* **1** To make such a sound. —*v.t.* **2** To express by purring. [Imit.]

purse (pûrs) *n.* **1** A small bag or pouch for money. **2** A receptacle carried usu. by women for holding personal articles, as a wallet, cosmetics, etc.; pocketbook. **3** Resources or means; a treasury. **4** A sum of money offered as a prize or gift. —*v.t.* **pursed, purs·ing** To contract into wrinkles or folds; pucker. [< Gk. *byrsa* a skin]

purs·er (pûr'sər) *n.* A ship's officer having charge of the accounts, records, payroll, etc.

purs·lane (pûrs'lin, -lān) *n.* Any of various prostrate, weedy plants with fleshy leaves and reddish stems. [< L *porcilaca,* var. of *portulaca*]

pur·su·ance (pər·sōō'əns) *n.* The act of pursuing; a following after or following through: in *pursuance* of the truth.

pur·su·ant (pər·sōō'ənt) *adj.* Pursuing. —**pursuant to** In accordance with; by reason of.

pur·sue (pər·sōō') *v.* **·sued, ·su·ing** *v.t.* **1** To follow in an attempt to overtake or capture; chase. **2** To seek to attain or gain: to *pursue* fame. **3** To advance along the course of, as a path or plan. **4** To apply one's energies to or have as one's profession. **5** To follow persistently; harass; worry. —*v.i.* **6** To follow. **7** To continue. [< L *pro-* forth + *sequi* follow] —**pur·su'er** *n.*

pur·suit (pər·sōōt') *n.* **1** The act of pursuing. **2** A continued employment, vocation, or preoccupation.

pur·sui·vant (pûr'swi·vənt) *n.* **1** An attendant upon a herald. **2** A follower; esp., a military attendant. [< OF *porsievre* pursue]

purs·y (pûr'sē) *adj.* **purs·i·er, purs·i·est 1** Short-breathed. **2** Fat. [< OF *polser* pant, gasp] —**purs'i·ness** *n.*

pu·ru·lent (pyŏŏr'ə·lənt, -yə·lənt) *adj.* Consisting of or secreting pus; suppurating. [< L *pus, puris* pus] —**pu'ru·lence** or **·len·cy** *n.* —**pu'ru·lent·ly** *adv.*

pur·vey (pər·vā') *v.t. & v.i.* To furnish or provide, as provisions. [< L *providere* foresee] —**pur·vey'or** *n.*

pur·vey·ance (pər·vā'əns) *n.* **1** The act of purveying. **2** Provisions.

pur·view (pûr'vyōō) *n.* **1** Extent or scope of anything, as of official authority. **2** Range of view, experience, or understanding; outlook. **3** *Law* The body or the scope or limit of a statute. [< OF *porveier* purvey]

pus (pus) *n.* A viscid, usu. yellowish fluid consisting of bacteria, leukocytes, serum, and dead cells from inflamed tissue.

push (poŏsh) *v.t.* **1** To exert force upon or against (an object) for the purpose of moving. **2** To force (one's way), as through a crowd. **3** To develop, advocate, or promote vigorously and persistently: to *push* a new product. **4** To bear hard upon; press: to be *pushed* for time. **5** *Informal* To approach or come close to: He's *pushing* fifty. **6** *Slang* To sell (narcotic or other drugs) illegally. —*v.i.* **7** To exert pressure against something so as to move it. **8** To move or advance vigorously or persistently. **9** To exert great effort. —*n.* **1** The act of pushing; a propelling or thrusting pressure. **2** Anything pushed to cause action. **3** Determined activity; energy; drive. **4** A vigorous and persistent advance or effort. **5** An emergency; exigency. [< L *pulsare* to push, beat] —**Syn.** *v.* **1** shove, thrust, press, propel, drive.

push button A button or knob which, on being pushed, opens or closes an electric switch. —**push′·but′ton** *adj.*

push·cart (poŏsh′kärt′) *n.* A wheeled cart pushed by hand.

push·er (poŏsh′ər) *n.* **1** One who or that which pushes; esp., an active, energetic person. **2** *Slang* One who sells narcotic or other drugs illegally.

push·ing (poŏsh′ing) *adj.* **1** Enterprising; energetic. **2** Too aggressive; impertinent. —**push′ing·ly** *adv.*

push·o·ver (poŏsh′ō′vər) *n.* *Slang* **1** Anything that can be done with little or no effort. **2** Someone easily defeated, overcome, outwitted, etc.; one who represents no challenge to one's aims.

Supermarket pushcart

push·y (poŏsh′ē) *adj.* **·i·er, ·i·est** Unpleasantly aggressive and persistent. —**push′i·ly** *adv.* —**push′i·ness** *n.*

pu·sil·lan·i·mous (pyōō′sə·lan′ə·məs) *adj.* Weak or cowardly in spirit; lacking strength of mind or courage. [< L *pusillus* very little + *animus* mind] —**pu′sil·la·nim′i·ty** (-lə-nim′ə-tē), **pu·sil·lan′i·mous·ness** *n.* —**pu·sil·lan′i·mous·ly** *adv.*

puss¹ (poos) *n.* **1** A cat. **2** A young girl: a term of affection. [?]

puss² (poos) *n.* *Slang* The mouth; face. [< Ir. *pus* mouth, lips]

pus·sy¹ (poos′ē) *n. pl.* **·sies** PUSS¹. **2** A fuzzy catkin, as of a willow.

pus·sy² (pus′ē) *adj.* **pus·si·er, pus·si·est** Full of or like pus. —**pus′si·ness** *n.*

pus·sy·foot (poos′ē·foot′) *v.i.* **1** To move softly and stealthily, as a cat does. **2** To act or proceed warily or tentatively, so as to be able to withdraw or change course before one's intentions are apparent. —**pus′sy·foot′er** *n.*

pus·sy willow (poos′ē) A small North American willow bearing velvety catkins in early spring.

pus·tu·late (pus′choō·lāt) *v.t. & v.i.* **·lat·ed, ·lat·ing** To form into or become pustules. —*adj.* (-lāt, -lit) Covered with pustules. —**pus′tu·la′tion** *n.*

pus·tule (pus′choōl) *n.* **1** A small, circumscribed elevation of the skin with an inflamed base containing pus. **2** Any elevation resembling a pimple or a blister. [< L *pustula*] —**pus′tu·lar, pus′tu·lous** *adj.*

put (poot) *v.* put, put·ting *v.t.* **1** To bring into or set in a specified or implied place or position; lay: *Put* the dishes in the sink. **2** To bring into a specified state, condition, or relation: to *put* someone to work; to *put* merchandise on sale. **3** To order or bring about the establishment or placement of: to *put* a new store in Dallas; to *put* a man on the moon. **4** To send or direct, as by projecting or thrusting: to *put* a dart in the bull's-eye. **5** To throw with a pushing motion: to *put* the shot. **6** To bring to bear; apply: They *put* pressure on her. **7** To impose: to *put* a tax on air travel. **8** To effect; carry out: I'll *put* a stop to that. **9** To express; state:

Pussy willow

to *put* it simply. **10** To subject: to *put* his loyalty to the test. **11** To incite; prompt: Who *put* him up to it? **12** To ascribe or attribute: to *put* the wrong interpretation on a remark. **13** To propose for debate, consideration, etc.: to *put* the question. **14** To estimate: to *put* the time at five o'clock. **15** To establish; fix, as a price. **16** To risk; bet: to *put* money on a horse. —*v.i.* **17** To go; proceed: to *put* to sea. —**put about 1** *Naut.* To change to the opposite tack. **2** To change direction. —**put across 1** To carry out successfully. **2** To manage to be understood. **3** To bring about through deceit. —**put aside** (or **by**) **1** To place in reserve; save. **2** To thrust aside; discard. —**put away 1** PUT ASIDE. **2** *Informal* To eat or drink. **3** *Informal* To kill, as an injured or sick animal. —**put down 1** To repress; crush. **2** To degrade; demote. **3** To write. **4** *Slang* To humble or deflate. **5** To preserve or can. —**put forth 1** To grow, as shoots or buds. **2** To set out; leave port. **3** To proffer; suggest. **4** To publish. **5** To exert. —**put forward** To advance; advocate, as a proposal. —**put in 1** To submit or advance, as a claim or application. **2** To interject; interpolate. **3** *Naut.* To enter a harbor. **4** *Informal* To devote; expend, as time. —**put off 1** To delay; postpone. **2** To discard. **3** To make uneasy or uncomfortable; disconcert. —**put on 1** To clothe oneself in; don. **2** To bring into operation; effectuate: to *put on* a light. **3** To add: to *put on* weight. **4** To stage, as a play. **5** To simulate; pretend: to *put on* a sad face. **6** *Slang* To fool or deceive mischievously. —**put out 1** To extinguish, as a flame. **2** To expel; eject. **3** To disconcert; embarrass. **4** To inconvenience. **5** PUT FORTH. **6** In baseball, to retire (a batter or base runner). **7** To publish or manufacture, as a book or magazine. **8** *Slang* To use extra effort; exert oneself. —**put over 1** To delay; postpone. **2** To carry out successfully. **3** To bring about through deceit. —**put through 1** To bring to successful completion. **2** To cause to perform. **3** To establish a telephone connection for. —**put up 1** To erect; build. **2** To provide (money, capital, etc.). **3** To preserve or can. **4** To sheathe, as a weapon. **5** To nominate as a candidate. **6** To provide accommodations for. **7** *Informal* To incite. —**put up with** To endure; tolerate. —*n.* The act of putting or casting, esp. the shot. —*adj. Informal* Settled in place; fixed: My hat won't stay *put*. [< OE *putian* place] —**put′ter** *n.*

pu·ta·tive (pyōō′tə·tiv) *adj.* Supposed; reported; reputed. [< L *putare* think] —**pu′ta·tive·ly** *adv.*

put-down (poot′doun′) *n. Slang* Something that humbles or deflates, as a cutting remark.

put-on (poot′on′) *n. Slang* A hoax; deception.

put-out (poot′out′) *n.* In baseball, the act of causing an out, as of a batter or base runner.

pu·tre·fac·tion (pyōō′trə·fak′shən) *n.* **1** The process of rotting or decomposing, as by bacterial action. **2** The state of being putrefied. —**pu′tre·fac′tive** *adj.*

pu·tre·fy (pyōō′trə·fī) *v.t. & v.i.* **·fied, ·fy·ing** To decay or cause to decay; rot. [< L *puter* rotten + *facere* make] —**pu′tre·fi′er** *n.*

pu·tres·cent (pyōō·tres′ənt) *adj.* **1** Becoming putrid. **2** Pertaining to putrefaction. [< L *putrescere* grow rotten] —**pu·tres′cence** *n.*

pu·trid (pyōō′trid) *adj.* **1** Being in a state of putrefaction; rotten. **2** Indicating or produced by putrefaction: a *putrid* smell. **3** Corrupt. [< L *putridus*] —**pu·trid·i·ty** (pyōō·trid′ə·tē), **pu′trid·ness** *n.*

putsch (pooch) *n. Often cap.* An outbreak or rebellion; an attempted coup d'état. [G]

putt (put) *n.* In golf, a light stroke made on a putting green to place the ball in or near the hole. —*v.t. & v.i.* To strike (the ball) with such a stroke. [Var. of PUT]

put·tee (put′ē, pu·tē′) *n.* A strip of cloth or leather gaiter fastened about the leg from knee to ankle. [< Skt. *paṭṭa* a strip of cloth]

put·ter¹ (put′ər) *n.* **1** One who putts. **2** A golf club used in putting. See GOLF.

put·ter² (put′ər) *v.i.* **1** To act, work, or proceed in a dawdling or ineffective manner. —*v.t.* **2** To waste or spend (time, etc.) in dawdling or puttering. [< OE *potion* push, kick]

put·ting green (put′ing) In golf, a smooth area of closely mown grass in which the hole is situated.

put·ty (put′ē) *n.* **1** A doughy mixture of clay and linseed oil, used to cement panes in windows, fill cracks, etc. **2** Any substance similar in properties or uses. —*v.t.* **·tied, ·ty·ing** To fill, stop, fasten, etc., with putty. [< OF *potee* calcined tin, lit., a potful] —**put′ti·er** *n.*

put-up (pŏŏt′up′) *adj. Informal* Prearranged or contrived; staged: a *put-up* job.

put-up·on (pŏŏt′ə·pon′) *adj.* Beset or harassed, as by impositions; abused.

puz·zle (puz′əl) *v.* **·zled, ·zling** *v.t.* **1** To confuse or perplex; mystify. **2** To solve by investigation and study, as something perplexing: with *out.* —*v.i.* **3** To be perplexed or confused. —**puzzle over** To attempt to understand or solve. —*n.* **1** Something difficult to understand or explain; an enigma or problem. **2** A device, as a toy, or a problem designed for recreation and requiring ingenuity to solve. **3** The state of being puzzled; perplexity. [?] —**puz′zle·ment, puz′zler** *n.*

Pvt. Private.

PW prisoner of war.

pwt. pennyweight.

PX post exchange.

py·e·mi·a (pī·ē′mē·ə) *n.* Septicemia caused by pus-producing microorganisms. Also **py·ae′mi·a.** [< Gk. *pyon* pus + *haima* blood] —**py·e′mic** *adj.*

pyg·my (pig′mē) *adj.* Diminutive; dwarfish. —*n. pl.* **·mies 1** Someone of no importance. **2** A dwarfish person or animal.

Pyg·my (pig′mē) *n. pl.* **·mies** A member of a Negroid people of equatorial Africa, ranging in height from four to five feet. [< Gk. *pygmalos* a dwarf]

py·ja·mas (pə·jä′məz, -jam′əz) *n.pl. Brit.* PAJAMAS.

py·lon (pī′lon) *n.* **1** *Archit.* A monumental gateway, as to an Egyptian temple or other large edifice. **2** A tall, mastlike structure, as for supporting high-tension wires or for marking a course for aircraft. [< Gk. *pylōn* a gateway]

py·lo·rus (pī·lôr′əs, -lō′rəs, pi-) *n. pl.* **·ri** (-rī) The muscularly controlled opening between the stomach and the duodenum. [< Gk. *pylōros* a gatekeeper] —**py·lor′ic** (-lôr′ik, -lor′ik) *adj.*

py·or·rhe·a (pī′ə·rē′ə) *n.* A discharge of pus; esp., inflammation and pus discharge affecting the gums and tooth sockets. Also **py′or·rhoe′a.** [< Gk. *pys, pyos* pus + *rheein* flow] —**py′or·rhe′al** *adj.*

pyr·a·mid (pir′ə·mid) *n.* **1** A solid structure of masonry with a square base and triangular sides meeting in an apex, such as those constructed by the ancient Egyptians as royal tombs. **2** Something having the form of a pyramid. **3** *Geom.* A solid having a polygonal base and triangular sides that meet in a common vertex. —*v.i.* **1** To increase in a series of steps; escalate. **2** To buy or sell stock with paper profits used as margin to finance succeeding transactions. —*v.t.* **3** To increase by steps. **4** To buy and sell (stock) with paper profits used as margin to

Egyptian pyramids

finance succeeding transactions. [< Gk. *pyramis*] —**py·ram·i·dal** (pi·ram′ə·dəl, pir′ə·mid′əl), **pyr′a·mid′ic** or **·i·cal** *adj.* —**pyr′a·mid′i·cal·ly** *adv.*

pyre (pīr) *n.* A heap of combustibles arranged for burning a dead body as a funeral rite. [< Gk. *pyr* a fire]

py·reth·rum (pī·reth′rəm, -rē′thrəm) *n.* **1** A species of chrysanthemum. **2** An insecticide prepared from the powdered flowers of certain chrysanthemums. [L, feverfew]

Py·rex (pī′reks) *n.* A type of heat-resistant glass: a trade name.

pyr·i·dox·ine (pir′ə·dok′sēn, -sin) *n.* A constituent of the vitamin B complex. [< Gk. *pyr* fire + -ID(E) + OX(Y)- + -INE]

py·rite (pī′rīt) *n.* A lustrous, pale yellow, mineral sulfide of iron. [< Gk. *pyritēs* flint]

py·ri·tes (pī·rī′tēz, pī′rīts) *n. pl.* **py·ri·tes** (pī·rī′tēz) Any of various mineral sulfides with a metallic sheen, including pyrite: copper *pyrites.* —**py·rit′ic** (-rit′ik) or **·i·cal** *adj.*

pyro- *combining form* Fire; heat: *pyromania.* Also **pyr-.** [< Gk. *pyr* fire]

py·ro·ma·ni·a (pī′rə·mā′nē·ə, -mān′yə) *n.* A compulsion to commit arson. —**py′ro·ma′ni·ac** (-ak) *adj., n.* —**py·ro·ma·ni·a·cal** (pī′rō·mə·nī′ə·kəl) *adj.*

py·rom·e·ter (pī·rom′ə·tər) *n.* A thermometer designed to measure high temperatures. —**py·ro·met·ric** (pī′rə·met′rik) or **·ri·cal** *adj.* —**py·rom′e·try** *n.*

py·ro·tech·nics (pī′rə·tek′niks) *n. pl. (construed as sing. in def. 1)* **1** The art of making or using fireworks. **2** A display of fireworks. **3** An ostentatious display, as of oratory; virtuosity. [< PYRO- + Gk. *technē* an art] —**py′ro·tech′nic** or **·ni·cal** *adj.*

py·rox·y·lin (pī·rok′sə·lin) *n.* A nitrocellulose that is more stable than guncotton, used in making quick-drying lacquers, etc. Also **py·rox′y·line** (-lēn, -lin). [< Gk. *pyr, pyros* fire + *xylon* wood + -INE]

Pyr·rhic victory (pir′ik) A victory gained at a ruinous cost, such as that of Pyrrhus over the Romans in 279 B.C.

Py·thag·o·re·an theorem (pi·thag′ə·rē′ən) *Math.* The theorem that the sum of the squares of the two sides of a right triangle is equal to the square of the hypotenuse. [< *Pythagoras,* c. 500 B.C., Greek philosopher]

Pyth·i·as (pith′ē·əs) See DAMON AND PYTHIAS.

py·thon (pī′thon, -thən) *n.* A large, nonvenomous snake that crushes its prey. [< Gk. *Pythōn* a serpent slain by Apollo]

Python

py·tho·ness (pī′thə·nis, pith′ə-) *n.* **1** The priestess of the Delphic oracle. **2** Any woman supposed to be possessed of the spirit of prophecy; a witch. [< Gk. *Pytho* a familiar spirit, orig. Delphi]

pyx (piks) *n.* A container for keeping the consecrated wafer of the Eucharist or for carrying it to the sick. [< L *pyxis* a box]

pyx·is (pik′sis) *n. pl.* **pyx·i·des** (pik′sə·dēz) *Bot.* A dehiscent seed vessel with the upper portion separating as a lid. Also **pyx·id·i·um** (pik·sid′ē·əm). [< L, a box]

Q

Q, q (kyōō) *n. pl.* **Q's, q's** or **Qs, qs** (kyōōz) **1** The 17th letter of the English alphabet. **2** Any spoken sound representing the letter *Q* or *q*. **3** Something shaped like a Q. —*adj.* Shaped like a Q.

Q queen (chess).

Q. Quebec.

q. quart; quarter; quarterly; quarto; quasi; queen; query; question

Qa·tar (kä′tär) *n.* A British protected sheikdom on the w coast of the Persian Gulf, 8,500 sq. mi., cap. Doha. • See map at SAUDI ARABIA.

qb., q.b. quarterback.

Q.C. Quartermaster Corps; Queen's Counsel.

q.e. which is (L *quod est*).

Q.E.D. which was to be demonstrated (L *quod erat demonstrandum*).

Q.E.F. which was to be done (L *quod erat faciendum*).

QM, Q.M. Quartermaster.

QMC, Q.M.C. Quartermaster Corps.

QMG, Q.M.G., Q.M.Gen. Quartermaster General.

Qq. quartos.

qq.v. which see (L *quos vide*).

qr. quarter; quarterly; quire.

q.s. as much as suffices (L *quantum sufficit*).

qt. quart; quantity.

q.t. *Slang* quiet, esp. **on the q.t.** in secret.

qto. quarto.

qts, qts. quarts.

qu. quart; quarter; queen; query; question.

quack¹ (kwak) *v.i.* To utter a harsh, croaking cry, as a duck. —*n.* The sound made by a duck, or a similar croaking noise [Imit.]

quack² (kwak) *n.* **1** A pretender to medical knowledge or skill. **2** A charlatan. —*adj.* Of or pertaining to quacks or quackery. —*v.i.* To play the quack. [Short for QUACKSALVER] —**quack′ish** *adj.* —**quack′ish·ly** *adv.*

quack·er·y (kwak′ər-ē) *n. pl.* **·er·ies** The deceitful practices of a quack.

quack·sal·ver (kwak′sal′vər) *n.* QUACK². [< MDu. *quacsalven* use home remedies]

quad¹ (kwod) *n. Informal.* A quadrangle, as of a college or prison.

quad² (kwod) *n. Printing* A piece of type metal lower than the letters, used for spacing. [ME *quadrat*, a square instrument]

quad³ (kwod) *adj.* QUADRAPHONIC.

quad. quadrangle; quadrant; quadrat; quadruple.

Quad·ra·ges·i·ma (kwod′rə·jes′ə·mə) *n.* The first Sunday in Lent. Also **Quadragesima Sunday.** [L, fortieth]

quad·ran·gle (kwod′rang·gəl) *n.* **1** *Geom.* A plane figure having four sides and four angles. **2** An area shaped like a quadrangle, esp. when it is enclosed by buildings. **3** The buildings that enclose such an area. [< L *quattuor* four + *angulus* angle] —**quad·ran′gu·lar** *adj.*

quad·rant (kwod′rənt) *n.* **1** A quarter part of a circle; also, its circumference, having an arc of 90°. **2** An instrument having a graduated arc of 90°, with a movable radius for measuring angles on it. [< L *quattuor* four] —**quad·ran·tal** (kwod·ran′təl) *adj.*

Quadrant

quad·ra·phon·ic (kwod′rə·fon′ik) *adj.* Of, pertaining to, or employing a system of sound reproduction that uses four transmission channels and loudspeakers. [< QUADR(I)- + PHONIC]

quad·rat (kwod′rət) *n.* QUAD².

quad·rate (kwod′rāt, -rit) *adj.* Square; four-sided. —*v.* (-rāt) **·rat·ed, ·rat·ing** *v.i.* **1** To correspond or agree: with *with.* —*v.t.* **2** To cause to conform; bring in accordance with. [< L *quadrare* to square < *quattuor* four]

quad·rat·ic (kwod·rat′ik) *adj.* **1** Pertaining to or resem-

bling a square. **2** Of or designating a quadratic equation. —*n. Math.* A quadratic equation.

quadratic equation An equation of the general form $ax^2 + bx + c = 0$, where *a, b, c* are constants.

quad·ra·ture (kwod′rə·chər) *n.* **1** The act or process of squaring. **2** The determining of the area of any surface.

quad·ren·ni·al (kwod·ren′ē·əl) *adj.* **1** Occurring once in four years. **2** Comprising four years. —*n.* A quadrennial period or event. [< QUADRI(I)- + L *annus* year]

quadri- *combining form* Four: *quadrilateral.* Also **quadr-.** [< L *quattuor* four]

quad·ri·lat·er·al (kwod′rə·lat′ər·əl) *adj.* Formed or bounded by four lines; four-sided. —*n.* **1** *Geom.* A polygon of four sides. **2** A space or area defended by four enclosing fortresses. [< QUADRI- + L *latus, lateris* side]

qua·drille (kwə·dril′) *n.* **1** A square dance for four couples. **2** Music for such a dance. [< L *quattuor* four]

quad·ril·lion (kwod·ril′yən) *n. & adj.* See NUMBER. [< F *quatre* four + *(m)illion* million]

quad·ri·ple·gi·a (kwod′rə·plē′jē·ə) *n.* Paralysis of the arms and legs.

quad·ri·va·lent (kwod′rə·vā′lənt) *adj. Chem.* Having a valence of four. [< QUADRI- + L *valere* be worth]

quad·roon (kwod·rōōn′) *n.* A person having one Negro and three white grandparents. [< Sp. *cuarto* fourth]

quad·ru·ped (kwod′rōō·ped) *n.* A four-footed animal, esp. a mammal. —*adj.* Having four feet. [< L *quattuor* four + *pes* foot] —**quad·ru·pe·dal** (kwod·rōō′pə·dəl, kwod′·rōō·ped′l) *adj.*

quad·ru·ple (kwod·rōō′pəl, -ru′-, kwod′rōō·pəl) *adj.* **1** Four times as great or as many. **2** Having four parts or members. **3** Marked by four beats to the measure. —*n.* A number or sum four times as great as another. —*v.t. & v.i.* **·pled, ·pling** To multiply by four. —*adv.* Fourfold. [< L *quadruplus*]

quad·ru·plet (kwod·rōō′plit, -ru′-, kwod′rōō-) *n.* A combination of four objects. **2** One of four offspring born of the same mother at one birth.

quad·ru·pli·cate (kwod·rōō′plə·kit, -kāt) *adj.* **1** FOURFOLD. **2** Raised to the fourth power. —*v.t.* (-kāt) **·cat·ed, ·cat·ing** To multiply by four; quadruple. —*n.* The fourth of four like things: to file a *quadruplicate.* —**in quadruplicate** In four identical copies. —**quad·ru′pli·ca′tion** *n.*

quaes·tor (kwes′tər, kwēs′-) *n.* Any of a number of public officials in ancient Rome. Also **ques′tor.** [L < *quaerere* seek, inqure] —**quaes′to′ri·al** *adj.* —**quaes′tor·ship** *n.*

quaff (kwaf, kwof, kwôf) *v.t. & v.i.* To drink, esp. copiously or with relish. —*n.* The act of quaffing; also, that which is quaffed. [?] —**quaff′er** *n.*

quag·gy (kwag′ē, kwog′ē) *adj.* **·gi·er, ·gi·est** **1** Yielding to or quaking under the foot, as soft, wet earth; boggy. **2** Soft; yielding; flabby. [< QUAGMIRE]

quag·mire (kwag′mīr′, kwog′-) *n.* **1** Marshy ground that gives way under the foot; bog. **2** A difficult situation. [? < earlier *quab-* wetness + MIRE] —**quag′mired′** *adj.*

qua·haug (kwô′hôg, -hog, kwə·hôg′, -hog′) *n.* An edible, thick-shelled clam of the Atlantic coast of North America. Also **qua′hog.** [< Algon.]

quail¹ (kwāl) *n.* **1** Any of various small game birds related to the partridge. **2** BOBWHITE. [< OF *quaille*]

quail² (kwāl) *v.i.* To shrink with fear; lose heart or courage. [ME *quailen*]

quaint (kwānt) *adj.* **1** Pleasingly different, fanciful, or old-fashioned. **2** Unusual; odd; curious. [< L *cognitus* known] —**quaint′ly** *adv.* —**quaint′ness** *n.*

quake (kwāk) *v.i.* **quaked, quak·ing 1** To shake, as with violent

Quail

emotion or cold; shudder; shiver. **2** To shake or tremble, as earth during an earthquake. —*n.* **1** A shaking or shuddering. **2** EARTHQUAKE. [< OE *cwacian* shake]

Quak·er (kwā′kər) *n.* A member of the Society of Friends: originally a term of derision, and still not used within the society. See SOCIETY OF FRIENDS. [< QUAKE, *v.*; with ref. to their founder's admonition to them to tremble at the word of the Lord] —**Quak′er·ish** *adj.* —**Quak′er·ism′** *n.*

quak·y (kwā′kē) *adj.* **quak·i·er, quak·i·est** Shaky; tremulous. —**quak′i·ly** *adv.* —**quak′i·ness** *n.*

qual·i·fi·ca·tion (kwol′ə·fə·kā′shən) *n.* **1** The act of qualifying, or the state of being qualified. **2** That which fits a person or thing for something. **3** A restriction; modification.

qual·i·fied (kwol′ə·fīd) *adj.* **1** Competent or eligible, as for public office. **2** Restricted or modified in some way. —**qual′i·fied′ly** *adv.*

qual·i·fy (kwol′ə·fī) *v.* **·fied, ·fy·ing** *v.t.* **1** To make fit or capable, as for an office, occupation, or privilege. **2** To make legally capable, as by the administration of an oath. **3** To limit, restrict, or lessen somewhat: He *qualified* his enthusiasm with a few criticisms. **4** To attribute a quality to; describe; characterize or name. **5** To make less strong or extreme; soften; moderate. **6** To change the strength or flavor of. **7** *Gram.* To modify. —*v.i.* **8** To be or become qualified. [< L *qualis* of such a kind + *facere* make] —**qual′i·fi′a·ble** *adj.* —**qual′i·fi′er** *n.*

qual·i·ta·tive (kwol′ə·tā′tiv) *adj.* Of or pertaining to quality. —**qual′i·ta′tive·ly** *adv.*

qualitative analysis The chemical identification of the elements or components in a compound or mixture.

qual·i·ty (kwol′ə·tē) *n. pl.* **·ties 1** That which makes a being or thing such as it is: a distinguishing element or characteristic: a *quality* of gases. **2** The basic nature or character of something: the *quality* of a summer's day. **3** Excellence: striving for *quality.* **4** Degree of excellence; relative goodness; grade: high *quality* of fabric. **5** A personal attribute, trait or characteristic: a woman with good and bad *qualities.* **6** *Archaic* Social rank; also, persons of rank, collectively. **7** *Music* That which distinguishes one tone from another, aside from pitch or loudness; timbre. —*adj.* Characterized by or having to do with quality: a *quality* product. [< L *qualis* of such a kind]

qualm (kwäm, kwôm) *n.* **1** A twinge of conscience; moral scruple. **2** A sensation of fear or misgiving. **3** A feeling of sickness. [? < OE *cwealm* death] —**qualm′ish, qualm′y** *adj.* —**qualm′ish·ly** *adv.* —**qualm′ish·ness** *n.*

quan·da·ry (kwon′dər·ē, -drē) *n. pl.* **·da·ries** A state of hesitation or perplexity; predicament. [?]

quan·ti·ta·tive (kwon′tə·tā′tiv) *adj.* **1** Of or pertaining to quantity. **2** Capable of being measured. —**quan′ti·ta′tive·ly** *adv.* —**quan′ti·ta′tive·ness** *n.*

quantitative analysis The precise determination of the relative amount of each chemical component in a compound or mixture.

quan·ti·ty (kwon′tə·tē) *n. pl.* **·ties 1** A definite or indefinite amount or number. **2** *pl.* Large amounts or numbers: *quantities* of food and drink. **3** That property of a thing which admits of exact measurement and numerical statement. **4** In prosody and phonetics, the relative period of time required to produce a given sound. [< L *quantus* how much, how large]

quan·tum (kwon′təm) *n. pl.* **·ta** (-tə) *Physics* A fundamental unit of energy or action as described in the quantum theory. [< L *quantus* how much]

quantum theory *Physics* A physical theory including as one of its essential features the postulate that energy is not continuous but divided into discrete packets, or quanta.

quar·an·tine (kwôr′ən·tēn, kwor′-) *n.* **1** A period of time fixed for the isolation and observation of persons, animals, or plants suspected of harboring an infectious disease. **2** A place for such isolation. **3** The isolation of subjects exposed to or infected with a communicable disease. —*v.t.* **·tined, ·tin·ing** To retain in quarantine. [< L *quadraginta* forty; a ref. to the original 40-day quarantine]

quark (kwärk) *n. Physics* Any of a group of three types of hypothetical fundamental particles proposed as the entities of which all other strongly interacting particles are composed. [Coined by M. Gell-Mann, born 1929, U.S. physicist]

quar·rel[1] (kwôr′əl, kwor′-) *n.* **1** An unfriendly, angry, or violent dispute. **2** A falling out or contention; breach of friendly relations: a lover's *quarrel.* **3** The cause for dispute. —*v.i.* **·reled** or **·relled, ·rel·ing** or **·rel·ling 1** To engage in a quarrel; dispute; contend; fight: to *quarrel* about money. **2** To break off a mutual friendship; fall out; disagree. **3** To find fault; cavil. [< L *querela* complaint] —**quar′rel·er** or **quar′rel·ler** *n.* —**Syn.** *n.* **1** altercation, bickering, brawl, controversy, feud, fracas, fray. **2** disagreement, fuss, misunderstanding, scene.

quar·rel[2] (kwôr′əl, kwor′-) *n.* **1** A dart or arrow with a four-edged head, formerly used with a crossbow. **2** A stonemason's chisel, glazier's diamond, or other tool having a several-edged point. [< L *quattuor* four]

quar·rel·some (kwôr′əl·səm, kwor′-) *adj.* Inclined to quarrel. —**quar′rel·some·ly** *adv.* —**quar′rel·some·ness** *n.*

quar·ri·er (kwôr′ē·ər, kwor′-) *n.* A workman in a stone quarry.

quar·ry[1] (kwôr′ē, kwor′ē) *n. pl.* **·ries 1** An animal being hunted down; game; prey. **2** Anything hunted, slaughtered, or eagerly pursued. [< L *corium* hide]

Quarrels
def. 1

quar·ry[2] (kwôr′ē, kwor′ē) *n. pl.* **·ries** An excavation from which stone is taken by cutting, blasting, or the like. —*v.t.* **·ried, ·ry·ing 1** To cut, dig, or take from or as from a quarry. **2** To establish a quarry in. [< LL *quadraria* place for squaring stone]

quart (kwôrt) *n.* **1 a** A U.S. measure of dry capacity equal to 2 pints or 1.10 liters. **b** A U.S. measure of fluid capacity equal to 2 pints or 0.946 liter. **2** A vessel of such capacity. [< L *quartus* fourth]

quar·ter (kwôr′tər) *n.* **1** One of four equal parts of something; a fourth. **2** Fifteen minutes or the fourth of an hour, or the moment with which it begins or ends. **3** A fourth of a year or three months. **4** A limb of a quadruped with the adjacent parts. **5** In the U.S. and Canada, a coin of the value of 25 cents. **6** *Astron.* **a** The time it takes the moon to make one fourth of its revolution around the earth. **b** Either of the phases of the moon between new moon and full moon. **7** *Nav.* One of the four principal points of the compass or divisions of the horizon; also, a point or direction of the compass. **8** A person, persons, or place, esp. as a source or origin of something: gossip coming from all *quarters.* **9** A particular division or district, as of a city. **10** *Usu. pl.* Proper or assigned station, position, or place, as of officers and crew on a warship. **11** *pl.* A place of lodging or residence. **12** *Naut.* The part of a vessel's after side, between the aftermost mast and the stern. **13** *Her.* Any of four equal divisions into which a shield is divided, or a figure or device occupying such a division. **14** Mercy shown to a vanquished foe by sparing his life; clemency. **15** One of the four periods into which a game, as football, is divided. —**at close quarters** Close by; at close range. —*adj.* **1** Consisting of a quarter. **2** Equal to a quarter. —*v.t.* **1** To divide into four equal parts. **2** To divide into a number of parts or pieces. **3** To cut the body of (an executed person) into four parts: He was hanged, drawn, and *quartered.* **4** To range from one side to the other of (a field, etc.) while advancing: The dogs *quartered* the field. **5** To furnish with quarters or shelter; lodge, station, or billet. **6** *Her.* **a** To divide (a shield) into quarters by vertical and horizontal lines. **b** To bear or arrange (different coats of arms) upon the quarters of a shield or escutcheon. —*v.i.* **7** To be stationed or lodged. **8** To range from side to side of an area, as dogs in hunting. **9** *Naut.* To blow on a ship's quarter: said of the wind. [< L *quartus* fourth]

quar·ter·back (kwôr′tər·bak′) *n.* In football, one of the backfield, who calls the signals and directs the offensive play of his team.

quarter day A day that begins a new quarter of the year, when quarterly payments, as of rent, etc., are due.

quar·ter·deck (kwôr′tər·dek′) *n. Naut.* The rear part of a ship's upper deck, reserved for officers.

quar·tered (kwôr′tərd) *adj.* 1 Divided into quarters. 2 Having quarters or lodgings. 3 Quartersawed.

quar·ter·ly (kwôr′tər·lē) *adj.* 1 Containing or being a quarter. 2 Occurring at intervals of three months. —*n. pl.* ·lies A publication issued once every three months. —*adv.* 1 Once in a quarter of a year. 2 In or by quarters.

quar·ter·mas·ter (kwôr′tər·mas′tər, -mäs′-) *n.* 1 The officer on an army post who is responsible for the supply of food, clothing, etc. 2 On shipboard, a petty officer who assists the master or navigator.

quar·tern (kwôr′tərn) *n. Chiefly Brit.* A fourth part, as of certain measures or weights. [< L *quartus* fourth]

quarter note *Music* A note with one fourth the time value of a whole note. • See NOTE.

quar·ter·saw (kwôr′tər·sô′) *v.t.* ·sawed, ·sawed or ·sawn, ·saw·ing To saw (a log) lengthwise into quarters and then into planks or boards, in order to show the wood grain advantageously.

quar·ter·sec·tion (kwôr′tər·sek′shən) *n.* A tract of land half a mile square, containing one fourth of a square mile; 160 acres.

quar·ter·ses·sions (kwôr′tər·sesh′ənz) *n.* 1 In the U.S., any of various courts with criminal jurisdiction and, sometimes, administrative functions. 2 In England, a local court held quarterly that has limited criminal and civil jurisdiction and, often, administrative functions.

quar·ter·staff (kwôr′tər·staf′, -stäf′) *n. pl.* ·staves (-stāvz′) A stout, iron-tipped staff about 6½ feet long, formerly used in England as a weapon.

quar·tet (kwôr·tet′) *n.* 1 A composition for four voices or instruments. 2 The four persons who render such a composition. 3 Any group of four persons or things. Also **quar·tette′**. [< Ital. *quarto* fourth]

quar·to (kwôr′tō) *adj.* Having four leaves or eight pages to the sheet: a *quarto* book. —*n. pl.* ·tos 1 The size of a piece of paper obtained by folding a sheet into four leaves. 2 Paper of this size; also, a page of this size. 3 A book made of pages of this size. [< L *(in) quarto* (in) fourth]

quartz (kwôrts) *n.* A hard mineral form of silicon dioxide occurring in many varieties, some of which are valued as gems. [< G *Quarz*]

qua·sar (kwā′zär, -sär) *n. Astron.* QUASI-STELLAR OBJECT. [< QUAS(I) - (STELL)AR RADIO SOURCE]

quash[1] (kwosh) *v.t. Law* To make void or set aside, as an indictment; annul. [< LL *cassare* to empty]

quash[2] (kwosh) *v.t.* To put down or suppress forcibly or summarily. [< L *quassare*, freq. of *quatere* shake]

qua·si (kwā′zī, -sī; kwä′zē, -sē) *adj.* More in resemblance than in fact: a *quasi* scholar. [L, as if]

quasi- *combining form* Resembling but not quite; in some ways or to some extent: *quasi-legal, quasi-official.* [< L *quasi* as if]

qua·si-stel·lar object (kwā′zī-stel′ər, -sī-, kwä′zē-, -sē-) Any of various starlike objects emitting vast amounts of radiation over a broad spectrum and having large red shifts. Also **quasi-stellar radio source.**

quas·si·a (kwosh′ē-ə, kwosh′ə) *n.* 1 Any of several tropical trees having bitter wood and bark. 2 A bitter extract obtained from a quassia tree, used to allay fever. 3 An insecticide obtained from the wood of a certain quassia tree. [< Graman *Quassi,* a Surinam Negro who discovered its use in 1730]

qua·ter·na·ry (kwot′ər·ner′ē, kwə·tûr′nə·rē) *adj.* Consisting of four. [< L *quaterni* by fours]

Qua·ter·na·ry (kwot′ər·ner′ē, kwə·tûr′nə·rē) *adj. & n.* See GEOLOGY.

quat·rain (kwot′rān, kwot·rān′) *n.* A stanza of four lines. [< F *quatre* four]

quat·re·foil (kat′ər·foil′, kat′rə-) *n.* 1 *Bot.* A leaf or flower with four leaflets or petals. 2 *Archit.* An ornament with four foils or lobes. [< OF *quatre* four + *foil* leaf]

Quatrefoil window

quat·tro·cen·to (kwät′trō·chen′tō) *n.* The 15th century, esp. in connection with Italian art and literature. —*adj.* Of or pertaining to the quattrocento. [< Ital., four hundred < *quattro* four + *cento* hundred]

qua·ver (kwā′vər) *v.i.* 1 To tremble or shake: said usu. of the voice. 2 To produce trills or quavers in singing or in playing a musical instrument. —*v.t.* 3 To utter or sing in a tremulous voice. —*n.* 1 A trembling or shaking, as in the voice. 2 A shake or trill, as in singing. 3 An eighth note. [< ME *cwafian* tremble] —**qua′ver·y** *adj.*

quay (kē) *n.* A wharf or artificial landing place where vessels load and unload. [F]

Que. Quebec.

quean (kwēn) *n.* A brazen woman; harlot; prostitute. [< OE *cwene* woman]

quea·sy (kwē′zē) *adj.* ·si·er, ·si·est 1 Feeling or causing nausea. 2 Easily nauseated; squeamish. 3 Causing or feeling uneasiness or discomfort. [ME *coysy*] —**quea′si·ly** *adv.* —**quea′si·ness** *n.*

Quech·ua (kech′wä) *n.* 1 One of a tribe of South American Indians which dominated the Inca empire prior to the Spanish conquest. 2 The language of the Quechuas. — **Quech′uan** *adj., n.*

queen (kwēn) *n.* 1 The wife of a king. 2 A female sovereign or monarch. 3 A woman preeminent in a given activity, accomplishment, etc. 4 A place or thing of great beauty, excellence, etc. 5 The most powerful piece in chess, capable of moving any number of squares in a straight or diagonal line. 6 A playing card bearing a conventional picture of a queen in her robes. 7 An egg-producing female in a colony of social insects, as bees, ants, etc. —*v.t.* 1 To make a queen of. —*v.i.* 2 To reign as or play the part of a queen: often with *it.* [< OE *cwēn* woman, queen] —**queen′ly** *adj., adv.* —**queen′li·ness** *n.*

Queen Anne's lace The wild carrot, having filmy white flowers resembling lace.

queen consort The wife of a reigning king.

queen dowager The widow of a king.

queen mother A queen dowager who is mother of a reigning sovereign.

queer (kwir) *adj.* 1 Different from the usual; strange; odd. 2 Of questionable character; open to suspicion; mysterious. 3 *Slang* Counterfeit. 4 Mentally unbalanced or eccentric. 5 Queasy or giddy. 6 *Slang* Homosexual: a contemptuous term. —*n. Slang* 1 Counterfeit money. 2 A homosexual, esp. a male homosexual: a contemptuous term. —*v.t. Slang* 1 To jeopardize or spoil. 2 To put into an unfavorable or embarrassing position. [< G *quer* oblique] —**queer′ly** *adv.* —**queer′ness** *n.* —**Syn.** *adj.* 1 bizarre, curious, droll, fantastic, grotesque, peculiar, singular. 2 suspect, suspicious. 4 peculiar, odd, deranged.

quell (kwel) *v.t.* 1 To put down or suppress by force; extinguish. 2 To quiet; allay, as pain. [< OE *cwellan* kill] —**quell′er** *n.*

quench (kwench) *v.t.* 1 To put out or extinguish, as a fire. 2 To slake or satisfy (thirst). 3 To suppress or repress, as emotions. 4 To cool, as heated iron or steel, by thrusting into water or other liquid. [ME *cwenken*] —**quench′a·ble** *adj.* —**quench′er** *n.*

quench·less (kwench′lis) *adj.* Incapable of being quenched; insatiable; irrepressible. —**quench′less·ly** *adv.* —**quench′less·ness** *n.*

quer·u·lous (kwer′ə·ləs, -yə·ləs) *adj.* 1 Disposed to complain or be fretful; faultfinding. 2 Indicating or expressing a complaint. [< L *queri* complain] —**quer′u·lous·ly** *adv.* —**quer′u·lous·ness** *n.* —**Syn.** 1 carping, captious, disparaging, critical, censorious.

que·ry (kwir′ē) *v.t.* ·ried, ·ry·ing 1 To inquire into; ask about. 2 To ask questions of; interrogate. 3 To express doubt concerning the correctness or truth of, esp., as in printing, by marking with a question mark. —*n. pl.* ·ries 1 An inquiry; question. 2 A doubt. 3 A question mark. [< L *quaerere* ask]

ques. question.

quest (kwest) *n.* 1 The act of seeking; a looking for something. 2 A search, as an adventure or expedition in medieval romance; also, the person or persons making the search. —*v.i.* To go on a quest. [< L *quaerere* ask, seek] —**quest′er** *n.*

ques·tion (kwes′chən) *n.* 1 An inquiry, esp. to obtain information, test knowledge, etc. 2 A written or vocal expression of such an inquiry; an interrogative sentence, clause, or expression. 3 A subject of debate or dispute. 4 An issue or problem: It's not a *question* of time. 5 A doubt or uncertainty: There is no *question* of his skill. —out of the question Not to be considered as a possibility. —*v.t.* 1 To put a question or questions to; interrogate. 2 To be uncertain of; doubt. 3 To make objection to; challenge; dispute. —*v.i.* 4 To ask a question or questions. [< L *quaerere* ask] —ques′tion·er *n.*

ques·tion·a·ble (kwes′chən·ə·bəl) *adj.* 1 Open to question; debatable. 2 Dubious or suspect, as regards morality, integrity, respectability, etc.: *questionable* motives. — ques′tion·a·bil′i·ty, ques′tion·a·ble·ness *n.* —ques′tion·a·bly *adv.*

question mark A punctuation mark (?) indicating that the sentence it closes is a direct question. A question mark is also used to denote that a fact, statement, etc., is uncertain or doubtful.

ques·tion·naire (kwes′chə·nâr′) *n.* A written or printed form comprising a series of questions submitted to one or more persons in order to obtain data, as for a survey or report. [F]

quet·zal (ket·säl′) *n. pl.* ·zals or ·zal·es (-sä′läs) A crested bird of Central America having long, upper tail feathers in the male. 2 The monetary unit of Guatemala. Also **que·zal** (kä·säl′). [< Nahuatl]

queue (kyōō) *n.* 1 A braid of hair hanging from the back of the head; a pigtail. 2 A line of persons or vehicles waiting in the order of their arrival. —*v.i.* **queued, queu·ing** To form such a line: usu. with *up*. [< L *cauda* a tail]

quib·ble (kwib′əl) *n.* 1 An evasion of a point or question; an equivocation. 2 A minor objection; cavil. —*v.i.* **·bled, ·bling** To use quibbles. [< L *quibus*, ablative pl. of *qui* who, which] —**quib′bler** *n.*

quiche (kēsh) *n.* Any of various nondessert, custardlike pies, having meat, cheese, vegetables, etc., as principal ingredients. [F]

quick (kwik) *adj.* 1 Done or occurring in a short time; expeditious; brisk; prompt; speedy: a *quick* answer. 2 Characterized by rapidity or readiness of movement or action; nimble; rapid; swift: a *quick* pace. 3 Alert; sensitive; perceptive: a *quick* ear; *quick* wit. 4 Responding readily; excitable; hasty: *quick-tempered*. 5 Lasting only a short time: a *quick* lunch. —*n.* 1 That which has life; those who are alive: chiefly in the phrase **the quick and the dead.** 2 The living flesh; esp., the tender flesh under a nail. 3 The most sensitive feelings: hurt to the *quick*. —*adv.* Quickly; rapidly. [< OE *cwic* alive]

quick bread Any bread, biscuits, etc., whose leavening agent makes immediate baking possible.

quick·en (kwik′ən) *v.t.* 1 To cause to move more rapidly; hasten or accelerate. 2 To make alive or quick; give or restore life to. 3 To excite or arouse; stimulate: to *quicken* the appetite. —*v.i.* 4 To move or act more quickly. 5 To come or return to life; revive. —**quick′en·er** *n.*

quick-freeze (kwik′frēz′) *v.t.* **-froze, -fro·zen, -freez·ing** To preserve by freezing rapidly and storing at a low temperature. —**quick′-fro′zen** *adj.*

quick·ie (kwik′ē) *n. Slang* Anything done hastily, as by short cuts or makeshift methods.

quick·lime (kwik′līm′) *n.* Unslaked lime.

quick·ly (kwik′lē) *adv.* In a quick manner; rapidly; soon.

quick·sand (kwik′sand′) *n.* A deep, wet bed of sand subjected to pressure by water below it and usu. incapable of supporting the weight of a person or animal.

quick·set (kwik′set′) *n.* 1 A slip, as of hawthorn, ready for planting. 2 A hedge made of such slips. —*adj.* Composed of quickset.

Quetzal

quick·sil·ver (kwik′sil′vər) *n.* Elemental mercury.

quick·step (kwik′step′) *n.* 1 A lively tune, esp. one in the rhythm of quick time. 2 A lively dance step, or a combination of such steps.

quick-tem·pered (kwik′tem′pərd) *adj.* Easily angered.

quick time A marching step of 120 paces a minute, each pace of 30 inches.

quick-wit·ted (kwik′wit′id) *adj.* Having a ready wit or quick discernment; keen; alert. —**quick′-wit′ted·ly** *adv.* — **quick′-wit′ted·ness** *n.*

quid[1] (kwid) *n.* A small portion, as of tobacco, to be chewed but not swallowed. [Var. of CUD]

quid[2] (kwid) *n. Brit. Slang* In England, a pound sterling, or a sovereign. [?]

quid·di·ty (kwid′ə·tē) *n. pl.* ·ties 1 The essence of a thing. 2 A quibble; cavil. [< L *quid* which, what]

quid·nunc (kwid′nungk′) *n.* A gossip; busybody. [< L *quid nunc* what now]

quid pro quo (kwid′ prō kwō′) A thing given or received for another thing. [L, lit., something for something]

qui·es·cent (kwī·es′ənt, kwē-) *adj.* Being in a state of repose or inaction; quiet; still. [< L *quiescere* be quiet] — **qui·es′cence** *n.* —**qui·es′cent·ly** *adv.*

qui·et (kwī′ət) *adj.* 1 Being in a state of repose; still; calm; motionless. 2 Free from turmoil, strife, or busyness; tranquil; peaceful. 3 Having or making little or no noise; silent. 4 Gentle or mild, as of disposition. 5 Undisturbed by din or bustle; secluded. 6 Not showy or obtrusive, as dress. —*n.* The condition or quality of being free from motion, disturbance, noise, etc.; peace; calm. —*v.t.* & *v.i.* To make or become quiet: often with *down*. —*adv.* In a quiet or peaceful manner. [< L *quies* rest, repose] —**qui′et·ly** *adv.* —**qui′et·ness** *n.*

qui·et·en (kwī′ə·tən) *v.t.* & *v.i. Brit. or Regional* To make or become quiet: often with *down*.

qui·e·tude (kwī′ə·t/ŏōd) *n.* A state or condition of calm or tranquillity; repose; rest.

qui·e·tus (kwī·ē′təs) *n.* 1 A final discharge or settlement, as of a debt. 2 A release from or extinction of activity or life; death. 3 Something that silences or suppresses. 4 Something that kills. [< L *quietus (est)* (he is) quiet]

quill (kwil) *n.* 1 A large, strong, wing or tail feather. 2 The hollow, horny stem of a feather. 3 Something made from this, as a pen or a plectrum. 4 A spine of a porcupine or hedgehog. [ME *quil*]

Quill

quilt (kwilt) *n.* 1 A bedcover made by stitching together two layers of cloth with a soft padding between them. 2 Any bedcover, esp. if thick. 3 A quilted skirt or other quilted article. —*v.t.* 1 To stitch together (two pieces of material) with a soft substance between. 2 To stitch in ornamental patterns or crossing lines. —*v.i.* 3 To make a quilt or quilted work. [< L *culcita* mattress] —**quilt′work′** *n.*

quilt·ing (kwilt′ting) *n.* 1 The act or process of making a quilt, or of stitching as in making a quilt. 2 Material for quiltwork. 3 A quilting bee or party.

quilting bee A social gathering of the women of a community for working on a quilt or quilts. Also **quilting party.**

quince (kwins) *n.* 1 A hard, acid, yellowish fruit, used for preserves. 2 The small tree, related to the apple, which bears quinces. [ME < Gk. *Kydōnia*, a town in Crete]

qui·nine (kwī′nīn, *esp. Brit.* kwi·nēn′) *n.* 1 A bitter alkaloid obtained from cinchona. 2 A medicinal compound of quinine, used to relieve the symptoms of malaria. [< Sp. *quina* cinchona bark + -INE]

Quin·qua·ges·i·ma (kwin′kwə·jes′ə·mə) *n.* The Sunday before Lent. Also **Quinquagesima Sunday.** [< L *quinquagesimus* fiftieth]

quin·sy (kwin′zē) *n.* An acute infection of the throat, esp. when suppurative. [< Gk. *kyōn* dog + *anchein* to choke]

quint (kwint) *n. Informal* A quintuplet. [< L *quinque* five]

quin·tal (kwin′təl) *n.* 1 A hundredweight. 2 In the metric system, 100 kilograms. [< Ar. *qintar*]

quin·tes·sence (kwin·tes′əns) *n.* 1 The essence of anything, esp. in its most pure, concentrated form. 2 The perfect manifestation or embodiment of anything. [< L *quinta essentia* fifth essence] —**quin·tes·sen·tial** (kwin′tə·sen′shəl) *adj.*

quin·tet (kwin·tet′) *n.* 1 A musical composition for five voices or instruments. 2 The five performers of such a composition. 3 Any group of five persons or things. Also **quin·tette′**. [< Ital. *quinto* fifth]

quin·til·lion (kwin·til′yən) *n. & adj.* See NUMBER. [< L *quintus* fifth + MILLION] —**quin·til′lionth** (-yənth) *adj., n.*

quin·tu·ple (kwin·t′y̅o̅o̅′pəl, -tup′əl, kwin′t′y̅o̅o̅·pəl) *v.t. & v.i.* **·pled**, **·pling** To multiply by five; make or become five times as large. —*adj.* 1 Consisting of five. 2 Being five times as much or as many. —*n.* A number or an amount five times as great as another. [< L *quintus* fifth + *-plex* -fold]

quin·tu·plet (kwin·tup′lit, -t′y̅o̅o̅′plit, -t′y̅o̅o̅′-, kwint′əp·lit) *n.* 1 Five things of a kind considered together. 2 One of five offspring born of the same mother at one birth.

quip (kwip) *n.* 1 A witty or sarcastic remark or retort; gibe. 2 A quibble. 3 An odd, fantastic action or object. —*v.i.* **quipped**, **quip·ping** To make a quip or quips. [< L *quippe* indeed] —**quip′pish** *adj.* —**quip′ster** *n.*

quire (kwīr) *n.* A set of 24 (or 25) sheets of paper of the same size and quality. [< L *quaterni* by fours]

Quir·i·nal (kwir′ə·nəl) *n.* One of the seven hills on which Rome stands, containing the **Quirinal palace**, formerly a papal residence, after 1870 the royal residence, now the residence of the president of Italy. —*adj.* Pertaining to or situated on the Quirinal.

quirk (kwûrk) *n.* 1 A peculiar mannerism or trait; idiosyncrasy. 2 An evasion; quibble. 3 A witticism; quip. 4 An abrupt curve or twist, as a flourish in writing. [?]

quirk·y (kwûrk′ē) *adj.* **quirk·i·er**, **quirk·i·est** Peculiar, unpredictable, and idiosyncratic: a *quirky* individual. —**quirk′i·ly** *adv.* —**quirk′i·ness** *n.*

quirt (kwûrt) *n.* A short-handled riding whip with a braided rawhide lash. —*v.t.* To strike with a quirt. [?]

quis·ling (kwiz′ling) *n.* One who betrays his country to the enemy and is then given political power by the conquerors. [< Vidkun *Quisling*, 1887–1945, Norwegian politician] —**quis′ling·ism** *n.*

quit (kwit) *v.* **quit** or **quit·ted**, **quit·ting** *v.t.* 1 To cease or desist from; discontinue. 2 To give up; renounce; relinquish: to *quit* a job. 3 To go away from; leave. 4 To let go of (something held). 5 To free; release. 6 To discharge; pay back. —*v.i.* 7 To resign from a position, etc. 8 To stop; cease; discontinue. 9 To leave; depart. —*adj.* Released, relieved, or absolved from something, as a duty, obligation, encumbrance, or debt; clear; free; rid. —*n.* The act of quitting. [< L *quies* rest, repose]

quit·claim (kwit′klām′) *n. Law* 1 The giving up of a claim, right, title, or interest. 2 An instrument by which one person gives up to another a claim or title to an estate. —*v.t.* To relinquish or give up claim or title to; release from a claim. [< QUIT + CLAIM]

quite (kwīt) *adv.* 1 Completely; fully; totally: not *quite* finished. 2 To a great or considerable extent; very: *quite* ill. 3 Positively; really: *quite* certain. [ME, rid of]

quit·tance (kwit′ns) *n.* 1 Discharge or release, as from a debt or obligation. 2 A document in evidence of this; receipt. 3 Something given or tendered by way of repayment. [< F *quiter* quit]

quit·ter (kwit′ər) *n.* One who quits needlessly; a shirker; slacker; coward.

quiv·er¹ (kwiv′ər) *v.i.* To shake with a slight, tremulous motion; vibrate; tremble. —*n.* The act or fact of quivering; a trembling or shaking. [?< QUAVER]

quiv·er² (kwiv′ər) *n.* A portable case or sheath for arrows; also, its contents. [< AF *quiveir*]

Quiver of arrows

qui vive? (kē vēv′) "Who goes there?": used by French sentinels. —**be on the qui vive** To be on the look-out; be wide-awake. [F, who lives?]

quix·ot·ic (kwik·sot′ik) *adj.* 1 Pertaining to or like Don Quixote, the hero of a Spanish romance ridiculing knight-errantry. 2 Ridiculously chivalrous or romantic; having high but impractical sentiments, aims, etc. —**quix·ot′i·cal·ly** *adv.* —**quix·ot·ism** (kwik′sə·tiz′əm) *n.*

quiz (kwiz) *n. pl.* **quiz·zes** 1 The act of questioning; specifically, a brief oral or written examination. 2 A. person given to ridicule or practical jokes. 3 A hoax; practical joke. —*v.t.* **quizzed**, **quiz·zing** 1 To examine by asking questions; question. 2 To make fun of; ridicule. [?] —**quiz′zer** *n.*

quiz program A television or radio program in which selected contestants or a panel of experts compete in answering questions.

quiz·zi·cal (kwiz′i·kəl) *adj.* 1 Mocking; teasing. 2 Perplexed; puzzled. 3 Queer; odd. —**quiz′zi·cal·ly** *adv.*

quod (kwod) *n. Brit. Slang* A prison. [?]

quoin (koin, kwoin) *n.* 1 An external angle of a building. 2 A large square stone forming such an angle. 3 A wedge-shaped stone, etc., as the keystone of an arch. [Var. of COIN]

quoit (kwoit, *esp. Brit.* koit) *n.* 1 A ring of iron or other material to be thrown over a stake, used in the game of quoits. 2 *pl.* A game played by throwing these disks at a short stake.

Quoins *def.* 2

quon·dam (kwon′dəm) *adj.* Having been formerly; former. [L]

Quon·set hut (kwon′sit) A prefabricated metal structure in the form of half a cylinder resting lengthwise on its flat surface: a trade name.

Quonset hut

quo·rum (kwôr′əm, kwō′rəm) *n.* The number of members of any deliberative or corporate body that is necessary for the legal transaction of business, usu., a majority. [L, of whom]

quot. quotation.

quo·ta (kwō′tə) *n.* A proportional part or share given to or required from a person, group, etc. [< L *quotus* how great]

quo·ta·tion (kwō·tā′shən) *n.* 1 The act of quoting. 2 The words quoted. 3 A price quoted or current, as of securities, etc. —**quo·ta′tion·al** *adj.* —**quo·ta′tion·al·ly** *adv.*

quotation mark One of a pair of marks (" " or ' ') placed at the beginning and end of a quoted word or passage, the single marks usu. being used to set off a quotation within a quotation.

quote (kwōt) *v.* **quot·ed**, **quot·ing** *v.t.* 1 To repeat or reproduce the words of. 2 To repeat or cite (a rule, author, etc.), as for authority or illustration. 3 In commerce: **a** To state (a price). **b** To give the current or market price of. —*v.i.* 4 To make a quotation, as from a book. —*n.* 1 QUOTATION. 2 QUOTATION MARK. [< Med. L *quotare* distinguish by number [< L *quot* how many] —**quot′a·bil′i·ty**, **quot′er** *n.* —**quot′a·ble** *adj.*

quoth (kwōth) *v.t. Archaic* Said or spoke; uttered: used only in the first and third persons, the subject always following the verb, as *quoth* he. [< OE *cwethan* say]

quo·tid·i·an (kwō·tid′ē·ən) *adj.* Recurring or occurring every day. —*n.* Something that returns every day, as a fever. [< L *quotidianus* daily]

quo·tient (kwō′shənt) *n. Math.* The result obtained by division; a factor by which a given number must be multiplied to produce a given product. [< L *quotiens* how often]

q.v. which see (L *quod vide*).

qy. query.

R

R, r (är) *n. pl.* **R's, r's, Rs, rs** (ärz) **1** The 18th letter of the English alphabet. **2** Any spoken sound representing the letter *R* or *r*. **3** Something shaped like an R. —**the three R's** Reading, writing, and arithmetic (regarded humorously as spelled *reading, 'riting,* and *'rithmetic*); the essential elements of a primary education. —*adj.* Shaped like an R.

R radical; ratio; Republican; rook (chess); registered (trademark).

R., r. rabbi; railroad; river; road; ruble; rupee.

r roentgen(s); radius.

r. range; rare; received; residence; retired; radius.

Ra (rä) The supreme Egyptian deity, the sun-god.

Ra radium.

rab·bet (rab'it) *n.* **1** A recess or groove in or near the edge of one piece of wood or other material to receive the edge of another piece. **2** A joint so made. —*v.t.* **1** To cut a rectangular groove in. **2** To unite in a rabbet. —*v.i.* **3** To be jointed by a rabbet. [< OF *rabattre* beat down]

rab·bi (rab'ī) *n. pl.* **·bis** **1** A Jew authorized to teach or expound Jewish law. **2** The official head of a Jewish congregation. [< Heb. *rabbī* my master]

Ra

rab·bin·i·cal (rə·bin'i·kəl) *adj.* Of or pertaining to the rabbis or to their opinions, languages, writings, etc. Also **rab·bin'ic.** —**rab·bin'i·cal·ly** *adv.*

rab·bit (rab'it) *n.* **1** Any of numerous small, herbivorous mammals having soft fur, long legs and ears, and a short tail. **2** HARE. **3** The pelt of a rabbit or hare. —*v.i.* To hunt rabbits. [ME *rabette*] —**rab'bit·er** *n.*

rabbit fever TULAREMIA.

rabbit foot The left hind foot of a rabbit carried as a good-luck charm. Also **rabbit's foot.**

rab·ble (rab'əl) *n.* A disorderly crowd; mob. —**the rabble** The common people: a contemptuous term. [?]

rab·ble-rous·er (rab'əl·rou'zər) *n.* One who tries to incite mobs by arousing prejudices and passions. —**Syn.** demagogue, instigator, agitator.

Rab·e·lai·si·an (rab'ə·lā'zē·ən, -zhən) *adj.* **1** Of, pertaining to, or like Rabelais or his works. **2** Humorously coarse and boisterous; bawdy. —**Rab'e·lai'si·an·ism** *n.*

rab·id (rab'id) *adj.* **1** Affected with, arising from, or pertaining to rabies; mad. **2** Unreasonably zealous; fanatical. **3** Furious; raging. [< L *rabere* be mad] —**ra·bid·i·ty** (rə·bid'ə·tē), **rab'id·ness** *n.* —**rab'id·ly** *adv.*

ra·bies (rā'bēz) *n. pl.* **·bies** An acute viral disease affecting the central nervous system of dogs, bats, and other warm-blooded animals and transmissible to man by the bite of an infected animal. [< L *rabere* rave]

rac·coon (ra·kōōn') *n.* **1** A North American nocturnal, tree-climbing mammal with a black face mask, long gray-brown fur, and a bushy, black-ringed tail. **2** The fur of this animal. Also **ra·coon'.** [< Algon.]

Raccoon

race¹ (rās) *n.* **1** A subdivision of mankind having a relatively constant set of physical traits, such as color of skin and eyes, stature, texture of hair, etc. **2** Any grouping of peoples according to geography, nation, etc. **3** A genealogical or family stock; clan: the *race* of MacGregor. **4** Any class of people having similar activities, interests, etc.: the *race* of lawyers. **5** *Biol.* A group of plants or animals within a species with distinct, inheritable characteristics; a variety. [< Ital. *razza*]

race² (rās) *n.* **1** A contest to determine the relative speed of the persons or animals which are in competition. **2** *pl.* A series of such contests, as for horses. **3** Any contest. **4** Duration of life; course; career. **5** A swift current of water or its channel. **6** A swift current or heavy sea. **7** A sluice or channel by which to conduct water to or from a waterwheel or around a dam. **8** Any guide or channel along which some part of a machine moves. **9** SLIPSTREAM. —*v.* **raced, rac·ing** *v.i.* **1** To take part in a race. **2** To move at great or top speed. **3** To move at an accelerated or too great speed, as an engine. —*v.t.* **4** To contend against in a race. **5** To cause to race. [< ON *rās*]

race·course (rās'kôrs', -kōrs') *n.* A course or track for racing.

ra·ceme (rā·sēm', rə-) *n. Bot.* A flower cluster having flowers on short stalks arranged at intervals along a central stalk. [< L *racemus* cluster] —**rac·e·mose** (ras'ə·mōs) *adj.* —**rac'e·mose·ly** *adv.*

rac·er (rā'sər) *n.* **1** One who races. **2** Anything having unusually rapid speed, as a car, yacht, etc. **3** Any of a genus of large, agile snakes of North America.

race riot A riot caused by racial hostility, as between two groups of different races.

race·track (rās'trak') *n.* A course or track for racing, esp. one for horse or dog racing.

Ra·chel (rā'chəl) In the Bible, the wife of Jacob and mother of Joseph.

ra·chi·tis (rə·kī'tis) *n.* RICKETS. [< Gk. *rhachitis* spinal inflammation] —**ra·chit'ic** (-kit'ik) *adj.*

ra·cial (rā'shəl) *adj.* **1** Of, pertaining to, characteristic of a race. **2** Existing between races: *racial* brotherhood. —**ra'cial·ly** *adv.*

ra·cial·ism (rā'shəl·iz'əm) *n.* **1** The belief in or practice of racial superiority. **2** RACISM.

ra·cism (rā'siz·əm) *n.* **1** An excessive and irrational belief in the superiority of one's own racial group. **2** A doctrine, program, or practice based on such belief. —**ra'cist** *adj., n.*

rack¹ (rak) *n.* **1** Something on which various articles can be hung, stored, or canned. **2** A triangular frame for arranging the balls on a billiard table. **3** *Mech.* A bar having teeth that engage those of a gearwheel or pinion. **4** A machine for stretching or making tense; esp., an instrument of torture which stretches the limbs of victims. **5** Intense mental or physical suffering or its cause. **6** A wrenching or straining, as from a storm. —**on the rack** In great physical or mental pain. —*v.t.* **1** To place or arrange in or on a rack. **2** To torture on the rack. **3** To torment. **4** To strain, as with the effort of thinking: to *rack* one's brains. **5** To raise (rents) excessively. —**rack up** *Informal* To gain or achieve: to *rack up* a good score. [Prob. < MDu. *recken* to stretch] —**rack'er** *n.*

Rack *def. 3* and pinion

rack² (rak) *n.* SINGLE FOOT. —*v.i.* To proceed or move with this gait. [? Var. of ROCK²]

rack³ (rak) *n.* Thin, flying, or broken clouds. [< Scand.]

rack⁴ (rak) *n.* Destruction: obsolete except in the phrase **go to rack and ruin.** [Var. of WRACK]

rack·et¹ (rak'it) *n.* **1** A bat consisting of an oval, wooden or metal hoop strung with catgut, nylon, etc., and having a handle, used in playing tennis, etc. **2** *pl. (construed as sing.)* A game resembling court tennis, played in a court with four walls: also **rac·quets** (rak'its). [< Ar. *rāha* palm of the hand]

rack·et² (rak'it) *n.* **1** A loud, clattering or confused noise. **2** *Informal* A scheme for getting money or other benefits by fraud, intimidation, or other illegitimate means. **3**

Slang Any business or occupation. —*v.i.* To make a loud, clattering noise. [?] —**rack′et·y** *adj.*

rack·et·eer (rak′ə·tir′) *n.* One who gets money or other benefits by fraud, intimidation, or other illegitimate means. —**rack′et·eer′ing** *n.*

rac·on·teur (rak′on·tûr′, *Fr.* rȧ·kôn̂·tœr′) *n.* A skilled storyteller. [F]

rac·y (rā′sē) *adj.* **rac·i·er, rac·i·est** **1** Full of spirit and vigor: a *racy* style. **2** Slightly immodest or risqué. **3** Spicy; piquant. [< RACE¹] —**rac′i·ly** *adv.* —**rac′i·ness** *n.*

rad (rad) *n.* A unit of absorbed radiation equivalent to 100 ergs of absorbed energy per gram of absorbing material. [< R(ADIATION) + A(BSORBED) + D(OSE)]

rad radian.

ra·dar (rā′där) *n.* *Electronics* A device which detects, locates, and indicates the speed and approximate nature of aircraft, ships, objects, etc., by means of reflected microwaves. [< RA(DIO) D(ETECTING) A(ND) R(ANGING)]

ra·di·al (rā′dē·əl) *adj.* **1** Pertaining to, consisting of, or resembling a ray or radius. **2** Extending from a center like rays. **3** *Anat.* Of, pertaining to, or near the radius or forearm. **4** Developing uniformly on all sides. —*n.* **1** A radiating part. **2** RADIAL TIRE. —**ra′di·al·ly** *adv.*

radial tire A pneumatic tire with plies of fabric laid at right angles to the direction of the tread. Also **ra·di·al·ply** **tire** (rā′dē·əl·plī′).

ra·di·an (rā′dē·ən) *n.* The angle subtended by an arc equal in length to the radius of the circle of which it is a part: a unit of measure. [< RADIUS]

ra·di·ance (rā′dē·əns) *n.* The quality or state of being radiant. Also **ra′di·an·cy, ra′di·ant·ness.**

ra·di·ant (rā′dē·ənt) *adj.* **1** Emitting rays of light or heat. **2** Beaming with brightness: a *radiant* smile. **3** Resembling rays. **4** Consisting of or transmitted by radiation: *radiant* heat. [< L *radiare* emit rays] —**ra′di·ant·ly** *adv.*

radiant energy *Physics* Energy transmitted by radiation, as electromagnetic waves.

ra·di·ate (rā′dē·āt) *v.* **·at·ed, ·at·ing** *v.i.* **1** To emit rays or radiation; be radiant. **2** To issue forth in rays. **3** To spread out from a center, as the spokes of a wheel. —*v.t.* **4** To send out or emit in rays. **5** To spread or show (joy, love, etc.) as if from a center. —*adj.* (·dē·it) Divided or separated into rays; having rays; radiating. [< L *radiare* emit rays] —**ra′di·a·tive** *adj.*

ra·di·a·tion (rā′dē·ā′shən) *n.* **1** The act or process of radiating or the state of being radiated. **2** That which is radiated, as energy in the form of particles or waves.

radiation sickness Sickness resulting from exposure to X-rays, nuclear explosions, etc.

ra·di·a·tor (rā′dē·ā′tər) *n.* **1** That which radiates. **2** A device for distributing heat, partly by radiation, as in heating or cooling systems.

rad·i·cal (rad′i·kəl) *adj.* **1** Thoroughgoing; extreme: *radical* measures. **2** Of, pertaining to, or professing policies and practices of extreme change, as in government. **3** Of or pertaining to the root or foundation; essential; basic. —*n.* **1** One who holds radical or extreme convictions. **2** In politics, one who advocates extreme governmental changes. **3** The primitive or underived part of a word; root. **4** *Math.* An indicated root of a number, expression, etc. **5** *Chem.* A group of atoms that act as a unit in a compound and remain together during a chemical reaction. [< L *radix, radicis* root] —**rad′i·cal·ly** *adv.* —**rad′i·cal·ness** *n.*

rad·i·cal·ism (rad′i·kəl·iz′əm) *n.* **1** The state of being radical. **2** Advocacy of radical or extreme measures.

rad·i·cal·ize (rad′i·kə·līz′) *v.t.* **·ized, ·iz·ing** To make radical, as in politics. —**rad·i·cal·i·za·tion** (rad′i·kə·lə·zā′shən) *n.*

radical sign *Math.* The symbol √ placed around a number or expression to indicate that its root is to be taken. A number above it, not written when equal to 2, shows what root is to be taken; thus ⁿ√a stands for the *n*th root of *a*.

rad·i·cle (rad′i·kəl) *n.* *Bot.* The embryonic root of a sprouting seed. [< L *radix, radicis* root]

ra·di·o (rā′dē·ō) *n. pl.* **·os** **1** The technology and process of communicating by means of radio waves. **2** A transmitter or receiver used in such communication. **3** The process, business, or industry of producing programs to be communicated in this way. —*adj.* Of, pertaining to, designat-

ing, employing, or produced by radiant energy, esp. electromagnetic waves: a *radio* beam. —*v.t.* & *v.i.* **·di·oed, ·di·o·ing** **1** To transmit (a message, etc.) by radio. **2** To communicate with (someone) by radio. [< RADIO(TELEGRAPHY)]

radio- *combining form* Radiation: *radioscopy.* [< L *radius* a ray]

ra·di·o·ac·tive (rā′dē·ō·ak′tiv) *adj.* Of, pertaining to, exhibiting, caused by, or characteristic of radioactivity.

ra·di·o·ac·tiv·i·ty (rā′dē·ō·ak·tiv′ə·tē) *n.* *Physics* The spontaneous disintegration of nuclei of certain elements and isotopes, with the emission of particles or rays.

radio astronomy The branch of astronomy which studies celestial phenomena by means of radio waves received from stars and other objects in space.

radio beacon A stationary radio transmitter which sends out signals for the guidance of ships and aircraft.

radio beam **1** A steady flow of radio signals concentrated along a given course or direction. **2** The narrow zone marked out for the guidance of aircraft by radio beacons.

ra·di·o·broad·cast (rā′dē·ō·brôd′kast′, -käst′) *v.t.* **·cast** or **·cast·ed, ·cast·ing** To broadcast by radio. —*n.* BROADCAST. —**ra′di·o·broad′cast′er** *n.* —**ra′di·o·broad′cast′·ing** *n.*

ra·di·o·car·bon (rā′dē·ō·kär′bən) *n.* CARBON 14.

radio frequency Any wave frequency from about 10 kilohertz to about 30,000 megahertz.

ra·di·o·gram (rā′dē·ō·gram′) *n.* **1** A message sent by wireless telegraphy. **2** RADIOGRAPH.

ra·di·o·graph (rā′dē·ō·graf′, -gräf′) *n.* An image made by means of X-rays or the products of radioactivity. —*v.t.* To make a radiograph of. —**ra′di·og′ra·pher** (-og′rə·fər), **ra′di·og′ra·phy** *n.* —**ra′di·o·graph′ic** or **·i·cal** *adj.*

ra·di·o·i·so·tope (rā′dē·ō·ī′sə·tōp) *n.* A radioactive isotope, usu. one of an element having also a stable isotope.

ra·di·ol·o·gy (rā′dē·ol′ə·jē) *n.* That branch of science concerned with radioactivity, X-rays, etc., esp. in diagnostic and therapeutic applications. —**ra·di·o·log·i·cal** (rā′dē·ə·loj′i·kəl) or **ra′di·o·log′ic** *adj.* —**ra′di·ol′o·gist** *n.*

ra·di·om·e·ter (rā′dē·om′ə·tər) *n.* An instrument for detecting and measuring radiant energy by noting the speed of rotation of blackened disks suspended in a partially evacuated chamber.

ra·di·o·phone (rā′dē·ō·fōn′) *n.* RADIO-TELEPHONE.

ra·di·o·pho·to (rā′dē·ō·fō′tō) *n.* A photograph or image transmitted by radio. Also **ra′di·o·pho′to·graph.**

ra·di·o·scope (rā′dē·ō·skōp′) *n.* An apparatus for detecting radioactivity or X-rays.

Radiometer

ra·di·os·co·py (rā′dē·os′kə·pē) *n.* Examination of bodies opaque to light by X-rays or other penetrating radiation. —**ra′di·o·scop′ic** (-skop′ik) or **·i·cal** *adj.*

ra·di·o·sonde (rā′dē·ō·sond′) *n.* *Meteorol.* A device, usu. attached to a small balloon and sent aloft, which measures the pressure, temperature, and humidity of the upper air and radios the data to the ground. [< RADIO + F *sonde* sounding]

radio star A star that emits a sizable part of its energy as radio waves.

ra·di·o·tel·e·gram (rā′dē·ō·tel′ə·gram) *n.* A message sent by radiotelegraphy.

ra·di·o·te·leg·ra·phy (rā′dē·ō·tə·leg′rə·fē) *n.* Telegraphic communication by means of radio waves. Also **ra′di·o·tel′e·graph** (-tel′ə·graf, -gräf). —**ra′di·o·tel′e·graph′ic** *adj.*

ra·di·o·tel·e·phone (rā′dē·ō·tel′ə·fōn′) *n.* A telephone set that uses radio waves to carry messages. —**ra′di·o·te·leph′o·ny** (-tə·lef′ə·nē) *n.*

radio telescope A sensitive radio receiver designed to receive radio waves from space.

Radiosonde

ra·di·o·ther·a·py (rā′dē·ō·ther′ə·pē) *n.* The use of X-rays and radioactivity in the treatment of disease.

radio wave Any electromagnetic wave of radio frequency.

rad·ish (rad′ish) n. 1 A tall, branching herb of the mustard family. 2 Its pungent, edible root, commonly eaten raw. [< L *radix, radicis* root]

ra·di·um (rā′dē·əm) n. A radioactive metallic element (symbol Ra) found in pitchblende as a disintegration product of uranium. [< L *radius* ray]

radium therapy The treatment of disease, esp. cancer, by means of radium.

ra·di·us (rā′dē·əs) n. pl. **·di·i** (-dē·ī) or **·di·us·es** 1 A straight line segment joining the surface of a sphere or circumference of a circle with its center. 2 *Anat.* The shorter of the two bones of the forearm. 3 *Zool.* A corresponding bone in the forelimb of other vertebrates. 4 *Bot.* A ray floret of a composite flower. 5 A raylike part, as a wheel spoke. 6 A circular area or boundary measured by its radius. 7 Sphere, scope, or limit, as of activity. 8 A fixed or circumscribed area or distance of travel. [L, spoke of a wheel, ray]

radius vector pl. **radius vectors** or **ra·di·i vec·to·res** (rā′dē·ī vek·tôr′ēz, -tō′rēz) *Math.* The distance in an indicated direction from a fixed origin to any point. *Radius def. 2*

ra·dix (rā′diks) n. pl. **rad·i·ces** (rad′ə·sēz, rā′də-) or **ra·dix·es** *Math.* A number or symbol used as the base of a system of numeration. [L, root]

ra·dome (rā′dōm) n. A housing, transparent to microwaves, for a radar assembly. [< RA(DAR) + DOME]

ra·don (rā′don) n. A gaseous, radioactive element (symbol Rn) resulting from the decay of radium and having a half-life of about four days. [< RAD(IUM) + (NE)ON]

RAF, R.A.F. Royal Air Force.

raf·fi·a (raf′ē·ə) n. 1 A cultivated palm of Madagascar. 2 Fiber made from the leaves of this palm, used for weaving baskets, etc. [< Malagasy *rafia*]

raff·ish (raf′ish) adj. 1 Tawdry; gaudy; vulgar. 2 Disreputable. [< ME *raf* rubbish + -ISH]

raf·fle (raf′əl) n. A form of lottery in which a number of people buy chances on an object. —v. **·fled, ·fling** v.t. 1 To dispose of by a raffle: often with *off.* —v.i. 2 To take part in a raffle. [< OF *rafle* a game of dice] —**raf′fler** n.

raft¹ (raft, räft) n. 1 A float of logs, planks, etc., fastened together for transportation by water. 2 A flat, often inflatable object, as of rubber, that floats on water. —v.t. 1 To transport on a raft. 2 To form into a raft. —v.i. 3 To travel by or work on a raft. [< ON *raptr* log] —**rafts′man** n.

raft² (raft, räft) n. *Informal* A large number or an indiscriminate collection of any kind. [< ME *raf* rubbish]

raft·er (raf′tər, räf′-) n. A timber or beam giving form, slope, and support to a roof. [< OE *ræfter*]

rag¹ (rag) v.t. **ragged, rag·ging** *Slang* 1 To tease or irritate. 2 To scold. —n. *Brit.* A prank. [?]

rag² (rag) n. 1 A waste, usu. torn piece of cloth. 2 A fragment of anything. 3 pl. Tattered or shabby clothing. 4 pl. Any clothing: a jocular use. 5 *Slang* A newspaper. —**chew the rag** *Slang* To talk or argue at length. —**glad rags** *Slang* One's best clothes. [< ON *rögg* tuft or strip of fur]

rag³ (rag) n. RAGTIME. —v.t. **ragged, rag·ging** To compose or play in ragtime.

ra·ga (rä′gə) n. One of a large number of traditional melodic patterns, used by Hindu musicians as the basis for improvisation. [< Skt. *rāga* (musical) color]

rag·a·muf·fin (rag′ə·muf′in) n. Anyone, esp. a child, wearing very ragged clothes. [< *Ragamoffyn*, demon in *Piers Plowman* (1393), a long allegorical poem]

rag·bag (rag′bag′) n. 1 A bag in which rags or scraps of cloth are kept. 2 A miscellaneous collection; potpourri.

rage (rāj) n. 1 Violent anger; wrath; fury. 2 Any great violence or intensity, as of a fever or a storm. 3 Extreme eagerness or emotion. 4 Something that arouses great enthusiasm; craze; vogue. —v.i. **raged, rag·ing** 1 To feel or show violent anger. 2 To act or proceed with great vio-

lence. 3 To spread or prevail uncontrolled, as an epidemic. [< L *rabies* madness]

rag·ged (rag′id) adj. 1 Torn or worn into rags; frayed. 2 Wearing worn, frayed, or shabby garments. 3 Of rough or uneven character or aspect: a *ragged* performance. 4 Naturally of a rough or shabby appearance. —**rag′ged·ly** adv. —**rag′ged·ness** n.

rag·ged·y (rag′id·ē) adj. Ragged in appearance.

rag·lan (rag′lən) n. An overcoat or topcoat, the sleeves of which extend in one piece up to the collar. —adj. Of or designating such a sleeve or a garment with such sleeves. [< Lord Fitzroy *Raglan*, 1788–1855, Eng. field marshal]

rag·man (rag′man′, -mən) n. pl. **·men** (-men′, -mən) One who buys and sells old rags and other waste; a ragpicker.

ra·gout (ra·gōō′) n. A highly seasoned dish of stewed meat and vegetables. —v.t. **ra·gouted** (-gōōd′), **ra·gout·ing** (-gōō′ing) To make into a ragout. [< F *ragoûter* revive the appetite]

rag·pick·er (rag′pik′ər) n. One who picks up and sells rags and other junk for a livelihood.

rag·time (rag′tīm′) n. 1 A kind of American dance music, popular 1890 to 1920, highly syncopated and in quick tempo. 2 The rhythm of this dance. [< *ragged time*]

rag·weed (rag′wēd′) n. Any of a genus of coarse, composite plants having pollen that often induces hay fever.

rag·wort (rag′wûrt′) n. GROUNDSEL (def. 1).

rah (rä) interj. Hurrah!: a cheer used esp. in school yells.

raid (rād) n. 1 A hostile or predatory attack, as by a rapidly moving body of troops. 2 AIR RAID. 3 Any sudden breaking into, invasion, or capture, as by the police. 4 A manipulative attempt to make stock prices fall by concerted selling. —v.t. 1 To make a raid on. —v.i. 2 To participate in a raid. [< OE *rād* a ride] —**raid′er** n.

rail¹ (rāl) n. 1 A bar, usu. of wood or metal, resting on supports, as in a fence, at the side of a stairway or roadway, or capping the bulwarks of a ship; a railing. 2 One of a series of parallel bars, of iron or steel, resting upon cross-ties, forming a support and guide for wheels, as of a railway. 3 A railroad: to ship by *rail.* —v.t. To furnish or shut in with rails; fence. [< L *regula* ruler]

rail² (rāl) n. Any of various small marsh and shore birds having short wings and tail. [< OF *raale, ralle*]

rail³ (rāl) v.i. To use scornful, insolent, or abusive language: with *at* or *against.* [< MF *railler* to mock]

rail·ing (rā′ling) n. 1 A series of rails; a balustrade. 2 Rails or material from which rails are made.

rail·ler·y (rā′lər·ē) n. pl. **·ler·ies** Merry jesting or teasing. [< F *raillerie* jesting]

Rail

rail·road (rāl′rōd′) n. 1 A graded road, having metal rails supported by ties, for the passage of trains or other rolling stock drawn by locomotives. 2 The system of tracks, stations, etc., used in transportation by rail. 3 The corporation or persons owning or operating such a system. —v.t. 1 To transport by railroad. 2 *Informal* To rush or force with great speed or without deliberation: to *railroad* a bill through Congress. 3 *Slang* To cause to be imprisoned on false charges or without fair trial. —v.i. 4 To work on a railroad. —**rail′road′er** n.

railroad flat An apartment having rooms arranged one after another in a straight line without hallways.

rail·split·ter (rāl′split′ər) n. One who splits logs into fence rails.

rail·way (rāl′wā′) n. 1 A railroad, esp. one using comparatively light vehicles. 2 *Brit.* RAILROAD. 3 Any track having rails for wheeled equipment.

rai·ment (rā′mənt) n. Wearing apparel; clothing; garb. [< ARRAY + -MENT]

rain (rān) n. 1 The condensed water vapor of the atmosphere falling in drops. 2 The fall of such drops. 3 A fall or shower of anything in the manner of rain. 4 A rainstorm; shower. 5 pl. The rainy season in a tropical country. —v.i. 1 To fall from the clouds in drops of water. 2 To fall like rain. **3** To send or pour down rain. —*v.t.* **4** To send down like rain; shower. [<OE *regn*]

rain·bow (rān′bō′) *n.* **1** An arch of light formed in the sky opposite the sun and exhibiting the colors of the spectrum. It is caused by refraction, reflection, and dispersion of sunlight in raindrops or mist. **2** Any brilliant display of color. **3** Any unfounded hope.

rain check 1 The stub of a ticket to an outdoor event entitling the holder to future admission if for any reason the event is called off. **2** Any postponed invitation.

rain·coat (rān′kōt′) *n.* A water-resistant coat giving protection against rain.

rain·drop (rān′drop′) *n.* A drop of rain.

rain·fall (rān′fôl′) *n.* **1** A fall of rain. **2** *Meteorol.* The amount of water precipitated in a given region over a stated time.

rain gauge An instrument for measuring rainfall.

rain·proof (rān′proōf′) *adj.* Shedding rain. —*v.t.* To make rainproof.

rain·storm (rān′stôrm′) *n.* A storm accompanied by heavy rain.

rain·wa·ter (rān′wô′tər, -wot′ər) *n.* Water that falls or has fallen as rain.

rain·y (rā′nē) *adj.* **rain·i·er, rain·i·est** Of, abounding in, or bringing rain. —**rain′i·ly** *adv.* —**rain′i·ness** *n.*

rainy day A time of need; hard times.

raise (rāz) *v.* **raised, rais·ing** *v.t.* **1** To cause to move upward or to a higher level; lift; elevate. **2** To place erect; set up. **3** To construct or build; erect. **4** To make greater in amount, size, or value: to *raise* the price of corn. **5** To advance or elevate in rank, estimation, etc. **6** To increase the strength, intensity, or degree of. **7** To breed; grow: to *raise* chickens or tomatoes. **8** To rear (children, a family, etc.). **9** To cause to be heard: to *raise* a hue and cry. **10** To cause; occasion, as a smile or laugh. **11** To stir to action or emotion; arouse. **12** To waken; animate or reanimate: to *raise* the dead. **13** To obtain or collect, as an army, capital, etc. **14** To bring up for consideration, as a question. **15** To cause to swell or become lighter; leaven. **16** To put an end to, as a siege. **17** In card games, to bid or bet more than. **18** *Naut.* To cause to appear above the horizon, as land or a ship, by approaching nearer. —*v.i.* **19** *Regional* To rise or arise. **20** In card games, to increase a bid or bet. —**raise Cain (or the devil, the dickens, a rumpus,** etc.) *Informal* to make a great disturbance; stir up confusion. —*n.* **1** The act of raising. **2** An increase, as of wages or a bet. [<ON *reisa* lift, set up]

raised (rāzd) *adj.* **1** Elevated in low relief. **2** Made with yeast or leaven.

rai·sin (rā′zən) *n.* A grape of a special sort dried in the sun or in an oven. [<L *racemus* bunch of grapes]

rai·son d'ê·tre (re·zôn′ de′tr′) *French* A reason or excuse for existing.

raj (räj) *n.* In India, sovereignty; rule [<Hind. *rāj*]

ra·ja (rä′jə) *n.* **1** A prince or chief of India. **2** A Malay or Javanese ruler. Also **ra′jah.** [<Skt. *rājan* king]

rake[1] (rāk) *n.* A long-handled, toothed implement for drawing together loose material, making a surface smooth, etc. — *v.* **raked, rak·ing** *v.t.* **1** To gather together with or as with a rake. **2** To smooth, clean, or prepare with a rake. **3** To gather by diligent effort. **4** To search or examine carefully. **5** To direct heavy gunfire along the length of. —*v.i.* **6** To use a rake. **7** To scrape or pass roughly or violently: with *across, over, etc.* **8** To make a search. —**rake in** *Informal* To earn or acquire (money, etc.) in large quantities. —**rake up** *Informal* To make public or bring to light: to *rake up* old gossip. [<OE *raca*]

Rakes
a. garden. b. broom.

rake[2] (rāk) *v.* **raked, rak·ing** *v.i.* **1** To lean from the perpendicular, as a ship's masts. —*v.t.* **2** To cause to lean; incline. —*n.* Inclination from the perpendicular or horizontal, as the edge of a cutting tool. [?] —**raked** *adj.*

rake[3] (rāk) *n.* A dissolute, lewd man. [Orig. *rakehell* < ME *rakel* rash, wild] —**Syn.** roué, libertine, lecher, profligate.

rake-off (rāk′ôf′, -of′) *n. Slang* A percentage, as of profits; commission or rebate, usu. illegitimate.

rak·ish[1] (rā′kish) *adj.* **1** Dashing; jaunty. **2** *Naut.* Having the masts unusually inclined, usu. connoting speed. [<RAKE[2]] —**rak′ish·ly** *adv.* —**rak′ish·ness** *n.*

rak·ish[2] (rā′kish) *adj.* Like a rake; dissolute. —**rak′ish·ly** *adv.* —**rak′ish·ness** *n.*

ral·len·tan·do (ral′ən·tän′dō, *Ital.* räl′len·tän′dō) *adj. & adv. Music* Gradually slower. [Ital., pr.p. of *rallentare* slow down]

ral·ly[1] (ral′ē) *v.* **-lied, -ly·ing** *v.t.* **1** To bring together and restore to effective discipline: to *rally* fleeing troops. **2** To summon up or revive: to *rally* one's spirits. **3** To bring together for common action. —*v.i.* **4** To return to effective discipline or action: The enemy *rallied.* **5** To unite for common action. **6** To make a partial or complete return to a normal condition. **7** In tennis, badminton, etc. to engage in a rally. —*n. pl.* **-lies 1** An assembly of people, esp. to arouse enthusiasm. **2** A quick recovery or improvement, as of health, spirits, vigor, etc. **3** A reassembling, as of scattered troops. **4** In tennis, badminton, etc., an exchange of several strokes before one side wins the point. **5** A competition for automobiles that emphasizes driving and navigational skills rather than speed. [<F *re-* again + *allier* join]

ral·ly[2] (ral′ē) *v.t. & v.i.* To tease or ridicule; banter. [<F *railler* banter]

ram (ram) *n.* **1** A male sheep. **2** BATTERING-RAM. **3** Any device for forcing or thrusting, as by heavy blows. **4** A device for raising water by pressure of its own flow; a hydraulic ram. —*v.t.* **rammed, ram·ming 1** To strike with or as with a ram; dash against. **2** To drive or force down or into something. **3** To cram; stuff. [<OE]

Ram (ram) *n.* ARIES.

RAM Random access memory, a kind of computer memory in which information may be stored and/or erased repeatedly.

ram·ble (ram′bəl) *v.i.* **-bled, -bling 1** To walk about freely and aimlessly; roam. **2** To write or talk aimlessly or without sequence of ideas. **3** To proceed with turns and twists; meander. —*n.* **1** The act of rambling. **2** A meandering path; maze. [?]

ram·bler (ram′blər) *n.* **1** One who or that which rambles. **2** Any of several varieties of climbing roses.

ram·bunc·tious (ram·bungk′shəs) *adj. Informal* Difficult to control or manage; unruly. [?]

ram·e·kin (ram′ə·kin) *n.* **1** Any of various food mixtures, usu. containing cheese, baked and served in individual dishes. **2** Any small or individual baking dish. Also **ram′e·quin.** [<F *ramequin*]

ram·i·fi·ca·tion (ram′ə·fə·kā′shən) *n.* **1** The act or process of ramifying. **2** An offshoot or branch. **3** A result or consequence; outgrowth, as of an action.

ram·i·fy (ram′ə·fī) *v.t. & v.i.* **-fied, -fy·ing** To divide or spread out into or as into branches. [<L *ramus* branch + *facere* make]

ram·jet (ram′jet′) *n.* A type of jet engine consisting of a duct whose forward motion provides compressed air which mixes with fuel that burns and provides an exhaust velocity high enough to create thrust.

ra·mose (rā′mōs, rə·mōs′) *adj.* **1** Branching. **2** Consisting of or having branches. [<L *ramus* branch]

ramp[1] (ramp) *n.* **1** An inclined passageway or roadway that connects different levels. **2** A movable stairway or passageway for entering or leaving an airplane. **3** *Archit.* A concave part at the top or cap of a railing, wall, or coping. [<F *ramper* to climb]

ramp[2] (ramp) *v.i.* **1** To rear up on the hind legs and stretch out the forepaws. **2** To act in a violent or threatening manner. —*n.* The act of ramping. [<OF *ramper* to climb]

ram·page (ram′pāj) *n.* An outbreak of boisterous or angry agitation or violence. —*v.i.* (ram·pāj′) **-paged, -pag·ing** To rush or act violently; storm; rage [Orig. Scot.,? < RAMP[2]]

ram·pant (ram′pənt) *adj.* **1** Exceeding all bounds; unrestrained; wild. **2** Widespread; unchecked, as an erroneous belief. **3** Standing on the hind legs; rearing: said of a quadruped. **4** *Her.* Standing on the hind legs, with both forelegs elevated. [<OF *ramper* to climb] —**ram′pan·cy** *n.* —**ram′pant·ly** *adv.*

Rampant lion

ram·part (ram′pärt, -pərt) *n.* **1** The embankment surrounding a fort, on which the parapet is raised. **2** A bulwark or defense. —*v.t.* To supply with or as with ramparts; fortify. [< OF *re-* again + *emparer* prepare]

ram·pike (ram′pīk′) *n. Can.* A bare, dead tree, esp. one destroyed by fire. [?]

ram·rod (ram′rod′) *n.* **1** A rod used to compact the charge of a muzzleloading firearm. **2** A similar rod used for cleaning the barrel of a rifle, etc.

ram·shack·le (ram′shak′əl) *adj.* About to go to pieces from age and neglect. [?] —*Syn.* dilapidated, unsteady, shaky, battered.

ran (ran) *p.t.* of RUN.

ranch (ranch) *n.* **1** An establishment for rearing or grazing cattle, sheep, horses, etc., in large herds. **2** The buildings, personnel, and lands connected with it. **3** A large farm. —*v.i.* To manage or work on a ranch. [< Sp. *rancho* group eating together, mess] —**ranch′er, ranch′man** *n.*

ranch house 1 A long, one-story residence having a low-pitched roof. **2** The main house on a ranch.

ran·cid (ran′sid) *adj.* Having the bad taste or smell of spoiled fats. [< L *rancere* be rancid] —**ran·cid·i·ty** (ran·sid′ə·tē), **ran′cid·ness** *n.*

ran·cor (rang′kər) *n.* Bitter and vindictive enmity. *Brit. sp.* **ran·cour.** [< L *rancere* be rank] —**ran′cor·ous** *adj.* —**ran′cor·ous·ly** *adv.* —**ran′cor·ous·ness** *n.* —*Syn.* malice, spite, hatred, hostility.

ran·dom (ran′dəm) *n.* Lack of definite purpose or intention: now chiefly in the phrase **at random,** without careful thought, planning, intent, etc.; haphazardly. —*adj.* **1** Done or chosen without deliberation or plan; chance; casual. **2** Chosen, determined, or varying without pattern, rule, or bias. [< OF *randonner, rander* move rapidly, gallop] —**ran′dom·ly** *adv.* —**ran′dom·ness** *n.*

ra·nee (rä′nē) *n.* RANI.

rang (rang) *p.t.* of RING².

range (rānj) *n.* **1** The area over which anything moves, operates, or is distributed. **2** An extensive tract of land over which cattle, sheep, etc., roam and graze. **3** Extent or scope: the whole *range* of political influence. **4** The extent of variation of anything: the temperature *range.* **5** A line, row, or series, as of mountains. **6** The horizontal distance between a gun and its target. **7** The horizontal distance covered by a projectile. **8** The maximum distance for which an airplane, ship, vehicle, etc., can be fueled. **9** The maximum effective distance, as of a weapon. **10** *Math.* The entire set of possible values of a dependent variable. **11** A place for shooting at a mark: a rifle *range.* **12** A large cooking stove. —*adj.* Of or pertaining to a range. —*v.* **ranged, rang·ing** *v.t.* **1** To place or arrange in definite order, as in rows. **2** To assign to a class, division, or category; classify. **3** To move about or over (a region, etc.), as in exploration. **4** To put (cattle) to graze on a range. **5** To adjust or train, as a telescope or gun. —*v.i.* **6** To move over an area in a thorough, systematic manner. **7** To rove; roam. **8** To occur; extend; be found: forests *ranging* to the east. **9** To vary within specified limits. **10** To lie in the same direction, line, etc. **11** To have a specified range. [< OF *ranger* arrange < *renc* row]

rang·er (rān′jər) *n.* **1** One who or that which ranges. **2** One of a group of mounted troops that protect large tracts of country. **3** One of a herd of cattle that feeds on a range. **4** A warden employed in patrolling forest tracts. **5** *Brit.* A government official in charge of a royal forest or park. **6** One of a group of soldiers trained esp. for raiding and close combat.

rang·y (rān′jē) *adj.* **rang·i·er, rang·i·est 1** Disposed to roam, or adapted for roving, as cattle. **2** Having long, slender limbs. **3** Roomy; spacious.

ra·ni (rä′nē) *n.* **1** The wife of a raja or prince. **2** A reigning Hindu queen or princess.

rank¹ (rangk) *n.* **1** A series of objects ranged in a line or row. **2** A degree of official standing: the *rank* of colonel. **3** A line of soldiers side by side in close order. **4** *pl.* An army; also, the common body of soldiers: to rise from the *ranks.* **5** Relative position in a scale; degree; grade: a writer of

low *rank.* **6** A social class or stratum: from all *ranks* of life. **7** High degree or position: a lady of *rank.* —*v.t.* **1** To place or arrange in a rank or ranks. **2** To assign to a position or classification. **3** To outrank: Sergeants *rank* corporals. —*v.i.* **4** To hold a specified place or rank. **5** To have the highest rank or grade. [< OF *ranc, renc*]

rank² (rangk) *adj.* **1** Flourishing and luxuriant in growth: *rank* weeds. **2** Strong and disagreeable to the taste or smell. **3** Utter; total: *rank* injustice. **4** Indecent; gross; vulgar. [< OE *ranc* strong] —**rank′ly** *adv.* —**rank′ness** *n.*

rank and file 1 The common soldiers of an army. **2** Those who form the main body of any organization, as distinguished from its leaders.

rank·ing (rangk′ing) *adj.* Taking precedence (over others): a *ranking* senator, officer, etc. —*Syn.* superior, senior.

ran·kle (rang′kəl) *v.* **·kled, ·kling** *v.i.* **1** To cause continued resentment, sense of injury, etc. **2** To become irritated or inflamed. —*v.t.* **3** To irritate; embitter. [< OF *rancler*]

ran·sack (ran′sak) *v.t.* **1** To search through every part of. **2** To search for plunder; pillage. [< ON *rann* house + *sækja* seek] —**ran′sack·er** *n.*

ran·som (ran′səm) *v.t.* **1** To secure the release of (a person, property, etc.) for a required price, as from captivity or detention. **2** To set free on payment of ransom. —*n.* **1** The price paid to ransom a person or property. **2** Release purchased, as from captivity. [< L *redimere* redeem] —**ran′som·er** *n.*

rant (rant) *v.i.* **1** To speak in loud, violent, or extravagant language. —*v.t.* **2** To exclaim or utter in a ranting manner. —*n.* Declamatory and bombastic talk. [< MDu. *ranten*] —**rant′er** *n.* —**rant′ing·ly** *adv.*

rap¹ (rap) *v.* **rapped, rap·ping** *v.t.* **1** To strike sharply and quickly; hit. **2** To utter in a sharp manner: with *out.* **3** *Slang* To criticize severely. —*v.i.* **4** To strike sharp, quick blows. **5** *Slang* To have a frank discussion; talk. —*n.* **1** A sharp blow. **2** A sound caused by or as by knocking. **3** *Slang* A severe criticism. **4** *Slang* Blame or punishment, as for wrongdoing: to take the *rap.* **5** *Slang* A prison sentence. **6** *Slang* A talk; discussion. —*adj. Slang* Marked by frank discussion: a *rap* session. [Imit.] —**rap′per** *n.*

rap² (rap) *n. Informal* The least bit: I don't care a *rap.* [?]

ra·pa·cious (rə·pā′shəs) *adj.* **1** Given to plunder or rapine. **2** Greedy; grasping. **3** Subsisting on prey seized alive, as hawks, etc. [< L *rapere* seize] —**ra·pa′cious·ly** *adv.* —**ra·pac·i·ty** (rə·pas′ə·tē), **ra·pa′cious·ness** *n.*

rape¹ (rāp) *v.* **raped, rap·ing** *v.t.* **1** To commit rape on. **2** To plunder or sack (a city, etc.). —*v.i.* **3** To commit rape. —*n.* **1** The act of a man who has sexual intercourse with a woman against her will or (called **statutory rape**) with a girl below the age of consent. **2** Any unlawful sexual intercourse or sexual connection by force or threat: homosexual *rape* in prison. **3** The plundering or sacking of a city, etc. **4** Any gross violation, assault, or abuse: the *rape* of natural forests. [< L *rapere* seize] —**rap′ist** *n.*

rape² (rāp) *n.* A plant related to mustard, grown for forage. [< L *rapum* turnip]

rape oil An oil obtained from seeds of the rape, used as a lubricant, etc. Also **rape·seed oil** (rāp′sēd′).

rap·id (rap′id) *adj.* **1** Having or done with great speed; swift; fast. **2** Marked by or characterized by rapidity. —*n. Usu. pl.* A swift-flowing descent in a river. [< L *rapidus* < *rapere* seize, rush] —**ra·pid·i·ty** (rə·pid′ə·tē), **rap′id·ness** *n.* —**rap′id·ly** *adv.*

rap·id-fire (rap′id·fīr′) *adj.* **1** Firing or designed to fire shots rapidly. **2** Characterized by speed: *rapid-fire* repartee. Also **rap′id-fir′ing.**

rapid transit An urban passenger railway system.

ra·pi·er (rā′pē·ər, rāp′yər) *n.* **1** A long, pointed, two-edged sword with a large cup hilt, used in dueling, chiefly for thrusting. **2** A shorter straight sword without cutting edge and therefore used for thrusting only. [< F *rapière*]

Rapier

rap·ine (rap'in) *n.* The taking of property by force, as in war. [<L *rapere* seize] —**Syn.** plunder, pillage, looting, spoiling.

rap·pel (ra·pel') *n.* A way of lowering oneself down a vertical surface, using a rope attached at the top and to the climber's body. —*v.i.* To lower oneself using a rappel. [<F]

rap·port (ra·pôr', -pôr', *Fr.* ra·pôr') *n.* Harmonious, sympathetic relationship; accord. —**en rapport** (äṅ ra·pôr') *French* In close accord. [<F *rapporter* refer, bring back]

rap·proche·ment (ra·prôsh·mäṅ') *n.* A state of harmony or reconciliation; restoration of cordial relations. [F]

rap·scal·lion (rap·skal'yən) *n.* A scamp; rascal. [Earlier *rascallion*<RASCAL]

rapt (rapt) *adj.* 1 Carried away with lofty emotion; enraptured; transported. 2 Deeply engrossed or intent. [<L *raptus*, pp. of *rapere* seize]

rap·to·ri·al (rap·tôr'ē·əl, -tō'rē-) *adj.* 1 Seizing and devouring living prey; predatory. 2 Having talons adapted for seizing prey: said esp. of hawks, vultures, eagles, owls, etc. [<L *raptus*, pp. of *rapere* seize]

rap·ture (rap'chər) *n.* 1 The state of being rapt or transported; ecstatic joy; ecstasy. 2 An expression of excessive delight. —*v.t.* ·tured, ·tur·ing To enrapture; transport with ecstasy. —**rap'tur·ous** *adj.* —**rap'tur·ous·ly** *adv.*

rare[1] (râr) *adj.* rar·er, rar·est 1 Occurring infrequently; not common, usual, or ordinary. 2 Excellent in quality, merit, etc. 3 Rarefied: now said chiefly of the atmosphere. [<L *rarus*] —**Syn.** 2 extraordinary, distinctive, fine, choice.

rare[2] (râr) *adj.* rar·er, rar·est Not thoroughly cooked, as roasted or broiled meat retaining its redness and juices. [<OE *hrēre* lightly boiled]

rare·bit (râr'bit) *n.* WELSH RABBIT. [Alter. of (WELSH) RABBIT]

rare earth Any of the oxides of the rare-earth elements.

rare-earth elements The series of metallic elements comprising atomic numbers 57 through 71. See PERIODIC TABLE OF ELEMENTS. Also **rare-earth metals.**

rar·e·fy (râr'ə·fī) *v.t. & v.i.* ·fied, ·fy·ing 1 To make or become rare, thin, or less dense. 2 To make or become more refined, pure, subtle, etc. [<L *rarus* rare + *facere* make] —**rar'e·fac'tion** (-fak'shən) *n.* —**rar'e·fac'tive** *adj.*

rare·ly (râr'lē) *adv.* 1 Not often; infrequently. 2 With unusual excellence or effect; finely. 3 Exceptionally; extremely.

rar·ing (râr'ing) *adj. Informal* Full of enthusiasm; intensely desirous; eager: used with an infinitive: *raring* to go. [<dial. E, var. of REAR[2], to raise]

rar·i·ty (râr'ə·tē) *n. pl.* ·ties 1 The quality or state of being rare, uncommon, or infrequent. 2 That which is exceptionally valued because scarce. 3 Thinness; tenuousness.

ras·cal (ras'kəl) *n.* 1 An unscrupulous person; scoundrel. 2 A mischievous person; tease; scamp. [<OF *rasque* filth, shavings] —**ras·cal'i·ty** (-kal'ə·tē) *n.* —**ras'cal·ly** *adj. & adv.*

rash[1] (rash) *adj.* 1 Acting without due caution or regard of consequences; reckless. 2 Exhibiting recklessness or precipitancy. [ME *rasch*] —**rash'ly** *adv.* —**rash'ness** *n.*

rash[2] (rash) *n.* A patch of redness, itchiness, or other usu. temporary skin lesion.

rash·er (rash'ər) *n.* 1 A thin slice of meat, esp. of bacon. 2 A serving of several such slices.[?]

rasp (rasp, räsp) *n.* A filelike tool having coarse, pointed projections. 2 The act or sound of rasping. —*v.t.* 1 To scrape with or as with a rasp. 2 To affect unpleasantly; irritate. 3 To utter in a rough voice. —*v.i.* 4 To grate; scrape. 5 To make a harsh, grating sound. [<OF *rasper* to scrape] —**rasp'er** *n.* —**rasp'y** *adj.* (·i·er, ·i·est)

rasp·ber·ry (raz'ber'ē, -bər·ē, räz'-) *n. pl.* ·ries 1 A sweet, edible fruit, composed of drupelets clustered around a fleshy receptacle. 2 Any of a genus of brambles yielding this fruit. 3 *Slang* BRONX CHEER. [Earlier *rasp, raspis* raspberry + BERRY]

rat (rat) *n.* 1 Any of a genus of long-tailed rodents of worldwide distribution, larger and more aggressive than the mouse. 2 Any of various similar animals. 3 *Slang* A contemptible person, esp. one who deserts or betrays his associates. 4 A pad over which a woman's hair is combed to give more fullness. —*v.i.* rat·ted, rat·ting 1 To hunt rats. 2

Slang To desert one's party, companions, etc. 3 *Slang* To betray or inform: with *on.* [<OE *ræt*]

rat·a·ble (rā'tə·bəl) *adj.* That may be rated or valued. Also **rate'a·ble.** —**rat'a·bil'i·ty** *n.* —**rat'a·bly** *adv.*

ra·tan (ra·tan') *n.* RATTAN.

ratch·et (rach'it) *n.* 1 A mechanism consisting of a notched wheel, the teeth of which engage with a pawl, permitting relative motion in one direction only. 2 The pawl or the wheel thus used. Also **ratchet wheel.** [< Ital. *rochetto* bobbin]

a. ratchet.
b. pawl.

rate[1] (rāt) *n.* 1 The quantity, quality, degree, etc., of a thing in relation to units of something else: a typing *rate* of 50 words per minute. 2 A price or value, esp. the unit cost of a commodity or service: the *rate* for electricity. 3 Rank or class: to be of the first *rate.* 4 A fixed ratio: the *rate* of exchange. 5 *Brit.* A local tax on property. —**at any rate** In any case; anyhow. —*v.* rat·ed, rat·ing *v.t.* 1 To estimate the value or worth of; appraise. 2 To place in a certain rank or grade. 3 To consider; regard: He is *rated* as a great statesman. 4 To fix the rate for the transportation of (goods), as by rail, water, or air. —*v.i.* 5 To have rank, rating, or value. [<L *ratus*, pp. of *reri* reckon] —**rat'er** *n.*

rate[2] (rāt) *v.t. & v.i.* rat·ed, rat·ing To reprove with vehemence; scold.[?]

rath·er (rath'ər, rä'thər) *adv.* 1 More willingly; preferably. 2 With more reason, justice, wisdom, etc.: We, *rather* than they, should leave first. 3 More accurately or precisely: my teacher, or *rather* my friend. 4 Somewhat; to a certain extent: *rather* tired. 5 On the contrary. —*interj. Chiefly Brit.* (ra'thûr', rä'-) Most assuredly; absolutely. [<OE *hrathor* sooner]

raths·kel·ler (rath'skel·ər, räts'kel·ər) *n.* A beer hall or restaurant, often located below the street level. [<G *Rat* town hall + *Keller* cellar]

rat·i·fy (rat'ə·fī) *v.t.* ·fied, ·fy·ing To give sanction to, esp. official sanction. [<L *ratus* fixed, reckoned + *facere* make] —**rat'i·fi·ca'tion, rat'i·fi'er** *n.* —**Syn.** confirm, approve, endorse, validate.

rat·ing (rā'ting) *n.* 1 A classification or evaluation based on a standard; grade; rank. 2 An evaluation of the financial standing of a business firm or an individual. 3 A classification of men in the armed services based on their specialties. 4 In radio and television, the popularity of a program as determined by polling public opinion. 5 Any of several classifications given a motion picture regarding the content or treatment of its subject matter.

ra·tio (rā'shō, -shē·ō) *n. pl.* ·tios 1 Relation of degree, number, etc., between two similar things; proportion; rate. 2 A fraction or indicated quotient, esp. one used to compare the magnitudes of numbers. [L, computation<*reri* think]

ra·ti·oc·i·nate (rash'ē·ōs'ə·nāt, -os'-, rat'ē-) *v.i.* ·nat·ed, ·nat·ing To make a deduction from premises; reason. [<L *ratiocinari* calculate, deliberate] —**ra'ti·oc'i·na'tion, ra'ti·oc'i·na'tor** *n.* —**ra'ti·oc'i·na'tive** *adj.*

ra·tion (rash'ən, rā'shən) *n.* 1 A portion; share. 2 A fixed allowance or portion of food or provisions, as alloted daily to a soldier, etc. 3 *pl.* Food or provisions, as for an army, expedition, etc. —*v.t.* 1 To issue rations to, as an army. 2 To give out or allot in rations. [<L *ratio* computation]

ra·tion·al (rash'ən·əl) *adj.* 1 Of, pertaining to, or attained by reasoning. 2 Able to reason; mentally sound; sane. 3 Sensible; judicious. 4 *Math.* **a** Of or being a rational number. **b** Denoting an algebraic expression, as $\sqrt{x^2 - y^2}$, containing a radical that can be solved. [<L *ratio* reckoning] —**ra'tion·al'i·ty** (-al'ə·tē) *n.* —**ra'tion·al·ly** *adv.*

ra·tion·ale (rash'ən·al') *n.* 1 A logical basis or reason for something. 2 A rational exposition of principles.

ra·tion·al·ism (rash'ən·əl·iz'əm) *n.* 1 The formation of opinions by relying upon reason alone. 2 *Philos.* The theory that truth and knowledge are attainable through reason alone rather than through experience or sense perception. —**ra'tion·al·ist** *adj., n.* —**ra'tion·al·is'tic** *adj.*

ra·tion·al·ize (rash'ən·əl·īz') *v.* ·ized, ·iz·ing *v.t.* 1 To explain (one's behavior) plausibly without recognizing the actual motives. 2 To explain or treat from a rationalistic point of view. 3 To make rational or reasonable. 4 *Math.*

To solve the radicals of (an expression or equation containing variables). —*v.i.* 5 To think in a rational or rationalistic manner. 6 To rationalize one's behavior. —**ra′tion-al·i·za′tion** (-ə-zā′shən, -ĭ-zā′shən) *n.*

ra·tion·al number A number expressible as a quotient of two integers; a fraction.

rat·ite (rat′ĭt) *adj.* Designating any of various large, flightless birds, as ostriches, kiwis, emus, etc. [< L *ratis* raft, in ref. to lack of a keel on the sternum]

rat·line (rat′lĭn) *n. Naut.* One of the small ropes fastened across the shrouds of a ship, used as a ladder for going aloft or descending. Also **rat′lin** (-lĭn), **rat′ling** (-lĭng). [?]

rat race *Slang* Frantic, usu. competitive activity or strife.

rats·bane (rats′bān′) *n.* Rat poison.

rat·tan (ra-tan′) *n.* 1 The long, tough, flexible stem of various climbing palms, used in wickerwork, etc. 2 Any of these palms. [< Malay *rotan*]

rat·ter (rat′ər) *n.* 1 A dog or cat that catches rats. 2 *Slang* A deserter or traitor.

rat·tle (rat′l) *v.* **·tled, ·tling** *v.i.* 1 To make a series of sharp noises in rapid succession. 2 To move or act with such noises. 3 To talk rapidly and foolishly; chatter. —*v.t.* 4 To cause to rattle. 5 To utter or perform rapidly or noisily. 6 *Informal* To confuse; disconcert. —*n.* 1 A series of short, sharp sounds in rapid succession. 2 A plaything, implement, etc., adapted to produce a rattling noise. 3 The series of jointed horny rings in the tail of a rattlesnake, or one of these. 4 Rapid and noisy talk; chatter. 5 A sound caused by the passage of air through mucus in the throat. [< ME *ratelen*]

rat·tle·brain (rat′l-brān′) *n.* A talkative, flighty person; foolish chatterer. Also **rat′tle·head** (-hed′), **rat′tle·pate** (-pāt′). —**rat′tle-brained′** *adj.*

rat·tler (rat′lər) *n.* 1 RATTLESNAKE. 2 One who or that which rattles.

rat·tle·snake (rat′l·snāk′) *n.* Any of various venomous American snakes with a tail ending in a series of horny rings that rattle when the tail is vibrated.

rat·tle·trap (rat′l·trap′) *n.* Any rickety, clattering, or worn-out vehicle or article.

rat·ty (rat′ē) *adj.* **·ti·er, ·ti·est** 1 Ratlike, or abounding in rats. 2 *Slang* Disreputable; treacherous. 3 *Slang* Rundown; shabby. —**rat′ti·ness** *n.*

rau·cous (rô′kəs) *adj.* 1 Rough in sound; hoarse; harsh. 2 Noisy and rowdy. [< L *raucus*] —**rau′cous·ly** *adv.* —**rau′cous·ness** *n.*

raunch·y (rôn′chē, rän′-) *adj. Slang* **raunch·i·er, raunch·i·est** 1 Sloppy; slovenly. 2 Sexually vulgar; lewd. 3 Lustful. [?] —**raunch′i·ly** *adv.* —**raunch′i·ness** *n.*

rav·age (rav′ij) *v.* **·aged, ·ag·ing** *v.t.* 1 To lay waste, as by pillaging or burning; despoil; ruin. 2 To wreak havoc; be destructive. —*n.* Violent and destructive action, or its result; ruin. [< F *ravir* ravish] —**rav′ag·er** *n.*

rave (rāv) *v.* **raved, rav·ing** *v.i.* 1 To speak wildly or incoherently. 2 To speak with extravagant enthusiasm. 3 To make a wild, roaring sound; rage. —*v.t.* 4 To utter wildly or incoherently. —*n.* 1 The act or state of raving. 2 *Informal* A highly favorable review. —*adj. Informal* Extravagantly enthusiastic: *rave* reviews. [< L *rabere* to rage] —**Syn.** 1 babble, rant, gibber.

rav·el (rav′əl) *v.* **·eled** or **·elled, ·el·ing** or **·el·ling** *v.t.* 1 To separate the threads or fibers of; unravel. 2 To make clear or plain; explain: often with *out.* —*v.i.* 3 To become separated, as threads or fibers; unravel; fray. —*n.* A raveled part or thread; a raveling. [? < MDu. *ravelen* to tangle] —**rav′el·er** or **rav′el·ler** *n.*

rav·el·ing (rav′əl·ĭng) *n.* A thread or threads raveled from a fabric. Also **rav′el·ling.**

ra·ven (rā′vən) *n.* A large, crowlike bird. —*adj.* Black and shining. [< OE *hræfn*]

rav·en·ing (rav′ən·ĭng) *adj.* 1 Seeking eagerly for prey; rapacious. 2 Mad. [< OF *raviner* ravage]

rav·en·ous (rav′ən·əs) *adj.* 1 Violently hungry; voracious. 2 Extremely eager; greedy; grasping: *ravenous* for praise. [< OF *ravine* rapine] —**rav′en·ous·ly** *adv.* —**rav′en·ous·ness** *n.*

Raven

ra·vine (rə-vēn′) *n.* A deep gorge or gully, esp. one worn by a flow of water. [F, small gully or torrent]

rav·ing (rā′vĭng) *adj.* 1 Furious; delirious; frenzied. 2 *Informal* Extraordinary; remarkable: a *raving* beauty. —*n.* Frenzied or irrational speech.

ra·vi·o·li (rä·vyō′lē, rä′vē·ō′lē, rav′ē-) *n.pl.* (*usu. construed as sing.*) Little envelopes of dough encasing meat, cheese, etc., which are boiled in broth and sauced. [Ital.]

rav·ish (rav′ish) *v.t.* 1 To fill with strong emotion, esp. delight; enrapture. 2 To rape. 3 To carry off by force. [< L *rapere* seize] —**rav′ish·er, rav′ish·ment** *n.*

rav·ish·ing (rav′ish·ĭng) *adj.* Very attractive, pleasing, etc. —**rav′ish·ing·ly** *adv.*

raw (rô) *adj.* 1 Not changed or prepared by cooking; uncooked. 2 In its original state or condition; not refined, processed, etc.: *raw* wool; *raw* sugar. 3 Having the skin torn or abraded: a *raw* wound. 4 Bleak; chilling: a *raw* wind. 5 Newly done; fresh: *raw* paint; *raw* work. 6 Inexperienced; undisciplined: a *raw* recruit. 7 Vulgar; off-color: a *raw* joke. 8 *Informal* Brutally harsh or unfair: a *raw* deal. —*n.* A sore or abraded spot. —**in the raw** 1 In a raw, unspoiled, or unrefined state. 2 *Informal* Nude. [< OE *hrēaw*] —**raw′ly** *adv.* —**raw′ness** *n.*

raw-boned (rô′bōnd′) *adj.* Bony; gaunt.

raw·hide (rô′hīd′) *n.* 1 An untanned cattle hide. 2 A whip made of such hide.

ray¹ (rā) *n.* 1 A narrow beam of light. 2 Any of several lines radiating from an object. 3 *Geom.* A straight line emerging from a point and extending in one direction only. 4 A slight amount or indication: a *ray* of hope. 5 *Zool.* a A supporting spine of a fish's fin. b Any of numerous parts radiating from a common center, as the arms of a starfish. 6 *Bot.* a RAY FLOWER. b One of the flower stalks of an umbel. 7 *Physics* A stream of particles or waves. —*v.i.* 1 To emit rays; shine. 2 To radiate. —*v.t.* 3 To send forth as rays. 4 To mark with rays or radiating lines. [< L *radius*]

ray² (rā) *n.* Any of an order of marine fishes having a cartilaginous skeleton and a horizontally flattened body, dorsally placed eyes, and a thin, usu. long tail. [< L *raia*]

ray flower *Bot.* Any of the straplike flowers encircling certain composite flower heads, as in the daisy or sunflower. Also **ray floret.**

Ray

ray·on (rā′on) *n.* 1 A synthetic fiber made from a cellulose solution that is forced through spinnerets to produce solidified filaments. 2 A fabric made from these fibers. [F, ray; in ref. to its sheen]

raze (rāz) *v.t.* **razed, raz·ing** 1 To tear down; demolish. 2 To scrape or shave off. [< L *rasum,* pp. of *radere* scrape]

ra·zor (rā′zər) *n.* A sharp cutting implement used for shaving off the beard or hair. [< OF *raser* to scrape]

ra·zor·back (rā′zər·bak′) *n.* 1 FINBACK WHALE. 2 A lean half-wild hog of SE U.S. 3 A sharp ridge. —**ra′zor·backed′** *adj.*

razz (raz) *n. Slang* BRONX CHEER. —*v.t.* To heckle; deride. [< RASPBERRY]

raz·zle-daz·zle (raz′əl·daz′əl) *n. Slang* Any bewildering, exciting, or dazzling activity or performance. [Varied reduplication of DAZZLE]

Rb rubidium.

RBI, rbi, r.b.i. run(s) batted in.

R.C. Red Cross; Roman Catholic.

RCAF, R.C.A.F. Royal Canadian Air Force.
RCMP, R.C.M.P. Royal Canadian Mounted Police.
RCN, R.C.N. Royal Canadian Navy.
RCP, R.C.P. Royal College of Physicians.
RCS, R.C.S. Royal College of Surgeons
R.D. Rural Delivery.
R & D, R. & D., R and D research and development.
re¹ (rā) *n. Music* In solmization, the second tone of a diatonic scale. [< L *re(sonare)* resound. See GAMUT.]
re² (rē, rā) *prep.* Concerning; about; in the matter of: used in business letters, etc. [L, ablative of *res* thing]
re- *prefix* **1** Back: *remit* (to send back). **2** Again; anew; again and again: *regenerate.* [< L *re-, red-* back, again] • In the list of words below, *re-* is used solely to mean *again, anew, again and again.* These words are for the most part written solid. A hyphen, however, is sometimes used: **a** To prevent confusion with a similarly spelled word having a different meaning, as in *retreat* (to go back) and *re-treat* (to treat again). **b** In the formation of nonce words, as in "We *reread* the contract and then *re-reread* it." Formerly, a hyphen was the rule before words beginning with *e*, as *re-edit*, but such words are now often written solid.

reabsorb	recharter	redraw
reabsorption	recheck	redrive
reaccess	rechoose	reecho
reaccommodate	rechristen	reedit
reaccredit	reclose	reelect
reaccuse	reclothe	reelection
readapt	recoin	reelevate
readdict	recoinage	reembark
readdress	recolonize	reembarkation
readjourn	recolor	reemerge
readjournment	recombination	reemergence
readjust	recombine	reemit
readjustment	recommence	reemphasize
readopt	recommission	reenact
readorn	recompose	reenaction
readvance	recompute	reenactment
readvertise	reconcentrate	reencourage
reaffirm	recondensation	reencouragement
realign	recondense	reendow
realignment	reconfirm	reengage
reanoint	reconjoin	reengagement
reappear	reconquer	reengrave
reappearance	reconquest	reenjoy
reapply	reconsecrate	reenjoyment
reappoint	reconsecration	reenlist
reappointment	reconsign	reenlistment
reapportion	reconsolidate	reenslave
reapportionment	reconsolidation	reenslavement
reargue	reconvene	reenter
reargument	reconvey	reenthrone
rearrest	recopy	reenthronement
reascend	recross	reentrance
reascension	recrystallization	reequip
reascent	recrystallize	reestablish
reassemblage	recultivate	reestablishment
reassemble	recultivation	reevaluate
reassert	redecorate	reevaluation
reassertion	rededicate	reexamination
reassign	rededication	reexamine
reassignment	redefine	reexchange
reassimilate	redeliberate	reexhibit
reassimilation	redeliver	reexpel
reassociate	redemand	reexperience
reattach	redemonstrate	reexport
reattachment	redeposit	reexportation
reattempt	redescend	reexpulsion
reavow	redescent	reface
reawake	redesign	refashion
reawakening	redesignate	refasten
rebaptism	redetermine	refertilize
rebaptize	redial	refind
rebid	redigest	reflavor
rebill	redirect	reflight
rebind	rediscover	reflorescence
rebloom	rediscovery	reflourish
reblossom	redispose	reflow
reboil	redissolve	reflower
reborn	redistill	refluctuation
rebottle	redistribute	refold
rebuild	redistribution	reformulate
recalibrate	redivide	refortification
recapitalize	redo	refortify
recharge	redraft	refreeze

refuel	reload	resegregate
refurbish	reloan	reseize
refurnish	relocate	reseizure
regalvanize	relocation	resell
regather	reman	resensitize
regerminate	remarriage	reseparate
regermination	remarry	re-serve
regild	remast	reset
regrade	remaster	resettle
regraft	remeasure	resettlement
regrant	remelt	reshape
regroup	remigrate	resharpen
rehandle	remigration	reshoot
rehang	remilitarize	reshuffle
rehearing	remix	re-sign
reheat	remold	resite
reheel	rename	resolder
rehire	renationalize	resole
rehybridize	renavigate	re-solve
rehydrate	renegotiate	re-sound
reimplant	renominate	resow
reimport	renomination	respeak
reimportation	renumber	respell
reimpose	renumerate	restart
reimposition	reobtain	restock
reimpress	reoccupation	restoke
reimprison	reoccupy	re-store
reinaugurate	reopen	restrengthen
reincorporate	reoppose	restress
reincur	reordain	restrike
reinduce	reorder	resubject
reinfect	reordination	resubjection
reinfection	reorient	resubjugate
reinflame	reorientation	resubmit
reinform	reossify	resummon
reinfuse	repacify	resummons
reingratiate	repack	resupply
reinhabit	repackage	resurprise
reinjure	repaint	resurvey
reinoculate	repartition	retake
reinoculation	repass	retarget
reinscribe	repassage	retell
reinsert	repeople	retool
reinsertion	rephrase	retrace
reinspect	replant	retrain
reinspection	replantation	re-treat
reinspire	replaster	retrial
reinstall	repledge	retrim
reinstruct	replunge	retry
reinsure	repolish	retune
reintegrate	repoll	re-turn
reintegration	repopulate	reunification
reinter	repopulation	reunify
reinterment	repossess	reurge
reintroduce	repour	reuse
reintroduction	re-press	reutilize
reinvest	reprocess	reutter
reinvestigate	reprogram	revaccinate
reinvestment	repropose	revaccination
reinvigorate	re-prove	revaluation
reinvigoration	republish	revalue
reinvitation	repurchase	revarnish
reinvite	repurify	revest
reinvolve	reread	re-view
reinvolvement	re-record	revindication
reissue	re-refer	revisit
rekindle	re-release	reweave
reknit	resail	reweigh
reland	resale	rewin
relaunch	resalute	rewind
relet	re-search	rewire
reliquidate	reseat	reword
reliquidation	reschool	rework

Re rhenium.

reach (rēch) *v.t.* **1** To stretch out or forth, as the hand. **2** To present or deliver; hand over. **3** To touch, grasp, or extend as far as: Can you *reach* the top shelf? **4** To arrive at or come to by motion or progress. **5** To achieve communication with; gain access to. **6** To amount to; total. **7** To have an influence on; affect. —*v.i.* **8** To stretch the hand, foot, etc., out or forth. **9** To attempt to touch or obtain something: He *reached* for his wallet. **10** To have extent in space, time, amount, influence, etc.: The ladder *reached* to the ceiling. **11** *Naut.* To sail on a tack with the wind on or forward of the beam. —*n.* **1** The act or power of reaching. **2** The distance one is able to reach, as with the hand, an instrument, or missile. **3** An extent or result attained by thought, influence, etc.; scope; range. **4** An unbroken stretch, as of a stream; a vista or expanse. **5** *Naut.* The sailing, or the distance sailed, by a vessel on one tack. [< OE *ræcan*] —**reach'er** *n.*

re·act (rē·akt') *v.i.* **1** To act in response, as to a stimulus. **2** To act in a manner contrary to some preceding act. **3** To be affected by a circumstance, influence, act, etc. **4** *Chem.* To undergo chemical change.

re·act (rē'akt') *v.t.* To act again.

re·ac·tance (rē·ak'təns) *n. Electr.* The component of impedance that results from the presence of capacitance or inductance.

re·ac·tion (rē·ak'shən) *n.* **1** Any response, as to a stimulus, event, influence, etc. **2** A trend or tendency toward a former state of things; esp., a trend toward an earlier, usu. outmoded social, political, or economic policy or condition. **3** Any change in an organism effected by an agent, as a drug, food, allergen, etc., or an environmental condition, as heat, cold, etc. **4** *Physics* The force exerted on an agent by the body acted upon. **5** Any process involving a change in the composition or structure of an atomic nucleus, as fission, fusion, or radioactive decay. **6** *Chem.* A molecular change undergone by two or more substances in contact. —**re·ac'tion·al** *adj.* —**re·ac'tion·al·ly** *adv.*

re·ac·tion·ar·y (rē·ak'shən·er'ē) *adj.* Of, relating to, favoring, or characterized by reaction (def. 2). —*n. pl.* **·ar·ies** One who generally opposes change or liberalism in political or social matters. Also **re·ac'tion·ist.**

re·ac·ti·vate (rē·ak'tə·vāt) *v.t.* **·vat·ed**, **·vat·ing** To make active or effective again. —**re·ac'ti·va'tion** *n.*

re·ac·tive (rē·ak'tiv) *adj.* **1** Tending to react, or resulting from reaction. **2** Responsive to a stimulus. —**re·ac'tive·ly** *adv.* —**re·ac'tiv'i·ty, re·ac'tive·ness** *n.*

re·ac·tor (rē·ak'tər) *n.* **1** One who or that which reacts. **2** An assembly of fissionable material, moderator, coolant, shielding, and other accessories, designed to control and utilize the energy released by atomic fission.

read (rēd) *v.* **read** (red), **read·ing** (rē'ding) *v.t.* **1** To apprehend the meaning of (a book, writing, etc.) by perceiving the form and relation of the printed or written characters. **2** To utter aloud (something printed or written). **3** To understand the significance of as if by reading: to *read* the sky. **4** To apprehend the meaning of something printed or written in (a foreign language). **5** To make a study of: to *read* law. **6** To discover the nature or significance of (a person, character, etc.) by observation or scrutiny. **7** To interpret (something read) in a specified manner. **8** To take as the meaning of something read. **9** To have or exhibit as the wording: The passage *reads* "principal," not "principle." **10** To indicate or register: The meter *reads* zero. **11** To extract (data) from storage: said of a computer or other information-retrieval system. **12** To bring into a specified condition by reading: I *read* her to sleep. —*v.i.* **13** To apprehend the characters of a book, musical score, etc. **14** To utter aloud the words or contents of a book, etc. **15** To gain information by reading: with *of* or *about.* **16** To learn by means of books; study. **17** To have a specified wording: The contract *reads* as follows. **18** To admit of being read in a specified manner. **19** To give a public reading or recital. —**read between the lines** To perceive or infer what is not expressed or obvious. —**read into** To discern (implicit meanings or implications) in a statement or position. —**read out** To expel from a religious body, political party, etc., by proclamation or concerted action. —**read up** (or **up on**) To learn by reading. —*adj.* (red) Informed by or acquainted with books or literature: *well-read.* [< OE *rædan* advise, read]

read·a·ble (rē'də·bəl) *adj.* **1** That can be read; legible. **2** Easy and pleasant to read. **3** MACHINE-READABLE. —**read'a·bil'i·ty, read'a·ble·ness** *n.* —**read'a·bly** *adv.*

read·er (rē'dər) *n.* **1** One who reads. **2** Any of various devices that provide readable images, as by projection on a screen, of material or microfilm, microcards, etc. **3** One who reads and criticizes manuscripts offered to publishers. **4** PROOFREADER. **5** A layman authorized to read the lesson in church services. **6** A professional reciter. **7** A textbook containing matter for exercises in reading.

read·ing (rē'ding) *n.* **1** The act or practice of one who reads. **2** The public recital of literary works. **3** Matter that is read or is designed to be read. **4** The datum indicated by an instrument, as a thermometer. **5** The form in which any passage or word appears in any copy of a work. **6** An interpretation, as of a musical composition. —*adj.* **1** Pertaining to or suitable for reading. **2** Inclined to read.

read·out (rēd'out') *n.* **1** A display in intelligible form of specific items of information derived from data that have been recorded automatically or processed by computer. **2** The information so displayed.

read·y (red'ē) *adj.* **read·i·er, read·i·est** **1** Prepared for use or action. **2** Prepared in mind; willing. **3** Likely or liable: with *to*: *ready* to sink. **4** Quick to act, follow, occur, or appear; prompt. **5** Immediately available; convenient; handy. **6** Designating the standard position in which a rifle is held just before aiming. **7** Quick to understand; alert; quick; facile: a *ready* wit. —*n.* The position in which a rifle is held before aiming. —*v.t.* **read·ied, read·y·ing** To make ready; prepare. [< OE *ræde, geræde*] —**read'i·ly** *adv.* —**read'i·ness** *n.*

read·y-made (red'ē·mād') *adj.* **1** Not made to order: *ready-made* clothing. **2** Not impromptu or original: *ready-made* opinions.

re·a·gent (rē·ā'jənt) *n.* Any substance used to induce a chemical reaction. [< RE- + AGENT]

re·al¹ (rē'əl, rēl) *adj.* **1** Having existence or actuality as a thing or state; not imaginary: a *real* event. **2** Not artificial or counterfeit; genuine. **3** Representing the true or actual, as opposed to the apparent or ostensible: the *real* reason. **4** Unaffected; unpretentious: a *real* person. **5** *Philos.* Having actual existence, and not merely possible, apparent, or imaginary. **6** *Law* Of or pertaining to things permanent and immovable: *real* property. **7** *Math.* Of or being a real number. —*n.* That which is real. —*adv. Informal* Very; extremely: to be *real* glad. [< Med. L *realis* < L *res* thing] —**re'al·ness** *n.*

re·al² (rē'əl, *Sp.* rā·äl') *n. pl.* **re·als** or **re·a·les** (rā·ä'lās) **1** A former small silver coin of Spain. **2** *pl.* **reis** (rās) A former Portuguese and Brazilian coin; one thousandth of a milreis. [Sp., lit., royal]

real estate Land, including whatever is made part of or attached to it by man or nature, as trees, houses, etc. —**re'al-es·tate'** *adj.*

re·al·ism (rē'əl·iz'əm) *n.* **1** A disposition to deal solely with facts and reality and to reject the impractical or visionary. **2** In literature and art, the principle of depicting persons and scenes as they actually exist, without any idealization. **3** *Philos.* **a** The doctrine that universals or abstract concepts have actual, objective existence. **b** The doctrine that things have reality apart from the conscious perception of them. —**re'al·ist** *adj., n.* —**re'al·is'tic** *adj.* —**re'al·is'ti·cal·ly** *adv.*

re·al·i·ty (rē·al'ə·tē) *n. pl.* **·ties** **1** The fact, state, or quality of being real, genuine, or true to life. **2** That which is real; an actual thing, situation, or event. **3** *Philos.* The absolute or the ultimate.

re·al·ize (rē'əl·īz) *v.* **·ized, ·iz·ing** *v.t.* **1** To understand or appreciate fully. **2** To make real or concrete. **3** To cause to appear real. **4** To obtain as a profit or return. **5** To obtain money in return for: He *realized* his holdings for a profit. —*v.i.* **6** To sell property for cash. —**re'al·iz'a·ble** *adj.* —**re'al·i·za'tion, re'al·iz'er** *n.*

re·al·ly (rē'ə·lē, rē'lē) *adv.* **1** In reality; actually. **2** Truly; genuinely: a *really* fine play. —*interj.* Oh: used to express surprise, doubt, etc.

realm (relm) *n.* **1** A kingdom. **2** Domain; sphere: the *realm* of imagination. [< L *regalis* royal]

real number A number whose square is greater than or equal to zero.

re·al·tor (rē'əl·tər, -tôr) *n.* **1** A person engaged in the real-estate business. **2** *Usu. cap.* A member of the National Association of Real Estate Boards: a trade name.

re·al·ty (rē'əl·tē) *n. pl.* **·ties** REAL ESTATE.

ream[1] (rēm) n. 1 A quantity of paper equal to 20 quires and consisting of 480, 500, or 516 sheets. 2 pl. Informal A prodigious amount. [< Ar. rizmah packet]

ream[2] (rēm) v.t. 1 To increase the size of (a hole), as with a rotating cutter or reamer. 2 To get rid of (a defect) by reaming. [< OE rēman enlarge, make room]

ream·er (rē′mər) n. 1 One who or that which reams. 2 A rotary tool with cutting edges for reaming. 3 A device with a ridged cone for extracting juice from citrus fruits.

Reamers

re·an·i·mate (rē·an′ə·māt) v.t. ·mat·ed, ·mat·ing 1 To bring back to life; resuscitate. 2 To revive; encourage. —re′an·i·ma′tion n.

reap (rēp) v.t. 1 To cut and gather (grain) with a scythe, reaper, etc. 2 To harvest a crop from: to reap a field. 3 To obtain as the result of action or effort. —v.i. 4 To harvest grain, etc. 5 To receive a return or result. [< OE repan] —reap′a·ble adj. —reap′ing n.

reap·er (rē′pər) n. 1 One who reaps. 2 A machine for reaping grain.

rear[1] (rir) n. 1 The back or hind part. 2 A place or position at the back of or behind anything. 3 That division of a military force which is farthest from the front. —adj. Being in the rear. [< ARREAR]

rear[2] (rir) v.t. 1 To place upright; raise. 2 To build; erect. 3 To care for and bring to maturity. 4 To breed or grow. —v.i. 5 To rise upon its hind legs, as a horse. 6 To rise high; tower, as a mountain. [< OE ræran set upright] —rear′er n.

rear admiral See GRADE.

rear guard A body of troops to protect the rear of an army.

re·arm (rē·ärm′) v.t. & v.i. 1 To arm again. 2 To arm with more modern weapons. —re·ar′ma·ment n.

rear·most (rir′mōst′) adj. Coming or stationed last.

re·ar·range (rē′ə·rānj′) v.t. & v.i. ·ranged, ·rang·ing To arrange again or in some new way. —re′ar·range′ment n. — Syn. reorder, redispose, reorganize, readjust.

rear·ward (rir′wərd) adj. Coming last or toward the rear; hindward. —adv. Toward or at the rear; backward: also rear′wards. —n. The rear; end.

rea·son (rē′zən) n. 1 A motive or basis for an action, opinion, etc. 2 A statement which explains or accounts for an action, belief, etc. 3 The ability to think logically and rationally. 4 Sound thinking or judgment; common sense. 5 Sanity. —by reason of Because of. —in (or within) reason Within reasonable limits or bounds. —it stands to reason It is logical. —with reason Justifiably. —v.i. 1 To think logically; obtain inferences or conclusions from known or presumed facts. 2 To talk or argue logically. — v.t. 3 To think out carefully and logically; analyze: with out. 4 To influence or persuade by means of reason. 5 To argue; debate. [< L ratio computation] —rea′son·er n.

rea·son·a·ble (rē′zən·ə·bəl, rēz′nə-) adj. 1 Conformable to reason. 2 Having the faculty of reason; rational. 3 Governed by reason. 4 Not extreme or excessive; moderate. — rea′son·a·bil′i·ty, rea′son·a·ble·ness n. —rea′son·a·bly adv.

rea·son·ing (rē′zən·ing) n. 1 The act or process of using one's rational faculties to draw conclusions from known or assumed facts. 2 The reasons or proofs resulting from this process.

re·as·sure (rē′ə·shŏŏr′) v.t. ·sured, ·sur·ing 1 To restore to courage or confidence. 2 To assure again. 3 To reinsure. — re′as·sur′ance n. —re′as·sur′ing·ly adv.

re·bate (rē′bāt, ri·bāt′) v.t. ·bat·ed, ·bat·ing 1 To allow as a deduction. 2 To make a deduction from. —n. A deduction from a gross amount; discount: also re·bate′·ment. [< OF rabattre beat down] —re′bat·er n.

re·bec (rē′bek) n. A medieval bowed instrument, somewhat like a violin. Also re′beck. [< Ar. rabāb]

Rebec

Re·bec·ca (ri·bek′ə) In the Bible, wife of Isaac and mother of Esau and Jacob.

re·bel (ri·bel′) v.i. ·belled, ·bel·ling 1 To resist or fight against any authority, established custom, etc. 2 To react with violent aversion: usu. with at. —n. (reb′əl) One who rebels. —adj. (reb′əl) 1 Rebellious; refractory. 2 Of rebels. [< L re- again + bellare make war]

re·bel·lion (ri·bel′yən) n. 1 The act of rebelling. 2 Organized resistance to a government or to any lawful authority.

re·bel·lious (ri·bel′yəs) adj. 1 Being in a state of rebellion; insubordinate. 2 Of or pertaining to a rebel or rebellion. 3 Resisting control; refractory: a rebellious temper. —re·bel′lious·ly adv. —re·bel′lious·ness n.

re·birth (rē·bûrth′, rē′bûrth′) n. 1 A new birth. 2 A revival or renaissance.

re·bound (ri·bound′) v.i. 1 To bounce or spring back after or as after hitting something. 2 To recover, as from a difficulty. 3 To reecho. —v.t. 4 To cause to rebound. —n. (rē′bound′, ri·bound′) 1 A bounding back; recoil. 2 Something that rebounds, as a basketball from a backboard. 3 Reaction after a disappointment: to fall in love on the rebound. [< F re- back + bondir bound]

re·broad·cast (rē·brôd′kast′, -käst′) v.t. ·cast or ·cast·ed, ·cast·ing To broadcast (the same program) again. —n. A program so transmitted.

re·buff (ri·buf′) v.t. 1 To reject or refuse abruptly or rudely. 2 To drive or beat back; repel. —n. 1 A sudden repulse; curt denial. 2 A sudden check; defeat. 3 A beating back. [< Ital. ribuffare]

re·buke (ri·byōōk′) v.t. ·buked, ·buk·ing To reprove sharply; reprimand. —n. A strong expression of disapproval. [< OF re- back + bucher beat] —re·buk′er n.

re·bus (rē′bəs) n. A representation of a word, phrase, or sentence by letters, numerals, pictures, etc., whose names suggest the same sounds as the words or phrases they represent. [L, ablative pl. of res thing]

Rebus meaning I can see.

re·but (ri·but′) v.t. ·but·ted, ·but·ting To dispute or show the falsity of, as by argument or by contrary evidence. [< OF re- back + bouter push, strike] —re·but′ter n. —Syn. disprove, refute, contradict.

re·but·tal (ri·but′l) n. The act of rebutting; refutation.

rec. receipt; recipe; record; recording.

re·cal·ci·trant (ri·kal′sə·trənt) adj. Not complying; obstinate; rebellious; refractory. —n. One who is recalcitrant. [< L re- back + calcitrare to kick] —re·cal′ci·trance, re·cal′ci·tran·cy n.

re·call (ri·kôl′) v.t. 1 To call back; order or summon to return. 2 To summon back in awareness or attention. 3 To recollect; remember. 4 To take back; revoke; countermand. —n. (ri·kôl′, rē′kôl′) 1 A calling back. 2 An ability to remember. 3 Revocation, as of an order. 4 A system whereby public officials may be removed from office by popular vote.

re·cant (ri·kant′) v.t. 1 To withdraw formally one's belief in (something previously believed or maintained). —v.i. 2 To disavow an opinion or belief previously held. [< L re- again + cantare sing] —re·can·ta·tion (rē′kan·tā′shən), re·cant′er n.

re·cap[1] (rē′kap′, rē·kap′) v.t. ·capped, ·cap·ping 1 To provide (a worn pneumatic tire) with a tread of new rubber. 2 To replace a cap on. —n. (rē′kap′) A tire which has been so treated. [< RE- + CAP]

re·cap[2] (rē′kap′) v.t. & v.i. ·capped, ·cap·ping RECAPITULATE. —n. RECAPITULATION (def. 2).

re·ca·pit·u·late (rē′kə·pich′ŏŏ·lāt) v.t. & v.i. ·lat·ed, ·lat·ing To restate or review briefly; sum up. [< LL re- again + capitulare draw up in chapters]

re·ca·pit·u·la·tion (rē′kə·pich′ŏŏ·lā′shən) n. 1 The act of recapitulating. 2 A brief summary. —re′ca·pit′u·la′tive, re′ca·pit′u·la·to′ry (-lə·tôr′ē, -tō′rē) adj.

re·cap·ture (rē·kap′chər) v.t. ·tured, ·tur·ing 1 To capture again. 2 To recall; remember. —n. The act of recapturing or the state of being recaptured.

re·cast (rē·kast′, -käst′) v.t. ·cast, ·cast·ing 1 To form anew; cast again. 2 To fashion anew by changing style, arrangement, etc., as a sentence. 3 To calculate anew. — n. (rē′kast′, -käst′) Something which has been recast.

recd. received.

re·cede (ri·sēd′) *v.i.* **·ced·ed, ·ced·ing** **1** To move back; withdraw, as flood waters. **2** To withdraw, as from an assertion, position, agreement, etc. **3** To slope backward: a *receding* forehead. **4** To become more distant or smaller. [< L *re-* back + *cedere* go]

re·cede (rē′sēd′) *v.t.* **·ced·ed, ·ced·ing** To cede back; grant or yield to a former owner.

re·ceipt (ri·sēt′) *n.* **1** The act or state of receiving anything: to be in *receipt* of good news. **2** *Usu. pl.* That which is received: cash *receipts.* **3** A written acknowledgment of the payment of money, of the delivery of goods, etc. **4** RECIPE. —*v.t.* **1** To give a receipt for the payment of. **2** To write acknowledgment of payment on, as a bill. —*v.i.* **3** To give a receipt, as for money paid. [< L *receptus,* pp. of *recipere* take back, receive]

re·ceiv·a·ble (ri·sē′və·bəl) *adj.* **1** Capable of being received; fit to be received, as legal tender. **2** Due to be paid. —*n. pl.* Outstanding accounts listed as business assets.

re·ceive (ri·sēv′) *v.* **·ceived, ·ceiv·ing** *v.t.* **1** To take into one's hand or possession (something given, offered, delivered, etc.). **2** To gain knowledge or information of. **3** To take from another by hearing or listening. **4** To bear; support. **5** To experience; meet with: to *receive* abuse. **6** To undergo; suffer: He *received* a wound in his arm. **7** To contain; hold. **8** To allow entrance to; admit; greet. **9** To perceive mentally: to *receive* a bad impression. **10** To regard in a specified way: The play was well *received.* —*v.i.* **11** To be a recipient. **12** To welcome visitors or callers. **13** *Telecom.* To convert incoming signals, as radio waves, into intelligible sounds or shapes, as in a radio or television set. [< L *re-* back + *capere* take]

re·ceived (ri·sēvd′) *adj. Chiefly Brit.* Accepted by established opinion or authority; standard.

re·ceiv·er (ri·sē′vər) *n.* **1** One who receives; a recipient. **2** An official assigned to receive money due. **3** *Law* A person appointed by a court to take into his custody the property or funds of another pending litigation. **4** One who knowingly buys or receives stolen goods. **5** Something which receives; a receptacle. **6** *Telecom.* An instrument designed to receive electric or electromagnetic signals and process them or transmit them to another stage.

re·ceiv·er·ship (ri·sē′vər·ship) *n.* **1** The office and functions pertaining to a receiver. **2** *Law* The state of being in the hands of a receiver.

re·cent (rē′sənt) *adj.* **1** Of or pertaining to a time not long past. **2** Occurring, formed, or characterized by association with a time not long past; modern; fresh; new. [< L *recens*] —**re′cent·ly** *adv.* —**re′cen·cy, re′cent·ness** *n.*

Re·cent (rē′sənt) *adj. & n.* See GEOLOGY.

re·cep·ta·cle (ri·sep′tə·kəl) *n.* **1** Anything that serves to contain or hold other things. **2** *Bot.* The base on which the parts of a flower grow. **3** An electric outlet. [< L *receptare,* freq. of *recipere* receive]

re·cep·tion (ri·sep′shən) *n.* **1** The act of receiving, or the state of being received. **2** A formal social entertainment of guests: a wedding *reception.* **3** The manner of receiving a person or persons: a warm *reception.* **4** *Telecom.* The act or process of receiving or, esp., the quality of reproduction achieved: poor radio *reception.*

re·cep·tion·ist (ri·sep′shən·ist) *n.* A person employed to receive callers, etc., as in a place of business.

re·cep·tive (ri·sep′tiv) *adj.* **1** Able or inclined to receive favorably; *receptive* to new ideas. **2** Able to contain or hold. —**re·cep′tive·ly** *adv.* —**re·cep·tiv·i·ty** (rē′sep·tiv′ə·tē), **re·cep′tive·ness** *n.*

re·cep·tor (ri·sep′tər) *n.* A sensory nerve ending adapted to receiving stimuli. [L, receiver]

re·cess (rē′ses, ri·ses′) *n.* **1** A depression or indentation in any otherwise continuous line or surface, esp. in a wall; niche. **2** A time of cessation from employment or occupation. **3** *Usu. pl.* A quiet and secluded spot; withdrawn or inner place: the *recesses* of the mind. —*v.* (*usu.* ri·ses′) *v.t.* **1** To place in or as in a recess. **2** To make a recess in. **3** To interrupt for a recess. —*v.i.* **4** To take a recess. [< L *recessus,* pp. of *recedere* go back]

re·ces·sion (ri·sesh′ən) *n.* **1** The act of receding; a withdrawal. **2** The procession of the clergy, choir, etc., as they leave the chancel after a church service. **3** A temporary economic setback occurring during a period of generally rising prosperity.

re·ces·sion (rē′sesh′ən) *n.* The act of ceding back, as to a former owner.

re·ces·sion·al (ri·sesh′ən·əl) *adj.* Of or pertaining to recession. —*n.* A hymn sung as the choir or clergy leave the chancel.

re·ces·sive (ri·ses′iv) *adj.* **1** Having a tendency to recede or go back. **2** *Genetics* Designating a hereditary factor that remains latent unless it is present in both members of a pair of chromosomes. —*n. Genetics* **1** A recessive factor or trait. **2** An organism having such factors or traits. —**re·ces′sive·ly** *adv.* —**re·ces′sive·ness** *n.*

re·cher·ché (rə·sher·shā′) *adj.* **1** Much sought after; choice; rare. **2** Elegant or refined, usu. to an excessive degree. [F]

re·cid·i·vism (rə·sid′ə·viz′əm) *n.* A tendency to relapse into a former state or condition, esp. into crime. [< L *recidivus* falling back] —**re·cid′i·vist** *adj., n.* —**re·cid′i·vis′tic, re·cid′i·vous** *adj.*

rec·i·pe (res′ə·pē) *n.* **1** A list of ingredients and directions for combining them, as in cooking, pharmacy, etc. **2** The means prescribed for attaining an end. [< L, imperative of *recipere* take]

re·cip·i·ent (ri·sip′ē·ənt) *adj.* Receiving or ready to receive; receptive. —*n.* One who or that which receives. —**re·cip′i·ence, re·cip′i·en·cy** *n.*

re·cip·ro·cal (ri·sip′rə·kəl) *adj.* **1** Done or given by each of two to the other; mutual. **2** Mutually interchangeable. **3** Related or corresponding, but in an inverse manner; opposite. **4** *Gram.* Expressive of mutual relationship or action: *One another* is a *reciprocal* phrase. **5** *Math.* Having a product of 1, as a pair of numbers. —*n.* **1** That which is reciprocal. **2** *Math.* Either of a pair of numbers having 1 as their product. [< L *reciprocus*] —**re·cip′ro·cal·ly** *adv.*

re·cip·ro·cate (ri·sip′rə·kāt) *v.* **·cat·ed, ·cat·ing** *v.t.* **1** To cause to move backward and forward alternately. **2** To give and receive mutually; interchange. **3** To give, feel, do, etc., in return. —*v.i.* **4** To move backward and forward. **5** To make a return in kind. **6** To give and receive favors, gifts, etc., mutually. [< L *reciprocare* move to and fro] —**re·cip′ro·ca′tion, re·cip′ro·ca′tor** *n.* —**re·cip′ro·ca′tive, re·cip′ro·ca·to′ry** (-kə·tôr′ē, -kə·tō′rē) *adj.*

rec·i·proc·i·ty (res′ə·pros′ə·tē) *n.* **1** Reciprocal obligation, action, or relation. **2** A trade relation between two countries by which each makes concessions favoring the importation of the products of the other.

re·cit·al (ri·sīt′l) *n.* **1** A retelling in detail of an event, etc.; a narration; also, that which is retold. **2** A public delivery of something memorized. **3** A musical or dance program by a single performer or by a small group.

rec·i·ta·tion (res′ə·tā′shən) *n.* **1** The act of publicly reciting something that has been memorized. **2** That which is recited. **3** The reciting of a lesson in school or the time during a class when this takes place.

rec·i·ta·tive (res′ə·tə·tēv′, rə·sit′ə·tiv) *n. Music* **1** A style of singing that approaches ordinary speech in its rhythms and lack of melodic variation, used in opera and oratorio. **2** A passage so sung. Also *Italian* **re·ci·ta·ti·vo** (rā′chē·tä·tē′vō) —*adj.* Having the character of a recitative. [< Ital. *recitativo*]

re·cite (ri·sīt′) *v.* **·cit·ed, ·cit·ing** *v.t.* **1** To declaim or say from memory, esp. formally, as in public or in a class. **2** To tell in particular detail; relate. **3** To enumerate. —*v.i.* **4** To declaim or speak something from memory. **5** To repeat or be examined in a lesson or part of a lesson in class. [< L *re-* again + *citare* cite] —**re·cit′er** *n.*

reck (rek) *v.t. & v.i. Archaic* **1** To heed; mind. **2** To be of concern or interest (to). [< OE *reccan*]

reck·less (rek′lis) *adj.* **1** Foolishly heedless of danger; rash. **2** Careless; irresponsible. [< OE *receléas*] —**reck′less·ly** *adv.* —**reck′less·ness** *n.*

reck·on (rek′ən) *v.t.* **1** To count; compute; calculate. **2** To

---

add, āce, câre, pälm; end, ēven; it, īce; odd, ōpen, ôrder; tōōk, pōōl; up, bûrn; ə = a in *above, u* in *focus;* yōō = u in *fuse;* oil; pout; check; go; ring; thin; this; zh, *vision.* < derived from; ? origin uncertain or unknown.

look upon as being; regard. **3** *Regional* To suppose or guess; expect. —*v.i.* **4** To make computation; count up. **5** To rely or depend: with *on* or *upon.* —**reckon with 1** To settle accounts with. **2** To take into consideration; consider. [< OE *recenian* explain] —**reck'on·er** *n.*

reck·on·ing (rek'ən·ing) *n.* **1** The act of counting; computation. **2** A settlement of accounts. **3** Account; bill, as at a hotel. **4** An appraisal or estimate. **5** *Naut.* The calculation of a ship's position.

re·claim (ri·klām') *v.t.* **1** To bring (a swamp, desert, etc.) into a condition to support cultivation or life, as by draining or irrigating. **2** To obtain (a substance) from used or waste products. **3** To cause to reform. —*n.* The act of reclaiming or state of being reclaimed. [< L *re-* against + *clamare* cry out] —**re·claim'a·ble** *adj.* —**re·claim'er, re·claim'ant** *n.*

re·claim (rē'klām') *v.t.* To claim again.

rec·la·ma·tion (rek'lə·mā'shən) *n.* **1** The act of reclaiming. **2** Restoration, as to ownership, usefulness, etc.

re·cline (ri·klīn') *v.t. & v.i.* ·clined, ·clin·ing To assume or cause to assume a recumbent position; lie or lay down or back. [< L *re-* back + *clinare* lean] —**rec·li·na·tion** (rek'lə·nā'shən) *n.*, **re·clin'er** *n.*

rec·luse (rek'lōōs, ri·klōōs') *n.* One who lives in solitude and seclusion; hermit. —*adj.* Secluded or retired from the world. [< L *recludere* shut off] —**re·clu'sion** *n.* —**re·clu'sive** *adj.*

rec·og·ni·tion (rek'əg·nish'ən) *n.* **1** The act of recognizing or the condition of being recognized. **2** Special notice or acknowledgment; attention: His work has received much *recognition.* **3** Acknowledgment and acceptance on the part of one government of the independence and validity of another. —**re·cog·ni·to·ry** (ri·kog'nə·tôr'ē, -tō'rē), **re·cog'ni·tive** *adj.*

re·cog·ni·zance (ri·kog'nə·zəns, -kon'ə-) *n.* *Law* **1** An acknowledgment or obligation of record, with condition to do some particular act, as to appear and answer. **2** A sum of money deposited as surety for fulfillment of such act or obligation, and forfeited by its nonperformance. [< L *recognoscere* call to mind] —**re·cog'ni·zant** *adj.*

rec·og·nize (rek'əg·nīz') *v.t.* ·nized, ·niz·ing **1** To perceive as identical with someone or something previously known. **2** To identify or know, as by previous experience or knowledge: I *recognize* the symptoms. **3** To perceive as true; realize: I *recognize* my error. **4** To acknowledge the independence and validity of, as a newly constituted government. **5** To indicate appreciation or approval of. **6** To regard as valid or genuine: to *recognize* a claim. **7** To give (someone) permission to speak, as in a legislative body. **8** To admit the acquaintance of; greet. [Back formation < RECOGNIZANCE] —**rec·og·niz·a·ble** (rek'əg·nīz'ə·bəl) *adj.* —**rec'og·niz·a·bly** *adv.* —**rec'og·niz'er** *n.* —Syn. **3** acknowledge, admit, allow.

re·coil (ri·koil') *v.i.* **1** To start back, as in fear or loathing; shrink. **2** To spring back, as from force of discharge or impact. **3** To return to the source; react: with *on* or *upon.* **4** To move; retreat. —*n.* (rē'koil') **1** A backward movement or impulse, as of a gun at the moment of firing. **2** A shrinking. [< OF *reculer*] —**re·coil'er** *n.*

re·coil (rē'koil') *v.t. & v.i.* To coil again.

rec·ol·lect (rek'ə·lekt') *v.t.* **1** To call back to the mind; remember. —*v.i.* **2** To have a recollection of something. [< L *recollectus,* pp. of *recolligere* gather together again]

re·col·lect (rē'kə·lekt') *v.t.* **1** To collect again, as things scattered. **2** To collect or recover (one's thoughts, strength, etc.). **3** To compose (oneself). Also, for defs. 2 & 3, **rec·ol·lect** (rek'ə·lekt'). —**re'·col·lec'tion** *n.*

rec·ol·lec·tion (rek'ə·lek'shən) *n.* **1** The act or power of recollecting. **2** Something remembered. —**rec'ol·lec'tive** *adj.* —**rec'ol·lec'tive·ly** *adv.* —**rec'ol·lec'tive·ness** *n.*

rec·om·mend (rek'ə·mend') *v.t.* **1** To commend or praise as desirable, worthy, etc. **2** To make attractive or acceptable. **3** To advise; urge. **4** To give in charge; commend. —**rec'om·mend'a·ble, rec'om·men·da·to·ry** (-də·tôr'ē, -tōr'ē) *adj.* —**rec'om·mend'er** *n.*

rec·om·men·da·tion (rek'ə·mən·dā'shən, -men-) *n.* **1** The act of recommending. **2** Something that recommends, as a letter or statement.

re·com·mit (rē'kə·mit') *v.t.* ·mit·ted, ·mit·ting **1** To commit

again. **2** To refer back to a committee, as a bill. —**re'com·mit'ment, re'com·mit'tal** *n.*

rec·om·pense (rek'əm·pens) *v.t.* ·pensed, ·pens·ing **1** To give compensation to; pay or repay; reward. **2** To give compensation for, as a loss. —*n.* An equivalent for anything given, done, or suffered; payment; compensation; reward. [< L *re-* again + *compensare* compensate]

rec·on·cil·a·ble (rek'ən·sī'lə·bəl, rek'ən·sī'-) *adj.* Capable of being reconciled, adjusted, or harmonized. —**rec'on·cil'a·bil'i·ty, rec'on·cil'a·ble·ness** *n.* —**rec'on·cil'a·bly** *adv.*

rec·on·cile (rek'ən·sīl) *v.t.* ·ciled, ·cil·ing **1** To bring back to friendship after estrangement. **2** To settle or adjust, as a quarrel. **3** To bring to acquiescence, content, or submission. **4** To make or show to be consistent or congruous; harmonize. [< L *re-* again + *conciliare* unite] —**rec'on·cile'ment, rec'on·cil'er, rec·on·cil·i·a·tion** (rek'ən·sil'ē·ā'-shən) *n.* —**rec'on·cil'i·a·to·ry** (-sil'ē·ə·tôr'ē, -tō'rē) *adj.*

rec·on·dite (rek'ən·dīt, ri·kon'dīt) *adj.* **1** Beyond ordinary or easy understanding or perception; abstruse. **2** Dealing in difficult matters. **3** Hidden; obscure. [< L *recondere* put away, hide] —**rec'on·dite'ly** *adv.* —**rec'on·dite'-ness** *n.*

re·con·di·tion (rē'kən·dish'ən) *v.t.* To put back into good or working condition, as by making repairs.

re·con·nais·sance (ri·kon'ə·səns, -säns) *n.* **1** An exploratory examination or survey, as of territory. **2** *Mil.* The act of obtaining information regarding the position, strength, and movement of enemy forces. [F]

re·con·noi·ter (rē'kə·noi'tər, rek'ə-) *v.t.* **1** To examine or survey, as for military, engineering, or geological purposes. —*v.i.* **2** To make a reconnaissance. *Brit. sp.* ·**noi'tre.** [< OF *reconoistre*] —**re'con·noi'ter·er, re'con·noi'trer** *n.*

re·con·sid·er (rē'kən·sid'ər) *v.t. & v.i.* To consider again, esp. with a view to a reversal of a previous action. —**re'·con·sid'er·a'tion** *n.*

re·con·sti·tute (rē'kon'stə·t(y)ōōt) *v.t.* ·tut·ed, ·tut·ing To constitute again, esp. to add water to a dehydrated or condensed substance. —**re'con'sti·tu'tion** *n.*

re·con·struct (rē'kən·strukt') *v.t.* To construct again. —Syn. rebuild, refashion, reestablish, remodel.

re·con·struc·tion (rē'kən·struk'shən) *n.* **1** The act of reconstructing. **2** Something reconstructed. **3** *Usu. cap.* **a** The restoration of the seceded s States as members of the Union after the American Civil War. **b** The period of this restoration, from 1867–1877. —**re'con·struc'tive** *adj.*

re·con·vert (rē'kən·vûrt') *v.t.* To change back, as to a former condition, form, religion, etc. —**re'con·ver'sion** (-vûr'zhən) *n.*

rec·ord (rek'ərd) *n.* **1** An account in written or other permanent form serving as evidence of a fact or event. **2** Something on which such an account is made, as a monument. **3** Information preserved and handed down: the heaviest rainfall on *record.* **4** The known career or performance of a person, animal, organization, etc. **5** The best listed achievement, as in a competitive sport. **6** *Law* **a** A written account of an act, statement, or transaction made by an officer acting under authority of law. **b** An official written account of a judicial or legislative proceeding. **7** A disk or cylinder, grooved so as to reproduce sounds that have been registered on its surface. —**go on record** To state publically or officially. —**off the rec·ord** Not for quotation or publication. —*adj.* Surpassing any previously recorded achievement or performance of its kind. —

re·cord (ri·kôrd') *v.t.* **1** To write down or otherwise inscribe, as for preservation, evidence, etc. **2** To indicate; register. **3** To offer evidence of. **4** To register and make permanently reproducible, as on tape, a phonograph record, etc. —*v.i.* **5** To record something. [< L *recordari* call to mind]

re·cord·er (ri·kôr'dər) *n.* **1** One who records. **2** A magistrate having criminal jurisdiction in a city or borough. **3** A type of flute blown at one end. **4** A device that records, as a tape recorder.

re·cord·ing (ri·kôr'ding) *n.* **1** The act or process of making a representation from which sound, video, data, etc., can be reproduced. **2** The material so represented.

Recorder
def. 3

record player A machine for reproducing sound from a record (def. 7).

re·count[1] (ri·kount′) v.t. 1 To relate the particulars of; narrate in detail. 2 To enumerate; recite. [< OF *reconter* relate] —**re·count′er** n.

re·count[2] (rē′kount′) v.t. To count again. —n. (rē′kount′) An additional count, esp. a second count of votes cast.

re·count·al (ri·koun′təl) n. A detailed narrative.

re·coup (ri·kōōp′) v.t. 1 To recover or make up for, as a loss. 2 To regain, as health. 3 To repay or reimburse. —n. The act of recouping. [< F *re-* again + *couper* to cut] —**re·coup′a·ble** adj. —**re·coup′ment** n.

re·course (rē′kôrs, -kōrs, ri·kôrs′, -kōrs′) n. 1 Resort to or application for help or security in trouble. 2 The person or thing resorted to. [< L *recursus* a running back]

re·cov·er (ri·kuv′ər) v.t. 1 To obtain again, as after losing; regain. 2 To make up for; retrieve, as a loss. 3 To restore (oneself) to natural balance, health, etc. 4 To reclaim, as land. 5 *Law* To gain or regain in judicial proceedings. —v.i. 6 To regain health, composure, etc. 7 *Law* To succeed in a lawsuit. [< L *recuperare*] —**re·cov′er·a·ble** adj.

re·cov·er (rē′kuv′ər) v.t. To cover again.

re·cov·er·y (ri·kuv′ər·ē) n. pl. **·er·ies** 1 The act, process, or an instance of recovering. 2 The duration of recovering. 3 Restoration from sickness or from any undesirable or abnormal condition. 4 The extraction of usable substances and materials from byproducts, waste, etc. 5 The retrieval of a flying object, as a balloon, space vehicle, meteorite, etc., after it has fallen to earth.

rec·re·ant (rek′rē·ənt) adj. 1 Unfaithful to a cause or pledge; false. 2 Craven; cowardly. —n. A cowardly or faithless person; also, a deserter. [< L *re-* back + *credere* believe] —**rec′re·ance, rec′re·an·cy** n. —**rec′re·ant·ly** adv.

rec·re·ate[1] (rek′rē·āt) v. **·at·ed, ·at·ing** v.t. 1 To impart fresh vigor to; refresh, esp. after toil. —v.i. 2 To take recreation. [< L *recreare* create anew] —**rec′re·a′tive** adj.

re·cre·ate[2] (rē′krē·āt′) v.t. **·at·ed, ·at·ing** To create anew. —**re′cre·a′tion** n.

rec·re·a·tion (rek′rē·ā′shən) n. 1 Refreshment of body or mind, esp. after work; diversion; amusement. 2 Any pleasurable exercise or occupation. —**rec′re·a′tion·al** adj.

re·crim·i·nate (ri·krim′ə·nāt) v. **·nat·ed, ·nat·ing** v.t. 1 To accuse in return. —v.i. 2 To repel one accusation by making another in return. [< L *re-* again + *criminare* accuse] —**re·crim′i·na′tor** n. —**re·crim′i·na′tive, re·crim·i·na·to·ry** (ri·krim′ə·nə·tôr′ē, -tō′rē) adj.

re·crim·in·a·tion (ri·krim′ə·nā′shən) n. 1 The act of recriminating. 2 An accusation made in response to another.

re·cru·desce (rē′krōō·des′) v.i. **·desced, ·desc·ing** To reappear after lying dormant. [< L *re-* again + *crudescere* become harsh, break out] —**re′cru·des′cence** n. —**re′cru·des′cent** adj.

re·cruit (ri·krōōt′) v.t. 1 To enlist (men or women) for service, as in a military organization or a police force. 2 To muster; raise, as an army, by enlistment. 3 To enlist the aid, services, or support of: to *recruit* new members for a political party. 4 To replenish. —v.i. 5 To enlist new personnel for service, as in an army or other organization. 6 To gain or raise new supplies of anything lost or needed. —n. 1 A newly enlisted person, as a soldier or sailor. 2 Any new adherent of a cause, organization, or the like. [< F *recrute*] —**re·cruit′er, re·cruit′ment** n.

rec. sec. recording secretary.

rect. receipt; rectangle; rector; rectory.

rec·tal (rek′təl) adj. Pertaining to, for, or in the region of the rectum.

rec·tan·gle (rek′tang′gəl) n. A parallelogram with all angles right angles. [< L *rectus* straight + *angulus* angle] • See PARALLELOGRAM.

rec·tan·gu·lar (rek·tang′gyə·lər) adj. 1 Having right angles. 2 Resembling a rectangle. —**rec·tan′gu·lar′i·ty** (-lar′ə·tē) n. —**rec·tan′gu·lar·ly** adv.

recti- *combining form* Straight: *rectilinear*. [< L *rectus* straight]

rec·ti·fi·er (rek′tə·fī′ər) n. 1 One who or that which recti-

fies. 2 *Electr.* A device that conducts in only one direction.

rec·ti·fy (rek′tə·fī) v.t. **·fied, ·fy·ing** 1 To make right; correct; amend. 2 *Chem.* To refine or purify, as a liquid, by distillation. 3 *Electr.* To change (an alternating current) into a direct current. 4 To allow for errors or inaccuracies in, as a compass reading. [< L *rectus* right + *facere* make] —**rec′ti·fi′a·ble** adj. —**rec′ti·fi·ca′tion** (-tə·fə·kā′shən) n.

rec·ti·lin·e·ar (rek′tə·lin′ē·ər) adj. Pertaining to, consisting of, moving in, or bounded by a straight line or lines; straight. Also **rec′ti·lin′e·al.** —**rec′ti·lin′e·ar·ly** adv.

rec·ti·tude (rek′tə·t/ōōd) n. 1 Uprightness in principles and conduct. 2 Correctness of judgment, method, etc. [< L *rectus* right]

rec·tor (rek′tər) n. 1 In the Church of England, a priest who has full charge of a parish. 2 In the Protestant Episcopal Church, a priest in charge of a parish. 3 In the Roman Catholic Church: a A priest in charge of a congregation or church. b The head of a seminary or university. 4 In certain universities, colleges, and schools, the headmaster or principal. [< L *rectus*, pp. of *regere* rule] —**rec′tor·ate** (-it) n. —**rec·to·ri·al** (rek·tôr′ē·əl, -tō′rē-) adj.

rec·to·ry (rek′tər·ē) n. pl. **·ries** 1 A rector's dwelling. 2 In England, a parish domain with its buildings, revenue, etc.

rec·tum (rek′təm) n. pl. **·tums** or **·ta** (-tə) The terminal part of the large intestine ending at the anus. [< NL *rectum (intestinum)* straight (intestine)]

re·cum·bent (ri·kum′bənt) adj. 1 Lying down, wholly or partly. 2 Resting; inactive. [< L *re-* back + *cumbere* lie] —**re·cum′bence, re·cum′ben·cy** n. —**re·cum′bent·ly** adv.

re·cu·per·ate (ri·k/ōō′pə·rāt) v. **·at·ed, ·at·ing** v.i. 1 To regain health or strength. 2 To recover from loss, as of money. —v.t. 3 To obtain again after loss; recover. 4 To restore to vigor and health. [< L *recuperare*] —**re·cu′per·a′tion, re·cu′per·a′tor** n. —**re·cu′per·a′tive** adj.

re·cur (ri·kûr′) v.i. **·curred, ·cur·ring** 1 To happen again or repeatedly. 2 To come back or return, as to the memory, in conversation, etc. [< L *re-* back + *currere* run]

re·cur·rent (ri·kûr′ənt) adj. 1 Happening or appearing again or repeatedly; recurring. 2 Turning back toward the source, as certain arteries and nerves. —**re·cur′rence, re·cur′ren·cy** n. —**re·cur′rent·ly** adv.

re·curve (ri·kûrv′) v.t. & v.i. **·curved, ·curv·ing** To curve or bend backward. [< L *re-* back + *curvus* curved] —**re·cur′vate** (-kûr′vit, -vāt) adj.

re·cy·cle (rē·sī′kəl) v.t. **·cy·cled, ·cy·cling** To reclaim (waste materials, as used newsprint, glass bottles, etc.) by using in the manufacture of new products. —**re·cy′cla·ble** adj.

red (red) adj. **red·der, red·dest** 1 Having or being of a bright color resembling blood. 2 Of a hue approximating red: *red* hair. 3 Ultraradical in politics, esp. communistic. —n. 1 One of the primary colors, occurring at the opposite end of the spectrum from violet; the color of fresh human blood. 2 A hue or tint that approximates primary red. 3 Any pigment or dye having or giving this color. 4 A red animal or object. 5 *Often cap.* An ultraradical or revolutionary in politics, esp. a communist: from the red banner of revolution. —**in the red** *Informal* Operating at a loss; owing money. —**see red** To be very angry. [< OE *rēad*] —**red′dish** adj. —**red′ly** adv. —**red′ness** n.

red. reduce; reduction.

re·dact (ri·dakt′) v.t. 1 To prepare, as for publication; edit; revise. 2 To draw up or frame, as a message or edict. [< L *redactus*, pp. of *redigere* lead back, restore] —**re·dac′tion, re·dac′tor** n.

red algae A class of marine algae having predominantly red pigment and usu. mosslike growth.

red·bait (red′bāt′) v.t. To denounce as being communist. —**red′bait′er** n.

red·bird (red′bûrd′) n. Any of various birds with red plumage in the male, as cardinals, certain tanagers, etc.

red·blood·ed (red′blud′id) adj. Having vitality and vigor. —**red′-blood′ed·ness** n.

red·breast (red′brest′) n. A robin.

red·cap (red′kap′) n. A porter, as in a railroad or airline terminal.

---

add, āce, câre, pälm; end, ēven; it, īce; odd, ōpen, ôrder; tōōk, pōōl; up, bûrn; ə = a in *above, u* in *focus*; yōō = u in *fuse*; oil; pout; check; go; ring; thin; this; zh, *vision*. < derived from; ? origin uncertain or unknown.

red carpet A long red carpet traditionally used for important guests to walk on. —**red′-car′pet** *adj.*

Red China *Informal* The People's Republic of China.

red·coat (red′kōt′) *n.* **1** A British soldier during the American Revolution and the War of 1812. **2** *Can.* MOUNTIE.

red corpuscle ERYTHROCYTE.

Red Cross 1 An international society for bringing aid to victims of a war or disaster. **2** Any national branch of this society. **3** Their emblem, a red Greek cross on a white ground, symbol of neutrality.

red deer 1 A common deer of Europe and Asia. **2** The white-tailed deer in its summer coat.

red·den (red′n) *v.t.* **1** To make red. —*v.i.* **2** To grow red, esp. to blush.

re·deem (ri·dēm′) *v.t.* **1** To regain possession of by paying a price. **2** To pay off, as a promissory note. **3** To convert into cash or a premium: to *redeem* stocks or trading stamps. **4** To set free; ransom. **5** *Theol.* To rescue from sin and its penalties. **6** To fulfill, as an oath or promise. **7** To make worthwhile. [< L *re-* back + *emere* buy] —**re·deem′a·ble, re·demp′ti·ble** (-demp′tə·bəl) *adj.*

re·deem·er (ri·dē′mər) *n.* One who redeems. —**the Re·deemer** Jesus Christ.

re·demp·tion (ri·demp′shən) *n.* **1** The act of redeeming, or the state of being redeemed. **2** The recovery of what is mortgaged or pawned. **3** The payment of a debt or obligation, esp. the paying of the value of its notes, warrants, etc., by a government. **4** Deliverance or rescue, as by paying a ransom. —**re·demp′tive, re·demp′to·ry** *adj.*

re·de·ploy (rē′di·ploi′) *v.t.* To transfer (troops) from one zone of combat to another. —**re′de·ploy′ment** *n.*

re·de·vel·op (rē′di·vel′əp) *v.t.* **1** To develop again. **2** To rebuild, as a slum area. **3** *Phot.* To intensify with chemicals and put through a second developing process. —*v.i.* **4** To develop again. —**re′de·vel′op·er, re′de·vel′op·ment** *n.*

red·eye (red′ī′) *n. Slang* Inferior whiskey.

red·hand·ed (red′han′did) *adj.* **1** Having just committed any crime. **2** Caught in the act of doing some particular thing. —**red′-hand′ed·ly** *adv.* —**red′-hand′ed·ness** *n.*

red·head (red′hed′) *n.* **1** A person with red hair. **2** A North American duck, the male of which has a red head. —**red′head′ed** *adj.*

redheaded woodpecker A North American woodpecker having a red head and neck.

red herring 1 Smoked herring. **2** An irrelevant topic introduced in order to divert attention from the main point under discussion.

red-hot (red′hot′) *adj.* **1** Heated to redness. **2** New; fresh. **3** Marked by excitement, agitation, or enthusiasm.

red·in·gote (red′ing·gōt′) *n.* An outer coat with long full skirts. [F< E *riding coat*]

re·dis·trict (rē′dis′trikt) *v.t.* To redraw the district boundaries of.

red lead (led) An oxide of lead, used as a red pigment.

red-let·ter (red′let′ər) *adj.* Happy or memorable: from the use on calendars of red letters to indicate holidays.

red light A traffic signal light meaning stop.

red-light district (red′līt′) That part of a city or town in which brothels are numerous: from the former use of red lights to mark brothels.

red man An American Indian.

red·neck (red′nek′) *n.* A white, usu. uneducated laborer of the South: a disparaging term. Also **red′-neck′.**

red·o·lent (red′ə·lənt) *adj.* **1** Fragrant; odorous. **2** Smelling: with *of:* a swamp *redolent* of decay. **3** Evocative: with *of: redolent* of the past. [< L *redolere* emit a smell] —**red′o·lence, red′o·len·cy** *n.* —**red′o·lent·ly** *adv.*

re·dou·ble (rē·dub′əl) *v.t. & v.i.* **-led, -ling 1** To make or become double. **2** To increase greatly. **3** To echo or re-echo. **4** To fold or double back again. **5** In bridge, to double (an opponent's double).

re·doubt (ri·dout′) *n.* **1** A temporary fortification, as to defend a pass, a hilltop, etc. **2** Any place providing protection; stronghold. [< Med. L *reductus,* lit., a refuge]

re·doubt·a·ble (ri·dou′tə·bəl) *adj.* **1** Inspiring fear; formidable. **2** Deserving respect or deference. Also **re·doubt′·ed.** [< L *re-* thoroughly + *dubitare* doubt] —**re·doubt′a·ble·ness** *n.* —**re·doubt′a·bly** *adv.*

re·dound (ri·dound′) *v.i.* **1** To have an effect or result. **2** To return; reflect. —*n.* A return by way of consequence; result. [< L *redundare* to overflow]

red pepper 1 Any of various capsicums having fruit that is red when ripe. **2** Such a fruit, or a condiment made from it, as cayenne, pimiento, etc.

red·poll (red′pōl′) *n.* A small finch of northern regions, having a reddish crown.

re·dress (ri·dres′) *v.t.* **1** To set right or make reparation for, as a wrong, by compensation or by punishment. **2** To make reparation to; compensate. **3** To remedy; correct. —*n.* (rē′dres, ri·dres′) **1** Satisfaction for wrong done; reparation; amends. **2** A restoration; correction. [< F *redresser* straighten] —**re·dress′er** or **re·dres′sor** *n.*

red shift *Astron.* Displacement toward the red or low-frequency end of the spectrum of light or radio waves from a celestial body that is receding at high velocity.

red snapper Any of various reddish, marine fish highly esteemed as food.

red·start (red′stärt′) *n.* Any of various small warblers having red markings. [< RED + obs. *start* tail]

Red snapper

red tape Rigid official regulations, forms, or procedure involving delay or inaction: from the former practice of tying public documents with red tape.

red·top (red′top′) *n.* Any of certain grasses used for lawns and pasturage.

re·duce (ri·dyōōs′) *v.* **-duced, -duc·ing** *v.t.* **1** To make less in size, amount, number, intensity, etc.; diminish. **2** To bring into a certain system or order; classify. **3** To bring to a lower condition; degrade. **4** To bring to submission; subdue; conquer. **5** To bring to a specified condition or state: with *to:* to *reduce* rock to powder; *reduced* to tears. **6** To thin (paint, etc.) with oil or turpentine. **7** *Math.* To change (an expression) to a more elementary form. **8** *Chem.* **a** To remove oxygen from (a compound). **b** To add electrons to (an atom). **c** To decrease the positive valence of (an atom). **9** *Phot.* To diminish the density of (a photographic negative). —*v.i.* **10** To become less in any way. **11** To decrease one's weight, as by dieting. [< L *re-* back + *ducere* lead] —**re·duc′er, re·duc′i·bil′i·ty** *n.* —**re·duc′i·ble** *adj.* —**re·duc′i·bly** *adv.*

reducing agent *Chem.* Any substance that reduces another substance and is thereby oxidized in a chemical reaction.

re·duc·ti·o ad ab·sur·dum (ri·duk′tē·ō ad ab·sûr′dəm, -shē·ō) Disproof of a proposition by showing that it is self-contradictory. [L, lit., reduction to absurdity]

re·duc·tion (ri·duk′shən) *n.* **1** The act or process of reducing. **2** Something that results from reducing. **3** The amount by which something is reduced. —**re·duc′tion·al, re·duc′tive** *adj.*

re·dun·dan·cy (ri·dun′dən·sē) *n. pl.* **·cies 1** The condition or quality of being redundant. **2** Something redundant, esp. unnecessary repetition. **3** Excess; surplus. **4** In information theory, repeated information in a message, used to lessen the probability of error. Also **re·dun′dance.**

re·dun·dant (ri·dun′dənt) *adj.* **1** Being more than is required; constituting an excess. **2** Unnecessarily repetitive or verbose. [< L *redundare* to overflow] —**re·dun′dant·ly** *adv.* —**Syn. 1** superfluous, excessive, inordinate, undue. **2** repetitious, iterative, reiterative, wordy.

re·du·pli·cate (ri·dyōō′plə·kāt) *v.* **·cat·ed, ·cat·ing** *v.t.* **1** To repeat again and again; copy; iterate. **2** *Ling.* To affix a reduplication to. —*v.i.* **3** To undergo reduplication. —*adj.* (-kit) Repeated again and again; duplicated. —**re·du′pli·ca′tive** *adj.*

re·du·pli·ca·tion (ri·dyōō′plə·kā′shən) *n.* **1** The act of reduplicating, or the state of being reduplicated; a redoubling. **2** *Ling.* **a** The repetition of an initial element or elements in a word. **b** The doubling of all or part of a word, often with vowel or consonant change, as in *fiddle-faddle.*

red·wing (red′wing′) *n.* **1** A North American blackbird with red and yellow wing patches in the male: also **red-winged blackbird. 2** An Old World thrush with reddish orange on its wings.

red·wood (red′wŏŏd′) *n.* **1** SEQUOIA. **2** Its wood.

reed (rēd) *n.* 1 The slender, frequently jointed stem of certain tall grasses growing in wet places; also, the grasses themselves. 2 *Music* **a** A thin, elastic plate of reed, wood, or metal nearly closing an opening, as in a pipe, used in reed organs, reed pipes of pipe organs, and some woodwind instruments, to produce a musical tone when vibrated by air. **b** An instrument having such a reed or reeds. 3 A crude musical pipe made of the hollow stem of a plant. 4 *Archit.* REEDING. 5 A comblike device on a loom that keeps the warp yarns evenly separated. —*v.t.* 1 To fashion into or decorate with reeds. 2 To thatch with reeds. —*adj. Music* Equipped with a reed or reeds. [< OE *hrēod*]

reed·ing (rē'ding) *n. Archit.* 1 Small, convex molding. 2 Parallel ornamentation using such molding.

reed organ A keyboard musical instrument sounding by means of reeds that vibrate freely in response to air currents.

re·ed·u·cate (rē·ej'ŏŏ·kāt) *v.t.* ·cat·ed, ·cat·ing 1 To educate again. 2 To rehabilitate, as a criminal, by education. —**re'ed·u·ca'tion** *n.*

reed·y (rē'dē) *adj.* reed·i·er, reed·i·est 1 Full of reeds. 2 Like a reed. 3 Having a tone like that of a reed instrument. —**reed'i·ness** *n.*

reef[1] (rēf) *n.* 1 A ridge of sand or rocks, or esp. of coral, at or near the surface of the water. 2 A lode, vein, or ledge. [< ON rif, reef] —**reef'y** *adj.* • See ATOLL.

reef[2] (rēf) *Naut. n.* 1 The part of a sail that is folded and secured or untied and let out in regulating its size on the mast. 2 The tuck taken in a sail when reefed. —*v.t.* 1 To reduce (a sail) by folding a part and tying it to a yard or boom. 2 To shorten or lower, as a topmast, by taking part of it in. [Prob. < ON *rif* rib]

reef·er[1] (rē'fər) *n.* 1 One who reefs. 2 A short, double-breasted coat or jacket.

reef·er[2] (rē'fər) *n. Slang* A marihuana cigarette. [?]

reef knot SQUARE KNOT.

reek (rēk) *v.i.* 1 To give off smoke, vapor, etc. 2 To give off a strong, offensive smell. 3 To be pervaded with anything offensive. —*v.t.* 4 To expose to smoke or its action. 5 To give off; emit. [< OE *rēocan*] —**reek'er** *n.* —**reek'y** *adj.* (·i·er, ·i·est)

reel[1] (rēl) *n.* 1 A rotatory device or frame for winding rope, cord, photographic film, or other flexible substance. 2 Such a device attached to a fishing rod. 3 The length of wire, film, thread, etc., wound on one reel. —*v.t.* 1 To wind on a reel or bobbin, as a line. 2 To draw in by reeling a line: with *in: to reel* a fish in. 3 To say, do, etc., easily and fluently: with *off.* [< OE *hrēol*] —**reel'a·ble** *adj.* —**reel'er** *n.*

Fishing reel

reel[2] (rēl) *v.i.* 1 To stagger, sway, or lurch, as when giddy or drunk. 2 To whirl round and round. 3 To have a sensation of giddiness or whirling: My head *reels.* 4 To waver or fall back, as attacking troops. —*v.t.* 5 To cause to reel. —*n.* A staggering motion; giddiness. [< REEL[1]] —**reel'er** *n.*

reel[3] (rēl) *n.* 1 A lively Scottish dance. 2 The music for such a dance. [?< REEL[1]]

re·en·force (rē'in·fôrs', -en-, -fōrs') *v.* ·forced, ·forc·ing REINFORCE.

re·en·try (rē·en'trē) *n.* 1 The act of entering again. 2 In whist and bridge, a card by which a player can regain the lead. 3 The return into the atmosphere of an object launched into space from the earth.

reeve[1] (rēv) *v.t.* reeved or rove (*for p.p. also* rov·en), reev·ing *Naut.* 1 To pass, as a rope or rod, through a hole, block, or aperture. 2 To fasten in such manner. 3 To pass a rope, etc., through (a block or pulley). [?< Du. *reven* reef a sail]

reeve[2] (rēv) *n.* In Canada, an elected official who presides over the council in certain villages and townships. [< OE *gerēfa* steward]

ref. reference; reference; referred; refining; reformed.

re·fec·tion (ri·fek'shən) *n.* 1 Refreshment by food and drink. 2 A light meal. [< L *refectus,* pp. of *reficere* remake, refresh]

re·fec·to·ry (ri·fek'tər·ē) *n. pl.* ·ries A room for eating, esp. in a monastery, convent, or college. [< Med. L *refectorium*]

re·fer (ri·fûr') *v.* ·ferred, ·fer·ring *v.t.* 1 To direct or send for information or other purpose. 2 To hand over for consideration, settlement, etc. 3 To assign or attribute to a source, cause, group, class, etc. —*v.i.* 4 To make reference; allude. 5 To turn, as for information, help, or authority. [< L *referre* back + *ferre* bear, carry] —**ref·er·a·ble** (ref'ər·ə·bəl, ri·fûr'-), **re·fer'ra·ble** or **re·fer'ri·ble** *adj.* —**re·fer'rer** *n.*

ref·e·ree (ref'ə·rē') *n.* 1 A person to whom a thing is referred for judgment or decision. 2 An official who sees that the rules of certain sports events are observed. —*v.t. & v.i.* To judge as a referee.

ref·er·ence (ref'ər·əns, ref'rəns) *n.* 1 The act of referring. 2 An incidental allusion or direction of the attention. 3 A note or other indication in a book, referring to some other book or passage. 4 One who or that which is or may be referred to. 5 A book or other source intended to be referred to for information, as a dictionary. 6 Relation: in *reference* to your inquiry. 7 A person to whom an employer may refer for information about a potential employee. 8 A written statement or testimonial referring to character or dependability. —**ref'er·en'tial** (-ər·en'shəl) *adj.* —**ref'er·en'tial·ly** *adv.*

ref·er·en·dum (ref'ə·ren'dəm) *n. pl.* ·dums or ·da (-də) 1 The submission of a proposed public measure or law, which has been passed upon by a legislature or convention, to a vote of the people for ratification or rejection. 2 The vote itself. [L, gerund of *referre* refer]

ref·er·ent (ref'ər·ənt) *n.* Something referred to, esp. the thing to which reference is made in any verbal statement.

re·fer·ral (ri·fûr'əl) *n.* 1 The act of referring or the condition of being referred. 2 One who has been referred.

re·fill (rē·fil') *v.t. & v.i.* To fill or become filled again. —*n.* (rē'fil') Any commodity packaged to fit and fill a container originally containing that commodity. —**re·fill'a·ble** *adj.*

re·fine (ri·fīn') *v.* ·fined, ·fin·ing *v.t.* 1 To make fine or pure. 2 To make more elegant, polished, etc. 3 To improve or perfect. —*v.i.* 4 To become fine or pure. 5 To become more polished or cultured. 6 To make fine distinctions; use subtlety in thought or speech. [< RE- + FINE[1], *v.*] —**re·fin'er** *n.*

re·fined (ri·fīnd') *adj.* 1 Characterized by refinement or polish. 2 Free from impurity. 3 Exceedingly precise or exact; subtle.

re·fine·ment (ri·fīn'mənt) *n.* 1 The act or process of refining. 2 The result of refining, esp. an improvement. 3 Fineness of thought, taste, language, etc.; freedom from coarseness or vulgarity. 4 A nice distinction; subtlety.

re·fin·er·y (ri·fī'nər·ē) *n. pl.* ·er·ies A plant for extracting useful products from raw material, as metal from ore.

re·fit (rē·fit') *v.t. & v.i.* ·fit·ted, ·fit·ting To make or be made fit or ready again, as by making or obtaining repairs, replacing equipment, etc. —*n.* The repair of damages or wear, esp. of a ship.

refl. reflection; reflex; reflexive.

re·flect (ri·flekt') *v.t.* 1 To turn or throw back, as rays of light, heat, or sound. 2 To produce a symmetrically reversed image of, as a mirror. 3 To cause or bring as a result: with *on: He reflects* credit on his teacher. 4 To show or manifest: His writings *reflect* great imagination. —*v.i.* 5 To send back rays, as of light or heat. 6 To return in rays. 7 To give back an image; also, to be mirrored. 8 To think carefully; ponder. 9 To bring blame, discredit, etc.: with *on* or *upon.* [< L *re-* back + *flectere* bend]

re·flec·tion (ri·flek'shən) *n.* 1 The act of reflecting, or the state of being reflected. 2 *Physics* The throwing off or back (from a surface) of impinging light, heat, sound, or any form of radiant energy. 3 Reflected rays or an image thrown by reflection. 4 Careful, serious thought or consideration. 5 The result of such thought. 6 Censure; discredit; also, a remark or action tending to discredit. —**re·flec'tion·al** *adj.*

re·flec·tive (ri·flek'tiv) *adj.* 1 Given to reflection or thought; meditative. **2** Of or caused by reflection. **3** That reflects. **—re·flec'tive·ly** adv. **—re·flec'tive·ness, re'flec·tiv'i·ty** n.

re·flec·tor (ri·flek'tər) n. One who or that which reflects, esp. a device for reflecting light, heat, sound, etc.

re·flex (rē'fleks) adj. **1** Turned, bent, directed, or thrown backward. **2** *Physiol.* Of, pertaining to, or produced by an involuntary action or response. **—n. 1** Reflection, as of light, or an image produced by reflection. **2** *Physiol.* An involuntary response to a stimulus: also **reflex action. 3** A habitual or automatic reaction. [< L *reflexus* reflected, pp. of *reflectere* bend back]

re·flex·ive (ri·flek'siv) adj. **1** REFLEX. **2** *Gram.* **a** Designating a verb whose object is identical with its subject, as "dresses" in "He dresses himself." **b** Designating a pronoun which is the direct object of a reflexive verb. **—n.** A reflexive verb or pronoun. **—re·flex'ive·ly** adv. **—re·flex'ive·ness, re·flex·iv·i·ty** (rē'flek·siv'ə·tē) n.

ref·lu·ent (ref'lōō·ənt) adj. Flowing back; ebbing, as the tide. [< L *re-* back + *fluere* flow] **—ref'lu·ence, ref'lu·en·cy** n.

re·flux (rē'fluks') n. A flowing back; ebb; return. [< L *refluxus,* pp. of *refluere* flow back]

re·for·est (rē·fôr'ist, -for'-) v.t. & v.i. To replant (an area) with trees. **—re'for·es·ta'tion** n.

re·form (ri·fôrm') v.t. **1** To make better by removing abuses, malpractice, etc. **2** To make better morally; persuade or educate from a sinful to a moral life. **3** To put an end to; stop (an abuse, malpractice, etc.). **—v.i. 4** To give up sin or error; become better. **—n.** A correction or improvement of social or personal evils or errors. [< L *re-* again + *formare* to form] **—re·form'a·tive** adj. **—re·form'er** n. **—re·form'ist** adj., n.

re-form (rē'fôrm') v.t. & v.i. To form again. **—re'-for·ma'tion** n.

ref·or·ma·tion (ref'ər·mā'shən) n. **1** The act of reforming. **2** The state of being reformed.

Ref·or·ma·tion (ref'ər·mā'shən) n. The religious revolution of the 16th century that began by trying to reform Catholicism and ended with the establishment of Protestantism.

re·form·a·to·ry (ri·fôr'mə·tôr'ē, -tō'rē) adj. Tending or aiming to reform. **—n. pl. ·ries** An institution for the reformation and instruction of juvenile offenders: also **reform school.**

re·fract (ri·frakt') v.t. **1** To deflect (a ray) by refraction. **2** *Optics* To determine the degree of refraction of (an eye or lens). [< L *refractus,* pp. of *refringere* turn aside]

re·frac·tion (ri·frak'shən) n. *Physics* The change of direction of a ray, as of light or heat, in oblique passage between media of different densities. **—re·frac'tive** adj. **—re·frac'tive·ness, re·frac·tiv·i·ty** (rē'frak·tiv'ə·tē), re·frac'tor n.

re·frac·to·ry (ri·frak'tər·ē) adj. **1** Hard to control; stubborn; obstinate. **2** Resisting heat. **3** Resisting treatment, as a disease. **—n. pl. ·ries 1** A refractory or obstinate person or thing. **2** Any of various highly heat-resistant materials. [< L *refractarius*] **—re·frac'to·ri·ly** adv. **—re·frac'to·ri·ness** n.

Light refraction **a.** air. **b.** glass prism.

re·frain[1] (ri·frān') v.i. To hold oneself back. [< L *refrenare* curb] **—re·frain'er** n. **—Syn.** abstain, forbear, forgo, renounce.

re·frain[2] (ri·frān') n. **1** A phrase or verse repeated at intervals in a poem or a song. **2** The music for a refrain. [< OF *refraindre* to check, repeat]

re·fran·gi·ble (ri·fran'jə·bəl) adj. Capable of being refracted, as light. [< RE- + L *frangere* to break] **—re·fran'gi·bil'i·ty, re·fran'gi·ble·ness** n.

re·fresh (ri·fresh') v.t. **1** To revive (a person), as with food or rest. **2** To make fresh, clean, cool, etc. **3** To stimulate, as the memory. **4** To renew or replenish with or as with new supplies. **—v.i. 5** To become fresh again; revive. **6** To take refreshment. **—re·fresh'er** n.

refresher course A course for reviewing and learning of recent developments in a profession or field of study.

re·fresh·ing (ri·fresh'ing) adj. **1** Serving to refresh. **2** Pleasing because new or unusual. **—re·fresh'ing·ly** adv.

re·fresh·ment (ri·fresh'mənt) n. **1** The act of refreshing, or the state of being refreshed. **2** That which refreshes. **3** pl. Food, or food and drink, served as a light meal.

re·frig·er·ant (ri·frij'ər·ənt) adj. **1** Cooling or freezing. **2** Allaying heat or fever. **—n. 1** Any medicine or material that reduces fever. **2** A substance used to produce refrigeration.

re·frig·er·ate (ri·frij'ə·rāt) v.t. **·at·ed, ·at·ing 1** To keep or cause to become cold; cool. **2** To freeze or chill for preservative purposes, as foodstuffs. [< L *re-* thoroughly + *frigerare* to cool] **—re·frig'er·a'tion** n. **—re·frig'er·a'tive** adj., n. **—re·frig'er·a·to'ry** adj.

re·frig·er·a·tor (ri·frij'ə·rā'tər) n. A box, cabinet, room, railroad car, etc., equipped with a cooling apparatus for preserving the freshness of perishable foods, etc.

ref·uge (ref'yōōj) n. **1** Shelter or protection, as from danger or distress. **2** A safe place; asylum. **3** Something that brings relief, lessens difficulties, etc. [< L *refugere* to retreat]

ref·u·gee (ref'yōō·jē', ref'yōō·jē') n. One who flees to find refuge in another land or place, as from persecution or political danger.

re·ful·gent (ri·ful'jənt) adj. Shining; radiant; resplendent. [< L *refulgere* reflect light] **—re·ful'gence, re·ful'gen·cy** n. **—re·ful'gent·ly** adv.

re·fund[1] (ri·fund') v.t. **1** To give or pay back (money, etc.). **2** To repay (a person). **—v.i. 3** To make repayment. **—n.** (rē'fund) A repayment; refunding; also, the amount repaid. [< L *refundere* pour back] **—re·fund'er, re·fund'ment** n.

re·fund[2] (rē'fund') v.t. To fund anew.

re·fus·al (ri·fyōō'zəl) n. **1** The act of refusing. **2** The privilege or opportunity of accepting or rejecting before others.

re·fuse[1] (ri·fyōōz') v. **·fused, ·fus·ing** v.t. **1** To decline to do, permit, take, or yield. **2** To decline to fulfill the request or desire of (a person). **3** To balk at jumping over (a ditch, hedge, etc.): said of a horse. **—v.i. 4** To decline to do, permit, take, or yield something. [< L *refusus,* pp. of *refundere* pour back] **—re·fus'er** n.

ref·use[2] (ref'yōōs) n. Anything worthless; rubbish. [< OF *refus* refused]

re·fute (ri·fyōōt') v.t. **·fut·ed, ·fut·ing 1** To prove the incorrectness or falsity of (a statement). **2** To prove (a person) to be in error; confute. [< L *refutare*] **—re·fut'a·ble** adj. **—re·fut'a·bly** adv. **—ref·u·ta·tion** (ref'yə·tā'shən), re·fu'tal, re·fut'er n.

reg. regiment; region; register; registered; regular; regulation.

re·gain (ri·gān') v.t. **1** To get possession of again. **2** To reach again; get back to. **—re·gain'er** n.

re·gal (rē'gəl) adj. Belonging to or fit for a king; royal, stately, magnificent, etc. [< L *rex, regis* king] **—re·gal·i·ty** (ri·gal'ə·tē) n. **—re'gal·ly** adv.

re·gale (ri·gāl') v. **·galed, ·gal·ing** v.t. **1** To give unusual pleasure to; delight. **2** To entertain royally or sumptuously; feast. **—v.i. 3** To feast. [< F *régaler*] **—re·gale'ment** n.

re·ga·li·a (ri·gā'lē·ə, -gāl'yə) n. pl. **1** The insignia and emblems of royalty, as the crown, scepter, etc. **2** The distinctive symbols, insignia, etc., of any society, order, or rank. **3** Fine clothes; fancy trappings.

re·gard (ri·gärd') v.t. **1** To look at or observe attentively. **2** To look on or think of in a certain way. **3** To take into account; consider. **4** To have relevance to. **—v.i. 5** To pay attention. **6** To gaze or look. **—n. 1** A look; gaze. **2** Careful attention; consideration. **3** Respect; esteem. **4** *Usu. pl.* Greetings; good wishes. **5** Reference; relation: with *regard* to your letter. [< OF *regarder* look at]

re·gard·ful (ri·gärd'fəl) adj. **1** Having or showing regard; heedful. **2** Respectful. **—re·gard'ful·ly** adv. **—re·gard'ful·ness** n.

re·gard·ing (ri·gär'ding) prep. In reference to; with regard to.

re·gard·less (ri·gärd'lis) adj. Having no regard or consideration; heedless; negligent. **—adv.** *Informal* In spite of everything. **—re·gard'less·ly** adv.

re·gat·ta (ri·gat'ə, -gä'tə) n. A boat race, or a series of such races. [Ital.]

re·gen·cy (rē'jən·sē) n. pl. **·cies 1** The government or office of a regent or body of regents. **2** The period during which a regent or body of regents governs. 3 A body of regents. 4 The district under the rule of a regent. Also **re'gent·ship.**

re·gen·er·ate (ri·jen'ə·rāt) v. ·at·ed, ·at·ing v.t. 1 To cause moral and spiritual reformation in. 2 To produce or form anew; reestablish; recreate. 3 Biol. To replace (a lost organ or tissue) with new growth. —v.i. 4 To form anew; be reproduced. 5 To become spiritually regenerate. 6 To effect regeneration. —adj. (ri·jen'ər·it) 1 Having new life; restored. 2 Spiritually renewed; regenerated. —re·gen'er·a·cy (-ər·ə·sē), re·gen'er·a'tion, re·gen'er·a'tor n.

re·gent (rē'jənt) n. 1 One who rules in the name and place of a sovereign. 2 One of various officers having charge of education, as of a university or state. [<L regens, pr.p. of regere rule]

reg·gae (reg'ā, rā'gā) n. A popular music of West Indian origin having a rhythm that suggests both blues and rock.

reg·i·cide (rej'ə·sīd) n. 1 The killing of a king. 2 The killer of a king. [<L rex, regis king + -CIDE] —reg'i·ci'dal adj.

re·gime (ri·zhēm') n. 1 System of government or administration. 2 A particular government or its duration of rule. 3 A social system. 4 REGIMEN. Also **ré·gime** (rā·zhēm'). [< F<L regimen]

reg·i·men (rej'ə·mən) n. A system of diet, exercise, etc., used for therapeutic purposes. [<L regimen<regere to rule]

reg·i·ment (rej'ə·mənt) n. A military unit larger than a battalion and smaller than a division. —v.t. 1 To form into a regiment or regiments; organize. 2 To assign to a regiment. 3 To form into well-defined or specific units or groups; systematize. 4 To make uniform. [<LL regimentum<L regere to rule] —reg'i·men'tal adj. —reg'i·men·ta'tion n.

reg·i·men·tals (rej'ə·men'təlz) n. pl. 1 Military uniform. 2 The uniform worn by the men and officers of a regiment.

re·gion (rē'jən) n. 1 An indefinite, usu. large portion of territory or space. 2 A specific area or place. 3 A specified area of activity, interest, etc.: the region of art. 4 A portion of the body. [<L regio<regere to rule]

re·gion·al (rē'jən·əl) adj. 1 Of or pertaining to a particular region; sectional; local: regional planning. 2 Of or pertaining to an entire region or section. —re'gion·al·ly adv.
• In this dictionary the label Regional is applied to terms used chiefly or exclusively within a particular region of the U.S., and constituting a part of that region's distinctive variety of speech or dialect. A user of regional speech should be aware that terms so labeled may be misunderstood or considered odd or illiterate in other parts of the country.

reg·is·ter (rej'is·tər) n. 1 An official record, as of names, events, transactions, etc. 2 The book containing such a record. 3 An item in such a record. 4 Any of various devices for adding or recording: a cash register. 5 REGISTRAR. 6 A device for regulating the admission of heated air to a room. 7 Music a The range or compass of a voice or instrument. b A series of tones of a particular quality or belonging to a particular portion of the compass of a voice or instrument. 8 Printing a Exact correspondence of the lines and margins on the opposite sides of a printed sheet. b Correct imposition of the colors in color printing. —v.t. 1 To enter in or as in a register; enroll or record officially. 2 To indicate on a scale. 3 To express or indicate: His face registered disapproval. 4 Printing To effect exact correspondence or imposition of. 5 To cause (mail) to be recorded, on payment of a fee, so as to insure delivery. —v.i. 6 To enter one's name in a register, poll, etc. 7 To have effect; make an impression. 8 Printing To be in register. [<L regestus, pp. of regerere record] —reg·is·tra·ble (rej'is·trə·bəl) adj. —reg'is·trant (-trənt) n.

reg·is·tered (rej'is·tərd) adj. 1 Recorded, as a birth, a voter, an animal's pedigree, etc. 2 Officially or formally qualified.

reg·is·trar (rej'is·trär) n. An authorized keeper of a register or of records, esp. of a college or court.

reg·is·tra·tion (rej'is·trā'shən) n. 1 The act of registering, as of voters, students, etc. 2 The number of persons registered. 3 An entry in a register.

reg·is·try (rej'is·trē) n. pl. ·tries 1 REGISTRATION. 2 A register, or the place where it is kept. 3 The nationality of a ship as entered in a register.

reg·nant (reg'nənt) adj. 1 Reigning in one's own right. 2 Predominant. 3 Widespread. [<L regnum reign]

re·gress (ri·gres') v.i. To go back; move backward; return. —n. (rē'gres) 1 A going back; return. 2 A return to a less perfect or lower state; retrogression. [<L regressus, pp. of regredi go back] —re·gres'sive adj. —re·gres'sive·ly adv. —re·gres'sor n.

re·gres·sion (ri·gresh'ən) n. 1 The act of regressing. 2 A return to a less perfect or lower state; retrogression. 3 Psychoanal. A retreat to earlier or infantile behavior.

re·gret (ri·gret') v.t. ·gret·ted, ·gret·ting 1 To look back upon with a feeling of distress or loss. 2 To feel sorrow or grief concerning. —n. 1 Distress of mind in recalling some past event, act, loss, etc. 2 Remorseful sorrow; compunction. 3 pl. A polite refusal in response to an invitation. [< OF regreter] —re·gret'ter n.

re·gret·ful (ri·gret'fəl) adj. Feeling, expressive of, or full of regret. —re·gret'ful·ly adv. —re·gret'ful·ness n. —Syn. sorry, remorseful, contrite, apologetic.

re·gret·ta·ble (ri·gret'ə·bəl) adj. Deserving regret; unfortunate. —re·gret'ta·bly adv.

regt. regiment.

reg·u·lar (reg'yə·lər) adj. 1 Made, formed, or arranged according to a rule, standard, or type; symmetrical; normal. 2 Methodical; orderly: regular habits. 3 Conforming to a fixed or proper procedure or principle. 4 Customary; habitual: his regular breakfast. 5 Officially authorized. 6 Without variation or abnormality: His pulse is regular. 7 Thorough; unmitigated: a regular bore. 8 Informal Pleasant, good, honest, etc.: a regular guy. 9 Gram. Undergoing the inflection that is normal or most common. 10 Bot. Having all similar parts or organs of the same shape and size: said mainly of flowers. 11 Eccl. Belonging to a religious order: the regular clergy. 12 Mil. Pertaining or belonging to the permanent army. 13 In politics, designating, nominated by, or loyal to the official party organization or platform. 14 Geom. Having equal sides and angles. 15 Math. Controlled or formed by one law or operation throughout. —n. 1 A soldier belonging to a permanent or standing army. 2 In sports, a starting member of a team. 3 An habitual customer, patron, etc. 4 A clothing size for those of average height and weight. 5 Eccl. A member of a religious order. 6 A person loyal to a certain political party. [<L regula rule] —reg'u·lar'i·ty n. —reg'u·lar·ly adv.

reg·u·lar·ize (reg'yə·lə·rīz') v.t. ·ized, ·iz·ing To make regular. —reg'u·lar·i·za'tion n.

reg·u·late (reg'yə·lāt) v.t. ·lat·ed, ·lat·ing 1 To direct, manage, or control according to certain rules, principles, etc. 2 To adjust according to a standard, degree, etc.: to regulate currency. 3 To adjust to accurate operation. 4 To put in order; set right. [<L regula a rule<regere rule, lead straight] —reg'u·la·tive, reg'u·la·to·ry (-lə·tôr'ē, -tō'rē) adj.

reg·u·la·tion (reg'yə·lā'shən) n. 1 The act of regulating, or the state of being regulated. 2 A prescribed rule of conduct or procedure. —adj. 1 Required by rule or regulation. 2 Normal; customary.

reg·u·la·tor (reg'yə·lā'tər) n. 1 One who or that which regulates. 2 A device for regulating the speed of a watch. 3 A contrivance for controlling motion, flow, voltage, etc.

re·gur·gi·tate (rē·gûr'jə·tāt) v. ·tat·ed, ·tat·ing v.i. 1 To flow backward. —v.t. 2 To cause to surge back, as partially digested food to the mouth from the stomach. [<LL reback + gurgitare flood, engulf] —re·gur'gi·tant adj. —re·gur'gi·ta'tion n.

re·ha·bil·i·tate (rē'hə·bil'ə·tāt, rē'ə-) v.t. ·tat·ed, ·tat·ing 1 To restore to a former state, capacity, privilege, rank, etc.; reinstate. 2 To restore to health or normal activity. [< Med. L rehabilitare] —re'ha·bil'i·ta'tion n.

re·hash (rē·hash') v.t. To work into a new form; go over again. —n. (rē'hash') The act or result of rehashing.

re·hears·al (ri·hûr′səl) n. 1 The act of rehearsing, as for a play. 2 The act of reciting or telling over again.

re·hearse (ri·hûrs′) v. **·hearsed, ·hears·ing** v.t. 1 To practice privately in preparation for public performance, as a play or song. 2 To instruct or direct (a person) by way of preparation. 3 To say over again; repeat aloud; recite. 4 To give an account of; relate. —v.i. 5 To rehearse a play, song, dance, etc. [< OF *reherser* harrow over, repeat] —**re·hears′er** n.

Reich (rīk, *Ger.* rīkh) n. Formerly, Germany, the German government, or its territory. —**Third Reich** The Nazi state under Adolf Hitler, 1933–45. [G]

reichs·mark (rīks′märk′, *Ger.* rīkhs′-) n. pl. **·marks** or **·mark** A monetary unit of Germany from 1924–48.

Reichs·tag (rīks′täg′, *Ger.* rīkhs′täkh′) n. The former legislative assembly of Germany.

reign (rān) n. 1 Sovereign power or rule; sovereignty. 2 The time or duration of a sovereign's rule. 3 Domination; sway: the *reign* of rationalism. —v.i. 1 To hold and exercise sovereign power. 2 To hold sway; prevail: Winter *reigns.* [< L *regnum* rule]

Reign of Terror The period of the French Revolution from May, 1793, to August, 1794, during which Louis XVI, Marie Antoinette, and thousands of others were guillotined.

re·im·burse (rē′im·bûrs′) v.t. **·bursed, ·burs·ing** 1 To pay back (a person) an equivalent for what has been spent or lost; recompense. 2 To pay back; refund. [< RE- + < L *in-* in + *bursa* purse] —**re′im·burs′a·ble** adj. —**re′im·burse′ment** n.

rein (rān) n. 1 *Usu. pl.* A strap attached to each end of a bit to control a horse or other draft animal. 2 Any means of restraint or control. —v.t. 1 To guide, check, or halt with or as with reins. —v.i. 2 To check or halt a horse by means of reins: with *in* or *up.* [< OF *resne*]

re·in·car·nate (rē′in·kär′nāt) v.t. **·nat·ed, ·nat·ing** To cause to undergo reincarnation.

re·in·car·na·tion (rē′in·kär·nā′shən) n. 1 The rebirth of a soul in a new body. 2 The Hindu doctrine that the soul, upon the death of the body, returns to earth in another body or a new form.

rein·deer (rān′dir′) n. pl. **·deer** A European form of caribou, often domesticated. [< ON *hreinn* reindeer + *dyr* deer]

re·in·force (rē′in·fôrs′, -fōrs′) v.t. **·forced, ·forc·ing** 1 To give new force or strength to. 2 *Mil.* To strengthen with more troops or ships. 3 To add some strengthening part or material to. 4 To increase the number of. [< RE- + *inforce,* var. of ENFORCE]

reinforced concrete Concrete containing metal bars, rods, or netting to increase its strength and durability.

re·in·force·ment (rē′in·fôrs′mənt, -fōrs′-) n. 1 The act of reinforcing. 2 Something that reinforces. 3 *Often pl. Mil.* A fresh body of troops or additional vessels.

re·in·state (rē′in·stāt′) v.t. **·stat·ed, ·stat·ing** To restore to a former state, position, etc. —**re′in·state′ment** n.

reis (rās) n.pl. of REAL² (def. 2).

re·it·er·ate (rē·it′ə·rāt) v.t. **·at·ed, ·at·ing** To say or do again and again. [< L *re-* again + *iterare* say] —**re·it′er·a′tion** n. —**re·it′er·a′tive** adj. —**re·it′er·a′tive·ly** adv. —**Syn.** iterate, repeat, retell, recapitulate.

re·ject (ri·jekt′) v.t. 1 To refuse to accept, recognize, believe, etc. 2 To refuse to grant; deny, as a petition. 3 To refuse (a person) recognition, acceptance, etc. 4 To expel; react against physiologically. 5 To cast away as worthless; discard. —n. (rē′jekt) A person or thing that has been rejected. [< L *re-* back + *jacere* to throw] —**re·ject′er** or **re·jec′tor, re·jec′tion** n.

re·joice (ri·jois′) v. **·joiced, ·joic·ing** v.i. 1 To feel joyful; be glad. —v.t. 2 To fill with joy; gladden. [< L *re-* again + *ex-* thoroughly + *gaudere* be joyous] —**re·joic′er, re·joic′ing** n. —**re·joic′ing·ly** adv.

re·join¹ (ri·join′) v.t. 1 To say in reply; answer. —v.i. 2 To answer. [< F *rejoindre*]

re·join² (rē′join′) v.t. 1 To come again into company with. 2 To join together again; reunite. —v.i. 3 To come together again.

re·join·der (ri·join′dər) n. 1 An answer to a reply. 2 Any reply or retort. [< F *rejoindre* to answer, reply]

re·ju·ve·nate (ri·jōō′və·nāt) v.t. **·nat·ed, ·nat·ing** To make young; give new vigor or youthfulness to. [< RE- again + L *juvenis* young + -ATE] —**re·ju′ve·na′tion** n.

rel. relating; relative; released; religion; religious.

re·lapse (ri·laps′) v.i. **·lapsed, ·laps·ing** 1 To lapse back, as into disease after partial recovery. 2 To return to bad habits or sin; backslide. —n. (*also* rē′laps) 1 The act or an instance of relapsing. 2 The return of an illness after apparent recovery. [< L *relapsus,* pp. of *relabi* slide back] —**re·laps′er** n.

re·late (ri·lāt′) v. **·lat·ed, ·lat·ing** v.t. 1 To tell the events or the particulars of; narrate. 2 To bring into connection or relation. —v.i. 3 To have relation: with *to.* 4 To have reference: with *to.* [< L *relatus,* pp. of *referre* to carry back] —**re·lat′er** n.

re·lat·ed (ri·lā′tid) adj. 1 Standing in relation; connected. 2 Of common ancestry; connected by blood or marriage; akin. 3 Narrated. —**re·lat′ed·ly** adv. —**re·lat′ed·ness** n.

re·la·tion (ri·lā′shən) n. 1 The fact or condition of being related or connected: the *relation* between poverty and disease. 2 Connection by blood or marriage; kinship. 3 A person connected by blood or marriage; a relative. 4 Reference; regard; allusion: in *relation* to your request. 5 *pl.* The contacts or dealings between or among individuals, groups, nations, etc.: race *relations;* political *relations.* 6 The act of relating or narrating; also, that which is related or told. —**re·la′tion·al** adj.

re·la·tion·ship (ri·lā′shən·ship) n. 1 The state or quality of being related; connection. 2 Kinship. 3 The kind or quality of association between people: a healthy *relationship.*

rel·a·tive (rel′ə·tiv) adj. 1 Having connection; pertinent: an inquiry *relative* to one's health. 2 Resulting from or depending upon a relation to or comparison with something else; comparative: a *relative* truth. 3 Intelligible only in relation to something else; not absolute. 4 *Gram.* Referring to or qualifying an antecedent: a *relative* pronoun. —n. 1 One who is related; a kinsman. 2 A relative word or term. —**rel′a·tive·ly** adv. —**rel′a·tive·ness** n.

relative clause *Gram.* A dependent clause introduced by a relative pronoun.

relative humidity At any given temperature, the percentage of the maximum possible water vapor content actually present in the air.

relative pronoun *Gram.* A pronoun that refers to an antecedent and introduces a dependent clause, as *who* in *We who knew him admired him.*

rel·a·tiv·i·ty (rel′ə·tiv′ə·tē) n. 1 The quality or condition of being relative; relativeness. 2 *Philos.* Existence viewed only as an object of, or in relation to, a thinking mind. 3 A condition of dependence or of close relation of one thing on or to another. 4 *Physics* The principle of the interdependence of matter, energy, space, and time, as mathematically formulated by Albert Einstein. The **special theory of relativity** states that the speed of light is the same in all frames of reference and that the same laws of physics hold in all frames of reference that are not accelerated. The **general theory of relativity** extends these principles to accelerated frames of reference and gravitational phenomena.

re·lax (ri·laks′) v.t. 1 To make lax or loose; make less tight or firm. 2 To make less stringent or severe, as discipline. 3 To abate; slacken, as efforts. 4 To relieve from strain or effort. —v.i. 5 To become lax or loose; loosen. 6 To become less stringent or severe. 7 To rest. 8 To unbend; become less formal. [< L *re-* again + *laxare* loosen] —**re·lax′a·ble** adj. —**re·lax′a·tion, re·lax′er** n.

re·lax·ant (ri·laks′ənt) adj. Pertaining to or causing relaxation. —n. A drug or other agent that reduces tension, esp. of muscles.

re·lay¹ (rē′lā) n. 1 A fresh set, as of men, horses, or dogs, to replace or relieve a tired set. 2 A supply of anything kept in store for anticipated use or need. 3 A relay race, or one of its laps or legs. 4 *Electr.* An electronically controlled switch. —v.t. (*also* ri·lā′) **·layed, ·lay·ing** 1 To send onward by or as by relays. 2 To provide with relays. 3 *Telecom.* To retransmit (a message or signal). [< Ital. *rilasciare* leave behind]

re·lay² (rē′lā′) v.t. **·laid, ·lay·ing** To lay again.

re·lay race (rē′lā) A race between teams, each runner of which runs only a set part of the course and is relieved by a teammate.

re·lease (ri·lēs′) *v.t.* **·leased, ·leas·ing** 1 To set free; liberate. 2 To deliver from worry, pain, obligation, etc. 3 To free from something that holds, binds, etc. 4 To permit the circulation, sale, performance, etc., of, as a motion picture, phonograph record, or news item. —*n.* 1 The act of releasing or setting free, or the state of being released. 2 A discharge from responsibility or penalty; also, a document authorizing this. *Law* An instrument of conveyance by which one person surrenders and relinquishes all claims or rights to another person. 4 The releasing of something to the public; also, that which is released, as a news item, motion picture, etc. 5 *Mech.* Any catch or device to hold and release something. [< L *relaxare* relax] — **re·leas′er** *n.*

re·lease (rē′lēs′) *v.t.* **·leased, ·leas·ing** To lease again.

rel·e·gate (rel′ə·gāt) *v.t.* **·gat·ed, ·gat·ing** 1 To send off or consign, as to an obscure position or place. 2 To assign, as to a particular class or sphere. 3 To refer (a matter) to someone for decision, action, etc. 4 To banish; exile. [< L *re-* away, back + *legare* send] —**rel′e·ga′tion** *n.*

re·lent (ri·lent′) *v.i.* To soften in temper; become more gentle or compassionate. [< L *relentescere* grow soft]

re·lent·less (ri·lent′lis) *adj.* 1 Unremitting; continuous. 2 Not relenting; pitiless. —**re·lent′less·ly** *adv.* —**re·lent′less·ness** *n.*

rel·e·vant (rel′ə·vənt) *adj.* Fitting; pertinent; applicable. [< Med. L *relevare* bear upon] —**rel′e·vance, rel′e·van·cy** *n.* —**rel′e·vant·ly** *adv.*

re·li·a·ble (ri·lī′ə·bəl) *adj.* That may be relied upon; worthy of confidence. —**re·li·a·bil′i·ty, re·li′a·ble·ness** *n.* —**re·li′a·bly** *adv.* —Syn. trustworthy, dependable, loyal, constant.

re·li·ance (ri·lī′əns) *n.* 1 The act of relying. 2 Confidence; trust; dependence. 3 That upon which one relies.

re·li·ant (ri·lī′ənt) *adj.* 1 Having or manifesting reliance. 2 Dependent: with *on.* —**re·li′ant·ly** *adv.*

rel·ic (rel′ik) *n.* 1 Some remaining portion or fragment of that which has vanished or is destroyed. 2 A custom, habit, etc., from the past. 3 A keepsake or memento. 4 The body or part of the body of a saint, or any sacred memento. 5 *pl.* A corpse; remains. [< L *reliquiae* remains < *relinquere* leave]

re·lief (ri·lēf′) *n.* 1 The act of relieving, or the state of being relieved. 2 That which relieves. 3 Charitable aid, as money or food. 4 Release, as from a post or duty; also, the person or persons who take over for those released. 5 In architecture and sculpture, the projection of a figure, ornament, etc., from a surface; also, any such figure. 6 In painting, the apparent projection of forms and masses. 7 *Geog.* a The unevenness of land surface, as caused by mountains, hills, etc. b The parts of a map which portray such unevenness.

Relief *def. 5*

re·lieve (ri·lēv′) *v.t.* **·lieved, ·liev·ing** 1 To free wholly or partly from pain, stress, pressure, etc. 2 To lessen or alleviate, as pain or pressure. 3 To give aid or assistance to. 4 To free from obligation, injustice, etc. 5 To release from duty by providing a substitute. 6 To make less monotonous, harsh, or unpleasant; vary. 7 To bring into prominence; display by contrast. [< L *relevare* lift up] —**re·liev′·a·ble** *adj.* —**re·liev′er** *n.*

re·lig·ion (ri·lij′ən) *n.* 1 A belief in a divine or superhuman power or principle, usu. thought of as the creator of all things. 2 The manifestation of such a belief in worship, ritual, conduct, etc. 3 Any system of religious faith or practice: the Jewish *religion.* 4 The religious or monastic life: to enter *religion.* 5 Anything that elicits devotion, zeal, dedication, etc.: Politics is his *religion.* [< L *religio*]

re·lig·i·os·i·ty (ri·lij′ē·os′ə·tē) *n.* The state or quality of being religious, esp. excessively or affectedly so.

re·lig·ious (ri·lij′əs) *adj.* 1 Feeling and manifesting religion; devout; pious. 2 Of or pertaining to religion: a *religious* teacher. 3 Faithful and strict in performance; conscientious: a *religious* loyalty. 4 Belonging to the monastic life. —*n. pl.* **·ious** A monk or nun. —**re·lig′ious·ly** *adv.* —**re·lig′ious·ness** *n.*

re·lin·quish (ri·ling′kwish) *v.t.* 1 To give up; abandon. 2 To renounce: to *relinquish* a claim. 3 To let go (a hold or something held). [< L *re-* back, from + *linquere* leave] — **re·lin′quish·er, re·lin′quish·ment** *n.*

rel·i·quar·y (rel′ə·kwer′ē) *n. pl.* **·quar·ies** A casket, shrine, or other repository for relics. [< L *reliquiae* remains]

rel·ish (rel′ish) *n.* 1 Appetite; appreciation; liking. 2 The flavor, esp. when agreeable, in food and drink. 3 The quality in anything that lends spice or zest: Danger gives *relish* to adventure. 4 A savory food or condiment served with other food to lend it flavor or zest. 5 A hint, trace, or suggestion of some quality or characteristic. —*v.t.* 1 To like; enjoy: to *relish* a dinner or a joke. —*v.i.* 2 To have an agreeable flavor; afford gratification. [< OF *relaisser* leave behind] —**rel′ish·a·ble** *adj.*

re·live (rē·liv′) *v.t.* **·lived, ·liv·ing** To experience again, as in one's memory.

re·luc·tance (ri·luk′təns) *n.* 1 The state of being reluctant; unwillingness. 2 *Electr.* Capacity for opposing magnetic induction. Also **re·luc′tan·cy.**

re·luc·tant (ri·luk′tənt) *adj.* 1 Disinclined; unwilling. 2 Marked by unwillingness. [< L *reluctari* fight back] —**re·luc′tant·ly** *adv.*

re·ly (ri·lī′) *v.i.* **·lied, ·ly·ing** To place trust or confidence: with *on* or *upon.* [< L *re-* again + *ligare* to bind] —Syn. lean, depend, count, bank (all with *on* or *upon*).

re·main (ri·mān′) *v.i.* 1 To stay or be left behind after the removal, departure, or destruction of other persons or things. 2 To continue in one place, condition, or character. 3 To be left as something to be done, dealt with, etc. 4 To endure or last; abide. [< L *re-* back + *manere* stay, remain]

re·main·der (ri·mān′dər) *n.* 1 That which remains; something left over. 2 *Math.* a The result of subtraction; difference. b The difference of the product of the quotient and divisor subtracted from the dividend in division. 3 *Law* An estate in expectancy, but not in actual possession and enjoyment. 4 A copy or copies of a book remaining with a publisher after sales have fallen off or ceased. —*adj.* Left over; remaining. —*v.t.* To sell as a remainder (def. 4).

re·mains (ri·mānz′) *n. pl.* 1 That which is left after a part has been removed or destroyed; remnants. 2 A corpse. 3 Unpublished writings at the time of an author's death. 4 Survivals of the past, as fossils, monuments, etc.

re·make (rē·māk′) *v.t.* **·made, ·mak·ing** To make again or in a different form: to *remake* a silent film. —*n.* (rē′māk) Something that is remade, esp. a motion picture.

re·mand (ri·mand′, -mänd′) *v.t.* 1 To order or send back. 2 *Law* a To recommit to custody, as an accused person after a preliminary examination. b To send (a case) back to a lower court. —*n.* The act of remanding or the state of being remanded. [< L *re-* back + *mandare* to order] — **re·mand′ment** *n.*

re·mark (ri·märk′) *n.* 1 A comment or saying; casual observation. 2 The act of noticing, observing, or perceiving. —*v.t.* 1 To say or write by way of comment. 2 To take particular notice of. —*v.i.* 3 To make remarks: with *on* or *upon.* [< F *re-* again + *marquer* to mark] —**re·mark′er** *n.*

re·mark·a·ble (ri·mär′kə·bəl) *adj.* 1 Worthy of special notice. 2 Extraordinary; unusual. —**re·mark′a·ble·ness** *n.* —**re·mark′a·bly** *adv.*

re·me·di·a·ble (ri·mē′dē·ə·bəl) *adj.* Capable of being cured or remedied. —**re·me′di·a·bly** *adv.*

re·me·di·al (ri·mē′dē·əl) *adj.* Of the nature of or adapted to be used as a remedy: *remedial* measures. —**re·me′di·al·ly** *adv.*

rem·e·dy (rem′ə·dē) *v.t.* **·died, ·dy·ing** 1 To cure or heal, as by medicinal treatment. 2 To make right; repair; correct. 3 To overcome or remove (an evil or defect). —*n. pl.* **·dies** 1 A medicine or remedial treatment. 2 A means of correcting an evil, fault, etc. 3 *Law* A legal mode for enforcing a right or redressing or preventing a wrong. [< L *re-* thoroughly + *mederi* heal, restore]

re·mem·ber (ri·mem′bər) *v.t.* **1** To bring back or present again to the mind or memory; recall. **2** To keep in mind carefully, as for a purpose. **3** To bear in mind with affection, respect, awe, etc. **4** To reward (someone) with a gift, legacy, tip, etc. —*v.i.* **5** To bring something back to or keep something in the mind. **6** To have or use one's memory. —**remember** (one) **to** To inform a person of the regard of: *Remember* me *to* your wife. [< L *re-* again + *memorare* bring to mind] —**re·mem′ber·er** *n.*

re·mem·brance (ri·mem′brəns) *n.* **1** The act or power of remembering or the state of being remembered. **2** The period within which one can remember. **3** That which is remembered. **4** A gift, memento, or keepsake. **5** An observance in commemoration.

re·mind (ri·mīnd′) *v.t.* To bring to (someone's) mind; cause to remember. —**re·mind′er** *n.* —**re·mind′ful** *adj.*

rem·i·nisce (rem′ə·nis′) *v.i.* **·nisced, ·nisc·ing** To recall incidents or events of the past; indulge in reminiscences. [Back formation < REMINISCENCE]

rem·i·nis·cence (rem′ə·nis′əns) *n.* **1** The recalling to mind of past incidents and events. **2** A written or oral account of past experiences. **3** Anything that serves as a reminder of something else. [< L *reminisci* recollect] —**rem′i·nis′cent** *adj.* —**rem′i·nis′cent·ly** *adv.*

re·miss (ri·mis′) *adj.* Lax or careless in matters requiring attention; negligent. [< L *remittere* send back, slacken] —**re·miss′ness** *n.*

re·mis·si·ble (ri·mis′ə·bəl) *adj.* Capable of being remitted or pardoned, as sins. —**re·mis′si·bil′i·ty** *n.*

re·mis·sion (ri·mish′ən) *n.* **1** The act of remitting, or the state of being remitted. **2** Pardon, as of sins or a crime. **3** Release from a debt, penalty, or obligation. **4** Temporary abatement, as of pain, symptoms, etc.

re·mit (ri·mit′) *v.* **·mit·ted, ·mit·ting** *v.t.* **1** To send, as money in payment for goods; transmit. **2** To refrain from exacting or inflicting, as a penalty. **3** To pardon; forgive. **4** To slacken; relax, as vigilance. **5** To restore; replace. **6** To put off; postpone. **7** *Law* To refer (a legal proceeding) to a lower court for further consideration. —*v.i.* **8** To send money, as in payment. **9** To diminish; abate. [< L *re-* back + *mittere* send] —**re·mit′ter** or **re·mit′tor** *n.*

re·mit·tal (ri·mit′l) *n.* REMISSION.

re·mit·tance (ri·mit′ns) *n.* **1** The act of remitting money or credit. **2** That which is remitted, as money.

re·mit·tent (ri·mit′nt) *adj.* Having temporary abatements: a *remittent* fever. —*n.* A remittent fever. [< L *remittere* remit] —**re·mit′tent·ly** *adv.*

rem·nant (rem′nənt) *n.* **1** That which remains of anything. **2** A piece of cloth, etc., left over after the last cutting. **3** A remaining trace or survival of anything: a *remnant* of faith. **4** A small remaining number or quantity, as of people. —*adj.* Remaining. [< OF *remaindre* remain]

re·mod·el (rē·mod′l) *v.t.* **·eled** or **·elled, ·el·ing** or **·el·ling** **1** To model again. **2** To make over or anew.

re·mon·e·tize (rē·mon′ə·tīz) *v.t.* **·tized, ·tiz·ing** To reinstate, esp. silver, as lawful money. [< RE- + L *moneta* money + -IZE] —**re·mon′e·ti·za′tion** *n.*

re·mon·strance (ri·mon′strəns) *n.* The act or an instance of remonstrating; protest.

re·mon·strant (ri·mon′strənt) *adj.* Protesting or opposing; expostulatory. —*n.* One who remonstrates.

re·mon·strate (ri·mon′strāt) *v.* **·strat·ed, ·strat·ing** *v.t.* **1** To say or plead in protest or opposition. —*v.i.* **2** To protest; object. [< L *re-* again + *monstrare* show] —**re·mon·stra·tion** (rē′mon·strā′shən, rem′ən-), **re·mon′stra′tor** *n.* —**re·mon′·stra·tive** (-strə·tiv) *adj.*

re·morse (ri·môrs′) *n.* The keen or hopeless anguish caused by a sense of guilt; distressing self-reproach. [< LL *remorsus* a biting back] —**re·morse′ful** *adj.* —**re·morse′ful·ly** *adv.* —**re·morse′ful·ness** *n.*

re·morse·less (ri·môrs′lis) *adj.* Having no remorse or compassion. —**re·morse′less·ly** *adv.* —**re·morse′less·ness** *n.* —**Syn.** pitiless, cruel, merciless, ruthless.

re·mote (ri·mōt′) *adj.* **1** Located far from a specified place. **2** Removed far from present time. **3** Having slight bearing on or connection with: a problem *remote* from our discussion. **4** Distant in relation to: a *remote* cousin. **5** Not

obvious; faint; slight: a *remote* likeness. **6** Cold; aloof: a *remote* manner. [< L *remotus*, p.p. of *removere* remove] —**re·mote′ly** *adv.* —**re·mote′ness** *n.*

remote control Control from a distance, as of a machine, apparatus, aircraft, etc.

re·mount (rē·mount′) *v.t. & v.i.* To mount again or anew. —*n.* (rē′mount′) **1** A new setting or framing. **2** A fresh riding horse.

re·mov·a·ble (ri·mōō′və·bəl) *adj.* Capable of being removed. —**re·mov′a·bil′i·ty, re·mov′a·ble·ness** *n.*

re·mov·al (ri·mōō′vəl) *n.* **1** The act of removing or the state of being removed. **2** Dismissal, as from office. **3** Changing of place, esp. of habitation.

re·move (ri·mōōv′) *v.* **·moved, ·mov·ing** *v.t.* **1** To take or move away or from one place to another. **2** To take off. **3** To get rid of; do away with: to *remove* abuses. **4** To kill. To displace or dismiss, as from office. **6** To take out; extract: with *from.* —*v.i.* **7** To change one's place of residence or business. **8** To go away; depart. —*n.* **1** The act of removing. **2** The distance or degree of difference between things: He is only one *remove* from a fool. [< L *re-* again + *movere* move] —**re·mov′er** *n.*

re·moved (ri·mōōvd′) *adj.* Separated, as by intervening space, time, or relationship, or by difference in kind: a cousin twice *removed.* —**re·mov·ed·ness** (ri·mōō′vid·nis) *n.*

re·mu·ner·ate (ri·myōō′nə·rāt) *v.t.* **·at·ed, ·at·ing** **1** To pay (a person) for something, as for services, losses, etc. **2** To compensate or reward for (work, diligence, etc.). [< L *remunerari*] —**re·mu′ner·a′tion, re·mu′ner·a′tor** *n.* —**re·mu′ner·a·tive** (-nər·ə·tiv, -nə·rā′tiv) *adj.* —**re·mu′ner·a·tive·ly** *adv.*

Re·mus (rē′məs) *Rom. Myth.* The twin brother of Romulus, by whom he was killed.

ren·ais·sance (ren′ə·säns′, -zäns′, ri·nā′səns) *n.* A new birth; resurrection; renascence. [F< *renaître* be reborn]

Ren·ais·sance (ren′ə·säns′, -zäns′, ri·nā′səns) *n.* **1** The revival of letters and art in Europe, marking the transition from the medieval to the modern world. **2** The period of this revival, from the 14th to the 16th century. **3** The style of art, literature, etc., marked by a classical influence, that was developed in and characteristic of this period. —*adj.* **1** Of, pertaining to, or characteristic of the Renaissance. **2** Pertaining to a style of architecture originating in Italy in the 15th century and based on the classical Roman style.

re·nal (rē′nəl) *adj.* Of or situated near the kidneys. [< L *renes* kidneys]

re·nas·cence (ri·nās′əns, -nas′-) *n.* A rebirth; revival. [< L *re-* again + *nasci* be born] —**re·nas′cent** *adj.*

Re·nas·cence (ri·nās′əns, -nas′-) *n.* RENAISSANCE.

rend (rend) *v.* **rent** or **rend·ed, rend·ing** *v.t.* **1** To tear apart forcibly. **2** To pull or remove forcibly: with *away, from, off,* etc. **3** To pass through (the air) violently and noisily. **4** To distress (the heart, etc.), as with grief or despair. —*v.i.* **5** To split; part. [< OE *rendan* tear, cut down] —**rend′er** *n.*

ren·der (ren′dər) *v.t.* **1** To give, present, or submit for action, approval, payment, etc. **2** To provide or furnish; give: to *render* aid. **3** To give as due: to *render* obedience. **4** To perform; do: to *render* great service. **5** To give or state formally. **6** To give by way of requital or retribution: to *render* good for evil. **7** To represent or depict, as in music or painting. **8** To cause to be: to *render* someone helpless. **9** To express in another language; translate. **10** To melt and clarify, as lard. **11** To give back; return: often with *back.* **12** To surrender; give up. [< L *reddere* give back] —**ren′der·a·ble** *adj.* —**ren′der·er** *n.*

ren·dez·vous (rän′dā·vōō, -də-) *n. pl.* **·vous** (-vōōz) **1** An appointed place of meeting. **2** A meeting or an appointment to meet. —*v.t. & v.i.* **·voused** (-vōōd), **·vous·ing** (-vōō′ing) To assemble or cause to assemble at a certain place or time. [< F *rendez-vous*, lit., betake yourself]

ren·di·tion (ren·dish′ən) *n.* **1** A version or interpretation of a text. **2** A performance or interpretation, as of a musical composition, role, etc. **3** The act of rendering. [< OF *rendre* render]

ren·e·gade (ren′ə·gād) *n.* **1** One who abandons a previous loyalty, as to a religion, political party, etc. **2** One who gives up conventional or lawful behavior. —*adj.* Traitorous. [< Sp. *renegar* deny]

re·nege (ri·nig′, -nĕg′, -nēg′) *v.i.* **-neged, -neg·ing 1** In card games, to fail to follow suit when able or required by rule to do so. **2** To fail to fulfill a promise. [< L *re-* again + *negare* deny] —**re·neg′er** *n.*

re·new (ri·n(y)ōō′) *v.t.* **1** To make new or as if new again. **2** To begin again; resume. **3** To repeat: to *renew* an oath. **4** To regain (vigor, strength, etc.). **5** To cause to continue in effect; extend: to *renew* a subscription. **6** To revive; reestablish. **7** To replenish or replace, as provisions. —*v.i.* **8** To become new again. **9** To begin or commence again. [< RE- + NEW] —**re·new′a·ble** *adj.* —**re·new′al, re·new′er** *n.* —**re·new′ed·ly** *adv.*

ren·i·form (ren′ə·fôrm, rē′nə-) *adj.* Kidney-shaped. [< L *renes* kidneys + -FORM]

ren·net (ren′it) *n.* **1** The mucous membrane lining the fourth stomach of a suckling calf or lamb. **2** An extract of this, used to curdle milk in making cheese, etc. **3** RENNIN. [< OE *rinnan* run together, coagulate]

ren·nin (ren′in) *n.* **1** A milk-curdling enzyme present in gastric juice. **2** This enzyme in partially purified form obtained from rennet.

re·nounce (ri·nouns′) *v.t.* **-nounced, -nounc·ing 1** To give up, esp. by formal statement. **2** To disown; repudiate. [< L *renuntiare* protest against] —**re·nounce′ment, re·nounc′er** *n.* —**Syn. 1** abjure, disavow, disclaim, forswear.

ren·o·vate (ren′ə·vāt) *v.t.* **-vat·ed, -vat·ing 1** To make as good as new, as by repairing, cleaning, etc. **2** To renew; refresh; reinvigorate. [< L *re-* again + *novare* make new] —**ren′o·va′tion, ren′o·va′tor** *n.*

re·nown (ri·noun′) *n.* The state of being widely known for great achievements; fame. [< L *re-* again + *nominare* to name] —**re·nowned′** *adj.*

rent[1] (rent) *n.* Compensation, esp. payment in money, made by a tenant to a landlord or owner for the use of property, as land, a house, etc., usu. due at specified intervals. —**for rent** Available in return for a rent. —*v.t.* **1** To obtain the temporary possession and use of in return for paying rent. **2** To grant the temporary use of for a rent. —*v.i.* **3** To be let for rent. [< L *reddita* what is given back or paid] —**rent′a·ble** *adj.* —**rent′er** *n.*

rent[2] (rent) A *p.t.* & *p.p.* of REND. —*n.* **1** A hole or slit made by rending or tearing. **2** A violent separation; schism.

rent·al (ren′təl) *n.* **1** An amount paid or due to be paid as rent. **2** The revenue derived from rented property. **3** The act of renting. —*adj.* **1** Of or pertaining to rent. **2** Engaged in the business of renting or supervising rents.

re·nun·ci·a·tion (ri·nun′sē·ā′shən, -shē-) *n.* **1** The act of renouncing; repudiation. **2** A declaration in which something is renounced. —**re·nun′ci·a′tive** (-sē·ā′tiv), **re·nun′ci·a·to′ry** *adj.*

re·o·pen (rē·ō′pən) *v.t.* & *v.i.* **1** To open again. **2** To begin again; resume.

re·or·gan·i·za·tion (rē·ôr·gən·ə·zā′shən, -ī·zā′-) *n.* **1** The act of reorganizing. **2** The legal reconstruction of a corporation, usu. to avert a failure.

re·or·gan·ize (rē·ôr′gən·īz) *v.t.* & *v.i.* **-ized, -iz·ing** To organize anew. —**re·or′gan·iz′er** *n.*

rep[1] (rep) *n.* A silk, cotton, rayon, or wool fabric having a crosswise rib. [< F *reps*]

rep[2] (rep) *n. Slang* **1** REPERTORY. **2** REPRESENTATIVE. **3** REPUTATION.

Rep. Representative; Republic; Republican.

re·pair[1] (ri·pâr′) *v.t.* **1** To restore to sound or good condition after damage, injury, decay, etc. **2** To make up, as a loss; compensate for. —*n.* **1** The act or instance of repairing. **2** Condition after use or after repairing: in good *repair*. [< L *re-* again + *parare* prepare] —**re·pair′er** *n.*

re·pair[2] (ri·pâr′) *v.i.* To betake oneself; go: to *repair* to the garden. [< LL *repatriare* repatriate]

re·pair·man (ri·pâr′man′, -mən) *n. pl.* **·men** (-men′, -mən) A man whose work is to make repairs.

rep·a·ra·ble (rep′ər·ə·bəl) *adj.* Capable of being repaired. —**rep′a·ra·bly** *adv.*

rep·a·ra·tion (rep′ə·rā′shən) *n.* **1** The act of making amends; atonement. **2** That which is done or paid by way of making amends. **3** *pl.* Indemnities paid by defeated

countries for acts of war. **4** The act of repairing, or the state of being repaired. —**re·par·a·tive** (ri·par′ə·tiv) *adj.*

rep·ar·tee (rep′är·tē′, -ər-, -tā′) *n.* **1** Conversation marked by quick and witty replies. **2** Skill in such conversation. **3** A witty reply. [< F *re-* again + *partir* depart]

re·past (ri·past′, -päst′, rē′past) *n.* Food taken at a meal; a meal. [< LL *repascere* feed again]

re·pa·tri·ate (rē·pā′trē·āt) *v.t.* & *v.i.* **·at·ed, ·at·ing** To send back to the country of birth, citizenship, or allegiance, as prisoners of war. —*n.* (rē·pā′trē·it) A person who has been repatriated. [< L *re-* again + *patria* native land] —**re·pa′tri·a′tion** *n.*

re·pay (ri·pā′) *v.* **·paid, ·pay·ing** *v.t.* **1** To pay back; refund. **2** To pay back or refund something to. **3** To make compensation or retaliation for. —*v.i.* **4** To make repayment or requital. —**re·pay′ment** *n.*

re·peal (ri·pēl′) *v.t.* To withdraw the authority to effect; rescind; revoke. —*n.* The act of repealing; revocation. [< OF *rapeler* recall] —**re·peal′a·ble** *adj.* —**re·peal′er** *n.*

re·peat (ri·pēt′) *v.t.* **1** To say again; reiterate. **2** To recite

Repeats *def. 2a*

from memory. **3** To say (what another has just said). **4** To tell, as a secret, to another. **5** To do, make, or experience again. —*v.i.* **6** To say or do something again. **7** To vote more than once at the same election. —*n.* **1** The act of repeating. **2** *Music* **a** A sign indicating that a passage is to be repeated. **b** A passage meant to be repeated. [< L *repetere* do or say again] —**re·peat′a·ble** *adj.*

re·peat·ed (ri·pē′tid) *adj.* Occurring or spoken again and again. —**re·peat′ed·ly** *adv.*

re·peat·er (ri·pē′tər) *n.* **1** One who or that which repeats. **2** A firearm that can discharge several shots without being reloaded. **3** One who illegally votes more than once at the same election. **4** One who has been repeatedly imprisoned for criminal offenses.

re·pel (ri·pel′) *v.* **·pelled, ·pel·ling** *v.t.* **1** To force or drive back; repulse. **2** To reject; refuse, as a suggestion. **3** To cause to feel distaste or aversion. **4** To fail to mix with or adhere to. —*v.i.* **5** To act so as to drive something back or away. **6** To cause distaste or aversion. [< L *re-* back + *pellere* drive] —**re·pel′ler** *n.*

re·pel·lent (ri·pel′ənt) *adj.* **1** Serving, tending, or having power to repel. **2** Exciting disgust; repugnant; repulsive. —*n.* Something that repels, as a substance that repels water, insects, etc. —**re·pel′len·cy, re·pel′lence** *n.*

re·pent (ri·pent′) *v.i.* **1** To feel remorse or regret, as for something done or undone; be contrite. **2** To change one's mind concerning past action: with *of.* —*v.t.* **3** To feel remorse or regret for (an action, sin, etc.). [< L *re-* again + *poenitere* cause to repent] —**re·pent′er** *n.*

re·pen·tance (ri·pen′təns) *n.* The act of repenting; sorrow for having done wrong. —**re·pen′tant** *adj.* —**re·pen′tant·ly** *adv.*

re·per·cus·sion (rē′pər·kush′ən) *n.* **1** *Usu. pl.* A long-range or unpredictable result, as of an event; aftereffect. **2** A reverberation; echo. [< L *repercussus,* p.p. of *repercutere* rebound] —**re′per·cus′sive** *adj.*

rep·er·toire (rep′ər·twär) *n.* **1** A list of works, as of music or drama, that a company or person is prepared to perform. **2** Such works collectively. **3** The aggregate of devices, methods, etc., used in a particular line of activity: the teacher's *repertoire* of visual aids. [< LL *repertorium* inventory]

rep·er·to·ry (rep′ər·tôr′ē, -tō′rē) *n. pl.* **·ries 1** A theatrical group having a repertoire of productions: also **repertory company, repertory theater. 2** REPERTOIRE. **3** A place where things are gathered in readiness for use. [< L *repertus,* p.p. of *reperire* find, discover]

rep·e·ti·tion (rep′ə·tish′ən) *n.* **1** The doing, making, or saying of something again. **2** That which is repeated; a copy. —**re·pet·i·tive** (ri·pet′ə·tiv) *adj.* —**re·pet′i·tive·ly** *adv.*

rep·e·ti·tious (rep′ə·tish′əs) *adj.* Characterized by or

containing repetition, esp. useless or tedious repetition. —
rep′e·ti′tious·ly adv. —**rep′e·ti′tious·ness** n.

re·pine (ri·pīn′) v.i. ·**pined,** ·**pin·ing** To be discontented or
fretful. [<RE- + PINE²] —**re·pin′er** n.

re·place (ri·plās′) v.t. ·**placed,** ·**plac·ing** 1 To put back in
place. 2 To take or fill the place of; supersede. 3 To refund;
repay. —**re·place′a·ble** adj. —**re·plac′er** n.

re·place·ment (ri·plās′mənt) n. 1 The act of replacing,
or the state of being replaced. 2 Something used to replace, as a substitute.

re·play (rē·plā′) v.t. 1 To play again. 2 To show a replay
of. —n. (rē′plā′) 1 The act of playing again. 2 The playing
of a television tape, often in slow motion and usu. immediately following the live occurrence of the action shown. 3
The action shown in such a replay.

re·plen·ish (ri·plen′ish) v.t. 1 To fill again. 2 To bring
back to fullness or completeness, as diminished supplies.
[<L re- again + plenus full] —**re·plen′ish·er, re·plen′ish·**
ment n.

re·plete (ri·plēt′) adj. 1 Full to the uttermost. 2 Gorged
with food or drink; sated. 3 Abundantly supplied or
stocked. [<L repletus, p.p. of replere fill again] —**re·ple′**
tion, re·plete′ness n.

rep·li·ca (rep′lə·kə) n. 1 A duplicate, as of a picture, executed by the original artist. 2 Any close copy or reproduction. [<L replicare to reply]

rep·li·cate (rep′lə·kāt) v.t. ·**cat·ed,** ·**cat·ing** 1 To make an
indeterminate number of copies of; duplicate. 2 To fold
over. —**rep′li·ca′tion** n.

re·ply (ri·plī′) v. ·**plied,** ·**ply·ing** v.i. 1 To give an answer. 2
To respond by some act, gesture, etc. 3 To echo. 4 Law To
file a pleading in answer to the statement of the defense.
—v.t. 5 To say in answer: She replied that she would do
it. —n. pl. ·**plies** Something said, written, or done by way
of answer. [<L replicare fold back, make a reply] —**re·**
pli′er n.

re·port (ri·pôrt′, -pōrt′) v.t. 1 To make or give an account
of; relate, as information obtained by investigation. 2 To
bear back or repeat to another, as an answer. 3 To complain about, esp. to the authorities. 4 To state the result
of consideration concerning: The committee reported the
bill. —v.i. 5 To make a report. 6 To act as a reporter. 7 To
present oneself, as for duty. —n. 1 That which is reported.
2 A formal statement of the result of an investigation. 3
Common talk; rumor. 4 Fame, reputation, or character. 5
A record of the transactions of a deliberative body. 6 An
account prepared for publication in the press. 7 An explosive sound: the report of a gun. [<L re- back + portare
carry] —**re·port′a·ble** adj. —Syn v. 1 describe, record, transcribe. n. 1, 2, 5, 6 account, statement, announcement. 3
gossip, hearsay.

re·port·age (ri·pôr′tij, -pōr′-, rep′ôr·täzh′) n. 1 The act
or art of reporting, as for publication. 2 Reports that deal
with events in a journalistic style. [F]

report card A periodic statement of a pupil's scholastic
record.

re·port·ed·ly (ri·pôr′tid·lē, -pōr′-) adv. According to report.

re·port·er (ri·pôr′tər, -pōr′-) n. 1 One who reports. 2 One
employed to gather and report news for publication or
broadcasting. —**rep·or·to·ri·al** (rep′ər·tôr′ē·əl, -tō′rē-) adj.

re·pose¹ (ri·pōz′) n. 1 The state of being at rest. 2 Sleep.
3 Freedom from excitement or anxiety; composure. 4 Dignified calmness; serenity; peacefulness. —v. ·**posed,** ·**pos·**
ing v.t. 1 To lay or place in a position of rest. —v.i. 2 To lie
at rest. 3 To lie in death. 4 To rely; depend: with on, upon,
or in. [<LL re- again + pausare to pause]— **re·pose′ful** adj.
—**re·pose′ful·ly** adv.

re·pose² (ri·pōz′) v.t. ·**posed,** ·**pos·ing** To place, as confidence or hope: with in. [<L repositus, p.p. of reponere put
back]

re·pos·i·to·ry (ri·poz′ə·tôr′ē, -tō′rē) n. pl. ·**ries** 1 A place
in which goods may be stored; a depository. 2 Anything
considered as a place of storage or assembly: a repository
of Indian lore. 3 A person to whom a secret is entrusted.
[<L repositorium]

re·pos·sess (rē′pə·zes′) v.t. To regain possession of, esp.
as a result of the default of payments due. —**re′pos·ses′**
sion n.

rep·re·hend (rep′ri·hend′) v.t. To criticize sharply; find
fault with. [<L re- back + prehendere hold] —**rep′re·hen′·**
sion n. —**rep′re·hen′sive** adj. —**rep′re·hen′sive·ly** adv.

rep·re·hen·si·ble (rep′ri·hen′sə·bəl) adj. Deserving
blame or censure. —**rep′re·hen′si·bil′i·ty, rep′re·hen′si·ble·**
ness n. —**rep′re·hen′si·bly** adv.

rep·re·sent (rep′ri·zent′) v.t. 1 To serve as the symbol,
expression, or designation of; symbolize: The dove represents peace. 2 To serve as an example, specimen, type, etc.,
of; typify: They represent the best in America. 3 To set
forth a likeness or image of; depict; portray. 4 To serve as
or be the delegate, agent, etc., of, as by legal authority or
by election. 5 To act the part of; impersonate. 6 To bring
before the mind; present clearly: Goya etchings that
represent the horrors of war. 7 To set forth in words, esp.
in a forceful and persuasive manner. 8 To describe as
being of a specified character or condition: to represent a
signature as authentic. [<L re- again + praesentare to
present]

rep·re·sen·ta·tion (rep′ri·zen·tā′shən) n. 1 The act of
representing, or the state of being represented. 2 A likeness or model. 3 A statement usu. purporting to be descriptive that represents a point of view and is intended
to influence judgment. 4 A dramatic performance. 5 Representatives collectively.

rep·re·sen·ta·tive (rep′ri·zen′tə·tiv) adj. 1 Typifying a
group or class. 2 Acting or having the power to act as an
agent. 3 Made up of representatives. 4 Based on the political principle of representation. 5 Presenting, portraying,
or representing. —n. 1 One who or that which is typical
of a group or class. 2 One who is authorized as an agent
or delegate. 3 Often cap. A member of a legislative body,
esp., in the U.S., a member of the lower house of Congress
or of a state legislature. —**rep′re·sen′ta·tive·ly** adv. —**rep′re·**
sen′ta·tive·ness n.

re·press (ri·pres′) v.t. 1 To keep under restraint or control. 2 To block the expression of: to repress a groan. 3 To
put down; quell, as a rebellion. [<L repressus, p.p. of re-
primere press back] —**re·press′er, re·pres′sive·ness** n. —**re·**
press′i·ble, re·pres′sive adj. —**re·pres′sive·ly** adv. —Syn. 1
curb, rein. 2 suppress, hold in.

re·pres·sion (ri·presh′ən) n. 1 The act of repressing, or
the condition of being repressed. 2 Psychoanal. The exclusion from consciousness of painful desires, memories, etc.,
and consequent manifestation through the unconscious.

re·prieve (ri·prēv′) v.t. ·**prieved,** ·**priev·ing** 1 To suspend
temporarily the execution of a sentence upon. 2 To relieve
for a time from suffering or trouble. —n. 1 The temporary
suspension of a sentence. 2 Temporary relief or cessation
of pain; respite. [<F reprendre take back]

rep·ri·mand (rep′rə·mand) v.t. To reprove sharply or formally. —n. Severe reproof or formal censure. [<L re-
primendus to be repressed]

re·print (rē′print′) n. A printing that is an exact copy of
a work already printed. —v.t. (rē·print′) To print again,
esp. without alteration. —**re·print′er** n.

re·pri·sal (ri·prī′zəl) n. Any action done in retaliation for
harm or injuries received, esp. an action involving the use
of force and sanctioned by a government or political
group. [<OF reprendre take back]

re·proach (ri·prōch′) v.t. To charge with or blame for
something wrong; rebuke. —n. 1 The act of or an expression of reproaching; censure; reproof. 2 A cause of blame
or disgrace. 3 Disgrace; discredit. [<OF reprochier] —**re·**
proach′ful adj. —**re·proach′ful·ly** adv. —**re·proach′ful·ness** n.

rep·ro·bate (rep′rə·bāt) adj. 1 Utterly depraved; profligate; corrupt. 2 Theol. Abandoned in sin; condemned. —n.
One who is reprobate. —v.t. ·**bat·ed,** ·**bat·ing** 1 To disap-
prove of heartily; condemn. 2 Theol. To abandon to damnation. [<LL reprobare reprove] —**rep′ro·ba′tion** n. —**rep′·**
ro·ba′tive adj.

re·pro·duce (rē′prə·dyōōs′) v. ·**duced,** ·**duc·ing** v.t. 1 To
make a copy or image of. 2 To bring (offspring) into existence by sexual or asexual generation. 3 To replace (a lost
part or organ) by regeneration. 4 To cause the reproduction of (plant life, etc.). 5 To produce again. 6 To recall to
the mind; recreate mentally. —v.i. 7 To produce offspring.
8 To undergo copying, reproduction, etc. —**re′pro·duc′er** n.
—**re′pro·duc′i·ble** adj.

re·pro·duc·tion (rē′prə·duk′shən) n. 1 The act or process of reproducing. 2 Any process by which animals or plants give rise to new organisms. 3 Something reproduced, as a photocopy. —re′pro·duc′tive adj. —re′pro·duc′· tive·ly adv. —re′pro·duc′tive·ness n.

re·prog·ra·phy (rē·prog′rə·fē) n. The reproduction of graphic material, esp. by electronic devices.

re·proof (ri·prōōf′) n. The act or an expression of reproving; censure.

re·prove (ri·prōōv′) v.t. ·proved, ·prov·ing 1 To censure, as for a fault; rebuke. 2 To express disapproval of (an act). [< L re- again + probare to test] —re·prov′er n. —re·prov′ing· ly adv. —Syn. 1 admonish, chasten, chide, reproach, scold.

rep·tile (rep′tīl, -til) n. 1 Any of a class of cold-blooded, air-breathing vertebrates having a scaly skin, as crocodiles, lizards, snakes, turtles, etc. 2 A groveling, abject person. —adj. 1 Of, like, or characteristic of a reptile. 2 Groveling, sly, base, etc. [< L reptus, p.p. of repere creep] —rep·til·i·an (rep·til′ē·ən) adj., n.

Reptile (crocodile)

re·pub·lic (ri·pub′lik) n. 1 A state in which the sovereignty resides in the people entitled to vote for officers who represent them in governing. 2 This form of government. [< L res thing + publicus public]

re·pub·li·can (ri·pub′li·kən) adj. Pertaining to, of the nature of, or suitable for a republic. —n. An advocate of a republican form of government. —re·pub′li·can·ism n.

Re·pub·li·can (ri·pub′li·kən) n. A member of the Republican Party in the U.S. —Re·pub′li·can·ism n.

Republican Party One of the two major political parties in the U.S.

re·pu·di·ate (ri·pyōō′dē·āt) v.t. ·at·ed, ·at·ing 1 To refuse to accept as valid, true, or authorized; reject. 2 To refuse to acknowledge or pay. 3 To cast off; disown, as a son. [< L repudium divorce] —re·pu′di·a′tion, re·pu′di·a′tor n.

re·pug·nance (ri·pug′nəns) n. 1 A feeling of strong distaste or aversion. 2 Contradiction; inconsistency.

re·pug·nant (ri·pug′nənt) adj. 1 Offensive to taste or feeling; exciting aversion. 2 Contradictory; inconsistent. [< L re back + pugnare to fight] —re·pug′nant·ly adv.

re·pulse (ri·puls′) v.t. ·pulsed, ·puls·ing 1 To drive back; repel, as an attacking force. 2 To repel by coldness, discourtesy, etc.; rebuff. 3 To excite disgust in. —n. 1 The act of repulsing, or the state of being repulsed. 2 Rejection; refusal. [< L repulsus, p.p. of repellere repel] —re·puls′er n.

re·pul·sion (ri·pul′shən) n. 1 The act of repelling, or the state of being repelled. 2 Aversion; repugnance. 3 Physics The mutual action of two bodies that tends to drive them apart.

re·pul·sive (ri·pul′siv) adj. 1 Exciting strong feelings of dislike or disgust; offensive. 2 Such as to discourage approach; forbidding. 3 Acting to repulse. —re·pul′sive·ly adv. —re·pul′sive·ness n.

rep·u·ta·ble (rep′yə·tə·bəl) adj. 1 Having a good reputation; estimable; honorable. 2 Complying with the usage of the best writers. —rep′u·ta·bil′i·ty n. —rep′u·ta·bly adv.

rep·u·ta·tion (rep′yə·tā′shən) n. 1 The general estimation in which a person or thing is held by others, either good or bad. 2 High regard or esteem. 3 A particular credit ascribed to a person or thing: a reputation for honesty. [< L reputare be reputed.]

re·pute (ri·pyōōt′) v.t. ·put·ed, ·put·ing To regard or consider: usu. in the passive: reputed to be clever. —n. REPUTATION (defs. 1 & 2). [< L re- again + putare think, count]

re·put·ed (ri·pyōō′tid) adj. Generally thought or supposed. —re·put′ed·ly adv.

re·quest (ri·kwest′) v.t. 1 To express a desire for, esp. politely. 2 To ask a favor of. —n. 1 The act of requesting; entreaty; petition. 2 That which is requested, as a favor. 3 The state of being requested: in request. [< L requisitus, p.p. of requirere seek again]

re·qui·em (rek′wē·əm, rē′kwē-) n. 1 Often cap. Any musical composition or service for the dead. 2 Often cap. A musical setting for such a service. [< L Requiem rest, the first word of a Roman Catholic mass for the dead]

req·ui·es·cat (rek′wē·es′kat) n. A prayer for the repose of the dead. [L, may he (or she) rest]

re·quire (ri·kwīr′) v. ·quired, ·quir·ing v.t. 1 To have need of; find necessary. 2 To call for, demand: Hunting requires patience. 3 To insist upon: to require absolute silence. 4 To command; order. —v.i. 5 To make a demand or request. [< L re- again + quaerere ask, seek] —re·quir′er n.

re·quire·ment (ri·kwīr′mənt) n. 1 That which is required, as to satisfy a condition; a requisite. 2 A need or necessity.

req·ui·site (rek′wə·zit) adj. Required by the nature of things or by circumstances; indispensable. —n. That which cannot be dispensed with. —req′ui·site·ly adv. —req′ui·site·ness n.

req·ui·si·tion (rek′wə·zish′ən) n. 1 A formal request, as for supplies or equipment. 2 The act of requiring or demanding, as that something be supplied. 3 The state of being required. —v.t. To make a requisition for or to.

re·qui·tal (ri·kwīt′l) n. 1 The act of requiting. 2 Adequate return for good or ill; reward, compensation, or retaliation.

re·quite (ri·kwīt′) v.t. ·quit·ed, ·quit·ing 1 To make equivalent return for, as kindness, service, or injury. 2 To compensate or repay in kind. [< RE- + quite, obs. var. of QUIT] —re·quit′er n.

rere·dos (rir′ə dos, rer′ə-, rir′dos) n. An ornamental screen behind an altar. [< OF arere at the back + dos back]

re·run (rē′run′) n. A running over again, esp. a showing of a film or videotape after the initial showing. —v.t. (rē·run′) ·ran, ·run·ning To run again.

res. research; reserve; residence; resolution.

re·scind (ri·sind′) v.t. To cancel or make void, as an order or an act. [< L re- back + scindere to cut] —re·scind′ment, re·scind′er n.

re·scis·sion (ri·sizh′ən) n. The act of rescinding. —re· scis′si·ble, re·scis′so·ry adj.

res·cue (res′kyōō) v.t. ·cued, ·cu·ing 1 To save or free from danger, captivity, evil, etc. 2 Law To take or remove forcibly from the custody of the law. —n. The act of rescuing. [< L re- again + excutere shake off] —res′cu·er n.

re·search (ri·sûrch′, rē′sûrch) n. Studious, systematic investigation or inquiry to ascertain, uncover, or assemble facts, used as a basis for conclusions or the formulation of theory. —v.t. 1 To do research on or for: to research an article. —v.i. 2 To do research; investigate. [< F recherche] —re·search′er n.

re·sect (ri·sekt′) v.t. To perform a resection on. [< L re- back + secare cut, amputate]

re·sec·tion (ri·sek′shən) n. The surgical removal of a part of a bone, organ, etc.

re·sem·blance (ri·zem′bləns) n. 1 The quality of similarlity in nature, appearance, etc.; likeness. 2 A point or degree of similarity. 3 That which resembles a person or thing; semblance.

re·sem·ble (ri·zem′bəl) v.t. ·bled, ·bling To be similar to in appearance, quality, or character. [< OF re- again + sembler seem]

re·sent (ri·zent′) v.t. To be indignant at, as an injury or insult. [< L re- again + sentire feel] —re·sent′ful adj. —re· sent′ful·ly adv. —re·sent′ful·ness n.

re·sent·ment (ri·zent′mənt) n. Anger and ill will caused by a feeling of injury or mistreatment.

res·er·va·tion (rez′ər·vā′shən) n. 1 A feeling of doubt or skepticism, expressed or unexpressed. 2 A qualification; condition; limitation. 3 An agreement to hold something back, as a hotel room, restaurant table, etc., for use at a particular time; also, a record of such an agreement. 4 The act of reserving. 5 A tract of public land set aside for some special purpose, as for the use of Indians or for the preservation of wildlife.

re·serve (ri·zûrv′) v.t. ·served, ·serv·ing, 1 To hold back or set aside for special or future use. 2 To arrange for ahead of time; have set aside for one's use. **3** To hold back or delay the determination or disclosure of: to *reserve* judgment. **4** To keep as one's own; retain: to *reserve* the right to quit. —*n.* **1** Something stored up for future use or set aside for a particular purpose. **2** A restrained quality of character or manner; reluctance to divulge one's feelings, thoughts, etc. **3** *Usu. pl.* **a** A military force held back from active duty to meet possible emergencies. **b** Members or units of such a force. **4** A substitute player on an athletic team. **5** Funds held back from investment, as in a bank, to meet regular demands. **6** The act of reserving; stint; qualification: without *reserve.* —**in reserve** Subject to or held for future use when needed. —*adj.* Constituting a reserve: a *reserve* supply. [< L *re-* back + *servare* keep] — **re·serv′er** *n.* —**Syn.** *n.* **2** reticence, diffidence, aloofness, modesty, restraint.

reserve clause In professional sports, the stipulation in a contract that commits a player to work for a particular team until released or traded by the employer or until retirement.

re·served (ri·zûrvd′) *adj.* **1** Showing or characterized by reserve of manner; undemonstrative. **2** Kept in reserve; held ready for use. —**re·serv·ed·ly** (ri·zûr′vid·lē) *adv.* —**re·serv′ed·ness** *n.*

re·serv·ist (ri·zûr′vist) *n.* A member of a military reserve.

res·er·voir (rez′ər·vwär, -vwôr -vôr) *n.* **1** A place where some material is stored for use, esp. a lake, usu. artificial, for collecting and storing water. **2** A receptacle for a fluid. **3** An extra supply; store.

re·shape (rē·shāp′) *v.t.* **·shaped, ·shap·ing** To give new form to; reorder the elements or structure of.

re·side (ri·zīd′) *v.i.* **·sid·ed, ·sid·ing** **1** To dwell for a considerable time; live. **2** To exist as an attribute or quality: with *in.* **3** To be vested: with *in.* [< L *residere* sit back]

res·i·dence (rez′ə·dəns) *n.* **1** The place or the house where one resides. **2** The act of residing. **3** The length of time one resides in a place. **4** The act or fact of residing. **5** The condition of residing in a particular place to perform certain duties or to pursue studies, often for a specified length of time.

res·i·den·cy (rez′ə·dən·sē) *n. pl.* **·cies 1** RESIDENCE. **2** A period of advanced training in a hospital, usu. in a medical specialty.

res·i·dent (rez′ə·dənt) *n.* **1** One who resides or dwells in a place. **2** A physician engaged in residency. **3** A diplomatic representative residing at a foreign seat of government. —*adj.* **1** Having a residence; residing. **2** Living in a place in connection with one's official work. **3** Not migratory: said of certain birds.

res·i·den·tial (rez′ə·den′shəl) *adj.* **1** Of, characteristic of, or suitable for residences. **2** Used by residents.

re·sid·u·al (ri·zij′ōō·əl) *adj.* **1** Pertaining to or having the nature of a residue or remainder. **2** Left over as a residue. —*n.* **1** That which is left over from a total, as after subtraction. **2** *Often pl.* A payment made to a performer for each rerun of taped or filmed TV material in which he or she has appeared. —**re·sid′u·al·ly** *adv.*

re·sid·u·ar·y (ri·zij′ōō·er′ē) *adj.* Entitled to receive the residue of an estate.

res·i·due (rez′ə·dyōō) *n.* **1** A remainder after a part has been separated or removed. **2** *Chem.* Matter left unaffected after combustion, distillation, evaporation, etc. **3** *Law* That portion of an estate which remains after all charges, debts, and particular bequests have been satisfied. [< L *residuus* remaining]

re·sid·u·um (ri·zij′ōō·əm) *n. pl.* **·sid·u·a** (-zij′ōō·ə) **1** RESIDUAL (def. 1). **2** RESIDUE (def. 3). [L]

re·sign (ri·zīn′) *v.t.* **1** To give up, as a position, office, or trust. **2** To relinquish (a privilege, claim, etc.). **3** To give over (oneself, one's mind, etc.), as to fate or domination. —*v.i.* **4** To resign a position, etc. [< OF< L *re-* back + *signare* to sign] —**re·sign′er** *n.*

res·ig·na·tion (rez′ig·nā′shən) *n.* **1** The act of resigning. **2** A formal notice of resigning. **3** The quality of being submissive; unresisting acquiescence.

re·signed (ri·zīnd′) *adj.* Characterized by resignation; submissive. —**re·sign·ed·ly** (ri·zī′nid·lē) *adv.* —**re·sign′ed·ness** *n.*

re·sil·ience (ri·zil′yəns) *n.* **1** The quality of being resilient; elasticity. **2** Cheerful buoyancy. Also **re·sil′ien·cy.**

re·sil·ient (ri·zil′yənt) *adj.* **1** Springing back to a former shape or position after being bent, compressed, etc. **2** Able to recover quickly; buoyant. [< L *resilire* to rebound] — **re·sil′ient·ly** *adv.*

res·in (rez′in) *n.* **1** A solid or semisolid, usu. translucent substance exuded from certain plants, used in varnishes, plastics, etc. **2** Any of various substances resembling this made by chemical synthesis. **3** ROSIN. —*v.t.* To apply resin to. [< Gk. *rhētinē*] —**res·i·na·ceous** (rez′ə·nā′shəs), **res′in·ous** *adj.*

re·sist (ri·zist′) *v.t.* **1** To stay the effect of; withstand; hold off: Steel *resists* corrosion. **2** To fight or struggle against; seek to foil or frustrate: to *resist* arrest; to *resist* temptation. —*v.i.* **3** To offer opposition. [< L *re-* back + *sistere,* causative of *stare* stand] —**re·sist′er, re·sist′i·bil′i·ty** *n.* —**re·sist′i·ble, re·sis′tive** *adj.* —**re·sist′i·bly** *adv.*

re·sis·tance (ri·zis′təns) *n.* **1** The act of resisting. **2** Any force tending to hinder motion. **3** The capacity of an organism to ward off the effects of potentially harmful substances, as toxins. **4** *Electr.* The opposition of a body to the passage through it of an electric current. **5** The underground and guerrilla movement in a conquered country opposing the occupying power. —**re·sis′tant** *adj.*

re·sis·tor (ri·zis′tər) *n.* *Electr.* A device whose principal property is resistance.

res·o·lute (rez′ə·lōōt) *adj.* Having a fixed purpose; determined. [< L *resolutus,* p.p. of *resolvere* to resolve] —**res′o·lute·ly** *adv.* —**res′o·lute·ness** *n.* —**Syn.** steady, constant, firm, decisive.

res·o·lu·tion (rez′ə·lōō′shən) *n.* **1** The act of resolving or of reducing to a simpler form. **2** The making of a resolve. **3** The purpose or course resolved upon. **4** Firmness of purpose. **5** An outcome or result that serves to settle a problem, uncertainty, or conflict. **6** A statement expressing the intention or judgment of an assembly or group. **7** *Music* **a** The conventional replacement of a dissonant tone, chord, etc., by one that is consonant. **b** The tone or chord replacing the dissonant one. **8** The capacity of a telescope, microscope, etc., to give separate images of objects close together.

re·solve (ri·zolv′) *v.* **·solved, ·solv·ing** *v.t.* **1** To decide; determine (to do something). **2** To cause to decide or determine. **3** To separate or break down into constituent parts; analyze. **4** To clear away or settle, as a problem, uncertainty, or conflict; explain or solve. **5** To state or decide by vote. **6** *Music* To cause (a dissonant tone, chord, etc.) to undergo resolution. **7** To make distinguishable, as with a telescope or microscope. —*v.i.* **8** To make up one's mind: with *on* or *upon.* **9** To become separated into constituent parts. **10** *Music* To undergo resolution. —*n.* **1** Fixity of purpose; determination. **2** Something resolved upon; a decision. **3** A formal expression of the intention or judgment of an assembly or group. [< L *resolvere* loosen again] —**re·solv′a·ble** *adj.* —**re·solv′er** *n.*

res·o·nance (rez′ə·nəns) *n.* **1** The state or quality of being resonant; resonant sound. **2** Prolongation and amplification of a sound or tone by reverberation. **3** *Physics* A property of oscillatory systems whereby excitation at certain frequencies produces response of greater amplitude than at other frequencies.

res·o·nant (rez′ə·nənt) *adj.* **1** Having the quality of prolonging and amplifying sound by reverberation; producing resonance. **2** Resounding; displaying resonance. **3** Full of or characterized by resonance: a *resonant* voice. [< L *resonare* resound, echo] —**res′o·nant·ly** *adv.*

res·o·nate (rez′ə·nāt) *v.i.* **·nat·ed, ·nat·ing** To exhibit or produce resonance.

res·o·na·tor (rez′ə·nā′tər) *n.* Any device used to produce resonance or to increase sound by resonance.

re·sor·cin·ol (ri·zôr′sin·ōl, -ol) *n.* A derivative of phenol, used as an antiseptic and in making dyes, plastics, etc. Also **re·sor′cin.** [< RES(IN) + *orcinol* a phenol]

re·sort (ri·zôrt′) *v.i.* **1** To go frequently or habitually; repair. **2** To have recourse: with *to.* —*n.* **1** A hotel or other place that provides recreational facilities and sometimes entertainment, esp. for those on vacation. **2** The use of something as a means; a recourse; refuge. **3** A person looked to for help. **4** A place frequented regularly. [< OF *re-* again + *sortir* go out] **—re·sort′er** *n.*

re·sound (ri·zound′) *v.i.* **1** To be filled with sound; echo; reverberate. **2** To make a loud, prolonged, or echoing sound. **3** To ring; echo. **4** To be famed or extolled. —*v.t.* **5** To give back (a sound, etc.); re-echo. **6** To celebrate; extol. [< L *resonare*]

re·source (rē′sôrs, -sōrs, -zôrs, -zōrs, ri·sôrs′, -sōrs′, -zôrs′, -zōrs′) *n.* **1** *Usu. pl.* That which can be drawn upon as a means of help or support. **2** *Usu. pl.* Natural advantages, esp. of a country, as forests, oil deposits, etc. **3** *pl.* Available wealth or property. **4** Skill or ingenuity in meeting any situation. **5** Any way or method of coping with a difficult situation. [< L *re-* back + *surgere* to rise, surge]

re·source·ful (ri·sôrs′fəl, -sōrs′-, -zôrs′, -zōrs′) *adj.* Having the ability to meet the demands of any situation; ingenious. **—re·source′ful·ly** *adv.* **—re·source′ful·ness** *n.*

re·spect (ri·spekt′) *v.t.* **1** To have deferential regard for; esteem. **2** To treat with propriety or consideration. **3** To avoid intruding upon; regard as inviolable. **4** To have reference to; concern. —*n.* **1** A high regard for and appreciation of worth; esteem. **2** Due regard or consideration: *respect* for the law. **3** Expressions of consideration; compliments: to pay one's *respects.* **4** The condition of being honored or respected. **5** A specific aspect or detail: In some *respects* the plan is impractical. **6** Reference or relation: usu. with *to:* with *respect* to profits. [< L *respectus,* p.p. of *respicere* look back, consider] **—re·spect′er** *n.*

re·spect·a·ble (ri·spek′tə·bəl) *adj.* **1** Deserving of respect. **2** Conventionally correct; socially acceptable. **3** Having a good appearance; presentable. **4** Moderate in quality, size, or amount; fair: a *respectable* talent. **—re·spect′a·bil′i·ty, re·spect′a·ble·ness** *n.* **—re·spect′a·bly** *adv.*

re·spect·ful (ri·spekt′fəl) *adj.* Characterized by or showing respect. **—re·spect′ful·ly** *adv.* **—re·spect′ful·ness** *n.*

re·spect·ing (ri·spek′ting) *prep.* In relation to.

re·spec·tive (ri·spek′tiv) *adj.* Relating separately to each of those under consideration; several.

re·spec·tive·ly (ri·spek′tiv·lē) *adv.* Singly in the order designated: to describe the duties of the judge and jury respectively.

res·pi·ra·tion (res′pə·rā′shən) *n.* **1** The act of inhaling air and expelling it; breathing. **2** The process by which an organism takes in and uses oxygen and gives off carbon dioxide and other waste products. **—re·spir·a·to·ry** (res′pər·ə·tôr′ē, ri·spīr′ə·tôr′ē) *adj.*

res·pi·ra·tor (res′pə·rā′tər) *n.* **1** A screen, as of fine gauze, worn over the mouth or nose, as a protection against dust, etc. **2** An apparatus for artificial respiration.

re·spire (ri·spīr′) *v.* **·spired, ·spir·ing** *v.i.* **1** To inhale and exhale air; breathe. —*v.t.* **2** To breathe. [< L *re-* again + *spirare* breathe]

res·pite (res′pit) *n.* **1** Postponement; delay. **2** Temporary relief from labor or effort; an interval of rest. [< Med. L *respectus* delay]

re·splen·dent (ri·splen′dənt) *adj.* Shining with brilliant luster; splendid; gorgeous. [< L *re-* again + *splendere* to shine] **—re·splen′dence, re·splen′den·cy** *n.* **—re·splen′dent·ly** *adv.*

re·spond (ri·spond′) *v.i.* **1** To give an answer; reply. **2** To act in reply or return. **3** To react favorably: to *respond* to treatment. —*v.t.* **4** To say in answer; reply. [< L *re-* back + *spondere* to pledge] **—re·spond′er** *n.*

re·spon·dent (ri·spon′dənt) *n.* **1** One who responds or answers. **2** *Law* The party called upon to answer an appeal or petition; a defendant. **—re·spon′dence, re·spon′den·cy** *n.*

re·sponse (ri·spons′) *n.* **1** Words or acts called forth as a reaction; an answer or reply. **2** *Eccl.* A portion of a church service said or sung by the congregation in reply to the officiating priest. **3** *Biol.* Any reaction resulting from a stimulus. **4** The action of a physical system when energized or disturbed.

re·spon·si·bil·i·ty (ri·spon′sə·bil′ə·tē) *n. pl.* **·ties 1** The state of being responsible or accountable. **2** That for which one is responsible; a duty or trust. Also **re·spon′si·ble·ness.**

re·spon·si·ble (ri·spon′sə·bəl) *adj.* **1** Subject to being called upon to account for or answer for something; accountable. **2** Able to discriminate between right and wrong. **3** Able to account or answer for something; able to meet one's obligations. **4** Being the cause: Rain was *responsible* for the delay. **—re·spon′si·bly** *adv.*

re·spon·sive (ri·spon′siv) *adj.* **1** Constituting a response. **2** Inclined to react with sympathy or understanding. **3** Containing responses. **—re·spon′sive·ly** *adv.* **—re·spon′sive·ness** *n.*

rest¹ (rest) *v.i.* **1** To cease working or exerting oneself for

Rests *def.* 8b
a. whole. b. half. c. quarter. d. eighth. e. sixteenth.
f. thirty-second. g. sixty-fourth.

a time; cease activity. **2** To obtain ease or refreshment by lying down, sleeping, etc. **3** To sleep. **4** To be still or quiet; cease all motion. **5** To be dead. **6** To be or lie in a specified place: The blame *rests* with me. **7** To be supported; stand, lean, lie, or sit: The rifle *rested* on the mantel. **8** To be founded or based: That *rests* on the assumption of his innocence. **9** To be directed, as the eyes. —*v.t.* **10** To give rest to; refresh by rest. **11** To put, lay, lean, etc., as for support or rest. **12** To found; base. **13** To direct (the gaze, eyes, etc.). **14** *Law* To cease presenting evidence in (a case). —*n.* **1** The act or state of resting. **2** A period of resting. **3** Freedom from disturbance or disquiet; peace; tranquility. **4** Sleep. **5** Death. **6** That on which anything rests; a support; basis. **7** A place for stopping or resting. **8** *Music* **a** A measured interval of silence. **b** A character representing this. **—at rest** In a state of rest; motionless, peaceful, asleep, or dead. [< OE *restan*] **—rest′er** *n.* **—Syn.** *n.* **1** repose, quiet, inactivity, relaxation. **2** respite. **3** serenity, peacefulness, calmness. **6** base, foundation.

rest² (rest) *n.* That which remains or is left over. **—the rest** That or those which remain; the remainder; the others. —*v.i.* To be and remain: Rest content. [< L *restare* stop, stand]

re·state (rē·stāt′) *v.t.* **·stat·ed, ·stat·ing** To state again or in a new way. **—re·state′ment** *n.*

res·tau·rant (res′tə·ränt, -tränt, -tər·ənt) *n.* A place where meals are prepared for sale and served on the premises. [F, lit., restoring]

res·tau·ra·teur (res′tər·ə·tûr′) *n.* The proprietor of a restaurant. [F]

rest·ful (rest′fəl) *adj.* **1** Full of or giving rest. **2** Being at rest; quiet. **—rest′ful·ly** *adv.* **—rest′ful·ness** *n.*

res·ti·tu·tion (res′tə·ty/ōō′shən) *n.* **1** The act of restoring something that has been taken away or lost. **2** Restoration or return to a rightful owner. **3** The act of making good for injury or loss. [< L *restituere* restore]

res·tive (res′tiv) *adj.* **1** Restless; fidgety: The audience grew *restive.* **2** Unwilling to submit to control; unruly; balky. [< F *rester* remain, balk] **—res′tive·ly** *adv.* **—res′tive·ness** *n.*

rest·less (rest′lis) *adj.* **1** Affording no rest or little rest; disturbed: a *restless* sleep. **2** Uneasy; impatient; unquiet: to feel *restless.* **3** Never resting; unending: the *restless* waves. **4** Constantly seeking change or activity; unable or unwilling to rest. **—rest′less·ly** *adv.* **—rest′less·ness** *n.*

res·to·ra·tion (res′tə·rā′shən) *n.* **1** The act of restoring, or the state of being restored. **2** The bringing back to an original or earlier condition, as a work of art or a building; also, the object so restored. **—the Restoration 1** The return of Charles II to the English throne in 1660. **2** The period following his return up to the revolution in 1688.

re·sto·ra·tive (ri·stôr′ə·tiv, -stō′rə-) *adj.* Tending or able to restore consciousness, strength, health, etc. —*n.* A restorative substance. **—re·sto′ra·tive·ly** *adv.* **—re·sto′ra·tive·ness** *n.*

re·store (ri·stôr′, -stōr′) *v.t.* **·stored, ·stor·ing 1** To bring into existence or effect again: to *restore* peace. **2** To bring back to a former or original condition, as a work of art or a building. **3** To put back in a former place or position; reinstate. **4** To bring back to health and vigor. **5** To give back (something lost or taken away); return. [< L *restaurare*] —re·stor′er *n.*

re·strain (ri·strān′) *v.t.* **1** To hold back from acting, proceeding, or advancing. **2** To restrict or limit. **3** To deprive of liberty, as by placing in a prison. [< L *re-* back + *stringere* draw tight] —re·strain′ed·ly (-strān′id·lē) *adv.* —re· strain′er *n.*

re·straint (ri·strānt′) *n.* **1** The act of restraining, or the state of being restrained. **2** Something that restrains, as a harness or similar device. **3** A restriction on conduct; stricture. **4** Control over the display of one's emotions, opinions, etc.; self-control.

re·strict (ri·strikt′) *v.t.* To hold or keep within limits or bounds; confine. [< L *re-* back + *stringere* draw tight]

re·strict·ed (ri·strik′tid) *adj.* **1** Limited or confined. **2** Available for use by certain persons or groups; also, excluding certain persons or groups.

re·stric·tion (ri·strik′shən) *n.* **1** The act of restricting, or the state of being restricted. **2** That which restricts; a limitation or restraint.

re·stric·tive (ri·strik′tiv) *adj.* **1** Serving, tending, or operating to restrict. **2** *Gram.* Limiting: a *restrictive* clause. —re·stric′tive·ly *adv.* • In *Will the man who spoke just now please stand up, who spoke just now* is a restrictive clause because it limits the application of *man*, which it modifies. It is not set off by commas, as in *The president, who will be 60 years old tomorrow, held a press conference today.*

rest room In a public building, a room or rooms provided with toilet facilities.

re·struc·ture (rē·struk′chər) *v.t.* ·tured, ·tur·ing To reorganize on a different basis or into a new pattern.

re·sult (ri·zult′) *n.* **1** The outcome of an action, course, or process. **2** A quantity or value derived by calculation. — *v.i.* **1** To be a result or outcome; follow: with *from*. **2** To have as a consequence; end: with *in*. [< L *resultare* spring back]

re·sul·tant (ri·zul′tənt) *adj.* Arising or following as a result. —*n.* **1** That which results; a consequence. **2** *Physics* A vector representing the sum of two or more other vectors.

re·sume (ri·zōōm′) *v.* ·sumed, ·sum·ing *v.t.* **1** To begin again after an interruption. **2** To take or occupy again: *Resume* your places. —*v.i.* **3** To continue after an interruption. [< L *resumere* take up again] —re·sum′er *n.*

rés·u·mé (rez′ŏŏ·mā, rez′ŏŏ·mā′) *n.* A summary, as of one's employment record, education, etc., used in applying for a new position. Also res·u·mé′, res·u·me′. [F]

re·sump·tion (ri·zump′shən) *n.* The act of resuming; a beginning again.

re·sur·face (rē·sûr′fis) *v.t.* ·faced, ·fac·ing **1** To provide with a new surface. —*v.i.* **2** To come into view again; become evident.

re·sur·gence (ri·sûr′jəns) *n.* A rising again, as from death, obscurity, or defeat; a surging back. Also re·sur′· gen·cy. —re·sur′gent *adj.*

res·ur·rect (rez′ə·rekt′) *v.t.* **1** To bring back to life. **2** To bring back into use or to notice.

res·ur·rec·tion (rez′ə·rek′shən) *n.* **1** Any revival or renewal, as of a practice or custom. **2** *Theol.* **a** A rising from the dead. **b** The state of those who have risen from the dead. —the Resurrection **1** The rising of Christ from the dead. **2** The rising again of all the dead at the day of final judgment. [< L *resurrectus*, p.p. of *resurgere*< *re-* again + *surgere* rise] —res′ur·rec′tion·al *adj.*

re·sus·ci·tate (ri·sus′ə·tāt) *v.t.* & *v.i.* ·tat·ed, ·tat·ing To revive from unconsciousness or apparent death. [< L *re-* again + *suscitare* revive] —re·sus′ci·ta′tion, re·sus′ci·ta′tor *n.* —re·sus′ci·ta′tive *adj.*

ret (ret) *v.t.* ret·ted, ret·ting To steep or soak, as flax, to separate the fibers. [ME *reten*]

ret. retired.

re·tail (rē′tāl) *n.* The selling of goods in small quantities directly to the consumer. —at retail **1** In small quantities to the consumer. **2** At retail prices. —*adj.* Of, pertaining

to, or engaged in the sale of goods at retail. —*adv.* AT RETAIL. —*v.t.* **1** To sell in small quantities directly to the consumer. **2** (ri·tāl′) To repeat, as gossip. —*v.i.* **3** To be sold at retail. [< OF *retailler* cut up] —re′tail·er *n.*

re·tain (ri·tān′) *v.t.* **1** To keep in one's possession; hold. **2** To maintain in use, practice, etc.: to *retain* one's standards. **3** To keep in a fixed condition or place. **4** To keep in mind; remember. **5** To hire or engage, as an attorney. [< L *re-* back + *tenere* to hold]

re·tain·er[1] (ri·tā′nər) *n.* **1** One employed in the service of a person of rank; servant. **2** One who or that which retains.

re·tain·er[2] (ri·tā′nər) *n.* **1** The fee paid to retain the services of an attorney or other adviser. **2** The act of retaining the services of an attorney, etc. [< OF *retenir* hold back]

retaining wall A wall to prevent a side of an embankment or cut from sliding.

re·tal·i·ate (ri·tal′ē·āt) *v.* ·at·ed, ·at·ing *v.i.* **1** To return like for like; esp., to repay evil with evil. —*v.t.* **2** To repay (an injury, wrong, etc.) in kind; revenge. [< L *re-* back + *talio* punishment in kind] —re·tal′i·a′tion *n.* —re·tal′i·a′tive, re· tal′i·a·to·ry *adj.*

re·tard (ri·tärd′) *v.t.* **1** To hinder the advance or course of; impede; delay. —*v.i.* **2** To be delayed. —*n.* Delay; retardation. [< L *re-* back + *tardus* slow] —re′tar·da′tion, re·tard′er *n.* —re·tard′a·tive *adj.*

re·tard·ant (ri·tär′dənt) *n.* Something that retards: a fire *retardant*. —*adj.* Tending to retard.

re·tar·date (ri·tär′dāt) *n.* A mentally retarded person.

re·tard·ed (ri·tärd′id) *adj.* Abnormally slow in development, esp. mental development.

retch (rech) *v.i.* To make an effort to vomit; strain; heave. [< OE *hræcan* bring up (blood or phlegm)]

retd. retained; returned; retired.

re·ten·tion (ri·ten′shən) *n.* **1** The act of retaining, or the state of being retained. **2** The ability to retain data, images, etc., in the mind subject to later recall. **3** *Med.* A retaining within the body of materials normally excreted.

re·ten·tive (ri·ten′tiv) *adj.* Having the power or tendency to retain, esp. to retain in the mind: a *retentive* memory. —re·ten′tive·ly *adv.* —re·ten′tive·ness, re·ten·tiv′i·ty *n.*

re·think (rē·thingk′) *v.t.* ·thought (-thôt), ·think·ing To think about again, esp. in order to reassess; reconsider.

ret·i·cent (ret′ə·sənt) *adj.* **1** Reluctant to speak or speak freely; habitually silent; reserved. **2** Subdued or restrained; shunning bold statement: *reticent* prose. [< L *re-* again + *tacere* be silent] —ret′i·cence, ret′i·cen·cy *n.* — ret′i·cent·ly *adv.*

re·tic·u·lar (ri·tik′yə·lər) *adj.* **1** Like a net. **2** Intricate. **3** Of or pertaining to a reticulum. [< L *reticulum* network]

re·tic·u·late (ri·tik′yə·lāt) *v.* ·lat·ed, ·lat·ing *v.t.* **1** To make a network of. **2** To cover with or as with lines of network. —*v.i.* **3** To form a network. —*adj.* (-lit, -lāt) Having the form or appearance of a network: also re·tic′u·lat′ed. —re· tic′u·late·ly *adv.* —re·tic′u·la′tion *n.*

ret·i·cule (ret′ə·kyōōl) *n.* A small handbag closed with a drawstring, formerly used by women. [< L *reticulum* network]

re·tic·u·lum (ri·tik′yə·ləm) *n. pl.* ·lums or ·la (-lə) The second stomach of a ruminant. [L, dim. of *rete* net]

ret·i·na (ret′ə·nə, ret′nə) *n. pl.* ·nas or ·nae (-nē) The light-sensitive membrane lining the back of the eyeball at the distal end of the optic nerve. [< L *rete* net] —ret′i·nal *adj.*

ret·i·nue (ret′ə·n'yōō) *n.* The group of retainers attending a person of rank. [< F *retenir* retain]

re·tire (ri·tīr′) *v.* ·tired, ·tir·ing *v.i.* **1** To withdraw oneself from business, public life, or active service. **2** To go away or withdraw, as for privacy, shelter, or rest. **3** To go to bed. **4** To fall back; retreat. **5** To

a. retina. b. lens. c. pupil. d. cornea. e. iris. f. optic nerve.

move back; recede. —*v.t.* **6** To remove from active service. **7** To pay off and withdraw from circulation: to *retire* bonds. **8** To withdraw (troops, etc.) from action. **9** In baseball, to put out, as a batter. [< F *re-* back + *tirer* draw]

re·tired (ri·tīrd′) *adj.* **1** Withdrawn from business, public life, or active service; esp., no longer actively engaged in one's occupation or profession because of having reached a certain age. **2** Of or for those in retirement. **3** Withdrawn from public view; secluded.

re·tir·ee (ri·tīr′ē′) *n.* A person who is retired.

re·tire·ment (ri·tīr′mənt) *n.* **1** The act of retiring, or the state of being retired. **2** A withdrawal from active engagement in one's occupation or profession, esp. because of age. **3** An age or date at which retirement is planned. **4** A secluded place.

re·tir·ing (ri·tīr′ing) *adj.* Shy; modest; reserved. —re·tir′-ing·ly *adv.*

re·tort[1] (ri·tôrt′) *v.t.* **1** To direct (a word or deed) back upon the originator. **2** To reply to, as an accusation or argument, by a similar one. **3** To say in reply. —*v.i.* **4** To answer, esp. sharply. **5** To respond to an accusation, etc., in kind. —*n.* A sharp or witty reply that turns back a previously expressed accusation, insult, etc., upon its originator. [<L *retorquere* twist back] —re·tort′er *n.* —Syn. *n.* rejoinder, riposte, comeback.

re·tort[2] (ri·tôrt′) *n.* A stoppered vessel with a side tube, for heating or distilling substances. [<L *retortus* bent back]

re·touch (rē·tuch′) *v.t.* **1** To modify by changing details; touch up, as a painting. **2** To change or improve, as a photographic print, by a hand process. —*n.* (*also* rē′- tuch′) A retouching, as of a picture. —re·touch′er *n.*

Retort

re·tract (ri·trakt′) *v.t.* & *v.i.* **1** To take back (an assertion, accusation, admission, etc.); disavow. **2** To draw back or in, as the claws of a cat. [<F<L *retractare* draw back] —re·tract′a·ble, re·trac′tive *adj.* —re·trac′tion, re·trac′tor *n.*

re·trac·tile (ri·trak′til) *adj.* *Zool.* Capable of being drawn back or in. —re·trac·til·i·ty (rē′trak·til′ə·tē) *n.*

re·tread (rē′tred′) *n.* A tire furnished with a new tread to replace a worn one. —*v.t.* (rē·tred′) To fit or furnish (a tire) with a new tread.

re·treat (ri·trēt′) *v.i.* **1** To go back or backward; withdraw. **2** To curve or slope backward. —*n.* **1** The act of retreating or drawing back, as from danger or conflict. **2** The retirement of an armed force from a position of danger. **3** In the armed forces, a signal, as by bugle, for the lowering of the flag at sunset. **4** A place of retirement or security; a refuge. **5** A period of religious contemplation and prayer by a group withdrawn from regular society. [<L *re-* again + *trahere* draw]

re·trench (ri·trench′) *v.t.* **1** To cut down or curtail (expenditures). **2** To cut off or away. —*v.i.* **3** To economize. [<MF *re-* back + *trencher* to cut] —re·trench′er, re·trench′ment *n.*

ret·ri·bu·tion (ret′rə·byōō′shən) *n.* **1** The impartial infliction of punishment, as for evil done. **2** That which is done or given in requital, as a reward or, esp., a punishment. [<L *re-* back + *tribuere* to pay] —re·trib·u·tive (ri·trib′yə·tiv), re·trib′u·to′ry *adj.* —re·trib′u·tive·ly *adv.*

re·triev·al (ri·trē′vəl) *n.* **1** The act or process of retrieving. **2** The power to restore or retrieve.

re·trieve (ri·trēv′) *v.* ·trieved, ·triev·ing *v.t.* **1** To get back; regain. **2** To restore; revive, as flagging spirits. **3** To make up for; remedy the consequences of. **4** To call to mind; remember. **5** To locate and provide access to (data) in computer storage. **6** In tennis, etc., to return (a ball, etc.) after a run. **7** To find and bring in (wounded or dead game): said of dogs. —*v.i.* **8** To retrieve game. —*n.* The act of retrieving; recovery. [<OF *re-* again + *trouver* find] —re·triev·a·bil′i·ty *n.* —re·triev′a·ble *adj.*

re·triev·er (ri·trē′vər) *n.* **1** Any of various breeds of dog usu. trained to retrieve game. **2** A person who retrieves.

retro- *prefix* Back; backward: *retrograde.* [<L *retro* backward]

ret·ro·ac·tive (ret′rō·ak′tiv, rē′trō-) *adj.* Effective or applicable to a period prior to the time of enactment: a *retroactive* ruling granting wage increases as of last May. —ret′ro·ac′tive·ly *adv.* —ret′ro·ac·tiv′i·ty *n.*

ret·ro·grade (ret′rə·grād) *adj.* **1** Going, moving, or tend-

ing backward. **2** Declining toward a worse state or character. **3** Inverted in order. —*v.* ·grad·ed, ·grad·ing *v.i.* **1** To move or appear to move backward. **2** To grow worse; decline; degenerate. [<L *retrogradus* a step backward] —ret′ro·gra·da′tion (-grā·dā′shən) *n.*

ret·ro·gress (ret′rə·gres) *v.i.* To go back to a more primitive or worse condition. [<L *retro-* backward + *gradi* walk] —ret′ro·gres′sion *n.* —ret′ro·gres′sive *adj.*

ret·ro·rock·et (ret′rō·rok′it) *n.* An auxiliary rocket that provides a backward thrust, as for reducing speed.

ret·ro·spect (ret′rə·spekt) *n.* A looking back on things past. —in retrospect In recalling or reviewing the past. [<L<*retro-* back + *specere* look] —ret′ro·spec′tion *n.*

ret·ro·spec·tive (ret′rə·spek′tiv) *adj.* **1** Looking back on the past. **2** RETROACTIVE. —*n.* An exhibition of works representing the entire period of an artist's productivity. —ret′ro·spec′tive·ly *adv.*

ret·ro·vi·rus (ret′rō·vī′rəs) *n.* A member of a family of viruses that contain RNA instead of DNA.

re·turn (ri·tûrn′) *v.i.* **1** To come or go back, as to or toward a former place or condition. **2** To come back or revert in thought or speech. **3** To revert to a former owner. **4** To answer; respond. —*v.t.* **5** To bring, carry, send, or put back; restore; replace. **6** To give in return, esp. with an equivalent: to *return* a favor. **7** To yield or produce, as a profit. **8** To send back; reflect, as light or sound. **9** To render (a verdict, etc.). **10** In sports, to throw, hit, or carry back (a ball). **11** In card games, to lead (a suit previously led by one's partner). —*n.* **1** The act of bringing back or restoring something to a former place or condition; restoration or replacement. **2** An appearing again; recurrence. **3** Something given or sent back, esp. in kind or as an equivalent; repayment. **4** Something, as an article of merchandise, returned for exchange or reimbursement. **5** *Often pl.* Profit or revenue; yield. **6** A response; answer; retort. **7** A formal or official report: a tax *return*. **8** *pl.* A report of the tabulated votes of an election. **9** In sports, the act of returning a ball. —in return In repayment; as an equivalent —*adj.* **1** Of or for a return: a *return* ticket. **2** Constituting a return or recurrence: a *return* engagement. **3** Returning. **4** Used for return: a *return* address. [<OF] —re·turn′er *n.*

re·un·ion (rē·yōōn′yən) *n.* **1** The act of reuniting. **2** A social gathering of persons who have been separated.

re·u·nite (rē′yōō·nīt′) *v.t.* & *v.i.* ·nit·ed, ·nit·ing To bring or come together after separation. —re′u·nit′er *n.*

rev (rev) *Informal n.* A revolution, as of a motor. —*v.t.* revved, rev·ving **1** To increase the speed of (an engine, motor, etc.,): often with *up.* **2** To increase in tempo or intensity with *up.* **3** To stimulate or excite: with *up.* —*v.i.* **4** To increase the speed of an engine, etc.: often with *up.* **5** To become stimulated or excited: with *up.*

Rev, Rev. Revelation; Reverend.

rev. revenue; reverse; review; revised; revision; revolution.

re·vamp (rē·vamp′) *v.t.* To make over or renovate.

re·vanch·ism (ri·vänsh′iz′əm) *n.* The revengeful desire to reacquire the land and power lost by a nation through war. [<F *revanche* revenge + -ISM] —re·vanch′ist *adj.*, *n.*

re·veal (ri·vēl′) *v.t.* **1** To make known; disclose; divulge. **2** To make visible; expose to view. [<L *revelare* unveil]

rev·eil·le (rev′i·lē) *n.* A morning signal by drum or bugle, notifying soldiers or sailors to rise. [<F *reveillez-vous,* imperative of *se reveiller* wake up]

rev·el (rev′əl) *v.i.* ·eled or ·elled, ·el·ing or ·el·ling **1** To take delight: with *in:* He *revels* in his freedom. **2** To make merry; engage in boisterous festivities. —*n.* **1** A boisterous festivity; celebration. **2** Merrymaking. [<OF<L *rebellare* to rebel] —rev′el·er or rev′el·ler *n.*

rev·e·la·tion (rev′ə·lā′shən) *n.* **1** The act of revealing. **2** That which is revealed, esp. news of a surprising nature. **3** *Theol.* **a** The act of revealing divine truth. **b** That which is so revealed.

Rev·e·la·tion (rev′ə·lā′shən) *n.* The Book of Revelation, the last book of the New Testament; the Apocalypse. Also Rev′e·la′tions.

rev·el·ry (rev′əl·rē) *n. pl.* **·ries** Noisy or boisterous merriment.

re·venge (ri·venj′) *v.* **1** The act of returning injury for injury to obtain satisfaction. **2** A means of avenging oneself or others. **3** The desire for vengeance. **4** An opportunity to obtain satisfaction, esp. to make up for a prior defeat, humiliation, etc. —*v.t.* **venged, veng·ing** **1** To inflict punishment, injury, or loss in return for. **2** To take or seek vengeance in behalf of. [MF < L *re-* again + *vindicare* vindicate] —**re·venge′ful** *adj.* —**re·venge′ful·ly** *adv.* —**re·veng′er** *n.*

rev·e·nue (rev′ə·nyōō) *n.* **1** Total current income of a government. **2** Income from any property or investment. **3** A source or an item of income. [< F *revenir* to return]

re·ver·ber·ate (ri·vûr′bə·rāt) *v.* **·at·ed, ·at·ing** *v.i.* **1** To resound or reecho. **2** To be reflected or repelled. **3** To rebound or recoil. —*v.t.* **4** To echo back (a sound); reecho. **5** To reflect. [< L *reverberare* strike back, cause to rebound < *re-* back + *verberare* to beat] —**re·ver′ber·ant** *adj.* —**re·ver′ber·a′tor** *n.*

re·ver·ber·a·tion (ri·vûr′bə·rā′shən) *n.* **1** The act of reverberating, or the state of being reverberated. **2** The rebound or reflection of light, heat, or sound waves. —**re·ver′ber·a′tive, re·ver′ber·a·to′ry** *adj.*

re·vere (ri·vir′) *v.t.* **·vered, ·ver·ing** To regard with profound respect and awe; venerate. [< L *re-* again and again + *vereri* to fear] —**re·ver′er** *n.*

rev·er·ence (rev′ər·əns) *n.* **1** A feeling of profound respect often mingled with awe and affection. **2** An act of respect; an obeisance, as a bow or curtsy. **3** The state of being revered. **4** A reverend person: used as a title. —*v.t.* **·enced, ·enc·ing** To regard with reverence. —**Syn.** *n.* **1** adoration, awe, homage, honor, veneration.

rev·er·end (rev′ər·ənd) *adj.* **1** Worthy of reverence. **2** *Usu. cap.* Being a clergyman: used as a title. **3** Of or pertaining to the clergy. —*n.* A clergyman. • In formal usage, *Reverend* follows *the* and precedes the clergyman's full name or title of address and last name: *the Reverend Donald Smith; the Rev. Mr.* (or *Dr.*) *Smith.* Less formally, *Reverend* is used as a title of address: *Reverend Smith.* The use of *reverend* as a noun should be avoided, esp. in writing: *The reverend's sermon was much admired.*

rev·er·ent (rev′ər·ənt) *adj.* Feeling or expressing reverence. —**rev′er·ent·ly** *adv.*

rev·er·en·tial (rev′ə·ren′shəl) *adj.* Proceeding from or expressing reverence. —**rev′er·en′tial·ly** *adv.*

rev·er·ie (rev′ər·ē) *n. pl.* **·er·ies** **1** Abstracted musing; daydreaming. **2** DAYDREAM. Also **rev′er·y.** [< F *rêver* dream]

re·vers (rə·vir′, -vâr′) *n. pl.* **·vers** (-virz′, -vârz′) A part of a garment folded over to show the inside, as the lapel of a coat. [< OF]

re·ver·sal (ri·vûr′səl) *n.* **1** The act of reversing. **2** A change to an opposite direction or course.

re·verse (ri·vûrs′) *adj.* **1** Turned backward; contrary or opposite in direction, order, etc. **2** Having the other side or back in view. **3** Causing backward motion. —*n.* **1** That which is directly opposite or contrary. **2** The back, rear, or secondary side or surface. **3** A change to an opposite position, direction, or state; reversal. **4** A change for the worse; a misfortune. **5** *Mech.* A gear that causes reverse motion. —*v.* **·versed, ·vers·ing** *v.t.* **1** To turn upside down or inside out. **2** To turn in an opposite direction. **3** To transpose; exchange. **4** To change completely or into something opposite: to *reverse* one's stand. **5** To set aside; annul: The higher court *reversed* the decision. **6** To apply (the charges for a telephone call) to the party receiving the call. **7** *Mech.* To cause to have an opposite motion or effect. —*v.i.* **8** To move or turn in the opposite direction. **9** To reverse its action: said of engines, etc. [< L *reversus,* p.p. of *revertere* turn around] —**re·verse′ly** *adv.* —**re·vers′er** *n.*

re·vers·i·ble (ri·vûr′sə·bəl) *adj.* **1** Capable of being worn or used with either side open to view, as a fabric, coat, rug, etc. **2** Capable of being reversed, as a chemical reaction. —*n.* A reversible coat, fabric, etc. —**re·vers′i·bil′i·ty** *n.* —**re·vers′i·bly** *adv.*

re·ver·sion (ri·vûr′zhən, -shən) *n.* **1** A return to some former condition or practice. **2** The act of reversing, or the state of being reversed. **3** *Biol.* The recurrence of ancestral characteristics; atavism. **4** *Law* The return of an estate to the grantor or his heirs after the expiration of the grant. —**re·ver′sion·ar′y, re·ver′sion·al** *adj.*

re·vert (ri·vûrt′) *v.i.* **1** To go or turn back to a former place, condition, attitude, topic, etc. **2** *Biol.* To return to or show characteristics of an earlier, primitive type. [< L *re-* back + *vertere* to turn]

re·vet·ment (ri·vet′mənt) *n.* A facing or retaining wall, as of masonry, for protecting earthworks, river banks, etc. [< F *revêtement*]

re·view (ri·vyōō′) *v.t.* **1** To go over or examine again: to *review* a lesson. **2** To look back upon, as in memory. **3** To study carefully; survey or evaluate: to *review* test scores. **4** To write or make a critical evaluation of, as a new book or film. **5** *Law* To examine (something done or adjudged by a lower court) so as to determine its legality or correctness. —*v.i.* **6** To go over material again. **7** To review books, films, etc. —*n.* **1** An examination or study of something; a retrospective survey. **2** A lesson studied again. **3** A careful study or survey. **4** A critical evaluation, as of a new book or film. **5** A periodical featuring critical reviews. **6** A formal inspection, as of troops. **7** *Law* The process by which the proceedings of a lower court are reexamined by a higher court. [< MF < L *re-* again + *videre* see] —**re·view′a·ble** *adj.* —**re·view′er** *n.*

re·vile (ri·vīl′) *v.* **·viled, ·vil·ing** *v.t.* **1** To assail with abusive language; attack verbally. —*v.i.* **2** To use abusive language. [< OF *reviler* treat as vile] —**re·vile′ment, re·vil′er** *n.* —**Syn.** abuse, vilify, malign, slander, defame.

re·vise (ri·vīz′) *v.t.* **·vised, ·vis·ing** **1** To read over so as to correct errors, make changes, etc. **2** To change; alter: to *revise* one's opinion. —*n.* **1** An instance of revising. **2** A corrected proof after having been revised. [< L *revisere* look back, see again] —**re·vis′er** *or* **re·vi′sor** *n.*

re·vi·sion (ri·vizh′ən) *n.* **1** The act or process of revising. **2** A revised version or edition. —**re·vi′sion·ar′y, re·vi′sion·al** *adj.*

re·vi·sion·ist (ri·vizh′ən·ist) *n.* **1** One who proposes a course of action regarded as a deviation from accepted ideas or established policy, as of a Communist state. **2** One who advocates revision. —*adj.* Of or characteristic of a revisionist. —**re·vi′sion·ism** *n.* —**re·vi′sion·is′tic** *adj.*

re·vi·tal·ize (rē·vī′təl·īz) *v.t.* **·ized, ·iz·ing** To restore vitality to; revive. —**re·vi′tal·i·za′tion** *n.*

re·viv·al (ri·vī′vəl) *n.* **1** The act of reviving, or the state of being revived. **2** A restoration or renewal after neglect or obscurity: the *revival* of radio drama. **3** An awakening of interest in religion. **4** A series of often emotional evangelical meetings.

re·viv·al·ist (ri·vī′vəl·ist) *n.* A preacher or leader of religious revivals. —**re·vi′val·ism** *n.* —**re·vi′val·is′tic** *adj.*

re·vive (ri·vīv′) *v.* **·vived, ·viv·ing** *v.t.* **1** To bring to life or consciousness again. **2** To give new vigor, health, etc., to. **3** To bring back into use or currency, as after a period of neglect or obscurity: to *revive* an old play. **4** To renew in the mind or memory. —*v.i.* **5** To return to consciousness or life. **6** To assume new vigor, health, etc. **7** To come back into use or currency. [< F < L *revivere* < *re-* again + *vivere* live] —**re·viv′er** *n.*

re·viv·i·fy (ri·viv′ə·fī) *v.t.* **·fied, ·fy·ing** To give new life or spirit to. [< L *re-* again + *vivificare* vivify] —**re·viv′i·fi·ca′tion, re·viv′i·fi·er** *n.*

rev·o·ca·ble (rev′ə·kə·bəl) *adj.* Capable of being revoked. —**rev′o·ca·bil′i·ty** *n.* —**rev′o·ca·bly** *adv.*

rev·o·ca·tion (rev′ə·kā′shən) *n.* The act of revoking, or the state of being revoked; repeal.

re·voke (ri·vōk′) *v.* **·voked, ·vok·ing** *v.t.* **1** To annul or make void; rescind. —*v.i.* **2** In card games, to fail to follow suit when possible and required by the rules. —*n.* In card games, neglect to follow suit. [< L *re-* back + *vocare* call] —**re·vok′er** *n.*

re·volt (ri·vōlt′) *n.* **1** An uprising against authority, esp. a government; a rebellion or insurrection. **2** An act of protest or refusal. —*v.i.* **1** To rise in rebellion against constituted authority. **2** To turn away in disgust or abhorrence. —*v.t.* **3** To cause to feel disgust or revulsion; repel. [< L *revolutus,* p.p. of *revolvere* revolve] —**re·volt′er** *n.*

re·volt·ing (ri·vōl′ting) *adj.* Abhorrent; loathsome; nauseating. —**re·volt′ing·ly** *adv.*

rev·o·lu·tion (rev′ə·lōō′shən) *n.* **1** The act or state of revolving. **2** A motion in a closed curve around a center, or a complete or apparent circuit made by a body in such a course. **3** Any turning, winding, or rotation about an axis. **4** A round or cycle of successive events or changes. **5** The period of space or time occupied by a cycle. **6** The overthrow and replacement of a government or political system by those governed. **7** Any extensive or drastic change.

rev·o·lu·tion·ar·y (rev′ə·lōō′shən·er′ē) *adj.* **1** Pertaining to or of the nature of revolution. **2** Causing or tending to produce a revolution. —*n. pl.* **·ar·ies** One who advocates or takes part in a revolution: also **rev′o·lu′tion·ist.**

Revolutionary War American Revolution.

rev·o·lu·tion·ize (rev′ə·lōō′shən·īz) *v.t.* **·ized, ·iz·ing** To bring about a radical or complete change in.

re·volve (ri·volv′) *v.* **·volved, ·volv·ing** *v.i.* **1** To move in a circle or closed path about a center. **2** To rotate. **3** To recur periodically. —*v.t.* **4** To cause to move in a circle or closed path. **5** To cause to rotate. **6** To turn over mentally. [< L *re-* back + *volvere* roll, turn]

re·volv·er (ri·vol′vər) *n.* A handgun with a cylinder that revolves to make possible successive discharges without reloading.

revolving door A door rotating like a turnstile and consisting of three or four adjustable panels.

Revolver
a. hammer. b. cylinder. c. barrel.
d. front sight. e. rifling. f. trigger.

re·vue (ri·vyōō′) *n.* A series of skits, songs, dances, etc., often comical or satirical in nature. [F, review]

re·vul·sion (ri·vul′shən) *n.* **1** A sudden change of feeling; a strong reaction. **2** Complete disgust or aversion; loathing. [< L *revulsus,* p.p. of *revellere* pluck away] —**re·vul′sive** *adj.*

re·ward (ri·wôrd′) *n.* **1** Something given or done in return, esp. to acknowledge and encourage merit, service, or achievement. **2** Money offered, as for the return of lost goods. —*v.t.* To give a reward to or for; recompense. [< AF *rewarder* look at] —**re·ward′er** *n.*

re·ward·ing (ri·wôrd′ing) *adj.* Yielding intangible rewards; satisfying: a *rewarding* career.

re·write (rē·rīt′) *v.t.* **·wrote, ·writ·ten, ·writ·ing 1** To write over again. **2** To revise or put into publishable form, as for a newspaper. —*n.* (rē′rīt′) A news item rewritten for publication.

RF, R.F., r.f. radio frequency.

RFD, R.F.D. Rural Free Delivery.

RH, R.H., r.h. right hand.

R.H. Royal Highness.

Rh rhodium.

r.h. relative humidity.

rhap·so·dize (rap′sə·dīz) *v.t. & v.i.* **·dized, ·diz·ing** To express or recite with exaggerated sentiment and enthusiasm. —**rhap′so·dist** *n.*

rhap·so·dy (rap′sə·dē) *n. pl.* **·dies 1** Any rapturous or highly enthusiastic utterance or writing. **2** *Music* An instrumental composition of free form. [< Gk. *rhaptein* stitch together + *ōidē* song] —**rhap·sod′ic** (rap·sod′ik) or **·i·cal** *adj.* —**rhap·sod′i·cal·ly** *adv.*

rhe·a (rē′ə) *n.* A ratite bird of South America, resembling but smaller than an ostrich, and having three toes. [NL]

rhe·ni·um (rē′nē·əm) *n.* A rare metallic element (symbol Re). [< L *Rhenus* Rhine]

rhe·o·stat (rē′ə·stat) *n. Electr.* A variable resistor used to control or limit current. [< Gk. *rheos* current + *statos* standing]

rhe·sus (rē′səs) *n.* A small macaque of India, widely used in research. Also **rhesus monkey.** [NL]

Rhe·sus factor (rē′səs) Rh factor.

rhet·o·ric (ret′ə·rik) *n.* **1** Skill in the use

Rhesus

of language, as in writing or speech. **2** The pretentious use of language. [< Gk. *rhētorikē (technē)* rhetorical (art)]

rhe·tor·i·cal (ri·tôr′i·kəl, -tor′-) *adj.* **1** Of the nature of rhetoric. **2** Designed for showy oratorical effect. —**rhe·tor′i·cal·ly** *adv.* —**rhe·tor′i·cal·ness** *n.*

rhetorical question A question put only for effect, the answer being implied in the question.

rhe·tor·i·cian (ret′ə·rish′ən) *n.* A master or teacher of rhetoric.

rheum (rōōm) *n.* **1** A watery discharge from the nose or eyes. **2** A cold in the head. [< Gk. *rheuma* a flow] —**rheum′y** *adj.* (·i·er, ·i·est)

rheu·mat·ic (rōō·mat′ik) *adj.* Of, causing, or affected with rheumatism. —*n.* One affected with rheumatism.

rheumatic fever A disease chiefly affecting young persons following streptococcal infection, characterized by swollen joints and fever.

rheu·ma·tism (rōō′mə·tiz′əm) *n.* Any of various painful disorders of the joints. [< Gk. *rheuma* rheum] —**rheu′ma·toid** (-toid) *adj.*

rheumatoid arthritis A chronic, crippling disease of the joints.

Rh factor (är′ach′) A genetically transmitted substance in the blood of most individuals (**Rh positive**) and which may cause hemolytic reactions under certain conditions, as during pregnancy, or following transfusions with blood lacking this factor (**Rh negative**). [< Rh(esus) monkey, the laboratory animal used in discovering this substance]

rhine·stone (rīn′stōn′) *n.* A highly refractive, colorless glass or paste, used as an imitation gemstone.

Rhine wine (rīn) A light, dry, white wine produced in the region of the Rhine River in w. cen. Europe.

rhi·ni·tis (rī·nī′tis) *n.* Inflammation of the mucous membrane of the nose. [< Gk. *rhis, rhinos* nose + -ITIS]

rhi·no (rī′nō) *n. pl.* **·nos** *Informal* A rhinoceros.

rhi·noc·e·ros (rī·nos′ər·əs) *n. pl.* **·ros·es** or **·ros** Any of various large, herbivorous, three-toed mammals of Africa and Asia, with one or two horns on the snout and a thick hide. [< Gk. *rhis, rhinos* nose + *keras* horn]

Indian rhinoceros

rhi·zome (rī′zōm) *n.* A specialized trailing or underground stem, producing roots from its lower surface and leaves or shoots from its upper surface or upturned tip. [< Gk. *rhizōma* mass of roots] —**rhi·zom·a·tous** (rī·zom′ə·təs, -zō′mə-) *adj.*

rho (rō) *n.* The 17th letter in the Greek alphabet (P,ρ).

Rhode Island Red (rōd) An American breed of chicken having reddish brown feathers.

Rho·de·sia (rō·dē′zhə, -zhē·ə) *n.* A British colony in cen. Africa; unilaterally declared independence in 1965; 150,333 sq. mi., cap. Salisbury. —**Rho·de′sian** *adj., n.* ● See map at Africa.

rho·di·um (rō′dē·əm) *n.* A hard, silvery metallic element (symbol Rh). [< Gk. *rhodon* rose; from the color of its salts]

Rhizome of bearded iris

rho·do·den·dron (rō′də·den′drən) *n.* Any of a genus of usu. evergreen shrubs or small trees with profuse clusters of flowers. [< Gk. *rhodon* rose + *dendron* tree]

rhom·boid (rom′boid) *n. Geom.* A parallelogram, esp. one with oblique angles, having unequal adjacent sides. —*adj.* Having the shape of a rhomboid or rhombus: also **rhom·boi′dal.** ● See parallelogram.

rhom·bus (rom′bəs) *n. pl.* **·bus·es** or **·bi** (-bī) *Geom.* An equilateral parallelogram, esp. one with oblique angles. [< Gk. *rhombos* spinning top, rhombus] —**rhom′bic** *adj.* ● See parallelogram.

rhu·barb (rōō′bärb) *n.* **1** Any of a genus of large-leaved perennial herbs. **2** The fleshy stalks of a species of rhubarb used in cooking. **3** *Slang* A heated argument or quarrel. [< Gk. *rha* rhubarb + *barbaron* foreign]

rhum·ba (rum′bə) *n. & v.* RUMBA.

rhyme (rīm) *n.* 1 A similarity of sounds of two or more words, esp. at the ends of lines of poetry. 2 A word wholly or partly similar in sound to another word. 3 A poem or verse employing such words, esp. at the ends of lines. 4 Poetry or verse in general. —*v.* **rhymed, rhy·ming** *v.i.* 1 To make rhymes or verses. 2 To be a rhyme. 3 To end in rhymes: said of verses. —*v.t.* 4 To write in rhyme. 5 To use as a rhyme. 6 To cause to be a rhyme or rhymes. [< Gk. *rhythmos* rhythm] —**rhym′er** *n.*

rhyme·ster (rīm′stər) *n.* A writer of light or inferior verse.

rhythm (rith′əm) *n.* 1 Movement or process characterized by the regular or harmonious recurrence of a beat, sound, action, development, etc.: the *rhythm* of the pulse; the *rhythm* of the seasons; the *rhythms* of speech. 2 a The property of music that arises from comparison of the relative duration and accents of sounds. b A particular arrangement of durations and accents: a dance *rhythm.* 3 In literature, drama, etc., a forward-moving or compelling development toward a particular end, effect, etc.: The *rhythm* of the play was all off. 4 In art, the regular or harmonious recurrence of colors, forms, etc. 5 In prosody: a The cadenced flow of sound as determined by the succession of accented and unaccented syllables. b A particular arrangement of such syllables: iambic *rhythm.* [< Gk. *rhythmos* < *rheein* flow] —**rhyth′mic** or **·mi·cal** *adj.* —**rhyth′mi·cal·ly** *adv.* —**rhyth′mist** *n.*

rhythm method A method of birth control that consists of sexual abstinence during the woman's monthly period of ovulation.

RI Rhode Island (P.O. abbr.).

R.I. King and Emperor (L *Rex et Imperator*); Queen and Empress (L *Regina et Imperatrix*); Rhode Island.

ri·al (rī′al) *n.* A silver coin, the basic monetary unit of Iran. [< OF *rial, real* royal]

ri·al·to (rē·al′tō) *n. pl.* **·tos** A market or place of exchange. [< *Rialto,* an island of Venice]

rib (rib) *n.* 1 *Anat.* One of the series of curved bones attached to the spine of most vertebrates, and enclosing the chest cavity. 2 Something, as a structural element, likened to a rib: the *rib* of an umbrella. 3 The curved piece of an arch; also, one of the intersecting arches in vaulting. 4 A curved side timber bending away from the keel in a boat or ship. 5 A raised wale or stripe in cloth or knit goods. 6 A vein or nerve of a leaf or insect's wing. 7 A cut of meat including one or more ribs. 8 A wife: in jocular allusion to the creation of Eve

Human ribs

from Adam's rib. *Gen.* 2:22. 9 *Slang* A practical joke. —*v.t.* **ribbed, rib·bing** 1 To make with ridges: to *rib* a piece of knitting. 2 To strengthen by or enclose within ribs. 3 *Slang* To make fun of; tease. [< OE *ribb*]

rib·ald (rib′əld) *adj.* Of or indulging in coarse, vulgar language or jokes. —*n.* A ribald person. [< OF *ribauld*] —Syn. *adj.* improper, unseemly, gross, obscene, impure.

rib·ald·ry (rib′əl·drē) *n. pl.* **·ries** Ribald language or jokes.

rib·bing (rib′ing) *n.* An arrangement of ribs, as in ribbed cloth, etc.

rib·bon (rib′ən) *n.* 1 A narrow strip of fabric made in a variety of weaves, used as trimming, for tying, etc. 2 Something shaped like or suggesting a ribbon. 3 *pl.* A narrow strip; a shred: torn to *ribbons.* 4 An ink-bearing strip of cloth in a typewriter. 5 A colored strip of cloth worn to signify the award of a prize, etc. 6 *Mil.* A strip of cloth worn to indicate campaigns served in, medals won, etc. —*v.t.* 1 To ornament with ribbons. 2 To tear into ribbons. [< OF *riban*]

ri·bo·fla·vin (rī′bō·flā′vin) *n.* A vitamin of the B complex found in many foods and essential for normal growth.

ri·bo·nu·cle·ic acid (rī′bō·n⁽ᵒᵒ⁾·klē′ik, -klā′ik) A substance that controls various processes within living cells, esp. the synthesis of proteins.

rice (rīs) *n.* 1 A cereal grass widely cultivated on wet land

in warm climates. 2 The edible, starchy seeds of this plant. —*v.t.* **riced, ric·ing** To reduce (a food) to ricelike grains. [< Gk. *oryza*]

rice paper 1 A thin paper made from rice straw. 2 A similar paper made from the pith of a Chinese shrub, the **rice-paper plant.**

ric·er (rī′sər) *n.* A utensil consisting of a perforated container through which cooked potatoes, etc., are pressed.

rich (rich) *adj.* 1 Having large possessions, as of money, goods, or lands; wealthy. 2 Abundantly supplied: with *in* or *with.* 3 Yielding abundant returns; plentiful: a *rich* source of oil. 4 Of precious materials, fine workmanship, etc.: *rich* fabrics. 5 Luxuriant; sumptuous. 6 Having many choice ingredients, as butter, cream, etc.: a *rich* dessert. 7 Pleasingly full and resonant: a *rich* tone. 8 Deep; intense: a *rich* color. 9 Very fragrant; pungent: a *rich* perfume. 10 Containing a high percentage of fuel to air: said of fuel mixtures. 11 Abounding in desirable qualities: *rich* soil. 12 *Informal* Very funny: a *rich* joke. [< OE *rīce*] —**rich′ly** *adv.* —**rich′ness** *n.*

rich·es (rich′iz) *n. pl.* 1 Abundant possessions; wealth. 2 Abundance of whatever is precious.

Rich·ter scale (rik′tər) A logarithmic measure of the estimated energy released by earthquakes according to which 1 represents an imperceptible tremor and 10 a theoretical maximum about one thousand times greater than any recorded earthquake. [< Charles R. *Richter,* born 1900, U.S. seismologist]

rick (rik) *n.* A stack, as of hay, having the top rounded and thatched to protect the interior from rain. —*v.t.* To pile in ricks. [< OE *hrēac*]

rick·ets (rik′its) *n. pl. (construed as sing.)* A children's disease in which the bones do not harden normally, usu. due to vitamin D deficiency. [?]

rick·ett·si·a (rik·et′sē·ə) *n. pl.* **·si·ae** (-si·ē) Any of a genus of pathogenic bacterialike organisms parasitic in certain ticks and lice and transmissible to other animals and man. [< H. T. *Ricketts,* 1871–1910, U.S. pathologist] —**rick·ett′si·al** *adj.*

rick·et·y (rik′it·ē) *adj.* 1 Ready to fall; tottering. 2 Affected with rickets. 3 Feeble; infirm. —**rick′et·i·ly** *adv.* —**rick′et·i·ness** *n.*

rick·ey (rik′ē) *n. pl.* **rick·eys** A drink consisting of liquor, usu. gin, sweetened lime juice, and carbonated water. [?]

rick·rack (rik′rak′) *n.* Flat braid in zigzag form, used as trimming. [Reduplication of RACK¹]

rick·shaw (rik′shô) *n.* JINRIKSHA. Also **rick′sha.**

ric·o·chet (rik′ə·shā′, *esp. Brit.* -shet′) *v.i.* **·cheted** (-shād′) or **·chet·ted** (-shet′id), **·chet·ing** (-shā′ing) or **·chet·ting** (-shet′ing) To glance or rebound obliquely from a surface. —*n.* 1 A richocheting. 2 Something that ricochets. [< OF]

ri·cot·ta (ri·kot′ə; *Ital.* rē·kôt′tä) *n.* An unripened cheese, Italian in origin and similar to cottage cheese but smoother. [< L *recoquere* to cook again]

rid (rid) *v.t.* **rid** or **rid·ded, rid·ding** To free, as from a burden or annoyance: usu. with *of.* —*adj.* Free; clear; quit: with *of:* We are well *rid* of him. [< ON *rythja* clear (land) of trees]

rid·dance (rid′ns) *n.* 1 A removal of something undesirable. 2 The state of being rid.

rid·den (rid′n) *p.p.* of RIDE.

rid·dle¹ (rid′l) *v.t.* **·dled, ·dling** 1 To perforate in numerous places, as with shot. 2 To sift through a coarse sieve. 3 To damage, injure, refute, etc., as if by perforating: to *riddle* a theory. —*n.* A coarse sieve. [< OE *hriddel* sieve] —**rid′dler** *n.*

rid·dle² (rid′l) *n.* 1 A puzzling question or conundrum. 2 Any mysterious object or person. —*v.* **·dled, ·dling** *v.t.* 1 To solve; explain. —*v.i.* 2 To utter or solve riddles; speak in riddles. [< OE *rædels*]

ride (rīd) *v.* **rode** (*Regional* rid), **rid·den** (*Regional* rid), **rid·ing** *v.i.* 1 To sit on and be borne along by a horse or other animal. 2 To be borne along as if on horseback. 3 To travel or be carried on or in a vehicle or other conveyance. 4 To be supported in moving: The wheel *rides* on a shaft. 5 To float; be borne: The ship *rides* on the waves. 6 To carry a rider, etc., in a specified manner: This car *rides* well. 7 To seem to float in space, as a star. 8 To lie at anchor, as a ship. 9 To overlap or overlie, as broken bones. 10 To depend: with *on*: Everything *rides* on him. **11** To be a bet: with *on*: They let their money *ride* on the filly. **12** *Informal* To continue unchanged: Let it *ride*. —*v.t.* **13** To sit on and control the motion of (a horse, bicycle, etc.). **14** To be borne or supported upon. **15** To overlap or overlie. **16** To travel or traverse (an area, certain distance, etc.) on a horse, in an automobile, etc. **17** To harass or bother oppressively: usu. in the past participle: *ridden* with shame. **18** To accomplish by riding: to *ride* a race. **19** To convey. **20** *Informal* To tease or torment by ridicule, criticisms, etc. **21** To keep somewhat engaged, usu. unnecessarily: to *ride* the brake. —**ride for a fall** To be headed for trouble, failure, etc. —**ride herd on** To control or supervise closely. —**ride out** To survive; endure successfully. —**ride up** To move upward out of place, as clothing. —*n.* **1** An excursion by any means of conveyance. **2** A means of transportation: to ask for a *ride*. **3** A manner of riding: a smooth *ride*. **4** A mechanical contrivance for riding, as at an amusement park. —**take for a ride** *Slang* **1** To remove (a person) to a place with the intent to murder. **2** To cheat; swindle. [< OE *rīdan*] —**rid′a·ble** *adj.*

rid·er (rī′dər) *n.* **1** One who or that which rides. **2** A piece of writing added to a document, contract, etc. **3** An addition to a legislative bill.

rid·er·less (rī′dər·lis) *adj.* Without a rider.

ridge (rij) *n.* **1** A raised mass of land long in proportion to its width and height. **2** A long, raised or top part of something, as the backbone of an animal, crest of a wave or mountain, ribbed part of a fabric, etc. **3** That part of a roof where the rafters meet the ridgepole. —*v.* **ridged, ridg·ing** *v.t.* **1** To mark with ridges. **2** To form into ridges. —*v.i.* **3** To form ridges. [< OE *hrycg* spine, ridge]

ridge·pole (rij′pōl′) *n.* A horizontal timber at the ridge of a roof. Also **ridge′beam′, ridge′piece′, ridge′plate′.**

rid·i·cule (rid′ə·kyōōl) *n.* Language or actions expressing amused contempt or scorn; derision; mockery. —*v.t.* **·culed, ·cul·ing** To make fun of; hold up as a laughingstock; deride. [< L *ridiculum* a jest] —**rid′i·cul′er** *n.* —**Syn.** *v.* banter, chaff, jeer, mock, taunt, satirize, scoff.

Ridgepole

ri·dic·u·lous (ri·dik′yə·ləs) *adj.* **1** Absurdly comical: a *ridiculous* costume. **2** Unworthy of consideration; preposterous. —**ri·dic′u·lous·ly** *adv.* —**ri·dic′u·lous·ness** *n.* —**Syn.** **1** droll, funny, grotesque, laughable. **2** absurd, nonsensical, foolish, stupid, asinine, senseless.

rid·ing¹ (rī′ding) *n.* The act of one who rides. —*adj.* **1** Suitable for riding: a *riding* horse. **2** To be used while riding: *riding* boots.

rid·ing² (rī′ding) *n.* **1** One of the three administrative divisions of Yorkshire, England. **2** Any similar administrative or electoral division, as in Canada, New Zealand, etc. [< OE *thrithing* the third part (of a county)]

rife (rīf) *adj.* **1** Prevalent; widespread. **2** Plentiful; abundant. **3** Containing in abundance: with *with*. [< OE *rīfe*]

riff (rif) *n.* In jazz music, a melodic phrase or motif played repeatedly as background or used as the main theme. —*v.i.* To perform a riff. [? Alter. of REFRAIN]

rif·fle (rif′əl) *n.* **1** A shoal or rocky obstruction lying beneath the surface of a stream and causing a stretch of choppy water. **2** Such a stretch of water. **3** A way of shuffling cards. —*v.t. & v.i.* **·fled, ·fling 1** To cause or form a riffle. **2** To shuffle (cards) by bending up adjacent corners of two halves of the pack, and permitting the cards to slip together as they are released. **3** To thumb through (the pages of a book). [?]

riff·raff (rif′raf′) *n.* **1** Low, disreputable persons; rabble. **2** Miscellaneous rubbish. [< OF *rif et raf* every bit]

ri·fle¹ (rī′fəl) *n.* **1** A firearm having spiral grooves on the surface of the bore for imparting rotation to the projectile. **2** Such a weapon fired from the shoulder. **3** *pl.* A

Automatic rifle (M-14)

body of soldiers equipped with rifles. —*v.t.* **·fled, ·fling** To cut a spirally grooved bore in (a firearm, etc.). [< OF *rifler* to scratch]

ri·fle² (rī′fəl) *v.t.* **·fled, ·fling 1** To search through and rob, as a safe. **2** To search and rob (a person). **3** To take away by force. [< OF *rifler* to scratch, plunder] —**ri′fler** *n.*

ri·fle·man (rī′fəl·mən) *n. pl.* **·men** (-mən) One armed or skilled with the rifle.

ri·fling (rī′fling) *n.* **1** The operation of forming the grooves in a rifle. **2** Such grooves collectively. • See REVOLVER.

rift (rift) *n.* **1** An opening made by splitting; a cleft; fissure. **2** A break in friendly relations. —*v.t. & v.i.* To rive; burst open; split. [< Scand.]

rig¹ (rig) *v.t.* **rigged, rig·ging 1** To fit out; equip. **2** *Naut.* **a** To fit, as a ship, with rigging. **b** To fit (sails, stays, etc.) to masts, yards, etc. **3** *Informal* To dress; clothe, esp. in finery: usu. with *out*. **4** To construct hurriedly or by makeshifts: often with *up*. **5** To prepare or arrange for special operation: controls *rigged* for the left hand only. —*n.* **1** The arrangement of sails, spars, etc., on a vessel. **2** *Informal* Dress or costume. **3** Gear, machinery, or equipment: an oil-well *rig*. **4** A carriage and its horse or horses. [< Scand.]

rig² (rig) *v.t.* **rigged, rig·ging** To control fraudulently: manipulate: to *rig* an election. [?]

rig·ger (rig′ər) *n.* One who rigs, esp. one who fits the rigging of ships, assembles lifting or hoisting gear, etc.

rig·ging (rig′ing) *n.* **1** *Naut.* The entire cordage system of a vessel. **2** Equipment or gear used in lifting, hauling, etc.

right (rīt) *adj.* **1** In accordance with some moral, just, or equitable law or standard; virtuous; upright. **2** Conformable to truth or fact; correct; accurate. **3** Proper; fitting; suitable. **4** Most desirable or preferable: to go to the *right* parties. **5** In an orderly or satisfactory state or condition: to put things *right*. **6** Sound; healthy; normal, as in mind or body. **7 a** Designating, being, or closest to that side of the body which is toward the south when one faces the sunrise. **b** Designating a corresponding side of anything. **8** Designating that surface or part of something designed to be worn outward or, when used, to be seen. **9** Politically conservative or reactionary. **10.** *Geom.* Formed by lines, segments, or planes perpendicular to a base. —*adv.* **1** According to some moral, just, or equitable law or standard. **2** Correctly; accurately. **3** In a straight line; directly: Go *right* home. **4** Precisely: He stood *right* in the doorway. **5** Suitably; properly: I can't fix it *right*. **6** Completely: burned *right* to the ground. **7** Thoroughly: He felt *right* at home. **8** Immediately: *right* after the storm. **9** Very: used regionally or in certain titles: a *right* nice day; the *Right* Reverend. **10** On or toward the right: to go *right*. —*n.* **1** That which is right, good, just, true, proper, etc. **2** Often *pl.* Any power or privilege to which a person has a moral, legal, or just claim: the *right* to vote. **3** *pl.* A claim or title to, or interest in, anything that is enforceable by law or custom: *rights* to property; fishing *rights*. **4** Something a person feels belongs justly or properly to him: a *right* to leave. **5** The correct or factual report or interpretation of something. **6** The right hand or side of a person or thing. **7** A direction to or a location on the right. **8** Something adapted for right-hand use or position. **9** In boxing: **a** A blow delivered with the right hand. **b** The right hand. **10** Often *cap.* In politics, a conservative or reactionary position, or a party or group advocating such a position, so designated because of the views of the party occupying seats on the right side of the presiding officer in certain European legislative bodies. —**by right** (or **rights**) Justly; properly. —**to rights** *Informal* Into a proper or orderly condition. —*v.t.* **1** To restore to an upright or normal position. **2** To put in order; set right. **3** To make correct or in accord with facts. **4** To make reparation for; redress or avenge: to *right* a wrong. **5** To make reparation to (a person); do justice to. —*v.i.* **6** To regain an upright or normal position. —*interj.* I agree! I understand! —**right on** *Informal* An interjectory phrase expressing enthusiastic agreement or encouragement: also used adjectivally: He was *right on* in that speech. [< OE *riht*]

right·a·bout (rīt′ə·bout′) *n.* A turning in or to the opposite direction, physically or mentally: also **right′a·bout′-face′** (-fās′).

right angle An angle with a measure of 90°. —**right′-an′-gled** *adj.* • See ANGLE.

right·eous (rī′chəs) *adj.* 1 Morally right and just. 2 Virtuous; blameless: a *righteous* man. 3 Justifiable; defensible: *righteous* anger. [< OE *riht* right + *wīs* wise] —**right′-eous·ly** *adv.* —**right′eous·ness** *n.*

right·ful (rīt′fəl) *adj.* 1 Owned or held by just or legal claim: *rightful* heritage. 2 Having a just or legal claim: the *rightful* heir. 3 Fair; upright; just. 4 Proper; suitable. —**right′ful·ly** *adv.* —**right′ful·ness** *n.*

right-hand (rīt′hand′) *adj.* 1 Of, pertaining to, or situated on the right side. 2 Of or for the right hand. 3 Most dependable or helpful: He was my *right-hand* man.

right-hand·ed (rīt′han′did) *adj.* 1 Using the right hand habitually or more easily than the left. 2 Done with the right hand. 3 Turning or moving from left to right, as the hands of a clock. 4 Adapted for use by the right hand, as a tool. —**right′-hand′ed·ness** *n.*

right·ism (rī′tiz·əm) *n.* Politically conservative or reactionary policies or principles. —**right′ist** *adj., n.*

right·ly (rīt′lē) *adv.* 1 Correctly. 2 Honestly; uprightly. 3 Properly; aptly.

right-mind·ed (rīt′mīn′did) *adj.* Having feelings or opinions that are right or sound.

right·ness (rīt′nis) *n.* The quality or condition of being right.

right of search 1 In international law, the right of a belligerent vessel in time of war to verify the nationality of a vessel and to ascertain, if neutral, whether it carries contraband goods. 2 A similar right in time of peace exercised to prevent piracy or to enforce revenue laws.

right of way 1 *Law* a The right, general or special, of a person to pass over the land of another. b The land over which such passage is made. 2 The strip of land over which a railroad, public highway, or high-tension power line is built. 3 The legal or customary precedence which allows one vehicle to cross in front of another. 4 Any right of precedence. Also **right′-of-way′.**

right triangle A triangle containing one right angle. • See TRIANGLE.

right whale Any of various large-headed, toothless whales that feed by straining water through whalebone plates in the mouth.

right wing 1 A political party or group advocating conservative or reactionary policies. 2 That part of any group advocating such policies. Also **Right Wing.** —**right′-wing′** *adj.* —**right′-wing′er** *n.*

rig·id (rij′id) *adj.* 1 Resisting change of form; stiff. 2 Rigorous; inflexible; severe; strict. 3 Precise; exact, as reasoning. [< L *rigere* be stiff] —**rig′id·ly** *adv.* —**ri·gid′i·ty, rig′id·ness** *n.*

rig·ma·role (rig′mə·rōl, rig′ə·mə-) *n.* Incoherent or uselessly complicated talk, writing, procedures, etc. [Alter. of *ragman roll* catalog, long list]

rig·or (rig′ər) *n.* 1 Harshness; strictness; severity, as of opinions, methods, temperament, etc. 2 Severe hardship, discomfort, etc. 3 Inclemency, as of the weather. 4 Exactitude; precision. 5 The condition of being stiff or rigid. *Brit. sp.* **rig′our.** [< L *rigere* be stiff] —**rig′or·is′tic** *adj.*

rig·or mor·tis (rig′ər môr′tis, rī′gər) The muscular stiffening that ensues within a few hours after death. [L, stiffness of death]

rig·or·ous (rig′ər·əs) *adj.* 1 Marked by or acting with rigor; severe. 2 Rigidly accurate; exact; strict. 3 Extremely difficult, arduous, or demanding. 4 Extremely variable, as weather; inclement. —**rig′or·ous·ly** *adv.* —**rig′or·ous·ness** *n.*

rile (rīl) *v.t. Informal* 1 To vex; irritate. 2 To roil; make muddy. [Var. of ROIL]

rill (ril) *n.* A small stream; rivulet. [< Du. *ril* or G *rille*]

rim (rim) *n.* 1 The edge or border of an object, usu. of a circular object. 2 The circumference of a wheel, esp., on an automobile wheel, the detachable, metal band over which the tire is fitted. —*v.t.* **rimmed, rim·ming** 1 To provide with or serve as a rim; border. 2 In sports, to roll around the edge of (the basket, cup, etc.) without falling in. [< OE *rima*]

rime¹ (rīm) *n., v.* **rimed, rim·ing** RHYME.

rime² (rīm) *n.* HOARFROST. —*v.t. & v.i.* **rimed, rim·ing** To cover with rime. [< OE *hrīm* frost] —**rim′y** *adj.*

rind (rīnd) *n.* The skin or outer coat that may be peeled or taken off, as of fruit, cheese, bacon, plants, etc. [< OE *rind* bark, crust]

ring¹ (ring) *n.* 1 Any object, line, or figure having the form of a circle or similar closed curve. 2 A rim or border of something circular. 3 A circular band of precious metal, worn on a finger. 4 Any metal or wooden band used for holding or carrying something: a napkin *ring.* 5 A group of persons or things in a circle. 6 A group of persons engaged in some common, often corrupt activity, business, etc.: a dope *ring.* 7 A place where the bark has been cut away around a branch or tree trunk. 8 A concentric layer of wood formed during a single year's growth in most trees and shrubs: also **annual ring.** 9 An area or arena, usu. circular, for exhibitions, etc.: a circus *ring.* 10 a A square area, usu. bordered with ropes, for boxing or wrestling matches. b The sport of prizefighting: with *the.* 11 Any field of competition or rivalry: He tossed his hat into the *ring.* —*v.* **ringed, ring·ing** *v.t.* 1 To surround with a ring; encircle. 2 To form into a ring or rings. 3 To provide or decorate with a ring or rings. 4 To cut a ring of bark from (a branch or tree); girdle. 5 To put a ring in the nose of (a pig, bull, etc.). 6 To hem in (cattle, etc.) by riding in a circle around them. 7 In certain games, to cast a ring over (a peg or pin). —*v.i.* 8 To form a ring or rings. 9 To move or fly in rings or spirals; circle. [< OE *hring*]

ring² (ring) *v.* **rang, rung, ring·ing** *v.i.* 1 To give forth a resonant sound, as a bell when struck. 2 To sound loudly or be filled with sound or resonance; reverberate; resound. 3 To cause a bell or bells to sound, as in summoning a servant. 4 To have or suggest, as by sounding, a specified quality: His story *rings* true. 5 To have a continued sensation of ringing or buzzing: My ears *ring.* —*v.t.* 6 To cause to ring, as a bell. 7 To produce, as a sound, by or as by ringing. 8 To announce or proclaim by ringing: to *ring* the hour. 9 To summon, escort, usher, etc., by or as by ringing: with *in* or *out:* to *ring* out the old year. 10 To strike (coins, etc.) on something so as to test their quality. 11 To call on the telephone: often with *up.* —*n.* 1 The sound produced by a bell. 2 A sound suggesting this: the *ring* of laughter. 3 Any loud, reverberating sound. 4 A telephone call. 5 A sound that is characteristic or indicative: with *of:* His words have the *ring* of truth. [< OE *hringan*] —**Syn.** *v.* 1 clang, sound, peal, toll, chime.

ring bolt A bolt having a ring through an eye in its head.

ringed (ringd) *adj.* 1 Wearing a ring or rings. 2 Encircled or marked by a ring or rings. 3 Composed of rings.

ring·er¹ (ring′ər) *n.* 1 One who or that which rings a bell, chime, etc. 2 *Slang* An athlete, horse, etc., illegally entered in a sports competition. 3 *Slang* A person who bears a marked resemblance to another.

ring·er² (ring′ər) *n.* 1 One who or that which rings or encircles. 2 A quoit or horseshoe that falls around one of the posts.

ring·lead·er (ring′lē′dər) *n.* A leader of any undertaking, esp. of an unlawful one.

ring·let (ring′lit) *n.* A long, spiral lock of hair; a curl.

ring·mas·ter (ring′mas′tər, -mäs′-) *n.* One who has charge of a circus ring and of the performances in it.

ring·side (ring′sīd′) *n.* 1 The space or seats immediately surrounding a ring, as at a prize fight. 2 Any area for close viewing.

ring·worm (ring′wûrm′) *n.* A contagious skin disease caused by certain fungi and marked by itchy lesions that spread ringlike from the site of infection.

rink (ringk) *n.* 1 A smooth surface of ice, used for sports, as ice-skating, hockey, curling, etc. 2 A smooth floor, used for roller-skating. 3 A building containing a surface for ice-skating or roller-skating. [< OF *renc* row, rank]

rinse (rins) *v.t.* **rinsed, rins·ing** 1 To remove soap, dirt, impurities, etc., from by immersing in or flooding with clear water. 2 To remove (soap, dirt, etc.) in this manner. 3 To wash lightly: often with *out.* 4 To use a rinse on (the hair). —*n.* 1 The act of rinsing. 2 A solution used for coloring the hair. [? < L *recens* recent, fresh] —**rins′er** *n.*

rins·ing (rin′sing) *n.* 1 A rinse. 2 *Usu. pl.* a The liquid in which anything is rinsed. **b** That which is removed by rinsing; dregs.

ri·ot (rī′ət) *n.* **1** A violent or tumultuous public disturbance by a large number of persons; uproar; tumult. **2** Any boisterous outburst: a *riot* of laughter. **3** A vivid show or display: a *riot* of color. **4** *Informal* An uproariously amusing person, thing, or performance. —**run riot 1** To act or move wildly and without restraint. **2** To grow profusely, as vines. —*v.i.* **1** To take part in a riot. **2** To live a life of unrestrained revelry. —*v.t.* **3** To spend (time, money, etc.) in riot or revelry. [< OF *riote*] —**ri′ot·er** *n.*

riot act Any forceful or vigorous warning or reprimand. —**read the riot act to** To reprimand bluntly and severely.

ri·ot·ous (rī′ət·əs) *adj.* **1** Of, pertaining to, like, or engaged in a riot. **2** Loud; boisterous. **3** Profligate: *riotous* spending. —**ri′ot·ous·ly** *adv.* —**ri′ot·ous·ness** *n.*

rip¹ (rip) *v.* **ripped, rip·ping** *v.t.* **1** To tear or cut apart, often roughly or violently. **2** To tear or cut from something else, often in a rough or violent manner: with *off, away, out,* etc. **3** To saw or split (wood) in the direction of the grain. —*v.i.* **4** To be torn or cut apart; split. **5** *Informal* To rush headlong. —**rip into** *Informal* To attack violently, as with blows or words. —**rip off** *Slang* **1** To steal or steal from. **2** To cheat, swindle, or dupe. —**rip out** *Informal* To utter with vehemence. —*n.* **1** A tear or split. **2** The act of ripping. [ME *rippen*] —**rip′per** *n.*

rip² (rip) *n.* **1** A ripple; a rapid in a river. **2** A riptide.

R.I.P. may he (she, or they) rest in peace (L *requiescat in pace*).

ri·par·i·an (ri·pâr′ē·ən, rī-) *adj.* Pertaining to, growing, or located on the banks of a river or other watercourse. [< L *ripa* bank of a river]

rip·cord (rip′kôrd′) *n.* The cord by which the canopy of a parachute is released from its pack.

ripe (rīp) *adj.* **rip·er, rip·est 1** Grown to maturity and fit for food, as fruit or grain. **2** Brought to a condition for use: *ripe* cheese. **3** Fully developed; matured; also, advanced, as in years. **4** In full readiness to do or try; prepared; ready: *ripe* for mutiny. **5** Resembling ripe fruit; rosy; luscious. **6** Ready for surgical treatment, as an abscess. [< OE *rīpe* ready for reaping] —**ripe′ly** *adv.* —**ripe′ness** *n.*

rip·en (rī′pən) *v.t. & v.i.* To make or become ripe; mature. —**rip′en·er** *n.*

rip-off (rip′of′, -ôf′) *n. Slang* **1** The act of ripping off; an act of stealing or cheating. **2** Anything dishonest, illegal, or exploitative.

ri·poste (ri·pōst′) *n.* **1** A return thrust, as in fencing. **2** A quick, clever reply or retort. Also **ri·post′.** [< L *respondere* to answer]

rip·ping (rip′ing) *adj. Brit. Slang* Splendid; excellent.

rip·ple (rip′əl) *v.* **·pled, ·pling** *v.i.* **1** To become slightly agitated on the surface, as water. **2** To flow with small waves or undulations. **3** To make a sound like water flowing in small waves. —*v.t.* **4** To cause to form ripples. —*n.* **1** A small wave or undulation on the surface of water. **2** Anything suggesting this in appearance. **3** Any sound like that made by rippling. [?] —**rip′pler** *n.* —**rip′pling** *adj.* —**rip′pling·ly** *adv.*

rip-roar·ing (rip′rôr′ing, -rōr′-) *adj. Slang* Excellent; exciting; boisterous.

rip·saw (rip′sô′) *n.* A saw designed for cutting wood in the direction of the grain.

rip·tide (rip′tīd′) *n.* Water violently agitated by conflicting tides or currents.

Ripsaw

rise (rīz) *v.* **rose, ris·en, ris·ing** *v.i.* **1** To move upward; go from a lower to a higher position. **2** To slope gradually upward: The ground *rises* here. **3** To have height or elevation; extend upward: The city *rises* above the plain. **4** To gain elevation in rank, status, fortune, or reputation. **5** To swell up: Dough *rises.* **6** To become greater in force, intensity, height, etc. **7** To become greater in amount, value, etc. **8** To become elated or more optimistic: Their spirits *rose.* **9** To become erect after lying down, sitting, etc.;

stand up. **10** To get out of bed. **11** To return to life. **12** To revolt; rebel: The people *rose* against the tyrant. **13** To adjourn: The House passed the bill before *rising.* **14** To appear above the horizon: The sun *rose.* **15** To come to the surface, as a fish after a lure. **16** To have origin; begin. **17** To become perceptible to the mind or senses: The scene *rose* in his mind. **18** To occur; happen. **19** To be able to cope with an emergency, danger, etc.: Will he *rise* to the occasion? —*v.t.* **20** To cause to rise. —**rise above** To prove superior to; show oneself indifferent to. —*n.* **1** A moving or sloping upward; ascent. **2** An elevated place, as a small hill. **3** Appearance above the horizon. **4** The height of a stair step or of a flight of stairs. **5** Advance, as in rank, status, prosperity, etc. **6** Increase, as in price, volume, intensity, etc. **7** An origin, source, or beginning. **8** *Informal* An emotional reaction; a response or retort, esp. in the phrase **get a rise out of** (someone). **9** *Brit.* An increase in salary. [< OE *rīsan*]

ris·er (rī′zər) *n.* **1** One who rises or gets up, as from bed: an early *riser.* **2** The vertical part of a step or stair.

ris·i·bil·i·ty (riz′ə·bil′ə·tē) *n. pl.* **·ties 1** A tendency to laughter. **2** *Usu. pl.* Appreciation of what seems laughable or ridiculous.

ris·i·ble (riz′ə·bəl) *adj.* **1** Having the power of laughing. **2** Of a nature to excite laughter. **3** Pertaining to laughter. [< L *risus,* p.p. of *ridere* to laugh] —**ris′i·bly** *adv.*

ris·ing (rī′zing) *adj.* **1** Increasing in wealth, rank, fame, etc. **2** Ascending: the *rising* moon. **3** Sloping upward: a *rising* hill. **4** Advancing to adult years; maturing: the *rising* generation. —*n.* **1** The act of one who or that which rises. **2** That which rises. **3** An uprising or revolt.

risk (risk) *n.* **1** A chance of encountering harm or loss; hazard; danger. **2** In insurance: **a** Chance of loss. **b** Degree of exposure to loss or injury. **c** An applicant for an insurance policy considered with regard to the hazard of insuring him. —*v.t.* **1** To expose to a chance of injury or loss; hazard. **2** To incur the risk of. [< Ital. *risicare* to dare] —**risk′er** *n.*

risk·y (ris′kē) *adj.* **risk·i·er, risk·i·est** Attended with risk; hazardous; dangerous. —**Syn.** perilous, ticklish, unsafe, uncertain, critical.

ris·qué (ris·kā′) *adj.* Bordering on or suggesting impropriety; somewhat daring or improper. [F] —**Syn.** indelicate, lewd, smutty, dirty, unseemly, unbecoming.

ri·tar·dan·do (rē′tär·dän′dō) *adj. & adv. Music* In a gradually slower tempo. [< Ital. *ritardare* to delay]

rite (rīt) *n.* **1** A solemn ceremony performed in a prescribed manner. **2** The words or acts accompanying such a ceremony. **3** Any formal practice or custom. [< L *ritus*]

rit·u·al (rich′ōō·əl) *n.* **1** A prescribed form or method for the performance of a rite. **2** The use or performing of such rites. **3** A book setting forth such a system of rites or observances. **4** Any act, observance, or custom performed somewhat regularly or formally. —*adj.* Of, pertaining to, or consisting of a rite or rites. —**rit′u·al·ly** *adv.*

rit·u·al·ism (rich′ōō·əl·iz′əm) *n.* **1** The use or performance of ritual. **2** Slavish devotion to ritual. —**rit′u·al·ist** *n.* —**rit′u·al·is′tic** *adj.* —**rit′u·al·is′ti·cal·ly** *adv.*

ritz·y (rit′sē) *adj.* **ritz·i·er, ritz·i·est** *Slang* Smart; elegant; luxurious. [< C. *Ritz,* 1850–1918, Swiss hotelier] —**Syn.** classy, posh, swank, chic.

ri·val (rī′vəl) *n.* **1** One who strives to equal or excel another; a competitor. **2** A person or thing equaling or nearly equaling another, in any respect. —*v.t.* **·valed** or **·valled, ·val·ing** or **·val·ling 1** To strive to equal or excel; compete with. **2** To be the equal of or a match for. —*adj.* Being a rival or rivals; competing. [< L *rivalis*]

ri·val·ry (rī′vəl·rē) *n. pl.* **·ries 1** The act of rivaling. **2** The state of being a rival or rivals; competition.

rive (rīv) *v.* **rived, rived** or **riv·en, riv·ing** *v.t.* **1** To split asunder by force; cleave. **2** To break (the heart, etc.). —*v.i.* **3** To become split. [< ON *rifa* tear, rend] —**riv·er** (rī′vər) *n.*

riv·er (riv′ər) *n.* **1** A large, natural stream of water, usu. fed by converging tributaries along its course and discharging into a larger body of water. **2** A large stream of any kind; copious flow. —**sell down the river** To betray;

deceive. **—send up the river** *Slang* To send to a penitentiary. [<L *riparius*]

river basin An area of land drained by a river and its branches.

riv·er·side (riv′ər·sīd′) *n.* The land adjacent to a river.

riv·et (riv′it) *n.* A metal bolt, having a head on one end, used to join objects, as metal plates, by passing the shank through holes and forming a head by flattening out the plain end. —*v.t.* **1** To fasten with or as with a rivet. **2** To fasten firmly. **3** To engross or attract (the eyes, attention, etc.). [<OF *river* to clench] **—riv′et·er** *n.*

riv·u·let (riv′yə·lit) *n.* A small stream or brook. [<L *rivus* brook]

RM, R.M., RM., r.m. Reichsmark(s).

rm. ream; room.

rms. reams; rooms.

R.N. registered nurse; Royal Navy.

Rn radon.

RNA ribonucleic acid.

R.N.R. Royal Naval Reserve.

R.N.W.M.P. Royal Northwest Mounted Police.

roach¹ (rōch) *n.* **1** A European freshwater fish of the carp family. **2** One of other related fishes, as the American freshwater sunfish. [<OF *roche*]

roach² (rōch) *n.* **1** COCKROACH. **2** *Slang* The butt of a marihuana cigarette.

road (rōd) *n.* **1** An open way for public passage; a highway. **2** Any course followed in a journey or a project. **3** A railroad. **—on the road 1** On tour: said of circuses, theatrical companies, athletic teams, etc. **2** Traveling, as a canvasser or salesman. [<OE *rād* a ride, a riding]

road·bed (rōd′bed′) *n.* The foundation of a railroad track or of a road.

road·block (rōd′blok′) *n.* **1** An obstruction, as of men or materials, for blocking passage, as along a road. **2** Any obstacle to progress or advancement.

road·house (rōd′hous′) *n.* A restaurant, bar, etc., located at the side of a suburban or rural road.

road·metal Broken stone or the like, used for making or repairing roads.

road·run·ner (rōd′run′ər) *n.* A long-tailed, very agile, crested ground cuckoo of SW North America.

road·stead (rōd′sted) *n. Naut.* A place of anchorage offshore, less sheltered than a harbor.

road·ster (rōd′stər) *n.* A light, open automobile having seats for two persons.

road·way (rōd′wā′) *n.* A road, esp. that part over which vehicles pass.

Roadrunner

roam (rōm) *v.i.* **1** To move about purposelessly from place to place; wander; rove. —*v.t.* **2** To wander over; range: to *roam* the fields. —*n.* The act of roaming. [ME *romen*] **—roam′er** *n.*

roan (rōn) *adj.* Of a color consisting of brown, reddish brown, black, or gray thickly interspersed with white hairs, as a horse. —*n.* **1** A roan color. **2** An animal of a roan color. [<Sp. *roano*]

roar (rôr, rōr) *v.i.* **1** To utter a deep, prolonged cry, as of rage or distress. **2** To make a loud noise or din, as a cannon. **3** To laugh loudly. **4** To move, proceed, or act noisily. —*v.t.* **5** To utter or express by roaring: The crowd *roared* its disapproval. —*n.* **1** A full, deep, resonant cry. **2** Any loud, prolonged sound, as of wind or waves. **3** Loud, boisterous laughter. [<OE *rārian*] **—roar′er** *n.*

roast (rōst) *v.t.* **1** To cook by subjecting to the action of heat, as in an oven or by placing in hot ashes, embers, etc. **2** To heat to an extreme degree. **3** To dry and parch: to *roast* coffee. **4** *Informal* To criticize or ridicule severely. —*v.i.* **5** To roast food in an oven, etc. **6** To be cooked or prepared by this method. **7** To be uncomfortably hot. —*n.* **1** Something prepared for roasting, or that is roasted. **2** A social gathering where food is roasted: a corn *roast*. **3** *Informal* Severe criticism or ridicule. —*adj.* Roasted. [< OHG *rōsten*]

roast·er (rōs′tər) *n.* **1** A person who roasts. **2** A pan for roasting. **3** Something suitable for roasting, as a chicken.

rob (rob) *v.* **robbed, rob·bing** *v.t.* **1** To seize and carry off the property of by unlawful violence or threat of violence. **2** To deprive (a person) of something belonging, necessary, due, etc.: *robbed* him of his honor. **3** To take something unlawfully from: to *rob* a store. **4** To steal: to *rob* gold. —*v.i.* **5** To commit robbery. [<OHG *roubon*] **—rob′ber** *n.*

rob·ber·y (rob′ər·ē) *n. pl.* **·ber·ies** The act of robbing, esp. the taking away of the property of another unlawfully by using force or intimidation.

robe (rōb) *n.* **1** A long, loose, flowing, outer garment. **2** *pl.* Such a garment worn as a badge of office or rank. **3** A bathrobe or dressing gown. **4** A blanket or covering: lap *robe*. —*v.* **robed, rob·ing** *v.t.* **1** To put a robe upon; clothe; dress. —*v.i.* **2** To put on robes. [<OHG *roub* robbery]

rob·in (rob′in) *n.* **1** A large North American thrush with reddish brown breast and underparts. **2** A small European songbird with cheeks and breast yellowish red. [Dim. of *Robert*]

Robin Hood A legendary, English outlaw of great skill in archery, who robbed the rich to relieve the poor.

rob·in's-egg blue (rob′inz·eg′) A pale greenish blue.

Rob·in·son Cru·soe (rob′in·sən krōō′sō) The hero of Daniel Defoe's *Robinson Crusoe* (1719), a sailor shipwrecked on a tropical island.

American robin

ro·bot (rō′bət, ·bot) *n.* **1** A machine designed to resemble a person and perform human tasks. **2** Any mechanical device that performs complex, often humanlike actions automatically or by remote control. **3** A person who lives or works mechanically, without spontaneity, etc. [<Czech *robota* work, compulsory service]

robot bomb An early form of jet-powered guided missile having an explosive charge.

ro·bot·ics (rō·bot′iks) *n.* The science of robots, their design, manufacture, and purposes.

ro·bust (rō·bust′, rō′bust) *adj.* **1** Possessing or characterized by great strength or endurance. **2** Requiring strength. **3** Boisterous; rude: *robust* humor. **4** Rich, as in flavor: a *robust* soup. [<L *robur, roboris*, a hard variety of oak, strength] **—ro·bust′ly** *adv.* **—ro·bust′ness** *n.*

roc (rok) *n.* In Arabian and Persian legend, an enormous and powerful bird of prey.

Ro·chelle salt (rō·shel′) A potassium and sodium salt of tartaric acid, used as a cathartic, etc. [<La *Rochelle*, France]

rock¹ (rok) *n.* **1** A large mass of stone or stony matter, often forming a peak or cliff. **2** A piece of stone of any size. **3** *Geol.* Solid mineral matter, such as that forming an essential part of the earth's crust. **4** Any strong, solid person or thing, often acting as a support, refuge, defense, etc. **5** *Slang* A precious gem, esp. a diamond. **—on the rocks** *Informal* **1** In a ruined or disastrous condition. **2** Bankrupt; destitute. **3** Served with ice cubes: said of an alcoholic beverage. —*adj.* Made or composed of rock; hard; stony. [<OF *roque*]

rock² (rok) *v.i.* **1** To move backward and forward or from side to side; sway. **2** To sway, reel, or stagger, as from a blow. —*v.t.* **3** To move backward and forward or from side to side, esp. so as to soothe or put to sleep. **4** To cause to sway or reel. —*n.* **1** The act of rocking or a rocking motion. **2** A type of popular music whose origins lie in jazz, country music, and blues, characterized by a strong, persistent rhythm, simple, often repeated melodies, and usu. performed by small, electronically amplified instrumental-singing groups: also **rock and roll, rock-and-roll, rock'n' roll.** [<OE *roccian*]

rock·a·by (rok′ə·bī) *interj.* Go to sleep: used to lull a child to slumber. Also **rock′a·bye, rock′-a-bye.**

rock bottom 1 The very bottom; the lowest possible level. **2** The basis of any issue. **—rock′-bot′tom** *adj.*

rock·bound (rok′bound′) *adj.* Encircled by or bordered with rocks.

rock candy Sugar candied in hard, clear crystals.

rock crystal Colorless transparent quartz.

rock·er (rok′ər) *n.* **1** One who or that which rocks. **2** One of the curved pieces on which a rocking chair or a cradle rocks. **3** ROCKING CHAIR.

rock·et (rok′it) *n.* **1 a** A usu. cylindrical firework, projectile, missile, or other device propelled by the reaction of ejected matter. **b** An engine that develops thrust by ejecting matter. **2** A vehicle propelled by rockets and designed for space travel. —*v.i. & v.t.* **1** To move or cause to move rapidly, as a rocket. **2** To rise or cause to rise rapidly: Her career *rocketed.* [< Ital. *rocchetta* spool]

rock·et·ry (rok′it·rē) *n.* The science and technology of rocket flight, design, and construction.

rock garden A garden with flowers and plants growing in rocky ground or among rocks arranged to imitate this.

rocking chair A chair having the legs set on rockers.

rocking horse A toy horse mounted on rockers.

rock 'n' roll (rok′ən·rōl′) ROCK[2] *n.* (def. 2).

rock-ribbed (rok′ribd′) *adj.* **1** Surrounded or edged by rocks. **2** Inflexible; unchangeable.

rock salt Salt found in large, rocklike masses; halite.

Rocking horse

rock·y[1] (rok′ē) *adj.* **rock·i·er, rock·i·est** **1** Consisting of, abounding in, or resembling rocks. **2** Marked by difficulties, obstacles, etc. **3** Tough; unfeeling; hard. —**rock′i·ness** *n.*

rock·y[2] (rok′ē) *adj.* **rock·i·er, rock·i·est** **1** Not firm; shaky; wobbly. **2** *Informal* Unsteady; dizzy. —**rock′i·ness** *n.*

Rocky Mountain goat MOUNTAIN GOAT.

ro·co·co (rə·kō′kō, rō′kə·kō′) *n.* **1** A style of decoration and architecture distinguished by profuse, elaborate, and delicately executed ornament, esp. prevalent during the 18th century. **2** Anything sometimes considered overly elaborate or delicate, as in literature, music, etc. —*adj.* **1** Having, or built in, the style of rococo. **2** Overelaborate; florid. [< F *rocaille* shellwork]

rod (rod) *n.* **1** A straight, usu. slim piece of wood, metal, etc. **2** A stick used to inflict punishment; also, the punishment itself. **3** A staff, wand, or scepter used as a badge of office, rank, rule, etc. **4** Dominion; rule; power, esp. if harsh. **5** FISHING ROD. **6** LIGHTNING ROD. **7** A measure of length, equal to 5.5 yards or 16.5 feet, or 5.03 meters. **8** A measuring rule. **9** One of the rodlike bodies of the retina sensitive to faint light. **10** *Slang* A pistol. [< OE *rod.*]

rode (rōd) *p.t.* of RIDE.

ro·dent (rōd′nt) *n.* Any of an order of gnawing mammals having incisors that grow continually, as a squirrel, beaver, or rat. —*adj.* **1** Gnawing. **2** Pertaining to the rodents. [< L *rodere* gnaw]

ro·de·o (rō′dē·ō, rō·dā′ō) *n. pl.* **·de·os** **1** A roundup of cattle. **2** A public performance in which the riding of broncos or bulls, roping of calves, lariat-throwing, etc., are presented. [< Sp. *rodear* go around]

rod·o·mon·tade (rod′ə·mon·tād′, rō′də-, -täd′) *n.* Vain boasting; bluster. —*adj.* Bragging. [< Ital. *rodomontata*]

roe[1] (rō) *n.* A mass of eggs of fish or of certain crustaceans, as lobsters. [< MDu. *roge*]

roe[2] (rō) *n.* A small, graceful deer of Europe and w Asia. Also **roe deer.** [< OE *rā*]

roe·buck (rō′buk′) *n.* The male of the roe deer.

Roent·gen ray (rent′gən, runt′-, ren′chən) X-RAY. [< W. K. *Roentgen,* 1845–1923, German physicist]

Ro·ga·tion days (rō·gā′shən) *Eccl.* The three days immediately preceding Ascension Day, observed by litanies, processions, etc. [< L *rogare* ask]

rog·er (roj′ər) *interj.* **1** *Often cap.* Message received: a code signal used in radiotelephone communication. **2** *Informal* All right; O.K. [< *Roger,* code word for *r* used in telecommunication]

rogue (rōg) *n.* **1** A dishonest and unprincipled person; scoundrel. **2** One who is innocently mischievous or playful. **3** A dangerous animal separated from the herd: also used adjectively: a *rogue* elephant. —*v.* **rogued, ro·guing** *v.t.* **1** To practice roguery upon; defraud. —*v.i.* **2** To live or act like a rogue. [?] —Syn. ne'er-do-well, dastard, good-for-nothing, scamp, knave, rascal.

ro·guer·y (rō′gər·ē) *n. pl.* **·guer·ies** **1** Knavery, cheating, or dishonesty. **2** Playful mischievousness.

rogues' gallery A collection of photographs of criminals taken to aid the police in their future identification.

ro·guish (rō′gish) *adj.* **1** Playfully mischievous. **2** Knavish; dishonest. —**ro′guish·ly** *adv.* —**ro′guish·ness** *n.*

roil (roil) *v.t.* **1** To make muddy, as a liquid, by stirring up sediment. **2** To irritate or anger. [?< F *rouiller* rust, make muddy] —**roil′y** *adj.*

roist·er (rois′tər) *v.i.* **1** To act in a blustery manner; swagger. **2** To engage in revelry. [< L *rusticus* rustic] —**roist′·er·er** *n.* —**roist′er·ing** *adj.*

ROK Republic of (South) Korea.

role (rōl) *n.* **1** A part or character taken by an actor. **2** Any assumed office or function. **3** A specific or acceptable pattern of behavior expected from those in a certain social status, profession, etc. Also **rôle.** [< F < Med. L *rotulus* roll of parchment]

roll (rōl) *v.i.* **1** To move upon a surface by turning round and round, as a wheel. **2** To move, be moved, travel about, etc., on or as on wheels. **3** To rotate wholly or partially: Her eyes *rolled.* **4** To assume the shape of a ball or cylinder by turning over and over upon itself. **5** To move or appear to move in undulations or swells, as waves or plains. **6** To sway or move from side to side, as a ship. **7** To rotate on a front-to-rear axis, as a projectile. **8** To walk with a swaying motion. **9** To make a sound as of heavy, rolling wheels; rumble: Thunder *rolled* across the sky. **10** To become spread or flat because of pressure applied by a roller, etc. **11** To perform a periodic revolution, as the sun. **12** To move ahead; progress. —*v.t.* **13** To cause to move by turning round and round or turning on an axis: to *roll* a ball; to *roll* a log. **14** To move, push forward, etc., on wheels or rollers. **15** To impel or cause to move onward with a steady, surging motion. **16** To begin to operate: *Roll* the presses. **17** To rotate, as the eyes. **18** To impart a swaying motion to. **19** To spread or make flat by means of a roller. **20** To wrap round and round upon itself. **21** To cause to assume the shape of a ball or cylinder by means of rotation and pressure: to *roll* a cigarette. **22** To wrap or envelop in or as in a covering. **23** To utter with a trilling sound: to *roll* one's r's. **24** To emit in a full and swelling manner, as musical sounds. **25** To beat a roll upon, as a drum. **26** To cast (dice) in the game of craps. **27** *Slang* To rob (a drunk or unconscious person). —**roll back** To cause (prices, wages, etc.) to return to a previous, lower level, as by government order. —**roll in 1** To arrive, usu. in large amounts: Money *rolled in.* **2** *Informal* To have large amounts of: *rolling in* money. —**roll out 1** To unroll. **2** *Informal* To get out of (bed, etc.). **3** To flatten by means of rollers. —**roll up 1** To assume or cause to assume the shape of a ball or cylinder by turning over and over upon itself. **2** To accumulate; amass: to *roll up* large profits. **3** To arrive, as in an automobile. —*n.* **1** The act or an instance of rolling. **2** Anything rolled up. **3** A list of names, a register of items, etc.: an honor *roll.* **4** A long strip of something rolled upon itself: a *roll* of carpet. **5** Any food rolled up in preparation for eating or cooking, esp. small, variously shaped pieces of baked bread dough. **6** A roller. **7** A rolling gait or movement. **8** A rotation on an axis from front to rear, as of an aircraft. **9** A reverberation, as of thunder. **10** A trill. **11** A rapid beating of a drum. **12** An undulation or swell, as of waves or land. **13** *Slang* A wad of paper money; also, money in general. [< L *rota* wheel]

roll·a·way (rōl′ə·wā′) *adj.* Mounted on rollers for easy movement into storage.

roll·back (rōl′bak′) *n.* A return, esp. by government order, to a lower level, as of prices, wages, or rents.

roll call 1 The act of calling out a list of names to ascertain who is present. **2** The time of or signal for this.

roll·er (rō′lər) *n.* **1** One who or that which rolls anything. **2** Any cylindrical device that rolls, as for smoothing, crushing, imprinting, etc. **3** The wheel of a caster or roller skate. **4** A rod on which something is rolled up, as a curtain, map, hair, etc. **5** One of a series of long, swelling waves which break on a coast.

roller bearing A bearing employing rollers to lessen friction between parts.

roller coaster A railway having many steep inclines and sharp curves over which open cars run, as at an amusement park.

roller derby A race between two teams on roller skates, in which points are scored when a player overtakes opponents after skating around a track within a given time.

roll·er·skate (rō'lər-skāt') v.i. **-skat·ed, -skat·ing** To go on roller skates. **—roller skater**

roller skate A metal frame on wheels, designed to be clamped to a shoe, or a shoe with wheels attached, for skating over a sidewalk, a wood floor, etc.

rol·lick·ing (rol'ik·ing) adj. Carelessly gay and frolicsome. Also **rol'lick·some** -(səm). [<earlier rollick, blend of ROMP and FROLIC]

rolling mill A machine or factory in which metal is rolled into sheets, bars, etc.

Roller skate

rolling pin A cylindrical roller of wood, glass, etc., for rolling out dough, etc.

rolling stock The wheeled transport equipment of a railroad.

roll·top (rōl'top') adj. Having a flexible cover which slides back: a rolltop desk.

ro·ly-po·ly (rō'lē-pō'lē) adj. Short and fat; pudgy; dumpy. —n. **1** Brit. A pudding made of a sheet of pastry dough spread with fruit, preserves, etc., rolled up and cooked. **2** A pudgy person.

ROM Read-only memory, a kind of computer memory from which information may only be read, not altered or erased.

Ro·ma·ic (rō·mā'ik) adj. Pertaining to the language or people of modern Greece. —n. Modern Greek. [<Gk. Rhōmaikos Roman]

ro·maine (rō·mān') n. A variety of lettuce having long leaves clustered in a head. [F, fem. of romain Roman]

ro·man (rō'mən) adj. Printing Designating a much-used style of type having serifs, and upright strokes thicker than horizontal strokes. —n. Roman type.

Ro·man (rō'mən) adj. **1** Of, pertaining to, or characteristic of Rome or its people. **2** Of the Roman Catholic Church. **3** LATIN. **4** Having a prominent, aquiline bridge: a Roman nose. —n. **1** A native, resident, or citizen of modern Rome or a citizen of ancient Rome. **2** A Roman Catholic.

ro·man à clef (rō·män' ä·klā') n. pl. **romans à clef** (-manz-) French A novel in which real persons or events appear under disguise; literally, novel with a key.

Roman calendar A calendar used by the ancient Romans. The day of the new moon (the calends), the full moon (the ides), and the ninth day before the ides (the nones) provided the bases for reckoning the day of the month.

Roman candle A tubular firework which discharges colored balls and sparks of fire.

Roman Catholic 1 A member of the Roman Catholic Church. **2** Of the Roman Catholic Church.

Roman Catholic Church The Christian church which recognizes the Pope as its supreme head on earth.

ro·mance (rō·mans', rō'mans) n. **1** Adventurous, fascinating, or picturesque nature or appeal: the romance of faraway places. **2** A disposition to delight in the mysterious, adventurous, sentimental, etc.: a child of romance. **3** A love affair. **4** A long narrative from medieval legend, usu. involving heroes in strange adventures and affairs of love. **5** Any fictitious narrative embodying adventure, love affairs, etc. **6** The class of literature consisting of romances (defs. 4 and 5). **7** An extravagant falsehood. —v. (rō·mans') **·manced, ·manc·ing** v.i. **1** To tell romances. **2** To think or act in a romantic manner. **3** Informal To make love. —v.t. **4** Informal To make love to; woo. [<OF romans a story written in French] **—ro·manc'er** n.

Ro·mance languages (rō·mans') The languages developed from the vulgar Latin speech, including French, Italian, Spanish, Portuguese, and Rumanian.

Roman Empire The empire of ancient Rome, established in 27 B.C. and continuing until A.D. 395.

Ro·man·esque (rō'mən·esk') adj. Of, pertaining to, or designating the style of architecture prevalent from the 5th to 12th centuries and characterized by the use of rounded arches and general massiveness. —n. Romanesque architecture.

Roman holiday Enjoyment or profit derived from the sufferings of others. [< gladiatorial contests of ancient Rome]

Ro·ma·nia (rō·mā'nē-ə, -mān'yə) n. RUMANIA. **—Ro·man'ian** adj. n.

Romanesque façade

Ro·man·ic (rō·man'ik) adj. **1** Roman. **2** Of or pertaining to the Romance languages.

Ro·man·ism (rō'mən·iz'əm) n. The dogmas, forms, etc., of the Roman Catholic Church: a term used chiefly in disparagement. **—Ro'man·ist** adj., n.

Ro·man·ize (rō'mən·īz) v.t. & v.i. **·ized, ·iz·ing 1** To make or become Roman or Roman Catholic. **2** To write or speak in a Latinized style. **—Ro'man·i·za'tion** n.

Roman numerals The letters used until the tenth century as symbols in arithmetical notation. The basic letters are I (1), V (5), X (10), L (50), C (100), D (500), and M (1000). Intermediate and higher numbers are formed according to the following rules: Any symbol following another of equal or greater value adds to its value, as II = 2, XI = 11; any symbol preceding one of greater value subtracts from its value, as IV = 4, IX = 9, XC = 90; when a symbol stands between two of greater value, it is subtracted from the second and the remainder added to the first, as XIV = 14, LIX = 59.

ro·man·tic (rō·man'tik) adj. **1** Of, like, characterized or influenced by romance. **2** Given to feelings or thoughts of romance, adventure, idealism, etc. **3** Characterized by or conducive to love or amorousness. **4** Visionary; fantastic; impractical: a romantic scheme. **5** Strangely wild or picturesque: romantic scenery. **6** Of, pertaining to, or characteristic of romanticism (def. 1). —n. **1** An adherent of romanticism; a romanticist. **2** A romantic person. [<F romance romance, novel] **—ro·man'ti·cal·ly** adv.

ro·man·ti·cism (rō·man'tə·siz'əm) n. **1** Often cap. In the late 18th and early 19th centuries, a social and esthetic movement, beginning as a reaction to neo-classicism, and characterized, in art, literature, music, etc., by freedom of form, spontaneity of feeling, flights of lyricism and imagination, and a fascination with the remote past, nature, the strange and picturesque, etc. **2** The quality or characteristic of being romantic. **—ro·man'ti·cist** n.

ro·man·ti·cize (rō·man'tə·sīz) v.t. **·cized, ·ciz·ing** To regard or interpret in a romantic manner.

Romantic Movement ROMANTICISM (def. 1).

Rom·a·ny (rom'ə·nē) n. pl. **·nies 1** GYPSY. **2** The Indic language of the Gypsies. [<Romany romani < rom man]

Ro·me·o (rō'mē·ō) n. **1** In Shakespeare's tragedy Romeo and Juliet, the hero of the play. **2** Any ardent male lover.

romp (romp) v.i. **1** To play boisterously. **2** To win easily. —n. **1** One, esp. a girl, who romps. **2** Noisy, exciting frolic or play. **3** An easy victory. [Var. of RAMP²]

romp·er (rom'pər) n. **1** One who romps. **2** pl. A combination of waist and bloomers, as worn by young children.

Rom·u·lus (rom'yə·ləs) Rom. Myth. The founder of Rome, who, with his twin brother Remus, was reared by a she-wolf.

ron·do (ron'dō, ron·dō') n. pl. **·dos** Music A composition or movement having a main theme that is repeated after each of several subordinate themes. [Ital., round]

rood (rood) n. **1** A cross or crucifix. **2** A square land measure, equivalent to one fourth of an acre, or 40 square rods. [<OE rōd rod]

roof (roof, roof) n. **1** The exterior upper covering of a building. **2** Any top covering, as of the mouth, a car, etc. **3** A house; home. **4** The most elevated part of anything; top; summit. —*v.t.* To cover with or as with a roof. [<OE *hrōf*] —**roof′er** *n.*

roof garden 1 A garden on the roof of a building. **2** A gardenlike space on a roof used for a nightclub, restaurant, etc.

roof·ing (rōō′fing, rōōf′ing) *n.* **1** Roofs collectively. **2** Material for roofs. **3** The act of covering with a roof.

rook[1] (rŏŏk) *n.* **1** An Old World bird similar to a crow. **2** A sharper; cheat; trickster. —*v.t. & v.i.* To cheat; defraud. [<OE *hrōc*]

rook[2] (rŏŏk) *n.* One of a pair of castle-shaped chessmen; a castle. [<Pers. *rukh*]

rook·er·y (rŏŏk′ər·ē) *n. pl.* **·er·ies 1** A place where rooks flock together and breed. **2** A breeding place of sea birds, seals, etc.

rook·ie (rŏŏk′ē) *n. Slang* **1** A raw recruit in the army, police, or any other service. **2** A first-year player in a major professional sport. [Prob. alter. of RECRUIT]

room (rōōm, rŏŏm) *n.* **1 a** A space for occupancy or use enclosed on all sides, as in a building. **b** The people in a room. **2** Space available or sufficient for some specified purpose: *room* to park. **3** Suitable or warrantable occasion; opportunity: *room* for doubt. **4** *pl.* Lodgings. —*v.i.* To occupy a room; lodge. [<OE *rūm* space]

room·er (rōō′mər, rŏŏm′ər) *n.* A lodger.

room·ette (rōō·met′, rŏŏm·et′) *n.* A compartment with a single bed in some railroad sleeping-cars.

room·ful (rōōm′fŏŏl′, rŏŏm′-) *n.* **1** As many or as much as a room will hold. **2** The number of persons in a room.

rooming house A house for roomers.

room·mate (rōōm′māt′, rŏŏm′-) *n.* One who occupies a room with another or others.

room·y (rōō′mē, rŏŏm′ē) *adj.* **room·i·er, room·i·est** Having abundant room; spacious. —**room′i·ly** *adv.* —**room′i·ness** *n.*

roor·back (rŏŏr′bak) *n. U.S.* A fictitious report circulated for political purposes. [< *Roorback*, purported author of a (nonexistent) book of travel]

roost (rōōst) *n.* **1 a** A perch upon which fowls rest at night. **b** Any place where birds resort to spend the night. **2** Any temporary resting place. —*v.i.* **1** To sit or perch upon a roost. **2** To come to rest; settle. [<OE *hrōst*]

roost·er (rōōs′tər) *n.* The male of the chicken; cock. [< ROOST + -ER[1]]

root[1] (rōōt, rŏŏt) *n.* **1** The descending axis of a plant, usu. growing underground, providing support and absorbing moisture from the soil. **2** Any underground growth, as a tuber or bulb. **3** Some rootlike part of an organ or structure: the *root* of a tooth, hair, nerve, etc. • See TOOTH. **4** That from which something derives its origin, growth, life, etc.: Money is the *root* of all evil. **5** *pl.* A mental or emotional attachment to some place or people, as through birth, childhood, etc. **6** The essence or basic part: the *root* of the problem. **7** *Ling.* A word or word part serving as the basic constituent element of a related group of words, as *know* in *unknown, knowledge, knowable,* and *knowingly.* **8** *Math.* A number or element that, taken a specified number of times as a factor, will produce a given number or element. **9** *Music* The principal tone of a chord. —*v.i.* **1** To put forth roots and begin to grow. **2** To be or become firmly fixed or established. —*v.t.* **3** To fix or implant by or as by roots. **4** To pull, dig, or tear up by or as by the roots; extirpate; eradicate: with *up* or *out.* [<OE *rōt*] —**root′y** *adj.*

root[2] (rōōt, rŏŏt) *v.t.* **1** To turn up or dig with the snout or nose, as swine. —*v.i.* **2** To turn up the earth with the snout. **3** To search for something; rummage. **4** To work hard; toil. [<OE *wrōtan* root up] —**root′er** *n.*

root[3] (rōōt, rŏŏt) *v.i. Informal* To give one's moral support to a contestant, team, cause, etc.: with *for.* [? < ROOT[2]] —**root′er** *n.*

Rooster

root beer A carbonated beverage flavored with the extracts of several roots.

root hair Any of numerous minute outgrowths on plant roots, having an absorbent function.

root·less (rōōt′lis, rŏŏt′-) *adj.* **1** Without roots. **2** Having no permanent or secure emotional attachment to a place, community, or culture. —**root′less·ness** *n.*

root·let (rōōt′lit, rŏŏt′-) *n.* A small root.

root·stock (rōōt′stok′, rŏŏt′-) *n.* RHIZOME.

rope (rōp) *n.* **1** An assembly of intertwined strands of fiber, wire, plastic, etc., forming a thick cord. **2** A collection of things plaited or united in a line. **3** A sticky or glutinous filament or thread of something, as of beaten egg yolks. **4 a** A cord or halter used in hanging. **b** Death by hanging. **5** LASSO. —*v.t.* **roped, rop·ing 1** To tie or fasten with or as with rope. **2** To enclose, border, or divide with a rope: usu. with *off*: He *roped* off the arena. **3** To catch with a lasso. **4** *Informal* To deceive: with *in.* [<OE *rāp*]

rop·y (rō′pē) *adj.* **rop·i·er, rop·i·est 1** That may be drawn into threads, as a glutinous substance; stringy. **2** Resembling ropes or cordage. —**rop′i·ly** *adv.* —**rop′i·ness** *n.*

Roque·fort cheese (rōk′fərt, *Fr.* rôk·fôr′) A strong cheese with a blue mold, made from ewe's and goat's milk. [< *Roquefort*, France, where first made]

ror·qual (rôr′kwəl) *n.* Any of various whales having a dorsal fin and marked lengthwise creases at the throat. [<Norw. *röyrkval*]

Rorqual

Ror·schach test (rôr′shäk, -shäkh, rôr′-) A psychological test based on the subject's interpretation of inkblot patterns. [< H. *Rorschach*, 1884–1922, Swiss psychiatrist]

ro·sa·ceous (rō·zā′shəs) *adj.* **1** Of, pertaining to, or designating the rose and related plants, as apple, hawthorn, etc. **2** Resembling a rose; rosy.

ro·sa·ry (rō′zə·rē) *n. pl.* **·ries** *Eccl.* **1** A string of beads for keeping count of a series of prayers, used esp. in Roman Catholicism. **2** The prayers. [< LL *rosarium* a rose garden]

rose[1] (rōz) *n.* **1** Any of a genus of hardy, erect or climbing shrubs with prickly stems and flowers of pink, red, white, yellow, etc. **2** The flower. **3** Any of various other plants or flowers having a likeness to the true rose. **4** A pinkish or purplish red color. **5** An ornamental knot, as of ribbon or lace; a rosette. **6** A form in which gems, esp. diamonds, are often cut. —*adj.* **1** Of, containing, or used for roses. **2** Of the color rose. **3** Rose-scented. [< L *rosa* < Gk. *rhodon*]

rose[2] (rōz) *p.t.* of RISE.

ro·se·ate (rō′zē·it, -āt) *adj.* **1** Of a rose color. **2** Optimistic; rosy. —**ro′se·ate·ly** *adv.*

rose·bud (rōz′bud′) *n.* The bud of a rose.

rose·bush (rōz′bŏŏsh′) *n.* A rose-bearing shrub.

rose chafer A hairy, fawn-colored beetle that feeds on the blossoms of roses and related plants. Also **rose beetle.**

rose fever A kind of hay fever that occurs in early summer when roses are in bloom. Also **rose cold.**

rose·mar·y (rōz′mâr′ē) *n. pl.* **·mar·ies 1** An evergreen, fragrant shrub related to mint. **2** Its leaves, used for their taste and aroma in cooking, perfumery, etc. [< L *ros* dew + *marinus* marine; infl. by *rose, Mary*]

rose of Sharon 1 In the Bible, an unidentified flower. **2** A species of hibiscus; althea. **3** A species of St. Johnswort.

ro·se·o·la (rō·zē·ō′lə, -zē′ə·lə) *n.* **1** A pink rash occurring as a symptom of various diseases. **2** A mild disease of infants, marked by fever and a pink rash. [< L *roseus* rosy]

Ro·set·ta stone (rō·zet′ə) A tablet containing an inscription in Egyptian hieroglyphics and in Greek, found near Rosetta, Egypt, in 1799. It supplied the key to the ancient inscriptions of Egypt.

ro·sette (rō·zet′) *n.* **1** A painted or sculptured architectural ornament with parts circularly arranged. **2** A ribbon badge shaped like a rose and worn to indicate possession of a certain military decoration. **3** Any flowerlike cluster as of leaves, markings, etc. [F, little rose]

rose water An aqueous extract of rose petals, used in perfumery and cooking. —**rose′·wa′ter** *adj.*

rose window A circular window filled with tracery that radiates from the center.

rose·wood (rōz′wŏŏd′) *n.* **1** The hard, dense, dark-colored wood of various tropical leguminous trees, valued for cabinet work. **2** Any tree yielding such a wood.

Rosh Ha·sha·na (rosh hə-shä′-nə, rōsh) The Jewish New Year, celebrated in September or early October. Also **Rosh Ha·sho′nah** (-shō′-). [< Hebrew *rōsh* head of + *hash-shānāh* the year]

Rose window

ros·in (roz′in) *n.* A hard, usu. amber-colored resin obtained from turpentine. —*v.t.* To apply rosin to. [Var. of RESIN] —**ros′in·y** *adj.*

ros·ter (ros′tər) *n.* **1** A list of officers and men enrolled for duty. **2** Any list of names. [< Du. *rooster* list]

ros·trum (ros′trəm) *n. pl.* **·trums** or **·tra** (-trə) **1** A stage or platform for public speaking. **2** Those speaking publically on a rostrum. **3** *pl.* **ros·tra** The orators' platform in the Roman forum. **4** A beak or snout. **5** One of various beaklike parts, as the prow of an ancient war galley. [< L *rostrum* beak]

ros·y (rō′zē) *adj.* **ros·i·er, ros·i·est 1** Like a rose in color. **2** Blushing. **3** Fresh and blooming. **4** Favorable; optimistic. —**ros′i·ly** *adv.* —**ros′i·ness** *n.*

rot (rot) *v.* **rot·ted, rot·ting** *v.i.* **1** To undergo decomposition. **2** To fall or pass by decaying: with *away, off,* etc. **3** To become morally rotten. —*v.t.* **4** To cause to decompose; decay. —*n.* **1** The process of rotting or the state of being rotten. **2** Any of various plant and animal diseases characterized by destruction of tissue. **3** *Informal* Nonsense; bosh. —*interj.* Nonsense. [< OE *rotian*]

rot. rotating; rotation.

ro·ta·ry (rō′tər·ē) *adj.* **1** Turning on an axis, as a wheel. **2** Having some part that so turns: a *rotary* press. [< L *rota* wheel]

rotary engine An engine, as a turbine, in which rotary motion is directly produced without reciprocating parts.

ro·tate (rō′tāt, rō-tāt′) *v.t. & v.i.* **·tat·ed, ·tat·ing 1** To turn or cause to turn on or as on its axis. **2** To alternate in a definite order or succession. [< L *rota* wheel] —**ro·tat′a·ble, ro′ta·tive** (-tə-tiv) *adj.* —**ro′ta·tor** *n.*

ro·ta·tion (rō-tā′shən) *n.* **1** The act or state of rotating. **2** Alternation or succession in some fixed order. **3** *Agric.* The practice of planting a field with a series of various crops to preserve the fertility of the field: also **crop rotation.** —**ro·ta′tion·al** *adj.*

ro·ta·to·ry (rō′tə·tôr′ē, -tō′rē) *adj.* **1** Of, pertaining to, or producing rotation. **2** Alternating or recurring.

ROTC, R.O.T.C. Reserve Officers' Training Corps.

rote (rōt) *n.* A routine, mechanical way of doing something. —**by rote** Mechanically; without intelligent attention: to learn *by rote*. [ME]

ro·ti·fer (rō′tə·fər) *n.* Any of numerous many-celled, aquatic microorganisms having rows of cilia at one end, which in motion resemble revolving wheels. [< L *rota* wheel + *ferre* to bear] —**ro·tif·er·al** (rō·tif′ər·əl), **ro·tif′er·ous** *adj.*

ro·tis·se·rie (rō·tis′ə·rē) *n.* **1** An establishment where meat is roasted and sold. **2** A device for roasting meat by rotating it on a spit before or over a source of heat. [< F *rôtir* to roast]

Rotifer

ro·to·gra·vure (rō′tə·grə·vyŏŏr′) *n.* **1** A printing process in which an impression is produced by rotating cylinders which have been etched from photographic plates. **2** Something printed by this process. [< L *rota* wheel + GRAVURE]

ro·tor (rō′tər) *n.* **1** A rotary part of a machine. **2** *Aeron.* The horizontally rotating airfoil assembly of a helicopter. [Contraction of ROTATOR]

rot·ten (rot′n) *adj.* **1** Decomposed; spoiled. **2** Smelling of decomposition or decay; putrid. **3** Untrustworthy; dishonest. **4** Weak or unsound, as if decayed. **5** *Informal* Disa-

greeable or very bad: a *rotten* disposition; a *rotten* movie. [< ON *rotinn*] —**rot′ten·ly** *adv.* —**rot′ten·ness** *n.*

rot·ter (rot′ər) *n. Chiefly Brit. Slang* A worthless or objectionable person.

ro·tund (rō·tund′) *adj.* **1** Rounded out, spherical, or plump. **2** Full-toned, as a voice or utterance. [< L *rota* wheel] —**ro·tun′di·ty, ro·tund′ness** *n.* —**ro·tund′ly** *adv.*

ro·tun·da (rō·tun′də) *n.* A circular building, room, hall, etc., esp. one with a dome. [< L *rotundus* round]

rou·ble (rōō′bəl) *n.* RUBLE.

rouche (rōōsh) *n.* RUCHE.

rou·é (rōō·ā′) *n.* A dissolute man; sensualist. [< F *rouer* break on the wheel]

Rotunda

rouge[1] (rōōzh) *n.* **1** Any cosmetic used for coloring the cheeks or lips. **2** A red powder, mainly ferric oxide, used in polishing. —*v.* **rouged, roug·ing** *v.t. & v.i.* To color with or apply rouge. [< L *rubeus* ruby]

rouge[2] (rōōzh) *n. Can.* A member of the Liberal party in Quebec. —*adj.* Of or pertaining to the Liberal party in Quebec.

rough (ruf) *adj.* **1** Having an uneven surface: a *rough* pavement. **2** Coarse in texture; shaggy: a *rough* tweed. **3** Disordered or ragged: a *rough* shock of hair. **4** Characterized by rude or violent action: *rough* sports. **5** Agitated; stormy: a *rough* passage. **6** Rude; coarse: a *rough* manner. **7** Lacking finish and polish; crude: a *rough* gem. **8** Done or made hastily and without attention to details: a *rough* sketch. **9** *Phonet.* Uttered with an aspiration, or *h* sound. **10** Harsh to the senses: *rough* sounds. **11** Without comforts or conveniences: the *rough* life of the poor. **12** Requiring physical strength: *rough* work. **13** *Informal* Difficult; trying: It's been a *rough* day. —**in the rough** In an unpolished or crude condition. —*n.* **1** Any rough ground. **2** A crude, incomplete, or unpolished object, material, or condition. **3** Any part of a golf course on which tall grass, bushes, etc., grow. **4** *Chiefly Brit.* A rude or violent person; ruffian. —*v.t.* **1** To make rough; roughen. **2** To treat roughly: often with *up.* **3** To make, cut, or sketch roughly: to *rough* in the details of a plan. —*v.i.* **4** To become rough. **5** To behave roughly. —**rough it** To live under or endure conditions that are hard, rustic, inconvenient, etc. —*adv.* In a rude manner. [< OE *rūh*] —**rough′ly** *adv.* —**rough′ness** *n.* —**Syn.** *adj.* **3** unkempt. **6** boorish, uncultivated.

rough·age (ruf′ij) *n.* Food containing bulky, indigestible constituents that stimulate peristalsis.

rough-and-read·y (ruf′ən·red′ē) *adj.* Crude or rough in quality but effective for a particular purpose.

rough-and-tum·ble (ruf′ən·tum′bəl) *adj.* Disregarding all rules of fighting; disorderly and violent. —*n.* A fight in which anything goes; a brawl.

rough-cast (ruf′kast′, -käst′) *v.t.* **-cast, -cast·ing 1** To shape or prepare in a preliminary or incomplete form. **2** To coat, as a wall, with coarse plaster. —*n.* **1** Very coarse plaster for the outside of buildings. **2** A rude model of a thing in its first rough stage. —**rough′-cast′er** *n.*

rough-dry (ruf′drī′) *v.t.* **-dried, -dry·ing** To dry (laundry) without ironing it afterward. —*adj.* Washed and dried but unironed.

rough·en (ruf′ən) *v.t. & v.i.* To make or become rough.

rough-hew (ruf′hyōō′) *v.t.* **-hewed, -hewed** or **-hewn, -hew·ing 1** To hew or shape roughly without smoothing. **2** To make crudely.

rough·house (ruf′hous′) *Slang n.* A noisy, boisterous disturbance; rough play. —*v.* (ruf′hous′, -houz′) **-housed, -hous·ing** *v.i.* **1** To engage in roughhouse. —*v.t.* **2** To handle or treat roughly, usu. without hostile intent.

rough·neck (ruf′nek′) *n. Slang* A rowdy.

rough-rid·er (ruf′rī′dər) *n.* One skilled in breaking horses for riding, or accustomed to hard, rough riding.

Rough Riders The 1st U.S. Volunteer Cavalry in the Spanish-American War of 1898, commanded by Theodore Roosevelt.

rough-shod (ruf′shod′) *adj.* Shod with rough shoes to prevent slipping, as a horse. —**ride rough-shod (over)** To treat harshly and without consideration.

rou·lette (roo·let′) *n.* **1** A gambling game in which participants place bets on which compartment of a rotating shallow bowl a small ball will fall into. **2** A toothed wheel for making marks or holes, as the tiny slits in a sheet of postage stamps. —*v.t.* **·let·ted, ·let·ting** To use a roulette upon. [< L *rota* wheel]

Rou·ma·ni·a (roo·mā′nē·ə, -mān′yə) *n.* RUMANIA. —**Rou·ma′ni·an** *adj., n.*

round (round) *adj.* **1** Having a shape like a ball, ring, or cylinder; spherical, circular, or cylindrical. **2** Semicircular: a *round* arch. **3** Plump. **4** Formed or moving in rotation or a circle: a *round* dance. **5** Approximate to the nearest ten, hundred, thousand, etc., as a number. **6** Pronounced with the lips forming a circle, as the vowel *o*. **7** Full; complete: a *round* dozen. **8** Large; ample; liberal: a good *round* fee. **9** Full in tone or resonance. **10** Free and easy; brisk: a *round* pace. —*n.* **1** Something round, as a globe, ring, or cylinder. **2** *Often pl.* A circular course or range; circuit; beat: to make one's *rounds*. **3** Motion in a circular path. **4** A series of recurrent actions; a routine: the daily *round* of life. **5** An outburst, as of applause. **6** In some sports and games, a division based on action or time. **7** A short canon for several voices. **8** A single shot fired by a weapon or by each of a number of weapons. **9** The ammunition used for such a shot. **10** ROUND DANCE (def. 1). **11** The state of being carved out on all sides: opposed to *relief*. **12** The state or condition of being circular; roundness. **13** A portion of a hind leg of beef, between the rump and lower leg. **14** A rung of a chair or ladder. —**go the rounds** to pass from person to person, as gossip, a rumor, etc. —*v.t.* **1** To make round or plump. **2** *Phonet.* To utter (a vowel) with the lips in a rounded position. **3** To travel or go around; make a circuit of. —*v.i.* **4** To become round or plump. **5** To make a circuit; travel a circular course. **6** To turn around. —**round off** (or **out**) **1** To make or become round. **2** To bring to perfection or completion. —**round up 1** To collect (cattle, etc.) in a herd, as for driving to market. **2** *Informal* To gather together; assemble. —*adv.* **1** On all sides; in such a manner as to encircle: A crowd gathered *round*. **2** In a circular path, or with a circular motion: The plane circled *round;* The wheel turns *round*. **3** To each of a number, one after the other: provisions enough to go *round*. **4** In circumference: a log three feet *round*. **5** From one position to another; here and there. **6** In the vicinity: to loiter *round*. **7** So as to complete a period of time: Will spring ever come *round* again? **8** In a circuitous or indirect way: Come *round* by way of the shopping center. **9** In the opposite direction: to turn *round*. —*prep.* **1** Enclosing; encircling: a belt *round* his waist. **2** On every side of; surrounding. **3** Toward every side of; about: He peered *round* him. **4** In the vicinity of: farms *round* the town. **5** To all or many parts of: driving friends *round* the city. **6** Here and there in: to look *round* a room. **7** So as to get to the other side of: walking *round* the corner. **8** In a group or mass surrounding: a rich socialite with hangers-on *round* him. [< L *rotundus*] —**round′ness** *n.*

round·a·bout (round′ə·bout′) *adj.* **1** Circuitous; indirect. **2** Encircling. —*n.* **1** A short, tight-fitting jacket for men and boys. **2** *Brit.* A merry-go-round.

round dance 1 A country dance in which the dancers form or move in a circle. **2** A dance with revolving or circular movements, as a waltz or polka, performed by two persons.

roun·de·lay (roun′də·lā) *n.* A simple song with a recurrent refrain. [< OF *rondel* round]

round·er (roun′dər) *n.* **1** *Informal* A dissolute person; wastrel. **2** A tool for rounding a surface or edge.

Round·head (round′hed′) *n.* A member of the Parliamentary party in England in the civil war of 1642–49.

round·house (round′hous′) *n.* **1** A cabin on the after part of the quarter-deck of a vessel. **2** A round building with a turntable in the center, used for housing and repairing locomotives.

round·ly (round′lē) *adv.* **1** In a round manner or form. **2** Severely; vigorously; bluntly. **3** Thoroughly; completely.

round robin 1 A petition, protest, etc., on which signa-

tures are written in a circle to avoid revealing the order of signing. **2** A tournament, as in tennis or chess, in which each player is matched with every other player.

round-shoul·dered (round′shōl′dərd) *adj.* Having the back rounded or the shoulders stooping.

round table 1 A group of persons meeting for a discussion. **2** Such a discussion. —**round′·ta′ble** *adj.*

Round Table 1 The table of King Arthur, made exactly circular so as to avoid any question of precedence among his knights. **2** King Arthur and his body of knights.

round trip A trip to a place and back again. —**round′-trip′** *adj.*

round·up (round′up′) *n.* **1** The bringing together of cattle scattered over a range for inspection, branding, etc. **2** The cowboys, horses, etc., employed in this work. **3** A bringing together, as of persons or things: a *roundup* of hobos.

round·worm (round′wûrm′) *n.* Any of a large phylum of worms with thin, cylindrical, unsegmented bodies; nematode worm.

rouse (rouz) *v.* **roused, rous·ing** *v.t.* **1** To cause to awaken from slumber, repose, unconsciousness, etc. **2** To excite to vigorous thought or action; stir up. **3** To startle or drive (game) from cover. —*v.i.* **4** To awaken from sleep or unconsciousness. **5** To become active. **6** To start from cover: said of game. —*n.* The act of rousing. [?] —**rous′er** *n.* —**Syn.** *v.* **2** animate, incite, arouse, stimulate.

rous·ing (rou′zing) *adj.* **1** Able to rouse or excite: a *rousing* speech. **2** Lively; vigorous: a *rousing* trade. **3** Exceptional; remarkable: a *rousing* success. —**rous′ing·ly** *adv.*

roust·a·bout (roust′ə·bout′) *n.* **1** A deck hand or dock worker. **2** An unskilled, semiskilled, or transient worker, as on an oil field or ranch. **3** A worker at a circus who helps to set up and dismantle tents, etc. [< *roust*, blend of ROUSE and ROUT]

rout[1] (rout) *n.* **1** A disorderly retreat or flight. **2** A boisterous and disorderly crowd; rabble. **3** An overwhelming defeat; debacle. —*v.t.* **1** To defeat disastrously. **2** To put to flight. [< L *ruptus*, p.p. of *rumpere* to break]

rout[2] (rout) *v.i.* **1** To turn up the earth with the snout, as swine. **2** To search; rummage. —*v.t.* **3** To dig or turn up with the snout. **4** To disclose to view; turn up as if with the snout: with *out*. **5** To hollow, gouge, or scrape, as with a scoop. **6** To drive or force out. [Var. of ROOT[2]]

route (root, rout) *n.* **1** A course or way taken in passing from one point to another. **2** A road; highway. **3** The established passage which is regularly traveled by a person who delivers mail, milk, etc. **4** A way or means of approach: the *route* to success. —*v.t.* **rout·ed, rout·ing 1** To send by a certain way, as passengers, goods, etc. **2** To arrange an itinerary for. [< L *rupta (via)* broken (road)] —**rout′er** *n.*

rou·tine (roo·tēn′) *n.* **1** A detailed method of procedure, prescribed or regularly followed. **2** Anything that has become customary or habitual. —*adj.* **1** Customary; habitual. **2** Uninspired; dull: a *routine* performance. [< F *route* way, road] —**rou·tine′ly** *adv.*

rove[1] (rōv) *v.* **roved, rov·ing** *v.i.* **1** To go from place to place without any definite destination. —*v.t.* **2** To roam over, through, or about. —*n.* The act of roving or roaming. [? < Du. *rooven* rob] —**Syn.** **1** ramble, roam, wander.

rove[2] (rōv) A *p.t.* & *p.p.* of REEVE[1].

row[1] (rō) *n.* An arrangement or series of persons or things in a continued line, as a street lined with buildings on both sides, or a line of seats in a theater. —**a long row to hoe** A hard task or undertaking. —*v.t.* To arrange in a row: with *up*. [< OE *rāw* line]

row[2] (rō) *v.i.* **1** To use oars, sweeps, etc., in propelling a boat. **2** To be propelled by or as if by oars. —*v.t.* **3** To propel across the surface of the water with oars, as a boat. **4** To transport by rowing. **5** To be propelled by (a specific number of oars): said of boats. **6** To take part in (a rowing race). **7** To row against in a race. —*n.* **1** A trip in a rowboat; also, the distance covered. **2** The act of rowing, or an instance of it. [< OE *rōwan*]

row[3] (rou) *n.* A noisy disturbance or quarrel; dispute; brawl; clamor. —*v.t.* & *v.i.* To engage in a row. [?]

---

add, āce, câre, pălm; end, ēven; it, īce; odd, ōpen, ôrder; tŏŏk, pōōl; up, bûrn; ə = a in *above*, u in *focus*; yōō = u in *fuse*; oil; pout; check; go; ring; thin; this; zh, *vision*. < derived from; ? origin uncertain or unknown.

row·an (rō′ən, rou′-) *n.* **1** Any of various related trees having compound pinnate leaves, white flowers and red berries, as the European or American mountain ash. **2** The fruit of these trees: also **row′an·ber′ry.** [< Scand.]

row·boat (rō′bōt′) *n.* A boat propelled by oars.

row·dy (rou′dē) *n. pl.* **·dies** One inclined to create disturbances or engage in rows; a rough, quarrelsome person. —*adj.* **·di·er, ·di·est** Rough and loud; disorderly. [?] —**row′di·ly** *adv.* —**row′di·ness, row′dy·ism** *n.* —**row′dy·ish** *adj.*

row·el (rou′əl) *n.* A spiked or toothed wheel, as on a spur. —*v.t.* **·eled** or **·elled, ·el·ing** or **·el·ling** To prick with a rowel; spur. [< L *rota* wheel]

row·lock (rō′lok′) *n. Brit.* OARLOCK.

roy. royal.

roy·al (roi′əl) *adj.* **1** Of, pertaining to, or being a king, queen, or other sovereign. **2** Of, pertaining to, or under the patronage or authority of a sovereign. **3** Like or suitable for a sovereign. **4** Of superior quality or size: *royal* octavo. —*n.* A small sail or mast next above the topgallant. [< L *regalis* kingly] —**roy′al·ly** *adv.* —**Syn.** *adj.* **3** imperial, kingly, noble, regal, stately.

Rowel of spur

royal blue A vivid purplish or reddish blue.

roy·al·ist (roi′əl·ist) *n.* A supporter of a king, queen, or other sovereign. —**roy′al·ism** *n.*

roy·al·ty (roi′əl·tē) *n. pl.* **·ties** **1** The rank, status, or authority of a sovereign. **2** A royal personage; also, royal persons collectively. **3** Royal nature or quality. **4** A share of proceeds paid to a proprietor, author, inventor, etc.

rpm, r.p.m. revolutions per minute.

rps, r.p.s. revolutions per second.

rpt. report.

R.R. railroad; Right Reverend.

R.S. Recording Secretary; Reformed Spelling; Revised Statutes.

R.S.F.S.R. Russian Soviet Federated Socialist Republic.

RSV Revised Standard Version (of the Bible).

R.S.V.P., r.s.v.p. please reply (F *répondez s'il vous plaît*).

Rt. Hon. Right Honorable.

Rt. Rev. Right Reverend.

Rts. rights.

Ru ruthenium.

rub (rub) *v.* **rubbed, rub·bing** *v.t.* **1** To move or pass over the surface of with pressure and friction. **2** To cause (something) to move or pass with friction. **3** To cause to become frayed, worn, or sore from friction: This collar *rubs* my neck. **4** To clean, shine, dry, etc., by means of pressure and friction, or by means of a substance applied thus. **5** To apply or spread with pressure and friction: to *rub* polish on a table. **6** To force by rubbing: with *in* or *into*: to *rub* oil into wood. **7** To remove or erase by friction: with *off* or *out.* —*v.i.* **8** To move along a surface with friction; scrape. **9** To exert pressure and friction. **10** To become frayed, worn, or sore from friction; chafe. **11** To undergo rubbing or removal by rubbing: with *off, out,* etc. —**rub down** To massage. —**rub it in** *Slang* To harp on someone's errors, faults, etc. —**rub out** *Slang* To kill. —**rub the wrong way** To irritate; annoy. —*n.* **1** A subjection to frictional pressure; rubbing: Give it a *rub.* **2** A hindrance or doubt: There's the *rub.* **3** Something that injures the feelings; a sarcasm. [ME *rubben*]

ru·ba·to (rōō·bä′tō) *Music adj. & adv.* With certain notes lengthened or shortened at the performer's discretion. —*n. pl.* **·tos** A rubato passage or manner of playing [Ital.]

rub·ber¹ (rub′ər) *n.* **1** A tough, resilient, elastic material made from the latex of certain tropical plants, or synthesized from coal, petroleum, etc. **2** An article made of this material, as: **a** A rubber overshoe. **b** A condom. **3** One who or that which rubs. —*adj.* Made of rubber. [< RUB] —**rub′ber·y** *adj.*

rub·ber² (rub′ər) *n.* **1** In bridge, whist, and other card games, a series of games (3, 5, or 7) played by the same partners against the same adversaries, terminated when one side has won a majority (2 out of 3, etc.). **2** The odd game which breaks a tie between the players. [?]

rubber band A continuous elastic band of rubber, stretched to encircle and bind articles, etc.

rub·ber·ize (rub′ər·īz) *v.t.* **·ized, ·iz·ing** To coat, impregnate, or cover with rubber or a rubber solution.

rub·ber·neck (rub′ər·nek′) *n. Slang* One who is extremely curious or inquisitive, as a tourist. —*v.i.* To look or listen with great curiosity.

rubber plant 1 Any of several plants yielding latex. **2** An Asian tree related to the fig, with oblong, leathery leaves, often kept as a house plant.

rub·ber-stamp (rub′ər·stamp′) *v.t.* **1** To endorse, initial, or approve with the mark made by a rubber stamping device. **2** *Informal* To pass or approve as a matter of course or routine.

rubber stamp 1 A stamp made of rubber which, when coated with ink, is used to print names, dates, etc. **2** A person or group of persons that approves something, as a policy or program, with little or no discussion, debate, etc. **3** Any routine approval.

rub·bish (rub′ish) *n.* **1** Waste refuse; garbage; trash. **2** Silly or worthless ideas, talk, etc.; nonsense. [?] —**rub′bish·y** *adj.* —**Syn.** **1** debris, litter. **2** absurdness, foolishness.

rub·ble (rub′əl) *n.* **1** Rough, irregular pieces of broken stone, brick, etc. **2** The debris to which buildings of brick, stone, etc., have been reduced by destruction or decay. **3** Masonry composed of irregular or broken stone: also **rub′ble·work′.**

rub·down (rub′doun′) *n.* A massage.

rube (rōōb) *n. Slang* An unsophisticated country person; rustic. [Abbr. of *Reuben*]

ru·bel·la (rōō·bel′ə) *n.* A contagious viral disease benign in children but linked to birth defects of children born of women infected in early pregnancy; German measles. [< L *rubellus* reddish, dim. of *ruber* red]

ru·be·o·la (rōō′bē·ō′lə, rōō·bē′ə·lə) *n.* A contagious viral disease usu. affecting children, marked by catarrh, fever, and a rash that persists for about a week; measles. [< L *rubeus* red] —**ru·be′o·lar** *adj.*

Ru·bi·con (rōō′bi·kon) *n.* A river in N CEN. Italy that formed the boundary separating Julius Caesar's province of Gaul from Italy; by crossing it under arms he committed himself to a civil war. —**cross the Rubicon** To commit oneself irrevocably to some course of action.

ru·bi·cund (rōō′bə·kənd) *adj.* Red, or inclined to redness; ruddy. [< L *rubicundus*] —**ru′bi·cun′di·ty** *n.*

ru·bid·i·um (rōō·bid′ē·əm) *n.* A soft, rare, metallic element (symbol Rb) resembling potassium. [< L *rubidus* red]

ru·ble (rōō′bəl) *n.* The basic monetary unit of the Soviet Union.

ru·bric (rōō′brik) *n.* **1** In early manuscripts and books, the heading of a chapter, an initial letter, etc., that appears in red, or in some distinctive type. **2** Any heading or title, as that of a statute. **3** A direction or rule as in a prayer book, missal, or breviary. [< L *ruber* red] —**ru′bri·cal** *adj.* —**ru′bri·cal·ly** *adv.*

ru·by (rōō′bē) *n. pl.* **·bies** **1** A translucent gemstone of a deep red color, a variety of corundum. **2** A rich red color like that of a ruby. —*adj.* Deep red. [< L *rubeus* red]

ruche (rōōsh) *n.* A pleated or gathered strip of fine fabric, worn about the neck or wrists of a woman's costume. [F< Med. L *rusca* tree bark]

ruch·ing (rōō′shing) *n.* **1** Material for ruches. **2** Ruches collectively.

ruck·sack (ruk′sak′, rŏŏk′-) *n.* KNAPSACK. [G, lit., back sack]

ruck·us (ruk′əs) *n. Slang* An uproar; commotion. [? blend of RUMPUS and *ruction,* alter. of INSURRECTION]

rud·der (rud′ər) *n.* **1** *Naut.* A broad, flat device hinged vertically at the stern of a vessel to direct its course. **2** Anything that guides or directs a course. **3** *Aeron.* A hinged or pivoted surface, used to turn an aircraft about its vertical axis. [< OE *rōthor* oar, scull] —**rud′der·less** *adj.*

a. rudder
def. 1.
b. screw.

rud·dy (rud′ē) *adj.* **·di·er, ·di·est** **1** Red or tinged with red. **2** Having a healthy glow; rosy: a *ruddy* complexion. [< OE *rudig*] —**rud′di·ly** *adv.* —**rud′di·ness** *n.*

rude (rōōd) *adj.* **rud·er, rud·est** **1** Offensively blunt or uncivil; impolite. **2** Characterized by lack of polish or refinement; uncouth. **3** Unskilfully made or done; crude. **4** Characterized by robust vigor; strong: *rude* health. **5** Barbarous; savage. **6**

Jarring to the ear; harsh; discordant. **7** Lacking skill, training, accuracy, etc. [< L *rudis* rough] —**rude′ly** *adv.* —**rude′ness** *n.* —Syn. **1** discourteous, impertinent. **2** boorish, uncultivated. **5** uncivilized.

ru·di·ment (rōō′də·mənt) *n.* **1** A first step, stage, or condition. **2** That which is undeveloped or partially developed. [< L *rudis* rough]

ru·di·men·ta·ry (rōō′də·men′tər·ē) *adj.* **1** Introductory; elementary: *rudimentary* knowledge. **2** Being in an imperfectly developed state; undeveloped. **3** Vestigial. Also **ru′di·men′tal.** —**ru′di·men′ta·ri·ly** *adv.* —**ru′di·men′ta·ri·ness** *n.*

rue[1] (rōō) *v.* **rued, ru·ing** *v.t.* **1** To feel sorrow or remorse for; regret extremely. —*v.i.* **2** To feel sorrow or remorse. —*n. Archaic* Sorrowful remembrance; regret. [< OE *hrēowan* be sorry] —**ru′er** *n.*

rue[2] (rōō) *n.* **1** A small, pungent shrub with bitter, ever-green leaves. **2** An infusion of rue leaves. [< Gk. *rhytē*]

rue·ful (rōō′fəl) *adj.* **1** Feeling or expressing sorrow, regret, or pity. **2** Causing sympathy or pity; pitiable. —**rue′-ful·ly** *adv.* —**rue′ful·ness** *n.*

ruff[1] (ruf) *n.* **1** A pleated, round, heavily starched collar popular in the 16th century. **2** A natural collar of projecting feathers or hair around the neck of a bird or mammal. **3** The male of a European species of sandpiper, which has a large ruff in the breeding season. [Short for RUF-FLE[1]] —**ruffed** *adj.*

ruff[2] (ruf) *n.* In a card game, the act of trumping. —*v.t. & v.i.* To trump. [< OF *roffle*]

ruffed grouse (ruft) A North American grouse having in the male a fan-shaped tail and a black ruff.

Ruff

ruf·fi·an (ruf′ē·ən, ruf′yən) *n.* A lawless, brutal person. —*adj.* Lawlessly or recklessly brutal or cruel. [< MF *rufian*] —**ruf′fi·an·ism** *n.* —**ruf′fi·an·ly** *adj.*

ruf·fle[1] (ruf′əl) *n.* **1** A pleated strip; frill, as for trim or ornament. **2** Anything resembling this, as a bird's ruff. **3** A disturbance; discomposure. **4** A ripple. —*v.* **·fled, ·fling** *v.t.* **1** To disturb or destroy the smoothness or regularity of: The wind *ruffles* the lake. **2** To draw into folds or ruffles; gather. **3** To furnish with ruffles. **4** To erect (the feathers) in a ruff, as a bird when frightened. **5** To disturb or irritate; upset. **6 a** To riffle (the pages of a book). **b** To shuffle (cards). —*v.i.* **7** To be or become rumpled or disordered. **8** To become disturbed or irritated. [ME *ruffelen* to ruffle]

ruf·fle[2] (ruf′əl) *n.* A low, continuous beat of a drum, not as loud as a roll. —*v.t.* **·fled, ·fling** To beat a ruffle upon, as a drum. [?]

rug (rug) *n.* **1** A covering for all or part of a floor, made of some heavy, durable fabric, strips of rag, animal skins, etc. **2** A warm covering, as of cloth, fur, etc., for the lap and feet.

rug·by (rug′bē) *n. Often cap.* A form of football. [< *Rugby* School, Rugby, England, where first played]

rug·ged (rug′id) *adj.* **1** Having a surface that is rough or uneven. **2** Rough; harsh: a *rugged* life. **3** Furrowed and irregular: *rugged* features. **4** Lacking polish and refinement. **5** Tempestuous; stormy: *rugged* weather. **6** Robust; sturdy: *rugged* health. [< Scand.] —**rug′ged·ly** *adv.* —**rug′-ged·ness** *n.*

ru·in (rōō′in) *n.* **1** Destruction, downfall, or decay. **2** A person or thing that has decayed, fallen, or been destroyed. **3** *Usu. pl.* That which remains of something that has decayed or been destroyed: the *ruins* of Dresden. **4** That which causes destruction, downfall, or decay: Gambling was his *ruin.* **5** The state of being destroyed, fallen, decayed, etc: to fall into *ruin.* —*v.t.* **1** To bring to ruin; destroy. **2** To bring to disgrace or bankruptcy. **3** To deprive of chastity; seduce. —*v.i.* **4** To fall into ruin. [< L *ruere* to fall] —**ru′in·er** *n.* —Syn. *n.* **1** collapse, devastation, dilapidation. *v.* **1** demolish, ravage, raze.

ru·in·a·tion (rōō′in·ā′shən) *n.* **1** The act of ruining. **2** The state of being ruined. **3** Something that ruins.

ru·in·ous (rōō′in·əs) *adj.* **1** Causing or tending to ruin. **2** Falling to ruin. —**ru′in·ous·ly** *adv.* —**ru′in·ous·ness** *n.*

rule (rōōl) *n.* **1** Controlling power, or its possession and exercise; government; reign; also, the period of time during which a ruler or government is in power. **2** A method or principle of action; regular course of procedure: I make early rising my *rule.* **3** An authoritative direction or regulation about something to do or the way of doing it. **4** The body of directions laid down by or for a religious order: the *rule* of St. Francis. **5** A procedure or formula for solving a given class of mathematical problems. **6** An established usage fixing the form of words: a *rule* for forming the plural. **7** Something in the ordinary course of events or condition of things: In some communities illiteracy is the *rule.* **8** *Law* A judicial decision on some specific question or point of law. **9** A straight-edged instrument for use in measuring, or as a guide in drawing lines; a ruler. **10** *Printing* A strip of type-high metal for printing a rule or line. —**as a rule** Ordinarily; usually. —*v.* **ruled, rul·ing** *v.t.* **1** To have authority or control over; govern. **2** To influence greatly; dominate. **3** To decide judicially or authoritatively. **4** To restrain; keep in check. **5** To mark lines on, as with a ruler. —*v.i.* **6** To have authority or control. **7** To form and express a decision: The judge *ruled* on that point. —**rule out 1** To eliminate or exclude. **2** To preclude; prevent. [< L *regula* ruler, rule]

rule of thumb 1 A rule based on experience or common sense instead of scientific knowledge. **2** A method of procedure that is practical but not precise.

rul·er (rōō′lər) *n.* **1** One who rules or governs, as a sovereign. **2** A straight-edged strip of wood, metal, etc., used in drawing lines and in measuring.

rul·ing (rōō′ling) *adj.* **1** Exercising control. **2** Prevalent; predominant. —*n.* A decision, as of a judge or chairman.

rum[1] (rum) *n.* **1** An alcoholic liquor distilled from fermented molasses. **2** Any alcoholic liquor. [?]

rum[2] (rum) *adj. Brit. Slang* Queer; strange. [?]

Rum. Rumania; Rumanian.

Ru·ma·ni·a (rōō·mā′nē·ə, -mān′yə) *n.* A republic of SE Europe, 91,671 sq. mi., cap. Bucharest. ● See map at BAL-KAN STATES.

Ru·ma·ni·an (rōō·mā′nē·ən, -mān′yən) *adj.* Of or pertaining to Rumania, its people, or their language. —*n.* **1** A native or citizen of Rumania. **2** The Romance language of the Rumanians.

rum·ba (rum′bə, *Sp.* rōōm′bä) *n.* **1** A dance originated by Cuban Negroes. **2** A ballroom dance based on this. **3** Music for such a dance. —*v.i.* To dance the rumba. [Sp.]

rum·ble (rum′bəl) *v.* **·bled, ·bling** *v.i.* **1** To make a low, heavy, rolling sound, as thunder. **2** To move or proceed with such a sound. —*v.t.* **3** To cause to make a low, heavy, rolling sound. **4** To utter with such a sound. —*n.* **1** A continuous low, heavy, rolling sound; a muffled roar. **2** A seat or baggage compartment in the rear of an automobile or carriage: also **rumble seat.** **3** *Slang* A street fight involving a group, usu. deliberately provoked. [< MDu. *rommelen*]

ru·men (rōō′men) *n. pl.* **ru·mi·na** (rōō′mə·nə) or **ru·mens** The first chamber of the stomach of a ruminant. [L, throat]

ru·mi·nant (rōō′mə·nənt) *n.* Any of a division of even-toed ungulates, as a deer, sheep, cow, etc., that graze and chew the cud, which is temporarily stored in the first of the four chambers of the stomach. —*adj.* **1** Chewing the cud. **2** Of or pertaining to ruminants. **3** Meditative or thoughtful. [< L *ruminare* chew the cud, think over]

ru·mi·nate (rōō′mə·nāt) *v.t. & v.i.* **·nat·ed, ·nat·ing 1** To chew (food previously swallowed and regurgitated) over again; chew (the cud). **2** To meditate or reflect (upon). —**ru′mi·nat′ing·ly, ru′mi·na′tive·ly** *adv.* —**ru′mi·na′tion, ru′mi·na′tor** *n.* —Syn. **2** brood, consider, contemplate, muse.

rum·mage (rum′ij) *v.* **·maged, ·mag·ing** *v.t.* **1** To search through (a place, box, etc.) by turning over and disarranging the contents; ransack. **2** To find or bring out by searching: with *out* or *up.* —*v.i.* **3** To make a thorough search. —*n.* **1** Any act of rummaging, esp., disarranging things by searching thoroughly. **2** Odds and ends. [< MF *arrumer* pack or arrange cargo] —**rum′mag·er** *n.*

rummage sale A sale of donated miscellaneous objects to raise money, as for some charity.

rum·my[1] (rum′ē) *n.* Any of several card games the object of which is to match cards into sets of three or four of the same denomination or into sequences in the same suit. [?]

rum·my[2] (rum′ē) *n. pl.* **·mies** *Slang* A drunkard. —*adj.* Of, pertaining to, or affected by rum.

ru·mor (rōō′mər) *n.* **1** A story or report circulating without known foundation or authority. **2** Common gossip; hearsay. —*v.t.* To tell or spread as a rumor; report abroad. *Brit. sp.* **ru′mour.** [L, noise]

rump (rump) *n.* **1** The upper part of the hindquarters of an animal. **2** A cut of beef from this part. **3** The buttocks. **4** A last, often unimportant or undesirable part.

rum·ple (rum′pəl) *v.t.* & *v.i.* **·pled, ·pling** To form into creases or folds; wrinkle. —*n.* An irregular fold or crease; wrinkle. [< MDu. *rumpelen*]

rum·pus (rum′pəs) *n. Informal* A usu. noisy disturbance or commotion. [?]

rumpus room A room used for recreation, games, etc.

rum-run·ner (run′run′ər) *n.* A person or ship involved in smuggling alcoholic liquor across or across a border.

run (run) *v.* **ran, run, run·ning** *v.i.* **1** To move by rapid steps, faster than walking. **2** To move rapidly; go swiftly. **3** To flee; take flight. **4** To make a brief or rapid journey: We *ran* over to Staten Island last night. **5** To make regular trips: This steamer *runs* between New York and Liverpool. **6 a** To take part in a race. **b** To be a candidate or contestant: to *run* for dogcatcher. **7** To finish a race in a specified position: I *ran* a poor last. **8** To move or pass easily: The rope *runs* through the pulley. **9** To pass or flow rapidly: watching the tide *run* out. **10.** To proceed in direction or extent: This road *runs* north. **11** To flow: His nose *runs.* **12** To become liquid and flow, as wax; also, to spread or mingle confusedly, as colors when wet. **13** To move or roam about freely and easily: to *run* around town with friends. **14** To pass into a specified condition: to *run* to seed. **15** To unravel, as a fabric. **16** To give forth a discharge or flow. **17** To leak. **18** To continue or proceed without restraint: The conversation *ran* on and on. **19** To be operative; work: Will the engine *run?* **20** To continue or extend, as in time or space: Our property *runs* down to the sea. **21** To be reported or expressed: The story *runs* as follows. **22** To migrate, as salmon from the sea to spawn. **23** To occur or return to the mind: An idea *ran* through his head. **24** To occur with specified variation of size, quality, etc.: The corn is *running* small this year. **25** To be performed or repeated in continuous succession: The play *ran* for forty nights. **26** To pass or spread, as from mouth to mouth or point to point: rumors *running* wild. **27** To creep or climb, as a vine. —*v.t.* **28** To run or proceed along, as a route or path. **29** To make one's way over, through, or past: to *run* rapids. **30** To perform or accomplish by or as by running: to *run* a race or an errand. **31** To compete against in or as in a race. **32** To become subject to; incur: to *run* the risk of failure. **33** To present and support as a candidate. **34** To hunt or chase, as game. **35** To bring to a specified condition by or as by running: to *run* oneself out of breath. **36** To drive or force: with *out of, off, into, through,* etc. **37** To cause to move, as in some manner or direction: They *ran* the ship into port. **38** To move (the eye, hand, etc.) quickly or lightly: He *ran* his hand over the table. **39** To cause to move, slide, etc., as into a specified position: to *run* up a flag. **40** To transport or convey in a vessel or vehicle. **41** To smuggle. **42** To cause to flow: to *run* water into a pot. **43** To trace back: trying to *run* a bit of gossip to its source. **44** To mold, as from melted metal; found. **45** To sew (cloth) in a continuous line, usu. by taking a number of stitches with the needle at a time. **46** To control the motion or operation of; operate: to *run* an engine. **47** To direct or control; manage. **48** To allow to continue or mount up, as a bill. **49** In games, to make (a number of points, strokes, etc.) successively. **50** To publish in a magazine or newspaper: to *run* an ad. **51** To mark, set down, or trace, as a boundary line. **52** To suffer from (a fever, etc.). —**run across** To meet by chance. —**run down 1** To pursue and overtake, as a fugitive. **2** To strike down while moving. **3** To exhaust or damage, as by abuse or overwork. **4** To speak of disparagingly. —**run for it** To run to avoid some-

thing, to escape, seek safety, etc. —**run in 1** To insert; include. **2** *Slang* To arrest and place in confinement. —**run into 1** To meet by chance. **2** To collide with. —**run off 1** To produce on a typewriter, printing press, etc. **2** To decide (a tied race, game, etc.) by the outcome of another, subsequent race, game, etc. —**run out** To be exhausted, as supplies. —**run out of** To exhaust one's supply of. —**run over 1** To ride or drive over; run down. **2** To overflow. **3** To go over, examine, or rehearse. —**run through 1** To squander. **2** To stab or pierce. **3** To rehearse quickly. —**run up** To make hurriedly, as on a sewing machine. —*n.* **1** The act, or an act, of running or going rapidly. **2** A running pace: to break into a *run.* **3** Flow; movement; sweep: the *run* of the tide. **4** A distance covered by running. **5** A journey or passage, esp. between two points, made by a vessel, train, etc. **6** A rapid journey or excursion: take a *run* into town. **7** A swift stream or brook. **8** A migration of fish, esp. to up-river spawning grounds; also, the fish that so migrate. **9** A grazing or feeding ground for animals: a sheep *run.* **10** The regular trail or path of certain animals: an elephant *run.* **11** The privilege of free use or access: to have the *run* of the place. **12** A runway. **13** *Music* A rapid succession of tones. **14** A series, sequence, or succession. **15** A trend or tendency: the general *run* of the market. **16** A continuous spell (of some condition): a *run* of luck. **17** A surge of demands, as those made upon a bank or treasury to meet its obligations. **18** A period of continuous performance, occurrence, popularity, etc.: a play with a long *run.* **19** Class or type; also, the usual or general class or type. **20** A period of operation of a machine or device: an experimental *run.* **21** The output during such a period. **22** A period during which a liquid is allowed to run. **23** The amount of liquid allowed to flow at one time. **24** A narrow, lengthwise ravel, as in a sheer stocking. **25** An approach to a target made by a bombing plane. **26** In baseball, a score made by a player who completes a circuit of the bases from home plate before three outs are made. **27** An unbroken series of successful shots, strokes, etc., as in billiards. —**in the long run** As the ultimate outcome of any train of circumstances. —**on the run 1** Hastily: to eat *on the run.* **2** Running, running away, or retreating. —*adj.* **1** Made liquid; melted. **2** That has been melted or cast: *run* metal. [< OE *rinnan* to flow]

run·a·bout (run′ə·bout′) *n.* **1** A light, open automobile. **2** A light, open wagon. **3** A small motorboat. **4** A person who wanders or runs about from place to place; gadabout.

run·a·round (run′ə·round′) *n. Informal* Evasive or deceptive action or treatment: to get the *runaround* from someone.

run·a·way (run′ə·wā′) *adj.* **1** Escaping or escaped from restraint or control. **2** Brought about by running away: a *runaway* marriage. **3** Easily won, as a horse race. —*n.* **1** One who or that which runs away or flees, as a fugitive or deserter, or a horse of which the driver has lost control. **2** An act of running away.

run·down (run′doun) *n.* **1** A summary; resumé. **2** In baseball, a play attempting to put out a base runner who is trapped between two bases.

run-down (run′doun′) *adj.* **1** Debilitated; tired out. **2** Dilapidated; shabby. **3** Stopped because not wound, as a watch. —*Syn.* **1** exhausted, weary. **2** decayed, ruined.

rune (rōōn) *n.* **1** A character of an ancient Germanic alphabet. **2** A Finnish or Old Norse poem; also, one of the sections of such a poem. **3** An obscure or mystic mark, song, poem, verse, or saying. [< ON *rūn* mystery, rune] —**ru′nic** *adj.*

Runes from an 11th-century tomb

rung[1] (rung) *n.* **1** A round crosspiece of a ladder or chair. **2** A spoke of a wheel. [< OE *hrung* crossbar]

rung[2] (rung) *p.p.* of RING[2].

run-in (run′in′) *n.* **1** A quarrel; bicker. **2** *Printing* Inserted or added matter. —*adj.* (run′in′) *Printing* That is inserted or added.

run·nel (run′əl) *n.* A little stream; a brook. Also **run′let** (-lit). [< OE *rinnan* to run]

run·ner (run′ər) *n.* **1** One who or that which runs. **2** One who operates or manages anything. **3** One who runs errands or goes about on any kind of business, as a messenger. **4** That part on which an object runs or slides: the *runner* of a skate. **5** *Bot.* A slender horizontal stem that takes root at the nodes to produce new plants, as in the strawberry. **6** A smuggler. **7** A long, narrow rug or carpeting, used in hallways, etc. **8** A narrow strip of cloth, usu. of fine quality, used on tables, dressers, etc.

run·ner-up (run′ər-up′) *n. pl.* **·ners-up** or **·ner-ups** A contestant or team finishing second in a contest.

run·ning (run′ing) *adj.* **1** Inclined or trained to a running gait, as certain horses. **2** Done in or started with a run: a *running* jump. **3** Following one another without intermission; successive: He talked for three hours *running*. **4** Continuous: a *running* battle. **5** Characterized by easy flowing curves; cursive: a *running* hand. **6** Discharging, as pus from a sore. **7** Fluid or flowing. **8** In operation, as an engine. **9** Measured in a straight line: the cost per *running* foot. —*n.* **1** The act or movement of one who or that which runs. **2** That which runs or flows. —**in the running** Having a chance to win. —**out of the running** Having no chance to win.

running board A footboard, as on the side of a locomotive, certain automobiles, etc.

running head A heading or title at the top of each page or of every other page of a book, etc.: also **running title.**

running knot A knot made so as to slip along a noose and tighten when pulled upon.

running mate A candidate running with another but for a lesser position, as one seeking to be vice-president.

run·ny (run′ē) *adj.* **·ni·er, ·ni·est** Having a tendency to discharge: a *runny* nose. —**run′ni·ness** *n.*

run-off (run′ôf′ -of′) *n.* **1** Rainfall that drains from a particular area rather than soaking into the soil. **2** A final, deciding contest, game, etc.

run-of-the-mill (run′əv-thə-mil′) *adj.* Average; ordinary.

run-on (run′on′, -ôn′) *Printing n.* Appended or added matter. —*adj.* That is appended or added.

runt (runt) *n.* **1** A stunted animal, esp. the smallest of a litter. **2** A small or stunted person. [?] —**runt′i·ness** *n.* —**runt′y** *adj.* (**·i·er, ·i·est**)

run-through (run′thrōō′) *n.* A rapid reading through or rehearsal, as of a musical composition or a dramatic work.

run·way (run′wā′) *n.* **1** A way on, in, along, or over which something runs. **2** The path over which animals pass to and from their places of feeding or watering. **3** An enclosed place, as for chickens. **4** A strip of surfaced ground used for the takeoff and landing of airplanes. **5** A long, narrow platform extending from a stage into an auditorium.

ru·pee (rōō·pē′, rōō′pe) *n.* The basic monetary unit of India, Pakistan, and Sri Lanka. [< Skt. *rūpya* silver]

ru·pi·ah (rōō·pē′ä) *n.* The basic monetary unit of Indonesia.

rup·ture (rup′chər) *n.* **1** The act of breaking apart or the state of being broken apart. **2** HERNIA. **3** Breach of peace and agreement between individuals or nations. —*v.t.* & *v.i.* **·tured, ·tur·ing** **1** To break apart. **2** To affect with or suffer a rupture. [< L *ruptus*, p.p. of *rumpere* to break]

ru·ral (rōōr′əl) *adj.* Of or pertaining to the country, country people, country life, or agriculture. [< L *rus, ruris* country] —**ru′ral·ism, ru′ral·ist, ru′ral·ness** *n.* —**ru′ral·ly** *adv.*

rural free delivery Free mail delivery by carrier in rural districts.

ru·ral·ize (rōōr′əl-īz) *v.* **·ized, ·iz·ing** *v.t.* To make rural. —*v.i.* To go into or live in the country; rusticate. —**ru′ral·i·za′tion** *n.*

Rus., Russ. Russia; Russian.

ruse (rōōs, rōōz) *n.* An action intended to mislead or deceive; a stratagem; trick. [< F *ruser* dodge, detour]

rush¹ (rush) *v.i.* **1** To move or go swiftly, impetuously, forcefully, or violently. **2** To make an attack; charge: with *on* or *upon*. **3** To proceed recklessly or rashly; plunge: with *in* or *into*. **4** To come, go, pass, act, etc. with suddenness or haste: Ideas kept *rushing* to her mind. **5** To advance a football in a running play. —*v.t.* **6** To move, push, drive,

etc. with haste, impetuosity, or violence. **7** To do, perform, deliver, etc. hastily or hurriedly: to *rush* one's work. **8** To make a sudden assault upon. **9** *Slang* To seek the favor of with assiduous attentions. **10** To advance (a football) in a running play. —*n.* **1** The act of rushing; a sudden turbulent movement, drive, surge, etc. **2** Frantic activity; haste: the *rush* of city life. **3** A sudden pressing demand; a run: a *rush* on foreign bonds. **4** A sudden exigency; urgent pressure: a *rush* of business. **5** A sudden flocking of people, as to some new location. **6** A general contest or scrimmage between students from different classes. **7** In football, an attempt to take the ball through the opposing linemen and toward the goal. **8** *Usu. pl.* In motion pictures, the first film prints of a scene or series of scenes, before editing or selection. —**with a rush** Suddenly and hastily. —*adj.* Requiring urgency or haste: a *rush* order. [< AF *russher* to push] —**rush′er** *n.* —**Syn.** *v.* **1** dash, hasten, hurry.

rush² (rush) *n.* **1** Any of various grasslike plants common in marshy ground. **2** The pliant stem of certain rush plants, used for mats, basketry, etc. [< OE *rysc*] —**rush′y** *adj.* (**·i·er, ·i·est**)

rush hour A time when large numbers of people are traveling, as to or from work. —**rush′-hour′** *adj.*

rush·light (rush′līt′) *n.* A candle made by dipping a rush in tallow: also **rush light, rush candle.**

rusk (rusk) *n.* **1** Plain or sweet bread that is sliced after baking and then toasted or baked a second time until it is brown and crisp. **2** A light, soft, sweet biscuit. [< Sp. *rosca,* twisted loaf of bread]

rus·set (rus′it) *n.* **1** Reddish brown or yellowish brown. **2** A coarse homespun cloth, russet in color, formerly used by country people. **3** A winter apple of russet color. —*adj.* **1** Reddish brown or yellowish brown. **2** Made of russet. [< L *russus* reddish] —**rus′set·y** *adj.*

Rus·sia (rush′ə) *n.* **1** Loosely, the Union of Soviet Socialist Republics. **2** The Russian Soviet Federated Socialist Republic.

Rus·sian (rush′ən) *n.* **1** Loosely, a citizen or native of the Union of Soviet Socialist Republics. **2** A citizen or native of Russia. **3** The language of Russia and the official language of the Union of Soviet Socialist Republics. —*adj.* **1** Loosely, of or pertaining to the Union of Soviet Socialist Republics. **2** Of or pertaining to Russia or its people. **3** Of or pertaining to Russian, the language.

Russian dressing Mayonnaise combined with chili sauce, chopped pickles, etc.

Rus·sian·ize (rush′ən-īz) *v.t.* **·ized, ·iz·ing** To make Russian. —**Rus′sian·i·za′tion** *n.*

Russian leather A smooth, well-tanned, high-grade leather, often dark red, of calfskin or light cattle hide, dressed with birch oil and having a characteristic odor.

Russian Orthodox Church An autonomous branch of the Eastern Orthodox Church.

Russian Revolution The uprising of 1917 that resulted in the overthrow of the czarist regime. The revolution had two phases: first, the establishment of a moderate, provisional government under Kerensky (the **February Revolution**), and, second, the seizure of power by the Bolsheviks (Communists) under Lenin (the **October Revolution**).

Russian thistle A large tumbleweed common on the central plains of North America.

Russian wolfhound BORZOI.

Russo- *combining form* **1** Russia. **2** Russian and: *Russo-*Egyptian.

rust (rust) *n.* **1** A reddish or yellow coating on iron or iron alloys due to spontaneous oxidation. **2** A corroded spot or film of oxide on any metal. **3** Any of various parasitic fungi living on higher plants. **4** A plant disease caused by such fungi, which form spots on stems and leaves. **5** Any spot or film resembling rust on metal. **6** Any of several shades of reddish brown. —*v.t.* & *v.i.* **1** To become or cause to become coated with rust. **2** To contract or cause to contract the plant disease rust. **3** To become or cause to become weakened because of disuse. [< OE *rūst*]

rus·tic (rus′tik) *adj.* **1** Of or pertaining to the country;

rural. **2** Uncultured; rude; awkward. **3** Unsophisticated; artless. **4** Made of the rough limbs of trees with the bark on them: *rustic* furniture. —*n.* **1** One who lives in the country. **2** An unsophisticated, coarse, or ignorant person, esp. one from a rural area. [< L *rus* country] —**rus'ti·cal·ly** *adv.*

rus·ti·cate (rus'tə·kāt) *v.* **·cat·ed**, **·cat·ing** *v.i.* **1** To go to or live in the country. —*v.t.* **2** To send or banish to the country. **3** *Brit.* To suspend (a student) temporarily from a college for punishment. —**rus'ti·ca'tion**, **rus'ti·ca'tor** *n.*

rus·tic·i·ty (rus·tis'ə·tē) *n. pl.* **·ties 1** The condition or quality of being rustic. **2** A rustic trait or peculiarity.

rus·tle[1] (rus'əl) *v.t. & v.i.* **·tled**, **·tling** To move or cause to move with a quick succession of small, light, rubbing sounds, as dry leaves or sheets of paper. —*n.* A rustling sound. [ME *rustelen*] —**rus'tler** *n.* —**rus'tling·ly** *adv.*

rus·tle[2] (rus'əl) *v.t. & v.i.* **·tled**, **·tling 1** *Informal* To act with or obtain by energetic or vigorous action. **2** *Informal* To steal (cattle, etc.). [? Blend of RUSH and HUSTLE]

rus·tler (rus'lər) *n.* **1** *Slang* A person who is active and bustling. **2** *Informal* A cattle thief.

rust·y (rus'tē) *adj.* **rust·i·er**, **rust·i·est 1** Covered or affected with rust. **2** Consisting of or produced by rust. **3** Having the color or appearance of rust; discolored; faded, etc. **4** Not working well or freely; lacking nimbleness; stiff. **5** Impaired or deficient by neglect or want of practice: *rusty* in math. —**rust'i·ly** *adv.* —**rust'i·ness** *n.*

rut[1] (rut) *n.* **1** A sunken track worn by a wheel, as in a road. **2** A groove, furrow, etc., in which something runs. **3** A settled and tedious routine. —*v.t.* **rut·ted**, **rut·ting** To wear or make a rut or ruts in. [? Var. of ROUTE] —**rut'ti·ness** *n.* —**rut'ty** *adj.* (**·i·er**, **·i·est**)

rut[2] (rut) *n.* The sexual excitement of various animals, esp. the male deer; also, the period during which it lasts. —*v.i.* **rut·ted**, **rut·ting** To be in rut. [< L *rugire* to roar]

ru·ta·ba·ga (rōō'tə·bā'gə) *n.* A variety of turnip having a large, yellowish root. [< dial. Sw. *rotabagge*]

ruth (rōōth) *n.* **1** Compassion; pity, mercy. **2** Grief; sorrow; remorse. [< OE *hrēow* sad]

Ruth (rōōth) In the Bible, a widow from Moab who left her people to live with her mother-in-law, Naomi. —*n.* The Old Testament book that tells her story.

ru·the·ni·um (rōō·thē'nē·əm) *n.* A rare metallic element (symbol Ru). [< *Ruthenia*, a region in the Ukraine]

ruth·less (rōōth'lis) *adj.* Having no compassion; merciless. —**ruth'less·ly** *adv.* —**ruth'less·ness** *n.*

R.V. Revised Version (of the Bible).

R.W. Right Worshipful; Right Worthy.

Rwan·da (rwän'də) *n.* A republic of CEN. Africa, 10,169 sq. mi., cap. Kigali. • See map at AFRICA.

Rx *symbol Med.* Take: the conventional heading for a prescription or formula. [Abbr. of L *recipe* take]

-ry Var. of -ERY.

Ry., ry. railway.

rye (rī) *n.* **1** A hardy, cultivated cereal grass. **2** The seeds of this grass. **3** Flour made from these seeds. **4** Whiskey consisting of a blend of bourbon and neutral spirits: also **rye whiskey**. [< OE *ryge*]

rye·grass (rī'gras', -gräs') *n.* A weedy grass sometimes cultivated for forage.

S

S, s (es) *n. pl.* **S's, s's, Ss, ss** (es'iz) **1** The 19th letter of the English alphabet. **2** Any spoken sound representing the letter S or s. **3** Something shaped like an S. —*adj.* Shaped like an S.

S Seaman; sulfur.

S. Sabbath; Saturday; Saxon; Senate; September; Signor; Sunday.

S., s. saint; school; senate; south; southern.

s. second; section; shilling; semi; series; shilling; son; southern; steamer; substantive; sun; surplus.

SA Seaman Apprentice.

S.A. Salvation Army; South Africa; South America.

Sab. Sabbath.

Sab·bath (sab'əth) *n.* **1** The seventh day of the week, a day of rest observed in Judaism and some Christian sects; Saturday. **2** The first day of the week as observed as a day of rest by Christians; Sunday. [< Heb. *shābath* to rest]

sab·bat·i·cal (sə·bat'i·kəl) *adj. Often cap.* Of the nature of or suitable for the Sabbath: also **sab·bat'ic.** —*n.* SABBATICAL YEAR (def. 2).

sabbatical year 1 In the ancient Jewish economy, every seventh year, in which the people were required to refrain from tillage. **2** In the U.S., a year of leave, or a shorter period, to be used for study and travel with full or partial salary, awarded to college faculty members, usu. every seven years: also **sabbatical leave.**

sa·ber (sā'bər) *n.* A heavy one-edged cavalry sword, often curved. —*v.t.* **·bered** or **·bred**, **·ber·ing** or **·bring** To strike, wound, kill, or arm with a saber. Also, and *Brit. sp.*, **sa'bre.** [< MHG *sabel*]

Sa·bine (sā'bīn) *n.* A member of an ancient people of CEN. Italy, conquered and absorbed by Rome in 290 B.C. —*adj.* Of or pertaining to the Sabines.

sa·ble (sā'bəl) *n.* **1** A N Eurasian species of marten bearing costly fur. **2** The dressed fur of a sable. **3** *pl.* Garments made wholly or partly of this fur. **4** The color black. —*adj.* **1** Black; dark. **2** Made of sable fur. [< Med. L *sabelum*]

Saber

or make a rut or ruts in. [? Var. of ROUTE] —**rut'ti·ness** *n.*

sa·bot (sab'ō, *Fr.* sả·bō') *n.* **1** A wooden shoe, as of a French peasant. **2** A shoe having a wooden sole but flexible shank. [F]

sab·o·tage (sab'ə·täzh) *n.* **1** A wasting of materials or damage to machinery, tools, etc., by workmen to make management comply with their demands. **2** The destruction of bridges, railroads, supply depots, etc., either by enemy agents or by underground resisters. **3** Any deliberate effort to obstruct plans or aims. —*v.t. & v.i.* **·taged**, **·tag·ing** To engage in, damage, or destroy by sabotage. [F < *saboter* work badly, damage]

sab·o·teur (sab'ə·tûr', *Fr.* sả·bô·tœr') *n.* One who engages in sabotage. [F]

sa·bra (sä'brə) *n. Often cap.* An Israeli born in Israel. [< Heb.]

sac (sak) *n.* A membranous pouch or cavity, often fluid-filled, in a plant or animal. [< L *saccus*]

SAC (sak) Strategic Air Command.

sac·cha·rin (sak'ər·in) *n.* A sweet compound derived from coal tar, used as a substitute for sugar. [< Gk. *sakcharon* sugar]

sac·cha·rine (sak'ər·in, -ə·rīn', -ə·rēn') *adj.* **1** Very sweet. **2** Cloyingly sweet: a *saccharine* voice. —*n.* SACCHARIN. —**sac'cha·rine·ly** *adv.* —**sac'cha·rin'i·ty** *n.*

sac·er·do·tal (sas'ər·dōt'l, sak'-) *adj.* Pertaining to a priest or priesthood; priestly. [< L *sacerdos* priest] —**sac'er·do'tal·ism** (-iz·əm) *n.* —**sac'er·do'tal·ly** *adv.*

sa·chem (sā'chəm) *n.* A North American Indian hereditary chief. [< Algon.]

sa·chet (sa·shā') *n.* **1** A small bag for perfumed powder, used to scent closets, dresser drawers, etc. **2** The perfumed powder so used. [< L *saccus* a sack]

sack[1] (sak) *n.* **1** A large bag for holding heavy articles. **2** Such a bag and its contents: a *sack* of potatoes. **3** A measure or weight of varying amount. **4** A loosely hanging dress without a waistline, often worn without a belt: also **sack dress. 5** A short, loosely fitting coatlike garment worn by women and children. **6** *Slang* Dismissal, esp. in the phrases **get the sack, give (someone) the sack. 7** In baseball slang, a base. **8** *Slang* A bed; mattress. —**hit the sack** *Slang* To go to bed; retire for the night. —*v.t.* **1** To put into a sack or sacks. **2** *Slang* To dismiss, as an employee. [< Gk. *sakkos* < Heb. *saq* sackcloth]

sack² (sak) *v.t.* To plunder or pillage (a town or city) after capturing. —*n.* The pillaging of a captured town or city. [< L *saccus* a sack (for carrying off plunder)] —**sack′er** *n.*

sack³ (sak) *n.* Any of several strong, light-colored, dry Spanish wines, esp. sherry. [< L *siccus* dry]

sack·but (sak′but) *n.* **1** An early instrument resembling the trombone. **2** In the Bible, a stringed instrument. [< OF *saquer* to pull + *bouter* to push]

sack·cloth (sak′klôth′, -kloth′) *n.* **1** A coarse cloth used for making sacks. **2** Coarse cloth or haircloth worn in penance or mourning.

sack coat A man's short, loose-fitting coat with no waist seam, for informal wear.

sack·ful (sak′fool′) *n. pl.* **·fuls** Enough to fill a sack.

sack·ing (sak′ing) *n.* A coarse cloth made of hemp or flax and used for sacks.

sacque (sak) *n.* A jacket for a baby.

sac·ra·ment (sak′rə·mənt) *n.* **1** A rite ordained by Christ or by the church as an outward sign of grace, as baptism, confirmation, marriage, etc. **2** *Often cap.* The Eucharist. **b** The consecrated bread and wine of the Eucharist: often with *the.* **3** Any solemn covenant or pledge. **4** Anything considered to have sacred significance. [< L *sacramentum* oath, pledge] —**sac′ra·men′tal** *adj.* —**sac′ra·men′tal·ly** *adv.*

sa·cred (sā′krid) *adj.* **1** Dedicated to religious use; hallowed. **2** Pertaining or related to religion: *sacred* books. **3** Consecrated by love or reverence: *sacred* to the memory of his father. **4** Dedicated to a person or purpose: a memorial *sacred* to those killed in battle. **5** Not to be profaned; inviolable: a *sacred* promise. [< L *sacer* holy] —**sa′cred·ly** *adv.* —**sa′cred·ness** *n.*

Sacred College COLLEGE OF CARDINALS.

sac·ri·fice (sak′rə·fīs) *n.* **1** The act of making an offering to a deity. **2** That which is sacrificed; a victim. **3** A giving up of something cherished or desired. **4** Loss incurred or suffered without return. **5** A reduction of price that leaves little profit or involves loss. **6** In baseball, a hit by which the batter is put out, but the base runner is advanced: also **sacrifice hit.** —*v.* **·ficed, ·fic·ing** *v.t.* **1** To give up (something valued) for the sake of something else: to *sacrifice* one's principles for expediency. **2** To sell or part with at a loss. **3** To make an offering, as to a god. **4** In baseball, to advance (one or more runners) by means of a sacrifice. —*v.i.* **5** To make a sacrifice. [< L *sacer* holy + *facere* to make] —**sac′ri·fic′er** *n.* —**sac′ri·fic′ing·ly** *adv.*

sac·ri·fi·cial (sak′rə·fish′əl) *adj.* Pertaining to, performing, or of the nature of a sacrifice. —**sac′ri·fi′cial·ly** *adv.*

sac·ri·lege (sak′rə·lij) *n.* The act of violating or profaning anything sacred. [< L *sacer* holy + *legere* to plunder]

sac·ri·le·gious (sak′rə·lij′əs, -lē′jəs) *adj.* Disrespectful or injurious to sacred persons or things. —**sac′ri·le′gious·ly** *adv.* —**sac′ri·le′gious·ness** *n.* —**Syn.** blasphemous, godless, impious, irreligious, profane.

sac·ris·tan (sak′ris·tən) *n.* A church official having charge of a sacristy and its contents. Also **sa′crist** (sā′krist). [< L *sacer* sacred]

sac·ris·ty (sak′ris·tē) *n. pl.* **·ties** A room in a church for the sacred vessels and vestments; a vestry. [< Med. L *sacrista* sacristan]

sac·ro·il·i·ac (sak′rō·il′ē·ak) *adj.* Pertaining to the sacrum and the ilium and the joint between them.

sac·ro·sanct (sak′rō·sangkt) *adj.* Exceedingly sacred; inviolable: sometimes used ironically. [< L *sacer* holy + *sanctus* holy] —**sac′ro·sanc′ti·ty** *n.*

sa·crum (sā′krəm, sak′rəm) *n. pl.* **·cra** (-krə) A triangular bone formed of fused vertebrae at the lower end of the spinal column and articulating with the hip bone. [< L *(os) sacrum* sacred (bone); from its being offered in sacrifices] • See PELVIS.

sad (sad) *adj.* **sad·der, sad·dest 1** Sorrowful or depressed in spirits; mournful. **2** Causing sorrow or pity; distressing. **3** *Informal* Very bad; awful: a *sad* situation. **4** Dark-hued; somber. [< OE *sæd* sated] —**sad′ly** *adv.* —**sad′ness** *n.* —**Syn. 1** dejected, despondent, disconsolate, miserable, un-

happy, depressed. **2** deplorable, grievous, lamentable, pitiful.

sad·den (sad′n) *v.t. & v.i.* To make or become sad.

sad·dle (sad′l) *n.* **1** A seat or pad for a rider, as on the back of a horse, bicycle, motorcycle, etc. **2** A padded cushion for a horse's back, as part of a harness or to support a pack, etc. **3.** The two hindquarters and part of the backbone of a carcass, as of mutton, venison, etc. **4** Some part or object like or likened to a saddle, as in form or position. —**in the saddle** In a position of control. —*v.t.* **·dled, ·dling 1** To put a saddle on. **2** To load, as with a burden. **3** To place (a burden or responsibility) on a person. [< OE *sadol*]

American stock saddle
a. pommel or saddle
horn. b. cinches.
c. stirrup.

sad·dle·bag (sad′l·bag′) *n.* A large pouch, usu. one of a pair connected by a strap or band and slung over an animal's back behind the saddle.

saddle block A form of anesthesia used esp. during childbirth, in which the patient is injected in the lower spinal cord.

sad·dle·bow (sad′l·bō′) *n.* The arched front upper part of a saddle.

sad·dle·cloth (sad′l·klôth′, -kloth′) *n.* A thick cloth laid on an animal's back under a saddle.

saddle horse A horse used or trained for riding.

sad·dler (sad′lər) *n.* A maker of saddles, harness, etc.

sad·dler·y (sad′lər·ē) *n. pl.* **·dler·ies 1** Saddles, harness, and fittings, collectively. **2** A shop or the work of a saddler.

saddle shoe A white sport shoe with a dark band of leather across the instep.

saddle soap A softening and preserving soap for leather, containing neat's-foot oil.

Sad·du·cee (saj′oo·sē, sad′yoo·sē) *n.* A member of an ancient Jewish sect, which during the time of Jesus rejected doctrines of the oral tradition, as resurrection, and adhered strictly to the Mosaic law. —**Sad′du·ce′an, Sad′du·cae′an** *adj.* —**Sad′du·cee′ism** *n.*

sad·i·ron (sad′ī′ərn) *n.* A heavy flatiron pointed at each end. [< SAD, in obs. sense "heavy" + IRON]

sad·ism (sā′diz·əm, sad′iz·əm) *n.* **1** The obtaining of sexual gratification by inflicting pain. **2** A morbid delight in cruelty. [< Comte Donatien de *Sade*, 1740–1814, French writer] —**sad·ist** (sā′dist, sad′ist) *n., adj.* —**sa·dis·tic** (sə·dis′tik, sā-) *adj.* —**sa·dis′ti·cal·ly** *adv.*

sad·o·mas·o·chism (sā′dō·mas′ə·kiz′m, sad′ō-, -maz′-) *n.* A tendency in one individual to be both a sadist and a masochist. [< SAD + -O- + MASOCHISM] —**sad′o·mas′o·chist** *n.* —**sad′o·mas′o·chis′tic** *adj.*

sad sack *Slang* A well-meaning but bungling person, esp. a soldier.

sa·fa·ri (sə·fä′rē) *n. pl.* **·ris** A hunting expedition or journey, esp. in E Africa. [< Ar. *safara* travel]

safe (sāf) *adj.* **saf·er, saf·est 1** Free or freed from danger. **2** Having escaped injury or damage. **3** Not involving risk or loss: a *safe* investment. **4** Not likely to disappoint: It is *safe* to promise. **5** Not likely to cause or do harm or injury: Is this ladder *safe?* **6** No longer in a position to do harm: a burglar *safe* in jail. **7** In baseball, having reached base without being retired. —*n.* **1** A strong iron-and-steel receptacle, usu. fireproof, for protecting valuables. **2** Any place of safe storage. [< L *salvus* whole, healthy] —**safe′ly** *adv.* —**safe′ness** *n.* —**Syn. 1** secure. **2** unharmed, unscathed. **3** dependable, reliable.

safe-con·duct (sāf′kon′dukt) *n.* **1** Permission to travel in foreign or enemy territories without risking arrest or injury. **2** An official document assuring such protection.

safe·crack·er (sāf′krak′ər) *n.* One who breaks into safes to rob them. —**safe′crack′ing** *n.*

safe-de·pos·it box (sāf′di·poz′it) A box, safe, or drawer, usu. fireproof, for valuable jewelry, papers, etc., generally located in a bank. Also **safe′ty-de·pos′it box.**

---

add, āce, câre, pälm; end, ēven; it, īce; odd, ōpen, ôrder; tōōk, pōōl; up, bûrn; ə = a in *above*, u in *focus*; yōō = u in *fuse*; oil; pout; check; go; ring; thin; this; zh, *vision*. < derived from; ? origin uncertain or unknown.

safe·guard (sāf′gärd′) *n.* **1** One who or that which guards or keeps in safety. **2** A mechanical device designed to prevent accident or injury. —*v.t.* To defend; guard.

safe·keep·ing (sāf′kē′ping) *n.* The act or state of keeping or being kept in safety; protection.

safe·ty (sāf′tē) *n. pl.* **·ties 1** Freedom from danger or risk. **2** Freedom from injury. **3** A device or catch designed as a safeguard. **4** In football, the touching of the ball to the ground behind the player's own goal line when the ball was propelled over the goal line by a member of his own team, scoring two points for the opposing team. **5** In baseball, a fair hit by which the batter reaches first base: also **base hit.** —*adj.* Providing protection.

safety belt 1 A strap that gives a workman needed freedom of movement and protection against falling. **2** SEAT BELT.

safety glass Glass strengthened by any of various methods to reduce the likelihood of its shattering upon impact.

safety match A match that ignites only if struck on a chemically prepared surface.

safety pin A pin whose point springs into place within a protecting sheath. • See PIN. **2** A pin which prevents the premature detonation of a hand grenade.

safety razor A razor in which the blade is fixed and provided with a guard to reduce the risk of cuts.

safety valve 1 *Mech.* A valve for automatically relieving excessive pressure. **2** Any outlet for pent-up energy or emotion.

saf·flow·er (saf′lou′ər) *n.* A thistlelike herb with composite orange-red flowers and seeds that yield edible **safflower oil.** [< Ital. *saffiore* saffron]

saf·fron (saf′rən) *n.* **1** A species of crocus with orange stigmas. **2** The dried stigmas, used in cookery. **3** A deep yellow orange: also **saffron yellow.** —*adj.* Of the color or flavor of saffron. [< Ar. *za'farān*]

S. Afr. South Africa; South African.

sag (sag) *v.* **sagged, sag·ging** *v.i.* **1** To droop from weight or pressure, esp. in the middle. **2** To hang unevenly. **3** To lose firmness; weaken, as from exhaustion, age, etc. **4** To decline, as in price or value. —*v.t.* **5** To cause to sag. —*n.* **1** A sagging. **2** A depressed or sagging place: a *sag* in a roof. [ME *saggen*] —**sag′ging·ly** *adv.*

sa·ga (sä′gə) *n.* **1** A medieval Scandinavian narrative dealing with legendary and heroic exploits. **2** A story having the saga form or manner. [ON, history, narrative]

sa·ga·cious (sə·gā′shəs) *adj.* **1** Ready and apt to apprehend and to decide on a course; intelligent. **2** Shrewd and practical. [< L *sagax* wise] —**sa·ga′cious·ly** *adv.* —**sa·ga′cious·ness** *n.* —**Syn. 1** acute, discerning, clear-sighted, keen, perspicacious.

sa·gac·i·ty (sə·gas′ə·tē) *n. pl.* **·ties** The quality or an instance of being sagacious; discernment or shrewdness.

sag·a·more (sag′ə·môr, -mōr) *n.* A lesser chief among the Algonquian Indians of North America. [< Algon.]

sage[1] (sāj) *n.* A venerable man of profound wisdom, experience, and foresight. —*adj.* **1** Characterized by or proceeding from calm, far-seeing wisdom and prudence: a *sage* observation. **2** Profound; learned; wise. [< L *sapere* be wise] —**sage′ly** *adv.* —**sage′ness** *n.*

sage[2] (sāj) *n.* **1** A plant of the mint family with aromatic, gray-green leaves that are used for flavoring meats. **2** Any of various related plants. **3** SAGEBRUSH. [< L *salvia*]

sage·brush (sāj′brush′) *n.* Any of various small, aromatic shrubs with composite flowers, native to the w U.S.

sage grouse A large grouse of the plains of the w U.S.

sage hen The sage grouse, esp. the female.

Sag·it·ta·ri·us (saj′ə·târ′ē·əs) *n.* A constellation and the ninth sign of the zodiac; the Archer. • See ZODIAC.

sag·it·tate (saj′ə·tāt) *adj.* Shaped like an arrowhead, as certain leaves. [< L *sagitta* an arrow] • See LEAF.

sa·go (sā′gō) *n. pl.* **·gos 1** Any of several varieties of East Indian palm. **2** The powdered pith of this palm, used as a thickening agent in puddings, etc. [< Malay *sāgū*]

sa·gua·ro (sə·gwä′rō, -wä′-) *n. pl.* **·ros** A giant cactus of the sw U.S.: also **sa·hua′ro** (-wä′-). [< Sp.]

sa·hib (sä′ib) *n.* Master; lord; Mr.; sir: formerly used in India by natives in speaking of or addressing Europeans. Also **sa′heb.** [< Ar. *sāhib* a friend]

said (sed) *p.t. & p.p.* of SAY. —*adj. Law* Previously mentioned.

sail (sāl) *n.* **1** *Naut.* A piece of canvas, etc., attached to a mast, spread to catch the wind, and thus to propel a craft through the water. **2** Sails collectively. **3** *pl.* **sail** A sailing vessel or craft. **4** A trip in any watercraft. **5** Anything resembling a sail in form or use, as a windmill arm. —**set sail** To begin a voyage. —**take in sail** To lower the sails of a craft. —**under sail** With sails spread and driven by the wind. —*v.i.* **1** To move across the surface of water by the action of wind or steam. **2** To travel over water in a ship or boat. **3** To begin a voyage. **4** To manage a sailing craft: Can you *sail?* **5** To move, glide, or float in the air; soar. **6** To move along in a stately or dignified manner: She *sailed* by haughtily. **7** *Informal* To pass rapidly. **8** *Informal* To proceed boldly into action: with *in.* —*v.t.* **9** To move or travel across the surface of (a body of water) in a ship or boat. **10** To navigate. —**sail into 1** To begin with energy. **2** To attack violently. [< OE *segl*]

sail·boat (sāl′bōt′) *n.* A small boat propelled by a sail or sails.

sail·cloth (sāl′klôth′, -kloth′) *n.* A very strong, firmly woven, cotton canvas suitable for sails.

sail·fish (sāl′fish′) *n. pl.* **·fish** or **·fish·es** Any of a genus of marine fishes allied to the swordfish, having a large dorsal fin likened to a sail.

Sailfish

sail·or (sā′lər) *n.* **1** An enlisted man in any navy. **2** One whose work is sailing. **3** One who works on a ship. **4** One skilled in sailing. **5** A passenger on a ship or boat, esp. in reference to seasickness: a good *sailor.* **6** A low-crowned, flat-topped hat with a brim. —**sail′or·ly** *adj.*

sail·plane (sāl′plān′) *n.* A light maneuverable glider used for soaring. —*v.i.* **·planed, ·plan·ing** To fly a sailplane.

saint (sānt) *n.* **1** A holy or sanctified person. **2** Such a person who has died and been canonized by certain churches, as the Roman Catholic. **3** *Often cap.* A member of any of certain religious sects calling themselves saints. **4** A very patient, unselfish person. —*v.t.* To canonize; venerate as a saint. —*adj.* Holy; canonized. [< L *sanctus* holy, consecrated] —**saint′hood** *n.*

Saint Ber·nard (bər·närd′) A working dog of great size and strength, originally bred in Switzerland to rescue travelers in the Swiss Alps.

saint·ed (sān′tid) *adj.* **1** Canonized. **2** Of holy character; saintly.

saint·ly (sānt′lē) *adj.* **·li·er, ·li·est 1** Like a saint; godly; holy. **2** Unusually good, kind, etc. —**saint′li·ness** *n.* —**Syn. 1** pious, sacred, blessed. **2** benevolent, charitable, kindly, righteous.

saith (seth, sā′ith) *Archaic* Present indicative third person singular of SAY.

sake[1] (sāk) *n.* **1** Purpose; motive; end: for the *sake* of peace and quiet. **2** Interest, regard, or consideration: for the *sake* of your children. [< OE *saccu* a (legal) case]

sa·ke[2] (sä′kē) *n.* A Japanese fermented alcoholic liquor made from rice: also **sa′ki.**

sal (sal) *n.* Salt: used esp. as a pharmaceutical term. [L]

sa·laam (sə·läm′) *n.* **1** An Oriental salutation resembling a low bow, the palm of the right hand being held to the forehead. **2** A respectful or ceremonious greeting. —*v.t. & v.i.* To make a salaam. [< Ar. *salām* peace]

sal·a·ble (sā′lə·bəl) *adj.* Such as can be sold; marketable. —**sal′a·bil′i·ty, sal′a·ble·ness** *n.* —**sal′a·bly** *adv.*

sa·la·cious (sə·lā′shəs) *adj.* Lascivious; lustful; lecherous. [< L *salire* to leap] —**sa·la′cious·ly** *adv.* —**sa·la′cious·ness, sa·lac′i·ty** (-las′ə·te) *n.*

sal·ad (sal′əd) *n.* **1** A dish of vegetables such as lettuce, cucumbers, tomatoes, etc., usu. uncooked and served with a dressing, sometimes mixed with chopped cold meat, fish, hard-boiled eggs, etc. **2** Any green vegetable that can be eaten raw. [< L *salare* to salt]

salad days Days of youth and inexperience.

salad dressing A sauce used on salads, as mayonnaise, oil and vinegar, etc.

sal·a·man·der (sal′ə·man′dər) *n.* 1 Any of an order of tailed amphibians having a smooth, moist skin. 2 A fabled reptile purportedly able to live in fire. [< L *salamandra*] **—sal′a·man′drine** (-drin) *adj.*

Salamander

sa·la·mi (sə·lä′mē) *n. pl.* **·mis** A salted, spiced sausage, originally Italian. [< L *sal* salt]

sal ammoniac AMMONIUM CHLORIDE. [L]

sal·a·ried (sal′ər·ēd) *adj.* 1 In receipt of a salary. 2 Yielding a salary.

sal·a·ry (sal′ər·ē) *n. pl.* **·ries** A periodic payment as compensation for official or professional services. **—v.t.** **·ried**, **·ry·ing** To pay or allot a salary to. [< L *salarium* money paid Roman soldiers for their salt]

sale (sāl) *n.* 1 The exchange or transfer of property for money or its equivalent. 2 A selling of merchandise at prices lower than usual. 3 An auction. 4 Opportunity of selling; market: Stocks find no *sale*. 5 *Usu. pl.* The amount sold: last year's *sales*. **—for sale** Offered or ready for sale. **—on sale** For sale at bargain rates. [< OE *sala*]

sale·a·ble (sā′lə·bəl) *adj.* SALABLE.

sal·er·a·tus (sal′ər·ā′təs) *n.* BAKING SODA. [< NL *sal aëratus* aerated salt]

sales·girl (sālz′gûrl′) *n.* A woman or girl hired to sell merchandise, esp. in a store.

sales·la·dy (sālz′lā′dē) *n. pl.* **·dies** *Informal* A woman or girl hired to sell merchandise, esp. in a store.

sales·man (sālz′mən) *n. pl.* **·men** (-mən) A man hired to sell goods, stock, etc., in a store or by canvassing.

sales·man·ship (sālz′mən·ship) *n.* 1 The work of a salesman. 2 Skill in selling.

sales·peo·ple (sālz′pē′pəl) *n.pl.* Salespersons.

sales·per·son (sālz′pûr′sən) *n.* A person hired to sell merchandise, esp. in a store: also **sales′clerk′** (-klûrk′).

sales resistance A resistance on the part of a potential customer to buying certain goods.

sales·room (sālz′rōōm′, -rōōm′) *n.* A room where merchandise is displayed for sale.

sales tax A tax on money received from sales of goods, usu. passed on to the buyer.

sales·wom·an (sālz′wōōm′ən) *n. pl.* **·wom·en** (-wim′in) A woman or girl hired to sell merchandise, esp. in a store.

Sal·ic (sal′ik) *adj.* Characterizing a law (the **Salic Law**) derived from Germanic sources in the fifth century, and providing that males only could inherit lands: later applied to the succession to the French and Spanish thrones.

sa·lic·y·late (sə·lis′ə·lāt, sal′ə·sil′āt) *n.* A salt or ester of salicylic acid.

sal·i·cyl·ic acid (sal′ə·sil′ik) A crystalline organic compound used in making aspirin and various analgesics. [< L *salix* willow]

sa·li·ent (sā′lē·ənt) *adj.* 1 Standing out prominently: a *salient* feature. 2 Extending outward; projecting: a *salient* angle. 3 Leaping; springing. **—n.** An extension, as of a fortification or a military line protruding toward the enemy. [< L *salire* to leap] **—sa′li·ence, sa′li·en·cy** *n.* **—sa′li·ent·ly** *adv.* **—Syn.** 1 conspicuous, noticeable, significant. 2 jutting.

sa·line (sā′lēn, sā′līn) *adj.* Constituting, consisting of, or characteristic of salt; salty. **—n.** 1 A metallic salt, esp. a salt of one of the alkalis or of magnesium. 2 A solution of sodium chloride or other salt. 3 A natural deposit of salt. [< L *sal* salt] **—sa·lin·i·ty** (sə·lin′ə·tē) *n.*

Salis·bur·y steak (sôlz′ber·ē, -brē) Ground beef mixed with bread crumbs, onion, seasoning, etc., cooked as patties and usu. served with gravy. [< J. H. *Salisbury*, 19th-century English physician]

Sa·lish (sā′lish) *n.* 1 A family of Indian languages of the NW U.S. and SW Canada. 2 A member of a tribe speaking any of these languages. **—adj.** Of or pertaining to the Salish languages or the people speaking them. Also **Sa′-lish·an** (-ən).

sa·li·va (sə·lī′və) *n.* A mixture of mucus and fluid secreted by glands in the cheeks and lower jaw. [L] **—sal·i·var·y** (sal′ə·ver′ē) *adj.*

sal·i·vate (sal′ə·vāt) *v.* **·vat·ed**, **·vat·ing** *v.i.* 1 To secrete saliva. **—v.t.** 2 To cause to secrete saliva, esp. excessively. **—sal′i·va′tion** *n.*

sal·low (sal′ō) *adj.* Of an unhealthy yellowish color or complexion. **—v.t.** To make sallow. [< OE *salo*] **—sal′low·ness** *n.*

sal·ly (sal′ē) *v.i.* **·lied**, **·ly·ing** 1 To rush out suddenly. 2 To set out energetically. 3 To go out, as from a room or building. **—n. pl.** **·lies** 1 A rushing forth, as of besieged troops against besiegers; sortie. 2 A going forth, as on a walk. A witticism or bantering remark. [< L *salire* to leap]

sal·ma·gun·di (sal′mə·gun′dē) *n.* 1 A dish of chopped meat, anchovies, eggs, onions, etc., mixed and seasoned. 2 Any medley or miscellany. [?< Ital. *salami conditi* pickled meats]

salm·on (sam′ən) *n.* 1 Any of various anadromous food and game fishes inhabiting cool ocean waters and certain landlocked lakes. 2 The pinkish orange color of the flesh of certain salmon: also **salm′on-pink′**. **—adj.** Having the color salmon: also **salm′on-pink′**. [< L *salmo*]

Salmon

sal·mo·nel·la (sal′mō·nel′ə) *n. pl.* **·lae** (lē) or **·las** Any of a genus of aerobic bacteria that cause food poisoning and some diseases, including typhoid fever. [< D. E. *Salmon*, U.S. pathologist, 1850–1914]

salmon trout Any of various salmonlike fish, as the European sea trout, the namaycush, etc.

Sa·lo·me (sə·lō′mē, sal·ə·mā′) The daughter of Herodias, who asked from Herod the head of John the Baptist in return for her dancing.

sa·lon (sə·lon′, sal′on, *Fr.* sȧ·lôṅ′) *n.* 1 A room in which guests are received; a drawing-room. 2 The periodic gathering of noted persons, under the auspices of some distinguished personage. 3 A hall or gallery used for exhibiting works of art. 4 An establishment devoted to some specific purpose: a beauty *salon*. [< Ital. *sala* a room, hall]

sa·loon (sə·lōōn′) *n.* 1 A place where alcoholic drinks are sold; a bar. 2 A large room for public use, as on a passenger ship: a dining *saloon*. [< F *salon* salon] •In the U.S., *saloon* (def. 1) is now used mainly in historical contexts dealing with the American western frontier or as a rough equivalent of *dive* in describing a squalid bar.

sa·loon-keep·er (sə·lōōn′kē′pər) *n.* One who keeps a saloon (def. 1).

sal·si·fy (sal′sə·fē, ·fī) *n.* A plant with purple, composite flowers and a white, edible root of an oysterlike flavor. [< F *salsifis*]

sal soda Sodium carbonate; washing soda.

salt (sôlt) *n.* 1 A white, soluble, crystalline compound of sodium and chlorine, widely distributed in nature and found in all living organisms: also **table salt, common salt.** 2 *Chem.* Any compound derived from an acid by replacement of all or part of the hydrogen by an electropositive radical or a metal. 3 *pl.* Any of various mineral compounds in common use, as Epsom salts, smelling salts, etc. 4 Piquant humor; dry wit. 5 That which preserves, corrects, or purifies: the *salt* of criticism. 6 A sailor. 7 A saltcellar. **—salt of the earth** A person or persons regarded as being fine, honest, kindly, etc. **—take with a grain of salt** To allow for exaggeration; have doubts about. **—worth one's salt** Worth one's pay or keep; hardworking. **—adj.** 1 Seasoned with salt; salty. 2 Cured or preserved with salt. 3 Containing, or growing or living in or near, salt water. **—v.t.** 1 To season with salt. 2 To preserve or cure with salt. 3 To furnish with salt: to *salt* cattle. 4 To add zest or piquancy to. 5 To add something to so as fraudulently to increase the value: to *salt* a mine with gold. **—salt away** 1 To pack in salt for preserving. 2 *Informal* To store up; save. [< OE *sealt*] **—salt′er** *n.*

SALT, S.A.L.T. (sôlt) Strategic Arms Limitation Talks.

salt·cel·lar (sôlt′sel′ər) *n.* A small receptacle for table salt. [< ME *salt saler* < *salt* salt + *saler* saltcellar < OF *saliere;* form infl. by CELLAR]

salt chuck *Can. Regional* The sea.

salt·ed (sôl′tid) *adj.* 1 Treated or preserved with salt. 2 *Informal* Experienced or expert.

salting out The injection of a saline solution into the amniotic fluid to terminate a pregnancy.

salt lick A place to which animals go to lick salt from superficial natural deposits.

salt marsh Low coastal land frequently overflowed by the tide, usu. covered with coarse grass: also **salt meadow**.

salt·pe·ter (sôlt′pē′tər) *n.* 1 POTASSIUM NITRATE. 2 CHILE SALTPETER. Also **salt′pe′tre**. [< L *sal* salt + *petra* rock]

salt·shak·er (sôlt′shā′kər) *n.* A container with small apertures for sprinkling table salt.

salt·wa·ter (sôlt′wô′tər, -wot′ər) *adj.* Of, composed of, or living in salt water.

salt·works (sôlt′wûrks′) *n. pl.* **·works** An establishment where salt is made commercially.

salt·wort (sôlt′wûrt′) *n.* Any of a genus of weedy plants adapted to saline soils.

salt·y (sôl′tē) *adj.* **salt·i·er, salt·i·est** 1 Tasting of or containing salt. 2 Piquant; sharp, as speech, etc. —**salt′i·ly** *adv.* — **salt′i·ness** *n.*

sa·lu·bri·ous (sə-lōō′brē-əs) *adj.* Conducive to health; healthful; wholesome. [< L *salus* health] —**sa·lu′bri·ous·ly** *adv.* —**sa·lu′bri·ty, sa·lu′bri·ous·ness** *n.*

sal·u·tar·y (sal′yə-ter′ē) *adj.* 1 Beneficial. 2 Wholesome; healthful. [< L *salus* health] —**sal′u·tar′i·ly** *adv.* —**sal′u·tar′i·ness** *n.*

sal·u·ta·tion (sal′yə-tā′shən) *n.* 1 The act of saluting. 2 Any form of greeting. 3 The opening words of a letter, as *Dear Sir* or *Dear Madam.*

sa·lu·ta·to·ri·an (sə-lōō′tə-tôr′ē-ən, -tō′rē-) *n.* In colleges and schools, the graduating student who delivers the salutatory at commencement.

sa·lu·ta·to·ry (sə-lōō′tə-tôr′ē, -tō′rē) *n. pl.* **·ries** An opening oration, as at a college commencement. —*adj.* Of or relating to a salutatory address. [< L *salutare* SALUTE]

sa·lute (sə-lōōt′) *v.* **·lut·ed, ·lut·ing** *v.t.* 1 To greet with an expression or sign of welcome, respect, etc.; welcome. 2 To honor in some prescribed way, as by raising the hand to the cap, presenting arms, firing cannon, etc. —*v.i.* 3 To make a salute. —*n.* 1 An act of saluting; a greeting, show of respect, etc. 2 The attitude assumed in giving a military hand salute. [< L *salutare* < *salus* health] —**sa·lut′er** *n.*

Sal·va·dor (sal′və-dôr′, *Sp.* säl′vä-thôr′) *n.* EL SALVADOR.

Sal·va·do·ri·an (sal′və-dôr′ē-ən, -dō′rē-) *n.* A citizen or native of El Salvador. —*adj.* Of or pertaining to El Salvador or its people: also **Sal′va·do′ran**.

sal·vage (sal′vij) *v.t.* **·vaged, ·vag·ing** 1 To save, as a ship or its cargo, from wreck, capture, etc. 2 To save (material) from something damaged or discarded for reuse: to *salvage* aluminum. —*n.* 1 The saving of a ship, cargo, etc., from loss. 2 Any act of saving property. 3 The compensation allowed to persons by whose exertions a vessel, its cargo, or the lives of those sailing on it are saved from loss. 4 That which is saved from a wrecked or abandoned vessel or from or after a fire. 5 Anything saved from destruction. [< OF *salver* to save] —**sal′vag·er** *n.*

sal·va·tion (sal-vā′shən) *n.* 1 The process or state of being saved. 2 A person or thing that delivers from evil, danger, or ruin. 3 *Theol.* Deliverance from sin and penalty; redemption. [< LL *salvare* to save]

Salvation Army A religious and charitable organization founded on semimilitary lines by William Booth in England in 1865. —**Sal·va′tion·ist** *n.*

salve[1] (sav, säv) *n.* 1 An emollient preparation for burns, cuts, etc. 2 Anything that heals, soothes, or mollifies. — *v.t.* **salved, salv·ing** 1 To dress with salve or ointment. 2 To soothe; appease, as conscience, pride, etc. [< OE *sealf*]

salve[2] (salv) *v.t.* **salved, salv·ing** To save from loss; salvage. [Back formation < SALVAGE]

sal·ver (sal′vər) *n.* A tray, as of silver. [< Sp. *salva*, orig. the foretasting of food, as for a king]

sal·vi·a (sal′vē-ə) *n.* 1 An ornamental species of sage with red flowers. 2 Any plant of the sage genus. [L]

sal·vo (sal′vō) *n. pl.* **·vos** or **·voes** 1 A simultaneous discharge of artillery, or of two or more bombs from an aircraft. 2 A sudden discharge or burst: a *salvo* of hail. 3 Tribute; praise. [< Ital. *salva* a salute]

sal vo·la·ti·le (sal vō·lat′ə·lē) Ammonium carbonate; smelling salts. [NL, volatile salt]

SAM (sam) surface-to-air missile.

S. Am., S. Amer. South America; South American.

sam·a·ra (sam′ər·ə, sə·mâr′ə) *n.* An indehiscent winged fruit, as of the elm or maple. [L, elm seed]

sa·mar·i·um (sə·mâr′ē·əm) *n.* A metallic element (symbol Sm) of the lanthanide series. [NL < Col. *Samarski*, 19th-century Russian mining official]

sam·ba (sam′bə, säm′bä) *n.* A dance of Brazilian origin in two-four time. —*v.i.* To dance the samba. [< a native African name]

Sam Browne belt (sam′ broun′) A military belt, with one or two light shoulder straps running diagonally across the chest from right to left. [< Sir Samuel J. Browne, 1824–1901, British army general]

same (sām) *adj.* 1 Identical; equal: They both are the *same* price. 2 Exactly alike; not different: The two children have the *same* first name. 3 Aforementioned; just spoken of. 4 Equal in degree of preference; indifferent. 5 Unchanged: The old place looks the *same.* —**all the same** 1 Nevertheless. 2 Equally acceptable or unacceptable. — **just the same** 1 Nevertheless. 2 Exactly identical or corresponding; unchanged. —*pron.* The identical person, thing, event, etc. —*adv.* In like manner; equally: with *the.* [< ON *samr, sami*] —**same′ness** *n.*

sam·i·sen (sam′i·sen) *n.* A three-stringed Japanese musical instrument played with a plectrum.

sa·mite (sā′mīt, sam′īt) *n.* A rich medieval fabric of silk, often interwoven with gold or silver. [< Gk. *hexamitos* woven with six threads]

Sa·mo·an (sə·mō′ən) *adj.* Of or pertaining to Samoa, its people, their language, culture, etc. —*n.* 1 A native or citizen of Samoa. 2 The language of the Samoans.

sam·o·var (sam′ə·vär) *n.* A metal urn containing a tube for charcoal for heating water, as for making tea. [Russ. < *samo*-self + *varit* boil]

Sam·o·yed (sam′ə·yed′) *n.* 1 One of a Mongoloid people inhabiting the Arctic coasts of Siberia. 2 A large Siberian dog with a thick white coat. —*adj.* Of or pertaining to the Samoyed people. Also **Sam′·o·yede′** (-yed′). —**Sam·o·yed′ic** *adj.*

Samovar

samp (samp) *n.* Coarsely ground Indian corn; also, a porridge made of it. [< Algon.]

sam·pan (sam′pan) *n.* Any of various small flat-bottomed boats used along rivers and coasts of China and Japan. [< Chin. *san* three + *pan* board]

sam·ple (sam′pəl) *n.* 1 A portion, part, or piece taken or shown as a representative of the whole. 2 An instance: This is a *sample* of his kindness. —*v.t.* **·pled, ·pling** To test or examine by means of a portion or sample. —*adj.* Serving as a sample: a *sample* dress. [< OF *essample* example]

Sampan

sam·pler (sam′plər) *n.* 1 One who tests by samples. 2 A device for removing a portion of a substance for testing. 3 A piece of needlework, designed to show a beginner's skill. [< L *exemplum* example]

Sam·son (sam′sən) In the Bible, a Hebrew judge of great physical strength, betrayed to the Philistines by Delilah.

sam·u·rai (sam′ōō·rī) *n. pl.* **·rai** Under the Japanese feudal system, a member of the soldier class of the lower nobility; also, the class itself. [Jap.]

san·a·tive (san′ə·tiv) *adj.* Healing; health-giving. [< L *sanare* heal]

san·a·to·ri·um (san′ə·tôr′ē·əm, -tō′rē-) *n. pl.* **·to·ri·ums** or **·to·ri·a** (-tôr′ē·ə, -tō′rē·ə) An institution for the treatment of chronic disorders, as mental illness, alcoholism, etc. [< LL *sanatorius* healthy]

sanc·ti·fy (sangk′tə·fī) *v.t.* **·fied, ·fy·ing** 1 To set apart as holy; consecrate. 2 To free of sin; purify. 3 To render sacred or inviolable, as a vow. [< L *sanctus* holy + *facere* to make] —**sanc′ti·fi·ca′tion, sanc′ti·fi′er** *n.*

sanc·ti·mo·ni·ous (sangk′tə·mō′nē·əs) *adj.* Making an

ostentatious display or a hypocritical pretense of sanctity. —**sanc'ti·mo'ni·ous·ly** *adv.* —**sanc'ti·mo'ni·ous·ness** *n.*

sanc·ti·mo·ny (sangk'tə-mō'nē) *n.* Assumed or outward sanctity; a show of devoutness. [< L *sanctimonia* holiness]

sanc·tion (sangk'shən) *v.t.* **1** To approve authoritatively; confirm; ratify. **2** To countenance; allow. —*n.* **1** Final and authoritative confirmation; justification or ratification. **2** A formal decree. **3** A provision for securing conformity to law, as by the enactment of rewards or penalties or both. **4** *pl.* In international law, a coercive measure adopted by several nations to force a nation to obey international law, by limiting trade relations, by military force and blockade, etc. [< L *sanctus,* p.p. of *sancire* make sacred]

sanc·ti·ty (sangk'tə-tē) *n. pl.* **·ties 1** The state of being sacred or holy. **2** Saintliness; holiness. **3** Something sacred or holy.

sanc·tu·ar·y (sangk'chōō·er'ē) *n. pl.* **·ar·ies 1** A holy or sacred place, esp. one devoted to the worship of a deity. **2** The most sacred part of a place in a sacred structure; esp. the part of a church where the principal altar is situated. **3** A place of refuge: a wildlife *sanctuary.* **4** Immunity from the law or punishment. [< L *sanctus* holy] —**Syn. 1** church, shrine, temple. **3** preserve, shelter.

sanc·tum (sangk'təm) *n. pl.* **·tums** or **·ta** (-tə) **1** A sacred place. **2** A private room where one is not to be disturbed. [L < *sanctus* holy]

sanc·tum sanc·to·rum (sangk'təm sangk·tôr'əm, -tō'rəm) **1** HOLY OF HOLIES. **2** A place of great privacy: often used humorously. [LL, holy of holies]

sand (sand) *n.* **1** A hard, granular rock material finer than gravel and coarser than dust. **2** *pl.* Stretches of sandy desert or beach. **3** *pl.* Sandy grains, as those of the hourglass. **4** *Slang* Endurance; grit. —*v.t.* **1** To sprinkle or cover with sand. **2** To smooth or abrade with sand or sandpaper. [< OE]

san·dal (san'dəl) *n.* **1** A foot covering, consisting usu. of a sole only, held to the foot by thongs or straps. **2** A light, openwork slipper. [< Gk. *sandalion*] —**san'daled** *adj.*

san·dal·wood (san'dəl·wŏŏd') *n.* **1** The fine-grained, dense, fragrant wood of any of several East Indian trees. **2** The similar wood of other trees. **3** Any tree yielding this wood. [< Med. L *sandalum* sandalwood + WOOD]

Sandal

sand·bag (sand'bag') *n.* **1** A bag filled with sand, used for building fortifications, for ballast, etc. **2** A small bag filled with sand and used as a club. —*v.t.* **·bagged, ·bag·ging 1** To fill or surround with sandbags. **2** To strike or attack with a sandbag. —**sand'bag'ger** *n.*

sand·bank (sand'bangk') *n.* A mound or ridge of sand.

sand·bar (sand'bär') *n.* A ridge of silt or sand in rivers, along beaches, etc., formed by the action of currents or tides.

sand·blast (sand'blast', -bläst') *n.* **1** An apparatus for propelling a jet of sand, as for etching glass or cleaning stone. **2** The jet of sand. —*v.t.* To clean or engrave by means of a sandblast. —**sand'blast'er** *n.*

sand·box (sand'boks') *n.* A box of sand for children to play in.

sand·er (san'dər) *n.* A device, esp. a machine powered by electricity, that smooths and polishes surfaces by means of a disk or belt coated with an abrasive: also **sanding machine.**

sand flea 1 CHIGOE. **2** Any of various tiny crustaceans that jump like fleas.

sand·hog (sand'hôg', -hog') *n.* One who works under air pressure, as in sinking caissons, building tunnels, etc.: also **sand hog.**

sand·lot (sand'lot') *n.* A vacant lot in or near an urban area. —*adj.* Of or played in such a lot: *sandlot* baseball.

sand·man (sand'man') *n.* In nursery lore, a mythical person supposed to make children sleepy by casting sand in their eyes.

sand·pa·per (sand'pā'pər) *n.* Strong paper coated with abrasive for smoothing or polishing. —*v.t.* To rub or polish with sandpaper.

sand·pi·per (sand'pī'pər) *n.* Any of certain small wading birds having long, thin bills and frequenting shores and marsh lands.

sand·stone (sand'stōn') *n.* A rock consisting chiefly of quartz sand cemented with other materials.

Sandpiper

sand·storm (sand'stôrm') *n.* A high wind by which clouds of sand or dust are carried along.

sand·wich (sand'wich, san'-) *n.* **1** Two or more slices of bread, having between them meat, cheese, etc. **2** Any combination of alternating dissimilar things pressed together. —*v.t.* To place between other persons or things. [< John Montagu, fourth Earl of *Sandwich,* 1718–92]

sandwich man *Informal* A man carrying boards, called **sandwich boards,** one in front and one behind, for the purpose of advertising or picketing.

sand·y (san'dē) *adj.* **sand·i·er, sand·i·est 1** Consisting of or characterized by sand; containing, covered with, or full of sand. **2** Yellowish red: a *sandy* beard. —**sand'i·ness** *n.*

sane (sān) *adj.* **san·er, san·est 1** Mentally sound; not deranged. **2** Proceeding from a sound mind. **3** Sensible; wise. [< L *sanus* whole, healthy] —**sane'ly** *adv.* —**sane'ness** *n.*

San·for·ize (san'fə·rīz) *v.t.* **·ized, ·iz·ing** To treat (cloth) by a special process so as to prevent more than slight shrinkage. [Back formation < *Sanforized,* a trade name]

sang (sang) *p.t.* of SING.

sang-froid (säng·frwä', *Fr.* sän·frwä') *n.* Calmness amid trying circumstances; composure. [F, lit., cold blood]

san·gui·nar·y (sang'gwə·ner'ē) *adj.* **1** Attended with bloodshed. **2** Prone to shed blood; bloodthirsty. [< L *sanguis* blood] —**san'gui·nar'i·ly** *adv.* —**san'gui·nar'i·ness** *n.*

san·guine (sang'gwin) *adj.* **1** Of buoyant disposition; hopeful. **2** Having the color of blood; ruddy: a *sanguine* complexion. **3** *Obs.* Bloodthirsty; sanguinary. Also **san·guin·e·ous** (sang·gwin'ē·əs). [< L *sanguis* blood] —**san'guine·ly** *adv.* —**san'guine·ness** *n.* —**Syn. 1** ardent, confident, enthusiastic, optimistic. **2** rubicund.

San·he·drin (san·hed'rən, -hēd'-, san'hi·drin, san'i-) *n.* In ancient times, the supreme council and highest court of the Jewish nation. Also **Great Sanhedrin.** [< Heb.]

san·i·tar·i·an (san'ə·târ'ē·ən) *n.* A person skilled in matters relating to sanitation and public health.

san·i·tar·i·um (san'ə·târ'ē·əm) *n. pl.* **·i·ums** or **·i·a** (-ē·ə) **1** A health resort. **2** SANATORIUM. [< L *sanitas* health]

san·i·tar·y (san'ə·ter'ē) *adj.* **1** Relating to the preservation of health and prevention of disease: *sanitary* measures. **2** Free from filth; clean; hygienic. —*n. pl.* **·tar·ies** A public toilet. [< L *sanitas* health] —**san'i·tar'i·ly** *adv.*

sanitary napkin An absorbent pad used by women during menstruation.

san·i·ta·tion (san'ə·tā'shən) *n.* **1** The science or process of establishing sanitary conditions, esp. as regards public health. **2** The removal of sewage, garbage, etc.

san·i·ta·tion·man (san'i·tā'shən·man') *n. pl.* **·men** (-mən) A person, esp. a municipal employee, whose work is the collection of refuse and trash.

san·i·tize (san'ə·tīz) *v.t.* **·tized, ·tiz·ing 1** To make sanitary, as by scrubbing, washing, or sterilizing. **2** To make acceptable or unobjectionable, as by deleting offensive parts: a *sanitized* fairy tale. —**san'i·ti·zer** *n.*

san·i·ty (san'ə·tē) *n.* **1** The state of being sane or sound; mental health. **2** Sane moderation or reasonableness. [< L *sanus* healthy] —**Syn. 1** rationality, saneness. **2** common sense, level-headedness, sensibleness.

sank (sangk) *p.t.* of SINK.

San Ma·ri·no (mä·rē'nō) *n.* A republic located in an enclave of NE Italy, 23 sq. mi., cap. San Marino.

sans (sanz, *Fr.* sän) *prep.* Without. [< OF *sens, sanz*]

sans·cu·lotte (sanz'kyŏŏ·lot', *Fr.* sän·kü·lôt') *n.* **1** A revolutionary: used by the aristocrats as a term of contempt for the poorly clad republicans who started the French Revolution of 1789. **2** Any revolutionary republican or radical. [F, lit., without knee breeches] **—sans′cu·lot′tic** *adj.* **—sans′cu·lot′tism** *n.*

san·se·vi·e·ri·a (san′sə·vir′ē·ə, -vi·ē′rē·ə) *n.* Any of a genus of succulent plants of the lily family with a cluster of tall, lance-shaped leaves. [< the Prince of *Sanseviero*, 1710–71, Italian scholar]

San·skrit (san′skrit) *n.* The ancient and classical language of the Hindus of India, belonging to the Indic branch of the Indo-Iranian subfamily of Indo-European languages: also **San′scrit.** [< Skt. *samskrita* well-formed]

sans ser·if (sanz ser′if) *Printing* A style of type without serifs.

San·ta Claus (san′tə klôz′) In folklore, a friend of children who brings presents at Christmas time: usu. represented as a fat, jolly old man in a red suit; St. Nicholas. [< dial. Du. *Sante Klaus* Saint Nicholas]

Santa Fe Trail The trade route, important from 1821 to 1880, between Independence, Missouri and Santa Fe, New Mexico.

sap[1] (sap) *n.* **1** The juices of plants, which contain and transport the materials necessary to growth. **2** Any vital fluid; vitality. **3** Sapwood. **4** *Slang* A foolish, stupid, or ineffectual person. [< OE *sæp*]

sap[2] (sap) *v.* **sapped, sap·ping** *v.t.* **1** To weaken or destroy gradually and insidiously. **2** To approach or undermine (an enemy fortification) by digging trenches. —*v.i.* To dig a sap or saps. —*n.* A deep, narrow trench dug so as to approach or undermine a fortification. [< MF *sappe* a spade] **—Syn.** *v.* **1** debilitate, disable, enervate, enfeeble.

sap·head (sap′hed′) *n. Slang* A stupid person; simpleton. **—sap′head′ed** *adj.*

sa·pi·ent (sā′pē·ənt, sap′ē-) *adj.* Wise; sagacious: often ironical. [< L *sapere* know, taste] **—sa′pi·ence, sa′pi·en·cy** *n.* **—sa′pi·ent·ly** *adv.*

sap·ling (sap′ling) *n.* **1** A young tree. **2** A young person. [Dim. of SAP[1]]

sap·o·dil·la (sap′ə·dil′ə) *n.* **1** A large tropical American evergreen tree which yields chicle and an edible fruit. **2** Its apple-shaped fruit: also **sapodilla plum.** [< Nahuatl *zapotl*]

sap·o·na·ceous (sap′ə·nā′shəs) *adj.* Soapy. [< L *sapo* soap] **—sap′o·na′ceous·ness** *n.*

sa·pon·i·fy (sə·pon′ə·fī) *v.t.* **·fied, ·fy·ing** To convert (a fat or oil) into soap by the action of an alkali. [< L *sapo* soap + *facere* to make] **—sa·pon′i·fi·ca′tion, sa·pon′i·fi′er** *n.*

sap·per (sap′ər) *n.* A soldier employed in making trenches, tunnels, and underground fortifications. [< SAP[2]]

sap·phire (saf′īr) *n.* **1** Any one of the hard, transparent, colored varieties of corundum, esp. a blue variety valued as a gem. **2** Deep blue. **—star sapphire** A sapphire cut without facets, showing six rays on the dome. **—adj.** Deep blue. [< Gk. *sappheiros* a gemstone]

sap·py (sap′ē) *adj.* **·pi·er, ·pi·est** **1** Full of sap; juicy. **2** *Slang* Immature; silly. **3** Vital; pithy. **—sap′pi·ness** *n.*

sap·ro·phyte (sap′rə·fīt) *n.* An organism that lives on dead or decaying organic matter, as certain bacteria, fungi, etc. [< Gk. *sapros* rotten + -PHYTE] **—sap′ro·phyt′ic** (-fit′ik) *adj.*

sap·suck·er (sap′suk′ər) *n.* A small woodpecker that taps trees and drinks sap.

sap·wood (sap′wood′) *n.* The new wood beneath the bark of a tree.

S.A.R. Sons of the American Revolution.

sar·a·band (sar′ə·band) *n.* **1** A stately Spanish dance in triple time, of the 17th and 18th centuries. **2** Music for this dance. Also **sar′a·bande.** [< Sp. *zarabanda*]

Sar·a·cen (sar′ə·sən) *n.* **1** Formerly, a Muslim enemy of the Crusaders. **2** An Arab. **—adj.** Of or pertaining to the Saracens. **—Sar′a·cen′ic** (-sen′ik) or **·i·cal** *adj.*

Sar·ah (sâr′ə) In the Bible, the wife of Abraham and the mother of Isaac.

Yellow-bellied sapsucker

Sa·ran (sə·ran′) *n.* A synthetic plastic material used as a textile fiber and as a transparent, moistureproof wrapping: a trade name.

sar·casm (sär′kaz·əm) *n.* **1** The use of keenly ironic or scornful remarks. **2** Such a remark. [< Gk. *sarkazein* tear flesh, speak bitterly] **—Syn.** **2** gibe, sneer, taunt.

sar·cas·tic (sär·kas′tik) *adj.* **1** Characterized by or of the nature of sarcasm. **2** Taunting. Also **sar·cas′ti·cal.** **—sar·cas′ti·cal·ly** *adv.*

sarce·net (särs′net) *n.* A fine, thin silk, used for linings. [< OF *drap sarrasinois*, lit. Saracen cloth]

sar·co·carp (sär′kō·kärp) *n.* The fleshy, usu. edible part of a drupe. [< Gk. *sarx* flesh + *karpos* a fruit]

sar·co·ma (sär·kō′mə) *n. pl.* **·mas** or **·ma·ta** (-mə·tə) A malignant tumor originating in connective tissue. [< Gk. *sarkaein* become fleshy] **—sar·co′ma·tous** (-kō′mə·təs) *adj.*

sar·coph·a·gus (sär·kof′ə·gəs) *n. pl.* **·gi** (-jī) or **·gus·es** **1** A stone coffin or tomb. **2** A large ornamental coffin of marble or other stone placed in a crypt or exposed to view. [< Gk. *sarx* flesh + *phagein* eat]

sard (särd) *n.* A deep brownish red variety of chalcedony, used as a gem. [< L *sarda*]

sar·dine (sär·dēn′) *n.* **1** A small fish preserved in oil as a delicacy. **2** The young of the herring or some like fish similarly prepared. [< Gk. *sarda* a kind of fish]

sar·don·ic (sär·don′ik) *adj.* Scornful or derisive; sneering; mocking; cynical. [< Gk. *sardanios* bitter, scornful] **—sar·don′i·cal·ly** *adv.* **—sar·don′i·cism** *n.*

sar·do·nyx (sär·don′iks, sär′də·niks) *n.* A variety of onyx, containing layers of light-colored chalcedony and sard. [< Gk. *sardios* sard + *onyx* onyx]

sar·gas·so (sär·gas′ō) *n.* Any of a genus of large, floating brown seaweed: also **sargasso weed, sar·gas′sum.** [< Pg. *sarga,* a kind of grape]

sa·ri (sä′rē) *n. pl.* **·ris** A length of cloth, constituting the principal garment of Hindu women, one end falling to the feet, and the other crossed over the bosom, shoulder, and sometimes over the head: also **sa′ree.** [< Skt. *śāṭī*]

sa·rong (sə·rong′) *n.* A rectangular piece of colored cloth worn as a skirt by both sexes in the Malay Archipelago. [< Malay *sārung*]

sar·sa·pa·ril·la (sas′pə·ril′ə, sär′sə·pə·ril′ə) *n.* **1** A tropical American vine with fragrant roots. **2** An extract of these roots, used as flavoring. **3** Any of various plants resembling sarsaparilla. [< Sp. *zarza* a bramble + *parilla* little vine]

sar·to·ri·al (sär·tôr′ē·əl, -tō′rē-) *adj.* **1** Pertaining to a tailor or his work. **2** Pertaining to men's clothes. [< L *sartor* tailor] **—sar·to′ri·al·ly** *adv.*

Sari

sash[1] (sash) *n.* An ornamental band or scarf, worn around the waist or over the shoulder. [< Ar. *shāsh* muslin, turban]

sash[2] (sash) *n.* A frame, as of a window, in which glass is set. **—v.t.** To furnish with a sash. [Alter. of CHASSIS, taken as a pl.]

sa·shay (sa·shā′) *v.i. Informal* To move or glide about, esp. ostentatiously. [< Fr. *chassé* a dance movement]

Sask. Saskatchewan.

sass (sas) *Informal n.* Impudence; back talk. **—v.t.** To talk to impudently. [Dial. alter. of SAUCE]

sas·sa·fras (sas′ə·fras) *n.* **1** A small North American tree related to laurel. **2** A flavoring agent made from the bark of its roots. [< Sp. *sasafrás*]

sas·sy (sas′ē) *adj.* **·si·er, ·si·est** *Informal* Saucy; impertinent. **—sas′si·ly** *adv.* **—sas′si·ness** *n.*

sat (sat) *p.t.* of SIT.

SAT Scholastic Aptitude Test.

Sat. Saturday; Saturn.

Sa·tan (sā′tən) In the Bible, the great adversary of God and tempter of mankind; the Devil. [< Heb. *sātān* an enemy] **—sa·tan·ic** (sā·tan′ik, sə-), **sa·tan′i·cal** *adj.* **—sa·tan′i·cal·ly** *adv.*

satch·el (sach′əl) *n.* A small bag for carrying books, clothing, etc. [< L *sacellus* little sack]

sate[1] (sāt) *v.t.* **sat·ed, sat·ing** **1** To satisfy the appetite of. **2** To indulge with too much so as to weary or sicken; satiate. [< OE *sadian*] **—Syn.** **1** gratify. **2** cloy, glut, stuff, surfeit.

sate[2] (sāt) *Archaic p.t.* of SIT.

sa·teen (sa·tēn′) *n.* A smooth, shiny cotton fabric resembling satin. [Alter. of SATIN]

sat·el·lite (sat'ə·līt) *n.* **1** A body held in orbit about a more massive one; a moon. **2** An artificial body propelled into orbit, esp. around the earth. **3** One who attends upon a person in power. **4** Any obsequious attendant. **5** A small nation dependent on a great power. [< L *satelles* an attendant]

sa·ti·a·ble (sā'shē·ə·bəl, -shə·bəl) *adj.* Capable of being satiated. **—sa'ti·a·bil'i·ty, sa'ti·a·ble·ness** *n.* **—sa'ti·a·bly** *adv.*

sa·ti·ate (sā'shē·āt) *v.t.* **·at·ed, ·at·ing 1** To satisfy the appetite or desire of; gratify. **2** To fill or gratify excessively; glut. **—adj.** Filled to satiety; satiated. [< L *satis* enough] **—sa'ti·a'tion** *n.*

sa·ti·e·ty (sə·tī'ə·tē, sā'shē·ə·tē) *n. pl.* **·ties** The state of being satiated; surfeit. [< L *satis* enough]

sat·in (sat'ən) *n.* A fabric of silk, rayon, etc., with glossy face and dull back. **—adj.** Of or similar to satin; glossy; smooth. [< OF] **—sat'in·y** *adj.*

sat·in·wood (sat'ən·wŏŏd') *n.* **1** The smooth, hard wood of various trees, used in cabinetwork. **2** Any tree yielding such wood.

sat·ire (sat'īr) *n.* **1** The use of sarcasm, irony, or wit in ridiculing and denouncing abuses, follies, customs, etc. **2** A literary work that ridicules in this manner. [< L *satira*]

sa·tir·i·cal (sə·tir'i·kəl) *adj.* **1** Given to or characterized by satire: a *satirical* writer. **2** Sarcastic; caustic; biting. Also **sa·tir'ic. —sa·tir'i·cal·ly** *adv.* **—sa·tir'i·cal·ness** *n.*

sat·i·rist (sat'ə·rist) *n.* **1** A writer of satire. **2** A person fond of satirizing or ridiculing.

sat·i·rize (sat'ə·rīz) *v.t.* **·rized, ·riz·ing** To subject to or criticize in satire. **—sat'i·riz'er** *n.*

sat·is·fac·tion (sat'is·fak'shən) *n.* **1** The act of satisfying, or the state of being satisfied. **2** The making of amends, reparation, or payment. **3** That which satisfies; compensation.

sat·is·fac·to·ry (sat'is·fak'tər·ē) *adj.* Giving satisfaction; answering expectations or requirements. **—sat'is·fac'to·ri·ly** *adv.* **—sat'is·fac'to·ri·ness** *n.* **—Syn.** adequate, gratifying, pleasing, sufficient.

sat·is·fy (sat'is·fī) *v.* **·fied, ·fy·ing** *v.t.* **1** To supply fully with what is desired, expected, or needed. **2** To please; gratify. **3** To free from doubt or anxiety; convince. **4** To give what is due to. **5** To pay or discharge (a debt, obligation, etc.). **6** To answer sufficiently or convincingly, as a question or objection. **7** To make reparation for; expiate. **—v.i. 8** To give satisfaction. [< L *satis* enough + *facere* do] **—sat'is·fi'er** *n.* **—sat'is·fy'ing·ly** *adv.*

sa·to·ri (sä·tō'rē) *n.* The sudden change of consciousness which is the goal of Zen Buddhism. [Jap.]

sa·trap (sā'trap, sat'rap) *n.* **1** A governor of a province in ancient Persia. **2** Any petty ruler under a despot. **3** A subordinate ruler or governor. [< O Pers. *shathraparan*, lit., a protector of a province]

sa·trap·y (sā'trə·pē, sat'rə·pē) *n. pl.* **·trap·ies** The territory or the jurisdiction of a satrap. Also **sa·trap·ate** (sā'·trə·pit, sat'rə-).

sat·u·rate (sach'ə·rāt) *v.t.* **·rat·ed, ·rat·ing** To soak or imbue thoroughly to the utmost capacity for absorbing or retaining. **—adj.** Saturated. [< L *satur* full] **—sat'u·ra'tor** or **sat'u·rat'er** *n.*

sat·u·rat·ed (sach'ə·rā'tid) *adj.* **1** Replete; incapable of holding more of a substance: a *saturated* solution. **2** *Chem.* Designating an organic compound having no free or multiple valence bonds available for direct union with additional atoms. **3** Tending to increase the cholesterol content of the blood: said of some edible fats.

sat·u·ra·tion (sach'ə·rā'shən) *n.* **1** A saturating or being saturated. **2** A massive concentration, in any given area, as of advertising, military force, etc., for a specific purpose: often used attributively: *saturation* bombing.

saturation point 1 The maximum possible degree of impregnation of one substance with another. **2** A condition in which a person has reached the limit of patience, toleration, etc.

Sat·ur·day (sat'ər·dē, -dā) *n.* The seventh or last day of the week; the day of the Jewish Sabbath. [< OE *Sæternesdæg* Saturn's day]

Sat·urn (sat'ərn) *Rom. Myth.* The god of agriculture. **—n.** The planet of the solar system sixth in distance from the sun. **•** See **PLANET. —Sa·tur·ni·an** (sə·tûr'nē·ən) *adj.* [< L *Saturnus*]

sat·ur·na·li·a (sat'ər·nā'lē·ə) *n.pl.* (*usu. construed as sing.*) Any season or period of general license or revelry. **—sat'ur·na'li·an** *adj.*

Sat·ur·na·li·a (sat'ər·nā'lē·ə) *n.pl.* The feast of Saturn held in ancient Rome in mid-December, and marked by wild reveling and abandon. **—Sat'ur·na'li·an** *adj.*

sat·ur·nine (sat'ər·nīn) *adj.* **1** Having a grave, gloomy, or morose disposition or character. **2** In astrology, born under the supposed dominance of Saturn. [< L *Saturnus* Saturn] **—sat'ur·nine·ly** *adv.* **—sat'ur·nine'ness** *n.*

sat·yr (sā'tər, sat'ər) *Gk. Myth.* A wanton woodland deity with a man's body and goatlike legs. **—n.** A lascivious man. [< Gk. *satyros*] **—sa·tyr·ic** (sə·tir'ik) or **·i·cal** *adj.*

sat·y·ri·a·sis (sat'ə·rī'ə·sis) *n.* An abnormally strong, insatiable sexual drive in males. [< Gk. *satyros* a satyr]

sauce (sôs) *n.* **1** An appetizing, usu. liquid relish for food to improve its taste. **2** A dish of fruit pulp stewed and sweetened: cranberry *sauce.* **3** *Informal* Pert or impudent language. **4** *Slang* Alcoholic liquor. **—v.t. sauced, sauc·ing 1** To flavor or dress with sauce. **2** *Informal* To be saucy to. [< L *salsus* salted]

sauce·pan (sôs'pan') *n.* A pan, usu. of metal or enamel, with projecting handle, for cooking food.

sau·cer (sô'sər) *n.* **1** A small dish for holding a cup. **2** Any round, shallow thing of similar shape. [< OF *sauce* sauce]

sau·cy (sô'sē) *adj.* **·ci·er, ·ci·est 1** Disrespectful to superiors; impudent. **2** Piquant; sprightly; amusing. **—sau'ci·ly** *adv.* **—sau'ci·ness** *n.*

Sau·di A·ra·bi·a (sou'dē ə·rä'bē·ə, sä·ōō'dē) A kingdom

of N CEN. Arabia, 927,000 sq. mi., cap. Riyadh. **—Sau'di A·ra'bi·an** *adj., n.*

sauer·kraut (sour'krout') *n.* Shredded and salted cabbage fermented in its own juice. [< G *sauer* sour + *kraut* cabbage]

Saul (sôl) In the Bible, the first king of Israel.

sau·na (sou'nə, sô'-) *n.* **1** A Finnish steam bath in which the steam is produced by running water over heated stones. **2** A bath in which the bather is exposed to very hot, dry air. **3** A room or enclosure for a sauna. [Finnish]

saun·ter (sôn'tər) *v.i.* To walk in a leisurely or lounging way; stroll. **—n. 1** A slow, aimless manner of walking. **2** An idle stroll. [< ME *santren* muse] **—saun'ter·er** *n.* **—saun'ter·ing·ly** *adv.*

sau·ri·an (sôr'ē·ən) *n.* Any of the suborder of reptiles comprising the lizards. **—adj.** Pertaining to or having the characteristics of lizards. [< Gk. *sauros* a lizard]

-saurus *combining form Zool.* Lizard: *brontosaurus.* [< Gk. *sauros* a lizard]

sau·sage (sô′sij) *n.* Finely chopped and highly seasoned meat, commonly stuffed into a prepared animal intestine or other casing. [< L *salsus* salted]

sau·té (sô·tā′, sō-) *v.t.* **·téed, ·té·ing** To fry quickly in a little fat. —*n.* A sautéed dish. [F, p.p. of *sauter* to leap]

sau·terne (sô·tûrn′, sō-; *Fr.* sō·tern′) *n.* A sweet, white wine. [< *Sauternes,* district in sw France]

sav·age (sav′ij) *adj.* 1 Of a wild and untamed nature; not domesticated. 2 Fierce; ferocious. 3 Living in or belonging to the most primitive condition of human society; uncivilized. 4 Remote and wild: *savage* mountain country. —*n.* 1 A primitive or uncivilized human being. 2 A brutal and cruel person. —*v.t.* **sav·aged, sav·a·ging** To beat or maul cruelly. [< L *silva* a wood] —**sav′age·ly** *adv.* —**Syn.** *adj.* 1 undomesticated, feral. 2 brutal, bloodthirsty, barbarous. 3 uncultivated.

sav·age·ry (sav′ij·rē) *n. pl.* **·ries** 1 The state of being savage. 2 Cruelty in disposition or action. 3 A savage act.

sa·van·na (sə·van′ə) *n.* A tract of level land covered with low vegetation; a treeless plain, esp. in or near the tropics: also **sa·van′nah.** [< Cariban]

sa·vant (sə·vänt′, sav′ənt; *Fr.* sá·vän′) *n.* A person of exceptional learning. [F < L *sapere* be wise]

save[1] (sāv) *v.* **saved, sav·ing** *v.t.* 1 To preserve or rescue from danger, harm, etc. 2 To keep from being spent, expended, or lost. 3 To set aside for future use; accumulate: often with *up.* 4 To treat carefully so as to avoid fatigue, harm, etc.: to *save* one's eyesight. 5 To prevent by timely action: A stitch in time *saves* nine. 6 *Theol.* To deliver from the consequences of sin; redeem. —*v.i.* 7 To be economical. 8 To preserve something from harm, etc. 9 To accumulate money. [< L *salvus* safe] —**sav′er** *n.*

save[2] (sāv) *prep.* Except; but. —*conj.* 1 Except; but. 2 *Archaic* Unless. [< OF *sauf* being excepted, orig. safe]

sav·ing (sā′ving) *adj.* 1 That saves or rescues: *lifesaving* equipment. 2 Economical; frugal. 3 Holding in reserve; qualifying: a *saving* clause. —*n.* 1 Preservation from loss or danger. 2 Avoidance of waste; economy. 3 Any reduction in cost, time, etc.: a *saving* of 16 percent. 4 *pl.* Sums of money saved, esp. those deposited in a bank. —*prep.* 1 With the exception of; save. 2 With due respect for: *saving* your presence. —*conj.* With the exception of. —**sav′ing·ly** *adv.* —**sav′ing·ness** *n.*

savings account An account drawing interest at a savings bank.

savings bank An institution for receiving and investing savings and paying interest on deposits.

sav·ior (sāv′yər) *n.* One who saves. —**the Savior** Jesus Christ. *Brit. sp.* **sav′iour.**

sa·voir faire (sá·vwár fâr′) Ability to see and to do the right thing; esp., sophisticated social poise. [F, lit., to know how to act]

sa·vor (sā′vər) *n.* 1 Taste and smell: a *savor* of garlic. 2 Specific or characteristic quality. 3 Relish; zest: The conversation had *savor.* —*v.i.* 1 To have savor; taste or smell: with *of.* 2 To have a specified savor or character: with *of.* —*v.t.* 3 To give flavor to; season. 4 To taste or enjoy with pleasure; relish. 5 To have the savor of. *Brit. sp.* **sa′vour.** [< L *sapere* taste, know] —**sa′vor·er** *n.* —**sa′·vor·ous** *adj.*

sa·vor·less (sā′vər·lis) *adj.* Tasteless; insipid.

sa·vor·y[1] (sā′vər·ē) *adj.* 1 Of an agreeable taste and odor; appetizing. 2 In good repute. —*n. pl.* **·vor·ies** *Brit.* A small, hot serving of tasty food, usu. eaten at the end of a dinner. *Brit. sp.* **sa′vour·y.** [< OF *savourer* to taste] —**sa′vor·i·ly** *adv.* —**sa′vor·i·ness** *n.* —**Syn.** *adj.* 1 flavorful, palatable, piquant, tasty, toothsome. 2 respectable.

sa·vor·y[2] (sā′vər·ē) *n.* A hardy, annual herb of the mint family used for seasoning. Also **summer savory.** [< OF *savoreie*]

sa·voy (sə·voi′) *n.* A variety of cabbage with wrinkled leaves and a compact head. [< F *(chou de) Savoie* (cabbage of) Savoy]

Sa·voy·ard (sə·voi′ərd, sav′oi·ärd′) *n.* An actor or actress in or an admirer or producer of the Gilbert and Sullivan operas. [< the *Savoy,* London theater]

sav·vy (sav′ē) *Slang v.i.* **·vied, ·vy·ing** To understand; comprehend. —*n.* Understanding; know-how. —*adj.* Having good sense or know-how. [Alter. of Sp. *¿ Sabe (usted)?* Do (you) know?]

saw[1] (sô) *n.* 1 A cutting tool with pointed teeth arranged continuously along the edge of a blade or disk. 2 A tool or machine having such teeth: a power *saw.* —*v.* **sawed, sawed** or **sawn, saw·ing** *v.t.* 1 To cut or divide with or as with a saw: 2 To shape or fashion with a saw. 3 To make a motion as if sawing: The speaker *saws* the air. —*v.i.* 4 To use a saw. 5 To cut: said of a saw. 6 To be cut with a saw: This wood *saws* easily. [< OE *sagu*] —**saw′er** *n.*

saw[2] (sô) *n.* A proverbial or familiar saying; old maxim. [< OE *sagu*]

saw[3] (sô) *p.t.* of SEE[1].

saw·bones (sô′bōnz′) *n. Slang* A surgeon.

saw·buck (sô′buk′) *n.* 1 A frame consisting of two X-shaped ends joined by connecting bars, for holding sticks of wood for sawing. 2 *Slang* A ten-dollar bill: from the resemblance of X, Roman numeral ten, to the ends of a sawbuck.

saw·dust (sô′dust′) *n.* Tiny particles of wood cut or torn out by sawing.

Sawbuck *def. 1*

saw·fish (sô′fish′) *n. pl.* **·fish** or **·fish·es** Any of a genus of large tropical fishes related to rays and having an elongated snout with teeth on each edge.

saw·fly (sô′flī′) *n. pl.* **·flies** A hymenopterous insect having in the female a pair of sawlike organs for piercing plants, wood, etc., in which to lay eggs.

saw·horse (sô′hôrs′) *n.* A frame consisting of a long wooden bar or plank supported by four extended legs.

saw·mill (sô′mil′) *n.* 1 An establishment for sawing logs with power-driven machinery. 2 A large sawing machine.

sawn (sôn) A *p.p.* of SAW[1].

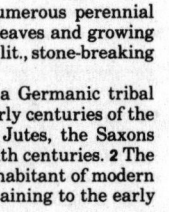

Sawhorse

saw-toothed (sô′tōōtht′) *adj.* Having teeth or toothlike processes similar to those of a saw; serrate. Also **saw′tooth′** (-tōōth′).

saw·yer (sô′yər) *n.* One who saws logs, esp. a lumberman who fells trees by sawing, or one who works in a sawmill.

sax (saks) *n. Informal* A saxophone.

sax·i·frage (sak′sə·frij) *n.* Any of numerous perennial plants usu. having a basal rosette of leaves and growing in rocky places. [< L *(herba) saxifraga,* lit., stone-breaking (herb)]

Sax·on (sak′sən) *n.* 1 A member of a Germanic tribal group living in NW Germany in the early centuries of the Christian era. With the Angles and Jutes, the Saxons conquered England in the fifth and sixth centuries. 2 The language of the early Saxons. 3 An inhabitant of modern Saxony in Germany. —*adj.* Of or pertaining to the early Saxons, or to their language.

sax·o·phone (sak′sə·fōn) *n.* Any of a group of reed instruments having a straight metal body equipped with finger keys and terminating in a curved, conical bore. [< A. J. *Sax,* 1814–94, Belgian instrument maker] —**sax′o·phon′ist** *n.*

say (sā) *v.* **said, say·ing** *v.t.* 1 To speak. 2 To express in words; tell. 3 To state positively: *Say* which you prefer. 4 To recite; repeat: to *say* one's prayers. 5 To allege: They *say* that he lied. 6 To assume: He is worth, *say,* a million. —*v.i.* 7 To make a statement; speak. —**say nothing of** Without mentioning. —**that is to say** In other words. —*n.* 1 What one has said or has to say: Let him have his *say.* 2 *Informal* Right or turn to speak or choose: Now it is my *say.* —**the say** *Informal* Authority: Who has *the say* in this office? —*interj.* A hail or exclamation to command attention: also *Brit.* **I say!** [< OE *secgan*] —**say′er** *n.* —**Syn.** *v.* 1 articulate, pronounce, utter. 2 declare, affirm. 5 assert.

Saxophone

say·ing (sā'ing) n. 1 An utterance. 2 A maxim or saw. — **go without saying** To be so evident as to require no explanation.

say-so (sā'sō') n. Informal 1 An unsupported assertion or decision. 2 Right or power to make decisions: He has the say-so.

Sb antimony (L stibium).

SBA Small Business Administration.

SbE south by east.

SbW south by west.

SC Security Council (of the United Nations); South Carolina (P.O. abbr.).

S.C. Signal Corps; South Carolina; Supreme Court.

Sc scandium; stratocumulus.

sc. he (or she) carved or engraved it (L sculpsit); namely (L scilicet); scale; scene; science; screw; scruple (weight).

s.c. small capitals (printing).

scab (skab) n. 1 A crust on a wound or sore. 2 A contagious disease of sheep. 3 Any of certain plant diseases marked by a roughened or warty exterior. 4 A worker who will not join a labor union. 5 A worker who does the job of a person on strike. —v.i. **scabbed, scab·bing** 1 To form or become covered with a scab. 2 To act or work as a scab. [< Scand.] —**scab'bi·ly** adv. —**scab'bi·ness** n. —**scab'by** adj. (·i·er, ·i·est)

scab·bard (skab'ərd) n. A sheath for a weapon, as for a bayonet or a sword. —v.t. To sheathe in a scabbard. [< OHG scar a sword + bergan hide, protect]

sca·bi·es (skā'bēz) n. A skin disease affecting man and various animals, caused by infestation by certain mites; the itch. [< L scabere to scratch, scrape] —**sca·bi·et·ic** (skā'bē·et'ik), **sca'bi·ous** (-əs) adj.

sca·bi·o·sa (skā'bē·ō'sə) n. Any of various plants related to the teasel, with showy, usu. prickly flowers. Also **sca'bi·ous** (-əs). [< Med. L (herba) scabiosa herb for scabies]

sca·brous (skā'brəs) adj. 1 Roughened with minute points. 2 Difficult to handle tactfully. 3 Suggestive; salacious. [< L scabere to scratch] —**sca'brous·ly** adv. —**sca'brous·ness** n.

scads (skadz) n.pl. Informal A large amount or quantity. [?]

scaf·fold (skaf'əld, -ōld) n. 1 A temporary elevated structure for the support of workmen, materials, etc., as in constructing, painting, or repairing a building. 2 A platform for the execution of criminals. 3 Any raised platform. —v.t. To furnish or support with a scaffold. [< OF escadafaut]

scaf·fold·ing (skaf'əl·ding) n. 1 A scaffold, or system of scaffolds. 2 The materials for constructing scaffolds.

scag (skag) n. Slang Heroin.

sca·lar (skā'lər) adj. Defined by a single number, as a quantity having only magnitude. —n. A scalar quantity. [< L scala a ladder]

scal·a·wag (skal'ə·wag) n. 1 Informal A worthless person; rascal. 2 A Southern white who became a Republican during the Reconstruction period: a contemptuous term. Also **scal'la·wag, scal'ly·wag**. [?]

scald¹ (skôld) v.t. 1 To burn with hot liquid or steam. 2 To cleanse or treat with boiling water. 3 To heat (a liquid) to a point just short of boiling. 4 To cook in a liquid which is just short of the boiling point. —v.i. 5 To be or become scalded. —n. 1 A burn due to a hot fluid or steam. 2 Surface injury of plant tissue due to various causes, as exposure to sun, fungi, etc. [< L ex- very + calidus hot]

scald² (skôld, skäld) n. SKALD. —**scal·dic** (skôl'dik, skäl'-) adj.

scale¹ (skāl) n. 1 One of the thin, horny, usu. overlapping, protective plates covering most fishes, reptiles, etc. 2 SCALE INSECT 3 A specialized leaf, as of a pine cone. 4 A flaky coating on metal, as from corrosion, etc. 5 Any thin, scalelike piece, as of skin. —v. **scaled, scal·ing** v.t. 1 To strip or clear of scale or scales. 2 To form scales on; cover with scales. 3 To take off in layers or scales; pare off. —v.i. 4 To come off in layers or scales; peel. 5 To shed scales. 6 To become incrusted with scales. [< OF escale a husk] —**scal'er** n.

Ascending chromatic scale def. 6

scale² (skāl) n. 1 An object bearing accurately spaced marks for use in measurement, or the series of marks so used. 2 Any system of units of measurement. 3 A proportion used in representing distances, as on a map or blueprint. 4 Math. A system of numeration in which the successive places determine the value of digits, as the decimal system. 5 Any progressive or graded series; a graduation: the social scale. 6 Music A series of tones arranged in a sequence of ascending or descending pitches according to any of various systems of intervals. 7 Phot. The range of light values which may be reproduced by a photographic paper. 8 A succession of steps or degrees: a salary scale. 9 A relative degree or extent: to live on a modest scale. —v. **scaled, scal·ing** v.t. 1 To climb to the top of. 2 To make according to a scale. 3 To regulate or adjust according to a scale or ratio: with up, down, etc. —v.i. To climb; ascend. 5 To rise, as in steps or stages: mountains scaling to the skies. [< L scala a ladder] —**scal'er** n.

scale³ (skāl) n. 1 The bowl, scoop, or platform of a weighing instrument or balance. 2 Usu. pl. The balance itself. —**the Scales** LIBRA. —**turn the scales** To determine; decide. —v. **scaled, scal·ing** v.t. 1 To weigh in scales. 2 To amount to in weight. —v.i. 3 To be weighed. [< ON skál a bowl]

scale insect Any of numerous plant-feeding insects of which the adult female is sedentary under a scalelike, waxy shield.

sca·lene (skā'lēn, skā·lēn') adj. Geom. Having no two sides equal: said of a triangle. [< Gk. skalēnos uneven] • See TRIANGLE.

scal·lion (skal'yən) n. 1 A young, tender onion with a small white bulb. 2 A shallot or leek. [< L (caepa) Ascalonia (onion) of Ashkelon, a Palestinian seaport]

scal·lop (skal'əp, skol'-) n. 1 Any of various mollusks having a hinged shell with radiating ribs and wavy edge. 2 The edible abductor muscle of certain scallops. 3 A scallop shell. 4 One of a series of semicircular curves along an edge, as for ornament. —v.t. 1 To shape the edge of with scallops for ornamentation. 2 To bake (food) in a casserole with a sauce, usu. topped with bread crumbs. [< MF escalope shell] — **scal'lop·er** n.

Scallop shell

scalp (skalp) n. 1 The skin of the top and back of the skull, usu. covered with hair. 2 A portion of this, cut or torn away as a trophy among certain North American Indians. —v.t. 1 To cut or tear the scalp from. 2 Informal To buy (tickets) and sell again at prices exceeding the established rate. 3 Informal To buy and sell quickly to make a small profit. —v.i. 4 Informal To scalp bonds, tickets, etc. [< Scand.] —**scalp'er** n.

scal·pel (skal'pəl) n. A small, sharp, surgical knife. [< L scalpere to cut]

scal·y (skā'lē) adj. **scal·i·er, scal·i·est** 1 Having a covering of scales or flakes. 2 Of the nature of a scale. 3 Incrusted with a flaking deposit. —**scal'i·ness** n.

scamp¹ (skamp) n. A confirmed rogue; rascal. [< obs. scamp to roam] —**scamp'ish** adj. —**scamp'ish·ness** n.

scamp² (skamp) v.t. To perform (work) carelessly or dishonestly. [?] —**scamp'er** n.

scam·per (skam'pər) v.i. To run quickly or hastily. —n. A hurried flight. [< L ex out + campus a plain, battlefield] —**scam'per·er** n.

scam·pi (skam'pē) n.pl. Large shrimp, usu. served in a garlic sauce. [Ital.]

---

scan (skan) *v.* **scanned, scan·ning** *v.t.* **1** To examine in detail; scrutinize closely. **2** To pass the eyes over quickly; glance at. **3** To separate (verse) into metrical feet. **4** *Electronics* To cause a beam, as of light, electrons, microwaves, etc., to pass systematically over a surface or through a region. —*v.i.* **5** To scan verse. **6** To conform to metrical rules: said of verse. [< LL *scandere* scan verses] —**scan′ner** *n.*

Scan., Scand. Scandinavia; Scandinavian.

scan·dal (skan′dəl) *n.* **1** A discreditable action or circumstance offensive to public morals or feelings. **2** Injury to reputation. **3** General criticism that injures reputation; malicious gossip. **4** A person whose conduct arouses public censure. [< Gk. *skandalon* a snare] —**Syn. 2** discredit, disgrace, disrepute. **3** calumny, defamation, slander.

scan·dal·ize (skan′dəl·īz) *v.t.* **·ized, ·iz·ing** To shock the moral feelings of; outrage. —**scan′dal·i·za′tion, scan′dal·iz′er** *n.*

scan·dal·ous (skan′dəl·əs) *adj.* **1** Causing or being a scandal; disgraceful. **2** Consisting of evil or malicious reports. —**scan′dal·ous·ly** *adv.* —**scan′dal·ous·ness** *n.*

Scan·di·na·vi·a (skan′də·nā′vē·ə) *n.* The region of NW Europe occupied by Sweden, Norway, and Denmark; 315,-156 sq. mi; Finland, Iceland, and the Faroe Islands are often included: total area, 485,539 sq. mi. —**Scan′di·na′vi·an** *adj., n.*

scan·di·um (skan′dē·əm) *n.* A rare metallic element of low density. [< L *Scandia* Scandinavia]

scan·sion (skan′shən) *n.* The act or art of scanning verse to show its metrical parts.

scant (skant) *adj.* **1** Meager in measure or quantity. **2** Being just short of the measure specified: a *scant* half-hour; a *scant* five yards. —**scant of** Insufficiently supplied with: to be *scant of* breath from running. —*v.t.* **1** To restrict or limit in supply; stint. **2** To treat briefly or inadequately. —*adv. Regional* Scarcely; barely. [< ON *skammr* short] —**scant′ly** *adv.* —**scant′ness** *n.*

scant·ling (skant′ling) *n.* **1** A small beam or timber, esp. an upright timber in a structure. **2** Such timbers collectively. [< OF *eschantillon* specimen]

scant·y (skan′tē) *adj.* **scant·i·er, scant·i·est 1** Too little; not enough: a *scanty* meal. **2** Scarcely enough for what is needed; insufficient. [< SCANT] —**scant′i·ly** *adv.* —**scant′i·ness** *n.* —**Syn. 1** deficient, poor, sparse. **2** limited, restricted.

scape·goat (skāp′gōt′) *n.* **1** In the Bible, the goat upon whose head Aaron symbolically laid the sins of the people on the day of atonement, after which it was led away into the wilderness. *Lev.* 16. **2** Any person bearing blame for the misdeeds of others. —*v.t. Informal* To make a scapegoat of. [< ESCAPE + GOAT]

scape·grace (skāp′grās′) *n.* A mischievous or incorrigible person.

s. caps. small capitals (printing).

scap·u·la (skap′yə·lə) *n. pl.* **·las** or **·lae** (-lē) Either of the two large, flat bones of the upper back; shoulder blade. [< L *scapulae* shoulder blades]

scap·u·lar (skap′yə·lər) *n.* **1** A garment of certain religious orders consisting of two strips of cloth hanging down front and back. **2** Two small rectangular pieces of cloth connected by strings, worn as a badge of membership by certain religious orders. Also **scap′u·lar·y** (-ler′ē). [< L *scapula* shoulder]

Scapula

scar (skär) *n.* **1** The mark left after the healing of a lesion. **2** Any lingering sign, as from hardship, misfortune, etc.: the *scars* of poverty. —*v.t. & v.i.* **scarred, scar·ring** To mark or become marked with a scar. [< LL *eschara* a scab]

scar·ab (skar′əb) *n.* **1** Any of various beetles, esp. a large, black beetle held sacred by the ancient Egyptians. **2** A gemstone or other ornament in the form of this beetle. Also **scar·a·bee** (skar′ə·bē). [< L *scarabaeus*] —**scar′a·boid** (-boid) *adj.*

scar·a·bae·us (skar′ə·bē′əs) *n. pl.* **·bae·us·es** or **·bae·i** (-bē′ī) SCARAB. Also **scar·a·be′us** —**scar·a·bae′id** *adj., n.*

scar·a·mouch (skar′ə·mouch, -mōōsh) *n.* **1** A boastful, cowardly person. **2** *Usu. cap.* A similar character in old Italian comedy. Also **scar′a·mouche.** [< Ital. *Scaramuccia,* lit., a skirmish]

scarce (skârs) *adj.* **scarc·er, scarc·est 1** Rare and unusual: *scarce* antiques. **2** Scant; insufficient. —**make oneself scarce** *Informal* To go or stay away. [< OF *eschars* scanty, insufficient] —**scarce′ness** *n.*

scarce·ly (skârs′lē) *adv.* **1** Only just; barely: so weary he could *scarcely* walk. **2** Rarely: He *scarcely* goes out now. **3** Certainly not; probably not: That's *scarcely* possible.

scar·ci·ty (skâr′sə·tē) *n. pl.* **·ties 1** Scantiness; insufficiency: a *scarcity* of truffles. **2** Rarity: the *scarcity* of genius.

scare (skâr) *v.* **scared, scar·ing** *v.t.* **1** To strike with sudden fear; frighten. **2** To drive or force by frightening: with *off* or *away.* —*v.i.* **3** To take fright; become scared. —**scare up** *Informal* To get together hurriedly; produce: *to scare up* a meal from leftovers. —*n.* A sudden fright; alarm. —*adj. Informal* Intended to provoke alarm or concern: *scare* tactics. [< ON *skiarr* shy] —**scar′er** *n.* —**scar′ing·ly** *adv.* —**Syn.** *v.* **1** alarm, startle, terrify. *n.* fright, panic.

scare·crow (skâr′krō′) *n.* **1** Any effigy set up to scare crows and other birds from growing crops. **2** A cause of false alarm. **3** A person who is ragged and tattered or thin and gangling.

scare·head (skâr′hed′) *n. Informal* A newspaper headline in large type for sensational news.

scarf¹ (skärf) *n. pl.* **scarfs 1** In carpentry, a lapped joint made as by notching two timbers at the ends, and bolting them together to form a single piece: also **scarf joint. 2** The notched end of either of the timbers so cut. —*v.t.* **1** To unite with a scarf joint. **2** To cut a scarf in. [ME]

Scarf joints

scarf² (skärf) *n. pl.* **scarfs** or **scarves** (skärvz) **1** A long and wide band, worn about the head, neck, shoulders, or waist. **2** A necktie or cravat with dangling ends. **3** A runner for a bureau or table. —*v.t.* To cover or decorate with a scarf. [< OF *escharpe*]

scar·i·fy (skar′ə·fī) *v.t.* **·fied, ·fy·ing 1** To make shallow scratches in; as the skin. **2** To criticize severely. **3** To stir the surface of, as soil. [< Gk. *skariphasthai* scratch an outline] —**scar′i·fi′er, scar′i·fi·ca′tion** *n.*

scar·la·ti·na (skär′lə·tē′nə) *n.* A mild form of scarlet fever.

scar·let (skär′lit) *n.* **1** A brilliant red, inclining to orange. **2** Cloth or clothing of a scarlet color. —*adj.* Brilliant red. [< Pers. *saqalāt* a rich, scarlet cloth]

scarlet fever An acute streptococcal infection marked by fever, sore throat, and a red rash.

scarlet letter A scarlet "A" which adulterous women were once condemned to wear.

scarlet runner A climbing bean with vivid red flowers and long seed pods. Also **scarlet runner bean.**

scarp (skärp) *n.* **1** Any steep slope. **2** A steep artificial slope, esp. the inner slope, about a fortification. —*v.t.* To cut to a steep slope. [< Ital. *scarpa*]

scarves (skärvz) A *pl.* of SCARF².

scar·y (skâr′ē) *adj.* **scar·i·er, scar·i·est** *Informal* **1** Easily scared. **2** Giving cause for alarm. —**scar′i·ness** *n.*

scat¹ (skat) *v.i.* **scat·ted, scat·ting** *Informal* To go away quickly: usu. in the imperative. [?]

scat² (skat) *n.* Jazz singing that employs improvised nonsense syllables. —*v.i.* **scat·ted, scat·ting** To sing scat. [?]

scathe (skāth) *v.t.* **scathed, scath·ing 1** To criticize severely. **2** *Archaic* To injure severely. [< ON *skatha*]

scathe·less (skāth′lis) *adj.* Without harm or injury.

scath·ing (skā′thing) *adj.* Blasting; withering: a *scathing* rebuke. —**scath′ing·ly** *adv.*

sca·tol·o·gy (ska·tol′ə·jē, skə-) *n.* **1** The scientific study of excrement. **2** Preoccupation with obscenity or with excrement, as in literature. [< Gk. *skōr, skatos* dung + -LOGY] —**scat·o·log·i·cal** (skat′ə·loj′i·kəl) *adj.* —**sca·tol′o·gist** *n.*

scat·ter (skat′ər) *v.t.* **1** To throw about in various places; strew. **2** To disperse; rout. **3** *Physics* To reflect (radiation) in more than one direction. —*v.i.* **4** To separate and go in different directions. —*n.* The act of scattering or the condition of being scattered. [ME *scateren*] —**scat'ter·er** *n.* — **Syn.** v. 1 disseminate, sow, spread, sprinkle. 2 drive away.

scat·ter·brain (skat'ər·brān') *n.* A heedless, flighty person. —**scat'ter·brained'** *adj.*

scat·ter·site (skat'ər·sīt) *adj.* Of or describing housing sponsored by government, esp. for low-income groups, located in various communities to avoid ghettoization.

scaup (skôp) *n.* A North American wild duck related to the canvasback, having the head and neck black in the male: also **scaup duck.** [Obs. var. of SCALP + DUCK]

scav·enge (skav'inj) *v.* **·enged, ·eng·ing** *v.t.* 1 To remove filth, rubbish, and refuse from, as streets. —*v.i.* 2 To act as a scavenger. 3 To search for food. [Back formation < SCAVENGER]

scav·en·ger (skav'in·jər) *n.* 1 Any organism that feeds on refuse, carrion, etc. 2 A person who removes refuse or unwanted things, as a garbage collector or a junkman. [< AF *scawage* inspection]

sce·nar·i·o (si·nâr'ē·ō, -nä'rē·ō) *n. pl.* **·nar·i·os** 1 The plot or outline of a dramatic work. 2 The written plot and arrangement of incidents of a motion picture. 3 An outline or plan of a projected series of actions or events. [< LL *scenarius* of stage scenes] —**sce·nar'ist** *n.*

scene (sēn) *n.* 1 A locality and all connected with it, as presented to view; a landscape. 2 The setting for a dramatic action. 3 The place and surroundings of any event, as in literature or art. 4 A division of an act of a play. 5 A specific incident or episode in a play, novel, motion picture, etc.: the ghost *scene* in *Hamlet.* 6 The painted canvas, hangings, etc., for the background for a play. 7 An unseemly display of anger or excited feeling, esp. in public. 8 *Slang* A place or realm of a currently popular activity: the country music *scene.* —**behind the scenes** 1 Out of sight of a theater audience; backstage. 2 Privately; in secret. [< Gk. *skēnē* a tent, a stage]

scen·er·y (sē'nər·ē) *n. pl.* **·er·ies** 1 The features of a landscape; view. 2 The painted backdrops, etc., used in the theater to represent a setting in a play.

sce·nic (sē'nik, sen'ik) *adj.* 1 Of or relating to beautiful natural scenery: a *scenic* spot. 2 In art, representing a situation, action, etc. 3 Relating to stage scenery. —**sce'·ni·cal·ly** *adv.*

scent (sent) *n.* 1 An odor. 2 The effluvium by which an animal can be tracked. 3 A clue aiding investigation. 4 A fragrant, fluid essence; perfume. 5 The sense of smell. —*v.t.* 1 To perceive by the sense of smell. 2 To form a suspicion of. 3 To cause to be fragrant; perfume. —*v.i.* 4 To hunt by the sense of smell. [< L *sentire* to sense]

scep·ter (sep'tər) *n.* 1 A staff or wand carried as the badge of command or sovereignty. 2 Kingly office or power. —*v.t.* To confer the scepter on; invest with royal power. Also, *esp. Brit.,* **scep'tre** (-tər). [< Gk. *skēptron* a staff]

scep·tic (skep'tik) *n.* SKEPTIC.

sched·ule (skej'ool, *Brit.* shed'yool) *n.* 1 A list specifying the details of some matter. 2 A timetable. 3 A detailed and timed plan for the steps in a procedure. —*v.t.* **·uled, ·ul·ing** 1 To place in or on a schedule. 2 To appoint or plan for a specified time or date: He *scheduled* his appearance for five o'clock. [< LL *scedula*]

sche·ma (skē'mə) *n. pl.* **sche·ma·ta** (skē'mə·tə) A synopsis, summary, diagram, etc. [< Gk. *schēma*]

sche·mat·ic (skē·mat'ik) *adj.* Of or relating to a scheme, diagram, or plan. —*n.* A schematic diagram or drawing.

Head of scepter

scheme (skēm) *n.* 1 A plan of something to be done; program. 2 An underhand plot: a *scheme* to defraud consumers. 3 A systematic arrangement: a color *scheme.* 4 An outline drawing; diagram. —*v.* **schemed, schem·ing** *v.t.* 1 To make a scheme for; plan. 2 To plan or plot in an underhand manner. —*v.i.* 3 To make schemes; plan. 4 To plot underhandedly. [< Gk. *schēma* a form, plan] —**schem'er** *n.*

scher·zo (sker'tsō) *n. pl.* **·zos** or **·zi** (-tsē) *Music* A playful or light movement, as in a symphony. [Ital., a jest]

Schick test (shik) A test that indicates susceptibility to diphtheria if reddening of the skin occurs at the site of an injection of toxin. [< B. *Schick,* 1877–1967, Austrian physician]

schil·ling (shil'ing) *n.* The basic monetary unit of Austria.

schism (siz'əm, skiz'əm) *n.* 1 A division of a church into factions because of differences in doctrine. 2 A splitting into antagonistic groups. [< Gk. *schizein* to split]

schis·mat·ic (siz·mat'ik, skiz'-) *adj.* 1 Of or being a schism. 2 Promoting or guilty of schism. Also **schis·mat'·i·cal.** —*n.* One who makes or participates in a schism. —**schis·mat'i·cal·ly** *adv.* —**schis·mat'i·cal·ness** *n.*

schist (shist) *n.* Any crystalline rock that readily splits or cleaves. [< Gk. *schizein* to split] —**schist'ous, schist·ose** (shis'tōs) *adj.*

schizo- *combining form* Split; divided: *schizophrenia.* [< Gk. *schizein* to split]

schiz·oid (skit'soid) *adj.* Pertaining to or resembling schizophrenia. —*n.* One having schizoid characteristics.

schiz·o·phre·ni·a (skit'sō·frē'nē·ə) *n.* Mental illness characterized in varying degrees by irrational thinking, disturbed emotions, bizarre behavior, etc. [< SCHIZO- + Gk. *phrēn* mind] —**schiz'o·phren'ic** (-fren'ik) *adj., n.*

schle·miel (shlə·mēl') *n. Slang* An inept, easily duped person. Also **schle·mihl'.** [Yiddish, an unlucky person]

schlep (shlep) *Slang v.* **schlepped, schlep·ping** *v.t.* 1 To drag awkwardly; lug. —*v.i.* 2 To drag something awkwardly. 3 To proceed wearily or heavily: to *schlep* uptown. —*n.* 1 A difficult journey. 2 A stupid, awkward person. Also **schlepp.** [Yiddish *shleppen* to drag] —**schlep'per** *n.*

schlock (shlok) *Slang n.* Shoddy, inferior merchandise. —*adj.* Of inferior quality; tawdry. [Yiddish] —**schlock'y** *adj.* (·i·er, ·i·est)

schmaltz (shmälts) *n. Slang* 1 Anything which is overly sentimental, as in music or literature. 2 Extreme sentimentalism. [< G *Schmalz,* lit., melted fat] —**schmaltz'y** *adj.* (·i·er, ·i·est)

schnapps (shnäps, shnaps) *n.* 1 A strong gin. 2 Any strong alcoholic liquor. Also **schnaps.** [G, a dram, a nip]

schnau·zer (shnou'zər) *n.* A breed of terrier having a wiry coat. [< G *Schnauze* snout]

schnor·kel (shnôr'kəl) *n.* SNORKEL.

schnoz·zle (shnoz'əl) *n. Slang* Nose. [< G *Schnauze*]

schol·ar (skol'ər) *n.* 1 A person eminent for learning. 2 An authority or specialist in an academic disicipline. 3 The holder of a scholarship. 4 One who learns under a teacher; a pupil. [< L *schola* school]

Schnauzer

schol·ar·ly (skol'ər·lē) *adj.* 1 Of or characteristic of a scholar: a *scholarly* mind. 2 Exhibiting great learning. 3 Devoted to learning. —*adv.* After the manner of a scholar. —**schol'ar·li·ness** *n.* —**Syn.** *adj.* 2 erudite, intellectual, learned, lettered. 3 bookish, studious.

schol·ar·ship (skol'ər·ship) *n.* 1 Learning; erudition. 2 A stipend or other aid given to a student to enable him to continue his studies.

scho·las·tic (skō·las'tik, skə-) *adj.* 1 Pertaining to or characteristic of scholars, education, or schools. 2 Pertaining to or characteristic of the medieval schoolmen. Also **scho·las'ti·cal.** —*n. Often cap.* 1 A schoolman of the Middle ages. 2 An advocate of scholasticism. [< Gk. *scholazein* devote leisure to study] —**scho·las'ti·cal·ly** *adv.*

scho·las·ti·cism (skō·las'tə·siz'əm, skə-) *n. Often cap.* 1 The systematized logic, philosophy, and theology of medieval scholars. 2 Any system of teaching which insists on traditional doctrines and forms.

school[1] (skool) *n.* 1 An educational institution. 2 The building or group of buildings in which formal instruction is given. 3 A period or session of an educational institution: *School begins tomorrow.* **4** The pupils and teachers in an educational institution. **5** A subdivision of a university devoted to a special branch of higher education: a medical *school.* **6** The training of any branch of the armed services: gunnery *school.* **7** A body of disciples of a teacher or a group of persons whose work shows a common style or influence: a painting of the Flemish *school.* **8** Any sphere or means of instruction: the *school* of hard knocks. **9** A group of people having similar opinions, patterns of behavior, interests, etc.: *He belongs to the old school.* — *v.t.* **1** To instruct in a school; train. **2** To subject to rule or discipline. [< Gk. *scholē* leisure, school]

school² (skōōl) *n.* A congregation of fish, whales, etc., that feed or swim together. — *v.i.* To come together in a school. [< MDu. *schōle*]

school board A legal board or committee in charge of public schools

school·book (skōōl′bŏŏk′) *n.* A book for use in school; textbook.

school·boy (skōōl′boi′) *n.* A boy attending school. — *adj.* Like or characteristic of a schoolboy.

school·fel·low (skōōl′fel′ō) *n.* A fellow pupil.

school·girl (skōōl′gûrl′) *n.* A girl attending school. — *adj.* Like or characteristic of a schoolgirl.

school·house (skōōl′hous′) *n.* A building in which a school is conducted.

school·ing (skōō′ling) *n.* **1** Instruction given at school. **2** The cost of educating and maintaining a student at a school. **3** The training of horses and riders.

school·man (skōōl′mən) *n. pl.* **·men** (-mən) One of the theologians of the Middle Ages.

school·marm (skōōl′märm′) *n. Informal* A woman schoolteacher, esp. one considered to be prudish.

school·mas·ter (skōōl′mas′tər, -mäs′-) *n.* A man who teaches in or is principal of a school.

school·mate (skōōl′māt′) *n.* A fellow pupil.

school·mis·tress (skōōl′mis′tris) *n.* A woman who teaches in or is principal of a school.

school·room (skōōl′rōōm′, -rŏŏm′) *n.* A room in which instruction is given.

school·teach·er (skōōl′tē′chər) *n.* One who teaches in a school below the college level.

schoon·er (skōō′nər) *n.* **1** A fore-and-aft rigged vessel having originally two masts, but later often three or more. **2** A large beer glass, holding about a pint. [< dial. *scoon* skim on water.]

Schooner

schtick (shtik) *n.* SHTICK.

schuss (shŏŏs) *v.i.* To ski down a steep slope at high speed. — *n.* **1** A straight, steep ski course. **2** The act of skiing down such a course. [G, lit., a shot] — **schuss′er** *n.*

schwa (shwä, shvä) *n.* **1** A weak or obscure central vowel sound occurring in most of the unstressed syllables in English speech, as that of the *a* in *alone* or the *u* in *circus.* **2** The symbol (ə) for this sound. [< Heb. *shewa*]

sci. science; scientific.

sci·at·ic (sī·at′ik) *adj.* Pertaining to, in the area of, or affecting the hip. — *n.* A large leg nerve originating at the hip: also **sciatic nerve.** [< Gk. *ischion* hip, hip joint]

sci·at·i·ca (sī·at′i·kə) *n.* **1** Severe pain affecting the sciatic nerve. **2** Any painful affection of the hip and leg.

sci·ence (sī′əns) *n.* **1** Knowledge as of facts, phenomena, laws, and proximate causes, gained and verified by exact observation, organized experiment, and analysis. **2** Any of the various branches of such knowledge, as biology, chemistry, physics (**natural sciences**); economics, history, sociology (**social sciences**); agriculture, engineering (**applied sciences**). **3** Any department of knowledge in which the results of investigation have been systematized in the form of hypotheses and general laws subject to verification. **4** Expertness; skill: the *science* of statesmanship. **5** Originally, knowledge. [< L *scire* know]

Sci·ence (sī′əns) *n.* CHRISTIAN SCIENCE.

science fiction Novels and short stories dealing with actual or imaginary scientific developments and their effect on society or individuals. — **sci′ence-fic′tion** *adj.*

sci·en·tif·ic (sī′ən·tif′ik) *adj.* **1** Of, pertaining to, discovered by, derived from, or used in science. **2** Agreeing with the rules, principles, or methods of science; systematic. **3** Versed in science or a science. — **sci′en·tif′i·cal·ly** *adv.*

sci·en·tist (sī′ən·tist) *n.* One trained or learned in science or devoted to scientific study or investigation.

Sci·en·tist (sī′ən·tist) *n.* A Christian Scientist.

sci·en·tol·o·gy (sī′ən·tol′ə·jē) *n. Often cap.* A religious and psychotherapeutic cult purporting to solve personal problems, cure mental and physical disorders, and increase intelligence. [< L *scientia* science + -LOGY] — **sci′en·tol′o·gist** *n.*

sci-fi (sī′fī′) *Informal n.* Science fiction. — *adj.* Science-fiction.

scil·i·cet (sil′ə·set) *adv.* Namely; that is to say. [< L *scire licet* it is permitted to know]

scim·i·tar (sim′ə·tər) *n.* A curved sword or saber used by Turks. Also **scim′i·ter.** [MF < Pers. *shamshīr*]

scin·til·la (sin·til′ə) *n.* **1** A spark. **2** A trace; iota: a *scintilla* of truth. [L]

scin·til·late (sin′tə·lāt) *v.* **·lat·ed, ·lat·ing** *v.i.* **1** To give off sparks. **2** To be witty and brilliant in conversation. **3** To twinkle, as a star. — *v.t.* **4** To give off as a spark or sparks. [< L *scintilla* a spark] — **scin′til·la′ting·ly** *adv.* — **scin′til·la′tion** *n.* — Syn. 1, 2 glitter, glow, shine, sparkle.

Scimitar

sci·o·lism (sī′ə·liz′əm) *n.* Pretentious, superficial knowledge. [< LL *sciolus* a smatterer] — **sci′o·list** *n.* — **sci′o·lis′tic** *adj.*

sci·on (sī′ən) *n.* **1** A child or descendant. **2** A bud or shoot from a plant or tree, used in grafting. [< OF *cion*]

scis·sion (sizh′ən, sish′-) *n.* **1** The act of cutting or splitting, or the state of being cut. **2** Any division. [< L *scissus,* p.p. of *scindere* to cut]

scis·sor (siz′ər) *v.t. & v.i.* To cut with scissors.

scis·sors (siz′ərz) *n.pl.* **1** A cutting implement with handles and a pair of blades pivoted face to face: sometimes a **pair of scissors.** **2** *(construed as sing.)* In wrestling, a hold secured by clasping the legs about the body or head of the opponent. [< LL *cisorium* a cutting instrument]

scissors kick In swimming, a kick in which both legs, bent at the knee, are thrust apart, then straightened and brought sharply together.

scis·sor·tail (siz′ər·tāl′) *n.* A flycatcher of the sw U.S. and Mexico having a forked tail.

scle·ra (skler′ə, sklir′ə) *n.* The firm, fibrous, white outer coat of the eyeball, continuous with the cornea: also **scle·rot·i·ca** (sklə·rot′i·kə). [< Gk. *sklēros* hard]

scle·ren·chy·ma (sklə·reng′kə·mə) *n. Bot.* Tissue composed of cells with hard, thick walls. [< Gk. *sklēros* hard + *enchyma* an infusion] — **scle·ren·chym·a·tous** (skler′en·kim′ə·təs, sklir′-, -kī′mə-) *adj.*

scle·ro·sis (sklə·rō′sis) *n.* Abnormal thickening and hardening of tissue. [< Gk. *sklēros* hard] — **scle·ro′sal** *adj.*

scle·rot·ic (sklə·rot′ik) *adj.* **1** Dense; firm, as the white of the eye. **2** Pertaining to or affected with sclerosis: also **scle·rosed** (-rōst′) [< Gk. *sklērotēs* hardness]

scoff (skôf, skof) *v.i.* **1** To speak with contempt or derision: often with *at.* — *v.t.* **2** To deride; mock. — *n.* **1** Words or actions of contempt. **2** A person or thing held in contempt. [ME *scof*] — **scoff′er** *n.* — **scoff′ing·ly** *adv.* — Syn. *v.* 1, 2 gibe, jeer, scorn, sneer, taunt.

scoff·law (skôf′lô, skof′-) *n.* A habitual or deliberate violator of traffic, safety, or public-health regulations.

scold (skōld) *v.t.* **1** To find fault with harshly. — *v.i.* **2** To find fault harshly or continuously. — *n.* One who scolds constantly: also **scold′er.** [< ON *skáld* a poet, satirist] — **scold′ing·ly** *adv.*

scol·lop (skol′əp) *n. & v.* SCALLOP.

sconce (skons) *n.* An ornamental wall bracket for holding a candle or other light. [< L *abscondere* to hide]

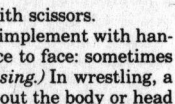

Wall sconce

scone (skōn, skon) *n.* **1** A thin oatmeal cake, baked on a griddle. **2** A teacake or soda biscuit. [?< MDu. *schoonbrot* fine bread]

scoop (skoōp) *n.* **1** The part of a dredge or steam shovel that lifts earth, sand, coal, etc. **2** A small shovellike implement for flour, sugar, ice cream, etc. **3** An implement for bailing, as water from a boat. **4** A spoon-shaped instrument for using in a cavity: a surgeon's *scoop.* **5** An act of scooping. **6** A scooping motion. **7** The amount scooped at once: a *scoop* of ice cream. **8** *Informal* A news story obtained and published ahead of rival papers. —*v.t.* **1** To take or dip out with a scoop. **2** To hollow out, as with a scoop; excavate. **3** *Informal* To heap up or gather in as if in scoopfuls; amass. **4** *Informal* To obtain and publish a news story before (a rival). [< MDu. *schōpe* a vessel for bailing out water] —**scoop′er** *n.*

scoop·ful (skoōp′fŏŏl′) *n. pl.* **·fuls** As much as a scoop will hold.

scoot (skoōt) *v.i. Informal* To go quickly; dart off. —*n.* The act of scooting. [? < Scand.]

scoot·er (skoō′tər) *n.* **1** A child's vehicle consisting of a board mounted on two wheels and steered by a handle attached to the front axle, the rider standing with one foot on the board, using the other to push. **2** A similar vehicle powered by an internal-combustion engine and having a driver's seat: also **motor scooter.**

scope (skōp) *n.* **1** A range of view or action. **2** Capacity for achievement. **3** End in view; aim. **4** *Informal* A telescope, microscope, oscilloscope, etc. [< Gk. *skopos* a watcher]

-scope *combining form* An instrument for viewing, observing, or indicating: *microscope.* [< Gk. *skopos* a watcher]

sco·pol·a·mine (skō·pol′ə·mēn, -min, skō′pə·lam′ēn, -in) *n.* A depressant drug related to belladonna which blocks the formation of memories and various other functions of the brain. [< G. A. *Scopoli,* 1723–88, Italian naturalist]

-scopy *combining form* Observation; viewing: *microscopy.* [< Gk. *skopeein* to watch]

scor·bu·tic (skôr·byoō′tik) *adj.* Of, like, or affected with scurvy. Also **scor·bu′ti·cal.** [< Med. L *scorbutus* scurvy] —**scor·bu′ti·cal·ly** *adv.*

scorch (skôrch) *v.t.* **1** To change the color, taste, etc., of, by slight burning. **2** To wither or shrivel by heat. **3** To criticize severely. —*v.i.* **4** To become scorched. **5** *Informal* To go at high speed. —*n.* **1** A superficial burn. **2** A mark caused by a slight burn. [ME *scorchen*] —**scorch′ing·ly** *adv.*

scorched-earth policy (skôrcht′ûrth′) The policy of destroying all crops, industrial equipment, dwellings, etc., before the arrival of an advancing enemy.

scorch·er (skôr′chər) *n.* **1** A person or thing that scorches. **2** *Informal* A very hot day. **3** *Informal* One who moves at great speed.

score (skōr, skôr) *n.* **1** The record of the winning points, counts, runs, etc., in competitive games. **2** A record of indebtedness; bill. **3** *Music* A printed or written copy of a musical composition in which all vocal and instrumental parts are shown on two or more connected staves one above another. **4** A group of 20. **5** *pl.* An indefinite large number. **6** A value assigned to an individual or group response to a test or series of tests, as of intelligence or performance. **7** *Slang* A success, esp. in making a purchase of narcotics. —**to pay off** (or **settle**) **old scores** To get even with someone for past wrongs, injuries, etc. —*v.* **scored, scor·ing** *v.t.* **1** To mark with notches, cuts, or lines. **2** To mark with cuts or lines for the purpose of keeping a tally. **3** To delete by means of a line drawn through: with *out.* **4** To make or gain, as points, runs, etc. **5** To count for a score of, as in games: A touchdown *scores* six points. **6** To rate or grade, as an examination paper. **7** *Music* **a** To orchestrate. **b** To arrange or adapt for an instrument. **8** *Informal* To criticize severely; scourge. **9** In cooking, to make superficial cuts in (meat, etc.). —*v.i.* **10** To make points, runs, etc., as in a game. **11** To keep score. **12** To make notches, cuts, etc. **13** To achieve a success. **14** *Slang* To purchase marihuana or narcotics. **15** *Slang* To succeed in having sexual intercourse with someone. [< ON *skora* a notch] —**scor′er** *n.*

sco·ri·a (skôr′ē·ə, skō′rē·ə) *n. pl.* **·ri·ae** (-i·ē) **1** The refuse of melted metal or reduced ore. **2** Lava that is loose and cinderlike. [< Gk. *skōr* dung] —**sco′ri·a′ceous** (-ā′shəs) *adj.*

scorn (skôrn) *n.* **1** A feeling of contempt. **2** An object of supreme contempt. —*v.t.* **1** To hold in or treat with contempt; despise. **2** To reject with scorn; spurn. [< OF *escarn*] —**scorn′er, scorn′ful·ness** *n.* —**scorn′ful** *adj.* —**scorn′ful·ly** *adv.* —**Syn.** *n.* **1** disdain, scoffing. *v.* **1** contemn, detest.

Scor·pi·o (skôr′pē·ō) *n.* A constellation and the eighth sign of the zodiac; the Scorpion. Also **Scor·pi·us** (-əs). [< Gk. *skorpios*] • See ZODIAC.

scor·pi·on (skôr′pē·ən) *n.* **1** Any of an order of arachnids with long segmented tails bearing a poisonous sting. **2** In the Bible, a whip or scourge. [< Gk. *skorpios*]

Scorpion *n.* SCORPIO.

scot (skot) *n.* An assessment or tax. [< ON *skot*]

Scot (skot) *n.* A native of Scotland. • See SCOTCH.

Indian scorpion

Scot. Scotland; Scots; Scottish.

scotch (skoch) *v.t.* **1** To cut; scratch. **2** To wound so as to maim or cripple. **3** To quash or suppress: to *scotch* a rumor. —*n.* **1** A superficial cut; a notch. **2** A line traced on the ground, as for hopscotch. [?]

Scotch (skoch) *n.* **1** The people of Scotland collectively. **2** One or all of the dialects spoken by the people of Scotland. **3** Scotch whisky. —*adj.* Of or pertaining to Scotland, its inhabitants, or their dialects. • **Scotch, Scots, Scottish; Scot, Scotchman, Scotsman** Of the three proper adjectives, the form *Scotch* is accepted in Scotland only as applying to *Scotch plaid, Scotch terriers, Scotch whisky,* etc. In Scotland and northern England, the forms *Scots* and *Scottish* are preferred as applying to the people, language, culture, and institutions of Scotland: *Scots* or *Scottish English, the Scottish church.* In referring to an inhabitant of Scotland, *Scot* and *Scotsman* are preferred over the chiefly U.S. term *Scotchman.*

Scotch·man (skoch′mən) *n. pl.* **·men** (-mən) A Scot; Scotsman. • See SCOTCH.

Scotch tape A rolled strip of transparent adhesive tape: a trade name.

Scotch terrier A small terrier with compact body, short legs, and a grizzled coat.

Scotch whisky Whiskey made in Scotland from malted barley and having a rather smoky flavor. • Scotch whisky is traditionally spelled without the "e."

Scotch terrier

sco·ter (skō′tər) *n.* Any of several large ducks of northern regions, having black or dark brown plumage. [?< dial. E *scote,* var. of SCOOT]

scot-free (skot′frē′) *adj.* **1** Free from any penalty, blame, or punishment. **2** Free from scot.

Scotland Yard **1** The headquarters of the London police: in full, **New Scotland Yard. 2** The London police force, esp. the detective bureau.

Scots (skots) *adj.* SCOTTISH. —*n.* The Scottish dialect of English. • See SCOTCH.

Scots·man (skots′mən) *n. pl.* **·men** (-mən) A Scot. • See SCOTCH.

Scot·ti·cism (skot′ə·siz′əm) *n.* A verbal usage or idiom peculiar to the Scottish people.

Scot·tish (skot′ish) *adj.* Pertaining to or characteristic of Scotland, its inhabitants, or their language. —*n.* **1** The dialect of English spoken in Scotland. **2** The people of Scotland collectively: with *the.* • See SCOTCH.

Scottish Gaelic The language of the Scottish Highlands.

Scottish terrier SCOTCH TERRIER. Also *Informal* **scot·tie** (skot′ē), **scot′ty.**

scoun·drel (skoun′drəl) *n.* An unscrupulous, dishonest person; villain. —*adj.* Villainous; base. [?] —**scoun′drel·ly** *adj.*

scour¹ (skour) *v.t.* **1** To clean or brighten by thorough washing and rubbing. **2** To remove dirt, grease, etc., from; clean. **3** To clear by means of a strong current of water; flush. —*v.i.* **4** To rub something vigorously so as to clean or brighten it. **5** To become bright or clean by rubbing. —*n.* **1** The act of scouring. **2** A cleanser used in scouring. **3** *Usu. pl.* A dysentery affecting cattle. [<OF *escurer*] —**scour′er** *n.* —**Syn.** *v.* **1** polish, scrub. **2** cleanse.

scour² (skour) *v.t.* **1** To range over or through, as in making a search. **2** To move or run swiftly over or along. —*v.i.* **3** To range swiftly about, as in making a search. [ME *scoure*]

scourge (skûrj) *n.* **1** A whip for inflicting suffering or punishment. **2** Any severe punishment. **3** Any means for causing suffering or death: the *scourge* of cholera. —*v.t.* **scourged, scourg·ing** **1** To whip severely; flog. **2** To punish severely; afflict. [<LL *excoriare* flay] —**scourg′er** *n.*

scout¹ (skout) *n.* **1** A person, plane, etc., sent out to observe and get information, as of the position or strength of an enemy in war. **2** The act of scouting. **3** A person in search of promising performers in athletics, entertainment, etc.: a talent *scout*. **4** A member of the Girl Scouts or the Boy Scouts. **5** A fellow; guy: usu. in the phrase **a good scout.** —*v.t.* **1** To observe or spy upon for the purpose of gaining information. —*v.i.* **2** To go or act as a scout. — **scout around** To go in search. [<L *auscultare* to listen] —**scout′er** *n.*

scout² (skout) *v.t. & v.i.* To reject with disdain. [<Scand.]

scout·mas·ter (skout′mas′tər, -mäs′-) *n.* The adult leader of a troop of Boy Scouts.

scow (skou) *n.* A large boat with a flat bottom and square ends, chiefly used to carry freight, garbage, etc. [<Du. *schouw*]

scowl (skoul) *n.* **1** A lowering of the brows, as in anger. **2** Gloomy aspect. —*v.i.* **1** To contract the brows in anger, sullenness, or disapproval. **2** To look threatening; lower. —*v.t.* **3** To affect or express by scowling. [?<Scand.]

scr. scrip; script; scruple (weight).

scrab·ble (skrab′əl) *v.* **·bled, ·bling** *v.i.* **1** To scratch, scrape, or paw. **2** To scribble. **3** To struggle or strive. —*v.t.* **4** To scrible on. **5** To scrape together. —*n.* **1** The act of scrabbling; a moving on hands and feet or knees. **2** A scrambling effort. [<Du. *schrabbelen*] —**scrab′bler** *n.*

scrag (skrag) *v.t.* **scragged, scrag·ging** *Informal* To wring the neck of; garrote. —*n.* **1** *Slang* The neck. **2** A lean, bony person or animal. [?<Scand.]

scrag·gly (skrag′lē) *adj.* **·gli·er, ·gli·est** Uneven; irregular; jagged: a *scraggly* beard.

scrag·gy (skrag′ē) *adj.* **·gi·er, ·gi·est** **1** SCRAGGLY. **2** Lean; scrawny. —**scrag′gi·ly** *adv.* —**scrag′gi·ness** *n.*

scram (skram) *v.i.* **scrammed, scram·ming** *Slang* To go away; leave quickly. [Short for SCRAMBLE]

scram·ble (skram′bəl) *v.* **·bled, ·bling** *v.i.* **1** To move by clambering or crawling. **2** To struggle in a disorderly manner; scuffle. **3** To strive for something in such a manner. —*v.t.* **4** To mix together haphazardly or confusedly. **5** To gather or collect hurriedly or confusedly. **6** To cook (eggs) with the yolks and whites stirred together. **7** *Telecom.* To encode (a message) so that a special decoder is needed to make it intelligible. —*n.* **1** A difficult climb, as over rough terrain. **2** A struggle for possession: a *scramble* for power. [?] —**scram′bler** *n.*

scrap¹ (skrap) *n.* **1** A small piece; fragment. **2** A small part of something written. **3** *pl.* Bits of unused food. **4** Old or refuse metal. —*v.t.* **scrapped, scrap·ping** **1** To break up into scrap. **2** To discard. —*adj.* Having the form of scraps: *scrap* metal. [<ON *skrap* scraps] —**Syn.** **1** bit, chip, segment, shard. **3** leftovers.

scrap² (skrap) *Informal v.i.* **scrapped, scrap·ping** To fight; quarrel. —*n.* A fight; quarrel; squabble. [?<SCRAPE, *n.* (def. 2)] —**scrap′per** *n.*

scrap·book (skrap′book′) *n.* **1** A blank book in which to paste pictures, cuttings from periodicals, etc. **2** A personal notebook.

scrape (skrāp) *v.* **scraped, scrap·ing** *v.t.* **1** To rub, as with something rough or sharp, so as to abrade. **2** To remove an outer layer thus: with *off, away*, etc. **3** To rub (a rough or sharp object) across a surface. **4** To rub roughly across or against (a surface). **5** To dig or form by scratching or scraping. **6** To gather or accumulate with effort or dif-

ficulty. —*v.i.* **7** To scrape something. **8** To rub with a grating noise. **9** To make a grating noise. **10** To draw the foot backward along the ground in bowing. **11** To manage or get along with difficulty. **12** To be very or overly economical. —*n.* **1** The act or effect of scraping; also, the noise made by scraping. **2** A difficult situation. **3** A quarrel or fight. **4** A scraping or drawing back of the foot in bowing. [<ON *skrapa*] —**scrap′er** *n.*

scrap·ing (skrā′ping) *n.* **1** The act of one who or that which scrapes. **2** The sound so produced. **3** *Usu. pl.* Something scraped off or together.

scrap·ple (skrap′əl) *n.* Cornmeal cooked with scraps of pork and spices and molded into a firm loaf to be sliced for frying.

scrap·py¹ (skrap′ē) *adj.* **·pi·er, ·pi·est** Composed of scraps; fragmentary. —**scrap′pi·ly** *adv.* —**scrap′pi·ness** *n.*

scrap·py² (skrap′ē) *adj.* **·pi·er, ·pi·est** *Informal* **1** Ready and willing to fight. **2** Strongly competitive; gritty; tough. — **scrap′pi·ly** *adv.* —**scrap′pi·ness** *n.*

scratch (skrach) *v.t.* **1** To tear or mark the surface of with something sharp or rough. **2** To scrape or dig with something sharp or rough. **3** To scrape lightly with the nails, etc., as to relieve itching. **4** To rub with a grating sound; scrape. **5** To write or draw awkwardly or hurriedly. **6** To erase or cancel by scratches or marks. **7** To withdraw (an entry) from a competition, race, etc. —*v.i.* **8** To use the nails or claws, as in fighting or digging. **9** To scrape the skin, etc., lightly, as to relieve itching. **10** To make a grating noise. **11** To manage or get along with difficulty. **12** To withdraw from a game, race, etc. —*n.* **1** A mark or incision made on a surface by scratching. **2** A slight flesh wound or cut. **3** The sound of scratching. **4** The line from which contestants start, as in racing. **5** *Slang* Money. —**from scratch** From the beginning; from nothing. —**up to scratch** *Informal* Meeting the standard or requirement. —*adj.* **1** Done by chance; haphazard. **2** Made for hurried notes, figuring, etc.: a *scratch* pad. **3** Chosen hastily and at random: a *scratch* team. [<MDu. *cratsen*] —**scratch′er** *n.*

scratch·y (skrach′ē) *adj.* **scratch·i·er, scratch·i·est** **1** Consisting of scratches: *scratchy* handwriting. **2** Making a scratching noise. **3** Causing itching: a *scratchy* sweater. —**scratch′i·ly** *adv.* —**scratch′i·ness** *n.*

scrawl (skrôl) *v.t. & v.i.* To write hastily or illegibly. —*n.* Irregular or careless writing. [?] —**scrawl′er** *n.*

scraw·ny (skrô′nē) *adj.* **·ni·er, ·ni·est** Lean and bony. [?] —**scraw′ni·ness** *n.*

scream (skrēm) *v.i.* **1** To utter a prolonged, piercing cry, as of pain, terror, or surprise. **2** To make a piercing sound: the wind *screamed* in the trees. **3** To laugh loudly or immoderately. **4** To use heated, hysterical language. —*v.t.* **5** To utter with a scream. —*n.* **1** A loud, shrill, prolonged cry or sound. **2** *Informal* A hugely entertaining person or thing. [<ON *skraema* to scare] —**scream′ing·ly** *adv.*

scream·er (skrē′mər) *n.* **1** One who or that which screams. **2** A South American wading bird, related to the ducks. **3** *Slang* A sensational headline in a newspaper.

screech (skrēch) *n.* A shrill, harsh cry; shriek. —*v.t.* **1** To utter with a screech. —*v.i.* **2** To shriek. [<ON *skrækja*] — **screech′er** *n.* —**screech′y** *adj.* (**·i·er, ·i·est**)

screech owl **1** Any of various small owls emitting a high-pitched wail. **2** The barn owl.

screed (skrēd) *n.* A prolonged spoken or written tirade; harangue. [<OE *scréade*]

screen (skrēn) *n.* **1** Something that separates or shelters, as a light partition. **2** A coarse or fine metal mesh used for sifting, or as protection: a window *screen*. **3** Something that serves to conceal or protect: a smoke *screen*. **4** A surface, as a canvas or curtain, on which motion pictures and slides may be shown. **5** The surface of a cathode-ray tube, on which television pictures, computer information or graphics, etc., may be viewed. —**the screen** Motion pictures. —*v.t.* **1** To shield or conceal with or as with a screen. **2** To pass through a screen or sieve; sift. **3** To classify or scan for suitability, qualifications, etc.: to *screen* applicants for a job. **4** To project on a motion-picture screen. **5** To photograph (a motion picture); shoot. **6** To adapt (a play, novel, story, etc.) for motion pictures. —*v.i.* **7** To be suitable for representation as a motion picture. [<OF *escren*]

screen·ing (skrēn'ing) n. 1 A meshlike material, as for a window screen. 2 A showing of a motion picture. 3 pl. The parts of anything passed through or retained by a sieve; siftings.

screw (skrōō) n. 1 A device resembling a nail but having a slotted head and a tapering or cylindrical spiral for driving into wood, metal, plaster, etc., or for insertion into a corresponding threaded part. 2 A cylindrical socket with a spiral groove or thread 3 Anything having the form of a screw. 4 SCREW PROpeller • See RUDDER. 5 A turn of or as of a screw. 6 Pressure; force. 7 Slang A prison guard. 8 Brit. Slang An old, worn-out, or bad-tempered horse. —**have a screw loose** Slang To be mentally deranged, eccentric, etc. —**put the screws on** (or to) Slang To exert pressure or force upon. —v.t. 1 To tighten, fasten, attach, etc., by a screw or screws. 2 To turn or twist. 3 To force; urge: to screw one's courage to the sticking point. 4 To contort, as one's features. 5 To practice oppression or extortion on; defraud. 6 To obtain by extortion. 7 Slang To act maliciously toward; harm. —v.i. 8 To turn as a screw. 9 To become attached or detached by means of twisting: with on, off, etc. 10 To twist or wind. 11 To practice oppression or extortion. —**screw up** Slang To botch; make a mess of: He screwed up his career. [< OF escroue nut] —**screw'er** n.

Screws
a. wood screw.
b. thumbscrew.
c. round-headed screw.

screw·ball (skrōō'bôl') n. 1 In baseball, a pitch thrown with a wrist motion opposite to that used for the outcurve. 2 Slang An unconventional or erratic person.

screw cap A cap or lid designed to screw onto the threaded top of a bottle, jar, or the like.

screw·driv·er (skrōō'drī'vər) n. A tool for turning screws.

screwed-up (skrōōd'up') adj. Slang 1 Disorganized or disorderly. 2 Mentally ill or emotionally distressed.

screw propeller An array of radial blades set at an angle on a rotary shaft to produce a spiral action in a fluid, used to propel ships, etc. • See RUDDER

screw thread The spiral ridge of a screw or nut.

screw·y (skrōō'ē) adj. screw·i·er, screw·i·est Slang Irrational; eccentric. —**screw'i·ly** adv. —**screw'i·ness** n.

scrib·ble (skrib'əl) v. ·bled, ·bling v.t. 1 To write hastily and carelessly. 2 To cover with careless or illegible writing. —v.i. 3 To write carelessly or hastily. 4 To make illegible or meaningless marks. —n. 1 Hasty, careless writing. 2 Meaningless lines and marks; scrawl. [< L scribere write] —**scrib'bler** n. —**scrib'bly** adj.

scribe (skrīb) n. 1 One who copied manuscripts and books before printing was invented. 2 A clerk, public writer, or amanuensis. 3 An author: used humorously. 4 An ancient Jewish teacher of the Mosaic law. [< L scribere write] —**scrib'al** adj.

scrim (skrim) n. A lightweight, open-mesh, usu. cotton fabric, used for curtains, etc. [?]

scrim·mage (skrim'ij) n. 1 A rough-and-tumble contest; fracas. 2 In American football, a mass play from the line of scrimmage after the ball has been placed on the ground and snapped back, the play ending when the ball is dead. —**line of scrimmage** In football, the hypothetic line, parallel to the goal lines, on which the ball rests and along which the opposing linemen take position at the start of play. —v.t. & v.i. ·maged, ·mag·ing To engage in a scrimmage. [Var. of SKIRMISH]

scrimp (skrimp) v.i. 1 To be very economical or stingy. —v.t. 2 To be overly sparing toward; skimp. 3 To cut too small, narrow, etc. [?] —**scrimp'er** n.

scrim·py (skrim'pē) adj. ·i·er, ·i·est Skimpy or meager. —**scrimp'i·ly** adv. —**scrimp'i·ness** n.

scrim·shaw (skrim'shô) n. 1 The carving and engraving of usu. whalebone or whale ivory, as by American sailors. 2 An article so made. —v.t. 1 To make into scrimshaw by carving or engraving. —v.i. 2 To create scrimshaw. [?]

scrip (skrip) n. 1 Writing. 2 Any of various certificates showing that a person is entitled to receive something, as a fractional share of stock, a share of jointly owned property, etc. 3 A piece of paper money less than a dollar, formerly issued during emergencies in the U.S. [<SCRIPT]

Scrip. Scriptural; Scripture(s).

script (skript) n. 1 Handwriting; also, a particular style of

This line is in script.

handwriting. 2 Printed matter in imitation of handwriting. 3 A manuscript or text. 4 The written text of a play, TV show, etc. [<L scribere write]

scrip·ture (skrip'chər) n. 1 The sacred writings of any people. 2 Any authoritative book or writing. [<L scribere write] —**scrip'tur·al** adj. —**scrip'tur·al·ly** adv.

Scripture (skrip'chər) n. 1 Usu. pl. The books of the Old and New Testaments; the Bible; also (the) Holy Scripture. 2 A passage from the Bible.

scriv·en·er (skriv'ən·ər, skriv'nər) n. 1 A clerk or scribe. 2 A notary. [<L scribere write]

scrod (skrod) n. A young codfish, esp. when split and prepared for broiling. [<MDu. schrode]

scrof·u·la (skrof'yə·lə) n. Tuberculosis of the lymph glands. [<LL scrofa a breeding sow] —**scrof'u·lous** adj. —**scrof'u·lous·ly** adv. —**scrof'u·lous·ness** n.

scroll (skrōl) n. 1 A roll of parchment, paper, etc., esp. one containing or intended for writing. 2 The writing on such a roll. 3 Anything resembling a parchment roll, as a convoluted ornament or part. —v.i. To move one or more lines of copy off the top of a computer screen, so that additional lines may be displayed at the bottom, or vice versa. [<AF escrowe]

scroll saw A narrow-bladed saw for cutting thin sheets of wood into curved or convoluted shapes.

scrooge (skrōōj) n. A miserly, misanthropic person. [<Ebenezer Scrooge, a miserly character in Dickens' A Christmas Carol]

scro·tum (skrō'təm) n. pl. ·ta (tə) or ·tums The pouch that contains the testes. [L] —**scro'tal** adj.

scrounge (skrounj) v.t. & v.i. scrounged, scoung·ing Slang 1 To hunt about and take (something); pilfer. 2 To mooch; sponge. [?] —**scroung'er** n.

scrub¹ (skrub) v. scrubbed, scrub·bing v.t. 1 To rub vigorously in washing. 2 To remove (dirt, etc.) by such action. —v.i. 3 To rub something vigorously in washing. —n. The act of scrubbing. [<MDu. schrobben] —**scrub'ber** n.

scrub² (skrub) n. 1 A stunted tree. 2 A tract of stunted trees or shrubs. 3 A domestic animal of inferior breed. 4 A poor, insignificant person. 5 In sports, a player not on the varsity or regular team. 6 A game of baseball contrived hastily by a few players. —adj. 1 Undersized or inferior. 2 Consisting of or participated in by untrained players or scrubs: scrub team. [Var. of SHRUB]

scrub·by (skrub'ē) adj. ·bi·er, ·bi·est 1 Of stunted growth. 2 Covered with or consisting of scrub or underbrush. —**scrub'bi·ly** adv. —**scrub'bi·ness** n.

scrub oak Any of various dwarf oaks.

scruff (skruf) n. The nape or outer back part of the neck. [Earlier scuff < ON skopt hair]

scruf·fy (skruf'ē) adj. ·i·er, ·i·est 1 Shabby; seedy. 2 Worthless. [<OE scruf scurf] —**scruf'fi·ly** adv. —**scruf'fi·ness** n.

scrump·tious (skrump'shəs) adj. Slang Elegant or stylish; splendid. [? Var. of SUMPTUOUS] —**scrump'tious·ly** adv.

scru·ple (skrōō'pəl) n. 1 Doubt or uncertainty about what one should do. 2 Reluctance arising from conscientious disapproval. 3 An apothecaries' weight of 20 grains. 4 A minute quantity. —v.t. & v.i. ·pled, ·pling To hesitate (doing) from considerations of right or wrong. [<L scrupulus a sharp stone]

scru·pu·lous (skrōō'pyə·əs) adj. 1 Cautious in action for fear of doing wrong; conscientious. 2 Resulting from the exercise of scruples; careful. —**scru'pu·lous·ly** adv. —**scru'pu·los'i·ty** (-los'ə·tē), **scru'pu·lous·ness** n. —**Syn.** 1 ethical, honest, upright. 2 exact, precise.

scru·ti·neer (skrōō'tə·nir') n. 1 One who scrutinizes. 2

Brit. & Can. One who oversees a polling place, checking voters against the registry, etc.

scru·ti·nize (skrōō′tə·nīz) *v.t.* **·nized, ·niz·ing** To observe carefully; examine in detail. **—scru′ti·niz′er** *n.* **—scru′ti·niz′ing·ly** *adv.*

scru·ti·ny (skrōō′tə·nē) *n. pl.* **·nies** Close investigation; careful inspection. [< L *scrutari* examine]

scu·ba (skyōō′bə) *n.* A device worn by a free-swimming diver to provide a supply of air for breathing. [< *s(elf-) c(ontained) u(nderwater) b(reathing) a(pparatus)*]

scuba diving Swimming under water with the aid of a scuba. **—scuba diver**

scud (skud) *v.i.* **scud·ded, scud·ding** To move, run, or fly swiftly. **—n.** **1** The act of scudding. **2** Light clouds driven rapidly before the wind. [?]

scuff (skuf) *v.i.* **1** To drag the feet in walking; shuffle. **—v.t.** **2** To scrape (the floor, ground, etc.) with the feet. **3** To roughen the surface by rubbing or scraping: to *scuff* one's shoes. **—n.** The act of scuffing; also, the noise so made. [? < ON *skūfa* shove]

scuf·fle (skuf′əl) *v.i.* **·fled, ·fling 1** To struggle roughly or confusedly. **2** To drag one's feet; shuffle. **—n.** A disorderly struggle; fracas. [? < Scand.] **—scuf′fler** *n.*

scull (skul) *n.* **1** A long oar worked from side to side over the stern of a boat. **2** A light oar, used in pairs by one person. **3** A small boat for sculling. **—v.t. & v.i.** To propel (a boat) by a scull or sculls. [ME *sculle*] **—scull′er** *n.*

scul·ler·y (skul′ər·ē) *n. pl.* **·ler·ies** A room where kitchen utensils are kept and cleaned. [< L *scutella* a tray]

scul·lion (skul′yən) *n. Archaic* A servant who scours dishes, pots, and kettles. [< OF *escouillon* a mop]

scul·pin (skul′pin) *n.* Any of a family of spiny fishes having a large head and fanlike pectoral fins. [< L *scorpaena*, a scorpionlike fish]

sculpt (skulpt) *v.t. & v.i. Informal* SCULPTURE.

sculp·tor (skulp′tər) *n.* A person who sculptures. **—sculp′tress** (-tris) *n. Fem.*

sculp·ture (skulp′chər) *n.* **1** The art of fashioning three-dimensional figures, busts, abstract pieces, etc., of stone, wood, clay, bronze, or other material. **2** A piece or group produced by sculpture. **—v.t. ·tured, ·tur·ing 1** To fashion, (stone, wood, metal, etc.) into sculpture. **2** To represent or portray by sculpture. **3** To embellish with sculpture. **4** To change (features on the surface of the earth) by erosion. **—v.i. 5** To work as a sculptor. [< L *sculpere* carve in stone] **—sculp′tur·al** *adj.* **—sculp′tur·al·ly** *adv.*

scum (skum) *n.* **1** A layer of impure or extraneous matter on the surface of a liquid. **2** Low, contemptible people. **—v. scummed, scum·ming** *v.t.* **1** To take scum from; skim. **—v.i. 2** To become covered with or form scum. [< MDu. *schuum*] **—scum′mi·ness** *n.* **—scum′my** *adj.* (·mi·er, ·mi·est)

scup (skup) *n.* A small porgy of the E coast of the U.S. [< Algon.]

scup·per (skup′ər) *n.* A hole or gutter bordering a ship's deck, to let water run off. [? < OF *escope* a bailing scoop]

scup·per·nong (skup′ər·nong) *n.* **1** A light-colored grape of the S U.S. **2** A sweet wine made from this grape. [< the *Scuppernong* River in N.C.]

scurf (skûrf) *n.* **1** Loose scales thrown off by the skin, as dandruff. **2** Any scaly matter adhering to a surface. [< OE] **—scurf′i·ness** *n.* **—scurf′y** *adj.* (·i·er, ·i·est)

scur·ri·lous (skûr′ə·ləs) *adj.* Grossly offensive or indecent; coarse and abusive: a *scurrilous* attack. [< L *scurra* a buffoon] **—scur·ril·i·ty** (skə·ril′ə·tē) (*pl.* ·ties), **scur′ri·lous·ness** *n.* **—scur′ri·lous·ly** *adv.*

scur·ry (skûr′ē) *v.i.* **·ried, ·ry·ing** To move or go hurriedly; scamper. **—n. pl. ·ries** The act or sound of scurrying. [?] **—Syn.** *v.* dart, dash, scoot, scuttle.

scur·vy (skûr′vē) A disease due to lack of vitamin C, marked by weakness, spotted skin, and bleeding gums. **—adj. ·vi·er, ·vi·est** Low or contemptible. [< SCURF] **—scur′vi·ly** *adv.* **—scur′vi·ness** *n.*

scut (skut) *n.* A short tail, as of a rabbit or deer. [ME, a tail, a hare]

scutch·eon (skuch′ən) *n.* ESCUTCHEON.

scu·tel·late (skyōō·tel′it, skyōō′tə·lāt) *adj. Zool.* Covered with small plates or scales: also **scu′tel·lat′ed** (-lā′tid). [< L *scutum* a shield]

scu·tel·lum (skyōō·tel′əm) *n. pl.* **·la** (-ə) A small protective plate or scale, as on the tarsus of a bird. [< L *scutum* a shield] **—scu·tel′lar** *adj.*

scut·tle[1] (skut′l) *n.* **1** A small opening or hatchway with movable lid or cover, esp. in the roof or wall of a house, or in the deck or side of a ship. **2** The lid closing such an opening. **—v.t. ·tled, ·tling 1** To sink (a ship) by making holes below the water line. **2** To wreck or destroy. [< MF *escoutille* a hatchway]

scut·tle[2] (skut′l) *n.* A metal vessel or hod for coal. [< OE *scutel* a dish, platter]

scut·tle[3] (skut′l) *v.i.* **·tled, ·tling** To run in haste; scurry. **—n.** A hurried run or departure. [?] **—scut′tler** *n.*

scut·tle·butt (skut′l·but) *n.* **1** A drinking fountain aboard ship. **2** *Slang* Rumor; gossip. [Orig. *scuttled butt*, a lidded cask for drinking water]

scu·tum (skyōō′təm) *n. pl.* **·ta** (-tə) **1** A large shield carried by Roman foot soldiers. **2** *Zool.* A large, horny protective plate or scale: also **scute.** [L] **—scu·tate** (skyōō′tāt) *adj.*

Scyl·la (sil′ə) *Gk. Myth.* A sea monster who dwelt in a cave on the Italian coast opposite the whirlpool Charybdis. **—between Scylla and Charybdis** Between two equally menacing situations, one of which must be dealt with.

scythe (sīth) *n.* A tool composed of a long curved blade fixed at an angle to a long handle, used for mowing, reaping, etc. **—v.t. scythed, scyth·ing** To cut with a scythe. [< OE *sithe*]

Scyth·i·a (sith′ē·ə) *n.* An ancient region of SE Europe, lying N of the Black Sea. **—Scyth′i·an** *adj., n.*

SD South Dakota (P.O. abbr.)

S.D., S. Dak. South Dakota.

SDR, S.D.R., SDRs, S.D.R.s Special Drawing Rights.

SE, S.E., se, s.e. southeast; southeastern.

Se selenium

sea (sē) *n.* **1** The great body of salt water covering most of the earth's surface; the ocean. **2** A large body of salt water partly or wholly enclosed by land: the Adriatic *Sea.* **3** An inland body of water, esp. if salty: the *Sea* of Galilee. **4** The state of the ocean with regard to the course, flow, swell, or turbulence of the waves. **5** A heavy wave or swell. **6** Anything vast or boundless that resembles or suggests the sea. **—at sea 1** On the ocean. **2** Bewildered. **—follow the sea** To follow the occupation of a sailor. **—put to sea** To sail away from the land [< OE *sæ*]

sea anemone Any of various soft-bodied, sessile marine polyps with tentacles resembling the petals of a flower.

sea bass Any of various carnivorous food fishes of U.S. coastal waters.

Sea·bee (sē′bē′) *n.* A member of one of the construction battalions of the U.S. Navy. [< *c(onstruction) b(attalion)*]

sea·board (sē′bôrd′, -bōrd′) *adj.* Bordering on the sea. **—n.** The seashore or seacoast and the adjoining region. [< SEA + *board* a border < OE *bord*]

Sea anemone
a. tentacles contracted. b. extended.

sea bread HARDTACK.

sea breeze A breeze blowing from the sea toward land.

sea calf A spotted seal of the E U.S. coast.

sea·coast (sē′kōst′) *n.* The land on or close to the sea.

sea cow 1 Any of various large aquatic mammals, as the manatee or the dugong. **2** WALRUS.

sea cucumber Any of various cylindrical echinoderms having a rosette of tentacles at the mouth.

sea dog 1 SEAL[2]. **2** DOGFISH. **3** A sailor with long experience at sea.

sea eagle Any of various fish-eating birds related to the bald eagle.

sea·far·er (sē′fâr′ər) *n.* A sailor; mariner.

sea·far·ing (sē′fâr′ing) *n.* **1** The occupation of a sailor. **2** Traveling over the sea. **—adj.** Of, pertaining to, given to, or engaged in seafaring.

sea·food (sē′fōōd′) *n.* Edible saltwater fish or shellfish.

sea·girt (sē′gûrt′) *adj.* Surrounded by the sea.

sea·go·ing (sē′gō′ing) *adj.* **1** Designed or adapted for use on the ocean. **2** SEAFARING.

sea green Bluish green.

sea gull A gull, esp. one of a widely distributed gregarious species.

sea horse 1 Any of various small fishes found in warm seas, having a long curled tail and a head resembling that of a horse. 2 A walrus. 3 A mythical creature, half horse and half fish.

sea king A viking pirate chief of the Middle Ages.

Sea horse

seal[1] (sēl) n. 1 An impression made on a letter, document, etc., to prove its authenticity. 2 A wax wafer, piece of paper, etc., bearing such an authenticating impression. 3 A device with a raised or cut initial, word, or design, used to make such an impression. 4 A stamp, ring, etc., bearing such a device. 5 Something used to close or secure a letter, door, lid, wrapper, joint, passage, etc., firmly. 6 Anything that confirms, ratifies, or guarantees; pledge. 7 A sign or indication; token. 8 An ornamental stamp for packages, etc. —v.t. 1 To affix a seal to, as to prove authenticity or prevent tampering. 2 To stamp or otherwise impress a seal upon in order to attest to weight, quality, etc. 3 To fasten or close with a seal: to *seal* a glass jar. 4 To confirm the genuineness or truth of, as a bargain. 5 To establish or settle finally. 6 To secure, set, or fill up, as with plaster. [< L *sigillum* a small picture, seal] —**seal'a·ble** *adj.* —**seal'er** *n.*

Great Seal of the United States

seal[2] (sēl) n. 1 Any of various species of sea mammals with a short tail and four webbed flippers, with which it swims and waddles ashore. 2 The commercially valued fur of the **fur seal**. 3 Leather made from the hide of a seal. —v.i. To hunt seals. [< OE *seolh*] —**seal'er** *n.*

Seal

sea legs The ability to walk aboard a ship in motion without losing one's balance or suffering from seasickness.

sea level The average level of the surface of the ocean.

sea lily CRINOID.

sealing wax A pigmented mixture of shellac and resin with turpentine that is fluid when heated but becomes solid as it cools: used to seal papers, etc.

sea lion One of various large, eared seals, esp. the California sea lion.

seal ring SIGNET RING.

seal·skin (sēl'skin') n. 1 The pelt or fur of the fur seal, often dyed dark brown or black. 2 An article made of this fur. —*adj.* Made of sealskin.

Sea·ly·ham terrier (sē'lē·ham, -əm) One of a breed of terriers with short legs, a wide skull, square jaws, and a wiry white coat. [Orig. bred in *Sealyham*, Wales]

seam (sēm) n. 1 A visible line of junction between parts, as the edges of two pieces of cloth sewn together. • See PINK[2]. 2 A line, ridge, or groove marking joined edges, as of boards. 3 Any similar line, ridge, etc., as that formed by a scar, wrinkle, etc. 4 A thin layer or stratum, as of rock or ore. —v.t. 1 To unite by means of a seam. 2 To mark with a cut, furrow, wrinkle, etc. —v.i. 3 To crack open; become fissured. [< OE *sēam*] —**seam'er** *n.*

sea·man (sē'mən) n. pl. **·men** (-mən) 1 An enlisted man in the navy or in the coast guard, graded according to his rank. 2 A mariner; sailor. —**sea'man·like'** (-līk') *adj.* —**sea'man·ly** *adj., adv.*

sea·man·ship (sē'mən·ship) n. The skill of a seaman in handling sea craft.

sea mew A gull, esp. the European mew.

sea·mount (sē'mount') n. A submarine mountain.

seam·stress (sēm'stris) n. A woman whose occupation is sewing. [< OE *sēam* seam + -ST(E)R + -ESS]

seam·y (sē'mē) adj. **seam·i·er, seam·i·est** 1 Like, formed by, or characterized by seams. 2 Showing an unworthy, unpleasant, or unpresentable aspect. —**seam'i·ness** n. —Syn. 2 sordid, degraded, squalid, disagreeable.

sé·ance (sā'äns) n. 1 A session or sitting. 2 A meeting of persons seeking to receive communications from spirits of the dead. [F < OF *seoir* sit]

sea·plane (sē'plān') n. An airplane that can take off from and land on the water.

sea·port (sē'pôrt', -pōrt') n. 1 A harbor or port accessible to seagoing ships. 2 A town or city located at such a place.

sea purse The leathery egg case of certain sharks, rays, etc.

sear (sir) v.t. 1 To wither; dry up. 2 To burn the surface of; scorch. 3 To burn or cauterize; brand. 4 To make callous; harden. —v.i. 5 To become withered; dry up. —*adj.* Dried or blasted; withered. —n. A scar or brand. [< OE *sēar* dry]

search (sûrch) v.t. 1 To look through or explore thoroughly in order to find something. 2 To subject (a person) to a search. 3 To examine with close attention; probe. 4 To penetrate or pierce: The wind *searches* my clothes. 5 To learn by examination or investigation: with *out*. —v.i. 6 To make a search. —n. 1 The act of searching. 2 An act of boarding and inspecting a ship in pursuance of the right to search. [< LL *circare* go round, explore] —**search'a·ble** *adj.* —**search'er** *n.*

search·ing (sûr'ching) adj. 1 Investigating thoroughly. 2 Keenly penetrating. —**search'ing·ly** *adv.* —**search'ing·ness** *n.*

search·light (sûrch'līt') n. 1 An apparatus consisting of a powerful light equipped with a reflector and mounted so that it can be projected in various directions. 2 The light so projected.

search warrant A warrant authorizing a police officer to search a house or other specified place, as for stolen goods.

sea·scape (sē'skāp') n. 1 A view of the sea. 2 A picture presenting such a view.

sea·shell (sē'shel') n. The shell of a marine mollusk.

sea·shore (sē'shôr', -shōr') n. Land bordering on the sea.

sea·sick (sē'sik') adj. Suffering from seasickness.

sea·sick·ness (sē'sik'nis) n. Nausea, dizziness, etc., caused by the motion of a ship at sea.

sea·side (sē'sīd') n. SEASHORE.

sea·son (sē'zən) n. 1 A division of the year as determined by the earth's position with respect to the sun: spring, summer, autumn, and winter. 2 A period of time. 3 A period of special activity or when a specified place is frequented: usu. with *the:* the opera *season;* the Palm Beach *season.* 4 A fit or suitable time. 5 The time of and surrounding a major holiday. —**in season** 1 At a time of availability and fitness, as for eating: Clams are *in season* during the summer. 2 In or at the right time. 3 Able to be killed or taken by permission of the law. 4 Ready to mate or breed: said of animals. —v.t. 1 To increase the flavor or zest of (food), as by adding spices, etc. 2 To add zest or piquancy to. 3 To render more suitable for use. 4 To make fit, as by discipline; harden. 5 To mitigate or soften; moderate. —v.i. 6 To become seasoned. [< LL *satio* sowing time] —**sea'son·er** *n.*

sea·son·a·ble (sē'zən·ə·bəl) adj. 1 Being in keeping with the season or circumstances. 2 Done or occurring at the proper or best time. —**sea'son·a·ble·ness** *n.* —**sea'son·a·bly** *adv.* —Syn. 1 timely, well-timed. 2 opportune, favorable, propitious, advantageous.

sea·son·al (sē'zən·əl) adj. Of, pertaining to, characteristic of, or happening during a season or the seasons. —**sea'son·al·ly** *adv.*

sea·son·ing (sē'zən·ing) n. 1 The process by which something is rendered fit for use. 2 Something added to give relish; esp., a condiment. 3 Something added to increase enjoyment, give zest, etc.

season ticket A ticket entitling the holder to something specified, as train trips, admission to entertainments, etc., during a certain period of time.

seat (sēt) n. **1** The thing on which one sits; a chair, bench, stool, etc. **2** That part of a thing upon which one rests in sitting, or upon which an object or another part rests. **3** That part of the person which sustains the weight of the body in sitting; buttocks. **4** That part of a garment which covers the buttocks. **5** The place where anything is situated or established: the *seat* of pain, the *seat* of a government. **6** A place of abode, esp. a large estate. **7** The privilege or right of membership in a legislative body, stock exchange, or the like. **8** The manner of sitting, as on horseback. **9** A surface or part upon which the base of anything rests. —*v.t.* **1** To place on a seat or seats; cause to sit down. **2** To have seats for; furnish with seats: The theater *seats* only 299 people. **3** To put a seat on or in; renew or repair the seat of. **4** To locate, settle, or center: usu. in the passive: The French government is *seated* in Paris. **5** To fix, set firmly, or establish in a certain position, place, etc. [< ON *sæti*]

seat belt A strap or harness that holds a passenger firmly in the seat, as while riding in a car or airplane.

seat·ing (sē′ting) n. **1** The act of providing with seats; also, the arrangement of such seats. **2** Fabric for upholstering seats. **3** A fitted support or base; a seat.

SEATO (sē′tō) Southeast Asia Treaty Organization.

sea urchin Any of various echinoderms shielded within a spine-covered, rounded case.

sea wall A wall for preventing erosion of the shore by the sea or for breaking the force of waves. —**sea-walled** (sē′wôld′) adj.

sea·ward (sē′wərd) adj. **1** Going or situated toward the sea. **2** Blowing, as wind, from the sea. —*adv.* In the direction of the sea: also **sea′wards**. —n. A direction or position toward the sea, away from land.

sea·way (sē′wā′) n. **1** A way or route over the sea. **2** An inland waterway that receives ocean shipping. **3** The headway made by a ship. **4** A rough sea.

sea·weed (sē′wēd′) n. Any marine plant or vegetation, esp. any multicellular alga.

sea·wor·thy (sē′wûr′thē) adj. In fit condition for a sea voyage. —**sea′wor′thi·ness** n.

se·ba·ceous (si·bā′shəs) adj. **1** Of, pertaining to, or resembling fat. **2** Secreting sebum. [< L *sebum* tallow]

se·bum (sē′bəm) n. An oily substance secreted by special glands in the skin. [L, tallow]

sec (sek) adj. *French* Dry: said of wines. Also *Italian* **sec·co** (sek′kō).

SEC, S.E.C. Securities and Exchange Commission.

sec. second(s); secondary; secretary; section(s); sector.

se·cant (sē′kant, -kənt) adj. Cutting, esp. into two parts; intersecting. —n. **1** *Geom.* A straight line intersecting a given curve. **2** *Trig.* A function equal to the reciprocal of the cosine. [< L *secare* to cut]

se·cede (si·sēd′) v.i. ·ced·ed, ·ced·ing To withdraw formally from a union, fellowship, etc., esp. from a political or religious organization. [< L *se-* apart + *cedere* go] — **se·ced′er** n.

se·ces·sion (si·sesh′ən) n. **1** The act of seceding. **2** *Usu. cap. U.S.* The withdrawal of the Southern States from the Union in 1860–61. —**se·ces′sion·al** adj. —**se·ces′·sion·ism, se·ces′sion·ist** n.

Ratio of AB to AD is the secant of angle BAD. AB is secant of arc CD.

Seck·el (sek′əl, sik′əl) n. A variety of small, sweet pear. Also **Seckel pear.** [< the Pennsylvania farmer who introduced it]

se·clude (si·klōōd′) v.t. ·clud·ed, ·clud·ing **1** To remove and keep apart from the society of others; isolate. **2** To screen or shut off, as from view. [< L *se-* apart + *claudere* to shut]

se·clud·ed (si·klōō′did) adj. **1** Separated; living apart from others. **2** Protected or screened. —**se·clud′ed·ly** adv. —**se·clud′ed·ness** n.

se·clu·sion (si·klōō′zhən) n. **1** The act of secluding, or the state or condition of being secluded; solitude; retirement. **2** A secluded place. —**se·clu′sive** adj. —**se·clu′sive·ly** adv. —**se·clu′sive·ness** n.

sec·ond¹ (sek′ənd) n. **1** A unit of time, 1/60 of a minute. **2** A unit of angular measure, 1/60 of a minute. **3** An instant; moment: Wait a *second*. [< Med. L *seconda (minuta)*, lit., second (minute), i.e., the result of the second sexagesimal division]

sec·ond² (sek′ənd) adj. **1** Next in order, authority, responsibility, etc., after the first. **2** Ranking next below the first or best. **3** Of lesser quality or value; inferior; subordinate. **4** Identical with another or preceding one; other. **5** *Music* Lower in pitch, or rendering a secondary part. —n. **1** The one next after the first, as in order, rank, importance, etc. **2** The element of an ordered set that corresponds to the number two. **3** An attendant who supports or aids another, as in a duel. **4** *Often pl.* An article of merchandise of inferior quality. **5** *Music* **a** The interval between any tone and another a whole step or half step away from or below it. **b** A subordinate part, instrument, or voice. **6** In parliamentary law, the act or declaration by which a motion is seconded: Do I hear a *second*? **7** *pl. Informal* A second portion of food. —*v.t.* **1** To act as a supporter or assistant of; promote; stimulate; encourage. **2** To support formally, as a motion, resolution, etc. —*adv.* In the second order, place, rank, etc. [< L *secundus* following]

sec·on·dar·y (sek′ən·der′ē) adj. **1** Of second rank, grade, or influence; subordinate. **2** Depending on, resulting from, or following what is primary. **3** Second in order of occurrence or development. **4** *Electr.* Of or pertaining to the output of a transformer. —n. pl. ·dar·ies **1** One who or that which is secondary or subordinate. **2** *Electr.* A secondary circuit or coil. —**sec′on·dar′i·ly** adv.

secondary accent See ACCENT.

secondary education Education beyond the elementary or primary, and below the college, level.

secondary school A school providing secondary education.

second best One who or that which is next after the best. —**sec′ond-best′** adj.

second childhood A time or condition of dotage; senility.

sec·ond-class (sek′ənd·klas′, -kläs′) adj. **1** Ranking next below the first or best; inferior, inadequate, etc. **2** Of, pertaining to, or belonging to a class next below the first: *second-class* mail, *second-class* ticket, etc. —*adv.* By using second-class travel accommodations or second-class mail.

sec·ond-guess (sek′ənd·ges′) v.t. **1** To use hindsight in criticizing (an action, decision, etc., or the person responsible for it). **2** OUTGUESS. —**sec′ond-guess′er** n.

sec·ond·hand (sek′ənd·hand′) adj. **1** Previously owned, worn, or used by another; not new. **2** Received from another; not direct from the original source: *secondhand* information. **3** Of, pertaining to, or dealing in merchandise that is not new. —*adv.* Indirectly.

second hand The hand that marks the seconds on a clock or a watch.

second lieutenant See GRADE.

sec·ond·ly (sek′ənd·lē) adv. In the second place; second.

second nature An acquired trait or habit so ingrained as to seem innate.

sec·ond-rate (sek′ənd·rāt′) adj. Second or inferior in quality, size, rank, importance, etc.; second-class. —**sec′·ond-rat′er** n.

second sight The supposed capacity to see objects not actually present, to see into the future, etc. —**sec′ond-sight′ed** adj.

sec·ond-sto·ry man (sek′ənd·stôr′ē, -stō′rē) *Informal* A burglar who enters a building through an upstairs window. Also **sec′ond-sto′ry-man.**

sec·ond-string (sek′ənd·string′) adj. *Informal* **1** In sports, being a substitute rather than a regular or starting player. **2** SECOND-RATE.

second thought A reevaluation or reconsideration of something following one's initial response or decision.

second wind **1** The return of easy breathing after a period of exertion or exercise. **2** A renewed capacity for the continuation of any effort.

se·cre·cy (sē′krə·sē) n. pl. ·cies **1** The condition or quality of being secret; concealment. **2** The character of being secretive.

se·cret (sē′krit) *adj.* 1 Kept separate or hidden from view or knowledge, or from all persons except the individuals concerned; unseen. 2 Affording privacy; secluded. 3 Good at keeping secrets; close-mouthed. 4 Unrevealed or unavowed: a *secret* partner. 5 Not revealed to everyone; mysterious; esoteric. —*n.* 1 Something known only by a few people. 2 Something that is not explained or is kept hidden; mystery. 3 An underlying reason; key. —**in secret** In privacy; in a hidden place. [< L *se-* apart + *cernere* to separate] —**se′cret·ly** *adv.*

sec·re·tar·i·at (sek′rə·târ′ē·it, -at) *n.* 1 A secretary's position. 2 The place where a secretary transacts business and keeps records. 3 The entire staff of secretaries in an office; esp., a department headed by a secretary-general.

sec·re·tar·y (sek′rə·ter′ē) *n. pl.* ·**tar·ies** 1 An employee who deals with correspondence, records, and clerical business for a person, business, committee, etc. 2 An official in a business, club, etc., who has overall responsibility for somewhat similar work. 3 An executive officer presiding over and managing a department of government. 4 A writing desk with a bookcase on top. [< L *secretum* a secret] —**sec′re·tar′i·al** (-târ′ē·əl) *adj.*

secretary bird A large, predatory African bird having a crest resembling quill pens stuck behind the ear.

secretary general *pl.* **secretaries general** A chief administrative officer, esp. the head of a secretariat.

sec·re·tar·y·ship (sek′rə·ter′ē·ship) *n.* The work or position of a secretary.

se·crete (si·krēt′) *v.t.* ·**cret·ed**, ·**cret·ing** 1 To remove or keep from observation; conceal; hide. 2 *Biol.* To form and release (an enzyme, hormone, etc.). [Alter. of obs. *secret*, to conceal] —**se·cre′tor** *n.*

se·cre·tion (si·krē′shən) *n.* 1 *Biol.* The cellular process by which materials are separated from blood or sap and converted into new substances: the *secretion* of milk, urine, etc. 2 The substance secreted. 3 The act of concealing or hiding.

se·cre·tive (sē′krə·tiv, si·krē′tiv) *adj.* 1 Having or showing a disposition to secrecy. 2 (si·krē′tiv) SECRETORY. —**se′cre·tive·ly** *adv.* —**se′cre·tive·ness** *n.*

se·cre·to·ry (si·krē′tər·ē) *adj.* Of, pertaining to, causing, or produced by secretion (def. 1).

secret service A department of the government concerned with work of a secret nature.

Secret Service A division of the U.S. Treasury Department concerned with the suppression of counterfeiting, the protection of the President, etc.

sect (sekt) *n.* 1 A religious denomination, esp. a body of dissenters from an ·established or older form of faith. 2 Adherents of a particular philosophical system or teacher, esp. a faction of a larger group. [< L *sequi* follow]

sect. section; sectional.

sec·tar·i·an (sek·târ′ē·ən) *adj.* 1 Of, pertaining to, or characteristic of a sect. 2 Having devotion to or prejudice in favor of a sect. 3 Narrow-minded; limited; parochial. —*n.* 1 A member of a sect. 2 A person who is blindly devoted to a sect or factional viewpoint. —**sec·tar′i·an·ism′** *n.*

sec·ta·ry (sek′tər·ē) *n. pl.* ·**ries** A member of a sect.

sec·tion (sek′shən) *n.* 1 The act of cutting; a separating by cutting. 2 A slice or portion separated by or as if by cutting. 3 A separate part or division, as of a book or chapter. 4 A distinct part of a country, community, etc. 5 *U.S.* An area of land one square mile in extent and constituting 1/36 of a township. 6 A portion of a railroad's right of way under the care of a particular crew of men. 7 In a sleeping-car, a space containing two berths. 8 A representation of an object, as if cut by an intersecting plane. —*v.t.* 1 To divide into sections. 2 To shade (a drawing) so as to designate a section or sections. [< L *sectus*, p.p. of *secare* to cut]

sec·tion·al (sek′shən·əl) *adj.* 1 Of, pertaining to, or characteristic of a section. 2 Made up of sections. —**sec′tion·al·ly** *adv.*

sec·tion·al·ism (sek′shən·əl·iz′əm) *n.* Exaggerated concern for a particular section of a country rather than the whole. —**sec′tion·al·ist** *n.*

sec·tor (sek′tər) *n.* 1 *Geom.* A part of a circle bounded by two radii and the arc subtended by them. 2 *Mil.* **a** A part of a front in contact with the enemy. **b** Any of the subdivisions of a defensive position. 3 A distinct part, as of a society. —*v.t.* To divide into sectors. [< L *sectus*, p.p. of *secare* to cut] —**sec·to·ri·al** (-tôr′ē·əl, -tō′rē-) *adj.*

ACB is a sector of the circle.

sec·u·lar (sek′yə·lər) *adj.* 1 Of or pertaining to this world; temporal; worldly. 2 Not controlled by the church; civil; not ecclesiastical. 3 Not concerned with religion; not sacred: *secular* art. 4 Not bound by monastic vows, and not living in a religious community. 5 Of or describing a trend or process continuing for a long, indefinite period of time. —*n.* 1 A member of the clergy who is not bound by monastic vows and who does not live in a religious community. 2 A layman as distinguished from a member of the clergy. [< L *saeculum* generation, age]

sec·u·lar·ism (sek′yə·lə·riz′əm) *n.* 1 Regard for worldly as opposed to spiritual matters. 2 The belief that religion should not be introduced into public education or public affairs. —**sec′u·lar·ist** *n.* —**sec′u·lar·is′tic** *adj.*

sec·u·lar·ize (sek′yə·lə·rīz′) *v.t.* ·**ized**, ·**iz·ing** 1 To make secular; convert from sacred to secular possession or uses. 2 To make worldly. 3 To change (a regular clergyman) to a secular. —**sec′u·lar·i·za′tion** *n.*

se·cure (si·kyo͝or′) *adj.* ·**cur·er**, ·**cur·est** 1 Free from or not likely to be exposed to danger, theft, etc.; safe. 2 Free from fear, apprehension, etc. 3 Confident; certain. 4 In a state or condition that will not break, come unfastened, etc.: Is the door *secure?* 5 Reliable; steady; dependable: a *secure* job. —*v.* ·**cured**, ·**cur·ing** *v.t.* 1 To make secure; protect. 2 To make firm, tight, or fast; fasten. 3 To make sure or certain; insure; guarantee. 4 To obtain possession of; get. —*v.i.* 5 To stop working: said of a ship's crew. 6 To berth; moor: said of a ship. [< L *se-* without + *cura* care] —**se·cur′a·ble** *adj.* —**se·cure′ly** *adv.* —**se·cure′ness, se·cur′er** *n.*

se·cu·ri·ty (si·kyo͝or′ə·tē) *n. pl.* ·**ties** 1 The state of being secure; freedom from danger, risk, care, poverty, doubt, etc. 2 One who or that which secures or guarantees; surety. 3 *pl.* Written promises or something deposited or pledged for payment of money, as stocks, bonds, etc. 4 Defense or protection against espionage, attack, escape, etc. 5 Measures calculated to provide such defense or protection. 6 An organization or division of one charged with providing for safety and protection.

Security Council A permanent organ of the United Nations charged with the maintenance of international peace and security.

secy., sec′y. secretary.

se·dan (si·dan′) *n.* 1 A closed automobile having one compartment, front and rear seats, and two or four doors. 2 A closed chair, for one passenger, carried by two men by means of poles at the sides: also **sedan chair.** [?]

Sedan def. 2

se·date (si·dāt′) *adj.* Not disturbed by excitement, passion, etc. [< L *sedare* make calm, settle] —**se·date′ly** *adv.* —**se·date′ness** *n.* —**Syn.** calm, composed, staid.

se·da·tion (si·dā′shən) *n.* The reduction of sensitivity to pain, stress, etc., by administering a sedative.

sed·a·tive (sed′ə·tiv) *adj.* Tending to calm or soothe; esp., acting to allay nervousness or emotional agitation. —*n.* A sedative medicine.

sed·en·tar·y (sed′ən·ter′ē) *adj.* 1 Accustomed to sit much or to work in a sitting posture. 2 Characterized by sitting. 3 Remaining in one place; not migratory. 4 Attached or fixed to an object. [< L *sedere* sit] —**sed′en·tar′i·ly** *adv.* —**sed′en·tar′i·ness** *n.*

Se·der (sā′dər) *n. pl.* **Se·da·rim** (sə·där′im) or **Se·ders** In Judaism, a ceremonial dinner commemorating the Exodus, held on the eve of the first day of Passover, and traditionally on the eve of the second day by Jews outside of Israel. [< Heb. *sēdher* order]

sedge (sej) *n.* Any of a large family of grasslike plants growing in wet ground and usu. having triangular, solid stems and tiny flowers in spikes. [< OE *secg*] —**sedged, sedg′y** *adj.*

sed·i·ment (sed′ə·mənt) *n.* 1 Matter that settles to the bottom of a liquid; dregs; lees. 2 *Geol.* Fragmentary material deposited by water, ice, or air. [< L *sedere* sit, settle] **sed′i·men·ta′tion** *n.*

sed·i·men·ta·ry (sed′ə·men′tər·ē) *adj.* 1 Of, pertaining to, or having the character of sediment. 2 *Geol.* Designating rocks composed of compacted sediment. Also **sed′i·men′tal.**

se·di·tion (si·dish′ən) *n.* The incitement and act of resistance to or revolt against lawful authority. [< L *sed-* aside + *itio* a going]

se·di·tious (si·dish′əs) *adj.* 1 Of, pertaining to, or having the character of sedition. 2 Inclined to, taking part in, or guilty of sedition. —**se·di′tious·ly** *adv.* —**se·di′tious·ness** *n.*

se·duce (si·dyoōs′) *v.t.* **·duced, ·duc·ing** 1 To lead astray, as from a proper or right course: *seduced* by quick profits. 2 To entice into wrong, disloyalty, etc.; tempt. 3 To induce to have sexual intercourse. [< L *se-* apart + *ducere* lead] —**se·duc′er** *n.* —**se·duc′i·ble** or **se·duce′a·ble** *adj.*

se·duc·tion (si·duk′shən) *n.* 1 The act of seducing or the condition of being seduced. 2 Something which seduces; an enticement. Also **se·duce′ment.**

se·duc·tive (si·duk′tiv) *adj.* Tending to seduce. —**se·duc′tive·ly** *adv.* —**se·duc′tive·ness** *n.*

sed·u·lous (sej′oō·ləs) *adj.* 1 Constant in application or attention; assiduous. 2 Diligent; industrious. [< L *se dolo* without guile] —**sed′u·lous·ly** *adv.* —**sed′u·lous·ness** *n.*

se·dum (sē′dəm) *n.* Any of a large genus of chiefly creeping or mat-forming plants with fleshy leaves, adapted to rocky terrain. [L, house leek]

see[1] (sē) *v.* **saw, seen, see·ing** *v.t.* 1 To perceive with the eyes; gain knowledge or awareness of by means of one's vision. 2 To perceive with the mind; comprehend. 3 To find out or ascertain; inquire about: *See* who is at the door. 4 To have experience or knowledge of; undergo: We have *seen* more peaceful times. 5 To encounter; chance to meet: I *saw* your husband today. 6 To have a meeting or interview with; visit or receive as a guest, visitor, etc.: The doctor will *see* you now. 7 To attend as a spectator; view. 8 To accompany; escort. 9 To take care; be sure: *See* that you do it! 10 In poker, to accept (a bet) or equal the bet of (a player) by betting an equal sum. —*v.i.* 11 To have or exercise the power of sight. 12 To find out; inquire. 13 To understand; comprehend. 14 To think; consider. 15 To take care; be attentive: *See* to your work. 16 To gain certain knowledge, as by awaiting an outcome: We will *see* if you are right. —**see about** 1 To inquire into the facts, causes, etc., of. 2 To take care of; attend to. —**see through** 1 To perceive the real meaning or nature of. 2 To aid or protect, as throughout a period of danger. 3 To finish. [< OE *sēon*]

see[2] (sē) *n.* 1 The official seat from which a bishop exercises jurisdiction. 2 The authority or jurisdiction of a bishop. [< L *sedes* a seat]

seed (sēd) *n.* 1 The ovule containing an embryo from which a plant may be reproduced. 2 That from which anything springs; source. 3 Offspring; children. 4 The male fertilizing element; semen; sperm. 5 Any small granular fruit, singly or collectively. —*v.t.* 1 To sow with seed. 2 To sow (seed). 3 To remove the seeds from: to *seed* raisins. 4 To strew (moisture-bearing clouds) with crystals, as of dry ice, silver iodide, etc., in order to initiate precipitation. 5 In sports: **a** To arrange (the drawing for positions in a tournament, etc.) so that the more skilled competitors meet only in the later events. **b** To rank (a skilled competitor) thus. —*v.i.* 6 To sow seed. 7 To grow to maturity and produce or shed seed. —**go to seed** 1 To develop and shed seed. 2 To become shabby, useless, etc.; deteriorate. [< OE *sæd*] —**seed′er** *n.* —**seed′less** *adj.*

seed·bed (sēd′bed′) *n.* 1 A protected bed of earth planted

with seeds for later transplanting. 2 A place of early growth or nurture.

seed·case (sēd′kās′) *n.* SEED VESSEL.

seed coat The integument of a seed. • See EMBRYO.

seed leaf COTYLEDON.

seed·ling (sēd′ling) *n.* 1 Any plant grown from seed. 2 A very small or young tree or plant.

seed oyster A young oyster, esp. one transplanted from one bed to another.

seed pearl A small pearl, esp. one used for ornamenting bags, etc., or in embroidery.

seed plant A plant which bears seeds.

seed vessel A pericarp, esp. one that is dry, as a pod.

seed·y (sē′dē) *adj.* **seed·i·er, seed·i·est** 1 Abounding with seeds. 2 Gone to seed. 3 Poor and ragged; shabby. 4 Feeling or looking wretched. —**seed′i·ly** *adv.* —**seed′i·ness** *n.*

see·ing (sē′ing) *conj.* Since; in view of the fact; considering.

Seeing Eye dog The name used for a dog trained to lead the blind, esp. one trained by an organization (Seeing Eye) in New Jersey: a trade name.

seek (sēk) *v.* **sought, seek·ing** *v.t.* 1 To go in search of; look for. 2 To strive for; try to get. 3 To endeavor or try: He *seeks* to mislead me. 4 To ask or inquire for; request: to *seek* information. 5 To go to; betake oneself to: to *seek* a warmer climate. —*v.i.* 6 To make a search or inquiry. [< OE *sēcan*] —**seek′er** *n.*

seem (sēm) *v.i.* 1 To give the impression of being; appear. 2 To appear to oneself: I *seem* to remember her face. 3 To appear to exist: There *seems* no reason for hesitating. 4 To be evident or apparent: It *seems* to be raining. [< ON *sæma* honor, conform to]

seem·ing (sē′ming) *adj.* Having the appearance of reality but often not so: Her *seeming* nonchalance was solely due to three martinis. —*n.* Appearance; semblance; esp., false show. —**seem′ing·ly** *adv.* —**seem′ing·ness** *n.*

seem·ly (sēm′lē) *adj.* **·li·er, ·li·est** 1 Befitting the proprieties; becoming; proper; decorous. 2 Handsome; attractive. —*adv.* Becomingly; appropriately. [< ON *sæmr* fitting] —**seem′li·ness** *n.*

seen (sēn) *p.p.* of SEE.

seep (sēp) *v.i.* To soak through pores or small openings; ooze. [< OE *sipian* soak] —**seep′y** *adj.*

seep·age (sē′pij) *n.* 1 The act or process of seeping; oozing; leakage. 2 The fluid that seeps.

seer (sē′ər *for def. 1;* sir *for def. 2*) *n.* 1 One who sees. 2 One who foretells events; a prophet. [< SEE[1] + -ER]

seer·suck·er (sir′suk′ər) *n.* A thin fabric, often striped, with crinkled surface. [< Pers. *shīr o shakkar*, lit., milk and sugar]

see·saw (sē′sô′) *n.* 1 A game or contest in which persons sit or stand on opposite ends of a board balanced at the middle and make it move up and down. 2 A board balanced for this sport. 3 Any up-and-down or to-and-fro movement, tendency, change, etc. —*v.t. & v.i.* To move on or as if on a seesaw. —*adj.* Moving up and down or to and fro. [Reduplication of SAW[1]]

seethe (sēth) *v.* **seethed, seeth·ing** *v.i.* 1 To boil. 2 To foam or bubble as if boiling. 3 To be agitated, as by rage. —*v.t.* 4 To soak in liquid; steep. 5 *Archaic* To boil. —*n.* The act or condition of seething. [< OE *sēothan*]

seg·ment (seg′mənt) *n.* 1 A part cut off or distinct from the other parts of anything: a section. 2 *Geom.* A part of a line or curve lying between two of its points. —*v.t. & v.i.* To divide into segments. [< L *secare* to cut] —**seg·men·tal** (seg·men′təl) *adj.* —**seg·men′tal·ly** *adv.* —**seg·men·tar·y** (seg′mən·ter′ē) *adj.*

seg·men·ta·tion (seg′mən·tā′shən) *n.* 1 Division into segments. 2 The process of repeated cleavage whereby a complex organism develops from a single cell.

se·go (sē′gō) *n. pl.* **·gos** 1 A perennial plant of the lily family, having bell-shaped flowers. 2 Its edible bulb. Also **sego lily.** [< Ute]

seg·re·gate (seg′rə·gāt) *v.* **·gat·ed, ·gat·ing** *v.t.* 1 To place apart from others or the rest; isolate. 2 To cause the separation of (a race, social class, etc.) from the general mass of society or from a larger group. —*v.i.* 3 To separate from a mass and gather about nuclei, as in crystallization. —*adj.* (-git) Separated or set apart from others; segregated.

[< L *se-* apart + *grex* a flock] —**seg're·ga'tive** *adj.* —**seg're·ga'tor** *n.*

seg·re·ga·tion (seg'rə·gā'shən) *n.* **1** A segregating or being segregated or process of segregating. **2** The act or policy of separating a race, social class, etc., from the general mass of society or from a larger group.

Seid·litz powders (sed'lits) An effervescent mixture of salts, used as a laxative. Also **Seidlitz powder.** [< similarity to spring water in *Seidlitz,* Czechoslovakia]

sei·gnior (sān·yôr', sān'yər) *n.* A man of rank, esp. a feudal lord. Also **sei·gneur** (sān'yər). [< L *senior* older] —**sei·gnio'ri·al** *adj.*

seign·ior·y (sān'yər·ē) *n. pl.* **·ior·ies** The territory, rights, or jurisdiction of a seignior.

seine (sān) *n.* Any long fishing net, having floats at the top edge and weights at the bottom. —*v.t. & v.i.* **seined, sein·ing** To fish or catch with a seine. [< Gk. *sagēnē* a fishing net]

seis·mic (sīz'mik, sīs'-) *adj.* Of, pertaining to, subject to, or produced by an earthquake or earthquakes. Also **seis'·mal, seis'mi·cal.** [< Gk. *seismos* earthquake.]

seismo- *combining form* Earthquake: *seismograph.* [< Gk. *seismos* an earthquake]

seis·mo·gram (sīz'mə·gram, sīs'-) *n.* The record made by a seismograph.

seis·mo·graph (sīz'mə·graf, -gräf, sīs'-) *n.* An instrument for automatically recording the movements of the earth's crust. —**seis'mo·graph'ic** *adj.* —**seis·mog·ra·pher** (sīz·mog'rə·fər, sīs-), **seis·mog'ra·phy** *n.*

seis·mol·o·gy (sīz·mol'ə·jē, sīs-) *n.* The science dealing with earthquakes and related phenomena. —**seis·mo·log·ic** (sīz'mə·loj'ik, sīs'-) or **·i·cal** *adj.* —**seis'mo·log'i·cal·ly** *adv.* —**seis·mol'o·gist** *n.*

seize (sēz) *v.* **seized, seiz·ing** *v.t.* **1** To take hold of suddenly and forcibly; clutch; grasp. **2** To grasp mentally; understand. **3** To take possession of by authority or right. **4** To take possession of by or as by force. **5** To take prisoner; capture. **6** To act upon with sudden and powerful effect; attack; strike. **7** To take advantage of immediately, as an opportunity. **8** *Naut.* To fasten or bind by turns of cord, line, or small rope; lash. —*v.i.* **9** To take hold or make use: usu. with *on* or *upon.* [< OF *saisir, seisir*] —**seiz'a·ble** *adj.* —**seiz'er** *n.*

sei·zure (sē'zhər) *n.* **1** The act of seizing or the state of being seized. **2** A sudden incapacitation, as by disease.

se·lah (sē'lə) *n.* A Hebrew word of unknown meaning in the Psalms, usu. considered as a direction to readers or musicians.

sel·dom (sel'dəm) *adv.* At widely separated intervals, as of time or space; infrequently; rarely. —*adj.* Infrequent; rare. [< OE *seldan*]

se·lect (si·lekt') *v.t.* **1** To take in preference to another or others; pick out; choose. —*v.i.* **2** To choose. —*adj.* **1** Chosen in preference to others. **2** Excellent; superior; choice. **3** Exclusive. **4** Very particular in selecting. [< L *se-* apart + *legere* choose] —**se·lect'ness, se·lec'tor** *n.*

se·lec·tee (si·lek'tē') *n.* One called up for military service under selective service.

se·lec·tion (si·lek'shən) *n.* **1** A selecting or being selected. **2** Anything selected. **3** *Biol.* Any process, natural or artificial, which determines the survival of specific characteristics.

se·lec·tive (si·lek'tiv) *adj.* **1** Of, pertaining to, or characterized by selection. **2** Having the power or tendency to select. **3** Having or characterized by good selectivity, as a radio receiver. —**se·lec·tive·ly** *adv.* —**se·lec'tive·ness** *n.*

selective service Compulsory military service according to specified conditions of age, fitness, etc. —**se·lec'·tive·ser'vice** *adj.*

se·lec·tiv·i·ty (si·lek'tiv'ə·tē) *n.* **1** The state or condition

Seismograph

a. concrete base. b. clock. c. seismogram. d. stylus. e. weight. f. spring suspension.

of being selective. **2** *Telecom.* That characteristic of a radio receiver or filter by which frequencies can be sharply discriminated.

se·lect·man (si·lekt'mən) *n. pl.* **·men** (-mən) One of a board of town officers, elected annually in New England, except in Rhode Island, to manage local affairs.

sel·e·nite (sel'ə·nīt) *n.* A crystalline form of gypsum. [< Gk. *selēnītēs (lithos),* lit., moon(stone); so called because it was thought to wax and wane with the moon]

se·le·ni·um (si·lē'nē·əm) *n.* A nonmetallic element (symbol Se) of variable electrical resistance under the influence of light and having several allotropic forms. [< Gk. *selēnē* the moon]

self (self) *n. pl.* **selves** **1** One's own person known or considered as the subject of his own consciousness. **2** The distinct and characteristic individuality or identity of any person or thing. **3** Personal interest or advantage. —*adj.* **1** Being uniform or of the same quality throughout. **2** Of the same kind (as in material, color, etc.,) as something else: a coat with a *self* belt. —*pron.* Myself, yourself, himself, or herself. [< OE]

self- *combining form* **1** Of oneself or itself: *self-analysis.* **2** By oneself or itself: *self-employed.* **3** In oneself or itself: *self-absorbed.* **4** To, with, for, or toward oneself: *self-satisfied.* **5** In or of oneself or itself inherently: *self-evident.*

self-ab·ne·ga·tion (self'ab'ni·gā'shən) *n.* The complete putting aside of self-interest. —**Syn.** self-sacrifice, self-denial, self-control, self-restraint.

self-a·buse (self'ə·byōōs') *n.* **1** The disparagement of one's own person or powers. **2** MASTURBATION.

self-ad·dressed (self'ə·drest') *adj.* Addressed to oneself.

self-as·sured (self'ə·shŏŏrd') *adj.* Confident in one's own abilities. —**self'-as·sur'ance** *n.*

self-cen·tered (self'sen'tərd) *adj.* Concerned exclusively with oneself and one's own needs and desires.

self-com·mand (self'kə·mand', -mänd') *n.* SELF-CONTROL.

self-con·fi·dence (self'kon'fə·dəns) *n.* Confidence in oneself or in one's own unaided powers, judgment, etc. — **self'-con'fi·dent** *adj.* —**self'-con'fi·dent·ly** *adv.*

self-con·scious (self'kon'shəs) *adj.* **1** Uncomfortably conscious that one is observed by others; ill at ease. **2** Displaying such consciousness: a *self-conscious* giggle. **3** Conscious of one's existence. —**self'-con'scious·ly** *adv.* — **self'-con'scious·ness** *n.*

self-con·tained (self'kən·tānd') *adj.* **1** Keeping one's thoughts and feelings to oneself; impassive. **2** Exercising self-control. **3** Having within oneself or itself all that is necessary for independent existence or operation.

self-con·tra·dic·tion (self'kon'trə·dik'shən) *n.* **1** The contradicting of oneself or itself. **2** A statement, proposition, etc., that contradicts itself. —**self'-con'tra·dic'to·ry** *adj.*

self-con·trol (self'kən·trōl') *n.* Control of one's impulses, emotions, etc.

self-de·fense (self'di·fens') *n.* Defense of oneself, one's property, one's reputation, etc. —**self'-de·fen'sive** *adj.*

self-de·ni·al (self'di·nī'əl) *n.* The restraining of one's desires, impulses, etc. —**self'-de·ny'ing** *adj.*

self-de·ter·mi·na·tion (self'di·tûr'mə·nā'shən) *n.* **1** The principle of free will; decision by oneself without extraneous force or influence. **2** Decision by the people of a country or section as to its future political status. —**self'-de·ter'mined, self'-de·ter'min·ing** *adj.*

self-de·vo·tion (self'di·vō'shən) *n.* The devoting of oneself to the service of a person or a cause.

self-ed·u·cat·ed (self'ej'ŏŏ·kā'tid) *adj.* Educated through one's own efforts with little or no formal instruction. —**self'-ed'u·ca'tion** *n.*

self-es·teem (self'es·tēm') *n.* **1** A good or just opinion of oneself. **2** An overestimate of oneself; conceit.

self-ev·i·dent (self'ev'ə·dənt) *adj.* Requiring no proof of its truth or validity. —**self'-ev'i·dence** *n.* —**self'-ev'i·dent·ly** *adv.*

self-ex·ist·ence (self'ig·zis'təns) *n.* Existence that is independent, without external cause. —**self'-ex·ist'ent** adj.

self-ex·plan·a·to·ry (self'ik·splan'ə·tôr·ē, -tō'rē) adj. Explaining itself; needing no explanation.

self-ex·pres·sion (self'ik·spresh'ən) n. Expression of one's own personality or individuality, as in art.

self-fer·til·i·za·tion (self'fûr'təl·ə·zā'shən, -ī·zā'shən) n. Fertilization of an organism by its own sperm or pollen.

self-gov·ern·ment (self'guv'ərn·mənt, -ər·mənt) n. 1 Self-control. 2 Government of a country or region by its own people. —**self'-gov'ern·ing, self'-gov'erned** adj.

self·heal (self'hēl') n. A weedy perennial herb reputed to cure disease.

self-im·age (self'im'ij) n. The image or idea one has of oneself or of one's position in life.

self-im·por·tance (self'im·pôr'təns) n. An excessively high appraisal of one's own importance; conceit. —**self'-im·por'tant** adj.

self-in·duced (self'in·dyōōst') adj. 1 Induced by oneself or by itself. 2 Produced by self-induction.

self-in·duc·tion (self'in·duk'shən) n. The production of an induced voltage in a circuit by the variation of the current in that circuit.

self-in·ter·est (self'in'trist, -in'tər·ist) n. Personal interest or advantage, or concern for it; selfishness. —**self'-in'ter·est·ed** adj.

self·ish (sel'fish) adj. 1 Motivated by personal needs and desires to the disregard of the welfare or wishes of others. 2 Proceeding from or characterized by undue concern for self. —**self'ish·ly** adv. —**self'ish·ness** n.

self·less (self'lis) adj. Having, showing, or prompted by a lack of concern for self. —**Syn.** unselfish, altruistic, self-sacrificing, self-denying.

self-load·ing (self'lō'ding) adj. Automatically reloading: said of a gun using the energy of recoil to eject and reload.

self-love (self'luv') n. Love of oneself; the desire or tendency to seek to promote one's own well-being.

self-made (self'mād') adj. 1 Having attained honor, wealth, etc., by one's own efforts. 2 Made by oneself.

self-pol·li·na·tion (self'pol'ə·nā'shən) n. Pollen transfer from stamens to pistils of the same flower, plant, or clone. —**self'-pol'li·na·ted** adj.

self-pos·ses·sion (self'pə·zesh'ən) n. The full possession or control of one's powers or faculties; presence of mind; self-control. —**self'-pos·sessed'** adj.

self-pres·er·va·tion (self'prez'ər·vā'shən) n. 1 The protection of oneself from injury or death. 2 The instinctive drive to protect oneself.

self-pro·nounc·ing (self'prə·noun'sing) adj. Having marks of pronunciation and stress applied to a word without phonetic alteration of the spelling.

self-re·li·ance (self'ri·lī'əns) n. Reliance on one's own abilities, resources, or judgment. —**self'-re·li'ant** adj. —**self'-re·li'ant·ly** adv.

self-re·spect (self'ri·spekt') n. A proper respect for oneself, one's standing, position, etc. —**self'-re·spect'ing, self'-re·spect'ful** adj. —**self'-re·spect'ful·ly** adv.

self-re·straint (self'ri·strānt') n. Restraint imposed by the force of one's own will; self-control. —**self'-re·strained'** adj.

self-right·eous (self'rī'chəs) adj. Having or showing a high, usu. smug, opinion of one's own moral superiority. —**self'-right'eous·ly** adv. —**self'-right'eous·ness** n.

self-ris·ing (self'rī'zing) adj. Rising without the addition of leaven, as some flours.

self-sac·ri·fice (self'sak'rə·fīs) n. The subordination of one's self or one's personal welfare or wishes for others' good, for duty, etc. —**self'-sac'ri·fic'ing** adj.

self·same (self'sām') adj. Exactly the same; identical. —**self'same'ness** n.

self-sat·is·fac·tion (self'sat'is·fak'shən) n. Satisfaction with one's own actions, characteristics, etc.; conceit. —**self'-sat'is·fied** adj. —**self'-sat'is·fy'ing** adj.

self-seek·ing (self'sē'king) adj. Given to the exclusive pursuit of one's own interests or gain. —n. Such a pursuit; selfishness. —**self'-seek'er** n.

self-ser·vice (self'sûr'vis) adj. Designating a particular type of café, restaurant, or store where patrons serve themselves.

self-serv·ing (self'sûr'ving) adj. Tending to justify or advance oneself, often at the expense of others.

self-start·er (self'stär'tər) n. 1 An engine or device with an automatic or semi-automatic starting mechanism; also, such a mechanism. 2 *Slang* One who requires no outside stimulus to start or accomplish work. —**self'-start'ing** adj.

self-styled (self'stīld') adj. Characterized (as such) by oneself: a *self-styled* gentleman.

self-suf·fi·cient (self'sə·fish'ənt) adj. 1 Able to support or maintain oneself without aid or cooperation from others. 2 Having too much confidence in oneself. Also **self'-suf·fic'ing** (-sə·fī'sing). —**self'-suf·fi'cien·cy** n.

self-sup·port·ing (self'sə·pôrt'ing) adj. 1 Capable of supporting itself or its own weight. 2 Able to provide for oneself, as with money, lodging, clothing, etc.

self-will (self'wil') n. Persistent adherence to one's own will or wish, esp. with disregard of the wishes of others; obstinacy. —**self'-willed'** adj.

self-wind·ing (self'wīn'ding) adj. Having an automatic winding mechanism, as some watches.

sell (sel) v. **sold, sell·ing** v.t. 1 To transfer (property) to another for a consideration; dispose of by sale. 2 To deal in; offer for sale. 3 To deliver, surrender, or betray in violation of duty or trust: often with *out*: to *sell* one's country. 4 *Informal* To cause to accept or approve something: They sold him on the scheme. 5 *Informal* To cause or promote the acceptance, approval, or sale of. 6 *Slang* To deceive; cheat. —v.i. 7 To engage in selling. 8 To be on sale or be sold. 9 To work as a salesperson. 10 To be popular with buyers, customers, etc. —**sell out** 1 To get rid of (one's goods, etc.) by sale. 2 *Informal* To betray one's trust, cause, associates, etc. —n. 1 *Slang* A trick; joke; swindle. 2 An act or instance of selling. [< OE *sellan* give]

sell·er (sel'ər) n. 1 One who sells. 2 An item that is being sold, considered in reference to its sales.

sell-out (sel'out') n. *Informal* 1 An act of selling out. 2 A performance for which all seats have been sold.

selt·zer (selt'sər) n. An artificially prepared mineral water that contains carbon dioxide. [< SELTZER]

Selt·zer (selt'sər) n. An effervescing mineral water. Also **Seltzer water.** [< Nieder *Selters,* a village in sw Prussia]

sel·vage (sel'vij) n. The edge of a woven fabric so finished that it will not ravel. Also **sel'vedge.** [< SELF + EDGE]

Sem. Seminary; Semitic.

se·man·tic (si·man'tik) adj. 1 Of or pertaining to meaning. 2 Of, relating to, or according to semantics. [< Gk. *sēmainein* signify]

se·man·tics (si·man'tiks) n. pl. (construed as sing.) 1 *Ling.* The study of the meanings of speech forms, esp. of the development and changes in meaning of words and word groups. 2 *Logic* The study of the relation between signs or symbols and what they signify. —**se·man'ti·cist** n.

sem·a·phore (sem'ə·fôr, -fōr) n. An apparatus for giving signals, as with movable arms, disks, flags, or lanterns. —v.t. To send by semaphore. [< Gk. *sēma* a sign + *pherein* carry] —**sem'a·phor'ic** (-fôr'ik, -for'ik) or **·i·cal** adj.

sem·blance (sem'bləns) n. 1 An outward, sometimes deceptive appearance; look. 2 A representation, likeness, or resemblance. 3 The barest trace; modicum. [< OF *sembler* seem]

se·men (sē'mən) n. The sperm-containing fluid of male animals. [< L *serere* sow]

Semaphore
a. clear. b. approach.
c. stop.

se·mes·ter (si·mes'tər) n. Either of the two periods of approximately 18 weeks into which an academic year is divided. [< L *sex* six + *mensis* month] —**se·mes'tral** adj.

semi- *prefix* 1 Partly; not fully: *semicivilized.* 2 Exactly half: *semicircle.* 3 Occurring twice (in the period specified): *semiweekly.* [< L]

sem·i·an·nu·al (sem'ē·an'yōō·əl, sem'ī-) adj. Occurring, issued, etc., twice a year or every six months. —**sem'i·an'nu·al·ly** adv.

sem·i·breve (sem′ē·brēv′, sem′ī-) *n. Music* WHOLE NOTE.

sem·i·cir·cle (sem′i·sûr′kəl, sem′ē-) *n.* 1 A half-circle; an arc of 180°. 2 Anything formed or arranged in a half-circle. —**sem′i·cir′cu·lar** *adj.* —**sem′i·cir′cu·lar·ly** *adv.*

semicircular canal Any of three fluid-filled tubes in the inner ear which serve as the organ of balance. • See EAR.

sem·i·civ·i·lized (sem′ē·siv′ə·līzd, sem′ī-) *adj.* Partly civilized.

sem·i·co·lon (sem′i·kō′lən, sem′ē-) *n.* A mark (;) of punctuation, indicating a greater degree of separation than the comma but less than the period. ·

sem·i·con·duc·tor (sem′ē·kən·duk′tər, sem′ī-) *n.* 1 One of a class of crystalline solids, as germanium or silicon, having an electrical conductivity intermediate between conductors and insulators, used in making transistors and related devices. 2 A transistor or related device.

sem·i·con·scious (sem′ē·kon′shəs, sem′ī-) *adj.* Partly conscious; not fully aware or responsive. —**sem′i·con′-scious·ly** *adv.* —**sem′i·con′scious·ness** *n.*

sem·i·de·tached (sem′ē·di·tacht′, sem′ī-) *adj.* Joined to another on one side only, as two houses built side by side with one common wall.

sem·i·fi·nal (sem′ē·fī′nəl, sem′ī-) *adj.* Next before the final, as in a series of competitions. —*n.* 1 A semifinal match. 2 A semifinal round. —**sem′i·fi′nal·ist** *n.*

sem·i·flu·id (sem′ē·flōō′id, sem′ī-) *adj.* Fluid, but thick and viscous. —*n.* A thick, viscous fluid.

sem·i·liq·uid (sem′ē·lik′wid, sem′ī-) *adj. & n.* SEMIFLUID.

sem·i·month·ly (sem′ē·munth′lē, sem′ī-) *adj.* Taking place, issued, etc., twice a month. —*n. pl.* **·lies** A publication issued twice a month. —*adv.* Twice monthly.

sem·i·nal (sem′ə·nəl) *adj.* 1 Of, pertaining to, or containing seed or semen. 2 Like seed in having or contributing to the potential for future development. [< L *semen,* seed] —**sem′i·nal·ly** *adv.* —**Syn.** 2 original, originative, germinal, germinative.

sem·i·nar (sem′ə·när) *n.* 1 A group of students at a college or university, meeting regularly with a professor for informal discussion of research problems. 2 A course thus conducted. 3 A room in which such a course is conducted. 4 Any informal meeting to discuss a particular topic, problem, etc. [< L *seminarium* seed plot]

sem·i·nar·y (sem′ē·ner′ē) *n. pl.* **·nar·ies** 1 A school of theology. 2 A boarding school, esp. for young women. 3 A place where anything is nurtured. [< L *seminarium* a seed plot]

sem·i·na·tion (sem′ə·nā′shən) *n.* 1 The act of sowing or spreading seeds. 2 Propagation. [< L *semen* a seed, semen]

sem·i·nif·er·ous (sem′ə·nif′ər·əs) *adj.* 1 Carrying or containing semen. 2 Seed-bearing.

Sem·i·nole (sem′ə·nōl) *n. pl.* **·noles** or **·nole** One of a Florida tribe of North American Indians of Muskhogean linguistic stock.

sem·i·of·fi·cial (sem′ē·ə·fish′əl, sem′ī-) *adj.* Having partial official authority or sanction; official to some extent. —**sem′i·of·fi′cial·ly** *adv.*

sem·i·per·me·a·ble (sem′ē·pûr′mē·ə·bəl, sem′ī-) *adj.* Selectively permeable; preventing passage of larger molecules, as membranes in osmosis.

sem·i·pre·cious (sem′ē·presh′əs, sem′ī-) *adj.* Designating a gem that is not as valuable as one classified precious.

sem·i·pri·vate (sem′ē·prī′vit, sem′ī-) *adj.* Partly private: said esp. of a hospital room with two, three, or four beds.

sem·i·pro (sem′ē·prō′, sem′ī-) *adj. & n.* SEMIPROFESSIONAL.

sem·i·pro·fes·sion·al (sem′ē·prə·fesh′ən·əl, sem′ī-) *adj.* 1 Taking part in a sport or other activity for pay but not on a full-time basis. 2 Engaged in by semiprofessional players. —*n.* A semiprofessional player, etc.

sem·i·qua·ver (sem′ē·kwā′vər, sem′ī-) *n.* SIXTEENTH NOTE.

sem·i·skilled (sem′ē·skild′, sem′ī-) *adj.* Partly skilled.

sem·i·sol·id (sem′ē·sol′id, sem′ī-) *adj.* Partly solid; highly viscous. —*n.* A semisolid substance.

Sem·ite (sem′īt, *esp. Brit.* sē′mīt) *n.* 1 A person considered as a descendant of Shem. 2 One of a people of sw Asia, now represented by the Jews and Arabs, but originally including the ancient Babylonians, Assyrians, Arameans, Phoenicians, etc.

Se·mit·ic (sə·mit′ik) *adj.* Of, pertaining to, or characteristic of the Semites or their languages. —*n.* 1 The Semitic family of languages. 2 Any of these languages, including Arabic, Hebrew, Amharic, Aramaic, etc.

Sem·i·tism (sem′ə·tiz′əm) *n.* 1 A Semitic word or idiom. 2 Semitic practices, opinions, or customs collectively. 3 Any political or economic policy favoring the Jews.

sem·i·tone (sem′ē·tōn′, sem′ī-) *n. Music* 1 The tone at an interval equal to half a tone in the standard diatonic scale. 2 Such an interval; a half step. —**sem′i·ton′ic** (-ton′-ik) *adj.*

sem·i·trop·i·cal (sem′ē·trop′i·kəl, sem′ī-) *adj.* Somewhat characteristic of the tropics.

sem·i·vow·el (sem′i·vou′əl) *n.* A vowellike sound used as a consonant, as (w), (y), and (r).

sem·i·week·ly (sem′ē·wēk′lē, sem′ī-) *adj.* Issued, occurring, done, etc., twice a week. —*n. pl.* **·lies** A publication issued twice a week. —*adv.* Twice a week.

sem·o·li·na (sem′ə·lē′nə) *n.* Coarse-ground wheat flour, used in making pasta. [< L *simila* fine flour]

sem·per fi·de·lis (sem′pər fi·dā′lis) *Latin* Always faithful: motto of the U.S. Marine Corps.

sem·per pa·ra·tus (sem′pər pə·rä′təs, -pə·rā′-) *Latin* Always prepared: motto of the U.S. Coast Guard.

sem·pi·ter·nal (sem′pə·tûr′nəl) *adj.* Enduring or existing to all eternity; everlasting. [< L *semper* always] —**sem′-pi·ter′nal·ly** *adv.* —**sem′pi·ter′ni·ty** *n.*

sen (sen) *n.* A Japanese coin or unit of currency, equal to 1/100 of a yen.

Sen., sen. senate; senator; senior.

sen·ate (sen′it) *n.* 1 *Usu. cap.* The upper branch of many national or state legislative bodies, as in the U.S. 2 A legislative body, as at a university; council. 3 A body of distinguished or venerable men often possessing legislative functions. 4 The highest governing body of the ancient Roman state. [< L *senatus,* lit., a council of old men]

sen·a·tor (sen′ə·tər) *n.* A member of a senate. —**sen′a·to′ri·al** *adj.* —**sen′a·to′ri·al·ly** *adv.* —**sen′a·tor·ship′** *n.*

send (send) *v.* **sent, send·ing** *v.t.* 1 To cause or enable to go: to *send* a messenger; to *send* one's daughter to medical school. 2 To cause to be conveyed; transmit; forward: to *send* a letter. 3 To cause to issue; emit or discharge, as heat, smoke, etc.: with *forth, out,* etc. 4 To drive by force; impel. 5 To cause to come, happen, etc.; grant: God *send* us peace. 6 To bring into a specified state or condition: The decision *sent* him into a panic. 7 To transmit, as an electric or magnetic signal. 8 *Slang* To thrill or delight. —*v.i.* 9 To dispatch an agent, messenger, or message. —**send for** To summon or order by a message or messenger. — **send packing** To dismiss abruptly or roughly. [< OE *sendan*] —**send′er** *n.*

send-off (send′ôf′, -of′) *n.* 1 The act of sending off; a start given to someone or something. 2 *Informal* A demonstration of friendship, enthusiasm, etc., toward someone beginning a new venture.

send-up (send′up′) *n. Brit. Slang* A parody; takeoff.

Sen·e·ca (sen′ə·kə) *n.* One of a tribe of North American Indians of Iroquoian stock, the largest tribe of the Five Nations, still living in New York and Ontario.

se·nes·cent (si·nes′ənt) *adj.* Growing old. [< L *senex* old] —**se·nes′cence** *n.*

sen·e·schal (sen′ə·shəl) *n.* A steward or major-domo in charge of the household of a medieval prince or noble. [< OF]

se·nile (sē′nīl, sen′īl) *adj.* Of, pertaining to, proceeding from, or characteristic of old age, esp. pertaining to or exhibiting certain mental infirmities often resulting from old age. [< L *senex* old] —**se′nile·ly** *adv.* —**se·nil·i·ty** (sə·nil′-ə·tē) *n.*

sen·ior (sēn′yər) *adj.* 1 Older in years; elder; after personal names (usu. abbreviated *Sr.*), to denote the elder of two related persons of the same name, esp. a father and his son. 2 Longer in service or superior in rank or dignity. 3 Of or pertaining to a senior or seniors. —*n.* 1 One older in years, longer in office, or more advanced in rank or dignity than another. 2 Any elderly person. 3 A member of a graduating class. [< L *senior* older]

senior citizen An elderly person, esp. one of or over the age of retirement.

sen·ior·i·ty (sēn·yôr′ə·tē, -yor′-) *n. pl.* **·ties** 1 The state or condition of being senior. 2 The status or priority one achieves by length of service (as in a business firm).

sen·na (sen′ə) *n.* 1 A cathartic obtained from certain species of cassia. 2 Any of various cassia plants. [< Ar. *sanā*]

se·ñor (sā·nyôr′) *n. pl.* **·ño·res** (-nyō′rās) *Spanish* 1 A title of courtesy equivalent to *Mr.* or *Sir.* 2 A man; gentleman.

se·ño·ra (sā·nyō′rä) *n. Spanish* 1 A title of courtesy equivalent to *Mrs.* or *Madam.* 2 A woman; lady.

se·ño·ri·ta (sā′nyō·rē′tä) *n. Spanish* 1 A title of courtesy equivalent to *Miss.* 2 An unmarried woman; young lady.

sen·sa·tion (sen·sā′shən) *n.* 1 a A mental event due to stimulation of a sense organ, as hearing, taste, etc. b The capacity to respond to such stimulation. 2 A state of mind induced by indeterminate stimuli: a *sensation* of fear. 3 A state of interest or excitement. 4 That which produces such a state of interest or excitement. [< L *sensus* sense]

sen·sa·tion·al (sen·sā′shən·əl) *adj.* 1 Of or pertaining to the senses or sensation. 2 Causing excitement; startling; thrilling. 3 Tending to shock, startle, etc., esp. by lurid or melodramatic details, techniques, etc. 4 *Informal* Excellent, great, etc. —**sen·sa′tion·al·ly** *adv.*

sen·sa·tion·al·ism (sen·sā′shən·əl·iz′əm) *n.* 1 *Philos.* The theory that all knowledge has a sensory basis. 2 The use of details, techniques, etc., that are intended to shock, or startle, as in literature, motion pictures, etc. —**sen·sa′tion·al·ist** *n.* —**sen·sa′tion·al·is′tic** *adj.*

sense (sens) *n.* 1 Any of the faculties of man and animals, specialized to receive and transmit external or internal stimuli, as sound, hunger, etc.; sight, touch, taste, hearing, and smell. 2 A perception or feeling produced by the senses. 3 A special capacity to perceive, appreciate, estimate, etc.: a *sense* of humor. 4 A somewhat vague perception or feeling; a *sense* of danger. 5 Rational perception or discrimination; awareness; realization: a *sense* of wrong. 6 Normal power of mind or understanding: The fellow has no *sense.* 7 That which is in accord with reason and good judgment: to talk *sense.* 8 Signification; meaning. 9 One of several meanings of the same word or phrase. 10 The opinion or judgment, as of a majority: the *sense* of the meeting. —*v.t.* **sensed, sens·ing** 1 To perceive; become aware of. 2 *Informal* To comprehend; understand. [< L *sensus* perception, p.p. of *sentire* feel]

sense·less (sens′lis) *adj.* 1 Unconscious; incapable of feeling or perception. 2 Devoid of good sense, knowledge, or meaning: a *senseless* remark. 3 Without apparent cause or reason: a *senseless* crime. —**sense′less·ly** *adv.* —**sense′·less·ness** *n.*

sense organ A structure specialized to receive sense impressions, as the eye, nose, ear, etc.

sen·si·bil·i·ty (sen′sə·bil′ə·tē) *n. pl.* **·ties** 1 The power to receive physical sensations. 2 A special susceptibility or sensitiveness to outside influences or mental impressions, as of pleasure or pain. 3 An awareness of and ability to respond to something (as an emotion or moral value). 4 Discriminating or excessive sensitivity in taste and emotion, with especial responsiveness to pathos.

sen·si·ble (sen′sə·bəl) *adj.* 1 Possessed of good mental perception; wise. 2 Capable of physical sensation; sensitive: *sensible* to pain. 3 Perceptible through the senses: *sensible* heat. 4 Perceptible to the mind. 5 Emotionally or mentally sensitive; aware. 6 Great enough to be perceived; appreciable. [< L *sensus,* p.p. of *sentire* feel, perceive] —**sen′si·ble·ness** *n.* —**sen′si·bly** *adv.*

sen·si·tive (sen′sə·tiv) *adj.* 1 Of or pertaining to the senses or sensation. 2 Receptive and responsive to sensations. 3 Responding readily to sensations, esp. of a particular kind: a *sensitive* ear. 4 Acutely receptive or responsive to the quality or strength of attitudes, feelings, or relationships. 5 Capable of appreciating aesthetic or intellec-

tual subtleties. 6 Easily irritated; tender: *sensitive* skin. 7 Hurt; sore. 8 Reacting excessively, as to an agent or substance: *sensitive* to insect bites. 9 Apt to take offense on slight provocation; touchy. 10 Capable of indicating very slight changes or differences; delicate: a *sensitive* barometer. 11 Readily fluctuating or tending to fluctuate: a *sensitive* stock market. [< L *sensus* sense] —**sen′si·tive·ly** *adv.* —**sen′si·tive·ness, sen′si·tiv′i·ty** *n.*

sensitive plant A tropical species of mimosa whose leaves close at a touch.

sen·si·tize (sen′sə·tīz) *v.t.* **·tized, ·tiz·ing** 1 To make sensitive, esp., in photography, to make sensitive to light, as a plate or film. 2 *Med.* To make susceptible to an allergen. —**sen′si·ti·za′tion, sen′si·tiz′er** *n.*

sen·so·ri·um (sen·sôr′ē·əm, -sō′rē-) *n. pl.* **·ri·a** (-ē-ə) The entire sensory apparatus of an organism. [< L *sensus* sense]

sen·so·ry (sen′sər·ē) *adj.* 1 Of or pertaining to the senses or sensation. 2 AFFERENT. Also **sen·so·ri·al** (sen·sôr′ē·əl, -sō′rē-).

sen·su·al (sen′shōō·əl) *adj.* 1 Of or pertaining to the senses or their gratification; fleshly; carnal. 2 Unduly indulgent to the appetites or senses. 3 Caused by or preoccupied with bodily or sexual pleasure. [< L *sensus* perception] —**sen′su·al·ly** *adv.*

sen·su·al·ism (sen′shōō·əl·iz′əm) *n.* 1 Frequent or excessive indulgence in sensual pleasures. 2 *Philos.* A system of ethics holding that sensual pleasures are the highest good. —**sen′su·al·ist** *n.* —**sen′su·al·is′tic** *adj.*

sen·su·al·i·ty (sen′shōō·al′ə·tē) *n.* 1 The state of being sensual. 2 Sensual indulgence; lewdness; lasciviousness.

sen·su·al·ize (sen′shōō·əl·īz′) *v.t.* **·ized, ·iz·ing** To make sensual. *Brit. sp.* **sen′su·al·ise′.** —**sen′su·al·i·za′tion** *n.*

sen·su·ous (sen′shōō·əs) *adj.* 1 Of, pertaining or appealing to, or perceived or caused by the senses. 2 Keenly appreciative of or susceptible to the pleasures of sensation. —**sen′su·ous·ly** *adv.* —**sen′su·ous·ness** *n.*

sent (sent) *p.t. & p.p.* of SEND.

sen·tence (sen′təns) *n.* 1 A determination; opinion, esp. one expressed formally. 2 A final judgment, esp. one pronounced by a court. 3 The penalty pronounced upon a convicted person. 4 *Gram.* A word or group of words expressing a complete thought in the form of a declaration, a question, a command, a wish or an exclamation, usu. beginning with a capital letter and concluding with proper end punctuation. —*v.t.* **·tenced, ·tenc·ing** To pass sentence upon; condemn to punishment. [< L *sententia* opinion< *sentire* feel, be of opinion] —**sen′tenc·er** *n.* —**sen·ten·tial** (sen·ten′shəl) *adj.*

sen·ten·tious (sen·ten′shəs) *adj.* 1 Saying much in few words; terse; pithy. 2 Habitually using or full of aphoristic language. 3 Habitually using or full of moralistic language. [< L *sententia* opinion] —**sen·ten′tious·ly** *adv.* —**sen·ten′tious·ness** *n.*

sen·ti·ent (sen′shē·ənt, -shənt) *adj.* Possessing the powers of feeling or perception. [< L *sentire* feel] —**sen′ti·ence** *n.* —**sen′ti·ent·ly** *adv.*

sen·ti·ment (sen′tə·mənt) *n.* 1 Noble, tender, or refined feeling; delicate sensibility, esp. as expressed in a work of art. 2 A complex of opinions and feelings used as a basis for judgment or action. 3 A mental attitude, judgment, or thought often conditioned by feeling more than reason. 4 SENTIMENTALITY. 5 The meaning of something said, as distinguished from its expression. 6 A thought or wish phrased in conventional language, as a toast. [< L *sentire* feel]

sen·ti·men·tal (sen′tə·men′təl) *adj.* 1 Of, pertaining to, caused by, having, or showing sentiment. 2 Experiencing, displaying, or given to sentiment in an extravagant or maudlin manner. —**sen′ti·men′tal·ism, sen′ti·men′tal·ist** *n.* —**sen′ti·men′tal·ly** *adv.*

sen·ti·men·tal·i·ty (sen′tə·men·tal′ə·tē) *n. pl.* **·ties.** 1 The state or quality of being overly sentimental, esp. in a superficial or maudlin way. 2 An expression of this.

sen·ti·men·tal·ize (sen′tə·men′təl·īz) *v.* **·ized, ·iz·ing** *v.t.* 1 To regard or treat with sentiment. —*v.i.* 2 To behave sentimentally.

sen·ti·nel (sen′tə·nəl) *n.* A guard, esp. a sentry. —*v.t.* **·neled** or **·nelled, ·nel·ing** or **·nel·ling** 1 To watch over as a sentinel. **2** To protect or furnish with sentinels. **3** To station or appoint as a sentinel. [< LL *sentinare* avoid danger < *sentire* perceive]

sen·try (sen′trē) *n. pl.* **·tries** **1** A guard, esp. a soldier placed on guard to see that only authorized persons pass his post and to give warning of approaching danger. **2** The guard kept by a sentry. [? var. of SENTINEL]

Sep. September; Septuagint.

sep. sepal; separate; separated.

se·pal (sē′pəl) *n. Bot.* Any of the individual leaves of a calyx. [< NL *sepa* covering + *petalum* a petal] —**sep·a·line** (sep′-ə·lin, -līn), **sep′a·lous, se′paled, se′palled** *adj.*

sep·a·ra·ble (sep′ər·ə·bəl, sep′-rə-) *adj.* Capable of being separated or divided. —**sep′a·ra·bil′i·ty, sep′a·ra·ble·ness** *n.* —**sep′a·ra·bly** *adv.*

Sepals of flower

sep·a·rate (sep′ə·rāt) *v.* **·rat·ed, ·rat·ing** *v.t.* **1** To set apart; sever; disjoin. **2** To keep apart; divide: The Hudson River *separates* New York from New Jersey. **3** To divide into components, parts, etc. **4** To isolate or obtain from a compound, mixture, etc.: to *separate* the wheat from the chaff. **5** To consider separately; distinguish between. **6** *Law* To part by separation. —*v.i.* **7** To become divided or disconnected; draw apart. **8** To part company; sever an association. **9** To cease living together as man and wife. **10** To break up into component parts, as a mixture. —*adj.* (sep′ər·it, sep′rit) **1** Existing or considered apart from others; distinct; individual. **2** Detached; disunited. **3** Existing independently; not related. —*n.pl.* Garments to be worn in various combinations, as skirts and blouses. [< L *se-* apart + *parare* prepare] —**sep′a·rate·ly** *adv.* —**sep′a·rate·ness, sep′a·ra′tor** *n.* —**sep′a·ra′tive** (-rā′tiv, -ə·rə·tiv) *adj.*

sep·a·ra·tion (sep′ə·rā′shən) *n.* **1** The act or process of separating. **2** The state of being separated. **3** A gap or dividing line. **4** *Law* Relinquishment of cohabitation between husband and wife by mutual consent.

sep·a·ra·tist (sep′ər·ə·tist, sep′rə-) *n.* One who advocates or upholds separation, esp. political, racial, or religious separation. Also **sep′a·ra′tion·ist.** —**sep′a·ra·tism** *n.*

Sep·a·ra·tist (sep′ər·ə·tist, sep′rə-) *n. Can.* One who believes in or supports the withdrawal of a province, esp. Quebec, from Confederation.

Se·phar·dim (si·fär′dim) *n. pl.* The Spanish and Portuguese Jews or their descendants. Also **Se·phar′a·dim** (-ə·dim). [< Hebrew *sephārādhīm* < *Sephārādh*, Obad. 1:20, a country identified with Spain] —**Se·phar′dic** *adj.*

se·pi·a (sē′pē·ə) *n.* **1** A reddish brown pigment prepared from the ink of certain cuttlefish. **2** The color of this pigment. **3** A picture done in this color. —*adj.* Executed in or colored like sepia. [< Gk. *sēpia* cuttlefish]

se·poy (sē′poi) *n.* Formerly, a native Indian soldier in the British or other European army. [< Pers. *sipāh* army]

sep·sis (sep′sis) *n.* The presence of pathogenic microorganisms or their toxins in the blood or tissues. [< Gk. *sēpein* make putrid]

sep·ta (sep′tə) *n. pl.* of SEPTUM.

Sep·tem·ber (sep·tem′bər) *n.* The ninth month of the year, containing 30 days. [< L *septem* seven]

sep·te·nar·y (sep′tə·ner′ē) *adj.* Consisting of, pertaining to, or being seven. —*n. pl.* **·nar·ies** A group of seven things of any kind. [< L *septeni* seven each]

sep·ten·ni·al (sep·ten′ē·al) *adj.* **1** Recurring every seven years. **2** Continuing or capable of lasting seven years. —**sep·ten′ni·al·ly** *adv.*

sep·tet (sep·tet′) *n.* **1** A group or set of seven, esp. seven musical performers. **2** *Music* A composition for such a group. Also **sep·tette′.** [< L *septem* seven]

sep·tic (sep′tik) *adj.* **1** Of, pertaining to, or caused by sepsis. **2** Productive of putrefaction; putrid. Also **sep′ti·cal.**

sep·ti·ce·mi·a (sep′tə·sē′mē·ə) *n.* BLOOD POISONING. Also **sep′ti·cae′mi·a.** [< Gk. *sēptikos* putrefactive + *haima* blood] —**sep′ti·ce′mic** (-sē′mik) *adj.*

septic tank A tank in which sewage is held until decomposed by anaerobic bacteria.

sep·til·lion (sep·til′yən) *n. & adj.* See NUMBER. [< L *sept(em)* + F *(m)illion* a million] —**sep·til′lionth** *adj., n.*

sep·tu·a·ge·nar·i·an (sep′tyōō·ə·jə·nâr′ē·ən, sep′tə·wäj′ə-) *n.* A person 70 years old, or between 70 and 80. [< L *septuaginta* seventy]

Sep·tu·a·ges·i·ma (sep′tə·wə·jes′ə·mə, -jā′zə-) *n.* The third Sunday before Lent. Also **Septuagesima Sunday.** [< L, seventieth]

Sep·tu·a·gint (sep′tyōō·ə·jint′, sep′tə·wə-) *n.* An ancient Greek version of the Old Testament, made between 280 and 130 B.C. [< L *septuaginta* seventy < a tradition that it was produced in 70 days by a group of 72 scholars]

sep·tum (sep′təm) *n. pl.* **·ta** (-tə) A partition between two masses of tissue or two cavities: the nasal *septum.* [< L *sepes* a hedge] —**sep′tal** *adj.*

sep·tu·ple (sep′tyōō·pəl, sep·tyōō′-) *adj.* **1** Consisting of seven; sevenfold. **2** Multiplied by seven; seven times repeated. —*v.t. & v.i.* **·pled, ·pling** To multiply by seven. —*n.* A number or sum seven times as great as another. [< L *septem* seven]

sep·ul·cher (sep′əl·kər) *n.* **1** A burial place; tomb; vault. **2** A receptacle for relics, esp. in an altar slab. —*v.t.* **·chered** or **·chred, ·cher·ing** or **·chring** To place in a grave; entomb; bury. Also **sep′ul·chre** (-kər). [< L *sepulcrum*]

se·pul·chral (si·pul′krəl) *adj.* **1** Of a sepulcher. **2** Dismal in color or aspect. **3** Low or melancholy in sound. —**se·pul′chral·ly** *adv.*

seq. sequel.

seq., seqq. the following (L *sequens, sequentia*).

se·quel (sē′kwəl) *n.* **1** Something which follows; a continuation; development. **2** A narrative which, though entire in itself, develops from a preceding one. **3** A consequence; result. [< L *sequi* follow]

se·quence (sē′kwəns) *n.* **1** The process or fact of following in space, time, or thought; succession or order. **2** Order of succession; arrangement. **3** A number of things following one another, considered collectively; a series. **4** An effect or consequence. **5** A section of motion-picture film presenting a single episode, without time lapses or interruptions. [< L *sequi* follow]

se·quent (sē′kwənt) *n.* That which follows; a consequence; result. —*adj.* **1** Following in the order of time; succeeding. **2** Consequent; resultant. [< L *sequi* follow]

se·quen·tial (si·kwen′shəl) *adj.* **1** Characterized by or forming a sequence, as of parts. **2** SEQUENT. —**se·quen·ti·al·i·ty** (si·kwen′shē·al′ə·tē) *n.* —**se·quen′tial·ly** *adv.* —Syn. **1** consecutive, orderly, serial.

se·ques·ter (si·kwes′tər) *v.t.* **1** To place apart; separate. **2** To seclude; withdraw: often used reflexively. **3** *Law* To take (property) into custody until a controversy, claim, etc., is settled. **4** In international law, to confiscate and control (enemy property) by preemption. [< LL *sequestrare* remove, lay aside] —**se·ques′tered** *adj.*

se·ques·trate (si·kwes′trāt) *v.t.* **·trat·ed, ·trat·ing** SEQUESTER. —**se·ques·tra·tor** (sē′·kwes·trā′tər, si·kwes′trā·tər) *n.*

se·quin (sē′kwin) *n.* A spangle or small coinlike ornament sewn on clothing. —*v.t.* **se·quined** or **se·quinned, se·quin·ing** or **se·quin·ning** To decorate with sequins. [< Ar. *sikka* a coining-die]

se·quoi·a (si·kwoi′ə) *n.* Either of two species of gigantic coniferous evergreen trees of the western U.S. [< *Sikwayi*, 1770?–1843, American Indian who invented the Cherokee alphabet]

ser. serial; series; sermon.

se·ra (sir′ə) A *pl.* of SERUM.

se·ra·glio (si·ral′yō, -räl′-) *n. pl.* **·glios** **1** That part of a sultan's palace where his harem lives. **2** The palace of a sultan. Also **se·rail** (se·rāl′). [< Ital. *serraglio* an enclosure]

Sequoia

se·ra·pe (se·rä′pē) n. A shawl or blanketlike outer garment worn in Latin America. [Sp.]

ser·aph (ser′əf) n. pl. **ser·aphs** or **ser·a·phim** (ser′ə·fim) An angel of the highest order, usu. represented as having six wings. [< Heb. *serāphīm*, pl.] —**se·raph·ic** (si·raf′ik) adj. —**se·raph′i·cal·ly** adv.

Ser·bo-Cro·a·tian (sûr′bō·krō·ā′shən) n. **1** The South Slavic language of Yugoslavia. **2** Any person whose native tongue is Serbo-Croatian. —adj. Of this language or people.

sere (sir) adj. Withered; dried up.

ser·e·nade (ser′ə·nād′) n. An evening piece, usu. the song of a lover beneath his lady's window. —v.t. & v.i. **·nad·ed, ·nad·ing** To entertain with a serenade. [< L *serenus* clear, serene] —**ser′e·nad′er** n.

Serape

ser·en·dip·i·ty (ser′ən·dip′ə·tē) n. The faculty of making fortunate discoveries by accident. [Coined by Horace Walpole (1754) after fairy tale characters] —**ser′en·dip′i·tous** adj.

se·rene (si·rēn′) adj. **1** Clear, bright, and fair; cloudless; untroubled. **2** Tranquil; calm; peaceful. **3** Usu. cap. Of exalted rank: used chiefly in royal titles: His *Serene* Highness. [< L *serenus*] —**se·rene′ly** adv. —**se·ren·i·ty** (si·ren′ə·tē), **se·rene′ness** n. —Syn. **2** composed, collected, placid.

serf (sûrf) n. **1** In feudal times, a person attached to the estate on which he lived. **2** Any person in servile subjection. [< L *servus* a slave] —**serf′dom, serf′age, serf′hood** n.

serge (sûrj) n. **1** A strong twilled woolen fabric woven with a diagonal rib on both sides. **2** A twilled silk or synthetic lining fabric. [< L *serica (lana)* (wool) of the Seres, an eastern Asian people]

ser·geant (sär′jənt) n. **1** See GRADE. **2** A police officer of rank next below a captain or lieutenant. **3** SERGEANT AT ARMS. [< L *servire* serve] —**ser′gean·cy, ser′geant·cy, ser′geant·ship** n.

sergeant at arms pl. **sergeants at arms** An officer in a legislative body, court, etc. who enforces order.

sergeant major pl. **sergeants major** See GRADE.

se·ri·al (sir′ē·əl) adj. **1** Of, like, or arranged in a series. **2** Published or presented in a series at regular intervals. **3** Of a serial or serials. **4** Of, pertaining to, or being atonal music consisting of a fixed series of tones based on the twelve-tone chromatic scale. —n. **1** A novel or other story regularly presented in successive installments, as in a magazine, on radio or television, or in motion pictures. **2** A periodical. —**se′ri·al·ly** adv.

se·ri·al·ism (sir′ē·əl·izm) n. Serial music. —**se′ri·al·ist** n.

se·ri·al·ize (sir′ē·əl·īz′) v.t. **·ized, ·iz·ing** To present in serial form. —**se′ri·al·i·za′tion** n.

serial number An identifying number assigned to a person, object, item of merchandise, etc.

se·ri·a·tim (sir′ē·ā′tim, ser′ē-) adv. One after another; in connected order; serially. [< L *series* series]

se·ries (sir′ēz) n. pl. **se·ries 1** An arrangement or connected succession of related things placed in space or happening in time one after the other: a *series* of games; a *series* of lakes. **2** Math. The indicated sum of any finite set of terms or of an ordered infinite set of terms. **3** Chem. A group of related compounds or elements showing an orderly succession of changes in composition or structure. **4** Electr. An arrangement of electric devices in which the current flows through each in order. [L < *serere* join]

ser·if (ser′if) n. Printing A light line or stroke crossing or projecting from the end of a main line or stroke in a letter. [< L *scribere* write]

se·ri·o·com·ic (sir′ē·ō·kom′ik) adj. Mingling the comic with the serious. Also **se′ri·o·com′i·cal.** —**se′ri·o·com′i·cal·ly** adv.

se·ri·ous (sir′ē·əs) adj. **1** Grave and earnest in quality, feeling, or disposition; thoughtful; sober. **2** Being or done in earnest; not jesting or joking. **3** Involving much work, thought, difficulty, etc.: a *serious* problem. **4** Of grave importance; weighty. **5** Attended with considerable danger or loss: a *serious* accident. [< L *serius*] —**se′ri·ous·ly** adv. —**se′ri·ous·ness** n. —Syn. **1** sedate, staid, solemn, grim. **3** complex, complicated, involved, hard, troublesome.

ser·jeant (sär′jənt) n. Brit. SERGEANT.

ser·mon (sûr′mən) n. **1** A discourse, usu. based on a passage or text of the Bible, delivered as part of a church service. **2** Any serious talk or exhortation, as on duty, morals, etc. [< L *sermo* talk] —**ser·mon·ic** (sər·mon′ik) adj.

ser·mon·ize (sûr′mən·īz) v.t. & v.i. **·ized, ·iz·ing** To deliver sermons (to). —**ser′mon·iz′er** n.

Sermon on the Mount The discourse of Jesus found recorded in Matt. 5–7.

se·rol·o·gy (si·rol′ə·jē) n. The science of serums and their actions. [< SER(UM) + -LOGY] —**se·ro·log·i·cal** (sir′ə·loj′i·kəl) adj.

se·rous (sir′əs) adj. Pertaining to, producing, or resembling serum.

ser·pent (sûr′pənt) n. **1** A snake, esp. a poisonous or large one. **2** A treacherous person. [< L *serpere* to creep]

ser·pen·tine (sûr′pən·tīn, -tēn) adj. **1** Of or like a serpent. **2** Winding; zigzag. **3** Subtle; cunning. —n. A massive or fibrous, often mottled green or yellow, magnesium silicate.

ser·rate (ser′āt, -it) adj. Having sawlike teeth, as the margins of certain leaves. Also **ser′rat·ed.** [< L *serra* a saw] • See LEAF.

ser·ra·tion (se·rā′shən) n. **1** The state of being edged as with saw teeth. **2** A single projection of a serrate edge, or a series of such projections. Also **ser·ra·ture** (ser′ə·chər). [< L *serra* a saw]

ser·ried (ser′ēd) adj. Compacted in rows or ranks, as soldiers in company formation. [< LL *serrare* to lock]

se·rum (sir′əm) n. pl. **se·rums** or **se·ra** (sir′ə) **1** The fluid constituent of blood. **2** The serum of the blood of an animal which has developed immunity to a specific pathogen. **3** WHEY. **4** Any watery plant or animal secretion. [L, whey]

ser·vant (sûr′vənt) n. **1** A person employed to assist in domestic matters, sometimes living within the employer's house. **2** A government worker. [< OF *servir* to serve]

serve (sûrv) v. **served, serv·ing** v.t. **1** To work for as a servant. **2** To be of service to; wait on. **3** To promote the interests of; aid; help: to *serve* one's country. **4** To obey and give homage to: to *serve* God. **5** To satisfy the requirements of; suffice for. **6** To perform the duties connected with, as a public office. **7** To go through (a period of enlistment, term of punishment, etc.). **8** To furnish or provide, as with a regular supply. **9** To offer or bring food or drink to (a guest, etc.); wait on at table. **10** To bring and place on the table or distribute among guests, as food or drink. **11** To operate or handle; tend: to *serve* a cannon. **12** To copulate with: said of male animals. **13** In tennis, etc., to put (the ball) in play by hitting it to one's opponent. **14** Law **a** To deliver (a summons or writ) to a person. **b** To deliver a summons or writ to. **15** Naut. To wrap (a rope, stay, etc.), as with wire, cordage, etc., so as to strengthen or protect. —v.i. **16** To be a servant. **17** To perform the duties of any employment, office, etc. **18** To go through a term of service, as in the army or navy. **19** To offer or give food or drink, as to guests. **20** To wait on customers. **21** To be suitable or usable, as for a purpose; perform a function. **22** To be favorable, as weather. **23** In tennis, etc., to put the ball in play. —n. In tennis, etc.: **a** The delivering of the ball by striking it toward an opponent. **b** The turn of one who serves. [< L *servus* a slave]

serv·er (sûr′vər) n. **1** One who serves, as an attendant aiding a priest at low mass. **2** That which is used in serving, as a tray.

serv·ice (sûr′vis) n. **1** The act or occupation of serving. **2** The manner in which one serves or is served. **3** A division of employment, esp. of public or governmental employment: the diplomatic *service*. **4** Any branch of the armed forces. **5** A facility for meeting some public need: electric *service*. **6** Installation, maintenance, and repair provided for the buyer of something. **7** Assistance; aid; benefit: to be of *service*. **8** Often pl. A useful result or product of labor which is not a tangible commodity: a doctor's *services*. **9** Often pl. A public exercise of worship. **10** A religious or civil ritual: the marriage *service*. **11** The music for a liturgical office or rite. **12** A set of articles for a particular purpose: a tea *service*. **13** Naut. The protective wire, cordage, etc., wrapped around a rope. **14** Law The legal communication of a writ, process, or summons to a designated person. **15** In animal husbandry, the copulation of a female. —*adj.* **1** Pertaining to or for service. **2** Of, for, or used by servants or tradespeople: a *service* entrance. **3** Of, pertaining to, or belonging to a military service: a *service* flag. **4** For rough or everyday usage. —*v.t.* **·viced, ·vic·ing 1** To maintain or repair: to *service* a car. **2** To supply service to. **3** SERVE (def. 12). [< L *servus* a slave]

ser·vice·a·ble (sûr′vis·ə·bəl) *adj.* **1** That can serve a useful purpose; beneficial. **2** Capable of rendering long service; durable. —**ser′vice·a·ble·ness, ser′vice·a·bil′i·ty** *n.* —**ser′vice·a·bly** *adv.* —**Syn. 1** practical, practicable, utilitarian, helpful.

ser·vice·man (sûr′vis·man′) *n. pl.* **·men** (-men′) **1** A member of one of the armed forces. **2** A man who performs services of maintenance, supply, repair, etc.: also **service man.**

service station 1 A place for supplying motor vehicles with gasoline, oil, etc., and often for doing auto maintenance and repair work. **2** A place for adjusting, repairing, or supplying parts for electrical and mechanical appliances.

ser·vi·ette (sûr′vē·et′, -vyet′) *n.* A table napkin. [< MF *servir* serve]

ser·vile (sûr′vīl, -vil) *adj.* **1** Having the spirit of a slave; slavish; abject. **2** Of, pertaining to, or appropriate for slaves or servants: *servile* employment. [< L *servus* a slave] —**ser′vile·ly** *adv.* —**ser·vil′i·ty, ser′vile·ness** *n.* —**Syn. 1** obsequious, fawning, groveling, cowering, submissive, cringing.

serv·ing (sûr′ving) *n.* **1** A portion of food for one person. **2** The act of one who or that which serves. —*adj.* Used for dealing out food.

ser·vi·tor (sûr′və·tər) *n.* One who waits upon and serves another; an attendant; follower; servant.

ser·vi·tude (sûr′və·tʸood) *n.* **1** The condition of a slave; slavery; bondage. **2** Enforced service as a punishment for crime: penal *servitude.* [< L *servus* a slave]

ser·vo·mech·a·nism (sûr′vō·mek′ə·niz′əm) *n.* Any of various devices using feedback in which a small input is amplified and used to control a machine, operation, process, etc. [< L *servus* slave + MECHANISM]

ses·a·me (ses′ə·mē) *n.* An East Indian plant bearing edible, oily seeds (**sesame seed**) that yield an oil (**sesame oil**) used in cooking. [< Gk. *sēsamon*]

ses·qui·cen·ten·ni·al (ses′kwi·sen·ten′ē·əl) *adj.* Of or pertaining to a century and a half. —*n.* A 150th anniversary, or its celebration. [< L *sesqui-* one half more + CENTENNIAL]

ses·sile (ses′il, -əl) *adj.* **1** *Bot.* Attached without a stalk, as a leaf. **2** *Zool. & Anat.* Attached at the base; sedentary. [< L *sessilis* sitting down, stunted] —**ses·sil′i·ty** *n.*

ses·sion (sesh′ən) *n.* **1** The sitting together of a legislative assembly, court, etc., for the transaction of business. **2** A single meeting or series of meetings of an assembly, court, etc. **3** In some schools, a term. **4** Any period of some specified activity: a *session* with the boss. [< L *sessus,* p.p. of *sedere* sit] —**ses′sion·al** *adj.* —**ses′sion·al·ly** *adv.*

ses·tet (ses·tet′) *n.* **1** The last six lines of a sonnet; also, any six-line stanza. **2** *Music* SEXTET. [< L *sextus* sixth]

set¹ (set) *v.* **set, set·ting** *v.t.* **1** To put in a certain place or position; place. **2** To put into a fixed, firm, or immovable position, condition, or state: to *set* brick; to *set* one's jaw. **3** To bring to a specified condition or state: *Set* your mind at ease; He *set* the barn afire; She has *set* her heart on being a doctor. **4** To restore to proper position for healing, as a broken bone. **5** To place in readiness for use: to *set* a trap. **6** To adjust according to a standard: to *set* a clock. **7** To adjust (an instrument, dial, etc.) to a particular calibration or position. **8** To place knives, forks, etc., on (a table) for a meal. **9** To bend the teeth of (a saw) to either side alternately. **10** To appoint or establish; prescribe: to *set* boundaries, regulations, fashions, etc. **11** To fix or establish a time for: We *set* our departure for noon. **12** To assign for performance, completion, etc.; to *set* a task. **13** To assign to some specific duty or function; appoint; sta-

tion: to *set* a guard. **14** To cause to sit. **15** To present or perform so as to be copied or emulated: to *set* the pace. **16** To give a specified direction to: He *set* his course for the Azores. **17** To put in place so as to catch the wind: to *set* the jib. **18** To place in a mounting or frame, as a gem. **19** To stud or adorn with gems: to *set* a crown with rubies. **20** To place (a hen) on eggs to hatch them. **21** To place (eggs) under a fowl or in an incubator for hatching. **22** To place (a price or value): with *by* or *on:* to *set* a price on an outlaw's head. **23** To arrange (hair), as with curlers, lotions, etc. **24** *Printing* **a** To arrange (type) for printing; compose. **b** To put into type, as a sentence, manuscript, etc. **25** *Music* To compose music for (words) or write words for (existing music). **26** To describe (a scene) as taking place: to *set* the scene in Monaco. **27** In the theater, to arrange (a stage) so as to depict a scene. **28** In some games, as bridge, to defeat. —*v.i.* **29** To go or pass below the horizon, as the sun. **30** To wane; decline. **31** To sit on eggs, as fowl. **32** To become firm; solidify; congeal. **33** To become fast, as a dye. **34** To begin to move, as on a journey: with *forth, out, off,* etc. **35** To begin: *Set* to work. **36** To have a specified direction; tend. **37** To hang or fit, as clothes. **38** To mend, as a broken bone. **39** *Regional* To sit. **40** *Bot.* To begin development or growth, as a rudimentary fruit. —**set against 1** To balance; compare. **2** To make unfriendly to; prejudice against. —**set off 1** To put apart by itself. **2** To serve as a contrast or foil for; enhance. **3** To make begin; set in motion. **4** To cause to explode. —**set out 1** To display; exhibit. **2** To lay out or plan. **3** To begin a journey. **4** To begin any enterprise. **5** To plant. —**set to 1** To start; begin. **2** To start fighting. —**set up 1** To place in an upright or high position. **2** To raise. **3** To place in power, authority, etc. **4 a** To construct or build. **b** To put together; assemble. **c** To found; establish. **5** To provide with the means to start a new business. **6** To cause to be heard: to *set up* a cry. **7** To propose or put forward (a theory, etc.). **8** To cause. **9** To work out a plan for. **10** To claim to be. **11 a** To pay for the drinks, etc., of; treat. **b** To pay for (drinks, etc.). **12** To encourage; exhilarate. —**set upon** To attack; assail. —*adj.* **1** Established by authority or agreement; prescribed; appointed: a *set* time or method. **2** Customary; conventional: a *set* phrase. **3** Deliberately and systematically conceived; formal: a *set* speech. **4** Fixed and motionless; rigid. **5** Firm in consistency. **6** Fixed in opinion or disposition; obstinate. **7** Formed; built; made: deep-*set* eyes. **8** Ready; prepared: to get *set.* —*n.* **1** The act or condition of setting. **2** Permanent change of form, as by bending, pressure, strain, etc. **3** The arrangement, tilt, or hang of a garment, hat, sail, etc. **4** Carriage or bearing: the *set* of his shoulders. **5** The sinking of a heavenly body below the horizon. **6** The direction of a current or wind. **7** A young plant ready for setting out. **8** Inclination of the mind; bent. **9** *Psychol.* A temporary condition assumed by an organism preparing for a particular response or activity. **10** An arrangement of the hair, as by curling. **11** In tennis, a group of games completed when one side wins six games, or, if tied at five games, wins either two more games consecutively or wins a tie breaker. [< OE *settan* cause to sit]

set² (set) *n.* **1** A number of persons regarded as associated through status, common interests, etc.: a new *set* of customers. **2** A social group having some exclusive character; coterie; clique: the fast *set.* **3** A number of things belonging together or customarily used together: a *set* of instruments. **4** A group of books or periodicals issued together or related by common authorship, subject, etc. **5** In jazz performances, the music played during one period of time without an intermission; also, the period of time. **6** In the theatre, motion pictures, etc., the complete assembly of properties, structures, etc., required in a scene. **7** Radio or television receiving equipment assembled for use. **8** *Math.* Any collection of elements, objects, or numbers. [< L *secta* a sect]

se·ta (sē′tə) *n. pl.* **·tae** (-tē) *Biol.* A bristle or bristlelike process. [< L] —**se·ta·ceous** (si·tā′shəs), **se′tose** *adj.*

set·back (set′bak′) *n.* **1** A misfortune or reversal, as in progress. **2** An indentation or steplike arrangement of the upper levels of a tall building.

Seth (seth) In the Bible, the third son of Adam.

set·off (set'ôf', -of') n. **1** Something that offsets, balances, or compensates for something else. **2** Something that contrasts with or sets off something else. **3** A counterclaim or the discharge of a debt by a counterclaim. **4** *Archit.* A ledge; offset.

set piece 1 Something, as a passage in literature, music, etc., aimed at creating a brilliant effect. **2** A fireworks display. **3** A piece of scenery for the stage.

set·screw (set'skrōō') n. **1** A screw so made that it can be screwed tightly against or into another surface to prevent movement. **2** A screw for regulating the tension of a spring or the opening of a valve.

set·tee (se·tē') n. **1** A long wooden seat with a high back. **2** A sofa suitable for two or three people. [?< SETTLE]

set·ter (set'ər) n. **1** One who or that which sets. **2** One of a breed of medium-sized, silky-coated dogs trained to indicate the location of game birds while standing rigid.

set·ting (set'ing) n. **1** The position, degree, etc., at which something is set. **2** A frame or mounting, as for a jewel. **3** Physical environment or surroundings. **4** The scene, time, background, etc., as of a novel or play. **5** A number of eggs placed together for hatching. **6** The music composed for a poem, set of words, etc. **7** The tableware set out for one person.

set·tle (set'l) v. **·tled, ·tling** v.t. **1** To put in order; set to rights; to *settle* affairs. **2** To establish or fix permanently or as if permanently: He *settled* himself on the couch. **3** To calm; quiet: to *settle* one's nerves. **4** To cause (sediment or dregs) to sink to the bottom. **5** To make firm or compact: to *settle* dust or ashes. **6** To make clear or transparent, as by causing sediment or dregs to sink. **7** To make quiet or orderly: One blow *settled* him. **8** To decide or determine finally, as an argument, legal case, etc. **9** To pay, as a debt; satisfy, as a claim. **10** To establish residents or residence in (a country, town, etc.). **11** To establish as residents. **12** To establish in a permanent occupation, home, etc. **13** *Law* To make over or assign (property) by legal act: with *on* or *upon*. —v.i. **14** To come to rest. **15** To sink gradually; subside. **16** To become clear by the sinking of sediment. **17** To become more firm by sinking. **18** To become established or located: The pain *settled* in his arm. **19** To establish one's abode or home. **20** To come to a decision; determine; resolve: with *on, upon,* or *with.* **21** To pay a bill, etc. —**settle down 1** To start living a regular, orderly life, esp. after a period of wandering or irresponsibility. **2** To become quiet or orderly. —n. A long, wooden, high-backed bench, usu. with arms and sometimes having a chest from seat to floor. [< OE *setl* a seat]

set·tle·ment (set'l·mənt) n. **1** The act of settling or the condition of being settled. **2** An area newly colonized. **3** A small, usu. remote village. **4** *Law* **a** The act of assigning property, money, etc., to someone. **b** That which is thus assigned. **5** An agreement or adjustment, as of differences. **6** An urban welfare institution that provides various educational or recreational services to a community or neighborhood: also **settlement house.**

set·tler (set'lər) n. **1** One who establishes himself in a colony or new country. **2** One who settles or decides.

set·tlings (set'lingz) n.pl. Dregs; sediment.

set-to (set'tōō') n. A bout at fighting, arguing, etc.

set-up (set'up') n. **1** A system or plan, as of a business operation, etc. **2** The arrangement or assembly of a machine, piece of equipment, etc. **3** The elements or circumstances of a situation or plan. **4** Carriage of the body; posture. **5** Ice, soda water, etc., provided for those who furnish their own liquor. **6** A table setting. **7** *Informal* **a** A contest or match arranged so as to result in an easy victory. **b** Anything easy to accomplish.

sev·en (sev'ən) n. **1** The sum of six plus one; 7; VII. **2** A set or group of seven members. [< OE *seofon*] —**sev'en** *adj., pron.*

seven deadly sins Pride, lust, envy, anger, covetousness, gluttony, and sloth.

Settle

sev·en·fold (sev'ən·fōld') *adj.* **1** Seven times as many or as great. **2** Made up of seven; septuple. **3** Folded seven times. —*adv.* In sevenfold manner or degree.

seven seas All the oceans of the world.

sev·en·teen (sev'ən·tēn') n. **1** The sum of 16 plus 1; 17; XVII. **2** A set or group of 17 members. —**sev'en·teen'** *adj., pron.*

sev·en·teenth (sev'ən·tēnth') *adj. & adv.* Next in order after the 16th. —n. **1** The element of an ordered set that corresponds to the number 17. **2** One of seventeen equal parts.

sev·enth (sev'ənth) *adj. & adv.* Next in order after the sixth. —n. **1** The element of an ordered set that corresponds to the number seven. **2** One of seven equal parts. **3** *Music* The interval between any tone and the seventh tone above or below in the diatonic scale. —*adv.* In the seventh order, place, or rank: also, in formal discourse, **sev'enth·ly.**

seventh heaven The highest condition of happiness. [< the highest heaven according to certain ancient cosmologies]

sev·en·ti·eth (sev'ən·tē·ith) *adj. & adv.* Tenth in order after the 60th. —n. **1** The element of an ordered set that corresponds to the number 70. **2** One of seventy equal parts.

sev·en·ty (sev'ən·tē) n. *pl.* **·ties 1** The product of seven and ten; 70; LXX. **2** A set or group of 70 members. **3** *pl.* The numbers, years, etc., between 70 and 80. —**sev'en·ty** *adj., pron.*

sev·er (sev'ər) v.t. **1** To put or keep apart; separate. **2** To cut or break into two or more parts. **3** To break off; dissolve, as a relationship. —v.i. **4** To come or break apart or into pieces. **5** To go away or apart; separate. [< L *separare* separate] —**sev'er·a·ble** *adj.* —**sev'er·er** n.

sev·er·al (sev'ər·əl, sev'rəl) *adj.* **1** Being of an indefinite number, more than one or two, yet not large; divers. **2** Considered individually; single; separate. **3** Individually different; various or diverse. [< L *separ* separate]

sev·er·al·ly (sev'ər·əl·ē, sev'rəl·ē) *adv.* **1** Individually; separately. **2** Respectively.

sev·er·ance (sev'ər·əns, sev'rəns) n. The act of severing, or the condition of being severed.

severance pay Additional pay sometimes given to an employee who has been discharged.

se·vere (si·vir') *adj.* **·ver·er, ·ver·est 1** Difficult; trying. **2** Unsparing; harsh; merciless: a *severe* punishment. **3** Conforming to rigid rules; extremely strict or accurate. **4** Serious and austere in disposition or manner; grave. **5** Austerely plain and simple, as in style, design, etc. **6** Causing sharp pain or anguish; extreme: *severe* hardship. —**se·vere'ness** n. [< L *severus*] —**se·vere'ly** *adv.*

se·ver·i·ty (si·ver'ə·tē) n. *pl.* **·ties** The quality or condition of being severe.

sew (sō) v. **sewed, sewed** or **sewn, sew·ing** v.t. **1** To make, mend, or fasten with needle and thread. **2** To enclose or secure by sewing. —v.i. **3** To work with needle and thread. —**sew up 1** To mend by sewing. **2** *Informal* **a** To achieve absolute control or use of. **b** To make or be totally successful. [< OE *siwan, siowian*]

sew·age (sōō'ij) n. The waste matter carried off in sewers. [< SEW(ER) + -AGE]

sew·er (sōō'ər) n. **1** A conduit, usu. laid underground, to carry off drainage and excrement. **2** Any large public drain. [< OF *seuwiere* a channel from a fish pond]

sew·er·age (sōō'ər·ij) n. **1** A system of sewers. **2** Systematic draining by sewers. **3** SEWAGE.

sew·ing (sō'ing) n. **1** The act, business, or occupation of one who sews. **2** Material worked with needle and thread; needlework.

sewing circle A group of women meeting periodically to sew, usu. for some charitable purpose.

sewing machine A machine for stitching or sewing cloth, leather, etc.

sewn (sōn) A *p.p.* of SEW.

sex (seks) n. **1** Either of two divisions, male and female, by which organisms are distinguished with reference to the reproductive functions. **2** Males or females collectively. **3** The character of being male or female. **4** The activity or phenomena of life concerned with sexual desire or reproduction. **5** *Informal* Any act affording sexual gratification, as sexual intercourse. —*adj. Informal* SEX-UAL. [< L *sexus*]

sex·a·ge·nar·i·an (sek′sə-jə-nâr′ē-ən) *adj.* Sixty years old, or between sixty and seventy. —*n.* A person of this age. [< L *sexageni* sixty each]

Sex·a·ges·i·ma (sek′sə-jes′ə-mə, -jā′zə-) *n.* The second Sunday before Lent. [L, sixtieth]

sex·a·ges·i·mal (sek′sə-jes′ə-məl) *adj.* Of or based on the number 60. [< L *sexagesimus* < *sexaginta* sixty]

sex appeal A physical quality or charm which attracts sexual interest.

sex chromosome Either of a pair of chromosomes associated with the determination of sex in plants and animals.

sex·ism (seks′iz-əm) *n.* Prejudice or discrimination against women. [< SEX + -ISM, on analogy with *racism*] —**sex′ist** *n, adj.*

sex·less (seks′lis) *adj.* **1** Having no sex; neuter. **2** Without sexual interest or qualities. —**sex′less·ly** *adv.* —**sex′·less·ness** *n.*

sex linkage The presence on a sex chromosome of genes for certain nonsexual characteristics, resulting in the development of those characteristics in one sex only. —**sex·linked** (seks′lingkt′) *adj.*

sex·ol·o·gy (seks-ol′ə-jē) *n.* The study of human sexual behavior. —**sex·o·log·ic** (sek′sə-loj′ik) or **-i·cal** *adj.* —**sex·ol′o·gist** *n.*

sex·ploi·ta·tion (seks′ploi-tā′shən) *n.* The commercial exploitation of interest in sex, as by means of pornography. [Blend of SEX + EXPLOITATION]

sex·pot (seks′pot) *n. Slang* A very sexy woman.

sext (sekst) *n.* One of the canonical hours; the office for the sixth hour or noon. [< L *sex* six]

sex·tant (seks′tənt) *n.* An instrument for measuring the angular distance between two objects, as between a heavenly body and the horizon, used esp. in determining latitude at sea. [< L *sextus* sixth]

sex·tet (seks-tet′) *n.* **1** A group of six musical performers. **2** A musical composition for such a group. **3** Any collection of six persons or things. Also **sex·tette′.** [Alter. of SESTET]

Sextant
a. eyepiece.

sex·til·lion (seks-til′yən) *n. & adj.* See NUMBER. [< L *sex* six + F *(m)illion* a million]

sex·ton (seks′tən) *n.* An officer of a church having charge of maintenance and also of ringing the bells, overseeing burials, etc. [< Med. L *sacristanus* sacristan]

sex·tu·ple (sek-st′ōōp′əl, -stup′-, seks′tōō-pəl) *adj.* **1** Sixfold. **2** Multiplied by six; six times repeated. **3** *Music* Having six beats to the measure. —*v.t.* **·pled, ·pling** To multiply by six. —*n.* A number or sum six times as great as another. [< L *sextus* sixth] —**sex′tu·ply** *adv.*

sex·tu·plet (seks-tup′lit, -tōō′plit, seks′tōō-plit) *n.* **1** A set of six similar things. **2** One of six offspring produced at a single birth.

sex·u·al (sek′shōō-əl) *adj.* **1** Of, pertaining or peculiar to, characteristic of, or affecting sex, the sexes, or the organs or functions of sex. **2** Characterized by or having sex. [< L *sexus* sex] —**sex′u·al′i·ty** (-al′ə-tē) *n.* —**sex′u·al·ly** *adv.*

sexual intercourse 1 The sexual act, esp. between humans, in which the erect penis is introduced into the vagina for the ejaculation of semen and sexual gratification. **2** Any act of sexual connection, esp. between humans.

sex·y (sek′sē) *adj.* **sex·i·er, sex·i·est 1** *Informal* Provocative of sexual desire: a *sexy* dress; a *sexy* woman. **2** *Informal* Concerned in large or excessive degree with sex: a *sexy* novel. **3** *Slang* Interesting, exciting, or stimulating: Crime was the *sexiest* issue of the political campaign.

sf., sfz. sforzando.

sfor·zan·do (sfôr-tsän′dō) *adj. & adv. Music* Accented with sudden explosive force. —*n.* A sforzando note or chord. Also **sfor·za′to** (-tsä′tō). [Ital. < *sforzare* to force]

sg. s.g. senior grade; specific gravity.

sgd. signed.

Sgt. Sergeant.

sh (sh) *interj.* An exclamation requesting silence.

sh. share; sheep; sheet; shilling.

Shab·bat (shä-bät′, shä′bəs) *n. pl.* **Shab·bat·im** (-bä′təm, -bô′səm) The Jewish Sabbath. [< Heb. *shabbāth*]

shab·by (shab′ē) *adj.* **·bi·er, ·bi·est 1** Threadbare, ragged. **2** Characterized by worn or ragged garments. **3** Mean; paltry. [< OE *sceabb* a scab] —**shab′bi·ly** *adv.* —**shab′bi·ness** *n.*

Sha·bu·oth (shä-vōō′ōth, shə-vōō′əs) *n.* The Jewish festival of Pentecost.

shack (shak) *n.* **1** A crudely built cabin or hut. **2** *Informal* A poorly built or designed house. —*v.i. Slang* To live or stay, usu. briefly, at a specific place. [?]

shack·le (shak′əl) *n.* **1** A bracelet or fetter for encircling and confining a limb or limbs. **2** *Usu. pl.* Any impediment or restraint. **3** One of various forms of fastenings, as a link for coupling railway cars. —*v.t.* **·led, ·ling 1** To restrain or confine with shackles; fetter. **2** To keep or restrain from free action or speech. **3** To connect or fasten with a shackle. [< OE *sceacul*] —**shack′ler** *n.*

Shackles

shad (shad) *n. pl.* **shad** Any of various anadromous fish related to the herring. [< OE *sceadd*]

shad·ber·ry (shad′ber′ē) *n. pl.* **·ries 1** SHADBUSH. **2** The fruit of the shadbush.

shad·bush (shad′bōōsh′) *n.* Any of various early-blooming shrubs with white flowers and edible purple berries. Also **shad′blow′** (-blō). [So called because it flowers when the shad appear in U.S. rivers]

shade (shād) *v.* **shad·ed, shad·ing** *v.t.* **1** To screen from light or heat. **2** To make dim with or as with a shadow; darken; **3** To screen or protect with or as with a shadow. **4** To cause to change, pass, blend, or soften, by gradations. **5 a** To represent (degrees of shade, colors, etc.) by gradations of light or shading. **b** To represent varying shades, colors, etc., in (a picture or painting). **6** To make slightly lower, as a price. —*v.i.* **7** To change or vary by degrees. —*n.* **1** Relative darkness caused by the interception or partial absence of rays of light. **2** A place having such relative darkness. **3** That part of a drawing, painting, etc. represented as being relatively dark or in shadow. **4** A gradation of darkness or blackness in a color. **5** A minute difference, variation, or degree: *shades* of meaning. **6** A screen or cover that partially or totally shuts off light: a lamp *shade.* **7** A ghost or phantom. **8** *pl. Slang* SUNGLASSES. —*in* (or *into*) *the shade* **1** In or into a shady place. **2** In or into a condition of inferiority, defeat, obscurity, etc. [< OE *sceadu* a shade]

shad·ing (shā′ding) *n.* **1** Protective against light or heat. **2** The representation pictorially of darkness, color, or depth. **3** A slight difference or variation.

shad·ow (shad′ō) *n.* **1** A comparative darkness within an illuminated area caused by the interception of light by an opaque body. **2** The dark figure or image thus produced on a surface: the *shadow* of a man. **3** The shaded portion of a picture. **4** A mirrored image: to see one's *shadow* in a pool. **5** A phantom, ghost, etc. **6** A faint representation or indication; a symbol: the *shadow* to things to come. **7** A remnant; vestige: *shadows* of his former glory. **8** An insignificant trace or portion: not a *shadow* of evidence. **9** Gloom or a saddening influence. **10** An inseparable companion. **11** One who trails or follows another, as a detective or spy. **12** A slight growth of beard, esp. in the phrase **five o'clock shadow.** —*v.t.* **1** To cast a shadow upon; shade. **2** To darken or make gloomy. **3** To represent or foreshow dimly or vaguely: with *forth* or *out*. **4** To follow closely or secretly; spy on. **5** To shade in painting, drawing, etc. —*adj.* Of or pertaining to a shadow cabinet. [< OE *sceadu* a shade] —**shad′ow·er** *n.*

shad·ow·box (shad′ō·boks′) *v.i.* To spar with an imaginary opponent as a form of exercise. —**shad′ow·box′ing** *n.*

shadow box A small, open, framed cabinet, usu. hung on a wall to display knickknacks, etc.

shadow cabinet In the British or other parliamentary government, a group of opposition leaders who would assume specific cabinet positions if the government in power should fall.

shad·ow·y (shad′ō-ē) adj. ·ow·i·er, ·ow·i·est 1 Dark; shady. 2 Vague; dim. 3 Unreal; ghostly. —**shad′ow·i·ness** n.

shad·y (shā′dē) adj. shad·i·er, shad·i·est 1 Full of shade; casting a shade. 2 Shaded or sheltered. 3 Morally questionable; suspicious. 4 Quiet; hidden. —**shad′i·ness** n.

shaft (shaft, shäft) n. 1 The long narrow rod of an arrow, spear, lance, harpoon, etc. 2 An arrow or spear. 3 Something hurled like or having the effect of an arrow or spear: *shafts* of ridicule. 4 A beam of light. 5 A long handle, as of a hammer, ax, etc. 6 *Mech.* A long and usu. cylindrical bar, esp. if rotating and transmitting motion. 7 *Archit.* **a** The portion of a column between capital and base. **b** A slender column, as an obelisk. 8 The stem of a feather. 9 The slender portion of a bone or the portion of a hair from root to the end. 10 A tall, narrow building or spire. 11 A narrow, vertical passage, as the entrance to a mine or an opening through a building for an elevator. 12 A conduit for the passage of air, heat, etc. 13 *Slang* Malicious or abusive treatment: with *the,* esp. in the phrases **get the shaft, give (someone) the shaft.** —v.t. *Slang* To act maliciously or abusively toward. [< OE *sceaft*]

shag (shag) n. 1 A rough coat or mass, as of hair. 2 A long, rough nap on cloth. 3 Cloth having a rough or long nap. 4 A coarse, strong tobacco: also **shag tobacco.** —v. **shagged, shag·ging** v.t. 1 To make shaggy or rough. —v.i. 2 To become shaggy or rough. [< OE *sceacga* wool]

shag·bark (shag′bärk′) n. 1 A species of hickory with rough, flaking bark. 2 Its edible nut. 3 Its wood.

shag·gy (shag′ē) adj. ·gi·er, ·gi·est 1 Having, consisting of, or resembling rough hair or wool. 2 Covered with any rough, tangled growth; fuzzy. 3 Unkempt. —**shag′gi·ly** adv. —**shag′gi·ness** n.

sha·green (shə-grēn′) n. 1 An abrasive leather made of the skin of various sharks and rays. 2 A rough-grained rawhide. [< Turk. *sāghrī* horse's hide]

shah (shä) n. An eastern ruler, esp. of Iran. [< Pers.]

shake (shāk) v. shook, shak·en, shak·ing v.t. 1 To cause to move to and fro or up and down with short, rapid movements. 2 To affect by or as by vigorous action: with *off, out, from,* etc.: to *shake* out a sail; to *shake* off a tackler. 3 To cause to tremble or quiver; vibrate: The blows *shook* the door. 4 To cause to stagger or totter. 5 To weaken or disturb: to *shake* one's determination. 6 To agitate or rouse; stir: often with *up.* 7 *Informal* To get rid of or away from. 8 To clasp (hands) as a form of greeting, agreement, etc. 9 *Music* TRILL. —v.i. 10 To move to and fro or up and down in short, rapid movements. 11 To be affected with vigorous action: with *off, out, from,* etc. 12 To tremble or quiver, as from cold or fear. 13 To become unsteady; totter. 14 To clasp hands. 15 *Music* TRILL. —**shake down** 1 To cause to fall by shaking. 2 To cause to settle by shaking. 3 To test or become familiar with (new equipment, etc.). 4 *Slang* To extort money from. —**shake up** 1 To mix or blend by shaking. 2 To agitate or rouse; stir. 3 To jar or jolt. 4 To effect or cause rather extensive changes or reorganization in. 5 *Slang* To cause to lose one's composure; disconcert. —n. 1 The act or an instance of shaking: a *shake* of the hand. 2 A tight fissure in rock or timber. 3 *pl. Informal* A fit of bodily shaking or trembling: usu. with *the.* 4 MILKSHAKE. 5 *Informal* EARTHQUAKE. 6 *Informal* An instant; jiffy. 7 *Informal* A deal: to get a fair *shake.* 8 *Music* TRILL. —**give (someone or something) the shake** To get away from (someone or something). [< OE *scacan*]

shake·down (shāk′doun′) n. 1 A thorough search. 2 *Slang* Extortion of money. 3 A testing or becoming familiar with something, as with a new ship. —adj. For the purpose of testing mechanical parts or familiarizing personnel: a *shakedown* cruise.

shak·er (shā′kər) n. One who or that which shakes: a *saltshaker,* cocktail shaker, etc.

Shak·er (shā′kər) n. One of a sect practicing celibacy and communal living: so called from their trembling movements during religious meetings. —**Shak′er·ism** n.

Shake·spear·i·an (shāk-spir′ē-ən) adj. Of, pertaining to, or characteristic of Shakespeare, his work, or his style. —n. A specialist on Shakespeare or his writings. Also **Shake·spear′e·an.**

shake-up (shāk′up′) n. A rather extensive change or reorganization, as in a business office, etc.

shak·o (shak′ō, shāk′-, shäk′-) n. pl. ·os A high, stiff military headdress, having a visor and an upright plume. [< Hung. *csākó*]

shak·y (shā′kē) adj. shak·i·er, shak·i·est 1 Not firm or solid. 2 Not well founded, thought out, etc.: a *shaky* theory. 3 Not dependable or reliable. 4 Characterized by shaking. 5 Weak; unsound, as in body. —**shak′i·ly** adv. —**shak′i·ness** n.

shale (shāl) n. A rock resembling slate, with fragile, uneven layers. [< G *Schale* shale] —**shal′y** adj.

Shako

shall (shal) v. p.t. **should.** Used now only as an auxiliary, *shall* expresses: 1 Simple futurity: I *shall* go next week. 2 That which seems inevitable or certain: I know I *shall* never leave. 3 Determination, promise, threat, or command: They *shall* not pass; You *shall* pay for this; You *shall* have it. 4 In laws, resolutions, etc., that which is obligatory: It *shall* be required to have identification. [< OE *sceal* I am obliged] • **shall, will** The traditional rule is that to express simple futurity *shall* is used with the first person and the auxiliary *will* with the second and third. To express determination, obligation, command, etc., *will* is used with the first person and *shall* with the second and third. This rule is now widely ignored, both in speech and in writing. *Will,* by far the more common auxiliary, occurs with all subjects and in all contexts. *Shall* is still often used with the first person, less so with the second and third, where its use is likely to appear stilted.

shal·lop (shal′əp) n. An open boat propelled by oars or sails. [< Du. *sloep* sloop]

shal·lot (shə-lot′, shal′ət) n. 1 A mild, onionlike vegetable allied to garlic. 2 SCALLION. [< OF *eschalotte*]

shal·low (shal′ō) adj. 1 Lacking depth. 2 Not extending far inwards or outwards: a *shallow* room. 3 Lacking intellectual depth; superficial. —n. *Usu. pl. but construed as sing. or pl.* A shallow place in a body of water; shoal. —v.t. & v.i. To make or become shallow. [ME *schalowe*] —**shal′low·ly** adv. —**shal′low·ness** n.

shalt (shalt) v. Archaic second person singular, present tense of SHALL: used with *thou.*

sham (sham) adj. False; pretended; counterfeit; mock. —n. 1 A person who shams. 2 A hoax; deception. 3 An imitation; counterfeit. 4 Cheap artificiality or pretension. 5 A decorative cover or the like for use over a household article: a pillow *sham.* —v. **shammed, sham·ming** v.t. 1 To counterfeit; feign. —v.i. 2 To make false pretenses; feign something. [? dial. var. of SHAME]

sha·man (shä′mən, shā′-, sham′ən) n. A priest of shamanism. [< Skt. *śamana* ascetic]

sha·man·ism (shä′mən·iz′əm, shā′-, sham′ən-) n. 1 A religion of NE Asia holding that supernatural spirits, etc., work for the good or ill of mankind only through the shamans. 2 Any similar religion, such as that practiced by certain Indians of the American Northwest. —**sha′man·ist** n. —**sha′man·is′tic** adj.

sham·ble (sham′bəl) v.i. ·bled, ·bling To walk with shuffling or unsteady gait. [? < SHAMBLES]

sham·bles (sham′bəlz) n.pl. (usu. construed as sing.) 1 SLAUGHTERHOUSE. 2 Any place of carnage or execution. 3 A place marked by great destruction, disorder, or confusion. [< OE *scamel* a bench.]

shame (shām) n. 1 A painful feeling caused by a sense of guilt, unworthiness, impropriety, etc. 2 Disgrace; humiliation. 3 A person or thing causing shame or humiliation. 4 Misfortune; outrage: It's a *shame* they didn't go. —**put to shame** 1 To disgrace; make ashamed. 2 To surpass or eclipse. —v.t. **shamed, sham·ing** 1 To cause to feel shame. 2 To bring shame upon; disgrace. 3 To impel by a sense of shame: with *into* or *out of.* [< OE *scamu*]

shame·faced (shām′fāst′) adj. 1 Showing shame; ashamed. 2 Bashful; modest. [< OE *scamfæst* abashed] —

shame·fac·ed·ly (shām′fā′sid·lē, shām′fāst′lē) *adv.* — **shame·fac′ed·ness** *n.*

shame·ful (shām′fəl) *adj.* 1 Bringing shame or disgrace; disgraceful; scandalous. 2 Indecent. —**shame′ful·ly** *adv.* — **shame′ful·ness** *n.* —**Syn.** 1 disreputable, dishonorable, ignoble, ignominious, base, despicable, contemptible, deplorable, vile, odious.

shame·less (shām′lis) *adj.* 1 Impudent; brazen; immodest. 2 Done without shame, indicating a want of decency. —**shame′less·ly** *adv.* —**shame′less·ness** *n.*

sham·my (sham′ē) *n.* CHAMOIS.

sham·poo (sham·pōō′) *v.t.* 1 To lather and wash (the hair and scalp) thoroughly. 2 To cleanse by rubbing. —*n.* The act or process of shampooing, or a preparation used for it. [< Hind. *chāmpnā* to press] —**sham·poo′er** *n.*

sham·rock (sham′rok) *n.* Any of several plants, with trifoliate leaves, accepted as the national emblem of Ireland, esp. the wood sorrel. [< Irish *seamar* trefoil]

shang·hai (shang′hī, shang·hī′) *v.t.* **·haied, ·hai·ing** 1 To drug or render unconscious and kidnap for service aboard a ship. 2 To cause to do something by force or deception. [< *Shanghai*]

Shamrock (wood sorrel)

Shan·gri-la (shang′grì·lä′) *n.* Any imaginary hidden utopia or paradise. [< *Shangri-la*, name of a utopian place in James Hilton's novel *Lost Horizon*, 1933]

shank (shangk) *n.* 1 The leg between the knee and the ankle. 2 The entire leg. 3 A cut of meat from the leg of an animal; the shin. 4 The stem, as of a tobacco pipe, key, anchor, etc. 5 The part of a tool connecting the handle with the working part; shaft. 6 The projecting piece or loop in the back of some buttons by which they are attached. 7 *Printing* The body of a type. 8 The narrow part of a shoe sole in front of the heel. • See SHOE. —**shank of the evening** *Informal* The early part of the evening. [< OE *sceanca*] —**shanked** *adj.*

shanks′ mare One's own legs as a means of conveyance.

shan′t (shant, shänt) Contraction of *shall not.*

shan·tung (shan′tung, shan·tung′) *n.* A fabric with a rough, nubby surface, originally made in China of silk, now often made of synthetic or cotton fiber. [< *Shantung,* China]

shan·ty¹ (shan′tē) *n. pl.* **·ties** A small, rickety shack or cabin. [< F (Canadian) *chantier* lumberer's shack]

shan·ty² (shan′tē) *n.* CHANTEY.

shape (shāp) *n.* 1 Outward form or contour. 2 Appearance of a body with reference only to its contour; figure. 3 Something that gives or determines shape, as a pattern or mold. 4 An assumed aspect or appearance; guise. 5 A developed or final expression or form: to put an idea into *shape.* 6 Any embodiment or form in which a thing may exist: the *shape* of a novel. 7 A ghost or phantom. 8 *Informal* The condition of a person or thing as regards health, orderliness, etc. —**in shape** In good physical condition or appearance. —**out of shape** In bad physical condition or appearance. —**take shape** To begin to have or assume definite form. —*v.* **shaped, shap·ing** *v.t.* 1 To give shape to; mold; form. 2 To adjust or adapt; modify. 3 To devise; prepare. 4 To give direction or character to: to *shape* one's course of action. 5 To put into or express in words. —*v.i.* 6 To take shape; develop; form: often with *up* or *into.* — **shape up** 1 To develop fully or appropriately; work out. 2 *Informal* To do, work, behave, etc., properly. [< OE *gesceap* creation] —**shap′er** *n.*

SHAPE (shāp) Supreme Headquarters Allied Powers, Europe.

shape·less (shāp′lis) *adj.* 1 Having no definite shape. 2 Lacking a pleasing shape or symmetry. —**shape′less·ly** *adv.* —**shape′less·ness** *n.*

shape·ly (shāp′lē) *adj.* **·li·er, ·li·est** Having a pleasing shape; well-formed. —**shape′li·ness** *n.*

shape-up (shāp′up′) *n.* The selection of a work crew, usu. on a day-to-day basis, from among a number of men assembled for a work shift.

shard (shärd) *n.* 1 A broken piece of a brittle substance, as of an earthen vessel. 2 *Zool.* A stiff covering, as the wing cover of a beetle. [< OE *sceard*]

share (shâr) *n.* 1 A portion alloted or due to a person or contributed by a person. 2 One of the equal parts into which the capital stock of a company or corporation is divided. 3 An equitable part of something used, done, or divided in common. —*v.* **shared, shar·ing** *v.t.* 1 To divide and give out in shares or portions; apportion. 2 To enjoy, use, participate in, endure, etc., in common. —*v.i.* 3 To have a part; participate: with *in.* 4 To divide something in equal parts: with *out* or *with.* [< OE *scearu*] —**shar′er** *n.*

share·crop·per (shâr′krop′ər) *n.* A tenant farmer who pays a share of his crop as rent for his land.

share·hold·er (shâr′hōl′dər) *n.* An owner of a share or shares of a company's stock.

sha·rif (shə·rēf′) *n.* SHERIF.

shark¹ (shärk) *n.* Any of a large order of mostly marine fishes having a cartilaginous skeleton, lateral gill slits, and a tough skin. —*v.i.* To fish for sharks. [?]

Great white shark

shark² (shärk) *n.* 1 A dishonest person, esp. a swindler. 2 *Slang* A person of exceptional skill or ability. [?< SHARK¹]

shark·skin (shärk′skin′) *n.* 1 Leather made of a shark's skin. 2 A summer fabric with a smooth surface. 3 A fabric with a pebbly surface.

sharp (shärp) *adj.* 1 Having a keen edge or an acute point; capable of cutting or piercing. 2 Not rounded; pointed; angular: *sharp* features. 3 Abrupt in change of direction: a *sharp* curve. 4 Distinct; well-defined: a *sharp* contrast. 5 Keen or quick in perception or discernment. 6 Keen or acute, as in seeing or hearing. 7 Shrewd, as in bargaining. 8 Quickly aroused; harsh: a *sharp* temper. 9 Heated; fiery: a *sharp* debate. 10 Vigilant; attentive: a *sharp* watch. 11 Quick; vigorous. 12 Keenly felt: *sharp* hunger pangs. 13 Intense or penetrating in effect; incisive to the point of being unsettling or wounding: a *sharp* look; a *sharp* tongue. 14 Shrill: a *sharp* sound. 15 Having an acid or pungent taste or smell. 16 *Slang* Stylishly dressed or well groomed. 17 *Music* Being above the proper or indicated pitch. —*adv.* 1 In a sharp manner. 2 Promptly; exactly: at 4 o'clock *sharp.* 3 *Music* Above the proper pitch. —*n.* 1 *Music* A character (♯) used on a natural degree of the staff to make it represent a tone a half-step higher; also, the tone so indicated. 2 A sewing needle of long, slender shape. 3 A cheat; sharper: a *cardsharp.* —*v.t.* 1 *Music* To raise in pitch, as by a half-step. —*v.i.* 2 *Music* To sing, play, or sound above the right pitch. [< OE *scearp*] —**sharp′ly** *adv.* —**sharp′ness** *n.*

sharp·en (shär′pən) *v.t. & v.i.* To make or become sharp. —**sharp′en·er** *n.*

sharp·er (shär′pər) *n.* A swindler; cheat.

sharp·ie (shär′pē) *n.* 1 A long, flat-bottomed sailboat having a centerboard and one or two masts. 2 *Informal* A shrewd, clever person, esp. in bargaining. [< SHARP]

sharp·shoot·er (shärp′shōō′tər) *n.* A skilled marksman. —**sharp′shoot′ing** *n.*

sharp-sight·ed (shärp′sī′tid) *adj.* Having keen vision. —**sharp′sight′ed·ly** *adv.* —**sharp′sight′ed·ness** *n.*

sharp-tongued (shärp′tungd′) *adj.* Bitter or caustic in speech.

sharp-wit·ted (shärp′wit′id) *adj.* Acutely intelligent; discerning.

Shas·ta daisy (shas′tə) A cultivated, daisylike variety of chrysanthemum having white-rayed flowers. [< Mt. *Shasta,* California]

shat·ter (shat′ər) *v.t.* 1 To break into pieces suddenly, as by a blow. 2 To break the health or well-being of, as the body or mind. 3 To damage or demolish. —*v.i.* 4 To break into pieces; burst. —*n. pl.* Shattered pieces or fragments, esp. in the phrase **in shatters.** [ME *schateren* to scatter]

shave (shāv) *v.* **shaved, shaved** or **shav·en, shav·ing** *v.i.* 1 To cut hair or beard close to the skin with a razor. —*v.t.* 2 To remove hair or beard from (the face, head, etc.) with a razor. 3 To cut (hair or beard) close to the skin with a razor: often with *off.* 4 To trim closely as if with a razor: to *shave* a lawn. 5 To cut thin slices or pieces from. 6 To touch or scrape in passing; graze; come close to. 7 *Informal* To lower or deduct from (a price, amount, etc.). —*n.* 1 The act or operation of shaving with a razor. 2 A thin slice or piece; shaving. 3 *Informal* The act of barely grazing something. [< OE *scafan*]

shav·en (shā′vən) A *p.p.* of SHAVE. —*adj.* 1 Shaved; also, tonsured. 2 Trimmed closely.

shav·er (shā′vər) *n.* 1 One who shaves. 2 An instrument for shaving: an electric *shaver.* 3 *Informal* A lad.

shave·tail (shāv′tāl′) *n. Slang* A second lieutenant, esp. one recently commissioned. [In allusion to young, unbroken army mules with bobbed tails]

Sha·vi·an (shā′vē·ən) *n.* An admirer of George Bernard Shaw, his writings, or his theories. —*adj.* Of or characteristic of George Bernard Shaw or his work.

shav·ing (shā′ving) *n.* 1 The act of one who or that which shaves. 2 A thin paring shaved from anything.

shawl (shôl) *n.* A wrap, as a square cloth, or large broad scarf, worn over the head or shoulders. [< Pers. *shāl*]

Shaw·nee (shô·nē′) *n.* One of a tribe of North American Indians of Algonquian stock, formerly living in Tennessee and South Carolina, now in Oklahoma. [< Algon.]

shay (shā) *n.* A light carriage; chaise. [Back formation < CHAISE, mistaking it for a plural]

she (shē) *pron.* 1 The female person or being previously mentioned or understood, in the nominative case. 2 Any woman. 3 Something personified as female: *She* is a great little car. —*n.* A female person or animal: often used in combination: a *she-lion.* [< OE *sēo*]

sheaf (shēf) *n. pl.* **sheaves** (shēvz) 1 Stalks of cut grain or the like, bound together. 2 Any collection of things, as papers, held together by a band or tie. —*v.t.* To bind in a sheaf; sheave. [< OE *scēaf*]

shear (shir) *n.* 1 Either of the blades of a pair of shears. 2 A cutting machine for sheet metal. 3 *Physics* **a** A deformation of a solid body, equivalent to a sliding over each other of adjacent layers. **b** A force or system of forces tending to cause this. 4 The act or result of shearing. —*v.* **sheared** (*Archaic* **shore**), **sheared** or **shorn**, **shear·ing** *v.t.* 1 To cut the hair, fleece, etc., from. 2 To remove by cutting or clipping: to *shear* wool. 3 To deprive; strip, as of power or wealth. 4 To cut or clip with shears or other sharp instrument: to *shear* a cable. —*v.i.* 5 To use shears or other sharp instrument. 6 To slide or break from a shear (def. 3). 7 To proceed by or as by cutting a way: with *through.* [< OE *sceran* to shear] —**shear′er** *n.*

shears (shirz) *n.pl.* Any large cutting or clipping instrument worked by the crossing of cutting edges. Also **pair of shears.**

shear·wa·ter (shir′wô′tər, -wot′ər) *n.* Any of various web-footed, far-ranging sea birds that usu. skim the water when flying.

sheath (shēth) *n.* 1 An envelope or case, as for a sword; scabbard. 2 *Biol.* Any structure that enfolds or encloses. [< OE *scæth*]

sheathe (shēth) *v.t.* **sheathed, sheath·ing** 1 To put into a sheath. 2 To plunge (a sword, etc.) into flesh. 3 To draw in, as claws. 4 To protect or conceal, as by covering: to *sheathe* plasterboard; to *sheathe* one's anger.

sheath·ing (shē′thing) *n.* 1 An outer covering, as of a building or ship's hull. 2 The material used for this. 3 The act of one who sheathes.

sheave¹ (shēv) *v.t.* **sheaved, sheav·ing** To gather into sheaves; collect.

sheave² (shēv) *n.* A grooved pulley wheel; also, a pulley wheel and its block. [ME]

sheaves (shēvz) *n.pl.* of SHEAF.

she·bang (shi·bang′) *n. Slang* Matter; concern; affair: tired of the whole *shebang.* [?]

shed¹ (shed) *v.* **shed, shed·ding** *v.t.* 1 To pour forth in drops; emit, as tears or blood. 2 To cause to pour forth. 3 To send forth or abroad; radiate: to *shed* light on a subject. 4 To throw off without allowing to penetrate, as rain; repel. 5 To cast off by natural process, as hair, skin, a shell, etc.

—*v.i.* 6 To cast off or lose hair, skin, etc., by natural process. 7 To fall or drop, as leaves or seed. —*n.* That which sheds, as a sloping surface or watershed. [< OE *scēadan* separate, part]

shed² (shed) *n.* 1 A small low building or lean-to, used for storage, etc. 2 A large hangarlike building, often with open front or sides. [Var. of SHADE]

she'd (shēd) Contraction of *she had* or *she would.*

shed·der (shed′ər) *n.* 1 One who sheds. 2 An animal that molts.

sheen (shēn) *n.* 1 A glistening brightness, as if from reflection. 2 Bright, shining attire. —*v.i.* To shine; gleam; glisten. [< OE *scēne* beautiful] —**sheen′y** *adj.*

sheep (shēp) *n. pl.* **sheep** 1 Any of a genus of woolly, medium-sized ruminants, esp. domesticated species grown for their fleece, flesh, and hide. 2 A meek or timid person. [< OE *scēap*]

Sheep

sheep·cote (shēp′kōt′) *n.* SHEEPFOLD. Also **sheep′cot′** (-kot′).

sheep dip Any insecticidal, medicinal, or cleansing solution used to bathe sheep.

sheep dog Any dog trained to guard and control sheep.

sheep·fold (shēp′fōld′) *n.* A pen for sheep.

sheep·herd·er (shēp′hûr′dər) *n.* A herder of sheep. —**sheep′herd′ing** *n.*

sheep·ish (shē′pish) *adj.* 1 Embarrassed; chagrined. 2 Meek; timid. —**sheep′ish·ly** *adv.* —**sheep′ish·ness** *n.*

sheep·skin (shēp′skin′) *n.* 1 A sheep's hide, or anything made from it, as parchment, an outdoor coat, etc. 2 A document written on parchment. 3 *Informal* A diploma.

sheep sorrel A low-growing weed related to buckwheat.

sheer¹ (shir) *v.i.* 1 To swerve from a course; turn aside. —*v.t.* 2 To cause to swerve. —*n.* 1 *Naut.* **a** The slight rise of the lengthwise lines of a vessel's hull. **b** A position of a vessel that enables it to swing clear of a single anchor. 2 A swerving course. [< SHEAR]

sheer² (shir) *adj.* 1 Having no modifying conditions; absolute; utter: *sheer* folly. 2 Exceedingly thin and fine: said of fabrics. 3 Perpendicular; steep: a *sheer* precipice. 4 Pure; pellucid. —*n.* Any very thin fabric used for clothes. —*adv.* 1 Entirely; utterly. 2 Perpendicularly. [ME *schere*] —**sheer′ly** *adv.* —**sheer′ness** *n.*

sheet (shēt) *n.* 1 A thin, broad, usu. rectangular piece of any material, as metal, glass, etc. 2 A broad, flat surface or expanse: a *sheet* of flame. 3 A large, usu. rectangular piece of cotton, linen, silk, etc., used as bedding. 4 A usu. rectangular piece of paper, used esp. for writing, printing, etc. 5 *Usu. pl. Printing* A printed signature for a book. 6 *Informal* A newspaper. 7 A sail: a literary use. 8 *Naut.* A rope or chain attached to the lower corner of a sail, used to regulate the angle of the sail to the wind. 9 The large, unseparated block of stamps printed by one impression of a plate. —*v.t.* To cover with, wrap in, or form into a sheet or sheets. —*adj.* Formed or cut into sheets: *sheet* metal. [< OE *scēte* linen cloth]

sheet anchor 1 An anchor used only in emergency. 2 A person or thing depended upon in an emergency.

sheet·ing (shē′ting) *n.* 1 Material for bed sheets. 2 Any material used for lining or covering a surface.

sheet metal Metal rolled and pressed into sheets.

sheet music Music printed on unbound sheets of paper.

sheik (shēk, shāk) *n.* The chief of an Arab tribe or family. Also **sheikh.** [< Ar. *shakha* grow old] —**sheik′dom, sheikh′·dom** *n.*

shek·el (shek′əl) *n.* 1 An ancient, esp. Hebrew unit of weight. 2 A coin having this weight. 3 *pl. Slang* Money; riches.

shel·drake (shel′drāk′) *n.* 1 Any of various Old World wild ducks with varicolored plumage. 2 MERGANSER. [< dial. E *sheld* dappled + DRAKE]

shelf (shelf) *n. pl.* **shelves** (shelvz) 1 A piece of material set horizontally into or against a wall, cabinet, closet, etc., to support articles. 2 The contents of a shelf. 3 Any flat projecting ledge, as of rock. 4 A reef; shoal. [< LG *schelf* set of shelves]

shell (shel) *n.* 1 The hard outer covering of a mollusk, lobster, egg, nut, etc. • See OYSTER. **2** Something like a shell in shape or function, as the outer framework of a building, a ship's hull, a hollow pastry or pie crust for filling, etc. **3** A sleeveless blouse or sweater. **4** A very light, long, and narrow racing rowboat. **5** A hollow metallic projectile filled with an explosive or chemical. **6** A metallic or paper cartridge case containing the powder, bullet, or shot for breechloading small arms. **7** Any case used to contain the explosives of fireworks. **8** A reserved or impersonal attitude: to come out of one's *shell*. —*v.t.* **1** To divest of or remove from a shell, husk, or pod. **2** To separate from the cob, as Indian corn. **3** To bombard with shells, as a fort. **4** To cover with shells. —*v.i.* **5** To shed or become freed from the shell or pod. **6** To fall off, as a shell or scale. [< OE *scell* shell] —**shell'er** *n.* —**shell'y** *adj.* (**·i·er, ·i·est**)

she'll (shēl) Contraction of *she will* or *she shall.*

shel·lac (shə·lak') *n.* **1** A purified lac in the form of thin flakes, used in varnish, insulators, etc. **2** A varnish made of shellac dissolved in alcohol. —*v.t.* **·lacked, ·lack·ing 1** To cover or varnish with shellac. **2** *Slang* **a** To beat. **b** To defeat utterly. Also **shel·lack'.** [< SHELL + LAC[1]]

shel·lack·ing (shə·lak'ing) *n. Slang* **1** A beating; assault. **2** A thorough defeat.

shell·back (shel'bak') *n.* **1** A veteran sailor. **2** Anyone who has crossed the equator on a ship.

shell·bark (shel'bärk') *n.* SHAGBARK.

shell·fire (shel'fīr') *n.* The firing of artillery shells.

shell·fish (shel'fish') *n. pl.* **·fish** or **·fish·es** An aquatic mollusk or crustacean, esp. if edible, as a clam, shrimp, etc.

shell game 1 A swindling game in which the victim bets on the location of a pea covered by one of three nutshells; thimblerig. **2** Any game in which the victim cannot win.

shell·proof (shel'prōōf') *adj.* Built to resist the destructive effect of projectiles and bombs.

shell shock COMBAT FATIGUE. —**shell-shocked** (shel'shokt') *adj.*

shel·ter (shel'tər) *n.* **1** That which covers or shields from exposure, danger, etc. **2** The state of being covered, protected, or shielded. —*v.t.* **1** To provide protection or shelter for; shield, as from danger or inclement weather. —*v.i.* **2** To take shelter. [?] —**shel'ter·er** *n.*

shelve (shelv) *v.* **shelved, shelv·ing** *v.t.* **1** To place on a shelf. **2** To postpone indefinitely; put aside. **3** To retire. **4** To provide or fit with shelves. —*v.i.* **5** To incline gradually.

shelves (shelvz) *n. pl.* of SHELF.

shelv·ing (shel'ving) *n.* **1** Shelves collectively. **2** Material for the construction of shelves.

Shem (shem) In the Bible, the eldest son of Noah.

Shem·ite (shem'īt) *n.* SEMITE.

she·nan·i·gan (shi·nan'ə·gən) *n. Usu. pl. Informal* **1** Trickery; foolery. **2** Deceitful or underhanded actions. [?]

She·ol (shē'ōl) *n.* In the Old Testament, a place where the dead were believed to go. [< Heb. *shā'al* dig]

shep·herd (shep'ərd) *n.* **1** A keeper or herder of sheep. **2** Figuratively, a pastor, leader, or guide. —*v.t.* To herd, guide, protect, or direct, as a shepherd. [< OE *scēaphyrde*] —**shep'herd·ess** *n. Fem.*

shepherd dog SHEEP DOG.

shepherd's purse A common weed related to mustard, bearing small white flowers and pouchlike pods.

Sher·a·ton (sher'ə·tən) *adj.* Denoting a style of furniture characterized by simplicity and pleasing proportions. [< T. *Sheraton*, 1751–1806, English designer]

sher·bet (shûr'bit) *n.* **1** A frozen dessert, usu. fruit-flavored, made with water or milk, gelatin, etc. **2** Originally, a Turkish drink, made of fruit juice sweetened and diluted with water. Also **sher'bert** (-bərt). [< Ar. *sharbah* a drink]

she·rif (shə·rēf') *n.* **1** A member of a princely Muslim family which claims descent from Mohammed. **2** The chief magistrate of Mecca. **3** An Arab chief. [< Ar. *sharîf* noble]

sher·iff (sher'if) *n.* **1** The chief law-enforcement officer of a county, who executes the mandates of courts, keeps order, etc. **2** In Canada, an official whose job is to enforce minor court orders, such as the eviction of persons for

nonpayment of rent. [< OE *scīr·gerēfa* shire reeve] —**sher'·iff·dom** *n.*

sher·ry (sher'ē) *n. pl.* **·ries** A fortified wine originally made in Spain. [< *Xeres*, former name of Jerez, Spain]

she's (shēz) Contraction of *she is* or *she has.*

Shet·land pony (shet'lənd) A small, shaggy breed of pony originally bred on the Shetland Islands.

shew (shō) *n. & v. Archaic* SHOW.

shew·bread (shō'bred') *n.* Unleavened bread formerly placed as an offering in Jewish temples.

SHF, S.H.F., shf, s.h.f. superhigh frequency.

shib·bo·leth (shib'ə·leth) *n.* A test word or pet phrase of a party; a watchword. [< Heb. *shibbōleth,* a word mispronounced by certain Hebrew spies, betraying them as aliens. *Judges* 12:4–6]

shied (shīd) *p.t. & p.p.* of SHY.

shield (shēld) *n.* **1** A broad piece of defensive armor, commonly carried on the left arm; a large buckler. **2** Anything that protects or defends. **3** Any of various devices that afford protection, as from machinery, electricity, radiation, etc. **4** Anything shaped like a shield, as a policeman's badge, decorative emblem, etc. **5** A heraldic escutcheon. —*v.t.* **1** To protect from danger; defend; guard. **2** To hide or screen from view. —*v.i.* **3** To act as a shield or safeguard. —**shield'er** *n.*

Shields
a. Anglo-Saxon.
b. Greek.

shield·ing (shēld'ing) *n.* A protective device or screen: radiation *shielding.*

shi·er (shī'ər) Comparative of SHY.

shi·est (shī'ist) Superlative of SHY.

shift (shift) *v.t.* **1** To change or move from one position, arrangement, place, etc., to another. **2** To change for another or others of the same class. —*v.i.* **3** To change position, place, attitude, etc. **4** To manage or get along. **5** To evade; equivocate. —*n.* **1** The act of shifting. **2** A change in position, place, direction, etc. **3** A change in attitude, loyalty, etc. **4** An action or recourse taken in an emergency; expedient. **5** A trick or evasion. **6** GEARSHIFT. **7** A relay of workers or their period of work: the night *shift.* **8** A woman's dress that is not belted or fitted at the waist. **9** *Archaic* A chemise or undergarment. [< OE *sciftan* divide] —**shift'er** *n.*

shift·less (shift'lis) *adj.* **1** Unable or unwilling to work or accomplish something; inefficient or lazy. **2** Inefficiently or incompetently done. —**shift'less·ly** *adv.* —**shift'·less·ness** *n.*

shift·y (shif'tē) *adj.* **shift·i·er, shift·i·est 1** Characterized by or showing deceit or trickery. **2** Full of expedients; resourceful. —**shift'i·ly** *adv.* —**shift'i·ness** *n.*

shill (shil) *n. Slang* The ally of a sidewalk peddler or gambler who makes a purchase or bet to encourage onlookers to buy or bet. [?]

shil·le·lagh (shi·lā'lē, -lə) *n.* In Ireland, a stout cudgel made of oak or blackthorn. Also **shil·la'lah, shil·lea'lah, shil·le'lah.** [< *Shillelagh,* a town in Ireland famed for its oaks]

shil·ling (shil'ing) *n.* **1** A current silver coin of Great Britain, equal to five (new) pence or 1/20 of a pound. **2** A former colonial American coin, varying in value from 12 to 16 cents. [< OE *scilling*]

shil·ly-shal·ly (shil'ē·shal'ē) *v.i.* **·lied, ·ly·ing** To act with indecision; vacillate. —*adj.* Irresolute; hesitating. —*n.* Weak or foolish vacillation; irresolution. —*adv.* In an irresolute manner. [Redupl. of *Shall I?*] —**shil'ly-shal'li·er** *n.*

shim (shim) *n.* A thin wedge of metal, wood, etc., used to fill out space. —*v.t.* **shimmed, shim·ming** To wedge up, fill out, or level by inserting a shim. [?]

shim·mer (shim'ər) *v.i.* To shine faintly; give off or emit a tremulous light; glimmer. —*n.* A tremulous shining or gleaming; glimmer. [< OE *scimerian*] —**shim'mer·y** *adj.*

shim·my (shim'ē) *n. pl.* **·mies 1** A jazz dance accompanied by shaking movements. **2** Undesired oscillation or vibration, as of automobile wheels. —*v.i.* **·mied, ·my·ing 1** To vibrate or wobble. **2** To dance the shimmy. [Alter. of CHE-MISE]

shin (shin) *n.* **1** The front part of the leg below the knee; also, the shinbone. **2** The lower foreleg: a *shin* of beef. —*v.t. & v.i.* **shinned, shin·ning** To climb (a pole) by gripping with the hands or arms and the shins or legs: usu. with *up.* [< OE *scinu*]

shin·bone (shin′bōn′) *n.* TIBIA.

shin·dig (shin′dig) *n. Slang* A dance or noisy party. [?]

shine (shīn) *v.i.* **shone** or *(esp. for def. 5)* **shined, shin·ing 1** To emit light; beam; glow. **2** To show or be conspicuous. **3** To excel; be preeminent. —*v.t.* **4** To cause to shine. **5** To brighten by rubbing or polishing. —*n.* **1** Radiance; luster; sheen. **2** Fair weather; sunshine. **3** *Informal* A liking or fancy. **4** *Informal* A smart trick or prank. **5** A gloss or polish, as on shoes. [< OE *scīnan*]

shin·er (shī′nər) *n.* **1** One who or that which shines. **2** Any of various species of minnows with silvery scales. **3** *Slang* A black eye.

shin·gle[1] (shing′gəl) *n.* **1** A thin, tapering piece of wood or other material, used in courses to cover roofs. **2** A small signboard bearing the name of a doctor, lawyer, etc., and placed outside his office. **3** A short haircut. —*v.t.* **·gled, ·gling 1** To cover (a roof, building, etc.) with shingles. **2** To cut (the hair) short. [< L *scandula* a shingle] —**shin′gler** *n.*

shin·gle[2] (shing′gəl) *n.* **1** Rounded, stones, coarser than gravel, found on the seashore. **2** A place strewn with shingle, as a beach. [?] —**shin′gly** *adj.*

shin·gles (shing′gəlz) *n. pl. (construed as sing.)* A painful viral disease marked by inflammation of sensory nerves and blistering, chiefly affecting the torso. [< L *cingulum* girdle]

shin·ing (shī′ning) *adj.* **1** Emitting or reflecting a continuous light; gleaming. **2** Of unusual excellence; conspicuous. —**shin′ing·ly** *adv.*

shin·ny[1] (shin′ē) *n.* A game resembling hockey, or one of the sticks or clubs used by the players. Also **shin′ney.** [< *shin ye*, a cry used in the game]

shin·ny[2] (shin′ē) *v.i.* **·nied, ·ny·ing** *Informal* To climb using one's shins: usu. with *up.*

Shin·to (shin′tō) *n.* The primary religion of Japan, consisting chiefly in ancestor worship, and formerly in the worship of the Emperor as a divinity. Also **Shin′to·ism.** [< Chin. *shin* god + *tao* way] —**Shin′to·ist** *n.*

shin·y (shī′nē) *adj.* **shin·i·er, shin·i·est 1** Glistening; glossy; polished. **2** Full of sunshine; bright. —**shin′i·ness** *n.*

ship (ship) *n.* **1** Any large vessel suitable for deep-water navigation. **2** The crew and officers of such a vessel. **3** An aircraft or spacecraft. —*v.* **shipped, ship·ping** *v.t.* **1** To transport by ship. **2** To send by any means of transportation, as by rail, truck, or air. **3** To hire and receive for service on board a vessel, as sailors. **4** To draw (oars) inside a boat. *Naut.* To receive over the side: to *ship* a wave. —*v.i.* **6** To go on board ship; embark. **7** To enlist as a seaman. [< OE *scip*]

-ship *suffix* **1** The state or quality of: *friendship.* **2** Office, rank, or dignity of: *kingship.* **3** The art or skill of: *marksmanship.* [< OE *-scipe*]

ship biscuit A hard, crackerlike biscuit; hardtack.

ship·board (ship′bôrd′, -bōrd′) *n.* A ship. —**on ship·board** In or on a ship.

ship·build·er (ship′bil′dər) *n.* One who designs or works at building ships. —**ship′build′ing** *n.*

ship·load (ship′lōd′) *n.* A load that a ship can carry.

ship·mas·ter (ship′mas′tər, -mäs′-) *n.* The captain or master of a merchant ship.

ship·mate (ship′māt′) *n.* A fellow sailor.

ship·ment (ship′mənt) *n.* **1** The act of shipping. **2** Goods shipped; a consignment.

ship·per (ship′ər) *n.* One who ships goods.

ship·ping (ship′ing) *n.* **1** The act, process, or business of shipping goods. **2** Ships collectively, esp. with respect to nationality or tonnage.

ship·shape (ship′shāp′) *adj.* Trim; orderly; neat. —*adv.* In a seamanlike manner; neatly.

ship·worm (ship′wûrm′) *n.* Any of various wormlike marine mollusks that undermine wooden piers, ships, etc., by boring into them.

ship·wreck (ship′rek′) *n.* **1** A ship or parts of it after

being wrecked. **2** The partial or total destruction of a ship at sea. **3** Utter destruction; ruin. —*v.t.* **1** To wreck, as a vessel. **2** To bring to disaster; destroy.

ship·wright (ship′rīt′) *n.* One whose work is to construct or repair ships.

ship·yard (ship′yärd′) *n.* An enclosure where ships are built or repaired.

shire (shīr) *n.* A territorial division of Great Britain; a county. [< OE *scīr*]

shirk (shûrk) *v.t.* **1** To avoid doing (something that should be done). —*v.i.* **2** To avoid work or evade obligation. —*n.* One who shirks: also **shirk′er.** [?]

shirr (shûr) *v.t.* **1** To gather (cloth) by parallel rows of small stitches. **2** To bake with crumbs in a buttered dish, as eggs. —*n.* A gathering of cloth made by shirring. [?]

shirt (shûrt) *n.* **1** A garment for the upper part of the body, usu. having a collar and cuffs and buttoning along the front. **2** UNDERSHIRT. —**lose one's shirt** *Slang* To lose everything. [< OE *scyrte* shirt, short garment]

shirt·ing (shûr′ting) *n.* Material used for making shirts, blouses, etc.

shirt-sleeve (shûrt′slēv′) *adj.* **1** Not wearing a jacket or coat; informally dressed: a *shirt-sleeve* audience. Also **shirt-sleeved. 2** Straightforward; plain; simple and direct in technique, approach, manner, etc.: *shirt-sleeve* diplomacy.

shirt·waist (shûrt′wāst′) *n.* A tailored blouse or shirt worn by women.

Shi·va (shē′və) SIVA.

shiv·er[1] (shiv′ər) *v.i.* To tremble, as with cold or fear. —*n.* The act of shivering; a shaking or quivering. —**shiv′er·y** *adj.* [ME *shiveren*]

shiv·er[2] (shiv′ər) *v.t. & v.i.* To break suddenly into fragments; shatter. —*n.* A splinter; silver. [ME *schivere*]

shlock (shlok) *n.* SCHLOCK. —**shlock′y** *adj.* (·i·er, ·i·est)

shoal[1] (shōl) *n.* **1** A shallow place in any body of water. **2** A bank or bar of sand, esp. one seen at low water. —*v.i.* To become shallow. [< OE *sceald* shallow]

shoal[2] (shōl) *n.* A thing or school, as of fish. —*v.i.* To gather in shoals. [< OE *scolu* shoal of fish.]

shoat (shōt) *n.* A young hog. [ME *shote*]

shock[1] (shok) *n.* **1** A violent collision or concussion; impact; blow. **2** The result of such a collision. **3** A sudden, severe effect on the mind or emotions; jolt: the *shock* of recognition. **4** Something causing such an effect. **5** An acute impairment of vital functions associated with failure of the circulatory system following grave trauma such as burns, poisoning, brain injury, massive bleeding, etc. **6** Involuntary muscular contraction caused by the passage of an electric current through the body. —*v.t.* **1** To disturb the emotions or mind of; horrify; disgust. **2** To subject to an electric shock. **3** To shake by sudden collison; jar. [< OF *choc*] —**shock′er** *n.* —**Syn.** *v.* **1** appall, take aback, surprise, astound.

shock[2] (shok) *n.* A number of sheaves of grain, stalks of corn, or the like, stacked for drying upright in a field. —*v.t. & v.i.* To gather (grain) into a shock or shocks. [ME *schokke*] —**shock′er** *n.*

shock[3] (shok) *adj.* Shaggy; bushy. —*n.* A coarse, tangled mass, as of hair. [?]

shock absorber *Mech.* A device designed to absorb the energy of sudden impacts, as in the suspension of an automobile.

shock·ing (shok′ing) *adj.* Causing sudden and violent surprise, horror, etc.: *shocking* news. —**shock′ing·ly** *adv.*

shock therapy A method of treating mental illness by inducing convulsions and unconsciousness with electric current or certain drugs. Also **shock treatment.**

shock wave *Physics* A powerful compression wave produced by a body moving faster than the speed of sound.

shod (shod) *p.t. & p.p.* of SHOE.

shod·dy (shod′ē) *n. pl.* **·dies 1** Reclaimed wool obtained by shredding waste materials. **2** Fiber or cloth manufactured of inferior material. **3** Vulgar display; sham. **4** Refuse; waste. —*adj.* **·di·er, ·di·est 1** Poorly made; inferior. **2** Made of or containing shoddy. **3** Cheaply pretentious; vulgar. **4** Nasty; mean: a *shoddy* remark. [?] —**shod′di·ly** *adv.* —**shod′di·ness** *n.* —**Syn.** *adj.* **1** tawdry, cheap, sloppy, second-rate.

shoe (shoo) *n.* **1** An outer covering, usu. of leather, for the human foot. **2** Something resembling a shoe in position or use. **3** A rim or plate of iron to protect the hoof of an animal. **4** The tread or outer covering of a pneumatic tire. **5** A braking device that stops or retards the motion of an object. —*v.t.* **shod** or **shoed, shoe·ing** To furnish with shoes or the like. [< OE *scōh*] —**sho′er** *n.*

Shoe
a. tongue. b. heel.
c. shank. d. vamp.

shoe·horn (shoo′hôrn′) *n.* A smooth curved implement as of metal, horn, etc., shaped to aid in putting on a shoe.

shoe·lace (shoo′lās) *n.* A cord or string used to fasten a shoe.

shoe·mak·er (shoo′mā′kər) *n.* One who makes or repairs shoes. —**shoe′mak′ing** *n.*

shoe·shine (shoo′shīn′) *n.* The waxing and polishing of a pair of shoes.

shoe·string (shoo′string) *n.* SHOELACE. —**on a shoestring** With meager or inadequate financial resources.

shoe·tree (shoo′trē′) *n.* A rigid form inserted in a shoe to hold its shape or to stretch it.

sho·far (shō′fär) A ram's horn used in Jewish ritual, sounded on solemn occasions. [< Heb. *shōphār*]

sho·gun (shō′gun) *n.* The hereditary commander in chief of the Japanese army until 1868. [< Chin. *chiang-chün* leader of an army] —**sho′gun·ate** (-it, -āt) *n.*

shone (shōn, shon) *p.t. & p.p.* of SHINE.

shoo (shoo) *interj.* Get away! —*v.t.* **1** To drive away by crying "shoo." —*v.i.* **2** To cry "shoo."

shoo-in (shoo′in′) *n. Informal* One who is virtually certain to win, as an election.

shook (shook) *p.t.* of SHAKE.

shoot (shoot) *v.* **shot, shoot·ing** *v.t.* **1** To hit, wound, or kill with a missile discharged from a weapon. **2** To discharge (a missile or weapon): to *shoot* an arrow or a gun. **3** To send forth, as questions, glances, etc. **4** To pass over or through swiftly: to *shoot* rapids. **5** To photograph or film. **6** To thrust out; dart; flick: with *out:* He *shot* out an arm in gesture. **7** To push into or out of the fastening, as the bolt of a door. **8** To propel, discharge, or dump, as down a chute or from a container. **9** *Slang* To inject (a drug, esp. a narcotic). **10** In games: **a** To score (a goal, point, total score, etc.). **b** To play (golf, craps, pool, etc.). **c** To propel (a basketball, puck, marble, etc.) to attempt a score. **d** To cast (dice). —*v.i.* **11** To discharge a missile from a firearm, bow, etc. **12** To go off; discharge. **13** To move swiftly; dart. **14** To extend or project. **15** To put forth buds, leaves, etc. **16** To record photographically. **17** In games, to make a play by propelling the ball, puck, etc., in a certain manner. — **shoot at** (or **for**) *Informal* To strive for; seek to attain. — **shoot the works** *Informal* To risk everything. —*n.* **1** A young branch or growth; offshoot. **2** The process of early growth. **3** A narrow passage in a stream; a rapid. **4** An inclined passage down which anything may be shot. **5** The act of shooting; a shot. **6** A shooting match, hunting party, etc. [< OE *scēotan*] —**shoot′er** *n.*

shooting star METEOR.

shoot-out (shoot′out′) *n.* A battle involving an exchange of gunfire.

shop (shop) *n.* **1** A place where goods and services are sold at retail: also **shoppe.** **2** A place for the carrying on of any skilled work: a machine *shop.* —**talk shop** To discuss one's work. —*v.i.* **shopped, shop·ping** To visit shops or stores to purchase or look at goods. [< OE *sceoppa* booth] —**shop′per** *n.* • *Shoppe* is an archaic spelling but is still used in the names of some establishments to suggest a quaint, old-fashioned character. However, the spelling *shop* has been in use since at least 1600, so it is hardly a novelty.

shop·keep·er (shop′kē′pər) *n.* One who owns or runs a shop.

shop·lift·er (shop′lif′tər) *n.* One who steals goods displayed for sale in a shop. —**shop′lift′ing** *n.*

shopping center A group of retail stores, restaurants, etc., including an ample parking area, usu. built as a unit and accessible chiefly by automobile.

shop steward A union worker elected to represent the union in conferences, etc., with management.

shop·worn (shop′wôrn′, -wōrn′) *adj.* **1** Soiled or damaged from having been handled or on display in a store. **2** Lacking freshness or originality: *shopworn* ideas.

sho·ran (shôr′an, shō′ran) *n.* A short-range electronic navigation system for ships and aircraft. [< *sho(rt) ra(nge) n(avigation)*]

shore¹ (shôr, shōr) *n.* **1** The land adjacent to an ocean, sea, lake, or large river. **2** Land, as distinguished from a body of water. [ME]

shore² (shôr, shōr) *v.t.* **shored, shor·ing** To prop, as a wall, by a vertical or sloping timber: usu. with *up.* —*n.* A beam set endwise as a prop, as against the side of a building. [ME *shoren*]

shore bird Any of various birds that feed and nest along the edges of lakes, oceans, rivers, etc.

shore·line (shôr′līn′, shōr′-) *n.* The line or contour of a shore.

shore patrol A detail of the U.S. Navy, Coast Guard, or Marine Corps assigned to police duties ashore.

shore·ward (shôr′wərd, shōr′-) *adj. & adv.* Toward the shore. Also **shore′wards.**

shor·ing (shôr′ing, shōr′ing) *n.* **1** The act of propping, as with shores. **2** Shores or their manner of use.

shorn (shôrn, shōrn) A *p.p.* of SHEAR.

short (shôrt) *adj.* **1** Having relatively little linear extension; not long. **2** Being below the average stature; not tall. **3** Having relatively little extension in time; brief. **4** Of no great distance: a *short* trip. **5** Less than the usual or standard duration, quantity, extent, etc.: on *short* notice; a *short* letter. **6** Having few items: a *short* list. **7** Not reaching or attaining a goal or requirement: an effort *short* of the mark. **8** Not retentive: a *short* memory. **9** Abrupt in manner; curt. **10** Having an inadequate supply: *short* of cash. **11** Quickly aroused or agitated: a *short* temper. **12** *Phonet.* **a** Of relatively brief duration. **b** Describing any vowel sound that contrasts with a long vowel, as the vowel sound in *mat* contrasted with that in *mate.* **13** In finance: **a** Not having in one's possession when selling, as stocks or commodities. **b** Describing a sale of stocks or commodities that the seller does not possess but anticipates procuring subsequently at a lower price for delivery as contracted. **14** In English prosody, unaccented. **15** Flaky or crisp: pastry made *short* with lard. —**for short** For brevity and ease of expression: The University of Connecticut is called Uconn *for short.* —**in short** In summary; briefly. —**in short order** Without delay; forthwith; promptly. —*n.* **1** Something short, as a garment, vowel, syllable, etc. **2** *pl.* Short trousers extending to the knee or above the knee. **3** *pl.* A man's undergarment resembling short trousers. **4** SHORT CIRCUIT. **5** SHORT SUBJECT. —*adv.* **1** Abruptly: to stop *short.* **2** In a curt manner. **3** So as to be short of a goal or mark. **4** By means of a short sale. — *v.t. & v.i.* **1** To give (someone) less than the amount due. **2** SHORT-CIRCUIT. [< OE *sceort*] —**short′ness** *n.*

short·age (shôr′tij) *n.* An inadequate supply; deficiency.

short·bread (shôrt′bred′) *n.* A rich, dry cake or cooky made with shortening.

short·cake (shôrt′kāk′) *n.* A dessert consisting of a cake or biscuit served with fruit and often topped with whipped cream.

short·change (shôrt′chānj′) *v.t.* **·changed, ·chang·ing 1** To give less change than is due to. **2** To give less than what is rightfully due; cheat. —**short′chang′er** *n.*

short-cir·cuit (shôrt′sûr′kit) *v.t. & v.i.* To make a short circuit (in).

short circuit *Electr.* An electrical connection of low resistance or impedance, esp. when accidental or unintended.

short·com·ing (shôrt′kum′ing) *n.* A defect; imperfection.

short·cut (shôrt′kut′) *n.* **1** A route between two places shorter than the regular way. **2** A means or method that saves time, effort, etc.

short·en (shôr′tən) *v.t.* **1** To make short or shorter; reduce; lessen. **2** To make flaky or crisp, as pastry. —*v.i.* **3** To become short or shorter. —**short′en·er** *n.*

short·en·ing (shôr′tən·ing, shôrt′ning) *n.* **1** Edible fat, esp. as used in bakery products. **2** An abbreviation.

short·fall (shôrt′fôl′) *n.* **1** A failure to meet an expectation or requirement. **2** The amount or extent of such a failure: a *shortfall* of 20 percent.

short·hand (shôrt′hand′) *n.* **1** Any of various systems of recording speech by writing symbols, abbreviations, etc.; stenography. **2** Any method of quick communication. —*adj.* **1** Written in shorthand. **2** Using shorthand.

short-hand·ed (shôrt′han′did) *adj.* Not having a sufficient number of assistants or workmen.

short·horn (shôrt′hôrn′) *n.* One of a breed of cattle with short horns.

short-lived (shôrt′līvd′, -livd′) *adj.* Living or lasting but a short time.

short·ly (shôrt′lē) *adv.* **1** In a short time; soon. **2** In few words; briefly. **3** Curtly; abruptly.

short shrift Little or no mercy or delay in dealing with a person or disposing of a matter.

short-sight·ed (shôrt′sī′tid) *adj.* **1** NEARSIGHTED. **2** Resulting from or characterized by lack of foresight. —**short′-sight′ed·ly** *adv.* —**short′-sight′ed·ness** *n.*

short·stop (shôrt′stop′) *n.* In baseball, an infielder stationed between second and third bases.

short story A narrative prose story shorter than a novel or novelette.

short subject A relatively brief film, as a documentary or animated cartoon.

short-tem·pered (shôrt′tem′pərd) *adj.* Easily aroused to anger.

short-term (shôrt′tûrm′) *adj.* Payable a short time after issue, as securities.

short ton 2,000 pounds avoirdupois.

short wave A radio wave having a wavelength of about 100 meters or less. —**short′-wave′** *adj.*

short-wind·ed (shôrt′win′did) *adj.* Becoming easily out of breath. —**short′-wind′ed·ness** *n.*

Sho·sho·ne (shō·shō′nē) *n.* One of a large tribe of North American Indians, formerly occupying parts of Wyoming, Idaho, Nevada, and Utah. Also **Sho·sho′ni.**

Sho·sho·ne·an (shō·shō′nē·ən, shō′shə·nē′ən) *n.* The largest branch of the Uto-Aztecan linguistic family of North American Indians. —*adj.* Of or pertaining to this linguistic branch. Also **Sho·sho′ni·an.**

shot¹ (shot) *n.* **1** The act of shooting, as a firearm. **2** Something likened to a shot, as a cutting remark. **3** *pl.* **shot a** Any of the lead pellets that comprise ammunition for a shotgun; also, the pellets collectively. **b** A solid missile, as a ball of iron, fired from a cannon or other gun. **4** A solid metal ball thrown for distance in sports competitions. **5** The range of a projectile. **6** One who shoots; a marksman. **7** A single effort, attempt, or opportunity to do a specific thing: to have a *shot* at getting the job. **8** In certain sports and games, the act or manner of shooting the ball, puck, etc., as in attempting a score. **9** A conjecture; guess. **10** A hypodermic injection, as of a drug, or the dose so administered. **11** An action or scene recorded on film. **12** The taking of a photograph; also, a photograph. **13** A blast, as in mining. —**like a shot** Very quickly. —*adj.* **1** Having a changeable or variegated appearance: purple fabric *shot* with gold. **2** *Informal* Utterly exhausted or ruined; washed-up. [< OE *scot*]

shot² (shot) *p.t.* & *p.p.* of SHOOT.

shote (shōt) *n.* SHOAT.

shot·gun (shot′gun′) *n.* A smoothbore gun, often double-barreled, adapted for the discharge of shot at short range. —*adj.* Coerced with, or as with, a shotgun.

Repeating shotgun

should (shŏŏd) **1** *p.t.* of SHALL. **2** An auxiliary expressing: **a** Obligation: You *should* write that letter. **b** Condition: If I *should* go, he would go too. **c** Futurity, as viewed from the past: She wondered how she *should* dress for the

party. **d** Expectation: I *should* be at home by noon. **e** Politeness or modesty in requests or statements of doubt: I *should* hardly think so. [< OE *scolde*, p.t. of *sculan* owe]

shoul·der (shōl′dər) *n.* **1** The part of the trunk between the neck and the arm or forelimb. **2** The joint connecting the arm or forelimb with the body. **3** *pl.* The area of the upper back including both shoulders. **4** The shoulders considered as a support for burdens or the seat of responsibility. **5** The part of a garment designed to cover the shoulder. **6** The forequarter of an animal. **7** Something resembling a shoulder in form, as the broadened part of a bottle below the neck. **8** Either edge of a road or highway. —**straight from the shoulder** *Informal* Candidly; straightforwardly. —*v.t.* **1** To assume as something to be borne: to *shoulder* the blame. **2** To bear upon the shoulders. **3** To push with or as with the shoulder. —*v.i.* **4** To push with the shoulder. —**shoulder arms** To rest a rifle against the shoulder, holding the butt with the hand on the same side. [< OE *sculder* shoulder]

shoulder blade SCAPULA.

should·n't (shŏŏd′nt) Contraction of *should not.*

shout (shout) *n.* A sudden and loud outcry. —*v.t.* **1** To utter with a shout; say loudly. —*v.i.* **2** To utter a shout; cry out loudly. [ME *shouten*] —**shout′er** *n.*

shove (shuv) *v.t.* & *v.i.* **shoved, shov·ing** **1** To push, as along a surface. **2** To press forcibly (against); jostle. —**shove off 1** To push along or away, as a boat. **2** *Informal* To depart. —*n.* The act of pushing or shoving. [< OE *scūfan*] —**shov′er** *n.*

shov·el (shuv′əl) *n.* A flattened scoop with a handle, as for digging, lifting earth, rock, etc. —*v.* **·eled** or **·elled, ·el·ing** or **·el·ling** *v.t.* **1** To take up and move or gather with a shovel. **2** To toss hastily or in large quantities as if with a shovel. **3** To clear or clean with a shovel, as a path. —*v.i.* **4** To work with a shovel. [< OE *scofl*] —**shov′el·er, shov′el·ler, shov′el·ful** *n.*

show (shō) *v.* **showed, shown** or **showed, show·ing** *v.t.* **1** To cause or permit to be seen; present to view. **2** To cause or allow (something) to be understood or known; explain. **3** To make known by behavior or expression; reveal: to *show* emotion. **4** To cause (someone) to understand or see; explain something to. **5** To confer; bestow: to *show* favor. **6** To make evident by the use of logic; prove. **7** To guide; lead, as into a room: Please *show* them in. **8** To enter in a show or exhibition. —*v.i.* **9** To become visible or known. **10** To appear; seem. **11** To make one's or its appearance. **12** To give a theatrical performance; appear. **13** In racing, to finish third or better. —**show off** To exhibit proudly; display ostentatiously. —**show up 1** To expose or be exposed, as faults. **2** To be evident or prominent. **3** To make an appearance. **4** *Informal* To be better than. —*n.* **1** A presentation, as of a film, television program, or live entertainment, for viewing by spectators. **2** An exhibition, as of merchandise or art. **3** A competition at which certain animals, as dogs, are displayed and judged. **4** Someone or something regarded as a spectacle to be viewed, as in wonder or amusement. **5** An act of showing; display or manifestation: a *show* of strength. **6** Pretense or semblance; also, ostentation: mere *show.* **7** A sign of metal, oil, etc., in a mining or drilling operation. **8** In racing, a finish of third place or better. [< OE *scēawian*] —**show′er** *n.* —Syn. *v.* **1** exhibit, manifest, display. **4** convince, teach. *n.* **1** viewing, showing. **5** mark, sign, indication.

show biz *Slang* SHOW BUSINESS.

show·boat (shō′bōt′) *n.* A boat on which an acting troupe gives performances in river towns.

show business The entertainment industry, esp. the theater, motion pictures, and television.

show·case (shō′kās′) *n.* A glass case for exhibiting and protecting articles for sale.

show·down (shō′doun′) *n.* *Informal* Any action that forces a resolution of an issue or dispute.

show·er (shou′ər) *n.* **1** A fall of rain, hail, or sleet, esp. of short duration. **2** A copious fall, as of tears, sparks, or other small objects. **3** A bath in which water is sprayed from an overhead nozzle: also **shower bath.** **4** A party for the giving of gifts, as to a bride. —*v.t.* **1** To sprinkle or wet with or as with showers. **2** To discharge in a shower; pour out. **3** To bestow upon in large numbers; overwhelm: to *shower* her with gifts. —*v.i.* **4** To fall as in a shower. **5** To take a shower bath. [< OE *scūr*] —**show′er·y** *adj.*

show·ing (shō′ing) *n.* **1** An act of presenting for public view, as a film. **2** A result of being shown, as in competition; record: a fine *showing.* **3** Presentation; statement, as of a subject.

show·man (shō′mən) *n. pl.* **·men** (-mən) **1** One who exhibits or produces shows. **2** One who is skilled at the art of effective performance. —**show′man·ship** *n.*

shown (shōn) *p.p.* of SHOW.

show·off (shō′ôf′) *n.* One who makes a pretentious display of himself.

show·piece (shō′pēs′) *n.* A prized object considered worthy of special exhibit.

show·place (shō′plās′) *n.* A place exhibited or noted for its beauty, historic interest, etc.

show·room (shō′rōōm′) *n.* A room for the display of merchandise.

show·y (shō′ē) *adj.* **show·i·er, show·i·est 1** Striking; splendid; brilliant. **2** Brilliant or conspicuous in a superficial or tasteless way; gaudy; meretricious. —**show′i·ly** *adv.* —**show′i·ness** *n.*

shpt. shipment.

shrank (shrangk) *p.t.* of SHRINK.

shrap·nel (shrap′nəl) *n. pl.* **·nel 1** A projectile for use against personnel, containing metal balls and a charge that expels them in mid-air. **2** Shell fragments. [< Henry *Shrapnel*, 1761–1842, British artillery officer]

shred (shred) *n.* **1** A long, irregular strip torn or cut off. **2** A fragment; particle. —*v.t.* **shred·ded** or **shred, shred·ding** To tear or cut into shreds. [< OE *scrēade* cutting] —**shred′der** *n.*

shrew (shrōō) *n.* **1** Any of numerous tiny mouselike mammals having a long pointed snout and soft fur. **2** A vexatious or nagging woman. [< OE *scrēawa*] —**shrew′ish** *adj.* —**shrew′ish·ly** *adv.* —**shrew′ish·ness** *n.*

Shrew

shrewd (shrōōd) *adj.* **1** Having keen insight, esp. in practical matters; clever; able. **2** Artful; sly. [< ME *shrew* malicious person] —**shrewd′ly** *adv.* —**shrewd′ness** *n.*

shriek (shrēk) *n.* A sharp, shrill cry or scream. —*v.i.* **1** To utter a shriek. —*v.t.* **2** To utter with a shriek. [< ON *skrækja*] —**shriek′er** *n.*

shrift (shrift) *n. Archaic* The act of shriving; confession. [< OE *scrift*]

shrike (shrīk) *n.* Any of various predatory birds with hooked bill and a slim tail. [< OE *scrīc* thrush]

shrill (shril) *adj.* **1** High-pitched and piercing, as a sound. **2** Emitting a sharp, piercing sound. **3** Harsh and immoderate: *shrill* criticism. —*v.t.* **1** To cause to utter a shrill sound. —*v.i.* **2** To make a shrill sound. [ME *shrille*] —**shrill′ness** *n.* —**shrill′y** *adv.* —Syn. **1** penetrating. **3** intemperate, hysterical, bitter.

shrimp (shrimp) *n. pl.* **shrimp** or **shrimps 1** Any of numerous small, long-tailed crustaceans having ten legs and a fused head and thorax covered with a carapace, esp. various edible marine species. **2** *Informal* A small or insignificant person. [ME *shrimpe*]

Shrimp

shrine (shrīn) *n.* **1** A receptacle for sacred relics. **2** A sacred tomb or chapel. **3** A thing or spot made sacred by historic or other association. [< L *scrinium* case]

shrink (shringk) *v.* **shrank** or **shrunk, shrunk** or **shrunk·en, shrink·ing** *v.i.* **1** To draw together; contract as from heat, cold, etc. **2** To become less or smaller; diminish. **3** To draw back, as from disgust or horror; recoil: with *from.* —*v.t.* **4** To cause to shrink, contract, or draw together. —*n.* **1** The act of shrinking. **2** *Slang* A psychiatrist or psychoanalyst. [< OE *scrincan*] —**shrink′a·ble** *adj.* —**shrink′er** *n.*

shrink·age (shringk′ij) *n.* **1** The act or process of shrinking; contraction. **2** The amount lost by contraction. **3** Decrease in value; depreciation.

shrive (shrīv) *v.* **shrove** (shrōv) or **shrived, shriv·en** (shriv′-) or **shrived, shriv·ing** *Archaic v.t.* **1** To receive the confession of and give absolution to. —*v.i.* **2** To make confession. **3** To hear confession. [< OE *scrīfan*] —**shriv′er** *n.*

shriv·el (shriv′əl) *v.t. & v.i.* **·eled** or **·elled, ·el·ing** or **·el·ling 1** To contract into wrinkles; shrink and wrinkle. **2** To make or become helpless or impotent; wither. [?]

shroud (shroud) *n.* **1** A cloth used to wrap a corpse for burial. **2** Something that envelops or conceals. **3** *Naut.* One of a set of ropes or wires stretched from a masthead to the sides of a ship, serving to strengthen the mast laterally. —*v.t.* **1** To clothe in a shroud. **2** To envelop or conceal; block from view. [< OE *scrūd* a garment]

shrove (shrōv) *p.t.* of SHRIVE.

Shrove·tide (shrōv′tīd′) *n.* The three days immediately preceding Ash Wednesday, on which confession is made in preparation for Lent.

shrub (shrub) *n.* A woody perennial of low stature, usu. with several stems. [< OE *scrybb* brushwood] —**shrub′bi·ness** *n.* —**shrub′by** *adj.* (**·bi·er, ·bi·est**)

shrub·ber·y (shrub′ər-ē) *n. pl.* **·ber·ies** A group of shrubs, as in a garden.

shrug (shrug) *v.t. & v.i.* **shrugged, shrug·ging** To draw up (the shoulders), as in displeasure, doubt, surprise, etc. —*n.* The act of shrugging the shoulders. [?]

shrunk (shrungk) *p.t. & p.p.* of SHRINK.

shrunk·en (shrungk′ən) *p.p.* of SHRINK. —*adj.* Contracted and atrophied.

shtick (shtik) *n. Slang* Something contrived to make one's personality distinct or memorable, as an actor's characteristic mannerism or a comedian's routine. [< Yiddish < G *stück* piece, bit]

sh. tn. short ton.

shuck (shuk) *n.* **1** A husk, shell, or pod, as of corn. • See WALNUT. **2** A shell of an oyster or a clam. **3** *Informal* Something of little or no value: not worth *shucks.* —*v.t.* **1** To remove the husk or shell from (corn, oysters, etc.). **2** *Informal* To take off or cast off, as an outer covering. [?] —**shuck′er** *n.*

shucks (shuks) *interj. Informal* A mild exclamation of annoyance, disgust, etc.

shud·der (shud′ər) *v.i.* To tremble or shake, as from fright or cold. —*n.* A convulsive shiver, as from horror or fear. [ME *shudren*] —Syn. *v.* shiver, quake. *n.* tremor.

shuf·fle (shuf′əl) *v.* **·fled, ·fling** *v.t.* **1** To shift about so as to mix up or confuse; disorder. **2** To change the order of by mixing, as cards in a pack. **3** To move (the feet) along with a dragging gait. **4** To change or move from one place to another. —*v.i.* **5** To scrape the feet along. **6** To change position; shift ground. **7** To resort to indirect or deceitful methods; prevaricate. **8** To shuffle cards. —*n.* **1** A dragging of the feet. **2** The act of shuffling, as cards. **3** A deceitful or evasive course; artifice. [< LG *schuffeln*] —**shuf′fler** *n.*

shuf·fle·board (shuf′əl·bôrd′, -bōrd′) *n.* A game in which disks are slid by means of a pronged cue along a smooth surface toward numbered spaces.

shun (shun) *v.t.* **shunned, shun·ning** To keep clear of; avoid. [< OE *scunian*] —**shun′ner** *n.*

shunt (shunt) *v.t.* **1** To turn aside. **2** In railroading, to switch, as a train or car, from one track to another. **3** *Electr.* **a** To connect a shunt in parallel with. **b** To be connected as a shunt for or of. **4** To put off on someone else, as a task. —*v.i.* **5** To move to one side. **6** *Electr.* To be diverted by a shunt: said of current. **7** To move back and forth; shuttle. —*n.* **1** The act of shunting. **2** A railroad switch. **3** *Electr.* A conductor joining two points in a circuit and diverting part of the current. —**shunt′er** *n.*

shush (shush) *interj.* Keep quiet! —*v.t.* To try to quiet.

shut (shut) *v.* **shut, shut·ting** *v.t.* **1** To bring into such position as to close an opening. **2** To close (an opening) so as to prevent passage or movement in or out. **3** To close and fasten securely, as with a lock. **4** To keep from entering or leaving: with *out* or *in.* **5** To close, fold, or bring together, as extended parts: to *shut* an umbrella. —*v.i.* **6** To be or become closed or in a closed position. —**shut down 1** To cease from operating, as a factory. **2** To lower;

come down close: The fog *shut down.* **—shut off 1** To cause to stop operating: to *shut off* a light. **2** To separate: usu. with *from: shut off* from all companionship. **—shut out** In sports, to keep (an opponent) from scoring during the course of a game. **—shut up 1** *Informal* To stop talking or cause to stop talking. **2** To close all the entrances to, as a house. **3** To imprison; confine. **—adj. 1** Made fast or closed. **2** *Regional* Freed, as from something disagreeable; rid: with *of.* [< OE *scyttan*]

shut·down (shut′doun′) *n.* The closing of a mine, industrial plant, etc.

shut·eye (shut′ī′) *n. Slang* Sleep.

shut·in (shut′in′) *n.* An invalid who has to stay at home. **—adj. 1** Obliged to stay at home. **2** Inclined to avoid people.

shut·out (shut′out′) *n.* In sports, a game in which one side is prevented from scoring.

shut·ter (shut′ər) *n.* **1** A hinged screen or cover, as for a window. **2** *Phot.* A mechanism for momentarily admitting light through a camera lens to a film or plate. **3** One who or that which shuts. **—v.t.** To furnish, close, or divide off with shutters.

shut·tle (shut′l) *n.* **1** A device used in weaving to carry the weft to and fro between the warp threads. **2** A similar device in a sewing machine. **3** A system of transportation for moving goods or passengers in both directions between two nearby points; also, the vehicle, as a bus, train, or airplane, operating between these points, usu. frequently. **—v.t. & v.i. ·tled, ·tling** To move back and forth frequently or like a shuttle. [< OE *scytel* missile]

shut·tle·cock (shut′l·kok′) *n.* A rounded piece of cork, with a crown of feathers, that is hit back and forth in the game of badminton.

shy¹ (shī) *adj.* **shy·er, shy·est,** or **shi·er, shi·est 1** Easily frightened or startled; timid. **2** Uneasy in the company of others; bashful; reserved. **3** Circumspect; watchful; wary. **4** Expressing or suggesting diffidence or reserve: a *shy* look. **5** *Informal* Having less than is called for or expected; short. **—v.t. shied, shy·ing 1** To start suddenly to one side, as a horse. **2** To draw back, as from doubt or caution: with *off* or *away.* **—n.** A starting aside, as in fear. [< OE *scēoh* timid] **—shy′ly** *adv.* **—shy′ness** *n.*

shy² (shī) *v.t. & v.i.* **shied, shy·ing 1** To throw with a swift, sidelong motion. **—n. pl. shies** A careless throw; a fling. [?]

shy·ster (shīs′tər) *n. Informal* Anyone, esp. a lawyer, who conducts his business in an unscrupulous or tricky manner. [?]

SI International System of Units (Le Système International d'Unités).

Si silicon.

Si·am (sī·am′) *n.* The former name for THAILAND. **—Si·a·mese** (sī′ə·mēz′, -mēs′) *adj., n.*

Siamese cat A breed of short-haired cat, typically fawn-colored or pale cream, with dark ears, tail, feet, and face, and blue eyes.

Siamese twins Any twins conjoined at birth. [< Eng and Chang (1811–74), conjoined twins born in Siam.]

sib (sib) *n.* **1** A blood relation, esp. a brother or sister. **2** Kinsmen collectively; relatives. **—adj.** Related by blood; akin. [< OE *sibb*]

sib·i·lant (sib′ə·lənt) *adj.* **1** Hissing. **2** *Phonet.* Describing those consonants which are uttered with a hissing sound, as (s), (z), (sh), and (zh). **—n.** *Phonet.* A sibilant consonant. [< L *sibilare* to hiss] **—sib′i·lance** *n.* **—sib′i·lant·ly** *adv.*

sib·ling (sib′ling) *n.* A brother or sister. [< OE, a relative]

sib·yl (sib′əl) *n.* **1** In ancient Greece and Rome, any of several women who prophesied future events. **2** A fortune-teller; sorceress. **—si·byl·ic** (si·bil′ik) or **si·byl′lic, sib′yl·line** (-īn) *adj.*

sic¹ (sik) *adv.* So; thus: used within brackets after something quoted, to indicate that the quotation is exactly reproduced, even though questionable or incorrect. [L]

sic² (sik) *v.t.* **sicked, sick·ing 1** To urge or attack: to *sic* a dog on a burglar. **2** To seek out or attack: used in the imperative esp. to a dog. [Var. of SEEK]

sick¹ (sik) *adj.* **1** Affected with disease; ill; ailing. **2** Of or used by sick persons. **3** Affected by nausea; nauseated. **4** Sickly; weak: a *sick* laugh. **5** Mentally or emotionally upset or ill: *sick* with grief. **6** Disposed to find offensive or wearisome from being surfeited: with *of: sick* of hearing transistor radios in public places. [< OE *sēoc*] **—sick′ish** *adj.* **—sick′ish·ly** *adv.* **—sick′ish·ness** *n.*

sick² (sik) *v.t.* SIC².

sick·bay (sik′bā′) *n.* That part of a ship or naval base set aside for the care of the sick.

sick·bed (sik′bed′) *n.* The bed upon which a sick person lies.

sick·en (sik′ən) *v.t. & v.i.* To make or become sick or disgusted. **—sick′en·er** *n.*

sick·en·ing (sik′ən·ing) *adj.* Disgusting; nauseating. **—sick′en·ing·ly** *adv.*

sick headache MIGRAINE.

sick·le (sik′əl) *n.* A cutting or reaping implement with a long, curved blade mounted on a short handle. **—v.t. ·led, ·ling** To cut with a sickle, as grass, hay, etc. [< OE *sicel*]

sick·le-cell anemia (sik′əl·sel′) A severe, hereditary anemia occurring among the offspring of parents who both have sickle-cell trait.

sickle-cell trait A tendency in erythrocytes to become deformed into a sickle shape and to clog small blood vessels, occurring chiefly among Negroes and due to the presence of a genetic hemoglobin abnormality inherited from one parent. Also **sickl·e·mi·a** (sik′əl·ē′mē·ə).

Sickle

sick·ly (sik′lē) *adj.* **·li·er, ·li·est 1** Habitually ailing; unhealthy; feeble. **2** Marked by the prevalence of sickness. **3** Nauseating; disgusting; sickening. **4** Of or characteristic of sickness: a *sickly* appearance. **5** Lacking in conviction; weak; unconvincing: a *sickly* excuse. **6** Faint; pallid. **—adv.** In a sick manner; poorly. **—v.t. ·lied, ·ly·ing** To make sickly, as in color. **—sick′li·ly** *adv.* **—sick′li·ness** *n.*

sick·ness (sik′nis) *n.* **1** The state of being sick; illness. **2** A particular form of disease. **3** Nausea. **4** Any disordered and weakened state.

side (sīd) *n.* **1** Any of the boundary lines of a surface or any of the surfaces of a solid: the *side* of a box. **2** A boundary line or surface, distinguished from the top and bottom or front and back. **3** Either of the surfaces of an object of negligible thickness, as a sheet of paper or a coin. **4** The right half or the left half of a human body, esp. of the torso, or of any animal. **5** The space beside someone. **6** A lateral part of a surface or object: the right *side* of a room. **7** The lateral half of a slaughtered animal: a *side* of beef. **8** One of two or more contrasted surfaces, parts, or places: the far *side* of a river. **9** A slope, as of a mountain. **10** An opinion, aspect, or point of view: the conservative *side* of the issue. **11** A group of competitors or partisans of a point of view. **12** Family connection, esp. by descent through one parent: my father's *side*. **—on the side** In addition to the main part or chief activity. **—side by side 1** Alongside one another. **2** In a spirit of cooperation; together. **—take sides** To give one's support to one of two sides engaged in a dispute. **—adj. 1** Situated at or on one side. **2** Being from one side: a *side* glance. **3** Incidental: a *side* issue. **4** Being in addition to the main dish: a *side* order. **—v.t.** To provide with a side or sides. **—side with** To range oneself on the side of; support, esp. in a dispute. [< OE]

side arms Weapons worn at the side, as pistols.

side·board (sīd′bôrd′, -bōrd′) *n.* **1** A piece of dining-room furniture for holding tableware. **2** *pl. Brit.* SIDEBURNS.

side·burns (sīd′bûrnz′) *n.pl.* **1** Whiskers grown on the cheeks; burnsides. **2** The hair growing on the sides of a man's face in front of the ears.

side·car (sīd′kär′) *n.* A one-wheeled passenger car attached to the side of a motorcycle.

side effect A secondary, often harmful effect, as of a drug.

side·kick (sīd′kik′) *n. Slang* A faithful subordinate or friend.

side·light (sīd′līt′) *n.* **1** A light coming from the side. **2** Incidental illustration or information.

side·line (sīd′līn′) *n.* **1** An auxiliary line of goods. **2** Any additional or secondary work differing from one's main job. **3** One of the lines bounding the two sides of an athletic field or court, as in football or tennis. **4** *pl.* The area just outside these lines. —*v.t.* **·lined, ·lin·ing** To make unfit or unavailable for active participation: Injuries *sidelined* him.

side·long (sīd′lông′, -long′) *adj.* Inclining or tending to one side; lateral. —*adv.* **1** In a lateral or oblique direction. **2** On the side.

side·man (sīd′man′) *n. pl.* **·men** (-men′) One of the supporting musicians, as distinguished from the featured performers, of a band, esp. a jazz band.

si·de·re·al (sī-dir′ē-əl) *adj.* **1** Of or relating to the stars. **2** Measured by means of the stars: *sidereal* time. [< L *sidus* star] —**si·de′re·al·ly** *adv.*

sid·er·ite (sid′ə-rīt) *n.* **1** A glassy ferrous carbonate mineral. **2** An iron meteorite. [< Gk. *sidēros* iron] —**sid′er·it′ic** (-rit′ik) *adj.*

side·sad·dle (sīd′sad′l) *n.* A saddle for a woman wearing skirts, designed to be ridden facing sideways, with both legs on the same side of the horse.

side·show (sīd′shō′) *n.* **1** A small show incidental to a major one, as in a circus. **2** Any subordinate issue or attraction.

side·split·ting (sīd′split′ing) *adj.* Provoking wild laughter; hilarious.

side·step (sīd′step′) *v.* **·stepped, ·step·ping** *v.i.* **1** To step to one side. **2** To avoid responsibility. —*v.t.* **3** To avoid, as an issue; dodge. —**side′step′per** *n.*

side step A step or movement to one side.

side·swipe (sīd′swīp′) *v.t. & v.i.* **·swiped, ·swip·ing** To strike or scrape along the side: to *sideswipe* a car while passing it. —*n.* **1** A glancing collision along the side. **2** *Informal* An oblique or parenthetical criticism.

side·track (sīd′trak′) *v.t. & v.i.* **1** To move to a siding, as a railroad train. **2** To divert from the main issue or subject. —*n.* A railroad siding.

side·walk (sīd′wôk′) *n.* A pavement at the side of the street for pedestrians.

side·ward (sīd′wərd) *adj.* Directed or moving toward or from the side; lateral. —*adv.* Toward or from the side: also **side′wards.**

side·ways (sīd′wāz′) *adv.* **1** From one side. **2** So as to incline with the side forward: Hold it *sideways.* **3** Toward one side; askance; obliquely. —*adj.* Moving to or from one side. Also **side′way′, side′wise′** (-wīz′).

side·wheel (sīd′hwēl′) *adj.* Describing a steamboat having a paddle wheel on either side. —**side′-wheel′er** *n.*

sid·ing (sī′ding) *n.* **1** A railway track by the side of the main track. **2** A material used to cover the side of a frame building, as paneling or shingles.

si·dle (sīd′l) *v.i.* **·dled, ·dling** To move sideways, esp. in a cautious or stealthy manner. —*n.* A sideways step or movement. [< obs. *sidling* sidelong] —**si′dler** *n.*

siege (sēj) *n.* **1** The surrounding of a town or fortified place in an effort to seize it, as after a blockade. **2** A steady attempt to win something. **3** A trying time: a *siege* of illness. —*v.t.* **sieged, sieg·ing** BESIEGE. [< L *sedere* sit]

si·en·na (sē-en′ə) *n.* **1** A yellowish brown pigment consisting of clay containing oxides of iron and manganese. **2** A yellowish brown color. **3** BURNT SIENNA. [< Ital. *(terra di) Siena* (earth of) Siena]

si·er·ra (sē-er′ə) *n.* A mountain range or chain, esp. one having a jagged outline. [< L *serra* a saw]

Si·er·ra Le·one (sē-er′rä lē-ōn′, sir′ə-) An independent member of the Commonwealth of Nations in w Africa, 27,925 sq. mi., cap. Freetown. • See map at AFRICA.

si·es·ta (sē-es′tə) *n.* A nap or rest taken in the afternoon. [Sp. < L *sexta (hora)* sixth (hour), noon]

sieve (siv) *n.* A utensil or apparatus for sifting, consisting of a frame provided with a bottom of mesh wire. —*v.t. & v.i.* **sieved, siev·ing** To sift. [< OE *sife* sieve]

sift (sift) *v.t.* **1** To pass through a sieve in order to separate the fine parts from the coarse. **2** To scatter by or as by a sieve. **3** To examine carefully. **4** To separate as if with a sieve; distinguish: to *sift* fact from fiction.

Sieve

—*v.i.* **5** To use a sieve. **6** To fall or pass through or as through a sieve: The light *sifts* through the trees. [< OE *siftan* sift] —**sift′er** *n.*

Sig., sig. signal; signature; signor.

sigh (sī) *v.i.* **1** To draw in and exhale a deep, audible breath, as in expressing sorrow, weariness, pain, or relief. **2** To make a sound suggestive of a sigh, as the wind. **3** To yearn; long: with *for.* —*v.t.* **4** To express with a sigh. —*n.* **1** The act of sighing. **2** A sound of sighing or one suggestive of sighing. [ME *sighen*] —**sigh′er** *n.*

sight (sīt) *n.* **1** The act or faculty of seeing; vision. **2** Something seen; an image perceived by the eye; spectacle: an inspiring *sight;* an ugly *sight.* **3** A view; glimpse: to catch *sight* of someone. **4** The range or scope of vision. **5** *Informal* Something remarkable or strange in appearance. **6** *Usu. pl.* A place or thing of particular interest, as to a tourist: seeing the *sights.* **7** A point of view; estimation. **8** Mental perception or awareness: Don't lose *sight* of the facts. **9** A device to assist aiming, as a gun or a leveling instrument. **10** An aim or observation taken with a telescope or other sighting instrument. —**at** (or **on**) **sight 1** As soon as seen. **2** On presentation for payment. —**out of sight 1** Beyond range of sight. **2** *Informal* Beyond expectation; too great or too much. **3** *Slang* Extraordinarily good. —*v.t.* **1** To catch sight of; discern with the eyes: to *sight* shore. **2** To look at through a sight, as a telescope; observe. **3** To adjust the sights of, as a gun. **4** To take aim with. —*v.i.* **5** To take aim. **6** To make an observation or sight. —*adj.* **1** Understood or performed on sight without previous familiarity or preparation: *sight* reading of music. **2** Payable when presented: a *sight* draft. [< OE *gesiht*]

sight·ed (sīt′əd) *adj.* Having (a specified kind of) sight or vision: *far-sighted.*

sight·less (sīt′lis) *adj.* **1** Blind. **2** Invisible. —**sight′less·ly** *adv.* —**sight′less·ness** *n.*

sight·ly (sīt′lē) *adj.* **·li·er, ·li·est 1** Pleasant to the view; comely. **2** Affording a grand view. —**sight′li·ness** *n.*

sight·see·ing (sīt′sē′ing) *n.* The practice of going to see places or things of interest, as in touring. —*adj.* Engaged in or for the purpose of sightseeing. —**sight′se′er** *n.*

sig·ma (sig′mə) *n.* The 18th letter in the Greek alphabet (Σ, σ, ς).

sign (sīn) *n.* **1** Anything that directs the mind or attention toward something: a *sign* of aging; a *sign* of intelligence. **2** A telltale mark or indication; trace: the first *sign* of spring. **3** A motion or action used to communicate a thought, desire, or command. **4** A symbol; token: black armbands as a *sign* of grief. **5** A conventional written or printed symbol representing a word or relation: $ is a dollar *sign;* = is an equal *sign.* **6** Information, directions, advertising, etc., publicly displayed. **7** A structure on which such information is printed or posted. **8** An occurrence taken to be miraculous and proof of divine commission. **9** One of the twelve equal divisions of the zodiac. —*v.t.* **1** To write one's signature on, esp. in acknowledging or attesting to the validity of a document. **2** To write (one's name). **3** To indicate or represent by a sign. **4** To mark or consecrate with a sign, esp. with a cross. **5** To engage by obtaining the signature of to a document. **6** To hire (oneself) out for work: often with *on.* —*v.i.* **7** To write one's signature. **8** To make signs or signals. —**sign off** To announce the end of a program from a broadcasting station and stop transmission. —**sign up** To enlist, as in a branch of military service. [< L *signum*] —**sign′er** *n.* —Syn. **2** vestige, evidence, spoor.

sig·nal (sig′nəl) *n.* **1** A sign or event agreed upon or understood as a call to action. **2** Any device, sound, gesture, etc., used to convey information or give direction or warning. **3** An event that incites to action or movement: His yawn was our *signal* to leave. **4** *Telecom.* A flow of energy that varies so as to transmit information. —*adj.* **1** Out of the ordinary; notable; distinguished. **2** Used to signal. —*v.* **·naled** or **·nalled, ·nal·ing** or **·nal·ling** *v.t.* **1** To inform or notify by signals. **2** To communicate by signals. —*v.i.* **3** To make a signal or signals. [< L *signum* sign] —**sig′nal·er** or **sig′nal·ler** *n.*

sig·nal·ize (sig′nəl·īz) *v.t.* **·ized, ·iz·ing 1** To make notable or distinguished. **2** To point out with care.

sig·nal·ly (sig′nəl·ē) *adv.* In a signal manner; extraordinarily.

sig·nal·man (sig′nəl·mən) *n. pl.* **·men** (-mən) One who operates or is responsible for signals, as for a railroad.

sig·na·to·ry (sig′nə·tôr′ē, -tō′rē) *n. pl.* **·ries** One who has signed or is bound by a document, esp. a nation so bound. —*adj.* Being a signatory. [< L *signum* a sign]

sig·na·ture (sig′nə·chər) *n.* **1** The name of a person written by himself. **2** The act of signing one's name. **3** Any identifying mark or sign, as a musical theme to signal the beginning and end of a television show. **4** *Printing* **a** A distinguishing mark or number on the first page of each sheet of pages to be gathered as a guide to the binder. **b** A printed sheet that when folded and trimmed constitutes a section of a book, as 32 pages. **5** *Music* A symbol or group of symbols at the beginning of a staff, indicating time or key. [< L *signum* sign]

sign·board (sīn′bôrd′, -bōrd′) *n.* A board displaying a sign, as an advertisement.

sig·net (sig′nit) *n.* **1** A seal used instead of a signature on a document to indicate its official nature. **2** An impression made by or as if by a seal. —*v.t.* To mark wth a signet or seal. [< L *signum* sign]

signet ring A finger ring bearing a signet, as a monogram.

sig·nif·i·cance (sig·nif′ə·kəns) *n.* **1** Importance; consequence. **2** That which is signified or intended to be expressed; meaning. **3** The state or character of being significant. Also **sig·nif′i·can·cy.**

sig·nif·i·cant (sig·nif′ə·kənt) *adj.* **1** Having or expressing a meaning; esp., rich in meaning: *significant* details. **2** Important; momentous. —**sig·nif′i·cant·ly** *adv.* —Syn. **1** meaningful, suggestive. **2** weighty, consequential.

sig·ni·fi·ca·tion (sig′nə·fə·kā′shən) *n.* **1** That which is signified; meaning; sense; import. **2** The act of signifying; communication.

sig·nif·i·ca·tive (sig·nif′ə·kā′tiv) *adj.* **1** Signifying. **2** Conveying a meaning; significant.

sig·ni·fy (sig′nə·fī) *v.* **·fied, ·fy·ing** *v.t.* **1** To represent; mean; suggest. **2** To make known by signs or words; express. —*v.i.* **3** To have some meaning or importance; matter. [< L *signum* sign + -FY] —**sig′ni·fi′er** *n.*

sign language A system of communication by means of signs, largely manual.

si·gnor (sēn·yôr′) *n. pl.* **si·gno·ri** (-ē) or **si·gnors** *Italian* **1** A title of courtesy equivalent to *Mr.* or *Sir.* **2** A man; gentleman. Also **si·gnior′.** [< L *senior* senior]

si·gno·ra (sē·nyô′rä) *n. pl.* **si·gno·re** (-rā) or **·ras** *Italian* **1** A title of courtesy equivalent to *Mrs.* or *Madam.* **2** A woman; lady.

si·gno·ri·na (sē′nyō·rē′nä) *n. pl.* **·ri·ne** (-nā) or **·nas** *Italian* **1** A title of courtesy equivalent to *Miss.* **2** An unmarried woman; young lady.

sign·post (sīn′pōst′) *n.* A post bearing a sign.

Sikh (sēk) *n.* An adherent of a religion of India characterized by monotheism and the rejection of caste. —*adj.* Of or pertaining to the Sikhs. [Hind., lit., disciple] —**Sikh′·ism** *n.*

si·lage (sī′lij) *n.* Succulent fodder stored in a silo.

si·lence (sī′ləns) *n.* **1** Absence of sound; stillness. **2** Abstinence from speech or from making any sound. **3** Failure to mention; oblivion; secrecy. —*v.t.* **·lenced, ·lenc·ing 1** To make silent. **2** To stop the activity or expression of; put to rest. —*interj.* Be silent. [< L *silere* be silent]

si·lenc·er (sī′lən·sər) *n.* **1** A device attached to the muzzle of a firearm to muffle the report. **2** One who or that which imposes silence.

si·lent (sī′lənt) *adj.* **1** Not making any sound or noise; noiseless. **2** Not speaking; mute. **3** Disinclined to talk; taciturn. **4** Present but not audible: *silent* tears. **5** Characterized by the absence of comment: His statement was *silent* on that point. **6** Free from activity, motion, or disturbance. **7** Written but not pronounced, as the *e* in *bake.* **8** Not accompanied by a sound track: a *silent* film. [< L *silere* be silent] —**si′lent·ly** *adv.* —**si′lent·ness** *n.*

silent partner A partner who shares in the financing of an enterprise but has no part in its management.

sil·hou·ette (sil′ōō·et′) *n.* **1** A profile drawing or portrait having its outline filled in with uniform color, usu. black. **2** The outline of a solid figure. —*v.t.* **·et·ted, ·et·ting** To cause to appear in silhouette; outline. [< Étienne de *Silhouette*, 1709–1767, French minister]

Silhouette of Abraham Lincoln

sil·i·ca (sil′i·kə) *n.* The dioxide of silicon, occurring pure as quartz and as an important constituent of rocks, sand, and clay. [< L *silex, silicis* flint]

sil·i·cate (sil′ə·kāt, -i·kit) *n.* Any of various compounds consisting of an oxide of silicon and a metallic radical.

sil·i·ceous (si·lish′əs) *adj.* Pertaining to or containing silica. Also **si·li′cious.**

si·lic·ic (si·lis′ik) *adj.* Pertaining to or derived from silica or silicon.

silicic acid Any of several gelatinous compounds of silica and water.

sil·i·con (sil′ə·kon′, -kən) *n.* A nonmetallic element (symbol Si) comprising about 25 percent of the earth's crust and forming many compounds analogous to those of carbon. [< L *silex, silicis* flint]

sil·i·cone (sil′ə·kōn′) *n.* Any of various synthetic compounds composed of chains of alternate silicon and oxygen atoms with hydrocarbon branches joined to the silicon.

sil·i·co·sis (sil′ə·kō′sis) *n.* A chronic lung disease due to inhalation of silica dust produced by stonecutting, etc.

silk (silk) *n.* **1** A soft, shiny fiber produced by various insect larvae, as silkworms, to form their cocoons. **2** Cloth or thread made of this fiber. **3** Anything resembling silk, as the fine strands of an ear of corn. **4** *Usu. pl.* A garment of silk, as the uniform of a jockey. —*adj.* Consisting of or like silk; silken. [< OE *seoloc*]

silk cotton The silky covering of the seeds of certain trees, used for filling cushions, etc.; kapok.

silk·en (sil′kən) *adj.* **1** Made of silk. **2** Like silk; glossy; smooth. **3** Suave; insinuating: *silken* speech. **4** Dressed in silk. **5** Luxurious.

silk-screen (silk′skrēn′) *adj.* Describing or made by a printing process which forces ink through the meshes of a silk screen prepared so that ink penetrates only in those areas to be printed. —*v.t.* To make or print by the silk-screen process.

silk-stock·ing (silk′stok′ing) *adj.* Marked by patrician elegance or extreme wealth. —*n.* A member of a silk-stocking social class.

silk·worm (silk′wûrm′) *n.* The larva of a moth that produces a dense silken cocoon.

silk·y (sil′kē) *adj.* **silk·i·er, silk·i·est 1** Like silk; soft; lustrous. **2** Made or consisting of silk; silken. **3** Smooth or insinuating. —**silk′i·ly** *adv.* —**silk′i·ness** *n.*

sill (sil) *n.* **1** A horizontal member or beam forming the foundation, or part of the foundation, of a structure, as at the bottom of a casing in a building. **2** The horizontal part at the bottom of a door or window frame. [< OE *syll*]

sil·ly (sil′ē) *adj.* **·li·er, ·li·est 1** Showing a lack of ordinary sense or judgment; foolish. **2** Trivial; frivolous. **3** *Informal* Stunned; dazed, as by a blow. —*n. pl.* **·lies** *Informal* A silly person. [< OE *gesælig* happy] —**sil′li·ly** or **sil′ly** *adv.* —**sil′li·ness** *n.*

si·lo (sī′lō) *n. pl.* **·los 1** A pit or tower in which fodder is stored. **2** An underground structure for the housing and launching of guided missiles. —*v.t.* **·loed, ·lo·ing** To put or preserve in a silo. [< Gk. *siros* pit for corn]

silt (silt) *n.* **1** An earthy sediment consisting of extremely fine particles suspended in and carried by water. **2** A deposit of such sediment. —*v.t. & v.i.* To fill or become filled or choked with silt: usu. with *up.* [ME *sylte*] —**sil·ta·tion** (sil·tā′shən) *n.* —**silt′y** *adj.* (**·i·er, ·i·est**)

Si·lu·ri·an (si·lŏŏr′ē·ən, sī-) *adj. & n.* See GEOLOGY.

sil·van (sil′vən) *adj.* SYLVAN.

sil·ver (sil′vər) *n.* **1** A pale gray, lustrous, malleable metallic element (symbol Ag), having great electric and thermal conductivity and forming various photosensitive salts. **2** Silver regarded as a commodity or as a standard of currency. **3** Silver coin considered as money. **4** Articles, as tableware, made of or plated with silver; silverware.

A luster or color resembling that of silver. —*adj.* **1** Made of or coated with silver. **2** Resembling silver; having a silvery grey color. **3** Relating to, connected with, or producing silver. **4** Having a soft, clear, bell-like tone. **5** Designating a 25th wedding anniversary. **6** Favoring the use of silver as a monetary standard. —*v.t.* **1** To coat or plate with silver or something resembling silver. —*v.i.* **2** To become silver or white, as with age. [< OE *siolfor*] —**sil′-ver·er** *n.* —**sil′ver·ly** *adv.*

sil·ver·fish (sil′vər·fish′) *n. pl.* **·fish** or **·fish·es** Any of numerous silvery, wingless insects having bristles on the tail and long feelers, usu. found in damp and dark places.

silver fox 1 A fox with white-tipped black fur. **2** The fur, or a garment made of it.

silver nitrate The salt of silver and nitric acid, used in industry, photography, and in medicine as an antiseptic.

sil·ver·smith (sil′vər·smith′) *n.* A maker of silverware.

silver standard A monetary standard or system based on silver.

sil·ver·ware (sil′vər·wâr′) *n.* Articles made of or plated with silver, esp. tableware.

sil·ver·y (sil′vər·ē) *adj.* **1** Containing silver. **2** Resembling silver, as in luster or hue. **3** Having a soft, clear, bell-like tone. —**sil′ver·i·ness** *n.*

sim·i·an (sim′ē·ən) *adj.* Like or pertaining to the apes and monkeys. —*n.* An ape or monkey. [< L *simia* ape]

sim·i·lar (sim′ə·lər) *adj.* **1** Bearing resemblance to one another or to something else. **2** Having like characteristics, nature, or degree. **3** *Geom.* Shaped alike, but differing in measure. [< L *similis* like] —**sim′i·lar·ly** *adv.*

sim·i·lar·i·ty (sim′ə·lar′ə·tē) *n. pl.* **·ties 1** The quality or state of being similar. **2** A point in which compared objects are similar.

sim·i·le (sim′ə·lē) *n.* A figure of speech expressing comparison or likeness by the use of such terms as *like* or *as.* [< L *similis* similar] • See METAPHOR.

si·mil·i·tude (si·mil′ə·t(y)ōōd) *n.* **1** Similarity; correspondence. **2** One who or that which is similar; counterpart. **3** A point of similarity. [< L *similis* like]

sim·i·tar (sim′ə·tər) *n.* SCIMITAR.

sim·mer (sim′ər) *v.i.* **1** To boil gently; be or stay at or just below the boiling point. **2** To be on the point of breaking forth, as with rage. —*v.t.* **3** To cook in a liquid at or just below the boiling point. —*n.* The state of simmering. [?]

si·mo·le·on (si·mō′lē·ən) *n. Slang* A dollar. [?]

Si·mon Le·gree (sī′mən lə·grē′) A harsh or brutal taskmaster. [< a character in Harriet Beecher Stowe's *Uncle Tom's Cabin,* 1851]

si·mon-pure (sī′mən·pyŏŏr′) *adj.* Real; genuine; authentic. [< a character in Susanna Centlivre's play, *A Bold Stroke for a Wife,* 1718]

si·mo·ny (sī′mə·nē, sim′ə-) *n.* The purchase or sale of sacred things, as ecclesiastical preferment. [< *Simon* (Magus), who offered Peter money for the gift of the Holy Spirit *Acts* 8:9–24]

si·moom (si·mōōm′, sī-) *n.* A hot, dry, dustladen, exhausting wind of the African and Arabian deserts. Also **si·moon′** (-mōōn′). [< Ar. *samūm*]

simp (simp) *n. Slang* A simpleton.

sim·per (sim′pər) *v.i.* **1** To smile in a silly, self-conscious manner; smirk. —*v.t.* **2** To say with a simper. —*n.* A silly, self-conscious smile. —**sim′per·er** *n.* —**sim′per·ing·ly** *adv.*

sim·ple (sim′pəl) *adj.* **·pler, ·plest 1** Easy to comprehend or do: a *simple* problem or task. **2** Not complex or complicated. **3** Without embellishment; plain; unadorned: a *simple* dress. **4** Having nothing added; mere: the *simple* truth. **5** Not luxurious or elaborate: a *simple* meal. **6** Consisting of one thing; single. **7** Free from affectation; artless: a *simple* soul. **8** Weak in intellect; silly or foolish. **9** Of humble rank or condition; ordinary. **10** *Bot.* Not divided: a *simple* leaf. —*n.* **1** One who is foolish or ignorant; simpleton. **2** A medicinal plant. [< L *simplex*] —**sim′ple·ness** *n.* —Syn. **4** bare, sheer. **5** frugal, austere. **7** guileless, unsophisticated.

simple fraction A fraction in which both numerator and denominator are integers.

simple interest Interest computed on the original principal alone.

simple machine Any one of certain basic mechanical devices, as the lever, the wedge, the inclined plane, the screw, the wheel and axle, and the pulley.

sim·ple-mind·ed (sim′pəl·mīn′did) *adj.* **1** Weak in intellect; foolish or feeble-minded. **2** Artless or unsophisticated. —**sim′ple-mind′ed·ly** *adv.* —**sim′ple-mind′ed·ness** *n.*

simple sentence A sentence consisting of one independent clause, without subordinate clauses.

sim·ple·ton (sim′pəl·tən) *n.* A weak-minded or silly person.

sim·plic·i·ty (sim·plis′ə·tē) *n. pl.* **·ties 1** The state of being simple; freedom from complexity or difficulty. **2** Freedom from ornament or ostentation. **3** Freedom from affectation; artlessness; sincerity. **4** Foolishness; stupidity.

sim·pli·fy (sim′plə·fī) *v.t.* **·fied, ·fy·ing** To make more simple or less complex. —**sim′pli·fi·ca′tion, sim′pli·fi′er** *n.*

sim·plis·tic (sim·plis′tik) *adj.* Tending to ignore or overlook underlying questions, complications, or details. —**sim·plis′ti·cal·ly** *adv.*

sim·ply (sim′plē) *adv.* **1** In a simple manner. **2** Merely; only. **3** Really; absolutely: *simply* adorable.

sim·u·la·crum (sim′yə·lā′krəm, -lak′rəm) *n. pl.* **·cra** (-krə) **1** A likeness; image. **2** An imaginary or shadowy semblance. [< L, image]

sim·u·late (sim′yə·lāt) *v.t.* **·lat·ed, ·lat·ing 1** To make a pretense of; imitate, esp. to deceive. **2** To assume or have the appearance or form of, without the reality. [< L *similis* like] —**sim′u·la′tive** *adj.* —**sim′u·la′tor** *n.*

sim·u·la·tion (sim′yə·lā′shən) *n.* **1** The act of simulating. **2** Something given the form or function of another, as in order to test or determine capability; model.

si·mul·cast (sī′məl·kast′, -käst′) *v.t.* **·cast, ·cast·ing** To broadcast by radio and television simultaneously. —*n.* A broadcast so transmitted.

si·mul·ta·ne·ous (sī′məl·tā′nē·əs, sim′əl-) *adj.* Occurring, done, or existing at the same time. [< L *simul* at the same time] —**si′mul·ta′ne·ous·ly** *adv.* —**si′mul·ta′ne·ous·ness, si′mul·ta·ne′i·ty** (-tə·nē′ə·tē) *n.*

sin (sin) *n.* **1** A transgression against moral or religious law or divine authority, esp. when deliberate. **2** The state of having thus transgressed; wickedness. **3** Any action or condition regarded as morally wrong or deplorable. —*v.* **sinned, sin·ning** *v.i.* **1** To commit a sin. **2** To do wrong. [< OE *synn*]

Si·nai (sī′nī), **Mount** The mountain where Moses received the law from God. *Ex.* 19.

since (sins) *adv.* **1** From a past time up to the present: traveling *since* last Monday. **2** At some time between the past and the present: He has *since* recovered from the illness. **3** Before now: long *since* forgotten. —*prep.* During the time following (a time in the past): Times have changed *since* you left. —*conj.* **1** During or within the time after which. **2** Continuously from the time when: She has been ill ever *since* she arrived. **3** Because of; inasmuch as. [< OE *siththan* afterwards]

sin·cere (sin·sir′) *adj.* **·cer·er, ·cer·est** Free from hypocrisy, deceit, or calculation; honest; genuine: a *sincere* friend; *sincere* regrets. [< L *sincerus* uncorrupted] —**sin·cere′ly** *adv.* —**sin·cere′ness** *n.*

sin·cer·i·ty (sin·ser′ə·tē) *n.* The state or quality of being sincere; honesty of purpose or character; freedom from hypocrisy.

sine (sīn) *n.* A function of an acute angle in a right triangle expressible as the ratio of the side opposite the angle to the hypotenuse. [< L *sinus* a bend]

si·ne·cure (sī′nə·kyŏŏr, sin′ə-) *n.* A position or office providing compensation or other benefits but requiring little or no responsibility or effort. [< L *sine* without + *cura* care]

BC/AB
= sine
of angle a

si·ne di·e (sī′nē dī′ē, sin′ā dē′ā) Without setting a date, as for another meeting; indefinitely: an adjournment *sine die.* [L, without a day]

si·ne qua non (sin′ə kwä nōn′, non′, sī′nē kwä nōn′) That which is absolutely indispensable; an essential element. [L, without which not]

sin·ew (sin′yōō) n. 1 TENDON. 2 Strength or power. 3 Often pl. A source of strength. —v.t. To strengthen, as with sinews. [< OE sinu, seonu] —sin′ew·less adj.

sin·ew·y (sin′yōō-ē) adj. 1 Of, like, or having sinews. 2 Having many sinews; tough. 3 Strong; brawny. 4 Vigorous; forceful.

sin·ful (sin′fəl) adj. Tainted with, full of, or characterized by sin. —sin′ful·ly adv. —sin′ful·ness n. —Syn. wicked, bad, immoral, evil.

sing (sing) v. sang or (now less commonly) sung, sung, sing·ing v.i. 1 To produce musical sounds with the voice. 2 To perform vocal compositions professionally or in a specified manner. 3 To produce melodious sounds, as a bird. 4 To make a continuous, melodious sound suggestive of singing, as a teakettle, the wind, etc. 5 To buzz or hum; ring: My ears are singing. 6 To be suitable for singing. 7 To relate or celebrate something in song or verse. 8 To compose poetry. 9 Slang To confess the details of a crime, esp. so as to implicate others. 10 To be joyous; rejoice. — v.t. 11 To perform (music) vocally. 12 To chant; intone. 13 To bring to a specified condition or place by singing: Sing me to sleep. 14 To relate, proclaim, praise, etc., in or as in verse or song. —n. Informal A singing, esp. by a group. [< OE singan] —sing′a·ble adj.

sing. singular.

singe (sinj) v.t. singed, singe·ing 1 To burn slightly. 2 To remove bristles or feathers from by passing through flame. 3 To burn the ends of (hair, etc.). —n. A slight or superficial burn; scorch. [< OE sengan] —sing′er n.

sing·er (sing′ər) n. 1 One who sings, esp. as a profession. 2 A poet. 3 A songbird.

Sin·gha·lese (sing′gə·lēz′, -lēs′) adj. Of or pertaining to a group of people in Sri Lanka or to their language. —n. 1 One of the Singhalese people. 2 Their language.

sin·gle (sing′gəl) adj. 1 Consisting of only one. 2 With no other or others; solitary; lone; alone. 3 Unmarried; also, pertaining to the unmarried state. 4 Of, pertaining to or involving only one person. 5 Consisting of only one part; simple. 6 Upright; sincere; honest. 7 Designed for use by only one person: a single bed. 8 Bot. Having only one row of petals, as a flower. —n. 1 One who or that which is single. 2 In baseball, a hit by which the batter reaches first base. 3 In cricket, a hit which scores one run. 4 pl. In tennis or similar games, a match with only one player on each side —v. ·gled, ·gling v.t. 1 To choose or select (one) from others: usually with out. —v.i. 2 In baseball, to make a single. [< L singulus] —sin′gle·ness n. —sin′gly adv.

sin·gle-breast·ed (sing′gəl·bres′tid) adj. Overlapping at the center of the front of the body just enough to allow for fastening by a single button or row of buttons.

single file 1 A line of people, animals, etc., moving one behind the other. 2 In such a line: to walk single file.

sin·gle-foot (sing′gəl·fōōt′) n. The gait of a horse in which the sequence in which the feet leave the ground is right hind, right fore, left hind, left fore. —v.i. To go at this gait.

sin·gle-hand·ed (sing′gəl·han′did) adj. 1 Done or working alone; without assistance; unaided. 2 Having but one hand. 3 Capable of being used with a single hand. —sin′· gle-hand′ed·ly adv.

sin·gle-heart·ed (sing′gəl·här′tid) adj. Sincere and undivided, as in purpose, dedication, feeling, etc. —sin′gle-heart′ed·ly adv.

sin·gle-mind·ed (sing′gəl·mīn′did) adj. 1 Having only one purpose or end in view. 2 Free from duplicity; ingenuous; sincere. —sin′gle-mind′ed·ly adv. —sin′gle-mind′ed·ness n.

sin·gle·stick (sing′gəl·stik′) n. 1 A wooden, swordlike stick used in fencing. 2 The art or an instance of fencing with such sticks.

sin·gle·ton (sing′gəl·tən) n. 1 A single card of a suit originally held in the hand of a player. 2 Any single thing, distinct from two or more of its group.

sin·gle-track (sing′əl·trak′) adj. 1 Having only one track. 2 Having a limited scope, outlook, flexibility, etc.

sin·gle·tree (sing′gəl·trē′) n. WHIFFLETREE.

sing·song (sing′sông′, -song′) n. 1 Monotonous regularity of rhythm and rhyme in verse. 2 Verse characterized by such regularity. 3 A voice, speech tones, etc., characterized by a monotonous rise and fall of pitch. — adj. Having a monotonous rhythm or rise and fall of pitch.

sin·gu·lar (sing′gyə·lər) adj. 1 Being the only one of its type; unique; separate; individual. 2 Extraordinary; remarkable; uncommon: a singular honor. 3 Odd; not customary or usual. 4 Gram. Of, pertaining to, or being a word form which denotes one person or thing. —n. Gram. The singular number, or a word form having this number. —sin′gu·lar·ly adv. —sin′gu·lar·ness n. —Syn. 1 peculiar, distinctive. 3 strange, conspicuous.

sin·gu·lar·i·ty (sing′gyə·lar′ə·tē) n. pl. ·ties 1 The state or quality of being singular. 2 Something of uncommon or remarkable character.

sin·gu·lar·ize (sing′gyə·lə·rīz′) v.t. ·ized, ·iz·ing To make singular.

Sin·ha·lese (sin′hə·lēz′, -lēs′) adj., n. SINGHALESE.

sin·is·ter (sin′is·tər) adj. 1 Malevolent; evil: a sinister expression on the face. 2 Boding or attended with misfortune or disaster; inauspicious. 3 Of, pertaining to, or situated on the left side or hand. 4 Her. On the wearer's left, the spectator's right. [L, left, unlucky] —sin′is·ter·ly adv. —sin′is·ter·ness n.

sink (singk) v. sank or sunk, sunk (Obs. sunk·en), sink·ing v.i. 1 To go beneath the surface or to the bottom, as of water or snow. 2 To go down, esp. slowly or by degrees. 3 To seem to descend, as the sun. 4 To incline downward; slope gradually, as land. 5 To pass into a specified state: to sink into a coma. 6 To approach death: He's sinking fast. 7 To become less in force, volume, or degree: His voice sank to a whisper. 8 To become less in value, price, etc. 9 To decline in quality or condition; retrogress; degenerate: usu. with into or to. 10 To penetrate or be absorbed: The oil sank into the wood. 11 To be impressed or fixed, as in the heart or mind: I think that lesson will sink in. —v.t. 12 To cause to go beneath the surface or to the bottom: to sink a fence post. 13 To cause or allow to fall or drop; lower. 14 To cause to penetrate or be absorbed. 15 To make (a mine shaft, well, etc.) by digging or excavating. 16 To reduce in force, volume, or degree. 17 To debase or degrade. 18 To suppress or hide; restrain. 19 To defeat; ruin. 20 To invest. 21 To invest and subsequently lose. 22 To pay up; liquidate. 23 In certain sports, to cause (a ball or other object) to go through or into a receptacle or hole. —n. 1 A basinlike receptacle with a drainpipe and usu. a water supply. 2 A sewer or cesspool. 3 A place where corruption and vice gather or are rampant. 4 A hollow place or depression in a land surface, esp. one in which water collects or disappears by evaporation or percolation. 5 A body or mechanism by which matter or energy is absorbed or dissipated: a heat sink. [< OE sincan] —sink′a·ble adj. —Syn. 2 descend, dwindle, diminish, lessen.

sink·er (singk′ər) n. 1 One who or that which sinks. 2 A weight for sinking a fishing or sounding line. 3 Informal A doughnut.

sinking fund A fund accumulated to pay off a debt at maturity.

sin·less (sin′lis) adj. Having no sin; guiltless; innocent. —sin′less·ly adv. —sin′less·ness n.

sin·ner (sin′ər) n. One who has sinned.

Sino- combining form 1 Of or pertaining to the Chinese people, language, etc. 2 Chinese and: Sino-Tibetan. [< LL Sinae the Chinese]

Si·no-Ti·bet·an (sī′nō·ti·bet′n) n. A family of languages spoken over a wide area in CEN. and SE Asia, including the languages of China, Burma, Tibet, and Thailand.

sin·u·ate (sin′yōō·it, -āt) adj. 1 Winding in and out; wavy. 2 Bot. Having a strongly indented, wavy margin, as some leaves. —v.i. (sin′yōō·āt) ·at·ed, ·at·ing To curve in and out; turn; wind. [< L sinus curve] —sin′u·ate·ly adv. —sin′u·a′tion n.

sin·u·ous (sin′yōō·əs) adj. 1 Characterized by turns or curves; winding; undulating; tortuous: a sinuous path. 2 Devious; indirect; not straightforward. [< L sinus bend] — sin′u·ous·ly adv. —sin·u·os·i·ty (sin′yōō·os′ə·tē) n. sin′u·ous·ness n.

si·nus (sī′nəs) *n.* 1 Any of the natural cavities in the skull that contain air and usu. connect with the nostrils. 2 A dilated part of a blood vessel. 3 Any narrow opening leading to an abscess. 4 *Bot.* A recess or depression between two adjoining lobes, as of a leaf. [L, curve, hollow]

si·nu·si·tis (sī′nə·sī′tis) *n.* Inflammation of a sinus or the sinuses of the skull.

Si·on (sī′ən) *n.* ZION.

Siou·an (sōō′ən) *n. pl.* **Siouan** or **Siouans** 1 A large family of languages spoken by Indians who formerly inhabited parts of CEN. and E North America. 2 A member of any of the peoples speaking a language of this family. —*adj.* Of or pertaining to this language family.

Sinuses
a. frontal.
b. maxillary.

Sioux (sōō) *n. pl.* **Sioux** One of a group of North American Indian tribes of Siouan linguistic stock formerly occupying parts of the Great Plains area in the Dakotas, Minnesota, and Nebraska.

sip (sip) *v.* **sipped, sip·ping** *v.t.* 1 To imbibe in small quantities. 2 To drink from by sips. 3 To take in; absorb. —*v.i.* 4 To drink in sips. —*n.* 1 A very small amount sipped. 2 The act of sipping. [< OE *sypian* drink in] —**sip·per** *n.*

si·phon (sī′fən) *n.* 1 A bent tube for transferring liquids from a higher to a lower level over an intervening barrier. 2 SIPHON BOTTLE. 3 *Zool.* A tubular structure in certain aquatic animals, as the squid, for drawing in or expelling liquids. —*v.t.* 1 To draw off by or cause to pass through or as through a siphon. —*v.i.* 2 To pass through a siphon. [< Gk. *siphōn*] —**si′phon·al** *adj.*

siphon bottle A bottle containing aerated or carbonated water, which is expelled through a bent tube in the neck of the bottle by the pressure of the gas when a valve in the tube is opened.

Siphon

sir (sûr) *n.* The conventional term of respectful address to a man: not followed by a proper name. [< SIRE]

Sir (sûr) *n.* A title of baronets and knights, used before the given name or the full name.

sire (sīr) *n.* 1 *Archaic* A father or forefather. 2 The male parent of an animal, esp. a domestic animal. 3 *Archaic* A man of high rank; also a form of address to a superior used esp. in addressing a king. —*v.t.* **sired, sir·ing** To beget; procreate: used chiefly of domestic animals. [< L *senior* older]

si·ren (sī′rən) *n.* 1 *Often cap. Gk. Myth.* One of a group of sea nymphs who lured sailors to destruction by their sweet singing. 2 A seductive, enticing woman. 3 A device for producing a series of loud tones, as for a warning, often consisting of a perforated rotating disk or disks through which sharp puffs of steam or compressed air are permitted to escape. —*adj.* Of or pertaining to a siren; seductive; enticing. [< Gk. *seirēn*]

Sir·i·us (sir′ē·əs) *n.* The Dog Star, the brightest star in the night sky, in the constellation of Canis Major. [< Gk. *seirios* scorching]

sir·loin (sûr′loin) *n.* A cut of meat, esp. of beef, from the upper portion of the loin. [< OF *sur-* above + *longe* loin]

si·roc·co (si·rok′ō) *n. pl.* **·cos** 1 A hot, dry, and dusty wind blowing from the Libyan deserts into s Europe, esp. to Italy, Sicily, and Malta. 2 Any hot or warm wind, esp. one blowing toward a center of low barometric pressure. [< Ar. *sharq* the east]

sir·up (sir′əp) *n.* SYRUP.

sis (sis) *n. Informal* Sister.

si·sal (sī′səl, -zəl, sis′əl) *n.* 1 A tough fiber obtained from the leaves of a species of agave. 2 The plant itself. Also **sisal hemp.** [< *Sisal,* town in Yucatán, Mexico]

sis·sy (sis′ē) *n. pl.* **·sies** *Informal* 1 An effeminate man or boy. 2 A timid person; weakling; coward. —*adj.* **·si·er, ·si·est** Being a sissy.[< SIS]

sis·ter (sis′tər) *n.* 1 A female person having the same parents as another person. 2 A female of the lower animals having one parent in common with another. 3 a HALF SISTER. b SISTER-IN-LAW. c A foster sister. 4 A woman or girl allied to another or others by race, creed, a common interest, membership in a society, etc. 5 *Eccl.* A member of a sisterhood; nun. 6 *Chiefly Brit.* A head nurse in the ward or clinic of a hospital; also, any nurse. 7 A person or thing having similar characteristics to another. —*adj.* Bearing the relationship of a sister or one suggestive of sisterhood. [< OE *swostor*] —**sis′ter·ly** *adj.*

sis·ter·hood (sis′tər·hŏŏd) *n.* 1 A body of women united by some bond. 2 *Eccl.* A community of women forming a religious order. 3 The sisterly relationship.

sis·ter-in-law (sis′tər·in·lô′) *n. pl.* **sis·ters-in-law** 1 A sister of one's husband or wife. 2 A brother's wife. 3 A brother-in-law's wife.

Sis·y·phus (sis′ə·fəs) *Gk. Myth.* A king of Corinth, condemned in Hades forever to roll uphill a huge stone that always rolled down again.

sit (sit) *v.* **sat, sit·ting** *v.i.* 1 To rest on the buttocks or haunches; be seated. 2 To perch or roost, as a bird. 3 To cover eggs so as to give warmth for hatching. 4 To pose, as for a portrait. 5 To be in session; hold a session. 6 To occupy a seat in a deliberative body. 7 To have or exercise judicial authority. 8 To fit or hang: That dress *sits* well. 9 To rest; lie: an obligation that *sat* heavily on her. 10 To be situated or located. 11 BABY-SIT. —*v.t.* 12 To have or keep a seat or a good seat upon: to *sit* a horse. 13 To seat (oneself): *Sit* yourself down. —**sit in (on)** 1 To join; participate: to *sit in on* a game of cards or a business deal. 2 To attend or take part in a discussion or music session. 3 To take part in a sit-in. —**sit on (or upon)** 1 To belong to (a jury, commission, etc.) as a member. 2 To hold discussions about or investigate. 3 *Informal* To suppress, squelch, or delay action on or consideration of. —**sit out** 1 To remain until the end of. 2 To sit during or take no part in: They *sat out* a dance. 3 To stay longer than. —**sit up** 1 To assume a sitting position. 2 To maintain an erect posture while seated. 3 To stay up later than usual at night. 4 To be startled or show interest. [< OE *sittan*]

si·tar (si·tär′) *n.* A stringed instrument used in Hindu music, somewhat resembling the lute, having a long neck, a resonating gourd or gourds, and a variable number of strings, some of which are plucked, others vibrating sympathetically. [< Hind. *sitār*]

sit·com (sit′kom′) *n. Slang* A situation comedy. [< SIT(UATION) + COM(EDY)]

sit-down (sit′doun′) *n.* 1 A strike during which strikers refuse to work or leave their place of employment until agreement is reached: also **sit-down strike.** 2 A form of civil disobedience in which demonstrators obstruct some activity by sitting down and refusing to move.

Sitar

site (sīt) *n.* 1 A plot of ground used for or considered for some specific purpose. 2 The place, scene, or location of something: the battle *site.* [< L *situs* position]

sit-in (sit′in′) *n.* 1 SIT-DOWN (def. 2). 2 An organized demonstration in which a protesting group occupies an area prohibited to them, as by taking seats in a restricted restaurant, etc. —**sit′-in·ner** *n.*

sit·ter (sit′ər) *n.* One who sits, esp. a baby sitter.

sit·ting (sit′ing) *n.* 1 The act or position of one who sits. 2 An uninterrupted period of being seated, as for the painting of a portrait. 3 A session or term. 4 An incubation; period of hatching. 5 The number of eggs on which a bird sits at one incubation. —*adj.* That sits or is seated.

sitting duck *Informal* An easy target or victim.

sit·ting room (sit′ting·rōōm′, -rŏŏm′) LIVING ROOM.

add, āce, câre, pälm; end, ēven; it, īce; odd, ōpen, ôrder; tŏŏk, pōōl; up, bûrn; ə = *a* in *above*, *u* in *focus*; yōō = *u* in *fuse*; oil; pout; check; go; ring; thin; ᵺis; zh, *vision.* < derived from; ? origin uncertain or unknown.

sit·u·ate (sich′ōō-āt) *v.t.* **·at·ed, ·at·ing** To place in a certain position; locate. [< L *situs* a place]

sit·u·at·ed (sich′ōō-ā′tid) *adj.* **1** Having a fixed location. **2** Placed in certain circumstances or conditions, esp. financially: He is well *situated.*

sit·u·a·tion (sich′ōō-ā′shən) *n.* **1** The way in which something is situated, relative to its surroundings; position; location. **2** A locality; site. **3** Condition as modified or determined by circumstances. **4** A salaried post of employment. **5** A combination of circumstances at a specific time; state of affairs. **6** An unusual, difficult, critical, or otherwise significant state of affairs. —**sit′u·a′tion·al** *adj.*

situation comedy A television or radio show typically centered about a few characters involved in comical situations and presented in separate episodes.

Si·va (sē′və, shē′-) The Hindu god of destruction and reproduction. —**Si′va·ism** *n.* —**Si′va·is′tic** *adj.*

six (siks) *n.* **1** The sum of five plus one; 6; VI. **2** A set or group of six members. —**at sixes and sevens** In a state of confusion and indecision. [< OE] —**six** *adj., pron.*

six-pack (siks′pak′) *n.* **1** A group of six cans or bottles packaged as a unit. **2** The contents of such a unit.

six·pence (siks′pəns) *n.* **1** A British coin worth six pence. **2** The sum of six pence.

six·pen·ny (siks′pen′ē, -pən-ē) *adj.* **1** Worth, or sold for sixpence. **2** Cheap; trashy. **3** Denoting a size of nails, usu. two inches long.

six-shoot·er (siks′shōō′tər) *n.* A revolver that will fire six shots without reloading.

six·teen (siks′tēn′) *n.* **1** The sum of 15 plus 1; 16; XVI. **2** A set or group of sixteen members. —**six′teen′** *adj., pron.*

six·teenth (siks′tēnth′) *adj. & adv.* Next in order after the 15th. —*n.* **1** The element of an ordered set that corresponds to the number 16. **2** One of 16 equal parts.

sixteenth note *Music* A note of one sixteenth of the time value of a whole note. • See NOTE.

sixth (siksth) *adj. & adv.* Next in order after the fifth. —*n.* **1** The element of an ordered set that corresponds to the number six. **2** One of six equal parts. **3** *Music* The interval between a tone and another five steps away in a diatonic scale.

sixth sense The power of intuitive perception, thought of as independent of the five senses.

six·ti·eth (siks′tē-ith) *adj. & adv.* Tenth in order after the 50th. —*n.* **1** The element of an ordered set that corresponds to the number 60. **2** One of sixty equal parts.

six·ty (siks′tē) *n. pl.* **·ties 1** The product of six and ten; 60; LX. **2** A set or group of 60 members. **3** *pl.* The numbers, years, etc., between 60 and 70. —**six′ty** *adj., pron.*

six·ty-fourth note (siks′tē-fôrth, -fōrth) *Music* A note of one sixty-fourth of the time value of a whole note. • See NOTE.

siz·a·ble (sī′zə-bəl) *adj.* Comparatively large. Also **size′a·ble.** —**siz′a·ble·ness** *n.* —**siz′a·bly** *adv.*

size¹ (sīz) *n.* **1** The dimensions of a thing as compared with some standard; physical magnitude or bulk. **2** Considerable amount, dimensions, etc. **3** One of a series of graded measures, as of hats, shoes, etc. **4** *Informal* State of affairs; true situation: That's the *size* of it. —*v.t.* **sized, siz·ing 1** To arrange or classify according to size. **2** To cut or otherwise make (an article) to a required size. —**size up** *Informal* **1** To form an opinion of. **2** To meet specifications. [< OF *assise* ASSIZE]

size² (sīz) *n.* A liquid preparation used to give a smooth finish to cloth, paper, or other porous surface. —*v.t.* **sized, siz·ing** To treat with size. [? < SIZE¹]

size³ (sīz) *adj.* SIZED (def. 1).

sized (sīzd) *adj.* **1** Having graded dimensions or a definite size: usu. in combination: large-*sized.* **2** Arranged according to size.

siz·ing (sī′zing) *n.* **1** SIZE². **2** The act or process of adding size to a fabric, yarn, etc.

siz·zle (siz′əl) *v.* **·zled, ·zling** *v.i.* **1** To emit a hissing sound under the action of heat. **2** To seethe with rage, resentment, etc. —*v.t.* **3** To cause to sizzle. —*n.* A hissing sound, as from frying. [Imit.]

S.J. Society of Jesus.

skald (skôld, skäld) *n.* A Scandinavian poet or bard of ancient times. [< ON *skáld* poet]

skate¹ (skāt) *n.* **1** A metal runner attached to a frame, with clamps or straps for fastening it to the sole of a boot or shoe, enabling the wearer to glide over ice. **2** A shoe or boot with such a runner permanently attached. **3** ROLLER SKATE. —*v.i.* **skat·ed, skat·ing** To glide or move over ice or some other smooth surface, on or as on skates. [< Du. *schaats*] —**skat′er** *n.*

skate² (skāt) *n.* Any of various flat-bodied, cartilaginous marine fishes with enlarged pectoral fins and ventral gill slits. [< ON *skata*]

skate·board (skāt′bôrd′, -bōrd′) *n.* A toy consisting of two pairs of skate wheels attached to a narrow board serving as a platform for riding. —**skate′board′er** *n.*

ske·dad·dle (ski-dad′l) *Informal v.i.* **·died, ·dling** To flee in haste. —*n.* A hasty flight. [?]

Skate

skeet (skēt) *n.* A variety of trapshooting in which clay targets, hurled in such a way as to resemble the flight of birds, are fired at from various angles. [?]

skein (skān) *n.* **1** A fixed quantity of yarn, thread, silk, wool, etc., wound in a loose coil. **2** Something like this: *skein* of hair. [< OF *escaigne*]

skel·e·ton (skel′ə·tən) *n.* **1** The supporting framework of a vertebrate, composed of bone and cartilage. **2** Any framework constituting the main supporting parts of a structure. **3** A mere sketch or outline of anything. **4** A very thin person or animal. —**skeleton in the closet** A secret source of shame or discredit. —*adj.* Of, pertaining to, or like a skeleton. [< Gk. *skeletos* dried up] —**skel·e·tal** *adj.*

skeleton key A key having a large part of the bit filed away to enable it to open many simple locks.

skep·tic (skep′tik) *n.* **1** A person characterized by skepticism, esp. in regard to religion. **2** A person who advocates or believes in philosophical skepticism. *Chiefly Brit. sp.* **scep′tic.** [< Gk. *skeptikos* reflective]

skep·ti·cal (skep′ti·kəl) *adj.* Of, pertaining to, characteristic of, or marked by skepticism. *Chiefly Brit. sp.* **scep′ti·cal.** —**skep′ti·cal·ly** *adv.* —**skep′ti·cal·ness** *n.*

skep·ti·cism (skep′tə·siz′əm) *n.* **1** A doubting or incredulous state of mind. **2** Doubt about basic religious doctrines such as immortality, revelation, etc. **3** The philosophical doctrine that absolute knowledge in any given area is unattainable, and that relative certainty can be approximated only by a continuous process of doubt, criticism, and suspended judgment. *Chiefly Brit. sp.* **scep′ti·cism.**

sketch (skech) *n.* **1** A rough or undetailed drawing or design, often done as a preliminary study. **2** A brief plan, description, or outline. **3** A short literary or musical composition. **4** A short scene, play, comical act, etc. —*v.t.* **1** To make a sketch or sketches of. —*v.i.* **2** To make a sketch or sketches. [< Gk. *schedios* impromptu] —**sketch′er** *n.*

sketch·book (skech′bŏok′) *n.* **1** A pad or book of drawing paper for sketching. **2** A printed volume of sketches.

sketch·y (skech′ē) *adj.* **sketch·i·er, sketch·i·est 1** Like or in the form of a sketch; roughly suggested without detail. **2** Incomplete; superficial. —**sketch′i·ly** *adv.* —**sketch′i·ness** *n.*

skew (skyōō) *v.i.* **1** To take an oblique direction. **2** To look sideways; squint. —*v.t.* **3** To give an oblique form or direction to. **4** To give a bias to; misrepresent; distort. —*adj.* **1** Placed, turned or running to one side; oblique; slanting. **2** ASYMMETRIC. —*n.* A deviation from straightness; an oblique direction or course. [< AF *eskiuer*]

skew·er (skyōō′ər) *n.* **1** A long pin of wood or metal, used for fastening meat while roasting. **2** Any of various articles of similar shape or use. —*v.t.* To run through or fasten with or as with a skewer. [?]

ski (skē, *Brit. also* shē) *n. pl.* **skis 1** One of a pair of flat, narrow runners of wood, metal, or other material, worn clamped to boots for gliding over snow. **2** WATER SKI. —*v.i.* **skied, ski·ing** *v.i.* **1** To glide or travel on skis. —*v.t.* **2** To glide or travel over on skis. [Norw. < ON *skidh* snowshoe] —**ski′er** *n.*

skid (skid) *n.* **1** A log, plank, etc., often one of a pair, used to support or elevate something or as an incline on which heavy objects can be rolled or slid. **2** A low, movable platform that holds material to be moved, temporarily stored, etc. **3** A shoe, drag, etc., used to prevent a wheel from turning. **4** A runner used in place of a wheel in the landing gear of an airplane or helicopter. **5** The act of skidding. — **on the skids** *Slang* Rapidly declining in prestige, power, etc. —*v.* **skid·ded, skid·ding** *v.i.* **1** To slide instead of rolling, as a wheel over a surface. **2** To slide due to loss of traction, as a vehicle. **3** *Aeron.* To slip sideways when turning. —*v.t.* **4** To put, drag, haul, or slide on skids. **5** To brake or hold back with a skid. [?] —**skid'der** *n.*

skid row *Slang* An urban section frequented by vagrants, derelicts, etc.

skiff (skif) *n.* **1** A light rowboat. **2** A small, light sailing vessel. [< OHG *scif* ship]

skill (skil) *n.* **1** Ability or proficiency in execution or performance. **2** A specific art, craft, trade, or job; also such an art, craft, etc., in which one has a learned competence. [< ON *skil* knowledge]

skilled (skild) *adj.* **1** Having skill. **2** Having or requiring a specialized ability, as in a particular occupation, gained by training or experience.

skil·let (skil'it) *n.* A frying pan. [ME *skelet*] • See APPLIANCE.

skill·ful (skil'fəl) *adj.* **1** Having skill. **2** Done with or requiring skill. Also **skil'ful.** —**skill'fully** *adv.* —**skill'ful·ness** *n.*

skim (skim) *v.* **skimmed, skim·ming** *v.t.* **1** To remove floating matter from the surface of (a liquid): to *skim* milk. **2** To remove (floating matter) from the surface of a liquid: to *skim* cream from milk. **3** To cover with a thin film, as of ice. **4** To move lightly and quickly across or over. **5** To cause to bounce and ricochet swiftly and lightly, as a coin across a pond. **6** To read or glance over hastily or superficially. —*v.i.* **7** To move quickly and lightly across or near a surface; glide. **8** To make a hasty and superficial perusal; glance: with *over* or *through.* **9** To become covered with a thin film. —*n.* **1** The act of skimming. **2** That which is skimmed off. **3** A thin layer or coating. —*adj.* Skimmed: *skim* milk. [< OF *escume* scum, foam] —**skim'mer** *n.*

skim milk Milk from which the cream has been removed. Also **skimmed milk.**

skimp (skimp) *v.i.* **1** To provide too little; scrimp. **2** To keep expenses at a minimum. —*v.t.* **3** To do poorly, hastily, or carelessly. **4** To be stingy in providing for. —*adj.* Scant; meager. [?] —**skimp'ing·ly** *adv.*

skimp·y (skim'pē) *adj.* **skimp·i·er, skimp·i·est** Scanty; insufficient. —**skimp'i·ly** *adv.* —**skimp'i·ness** *n.*

skin (skin) *n.* **1** The membranous outer covering of an animal body. **2** The pelt or hide of an animal. **3** A vessel for holding liquids, made of the skin of an animal. **4** Any outside layer, coat, or covering resembling skin, as fruit rind. —**by the skin of one's teeth** *Informal* Very closely or narrowly; barely. —**get under one's skin 1** To provoke one. **2** To be a source of excitement, emotion, etc., to one. —**have a thick (thin) skin** To be very insensitive (or sensitive), as to insult, criticism, etc. —**save one's skin** *Informal* To avoid harm or death. —*v.* **skinned, skin·ning** *v.t.* **1** To remove the skin of; peel. **2** To cover with or as with skin. **3** To remove as if taking off skin: to *skin* a dollar from a roll of bills. **4** *Informal* To cheat or swindle. —*v.i.* **5** To become covered with skin. **6** To climb up or down; shin. [< ON *skinn*] —**skin·ner** *n.*

skin-deep (skin'dēp') *adj.* **1** Penetrating only as deep as the skin. **2** Of little significance; superficial.

skin diving Underwater swimming in which the swimmer is equipped with a breathing apparatus, as a snorkel, goggles, and with various other equipment as foot fins, rubber garments, etc. —**skin diver**

skin·flint (skin'flint) *n.* One who tries to get or save money in any possible way. —**Syn.** miser, niggard, scrooge.

skink (skingk) *n.* One of a group of lizards with short limbs and smooth, flat, shiny scales. [< Gk. *skinkos,* a kind of lizard]

skin·ner (skin'ər) *n.* **1** One who strips or processes the skins of animals. **2** A dealer in skins. **3** *Informal* A mule driver.

skin·ny (skin'ē) *adj.* **·ni·er, ·ni·est** **1** Consisting of or like skin. **2** Without sufficient flesh; too thin. **3** Lacking

normal or desirable quality, quantity, size, etc. —**skin'ni·ly** *adv.* —**skin'ni·ness** *n.*

skin·ny-dip (skin'ē-dip') *Informal v.i.* **·dipped, ·dip·ping** To swim in the nude. —*n.* A swim in the nude. —**skin·ny-dip·per** *n.*

skin-tight (skin'tīt') *adj.* Fitting tightly to the skin, as a garment.

skip (skip) *v.* **skipped, skip·ping** *v.i.* **1** To move with springing steps, esp. by a series of light hops on alternate feet. **2** To be deflected from a surface; ricochet. **3** To pass from one point to another without noticing what lies between. **4** *Informal* To leave or depart hurriedly; flee. **5** To be advanced in school beyond the next grade in order —*v.t.* **6** To leap lightly over. **7** To cause to ricochet. **8** To pass over or by without notice. **9** *Informal* To leave (a place) hurriedly. **10** To fail to attend a session or sessions of (church, school, etc.) **11** To cause to be advanced in school beyond the next grade in order —*n.* **1** A light bound or spring, esp. any of a series of light hops on alternate feet. **2** A passing over without notice. [Prob. < Scand.]

skip-jack (skip'jak) *n.* Any of various fishes that jump above or play along the surface of the water.

skip·per¹ (skip'ər) *n.* **1** One who or that which skips. **2** Any of various insects that make erratic, skipping movements.

skip·per² (skip'ər) *n.* **1** The master or captain of a vessel, esp. of a small ship or boat. **2** One who is in charge of any endeavor. —*v.t.* To act as the skipper of (a vessel, etc.) [< Du. *schip* ship]

skirl (skûrl, skirl) *v.i.* **1** To shriek shrilly, as a bagpipe. — *v.t.* **2** To play on the bagpipe. —*n.* A high, shrill sound, as of a bagpipe. [< Scand.]

skir·mish (skûr'mish) *n.* **1** A minor fight or encounter, usu. an incident in a larger conflict. **2** Any unimportant dispute, argument, etc. —*v.i.* To take part in a skirmish. [< OF *eskermir* to fence, fight] —**skir'mish·er** *n.*

skirt (skûrt) *n.* **1** That part of a dress, gown, etc., that hangs from the waist down. **2** A separate garment for women or girls that hangs from the waist down. • See PLEAT. **3** Anything that hangs or covers like a skirt: the *skirt* of a dressing table. **4** *Slang* A girl; woman. **5** The margin, border, or outer edge of anything. **6** *pl.* The border, fringe, or edge of a particular area; outskirts. —*v.t.* **1** To lie along or form the edge of; to border. **2** To surround or border: with *with.* **3** To pass around or about, usu. to avoid crossing: to *skirt* the town. —*v.i.* **4** To be on or pass along the edge or border. [< ON *skyrt* shirt]

skit (skit) *n.* **1** A short theatrical sketch, usu. humorous or satirical. **2** A short piece of writing, humorous or satirical in tone. [?]

skit·ter (skit'ər) *v.i.* **1** To glide or skip along a surface lightly and quickly. **2** To draw a lure or baited hook along the surface of the water with a skipping or twitching movement. —*v.t.* **3** To cause to skitter.

skit·tish (skit'ish) *adj.* **1** Easily frightened, as a horse. **2** Very playful or lively. **3** Unreliable; fickle. [ME] —**skit'tish·ly** *adv.* —**skit'tish·ness** *n.*

skit·tle (skit'l) *n.* **1** *pl.* (construed as sing.) A British version of the game of ninepins, in which a wooden disk or ball is thrown to knock down the pins. **2** One of the pins used in this game. —**beer and skittles** Carefree, unruffled enjoyment: usu. with a negative: Life is not all *beer and skittles.* [?]

skiv·vy (skiv'ē) *n. pl.* **·vies** *Slang* **1** A man's T-shirt. **2** *pl.* Men's underwear. [?]

skoal (skōl) *interj.* Good health, good luck, etc.: used as a toast. [< Dan. and Norw. *skaal* cup < ON *skāl* bowl]

Skr. Sanskrit.

Skt. Sanskrit.

sku·a (skyōō'ə) *n.* A predatory sea bird. Also **skua gull.** [< ON *skūfr*]

skul·dug·ger·y (skul·dug'ər-ē) *n.* Dishonesty; trickery; underhandedness. [?]

skulk (skulk) *v.i.* **1** To move about furtively or slily; sneak. **2** *Chiefly Brit.* To shirk; evade work or responsibility. —*n.* One who skulks. [< Scand.] —**skulk'er** *n.*

skull (skul) *n.* **1** The bony framework of the head of a vertebrate animal; the cranium. **2** The head considered as the seat of intelligence; mind. [< Scand.]

skull and crossbones A representation of the human skull over two crossed thighbones, used as a warning label on poison and, formerly, as an emblem of piracy.

Bones of the human skull
a. frontal. b. sphenoid.
c. superior maxillary. d. inferior maxillary. e. mastoid process.
f. occipital. g. temporal.
h. parietal.

skull·cap (skul′kap′) *n.* A cap closely fitting the skull and having no brim or peak.

skunk (skungk) *n.* **1** A small nocturnal carnivore of North America, usu. black with a white stripe down the back, and ejecting an offensive odor when attacked. **2** *Informal* A low, contemptible person. —*v.t. Slang* To defeat, as in a contest, esp. to defeat so thoroughly as to keep from scoring. [< Algon. *seganku*]

skunk cabbage A stemless perennial herb growing in marshy terrain and having a strong, skunklike odor. Also **skunk′weed′** (-wēd′).

Skunk

sky (skī) *n. pl.* **skies 1** The blue vault that seems to bend over the earth; the firmament. **2** *Often pl.* The upper atmosphere, esp. in regard to its appearance: cloudy *skies.* **3** The celestial regions; heaven. **4** Climate; weather. —**out of a clear (or blue) sky** Without any warning. —**to the skies** Without reservations: to praise something *to the skies.* —*v.t.* **skied** or **skyed, sky·ing** *Informal* **1** To hit, throw, bat, etc., high into the air. **2** To hang, as a picture, esp. at an exhibition, above eye level. [< ON *skȳ* cloud]

sky blue A blue like the color of the sky; azure. —**sky′-blue′** *adj.*

sky·dive (skī′dīv′) *v.i.* **·dived, ·div·ing** To engage in skydiving. —**sky′div′er** *n.*

sky·div·ing (skī′dī′ving) *n.* The sport of jumping from an airplane and performing various maneuvers before opening a parachute.

sky·jack (skī′jak′) *v.t.* HIJACK (def. 3). [< SKY + (HI)JACK] —**sky′jack′er** *n.*

sky·lark (skī′lärk′) *n.* A lark noted for singing as it flies. —*v.i.* To indulge in hilarious or boisterous frolic. —**sky′-lark′er** *n.*

sky·light (skī′līt′) *n.* A window facing skyward.

sky·line (skī′līn′) *n.* **1** The line where earth and sky appear to meet; horizon. **2** The outline of buildings, trees, etc., against the sky.

sky·rock·et (skī′rok′it) *n.* A rocket that is shot high into the air. —*v.t. & v.i.* To rise or cause to rise or ascend steeply, like a skyrocket, as wages, prices, etc.

sky·sail (skī′səl, -sāl′) *n. Naut.* A small sail above the royal in a square-rigged vessel.

sky·scrap·er (skī′skrā′pər) *n.* A very high building.

sky·ward (skī′wərd) *adv.* Toward the sky. Also **sky′-wards.** —**sky′ward** *adj.*

sky·writ·ing (skī′rī′ting) *n.* The forming of words in the air by the release of a substance, as a jet of vapor, from an airplane. —**sky′writ′er** *n.*

slab (slab) *n.* **1** A fairly thick, flat piece or slice, as of metal, stone, meat, etc. **2** An outer piece cut from a log. —*v.t.* **slabbed, slab·bing 1** To saw slabs from, as a log. **2** To form into a slab or slabs. [ME]

slack[1] (slak) *adj.* **1** Hanging loosely. **2** Careless; remiss; slovenly; slow. **3** Weak; loose: a *slack* mouth. **4** Lacking activity; not brisk or busy; slow or sluggish: a *slack* season. **5** Listless; limp: a *slack* grip. **6** Flowing sluggishly, as water. —*v.t.* **1** To make slack. **2** To slake, as lime. —*v.i.* **3** To be or become slack. **4** To become less active or less busy: usu. with *off.* —*n.* **1** The part of anything, as a rope, that is slack. **2** A period of inactivity. **3** A cessation of movement, as in a current. —*adv.* In a slack manner. [< OE *slæc*] —**slack′ly** *adv.* —**slack′ness** *n.*

slack[2] (slak) *n.* A mixture of coal dust, dirt, and small pieces of coal left after coal has been screened. [ME *sleck*]

slack·en (slak′ən) *v.t. & v.i.* To make or become slack.

slack·er (slak′ər) *n.* One who shirks his duties, esp. one who avoids military service in wartime.

slacks (slaks) *n.pl.* Trousers, esp. for informal wear.

slag (slag) *n.* **1** *Metall.* The fused residue separated in the reduction of ores. **2** Volcanic scoria. —*v.t. & v.i.* **slagged, slag·ging** To form into slag. [< MLG *slagge*] —**slag′gy** *adj.*

slain (slān) *p.p.* of SLAY.

slake (slāk) *v.* **slaked, slak·ing** *v.t.* **1** To lessen the force of; quench: to *slake* thirst or flames. **2** To mix (an oxide, as lime, etc.) with water; to hydrate. —*v.i.* **3** To become hydrated; said of lime. [< OE *slacian* retard]

slaked lime Calcium hydroxide produced by mixing calcium oxide and water.

sla·lom (slä′ləm, slä′-) *n.* In skiing, a race over a zigzag course laid out between upright obstacles. —*v.i.* To ski in or as in a slalom. [Norw.]

slam[1] (slam) *v.* **slammed, slam·ming** *v.t.* **1** To shut with violence and noise. **2** To put, dash, throw, etc., with violence. **3** *Slang* To strike with the fist. **4** *Informal* To criticize severely. —*v.i.* **5** To shut or move with force. —*n.* **1** A closing or striking with a bang; the act or noise of slamming. **2** *Informal* Severe criticism. [? < Scand.]

slam[2] (slam) *n.* **1** GRAND SLAM (def. 1). **2** LITTLE SLAM. [?]

slam-bang (slam′bang′) *Informal adv.* Vigorously, violently, or noisily. —*adj.* Vigorous, violent, or noisy.

slan·der (slan′dər) *n.* **1** The uttering of false statements or misrepresentations which defame and injure the reputation of another. **2** Such a statement. —*v.t.* **1** To injure by uttering a false statement, etc.; defame. —*v.i.* **2** To utter slander. [< L *scandalum* scandal] —**slan′der·er** *n.* • Popularly, *slander* and *libel* are used synonomously to mean defamation. Legally, however, *slander* refers to oral defamation and *libel* to defamation by any other means, as writing, pictures, effigies, etc.

slan·der·ous (slan′dər·əs) *adj.* **1** Uttering slander. **2** Containing or constituting slander. —**slan′der·ous·ly** *adv.* —**slan′der·ous·ness** *n.*

slang (slang) *n.* **1** A type of popular language comprised of words and phrases of a vigorous, colorful, or facetious nature, which are invented or derived from the unconventional use of the standard vocabulary. **2** The special vocabulary of a certain class, group, profession, etc.; argot; jargon. [?] —**slang′i·ness** *n.* —**slang′y** *adj.*

slant (slant) *v.t.* **1** To give a sloping direction to. **2** To write or edit (news or other literary matter) so as to express a special attitude or appeal to a particular group, interest, etc. —*v.i.* **3** To have or take an oblique or sloping direction. —*adj.* Sloping —*n.* **1** A slanting direction, course, line, etc.; incline. **2** A point of view, esp. one that is personal or peculiar. [< Scand.] —**slant′ing** *adj.* —**slant′ing·ly** *adv.* —**slant′ing·ness** *n.*

slant·wise (slant′wīz) *adj.* Slanting; oblique. —*adv.* At a slant or slope; obliquely. Also **slant′ways′** (-wāz′).

slap (slap) *n.* **1** A blow delivered with the open hand or with something flat. **2** The sound made by such a blow, or a sound like it. **3** An insult or rebuff. —*v.* **slapped, slap·ping** *v.t.* **1** To strike with the open hand or with something flat. **2** To put, place, throw, etc., violently or carelessly. —*adv.* **1** Suddenly; abruptly. **2** Directly; straight: *slap* into his face. [< LG *slapp*] —**slap′per** *n.*

slap-dash (slap′dash′) *adj.* Done or acting in a hasty or careless way. —*n.* Something done in a hasty or careless manner. —*adv.* In a slap-dash manner.

slap-hap·py (slap′hap′ē) *adj. Slang* **1** Confused or dazed, as by blows to the head. **2** Giddy or silly.

slap·jack (slap′jak) *n.* PANCAKE.

slap·stick (slap′stik′) *n.* **1** A flexible, double paddle formerly used in farces and pantomimes to make a loud report when an actor was struck with it. **2** The type of comedy which depends on farce, violent activity, etc. —*adj.* Using or suggestive of such comedy.

slash (slash) *v.t.* **1** To cut violently with or as with an edged instrument; gash. **2** To strike with a whip; lash; scourge. **3** To slit, as a garment, so as to expose ornamental material or lining in or under the slits. **4** To criticize severely. **5** To reduce sharply, as salaries. —*v.i.* **6** To make a long sweeping stroke with or as with something sharp; cut. —*n.* **1** The act of slashing. **2** The result of slashing; cut; slit; gash. **3** An ornamental slit cut in a garment. **4** An opening in a forest, covered with debris, as from cutting timber. **5** Such debris. [? < OF *esclashier* to break] —**slash′er** *n.*

slash·ing (slash′ing) *adj.* **1** Severely critical; merciless. **2** Spirited; dashing; impetuous. **3** *Informal* Tremendous; great. —*n.* A slash. —**slash′ing·ly** *adv.* —**slash′ing·ness** *n.*

slat (slat) *n.* Any thin, narrow strip of wood or metal; lath. —*v.t.* **slat·ted, slat·ting** To provide or make with slats. [< OF *esclat* splinter, chip]

slat (slāt) *n.* **1** A rock that splits readily into thin and even sheets or layers. **2** A piece, slab, or plate of slate used for roofing, writing upon, etc. **3** A list of candidates, as for nomination or election. **4** A dull bluish gray color resembling that of slate: also **slate gray.** —**a clean slate** A record unmarred by dishonor or dishonesty. —*v.t.* **slat·ed, slat·ing** **1** To cover with or as with slate. **2** To put on a political slate or a list of any sort. [< OF *esclat* a chip, splinter] —**slat′er** *n.* —**slat′y** *adj.* (**·i·er, ·i·est**)

slat·tern (slat′ərn) *n.* An untidy or slovenly woman. [?]

slat·tern·ly (slat′ərn·lē) *adj.* Of, pertaining to, characteristic of, or fit for a slattern. —*adv.* In the manner of a slattern. —**slat′tern·li·ness** *n.* —**Syn.** *adj.* untidy, dowdy, frowzy, sluttish.

slaugh·ter (slô′tər) *n.* **1** The act of killing, esp. the butchering of animals for market. **2** The wanton or savage killing of one or more human beings, esp. of a great number in battle. —*v.t.* **1** To kill for the market; butcher. **2** To kill wantonly or savagely, esp. in large numbers. [< ON *slátr* butcher's meat] —**slaugh′ter·er** *n.* —**slaugh′ter·ous** *adj.* —**slaugh′ter·ous·ly** *adv.*

slaugh·ter·house (slô′tər·hous′) *n.* A place where animals are butchered.

Slav (släv, slav) *n.* A member of any of the Slavic-speaking peoples of E, SE, or CEN. Europe.

Slav. Slavic.

slave (slāv) *n.* **1** A person who is owned by and completely subject to another; one bound by slavery. **2** A person who is totally subject to some habit, influence, etc. **3** One who labors like a slave; drudge. **4** A machine or device that is controlled by another machine or device. **5** SLAVE ANT. —*v.i.* **slaved, slav·ing** To work like a slave; toil; drudge. [< Med. L *sclavus* Slav]

slave ant An ant enslaved by members of a slave-making ant species.

slave-driv·er (slāv′drī′vər) *n.* **1** An overseer of slaves at work. **2** Any severe or exacting taskmaster.

slave-hold·er (slāv′hōl′dər) *n.* An owner of slaves. —**slave′hold′ing** *adj.* *n.*

slav·er¹ (slā′vər) *n.* A person or a vessel engaged in the slave trade.

slav·er² (slav′ər) *v.i.* To dribble saliva; drool. —*n.* Saliva dribbling from the mouth. [? < ON *slafra*] —**slav′er·er** *n.*

slav·er·y (slā′vər·ē, slāv′rē) *n.* **1** The legalized social institution in which humans are held as property or chattels. **2** The condition of being a slave. **3** Submission to some habit, influence, etc. **4** Slavish toil; drudgery.

slave trade The business of dealing in slaves, esp. the procurement, transportation, and sale of black Africans.

slav·ey (slā′vē, slav′ē) *n. pl.* **slav·eys** *Chiefly Brit. Informal* A drudge, usu. a maidservant.

Slav·ic (slä′vik, slav′ik) *adj.* Of or pertaining to the Slavs or their languages. —*n.* A branch of the Indo-European language family including Byelorussian, Bulgarian, Czech, Polish, Serbo-Croatian, Slovene, Russian, and Ukrainian.

slav·ish (slā′vish) *adj.* **1** Of, pertaining to, or characteristic of a slave; servile. **2** Having no originality; imitative. —**slav′ish·ly** *adv.* —**slav′ish·ness** *n.*

slaw (slô) *n.* COLESLAW. [< Du. *sla*, short for *salade* salad]

slay (slā) *v.t.* **slew, slain, slay·ing 1** To kill violently; slaughter. **2** *Informal* To amuse, impress, etc., in an overwhelming way. [< OE *slēan*] —**slay′er** *n.*

slea·zy (slē′zē, slā′-) *adj.* **·zi·er, ·zi·est 1** Lacking firmness of texture or substance. **2** Cheap in character or quality; shoddy, shabby, etc.: a *sleazy* novel; a *sleazy* dress. [?] —**slea′zi·ly** *adv.* —**slea′zi·ness** *n.*

sled (sled) *n.* **1** A vehicle on runners, designed for carrying people or loads over snow and ice. **2** A small sled used esp. by children for sliding on snow and ice. —*v.* **sled·ded, sled·ding** *v.t.* **1** To convey on a sled. —*v.i.* **2** To ride on or use a sled. [< MLG *sledde*] —**sled′der** *n.*

sled·ding (sled′ing) *n.* **1** The act of using or riding on a sled. **2** The conditions under which one uses a sled. **3** *Informal* The conditions under which one pursues any goal; going; progress.

sledge¹ (slej) *n.* A vehicle mounted on low runners for moving loads, esp. over snow and ice. —*v.t. & v.i.* **sledged, sledg·ing** To travel or convey on a sledge. [< MDu. *sleedse*]

Sledge

sledge² (slej) *n. & v.t., v.i.* **sledged, sledg·ing** SLEDGEHAMMER. [< OE *slecg*]

sledge·ham·mer (slej′ham′ər) *n.* A long, heavy hammer, usu. wielded with both hands. —*v.t. & v.i.* To strike with or as with such a hammer. —*adj.* Like a sledgehammer; extremely powerful; crushing.

sleek (slēk) *adj.* **1** Smooth and glossy. **2** Well-groomed or well-fed. **3** Smooth-spoken and polished in behavior, esp. in a specious way. —*v.t.* **1** To make smooth or glossy; polish. **2** To soothe; mollify. [Var. of SLICK] —**sleek′ly** *adv.* —**sleek′ness** *n.*

sleep (slēp) *n.* **1** A natural, recurrent physiological state characterized by cessation of voluntary movement and inattention to external stimuli. **2** A period of sleep. **3** Any condition of inactivity or rest. —**last sleep** Death. —*v.* **slept, sleep·ing** *v.i.* **1** To be or fall asleep; slumber. **2** To be in a state resembling sleep. —*v.t.* **3** To rest or repose in: to *sleep* the sleep of the dead. **4** To provide with sleeping quarters; lodge: The hotel can *sleep* a hundred guests. —**sleep away** To pass or spend in sleeping. —**sleep in** To sleep in the house where one works. —**sleep off** To get rid of by sleeping: He *slept off* a headache. —**sleep on** To postpone a decision upon. [< OE *slēp*]

sleep·er (slē′pər) *n.* **1** One who or that which sleeps. **2** A railroad sleeping car. **3** A heavy beam resting on or in the ground, as a support for a roadway, rails, etc. **4** *Informal* Someone or something thought to be unpromising that unexpectedly attains value, importance, notoriety, etc.

sleeping bag A large, warmly-lined bag, usu. zippered and often padded, for sleeping in esp. outdoors.

sleeping car A passenger railroad car with accommodations for sleeping.

sleeping sickness 1 Any of several often fatal tropical diseases caused by protozoans transmitted by the bites of certain insects, as the tsetse fly in Africa, and marked by fever and progressive lethargy. **2** A form of encephalitis.

sleep·less (slēp′lis) *adj.* **1** Unable to sleep; wakeful; restless. **2** Marked by or giving no sleep. **3** Always active or moving. —**sleep′less·ly** *adv.* —**sleep′less·ness** *n.*

sleep·walk·er (slēp′wô′kər) *n.* A person who walks in his sleep; somnambulist. —**sleep′walk′ing** *n.*

sleep·y (slē′pē) *adj.* **sleep·i·er, sleep·i·est 1** Inclined to or ready for sleep; drowsy. **2** Lethargic, inactive, sluggish, or dull. **3** Conducive to sleep. —**sleep′i·ly** *adv.* —**sleep′i·ness** *n.*

sleet (slēt) *n.* **1** A mixture of snow or hail and rain. **2** Partly frozen rain. **3** A thin coating of ice, as on rails, wires, roads, etc. —*v.i.* To pour or shed sleet. [ME *slete*] —**sleet′y** *adj.*

sleeve (slēv) *n.* **1** The part of a garment that serves as a

Sledge-hammers

covering for the arm. 2 *Mech.* A tube or tubelike part surrounding another part or into which another part fits. **—up one's sleeve** Hidden but at hand **—***v.t.* **sleeved, sleev·ing** To furnish with a sleeve or sleeves. [< OE *slēfe*]

sleigh (slā) *n.* A light vehicle with runners, used esp. for transporting people on snow and ice. **—***v.i.* To ride or travel in a sleigh. [< Du. *slee,* contraction of *slede* sledge[1]] **—sleigh'er** *n.*

sleight (slīt) *n.* **1** Deftness; skill; dexterity. **2** Craft; cunning. [< ON *slægdh* slyness]

Sleigh

sleight of hand **1** Skill in performing magical tricks or in juggling. **2** An instance of such skill in performing.

slen·der (slen'dər) *adj.* **1** Having a small width or circumference, in proportion to length or height; long and thin. **2** Having a slim figure; attractively slight. **3** Having slight force or foundation. **4** Small or inadequate. [ME *slendre*] **—slen'der·ly** *adv.* **—slen'der·ness** *n.*

slen·der·ize (slen'də·rīz) *v.t. & v.i.* **·ized, ·iz·ing** To make or become slender.

slept (slept) *p.t. & p.p.* of SLEEP.

sleuth (slooth) *n.* **1** *Informal* A detective. **2** A bloodhound: also **sleuth'hound.** **—***v.i.* To act as a detective. [< ON *slōdh* track]

slew[1] (sloo) *p.t.* of SLAY.

slew[2] (sloo) *n.* SLOUGH[1] (def. 2).

slew[3] (sloo) *n. Informal* A large number or amount. [< Ir. *sluagh*]

slew[4] (sloo) *v. & n.* SLUE[1].

slice (slīs) *n.* **1** A thin, broad piece cut off from a larger body. **2** A share or portion. **3** Any of various implements with a thin, broad blade, as a spatula. **4 a** The course of a ball so hit that it curves in the direction of the dominant hand of the player who propels it. **b** The ball that follows such a course. **—***v.* **sliced, slic·ing** *v.t.* **1** To cut or remove from a larger piece: often with *off, from,* etc. **2** To cut, separate, or divide into parts, shares, or thin, broad pieces. **3** To stir, spread, etc. with a slice. **4** To hit (a ball) so as to produce a slice. **—***v.i.* **5** To cut with or as with a knife. **6** To slice a ball, as in golf. [< OHG *slizan* to slit] **—slic'er** *n.*

slick (slik) *adj.* **1** Smooth, slippery, or sleek. **2** *Informal* Deceptively clever; tricky; smooth. **3** Clever; deft; adept. **4** *Informal* Technically skillful but shallow and insignificant: a *slick* novel. **5** *Slang* Very good, attractive, enjoyable, etc. **—***n.* **1** A smooth place on a surface of water, as from oil. **2** A film of oil on the surface of water. **3** *Informal* A magazine printed on glossy paper. **—***adv. Slang* In a slick or smooth manner; deftly, cleverly, smoothly, etc. **—***v.t.* **1** To make smooth, trim, or glossy. **2** *Informal* To make smart or presentable: often with *up.* [< OE *slician* make smooth]

slick·er (slik'ər) *n.* **1** A long, loose waterproof coat of oilskin. **2** *Informal* A clever, deceptive, crooked person.

slide (slīd) *v.* **slid, slid** or **slid·den, slid·ing** *v.i.* **1** To pass along a surface with a smooth movement. **2** To move smoothly over snow or ice. **3** To move or pass stealthily or imperceptibly. **4** To proceed in a natural way; drift: to let the matter *slide.* **5** To pass or fall gradually (into a specified condition). **6** To slip from a position: The cup *slid* off the saucer. **7** To slip or fall by losing one's equilibrium or foothold. **8** In baseball, to throw oneself along the ground toward a base. **—***v.t.* **9** To cause to slide, as over a surface. **10** To move, put, enter, etc., with quietness or dexterity: with *in* or *into.* **—***n.* **1** An act of sliding. **2** An inclined plane, channel, etc., on which persons, goods, logs, etc., slide downward to a lower level. **3** A small plate of glass on which a specimen is mounted and examined through a microscope. **4** A small plate of transparent material bearing a single image for projection on a screen. **5** A part or mechanism that slides, as the U-shaped portion of the tubing which is pushed in and out to vary the pitch of a trombone. **6** The slipping of a mass of earth, snow, etc., from a higher to a lower level. **7** The mass that slips down. [< OE *slīdan*] **—slid'er** *n.*

slide fastener ZIPPER.

slide rule A device consisting of a rigid ruler with a central sliding piece, both graduated, used in calculation.

sliding scale A schedule affecting imports, prices, or wages, varying under conditions of consumption, demand, or market price.

slight (slīt) *adj.* **1** Of small importance or degree: a *slight* illness. **2** Slender in build: a *slight* figure. **3** Frail; fragile: a *slight* structure. **—***v.t.* **1** To omit due courtesy toward or respect for: to *slight* a friend. **2** To do carelessly or thoughtlessly; shirk. **3** To treat as trivial or insignificant. **—***n.* An act of discourtesy or disrespect. [< ON *slēttr* smooth] **—slight'er, slight'ness** *n.* **—slight'ly** *adv.*

sli·ly (slī'lē) *adv.* SLYLY.

slim (slim) *adj.* **slim·mer, slim·mest** **1** Small in thickness in proportion to height or length. **2** Slight; meager: a *slim* chance of survival. **—***v.t. & v.i.* **slimmed, slim·ming** To make or become thin or thinner. [< Du. *slim* bad] **—slim'ly** *adv.* **—slim'ness** *n.*

slime (slīm) *n.* **1** Soft, moist, adhesive mud or earth; muck. **2** A mucous exudation from the bodies of certain organisms. **3** An offensive, digusting substance or quality. **—***v.t.* **slimed, slim·ing** **1** To smear with or as with slime. **2** To remove slime from, as fishes. [< OE *slīm*]

slim·y (slī'mē) *adj.* **slim·i·er, slim·i·est** **1** Covered with slime. **2** Containing slime. **3** Filthy; foul. **—slim'i·ly** *adv.* **—slim'i·ness** *n.*

sling (sling) *n.* **1** A strap or pocket with a string attached to each end, for hurling a stone. **2** One of various devices for holding up an injured arm. **3** A device, as a band or chain, for lifting or moving heavy objects. **4** The act of slinging; a sudden throw. **5** A drink made of sugar, liquor, and water: a gin *sling.* **—***v.t.* **slung, sling·ing** **1** To fling; hurl. **2** To move or hoist, as by a rope or tackle. **3** To suspend loosely in a sling. [? < ON *slyngva* hurl] **—sling'er** *n.*

sling·shot (sling'shot') *n.* A forked stick with an elastic strap attached to the prongs for hurling small missiles.

slink (slingk) *v.* **slunk** or **slinked, slink·ing** *v.i.* To move or go furtively or stealthily. [< OE *slincan*] **—slink'ing·ly** *adv.* **—Syn.** creep, steal, sneak, skulk.

slink·y (slingk'ē) *adj.* **slink·i·er, slink·i·est** **1** Sneaking; stealthy. **2** *Slang* Sinuous or feline in movement or form. **—slink'i·ly** *adv.* **—slink'i·ness** *n.*

slip[1] (slip) *v.* **slipped, slip·ping** *v.t.* **1** To cause to glide or slide. **2** To put on or off easily, as a loose garment. **3** To convey slyly or secretly. **4** To free oneself or itself from. **5** To unleash, as hounds. **6** To release from its fastening and let run out, as a cable. **7** To dislocate, as a bone. **8** To escape or pass unobserved: It *slipped* my mind. **—***v.i.* **9** To slide so as to lose one's footing. **10** To fall into an error. **11** To escape. **12** To move smoothly and easily. **13** To go or come stealthily: often with *off, away,* or *from.* **14** To overlook: to let an opportunity *slip.* **—let slip** To say without intending to. **—slip one over on** *Informal* To take advantage of by trickery. **—slip up** *Informal* To make a mistake. **—***n.* **1** A sudden slide. **2** A slight mistake. **3** A narrow space between two wharves. **4** A pier. **5** An inclined plane leading down to the water, on which vessels are repaired or constructed. **6** A woman's undergarment approximately the length of a dress. **7** A pillowcase. **8** A leash containing a device which permits quick release of the dog. **9** Undesired relative motion, as between a wheel and the road; also, the amount of this. **—give (someone) the slip** To elude (someone). [< MLG *slippen*]

slip[2] (slip) *n.* **1** A cutting from a plant for planting or grafting. **2** A small, slender person, esp. a youthful one. **3** A small piece of something, as of paper. **—***v.t.* **slipped, slip·ping** To cut off for planting; make a slip or slips of. [< MDu. *slippe*]

slip·cov·er (slip'kuv'ər) *n.* A fitted cloth cover for a piece of furniture, that can be readily removed.

slip·knot (slip'not') *n.* **1** A knot so made that it will slip along the rope or cord around which it is formed. **2** A knot easily untied by pulling. Also **slip knot.**

slip-on (slip'on', -ôn') *adj.* **1** Designating a garment or accessory that can be easily donned or taken off. **2** Designating a garment, esp. a sweater, that is put on and taken off over the head: also **slip'o'ver** (-ō'vər). **—***n.* A slip-on garment, glove, shoe, etc.

slip·per (slip'ər) *n.* A low, light shoe into or out of which the foot is easily slipped. **—slip'pered** *adj.*

slip·per·y (slip′ər·ē) *adj.* **·per·i·er, ·per·i·est 1** Having a surface so smooth that bodies slip or slide easily on it. **2** That evades one's grasp; elusive. **3** Unreliable; tricky. —**slip′per·i·ness** *n.*

slippery elm 1 A species of small elm with mucilaginous inner bark. **2** Its wood or inner bark.

slip·shod (slip′shod′) *adj.* **1** Wearing shoes or slippers down at the heels. **2** Slovenly; sloppy. **3** Performed carelessly: *slipshod* work.

slip·stream (slip′strēm′) *n. Aeron.* The stream of air driven backwards by the propeller of an aircraft.

slip-up (slip′up′) *n. Informal* A mistake; error.

slit (slit) *n.* A relatively straight cut or a long, narrow opening. —*v.t.* **slit, slit·ting 1** To make a long incision in; slash. **2** To cut lengthwise into strips. **3** To sever. [ME *slitten*] —**slit′ter** *n.*

slith·er (slith′ər) *v.i.* **1** To slide; slip, as on a loose surface. **2** To glide, as a snake. —*v.t.* **3** To cause to slither. —*n.* A sinuous, gliding movement. [< OE *slidrian*] —**slith′er·y** *adj.*

sliv·er (sliv′ər) *n.* **1** A slender piece, as of wood, cut or torn off lengthwise; a splinter. **2** Corded textile fibers drawn into a fleecy strand. —*v.t. & v.i.* To cut or be split into long thin pieces. [< ME *sliven* to cleave] —**sliv′er·er** *n.*

slob (slob) *n.* **1** Mud; mire. **2** *Slang* A careless or unclean person. [< Ir. *slab*]

slob·ber (slob′ər) *v.t.* **1** To wet with liquids oozing from the mouth. **2** To shed or spill, as liquid food, in eating. —*v.i.* **3** To drivel; slaver. **4** To talk or act gushingly. —*n.* **1** Liquid spilled as from the mouth. **2** Gushing, sentimental talk. [ME *sloberen*] —**slob′ber·er** *n.* —**slob′ber·y** *adj.*

sloe (slō) *n.* **1** A small, plumlike, astringent fruit. **2** The shrub that bears it; the blackthorn. [< OE *slā*]

sloe gin A cordial with a gin base, flavored with sloes.

slog (slog) *v.t. & v.i.* **slogged, slog·ging 1** To slug, as a pugilist. **2** To plod (one's way). —*n.* A heavy blow. [?] —**slog′ger** *n.*

slo·gan (slō′gən) *n.* **1** A catchword or motto adopted by a political party, advertiser, etc. **2** A battle or rallying cry. [< Scot. Gael. *sluagh* army + *gairm* yell]

slo·gan·eer (slō′gə·nir′) *Informal n.* One who coins or uses slogans. —*v.i.* To coin or use slogans.

sloop (slo̅o̅p) *n.* A small sailboat with a single mast and at least one jib. [< Du. *sloep*]

slop[1] (slop) *v.* **slopped, slop·ping** *v.i.* **1** To splash or spill. **2** To walk or move through slush. —*v.t.* **3** To cause (a liquid) to spill or splash. **4** To feed (a domestic animal) with slops. —**slop over 1** To overflow and splash. **2** *Slang* To show too much zeal, emotion, etc. —*n.* **1** Slush or watery mud. **2** An unappetizing liquid or watery food. **3** *pl.* Refuse liquid. **4** *pl.* Waste food or swill. [< ME *sloppe* mud]

Sloop

slop[2] (slop) *n.* **1** A loose outer garment, as a smock. **2** *pl.* Articles of clothing and other merchandise sold to sailors on shipboard. [ME *sloppe*]

slope (slōp) *v.* **sloped, slop·ing** *v.i.* **1** To be inclined from the level; slant downward or upward. **2** To go obliquely. —*v.t.* **3** To cause to slope. —*n.* **1** Any slanting surface or line. **2** The degree of inclination of a line or surface from the plane of the horizon. [< OE *aslupan* slip away] —**slop′er, slop′ing·ness** *n.* —**slop′ing·ly** *adv.*

slop·py (slop′ē) *adj.* **·pi·er, ·pi·est 1** Slushy; splashy; wet. **2** Watery or pulpy. **3** Splashed with liquid or slops. **4** *Informal* Messy; slovenly; careless. **5** *Informal* Maudlin; overly sentimental. —**slop′pi·ly** *adv.* —**slop′pi·ness** *n.*

slosh (slosh) *v.t.* **1** To throw about, as a liquid. —*v.i.* **2** To splash; flounder: to *slosh* through a pool. —*n.* Slush. [Var. of SLUSH]

slot (slot) *n.* **1** A long narrow groove or opening; slit. **2** A narrow depression cut to receive some corresponding part in a mechanism. **3** *Informal* An opening or position, as in an organization, or a place in a sequence. —*v.t.* **slot·ted, slot·ting** To cut a slot or slots in. [< OF *esclot* the hollow between the breasts]

sloth (slōth, slôth, sloth) *n.* **1** Disinclination to exertion; laziness. **2** Any of several slow-moving, arboreal mammals of South America. [< SLOW]

sloth·ful (slōth′fəl, slôth′-, sloth′-) *adj.* Inclined to or characterized by sloth. —**sloth′ful·ly** *adv.* —**sloth′ful·ness** *n.* —*Syn.* lazy, indolent, sluggish, shiftless.

slot machine A vending machine or gambling machine having a slot in which a coin is dropped to cause operation.

Three-toed sloth

slouch (slouch) *v.i.* **1** To have a downcast or drooping gait, look, or posture. **2** To hang or droop carelessly. —*n.* **1** A drooping movement or appearance caused by depression or carelessness. **2** An awkward or incompetent person. [?] —**slouch′y** *adj.* (·i·er, ·i·est) — **slouch′i·ly** *adv.* —**slouch′i·ness** *n.*

slough[1] (slou; slo̅o̅ *esp. for def. 2*) *n.* **1** A place of deep mud or mire. **2** A stagnant swamp, backwater, etc. **3** A state of great despair or degradation. [< OE *slōh*] —**slough′y** *adj.*

slough[2] (sluf) *n.* **1** Dead tissue separated and thrown off from living tissue. **2** The skin of a serpent that has been or is about to be shed. —*v.t.* **1** To cast off; shed. **2** To discard; shed, as a habit or a growth. —*v.i.* **3** To be cast off. **4** To cast off a slough or tissue. [ME *slouh*] —**slough′y** *adj.*

Slo·vak (slō′väk, slō′vak) *n.* **1** One of a Slavic people of NW Hungary and parts of Moravia. **2** The language spoken by the Slovaks. —*adj.* Of or pertaining to the Slovaks or to their language. Also **Slo·vak′i·an.**

slov·en (sluv′ən) *n.* One who is habitually untidy, careless, or dirty. [ME *sloveyn*]

Slo·vene (slō′vēn, slō·vēn′) *n.* One of a group of s Slavs now living in NW Yugoslavia. —*adj.* Of or pertaining to the Slovenes or to their language. —**Slo·ve′ni·an** *adj., n.*

slov·en·ly (sluv′ən·lē) *adj.* **·li·er, ·li·est** Untidy and careless in appearance, work, habits, etc. —*adv.* In a slovenly manner. —**slov′en·li·ness** *n.*

slow (slō) *adj.* **1** Taking a long time to move, perform, or occur. **2** Behind the correct time: said of a timepiece. **3** Not hasty: *slow* to anger. **4** Dull in comprehending: a *slow* student. **5** Uninteresting; tedious: a *slow* drama. **6** Denoting a condition of a racetrack that retards the horses' speed. **7** Heating or burning slowly; low: a *slow* flame. **8** Not brisk; slack: Business is *slow.* —*v.t. & v.i.* To make or become slow or slower: often with *up* or *down.* —*adv.* In a slow manner. [< OE *slāw*] —**slow′ly** *adv.* —**slow′ness** *n.*

slow-mo·tion (slō′mō′shən) *adj.* **1** Moving or acting at less than normal speed. **2** Denoting a television or motion picture filmed at greater than standard speed so that the action appears slow in normal projection.

sludge (sluj) *n.* **1** Soft, water-soaked mud. **2** A slush of snow or broken or half-formed ice. **3** Muddy or pasty refuse, sediment, etc. [?] —**sludg′y** *adj.* (·i·er, ·i·est)

slue[1] (slo̅o̅) *v.* **slued, slu·ing** *v.t.* **1** To cause to swing, slide, or skid to the side. **2** To cause to twist or turn. —*v.i.* **3** To move sidewise. —*n.* The act of skidding or pivoting. [?]

slue[2] (slo̅o̅) *n. Informal* SLEW[3].

slue[3] (slo̅o̅) *n.* SLOUGH[1] (def. 2).

slug[1] (slug) *n.* **1** A bullet. **2** *Printing* **a** A strip of type metal between words or letters. **b** A metal strip bearing a line of type in one piece. **3** Any small chunk of metal; esp., one used in place of a coin in automatic machines.

slug[2] (slug) *n.* **1** Any of numerous land mollusks related to the snail, having an elongated body and a rudimentary shell. **2** The sluglike larvae of certain insects. [ME *slugge* a sluggard]

slug[3] (slug) *Informal n.* A heavy blow, as with the fist. —*v.t.* **slugged, slug·ging** To strike heavily, as with the fist. [?] —**slug′ger** *n.*

Slug

slug⁴ (slug) *n. Slang* A single drink, esp. of undiluted alcoholic liquor. [< Du. *sluck* a swallow]

slug·gard (slug′ərd) *n.* A person habitually lazy. —*adj.* Lazy; sluggish. [< SLUG²] —**slug′gard·ly** *adv.*

slug·gish (slug′ish) *adj.* 1 Having little motion; inactive; torpid. 2 Habitually idle and lazy. —**slug′gish·ly** *adv.* —**slug′gish·ness** *n.*

sluice (slōōs) *n.* 1 Any artificial channel for conducting water. 2 A device for controlling the flow of water; a floodgate: also **sluice gate.** 3 The water held back by such a gate. 4 Something through which anything issues or flows. 5 A sloping trough in which gold is washed from sand. —*v.* **sluiced, sluic·ing** *v.t.* 1 To drench or cleanse by a flow of water. 2 To wash in or by a sluice. 3 To draw out or conduct by or through a sluice. 4 To send (logs) down a sluiceway. —*v.i.* 5 To flow out or issue from a sluice. [< L *excludere* shut out]

sluice·way (slōōs′wā′) *n.* An artificial channel for the passage of water.

slum (slum) *n.* A squalid, dirty, overcrowded street or section of a city. —*v.i.* **slummed, slum·ming** To visit slums, as for reasons of curiosity. [?] —**slum′mer** *n.*

slum·ber (slum′bər) *v.i.* 1 To sleep lightly or quietly. 2 To be inactive; stagnate. —*v.t.* 3 To spend or pass in sleeping. —*n.* Quiet sleep. [< OE *slūma* sleep] —**slum′ber·er** *n.* —**slum′ber·ing·ly** *adv.*

slum·ber·ous (slum′bər-əs) *adj.* 1 Inviting to slumber. 2 Drowsy; sleepy. 3 Quiet; peaceful: a hot, *slumberous* afternoon. Also **slum·brous** (slum′brəs). —**slum′ber·ous·ly** *adv.* —**slum′ber·ous·ness** *n.*

slum·lord (slum′lôrd′) *n.* A landlord who derives high profits from run-down property, esp. housing. [< SLUM + (LAND)LORD]

slump (slump) *v.i.* 1 To fall or fail suddenly. 2 To stand, walk, or proceed with a stooping posture; slouch. —*n.* 1 The act of slumping. 2 A collapse or decline: a *slump* in the stock market. [Prob. < Scand.]

slung (slung) *p.t. & p.p.* of SLING.

slunk (slungk) *p.t. & p.p.* of SLINK.

slur (slûr) *v.t.* **slurred, slur·ring** 1 To slight; disparage; depreciate. 2 To pass over lightly or hurriedly. 3 To pronounce hurriedly and indistinctly. 4 *Music* **a** To sing or play as indicated by the slur. **b** To mark with a slur. —*n.* 1 A disparaging remark or insinuation. 2 *Music* **a** A curved line (‿ or ⁀) indicating that tones so tied are to be performed without a break between them. **b** The legato effect indicated by this mark. 3 A slurred pronunciation. [< ME *sloor* mud] —**slur′ring·ly** *adv.*

slurb (slûrb) *n. Slang* A suburban area so poorly planned and developed as to seem like a slum. [< SL(UM) + (SUB)URB]

slurp (slûrp) *v.t. & v.i. Slang* To sip noisily. [Imit.]

slush (slush) *n.* 1 Soft, sloppy material, as melting snow or soft mud. 2 Greasy material used for lubrication, etc. 3 Sentimental talk or writing. [ME *sloche*] —**slush′y** *adj.*

slush fund Money collected or spent for bribery, lobbying, political pressure, etc.

slut (slut) *n.* 1 A slatternly woman. 2 A sexually promiscuous woman; whore. 3 A female dog. [?] —**slut′tish** *adj.* —**slut′tish·ly** *adv.* —**slut′tish·ness** *n.*

sly (slī) *adj.* **sli·er** or **sly·er, sli·est** or **sly·est** 1 Artfully dexterous in doing things secretly. 2 Playfully clever; roguish. 3 Meanly or stealthily clever; crafty. 4 Done with or marked by artful secrecy: a *sly* trick. —**on the sly** In a stealthy way. [< ON *slægr*] —**sly′ly** *adv.* —**sly′ness** *n.*

Sm samarium.

smack¹ (smak) *n.* 1 A quick, sharp sound, as of the lips when separated rapidly. 2 A noisy kiss. 3 A sounding blow or slap. —*v.t.* 1 To separate (the lips) rapidly. 2 To kiss noisily. 3 To slap. —*v.i.* 4 To make a smacking noise, as in tasting, kissing, striking, etc. —*adv.* Directly; exactly: also **smack′·dab′** (-dab′). [< MDu. *smack* a blow]

smack² (smak) *v.i.* 1 To have a slight taste or flavor: usu. with *of.* 2 To have, keep, or disclose a slight suggestion: with *of.* —*n.* 1 A suggestive flavor. 2 A mere taste; smattering. [< OE *smæc* a taste]

smack³ (smak) *n.* A small sailing vessel used chiefly for fishing; esp. one having a well for fish in its hold. [< Du. *smak, smacke*]

smack⁴ (smak) *n. Slang* HEROIN.

smack·er (smak′ər) *n.* 1 One who or that which smacks. 2 *Slang* A dollar.

smack·ing (smak′ing) *adj.* Brisk; lively, as a breeze.

small (smôl) *adj.* 1 Not as large as other things of the same kind; little. 2 Being of slight degree, weight, or importance. 3 Ignoble; mean: a *small* nature. 4 Of humble background; poor. 5 Acting or transacting business in a limited way: a *small* shopkeeper. 6 Weak in characteristic properties: *small* beer. 7 Having little body or volume. 8 Not capital: said of letters. —**feel small** To feel humiliated or ashamed. —*adv.* 1 In a low or faint tone: to sing *small.* 2 Into small pieces. 3 In a small way; trivially. —*n.* 1 A small or slender part: the *small* of the back. 2 A small thing or quantity. [< OE *smæl*] —**small′ness** *n.*

small arms Arms that may be carried on the person, as a rifle, automatic pistol, or revolver.

small calorie See CALORIE.

small capital A capital letter cut slightly larger than the lower-case letters of a specified type and slightly smaller than the regular capital.

small fry 1 Small, young fish. 2 Young children. 3 Small or insignificant people or things.

small hours The early hours after midnight.

small-minded (smôl′mīn′did) *adj.* Having a petty mind; intolerant; ungenerous.

small potatoes *Informal* Unimportant, insignificant persons or things.

small-pox (smôl′poks′) *n.* An acute, highly contagious viral disease characterized by a rash that leaves pitted scars.

small talk Unimportant or casual conversation.

small-time (smôl′tīm′) *adj. Slang* Petty; unimportant: a *small-time* gambler.

smart (smärt) *v.i.* 1 To experience a stinging sensation. 2 To cause a stinging sensation. 3 To experience remorse, grief, hurt feelings, etc. —*v.t.* 4 To cause to smart. —*adj.* 1 Quick in thought; clever. 2 Impertinently witty. 3 Harsh; severe: a *smart* slap. 4 Brisk: to go at a *smart* pace. 5 Keen or sharp, as at trade; shrewd. 6 *Informal* or *Regional* Large; considerable: a *smart* crop of wheat. 7 Sprucely dressed. 8 Fashionable; chic. —*n.* 1 An acute stinging sensation, as from a scratch or an irritant. 2 Any mental or emotional suffering. [< OE *smeortan*] —**smart′ly** *adv.* —**smart′ness** *n.*

smart al·eck (al′ik) *Informal* A cocky, conceited person. —**smart-al·eck·y** (smärt′al′ik-ē) *adj.*

smart bomb *Slang* A bomb capable of being guided, as by a laser beam, to a target.

smart·en (smär′tən) *v.t.* 1 To improve in appearance. 2 To make alert or lively. —*v.i.* 3 To improve one's appearance: with *up.*

smart set Fashionable, sophisticated society.

smart·weed (smärt′wēd′) *n.* Any of several species of knotgrass having an acrid taste, growing usu. in wet soil.

smash (smash) *v.t.* 1 To break in many pieces suddenly. 2 To flatten; crush. 3 To dash or fling violently so as to break in pieces. 4 To strike with a sudden blow. 5 To destroy; ruin. 6 In tennis, to strike (the ball) with a hard, swift, overhand stroke. —*v.i.* 7 To be ruined; fail. 8 To move or be moved with force; collide. —**go to smash** *Informal* To be ruined; fail. —*n.* 1 An instance or sound of smashing. 2 Any disaster or sudden collapse, esp. financial ruin. 3 In tennis, a strong overhand shot. 4 *Informal* An outstanding public success. —*adj.* Outstandingly successful: a *smash* hit. [?] —**smash′er** *n.*

smash·ing (smash′ing) *adj.* 1 That smashes: a *smashing* blow. 2 *Informal* Extremely impressive; overwhelmingly good. —*interj. Chiefly Brit.* An exclamation expressing approval, enthusiasm, etc.

smash-up (smash′up′) *n.* A violent collision; a wreck.

smat·ter (smat′ər) *n.* A slight knowledge. [< ME *smateren* to dabble]

smat·ter·ing (smat′ər·ing) *n.* 1 A superficial or fragmentary knowledge. 2 A little bit or a few.

sm. c., sm. caps small capitals (printing).

smear (smir) *v.t.* 1 To rub or soil with grease, paint, dirt, etc. 2 To spread or apply in a thick layer or coating. 3 To harm the reputation of; slander. 4 *Slang* To defeat utterly. —*v.i.* 5 To become smeared. —*n.* 1 A soiled spot; stain. 2

A specimen, as of blood, tissue cells, etc., spread on a slide for microscopic examination. 3 A slanderous attack. [< OE *smeoru* grease] —**smear′y** adj. —**smear′i·ness** n.

smell (smel) v. **smelled** or **smelt, smell·ing** v.t. 1 To perceive by means of the nose and its olfactory nerves. 2 To perceive the odor of. 3 To test by odor or smell. 4 To discover or detect, as if by smelling. —v.i. 5 To give off a particular odor: to *smell* of roses. 6 To have an unpleasant odor. 7 To give indications of: to *smell* of treason. 8 To use the sense of smell. —n. 1 The sense by means of which odors are perceived. 2 That which is smelled; odor. 3 An unpleasant odor. 4 A faint suggestion; hint. 5 An act of smelling. [ME *smellen*] —**smel′ler** n. —**smel′ly** adj. (·i·er, ·i·est) —**Syn.** n. 2 aroma, fragrance, scent. 3 reek, stench, stink.

smelling salts A pungent preparation, as ammonium carbonate, used to relieve faintness, etc.

smelt[1] (smelt) v.t. *Metall.* 1 To reduce (ores) by fusion in a furnace. 2 To obtain (a metal) from the ore by a process including fusion. —v.i. 3 To melt or fuse, as a metal. [< MDu. *smelten* melt]

smelt[2] (smelt) n. pl. **smelts** or **smelt** Any of various small, silvery, anadromous or landlocked food fishes. [< OE]

smelt[3] (smelt) A p.t. & p.p. of SMELL.

smelt·er (smel′tər) n. 1 One engaged in smelting ore. 2 An establishment for smelting: also **smelt′er·y.**

smidg·en (smij′ən) n. *Informal* A tiny bit or part. [?]

smi·lax (smī′laks) n. 1 Any of a large genus of woody vines having oval leaves and globular fruit. 2 A twining plant of the lily family, with greenish flowers, used for bouquets, etc. [< Gk. *smilax* yew]

smile (smīl) n. 1 A pleased or amused expression of the face, formed by curling the corners of the mouth upward. 2 A favorable appearance or aspect: the *smile* of fortune. —v. **smiled, smil·ing** v.i. 1 To exhibit a smile; appear cheerful. 2 To show approval or favor: often with *upon.* —v.t. 3 To express by means of a smile. [ME *smilen.*] —**smil′er** n. —**smil′ing·ly** adv.

Smilax

smirch (smûrch) v.t. 1 To soil, as by contact with grime; smear. 2 To defame; dishonor: to *smirch* a reputation. — n. 1 A smutch; smear. 2 A moral stain. [ME *smorchen*]

smirk (smûrk) v.i. To smile in a self-complacent, affected manner. —n. An affected or artificial smile. [< OE *smercian*] —**smirk′er** n. —**smirk′ing·ly** adv.

smite (smīt) v. **smote, smit·ten** or **smote, smit·ing** v.t. 1 To strike (something) hard. 2 To strike a blow with (something); cause to strike. 3 To kill with a sudden blow. 4 To strike with disaster; afflict. 5 To affect or impress suddenly and powerfully. —v.i. 6 To strike a blow with or as if with sudden force. [< OE *smītan*] —**smit′er** n.

smith (smith) n. 1 One whose work is shaping metals, esp. a blacksmith. 2 A maker: used in combination: *gunsmith; wordsmith.* [< OE]

smith·er·eens (smith′ə·rēnz′) n.pl. *Informal.* Fragments produced as by a blow. Also **smith′ers.** [< Ir. *smidirin* a fragment]

smith·y (smith′ē, smith′ē) n. pl. **smith·ies** A blacksmith's shop.

smit·ten (smit′n) A p.p. of SMITE.

smock (smok) n. A loose outer garment worn to protect one's clothes. —v.t. To decorate (fabric) with smocking. [< OE *smoc*]

smock·ing (smok′ing) n. Shirred work; stitching that forms a gathered pattern.

smog (smog) n. A noxious mist resulting from the action of sunlight on atmospheric pollutants. [< SM(OKE) + (F)OG]

smoke (smōk) n. 1 The vaporous products of the combustion of an organic compound, as coal, wood, etc., charged with fine particles of carbon or soot. 2 Any system of solid particles dispersed in a gas. 3 The act of or time taken in smoking tobacco. 4 *Informal* A cigarette, cigar, or

Smocking

pipeful of tobacco. —v. **smoked, smok·ing** v.i. 1 To emit or give out smoke. 2 To emit smoke excessively, as a stove or lamp. 3 To inhale and exhale the smoke of tobacco. —v.t. 4 To inhale and exhale the smoke of (tobacco, opium, etc.). 5 To use, as a pipe, for this purpose. 6 To treat, cure, or flavor with smoke. 7 To drive away or force out of hiding by or as if by the use of smoke: *smoke* bees; *smoke* out the enemy. 8 To change the color of (glass, etc.) by darkening with smoke. [< OE *smoca*]

smoke·house (smōk′hous′) n. A building or room in which meat, fish, hides, etc., are smoked.

smoke·less (smōk′lis) adj. Having or emitting little or no smoke: *smokeless* powder.

smok·er (smō′kər) n. 1 One who smokes tobacco habitually. 2 A railroad car in which smoking is allowed. 3 A social gathering for men only.

smoke screen 1 A dense cloud of smoke emitted to screen an attack or cover a retreat. 2 Anything intended to conceal or mislead.

smoke·stack (smōk′stak′) n. An upright pipe through which combustion gases from a furnace are discharged into the air.

smok·y (smō′kē) adj. **smok·i·er, smok·i·est** 1 Giving forth smoke, esp. excessively or unpleasantly. 2 Containing smoke: *smoky* air. 3 Like or suggestive of smoke: a *smoky* flavor. 4 Discolored by smoke. 5 Smoke-colored. —**smok′i·ly** adv. —**smok′i·ness** n.

smol·der (smōl′dər) v.i. 1 To burn showing little smoke and no flame. 2 To show suppressed feeling. 3 To exist in a latent state or inwardly. —n. A smoldering fire or thick smoke. *Brit. sp.* **smoul′der.** [ME *smolderen*]

smolt (smōlt) n. A young salmon on its first descent from the river to the sea. [ME]

smooch (smōōch) v.i. *Slang* To kiss and caress; neck. — **smooch′er** n. [?]

smooth (smōōth) adj. 1 Having no surface irregularities; continuously even. 2 Free from obstructions, shocks, or jolts. 3 Without lumps; well blended. 4 Free from hair. 5 Flowing or moving evenly and without interruption. 6 Mild-mannered; calm. 7 Suave and flattering, usu. in a deceitful way: a *smooth* talker. 8 Pleasant-tasting; mild: a *smooth* wine. 9 *Phonet.* Having no aspiration. —adv. Calmly; evenly. —v.t. 1 To make smooth or even on the surface. 2 To free from obstructions. 3 To soften the worst features of: usu. with *over.* 4 To make calm; mollify. —v.i. 5 To become smooth. —n. 1 The smooth portion or surface of anything. 2 The act of smoothing. [< OE *smōth*] — **smooth′er, smooth′ness** n. —**smooth′ly** adv. —**Syn.** adj. 1 glossy, polished, sleek. 6 collected, placid, unruffled. v. 3 extenuate, palliate. 4 soothe.

smooth·bore (smōōth′bôr′, -bōr′) n. A firearm with an unrifled bore: also **smooth bore.** —adj. Having no rifling: said of firearms.

smooth muscle Muscle tissue consisting of flat sheets of spindle-shaped cells, by which involuntary movement is effected in blood vessels, viscera, etc.

smor·gas·bord (smôr′gəs·bôrd; *Sw.* smœr′gōs·bôrd) n. A Scandinavian buffet. Also **smör′gås·bord.** [Sw.]

smote (smōt) p.t. of SMITE.

smoth·er (smuth′ər) v.t. 1 To prevent (someone) from breathing. 2 To kill by such means; suffocate. 3 To cover, or cause to smolder, as a fire. 4 To hide or suppress: to *smother* a scandal. 5 To cook in a covered pan or under a blanket of some other substance. —v.i. 6 To be covered without vent or air, as a fire. 7 To be hidden or suppressed, as wrath. —n. That which smothers, as stifling vapor or dust. [< OE *smorian*] —**smoth′er·er** n. —**smoth′er·y** adj.

smudge (smuj) v. **smudged, smudg·ing** v.t. 1 To smear; soil. —v.i. 2 To be or become smudged. —n. 1 A smear; stain. 2 A smoky fire or smoke for driving away insects, preventing frost, etc. [? var. of SMUTCH] —**smudg′i·ly** adv. —**smudg′i·ness** n. —**smudg′y** adj. (·i·er, ·i·est)

smug (smug) adj. **smug·ger, smug·gest** 1 Self-satisfied or extremely complacent. 2 Trim; neat; spruce. [?< LG *smuk* neat] —**smug′ly** adv. —**smug′ness** n.

smug·gle (smug′əl) v. **·gled, ·gling** v.t. 1 To take (merchandise) into or out of a country illegally. 2 To bring in or introduce illicitly or secretly. —*v.i.* 3 To engage in or practice smuggling. [< LG *smuggeln*] —**smug′gler** *n.*

smut (smut) *n.* 1 The blackening made by soot, smoke, etc. 2 Obscene writing, speech, or illustration. 3 Any of various fungus diseases of plants, characterized by patches of powdery black spores. 4 The parasitic fungus causing such a disease. —*v.t.* & *v.i.* **smut·ted, smut·ting** To make or become smutty. [< LG *schmutt* dirt]

smutch (smuch) *n.* A stain or smear. —*v.t.* To smear; smudge. [?] —**smutch·y** *adj.* (**·i·er, ·i·est**)

smut·ty (smut′ē) *adj.* **·ti·er, ·ti·est** 1 Soiled with smut; stained. 2 Affected by smut: *smutty* corn. 3 Obscene; indecent. —**smut′ti·ly** *adv.* —**smut′ti·ness** *n.* —Syn. 1 blackened, dirty. 3 coarse, earthy, suggestive.

Sn tin (L *stannum*).

Sn. sanitary.

snack (snak) *n.* A light meal. —*v.i.* To eat a snack. [< MDu. *snacken* to bite, snap]

snaf·fle (snaf′əl) *n.* A horse's bit without a curb, jointed in the middle. —*v.t.* **·fled, ·fling** To control with a snaffle. [?< Du. *snavel* muzzle]

sna·fu (sna·fōō′) *Slang adj.* In a state of utter confusion; chaotic. —*v.t.* **·fued, ·fu·ing** To put into a confused or chaotic condition. —*n.* A confused or chaotic situation. [< S(ITUATION) N(ORMAL) A(LL) F(UCKED) U(P)]

snag (snag) *n.* 1 A jagged or sharp protuberance, esp. the stumpy base of a branch left in pruning. 2 A snaggletooth. 3 The trunk of a tree fixed in a river, bayou, etc., which presents a danger to navigation. 4 Any hidden obstacle or difficulty. —*v.t.* **snagged, snag·ging** To injure, destroy, or impede by or as by a snag. [< Scand.] —**snag′gy** *adj.*

snag·gle·tooth (snag′əl·tōōth′) *n.* A tooth that is broken or out of alignment with the others. —**snag′gle·toothed′** (-tōōtht′, -tōōthd′) *adj.*

snail (snāl) *n.* 1 Any of numerous slow-moving, terrestrial or aquatic gastropod mollusks with a spiral shell. 2 A slow or lazy person. [< OE *snægl*]

snake (snāk) *n.* 1 Any of a large variety of limbless reptiles having a scaly body, no eyelids, having a specialized swallowing apparatus. 2 A treacherous person. 3 A flexible wire used to clean clogged drains, etc. —*v.* **snaked, snak·ing** *v.t.* *Informal* 1 To drag or pull forcibly; haul, as a log. —*v.i.* 2 To wind or move like a snake. [< OE *snaca*]

Snail

snake·bird (snāk′bûrd′) *n.* Any of several birds with a long sinuous neck, frequenting southern U.S. swamps.

snak·y (snā′kē) *adj.* **snak·i·er, snak·i·est** 1 Of or like a snake. 2 Cunning; treacherous. 3 Full of snakes. 4 Winding; serpentine. —**snak′i·ly** *adv.* —**snak′i·ness** *n.*

snap (snap) *v.* **snapped, snap·ping** *v.i.* 1 To make a sharp, quick sound, as of twigs breaking. 2 To break suddenly with a crackling noise. 3 To close, fasten, etc., with a snapping sound. 4 To bite or snatch with a sudden, grasping motion: often with *up* or *at.* 5 To speak sharply: often with *at.* 6 To move or act with sudden, neat

Snakebird

gestures: He *snapped* to attention. 7 To give way suddenly, as under mental pressure. —*v.t.* 8 To seize suddenly or eagerly; snatch: often with *up.* 9 To sever with a snapping sound. 10 To cause to make a sharp, quick sound. 11 To close, fasten, etc., with a snapping sound. 12 To take (a photograph). —**snap out of it** *Informal* 1 To recover quickly. 2 To change a mood, attitude, etc., quickly. —*n.* 1 The act of snapping or a sharp, quick sound produced by it. 2 A sudden breaking or release of anything or the sound so produced. 3 Any catch, fastener, etc., that closes or springs into place with a snapping sound. 4 A small, thin, crisp cake, esp. a gingersnap. 5 Brisk energy; zip. 6

A brief spell: said chiefly of cold weather. 7 Any easy task or duty. 8 A snapshot. —*adj.* 1 Made or done suddenly: a *snap* judgment. 2 Fastening with a snap. 3 *Informal* Easy. —*adv.* Briskly; quickly. [< MDu. *snappen* bite at]

snap·drag·on (snap′drag′ən) *n.* Any of several varieties of plants having racemes of flowers with a saclike, double-lipped corolla.

snap·per (snap′ər) *n.* 1 One who or that which snaps. 2 Any of various voracious marine food fishes. • See RED SNAPPER. 3 A snapping turtle.

snapping turtle Any of various large voracious freshwater turtles having powerful jaws, a small plastron, and a tail with erect bony scales.

Snapping turtle

snap·pish (snap′ish) *adj.* 1 Apt to speak crossly. 2 Disposed to snap or bite, as a dog. —**snap′pish·ly** *adv.* —**snap′pish·ness** *n.*

snap·py (snap′ē) *adj.* **·pi·er, ·pi·est** 1 *Informal* Brisk and energetic. 2 *Informal* Smart or stylish. 3 Snappish. —**snap′pi·ly** *adv.* —**snap′pi·ness** *n.*

snap·shot (snap′shot′) *n.* A photograph taken with a small, simple camera.

snare[1] (snâr) *n.* 1 A device, as a noose, for catching birds or other animals; a trap. 2 Anything that misleads, entangles, etc. —*v.t.* **snared, snar·ing** 1 To catch with a snare; entrap. 2 To capture by trickery; entice. [< ON *snara*] —**snar′er** *n.*

snare[2] (snâr) *n.* 1 A cord that produces a rattling on a drumhead. 2 A snare drum. [< MDu. *snare* a string]

snare drum A small drum to be beaten on one head and having snares stretched across the other. • See DRUM.

snarl[1] (snärl) *n.* A sharp, angry growl. —*v.i.* 1 To growl harshly, as a dog. 2 To speak angrily and resentfully. —*v.t.* 3 To utter or express with a snarl. [< MLG *snarren* to growl] —**snarl′er** *n.* —**snarl′ing·ly** *adv.* —**snarl′y** *adj.*

snarl[2] (snärl) *n.* 1 A tangle, as of hair or yarn. 2 Any complication or entanglement. —*v.i.* 1 To become entangled or confused. —*v.t.* 2 To put into a snarl. [?< SNARE[1]] —**snarl′er** *n.* —**snarl′y** *adj.*

snatch (snach) *v.t.* 1 To seize, take, grasp, etc., suddenly or eagerly. 2 To take or obtain as the opportunity arises: to *snatch* a few hours of sleep. —*v.i.* 3 To attempt to seize swiftly and suddenly: with *at.* —*n.* 1 A hasty grab or grasp: usu. with *at.* 2 A small amount; fragment: *snatches* of a conversation. [ME *snacchen*] —**snatch′er** *n.*

snatch·y (snach′ē) *adj.* **snatch·i·er, snatch·i·est** Interrupted; spasmodic.

sneak (snēk) *v.i.* 1 To move or go in a stealthy manner. 2 To act slyly or with cowardice. —*v.t.* 3 To put, give, move, etc., secretly or stealthily. 4 *Informal* To pilfer. —**sneak out of** To avoid (work, etc.) by sly means. —*n.* 1 One who sneaks; a stealthy, despicable person. 2 *pl. Informal* Sneakers. 3 A stealthy movement. —*adj.* Stealthy; covert: a *sneak* attack. [?] —**sneak′i·ly, sneak′ing·ly** *adv.* —**sneak′i·ness** *n.* —**sneak′y** *adj.* (**·i·er, ·i·est**)

sneak·er (snē′kər) *n.* 1 *pl.* Rubber-soled canvas shoes. 2 One who sneaks; a sneak.

sneer (snir) *n.* 1 A grimace of contempt or scorn. 2 A mean or contemptuous sound, word, etc. —*v.i.* 1 To show contempt or scorn by a sneer. 2 To express contempt in speech, writing, etc. —*v.t.* 3 To utter with a sneer. [ME *sneren*] —**sneer′er** *n.* —**sneer′ing·ly** *adv.* —Syn. *v.* 2 gibe, jeer, scoff, taunt.

sneeze (snēz) *v.i.* **sneezed, sneez·ing** To drive air forcibly and audibly out of the mouth and nose by a spasmodic involuntary action. —**not to be sneezed at** *Informal* Entitled to consideration; not to be ignored. —*n.* An act of sneezing. [ME *fnesen*] —**sneez′er** *n.*

snick·er (snik′ər) *n.* A half-suppressed or smothered laugh, usu. scornful. —*v.i.* 1 To utter a snicker. —*v.t.* 2 To utter or express with a snicker. [Imit.]

snide (snīd) *adj.* **snid·er, snid·est** Malicious; nasty. [?] —**snide′ly** *adv.* —**snide′ness** *n.*

sniff (snif) *v.i.* 1 To breathe through the nose in short, quick, audible inhalations. 2 To express contempt, etc., by sniffing: often with *at.* 3 To inhale a scent in sniffs. —*v.t.* 4 To inhale. 5 To smell or attempt to smell with sniffs. 6 To perceive as if by sniffs. —*n.* 1 An act or the sound of sniffing. 2 Something perceived by sniffing; an odor. [ME *sniffen*]

snif·fle (snif'əl) *v.i.* **·fled, ·fling** 1 To breathe through a partially obstructed nose noisily and with difficulty. 2 To snivel or whimper. —*n.* The act of sniffling, or the sound made by it. —**the sniffles** A clogged condition of the nose caused by a cold, allergy, etc. [Freq. of SNIFF] —**snif'fler** *n.*

snig·ger (snig'ər) *n.* SNICKER. —*v.i.* SNICKER. [Var. of SNICKER] —Syn. *n.,v.* giggle, smirk, snort, titter.

snip (snip) *v.* **snipped, snip·ping** *v.t.* 1 To clip, remove, or cut with a short, light stroke or strokes, as of shears: often with *off*. —*v.i.* 2 To cut with small, quick strokes. —*n.* 1 An act of snipping. 2 A small piece snipped off. 3 *Informal* A small or insignificant person. [< Du. *snippen*] —**snip'per** *n.*

snipe (snīp) *n. pl.* **snipe** or **snipes** Any of various marsh and shore birds having a long, flexible bill. —*v.i.* **sniped, snip·ing** 1 To hunt or shoot snipe. 2 To shoot at individuals, as of an enemy force, from a place of concealment. 3 To attack a person in an underhanded, malicious manner: with *at*. [< ON *snīpa*]

snip·er (snī'pər) *n.* One who shoots at individuals, as of an enemy force, from a place of concealment.

snip·pet (snip'it) *n.* 1 A small piece snipped off. 2 A small or insignificant person.

snip·py (snip'ē) *adj.* **·pi·er, ·pi·est** *Informal* 1 Supercilious; impertinent. 2 Fragmentary. —**snip'pi·ly** *adv.* —**snip'pi·ness** *n.*

snit (snit) *n. Informal* A state of irritability or agitation.

snitch (snich) *Slang v.t.* 1 To grab quickly; steal. —*v.i.* 2 To inform; tattle: usu. with *on.* [?]

sniv·el (sniv'əl) *v.i.* **·eled** or **·elled, ·el·ing** or **·el·ling** To cry in a snuffling manner. —*n.* The act of sniveling. [< OE (assumed) *snyflan*] —**sniv'el·er** or **sniv'el·ler** *n.*

snob (snob) *n.* 1 One who regards wealth and elevated social position as of paramount importance and who typically seeks to improve his station by associating with the rich or powerful or popular and by avoiding or behaving with condescension to those with whom association is inexpedient. 2 One who affects to be superior, as in taste or learning: an intellectual *snob*. [?] —**snob'ber·y** (*pl.* **·ies**), **snob'bish·ness** *n.* —**snob'bish** *adj.* —**snob'bish·ly** *adv.*

snood (snōōd) *n.* A small meshlike cap or bag worn by women to keep the hair in place at the back of the head. —*v.t.* To bind with a snood. [< OE *snōd*]

snoop (snōōp) *Informal v.i.* To pry into things with which one has no business. —*n.* One who snoops. [< Du. *snoepen* eat goodies on the sly] —**snoop'er** *n.* —**snoop'y** *adj.* (**·i·er, ·i·est**)

snoot (snōōt) *n. Informal* The nose or face. [Var. of SNOUT]

snoot·y (snōō'tē) *adj.* **snoot·i·er, snoot·i·est** *Informal* Haughty; snobbish. —**snoot'i·ly** *adv.* —**snoot'i·ness** *n.*

snooze (snōōz) *Informal v.i.* **snoozed, snooz·ing** To sleep lightly; doze. —*n.* A short, light sleep. [?]

snore (snôr, snōr) *v.i.* **snored, snor·ing** To breathe with loud, snorting noises while asleep. —*n.* An act or sound of snoring. [Imit.] —**snor'er** *n.*

snor·kel (snôr'kəl) *n.* 1 A long ventilating tube capable of extending from a submerged submarine to the surface of the water. 2 A similar device used for underwater breathing. —*v.i.* To swim with a snorkel. [< G *Schnorchel*] —**snor'kel·er** *n.*

snort (snôrt) *v.i.* 1 To force the air violently and noisily through the nostrils, as a horse. 2 To express indignation, ridicule, etc., by a snort. —*v.t.* 3 To utter or express by snorting. —*n.* 1 The act or sound of snorting. 2 *Slang* A small drink of liquor. [ME *snorten*] —**snort'er** *n.*

snot (snot) *n.* 1 Mucus from or in the nose: a vulgar usage. 2 *Slang* A snotty person. [< OE *gesnot*]

snot·ty (snot'ē) *adj.* **·ti·er, ·ti·est** 1 Dirtied with snot: a vulgar usage. 2 *Slang* Contemptible; nasty. 3 *Slang* Impudent. —**snot'ti·ly** *adv.* —**snot'ti·ness** *n.*

snout (snout) *n.* 1 The projecting muzzle of a vertebrate. 2 Some similar anterior prolongation of the head, as that of a gastropod, skate, weevil, etc. 3 A person's nose, esp. a large one. [ME *snute*]

snow (snō) *n.* 1 Precipitation in the form of ice crystals formed from water vapor in the air when the temperature is below 32° F., usu. falling in irregular masses or flakes. 2 A fall of snow. 3 Flickering light or dark spots appearing on a television or radar screen. 4 *Slang* Cocaine. —*v.i.* 1 To fall as snow. —*v.t.* 2 To cause to fall as or like snow. 3 *Slang* To overpower with insincere or flattering talk. —**snow in** To close in or obstruct with snow.

Snow crystals

—**snow under** 1 To cover with snow. 2 *Informal* To overwhelm: *snowed under with* work. [< OE *snāw*]

snow·ball (snō'bôl') *n.* 1 A small round mass of snow to be thrown. 2 A shrub related to honeysuckle, having globular clusters of sterile white flowers: also **snowball bush** or **tree**. —*v.i.* 1 To throw snowballs. 2 To gain in size, importance, etc. —*v.t.* 3 To throw snowballs at.

snow bank A large mound or heap of snow.

snow·ber·ry (snō'ber'ē) *n. pl.* **·ries** Any of various shrubs bearing white berries.

snow·bird (snō'bûrd') *n.* 1 A junco. 2 SNOW BUNTING.

snow blindness A temporary or partial impairment of vision, caused by long exposure to the glare of snow. —**snow'-blind'** *adj.*

snow·bound (snō'bound') *adj.* Forced to remain in a place because of heavy snow.

snow bunting A sparrowlike bird of northern regions, having white plumage with black or rust-colored markings.

snow·capped (snō'kapt') *adj.* Having its top covered with snow, as a mountain.

snow·drift (snō'drift') *n.* A pile of snow heaped up by the wind.

snow·drop (snō'drop') *n.* A low, early-blooming bulbous plant bearing a single, white, drooping flower.

snow·fall (snō'fôl') *n.* 1 A fall of snow. 2 The amount of snow that falls in a given period.

snow·flake (snō'flāk') *n.* 1 A flake or crystal of snow. 2 Any of various plants allied to and resembling the snowdrop.

snow job *Slang* An attempt to overpower with a flow of insincere talk, esp. flattery.

snow line The limit of perpetual snow on the sides of mountains. Also **snow limit.**

snow·mo·bile (snō'mō-bēl') *n.* A motorized vehicle used for traveling over snow, ice, etc. —**snow'mo·bil'er, snow'mo·bil'ing** *n.*

snow·plow (snō'plou') *n.* Any large, plowlike device for removing snow from roads, railroad tracks, etc.

snow·shoe (snō'shōō') *n.* A device, usu. a network of sinew in a wooden frame, to be fastened on the foot and used to prevent sinking in soft snow when walking. —*v.i.* **·shoed, ·shoe·ing** To walk on snowshoes.

Snowshoe

snow·slide (snō'slīd') *n.* An avalanche of snow.

snow·storm (snō'stôrm') *n.* A storm with a heavy fall of snow.

snow·y (snō'ē) *adj.* **·i·er, ·i·est** 1 Abounding in or covered with snow. 2 White as snow. —**snow'i·ly** *adv.* —**snow'i·ness** *n.*

snub (snub) *v.t.* **snubbed, snub·bing** 1 To treat with contempt or disdain. 2 To stop or check, as the movement of a rope in running out. —*n.* 1 An act of snubbing; a deliberate slight. 2 A sudden checking, as of a running rope or cable. —*adj.* Short and slightly turned-up: said of the nose. [< ON *snubba*] —**snub'ber** *n.* —Syn. *v.* 1 cut, high-hat, ignore, rebuff, slight.

snub-nosed (snub'nōzd') *adj.* Having a snub nose.

snuff¹ (snuf) *v.t.* 1 To draw in (air, etc.) through the nose.

2 To smell; sniff. —*v.i.* **3** To snort; sniff. —*n.* An act of snuffing. [?< MDu. *snuffen*] —**snuf′fi·ness** *n.* —**snuf′fy** *adj.*

snuff² (snuf) *n.* The charred portion of a wick. —*v.t.* **1** To crop the snuff from (a wick). **2** To put out or extinguish: with *out.* [ME *snoffe*]

snuff³ (snuf) *n.* **1** Pulverized tobacco to be inhaled into the nostrils. **2** The quantity of it taken at one time. —**up to snuff** *Informal* Meeting the usual standard, as in quality, health, etc. —*v.i.* To take or use snuff. [< Du. *snuf*]

snuf·fer (snuf′ər) *n.* **1** One who or that which snuffs (a candle). **2** *pl.* A scissorlike instrument for removing the snuff from a candle.

snuf·fle (snuf′əl) *v.* **·fled, ·fling** *v.i.* **1** SNIFFLE. **2** To talk through the nose. —*v.t.* **3** To utter in a nasal tone. —*n.* An act of snuffling, or the sound made by it. —**the snuffles** THE SNIFFLES. See SNIFFLE. [Freq. of SNUFF¹] —**snuf′fler** *n.*

snug (snug) *adj.* **snug·ger, snug·gest 1** Comfortable and cozy. **2** Well-built and compact; trim: said of a ship. **3** Fitting closely, as a garment. —*v.* **snugged, snug·ging** —*v.t.* **1** To make snug. —*v.i.* **2** SNUGGLE. —**snug down** To prepare (a vessel) for a storm, as by lashing down movables. [?] —**snug′ly** *adv.* —**snug′ness** *n.*

snug·gle (snug′əl) *v.t. & v.i.* **·gled, ·gling** To nestle; cuddle; often with *up* or *together.* [Freq. of SNUG]

so¹ (sō) *adv.* **1** To this or that or such a degree; to this or that extent: Don't talk *so* much. **2** In this, that, or such a manner: Hold the flag *so.* **3** To such a great extent: I love him *so.* **4** Just as said, directed, suggested, or implied; consequently; therefore. **5** To an extreme degree; very: He is *so* tall. **6** About as many or as much as stated; thereabouts: I shall stay a day or *so.* **7** Too; also: and *so* do I. **8** According to the truth of what is sworn to or averred: *So* help me God. —*adj.* True: It isn't *so.* —*conj.* **1** With the purpose that: often with *that.* **2** As a consequence of which: He consented, *so* they went away. —*interj.* An expression of surprise, disapproval, triumph, etc. [< OE *swā*]

so² (sō) *n.* SOL.

So. South; southern.

soak (sōk) *v.t.* **1** To place in liquid till thoroughly saturated; steep. **2** To wet thoroughly; drench. **3** *Informal* To drink, esp. to excess. **4** *Slang* To charge exorbitantly. —*v.i.* **5** To remain or be placed in liquid till saturated. **6** To penetrate; pass: with *in* or *into.* **7** *Slang* To drink to excess. —**soak up 1** To take up; absorb. **2** *Informal* To take eagerly into the mind. —*n.* **1** The process or act of soaking, or state of being soaked. **2** Liquid in which something is soaked. **3** *Slang* A hard drinker. [< OE *socian*] —**soak′er** *n.* —**soak′ing·ly** *adv.*

so-and-so (sō′ən·sō′) *n. pl.* **·sos** An unnamed or undetermined person or thing: often a euphemism for offensive epithets.

soap (sōp) *n.* **1** *Chem.* A metallic salt of a fatty acid. **2** A cleansing agent consisting of a sodium or potassium salt of a fatty acid made by boiling a fat or oil with a lye. **3** *Slang* Money used for bribes. —**no soap** *Slang* It's not possible or acceptable. —*v.t.* To rub or treat with soap. [< OE *sāpe*] —**soap′i·ly** *adv.* —**soap′i·ness** *n.* —**soap′y** *adj.*

soap·ber·ry (sōp′ber′ē) *n. pl.* **·ries 1** A berrylike fruit containing a substance that forms a detergent lather with water. **2** Any of various related trees of s U.S. and tropical America that yield soapberries.

soap·box (sōp′boks′) *n.* Any box or crate used as a platform by street orators. —*adj.* Of or pertaining to such orators or oratory. —*v.i.* To make a speech to a street audience.

soap opera A daytime television or radio drama presented serially and usu. dealing with highly emotional domestic themes.

soap·stone (sōp′stōn′) *n.* STEATITE.

soap·suds (sōp′sudz′) *n.pl.* Soapy water, esp. when worked into a foam.

soar (sôr, sōr) *v.i.* **1** To float aloft through the air on wings, as a bird. **2** To sail or glide through the air. **3** To rise above any usual level: Prices *soared.* —*n.* **1** An act of soaring. **2** A range of upward flight. [< L *ex* out + *aura* breeze, air] —**soar′er** *n.* —**soar′ing·ly** *adv.*

sob (sob) *v.* **sobbed, sob·bing** *v.i.* **1** To weep with audible, convulsive catches of the breath. **2** To make a sound like a sob, as the wind. —*v.t.* **3** To utter with sobs. **4** To bring

to a specified condition by sobbing: to *sob* oneself to sleep. —*n.* The act or sound of sobbing. [Imit.] —**sob′bing·ly** *adv.*

so·ber (sō′bər) *adj.* **1** Moderate in or abstaining from the use of alcoholic beverages. **2** Not drunk. **3** Temperate in action or thought; rational. **4** Not frivolous; straightforward. **5** Solemn; serious: a *sober* expression. **6** Of subdued or modest color. —*v.t.* **1** To make sober. —*v.i.* **2** To become sober, as after intoxication: with *up.* [< L *sobrius*] —**so′ber·ly** *adv.* —**so′ber·ness** *n.* —**Syn.** *n.* **1** abstemious. **3** calm, dispassionate, staid, steady.

so·bri·e·ty (sō·brī′ə·tē) *n. pl.* **·ties 1** The state or quality of being moderate, serious, or sedate. **2** Abstinence from alcoholic drink.

so·bri·quet (sō′bri·kā, sō·bri·kā′) *n.* A fanciful or humorous appellation; a nickname. [F]

sob story *Slang* A sad personal narrative told to elicit pity or sympathy.

soc. socialist; society.

so-called (sō′kôld′) *adj.* **1** Popularly or generally named or known (by the following term): the *so-called* black market. **2** Called (by the following term): an ironic use, implying that the designated term is unjustified or unsuitable: his *so-called* wittiness.

soc·cer (sok′ər) *n.* A form of football in which the ball is propelled toward the opponents' goal by kicking or by striking with the body or head, but never with the hands. [Alter. of *association (football)*, original name]

so·cia·ble (sō′shə·bəl) *adj.* **1** Inclined to seek company; friendly. **2** Characterized by or affording occasion for agreeable conversation and friendliness. —*n.* An informal social gathering. [< L *socius* friend] —**so′cia·bil′i·ty, so′cia·ble·ness** *n.* —**so′cia·bly** *adv.*

so·cial (sō′shəl) *adj.* **1** Of or pertaining to society or its organization: *social* questions. **2** Friendly toward others; sociable. **3** Living in a society: *social* beings. **4** Of or pertaining to public welfare: *social* work. **5** Pertaining to or characteristic of fashionable, wealthy people: the *social* register. **6** Living in communities: *social* ants. **7** Grouping compactly, as individual plants. **8** Partly or wholly covering a large area of land: said of plant species. —*n.* An informal social gathering. [< L *socius* ally]

social disease Venereal disease: a euphemism.

so·cial·ism (sō′shəl·iz′əm) *n.* **1** The theory of public collective ownership or control of the basic means of production, distribution, and exchange, with the avowed aim of operating for use rather than for profit. **2** A political system or party advocating or practicing this theory. —**so′·cial·ist** *adj., n.* —**so′cial·is′tic** *adj.*

Socialist party A political party advocating socialism, esp. a U.S. party formed in 1901.

so·cial·ite (sō′shəl·īt) *n.* A person prominent in fashionable society.

so·cial·ize (sō′shəl·īz) *v.* **·ized, ·iz·ing** *v.t.* **1** To make friendly, cooperative, or sociable. **2** To put under group control; esp. to regulate according to socialistic principles. **3** To adopt for the uses and needs of society. —*v.i.* **4** To take part in social activities. *Brit. sp.* **so′cial·ise.** —**so′cial·i·za′tion** *n.*

socialized medicine The provision of comprehensive medical services at public expense.

social register A directory of persons prominent in fashionable society.

social science 1 The body of knowledge dealing with society, its members, organizations, interrelationships, etc. **2** Any of the fields into which this body of knowledge is divided, as economics, history, sociology, politics, etc.

social security A federal program of old-age pensions, unemployment benefits, disability insurance, survivors' benefits, etc., paid jointly by workers, employers, and the U.S. government.

social work Any of various activities for improving community welfare, as services for health, rehabilitation, counseling, recreation, adoptions, etc. Also **social service.** —**social worker**

so·ci·e·ty (sə·sī′ə·tē) *n. pl.* **·ties 1** A group of people, usu. having geographical boundaries and sharing certain characteristics, as language, culture, etc. **2** The people making up such a group. **3** The fashionable, usu. wealthy portion of a community. **4** A body of persons associated for a common purpose; an association, club, or fraternity. **5** Association based on friendship or intimacy: to enjoy the *society* of one's neighbors. [< L *socius* a friend]

Society of Friends A Christian religious group, founded in seventeenth-century England, noted for its repudiation of ritual and its opposition to military service and to violence.

Society of Jesus The Jesuits.

socio- *combining form* **1** Society; social: *sociology.* **2** Sociology; sociological: *socioeconomic.* [< F < L *socius* a companion]

so·ci·o·bi·ol·o·gy (sō′sē-ō-bī-ol′ə-jē) *n.* The study of social behavior in animals and humans, as determined by their biological characteristics.

so·ci·o·ec·o·nom·ic (sō′sē-ō-ek′ə-nom′ik, sō′shē-, -ē′kə-) *adj.* Based upon the interrelationship of social and economic factors. —**so′ci·o·ec′o·nom′i·cal·ly** *adv.*

so·ci·o·lin·guis·tics (sō′sē-ō-ling-gwis′tiks, sō′shē-) *n. pl.* (*construed as sing.*) The study of language as a social instrument and in its social context. [< SOCIO- + LINGUISTICS] —**so′ci·o·lin·guis′tic** *adj.* —**so′ci·o·lin·guis′ti·cal·ly** *adv.*

so·ci·ol·o·gy (sō′sē-ol′ə-jē, sō′shē-) *n.* The science dealing with the origin, evolution, and development of human society and its organization, institutions, and functions. —**so′ci·o·log′i·cal** *adj.* —**so′ci·o·log′i·cal·ly** *adv.* —**so·ci·ol′o·gist** *n.*

sock[1] (sok) *n.* A short stocking reaching part way to the knee. [< L *soccus* slipper]

sock[2] (sok) *Slang v.t.* To strike or hit, esp. with the fist. —*n.* A hard blow. [?]

sock·et (sok′it) *n.* A cavity into which a corresponding part fits: an electric light *socket;* the eye *socket.* [< OF *soc* a plowshare]

sock·eye (sok′ī′) *n.* A red salmon of the Pacific coast, highly valued as a food fish. [Alter. of Salishan *sukkegh*]

So·crat·ic method (sə-krat′ik, sō-) The method of instruction by questions and answers, as adopted by Socrates in his disputations, leading the pupil either to a foreseen conclusion or to contradict himself.

sod (sod) *n.* **1** Grassy surface soil held together by the matted roots of grass and weeds. **2** A piece of such soil. —*v.t.* **sod·ded, sod·ding** To cover with sod. [< MDu. *sode* piece of turf]

so·da (sō′də) *n.* **1** Any of several sodium compounds in common use, as sodium bicarbonate, carbonate, hydroxide, etc. **2** SODA WATER **3** A soft drink containing soda water and flavoring and sometimes ice cream. [< Ital. *soda (cenere)* solid (ash)]

soda ash Anhydrous sodium carbonate.

soda cracker A thin, crisp, usu. salted wafer of flour leavened with baking soda.

soda fountain 1 An apparatus from which soda water is drawn, usu. containing receptacles for syrups, ice, and ice cream. **2** A counter at which soft drinks and ice cream are dispensed.

soda jerk *Slang* A clerk who serves at a soda fountain.

so·dal·i·ty (sō-dal′ə-tē) *n. pl.* **·ties** A brotherhood or fraternity; esp., one for devotional or charitable purposes. [< L *sodalis* companion]

soda water An effervescent drink consisting of water charged under pressure with carbon dioxide, formerly generated from sodium bicarbonate.

sod·den (sod′n) *adj.* **1** Soaked; saturated. **2** Doughy; soggy, as undercooked bread. **3** Dull or stupid, as from drink. [ME *sothen,* pp. of *sethen* seethe] —**sod′den·ly** *adv.*

so·di·um (sō′dē-əm) *n.* A soft, silver-white, highly reactive metallic element (symbol Na) whose compounds are abundant in nature and essential to life. [< Med. L *soda* soda]

sodium bicarbonate A white crystalline compound that reacts with acids to liberate carbon dioxide; baking soda.

sodium carbonate The strongly alkaline sodium salt of carbonic acid, in crystalline hydrated form known as washing soda.

sodium chloride Common salt.

sodium cyanide A white, very poisonous salt of hydrocyanic acid, used in electroplating, as a fumigant, etc.

sodium hydroxide A white, deliquescent compound forming a strongly alkaline solution in water; caustic soda.

sodium hypochlorite An unstable compound of sodium, oxygen, and chlorine, used in weak aqueous solution as a laundry bleach.

sodium nitrate A white compound occurring naturally and produced synthetically, used as a fertilizer and in the manufacture of nitric acid and explosives.

sodium thiosulfate A crystalline compound of sodium, sulfur, and oxygen, used in photography as a fixing agent. Also, erroneously, **sodium hyposulfite.**

Sod·om (sod′əm) *n.* In the Bible, a city on the Dead Sea, destroyed with Gomorrah because of the wickedness of its people. *Gen.* 13:10.

sod·om·ite (sod′əm-īt) *n.* A person who practices sodomy.

sod·om·y (sod′əm-ē) *n.* Anal copulation, esp. between male persons or with animals. [< LL *Sodoma* Sodom]

so·ev·er (sō-ev′ər) *adv.* To or in any degree at all. • *Soever* is usu. added to *who, which, what, where, when, how,* etc., to form the compounds *whosoever,* etc., giving them emphasis or specific force. When used separately, as in "how great *soever* he might be," *soever* tends to sound stilted and literary.

so·fa (sō′fə) *n.* A long upholstered couch having a back and arms. [< Ar. *soffah* a part of a floor raised to form a seat]

Sofa

soft (sôft, soft) *adj.* **1** Easily changed in shape by pressure. **2** Easily worked: *soft* wood. **3** Less hard than other things of the same kind: *soft* rock. **4** Smooth and delicate to the touch: *soft* skin. **5** Not loud or harsh: a *soft* voice. **6** Mild; gentle: a *soft* breeze. **7** Not glaring; subdued: *soft* colors. **8** Expressing mildness or sympathy: *soft* words. **9** Easily touched in feeling: a *soft* heart. **10** Out of condition: *soft* muscles. **11** *Informal* Weak-minded: *soft* in the head. **12** *Informal* Overly lenient: a judge *soft* on criminals. **13** Free from mineral salts that form insoluble compounds with soap: said of water. **14** Biodegradable: said of detergents. **15** Regarded as being nonaddicting and less harmful than hard narcotics: said of drugs, esp. marihuana. **16** *Phonet.* Describing *c* and *g* when articulated fricatively as in *cent* and *gibe.* **17** *Informal* Easy: a *soft* job. —*n.* That which is soft; a soft part or material. —*adv.* **1** Softly. **2** Quietly; gently. —*interj. Archaic* Hush! Stop!. [< OE *sōfte*] —**soft′ly** *adv.* —**soft′ness** *n.* —**Syn.** *adj.* **1** flexible, malleable, pliable. **5** low. **9** compassionate, kind, sympathetic.

soft·back (sôft′bak′, soft′-) *adj.* SOFT·COVER. —*n.* A soft-cover book.

soft·ball (sôft′bôl′, soft′-) *n.* **1** A variation of baseball requiring a smaller diamond and a larger, softer ball. **2** The ball used in this game.

soft-boiled (sôft′boild′) *adj.* Boiled so that the yolk and white are soft or semiliquid: said of eggs.

soft coal Bituminous coal.

soft-cov·er (sôft′kuv′ər, soft′-) *adj.* Designating a book having flexible sides, as of paper. Also **soft′bound′** (-bound′).

soft drink A nonalcoholic beverage, esp. a carbonated drink.

sof·ten (sôf′ən, sof′-) *v.t. & v.i.* To make or become soft or softer. —**sof′ten·er** *n.*

soft-heart·ed (sôft′här′tid, soft′-) *adj.* Full of kindness, tenderness, and compassion. —**soft′heart′ed·ly** *adv.*

soft palate The fleshy back part of the roof of the mouth. • See MOUTH.

soft-shell (sôft′shel′, soft′-) *adj.* Having a soft shell, as a crab after shedding its shell: also **soft′-shelled′.** —*n.* A crab that has shed its shell: also **soft-shelled crab.**

soft-soap (sôft′sōp′, soft′-) *v.t. Informal* To flatter.

soft soap 1 Fluid or semifluid soap. **2** *Informal* Flattery.

soft·ware (sôft′wâr′, soft′-) *n.* In a digital computer, any of the programs designed to control various aspects of the operation of the machine, such as input and output operations.

soft·wood (sôft′wŏŏd′, soft′-) *n.* **1** A coniferous tree or its wood. **2** Any light, loosely structured wood, or any tree with such wood.

soft·y (sôf′tē, sof′-) *n. pl.* **soft·ies** *Informal* **1** An extremely sentimental person. **2** A person who is easily taken advantage of. Also **soft′ie.**

sog·gy (sog′ē) *adj.* **·gi·er, ·gi·est 1** Saturated with water or moisture; soaked. **2** Heavy and wet: said of pastry. [< dial. E *sog* a swamp, bog] **—sog′gi·ly** *adv.* **—sog′gi·ness** *n.*

soil¹ (soil) *n.* **1** Finely divided rock mixed with decayed vegetable or animal matter, constituting the portion of the surface of the earth in which plants grow. **2** Region, land, or country. [< L *solium* a seat, mistaken for *solum* the ground]

soil² (soil) *v.t.* **1** To make dirty; smudge. **2** To disgrace; defile. *—v.i.* **3** To become dirty. *—n.* A spot or stain. [< L *suculus,* dim. of *sus* a pig]

soi·rée (swä·rā′) *n.* An evening party or reception. Also **soi·ree′.** [F< *soir* evening]

so·journ (sō′jûrn, sō·jûrn′) *v.i.* To stay or live temporarily. *—n.* (sō′jûrn) A temporary residence or short visit. [< OF *sojourner*] **—so′journ·er** *n.*

sol (sōl) *n. Music* In solmization, the fifth note of a diatonic scale. [See GAMUT.]

Sol (sol) *Rom. Myth.* The god of the sun. *—n.* The sun. [L]

Sol. Solomon.

sol. solicitor; soluble; solution.

sol·ace (sol′is) *v.t.* **·aced, ·ac·ing 1** To comfort in trouble or grief; console. **2** To alleviate, as grief; soothe. *—n.* **1** Comfort in grief, trouble, or calamity. **2** Anything that supplies such comfort. [< L *solacium*] **—sol′ac·er** *n.* **—Syn.** *v.* **2** assuage, ease, mitigate. *n.* **1** cheer, consolation.

so·lar (sō′lər) *adj.* **1** Of, from, reckoned by, or pertaining to the sun. **2** Using energy from the sun: *solar* heat. [< L *sol* sun]

solar energy 1 Energy emitted by the sun as radiation over the entire electromagnetic spectrum. **2** Radiation from the sun, esp. in the infrared range, technologically convertible to domestic and industrial uses.

so·lar·i·um (sō·lâr′ē·əm) *n. pl.* **·i·a** (-ē-ə) or **·ums** A room, porch, etc., in which people can sit in the sun. [L]

solar plexus 1 A network of sympathetic nerves serving the abdominal viscera. **2** *Informal* The pit of the stomach.

solar system The sun and the bodies that orbit it. • See PLANET.

sold (sōld) *p.t.* & *p.p.* of SELL.

sol·der (sod′ər) *n.* **1** An easily melted alloy used for joining metal parts. **2** Anything that unites or cements. *—v.t.* **1** To unite or repair with solder. **2** To join together; bind. *—v.i.* **3** To work with solder. **4** To be united by or as by solder. [< L *solidus* firm, hard] **—sol′der·er** *n.*

sol·dier (sōl′jər) *n.* **1** A person serving in an army. **2** An enlisted man in an army, as distinguished from a commissioned officer. **3** A brave, skillful, or experienced warrior. **4** One who serves a cause loyally. *—v.i.* **1** To be or serve as a soldier. **2** To shirk: to *soldier* on the job. [< LL *solidus*] **—sol′dier·ly** *adj.* **—sol′dier·li·ness** *n.*

soldier of fortune A soldier willing to serve any government for money or adventure.

sol·dier·y (sōl′jər·ē) *n. pl.* **·ies 1** Soldiers collectively. **2** Military service.

sole¹ (sōl) *n.* **1** The bottom surface of the foot. **2** The bottom surface of a shoe, boot, etc. **3** The lower part or bottom of anything. *—v.t.* **soled, sol·ing** To furnish with a new sole, as a shoe. [< L *solea* a sandal]

sole² (sōl) *n.* Any of several marine flatfishes allied to the flounders, highly esteemed as food. [< L *solea* sole¹, fish]

sole³ (sōl) *adj.* **1** Being the only one: a *sole* survivor. **2** Only: His *sole* desire was for sleep. **3** *Law* Unmarried; single. **4** Of or for only one person or group. **5** Acting or accomplished without another. [< L *solus* alone] **—sole′ness** *n.*

Sole

sol·e·cism (sol′ə·siz′əm) *n.* **1** A grammatical error or a violation of approved idiomatic usage. **2** Any impropriety or incongruity. [< Gk *soloikos* speaking incorrectly] **—sol′e·cist** *n.* **—sol′e·cis′tic** or **·ti·cal** *adj.*

sole·ly (sōl′lē) *adv.* **1** By oneself or itself alone; singly. **2** Completely; entirely. **3** Only.

sol·emn (sol′əm) *adj.* **1** Characterized by majesty, mystery, or power; awe-inspiring. **2** Characterized by ceremonial observances; sacred. **3** Marked by gravity; earnest. [< L *solemnis*] **—sol′emn·ly** *adv.* **—sol′emn·ness** *n.* **—Syn. 1** impressive. **3** grave, sedate, serious, somber.

so·lem·ni·ty (sə·lem′nə·tē) *n. pl.* **·ties 1** The state or quality of being solemn. **2** A solemn rite or observance.

sol·em·nize (sol′əm·nīz) *v.t.* **·nized, ·niz·ing 1** To perform according to legal or ritual forms: to *solemnize* a marriage. **2** To celebrate with formal ritual. **3** To make solemn, grave, or serious. **—sol′em·ni·za′tion, sol′em·niz′er** *n.*

so·le·noid (sō′lə·noid) *n. Electr.* A conducting wire in the form of a cylindrical coil, used to produce a magnetic field. [< Gk. *sōlēn* a channel + -OID] **—so′le·noi′dal** *adj.* **—so′le·noi′dal·ly** *adv.*

Solenoid

sol·fa (sōl′fä′) *Music v.t.* & *v.i.* **·faed, ·fa·ing** To sing using the sol-fa instead of words. *—n.* **1** The syllables used in solmization. **2** The act of singing them. [< Ital. *solfa.* See GAMUT.] **—sol′fa′ist** *n.*

sol·feg·gio (sōl·fej′ō) *n. pl.* **·feg·gi** (-fej′ē) or **·feg·gios** *Music* **1** A florid singing exercise using arbitrary vowels and consonants. **2** Solmization. [< Ital. *solfa* sol-fa]

so·lic·it (sə·lis′it) *v.t.* **1** To ask for earnestly; beg or entreat. **2** To seek to obtain, as by persuasion. **3** To entice (one) to an unlawful or immoral act. *—v.i.* **4** To make a petition. [< L *sollicitare* agitate] **—so·lic′i·ta′tion** *n.*

so·lic·i·tor (sə·lis′ə·tər) *n.* **1** A person who solicits money for causes, subscriptions, etc. **2** The chief law officer of a city, town, etc. **3** In England, a lawyer who may appear as an advocate in the lower courts only. **—so·lic′i·tor·ship′** *n.*

Solicitor General *pl.* **Solicitors General 1** A law officer ranking below the Attorney General and assisting him. **2** The principal law officer in some of the states, corresponding to the Attorney General in others.

so·lic·i·tous (sə·lis′ə·təs) *adj.* **1** Full of anxiety or concern. **2** Full of eagerness. **—so·lic′i·tous·ly** *adv.* **—so·lic′i·tous·ness** *n.*

so·lic·i·tude (sə·lis′ə·t/y/ōōd′) *n.* **1** The state of being solicitous. **2** That which makes one solicitous.

sol·id (sol′id) *adj.* **1** Having a definite shape and volume; resistant to stress; not fluid. **2** Filling the whole of the space occupied by its form; not hollow. **3** Of the same substance throughout: *solid* marble. **4** Three-dimensional. **5** Well-built; firm: a *solid* building. **6** United or unanimous: a *solid* base of support. **7** Financially safe; sound. **8** Continuous; unbroken: a *solid* hour. **9** Written without a hyphen: said of a compound word. **10** Carrying weight or conviction: a *solid* argument. **11** Serious; reliable: a *solid* citizen. **12** *Informal* Being on good terms: They were *solid* with the boss. **13** *Slang* Excellent. **14** *Printing* Having no leads or slugs between the lines; not open. *—n.* **1** A mass of matter that has a definite shape which resists change. **2** A three-dimensional figure or object. [< L *solidus*] **—sol′id·ly** *adv.* **—so·lid′i·ty** (*pl.* **·ties**), **sol′id·ness** *n.*

solid angle The angle formed at the vertex of a cone or subtended at the point of intersection of three or more planes.

sol·i·dar·i·ty (sol′ə·dar′ə·tē) *n. pl.* **·ties** Unity of purpose, relations, or interests, as of a race, class, etc.

solid geometry The geometry of a space of three dimensions.

so·lid·i·fy (sə·lid′ə·fī) *v.t.* & *v.i.* **·fied, ·fy·ing 1** To make or become solid, hard, firm, or compact. **2** To bring or come together in unity. **—so·lid′i·fi·ca′tion** *n.*

solid state physics The physics of solid substances, esp. their properties and structure.

sol·i·dus (sol′ə·dəs) *n. pl.* **·di** (-dī) **1** A gold coin of the Byzantine Empire. **2** The sign (/) used to divide shillings from pence: 10/6 (10*s.* 6*d.*) or sometimes used to express fractions: 3/4. [L, solid]

so·lil·o·quize (sə·lil′ə·kwīz) *v.i.* **·quized, ·quiz·ing** To utter a soliloquy. **—so·lil′o·quist** (-kwist), **so·lil′o·quiz′er** *n.* **—so·lil′o·quiz′ing·ly** *adv.*

so·lil·o·quy (sə-lil′ə-kwē) *n. pl.* **·quies** 1 A talking to oneself. 2 A speech made by an actor while alone on the stage, revealing his thoughts to the audience. [< L *solus* alone + *loqui* to talk]

sol·ip·sism (sol′ip-siz′əm) *n.* The theory that only knowledge of the self is possible, that, for each individual, only the self exists, and therefore that reality is subjective. **—sol′ip·sist** *n.* **—sol′ip·sis′tic** *adj.*

sol·i·taire (sol′ə-târ′) *n.* 1 A diamond or other gem set alone. 2 Any of various card games played by one person. [< L *solitarius* solitary]

sol·i·tar·y (sol′ə-ter′ē) *adj.* 1 Living, being, or going alone. 2 Made, done, or passed alone: a *solitary* life. 3 Remote; secluded. 4 Lonesome; lonely. 5 Single; one; sole: Not a *solitary* soul was there —*n.* 1 *pl.* **·tar·ies** One who lives alone; a hermit. 2 *Informal* Solitary confinement in prison, usu. directed as a punishment. [< L *solus* alone] **—sol′i·tar′i·ly** *adv.* **—sol′i·tar′i·ness** *n.*

sol·i·tude (sol′ə-t/ood) *n.* 1 A being alone; seclusion. 2 Loneliness. 3 A deserted or lonely place. [< L *solus* alone] **—Syn.** 1 privacy, retirement. 2 isolation, lonesomeness.

sol·mi·za·tion (sol′mə-zā′shən) *n. Music* The use of syllables as names for the tones of the scale, now commonly *do, re, mi, fa, sol, la, ti.* [< SOL + MI]

so·lo (sō′lō) *n. pl.* **·los** or **·li** (-lē) 1 A musical composition or passage for a single voice or instrument, with or without accompaniment. 2 Any of several card games, esp. one in which a player plays alone against others. 3 Any performance accomplished alone or without assistance. —*adj.* 1 Performed or composed to be performed as a solo. 2 Done by a single person alone: a *solo* flight. —*v.i.* **·loed, ·lo·ing** To fly an airplane alone, esp. for the first time. [< L *solus* alone] **—so′lo·ist** *n.*

Sol·o·mon (sol′ə-mən) In the Bible, king of Israel, successor to his father David. —*n.* Any very wise man.

Sol·o·mon's-seal (sol′ə-mənz-sēl′) *n.* Any of several perennial herbs of the lily family, having tubular greenish flowers.

so long *Informal* Good-by.

sol·stice (sol′stis) *n.* Either of the times of year when the sun is farthest from the celestial equator, either north or south. In the northern hemisphere the **summer solstice** occurs about June 22, the **winter solstice** about December 22. [< L *solstitium*] **—sol·sti·tial** (sol·stish′əl) *adj.*

sol·u·ble (sol′yə-bəl) *adj.* 1 Capable of being dissolved. 2 Capable of being solved or explained. [< L *solvere* solve, dissolve] **—sol′u·bil′i·ty, sol′u·ble·ness** *n.* **—sol′u·bly** *adv.*

sol·ute (sol′yōōt, sō′lōōt) *n.* The dissolved substance in a solution.

so·lu·tion (sə-lōō′shən) *n.* 1 A homogeneous mixture of varying proportions, formed by dissolving one or more substances, whether solid, liquid, or gaseous, in another substance, usu. liquid but sometimes gaseous or solid. 2 The act or process by which such a mixture is made. 3 The act or process of explaining, settling, or solving a difficulty, problem, or doubt. 4 The answer or explanation reached in such a process. [< L *solutus,* pp. of *solvere* dissolve]

solve (solv) *v.t.* **solved, solv·ing** To arrive at or work out the correct solution or the answer to; resolve. [< L *solvere* solve, loosen] **—sol′va·ble** *adj.* **—sol′va·bil′i·ty, sol′ver** *n.*

sol·vent (sol′vənt) *adj.* 1 Having means sufficient to pay all debts. 2 Capable of dissolving. —*n.* 1 That which solves. 2 A substance, usu. a liquid, capable of dissolving other substances. [< L *solvere* solve, loosen] **—sol′ven·cy** *n.*

Som. Somaliland.

So·ma·lia (sō-mä′lyə) *n.* A republic of E Africa, 262,000 sq. mi., cap. Mogadiscio. • See map at AFRICA. **—So·ma′li** (-lē) *adj., n.*

so·mat·ic (sō-mat′ik) *adj.* 1 Of or relating to the body; corporeal. 2 Of or pertaining to the walls of a body, as distinguished from the viscera. 3 Pertaining to those elements or processes of an organism which are concerned with the maintenance of the individual as distinguished

from the reproduction of the species: *somatic* cells. [< Gk. *sōma* body] **—so·mat′i·cal·ly** *adv.*

som·ber (som′bər) *adj.* 1 Dark; gloomy. 2 Somewhat melancholy; sad. *Brit. sp.* **som′bre.** [< F *sombre*] **—som′ber·ly** *adv.* **—som′ber·ness** *n.* **—Syn.** 1 cloudy, dusky, murky.

som·bre·ro (som-brâr′ō) *n. pl.* **·ros** A broad-brimmed hat, usu. of felt, worn in Spain and Latin America. [< Sp. *sombra* shade]

Sombrero

some (sum) *adj.* 1 Of indeterminate quantity: Have *some* candy. 2 Of an unspecified number: It happened *some* days ago. 3 Not definitely specified: *Some* people dislike cats. 4 *Informal* Worthy of notice; extraordinary: That was *some* cake. —*pron.* 1 A certain undetermined quantity or part: Please take *some.* 2 Certain ones not named: *Some* believe it is true. —*adv.* 1 *Informal* Approximately; about: *Some* eighty people were present. 2 *Informal* Somewhat. [< OE *sum* some]

-some¹ *suffix of adjectives* Characterized by, or tending to be: *blithesome.* [< OE *-sum* like, resembling]

-some² *suffix of nouns* A group consisting of (a specified number): *twosome.* [< SOME]

some·bod·y (sum′bod′ē, -bəd·ē) *pron.* An unknown or unnamed person. —*n. pl.* **·bod·ies** *Informal* A person of consequence or importance.

some·day (sum′dā′) *adv.* At some future time.

some·how (sum′hou′) *adv.* In some unspecified way.

some·one (sum′wun′, -wən) *pron.* Some person; somebody.

som·er·sault (sum′ər-sôlt) *n.* An acrobatic roll in which a person turns heels over head. —*v.i.* To perform a somersault. [< OF *sobresault*]

some·thing (sum′thing) *n.* 1 A thing not determined or stated. 2 A person or thing of importance. 3 An indefinite quantity or degree: He is *something* of an artist. —*adv.* Somewhat: *something* like his brother.

some·time (sum′tīm′) *adv.* 1 At some future time not precisely stated. 2 At some indeterminate time or occasion. —*adj.* 1 Former: a *sometime* student at Oxford. 2 *Informal* Occasional; sporadic: a *sometime* thing.

some·times (sum′tīmz′) *adv.* At times; occasionally.

some·way (sum′wā′) *adv.* In some way; somehow: also **some way, some′ways′.**

some·what (sum′ʰwot′, -ʰwət) *adv.* To some degree. —*n.* An uncertain quantity or degree.

some·where (sum′ʰwâr′) *adv.* 1 In, at, or to some unspecified or unknown place. 2 At some unspecified time: *somewhere* around noon. 3 Approximately. —*n.* An unspecified or unknown place.

some·wheres (sum′ʰwârz′) *adv. Chiefly Regional* Somewhere.

som·nam·bu·late (som-nam′byə-lāt) *v.* **·lat·ed, ·lat·ing** *v.i.* To walk about while asleep. [< L *somnus* sleep + AMBULATE] **—som·nam′bu·la′tion** *n.*

som·nam·bu·lism (som-nam′byə-liz′əm) *n.* The act or state of walking during sleep. **—som·nam′bu·lant** (-lənt), **som·nam′bu·lis′tic** *adj.* **—som·nam′bu·list** *n.*

som·nif·er·ous (som-nif′ər-əs) *adj.* Tending to produce sleep; narcotic. [< L *somnus* sleep + -FEROUS]

som·no·lent (som′nə-lənt) *adj.* 1 Inclined to sleep; drowsy. 2 Tending to induce drowsiness. [< L *somnus* sleep] **—som′no·lence** or **·len·cy** *n.* **—som′no·lent·ly** *adv.*

son (sun) *n.* 1 A male child considered in his relationship to one parent or both. 2 Any male descendant. 3 One who occupies the place of a son, as by adoption, marriage, or regard. 4 Any male associated with a particular country, place, or idea: a *son* of liberty; a native *son.* 5 A familiar term of address to a young man or boy. **—the Son** Jesus Christ. [< OE *sunu*]

so·nant (sō′nənt) *Phonet. adj.* Voiced. —*n.* 1 A voiced speech sound. 2 A syllabic sound. [< L *sonare* resound]

so·nar (sō′när) *n.* A system or device for using underwater sound waves for sounding, range finding, detection of submerged objects, communication, etc. [< *so(und) na(vigation and) r(anging)*]

so·na·ta (sə-nä′tä) *n. Music* An instrumental composition written in three or four movements. [< Ital. *sonare* to sound]

song (sông, song) *n.* 1 The act of singing. 2 Any melodious utterance, as of a bird. 3 A short musical composition for voice. 4 A short poem; a lyric or ballad. 5 Poetry; verse. —**for a song** At a very low price. —**song and dance** *Slang* A long, usu. repetitive statement or explanation, often untrue or not pertinent to the subject under discussion. [< OE]

song·bird (sông′bûrd′, song′-) *n.* Any of a large number of small, perching birds, having complex musical songs characteristic of each species.

Song of Solomon A book of the Old Testament, consisting of a dramatic love poem, attributed to Solomon. Also **Song of Songs.**

song sparrow A common North American sparrow noted for its song.

song·ster (sông′stər, song′-) *n.* 1 A person or bird given to singing. 2 A writer of songs. —**song′stress** (-stris) *n. Fem.*

son·ic (son′ik) *adj.* Of, pertaining to, determined, or affected by sound: *sonic* speed. [< L *sonus* sound]

sonic barrier *Aeron.* The effects, such as drag and turbulence, that hinder flight at or near the speed of sound.

son-in-law (sun′in-lô′) *n. pl.* **sons-in-law** The husband of one's daughter.

son·net (son′it) *n.* A poem of 14 lines in any of several fixed verse and rhyme schemes. [< Prov. *son* a sound]

son·net·eer (son′ə-tir′) *n.* A composer of sonnets. —*v.i.* To compose sonnets.

son·ny (sun′ē) *n. pl.* **·nies** *Informal* Little boy: a familiar form of address.

so·no·rous (sə-nôr′əs, -nō′rəs, son′ə-rəs) *adj.* 1 Productive or capable of producing sound vibrations. 2 Loud and full-sounding; resonant. 3 High-sounding: *sonorous* verse. [< L *sonare* resound] —**so·nor·i·ty** (sə-nôr′ə-tē, -nor-, son′·ôr′ə-tē), **so·nor′ous·ness** *n.* —**so·no′rous·ly** *adv.*

soon (sōōn) *adv.* 1 In the near future; shortly. 2 Without delay. 3 Early: He awoke too *soon.* 4 In accord with one's inclination; willingly: I would as *soon* go as not; I'd *sooner* quit than accept a demotion. —**had sooner** Would rather. —**sooner or later** Eventually; in time; sometime. [< OE *sōna* immediately]

soot (sōōt, sōōt) *n.* A black deposit of finely divided carbon from the incomplete combustion of wood, coal, etc. —*v.t.* To soil or cover with soot. [< OE *sōt*] —**soot′i·ness** *n.* —**soot′y** *adj.* (**·i·er, ·i·est**)

sooth (sōōth) *Archaic adj.* True; real. —*n.* Truth. —**in sooth** *Archaic* Truly. [< OE *sōth*] —**sooth′ly** *adv.*

soothe (sōōth) *v.* **soothed, sooth·ing** *v.t.* 1 To restore to a quiet or normal state; calm. 2 To mitigate, soften, or relieve, as pain or grief. —*v.i.* 3 To afford relief. [< OE *sōthian* verify] —**sooth′er** *n.* —**sooth′ing·ly** *adv.* —**Syn.** 1 compose, pacify, tranquilize. 2 allay, alleviate, ease.

sooth·say·er (sōōth′sā′ər) *n.* A person who claims to be able to foretell events. —**sooth′say·ing** *n.*

sop (sop) *v.* **sopped, sop·ping** *v.t.* 1 To dip or soak in a liquid. 2 To take up by absorption: often with *up.* —*v.i.* 3 To be absorbed; soak in. 4 To become saturated or drenched. —*n.* 1 Anything softened in liquid, as bread. 2 Anything given to pacify, as a bribe. [< OE *sopp*]

SOP, S.O.P. standard operating procedure; *(Mil.)* standing operating procedure.

sop. soprano.

soph·ism (sof′iz-əm) *n.* 1 A false argument seemingly correct but actually misleading. 2 A fallacy. [< Gk. *sophos* wise]

soph·ist (sof′ist) *n.* 1 A learned person; thinker. 2 One who argues cleverly and deviously. 3 *Often cap.* A member of a certain school of early Greek philosophy, preceding the Socratic school. 4 *Often cap.* One of the later Greek teachers of philosophy and rhetoric, skilled in subtle disputation. [< Gk. *sophos* wise] —**so·phis′tic** or **·ti·cal** *adj.* —**so·phis′ti·cal·ly** *adv.* —**so·phis′ti·cal·ness** *n.*

so·phis·ti·cate (sə·fis′tə·kāt) *v.* **·cat·ed, ·cat·ing** *v.t.* 1 To make less simple or ingenuous; render worldly-wise. 2 To

mislead or corrupt. —*v.i.* 3 To indulge in sophistry. —*n.* (-kit, -kāt) A sophisticated person. [< Gk. *sophos* wise] —**so·phis′ti·ca′tor** *n.*

so·phis·ti·cat·ed (sə·fis′tə·kā′tid) *adj.* 1 Worldly-wise. 2 Of a kind that appeals to the worldly-wise. 3 Very complicated in design, function, etc.: a *sophisticated* machine.

so·phis·ti·ca·tion (sə·fis′tə·kā′shən) *n.* 1 Worldly experience; urbanity, usu. with a loss of simplicity. 2 The state of being sophisticated. 3 Sophistry.

soph·is·try (sof′is·trē) *n. pl.* **·tries** 1 Subtly fallacious reasoning or disputation. 2 The art or methods of the Sophists.

soph·o·more (sof′ə-môr, -mōr) *n.* A second-year student in an American high school or college. —*adj.* Of or pertaining to second-year students or studies. [Earlier *sophomer* a dialectician< *sophom,* var. of **SOPHISM**]

soph·o·mor·ic (sof′ə-môr′ik, -mōr′-) *adj.* 1 Of, pertaining to, or like a sophomore. 2 Shallow and pretentious. 3 Immature; inexperienced. Also **soph′o·mor′i·cal.** —**soph′o·mor′i·cal·ly** *adv.*

-sophy *combining form* Knowledge or a system of knowledge: *philosophy.* [< Gk. *sophia* wisdom]

sop·o·rif·ic (sop′ə-rif′ik, sō′pə-) *adj.* 1 Causing or tending to cause sleep. 2 Drowsy; sleepy. —*n.* A medicine that produces sleep. [< L *sopor* sleep]

sop·ping (sop′ing) *adj.* Drenched; soaking.

sop·py (sop′ē) *adj.* **·pi·er, ·pi·est** Saturated and softened with moisture; soft and sloppy. —**sop′pi·ness** *n.*

so·pran·o (sə·pran′ō, -prä′nō) *n. pl.* **so·pran·os** or **so·pra·ni** (sə·prä′nē) 1 A part or singing voice of the highest range. 2 The music for such a voice. 3 A person having such a voice or singing such a part. —*adj.* Of or pertaining to a soprano voice or part. [< Ital. *sopra* above]

so·ra (sôr′ə, sō′rə) *n.* A grayish brown crake with a short yellow bill. Also **sora rail.** [?< N. Am. Ind.]

sor·cer·er (sôr′sər-ər) *n.* A wizard; magician.

sor·cer·ess (sôr′sər-es) *n.* A woman who practices sorcery; witch.

sor·cer·y (sôr′sər-ē) *n. pl.* **·cer·ies** Use of supernatural agencies; magic; witchcraft. [< L *sors* fate] —**sor′cer·ous** *adj.* —**sor′cer·ous·ly** *adv.*

sor·did (sôr′did) *adj.* 1 Of degraded character; vile; base. 2 Dirty; squalid. 3 Mercenary; selfish. [< L *sordidus* squalid] —**sor′did·ly** *adv.* —**sor′did·ness** *n.*

sore (sôr, sōr) *n.* 1 A place on an animal body where the skin or flesh is bruised, broken, or inflamed. 2 Anything that causes pain or trouble. —*adj.* **sor·er, sor·est** 1 Having a sore or sores; tender. 2 Pained or distressed. 3 Irritating; distressing. 4 Very great; extreme: in *sore* need of money. 5 *Informal* Offended; angry. —*adv. Archaic* Sorely. [< OE *sār*] —**sore′ness** *n.* —**Syn.** *n.* 1 cut, scrape, wound.

sore·head (sôr′hed′, sōr′-) *n. Informal.* A disgruntled person.

sore·ly (sôr′lē, sōr′-) *adv.* 1 Grievously; distressingly. 2 Greatly: His aid was *sorely* needed.

sor·ghum (sôr′gəm) *n.* 1 A canelike tropical grass cultivated for fodder and its sugary sap. 2 Syrup prepared from the sap of the plant. [< L *Syricus* of Syria, where originally grown]

so·ror·i·ty (sə·rôr′ə·tē, -ror′-) *n. pl.* **·ties** A women's organization having chapters at colleges, universities, etc. [< L *soror* a sister]

sor·rel[1] (sôr′əl, sor′-) *n.* Any of various plants with acid leaves. [< OF *sur* sour]

sor·rel[2] (sôr′əl, sor′-) *n.* 1 A reddish brown color. 2 An animal of this color. —*adj.* Reddish brown. [< OF *sor* a hawk with red plumage]

Sorghum

sor·row (sor′ō, sôr′ō) *n.* 1 Pain or distress because of loss, injury, misfortune, or grief. 2 An event that causes such pain or distress; affliction. 3 The expression of grief; mourning. —*v.i.* To feel or express sorrow; grieve. [< OE *sorg* care] —**sor′row·er** *n.*

sor·row·ful (sor′ə-fəl, sôr′-) *adj.* 1 Full of or showing sorrow or grief. 2 Causing sorrow: a *sorrowful* occasion. —**sor′row·ful·ly** *adv.* —**sor′row·ful·ness** *n.*

sor·ry (sor′ē, sôr′ē) *adj.* **·ri·er, ·ri·est 1** Feeling or showing regret or remorse. **2** Affected by sorrow; grieved. **3** Causing sorrow; melancholy. **4** Pitiable or worthless; paltry. [< OE *sārig* < *sār* sore] —**sor′ri·ly** *adv.* —**sor′ri·ness** *n.*

sort (sôrt) *n.* **1** A collection of persons or things characterized by similar qualities; a kind. **2** Character; nature. **3** Manner; way; style. **4** A person of a certain type: He's a good *sort.* —**of sorts** Of a poor or unsatisfactory kind: an actor *of sorts.* —**out of sorts** Slightly ill or ill-humored. —**sort of** *Informal* Somewhat. —*v.t.* To arrange or separate into grades, kinds, or sizes; assort. [< L *sors* lot, condition] —**sort′er** *n.*

sor·tie (sôr′tē) *n.* **1** A sudden attack by troops from a besieged place. **2** A single trip of an aircraft on a military mission. [< F *sortir* go forth]

S O S (es′ō·es′) **1** The international signal of distress in the Morse code (. . . – – – . . .), used by airplanes, ships, etc. **2** *Informal* Any call for assistance.

so-so (sō′sō′) *adj.* Passable; mediocre. —*adv.* Indifferently; tolerably. Also **so′so′, so so.**

sot (sot) *n.* A habitual drunkard. [< OE *sott* a fool] —**sot′· tish** *adj.* —**sot′tish·ly** *adv.* —**sot′tish·ness** *n.*

sot·to vo·ce (sot′ō vō′chē, *Ital.* sôt′tō vō′chä) Softly; in an undertone; privately. [Ital., lit., under the voice]

sou (sōō) *n.* **1** Any of several former French coins of varying value, esp. one equal to 12 deniers. **2** A coin equal to five centimes. [< LL *solidus*, a gold coin]

sou·brette (sōō·bret′) *n.* **1** The part of a frivolous or flirtatious young woman, often a maidservant, in a play or light opera. **2** An actress who portrays such parts. [< Prov. *soubret* shy] —**sou·bret′tish** *adj.*

sou·bri·quet (sōō′bri·kā, sōō·bri·kā′) *n.* SOBRIQUET.

souf·flé (sōō·flā′) *adj.* Made light and frothy, and fixed in that condition by heat: also **souf·fléed′** (-flād′). —*n.* A light, baked dish made of a sauce, beaten egg whites, and various flavorings and ingredients. [F < L *sub-* under + *flare* to blow]

sough (suf, sou) *v.i.* To make a sighing sound, as the wind. —*n.* A deep, murmuring sound. [< OE *swōgan* sound]

sought (sôt) *p.t.* & *p.p.* of SEEK.

soul (sōl) *n.* **1** That essence or entity of the human person which is regarded as being immortal, invisible, and the source or origin of spirituality, emotion, volition, etc. **2** The moral or spiritual part of man. **3** Emotional or spiritual force, vitality, depth, etc.: His acting lacks *soul.* **4** The most essential or vital element or quality of something: Justice is the *soul* of law. **5** The leading figure or inspirer of a cause, movement, etc. **6** Embodiment: the *soul* of generosity. **7** A person: Every *soul* trembled at the sight. **8** The disembodied spirit of one who has died. **9** Among U.S. Negroes: **a** The awareness of a black African heritage. **b** A strongly emotional pride and solidarity based on this awareness. **c** The qualities that arouse such feelings, esp. as exemplified in black culture and art. **10** SOUL MUSIC. **11** SOUL FOOD. —*adj.* Of or pertaining to soul (def. 9). [< OE *sāwol*]

soul brother A Negro male: used by other Negroes.

soul food Any of various Southern foods or dishes popular with American Negroes, as fried chicken, ham hocks, chitterlings, yams, etc.

soul·ful (sōl′fəl) *adj.* Full of emotion or feeling. —**soul′ful· ly** *adv.* —**soul′ful·ness** *n.* —**Syn.** deep-felt, heartfelt, deep, profound, moving, emotional.

soul kiss A kiss with the mouth open and the tongues touching.

soul·less (sōl′lis) *adj.* **1** Having no soul. **2** Without feeling or emotion; cold. —**soul′less·ly** *adv.* —**soul′less·ness** *n.*

soul music A type of popular music strongly emotional in character and influenced chiefly by the blues and gospel hymns.

soul-search·ing (sōl′sûrch′ing) *n.* A deep examination of one's motives, desires, actions, etc.

soul sister A Negro female: used by other Negroes.

sound[1] (sound) *n.* **1** Energy in the form of a disturbance, usually periodic, in the pressure and density of a fluid or the elastic strain of a solid, detectable by human organs of hearing when between about 20Hz and 20kHz in frequency. **2** The sensation produced by such energy. **3** Any noise, tone, voice, etc., of a specified quality or source: the *sound* of a door slamming shut. **4** Sounding or hearing distance; earshot: within *sound* of the battle. **5** Significance; implication: The story has a sinister *sound.* **6** Mere noise without significance: full of *sound* and fury. —*v.i.* **1** To give forth a sound or sounds. **2** To give a specified impression; seem: The story *sounds* true. —*v.t.* **3** To cause to give forth sound: to *sound* a bell; also, to give forth the sound of: to *sound* A on the violin. **4** To give a signal or order for or announcement of: to *sound* retreat. **5** To utter audibly; pronounce. **6** To make known or celebrated. **7** To test or examine by sound; auscultate. [< OF *son* < L *sonus*]

sound[2] (sound) *adj.* **1** Functioning without impairment; healthy. **2** Free from injury, flaw, or decay: *sound* timber. **3** Correct, logical, or sensible in reasoning, judgment, etc.: *sound* advice. **4** Not unorthodox; established: a *sound* belief. **5** Financially solid or solvent. **6** Stable; safe; secure: a *sound* investment. **7** Complete and effectual; thorough: a *sound* beating. **8** Deep; unbroken: *sound* sleep. **9** Legally valid. [< OE *gesund*] —**sound′ly** *adv.* —**sound′ness** *n.*

sound[3] (sound) *n.* **1** A long, narrow body of water connecting larger bodies of water or separating an island from the mainland. **2** The air bladder of a fish. [< OE *sund* sea and ON *sund* a strait]

sound[4] (sound) *v.t.* **1** To test the depth of (water, etc.), esp. by means of a lead weight at the end of a line. **2** To measure (depth) thus. **3** To explore or examine (the bottom of the sea, the atmosphere, etc.) by means of various probing devices. **4** To discover or try to discover the views and attitudes of (a person) by means of conversation, subtle questions, etc.: usu. with *out.* **5** To try to ascertain or determine (beliefs, attitudes, etc.) in such a manner. **6** *Surg.* To examine, as with a sound. —*v.i.* **7** To measure depth, as with a sounding lead. **8** To dive down suddenly and deeply, as a whale when harpooned. **9** To make investigation; inquire. —*n. Surg.* An instrument for exploring a cavity; a probe. —*adv.* Deeply: *sound* asleep. [< OF *sonder*] —**sound′a·ble** *adj.* —**sound′er** *n.*

sound barrier SONIC BARRIER.

sound effects In motion pictures, radio, on the stage, etc., the imitative sounds, as of rain, hoofbeats, fire, etc., produced by various methods.

sound·ing[1] (soun′ding) *adj.* **1** Giving forth a full sound; sonorous. **2** Noisy and empty. —**sound′ing·ly** *adv.*

sound·ing[2] (soun′ding) *n.* **1** Measurement of the depth of water. **2** *pl.* The depth of water as sounded. **3** Water of such depth that the bottom may be reached by sounding. **4** Measurement or examination of the atmosphere, space, etc. at various heights. **5** A sampling of public opinion.

sounding board 1 A structure over a pulpit or speaker's platform to amplify and clarify the speaker's voice. **2** A thin board, as the belly of a violin, used to increase the resonance of the sound: also **sound′board′. 3** Any person, group, device, etc., used to propagate opinions. **4** A person or group on whom one tests the validity or effectiveness of something.

sound·less (sound′lis) *adj.* Making no sound; silent. —**sound′less·ly** *adv.* —**sound′less·ness** *n.*

sound·man (sound′man′) *n. pl.* **·men** (-men′) A man who has charge of sound effects.

sound·proof (sound′prōōf′) *adj.* Resistant to the penetration or spread of sound. —*v.t.* To make soundproof.

sound track That portion along the edge of a motion-picture film which carries the sound record.

soup (sōōp) *n.* **1** A food made of meat or fish, vegetables, etc., cooked and served, either whole or puréed, in water, stock, or other liquid. **2** *Slang* A heavy fog. **3** *Slang* Nitroglycerin. —**in the soup** *Slang* In difficulties; in a quandary. —**soup up** *Slang* To supercharge or otherwise modify (an engine) for high speed. [< F *soupe*]

soup·çon (sōōp·sôn′) *n.* A minute quantity; a taste. [F, lit., a suspicion]

soup·y (sōō′pē) *adj.* **soup·i·er, soup·i·est 1** Like soup in consistency. **2** Very foggy or cloudy. **3** Overly sentimental.

sour (sour) *adj.* 1 Sharp, acid, or tart to the taste, like vinegar. 2 Having an acid or rancid taste or smell as the result of fermentation. 3 Of or pertaining to fermentation. 4 Cross; morose: a *sour* smile. 5 Bitterly disenchanted. 6 Bad in quality, performance, etc.: an athlete gone *sour*. 7 Wrong or unpleasant in pitch or tone: a *sour* note. 8 Unpleasant. 9 Acid: said of soil. —*v.t. & v.i.* To become or make sour. —*n.* 1 Something sour. 2 A cocktail, made usu. with lemon juice, fruit garnishes, etc.: a whiskey *sour.* [< OE *sūr*] —**sour′ly** *adv.* —**sour′ness** *n.* —**Syn.** 4 dour, acid, bitter, unhappy.

source (sôrs, sōrs) *n.* 1 That from which something originates or is derived. 2 A cause or agency: a *source* of joy. 3 The spring or fountain from which a stream of water originates. 4 A person, writing, or agency from which information is obtained. [< L *surgere* to rise]

sour cream A food product made of cream soured and thickened by the action of lactic acid bacteria.

sour·dough (sour′dō′) *n.* 1 Fermented dough for use as leaven in making bread. 2 A pioneer or prospector in Alaska or Canada: from the practice of carrying fermented dough to make bread.

sour grapes That which a person affects to despise, because it is unattainable: an allusion to Aesop's fable of the fox and the grapes.

sour·gum (sour′gum′) *n.* TUPELO.

sour·puss (sour′pŏŏs′) *n.* *Slang* A person with a sullen, peevish expression or disposition.

souse (sous) *v.t. & v.i.* **soused, sous·ing** 1 To dip or steep in a liquid. 2 To pickle. 3 To make or become thoroughly wet. 4 *Slang* To make or get drunk. —*n.* 1 Pickled meats, esp. the feet and ears of a pig. 2 A plunge in water. 3 Brine. 4 *Slang* A drunkard. [< OHG *sulza* brine]

sou·tane (sŏŏ·tän′, -tan′) *n.* CASSOCK. [< Ital. *sottana*]

south (south) *n.* 1 The general direction to the right of sunrise. 2 The point of the compass at 180°, directly opposite north. 3 A region or point lying in this direction. — *adj.* 1 Situated in a southern direction relatively to the observer or to any given place or point. 2 Facing south. 3 Belonging to or proceeding from the south. —*v.i.* To turn southward. —*adv.* 1 Toward or at the south. 2 From the south. —**the South** 1 In the U.S., those states lying south of Pennsylvania and the Ohio River and east of the Mississippi. 2 The Confederacy. [< OE *sūth*]

South Africa A republic of s Africa, 472,359 sq. mi., cap. Pretoria, legislative center Cape Town.

South African A native or citizen of South Africa, esp. an Afrikaner. —*adj.* Of or pertaining to South Africa or its people.

South African Dutch AFRIKAANS.

South America The southern continent of the western hemisphere, about 6,900,000 square miles. —**South American**

south·bound (south′bound′) *adj.* Going southward.

south·east (south′ēst′, *in nautical usage* sou′ēst′) *n.* 1 The direction or compass point midway between south and east. 2 Any region lying in this direction. —*adj.* Of, pertaining to, toward, or from the southeast. —*adv.* Toward or from the southeast. —**south′east′ern, south′east′ern·most** *adj.*

south·east·er (south′ēs′tər, *in nautical usage* sou′ēs′tər) *n.* A gale from the southeast.

south·east·er·ly (south′ēs′tər·lē, *in nautical usage* sou′ēs′tər·lē) *adj. & adv.* 1 Toward the southeast. 2 From the southeast: said of wind.

south·east·ward (south′ēst′wərd) *adj. & adv.* Toward the southeast. —*n.* A southeastward point or direction — **south′east′ward·ly, south′east′wards** *adv.*

south·er (sou′thər) *n.* A strong wind from the south.

south·er·ly (suth′ər·lē) *adj.* 1 Situated in or tending toward the south. 2 From the south: a *southerly* wind. —*adv.* Toward or from the south. —**south′er·li·ness** *n.*

south·ern (suth′ərn) *adj.* 1 Of, in, or facing the south. 2 From the south, as a wind. 3 *Often cap.* Of, from, or char-

acteristic of the South: *southern* cooking. —**south′ern·ly** *adv.* —**south′ern·most** *adj.*

Southern Cross A southern constellation having four bright stars in the form of a cross.

South·ern·er (suth′ərn·ər) *n.* A native or inhabitant of the s regions of the U.S.

Southern Hemisphere See HEMISPHERE.

southern lights AURORA AUSTRALIS.

Southern Yemen YEMEN, PEOPLE'S DEMOCRATIC REPUBLIC OF.

South Korea See KOREA.

south·land (south′land′) *n.* 1 A region situated to the south. 2 *Often cap.* The southern U.S. —**south′land′er** *n.*

south·paw (south′pô′) *Slang n.* 1 In baseball, a left-handed pitcher. 2 Any left-handed person or player. — *adj.* Left-handed.

South Pole The southern extremity of the earth's axis; the 90th degree of south latitude.

south-south·east (south′south′ēst′, *in nautical usage* sou′sou′ēst′) *n.* The direction or compass point midway between south and southeast. —*adj.* Of, pertaining to, toward, or from this direction. —*adv.* Toward or from this direction.

south-south·west (south′south′west′, *in nautical usage* sou′sou′west′) *n.* The direction or compass point midway between south and southwest. —*adj.* Of, pertaining to, toward, or from this direction. —*adv.* Toward or from this direction.

South Vietnam See VIETNAM.

south·ward (south′wərd, *in nautical usage* suth′ərd) *adj.* Situated in or toward the south. —*adv.* In a southerly direction: also **south′ward·ly, south′wards.** —*n.* The direction of south; also, a region to the south.

south·west (south′west′, *in nautical usage* sou′west′) *n.* 1 The direction or compass point midway between south and west. 2 Any region lying in this direction. —*adj.* Of, pertaining to, toward or from the southwest. —*adv.* Toward or from the southwest. —**the Southwest** The sw part of the U.S., generally including Oklahoma, Texas, New Mexico, Arizona, and southern California. —**south′west′ern, south′west′ern·most** *adj.*

south·west·er (south′wes′tər, *in nautical usage* sou′wes′tər) *n.* 1 A wind, gale, or storm from the southwest. 2 A waterproof hat of oilskin, canvas, etc., with a broad protective brim behind. Also **sou′west′er.**

south·west·er·ly (south′wes′tər·lē, *in nautical usage* sou′wes′tər·lē) *adj. & adv.* 1 Toward the southwest. 2 From the southwest: said of wind.

south·west·ward (south′west′- wərd) *adj. & adv.* Toward the Southwester *def.* 2 southwest. —*n.* A southwestward point or direction. — **south′west′ward·ly, south′west′wards** *adv.*

sou·ve·nir (sŏŏ′və·nir′, sŏŏ′və·nir) *n.* A token of remembrance; memento. [< L *subvenire* come to mind]

sov·er·eign (sov′rin, -ə·rən, -ərn, suv′-) *adj.* 1 Exercising or possessing supreme jurisdiction or power. 2 Free; independent; autonomous: a *sovereign* state. 3 Supremely excellent, great, or exalted. 4 Extremely potent or effective: a *sovereign* remedy. 5 Total; unmitigated: *sovereign* hate. 6 Of chief importance, supremacy, etc.: *sovereign* claims. —*n.* 1 One who possesses sovereign authority; a monarch. 2 A body of persons in whom sovereign power is vested. 3 An English gold coin equivalent to one pound sterling. [< L *super* above] —**sov′er·eign·ly** *adv.*

sov·er·eign·ty (sov′rin·tē, -ə·rən-, -ərn-, suv′-) *n. pl.* **·ties** 1 The state or quality of being sovereign. 2 The ultimate, supreme power in a state. 3 A sovereign state. 4 The status or power of a sovereign.

so·vi·et (sō′vē·et, sō′vē·et′, sov′ē-, -ē·it) *n.* 1 In the Soviet Union, any of the elected legislative councils existing at various governmental levels. 2 Any of various similar socialist legislative councils. [< Russ. *sovyet* a council]

So·vi·et (sō′vē·et, sō′vē·et′, sov′ē-, -ē·it) *adj.* Of or pertaining to the Union of Soviet Socialist Republics. —*n.pl.* The Soviet people, esp. the officials of the government.

so·vi·et·ize (sō′vē·ə·tīz′, sov′ē-) v.t. **-ized, -iz·ing** To bring under a soviet form of government. —**so′vi·et·i·za′tion** n.

Soviet Russia 1 UNION OF SOVIET SOCIALIST REPUBLICS. 2 RUSSIAN SOVIET FEDERATED SOCIALIST REPUBLIC.

Soviet Union UNION OF SOVIET SOCIALIST REPUBLICS.

sow[1] (sō) v. **sowed, sown** or **sowed, sow·ing** v.t. 1 To scatter (seed) over land for growth. 2 To scatter seed over (land). 3 To disseminate; implant: to *sow* the seeds of distrust. — v.i. 4 To scatter seed. [< OE *sāwan*] —**sow′er** n.

sow[2] (sou) n. A female hog. [< OE *sū*]

sow·bel·ly (sou′bel′ē) n. *Informal* SALT PORK.

soy (soi) n. A dark brown salty liquid condiment made from fermented soybeans. Also **soy sauce.** [Japanese]

soy·bean (soi′bēn′) n. 1 A small leguminous forage plant native to Asia. 2 Its edible bean, a source of oil, flour, and other products. Also, *esp. Brit.,* **soy·a** (soi′ə).

SP Shore Patrol; Submarine Patrol.

Sp. Spain; Spaniard; Spanish.

sp. special; specialist; species; specific; spelling; spirit(s).

s.p. without issue (L *sine prole*).

spa (spä) n. 1 Any locality frequented for its mineral springs. 2 A mineral spring. 3 A fashionable resort or resort hotel. [< *Spa,* a Belgian watering town]

space (spās) n. 1 The three-dimensional expanse that is considered as coextensive with the universe. 2 A limited or measurable distance or area, as that between or within points or objects. 3 A specific area designated for a particular purpose: landing *space.* 4 OUTER SPACE. 5 An interval or period of time. 6 One of the degrees of a musical staff between two lines. 7 *Printing* **a** A blank piece of type metal, used for spacing between lines, characters, etc. **b** The area occupied by such pieces. 8 Reserved accommodations, as on a ship or airliner. —*adj.* Of or pertaining to space, esp. to outer space. —*v.t.* **spaced, spac·ing** 1 To separate by spaces. 2 To divide into spaces. [< L *spatium*] —**space′less** *adj.* —**spac′er** n.

space·craft (spās′kraft′, -kräft′) n. Any vehicle, manned or unmanned, designed for flight in outer space.

spaced-out (spāst′out′) *adj. Slang* Dazed or drugged, by or as by the use of narcotics.

space-flight (spās′flīt′) n. Flight in outer space.

space·ship (spās′ship′) n. Any vehicle designed to travel outside the earth's atmosphere.

space station A large, usu. manned satellite orbiting the earth and used for observation, experiments, as a relay station, etc.

space-time (spās′tīm′, -tīm′) n. A four-dimensional continuum in which each point is identified by three position coordinates and one coordinate of time. Also **space-time continuum.**

spa·cial (spā′shəl) *adj.* SPATIAL.

spac·ing (spā′sing) n. 1 The arrangement of spaces. 2 A space or spaces, as in a line of print.

spa·cious (spā′shəs) *adj.* 1 Of large or ample extent; not cramped or crowded; roomy. 2 Large or great in scale or scope. —**spa′cious·ly** *adv.* —**spa′cious·ness** n. —Syn. 1 extensive, ample, sizable, capacious, commodious.

spack·le (spak′əl) v.t. **-led, -ling** To apply Spackle to.

Spack·le (spak′əl) n. A powder which, moistened to form a paste, is used for filling cracks, etc. before painting: a trade name.

spade[1] (spād) n. An implement used for digging in the ground, heavier than a shovel and having a flatter blade. —**call a spade a spade** 1 To call a thing by its right name. 2 To speak the plain truth. —*v.t.* **spad·ed, spad·ing** To dig or cut with a spade. [< OE *spadu*] —**spade′ful** n. **spad′er** n.

spade[2] (spād) n. 1 A figure, resembling a heart with a triangular handle, on a playing card. 2 A card so marked. 3 *Usu. pl.* The suit of cards so marked. [< Gk. *spathē* broad sword]

spade·work (spād′wûrk′) n. Any preliminary work necessary to get a project under way.

spa·dix (spā′diks) n. *pl.* **spa·di·ces** (spā′də·sēz) *Bot.* A spike of tiny flowers on a fleshy axis, usu. enclosed within a spathe. [L, branch torn from palm tree < Gk.]

spa·ghet·ti (spə·get′ē) n. 1 A thin, cordlike pasta. 2 Insulated tubing through which bare wire is passed, as in a radio circuit. [< Ital. *spago* a small cord]

Spain (spān) n. A nominal constitutional monarchy in sw Europe, 194,368 sq. mi., capital Madrid.

spake (spāk) *Archaic p.t.* of SPEAK.

span[1] (span) v.t. **spanned, span·ning** 1 To measure, esp. with the hand with the thumb and little finger extended. 2 To extend in time across: His influence *spanned* two centuries. 3 To extend over or from side to side of: This road *spans* the continent. 4 To provide with something that stretches across or extends over. —n. 1 The distance or measure between two points, ends, or extremities: the *span* of an eagle's wing. 2 The space or distance between the supports of an arch, abutments of a bridge, etc. 3 The part that spans such a space or distance: the graceful *spans* of Brooklyn Bridge. 4 A period of time or duration: life *span.* 5 The extreme space over which the hand can be expanded, usu. considered to be nine inches. [< OE *spann* distance]

span[2] (span) n. A pair of matched horses, oxen, etc., used as a team. [< MDu. *spannen* join together]

span·gle (spang′gəl) n. 1 A small bit of brilliant metal foil, plastic, etc., used for decoration, esp. on theatrical costumes. 2 Any small sparkling object. —v. **-gled, -gling** v.t. 1 To adorn with or as with spangles; cause to glitter. —v.i. 2 To sparkle as spangles; glitter. [< MDu. *spang* a clasp, brooch] —**span′gly** *adj.*

Span·iard (span′yərd) n. A native or citizen of Spain.

span·iel (span′yəl) n. 1 A small or medium-sized dog having large pendulous ears and long silky hair. • See SPRINGER. 2 An obsequious follower. [< OF *espaignol* Spanish (dog)]

Span·ish (span′ish) n. 1 The language of Spain and many of the countries of the Western Hemisphere. 2 The people of Spain collectively: used with *the.* —*adj.* Of or pertaining to Spain, its people, their language, etc.

Spanish America Those countries of the Western Hemisphere in which Spanish is the common language. —**Span′ish-A·mer′i·can** *adj.*

Spanish American A native or inhabitant of Spanish America.

Spanish moss An epiphytic plant related to pineapple, growing in pendulous tufts on trees in s U.S. and tropical America.

spank (spangk) v.t. 1 To slap or strike, esp. on the buttocks with the open hand as a punishment. —v.i. 2 To move briskly. —n. A smack on the buttocks. [Imit.]

spank·er (spangk′ər) n. 1 One who spanks. 2 *Naut.* A fore-and-aft sail extended by a boom and a gaff from the mizzenmast of a ship or bark.

spank·ing (spangk′ing) *adj.* 1 Moving or blowing rapidly; swift; lively. 2 *Informal* Uncommonly large or fine. —n. A series of slaps on the buttocks. —*adv. Informal* Very: a *spanking* new bike. [?]

span·ner (span′ər) n. 1 One who or that which spans. 2 *Brit.* WRENCH.

spar[1] (spär) n. 1 *Naut.* A pole for extending a sail, as a mast, yard, or boom. 2 A similar heavy, round beam forming part of a derrick, crane, etc. 3 That part of an airplane wing which supports the ribs. —v.t. **sparred, spar·ring** To furnish with a beam. [< ON *sparri* a beam]

spar[2] (spär) v.i. **sparred, spar·ring** 1 To box, esp. with care and adroitness, as in practice. 2 To bandy words; wrangle. 3 To fight, as cocks, by striking with spurs. —n. The act or practice of boxing: also **spar′ring.** [< L *parare* prepare]

spar[3] (spär) n. Any of various vitreous, crystalline, easily cleavable, lustrous minerals. [< MDu.]

Spar (spär) n. A member of the women's reserve of the U.S. Coast Guard. Also **SPAR.** [< L *s(emper) par(atus)* always ready, the motto of the U.S. Coast Guard]

spare (spâr) v. **spared, spar·ing** v.t. **1** To refrain from injuring, molesting, or killing; treat mercifully. **2** To free or relieve (someone) from (pain, expense, etc.): *Spare* us the sight. **3** To use frugally; refrain from using or exercising. **4** To dispense or dispense with; do without: Can you *spare* a dime? —v.i. **5** To be frugal. **6** To be lenient or forgiving. —adj. **spar·er, spar·est 1** That is over and above what is necessary, used, filled, etc.: *spare* time. **2** Held in reserve; additional; extra. **3** Thin; lean. **4** Not abundant or plentiful; scanty. **5** Not elaborate or fussy: a *spare* style of writing. —n. **1** A duplicate of something that has been saved for future use. **2** An extra tire usu. carried in or on a vehicle as a replacement in the event of a flat tire: also **spare tire. 3** In bowling, the act of overturning all the pins with the first two balls; also, the score thus made. [< OE *sparian* to spare] —**spare'ly** adv. —**spare'ness, spar'er** n.

spare·ribs (spâr'ribz') n.pl. A cut of pork ribs somewhat closely trimmed.

spar·ing (spâr'ing) adj. **1** Scanty; slight. **2** Frugal; stingy. —**spar'ing·ly** adv. —**spar'ing·ness** n.

spark (spärk) n. **1** An incandescent particle, esp. one thrown off by a fire. **2** Any similar glistening or brilliant point or particle. **3** A small trace or indication: a *spark* of wit. **4** Anything that kindles or animates. **5** *Electr.* The luminous effect of an electric discharge, or the discharge itself. —v.i. **1** To give off sparks. **2** In an internal-combustion engine, to have the electric ignition operating. —v.t. **3** To activate or cause: The shooting *sparked* a revolution. [< OE *spearca*] —**spark'er** n.

spar·kle (spär'kəl) v.i. **·kled, ·kling 1** To give off flashes or bright points of light; glitter. **2** To emit sparks. **3** To effervesce, as certain wines, etc. **4** To be brilliant or vivacious. —n. **1** A spark; gleam. **2** Brilliance; vivacity. [Freq. of SPARK]

spar·kler (spär'klər) n. **1** One who or that which sparkles. **2** *Informal* A sparkling gem, as a diamond. **3** A thin, rodlike firework that emits sparks.

spark plug A device for igniting the charge in an internal-combustion engine by means of an electric spark.

spar·row (spar'ō) n. **1** Any of various small, plainly colored, passerine birds related to the finches, as the English sparrow. **2** Any of numerous similar birds, as the song sparrow. [< OE *spearwa*]

sparrow hawk **1** A small North American falcon with rufous back and tail. **2** A small European hawk.

sparse (spärs) adj. **spars·er, spars·est** Thinly spread or scattered; not dense: a *sparse* crowd. [< L *sparsus*, pp. of *spargere* sprinkle] —**sparse'ly** adv. —**sparse'ness, spar·si·ty** (spär'sə·tē) n.

Spar·ta (spär'tə) n. An ancient city in the Peloponnesus, s Greece, capital of ancient Laconia.

Spar·tan (spär'tən) adj. **1** Of Sparta or the Spartans. **2** Characterized by austerity, simplicity, self-denial, self-discipline, etc. **3** Heroically brave and enduring. —n. **1** A native or citizen of Sparta. **2** One of exceptional valor and fortitude. —**Spar'tan·ism** n.

spasm (spaz'əm) n. **1** A sudden, involuntary muscular contraction. **2** Any sudden action or effort. [< Gk. *spasmos* < *spaein* draw, pull]

spas·mod·ic (spaz·mod'ik) adj. **1** Of the nature of a spasm; intermittent; temporary; transitory. **2** Violent or impulsive. Also **spas·mod'i·cal.** —**spas·mod'i·cal·ly** adv.

spas·tic (spas'tik) adj. Of, pertaining to, or characterized by spasms. —n. A person afflicted with cerebral palsy or similar disability. —**spas'ti·cal·ly** adv.

spat[1] (spat) p.t. & p.p. of SPIT[1].

spat[2] (spat) n. **1** Spawn of a bivalve mollusk, esp. the oyster. **2** A young oyster, or young oysters collectively. [?]

spat[3] (spat) n. **1** *Informal* A petty dispute or quarrel. **2** A splash, as of rain; spatter. —v. **spat·ted, spat·ting** v.i. **1** To strike with a slight sound. **2** *Informal* To engage in a petty quarrel. —v.t. **3** To slap. [Imit.]

spat[4] (spat) n. A short gaiter worn over a shoe and fastened underneath with a strap. [Short for SPATTERDASH]

Spats[4]

spate (spāt) n. **1** A flood or overflow. **2** A large amount or incidence. **3** A sudden outpouring, as of words. [?]

spathe (spāth) n. *Bot.* A large bract or pair of bracts sheathing a flower cluster, as a spadix. [< Gk. *spathē* broad sword]

spa·tial (spā'shəl) adj. Of, involving, occupying, or having the nature of space. [< L *spatium* space] —**spa·ti·al·i·ty** (spā'shē·al'ə·tē) n. —**spa'tial·ly** adv.

spat·ter (spat'ər) v.t. **1** To scatter in drops or splashes, as mud or paint. **2** To splash with such drops; bespatter. **3** To defame. —v.i. **4** To throw off drops or splashes. **5** To fall in a shower, as raindrops. —n. **1** The act of spattering or the condition of being spattered. **2** The mark or soiled place caused by spattering. **3** The sound of spattering. **4** A small amount or number. [? < OE *spatlian* spit out]

spat·ter·dash (spat'ər·dash') n. A knee-high legging worn as a protection from mud, esp. when riding.

spat·u·la (spach'oo·lə) n. A knifelike instrument with a dull, flexible, rounded blade, used to spread plaster, cake icing, etc. [L]

spav·in (spav'in) n. A laming disease of the hock joint of horses. [< OF *espavain*] —**spav'ined** adj.

spawn (spôn) n. **1** The eggs of fishes, amphibians, mollusks, etc., esp. in masses. **2** A great number of offspring: usu. derisive. **3** Any large quantity or yield. —v.i. **1** To produce spawn; deposit eggs or roe. **2** To come forth as or like spawn. —v.t. **3** To produce (spawn). **4** To give rise to; originate. [< L *expandere* expand]

spay (spā) v.t. To remove the ovaries from (a female animal). [< OF *espeer* cut with a sword]

S.P.C.A. Society for the Prevention of Cruelty to Animals.

speak (spēk) v. **spoke** (*Archaic* **spake**), **spo·ken** (*Archaic* **spoke**), **speak·ing** v.i. **1** To employ the vocal organs in ordinary speech; utter words. **2** To express or convey ideas, opinions, etc., in or as in speech: Actions *speak* louder than words. **3** To make a speech; deliver an address. **4** To converse. **5** To make a sound; also, to bark, as a dog. —v.t. **6** To express or make known in or as in speech. **7** To utter in speech: to *speak* words of love. **8** To use or be capable of using (a language) in conversation. —**so to speak** In a manner of speaking. —**speak for 1** To speak in behalf of; represent officially. **2** To reserve or request: usu. used in the passive voice: Has that appointment been *spoken for?* [< OE *specan*] —**speak'a·ble** adj.

speak·eas·y (spēk'ē'zē) n. pl. **·eas·ies** A place where liquor is sold contrary to law, esp. such a place in the U.S. during prohibition.

speak·er (spē'kər) n. **1** One who speaks, esp. in public. **2** The presiding officer in a legislative body. **3** LOUDSPEAKER.

speak·ing (spē'king) adj. **1** Able to speak. **2** Of, pertaining to, or for speech. **3** Using a specified language: a French-*speaking* colony. **4** Vividly lifelike: the *speaking* image of his father. —n. **1** The act or technique of one who speaks. **2** Something spoken. —**speak'ing·ly** adv.

spear (spir) n. **1** A weapon consisting of a pointed head on a long shaft. **2** A similar instrument, barbed and usu. forked, as for spearing fish. **3** A leaf or slender stalk, as of grass. —v.t. **1** To pierce or capture with or as with a spear. —v.i. **2** To pierce or wound with or as with a spear. **3** To send forth spears, as a plant. [< OE *spere*] —**spear'er** n.

spear·head (spir'hed') n. **1** The point of a spear or lance. **2** The person, group, etc., that leads an action or undertaking. —v.t. To be in the lead of (an attack, etc.).

spear·man (spir'mən) n. pl. **·men** (-mən) A man armed with a spear. Also **spears'man.**

spear·mint (spir'mint') n. An aromatic herb similar to peppermint.

spe·cial (spesh'əl) adj. **1** Out of the ordinary; uncommon; unique; different: a *special* problem. **2** Designed for or assigned to a specific purpose, occasion, etc.: a *special* permit. **3** Memorable; notable: a very *special* occasion. **4** Extra or additional: a *special* bonus. **5** Intimate; esteemed; beloved: a *special* favorite. —n. **1** Something made, detailed for, or appropriated to a specific service, occasion, etc., as a train, newspaper edition, sales item, featured dish, etc. **2** A television show produced and scheduled for a single presentation only. [< L *species* kind, species] —**spe·cial·ly** adv. —**Syn.** adj. **1** peculiar, particular, distinctive, singular, original, unusual. **3** noteworthy, unforgettable, extraordinary, exceptional, rare.

special delivery Mail delivery by special courier for an additional fee.

Special Drawing Rights International monetary credit that can be drawn by member nations from the International Monetary Fund to be used in lieu of gold.

spe·cial·ist (spesh′əl·ist) *n.* A person devoted to one line of study, occupation, or professional work. —**spe′cial·ism** *n.* —**spe′cial·is′tic** *adj.*

spe·ci·al·i·ty (spesh′ē·al′ə·tē) *n. pl.* **·ties** *Chiefly Brit.* SPE-CIALTY.

spe·cial·ize (spesh′əl·īz) *v.* **·ized, ·iz·ing** *v.i.* **1** To concentrate on one particular activity or subject. **2** To take on a form or forms adapted to special conditions or functions. —*v.t.* **3** To make specific or particular; particularize. **4** To adapt for or direct toward some special use or purpose. *Brit. sp.* **·ise.** —**spe′cial·i·za′tion** *n.*

spe·cial·ty (spesh′əl·tē) *n. pl.* **·ties** **1** Something, as a trade, study, activity, etc., in which one specializes. **2** A product or article possessing a special quality, excellence, character, etc.: Fish is the *specialty* of this restaurant. **3** A special mark, quality, or characteristic. **4** The state of being special.

spe·cie (spē′shē) *n.* Coined money; coin. —**in specie 1** In coin. **2** In kind. [< L (*in) specie* (in) kind]

spe·cies (spē′shēz, -shiz) *n. pl.* **·cies 1** A category of animals or plants subordinate to a genus and comprising similar organisms usu. with the capacity of interbreeding only among themselves. **2** A group of individuals or objects having in common certain attributes and designated by a common name. **3** A kind; sort; variety; form. **4** *Eccl.* **a** The visible form of bread or of wine retained by the eucharistic elements after consecration. **b** The consecrated elements of the Eucharist. [L, kind]

spe·cif·ic (spi·sif′ik) *adj.* **1** Distinctly and plainly set forth; explicit. **2** Special; definite; particular; distinct: He took no *specific* action. **3** Belonging to or distinguishing a species. **4** Having some distinct medicinal or pathological property: a *specific* germ. **5** Designating a particular property, composition, ratio, or quantity serving to identify a given substance or phenomenon: *specific* gravity. —*n.* **1** Anything adapted to effect a specific result. **2** A medicine affecting a specific condition or pathogen. **3** *Usu. pl.* A particular item or detail. [< L *species* kind + -FIC] —**spe·cif′i·cal·ly** *adv.* —**spec′i·fic·i·ty** (spes′ə·fis′ə·tē) *n.*

spec·i·fi·ca·tion (spes′ə·fə·kā′shən) *n.* **1** The act of specifying. **2** A definite and complete statement, as in a contract; also, one detail in such a statement. **3** In patent law, the detailed description of an invention. **4** *Usu. pl.* A description of dimensions, types of material, capabilities, etc., of a device, building project, etc. **5** A single item in such a description.

specific gravity The ratio of the mass of a substance to that of an equal volume of some standard substance, water in the case of solids and liquids, and air or hydrogen in the case of gases.

spec·i·fy (spes′ə·fī) *v.t.* **·fied, ·fy·ing 1** To mention or state in full and explicit detail. **2** To include as an item in a specification.

spec·i·men (spes′ə·mən) *n.* **1** A person or thing regarded as representative of a class. **2** A sample, as of blood, sputum, etc., for laboratory analysis. **3** *Informal* A person of a specified type or character. [< L *specere* look at]

spe·cious (spē′shəs) *adj.* Apparently good, right, logical, etc., but actually without merit or foundation: *specious* reasoning. [< L *speciosus* fair] —**spe′cious·ly** *adv.* —**spe′cious·ness** *n.*

speck (spek) *n.* **1** A small spot or stain. **2** Any very small thing; particle. —*v.t.* To mark with specks. [< OE *specca*]

speck·le (spek′əl) *v.t.* **·led, ·ling** To mark with specks. —*n.* A speck.

specs (speks) *n.pl. Informal* **1** EYEGLASSES. **2** Specifications. See SPECIFICATION (def. 4).

spec·ta·cle (spek′tə·kəl) *n.* **1** A grand or unusual sight or public display, as a pageant, parade, natural phenome-

non, etc. **2** An embarrassing or deplorable exhibition. **3** *pl.* EYEGLASSES. [< L *specere* see] —**spec′ta·cled** (-kəld) *adj.*

spec·tac·u·lar (spek·tak′yə·lər) *adj.* Of or like a spectacle; unusually wonderfully, exciting, etc. —*n.* Something spectacular, esp. a lavish television production. —**spec·tac′u·lar·ly** *adv.* —**spec·tac′u·lar′i·ty** (-lar′ə·tē) *n.*

spec·ta·tor (spek′tā·tər, spek·tā′-) *n.* **1** One who beholds; an eyewitness. **2** One who is present at and views a show, game, spectacle, etc. [L < *spectare* look at]

spec·ter (spek′tər) *n.* A phantom; apparition. Also *esp. Brit.* **spec′tre.** [< L *spectrum* vision]

spec·tra (spek′trə) A *pl.* of SPECTRUM.

spec·tral (spek′trəl) *adj.* **1** Pertaining to a specter; ghostly. **2** Pertaining to a spectrum. —**spec′tral·ly** *adv.*

spectro- *combining form* Spectrum: *spectroscope.*

spec·tro·gram (spek′trə·gram) *n.* A photograph or other record of a spectrum.

spec·tro·graph (spek′trə·graf, -gräf) *n.* A device for displaying and recording spectra.

spec·tro·scope (spek′trə·skōp) *n.* An instrument for sorting out into a spectrum the wavelengths in a beam of light or other radiation. —**spec′tro·scop′ic** (-skop′ik) or **·i·cal** *adj.* —**spec′tro·scop′i·cal·ly** *adv.*

spec·tros·co·py (spek·tros′kə·pē) *n.* **1** The science treating of the phenomena observed with the spectroscope. **2** The art of using the spectroscope.

spec·trum (spek′trəm) *n. pl.* **·tra** (-trə) or **·trums 1** The continuous band of colors observed when a beam of white light is diffracted, as by a prism, according to wavelength, ranging from red, the longest visible rays, to violet, the shortest. **2** Any array of radiant energy ordered according to a varying characteristic, as frequency, wavelength, etc. **3** A band of wave frequencies: the radio *spectrum.* **4** A series or range within limits: a wide *spectrum* of activities. [L, a vision]

spec·u·late (spek′yə·lāt) *v.i.* **·lat·ed, ·lat·ing 1** To weigh mentally or conjecture; ponder; theorize. **2** To make a risky investment with hope of gain. [< L *speculari* look at, examine] —**spec′u·la′tor** *n.* —**spec′u·la·to′ry** (-lə·tôr′ē, -tō′-rē) *adj.* —**Syn. 1** guess, presume, surmise, venture, hazard.

spec·u·la·tion (spek′yə·lā′shən) *n.* **1** The act of speculating or conjecturing. **2** A theory or conjecture. **3** An investment or business transaction involving risk with hope of large profit.

spec·u·la·tive (spek′yə·lə·tiv, -lā′tiv) *adj.* **1** Of, pertaining to, engaged in, or given to speculation or conjecture. **2** Strictly theoretical; not practical. **3** Engaging in or involving financial speculation. **4** Risky; doubtful. —**spec′u·la·tive·ly** *adv.* —**spec′u·la·tive·ness** *n.*

spec·u·lum (spek′yə·ləm) *n. pl.* **·la** (-lə) or **·lums 1** A mirror usu. of polished metal, used for telescope reflectors, etc. **2** *Med.* An instrument that dilates a passage of the body for examination. [L, mirror < *specere* see]

sped (sped) A *p.t.* & *p.p.* of SPEED.

speech (spēch) *n.* **1** The act of speaking; faculty of expressing thought and emotion by spoken words. **2** The power or capability of speaking. **3** That which is spoken; conversation; talk. **4** A public address. **5** A characteristic manner of speaking. **6** A particular language, idiom, or dialect: American *speech.* **7** The study or art of oral communication. [< OE *specan* speak]

speech·i·fy (spē′chə·fī) *v.i.* **·fied, ·fy·ing** To make speeches: often used derisively. —**speech′i·fi′er** *n.*

speech·less (spēch′lis) *adj.* **1** Temporarily unable to speak because of physical weakness, strong emotion, etc.: *speechless* with rage. **2** Mute; dumb. **3** Silent; reticent. **4** Inexpressible in words: *speechless* joy. —**speech′less·ly** *adv.* —**speech′less·ness** *n.*

speed (spēd) *n.* **1** Rapidity of motion; swiftness. **2** Rate of motion: *speed* of light. **3** Rate or rapidity of any action or performance. **4** A transmission gear in a motor vehicle. **5** *Informal* A characteristic interest, life style, etc. **6** *Slang* An amphetamine drug, esp. methamphetamine. **7** *Archaic* Good luck; success: They wished him good *speed.* —*v.* **sped** or **speed·ed, speed·ing** *v.i.* **1** To move or go with speed. **2** To exceed the legal driving limit, esp. on highways. —*v.t.* 3 To promote the forward progress of: *speed* a letter. 4 To cause to move or go with speed. 5 To promote the success of. 6 To wish Godspeed to: *Speed* the parting guest. —**speed up** To accelerate in speed or action. —*adj.* Of, pertaining to, or indicating speed. [< OE *spēd* power]

speed·boat (spēd′bōt′) *n.* A motorboat capable of high speed.

speed·er (spē′dər) *n.* A person or thing that speeds; esp., a motorist who drives at a speed exceeding a safe or legal limit.

speed·om·e·ter (spi·dom′ə·tər) *n.* A device for indicating the speed of a vehicle.

speed·ster (spēd′stər) *n.* A speeder.

speed·up (spēd′up′) *n.* An acceleration in work, output, movement, etc.

speed·way (spēd′wā′) *n.* 1 A racetrack for automobiles or motorcycles. 2 A road for vehicles traveling at high speed.

speed·well (spēd′wel) *n.* Any of various herbs of the figwort family, usu. bearing blue or white flowers.

speed·y (spē′dē) *adj.* **speed·i·er, speed·i·est** 1 Characterized by speed. 2 Without delay. —**speed′i·ly** *adv.* —**speed′·i·ness** *n.*

spe·le·ol·o·gy (spē′lē·ol′ə·jē, spel′ē-) *n.* 1 The scientific study of caves. 2 The exploration of caves. [< L *spelaeum* a cave + -LOGY] —**spe′le·o·log′i·cal** (-ə·loj′i·kəl) *adj.* —**spe′le·ol′o·gist** *n.*

spell[1] (spel) *v.* **spelled** or **spelt, spell·ing** *v.t.* 1 To pronounce or write the letters of (a word); esp., to do so correctly. 2 To form or be the letters of: C-a-t *spells* cat. 3 To signify; mean. —*v.i.* 4 To form words out of letters, esp. correctly. —**spell out** 1 To read each letter of, usu. with difficulty. 2 To puzzle out and learn. 3 To make explicit and detailed. [< OF *espeler*]

spell[2] (spel) *n.* 1 A magical word or formula. 2 A state of enchantment. 3 An irresistible power or fascination. [< OE, story]

spell[3] (spel) *n.* 1 *Informal* A period of time, usu. of short duration. 2 *Informal* A continuing type of weather. 3 *Informal* A short distance. 4 *Informal* A fit of illness, debility, etc. 5 A turn of duty in relief of another. 6 A period of work or employment. —*v.t.* 1 To relieve temporarily from some work or duty. 2 *Austral.* To give a rest to, as a horse. —*v.i.* 3 *Austral.* To take a rest. [< OE *gespelia* a substitute]

spell·bind (spel′bīnd′) *v.t.* **·bound, ·bind·ing** To bind or enthrall, as if by a spell. —**spell′bind·er** *n.*

spell·bound (spel′bound′) *adj.* Enthralled or fascinated by or as by a spell. —**Syn.** astonished, amazed, aghast, agog, bewitched, enchanted, charmed.

spell·er (spel′ər) *n.* 1 One who spells. 2 A spelling book.

spell·ing (spel′ing) *n.* 1 The act of one who spells. 2 The art of correct spelling; orthography. 3 The way in which a word is spelled.

spelling bee A spelling competition.

spelt[1] (spelt) A *p.t. & p.p.* of SPELL[1].

spelt[2] (spelt) *n.* A species of wheat. [< OE]

spe·lun·ker (spē·lung′kər) *n.* An enthusiast in the exploration and study of caves; a speleologist. [< L *spelunca* a cave]

spend (spend) *v.* **spent, spend·ing** *v.t.* 1 To pay out or disburse (money). 2 To expend by degrees; use up. 3 To apply or devote, as thought or effort, to some activity, purpose, etc. 4 To pass: to *spend* one's life in jail. 5 To use wastefully; squander. —*v.i.* 6 To pay out or disburse money, etc. [< OE *aspendan*] —**spend′er** *n.*

spend·thrift (spend′thrift′) *n.* One who is wastefully lavish of money. —*adj.* Excessively lavish; prodigal.

spent (spent) *p.t. & p.p.* of SPEND. —*adj.* 1 Worn out or exhausted. 2 Deprived of force.

sperm[1] (spûrm) *n.* 1 The male fertilizing fluid; semen. 2 A male reproductive cell; spermatozoon. [< Gk. *sperma* a seed]

sperm[2] (spûrm) *n.* 1 SPERM WHALE. 2 SPERMACETI. 3 SPERM OIL.

-sperm *combining form Bot.* A seed (of a specified kind): *gymnosperm.* [< Gk. *sperma* a seed]

sper·ma·ce·ti (spûr′mə·sē′tē, -set′ē) *n.* A white, waxy substance separated from the oil contained in the head of

the sperm whale, used for making candles, ointments, etc. [< L *sperma ceti* seed of a whale]

sper·mat·ic (spûr·mat′ik) *adj.* Of or pertaining to sperm or the male sperm-producing gland.

sper·ma·to·phyte (spûr′mə·tə·fīt′) *n.* Any seed-bearing plant; an angiosperm or a gymnosperm. [< Gk. *sperma* seed + *phylos* plant] —**sper′ma·to·phyt′ic** (-fit′ik) *adj.*

sper·ma·to·zo·on (spûr′mə·tə·zō′on) *n. pl.* **·zo·a** (-zō′ə) A male reproductive cell of an animal, which carries half the complement of genetic material normal for its species. [< Gk. *sperma* seed + *zōion* an animal] —**sper′ma·to·zo′al, sper′ma·to·zo′an, sper′ma·to·zo′ic** *adj.*

sperm oil A pale yellow lubricating oil obtained from the sperm whale.

sperm whale A large, toothed whale of warm seas, having a huge truncate head containing a reservoir of sperm oil.

Sperm whale

spew (spyōō) *v.i.* 1 To throw up; vomit. 2 To come or issue forth. —*v.t.* 1 To throw up; vomit. 2 To eject or send forth. —*n.* That which is spewed. [< OE *spīwan*]

sp. gr. specific gravity.

sphag·num (sfag′nəm) *n.* 1 Any of a genus of whitish gray mosses; peat moss. 2 This moss in dried form, used by florists for potting plants, etc. [< Gk. *sphagnos* kind of moss] —**sphag′nous** *adj.*

sphe·noid (sfē′noid) *n.* An irregular, wedge-shaped bone forming part of the orbit. —*adj.* Wedge-shaped. [< Gk. *sphēn* wedge] —**sphe·noi·dal** (sfi·noid′l) *adj.* •See SKULL.

sphere (sfir) *n.* 1 A round body in which every point on its surface is equidistant from the center; globe. 2 A planet, sun, star, etc. 3 CELESTIAL SPHERE. 4 The apparent outer dome of the sky. 5 The field or place of activity, experience, influence, etc.; scope; province. 6 Social rank or position. —*v.t.* **sphered, spher·ing** 1 To place in or as in a sphere; encircle. 2 To set among the celestial spheres. 3 To make spherical. [< Gk. *sphaira* a ball]

-sphere *combining form* Denoting an enveloping spherical mass: *atmosphere.*

spher·i·cal (sfer′i·kəl) *adj.* 1 Shaped like a sphere; globular. 2 Pertaining to a sphere or spheres. Also **spher′ic.** —**spher′i·cal·ly** *adv.* —**spher′i·cal·ness** *n.*

sphe·roid (sfir′oid) *n.* A body having approximately the form of a sphere; an ellipsoid. —**sphe·roi′dal** (sfi·roid′l), **sphe·roi′dic** or **-di·cal** *adj.* —**sphe·roi′dal·ly** *adv.*

sphinc·ter (sfingk′tər) *n. Anat.* A ring of muscle serving to open and close an opening in the body. [< Gk. *sphingein* to close] —**sphinc′ter·al** *adj.*

sphinx (sfingks) *n. pl.* **sphinx·es** or **sphin·ges** (sfin′jēz) 1 *Egypt. Myth* A wingless monster with a lion's body and the head of a man, a ram, or a hawk. 2 *Gk. Myth. Usu. cap.* A winged monster with a woman's head and breasts and a lion's body, that destroyed those unable to guess her riddle. 3 A mysterious or enigmatical person. [< Gk.]

Sphinx *def. 2*

sphyg·mo·ma·nom·e·ter (sfig′mō·mə·nom′ə·tər) *n.* An instrument for measuring blood pressure. Also **sphyg·mom′e·ter** (-mom′ə·tər). [< Gk. *sphygmos* pulse + MANOMETER]

spi·cate (spī′kāt) *adj.* 1 Arranged in spikes: said of flowers. 2 Having a spur, as the legs of some birds. Also **spi′·cat·ed.** [< L *spica* spike]

spice (spīs) *n.* 1 An aromatic vegetable substance, as cinnamon, cloves, etc., used for flavoring. 2 Such substances collectively. 3 That which gives zest or adds interest. 4 An aromatic odor; an agreeable perfume. —*v.t.* **spiced, spic·ing** 1 To season with spice. 2 To add zest or piquancy to. [< L *species* kind] —**spic′er** *n.*

spice·bush (spīs′bŏŏsh′) *n.* An aromatic deciduous shrub related to laurel. Also **spice′wood′** (-wŏŏd′).

spick-and-span (spik′ən·span′) *adj.* **1** Neat and clean. **2** Perfectly new, or looking as if new. Also **spic′-and-span′**. [Var. of SPIKE¹ + ON *spánn* chip]

spic·ule (spik′yōōl) *n.* **1** A small, slender, sharp-pointed body; a spikelet. **2** *Zool.* One of the small, hard, needlelike growths supporting the soft tissues of certain invertebrates, as sponges. Also **spic·u·la** (spik′yə·lə). [< L *spicum* point, spike] —**spic′u·lar, spic′u·late** (-lāt, -lit) *adj.*

spic·u·lum (spik′yə·ləm) *n. pl.* **·la** (-lə) **1** SPICULE. **2** *Zool.* A small, pointed organ, as a spine of a sea urchin. [L]

spic·y (spī′sē) *adj.* **spic·i·er, spic·i·est** **1** Containing, flavored, or fragrant with spices. **2** Producing spices. **3** Full of spirit and zest; lively. **4** Somewhat improper or risqué. —**spic′i·ly** *adv.* —**spic′i·ness** *n.*

spi·der (spī′dər) *n.* **1** Any of numerous wingless arachnids capable of spinning silk into webs for the capture of prey. **2** A long-handled iron frying pan, often having legs. **3** Any of various devices with radiating, leglike projections. [< OE *spīthra*] —**spi′der·y** *adj.*

spider crab Any of various ocean crabs with long legs and spiny growths on the carapace.

Garden spider

spider monkey An arboreal Central and South American monkey with very long, slender limbs and a long prehensile tail.

spi·der·wort (spī′dər·wûrt′) *n.* Any of several plants with grasslike leaves and usu. blue, three-petaled flowers.

spiel (spēl) *Slang n.* An informal but purposeful speech or talk, usu. rehearsed, as by a politician or salesman. —*v.i.* To deliver a spiel. [< G *spielen* to play]

spi·er (spī′ər) *n.* One who spies.

spif·fy (spif′ē) *adj.* **·fi·er, ·fi·est** *Slang* Smartly dressed; spruce. —**spif′fi·ness** *n.* [?]

spig·ot (spig′ət, spik′-) *n.* **1** A plug for the bunghole of a cask. **2** A turning plug or valve fitting into a faucet; also, the faucet itself. [ME *spigote*]

spike¹ (spīk) *n.* **1** A very large, thick nail. **2** A slender, pointed piece of metal, as used along the top of an iron fence. **3** A projecting, pointed piece of metal in the soles of shoes to keep the wearer from slipping. **4** A very high, slender heel on a woman's shoe. **5** A straight, unbranched antler, as of a young deer. —*v.t.* **spiked, spik·ing 1** To fasten with spikes. **2** To set or provide with spikes. **3** To block; put a stop to. **4** To pierce with or impale on a spike. **5** *Informal* To add alcoholic liquor to. [ME] —**spik′er** *n.* —**spik′y** *adj.*

spike² (spīk) *n.* **1** An ear of corn, barley, wheat, or other grain. **2** *Bot.* A flower cluster in which the flowers are closely attached to the stalk. [< L *spica* ear of grain]

spike·let (spīk′lit) *n. Bot.* A small spike.

spike·nard (spīk′nərd, -närd) *n.* **1** An ancient fragrant and costly ointment. **2** A perennial East Indian herb of the valerian family yielding this ointment. [< L *spica* spike + *nardus* nard]

spile (spīl) *n.* **1** A large timber or stake driven into the ground as a foundation; a pile. **2** A wooden spigot or plug used in a cask. **3** A spout driven into a sugar-maple tree to lead the sap to a bucket. —*v.t.* **spiled, spil·ing 1** To pierce for and provide with a spile. **2** To drive spiles into. [< MDu., skewer]

spill¹ (spil) *v.* **spilled** or **spilt, spill·ing** *v.t.* **1** To allow or cause to fall or run out or over, as a liquid or a powder. **2** To shed, as blood. **3** *Naut.* To empty (a sail) of wind. **4** *Informal* To cause to fall, as from a horse. **5** *Informal* To divulge; make known, as a secret. —*v.i.* **6** To fall or run out or over: said of liquids, etc. —*n.* **1** The act of spilling. **2** That which is spilled. **3** *Informal* A fall to the ground, as from a horse or vehicle. **4** SPILLWAY. [< OE *spillan* destroy] —**spill′age, spill′er** *n.*

spill² (spil) *n.* **1** A slip of wood, or rolled strip of paper, used for lighting lamps, etc. **2** A splinter. **3** A slender peg, pin, or bar of wood, esp. for stopping up a hole. [Var. of SPILE¹]

spill·way (spil′wā′) *n.* A passageway in or about a dam

to release the water in a reservoir. **2** The paved upper surface of a dam over which surplus water escapes.

spilt (spilt) A *pt. & p.p.* of SPILL¹.

spin (spin) *v.* **spun, spin·ning** *v.t.* **1** To draw out and twist into threads; also, to draw out and twist fiber into (threads, yarn, etc.). **2** To make or produce (a web or cocoon) as if by spinning. **3** To tell, as a story or yarn. **4** To protract; prolong, as a story by additional details: with *out*. **5** To cause to whirl rapidly. —*v.i.* **6** To make thread or yarn. **7** To extrude filaments of a viscous substance from the body: said of spiders, etc. **8** To whirl rapidly; rotate. **9** To seem to be whirling, as from dizziness. **10** To move rapidly. —*n.* **1** An act or instance of spinning. **2** A rapid whirling. **3** Any rapid movement or action. **4** A ride, as in an automobile. **5** The uncontrolled, spiral descent of an airplane after a stall. [< OE *spinnan*]

spin·ach (spin′ich) *n.* **1** An edible garden plant of the goosefoot family. **2** Its edible leaves. [< Ar. *isbānah*]

spi·nal (spī′nəl) *adj.* **1** Of or pertaining to the spine or spinal cord. **2** Of or pertaining to spines or a spiny process.

spinal column A series of hollow, articulated bones that enclose the spinal cord and form the axis of the skeleton of a vertebrate animal.

spinal cord The thick, soft cord of nerve tissue enclosed by the spinal column.

spin·dle (spin′dəl) *n.* **1** In hand spinning, a notched, tapered rod used to twist into thread the fibers pulled from the distaff. **2** The slender rod in a spinning wheel by the rotation of which the thread is twisted and wound on a spool or bobbin on the same rod. **3** A small rod or pin bearing the bobbin of a spinning machine. **4** A rotating rod, pin, axis, arbor, or shaft, esp. when small and bearing something that rotates: the *spindle* of a lathe. **5** The tapering end of a vehicle axle that enters the hub. **6** A small shaft passing through the lock of a door and bearing the knobs or handles. **7** Any decorative, often tapered rod, used in the back of a chair, etc. **8** A needlelike rod mounted on a weighted base, for impaling bills, checks, etc. —*v.* **·dled, ·dling** *v.i.* **1** To grow into a long, slender stalk or body. —*v.t.* **2** To form into or as into a spindle. **3** To provide with a spindle. [< OE *spinel*]

spin·dle-leg·ged (spin′dəl·leg′id, -legd′) *adj.* Having long, slender legs. Also **spin′dle-shanked′** (-shangkt′).

spin·dle-legs (spin′dəl·legz′) *n.* **1** Long, slender legs. **2** *Informal* A person having long, slender legs. Also **spin′dle-shanks′** (-shangks′).

spin·dling (spind′ling) *adj.* SPINDLY.

spin·dly (spind′lē) *adj.* **·dli·er, ·dli·est** Of a slender, lanky growth or form, suggesting weakness.

spin·drift (spin′drift) *n.* Blown spray or scud. [Var. of SPOONDRIFT]

spine (spīn) *n.* **1** SPINAL COLUMN. **2** Any of various hard, pointed outgrowths on the bodies of certain animals, as the porcupine and starfish. **3** A thorny projection on the stems of certain plants, as the cactus. **4** The back of a bound book. **5** A projecting eminence or ridge. [< L *spina* spine, thorn]

spi·nel (spi·nel′, spin′əl) *n.* Any of various hard minerals, a red variety, the **ruby spinel**, being used as a gem. [< Ital. *spina* thorn]

spine·less (spīn′lis) *adj.* **1** Having no spine or backbone; invertebrate. **2** Lacking spines. **3** Having a very flexible backbone; limp. **4** Weak-willed; irresolute. —**spine′less·ness** *n.*

spin·et (spin′it) *n.* **1** A small harpsichord. **2** A small upright piano. **3** A small electronic organ. [< Ital. *spinetta*]

spin·na·ker (spin′ə·kər) *n. Naut.* A large jib-shaped sail set on the mainmast of a racing vessel, opposite the mainsail, and used when sailing before the wind. [?]

spin·ner (spin′ər) *n.* **1** One who or that which spins, as a spider or a machine. **2** In angling, a whirling spoon bait.

spin·ner·et (spin′ə·ret′) *n.* **1** An organ, as of spiders and silkworms, for spinning their silky threads. **2** A metal plate pierced with holes through which filaments of plastic material are forced, as in the making of rayon fibers.

spin·ning (spin′ing) *n.* **1** The action of converting fibers into thread or yarn. **2** The product of spinning. —*adj.* That spins or is used in the process of spinning.

spinning jenny A machine for spinning more than one strand of yarn at a time.

spinning wheel A former household implement for spinning yarn or thread, consisting of a rotating spindle operated by a treadle and flywheel.

spin-off (spin′ôf′, -of′) *n.* **1** A secondary product, application, or result derived from another product or activity; by-product: industrial *spin-offs* from military technological research. **2** The distribution by a corporation to its stockholders of stocks or assets obtained from a subsidiary company. Also **spin′off′**.

Spinning wheel

spi·nose (spī′nōs) *adj.* Bearing, armed with, or having spines. Also **spi·nous** (-nəs). —**spi′nose·ly** *adv.* —**spi·nos′i·ty** (-nos′ə·tē) *n.*

spin·ster (spin′stər) *n.* **1** A woman who has never married, esp. an elderly one. **2** A woman who spins; a spinner. [< SPIN + -STER] —**spin′ster·hood** *n.* —**spin′ster·ish** *adj.*

spin·y (spī′nē) *adj.* **spin·i·er, spin·i·est 1** Having spines; thorny. **2** Difficult; perplexing. —**spin′i·ness** *n.*

spiny anteater ECHIDNA.

spir·a·cle (spir′ə·kəl, spī′rə-) *n.* **1** Any of numerous external openings through which air enters the tracheae of insects, etc. **2** The blowhole of a cetacean. [< L *spiraculum* airhole]

spi·ral (spī′rəl) *adj.* **1** Winding about and constantly receding from or advancing toward a center. **2** Winding and advancing; helical. **3** Winding and rising in a spire, as some springs. **4** Continuously increasing or developing. — *n.* **1** *Geom.* Any plane curve formed by a point that moves around a fixed center at a distance that is always increasing. **2** A curve winding like a screw thread. **3** Something wound as a spiral or having a spiral shape. **4** A continuously developing increase or decrease: price *spirals.* —*v.* **·raled** or **·ralled, ·ral·ing** or **·ral·ling** *v.t.* **1** To cause to take a spiral form or course. —*v.i.* **2** To take a spiral form or course. **3** To increase or decrease continuously or sharply, as prices, costs, etc. [< L *spira* coil] —**spi′ral·ly** *adv.* • The use of the intransitive verb (def. 3) without any accompanying modifier almost always means "to increase," as *Prices spiraled in June.* If "to decrease" is meant, an adverb should be used to prevent ambiguity, as *Prices spiraled downward in June.*

spi·rant (spī′rənt) *n. & adj. Phonet.* FRICATIVE. [< L *spirare* breathe]

spire (spīr) *n.* **1** The tapering or pyramidal roof of a tower; also, a steeple. **2** A slender stalk or blade. **3** The summit or tapering end of anything. —*v.* **spired, spir·ing** *v.t.* **1** To furnish with a spire or spires. —*v.i.* **2** To shoot or point up in or as in a spire. **3** To put forth a spire or spires; sprout. [< OE *spīr* stem] —**spired** *adj.*

spi·re·a (spī·rē′ə) *n.* Any of a genus of ornamental shrubs of the rose family, having small, white or pink flowers. Also **spi·rae′a.** [< Gk. *speira* coil]

Spire

spir·it (spir′it) *n.* **1** The animating principle of life and energy in man and animals. **2** SOUL (def. 1). **3** That part of a human being characterized by intelligence, emotion, will, etc.; the mind. **4 a** A supernatural being without a material body, as an angel, demon, etc. **b** Such a being regarded as having a certain character, abode, etc.: an evil *spirit.* **c** A supernatural being regarded as having a visible form, power of speech, etc.; ghost; specter. **5** A state of mind; mood; disposition: low *spirits.* **6** Vivacity, energy, courage, positiveness, etc.: to have *spirit.* **7** A characteristic or prevailing feeling, attitude, motivation, quality, etc.: in the *spirit* of fun; the *spirit* of the Reformation. **8** A person regarded with reference to any specific activity, characteristic, or temper: a

blithe *spirit.* **9** True intent or meaning: the *spirit* of the law. **10** Ardent loyalty or devotion: school *spirit.* **11** *pl.* A strong alcoholic liquor or liquid obtained by distillation. **12** *Usu. pl.* A distilled extract: *spirits* of turpentine. **13** *Usu. pl.* A solution of a volatile principle in alcohol; essence: *spirits* of ammonia. —**the Spirit** HOLY GHOST. — *v.t.* **1** To carry off secretly or mysteriously: with *away, off,* etc. **2** To infuse with spirit or animation; inspirit. —*adj.* **1** Of or pertaining to ghosts or disembodied entities. **2** Operated by the burning of alcohol: a *spirit* lamp. [< L *spiritus* breathing, breath of a god]

spir·it·ed (spir′it·id) *adj.* **1** Full of spirit; lively; animated. **2** Having a specific characteristic, temper, etc.: *high-spirited, mean-spirited.* —**spir′it·ed·ly** *adv.* —**spir′it·ed·ness** *n.*

spir·it·less (spir′it·lis) *adj.* Lacking enthusiasm, energy, or courage. —**spir′it·less·ly** *adv.* —**spir′it·less·ness** *n.*

spirit level An instrument for indicating the horizontal or perpendicular by reference to the position of a bubble of air in a tube of liquid.

spir·it·ous (spir′i·təs) *adj.* SPIRITUOUS.

spir·it·u·al (spir′i·chōō·əl, -ich·əl) *adj.* **1** Of or pertaining to spirit, as distinguished from matter. **2** Of or consisting of spirit; incorporeal. **3** Of, pertaining to, or affecting the highest or purest moral or intellectual qualities of man; not earthly or sensual. **4** Sacred or religious; not lay or temporal. **5** Supernatural. —*n.* **1** Anything pertaining to spirit or to sacred matters. **2** A religious folk song originating among the Negroes of the s U.S. —**spir′it·u·al′i·ty, spir′it·u·al·ness** *n.* —**spir′it·u·al·ly** *adv.* —**Syn.** *adj.* **3** otherworldly, unworldly, unearthly, pure, heavenly, angelic.

spir·it·u·al·ism (spir′i·chōō·əl·iz′əm) *n.* **1** The belief that the spirits of the dead can communicate with the living, usu. through the agency of a person called a medium. **2** *Usu. cap.* A religious movement based on this belief. **3** A philosophy that identifies ultimate reality as basically spiritual. —**spir′it·u·al·ist** *n.* —**spir′it·u·al·is′tic** *adj.*

spir·it·u·al·ize (spir′i·chōō·əl·īz′, -ich·ə·līz′) *v.t.* **·ized, ·iz·ing 1** To make spiritual. **2** To treat as having a spiritual meaning or sense. *Brit. sp. ·ise.* —**spir′it·u·al·i·za′tion, spir′it·u·al·iz′er** *n.*

spir·i·tu·el (spir′i·chōō·el′, *Fr.* spē·rē·tü·el′) *adj.* Characterized by esprit, or wit, and by the higher and finer qualities of the mind generally. [F] —**spir′i·tu·elle′** *adj. Fem.*

spir·it·u·ous (spir′i·chōō·əs, -ich·əs, -ət·əs) *adj.* Containing alcohol, esp. distilled alcohol. —**spir′it·u·ous·ness** *n.*

spiro- *combining form* Spiral; coiled: *spirochete.* [< Gk. *speira* a coil]

spi·ro·chete (spī′rə·kēt) *n.* **1** Any of a genus of spiral-shaped bacteria usu. found in water. **2** Any similar microorganisms including those which cause syphilis, yaws, etc. Also **spi′ro·chaete.** [< Gk. *speira* coil + *chaitē* bristle] —**spi′ro·che′tal** *adj.* • See BACTERIUM.

spirt (spûrt) *n. & v.* SPURT.

spit¹ (spit) *v.* **spat** or **spit, spit·ting** *v.t.* **1** To eject (saliva, blood, etc.) from the mouth. **2** To throw off, eject, or utter by or as if by spitting: often with *out:* to *spit* out an oath. **3** To light, as a fuse. —*v.i.* **4** To eject saliva from the mouth. **5** To make a hissing noise, as an angry cat. **6** To fall in scattered drops or flakes, as rain or snow. —**spit on** *Informal* To treat with contempt. —*n.* **1** Spittle; saliva. **2** An act of spitting or expectorating. **3** A frothy, spitlike secretion of a spittle insect; also, a spittle insect. **4** A light, scattered fall of snow or rain. **5** *Informal* SPITTING IMAGE. [< OE *spittan*] —**spit′ter** *n.*

spit² (spit) *n.* **1** A pointed rod on which meat is skewered and roasted before a fire. **2** A point of low land, or a long, narrow shoal, extending into the water. —*v.t.* **spit·ted, spit·ting** To transfix or impale with or as with a spit. [< OE *spitu*]

spit·ball (spit′bôl′) *n.* **1** Paper chewed in the mouth and shaped into a ball for use as a missile. **2** In baseball, an illegal pitch of a ball moistened on one side with saliva, etc.

spite (spīt) *n.* **1** Malicious bitterness or resentment, usu. resulting in mean or vicious acts. **2** That which is done in spite. —**in spite of** (or **spite of**) In defiance of; notwithstanding. —*v.t.* **spit·ed, spit·ing** To show one's spite toward; vex maliciously; thwart. [Short for DESPITE] —**spite′ful** *adj.* —**spite′ful·ly** *adv.* —**spite′ful·ness** *n.*

spit·fire (spit′fīr′) *n.* A quick-tempered person.

spitting image *Informal* An exact likeness or counterpart. Also **spit and image.**

spit·tle (spit′l) *n.* 1 SALIVA. 2 SPIT¹ *n.* (def. 3). [< OE *spātl*]

spittle insect Any of various jumping insects whose nymphs excrete frothy matter.

spit·toon (spi-tōōn′) *n.* A receptacle for spit; a cuspidor.

spitz (spitz) *n.* One of a breed of small dogs with a tapering muzzle; a Pomeranian. Also **spitz dog.** [G, pointed]

spiv (spiv) *n.* *Brit. Informal* A flashy chiseler, sharper, or one who lives by his wits. [?]

splash (splash) *v.t.* 1 To dash or spatter (a liquid, etc.) about. 2 To spatter, wet, or soil with a liquid dashed about. 3 To make with splashes: to *splash* one's way. 4 To decorate or mark with or as with splashed colors. 5 To display prominently: His name was *splashed* all over the front page. —*v.i.* 6 To make a splash or splashes. 7 To move, fall, or strike with a splash or splashes. —*n.* 1 The act or noise of splashing liquid. 2 Something splashed, as a spot of liquid. 3 A small area or spot of color, light, etc. 4 A small amount; dash: a *splash* of bitters. 5 A brilliant or ostentatious display. —**make a splash** *Informal* To attract notice or become conspicuous, usu. briefly. [Var. of PLASH] —**splash′er** *n.* —**splash′y** *adj.* (·i·er, ·i·est)

splash·down (splash′doun′) *n.* The landing of a spacecraft, or a part of it, in the seas following its flight.

splat (splat) *n.* A thin, broad piece of wood, as that forming the middle of a chair back. [?]

splat·ter (splat′ər) *v.t. & v.i.* To spatter or splash. —*n.* A spatter; splash. [Blend of SPLASH and SPATTER]

splay (splā) *adj.* 1 Spread or turned outward. 2 Clumsily formed; ungainly. —*n.* *Archit.* A slanted surface or beveled edge. —*v.t.* 1 To make with a splay. 2 To open to sight; spread out. —*v.i.* 3 To spread out; open. 4 To slant; slope. [Var. of DISPLAY]

splay·foot (splā′fōōt′) *n.* 1 Abnormal flatness and turning outward of a foot or feet. 2 A foot so affected. —**splay′-foot′ed** *adj.*

spleen (splēn) *n.* *Anat.* 1 A highly vascular, ductless organ near the stomach of most vertebrates, which modifies, filters, and stores blood. 2 Ill temper; spitefulness: to vent one's *spleen.* [< Gk. *splēn*]

spleen·ful (splēn′fəl) *adj.* Irritable; peevish; ill-tempered. Also **spleen′ish, spleen′y.** —**spleen′ful·ly** *adv.*

splen·did (splen′did) *adj.* 1 Magnificent; imposing. 2 Conspicuously great or illustrious; glorious: a *splendid* achievement. 3 Giving out or reflecting brilliant light; shining. 4 *Informal* Very good; excellent: a *splendid* offer. [< L *splendere* to shine] —**splen′did·ly** *adv.* —**splen′did·ness** *n.* —**Syn.** 1 majestic, dazzling, sublime, superb, grand. 2 outstanding, renowned, celebrated, marvelous.

splen·dif·er·ous (splen·dif′ər·əs) *adj.* *Informal* Exhibiting great splendor; very magnificent: a facetious usage.

splen·dor (splen′dər) *n.* 1 Exceeding brillance or brightness. 2 Magnificence; greatness; grandeur. *Brit. sp.* **·dour.** —**splen′dor·ous, splen′drous** *adj.*

sple·net·ic (spli-net′ik) *adj.* Fretfully spiteful; peevish; irritable. —*n.* A peevish person. —**sple·net′i·cal·ly** *adv.*

splen·ic (splen′ik, splē′nik) *adj.* Of or pertaining to the spleen.

splice (splīs) *v.t.* **spliced, splic·ing** 1 To unite, as two ropes or parts of a rope, so as to form one continuous piece, by intertwining the strands. 2 To connect, as timbers, by beveling, scarfing, or overlapping at the ends. 3 *Slang* To join in marriage. —*n.* A joining or joint made by splicing. [< MDu. *splissen*] —**splic′er** *n.*

splint (splint) *n.* 1 SPLINTER. 2 A thin, flexible strip of split wood used for basket-making, chair bottoms, etc. 3 An appliance for supporting or immobilizing a part of the body. —

Splices
a. cut. b, c. long.

v.t. To confine, support, or brace, as a fractured limb, with or as with splints. [< MDu. *splinte*]

splin·ter (splin′tər) *n.* 1 A thin, sharp piece of wood, glass, metal, etc., split or torn off lengthwise; a sliver. 2 SPLINTER GROUP. —*v.t. & v.i.* 1 To split into thin sharp pieces or fragments; shatter; shiver. 2 To separate into smaller groups or factions. [< MDu.] —**splin′ter·y** *adj.*

splinter group A group or faction that has broken away from a parent group or organization, usu. because of disagreements.

split (split) *v.* **split, split·ting** *v.t.* 1 To separate into two or more parts by or as by force. 2 To break or divide lengthwise or along the grain. 3 To divide or separate: The mountains *split* the state down the middle. 4 To divide and distribute by portions or shares. 5 To divide into groups or factions. 6 To cast (a vote) for candidates of different parties. 7 To act upon as if by splitting or breaking: Thunder *split* the air. —*v.i.* 8 To break apart or divide lengthwise or along the grain. 9 To become divided through disagreement, etc. 10 To share something with others. 11 *Slang* To leave quickly or abruptly. —**split off** 1 To break off by splitting. 2 To separate by or as by splitting. —**split up** 1 To separate into parts and distribute. 2 To cease association; separate. —*n.* 1 The act of splitting. 2 The result of splitting, as a crack, tear, rent, etc. 3 A separation into factions or groups, usu. because of disagreements. 4 A sliver; splinter. 5 A share or portion, as of loot or booty. 6 A small, usu. six-ounce, bottle of wine, soft drink, etc. 7 A wooden strip, as of osier, used in weaving baskets. 8 A confection made of a sliced banana, ice cream, syrup, chopped nuts, and whipped cream. 9 A single thickness of a skin or hide split horizontally. 10 In bowling, the position of two or more pins left standing on such spots that a spare is nearly impossible. 11 An acrobatic trick in which the legs are fully extended to the front and back and at right angles to the body. 12 *Slang* A quick departure. —*adj.* 1 Divided or separated longitudinally or along the grain. 2 Divided, as to agreement, unanimity, etc.: a *split* ballot; a *split* decision. [< MDu. *splitten*] —**split′ter** *n.*

split infinitive A verbal phrase in which the sign of the infinitive "to" is separated from its verb by an intervening word, usu. an adverb, as in "to quickly return." ● Although this construction is often condemned by purists, it is sometimes justified to avoid ambiguity or awkwardness.

split-lev·el (split′lev′əl) *adj.* Designating a type of dwelling in which the floors of adjoining parts are at different levels, connected by short flights of stairs. —*n.* A split-level dwelling.

split pea A dried, hulled pea that has split naturally into two parts, used mainly for soup.

split personality A psychological condition in which a person intermittently exhibits traits, mannerisms, attitudes, etc., of two or more unrelated personalities.

split second A very small instant of time. —**split′-sec′-ond** *adj.*

split ticket A ballot on which the voter has distributed his votes among candidates of different parties.

split·ting (split′ing) *adj.* Acute or extreme in kind or degree: a *splitting* headache.

splotch (sploch) *n.* A spot or daub, as of ink, etc. —*v.t.* To soil or mark with a splotch or splotches. [?] —**splotch′y** *adj.*

splurge (splûrj) *Informal n.* 1 An ostentatious display. 2 An extravagant expenditure. —*v.i.* **splurged, splurg·ing** 1 To show off; be ostentatious. 2 To spend money lavishly or wastefully. [?]

splut·ter (splut′ər) *v.i.* 1 To make a series of slight, explosive sounds, or throw off small particles, as meat frying in fat. 2 To speak hastily, confusedly, or incoherently, as from surprise or indignation. —*v.t.* 3 To utter excitedly or confused; sputter. 4 To spatter or bespatter. —*n.* A spluttering noise or utterance. [Blend of SPLASH and SPUTTER] —**splut′ter·er** *n.*

spoil (spoil) *v.* **spoiled** or **spoilt, spoil·ing** *v.t.* 1 To impair or destroy the value, beauty, enjoyment, etc., of.

2 To weaken or impair the character or personality of, esp. by overindulgence. —*v.i.* **3** To lose normal or useful qualities; specifically, to become tainted or decayed, as food. —*n.* **1** *Usu. pl.* Plunder seized by violence; booty; loot. **2** *Usu. pl.* The jobs in government awarded by a winning political party to its faithful supporters. **3** An object of plunder. **4** Material removed in digging. [< L *spolium* booty] —**spoil′er** *n.* —**Syn.** *v.* **1** damage, injure, harm, mar, mutilate, disfigure, maim, botch, bungle. **2** indulge, humor. **3** decay, decompose, mold, rot, putrefy.

spoil·age (spoi′lij) *n.* **1** The act or process of spoiling. **2** Something spoiled. **3** Waste or loss due to spoilage.

spoils·man (spoilz′mən) *n. pl.* **·men** (-mən) One who works for a political party for spoils.

spoil·sport (spoil′spôrt′, -spōrt′) *n.* A person who spoils the pleasures of others.

spoils system The practice of giving public offices or other awards to supporters of a victorious political party.

spoke¹ (spōk) *n.* **1** One of the members of a wheel which brace the rim by connecting it to the hub. **2** One of the radial handles of a ship's steering wheel. **3** A rung of a ladder. —*v.t.* **spoked, spok·ing** To provide with spokes. [< OE *spāca*]

spoke² (spōk) *p.t.* & a *p.p.* of SPEAK.

spo·ken (spō′kən) *p.p.* of SPEAK. —*adj.* **1** Uttered as opposed to written. **2** Having a specified kind of speech: *smooth-spoken.*

spoke·shave (spōk′shāv′) *n.* A wheelwright's tool having a blade set between two handles, used with a drawing motion in rounding and smoothing wooden surfaces.

spokes·man (spōks′mən) *n. pl.* **·men** (-mən) One who speaks in the name and on behalf of another or others. — **spokes′wom′an** (-wŏŏm′ən) *n. Fem.*

spo·li·a·tion (spō′lē·ā′shən) *n.* **1** The act of plundering or robbing. **2** The act of spoiling or damaging. [< L *spoliare* despoil] —**spo′li·a′tor** *n.*

spon·dee (spon′dē) *n.* A metrical foot consisting of two long or accented syllables. [< Gk. *spondeios* (*pous*)/libation (meter)] —**spon·da′ic** (-dā′ik) *adj.*

sponge (spunj) *n.* **1** Any of a phylum of plantlike animals having a fibrous skeleton and growing underwater in large colonies. **2** The light, porous, extremely absorbent skeleton of such animals, used for bathing, cleaning, etc. **3** Any of various absorbent substances or materials used to clean, soak up liquids, etc. **4** Leavened dough. **5** A porous mass of metal, as platinum. **6** *Informal* SPONGER (def. 3). —**throw** (or **toss**) **up** (or **in**) **the sponge** *Informal* To yield; give up; abandon the struggle. —*v.* **sponged, spong·ing** *v.t.* **1** To wipe, wet, or clean with a sponge. **2** To wipe out; expunge; erase. **3** To absorb; suck in, as a sponge does. **4** *Informal* To get by imposing at another's expense. — *v.i.* **5** To be absorbent. **6** To gather or fish for sponges. **7** *Informal* To be a sponger (def. 3): often with *off* or *on.* [< OE < Gk. *spongos*] —**spong′i·ness** *n.* —**spong′y** *adj.*

sponge cake A light cake of sugar, eggs, flour, etc., but containing no shortening.

spong·er (spun′jər) *n.* **1** One who uses a sponge, as for cleaning, etc. **2** A person or vessel that gathers sponges. **3** *Informal* A person who obtains something from others by taking advantage of their generosity, good nature, etc.

spon·son (spon′sən) *n.* **1** A curved projection from the hull of a vessel or seaplane, to increase its stability or surface area. **2** A similar protuberance on a ship or tank, for storage purposes or for the training of a gun. **3** An air tank built into the side of a canoe, to improve stability and prevent sinking. [?]

spon·sor (spon′sər) *n.* **1** A person who acts as surety for another, as in a loan, debt, etc. **2** A person or group who helps establish or finance something, as a club, activity, etc. **3** GODPARENT. **4** A business firm or enterprise that assumes all or part of the costs of a radio or television program which advertises its product or service. —*v.t.* To act as a sponsor for. [< L *spondere* to pledge] —**spon·so·ri·al** (spon·sôr′ē·əl, -sō′rē-) *adj.* —**spon′sor·ship** *n.*

spon·ta·ne·i·ty (spon′tə·nē′ə·tē, -nā-) *n. pl.* **·ties** **1** The state or quality of being spontaneous. **2** Something spontaneous, as an action, manner of behavior, etc.

spon·ta·ne·ous (spon·tā′nē·əs) *adj.* **1** Acting or arising naturally and without constraint from an inner impulse, prompting, or desire; not planned or contrived. **2** Apparently arising independently without external cause, stimulus, influence, or condition. **3** Produced without human labor; wild; indigenous. [< L *sponte* of free will] —**spon·ta′ne·ous·ly** *adv.* —**spon·ta′ne·ous·ness** *n.*

spontaneous combustion Ignition resulting from the accumulation of heat generated by slow oxidation.

spontaneous generation *Biol.* ABIOGENESIS.

spoof (spōōf) *Informal v.t.* & *v.i.* **1** To deceive or hoax; joke. **2** To satirize in a good-natured manner. —*n.* **1** A deception; hoax. **2** A playful parody or satire. [< a game invented by A. Roberts, 1852-1933, English comedian]

spook (spōōk) *Informal n.* A ghost; apparition; specter. — *v.t.* **1** To haunt (a person or place). **2** To frighten, disturb, or annoy. **3** To startle or frighten (an animal) into flight, stampeding, etc. [< Du.] —**spook′ish** *adj.*

spook·y (spōō′kē) *adj.* **spook·i·er, spook·i·est** *Informal* **1** Of or like a spook; ghostly; eerie. **2** Frightened; nervous; skittish. —**spook′i·ly** *adv.* —**spook′i·ness** *n.*

spool (spōōl) *n.* **1** A cylinder having a projecting rim at each end, on which is wound thread, wire, etc., and a hole from one end to the other, as for mounting on a spindle. **2** The quantity of thread, wire, etc., held by a spool. **3** Anything resembling a spool in shape or purpose. —*v.t.* To wind on a spool. [< MLG *spole*]

spoon (spōōn) *n.* **1** A utensil having a shallow, generally ovoid bowl and a handle, used in preparing, serving, or eating food. **2** Something resembling a spoon or its bowl. **3** A metallic lure attached to a fishing line: also **spoon bait**. **4** A wooden golf club with lofted face and comparatively short, stiff shaft. —*v.t.* **1** To lift up or out with a spoon. **2** To play or hit (a ball) with a weak shoving or scooping movement. —*v.i.* **3** To spoon a ball. **4** *Informal* To kiss and caress, as lovers. [< OE *spōn* chip]

spoon·bill (spōōn′bil′) *n.* **1** A wading bird related to the ibis, having a spoon-shaped bill. **2** A duck having the bill broad and flattened; a shoveler. —**spoon′-billed′** *adj.*

spoon·drift (spōōn′drift) *n.* SPINDRIFT. [< *spoon*, var. of SPUME + DRIFT]

spoon·er·ism (spōō′nə·riz′əm) *n.* The unintentional transposition of sounds or of parts of words in speaking, as in "half-*w*armed *f*ish" for "half-*f*ormed *w*ish". [< W. A. *Spooner*, 1844-1930, of New College, Oxford]

Spoonbill *def. 1*

spoon·feed (spōōn′fēd′) *v.t.* **·fed, ·feed·ing** **1** To feed with a spoon. **2** To pamper; spoil. **3** To present (information) in such a manner that little or no thought, initiative, etc., is required of the recipient. **4** To instruct or inform (a person or group) in this manner.

spoon·ful (spōōn′fŏŏl′) *n. pl.* **·fuls** As much as a spoon will hold.

spoon·y (spōō′nē) *adj.* **spoon·i·er, spoon·i·est** *Informal* Sentimental or silly, as in lovemaking. Also **spoon′ey**.

spoor (spŏŏr) *n.* Footprints, droppings, or other traces of a wild animal. —*v.t.* & *v.i.* To track by or follow a spoor. [< MDu.]

spo·rad·ic (spə·rad′ik) *adj.* **1** Occurring infrequently; occasional. **2** Not widely diffused; occurring in isolated cases: a *sporadic* infection. Also **spo·rad′i·cal**. [< Gk. *sporas* scattered] —**spo·rad′i·cal·ly** *adv.* —**spo·rad′i·cal·ness** *n.* — **Syn. 1** irregular, fitful, spasmodic, intermittent.

spo·ran·gi·um (spô·ran′jē·əm, spō-) *n. pl.* **·gi·a** (-jē·ə) A sac or single cell in which spores are produced. [< SPOR(O)- + Gk. *angeion* a vessel] —**spo·ran′gi·al** *adj.*

spore (spôr, spōr) *n.* **1** The reproductive body in plants that bear no seeds, as bacteria, algae, ferns, etc. **2** A minute body that develops into a new individual; any minute organism; a germ. —*v.i.* **spored, spor·ing** To develop spores: said of plants. [< Gk. *spora* seed, sowing] —**spo·ra·ceous** (spô·rā′shəs, spō-) *adj.*

spore case SPORANGIUM.

sporo- *combining form* Seed; spore: *sporophyte*.

spo·ro·phyll (spôr′ə·fil, spō′rə-) *n.* A leaf, or modified leaf, which bears sporangia. Also **spo′ro·phyl**.

sporophyte   711   spread

spo·ro·phyte (spôr′ə·fīt, spō′rə-) *n.* The spore-bearing generation in plants which have a distinct reproductive phase.

spor·ran (spor′ən, spôr′-) *n.* A skin pouch, usu. with the fur on, worn in front of the kilt by Highlanders. [< Scots Gaelic *sporan*] • See KILT.

sport (spôrt, spōrt) *n.* 1 A diversion; pastime. 2 A particular game or physical activity pursued for diversion, esp. an outdoor or athletic game, as baseball, football, track, tennis, swimming, etc. 3 A spirit of jesting or raillery. 4 An object of derision; a laughingstock; butt. 5 An animal or plant that exhibits sudden variation from the normal type; a mutation. 6 *Informal* A gambler. 7 *Informal* One who lives a fast, gay, or flashy life. 8 A person characterized by his observance of the rules of fair play, or by his ability to get along with others: a good *sport.* 9 *Archaic* Amorous or sexual play. —*v.i.* 1 To amuse oneself; play; frolic. 2 To participate in games. 3 To make sport or jest; trifle. 4 To vary suddenly or spontaneously from the normal type; mutate. 5 *Archaic & Regional* To make love, esp. in a trifling manner. —*v.t.* 6 *Informal* To display or wear ostentatiously. —*adj.* Of, pertaining to, or fitted for sports; also, appropriate for casual wear: a *sport* coat: also **sports.** [Var. of DISPORT] —**sport′ful** *adj.* —**sport′ful·ly** *adv.*

sport·ing (spôr′ting, spōr′-) *adj.* 1 Pertaining to, engaged in, or used in athletic games or field sports. 2 Characterized by or conforming to the spirit of sportsmanship. 3 Interested in or associated with gambling or betting. —**sport′ing·ly** *adv.*

sporting chance *Informal* A chance involving the likelihood of loss but also the possibility of success.

spor·tive (spôr′tiv, spōr′-) *adj.* 1 Relating to or fond of sport or play; frolicsome. 2 Interested in, active in, or related to sports. —**spor′tive·ly** *adv.* —**spor′tive·ness** *n.*

sports·man (spôrts′mən, spōrts′-) *n. pl.* **·men** (-mən) 1 One who pursues field sports, esp. hunting and fishing. 2 One who abides by a code of fair play. —**sports′man·like′, sports′man·ly** *adj.*

sports·man·ship (spôrts′mən·ship, spōrts′-) *n.* 1 The art or practice of field sports. 2 Honorable or sportsmanlike conduct.

sports·wear (spôrts′wâr′, spōrts′-) *n.* Clothes made for informal or outdoor activities.

sports·wom·an (spôrts′wŏŏm′ən, spōrts′-) *n. pl.* **·wom·en** (-wim′in) A woman who participates in sports.

sport·y (spôr′tē, spōr′-) *adj.* **sport·i·er, sport·i·est** *Informal* 1 Relating to or characteristic of a sport. 2 Colorful; gay; loud, as clothes. —**sport′i·ly** *adv.* —**sport′i·ness** *n.*

spor·ule (spôr′yŏŏl, spor′-) *n.* A little spore. [Dim. of SPORE]

spot (spot) *n.* 1 A particular place or locality. 2 Any small portion of a surface differing as in color from the rest, as a mark, speck, blotch, etc. 3 A stain or blemish on character; a fault; a reproach. 4 A food fish of the Atlantic coast of the U.S. 5 One of the figures or pips with which a playing card is marked; also, a card having (a certain number of) such marks: the five *spot* of clubs. 6 *Slang* Paper money having a specified value: a ten *spot.* 7 *Chiefly Brit.* A portion or bit: a *spot* of tea. 8 *Informal* Place or allotted time, as on a list, schedule, etc. 9 *Informal* Position, job, or situation. 10 *Informal* SPOTLIGHT. 11 *Slang* NIGHTCLUB. 12 *Informal* A brief commercial or announcement, usu. scheduled between regular radio or television programs. —**hit the spot** *Slang* To gratify an appetite or need. —**in a spot** *Slang* In a difficult or embarrassing situation; in trouble. —**on the spot** 1 At once; immediately. 2 At the very place of occurrence. 3 *Slang* a In trouble, danger, difficulty, etc. b Accountable for some action, mistake, etc. —*v.* **spot·ted, spot·ting** *v.t.* 1 To mark or soil with spots. 2 To remove spots from. 3 To place or locate in or at a designated spot or spots. 4 To recognize or detect; identify; see. 5 To sully or disgrace, as the reputation of. 6 To schedule or list. 7 To shine a spotlight on. 8 *Informal* To yield (an advantage or handicap) to someone. —*v.i.* 9 To become marked or soiled with spots. 10 To make a stain or discoloration. —*adj.* 1 Paid or ready to be paid for at

once: *spot* cash. 2 Ready for instant delivery following sale. 3 Involving cash payment only. 4 Made or selected at random or according to a prearranged plan: a *spot* check. 5 Broadcast between regular programs: a *spot* announcement. 6 Televised or broadcast on the spot or from a specific spot. [< LG] —**spot′ta·ble** *adj.*

spot-check (spot′chek′) *v.t. & v.i.* To sample or examine at random or according to a prearranged plan.

spot·less (spot′lis) *adj.* 1 Free from spots, dirt, etc.: a *spotless* house. 2 Pure; unsullied: a *spotless* life. —**spot′less·ly** *adv.* —**spot′less·ness** *n.*

spot·light (spot′līt′) *n.* 1 A bright, powerful beam of light used to illuminate a person, group, building, etc. 2 A device that produces such a light. 3 Public notice or acclaim. —*v.t.* To light up or make prominent with or as with a spotlight.

spot·ted (spot′id) *adj.* 1 Discolored in spots; soiled. 2 Characterized or marked by spots.

spotted fever Any of various infectious diseases marked by fever and skin rash.

spot·ter (spot′ər) *n.* 1 In drycleaning, one who removes spots. 2 A detective hired to watch for theft, etc., as in a department store. 3 Anyone who keeps watch for something.

spot·ty (spot′ē) *adj.* **·ti·er, ·ti·est** 1 Having many spots. 2 Uneven or irregular, as in quality, performance, etc. —**spot′ti·ly** *adv.* —**spot′ti·ness** *n.*

spous·al (spou′zəl) *adj.* Pertaining to marriage. —*n.* Marriage; espousal.

spouse (spouz, spous) *n.* A partner in marriage; one's husband or wife. [< L *sponsus,* pp. of *spondere* to promise, betroth]

spout (spout) *v.i.* 1 To pour out copiously and forcibly, as a liquid under pressure. 2 To speak pompously, somewhat angrily, or at length. —*v.t.* 3 To cause to pour or shoot forth. 4 To utter pompously, somewhat angrily, or at length. —*n.* 1 A tube, trough, etc., for the discharge of a liquid. 2 A continuous stream of fluid. [ME *spoute*] —**spout′er** *n.*

spp. species (plural).

sprain (sprān) *n.* 1 A violent straining or twisting of the ligaments surrounding a joint. 2 The condition due to such strain. —*v.t.* To cause a sprain in. [< OF *espreindre* to squeeze]

sprang (sprang) A *p.t.* of SPRING.

sprat (sprat) *n.* Any of various small herringlike fish. [< OE *sprott*]

sprawl (sprôl) *v.i.* 1 To sit or lie with the limbs stretched out ungracefully. 2 To be stretched out ungracefully, as the limbs. 3 To move with awkward motions of the limbs. 4 To spread out in a straggling manner, as handwriting, vines, etc. —*v.t.* 5 To cause to spread or extend awkwardly or irregularly. —*n.* 1 The act or position of sprawling. 2 An unplanned or disorderly group, as of houses, spread out over a broad area: urban *sprawl.* [< OE *sprēawlian* move convulsively] —**sprawl′er** *n.*

spray¹ (sprā) *n.* 1 Liquid dispersed in fine particles. 2 An instrument for discharging small particles of liquid; an atomizer. 3 Something like a spray of liquid. —*v.t.* 1 To disperse (a liquid) in fine particles. 2 To apply spray to. —*v.i.* 3 To send forth or scatter spray. 4 To go forth as spray. [< MDu. *sprayen*] —**spray′er** *n.*

spray² (sprā) *n.* 1 A small branch bearing dependent branchlets or flowers. 2 Any ornament or pattern like this. [ME]

spread (spred) *v.* **spread, spread·ing** *v.t.* 1 To open or unfold to full width, extent, etc., as wings, sail, a map, etc. 2 To distribute over a surface, esp. in a thin layer. 3 To cover with something. 4 To force apart or farther apart. 5 To distribute over a period of time or among a group. 6 To make more widely known, active, etc.; promulgate or diffuse: to *spread* a rumor. 7 To set (a table, etc.), as for a meal. 8 To arrange or place on a table, etc., as a meal or feast. 9 To set forth or record in full. —*v.i.* 10 To be extended or expanded; increase in size, width, etc. 11 To be distributed or dispersed, as over a surface or area; scatter.

add, āce, câre, pălm; end, ēven; it, īce; odd, ōpen, ôrder; tŏŏk, pōōl; up, bûrn; ə = *a* in *above, u* in *focus;* yŏŏ = *u* in *fuse;* oil; pout; check; go; ring; thin; this; zh, *vision.* < derived from; ? origin uncertain or unknown.

12 To become more widely known, active, etc. **13** To be forced farther apart; separate. —*n.* **1** The act of spreading. **2** The limit, distance, or extent of spreading, expansion, etc. **3** A cloth or covering for a table, bed, etc. **4** Something used for spreading: a cheese *spread.* **5** *Informal* A feast or banquet; also, a table with a meal set out on it. **6** A prominent presentation in a periodical. **7** Two pages of a magazine or newspaper facing each other and covered by related material; also, the material itself. —*adj.* Expanded; outstretched. [<OE *spraedan*] —**spread′er** *n.*

spread-ea·gle (spred′ē′gəl) *adj.* **1** Having the arms and legs spread wide apart. **2** Extravagant; bombastic: said of excessively patriotic oratory in the U.S. —*v.* **-ea·gled, -ea·gling** *v. t.* **1** To force to assume a spread-eagle position.

spread eagle 1 The figure of an eagle with extended wings, used as an emblem of the U.S. **2** Any position or movement resembling this, as a figure in skating.

spread·sheet (spred′shēt′) *n.* A kind of computer program that processes numerical data for detailed financial calculations of various kinds.

spree (sprē) *n.* **1** A period of heavy drinking. **2** Any period of fun, activity, etc. [?]

sprig (sprig) *n.* **1** A shoot or sprout of a plant. **2** An ornament in this form. **3** An heir or offspring of a family, esp. a young man. [ME *sprigge*] —**sprig′ger** *n.*

spright·ly (sprīt′lē) *adj.* **-li·er, -li·est** Full of animation and spirits; vivacious; lively. —*adv.* Spiritedly; briskly; gaily. [<*spright*, var. of SPRITE] —**spright′li·ness** *n.* —**Syn.** *adj.* animated, brisk, bustling, cheerful, nimble, spry, quick.

spring (spring) *v.* **sprang** or **sprung, sprung, spring·ing** *v.i.*
1 To move or rise suddenly and rapidly; leap; dart. **2** To move suddenly as by elastic reaction; snap. **3** To happen or occur suddenly or immediately: An angry retort *sprang* to his lips. **4** To work or snap out of place, as a mechanical part. **5** To become warped or bent, as boards. **6** To rise above surrounding objects. **7** To come into being: New towns have *sprung* up. **8** To originate; proceed, as from a source. **9** To develop; grow, as a plant. **10** To be descended: He *springs* from good stock. —*v.t.* **11** To cause to spring or leap. **12** To cause to act, close, open, etc., unexpectedly or suddenly, as by elastic reaction: to *spring* a trap. **13** To cause to happen, become known, or appear suddenly: to *spring* a surprise. **14** To leap over; vault. **15** To start (game) from cover; flush. **16** To explode (a mine). **17** To warp or bend; split. **18** To cause to snap or work out of place. **19** To force into place, as a beam or bar. **20** To suffer (a leak). **21** *Slang* To obtain the release of (a person) from prison or custody. —*n.* **1** *Mech.* An elastic device that yields under stress, and returns to normal form when the stress is removed. **2** Elastic quality or energy. **3** The act of flying back from a position of tension; recoil. **4** A cause of action; motive. **5** Any source or origin. **6** A flow or fountain, as of water. **7** The act of leaping up or forward suddenly; a jump; bound. **8** The season in which vegetation starts anew; in the north temperate zone, the three months of March, April, and May; in the astronomical year, the period from the vernal equinox to the summer solstice. —*adj.* **1** Of or pertaining to the season of spring. **2** Resilient; acting like or having a spring. **3** Hung on springs. **4** Coming from or housing a spring of water. [<OE *springan*]

Springs

spring·board (spring′bôrd′, -bōrd′) *n.* **1** A flexible board used to give impetus, as to a dive, acrobatic leap, etc. **2** Anything that gives impetus, as to an activity.

spring·bok (spring′bok′) *n. pl.* **·bok** or **·boks** A small African gazelle noted for its ability to leap high in the air. Also **spring′buck′** (-buk′). [<Afrikaans]

spring chicken 1 A young chicken. **2** *Informal* A young person, esp. a girl: usu. with a negative: She's no *spring chicken.*

Springbok

spring·er (spring′ər) *n.* **1** One who or that which springs. **2** A young chicken. **3** A spaniel valuable for flushing game; also **springer spaniel.**

spring fever The listlessness that overtakes a person with the first warm days of spring.

spring tide 1 A high tide occurring about new moon and full moon. **2** Any great wave of feeling, etc.

Springer spaniel

spring·time (spring′tīm′) *n.* **1** The season of spring. **2** Any early or youthful period. Also **spring′tide′** (-tīd′).

spring·y (spring′ē) *adj.* **spring·i·er, spring·i·est 1** Elastic; resilient. **2** Having many water springs; wet. —**spring′i·ly** *adv.* —**spring′i·ness** *n.*

sprin·kle (spring′kəl) *v.* **·kled, ·kling** *v.t.* **1** To scatter in drops or small particles. **2** To scatter over or upon: *Sprinkle* the top with flour. —*v.i.* **3** To fall or rain in scattered drops. —*n.* **1** The act of sprinkling. **2** A small quantity. **3** A light rain. [ME *sprenkelen*] —**sprin′kler** *n.*

sprin·kling (spring′kling) *n.* **1** The act of one who or that which sprinkles. **2** A small amount or number: a *sprinkling* of people.

sprint (sprint) *n.* **1** The act of sprinting. **2** A short race run at top speed. **3** A brief period, as of speed. —*v.i.* To go or run fast, as in a sprint. [<Scand.] —**sprint′er** *n.*

sprit (sprit) *n.* A small spar reaching diagonally from a mast to the peak of a fore-and-aft sail. [<OE *sprēot* pole]
• See SPRITSAIL.

sprite (sprīt) *n.* **1** A fairy, elf, or goblin. **2** A small, elflike person. **3** A ghost. [<L *spiritus*]

sprit·sail (sprit′səl, sprit′sāl′) *n.* A sail extended by a sprit.

sprock·et (sprok′it) *n.* **1** A projection, as on the rim of a wheel, for engaging with the links of a chain. **2** A wheel bearing such projections: also **sprocket wheel.** [?]

a. spritsail. b. sprit.

sprout (sprout) *v.i.* **1** To put forth shoots; begin to grow; germinate. **2** To develop or grow rapidly. —*v.t.* **3** To cause to sprout. **4** To remove shoots from. —*n.* **1** A new shoot or bud on a plant. **2** Something like or suggestive of a sprout, as a young person. **3** *pl.* BRUSSELS SPROUTS. [<OE *sprūtan*]

spruce[1] (sprōōs) *n.* **1** Any of a genus of evergreen trees of the pine family, having needle-shaped leaves and pendulous cones. **2** The wood of any of these trees. [<Med. L *Prussia* Prussia]

spruce[2] (sprōōs) *adj.* **spruc·er, spruc·est** Smart, trim, and neat in appearance. —*v.* **spruced, spruc·ing** *v.t.* **1** To make spruce: often with *up.* —*v.i.* **2** To make oneself spruce: usu. with *up.* [<earlier *spruce,* a kind of superior Prussian leather] —**spruce′ly** *adv.* —**spruce′ness** *n.*

sprung (sprung) *p.p.* & *a. p.t.* of SPRING.

spry (sprī) *adj.* **spri·er** or **spry·er, spri·est** or **spry·est** Quick and active; agile. [<Scand.] —**spry′ly** *adv.* —**spry′ness** *n.*

spt. seaport.

spud (spud) *n.* **1** A spadelike tool with narrow blade or prongs for uprooting weeds. **2** *Informal* A potato. —*v.t.* **spud·ded, spud·ding** To remove, as weeds, with a spud. [ME *spuddle*]

spume (spyōōm) *n.* Froth; foam; scum. —*v.i.* **spumed, spum·ing** To foam; froth. [<L *spuma* foam] —**spu′mous, spum′y** *adj.*

spu·mo·ni (spyōō·mō′nē) *n.* A frozen dessert of Italian origin, containing ice cream in layers of various colors and usu. candied fruit and nuts. Also **spu·mo′ne.** [<L *spuma* foam]

spun (spun) *p.t.* & *p.p.* of SPIN.

spunk (spungk) *n.* **1** A slow-burning tinder, as punk. **2** *Informal* Mettle; pluck; courage. [<L *spongia* sponge]

spunk·y (spungk′ē) *adj.* **spunk·i·er, spunk·i·est** *Informal* Spirited; courageous. —**spunk′i·ly** *adv.* —**spunk′i·ness** *n.*

spur (spûr) *n.* **1** Any of various pricking or goading instruments worn on the heel of a horseman. **2** Anything that incites or urges; incentive. **3** A part or attachment like a spur, as a steel gaff fastened to a gamecock's leg, a climbing iron used by linemen, etc. **4** A stiff, sharp spine on the legs or wings of certain birds. **5** A crag or ridge extending laterally from a mountain or range. **6** A branch of a railroad, lode, etc. **7** A buttress or other offset from a wall. **8** A brace reinforcing a rafter or post. **9** A tubular extension of a part of a flower, usu. containing the nectar. **—on the spur of the moment** Hastily; impulsively. **—win one's spurs** To gain recognition or reward, esp. for the first time. **—v. spurred, spur·ring** *v.t.* **1** To prick or urge with or as with spurs. **2** To furnish with spurs. **3** To injure or gash with the spur, as a gamecock. **—v.i. 4** To spur one's horse. **5** To hasten; hurry. [< OE *spura*] **—spur'rer** *n.*

spurge (spûrj) *n.* Any of several flowering shrubs yielding a milky juice of bitter taste. [< OF *espurgier* to purge]

spu·ri·ous (spyŏŏr'ē-əs) *adj.* **1** Seemingly real or genuine, but actually not; false; counterfeit. **2** Illegitimate, as of birth. [< L *spurius*] **—spu'ri·ous·ly** *adv.* **—spu'ri·ous·ness** *n.*

spurn (spûrn) *v.t.* **1** To reject with disdain; scorn. **2** To strike with the foot; kick. **—v.i. 3** To reject something with disdain. **—n.** The act or an instance of spurning. [< OE *spurnan*] **—spurn'er** *n.*

spurred (spûrd) *adj.* Wearing or having spurs.

spurt (spûrt) *n.* **1** A sudden gush of liquid. **2** Any sudden, short-lived outbreak, as of anger, energy, etc. **—v.i. 1** To come out in a jet; gush forth. **2** To make a sudden, forceful effort. **—v.t. 3** To squirt. [< OE *spryttan* come forth]

sput·nik (spoot'nik, sput'-) *n.* An artificial earth satellite, esp. the first, called Sputnik I, launched in October, 1957, by the U.S.S.R. [Russ., lit., fellow traveler]

sput·ter (sput'ər) *v.i.* **1** To throw off solid or fluid particles in a series of slight explosions. **2** To speak excitedly and incoherently. **3** To make crackling or popping sounds, as burning wood, frying fat, etc. **—v.t. 4** To throw off in small particles. **5** To utter excitedly or incoherently. **—n. 1** The act or sound of sputtering; esp. excited talk; jabbering. **2** That which is thrown out in sputtering. [< Du. *sputteren*] **—sput'ter·er** *n.*

spu·tum (spyoo'təm) *n. pl.* **·ta** (-tə) Mucus from the respiratory tract, usu. mixed with saliva; expectorated matter. [< L *spuere* to spit]

spy (spī) *n. pl.* **spies 1** One who is hired to get secret information from or about an enemy, another government, etc.; a secret agent. **2** One who watches another or others secretly. **—v. spied, spy·ing** *v.i.* **1** To keep watch closely or secretly; act as a spy. **2** To make careful examination; pry: with *into*. **—v.t. 3** To observe stealthily and usu. with hostile intent: often with *out*. **4** To catch sight of; see; espy. [< OF *espier* espy]

spy·glass (spī'glas', -gläs') *n.* A small telescope.

Sq. Squadron; Square (street).

sq. square; sequence; the following (L *sequentia*).

sq. ft. square foot; square feet.

sq. in. square inch(es).

sq. mi. square mile(s).

squab (skwob) *n.* **1** A young nestling pigeon about four weeks old. **2** A fat, short person. **—adj. 1** Fat and short; squat. **2** Unfledged or but half-grown. [< Scand.]

squab·ble (skwob'əl) *v.i.* **·bled, ·bling** To engage in a petty quarrel; bicker. **—n.** A petty quarrel. [< Scand.] **—squab'bler** *n.*

squad (skwod) *n.* **1** A small group of persons organized to do a special job; esp., the smallest tactical unit in the infantry of the U.S. Army. **2** A team: a football *squad.* **—v.t. squad·ded, squad·ding 1** To form into a squad or squads. **2** To assign to a squad. [< L *quattuor* four]

squad car An automobile used by police for patrolling, and equipped with radiotelephone for communicating with headquarters.

squad·ron (skwod'rən) *n.* **1** An assemblage of war vessels smaller than a fleet. **2** A division of a cavalry regiment. **3** The basic unit of the U.S. Air Force, usu. consisting of two or more flights operating as a unit. **4** Any regularly arranged or organized group. **—v.t.** To arrange in a squadron or squadrons. [< Ital. *squadra* squad]

squal·id (skwol'id) *adj.* **1** Having a dirty, neglected, or poverty-stricken appearance. **2** Sordid; base. [< L *squalere* be foul] **—squal'id·ly** *adv.* **—squal'id·ness, squa·lid·i·ty** (skwo·lid'ə·tē) *n.* **—Syn. 1** foul, filthy, wretched, untidy.

squall[1] (skwôl) *n.* A loud, screaming outcry. **—v.i.** To cry loudly; scream; bawl. [< Scand.] **—squall'er** *n.*

squall[2] (skwôl) *n.* **1** A sudden, violent burst of wind, often accompanied by rain or snow. **2** A brief disturbance or commotion. **—v.i.** To blow a squall. [< Scand.] **—squall'y** *adj.* (·i·er, ·i·est)

squal·or (skwol'ər) *n.* The state of being squalid; wretched filth or poverty.

squa·ma (skwā'mə) *n. pl.* **·mae** (-mē) A thin, scalelike structure; a scale. [L] **—squa'mate** (-māt), **squa'mose, squa'mous** *adj.*

squan·der (skwon'dər) *v.t.* To spend (money, time, etc.) wastefully. **—n.** Prodigality; wastefulness. [?] **—squan'der·er** *n.* **—squan'der·ing·ly** *adv.* **—Syn. v.** dissipate, waste, lavish, run through, throw away.

square (skwâr) *n.* **1** A parallelogram having four equal sides and four right angles. **2** Any object, part, or surface that is square or nearly so, as one of the spaces on a checkerboard. **3** An L- or T-shaped instrument by which to test or lay out right angles. **4** An open area bordered by streets or formed by their intersection. **5** A town or city block; also, the distance between one street and the next. **6** *Math.* The product of a number or element multiplied by itself. **7** *Slang* A person of excessively conventional tastes or habits. **—on the square 1** At right angles. **2** *Informal* Honest, fair, true, etc.; also, honestly, fairly, truly, etc. **—out of square** Not at right angles; obliquely. **—adj. squar·er, squar·est 1** Having four equal sides and four right angles. **2** Approaching a square or a cube in form: a *square* box. **3** Forming a right angle: a *square* nook. **4** Adapted to forming squares or computing in squares: a *square* measure. **5** Being a square with each side of specified length: two inches *square.* **6** Perfectly adjusted, aligned, balanced, etc. **7** Even; settled: said of debts, etc. **8** Tied, as a score. **9** Honest; fair; just. **10** *Informal* Solid; full; satisfying: a *square* meal. **11** Broad; solid; muscular: a *square* build. **12** *Slang* Excessively conventional or conservative; not sophisticated. **13** *Naut.* At right angles to the mast and keel. **—v. squared, squar·ing** *v.t.* **1** To make square. **2** To shape or adjust so as to form a right angle. **3** To mark with or divide into squares. **4** To test for the purpose of adjusting to a straight line, right angle, or plane surface. **5** To bring to a position suggestive of a right angle: *Square* your shoulders. **6** To make satisfactory settlement or adjustment of: to *square* accounts. **7** To make equal, as a game score. **8** To cause to conform; adapt: to *square* one's opinions to the times. **9** To reconcile or set right. **10** *Math.* **a** To multiply (a number or element) by itself. **b** To determine the area of. **11** *Slang* To bribe. **—v.i. 12** To be at right angles. **13** To conform; agree; harmonize: with *with*. **—square away 1** *Naut.* To set (the yards) at right angles to the keel. **2** To put into good order; make ready. **3** SQUARE OFF. **—square off** To assume a position for attack or defense; prepare to fight. **—square up** To adjust or settle satisfactorily. **—adv. 1** So as to be square, or at right angles. **2** Honestly; fairly. **3** Directly; firmly. [< OF *esquarre*] **—square'ness, squar'er** *n.* • See PARALLELOGRAM.

square dance Any dance, as a quadrille, in which the couples form sets in squares.

square knot A common knot, formed of two overhand knots. • See KNOT.

square·ly (skwâr'lē) *adv.* **1** In a direct or straight manner: He looked her *squarely* in the eyes. **2** Honestly; fairly. **3** Plainly; unequivocally. **4** In a square form: *squarely* built. **5** At right angles (to a line or plane).

square measure A unit or system of units for measuring areas. • See MEASURE.

square-rigged (skwâr'rigd') *adj.* Having the principal sails extended by horizontal yards at right angles to the masts.

square-rig·ger (skwâr'rig'ər) *n.* A square-rigged ship.

square root *Math.* A number or element whose square is equal to a given quantity.

square sail A four-sided sail usu. rigged on a horizontal yard set at right angles to the mast.

square shooter *Informal* One who acts honestly and justly.

squash[1] (skwosh) *v.t.* **1** To squeeze or press into a pulp or soft mass; crush. **2** To quell or suppress. **3** *Informal* To silence or humiliate quickly and thoroughly; squelch. — *v.i.* **4** To be smashed or squashed. **5** To make a splashing or sucking sound. —*n.* **1** A crushed mass. **2** The sudden fall of a heavy, soft, or bursting body; also, the sound made by such a fall. **3** The sucking, squelching sound made by walking through ooze or mud. **4** Either of two games played on an indoor court with rackets and a ball. In one (**squash rackets**), a slow rubber ball is used; in the other (**squash tennis**), a livelier, smaller ball. **5** *Brit.* A fruit-flavored beverage. —*adv.* With a squelching, oozy sound. [< L *ex-* thoroughly + *quassare* crush] —**squash′er** *n.*

squash[2] (skwosh) *n.* **1** Any of various edible gourds usu. cooked and served as a vegetable. **2** The plant that bears it. [< Algon.]

squash·y (skwosh′ē) *adj.* **squash·i·er, squash·i·est 1** Soft and moist. **2** Easily squashed. —**squash′i·ly** *adv.* —**squash′i·ness** *n.*

squat (skwot) *v.* **squat·ted** or **squat, squat·ting** *v.i.* **1** To sit on the heels or hams, or with the legs near the body. **2** To crouch or cower down, as to avoid being seen. **3** To settle on a piece of land without title or payment. **4** To settle on government land in accordance with certain government regulations that will eventually give title. —*v.t.* **5** To cause (oneself) to squat. —*adj.* **squat·ter, squat·test 1** Short and thick. **2** Being in a squatting position. —*n.* A squatting attitude or position. [< OF *esquatir*] —**squat′ter** *n.*

squat·ty (skwot′ē) *adj.* **·ti·er, ·ti·est** Short and thickset; squat.

squaw (skwô) *n.* An American Indian woman or wife.

squawk (skwôk) *v.i.* **1** To utter a shrill, harsh cry, as a parrot. **2** *Slang* To utter loud complaints or protests. —*n.* **1** A shrill, harsh cry. **2** *Slang* A shrill complaint. [Imit.] —**squawk′er** *n.*

squeak (skwēk) *n.* **1** A thin, sharp, penetrating sound. **2** *Informal* An escape, in the phrase **a narrow** (or **close**) **squeak.** —*v.i.* **1** To make a squeak. **2** *Informal* To let out information; squeal. **3** To succeed or otherwise progress after narrowly averting failure: to *squeak* through. —*v.t.* **4** To utter or effect with a squeak. **5** To cause to squeak. [Prob. < Scand.] —**squeak′y** *adj.* **·i·er, ·i·est**) —**squeak′i·ly** *adv.* —**squeak′i·ness** *n.*

squeal (skwēl) *v.i.* **1** To utter a sharp, shrill, somewhat prolonged cry. **2** *Slang* To turn informer; betray an accomplice or a plot. —*v.t.* **3** To utter with or cause to make a squeal. —*n.* A shrill, prolonged cry, as of a pig. [Imit.] —**squeal′er** *n.*

squeam·ish (skwē′mish) *adj.* **1** Easily disgusted or shocked. **2** Overly scrupulous. **3** Nauseated; also, easily nauseated. [< AF *escoymous*] —**squeam′ish·ly** *adv.* —**squeam′ish·ness** *n.*

squee·gee (skwē′jē) *n.* **1** An implement having a straight-edged strip of rubber, etc., used for removing water from window panes, etc., after washing them. **2** *Phot.* A smaller similar implement, often made in the form of a roller, used for pressing a film closer to its mount, etc. —*v.t.* **·geed, ·gee·ing** To use a squeegee on. [Var. of SQUEEZE]

squeeze (skwēz) *v.* **squeezed, squeez·ing** *v.t.* **1** To press hard upon; compress. **2** To extract something from by pressure: to *squeeze* oranges. **3** To get or draw forth by pressure: to *squeeze* juice from apples. **4** To force, push, maneuver, etc., by or as by pressure: He *squeezed* his car into the narrow space. **5** To oppress, as with burdensome taxes. **6** To exert pressure upon (someone) to act as one desires, as by blackmailing. **7** To embrace; hug. —*v.i.* **8** To apply pressure. **9** To force one's way; push: with *in, through,* etc. **10** To be pressed; yield to pressure. — **squeeze by, through,** etc. *Informal* To avoid failure, defeat, trouble, etc., by the narrowest margin. —*n.* **1** The act or process of squeezing; pressure. **2** A handclasp; also, an embrace; hug. **3** A quantity of something, as juice, etc., extracted or expressed. **4** The state or condition of being

squeezed; crush. **5** A time of trouble, scarcity, difficulty, etc. **6** SQUEEZE PLAY. **7** *Informal* Pressure exerted for the extortion of money or favors; also, financial pressure. [< OE *cwēsan* to crush] —**squeez′a·ble** *adj.* —**squeez′er** *n.*

squeeze play 1 In baseball, a play in which the batter bunts the ball so that a man on third base may score by starting while the pitcher is about to deliver the ball. **2** Any attempt or maneuver to realize some end or goal by coercion.

squelch (skwelch) *v.t.* **1** To crush; squash. **2** *Informal* To subdue utterly; silence, as with a crushing reply. —*v.i.* **3** To make or move with a splashing or sucking noise. —*n.* **1** A noise, as made when walking in wet boots. **2** A heavy fall or blow. **3** *Informal* A crushing retort or reply. [Imit.] —**squelch′er** *n.*

squib (skwib) *n.* **1** A brief news item. **2** A short witty or satirical speech or writing. **3** A broken firecracker that burns with a spitting sound. —*v.* **squibbed, squib·bing** *v.i.* **1** To write or use squibs. **2** To fire a squib. **3** To explode or sound like a squib. —*v.t.* **4** To attack with squibs; lampoon. [?]

squid (skwid) *n.* One of various ten-armed marine cephalopods with a long, slender body, ink sac, and broad caudal fins. [?]

squill (skwil) *n.* **1** A bulbous plant of the lily family. **2** Its bulb, containing various medicinal and poisonous alkaloids. [< Gk. *skilla* sea onion]

Squid

squint (skwint) *v.i.* **1** To look with half-closed eyes, as into bright light. **2** To look with a side glance; look askance. **3** To be cross-eyed. **4** To incline or tend: with *toward,* etc. —*v.t.* **5** To hold (the eyes) half shut, as in glaring light. **6** To cause to squint. —*adj.* **1** Affected with strabismus. **2** Looking obliquely or askance; indirect. —*n.* **1** An affection of the eyes in which their axes are differently directed; strabismus. **2** The act or habit of squinting. [?] —**squint′er** *n.*

squire (skwīr) *n.* **1** A knight's attendant; an armor bearer. **2** In England, the chief landowner of a district. **3** In the U.S., a title applied esp. to village lawyers and justices of the peace. **4** A gentleman who escorts a lady in public; a gallant. —*v.t.* **squired, squir·ing** To be a squire to (someone); escort. [Var. of ESQUIRE]

squirm (skwûrm) *v.i.* **1** To bend and twist the body; wriggle; writhe. **2** To show signs of pain or distress. —*n.* A squirming motion. [?] —**squirm′y** *adj.* **(·i·er, ·i·est)**

squir·rel (skwûr′əl *Brit.* skwir′əl) *n.* **1** Any of various slender rodents with a long bushy tail, living mainly in trees and feeding chiefly on nuts. The **red squirrel,** the **gray squirrel,** and the **fox squirrel** are North American types. **2** One of various related rodents, as the woodchuck, ground squirrel, etc. The fur of a squirrel. —*v.t.* **squirreled** or **·relled, squir·rel·ing** or **·rel·ling** To take away and hide (something) for possible use in the future: often with *away.* [< Gk. *skia* shadow + *oura* tail]

Gray squirrel

squirt (skwûrt) *v.i.* **1** To come forth in a thin stream or jet; spurt out. —*v.t.* **2** To eject (water or other liquid) forcibly and in a jet. **3** To wet or bespatter with a squirt or squirts. —*n.* **1** The act of squirting or spurting; also, a jet of liquid squirted forth. **2** A syringe or squirt gun. **3** *Informal* A youngster, esp. a mischievous one. [ME *swirten*] —**squirt′er** *n.*

squirt gun An instrument or toy shaped like a gun and used for squirting.

squish (skwish) *v.t. & v.i.* SQUASH[1]. —*n.* A squashing sound. [Var. of SQUASH[1]] —**squish′y** *adj.* **(·i·er, ·i·est)**

sq. yd. square yard(s).

Sr strontium.

Sr. Senior; Señor; Sir; Sister.

sr steradian.

Sra. Señora.

Sri Lank·a (srē langk′ə) An island south of India, an independent state of the Commonwealth of Nations, 25,-332 sq. mi., cap. Colombo: formerly Ceylon. • See map at INDIA.

S.R.O. standing room only.

Srta. Señorita.

SS, SS. Nazi special police (G *Schutzstaffel*).

SS, S.S., S/S steamship.

SS. Saints.

S.S. Sunday School; written above (L *supra scriptum*).

ss, ss., s.s. shortstop.

SSA, S.S.A. Social Security Administration.

SSB, S.S.B. Social Security Board.

SSE, S.S.E., sse, s.s.e. south-southeast.

S.Sgt., S/Sgt Staff Sergeant.

SSR, S.S.R. Soviet Socialist Republic.

SSS Selective Service System.

SST supersonic transport.

SSW, S.S.W., ssw, s.s.w. south-southwest.

St. Saint; Strait; Street.

St., st. statute(s); stratus (clouds).

st. stanza; stet; stitch; stone (weight); street.

s.t. short ton.

Sta. Santa; Station.

sta. station; stationary.

stab (stab) *v.* **stabbed, stab·bing** *v.t.* **1** To pierce with a pointed weapon; wound, as with a dagger. **2** To thrust (a dagger, etc.), as into a body. **3** To penetrate; pierce. —*v.i.* **4** To thrust or wound with or as with a pointed weapon. —*n.* **1** A thrust or wound made with a pointed weapon. **2** A sharp painful or poignant sensation: a *stab* of grief. **3** *Informal* An effort; attempt. [ME *stabbe*] —**stab′ber** *n.*

sta·bile (stā′bil, -bīl) *adj.* **1** Stable; fixed. **2** *Med.* Not affected by moderate heat. —*n.* (stā′bēl) A piece of stationary abstract sculpture, usu. of sheet metal, wood, wire, etc. [< L *stabilis*]

sta·bil·i·ty (stə·bil′ə·tē) *n. pl.* **·ties 1** The condition of being stable; steadiness. **2** Steadfastness of purpose or resolution; constancy. **3** *Physics* The ability of an object or system to resume equilibrium after a disturbance.

sta·bi·lize (stā′bə·līz) *v.* **·lized, ·liz·ing** *v.t.* **1** To make stable. **2** To keep from fluctuating, as currency: to *stabilize* prices. —*v.i.* **3** To become stable. —**sta′bi·li·za′tion** *n.*

sta·bi·liz·er (stā′bə·lī′zər) *n.* Something that stabilizes, esp. an auxiliary airfoil of an aircraft. • See AIRPLANE.

sta·ble[1] (stā′bəl) *adj.* **·bler, ·blest 1** Standing firmly in place; not easily moved, shaken, or overthrown; fixed. **2** Marked by firmness of purpose; steadfast. **3** Having durability or permanence; abiding. **4** Resistant to chemical change. **5** *Physics* Of, having, or exhibiting stability. [< L *stabilis*] —**sta′bly** *adv.* —**sta′ble·ness** *n.*

sta·ble[2] (stā′bəl) *n.* **1** A building for lodging and feeding horses or cattle. **2** Racehorses belonging to a particular owner; also, the personnel who take care of such racehorses. **3** *Informal* Those performers, writers, athletes, etc., who are under the same management or agency. —*v.t. & v.i.* **·bled, ·bling** To put or lodge in or as in a stable. [< L *stabulum*]

sta·ble·boy (stā′bəl·boi′) *n.* A boy employed in a stable.

stac·ca·to (stə·kä′tō) *adj.* **1** *Music* Played, or to be played, with brief pauses between each note. **2** Marked by abrupt, sharp sounds or emphasis: a *staccato* style of speaking. —*adv.* So as to be staccato. —*n.* Something staccato. [< Ital. *staccare* detach]

stack (stak) *n.* **1** A large, orderly pile of unthreshed grain, hay, or straw, usu. conical. **2** Any pile or heap of things arranged somewhat neatly or systematically. **3** A group of rifles (usu. three) set upright and supporting one another. **4** *pl.* That part of a library where most of the books are shelved; also, the bookshelves. **5** A chimney; smokestack; also, a collection of such chimneys or flues. **6** *Informal* A great amount; plenty. —*v.t.* **1** To gather or pile up in a stack. **2** To plan or arrange dishonestly beforehand so as to assure a certain result or outcome. **3** To assign (an airplane) to a pattern of designated altitudes while awaiting clearance to land: often with *up.* —**stack up 1** To total. **2** To compare: often with *against.* [< ON *stakkr*] —**stack′er** *n.*

sta·di·um (stā′dē·əm) *n. pl.* **·di·ums,** for def. 2 **·di·a** (-dē·ə) **1** A large modern structure for sports events, having seats arranged in tiers. **2** In ancient Greece and Rome: **a** A course for footraces, with banked seats for spectators. **b** A measure of length, equaling 606.75 feet. [< Gk. *stadion,* a measure of length]

staff (staf) *n. pl.* **staffs;** *also for defs. 1–3* **staves** (stāvz). **1** A stick or piece of wood carried for some special purpose, as an aid in climbing, as a cudgel, or as an emblem of authority. **2** A shaft or pole that forms a support or handle: the *staff* of a flag. **3** A stick used in measuring or testing, as a surveyor's leveling rod. **4** A group of people who function as assistants or advisors to a leader, director, president, etc. **5** A body of persons working together in some specific task, occupation, or enterprise: the hospital *staff;* the editorial *staff.* **6** *Mil.* A body of officers not having command but attached in an executive or advisory capacity to a military unit as assistants to the officer in command. **7** *Music* The five horizontal lines and the spaces between them on which notes are written. —*v.t.* To provide (an office, etc.) with a staff. [< OE *stæf* stick]

staff·er (staf′ər) *n.* A member of a staff, as of a periodical.

staff officer An officer serving on a military staff.

stag (stag) *n.* **1** The adult male of various deer, esp. the red deer. **2** A castrated bull or boar. **3** A man at a party, dance, etc., who is unaccompanied by a woman. **4** A social gathering for men only. —*adj.* Of or for men only. [< OE *stagga*]

Stag head

stage (stāj) *n.* **1** The platform on which plays, operas, etc., are given. **2** The area on the adjacent sides and in back of this platform, including the wings, backstage, etc. **3** The profession of acting: with *the.* **4** Any of the activities or occupations having to do with the theater or drama: with *the.* **5** Any raised platform or floor, esp. a scaffold for workmen. **6** A horizontal level, section, or story of a building. **7** The scene of, or plan of action for, an event or events. **8** A center of attention. **9** A distinct period or step in some development, progress, or process. **10** A water level: flood *stage.* **11** A regular stopping place on a journey, esp. a journey by stagecoach. **12** STAGECOACH. **13** The distance traveled between two stopping points; leg. **14** *Electronics* One of a series of modules through which a signal passes. **15** One of the series of propulsion units used by a rocket vehicle. —*v.t.* **staged, stag·ing 1** To put or exhibit on the stage. **2** To plan, conduct, or carry out: to *stage* a rally. **3** To organize, perform, or carry out so as to appear authentic, legitimate, or spontaneous, when actually not so: The entire incident was *staged* for the press photographers. [< OF *estage*]

stage·coach (stāj′kōch′) *n.* A horse-drawn, passenger and mail vehicle having a regular route between towns.

stage·craft (stāj′kraft′, -kräft′) *n.* Skill in writing or staging plays.

stage door A door to a theater which leads to the stage or behind the scenes.

stage·hand (stāj′hand′) *n.* A worker in a theater who handles scenery and props, etc.

stage-man·age (stāj′man′ij) *v.t.* **·aged, ·ag·ing 1** To be a stage manager for. **2** To direct, organize, or carry out so as to achieve maximum effectiveness, publicity, etc.

stage manager One who assists a director in the production of a play and, during its performance, superintends the stage area, actors, and technicians.

stage·struck (stāj′struk′) *adj.* **1** Fascinated by the theater. **2** Longing to become an actor or actress.

stage whisper A loud whisper, as one uttered on the stage for the audience to hear.

stag·fla·tion (stag′flā′shən) *n. Econ.* Inflation combined with abnormally slow economic growth, resulting in high unemployment. [< *stag(nation)* + *(in)flation*]

stag·ger (stag′ər) *v.i.* **1** To move unsteadily; totter; reel. **2** To become less confident or resolute; waver; hesitate. —*v.t.* **3** To cause to stagger. **4** To affect strongly; overwhelm, as with surprise or grief. **5** To place in alternating rows or groups. **6** To arrange or distribute so as to prevent congestion or confusion: to *stagger* lunch hours. —*n.* The act of staggering. —**the (blind) staggers** Any of various diseases of domestic animals marked by staggering, falling, etc. [< ON *stakra*] —**stag′ger·er** *n.* —**stag′ger·ing·ly** *adv.*

stag·ing (stā′jing) *n.* **1** A scaffolding or temporary platform. **2** The act of putting a play, opera, etc., upon the stage. **3** The act of jettisoning a rocket stage from a space vehicle. **4** The business of running stagecoaches. **5** Traveling by stagecoach.

stag·nant (stag′nənt) *adj.* **1** Standing still; not flowing: said of water. **2** Foul from long standing. **3** Dull; inert; sluggish. [< L *stagnum* a pool] —**stag′nan·cy** *n.* —**stag′nant·ly** *adv.*

stag·nate (stag′nāt) *v.i.* **·nat·ed, ·nat·ing** To be or become stagnant. —**stag·na′tion** *n.*

stag·y (stā′jē) *adj.* **stag·i·er, stag·i·est 1** Of or suited to the stage. **2** Excessively theatrical; artificial. —**stag′i·ly** *adv.* —**stag′i·ness** *n.*

staid (stād) *adj.* Sedate; sober; serious. [Orig. p.t. and p.p. of STAY¹] —**staid′ly** *adv.* —**staid′ness** *n.*

stain (stān) *n.* **1** A discoloration or spot from foreign matter. **2** A dye or thin pigment used in staining. **3** A moral blemish or taint. —*v.t.* **1** To make a stain upon; discolor; soil. **2** To color with a dye or stain. **3** To bring a moral stain upon; blemish. —*v.i.* **4** To take or impart a stain. [< OF *desteindre* to deprive of color] —**stain′a·ble** *adj.* —**stain′er** *n.*

stained glass Glass colored by the addition of pigments, usu. in the form of metallic oxides which are fused throughout the glass or burned onto its surface. —**stained′-glass′** *adj.*

stain·less (stān′lis) *adj.* **1** Without a stain. **2** Resistant to stain. **3** Made of stain-resistant materials. —*n.* Tableware made of stainless steel. —**stain′less·ly** *adv.*

stainless steel A corrosion-resistant steel alloyed with chromium and often other elements, esp. nickel.

stair (stâr) *n.* **1** A step, or one of a series of steps, for mounting or descending from one level to another. **2** *Usu. pl.* A series of steps. [< OE *stæger*]

stair·case (stâr′kās′) *n.* A flight of stairs, complete with the supports, balusters, etc.

stair·way (stâr′wā′) *n.* One or more flights of stairs.

stair·well (stâr′wel′) *n.* A vertical shaft enclosing a staircase.

stake (stāk) *n.* **1** A stick or post, as of wood or metal, sharpened for driving into the ground. **2** A post to which a person is bound to be burned alive; also, death by burning at the stake. **3** A post or stick set upright in the floor of a car or wagon, to confine loose material. **4** *Often pl.* Something wagered or risked, as the money bet on a race. **5** *Often pl.* A prize in a contest. **6** An interest or share, as in an enterprise. **7** GRUBSTAKE. —**at stake** In hazard or jeopardy. —*v.t.* **staked, stak·ing 1** To fasten or support by means of a stake. **2** To mark the boundaries of with stakes: often with *off* or *out.* **3** *Informal* To wager; risk. **4** *Informal* To supply with money, equipment, etc.; back. [< OE *staca*]

sta·lac·tite (stə·lak′tīt′, stal′ək-) *n.* **1** An elongated, hanging cone of calcium carbonate formed by slow dripping from the roof of a cave. **2** Any similar formation. [< Gk. *stalaktitos* dripping] —**sta·lac·tit·ic** (stal′ək·tit′ik) or **·i·cal** *adj.*

sta·lag·mite (stə·lag′mīt′, stal′· əg-) *n.* **1** A usu. conical mound deposited on a cave floor by dripping from a stalactite. **2** Any similar formation. [< Gk. *stalagmos* a dripping] —**sta·lag·mit·ic** (stal′· əg·mit′ik) or **·i·cal** *adj.* • See STALACTITE.

a. stalactite.
b. stalagmite.

stale (stāl) *adj.* **stal·er, stal·est 1** Having lost freshness; slightly changed or deteriorated, as air, beer, old bread, etc. **2** Lacking in interest from age or familiarity; trite: a *stale* joke. **3** Lacking effectiveness, energy, spontaneity, etc., from too little or too much activity or practice. —*v.t. & v.i.* **staled, stal·ing** To make or become stale. [?] —**stale′ly** *adv.* —**stale′ness** *n.*

stale·mate (stāl′māt′) *n.* **1** In chess, a position in which a player can make no move without putting his king in check. The result is a draw. **2** Any tie, standstill, or deadlock. —*v.t.* **·mat·ed, ·mat·ing 1** To put into a condition of stalemate. **2** To bring to a standstill. [< AF *estale* a fixed position + MATE²]

stalk¹ (stôk) *n.* **1** The stem or axis of a plant. **2** Any support on which an organ is borne, as a pedicel. **3** A supporting part or stem: the *stalk* of a quill. **4** Any stem or main axis, as of a goblet. [ME *stalke*] —**stalked, stalk′less** *adj.*

stalk² (stôk) *v.i.* **1** To approach game, etc., stealthily. **2** To walk in a stiff or haughty manner. —*v.t.* **3** To approach (game, etc.) stealthily. **4** To invade or permeate: Famine *stalked* the countryside. —*n.* **1** The act of stalking game. **2** A stalking step or walk. [< OE *bestealcian* move stealthily] —**stalk′er** *n.*

stalk·ing-horse (stô′king·hôrs′) *n.* **1** A horse behind which a hunter conceals himself in stalking game. **2** Anything serving to conceal one's intention.

stall (stôl) *n.* **1** A compartment in which a horse or bovine animal is confined and fed. **2** A small booth or compartment in a street, market, etc., for the sale or display of small articles. **3** A partially enclosed seat, as in the choir of a cathedral. **4** *Brit.* A seat very near the stage of a theater. **5** A small compartment, as for showering. **6** An evasive or delaying action. **7** A condition in which a motor temporarily stops functioning. **8** A condition in which an airplane loses the air speed needed to produce sufficient lift to keep it flying. —*v.t.* **1** To place or keep in a stall. **2** To bring to a standstill; halt the progress of. **3** To stop, usu. unintentionally, the operation or motion of. **4** To put (an airplane) into a stall. **5** To cause to stick fast in mud, snow, etc. —*v.i.* **6** To come to a standstill; stop, esp. unintentionally. **7** To stick fast in mud, snow, etc. **8** To make delays; be evasive: *stall* for time. **9** To live or be kept in a stall. **10** *Aeron.* To go into a stall. [< OE *steall*]

stall-feed (stôl′fēd′) *v.t.* **-fed, -feed·ing** To feed (cattle) in a stall so as to fatten them. —**stall′-fed′** *adj.*

stal·lion (stal′yən) *n.* An uncastrated male horse. [< OHG *stal* stable]

stal·wart (stôl′wərt) *adj.* **1** Strong and robust. **2** Resolute; determined. **3** Brave; courageous. —*n.* **1** An uncompromising partisan, as in politics. **2** One who is stalwart. [< OE *stæl* place + *wierthe* worth] —**stal′wart·ly** *adv.* —**stal′wart·ness** *n.*

sta·men (stā′mən) *n. pl.* **sta·mens** or **stam·i·na** (stam′ə·nə) One of the pollen-bearing organs of a flower, consisting of a filament supporting an anther. [L, warp, thread] —**stam·i·nal** (stam′· ə·nəl) *adj.*

Stamen (a, b, c)
a. pollen. b. anther.
c. filament. d. pistil.

stam·i·na (stam′ə·nə) *n.* Strength and endurance, as in withstanding hardship or difficulty. [L, pl. of *stamen* warp, thread] —**stam′i·nal** *adj.*

stam·i·nate (stam′ə·nit, -nāt) *adj.* **1** Having stamens but no pistil, as male flowers. **2** Having stamens.

stam·mer (stam′ər) *v.t. & v.i.* To speak or utter with nervous repetitions or prolongations of a sound or syllable, and involuntary pauses. —*n.* The act or habit of stammering. [< OE *stamerian*] —**stam′mer·er** *n.*

stamp (stamp) *v.t.* **1** To strike heavily with the sole of the foot. **2** To bring down (the foot) heavily and noisily. **3** To affect in a specified manner by or as by stamping with the foot: to *stamp* out opposition. **4** To make, form, cut out, etc., with a stamp or die: often with *out:* to *stamp* out a circle from the steel. **5** To imprint or impress with a die, stamp, etc.: to *stamp* the date on a letter. **6** To fix or imprint permanently: The deed was *stamped* on his memory. **7** To characterize; brand: to *stamp* a story false. **8** To affix an official seal, stamp, etc., to. **9** To crush or pulverize, as ore. —*v.i.* **10** To strike the foot heavily on the ground. **11** To walk with heavy, resounding steps. —*n.* **1** The act of stamping. **2** A machine or tool, as a die, that cuts out or shapes a form. **3** An implement or device that imprints a design, character, mark, etc., on something; also, the design, character, mark, etc., so imprinted. **4** A printed device of paper to be attached to something to show that a tax or fee has been paid: a postage *stamp*. **5** TRADING STAMP. **6** A specific impression or effect: the *stamp* of genius. **7** Characteristic quality or form; kind; sort: I dislike men of his *stamp*. [ME *stampen*] —**stamp′er** *n.*

stam·pede (stam-pēd′) *n.* **1** A sudden starting and rushing off through panic: said primarily of a herd of cattle, horses, etc. **2** Any sudden, impulsive rush or movement of a crowd, as of a mob. **3** A spontaneous mass impulse, trend, or movement, as toward the support of a political candidate. **4** *Can.* RODEO. —*v.* ·ped·ed, ·ped·ing *v.t.* **1** To cause a stampede in. —*v.i.* **2** To engage in a stampede. [< Am. Sp. *estampar* to stamp] —**stam·ped′er** *n.*

stamping ground A favorite or habitual gathering place.

stance (stans) *n.* **1** Mode of standing; posture, esp. with reference to the placing of the feet. **2** Attitude; point of view: a moral *stance*. [< L *stans* pr. p. of *stare* to stand]

stanch (stanch, stänch) *v.t.* **1** To stop or check the flow of (blood, tears, etc.). **2** To stop the flow of blood from (a wound). **3** To check or put an end to. —*adj.* STAUNCH. [< OF *estanchier* to halt] —**stanch′er** *n.* • The spelling *stanch* is usu. preferred for the verb in both England and the U.S., and *staunch* for the adjective. Many writers, however, use one or the other spelling for both.

stan·chion (stan′shən) *n.* **1** An upright bar forming a principal support. **2** A device that fits around a cow's neck, used to restrain movement in a stall. —*v.t.* To provide, restrain, or support with stanchions. [< OF *estanchon*]

stand (stand) *v.* **stood, stand·ing** *v.i.* **1** To assume or maintain an erect position on the feet. **2** To be in a vertical position: The oars *stood* in the corner. **3** To measure a specified height when standing: He *stands* six feet. **4** To assume a specified position: to *stand* aside. **5** To be situated; have position or location; lie: The factory *stands* on a hill. **6** To have or be in a specified state, condition, or relation: We *stand* to gain everything by not fighting; He *stood* in fear of his life. **7** To assume an attitude for defense or offense: *Stand* and fight! **8** To maintain one's attitude, opinions, etc.: *Stand* firm. **9** To be or exist in a printed or written form: Photograph the letter just as it *stands*. **10** To remain unimpaired, unchanged, or valid: My decision still *stands*. **11** To collect and remain: Tears *stood* in her eyes. **12** To be of a specified rank or class: He *stands* third. **13** To stop or pause; halt. **14** *Naut.* To take a direction; steer. **15** *Brit.* To be a candidate, as for election. —*v.t.* **16** To place upright; set in an erect position. **17** To put up with; endure; tolerate. **18** To be subjected to; undergo: He must *stand* trial. **19** To withstand or endure successfully: to *stand* the test of time. **20** To carry out the duty of: to *stand* watch. **21** *Informal* **a** To treat: I'll *stand* you to a drink. **b** To bear the expense of: to *stand* a dinner. —**stand a chance** To have a chance. —**stand by 1** To stay near and be ready to help or operate. **2** To help; support. **3** To abide by; make good; adhere to. **4** To remain passive, as when help is needed. **5** *Telecom.* To keep tuned in, as for the continuance of an interrupted transmission. —**stand for 1** To represent; symbolize. **2** To put up with; tolerate. —**stand in for** To act as a substitute for. —**stand off 1** To keep at a distance. **2** To fail to agree or comply. **3** To put off; evade, as a creditor. —**stand on 1** To be based on or grounded in; rest. **2** To insist on observance of: to *stand on* ceremony. **3** *Naut.* To keep on the same tack or course. —**stand out 1** To stick out; project or protrude. **2** To be prominent or conspicuous. **3** To be outstanding, remarkable, etc. **4** To refuse to consent or agree. —**stand pat 1** In poker, to play one's hand as dealt, without drawing new cards. **2** To resist change. —**stand to reason** To conform to reason. —**stand up 1** To stand erect. **2** To withstand wear, criticism, analysis, etc. **3** *Slang* To fail, usu. intentionally, to keep an appointment with. —**stand up for** To side with; take the part of. —**stand up to** To confront courageously; face. —*n.* **1** The act or condition of standing, esp. of halting or stopping, as: **a** A stopping or halt, as in a retreat, to fight back or resist. **b** A stop for a performance, made by a theatrical company while on

tour; also, the place stopped at. **2** The place or location where one stands or is assigned to stand; position. **3** Any place where something stands: a taxi *stand*. **4** An opinion, attitude, point of view, etc.: to take a *stand*. **5** A structure upon which persons may sit or stand, as: **a** *Often pl.* A series of raised seats or benches, as at an athletic contest. **b** A platform: a reviewing *stand*. **c** A small platform in court from which a witness testifies. **6** A small table. **7** A rack or other structure for holding something: an umbrella *stand*. **8** A stall, counter, or the like where merchandise is displayed or sold. **9** A vertical growth of trees or plants. [< OE *standan*] —**stand′er** *n.*

stan·dard (stan′dərd) *n.* **1** A flag, ensign, or banner, used as an emblem of a government, body of men, head of state, etc. **2** A figure or image adopted as an emblem or symbol. **3** Something established and generally accepted as a model, example, or test of excellence, attainment, etc.; criterion. **4** Something established as a measure or reference of weight, extent, quantity, quality, or value. **5** In coinage, the established proportion by weight of pure gold or silver and an alloy. **6** The measurable basis of value in a monetary system. **7** An upright structure, timber, post, etc., used as a support. **8** A musical composition whose popularity has become firmly established over the years. **9** A plant growing on a vigorous, unsupported, upright stem. —*adj.* **1** Having the accuracy or authority of a standard; serving as a gauge or criterion. **2** Of recognized excellence, popularity, reliability, etc.: the *standard* repertoire of symphonies. **3** Not unusual or special in any way; ordinary; typical; regular: *standard* procedure; *standard* equipment. [< OF *estandard* banner]

stan·dard-bear·er (stan′dərd-bâr′ər) *n.* **1** The person who carries the flag or standard of a group, esp. of a regiment or other military body. **2** The official leader or representative of a group, as a presidential nominee.

standard gauge 1 A railroad track width of 56½ inches, considered as standard. **2** A railroad having such a gauge. —**stan′dard-gauge′** *adj.*

stan·dard·ize (stan′dər-dīz) *v.t.* **·ized, ·iz·ing** To make conform to, regulate, or test by a standard. —**stan′dard·i·za′tion, stan′dard·iz′er** *n.*

standard of living The average manner of day-to-day living of a country, group, or person, with reference to food, housing, clothing, comforts, etc.

standard time The official time for any region or country. Mean solar time is reckoned, east or west, from the meridian of Greenwich, England, each time zone comprising a sector of 15 degrees of longitude and representing a time interval of one hour. In the conterminous U.S., the four time zones, **Eastern Standard Time, Central Standard Time, Mountain Standard Time,** and **Pacific Standard Time** represent the 75th, 90th, 105th, and 120th meridians west of Greenwich, and are accordingly 5, 6, 7, and 8 hours earlier than Greenwich time. Therefore, noon in London corresponds to 7 A.M. in New York, 6 A.M. in Chicago, 5 A.M. in Denver, and 4 A.M. in San Francisco.

stand·by (stand′bī′) *n. pl.* **·bys 1** A person who can be relied on, as in an emergency. **2** Something that always pleases, is always effective, etc. **3** A person or thing waiting and ready to replace another person or thing; substitute.

stand·ee (stan-dē′) *n.* A person who must stand for lack of chairs or seats, as at a theater or on a train.

stand·in (stand′in′) *n.* **1** A person who substitutes for a motion-picture or television performer while lights are arranged, camera angles set, etc. **2** Any substitute for another person.

stand·ing (stan′ding) *adj.* **1** That is upright or erect. **2** Continuing for regular or permanent use; not special or temporary: a *standing* rule. **3** Stagnant; not flowing: *standing* water. **4** Begun or done while standing: a *standing* ovation; a *standing* high jump. **5** Not in use; idle: *standing* machinery. **6** Not movable. —*n.* **1** The act or condition of one who stands. **2** A place to stand in. **3** Relative place or position, as on a graded list of excellence, achievement, etc. **4** Reputation, esp. good reputation. **5** Duration; continuance: a feud of long *standing.*

standing room Place in which to stand, as in a theater when the seats are all occupied.

stand-off (stand′ôf′, -of′) *n.* **1** A draw or tie, as in a game. **2** A counterbalancing or neutralizing effect. —*adj.* **1** That stands off. **2** STANDOFFISH.

stand-off-ish (stand′ôf′ish) *adj.* Aloof; cool. —**stand′off′· ish-ly** *adv.* —**stand′off′ish-ness** *n.*

stand-out (stand′out′) *Informal n.* A person or thing that is unusually good or excellent. —*adj.* Unusually good or excellent.

stand-pat (stand′pat′) *adj. Informal* Resistant to change; conservative. —**stand′pat′ter, stand′pat′tism** *n.*

stand-pipe (stand′pīp′) *n.* A high vertical pipe or water tower, as at a reservoir, into which the water is pumped to create pressure.

stand-point (stand′point′) *n.* Point of view; position; stance.

stand-still (stand′stil′) *n.* A stopping; cessation; halt.

stand-up (stand′up′) *adj.* **1** Having an erect or vertical position: a *stand-up* collar. **2** Done, consumed, etc., while standing.

stan-hope (stan′hōp) *n.* A light, open, one-seated carriage. [< F. *Stanhope,* 1787–1864, English clergyman]

stank (stangk) *p.t.* of STINK.

stan-nic (stan′ik) *adj. Chem.* Of, pertaining to, or containing tin, esp. in its higher valence. [< L *stannum* tin]

stan-nous (stan′əs) *adj.* Of, pertaining to, or containing tin, esp. in its lower valence. [< L *stannum* tin]

stan-za (stan′zə) *n.* A certain number of lines of verse grouped together and forming a definite division of a poem. [Ital., room, stanza] —**stan-za-ic** (stan-zā′ik) *adj.*

sta-pes (stā′pēz) *n. pl.* **sta-pes** or **sta-pe-des** (stə-pē′dēz, stā′pə-dēz′) *Anat.* The innermost small bone of the middle ear of mammals. [LL, a stirrup] —**sta-pe-di-al** (stə-pē′· dē-əl) *adj.*

staph (staf) *n.* STAPHYLOCOCCUS.

staph-y-lo-coc-cus (staf′ə-lō-kok′əs) *n. pl.* **-coc-ci** (-kok′sī, -sē, -ī, -ē) Any of a group of spherical bacteria occurring singly, in pairs, or in irregular clusters and often acting as infective agents. [< Gk. *staphylos* bunch of grapes + *kokkos* a berry] —**staph′y-lo-coc′cic** (-kok′sik, -kok′ik) *adj.* • See BACTERIUM.

sta-ple¹ (stā′pəl) *n.* **1** A principal commodity or product of a country or region. **2** A chief item, element, or main constituent of anything. **3** A product that is constantly sold and used, as sugar or salt. **4** Raw material. **5** The corded or combed fiber of cotton, wool, or flax, with reference to its length. **6** A source of supply; storehouse. —*adj.* **1** Regularly and constantly produced, consumed, or sold. **2** Main; chief. —*v.t.* **·pled, ·pling** To sort or classify according to length, as wool fiber. [< MDu. *stapel* market]

sta-ple² (stā′pəl) *n.* A U-shaped piece of metal or thin wire, having pointed ends and driven into a surface, as wood or paper, to serve as a fastening. —*v.t.* **·pled, ·pling** To fix or fasten by a staple or staples. [< OE *stapol* post]

sta-pler¹ (stā′plər) *n.* **1** A person who staples wool, etc. **2** A person who deals in staple goods.

sta-pler² (stā′plər) *n.* A device for driving staples into a surface.

star (stär) *n.* **1** *Astron.* Any of the numerous celestial objects that emit radiant energy, including visible light, generated by nuclear reactions. **2** Loosely, any of the luminous bodies regularly seen as points of light in the night sky. **3** A conventional figure having five or more radiating points. **4** Something resembling such a figure, as an emblem or device. **5** An asterisk (*). **6** A person of outstanding talent or accomplishment and a quality of personality that attracts wide public interest or attention. **7** A performer who plays the leading role in a play, opera, etc. **8** *Often pl.* Any of the planets or their configuration considered as influencing one's fate. **9** Fortune; destiny. —*v.* **starred, star-ring** *v.t.* **1** To set, mark, or adorn with stars. **2** To mark with an asterisk. **3** To present as a star in an entertainment. —*v.i.* **4** To be prominent or brilliant. **5** To play the leading part; be the star. —*adj.* **1** Of or pertaining to a star or stars. **2** Prominent; brilliant: a *star* football player. [< OE *steorra*] —**star′less, star′like** *adj.*

star-board (stär′bərd) *n.* The right-hand side of a vessel or aircraft as one faces the front or forward. —*adj.* Of, pertaining to, or on the starboard. —*adv.* Toward the starboard side. —*v.t.* To put, move, or turn (the helm) to the starboard side. [< OE *steorbord* steering side]

starch (stärch) *n.* **1** A complex, insoluble carbohydrate produced by photosynthesis and usu. stored in roots, tubers, seeds, etc. **2** A white, powdery substance consisting of purified starch extracted from potatoes, corn, etc. **3** Any starchy foodstuff. **4** A fabric stiffener made of starch suspended in water. **5** A stiff or formal manner. **6** *Informal* Energy; vigor. —*v.t.* To apply starch to; stiffen with or as with starch. [< OE *stearc* stiff]

starch-y (stär′chē) *adj.* **starch-i-er, starch-i-est** **1** Stiffened with starch; stiff. **2** Primly formal or stiff. **3** Containing a large proportion of starch: a *starchy* vegetable. —**starch′· i-ly** *adv.* —**starch′i-ness** *n.*

star-crossed (stär′krôst′, -krost′) *adj.* Doomed; ill-fated: a *star-crossed* love affair.

star-dom (stär′dəm) *n.* **1** The status of a person who is a star. **2** Stars of the stage, screen, etc., collectively.

stare (stâr) *v.* **stared, star-ing** *v.i.* **1** To gaze fixedly, usu. with the eyes open wide, as from admiration, fear, or insolence. **2** To be conspicuous or unduly apparent; glare. —*v.t.* **3** To gaze fixedly at. **4** To affect in a specified manner by a stare: to *stare* a person into silence. —**stare down** To gaze back fixedly (at a person) until he turns his eyes away. —**stare one in the face** To be perfectly plain or obvious. —*n.* A steady, fixed gaze. [< OE *starian*] — **star′er** *n.*

star-fish (stär′fish′) *n. pl.* **·fish** or **·fish-es** Any of various radially symmetrical echinoderms with a star-shaped body having five or more arms.

star-gaze (stär′gāz′) *v.i.* **·gazed, ·gaz-ing** **1** To gaze at or study the stars. **2** To daydream. —**star′gaz′· er** *n.*

stark (stärk) *adj.* **1** Deserted; barren; bleak: a *stark* landscape. **2** Severe; irregular: *stark* measures. **3** With little or no ornamentation, color, etc.: a *stark* room. **4** Blunt; grim; pitiless: *stark* reality. **5** Complete; utter: *stark* madness. **6** Stiff or rigid, as in death. **7** Sharp and bare, as of outline. —*adv.* **1** In a stark manner. **2** Completely; utterly: *stark* naked. [< OE *stearc* stiff] —**stark′ly** *adv.* —**stark′ness** *n.*

Starfish

star-let (stär′lit) *n. Informal* A young movie actress being prepared for stardom.

star-light (stär′līt) *n.* The light given by a star or stars. —*adj.* Lighted by or only by the stars: also **star′lit′** (-lit′).

star-ling (stär′ling) *n.* **1** A chubby, gregarious, aggressive bird with iridescent black plumage, introduced from Europe and now common in North America. **2** Any of various related European birds. [< OE *stærling*]

star of David The six-pointed star used as a symbol of Judaism.

starred (stärd) *adj.* **1** Spangled or marked with stars. **2** Marked with an asterisk. **3** Affected by astral influence: used chiefly in combination: *ill-starred.* **4** Presented or advertised as the star of an entertainment.

star-ry (stär′ē) *adj.* **·ri-er, ·ri-est** **1** Set or marked with stars. **2** Shining as or like stars. **3** Star-shaped. **4** Lighted by or abounding in stars. **5** Of, from, having to do with, or like stars. —**star′ri-ness** *n.*

Star of David

star-ry-eyed (stär′ē-īd′) *adj.* Excited by or given to fanciful thoughts of romance, adventure, etc.

Stars and Stripes The flag of the U.S., having 13 alternating horizontal stripes of red and white, and in the upper left-hand corner 50 white stars against a blue ground.

star-span-gled (stär′spang′gəld) *adj.* Spangled with stars or starlike spots or points.

Star-Spangled Banner **1** The flag of the U.S. **2** The national anthem of the U.S., with words written by Francis Scott Key in 1814.

start (stärt) *v.i.* **1** To make an involuntary, startled movement, as from fear or surprise. **2** To move suddenly, as with a spring, leap, or bound. **3** To begin an action, undertaking, trip, etc.: They *started* early on their vacation. **4** To become active, operative, etc.: School *starts* in the fall. **5** To be on the team, lineup, etc., that begins a game or contest. **6** To protrude; seem to bulge: His eyes *started* from his head. **7** To be displaced or dislocated; become loose, warped, etc. —*v.t.* **8** To set in motion, activity, etc.: to *start* an engine; to *start* a rumor. **9** To begin; commence: to *start* a lecture. **10** To put on the team, lineup, etc., that begins a game or contest: I'm *starting* the new players today. **11** To set up; establish. **12** To introduce (a subject) or propound (a question). **13** To displace or dislocate; loosen, warp, etc.: The collision *started* the ship's seams. **14** To rouse from cover; cause to take flight; flush, as game. **15** To draw the contents from; tap, as a cask. —**start up 1** To rise or appear suddenly. **2** To begin; come into being. **3** To begin the operation of (a motor, etc.). —**to start with** In the first place. —*n.* **1** A quick, startled movement or reaction. **2** A temporary or spasmodic action or attempt: by fits and *starts.* **3** A beginning or commencement, as of an action, undertaking, etc. **4** Advantage; lead, as in a race. **5** A place or time of beginning. **6** A loosened place or condition; crack: a *start* in a ship's planking. [ME *sterten* start, leap]

start·er (stär′tər) *n.* **1** One who or that which starts, esp.. **a** A competitor or member of a team at the start of a race or contest. **b** A person giving the starting signal for a race or contest. **c** A person whose job is to see to it that buses, trolleys, etc., leave on schedule. **d** Any mechanical device that initiates movement in an engine or the like. **2** A substance or mixture that initiates a chemical reaction, esp. in food: a *starter* for bread.

star·tle (stärt′əl) *v.* **·tled, ·tling** *v.t.* **1** To arouse or excite suddenly; alarm. —*v.i.* **2** To be aroused or excited suddenly; take alarm. —*n.* A sudden fright or shock; a scare. [< OE *steartlian* to kick] —**star′tler** *n.*

star·tling (stärt′ling) *adj.* Rousing sudden surprise, alarm, or the like. —**star′tling·ly** *adv.*

star·va·tion (stär·vā′shən) *n.* **1** The act of starving. **2** The state of being starved. —*adj.* Insufficient to sustain life or to purchase basic necessities: a *starvation* diet; *starvation* wages.

starve (stärv) *v.* **starved, starv·ing** *v.i.* **1** To die or perish from lack of food. **2** To suffer from extreme hunger. **3** To suffer from lack or need: to *starve* for friendship. —*v.t.* **4** To cause to die of hunger. **5** To deprive of food. **6** To bring to a specified condition by starving: to *starve* an enemy into surrender. [< OE *steorfan* die] —**starv′er** *n.*

starve·ling (stärv′ling) *n.* A person or animal that is starving, starved, or emaciated.

stash (stash) *v.t. Informal* To hide or conceal (money or valuables), for future use or safe-keeping: often with *away.* —*n. Slang* **1** A place where things are stashed away. **2** Something stashed away. [?]

-stat *combining form* A device which stops or makes constant: *thermostat.* [< Gk. *-statēs* causing to stand]

state (stāt) *n.* **1** A mode or condition of being or existing: a *state* of war. **2** A particular physical or chemical stage or condition of something: Ice is the solid *state* of water. **3** Frame of mind: a *state* of utter peace. **4** Any extreme mental condition, as of excitement, nervousness, etc. **5** Social status or position. **6** A grand, ceremonious, or luxurious style of living or doing: to arrive in *state.* **6** A sovereign political community; nation. **7** A political and territorial unit within such a community: the *state* of Maine. —**lie in state** To be placed on public view before burial. —*adj.* **1** Of or pertaining to a state, nation, or government. **2** Intended for use on occasions of ceremony. —*v.t.* **stat·ed, stat·ing 1** To set forth explicitly in speech or writing; declare. **2** To fix; settle: to *state* terms. [< L *status* condition, state < *stare* to stand] —**Syn.** *n.* **1** circumstances. **5** standing. *v.* **1** affirm, assert, aver.

state·craft (stāt′kraft′, -kräft′) *n.* The art of conducting affairs of state.

stat·ed (stā′tid) *adj.* **1** Regular; fixed. **2** Told; asserted: a *stated* fact. —**stat′ed·ly** *adv.*

state·house (stāt′hous′) *n. Often cap.* A building used for sessions of a state legislature. Also **state house.**

state·ly (stāt′lē) *adj.* **·li·er, ·li·est 1** Dignified; majestic: a *stately* mansion. **2** Slow; measured: a *stately* march. —*adv.* Loftily. —**state′li·ness** *n.* —**Syn. 1** imposing, grand, awesome, impressive.

state·ment (stāt′mənt) *n.* **1** The act of stating. **2** That which is stated. **3** A summary of assets and liabilities, showing the balance due. **3** A major or dominant idea expressed in the composition of a creative work, as in art, music, or design; motif. **4** The expression of such an idea.

state·room (stāt′rōōm′, -rŏŏm′) *n.* A small private bedroom on a passenger ship or railroad train.

state's evidence Testimony for the prosecution in a U.S. federal or state court, esp. that of a criminal against his accomplices. —**turn state's evidence** To offer state's evidence.

state·side (stāt′sīd′) *adj. Informal* Of or in the continental U.S. —*adv.* In or to the continental U.S.

states·man (stāts′mən) *n. pl.* **·men** (-mən) A person skilled in the science of government and prominent in national and foreign affairs. —**states′man·ly** *adv.* —**states′·man·ship** *n.*

state socialism A political theory advocating government ownership of utilities and industries.

States' rights The powers not vested in the U.S. federal government by the Constitution nor prohibited by it to the states. Also **State rights.**

states·wom·an (stāts′wŏŏm′ən) *n. pl.* **·wom·en** (-wim′in) A woman skilled in the science of government and prominent in national and foreign affairs.

state-wide (stāt′wīd′) *adj. & adv.* Throughout a state.

stat·ic (stat′ik) *adj.* **1** Pertaining to bodies at rest or forces in equilibrium. **2** *Physics* Not involved in or with motion: *static* pressure. **3** *Electr.* Of or caused by stationary electric charges. **4** At rest; not active. **5** Of or pertaining to nonactive elements. **6** Dealing with fixed or stable conditions. Also **stat′i·cal.** —*n. Electronics* Electrical noise, esp. atmospheric, that interferes with radio communications. [< Gk *statikos* causing to stand] —**stat′i·cal·ly** *adv.*

stat·ics (stat′iks) *n.pl.* *(construed as sing.)* The mechanics of bodies at rest.

sta·tion (stā′shən) *n.* **1** A place where a person or thing usu. stands. **2** The headquarters of some official person or body of men: a police *station.* **3** A starting point or stopping place of a railroad or bus line. **4** A building for the accommodation of passengers or freight, as on a railroad or bus line; depot. **5** Social rank; standing. **6** *Mil.* The place to which an individual, unit, or ship is assigned for duty. **7** The installations of a radio or television broadcasting unit. —*v.t.* To assign to a station; set in position. [< L *stare* to stand]

sta·tion·ar·y (stā′shə·ner′ē) *adj.* **1** Remaining in one place. **2** Fixed; not portable. **3** Exhibiting no change of character or condition.

sta·tion·er (stā′shə·nər) *n.* A dealer in stationery and related goods. [< Med. L *stationarius* stationary, having a fixed location (for business)]

sta·tion·er·y (stā′shə·ner′ē) *n.* Paper, pens, pencils, ink, notebooks, and other related goods.

station wagon An automotive vehicle with one or more rows of seats behind the front seat and with a hinged tailgate for admitting luggage, etc.

stat·ism (stā′tiz·əm) *n.* A theory of government which advocates the concentration of economic planning, control, etc., in a centralized government. —**stat′ist** *n.*

sta·tis·tic (stə·tis′tik) *n.* Any element entering into a statistical statement. —*adj.* STATISTICAL.

sta·tis·ti·cal (stə·tis′tə·kəl) *adj.* **1** Of or pertaining to statistics. **2** Composed of statistics. —**sta·tis′ti·cal·ly** *adv.*

stat·is·ti·cian (stat′is·tish′ən) *n.* One skilled in collecting and tabulating statistical data.

sta·tis·tics (stə·tis′tiks) *n.pl.* **1** A collection of quantitative data or facts. **2** *(construed as sing.)* The branch of mathematics that deals with the collection and analysis of quantitative data. [< L *status* position, state]

stat·u·ar·y (stach′ŏŏ·er′ē) *n. pl.* **·ar·ies** Statues collectively. —*adj.* Of or suitable for statues. [< L *statua* statue]

stat·ue (stach′ŏŏ) *n.* A three-dimensional representation of a human or animal figure modeled in clay or wax, cast in bronze or plaster, or carved in wood or stone. [< L *status,* pp. of *stare* stand]

stat·u·esque (stach′ŏŏ·esk′) *adj.* 1 Resembling a statue, as in grace or dignity. 2 Shapely; comely. —**stat′u·esque′ly** *adv.* —**stat′u·esque′ness** *n.*

stat·u·ette (stach′ŏŏ·et′) *n.* A small statue. [F]

stat·ure (stach′ər) *n.* 1 The natural height of a body. 2 The height of anything, as a tree. 3 Status or reputation resulting from development or growth: artistic *stature.* [< L *status* condition, state]

sta·tus (stā′təs, stat′əs) *n.* 1 State, condition, or relation. 2 Relative position or rank. [< L *stare* to stand]

sta·tus quo (stā′təs kwō, stat′əs) The actual or existing condition or state. Also **status in quo.** [L]

stat·ute (stach′ŏŏt) *n.* 1 *Law* A legislative enactment. 2 An established law or regulation. [< L *statutus,* pp. of *statuere* constitute]

statute law The law as set forth in statutes.

statute mile MILE (def. 1).

statute of limitations A statute which imposes time limits upon the right of action in certain cases.

stat·u·to·ry (stach′ə·tôr′ē, -tō′rē) *adj.* 1 Pertaining to a statute. 2 Created by or based upon legislative enactment.

statutory rape See RAPE.

staunch (stônch, stänch) *adj.* 1 Firm in principle; constant; trustworthy. 2 Stout; seaworthy: a *staunch* ship. —*v.t.* STANCH. [< OF *estanchier* make stand] —**staunch′ly** *adv.* —**staunch′ness** *n.* —**Syn.** *adj.* 1 faithful, loyal, trusty. 2 sound, trim. • See STANCH.

stave (stāv) *n.* 1 A curved strip of wood, forming a part of the sides of a barrel, tub, or the like. 2 *Music* A staff. 3 A stanza; verse. 4 A rod, cudgel, or staff. 5 A rung of a rack or ladder. —*v.* **staved** or **stove, stav·ing** *v.t.* 1 To break or make (a hole) by crushing or collision. 2 To furnish with staves. —*v.i.* 1 To be broken in, as a vessel's hull. —**stave off** To ward off: to *stave off* bankruptcy. [< *staves,* pl. of STAFF]

Barrel stave

staves (stāvz) *n.* 1 A *pl.* of STAFF. 2 *pl.* of STAVE.

stay[1] (stā) *v.i.* 1 To stop; halt: *Stay* where you are. 2 To continue in a specified place or condition: to *stay* home; to *stay* healthy. 3 To remain temporarily as a guest or resident. 4 To tarry: I'll *stay* a few more minutes. 5 *Informal* To have endurance; last. 6 *Informal* To keep pace with a competitor, as in a race. —*v.t.* 7 To bring to a stop; halt. 8 To hinder; delay. 9 To put off; postpone. 10 To satisfy the demands of temporarily; appease: to *stay* the pangs of hunger. 11 To remain for the duration of: to *stay* the night. —*n.* 1 The act or time of staying: a week's *stay* at the beach. 2 A deferment or suspension of judicial proceedings: The court granted a *stay* of sentencing. 3 *Informal* Staying power; endurance. [< L *stare* stand] —**stay′er** *n.*

stay[2] (stā) *v.t.* To be a support to; prop or hold up. —*n.* 1 Anything which props or supports. 2 *pl.* A corset stiffened, as with steel strips or whalebone. [< OF *estayer*]

stay[3] (stā) *Naut. n.* 1 A large, strong rope or wire, used to brace a mast or spar. 2 Any rope having a similar use. —*v.t.* 1 To support with a stay or stays. 2 To put (a vessel) on the opposite tack. —*v.i.* 3 To tack: said of vessels. [< OE *stæg*]

staying power The ability to endure.

stay·sail (stā′sāl′, -səl) *n. Naut.* A sail, usu. triangular, extended on a stay.

Ste. Sainte (female) [F *Sainte*).

stead (sted) *n.* Place of another person or thing as assumed by a substitute or a successor: My sister went in my *stead.* —**stand (one) in good stead** To give (one) good service, support, etc. [< OE *stede* place]

stead·fast (sted′fast′, -fäst′, -fəst) *adj.* 1 Firmly fixed in faith or devotion to duty. 2 Directed fixedly at one point, as the gaze. [< OE *stedefæst*] —**stead′fast′ly** *adv.* —**stead′fast′ness** *n.*

stead·y (sted′ē) *adj.* **stead·i·er, stead·i·est** 1 Stable; not liable to shake or totter: a *steady* ladder. 2 Unfaltering; constant: a *steady* light; *steady* loyalty. 3 Calm; unruffled: *steady* nerves. 4 Free from intemperance and dissipation: *steady* habits. 5 Regular: a *steady* customer. 6 Of a ship, keeping more or less upright in rough seas. —**go steady** *Informal* To date exclusively. —*v.t. & v.i.* **stead·ied, stead·y·ing** To make or become steady. —*interj.* Not so fast; keep calm. —*n. Slang* A sweetheart or constant companion. [< STEAD] —**stead′i·ly** *adv.* —**stead′i·ness** *n.*

steak (stāk) *n.* A slice of meat or fish, esp. of beef, usu. broiled or fried. [< ON *steik*]

steal (stēl) *v.* **stole, sto·len, steal·ing** *v.t.* 1 To take from another without right or permission. 2 To take or obtain in a subtle manner: He has *stolen* the hearts of the people. 3 In baseball, to reach (another base) without the aid of a hit or error: said of a base runner. —*v.i.* 4 To move quietly and stealthily: to *steal* away in the night. 5 To commit theft. 6 To move secretly or furtively. —*n. Informal* 1 The act of stealing or that which is stolen. 2 Any underhanded financial deal that benefits the originators. 3 A bargain: a *steal* at $3.99. [< OE *stelan*] —**steal′er** *n.* —**Syn.** *v.* 1 filch, pilfer, purloin. 4 skulk, slink.

stealth (stelth) *n.* Secret or furtive action, movement, or behavior. [< OE *stelan* steal]

stealth·y (stel′thē) *adj.* **stealth·i·er, stealth·i·est** Marked by stealth; designed to elude notice. —**stealth′i·ly** *adv.* —**stealth′i·ness** *n.*

steam (stēm) *n.* 1 Water in the form of a gas, esp. above the boiling point of the liquid. 2 The visible mist formed by sudden cooling of hot steam. 3 Any kind of vaporous exhalation. 4 Energy or power derived from hot water vapor under pressure. 5 *Informal* Vigor; force; speed. —**let off steam** To give expression to pent-up emotions or opinions. —*v.i.* 1 To emit steam or vapor. 2 To rise or pass off as steam. 3 To become covered with condensed water vapor: often with *up.* 4 To generate steam. 5 To move or travel by the agency of steam. —*v.t.* 6 To treat with steam, as in softening, cooking, cleaning, etc. —*adj.* 1 Of, driven, or operated by steam. 2 Producing or containing steam: a *steam* boiler; a *steam* pipe. 3 Treated by steam. 4 Using steam: *steam* heat. [< OE *stēam*] —**steam′i·ness** *n.* —**steam′y** *adj.* (**·i·er, ·i·est**)

steam·boat (stēm′bōt′) *n.* A boat propelled by steam.

steam engine An engine that derives its force from the pressure of hot steam.

steam·er (stē′mər) *n.* 1 A steamship or steamboat. 2 A pot or container in which something is steamed.

steam·fit·ter (stēm′fit′ər) *n.* A man who sets up or repairs steam pipes and their fittings. —**steam′fit′ting** *n.*

steam·roll·er (stēm′rōl′ər) *n.* 1 A machine having a heavy roller for flattening asphalt surfaces. 2 *Informal* Any force that ruthlessly overcomes opposition. —*v. Informal v.t.* 1 To crush ruthlessly. —*v.i.* 2 To move with crushing force. Also **steam′roll′.**

steam·ship (stēm′ship′) *n.* A large vessel used for ocean traffic and propelled by steam.

steam shovel A power-operated machine for digging and excavation.

ste·ap·sin (stē·ap′sin) *n.* A pancreatic enzyme that aids in the digestion of fat. [< STEA(RIN) + (PE)PSIN]

ste·ar·ic acid (stē·ar′ik, stir′ik) A fatty acid common in solid animal fats, used in making soap. Also **ste′a·rin.** [< Gk. *stear* suet]

ste·a·tite (stē′ə·tīt) *n.* Massive talc found in extensive beds and used for electric insulation. [< Gk. *stear, steatos* suet, tallow] —**ste′a·tit′ic** (-tit′ik) *adj.*

sted·fast (sted′fast′, -fäst′, -fəst) *adj.* STEADFAST.

steed (stēd) *n.* A horse; esp., a spirited horse. [< OE *stēda* studhorse]

steel (stēl) *n.* 1 Any of various alloys of iron containing carbon in amounts up to about 2 percent, often with other components that give special properties. 2 Something made of steel, as an implement or weapon. 3 Hardness of character. 4 *Can.* A railway track or line. —*adj.* 1 Made or composed of steel. 2 Adamant; unyielding. —*v.t.* 1 To cover with steel. 2 To make strong; harden: to *steel* one's heart against misery. [< OE *stēl*] —**steel′i·ness** *n.* —**steel′y** *adj.* (**·i·er, ·i·est**)

steel wool Steel fibers matted together for use in cleaning and polishing.

steel·work·er (stēl′wûr′kər) *n.* One who works in a steel mill.

steel·yard (stēl′yärd′, stil′yərd) *n.* A device for weighing, consisting of a scaled beam, a movable counterpoise, and hooks to hold the article to be weighed. Also **steel′yards.**

steen·bok (stēn′bok, stän′) *n. pl.* **·bok** or **·boks** A small African antelope with short horns in the male. [< MDu. *steen* stone + *boc* buck]

steep[1] (stēp) *adj.* **1** Sloping sharply; precipitous. **2** *Informal* Exorbitant; high, as a price. —*n.* A cliff; a precipitous place. [< OE *stēap*] —**steep′ly** *adv.* —**steep′ness** *n.* —Syn. *adj.* **1** abrupt, high, sharp, sheer.

steep[2] (stēp) *v.t.* **1** To soak in a liquid, as for softening, cleansing, etc. **2** To imbue thoroughly: *steeped* in crime. —*v.i.* **3** To undergo soaking in a liquid. —*n.* **1** The process of steeping, or the state of being steeped. **2** A liquid or bath in which anything is steeped. [< ON *steypa* pour] —**steep′er** *n.*

Steenbok

steep·en (stē′pən) *v.t. & v.i.* To make or become steep or steeper.

stee·ple (stē′pəl) *n.* A lofty structure rising above the roof of a church, usu. having a spire. [< OE *stēpel*]

stee·ple·chase (stē′pəl·chās′) *n.* **1** A race on horseback across country. **2** A race over a course with hedges, rails, and water jumps. —**stee′ple·chas′er** *n.*

stee·ple·jack (stē′pəl·jak′) *n.* A man whose occupation is to climb steeples and other tall structures to inspect or make repairs.

steer[1] (stir) *v.t.* **1** To direct the course of (a vessel or vehicle). **2** To follow (a course). **3** To direct; guide; control. —*v.i.* **4** To direct the course of a vessel, vehicle, etc. **5** To undergo guiding or steering. **6** To follow a course: to *steer* for land. —**steer clear of** To avoid; keep away from. —*n. Slang* A tip; piece of advice. [< OE *stēoran*] —**steer′er** *n.*

steer[2] (stir) *n.* **1** A young castrated bovine. **2** Any male cattle raised for beef. [< OE *stēor*]

steer·age (stir′ij) *n.* That part of an ocean passenger vessel allotted to passengers paying the lowest fares.

steers·man (stirz′mən) *n. pl.* **·men** (-mən) One who steers a boat or a ship; a helmsman.

stein (stīn) *n.* A beer mug. [G]

stein·bok (stīn′bok) *n.* STEENBOK.

stel·lar (stel′ər) *adj.* **1** Of or pertaining to the stars; astral. **2** Chief; principal: a *stellar* role in a play. [< L *stella* star]

stel·late (stel′it, -āt) *adj.* Star-shaped; having rays pointing outward from a center. Also **stel·lat·ed** (stel′ā·tid). [< L *stella* star] —**stel′late·ly** *adv.*

St. El·mo's fire (sānt el′mōz) A luminous discharge of static electricity sometimes appearing on the superstructure of ships, on the tips of airplane wings, etc. Also **St. El·mo's light.**

stem[1] (stem) *n.* **1** The main ascending axis of a plant, serving to transport water and nutrients, to hold up the leaves to air and light, etc. **2** A subsidiary stalk supporting a fruit, flower, or leaf. **3** The slender upright support of a goblet, wine glass, vase, etc. **4** In a watch, the small projecting rod used for winding the mainspring. **5** *Music* The line attached to the head of a written musical note. **6** *Ling.* The unchanged element common to all the members of a given inflection. **7** The bow of a boat. —**from stem to stern** From one end of a ship to the other. **2** Throughout; thoroughly. —*v.t.* **stemmed, stem·ming** To remove the stems of or from. —**stem from** To be descended or derived. [< OE *stemm, stemn*] —**stem′mer** *n.*

stem[2] (stem) *v.t.* **stemmed, stem·ming 1** To stop, hold back, or dam up, as a current. **2** To make progress against, as a current, opposing force, etc. [< ON *stemma* stop]

stem·wind·er (stem′wīn′der) *n.* **1** A stemwinding watch. **2** *Slang* A very superior person or thing.

stem·wind·ing (stem′wīn′ding) *adj.* Wound, as a watch, by turning a knob at the outermost end of the stem.

stench (stench) *n.* A foul or offensive odor. [< OE *stenc*] —**stench′y** *adj.* —Syn. fetidness, miasma, reek, stink.

sten·cil (sten′səl) *n.* **1** A thin sheet or plate in which a written text or a pattern is cut through which applied paint or ink penetrates to a surface beneath. **2** Produced by stenciling. —*v.t.* **·ciled** or **·cilled, ·cil·ing** or **·cil·ling** To mark with a stencil. [< OF *estenceler*] —**sten′cil·er** or **sten′cil·ler** *n.*

sten·o (sten′ō) *n. pl.* **sten·os 1** STENOGRAPHER. **2** STENOGRAPHY.

steno- *combining form* Tight; contracted: *stenography.* [< Gk. *stenos* narrow]

steno., stenog. stenographer; stenography.

ste·nog·ra·pher (stə·nog′rə·fər) *n.* One who is skilled in shorthand.

ste·nog·ra·phy (stə·nog′rə·fē) *n.* **1** The method of rapid writing by the use of contractions or arbitrary symbols; shorthand. **2** The act of using stenography. —**sten·o·graph·ic** (sten′ə·graf′ik) or **·i·cal** *adj.* —**sten′o·graph′i·cal·ly** *adv.*

sten·o·type (sten′ə·tīp) *n.* A keyboard-operated machine for recording on paper tape symbols representing speech.

sten·o·typ·y (sten′ə·tī′pē) *n.* A system of shorthand utilizing a keyboard-operated machine to record letters in various combinations that represent sounds, words, or phrases. —**sten′o·typ′ist** *n.*

sten·to·ri·an (sten·tôr′ē·ən, -tō′rē-) *adj.* Extremely loud. [< *Stentor,* a herald in the *Iliad,* famous for his loud voice] —**sten·to′ri·an·ly** *adv.*

step (step) *n.* **1** A change in location or position accomplished by lifting the foot and putting it down in a different place. **2** The distance passed over in making such a motion. **3** Any space easily traversed. **4** A stair or ladder rung. **5** A single action or proceeding regarded as leading to something. **6** A grade or degree: They advanced him a *step.* **7** The sound of a footfall. **8** A footprint; track. **9** *pl.* Progression by walking. **10** A combination of foot movements in dancing. **11** *Music* An interval approximately equal to that between the first two tones of a diatonic scale. —**in step 1** Walking or dancing evenly with another by taking corresponding steps. **2** Conforming; in agreement. —**out of step 1** Not in step. **2** Not conforming or agreeing. —**step by step** In slow stages. —**take steps** To adopt measures, as to attain an end. —**watch one's step** To be cautious. —*v.* **stepped, step·ping** *v.i.* **1** To move forward or backward by taking a step or steps. **2** To walk a short distance. **3** To move with measured, dignified, or graceful steps. **4** To move or act quickly or briskly. **5** To pass into a situation, circumstance, etc.: He *stepped* into a fortune. —*v.t.* **6** To take (a pace, stride, etc.). **7** To perform the steps of: to *step* a quadrille. **8** To place or move (the foot) in taking a step. **9** To measure by taking steps: often with *off.* **10** To cut or arrange in steps. —**step down 1** To decrease gradually. **2** To resign from an office or position; abdicate. —**step in** To begin to take part; intervene. —**step on** (or **upon**) **1** To tread upon. **2** To put the foot on so as to activate, as a brake or treadle. **3** *Informal* To reprove or subdue. —**step on it** *Informal* To hurry; hasten. —**step out 1** To go outside. **2** *Informal* To go out for fun or entertainment. **3** To step down. **4** To walk with long strides. —**step up** To increase; raise. [< OE *stæpe*] —Syn. *n.* **6** stage, level, position, notch.

step- *combining form* Related through the previous marriage of a parent or spouse, but not by blood: *stepchild.* [< OE *steop-*]

step·broth·er (step′bruth′ər) *n.* The son of one's stepparent by a former marriage.

step·child (step′chīld′) *n. pl.* **·chil·dren** The child of one's husband or wife by a former marriage.

step·daugh·ter (step′dô′tər) *n.* A female stepchild.

step-down (step′doun′) *adj.* **1** That decreases gradually. **2** *Electr.* Designating a transformer whose output voltage is less than its input voltage. **3** Designating a speed-reducing gear.

step·fa·ther (step′fä′thər) *n.* A man who has married one's mother after the decease or divorce of one's own father.

step-in (step′in′) *adj.* Put on, as undergarments or shoes, by being stepped into.

step·lad·der (step′lad′ər) *n.* A set of portable, usu. flat steps with a hinged frame at the back for support.

step·moth·er (step′muth′ər) *n.* A woman who has married one's father after the decease or divorce of one's own mother.

step·par·ent (step′pâr′ənt) *n.* A stepfather or stepmother.

steppe (step) *n.* **1** A vast plain devoid of forest. **2** One of the extensive plains in SE Europe and Asia. [< Russ. *step′*]

stepped-up (stept′up′) *adj. Informal* Speeded up; increased: *stepped-up* production.

step·per (step′ər) *n.* **1** One who or that which steps. **2** *Slang* A dancer.

step·ping-stone (step′ing-stōn′) *n.* **1** A stone forming a footrest, as for crossing a stream, etc. **2** That by which one advances or rises.

step·sis·ter (step′sis′tər) *n.* The daughter of one's stepparent by a former marriage.

step·son (step′sun′) *n.* A male stepchild.

step-up (step′up′) *adj.* **1** Increasing by stages. **2** Designating a transformer whose output voltage exceeds its input voltage. **3** Designating a speed-increasing gear. —*n.* An increase, as in intensity, amount, etc.

-ster *suffix of nouns* **1** One who makes or is occupied with: *songster.* **2** One who belongs or is related to: *gangster.* **3** One who is: *youngster.* [< OE *-estre*]

ster., stg. Sterling.

ste·ra·di·an (sti·rā′dē·ən) *n.* A solid angle with its vertex at the center of a sphere which encloses a surface equivalent to the square of the radius of the sphere: a unit of measure. [< Gk. *stereos* solid + RADIAN]

stere (stir) *n.* A cubic meter. [< Gk. *stereos* solid]

ster·e·o (ster′ē·ō, stir′-) *n. pl.* **·e·os** **1** A stereophonic record player, record, tape, etc. **2** Stereophonic sound. **3** STEREOTYPE (defs. 1 & 2). **4** A stereoscopic method; also, a stereoscopic photograph. —*adj.* **1** STEREOPHONIC. **2** STEREOTYPED (def. 1). **3** Of or pertaining to the stereoscope; stereoscopic.

stereo- *combining form* Solid; firm; three-dimensional: *stereoscope.* [< Gk. *stereos* hard]

ster·e·o·phon·ic (ster′ē·ə·fon′ik, stir′-) *adj.* Of, for, or designating a system of sound reproduction in which two independent channels are used so as to present different sounds to each of a listener's ears. —**ster′e·o·phon′i·cal·ly** *adv.*

ster·e·o·scope (ster′ē·ə·skōp′, stir′-) *n.* An instrument for presenting different images of an object to each eye, so as to produce a three-dimensional illusion. —**ster′e·o·scop′ic** (-skop′ik) or **·i·cal** *adj.* —**ster′e·o·scop′i·cal·ly** *adv.* — **ster·e·os·co·pist** (ster′ē·os′kə·pist, stir-) *n.*

ster·e·o·type (ster′ē·ə·tīp′, stir′-) *n.* **1** A printing plate cast in metal from a matrix molded from a raised surface, as type. **2** Anything made or processed in this way. **3** A conventional or hackneyed expression, custom, or mode of thought. —*v.t.* **·typed, ·typ·ing** **1** To make a stereotype of. **2** To print from stereotypes. **3** To give a fixed or unalterable form to. —**ster′e·o·typ′er, ster′e·o·typ′ist** *n.*

ster·e·o·typed (ster′ē·ə·tīpt′, stir′-) *adj.* **1** Produced from a stereotype. **2** Hackneyed; without originality.

ster·ile (ster′əl, *Chiefly Brit.* -īl) *adj.* **1** Having no reproductive power; barren. **2** Lacking productiveness: *sterile* soil. **3** Containing no microorganisms; aseptic: a *sterile* fluid. **4** Lacking vigor or interest; *sterile* prose. **5** Without results; futile: *sterile* hopes. [< L *sterilis*] —**ster′ile·ly** *adv.* —**ste·ril·i·ty** (stə·ril′ə·tē), **ster′ile·ness** *n.*

ster·il·ize (ster′əl·īz) *v.t.* **·ized, ·iz·ing** **1** To render incapable of reproduction, esp. by surgery. **2** To destroy microorganisms. **3** To make barren. —**ster′i·li·za′tion, ster′il·iz′er** *n.*

ster·ling (stûr′ling) *n.* **1** British money. **2** The official standard of fineness for British coins. **3** Sterling silver as used in manufacturing articles, as tableware, etc. **4** Articles made of sterling silver collectively. —*adj.* **1** Made of or payable in sterling: pounds *sterling.* **2** Made of sterling silver. **3** Having great worth; genuine: *sterling* qualities. [Prob. < OE *steorra* star + -LING]

sterling silver An alloy of 92.5 percent silver and usu. 7.5 percent copper.

stern¹ (stûrn) *adj.* **1** Marked by severity or harshness: a *stern* command. **2** Having an austere disposition: a *stern* judge. **3** Inspiring fear. **4** Resolute: a *stern* resolve. [< OE *styrne*] —**stern′ly** *adv.* —**stern′ness** *n.*

stern² (stûrn) *n.* **1** *Naut.* The aft part of a ship, boat, etc. **2** The hindmost part of any object. —*adj.* Situated at or belonging to the stern. [< ON *styra* steer] —**stern′most′** (-mōst′) *adj.*

ster·num (stûr′nəm) *n. pl.* **·na** (-nə) or **·nums** The structure of bone and cartilage that forms the ventral support of the ribs in vertebrates. [< Gk. *sternon* breast] —**stern·al** (stûr′nal) *adj.*

ster·nu·ta·tion (stûr′nyə·tā′shən) *n.* **1** The act of sneezing. **2** A sneeze or the noise produced by it. [< L *sternuere* to sneeze] —**ster·nu·ta·to·ry** (ster·nyōō′tə·tôr′ē, -tō′ri) *adj.*

stern-wheel·er (stûrn′hwē′lər) *n.* A steamboat propelled by one large paddle wheel at the stern.

ster·oid (ster′oid) *n.* Any of a large group of structurally similar organic compounds found in plants and animals, including many hormones and the precursors of certain vitamins. [< STER(OL) + -OID]

ster·ol (ster′ōl, -ol) *n.* Any of a class of steroids comprising solid, fat-soluble alcohols, as cholesterol. [Contraction of CHOLESTEROL]

ster·tor·ous (stûr′tər·əs) *adj.* Characterized or accompanied by a snoring sound: *stertorous* breathing. [< L *stertere* to snore] —**ster′tor·ous·ly** *adv.* —**ster′tor·ous·ness** *n.*

stet (stet) Let it stand: a direction used in proofreading to indicate that a word, letter, etc., marked for omission is to remain. —*v.t.* **stet·ted, stet·ting** To mark for retention with the word *stet.* [< L *stare* to stand]

steth·o·scope (steth′ə·skōp) *n.* An apparatus for conducting sounds from the human body to the ears of an examiner. [< Gk. *stēthos* breast + -SCOPE] —**steth′o·scop′ic** (-skop′ik) *adj.* —**steth′o·scop′i·cal·ly** *adv.* —**ste·thos·co·py** (ste·thos′kə·pē) *n.*

stet·son (stet′sən) *n. Often cap.* A man's hat, usu. of felt, with a high crown and a broad brim, popular in the w U.S. [< *Stetson,* a trade name]

ste·ve·dore (stē′və·dôr, -dōr) *n.* One whose business is loading or unloading ships. —*v.t. & v.i.* **·dored, ·dor·ing** To load or unload (a vessel or vessels). [< L *stipare* compress, stuff]

stew (styōō) *v.t. & v.i.* **1** To boil slowly and gently. **2** *Informal* To worry. —*n.* **1** Stewed food, esp. a preparation of meat or fish and vegetables cooked by stewing. **2** *Informal* Mental agitation; worry. [< OF *estuver*]

stew·ard (styōō′ərd) *n.* **1** A person entrusted with the management of the affairs of others. **2** A person put in charge of services for a club, ship, railroad train, etc. **3** On shipboard, a person who waits on table and takes care of passengers' staterooms. **4** SHOP STEWARD. [< OE *stī* hall + *weard* ward, keeper] —**stew′ard·ship** *n.*

stew·ard·ess (styōō′ər·dis) *n.* A woman whose occupation is that of a steward, esp. one who is employed on an airplane to attend passengers.

stewed (styōōd) *adj.* **1** Cooked by stewing. **2** *Slang* Drunk.

stge. storage.

stick (stik) *n.* **1** A stiff shoot or branch cut or broken off from a tree or bush. **2** Any relatively long and thin piece of wood. **3** A piece of wood fashioned for a specific use: a walking *stick;* a hockey *stick.* **4** Anything resembling a stick in form: a *stick* of dynamite. **5** A piece of wood of any size, cut for fuel, lumber, or timber. **6** *Aeron.* The lever of an airplane that controls pitching and rolling. **7** A poke, stab, or thrust with a stick or pointed implement. **8** The state of being stuck together; adhesion. **9** *Informal* A stiff, inert, or dull person. —**the sticks** *Informal* An obscure rural district. —*v.* **stuck, stick·ing** *v.t.* **1** To pierce or penetrate with a pointed object. **2** To stab. **3** To thrust or force, as a sword or pin, into or through something else. **4** To force the end of (a nail, etc.) into something. **5** To fasten in place with or as with pins, nails, etc. **6** To cover with objects piercing the surface: a paper *stuck* with pins. **7** To impale; transfix. **8** To put or thrust: He *stuck* his hand into his pocket. **9** To fasten to a surface by or as by an adhesive substance. **10** To bring to a standstill: We were *stuck* in Rome. **11** *Informal* To smear with something sticky. **12** *Informal* To baffle; puzzle. **13** *Slang* To cheat. **14** *Slang* To force great expense, an unpleasant task, responsibility, etc., upon. —*v.i.* **15** To be or become fixed in place by being thrust in: The pins are *sticking* in the cushion. **16** To adhere; cling. **17** To come to a standstill; halt. **18** *Informal* To be baffled or disconcerted. **19** To hesitate; scruple: with *at* or *to*. **20** To persevere, as in a task or undertaking: with *at* or *to*. **21** To remain faithful, as to an ideal or bargain. **22** To protrude: with *out, through, up,* and so on. —**be stuck on** *Informal* To be enamored of. —**stick around** *Slang* To remain near or near at hand. —**stick by** To remain loyal to. —**stick it out** To persevere to the end. —**stick up** *Slang* To stop and rob. —**stick up for** *Informal* To take the part of; defend. [< OE *sticca*]

stick·er (stik′ər) *n.* **1** One who or that which sticks. **2** A gummed label. **3** *Informal* Anything that confuses; a puzzle. **4** A prickly stem, thorn, or bur.

sticking plaster An adhesive material for covering slight cuts, etc.

stick·le (stik′əl) *v.i.* **·led, ·ling** **1** To contend about trifles. **2** To hesitate for petty reasons. [< OE *stihtan* arrange]

stick·le·back (stik′əl·bak′) *n.* Any of various small, nest-building fresh- or salt-water fishes having sharp dorsal spines.

Stickleback

stick·ler (stik′lər) *n.* **1** One who insists upon exacting standards, as of behavior: with *for*: a *stickler* for punctuality. **2** A baffling problem.

stick·pin (stik′pin′) *n.* An ornamental pin for a necktie.

stick-to-it-ive-ness (stik′tōō′ə·tiv·nis) *n.* *Informal* Perseverance; diligence.

stick·up (stik′up′) *n.* *Slang* A robbery or hold-up.

stick·y (stik′ē) *adj.* **stick·i·er, stick·i·est** **1** Adhering to a surface; adhesive. **2** Warm and humid. **3** *Informal* Unpleasant or complicated: a *sticky* situation. —**stick′i·ly** *adv.* —**stick′i·ness** *n.* —Syn. **1** gluey, mucilaginous, viscous.

stiff (stif) *adj.* **1** Resistant to bending; rigid. **2** Not easily worked or moved: a *stiff* bolt. **3** Moving with difficulty or pain: a *stiff* back. **4** Not natural, graceful, or easy: a *stiff* bow. **5** Taut; tightly drawn: a *stiff* rope. **6** Strong and steady: a *stiff* breeze. **7** Thick; viscous: a *stiff* batter. **8** Harsh; severe: a *stiff* penalty. **9** High; dear: *stiff* prices. **10** Difficult; hard: a *stiff* examination. **11** Stubborn; unyielding: *stiff* resistance. **12** Awkward or noticeably formal; not relaxed or easy; wooden. **13** Strong; potent: a *stiff* drink. **14** Difficult; arduous: a *stiff* climb. —*n.* *Slang* **1** A corpse. **2** An awkward or unresponsive person. **3** A person; fellow: a working *stiff*. **4** A rough person. [< OE *stīf*] —**stiff′ly** *adv.* —**stiff′ness** *n.*

stiff·en (stif′ən) *v.t.* & *v.i.* To make or become stiff or stiffer. —**stiff′en·er** *n.*

stiff-necked (stif′nekt′) *adj.* **1** Suffering from a stiff neck. **2** Stubborn; obstinate.

sti·fle (stī′fəl) *v.* **·fled, ·fling** *v.t.* **1** To kill by stopping respiration; choke. **2** To suppress or repress, as sobs. —*v.i.* **3** To die of suffocation. **4** To experience difficulty in breathing, as in a stuffy room. [ME *stuflen*] —**sti′fler** *n.* —**sti′fling·ly** *adv.*

stig·ma (stig′mə) *n. pl.* **stig·ma·ta** (stig·mä′tə, stig′mə·tə) or (*esp. for def. 2*) **stig·mas** **1** A mark of disgrace. **2** *Bot.* That part of a pistil which receives the pollen. **3** *Biol.* Any spot or small opening. **4** A spot or scar on the skin. **5** *Med.* Any physical sign of diagnostic value. **6** *pl.* The wounds that Christ received at the Crucifixion. [L, mark, brand] —**stig·mat·ic** (-mat′ik) *adj.* —Syn. **1** blemish, blot, stain.

stig·ma·tize (stig′mə·tīz) *v.t.* **·tized, ·tiz·ing** **1** To characterize as disgraceful. **2** To mark with a stigma. *Brit. sp.* **stig′ma·tise.** —**stig′ma·ti·za′tion, stig′ma·tiz′er** *n.*

stile (stīl) *n.* A step, or series of steps, on each side of a fence or wall to enable one to climb over. [< OE *stigel*]

Stile

sti·let·to (sti·let′ō) *n. pl.* **·tos** or **·toes** A small dagger with a slender blade. —*v.t.* **·toed, ·to·ing** To pierce with a stiletto; stab. [< Ital. *stilo* dagger]

still¹ (stil) *adj.* **1** Being without movement; motionless. **2** Free from disturbance or agitation. **3** Making no sound; silent. **4** Low in sound; hushed. **5** Subdued; soft. **6** Dead; inanimate. **7** Having no effervescence: said of wines. **8** *Phot.* Not capable of showing movement. —*n.* **1** Absence of sound or noise. **2** *Phot.* A still photograph; esp. one taken on a motion-picture set, for advertising purposes. —*adv.* **1** Up to this or that time; yet: He is *still* here. **2** After or in spite of something; nevertheless. **3** In increasing degree; even yet: *still* more. **4** *Archaic* or *Regional* Always; constantly. —*conj.* Nevertheless. —*v.t.* **1** To cause to be still or calm. **2** To silence or hush. **3** To allay, as fears. —*v.i.* **4** To become still. [< OE *stille*] —**still′ness** *n.* —Syn. *adj.* **2** peaceful, tranquil, undisturbed. *v.* **1** soothe, tranquillize. **2** quiet.

Still²

still² (stil) *n.* **1** An apparatus for distilling liquids, esp. alcoholic liquors. **2** DISTILLERY. —*v.t.* & *v.i.* To distill. [< L *stilla* a drop]

still·born (stil′bôrn′) *adj.* Dead at birth. —**still′birth′** (-bûrth′) *n.*

still life *pl.* **lifes** **1** In painting, the representation of inanimate objects. **2** A picture of such objects. —**still′-life′** *adj.*

Still·son wrench (stil′sən) A wrench resembling a monkey wrench, but with one serrated jaw capable of slight angular movement, so that the grip is tightened by pressure on the handle: a trade name. [< D. *Stillson,* its U.S. inventor in 1869]

Stillson wrench

still·y (stil′ē) *adj.* **·i·er, ·i·est** Quiet; calm. —*adv.* (stil′lē) Calmly; quietly.

stilt (stilt) *n.* **1** One of a pair of slender poles made with a projection above the ground to support the foot in walking. **2** A tall post or pillar used as a support for a dock or building. **3** Any of various shore birds with thin bills and long legs. [ME *stilte*]

stilt·ed (stil′tid) *adj.* Excessively formal or stuffy: *stilted* prose. —**stilt′ed·ly** *adv.* —**stilt′ed·ness** *n.*

stim·u·lant (stim′yə·lənt) *n.* **1** A drug that stimulates the rate or intensity of vital functions, esp. in the central nervous system. **2** Something that stimulates one to activity.

stim·u·late (stim′yə·lāt) *v.* **·lat·ed, ·lat·ing** *v.t.* **1** To rouse to activity; spur. **2** To increase action in by applying some form of stimulus: to *stimulate* the heart. **3** To affect by intoxicants. —*v.i.* **4** To act as a stimulus or stimulant. [< L *stimulus* a goad] —**stim′u·lat′er, stim′u·la′tor, stim′u·la′tion** *n.*

stim·u·la·tive (stim′yə·lā′tiv) *adj.* Having the power to stimulate. —*n.* Something that stimulates.

stim·u·lus (stim′yə·ləs) *n. pl.* **·li** (-lī, -lē) **1** Anything that rouses to activity, as a stimulant, incentive, etc. **2** Any agent that influences activity in an organism. [< L]

sting (sting) *v.* **stung, sting·ing** *v.t.* **1** To pierce or prick painfully: The bee *stung* me. **2** To cause to suffer sharp, smarting pain. **3** To cause to suffer mentally: to be *stung* with remorse. **4** To stimulate or rouse as if with a sting; goad. **5** *Slang* To overcharge. —*v.i.* **6** To have or use a sting, as a bee. **7** To suffer a sharp, smarting pain. **8** To suffer mental distress. —*n.* **1** A sharp offensive or defensive organ, as of a bee, capable of introducing an allergen or a venom into a victim's skin. **2** The act of stinging. **3** A wound made by a sting. **4** The pain caused by such a wound. **5** Any sharp, smarting sensation. **6** A keen stimulus; spur. [< OE *stingan*] —**sting′er** *n.* —**sting′ing·ly** *adv.*

sting ray Any of various flat-bodied fishes with a whip-like tail having one or more stinging spines. Also **sting′ray, sting·a·ree** (sting′ə·rē, sting′rē′)

Sting ray

stin·gy (stin′jē) *adj.* ·**gi·er**, ·**gi·est** **1** Extremely penurious or miserly. **2** Scanty; meager: a *stingy* portion. [?] —**stin′gi·ly** *adv.* —**stin′·gi·ness** *n.* —**Syn. 1** avaricious, niggardly, parsimonious, tight-fisted.

stink (stingk) *n.* A strong, foul odor; stench. —*v.* **stank** or **stunk, stunk, stink·ing** *v.i.* **1** To give forth a foul odor. **2** To be extremely offensive or hateful. —*v.t.* **3** To cause to stink. [< OE *stincan*] —**stink′er** *n.* —**stink′ing·ly** *adv.* —**stink′y** *adj.* (·**i·er, ·i·est**)

stink·bug (stingk′bug′) *n.* Any of certain hemipterous insects with a sickening odor.

stink·weed (stingk′wēd′) *n.* Any of various plants with foul-smelling flowers or leaves.

stint (stint) *v.t.* **1** To limit, as in amount. —*v.i.* **2** To be frugal or sparing. —*n.* **1** A task to be performed within a specified time: a weekly *stint*. **2** A bound; restriction. [< OE *styntan* stupefy] —**stint′er** *n.* —**stint′ing·ly** *adv.*

stipe (stīp) *n.* A stalklike support, esp. that of a fern frond, a pistil, or a mushroom cap. [< L *stipes* branch]

sti·pend (stī′pend, -pənd) *n.* A regular, fixed allowance or salary. [< L *stips* payment in coin + *pendere* weigh, pay out]

sti·pen·di·ar·y (stī·pen′dē·er′ē) *adj.* **1** Receiving a stipend. **2** Performing services for a fixed payment. —*n. pl.* ·**ar·ies** One who receives a stipend.

stip·ple (stip′əl) *v.t.* ·**pled, ·pling** To draw, paint, or engrave with dots. —*n.* **1** In painting, etching, etc., a method of representing light and shade by employing dots instead of lines. **2** The effect resulting from this method. **3** Stippled work. Also **stip′pling.** [< Du. *stip* dot] —**stip′pler** *n.*

stip·u·late (stip′yə·lāt) *v.* ·**lat·ed, ·lat·ing** *v.t.* **1** To specify as the terms of an agreement, contract, etc. **2** To specify as a requirement for agreement. —*v.i.* **3** To demand something as a requirement or condition. [< L *stipulari* to bargain] —**stip′u·la′tor** *n.* —**stip′u·la·to·ry** (-lə·tôr′ē, -tō′rē) *adj.*

stip·u·la·tion (stip′yə·lā′shən) *n.* **1** The act of stipulating. **2** An agreement or contract.

stip·ule (stip′yōol) *n.* One of a pair of leaflike appendages at the base of the petiole of certain leaves. [< L *stipula* stalk] —**stip′u·lar, stip′u·late, stip′u·lat′ed** *adj.*

stir¹ (stûr) *v.* **stirred, stir·ring** *v.t.* **1** To mix thoroughly by giving a circular motion to, as with a spoon, fork, etc.: to *stir* soup. **2** To cause to move, esp. slightly. **3** To move vigorously; bestir: *Stir* yourself! **4** To rouse, as from sleep, indifference, or inactivity. **5** To incite; provoke: often with *up*. **6** To affect strongly; move with emotion. —*v.i.* **7** To move, esp. slightly: The log wouldn't *stir*. **8** To be active; move about. **9** To take place; happen. **10** To undergo stirring: This molasses *stirs* easily. —*n.* **1** The act of stirring. **2** Movement. **3** Public interest; excitement. **4** A poke; nudge. [< OE *styrian*] —**stir′rer** *n.*

stir² (stûr) *n. Slang* A jail; prison. [?]

stir·ring (stûr′ing) *adj.* **1** Stimulating; inspiring. **2** Full of activity. —**stir′ring·ly** *adv.* —**Syn. 1** exciting, rousing. **2** animated, lively, sprightly.

stir·rup (stûr′əp, stir′-) *n.* **1** A loop of metal or wood suspended from a saddle to support a horseback rider's foot. **2** A similar device used as a support, as for a beam. [< OE *stigrāp* mounting rope] • See SADDLE.

stirrup bone STAPES.

stitch (stich) *n.* **1** A single passage of a threaded needle or other implement through fabric and back again, as in sewing. **2** A single turn of thread or yarn around a needle or other implement, as in knitting or crocheting. **3** Any individual arrangement of a thread or threads used in sewing: a chain *stitch*. **4** A sharp sudden pain. **5** *Informal* A garment: I haven't a *stitch* to wear. —**be in stitches** To

be overcome with laughter. —*v.t.* **1** To join together with stitches. **2** To ornament with stitches. —*v.i.* **3** To make stitches; sew. [< OE *stice* prick]

sti·ver (stī′vər) *n.* **1** A small Dutch coin, 1/20 of a guilder. **2** Anything of little value.

St. Johns·wort (sānt jonz′wûrt′) Any of various small, woody perennials, usu. with yellow flowers. Also **Saint Johnswort, St. John's-wort.**

stk. stock.

sto·a (stō′ə) *n. pl.* **sto·ae** (stō′ē) or **sto·as** In Greek architecture, a covered colonnade, portico, cloister, or promenade. [Gk., porch]

stoat (stōt) *n. pl.* **stoats** or **stoat** The ermine, esp. in its brown summer coat. [ME *stote*]

stock (stok) *n.* **1** The goods a store or merchant has on hand. **2** A quantity of something acquired or kept for future use: a *stock* of provisions. **3** LIVESTOCK. **4** The original, as a man, race, or language, from which others are descended or derived. **5** A line of familial descent. **6** An ethnic group; race. **7** A related group of plants or animals. **8** A group of related languages; also, a language family. **9** The trunk or main stem of a tree or other plant. **10 a** A plant stem from which cuttings are taken for grafting. **b** A plant stem upon which a graft is made. **11** In finance: **a** The capital raised by a corporation through the sale of shares that entitle the holder to interest or dividends. **b** The part of this capital credited to an individual stock holder. **c** The certificate or certificates indicating this. **12** A fund or debt owed (as by a nation, city, etc.) to individuals who receive a fixed interest rate. **13** The part of a device that functions as a support and to which other parts are attached, as the wooden portion or handle of a firearm, whip, etc. **14** Raw material: paper *stock*. **15** The broth from boiled vegetables, meat, or fish, used in preparing soups, gravies, etc. **16** Something lacking life, feeling, or motion. **17** The group of plays produced by a theatrical company at one theater. **18** A broad, heavily starched band, formerly worn as a cravat. —**in stock** Available for purchase. —**out of stock** Not available; all sold out. —**stock in trade** One's abilities, talents, or resources. —**take stock 1** To take an inventory. **2** To size up a situation. —**take stock in** *Informal* To have trust or belief in. —**the stocks 1** A former device for public punishment consisting of a timber frame for confining the ankles, or the ankles and wrists. **2** The timber frame on which a ship or boat is built. —*v.t.* **1** To supply with cattle, as a farm. **2** To supply (a store) with merchandise. **3** To keep for sale: to *stock* avocados. **4** To supply with wildlife: to *stock* a pond. **5** To put aside for future use. **6** To provide with a handle or stock. —*v.i.* **7** To lay in supplies or stock: often with *up*. —*adj.* **1** Kept on hand: a *stock* size. **2** Banal; commonplace: a *stock* phrase. **3** Of or pertaining to the breeding and raising of livestock. **4** Employed in handling or caring for the stock: a *stock* clerk. **5** Of or pertaining to a stock or stocks (def. 9). [< OE *stocc*]

stock·ade (sto·kād′) *n.* **1** A defense consisting of a strong, high barrier of upright posts, stakes, etc. **2** The area enclosed by such a barrier. **3** A similar area used to confine prisoners, esp. in military installations. —*v.t.* ·**ad·ed, ·ad·ing** To surround or fortify with a stockade. [< OF *estaque* a stake]

stock·bro·ker (stok′brō′kər) *n.* One who buys and sells stocks or securities for others.

stock car 1 An automobile, usu. a sedan, modified for racing. **2** A railroad car used for transporting cattle.

stock company 1 An incorporated company that issues stock. **2** A theatrical company under one management that presents a series of plays.

stock exchange 1 A place where securities are bought and sold. **2** An association of stockbrokers.

stock farm A farm that specializes in the breeding of livestock.

stock·hold·er (stok′hōl′dər) *n.* One who holds stocks or shares in a company.

stock·i·net (stok′i·net′) *n.* An elastic knitted fabric used chiefly for undergarments. [< STOCKING]

stock·ing (stok′ing) *n.* **1** A close-fitting knitted covering for the foot and leg. **2** Something resembling such a covering. [< STOCK, in obs. sense of "a stocking"]

stocking cap A long knitted cap, tapered and often having a pompon or tassel at the end.

stock·man (stok′mən) *n. pl.* **·men** (-mən) **1** One who raises or owns livestock; a cattleman. **2** A man having charge of goods, as in a warehouse.

stock market 1 STOCK EXCHANGE. **2** The business transacted in such a place: The *stock market* was active.

stock·pile (stok′pīl′) *n.* A storage pile of materials or supplies. Also **stock pile.** —*v.t. & v.i.* **·piled, ·pil·ing** To accumulate a supply or stockpile (of).

stock raising The breeding and raising of livestock.

stock·room (stok′rōōm′, -rōōm′) *n.* A room where reserve stocks of goods are stored.

stock·still (stok′stil′) *adj.* Completely motionless.

stock·y (stok′ē) *adj.* **stock·i·er, stock·i·est** Short and stout. —**stock′i·ly** *adv.* —**stock′i·ness** *n.*

stock·yard (stok′yärd′) *n.* A large yard with pens, stables, etc., where cattle are kept ready for shipping, slaughter, etc.

stodg·y (stoj′ē) *adj.* **stodg·i·er, stodg·i·est 1** Dull; boring. **2** Indigestible; heavy. [?] —**stodg′i·ly** *adv.* —**stodg′i·ness** *n.*

sto·gy (stō′gē) *n. pl.* **·gies** A long, slender, inexpensive cigar. Also **sto′gie.** [< *Conestoga,* Pennsylvania]

sto·ic (stō′ik) *n.* A person apparently unaffected by pleasure or pain. —*adj.* Indifferent to pleasure or pain; impassive: also **sto′i·cal.** [< STOIC] —**sto′i·cal·ly** *adv.* —**sto′i·cal·ness** *n.*

Sto·ic (stō′ik) *n.* A member of a school of Greek philosophy founded by Zeno about 308 B.C., holding the belief that wisdom lies in being superior to passion, joy, grief, etc. —*adj.* Of or pertaining to the Stoics or Stoicism. [< Gk. *Stoa,* the colonnade at Athens where Zeno taught]

sto·i·cism (stō′ə·siz′əm) *n.* Indifference to pleasure or pain.

Sto·i·cism (stō′ə·siz′əm) *n.* The doctrines of the Stoics.

stoke (stōk) *v.t.* **stoked, stok·ing 1** To supply (a furnace) with fuel. **2** To stir up; intensify. —*v.i.* **3** To tend a fire. [Back formation < STOKER]

stoke·hole (stōk′hōl′) *n.* **1** The space about the mouth of a furnace; the fireroom. **2** The mouth of a furnace.

stok·er (stō′kər) *n.* **1** A person who tends a furnace or boiler. **2** A mechanical device for feeding coal to a furnace. [< Du. *stoken* stir a fire]

STOL, S.T.O.L. short takeoff and landing.

stole[1] (stōl) *n.* **1** *Eccl.* A long, narrow band, usu. of decorated silk or linen, worn about the shoulders by priests and bishops. **2** A fur, scarf, or garment resembling a stole, worn by women. [< Gk. *stolē* a garment] — **stoled** *adj.*

stole[2] (stōl) *p.t.* of STEAL.

sto·len (stō′lən) *p.p.* of STEAL.

stol·id (stol′id) *adj.* Expressing no feeling; impassive. [< L *stolidus* dull] —**sto·lid·i·ty** (stə·lid′ə·tē), **stol′id·ness** *n.* —**stol′id·ly** *adv.*

sto·ma (stō′mə) *n. pl.* **sto·ma·ta** (stō′mə·tə, stom′ə·tə) or **sto·mas** A small, mouthlike opening, esp. any of the minute epidermal breathing pores on a plant leaf. Also **sto′mate** (stō′māt′). [< Gk. *stoma* mouth] —**sto′ma·tal** *adj.*

Stole

stom·ach (stum′ək) *n.* **1** A pouchlike dilation of the alimentary canal, situated in most vertebrates next to the esophagus and serving as one of the principal organs of digestion. **2** Any digestive cavity, as of an invertebrate. **3** The abdomen; belly. **4** Desire for food; appetite. **5** Any desire or inclination. —*v.t.* **1** To put up with; endure. **2** To take into and retain in the stomach; digest. [< Gk. *stomachos*] —**stom′ach·al** *adj.* —**sto·mach·ic** (stō·mak′ik), **sto·mach′i·cal** *adj., n.* ● See LIVER.

stom·ach·er (stum′ək·ər) *n.* A former article of clothing worn, esp. by women, over the breast and stomach.

stomp (stomp) *v.t. & v.i.* To stamp; tread heavily (upon).

—*n.* A jazz dance involving heavy stamping. [Var of STAMP] —**stomp′er** *n.*

stone (stōn) *n. pl.* **stones** or *for def. 8* **stone 1.** ROCK (def. 3). **2** A small piece of rock, as a pebble. **3** A piece of shaped or hewn rock, as a gravestone. **4** A jewel; gem. **5** Something like a stone in shape or hardness: a *hailstone.* **6** An abnormal, hard concretion in the body. **7** The hard inner part of a drupe. **8** *Brit.* A measure of weight equal to 14 pounds. —**cast the first stone** To be the first to blame (someone). —**leave no stone unturned** To do everything within possibility. —*adj.* **1** Made of stone: a *stone* ax. **2** Made of coarse, hard earthenware: a *stone* bottle. —*v.t.* **stoned, ston·ing 1** To hurl stones at. **2** To kill by throwing stones at. **3** To remove the stones or pits from. **4** To furnish or line with stone. [< OE *stān*] —**ston′er** *n.*

Stone Age The earliest known period of human cultural evolution, marked by the creation of stone implements.

stone-blind (stōn′blīnd′) *adj.* Completely blind.

stone-broke (stōn′brōk′) *adj. Informal* Without any money; having no funds. Also **ston′y-broke′.**

stone·crop (stōn′krop′) *n.* SEDUM.

stone·cut·ter (stōn′kut′ər) *n.* One who or that which cuts stone; esp. a machine for facing stone. —**stone′cut′ting** *n.*

stoned (stōnd) *adj. Slang* **1** Drunk. **2** Under the influence of a drug or narcotic.

stone-deaf (stōn′def′) *adj.* Completely deaf.

stone·ma·son (stōn′mā′sən) *n.* One whose trade is to prepare and lay stones in building. —**stone′ma′son·ry** *n.*

stone's throw 1 The distance a stone may be cast by hand. **2** A short distance.

stone·wall (stōn′wôl′) *Slang v.i.* **1** To act in a calculatedly obstructive way, as by lying or failing to respond to inquiry. —*v.t.* **2** To respond to in such a way.

stone·ware (stōn′wâr′) *n.* A very hard, glazed pottery, made from siliceous clay or clay mixed with flint or sand.

stone·work (stōn′wûrk′) *n.* **1** The art or process of cutting or setting stone. **2** Work built or made of stone. **3** *pl.* A place where stone is shaped. —**stone′work′er** *n.*

ston·y (stō′nē) *adj.* **ston·i·er, ston·i·est 1** Abounding in stone or stones. **2** Made or consisting of stone. **3** Hard as stone; unfeeling. **4** Like stone. **5** *Slang* Having no money. —**ston′i·ly** *adv.* —**ston′i·ness** *n.* —**Syn. 3** chilly, cold, pitiless.

stood (stōōd) *p.t. & p.p.* of STAND.

stooge (stōōj) *n.* **1** *Informal* An actor who feeds lines to the principal comedian, acts as a foil for his jokes, etc. **2** Anyone who acts as or is the tool or dupe of another. —*v.i.* **stooged, stoog·ing** To act as a stooge: usu. with *for.* [?]

stool (stōōl) *n.* **1** A backless and armless seat intended for one person. **2** A low bench or portable support for the feet or for kneeling. **3** A seat or place used as a toilet. **4** The matter evacuated from the bowels; feces. **5** A stump or root from which suckers or sprouts shoot up. [< OE *stōl*]

stool pigeon 1 A living or artificial pigeon used to decoy others into a trap. **2** *Slang* An informer, as for the police.

stoop[1] (stōōp) *v.i.* **1** To lean the body forward and down. **2** To stand or walk with the upper part of the body habitually bent forward; slouch. **3** To bend: said of trees, cliffs, etc. **4** To lower or degrade oneself. —*v.t.* **5** To bend (one's head, shoulders, etc.) forward. —*n.* **1** A downward and forward bending of the body. **2** A habitual forward inclination of the head and shoulders. [< OE *stūpian*]

stoop[2] (stōōp) *n.* A small porch or platform at the entrance to a house. [< Du. *stoep*]

stop (stop) *v.* **stopped, stop·ping** *v.t.* **1** To bring (something in motion) to a halt: to *stop* an automobile. **2** To prevent the doing or completion of: to *stop* a revolution. **3** To prevent (a person) from doing something; restrain. **4** To withhold or cut off, as wages or supplies. **5** To cease doing: *Stop* that! **6** To check, as a flow of blood from a wound. **7** To obstruct (a passage, road, etc.). **8** To fill in or otherwise close, as a hole, cavity, etc. **9** To close (a bottle, barrel, etc.) with a cork, plug, etc. **10** To order a bank not to pay or honor: to *stop* a check. **11** *Music* To press down (a string) or close (a finger hole) to change the pitch of. **12** In boxing, etc., to parry. —*v.i.* **13** To come to a halt; cease progress or motion. **14** To cease doing something. —**stop off** To stop for a brief stay before continuing on a trip. —**stop over** *Informal* To stop briefly, as for a visit or a rest during a journey. —*n.* **1** The act of stopping, or the state of being stopped. **2** That which stops or limits the range or time of a movement; an obstruction. **3** *Music* **a** The pressing down of a string or the closing of an aperture to change the pitch. **b** A key, lever, or handle for stopping a string or an aperture. **4** *Music* In an organ, a set of pipes producing tones of the same timbre. **5 a** *Brit.* A punctuation mark; a period. **b** In cables, etc., a period. **6** *Phonet.* **a** Complete blockage of the breath stream, as with the lips or tongue, followed by a sudden release. **b** A consonant so produced, as *p, b, t, d, k,* and *g.* —**put a stop to** To end; terminate. [< OE *-stoppian*] —**Syn** *v.* **2** deter, quash. **4** discontinue.

stop·cock (stop′kok′) *n.* A faucet or valve.

stop·gap (stop′gap′) *n.* A person or thing serving as a temporary substitute. —*adj.* Being a stopgap.

stop·o·ver (stop′ō′vər) *n.* The act of stopping over, or permission to stop over on a journey and continue later, using the ticket issued for the whole journey.

stop·page (stop′ij) *n.* **1** The act of stopping or the state of being stopped. **2** A blocking or obstruction.

stop·per (stop′ər) *n.* **1** One who or that which stops or brings to a stop. **2** A plug or cork for a container, as a bottle. —*v.t.* To secure or close with a stopper.

stop·ple (stop′əl) *n.* A stopper, plug, cork, or bung. —*v.t.* **·pled, ·pling** To close with or as with a stopple. [< ME *stoppen* stop]

stop·watch (stop′woch′) *n.* A watch with a hand indicating fractions of a second which may be stopped or started instantly, used for timing races, etc.

stor·age (stôr′ij, stō′rij) *n.* **1** The depositing of articles in a place for their safekeeping. **2** Space for storing goods. **3** A charge for storing. **4** A section of a computer in whch data is held for later use; memory.

storage battery A connected group of two or more electrolytic cells that can be reversibly charged and discharged.

store (stôr, stōr) *v.t.* **stored, stor·ing 1** To put away for future use. **2** To furnish or supply; provide. **3** To place in a warehouse or other place for safekeeping. —*n.* **1** That which is stored or laid up against future need. **2** *pl.* Supplies, as of food, arms, or clothing. **3** A storehouse; warehouse. **4** A place where merchandise of any kind is kept for sale; a shop. —**in store** Set apart for the future; impending. —**set store by** To value or esteem. [< L *instaurare* restore, erect]

store·front (stôr′frunt′, stōr′-) *n.* **1** The front or facade of a store, usu. opening directly out onto a pedestrian sidewalk. **2** A public service or other facility, often temporary, situated on the site of a former store. —*adj.* Characteristic of or being a storefront.

store·house (stôr′hous′, stōr′-) *n.* A place in which goods are stored; depository.

store·keep·er (stôr′kē′pər, stōr′-) *n.* A person who keeps a retail store or who is in charge of supplies.

store·room (stôr′rōōm′, -rōōm′, stōr′-) *n.* A room in which things are stored.

sto·rey (stôr′ē, stōr′ē) *n. pl.* **·reys** *Chiefly Brit.* STORY².

sto·ried¹ (stôr′ēd, stōr′ēd) *adj.* Having or consisting of stories: a *six-storied* house.

sto·ried² (stôr′ēd, stōr′ēd) *adj.* **1** Having a notable history. **2** Ornamented with designs representing scenes from history or story.

stork (stôrk) *n.* A large wading bird with a long neck and long legs, related to the herons. [< OE *storc*]

storm (stôrm) *n.* **1** A disturbance of the atmosphere that creates strong winds, often with heavy precipitation of rain, snow, dust, etc. **2** Any heavy, prolonged precipitation of snow, rain, etc. **3** Anything similar to a storm: a *storm* of missiles. **4** A violent outburst: a *storm* of applause. **5** A violent and rapid assault. —*v.i.* **1** To blow with violence; rain, snow,

White stork

hail, etc., heavily. **2** To be very angry; rage. **3** To rush with violence or rage: He *stormed* about the room. —*v.t.* **4** To attack: to *storm* a fort. [< OE]

storm cellar An underground shelter adapted for use during cyclones, hurricanes, etc.

storm door An additional outer door used to conserve heat during cold weather.

storm petrel Any of certain petrels thought to portend storm.

storm troops A Nazi party militia unit, the *Sturmabteilung,* established in 1924. —**storm trooper**

storm window An extra window outside the ordinary one for greater insulation against cold.

storm·y (stôr′mē) *adj.* **storm·i·er, storm·i·est 1** Characterized by storms; turbulent. **2** Violent; rough. —**storm′i·ly** *adv.* —**storm′i·ness** *n.* —**Syn. 1** blustery, tempestuous. **2** disturbed, passionate, vehement.

stormy petrel 1 STORM PETREL. **2** A person thought to portend or foment trouble.

sto·ry¹ (stôr′ē, stōr′ē) *n. pl.* **·ries 1** A narrative or recital of an event, or a series of events. **2** A narrative intended to entertain a reader or hearer. **3** An account of the facts relating to a particular person, thing, or incident. **4** A news article in a newspaper or magazine. **5** The material for a news article. **6** An anecdote. **7** *Informal* A lie; falsehood. **8** The series of events in a novel, play, etc. —*v.t.* **·ried, ·ry·ing 1** *Archaic* To relate as a story. **2** To adorn with designs representing scenes from history, legend, etc. [< L *historia*]

sto·ry² (stôr′ē, stōr′ē) *n. pl.* **·ries 1** A division in a building comprising the space between two successive floors. **2** All the rooms on one level of a building. [< Med. L *historia* story (painted on a row of windows)]

sto·ry·tell·er (stôr′ē·tel′ər, stōr′ē-) *n.* **1** One who relates stories or anecdotes. **2** *Informal* A prevaricator; fibber. —**sto·ry·tell·ing** *n., adj.*

stoup (stōōp) *n.* **1** *Eccl.* A basin for holy water at the entrance of a church. **2** A flagon, tankard, or large drinking glass. [< ON *staup* bucket]

stout (stout) *adj.* **1** Fat; thick-set. **2** Firmly built; strong: a *stout* fence. **3** Courageous: a *stout* heart. **4** Stubborn; unyielding: a *stout* denial. —*n.* **1** A stout person. **2** *Usu. pl.* Clothing made for stout or big people. **3** A strong, very dark porter or ale. [< OF *estout* bold, strong] —**stout′ly** *adv.* —**stout′ness** *n.*

stout·heart·ed (stout′här′tid) *adj.* Brave; courageous. —**stout′heart′ed·ly** *adv.* —**stout′heart′ed·ness** *n.*

stove¹ (stōv) *n.* An apparatus, usu. of metal, in which fuel is consumed for heating or cooking. [< OE *stofa* a heated room]

stove² (stōv) A *p.t. & p.p.* of STAVE.

stove·pipe (stōv′pīp′) *n.* **1** A pipe for conducting the smoke from a stove to a chimney flue. **2** *Informal* A tall silk hat: also **stovepipe hat.**

stow (stō) *v.t.* **1** To place or arrange compactly; pack. **2** To fill by packing. —**stow away 1** To put in a place of safekeeping, hiding, etc. **2** To be a stowaway. [< OE *stōw* a place]

stow·age (stō′ij) *n.* **1** The act of stowing. **2** Space for stowing goods. **3** Charge for stowing goods. **4** The goods stowed.

stow·a·way (stō′ə·wā′) *n.* One who conceals himself on a ship, train, airplane, etc., to obtain free passage, to escape, or to cross a border illegally.

STP (es′tē′pē′) *n.* A hallucinogenic drug chemically related to mescaline and amphetamine. [< STP, a trade name for a gasoline additive supposed to increase engine power.]

STP standard temperature and pressure.

str. steamer; strait; string(s).

stra·bis·mus (strə·biz′məs) *n.* Inability to focus the eyes simultaneously on the same spot because of a disorder of the eye muscles. [< Gk. *strabizein* to squint] —**stra·bis′mal, stra·bis′mic** or **-mi·cal** *adj.*

strad·dle (strad′l) *v.* **·dled, ·dling** *v.i.* **1** To stand, walk, or sit with the legs spread apart. **2** To be spread apart: said of the legs. **3** *Informal* To appear to favor both sides of an issue. —*v.t.* **4** To stand, walk, or sit with the legs on either side of. **5** To spread (the legs) wide apart. **6** *Informal* To appear to favor both sides of (an issue). —*n.* **1** The act of straddling. **2** The distance between the legs in strad- dling. **3** *Informal* A noncommital position on an issue. [Freq. of STRIDE] **—strad′dler** *n.* **—strad′dling·ly** *adv.*

Strad·i·var·i·us (strad′i·vâr′ē·əs) *n.* One of the violins, cellos, etc., made by Antonio Stradivari (1644–1737), Ital- ian violin maker.

strafe (strāf, sträf) *v.t.* **strafed, straf·ing 1** To attack (troops, emplacements, etc.) with machine-gun fire from low-flying airplanes. **2** To bombard or shell heavily. **3** *Slang* To punish. [< G *strafen* punish] **—straf′er** *n.*

strag·gle (strag′əl) *v.i.* **·gled, ·gling 1** To wander from the road, main body, etc.; stray. **2** To wander aimlessly about; ramble. **3** To occur at irregular intervals. [ME *straglen*] **—strag′gler** *n.* **—strag′gling·ly** *adv.* **—strag′gly** *adj.* **(·i·er, ·i·est)**

straight (strāt) *adj.* **1** Extending uniformly in the same direction without curve or bend. **2** Free from kinks; not curly, as hair. **3** Not stooped; erect. **4** Not deviating from truth, fairness, or honesty. **5** Free from obstruction; unin- terrupted. **6** Correctly ordered or arranged. **7** Sold without discount for number or quantity taken. **8** *Informal* Ac- cepting the whole, as of a plan, party, or policy: a *straight* ticket. **9** In poker, consisting of five cards forming a se- quence. **10** Having nothing added: *straight* whiskey. **11** *Slang* Conforming to what is accepted as usual, normal, or conventional, esp. according to middle-class standards. **12** *Slang* HETEROSEXUAL. **—***n.* **1** A straight part or piece. **2** The part of a racecourse between the winning post and the last turn. **3** In poker, a numerical sequence of five cards. **4** *Slang* A conventional person. **5** *Slang* HETEROSEX- UAL. **—***adv.* **1** In a straight line or a direct course. **2** Closely in line; correspondingly. **3** At once: Go *straight* to bed. **4** Uprightly: to live *straight.* **5** Correctly: I can't think *straight.* **6** Without restriction or qualification: Tell it *straight.* **—go straight** To reform after having led the life of a criminal. **—straight away** or **off** At once; right away. [< OE *streht,* pp. of *streccan* stretch] **—straight′ness** *n.*

straight angle An angle of 180°.

straight·a·way (strāt′ə·wā′) *adj.* Having no curve or turn. **—***n.* A straight course or track. **—***adv.* At once; straightway.

straight·en (strāt′n) *v.t.* **1** To make straight. **—***v.i.* **2** To become straight. **—straighten out** To restore order to; rectify. **—straighten up 1** To make neat; tidy. **2** To stand in erect posture. **3** To reform. **—straight′en·er** *n.*

straight face A sober, expressionless, or unsmiling face. **—straight-faced** (strāt′fāst′) *adj.*

straight·for·ward (strāt′fôr′wərd) *adj.* **1** Candid; hon- est. **2** Proceeding in a straight course. **—***adv.* In a straight course or direct manner: also **straight′for′wards** (-wərdz). **—straight′for′ward·ly** *adv.* **—straight′for′ward·ness** *n.* **—Syn. 1** aboveboard, frank, open, sincere. **2** direct.

straight man *Informal* An entertainer who acts as a foil for a comedian.

straight-out (strāt′out′) *adj.* *Informal* **1** Unreserved; unrestrained. **2** Thorough; complete.

straight·way (strāt′wā′) *adv.* Immediately.

strain¹ (strān) *v.t.* **1** To pull or draw tight. **2** To exert to the utmost. **3** To injure by overexertion; sprain. **4** To de- form in structure or shape as a result of stress. **5** To stretch beyond the true intent, proper limit, etc.: to *strain* a point. **6** To embrace tightly; hug. **7** To pass through a strainer. **8** To remove by filtration. **—***v.i.* **9** To make vio- lent efforts; strive. **10** To be or become wrenched or twisted. **13** To filter, trickle, or percolate. **—strain at 1** To push or pull with violent efforts. **2** To strive for. **3** To scruple or balk at accepting. **—***n.* **1** An act of straining or the state of being strained. **2** Any very taxing demand on strength, emotions, etc.: the *strain* of city life. **3** Any vio- lent effort or exertion. **4** The injury resulting from exces- sive tension or effort. **5** *Physics* The change of shape or structure of a body produced by the action of a stress. [< L *stringere* bind tight]

strain² (strān) *n.* **1** Line of descent, or the individuals, collectively, in that line. **2** Inborn or hereditary disposi- tion; natural tendency. **3** A line of plants or animals selec- tively bred to perpetuate distinctive traits. **4** *Often pl.* A

melody; tune. **5** Prevailing tone, style, or manner. [< OE *strēon* offspring]

strain·er (strā′nər) *n.* A utensil or device that filters, strains, or sifts.

strait (strāt) *n.* **1** *Often pl.* A narrow passage of water connecting two larger bodies of water. **2** Any narrow pass or passage. **3** *Often pl.* Distress; embarrassment: financial straits. **—***adj.* Archaic **1** Narrow. **2** Strict. [< L *strictus,* p.p. of *stringere* bind tight.] **—strait′ly** *adv.* **—strait′ness** *n.*

strait·en (strāt′n) *v.t.* **1** To make strait or narrow; re- strict. **2** To embarrass, or restrict, as in finances.

strait·jack·et (strāt′jak′it) *n.* **1** A jacket with long, closed sleeves for confining the arms of a violent patient or pris- oner. **2** Anything that unduly confines or restricts. **—***v.t.* To confine in or as if in a straitjacket.

strait-laced (strāt′lāst′) *adj.* **1** Formerly, tightly laced, as corsets. **2** Strict, esp. in morals or manners; prudish.

strand¹ (strand) *n.* A shore or beach, esp. on the ocean. **—***v.t.* & *v.i.* **1** To drive or run aground, as a ship. **2** To leave or be left in difficulties or helplessness: *stranded* in a strange city. [< OE]

strand² (strand) *n.* **1** Any of the fibers, wires, or threads twisted or plaited together to form a rope, cable, cord, etc. **2** A single hair or similar filament. **3** Any of various rope- like objects: a *strand* of pearls. **—***v.t.* To break a strand of (a rope). [ME *strond*]

strange (strānj) *adj.* **strang·er, strang·est 1** Previously un- known, unseen, or unheard of. **2** Peculiar; out of the ordi- nary: a *strange* experience. **3** Foreign; alien. **4** Out of place: to feel *strange* in a new school. **5** Inexperienced: *strange* to a new job. [< L *extraneus* foreign] **—strange′ly** *adv.* **—strange′ness** *n.* **—Syn. 1** unfamiliar. **2** odd, queer, unusual. **4** unaccustomed.

stran·ger (strān′jər) *n.* **1** One who is not an acquaint- ance. **2** An unfamiliar visitor; guest. **3** A foreigner. **4** One unacquainted with something specified: with *to:* a *stranger* to higher mathematics.

stran·gle (strang′gəl) *v.* **·gled, ·gling** *v.t.* **1** To choke to death; throttle. **2** To repress; suppress. **—***v.i.* **3** To suffer or die from strangulation. [< Gk. *strangalaein*] **—stran′gler** *n.*

stran·gle·hold (strang′gəl·hōld′) *n.* **1** In wrestling, an illegal hold which chokes one's opponent. **2** Anything that chokes freedom or progress.

stran·gu·late (strang′gyə·lāt) *v.t.* **·lat·ed, ·lat·ing 1** STRAN- GLE. **2** *Pathol.* To constrict so as to cut off circulation of the blood. [< L *strangulare*] **—stran′gu·la′tion** *n.*

strap (strap) *n.* **1** A long, narrow, and flexible strip of leather, webbing, etc., for binding or fastening things together. **2** A razor strop. **3** Something used as a strap: a shoulder *strap.* **—***v.t.* **strapped, strap·ing 1** To fasten or bind with a strap. **2** To beat with a strap. **3** To sharpen or strop. **4** To embarrass financially. [Var. of STROP]

strap·hang·er (strap′hang′ər) *n.* *Informal* A standing passenger on a bus or train who keeps his balance by holding on to a strap, bar, etc.

strap·ping (strap′ing) *adj.* *Informal* Large and muscu- lar; robust.

stra·ta (strā′tə, strat′ə) *n.pl.* of STRATUM.

strat·a·gem (strat′ə·jəm) *n.* **1** A maneuver designed to deceive or outwit an enemy. **2** Any device or trick for obtaining advantage. [< Gk. *stratēgēma* piece of general- ship] **—Syn. 2** artifice, deception, ruse, trick.

stra·te·gic (strə·tē′jik) *adj.* **1** Of or based on strategy. **2** Important in strategy. **3** Having to do with materials es- sential for conducting a war. **4** Assigned to destroy impor- tant enemy installations: a *strategic* air force. Also **stra- te′gi·cal. —stra·te′gi·cal·ly** *adv.*

strat·e·gist (strat′ə·jist) *n.* One skilled in strategy.

strat·e·gy (strat′ə·jē) *n. pl.* **·gies 1** The science of planning and conducting military campaigns on a broad scale. **2** Any plan based on this. **3** The use of stratagem or artifice, as in business, politics, etc. **4** Skill in management. **5** An ingenious plan or method. [< Gk. *stratēgos* general]

strat·i·fy (strat′ə·fī) *v.* **·fied, ·fy·ing** *v.t.* **1** To form or ar- range in strata or layers. **—***v.i.* **2** To form in strata. **3** To

---

add, āce, câre, pälm; end, ēven; it, īce; odd, ōpen, ôrder; tŏŏk, pōōl; up, bûrn; ə = a in *above,* u in *focus;* yōō = u in *fuse;* oil; pout; check; go; ring; thin; this; zh, *vision.* < derived from; ? origin uncertain or unknown.

be formed in strata. [< L *stratum* layer + -FY] —**strat′i·fi·ca′tion** *n.*

stra·to·cu·mu·lus (strāt′ō·kyōō′myə·ləs, strat′-) *n. pl.* **-li** (-lī) *Meteorol.* A type of dark, low-lying cloud, characterized by horizontal bases and high, rounded summits.

strat·o·sphere (strat′ə·sfir) *n. Meteorol.* The portion of the atmosphere beginning at about six miles above the earth, where a more or less uniform temperature prevails. —**strat′o·spher′ic** (-sfer′ik) or **-i·cal** *adj.*

stra·tum (strā′təm, strat′əm) *n. pl.* **·ta** (-tə) or **·tums** 1 A natural or artificial layer. 2 *Geol.* A more or less homogeneous layer of rock. 3 A level of society, having similar educational, cultural, and usu. economic backgrounds. [< L *stratus,* p.p. of *sternere* to spread]

stra·tus (strā′təs, strat′əs) *n. pl.* **·ti** (-tī) *Meteorol.* A low-lying, foglike cloud. [L, orig. p.p. of *sternere* to spread]

Rock strata

straw (strô) *n.* 1 A dry stalk of grain. 2 Stems or stalks of grain after being threshed, used for fodder, etc. 3 A mere trifle. 4 A slender tube made of paper, glass, etc., used to suck up a beverage. —**catch** (or **grab**) **at a straw** To try anything as a last resort. —**straw in the wind** A sign of the course of future events. —*adj.* 1 Made of or like straw, as in color. 2 Worthless; sham. [< OE *strēaw* straw]

straw·ber·ry (strô′ber′ē, -bər-ē) *n. pl.* **·ries** 1 Any of a genus of stemless perennials of the rose family, with trifoliolate leaves, usu. white flowers and slender runners by which it propagates: also **strawberry vine.** 2 Its edible fruit, consisting of a red, fleshy receptacle bearing many achenes. [< STRAW + BERRY]

strawberry blond A person having reddish blond hair.

straw boss *Informal* A worker acting as an assistant foreman.

straw vote An unofficial test vote.

stray (strā) *v.i.* 1 To wander from the proper course; roam. 2 To deviate from right or goodness; go astray. —*adj.* 1 Having strayed; straying: a *stray* dog. 2 Irregular; occasional: He made a few *stray* remarks. —*n.* A domestic animal that has strayed. [< L *extra vagare* wander outside] —**stray′er** *n.*

streak (strēk) *n.* 1 A long, narrow mark or stripe: a *streak* of lightning. 2 A trace or characteristic: a *streak* of meanness. 3 A layer or strip: meat with a *streak* of fat and a *streak* of lean. 4 *Informal* A period or interval: a winning *streak.* 5 *Slang* The act or an instance of streaking (v. def. 3). —**like a streak** *Informal* As rapidly as possible. —*v.i.* 1 To form a streak or streaks. 2 To move at great speed. 3 *Slang* To appear naked in a public place, usu. briefly and esp. while running, as for a thrill. —*v.t.* 4 To form streaks in or on. 5 *Slang* To appear naked in (a public place), usu. briefly and esp. while running, as for a thrill. [< OE *strica*] —**streak′y** *adj.* (**·i·er, ·i·est**) —**streak′i·ly** *adv.* —**streak′er, streak′i·ness** *n.*

stream (strēm) *n.* 1 A current or flow of water, esp. a small river. 2 Any continuous flow or current: a *stream* of invective. —*v.i.* 1 To pour forth or issue in a stream. 2 To pour forth in a stream: eyes *streaming* with tears. 3 To proceed uninterruptedly, as a crowd. 4 To float with a waving movement, as a flag. 5 To move with a trail of light, as a meteor. 6 To come or arrive in large numbers. [< OE *strēam*] —**Syn.** *n.* 1 brook, course, creek, rill, rivulet.

stream·er (strē′mər) *n.* 1 An object that streams forth, or hangs extended. 2 A long, narrow flag or standard. 3 A stream or shaft of light. 4 A newspaper headline that runs across the whole page.

stream·let (strēm′lit) *n.* RIVULET.

stream·line (strēm′līn′) *n.* 1 A line in a mass of fluid such that each of its tangents coincides with the local velocity of the fluid. 2 Any shape or contour designed to lessen resistance to motion of a solid in a fluid. —*adj.* 1 Designating an uninterrupted flow or drift. 2 Denoting a

form or body designed to minimize turbulence in the flow of fluid around it. —*v.t.* **-lined, -lin·ing** 1 To design with a streamline shape. 2 To make more up-to-date, esp. by reorganization.

stream·lined (strēm′līnd′) *adj.* 1 STREAMLINE. 2 Improved in efficiency; modernized.

street (strēt) *n.* 1 A public way in a city, town, or village, usu. with buildings on one or both sides. 2 Such a public way as set apart for vehicles: Don't play in the *street.* 3 *Informal* The people living on a specific street. —*adj.* 1 Working in the streets: a *street* musician. 2 Opening onto the street: a *street* door. 3 Performed or taking place on the street: *street* crime. 4 Habituated to the ways of life in the streets, esp. in cities: *street* people. [< LL *strata (via)* paved (road)]

street Arab A homeless or outcast child who lives in the streets; gamin.

street·car (strēt′kär′) *n.* A passenger car that runs on rails laid on the surface of the streets.

street people Young people, esp. of the late 1960s, usu. without a permanent residence and having a life style marked by the rejection of middle-class values and by the use of drugs.

street·walk·er (strēt′wô′kər) *n.* A prostitute who solicits in the streets. —**street′walk′ing** *n.*

strength (strength) *n.* 1 The quality or property of being physically strong: the *strength* of a weight lifter. 2 The capacity to sustain the application of force without yielding or breaking. 3 Effectiveness: the *strength* of an argument. 4 Binding force or validity, as of a law. 5 Vigor or force of style: a drama of great *strength.* 6 Available numerical force in a military unit or other organization. 7 Degree of intensity, as of color, light, or sound. 8 Potency, as of a drug, chemical, or liquor; concentration. 9 A support; aid: He is our *strength.* —**on the strength of** Relying on; on the basis of. [< OE *strang* strong] —**Syn.** 1 force, power, vigor. 2 solidity, tenacity, toughness.

strength·en (streng′thən) *v.t.* 1 To make strong. 2 To encourage; hearten. —*v.i.* 3 To become or grow strong or stronger. —**strength′en·er** *n.*

stren·u·ous (stren′yōō·əs) *adj.* Necessitating or marked by strong effort or exertion. [< L *strenuus*] —**stren′u·ous·ly** *adv.* —**stren′u·ous·ness** *n.*

strep throat (strep) A streptococcal throat infection.

strep·to·coc·cus (strep′tə·kok′əs) *n. pl.* **·coc·ci** (-kok′sī, -sē, -ī, -ē) Any of a large group of spherical bacteria that grow together in long chains, including a few pathogens. [< Gk. *streptos* twisted + COCCUS] —**strep′to·coc′cal** (-kok′əl), **strep′to·coc′cic** (-kok′sik, -kok′ik) *adj.*

strep·to·my·cin (strep′tō·mī′sin) *n.* A potent antibiotic isolated from a mold. [< Gk. *streptos* twisted + *mykēs* fungus]

stress (stres) *n.* 1 Special weight, importance, or significance. 2 Physical or emotional tension. 3 *Mech.* A force tending to deform a body on which it acts. 4 Emphasis. 5 In pronunciation, the relative force with which a sound, syllable, or word is uttered. —*v.t.* 1 To subject to stress. 2 To accent, as a syllable. 3 To give emphasis or weight to. [< L *strictus,* p.p. of *stringere* draw tight] —**stress′ful** *adj.*

-stress *suffix of nouns* Feminine form of -STER: *songstress.*

stretch (strech) *v.t.* 1 To extend or draw out, as to full length or width. 2 To draw out forcibly, esp. beyond normal or proper limits. 3 To cause to reach, as from one place to another. 4 To put forth, hold out, or extend (the hand, an object, etc.). 5 To tighten, strain, or exert to the utmost: to *stretch* every nerve. 6 To adjust or adapt to meet specific needs, circumstances, etc.: to *stretch* the truth; to *stretch* food. 7 *Slang* To fell with a blow. —*v.i.* 8 To reach or extend from one place to another. 9 To become extended, esp. beyond normal limits. 10 To extend one's body or limbs, as in relaxing. 11 To lie down: usu. with *out.* —*n.* 1 An act of stretching, or the state of being stretched. 2 Extent to which something can be stretched. 3 A continuous extent of space or time: a *stretch* of woodland; a *stretch* of two years. 4 In racing, the straight part of the track. 5 *Slang* A term of imprisonment. —*adj.* Capable of being easily stretched, as clothing: *stretch* socks. [< OE *streccan* stretch] —**stretch′i·ness** *n.* —**stretch′y** *adj.*

stretch·er (strech′ər) *n.* 1 Any device for stretching: a shoe *stretcher.* 2 A portable, often webbed frame for carrying the injured, sick, or dead.

stretch-out (strech′out′) *n. Informal* A system of industrial operation in which employees are required to perform more work per unit of time worked, usu. without increase in pay.

strew (strōō) *v.t.* **strewed, strewed** or **strewn, strew·ing** 1 To spread about at random; sprinkle. 2 To cover with something scattered or sprinkled. 3 To be scattered over (a surface). [< OE *strēawian*]

stri·a·ted (strī′ā·tid) *adj.* Striped, grooved, or banded: *striated* muscle. [< L *striatus,* p.p. of *striare* to groove] — **stri′a·tion** *n.*

strick·en (strik′ən) *adj.* 1 Struck down by injury, disease, calamity, remorse, etc. 2 Advanced or far gone, as in age: *stricken* in years. [< OE *stricen,* p.p. of *strican* to strike]

strict (strikt) *adj.* 1 Observing or enforcing rules exactly: a *strict* church. 2 Containing severe rules or provisions; exacting. 3 Harsh; stern: a *strict* teacher. 4 Exactly defined or applied: the *strict* truth. 5 Devout; orthodox: a *strict* Catholic. 6 Absolute: in *strict* confidence. [< L *strictus,* p.p. of *stringere* draw tight] —**strict′ly** *adv.* —**strict′·ness** *n.*

stric·ture (strik′chər) *n.* 1 Severe criticism. 2 Something that checks or restricts. 3 Closure or narrowing of a duct or passage of the body. [< L *strictus* strict]

stride (strīd) *n.* 1 A long and measured step. 2 The space passed over by such a step. —**hit one's stride** To attain one's normal speed. —**make rapid strides** To make quick progress. —**take (something) in one's stride** To do or accept (something) without undue effort or without becoming upset. —*v.* **strode, strid·den, strid·ing** *v.i.* 1 To walk with long steps, as from haste. —*v.t.* 2 To walk through, along, etc., with long steps. 3 To pass over with a single stride. 4 To straddle; bestride. [< OE *strīdan* to stride] —**strid′er** *n.*

stri·dent (strīd′nt) *adj.* Having a loud and harsh sound; grating. [< L *stridere* to creak] —**stri′dence, stri′den·cy** *n.* —**stri′dent·ly** *adv.*

strid·u·late (strij′ŏŏ·lāt) *v.i.* **·lat·ed, ·lat·ing** To make a chirping, nonvocal noise, as a cricket, etc. [< L *stridere* to rattle, rasp] —**strid′u·la′tion** *n.* —**strid′u·la·to′ry** (-lə·tôr′ē, -tō′rē), **strid′u·lous** *adj.*

strife (strīf) *n.* 1 Angry contention; fighting. 2 Any contest or rivalry. 3 The act of striving; strenuous endeavor. [< OF *estriver* strive]

strike (strīk) *v.* **struck, struck** (*chiefly Archaic* **strick·en**), **strik·ing** *v.t.* 1 To hit with a blow; deal a blow to. 2 To crash into: The car *struck* the wall. 3 To deal (a blow, etc.). 4 To cause to hit forcibly: He *struck* his hand on the table. 5 To attack; assault. 6 To ignite (a match, etc.) 7 To form by stamping, printing, etc. 8 To announce; sound: The clock *struck* two. 9 To reach: A sound *struck* his ear. 10 To affect suddenly or in a specified manner: He was *struck* speechless. 11 To occur to: An idea *strikes* me. 12 To impress in a specified manner. 13 To attract the attention of: The dress *struck* her fancy. 14 To assume: to *strike* an attitude. 15 To cause to enter deeply or suddenly: to *strike* dismay into one's heart. 16 To lower or haul down, as a sail or a flag. 17 To cease working at in order to compel compliance to a demand, etc. 18 To make and confirm, as a bargain. —*v.i.* 19 To come into violent contact; crash; hit. 20 To deal or aim a blow or blows. 21 To make an assault or attack. 22 To sound from a blow or blows. 23 To be indicated by the sound of blows or strokes: Noon has just *struck.* 24 To ignite. 25 To lower a flag in token of surrender. 26 To take a course; start and proceed: to *strike* for home. 27 To cease work in order to enforce demands, etc. 28 To snatch at or swallow the lure: said of fish. —**strike camp** To take down the tents of a camp. —**strike down** 1 To fell with a blow. 2 To incapacitate completely. —**strike dumb** To astonish; amaze. —**strike home** 1 To deal an effective blow. 2 To have telling effect. —**strike it rich** 1 To find a valuable pocket of ore. 2 To come into wealth or good fortune. —**strike off** 1 To remove or take off by or as by a blow or stroke. 2 To deduct. —**strike oil**

1 To find oil while drilling. 2 *Slang* To meet with unexpected good fortune. —**strike out** 1 To aim a blow or blows. 2 To cross out or erase. 3 To begin; start. 4 In baseball, to put out (the batter) by pitching three strikes. —**strike up** 1 To begin to play, as a band. 2 To start up; begin, as a friendship. —*n.* 1 An act of striking. 2 In baseball, an unsuccessful attempt by the batter to hit the ball. 3 In bowling, the knocking down of all the pins with the first bowl. 4 The quitting of work by a body of workers to secure some demand from management. 5 A new discovery, as of oil or ore. 6 Any unexpected or complete success. 7 The sudden rise and taking of the bait by a fish. —**on strike** Refusing to work in order to secure higher pay, better working conditions, etc. [< OE *strican* stroke, move]

strike·break·er (strīk′brā′kər) *n.* One who takes the place of a worker on strike or who seeks to intimidate or replace the strikers with other workers. —**strike′break′ing** *n.*

strik·er (strī′kər) *n.* 1 One who or that which strikes. 2 An employee who is on strike.

strik·ing (strī′king) *adj.* 1 Notable; impressive: a *striking* girl. 2 On strike. 3 That strikes: a *striking* clock. —**strik′ing·ly** *adv.* —**strik′ing·ness** *n.*

string (string) *n.* 1 A slender line, thinner than a cord and thicker than a thread, used for tying parcels, lacing, etc. 2 A cord of catgut, nylon, wire, etc., for musical instruments, bows, tennis rackets, etc. 3 A stringlike formation, as of certain vegetables. 4 A series of things hung on a small cord: a *string* of pearls. 5 A connected series or succession, as of things, acts, or events. 6 A drove or small collection of stock, esp. of saddle horses. 7 *pl.* Stringed instruments, esp., the section of violins, cellos, etc., in a symphony orchestra. 8 In sports, a group of contestants ranked as to skill. 9 *Informal* Often *pl.* A condition or restriction attached to an offer or gift. —**on a string** Under control or domination. —**pull strings** 1 To control the actions of others, usu. secretly. 2 To influence others to gain an advantage. —*v.* **strung, string·ing** *v.t.* 1 To thread, as beads, on or as on a string. 2 To fit with a string or strings, as a guitar or bow. 3 To bind, fasten, or adorn with a string or strings. 4 To tune the strings of (a musical instrument). 5 To brace; strengthen. 6 To make tense or nervous. 7 To arrange or extend like a string. 8 To remove the strings from (vegetables). —*v.i.* 9 To extend or proceed in a line or series. 10 To form into strings. —**string along** *Slang* 1 To cooperate with. 2 To deceive; cheat. 3 To keep (someone) on tenterhooks. —**string out** *Informal* To protract; prolong: to *string out* an investigation. —**string up** *Informal* To hang. [< OE *streng* string]

string bean 1 The unripe edible seed pod of several varieties of bean. 2 The plants bearing these pods. 3 *Informal* A tall, skinny person.

stringed instrument (stringd) A musical instrument provided with strings or wires, as a violin, guitar, etc.

strin·gent (strin′jənt) *adj.* 1 Rigid; severe, as regulations. 2 Hampered by scarcity of money: said of a market. 3 Convincing; forcible. [< L *stringens,* pr.p of *stringere* draw tight] —**strin′gen·cy, strin′gent·ness** *n.* —**strin′gent·ly** *adv.*

string·er (string′ər) *n.* 1 One who strings. 2 A heavy timber supporting other members of a structure. 3 A newsman employed on a free-lance basis, often in out-of-town or foreign locations. 4 A person having a specific rating as to excellence, skill, etc.: used in combination: a *second-stringer.*

string·halt (string′hôlt′) *n.* In horses, lameness marked by spasmodic movement of the hind legs.

string·y (string′ē) *adj.* **string·i·er, string·i·est** 1 Of or like a string or strings: *stringy* hair. 2 Containing fibrous strings. 3 Forming in strings, as thick glue; ropy. 4 Tall and wiry in build. —**string′i·ly** *adv.* —**string′i·ness** *n.*

strip¹ (strip) *n.* 1 A narrow piece, comparatively long, as of cloth, wood, etc. 2 A number of stamps attached in a row. 3 A narrow piece of land used as a runway for airplanes. 4 A comic strip. [?]

strip² (strip) *v.* **stripped** or **stript, strip·ping** *v.t.* 1 To pull the covering, clothing, leaves, etc., from; lay bare. **2** To pull off (the covering, etc.). **3** To rob or plunder; spoil. **4** To make bare or empty. **5** To take away. **6** To deprive of something; divest. **7** To damage the teeth, thread, etc., of (a gear, bolt, etc.). —*v.i.* **8** To undress. [< OE *bestrȳpan* plunder]

stripe¹ (strīp) *n.* **1** A line, band, or long strip of material differing in color or finish from its adjacent surfaces. **2** Distinctive quality or character: a man of artistic *stripe*. **3** Striped cloth. **4** *pl.* Prison uniform. **5** A piece of material or braid on a uniform to indicate rank. —*v.t.* **striped, strip·ing** To mark with a stripe or stripes. [< MDu.]

stripe² (strīp) *n.* **1** A blow struck with a whip or rod. **2** A weal or welt on the skin caused by such a blow. [Prob. < LG]

strip·ling (strip'ling) *n.* A mere youth; a lad. [?]

strip mine A mine, esp. a coal mine, the seams of which are close to the surface of the earth and which is worked by stripping away the topsoil and the material beneath it. —**strip'-mine'** *v.t.* (**-mined, -min·ing**) —**strip miner**

strip·per (strip'ər) *n.* **1** One who or that which strips. **2** *Slang* A female performer of a striptease.

strip·tease (strip'tēz') *n.* An act, usu. in burlesque, in which a female performer gradually disrobes before an audience. —**strip'teas'er** *n.*

strive (strīv) *v.i.* **strove, striv·en** (striv'ən) or **strived, striv·ing** **1** To make earnest effort. **2** To engage in strife; fight: to *strive* against an enemy. [< OF *estriver*] —**striv'er** *n.* —**Syn.** **1** endeavor, try. **2** contend, struggle.

strobe (strōb) *n.* **1** STROBOSCOPE. **2** An electronically controlled device that emits light in very brief, brilliant flashes, used in photography, in the theater, etc.: also **strobe light.**

strob·o·scope (strōb'ə·skōp) *n.* An instrument for studying the motion of an object by making the object appear to be stationary, as by periodic instantaneous illumination or observation. [< Gk. *strobos* twirling + -SCOPE] —**strob'o·scop'ic** (-skop'ik) or **·i·cal** *adj.* —**strob·os·co·py** (strō·bos'kə·pē) *n.*

strode (strōd) *p.t.* of STRIDE.

stroke (strōk) *n.* **1** The act or movement of striking. **2** One of a series of recurring movements, as of oars, arms in swimming, a piston, etc. **3** A rower who sets the pace for the rest of the crew. **4** A single movement of a pen or pencil. **5** A mark made by such a movement. **6** Any ill effect: a *stroke* of misfortune. **7** APOPLEXY. **8** A sound of a striking mechanism, as a clock. **9** A sudden or brilliant mental act: a *stroke* of wit. **10** A light caressing movement; a stroking. —**keep stroke** To make strokes simultaneously, as oarsmen. —*v.t.* **stroked, strok·ing** **1** To pass the hand over gently or caressingly. **2** To set the pace for (a rowboat or its crew). [< OE *strācian* strike] —**strok'er** *n.*

stroll (strōl) *v.i.* **1** To walk in a leisurely manner; saunter. **2** To go from place to place. —*n.* A leisurely walk. [?]

stroll·er (strō'lər) *n.* **1** A small, light baby carriage, often collapsible. **2** One who strolls. **3** An actor who travels from place to place to perform.

strong (strông, strong) *adj.* **1** Physically powerful; muscular. **2** Healthy; robust: a *strong* constitution. **3** Resolute; courageous. **4** Mentally powerful or vigorous. **5** Especially competent or able: *strong* in mathematics. **6** Abundantly supplied: *strong* in trumps. **7** Solidly made or constituted: *strong* walls. **8** Powerful, as a rival or combatant. **9** Easy to defend: a *strong* position. **10** In numerical force: an army 20,000 *strong.* **11** Well able to exert influence, authority, etc. **12** Financially sound: a *strong* market. **13** Powerful in effect: *strong* poison. **14** Not diluted or weak: *strong* coffee. **15** Containing much alcohol: a *strong* drink. **16** Powerful in flavor or odor: a *strong* breath. **17** Intense in degree or quality: a *strong* light. **18** Loud and firm: a *strong* voice. **19** Firm; tenacious: a *strong* will. **20** Fervid: a *strong* desire. **21** Cogent; convincing: *strong* evidence. **22** Distinct; marked: a *strong* resemblance. **23** Extreme: *strong* measures. **24** Emphatic: *strong* language. **25** Moving with great force: said of a wind, stream, or tide. **26** *Phonet.* Stressed. **27** *Gram.* Of verbs, indicating changes in tense by means of vowel changes, rather than by inflectional endings, as *drink, drank, drunk.* —*adv.* In a firm, vigorous manner. [< OE] —**strong'ly** *adv.* —**strong'ness** *n.*

strong-arm (strông'ärm', strong'-) *Informal adj.* Using

physical or coercive power: *strong-arm* tactics. —*v.t.* **1** To use physical force upon; assault. **2** To coerce; compel.

strong·box (strông'boks', strong'-) *n.* A chest or safe for keeping valuables.

strong drink Alcoholic liquors.

strong·hold (strông'hōld', strong'-) *n.* A strongly defended place; fortress.

strong·man (strông'man', strong'-) *n. pl.* **·men** (-mən) A political leader having preeminent power, as from a military coup or other extralegal means.

strong-mind·ed (strông'mīn'did, strong'-) *adj.* **1** Having an active, vigorous mind. **2** Determined; resolute. —**strong'-mind'ed·ly** *adv.* —**strong'-mind'ed·ness** *n.*

strong-willed (strông'wild', strong'-) *adj.* Having a strong will; obstinate.

stron·ti·um (stron'chē·əm, -chəm, -tē·əm) *n.* A metallic element (symbol Sr) chemically resembling calcium, used in pyrotechnics. [< *Strontian,* Argyll, Scotland, where first discovered] —**stron'tic** (-tik) *adj.*

strop (strop) *n.* A strip of leather on which to sharpen a razor. —*v.t.* **stropped, strop·ping** To sharpen on a strop. [< Gk. *strophos* band]

stro·phe (strō'fē), *n.* **1** In ancient Greece, the verses sung by the chorus in a play while moving from right to left. **2** A stanza of a poem. [< Gk. *strophē* a turning, twist] —**stroph·ic** (strof'ik, strō'fik) or **·i·cal** *adj.*

strove (strōv) *p.t.* of STRIVE.

struck (struk) *p.t. & p.p.* of STRIKE.

struc·tur·al (struk'chər·əl) *adj.* **1** Of, pertaining to, or characterized by structure. **2** Used in or essential to construction. —**struc'tur·al·ly** *adv.*

Strop

structural steel Rolled steel shaped and adapted for use in construction.

struc·ture (struk'chər) *n.* **1** That which is constructed, as a building. **2** Something based upon or organized according to a plan or design: the political *structure* of a republic. **3** The manner of such organization: a hierarchical *structure.* **4** The arrangement and relationship of the parts of a whole, as organs in a plant or animal, atoms in a molecule, etc. —*v.t.* **·tured, ·tur·ing** **1** To form or organize into a structure; build. **2** To conceive as a structural whole. [< L *structus,* p.p. of *struere* build]

stru·del (strōōd'l) *n.* A kind of pastry with a filling of fruit, nuts, etc. [G, lit., eddy]

strug·gle (strug'əl) *n.* **1** A violent effort or series of efforts. **2** A war; battle. —*v.i.* **·gled, ·gling** **1** To contend with an adversary in physical combat; fight. **2** To strive: to *struggle* against odds. **3** To make one's way by violent efforts: to *struggle* through mud. [ME *strogelen*] —**strug'gler** *n.* —**strug'gling·ly** *adv.*

strum (strum) *v.t. & v.i.* **strummed, strum·ming** To play idly or carelessly (on a stringed instrument). —*n.* The act of strumming. [Prob. Imit.] —**strum'mer** *n.*

strum·pet (strum'pit) *n.* A whore; prostitute. [ME]

strung (strung) *p.t. & p.p.* of STRING.

strung out *Slang* **1** Sick or in weakened health from prolonged use of drugs. **2** Addicted to narcotics.

strut (strut) *n.* **1** A proud or pompous step or walk. **2** A supporting piece in a framework, keeping two others from approaching nearer together. —*v.* **strut·ted, strut·ting** *v.i.* **1** To walk pompously and affectedly. —*v.t.* **2** To brace or support with a brace or strut. [< OE *strūtian* be rigid, stand stiffly] —**strut'ter** *n.* —**strut'ting·ly** *adv.*

strych·nine (strik'nīn, -nən, -nēn) *n.* A poisonous alkaloid obtained from nux vomica, used in medicine as a stimulant. Also **strych'ni·a** (-nē·ə) [< Gk. *strychnos* nightshade] —**strych'nic** *adj.*

stub (stub) *n.* **1** Any short remnant, as of a pencil, candle, cigarette, cigar, or broken tooth. **2** In a checkbook, the short piece on which the amount of a check is recorded and that remains when the check is detached. **3** A tree stump. —*v.t.* **stubbed, stub·bing** **1** To strike, as the toe, against a low obstruction or projection. **2** To clear or remove the stubs or roots from. [< OE *stubb*] —**stub'ber** *n.*

stub·ble (stub'əl) *n.* **1** The stubs of plants covering a field after reaping. **2** The field itself. **3** Any surface or growth resembling stubble, as short bristly hair or beard. [< L *stipula* stalk] —**stub'bly** *adj.* (**·bli·er, ·bli·est**)

stub·born (stub′ərn) *adj.* 1 Inflexible in opinion or intention. 2 Determined to have one's own way. 3 Not easily handled, bent, or overcome. 4 Characterized by perseverance or persistence: *stubborn* fighting. [ME *stoborne*] — **stub′born·ly** *adv.* —**stub′born·ness** *n.* —Syn. 1 opinionated, unyielding. 2 headstrong, obdurate, obstinate.

stub·by (stub′ē) *adj.* **·bi·er, ·bi·est** 1 Short, stiff, and bristling: a *stubby* beard. 2 Short and thick: a *stubby* pencil. 3 Short and thick-set: a *stubby* man. —**stub′bi·ly** *adv.* — **stub′bi·ness** *n.*

stuc·co (stuk′ō) *n. pl.* **·coes** or **·cos** 1 Any plaster or cement used for the external coating of buildings. 2 Work done in stucco: also **stuc′co·work′**. —*v.t.* **·coed, ·co·ing** To apply stucco to; decorate with stucco. [Ital.] —**stuc′co·er** *n.*

stuck (stuk) *p.t. & p.p.* of STICK.

stuck-up (stuk′up′) *adj. Informal* Conceited; very vain.

stud¹ (stud) *n.* 1 Any of a series of small knobs, round-headed nails, or small protuberant ornaments. 2 A small, removable button such as is used in a shirt front. 3 A post to which laths are nailed in a building frame. 4 STUD POKER. —*v.t.* **stud·ded, stud·ding** 1 To set thickly with small points, projections, or knobs. 2 To be scattered over: Daisies *stud* the meadows. 3 To support or stiffen by means of studs or upright props. [< OE *studu* post]

stud² (stud) *n.* 1 A collection of horses and mares for breeding, riding, hunting, or racing. 2 The place where they are kept. 3 A stallion. —**at stud** Available for breeding purposes: said of male animals. —*adj.* Of or pertaining to a stud. [< OE *stōd*]

stu·dent (st(y)ōōd′nt, -ənt) *n.* 1 A person engaged in a course of study, esp. in an educational institution. 2 One who closely examines or investigates. [< L *studere* be eager, apply oneself, study]

stud·horse (stud′hôrs′) *n.* A stallion kept for breeding. Also **stud horse.**

stud·ied (stud′ēd) *adj.* 1 Deliberately planned; premeditated: a *studied* insult. 2 Acquired or prepared by study. —**stud′ied·ly** *adv.* —**stud′ied·ness** *n.*

stu·di·o (st(y)ōō′dē·ō) *n. pl.* **·di·os** 1 The workroom of an artist, photographer, etc. 2 A place where motion pictures are filmed. 3 A room or rooms where radio or television programs are broadcast or recorded. 4 A room or place in which music is recorded. [< L *studere* apply oneself, be diligent]

stu·di·ous (st(y)ōō′dē·əs) *adj.* 1 Given to or fond of study. 2 Considerate; careful; attentive. —**stu′di·ous·ly** *adv.* — **stu′di·ous·ness** *n.*

stud poker A game of poker in which the cards of the first round are dealt face down and the rest face up.

stud·y (stud′ē) *v.* **stud·ied, stud·y·ing** *v.t.* 1 To acquire a knowledge of: to *study* physics. 2 To examine; search into: to *study* a problem. 3 To scrutinize: to *study* one's reflection. 4 To memorize, as a part in a play. —*v.i.* 5 To apply the mind in acquiring knowledge. 6 To be a student. — **study up on** To acquire more complete information concerning. —*n. pl.* **stud·ies** 1 The process of acquiring information. 2 A particular instance or form of mental work. 3 A branch or department of knowledge. 4 A specific product of studious application: his *study* of plankton. 5 An examination or consideration of a problem, proposal, etc. 6 In art, a first sketch. 7 A careful literary treatment of a subject. 8 A room set aside for study, reading, etc. 9 A thoughtful state of mind: a brown *study*. 10 *Music* A composition designed to develop technique; an étude. [< L *studium* zeal] —Syn. *v.* 1 grasp, learn. 2 investigate, ponder, analyze.

stuff (stuf) *v.t.* 1 To fill completely; pack. 2 To plug. 3 To obstruct or stop up. 4 To fill with padding, as a cushion. 5 To fill (a fowl, roast, etc.) with stuffing. 6 In taxidermy, to fill the skin of (a bird, animal, etc.) with a material preparatory to mounting. 7 To fill too full; cram: He *stuffed* himself with cake. 8 To fill with knowledge, ideas, or attitudes, esp. unsystematically. —*v.i.* 9 To eat to excess. —*n.* 1 The material or matter out of which something is or may be shaped or made. 2 The fundamental element of anything: the *stuff* of genius. 3 *Informal* A

specific skill, field of knowledge, etc.: That editor knows her *stuff.* 4 Personal possessions generally. 5 Unspecified material, matter, etc.: They carried away tons of the *stuff.* 6 A miscellaneous collection of things. 7 Nonsense; foolishness. 8 Woven material, esp. of wool. 9 Any textile fabric. [< OF *estoffer* cram] —**stuff′er** *n.*

stuffed shirt *Informal* A pretentious, pompous person.

stuff·ing (stuf′ing) *n.* 1 The material with which anything is stuffed. 2 A mixture, as of crumbs with seasoning, used in stuffing fowls, etc. 3 The process of stuffing anything.

stuff·y (stuf′ē) *adj.* **stuff·i·er, stuff·i·est** 1 Badly ventilated. 2 Filled up so as to impede respiration: a *stuffy* nose. 3 Dull; uninspired: a *stuffy* speech. 4 Strait-laced; stodgy. — **stuff′i·ly** *adv.* —**stuff′i·ness** *n.*

stul·ti·fy (stul′tə·fī′) *v.t.* **·fied, ·fy·ing** 1 To cause to appear absurd. 2 To make useless or futile. [< L *stultus* foolish + -FY] —**stul′ti·fi·ca′tion, stul′ti·fi′er** *n.*

stum·ble (stum′bəl) *v.* **·bled, ·bling** *v.i.* 1 To miss one's step in walking or running; trip. 2 To speak or act in a blundering manner: The student *stumbled* through his recitation. 3 To happen upon something by chance: with *across, on, upon,* etc. 4 To do wrong; err. —*v.t.* 5 To cause to stumble. —*n.* The act of stumbling. [ME *stumblen*] —**stum′bler** *n.* — **stum′bling·ly** *adv.*

stum·bling·block (stum′bling·blok′) *n.* Any obstacle or hindrance.

stump (stump) *n.* 1 That portion of the trunk of a tree left standing when the tree is felled. 2 The part of a limb, etc., that remains when the main part has been removed. 3 *pl. Informal* The legs. 4 A place or platform where a political speech is made. 5 A short, thick-set person or animal. 6 A heavy step; a clump. —**take the stump** To electioneer in a political campaign. —**up a stump** In trouble or in a dilemma. —*adj.* 1 Being or resembling a stump. 2 Of or pertaining to political oratory or campaigning: a *stump* speaker. —*v.t.* 1 To reduce to a stump; lop. 2 To remove stumps from (land). 3 To canvass (a district) by making political speeches. 4 *Informal* To bring to a halt by real or fancied obstacles. 5 To stub, as one's toe. —*v.i.* 6 To walk heavily. [< MLG] —**stump′i·ness** *n.* —**stump′y** *adj.*

stun (stun) *v.t.* **stunned, stun·ning** 1 To render unconscious or incapable of action. 2 To astonish; astound. 3 To daze or overwhelm. —*n.* The act of stunning or the condition of being stunned. [< OF *estoner*]

stung (stung) *p.t. & p.p.* of STING.

stunk (stungk) *p.p.* and alternative *p.t.* of STINK.

stun·ner (stun′ər) *n.* 1 A person or blow that stuns. 2 *Slang* A person or thing of extraordinary qualities, such as beauty.

stun·ning (stun′ing) *adj.* 1 That stuns or astounds. 2 *Informal* Surprising; impressive; beautiful. —**stun′ning·ly** *adv.*

stunt¹ (stunt) *v.t.* To check the natural development of; dwarf; cramp. —*n.* 1 A check in growth, progress, or development. 2 A stunted animal or person. [< OE, dull, foolish] —**stunt′ed·ness** *n.*

stunt² (stunt) *Informal n.* 1 A sensational feat, as of bodily skill. 2 Any remarkable feat. —*v.i.* 1 To perform a stunt or stunts. —*v.t.* 2 To perform stunts with (an airplane, etc.). [?]

stunt man In motion pictures, a person employed to substitute for an actor when dangerous jumps, falls, etc., must be made.

stu·pe·fac·tion (st(y)ōō′pə·fak′shən) *n.* The act of stupefying or state of being stupefied.

stu·pe·fy (st(y)ōō′pə·fī′) *v.t.* **·fied, ·fy·ing** 1 To dull the senses or faculties of; stun. 2 To amaze; astound. [< L *stupere* be stunned + -FY] —**stu′pe·fi′er** *n.*

stu·pen·dous (st(y)ōō·pen′dəs) *adj.* 1 Of prodigious size, bulk, or degree. 2 Astonishing; marvelous. [< L *stupere* be stunned] —**stu·pen′dous·ly** *adv.* —**stu·pen′dous·ness** *n.*

stu·pid (st(y)ōō′pid) *adj.* 1 Very slow in understanding; lacking in intelligence; dull-witted. 2 Affected with stupor; stupefied. 3 Dull and profitless; tiresome: to regard rote learning as *stupid*. 4 Resulting from slowness in understanding or a lack of intelligence. 5 *Informal* Annoying; bothersome: This *stupid* nail won't go in straight. [< L *stupidus* struck dumb] —stu·pid·i·ty (stʸoo·pid′ə·tē) (*pl.* ·ties), stu′pid·ness *n.* —stu′pid·ly *adv.*

stu·por (stʸoo′pər) *n.* 1 Abnormal lethargy due to shock, drugs, etc. 2 Extreme intellectual dullness. [< L *stupere* be stunned] —stu′por·ous *adj.*

stur·dy (stûr′dē) *adj.* ·di·er, ·di·est 1 Possessing rugged health and strength. 2 Firm and resolute: a *sturdy* defense. [< OF *estourdir* stun, amaze] —stur′di·ly *adv.* — stur′di·ness *n.* —Syn. 1 hardy, lusty, robust, vigorous. 2 determined, unyielding.

stur·geon (stûr′jən) *n.* Any of various large edible fishes of northern regions, valued as the source of caviar. [< Med. L *sturio*]

Sturgeon

stut·ter (stut′ər) *v.t. & v.i.* To utter or speak with spasmodic repetition, blocking, and prolongation of sounds and syllables. —*n.* The act or habit of stuttering. [Freq. of ME *stutten* stutter] —stut′ter·er *n.* —stut′ter·ing·ly *adv.*

St. Vi·tus's dance (sānt vī′təs·iz) CHOREA. Also St. Vitus dance. [< *St. Vitus,* third-century Christian child martyr]

sty¹ (stī) *n. pl.* sties 1 A pen for swine. 2 Any filthy habitation. [< OE *stī, stig*]

sty² (stī) *n. pl.* sties A pustule on the edge of an eyelid. Also stye. [< OE *stīgan* rise + *ye* eye]

Styg·i·an (stij′ē·ən) *adj.* 1 Pertaining to or like the river Styx or the lower world. 2 Dark and gloomy.

style (stīl) *n.* 1 A fashionable manner or appearance: to be in *style.* 2 Fashion: the latest *style* in shirts. 3 A particular fashion in clothing. 4 A distinctive form of expression: a florid *style.* 5 An effective way of expression: His drawings have *style.* 6 Manner: a church in the Romanesque *style* of architecture. 7 A way of living or behaving: Domestic life is not his *style.* 8 A pointed instrument for marking or engraving. 9 An indicator on a dial. 10 *Printing* The typography, spelling, design, etc., used in a given published text. 11 *Bot.* The slender part of a carpel between stigma and ovary. 12 A system of arranging the calendar years so as to average that of the true solar year. Our calendar, adopted in 1752, is called New Style, while Old Style dates are 13 days earlier. —*v.t.* styled, styl·ing 1 To name; give a title to: Richard I was *styled* "the Lion-Hearted." 2 To cause to conform to a specific style: to *style* a manuscript. [< L *stylus* writing instrument] —styl′er *n.*

style·book (stīl′book′) *n.* A book setting forth rules of capitalization, punctuation, etc., for the use of printers, writers, and editors. Also style manual.

styl·ish (stī′lish) *adj.* 1 Having style. 2 Very fashionable. —styl′ish·ly *adv.* —styl′ish·ness *n.*

styl·ist (stī′list) *n.* 1 One who is a master of style: a literary *stylist.* 2 An adviser on or a creator of styles: a hair *stylist.* —sty·lis′tic *adj.* —sty·lis′ti·cal·ly *adv.*

styl·ize (stī′līz) *v.t.* ·ized, ·iz·ing To conform to or create in a distinctive or specific style. *Brit. sp.* styl′ise. —styl′i·za′tion (stī′lə·za′shən), styl′iz·er *n.*

sty·lus (stī′ləs) *n. pl.* ·lus·es or ·li (lī) 1 An ancient instrument for writing on wax tablets. 2 A tiny, usu. jewel-tipped needle whose vibrations in tracing the groove in a phonograph record transmit sound. [L]

sty·mie (stī′mē) *n.* A condition in golf in which an opponent's ball lies in the line of the player's putt on the green. —*v.t.* ·mied, ·my·ing 1 To block (an opponent) by or as by a stymie. 2 To baffle or perplex. [?]

styp·tic (stip′tik) *adj.* Tending to halt bleeding; astringent: also styp′ti·cal. —*n.* A styptic substance. [< Gk. *styp-sis* a contraction] —styp·tic·i·ty (stip·tis′ə·tē) *n.*

Sty·ro·foam (stī′rə·fōm) *n.* A lightweight, rigid, cellular material formed from a synthetic hydrocarbon polymer: a trade name.

Styx (stiks) *n. Gk. Myth.* The river across which the dead were ferried to Hades.

sua·sion (swā′zhən) *n.* The act of persuading: usu. in the phrase moral suasion. [< L *suadere* persuade] —sua·sive (swā′siv), sua·so·ry (swā′sər·ē) *adj.* —sua′sive·ly *adv.* — sua′sive·ness *n.*

suave (swäv) *adj.* Smooth and pleasant in manner, often superficially so. [< L *suavis* sweet] —suave′ly *adv.* — suave′ness, suav′i·ty (*pl.* ·ties) *n.*

sub (sub) *n. Informal* 1 SUBSTITUTE. 2 A subordinate or subaltern. 3 SUBMARINE. —*v.i.* subbed, sub·bing To act as a substitute for someone.

sub- *prefix* 1 Under; beneath; below: *subcutaneous.* 2 Almost; nearly: *subtropical.* 3 Further; again: *subdivide.* 4 Lower in rank or grade: *subordinate.* 5 Having less importance; secondary: *subtitle.* 6 Forming a further division: *subcommittee.* [< L *sub* under] •See TAXONOMY.

sub. subaltern; submarine; subscription; substitute; suburb; suburban.

sub·al·tern (sub·ôl′tərn, *esp. Brit.* sub′əl·tərn) *adj.* 1 *Brit. Mil.* Ranking below a captain. 2 Of inferior rank or position. —*n.* 1 A person of subordinate rank or position. 2 *Brit. Mil.* An officer ranking below a captain. [< L *sub-* under + *alternus* alternate]

sub·ant·arc·tic (sub′ant·ärk′tik, -är′tik) *adj.* Denoting or pertaining to a region surrounding the Antarctic Circle.

sub·arc·tic (sub·ärk′tik, -är′tik) *adj.* Denoting or pertaining to a region surrounding the Arctic Circle.

sub·a·tom·ic (sub′ə·tom′ik) *adj.* 1 Of or pertaining to the constituent parts of an atom. 2 Smaller than an atom.

sub·com·mit·tee (sub′kə·mit′ē) *n.* A small committee appointed from a larger committee for special work.

sub·con·scious (sub·kon′shəs) *adj.* 1 Only dimly conscious; not fully aware. 2 Not attended by full awareness, as an automatic action. —*n.* That portion of mental activity not in the focus of consciousness. —sub·con′scious·ly *adv.* —sub·con′scious·ness *n.*

sub·con·tract (sub·kon′trakt) *n.* A contract subordinate to another contract and assigning part of the work to a third party. —*v.t. & v.i.* (sub′kən·trakt′) To make a subcontract (for). —sub·con·trac·tor (sub′kon′trak′tər, sub′·kən·trak′-) *n.*

sub·cul·ture (sub′kul·chər) *n.* A group having specific patterns of behavior that set it off from other groups within a culture or society.

sub·cu·ta·ne·ous (sub′kyoo·tā′nē·əs) *adj.* Situated or applied beneath the skin. [< L *sub-* under + *cutis* skin] — sub′cu·ta′ne·ous·ly *adv.*

subd. subdivision.

sub·deb (sub′deb′) *n. Informal* 1 A young girl during the period before she becomes a debutante. 2 Any young girl of the same age.

sub·di·vide (sub′di·vīd′, sub′di·vīd′) *v.t. & v.i.* ·vid·ed, ·vid·ing 1 To divide again. 2 To divide (land) into lots for sale or improvement.

sub·di·vi·sion (sub′di·vizh′ən, sub′di·vizh′ən) *n.* 1 Division following upon division. 2 A part, as of land, resulting from subdividing.

sub·due (sub·dʸoo′) *v.t.* ·dued, ·du·ing 1 To gain dominion over, as by war or force. 2 To overcome by training, influence, or persuasion. 3 To repress (emotions, impulses, etc.). 4 To reduce the intensity of. [< L *subducere* lead away] —sub·du′ed·ly *adv.* —sub·du′er *n.* —Syn. 1 conquer, subjugate, vanquish. 2 master, tame. 4 lessen, soften.

sub·group (sub′groop′) *n.* A subdivision of a group.

sub·head (sub′hed′) *n.* 1 A heading or title of a subdivision of a chapter, etc. 2 A subordinate title. Also sub′·head·ing.

sub·hu·man (sub·hʸoo′mən) *adj.* Less than or imperfectly human.

subj. subject; subjective; subjunctive.

sub·ja·cent (sub·jā′sənt) *adj.* Situated underneath; underlying. [< L *sub-* under + *jacere* to lie] —sub·ja′cen·cy *n.* —sub·ja′cent·ly *adv.*

sub·ject (sub′jikt) *adj.* 1 Being under the power of another. 2 Exposed: *subject* to criticism. 3 Having a tendency: *subject* to colds. 4 Conditional upon: *subject* to your consent. —*n.* 1 One who is under the governing power of another, as of a ruler. •See CITIZEN. 2 One who or that which is employed or treated in a specified way, as in an experiment. 3 The theme or topic of a discussion. 4 Something described or depicted in a literary or artistic work. 5 *Gram.* The word, phrase, or clause of a sentence about which something is stated or asked in the predicate. 6

Music The melodic phrase on which a composition or a part of it is based. **7** A branch of learning. —*v.t.* (səb·jekt′) **1** To bring under dominion or control; subjugate. **2** To cause to undergo some experience or action. **3** To make liable; expose: His inheritance was *subjected* to heavy taxation. [< L *sub-* under + *jacere* throw] —**sub·jec′tion** *n.*

sub·jec·tive (səb·jek′tiv) *adj.* **1** Of or belonging to that which is within the mind and not subject to independent verification. **2** Expressing very personal feelings or opinions: a *subjective* piece of writing. **3** Highly influenced by the emotions or by prejudice. **4** *Med.* Of the kind of which only the patient is aware: said of symptoms. **5** *Gram.* Designating the case and function of the subject of a sentence. —**sub·jec′tive·ly** *adv.* —**sub·jec′tive·ness, sub·jec·tiv·i·ty** (sub′jek·tiv′ə·tē) *n.*

sub·join (sub·join′) *v.t.* To add at the end; affix. [< L *sub-* in addition + *jungere* join] —**sub·join′der** (-dər) *n.*

sub·ju·gate (sub′jŏō·gāt) *v.t.* **·gat·ed, ·gat·ing** **1** To bring under dominion; conquer. **2** To make subservient or submissive. [< L *sub-* under + *jugum* a yoke] —**sub′ju·ga′tion, sub′ju·ga′tor** *n.*

sub·junc·tive (səb·jungk′tiv) *Gram. adj.* Of or pertaining to that mood of the finite verb that is used to express a future contingency, a supposition, or a wish or desire. —*n.* **1** The subjunctive mood. **2** A verb form or construction in this mood. [< L *subjunctus* p.p. of *subjungere* subjoin] —**sub·junc′tive·ly** *adv.*

sub·lease (sub·lēs′) *v.t.* **·leased, ·leas·ing** To obtain or let (property) on a sublease. —*n.* (sub′lēs′) A lease of property from a tenant.

sub·let (sub·let′, sub′let′) *v.t.* **·let, ·let·ting** **1** To let to another (property held on a lease). **2** To let (work that one has contracted to do) to a subordinate contractor. —*n.* Property, esp. dwellings, that is subleased or available for subleasing.

sub·li·mate (sub′lə·māt) *v.* **·mat·ed, ·mat·ing** *v.t.* **1** To refine; purify. **2** *Psychol.* To convert (a primitive impulse) into socially acceptable behavior. **3** *Chem.* SUBLIME. —*v.i.* **4** To undergo or engage in sublimation. —*adj.* Sublimated; refined. —*n. Chem.* The product of sublimation. [< L *sublimis* uplifted, sublime]

sub·li·ma·tion (sub′lə·mā′shən) *n.* **1** The act or process of sublimating. **2** *Chem.* A change of state from solid to vapor or from vapor to solid without liquefaction.

sub·lime (sə·blīm′) *adj.* **1** Characterized by or eliciting feelings of grandeur, nobility, or awe. **2** *Informal* Outstandingly excellent; supreme: a *sublime* meal. —*v.* **·limed, ·lim·ing** *v.t.* **1** To make sublime; ennoble. **2** *Chem.* To purify by the process of sublimation. —*v.i.* **3** *Chem.* To undergo sublimation. [< L *sublimis* lofty] —**sub·lime′ly** *adv.* —**sub·lim·i·ty** (sə·blim′ə·tē), **sub·lime′ness** *n.* —Syn. *adj.* **1** grand, magnificent, solemn. **2** noble.

sub·lim·i·nal (sub·lim′ə·nəl) *adj.* **1** Below or beyond the threshold of consciousness: a *subliminal* stimulus. **2** Too slight or weak to be felt or perceived. [< L *sub-* under + *limen* threshold] —**sub·lim′i·nal·ly** *adv.*

sub·ma·chine gun (sub′mə·shēn′) A lightweight, automatic or semi-automatic gun, designed for firing from the shoulder or hip.

sub·mar·gin·al (sub·mär′jən·əl) *adj.* **1** Below the margin. **2** Not productive enough to develop, cultivate, etc.: *submarginal* land.

sub·ma·rine (sub′mə·rēn′) *adj.* Existing, done, or operating beneath the surface of the sea. —*n.* (sub′mə·rēn) **1** A vessel, usu. a warship, designed to operate both on and below the surface of the water. **2** HERO (def. 6).

sub·max·il·lar·y (sub·mak′sə·ler′ē) *adj.* Of, pertaining to, or situated in the lower jaw. —*n. pl.* **·lar·ies** A submaxillary salivary gland, nerve, artery, etc.

sub·merge (səb·mûrj′) *v.* **·merged, ·merg·ing** *v.t.* **1** To place under or plunge into water. **2** To cover; hide. —*v.i.* **3** To sink or dive beneath the surface of the water. [< L *sub-* under + *mergere* to plunge] —**sub·mer′gence** *n.*

sub·merse (səb·mûrs′) *v.t.* **·mersed, ·mers·ing** SUBMERGE. [< L *submergere* submerge] —**sub·mer′sion** *n.*

sub·mers·i·ble (səb·mûr′sə·bəl) *adj.* That may be sub-

merged. —*n.* **1** SUBMARINE (def. 1). **2** Any of various, usu. small, underwater craft used for naval observation, scientific study, etc.

sub·mis·sion (səb·mish′ən) *n.* **1** A yielding to the power or authority of another. **2** Acquiescence or obedience. **3** The act of referring a matter of controversy to consideration, arbitration, etc. —Syn. **1** surrender. **2** compliance, humbleness.

sub·mis·sive (səb·mis′iv) *adj.* Willing or inclined to submit; docile. —**sub·mis′sive·ly** *adv.* —**sub·mis′sive·ness** *n.*

sub·mit (səb·mit′) *v.* **·mit·ted, ·mit·ting** *v.t.* **1** To place under or yield to the authority of another. **2** To present for the consideration of others; refer. **3** To present as one's opinion; suggest. —*v.i.* **4** To give up; surrender. **5** To be obedient. [< L *sub-* under + *mittere* send] —**sub·mit′tal** *n.*

sub·nor·mal (sub·nôr′məl) *adj.* Below the normal; of less than normal intelligence, development, etc. —*n.* A subnormal individual. —**sub·nor·mal·i·ty** (sub′nôr·mal′ə·tē) *n.* —**sub·nor′mal·ly** *adv.*

sub·or·di·nate (sə·bôr′də·nit) *adj.* **1** Secondary; minor. **2** Lower in rank. **3** Subject or subservient to another. **4** *Gram.* Used within a sentence as a noun, adjective, or adverb: said of a clause. —*n.* One who or that which is subordinate. —*v.t.* (-nāt) **·nat·ed, ·nat·ing** **1** To assign to a lower order or rank. **2** To make subject or subservient. [< L *sub-* under + *ordinare* to order] —**sub·or′di·nate·ly** *adv.* —**sub·or′di·nate·ness, sub·or′di·na′tion** *n.*

sub·orn (sə·bôrn′) *v.t.* **1** To bribe (someone) to commit perjury. **2** To incite or instigate to an evil act. [< L *sub-* secretly + *ornare* equip] —**sub·orn′er, sub·or·na·tion** (sub′ôr·nā′shən) *n.*

sub·poe·na (sə·pē′nə) *n.* A writ requiring a person to appear at court at a specified time and place. —*v.t.* **·naed, ·na·ing** To summon by subpoena. Also **sub·pe′na.** [< L *sub-* under + *poena* penalty]

sub·ro·gate (sub′rō·gāt) *v.t.* **·gat·ed, ·gat·ing** To substitute (one person, esp. one creditor) for another. [< L *sub-* in place of + *rogare* ask] —**sub′ro·ga′tion** *n.*

sub ro·sa (sub rō′zə) Confidentially; in secret. [L, under the rose, a symbol of silence]

sub·rou·tine (sub′rŏō·tēn′) *n.* A part of a computer program, especially a sequence of instructions to perform a specific task.

sub·scribe (səb·skrīb′) *v.* **·scribed, ·scrib·ing** *v.t.* **1** To write, as one's name, at the end of a document; sign. **2** To sign one's name to as an expression of assent. **3** To promise, esp. in writing, to pay or contribute (a sum of money). —*v.i.* **4** To write one's name at the end of a document. **5** To give approval; agree. **6** To promise to contribute money. **7** To pay in advance for a series of periodicals, tickets to performances, etc. with *to*. [< L *sub-* under + *scribere* write] —**sub·scrib′er** *n.*

sub·script (sub′skript) *adj.* **1** Written following and slightly beneath, as a small letter or number. —*n.* A subscript number, symbol, or letter, as the *2* in H_2O. [< L *subscriptus*, p.p. of *subscribere* subscribe]

sub·scrip·tion (səb·skrip′shən) *n.* **1** The act of subscribing; confirmation or agreement. **2** That which is subscribed; a signed paper or statement. **3** A signature written at the end of a document. **4** The total subscribed for any purpose. **5** The purchase in advance of a series of periodicals, tickets to performances, etc.

sub·sec·tion (sub·sek′shən, sub′sek′shən) *n.* A subdivision of a section.

sub·se·quent (sub′sə·kwənt) *adj.* Following in time, place, or order, or as a result. —**subsequent to** Following; after. [< L *sub-* next below + *sequi* follow] —**sub·se·quence** (sub′sə·kwəns), **sub′se·quen·cy, sub′se·quent·ness** *n.* —**sub′se·quent·ly** *adv.*

sub·serve (səb·sûrv′) *v.t.* **·served, ·serv·ing** **1** To be of use or help in furthering (a process, cause, etc.); promote. **2** To serve as a subordinate to (a person). [< L *sub-* under + *servire* serve]

sub·ser·vi·ent (səb·sûr′vē·ənt) *adj.* **1** Servile; obsequious; truckling. **2** Adapted to promote some end or purpose, esp. in a subordinate capacity. —*n.* One who or that which subserves. **—sub·ser′vi·ent·ly** *adv.* **—sub·ser′vi·ent·ness, sub·ser′vi·ence, sub·ser′vi·en·cy** *n.*

sub·set (sub′set) *n. Math.* A set comprising some or all of the elements of another set.

sub·side (səb·sīd′) *v.i.* **·sid·ed, ·sid·ing 1** To sink to a lower level. **2** To become calm or quiet; abate. **3** To sink to the bottom, as sediment; settle. [< L *sub-* under + *sidere* to settle] **—sub·sid·ence** (səb·sīd′ns, sub′sə·dəns) *n.* **—Syn. 1** fall. **2** decrease, diminish, ebb, wane.

sub·sid·i·ar·y (səb·sid′ē·er′ē, -sid′ə·rē) *adj.* **1** Assisting; supplementary; auxiliary. **2** Of, pertaining to, or in the nature of a subsidy. **—***n. pl.* **·ar·ies 1** One who or that which furnishes supplemental aid or supplies. **2** A business enterprise with over half of its assets or stock owned by another company. **—sub·sid·i·ar·i·ly** (səb·sid′ē·er′ə·lē) *adv.*

sub·si·dize (sub′sə·dīz) *v.t.* **·dized, ·diz·ing 1** To grant a regular allowance or financial aid to. **2** To obtain the assistance of by a subsidy. *Brit. sp.* **sub′si·dise. —sub′si·di·za′tion, sub′si·diz′er** *n.*

sub·si·dy (sub′sə·dē) *n. pl.* **·dies 1** Financial aid directly granted by government to a person or commercial enterprise whose work is deemed beneficial to the public. **2** Any financial assistance granted by one government to another. [< L *subsidium* auxiliary forces, aid < *subsidere* subside]

sub·sist (səb·sist′) *v.i.* **1** To continue to exist. **2** To remain alive; manage to live: to *subsist* on a meatless diet. **3** To continue unchanged; abide. [< L *sub-* under + *sistere* cause to stand] **—sub·sist′er** *n.*

sub·sis·tence (səb·sis′təns) *n.* **1** The act of subsisting. **2** That on which or by which one subsists; sustenance; livelihood. [< LL *subsistentia* < *subsistere* SUBSIST] **—sub·sis′tent** *adj.*

sub·soil (sub′soil′) *n.* The stratum of earth just beneath the surface soil.

sub·son·ic (sub·son′ik) *adj.* Designating those sound waves beyond the lower limits of human audibility.

subst. substantive; substitute.

sub·stance (sub′stəns) *n.* **1** The material of which anything is made or constituted. **2** The essential meaning of anything said or written. **3** Material possessions; wealth; property. **4** The quality of stability or solidity: an argument lacking *substance*. **5** A distinct but unidentified kind of matter: a gaseous *substance*. **6** Essential components or ideas: The *substance* of the two arguments is the same. **— in substance 1** Essentially; chiefly. **2** Really; actually. [< L *substare* be present]

sub·stan·dard (sub·stan′dərd) *adj.* **1** Below an accepted standard; inferior: *substandard* housing. **2** Lower than the established legal standard. **3** Not conforming to the standard language usage of educated speakers and writers: "He don't want none" is *substandard*.

sub·stan·tial (səb·stan′shəl) *adj.* **1** Solid; strong; firm: a *substantial* bridge. **2** Of real worth and importance: a *substantial* profit. **3** Possessed of wealth or sufficient means. **4** Having real existence; not illusory. **5** Containing or conforming to the essence of a thing: in *substantial* agreement. **6** Ample and nourishing: a *substantial* meal. **—sub·stan′ti·al′i·ty** (-shē·al′ə·tē), **sub·stan′tial·ness** *n.* **—sub·stan′tial·ly** *adv.*

sub·stan·ti·ate (səb·stan′shē·āt) *v.t.* **·at·ed, ·at·ing 1** To establish by evidence; verify. **2** To give form or substance to. [< L *substantia* substance] **—sub·stan′ti·a′tion** *n.* **—sub·stan′ti·a′tive** *adj.*

sub·stan·tive (sub′stən·tiv) *n.* **1** A noun or pronoun. **2** A verbal form, phrase, or clause used in place of a noun. **— *adj.* 1** Capable of being used as a noun. **2** Expressive of or denoting existence: The verb "to be" is called the *substantive* verb. **3** Having substance or reality. **4** Being an essential part or constituent. **5** Having distinct individuality. **6** Independent. [< L *substantia* substance] **—sub·stan′ti·val** (sub′stən·tī′vəl) *adj.* **—sub′stan·ti·val·ly, sub′stan·tive·ly** *adv.* **—sub′stan·tive·ness** *n.*

sub·sta·tion (sub′stā′shən) *n.* A subsidiary station, as for electric power or postal service.

sub·sti·tute (sub′stə·tyōōt) *v.* **·tut·ed, ·tut·ing** *v.t.* **1** To put in the place of another person or thing. **2** To take the place of. **—***v.i.* **3** To act as a substitute. **—***n.* One who or that which takes the place of another. **—***adj.* Situated in or

taking the place of another: a *substitute* teacher. [< L *sub-* in place of + *statuere* set up]

sub·sti·tu·tion (sub′stə·tyōō′shən) *n.* **1** The act of substituting, or the state of being substituted. **2** A substitute. **—sub′sti·tu′tion·al** *adj.* **—sub′sti·tu′tion·al·ly** *adv.*

sub·stra·tum (sub·strā′təm, -strat′əm) *n. pl.* **·stra·ta** (-strā′tə, -strat′ə) or **·stra·tums 1** An underlying stratum or layer, as of earth or rock. **2** A foundation or basis. [< L, p.p. neut. of *substernere* spread underneath] **—sub·stra′tal, sub·stra′tive** *adj.*

sub·struc·ture (sub′struk′chər, sub·struk′-) *n.* A structure serving as a foundation. **—sub·struc′tur·al** *adj.*

sub·ten·ant (sub·ten′ənt) *n.* A person who rents or leases from a tenant. **—sub·ten′an·cy** *n.*

sub·tend (sub·tend′) *v.t.* **1** *Geom.* To extend under or opposite to, as the chord of an arc or the side of a triangle opposite to an angle. **2** *Bot.* To enclose in its axil: A leaf *subtends* a bud. [< L *sub-* underneath + *tendere* stretch]

sub·ter·fuge (sub′tər·fyōōj′) *n.* Any plan or trick to escape something unpleasant. [< L *subter-* below, in secret + *fugere* flee, take flight]

sub·ter·ra·ne·an (sub′tə·rā′nē·ən) *adj.* **1** Situated or occurring below the surface of the earth. **2** Hidden. Also **sub′ter·ra′ne·ous.** [< L *sub-* under + *terra* earth] **—sub′ter·ra′ne·an·ly, sub′ter·ra′ne·ous·ly** *adv.*

sub·tile (sut′l, sub′til) *adj.* **1** Elusive; subtle. **2** Crafty; cunning. [< L *subtilis*] **—sub′tile·ly** *adv.* **—sub′tile·ness, sub·til·i·ty** (sub·til′ə·tē) *n.*

sub·ti·tle (sub′tīt′l) *n.* **1** A subordinate or explanatory title, as in a book, play, or document. **2** *pl.* In motion pictures, printed translations of foreign-language dialogue, usu. appearing at the bottom of the screen.

sub·tle (sut′l) *adj.* **sub·tler** (sut′lər, sut′l·ər), **sub·tlest 1** Not easily detected; elusive; delicate: a *subtle* aroma. **2** Characterized by or requiring keenness of mind, vision, hearing, etc.: *subtle* humor; *subtle* variations in sound. **3** Very skillful or ingenious: a *subtle* craftsman. **4** Not direct or obvious: a *subtle* hint. [< L *subtilis* fine] **—sub′tle·ness** *n.* **—sub′tly** *adv.*

sub·tle·ty (sut′l·tē) *n. pl.* **·ties 1** The state or quality of being subtle. **2** Something that is subtle.

sub·tract (səb·trakt′) *v.t. & v.i.* To take away or deduct, as a portion from the whole, or one quantity from another. [< L *sub-* away + *trahere* draw] **—sub·tract′er, sub·trac′tion** *n.* **—sub·trac′tive** *adj.*

sub·tra·hend (sub′trə·hend) *n. Math.* That which is to be subtracted from a number or quantity to give the difference.

sub·treas·ur·y (sub·trezh′ər·ē) *n. pl.* **·ur·ies 1** A branch office of the U.S. Treasury Department. **2** Any branch treasury. **—sub·treas′ur·er** *n.*

sub·trop·i·cal (sub·trop′i·kəl) *adj.* Of, pertaining to, or designating regions adjacent to the tropical zone. Also **sub·trop′ic. —sub·trop′ics** *n.pl.*

sub·urb (sub′ûrb) *n.* **1** A district or town adjacent to a city. **2** Outlying districts; environs. **—the suburbs** Residential areas near or within commuting distance of a city. [< L *sub-* near to + *urbs* a city]

sub·ur·ban (sə·bûr′bən) *adj.* Of or pertaining to a suburb or its residents.

sub·ur·ban·ite (sə·bûr′bən·īt) *n.* A resident of a suburb.

sub·ur·ban·ize (sə·bûr′bə·nīz′) *v.t.* **·ized, ·iz·ing** To make suburban or give a suburban character to. **—sub·ur′ban·i·za′tion** *n.*

sub·ur·bi·a (sə·bûr′bē·ə) *n.* **1** The social and cultural world of suburbanites. **2** Suburbs or suburbanites collectively.

sub·ven·tion (səb·ven′shən) *n.* A grant of money made, esp. by a government, to an institution, cause, or study; subsidy. [< L *subvenire*] **—sub·ven′tion·ar′y** (-er′ē) *adj.*

sub·ver·sion (səb·vûr′shən, -zhən) *n.* **1** The act of subverting; demolition; overthrow. **2** A cause of ruin. **—sub·ver′sion·ar′y** (-er′ē) *adj.*

sub·ver·sive (səb·vûr′siv) *adj.* Tending to subvert or overthrow. **—***n.* A person regarded as desiring to weaken or overthrow a government, organization, etc. **—sub·ver′sive·ly** *adv.* **—sub·ver′sive·ness** *n.*

sub·vert (səb·vûrt′) *v.t.* **1** To overthrow from the very foundation; destroy utterly. **2** To corrupt; undermine the principles or character of. [< L *subvertere* overturn] — **sub·vert'er** n.

sub·way (sub'wā) n. 1 A passage below the surface of the ground. 2 An underground railroad beneath city streets for local transportation; also, the tunnel through which it runs. 3 UNDERPASS.

suc·ceed (sak·sēd') v.i. 1 To accomplish what is attempted or intended. 2 To come next in order or sequence. 3 To come after another into office, ownership, etc. —v.t. 4 To be the successor or heir of. 5 To come after in time or sequence; follow. [< L *succedere* go under, follow after] —**suc·ceed'er** n.

suc·cess (sak·ses') n. 1 A favorable course or termination of anything attempted. 2 The gaining of position, fame, wealth, etc. 3 A person or thing that is successful. 4 The degree of succeeding: Did you have any *success* in getting an appointment? [< L *succedere* succeed] —Syn. 1 achievement, satisfaction. 2 prosperity, eminence, station.

suc·cess·ful (sak·ses'fal) adj. 1 Having achieved success. 2 Ending in success: a *successful* venture. —**suc·cess'ful·ly** adv. —**suc·cess'ful·ness** n.

suc·ces·sion (sak·sesh'an) n. 1 The act of following consecutively. 2 A group of things that succeed in order; a series or sequence. 3 The act or right of legally or officially coming into a predecessor's office, possessions, position, etc. 4 A group or hierarchy of persons having the right to succeed. —**in succession** One after another. —**suc·ces'·sion·al** adj. —**suc·ces'sion·al·ly** adv.

suc·ces·sive (sak·ses'iv) adj. Following in succession; consecutive. —**suc·ces'sive·ly** adv. —**suc·ces'sive·ness** n.

suc·ces·sor (sak·ses'ar) n. One who or that which follows in succession; esp. a person who succeeds to an office, position, or property.

suc·cinct (sak·singkt') adj. Reduced to a minimum number of words; concise; terse. [< L *sub-* underneath + *cingere* gird] —**suc·cinct'ly** adv. —**suc·cinct'ness** n.

suc·cor (suk'ar) n. 1 Help rendered in danger, difficulty, or distress. 2 One who or that which affords relief. —v.t. To go to the aid of; help. *Brit. sp.* **suc'cour.** [< L *sub-* up from under + *currere* to run] —**suc'cor·er** n. —Syn. n. 1 aid, rescue, relief, support.

suc·co·tash (suk'a·tash) n. A dish of corn kernels and beans, usu. lima beans, cooked together. [< Algon.]

suc·cu·bus (suk'ya·bas) n. pl. **·bi** (-bī, -bē) One of a class of demons in female form fabled to have intercourse with sleeping men. [< LL *succuba* a strumpet]

suc·cu·lent (suk'ya·lant) adj. 1 Juicy; full of juice. 2 *Bot.* Composed of fleshy, juicy tissue: a *succulent* leaf. 3 Absorbing; interesting. —n. A succulent plant. [< L *succus* juice] —**suc'cu·lence, suc'cu·len·cy** n. —**suc'cu·lent·ly** adv.

suc·cumb (sa·kum') v.i. 1 To give way; yield, as to force or persuasion. 2 To die. [< L *sub-* underneath + *cumbere* lie]

such (such) adj. 1 Being the same or similar in kind or quality; of a kind mentioned or indicated: a book *such* as this; screws, bolts, and other *such* items. 2 Indicated but not specified: some *such* place. 3 Extreme in degree, quality, etc.: *such* an uproar. —**such as** As an example or examples of the kind indicated: flowers *such as* dandelions. —pron. 1 Such a person or thing or such persons or things. 2 The same as implied or indicated: *Such* was the result. —**as such** As the particular thing or kind it is, regardless of others: People *as such* deserve compassion. —adv. 1 So: *such* destructive criticism. 2 Especially; very: She's in *such* good spirits today. [< OE *swelc, swylc*]

such and such Understood to be specific but not specified: to consult *such and such* an expert.

such·like (such'līk') adj. Of a like or similar kind. — pron. Persons or things of that kind.

suck (suk) v.t. 1 To draw into the mouth by means of a partial vacuum created by action of the lips and tongue. 2 To draw in or take up by suction. 3 To draw liquid or nourishment from with the mouth: to *suck* an orange or a lollipop. 4 To take and hold in the mouth as if to do this: to *suck* one's thumb. 5 To pull or draw into an association: with *in* or *into:* The lure of quick profits *sucked* him in. —

v.i. 6 To draw in liquid, air, etc., by suction. 7 To draw in milk from a breast or udder by sucking. 8 To make a sucking sound. —n. 1 The act or sound of sucking. 2 That which is sucked. [< OE *sūcan*]

suck·er (suk'ar) n. 1 One who or that which sucks. 2 Any of various freshwater fishes having thick, fleshy lips. 3 A mouth adapted for clinging and sucking, as that of a leech, tapeworm, etc. 4 *Slang* A person easily deceived. 5 *Bot.* An adventitious shoot. 6 A tube or pipe used for suction. 7 A lollipop. —v.t. 1 To strip (a plant) of suckers. —v.i. 2 To form or send out suckers or shoots.

Sucker *def.* 2

suck·le (suk'al) v. **·led, ·ling** v.t. 1 To nourish at the breast; nurse. 2 To bring up; nourish. —v.i. 3 To suck at the breast. —**suck'ler** n.

suck·ling (suk'ling) n. An unweaned mammal.

su·cre (sōō'krā) n. The monetary unit of Ecuador.

su·crose (sōō'krōs) n. The sweet, soluble, crystalline carbohydrate familiar as the common white sugar of commerce, and consisting of fructose and glucose in chemical combination. [< F *sucre* sugar]

suc·tion (suk'shan) n. 1 The act or process of sucking. 2 The production of a partial vacuum in a space connected with a fluid or gas under reduced pressure. —adj. Creating or operating by suction.

suc·to·ri·al (suk·tôr'ē·al, -tōr'-) adj. 1 Adapted for sucking or suction. 2 *Zool.* Living by sucking; having organs for sucking.

Su·dan (sōō·dan') n. A republic of NE Africa, 967,500 sq. mi., cap. Khartoum. —**Su·da·nese** (sōō'da·nēz') adj., n. • See map at AFRICA.

sud·den (sud'n) adj. 1 Happening quickly and without warning. 2 Causing surprise; unexpected: a *sudden* development. 3 Hurried; hasty; rash. —**all of a sudden** Without warning; suddenly. [< L *subitus,* p.p. of *subire* come or go stealthily] —**sud'den·ly** adv. —**sud'den·ness** n.

suds (sudz) n.pl. 1 Soapy water. 2 Froth; foam. 3 *Slang* Beer. [< MDu. *sudde, sudse* a marsh] —**suds'y** adj.

sue (sōō) v. **sued, su·ing** v.t. 1 To institute legal proceedings against, as for the redress of some wrong. 2 To prosecute (a legal action). —v.i. 3 To institute legal proceedings. 4 To seek to persuade someone by entreaty: with *for:* to *sue* for peace. [< AF *suer* pursue, sue] —**su'er** n.

suede (swād) n. Leather or a fabric having a napped surface. Also **suède.** [< F *gants de Suède* Swedish gloves]

su·et (sōō'it) n. The white, solid fatty tissue of beef, lamb, etc. [< L *sebum* fat] —**su'et·y** adj.

suf., suff. suffix.

suf·fer (suf'ar) v.i. 1 To feel pain or distress. 2 To sustain loss, injury, or detriment. 3 To undergo punishment, esp. death. —v.t. 4 To have inflicted on one; sustain, as an injury or loss: to *suffer* a fracture of the arm; to *suffer* a business reversal. 5 To undergo; pass through, as change. 6 To bear; endure: He never could *suffer* incompetence. 7 To allow; permit. [< L *sub-* up from under + *ferre* bear] —**suf'fer·a·ble** adj. —**suf'fer·a·bly** adv. —**suf'fer·er** n.

suf·fer·ance (suf'ar·ans, suf'rans) n. 1 Permission given or implied by failure to prohibit. 2 The capacity for suffering or tolerating pain or distress. —**on sufferance** Tolerated or suffered but not encouraged.

suf·fer·ing (suf'ar·ing, suf'ring) n. 1 The state of anguish or pain of one who suffers. 2 The pain suffered; loss; injury.

suf·fice (sa·fīs', -fīz') v. **·ficed, ·fic·ing** v.i. To be sufficient or adequate. [< L *sub-* under + *facere* make]

suf·fi·cien·cy (sa·fish'an·sē) n. pl. **·cies** 1 The state of being sufficient. 2 That which is sufficient; esp., adequate means or income.

suf·fi·cient (sa·fish'ant) adj. Being all that is needed; adequate; enough. [< L *sufficere* substitute, suffice] —**suf·fi'cient·ly** adv. —Syn. ample, satisfactory, fitting.

suf·fix (suf'iks) n. A letter or letters added to the end of a word or root, forming a new word or functioning as an inflectional element, as *-ful* in faithful and *-ed* in loved.

—*v.t.* To add as a suffix. [< L *suffixus*, p.p. of *suffigere* fasten underneath] —**suf′fix·al** *adj.*

suf·fo·cate (suf′ə·kāt′) *v.* ·**cat·ed**, ·**cat·ing** *v.t.* **1** To kill by obstructing respiration in any manner. **2** To cause distress in by depriving of an adequate supply or quality of air. **3** To stifle or smother, as a fire. —*v.i.* **4** To die from suffocation. **5** To be distressed by an inadequate supply or quality of air. [< L *sub-* under + *fauces* throat] —**suf′fo·cat′ing·ly** *adv.* —**suf′fo·ca′tion** *n.* —**suf′fo·ca′tive** *adj.*

suf·fra·gan (suf′rə·gən, -jən) *n.* **1** An auxiliary or assistant bishop. **2** Any bishop subordinate to an archbishop. —*adj.* Assisting; auxiliary. [< L *suffragium* vote] —**suf′fra·gan·ship′** *n.*

suf·frage (suf′rij) *n.* **1** A vote in support of someone or something. **2** The right or privilege of voting; franchise. **3** Any short intercessory prayer. [< L *suffragium* a vote]

suf·fra·gette (suf′rə·jet′) *n.* A woman who advocates female suffrage. —**suf′fra·get′tism** *n.*

suf·fra·gist (suf′rə·jist) *n.* An advocate of suffrage, esp. for women.

suf·fuse (sə·fyo͞oz′) *v.t.* ·**fused**, ·**fus·ing** To spread over, as with a fluid, light, or color. [< L *suffusus*, p.p. of *suffundere* pour underneath] —**suf·fu′sion** *n.* —**suf·fu′sive** *adj.*

sug·ar (sho͝og′ər) *n.* **1** A sweet, crystalline foodstuff obtained chiefly from sugar cane and sugar beets; sucrose. **2** Any of a large class of mostly sweet and water-soluble carbohydrates widely distributed in plants and animals, as lactose, glucose, fructose, etc. —*v.t.* **1** To sweeten, cover, or coat with sugar. **2** To make less distasteful, as by flattery. —*v.i.* **3** To make maple sugar by boiling down maple syrup: usu. with *off.* **4** To form or produce sugar; granulate. [< Ar. *sukkar*] —**sug′ar·less** *adj.*

sugar beet A variety of beet cultivated as a commercial source of sugar.

sugar cane A tall tropical grass with a solid jointed stalk rich in sugar.

sug·ar-coat (sho͝og′ər·kōt′) *v.t.* **1** To cover with sugar. **2** To cause to appear attractive or less distasteful. —**sug′ar-coat′ing** *n.*

sug·ar-cured (sho͝og′ər·kyo͝ord′) *adj.* Treated with a sweetened brine, as ham or pork.

sug·ar·plum (sho͝og′ər·plum′) *n.* A small ball or disk of candy.

sug·ar·y (sho͝og′ər·ē) *adj.* **1** Of, like, or composed of sugar; sweet. **2** Honeyed or complaisant; esp., excessively sweet or sentimental. —**sug′ar·i·ness** *n.*

sug·gest (səg·jest′, sə·jest′) *v.t.* **1** To bring or put forward for consideration, action, or approval; propose. **2** To arouse in the mind by association or connection: Gold *suggests* wealth. **3** To give a hint of; intimate: Her gesture *suggested* indifference. [< L *suggerere* carry underneath, suggest] —**sug·gest′er** *n.*

sug·gest·i·ble (səg·jes′tə·bəl, sə-) *adj.* **1** That can be suggested. **2** Responding readily to suggestions; easily led. —**sug·gest′i·bil′i·ty** *n.*

sug·ges·tion (səg·jes′chən, sə·jes′-) *n.* **1** The act of suggesting. **2** Something suggested. **3** A hint; trace; touch: a *suggestion* of irony. **4** An association of thoughts or ideas, esp. if based upon incidental or fortuitous similarities rather than a logical or rational relationship.

sug·ges·tive (səg·jes′tiv, sə-) *adj.* **1** Tending to suggest; stimulating thought or reflection. **2** Suggesting or hinting at something improper or indecent. —**sug·ges′tive·ly** *adv.* —**sug·ges′tive·ness** *n.*

su·i·cide (so͞o′ə·sīd) *n.* **1** The intentional taking of one's own life. **2** One who takes or tries to take one's own life. **3** Personal or professional ruin brought on by one's own actions. [< L *sui* of oneself + *caedere* kill] —**su·i·ci·dal** (so͞o′ə·sīd′l) *adj.* —**su′i·ci′dal·ly** *adv.*

su·i gen·er·is (so͞o′ī jen′ər·is, so͞o′ē, gen′-) Of his (her, its) particular kind; unique. [L]

suit (so͞ot) *n.* **1** A set of garments worn together; esp., a coat and trousers or skirt, made of the same fabric. **2** An outfit or garment for a particular purpose: a bathing *suit.* **3** A group of like things; a set. **4** Any of the four sets of thirteen cards each that make up a deck of cards. **5** A proceeding in a court of law for the recovery of a right or the redress of a wrong. **6** The courting of a woman. —**follow suit 1** To play a card identical in suit to the card

led. **2** To follow an example set by another. —*v.t.* **1** To meet the requirements of or be appropriate to; befit. **2** To please; satisfy. **3** To render appropriate; adapt. **4** To furnish with clothes. —*v.i.* **5** To agree; accord. **6** To be or prove satisfactory. **7** To put on a protective suit or uniform: with *up:* ballplayers *suiting up* before a game. [< OF *sieute* < L *sequi* follow]

suit·a·ble (so͞o′tə·bəl) *adj.* Appropriate; proper; fitting. —**suit′a·bil′i·ty, suit′a·ble·ness** *n.* —**suit′a·bly** *adv.*

suit·case (so͞ot′kās′) *n.* A case for carrying clothing, etc., esp. one that is flat and rectangular.

suite (swēt; *for def. 2, also* so͞ot) *n.* **1** A set of things intended to go or be used together, as a number of connected rooms forming an apartment or leased as a unit in a hotel. **2** A set of matched furniture. **3** A company of attendants; a retinue. **4** *Music* An instrumental composition consisting of a series of short pieces. [< OF *sieute.* See SUIT.]

suit·ing (so͞o′ting) *n.* Cloth used in making suits of clothes.

suit·or (so͞o′tər) *n.* **1** One who institutes a suit in court. **2** A man who courts a woman. **3** A petitioner.

su·ki·ya·ki (so͞o′kē·yä′kē, skē·yä′kē) *n.* A Japanese dish of thinly sliced meat and vegetables fried together and served with condiments. [Jap.]

Suk·koth (so͝ok′ōth, so͝ok′ōs) *n.* A Jewish holiday, originally a harvest festival, occurring in late September or in October. Also **Suk′kos, Suk′kot.** [< Hebrew *sūkōth* tabernacles, booths]

sulfa- *combining form Chem.* Sulfur; related to or containing sulfur. Also **sulf-, sulfo-.** [< SULFUR]

sul·fa drug (sul′fə) Any of various sulfonamide derivatives effective in the treatment of certain bacterial infections.

sul·fate (sul′fāt) *n.* A salt of sulfuric acid. —*v.* ·**fat·ed**, ·**fat·ing** *v.t.* **1** To convert into a sulfate. **2** To treat with a sulfate or sulfuric acid. **3** *Electr.* To form a coating of lead sulfate on (the plate of a storage battery). —*v.i.* **4** To become sulfated. Also **sul′phate.** [< L *sulfur* sulfur] —**sul·fa′tion** *n.*

sul·fide (sul′fīd) *n.* A compound of sulfur with an element or radical. Also **sul′phide.**

sul·fite (sul′fīt) *n.* A salt or ester of sulfurous acid. Also **sul′phite.** —**sul·fit′ic** (-fit′ik) *adj.*

sul·fon·a·mide (sul·fon′ə·mīd, -mid) *n.* Any of a group of organic sulfur compounds containing a univalent amide radical.

sul·fur (sul′fər) *n.* **1** An industrially important, abundant nonmetallic element (symbol S), occurring in three allotropic forms and found in both free and combined states. **2** Any of various small yellow butterflies. Also, and for def. 2 always, **sul′phur.** —**sul′fur·y** *adj.*

sul·fu·rate (sul′fyə·rāt) *v.t.* ·**rat·ed**, ·**rat·ing** SULFURIZE. —**sul′fu·ra′tion** *n.*

sulfur dioxide A colorless gas with a sharp odor, very soluble in water, used in manufacturing sulfuric acid, in bleaching, etc.

sul·fu·re·ous (sul·fyo͝or′ē·əs) *adj.* **1** Of or like sulfur. **2** Greenish yellow.

sul·fu·ret (sul′fyə·ret) *v.t.* ·**ret·ed** or ·**ret·ted**, ·**ret·ing** or ·**ret·ting** SULFURIZE. —*n.* SULFIDE.

sul·fu·ric (sul·fyo͝or′ik) *adj.* Pertaining to or derived from sulfur, esp. in its higher valence.

sulfuric acid A colorless, exceedingly corrosive, syrupy liquid with a strong affinity for water, used extensively in the chemical industry.

sul·fur·ize (sul′fyə·rīz) *v.t.* ·**ized**, ·**iz·ing** To impregnate, treat with, or subject to the action of sulfur. —**sul′fur·i·za′tion** *n.*

sul·fur·ous (sul′fər·əs, *for def. 1 esp.* sul·fyo͝or′əs) *adj.* **1** Pertaining to or derived from sulfur, esp. in its lower valence. **2** Resembling burning sulfur; fiery. **3** Biting; vitriolic: *sulfurous* criticism. **4** Blasphemous, as language. —**sul′fur·ous·ly** *adv.* —**sul′fur·ous·ness** *n.*

sulfurous acid (sul·fyo͝or′əs) An unstable acid formed by dissolving sulfur dioxide in water.

sulk (sulk) *v.i.* To be sullen in mood and tend to shun others. —*n.* A sulky mood or humor. [Back formation < SULKY]

sulk·y[1] (sul′kē) *adj.* **sulk·i·er, sulk·i·est** Sulking or tending to sulk. [? < OE *(ā)seolcan* be weak or slothful] —**sulk′i·ly** *adv.* —**sulk′i·ness** *n.*

sulk·y[2] (sul′kē) *n. pl.* **sulk·ies** A light, two-wheeled, one-horse vehicle for one person. [< SULKY[1]; so called because one rides alone]

Sulky

sul·len (sul′ən) *adj.* **1** Showing ill-humor, as from dwelling upon a grievance; morose; glum. **2** Depressing; somber: *sullen* clouds. **3** Slow; sluggish. **4** Melancholy; mournful. [< AF *solein* sullen, alone] —**sul′len·ly** *adv.* —**sul′len·ness** *n.* —**Syn. 1** gloomy, sad, sulky, moody.

sul·ly (sul′ē) *v.* **·lied, ·ly·ing** *v.t.* To mar the brightness or purity of; soil; defile. [< MF *souiller* to soil]

sulph- For all words so spelled, see SULF-.

sul·tan (sul′tən) *n.* A Muslim ruler. [< Ar. *sultān* a sovereign, dominion]

sul·tan·a (sul·tan′ə, -tä′nə) *n.* **1** A sultan's wife, daughter, sister, or mother. **2** A white, seedless variety of grape or raisin.

sul·tan·ate (sul′tən·āt, -it) *n.* **1** The authority of a sultan. **2** The domain of a sultan. Also **sul′tan·ship.**

sul·try (sul′trē) *adj.* **·tri·er, ·tri·est 1** Hot, moist, and still; close: said of weather. **2** Oppressively hot; burning. **3** Inflamed with passion. **4** Expressing or tending to excite sexual interest; sensual. [< obs. *sulter*, var. of SWELTER] —**sul′tri·ly** *adv.* —**sul′tri·ness** *n.*

sum (sum) *n.* **1** An amount of money. **2** The result obtained by the addition of numbers or quantities. **3** A problem in arithmetic. **4** The entire quantity, number, or substance; the whole: The *sum* of his effort came to naught. **5** Essence or core; summary: In *sum,* the issue is one of trust; the *sum* of an argument. **6** The highest or furthest point; summit. —*v.* **summed, sum·ming** *v.t.* **1** To present as a summary; recapitulate; summarize: usu. with *up.* **2** To add into one total: often with *up.* —*v.i.* **3** To give a summary; recapitulate: usu. with *up.* **4** To calculate a sum: often with *up.* [< L *summa (res)* highest (thing)]

su·mac (soō′mak, shoō′-) *n.* **1** Any of a genus of woody plants related to the cashew. **2** A species of sumac with hairy red fruit and compound leaves turning brilliant red in autumn: also **smooth sumac. 3** The dried and powdered leaves of certain species of sumac, used for tanning and dyeing. Also **su′mach.** [< Ar. *summāq*]

sum·ma cum lau·de (soom′ə koom lou′də, -dē, soō′mə, sum′ə kum lô′dē) *Latin* With the greatest praise: to be graduated *summa cum laude.*

sum·ma·rize (sum′ə·rīz) *v.t.* **·rized, ·riz·ing** To make a summary of. *Brit. sp.* **·rise.** —**sum′ma·ri·za′tion** *n.*

sum·ma·ry (sum′ə·rē) *n. pl.* **·ries** A brief account of the substance or essential points of something spoken or written; recapitulation. —*adj.* **1** Giving the substance or essential points; concise. **2** Performed without ceremony or delay; instant: *summary* execution. [< L *summa.* See SUM.] —**Syn.** *n.* condensation, abridgment, epitome, précis, compendium. —**sum·ma·ri·ly** (sə·mer′ə·lē, sum′ər·ə·lē) *adv.*

sum·ma·tion (sum·ā′shən) *n.* **1** The act or operation of obtaining a sum; addition. **2** A sum or total. **3** A summing up of the main points of an argument, as the final speech in behalf of one of the parties in a court trial.

sum·mer (sum′ər) *n.* **1** The warmest season of the year, including, in the northern hemisphere, June, July, and August. **2** A year of life. **3** A bright or prosperous period. —*v.i.* **1** To pass the summer. —*v.t.* **2** To keep or care for through the summer. —*adj.* **1** Of, pertaining to, or occurring in summer. **2** Used or intended for use in the summer: a *summer* house. [OE *sumor, sumer*] —**sum′mer·y** *adj.*

sum·mer·sault (sum′ər·sôlt) *n. v.i.* SOMERSAULT.

summer squash Any of various small squashes with a soft rind, usu. eaten before they ripen.

sum·mer·time (sum′ər·tīm′) *n.* Summer; the summer season.

sum·mit (sum′it) *n.* **1** The highest part; the top; vertex.

2 The highest degree; maximum. **3** The highest level or office, as of a government or business organization. **4** A meeting of executives of the highest level, as heads of government. —*adj.* Of or involving those at the highest level: a *summit* conference. [< L *summus* highest]

sum·mit·ry (sum′it·rē) *n.* **1** Meetings of officials of the highest rank, as heads of government. **2** The use or dependency upon such meetings to solve international problems.

sum·mon (sum′ən) *v.t.* **1** To order to come; send for. **2** To call together; cause to convene, as a legislative assembly. **3** To order (a person) to appear in court by a summons. **4** To call forth or into action; arouse: usu. with *up:* to *summon* up courage. **5** To call on for a specific act. [< L *summonere* suggest, hint] —**sum′mon·er** *n.*

sum·mons (sum′ənz) *n. pl.* **sum·mons·es 1** An order or call to attend or act at a particular place or time. **2** *Law* **a** A notice to a defendant summoning him to appear in court. **b** A notice to appear in court as a witness or as a juror. [< OF *somondre* summon]

su·mo (soō′mō) *n.* A highly stylized form of wrestling popular in Japan. [< Japanese *sumō*]

sump (sump) *n.* A pit or reservoir in which liquids are received by drainage, as a cesspool. [< MDu. *somp, sump* a marsh]

sump·ter (sump′tər) *n.* A pack animal. [< OF *sometier* a driver of a pack horse]

sump·tu·ar·y (sump′choo·er′ē) *adj.* Limiting or regulating expenditure. [< L *sumptus* expenditure < *sumere* take]

sump·tu·ous (sump′choo·əs) *adj.* **1** Involving or showing lavish expenditure. **2** Luxurious; magnificent. [< L *sumptus* expense] —**sump′tu·ous·ly** *adv.* —**sump′tu·ous·ness** *n.*

sun (sun) *n.* **1** The star that is the gravitational center and the main source of energy for the solar system, about 93,000,000 miles distant from the earth, with a diameter of 864,000 miles and a mass 332,000 times that of the earth. **2** Any star, esp. one with a planetary system. **3** The light and heat from the sun; sunshine. **4** Anything brilliant and magnificent; a source of splendor. **5** A day or a year. —*v.* **sunned, sun·ning** *v.t.* **1** To expose to the light or heat of the sun. —*v.i.* **2** To bask in the sun; sun oneself. [< OE *sunne*]

Sun. Sunday.

sun·bathe (sun′bāth′) *v.i.* **·bathed, ·bath·ing** To bask in the sun. —**sun′·bath′er** *n.*

sun·beam (sun′bēm′) *n.* A ray or beam of the sun.

Sun·belt (sun′belt′) *n.* The southeastern and southwestern states of the U.S., ranging from Virginia south to Florida and west to California.

sun·bon·net (sun′bon′it) *n.* A wide-brimmed bonnet sometimes having a flap covering the neck.

sun·burn (sun′bûrn′) *n.* Injury to the skin by ultraviolet radiation from the sun. —*v.t. & v.i.* **·burned** or **·burnt** (bûrnt), **·burn·ing** To affect or be affected with sunburn.

sun·dae (sun′dē) *n.* Ice cream topped with crushed fruit, flavoring, syrup, nuts, etc. [? < *Sunday*]

Sun·day (sun′dē, -dā) *n.* The first day of the week; the Christian Sabbath. [< OE *sunnan dæg* day of the sun]

Sunday school A school meeting on Sundays for religious instruction, esp. of the young.

sun·der (sun′dər) *v.t. & v.i.* To break apart; sever. [< OE *syndrian, sundrian*]

sun·di·al (sun′dī′əl, -dīl) *n.* A device that shows the time of day by the shadow of a style or gnomon cast on a dial in sunlight.

sun·down (sun′doun′) *n.* SUNSET (def. 2).

sun·dries (sun′drēz) *n. pl.* Various or miscellaneous articles. [< SUNDRY]

sun·dry (sun′drē) *adj.* Various; several; miscellaneous. [< OE *syndrig* separate]

sun·fish (sun′fish′) *n. pl.* **·fish** or

Sundial

·fish·es 1 Any of several North American freshwater perchlike fishes, usu. with narrow bodies. 2 Any of various large fishes of warm seas, having a deep compressed body.

sun·flow·er (sun'flou'ər) n. Any of a genus of tall plants with large leaves and large composite flower heads encircled with a ring of bright yellow ray flowers.

sung (sung) p.p. of SING.

sun·glasses (sun'glas'iz, -gläs'-) n. pl. Eyeglasses having colored lenses that protect the eyes from the glare of the sun.

sunk (sungk) p.p. & a p.t. of SINK.

sunk·en (sung'kən) A p.p. of SINK. —adj. 1 Lying at the bottom of a body of water. 2 Located beneath a surface. 3 Lower than the surrounding or usual level: *sunken* gardens. 4 Deeply depressed or fallen in: *sunken* cheeks.

Sunflower

sun·lamp (sun'lamp') n. An electric lamp radiating ultraviolet rays, used esp. for the therapeutic treatments.

sun·less (sun'lis) adj. Dark; cheerless. —**sun'less·ness** n.

sun·light (sun'līt') n. The light of the sun.

sun·lit (sun'lit') adj. Lighted by the sun.

sun·ny (sun'ē) adj. ·ni·er, ·ni·est 1 Characterized by bright sunlight. 2 Filled with sunlight: a *sunny* room. 3 Cheerful; genial: a *sunny* smile. —**sun'ni·ly** adv. —**sun'ni·ness** n.

sun parlor A room enclosed in glass and having a sunny exposure. Also **sun porch, sun room.**

sun·rise (sun'rīz') n. 1 The daily first appearance of the sun above the horizon. 2 The time at which the sun rises.

sun·set (sun'set') n. 1 The apparent daily descent of the sun below the horizon. 2 The time at which the sun sets. 3 A final period or decline, as of life.

sun·shade (sun'shād') n. Something used as protection from the sun, as a parasol or an awning.

sun·shine (sun'shīn') n. 1 The direct light of the sun. 2 The light and warmth of sunlight. 3 Brightness or warmth, as of feeling. —**sun'shin'y** adj.

sun·spot (sun'spot') n. One of many dark irregular spots appearing sometimes on the surface of the sun.

sun·stroke (sun'strōk') n. Prostration and fever induced by heat and exposure to the sun. —**sun'struck'** (-struk') adj.

sun·tan (sun'tan') n. A darkened coloration of the skin induced by exposure to ultraviolet light. —**sun'tanned'** '(-tand') adj.

sun·up (sun'up') n. SUNRISE.

sun·ward (sun'wərd) adj. Facing toward the sun. —adv. Toward the sun: also **sun'wards.**

sup[1] (sup) v.t. & v.i. **supped, sup·ping** To take (fluid food) a little at a time; sip. —n. A mouthful or sip of liquid or semiliquid food. [<OE sūpan drink]

sup[2] (sup) v. **supped, sup·ping** v.i. To eat supper. [<OF soper<soupe soup]

sup. above (L supra); superior, superlative; supplement; supplementary; supply.

su·per (sōō'pər) adj. 1 Surpassing others of its class, as in power or size: a *super* bomb; a *super* city. 2 *Informal* Outstanding; superb: a *super* performance. 3 *Slang* Great; wonderful: He's *super!* 4 More than normal or warranted. —n. 1 A superintendent (def. 2). 2 SUPERNUMERARY (esp. def. 2). 3 An article of superior size or quality.

super- prefix 1 Above in position; over: *superstructure.* 2 More than; above or beyond: *supersonic.* 3 More than normal or warranted; inordinate or inordinately: *superintelligent; superpatriot.* 4 Surpassing others in its class, as in power, size, or skill; superior: *superhighway.* 5 Extra: *supertax.* [<L super above, beyond] • See TAXONOMY.

su·per·a·ble (sōō'pər·ə·bəl) adj. That can be surmounted, overcome, or conquered. [<L superare overcome<super over] —**su'per·a·bil'i·ty** n. —**su'per·a·bly** adv.

su·per·a·bound (sōō'pər·ə·bound') v.i. To abound to excess. [<L super- exceedingly + abundare overflow]

su·per·a·bun·dant (sōō'pər·ə·bun'dənt) adj. More than sufficient; excessive. [<LL superabundare to superabound] —**su'per·a·bun'dance** n. —**su'per·a·bun'dant·ly** adv.

su·per·an·nu·at·ed (sōō'pər·an'yōō·wāt'id) adj. 1 Re-

lieved of active work on account of age; retired. 2 Set aside or discarded as obsolete or too old. [<L super beyond + annus a year]

su·perb (sōō-pûrb', sōō-) adj. 1 Extraordinarily good; excellent: a *superb* wine. 2 Having grand, impressive beauty; majestic: a *superb* cathedral. 3 Luxurious; elegant. [<L superbus proud] —**su·perb'ly** adv. —**su·perb'ness** n.

su·per·block (sōō'pər·blok') n. A large block of commercial buildings or residences from which motor traffic is barred, often landscaped as a unit and joined by pedestrian walks.

su·per·car·go (sōō'pər·kär'gō) n. pl. ·goes or ·gos An officer on board ship in charge of the cargo and its sale and purchase.

su·per·charge (sōō'pər·chärj') v.t. ·charged, ·charg·ing 1 To adapt (an engine) to develop more power, as by fitting with a supercharger. 2 To charge excessively, as with emotion.

su·per·charg·er (sōō'pər·chär'jər) n. A compressor for supplying extra air or fuel mixture to an internal-combustion engine.

su·per·cil·i·ous (sōō'pər·sil'ē·əs) adj. Haughtily contemptuous; arrogant. [<L supercilium eyebrow, pride] —**su'per·cil'i·ous·ly** adv. —**su'per·cil'i·ous·ness** n.

su·per·col·lid·er (sōō'pər·kə·līd·er) n. A very large particle accelerator.

su·per·con·duc·ting (sōō'pər·kən·duk'ting) adj. Having the property, when cooled to temperatures near absolute zero, of conducting electricity continuously without resistance: said of certain metals and alloys. —**su'per·con·duc'tive** adj. —**su'per·con·duc·tiv'i·ty** (-kon'duk·tiv'ə·tē), **su'per·con·duc'tor** n.

su·per·e·go (sōō'pər·ē'gō, -eg'ō) n. pl. ·gos Psychoanal. A largely unconscious element of the personality, acting principally as conscience and critic.

su·per·er·o·ga·tion (sōō'pər·er'ə·gā'shən) n. The performance of an act in excess of the demands or requirements of duty. [<L super- above + erogare pay out]

su·per·e·rog·a·to·ry (sōō'pər·ə·rog'ə·tôr'ē, -tō'rē) adj. 1 Of the nature of supererogation. 2 SUPERFLUOUS.

su·per·fi·cial (sōō'pər·fish'əl) adj. 1 Of, lying near, or on the surface: a *superficial* wound. 2 Of or pertaining to only the ordinary and the obvious; not profound; shallow. 3 Hasty; cursory: a *superficial* examination. 4 Apparent only; not real or genuine. [<L super- above + facies a face] —**su'per·fi·ci·al'i·ty** (-fish'ē·al'ə·tē), **su'per·fi'cial·ness** n. —**su'per·fi'cial·ly** adv.

su·per·fine (sōō'pər·fīn') adj. 1 Of the best quality; very fine and delicate. 2 Unduly elaborate. —**su'per·fine'ness** n.

su·per·flu·i·ty (sōō'pər·flōō'ə·tē) n. pl. ·ties 1 The state of being superfluous. 2 That which is superfluous.

su·per·flu·ous (sōō·pûr'flōō·əs) adj. Exceeding what is needed; surplus. [<L super- above + fluere to flow] —**su·per'flu·ous·ly** adv. —**su·per'flu·ous·ness** n.

su·per·heat (sōō'pər·hēt') v.t. 1 OVERHEAT. 2 To raise the temperature of (a vapor not in contact with its liquid) above the saturation point for a given pressure. 3 To heat (a liquid) above the boiling point without conversion into vapor. —**su'per·heat'er** n.

su·per·het·er·o·dyne (sōō'pər·het'ər·ə·dīn') adj. Electronics Pertaining to or designating radio reception in which the incoming signals are converted to an intermediate frequency, and are then amplified and demodulated. —n. A radio receiver of this type. [<SUPER(SONIC) + HETERODYNE]

su·per·high·way (sōō'pər·hī'wā') n. A highway for high-speed traffic, usu. with four or more lanes.

su·per·hu·man (sōō'pər·ʰyōō'mən) adj. 1 Above and beyond what is human; miraculous; divine. 2 Beyond normal human ability or power. —**su'per·hu'man·ly** adv.

su·per·im·pose (sōō'pər·im·pōz') v.t. ·posed, ·pos·ing 1 To lay or impose something else. 2 To add as an incidental or superfluous feature. —**su'per·im'po·si'tion** (-im'pə·zish'ən) n.

su·per·in·duce (sōō'pər·in·dʸōōs') v.t. ·duced, ·duc·ing To introduce additionally. [<L super- over + inducere lead in] —**su'per·in·duc'tion** (-duk'shən) n.

su·per·in·tend (sōō'pər·in·tend') v.t. To have the charge and direction of; supervise. [<LL super- over + intendere

direct, aim at] —**su′per·in·ten′dence, su′per·in·ten′den·cy** n.

su·per·in·ten·dent (sŏŏ′pər·in·ten′dənt) n. **1** One who has charge of an institution or undertaking; director. **2** One responsible for the maintenance and repair of a building. —adj. Superintending.

su·pe·ri·or (sə·pir′ē·ər, sŏŏ-) adj. **1** Higher in rank, quality, or degree; better or excellent: superior vision; superior talent. **2** Greater in quantity: a superior supply. **3** Higher in relation to other things; upper. **4** Printing Set above the line, as 1 in x¹. **5** Serenely unaffected or indifferent: with to: superior to pettiness. **6** Affecting or suggesting an attitude of contemptuous indifference or disdain: superior airs. —n. **1** One who is superior, as in rank or excellence. **2** The head of an abbey, convent, or monastery. [< L superus higher < super above] —**su·pe·ri·or·i·ty** (sə·pir′ē·ôr′ə·tē, - or′-, sŏŏ-) n. —**su·pe′ri·or·ly** adv.

su·per·la·tive (sə·pûr′lə·tiv, sŏŏ-) adj. **1** Being of the highest degree; most excellent or eminent. **2** Gram. Expressing the highest or extreme degree of the quality expressed by the positive degree of an adjective or adverb: "Wisest" is the superlative form of "wise." **3** Exaggerated. —n. **1** That which is superlative. **2** The highest degree; apex. **3** Gram. **a** The superlative degree. **b** A form in the superlative degree. [< L superlatus excessive < super- above + latus carried] —**su·per′la·tive·ly** adv. —**su·per′la·tive·ness** n.

su·per·man (sŏŏ′pər·man′) n. pl. **·men** (-men′) **1** A man of superhuman powers. **2** An intellectually and morally superior man.

su·per·mar·ket (sŏŏ′pər·mär′kit) n. A large, chiefly self-service store selling food and household supplies.

su·per·nal (sŏŏ·pûr′nəl) adj. **1** Heavenly; celestial. **2** Coming from above or from the sky. [< L supernus < super over] —**su·per′nal·ly** adv.

su·per·nat·u·ral (sŏŏ′pər·nach′ər·əl, -rəl) adj. **1** Existing or occurring through some agency beyond the known forces of nature. **2** Of or concerning phenomena of this kind: supernatural tales. **3** Believed to be miraculous or divine. **4** Suggestive of ghosts, demons, or other agents unconstrained by natural law. —n. That which is supernatural. [< L super- above + natura nature] —**su′per·nat′u·ral·ism, su′per·nat′u·ral·ness** n. —**su′per·nat′u·ral·ist** adj., n. —**su′per·nat′u·ral·is′tic** adj. —**su′per·nat′u·ral·ly** adv.

su·per·nu·mer·a·ry (sŏŏ′pər·nyŏŏ′mə·rer′ē) adj. **1** Being beyond a fixed or usual number. **2** Beyond a necessary number; superfluous. —n. pl. **·ar·ies 1** A supernumerary person or thing. **2** A stage performer without any speaking part. [< L super over + numerus a number]

su·per·pa·tri·ot (sŏŏ′pər·pā′trē·ət, -ot) n. A person who is or claims to be a great patriot, often one whose patriotic fervor is marked by a readiness to regard dissent as unpatriotic or subversive. —**su′per·pa′tri·ot′ic** adj. —**su′per·pa′tri·ot·ism** n.

su·per·pose (sŏŏ′pər·pōz′) v.t. **·posed, ·pos·ing** To lay over or upon something else. —**su′per·pos′a·ble** adj. —**su′per·po·si′tion** (-pə·zish′ən) n.

su·per·pow·er (sŏŏ′pər·pou′ər) n. One of a few great, dominant nations characterized by superior economic or military strength and by large population.

su·per·sat·u·rate (sŏŏ′pər·sach′ŏŏ·rāt) v.t. **·rat·ed, ·rat·ing** To cause (a solution) to hold more of a solute than it can normally hold at the given temperature. —**su′per·sat′u·ra′tion** n.

su·per·scribe (sŏŏ′pər·skrīb′) v.t. **·scribed, ·scrib·ing 1** To write or engrave on the outside or on the upper part of. **2** To address, as a letter. [< L super- over + scribere write] —**su′per·scrip′tion** (-skrip′shən) n.

su·per·script (sŏŏ′pər·skript′) adj. Written above or overhead. —n. A letter, index, or other mark following and above a letter or figure, as in a³ or c′. [< LL superscriptus, p.p. of superscribere superscribe]

su·per·sede (sŏŏ′pər·sēd′) v.t. **·sed·ed, ·sed·ing 1** To take the place of, as by reason of superiority or right; replace. **2** To put something in the place of; set aside. [< L super- above + sedere sit] —**su′per·sed′er, su′per·se′dure** (-sē′jər) n.

su·per·son·ic (sŏŏ′pər·son′ik) adj. **1** Of or capable of moving at a speed greater than that of sound. **2** Moving at such a speed. **3** ULTRASONIC. —**su′per·son′i·cal·ly** adv.

su·per·star (sŏŏ′pər·stär′) n. A public performer, as an actor, singer, or professional athlete, regarded as one of the best or most popular. —**su′per·star′dom** n.

su·per·sti·tion (sŏŏ′pər·stish′ən) n. **1** An ignorant or irrational belief, often provoked by fear, and based upon assumptions of cause and effect contrary to known scientific facts and principles. **2** Any practice inspired by such belief. **3** Any unreasonable belief or impression. [< L superstitio excessive fear of the gods, amazement]

su·per·sti·tious (sŏŏ′pər·stish′əs) adj. **1** Disposed to believe in or be influenced by superstitions. **2** Of, based upon, or manifesting superstition. —**su′per·sti′tious·ly** adv. —**su′·per·sti′tious·ness** n.

su·per·struc·ture (sŏŏ′pər·struk′chər) n. **1** Any structure above the basement or considered in relation to its foundation. **2** Any structure built on top of another. **3** The parts of a ship's structure above the main deck.

su·per·tank·er (sŏŏ′pər·tangk′ər) n. A very large tanker capable of carrying a vast cargo, as of oil.

su·per·tax (sŏŏ′pər·taks′) n. An extra tax in addition to the normal tax; a surtax.

su·per·vene (sŏŏ′pər·vēn′) v.i. **·vened, ·ven·ing** To follow closely upon something as an extraneous or additional circumstance. [< L super- over and above + venire come] —**su′per·ven′ient** (-vēn′yənt) adj. —**su′per·ven′tion** (-ven′·shən) n.

su·per·vise (sŏŏ′pər·vīz′) v.t. **·vised, ·vis·ing** To have charge of; direct. [< L super- over + videre see] —**Syn.** manage, run, oversee, superintend.

su·per·vi·sion (sŏŏ′pər·vizh′ən) n. The act or process of supervising; direction, control, or guidance.

su·per·vi·sor (sŏŏ′pər·vī′zər) n. **1** One who supervises; a superintendent or manager. **2** In education, an official supervising teachers and responsible for curricula, etc., in a particular subject. —**su′per·vi′sor·ship** n. —**su·per·vi·so·ry** (sŏŏ′pər·vī′zər·ē) adj.

su·pine (sŏŏ·pīn′, sə-) adj. **1** Lying on the back, or with the face turned upward. **2** Having no interest or care; listless. [< L supinus] —**su·pine′ly** adv. —**su·pine′ness** n.

supp., suppl. supplement; supplementary.

sup·per (sup′ər) n. **1** The last meal of the day; the evening meal. **2** A social event including the serving of supper: a church supper. [< OF soper sup] —**sup′per·less** adj.

sup·plant (sə·plant′, -plänt′) v.t. **1** To take the place of, as of something inferior or out of date; displace. **2** To take the place of (someone) by scheming, treachery, etc. **3** To replace (one thing) with another: to supplant naive expectations with realistic goals. [< L supplantare trip up] —**sup·plan·ta·tion** (sup′lan·tā′shən), **sup·plant′er** n.

sup·ple (sup′əl) adj. **sup·pler** (sup′lər, -əl·ər), **sup·plest 1** Easily bent; flexible; pliant: supple leather. **2** Agile or graceful in movement; limber. **3** Yielding readily to the wishes of others; compliant. **4** Servile; obsequious. **5** Quick to respond or adjust, as the mind; adaptable. —v.t. & v.i. **·pled, ·pling** To make or become supple. [< L supplex, lit., bending under] —**sup′ple·ly** (sup′əl·ē, sup′lē) or **sup′ply** (sup′lē) adv. —**sup′ple·ness** n. —**Syn.** 2 lithe, deft, nimble.

sup·ple·ment (sup′lə·mənt) n. **1** Something added that supplies a deficiency. **2** An addition to a publication, as a section providing additional information added to a book. —v.t. To make additions to; provide for what is lacking in. [< L supplere. See SUPPLY.] —**sup·ple·ment·al** (sup′lə·men′·təl) adj. • Both supplement and complement refer to something added to make up for a lack or deficiency. Complement (not to be confused with compliment, an expression of praise) emphasizes the correction or adjustment of something unfinished or imperfect, and often implies a balancing of elements: The design of the housing project called for low buildings to complement the high-rises. In the case of supplement, the fact of being added is more emphatic, and the expected result is one of improvement rather than completion: Student teachers supplemented the regular teaching staff, freeing them to give more individual help to slow learners.

sup·ple·men·ta·ry (sup'lə·men'tər·ē, -trē) *adj.* Added as a supplement; additional.

sup·pli·ant (sup'lē·ənt) *adj.* Entreating earnestly and humbly. —*n.* One who supplicates. [< L *supplicare* supplicate] —**sup'pli·ant·ly** *adv.* —**sup'pli·ant·ness** *n.*

sup·pli·cant (sup'lə·kənt) *n.* One who supplicates. —*adj.* Asking or entreating humbly. [< L *supplicare* supplicate]

sup·pli·cate (sup'lə·kāt) *v.* **·cat·ed, ·cat·ing** *v.t.* 1 To ask for humbly or by earnest prayer. 2 To beg something of; entreat. —*v.i.* 3 To make an earnest request. [< L *sub-* under + *plicare* bend, fold] —**sup'pli·ca'tion** *n.* —**sup'pli·ca·to·ry** (-kə·tôr'ē, -tō'rē) *adj.*

sup·ply (sə·plī') *v.* **·plied, ·ply·ing** *v.t.* 1 To make available; provide or furnish: to *supply* electricity to a remote area. 2 To furnish with what is needed: to *supply* an army with weapons. 3 To provide for adequately; satisfy. 4 To make up for; compensate for. 5 To fill (the place of another). —*v.i.* 6 To take the place of another temporarily. —*n. pl.* **·plies** 1 That which is or can be supplied. 2 A store or quantity on hand. 3 *pl.* Accumulated stores, as for an army. 4 The amount of a commodity offered at a given price or available for meeting a demand. 5 The act of supplying. [< L *supplere* < *sub-* up from under + *plere* fill] —**sup·pli'er** *n.*

sup·port (sə·pôrt', -pōrt') *v.t.* 1 To bear the weight of, esp. from underneath; hold in position; keep from falling, sinking, etc. 2 To bear or sustain (weight, etc.). 3 To provide money or necessities for; provide with the means of subsistence. 4 To give approval or assistance to; uphold. 5 To serve to uphold or corroborate; substantiate: His testimony *supports* our position. 6 To endure patiently; tolerate. 7 To provide with the means to endure; keep from collapsing or yielding: Faith *supported* her. 8 To carry on; keep up: to *support* a war. 9 In the theater, etc., to act in a subordinate role to. —*n.* 1 The act of supporting. 2 One who supports. 3 That which supports, as a brace or girdle for the body. [< L *sub-* up from under + *portare* carry] —**sup·port'a·ble** *adj.* —**sup·port'a·bly** *adv.* —**Syn.** 4 advocate, endorse, help, aid, assist. 5 verify, bear out. 6 bear, suffer. 7 sustain.

sup·port·er (sə·pôr'tər, -pōr'-) *n.* 1 One who or that which supports. 2 An elastic or other support for some part of the body.

sup·por·tive (sə·pôr'tiv, -pōr'-) *adj.* 1 Tending or intended to support. 2 Contributing importantly to the stability of one's physical or emotional health: *supportive* treatment. —**sup·por'tive·ly** *adv.*

sup·pose (sə·pōz') *v.* **·posed, ·pos·ing** *v.t.* 1 To believe to be true or probable; presume. 2 To assume as true for the sake of argument or illustration. 3 To expect: I am *supposed* to follow. 4 To presuppose; imply: Mercy *supposes* a sense of compassion. —*v.i.* 5 To make a supposition. [< L *supponere* substitute, put under] —**sup·pos'a·ble** *adj.* —**sup·pos'a·bly** *adv.* —**sup·pos'er** *n.*

sup·posed (sə·pōzd') *adj.* 1 Accepted as genuine; believed. 2 Imagined only, instead of actually experienced. —**sup·pos·ed·ly** (sə·pō'zid·lē) *adv.*

sup·po·si·tion (sup'ə·zish'ən) *n.* 1 Something supposed; a conjecture or hypothesis. 2 The act of supposing. —**sup'po·si'tion·al** *adj.* —**sup'po·si'tion·al·ly** *adv.*

sup·pos·i·to·ry (sə·poz'ə·tôr'ē, -tō'rē) *n. pl.* **·ries** A small mass of a usu. medicated substance that melts at body temperature, for introduction into a body cavity, as the rectum or vagina. [< LL *suppositorius* placed underneath or up < L *supponere* put under]

sup·press (sə·pres') *v.t.* 1 To put an end or stop to; crush, as a rebellion. 2 To stop or prohibit the activities of. 3 To withhold from knowledge or publication, as a book, news, etc. 4 To hold back or repress. 5 To stop or check (a hemorrhage, etc.). [< L *suppressus,* p.p. of *supprimere* press down] —**sup·press'er, sup·pres'sor** *n.* —**sup·press'i·ble, sup·pres'sive** *adj.*

sup·pres·sion (sə·presh'ən) *n.* 1 The act of suppressing, or the state of being suppressed. 2 The deliberate exclusion from consciousness of unacceptable ideas, memories, etc.

sup·pu·rate (sup'yə·rāt) *v.i.* **·rat·ed, ·rat·ing** To discharge or generate pus. [< L *sub-* under + *pus, puris* pus] —**sup'pu·ra'tion** *n.* —**sup'pu·ra·tive** (-rə·tiv, -rā'-) *adj.*

su·pra (sōō'prə) *adv.* Above. [L]

supra- *prefix* Above; beyond: *supranational.* [< L *supra* above, beyond]

su·pra·na·tion·al (sōō'prə·nash'ə·nəl) *adj.* Of or concerning several or a number of nations; involving more than one nation. —**su'pra·na'tion·al·ism** *n.* —**su'pra·na'tion·al·ist** *adj., n.*

su·pra·re·nal (sōō'prə·rē'nəl) *adj.* Situated above the kidneys; adrenal. —*n.* An adrenal gland. [< L *supra-* above + *renalis* renal]

su·prem·a·cy (sə·prem'ə·sē, sōō-) *n. pl.* **·cies** 1 The state of being supreme. 2 Supreme power or authority.

su·preme (sə·prēm', sōō-) *adj.* 1 Highest in power or authority; dominant. 2 Highest or greatest, as in degree; utmost: *supreme* devotion. 3 Ultimate; last and greatest. [< L *supremus,* superl. of *superus* < *super* above] —**su·preme'ly** *adv.* —**su·preme'ness** *n.*

Supreme Being God.

Supreme Court 1 The highest Federal court. 2 The highest court in many states.

Supreme Soviet The legislature of the Soviet Union.

supt. superintendent.

sur- *prefix* Over; beyond: *surtax.* [< OF *sur-* < L *super-*]

su·rah (sŏŏr'ə) *n.* A soft, usu. twilled, silk or silk and rayon fabric. [< *Surat,* India]

sur·base (sûr'bās') *n.* A border or molding above the top of a base, as of a pedestal.

sur·cease (sûr·sēs', sûr'sēs) *n.* Cessation; end. —*v.t. & v.i.* **·ceased, ·ceas·ing** To end. [< AF *surseoir* to refrain < L *supersedere* to sit above]

sur·charge (sûr'chärj') *n.* 1 An additional amount charged or imposed. 2 An excessive burden, load, or charge. 3 OVERCHARGE. 4 A new valuation or something additional printed on a postage or revenue stamp. —*v.t.* (sûr·chärj') **·charged, ·charg·ing** 1 OVERCHARGE. 2 To fill or load to excess. 3 To imprint a surcharge on (postage stamps). —**sur·charg'er** *n.*

sur·cin·gle (sûr'sing·gəl) *n.* A strap encircling the body of a horse, for holding a saddle, blanket, etc. [< SUR- + L *cingulum* a belt]

sur·coat (sûr'kōt') *n.* An outer coat or garment, esp., in the Middle Ages, one worn over armor.

surd (sûrd) *n.* 1 *Math.* An irrational number, esp. an indicated root, as $\sqrt{2}$. 2 *Phonet.* A voiceless speech sound. —*adj.* 1 *Math.* IRRATIONAL. 2 *Phonet.* VOICELESS. [< L *surdus* deaf, silent]

sure (shŏŏr) *adj.* **sur·er, sur·est** 1 Not subject to uncertainty or doubt; beyond all question; indisputable. 2 Characterized by freedom from doubt or uncertainty; firm: *sure* convictions; a *sure* grasp of his subject. 3 Certain or confident; positive: I was *sure* I had seen her before. 4 Not liable to fail or disappoint; reliable; sound: a *sure* memory. 5 Bound to happen or be: a *sure* winner. 6 *Obs.* Safe; secure. —*adv. Informal* Surely; certainly. —**for sure** Certainly; beyond all question. —**to be sure** Indeed; certainly; quite so. [< L *securus*] —**sure'ness** *n.* —**Syn.** 1 unquestionable, unimpeachable, indubitable. 4 trustworthy, dependable, true.

Surcoat

sure-foot·ed (shŏŏr'fŏŏt'id) *adj.* Not liable to fall or stumble. —**sure'-foot'ed·ly** *adv.* —**sure'-foot'ed·ness** *n.*

sure·ly (shŏŏr'lē) *adv.* 1 In a sure manner. 2 Without doubt; certainly. 3 Really; certainly: used as an intensive to express strong probability: He *surely* knew that.

sure·ty (shŏŏr'ə·tē, shŏŏr'tē) *n. pl.* **·ties** 1 The state of being sure; certainty. 2 Security against loss or damage. 3 One who assumes the debts, responsibilities, etc. of another; a guarantor. [< L *securus* secure] —**sure'ty·ship** *n.*

surf (sûrf) *n.* 1 The swell of the sea that breaks upon a shore. 2 The foam caused by the billows. —*v.i.* To ride the surf on a surfboard; engage in surfing. [?] —**surf'er** *n.*

sur·face (sûr'fis) *n.* 1 The outer part or face of an object. 2 That which has area but not thickness. 3 A superficial aspect; external appearance. —v. ·faced, ·fac·ing v.t. 1 To put a surface on; esp., to make smooth, even, or plain. 2 To cause to rise to the surface, as a submarine. —v.i. 3 To rise to the surface. 4 To come to public notice, esp. something formerly kept secret. [< SUR- + FACE] —sur′fac·er n.

sur·face-ac·tive (sûr′fis·ak′tiv) adj. Effective in changing the properties of a substance, esp. surface tension, at the area of contact with another substance: surface-active detergents.

surface tension That property of a liquid by which the surface molecules exert a strong cohesive force, thus forming an elastic skin that tends to contract.

sur·fac·tant (sûr·fak′tənt) n. A surface-active substance, as a detergent. [< SURF(ACE)-ACT(IVE) + -ANT]

surf·board (sûrf′bôrd′, -bōrd′) n. A long, narrow board used in surfing. —v.i. SURF. —surf′board′er n.

surf·boat (sûrf′bōt′) n. A boat of extra strength and buoyancy, for launching and landing through surf.

sur·feit (sûr′fit) v.t. 1 To feed or supply to fullness or to excess. —v.i. 2 To overindulge in food or drink. —n. 1 Excess in eating or drinking. 2 The result of such excess; satiety. 3 Any excessive amount: a surfeit of praise. [< OF surfaire overdo]

surf·ing (sûrf′ing) n. A water sport in which a person standing on a surfboard is borne by the surf toward the shore. Also surf·rid·ing (sûrf′rī′ding).

surg. surgeon; surgery; surgical.

surge (sûrj) v. surged, surg·ing v.i. 1 To rise and roll with a powerful, swelling motion, as waves. 2 To be tossed about by waves. 3 To move or go in a powerful, wavelike motion: The mob surged through the square. 4 To increase or vary suddenly, as an electric current. —n. 1 A large swelling wave; billow. 2 A great swelling or rolling movement, as of waves. 3 Electr. A sudden, transient rise in current flow. 4 Any sudden, sharp increase. [< L surgere]

sur·geon (sûr′jən) n. One who practices surgery. [< OF cirurgie surgery] —sur′geon·cy (-sē) n.

sur·ger·y (sûr′jər·ē) n. pl. ·ger·ies 1 The treatment of disease, injury, etc., by manual and operative means. 2 The branch of medicine concerned with surgical treatment. 3 A place where surgery is performed; an operating room. 4 Brit. A physician's office. [< Gk. cheirourgia a handicraft < cheir the hand + ergein to work] —sur·gi·cal (sûr′ji·kəl) —sur′gi·cal·ly adv.

sur·ly (sûr′lē) adj. ·li·er, ·li·est Rude and ill-humored, esp. in response; gruff or insolent. [Earlier sirly like a lord < sir a lord] —sur′li·ly adv. —sur′li·ness n.

sur·mise (sər·mīz′) v. ·mised, ·mis·ing v.t. & v.i. To infer (something) on slight evidence; guess. —n. (sər·mīz′, sûr′mīz) A conjecture made on slight evidence; supposition. [< OF surmettre accuse < sur- upon + mettre put] —Syn. v. suppose, assume, conjecture.

sur·mount (sər·mount′) v.t. 1 To overcome; prevail over (a difficulty, etc.). 2 To mount to the top or cross to the other side of, as an obstacle. 3 To be or lie over or above. 4 To place something above or on top of; cap. [< L super- over + mons, montis a hill, mountain]

sur·name (sûr′nām′) n. 1 A last name; family name. 2 A name added to one's real name, as Ethelred the Unready. —v.t. (sûr′nām′, sûr·nām′) ·named, ·nam·ing To give a surname to; call by a surname. [< OF sur- above, beyond + nom a name]

sur·pass (sər·pas′, -päs′) v.t. 1 To go beyond or past in degree or amount; exceed or excel. 2 To be beyond the reach or powers of; transcend. —sur·pass·a·ble adj. —sur·pass′er n. —Syn. 1 eclipse, outdo, outstrip.

sur·pass·ing (sər·pas′ing, -päs′-) adj. Exceptional; excellent. —sur·pass′ing·ly adv.

sur·plice (sûr′plis) n. A loose white vestment with full sleeves, worn over the cassock by the clergy and choristers of some churches. [< Med. L superpellicium (vestimentum) an overgarment]

Surplice

sur·plus (sûr′plus) n. 1 That which remains over and above what is used or required. 2 Assets in excess of liabilities. —adj. Being in excess of what is used or needed. [< L super- over and above + plus more] —sur′plus·age (-ij) n.

sur·prise (sər·prīz′, sə-) v.t. ·prised, ·pris·ing 1 To cause to feel wonder or astonishment, esp. because unusual or unexpected. 2 To come upon suddenly or unexpectedly; take unawares. 3 To attack suddenly and without warning. 4 To lead unawares, as into doing something not intended: with into. —n. 1 The state of being surprised; astonishment. 2 Something that causes surprise, as a sudden and unexpected event. 3 A sudden attack or capture. [< L super- over + prehendere take] —sur·pris′er n.

sur·pris·ing (sər·prī′zing, sə-) adj. Causing surprise or wonder. —sur·pris′ing·ly adv. —Syn. amazing, startling.

sur·re·al·ism (sə·rē′əl·iz′əm) n. A 20th-century movement in art and literature characterized chiefly by the incongruous juxtaposition or use of dreamlike elements, in theory an expression of the unconscious mind. —sur·re·al·ist adj., n. —sur·re·al·is·tic adj. —sur·re·al·is·ti·cal·ly adv.

sur·ren·der (sə·ren′dər) v.t. 1 To yield possession of or power over to another because of demand or compulsion. 2 To give up or relinquish, esp. in favor of another; resign; abandon. 3 To give (oneself) over to a passion, influence, etc. —v.i. 4 To give oneself up, as to an enemy in warfare. —n. The act of surrendering. [< OF surrendre < sur- over + rendre give, render]

sur·rep·ti·tious (sûr′əp·tish′əs) adj. 1 Accomplished by secret or improper means; clandestine. 2 Acting secretly or by stealth. [< L subreptus, p.p. of subripere steal] —sur′rep·ti′tious·ly adv. —sur′rep·ti′tious·ness n.

sur·rey (sûr′ē) n. A vehicle having two seats facing forward and sometimes a top. [< Surrey, England]

Surrey

sur·ro·gate (sûr′ə·gāt, -git) n. 1 Someone or something taking the place of another; substitute. 2 In some U.S. states, a probate court judge. —v.t. (sûr′ə·gāt) ·gat·ed, ·gat·ing To put in the place of another; deputize or substitute. [< L subrogare < sub- in place of another + rogare ask]

sur·round (sə·round′) v.t. 1 To extend or place completely around; encircle or enclose. 2 To enclose on all sides so as to cut off communication or retreat. 3 To be or cause something to become a significant part of the environment or experience of: surrounded by lies; to surround oneself with the best legal talent. —n. Chiefly Brit. That which surrounds, as a border. [< LL super- over + undare rise in waves]

sur·round·ings (sə·roun′dingz) n.pl. The conditions, objects, etc., that constitute one's environment.

sur·tax (sûr′taks) n. An extra or additional tax.

sur·tout (sər·tōō′, sûr′tōō′) n. A man's long, close-fitting overcoat. [F < sur- above + tout all]

sur·veil·lance (sər·vā′ləns, -väl′yəns) n. A careful watching of someone or something, usu. carried on secretly or discreetly: to keep a suspect under surveillance. [F < sur- over + veiller watch] —sur·veil′lant adj.

sur·vey (sər·vā′, sûr′vā) v.t. 1 To look at in its entirety; view comprehensively, as from a height. 2 To look at carefully and minutely; scrutinize. 3 To determine accurately the area, contour, or boundaries of according to the principles of geometry and trigonometry. 4 To make a survey of. —v.i. 5 To survey land. —n. (usu. sûr′vā) 1 The operation, act, process, or results of surveying land. 2 A systematic inquiry to collect data for analysis, used esp. for the preparation of a comprehensive report or summary. 3 The result of such an inquiry; a comprehensive report. 4 A general or overall view; overview: a *survey* of contemporary theater. [< L *super-* over + *videre* look]

sur·vey·ing (sər·vā′ing) *n.* 1 The science and art of surveying portions of the surface of the earth and representing them on maps. 2 The work of one who surveys.

sur·vey·or (sər·vā′ər) *n.* One who surveys, esp. one engaged in land surveying.

sur·viv·a·ble (sûr·vī′və·bəl) *adj.* Not precluding survival: a *survivable* accident. —**sur·viv′a·bil·i·ty** *n.*

sur·viv·al (sər·vī′vəl) *n.* 1 The act or fact of surviving; a continuation of life or existence. 2 The fact of living or lasting beyond another. 3 One who or that which survives.

sur·vive (sər·vīv′) *v.* **·vived, ·viv·ing** 1 *v.i.* To live or continue beyond the death of another, the occurrence of an event, etc.; remain alive or in existence. —*v.t.* 2 To live or exist beyond the death, occurrence, or end of; outlive or outlast. 3 To go on living after or in spite of: to *survive* a flood. [< L *super-* above, beyond + *vivere* live] —**sur·vi′vor, sur·viv′er** *n.*

sus·cep·ti·ble (sə·sep′tə·bəl) *adj.* 1 Readily affected; especially subject or vulnerable: with *to: susceptible* to infection; lax supervision *susceptible* to abuse. 2 Capable of being influenced or determined; liable: with *of* or *to: susceptible* of proof. 3 Easily affected in feeling or emotion; sensitive. [< L *suscipere* receive, undertake] —**sus·cep·ti·bil·i·ty** (sə·sep′tə·bil′ə·tē), **sus·cep′ti·ble·ness** *n.* —**sus·cep′ti·bly** *adv.* —**Syn.** 1 unresistant, open. 2 admitting. 3 tender, impressionable.

sus·pect (sə·spekt′) *v.t.* 1 To think (a person) guilty without evidence or proof. 2 To have distrust of; doubt: to *suspect* one's motives. 3 To have an inkling or suspicion of; think possible. —*v.i.* 4 To have suspicions. —*adj.* (sus′pekt, sə·spekt′) Suspected; exciting suspicion. —*n.* (sus′pekt) A person suspected, esp. of a crime. [< F *suspecter* < L *suspectus,* p.p. of *suspicere* look under, mistrust] —**sus·pect′er** *n.*

sus·pend (sə·spend′) *v.t.* 1 To bar for a time from a privilege or office as a punishment. 2 To cause to cease for a time; interrupt: to *suspend* telephone service. 3 To withhold or defer action on: to *suspend* a sentence. 4 To hang from a support so as to allow free movement. 5 To keep in suspension, as dust particles in the air. —*v.i.* 6 To stop for a time. 7 To fail to meet obligations; stop payment. [< L *sub-* under + *pendere* hang]

sus·pend·er (sə·spen′dər) *n.* 1 One who or that which suspends. 2 *pl.* A pair of straps for supporting trousers. 3 *Brit.* A garter.

sus·pense (sə·spens′) *n.* 1 Anxiety caused by an uncertainty, as to the outcome of an event. 2 Excited interest caused by the progressive unfolding of events or information leading to a climax or resolution. 3 The state of being uncertain or indecisive. [< L *suspensus,* p.p. of *suspendere* suspend]

sus·pen·sion (sə·spen′shən) *n.* 1 The act of suspending, or the state of being suspended. 2 A temporary removal from office or position or withdrawal of privilege. 3 An interruption; cessation: *suspension* of normal procedure. 4 A deferment of action. 5 The state of hanging freely from a support. 6 A dispersion in a liquid or gas of insoluble particles that slowly settle on standing; also, a substance in this condition. 7 *Mech.* A system, as of springs or other absorbent parts, by which the chassis and body of a vehicle is insulated against shocks when moving. 8 a *Music* The prolongation of one or more tones of a chord into the succeeding chord, causing a transient dissonance. b The note so prolonged.

suspension bridge A bridge having its roadway suspended from cables supported by towers and anchored at either end.

sus·pen·sive (sə·spen′siv) *adj.* 1 Tending to suspend or keep in suspense. 2 Suspending or deferring operation or effect: a *suspensive* veto. —**sus·pen′sive·ly** *adv.*

sus·pen·so·ry (sə·spen′sər·ē) *adj.* 1 Acting to support or sustain. 2 Suspending or delaying. —*n. pl.* **·ries** Something that supports or sustains, esp. a truss for the scrotum.

sus·pi·cion (sə·spish′ən) *n.* 1 The act of suspecting; an uncertain but often tenacious feeling or belief in the likelihood of another's guilt, wrongdoing, etc., without evidence or proof. 2 *Informal* A slight amount; trace, as

of a flavor. —*v.t. Regional* To suspect. [< L *suspicere.* See SUSPECT.]

sus·pi·cious (sə·spish′əs) *adj.* 1 Tending to arouse suspicion; questionable. 2 Having or disposed to have suspicions. 3 Indicating suspicion. —**sus·pi′cious·ly** *adv.* —**sus·pi′cious·ness** *n.*

sus·tain (sə·stān′) *v.t.* 1 To keep up or maintain; keep in effect or being. 2 To maintain by providing with food and other necessities. 3 To keep from sinking or falling, esp. by bearing up from below. 4 To endure without succumbing; withstand. 5 To suffer, as a loss or injury; undergo. 6 To uphold or support as being true or just. 7 To prove the truth or correctness of; confirm. [< L *sub-* up from under + *tenere* to hold] —**sus·tain′a·ble** *adj.* —**sus·tain′er, sus·tain′ment** *n.* —**Syn.** 7 corroborate, establish.

sus·te·nance (sus′tə·nəns) *n.* 1 The act or process of sustaining; esp., maintenance of life or health; subsistence. 2 That which sustains, as food. 3 Means of support; livelihood.

sut·ler (sut′lər) *n.* Formerly, a peddler or tradesman who followed an army to sell goods and food to the soldiers. [< Du. *soeteler*] —**sut′ler·ship** *n.*

sut·tee (su·tē′, sut′ē) *n.* 1 The former custom in which a Hindu woman willingly cremated herself on the funeral pyre of her husband: also **sut·tee′ism.** 2 The widow so cremated. [< Hind. *satī* < Skt., faithful wife, fem. of *sat* good, wise]

su·ture (sōō′chər) *n.* 1 The junction of two edges by or as by sewing. 2 *Anat.* The fusion of two bones at their edges, as in the skull. 3 *Surg.* a The act or operation of joining the edges of an incision, wound, etc. b The thread, wire, or other material used in this operation. —*v.t.* **·tured, ·tur·ing** To unite by means of sutures; sew together. [< L *sutus,* p.p. of *suere* sew] —**su′tur·al** *adj.* —**su′tur·al·ly** *adv.*

su·ze·rain (sōō′zə·rin, -rān) *n.* 1 A feudal lord. 2 A nation having paramount control over a locally autonomous state. [< L *susum* upwards] —**su′ze·rain·ty** *n.* (*pl.* **·ties**)

svelte (svelt) *adj.* 1 Slender; willowy: a *svelte* fashion model. 2 Sophisticated; smart; chic. [< Ital. *svelto* stretched, slender]

SW, S.W., sw, s.w. southwest; southwestern.

Sw. Sweden; Swedish.

swab (swob) *n.* 1 A soft, absorbent substance, as of cotton or gauze, usu. secured at the end of a small stick, for applying medication, cleansing a body surface, etc. 2 *Med.* A specimen of mucus, etc., taken for examination with a swab. 3 A mop for cleaning decks, floors, etc. 4 A cylindrical brush for cleaning firearms. 5 *Slang* An oaf; lout. —*v.t.* **swabbed, swab·bing** To clean or apply with a swab. [< MDu. *zwabben* swab] —**swab′ber** *n.*

swad·dle (swod′l) *v.t.* **·dled, ·dling** 1 To wrap (an infant) in swaddling clothes. 2 To wrap with or as if with a bandage; swathe; bind. —*n.* A band or cloth used for swaddling. [< OE *swathian* swathe]

swaddling clothes Bands or strips of linen or cloth formerly wound around a newborn infant. Also **swaddling bands.**

swag (swag) *n.* 1 A curved decoration, as a hanging fastened at either end or a carved motif on a building. 2 *Slang* Property obtained by robbery or theft; plunder. 3 *Austral.* A bundle or pack containing belongings. 4 A swaying; a lurch. [? < Scand.]

swage (swāj) *n.* A tool or form for shaping metal by hammering or pressure. —*v.t.* **swaged, swag·ing** To shape (metal) with or as with a swage. [< OF *souage*]

swag·ger (swag′ər) *v.i.* 1 To walk with an air of conspicuous self-satisfaction and usu. of masculine vanity. 2 To behave in a blustering or self-satisfied manner. 3 To boast; brag. —*n.* 1 A swaggering gait or manner. 2 Verve; dash; bravado. —*adj.* Showy or stylish; smart. [< SWAG] —**swag′ger·er** *n.* —**swag′ger·ing·ly** *adv.*

swagger stick A short, lightweight stick, usu. tipped with metal, carried by some military officers as a mark of elegance or authority.

Swa·hi·li (swä·hē′lē) *n. pl.* **·li** or **·lis** 1 One of a Bantu people of Zanzibar and the adjacent coast. 2 The language of this people, now widely used in E and central Africa.

swain (swān) *n.* 1 A rustic youth. 2 A lover; wooer. [< ON *sveinn* a boy, servant]

swal·low[1] (swol′ō) v.t. 1 To cause (food, etc.) to pass from the mouth into the stomach by means of muscular action of the esophagus. 2 To take in or engulf in a manner suggestive of this; absorb; envelop: often with *up*. 3 To put up with or endure; submit to, as insults. 4 To refrain from expressing; suppress: to *swallow* one's pride. 5 To take back: to *swallow* one's words. 6 *Informal* To believe (something improbable or incredible) to be true. —v.i. 7 To perform the act or the motions of swallowing. —n. 1 The act of swallowing. 2 An amount swallowed at once; a mouthful. [< OE *swelgan* swallow] —**swal′low·er** n.

swal·low[2] (swol′ō) n. 1 Any of various small birds with short bill, long, pointed wings, and forked tail, noted for swiftness of flight and migratory habits. 2 A similar bird, as the swift. [< OE *swealwe*]

swal·low·tail (swol′ō·tāl′) n. 1 A man's dress coat with two long, tapering skirts or tails. 2 A butterfly having a tapering prolongation on each hind wing. —**swal′low·tailed′** adj.

swam (swam) p.t. of SWIM.

swa·mi (swä′mē) n. pl. **·mis** Master; lord: a Hindu title of respect, esp. for a religious teacher.

swamp (swomp, swômp) n. A tract or region of low land saturated with water; a bog. Also **swamp′land** (-land′). — v.t. 1 To drench or submerge with water or other liquid. 2 To overwhelm with difficulties; crush; ruin. 3 To sink or fill (a boat) with water. —v.i. 4 To sink in water, etc.; become swamped. [?< LG] —**swamp′y** adj. (·i·er, ·i·est)

swamp fever MALARIA.

swan (swon, swôn) n. Any of several large, web-footed, long-necked birds allied to but heavier than the goose. [< OE]

swan dive A dive performed with the head tilted back and the arms held sideways and brought together as the water is entered.

swank (swangk) n. 1 Ostentatious display, as in taste or manner; swagger. 2 Stylishness; smartness. —adj. 1 Ostentatiously fashionable. 2 Stylish; smart. —v.i. *Slang* To swagger; bluster. [?< MHG *swanken* sway]

Trumpeter swan

swank·y (swangk′ē) adj. **swank·i·er, swank·i·est** *Informal* Ostentatiously or extravagantly fashionable. —**swank′i·ly** adv. —**swank′i·ness** n.

swan's-down (swonz′doun′, swônz′-) n. 1 The down of a swan, used for trimming, powder puffs, etc. 2 Any of various fine, soft fabrics, usu. with a nap. Also **swans′·down′**.

swan song A last work, utterance, or performance, as before retirement or death. [< the ancient fable that the swan sings a last song before dying]

swap (swop) v.t. & v.i. **swapped, swap·ping** *Informal* To exchange (one thing for another); trade. —n. The act or an instance of swapping. [< ME *swappen* strike (a bargain), slap] —**swap′per** n.

sward (swôrd) n. Land thickly covered with grass; turf. — v.t. To cover with sward. [< OE *sweard* a skin]

swarm[1] (swôrm) n. 1 A large number of bees moving together with a queen to form a new colony. 2 A hive of bees. 3 A large crowd or mass, esp. one in apparent overall movement; throng. —v.i. 1 To leave the hive in a swarm: said of bees. 2 To come together, move, or occur in great numbers: The crowd *swarmed* out of the stadium; gnats *swarming* about. 3 To be crowded or overrun; teem: with *with: swarming* with tourists. —v.t. 4 To fill with a swarm or crowd. [< OE *swearm*] —**swarm′er** n.

swarm[2] (swôrm) v.t. & v.i. To climb (a tree, etc.) by clasping it with the hands and limbs. [?]

swart (swôrt) adj. Swarthy. [< OE *sweart*] —**swart′ness** n.

swarth·y (swôr′thē) adj. **swarth·i·er, swarth·i·est** Having a dark complexion; tawny. [Var. of obs. *swarty* < SWART] —**swarth′i·ly** adv. —**swarth′i·ness** n.

swash (swosh, swôsh) v.i. 1 To move with a splashing sound, as waves. —v.t. 2 To splash (water, etc.). 3 To splash or dash water, etc., upon or against. —n. The splash of a liquid. [Imit.] —**swash′er** n. —**swash′ing·ly** adv.

swash·buck·ler (swosh′buk′lər, swôsh′-) n. A swaggering soldier, adventurer, daredevil, etc. [< SWASH + BUCK-LER] —**swash′buck′ler·ing** n. —**swash′buck′ling** adj., n.

swas·ti·ka (swos′ti·kə) n. 1 A primitive ornament or symbol in the form of a cross with arms of equal length, bent at the ends at right angles. 2 Such a figure with the arms extended clockwise, used as the emblem of the Nazis. Also **swas′ti·ca**. [< Skt. *sú* good + *astí* being < *as* be]

Nazi swastika

swat (swot) v.t. **swat·ted, swat·ting** To hit with a sharp, quick, or violent blow. —n. A sharp, quick, or violent blow. [Var. of SQUAT] —**swat′ter** n. —**Syn.** v. smack, strike, whack.

swatch (swoch) n. A strip, as of fabric, esp. one cut off for a sample. [?]

swath (swoth, swôth) n. 1 A row or line of cut grass or grain. 2 The space cut by a machine or implement in a single course. 3 A strip, track, row, etc. —**cut a wide swath** To make a fine impression. [< OE *swæth* a track]

swathe[1] (swāth, swäth) v.t. **swathed, swath·ing** 1 To bind or wrap, as in bandages; swaddle. 2 To envelop; enwrap. —n. A bandage for swathing. [< OE *swathian*] —**swath′er** n.

swathe[2] (swāth, swäth) n. SWATH.

sway (swā) v.i. 1 To swing from side to side or to and fro; oscillate. 2 To bend or incline to one side. 3 To incline in opinion, sympathy, etc. 4 To control; rule. —v.t. 5 To cause to swing from side to side. 6 To cause to bend or lean to one side. 7 To cause (a person, opinion, etc.) to tend in a given way; influence. 8 To deflect or divert, as from a course of action. —n. 1 Power; influence. 2 A sweeping, swinging, or turning from side to side. [Prob. < ON *sveigja* bend] —**Syn.** v. 2 lean, veer. 4 govern, influence. n. 1 control, dominion.

sway·back (swā′bak′) n. A hollow or sagging condition of the back, as in a horse. —adj. Having such a back: also **sway′backed′** (-bakt′).

Swa·zi·land (swä′zē·land) n. An independent kingdom of the Commonwealth of Nations in SE Africa, 6,704 sq. mi., cap. Mbabane. • See map at AFRICA.

swear (swâr) v. **swore, sworn, swear·ing** v.i. 1 To make a solemn affirmation with an appeal to God or some other deity or to something held sacred. 2 To make a vow. 3 To use profanity; curse. 4 *Law* To give testimony under oath. —v.t. 5 To affirm or assert solemnly by invoking sacred beings or things. 6 To promise with an oath; vow. 7 To declare or affirm, earnestly or emphatically: I *swear* he's a liar. 8 To take or utter (an oath). —**swear by** 1 To appeal to by oath. 2 To have complete confidence in. —**swear in** To administer a legal oath to. —**swear off** *Informal* To promise to give up: to *swear off* drink. —**swear out** To obtain (a warrant for arrest) by making a statement under oath. [< OE *swerian*] —**swear′er** n.

swear·word (swâr′wûrd′) n. A word used in profanity or cursing.

sweat (swet) v. **sweat** or **sweat·ed, sweat·ing** v.i. 1 To exude or excrete salty moisture from the pores of the skin; perspire. 2 To exude moisture in drops. 3 To gather and condense moisture in drops on its surface. 4 To pass through pores or interstices in drops. 5 To ferment, as tobacco leaves. 6 To come forth, as through a porous surface; ooze. 7 *Informal* To work hard; toil; drudge. 8 *Informal* To suffer, as from anxiety. —v.t. 9 To exude (moisture) from the pores or a porous surface. 10 To gather or condense drops of (moisture). 11 To soak or stain with sweat. 12 To cause to sweat. 13 To cause to work hard. 14 *Informal* To force (employees) to work for low wages and under unfavorable conditions. 15 To heat (solder, etc.) until it melts. 16 To join, as metal objects with solder. 17 *Metall.* To heat so as to extract an element that is easily fusible; also, to extract thus. 18 To subject to fermentation, as hides or tobacco. 19 *Slang* To subject to torture or rigorous interrogation to extract information. —**sweat (something) out** *Slang* To wait through anxiously; endure. —*n.* **1** Moisture in minute drops on the skin. **2** The act or state of sweating. **3** Hard labor; drudgery. **4** *Informal* Impatience, anxiety, or hurry. [< OE *swætan*] —**sweat′i·ly** *adv.* —**sweat′i·ness** *n.* —**sweat′y** *adj.* (**·i·er, ·i·est**)

sweat·band (swet′band′) *n.* **1** A band, usu. of leather, inside a hat to protect it from sweat. **2** An absorbent cloth band worn over the forehead or around the wrist.

sweat·er (swet′ər) *n.* **1** One who or that which sweats. **2** A knitted or crocheted garment with or without sleeves.

sweat gland One of the numerous minute subcutaneous glands that secrete sweat.

sweat shirt A loose-fitting, usu. long-sleeved pullover of soft, absorbent material, sometimes hooded.

sweat·shop (swet′shop′) *n.* A place where work is done under poor conditions, for insufficient wages, and for long hours.

sweat·suit (swet′sōōt′) *n.* A sweat shirt and matching pants (**sweat pants**) worn esp. by athletes when warming up or just after competing.

Swed. Sweden; Swedish.

Swede (swēd) *n.* A native or citizen of Sweden.

Swe·den (swē′dən) *n.* A constitutional monarchy of N Europe, 173,577 sq. mi., cap. Stockholm.

Swed·ish (swē′dish) *adj.* Of or pertaining to Sweden, the Swedes, or their language. —*n.* **1** The North Germanic language of Sweden. **2** The inhabitants of Sweden collectively: with *the.*

sweep (swēp) *v.* **swept, sweep·ing** *v.t.* **1** To collect or clear away with a broom, brush, etc. **2** To clear or clean with a broom, etc.: to *sweep* a floor. **3** To touch or brush with a motion as of sweeping: to *sweep* the strings of a harp. **4** To pass over swiftly: The searchlight *swept* the sky. **5** To move, carry, bring, etc., with force: The flood *swept* the bridge away. **6** To move over or through with force: The gale *swept* the bay. **7** To drag the bottom of (a body of water, etc.). **8** To win totally or overwhelmingly. —*v.i.* **9** To clean a floor or other surface with a broom, etc. **10** To move or go strongly and evenly: The train *swept* by. **11** To walk with great dignity: She *swept* into the room. **12** To trail, as a skirt. **13** To extend with a long reach or curve: The road *sweeps* along the lake shore on the north. —*n.* **1** The act or result of sweeping. **2** A long stroke or movement: a *sweep* of the hand. **3** The act of clearing out or getting rid of. **4** An unbroken stretch or extent: a *sweep* of beach. **5** A total or overwhelming victory, as in an election. **6** The range, area, or compass reached by sweeping. **7** One who sweeps chimneys, streets, etc. **8** A curving line; flowing contour. **9** A long, heavy oar. **10** A long pole on a pivot, having a bucket suspended from one end, for use in drawing water. **11** *pl.* Sweepings. **12** *pl. Informal* Sweepstakes. [< OE *swāpan*] —**sweep′er** *n.*

sweep·ing (swē′ping) *adj.* **1** Extending in a long line or over a wide area: a *sweeping* glance. **2** Covering a wide area; comprehensive: *sweeping* reforms. —*n.* **1** The action of one who or that which sweeps. **2** *pl.* Things swept up, as refuse. —**sweep′ing·ly** *adv.* —**sweep′ing·ness** *n.*

Sweep *def. 10*

sweep·stakes (swēp′stāks′) *n. pl.* **·stakes** (construed as *sing.* or *pl.*) **1** A type of lottery in which all the sums staked may be won by one or by a few of the betters, as in a horse race. **2** A race, contest, etc., to determine the outcome of such a lottery. **3** A prize in such a lottery. Also **sweep′stake′.**

sweet (swēt) *adj.* **1** Having a flavor like that of sugar, often due to the presence of sugar in some form. **2** Not salted, sour, rancid, or spoiled. **3** Gently pleasing to the senses; agreeable to the taste, smell, etc. **4** Agreeable or delightful to the mind or the emotions. **5** Having gentle, pleasing, and winning qualities. **6** Sound; rich; productive: said of soil. —*n.* **1** The quality of being sweet; sweetness. **2** Something sweet, agreeable, or pleasing. **3** *Usu. pl.* Confections, preserves, candy, etc. **4** A beloved person. **5** *Brit.* DESSERT. [< OE *swēte*] —**sweet′ly** *adv.* —**sweet′ness** *n.*

sweet alyssum A small plant related to mustard having spikes of fragrant white blossoms.

sweet·bread (swēt′bred′) *n.* The pancreas (**stomach sweetbread**) or the thymus (**neck sweetbread** or **throat sweetbread**) of a calf or other animal, when used as food.

sweet·bri·er (swēt′brī′ər) *n.* A species of rose with dense, prickly branches and fragrant leaves. Also **sweet′·bri′ar.**

sweet clover Any of several leguminous forage plants having fragrant white or yellow flowers.

sweet corn Any of several varieties of maize rich in sugar, cultivated for use as a vegetable.

sweet·en (swēt′n) *v.t.* **1** To make sweet or sweeter. **2** To make more endurable; alleviate; lighten. **3** To make pleasant or gratifying. —**sweet′en·er** *n.*

sweet·en·ing (swēt′n·ing) *n.* **1** The act of making sweet. **2** That which sweetens.

sweet flag A marsh-dwelling plant with sword-shaped leaves and a fragrant rhizome.

sweet gum **1** A large North American tree with maple-like leaves and bark exuding a fragrant gum. **2** The balsam or gum yielded by it.

sweet·heart (swēt′härt′) *n.* **1** Darling: a term of endearment. **2** A lover.

sweetheart contract An agreement made between an employer and union officials, the terms of which are disadvantageous to union members. Also **sweetheart agreement.**

sweet·meat (swēt′mēt′) *n. Usu. pl.* A highly sweetened food, as candy, cake, candied fruit, etc.

sweet pea A climbing leguminous plant cultivated for its fragrant, varicolored flowers.

sweet pepper A mild variety of capsicum used for pickling and as a vegetable.

sweet potato **1** A perennial tropical vine of the morning-glory family, with a fleshy tuberous root. **2** The sweet yellow or orange root, eaten as a vegetable.

sweet-talk (swēt′tôk′) *Informal v.t.* **1** To persuade by coaxing or flattering. —*v.i.* **2** To flatter or coax someone. —**sweet talk**

sweet tooth *Informal* A fondness for candy or sweets.

sweet wil·liam (wil′yəm) A perennial species of pink with fragrant, closely clustered flowers. Also **sweet William.**

swell (swel) *v.* **swelled, swelled** or **swol·len, swell·ing** *v.i.* **1** To increase in size or volume, as by inflation with air or by absorption of moisture. **2** To increase in amount, degree, force, intensity, etc. **3** To rise above the usual or surrounding level, surface, etc. **4** To rise in waves or swells, as the sea. **5** To bulge. **6** *Informal* To become puffed up with pride. —*v.t.* **7** To cause to increase in size or volume. **8** To cause to increase in amount, degree, force, intensity, etc. **9** To cause to bulge. **10** To puff with pride. —*n.* **1** The act, process, or effect of swelling; expansion. **2** A long continuous wave without a crest. **3** A rise of, or undulation in, the land. **4** Any bulge or protuberance. **5** *Music* A crescendo and diminuendo in succession; also, the signs (< >) indicating it. **6** A device by which the loudness of an organ may be varied. **7** *Informal* A person who is very fashionable, elegant, or social. —*adj.* **1** *Informal* Very fashionable, elegant, or social. **2** *Slang* Very fine; first-rate; excellent. [< OE *swellan*] —**Syn.** *v.* **1** bulge, dilate, distend, enlarge, expand.

swell·ing (swel′ing) *n.* **1** The act or process by which a person or thing swells. **2** The condition of being swollen. **3** Something swollen, esp. an abnormal enlargement of a part of the body. —*adj.* That swells; increasing, bulging, puffing up, etc.

swel·ter (swel′tər) *v.i.* **1** To perspire or suffer from oppressive heat. —*v.t.* **2** To cause to swelter. —*n.* A sweltering condition; oppressive heat. [< OE *sweltan* die] **—swel'·ter·ing·ly** *adv.*

swept (swept) *p.t. & p.p.* of SWEEP.

swept·back (swept'bak') *adj. Aeron.* Having the front edge (of a wing) tilted backward from the lateral axis, as an airplane.

swerve (swûrv) *v.t. & v.i.* **swerved, swerv·ing** To turn or cause to turn aside from a course; deflect. **—n.** The act of swerving; a sudden turning aside. [< OE *sweorfan* file or grind away]

swift[1] (swift) *adj.* **1** Moving with great speed; rapid; quick. **2** Capable of quick motion; fleet. **3** Happening, coming, finished, etc., in a brief time. **4** Quick to act or respond; prompt. **—adv.** In a swift manner. [< OE] **—swift'ly** *adv.* **—swift'ness** *n.*

swift[2] (swift) *n.* Any of various swallowlike birds with extraordinary powers of flight, as the chimney swift. [< SWIFT[1]]

swig (swig) *n. Informal* A great gulp; deep draft. **—v.t. & v.i.** **swigged, swig·ging** *Informal* To take swigs (of). [?]

swill (swil) *v.t.* **1** To drink greedily or to excess. **2** To drench, as with water; rinse; wash. **3** To fill with, as drink. **—v.i.** **4** To drink greedily or to excess. **—n.** **1** Semiliquid food for domestic animals, as the mixture of edible refuse and liquid fed to pigs. **2** Garbage. **3** Unappetizing food. **4** A great gulp; swig. [< OE *swillan* to wash]

Chimney swift

swim[1] (swim) *v.* **swam** (*Regional* **swum**), **swum, swim·ming** *v.i.* **1** To move through water by working the legs, arms, fins, etc. **2** To float. **3** To move with a smooth or flowing motion. **4** To be flooded. **—v.t.** **5** To cross or traverse by swimming. **6** To cause to swim. **—n.** **1** The action or pastime of swimming. **2** The distance swum or to be swum. **3** The air bladder of a fish: also **swim bladder, swimming bladder.** **—in the swim** Active in current affairs, esp. those involved with fashion, socializing, etc. [< OE *swimman*] **—swim'mer** *n.*

swim[2] (swim) **swam** (*Regional* **swum**), **swum, swim·ming** *v.i.* **1** To be dizzy. **2** To seem to go round; reel. [< OE *swima* dizziness]

swimming hole A deep hole or pool in a stream, used for swimming.

swim·ming·ly (swim'ing·lē) *adv.* Easily and successfully.

swim·suit (swim'soot') *n.* A garment designed to be worn while swimming.

swin·dle (swin'dəl) *v.* **·dled, ·dling** *v.t.* **1** To cheat; defraud. **2** To obtain by such means. **—v.i.** **3** To practice fraud. **—n.** The act or process of swindling. [< G *schwindeln* cheat] **—swin'dler** *n.* **—Syn.** *v.* **1** deceive, dupe, rook.

swine (swīn) *n. pl.* **swine** **1** A pig or hog: usu. used collectively. **2** A low, greedy, or vicious person. [< OE *swīn*] **—swin'ish** *adj.* **—swin'ish·ly** *adv.* **—swin'ish·ness** *n.*

swine·herd (swīn'hûrd') *n.* A tender of swine.

swing (swing) *v.* **swung, swing·ing** *v.i.* **1** To move to and fro or backward and forward rhythmically, as something suspended. **2** To ride in a swing. **3** To move with an even, swaying motion. **4** To turn; pivot: We *swung* around and went home. **5** To be suspended; hang. **6** *Informal* To be executed by hanging. **7** *Slang* To be very up-to-date and sophisticated, esp. in one's amusements and pleasures. **8** *Informal* To sing or play with or to have a compelling, usu. jazzlike rhythm. **9** *Slang* To be sexually promiscuous. **—v.t.** **10** To cause to move to and fro or backward and forward. **11** To brandish; flourish: to *swing* an ax. **12** To cause to turn on or as on a pivot or central point. **13** To lift, hoist, or hang: They *swung* the mast into place. **14** *Informal* To bring to a successful conclusion: to *swing* a deal. **15** *Informal* To sing or play in the style of swing (*n.,* def. 8). **—n.** **1** The action process, or manner of swinging. **2** A free swaying motion. **3** A contrivance of hanging ropes with a seat on which a person may move to and fro through the air. **4** Freedom of action. **5** The arc or range of something that swings. **6** A swinging blow or stroke. **7**

A trip or tour: a *swing* through the west. **8** A type of jazz music played by big bands, achieving its effect by lively, compelling rhythms, contrapuntal styles, and arranged ensemble playing: also **swing music.** **—in full swing** In full and lively operation. [< OE *swingan* scourge, beat up]

swinge (swinj) *v.t.* **swinged, swinge·ing** *Archaic* To flog; chastise. [< OE *swengan* shake, beat] **—swing'er** *n.*

swinge·ing (swin'jing) *adj. Chiefly Brit. Informal* Very large, good, or first-rate. [< SWINGE]

swing·er (swing'ər) *n. Slang* **1** A lively and up-to-date person. **2** A person who indulges freely in sex.

swing·ing (swing'ing) *adj. Slang* **1** Lively and compelling in effect: a *swinging* jazz quartet. **2** Modern; modish.

swin·gle (swing'gəl) *n.* A large, knifelike wooden implement for beating and cleaning flax: also **swing'knife.** **—v.t.** **·gled, ·gling** To cleanse, as flax, by beating with a swingle. [< MDu. *swinghel*]

swin·gle·tree (swing'gəl·trē') *n.* WHIFFLETREE.

swing shift An evening work shift, usu. lasting from about 4 p.m. to midnight. **—swing shifter**

swipe (swīp) *v.* **swiped, swip·ing** **—v.t.** **1** *Informal* To strike with a sweeping motion. **2** *Slang* To steal; snatch. **—v.i.** **3** To hit with a sweeping motion. **—n.** *Informal* A hard blow. [Var. of SWEEP]

swirl (swûrl) *v.t. & v.i.* To move or cause to move along in irregular eddies; whirl. **—n.** **1** A whirling along, as in an eddy. **2** A curl or twist; spiral. [ME *swyrl*] **—swirl'y** *adj.*

swish (swish) *v.i.* **1** To move with a hissing or whistling sound. **—v.t.** **2** To cause to swish. **—n.** **1** A swishing sound. **2** A movement producing such a sound. [Imit.]

Swiss (swis) *n.* **1** A citizen or native of Switzerland. **2** The people of Switzerland collectively: used with *the.* **—adj.** Of or pertaining to Switzerland or its people.

Swiss chard Chard.

Swiss cheese A pale yellow cheese with many large holes, originally made in Switzerland.

Swiss steak A cut of steak floured and cooked, often with a sauce of tomatoes, onions, etc.

Swit., Switz., Swtz. Switzerland.

switch (swich) *n.* **1** A small flexible rod, twig, or whip. **2** A tress of false hair, worn by women in building a coiffure. **3** A mechanism for shifting a railway train from one track to another. **4** The act or operation of switching, shifting, or changing. **5** The tuft of hair at the end of the tail in certain animals, as a cow. **6** *Electr.* A device used to start or stop a flow of current. **7** A blow with or as with a switch. **—v.t.** **1** To whip or lash. **2** To move, jerk, or whisk suddenly or sharply. **3** To turn aside or divert; shift. **4** To exchange: They *switched* plates. **5** To shift, as a railroad car, to another track. **6** *Electr.* To connect or disconnect with a switch. **—v.i.** **7** To turn aside; change; shift. **8** To swing back and forth or from side to side. **9** To shift from one track to another. [?] **—switch'er** *n.*

switch·back (swich'bak') *n.* **1** A zigzag road or railroad up a steep incline. **2** *Brit.* ROLLER COASTER.

switch·board (swich'bôrd', -bōrd') *n.* A panel bearing switches or controls for several electric circuits, as a telephone exchange.

switch·man (swich'mən) *n. pl.* **·men** (-mən) One who handles switches, esp. on a railroad.

switch·yard (swich'yärd') *n.* A railroad yard in which trains are stored, maintained, assembled, etc.

Swit·zer·land (swit'sər·lənd) *n.* A republic of CEN. Europe, 15,940 sq. mi., cap. Bern. •See map at ITALY.

swiv·el (swiv'əl) *n.* **1** A coupling or pivot that permits parts, as of a mechanism, to rotate independently. **2** Anything that turns on a pin or headed bolt. **3** A cannon that swings on a pivot: also **swivel gun.** **—v.** **·eled** or **·elled, ·el·ing** or **·el·ling** *v.t.* **1** To turn on or as on a swivel. **2** To provide with or secure by a swivel. **3** To turn or swing on or as on a swivel. [< OE *swīfan* revolve]

swivel chair A chair whose seat turns freely on a swivel.

swob (swob) *n. & v.* **swobbed, swob·bing** SWAB.

swol·len (swō'lən) A *p.p.* of SWELL.

swoon (swoon) *v.i.* To faint. **—n.** A fainting fit. [< OE *swōgan* suffocate]

---

swoop (swoōp) *v.i.* **1** To drop or descend suddenly, as a bird pouncing on its prey. —*v.t.* **2** To take or seize suddenly; snatch. —*n.* The act of swooping. [< OE *swāpan* sweep]

swop (swop) *n. & v.* **swopped, swop·ping** SWAP.

sword (sôrd, sōrd) *n.* A weapon consisting of a long blade fixed in a hilt. —**at swords' points** Very unfriendly; hostile. —**cross swords 1** To quarrel; argue. **2** To fight. —**put to the sword** To kill with a sword. —**the sword 1** Military power. **2** War. [< OE *sweord*]

sword·fish (sôrd'fish', sōrd'-) *n. pl.* **·fish** or **·fish·es** A large fish of the open sea having the upper jaw elongated into a swordlike process.

Swordfish

sword·grass (sôrd'gras', -gräs', sōrd'-) *n.* Any of several grasses or sedges with serrated or swordlike leaves.

sword·knot (sôrd'not', sōrd'-) *n.* An ornamental tassel of leather, cord, etc., tied to a sword hilt.

sword play The act, technique, or skill of using a sword, esp. in fencing. —**sword'-play'er** *n.*

swords·man (sôrdz'mən, sōrdz'-) *n. pl.* **·men** (-mən) One skilled in the use of or armed with a sword, esp. a fencer. Also **sword'man.** —**swords'man·ship, sword'man·ship** *n.*

swore (swôr, swōr) *p.t.* of SWEAR.

sworn (swôrn, swōrn) *p.p.* of SWEAR.

swot (swot) *n. & v.* **swot·ted, swot·ting** SWAT.

swounds (zwoundz, zoundz) *interj.* ZOUNDS.

swum (swum) *p.p. & regional p.t.* of SWIM.

swung (swung) *p.t. & p.p.* of SWING.

syb·a·rite (sib'ə-rīt) *n.* A person devoted to luxury or sensuality; voluptuary. [< *Sybaris,* an ancient Greek city in southern Italy] —**syb·a·rit·ic** (sib'ə-rit'ik), **syb·a·rit'i·cal** *adj.* —**syb'a·rit'i·cal·ly** *adv.*

syc·a·more (sik'ə-môr, -mōr) *n.* **1** A medium-sized tree of Syria and Egypt allied to the fig. **2** Any of various plane trees widely distributed in North America. **3** An ornamental maple tree: also **sycamore maple.** [< Gk. *sykon* a fig + *moron* a mulberry]

syc·o·phant (sik'ə-fənt, -fant) *n.* A servile flatterer; toady. [< Gk. *sykon* fig + *phainein* to show] —**syc'o·phan·cy** (-sē) (*pl.* **·cies**) *n.* —**syc'o·phan'tic** (-fan'tik), **syc'o·phan'·ti·cal** *adj.* —**syc'o·phan'ti·cal·ly** *adv.*

syl·la·bar·y (sil'ə-ber'ē) *n. pl.* **·bar·ies** A list of syllables; esp., a list of written characters representing syllables.

syl·lab·ic (si·lab'ik) *adj.* **1** Of, pertaining to, or consisting of syllables. **2** *Phonet.* Designating a consonant capable of forming a complete syllable, as *l* in *middle* (mid'l). **3** Having every syllable distinctly pronounced. Also **syl·lab'i·cal.** —*n. Phonet.* A syllabic sound. —**syl·lab'i·cal·ly** *adv.*

syl·lab·i·cate (si·lab'ə·kāt) *v.t.* **·cat·ed, ·cat·ing** SYLLABIFY. —**syl·lab'i·ca'tion** *n.*

syl·lab·i·fy (si·lab'ə·fī) *v.t.* **·fied, ·fy·ing** To form or divide into syllables. —**syl·lab'i·fi·ca'tion** *n.*

syl·la·ble (sil'ə·bəl) *n.* **1** *Phonet.* A word or part of a word uttered in a single vocal impulse. **2** A part of a written or printed word corresponding to the spoken division. **3** The least detail or mention: Please don't repeat a *syllable* of what you've heard here. —*v.* **·bled, ·bling** *v.t.* **1** To pronounce the syllables of. —*v.i.* **2** To pronounce syllables. [< Gk. *syn-* together + *lambanein* take]

syl·la·bus (sil'ə·bəs) *n. pl.* **·bus·es** or **·bi** (-bī) A concise statement or outline, esp. of a course of study. [< Gk. *sittyba* label on a book] —**Syn.** abstract, epitome, synopsis.

syl·lo·gism (sil'ə·jiz'əm) *n.* **1** *Logic* A form of reasoning consisting of three propositions. The first two propositions, called *premises,* have one term in common furnishing a relation between the two other terms, which are linked in the third, called the *conclusion.* Example: All men are mortal (*major premise*); kings are men (*minor premise*); therefore, kings are mortal (*conclusion*). **2** Reasoning that makes use of this form; deduction. [< Gk. *syn-* together + *logizesthai* infer] —**syl'lo·gis'tic, syl'lo·gis'ti·cal** *adj.* —**syl'lo·gis'ti·cal·ly** *adv.*

sylph (silf) *n.* **1** A being, mortal but without a soul, living in and on the air. **2** A slender, graceful young woman or girl. [< NL *sylphus*]

syl·van (sil'vən) *adj.* **1** Of, pertaining to, or located in a forest or woods. **2** Composed of or abounding in trees or woods. —*n.* A person or animal living in or frequenting forests or woods. [< L *silva* a wood]

sym. symbol; symmetrical; symphony.

sym·bi·o·sis (sim'bī·ō'sis, -bē-) *n.* An intimate and mutually advantageous partnership of dissimilar organisms, as of algae and fungi in lichens. [< Gk. *syn-* together + *bios* life] —**sym'bi·ot'ic** (-ot'ik) or **·i·cal** *adj.* —**sym'bi·ot'i·cal·ly** *adv.*

sym·bol (sim'bəl) *n.* **1** Something chosen to stand for or represent something else, as an object used to typify a quality, idea, etc.: The lily is a *symbol* of purity. **2** A character, mark, abbreviation, letter, etc., that represents something else. —*v.t.* **sym·boled** or **·bolled, sym·bol·ing** or **·bol·ling** SYMBOLIZE. [< Gk. *syn-* together + *ballein* throw]

sym·bol·ic (sim·bol'ik) *adj.* **1** Of, pertaining to, or expressed by a symbol. **2** Used as a symbol: with *of.* **3** Characterized by or involving the use of symbols or symbolism: *symbolic* poetry. Also **sym·bol'i·cal.** —**sym·bol'i·cal·ly** *adv.* —**sym·bol'i·cal·ness** *n.*

sym·bol·ism (sim'bəl·iz'əm) *n.* **1** The use of symbols to represent things; the act or art of investing things with a symbolic meaning. **2** A system of symbols or symbolical representation. **3** Symbolic meaning or character.

sym·bol·ist (sim'bəl·ist) *n.* One who uses symbols or symbolism, esp. an artist or writer skilled in the use of symbols.

sym·bol·is·tic (sim'bəl·is'tik) *adj.* Of or pertaining to symbolism or symbolists. —**sym'bol·is'ti·cal·ly** *adv.*

sym·bol·ize (sim'bəl·īz) *v.* **·ized, ·iz·ing** *v.t.* **1** To be a symbol of; represent symbolically; typify. **2** To represent by a symbol or symbols. **3** To treat as symbolic or figurative. —*v.i.* **4** To use symbols. *Brit. sp.* **sym'bol·ise.** —**sym'bol·i·za'·tion, sym'bol·i·zer** *n.*

sym·me·try (sim'ə·trē) *n. pl.* **·tries 1** Corresponding arrangement or balancing of the parts or elements of a whole in respect to size, shape, and position on opposite sides of an axis or center. **2** The element of beauty and harmony in nature or art that results from such arrangement and balancing. **3** *Math.* An arrangement of points in a system such that the system appears unchanged after certain partial rotations. [< Gk. *syn-* together + *metron* a measure] —**sym·met·ric** (si·met'rik), **sym·met'ri·cal** *adj.* —**sym·met'ri·cal·ly** *adv.* —**sym·met'ri·cal·ness** *n.*

sym·pa·thet·ic (sim'pə·thet'ik) *adj.* **1** Pertaining to, expressing, or proceeding from sympathy. **2** Having a compassionate feeling for others; sympathizing. **3** Being in accord or harmony; congenial. **4** Of, proceeding from, or characterized by empathy. **5** Referring to sounds produced by responsive vibrations. Also **sym'pa·thet'i·cal.** —**sym'pa·thet'i·cal·ly** *adv.*

sympathetic nervous system The part of the autonomic nervous system that controls such involuntary actions as the dilation of pupils, constriction of blood vessels and salivary glands, and increase of heartbeat.

sym·pa·thize (sim'pə·thīz) *v.i.* **·thized, ·thiz·ing 1** To experience or understand the sentiments or ideas of another. **2** To feel or express compassion, as for another's sorrow or affliction: with *with.* **3** To be in harmony or agreement. *Brit. sp.* **sym'pa·thise.** —**sym'pa·thiz'er** *n.* —**sym'pa·thiz'ing·ly** *adv.*

sym·pa·thy (sim'pə·thē) *n. pl.* **·thies 1** The fact or condition of an agreement in feeling: The *sympathy* between husband and wife was remarkable. **2** A feeling of compassion for another's sufferings. **3** Agreement or accord: to be in *sympathy* with an objective. **4** Support; loyalty; approval: trying to enlist my *sympathies.* [< Gk. *syn-* together + *pathos* a feeling, passion] —**Syn. 1** affinity, concord. **2** commiseration, condolence, pity.

sympathy strike A strike in which the strikers support the demands of another group of workers. Also **sympathetic strike.**

sym·pho·ny (sim'fə·nē) *n. pl.* **·nies 1** A harmonious or agreeable mingling of sounds. **2** Any harmony or agreeable blending, as of color. **3** A composition for orchestra, consisting usu. of four extensive movements. **4** SYMPHONY ORCHESTRA. [< Gk. *syn-* together + *phōnē* a sound] —**sym·phon·ic** (sim·fon'ik) *adj.* —**sym·phon'i·cal·ly** *adv.*

symphony orchestra A large orchestra composed usu. of string, brass, woodwind, and percussion instruments.

sym·po·si·um (sim-pō′zē-əm) *n. pl.* **·si·ums, ·si·a** (-zē-ə) 1 A meeting for discussion of a particular subject or subjects. 2 A collection of comments, opinions, essays, etc. on the same subject. [< Gk. *syn-* together + *posis* drinking] — **sym·po′si·ac** (-ak) *adj.*

symp·tom (simp′təm) *n.* 1 An organic or functional condition indicating the presence of disease, esp. when regarded as an aid in diagnosis. 2 A sign or indication that serves to point out the existence of something else: *symptoms* of civil unrest. [< Gk. *syn-* together + *piptein* fall] — **symp′to·mat′ic** (-tə-mat′ik), **symp′to·mat′i·cal** *adj.* —**symp′·to·mat′i·cal·ly** *adv.* —**Syn.** 2 earmark, mark, signal, token.

syn- *prefix* With; together; associated; at the same time: *syncarp.* [< Gk. *syn* together]

syn. synchronize; synonym; synonymous; synonymy.

syn·a·gogue (sin′ə-gôg, -gog) *n.* 1 A place of meeting for Jewish worship and religious instruction. 2 A Jewish congregation or assemblage for religious instruction and observances. Also **syn′a·gog.** [< Gk. *synagōgē* an assembly]

syn·apse (sin′aps′, sə-naps′) *n.* The junction point of two neurons, across which a nerve impulse passes. Also **syn·ap·sis** (sə-nap′səs) *pl.* **·ap·ses** (-sēz). [< Gk. *syn-* together + *hapsis* a joining] —**syn·ap·tic** (-nap′tik) *adj.*

sync (singk) *n. & v.* **synced, sync·ing** SYNCH.

syn·carp (sin′kärp) *n.* A multiple or fleshy aggregate fruit, as the blackberry. [< Gk. *syn-* together + *karpos* a fruit] — **syn·car·pous** (sin-kär′pəs) *adj.*

synch (singk) *Slang v.i. & v.t.* **synched, synch·ing** To synchronize or cause to be synchronized. —*n.* Synchronization: usu. in phrases **in synch** and **out of synch.** [< SYNCHRONIZATION]

syn·chro·mesh (sing′kro-mesh′, sin′-) *n. Mech.* 1 A gear system in which parts are synchronized before engagement. 2 The synchronizing mechanism thus used.

Syncarp (blackberry)

syn·chro·nism (sing′krə-niz′əm, sin′-) *n.* 1 The state of being synchronous; concurrence. 2 A grouping of historic personages or events according to their dates. —**syn′chro·nis′tic, syn′chro·nis′ti·cal** *adj.* —**syn′chro·nis′ti·cal·ly** *adv.*

syn·chro·ni·za·tion (sing′krə-nə-zā′shən) *n.* 1 The state of being synchronous. 2 The act of synchronizing, or the state of being synchronized.

syn·chro·nize (sing′krə-nīz, sin′-) *v.* **·nized, ·niz·ing** *v.i.* 1 To occur at the same time; coincide. 2 To move or operate in unison. —*v.t.* 3 To cause to operate synchronously: to *synchronize* watches. 4 To cause (the appropriate sound of a motion picture) to coincide with the action. 5 To assign the same date or period to; make contemporaneous. [< SYNCHRONOUS] —**syn′chro·niz′er** *n.*

syn·chro·nous (sing′krə-nəs, sin′-) *adj.* 1 Occurring at the same time; concurrent; simultaneous. 2 *Physics* Having the same period or frequency. 3 *Electr.* Normally operating at a speed proportional to the frequency of the current in the power line, as a motor. Also **syn′chro·nal.** [< Gk. *syn-* together + *chronos* time] —**syn′chro·nous·ly** *adv.* —**syn′chro·nous·ness** *n.*

syn·cline (sin′klīn) *n. Geol.* A trough or fold of stratified rock in which the layers dip downward on each side toward the axis of the fold. [< Gk. *syn-* together + *klinein* to incline] —**syn·cli′nal** (sin-klī′nəl) *adj.*

syn·co·pate (sing′kə-pāt, sin′-) *v.t.* **·pat·ed, ·pat·ing** 1 To contract, as a word, by syncope. 2 *Music* To treat or modify (a rhythm, melody, etc.) by syncopation. [< LL *syncope syncope*]

syn·co·pa·tion (sing′kə-pā′shən, sin′-) *n.* 1 The act of syncopating or state of being syncopated; also, that which is syncopated. 2 *Music* The suppression of an expected rhythmic accent by the continuation of an unaccented tone that begins just before it. 3 Any music featuring syncopation, as ragtime, jazz, etc. 4 Syncope of a word, or an example of it.

syn·co·pe (sing′kə-pē, sin′-) *n.* 1 The elision of a sound or syllable in the middle part of a word, as *e'er* for *ever.* 2 *Music* Syncopation. 3 Temporary loss of consciousness; fainting. [< Gk. *syn-* together + *koptein* to cut] —**syn′co·pal, syn·cop·ic** (sin-kop′ik) *adj.*

syn·cre·tize (sin′krə-tīz, sing′-) *v.t.* **·tized, ·tiz·ing** To attempt to blend and reconcile. [< Gk. *synkrētizein* combine] —**syn′cre·tism** *n.*

syn·dic (sin′dik) *n.* 1 The business agent of a university or other corporation. 2 A government official, as a civil magistrate, with varying powers in different countries. [< Gk. *syn-* together + *dikē* judgment] —**syn′di·cal** *adj.*

syn·di·cal·ism (sin′di-kəl-iz′əm) *n.* A social and political theory proposing the taking over of the means of production by federations of labor unions through the staging of general strikes, etc. [< F *(chambre) syndicale* a labor union] —**syn′di·cal·ist** *n.* —**syn′di·cal·is′tic** *adj.*

syn·di·cate (sin′də-kit) *n.* 1 An association of individuals united to negotiate some business or to engage in some enterprise, often one requiring large capital. 2 An association for purchasing feature articles, etc., and selling them again to a number of periodicals, as newspapers, for simultaneous publication. 3 The office or jurisdiction of a syndic; also, a body of syndics. —*v.t.* (-kāt) **·cat·ed, ·cat·ing** 1 To combine into or manage by a syndicate. 2 To sell for publication in many newspapers or magazines. [< F *syndic* syndic] —**syn′di·ca′tion, syn′di·ca′tor** *n.*

syn·drome (sin′drōm) *n.* 1 The aggregate of symptoms and signs characteristic of a specific disease or condition. 2 A group of traits regarded as being characteristic of a certain type, condition, etc. [< Gk. *syn-* together + *dramein* run] —**syn·drom·ic** (sin-drom′ik) *adj.*

sy·nec·do·che (si-nek′də-kē) *n.* A figure of speech in which a part stands for a whole or a whole for a part, a material for the thing made of it, etc., as *bronze* for a *statue.* [< Gk. *syn-* together + *ekdechesthai* take from]

syn·er·gism (sin′ər-jiz′əm) *n.* The mutually reinforcing action of separate substances, organs, agents, etc., which together produce an effect greater than that of all of the components acting separately. Also **syn′er·gy.** [< Gk. *synergos* working together] —**syn′er·gis′tic** or **·ti·cal** *adj.*

syn·fu·el (sin′fyōō′əl) *n.* Synthetic fuel.

syn·od (sin′əd, -od) *n.* 1 An ecclesiastical council. 2 Any assembly, council, etc. [< Gk. < *syn-* together + *hodos* a way]

sy·nod·i·cal (si-nod′i-kəl) *adj.* 1 Of, pertaining to, or of the nature of a synod; transacted in a synod. 2 *Astron.* Pertaining to the conjunction of two celestial bodies or to the interval between two successive conjunctions of the same celestial bodies. Also **syn·od·al** (sin′ə-dəl, si-nod′əl), **sy·nod′ic.** —**sy·nod′i·cal·ly** *adv.*

syn·o·nym (sin′ə-nim) *n.* 1 A word having the same or almost the same meaning as some other or others in the same language. 2 A word used in metonymy to substitute for another. [< Gk. *syn-* together + *onyma* a name] — **syn′o·nym′ic, syn′o·nym′i·cal** *adj.* —**syn′o·nym′i·ty** *n.*

sy·non·y·mous (si-non′ə-məs) *adj.* Being equivalent or similar to meaning. —**sy·non′y·mous·ly** *adv.*

sy·non·y·my (si-non′ə-mē) *n. pl.* **·mies** 1 The quality of being synonymous. 2 The study of synonyms. 3 The discrimination of synonyms. 2 A list or collection discriminating the meanings of synonyms or of allied terms.

sy·nop·sis (si-nop′sis) *n. pl.* **·ses** (-sēz) A general view or condensation, as of a story, book, etc.; summary. [< Gk. *syn-* together + *opsis* a view] —**Syn.** abridgment, abstract, digest, précis.

sy·nop·tic (si-nop′tik) *adj.* 1 Giving a general view. 2 Presenting the same or a similar point of view: said of the first three Gospels (**Synoptic Gospels**). Also **sy·nop′ti·cal.** — **sy·nop′ti·cal·ly** *adv.*

sy·no·vi·a (si-nō′vē-ə) *n.* The viscid, transparent, lubricating fluid secreted by a membrane in the interior of joints. [< Gk. *syn-* together + L *ovum* an egg] —**sy·no′vi·al** *adj.*

syn·tax (sin′taks) *n.* 1 The arrangement and interrelationship of words in grammatical constructions. 2 The branch of grammar which deals with this. [< Gk. *syn-* together + *tassein* arrange] —**syn·tac·tic** (sin·tak′tik), **syn·tac′ti·cal** *adj.* —**syn·tac′ti·cal·ly** *adv.*

syn·the·sis (sin′thə·sis) *n. pl.* **·ses** (-sēz) 1 The assembling of separate or subordinate parts into a new form. 2 The complex whole resulting from this. 3 *Chem.* The building up of a compound by the direct union of its elements or of simpler compounds. [< Gk. *syn-* together + *tithenai* to place] —**syn′the·sist** *n.*

syn·the·size (sin′thə·sīz) *v.t.* **·sized**, **·siz·ing** 1 To unite or produce by synthesis. 2 To apply synthesis to. *Brit. sp.* **syn′the·sise**.

syn·the·siz·er (sin′thə·sīz′ər) *n.* Any of various complex electronic devices by which a musician can create and manipulate a wide variety of tones.

syn·thet·ic (sin·thet′ik) *adj.* 1 Of, pertaining to, or using synthesis. 2 Produced artificially by chemical synthesis. 3 Artificial; spurious. Also **syn·thet′i·cal.** —*n.* Anything produced by synthesis, esp. by chemical synthesis, as a material. [< Gk. *syn-* together + *tithenai* to place] —**syn·thet′i·cal·ly** *adv.*

syph·i·lis (sif′ə·lis) *n.* An infectious, chronic, venereal disease caused by a spirochete transmissible by direct contact or congenitally. [< *Syphilus*, a shepherd in a 16th-century Latin poem who had the disease] —**syph·i·lit·ic** (sif′ə·lit′ik) *adj., n.*

syphon (sī′fən) *n. & v.* SIPHON.

Syr. Syria; Syriac; Syrian.

syr. syrup (pharmacy).

Syr·i·a (sir′ē·ə) *n.* A republic of sw Asia, 72,234 sq. mi., cap. Damascus. • See map at JORDAN.

Syr·i·ac (sir′ē·ak) *n.* The language of the ancient Syrians, a dialect of Aramaic.

Syr·i·an (sir′ē·ən) *adj.* Of or pertaining to Syria, its people, or their language. —*n.* 1 A citizen or native of Syria. 2 The Arabic dialect spoken in modern Syria.

sy·rin·ga (si·ring′gə) *n.* 1 LILAC (defs. 1 and 2) 2 MOCK ORANGE. [< Gk. *syrinx* a pipe]

syr·inge (si·rinj′, sir′inj) *n.* 1 An instrument used to remove fluids from or inject fluids into body cavities. 2 HYPODERMIC SYRINGE. —*v.t.* **·inged**, **·ing·ing** To spray, cleanse, inject, etc. with a syringe. [< Gk. *syrinx* a pipe]

syr·inx (sir′ingks) *n. pl.* **sy·rin·ges** (sə·rin′jēz), **syr·inx·es** 1 A modification of the windpipe in songbirds serving as the vocal organ. 2 *pl.* PANPIPES. [Gk., a pipe] —**sy·rin·ge·al** (si·rin′jē·əl) *adj.*

syr·up (sir′əp) *n.* A thick, sweet liquid, as the boiled juice of fruits, sugar cane, etc. [< OF sirop < Turkish *sharbat* sherbet] —**syr′up·y** *adj.*

syst. system; systematic.

sys·tem (sis′təm) *n.* 1 A group or arrangement of parts, facts, phenomena, etc., that relate to or interact with each other in such a way as to form a whole: the solar *system;* the nervous *system.* 2 Any orderly group of logically related facts, principles, beliefs, etc.: the democratic *system.* 3 An orderly method, plan, or procedure: a betting *system* that really works. 4 A method of classification, organization, arrangement, etc.: books classified according to the Dewey decimal *system.* 5 The body, considered as a functional whole. —**the system** The dominant political, economic, and social institutions and their leaders, regarded as resistant to change or to effective influence. [< Gk. *systēma* an organized whole]

sys·tem·at·ic (sis′tə·mat′ik) *adj.* 1 Of, pertaining to, or characterized by system or classification. 2 Acting by or carried out with system or method; methodical. 3 Forming or based on a system. Also **sys′tem·at′i·cal.** —**sys′tem·at′i·cal·ly** *adv.* —**Syn.** 2 orderly, organized, procedural, routine. 3 organizational, bureaucratic.

sys·tem·a·tize (sis′tə·mə·tīz′) *v.t.* **·tized**, **·tiz·ing** To make into a system; organize methodically. Also **sys′tem·ize.** *Brit. sp.* **sys′tem·a·tise′.** —**sys′tem·a·ti·za′tion, sys′tem·i·za′·tion** *n.* —**sys′tem·a·tiz′er, sys′tem·iz′er** *n.*

sys·tem·ic (sis·tem′ik) *adj.* 1 Of or pertaining to a system; systematic. 2 Pertaining to or affecting the body as a whole: a *systemic* poison. —**sys·tem′i·cal·ly** *adv.*

systems analysis The technique of reducing complex processes, as of industry, government, research, etc., to basic operations that can be treated quantitatively and reordered into sequences amenable to control.

sys·to·le (sis′tə·lē) *n.* 1 The rhythmic contraction of the heart, esp. of the ventricles, that impels the blood outward. 2 The shortening of a syllable that is naturally or by position long. [< Gk. *syn-* together + *stellein* send] —**sys·tol·ic** (sis·tol′ik) *adj.*

T

T, t (tē) *n. pl.* **T's, t's** or **Ts, ts, tees** (tēz) 1 The 20th letter of the English alphabet. 2 Any spoken sound representing the letter *T* or *t.* 3 Something shaped like a T. —**to a T** Precisely; perfectly. —*adj.* Shaped like a T.

't Contraction of IT: used initially, as in *'tis,* and finally, as in *on't.*

-t Inflectional ending used to indicate past participles and past tenses, as in *bereft, lost, spent:* equivalent to *-ed.*

T Technician; temperature (absolute); tension (surface); time (of firing or launching).

T. tablespoon (s); Testament; Tuesday.

t. in the time of (L *tempore*); teaspoon(s); time; ton(s); transitive; troy.

Ta tantalum.

tab¹ (tab) *n.* A flap, strip, tongue, or projection of something, as a garment, file card, etc. —*v.t.* **tabbed, tab·bing** To provide with a tab or tabs. [?]

tab² (tab) *n. Informal* 1 A check or bill; also, the total cost of something. 2 Close watch: to keep *tabs* on someone's activities. [? Short for TABULATION]

tab. table(s); tablet(s).

tab·ard (tab′ərd) *n.* 1 Formerly, a short, sleeveless or short-sleeved outer garment. 2 A

knight's cape or cloak, worn over his armor and emblazoned with his own arms. 3 A similar garment worn by a herald and embroidered with his lord's arms. [< OF]

Ta·bas·co (tə·bas′kō) *n.* A pungent sauce made from capsicum: a trade name.

tab·by (tab′ē) *n. pl.* **·bies** 1 A silk taffeta, esp. one that is striped or watered. 2 A brown or gray domestic cat with dark stripes. 3 Any domestic cat, esp. a female. 4 A gossiping woman. —*adj.* 1 Of, pertaining to, or made of tabby. 2 Brindled. [< *Attabi,* a quarter of Baghdad where it was manufactured]

tab·er·nac·le (tab′ər·nak′əl) *n.* 1 A tent or similar temporary structure. 2 *Usu. cap.* In the Old Testament, the portable sanctuary used by the Israelites in the wilderness. 3 *Usu. cap.* The Jewish temple. 4 Any house of worship, esp. one of large size. 5 The human body as the dwelling place of the soul. 6 The ornamental receptacle for the consecrated eucharistic elements. [< L *taberna* shed] —**tab·er·nac·u·lar** (tab′ər·nak′yə·lər) *adj.*

ta·ble (tā′bəl) *n.* 1 An article of furniture with a flat top, usu. fixed on legs. 2 Such a table on which food is set for a meal. 3 The food served at a meal. 4 The persons present at a meal. 5 A gaming table, as for roulette. 6 A collection of related numbers, values, signs, or items of any kind, arranged for ease of reference or comparison, often in parallel columns. 7 A compact listing: *table* of contents. 8 A tableland; plateau. 9 Any flat horizontal rock, surface,

Tabard *def. 3*

tableau　　　　　　　749　　　　　　　**tag**

etc. **10** A tablet or slab bearing an inscription. —**the Ta-bles** Laws inscribed on tablets, as the Ten Commandments. —**turn the tables** To reverse a situation. —*v.t.* **·bled, ·bling 1** To place on a table. **2** To postpone discussion of (a resolution, bill, etc.). [< L *tabula* board]

tab·leau (tab′lō, ta·blō′) *n. pl.* **·leaux** (-lōz) or **·leaus** (-lōz) **1** Any picture or picturesque representation. **2** A scene reminiscent of a picture, usu. presented by persons motionless on a stage. [F, lit., small table]

ta·ble·cloth (tā′bəl·klôth′, -kloth′) *n.* A cloth covering for a table.

tab·le d'hôte (tab′əl dōt′, tä′bəl) *pl.* **tab·les d'hote** (tab′-əlz dōt′, tä′bəlz) A complete meal of several specified courses, served in a restaurant at a fixed price. [F, lit., table of the host]

ta·ble·land (tā′bəl·land′) *n.* A broad, level, elevated region; a plateau.

ta·ble·spoon (tā′bəl·spoon′, -spoon′) *n.* **1** A measuring spoon with three times the capacity of a teaspoon. **2** A tablespoonful.

ta·ble·spoon·ful (tā′bəl·spoon·fool′, -spoon-) *n. pl.* **·fuls** The amount a tablespoon will hold; ½ fluid ounce.

tab·let (tab′lit) *n.* **1** A small, flat or nearly flat piece of some prepared substance, as a drug. **2** A pad, as of writing paper or note paper. **3** A small flat surface designed for or containing an inscription or design. **4** A thin leaf or sheet of ivory, wood, etc., for writing, painting, or drawing. **5** A set of such leaves joined together at one end. [< OF *tablete*, lit., small table]

table tennis A game resembling tennis in miniature, played indoors with a small celluloid ball and wooden paddles on a large table.

ta·ble·ware (tā′bəl·wâr′) *n.* Dishes, knives, forks, spoons, etc., used to set a table.

tab·loid (tab′loid) *n.* A newspaper, usu. one half the size of an ordinary newspaper, in which the news is presented concisely, often sensationally, and with many pictures. —*adj.* Compact; concise. [< TABL(ET) + -OID]

ta·boo (tə·boo′, ta-) *n. pl.* **·boos 1** A religious or social prohibition against touching or mentioning someone or something or doing something because such persons or things are considered sacred, dangerous, etc. **2** The practice of such prohibitions. **3** Any restriction or ban based on custom or convention. —*adj.* Restricted, prohibited, or excluded by taboo, custom, or convention. —*v.t.* **1** To place under taboo. **2** To avoid as taboo. Also **ta·bu′.** [< Tongan]

ta·bor (tā′bər) *n.* A small drum on which a fife player beats his own accompaniment. Also **ta′bour.** [< Pers. *tabī-rah* drum]

tab·o·ret (tab′ə·ret′, -rā′) *n.* **1** A small tabor. **2** A stool or small seat, usu. without arms or back. **3** A small table or stand. **4** An embroidery frame. Also **tab′ou·ret.**

tab·u·lar (tab′yə·lər) *adj.* **1** Of, pertaining to, or arranged in a table or list. **2** Computed from or with a mathematical table. **3** Having a flat surface. —**tab′u·lar·ly** *adv.*

tab·u·late (tab′yə·lāt) *v.t.* **·lat·ed, ·lat·ing** To arrange in a table or list. —*adj.* Having a flat surface or surfaces; broad and flat. —**tab′u·la′tion, tab′u·la′tor** *n.*

tac·a·ma·hac (tak′ə·mə·hak′) *n.* **1** A resinous substance with a strong odor, used in ointments and incense. **2** Any of the trees producing this substance. Also **tac′a·ma·hac′a** (-hak′ə), **tac′ma·hack′.** [< Nahuatl *tecomahca*]

ta·chom·e·ter (tə·kom′ə·tər) *n.* A device for indicating the speed of rotation of an engine, centrifuge, etc. [< Gk. *tachos* speed + -METER]

tach·y·car·di·a (tak′i·kär′dē·ə) *n.* Abnormal rapidity of the heartbeat. [< Gk. *tachys* swift + *kardia* heart]

tac·it (tas′it) *adj.* **1** Existing, inferred, or implied without being directly stated. **2** Not spoken; silent. **3** Emitting no sound. [< L *tacitus*, pp. of *tacere* be silent] —**tac′it·ly** *adv.*

tac·i·turn (tas′ə·tûrn) *adj.* Habitually silent or reserved. [< L *tacitus.* See TACIT.] —**tac·i·tur·ni·ty** (tas′ə·tûr′nə·tē) *n.* —**tac′i·turn·ly** *adv.* —**Syn.** uncommunicative, reticent.

tack (tak) *n.* **1** A small sharp-pointed nail, usu. with a relatively broad, flat head. **2** *Naut.* **a** A rope which holds down the lower outer corner of some sails. **b** The corner so held. **c** The direction in which a vessel sails when sailing closehauled, considered in relation to the position of its sails. **d** A change in a ship's direction made by a change in the position of its sails. **3** A policy or course of action. **4** A temporary fastening, as any of various stitches in sewing. —*v.t.* **1** To fasten or attach with tacks. **2** To secure temporarily, as with long stitches. **3** To attach as supplementary; append. **4** *Naut.* **a** To change the course of (a vessel) by turning into the wind. **b** To navigate (a vessel) to windward by making a series of tacks. —*v.i.* **5** *Naut.* **a** To tack a vessel. **b** To sail to windward by a series of tacks. **6** To change one's course of action. **7** ZIGZAG. [< OF *tache* a nail] —**tack′er** *n.*

tack·le (tak′əl) *n.* **1** A rope and pulley or combination of ropes and pulleys, used for hoisting or moving objects. **2** The rigging of a ship. **3** The equipment used in any work or sport; gear. **4** The act of tackling. **5** In football, either of two linemen stationed between the guard and end. —*v.t.* **·led, ·ling 1** To fasten with or as if with tackle. **2** To harness (a horse). **3** To undertake to master, accomplish, or solve: *tackle* a problem. **4** To seize suddenly and forcefully. **5** In football, to seize and stop (an opponent carrying the ball). [< MLG *taken* seize] —**tack′ler** *n.*

Tackles

tack·y¹ (tak′ē) *adj.* **tack·i·er, tack·i·est** Slightly sticky, as partly dried varnish. [< TACK, *v.*]

tack·y² (tak′ē) *adj.* **tack·i·er, tack·i·est 1** *Informal* Unfashionable; in bad taste. **2** Without good breeding; common. [?]

ta·co (tä′kō) *n. pl.* **·cos** A fried tortilla folded around any of several fillings, as chopped meat or cheese. [< Sp., wad]

tact (takt) *n.* **1** A quick or intuitive appreciation of what is fit, proper, or right; facility in saying or doing the proper thing. **2** A delicate sense of discrimination, esp. in aesthetics. [< L *tactus* sense of touch, pp. of *tangere* touch]

tact·ful (takt′fəl) *adj.* Having or showing tact. —**tact′ful·ly** *adv.* —**tact′ful·ness** *n.*

tac·ti·cal (tak′ti·kəl) *adj.* **1** Of or pertaining to tactics. **2** Showing adroitness in planning and maneuvering. —**tac′ti·cal·ly** *adv.*

tac·ti·cian (tak·tish′ən) *n.* An expert in tactics.

tac·tics (tak′tiks) *n.pl.* **1** *(construed as sing.)* The science and art of handling troops in securing military and naval objectives. **2** Any adroit maneuvering to gain an end. [< Gk. *taktikos* suitable for arranging]

tac·tile (tak′təl, -tīl) *adj.* **1** Of, pertaining to, or having the sense of touch. **2** That may be touched; tangible. [< L *tactus.* See TACT.] —**tac·til·i·ty** (tak·til′ə·tē) *n.*

tact·less (takt′lis) *adj.* Showing or characterized by a lack of tact. —**tact′less·ly** *adv.* —**tact′less·ness** *n.*

tad·pole (tad′pōl) *n.* The aquatic larva of an amphibian, as a frog or toad, having gills and a tail. [< ME *tadde* toad + *pol* head, poll]

tael (tāl) *n.* **1** Any of several units of weight of E Asia. **2** A Chinese monetary unit. [< Pg. < Malay *tahil*]

taf·fe·ta (taf′ə·tə) *n.* A fine, glossy, somewhat stiff fabric woven of silk, rayon, nylon, etc. —*adj.* Made of or resembling taffeta. [< Pers. *tāftah*]

Development of a tadpole

taff·rail (taf′rāl′) *n.* The rail around a vessel's stern. [< MDu. *tafereel* panel, lit., small table]

taf·fy (taf′ē) *n. pl.* **taf·fies 1** A chewy confection made usu. of brown sugar or molasses, boiled down, and pulled until it cools. **2** *Informal* Flattery; blarney. [?]

tag¹ (tag) *n.* **1** Something attached to something else, to identify, price, classify, etc.; a label. **2** A loose, ragged edge, esp. of a piece of cloth. **3** The metal sheath at the end of a lace, cord etc. **4** The final lines of a speech, song, or poem. —*v.* **tagged, tag·ging** *v.t.* **1** To supply, adorn, fit, mark, or label with a tag. 2 *Informal* To follow closely or persistently. —*v.i.* 3 *Informal* To follow closely at one's heels: with *along, behind,* etc. [? < Scand.]

tag² (tag) *n.* A children's game in which a player, called "it," chases other players until he touches one of them, that person in turn becoming the one who must pursue another. —*v.t.* **tagged, tag·ging** To overtake and touch, as in the game of tag. [?]

Ta·ga·log (tə·gäl′əg, -gä′lôg) *n.* 1 A member of a people native to the Philippines. 2 The Austronesian language of this people, the official language of the Philippines.

tail¹ (tāl) *n.* 1 The rear end of an animal's body, esp. when prolonged to form a flexible appendage. 2 Anything similar in appearance, as a pigtail. 3 *Astron.* The luminous cloud extending from a comet. 4 The hind, back, or inferior portion of anything. 5 *Often pl. Informal* The reverse side of a coin. 6 A body of persons in single file. 7 A group of attendants; retinue. 8 *Aeron.* A system of airfoils placed some distance to the rear of the main bearing surfaces of an airplane. 9 *pl. Informal* A man's full-dress suit; also, a swallow-tailed coat. 10 *Informal* A person, as a detective, who follows another in surveillance. 11 *Informal* A trail or course, as one taken by a fugitive. —*v.t.* 1 To furnish with a tail. 2 To cut off the tail of. 3 To be the tail or end of. 4 To join (one thing) to the end of another. 5 To insert and fasten by one end. 6 *Informal* To follow secretly and stealthily; shadow. —*v.i.* 7 To form or be part of a tail. 8 *Informal* To follow close behind. 9 To diminish gradually: with *off.* —*adj.* 1 Rearmost; hindmost: the *tail* end. 2 Coming from behind: a *tail* wind. [< OE *tægl*]

tail² (tāl) *Law adj.* Restricted in some way, as to particular heirs: an estate *tail.* —*n.* A limiting of the inheritance of an estate, as to particular heirs. [< OF *taillié,* p.p. of *taillier* to cut]

tail·gate (tāl′gāt′) *n.* A hinged or removable board or gate closing the back end of a truck, wagon, etc. Also **tail·board** (tāl′bôrd′, -bōrd′). —*v.t. & v.i.* **·gat·ed, ·gat·ing** To drive too close for safety behind (another vehicle).

tail·light (tāl′līt′) *n.* A warning light, usu. red, attached to the rear of a vehicle. Also **tail lamp.**

tai·lor (tā′lər) *n.* One who makes or repairs garments. —*v.i.* 1 To do a tailor's work. —*v.t.* 2 To fit with garments. 3 To make, work at, or style by tailoring. 4 To form or adapt to meet certain needs or conditions. [< LL *taliare* split, cut] —**tai′lor·ing** *n.*

tai·lor·bird (tā′lər·bûrd′) *n.* Any of various small birds of Asia and Africa that stitch leaves together so as to conceal the nest. • See NEST.

tai·lor-made (tā′lər·mād′) *adj.* 1 Made by or looking as if made by a tailor. 2 Right or suitable for a particular person, specific conditions, etc.

tail·piece (tāl′pēs′) *n.* 1 Any endpiece or appendage. 2 In a violin or similar instrument, a piece of wood at the sounding-board end, having the strings fastened to it. 3 *Printing* An ornamental design at the end of a chapter or the bottom of a short page. 4 A short beam or rafter tailed into a wall.

tail·spin (tāl′spin′) *n.* 1 *Aeron.* The uncontrolled descent of an airplane along a helical path at a steep angle. 2 *Informal* A sudden, sharp, mental or emotional upheaval.

tail wind A wind blowing in the same direction as the course of an aircraft or ship.

taint (tānt) *v.t.* 1 To affect with decay or contamination. 2 To render morally corrupt. —*v.i.* 3 To be or become tainted. —*n.* A cause or result of contamination or corruption. [< OF *teint,* pp. of *teindre* to tinge, color]

take (tāk) *v.* **took, tak·en, tak·ing** *v.t.* 1 To lay hold of; grasp. 2 To get possession of; seize; capture; catch. 3 To gain, capture, or win, as in a game or in competition. 4 To choose; select. 5 To buy. 6 To rent or hire; lease. 7 To subscribe to, as a periodical. 8 To assume occupancy of: to *take* a chair. 9 To assume the responsibilities of: to *take* office. 10 To accept into some relation to oneself: He *took* a wife. 11 To assume as a symbol or badge: to *take* the veil. 12 To subject oneself to: to *take* a vow. 13 To remove or carry off: with *away.* 14 To steal. 15 To remove by death. 16 To subtract or deduct. 17 To be subjected to; undergo: to *take* a beating. 18 To submit to; accept passively: to *take* an insult. 19 To become affected with; contract: He *took*

cold. 20 To affect: The fever *took* him at dawn. 21 To captivate; charm or delight: The dress *took* her fancy. 22 To react to: How did she *take* the news? 23 To undertake to deal with; contend with; handle: to *take* an examination. 24 To consider; deem: I *take* him for an honest man. 25 To understand; comprehend: I couldn't *take* the meaning of her remarks. 26 To hit: The blow *took* him on the forehead. 27 *Informal* To aim or direct: He *took* a shot at the target. 28 To carry with one: *Take* your umbrella! 29 To lead: This road *takes* you to town. 30 To escort. 31 To receive into the body, as by eating, inhaling, etc.: *Take* a deep breath. 32 To accept or assume as if due or granted: to *take* credit. 33 To require: it *takes* courage. 34 To let in; admit; accommodate: The car *takes* only six people. 35 To occupy oneself in; enjoy: to *take* a nap. 36 To perform, as an action: to *take* a stride. 37 To confront and get over: The horse *took* the hurdle. 38 To avail oneself of (an opportunity, etc.). 39 To put into effect; adopt: to *take* measures. 40 To use up or consume: The piano *takes* too much space. 41 To make use of; apply: to *take* pains. 42 To travel by means of: to *take* a train. 43 To seek: to *take* cover. 44 To ascertain by measuring, computing, etc.: to *take* a census. 45 To obtain or derive from some source. 46 To write down or copy: to *take* notes. 47 To obtain (a likeness or representation of) by photographing. 48 To conceive or feel: She *took* a dislike to him. 49 *Slang* To cheat; deceive. 50 *Gram.* To require by construction or usage: The verb *takes* a direct object. —*v.i.* 51 To get possession. 52 To engage; catch, as mechanical parts. 53 To begin to grow; germinate. 54 To have the intended effect: The vaccination *took.* 55 To gain favor, as a play. 56 To detract: with *from.* 57 To become (ill or sick). —**take after** 1 To resemble. 2 To follow in pursuit. —**take amiss** To be offended by. —**take back** To retract. —**take down** 1 To humble. 2 To write down. —**take for** To consider to be. —**take in** 1 To admit; receive. 2 To lessen in size or scope. 3 To include; embrace. 4 To understand. 5 To cheat or deceive. 6 To visit. —**take it** To endure hardship, abuse, etc. —**take off** 1 To mimic; burlesque. 2 To rise from a surface, esp. to begin a flight, as an airplane or rocket. 3 To leave; depart. 4 To begin: often used to refer to that point in an economic venture when growth becomes a self-generating and self-sustaining process. —**take on** 1 To hire; employ. 2 To undertake to deal with. 3 *Informal* To exhibit violent emotion. —**take over** To assume control of (a business, nation, etc.) —**take place** To happen. —**take to** 1 To become fond of. 2 *Informal* To adopt a way of doing, using, etc.: He has *taken* to walking to work. 3 To flee: to *take to* the hills. —**take up** 1 To make smaller or less; shorten or tighten. 2 To pay, as a note or mortgage. 3 To accept as stipulated: to *take up* an option. 4 To begin or begin again. 5 To occupy, engage, or consume, as space or time. 6 To develop an interest in or devotion to: to *take up* a cause. —**take up with** *Informal* To become friendly with; associate with. —*n.* 1 The act of taking or that which is taken. 2 *Slang* An amount of money received; receipts; profit. 3 A quantity collected at one time: the *take* of fish. 4 An uninterrupted run of the camera in photographing a movie or television scene. 5 A scene so photographed. 6 The process of making a sound recording. 7 A recording made in a single recording session. [< OE *tacan* < ON *taka*] —**tak′er** *n.* • See BRING.

take-home pay (tāk′hōm′) Net wages after tax and other deductions.

take·off (tāk′ôf′, -of′) *n.* 1 *Informal.* A satirical representation; caricature. 2 The act of taking off, as in flight. 3 The place from which one takes off. 4 A point at which something begins.

take·o·ver (tāk′ō′vər) *n.* The act or an instance of taking over, esp. the assumption of power in a business, nation, etc.

tak·ing (tā′king) *adj.* Fascinating; captivating. —*n.* 1 The act of one who takes. 2 The thing or things taken; catch. 3 *pl.* Receipts, as of money. —**tak′ing·ly** *adv.* —**tak′ing·ness** *n.*

talc (talk) *n.* A soft mineral magnesium silicate, used in making talcum powder, lubricants, etc. —*v.t.* **talcked** or **talced, talck·ing** or **talc·ing** To treat with talc. [< Ar. *talq*]

tal·cum (tal′kəm) *n.* TALC.

talcum powder Finely powdered, purified, and usu. perfumed talc, used as a face and body powder.

tale (tāl) *n.* 1 A story that is told or written; a narrative of real or fictitious events. 2 An idle or malicious piece of gossip. 3 A lie. 4 *Archaic* A tally or amount; total. [< OE *talu* speech, narrative]

tale·bear·er (tāl'bâr'ər) *n.* One who gossips, spreads rumors, tells secrets, etc. —**tale'bear'ing** *adj., n.* —Syn. gossip, scandalmonger, newsmonger.

tal·ent (tal'ənt) *n.* 1 *pl.* A person's natural abilities. 2 A particular aptitude for some special work, artistic endeavor, etc. 3 A person, or people collectively with skill or ability. 4 Any of various ancient weights and denominations of money, used in ancient Greece, Rome, and the Middle East. [< L *talentum*, a sum of money] —**tal'ent·ed** *adj.*

ta·ler (tä'lər) *n.* A former German silver coin. [< G *Taler*]

tales·man (tālz'mən) *n. pl.* ·men (-mən) One summoned to fill a vacancy in a jury when the regular panel has become deficient in number. [< ML *tales (de circumstantibus)* such (of the bystanders) + MAN]

tale·tel·ler (tāl'tel'ər) *n.* 1 RACONTEUR. 2 TALEBEARER. — **tale'tell'ing** *adj., n.*

ta·li (tā'lī) *n.pl.* of TALUS[1].

tal·i·pes (tal'ə·pēz) *n.* Congenital deformity of one or both feet. [< L *talus* ankle + *pes* foot]

tal·i·pot (tal'ə·pot) *n.* An East Indian palm crowned by large leaves often used as fans, umbrellas, etc. Also **talipot palm.** [< Skt. *tālī* fan palm + *pattra* leaf]

tal·is·man (tal'is·mən, -iz-) *n. pl.* ·mans 1 An object, as a ring or amulet, supposed to ward off evil, bring good luck, etc. 2 Anything supposed to have a magical effect. [< LGk. *telesma* a sacred rite] —**tal'is·man'ic** (·man'ik) *adj.*

talk (tôk) *v.i.* 1 To express or exchange thoughts in audible words; speak or converse. 2 To communicate by means other than speech: to *talk* with one's fingers. 3 To chatter. 4 To confer; consult. 5 To gossip. 6 To make sounds suggestive of speech. 7 *Informal* To give information; inform. — *v.t.* 8 To express in words; utter. 9 To converse in: to *talk* Spanish. 10 To discuss: to *talk* business. 11 To bring to a specified condition or state by talking: to *talk* one into doing something. —**talk back** To answer impudently. — **talk down** To silence by talking. —**talk down to** To speak to patronizingly. —**talk shop** To talk about one's work. —*n.* 1 The act of talking; conversation; speech. 2 A speech, either formal or informal. 3 Report; rumor: *talk* of war. 4 A subject of conversation. 5 A conference or discussion. 6 Mere words; empty conversation, discussion, etc. 7 A special kind of speech; lingo: baseball *talk*. 8 Sounds suggestive of speech, as made by a bird or animal. [Prob. < OE *talian* reckon, tell]

talk·a·thon (tô'kə·thon') *n. Informal* A prolonged session of talking, debating, etc. [< TALK + (MAR)ATHON]

talk·a·tive (tô'kə·tiv) *adj.* Given to or fond of much talking. —**talk'a·tive·ly** *adv.* —**talk'a·tive·ness** *n.* —Syn. garrulous, loquacious, voluble, windy.

talk·ie (tô'kē) *n.* Formerly, a motion picture with a sound track, as distinguished from a silent film.

talk·ing-to (tô'king·tōō') *n. pl.* ·tos *Informal* A scolding.

tall (tôl) *adj.* 1 Having more than average height; high. 2 Having a specified height: five feet *tall*. 3 *Informal* Extravagant; boastful; exaggerated: a *tall* story. 4 Large; extensive: a *tall* order. —*adv. Informal* Proudly: to walk *tall*. [< OE *getæl* swift, prompt] —**tall'ish** *adj.* —**tall'ness** *n.*

tal·lith (tal'ith, tä'lis) *n. pl.* **tal·li·thim** (tal'ə·sēm', -thēm) A fringed shawl worn by Jewish men during morning prayer. [< Heb. *tallith* cover]

tal·low (tal'ō) *n.* Solid, rendered animal fats, as of beef or mutton, refined for making candles, soaps, etc. —*v.t.* To smear with tallow. [< MLG *talg, talch*] —**tal'low·y** *adj.*

tal·ly (tal'ē) *n. pl.* ·lies 1 A piece of wood on which notches or scores are cut as marks of number. 2 A score or mark. 3 A reckoning; account. 4 A counterpart; duplicate. 5 A mark indicative of number. 6 A label; tag. —*v.* ·lied, ·ly·ing *v.t.* 1 To score on a tally; mark. 2 To reckon; count: often with *up*. 3 To register, as points in a game; score.

4 To cause to correspond. —*v.i.* 5 To make a tally. 6 To agree precisely: His story *tallies* with yours. 7 To keep score. 8 To score, as in a game. [< L *talea* rod, cutting] — **tal'li·er** *n.*

tal·ly·ho (tal'ə·hō') *interj.* A huntsman's cry to hounds when the quarry is sighted. —*n.pl.* ·hos 1 The cry of "tallyho." 2 A kind of coach drawn by four horses. —*v.t.* 1 To urge on, as hounds, with the cry of "tallyho." —*v.i.* 2 To cry "tallyho." [? < F *taïaut*, a hunting cry]

Tal·mud (tal'mud, täl'mŏŏd) *n.* The written body of Jewish civil and religious law. [< Heb. *talmūdh* instruction] —**Tal·mud'ic** or ·i·cal *adj.* —**Tal'mud·ist** *n.*

tal·on (tal'ən) *n.* 1 The claw of a bird or other animal, esp. a bird of prey. 2 A human finger or hand thought of as resembling a claw. [< L *talus* heel] —**tal'oned** *adj.*

ta·lus[1] (tā'ləs) *n. pl.* ·li (-lī) or ·lus·es 1 The upper, pivotal bone of the ankle. 2 The entire ankle. [L, ankle]

ta·lus[2] (tā'ləs, tal'əs) *n.* 1 A slope, as of a tapering wall. 2 *Geol.* The sloping mass of rock fragments at the foot of a cliff. 3 The slope given to the face of a wall, as in a fortification. [F < L *talutium* slope bearing signs of the presence of gold]

tam (tam) *n.* TAM-O'-SHANTER.

ta·ma·le (tə·mä'lē) *n.* A Mexican dish made of ground meat seasoned with red pepper, rolled in cornmeal, wrapped in corn husks, and steamed. [< Naḥuatl *tamalli*]

tam·a·rack (tam'ə·rak) *n.* 1 A species of larch common in N North America. 2 Its wood. [< Algon.]

tam·a·rind (tam'ə·rind) *n.* 1 A tropical tree of the bean family, with yellow flowers. 2 The edible fruit of this tree, a pod with acid pulp. [< Ar. *tamr hindi* Indian date]

tam·bour (tam'bŏŏr) *n.* 1 A drum. 2 A light wooden frame, usu. circular, esp. a set of two hoops between which fabric is stretched for embroidering. —*v.t. & v.i.* To embroider on a tambour. [< Ar. *tanbūr* drum]

tam·bou·rine (tam'bə·rēn') *n.* A musical instrument like the head of a drum, with metal disks in the rim, played by striking it with the hand. [F, lit., small tambour]

tame (tām) *adj.* **tam·er, tam·est** 1 Having lost its native wildness; domesticated. 2 Docile; tractable; subdued; submissive. 3 Lacking in spirit; uninteresting; dull. —*v.t.* **tamed, tam·ing** 1 To make tame; domesticate. 2 To bring into subjection or obedience. 3 To tone down; soften. [< OE *tam*] —**tam'a·ble** or **tame'a·ble** *adj.* —**tame'ly** *adv.* — **tame'ness, tam'er** *n.*

tame·less (tām'lis) *adj.* Untamable or not tamed.

Tam·il (tam'əl) *n.* 1 A member of a Dravidian people of S India and N Sri Lanka. 2 Their language.

Tam·ma·ny (tam'ə·nē) *n.* A fraternal society in New York City (founded 1789) serving as the central organization of the city's Democratic party, located in **Tammany Hall.** [< *Tamanend*, a 17th c. Delaware Indian chief]

tam-o'-shan·ter (tam'ə·shan'tər) *n.* A Scottish cap with a round flat top, sometimes with a center pompon. [< the hero of a poem by Robert Burns]

tamp (tamp) *v.t.* 1 To force down or pack closer by repeated blows. 2 In blasting, to pack matter around a charge in order to increase the explosive effect. [Back formation < TAMPION] —**tam'per** *n.*

tam·per (tam'pər) *v.i.* 1 To meddle; interfere: usu. with *with.* 2 To make changes, esp. so as to damage, falsify, etc.: with *with.* 3 To use secret or improper measures, as bribery. [Var. of TEMPER] —**tam'per·er** *n.*

tam·pi·on (tam'pē·ən) *n.* A plug or cover for the muzzle of a gun. [< OF *tapon, tape* a bung]

tam·pon (tam'pon) *n.* A plug of absorbent material for insertion in a body cavity or wound to stop bleeding or absorb secretions. —*v.t.* To plug up, as a wound, with a tampon. [< OF *tapon, tape* a bung]

tan (tan) *v.* **tanned, tan·ning** *v.t.* 1 To convert into leather, as hides or skins, by treating with tannin. 2 To darken, as the skin, by exposure to sunlight. 3 *Informal.* To thrash; flog. —*v.i.* 4 To become tanned. —*n.* 1 TANBARK. 2 TANNIN. 3 A yellowish brown color tinged with red. 4 A dark coloring of the skin, resulting from exposure to the sun. —*adj.*

1 Of the color tan. 2 Of, pertaining to, or used for tanning. [< Med. L *tanum* tanbark]

tan tangent.

tan·a·ger (tan'ə·jər) *n.* Any of a family of American songbirds related to finches and noted for the brilliant plumage of the male. [< Pg. *tangara* < Tupi] —**tan'a·grine** (-grēn) *adj.*

tan·bark (tan'bärk') *n.* 1 The bark of certain trees used as a source of tannin. 2 Shredded bark from which the tannin has been removed, used on circus rings, racetracks, etc.

tan·dem (tan'dəm) *adv.* One behind the other. —*n.* 1 A team, as of horses, harnessed one behind the other. 2 A two-wheeled carriage drawn in such a way. 3 A bicycle with two or more seats one behind the other. —*adj.* Having parts or things arranged one behind another. [L, at length (of time)]

Tandem bicycle

tang (tang) *n.* 1 A sharp, penetrating taste, flavor or odor. 2 Any distinctive quality or flavor. 3 A trace or hint. 4 A slender shank or tongue projecting from the end of a sword blade, chisel, etc., for fitting into a handle, hilt, etc. [< ON *tongi* a point] —**tang'y** *adj.* (·i·er, ·i·est)

tan·gent (tan'jənt) *adj.* 1 *Geom.* Coinciding at a point or along a line without intersection, as a curve and line, surface and plane, etc. 2 Touching; in contact. —*n.* 1 *Geom.* A line tangent to a curve at any point. 2 *Trig.* A function of an angle, equal to the quotient of its sine divided by its cosine. 3 A sharp change in course or direction. —**fly (or go) off on a tangent** *Informal* To make a sharp or sudden change, as in a course of action or train of thought. [< L *tangere* to touch] —**tan·gen·cy** (tan'jən·sē) *n.*

tan·gen·tial (tan·jen'shəl) *adj.* 1 Of, pertaining to, like, or in the direction of a tangent. 2 Touching slightly. 3 Divergent. —**tan·gen'ti·al'i·ty** (-shē·al'ə·tē) *n.* —**tan·gen'tial·ly** *adv.*

tan·ger·ine (tan'jə·rēn, tan'jə·rēn') *n.* 1 A variety of orange with a loose skin and easily separated segments. 2 A burnt orange color like that of the tangerine. [< *Tangier*, a city in Morocco]

tan·gi·ble (tan'jə·bəl) *adj.* 1 Perceptible by touch. 2 Not elusive or unreal; objective; concrete: *tangible* evidence. 3 Having value that can be appraised. —*n. pl.* Things having value that can be appraised. [< L *tangere* to touch] —**tan'gi·bil'i·ty, tan'gi·ble·ness** *n.* —**tan'gi·bly** *adv.*

tan·gle (tang'gəl) *v.* ·gled, ·gling *v.t.* 1 To twist in a confused and not readily separable mass. 2 To ensnare as in a tangle; trap; enmesh. 3 To involve in such a way as to confuse, obstruct, etc. —*v.i.* 4 To be or become entangled. —**tangle with** *Informal* To become involved or fight with. —*n.* 1 A confused intertwining, as of threads or hairs; a snarl. 2 State of confusion or complication. 3 A state of bewilderment. [Prob. < Scand.] —**tan'gler** *n.*

tan·go (tang'gō) *n. pl.* ·gos 1 A Latin American dance characterized by deliberate gliding steps and low dips. 2 The music for such a dance. —*v.i.* To dance the tango. [< Sp.]

tank (tangk) *n.* 1 A large vessel, basin, or receptacle for holding a fluid. 2 A natural or artificial pool or pond. 3 An armored combat vehicle that rides on treads and has mounted guns. 4 *Slang* A jail cell, esp. one for receiving prisoners. —*v.t.* To place or store in a tank. [? < Pg. *estanque*]

tank·age (tangk'ij) *n.* 1 The act or process of

storing in tanks. 2 The price for storage in tanks. 3 The capacity or contents of a tank. 4 Slaughterhouse waste from which the fat has been rendered in tanks, used, when dried, as fertilizer or feed.

tank·ard (tangk'ərd) *n.* A large, one-handled drinking cup, often with a cover. [ME]

tank·er (tangk'ər) *n.* 1 A cargo ship for the transport of oil or other liquids. 2 A cargo plane used to carry gasoline and to refuel other planes in flight.

tank farm An area where oil is stored in tanks.

tan·ner (tan'ər) *n.* One who tans hides.

tan·ner·y (tan'ər·ē) *n. pl.* ·ner·ies A place where leather is tanned.

tan·nic (tan'ik) *adj.* Of, pertaining to, or derived from tannin or tanbark.

tan·nin (tan'in) *n.* A yellowish, astringent substance extracted from tanbark, gallnut, etc., used in dyeing, tanning, etc. Also **tannic acid.** [< F *tanin* < *tanner* to tan]

tan·sy (tan'zē) *n. pl.* ·sies Any of a genus of coarse perennial herbs, esp. a species with yellow flowers and pungent foliage. [< Gk. *athanasia* immortality]

tan·ta·lize (tan'tə·līz') *v.t.* ·lized, ·liz·ing To tease or torment by promising or showing something desirable and then denying access to it. *Brit. sp.* ·lise'. [< TANTALUS] —**tan'ta·li·za'tion, tan'ta·liz'er** *n.* —**tan'ta·liz'ing·ly** *adv.*

tan·ta·lum (tan'tə·ləm) *n.* A hard, corrosion-resistant metallic element (symbol Ta). [< TANTALUS, from its inability to react with most acids]

Tan·ta·lus (tan'tə·ləs) *Gk. Myth.* A king who was punished in Hades by being made to stand in water that receded when he tried to drink and under fruit-laden branches he could not reach.

tan·ta·mount (tan'tə·mount) *adj.* Equivalent: with *to.* [< L *tantus* as much + OF *amonter* to amount]

tan·trum (tan'trəm) *n.* A violent fit of temper. [?]

Tan·za·ni·a (tan'zə·nē'ə) *n.* A republic of the Commonwealth of Nations in E Africa, 362,800 sq. mi., cap. Dar es Salaam. —**Tan'za·ni'an** *adj., n.* • See map at AFRICA.

Tao·ism (dou'iz·əm, tou'-) *n.* One of the principal religions or philosophies of China, founded in the sixth century B.C. by Lao-tse. [< Chin. *tao* way] —**Tao'ist** *adj., n.* —**Tao·is'tic** *adj.*

tap¹ (tap) *n.* 1 A spout through which liquid is drawn, as from a cask. 2 FAUCET. 3 A plug or stopper to close an opening, as in a cask. 4 Liquor drawn from a tap, esp. of a particular quality or brew. 5 A tool for cutting internal screw threads. 6 A point of connection for an electrical circuit. 7 The act or an instance of wiretapping. —**on tap** 1 Contained in a cask; ready for tapping: beer *on tap.* 2 *Informal* Available; ready. —*v.t.* **tapped, tap·ping** 1 To provide with a tap or spigot. 2 To pierce or open so as to draw liquid from. 3 To draw (liquid) from a container, body cavity, etc. 4 To make connection with: to *tap* a gas main. 5 To draw upon; utilize: to *tap* new sources of energy. 6 To make connection with secretly: to *tap* a telephone wire. 7 To make an internal screw thread in with a tap. [< OE *tæppa*]

tap² (tap) *v.* **tapped, tap·ping** *v.t.* 1 To touch or strike gently. 2 To strike gently with. 3 To make or produce by tapping. 4 To apply a tap to (a shoe) —*v.i.* 5 To strike a light blow or blows, as with the finger tip. 6 To walk with a light, tapping sound. 7 TAP-DANCE. —*n.* 1 The act or sound of striking gently. 2 Leather, metal, etc., affixed to a shoe sole or heel, for repair or tap-dancing. 3 *pl.* A military signal sounded on a trumpet or drum for the extinguishing of all lights in soldiers' quarters. [< OF *taper*]

ta·pa (tä'pä) *n.* 1 The inner bark of an Asian tree related to the mulberry. 2 A cloth made of this bark: also **tapa cloth.** [< native Polynesian name]

tap-dance (tap'dans', -däns') *v.i.* ·danced, ·danc·ing To dance a tap dance. —**tap'-danc'er** *n.*

tap dance A dance in which the dancer taps out a rhythm with the heels and toes of shoes.

tape (tāp) *n.* 1 A narrow strip of woven fabric. 2 Any long, narrow, flat strip of paper, metal, plastic, etc., as the magnetic strip used in a tape recorder. 3 TAPE MEASURE. 4 A string stretched across the finishing point of a racetrack and broken by the winner of the race. —*v.t.* **taped, tap·ing** 1 To wrap or secure with tape. 2 To measure with a tape measure. **3** To record on magnetic tape. [< OE *tæppe* strip of cloth] —**tap′er** *n.*

tape deck An assembly of magnetic head, tape reels, and drive for tape recording and playback.

tape measure A tape marked in inches, feet, etc., for measuring. Also **tape-line** (tāp′lĭn′) *n.*

ta-per (tā′pər) *n.* **1** A slender candle. **2** A long wax-coated wick used to light candles, lamps, etc. **3** A weak light. **4** A gradual diminution of size in an elongated object; also, any tapering object, as a cone. **5** Any gradual decrease. — *v.t. & v.i.* **1** To make or become smaller or thinner toward one end. **2** To lessen gradually: with *off.* —*adj.* Growing smaller toward one end. [< OE]

tape-re-cord (tāp′rĭ-kôrd′) *v.t.* TAPE (*v.*, def. 3).

tape recorder An electromagnetic apparatus which can record sound on magnetic tape and play it back.

tap-es-try (tap′is-trē) *n. pl.* **-tries 1** A heavy woven textile with a pictorial design, used for hangings, upholstery, etc. **2** Something like this, as in complexity of design. —*v.t.* **-tried, -try-ing 1** To hang or adorn with tapestry. **2** To depict or weave in a tapestry. [< Gk. *tapētion,* dim. of *tapēs* rug]

tape-worm (tāp′wûrm′) *n.* Any of various long flat-worms parasitic in the intestines of man and various animals.

tap-i-o-ca (tap′ē-ō′kə) *n.* A starchy, granular foodstuff obtained from cassava, used in puddings, as a thickener for soups, etc. [< Tupi *tipioca*]

ta-pir (tā′pər) *n.* Any of various hoofed, herbivorous mammals of tropical America and SE Asia, having short stout limbs and a flexible snout. [< Tupi *tapy′ra*]

tap-room (tap′rōōm′, -rōōm′) *n.* BARROOM.

tap-root (tap′rōōt′, -rōōt′) *n.* A type of plant root having one main descending part. —**tap′root′ed** *adj.*

tar¹ (tär) *n.* A dark, usu. pungent, viscid mixture of hydrocarbons obtained by the dry distillation of wood, coal, etc. —*v.t.* **tarred, tar-ring** To cover with or as with tar. —**tar and feather** To smear with tar and then cover with feathers as a punishment. —*adj.* Made of, derived from, or resembling tar. [< OE *teru*]

tar² (tär) *n. Informal* A sailor. [Short for TARPAULIN]

tar-an-tel-la (tar′ən-tel′ə) *n.* **1** A lively Neapolitan dance. **2** Music for this dance. [< *Taranto,* a port in SE Italy]

ta-ran-tu-la (tə-ran′chōō-lə, -tə-lə) *n. pl.* **-las** or **-lae** (-lē) **1** A large, hairy, venomous spider of s Europe. **2** Any of various large, hairy American spiders capable of inflicting a painful but not dangerous bite. [< *Taranto,* Italy]

Tarantula *def. 1*

tar-dy (tär′dē) *adj.* **-di-er, -di-est 1** Not coming, happening, etc., at the scheduled or proper time. **2** Moving, acting, etc., at a slow pace. [< L *tardus* slow] —**tar′di-ly** *adv.* —**tar′di-ness** *n.* —**Syn. 1** late, dilatory, overdue, delayed. **2** slow, sluggish, leisurely, torpid.

tare¹ (târ) *n.* **1** In the Bible, a weed that grows among wheat, supposed to be the darnel. **2** Any one of various species of vetch. [?]

tare² (târ) *n.* **1** The deduction of the weight of a container, used to calculate the weight of its contents if the gross weight of the container and contents is determined. **2** The weight of the container. —*v.t.* **tared, tar-ing** To weigh, as a vessel or package, in order to determine the tare. [< Ar. *tarhah*]

tar-get (tär′git) *n.* **1** An object presenting a usu. marked surface that is to be aimed and shot at, as in archery practice. **2** Anything that is shot at. **3** One who or that which is made an object of ridicule, criticism, etc.; butt. **4** A goal; objective. **5** A small round shield. —*v.t.* **1** To make a target of. **2** To establish as a goal. [< OF *targe* shield] —**tar′get-a-ble** *adj.*

tar-iff (tar′if) *n.* **1** A schedule of government-imposed duties to be paid for the importation or exportation of goods. **2** A duty of this kind, or its rate. **3** Any schedule of charges, prices, etc. —*v.t.* **1** To make a list of duties on. **2** To fix a price or tariff on. [< Ar. *ta′rif* information]

tarn (tärn) *n.* A small mountain lake. [< ON *tjörn*]

tar-nish (tär′nish) *v.t.* **1** To dim the luster of. **2** To sully, mar, debase, etc. —*v.i.* **3** To become tarnished. —*n.* **1** The condition of being tarnished; stain, blemish, loss of luster, etc. **2** The thin discolored film on the surface of tarnished metal. [< OF *ternir*] —**tar′nish-a-ble** *adj.*

ta-ro (tä′rō, tar′ō) *n. pl.* **-ros** Any of several tropical plants having starchy, edible rootstocks. [< native Polynesian name]

tar-ot (tar′ō, -ət, tar-ō′) *n.* Any of a set of old Italian figured playing cards, now used chiefly in fortunetelling.

tar-pau-lin (tär-pô′lin, tär′pə-) *n.* A waterproof material, esp. canvas, used as a covering for exposed objects. [?< TAR¹ + *palling,* pr.p. of PALL¹]

tar-pon (tär′pon, -pən) *n. pl.* **-pon** or **-pons** A large game fish of the West Indies and the coast of Florida. [?]

tar-ra-gon (tar′ə-gon) *n.* **1** A European perennial plant allied to wormwood. **2** The fragrant leaves of this plant, used for seasoning. [< Ar. *tarkhun*]

tar-ry¹ (tar′ē) *v.* **-ried, -ry-ing** *v.i.* **1** To put off going or coming; linger. **2** To remain in the same place; stay. **3** To wait. —*v.t.* **4** *Archaic* To wait for. [< L *tardare* to delay]

tar-ry² (tär′ē) *adj.* **tar-ri-er, tar-ri-est** Of, like, or covered with tar. —**tar′ri-ness** *n.*

tar-sal (tär′səl) *adj.* Of, pertaining to, or situated near the tarsus or ankle. —*n.* A tarsal part, as a bone.

tar-si-er (tär′sē-ər) *n.* A small, arboreal, nocturnal East Indian primate with large eyes and ears, long tail, and elongated digits. [< F < *tarse* tarsus]

tar-sus (tär′səs) *n. pl.* **-si** (-sī) **1** *Anat.* **a** The ankle. **b** In man, the seven bones of the ankle and heel. **2** *Zool.* **a** The shank of a bird's leg. **b** The distal part of the leg of certain arthropods. [< Gk. *tarsos* flat of the foot, any flat surface]

Tarsier

tart¹ (tärt) *adj.* **1** Having a sharp, sour taste. **2** Severe; caustic: a *tart* remark. [< OE *teart*] —**tart′ly** *adv.* —**tart′ness** *n.* —**Syn. 1** acid, bitter. **2** cutting, biting, acrimonious, sarcastic.

tart² (tärt) *n.* **1** A small open pastry shell filled with fruit, jelly, custard, etc. **2** *Slang* A girl or woman of loose morality. [< OF *tarte*]

tar-tan (tär′tən) *n.* **1** A woolen plaid fabric, esp. one with a pattern distinctive to a particular clan of the Scottish Highlands. **2** A fabric made to look like this. **3** Any plaid. —*adj.* Made of or like tartan. [? < OF *tiretaine* linsey-woolsey] See PLAID.

tar-tar¹ (tär′tər) *n.* **1** A hard deposit of potassium tartrate that forms in wine casks. **2** A yellowish incrustation on teeth, chiefly calcium phosphate. [< Med. Gk. *tartaron*] —**tar-tar′e-ous** *adj.*

tar-tar² (tär′tər) *n.* A person of intractable or violent disposition.

Tar-tar (tär′tər) *n.* TATAR. —*adj.* Of or pertaining to the Tatars or Tatary.

tartar emetic A poisonous tartrate of antimony and potassium, used in medicine and in dyeing.

tar-tar-ic (tär-tar′ik, -tär′ik) *adj.* Pertaining to or derived from tartar or tartaric acid.

tartaric acid A white, crystalline organic acid present in grapes and other fruits.

Tar-ta-rus (tär′tər-əs) *Gk. Myth.* **1** The abyss below Hades where Zeus confined the Titans. **2** HADES (def. 2).

Tar-ta-ry (tär′tər-ē) *n.* TATARY.

task (task, täsk) *n.* **1** A piece of work, esp. one imposed by authority or required by duty or necessity. **2** Any unpleasant or difficult assignment; burden. —**take to task** To reprove; lecture. —*v.t.* **1** To assign a task to. **2** To burden. [< L *taxare* appraise]

task force 1 A military unit specially trained to execute a specific mission. **2** Any group assigned to handle a specific task.

task-mas-ter (task′mas′tər, täsk′mäs′tər) *n.* One who assigns tasks, esp. burdensome ones.

tas·sel (tas′əl) n. 1 A tuft of loosely hanging threads or cords used as an ornament for curtains, cushions, etc. 2 Something resembling a tassel, as the inflorescence on Indian corn. —v. ·seled or ·selled, ·sel·ing or ·sel·ling v.t. 1 To provide or adorn with tassels. 2 To form in a tassel or tassels. —v.i. 3 To put forth tassels, as Indian corn. [< OF, clasp]

taste (tāst) v. tast·ed, tast·ing v.t. 1 To perceive the flavor of (something) by taking into the mouth or touching with the tongue. 2 To eat or drink a little of. 3 To recognize by the sense of taste. 4 To experience. —v.i. 5 To recognize a flavor by the sense of taste. 6 To take a small quantity into the mouth: usu. with of. 7 To have experience or enjoyment: with of: taste of great sorrow. 8 To have a specified flavor when in the mouth: Sugar tastes sweet. — n. 1 The sensation associated with stimulation of the taste buds by foods or other substances. 2 The quality thus perceived; flavor. 3 A small quantity tasted. 4 A slight experience; sample. 5 Special fondness and aptitude; inclination: a taste for music. 6 Appreciation of the beautiful in nature, art, and literature. 7 Style or form with respect to the rules of propriety or etiquette. 8 Individual preference or liking. 9 The act of tasting. [< L taxare touch, handle, appraise]

taste bud Any of numerous clusters of receptors located on the tongue and capable of stimulation by sweet, salt, sour or bitter substances.

taste·ful (tāst′fəl) adj. Having, showing, or conforming to good taste. —taste′ful·ly adv. —taste′ful·ness n. —Syn. elegant, aesthetic, artistic, graceful.

taste·less (tāst′lis) adj. 1 Having no flavor; insipid; dull. 2 Uninteresting; dull. 3 Lacking or showing a lack of good taste. —taste′less·ly adv. —taste′less·ness n.

tast·er (tās′tər) n. 1 One who tastes, esp. to test the quality of something. 2 A device for testing or sampling, as the small, shallow, metal vessel used in testing wines.

tast·y (tās′tē) adj. tast·i·er, tast·i·est 1 Having a fine flavor. 2 Tasteful. —tast′i·ly adv. —tast′i·ness n.

tat (tat) v. tat·ted, tat·ting v.t. 1 To make (edging) by tatting. —v.i. 2 To make tatting. [Back formation < TATTING] —tat′ter n.

Ta·tar (tä′tər) n. 1 A member of any of the Mongolian and Turkic tribes that invaded much of w Asia and E Europe in the Middle Ages. 2 A member of a chiefly Turkic people now living in the Russian Soviet Federated Socialist Republic and Soviet Central Asia. 3 Any of the Turkic languages of the Tatars, as Uzbek. —adj. Of or pertaining to the Tatars or Tatary. —Ta·tar′i·an (tä·târ′ē·ən) adj., n. —Ta·tar′ic adj.

Ta·ta·ry (tä′tər·ē) n. A region of indefinite extent in Asia and E Europe invaded and inhabited by Tatars in the Middle Ages.

tat·ter (tat′ər) n. 1 A torn and hanging shred; rag. 2 pl. Ragged clothing. —v.t. 1 To tear into tatters. —v.i. 2 To become ragged. [< ON töturr rags]

tat·ting (tat′ing) n. 1 A kind of lace made by looping and knotting a single thread that is wound on a shuttle. 2 The act or process of making it. [?]

tat·tle (tat′l) v. ·tled, ·tling v.i. 1 To talk idly; chatter. 2 To tell secrets, plans, etc.; gossip. —v.t. 3 To reveal by gossiping. —n. Idle talk or gossip. [< MDu. tatelen] —tat′tler n.

tat·tle·tale (tat′l·tāl′) n. A talebearer; tattler. —adj. Revealing; betraying.

tat·too¹ (ta·to̅o̅′) v.t. ·tooed, ·too·ing 1 To mark (the skin) in patterns with indelible pigments. 2 To mark the skin with (designs, etc.) in this way. —n. pl. ·toos 1 A pattern or design so made. 2 The act of tattooing or the condition of being tattooed. [< Polynesian] —tat·too′er n.

tat·too² (ta·to̅o̅′) n. pl. ·toos 1 A continuous beating or drumming. 2 A signal by drum or bugle to soldiers to repair to quarters. —v.t. & v.i. ·tooed, ·too·ing To beat or rap on (a drum, etc.). [< Du. < tap tap, faucet + toe shut]

tau (tou) n. The nineteenth letter in the Greek alphabet (T, τ).

taught (tôt) p.t. & p.p. of TEACH.

taunt (tônt) n. A sarcastic, biting remark; insult; jibe. — v.t. 1 To reproach or challenge with sarcastic or contemptuous words. 2 To provoke with taunts. [? < OF tanter provoke] —taunt′er n. —taunt′ing·ly adv.

taupe (tōp) n. The color of moleskin; dark brownish gray. [< L talpa mole]

Tau·rus (tôr′əs) n. A constellation and the second sign of the zodiac; the Bull. [L, bull] • See ZODIAC.

taut (tôt) adj. 1 Stretched tight. 2 In proper shape; trim; tidy. 3 Tense; tight: taut muscles. [? < OE togian, to pull, tow] —taut′ly adv. —taut′ness n.

tau·tog (tô·tôg′, -tog′) n. Any of various blackish, edible fishes of the North American Atlantic coast. [< Algon.]

tau·tol·o·gy (tô·tol′ə·jē) n. pl. ·gies 1 Unnecessary repetition of the same idea in different words. 2 An instance of this. [< Gk. tautos identical + logos discourse] —tau·to·log·ic (tô′tə·loj′ik) or ·i·cal adj. —tau′to·log′i·cal·ly adv.

tav·ern (tav′ərn) n. 1 An inn. 2 A place licensed to sell liquor, beer, etc., to be drunk on the premises. [< OF < L taberna hut, booth]

taw (tô) n. 1 A game of marbles. 2 The line from which marble players shoot. 3 A fancy marble used for shooting. [?]

taw·dry (tô′drē) adj. ·dri·er, ·dri·est Pretentiously showy without taste or quality. [< St. Audrey, designating a cheap type of lace sold at St. Audrey's Fair at Ely, England] —taw′dri·ly adv. —taw′dri·ness n. —Syn. cheap, gaudy, meretricious, flashy.

taw·ny (tô′nē) adj. ·ni·er, ·ni·est Tan-colored; brownish yellow. —n. The color tan or brownish yellow. [< OF tanner to tan] —taw′ni·ness n.

tax (taks) n. 1 A compulsory contribution levied upon persons, property, or business for the support of government. 2 A heavy demand, as on one's powers or resources; a burden. —v.t. 1 To impose a tax on. 2 To settle or fix (amounts) chargeable in any judicial matter. 3 To impose a burden upon; task. 4 To charge; blame: usu. with with. [< L taxare estimate, appraise]

tax·a·ble (taks′ə·bəl) adj. Liable to be taxed: taxable income. —tax′a·bil′i·ty n.

tax·a·tion (tak·sā′shən) n. 1 The act of taxing. 2 The amount assessed as a tax. 3 Revenue raised from taxes.

tax·i (tak′sē) n. pl. tax·is or tax·ies TAXICAB. —v. tax·ied, tax·i·ing or tax·y·ing v.i. 1 To ride in a taxicab. 2 To move along the ground or on the surface of the water, as an airplane before taking off or after landing. —v.t. 3 To cause (an airplane) to taxi.

tax·i·cab (tak′sē·kab′) n. A passenger vehicle, usu. fitted with a taximeter, available for hire. [< TAXIMETER + CAB]

tax·i·der·my (tak′sə·dûr′mē) n. The art of stuffing and mounting the skins of dead animals to simulate their appearance when alive. [< Gk. taxis arrangement + derma skin] —tax′i·der′mal, tax′i·der′mic adj. —tax′i·der′·mist n.

tax·i·me·ter (tak′si·mē′tər) n. An instrument for recording fares in a taxicab. [< F < taxe tariff + mètre a meter]

tax·on·o·my (tak·son′ə·mē) n. 1 The laws and principles of classification. 2 Biol. The systematic classification of plant and animal life into successive subgroups, as kingdom, phylum or division, class, order, family, genus, and species. [< Gk. taxis arrangement + nomos law] —tax·o·nom·ic (tak′sə·nom′ik) or ·i·cal adj. —tax′o·nom′i·cal·ly adv. —tax·on′o·mist n. • The prefixes sub-, meaning next below, and super-, meaning next above, are often used with the taxonomic categories specified in def. 2. Thus a suborder ranks next below an order but above a family (or a superfamily), whereas a superorder ranks above an order but below a class (or a subclass).

tax·pay·er (taks′pā′ər) n. One who pays or is liable to pay taxes.

TB, T.B., tb, t.b. tubercle bacillus; tuberculosis.

Tb terbium.

tbs. tbsp. tablespoon(s).

Tc technetium.

Te tellurium.

tea (tē) n. 1 An evergreen Asian plant having white flowers. 2 The prepared leaves of this plant, or an infusion of them used as a beverage. 3 A similar potable infusion of plant leaves or animal extract: beef tea. 4 Brit. A light evening or afternoon meal. 5 A social gathering at which tea is served. 6 Slang MARIHUANA. [< dial. Chinese t'e]

tea bag A small porous sack of cloth or paper containing tea leaves, which is immersed in water to make tea.

teach (tēch) v. **taught, teach·ing** v.t. 1 To give instruction to: *teach* a class. 2 To give instruction in: *teach* French. 3 To train by example, practice, or exercise. —v.i. 4 To act as a teacher; impart knowledge or skill. [< OE *tæcan*] —teach'a·bil'i·ty, teach'a·ble·ness n. —teach'a·ble adj.

teach·er (tē'chər) n. One who teaches, esp. as an occupation.

teach·in (tēch'in') n. An extended meeting, as at a college or university, during which faculty and students participate in lectures, discussions, etc., on a controversial issue, esp. as a form of social protest.

teach·ing (tē'ching) n. 1 The act or occupation of a teacher. 2 That which is taught.

teaching machine Any of various mechanical devices that present educational material to a student, enabling him to learn at his own rate by a system of corrective feedback.

tea·cup (tē'kup') n. 1 A small cup suitable for serving tea. 2 The amount a teacup will hold: also **tea'cup·ful'** (-fŏŏl')

teak (tēk) n. 1 A large tree of SE Asia yielding a hard, durable timber highly prized for furniture, etc. 2 The wood of this tree: also **teak'wood.** [< Pg. *teca* < Malayalam *tēkka*]

tea·ket·tle (tē'ket'l) n. A kettle with a spout, used for boiling water.

teal (tēl) n. Any of several small, short-necked, wild ducks. [ME *tele*]

team (tēm) n. 1 Two or more beasts of burden harnessed together. 2 A group of people working or playing together as a unit, esp. a group forming one side in a contest. —v.t. 1 To convey with a team. 2 To harness together in a team. —v.i. 3 To drive a team. 4 To form or work as a team: to *team* up. [< OE *tēam* offspring, team]

team·mate (tēm'māt') n. A fellow player on a team.

team·ster (tēm'stər) n. One who drives a team or a truck, esp. as an occupation.

team·work (tēm'wûrk') n. 1 Work done by a team. 2 Unity of action, as by the players on a team.

tea·pot (tē'pot') n. A vessel with a spout, handle, and lid, in which tea is brewed and from which it is served.

tear¹ (târ) v. **tore, torn, tear·ing** v.t. 1 To pull apart, as cloth; rip. 2 To make by tearing: *tear* a hole in. 3 To injure or lacerate. 4 To divide or disrupt: a party *torn* by dissension. 5 To distress or torment: The sight *tore* his heart. —v.i. 6 To become torn or rent. 7 To move with haste and energy. —**tear down** 1 To demolish, as a building. 2 To take apart, as a machine for repair. 3 *Informal* To attack or abuse verbally. —**tear into** To attack violently or with impetuous haste. —n. 1 The act of tearing. 2 A fissure made by tearing. 3 *Slang* A spree; frolic. 4 A rushing motion. 5 A violent outburst, as of anger. [< OE *teran*]

tear² (tir) n. 1 A drop of the saline liquid that normally lubricates the eyeball and in weeping flows from the eyes. 2 Something resembling this. 3 *pl.* Sorrow. 4 *pl.* The act of weeping: to burst into *tears.* —v.i. To fill with tears. [< OE *tēar*] —**tear'less, tear'y** adj.

tear·drop (tir'drop') n. A tear. —adj. Shaped like a falling tear: a *teardrop* earring.

tear·ful (tir'fəl) adj. 1 Weeping. 2 Causing tears. 3 Accompanied by tears: a *tearful* confession. —**tear'ful·ly** adv. —**tear'ful·ness** n. —Syn. 1 sobbing, crying, blubbering. 2 sad, pathetic, mournful.

tear gas (tir) A gas or other agent that causes the eyes to tear.

tear-jerk·er (tir'jûr'kər) n. *Slang* A story, play, film, etc., charged with sentimental sadness.

tea·room (tē'rŏŏm', -rŏŏm') n. A restaurant serving tea and other light refreshments.

tease (tēz) v. **teased, teas·ing** v.t. 1 To annoy or harass; pester. 2 To raise the nap, as with teasels. 3 To coax or beg. 4 To comb or card, as wool or flax. 5 To comb (hair) in such a way as to form fluffy layers. —v.i. 6 To annoy a person in a facetious or petty way. —n. 1 One who teases. 2 The act of teasing or the state of being teased. [< OE *tǣsan* tease, pluck apart] —**teas'er** n. —**teas'ing·ly** adv.

tea·sel (tē'zəl) n. 1 Any of various coarse, prickly herbs having the flower heads covered with hooked bracts, esp. the **fuller's teasel.** 2 The dried flower head of this plant, or a mechanical substitute, used to raise a nap on cloth. —v.t. **·seled** or **·selled, ·sel·ing** or **·sel·ling** To raise the nap of with a teasel. Also **tea'zel, tea'zle.** [< OE *tǣsel*] —**tea'sel·er** or **tea'·sel·ier** n.

Teasel

tea·spoon (tē'spōōn', -spŏŏn') n. 1 A small spoon used for stirring tea, etc. 2 The amount a teaspoon will hold, ⅓ of a tablespoon: also **tea'spoon·ful** (-fŏŏl').

teat (tit, tēt) n. 1 The protuberance on the breast or udder of most female mammals, through which milk is drawn; a nipple. 2 A small protuberance like a teat. [< OF *tete*]

teched (techt) adj. TETCHED.

tech·ne·ti·um (tek·nē'shē·əm) n. A synthetic radioactive metallic element (symbol Tc) occupying a former gap after molybdenum in the periodic table. [< Gk. *technētos* artificial]

tech·nic (tek'nik) n. TECHNIQUE. —adj. TECHNICAL.

tech·ni·cal (tek'ni·kəl) adj. 1 Of or pertaining to some particular art, science, or trade, esp. to the practical arts or applied sciences. 2 Of, characteristic of, used or skilled in a particular art, science, profession, etc. 3 Of, in, or exhibiting technique. 4 According to an accepted body of rules and regulations: a *technical* defeat. [< Gk. *technē* art] —**tech'ni·cal·ly** (-kə·lē, -klē) adv. —**tech'ni·cal·ness** n.

tech·ni·cal·i·ty (tek'ni·kal'ə·tē) n. pl. **·ties** 1 The state or quality of being technical. 2 A technical point peculiar to some art, trade, etc. 3 A petty, formal, or highly specialized distinction or detail.

technical sergeant See GRADE.

tech·ni·cian (tek·nish'ən) n. One skilled in carrying out operations in a specific field.

Tech·ni·col·or (tek'ni·kul'ər) n. Brilliant or realistic color. [< *Technicolor*] —**tech'ni·col'ored** adj.

Tech·ni·col·or (tek'ni·kul'ər) n. A process used in making color films: a trade name. Also **tech'ni·col'or.**

tech·nics (tek'niks) n.pl. (construed as sing.) The principles or study of an art or of the arts, esp. the industrial or mechanical arts.

tech·nique (tek·nēk') n. 1 The way in which an artist, craftsman, scientist, etc., handles technical details or uses basic skills. 2 The degree of excellence in doing these things. 3 Any method of accomplishing something. [< Gk. *technikos* technical]

tech·noc·ra·cy (tek·nok'rə·sē) n. pl. **·cies** A government controlled by technicians, as scientists, engineers, etc. —**tech'no·crat** (tek'nə·krat) n. —**tech'no·crat'ic** adj.

tech·nol·o·gy (tek·nol'ə·jē) n. 1 The sum total of the technical means employed to meet the material needs of a society. 2 Applied science. 3 The technical terms used in a science, art, etc. [< Gk. *technē* skill + -LOGY] —**tech'no·log'ic** or **·i·cal** adj. —**tech'no·log'i·cal·ly** adv. —**tech·nol'o·gist** n.

tec·ton·ics (tek·ton'iks) n.pl. (construed as singular) 1 The science or art of constructing buildings or things. 2 The branch of geology relating to the continuing structural evolution of the earth's crust. [< Gk. *tektōn* carpenter] —**tec·ton'ic** adj. —**tec·ton'i·cal·ly** adv.

ted (ted) v.t. **ted·ded, ted·ding** To scatter or spread for drying, as newly mown grass. [? < ON *tethja* spread manure]

ted·dy bear (ted'ē) A toy bear. [< *Teddy*, a nickname for Theodore Roosevelt, 26th U.S. president, 1858–1919]

Te De·um (tē dē'əm) 1 An ancient Christian hymn beginning with the words *Te Deum.* 2 The music for this hymn. [< L *Te Deum (laudamus)* (we praise) Thee, O God]

te·di·ous (tē'dē·əs) adj. Fatiguing or boring, as because of lack of interest or repetitiousness. [< L *taedium* tedium] —**te'di·ous·ly** adv. —**te'di·ous·ness** n.

te·di·um (tē'dē·əm) n. The quality or state of being boring, wearisome, monotonous, etc. [< L *taedere* vex, weary]

tee[1] (tē) n. 1 The letter T. 2 Something resembling the form of the letter T. —adj. Shaped like a T.

tee[2] (tē) n. 1 A little peg or cone-shaped mound on which a golf ball is placed in making the first play to a hole. 2 In golf, the area from which a player makes his first stroke at the beginning of play for each hole. —v.t. & v.i. ·teed, tee·ing To place (the ball) on the tee before striking it. —tee off 1 To strike (a golf ball) in starting play. 2 To begin. 3 Slang To make angry or resentful.[?]

tee[3] (tē) n. In certain games, a mark toward which the balls, quoits, etc., are directed. [?<TEE[1]]

teem (tēm) v.i. To be full to overflowing; abound. [<OE *tīeman*]

teen·age (tēn'āj') adj. Of, being in, or related to the years from 13 to 19 inclusive. —teen'ag'er n.

teens (tēnz) n. pl. 1 The numbers from 13 to 19 inclusive. 2 The years of one's age from 13 to 19 inclusive. [<OE *tēne* ten]

tee·ny (tē'nē) adj. ·ni·er, ·ni·est Informal Tiny. [Alter. of TINY]

teen·y·bop·per (tē'nē·bop'ər) n. Slang A modern, hip teen-ager of the 1960's, esp. a girl.

tee·pee (tē'pē) n. TEPEE.

tee shirt (tē) T-SHIRT.

tee·ter (tē'tər) v.i. 1 SEESAW. 2 To walk or move with a swaying or tottering motion. 3 To vacillate; waver. —v.t. 4 To cause to teeter. —n. SEESAW. [?<ON *titra* tremble]

tee·ter-tot·ter (tē'tər·tot'ər) n. SEESAW.

teeth (tēth) n. pl. of TOOTH.

teethe (tēth) v.i. teethed, teeth·ing To develop teeth; cut one's teeth.

tee·to·tal (tē'tōt'l) adj. 1 Of, pertaining to, or practicing total abstinence from alcoholic beverages. 2 Total; entire. [<TOTAL, with emphatic repetition of initial letter] —tee·to'tal·ism n. —tee·to'tal·ly adv.

tee·to·tal·er (tē·tōt'l·ər) n. One who abstains totally from alcoholic beverages. Also tee·to'tal·ist, tee·to'tal·ler.

Tef·lon (tef'lon) n. A tough, slippery, heat-resistant, chemically inert, synthetic polymer having many industrial and household applications: a trade name.

tel. telegram; telegraph; telephone.

tele- combining form 1 At, from, over, or to a distance; distant: *telegraph*. 2 Of, in, pertaining to, or transmitted by television: *telecast*. [<Gk. *tēle* far]

tel·e·cast (tel'ə·kast, -käst) v.t. & v.i. ·cast or ·cast·ed, ·cast·ing To broadcast by television. —n. A program broadcast by television.

tel·e·com·mu·ni·ca·tion (tel'ə·kə·myōō'nə·kā'shən) n. The technology of communicating at a distance, as in radio, television, telegraphy, etc. Also **tel'e·com·mu'ni·ca'tions** (construed as sing. or pl.).

tel·e·com·mut·ing (tel'ə·kə·myōōt'ing) n. Working at home by means of a home computer terminal connected by telephone line to a main computer.

tel·e·gram (tel'ə·gram) n. A message sent by telegraph.

tel·e·graph (tel'ə·graf, -gräf) n. Any of various devices, systems, or processes for transmitting messages to a distance, esp. by means of coded electric impulses conducted by wire. —v.t. 1 To send (a message) by telegraph. 2 To communicate with by telegraph. —v.i. 3 To transmit a message by telegraph. —te·leg·ra·pher (tə·leg'rə·fər) n.

tel·e·graph·ic (tel'ə·graf'ik) adj. 1 Of, pertaining to, or transmitted by the telegraph. 2 Concise, as a telegram. Also **tel'e·graph'i·cal.** —**tel'e·graph'i·cal·ly** adv.

te·leg·ra·phy (tə·leg'rə·fē) n. 1 The process of conveying messages by telegraph. 2 The technology used in doing this.

Te·lem·a·chus (tə·lem'ə·kəs) Gk. Myth. The son of Odysseus and Penelope, who helped his father kill his mother's suitors.

tel·e·mar·ket·ing (tel'ə·mär'kə·ting) n. The marketing of products and services over the telephone or on television.

te·lem·e·ter (tel'ə·mē'tər, tə·lem'ə·tər) n. An apparatus for indicating or measuring various quantities and for transmitting the data to a distant point. —v.t. & v.i. To transmit by telemeter. —te·lem'e·try n.

tel·e·ol·o·gy (tel'ē·ol'ə·jē, tē'lē-) n. 1 The study of final causes. 2 The belief that natural phenomena can be explained in terms of an overall design as well as by me-

chanical causes. 3 The study of evidence supporting this belief. 4 The explanation of nature in terms of utility or purpose. [<Gk. *telos, teleos* end + -LOGY] —tel'e·o·log'i·cal (-ə·loj'i·kəl) adj. —tel'e·ol'o·gist n.

te·lep·a·thy (tə·lep'ə·thē) n. The supposed communication of one mind with another by other than normal sensory means. —tel·e·path·ic (tel'ə·path'ik) adj. —tel'e·path'i·cal·ly adv. —te·lep'a·thist n.

tel·e·phone (tel'ə·fōn) n. An instrument for reproducing sound or speech at a distant point, using electric impulses transmitted by wire. —v. ·phoned, ·phon·ing —v.t. 1 To send by telephone, as a message. 2 To communicate with by telephone. —v.i. 3 To communicate by telephone. —tel'e·phon'ic (-fon'ik) adj. —tel'e·phon'i·cal·ly adv.

te·leph·o·ny (tə·lef'ə·nē) n. The technology of telephone communication.

tel·e·pho·to (tel'ə·fō'tō) adj. 1 Denoting a system of lenses which produces a large image of a distant object in a camera. 2 Of, pertaining to, or being telephotography.

tel·e·pho·to·graph (tel'ə·fō'tə·graf, -gräf) n. 1 A picture transmitted by wire or radio. 2 A picture made with a telephoto lens. —v.t. & v.i. To take or transmit (photographs) by telephotography. —tel'e·pho'to·graph'ic adj.

tel·e·pho·tog·ra·phy (tel'ə·fə·tog'rə·fē) n. 1 The technique of producing magnified photographs of distant objects. 2 The transmission of photographs or other visual material by radio or wire.

tel·e·proc·ess·ing (tel'ə·pros'es·ing) n. Data processing by a computer which collects data from distant locations by means of communications lines.

Tel·e·promp·ter (tel'e·promp'tər) n. A prompting device for television whereby a magnified script, unseen by the audience, is unrolled for a speaker or performer, line by line: a trade name.

tel·e·scope (tel'ə·skōp) n. An optical instrument for enlarging the image of a distant object. —v. ·scoped, ·scop·ing v.t. 1 To put together so that one part fits into another. 2 To shorten, condense, or compress. —v.i. 3 To slide or be forced one into another, as the cylindrical tubes of a collapsible telescope or railroad cars in a collision.

tel·e·scop·ic (tel'ə·skop'ik) adj. 1 Of, pertaining to, or done with a telescope. 2 Visible through or obtained by a telescope. 3 Visible only through a telescope. 4 Far-seeing. 5 Having sections that slide within or over one another. Also **tel'e·scop'i·cal.**

te·les·co·py (tə·les'kə·pē) n. The technology of using or making telescopes. —te·les'co·pist n.

Refracting telescope

tel·e·text (tel'ə·tekst') n. A communications system that transmits information over a television broadcast signal, to be viewed on a television screen.

tel·e·thon (tel'ə·thon) n. A long telecast, usu. to raise funds for a charity. [<TELE- + (MARA)THON]

Tel·e·type (tel'ə·tīp) n. A teletypewriter: a trade name.

tel·e·type·writ·er (tel'ə·tīp·rī'tər) n. A telegraphic instrument resembling a typewriter, by which the work done on one is simultaneously typed on others, electrically connected but a distance away.

tel·e·view (tel'ə·vyōō) v.t. & v.i. To observe by means of television. —tel'e·view'er n.

tel·e·vise (tel'ə·vīz) v.t. & v.i. ·vised, ·vis·ing To transmit or receive by television.

tel·e·vi·sion (tel'ə·vizh'ən) n. 1 An optical and electric system for continuous transmission of visual images and sound that may be instantaneously received at a distance. 2 The technology of television transmission. 3 A television receiving set. 4 Television as an industry, an art form, or a medium of communications. 5 A show transmitted by television: to watch *television*.

tel·ex (tel'eks) n. 1 A communication system using teletypewriters connected by wire through exchanges which operate automatically. **2** A message sent by such a system. —*v.t.* To send by telex. [< TEL(ETYPEWRITER) + EX(CHANGE)]

tell (tel) *v.* **told, tell·ing** *v.t.* **1** To relate in detail; narrate, as a story. **2** To make known by speech or writing; express in words; communicate; utter; say. **3** To divulge; reveal; disclose: to *tell* secrets. **4** To decide; ascertain: I cannot *tell* who is to blame. **5** To distinguish; recognize: to *tell* right from wrong. **6** To command; direct; order: I *told* him to go home. **7** To let know; report to; inform. **8** To state or assure emphatically: It's cold out, I *tell* you! **9** To count; enumerate: to *tell* one's beads. —*v.i.* **10** To give an account or description: usu. with *of.* **11** To serve as indication or evidence: with *of:* Their rags *told* of their poverty. **12** To produce a marked effect: Every blow *told.* —**tell off 1** To count and set apart. **2** *Informal* To reprimand severely. —**tell on 1** To wear out; tire; exhaust. **2** *Informal* To tattle on; inform against. [< OE *tellan*] —**Syn. 1** recount, recite. **2** state, aver. **4** discriminate.

tell·er (tel′ər) *n.* **1** One who tells, as a story; narrator. **2** One who receives or pays out money, as in a bank. **3** One who counts, esp. one appointed to count votes.

tell·ing (tel′ing) *adj.* Producing a great effect. —**tell′ing·ly** *adv.* —**Syn.** striking, effective, impressive, forceful.

tell·tale (tel′tāl′) *adj.* Betraying or revealing. —*n.* **1** One who gives information about others; a tattler. **2** That which conveys information; an outward sign or indication. **3** An instrument or device for giving or recording information, as a time clock.

tel·lu·ri·um (te·lŏŏr′ē·əm, tel·yŏŏr′-) *n.* A rare, very poisonous, semimetallic element (symbol Te) resembling sulfur and selenium. [< L *tellus* the earth]

tel·ly (tel′ē) *n. pl.* **tel·lies** *Chiefly Brit. Informal* Television.

Tel·star (tel′stär′) *n.* Any of several U.S. comsats, the first of which was launched July 10, 1962.

te·mer·i·ty (tə·mer′ə·tē) *n.* Foolish boldness; rashness; foolhardiness. [< L *temeritas*] —**Syn.** audacity, heedlessness, recklessness, presumption, venturesomeness.

temp. temperature; temporary; in the time of (L *tempore*).

tem·per (tem′pər) *n.* **1** A fit of anger; rage. **2** A tendency to become easily angered. **3** State of mind or feeling; mood. **4** TEMPERAMENT (def. 1). **5** Equanimity; self-control: used only in the phrases **lose** (or **keep**) **one's temper. 6** The hardness and strength of a metal, esp. when produced by heat treatment. **7** Something used to temper a substance or mixture. —*v.t.* **1** To moderate or make suitable, as by adding another quality; free from excess; mitigate: to *temper* justice with mercy. **2** To bring to the proper consistency, texture, etc., by moistening and working: to *temper* clay. **3** To bring (metal) to a required hardness and elasticity by controlled heating and cooling. **4** To make experienced; toughen, as by difficulties, hardships, etc. **5** *Music* To tune (an instrument) by temperament. —*v.i.* **6** To be or become tempered. [< L *temperare* combine in due proportion] —**tem′per·a·bil′i·ty** *n.* —**tem′per·a·ble** *adj.*

tem·per·a (tem′pər·ə) *n.* **1** An aqueous painting medium in which the pigment is laid down in a matrix of casein, size, egg, etc. **2** The method of painting in this medium; also a painting done in tempera. **3** A water-soluble paint used for posters. [< Ital. *temperare* to temper]

tem·per·a·ment (tem′pər·ə·mənt, -prə-) *n.* **1** The characteristic nature or disposition of a person. **2** A nature or disposition that is exceedingly dramatic, excitable, moody, etc. **3** *Music* The tuning of an instrument of fixed intonation to a slightly modified chromatic scale so that it is in tune for all keys. [< L *temperamentum* proper mixture]

tem·per·a·men·tal (tem′pər·ə·men′təl, -prə-) *adj.* **1** Of or pertaining to temperament. **2** Exceedingly excitable, moody, capricious, etc. **3** Unpredictable or erratic, as in performance. —**tem′per·a·men′tal·ly** *adv.*

tem·per·ance (tem′pər·əns) *n.* **1** Habitual moderation and self-control, esp. in the indulgence of any appetite. **2** The principle and practice of moderation or total abstinence from intoxicants. —*adj.* Of, relating to, practicing,

or promoting total abstinence from intoxicants. [< L *temperare* mix in due proportions]

tem·per·ate (tem′pər·it, tem′prət) *adj.* **1** Characterized by moderation or the absence of extremes; not excessive. **2** Calm; restrained; self-controlled. **3** Observing moderation or self-control, esp. in the use of intoxicating liquors. **4** Moderate as regards temperature; mild. [< L *temperare* mix in due proportions] —**tem′per·ate·ly** *adv.* —**tem′per·ate·ness** *n.*

temperate zone Either of two zones of the earth, the one between the Tropic of Capricorn and the Antarctic Circle and the other between the Tropic of Cancer and the Arctic Circle. • See ZONE.

tem·per·a·ture (tem′pər·ə·chər, -prə-) *n.* **1** The degree of heat in the atmosphere as measured on a thermometer.

TEMPERATURE CONVERSION TABLE

This table provides approximate conversion figures from the Fahrenheit to the Celsius temperature scales and vice versa. On the Celsius scale, water boils at about 100° and freezes at about 0°. On the Fahrenheit scale, water boils at about 212° and freezes at about 32°. One Fahrenheit degree = 5/9° Celsius. To convert from Fahrenheit to Celsius, subtract 32 from the Fahrenheit reading, multiply by 5, and divide the product by 9. *Example:* 65°F − 32 = 33; 33 × 5 = 165; 165 ÷ 9 = 18.3°C. To convert from Celsius to Fahrenheit, multiply the Celsius reading by 9, divide the product by 5, and add 32. *Example:* 35°C × 9 = 315; 315 ÷ 5 = 63; 63 + 32 = 95°F.

Fahrenheit	Celsius	Fahrenheit	Celsius
500	260.0	0	−17.8
400	204.4	−10	−23.3
300	149.0	−20	−28.9
212	100.0	−30	−34.4
200	93.3	−40	−40.0
100	37.8	−50	−45.6
90	32.2	−60	−51.1
80	26.7	−70	−56.7
70	21.1	−80	−62.2
60	15.6	−90	−67.8
50	10.0	−100	−73.3
40	4.4	−200	−129.0
32	0.0	−300	−184.0
30	−1.1	−400	−240.0
20	−6.6	−459.4*	−273.0
10	−12.2		*Absolute zero.

Celsius	Fahrenheit	Celsius	Fahrenheit
500	932	0	32
400	752	−10	14
300	572	−20	−4
200	392	−30	−22
100	212	−40	−40
90	194	−50	−58
80	176	−60	−76
70	158	−70	−94
60	140	−80	−112
50	122	−90	−130
40	104	−100	−148
30	86	−200	−328
20	68	−273*	−459.4
10	50		*Absolute zero.

---

2 The degree or intensity of heat in a living body; also, the excess of this above the normal. **3** The intensity of heat or cold in any substance. [< L *temperatura* due measure]

tem·pered (tem′pərd) *adj.* **1** Having a particular kind of temper: used mostly in combination: *quick-tempered, ill-tempered.* **2** Moderated or changed by the addition of something else: love *tempered* with discipline. **3** *Music* Adjusted in pitch to some temperament. **4** Having the right degree of hardness, elasticity, etc.

tem·pest (tem′pist) *n.* **1** An extensive and violent wind, usu. attended with rain, snow, or hail. **2** A violent commotion or tumult. [< L *tempestas* space of time, weather < *tempus* time]

tem·pes·tu·ous (tem·pes′chōō·əs) *adj.* Stormy; turbulent; violent. —**tem·pes′tu·ous·ly** *adv.* —**tem·pes′tu·ous·ness** *n.*

---

add, āce, câre, pālm; end, ēven; it, īce; odd, ōpen, ôrder; tŏŏk, pōōl; up, bûrn; ə = *a* in *above, u* in *focus;* yōō = *u* in *fuse;* oil; pout; check; go; ring; thin; this; zh, *vision.* < derived from; ? origin uncertain or unknown.

Tem·plar (tem′plər) *n.* KNIGHT TEMPLAR.

tem·plate (tem′plit) *n.* 1 A pattern, as of wood or metal, used as a guide in shaping or making something. 2 In building, a stout stone or timber for distributing weight or thrust. [< OF *temple* small timber]

tem·ple¹ (tem′pəl) *n.* 1 An edifice consecrated to the worship of one or more deities. 2 An edifice dedicated to public worship; esp., in the U.S.: **a** A synagogue. **b** A Mormon church. 3 Any usu. large or imposing building dedicated or used for a special purpose: a *temple* of learning. [< L *templum* temple]

tem·ple² (tem′pəl) *n.* The region on each side of the head above the cheek bone. [< L *tempus* temple]

tem·po (tem′pō) *n. pl.* **-pos** or **-pi** (-pē) 1 *Music* Relative speed at which a composition is played or is supposed to be played. 2 Characteristic rate of speed; pace. [< L *tempus* time]

tem·po·ral¹ (tem′pər·əl) *adj.* 1 Of or pertaining to the present as opposed to a future life. 2 Worldly; material, as opposed to spiritual. 3 Ephemeral; transitory, as opposed to eternal. 4 Of or relating to time. 5 *Gram.* Of, pertaining to, or denoting time: *temporal* conjunctions. [< L *tempus, temporis* time] —**tem·po·ral·i·ty** (tem′pə·ral′ə·tē), **tem′po·ral·ness** *n.* —**tem′po·ral·ly** *adv.*

tem·po·ral² (tem′pər·əl) *adj.* Of, pertaining to, or situated at the temple or temples of the head.

temporal bone The compound bone forming either side of the skull. • See SKULL.

tem·po·rar·y (tem′pə·rer′ē) *adj.* Lasting, to be used, etc., for a time only; not permanent. [< L *tempus, temporis* time] —**tem′po·rar·i·ly** *adv.* —**tem′po·rar′i·ness** *n.*

tem·po·rize (tem′pə·rīz) *v.i.* **-rized, -riz·ing** 1 To act evasively so as to gain time or put off commitment. 2 To comply with or yield to the situation, circumstances, etc.; compromise. [< L *tempus, temporis* time] —**tem′po·ri·za′·tion,** **tem′po·riz′er** *n.* —**tem′po·riz′ing·ly** *adv.*

tempt (tempt) *v.t.* 1 To attempt to persuade (a person) to do wrong, as by promising pleasure or gain. 2 To be attractive to; invite: Your offers do not *tempt* me. 3 To provoke or risk provoking: to *tempt* fate. 4 To incline or dispose: They were *tempted* to leave at once. [< L *temptare, tentare* test, try] —**tempt′a·ble** *adj.* —**tempt′er** *n.* —**tempt′ress** *n. Fem.*

temp·ta·tion (temp·tā′shən) *n.* 1 That which tempts. 2 The state of being tempted.

tempt·ing (temp′ting) *adj.* Alluring; attractive; seductive. —**tempt′ing·ly** *adv.* —**tempt′ing·ness** *n.*

tem·pu·ra (tem·pŏŏr′ə, tem′pŏŏr′ə, -pŏŏ·rä′) *n.* A Japanese dish of seafood or vegetables, dipped in batter and deep-fried. [Jap., fried food]

tem·pus fu·git (tem′pəs fyŏŏ′jit) *Latin* Time flies.

ten (ten) *n.* 1 The sum of nine plus one; 10; X. 2 A set or group of ten members. [< OE *tēne*] —**ten** *adj., pron.*

ten. tenement; tenor; tenuto (music).

ten·a·ble (ten′ə·bəl) *adj.* Capable of being held, maintained, or defended. [< L *tenere* to hold] —**ten′a·bil′i·ty, ten′a·ble·ness** *n.* —**ten′a·bly** *adv.*

te·na·cious (ti·nā′shəs) *adj.* 1 Having great cohesiveness; tough. 2 Adhesive; sticky. 3 Stubborn; obstinate; persistent. 4 Strongly retentive: a *tenacious* memory. [< L *tenax* holding fast] —**te·na′cious·ly** *adv.* —**te·na′cious·ness, te·nac·i·ty** (tə·nas′ə·tē) *n.*

ten·an·cy (ten′ən·sē) *n. pl.* **-cies** 1 The holding of lands or estates by any form of title; occupancy. 2 The period of being a tenant. 3 The property occupied by a tenant.

ten·ant (ten′ənt) *n.* 1 A person who rents a house, land, etc., for his own use. 2 One who holds or possesses lands or property by any kind of title. 3 A dweller in any place; an occupant. —*v.t.* 1 To hold as tenant; occupy. —*v.i.* 2 To be a tenant. [< F *tenir* to hold] —**ten′ant·a·ble** *adj.*

tenant farmer One who farms land owned by another and pays rent either in cash or in a share of the crops.

ten·ant·ry (ten′ən·trē) *n. pl.* **-ries** 1 Tenants collectively. 2 The state of being a tenant.

ten-cent store (ten′sent′) FIVE-AND-TEN-CENT STORE.

Ten Commandments In the Old Testament, the ten rules of conduct given by God to Moses on Mount Sinai.

tend¹ (tend) *v.i.* 1 To have an aptitude, tendency, or disposition; incline. 2 To lead or conduce: Education *tends* to

refinement. 3 To go in a certain direction. [< L *tendere* extend, tend]

tend² (tend) *v.t.* 1 To attend to the needs or requirements of; take care of; minister to: to *tend* children. 2 To watch over or be in charge of: to *tend* a store. —*v.i.* 3 To be in attendance; serve or wait: with *on* or *upon.* 4 To give attention or care: with *to.* [Alter. of ATTEND]

ten·den·cy (ten′dən·sē) *n. pl.* **-cies** 1 Inclination; propensity; bent: a *tendency* to lie. 2 A movement or course toward some purpose, end, or result. 3 The purpose or trend of a speech or story. [< L *tendere* extend, tend] —**Syn.** 1 aptitude, proclivity, disposition, leaning, predilection.

ten·den·tious (ten·den′shəs) *adj.* Disposed to promote a particular view or opinion; lacking in detachment. —**ten·den′tious·ly** *adv.* —**ten·den′tious·ness** *n.*

ten·der¹ (ten′dər) *adj.* 1 Easily crushed, bruised, broken, etc.; delicate; fragile. 2 Easily chewed or cut: said of food. 3 Physically weak; not strong or hardy. 4 Youthful and delicate; not strengthened by maturity: a *tender* age. 5 Characterized by gentleness, care, consideration, etc.: a *tender* respect for the aged. 6 Kind; affectionate; loving: a *tender* father. 7 Sensitive to impressions, feelings, etc.: a *tender* conscience. 8 Sensitive to pain, discomfort, roughness, etc.: a *tender* skin. 9 Of delicate quality: a *tender* color. 10 Capable of arousing sensitive feelings; touching: *tender* memories. 11 Requiring deft or delicate treatment; ticklish; touchy: a *tender* subject. —*v.t.* To make tender; soften. [< L *tener*] —**ten′der·ly** *adv.* —**ten′der·ness** *n.*

ten·der² (ten′dər) *v.t.* 1 To present for acceptance, as a resignation; offer. 2 To proffer, as money, in payment of a debt, etc. —*n.* 1 The act of tendering; an offer. 2 That which is offered as payment, esp. money. [< L *tendere* extend, tend] —**ten′der·er** *n.*

tend·er³ (ten′dər) *n.* 1 A boat used to bring supplies, passengers, and crew to and from a ship anchored near the shore. 2 A vessel that services ships at sea, lighthouses, seaplanes, etc. 3 A vehicle attached to the rear of a steam locomotive to carry fuel and water for it. 4 One who tends or ministers to.

ten·der·foot (ten′dər·fŏŏt′) *n. pl.* **·feet** (-fēt′) or **·foots** 1 A newcomer, esp. to a rough or unsettled region. 2 Any inexperienced person or beginner. 3 A Boy Scout in the beginning group. —*adj.* Inexperienced.

ten·der·heart·ed (ten′dər·här′tid) *adj.* Compassionate; sympathetic. —**ten′der·heart′ed·ly** *adv.* —**ten′der·heart′ed·ness** *n.*

ten·der·ize (ten′də·rīz) *v.t.* **-ized, -iz·ing** To make (meat) tender by some process or substance that softens the tough fibers and connective tissues. —**ten′der·iz′er** *n.*

ten·der·loin (ten′dər·loin′) *n.* 1 The tender part of the loin of beef, pork, etc., that lies parallel to the backbone. 2 *Often cap.* A city district noted for its high incidence of crime, corruption, and police leniency.

ten·don (ten′dən) *n.* One of the bands of tough, fibrous tissue attaching a voluntary muscle to a bone. [< Gk. *tenōn* a sinew < *tenein* stretch] —**ten′di·nous** *adj.*

ten·dril (ten′dril) *n.* One of the slender, threadlike, usu. coiling organs serving to attach a climbing plant to a supporting surface. [< OF *tendron* sprout] —**ten′driled** or **ten′drilled, ten′dril·ous** *adj.*

ten·e·ment (ten′ə·mənt) *n.* 1 A room, or set of rooms, designed for one family; apartment; flat. 2 TENEMENT HOUSE. 3 *Law* Anything, as land, houses, offices, franchises, etc., held of another by tenure. [< LL *tenementum* tenure < L *tenere* to hold] —**ten′e·men′ta·ry** (-men′tər·ē), **ten′e·men′tal** (-men′təl) *adj.*

tenement house A run-down building or house, usu. an apartment house, situated in a poor section of a city.

ten·et (ten′it, tē′nit) *n.* A principle, dogma, or doctrine, esp. one held by a group or profession. [L, he holds]

ten·fold (ten′fōld′) *adj.* 1 Made up of ten. 2 Ten times as many or as much. —*adv.* In a tenfold manner or degree.

Tenn. Tennessee.

ten·nis (ten′is) *n.* 1 A game in which two opposing players or pairs of players strike a ball with rackets over a low net on a court (**tennis court**), as of clay or synthetic materials, usu. outdoors. 2 An old form of tennis played in an interior space: also **court tennis.** [< AF *tenetz* take, receive, imperative of *tenir* hold]

ten·on (ten′ən) n. A projection on the end of a timber, etc., for inserting into a mortise to form a joint. —v.t. 1 To form a tenon on. 2 To join by a mortise and tenon. [< OF *tenir* to hold] • See MORTISE.

ten·or (ten′ər) n. 1 General intent or purport; substance: the *tenor* of the speech. 2 General course or tendency: the even *tenor* of their ways. 3 General character or nature. 4 A man's voice singing higher than a baritone and lower than an alto; also, a singer having, or a part to be sung by, such a voice. —adj. 1 Of or pertaining to a tenor. 2 Having a range of or similar to a tenor voice. [< L, a course < *tenere* to hold]

ten·pins (ten′pinz′) n.pl. 1 (construed as sing.) A game of bowling in which the players attempt to bowl down ten pins. 2 The pins.

tense¹ (tens) adj. **tens·er, tens·est** 1 Stretched tight; taut. 2 Under mental or nervous strain; apprehensive. 3 *Phonet.* Pronounced with the tongue and its muscles taut, as (ē) and (o͞o). —v.t. & v.i. **tensed, tens·ing** To make or become tense. [< L *tensus,* pp. of *tendere* to stretch] —**tense′ly** adv. —**tense′ness** n. —**Syn.** 2 anxious, nervous, restless, jittery, restive, fidgety.

tense² (tens) n. 1 Any of the forms of a verb that indicate when or how long the expressed action took place or the state of being existed. 2 A specific set of such verb forms: the past *tense* of *to see.* [< L *tempus* time, tense]

ten·sile (ten′sil, *Brit.* ten′sīl) adj. 1 Of or pertaining to tension. 2 Capable of tension. —**ten·sil·i·ty** (ten·sil′ə·tē) n.

tensile strength The resistance of a material to forces of rupture and longitudinal stress: usu. expressed in pounds or tons per square inch.

ten·sion (ten′shən) n. 1 The act of stretching or the condition of being stretched tight; tautness. 2 Mental or nervous strain or anxiety. 3 Any strained relation, as between governments. 4 *Physics* **a** A stress that tends to lengthen a body. **b** The condition of a body when acted on by such stress. 5 A device to regulate the tightness or tautness of something, esp. the thread in a sewing machine. 6 A condition of balance or symmetry produced by opposing elements, as in an artistic work. 7 Electric potential. —**ten′sion·al** adj.

ten·sor (ten′sər, -sôr) n. Any muscle that makes tense or stretches a part.

tent (tent) n. A shelter of canvas or the like, supported by poles and fastened by cords to pegs (called **tent pegs**) driven into the ground. —v.t. 1 To cover with or as with a tent. —v.i. 2 To pitch a tent; camp out. [< L *tendere* stretch]

ten·ta·cle (ten′tə·kəl) n. 1 *Zool.* Any of various long, slender, flexible appendages of animals, esp. invertebrates, functioning as organs of touch, motion, etc. • See SEA ANEMONE. 2 *Bot.* A sensitive hair, as on the leaves of some plants. [< L *tentaculum* < *tentare* to touch, try] —**ten·tac′u·lar** (ten·tak′yə·lər) adj.

ten·ta·tive (ten′tə·tiv) adj. 1 Not definite or final; subject to change. 2 Somewhat uncertain or timid: a *tentative* glance. [< L *tentatus,* pp. of *tentare* to try, probe] —**ten′ta·tive·ly** adv. —**ten′ta·tive·ness** n.

tent caterpillar The gregarious larva of several moths that form colonies in large silken webs in the branches of trees, etc.

ten·ter (ten′tər) n. A frame or machine for stretching cloth to prevent shrinkage while drying. [< L *tentus* extended]

ten·ter·hook (ten′tər·ho͝ok′) n. A sharp hook for holding cloth while being stretched on a tenter. —**be on tenterhooks** To be in a state of anxiety or suspense.

tenth (tenth) adj. & adv. Next in order after the ninth. —n. 1 The element of an ordered set that corresponds to the number ten. 2 One of ten equal parts.

ten·u·ous (ten′yo͞o·əs) adj. 1 Without much substance; slight; weak: *tenuous* arguments. 2 Thin; slender. 3 Having slight density; rare. [< L *tenuis* thin] —**ten′u·ous·ly** adv. —**ten′u·ous·ness, ten·u·i·ty** (te·n′yo͞o′ə·tē, tə-) n.

ten·ure (ten′yər) n. 1 The act, right, length of time, or manner of holding something, as land, elected office, or a

position. 2 The permanent status of a teacher, civil servant, etc., after fulfilling certain requirements. [< L *tenere* to hold] —**ten′ured, ten·u·ri·al** (ten·yo͝or′ē·əl) adj. —**ten·u′ri·al·ly** adv.

te·pee (tē′pē) n. A conical tent of the North American Plains Indians, usu. covered with skins.

tep·id (tep′id) adj. 1 Moderately warm, as a liquid. 2 Not enthusiastic. [< L *tepere* be lukewarm] —**te·pid·i·ty** (tə·pid′ə·tē), **tep′id·ness** n. —**tep′id·ly** adv.

te·qui·la (tə·kē′lə) n. A Mexican alcoholic liquor made from the maguey. [< *Tequila,* a district in Mexico]

Tepee

ter., terr. terrace; territorial; territory.

ter·a·tism (ter′ə·tiz′əm) n. *Biol.* A monstrosity, esp. a malformed human or animal fetus. [< Gk. *teras* monster]

ter·a·to·gen·ic (ter′ə·tō·jen′ik) adj. Tending to cause malformations, as in a developing fetus.

ter·bi·um (tûr′bē·əm) n. A rare-earth metal (symbol Tb). [< *Ytterby,* a town in Sweden]

ter·cen·te·nar·y (tûr′sen·ten′ər·ē, -sent′ən·er′ē) adj. Of or pertaining to a 300th anniversary. —n. pl. **·nar·ies** The 300th anniversary. Also **ter·cen·ten·ni·al** (tûr′sen·ten′ē·əl).

ter·gi·ver·sate (tər·jiv′ər·sāt′, -giv′-) v.i. **·sat·ed, ·sat·ing** 1 To be evasive; equivocate. 2 To change sides, attitudes, etc.; apostatize. [< L *tergum* back + *versare* to turn] —**ter′gi·ver·sa′tor, ter′gi·ver·sa′tion** n.

ter·i·ya·ki (ter′ē·yä′kē) n. A Japanese dish of meat or fish marinated in soy sauce, ginger, etc., then fried, broiled, or grilled. [< Jap.]

term (tûrm) n. 1 A word or expression used to designate some definite thing in a science, profession, art, etc.: a medical *term.* 2 *Often pl.* Any word or expression conveying some conception or thought: a *term* of reproach; to speak in general *terms.* 3 *pl.* The conditions or stipulations according to which something is to be done or acceded to: the *terms* of a contract; peace *terms.* 4 *pl.* Mutual relations; footing: usu. preceded by *on* or *upon:* to be on friendly *terms.* 5 *Math.* **a** The numerator or denominator of a fraction. **b** One of the units of an algebraic expression that are connected by the plus and minus signs. 6 *Logic* **a** In a proposition, either of the two parts, the subject and predicate, which are joined by a copula. **b** Any of the three elements of a syllogism. 7 A fixed or definite period of time, esp. of duration: a *term* of office. 8 A school semester or quarter. 9 End; conclusion. 10 *Law* **a** One of the prescribed periods of the year during which a court may hold a session. **b** A specific extent of time during which an estate may be held. **c** A space of time allowed a debtor to meet his obligation. 11 *Med.* The time for the normal termination of a pregnancy. —**in terms of** With respect to; as relating to. —v.t. To designate by means of a term; name or call. [< L *terminus* a limit]

term. terminal; termination; terminology.

ter·ma·gant (tûr′mə·gənt) n. A scolding or abusive woman; shrew. —adj. Violently abusive and quarrelsome; vixenish. [< ME < *Termagant,* an imaginary Muslim deity] —**ter′ma·gan·cy** n.

term·er (tûr′mər) n. A person serving or attending a certain term, as in a prison or school: used in combination: a *second-termer.*

ter·mi·na·ble (tûr′mə·nə·bəl) adj. That may be terminated; not perpetual. —**ter′mi·na·bil′i·ty, ter′mi·na·ble·ness** n. —**ter′mi·na·bly** adv.

ter·mi·nal (tûr′mə·nəl) adj. 1 Situated at or forming the end, limit, or boundary of something: a *terminal* bus station. 2 Situated or occurring at the end of a series or period of time; final: a *terminal* experiment. 3 At, undergoing, or causing the termination of life: *terminal* cancer; a *terminal* patient. 4 Of or occurring regularly in or at the end of a term or period of time: *terminal* payments. 5

Borne at the end of a stem or branch. —*n.* **1** A terminating point or part; termination; end. **2 a** Either end of a railroad line, bus line, airline, etc. **b** A passenger or freight station located at these end points. **c** Any large passenger or freight station serving an area of considerable size. **3 a** A point in an electric circuit at which it is usual to make or break a connection. **b** A connector designed to facilitate this. **4** An electronic device by means of which a user may communicate with a computer, usually including a cathode-ray tube, a keyboard, and a printer. [<L *terminus* boundary] —**ter′mi·nal·ly** *adv.*

ter·mi·nate (tûr′mə·nāt) *v.* **·nat·ed, ·nat·ing** *v.t.* **1** To put an end or stop to. **2** To form the conclusion of; finish. **3** To bound or limit. —*v.i.* **4** To have an end; come to an end. [<L *terminus* a limit] —**ter′mi·na′tive** *adj.*

ter·mi·na·tion (tûr′mə·nā′shən) *n.* **1** The act of terminating or the condition of being terminated. **2** That which bounds or limits in time or space; close; end. **3** Outcome; result; conclusion. **4** The final letters or syllable of a word; a suffix. —**ter′mi·na′tion·al** *adj.*

ter·mi·na·tor (tûr′mə·nā′tər) *n.* **1** One who or that which terminates. **2** *Astron.* The boundary between the illuminated and dark portions of the moon or of a planet.

ter·mi·nol·o·gy (tûr′mə·nol′ə·jē) *n. pl.* **·gies** The technical terms relating to a particular subject, as a science, art, trade, etc. [<L *terminus* a limit + -LOGY] —**ter′mi·no·log′i·cal** (-nə·loj′i·kəl) *adj.* —**ter′mi·no·log′i·cal·ly** *adv.*

ter·mi·nus (tûr′mə·nəs) *n. pl.* **·nus·es** or **·ni** (-nī, -nē) **1** The final point or goal; end; terminal. **2** Either end of a railroad or bus line, airline, etc.; also, a town or station located at either end [L]

ter·mite (tûr′mīt) *n.* Any of an order of whitish, soft-bodied insects resembling ants and noted for boring into and destroying wooden structures, furniture, etc. [<L *termes, termitis*]

tern (tûrn) *n.* Any of several birds resembling gulls, but smaller, with a sharply pointed bill and a deeply forked tail. [<Scand.]

ter·na·ry (tûr′nər·ē) *adj.* **1** Formed or consisting of three; grouped in threes. **2** Third in order, importance, etc. —*n. pl.* **·ries** A group of three; a triad. [<L *terni* by threes]

ter·pene (tûr′pēn) *n.* Any of various isomeric hydrocarbons contained in essential oils, resins, etc. [<*terp(entin)*, earlier form of TURPENTINE + -ENE]

Terp·sich·o·re (tûrp·sik′ə·rē) *Gk. Myth.* The Muse of dancing. [<Gk. *terpsis* enjoyment + *choros* dance]

terp·si·cho·re·an (tûrp′si·kə·rē′ən, -sə·kôr′ē-, -kō′rē-) *adj.* Of or relating to dancing. Also **terp′si·cho·re′al.**

ter·race (ter′is) *n.* **1** A raised level space, as of lawn, usu. with sloping sides; also, such levels collectively. **2** A raised street supporting a row of houses; also, the houses occupying such a street. **3** A flat roof, esp. of an Oriental or Spanish house. **4** An open, paved area connected to a house, apartment, or building, usu. with places for seating, plantings, etc. **5** A balcony. **6** A parklike area extending down the middle of a wide street or boulevard. **7** A relatively narrow step in the face of a steep natural slope. —*v.t.* **·raced, ·rac·ing** To form into or provide with a terrace or terraces. [<L *terra* earth]

ter·ra cot·ta (ter′ə kot′ə) **1** A hard, kiln-burnt clay, reddish brown and usu. unglazed, used for pottery, sculpture, etc. **2** A statue made of this clay. **3** A brownish red color. [Ital., lit, cooked earth]

ter·ra fir·ma (ter′ə fûr′mə) Solid ground, as distinguished from the sea or the air. [L]

ter·rain (te·rān′, ter′ān) *n.* **1** Battleground, or a region suited for defense, fortifications, etc. **2** A land area viewed with regard to some particular characteristic: marshy *terrain.* [<L *terrenus* earthen < *terra* earth]

Ter·ra·my·cin (ter′ə·mī′sin) *n.* An antibiotic effective against a wide variety of pathogenic organisms: a trade name.

ter·ra·pin (ter′ə·pin) *n.* **1** One of the several North American edible tortoises, esp. the diamond-back. **2** Its flesh. [<Algon.]

ter·rar·i·um (te·râr′ē·əm) *n. pl.* **·rar·i·ums** or **·rar·i·a** (-râr′ē·ə) **1** A glass enclosure for growing a collection of small plants. **2** A

Terrapin

vivarium for small land animals. [<L *terra* earth + -arium, on analogy with *aquarium*]

ter·res·tri·al (tə·res′trē·əl) *adj.* **1** Belonging to the planet earth. **2** Pertaining to land or earth. **3** Living or growing in earth. **4** Belonging to or consisting of land, as distinct from water, air, etc. **5** Worldly; mundane. —*n.* An inhabitant of the earth. [<L *terra* land] —**ter·res′tri·al·ly** *adv.*

ter·ret (ter′it) *n.* One of two metal rings on a harness, through which the reins are passed. [<OF *touret* small wheel]

ter·ri·ble (ter′ə·bəl) *adj.* **1** Causing extreme fear, dread, or terror. **2** Severe; extreme: a *terrible* headache. **3** Awesome: a *terrible* burden of guilt. **4** Very bad; dreadful; awful: a *terrible* play. [<L *terribilis* < *terrere* terrify] —**ter′ri·ble·ness** *n.* —**ter′ri·bly** *adv.*

ter·ri·er (ter′ē·ər) *n.* Any of several breeds of small, active, wiry dogs, formerly used to hunt burrowing animals. [<L *terrarius* pertaining to earth]

ter·rif·ic (tə·rif′ik) *adj.* **1** Arousing great terror or fear; frightening. **2** *Informal* **a** Very great; extraordinary; tremendous. **b** Unusually good; excellent. —**ter·rif′i·cal·ly** *adv.*

ter·ri·fy (ter′ə·fī) *v.t.* **·fied, ·fy·ing** To fill with terror; frighten severely. [<L *terrere* frighten + -FY]

ter·ri·to·ri·al (ter′ə·tôr′ē·əl, -tō′rē-) *adj.* **1** Of or pertaining to a territory or territories. **2** Of, restricted to, or under the jurisdiction of a particular territory, region, or district. **3** *Often cap.* Organized or intended primarily for home defense: the British *Territorial* Army. —**ter′ri·to′ri·al·ism′, ter′ri·to′ri·al·ist** *n.* —**ter′ri·to′ri·al·ly** *adv.*

ter·ri·to·ri·al·i·ty (ter′ə·tôr′ē·al′ə·tē, -tō′rē-) *n.* Territorial condition, status, or position.

ter·ri·to·ry (ter′ə·tôr′ē, -tō′rē) *n. pl.* **·ries 1** The domain over which a nation, state, etc., exercises jurisdiction. **2** Any considerable tract of land; a region; district. **3** A region having a certain degree of self-government, but not having the status of a state or province. **4** A special sphere or province of activity, knowledge, etc. **5** A specific area used by or assigned to a person, group, etc.: a salesman's *territory.* [<L *terra* earth]

ter·ror (ter′ər) *n.* **1** Overwhelming fear. **2** A person or thing that causes extreme fear. **3** *Informal* A difficult or annoying person, esp. a child. **4** TERRORISM. [<L *terrere* frighten]

ter·ror·ism (ter′ə·riz′əm) *n.* The act or practice of terrorizing, esp. by violence committed for political purposes, as by a government seeking to intimidate a populace or by revolutionaries seeking to overthrow a government, compel the release of prisoners, etc. —**ter′ror·ist** *n.* —**ter′ror·is′tic** *adj.*

ter·ror·ize (ter′ə·rīz) *v.t.* **·ized, ·iz·ing 1** To reduce to a state of terror; terrify. **2** To coerce or intimidate through terrorism. —**ter′ror·i·za′tion, ter′ror·iz′er** *n.*

ter·ry (ter′ē) *n. pl.* **·ries** A very absorbent pile fabric in which the loops are uncut, used for towels, etc. Also **terry cloth.** [?]

terse (tûrs) *adj.* **ters·er, ters·est** Short and to the point; succinct. [<L *tersus*, pp. of *tergere* rub off, rub down] —**terse′ly** *adv.* —**terse′ness** *n.* —**Syn.** brief, concise, pithy, curt, laconic.

ter·tian (tûr′shən) *adj.* Recurring every other day: said of a fever or disease causing such a fever, as certain forms of malaria. [<L *tertius* third (recurring every third day, reckoned inclusively)]

ter·ti·ar·y (tûr′shē·er′ē, -shə·rē) *adj.* Third in point of time, importance, rank, or value. —*n. pl.* **·ar·ies** Any of the third row of wing feathers of a bird. [<L *tertius* third]

Ter·ti·ar·y (tûr′shē·er′ē, -shə·rē) *n. & adj.* See GEOLOGY.

tes·sel·late (tes′ə·lāt) *v.t.* **·lat·ed, ·lat·ing** To lay or adorn with small squares or mosaic tiles, as pavement. —*adj.* Adorned or laid with mosaic patterns: also **tes′sel·lat′ed.** [<L *tessellatus* checkered] —**tes′sel·la′tion** *n.*

tes·si·tu·ra (tes′i·tŏor′ə) *n.* The average range of a melody or vocal composition. [Ital., lit., texture]

test (test) *v.t.* **1** To subject to an examination or proof; try. —*v.i.* **2** To undergo or give an examination or test: usu. with *for:* to *test* for accuracy. **3** To receive a rating as a result of testing: The alcohol *tested* 75 percent. —*n.* **1** An examination or observation to find out the real nature of something or to prove or disprove its value or validity. **2** A method or technique employed to do this. **3** A criterion or standard of judgment or evaluation. **4** An undergoing of or subjection to certain conditions that disclose the character, quality, nature, etc., of a person or thing: a *test* of will. **5** A series of questions, problems, etc., intended to measure knowledge, aptitudes, intelligence, etc. **6** *Chem.* **a** A reaction by means of which a compound or ingredient may be identified. **b** Its agent or the result. [< L *testum* an earthen vessel < *testa* potsherd, shell] —**test'a·ble** *adj.* —**test'er** *n.*

Test. Testament.

tes·ta (tes'tə) *n. pl.* **·tae** (-tē) The outer, usu. hard and brittle coat of a seed. [L, shell]

tes·ta·ment (tes'tə·mənt) *n.* **1** The written declaration of one's last will: now usu. in the phrase **last will and testament**. **2** A statement testifying to some belief or conviction; credo. **3** Proof; evidence: a *testament* to their courage. **4** In Biblical use, a covenant; dispensation. [< L *testari* testify] —**tes'ta·men'tal, tes'ta·men'ta·ry** (-men'tər·ē) *adj.*

Tes·ta·ment (tes'tə·mənt) *n.* Either of the two parts of the Bible, distinguished as the **Old** and the **New Testament**.

tes·tate (tes'tāt) *adj.* Having made a will before decease. [< L *testari* be a witness]

tes·ta·tor (tes·tā'tər, tes'tā·tər) *n.* One who has died leaving a will. [< L] —**tes·ta'trix** (-triks) *n. Fem.*

tes·ti·cle (tes'ti·kəl) *n.* One of the two sex glands of the male which secrete sex hormones and spermatozoa. [< L *testiculus,* dim. of *testis* testicle]

tes·ti·fy (tes'tə·fī) *v.* **·fied, ·fy·ing** *v.i.* **1** To make solemn declaration of truth or fact. **2** *Law* To give testimony; bear witness. **3** To serve as evidence or indication. —*v.t.* **4** To bear witness to; affirm. **5** *Law* To state or declare on oath or affirmation. **6** To be evidence or indication of. **7** To make known publicly; declare. [< L *testis* witness + -FY] —**tes'ti·fi·ca'tion, tes'ti·fi'er** *n.*

tes·ti·mo·ni·al (tes'tə·mō'nē·əl) *n.* **1** A statement, often a letter, recommending the character, value, etc., of a person or thing. **2** An act, statement, event, etc., that gives public acknowledgment of esteem or appreciation. —*adj.* Pertaining to or constituting testimony or a testimonial.

tes·ti·mo·ny (tes'tə·mō'nē) *n. pl.* **·nies** **1** An oral statement of a witness under oath in a court, usu. made in answer to questioning by a lawyer or judge. **2** Any public acknowledgment or declaration, as of a religious experience. **3** Proof of something; evidence. [< L *testimonium* < *testis* a witness]

tes·tis (tes'tis) *n. pl.* **·tes** (-tēz) TESTICLE. [L]

tes·tos·ter·one (tes·tos'tə·rōn) *n.* A natural or synthetic male sex hormone. [< TESTIS + STER(OL) + -ONE]

test-tube (tes't'ʹyōōb') *adj.* **1** Experimental in nature. **2** Produced by artificial insemination.

test tube A tubular glass vessel used in making chemical or biological tests.

tes·ty (tes'tē) *adj.* **·ti·er, ·ti·est** Irritable; touchy. [< AF *testif* heady < OF *teste* head] —**tes'ti·ly** *adv.* —**tes'ti·ness** *n.* —**Syn.** irascible, peevish, petulant, querulous, snappish, crabby, grouchy.

tet·a·nus (tet'ə·nəs) *n.* An acute and often fatal infectious bacterial disease marked by spasmodic contraction of voluntary muscles, esp. the muscles of the jaw. [< Gk. *tetanos* spasm < *teinein* to stretch] —**te·tan·ic** (ti·tan'ik) *adj.*

tetched (techt) *adj. Regional* Slightly unbalanced mentally. [Alter. of *touched*]

tetch·y (tech'ē) *adj.* **tetch·i·er, tetch·i·est** Irritable; peevish; touchy. [< OF *teche* mark, quality] —**tetch'i·ly** *adv.* —**tetch'i·ness** *n.*

tête-à-tête (tāt'ə·tāt', *Fr.* tet·à·tet') *adj.* Confidential, as between two persons. —*n.* **1** A confidential chat between two persons. **2** An S-shaped sofa on which two persons may face each other. —*adv.* In private or personal talk. [F, lit., head to head]

teth·er (teth'ər) *n.* **1** Something used to check or confine, as a rope for fastening an animal. **2** The limit of one's

powers or field of action. —**at the end of one's tether** At the extreme limit of one's resources, patience, etc. [< Scand.]

tetra- *combining form* Four; fourfold: *tetrachloride.* [< Gk.]

tet·ra·chlo·ride (tet'rə·klôr'īd, -id, -klō'rīd, -rid) *n.* A compound containing four atoms of chlorine per molecule.

tet·ra·eth·yl lead (tet'rə·eth'il led) A poisonous organic antiknock compound.

tet·ra·he·dron (tet'rə·hē'drən) *n. pl.* **·drons** or **·dra** (-drə) A solid bounded by four plane triangular faces. [< Gk. *tetra-* four + *hedra* base] —**tet'ra·he'dral** *adj.*

te·tral·o·gy (te·träl'ə·jē, -tral'-) *n. pl.* **·gies** **1** A group of four dramas presented together at the festivals of Dionysus at Athens. **2** Any series of four related novels, plays, operas, etc. [< TETRA- + -LOGY]

Tetrahedron

te·tram·e·ter (te·tram'ə·tər) *n.* In English verse, a line having four metrical feet. [< TETRA + -METER]

tet·rarch (tet'rärk, tē'trärk) *n.* **1** In the Roman Empire, the governor of one of four divisions of a province. **2** A subordinate ruler. [< Gk. *tetra-* four + *archos* ruler] —**tet·rar·chy** (tet'rär·kē, tē'trär-), **tet·rarch·ate** (tet'rär·kāt, -kit, tē'trär-) *n.*

tet·ra·va·lent (tet'rə·vā'lənt) *adj.* QUADRIVALENT. —**tet'ra·va'lence, tet'ra·va'len·cy** *n.*

te·trox·ide (te·trok'sīd, -sid) *n.* Any oxide having four atoms of oxygen per molecule. [< TETR(A)- + OXIDE]

Teu·ton (tyōōt'n) *n.* **1** One of an ancient German tribe that dwelt in Jutland north of the Elbe, appearing in history as **Teu·to·nes** (tyōō'tə·nēz). **2** One belonging to any of the Teutonic peoples, esp. a German.

Teu·ton·ic (tyōō·ton'ik) *adj.* **1** Of or pertaining to the Teutons. **2** Of or pertaining to Germany or the Germans. **3** Of or pertaining to the peoples of northern Europe, including the English, Scandinavians, Dutch, etc. —**Teu·ton'i·cal·ly** *adv.*

Tex. Texan; Texas.

Texas leaguer In baseball, a looping fly ball that falls safe between an infielder and an outfielder.

text (tekst) *n.* **1** The actual or original words of an author or speaker, as distinguished from notes, commentary, illustrations, etc. **2** Any of the written or printed versions or editions of a piece of writing. **3** The main body of written or printed matter of a book or a single page, as distinguished from notes, indexes, illustrations, etc. **4** The words of a song, opera, etc. **5** A verse of Scripture, esp. when cited as the basis of a sermon. **6** Any subject of discourse; a topic; theme. **7** One of several styles of letters or types. **8** TEXTBOOK. [< L *textus* fabric, structure < *texere* to weave]

text·book (tekst'book') *n.* A book used as a standard work or basis of instruction in any branch of knowledge; schoolbook; manual.

tex·tile (teks'tīl, -til) *adj.* **1** Pertaining to weaving or woven fabrics. **2** Such as may be woven; manufactured by weaving. —*n.* **1** A fabric, esp. if woven or knitted; cloth. **2** Material, as a fiber, yarn, etc., capable of being woven. [< L *textus* fabric. See TEXT.]

tex·tu·al (teks'chōō·əl) *adj.* **1** Pertaining to, contained in, or based on a text. **2** Literal; word for word. —**tex'tu·al·ly** *adv.*

tex·ture (teks'chər) *n.* **1** The arrangement or characteristics of the threads, etc., of a fabric: a tweed having a rough *texture.* **2** The arrangement or characteristics of the constituent elements of anything, esp. as regards surface appearance or tactile qualities: the *texture* of bread. **3** The overall or characteristic structure, form, or interrelatedness of parts of a work of art, music, literature, etc.: the tightly-knit *texture* of his poems. **4** The basic nature or structure of something: the *texture* of rural life. [< L *textus* fabric. See TEXT.] —**tex'tur·al** *adj.* —**tex'tur·al·ly** *adv.*

T-group (tē'grōōp) *n.* A group of people, often business or industrial personnel, who meet with a trained leader whose function is to guide them to a more insightful awareness of themselves and others through the free and uninhibited expression of their thoughts, feelings, prejudices, etc. [< *t(raining) group*]

-th[1] *suffix of nouns* **1** The act or result of the action: *growth.* **2** The state or quality of being or having: *health.* [< OE *-thu, -tho*]

-th[2] *suffix* Used in ordinal numbers: *tenth.* Also **-eth.** [< OE *-tha, -the*]

-th[3] See -ETH[1].

Th thorium.

Th., Thur., Thurs. Thursday.

Thai (tī) *n.* **1** *pl.* **Thai** or **Thais a** A native or citizen of Thailand. **b** A member of the majority ethnic group of Thailand. **2** Any one of a group of related languages used in Thailand. —*adj.* Of or pertaining to Thailand, its people, or their languages.

Thai·land (tī′land) *n.* A constitutional monarchy in SE Asia, 198,404 sq. mi., cap. Bangkok. •See map at INDO-CHINA.

thal·a·mus (thal′ə·məs) *n. pl.* ·**mi** (-mī, mē) **1** A mass of gray matter at the base of the brain, involved in sensory transmission. **2** The receptacle of a flower. [< Gk. *thalamos* chamber] —**tha·lam·ic** (thə·lam′ik) *adj.*

Tha·li·a (thə·lī′ə, thā′lē·ə, thāl′yə) *Gk. Myth.* **1** The Muse of comedy and pastoral poetry. **2** One of the three Graces. [< Gk. *thallein* to bloom]

thal·li·um (thal′ē·əm) *n.* A soft, rare, highly poisonous metallic element (symbol Tl), used in rat poison, insecticides, and in making optical glass. [< Gk. *thallos* a green shoot; from the bright green line in its spectrum]

thal·lo·phyte (thal′ə·fīt) *n.* Any of a major division of plants without roots, stems, or leaves, comprising the bacteria, fungi, algae, and lichens. [< THALLUS + -PHYTE] —**thal′lo·phyt′ic** (-fit′ik) *adj.*

thal·lus (thal′əs) *n. pl.* ·**lus·es** or ·**li** (-ī) *Bot.* A plant body without true root, stem, or leaf, as in thallophytes. [< Gk. *thallos* a shoot]

than (than, *unstressed* thən) *conj.* **1** When, as, or if compared with: after an adjective or adverb to express comparison between what precedes and what follows: I am stronger *than* he (is); I know her better *than* (I know) him. **2** Except; but: used after *other, else, else:* no other *than* you. **3** When: usu. used after *scarcely, hardly, barely:* Scarcely had we got settled *than* we had to leave. —*prep.* Compared to: used only in the phrases *than whom, than which:* An eminent judge *than whom* no other is finer. [< OE *thanne*] • The case of a word following *than* can be either nominative or objective, depending on the word's function in the elliptical clause introduced by *than: You owe him more money than I* (owe him) or *You owe him more money than (you owe) me.* However, in informal writing and speech, the objective case is acceptable following *than* whether or not it agrees with the ellipsis: *He is younger than me.*

thane (thān) *n.* **1** In Anglo-Saxon England, a man who ranked above an ordinary freeman but below an earl or nobleman and who held land of the king or a noble in exchange for military service. **2** The chief of a Scottish clan, a baron in the service of the king. [< OE *thegn*]

thank (thangk) *v.t.* **1** To express gratitude to; give thanks to. **2** To hold responsible; blame: often used ironically: We have him to *thank* for this mess. —**thank you** An expression of gratitude or in acknowledgment of a service rendered. [< OE *thancian*]

thank·ful (thangk′fəl) *adj.* Feeling or manifesting thanks or gratitude; grateful. —**thank′ful·ly** *adv.* —**thank′ful·ness** *n.*

thank·less (thangk′lis) *adj.* **1** Not feeling or expressing gratitude; ungrateful. **2** Not gaining or likely to gain thanks; unappreciated. —**thank′less·ly** *adv.* —**thank′less·ness** *n.*

thanks (thangks) *n.pl.* An expression of gratitude or appreciation. —*interj.* I thank you. —**thanks to 1** Thanks be given to. **2** Because of.

thanks·giv·ing (thangks′giv′ing) *n.* **1** The act of giving thanks. **2** A manner of expressing thanks, as a prayer, public celebration, etc.

Thanksgiving Day 1 In the U.S., the fourth Thursday in November, set apart as a legal holiday for giving

thanks for the year's blessings. Also **Thanksgiving. 2** In Canada, a similar holiday celebrated the second Monday in October.

that (that, *unstressed* thət) *adj. pl.* **those 1** Pertaining to some person or thing previously mentioned, understood, or specifically designated: *that* man. **2** Denoting something more remote in place, time, or thought than the thing with which it is being compared: This winter was colder than *that* one. —*pron. pl.* **those 1** As a demonstrative pronoun: **a** The person or thing implied, mentioned, or understood. **b** The thing further away or more remote: This will happen sooner than *that* will. **2** As a relative pronoun, *that* is used to introduce restrictive clauses and, as such, has a variety of meanings, as *who, whom, which, where, at which, with which,* etc.: The man *that* (whom) I saw is not here; The house *that* (which) you lived in was torn down. **3** Something: There is *that* to be said for him. —*adv.* **1** To that extent; so: I can't see *that* far. **2** *Informal* In such a manner or degree: It really is *that* bad! —*conj.* *That* is used primarily to connect a subordinate clause with its principal clause, with the following meanings: **1** As a fact that: introducing a fact: I tell you *that* it is so. **2** So that; in order that: I tell you *that* you may know. **3** For the reason that; because: She wept *that* she was growing old. **4** As a result: introducing a result, consequence, or effect: He bled so profusely *that* he died. **5** At which time; when: It was only yesterday *that* I saw him. **6** Introducing an exclamation: O *that* he would come! —**so that 1** To the end that. **2** With the result that. **3** Provided. [< OE *thæt*] •See WHO.

thatch (thach) *n.* **1** A covering of reeds, straw, etc., arranged on a roof so as to shed water. **2** Any of various palm leaves or coarse grasses so used. Also **thatching.** —*v.t.* To cover with a thatch. [< OE *thæc* cover] —**thatch′er** *n.* —**thatch′y** *adj.* (**thatch·i·er, thatch·i·est**)

thau·ma·tur·gy (thô′mə·tûr′jē) *n.* Magic; the performance or working of wonders or miracles. [< Gk. *thauma* wonder + *ergon* work] —**thau′ma·turge, thau′ma·tur′gist** *n.* —**thau′ma·tur′gic** or -**gi·cal** *adj.*

thaw (thô) *v.i.* **1** To melt or dissolve, as snow or ice. **2** To lose the effects of coldness or of having been frozen: often with *out.* **3** To rise in temperature so as to melt ice and snow: said of weather: It *thawed* last night. **4** To become less aloof, unsociable, rigid in opinions, etc. —*v.t.* **5** To cause to thaw. —*n.* **1** The act of thawing. **2** Warmth of weather such as melts things frozen. **3** A becoming less aloof, unsociable, etc. [< OE *thāwian*] —**thaw′er** *n.*

Th.B. Bachelor of Theology.

Th.D. Doctor of Theology.

the[1] (*stressed* thē; *unstressed before a consonant* thə; *unstressed before a vowel* thē, thi) *definite article. The* is opposed to the indefinite article *a* or *an,* and is used specifically: **1** When reference is made to a particular person, thing, or group: *The* children are getting restless; He left *the* room. **2** To give an adjective substantive force, or render a notion abstract: *the* quick and *the* dead; *the* doing of the deed. **3** Before a noun to make it generic: *The* dog is a friend of man. **4** With the force of a possessive pronoun: He kicked me in *the* (my) leg. **5** To give distributive force: equivalent to *a, per, each,* etc.: a dollar *the* bushel. **6** To designate the whole of a specific time period: *The* children are getting restless; in *the* Middle Ages; in *the* forties. **7** To designate a particular one as emphatically outstanding: usu. stressed in speech and italicized in writing: He is *the* officer for the command. **8** As part of a title: *The* Duke of York. **9** Before the name of a well-known place, thing, etc.: *the* Grand Canyon; *the* Eiffel Tower. [< OE]

the[2] (thə) *adv.* By that much; to this extent: *the* more, *the* merrier: used to modify words in the comparative degree. [< OE *thȳ*]

the·a·ter (thē′ə·tər) *n.* **1** A structure for the indoor or outdoor presentation of plays, operas, motion pictures, etc. **2** A place resembling such a structure, used for lectures, surgical demonstrations, etc. **3** The theatrical world and everything relating to it, esp.: **a** The legitimate stage, as distinguished from motion pictures, television, etc. **b** The works written for or the arts connected with the theater. **4** Theatrical effectiveness: The play was not good *theater.* **5** Any place that is the scene of events or action:

a *theater* of war operations. Also **the′a·tre**. [< Gk. *theatron* < *theasthai* behold]

the·a·ter-in-the-round (thē′ə·tər·in·thə·round′) *n.* A theater having a central stage and no proscenium, with seats surrounding the stage.

theater of the absurd A form of drama that concerns itself with the tragic or comic absurdities of man's condition and his futile efforts to deal with or resolve such absurdities.

the·at·ri·cal (thē·at′ri·kəl) *adj.* 1 Of or pertaining to the theater or things of the theater, as plays, actors, costumes, etc. 2 Dramatically effective or compelling. 3 Artificially dramatic, esp. in a pretentious or showy way. Also **the·at′ric**. —*n.pl.* Dramatic performances, esp. when given by amateurs. —**the·at′ri·cal·ism, the·at′ri·cal′i·ty** *n.* — **the·at′ri·cal·ly** *adv.*

the·at·rics (thē·at′riks) *n.pl.* *(construed as sing.)* The art of the theater. 2 Exaggeratedly dramatic or showy behavior, mannerisms, etc.

thee (thē) *pron.* 1 The objective case of *thou.* 2 Thou: used generally by Quakers with a verb in the third person singular: *Thee* knows my mind. [< OE *thē*]

theft (theft) *n.* 1 The act or an instance of stealing; larceny. 2 That which is stolen. [< OE *thēoft*]

the·ine (thē′ən) *n.* The alkaloid identical with caffeine, found in tea. [< NL *thea* tea]

their (thâr) *pronominal adj.* The possessive case of the pronoun *they* used attributively; belonging or pertaining to them: *their* homes. [< ON *theirra* of them]

theirs (thârz) *pron.* 1 The possessive case of *they*, used predicatively; belonging or pertaining to them: That house is *theirs.* 2 The things or persons belonging or relating to them: our country and *theirs.* —**of theirs** Belonging or pertaining to them.

the·ism (thē′iz·əm) *n.* 1 Belief in a god or gods. 2 Belief in a personal God as creator and supreme ruler of the universe. [< Gk. *theos* god] —**the′ist** *n.* —**the·is′tic** or **·ti·cal** *adj.* —**the·is′ti·cal·ly** *adv.*

them (them, *unstressed* thəm) *pron.* The objective case of *they.* [< ON *theim*]

theme (thēm) *n.* 1 A main subject or topic, as of a poem, novel, play, speech, etc. 2 A short essay, often written as an exercise. 3 In a musical composition, a melodic, harmonic, or rhythmic subject or phrase, usu. developed with variations. 4 THEME SONG. [< Gk. *thema*] —**the·mat′ic** (-mat′ik) or **·i·cal** *adj.* —**the·mat′i·cal·ly** *adv.*

theme song 1 A musical motif recurring in a film, television presentation, etc. 2 The brief melody identifying a radio or television presentation, a dance band, etc.

them·selves (them′selvz′, *unstressed* thəm-) *pron.* A form of the third person, plural pronoun, used: 1 As a reflexive: They forced *themselves* to go. 2 As an intensive: They *themselves* are responsible. 3 As an indication of their normal, true, or proper selves: They were not *themselves* when they said it.

then (then) *adv.* 1 At that time. 2 Soon afterward; next in time: We dressed and *then* ate. 3 Next in space or order: Add the flour, *then* the butter. 4 At another time: often introducing a sequential statement following *now, at first,* etc.: At first she laughed, *then* she cried. —*conj.* 1 For that reason; as a consequence; accordingly: If we leave now, *then* you can go to bed. 2 In that case: I will *then,* since you won't. —*adj.* Being or acting in, or belonging to, that time: the *then* secretary of state. —*n.* A specific time already mentioned or understood; that time: We will be gone by *then.* [< OE *thanne*]

thence (thens) *adv.* 1 From that place. 2 From the circumstance, fact, or cause; therefore. 3 From that time; after that time. [< OE *thanon* from there]

thence·forth (thens′fôrth′, -fōrth′) *adv.* From that time on; thereafter. Also **thence′for′ward** (-fôr′wərd), **thence′·for′wards.**

theo- *combining form* God or a god: *theocracy.* [< Gk. *theos* a god]

the·o·cen·tric (thē′ə·sen′trik) *adj.* Having God for its center; proceeding from God.

the·oc·ra·cy (thē·ok′rə·sē) *n. pl.* **·cies** 1 A state, polity, or group of people that claims a deity as its ruler. 2 Government by a priestly class claiming to have divine authority, as in the Papacy. [< Gk. *theos* god + *krateein* rule] —**the·o·crat** (thē′ə·krat) *n.* —**the·o·crat·ic** (thē′ə·krat′ik) or **·i·cal** *adj.* —**the′o·crat′i·cal·ly** *adv.*

the·od·o·lite (thē·od′ə·līt) *n.* A surveying instrument having a small telescope for measuring angles. [?]

theol. theologian; theological; theology.

the·o·lo·gi·an (thē′ə·lō′jən) *n.* One versed in theology.

the·o·log·i·cal (thē′ə·loj′i·kəl) *adj.* Of, pertaining to, based on, or teaching theology. Also **the′o·log′ic.** —**the′o·log′i·cal·ly** *adv.*

the·ol·o·gize (thē·ol′ə·jīz) *v.* **·gized, ·giz·ing** *v.t.* 1 To devise or fit (something) into a system of theology. —*v.i.* 2 To reason theologically.

the·ol·o·gy (thē·ol′ə·jē) *n. pl.* **·gies** 1 The study of God, his attributes, and his relationship with man and the universe, esp. such studies as set forth by a specific church, religious group, or theologian. 2 The study of religion and religious doctrine, culminating in a synthesis or philosophy of religion. [< Gk. *theos* god + *logos* discourse]

the·o·rem (thē′ər·əm, thir′əm) *n.* 1 A proposition demonstrably true or so universally acknowledged as such as to become part of a general theory. 2 *Math.* A proposition to be proved or which has been proved. [< Gk. *theōrēma* sight, theory] —**the·o·re·mat·ic** (thē′ər·ə·mat′ik) *adj.*

the·o·ret·i·cal (thē′ə·ret′i·kəl) *adj.* 1 Of, relating to, or consisting of theory. 2 Existing only in theory; not applied; speculative; hypothetical. 3 Addicted to theorizing. Also **the′o·ret′ic.** —**the′o·ret′i·cal·ly** *adv.*

the·o·re·ti·cian (thē′ər·ə·tish′ən) *n.* One who theorizes. Also **the·o·rist** (thē′ər·ist).

the·o·rize (thē′ə·rīz) *v.i.* **·rized, ·riz·ing** To form or express theories; speculate. —**the′o·ri·za′tion, the′o·riz′er** *n.*

the·o·ry (thē′ər·ē, thir′ē) *n. pl.* **·ries** 1 A plan, scheme, or procedure intended or to be used as a basis or technique for doing something. 2 A merely speculative or an ideal circumstance, principle, mode of action, etc.: often with *in:* In *theory,* the plan worked. 3 A body of fundamental or abstract principles underlying a science, art, etc.: a *theory* of modern architecture. 4 A proposed explanation or hypothesis designed to account for any phenomenon. 5 Loosely, mere speculation, conjecture, or guesswork. [< Gk. *theōria* view, speculation]

theos. theosophical; theosophist; theosophy.

the·os·o·phy (thē·os′ə·fē) *n.* 1 Any of several religious or philosophical systems claiming to have mystical insight into the nature of God and the universe. 2 *Usu. cap.* The religious system of a modern religious sect (**Theosophical Society**) that is strongly Buddhist or Brahmanic in character and claims to have and to be able to teach such mystical insights. [< Gk. *theos* god + *sophos* wise] —**the·o·soph·ic** (thē′ə·sof′ik) or **·i·cal** *adj.* —**the′o·soph′i·cal·ly** *adv.* —**the·os′o·phist** *n.*

ther·a·peu·tic (ther′ə·pyōō′tik) *adj.* 1 Having healing qualities; curative. 2 Pertaining to therapeutics. Also **ther′a·peu′ti·cal.** [< Gk. *therapeuein* serve, take care of] — **ther′a·peu′ti·cal·ly** *adv.*

ther·a·peu·tics (ther′ə·pyōō′tiks) *n.pl.* *(construed as sing.)* The branch of medicine that treats of remedies for disease. —**ther′a·peu′tist** *n.*

ther·a·py (ther′ə·pē) *n. pl.* **·pies** 1 The treatment of disease or any bodily disorder or injury by drugs, physical exercise, etc. 2 PSYCHOTHERAPY. [< Gk. *therapeuein* take care of] —**ther′a·pist** *n.*

there (thâr) *adv.* 1 In or at that place; in a place other than that of the speaker. 2 To, toward, or into that place; thither. 3 At that stage or point of action or proceeding. 4 In that respect, relation, or connection. —*n.* That place, position, or point: We moved it from *there* to here. [< OE *thær*] • *There* is also used: **a** As a pronominal expletive introducing a clause or sentence, the subject usually following the verb: *There* once lived three bears. **b** With independent phrases or clauses, as an equivalent of *that,* expressing encouragement, approval, etc.: *There's* a little dear. **c** As an exclamation expressing triumph, etc.: *There!* I told you so.

there·a·bouts (thâr′ə·bouts′, thâr′ə·bouts′) *adv.* Near that number, quantity, degree, place, or time; approximately. Also **there′a·bout** (-bout′).

there·af·ter (thâr′af′tər, -äf′-) *adv.* **1** Afterward; from that time on. **2** Accordingly.

there·at (thâr′at′) *adv.* At that event, place, or time; at that incentive; upon that.

there·by (thâr′bī′, thâr′bī′) *adv.* **1** Through the agency of that. **2** Connected with that. **3** Conformably to that. **4** Nearby; thereabout. **5** By it or that; into possession of it or that: How did you come *thereby?*

there·for (thâr′fôr′) *adv.* For this, that, or it; in return or requital for this or that: We return thanks *therefor.*

there·fore (thâr′fôr′, -fōr′) *adv. & conj.* **1** For that or this reason. **2** Consequently: He did not run fast enough; *therefore* he lost the race.

there·from (thâr′frum′, -from′) *adv.* From this, that, or it; from this or that time, place, state, event, or thing.

there·in (thâr′in′) *adv.* **1** In that place. **2** In that time, matter, or respect.

there·in·af·ter (thâr′in·af′tər, -äf′-) *adv.* In a subsequent part of that (book, document, speech, etc.).

there·in·to (thâr′in·tōō′, thâr·in′tōō) *adv.* Into this, that, or it.

there·of (thâr′uv′, -ov′) *adv.* **1** Of or relating to this, that, or it. **2** From or because of this or that cause or particular; therefrom.

there·on (thâr′on′, -ôn′) *adv.* **1** On this, that, or it. **2** Thereupon; thereat.

there's (thârz) Contraction of *there is.*

there·to (thâr′tōō′) *adv.* **1** To this, that, or it. **2** In addition; furthermore. Also **there·un·to** (thâr′un′tōō, -un·tōō′).

there·to·fore (thâr′tə·fôr′, -fōr′, thâr′tə·fôr′, -fōr′) *adv.* Before this or that; previously to that.

there·un·der (thâr′un′dər) *adv.* **1** Under this or that. **2** Less, as in number. **3** In a lower or lesser status or rank.

there·up·on (thâr′ə·pon′, -pôn′, thâr′ə·pon′, -ə·pôn′) *adv.* **1** Upon that; upon it. **2** Following upon or in consequence of that. **3** Immediately following; at once.

there·with (thâr′with′, -with′) *adv.* **1** With this, that, or it. **2** Thereupon; thereafter; immediately afterward.

there·with·al (thâr′with·ôl′) *adv.* With all this or that; besides.

ther·mal (thûr′məl) *adj.* **1** Of, coming from, or having hot springs. **2** Of, relating to, or caused by heat. **3** Hot or warm: a *thermal* draft. **4** Aiding to conserve body heat: *thermal* fabrics. Also **ther′mic.** —*n.* A rising current of warm air in the atmosphere. [< Gk. *thermē* heat]

thermo- *combining form* Heat; of, related to, or caused by heat: *thermodynamics.* [< Gk. *thermos* heat, warmth]

ther·mo·dy·nam·ics (thûr′mō·dī·nam′iks, -di-) *n.pl. (construed as sing.)* The branch of physics that deals with the relations between heat, other forms of energy, and work. —**ther′mo·dy·nam′ic** or **·i·cal** *adj.* —**ther′mo·dy·nam′i·cist** (-nam′ə·sist) *n.*

ther·mo·e·lec·tric·i·ty (thûr′mō·i·lek′tris′ə·tē) *n.* Electricity generated by heat. —**ther′mo·e·lec′tric** or **·tri·cal** *adj.* —**ther′mo·e·lec′tri·cal·ly** *adv.*

ther·mo·gram (thûr′mə·gram) *n.* The record made by a thermograph.

ther·mo·graph (thûr′mə·graf, -gräf) *n.* **1** An instrument for detecting and recording temperature gradations across a surface. **2** A self-registering thermometer.

ther·mog·ra·phy (thər·mog′rə·fē) *n.* **1** The process of recording temperature variations with a thermograph. **2** A process that produces raised lettering on paper, as on stationery, by applying a powder to the lettering and then subjecting it to heat. —**ther·mo·graph·ic** (thûr′mə·graf′ik) *adj.*

ther·mom·e·ter (thər·mom′ə·tər) *n.* An instrument for measuring temperature, often consisting of a tube with a bulb containing a liquid which expands or contracts so that its height in the tube is proportional to the temperature. —**ther·mo·met·ric** (thûr′mō·met′rik) or **·ri·cal** *adj.* —**ther′mo·met′ri·cal·ly** *adv.*

ther·mo·nu·cle·ar (thûr′mō·nyōō′klē·ər) *adj. Physics* Pertaining to or characterized by reactions involving the fusion of light atomic nuclei subjected to very high temperatures.

ther·mo·plas·tic (thûr′mō·plas′tik) *adj.* Becoming soft when heated, as certain synthetic resins. —*n.* A thermoplastic substance or material.

Ther·mop·y·lae (thər·mop′ə·lē) *n.* A narrow mountain pass in Greece; scene of a battle, 480 B.C., in which the Spartans held off the Persians and finally died to the last man rather than yield.

ther·mos (thûr′məs) *n.* A container having two walls separated by a vacuum which serves to retard transfer of heat to or from the contents. Also **thermos bottle.** [< *Thermos,* a trade name]

ther·mo·set·ting (thûr′mō·set′ing) *adj.* Permanently assuming a fixed shape when heated, as certain synthetic resins.

ther·mo·stat (thûr′mə·stat) *n.* An automatic control device used to maintain a desired temperature. [< THERMO- + Gk. *statos* standing] —**ther′mo·stat′ic** *adj.* —**ther′mo·stat′i·cal·ly** *adv.*

ther·mot·ro·pism (thər·mot′rə·piz′əm) *n. Biol.* Movement or growth in a direction determined by the location of a heat source. —**ther·mo·trop·ic** (thûr′mō·trop′ik) *adj.* —**ther′mo·trop′i·cal·ly** *adv.*

the·sau·rus (thi·sôr′əs) *n. pl* **·sau·ri** (-sôr′ī) or **sau·rus·es** **1** A book containing words and their synonyms grouped together. **2** A book containing words or facts dealing with a specific subject or field. [< Gk. *thēsauros* treasure]

these (thēz) *pl.* of THIS.

The·seus (thē′sōōs, -sē·əs) *Gk. Myth.* The chief hero of Attica, celebrated chiefly for killing the Minotaur, and for unifying Attica with Athens as its capital. —**The′se·an** (-sē·ən) *adj.*

the·sis (thē′sis) *n. pl.* **·ses** (-sēz) **1** A proposition, esp. a formal proposition advanced and defended by argumentation. **2** A formal treatise on a particular subject, esp. a dissertation presented by a candidate for an advanced academic degree. **3 a** *Logic* An affirmative proposition. **b** An unproved premise or postulate, as opposed to a hypothesis. [< Gk., a placing, proposition]

thes·pi·an (thes′pē·ən) *adj. Often cap.* Of or relating to drama; dramatic. —*n.* An actor or actress. [< *Thespis,* 6th-c. B.C. Gk. poet]

Thess. Thessalonians.

Thes·sa·lo·ni·ans (thes′ə·lō′nē·ənz) *n.pl. (construed as sing.)* Either of two epistles in the New Testament (**First** and **Second Thessalonians**) written by St. Paul to the Christians of Thessalonica.

Thes·sa·lo·ni·ca (thes′ə·lə·nī′kə, -lon′i·kə) *n.* An ancient city of N Greece.

the·ta (thā′tə, thē′tə) *n.* The eighth letter in the Greek alphabet (Θ, ϑ, θ).

thew (thyōō) *n.* **1** A sinew or muscle. **2** *pl.* Bodily strength or vigor. [< OE *thēaw* habit, characteristic quality]

they (thā) *pron.* **1** The persons, beings, or things previously mentioned or understood: the nominative plural of *he, she, it.* **2** People in general: *They* say that the fishing is excellent in this area. [< ON *their*]

they'd (thād) Contraction of *they had* or *they would.*

they'll (thāl) Contraction of *they shall* or *they will.*

they're (thâr) Contraction of *they are.*

they've (thāv) Contraction of *they have.*

T.H.I., T.-H.I. temperature-humidity index.

thi·a·mine (thī′ə·min, -mēn) *n.* Vitamin B$_1$, a compound found in cereal grains, liver, egg yolk, etc., and also made synthetically. Also **thi′a·min** (-min). [< THI(O)- + -AMINE]

thick (thik) *adj.* **1** Relatively large in depth or extent from one surface to its opposite; not thin. **2** Having a specified dimension of this kind, whether great or small: an inch *thick.* **3** Having the constituent or specified elements growing, packed, arranged, etc., close together: a field *thick* with daisies. **4** Viscous in consistency: a *thick* sauce. **5** Heavy; dense: a *thick* fog. **6** Foggy, hazy, smoky, etc. **7** Very dark; impenetrable: a *thick* gloom. **8** Indistinct; muffled; guttural, as speech. **9** Very noticeable; decided: a *thick* German accent. **10** *Informal* Dull; stupid. **11** *Informal* Very friendly; intimate. **12** *Informal* Going beyond what is tolerable; excessive. —*adv.* In a thick manner. —

n. The thickest or most intense time or place of anything: the *thick* of the fight. [< OE *thicce*] —**thick′ish** *adj.* — **thick′ly** *adv.* —**thick′ness** *n.*

thick·en (thik′ən) *v.t. & v.i.* **1** To make or become thick or thicker. **2** To make or become more intricate or intense: The plot *thickens.* —**thick′en·er** *n.*

thick·en·ing (thik′ən·ing) *n.* **1** The act of making or becoming thick. **2** Something added to a liquid to make it thicker. **3** That part which is or has been thickened.

thick·et (thik′it) *n.* A thick growth, as of underbrush. [< OE *thiccet* < *thicce* thick]

thick·head (thik′hed′) *n.* A stupid person. —**thick′head′ed** *adj.* —**thick′head′ed·ness** *n.*

thick·set (thik′set′) *adj.* **1** Having a short, thick body; stocky. **2** Closely planted.

thick-skinned (thik′skind′) *adj.* **1** Having a thick skin, as a pachyderm. **2** Insensitive; callous to hints or insults.

thick-wit·ted (thik′wit′id) *adj.* Stupid; obtuse.

thief (thēf) *n. pl.* **thieves** (thēvz) One who takes something belonging to another, esp. secretly. [< OE *thēof*]

thieve (thēv) *v.* **thieved, thiev·ing** *v.t.* To take by theft; purloin; steal. —*v.i.* To be a thief; commit theft. [< OE *thēofian*]

thiev·er·y (thē′vər·ē) *n. pl.* **·er·ies** The practice or act of thieving; theft; also, an instance of thieving. —**thiev′ish** *adj.* —**thiev′ish·ly** *adv.* —**thiev′ish·ness** *n.*

thigh (thī) *n.* **1** The human leg between the hip and the knee. **2** The corresponding portion in other animals. [< OE *thēoh*]

thigh·bone (thī′bōn′) *n.* FEMUR. Also **thigh bone.**

thim·ble (thim′bəl) *n.* **1** In sewing, a pitted cover worn to protect the finger that pushes the needle. **2** Any similar device, esp. a ring on a rope to prevent chafing. [< OE *thȳmel* < *thūma* thumb]

thin (thin) *adj.* **thin·ner, thin·nest** **1** Having opposite surfaces relatively close to each other; being of little depth or width; not thick. **2** Lean and slender of figure. **3** Having the component parts or particles scattered or diffused; rarefied: a *thin* gas. **4** Not large or abundant, as in number: a *thin* audience. **5** Lacking thickness of consistency: a *thin* sauce. **6** Not dense or heavy: a *thin* fog. **7** Having little intensity or richness: a *thin* red. **8** Having little volume or resonance; shrill, as a voice. **9** Of a loose or light texture: *thin* clothing. **10** Insufficient; flimsy: a *thin* excuse. **11** Lacking essential ingredients or qualities: *thin* blood. **12** Meager; scant: *thin* hair. **13** Lacking vigor, force, substance, complexity, etc.; superficial; slight: *thin* humor. —*adv.* In a thin way: Slice the sausage *thin.* —*v.t. & v.i.* **thinned, thin·ning** To make or become thin or thinner. [< OE *thynne*] —**thin′ly** *adv.* —**thin′ness** *n.*

thine (thīn) *pron. Archaic* The things or persons belonging to thee: thou and *thine.* —*pronominal adj. Archaic* Thy: *thine* eyes. [< OE *thīn*]

thing (thing) *n.* **1** That which exists or is conceived to exist as a separate entity: all the *things* in the world. **2** That which is designated, as contrasted with the word or symbol used to denote it. **3** A matter or circumstance: *Things* have changed. **4** An act, deed, event, etc.: That was a shameless *thing* to do. **5** A procedure or step, as in an ordered course or process: the first *thing* to do. **6** An item, particular, detail, etc.: each *thing* on the schedule. **7** A statement or expression; utterance: to say the right *thing.* **8** An idea; opinion; notion: Stop putting *things* in her head. **9** A quality; attribute; characteristic: Kindness is a precious *thing.* **10** An inanimate object. **11** An object that is not or cannot be described or particularized: What kind of *thing* is that? **12** A person, regarded in terms of pity, affection, or contempt: that poor *thing.* **13** *pl.* Possessions; belongings: to pack one's *things.* **14** *pl.* Clothes; esp. outer garments. **15** A piece of clothing, as a dress: not a *thing* to wear. **16** A piece of literature, art, music, etc.: He read a few *things* by Byron. **17** The proper or befitting act or result: with *the:* That was not the *thing* to do. **18** The important point, attitude, etc.: with *the:* The *thing* one learns from travel is how to combat fatigue. **19** *Informal* A point; issue; case: He always makes a big *thing* out of

dividing up the bill. **20** *Informal* A strong liking, disliking, fear, attraction, etc.: to have a *thing* for tall girls. **21** *Law* A subject or property or dominion, as distinguished from a person. —**do one's (own) thing** *Slang* To express oneself by doing what one wants to do or can do well or is in the habit of doing. [< OE, thing, cause, assembly]

thing·a·ma·bob (thing′ə·mə·bob′) *n. Informal* THINGAMAJIG. Also **thing′um·a·bob′, thing′um·bob.**

thing·a·ma·jig (thing′ə·mə·jig′) *n. Informal* A thing the specific name of which is unknown or forgotten. Also **thing′um·a·jig′.**

think¹ (thingk) *v.* **thought** (thôt), **think·ing** *v.t.* **1** To produce or form in the mind; conceive mentally: to *think* evil thoughts. **2** To examine in the mind; meditate upon, or determine by reasoning: to *think* a plan through. **3** To believe; consider: I *think* him guilty. **4** To expect; anticipate: They did not *think* to meet us. **5** To bring to mind; remember; recollect: I cannot *think* what he said. **6** To have the mind preoccupied by: to *think* business morning, noon, and night. **7** To intend; purpose: Do they *think* to rob me? —*v.i.* **8** To use the mind or intellect in exercising judgment, forming ideas, etc.; engage in rational thought; reason. **9** To have a particular opinion, sentiment, or feeling: I don't *think* so. —**think of** (or **about**) **1** To bring to mind; remember; recollect. **2** To conceive in the mind; invent; imagine. **3** To have a specified opinion or attitude toward; regard. **4** To be considerate of; have regard for. — **think over** To reflect upon; ponder. —**think up** To devise, arrive at, or invent by thinking. —*n. Informal* The act of thinking. [< OE *thencan*] —**think′er** *n.*

think² (thingk) *v.i.* To seem; appear: now obsolete except with the pronoun as indirect object in the combinations *methinks, methought.* [< OE *thyncan* seem]

think·a·ble (thingk′ə·bəl) *adj.* **1** Susceptible of being thought; conceivable. **2** Possible.

think·ing (thingk′ing) *adj.* Using or given to using the mind; intellectually active. —*n.* **1** The act or process of using the mind to think. **2** A result of thought; opinion or position. —**think′ing·ly** *adv.*

think tank *Informal* **1** A group of people (**think tankers**), usu. academics, business executives, or government employees, organized for the investigation and study of social, scientific, and technological problems. **2** The place in which such a group works.

thin·ner (thin′ər) *n.* One who or that which thins, esp. a liquid added to a viscid substance to thin it.

thin-skinned (thin′skind′) *adj.* **1** Having a thin skin. **2** Easily offended; sensitive.

thio- *combining form* Containing sulfur: *thiosulfate.* [< Gk. *theion* sulfur]

thi·o·sul·fate (thī′ō·sul′fāt) *n.* Any salt of thiosulfuric acid, esp. sodium thiosulfate.

thi·o·sul·fu·ric acid (thī′ō·sul·fyŏŏr′ik) An unstable acid, known chiefly by its salts, which are used in bleaching and photography.

third (thûrd) *adj. & adv.* **1** Next in order after the second. **2** Being one of three equal parts. —*n.* **1** The element of an ordered set that corresponds to the number three. **2** One of three equal parts. **3** *Music* The interval between any tone and another two steps away in a diatonic scale. **4** In baseball, the third base. [< OE *thridda*]

third-class (thûrd′klas′, -kläs′) *adj.* **1** Ranking next below the second or second best. **2** Of, pertaining to, or belonging to a class next below the second: *third-class* mail. —*adv.* By third-class accommodations or mail.

third degree *Informal* Severe or brutal examination of a prisoner for the purpose of securing information or a confession.

third estate The common people, traditionally ranked after the nobility and the clergy.

third·ly (thûrd′lē) *adv.* Third.

third person The form of the pronoun, as *he, she, it,* to indicate the person or thing spoken of, or the grammatical form of the verb referring to such person or thing.

third rail An insulated rail on an electric railway for supplying current to the trains or cars.

add, āce, câre, pälm; end, ēven; it, īce; odd, ōpen, ôrder; tōŏk, pōōl; up, bûrn; ə = *a* in *above, u* in *focus;* yōō = *u* in *fuse;* oil; pout; check; go; ring; thin; ᵗhis; zh, *vision.* < derived from; ? origin uncertain or unknown.

third-rate (thûrd′rāt′) *adj.* **1** Third in rating or class. **2** Of poor quality; inferior.

third world **1** Any or all of the underdeveloped countries in the world, esp. such countries in Asia or Africa that are not aligned with either the Communist or non-Communist nations. **2** Those not resident in the countries of the third world but collectively identified with their peoples, as because of ideology, ethnic background, or disadvantaged status. Also **Third World.**

thirst (thûrst) *n.* **1** Discomfort or distress due to a need for water. **2** A craving or taste for any specified liquid: a *thirst* for alcohol. **3** Any longing or craving: a *thirst* for glory. — *v.i.* **1** To feel thirst; be thirsty. **2** To have an eager desire or craving. [< OE *thurst*] —**thirst′er** *n.*

thirst·y (thûrs′tē) *adj.* **thirst·i·er, thirst·i·est** **1** Affected with thirst. **2** Lacking moisture; arid; parched. **3** Eagerly desirous. **4** *Informal* Causing thirst. [< OE *thurstig*] —**thirst′i·ly** *adv.* —**thirst′i·ness** *n.*

thir·teen (thûr′tēn′) *n.* **1** The sum of 12 plus 1; 13; XIII. **2** A set or group of 13 members. [< OE *thrēotēne*] —**thir′teen′** *adj., pron.*

thir·teenth (thûr′tēnth′) *adj. & adv.* Next in order after the 12th. —*n.* **1** The element of an ordered set that corresponds to the number 13. **2** One of 13 equal parts.

thir·ti·eth (thûr′tē·ith) *adj. & adv.* Tenth in order after the 20th. —*n.* **1** The element of an ordered set that corresponds to the number 30. **2** One of 30 equal parts.

thir·ty (thûr′tē) *n. pl.* **·ties** **1** The product of three and ten. **2** A set or group of 30 members. **3** *pl.* The numbers, years, etc. from 30 to 40. [< OE *thrītig*] —**thir′ty** *adj., pron.*

thir·ty-sec·ond note (thûr′tē·sek′ənd) *Music* A note having one thirty-second of the time value of a whole note. • See NOTE.

this (this) *adj. pl.* **these** **1** That is near or present, either actually or in thought: *This* house is for sale; I shall be there *this* evening. **2** That is understood or has just been mentioned: *This* offense justified my revenge. **3** That is nearer than or contrasted with something else: opposed to *that: This* tree is still alive, but that one is dead. —*pron. pl.* **these** **1** The person or thing near or present, being understood or just mentioned: *This* is where I live; *This* is the guilty man. **2** The person or thing nearer than or contrasted with something else: opposed to *that: This* is a better painting than that. **3** The idea, statement, etc., about to be made clear: I will say *this:* he is a hard worker. —*adv.* To this degree; thus or so: I was not expecting you *this* soon. [< OE]

this·tle (this′əl) *n.* Any of various prickly plants with cylindrical or globular heads of composite flowers. [< OE *thistel*] —**this′tly** *adj.*

this·tle·down (this′əl·doun′) *n.* The silky fibers of the ripening flower of a thistle.

thith·er (thith′ər, thith′-) *adv.* To that place; in that direction. —*adj.* Situated or being on the other side; more distant. [< OE *thider*]

thith·er·to (thith′ər·tōō′, thith′-) *adv.* Up to that time.

thith·er·ward (thith′ər·wərd, thith′-) *adv.* In that direction; toward that place. Also **thith′er·wards.**

tho (thō) *conj. & adv.* THOUGH.

thole (thōl) *n.* A pin or pair of pins serving as a fulcrum for an oar in rowing. Also **thole pin.** [< OE *thol*]

Tho·mism (tō′miz·əm) *n.* The theological and philosophical doctrines of St. Thomas Aquinas. [< St. *Thomas* Aquinas] —**Tho′mist** *adj., n.*

thong (thông, thong) *n.* **1** A narrow strip, usu. of leather, as for fastening. **2** A lash of a whip. [< OE *thwang* thong]

Thor (thôr, tôr) *Norse Myth.* The god of war and thunder and son of Odin.

tho·rax (thôr′aks, thō′raks) *n. pl.* **tho·rax·es** or **tho·ra·ces** (thôr′ə·sēz, thō′rə-) **1** The part of the body between the neck and the abdomen, enclosed by the ribs. **2** The middle segment between the head and abdomen of an insect. • See INSECT. [< Gk. *thōrax*] —**tho·rac·ic** (thô·ras′ik) *adj.*

tho·ri·um (thôr′ē·əm, thō′rē-) *n.* A rare, radioactive, metallic element (symbol Th), used as a fuel in certain nuclear reactors. [< THOR] —**tho′ric** *adj.*

Thistle

thorn (thôrn) *n.* **1** A sharp, rigid outgrowth from a plant stem. **2** Any of various thorn-bearing shrubs or trees. **3** A cause of discomfort, pain, or annoyance. **4** The name of the Old English rune þ, equivalent to *th*, as in *thorn*, from which it derives its name. —*v.t.* To pierce or prick with a thorn. [< OE] —**thorn′less** *adj.*

thorn apple **1** JIMSONWEED. **2** HAW².

thorn·y (thôr′nē) *adj.* **thorn·i·er, thorn·i·est** **1** Full of thorns; spiny. **2** Sharp like a thorn. **3** Full of difficulties or trials; painful; vexatious. —**thorn′i·ness** *n.*

tho·ron (thôr′on, thō′ron) *n.* A radioactive isotope of radon, resulting from the disintegration of thorium and having a half-life of 54.5 seconds.

thor·ough (thûr′ō, thûr′ə) *adj.* **1** Complete; exhaustive: a *thorough* search. **2** Attentive to details and accuracy; painstaking: a *thorough* worker. **3** Completely (such and such); through and through: a *thorough* nincompoop. [Emphatic var. of THROUGH] —**thor′ough·ly** *adv.* —**thor′ough·ness** *n.* —**Syn.** **1** comprehensive, sweeping, out-and-out, total. **2** exact, precise, meticulous, careful, conscientious. **3** absolute, downright, utter, unmitigated, perfect.

thor·ough·bred (thûr′ə·bred′) *adj.* **1** Bred from pure stock; pedigreed. **2** Possessing or showing excellence, as in training, education, manners, culture, etc.; first-rate. —*n.* **1** A thoroughbred animal. **2** A person of culture and good breeding.

Thor·ough·bred (thûr′ə·bred′) *n.* A breed of English race horse, originally developed by mating Arabian stallions with English mares.

thor·ough·fare (thûr′ō·fâr′, thûr′ə-) *n.* **1** A much frequented road or street through which the public have unobstructed passage. **2** A passage: now chiefly in the phrase **no thoroughfare.** [< OE *thurh* through + *faru* going]

thor·ough·go·ing (thûr′ō·gō′ing, thûr′ə-) *adj.* **1** Characterized by extreme thoroughness or efficiency. **2** Unmitigated; out-and-out.

those (thōz) *adj. & pron. pl.* of THAT. [< OE *thās*]

thou (thou) *pron.* The person spoken to, as denoted in the nominative case: archaic except in religious or poetic language, or in certain dialects. [< OE *thū*]

though (thō) *conj.* **1** Notwithstanding the fact that; although: *Though* he was sleepy, he stayed awake. **2** Granting that; even if: *Though* she may win, she will have lost her popularity. **3** And yet; still; however: I am well, *though* I do not feel very strong. —*adv.* Notwithstanding; nevertheless: It's not a good play, but I like it *though.* [< ON *thō*]

thought¹ (thôt) *n.* **1** The act or process of thinking. **2** The product of thinking, as an idea, concept, judgment, opinion, or the like. **3** Intellectual activity of a specific kind, time, place, etc.: Greek *thought*. **4** Consideration; attention; heed: Give the plan some *thought*. **5** Intention; plan; design: All *thought* of returning was abandoned. **6** Expectation; anticipation: He had no *thought* of finding her there. **7** A trifle; a small amount: Be a *thought* more cautious. [< THOUGHT²]

thought² (thôt) *p.t. & p.p.* of THINK. [< OE *thōht*]

thought·ful (thôt′fəl) *adj.* **1** Full of thought; meditative. **2** Showing, characterized by, or promoting thought. **3** Attentive; careful, esp. manifesting regard for others; considerate. —**thought′ful·ly** *adv.* —**thought′ful·ness** *n.*

thought·less (thôt′lis) *adj.* **1** Manifesting lack of thought or care; careless. **2** Not considerate of others. **3** Giddy; flighty. —**thought′less·ly** *adv.* —**thought′less·ness** *n.*

thou·sand (thou′zənd) *n.* **1** The product of ten times a hundred. **2** *Usu. pl.* An indefinitely large number. —*adj.* Consisting of a hundred times ten. [< OE *thūsend*] —**thou′sand·fold′** (-fōld′) *adj., adv.*

thou·sandth (thou′zəndth) *adj.* **1** Last in a series of a thousand. **2** Being one of a thousand equal parts. —*n.* **1** The element of an ordered set that corresponds to the number 1000. **2** One of a thousand equal parts.

thrall (thrôl) *n.* **1** A person in bondage; a slave; serf. **2** One controlled by a passion or vice. **3** Slavery. [< ON *thræl*]

thrall·dom (thrôl′dəm) *n.* **1** The state of being a thrall. **2** Any sort of bondage or servitude. Also **thral′dom.**

thrash (thrash) *v.t.* **1** To thresh, as grain. **2** To beat as if with a flail; flog; whip. **3** To move or swing with flailing, violent motions. **4** To defeat utterly. —*v.i.* **5** To move or swing about with flailing, violent motions. **6** To make one's way by thrashing. —**thrash out** (or **over**) To discuss fully and usu. come to a conclusion. —*n.* The act of thrashing. [Dial. var. of THRESH]

thrash·er[1] (thrash′ər) *n.* **1** One who or that which thrashes. **2** A machine for threshing grain. **3** THRESHER (def. 2).

thrash·er[2] (thrash′ər) *n.* Any of several long-tailed American songbirds resembling the thrushes and related to the mockingbirds. [?< THRUSH[1]]

thread (thred) *n.* **1** A very slender cord or line composed of two or more filaments, as of flax, cotton, silk, nylon, etc., twisted together. **2** A filament of metal, glass, etc. **3** A fine beam: a *thread* of light. **4** Something that runs a continuous course through a series or whole: the *thread* of his discourse. **5** *Mech.* The helical ridge of a screw. —*v.t.* **1** To pass a thread through the eye of: to *thread* a needle. **2** To string on a thread, as beads. **3** To cut a thread on or in, as a screw. **4** To make one's way through or over: to *thread* a maze. **5** To make (one's way) carefully. —*v.i.* **6** To make one's way carefully. **7** To fall from a fork or spoon in a fine thread: said of boiling syrup. [< OE *thræd*] —**thread′er** *n.*

thread·bare (thred′bâr′) *adj.* **1** Worn so that the threads show, as a rug or garment. **2** Clad in worn garments. **3** Commonplace; hackneyed. —**thread′bare′ness** *n.* —**Syn.** **2** shabby. **3** common, stale, stereotyped, trite.

thread·y (thred′ē) *adj.* **thread·i·er, thread·i·est 1** Like a thread; stringy. **2** Forming threads, as some liquids. **3** Weak; lacking vigor: a *thready* pulse. —**thread′i·ness** *n.*

threat (thret) *n.* **1** A declaration of an intention to inflict injury or pain. **2** Any menace or danger. [< OE *threat* crowd, oppression]

threat·en (thret′n) *v.t.* **1** To utter threats against. **2** To be menacing or dangerous to. **3** To portend (something unpleasant or dangerous). **4** To utter threats of (injury, vengeance, etc.). —*v.i.* **5** To utter threats. **6** To have a menacing aspect; lower. —**threat′en·er** *n.* —**threat′en·ing·ly** *adv.*

three (thrē) *n.* **1** The sum of two plus one; 3, III. **2** A set or group of three members. [< OE *thri*] —**three** *adj., pron.*

three-D (thrē′dē′) *adj.* THREE-DIMENSIONAL. —*n.* A technique, medium, or process giving the appearance of three dimensions to visual images. Also **3-D.**

three-deck·er (thrē′dek′ər) *n.* **1** A vessel having three decks or gun decks. **2** Anything having three levels.

three-di·men·sion·al (thrē′də·men′shən·əl) *adj.* **1** Of or having three dimensions. **2** Appearing to have depth as well as height and width.

three·fold (thrē′fōld′) *adj.* **1** Made up of three parts. **2** Having three times as many or as much. —*adv.* Triply; in a threefold manner.

three-mile limit (thrē′mīl′) A distance of three geographic miles from the shore line seaward, allowed by international law for territorial jurisdiction.

three·pence (thrip′əns, threp′-, thrup′-) *n. Brit.* **1** The sum of three pennies. **2** A small coin of Great Britain worth three pennies: also **thrip′pence** (thrip′əns).

three-ply (thrē′plī′) *adj.* Consisting of three thicknesses, strands, layers, etc.

three R's Reading, writing, and arithmetic.

three·score (thrē′skôr′, -skōr′) *adj. & n.* Sixty.

three·some (thrē′səm) *n.* **1** A group of three people. **2** A game played by three people; also, the players.

thren·o·dy (thren′ə·dē) *n. pl.* **·dies** An ode or song of lamentation; a dirge. Also **thren′ode** (-ōd). [< Gk. *thrēnos* lament + *ōidē* song] —**thre·nod·ic** (thri·nod′ik) *adj.* —**thren′o·dist** *n.*

thresh (thresh) *v.t.* **1** To beat stalks of (ripened grain) with a flail so as to separate the grain from the husks. —*v.i.* **2** To thresh grain. **3** To move or thrash about. —**thresh out** To discuss fully and to a conclusion. —**thresh over** To discuss over and over. [< OE *therscan*]

thresh·er (thresh′ər) *n.* **1** One who or that which threshes, esp. a machine for threshing. **2** A large shark having an extremely long tail: also **thresher shark.**

thresh·old (thresh′ōld, -hōld) *n.* **1** The plank, timber, or stone lying under the door of a building; doorsill. **2** The entering point or beginning of anything: the *threshold* of the 20th century. **3** The minimum degree of stimulation necessary to produce a response or to be perceived. [< OE *therscold*]

threw (thrōō) *p.t.* of THROW.

thrice (thrīs) *adv.* **1** Three times. **2** Fully; extremely. [< OE *thriwa* thrice]

thrift (thrift) *n.* Care and wisdom in the management of one's resources; frugality. [< ON] —**thrift′less** *adj.* —**thrift′less·ly** *adv.* —**thrift′less·ness** *n.*

thrift·y (thrif′tē) *adj.* **thrift·i·er, thrift·i·est 1** Displaying thrift or good management; frugal. **2** Prosperous; thriving. —**thrift′i·ly** *adv.* —**thrift′i·ness** *n.* —**Syn. 1** economical, provident, prudent, saving.

thrill (thril) *v.t.* **1** To cause to feel a great or tingling excitement. —*v.i.* **2** To feel a sudden wave of emotion. **3** To vibrate or tremble; quiver. —*n.* **1** A feeling of excitement. **2** A thrilling quality. **3** A pulsation; quiver. [< OE *thyrlian* pierce] —**thrill′ing·ly** *adv.*

thrill·er (thril′ər) *n.* **1** One who or that which thrills. **2** *Informal* An exciting book, play, etc.

thrive (thrīv) *v.i.* **throve** (thrōv) or **thrived, thrived** or **thriv·en** (thriv′ən), **thriv·ing 1** To prosper; be successful. **2** To flourish. [< ON *thrifast* reflexive of *thrifa* grasp] —**thriv′er** *n.* —**thriv′ing·ly** *adv.*

throat (thrōt) *n.* **1** The front part of the neck. **2** The passage extending from the back of the mouth and containing the epiglottis, larynx, trachea, and pharynx. **3** Any narrow passage resembling a throat. —**jump down one's throat** To scold or criticize with sudden violence. —**lump in the throat** A feeling of tightness in the throat, as from strong emotion. —**stick in one's throat** To be difficult or painful to say. [< OE *throte*]

Throat
a. soft palate. b. pharynx. c. epiglottis. d. esophagus. e. trachea.

throat·y (thrō′tē) *adj.* **throat·i·er, throat·i·est** Uttered in the throat; guttural. —**throat′i·ly** *adv.* —**throat′i·ness** *n.*

throb (throb) *v.i.* **throbbed, throb·bing 1** To pulsate rhythmically, as the heart. **2** To feel or show emotion by trembling. —*n.* **1** The act or state of throbbing. **2** A pulsation, esp. one caused by excitement or emotion. [Imit.] —**throb′ber** *n.*

throe (thrō) *n.* **1** A violent pang or pain. **2** *pl.* The pains of death or childbirth. **3** Any agonized or agonizing activity. [< OE *thrawe*]

throm·bin (throm′bin) *n.* An enzyme in blood serum that promotes clotting. [< Gk. *thrombos* clot]

throm·bo·sis (throm·bō′sis) *n.* The formation of a blood clot inside the heart or a blood vessel. [< Gk. *thrombos* clot] —**throm·bot′ic** (-bot′ik) *adj.*

throne (thrōn) *n.* **1** The chair occupied by a king, pope, etc., on state occasions. **2** The rank or authority of a king, queen, etc. —*v.t. & v.i.* **throned, thron·ing** To enthrone; exalt. [< Gk. *thronos* seat]

throng (thrông, throng) *n.* **1** A closely crowded multitude. **2** Any numerous collection. —*v.t.* **1** To crowd into and occupy fully; jam. **2** To crowd upon. —*v.i.* **3** To collect or move in a throng. [< OE *gethrang*] —**Syn.** *n.* **1** crowd, host, jam, mass, press.

throt·tle (throt′l) *n.* **1** A valve controlling the supply of fuel or steam to the cylinders of an engine: also **throttle valve. 2** The lever which operates the throttle valve: also **throttle lever.** —*v.t.* **throt·tled, throt·tling 1** To strangle, choke or suffocate. **2** To silence, stop, or suppress. **3** To reduce or shut off the flow of (steam or fuel to the cylinders of an engine). **4** To reduce the speed of by means of a throttle. —*v.i.* **5** To suffocate; choke. [Dim. of ME *throte* throat] —**throt′tler** *n.*

through (thrōō) *prep.* **1** From end to end, side to side, or limit to limit of; into at one side, end, or point, and out of at another. **2** Covering, entering, or penetrating all parts of; throughout. **3** From the first to the last of: *through the day.* **4** Here and there upon or in. **5** By way of: He departed *through* the door. **6** By the instrumentality or aid of. **7** Having reached the end of: He got *through* his examinations. —*adv.* **1** From one end, side, surface, etc., to or beyond another. **2** From beginning to end. **3** To a termination or conclusion: to pull *through.* **4** Completely; entirely: He is wet *through.* —**through and through** Thoroughly; completely. —*adj.* **1** Going to its destination without stops: a *through* train. **2** Usable or valid for an entire trip: a *through* ticket. **3** Extending from one side or surface to another. **4** Allowing unobstructed or direct passage: a *through* road. **5** Finished: Are you *through* with my pen? [< OE *thurh*]

through·out (thrōō·out′) *adv.* Through or in every part. —*prep.* All through; everywhere in.

throve (thrōv) *p.t.* of THRIVE.

throw (thrō) *v.* **threw** (thrōō), **thrown, throw·ing** *v.t.* **1** To propel through the air by means of a sudden straightening or whirling of the arm. **2** To propel or hurl. **3** To put hastily or carelessly: He *threw* a coat over his shoulders. **4** To direct or project (light, shadow, a glance, etc.). **5** To bring to a specified condition or state: to *throw* the enemy into a panic. **6** To cause to fall: The horse *threw* its rider. **7** In wrestling, to force the shoulders of (an opponent) to the ground. **8** To cast (dice). **9** To make (a specified cast) with dice. **10** To shed; lose: The horse *threw* a shoe. **11** *Informal* To lose purposely, as a race. **12** To move, as a lever or switch. **13** *Slang* To give (a party, etc.). **14** In ceramics, to shape on a potter's wheel. —*v.i.* **15** To cast or fling something. —**throw away 1** To cast off; discard. **2** To squander. —**throw cold water on** To discourage. —**throw off 1** To reject; spurn. **2** To rid oneself of. **3** To do or utter in an offhand manner. **4** To emit; discharge. **5** To confuse; mislead. **6** To elude (a pursuer). —**throw oneself at** To strive to gain the affection or love of. —**throw oneself into** To take part in vigorously. —**throw oneself on** (or **upon**) To rely on utterly. —**throw open 1** To open suddenly, as a door. **2** To free from restrictions or obstacles. —**throw out 1** To emit. **2** To discard; reject. **3** To utter as if accidentally: to *throw out* hints. **4** In baseball, to retire (a runner) by throwing the ball to the base toward which he is advancing. —**throw over 1** To overturn. **2** To jilt. —**throw together** To put together carelessly. —**throw up 1** To vomit. **2** To erect hastily. **3** To give up. **4** *Informal* To mention (something) repeatedly and reproachfully; taunt. —*n.* **1** An act of throwing. **2** The distance over which a missile may be thrown: a long *throw.* **3** A cast of dice, or the resulting number. **4** A scarf or other light covering. **5** In wrestling, a flooring of one's opponent so that both his shoulders touch the mat simultaneously for ten seconds. [< OE *thrāwan* to turn, twist, curl] —**throw′er** *n.* —**Syn.** *v.* **1** fling, heave, hurl, pitch.

throw·back (thrō′bak′) *n.* **1** An atavism. **2** A throwing back.

thru (thrōō) *adj., adv. & prep.* THROUGH.

thrum (thrum) *v.* **thrummed, thrum·ming** *v.t.* **1** To play on (a stringed instrument), esp. idly; strum. **2** To drum on monotonously with the fingers. —*v.i.* **3** To strum a stringed instrument. —*n.* The sound made by thrumming. [Prob. imit.]

thrush¹ (thrush) *n.* Any of many species of migratory songbirds, usu. having long wings and spotted under parts, as the **hermit thrush,** the **wood thrush,** the **robin,** and the **bluebird.** [< OE *thrysce*]

thrush² (thrush) *n.* A disease of the mouth, lips, and throat caused by a yeastlike fungus. [?]

Wood thrush

thrust (thrust) *v.* **thrust, thrust·ing** *v.t.* **1** To push or shove with force. **2** To pierce with a sudden forward motion, as with a sword. **3** To interpose. —*v.i.* **4** To make a sudden push or thrust. **5** To force oneself on or ahead: to *thrust* through a crowd. —*n.* **1** A sudden and forcible push, esp. with a pointed weapon. **2** A vigorous attack; sharp onset. **3** A force that drives or propels. **4** Salient force or mean-

ing: the *thrust* of his remarks. [< ON *thrȳsta*] —**thrust′er** *n.* —**Syn.** *v.* **1** lunge. **2** stab, stick. *n.* **4** import, intention, significance, sense, gist.

thru·way (thrōō′wā′) *n.* EXPRESSWAY.

thud (thud) *n.* **1** A dull, heavy sound. **2** A blow causing such a sound; a thump. —*v.i.* **thud·ded, thud·ding** To strike or fall with a thud. [< OE *thyddan* strike, thrust, press]

thug (thug) *n.* **1** Formerly, one of an organization of religious assassins in India. **2** Any assassin or ruffian. [< Skt. *sthaga* swindler]

thu·li·um (thōō′lē·əm) *n.* A metallic element (symbol Tm) of the lanthanide series. [< *Thule,* the northernmost limit of the habitable world in ancient geography]

thumb (thum) *n.* **1** The short, thick digit of the human hand. **2** A similar part in certain animals. **3** The division in a glove or mitten that covers the thumb. —**all thumbs** Clumsy with the hands. —**thumbs down** A signal of negation or disapproval. —**thumbs up** A signal of approval. —**under one's thumb** Under one's influence or power. —*v.t.* **1** To rub, soil, or wear with the thumb in handling. **2** To handle clumsily. **3** To run through the pages of (a book, etc.) rapidly. —**thumb a ride** To get a ride by signaling with the thumb. [< OE *thūma*]

thumb index A series of scalloped indentations cut along the front edge of a book and labeled to indicate its various sections. —**thumb′-in′dex** *v.t.*

thumb·nail (thum′nāl′) *n.* **1** The nail of the thumb. **2** Anything as small as a thumbnail. —*adj.* Very brief: a *thumbnail* sketch.

thumb·screw (thum′skrōō′) *n.* **1** A screw to be turned by thumb and fingers. • See SCREW. **2** An instrument of torture for compressing the thumb or thumbs.

thumb·tack (thum′tak′) *n.* A broad-headed tack that may be pushed in with the thumb.

thump (thump) *n.* **1** A blow with a blunt or heavy object. **2** The sound made by such a blow; a thud. —*v.t.* **1** To beat or strike so as to make a heavy thud or thuds. **2** *Informal* To beat or defeat severely. —*v.i.* **3** To strike with a thump. **4** To pound or throb, as the heart. [Imit.] —**thump′er** *n.*

thun·der (thun′dər) *n.* **1** The sound that accompanies lightning, caused by the explosive effect of the electric discharge. **2** Any loud noise resembling thunder. **3** A vehement or powerful utterance. —**steal one's thunder** To undermine the effectiveness of an opponent by anticipating his next move, argument, etc. —*v.i.* **1** To give forth peals of thunder: It is *thundering.* **2** To make a noise like thunder. **3** To utter vehement denunciations. —*v.t.* **4** To utter or express with a noise like thunder: The cannon *thundered* defiance. [< OE *thunor*] —**thun′der·er** *n.*

thun·der·bolt (thun′dər·bōlt′) *n.* **1** A lightning flash accompanied by a clap of thunder. **2** A person or thing acting with great force, speed, or destructiveness.

thun·der·clap (thun′dər·klap′) *n.* **1** A sharp, violent detonation of thunder. **2** Anything violent or sudden.

thun·der·cloud (thun′dər·kloud′) *n.* A dark, heavy mass of electrically charged cloud.

thun·der·head (thun′dər·hed′) *n.* A rounded mass of silvery cumulus cloud, often developing into a thundercloud.

thun·der·ous (thun′dər·əs) *adj.* Producing or emitting thunder or a sound like thunder. —**thun′der·ous·ly** *adv.*

thun·der·show·er (thun′dər·shou′ər) *n.* A shower of rain with thunder and lightning.

thun·der·storm (thun′dər·stôrm′) *n.* A local storm accompanied by lightning and thunder.

thun·der·struck (thun′dər·struk′) *adj.* Amazed, astonished, or confounded. Also **thun′der·strick′en** (-strik′ən).

Thur., Thurs. Thursday.

thu·ri·ble (thōōr′ə·bəl) *n.* CENSER. [< L *thus, thuris* frankincense]

Thurs·day (thûrz′dē, -dā) *n.* The fifth day of the week. [< OE *Thunres dæg* day of Thor]

thus (thus) *adv.* **1** In this or that or the following way. **2** To such degree or extent; so: *thus* far. **3** In this case; therefore. [< OE]

thwack (thwak) *v.t.* To strike heavily with something flat; whack. —*n.* A blow with something flat. [Prob. imit.] —**thwack′er** *n.*

thwart (thwôrt) *v.t.* To obstruct (a plan, a person, etc.) as by interposing an obstacle; frustrate. —*n.* **1** An oarsman's seat extending athwart a boat. **2** A brace athwart a canoe. —*adj.* Lying, moving, or extending across something; transverse. —*adv. & prep.* Athwart. [< ON *thvert*, neut. of *thverr* transverse] —**thwart′er** *n.*

thy (thī) *pronominal adj.* Belonging or pertaining to thee: *Thy* kingdom come. [< OE *thīn* THINE]

thyme (tīm) *n.* **1** Any of various small shrubby plants of the mint family, having aromatic leaves. **2** The dried leaves of certain thyme plants, used for seasoning in cookery. [< Gk. *thymon*] —**thy·mic** (-mik), **thym′y** *adj.*

thy·mus (thī′məs) *n.* A ductless glandlike structure situated at the root of the neck and usu. becoming atrophied after early childhood. [< Gk. *thymos*] • See THYROID.

thy·roid (thī′roid) *adj.* **1** Of or pertaining to the cartilage of the larynx which forms the Adam's apple. **2** Of, pertaining to, or describing a large ductless gland situated near the larynx on each side of the trachea and secreting thyroxin. —*n.* **1** The thyroid cartilage. **2** The thyroid gland. [< Gk. *thyreoeidēs* shield-shaped]

thy·rox·in (thī·rok′sin) *n.* **1** A vital hormone, secreted by the thyroid gland, which regulates growth and metabolism. **2** A white, crystalline compound, obtained from the thyroid glands of animals and also made synthetically, used in the treatment of thyroid disorders. Also **thy·rox′ine** (-sēn, -sin).

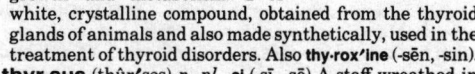

a. thyroid. b. thymus.

thyr·sus (thûr′səs) *n. pl.* **·si** (-sī, -sē) A staff wreathed in ivy and crowned with a pine cone or a bunch of ivy leaves, borne by Dionysus and the satyrs. [< Gk. *thyrsos*]

thy·self (thī·self′) *pron.* Emphatic or reflexive form of *thou:* I love thee for *thyself.*

ti (tē) *n. Music* In solmization, the seventh note of a diatonic scale. [Ital. See GAMUT.]

Ti titanium.

ti·ar·a (tē·âr′ə, -är′ə) *n.* **1** The pope's triple crown. **2** The upright headdress worn by the ancient Persian kings. **3** A jeweled head ornament or coronet worn by women on very formal or state occasions. [Gk., Persian headdress]

Ti·bet·an (ti·bet′n) *adj.* Of or pertaining to Tibet, the Tibetans, or to their language. —*n.* **1** An inhabitant or citizen of Tibet. **2** The language of Tibet.

Tibia

tib·i·a (tib′ē·ə) *n. pl.* **tib·i·as** or **tib·i·ae** (tib′· ē·ē, -ē·ī) The inner and larger of the two bones of the leg below the knee; the shinbone. —**tib′i·al** *adj.*

tic (tik) *n.* Any involuntary, recurrent muscular spasm. [F]

tick[1] (tik) *n.* **1** A light recurring sound made by a watch, clock, etc. **2** *Informal* The time elapsing between two ticks of a clock; an instant. **3** A mark, as a dot or dash, used in checking off something. —*v.i.* **1** To sound a tick or ticks. —*v.t.* **2** To mark or check with ticks. [Prob. imit.]

tick[2] (tik) *n.* **1** Any of numerous small, bloodsucking arachnids, parasitic on warm-blooded animals and often harboring and transmitting pathogenic microorganisms. **2** Any of certain usu. wingless parasitic insects. [< OE *ticia*]

tick[3] (tik) *n.* **1** The stout outer covering of a mattress; also, the material for such covering. **2** *Informal* Ticking. [< Gk. *thēke* a case]

Tick

tick[4] (tik) *n. Brit. Informal* Credit; trust: to buy merchandise on *tick.* [Short for TICKET]

tick·er (tik′ər) *n.* **1** One who or that which ticks. **2** Formerly, a telegraphic instrument that printed stock quotations on paper ribbon (**ticker tape**). **3** *Slang* The heart.

tick·et (tik′it) *n.* **1** A printed card showing that the holder is entitled to something, as transportation in a public vehicle, admission to a theater, etc. **2** A label or tag: a price *ticket.* **3** A list of candidates of a single party on a ballot: the Democratic *ticket.* **4** *Informal* A court summons for a traffic violation, usu. involving a fine. —*v.t.* **1** To fix a ticket to; label. **2** To furnish with a ticket. [< OF *estiquette*]

ticket of leave *Brit.* Formerly, a written permit granted to a convict to be at large before the expiration of his sentence.

tick·ing (tik′ing) *n.* A strong, closely woven cotton or linen fabric, used for mattress covering, awnings, etc. [< TICK[3]]

tick·le (tik′əl) *v.* **·led**, **·ling** *v.t.* **1** To excite the nerves of by touching or scratching on some sensitive spot, producing a sensation resulting in spasmodic laughter or twitching. **2** To please: Compliments *tickle* our vanity. **3** To amuse or entertain; delight. **4** To move, stir, or get by tickling. —*v.i.* **5** To have a tingling sensation: My foot *tickles.* **6** To be ticklish. —*n.* **1** The sensation produced by tickling. **2** The touch or action producing such sensation. [ME *tikelen*]

tick·ler (tik′lər) *n.* **1** One who or that which tickles. **2** A memorandum book or file used as a reminder to attend to matters on certain dates in the future.

tick·lish (tik′lish) *adj.* **1** Sensitive to tickling. **2** Liable to be upset. **3** Easily offended; sensitive. **4** Requiring tact in handling; delicate: a *ticklish* situation. —**tick′lish·ly** *adv.* —**tick′lish·ness** *n.*

tick-tock (tik′tok′) *n.* The oscillating sound of a clock. —*v.i.* To make this sound. [Imit.]

tick·y tack·y (tik′ē tak′e) *Slang* **1** Shoddy, inferior materials: rows of little houses built of *ticky tacky.* **2** Dull, tedious uniformity. —**tick′y-tack′y** *adj.*

tid·al (tīd′l) *adj.* **1** Of, pertaining to, or influenced by the tides. **2** Dependent on the tide.

tidal wave **1** A great incoming rise of waters along a shore, caused by heavy winds and very high tides. **2** TSUNAMI. **3** A great upsurge, as of popular sentiment.

tid·bit (tid′bit′) *n.* A choice bit, as of food. [< dial. E *tid* a small object + BIT[1]]

tide (tīd) *n.* **1** The periodic rise and fall of the surface of the ocean caused by the gravitational attraction of moon and sun. **2** Anything that comes like the tide at flood. **3** The natural drift or tendency of events. **4** A current; stream: the *tide* of public feeling. **5** Season; time: Eastertide. —**turn the tide** To reverse a condition completely. —*v.i.* **tid·ed**, **tid·ing** To ebb and flow like the tide. —**tide over** **1** To give or act as temporary help, as in a difficulty. **2** To surmount. [< OE *tīd* a period, season]

tide·land (tīd′land′) *n.* **1** Land alternately covered and uncovered by the tide. **2** *Often pl.* Offshore land lying completely under the ocean, but within the limits of a nation's territorial waters.

tide·wa·ter (tīd′wô′tər, -wot′ər) *n.* **1** Water affected by the tide on the seacoast or in a river. **2** A region in which water is affected by the tide. —*adj.* Pertaining to or along a tidewater.

ti·dings (tī′dingz) *n.pl. (sometimes construed as sing.)* Information; news. [< OE *tīdung*]

ti·dy (tī′dē) *adj.* **·di·er**, **·di·est** **1** Neat in appearance; orderly: a *tidy* desk. **2** Keeping things in order: a *tidy* housekeeper. **3** *Informal* Moderately large: a *tidy* sum. **4** *Informal* Fairly good. —*v.t. & v.i.* **ti·died**, **ti·dy·ing** To put (things) in order. —*n. pl.* **·dies** An antimacassar. [< OE *tīd* time] —**ti′di·ly** *adv.* —**ti′di·ness** *n.* —**Syn.** *adj.* **1** shipshape, spruce, trim, well-kept.

tie (tī) *v.* **tied**, **ty·ing** *v.t.* **1** To fasten with cord, rope, etc., the ends of which are then knotted. **2** To draw the parts of together by a cord fastened with a knot: to *tie* one's shoes. **3** To form (a knot). **4** To form a knot in, as string. **5** To fasten, or join in any way. **6** To restrict; bind. **7 a** To equal (a competitor) in score or achievement. **b** To equal (a competitor's score). **8** *Informal* To unite in marriage. **9** *Music* To unite by a tie. —*v.i.* **10** To make a tie or connection. **11** To make the same score; be equal. —**tie down** To hinder;

restrict. **—tie up 1** To fasten with rope, string, etc. **2** To wrap, as with paper, and fasten with string, cord, etc. **3** To moor (a vessel). **4** To block; hinder. **5** To be previously committed, so as to be unavailable: *His money is tied up in real estate.* **—n. 1** A flexible bond or fastening secured by drawing the ends into a knot or loop. **2** Any bond or obligation. **3** In a contest, a draw; also, the point at which this occurs. **4** Something that is tied or intended for tying, as a shoelace, necktie, etc. **5** *Engin.* A structural member fastening parts together. **6** *Music* A curved line joining two notes of the same pitch to make them represent one tone. **7** One of a set of timbers laid crosswise on the ground as supports for railroad tracks. **8** *pl.* Low shoes with laces. [< OE *tīgan* bind] **—tī′er** *n.*

tie-dye (tī′dī′) *v.t.* **-dyed, -dye·ing** To create designs on fabric by tying parts of it in clumps that will not absorb the dye. **—n. 1** The process of decorating fabrics by tie-dyeing. **2** Fabric so decorated; also, a design so made.

tie-in (tī′in′) *n.* Something that connects or associates.

tier (tir) *n.* A rank or row in a series of things placed one above another. **—v.t. & v.i.** To place or rise in tiers. [< OF, a sequence]

tierce (tirs) *n.* **1** Formerly, a third of anything. **2** The third canonical hour. [< OF, a third < L *tertius*]

tie-up (tī′up′) *n.* **1** A temporary stoppage of services, operations, progress of traffic, etc. **2** *Informal* Connection; linkage.

tiff (tif) *n.* A slight quarrel; a spat. **—v.i.** To be in or have a tiff. [?]

tif·fin (tif′ən) *Brit. n.* Midday luncheon. **—v.i.** To lunch. [< Anglo-Indian *tiffing* drinking]

ti·ger (tī′gər) *n.* **1** A large carnivorous feline of Asia, with black stripes on a tawny body. **2** A fiercely determined, spirited, or energetic person or quality. [< Gk. *tigris*] **—tī′gress** *n. Fem.* **—tī′ger·ish, tī′grish** *adj.*

tiger beetle Any of certain active, usu. striped or spotted beetles having larvae that feed on other insects.

ti·ger·eye (tī′gər-ī′) *n.* A semiprecious stone, usu. shimmering yellow and brown. Also **tī′ger's-eye′.**

tiger lily Any of various lilies having orange flowers with recurved petals spotted with black. • See LILY.

tiger moth A stout-bodied moth with striped or spotted wings.

tight (tīt) *adj.* **1** Impervious to fluids; not leaky: often used in combination: *watertight.* **2** Firmly fixed or fastened in place; secure. **3** Fully stretched; taut: *tight* as a drum. **4** Strict; stringent: a *tight* schedule. **5** Fitting closely; esp. too closely: *tight* shoes. **6** *Informal* Difficult to cope with; troublesome: a *tight* spot. **7** *Informal* Stingy. **8** *Slang* Intoxicated. **9** Evenly matched: said of a race or contest. **10** Difficult to obtain because of scarcity or financial restrictions: said of money or of commodities. **—adv. 1** Firmly; securely: Hold on *tight.* **2** With much constriction: The dress fits too *tight.* **—sit tight** To remain firm in one's position or opinion. [?< ON *thēttr* dense] **—tight′ly** *adv.* **—tight′ness** *n.*

tight·en (tīt′n) *v.t. & v.i.* To make or become tight or tighter. **—tight′en·er** *n.*

tight-fist·ed (tīt′fis′tid) *adj.* Stingy.

tight-lipped (tīt′lipt′) *adj.* **1** Having the lips held tightly together. **2** Reticent; uncommunicative.

tight·rope (tīt′rōp′) *n.* A tightly stretched rope on which acrobats perform. **—adj.** Pertaining to or performing on a tightrope.

tights (tīts) *n.pl.* A close-fitting garment for the lower torso and legs, worn by dancers, acrobats, etc.

tight·wad (tīt′wod′) *n. Slang* A miser.

tike (tīk) *n.* TYKE.

til·bur·y (til′ber-ē) *n. pl.* **-bur·ies** A light, two-wheeled carriage seating two persons. [< *Tilbury,* 19th-c. London coachmaker]

til·de (til′də, -dē) *n.* A sign (˜) used in Spanish over *n* to indicate the sound of *ny,* as in *cañon,* canyon. [Sp.< L *titulus* superscription, title]

tile (tīl) *n.* **1** A thin piece of baked clay, stone, etc., used for covering roofs, floors, etc., and as an ornament. **2** A thin piece of linoleum, plastic, cork, etc., for covering walls and floors. **3** A short earthenware pipe, as used in forming sewers. **4** Tiles collectively; tiling. **5** Any of the pieces in

the game of mah jong. **—v.t. tiled, til·ing** To cover with tiles. [< L *tegula* < *tegere* to cover] **—til′er** *n.*

til·ing (tī′ling) *n.* **1** The work of one who covers with tiles. **2** Tiles collectively. **3** Something made of or faced with tiles.

till¹ (til) *v.t. & v.i.* To put and keep (soil) in order for the production of crops, as by plowing, hoeing, etc.; cultivate. [< OE *tilian* strive, acquire] **—till′er** *n.*

till² (til) *prep & conj.* UNTIL. [< OE *til*] • *Till* and *until* have exactly the same meaning and may usu. be used interchangeably. However, *until* is the preferred form at the beginning of a sentence: *Until today, the weather has been bad; It won't be long till winter.*

till³ (til) *n.* **1** A money drawer behind the counter of a store. **2** The money in such a drawer; also, available cash. **3** Formerly, a drawer for holding valuables. [ME *tillen*]

till·age (til′ij) *n.* **1** The cultivation of land. **2** The state of being tilled. **3** Land that has been tilled. **4** Crops growing on such land. [< TILL¹ + -AGE]

till·er (til′ər) *n.* **1** A lever to turn a rudder. **2** A means of guidance. [< Med. L *telarium* a weaver's beam]

tilt (tilt) *v.t.* **1** To cause to rise at one end or side; slant. **2** To aim or thrust, as a lance. **3** To charge or overthrow in a tilt or joust. **—v.i. 4** To incline at an angle; lean. **5** To contend with the lance; joust. **6** To argue; debate. **—n. 1** A slant or slope. **2** The act of tilting something. **3** A medieval sport in which mounted knights, charging with lances, endeavored to unseat each other. **4** A quarrel or dispute. **5** *Can.* In certain provinces, a seesaw. **—at full tilt** At full speed. [ME *tylten* be overthrown, totter] **—tilt′er** *n.*

tilth (tilth) *n.* **1** The act of tilling; cultivation. **2** Cultivated land.

tim·bal (tim′bəl) *n.* A kettledrum. [< Ar. *aṭ ṭabl* the drum]

tim·bale (tim′bəl, *Fr.* taṅ·bál′) *n.* **1** A dish made of chicken, fish, cheese, or vegetables, mixed with eggs, sweet cream, etc., cooked in a drum-shaped mold. **2** A small cup made of fried pastry, in which food may be served. [F, timbal]

tim·ber (tim′bər) *n.* **1** Wood suitable for building or constructing things. **2** Growing or standing trees; forests. **3** A single piece of squared wood prepared for use or already in use. **4** Any principal beam in a ship. **—v.t.** To provide or shore with timber. [< OE] **—tim′ber·er** *n.*

timber hitch A knot by which a rope is fastened around a spar, post, etc.

tim·ber·land (tim′bər-land′) *n.* Land covered with forests.

timber line The boundary of tree growth on mountains and in arctic regions; the line above which no trees grow. **—tim′ber-line′** (-līn′) *adj.*

timber wolf The large gray wolf of northern forest areas. • See WOLF.

tim·bre (tam′bər, tim′-; *Fr.* taṅ′br′) *n.* The distinctive quality of sound, produced chiefly by overtones, that characterizes or identifies a singing voice, a musical instrument, or a voiced speech sound. [F < L *tympanum* kettledrum]

tim·brel (tim′brəl) *n.* An ancient Hebrew instrument resembling a tambourine. [< OF *timbre,* a small bell]

time (tīm) *n.* **1** The general idea, relation, or fact of continuous or successive existence; the past, present, and future. **2** A definite moment, hour, period, etc.: *The time is 3:30.* **3** Epoch; era: *the time of the Vikings.* **4** The portion of duration allotted to some specific happening, condition, etc. **5** Leisure: *He has no time to play golf.* **6** Experience on a specific occasion: *to have a good time.* **7** A point in duration; occasion: *Your time has come!* **8** A period considered as having some quality of its own: *Times are hard.* **9** A system of reckoning or measuring duration: daylight-saving time. **10** A case of recurrence or repetition: three *times* a day. **11** *Music* The division of a musical composition into measures; meter. **12** Period during which work has been or remains to be done; also, the amount of pay due one: *time* and a half for overtime. **13** Rate of movement, as in dancing, marching, etc.; tempo. **14** Fit or proper occasion: *This is no time to quibble.* **—against time** As quickly as possible so as to finish within the allotted time. **—at the same time 1** At the same moment. **2**

Despite that; nevertheless. —**at times** Now and then. —**behind the times** Out-of-date; passé. —**for the time being** For the present time. —**from time to time** Now and then; occasionally. —**in good time** 1 Soon. 2 At the right time. —**in time** 1 While time permits or lasts. 2 Ultimately. —**keep time** 1 To indicate time correctly, as a clock. 2 To make regular or rhythmic movements in unison with another or others. 3 To render a musical composition in proper time or rhythm. 4 To make a record of the number of hours worked by an employee. —**on time** 1 Promptly. 2 Paid for, or to be paid for, later or in installments. —**time after time** Again and again. —*adj.* 1 Of or pertaining to time. 2 Devised so as to operate, explode, etc., at a specified time: a *time* bomb, *time* lock. 3 Payable at, or to be paid for at, a future date. —*v.t.* **timed, tim·ing** 1 To record the speed or duration of: to *time* a race. 2 To cause to correspond in time: They *timed* their steps to the music. 3 To arrange the time or occasion for: He *timed* his arrival for five o'clock. 4 To mark the rhythm or measure of. [<OE *tīma*]

time·card (tīm′kärd′) *n.* A card for recording the arrival and departure times of an employee.

time clock A clock equipped to record times of arrival and departure of employees.

time exposure A long film exposure made by two separate manual operations of the shutter.

time-hon·ored (tīm′on′ərd) *adj.* Honored or accepted because of long-established usage or custom.

time·keep·er (tīm′kē′pər) *n.* 1 One who or that which keeps time. 2 TIMEPIECE.

time·less (tīm′lis) *adj.* 1 Eternal; unending. 2 Not assigned or limited to any special time, era, or epoch. —**time′less·ly** *adv.* —**time′less·ness** *n.*

time·ly (tīm′lē) *adj.* **-li·er, -li·est** Being or occurring in good or proper time. —**time′li·ness** *n.* —**Syn.** convenient, fitting, opportune, suitable.

time·piece (tīm′pēs′) *n.* A clock or watch.

tim·er (tī′mər) *n.* 1 A timekeeper. 2 A stopwatch. 3 A device similar to a stopwatch for timing various processes: a kitchen *timer.* 4 A device that begins operations in sequence or after measured intervals of time.

times (tīmz) *prep.* Multiplied by: four *times* two is eight.

time·serv·ing (tīm′sûr′ving) *adj.* Conducting oneself so as to conform to the demands and opinions of the times and of those in power, usu. for personal advantage. —*n.* The actions of a timeserving person. —**time′serv′er** *n.*

time-shar·ing (tīm′shâr′ing) *n.* The simultaneous use of a single large computer by many people at once, by means of individual terminals.

time signature A sign, usu. two numerals placed one above the other on a musical staff, to indicate meter.

time·ta·ble (tīm′tā′bəl) *n.* A schedule showing the times at which trains, boats, airplanes, buses, etc., arrive and depart.

time-worn (tīm′wôrn, -worn′) *adj.* Made worn and ineffective by long existence or use.

time zone One of the 24 established divisions or sectors into which the earth is divided for convenience in reckoning time: each sector represents 15 degrees of longitude, or a time interval of 1 hour.

tim·id (tim′id) *adj.* 1 Easily frightened; fearful. 2 Lacking self-confidence. [<L *timere* to fear] —**ti·mid·i·ty** (ti·mid′ə·tē), **tim′id·ness** *n.* —**tim′id·ly** *adv.* —**Syn.** 2 retiring, shrinking, shy, timorous.

tim·ing (tī′ming) *n.* The art or act of regulating the speed at which something is performed to secure maximum effects.

tim·or·ous (tim′ər·əs) *adj.* Fearful and anxious; timid. [<L *timor* fear] —**tim′or·ous·ly** *adv.* —**tim′or·ous·ness** *n.*

tim·o·thy (tim′ə·thē) *n.* A perennial fodder grass having its flowers in a dense cylindrical spike. Also **timothy grass.** [<*Timothy* Hanson, who took the seed from New York to the Carolinas about 1720]

Tim·o·thy (tim′ə·thē) A convert and companion of the apostle Paul. —*n.* Either of two epistles in the New Testament, written to Timothy by Paul.

tim·pa·ni (tim′pə·nē) *n. pl. (construed as sing. or pl.)* Kettledrums. [<Ital., pl. of *timpano* a kettledrum <L *tympanum* a drum] —**tim′pa·nist** *n.*

tin (tin) *n.* 1 A soft, silvery white, corrosion-resistant metallic element (symbol Sn) usu. found combined with oxygen; used in making alloys. 2 Tin plate. 3 *Chiefly Brit.* A can, as of preserved food. —*v.t.* **tinned, tin·ning** 1 To coat or cover with tin, solder, or tin plate. 2 *Chiefly Brit.* To pack or preserve (food) in cans. —*adj.* Made of tin. [<OE]

tinc·ture (tingk′chər) *n.* 1 A medicinal solution, usu. in alcohol. 2 A tinge of color; tint. 3 A slight trace. [<L *tinctura* a dyeing]

tin·der (tin′dər) *n.* Any dry, readily combustible substance that will ignite on contact with a spark. [<OE *tynder*] —**tin′der·y** *adj.*

tin·der·box (tin′dər·boks′) *n.* 1 A box containing tinder, flint, and steel for starting a fire. 2 A highly flammable mass of material. 3 An excitable, temperamental person.

tine (tīn) *n.* A spike or prong, as of a fork or of an antler. [<OE *tind*] —**tined** *adj.*

tin·foil (tin′foil′) *n.* 1 Tin or an alloy of tin made into very thin sheets. 2 A similar sheeting made of rolled aluminum, commonly used as wrapping material.

ting (ting) *n.* A high metallic sound, as of a small bell.

tinge (tinj) *v.t.* **tinged, tinge·ing** or **ting·ing** 1 To imbue with a faint trace of color. 2 To impart a slight trace of a quality to. —*n.* 1 A faint trace of added color. 2 A slight trace, as of a quality. [<L *tingere* to dye] —**Syn.** *n.* 1, 2 dash, hint, soupçon, tincture, touch.

tin·gle (ting′gəl) *v.* **-gled, -gling** *v.i.* 1 To experience a prickly, stringing sensation. 2 To cause such a sensation. 3 To jingle; tinkle. —*v.t.* 4 To cause to tingle. —*n.* 1 A prickly, stinging sensation. 2 A jingle or tinkling. [Appar. var. of TINKLE] —**tin′gler** *n.* —**tin′gly** *adj.*

tin·horn (tin′hôrn′) *adj. Slang* Cheap, vulgar, and pretentious: a *tinhorn* politician. [With ref. to the fine appearance but poor sound of a tin horn]

tink·er (tingk′ər) *n.* 1 A mender of pots and pans, etc. 2 A clumsy workman; a botcher. 3 Work done hastily and carelessly. —*v.i.* 1 To work as a tinker. 2 To work in a clumsy, makeshift fashion. 3 To potter; fuss. —*v.t.* 4 To mend as a tinker. 5 To repair clumsily or inexpertly. [Var. of earlier *tinekere* a worker in tin]

tinker's damn *Slang* Any useless or worthless thing: usu. in the phrase **not worth a tinker's damn.** Also **tinker's dam.** [<TINKER + DAMN; with ref. to the reputed profanity of tinkers]

tin·kle (ting′kəl) *v.* **-kled, -kling** *v.i.* 1 To produce slight, sharp, metallic sounds, as a small bell. —*v.t.* 2 To cause to tinkle. 3 To summon or signal by a tinkling. —*n.* A sharp, clear, tinkling sound. [Imit.] —**tin′kly (-kli·er, -kli·est)** *adj.*

tin·ner (tin′ər) *n.* 1 A miner employed in tin mines. 2 A tinsmith.

tin·ni·tus (ti·nī′təs) *n.* A ringing, buzzing, or clicking sound in the ears, not caused by external stimuli. [<L *tinnire* to ring]

tin·ny (tin′ē) *adj.* **-ni·er, -ni·est** 1 Made of or containing tin. 2 Like tin in cheapness and brightness. 3 Having a thin, flat sound like that of tin being struck. —**tin′ni·ly** *adv.* —**tin′ni·ness** *n.*

Tin Pan Alley 1 A section of a city, esp. New York, frequented by musicians, song writers, and publishers of popular music. 2 The musicians, writers, publishers, etc., of popular music.

tin plate Sheet iron or steel plated with tin. —**tin′-plate′ (-plat·ed, -plat·ing)** *v.t.* —**tin′-plat′er** *n.*

tin·sel (tin′səl) *n.* 1 Very thin glittering bits of metal or plastic used for display and ornament. 2 Anything sparkling and showy, but with little real worth. —*adj.* 1 Made or covered with tinsel. 2 Like tinsel; superficially brilliant. —*v.t.* **-seled** or **-selled, -sel·ing** or **-sel·ling** 1 To adorn or decorate with or as with tinsel. 2 To give a false attractiveness to. [<L *scintilla* a spark]

tin·smith (tin′smith′) *n.* One who works with tin or tin plate.

tint (tint) *n.* **1** A variety of color; tinge: red with a blue *tint.* **2** A gradation of a color made by dilution with white. **3** A pale or delicate color. **4** In engraving, uniform shading produced by parallel lines or hatching. —*v.t.* To give a tint to. [< L *tinctus* a dyeing] —**tint′er** *n.*

tin·tin·nab·u·la·tion (tin′ti·nab′yə·lā′shən) *n.* The pealing, tinkling, or ringing of bells. [< L *tintinnare* to ring]

tin·type (tin′tīp′) *n.* An old type of photograph taken on a sensitized plate of enameled tin or iron.

tin·ware (tin′wâr′) *n.* Articles made of tin plate.

ti·ny (tī′nē) *adj.* **·ni·er, ·ni·est** Very small; minute. [< obs. *tine* a small amount, bit] —**ti′ni·ness** *n.*

-tion *suffix of nouns* **1** Action or process of: *rejection.* **2** Condition or state of being: *completion.* **3** Result of: *connection.* [< L *-tio, -tionis*]

tip[1] (tip) *n.* A slanting position; a tilt. —*v.* **tipped, tip·ping** *v.t.* **1** To cause to lean; tilt. **2** To put at an angle: to *tip* one's hat. **3** To overturn or upset: often with *over.* —*v.i.* **4** To become tilted; slant. **5** To overturn; topple: with *over.* [ME *tipen* overturn] —**tip′per** *n.*

tip[2] (tip) *v.t.* **tipped, tip·ping** **1** To strike lightly; tap. **2** In baseball, to strike (the ball) a light, glancing blow. —*n.* A tap; light blow. [Prob. < LG *tippe*]

tip[3] (tip) *n.* **1** A small gift of money for services rendered. **2** A helpful hint. **3** A piece of confidential information: a *tip* on a horse race. —*v.* **tipped, tip·ping** *v.t.* **1** To give a small gratuity to. **2** *Informal* To give secret information to, as in betting, etc. —*v.i.* **3** To give gratuities. —**tip off** *Informal* **1** To give secret information to. **2** To warn. [? < TIP[2]] —**tip′per** *n.*

tip[4] (tip) *n.* **1** The point or extremity of anything tapering: the *tip* of the tongue. **2** A piece made to form the end of something, as a nozzle, ferrule, etc. **3** The uppermost part; top: the *tip* of a flagpole. —*v.t.* **tipped, tip·ping** **1** To furnish with a tip. **2** To form the tip of. **3** To cover or adorn the tip of. [Prob. < MDu., a point]

tip-off (tip′ôf′, -of′) *n. Informal* A hint or warning, usu. given confidentially.

tip·pet (tip′it) *n.* **1** Formerly, a long hanging strip of cloth attached to the sleeve or hood. **2** A covering, usu. of fur, velvet, etc., for the neck and shoulders, hanging well down in front. [Prob. dim. of TIP[4]]

tip·ple (tip′əl) *v.t. & v.i.* **·pled, ·pling** To drink (alcoholic beverages) frequently and habitually. —*n.* Liquor consumed in tippling. [< earlier *tipler* bartender]

tip·ster (tip′stər) *n. Informal* One who sells tips for betting, as on a race.

tip·sy (tip′sē) *adj.* **·si·er, ·si·est** **1** Mildly intoxicated. **2** Shaky; unsteady. [< TIP[1]] —**tip′si·ly** *adv.* —**tip′si·ness** *n.*

Tippet *def. 1*

tip·toe (tip′tō′, -tō′) *n.* The tip of a toe, or the tips of all the toes. —**on tiptoe** **1** On one's tiptoes. **2** Expectantly; eagerly. **3** Stealthily; quietly. —*v.i.* **·toed, ·toe·ing** To walk on tiptoe; go stealthily or quietly. —*adv.* On tiptoe.

tip-top (tip′top′) *adj.* **1** At the very top. **2** *Informal* Best of its kind; first-rate. —*n.* The highest point. —**tip′-top′per** *n.*

ti·rade (tī′rād, tī·rād′) *n.* A prolonged declamatory outpouring, as of censure. [< Ital. *tirata* a volley]

tire[1] (tīr) *v.* **tired, tir·ing** *v.t.* **1** To reduce the strength of, as by exertion. **2** To reduce the interest or patience of, as with monotony. —*v.i.* **3** To become weary or exhausted. **4** To lose patience, interest, etc. —**tire of** To become bored or impatient with. —**tire out** To weary completely. [< OE *tīorian*] —**Syn. 1** exhaust, fag, fatigue, wear out, weary.

tire[2] (tīr) *n.* **1** A band or hoop surrounding the rim of a wheel. **2** A tough, flexible tube, usu. of inflated rubber, set around the rims of the wheels of automobiles, bicycles, etc. —*v.t.* **tired, tir·ing** To put a tire on. *Brit. sp.* **tyre.** [Prob. < obs. *tire* to attire]

tired (tīrd) *adj.* Weary; fatigued. [Orig. pp. of TIRE[1]] —**tired′ly** *adv.* —**tired′ness** *n.*

tire·less (tīr′lis) *adj.* **1** Not becoming easily fatigued; untiring. **2** Ceaseless; *tireless* zeal. —**tire′less·ly** *adv.* —**tire′less·ness** *n.*

tire·some (tīr′səm) *adj.* Tending to tire, or causing one to tire; tedious. —**tire′some·ly** *adv.* —**tire′some·ness** *n.*

ti·ro (tī′rō) *n.* TYRO.

'tis (tiz) Contraction of *it is.*

tis·sue (tish′ōō) *n.* **1** Any light or gauzy textile fabric. **2** *Biol.* An aggregate of cells and intercellular material having a particular function: nerve *tissue.* **3** A network; chain: a *tissue* of lies. **4** TISSUE PAPER. **5** A disposable square of soft absorbent paper for use as a handkerchief, etc. [< OF *tistre* to weave]

tissue paper Very thin, unsized, translucent paper for wrapping delicate articles, protecting engravings, etc.

tit[1] (tit) *n.* A titmouse, titlark, etc.

tit[2] (tit) *n.* Teat; breast; nipple. [< OE *titt*]

ti·tan (tīt′n) *n.* Any person having gigantic strength or size; a giant. —**ti·tan′ic** *adj.* [< TITAN]

Ti·tan (tīt′n) *Gk. Myth.* One of a race of giant gods, who were succeeded by the Olympian gods. —**Ti·tan′ic** *adj.*

Ti·ta·ni·a (ti·tā′nē·ə, tī-, -tan′yə) In folklore, the queen of fairyland and wife of Oberon.

ti·ta·ni·um (tī·tā′nē·əm) *n.* A widely distributed lightweight metallic element (symbol Ti) resembling aluminum in appearance, used to make tough, heat-resistant alloys. [< L *Titani* the Titans]

tit·bit (tit′bit′) *n.* TIDBIT.

tit for tat Retaliation in kind; blow for blow. [?]

tithe (tīth) *n.* **1** One tenth. **2** *Usu. pl.* A tax of one tenth part of yearly income arising from lands and from the personal industry of the inhabitants, for the support of the clergy and the church. **3** A small part. **4** Loosely, any tax or levy. —*v.t.* **tithed, tith·ing** **1** To give or pay a tithe, or tenth part of. **2** To tax with tithes. [< OE *tēotha, tēogotha* a tenth] —**tith′er** *n.*

ti·tian (tish′ən) *n.* A reddish yellow color much used by Titian, esp. in painting women's hair. —*adj.* Having the color titian. [< *Titian,* Venetian artist, 1477–1576]

tit·il·late (tit′ə·lāt) *v.t.* **·lat·ed, ·lat·ing** **1** To cause a tickling sensation in. **2** To excite pleasurably. [< L *titillare* to tickle] —**tit′il·lat′er, tit′il·la′tion** *n.* —**tit′il·la′tive** *adj.*

tit·i·vate (tit′ə·vāt) *v.t. & v.i.* **·vat·ed, ·vat·ing** *Informal* To smarten; dress up. Also **tit′ti·vate.** [Earlier *tidivate* ? < TIDY, on analogy with *cultivate*] —**tit′i·va′tion, tit′i·va′tor** *n.*

tit·lark (tit′lärk′) *n.* A pipit. [ME *tit* a little thing + LARK]

ti·tle (tīt′l) *n.* **1** The name of a book, play, motion picture, song, etc. **2** A title page, as of a book. **3** A descriptive name; epithet. **4 a** An appellation showing rank, office, profession, station in life, etc. **b** In some countries, a designation of nobility or one conferred for unusual distinction. **5** In some sports, championship: to win the *title.* **6** *Law* **a** The legal right to own property. **b** Legal evidence of such a right. **c** A document setting forth such evidence. —*v.t.* **·tled, ·tling** To give a name to; entitle. [< L *titulus* a label, inscription]

ti·tled (tīt′ld) *adj.* Having a title, esp. of nobility.

title page A page containing the title of a work, its author, its publisher, etc.

title role The character in a play, opera, or motion picture for whom it is named.

tit·mouse (tit′mous′) *n. pl.* **·mice** (-mīs′) Any of numerous small birds related to the nuthatches. [< ME *tit-* little + *mose* < OE *mase* a titmouse]

ti·trate (tī′trāt) *v.t. & v.i.* **·trat·ed, ·trat·ing** To analyze (a substance) by titration. [< F *titrer*]

ti·tra·tion (tī·trā′shən, ti-) *n.* Quantitative analysis of a substance in solution by the completion of a specific reaction with a measured volume of a standard solution.

Titmouse

tit·ter (tit′ər) *v.i.* To laugh in a suppressed way. —*n.* The act of tittering. [Imit.] —**tit′ter·er** *n.* —**tit′ter·ing·ly** *adv.* —**Syn.** *v.* chuckle, giggle, snicker, snigger, snort.

tit·tle (tit′l) *n.* **1** The minutest quantity; iota. **2** A very small diacritical mark in writing, as the dot over an *i,* etc. [< L *titulus* title]

tit·tle-tat·tle (tit′l-tat′l) *n.* **1** Trivial talk; gossip. **2** An idle talker. —*v.i.* **·tled, ·tling** To gossip; chatter. [Reduplication of TATTLE]

tit·u·lar (tich′ŏŏ·lər, tit′yə-) *adj.* **1** Existing in name or title only: a *titular* ruler. **2** Pertaining to a title. **3** Having a title. [< L *titulus* a title] —**tit′u·lar·ly** *adv.*

Ti·tus (tī′təs) A disciple of the apostle Paul. —*n.* The epistle in the New Testament addressed to Titus and attributed to Paul.

tiz·zy (tiz′ē) *n. pl.* **·zies** *Slang* A bewildered or excited state of mind; a dither. [?]

TKO, T.K.O., t.k.o. technical knockout.

Tl thallium.

T.L. trade last.

T/L time loan.

Tm thulium.

TN Tennessee (P.O. abbr.).

Tn thoron.

tn. ton; train.

tng. training.

TNT, T.N.T. trinitrotoluene.

to (tŏŏ, *unstressed* tə) *prep.* **1** Toward or terminating in: going *to* town. **2** Opposite or near: face *to* face; Hold me *to* your breast. **3** Intending or aiming at: Come *to* my rescue. **4** Resulting in: frozen *to* death. **5** Belonging with; of: the key *to* the barn. **6** In honor of: Drink *to* our victory. **7** In comparison with: 9 is *to* 3 as 21 is *to* 7. **8** Until: five minutes *to* one. **9** For the utmost duration of: a miser *to* the end of his days. **10** Concerning: blind *to* her faults. **11** In close application toward: Get down *to* work. **12** For: The contest is open *to* everyone. **13** Noting action toward: Give the ring *to* me. **14** By: known *to* the world. **15** From the point of view of: It seems *to* me. **16** About; involved in: That's all there is *to* it. **17** On; against: Nail the sign *to* the post. **18** In: four quarts *to* a gallon. **19** Into: The house was reduced *to* ashes. —*adv.* **1** Forward: He wore his sweater back side *to*. **2** In a direction or position, esp. closed: Pull the door *to*. **3** Into a normal condition or consciousness: She soon came *to*. **4** Into action or operation: They fell *to* eagerly. —**to and fro** In opposite or different directions; back and forth. [< OE *tō*] • *To* is also used before a verb to indicate the infinitive: It is good *to* see you; You can go if you want *to* (go).

toad (tōd) *n.* **1** Any of various tailless, jumping, insectivorous amphibians resembling the frog but usu. having a warty skin and resorting to water only to breed. **2** A contemptible or loathsome person. [< OE *tādige*]

toad·fish (tōd′fish′) *n. pl.* **·fish** or **·fish·es** Any of a family of fishes with scaleless skin and a toadlike head.

toad·stool (tōd′stōōl′) *n.* An inedible or poisonous mushroom.

Toad

toad·y (tō′dē) *n. pl.* **toad·ies** An obsequious flatterer; a sycophant. —*v.t. & v.i.* **toad·ied, toad·y·ing** To act the toady (to). [< earlier *toad-eater*, a charlatan's attendant who pretended to eat toads] —**toad′y·ism** *n.*

to-and-fro (tōō′ən-frō′) *adj.* Moving back and forth or from one position to another. —*adv.* In a to-and-fro motion.

toast¹ (tōst) *v.t.* **1** To brown the outside of (a piece of bread, etc.) by heating in an oven, toaster, etc. **2** To warm thoroughly. —*v.i.* **3** To become warm or toasted. —*n.* Toasted bread. [< L *tostus* < *torrere* parch, roast]

toast² (tōst) *n.* **1** The act of drinking to someone's health or to some thing. **2** The person or thing thus named. —*v.t. & v.i.* To drink a toast or toasts (to). [< TOAST¹, from a custom of flavoring a drink with a spiced piece of toast] —**toast′er** *n.*

toast·er (tōst′ər) *n.* An electrical device for toasting bread.

toast·mas·ter (tōst′mas′tər, -mäs′tər) *n.* A person who, at public dinners, announces the toasts, calls upon the speakers, etc.

to·bac·co (tə-bak′ō) *n. pl.* **·cos** or **·coes** **1** Any of various plants of the nightshade family, with large sticky leaves and yellow, white, or purple flowers. **2** The leaves of several of these plants, processed for smoking, chewing, etc. **3** The various products prepared from tobacco leaves, as cigarettes, cigars, etc. [< Sp. *tabaco*]

to·bac·co·nist (tə-bak′ə-nist) *n. Brit.* One who deals in tobacco.

To·bit (tō′bit) *n.* A book of the Apocrypha of the Old Testament. Also **To·bi·as** (tō-bī′əs).

to·bog·gan (tə-bog′ən) *n.* A long sledlike vehicle without runners, consisting of thin boards curved upward in front. —*v.i.* **1** To coast on a toboggan. **2** To descend swiftly: Wheat prices *tobogganed*. [< Algon.] —**to·bog′gan·er, to·bog′gan·ist** *n.*

Tobacco plant

to·by (tō′bē) *n. pl.* **·bies** *Often cap.* A mug or jug for ale or beer, often made in the form of an old man wearing a three-cornered hat. Also **toby jug.** [< *Toby*, dim. of the name *Tobias*]

toc·ca·ta (tə-kä′tə, *Ital.* tôk·kä′tä) *n.* An elaborate composition for piano, organ, etc. often preceding a fugue. [Ital., lit., a touching]

To·char·i·an (tō-kâr′ē·ən, -kär′-) *n.* **1** One of an ancient people who inhabited central Asia in the first Christian millennium. **2** The language of the Tocharians, two dialects of which are known.

to·coph·er·ol (tō-kof′ə·rōl, -rol) *n.* Vitamin E. [< Gk. *tokos* offspring + *pherein* to bear]

toc·sin (tok′sin) *n.* **1** A signal sounded on a bell; alarm. **2** An alarm bell. [< Prov. *tocar* to strike, touch + *senh* a bell]

to·day (tə-dā′) *adv.* **1** On or during this present day. **2** At the present time. —*n.* The present day or age. Also **to·day′.** [< OE *tō* + *dæg* day]

tod·dle (tod′l) *v.i.* **·dled, ·dling** To walk unsteadily and with short steps, as a little child. —*n.* The act of toddling. —**tod′dler** *n.*

tod·dy (tod′ē) *n. pl.* **·dies** **1** A drink made with whiskey, brandy, etc., and hot water and sugar. **2** The fermented sap of certain East Indian palms (**toddy palms**). [< Skt. *tāla* a palm tree]

to-do (tə-dōō′) *n. Informal* A stir; fuss. —**Syn.** bustle, commotion, confusion, disturbance.

toe (tō) *n.* **1** One of the five digits of the foot. **2** The forward part of the foot. **3** That portion of a shoe, boot, sock, etc., that covers or corresponds to the toes. **4** Anything resembling a toe in contour, function, position, etc. —**on one's toes** Alert. —**tread on (someone's) toes** To trespass on (someone's) feelings, prejudices, etc. —*v.* **toed, toe·ing** *v.t.* **1** To touch or kick with the toes. **2** To furnish with a toe. **3** To drive (a nail or spike) obliquely. **4** To attach by nails driven thus. —*v.i.* **5** To stand or walk with the toes pointing in a specified direction: to *toe* out. —**toe the mark** (or **line**) **1** To touch a certain line with the toes preparatory to starting a race. **2** To conform to a discipline or a standard. [< OE *tā*]

toed (tōd) *adj.* **1** Having (a specified kind or number of) toes: used in combination: *pigeon-toed; three-toed.* **2** Fastened or fastening by obliquely driven nails. **3** Driven in obliquely, as a nail.

toe dance Dancing on the tips of the toes, as in ballet. —**toe′-dance′** (**-danced, -danc·ing**) *v.i.* —**toe′-danc′er** *n.*

toe·hold (tō′hōld′) *n.* **1** In climbing, a small space which supports the toes. **2** Any means of entrance, support, or the like; a footing. **3** A hold in which a wrestler bends back the foot of his opponent.

toe·nail (tō′nāl′) *n.* **1** The nail growing on a toe. **2** A nail driven obliquely. —*v.t.* To fasten with obliquely driven nails.

tof·fee (tôf′ē, tof′ē) *n.* TAFFY. Also **tof′fy.**

tog (tog) *Informal n. pl.* Clothes. —*v.t.* **togged, tog·ging** To clothe: often with *up* or *out.* [< L *toga* toga]

---

to·ga (tō′gə) n. pl. **·gas** or **·gae** (-gī) 1 The loose, flowing outer garment worn in public by a citizen of ancient Rome. 2 Any robe characteristic of a calling. [< L < tegere to cover] **—to′· gaed** adj.

to·geth·er (tŏŏ·geth′ər, tə-) adv. 1 In company: We were sitting together. 2 In or into one group, mass, unit, etc.: They put the jigsaw puzzle together. 3 Into contact with each other: Glue these two pieces together. 4 Simultaneously: Let's sing it together. 5 With one another; mutually: They discussed it together. 6 In agreement or harmony: The tie and shirt go well together. 7 Considered collectively: He has more courage than all of us together. 8 Without cessation: He talked for hours together. **—get it all together** Slang To achieve a positive outlook on life; free oneself from anxiety. **—together with** Along with. [< OE tōgædere]

Roman toga

tog·ger·y (tog′ər·ē) n. Informal Clothing; togs.

tog·gle (tog′əl) n. 1 A pin, or short rod, properly attached in the middle, as to a rope, and designed to be passed through a hole or eye and turned. 2 A toggle joint. **—v.t. ·gled, ·gling** To fix, fasten, or furnish with a toggle or toggles. [?]

toggle joint A joint having a central hinge like an elbow, and operable by applying the force at the junction, thus changing the direction of motion.

toggle switch Electr. A switch connected to its actuating lever by a toggle joint loaded by a spring.

To·go (tō′gō) n. A republic of w Africa, 21,500 sq. mi., cap. Lomé. **—To′go·lese′** (-lēs, -lēz) adj., n. • See map at AFRICA.

Toggle joint

toil[1] (toil) n. 1 Fatiguing work; labor. 2 Any work accomplished by great labor. **—v.i.** 1 To work strenuously and tiringly. 2 To make one's way laboriously: to toil up a hill. **—v.t.** 3 To accomplish with great effort: to toil one's way. [< L tudiculare stir about] **—toil′er** n. **—Syn.** v. 1 drudge, labor, slave, travail.

toil[2] (toil) n. Archaic A net, snare, or other trap. 2 pl. Anything that binds or entraps: the toils of remorse. [< L tela a web]

toi·let (toi′lit) n. 1 A fixture in the shape of a bowl, used for urination and defecation and equipped with a device for flushing and discharging with water. 2 A room containing such a fixture or fixtures. 3 PRIVY. 4 The act or process of bathing, grooming, and dressing oneself. 5 Formerly, a woman's attire or costume: also **toi·lette** (twa·let′). **—adj.** Used in dressing or grooming: toilet articles. [< F toilette orig. a cloth dressing gown, dim. of toile cloth]

toi·let·ry (toi′lit·rē) n. pl. **·ries** Soap, powder, cologne, etc., used in bathing and grooming oneself.

toilet water A scented liquid applied after the bath, after shaving, etc.

toil·some (toil′səm) adj. Involving hard work; laborious; difficult. **—toil′some·ly** adv. **—toil′some·ness** n.

toil·worn (toil′wôrn′, -wōrn′) adj. Exhausted by toil; showing the effects of toil.

To·kay (tō·kā′) n. 1 A large, sweet grape originally from Tokay, Hungary. 2 A wine made from it.

to·ken (tō′kən) n. 1 A visible sign; indication: This gift is a token of my affection. 2 Some tangible proof or evidence of one's identity, authority, etc. 3 A keepsake; souvenir. 4 A characteristic mark or feature. 5 A piece of metal issued as currency and having a face value greater than its actual value: a bus token. **—by the same token** Moreover; furthermore. **—in token of** As a sign or evidence of. **—adj.** 1 Having only the appearance of; nominal; minimal: token resistance; token submission. 2 Partial or very small: a token payment. [< OE tācen]

to·ken·ism (tō′kən·iz·əm) n. The policy of attempting to meet certain obligations or conditions by partial, symbolic, or token efforts.

To·khar·i·an (tō·kâr′ē·ən, -kär′-) n. TOCHARIAN.

told (tōld) p.t. & p.p. of TELL.

To·le·do (tə·lē′dō) n. pl. **·dos** A sword or sword blade from Toledo, Spain. Also **to·le′do.**

tol·er·a·ble (tol′ər·ə·bəl) adj. 1 Endurable; bearable. 2 Fairly good: tolerable health. [< L tolerare endure] **—tol′· er·a·ble·ness** n. **—tol′er·a·bly** adv.

tol·er·ance (tol′ər·əns) n. 1 The character, state, or quality of being tolerant. 2 Freedom from prejudice; open-mindedness. 3 The act of enduring, or the capacity for endurance. 4 An allowance for variations from specified measure, as of machine parts. 5 Med. Ability to withstand large or increasing amounts of a specified substance or stimulus.

tol·er·ant (tol′ər·ənt) adj. 1 Of a long-suffering disposition. 2 Indulgent; liberal. 3 Med. Resistant to the effects of a specific substance or stimulus. [< L tolerare endure] **—tol′er·ant·ly** adv.

tol·er·ate (tol′ə·rāt) v.t. **·at·ed, ·at·ing** 1 To allow without opposition. 2 To concede, as the right to opinions or participation. 3 To bear or be capable of bearing. 4 Med. To be tolerant. [< L tolerare endure] **—tol′er·a′tive** adj. **—tol′· er·a′tion, tol′er·a′tor** n. **—Syn.** 1 permit. 3 endure, sustain.

toll[1] (tōl) n. 1 A tax or charge for some privilege granted, esp. for passage on a bridge or turnpike. 2 The right to levy such a charge. 3 A charge for a special service, as for a long-distance telephone call. 4 The number or amount lost, as in a disaster: The wreck took a toll of nine lives. **—v.t.** 1 To take as a toll. **—v.i.** 2 To exact a toll. [< OE]

toll[2] (tōl) v.t. 1 To sound (a church bell) slowly and at regular intervals. 2 To announce (a death, funeral, etc.) by tolling a church bell. 3 To call or summon by tolling. **—v.i.** 4 To sound slowly and at regular intervals. **—n.** 1 The act of tolling. 2 The sound of a bell rung slowly and regularly. [ME tollen] **—toll′er** n.

toll bridge A bridge at which toll for passage is paid.

toll call A long-distance telephone call.

toll·gate (tōl′gāt′) n. A gate at the entrance to a bridge, or on a road, at which toll is paid.

toll·keep·er (tōl′kē′pər) n. One who collects the tolls at a tollgate.

Tol·tec (tōl′tek, tol′-) n. Any of certain ancient Nahuatlan tribes that dominated Mexico about 900–1100 before the Aztecs. **—adj.** Of or pertaining to the Toltecs: also **Tol′tec·an.**

tol·u·ene (tol′yŏŏ·ēn) n. A hydrocarbon obtained from coal tar, used in making dyes, drugs, and explosives. Also **tol′u·ol** (-yŏŏ-wôl, -wōl).

tom (tom) n. 1 The male of various animals, esp. the cat. 2 Often cap. Slang UNCLE TOM. **—adj.** Male: a tom turkey.

tom·a·hawk (tom′ə·hôk) n. An ax used as a tool and as a war weapon by the Algonquian Indians. **—v.t.** To strike or kill with a tomahawk. [< Algon.]

to·ma·to (tə·mā′tō, -mä′-) n. pl. **·toes** 1 The pulpy edible berry, yellow or red when ripe, of a tropical American plant related to the potato, used as a vegetable. 2 The plant itself. 3 Slang An attractive girl or woman. [< Nah. tomatl]

North American Indian tomahawks

tomb (tŏŏm) n. 1 A burial place; grave. 2 A tombstone or monument. **—the tomb** Death. **—v.t.** To entomb; bury. [< Gk. tymbos a mound]

tom·boy (tom′boi′) n. A young girl who behaves like a lively, active boy. [< TOM + BOY] **—tom′boy·ish** adj. **—tom′boy·ish·ness** n.

tomb·stone (tŏŏm′stōn′) n. A stone, usu. inscribed, marking a place of burial.

tom·cat (tom′kat′) n. A male cat. **—v.i. ·cat·ted, ·cat·ting** Slang To engage in sexual relations indiscriminately: said of a man. [< Tom, hero of The Life and Adventures of a Cat, 1760, a popular anonymous work]

tome (tōm) n. A large, heavy book. [< Gk. tomos a fragment, volume]

tom·fool (tom′fŏŏl′) n. An idiotic or silly person. **—adj.** Foolish; stupid. [< Tom Fool, a name formerly applied to mental defectives]

tom·fool·er·y (tom′fŏŏl′ər·ē) n. pl. **·er·ies** Nonsensical behavior; silliness.

tom·my (tom'ē) *n. pl.* **·mies** A British soldier. Also **Tom'·my**. [Short for TOMMY ATKINS]

Tommy At·kins (at'kinz) A British private of the regular army. [< *Thomas Atkins*, a name used on British Army specimen forms]

Tommy gun *Informal* A type of submachine gun. [< J. Thompson, d. 1940, U.S. army officer]

to·mor·row (tə-môr'ō, -mor'ō) *adv.* On or for the next day after today. —*n.* The next day after today. Also **to·mor'row**. [< OE *tō* to + *morgen* morning, morrow]

Tom Thumb 1 In English folklore, a hero as big as his father's thumb. 2 Any midget or dwarf.

tom·tit (tom'tit') *n.* A titmouse or other small bird. [< the name *Tom* + TIT']

tom-tom (tom'tom') *n.* Any of various drums, as of American Indian and African tribes, usu. beaten with the hands. [< Hind. *tamtam*, imit.]

-tomy *combining form* A cutting of a (specified) part or tissue: *lobotomy*. [< Gk. *tomē* a cutting]

ton (tun) *n.* 1 Any of several measures of weight; esp. the **short ton** of 2000 pounds avoirdupois; the **long ton** of 2240 pounds; or the **metric ton** of 1000 kilograms. 2 A unit for reckoning the displacement of vessels, equal to 35 cubic feet, or about one long ton of sea water: called **displacement ton.** 3 A unit for reckoning the freight capacity of a ship, usu. equivalent to 40 cubic feet of space: called **freight ton, measurement ton.** 4 A unit for reckoning the capacity of merchant vessels for purposes of registration, equivalent to 100 cubic feet or 2.832 cubic meters: called **register ton.** 5 *Informal* Any large amount, weight, etc. [Var. of TUN]

to·nal (tō'nəl) *adj.* 1 Of or pertaining to tone or tonality. 2 Having a keynote or tonic. —**to'nal·ly** *adv.*

to·nal·i·ty (tō-nal'ə-tē) *n. pl.* **·ties** 1 The existence of a keynote or tonic in music; also a key or mode. 2 The general color scheme or collective tones of a painting.

tone (tōn) *n.* 1 A vocal or musical sound; also, the quality of such a sound. 2 *Music* **a** A sound having a definite pitch, loudness, and timbre. **b** WHOLE STEP. 3 A predominating disposition; mood. 4 Characteristic tendency; quality: a want of moral *tone.* 5 Style or elegance: The party had *tone.* 6 Vocal inflection: a *tone* of pity. 7 The acoustical pitch, or change in pitch, of a phrase or sentence: A question is indicated by a rising *tone.* 8 The effect of light, shade, and color as combined in a picture. 9 A shade of a particular color: a deep *tone* of yellow. 10 Tonicity. —*v.* **toned, ton·ing** *v.t.* 1 To give tone to; modify in tone. 2 INTONE. —*v.i.* 3 To assume a certain tone or hue. 4 To blend or harmonize, as in tone or shade. —**tone down** 1 To subdue the tone of. 2 To moderate in quality or tone. — **tone up** 1 To raise in quality or strength. 2 To elevate in pitch. 3 To gain in vitality. [< Gk. *tonos* a pitch of voice, a stretching] —**ton'er** *n.*

tone·less (tōn'lis) *adj.* Lifeless; flat: a *toneless* voice. — **tone'less·ly** *adv.* —**tone'less·ness** *n.*

tong (tông, tong) *n.* 1 A Chinese association or closed society. 2 In the U.S., a former secret society composed of Chinese. [< Chin. *t'ang* a hall, meeting place]

Ton·ga (tong'gə) *n.* An independent kingdom in the Commonwealth of Nations situated on an archipelago E of Fiji, 270 sq. mi., cap. Nukualofa.

Ton·gan (tong'gən) *n.* 1 One of the Polynesian inhabitants of Tonga. 2 The language of Tonga.

tongs (tôngz, tongz) *n.pl. (sometimes construed as sing.)* An implement for grasping, holding, or lifting objects, consisting usu. of a pair of pivoted levers. Also **pair of tongs.** [< OE *tange*]

tongue (tung) *n.* 1 A muscular organ attached to the floor of the mouth of most vertebrates, important in masticating and tasting food, and in man as an organ of speech. • See MOUTH. 2 A similar organ in various insects, etc. 3 An animal's tongue, as of beef,

Tongs
a. blacksmith's.
b. ice.

prepared as food. 4 The power of speech: Have you lost your *tongue?* 5 Manner or style of speaking: a smooth *tongue.* 6 Utterance; talk. 7 A language or dialect. 8 Anything resembling a tongue in appearance, shape, or function. 9 A slender projection of land. 10 A long narrow bay or inlet. 11 A jet of flame. 12 A strip of leather for closing the gap in front of a laced shoe. • See SHOE. 13 The free or vibrating end of a reed in a wind instrument. 14 The clapper of a bell. 15 The harnessing pole of a horse-drawn vehicle. 16 The projecting edge of a tongue-and-groove joint. —**hold one's tongue** To keep silent. —**on the tip of one's tongue** On the verge of being remembered or uttered. —**with tongue in cheek** Facetiously, insincerely, or ironically. —*v.* **tongued, tongu·ing** *v.t.* 1 To use the tongue to attack or separate (notes) in playing a wind instrument. 2 To touch or lap with the tongue. 3 In carpentry: **a** To cut a tongue on (a board). **b** To join by a tongue-and-groove joint. —*v.i.* 4 To use the tongue to attack or separate notes in playing a wind instrument. 5 To extend as a tongue. [< OE *tunge*]

tongue-and-groove joint (tung'ən-grōōv') In carpentry, a joint in which a projecting edge, or tongue, of one board is inserted into a corresponding groove of another board.

tongue-in-cheek (tung'ən-chĕk') *adj.* Said or meant insincerely, ironically, or facetiously.

tongue-tie (tung'tī') *n.* Abnormal shortness of the membrane under the tongue, whereby its motion is impeded. —*v.t.* **·tied, ·ty·ing** 1 To deprive of speech or the power of speech. 2 To bewilder or amaze so as to render speechless.

Tongue-and-groove joint

tongue twister A word or phrase difficult to articulate quickly: "Miss Smith's fish-sauce shop" is a *tongue-twister.*

ton·ic (ton'ik) *adj.* 1 Having power to invigorate or build up; bracing. 2 Pertaining to tone or tones; in music, of the principal tone of a scale or tonal system. 3 *Physiol.* Of or pertaining to tension, esp. muscular tension. 4 *Pathol.* Rigid; unrelaxing: *tonic* spasm. 5 Of or pertaining to musical intonations or modulations of words, sentences, etc. 6 *Phonet.* Accented or stressed. —*n.* 1 *Med.* A medicine that promotes physical well-being. 2 Whatever imparts vigor or tone. 3 The basic tone of a key or tonal system. [< Gk. *tonos* sound, tone]

to·nic·i·ty (tō-nis'ə-tē) *n.* 1 The state of being tonic; tone. 2 The normal tension of muscle tissue. 3 Health and vigor.

to·night (tə-nīt') *adv.* In or during the present or coming night. —*n.* The night that follows this day; also, the present night. Also **to·night'.** [< OE *tō* to + *niht* night]

ton·nage (tun'ij) *n.* 1 Weight, as expressed in tons. 2 Capacity, as of a vessel or vessels, expressed in tons. 3 A tax levied at a given rate per ton. [< OF *tonne* a ton, tun]

ton·neau (tu-nō') *n. pl.* **·neaus** (-nōz') or **·neaux** (-nōz') The rear part of an early type of automobile enclosing the seats for passengers. [F, lit., barrel]

ton·sil (ton'səl) *n.* Either of two oval lymphoid organs situated on either side of the passage from the mouth to the pharynx. [< L *tonsillae* tonsils] —**ton'sil·lar, ton'sil·ar** *adj.* • See MOUTH.

ton·sil·lec·to·my (ton'sə-lek'tə-mē) *n. pl.* **·mies** Removal of the tonsils by surgery.

ton·sil·li·tis (ton'sə-lī'tis) *n.* Inflammation of the tonsils. —**ton'sil·lit'ic** (-lit'ik) *adj.*

ton·so·ri·al (ton-sôr'ē-əl, -sō'rē-) *adj.* Pertaining to a barber or to barbering: chiefly humorous. [< L *tonsor* a barber]

ton·sure (ton'shər) *n.* 1 The shaving of the head, or of the crown of the head, as of a priest or monk. 2 That part of a priest's or monk's head left bare by shaving. —*v.t.* **·sured, ·sur·ing** To shave the head of. [< L *tonsura* a shearing]

ton·tine (ton'tēn, ton·tēn') *n.* A form of collective life annuity, the individual profits of which increase as the number of survivors diminishes, the final survivor taking the whole. —*adj.* Of or pertaining to such an annuity. [< Lorenzo *Tonti*, a 17th-c. Neapolitan banker]

to·nus (tō′nəs) *n. Physiol.* The slightly contracted state of a muscle at rest. [L, tone]

ton·y (tō′nē) *adj.* **ton·i·er, ton·i·est** *Informal* Aristocratic; fashionable. [< TONE]

too (tōō) *adv.* 1 In addition; also. 2 In excessive quantity or degree: *too* long. 3 Very; extremely: I am *too* happy for you. 4 *Informal* Indeed: an intensive: You are *too* going! [< OE *tō* to]

took (tōōk) *p.t.* of TAKE.

tool (tōōl) *n.* 1 A simple implement, as a hammer, saw, spade, chisel, etc., used in work. 2 A power-driven apparatus used for cutting, shaping, boring, etc. 3 The active part of such an apparatus. 4 *Often pl.* Something necessary to the performance of a profession, vocation, etc.: Paints and brushes are an artist's *tools.* 5 A person used to carry out the designs of another or others, esp. when such designs are unethical or unlawful. —*v.t.* 1 To shape or work with a tool. 2 To provide, as a factory, with machinery and tools. 3 In bookbinding, to ornament or impress designs upon with a tool. —*v.i.* 4 To work with a tool. 5 *Informal* To drive or travel in a vehicle: usu. with *along.* 6 To install, as in a factory, equipment, tools, etc; usu. with *up.* [< OE *tōl*] —**tool′er** *n.* —Syn. *n.* 1 appliance, device, instrument, utensil. 5 dupe, stooge.

tool·ing (tōō′ling) *n.* Ornamentation or work done with tools.

toot (tōōt) *v.i.* 1 To blow a horn, whistle, etc., with short blasts. 2 To give forth a short blast. —*v.t.* 3 To sound (a horn, etc.) with short blasts. 4 To sound (a blast, etc.). — *n.* 1 A short blast on a horn, whistle, etc. 2 *Slang* A drinking spree. [? < MLG *tūten*] —**toot′er** *n.*

tooth (tōōth) *n. pl.* **teeth** (tēth) 1 One of the hard, dense

Teeth of human adult
A. cross-section of a molar. B. left upper jaw. C. left lower jaw. A.a. crown. b. enamel. c. pulp cavity. d. dentine. e. cement. f. roots. B. & C. g. incisors. h. canines. i. bicuspids. j. molars. k. wisdom teeth.

structures in the mouth of most vertebrates, used for seizing and chewing food, as offensive and defensive weapons, etc. 2 One of various hard bodies of the oral or gastric regions of invertebrates. 3 Something resembling a tooth in form or use, as a projection on a saw, comb, rake, or gearwheel. 4 Appetite or taste (for something): She has a sweet *tooth.* —**armed to the teeth** Completely or heavily armed. —**in the teeth of** Counter to or in defiance of. — **put teeth into** To make effective: to *put teeth into* a law. —**tooth and nail** With all one's strength and skill. —*v.t.* 1 To supply with teeth, as a rake or saw. 2 To give a serrated edge to; indent. —*v.i.* 3 To become interlocked, as gearwheels. [< OE *tōth*]

tooth·ache (tōōth′āk′) *n.* Pain in a tooth or in the nearby area.

tooth·brush (tōōth′brush′) *n.* A small brush used for cleaning the teeth.

toothed (tōōtht, tōōthd) *adj.* 1 Having (a specified type or number of teeth): used in combination: *sharp-toothed.* 2 Notched; serrated.

tooth·paste (tōōth′pāst′) *n.* A paste applied to a toothbrush and used in cleaning the teeth.

tooth·pick (tōōth′pik′) *n.* A small sliver, as of wood, used for removing particles of food from between the teeth.

tooth·some (tōōth′səm) *adj.* Having a pleasant taste. — **tooth′some·ly** *adv.* —**tooth′some·ness** *n.* —Syn. appetizing, delicious, savory, tasty.

too·tle (tōōt′l) *v.i.* **·tled, ·tling** 1 To toot lightly or continuously, as on a flute, whistle, etc. —*v.t.* 2 To toot (a flute, whistle, etc.) lightly and continuously. —*n.* The sound of tootling. [Freq. of TOOT]

top¹ (top) *n.* 1 The uppermost or highest part: the *top* of a hill. 2 The higher or upper surface: the *top* of a bureau. 3 A lid or cover: a bottle *top.* 4 The roof of a vehicle, as an automobile. 5 The crown of the head. 6 *pl.* The aboveground part of a root vegetable. 7 The highest degree or reach: at the *top* of one's voice. 8 The most prominent place or rank: at the *top* of one's profession. 9 One who is highest in rank: the *top* of one's class. 10 The choicest or best part: the *top* of the crop. 11 The upper part of a shoe or boot. —**blow one's top** *Slang* To break out in a rage. —**from top to toe** 1 From head to foot. 2 Completely. — **on top** 1 Successful. 2 With success; victoriously. —**over the top** Over the upper edge of a trench so as to attack. —*adj.* 1 Of or pertaining to the top. 2 Forming or comprising the top. 3 Most important; chief: *top* authors. 4 Greatest in amount or degree: *top* prices; *top* speed. —*v.* **topped, top·ping** *v.t.* 1 To remove the top of; prune: to *top* a tree. 2 To provide with a top, cap, etc. 3 To form the top of. 4 To reach the top of; surmount: to *top* a wave. 5 To surpass or exceed: Can you *top* this? 6 In golf, tennis, etc., to hit the upper part of (the ball) in making a stroke. —*v.i.* 7 To top someone or something. —**top off** To complete, esp. with a finishing touch. [< OE]

top² (top) *n.* A toy of wood, plastic, metal, etc., with a point on which it is made to spin, as by the unwinding of a string. [< OE]

to·paz (tō′paz) *n.* 1 A yellow or brownish yellow crystalline mineral, valued as a gemstone. 2 A yellow sapphire. 3 A yellow variety of quartz resembling topaz. [< Gk. *topazos*]

top boot A boot with a high top, sometimes ornamented with materials different from the rest of the boot. —**top′boot′ed** *adj.*

top·coat (top′kōt′) *n.* A lightweight overcoat.

top·drawer (top′drôr′) *adj. Informal* Of the highest quality, rank, or status.

top·flight (top′flīt′) *adj. Informal* Of the highest quality; outstanding; superior.

top·gal·lant (top′gal′ənt, tə·gal′ənt) *Naut. n.* The mast, sail, yard, or rigging immediately above the topmast and topsail. —*adj.* Pertaining to the topgallants.

top hat A man's formal hat, usu. black and made of silk, having a tall, cylindrical crown.

top·heav·y (top′hev′ē) *adj.* **·heav·i·er, ·heav·i·est** 1 Too heavy at the top and liable to topple: a *topheavy* bookcase. 2 Having too many in positions of high rank, as an organization. —**top′heav′i·ly** *adv.* —**top′heav′i·ness** *n.*

top·ic (top′ik) *n.* 1 A subject treated of in speech or writing. 2 A theme for discussion. 3 A subdivision of an outline or a treatise. [< L *Topica*, title of a work by Aristotle] — Syn. 1 issue, matter, point, question.

top·i·cal (top′i·kəl) *adj.* 1 Of or belonging to a place or spot; local. 2 Of or relating to matters of present or local interest; limited in relevance to a time or place. 3 Of or pertaining to a topic. 4 *Med.* Pertaining to a restricted area of the body. —**top′i·cal·ly** *adv.*

top kick *Slang* A top sergeant.

top·knot (top′not′) *n.* 1 A tuft or knot of hair or feathers on the top of the head. 2 A bow or other ornament worn as a headdress.

top·less (top′lis) *adj.* 1 Lacking a top. 2 Nude from the waist up. 3 Being without a covering for the breasts. 4 Presenting topless waitresses, dancers, etc., as a bar. 5 So high that no top can be seen. —**top′less·ness** *n.*

top·lev·el (top′lev′əl) *adj.* Of the highest rank or importance.

top·loft·y (top′lôf′tē) *adj.* **·i·er, ·i·est** Very proud or haughty. —**top′loft′i·ness** *n.*

top·mast (top′mast′, -məst) *n. Naut.* The mast next above the lower mast.

top·most (top′mōst′) *adj.* Being at the very top.

top·notch (top′noch′) *adj. Informal* Best or highest, as in quality, merit, or performance. —**top′-notch′er** *n.*

to·pog·ra·phy (tə·pog′rə·fē) *n. pl.* **·phies** 1 The art of representing on a map or chart the physical features of a place, as mountains, lakes, canals, usu. with indications of elevation. **2** The physical features of a region. **3** Topographic surveying. [< Gk. *topos* place + -GRAPHY] —**to·pog′ra·pher** *n.* —**top·o·graph·ic** (top′ə·graf′ik) or **-i·cal** *adj.* —**top′o·graph′i·cal·ly** *adv.*

top·per (top′ər) *n.* **1** One who or that which tops. **2** *Slang* One who or that which is of supreme quality. **3** *Informal* A top hat. **4** *Informal* A topcoat.

top·ping (top′ing) *adj.* **1** Towering high above. **2** Eminent; distinguished. **3** *Brit. Informal* Excellent; first-rate. —*n.* That which forms a top.

top·ple (top′əl) *v.* **·pled, ·pling** *v.i.* **1** To fall, top foremost, by or as if by its own weight. **2** To seem to be about to fall; totter. —*v.t.* **3** To cause to totter or fall. **4** To cause to collapse; overthrow: to *topple* a government. [Freq. of TOP[1], *v.*]

tops (tops) *adj. Slang* Excellent; first-rate.

top·sail (top′sāl′, -səl) *n. Naut.* **1** In a square-rigged vessel, a square sail set next above the lowest sail of a mast. **2** In a fore-and-aft-rigged vessel, a sail above the gaff of a lower sail.

top-se·cret (top′sē′krit) *adj.* Designating information requiring the strictest secrecy.

top sergeant *Informal* FIRST SERGEANT. See GRADE.

top·side (top′sīd′) *n.* **1** The portion of a ship above the main deck. **2** *pl.* The side of a ship above the waterline. —*adv.* To or on the upper parts of a ship.

top·soil (top′soil′) *n.* The surface soil of land.

top·sy-tur·vy (top′sē-tûr′vē) *adv.* **1** Upside down. **2** In utter confusion. —*adj.* **1** Being in an upset or disordered condition. **2** Upside-down. —*n.* A state of being topsy-turvy; disorder. [Earlier *topsy-tervy,* ? < TOP[1] + obs. *terve* overturn] —**top′sy-tur′vi·ly** *adv.* —**top′sy-tur′vi·ness** *n.*

toque (tōk) *n.* **1** A small, close-fitting, brimless hat worn by women. **2** TUQUE. [< Sp. *toca*]

To·rah (tôr′ə, tō′rə) *n.* In Judaism: **1** The Pentateuch. **2** A scroll, as of parchment, containing the Pentateuch. **3** The whole of Jewish law, including the Old Testament and the Talmud. [< Hebrew *tōrāh* an instruction, law]

torch (tôrch) *n.* **1** A stick of wood or some material dipped in tallow or oil and set ablaze at the end to provide a light that can be carried about. **2** Anything that illuminates or brightens. **3** A portable device giving off an intensely hot flame and used for burning off paint, melting solder, etc. **4** *Brit.* A flashlight. [< OF *torche*]

torch·bear·er (tôrch′bâr′ər) *n.* **1** One who carries a torch. **2** One who conveys knowledge, truth, etc. **3** A leader of a cause or movement.

torch·light (tôrch′līt′) *n.* The light of a torch or torches. —*adj.* Lighted by torches.

torch song A popular love song, usu. melancholy and expressing hopeless yearning. —**torch singer**

tore (tôr, tōr) *p.t.* of TEAR[1].

tor·e·a·dor (tôr′ē·ə·dôr′, tō′rē-) *n.* One who engages in a bullfight, esp. on horseback. [< Sp. < *toro* a bull]

to·ri·i (tôr′ē·ē, tōr′-) *n. pl.* **to·ri·i** The gateway of a Shinto shrine. [Jap.]

tor·ment (tôr′mənt, -mənt) *n.* **1** Intense bodily pain or mental anguish. **2** A source of pain or anguish, or a persistent annoyance. **3** The inflicting of torture. —*v.t.* (tôr·ment′) **1** To subject to intense or persistent physical or mental pain; make miserable. **2** To harass or vex. **3** To disturb; agitate; stir up. [< L *tormentum* a rack] —**tor·men′tor, tor·men′ter** *n.*

Japanese torii

—*Syn.* **n. 1** agony, torture, suffering, misery.

torn (tôrn, tōrn) *p.p.* of TEAR[1].

tor·na·do (tôr·nā′dō) *n. pl.* **·does** or **·dos** **1** A whirling wind of exceptional force and violence, accompanied by a funnel-shaped cloud marking the narrow path of greatest destruction. **2** Any hurricane or violent windstorm. [Alter. of Sp. *tronada* a thunderstorm < *tronar* to thunder] —**tor·nad′ic** (-nad′ik) *adj.*

tor·pe·do (tôr·pē′dō) *n. pl.* **·does** **1** A self-propelled, tube-shaped underwater missile with an explosive warhead. **2** Any of various devices containing an explosive, as a submarine mine. —*v.t.* **·doed, ·do·ing** **1** To damage or sink (a vessel) with a torpedo. **2** *Informal* To destroy utterly; demolish: Publicity could *torpedo* the agreement. **3** ELECTRIC RAY. [L, stiffness, numbness < *torpere* be numb]

torpedo boat A swift, lightly armed boat equipped to discharge torpedoes.

tor·pid (tôr′pid) *adj.* **1** Having lost sensibility or power of motion, partially or wholly, as a hibernating animal; dormant; numb. **2** Slow to act or respond; sluggish. **3** Apathetic; spiritless; dull. [< L *torpidus* < *torpere* be numb] —**tor·pid·i·ty** (tôr·pid′ə·tē), **tor′pid·ness** *n.* —**tor′pid·ly** *adv.*

tor·por (tôr′pər) *n.* **1** Complete or partial loss of sensibility or power of motion; stupor. **2** Apathy; listlessness; dullness. [< L *torpere* be numb] —**tor·po·rif·ic** (tôr′pə·rif′ik) *adj.*

torque (tôrk) *n.* That which causes or tends to cause twisting or rotational acceleration; the moment of a force. [< L *torquere* to twist]

tor·rent (tôr′ənt, tor′-) *n.* **1** A stream of liquid, esp. water, flowing rapidly and turbulently. **2** Any violent or tumultuous flow; a gush: a *torrent* of abuse. [< L *torrens,* lit., boiling, burning, pr.p. of *torrere* parch]

tor·ren·tial (tô·ren′shəl, to-) *adj.* **1** Of, like, or resulting in a torrent. **2** Resembling a torrent. —**tor·ren′tial·ly** *adv.*

tor·rid (tôr′id, tor′-) *adj.* **1** Parched or hot from exposure to heat, esp. of the sun. **2** Intensely hot and dry; scorching. **3** Passionate. [< L *torridus* < *torrere* parch] —**tor·rid·i·ty** (tô·rid′ə·tē, to-), **tor′rid·ness** *n.* —**tor′rid·ly** *adv.*

torrid zone That part of the earth's surface on both sides of the equator between the tropics of Cancer and Capricorn. • See ZONE.

tor·sion (tôr′shən) *n.* **1** The act of twisting, or the state of being twisted. **2** *Mech.* Deformation or stress caused by twisting. [< L *tortus,* p.p. of *torquere* twist] —**tor′sion·al** *adj.* —**tor′sion·al·ly** *adv.*

tor·so (tôr′sō) *n. pl.* **·sos** or **·si** (-sē) **1** The trunk of a human body. **2** The part of a sculptured human figure corresponding to the trunk, esp. when the head and limbs are missing. [Ital., a stalk, trunk of a body]

tort (tôrt) *n. Law* Any civil wrong by act or omission for which a suit can be brought, exclusive of a breach of contract. [< L *tortus* twisted]

torte (tôrt, tôr′tə) *n. pl.* **tortes** or **tor·ten** (tôr′tən) A rich cake variously made of butter, eggs, fruits, and nuts. [G]

tor·til·la (tôr·tē′ə) *n.* A small, flat cake made of coarse cornmeal and baked on a griddle, common in Mexico. [Sp., dim. of *torta* a cake]

tor·toise (tôr′təs) *n.* A turtle, esp. one living on land. [< Med. L *tortuca*]

tortoise shell 1 The mottled yellow and brown shell of certain turtles, formerly used to make eyeglass frames, combs, etc. **2** A plastic imitation of this. —**tor′toise-shell′** *adj.*

Giant tortoise

tor·tu·ous (tôr′chōō·əs) *adj.* **1** Abounding in bends, twists, or turns; winding. **2** Not straightforward; devious: *tortuous* logic. [< L *tortus* twisted. See TORSION.] —**tor′tu·ous·ly** *adv.* —**tor′tu·ous·ness** *n.*

tor·ture (tôr′chər) *n.* **1** The infliction of extreme pain on one held captive, as in punishment, to obtain a confession or information, or to deter others from a course of action. **2** Intense physical or mental suffering; agony. **3** Something that causes severe pain. **4** *Informal* Something intensely annoying, embarrassing, or intolerable: Sitting through his speech was sheer *torture.* —*v.t.* **·tured, ·tur·ing** **1** To inflict extreme pain upon; subject to torture. **2** To cause to suffer keenly in body or mind. **3** To twist or turn into an abnormal form; distort; wrench. [< L *tortura,* lit., a twisting < *tortus.* See TORSION.] —**tor′tur·er** *n.*

---

add, āce, câre, pälm; end, ēven; it, īce; odd, ōpen, ôrder; tŏŏk, pōōl; up, bûrn; ə = a in above, u in focus; yōō = u in fuse; oil; pout; check; go; ring; thin; this; zh, vision. < derived from; ? origin uncertain or unknown.

To·ry (tôr′ē, tō′rē) *n. pl.* **To·ries** 1 A historical English political party, opposed to the Whigs, now called the Conservative party. 2 One who adhered to the British cause at the time of the American Revolution. 3 A very conservative person: also **tory.** —**To′ry·ism** *n.*

toss (tôs, tos) *v.t.* 1 To throw, pitch, or fling about: *tossed* in a small boat on the open sea. 2 To throw or cast upward or toward another: to *toss* a ball. 3 To throw, esp. casually or indifferently: to *toss* clothes on a chair. 4 To remove from abruptly or violently: with *out:* He was *tossed* out of a job. 5 To throw (a coin) in the air to decide a question by comparing the side facing up, upon landing, with a previous call. 6 To lift with a quick motion, as the head. 7 To insert or interject casually or carelessly: to *toss* in impressive but irrelevant statistics. 8 To utter, write, or do easily or in an offhand manner: with *off.* 9 To bandy about, as something discussed. 10 To turn over and mix the contents of: to *toss* a salad. 11 To make restless; agitate. 12 To drink at one draft: often with *off.* —*v.i.* 13 To be moved or thrown about, as a ship in a storm. 14 To roll about restlessly or from side to side, as in sleep. 15 To go quickly or angrily, as with a toss of the head. 16 To toss a coin. —*n.* 1 The act of tossing, as a throw or pitch. 2 A quick movement, as of the head. 3 The state of being tossed. 4 TOSS-UP (def. 1). [Prob. < Scand.] —**toss′er** *n.* —**Syn.** *v.* 2 flip, flick, hurl. 12 quaff, swallow, gulp.

toss-up (tôs′up′, tos′-) *n.* 1 The tossing of a coin to decide a question. 2 An even chance.

tot[1] (tot) *n.* A little child; toddler. [Prob. < Scand.]

tot[2] (tot) *v.* **tot·ted, tot·ting** *Informal v.t.* 1 To add; total: with *up.* —*v.i.* 2 To add. [Short for TOTAL]

to·tal (tōt′l) *n.* The whole sum or amount. —*adj.* 1 Constituting or comprising a whole. 2 Complete: a *total* loss. —*v.* **·taled** or **·talled, ·tal·ing** or **·tal·ling** *v.t.* 1 To ascertain the total of. 2 To come to or reach as a total; amount to. 3 *Slang* To wreck completely; demolish, esp. a car. —*v.i.* 4 To amount: often with *to.* [< L *totus* all] —**to′tal·ly** *adv.*

to·tal·i·tar·i·an (tō·tal′ə·târ′ē·ən) *adj.* 1 Designating or characteristic of a government controlled exclusively by one party or faction that suppresses political dissent by force or intimidation and whose power to control the economic, social, and intellectual life of the individual is virtually unlimited. 2 Tyrannical; despotic. —*n.* An adherent of totalitarian government. —**to·tal′i·tar′i·an·ism** *n.*

to·tal·i·ty (tō·tal′ə·tē) *n. pl.* **·ties** 1 A total amount; aggregate; sum. 2 The state of being whole or entire.

tote (tōt) *Informal v.t.* **tot·ed, tot·ing** 1 To carry or bear on the person; transport; haul. 2 To carry habitually: He *totes* a gun. —*n.* 1 The act of toting. 2 A load or haul. [?] —**tot′er** *n.*

tote bag A large handbag for personal articles, carried esp. by women.

to·tem (tō′təm) *n.* 1 An animal, plant, or other natural object believed to be ancestrally related to a tribe, clan, or family group, and serving as its emblem, as among the North American Indians. 2 A representation of such an emblem. [< Algon.] —**to·tem·ic** (tō·tem′ik) *adj.* —**to′·tem·ism** *n.*

totem pole A pole carved or painted with totemic symbols, erected outside the houses of Indians along the NW coast of North America.

tot·ter (tot′ər) *v.i.* 1 To shake or waver, as if about to fall; be unsteady. 2 To walk unsteadily. —*n.* An unsteady or wobbly manner of walking. [Prob. < Scand.] —**tot′ter·er** *n.* —**tot′ter·ing·ly** *adv.* —**tot′ter·y** *adj.*

tou·can (tōō′kan, tōō·kän′) *n.* A fruit-eating bird of tropical America with brilliant plumage and a very large beak. [< Tupi *tucana*]

touch (tuch) *v.t.* 1 To place the hand, finger, or other body part in contact with; perceive by feeling. 2 To be or come in contact with. 3 To bring into contact with something else. 4 To hit or strike lightly; tap. 5 To lay the hand or hands on: Please don't *touch* the paintings. 6 To border on; adjoin. 7 To come to; reach: The temperature *touched* 90°. 8 To rival or equal: As a salesman, nobody could *touch* him. 9 To color slightly: The sun *touched* the clouds with gold. 10 To

Toucan

affect the emotions of, esp. so as to feel compassion or gratitude; move: She was *touched* by their concern for her health. 11 To hurt the feelings of. 12 To relate to; concern; affect: The war *touches* us all. 13 To have to do with, use, or partake of: He never *touches* anything stronger than ginger ale. 14 To affect injuriously; taint: vegetables *touched* by frost. 15 *Slang* To borrow money from. —*v.i.* 16 To touch someone or something. 17 To come into or be in contact. —**touch at** To stop briefly at (a port or place) in the course of a journey or voyage. —**touch down** To land after flight. —**touch off** 1 To cause to explode; detonate; fire. 2 To provoke or initiate, esp. a violent reaction. —**touch on** (or **upon**) 1 To relate to; concern: That *touches on* another question. 2 To treat or discuss briefly or in passing. —**touch up** To add finishing touches or corrections to, as a work of art or writing. —*n.* 1 The act or fact of touching; a coming into contact, as a tap. 2 The sense stimulated by touching; the tactile sense by which a surface or its characteristics, as of pressure or texture, may be perceived. 3 A sensation conveyed by touching: a silky *touch.* 4 Communication or contact: Let's keep in *touch.* 5 A distinctive manner or style, as of an artist, author, or craftsman: a master's *touch.* 6 Delicate sensitivity, appreciation, or understanding: a fine *touch* for collecting rare china. 7 Any slight or delicate detail that helps to finish or perfect something, as a work of art or writing: to apply the finishing *touches.* 8 A trace; hint: a *touch* of irony. 9 A slight attack; twinge: a *touch* of rheumatism. 10 A small quantity; dash: a *touch* of perfume. 11 The resistance to motion offered by the keys of a piano, typewriter, etc. 12 The manner in which something is struck or touched, as the keys of a piano. 13 *Slang* Borrowed money, or a request to borrow money. 14 *Slang* A person from whom money may be borrowed, esp. easily: a soft *touch.* [< OF *tochier*] —**touch′a·ble** *adj.* —**touch′er** *n.*

touch and go An uncertain, risky, or precarious state of things. —**touch′-and-go′** *adj.*

touch·back (tuch′bak′) *n.* In football, the act of touching the ball to the ground behind the player's own goal line when the ball was propelled over the goal line by an opponent.

touch·down (tuch′doun′) *n.* 1 A scoring play in football in which a player has possession of the ball on or over the opponent's goal line. 2 The act of touching down, as an aircraft or spacecraft.

tou·ché (tōō·shā′) *interj.* A term used in fencing to indicate a touch scored by one's opponent, and otherwise to acknowledge the wit or effectiveness of a point made in argument or conversation. [F]

touched (tucht) *adj.* 1 Affected emotionally; moved. 2 Slightly unbalanced in mind; crack-brained.

touch·ing (tuch′ing) *adj.* Appealing to the emotions; esp., inspiring tenderness or sympathy. —*prep.* With regard to; concerning. —**touch′ing·ly** *adv.* —**touch′ing·ness** *n.*

touch-me-not (tuch′mē·not′) *n.* Any of various plants, the ripe seed capsules of which explode when touched.

touch·stone (tuch′stōn′) *n.* 1 A dark stone formerly used to test the purity of gold by the color of the streak made on the stone by the metal. 2 Any criterion or standard by which quality or value may be tested.

touch·wood (tuch′wŏŏd′) *n.* PUNK[1] (def. 1).

touch·y (tuch′ē) *adj.* **touch·i·er, touch·i·est** 1 Apt to take offense on very little provocation. 2 Liable to cause hurt feelings or contention: a *touchy* subject. —**touch′i·ly** *adv.* —**touch′i·ness** *n.* —**Syn.** 1 sensitive, thin-skinned, volatile. 2 delicate, sensitive.

tough (tuf) *adj.* 1 Capable of bearing tension or strain without breaking, esp. because strong in texture or composition. 2 Difficult to cut or chew. 3 Strong in body or mind, esp. in resisting or enduring stress. 4 Requiring determined or intense effort; difficult: a *tough* assignment. 5 Resolute; unyielding; inflexible: a *tough* stand in the negotiations. 6 Severe; harsh: a *tough* punishment. 7 Given to or characterized by violence or rowdyism: a *tough* neighborhood. 8 *Informal* Unfortunate; regrettable. 9 *Slang* Great; fine. —*n.* A ruffian; rowdy. —*v.t. Informal* To manage to get through; endure: often with *out:* to *tough out* a recession. [< OE *tōh*] —**tough′ly** *adv.* —**tough′ness** *n.* —**Syn.** 5 uncompromising, stubborn, militant.

tough·en (tuf′ən) *v.t. & v.i.* To make or become tough or tougher. —**tough′en·er** *n.*

tou·pee (tōō·pā′) *n.* A man's small wig worn to cover a bald spot. [< OF *toup, top* a tuft of hair]

tour (tōōr) *n.* 1 An excursion or journey, as for sightseeing. 2 A trip, usu. over a planned course, as to conduct business, present theatrical performances, etc. 3 A set period of time, as of service in a particular place; turn or shift. 4 A brief survey; circuit: a *tour* of the grounds. —*v.t.* 1 To make a tour of; travel. 2 To present on a tour: to *tour* a play. —*v.i.* 3 To go on a tour. [< OF *tor* a turn < L *tornus* a lathe]

tour de force (tōōr də fôrs′) *pl.* **tours de force** (tōōr) A remarkable feat, as of skill, creativity, or industry. [F, lit., feat of strength]

touring car An old type of large, open automobile with a capacity for five or more passengers.

tour·ism (tōōr′iz·əm) *n.* 1 Recreational travel, considered esp. as an industry or source of income. 2 The organization and guidance of tourists. —**tour·is′tic** *adj.*

tour·ist (tōōr′ist) *n.* One who makes a tour or a pleasure trip. —*adj.* Of or suitable for tourists. —**tour′ist·y** *adj.*

tour·ma·line (tōōr′mə·lən, -lēn′) *n.* A complex mineral with a vitreous to resinous luster, found in various colors and valued in its transparent varieties as a gemstone. Also **tour′ma·lin** (-lin). [< F]

tour·na·ment (tûr′nə·mənt, tōōr′-) *n.* 1 A series of competitive sports events or games for prizes or cash awards and often for a championship: a golf or bridge *tournament.* 2 In medieval times, a pageant in which two opposing parties of men in armor contended on horseback with blunted weapons, esp. lances. [< OF < *torneier* to tourney]

tour·ney (tûr′nē, tōōr′-) *v.i.* To take part in a tournament. —*n.* TOURNAMENT. [< OF *torneier*]

tour·ni·quet (tōōr′nə·kit, tûr′-) *n.* A device for controlling arterial bleeding by tightening a nooselike bandage. [< F *tourner* to turn]

tou·sle (tou′zəl) *v.t.* ·**sled**, ·**sling** To disarrange or dishevel; rumple. —*n.* A tousled mass, esp. of hair. [Freq. of ME *tousen*]

tout (tout) *Informal v.i.* 1 To solicit patronage, customers, votes, etc. 2 To sell information, as to a bettor, about horses entered in a race. —*v.t.* 3 To solicit; importune. 4 To praise highly or proclaim: *touted* as the world's fastest human. 5 To sell information concerning (a race horse). —*n.* 1 One who touts. 2 One who solicits business. [< OE *tōtian, tȳtan* peep, look out]

tout à fait (tōō tà fe′) *French* Entirely; quite.

tout de suite (tōōt swēt) Immediately; at once. [F]

tout en·sem·ble (tōō tän sän′bl′) *French* All in all; everything considered.

tow¹ (tō) *n.* A short, coarse hemp or flax fiber prepared for spinning. [Prob. < OE *tōw-* spinning]

tow² (tō) *v.t.* To pull or drag, as by a rope or chain. —*n.* 1 The act of towing, or the state of being towed. 2 That which is towed, as a barge. 3 TOWLINE. —**in tow** 1 In the condition of being towed. 2 Drawn along as if being towed: a film star with her fans *in tow.* 3 Under one's protection or care: took the orphan *in tow.* [< OE *togian*]

tow·age (tō′ij) *n.* 1 The charge for towing. 2 The act of towing.

to·ward (tôrd, tōrd, tə·wôrd′) *prep.* 1 In the direction of; facing. 2 With respect to; regarding. 3 In anticipation of or as a contribution to; for: He is saving *toward* his education. 4 Near in point of time; approaching: *toward* evening. 5 Tending or designed to result in. Also **to·wards′.** —*adj.* (tôrd, tōrd) Impending or imminent. [< OE *tō* to + -*weard* -ward] —**to·ward′ness** *n.*

tow·el (toul, tou′əl) *n.* A cloth or paper for drying anything by wiping. —*v.t.* ·**eled** or ·**elled**, ·**el·ing** or ·**el·ling** To wipe or dry with a towel. [< OF *toaille*]

tow·el·ing (tou′ling, tou′əl·ing) *n.* Material for towels. Also **tow·el·ling.**

tow·er (tou′ər) *n.* 1 A structure very tall in proportion to its other dimensions, and either standing alone or forming part of a building. 2 A place of security or defense;

citadel. 3 Someone or something likened to a tower in strength or command. —*v.i.* To rise or stand like a tower; extend to a great height. [< L *turris*]

tow·er·ing (tou′ər·ing) *adj.* 1 Very high or very great: a *towering* figure in modern drama. 2 Rising to a high pitch of violence or intensity: a *towering* rage.

tow·head (tō′hed′) *n.* 1 A head of very light-colored or flaxen hair. 2 A person having such hair. [< TOW¹ + HEAD] —**tow′-head′ed** *adj.*

tow·hee (tō′ē, tō′hē) *n.* Any of various American finches related to the buntings and the sparrows. Also **towhee bunting.** [Imit.]

tow·line (tō′līn′) *n.* A line, rope, or chain used in towing.

town (toun) *n.* 1 Any collection of dwellings and other buildings larger than a village and smaller than a city. 2 A closely settled urban district, as contrasted with less populated or suburban areas or with the open country. 3 A city of any size. 4 The inhabitants or voters of a town. 5 TOWNSHIP. 6 Those residents of a town who are not associated educationally or administratively with a college or university situated in the town: *town* and *gown.* —**go to town** *Slang* To work or proceed with dispatch; get busy. —**on the town** *Slang* On a round of bars, nightclubs, etc., in the city in search of diversion or excitement. —**paint the town red** *Slang* To go on a spree; carouse. —*adj.* Of, situated in, or for a town. [< OE *tūn, tuun* an enclosure, group of houses]

Towhee

town clerk An official who keeps the records of a town.

town crier Formerly, a person appointed to make proclamations through the streets of a town.

town hall A building in a town containing the public offices and often a place for meetings.

town house 1 A residence in a town or city, esp. when owned by one who also owns a house in the country. 2 A two- or three-story house, usu. for one family, contiguous to one or more similar houses.

town meeting A meeting of residents or voters of a town for the purpose of transacting town business.

town·ship (toun′ship) *n.* 1 In the U.S. and Canada, a territorial subdivision of a county with certain corporate powers of municipal government for local purposes. 2 In New England, a local political unit governed by a town meeting.

towns·man (tounz′mən) *n. pl.* ·**men** (-mən) 1 A resident of a town. 2 A fellow citizen of a town. 3 A permanent resident of a town, as contrasted with a student or teacher in a school or college situated in the town.

towns·peo·ple (tounz′pē′pəl) *n.pl.* People who live in towns or in a particular town or city. Also **towns′folk′** (-fōk′).

town·y (toun′ē) *n. pl.* **town·ies** *Informal* TOWNSMAN (def. 3). Also **town′ie.**

tow·path (tō′path′, -päth′) *n.* A path along a river or canal used by men, horses, or mules towing boats.

tow·rope (tō′rōp′) *n.* A heavy rope or cable for towing.

tow truck (tō) A truck equipped to tow other vehicles.

tox·e·mi·a (tok·sē′mē·ə) *n.* The presence in the blood of toxins from a local source of infection. Also **tox·ae′mi·a.** [< TOX(IC) + Gk. *haima* blood] —**tox·e′mic** *adj.*

tox·ic (tok′sik) *adj.* 1 Poisonous. 2 Due to or caused by poison or a toxin. [< Gk. *toxicon (pharmakon)* (a poison) for arrows < *toxon* a bow] —**tox′i·cal·ly** *adv.* —**tox·ic′i·ty** (-sis′ə·tē) *n.*

toxico- *combining form* Poison; of or pertaining to poison or poisons: *toxicology.* Also **toxic-.** [< Gk. *toxicon* poison]

tox·i·col·o·gy (tok′sə·kol′ə·jē) *n.* The science that deals with poisons, their detection, antidotes, etc. —**tox′i·co·log′ic** (-kə·loj′ik) or ·**i·cal** *adj.* —**tox′i·co·log′i·cal·ly** *adv.* —**tox′i·col′o·gist** *n.*

tox·in (tok′sin) *n.* 1 Any of various poisonous compounds produced by living organisms and acting as causative agents in many diseases. 2 Any toxic matter generated in living or dead organisms. [< TOX(IC) + -IN]

toy (toi) *n.* 1 Something designed or serving as a plaything for children. 2 Something trifling or unimportant. 3 An ornament; trinket. 4 A small animal, esp. one of a breed characterized by small size. —*v.i.* 1 To act or consider something without seriousness or conviction; trifle: to *toy* with an idea. 2 To use someone or something for one's amusement. 3 To act flirtatiously. —*adj.* 1 Designed as a toy. 2 Resembling a toy; esp., of miniature size: a *toy* dog. [Prob. < ME *toye* flirtation, sport] —**toy′er** *n.*

tp. township.

tpk. turnpike.

tr. translated; translation; translator; transpose; transitive; treasurer.

trace¹ (trās) *n.* 1 A vestige or mark left by some past event or by a person or thing no longer present. 2 An imprint or mark indicating the passage of a person or thing, as a footprint, etc. 3 A path or trail beaten down by men or animals. 4 A barely detectable quantity, quality, or characteristic. 5 A lightly drawn line; something traced. —*v.* **traced, trac·ing** *v.t.* 1 To follow the tracks or trail of. 2 To follow the course or development of, esp. by investigation of a series of events. 3 To find out or determine by investigation. 4 To follow (tracks, a course of development, etc.). 5 To draw; sketch. 6 To copy (a drawing, etc.) on a superimposed transparent sheet. 7 To form (letters, etc.) painstakingly. —*v.i.* 8 To have its origin; go back in time. 9 To follow a track, course of development, etc. [< OF *tracier* to trace] —**trace′a·bil′i·ty, trace′a·ble·ness** *n.* —**trace′a·ble** *adj.* —**trace′a·bly** *adv.* —**Syn.** 1 remnant, sign, aftermath, token, clue.

trace² (trās) *n.* One of two side straps or chains connected to a draft animal's harness and to the vehicle to be pulled. —**kick over the traces** To throw off control; become unmanageable. [< OF *trait* a dragging, a leather harness]

trac·er (trā′sər) *n.* 1 One who or that which traces. 2 An inquiry forwarded from one point to another, to trace missing mail, etc. 3 A substance, as a radioisotope, introduced into a system in minute amount as an indicator of the course of a process, reaction, disease, etc. 4 A bullet or shell that indicates its course by leaving a trail of smoke or fire.

trac·er·y (trā′sər·ē) *n. pl.* **·er·ies** 1 Ornamental stonework formed of branching lines, as in a Gothic window. 2 Any delicate ornamentation resembling this.

tra·che·a (trā′kē·ə) *n. pl.* **·che·ae** (-kē·ē, -kē·ī) or **·che·as** 1 In vertebrates, the duct by which air passes from the larynx to the bronchi and the lungs; the windpipe. 2 Any of the air passages in air-breathing arthropods. [< Gk. *(artēria) tracheia* a rough (artery)] —**tra′che·al** *adj.*

tra·che·ot·o·my (trā′kē·ot′ə·mē) *n. pl.* **·mies** *Surg.* An incision into the trachea. Also **tra′che·ost′·o·my** (-ost′ə·mē).

Trachea

tra·cho·ma (trə·kō′mə) *n.* A contagious virus disease of the eye characterized by granular excrescences on the inner surface of the eyelids. [< Gk. *trachōma* roughness] —**tra·chom·a·tous** (trə·kom′ə·təs) *adj.*

trac·ing (trā′sing) *n.* 1 The act of one who traces. 2 Something traced, as a copy made by tracing on transparent paper. 3 A record made by a self-registering instrument.

track (trak) *n.* 1 A mark or trail left by the passage of anything, as a series of footprints. 2 A path or way marked or worn out by the repeated passage of people, animals, or vehicles. 3 Any course or path, esp. one describing movement: the *track* of a missile or a comet. 4 A pair of parallel rails, usu. including the ties, that guide the wheels of a train, trolley, etc. 5 A usu. elliptical course for racing. 6 A sport in which footraces of various distances are held on a track. 7 TRACK AND FIELD. 8 A sequence of events; a succession of ideas. 9 Awareness of the progress or sequence; count; record: to lose *track* of an old friend; to keep *track* of expenses. 10 An endless metal belt, usu. one of a pair, by means of which certain vehicles are capable of moving over soft, slippery, or uneven surfaces. 11 The distance between the front or rear wheels of a vehicle, usu. measured from the center of the treads. 12

SOUND TRACK. 13 In education, any of two or more classes covering the same course of study in which students are placed according to their preparation and ability. —**in one's tracks** Right where one is; on the spot. —**make tracks** *Informal* To run away in haste; hurry. —**on** (or **off**) **the track** Keeping in view (or losing sight of) the subject or objective. —*v.t.* 1 To follow the tracks of; trail. 2 To discover or apprehend by following up marks, clues, or other evidence: with *down*: to *track* down a suspect; to *track* down a shipment of contaminated canned food. 3 To observe or plot the course of (an aircraft, spacecraft, etc.). 4 To make tracks upon or with: to *track* mud into a house. 5 To go through or traverse, as on foot: to *track* the wilderness. 6 To furnish with rails or tracks. —*v.i.* 7 To measure a certain distance between front or rear wheels. 8 To run in the same track or groove; be in alignment. 9 To leave tracks. —*adj.* Pertaining to or performed on a track, esp. a track for racing: *track* events. [< OF *trac*] —**track′er** *n.* —**track′less** *adj.*

track·age (trak′ij) *n.* 1 Railroad tracks collectively. 2 The right of one company to use the tracks of another. 3 The charge for this right.

track and field A sport consisting of footraces on a track and contests on a field, as in hurling, throwing, or leaping. —**track′-and-field′** *adj.*

trackless trolley TROLLEY BUS.

track record *Informal* A record of achievements.

tract¹ (trakt) *n.* 1 An extended area, as of land or water; stretch or expanse. 2 A system of parts or organs in an animal, having a distinct function: the alimentary *tract*. [< L *tractus* a drawing out < *trahere* draw]

tract² (trakt) *n.* A short treatise or pamphlet, as on religion or morals. [< L *tractatus* a handling]

tract·a·ble (trak′tə·bəl) *adj.* 1 Easily led or controlled; docile. 2 Readily worked or handled; malleable. [< L *tractare* handle, freq. of *trahere* draw] —**tract′a·bly** *adv.* —**tract′a·ble·ness, tract′a·bil′i·ty** *n.* —**Syn.** 1 manageable, compliant, mild, submissive.

trac·tile (trak′til, -tīl) *adj.* That can be drawn out; ductile. [< L *tractus.* See TRACT¹.] —**trac·til′i·ty** *n.*

trac·tion (trak′shən) *n.* 1 The act of drawing, as by motive power over a surface. 2 The state of being pulled or drawn: to place a fractured limb in *traction*. 3 The power employed in pulling or drawing. 4 Adhesive or rolling friction, as of tires on a road. [< L *tractus.* See TRACT¹.] —**trac′tion·al, trac·tive** (trak′tiv) *adj.*

trac·tor (trak′tər) *n.* 1 A powerful, self-propelled vehicle used to pull farm machinery. 2 An automotive vehicle with a driver's cab, used to haul trailers, etc. 3 An airplane with the propeller or propellers situated in front of the lifting surfaces. [< L *tractus.* See TRACT¹.]

Tractor *def.* 1

trad (trad) *adj. Slang* Traditional: *trad* jazz.

trade (trād) *n.* 1 A business or occupation. 2 A skilled or specialized line of work, as a craft. 3 The people or companies engaged in a particular business. 4 The buying and selling or exchange of commodities; also, an instance of such commerce. 5 A firm's customers. 6 An exchange of personal articles; swap. 7 Any exchange of things or people having negotiable value: a baseball *trade*. 8 Usu. pl. TRADE WIND. —*adj.* 1 Of or pertaining to a trade. 2 Used by or intended for the members of a particular trade: a *trade* journal. —*v.t.* **trad·ed, trad·ing** 1 To give in exchange for something else. 2 To barter or exchange. —*v.i.* 3 To engage in commerce or in business transactions. 4 To make an exchange. 5 *Informal* To do one's shopping: with *at*: to *trade* at a store. —**trade in** To give in exchange as payment or part payment. —**trade off** To match or correlate, as incompatible elements or objectives, in the process of reaching a solution or compromise. —**trade on** To take advantage of. [< MLG, a track] —**trad′er** *n.*

trade-in (trād′in′) *n.* Used merchandise accepted in payment or part payment for other, esp. new, merchandise.

trade-last (trād′last′, -läst′) *n. Informal* A favorable remark that one has heard and offers to repeat to the person complimented in return for a similar remark.

trade·mark (trād′märk′) *n.* 1 A name, symbol, design, device, or word used by a merchant or manufacturer to identify his product and distinguish it from that of others. 2 Any distinctive or characteristic feature. —*v.t.* 1 To label with a trademark. 2 To register and bring under legal protection as a trademark.

trade name 1 The name by which an article, process, etc., is designated in trade. 2 A name given by a manufacturer to designate a proprietary article, sometimes having the status of a trademark. 3 The name of a business concern.

trade-off (trād′ôf′, -of′) *n.* 1 A giving up of something, as an objective or advantage, in exchange for something else: a *trade-off* of higher pay for longer vacations. 2 The relationship that characterizes such an exchange; a compromise or adjustment between opposing elements or positions: the *trade-off* between taxation and improved public services.

trade school A school where practical skills or trades are taught.

trades·man (trādz′mən) *n. pl.* **·men** (-mən) A retail dealer; shopkeeper. —**trades′wom·an** *n. Fem.*

trade union LABOR UNION. Also **trades union.** —**trade unionism** —**trade unionist**

trade wind Either of two steady winds blowing toward the equator, one from the northeast on the north, the other from the southeast on the south side of the equatorial line.

trading post A building or small settlement in unsettled territory used as a station for barter, as for furs.

trading stamp A stamp of fixed value given as a premium with a purchase and exchangeable, in quantity, for merchandise.

tra·di·tion (trə·dish′ən) *n.* 1 The transmission of knowledge, opinions, customs, practices, etc., from generation to generation, esp. by word of mouth and by example. 2 The body of beliefs and usages so transmitted; also, any particular story, belief, or usage of this kind. 3 A custom so long continued that it has almost the force of a law. [< L *traditus,* p.p. of *tradere* deliver] —**tra·di′tion·al** *adj.* —**tra·di′tion·al·ly** *adv.*

tra·duce (trə·d′ōōs′) *v.t.* **·duced, ·duc·ing** To misrepresent willfully the conduct or character of; defame; slander. [< L *traducere* transport, bring into disgrace] —**tra·duce′·ment, tra·duc′er** *n.*

traf·fic (traf′ik) *n.* 1 The passing of pedestrians, vehicles, aircraft, messages, etc., in a limited space or between certain points. 2 The people, vehicles, messages, etc., so moving. 3 The business of buying and selling commodities; trade. 4 Unlawful or improper trade: *traffic* in stolen goods. 5 The people or freight transported by a carrier, as a railroad. 6 The business of transportation. 7 Communication or contact; connection. —*v.i.* **·ficked, ·fick·ing** 1 To engage in buying and selling illegally: with *in:* to *traffic* in narcotic drugs. 2 To have dealings with: with *with.* [< MF < Ital. *traffico*] —**traf′fick·er** *n.*

traffic light A set of colored signal lights used to control the passage of automotive traffic.

tra·ge·di·an (trə·jē′dē·ən) *n.* 1 An actor of tragedy. 2 A writer of tragedies.

tra·ge·di·enne (trə·jē′dē·en′) *n.* An actress of tragedy.

trag·e·dy (traj′ə·dē) *n. pl.* **·dies** 1 A form of drama in which the protagonist comes to disaster, as through a flaw in character, and in which the ending is usu. marked by sorrow or pity. 2 A play, film, etc., of this kind. 3 Any tragic or disastrous incident or series of incidents. 4 *Informal* A misfortune. [< Gk. *tragōidia*]

trag·ic (traj′ik) *adj.* 1 Of or having the nature of tragedy. 2 Appropriate to or suggestive of tragedy: a *tragic* manner. 3 Causing or likely to cause suffering, sorrow, or death: a *tragic* accident. [< Gk. *tragikos* pertaining to tragedy] —**trag′i·cal·ly** *adv.*

trag·i·com·e·dy (traj′i·kom′ə·dē) *n. pl.* **·dies** 1 A drama having characteristics of both tragedy and comedy. 2 An

incident or series of incidents of this nature. —**trag′i·com′ic** or **·i·cal** *adj.* —**trag′i·com′i·cal·ly** *adv.*

trail (trāl) *v.t.* 1 To draw along lightly over a surface. 2 To drag or draw after: to *trail* oars; to *trail* an injured leg. 3 To follow the track of; trace: to *trail* game. 4 To be or come along behind. 5 To follow behind, as in pursuit or to keep under surveillance: to *trail* a suspect. —*v.i.* 6 To hang or extend loosely so as to drag over a surface. 7 To grow extensively and usu. irregularly along the ground or over rocks, etc. 8 To be or come along behind. 9 To move or walk heavily or ponderously; trudge. 10 To lag behind: to *trail* by 30,000 votes; to *trail* in the development of auto safety standards. 11 To flow or extend, as in a stream. —*n.* 1 The track left by something that has moved or been drawn or dragged over a surface. 2 The track, scent, etc., indicating the passage of someone or something. 3 The path worn by persons or by animals, esp. through a wilderness. 4 Something that trails or is trailed behind, as the train of a dress or the track of a meteor. 5 A sequence of results or conditions following after something: left a *trail* of broken hearts. [< AF *trailler* haul, tow a boat]

trail·er (trā′lər) *n.* 1 One who or that which trails. 2 A vehicle drawn by a cab or tractor having motive power. 3 A vehicle usu. drawn by an automobile or truck and equipped to serve as living quarters. 4 PREVIEW (def. 2).

trailing arbutus A prostrate evergreen shrub bearing clusters of fragrant pink flowers.

train¹ (trān) *n.* 1 A series of connected railway cars, often drawn by a locomotive. 2 Anything drawn along behind, as a trailing part of a skirt. 3 A line or group of followers; retinue. 4 A moving line of people, animals, vehicles, etc.; procession. 5 A series, succession, or set of connected things; sequence: a *train* of thought. 6 Something, as a period of time or set of circumstances, following after something else; aftermath: The argument left bitter feelings in its *train.* 7 *Mech.* A series of parts acting on each other, as for transmitting motion. —*v.t.* 1 To bring to a desired standard by careful instruction; esp., to guide in morals or manners. 2 To make skillful or proficient: to *train* soldiers. 3 To make obedient to orders or capable of performing tricks, as an animal. 4 To lead into taking a particular course; develop into a fixed shape: to *train* a plant on a trellis; to *train* the hair to lie flat. 5 To put or point in an exact direction; aim: to *train* a rifle or a gaze on someone. —*v.i.* 6 To undergo a course of training. [< OF *trahiner* to draw] —**train′a·ble** *adj.* —**train′er** *n.* —**Syn.** *v.* 1 educate, instruct, rear, bring up, mold.

train² (trān) *n. Can.* A large sled, having a shape like a toboggan. [< F *traineau* sled]

train·ee (trā·nē′) *n.* One who is being trained, as a new employee.

train·ing (trā′ning) *n.* 1 Systematic instruction and drill. 2 The method or action of one who trains, as for an athletic contest.

train·man (trān′mən) *n. pl.* **·men** (-mən) A railway employee serving on a train.

traipse (trāps) *v.i.* **traipsed, traips·ing** To walk or wander about; gad. —*n.* The act of traipsing. [Prob. < OF *trapasser,* var. of *trespasser* trespass]

trait (trāt) *n.* A distinguishing feature or quality, as of character. [< L *tractus* a drawing out < *trahere* draw]

trai·tor (trā′tər) *n.* 1 One who commits treason. 2 One who betrays a trust or acts deceitfully and disloyally. [< L *tradere* betray] —**trai′tress** (-tris) *n. Fem.*

trai·tor·ous (trā′tər·əs) *adj.* 1 Of, constituting, or resembling treason. 2 Of or characteristic of a traitor; treacherous. —**trai′tor·ous·ly** *adv.* —**trai′tor·ous·ness** *n.*

tra·jec·to·ry (trə·jek′tər·ē) *n. pl.* **·ries** The path described by an object or body moving in space, as of a comet or a bullet. [< L *trajectus,* p.p. of *trajicere* throw over]

tram (tram) *n.* 1 *Brit.* STREETCAR. 2 An open vehicle running on rails, used to carry coal in a mine. Also **tram′car′** (-kär′). [< dial. *tram* a rail]

tram·mel (tram′əl) *n.* 1 *Usu. pl.* That which limits freedom or activity; hindrance. 2 A fetter or shackle, esp. one used in teaching a horse to amble. 3 An instrument for drawing ellipses. **4** An adjustable hook used to suspend cooking pots from a fireplace crane. **5** A net formed of three layers, the central one of finer mesh, to trap fish passing through either of the others: also **trammel net.** —*v.t.* **·meled** or **·melled**, **·mel·ing** or **·mel·ling** **1** To hinder or obstruct; restrict. **2** To entangle in or as in a snare; imprison. [< LL *tremaculum* net < L *tri-* three + *macula* a mesh] —**tram′mel·er** or **tram′mel·ler** *n.*

tramp (tramp) *v.i.* **1** To walk or wander about, esp. as a tramp or hobo. **2** To walk heavily or firmly. —*v.t.* **3** To walk or wander through. **4** To walk on heavily; trample. —*n.* **1** One who travels from place to place, usu. on foot and destitute and dependent on charity for a living. **2** The sound of heavy marching or walking. **3** A long stroll; hike. **4** A steam vessel that goes from port to port picking up freight wherever it can: also **tramp steamer. 5** *Slang* A sexually promiscuous woman. [ME *trampen*] —**tramp′er** *n.* — **Syn** *n.* **1** vagrant, vagabond, hobo, bum.

tram·ple (tram′pəl) *v.* **·pled**, **·pling** *v.i.* **1** To tread heavily, esp. so as to crush. **2** To injure or encroach upon someone or something by or as by tramping: with *on:* to *trample* on someone's rights. —*v.t.* **3** To tread heavily or ruthlessly on. —*n.* The sound of treading under foot. [< ME *trampen* tramp] —**tram′pler** *n.*

tram·po·line (tram′pə·lēn′, tram′pə·lēn′) *n.* A heavy canvas stretched to a frame by springs and used for its resiliency in tumbling. Also **tram′po·lin.** [< Ital. *trampoli* stilts]

tram·way (tram′wā′) *n. Brit.* A streetcar line.

trance (trans, träns) *n.* **1** A state in which one appears to be unable to act consciously, as though hypnotized or governed by a supernatural force. **2** A dreamlike or sleepy state, as that induced by hypnosis. **3** A state of profound concentration marked by lack of awareness of one's surroundings; deep abstraction. [< OF *transir* pass, die]

tran·quil (trang′kwil) *adj.* **1** Free from agitation or disturbance; calm: a *tranquil* mood. **2** Quiet and motionless: a *tranquil* scene. [< L *tranquillus* quiet] —**tran′quil·ly** *adv.* —**tran′quil·ness** *n.* —**Syn.** **1** relaxed, serene. **2** placid.

tran·quil·ize (trang′kwəl·īz) *v.t.* & *v.i.* **·ized**, **·iz·ing** To make or become tranquil, esp. by using a drug. Also **tran′· quil·lize.** *Brit. sp.* **·lise.** —**tran′quil·i·za′tion** *n.*

tran·quil·iz·er (trang′kwəl·ī′zər) *n.* **1** One who or that which tranquilizes. **2** Any of various drugs that calm mental agitation without impairing consciousness. Also **tran′· quil·liz′er.**

tran·quil·li·ty (trang·kwil′ə·tē) *n.* The state of being tranquil; peacefulness; quiet. Also **tran·quil′i·ty.**

trans- *prefix* **1** Across; beyond; on the other side of: *transatlantic; transmigrate.* **2** Through: *transfix.* **3** Through and through; changing completely: *transform.* [< L *trans* across, beyond, over]

trans. transactions; transferred; transitive; translated; translation; translator.

trans·act (trans·akt′, tranz-) *v.t.* **1** To carry through; accomplish; do. —*v.i.* **2** To do business. [< L *transactus,* p.p. of *transigere* drive through, accomplish] —**trans·ac′tor** *n.*

trans·ac·tion (trans·ak′shən, tranz-) *n.* **1** The act or process of transacting. **2** Something transacted; esp., a business deal. **3** *pl.* Published reports, as of a society. —**trans· ac′tion·al** *adj.*

trans·at·lan·tic (trans′ət·lan′tik, tranz′-) *adj.* **1** Across or crossing the Atlantic Ocean: a *transatlantic* flight. **2** On the other side of the Atlantic.

tran·scend (tran·send′) *v.t.* **1** To go or pass beyond the limits of: knowledge that *transcends* reason. **2** To rise above in excellence or degree. —*v.i.* **3** To be surpassing; excel. [< L *trans-* beyond, over + *scandere* to climb]

tran·scen·dent (tran·sen′dənt) *adj.* **1** TRANSCENDENTAL (def. 1). **2** *Theol.* Existing apart from and above the material universe: said of God. [< L *transcendere* transcend] — **tran·scen′dence, tran·scen′den·cy** *n.* —**tran·scen′dent·ly** *adv.*

tran·scen·den·tal (tran′sen·den′təl) *adj.* **1** Rising above or going beyond ordinary limits; surpassing. **2** Beyond natural experience; supernatural. **3** Of or pertaining to transcendentalism. —**tran·scen·den′tal·ly** *adv.*

tran·scen·den·tal·ism (tran′sen·den′təl·iz′əm) *n.* The philosophical doctrine that man can attain knowledge which goes beyond or transcends appearances or sensory

phenomena. —**tran′scen·den′tal·ist** *adj., n.* —**tran′scen·den′· tal·is′tic** *adj.*

transcendental number An irrational number, such as pi, that cannot result from any finite set of algebraic equations having rational coefficients.

trans·con·ti·nen·tal (trans′kon·tə·nen′təl) *adj.* Extending or passing across a continent.

tran·scribe (tran·skrīb′) *v.t.* **·scribed**, **·scrib·ing** **1** To write over again; copy from an original. **2** To make a record of in handwriting or typewriting, as of something spoken. **3** To translate (shorthand notes, etc.) into standard written form. **4** To make a recording of for use in a later broadcast. **5** To adapt (a musical composition) for a change of instrument or voice. [< L *trans-* over + *scribere* write] —**tran· scrib′er** *n.*

tran·script (tran′skript) *n.* **1** Something transcribed, as from a stenographer's notes. **2** Any copy, esp., an official copy of a student's academic record. [< L *transcribere* transcribe]

tran·scrip·tion (tran·skrip′shən) *n.* **1** The act of transcribing. **2** Something transcribed; a copy; transcript. **3** A recording made for a later broadcast. **4** *Music* The adaptation of a composition for a different instrument or voice. —**tran·scrip′tion·al** *adj.*

tran·sept (tran′sept) *n.* A projecting part of a cruciform church crossing at right angles to the longer part and situated between the nave and choir; also, its projecting ends. [< L *transversus* transverse + *septum* an enclosure] —**tran·sep′tal** *adj.*

Transepts

trans·fer (trans·fûr′, trans′fər) *v.* **·ferred**, **·fer·ring** *v.t.* **1** To carry, or cause to pass, from one person, place, etc., to another. **2** To make over possession of to another. **3** To convey (a drawing) from one surface to another. —*v.i.* **4** To transfer oneself. **5** To be transferred. **6** To change from one vehicle or line to another. —*n.* (trans′fər) **1** The act of transferring, or the state of being transferred. **2** That which is transferred, as a design conveyed from one surface to another. **3** A place, method, or means of transfer. **4** A ticket entitling a passenger on one vehicle to ride on another. **5** A delivery of title or property from one person to another. **6** A person transferred from one organization or position to another. [< L *trans-* across + *ferre* carry] —**trans·fer′a·bil′i·ty, trans·fer′ence, trans·fer′rer** *n.* —**trans·fer′a·ble, trans·fer′ra·ble** *adj.*

trans·fer·al (trans·fûr′əl) *n.* The act or an instance of transferring. Also **trans·fer′ral.**

trans·fig·u·ra·tion (trans·fig′yə·rā′shən) *n.* A change in shape or appearance. —**the Transfiguration 1** The supernatural transformation of Christ on the mount. **2** A festival commemorating this, August 6.

trans·fig·ure (trans·fig′yər) *v.t.* **·ured**, **·ur·ing** **1** To change the outward form or appearance of. **2** To make glorious. [< L *trans-* across + *figura* shape] —**trans·fig′ure·ment** *n.*

trans·fix (trans·fiks′) *v.t.* **1** To pierce through, as with a pointed implement; impale. **2** To fix in place by impaling. **3** To make motionless, as with horror, amazement, etc. [< L *trans-* through, across + *figere* fasten] —**trans·fix′ion** (-fik′shən) *n.*

trans·form (trans·fôrm′) *v.t.* **1** To change the form or appearance of. **2** To change the nature or character of; convert. **3** *Electr.* To subject to the action of a transformer. —*v.i.* **4** To be or become changed in form or character. [< L *trans-* over + *forma* a form] —**trans·form′a·ble, trans· form′a·tive** *adj.*

trans·for·ma·tion (trans′fər·mā′shən) *n.* **1** The act of transforming or the state of being transformed. **2** *Ling.* Any of the systematic processes by which grammatical sentences of a language may be derived from underlying constructions. —**trans′for·ma′tion·al** *adj.*

trans·form·er (trans·fôr′mər) *n.* **1** One who or that which transforms. **2** *Electr.* A device that couples electricity from one alternating-current circuit to another by electromagnetic induction, often with a change in the ratio of current to voltage and always with a small power loss.

trans·fuse (trans·fyōōz′) *v.t.* **·fused**, **·fus·ing** **1** To cause to flow or pass from one person or thing to another. **2** *Med.* **a** To transfer (blood, plasma, etc.) from one person or animal to another. **b** To give a transfusion to. **3** To pass into; permeate. [< L *transfusus,* p.p. of *transfundere*] — **trans·fus′er** *n.* —**trans·fus′i·ble, trans·fu·sive** (trans-fyōō′siv) *adj.*

trans·fu·sion (trans-fyōō′zhən) *n.* **1** The act or an instance of transfusing. **2** *Med.* The introduction of a fluid, as saline solution, blood, blood plasma, etc., into the blood stream.

trans·gress (trans-gres′, tranz-) *v.t.* **1** To disregard and go beyond the bounds of, as a divine or traditional law; violate. **2** To pass beyond or over (limits); exceed. —*v.i.* **3** To break a law; sin. [< L *transgressus,* p.p. of *transgredi* step across] —**trans·gres′sor** *n.*

trans·gres·sion (trans-gresh′ən, tranz-) *n.* The act or an instance of transgressing, esp. a sin.

tran·ship (tran-ship′) *v.t.* **·shipped, ·shipping** TRANSSHIP. — **tran·ship′ment** *n.*

tran·sient (tran′shənt, tranch′ənt, tranz′ē·ənt) *adj.* **1** Occurring or existing only for a time; not permanent; transitory. **2** Brief; fleeting; momentary. **3** Residing or staying in a place temporarily: a large *transient* population. —*n.* One who or that which is transient, esp. a temporary resident. [< L *transire* go across] —**tran′sience, tran′sien·cy** *n.* —**tran′sient·ly** *adv.* —**Syn. 1** temporary, passing. **2** ephemeral, fugitive, evanescent. **3** casual.

tran·sis·tor (tran·zis′tər, -sis′-) *n. Electronics* **1** A semiconductor device having three terminals and the property that the current between one pair of them is a function of the current between another pair. **2** A transistorized radio. [< TRANS(FER) (RES)ISTOR]

tran·sis·tor·ize (tran·zis′tər·īz, -sis′-) *v.t.* **·ized, ·iz·ing** To equip with transistors. —**tran·sis′tor·i·za′tion** *n.*

tran·sit (tran′sit, -zit) *n.* **1** The act of passing over or through; passage. **2** The process of change; transition. **3** The act of carrying across or through; conveyance. **4** Transportation, esp. for carrying large numbers of people, as in a city: public *transit.* **5** *Astron.* **a** The passage of one celestial body over the disk of another. **b** The passage of a celestial body across the meridian. **6** A surveying instrument resembling a theodolite. [< L *transire* go across]

tran·si·tion (tran·sish′ən, tranz-) *n.* **1** Passage from one place, condition, or stage to another; change. **2** Something, as a period of time or a situation, that leads from one stage or period to another. **3** *Music* A passage or modulation connecting sections of a composition. —**tran·si′tion·al** *adj.* —**tran·si′tion·al·ly** *adv.*

tran·si·tive (tran′sə·tiv) *adj.* **1** *Gram.* Having, requiring, or completed by a direct object: said of a verb. **2** Of or pertaining to transition. —*n. Gram.* A transitive verb. [< L *transitus* transit] —**tran′si·tive·ly** *adv.* —**tran′si·tive·ness, tran′si·tiv′i·ty** *n.*

tran·si·to·ry (tran′sə·tôr′ē, -tō′rē) *adj.* **1** Existing for a short time only; soon extinguished or annulled. **2** Brief; ephemeral. —**tran′si·to′ri·ly** *adv.* —**tran′si·to′ri·ness** *n.*

trans·late (trans·lāt′, tranz-, trans′lāt, tranz′-) *v.* **·lat·ed, ·lat·ing** *v.t.* **1** To change into another language. **2** To change from one form, condition, or place to another. **3** To explain in other words; interpret. **4** *Mech.* To change the position of in space, esp. without rotation. —*v.i.* **5** To change the words of one language into those of another, esp. as an occupation. **6** To admit of translation. [< L *translatus,* lit., carried across] —**trans·lat′a·ble** *adj.* —**trans·la′tor** *n.*

trans·la·tion (trans·lā′shən, tranz-) *n.* **1** The act of translating, or the state of being translated. **2** Something translated; esp., a reproduction of a work in a language different from the original. **3** *Mech.* Motion in which all the parts of a body follow identical courses. —**trans·la′tion·al** *adj.*

trans·lit·er·ate (trans·lit′ə·rāt, tranz-) *v.t.* **·at·ed, ·at·ing** To represent, as a word, by the characters of another alphabet. [< TRANS- + L *litera* a letter] —**trans·lit′er·a′tion** *n.*

trans·lu·cent (trans·lōō′sənt, tranz-) *adj.* Allowing the passage of light, but not permitting a clear view of any

object. [< L *trans-* through, across + *lucere* to shine] — **trans·lu′cence, trans·lu′cen·cy** *n.* —**trans·lu′cent·ly** *adv.*

trans·mi·grate (trans·mī′grāt, tranz-, trans′mī-, tranz′·mī-) *v.i.* **·grat·ed, ·grat·ing** **1** To pass into another body, as the soul at death. **2** To migrate, as from one country or jurisdiction to another. —**trans·mi·gra·tion** (trans′mī·grā′·shən, tranz′-), **trans·mi′gra·tor** *n.* —**trans·mi′gra·to·ry** (-mī′·grə·tôr′ē, -tō′rē) *adj.*

trans·mis·si·ble (trans·mis′ə·bəl, tranz-) *adj.* Capable of being transmitted. —**trans·mis′si·bil′i·ty** *n.*

trans·mis·sion (trans·mish′ən, tranz-) *n.* **1** The act of transmitting, or the state of being transmitted. **2** That which is transmitted. **3** *Mech.* A device that transmits power from its source to its point of application, as from the engine of an automobile to the wheels. —**trans·mis′sive** *adj.*

trans·mit (trans·mit′, tranz-) *v.t.* **·mit·ted, ·mit·ting** **1** To send from one place or person to another; convey. **2** To pass on (a gene, a virus, etc.) from one organism to another. **3** To cause (light, sound, etc.) to pass through space or a medium. **4** To send out, as by means of radio waves. **5** To serve as a medium of passage for; conduct: Iron *transmits* heat. **6** *Mech.* To convey (force, motion, etc.) from one part or mechanism to another. [< L *trans-* across + *mittere* send] —**trans·mit′ta·ble** *adj.* —**trans·mit′tal, trans·mit′tance** *n.*

trans·mit·ter (trans·mit′ər, tranz-) *n.* **1** One who or that which transmits. **2** The part of a telephone into which a person talks. **3** The part of a telegraph for sending messages. **4** *Telecom.* A device that modulates a carrier with a signal and sends the carrier forth, as in radio, telephony, or telegraphy.

trans·mog·ri·fy (trans·mog′rə·fī, tranz-) *v.t.* **·fied, ·fy·ing** To make into something altogether different; transform radically: often used humorously. [?] —**trans·mog′ri·fi·ca′·tion** *n.*

trans·mu·ta·tion (trans′myōō·tā′shən, tranz′-) *n.* **1** The act of transmuting, or the state of being transmuted. **2** The conversion of an atom of an element into an atom of a different element, as by radioactive decay, nuclear fission, etc. **3** The supposed conversion of a base metal into gold or silver. —**trans′mu·ta′tion·al, trans·mu·ta·tive** (trans·myōō′tə·tiv, tranz-) *adj.*

trans·mute (trans·myōōt′, tranz-) *v.t.* **·mut·ed, ·mut·ing** To change in nature or form. Also **trans·mu′tate.** [< L *trans-* across + *mutare* to change] —**trans·mut′a·ble** *adj.* —**trans·mut′a·bil′i·ty, trans·mut′a·ble·ness, trans·mut′er** *n.* —**trans·mut′a·bly** *adv.*

trans·o·ce·an·ic (trans′ō·shē·an′ik, tranz′-) *adj.* **1** Crossing or traversing the ocean. **2** Lying beyond or over the ocean.

tran·som (tran′səm) *n.* **1** A horizontal piece framed across an opening; a lintel. **2** A small window above and often hinged to such a bar, usu. situated above a door. **3** The horizontal crossbar of a gallows or cross. [< L *transtrum* a crossbeam] —**tran′somed** *adj.*

transp. transportation.

trans·pa·cif·ic (trans′pə·sif′ik) *adj.* **1** Across or crossing the Pacific Ocean. **2** On the other side of the Pacific.

trans·par·en·cy (trans·pâr′ən·sē, -par′-) *n. pl.* **·cies** **1** The state or quality of being transparent. **2** Something whose transmission of light defines an image, esp. a piece of photographic film, often mounted as a slide and viewed by projecting its image on a screen or other surface.

trans·par·ent (trans·pâr′ənt, -par′-) *adj.* **1** Allowing the passage of light and of clear views of objects beyond. **2** Having a texture fine enough to be seen through; diaphanous. **3** Easy to understand. **4** Without guile; frank; candid. **5** Easily detected; obvious: a *transparent* lie. [< L *trans-* across + *parere* appear, be visible] —**trans·par′ent·ly** *adv.* —**trans·par′ence, trans·par′ent·ness** *n.*

tran·spi·ra·tion (trans′pə·rā′shən) *n.* A transpiring or exhalation, as the loss of water from a plant by evaporation.

tran·spire (trans·pīr′) *v.* **·spired, ·spir·ing** *v.t.* **1** To give off through permeable tissues, as of the skin and lungs or of leaf surfaces. —*v.i.* **2** To be emitted, as through the skin; be exhaled, as moisture or odors. **3** To become known. **4** To happen; occur. [< L *trans-* across, through + *spirare* breathe] • An accepted meaning of *transpire* is to become known or leak out: *It transpired that he had died penniless.* The word is more commonly used today, however, with the sense of "to happen": *We shall never know what transpired at that meeting.* The latter usage still strikes the more traditionally inclined as improper or ignorant. That judgment may be unduly harsh, but as a matter of style the usage is almost always inelegant and often pretentious.

trans·plant (trans-plant´) *v.t.* **1** To remove and plant in another place. **2** To remove and settle for residence in another place. **3** *Surg.* To transfer (an organ or tissue) from its original site to another part of the body or to another individual. —*v.i.* **4** To admit of being transplanted. —*n.* (trans´plant´) **1** That which is transplanted, as a seedling or an organ of the body. **2** The act of transplanting. —**trans´plan·ta´tion, trans·plant´er** *n.*

trans·port (trans-pôrt´, -pōrt´) *v.t.* **1** To carry or convey from one place to another. **2** To carry away with emotion, as with delight; enchant. **3** To banish to another country. —*n.* (trans´pôrt, -pōrt) **1** The act or a means of transporting; transportation. **2** A state of emotional rapture; intense delight. **3** A ship, train, truck, etc., used to transport troops, supplies, etc. **4** A system of transportation. **5** A deported convict. [< L *trans-* across + *portare* carry] —**trans·port´a·bil´i·ty, trans·port´er** *n.* —**trans·port´able** *adj.*

trans·por·ta·tion (trans´pər-tā´shən) *n.* **1** The act of transporting. **2** A means of transporting or traveling. **3** The conveying of passengers or freight, esp. as an industry. **4** Money, a pass, etc., used for being transported.

trans·pose (trans-pōz´) *v.t.* **·posed, ·pos·ing 1** To reverse the order or change the place of: to *transpose* two numerals or a word in a sentence. **2** *Math.* To transfer (a term) from one side of an algebraic equation to the other with reversed sign. **3** *Music* To write or play in a different key. [< L *trans-* over + OF *poser* put] —**trans·pos´a·ble** *adj.* —**trans·po´sal, trans·pos´er, trans·po·si·tion** (trans´pə-zish´ən) *n.*

trans·sex·u·al (trans-sek´shōō-əl, -sek´shəl) *n.* A person who is genetically and physically of one sex but who identifies psychologically with the other and may seek treatment by surgery or with hormones to bring the physical sexual characteristics into conformity with the psychological preference. —*adj.* Of, for, or characteristic of transsexuals. —**trans·sex´u·al·ism** *n.*

trans·ship (trans-ship´) *v.t. & v.i.* **·shipped, ·ship·ping** To transfer from one conveyance or means of transport to another for further shipment. —**trans·ship´ment** *n.*

tran·sub·stan·ti·ate (tran´səb-stan´shē-āt) *v.t.* **·at·ed, ·at·ing 1** To change from one substance into another; transmute; transform. **2** *Theol.* To change the substance of (bread and wine) in the rite of transubstantiation.

tran·sub·stan·ti·a·tion (tran´səb-stan´shē-ā´shən) *n.* In the Roman Catholic and Eastern Orthodox churches, the conversion of the substance of the bread and wine of the Eucharist into that of Christ's body and blood.

trans·u·ra·ni·um (trans´yōō-rā´nē-əm, tranz´-) *adj.* Of or pertaining to elements having an atomic number greater than that of uranium. Also **trans´u·ran´ic** (-ran´ik).

trans·ver·sal (trans-vûr´səl, tranz-) *adj.* TRANSVERSE. —*n. Geom.* A straight line intersecting a system of lines.

trans·verse (trans-vûrs´, tranz-) *adj.* Lying or being across or from side to side. —*n.* (*also* trans´vûrs, tranz´-) That which is transverse. [< L *transversus* lying across] —**trans·verse´ly** *adv.*

trans·ves·tite (trans-ves´tīt, tranz-) *n.* One who wears the clothes of the opposite sex. [< L *trans-* over + *vestire* to clothe + -ITE] —**trans·ves´tism, trans·ves´ti·tism** (-ves´tə-tiz´əm) *n.*

trap¹ (trap) *n.* **1** A device for catching game or other animals, as a pitfall or a baited contrivance set to spring shut on being slightly jarred or moved. **2** A devious plan or trick by which a person may be caught or taken unawares. **3** A device for hurling clay pigeons into the air, used in trapshooting. **4** Any of various devices that collect residual material or that form a seal to stop a return flow of noxious gas, etc., as a water-filled U- or S-bend in a pipe. **5** In golf, an obstacle or hazard: a sand *trap.* **6** TRAPDOOR. **7** A light, two-wheeled carriage suspended by springs. **8** *pl.* Percussion instruments, as drums, cymbals, etc. **8** *Slang* The mouth. —*v.* **trapped, trap·ping** *v.t.* **1** To catch in or as if in a trap. **2** To provide with a trap. **3** To stop or hold by the formation of a seal. **4** To catch (a ball) just as or after it strikes the ground. —*v.i.* **5** To set traps for game; be a trapper. [< OE *træppe*]

trap² (trap) *n. Geol.* A dark, fine-grained igneous rock, often of columnar structure, as basalt. Also **trap´rock´**. [< Sw. *trappa* a stair]

trap·door (trap´dôr´, -dōr´) *n.* A door, hinged or sliding, to cover an opening, as in a floor or roof.

tra·peze (tra-pēz´, trə-) *n.* A short swinging bar suspended by two ropes, for gymnastic exercises and acrobatic stunts. [< NL *trapezium* a trapezium]

tra·pe·zi·um (trə-pē´zē-əm) *n. p.* **·zi·ums** or **·zi·a** (-zē-ə) *Geom.* A four-sided plane figure of which no two sides are parallel. **2** *Brit.* TRAPEZOID (def. 1). [< Gk. *trapeza* a table, lit., a four-footed (bench)]

Trapezium def. 1

Trapezoid def. 1

trap·e·zoid (trap´ə-zoid´) *n. Geom.* **1** A quadrilateral of which two sides are parallel. **2** *Brit.* TRAPEZIUM (def. 1). [< Gk. *trapeza* a table + *eidos* a form] —**trap´e·zoi´dal** *adj.*

trap·per (trap´ər) *n.* One whose occupation is the trapping of fur-bearing animals.

trap·pings (trap´ingz) *n. pl.* **1** An ornamental covering or harness for a horse; caparison. **2** Adornments of any kind; embellishments. **3** The superficial signs or perquisites; marks: the *trappings* of success. [< ME *trappe*]

Trap·pist (trap´ist) *n.* A monk belonging to an ascetic order noted for silence. —*adj.* Of this order. [< *La Trappe,* France, site of the order's establishment in 1664]

trap·shoot·ing (trap´shōō´ting) *n.* The sport of shooting clay pigeons sent up from spring traps. —**trap´shoot´er** *n.*

trash (trash) *n.* **1** Worthless or waste matter; rubbish. **2** That which is broken or lopped off, as twigs and branches. **3** Foolish or idle talk. **4** Anything worthless, shoddy, or without merit: literary *trash.* **5** A person regarded as worthless or of no account. —*v.t. & v.i. Slang* To wreck or destroy (something) purposefully but often indiscriminately as an expression of alienation or rebellion. [?] —**trash´i·ness** *n.* —**trash´y** (·i·er, ·i·est) *adj.*

trau·ma (trou´mə, trô´-) *n. pl.* **·mas** or **·ma·ta** (-mə-tə) **1** Any physical injury resulting from force. **2** A severe emotional shock having a deep effect upon the personality. [< Gk., a wound] —**trau·mat·ic** (trou-mat´ik, trô´-) *adj.* —**trau·mat´i·cal·ly** *adv.*

trau·ma·tize (trô´mə-tīz) *v.t.* **·tized, ·tiz·ing** To cause trauma to or in.

trav·ail (trə-vāl´, trav´āl) *n.* **1** Pain, anguish, or distress encountered in an effort or achievement. **2** Labor in childbirth. **3** Hard or wearisome labor. **4** Physical agony. —*v.i.* **1** To suffer the pangs of childbirth. **2** To toil; labor. [< OF < *travailler* to labor, toil]

trav·el (trav´əl) *v.* **trav·eled** or **·elled, trav·el·ing** or **·el·ling** *v.i.* **1** To go from one place to another or from place to place; make a journey or tour. **2** To proceed; advance. **3** To go about from place to place as a traveling salesman. **4** *Informal* To move with speed. **5** To pass or be transmitted, as light, sound, etc. **6** *Mech.* To move in a fixed path, as a machine part. **7** In basketball, to commit the infraction of failing to dribble while moving with the ball. —*v.t.* **8** To move or journey across or through: traverse. —*n.* **1** The act of traveling. **2** *Often pl.* A journey or tour, usu. extensive. **3** Passage to, over, or past a certain place. **4** Distance traveled, as by a machine part. [< OF *travailler* to travail]

trav·eled (trav´əld) *adj.* **1** Having made many journeys. **2** Frequented or used by travelers. Also **trav´elled.**

trav·e·logue (trav·ə-lôg, -log) *n.* **1** A documentary film about a traveled place. **2** A lecture or talk on travel, usu. illustrated pictorially. Also **trav´e·log.**

tra·verse (trə-vûrs´, tra-) *v.* **·ersed, ·ers·ing** *v.t.* **1** to pass over, across, or through. **2** To move back and forth over or along. **3** To examine carefully; scrutinize. **4** To oppose; thwart. **5** *Law* To make denial of. —*v.i.* **6** To move back and forth. **7** To move across; cross. —**trav·erse** (trav′ərs) *n.* **1** Something that traverses, as a crosspiece of a machine or structure. **2** Something serving as a screen or barrier. **3** The act of traversing or denying; a denial. —*adj.* (trav′. ərs) Lying or being across; transverse. [< L *transversus* transverse] —**tra·vers·a·ble** *adj.* —**tra·vers′al, tra·vers′er** *n.*

trav·erse rod (trav′ərs) A curtain rod equipped with a sliding mechanism for drawing a pair of curtains together or apart with a cord.

trav·es·ty (trav′is·tē) *n. pl.* **·ties 1** A grotesque imitation, as of a lofty subject; burlesque. **2** A distorted or absurd rendering or example, as if in mockery: a *travesty* of justice. —*v.t.* **·tied, ·ty·ing** To make a travesty of; burlesque; parody. [< Ital. *travestire* to disguise]

trawl (trôl) *n.* **1** A large net for towing on the bottom of the ocean by a fishing boat. **2** A stout fishing line, anchored and buoyed, from which many lines bearing baited hooks may be secured. —*v.i.* **1** To fish with a trawl. —*v.t.* **2** To drag, as a net, to catch fish. [?]

trawl·er (trô′lər) *n.* A boat used for trawling.

tray (trā) *n.* **1** A flat, shallow utensil with raised edges, used to hold or carry several or a number of articles, as dishes. **2** A tray and the articles on it. **3** A shallow, topless box serving as a compartment, as in a tool or sewing box. [< OE *trēg* a wooden board] —**tray′ful** (-fool′) *n.*

treach·er·ous (trech′ər·əs) *adj.* **1** Likely to betray allegiance or confidence; untrustworthy. **2** Of the nature of treachery; perfidious. **3** Apparently safe or secure, but in fact dangerous or unreliable: *treacherous* footing. — **treach′er·ous·ly** *adv.* —**treach′er·ous·ness** *n.*

treach·er·y (trech′ər·ē) *n. pl.* **·er·ies** Violation of allegiance, confidence, or faith; treason. [< OF *tricher* cheat]

trea·cle (trē′kəl) *n.* **1** Molasses, esp. that obtained in refining sugar. **2** Saccharine speech or sentiments. **3** Formerly, a compound used as an antidote for poison. [< Gk. *thēriakē* a remedy for poisonous bites] —**trea′cly** *adj.*

tread (tred) *v.* **trod, trod·den** or **trod, tread·ing** *v.t.* **1** To step or walk on, over, along, etc. **2** To press with the feet; trample. **3** To crush or oppress harshly. **4** To accomplish in walking or in dancing: to *tread* a measure. **5** To copulate with: said of male birds. —*v.i.* **6** To place the foot down; walk. **7** To press the ground or anything beneath the feet: usu. with *on*. —**tread water** In swimming, to keep the body erect and the head above water by moving the feet and arms. —*n.* **1** The act, manner, or sound of treading; a walking or stepping. **2** The part of a wheel or automobile tire that comes into contact with the road or rails. **3** The impression made by a foot, a tire, etc. **4** The horizontal part of a step in a stairway. [< OE *tredan*] — **tread′er** *n.*

tread·le (tred′l) *n.* A lever operated by the foot, usu. to cause rotary motion. —*v.i.* **·led, ·ling** To work a treadle. [< OE *tredel* < *tredan* tread] • See POTTER'S WHEEL.

tread·mill (tred′mil′) *n.* **1** A mechanism rotated by the walking motion of one or more persons or animals. **2** Monotonous routine; tedious and unrewarding effort.

treas. treasurer; treasury.

trea·son (trē′zən) *n.* **1** Betrayal, treachery, or breach of allegiance toward a sovereign or government. **2** A breach of faith; treachery. [< L *traditio* a betrayal, delivery] — **trea′son·ous** *adj.* —**trea′son·ous·ly** *adv.*

trea·son·a·ble (trē′zən·ə·bəl) *adj.* Of, involving, or characteristic of treason. —**trea′son·a·ble·ness** *n.* —**trea′son·a·bly** *adv.*

treas·ure (trezh′ər) *n.* **1** Riches accumulated or possessed, as a store of precious metals, jewels, or money. **2** Someone or something very precious. —*v.t.* **·ured, ·ur·ing 1** To set a high value upon; prize. **2** To lay up in store; accumulate. [< L *thesaurus*] —**Syn.** *v.* **1** cherish, esteem, value, venerate. **2** hoard.

treas·ur·er (trezh′ər·ər) *n.* **1** An officer authorized to receive, care for, and disburse revenues, as of a government, business corporation, or society. **2** A similar custodian of the funds of a society or a corporation.

treas·ure-trove (trezh′ər·trōv′) *n.* **1** *Law* Money, gold, etc., found hidden, the owner being unknown. **2** Any rich or rewarding discovery. Also **treasure trove**. [< AF *tresor* treasure + *trover* to find]

treas·ur·y (trezh′ər·ē) *n. pl.* **·ur·ies 1** A place of receipt and disbursement of public revenue or private funds. **2** The revenue or funds. **3** The place where a treasure is stored. **4** A department of government concerned with finances, the issuance of money, etc. [< OF *tresor* treasure]

treat (trēt) *v.t.* **1** To conduct oneself toward (a person, animal, etc.) in a specified manner. **2** To look upon or regard in a specified manner: They *treat* it as a childhood prank. **3** To give medical or surgical attention to. **4** To deal with in writing or speaking. **5** To depict or express artistically in a specified style. **6** To pay for the entertainment, food, or drink of. —*v.i.* **7** To deal with a subject in writing or speaking: usu. with *of*. **8** To carry on negotiations; negotiate. **9** To pay for another's entertainment. —*n.* **1** Something that gives unusual pleasure. **2** Entertainment of any kind furnished gratuitously to another. **3** *Informal* One's turn to pay for refreshment or entertainment. [< OF *tretier, traitier*] —**treat′er** *n.*

trea·tise (trē′tis) *n.* A formal, systematic, written exposition of a serious subject: a *treatise* on labor relations. [< OF *traitier*]

treat·ment (trēt′mənt) *n.* **1** The act, manner, or process of treating anything. **2** The therapeutic measures designed to cure a disease or abnormal condition.

trea·ty (trē′tē) *n. pl.* **·ties** A formal agreement or compact between two or more nations. [< OF *traitié*, p.p. of *traitier* treat]

tre·ble (treb′əl) *v.t. & v.i.* **·led, ·ling** To multiply by three; triple. —*adj.* **1** Threefold. **2** *Music* **a** Of the highest range. **b** Soprano. —*n.* **1 a** *Music* A part or instrument of the highest range. **b** A soprano singer. **2** High, piping sound. [< L *triplus* triple] —**treb′ly** *adv.*

tree (trē) *n.* **1** A woody perennial plant having a distinct trunk with branches and foliage at some distance above the ground. **2** Any shrub or plant with a treelike shape or dimensions. **3** Something whose outline resembles the spreading branches of a tree, as a diagram: a genealogical *tree*. **4** A timber, post, or piece of wood used for a particular purpose. —*v.t.* **treed, tree·ing 1** To force to climb or take refuge in a tree: to *tree* an opossum. **2** *Informal* To get the advantage of; corner. [< OE *trēow*]

tree fern Any of various treelike ferns with woody trunks.

tree frog Any of various arboreal frogs having adhesive disks on the toes. Also **tree toad**.

tree·nail (trē′nāl′, tren′əl, trun′əl) *n.* A wooden peg or nail of dry, hard wood which swells when moist, used for fastening timbers.

tree of heaven AILANTHUS.

tree surgery The treatment of damaged trees by pruning, cementing cavities, etc. —**tree surgeon**

Trefoil def. 2

tre·foil (trē′foil) *n.* **1** Any of various plants having threefold leaves, as clover. **2** An architectural ornament having the form of a three-lobed leaf. [< L *trifolium*]

trek (trek) *v.* **trekked, trek·king** *v.i.* **1** To move along with effort or slowly, esp. on foot. **2** To make a journey; travel. **3** In South Africa, to travel by ox wagon. —*v.t.* **4** To transport. **5** In South Africa, to draw (a vehicle or load): said of an ox. —*n.* **1** A journey or a stage in a journey. **2** The act of trekking. **3** In South Africa, an organized migration. [< Du. *trekken* draw, travel < MDu. *trecken*] —**trek′ker** *n.*

trel·lis (trel′is) *n.* A grating or lattice, often of wood, used as a screen or a support for vines, etc.

Trellis

—*v.t.* 1 To interlace so as to form a trellis. 2 To furnish with or fasten on a trellis. [<L *trilix* of three threads]

trem·a·tode (trem′ə-tōd, trē′mə-) *n.* Any of a class of parasitic flatworms, as the liver fluke. [<Gk. *trēma* a hole + *eidos* form] —**trem′a·toid** (-toid) *adj.*

trem·ble (trem′bəl) *v.i.* ·bled, ·bling 1 To shake involuntarily, as with fear or weakness. 2 To move slightly or vibrate, as from some jarring force: The building *trembled.* 3 To feel anxiety or fear. 4 To quaver, as the voice. —*n.* The act or state of trembling. [<LL *tremulus* tremulous] —**trem′bler** *n.* —**trem′bling·ly** *adv.* —**trem′bly** *adj.* — **Syn.** *v.* 2 quiver, shake, totter, quake.

tre·men·dous (tri-men′dəs) *adj.* 1 Extraordinarily large or extensive; enormous; great. 2 Causing astonishment by its magnitude, force, etc.; awe-inspiring. 3 *Informal* Wonderful; marvelous. [<L *tremendus* to be trembled at] —**tre·men′dous·ly** *adv.* —**tre·men′dous·ness** *n.*

trem·o·lo (trem′ə-lō) *n. pl.* ·los *Music* 1 A rapid, periodic variation in the loudness of a tone. 2 The mechanism for causing this in organ tones. [Ital., trembling]

trem·or (trem′ər, trē′mər) *n.* 1 A quick, vibratory movement; a shaking. 2 Any involuntary quivering or trembling, as of a muscle. 3 A state of agitation or excitement, as in anticipation of something. [<OF *tremour* fear, a trembling]

trem·u·lous (trem′yə-ləs) *adj.* 1 Characterized or affected by trembling: *tremulous* speech. 2 Showing timidity and irresolution. 3 Characterized by mental excitement. Also **trem′u·lant.** [<L *tremulus*] —**trem′u·lous·ly** *adv.* —**trem′u·lous·ness** *n.*

tre·nail (trē′nāl, tren′əl, trun′əl) *n.* TREENAIL.

trench (trench) *n.* 1 A long narrow ditch, esp. one lined with a parapet of the excavated earth, to protect troops. 2 A long, narrow region much deeper than the adjacent surfaces, as along the ocean floor. —*v.t.* 1 To dig a trench or trenches in. 2 To fortify with trenches. 3 To cut deep furrows in. —*v.i.* 4 To cut or dig trenches. 5 To cut; carve. 6 To encroach. [<OF *trenchier* to cut] —**trench′er** *n.*

trench·ant (tren′chənt) *adj.* 1 Clear, vigorous, and effective: a *trenchant* rebuttal. 2 Cutting, as sarcasm; biting. 3 Incisive; sharp; keen: *trenchant* wit. 4 *Archaic* Cutting deeply and quickly: a *trenchant* sword. [<OF *trenchier*]

trench coat A raincoat with a belt, straps on the shoulders, and several pockets.

trench·er (tren′chər) *n.* A wooden plate or board used to serve food or as a surface for cutting it. [<OF *trenchier* to cut]

trench·er·man (tren′chər·mən) *n. pl.* ·men (-mən) A person who eats heartily.

trench fever A relapsing fever transmitted by body lice.

trench foot A foot condition resembling frostbite, due to continued dampness and cold.

trench mouth A mildly contagious disease of the gums, and sometimes the larynx and tonsils, caused by a soil bacillus.

trend (trend) *n.* 1 A prevailing or probable tendency; predominant or likely course or direction; drift: a *trend* toward smaller families; investment *trends;* to study *trends* in education. 2 A popular preference or inclination: fashion *trends.* 3 The general course or direction, as of a coast; bent. —*v.i.* 1 To have or follow a general course or direction. 2 To exhibit a tendency; move: wheat prices *trending* upward. [<OE *trendan* to roll]

trend·y (tren′dē) *adj. Slang* trend·i·er, trend·i·est In step with current fashion; voguish. —*n. pl.* trend·ies *Chiefly Brit.* A trendy person or thing. —**trend′i·ness** *n.*

tre·pan (tri-pan′) *n.* 1 An early form of the trephine. 2 A large rock-boring tool —*v.t.* ·panned, ·pan·ning To use a trepan upon. [<Gk. *trypanon* a borer]

tre·phine (tri-fīn′, -fēn′) *n. Surg.* A cylindrical saw for removing a disk of tissue, as from the skull, cornea, etc. —*v.t.* ·phined, ·phin·ing To operate on with a trephine. [< L *tres fines* three ends]

trep·i·da·tion (trep′ə-dā′shən) *n.* 1 Tremulous agitation caused by fear; apprehension. 2 *Archaic* An involuntary trembling; tremor. [<L *trepidare* hurry, be alarmed]

tres·pass (tres′pəs, -pas′) *v.i.* 1 To violate the personal or property rights of another; esp., to go unlawfully onto another's land. 2 To go beyond the bounds of what is right

or proper; transgress. 3 To intrude; encroach: to *trespass* on one's privacy. —*n.* 1 *Law* **a** Any act accompanied by actual or implied force in violation of another's person, property, or rights. **b** An action for injuries sustained because of this. 2 Any transgression of law or moral duty. 3 An intrusion; encroachment. [<Med. L *trans-* across, beyond + *passare* to pass] —**tres′pass·er** *n.*

tress (tres) *n.* 1 A lock or curl of human hair. 2 *pl.* The hair of a woman or girl, esp. when long and worn loose [<OF *tresce* (trest) *adj.*

tres·tle (tres′əl) *n.* 1 A beam or bar braced by two pairs of divergent legs, used to support tables, platforms, etc. 2 A braced framework functioning like a bridge in supporting a roadway or railway over a short span. [<L *transtrum* crossbeam]

trey (trā) *n.* A card, domino, or die having three spots or pips. [<L *tres* three]

tri- *prefix* 1 Three; threefold; thrice: *tricycle.* 2 *Chem.* Containing three atoms, radicals, groups, etc.: *trioxide.* 3 Occurring three times within a (specified) interval: *triweekly.* [<L *tri-* threefold]

tri·ad (trī′ad) *n.* 1 A group of three persons or things. 2 *Music* A chord of three tones, esp. a tone with its third and fifth. [<Gk. *trias*<*treis* three] —**tri·ad′ic** *adj., n.*

tri·al (trī′əl, trīl) *n.* 1 The examination in a court of law, often before a jury, of the facts of a case in order to determine its disposition. 2 The act of testing or proving by experience or use. 3 The state of being tried or tested. 4 An experience, person, or thing that puts strength, patience, or faith to the test. 5 An attempt or effort to do something. 6 Hardship; difficulty: the *trials* of poverty. —**on trial** In the process of being tried or tested. —**trial and error** The trying of one thing after another until something succeeds. —*adj.* 1 Of or pertaining to a trial or trials. 2 Made or used in the course of trying or testing. [<AF<*trier* to try] —**Syn.** *n.* 2 examination, experiment. 5 endeavor. 6 misfortune, trouble.

trial balance In double-entry bookkeeping, a draft of the debit and credit balances of each account in the ledger.

trial jury A jury of 12 persons impaneled to decide a civil or criminal case; petit jury.

tri·an·gle (trī′ang·gəl) *n.* 1 *Geom.* A figure, esp. a plane figure, bounded by three sides, and having three angles. 2 Something resembling such a figure in shape. 3 A situation involving three persons: the eternal *triangle.* 4 *Music* A percussion instrument consisting of a resonant metal bar bent into a triangle and sounded by striking with a small metal rod. [<L *tri-* three + *angulus* an angle]

Triangles
a. equilateral. b. isosceles.
c. scalene. d. right-angle.

tri·an·gu·lar (trī·ang′gyə·lər) *adj.* 1 Pertaining to, like, or bounded by a triangle. 2 Concerned with or pertaining to three things, parties, or persons. —**tri·an′gu·lar′i·ty** (-lar′ə·tē) *n.* —**tri·an′gu·lar·ly** *adv.*

tri·an·gu·late (trī·ang′gyə·lāt) *v.t.* ·lat·ed, ·lat·ing 1 To divide into triangles. 2 To measure or determine by means of trigonometry. 3 To give triangular shape to. —*adj.* Marked with triangles. —**tri·an·gu·la′tion** *n.*

Tri·as·sic (trī·as′ik) *adj. & n.* See GEOLOGY. [<LL *trias* triad]

tri·ath·lon (trī·ath′lon) *n.* An athletic event comprising swimming, bicycle riding, and long-distance running. [<Gk. *tri-* three + *athlon* a contest]

tri·bal·ism (trī′bəl·iz′əm) *n.* Tribal organization, culture, or relations.

tribe (trīb) *n.* 1 A group of people, under one chief or ruler, united by common ancestry, language, and culture. 2 In ancient Israel, any of the 12 divisions of the Hebrews. 3 In ancient Rome, any of the three clans making up the Roman people. 4 A number of persons of any class or profession taken together: often contemptuous. 5 *Biol.* **a** A group of closely related genera. **b** Any group of plants or animals. [<L *tribus*] —**tri′bal** *adj.* —**tri′bal·ly** *adv.*

tribes·man (trībz′mən) *n. pl.* ·men (-mən) A member of a tribe.

trib·u·la·tion (trib'yə·lā'shən) *n.* **1** A condition of distress; suffering. **2** The cause of such distress. [< L *tribulare* thrash] —**Syn.** **1** misery, oppression, sorrow, trouble.

tri·bu·nal (trī·byōō'nəl, tri-) *n.* **1** A court of justice. **2** Any judicial body, as a board of arbitrators. **3** The seat set apart for judges, magistrates, etc. [< L *tribunus* tribune]

trib·une[1] (trib'yōōn, trib·yōōn') *n.* **1** In ancient Rome, a magistrate chosen by the plebeians to protect them against patrician oppression. **2** Any champion of the people. [< L *tribunus*, lit., head of a tribe < *tribus* a tribe] —**trib'u·nar'y** (-yə·ner'ē), **trib'u·ni'tial** (-yə·nish'əl) *adj.*

trib·une[2] (trib'yōōn) *n.* A rostrum or platform. [< L *tribunal* a tribunal]

trib·u·tar·y (trib'yə·ter'ē) *adj.* **1** Supplying a larger body, as a stream flowing into a river. **2** Paying tribute. —*n. pl.* **·tar·ies** **1** A stream flowing into a larger one. **2** A person or state paying tribute. [< L *tributum*. See TRIBUTE.]

trib·ute (trib'yōōt) *n.* **1** Money or other valuables paid by one state to another as the price of peace and protection, or by virtue of some treaty. **2** Any obligatory payment, as a tax. **3** Anything given that is due to worth, affection, or duty: a *tribute* of praise. [< L *tributum*, neut. p.p. of *tribuere* pay, allot]

trice (trīs) *v.t.* **triced, tric·ing** To raise with a rope: usu. with *up.* —*n.* An instant: only in the phrase **in a trice.** [< MDu. *trisen* to hoist]

tri·ceps (trī'seps) *n. pl.* **·cep·ses** (-sep·sēz) or **·ceps** The large muscle at the back of the upper arm which straightens the arm when it contracts. [L, three-headed]

tri·chi·na (tri·kī'nə) *n. pl.* **·nae** (-nē) or **·nas** A roundworm whose larvae cause trichinosis. [< Gk. *trichinos* of hair]

trich·i·no·sis (trik'ə·nō'sis) *n.* A disease usu. resulting from eating undercooked infected pork and marked by encysted trichina larvae in the muscles. Also **trich'i·ni'a·sis** (-nī'ə·sis). —**trich'i·nosed** (-nōzd, -nōst), **trich'i·nous** (-ə·nəs) *adj.*

Triceps

trick (trik) *n.* **1** A deception; a petty artifice. **2** A malicious or annoying act: a dirty *trick.* **3** A practical joke; prank. **4** A particular characteristic; trait: a *trick* of tapping her foot. **5** A peculiar skill or knack. **6** A feat of jugglery. **7** In card games, the whole number of cards played in one round. **8** A turn or spell of duty. **9** *Informal* A child or young girl. —**do** (or **turn**) **the trick** *Slang* To produce the desired result. —*v.t.* **1** To deceive or cheat; delude. —*v.i.* **2** To practice trickery or deception. [< OF *trichier* cheat] —**trick'er** *n.* —**Syn.** *n.* **1** ruse, stratagem, subterfuge, device.

trick·er·y (trik'ər·ē) *n. pl.* **·er·ies** The practice of tricks; artifice; wiles.

trick·le (trik'əl) *v.* **·led, ·ling** *v.i.* **1** To flow or run drop by drop or in a very thin stream. **2** To move, come, go, etc., bit by bit. —*v.t.* **3** To cause to trickle. —*n.* **1** The act or state of trickling. **2** A thin stream. [ME *triklen*]

trick·ster (trik'stər) *n.* One who plays tricks.

trick·y (trik'ē) *adj.* **trick·i·er, trick·i·est** **1** Given to tricks; crafty; deceitful. **2** Intricate; requiring adroitness or skill. —**trick'i·ly** *adv.* —**trick'i·ness** *n.*

tri·col·or (trī'kul'ər) *adj.* Having or characterized by three colors: also **tri'col'ored.** —*n.* The French national flag. *Brit. sp.* **tri'col'our.**

tri·corn (trī'kôrn) *n.* A hat with the brim turned up on three sides. —*adj.* Three-horned; three-pronged. [< L *tricornis* three-horned]

tri·cot (trē'kō, trī'kət) *n.* **1** A hand-knitted or woven fabric, or a machine-made imitation thereof. **2** A soft ribbed cloth. [< F *tricoter* knit]

tri·cus·pid (trī·kus'pid) *adj.* **1** Having three cusps or points, as a molar tooth: also **tri·cus'pi·date.** **2** Having three segments, as the valve between the right auricle and right ventricle of the heart: also **tri·cus'pi·dal.** [< L *tricuspis* three-pointed]

tri·cy·cle (trī'sik·əl) *n.* A three-wheeled vehicle worked by pedals, esp. one used by children.

tri·dent (trīd'nt) *n.* A three-pronged implement or weapon, the emblem of Neptune (Poseidon). —*adj.* Having three teeth or prongs: also **tri·den·tate** (trī·den'tāt), **tri·den'tat·ed.** [< L *tri-* three + *dens* a tooth]

tried (trīd) *p.t. & p.p.* of TRY. —*adj.* **1** Tested; trustworthy. **2** Freed of impurities.

tri·en·ni·al (trī·en'ē·əl) *adj.* **1** Taking place every third year. **2** Lasting three years. —*n.* **1** A ceremony celebrated every three years. **2** A plant lasting three years. [< L *tri-* three + *annus* year] —**tri·en'ni·al·ly** *adv.*

tri·fle (trī'fəl) *v.* **·fled, ·fling** *v.i.* **1** To treat or speak of something as of no value or importance: with *with.* **2** To play; toy. —*v.t.* **3** To spend (time, money, etc.) idly and purposelessly: He *trifled* away his entire fortune. —*n.* **1** Anything of very little value or importance. **2** A dessert, popular in England, made of layers of macaroons or ladyfingers with sugared fruit, custard, and meringue or whipped cream. **3** A small amount: It costs only a *trifle.* —**a trifle** Slightly; to a small extent: a *trifle* short. [< OF *truffer* deceive, jeer at] —**tri'fler** *n.*

tri·fling (trī'fling) *adj.* **1** Frivolous. **2** Insignificant. —**tri'·fling·ly** *adv.*

tri·fo·cal (trī·fō'kəl) *adj. Optics* Of or describing a lens with three segments, for near, intermediate, and far vision respectively. —*n.* A trifocal lens.

tri·fo·li·ate (trī·fō'lī·it, -āt) *adj. Bot.* Having three leaves or leaflike processes. Also **tri·fo'li·at·ed.**

tri·fo·li·o·late (trī·fō'lē·ə·lāt') *adj. Bot.* Having three leaflets, as a clover leaf.

tri·fo·ri·um (trī·fôr'ē·əm, -fō'rē-) *n. pl.* **·fo·ri·a** (-fôr'ē·ə, -fō'rē·ə) *Archit.* A gallery above the arches of the nave or transept in a church. [< L *tri-* three + *foris* a door] —**tri·fo'ri·al** *adj.*

trig[1] (trig) *adj.* **1** Characterized by tidiness; trim; neat. **2** Strong; sound; firm. —*v.t.* **trigged, trig·ging** To make trig or neat; often with *out* or *up.* [< ON *tryggr* true, trusty] —**trig'ly** *adv.* —**trig'ness** *n.*

trig[2] (trig) *n.* TRIGONOMETRY.

Triforium

trig., trigon. trigonometric; trigonometry.

trig·ger (trig'ər) *n.* **1** A lever of a gun activating the firing mechanism when moved by a finger. • See REVOLVER. **2** Any one of various devices designed to activate other devices or systems. —**quick on the trigger** **1** Quick to shoot a gun. **2** Quick-witted; alert. —*v.t.* *Informal* To cause or set off (an action). [< Du. *trekken* pull, tug at]

trigonometric functions *Math.* Any of various functions of an angle or arc, principally the sine, cosine, tangent, cotangent, secant, and cosecant.

trig·o·nom·e·try (trig'ə·nom'ə·trē) *n.* The branch of mathematics based on the use of trigonometric functions, as in studying the relations of the sides and angles of triangles. [< Gk. *trigōnon* a triangle + *metron* measure] —**trig·o·no·met·ric** (trig'ə·nə·met'rik) or **·ri·cal** *adj.* —**trig'o·no·met'ri·cal·ly** *adv.*

tri·he·dron (trī·hē'drən) *n. pl.* **·dra** (-drə) *Geom.* A figure having three plane surfaces meeting at a point. [< Gk. *tri-* three + *hedra* a base] —**tri·he'dral** *adj.*

tri·lat·er·al (trī·lat'ər·əl) *adj.* Having three sides. [< L *tri-* three + *latus, lateris* a side] —**tri·lat'er·al·ly** *adv.*

trill (tril) *v.t.* **1** To sing or play in a quavering or tremulous tone. **2** *Phonet.* To articulate with a trill. —*v.i.* **3** To utter a quavering or tremulous sound. **4** *Music* To execute a trill. —*n.* **1** A tremulous utterance of successive tones, as of certain insects or birds; a warble. **2** *Music* A quick alternation of two notes either a tone or a semitone apart. **3** *Phonet.* A rapid vibration of a speech organ, as of the tip of the tongue. **4** A consonant or word so uttered. [< Ital. *trillare*] —**tril'ler** *n.*

tril·lion (tril'yən) *n. & adj.* See NUMBER. [< MF *tri-* three + *million* million] —**tril'lionth** *adj., n.*

tril·li·um (tril'ē·əm) *n.* Any of a genus of perennial plants of the lily family, bearing a whorl of three leaves and a solitary flower. [< L *tri-* three]

tri·lo·bate (trī·lō′bāt, trī′lə·bāt) *adj.* Having three lobes. Also **tri·lo′bal, tri·lo′bat·ed, tri·lobed** (trī′lōbd′).

tri·lo·bite (trī′lə·bīt) *n.* Any of various fossilized extinct marine arthropods found in abundance in Paleozoic rocks, characterized by two lengthwise grooves forming three ridges. [< Gk. *tri-* three + *lobos* a lobe] **—tri′lo·bit′ic** (-bit′ik) *adj.*

tril·o·gy (tril′ə·jē) *n. pl.* **·gies** A group of three literary or dramatic compositions, each complete in itself, but connected into a whole through theme and subject matter. [< Gk. *tri-* three + *logos* a discourse]

trim (trim) *v.* trimmed, trim·ming *v.t.* 1 To make neat by clipping, pruning, etc. 2 To remove by cutting: usu. with *off* or *away.* 3 To put ornaments on; decorate. 4 In carpentry, to smooth; dress. 5 *Informal* a To chide; rebuke. b To punish. c To defeat. 6 *Naut.* a To adjust (sails or yards) for sailing. b To cause (a ship) to sit well in the water by adjusting cargo, ballast, etc. 7 To bring (an airplane) to stable flight by adjusting controls. —*v.i.* 8 *Naut.* a To be or remain in equilibrium. b To adjust sails or yards for sailing. 9 To act so as to appear to favor opposing sides in a controversy. —*n.* 1 State of adjustment or preparation; fitting condition. 2 Good physical condition: in *trim* to play tennis. 3 *Naut.* Fitness for sailing. 4 *Naut.* Actual or comparative degree of immersion. 5 The moldings, etc., as about the doors of a building. 6 Ornament, as on a dress; trimming. 7 The attitude of an aircraft in flight. —*adj.* trim·mer, trim·mest Having a smart appearance; spruce. —*adv.* In a trim manner: also **trim′ly.** [< OE *trymman* arrange, strengthen] **—trim′ness** *n.* —**Syn.** *v.* 1 cut, lop. 2 pare. 3 adorn, garnish.

tri·mes·ter (trī·mes′tər, trī′mes·tər) *n.* 1 A three-month period; quarter, as of an academic year. 2 Any of the three three-month periods used to identify the progress of a pregnancy. [< L *trimestris* < *tri-* three + *mensis* a month] **—tri·mes′tral, tri·mes′tri·al** *adj.*

trim·e·ter (trim′ə·tər) *adj.* In prosody, consisting of three measures or of lines containing three measures. —*n.* A line of verse having three measures.

trim·ming (trim′ing) *n.* 1 Something added for ornament or to give a finished appearance or effect. 2 *pl. Informal* The proper accompaniments or condiments of an article or food. 3 Parts or pieces trimmed away. 4 A severe reproof or a chastisement. 5 *Informal* A defeat.

tri·month·ly (trī·munth′lē) *adj. & adv.* Done or occurring every third month.

Trin·i·dad and To·ba·go (trin′ə·dad, tō·bā′gō) An independent member of the Commonwealth of Nations on two islands N of Venezuela, 1,980 sq. mi., cap. Port-of-Spain.

Trin·i·tar·i·an (trin′ə·târ′ē·ən) *adj.* 1 Of or pertaining to the Trinity. 2 Holding or professing belief in the Trinity. —*n.* A believer in the doctrine of the Trinity. **—Trin′i·tar′i·an·ism** *n.*

tri·ni·tro·tol·u·ene (trī·nī′trō·tol′yōō·ēn) *n.* An explosive made by treating toluene with nitric acid. Also **tri·ni′tro·tol′u·ol** (-yōō·ōl, -ol). [< TRI- + NITRO- + TOLUENE]

trin·i·ty (trin′ə·tē) *n. pl.* **·ties** 1 The state or character of being three. 2 The union of three parts or elements in one; a triad. [< L *trinitas* a triad]

Trin·i·ty (trin′ə·tē) *n.* In Christian theology, the union in one divine nature of Father, Son, and Holy Spirit.

trin·ket (tring′kit) *n.* 1 Any small ornament, as of jewelry. 2 A trifle; trivial object. [< AF *trenquet*]

tri·no·mi·al (trī·nō′mē·əl) *adj.* 1 *Biol.* Of, having, or employing three terms or names. 2 *Math.* Expressed as a sum of three terms. —*n.* 1 *Math.* A trinomial expression in algebra. 2 A trinomial name. Also **tri·nom′i·nal** (-nom′ə·nəl). [< TRI- + (BI)NOMIAL] **—tri·no′mi·al·ly** *adv.*

tri·o (trē′ō) *n. pl.* **tri·os** 1 Any three things grouped or associated together. 2 *Music* a A composition for three performers. b A group of three musicians who perform trios. [< Ital. *tre* three]

tri·ox·ide (trī·ok′sīd) *n.* An oxide containing three atoms of oxygen per molecule.

trip (trip) *n.* 1 A journey; excursion. 2 A misstep or stumble. 3 An active, nimble step or movement. 4 A catch or similar device for starting or stopping a movement, as in a mechanism. 5 A sudden catch of the legs or feet to make

a person fall. 6 A blunder; mistake. 7 *Slang* a The hallucinations and other sensations experienced by a person taking a psychedelic drug. b Any intense, usu. personal experience. —*v.* tripped, trip·ping *v.i.* 1 To stumble. 2 To move quickly and lightly. 3 To make an error. 4 To run past the nicks or dents of the ratchet escape wheel of a timepiece. 5 *Slang* To experience the effects of a psychedelic drug: often with *out.* —*v.t.* 6 To cause to stumble or make a mistake: often with *up.* 7 To perform (a dance) lightly. 8 *Mech.* To activate by releasing a catch, trigger, etc. —**trip it** To dance. [< OF *treper, triper* leap, trample] —**Syn.** *n.* 1 jaunt, tour, sojourn, voyage.

tri·par·tite (trī·pär′tīt) *adj.* 1 Divided into three parts. 2 Having three corresponding parts or copies. 3 Made between three persons: a *tripartite* pact. [< L *tri-* three + *partitus,* p.p. of *partiri* to divide] **—tri·par′tite·ly** *adv.* **—tri′·par·ti′tion** (-tish′ən) *n.*

tripe (trīp) *n.* 1 A part of the stomach wall of a ruminant used for food. 2 *Informal* Contemptible or worthless stuff; nonsense. [< OF]

trip·ham·mer (trip′ham′ər) *n.* A heavy power hammer that is raised mechanically and allowed to drop by a tripping action.

tripl. triplicate.

trip·le (trip′əl) *v.* **·led, ·ling** *v.t.* 1 To make threefold in number or quantity. —*v.i.* 2 To be or become three times as many or as large. 3 In baseball, to make a triple. —*adj.* 1 Consisting of three things united. 2 Multiplied by three; thrice said or done. —*n.* 1 A set or group of three. 2 In baseball, a fair hit that enables the batter to reach third base without the help of an error. [< Gk. *triploos* threefold] **—trip′ly** *adv.*

triple play In baseball, a play during which three men are put out.

trip·let (trip′lit) *n.* 1 A group of three of a kind. 2 Any of three children born at one birth. 3 *Music* A group of three notes that divide the time usu. taken by two. [< TRIPLE]

triple time *Music* A rhythm having three beats to the measure with the accent on the first beat.

trip·li·cate (trip′lə·kit) *adj.* Threefold; made in three copies. —*n.* One of three precisely similar things. **—in triplicate** In three identical copies. —*v.t.* (-kāt) **·cat·ed, ·cat·ing** To make three times; triple. [< L *triplicare* to triple] **—trip′li·cate·ly** *adv.* **—trip′li·ca′tion** *n.*

tri·pod (trī′pod) *n.* A three-legged frame or stand, as for supporting a camera, etc. [< Gk. *tri-* three + *pous* foot] **—trip·o·dal** (trip′ə·dəl), **tri·pod·ic** (trī·pod′ik) *adj.*

Tripod

trip·per (trip′ər) *n.* 1 A person or thing that trips. 2 *Brit. Informal* A tourist or traveler. 3 *Mech.* A trip or tripping mechanism, as a cam, pawl, etc. 4 *Slang* A person who frequently uses psychedelic drugs.

trip·ping (trip′ing) *adj.* Light; nimble. **—trip′ping·ly** *adv.*

trip·tych (trip′tik) *n.* 1 A picture, carving, or work of art on three panels side by side. 2 A writing tablet in three sections. [< Gk. *tri-* three + *ptyx, ptychos* a fold]

tri·reme (trī′rēm′) *n.* An ancient warship with three banks of oars on each side. [< L *tri-* three + *remus* an oar]

tri·sect (trī·sekt′) *v.t.* To divide into three parts, esp., as in geometry, into three equal parts. [< TRI- + L *sectus,* p.p. of *secare* to cut] **—tri·sec′tion** (-sek′shən), **tri·sec′tor** *n.*

triste (trēst) *adj.* Sorrowful; sad. [F]

tri·syl·la·ble (trī·sil′ə·bəl) *n.* A word of three syllables. **—tri·syl·lab·ic** (trī·si·lab′ik) *adj.* **—tri′syl·lab′i·cal·ly** *adv.*

trite (trīt) *adj.* trit·er, trit·est Made commonplace or hackneyed by frequent repetition. [< L *tritus,* p.p. of *terere* to rub] **—trite′ly** *adv.* **—trite′ness** *n.* —**Syn.** stale, stereotyped, threadbare, cliché, shopworn, tired, stock.

trit·i·um (trit′ē·əm, trish′ē·əm) *n.* The radioactive hydrogen isotope of atomic mass 3, having a half-life of 12.5 years. [< Gk. *tritos* third]

tri·ton (trīt′n) *n.* A marine snail with a trumpet-shaped shell. [< TRITON]

Triton

Tri·ton (trīt'n) *Gk. Myth.* A sea god having a man's head and upper body and a dolphin's tail.

trit·u·rate (trich'ə·rāt) *v.t.* ·rat·ed, ·rat·ing To reduce to a fine powder or pulp by grinding or rubbing; pulverize. — *n.* That which has been triturated. [< L *tritura* a rubbing, threshing < *tritus.* See TRITE.] *adj.* —**trit'u·ra'tor, trit'u·ra'·tion** *n.*

tri·umph (trī'əmf) *v.i.* 1 To win a victory. 2 To be successful. 3 To rejoice over a victory; exult. —*n.* 1 A victory or conquest: a *triumph* of will power. 2 An important success: the *triumphs* of modern medicine. 3 Exultation over a victory. 4 In ancient Rome, a pageant welcoming a victorious general. [< Gk. *thriambos* a processional hymn to Dionysus] —**tri·um·phal** (trī·um'fəl) *adj.* —**tri·um'phal·ly** *adv.* —**tri'umph·er** *n.*

tri·um·phant (trī·um'fənt) *adj.* 1 Exultant for or as for victory. 2 Crowned with victory; victorious. —**tri·um'phant·ly** *adv.*

tri·um·vir (trī·um'vər) *n. pl.* ·virs or ·vi·ri (-və·rī', -rē') In ancient Rome, one of three men united in public office or authority. [< L *trium virorum* of three men] —**tri·um'vi·ral** *adj.*

tri·um·vi·rate (trī·um'vər·it, -və·rāt) *n.* 1 A group or coalition of three men who govern. 2 The office of a triumvir. 3 The triumvirs collectively. 4 A group of three persons; a trio. [< L *triumvir* triumvir]

tri·une (trī'yōōn) *adj.* Three in one: said of the Godhead. [< TRI- + L *unus* one] —**tri·un·i·ty** (trī·yōō'nə·tē) *n.*

tri·va·lent (trī·vā'lənt) *adj. Chem.* Having a valence or combining value of three. [< TRI- + L *valens,* pr.p. of *valere* be strong] —**tri·va'lence, tri·va'len·cy** *n.*

triv·et (triv'it) *n.* A short, usu. three-legged stand for holding cooking vessels in a fireplace, a hot dish on a table, or a heated iron. [< L *tri-* three + *pes, pedis* a foot]

triv·i·a (triv'ē·ə) *n.pl.* Insignificant or unimportant matters; trifles. [< L *trivialis* trivial]

triv·i·al (triv'ē·əl) *adj.* 1 Of little value or importance; insignificant. 2 *Archaic* Ordinary; commonplace. [< L *trivialis* of the crossroads, commonplace] —**triv'i·al·ism** *n.* —**triv'i·al·ly** *adv.* —**Syn.** 1 slight, mean, paltry, inconsiderable, piddling.

triv·i·al·i·ty (triv'ē·al'ə·tē) *n. pl.* ·ties 1 The state or quality of being trivial. 2 A trivial matter.

triv·i·al·ize (triv'ē·ə·līz) *v.t.* ·ized, ·iz·ing To treat as or make trivial; regard as unimportant. —**triv'i·al·i·za'tion** *n.*

tri·week·ly (trī·wēk'lē) *adj. & adv.* 1 Occurring three times a week. 2 Done or occurring every third week. —*n. pl.* ·lies A triweekly publication.

tro·che (trō'kē) *n.* A small medicated lozenge, usu. circular. [< Gk. *trochiskos* a small wheel, a lozenge]

tro·chee (trō'kē) *n.* In prosody, a foot comprising a long and short syllable (‾ �‌), or an accented syllable followed by an unaccented one. [< Gk. *trochaios (pous)* a running (foot) < *trechein* to run] —**tro·cha·ic** (trō·kā'ik) *adj.*

trod (trod) *p.t. & alternative p.p.* of TREAD.

trod·den (trod'n) *p.p.* of TREAD.

trog·lo·dyte (trog'lə·dīt) *n.* 1 A prehistoric cave man. 2 A person with primitive habits. 3 A hermit. [< Gk. *trōglodytēs*] —**trog'lo·dyt'ic** (-dit'ik), **trog'lo·dyt'i·cal** *adj.*

Tro·jan (trō'jən) *n.* 1 A native of Troy. 2 A brave, persevering person. —*adj.* Of or pertaining to ancient Troy or to its people.

Trojan horse 1 *Gk. Myth.* During the Trojan War, a large, hollow wooden horse filled with Greek soldiers and brought within the walls of Troy, thus bringing about the downfall of the city. 2 *Mil.* The infiltration of military men into enemy territory to commit sabotage against industry and military installations.

Trojan War *Gk. Myth.* The ten years' war waged by the Greeks against the Trojans to recover Helen, the wife of Menelaus, who had been abducted by Paris.

troll[1] (trōl) *v.t.* 1 To sing in succession, as in a round. 2 To sing in a full, hearty manner. 3 To fish for with a moving lure, as from a moving boat. —*v.i.* 4 To roll; turn. 5 To sing a tune, etc., in a full, hearty manner. 6 To fish with a moving lure. —*n.* 1 A song taken up at intervals by sev-

eral voices; round. 2 A rolling movement or motion. 3 In fishing, a spoon or other lure. [?] —**troll'er** *n.*

troll[2] (trōl) *n.* In Scandinavian folklore, a giant or dwarf living in caves or underground. [< ON]

trol·ley (trol'ē) *n. pl.* ·leys 1 A device that rolls or slides along an electric conductor to carry current to an electric vehicle. 2 A trolley car; also, a system of trolley cars. 3 A small truck or car suspended from an overhead track and used to convey material, as in a factory, mine, etc. —*v.t. & v.i.* To convey or travel by trolley. [< TROLL[1]]

trolley bus A passenger conveyance operating without rails, propelled electrically by current taken from an overhead wire by means of a trolley.

trolley car A car arranged with a trolley and motor for use on an electric railway.

trol·lop (trol'əp) *n.* 1 A slatternly woman. 2 A prostitute. [?]

trom·bone (trom·bōn', trom'bōn) *n.* A brass wind instrument of the trumpet family in the tenor range, usu. equipped with a slide for changing pitch. [< Ital. *tromba* a trumpet] —**trom·bon'ist** *n.*

Trombone

troop (trōōp) *n.* 1 A gathering of people. 2 A flock or herd, as of animals. 3 A unit of cavalry having 60 to 100 men and corresponding to a company in other military branches. 4 *pl.* Soldiers. 5 A unit of Boy Scouts or Girl Scouts. —*v.i.* 1 To move along as a group: shoppers *trooping* through a store. 2 To go: to *troop* across the street. —*v.t.* 3 To form into troops. [< LL *troppus* a flock] —**Syn.** 1 company, crowd, multitude, throng.

troop·er (trōō'pər) *n.* 1 A cavalryman. 2 A mounted policeman. 3 A troop horse. 4 *Informal* A state policeman.

troop·ship (trōōp'ship') *n.* A ship for carrying troops.

trope (trōp) *n.* 1 The figurative use of a word or phrase. 2 A figure of speech. 3 Figurative language in general. [< L *tropus* a figure of speech < Gk. *tropos* a turn]

tro·phy (trō'fē) *n. pl.* ·phies 1 Anything taken from an enemy and displayed or treasured in proof of victory. 2 A prize representing victory or achievement: a tennis *trophy.* 3 An animal skin, mounted head, etc., kept to show skill in hunting. 4 Any memento. [< Gk. *tropē* a defeat, turning] —**tro'phied** *adj.*

trop·ic (trop'ik) *n.* 1 *Geog.* Either of two parallels of latitude, the **tropic of Cancer** at 23° 27' north of the equator and the **tropic of Capricorn** 23° 27' south of the equator, between which lies the torrid zone. 2 *Astron.* Either of two corresponding parallels in the celestial sphere similarly named, and respectively 23° 27' north or south from the celestial equator. 3 *pl.* The regions in the torrid zone. — *adj.* Of or pertaining to the tropics; tropical. [< Gk. *tropikos (kyklos)* the tropical (circle), pertaining to the turning of the sun at the solstice.]

-tropic *combining form* Having a (specified) tropism: *geotropic.* [< Gk. *tropos* a turn]

trop·i·cal (trop'i·kəl) *adj.* 1 Of, pertaining to, or characteristic of the tropics. 2 Of the nature of a trope or metaphor. —**trop'i·cal·ly** *adv.*

tropical fish Any of various small, usu. brightly colored fishes originating in the tropics and adapted to living in an aquarium (**tropical aquarium**) kept at a constant warm temperature.

tro·pism (trō'piz·əm) *n.* 1 A tendency in an organism to grow or move toward or away from a given stimulus. 2 An instance of such growth or movement. [< Gk. *tropē* a turning] —**tro·pis·tic** (trō·pis'tik) *adj.*

-tropism *combining form* A (specified) tropism: *phototropism.* Also **-tropy.**

trop·o·sphere (trōp'ə·sfir, trop'-) *n. Meteorol.* The region of the atmosphere extending from six to twelve miles above the earth's surface, characterized by decreasing temperature with increasing altitude. [< Gk. *tropos* a turning + SPHERE]

trot (trot) *n.* 1 The gait of a quadruped, in which each diagonal pair of legs is moved alternately. 2 The sound of this gait. 3 A slow running gait of a person. 4 A little child. 5 *Informal* A literal translation of a foreign-language text, used by students, often dishonestly. —the trots *Slang* Diarrhea. —*v.* trot·ted, trot·ting *v.i.* 1 To go at a trot. 2 To go quickly; hurry. —*v.t.* 3 To cause to trot. 4 To ride at a trotting gait. —trot out *Informal* To bring forth for inspection, approval, etc. [< OHG *trottōn* to tread]

troth (trôth, trōth) *n.* 1 Good faith; fidelity. 2 The act of pledging fidelity. 3 Truth; verity. —plight one's troth To promise to marry or be faithful to. [< OE *trēowth* truth]

Trot·sky·ism (trot'skē·iz'əm) *n.* The doctrines of Trotsky and his followers who opposed Stalin and believed that Communism to succeed must be international. [< L. *Trotsky*, 1879–1940, Russian Bolshevist leader] —Trot'sky·ist, Trot'sky·ite *n., adj.*

trot·ter (trot'ər) *n.* 1 One who or that which trots; a trotting horse, esp. one trained to trot in races. 2 *Informal* An animal's foot: a pig's *trotters.*

trou·ba·dour (trōō'bə·dôr, -dōr, -dŏŏr) *n.* One of a class of lyric poets, sometimes including wandering minstrels, flourishing in parts of France, Italy, and Spain during the 12th and 13th centuries. [< Prov. *trobador* < *trobar* compose, invent]

trou·ble (trub'əl) *n.* 1 The state of being distressed or worried. 2 A person, circumstance, or event that occasions difficulty or perplexity. 3 A condition of difficulty: to be in *trouble* at school; money *troubles.* 4 A disease or ailment: heart *trouble.* 5 Bother; effort: They took the *trouble* to drive me home. 6 Agitation; unrest: *trouble* in the streets. —*v.* ·led, ·ling *v.t.* 1 To distress; worry. 2 To stir up or roil, as water. 3 To inconvenience. 4 To annoy. 5 To cause physical pain or discomfort to. —*v.i.* 6 To take pains; bother. [< OF *turbler* to trouble] —troub'ler *n.*

troub·le·mak·er (trub'əl·mā'kər) *n.* One who habitually stirs up trouble for others.

troub·le·shoot·er (trub'əl·shōōt'ər) *n.* 1 A skilled workman able to analyze and repair breakdowns in machinery, electronic equipment, etc. 2 A person assigned to eliminate sources of difficulty or to mediate disputes, esp. in diplomacy and politics. —troub'le·shoot'ing *n.*

troub·le·some (trub'əl·səm) *adj.* 1 Causing trouble; trying. 2 Difficult: a *troublesome* task. —troub'le·some·ly *adv.* —troub'le·some·ness *n.* —Syn. 1 burdensome, disturbing, galling, harassing.

troub·lous (trub'ləs) *adj.* 1 Uneasy; restless: *troublous* times. 2 Troublesome.

trough (trôf, trof) *n.* 1 A long, narrow receptacle for food or water for animals. 2 A similarly shaped receptacle, as for mixing dough. 3 A long, narrow depression, as between waves. 4 A gutter for rain water fixed under the eaves of a building. 5 *Meteorol.* An elongated region of relatively low atmospheric pressure. [< OE *trog*]

trounce (trouns) *v.t.* trounced, trounc·ing 1 To beat or thrash severely; punish. 2 *Informal* To defeat. [?]

troupe (trōōp) *n.* A company of actors or other performers. —*v.i.* trouped, troup·ing To travel as one of a company of actors or entertainers. [< OF *trope* troop]

troup·er (trōōp'ər) *n.* 1 A member of a theatrical company. 2 An older actor of long experience.

trou·sers (trou'zərz) *n.pl.* A two-legged garment, covering the body from the waist to the ankles or knees. [Blend of obs. *trouse* breeches and DRAWERS]

trous·seau (trōō'sō, trōō·sō') *n. pl.* ·seaux (-sōz, -sōz') or ·seaus A bride's outfit, esp. of clothing. [F < OF, dim. of *trousse* a packed collection of things]

trout (trout) *n.* Any of various fishes of the salmon family found mostly in fresh waters and esteemed as a game and food fish. [< OE *trūht*]

trow·el (trou'əl, troul) *n.* 1 A flat-bladed, sometimes pointed implement, used by masons, plasterers, and molders. 2 A small concave scoop with a handle, used in digging about small plants. —*v.t.* ·eled or ·elled, ·el·ing or ·el·ling To apply, smooth, or dig

Trowels
a. garden. b. plastering. c. brick.

with a trowel. [< L *trulla*, dim. of *trua* a stirring spoon] —trow'el·er or trow'el·ler *n.*

troy (troi) *adj.* Measured or expressed in troy weight. [< *Troyes*, France; with ref. to a weight used at a fair held there]

troy weight A system of weights in which 12 ounces or 5,760 grains equal a pound, and the grain is identical with the avoirdupois grain. • See MEASURE.

tru·ant (trōō'ənt) *n.* 1 A pupil who stays away from school without leave. 2 A person who shirks responsibilities or work. —play truant 1 To be absent from school without leave. 2 To shirk responsibilities or work. —*adj.* 1 Being truant; idle. 2 Relating to or characterizing a truant. [< OF, a vagabond] —tru·an·cy (trōō'ən·sē) *n.* (*pl.* ·cies)

truce (trōōs) *n.* 1 An agreement for a temporary suspension of hostilities; an armistice. 2 A temporary stopping, as from pain, etc.; respite. [< OE *truwa* faith, a promise]

Tru·cial States (trōō'shəl) A group of sheikdoms, bound by treaties with Great Britain, in E Arabia, 32,300 sq. mi.

truck[1] (truk) *n.* 1 Any of several types of strongly built motor vehicles designed to transport heavy loads, bulky articles, freight, etc. 2 A two-wheeled barrowlike vehicle for moving barrels, boxes, etc., by hand. 3 A small wheeled vehicle used for moving baggage, goods, etc. 4 A disk at the upper extremity of a mast or flagpole through which the halyards of signals are run. 5 A small wheel. —*v.t.* 1 To carry on a truck. —*v.i.* 2 To carry goods on a truck. 3 To drive a truck. [< Gk. *trochos* a wheel]

truck[2] (truk) *v.t. & v.i.* To exchange or barter. —*n.* 1 Commodities for sale. 2 Garden produce for market. 3 *Informal* Rubbish; worthless articles. 4 Barter. 5 *Informal* Dealings: I will have no *truck* with him. [< OF *troquer* to barter]

truck·age (truk'ij) *n.* 1 The conveyance of goods on trucks. 2 The charge for this. [< TRUCK[1]]

truck·er (truk'ər) *n.* One who drives or supplies trucks or moves commodities in trucks.

truck farm A farm on which vegetables are produced for market. —truck farmer, truck farming

truck·ing (truk'ing) *n.* The act or business of transportation by trucks.

truck·le (truk'əl) *v.* ·led, ·ling *v.i.* 1 To yield or submit weakly: with *to.* 2 To move on rollers or casters. —*v.t.* 3 To cause to move on rollers or casters. —*n.* A small wheel. [< L *trochlea* system of pulleys] —truck'ler *n.*

truckle bed TRUNDLE BED.

truck·man (truk'mən) *n. pl.* ·men (mən) 1 A truck driver. 2 One engaged in the business of trucking.

truc·u·lent (truk'yə·lənt) *adj.* Of savage character; cruel; ferocious. [< L *trux, trucis* fierce] —truc·u·lence (truk'yə·ləns), truc'u·len·cy *n.* —truc'u·lent·ly *adv.* —Syn. barbarous, brutal, fierce, ruthless, vicious.

trudge (truj) *v.i.* trudged, trudg·ing To walk wearily or laboriously; plod. —*n.* A tiresome walk or tramp. [?] —trudg'er *n.*

true (trōō) *adj.* tru·er, tru·est 1 Faithful to fact or reality. 2 Being real; genuine, not counterfeit: *true* gold. 3 Faithful to friends, promises, or principles; loyal. 4 Exact: a *true* copy. 5 Accurate, as in shape, or position: a *true* fit. 6 Faithful to the requirements of law or justice; legitimate: the *true* king. 7 Faithful to truth; honest: a *true* man. 8 Faithful to the promise or predicted event: a *true* sign. 9 *Biol.* Possessing all the attributes of its class: a *true* root. 10 *Music* Exactly in tune. —come true To turn out as hoped for or imagined. —*n.* The state or quality of being true; also, something that is true: usu. with *the.* —in (or out of) true In (or not in) line of adjustment. —*adv.* 1 In truth; truly. 2 Within proper tolerances: The wheel runs *true.* —*v.t.* trued, tru·ing To bring to conformity with a standard or requirement: to *true* a frame. [< OE *trēowe*] —true'ness *n.*

true bill *Law* A bill of indictment found by a grand jury to be sustained by the evidence.

true-blue (trōō'blōō') *adj.* Staunch; faithful.

true-love (trōō'luv') *n.* One truly beloved; a sweetheart.

truf·fle (truf'əl, trōō'fəl) *n.* Any of various fleshy underground edible fungi regarded as a delicacy. [< OF *truffe*]

tru·ism (trōō'iz·əm) *n.* An obvious or self-evident truth; a platitude.

trull (trul) *n.* A prostitute. [< G *Trolle*]

tru·ly (trōō′lē) *adv.* 1 In conformity with fact. 2 With accuracy. 3 With loyalty.

trump (trump) *n.* 1 In various card games, a card of the suit selected to rank above all others temporarily. 2 The suit thus determined. 3 *Informal* A fine, reliable person. —*v.t.* 1 To take (another card) with a trump. 2 To surpass; excel; beat. —*v.i.* 3 To play a trump. —**trump up** To invent for a fraudulent purpose. [Alter. of TRIUMPH]

trump·er·y (trum′pər·ē) *n. pl.* **·er·ies** 1 Worthless finery. 2 Rubbish; nonsense. —*adj.* Having a showy appearance, but valueless. [< OF *tromper* to cheat]

trum·pet (trum′pit) *n.* 1 A soprano brass wind instrument with a flaring bell and a long metal tube. 2 Something resembling a trumpet in form. 3 A tube for collecting and conducting sounds to the ear; an ear trumpet. 4 A loud penetrating sound like that of a trumpet. —*v.t.* 1 To sound or publish abroad. —*v.i.* 2 To blow a trumpet. 3 To give forth a sound as if from a trumpet, as an elephant. [< OF *trompette*]

Trumpet

trum·pet·er (trum′pə·tər) *n.* 1 One who plays a trumpet. 2 One who publishes something loudly abroad. 3 A large South American bird, related to the cranes. 4 A large North American wild swan having a clarionlike cry: also **trumpeter swan.** • See SWAN. 5 A breed of domestic pigeons.

trun·cate (trung′kāt) *v.t.* **·cat·ed, ·cat·ing** To cut the top or end from. —*adj. Biol.* Ending abruptly, as though cut off: a *truncate* leaf. [< L *truncare*] —**trun′cate·ly** *adv.* —**trun·ca·tion** (trung·kā′shən) *n.*

trun·cheon (trun′chən) *n.* 1 A short, heavy stick, esp. a policeman's club. 2 Any baton of office or authority. —*v.t.* To beat as with a truncheon; cudgel. [< OF *tronchon* a stump]

trun·dle (trun′dəl) *n.* 1 A small broad wheel, as of a caster. 2 The act, motion, or sound of trundling. 3 TRUNDLE BED. —*v.* **·dled, ·dling** *v.t.* 1 To propel by rolling along: to *trundle* a wheelbarrow. 2 To haul or carry in a wheeled vehicle. —*v.i.* 3 To move ahead by revolving. 4 To progress on wheels. [< OE *trendel* a circle] —**trun′dler** *n.*

trundle bed A bed with very low frame resting upon casters, so that it may be rolled under another bed.

trunk (trungk) *n.* 1 The main stem or stock of a tree. 2 An animal or human body, apart from the head and limbs; the torso. 3 The thorax of an insect. 4 The main stem of a nerve, blood vessel, or lymphatic. 5 A main line of communication or transportation, as the circuit connecting two telephone exchanges. 6 A proboscis, as of an elephant. 7 A large box or case used for packing and carrying clothes or other articles. 8 *pl.* Very short, close-fitting trousers worn by swimmers, athletes, etc. 9 *Archit.* The shaft of a column. 10 A compartment in an automobile, opposite the end housing the motor, for carrying luggage, tools, etc. —*adj.* Being or belonging to a trunk or main body: a *trunk* railroad. [< L *truncus* stem, trunk]

trunk·fish (trungk′fish′) *n. pl.* **·fish** or **·fish·es** Any of a family of fishes characterized by a body covering of hard, bony plates.

truss (trus) *n.* 1 A supporting framework, as for a roof or bridge. 2 A bandage or support for a hernia. 3 A bundle or package. 4 *Naut.* A heavy iron piece by which a lower yard is attached to a mast. —*v.t.* 1 To tie or bind; fasten: often with *up.* 2 To support or brace (a roof, bridge, etc.) with trusses. 3 To fasten the wings of (a fowl) before cooking. [< OF *trousser, trusser* pack up, bundle] —**truss′er** *n.*

trust (trust) *n.* 1 A reliance on the integrity, veracity, or reliability of a person or thing. 2 Something committed to one's care for use or safekeeping. 3 The state or position

of one who has received an important charge. 4 Confident expectation; hope. 5 In commerce, credit. 6 *Law* a The confidence reposed in a person to whom the legal title to property is conveyed for the benefit of another. b The property or thing held in trust. c The relation subsisting between the holder and the property so held. 7 A combination of business firms formed to control production and prices of some commodity. —**in trust** In the charge or care of another or others. —**on trust** 1 On credit. 2 Without investigating: to accept a statement *on trust.* —*v.t.* 1 To rely upon. 2 To commit to the care of another; entrust. 3 To commit something to the care of: with *with.* 4 To allow to do something without fear of the consequences. 5 To expect; hope. 6 To believe. 7 To allow business credit to. —*v.i.* 8 To place trust or confidence; rely: with *in.* 9 To allow business credit. —**trust to** To depend upon; confide in. —*adj.* Held in trust: *trust* property. [< ON *traust,* lit., firmness] —**trust′er** *n.* —**Syn.** *n.* 1 confidence, credence, faith.

trus·tee (trus·tē′) *n.* 1 One who is entrusted with the property of another. 2 One of a body of persons, often elective, who hold the property and manage the affairs of a company or institution.

trus·tee·ship (trus·tē′ship) *n.* 1 The post or function of a trustee. 2 Supervision and control of a trust territory by a country or countries commissioned by the United Nations.

trust·ful (trust′fəl) *adj.* Disposed to trust. —**trust′ful·ly** *adv.* —**trust′ful·ness** *n.*

trust fund Money, securities, or similar property held in trust.

trust·ing (trus′ting) *adj.* Having trust; trustful. —**trust′ing·ly** *adv.* —**trust′ing·ness** *n.*

trust territory An area, usu. a former colonial possession, governed by a member state of the United Nations.

trust·wor·thy (trust′wûr′thē) *adj.* Worthy of confidence; reliable. —**trust′wor′thi·ly** (-wûr′thə·lē) *adv.* —**trust′wor′thi·ness** *n.*

trust·y (trus′tē) *adj.* **trust·i·er, trust·i·est** 1 Faithful to duty or trust. 2 Staunch; firm. —*n. pl.* **trust·ies** A trustworthy person; esp. a convict to whom special privileges are granted. —**trust′i·ly** *adv.* —**trust′i·ness** *n.*

truth (trōōth) *n. pl.* **truths** (trōōthz, trōōths) 1 The state or character of being true. 2 That which is true. 3 Conformity to fact or reality. 4 The quality of being true; fidelity; constancy. —**in truth** Indeed; in fact. [< OE *treowe* true]

truth·ful (trōōth′fəl) *adj.* 1 Conforming to fact; veracious. 2 Telling the truth. —**truth′ful·ly** *adv.* —**truth′ful·ness** *n.*

try (trī) *v.* **tried, try·ing** *v.t.* 1 To make an attempt to do or accomplish. 2 To make experimental use or application of: to *try* a new pen. 3 To subject to a test; put to proof. 4 To put severe strain upon; tax: to *try* one's patience. 5 To subject to trouble or tribulation. 6 To extract by rendering or melting; refine. 7 *Law* To determine the guilt or innocence by judicial trial. —*v.i.* 8 To make an attempt; put forth effort. 9 To make an examination or test. —**try on** To put on (a garment) to test it for fit or appearance. —**try out** 1 To attempt to qualify: He *tried out* for the team. 2 To test the result or effect of. —*n. pl.* **tries** The act of trying; trial. [< OF *trier* sift, pick out] —**tri′er** *n.* • **try and, try to** These constructions are both standard in modern English: *Try and meet me at six; Try to finish your work on time.* However, *try to* is usu. preferable in precise, formal writing.

try·ing (trī′ing) *adj.* Testing severely; hard to endure. —**try′ing·ly** *adv.* —**try′ing·ness** *n.* —**Syn.** arduous, difficult, onerous, troublesome.

try·out (trī′out′) *n. Informal* A test of ability, as of an actor or athlete.

tryp·sin (trip′sin) *n.* A pancreatic enzyme that helps to digest proteins. [< Gk. *tripsis* a rubbing + (PEP)SIN] —**tryp′tic** (-tik) *adj.*

try square A device for marking off right angles and testing the accuracy of anything square.

tryst (trist, trīst) *n.* 1 An appointment to meet at a specified time or place. 2 The meeting place agreed upon. 3 The meeting so agreed upon. [< OF *triste, tristre* an appointed station in hunting]

tsar (zär, tsär) *n.* CZAR.

tset·se (tset′sē, tsē′tsē) *n.* Any of several bloodsucking flies of Africa, including species that carry and transmit pathogenic organisms to humans and animals. Also **tsetse fly.** [< Bantu]

T. Sgt., T/Sgt Technical Sergeant.

T-shirt (tē′shûrt′) *n.* A knitted cotton undershirt with short sleeves.

tsp. teaspoon(s); teaspoonful(s).

T-square (tē′skwâr′) *n.* A device used to measure out right angles or parallel lines, consisting usu. of a flat strip with a shorter head at right angles to it.

tsu·na·mi (tsŏŏ-nä′mē) *n.* An immense wave generated by a submarine earthquake. [Jap. < *tsu* port, harbor + *nami* wave]

Tu., Tues. Tuesday.

tub (tub) *n.* 1 A broad, open-topped vessel of metal, wooden staves, etc., for washing and bathing. 2 A bathtub. 3 *Informal* A bath taken in a tub. 4 The amount that a tub contains. 5 Anything resembling a tub, as a broad, clumsy boat. 6 *Informal* A small cask. —*v.t. & v.i.* **tubbed, tub·bing** To wash or bathe in a tub. [< MDu. *tubbe*] —**tub′ber** *n.*

tu·ba (tyŏŏ′bə) *n. pl.* **·bas** or **·bae** (-bē) A large bass instrument of the bugle family. [< L, a war trumpet]

tub·by (tub′ē) *adj.* **·bi·er, ·bi·est** Resembling a tub in form; round and fat. —*Syn.* chubby, chunky, corpulent, rotund.

tube (tyŏŏb) *n.* 1 A long hollow cylindrical body of metal, glass, rubber, etc., generally used to convey or hold a liquid or gas. 2 Any device having a tube or tubelike part, as a telescope. 3 *Biol.* Any elongated hollow part or organ. 4 A subway or subway tunnel. 5 An electron tube. 6 A collapsible metal or plastic cylinder for containing paints, toothpaste, glue, and the like. —**the tube** *Slang* Television. —*v.t.* **tubed, tub·ing** 1 To fit or furnish with a tube. 2 To make tubular. [< L *tubus*] —**tu′bal** *adj.*

tu·ber (tyŏŏ′bər) *n.* 1 A short, thickened portion of an underground stem, as a potato. 2 A tubercle. [L, a swelling]

tu·ber·cle (tyŏŏ′bər-kəl) *n.* 1 A small rounded eminence or nodule. 2 *Bot.* A small wartlike swelling, usu. due to symbiotic microorganisms, as on the roots of certain legumes. 3 *Pathol.* A small granular tumor within an organ. [< L *tuber* a swelling]

tubercle bacillus The rod-shaped bacterium that causes tuberculosis.

tu·ber·cu·lar (tyŏŏ-bûr′kyə-lər) *adj.* 1 Affected with tubercles. 2 Tuberculous. —*n.* One affected with tuberculosis.

tu·ber·cu·lin (tyŏŏ-bûr′kyə-lin) *n.* A substance derived from tubercle bacilli, used in a diagnostic test for tuberculosis. [< L *tuberculum* TUBERCLE + -IN]

tu·ber·cu·lo·sis (tyŏŏ-bûr′kyə-lō′sis) *n.* A communicable disease caused by the tubercle bacillus and characterized by tubercles in the lungs or other organs or tissues of the body. —**tu·ber′cu·lous** (tyŏŏ-bûr′kyə-ləs) *adj.*

tube·rose (tyŏŏb′rōz′, tyŏŏ′bə-rōs′) *n.* A bulbous plant of the amaryllis family, bearing a spike of fragrant white flowers. [< L *tuberosus* knobby < *tuber* a swelling]

tu·ber·ous (tyŏŏ′bər-əs) *adj.* 1 Bearing projections or prominences. 2 Resembling tubers. 3 *Bot.* Bearing tubers: also **tu′ber·ose.** —**tu·ber·os·i·ty** (tyŏŏ′bə-ros′ə-tē) *n.* (*pl.* **·ties**)

tub·ing (tyŏŏ′bing) *n.* 1 Tubes collectively. 2 A piece of tube or material for tubes.

tu·bu·lar (tyŏŏ′byə-lər) *adj.* 1 Having the form of a tube. 2 Of or pertaining to a tube or tubes.

tuck (tuk) *v.t.* 1 To thrust or press in the ends or edges of: to *tuck* in a blanket. 2 To wrap or cover snugly. 3 To thrust or press into a close place; cram. 4 To make tucks in, by folding and stitching. —*v.i.* 5 To contract; draw together. 6 To make tucks. —*n.* 1 A fold sewed into a garment. 2 Any inserted or folded thing. 3 A position in diving in which the knees are bent and the upper legs pressed against the chest. [< OE *tūcian* ill-treat, lit., tug]

tuck·er¹ (tuk′ər) *n.* 1 One who or that which tucks. 2 A

covering of muslin, lace, etc., formerly worn over the neck and shoulders by women. 3 A device on a sewing machine to make tucks.

tuck·er² (tuk′ər) *v.t. Informal* To weary completely; exhaust: usu. with *out.* [?]

Tu·dor (tyŏŏ′dər) *adj.* 1 Of or pertaining to the English royal family (1485–1603) descended from Sir Owen Tudor. 2 Designating or pertaining to the architecture, poetry, etc., developed during the reigns of the Tudors.

Tues·day (tyŏŏz′dē, -dā) *n.* The third day of the week. [< OE *tīwesdæg* day of Tiw, a god of war]

tuft (tuft) *n.* 1 A collection or bunch of small, flexible parts, as hair, grass, or feathers, held together at the base. 2 A clump or knot. —*v.t.* 1 To provide (a mattress, upholstery, etc.) with tightly drawn tufts or buttons to keep the padding in place. 2 To cover or adorn with tufts. —*v.i.* 3 To form or grow in tufts. [< OF *tuffe*] —**tuft′er** *n.*

tuft·ed (tuf′tid) *adj.* 1 Having or adorned with a tuft or crest. 2 Forming a tuft or dense cluster.

tug (tug) *v.* **tugged, tug·ging** *v.t.* 1 To pull at with effort; strain at. 2 To pull or drag with effort. 3 To tow with a tugboat. —*v.i.* 4 To pull strenuously: to *tug* at an oar. 5 To strive; struggle. —*n.* 1 A violent pull. 2 A strenuous contest. 3 A tugboat. 4 A trace of a harness. [< OE *tēon* tow] —**tug′ger** *n.* —*Syn. v.* 2 draw, haul, heave, lug.

tug·boat (tug′bōt′) *n.* A small, compact, ruggedly built vessel designed for towing or pushing barges and larger vessels.

tug of war 1 A contest in which a number of persons at one end of a rope pull against a like number at the other end. 2 A laborious effort; supreme contest. Also **tug-of-war** (tug′uv-wôr′, tug′ə-) *n.* (*pl.* **tugs-of-war**).

tu·i·tion (tyŏŏ-ish′ən) *n.* 1 The act or business of teaching. 2 The charge or payment for instruction. [< L *tuitio* a guard, guardianship] —**tu·i′tion·al, tu·i′tion·ar′y** (-er′ē) *adj.*

tu·la·re·mi·a (tyŏŏ′lə-rē′mē-ə) *n.* An acute bacterial infection that can be transmitted to man from infected rabbits, squirrels, or other animals by the bite of certain flies or by direct contact. Also **tu′la·rae′mi·a.** [< *Tulare* County, California + Gk. *haima* blood]

tu·lip (tyŏŏ′lip) *n.* 1 Any of numerous bulbous plants of the lily family, bearing variously colored cup-shaped flowers. 2 A bulb or flower of this plant. [< Turkish *tuliband* turban]

tulip tree A large North American forest tree related to magnolia, with greenish cup-shaped flowers.

tu·lip·wood (tyŏŏ′lip-wŏŏd′) *n.* 1 The soft, light wood of the tulip tree. 2 Any of several ornamental cabinet woods. 3 Any of the trees yielding these woods.

tulle (tŏŏl, *Fr.* tül) *n.* A fine, silk, open-meshed material, used for veils, etc. [< *Tulle,* a city in sw France]

tum·ble (tum′bəl) *v.* **·bled, ·bling** *v.i.* 1 To roll or toss about. 2 To perform acrobatic feats, as somersaults, etc. 3 To fall violently or awkwardly. 4 To move in a careless or headlong manner; stumble. 5 *Informal* To understand; comprehend: with *to.* —*v.t.* 6 To toss carelessly; cause to fall. 7 To throw into disorder; rumple. —*n.* 1 The act of tumbling; a fall. 2 A state of disorder or confusion. [< OE *tumbian* fall, leap]

tum·ble·bug (tum′bəl-bug′) *n.* Any of several beetles that roll up a ball of dung to enclose their eggs.

tum·ble-down (tum′bəl-doun′) *adj.* Rickety, as if about to fall in pieces; dilapidated.

tum·bler (tum′blər) *n.* 1 A drinking glass without a foot or stem; also, its contents. 2 One who or that which tumbles, as an acrobat or contortionist. 3 One of a breed of domestic pigeons noted for turning somersaults during flight. 4 In a lock, a latch that engages and immobilizes a bolt unless raised by the key bit. 5 A revolving device the contents of which are tumbled about, as certain dryers for clothes.

tum·ble·weed (tum′bəl-wēd′) *n.* Any of various plants which break off in autumn and are driven about by the wind.

Tumbrel

tum·brel (tum′brəl) *n.* 1 A farmer's cart. 2 A rude cart in which prisoners were taken to the guillotine during the French

Revolution. **3** A military cart for carrying tools, ammunition, etc. Also **tum′bril.** [< OE *tomberel*]

tu·me·fy (tʸoō′mə·fī) *v.t.* & *v.i.* **·fied, ·fy·ing** To swell or puff up. [< L *tumere* swell + *facere* make] —**tu·me·fac·tion** (tʸoō′mə·fak′shən) *n.*

tu·mes·cent (tʸoō·mes′ənt) *adj.* Swelling; somewhat tumid. [< L *tumescere* to swell up] —**tu·mes′cence** *n.*

tu·mid (tʸoō′mid) *adj.* **1** Swollen; enlarged, protuberant. **2** Inflated or pompous. [< L *tumidus* < *tumere* swell] —**tu·mid′i·ty, tu′mid·ness** *n.*

tum·my (tum′ē) *n. pl.* **·mies** *Colloq.* The stomach or abdomen.

tu·mor (tʸoō′mər) *n.* A local swelling on or in the body, esp. from growth of tissue having no physiological function. *Brit. sp.* **tu′mour.** [< L *tumere* to swell] —**tu′mor·ous** *adj.*

tu·mult (tʸoō′mult) *n.* **1** The commotion, disturbance, or agitation of a multitude; an uproar. **2** Any violent commotion. **3** Mental or emotional agitation. [< L *tumultus* < *tumere* swell] —**Syn.** ferment, hubbub, racket, turbulence.

tu·mul·tu·ous (tʸoō·mul′choō·əs) *adj.* **1** Characterized by tumult; disorderly; violent. **2** Greatly agitated or disturbed. **3** Stormy; tempestuous. —**tu·mul′tu·ous·ly** *adv.* —**tu·mul′tu·ous·ness** *n.*

tun (tun) *n.* **1** A large cask. **2** A varying measure of capacity for wines, etc., usu. equal to 252 gallons. —*v.t.* **tunned, tun·ning** To put into a cask or tun. [< OE *tunne*]

tu·na (tʸoō′nə) *n. pl.* **tu·na** or **tu·nas** Any of various large marine food and game fishes related to mackerel. Also **tuna fish.** [Am. Sp., ult. < *thunnus* tunny]

tun·dra (tun′drə, toōn′-) *n.* A rolling, treeless, often marshy plain of Siberia, arctic North America, etc. [Russ.]

tune (tʸoōn) *n.* **1** A coherent succession of musical tones; a melody or air. **2** Correct musical pitch or key. **3** Fine adjustment: the *tune* of an engine. **4** State of mind; humor: He will change his *tune.* **5** Concord; agreement: to be out of *tune* with the times. —**sing a difficult tune** To assume a different style or attitude. —**to the tune of** *Informal* To the amount of: *to the tune of* ten dollars. —*v.* **tuned, tun·ing** *v.t.* **1** To put into tune; adjust precisely. **2** To adapt to a particular tone, expression, or mood. **3** To bring into harmony or accord. —*v.i.* **4** To be in harmony. —**tune in 1** To adjust a radio or television receiver to (a station, program, etc.). **2** *Slang* To become or cause to become aware, knowing, or sophisticated. —**tune out 1** To adjust a radio or television receiver to exclude (interference, a station, etc.). **2** *Slang* To turn one's interest or attention away from. —**tune up 1** To bring (musical instruments) to a common pitch. **2** To adjust (a machine, engine, etc.) to proper working order. [< ME *tone* tone] —**tun′er** *n.*

tune·ful (tʸoōn′fəl) *adj.* Melodious; musical. —**tune′ful·ly** *adv.* —**tune′ful·ness** *n.*

tune·less (tʸoōn′lis) *adj.* **1** Not being in tune. **2** Lacking in melody. —**tune′less·ly** *adv.* —**tune′less·ness** *n.*

tune-up (tʸoōn′up′) *n.* A precise adjustment of an engine or other device.

tung oil (tung) A fast-drying oil extracted from the seeds of the subtropical **tung tree,** used in paints, varnishes, etc. [Chin. *t′ung* the tung tree]

tung·sten (tung′stən) *n.* A hard, heavy metallic element (symbol W), having a high melting point, used to make filaments for electric lamps and various alloys. [Sw. < *tung* weighty + *sten* stone]

tu·nic (tʸoō′nik) *n.* **1** Among the ancient Greeks and Romans, a loose body garment, with or without sleeves, reaching to the knees. **2** A modern outer garment gathered at the waist, as a short overskirt or a blouse. **3** A short coat worn as part of a uniform. **4** *Biol.* A mantle of tissue covering an organism or a part: also **tu′ni·ca** (-kə) [< L *tunica*]

tuning fork A fork-shaped piece of steel that produces a fixed tone when struck.

Tu·ni·sia (tʸoō·nē′zhə, -nish′ə, -nish′ē·ə) *n.* A republic of N Africa, 48,195 sq. mi., cap. Tunis. —**Tu·ni′sian** *adj., n.* • See map at AFRICA.

tun·nage (tun′ij) *n. Brit.* TONNAGE.

tun·nel (tun′əl) *n.* **1** An underground passageway or gallery, as for a railway or roadway. **2** Any similar passageway under or through something. **3** A burrow. —*v.* **·neled** or **·nelled, ·nel·ing** or **·nel·ling** *v.t.* **1** To make a tunnel or similar passage through or under. **2** To proceed by digging or as if by digging a tunnel. —*v.i.* **3** To make a tunnel. [< OF *tonne* a cask] —**tun′nel·er** or **tun′nel·ler** *n.*

tun·ny (tun′ē) *n. pl.* **·nies** or **·ny** TUNA. [< Gk. *thynnos*]

tup (tup) *n.* A ram, or male sheep. —*v.t.* & *v.i.* **tupped, tup·ping** To copulate with (a ewe). [Prob. < Scand.]

tu·pe·lo (tʸoō′pə·lō) *n. pl.* **·los** Any of several North American gum trees having smooth, oval leaves and brilliant red autumn foliage. [< Muskhogean]

Tu·pi (toō·pē′, toō·pē′) *n. pl.* **Tu·pis** or **Tu·pi 1** A member of any of a group of South American Indian tribes comprising the N branch of the Tupian stock. **2** The language spoken by the Tupis: also **Tu·pi′-Gua·ra·ni′** (-gwä·rä·nē′).

Tu·pi·an (toō·pē′ən) *adj.* Of or pertaining to the Tupis or their language. —*n.* A large linguistic stock of South American Indians.

tup·pence (tup′əns) *n.* TWOPENCE.

tuque (tʸoōk) *n. Can.* A knitted stocking cap. [F (Canadian) < F *toque* < Sp. *toca*]

tur·ban (tûr′bən) *n.* **1** A head covering consisting of a sash or shawl, twisted about the head or about a cap, worn by men in the Orient. **2** Any similar headdress. [< Pers. *dulband* < *dul* a turn + *band* a band] —**tur′baned** (-bənd) *adj.*

tur·bid (tûr′bid) *adj..* **1** Muddy or opaque: a *turbid* stream. **2** Dense; heavy: *turbid* clouds of smoke. **3** Confused; disturbed. [< L *turbidus* < *turbare* to trouble] —**tur′bid·ly** *adv.* —**tur′bid·ness, tur·bid·i·ty** (tûr·bid′ə·tē) *n.* • **turbid, turgid** Because these words sound alike, they are often confused: *Turbid* usu. refers to water, smoke, etc., so filled with sediment or particles as to be opaque. *Turgid* means abnormally swollen or inflated.

tur·bine (tûr′bin, -bīn) *n.* An engine consisting of one or more rotary units, mounted on a shaft and provided with a series of vanes, actuated by steam, water, gas, or other fluid under pressure. [< L *turbo* a whirlwind, top]

turbo- *combining form* Pertaining to, consisting of, or driven by a turbine: *turbojet.* [< L *turbo* a top]

tur·bo·fan (tûr′bō·fan′) *n. Aeron.* A jet engine with turbine-driven fans that augment its thrust.

tur·bo·jet (tûr′bō·jet′) *n. Aeron.* A jet engine that uses a gas turbine to drive the air compressor.

tur·bo·prop (tûr′bō·prop′) *n. Aeron.* A jet engine in which part of the thrust is produced by a turbine-driven propeller.

tur·bot (tûr′bət) *n. pl.* **·bot** or **·bots 1** A large, edible European flatfish. **2** Any of various flatfishes, as the flounder, halibut, etc. [< OF *tourbout*]

tur·bu·lent (tûr′byə·lənt) *adj.* **1** Violently disturbed or agitated: a *turbulent* sea. **2** Inclined to rebel; insubordinate. **3** Having a tendency to disturb. [< L *turbulentus* full of disturbance] —**tur′bu·lence, tur′bu·len·cy** *n.* —**tur′bu·lent·ly** *adv.* —**Syn. 1** stormy, tumultuous, wild. **2** obstreperous, unruly.

tu·reen (tʸoō·rēn′) *n.* A large, deep, covered dish, as for soup. [< F *terrine*]

turf (tûrf) *n. pl.* **turfs** (*Archaic* **turves**) **1** A mass of grass and its matted roots. **2** A plot of grass. **3** Peat. **4** *Slang* **a** A home territory, esp. that of a youthful street gang, defended against invasion by rival gangs. **b** Any place regarded possessively as the center of one's activity or interest: *Philadelphia is his home turf.* —**the turf 1** A racecourse. **2** Horse racing. —*v.t.* To cover with turf; sod. [< OE]

turf·man (tûrf′mən) *n. pl.* **·men** (-mən) A man who is connected with horseracing.

tur·ges·cent (tur·jes′ənt) *adj.* Being or becoming swollen or inflated. [< L *turgere* swell] —**tur·ges′cence, tur·ges′cen·cy** *n.* —**tur·ges′cent·ly** *adv.*

tur·gid (tûr′jid) *adj.* **1** Unnaturally distended; swollen. **2** Using high-flown laguage; bombastic: *turgid* prose. [< L *turgere* swell] —**tur·gid·i·ty** (tər·jid′ə·tē), **tur′gid·ness** *n.* —**tur′gid·ly** *adv.* • See TURBID.

---

add, ăce, câre, pălm; end, ĕven; ĭt, īce; odd, ōpen, ôrder; tŏŏk, pōōl; up, bûrn; ə = *a* in *above; u* in .*focus*; yōō = *u* in *fuse;* oil; pout; check; go; ring; thin; ᵺis; zh, *vision.* < derived from; ? origin uncertain or unknown.

Turk (tûrk) *n.* A citizen or native of Turkey.

Turk. Turkey; Turkish.

tur·key (tûr'kē) *n. pl.* **·keys** 1 A large North American bird related to the pheasant, having the head naked and a spreading tail. 2 The edible flesh of this bird. 3 *Slang* A play or a motion picture that fails. [From mistaken identification with a guinea fowl originating in *Turkey*]

Turkey

Tur·key (tûr'kē) *n.* A republic of s Eurasia, 296,108 sq. mi., cap. Ankara.

turkey buzzard A black vulture of temperate and tropical America with a naked red head and neck. Also **turkey vulture.**

Turk·ic (tûr'kik) *n.* A subfamily of the Altaic family of languages. —*adj.* Pertaining to this linguistic subfamily, or to any of the peoples speaking its languages.

Turk·ish (tûr'kish) *n.* The language of Turkey. —*adj.* Of or pertaining to Turkey, its people, or their language.

Turkish bath A bath in which sweating is induced by exposure to high temperature, usu. in a room heated by steam.

Turkish Empire OTTOMAN EMPIRE.

Turkish towel A heavy, rough towel with loose, uncut pile. Also **turkish towel.**

tur·mer·ic (tûr'mər·ik, t$\overline{oo}$'mə·rik) *n.* 1 The orange-red, aromatic root of an East Indian plant; used as a condiment, dyestuff, etc. 2 The plant. 3 Any of several plants resembling turmeric. [? < F *terre mérite* deserving earth]

tur·moil (tûr'moil) *n.* Confused motion; disturbance; tumult. [?]

turn (tûrn) *v.t.* 1 To cause to rotate, as about an axis. 2 To change the position of, as by rotating: to *turn* a trunk on its side. 3 To move so that the upper side becomes the under: to *turn* a page. 4 To reverse the arrangement or order of; cause to be upside down. 5 To ponder: often with *over.* 6 To sprain or strain: to *turn* one's ankle in running. 7 To make sick or disgusted: The sight *turns* my stomach. 8 To shape in a lathe. 9 To give rounded or curved form to. 10 To give graceful or finished form to: to *turn* a phrase. 11 To perform by revolving: to *turn* cartwheels. 12 To bend, curve, fold, or twist. 13 To bend or blunt (the edge of a knife, etc.). 14 To change or transform: to *turn* water into wine. 15 To translate: to *turn* French into English. 16 To exchange for an equivalent: to *turn* stocks into cash. 17 To cause to become as specified: The sight *turned* him sick. 18 To make sour or rancid; ferment or curdle. 19 To change the direction of. 20 To change the direction or focus of (thought, attention, etc.). 21 To deflect or divert: to *turn* a blow. 22 To repel: to *turn* a charge. 23 To go around: to *turn* a corner. 24 To pass or go beyond: to *turn* twenty-one. 25 To compel to go; drive: to *turn* a beggar from one's door. —*v.i.* 26 To rotate; revolve. 27 To move completely or partially on or as if on an axis: He *turned* and ran. 28 To change position, as in bed. 29 To take a new direction: We *turned* north. 30 To reverse position; become inverted. 31 To reverse direction or flow: The tide has *turned.* 32 To change the direction of one's thought, attention, etc.: Let us *turn* to the next problem. 33 To depend; hinge: with *on* or *upon.* 34 To be affected with giddiness; whirl, as the head. 35 To become upset, as the stomach. 36 To change attitude, sympathy, or allegiance: to *turn* on one's neighbors. 37 To become transformed; change: The water *turned* into ice. 38 To become as specified: His hair *turned* gray. 39 To change color: said esp. of leaves. 40 To become sour or fermented, as milk or wine. —**turn against** To become or cause to become opposed or hostile to. —**turn down** 1 To diminish the flow, volume, etc., of: *Turn down* the gas. 2 *Informal.* **a** To reject or refuse, as a proposal, or request. **b** To refuse the request, proposal, etc., of. —**turn in** 1 To fold or double. 2 To bend or incline inward. 3 To deliver; hand over. 4 *Informal* To go to bed. —**turn off** 1 To stop the operation, flow, etc., of. 2 To leave the direct road; make a turn. 3 To deflect or

divert. 4 *Slang* To cause (a person) to lose interest in or liking for. —**turn on** 1 To set in operation, flow, etc.: to *turn on* an engine. 2 *Slang* To experience the effects of taking a psychedelic drug. 3 *Slang* To arrange for (someone) to take such a drug. 4 *Slang* To evoke in (someone) a profound or rapt response. —**turn out** 1 To turn inside out. 2 To eject or expel. 3 To bend or incline outward. 4 To produce or make. 5 To come or go out: to *turn out* for a meeting. 6 To prove (to be). 7 To equip or fit; dress. 8 *Informal* To get out of bed. —**turn over** 1 To change the position of. 2 To upset; overturn. 3 To hand over; transfer. 4 To do business to the amount of. 5 To invest and get back (capital). —**turn to** 1 To set to work. 2 To seek aid from. 3 To refer or apply to. —**turn up** 1 To fold the under side upward. 2 To incline upward. 3 To find or be found: to *turn up* new evidence. 4 To increase the flow, volume, etc., of. 5 To arrive. —*n.* 1 The act of turning, or the state of being turned. 2 A change to another direction or position: a *turn* of the tide. 3 A deflection from a course; a bend. 4 The point at which a change takes place: a *turn* for the better. 5 A rotation or revolution: the *turn* of a crank. 6 A regular time or chance in some sequence of action: It's his *turn* at bat. 7 Characteristic form or style. 8 Disposition; tendency: a humorous *turn.* 9 A deed: an ill *turn.* 10 A walk or drive: a *turn* in the park. 11 A round in a skein or coil. 12 *Music* An ornament in which the main tone alternates with the seconds above and below. 13 *Informal* A spell of dizziness or nervousness: The explosion gave me quite a *turn.* 14 A variation or difference in type or kind. 15 A short theatrical act. 16 A twist, as of a rope, around a tree or post. 17 A business transaction. —**at every turn** On every occasion; constantly. —**by turns** 1 In alternation or sequence: also **turn by turn.** 2 At intervals. —**in turn** One after another. —**out of turn** Not in proper order or sequence. —**to a turn** Just right: meat browned *to a turn.* —**take turns** To act, play, etc. in proper order. [< L *tornare* turn in a lathe < *turnus* a lathe] —**turn'er** *n.*

turn·a·bout (tûrn'ə·bout') *n.* 1 The act of turning about so as to face the opposite direction. 2 An about-face in allegiance, opinion, etc.

turn·a·round (tûrn'ə·round') *n.* 1 The time required for maintenance, refueling, discharging or loading cargo, etc., during a round trip of a ship, aircraft, etc. 2 A space, as in a driveway, large enough for the turning around of a vehicle. 3 A shift or reversal of a trend, procedure, development, etc.

turn·buck·le (tûrn'buk'əl) *n. Mech.* A threaded coupling that receives a threaded rod at each end so that it may be turned to regulate the distance between them.

turn·coat (tûrn'kōt') *n.* One who goes over to the opposite side or party; a renegade.

turn·down (tûrn'doun') *adj.* Folded down or able to be folded down, as a collar. —*n.* 1 A rejection. 2 A decline: a *turndown* in prices.

turn·ing (tûr'ning) *n.* 1 The art of shaping wood, metal, etc., in a lathe. 2 *pl.* Spiral shavings produced by turning wood or metal on a lathe. 3 A winding; bend.

turning point The point of decisive change, as in progress, decline, etc.

tur·nip (tûr'nip) *n.* 1 The fleshy, yellow or white edible root of certain plants related to cabbage. 2 Any of these plants. [< Earlier *turnepe*]

turn·key (tûrn'kē') *n.* One who has charge of the keys of a prison; a jailer. —*adj.* Of, pertaining to, or being, by prearrangement with a buyer, a product or service in complete readiness for use when purchased: a *turnkey* housing project.

turn·out (tûrn'out') *n.* 1 A turning out. 2 An assemblage of persons, as at a meeting: a good *turnout.* 3 A quantity produced; output. 4 Array; equipment; outfit. 5 A railroad siding. 6 A carriage or wagon with its horses and equipage.

turn·o·ver (tûrn'ō'vər) *n.* 1 An upset. 2 A change or revolution: a *turnover* in affairs. 3 A tart made by covering half of a circular crust with fruit, jelly, etc., and turning the other half over on top. 4 The amount of money taken in and paid out in a business within a given period. 5 The selling out and restocking of goods, as in a store. 6 The rate at which persons hired within a given period are

replaced by others; also, the number of persons hired. —
adj. Turning over, or capable of being turned over.

turn·pike (tûrn′pīk′) *n.* 1 A road on which there are, or formerly were, tollgates: also **turnpike road. 2 TOLLGATE.** [ME *turnpyke* a spiked road barrier < TURN, *v.* + PIKE¹]

turn·stile (tûrn′stīl′) *n.* A kind of gate consisting of a vertical post and horizontal arms which by revolving permit persons to pass.

turn·stone (tûrn′stōn′) *n.* A ploverlike migratory bird that turns over stones when searching for food.

turn·ta·ble (tûrn′tā′bəl) *n.* 1 A rotating platform, usu. circular, on which to turn a locomotive or other vehicle around. 2 The revolving disk of a phonograph on which records are played.

tur·pen·tine (tûr′pən·tīn) *n.* 1 A resinous, oily liquid obtained from any of several coniferous trees. 2 The colorless essential oil (**oil of turpentine**) formed when turpentine is distilled, widely used in industry, medicine, and in mixing paints. —*v.t.* **·tined, ·tin·ing** To treat or saturate with turpentine. [< L *terebinthus* a Mediterranean tree]

tur·pi·tude (tûr′pə·t/ōōd) *n.* Inherent baseness; depravity. [< L *turpis* vile] —**Syn.** corruption, degeneracy, vileness, wickedness.

tur·quoise (tûr′koiz, -kwoiz) *n.* 1 A blue or blue-green stone, esteemed as a gemstone when highly polished. 2 A light, greenish blue: also **turquoise blue.** —*adj.* Light, greenish blue. [< MF *(pierre) turquoise* Turkish (stone)]

tur·ret (tûr′it) *n.* 1 A small projecting tower, usu. at the corner of a building. 2 *Mil.* A rotating armed structure containing guns and gunners, forming part of a warship or tank. 3 A structure for a gunner on a combat airplane, usu. enclosed in transparent plastic material. [< OF *tor* tower] —**tur′ret·ed** *adj.*

tur·tle (tûr′təl) *n.* 1 Any of numerous four-limbed, terrestrial or aquatic reptiles having a toothless beak and a soft body encased in a shell. 2 The edible flesh of certain turtles. —**turn turtle** To overturn; capsize. [?< Sp. *tortuga* < Med. L *tortuca* tortoise] • See SNAPPING TURTLE.

tur·tle·dove (tûr′təl·duv′) *n.* 1 A dove noted for its plaintive cooing. 2 The mourning dove. [< L *turtur* turtledove]

Turtle

tur·tle·neck (tûr′təl·nek′) *n.* 1 A pullover sweater or knitted shirt with a high, close-fitting, turnover collar. 2 Such a collar.

tusk (tusk) *n.* A long, projecting tooth, as in the boar, walrus, or elephant. —*v.t.* To use the tusks to gore, root up, etc. [< OE *tūx*]

tus·sah (tus′ə) *n.* 1 An Asian silkworm that spins large cocoons of brownish or yellowish silk. 2 The silk, or the fabric woven from it. [< Skt. *tasara* a shuttle]

tus·sle (tus′əl) *v.t. & v.i.* **·sled, ·sling** 1 To scuffle or struggle. 2 To argue. —*n.* 1 A scuffle or struggle. 2 An argument. [Var. of TOUSLE]

tus·sock (tus′ək) *n.* 1 A tuft or clump of grass or sedge. 2 A tuft, as of hair or feathers. [?] —**tus′sock·y** *adj.*

tut (tut) *interj.* An exclamation to express impatience.

tu·te·lage (t/ōō′tə·lij) *n.* 1 The state of being under the care of a tutor or guardian. 2 The act or office of a guardian. 3 The act of tutoring; instruction. [< L *tutela* a watching, guardianship]

tu·te·lar·y (t/ōō′tə·ler′ē) *adj.* 1 Watching over; protecting. 2 Of or pertaining to a guardian. Also **tu′te·lar.** —*n. pl.* **·ar·ies** A guardian spirit, divinity, or saint.

tu·tor (t/ōō′tər) *n.* 1 A private teacher. 2 A college teacher who gives individual instruction. 3 *Brit.* A college official entrusted with the tutelage and care of undergraduates assigned to him. —*v.t.* 1 To act as tutor to; train. 2 To treat sternly; discipline. —*v.i.* 3 To do the work of a tutor. 4 To be tutored or instructed. [< L, a watcher, guardian]

tu·to·ri·al (t/ōō·tôr′ē·əl) *adj.* Of or involving tutors, or based upon their participation: the *tutorial* system. —*n.* A small class of students guided by a tutor.

tut·ti (tōō′tē) *Music adj.* All: used to indicate that all performers take part. —*n.* A passage or section to be performed by all the voices and instruments together. [< Ital. *tutto* all]

tut·ti-frut·ti (tōō′tē-frōō′tē) *n.* A confection, chewing gum, ice cream, etc., made or flavored with mixed fruits. —*adj.* Flavored with mixed fruits. [Ital., all fruits]

tu·tu (tōō′tōō; *Fr.* tü′tü) *n.* A short, projecting, layered skirt worn by ballet dancers. [F]

tux·e·do (tuk·sē′dō) *n. pl.* **·dos** 1 A man's semiformal dinner or evening jacket without tails. 2 The suit of which the jacket is a part. Also **Tux·e′do.** [< *Tuxedo* Park, N.Y.]

TV (tē′vē′) *n.* TELEVISION.

TV terminal velocity.

TVA, T.V.A. Tennessee Valley Authority.

TV dinner A frozen meal in a partitioned tray, ready to be heated and served.

twad·dle (twod′l) *v.t. & v.i.* **·dled, ·dling** To talk foolishly and pretentiously. —*n.* Pretentious, silly talk. [?] —**twad′·dler** *n.*

twain (twān) *adj. & n. Archaic* Two. [< OE *twēgen* two]

twang (twang) *v.t. & v.i.* **twanged, twang·ing** 1 To make or cause to make a sharp, vibrant sound. 2 To utter or speak with a harsh, nasal sound. —*n.* 1 A sharp, vibrating sound. 2 A sharp, nasal sound of the voice. 3 A sound resembling these. [Imit.] —**twang′y** *adj.* (**·i·er, ·i·est**)

tweak (twēk) *v.t.* To pinch and twist sharply. —*n.* A twisting pinch. [< OE *twiccan* twitch]

tweed (twēd) *n.* 1 A woolen fabric often woven in two or more colors to effect a check or plaid pattern. 2 *pl.* Clothes made of tweed. [< Scot. *tweel*, var. of TWILL]

twee·dle (twēd′l) *v.* **·dled, ·dling** *v.t.* 1 To play (a musical instrument) casually or carelessly. —*v.i.* 2 To produce a series of shrill tones. 3 To play a musical instrument casually or carelessly. —*n.* A sound so produced. [Imit. of the sound of a reed pipe]

tweet (twēt) *v.i.* To utter a thin, chirping note. —*n.* A twittering or chirping. [Imit.]

tweet·er (twē′tər) *n.* A loudspeaker specially designed to reproduce only high-frequency sounds.

tweeze (twēz) *v.t.* **tweezed, tweez·ing** *Informal* To handle, pinch, pluck, etc., with tweezers.

tweez·ers (twē′zərz) *n.pl.* (*construed as sing. or pl.*) Small pincers for picking up or extracting tiny objects. Also **pair of tweezers.** [< F *étui* a small case]

twelfth (twelfth) *adj. & adv.* Next in order after the 11th. —*n.* 1 The element of an ordered set that corresponds to the number 12. 2 One of 12 equal parts. [< OE *twelfta*]

Twelfth Day The twelfth day after Christmas; Epiphany.

twelve (twelv) *n.* 1 The sum of eleven plus one; 12; XII. 2 A set or group of 12 members. —**the Twelve** The twelve apostles. [< OE *twelf*] —**twelve** *adj., pron.*

Twelve Apostles The twelve original disciples of Jesus.

twelve·month (twelv′munth′) *n.* A year.

twelve-tone (twelv′tōn′) *adj. Music* Of, pertaining to, or composed in a system in which any series of all twelve tones of the chromatic scale is used as the basis of composition.

twen·ti·eth (twen′tē·ith) *adj. & adv.* Tenth in order after the tenth. —*n.* 1 The element of an ordered set that corresponds to the number 20. 2 One of 20 equal parts.

twen·ty (twen′tē) *n. pl.* **·ties** 1 The sum of 19 plus 1; 20; XX. 2 A set or group of 20 members. 3 The numbers, years, etc., from 20 to 30. [< OE *twentig*] —**twen′ty** *adj., pron.*

twen·ty-one (twen′tē·wun′) *n.* BLACKJACK (def. 3).

twice (twīs) *adv.* 1 Two times. 2 In double measure; doubly. [< OE *twiga*]

twid·dle (twid′l) *v.* **·dled, ·dling** *v.t.* 1 To twirl idly; play with. —*v.i.* 2 To toy with something idly. 3 To be busy about trifles. —**twiddle one's thumbs** 1 To rotate one's thumbs around each other. 2 To do nothing; be idle. —*n.* A gentle twirling. [Prob. < ON *tridla* stir] —**twid′dler** *n.*

twig (twig) *n.* A small shoot or branch of a woody plant. [< OE *twigge*]

twi·light (twī′līt′) n. 1 The light diffused over the sky after sunset and before sunrise. 2 The period during which this light prevails. 3 Any faint light; shade. 4 An obscure condition following the waning of past glory, achievements, etc. —adj. Pertaining or peculiar to twilight. [< OE < twa two + LIGHT]

twilight sleep A light anesthesia induced by morphine and scopolamine, formerly used in childbirth.

twill (twil) n. 1 Cloth woven in such a way as to produce diagonal, parallel ribs or lines. 2 The pattern formed by such weaving. —v.t. To weave (cloth) with a twill. [< OE twili a twilled fabric]

Twill

twin (twin) n. 1 Either of two young produced at the same birth. 2 Either of two persons or things greatly alike. —the Twins GEMINI. —adj. 1 Being a twin or twins: twin boys. 2 Being one of a pair of similar and closely related people or things. —v. twinned, twin·ning v.i. 1 To bring forth twins. 2 To be matched or equal. —v.t. 3 To bring forth as twins. 4 To couple; match. [< OE twinn, getwinn]

twine (twīn) v. twined, twin·ing v.t. 1 To twist together, as threads. 2 To form by such twisting. 3 To coil or wrap about something. 4 To encircle by winding or wreathing. —v.i. 5 To interlace. 6 To proceed in a winding course; meander. —n. 1 A string composed of two or more strands twisted together. 2 The act of twining or entwining. 3 A thing produced by twining. [< OE twīn a twisted double thread < twa two] —twin′er n. —twin′ing·ly adv.

twinge (twinj) v.t. & v.i. twinged, twing·ing To affect with or suffer a sudden pain. —n. 1 A sharp, darting, local pain. 2 A mental pang. [< OE twengan pinch] —Syn. n. 1 ache, cramp, throe.

twin·kle (twing′kəl) v. ·kled, ·kling v.i. 1 To shine with fitful, intermittent gleams. 2 To be bright, as with amusement: Her eyes twinkled. 3 To wink or blink. 4 To move rapidly to and fro; flicker: twinkling feet. —v.t. 5 To cause to twinkle. 6 To emit (light) in fitful, intermittent gleams. —n. 1 A tremulous gleam of light; glimmer. 2 A quick or repeated movement of the eyelids. 3 An instant; a twinkling. [< OE twinclian] —twin′kler n.

twin·kling (twing′kling) n. 1 The act of something that twinkles. 2 A wink or twinkle. 3 An instant; moment. — twink′ling·ly adv.

twirl (twûrl) v.t. & v.i. 1 To whirl or rotate rapidly. 2 To twist or curl. 3 In baseball, to pitch. —n. 1 A whirling motion. 2 A curl; twist; coil. [?] —twirl′er n.

twist (twist) v.t. 1 To wind (strands, etc.) around each other. 2 To form by such winding: to twist thread. 3 To give a spiral shape to. 4 To deform or distort, esp. by means of torque. 5 To distort the meaning of. 6 To confuse; perplex. 7 To wreathe, twine, or wrap. 8 To cause to revolve or rotate. 9 To impart spin to (a ball) so that it moves in a curve. —v.i. 10 To become twisted. 11 To move in a winding course. 12 To squirm; writhe. —n. 1 The act, manner, or result of twisting. 2 The state of being twisted. 3 Physics A torsional strain. 4 A curve; turn; bend. 5 A wrench; strain, as of a joint or limb. 6 A peculiar inclination or attitude: a mind with a criminal twist. 7 An unexpected turn or development. 8 A variant or novel approach or method: a mystery novel with a new twist. 9 Thread or cord made of tightly twisted or braided strands. 10 A twisted roll of bread. 11 A spin given to a ball by a certain stroke or throw. [< OE -twist a rope]

twist·er (twis′tər) n. 1 One who or that which twists. 2 In baseball, a curve. 3 A tornado; cyclone.

twit (twit) v.t. twit·ted, twit·ting To taunt. —n. A taunting allusion; reproach. [< OE ætwitan] —twit′ter n. —Syn. v. gibe, jeer, scoff, tease.

twitch (twich) v.t. 1 To pull sharply; pluck with a jerky movement. —v.i. 2 To move with a quick, spasmodic jerk, as a muscle. —n. 1 A sudden involuntary contraction of a muscle. 2 A sudden jerk or pull. [ME twicchen]

twit·ter (twit′ər) v.i. 1 To utter a series of light chirping or tremulous notes, as a bird. 2 To titter. 3 To be excited.

—v.t. 4 To utter or express with a twitter. —n. 1 A succession of light, tremulous sounds. 2 A state of excitement. [Imit.]

'twixt (twikst) prep. Betwixt.

two (tōō) n. 1 The sum of one plus one; 2; II. 2 A set or group of two members. —in two Bisected; asunder —put two and two together To draw an obvious conclusion by considering the facts. [< OE twā, tū] —two adj., pron.

two-base hit (tōō′bās′) In baseball, a hit in which the batter reaches second base without benefit of an error. Also two′-bag′ger (-bag′ər).

two-bit (tōō′bit′) adj. Slang Cheap; small-time: a two-bit gambler.

two bits Informal Twenty-five cents.

two-by-four (tōō′bī·fôr′, -fōr′) adj. 1 Measuring two inches by four inches. 2 Slang Narrow or cramped: a two-by-four kitchen. —n. (tōō′bī·fôr′, -fōr′) A timber measuring two inches in thickness and four inches in width before finishing.

two-edged (tōō′ejd′) adj. 1 Having an edge on each side; cutting both ways. 2 Having a double meaning.

two-faced (tōō′fāst′) adj. 1 Having two faces. 2 Double-dealing; insincere. —two′-fac′ed·ly (-fā′sid·lē, -fāst′lē) adv. —two′fac′ed·ness n.

two-fer (tōō′fər) n. 1 An article sold at two for the price of one. 2 A free coupon entitling the holder to buy two theater tickets for the price of one.

two-fold (tōō′fōld′) adj. Double. —adv. In a twofold manner or degree; doubly.

two-hand·ed (tōō′han′did) adj. 1 Requiring the use of both hands at once. 2 Constructed for use by two persons: a two-handed saw. 3 Ambidextrous. 4 Having two hands. 5 Played by two people: a two-handed card game.

two·pence (tup′əns) n. Brit. 1 Two pennies. 2 A silver coin of the same value, now issued only for alms money on Maundy Thursday. 3 A trifle; small amount.

two·pen·ny (tup′ən·ē) adj. Brit. 1 Of the value of twopence. 2 Cheap; worthless.

two-ply (tōō′plī′) adj. 1 Woven double: a two-ply carpet. 2 Made of two strands or thicknesses of material.

two·some (tōō′səm) n. 1 Two persons together. 2 A game played by two persons. 3 The players.

two-step (tōō′step′) n. 1 A ballroom dance step in 2/4 time. 2 The music for it. —v.i. To do the two-step.

two-time (tōō′tīm′) v.t. -timed, -tim·ing Slang 1 To be unfaithful to. 2 DOUBLE-CROSS. —two′-tim′er n.

two-way (tōō′wā′) adj. 1 Permitting vehicles to go in opposite directions simultaneously: a two-way street. 2 Involving mutual or reciprocal exchanges, duties, obligations, etc.: a two-way agreement. 3 Involving two persons, groups, etc.: a two-way contest. 4 Capable of both sending and receiving communications: a two-way radio. 5 Made or fashioned so as to be used or worn in two ways: a two-way jacket.

twp. township.

TX Texas (P.O. abbr.)

-ty¹ suffix of nouns The state or condition of being: sanity. [< L -tas]

-ty² suffix Ten; ten times: used in numerals, as thirty, forty, etc. [< OE -tig ten]

Ty. Territory.

ty·coon (tī·kōōn′) n. 1 Informal A wealthy and powerful business leader. 2 A Japanese shogun. [< Japanese taikun a mighty lord]

ty·ing (tī′ing) pr.p. of TIE.

tyke (tīk) n. 1 A mongrel dog. 2 Informal A small mischievous child. [< ON tik bitch]

tym·pa·ni (tim′pə·nē) n.pl. TIMPANI.

tympanic membrane The membrane separating the middle ear from the external ear; the eardrum.

tym·pa·nist (tim′pə·nist) n. One who plays the timpani.

tym·pa·num (tim′pə·nəm) n. pl. ·na (-nə) or ·nums 1 Anat. a The cavity of the middle ear lined with the tympanic membrane. b TYMPANIC MEMBRANE. 2 A drum. 3 Archit. a A recessed, usu. triangular, space bounded by the sides of a pediment or gable at the end of a building. b A similar space over a door or window, between the lintel and the arch. [< Gk. tympanon a drum] —tym·pan·ic (tim·pan′ik) adj.

typ., typo., typog. typographer; typographic; typography.

type (tīp) *n.* 1 A class or group having traits and characteristics in common: an old *type* of car. 2 A standard or model. 3 The characteristic plan, form, style, etc., of a given class or group. 4 A person, animal, or object embodying the characteristics of a class or group. 5 *Printing* a A piece or block of metal or of wood bearing, usu. in relief, a letter or character for use in printing. b Such pieces collectively. 6 Typewritten or printed letters and numerals. 7 The characteristic device on either side of a medal or coin. —*v.* **typed, typ·ing** *v.t.* 1 To represent; typify. 2 To determine the type of; identify: to *type* a blood sample. 3 TYPEWRITE. 4 To prefigure. —*v.i.* 5 TYPEWRITE. [< Gk. *typos* an impression, figure, type]

-type *combining form* 1 Representative form; stamp; type: *prototype.* 2 Used in or produced by duplicating processes or by type: *Linotype.* [< Gk. *typos* stamp]

type·face (tīp′fās′) *n.* 1 A set of type of a particular design. 2 The face or impression of a type.

type·set·ter (tīp′set′ər) *n.* 1 One who sets type. 2 A machine for setting type. —**type′set′ting** *adj., n.*

type·write (tīp′rīt′) *v.t. & v.i.* **·wrote, ·writ·ten, ·writ·ing** To write with a typewriter.

type·writ·er (tīp′rī′tər) *n.* 1 A keyboard machine for producing characters, as letters, numbers, etc., that have the appearance of printer's type. 2 A typist.

ty·phoid (tī′foid) *adj.* 1 Pertaining to or resembling typhoid fever: also **ty·phoi′dal.** 2 Resembling typhus. —*n.* TYPHOID FEVER.

typhoid fever A serious infectious disease caused by a bacillus transmitted in contaminated water or food and characterized by high fever, severe intestinal disturbances, and prostration.

ty·phoon (tī·fōōn′) *n.* A violent tropical storm, occurring in the w Pacific. [< Chin. *tai feng,* lit., big wind]

ty·phus (tī′fəs) *n.* Any of a group of contagious rickettsial diseases marked by high fever, a rash, nervous and mental disorders, and extreme prostration. [< Gk. *typhos* smoke, a stupor] —**ty′phous** *adj.*

typ·i·cal (tip′i·kəl) *adj.* 1 Having the nature or character of a type: a *typical* schoolboy. 2 Characteristic or representative of a group, class, etc.: *typical* middle-class values. [< Gk. *typos* TYPE] —**typ′i·cal·ly** *adv.* —**typ′i·cal·ness** *n.*

typ·i·fy (tip′ə-fī) *v.t.* **·fied, ·fy·ing** 1 To represent by a type. 2 To serve as a characteristic example of. —**typ′i·fi·ca′tion** (-fə·kā′shən), **typ′i·fi′er** *n.*

typ·ist (tī′pist) *n.* 1 One who uses a typewriter. 2 A person whose work is operating a typewriter.

ty·po (tī′pō) *n. pl.* **ty·pos** *Informal* An error made by a printer or a typist. [< *typo(graphical error)*]

ty·pog·ra·pher (tī·pog′rə-fər) *n.* An expert in typography, esp. a printer or compositor.

ty·po·graph·i·cal (tī′pə-graf′i·kəl) *adj.* Of or pertaining to printing. Also **ty′po·graph′ic.** —**ty′po·graph′i·cal·ly** *adv.*

ty·pog·ra·phy (tī·pog′rə-fē) *n.* 1 The arrangement, style, and appearance of printed matter. 2 The act or art of composing and printing from types.

typw. typewriter; typewritten.

ty·ran·ni·cal (ti-ran′i·kəl, tī-) *adj.* Of or like a tyrant; despotic; arbitrary. Also **ty·ran′nic.** —**ty·ran′ni·cal·ly** *adv.* —**ty·ran′ni·cal·ness** *n.*

ty·ran·ni·cide (ti-ran′ə·sīd, tī-) *n.* 1 The slayer of a tyrant. 2 The slaying of a tyrant.

tyr·an·nize (tir′ə·nīz) *v.* **·nized, ·niz·ing** *v.i.* 1 To exercise power cruelly or unjustly. 2 To rule as a tyrant; have absolute power. —*v.t.* 3 To treat tyrannically; domineer. —**tyr′an·niz′er** *n.*

tyr·an·nous (tir′ə·nəs) *adj.* Despotic; tyrannical. —**tyr′an·nous·ly** *adv.* —**tyr′an·nous·ness** *n.*

tyr·an·ny (tir′ə·nē) *n. pl.* **·nies** 1 The office, power, or jurisdiction of a tyrant. 2 A government or ruler having absolute power; despot or despotism. 3 Power used in a cruel or oppressive manner. 4 Harsh rigor; severity. 5 A tyrannical act. [< L *tyrannus* a tyrant]

ty·rant (tī′rənt) *n.* 1 One who rules oppressively or cruelly; a despot. 2 Any person who exercises power or authority in a harsh, cruel manner. [< Gk. *tyrannos* a master, a usurper]

tyre (tīr) *n. Brit. sp.* of TIRE².

Tyre (tīr) *n.* A port and capital of ancient Phoenicia, now in sw Lebanon.

ty·ro (tī′rō) *n. pl.* **·ros** One who is beginning to learn or study something; novice. [< L *tiro* a recruit]

tzar (tsär) *n.* CZAR.

tzet·ze (tset′sē) *n.* TSETSE.

tzi·gane (tsē·gän′) *n.* A Gypsy, esp. a Hungarian Gypsy. [F < Hung. *czigány*]

U

U, u (yōō) *n. pl.* **U's, u's, Us, us** (yōōz) 1 The twenty-first letter of the English alphabet. 2 Any spoken sound representing the letter *U* or *u.* 3 Something shaped like a U. —*adj.* Shaped like a U.

U uranium.

U., u. uncle; union; unit; university.

U.A.R. United Arab Republic.

UAW, U.A.W. United Automobile Workers; (officially) United Automobile, Aerospace, and Agricultural Implement Workers of America.

u·biq·ui·tous (yōō·bik′wə·təs) *adj.* Existing, or seeming to exist, everywhere at once; omnipresent. —**u·biq′ui·tous·ly** *adv.* —**u·biq′ui·tous·ness** *n.*

u·biq·ui·ty (yōō·bik′wə·tē) *n.* The state of being or seeming to be everywhere at the same time; omnipresence, real or seeming. [< L *ubique* everywhere]

U-boat (yōō′bōt′) *n.* A German submarine. [< G *U-boot,* contraction of *Unterseeboot,* lit., undersea boat]

u.c. upper case (printing).

ud·der (ud′ər) *n.* A large, pendulous, milk-secreting gland having nipples or teats for the suckling of offspring, as in cows. [< OE *ūder*]

UFO (yōō′ef·ō′) *n. pl.* **UFOs, UFO's** Any of various unidentified flying objects alleged to have been seen traveling at speeds and following courses that would be impossible for any aircraft to duplicate. [< *u(nidentified) f(lying) o(bject)*]

U·gan·da (yōō·gan′də, ōō·gän′dä), *n.* An independent member of the Commonwealth of Nations in CEN. Africa, 93,981 sq. mi., cap. Kampala. • See map at AFRICA.

ugh (ug, ukh, u, ŏŏkh, ōō) *interj.* An exclamation of repugnance or disgust. [Imit.]

ug·li·fy (ug′lə·fī′) *v.t.* **·fied, ·fy·ing** To make ugly. —**ug′li·fi·ca′tion** (-fə·kā′shən) *n.*

ug·ly (ug′lē) *adj.* **·li·er, ·li·est** 1 Distasteful in appearance; unsightly. 2 Distasteful to any of the senses. 3 Morally revolting or repulsive. 4 Bad in character or consequences, as a rumor or a wound. 5 Ill-tempered; quarrelsome. 6 Portending storms; threatening. [< ON *uggligr* dreadful < *uggr* fear] —**ug′li·ly** *adv.* —**ug′li·ness** *n.* —**Syn.** 1 homely, ill-looking, unlovely, unseemly. 2 repulsive, repellent, repugnant, revolting, abhorrent, disgusting. 5 ill-humored, irascible, irritable, testy, querulous.

ugly duckling Any ill-favored or unpromising child who unexpectedly grows into a beauty or a wonder. [< *The Ugly Duckling,* a story by Hans Christian Andersen]

U·gri·an (ōō′grē·ən, yōō′-) *n.* 1 A member of any of the Finno-Ugric peoples of Hungary and w Siberia. 2 UGRIC.

—*adj.* Of or pertaining to the Ugrians or their languages.

U·gric (ōō'grik, yōō'-) *n.* A branch of the Finno-Ugric subfamily of languages including Magyar (Hungarian). —*adj.* UGRIAN.

UHF, U.H.F., uhf, u.h.f. ultrahigh frequency.

ult·land·er (ĭt'lan·dər, oit'-; *Afrikaans* œit'län·dər) *n.* Often *cap.* A foreigner; outlander. [Afrikaans]

U.K. United Kingdom.

u·kase (yōō·kās', -kāz', yōō'kās, ōō·koz') *n.* 1 In imperial Russia, an edict or decree of the czar. 2 Any official decree. [<Russ. *ukaz*]

U·krain·i·an (yōō·krā'nē·ən, -krī'-) *adj.* Of or pertaining to the Ukraine, its people, or their language. —*n.* 1 A native or inhabitant of the Ukraine. 2 An East Slavic language spoken in the Ukraine.

u·ku·le·le (yōō'kə·lā'lē; *Hawaiian* ōō'kōō·lā'lä) *n.* A small, guitarlike musical instrument having four strings. [Hawaiian <*uku* insect + *lele* jump; from the movements of the fingers in playing]

Ukulele

ul·cer (ul'sər) *n.* 1 An open sore on skin or mucous membrane with disintegration of tissue. 2 Any evil or corrupt condition or vice. [<L *ulcus, ulceris*] —**ul'cer·ous** *adj.* —**ul'cer·ous·ly** *adv.*

ul·cer·ate (ul'sə·rāt) *v.t.* & *v.i.* **·at·ed, ·at·ing** To make or become ulcerous. —**ul'cer·a'tion** *n.* —**ul'cer·a'tive** *adj.*

-ule *suffix* Small; little: used to form diminutives: *granule.* [<L *-ulus*]

-ulent *suffix* Abounding in; full of (what is indicated in the main element): *opulent, truculent.* [<L *-ulentus*]

ul·na (ul'nə) *n. pl.* **·nae** (-nē) *or* **·nas** 1 The larger of the two bones of the forearm on the same side as the little finger. 2 The homologous bone in the foreleg of a quadruped. [< L, elbow] —**ul'nar** *adj.* • See HUMERUS.

ul·ster (ul'stər) *n.* A long, loose overcoat, sometimes belted at the waist, made originally of Irish frieze. [< *Ulster,* Ireland]

ult. ultimate; ultimately.

ul·te·ri·or (ul·tir'ē·ər) *adj.* 1 Not as pertinent as something else: *ulterior* considerations. 2 Intentionally unrevealed; hidden: *ulterior* motives. 3 Later in time, or secondary in importance; following; succeeding. 4 Lying beyond or on the farther side of a certain bounding line. [<L, compar. of *ulter* beyond] —**ul·te'ri·or·ly** *adv.*

ul·ti·ma (ul'tə·mə) *n.* The last syllable of a word. [<L, fem. of *ultimus* last]

ul·ti·mate (ul'tə·mit) *adj.* 1 Beyond which there is no other; maximum, greatest, utmost, etc. 2 Last; final, as of a series. 3 Most distant or remote; farthest. 4 Not susceptible of further analysis; elementary; primary. —*n.* The best, latest, most fundamental, etc., of something. [<L *ultimus* farthest, last, superl. of *ulter* beyond] —**ul'ti·mate·ness** *n.*

ul·ti·mate·ly (ul'tə·mit·lē) *adv.* In the end; at last; finally.

ul·ti·ma Thu·le (ul'tə·mə thōō'lē, tōō'lē) 1 In ancient geography, Thule, the northernmost habitable regions of the earth. 2 Any distant, unknown region. 3 The farthest possible point, degree, or limit.

ul·ti·ma·tum (ul'tə·mā'təm, -mä'-) *n. pl.* **·tums** *or* **·ta** (-tə) A final statement of terms, demands, or conditions, the rejection of which usu. results in a breaking off of all negotiations, a resorting to force, etc. [<L *ultimus* last, ultimate]

ul·ti·mo (ul'tə·mō) *adv.* In the month preceding the present month. [L]

ul·tra (ul'trə) *adj.* Going beyond the bounds of moderation; extreme. —*n.* One who holds extreme opinions. [<L, beyond, on the other side]

ultra- *prefix* 1 On the other side of; beyond in space: *ultramarine.* 2 Going beyond the limits or range of: *ultrasonic.* 3 Beyond what is usual or natural; extremely or excessively; *ultraconservative.*

ul·tra·high frequency (ul'trə·hī') Any wave frequency between 300 and 3,000 megahertz.

ul·tra·ist (ul'trə·ist) *n.* One who goes to extremes in opinions, conduct, etc.; extremist. —*adj.* Radical; extreme: also **ul'tra·is'tic.** —**ul'tra·ism** *n.*

ul·tra·light (ul'trə·līt') *adj.* Extremely light in weight. —*n.* An extremely lightweight airplane.

ul·tra·ma·rine (ul'trə·mə·rēn') *n.* 1 A deep purplish blue pigment. 2 The color of ultramarine. —*adj.* Beyond or across the sea. [<L *ultra* beyond + *mare* sea]

ul·tra·mi·cro·scope (ul'trə·mī'krə·skōp') *n.* A microscope in which objects too small to be seen by the transmitted light of an ordinary microscope are examined against a dark background by means of refracted light.

ul·tra·mi·cro·scop·ic (ul'trə·mī'krə·skop'ik) *adj.* 1 Too minute to be seen by an ordinary microscope. 2 Relating to the ultramicroscope. Also **ul'tra·mi'cro·scop'i·cal.**

ul·tra·mod·ern (ul'trə·mod'ərn) *adj.* Extremely modern, as in tastes, design, etc. —**ul'tra·mod'ern·ist** *n.*

ul·tra·son·ic (ul'trə·son'ik) *adj.* Pertaining to or designating sound waves having a frequency above the limits of audibility.

ul·tra·vi·o·let (ul'trə·vī'ə·lit) *adj.* Having wavelengths shorter than those of visible violet light and longer than those of X-rays.

ul·u·late (ul'yə·lāt', yōōl'yə·lāt') *v.i.* **·lat·ed, ·lat·ing** To howl, hoot, or wail. [<L *ululare*] —**ul'u·lant** *adj.*

U·lys·ses (yōō·lis'ēz) ODYSSEUS.

um·bel (um'bəl) *n.* A flower cluster having pedicels arising from a single point. [<L *umbella* a parasol, dim. of *umbra* shadow] —**um·bel·late** (um'bə·lit, -lāt), **um'bel·lat'ed** *adj.*

um·ber (um'bər) *n.* 1 A chestnut- to liver-brown iron oxide earth, used as a pigment. 2 The color of umber, either in its natural state (**raw umber**), or heated, so as to produce a reddish brown (**burnt umber**). —*adj.* 1 Of or pertaining to umber. 2 Of the color of umber. —*v.t.* To color with umber. [<F *(terre d')ombre*<Ital. *ombra*<L *umbra* shade, shadow]

um·bil·i·cal (um·bil'i·kəl) *adj.* 1 Pertaining to or situated near the umbilicus. 2 Placed near the navel; central. —*n.* 1 A long, flexible tube that serves as a connecting device, conduit for air, power, communication, etc., for an astronaut or aquanaut when outside the craft. 2 A similar device used as a source of fuel, etc., for a spacecraft before launching. [<L *umbilicus* navel]

umbilical cord 1 The ropelike structure connecting the navel of a fetus with the placenta. 2 UMBILICAL (*n.*).

um·bil·i·cus (um'bə·lī'kəs, -bil'i-) *n. pl.* **·ci** (-kī, -sī) 1 NAVEL. 2 A navel-shaped depression. [<L]

um·bra (um'brə) *n. pl.* **·bras** *or* **·brae** (-brē, -brī) 1 A shadow. 2 The cone of shadow cast at all times by a celestial body in the solar system. When the umbra of the moon strikes the earth, it creates an area of total solar eclipse. 3 The inner dark portion of a sunspot. [L, shadow]

um·brage (um'brij) *n.* 1 A feeling of anger or resentment, esp. in the phrase **take umbrage,** to have such feelings. 2 That which gives shade, as a leafy tree. 3 Shade or shadow. [<L *umbraticus* shady<*umbra* shade] —**um·bra'geous** (-brā'jəs) *adj.* —**um·bra'geous·ly** *adv.*

um·brel·la (um·brel'ə) *n.* 1 A light portable canopy on a folding frame, carried as a protection against sun or rain. 2 A usu. radial formation of military aircraft, used as a protective screen for operations on the ground or on water. 3 Something serving as a cover or shield, or as a means of linking together various things under a common name or sponsor: the expanding *umbrella* of nuclear power. [<L *umbella* parasol, dim. of *umbra* shadow]

umbrella tree A magnolia of the s U.S., with white flowers and umbrellalike whorls of leaves at the ends of the branches.

u·mi·ak (ōō'mē·ak') *n.* A large, open boat made of skins on a wooden frame. Also **u'mi·ack.** [Eskimo]

Umiak

um·laut (o͞om′lout) n. **1** Ling. **a** The change in quality of a vowel sound caused by its partial assimilation to a vowel or semivowel (often later lost) in the following syllable. **b** A vowel which has been so altered, as ä, ö, and ü in German. **2** In German, the two dots (ö) put over a vowel modified by umlaut. —v.t. To modify by umlaut. [G, change of sound < um about + laut sound]

um·pir·age (um′pīr·ij, -pə·rij) n. The office, function, or decision of an umpire. Also **um′pire·ship.**

um·pire (um′pīr) n. **1** A person called upon to settle a disagreement or dispute. **2** In various games, as baseball, a person chosen to enforce the rules of the game and to settle disputed points. —v.t. & v.i. **·pired, ·pir·ing** To act as umpire (of or in). [Alter. of ME noumpere]

ump·teen (ump′tēn′) adj. Slang Indeterminately large in number; very many. —**ump′teenth′** adj.

UMW, U.M.W. United Mine Workers.

un-¹ prefix Used in forming adjectives, adverbs, and less often nouns, to indicate: **1** Not; opposed or contrary to: unable, unmannerly. **2** Lack of: unease. [< OE] • See **UN-².**

un-² prefix Used in forming verbs to indicate: **1** Reversal of an action: untie. **2** Removal from something: unearth. **3** Deprivation of a condition or quality: unman; unnerve. **4** Intensification: unloose. [< OE un-, on-, and-] • Beginning at the bottom of this page is a partial list of words formed with **un-¹** and **un-².** Other words formed with these prefixes, having strongly positive, specific, or special meanings, will be found in vocabulary place.

UN, U.N. United Nations.

un·a·ble (un·ā′bəl) adj. **1** Not able; incompetent. **2** Helpless; ineffectual.

un·ac·count·a·ble (un′ə·koun′tə·bəl) adj. **1** Impossible to be explained or accounted for; inexplicable. **2** Not responsible. —**un′ac·count′a·ble·ness** n. —**un′ac·count′a·bly** adv.

un·ac·cus·tomed (un′ə·kus′təmd) adj. **1** Not accustomed or familiar: usu. with to: unaccustomed to hard-ship. **2** Not common; strange: an unaccustomed sight. —**un′ac·cus′tomed·ness** n.

un·ad·vised (un′əd·vīzd′) adj. **1** Not having received advice. **2** Rash or imprudent. —**un′ad·vis′ed·ly** (-vī′zid·lē) adv. —**un′ad·vis′ed·ness** n.

un·af·fect·ed (un′ə·fek′tid) adj. **1** Not showing affectation; natural; sincere. **2** Not influenced or changed. —**un′·af·fect′ed·ly** adv. —**un′af·fect′ed·ness** n.

un-A·mer·i·can (un′ə·mer′ə·kən) adj. Not American, esp. not consistent with or opposed to the institutions, ideals, objectives, etc. of the U.S. —**un′-A·mer′i·can·ism** n.

u·nan·i·mous (yo͞o·nan′ə·məs) adj. **1** Sharing the same views or sentiments. **2** Showing or resulting from the assent of all concerned: the unanimous voice of the jury. [< L unus one + animus mind] —**u·na·nim·i·ty** (yo͞o′nə·nim′ə·tē) n. —**u·nan′i·mous·ly** adv.

un·ap·proach·a·ble (un′ə·prō′chə·bəl) adj. **1** Not easy to know or contact; aloof; reserved. **2** Inaccessible. —**un′ap·proach′a·bil′i·ty, un′ap·proach′a·ble·ness** n. —**un′ap·proach′·a·bly** adv.

un·armed (un·ärmd′) adj. Having no firearms, esp. on one's person.

un·as·sail·a·ble (un′ə·sāl′ə·bəl) adj. **1** That cannot be disproved or contested successfully. **2** Resistant to attack; impregnable. —**un′as·sail′a·ble·ness, un′as·sail′a·bil′i·ty** n. —**un′as·sail′a·bly** adv.

un·as·sum·ing (un′ə·so͞o′ming) adj. Not pretentious; modest. —**un′as·sum′ing·ly** adv.

un·at·tached (un′ə·tacht′) adj. **1** Not attached. **2** Not connected with any particular group; independent. **3** Not married or engaged. **4** Law Not held or seized, as in satisfaction of a judgment.

un·a·vail·ing (un′ə·vā′ling) adj. Not effective; futile. —**un′a·vail′ing·ly** adv.

un·a·void·a·ble (un′ə·voi′də·bəl) adj. That cannot be avoided; inevitable. —**un′a·void′a·ble·ness** n. —**un′a·void′a·bly** adv.

---

unabashed	unarguable	unbloody	unchastity	unconfirmed	uncreated
unabated	unarm	unboastful	unchecked	uncongeal	uncredited
unabridged	unarmored	unboned	unchewed	uncongealed	uncritical
unaccented	unashamed	unbought	unchilled	uncongenial	uncross
unacceptable	unashamedly	unbound	unchivalrous	unconnected	uncrowded
unaccommodating	unasked	unbranched	unchlorinated	unconnectedly	uncrown
unaccompanied	unaspirated	unbranded	unchristened	unconquerable	uncrowned
unaccredited	unassailable	unbreakable	unclaimed	unconquerably	uncrystalline
unachievable	unassailably	unbreathable	unclassifiable	unconquered	uncrystallizable
unacknowledged	unassignable	unbridgeable	unclassified	unconscientious	uncrystallized
unacquainted	unassigned	unbridle	uncleaned	unconsecrated	uncultivated
unadorned	unassimilable	unbudging	unclear	unconsenting	uncultured
unadulterated	unassimilated	unburied	unclench	unconsidered	uncurbed
unadvisable	unassisted	unburnt	unclog	unconsoled	uncurdled
unaesthetic	unathletic	unbusinesslike	unclogged	unconsolidated	uncured
unaffiliated	unattainable	unbuttoned	unclouded	unconstituted	uncurl
unafraid	unattained	uncage	uncoated	unconstrained	uncurled
unaggressive	unattempted	uncalculating	uncock	unconsumed	uncursed
unaided	unattended	uncalendered	uncoerced	uncontaminated	uncurtained
unaligned	unattested	uncanceled	uncoined	uncontested	uncushioned
unalike	unattractive	uncared-for	uncollectable	uncontradicted	undamaged
unallied	unauthenticated	uncaring	uncollected	uncontrite	undamped
unalloyed	unauthorized	uncarpeted	uncollectible	uncontrollable	undated
unalluring	unavailable	uncastrated	uncolored	uncontrollably	undecayed
unalterable	unavenged	uncaught	uncombed	uncontrolled	undecaying
unaltered	unavowed	uncaused	uncomforted	unconversant	undecipherable
unambiguous	unavowedly	unceasing	uncommercial	unconverted	undeciphered
unambitious	unawakened	unceasingly	uncommissioned	unconvinced	undeclared
unamusing	unawed	uncensored	uncommitted	unconvincing	undeclinable
unannealed	unbacked	uncensured	uncompetitive	uncooked	undeclined
unannounced	unbaked	uncertified	uncomplaining	uncooperative	undecomposed
unanswerable	unbanked	unchallenged	uncompleted	uncoordinated	undecorated
unanswerably	unbaptized	unchangeable	uncomplicated	uncorked	undefaced
unanswered	unbeaten	unchanged	uncomplimentary	uncorrected	undefeated
unanticipated	unbelt	unchanging	uncomprehending	uncorroborated	undefended
unapparent	unbetrayed	unchangingly	uncomprehendingly	uncorrupt	undefiled
unappeasable	unbetrothed	unchaperoned	uncompressed	uncorrupted	undefinable
unappeased	unbleached	uncharged	uncompromised	uncounseled	undefined
unappetizing	unblemished	uncharted	uncomputed	uncountable	undeformed
unappreciative	unblest	unchartered	unconcealable	uncourteous	undelayed
unappropriated	unblinking	unchaste	unconcealed	uncourtly	undeliverable
unapproved	unblinkingly	unchastened	unconfined	uncovered	undelivered

---

un·a·ware (un'ə·wâr') *adj.* 1 Not aware or cognizant, as of something specified. 2 Carelessly unmindful; inattentive; heedless. —*adv.* UNAWARES.

un·a·wares (un'ə·wârz') *adv.* 1 Unexpectedly. 2 Without premeditation; unwittingly.

un·bal·ance (un·bal'əns) *v.t.* **·anced, ·anc·ing** 1 To deprive of balance. 2 To disturb or derange mentally. —*n.* The state or condition of being unbalanced.

un·bal·anced (un·bal'ənst) *adj.* 1 Not in a state of equilibrium. 2 In bookkeeping, not adjusted so as to balance. 3 Lacking mental balance; unsound; erratic.

un·bar (un·bär') *v.t.* **·barred, ·bar·ring** To remove the bar from.

un·bear·a·ble (un'bâr'ə·bəl) *adj.* Not to be borne; intolerable; insufferable. —**un'bear'a·bly** *adv.*

un·beat·a·ble (un'bēt'ə·bəl) *adj.* 1 Not to be defeated. 2 *Slang* First-rate; excellent.

un·be·com·ing (un'bi·kum'ing) *adj.* 1 Not becoming or appropriate, as a dress. 2 Not fitting or decorous; improper. —**un'be·com'ing·ly** *adv.* —**un'be·com'ing·ness** *n.*

un·be·known (un'bi·nōn') *adj.* Unknown: used with *to.* Also **un'be·knownst'** (-nōnst').

un·be·lief (un'bi·lēf') *n.* 1 Absence of positive belief; incredulity. 2 A refusal to believe; disbelief, as in religion.

un·be·liev·a·ble (un'bə·lēv'ə·bəl) *adj.* Too unusual or astonishing to be believed; incredible. —**un'be·liev'a·bly** *adv.* —**Syn.** inconceivable, untenable, staggering, improbable.

un·be·liev·er (un'bi·lē'vər) *n.* 1 One who does not believe; skeptic; doubter. 2 One who has no religious belief.

un·be·liev·ing (un'bi·lē'ving) *adj.* Doubting; skeptical. —**un'be·liev'ing·ly** *adv.* —**un'be·liev'ing·ness** *n.*

un·bend (un·bend') *v.* **·bent, ·bend·ing** *v.t.* 1 To relax, as from exertion or formality. 2 To straighten (something bent or curved). 3 To relax, as a bow, from tension. 4 *Naut.* To loose or detach, as a rope or sail. —*v.i.* 5 To become free of restraint or formality; relax. 6 To become straight or nearly straight again.

un·bend·ing (un·ben'ding) *adj.* 1 Not bending easily. 2 Resolute; firm. 3 Not relaxed socially; stiff. —**un·bend'ing·ly** *adv.* —**un·bend'ing·ness** *n.*

un·bi·ased (un·bī'əst) *adj.* Having no bias; not prejudiced; impartial. Also **un·bi'assed.** —**un·bi'ased·ly** *adv.* —**un·bi'ased·ness** *n.*

un·bid·den (un·bid'n) *adj.* 1 Not commanded or invited. 2 Spontaneous: *unbidden* thoughts.

un·blush·ing (un·blush'ing) *adj.* Not blushing; immodest; shameless. —**un·blush'ing·ly** *adv.*

un·born (un·bôrn') *adj.* 1 Not yet born. 2 Of a future time or generation; future. 3 Not in existence.

un·bos·om (un·bŏŏz'əm, -bŏŏ'zəm) *v.t.* 1 To reveal, as one's thoughts or secrets: often used reflexively. —*v.i.* 2 To say what is troubling one; tell one's thoughts, feelings, etc.

un·bound·ed (un·boun'did) *adj.* 1 Having no bounds or limits; boundless. 2 Going beyond bounds; unrestrained. —**un·bound'ed·ly** *adv.* —**un·bound'ed·ness** *n.*

un·bowed (un·boud') *adj.* 1 Not bent or bowed. 2 Not broken or subdued by defeat or adversity.

un·brace (un·brās') *v.t.* **·braced, ·brac·ing** 1 To free from bands or braces. 2 To free from tension; loosen. 3 To weaken.

un·bri·dled (un·brīd'ld) *adj.* 1 Having no bridle on. 2 Without restraint; unrestrained: an *unbridled* tongue.

un·bro·ken (un·brō'kən) *adj.* 1 Not broken; whole; entire. 2 Not violated: an *unbroken* promise. 3 Uninterrupted; continuous. 4 Not tamed or trained. 5 Not bettered or surpassed. 6 Not disarranged or thrown out of order.

un·bur·den (un·bûr'dən) *v.t.* 1 To free from a burden. 2 To relieve (oneself, one's mind, etc.) from cares, worries, etc. 3 To make known (one's cares, worries, guilt, etc.) in order to gain relief.

un·called-for (un·kôld'fôr') *adj.* 1 Not needed; unnecessary. 2 Not justified by circumstances; unprovoked.

un·can·ny (un·kan'ē) *adj.* 1 Weird; unnatural; eerie. 2 So

undemocratic	undissected	unendurable	unexported	unforgetful	ungrammatical
undemonstrable	undisseminated	unenforceable	unexposed	unforgetting	ungrammatically
undemonstrative	undissolved	unenforced	unexpressed	unforgivable	ungranted
undenominational	undistilled	unenfranchised	unexpressive	unforgiven	ungratified
undependable	undistinguished	unengaged	unexpurgated	unforgiving	ungrounded
underived	undistracted	unengaging	unextended	unforgotten	ungrudging
underserved	undistributed	un-English	unextinguished	unformed	unguided
undeservedly	undisturbed	unenjoyable	unfaded	unformulated	unhackneyed
undeserving	undiversified	unenlightened	unfading	unforsaken	unhampered
undesignated	undiverted	unenlivened	unfallen	unfortified	unhang
undesigned	undivided	unenriched	unfaltering	unfought	unhanged
undesirable	undivorced	unenrolled	unfashionable	unfound	unharbored
undesirably	undocking	unenslaved	unfashionably	unfractured	unharmed
undesired	undogmatic	unentangled	unfastened	unframed	unharnessed
undesirous	undomesticated	unentered	unfathomable	unfranchised	unharrowed
undetached	undoubting	unenterprising	unfavored	unfree	unharvested
undetected	undramatic	unenthralled	unfeared	unfreedom	unhasty
undetermined	undramatized	unenthusiastic	unfearing	unfrozen	unhatched
undeterred	undrape	unenthusiastically	unfeasible	unfruitful	unhealed
undeveloped	undraped	unenviable	unfed	unfulfilled	unhealthful
undeviating	undreamed	unenvied	unfederated	unfunded	unheated
undifferentiated	undreamt	unenvious	unfelt	unfunny	unheeded
undiffused	undried	unequipped	unfeminine	unfurnished	unheedful
undigested	undrinkable	unerased	unfenced	unfussy	unheeding
undignified	undutiful	unerotic	unfermented	ungallant	unheedingly
undilated	undyed	unestablished	unfertilized	ungarnished	unhelpful
undiluted	uneatable	unethical	unfetter	ungenerous	unheralded
undiminished	uneaten	unexaggerated	unfettered	ungentle	unheroic
undimmed	uneconomic	unexalted	unfilled	ungentlemanly	unhesitating
undiplomatic	uneconomical	unexamined	unfilmed	ungently	unhesitatingly
undirected	unedifying	unexcavated	unfiltered	ungenuine	unhindered
undiscernible	uneducable	unexcelled	unfinished	ungifted	unhired
undiscerning	uneducated	unexchangeable	unfired	ungird	unhistoric
undischarged	unelectrified	unexcited	unfixed	ungirt	unhomogeneous
undisciplined	unembarrassed	unexciting	unflattered	unglazed	unhonored
undisclosed	unembellished	unexcused	unflattering	unglossed	unhousebroken
undiscouraged	unemotional	unexpanded	unflavored	unglove	unhoused
undiscoverable	unemotionally	unexpended	unfocus	ungloved	unhurried
undiscovered	unemphatic	unexpiated	unforbidden	unglue	unhurt
undiscriminating	unencumbered	unexpired	unforced	ungoverned	unhusk
undiscussed	unendangered	unexplainable	unfordable	ungraced	unhygienic
undisguised	unending	unexplained	unforeseeable	ungraceful	unhyphenated
undismayed	unendingly	unexploded	unforetold	ungraded	unhypocritical
undispelled	unendorsed	unexploited	unforfeited	ungrafted	unidentified
undisputed	unendowed	unexplored	unforged	ungrained	unidiomatic

good as to seem almost supernatural in origin: *uncanny* accuracy. —**un·can'ni·ly** *adv.* —**un·can'ni·ness** *n.*

un·cer·e·mo·ni·ous (un'ser·ə·mō'nē·əs) *adj.* 1 Not ceremonious; informal. 2 Abruptly rude or discourteous. — **un'cer·e·mo'ni·ous·ly** *adv.* —**un'cer·e·mo'ni·ous·ness** *n.*

un·cer·tain (un·sûr'tən) *adj.* 1 Not yet determined; indefinite: The date is *uncertain.* 2 Not to be relied upon; unpredictable: *uncertain* weather. 3 Not definitely or exactly known. 4 Not sure or convinced; doubtful; dubious. 5 Not constant; fitful; changeable. 6 Not clear, forceful, steady, etc.: His delivery of the speech was very *uncertain.* —**un·cer'tain·ly** *adv.*

un·cer·tain·ty (un·sûr'tən·tē) *n. pl.* **·ties** 1 The state of being uncertain; doubt. 2 Something uncertain.

un·char·i·ta·ble (un·char'ə·tə·bəl) *adj.* Not forgiving or charitable, as in judgment; censorious. —**un·char'i·ta·ble·ness** *n.* —**un·char'i·ta·bly** *adv.*

un·char·ted (un·chär'tid) *adj.* 1 Not marked or charted on a map. 2 Not explored; unknown.

un·chris·tian (un·kris'chən) *adj.* 1 Not according with Christian principles, attitudes, etc. 2 Not Christian.

un·church (un·chûrch') *v.t.* 1 To deprive of membership in a church; excommunicate. 2 To deny the status of a church to (a sect, etc.).

un·cir·cum·cised (un·sûr'kəm·sīzd) *adj.* 1 Not circumcised. 2 Not Jewish; Gentile.

un·civ·il (un·siv'əl) *adj.* Wanting in civility; discourteous; ill-bred. —**un·civ'il·ly** *adv.*

un·civ·i·lized (un·siv'ə·līzd) *adj.* 1 Not civilized; barbarous. 2 Uncouth; rude; gross. 3 Remote from civilization. —**Syn.** 1 savage, brutish, brutal, ferocious. 2 crude, cross, boorish, churlish, vulgar, coarse.

un·clad (un·klad') *adj.* Without clothes; naked.

un·cle (ung'kəl) *n.* 1 The brother of one's father or mother. 2 The husband of one's aunt. 3 *Informal* An elderly man; used in direct address. 4 *Slang* A pawnbroker. [< L *avunculus* a mother's brother]

un·clean (un·klēn') *adj.* 1 Not clean; foul. 2 Morally impure. 3 Ceremonially impure. —**un·clean'ness** *n.*

un·clean·ly[1] (un·klen'lē) *adj.* 1 Lacking cleanliness. 2 Morally impure. —**un·clean'li·ness** *n.*

un·clean·ly[2] (un·klēn'lē) *adv.* In an unclean manner.

Uncle Sam The personification of the government or the people of the U.S., represented as a tall, lean man with chin whiskers, wearing a plug hat, blue swallow-tailed coat, and red-and-white striped pants.

Uncle Tom *Informal* A Negro who acts in an obsequious or servile manner towards whites: a contemptuous term. —*v.i.* **Uncle Tommed, Uncle Tom·ming** To behave like an Uncle Tom. [< *Uncle Tom,* the faithful Negro slave in H. B. Stowe's *Uncle Tom's Cabin*] —**Uncle Tom'ism** *n.*

un·cloak (un·klōk') *v.t.* 1 To remove the cloak or covering from. 2 To unmask; expose.

un·close (un·klōz') *v.t. & v.i.* **·closed, ·clos·ing** 1 To open or set open. 2 To reveal; disclose.

un·clothe (un·klōth') *v.t.* **·clothed** or **·clad, ·cloth·ing** 1 To remove the clothes from; undress. 2 To divest; uncover.

un·com·fort·a·ble (un·kum'fər·tə·bəl, -kumf'tə·bəl) *adj.* 1 Not at ease; feeling discomfort. 2 Causing uneasiness; disquieting. —**un·com'fort·a·ble·ness** *n.* —**un·com'fort·a·bly** *adv.*

un·com·mon (un·kom'ən) *adj.* 1 Not usual or common. 2 Strange; remarkable. —**un·com'mon·ly** *adv.* —**un·com'mon·ness** *n.*

un·com·mu·ni·ca·tive (un'kə·myōō'nə·kə·tiv, -kāt'iv) *adj.* Not communicative; not disposed to talk, to give information, etc.; reserved; taciturn. —**un'com·mu'ni·ca·tive·ly** *adv.* —**un'com·mu'ni·ca·tive·ness** *n.*

un·com·pro·mis·ing (un·kom'prə·mī'zing) *adj.* Making or admitting of no compromise; inflexible; strict. — **un·com'pro·mis'ing·ly** *adv.* —**Syn.** resolute, steadfast, firm, indomitable, inexorable, tenacious, obstinate.

un·con·cern (un'kən·sûrn') *n.* 1 Lack of anxiety, concern, or worry. 2 Lack of interest; indifference.

unilluminated	unintentional	unlisted	unmold	unorthodox	unplanted
unillumined	unintentionally	unlit	unmolested	unostentatious	unplayed
unillustrated	uninteresting	unliteral	unmollified	unostentatiously	unpleasing
unimaginable	uninterpreted	unliveliness	unmortgaged	unowned	unpledged
unimaginably	uninterrupted	unlively	unmotivated	unoxidized	unplowed
unimaginative	unintimidated	unlocked	unmounted	unpacified	unplucked
unimagined	unintoxicated	unlovable	unmourned	unpaginated	unplugged
unimbued	uninvited	unloved	unmoved	unpaid	unpoetic
unimitated	uninviting	unlovely	unmown	unpaired	unpoetical
unimmunized	uninvoked	unloving	unmuffle	unpalatable	unpointed
unimpaired	uninvolved	unlubricated	unmusical	unpardonable	unpolarized
unimpeded	unissued	unmagnified	unmuzzle	unpardonably	unpolished
unimportance	unitemized	unmanageable	unmuzzled	unparliamentary	unpolitical
unimportant	unjaded	unmanful	unnamable	unparted	unpolluted
unimposing	unjoined	unmanicured	unnameable	unpartisan	unpopulated
unimpressed	unjointed	unmannerly	unnamed	unpasteurized	unposted
unimpressionable	unjustifiable	unmarked	unnaturalized	unpatched	unpractical
unimpressive	unjustifiably	unmarketable	unnavigable	unpatented	unpredictable
unincorporated	unkennel	unmarred	unnavigated	unpatriotic	unpredictably
unindemnified	unkept	unmarriageable	unneeded	unpaved	unprejudiced
unindustrialized	unkindled	unmarried	unneighborly	unpeaceable	unpremeditated
uninfected	unkissed	unmasculine	unnoted	unpeaceful	unprepared
uninfested	unknowable	unmastered	unnoticed	unpedigreed	unprepossessing
uninflammable	unknowing	unmatched	unobjectionable	unpensioned	unpressed
uninflected	unlabeled	unmated	unobliging	unpeopled	unpretentious
uninfluenced	unlabored	unmatted	unobservant	unperceived	unpretentiously
uninformed	unladylike	unmeant	unobserved	unperfected	unpretentiousness
uninhabitable	unlamented	unmechanical	unobserving	unperforated	unpriced
uninhabited	unlash	unmedicated	unobstructed	unperformed	unprimed
uninhibited	unlasting	unmemorable	unobtainable	unpersuaded	unprinted
uninitiated	unlaundered	unmercenary	unobtrusive	unpersuasive	unprivileged
uninjured	unleaded	unmerited	unobtrusively	unperturbed	unprocessed
uninspired	unleased	unmethodical	unobtrusiveness	unphilosophical	unproductive
uninspiring	unlevel	unmilitary	unoffending	unphonetic	unprofitable
uninstructed	unlevied	unmilled	unoffered	unphotogenic	unprofitably
uninsurable	unlicensed	unmindful	unoiled	unphysical	unprogramed
uninsured	unlifelike	unmistaken	unopen	unpicturesque	unpromising
unintellectual	unlighted	unmixed	unopened	unpile	unpronounceable
unintelligent	unlikable	unmodified	unopposed	unpitying	unpropitious
unintelligible	unlikeable	unmodish	unoppressed	unplaced	unprosperous
unintelligibly	unlined	unmodulated	unordained	unplait	unprotected
unintended	unlink	unmoistened	unoriginal	unplanned	unproved

un·con·cerned (un′kən·sûrnd′) *adj.* **1** Not anxious or worried. **2** Not interested; indifferent. —**un′con·cern′ed·ly** (-sûr′nid·lē) *adv.* —**un′con·cern′ed·ness** *n.*

un·con·di·tion·al (un′kən·dish′ən·əl) *adj.* Limited by no conditions; absolute. —**un′con·di′tion·al·ly** *adv.*

un·con·di·tioned (un′kən·dish′ənd) *adj.* **1** Not restricted; unconditional. **2** *Psychol.* Not acquired; natural.

un·con·scion·a·ble (un·kon′shən·ə·bəl) *adj.* **1** Unbelievably bad, wrong, inequitable, etc.: an *unconscionable* error. **2** Wholly unscrupulous. —**un·con′scion·a·ble·ness** *n.* —**un·con′scion·a·bly** *adv.*

un·con·scious (un·kon′shəs) *adj.* **1** Temporarily deprived of consciousness. **2** Not cognizant; unaware: with *of*: *unconscious* of his charm. **3** Not produced or accompanied by conscious effort; not intended or known: an *unconscious* pun. **4** Not endowed with consciousness or a mind. **5** Of or having to do with the unconscious. —*n.* That area of the psyche which is not in the immediate field of awareness and whose content may become manifest through dreams, morbid fears and compulsions, etc.: with *the*. —**un·con′scious·ly** *adv.* —**un·con′scious·ness** *n.*

un·con·sti·tu·tion·al (un′kon·sti·t′ōō′shən·əl) *adj.* Contrary to or violating the precepts of a constitution. —**un′·con·sti·tu′tion·al′i·ty** *n.* —**un·con′sti·tu′tion·al·ly** *adv.*

un·con·ven·tion·al (un′kən·ven′shən·əl) *adj.* Not adhering to conventional rules, practices, etc.; informal; free. —**un′con·ven′tion·al′i·ty** *n.* —**un′con·ven′tion·al·ly** *adv.*

un·count·ed (un·koun′tid) *adj.* **1** Not counted. **2** Beyond counting; innumerable.

un·coup·le (un·kup′əl) *v.t.* **·led, ·ling 1** To disconnect or unfasten. **2** To set loose; unleash (dogs). —**un·coup′led** (-kup′əld) *adj.*

un·couth (un·kōōth′) *adj.* **1** Marked by awkwardness or oddity; outlandish. **2** Coarse, boorish, or unrefined, as in manner or speech. [< OE *uncūth* unknown] —**un·couth′ly** *adv.* —**un·couth′ness** *n.*

un·cov·er (un·kuv′ər) *v.t.* **1** To remove a covering from.

2 To make known; disclose. —*v.i.* **3** To remove a covering. **4** To raise or remove the hat, as in token of respect.

unc·tion (ungk′shən) *n.* **1** The act of anointing, as for religious or medicinal purposes. **2** A substance used in anointing, as oil. **3** Anything that soothes or palliates. **4** A quality of speech, esp. in religious discourse, that awakens or is intended to awaken deep sympathetic feeling. **5** Excessive or affected sincerity or sympathy in speech or manner. [< L *unctio* < *ungere* anoint]

unc·tu·ous (ungk′chōō·əs) *adj.* **1** Like an unguent; greasy. **2** Greasy or soapy to the touch, as certain minerals. **3** Characterized by excessive or affected sincerity, sympathy, concern, etc. **4** Unduly smooth or suave in speech or manner. **5** Having plasticity, as clay. [< L *unctum* ointment, orig. neut. p.p. of *ungere* anoint] —**unc′tu·ous·ly** *adv.* —**unc′tu·ous·ness, unc′tu·os′i·ty** (-chōō·os′ə·tē) *n.*

un·cut (un·kut′) *adj.* **1** Not cut. **2** In bookbinding, having untrimmed margins. **3** Not ground, as a gem. **4** Not shortened or abridged.

un·daunt·ed (un·dôn′tid, -dän′-) *adj.* Not daunted; fearless; intrepid. —**un·daunt′ed·ly** *adv.* —**un·daunt′ed·ness** *n.*

un·de·cid·ed (un′di·sī′did) *adj.* **1** Not having the mind made up; irresolute. **2** Not decided upon or determined. —**un′de·cid′ed·ly** *adv.*

un·de·ni·a·ble (un′di·nī′ə·bəl) *adj.* **1** That cannot be denied; indisputably true. **2** Unquestionably good; excellent: His reputation was *undeniable*. —**un′de·ni′a·bly** *adv.*

un·der (un′dər) *prep.* **1** Beneath; covered by: dust *under* the rug. **2** In a place lower than; at the foot or bottom of: *under* the hill. **3** Beneath the shelter of: *under* the paternal roof. **4** Beneath the concealment, guise, or assumption of: *under* a false name. **5** Less than in number, degree, age, value, or amount: *under* 10 tons. **6** Inferior to in quality, character, or rank. **7** Beneath the domination of; subordinate or subservient to: *under* the British flag. **8** Subject to the guidance, tutorship, or direction of: He studied *under* Mendelssohn. **9** Subject to the moral obligation of: a state-

unproven	unrelieved	unrevealed	unscholarly	unsinkable	unstitched
unprovided	unremarkable	unrevenged	unschooled	unsized	unstopped
unprovoked	unremarked	unrevised	unscientific	unskeptical	unstopper
unpruned	unremedied	unrevoked	unscratched	unslaked	unstrap
unpublishable	unremembered	unrewarded	unscreened	unsling	unstratified
unpublished	unremitted	unrhymed	unsealed	unsmiling	unstressed
unpunctual	unremorseful	unrhythmic	unseamed	unsmilingly	unstriated
unpunished	unremunerated	unrhythmical	unseasoned	unsmoked	unstriped
unpurified	unremunerative	unrighted	unseaworthy	unsnobbish	unstructured
unpuritanical	unrenewed	unripened	unseconded	unsocial	unstuck
unqualifying	unrented	unrisen	unsecret	unsoiled	unstudied
unquenchable	unrepaid	unroasted	unsecretive	unsold	unstuffed
unquestioning	unrepairable	unromantic	unsectarian	unsoldierly	unsubsidized
unrated	unrepaired	unromantically	unsecured	unsolicited	unsubstantiated
unratified	unrepealed	unroof	unseeing	unsolicitous	unsubtle
unreachable	unrepeatable	unruled	unseen	unsoluble	unsuccessful
unreadable	unrepentant	unsafe	unsegmented	unsolvable	unsuccessfully
unrealizable	unrepented	unsafely	unselected	unsolved	unsuited
unrealized	unrepenting	unsafeness	unselective	unsorted	unsullied
unrebuked	unreplaced	unsaintly	unself-conscious	unsought	unsupportable
unreceipted	unreplenished	unsalability	unselfish	unsown	unsupported
unreceivable	unreported	unsalable	unselfishly	unspecialized	unsuppressed
unreceived	unrepresentative	unsalaried	unselfishness	unspecified	unsure
unreceptive	unrepresented	unsaleability	unsent	unspectacular	unsurmountable
unreciprocated	unrepressed	unsaleable	unsentimental	unspent	unsurpassed
unreclaimed	unrequested	unsalted	unserviceable	unspilled	unsurprising
unrecognizable	unrequited	unsalvageable	unset	unspiritual	unsurveyed
unrecognized	unresented	unsanctified	unsew	unspoiled	unsurvivable
unreconciled	unreserve	unsanctioned	unsewn	unspoken	unsusceptible
unrecorded	unresigned	unsanitary	unsexual	unsponsored	unsuspected
unrecounted	unresistant	unsated	unshaded	unsportsmanlike	unsuspecting
unredeemed	unresisting	unsatiated	unshakable	unstack	unsuspicious
unrefined	unresistingly	unsatiating	unshaken	unstained	unswathe
unreflecting	unresolved	unsatisfactorily	unshaven	unstamped	unswear
unreflective	unrespectful	unsatisfactory	unsheathed	unstandardized	unsweetened
unreformable	unresponsive	unsatisfied	unsheltered	unstarched	unswept
unreformed	unresting	unsatisfying	unshod	unstarred	unsworn
unrefreshed	unrestless	unsaved	unshorn	unstartling	unsymmetrical
unregistered	unrestrained	unsayable	unshrinkable	unstatesmanlike	unsympathetic
unregretted	unrestrainedly	unscaled	unshriven	unstemmed	unsympathetically
unregulated	unrestraint	unscanned	unshrouded	unstereotyped	unsystematic
unrehearsed	unrestricted	unscarred	unshut	unsterile	untack
unrelated	unretentive	unscenic	unsifted	unsterilized	untactful
unrelaxed	unretracted	unscented	unsighted	unstick	untactfully
unrelievable	unreturned	unscheduled	unsigned	unstimulating	untainted

ment *under* oath. **10** With the liability or certainty of incurring: *under* penalty of the law. **11** Subject to the influence or pressure of: *under* the circumstances. **12** Swayed or impelled by: *under* fear of death. **13** Driven or propelled by: *under* sail. **14** Included in the group or class of; found in the matter titled or headed: See *under* History. **15** Being the subject of: the matter *under* discussion. **16** During the period of; in the reign of. **17** By virtue of; authorized, substantiated, attested, or warranted by: *under* his own signature. **18** In conformity to or in accordance with; having regard to. **19** Planted or sowed with: an acre *under* wheat. —*adv.* **1** In or into a position below something; underneath. **2** In or into an inferior or subordinate condition, rank, etc. **3** So as to be covered or hidden. **4** Less in amount, value, time, etc.: We did it in ten minutes or *under*. —*adj.* **1** Situated or moving under something else; lower or lowermost: an *under* layer. **2** Subordinate; lower in rank or authority. **3** Less than usual, standard, or prescribed. **4** Held in subjection or restraint: used predicatively. [< OE]

under- *combining form* **1** Below in position; situated or directed beneath; on the underside: *undercarriage.* **2** Below or beneath another surface or covering: *undergarment.* **3** Inferior in rank or importance; subordinate: *undergraduate.* **4** Less than is usual or proper; not enough; insufficient(ly): *underdeveloped.* **5** At a lower rate; less in degree or amount: *underpay.*

un·der·a·chieve (un′dər·ə·chēv′) *v.i.* ·chieved, ·chiev·ing To fail to achieve the approximate level of performance, esp. in school studies, commensurate with one's abilities as indicated by testing. —**un′der·a·chieve′ment, un′der·a·chiev′er** *n.*

un·der·act (un′dər·akt′) *v.t. & v.i.* To perform (a role, scene, etc.) in a somewhat less dramatic or emphatic way than might naturally be expected.

un·der·age (un′dər·āj′) *adj.* Not of a requisite or legal age.

untaken	untranslated	unwarlike
untalented	untrapped	unwarmed
untamable	untraveled	unwarned
untame	untraversed	unwarranted
untameable	untread	unwashed
untamed	untreatable	unwasted
untangled	untreated	unwatched
untaped	untried	unwavering
untapped	untrim	unwaveringly
untarnished	untrodden	unweakened
untasted	untroubled	unweaned
untaxable	untrustworthy	unwearable
untaxed	untuck	unweary
unteachable	untufted	unwearying
untechnical	untuned	unweathered
untempered	untuneful	unweave
untenable	unturned	unwed
untenanted	untwilled	unwedded
untended	untwisted	unweeded
untenured	untypical	unwelcome
untested	unusable	unwelded
untether	unutilized	unwhetted
unthatched	unuttered	unwhipped
untheatrical	unvaccinated	unwilled
unthinkable	unvalued	unwished
unthoughtful	unvanquished	unwithered
unthreshed	unvaried	unwitnessed
unthrifty	unvarying	unwomanly
unthrone	unvaryingly	unwooded
untilled	unveiled	unwooed
untinged	unventilated	unworkable
untired	unverifiable	unworked
untiring	unverified	unworkmanlike
untiringly	unversed	unworldly
untitled	unvitrified	unworn
untouched	unvocal	unworshiped
untracked	unvoiced	unwounded
untrained	unvolatilized	unwoven
untrammeled	unvulcanized	unwrinkled
untransferable	unwakened	unwrought
untransferred	unwalled	unyielding
untranslatable	unwanted	unzealous

un·der·arm (un′dər·ärm′) *adj.* **1** Situated, placed, or used under the arm. **2** UNDERHAND (def. 2). —*n.* ARMPIT.

un·der·bid (un′dər·bid′) *v.t.* ·bid, ·bid·ding **1** To bid lower than, as in a competition. **2** In bridge, to fail to bid the full value of (a hand). —**un′der·bid′der** *n.*

un·der·brush (un′dər·brush′) *n.* Small trees and shrubs growing beneath forest trees; undergrowth. Also **un′der·bush′** (-bŏŏsh′).

un·der·buy (un′dər·bī′) *v.t.* ·bought, ·buy·ing **1** To buy at a price lower than that paid by (another). **2** To pay less than the value for. **3** To buy less of (something) than is required.

un·der·car·riage (un′dər·kar′ij) *n.* **1** The framework supporting the body of a structure, as an automobile. **2** The principal landing gear of an aircraft.

Undercarriage *def.* 2

un·der·charge (un′dər·chärj′) *v.t.* ·charged, ·charg·ing **1** To make an inadequate charge for. **2** To load with an insufficient charge, as a gun. —*n.* (un′dər·chärj′) An inadequate or insufficient charge.

un·der·class·man (un′dər·klas′mən, -kläs′-) *n. pl.* ·men (-mən) A freshman or sophomore.

un·der·clothes (un′dər·klōz′, -klōthz′) *n.pl.* UNDERWEAR. Also **un′der·cloth′ing.**

un·der·coat (un′dər·kōt′) *n.* **1** A coat worn under another. **2** A layer of paint, varnish, etc., beneath another layer; also, a protective coating applied to the undersurface of a vehicle: also **un′der·coat′ing.** —*v.t.* To provide with an undercoat (def. 2).

un·der·cov·er (un′dər·kuv′ər) *adj.* Secret; surreptitious; esp., engaged in spying.

un·der·cur·rent (un′dər·kûr′ənt) *n.* **1** A current, as of water or air, below another or below the surface. **2** A hidden drift or tendency, as of popular sentiments.

un·der·cut (un′dər·kut′) *n.* **1** The act or result of cutting away a part, section, etc., from the lower or under surface of something. **2** *Brit.* TENDERLOIN. **3** A notch cut in the side of a tree so that it will fall toward that side when sawed through. **4** In sports, a cut or backspin imparted to the ball by an underhand stroke. —*v.t.* (un′dər·kut′) ·cut, ·cut·ting **1** To cut away the underpart of. **2** To cut away a lower portion of so as to leave a part overhanging. **3** To work or sell for lower payment than (a rival). **4** In sports, to hit (a ball) with an oblique downward or underhand stroke so as to give the ball a backspin. **5** To lessen or destroy the effectiveness or impact of; undermine. —*adj.* **1** Having the parts in relief cut under. **2** Done by undercutting.

un·der·de·vel·oped (un′dər·di·vel′əpt) *adj.* **1** Not sufficiently developed. **2** Below a normal or adequate standard in the development of industry, resources, agriculture, etc.: an *underdeveloped* country.

un·der·dog (un′dər·dôg′, -dog′) *n.* **1** The one that is losing, has lost, or is at a disadvantage in a contest. **2** The weaker, subservient, or exploited person.

un·der·done (un′dər·dun′) *adj.* Not cooked to the fullest degree.

un·der·em·ployed (un′dər·əm·ploid′) *adj.* Employed only part of the time or for too few hours to assure an adequate income. —**un′der·em·ploy′ment** *n.*

un·der·es·ti·mate (un′dər·es′tə·māt) *v.t.* ·mat·ed, ·mat·ing To put too low an estimate or valuation upon (things or people). —*n.* (-mit) An estimate below the just value, expense, opinion, etc. —**un′der·es·ti·ma′tion** *n.*

un·der·ex·pose (un′dər·ik·spōz′) *v.t.* ·posed, ·pos·ing *Phot.* To expose (a film) to less light than is required for a clear image. —**un′der·ex·po′sure** (-spō′zhər) *n.*

un·der·feed (un′dər·fēd′) *v.t.* ·fed, ·feed·ing To feed insufficiently.

un·der·foot (un′dər·fŏŏt′) *adv.* **1** Beneath the feet; down on the ground. **2** In the way.

un·der·gar·ment (un′dər·gär′mənt) *n.* A garment to be worn beneath outer garments.

un·der·go (un′dər·gō′) *v.t.* ·went, ·gone, ·go·ing **1** To be subjected to; have experience of; suffer. **2** To bear up under; endure.

un·der·grad·u·ate (un′dər·graj′oo·it) *n.* A student of a university or college who has not taken the bachelor's degree. —*adj.* Of, being, or for an undergraduate.

un·der·ground (un′dər·ground′) *adj.* **1** Situated, done, or operated beneath the surface of the ground. **2** Done in secret; clandestine. **3** Of, relating to, or characterized by the underground (defs. 3 and 4), their works, actions, etc. —*n.* **1** That which is beneath the surface of the ground, as a passage or space. **2** *Brit.* SUBWAY. **3** A group usually organized to resist or oppose those in control of a government or country: usu. with *the.* **4** An avant-garde movement in art, cinema, journalism, etc., generally considered to be in opposition to conventional culture or society and whose works are usu. experimental, erotic, or radical in style, content, or purpose: usu. with *the.* —*adv.* (un′dər·ground′) **1** Beneath the surface of the ground. **2** In or into hiding, secrecy, etc.

Underground Railroad A system of cooperation among antislavery people, before 1861, for assisting fugitive slaves to escape to Canada and the free states.

un·der·growth (un′dər·grōth′) *n.* UNDERBRUSH.

un·der·hand (un′dər·hand′) *adj.* **1** Done or acting in a sly or treacherously secret manner. **2** In certain sports, done or delivered with the hand and forearm lower than the elbow or shoulder. —*adv.* **1** In a secret, sly manner. **2** With an underhand motion.

un·der·hand·ed (un′dər·han′did) *adj. & adv.* UNDERHAND. —**un′der·hand′ed·ly** *adv.* —**un′der·hand′ed·ness** *n.*

un·der·lay (un′dər·lā′) *v.t.* **·laid, ·lay·ing 1** To place (one thing) under another. **2** To furnish with a base or lining. **3** To support or elevate with something placed beneath. —*n.* (un′dər·lā′) Something laid beneath something else, esp., in printing, a piece of paper, etc., placed under type, etc., in order to raise it.

un·der·lie (un′dər·lī′) *v.t.* **·lay, ·lain, ·ly·ing 1** To lie below or under. **2** To be the basis or reason for: *What motives underlie his refusal to go?* **3** To constitute a first or prior claim or lien over.

un·der·line (un′dər·līn′) *v.t.* **·lined, ·lin·ing 1** To mark with a line underneath; underscore. **2** To emphasize. —*n.* A line underneath a word or passage, as for emphasis.

un·der·ling (un′dər·ling) *n.* A subordinate; inferior.

un·der·ly·ing (un′dər·lī′ing) *adj.* **1** Lying under: *underlying* strata. **2** Basic; fundamental: *underlying* principles. **3** Not obvious; implicit: *underlying* reasons.

un·der·mine (un′dər·mīn′; un′dər·mīn) *v.t.* **·mined, ·min·ing 1** To excavate beneath; dig a mine or passage under. **2** To weaken by wearing away at the base. **3** To weaken or impair secretly, insidiously, or by degrees.

un·der·most (un′dər·mōst′) *adj.* Having the lowest place or position.

un·der·neath (un′dər·nēth′) *adv.* **1** In a place below. **2** On the under or lower side. —*prep.* **1** Beneath; under; below. **2** Under the form or appearance of. **3** Under the authority of; in the control of. —*adj.* Lower. —*n.* The lower or under part or side. [< OE *underneothan*]

un·der·nour·ish (un′dər·nûr′ish) *v.t.* To provide with insufficient nourishment. —**un′der·nour′ished** *adj.* —**un′der·nour′ish·ment** *n.*

un·der·pass (un′dər·pas′, -päs′) *n.* A road, passageway, etc., that runs beneath something, esp. a road that passes under railway tracks or under another road.

un·der·pay (un′dər·pā′) *v.t.* **·paid, ·pay·ing** To pay insufficiently.

un·der·pin·ning (un′dər·pin′ing) *n.* **1** Material or framework used to support a wall or building from below. **2** *Often pl.* Something used or functioning as a basis or foundation: the *underpinnings* of guilt in our society.

Underpass

un·der·play (un′dər·plā′) *v.t. & v.i.* **1** UNDERACT. **2** To behave, react to, etc., in a deliberately restrained manner.

un·der·priv·i·leged (un′dər·priv′ə·lijd) *adj.* **1** Deprived socially and economically of enjoying certain fundamental rights theoretically possessed by all members of a community or nation. **2** Of or pertaining to people who are underprivileged.

un·der·rate (un′dər·rāt′) *v.t.* **·rat·ed, ·rat·ing** To rate too low; underestimate.

un·der·score (un′dər·skôr′, -skōr′) *v.t.* **·scored, ·scor·ing** To draw a line below, as for emphasis; underline. —*n.* (un′dər·skôr′, -skōr′) A line drawn beneath a word, etc., as for emphasis.

un·der·sea (un′dər·sē′) *adj.* Being, carried on, or designed for use beneath the surface of the sea. —*adv.* (un′dər·sē′) Beneath the surface of the sea: also **un·der·seas** (un′dər·sēz′).

under secretary The assistant secretary of a principal secretary in government.

un·der·sell (un′dər·sel′) *v.t.* **·sold, ·sell·ing 1** To sell at a lower price than. **2** To present or promote, as a point of view or commodity, in an understated manner.

un·der·shirt (un′dər·shûrt′) *n.* A collarless undergarment, usu. without sleeves, worn beneath a shirt.

un·der·shoot (un′dər·shōōt′) *v.* **·shot, ·shoot·ing** *v.t.* **1** To shoot short of or below (a target). **2** To land an airplane short of (the runway). —*v.i.* **3** To shoot or land short of the mark.

un·der·shot (un′dər·shot′) *adj.* **1** Propelled by water that flows underneath, as a water wheel. **2** Having a projecting lower jaw or teeth.

un·der·side (un′dər·sīd′) *n.* The lower or under side or surface.

un·der·signed (un′dər·sīnd′) *n.* The person or persons who have signed their names at the end of a document, letter, etc.

un·der·sized (un′dər·sīzd′) *adj.* Of less than the normal, legal, or average size.

Undershot water wheel

un·der·slung (un′dər·slung′) *adj.* Having the springs fixed to the axles from below, as certain automobiles.

un·der·stand (un′dər·stand′) *v.* **·stood, ·stand·ing** *v.t.* **1** To come to know the meaning or import of. **2** To perceive the nature or character of: *I do not understand her.* **3** To have comprehension or mastery of: *Do you understand German?* **4** To be aware of; realize: *She understands her position.* **5** To have been told; believe: *I understand that she went home.* **6** To take or interpret: *How am I to understand that remark?* **7** To accept as a condition or stipulation: *It is understood that the tenant will provide his own heat.* —*v.i.* **8** To have understanding; comprehend. **9** To grasp the meaning, significance, etc., of something. **10** To believe or assume something to be the case. **11** To have a sympathetic attitude or tolerance toward something. [< OE *under-* under + *standan* stand] —**un′der·stand′a·ble** *adj.* —**un′der·stand′a·bly** *adv.*

un·der·stand·ing (un′dər·stan′ding) *n.* **1** An intellectual grasp of something; comprehension. **2** The power or capacity to think, acquire and retain knowledge, interpret experience, etc.; intelligence. **3** An agreement or settlement of differences. **4** An informal or confidential compact or agreement. **5** An individual viewpoint, interpretation, or opinion. **6** A sympathetic comprehension of or tolerance for the feelings, actions, attitudes, etc., of others. —*adj.* Possessing or characterized by comprehension, compassion, etc. —**un′der·stand′ing·ly** *adv.*

un·der·state (un′dər·stāt′) *v.t.* **·stat·ed, ·stat·ing 1** To state with less force than the actual truth warrants. **2** To state or describe in a deliberately restrained manner in order to achieve greater force or effectiveness. —**un′der·state′·ment** *n.*

un·der·stat·ed (un′dər·stāt′əd) *adj.* Stated, executed, designed, etc., in an unemphatic, restrained, or simple manner.

un·der·stood (un′dər·stōōd′) *p.t. & p.p.* of UNDERSTAND. —*adj.* **1** Grasped mentally; comprehended. **2** Taken for granted. **3** Agreed upon by all.

un·der·stud·y (un′dər·stud′ē) *v.t. & v.i.* **·stud·ied, ·stud·y·ing** 1 To study (a part) in order to be able, if necessary, to substitute for the actor playing it. 2 To act as an understudy to (another actor). —*n. pl.* **·stud·ies** 1 An actor or actress who can substitute for another actor in a given role. 2 A person prepared to perform the work or fill the position of another.

un·der·take (un′dər·tāk′) *v.t.* **·took, ·tak·en, ·tak·ing** 1 To take upon oneself; agree or attempt to do. 2 To contract to do; pledge oneself to. 3 To guarantee or promise. 4 To take under charge or guidance.

un·der·tak·er (un′dər·tā′kər *for def. 1*; un′dər·tā′kər *for def. 2*) *n.* 1 One who undertakes any work or enterprise; esp. a contractor. 2 One whose business it is to prepare a dead person for burial and to conduct funerals.

un·der·tak·ing (un′dər·tā′king, *esp. for def. 3*, un′dər·tā′king) *n.* 1 The act of one who undertakes any task or enterprise. 2 The thing undertaken; an enterprise; task. 3 The business of an undertaker (def. 2). 4 An engagement, promise, or guarantee.

un·der·tone (un′dər·tōn′) *n.* 1 A low or subdued tone, esp. a vocal tone, as a whisper. 2 A subdued color, esp. one with other colors imposed on it. 3 A meaning, suggestion, quality, etc., that is implied but not expressed.

un·der·tow (un′dər·tō′) *n.* A flow of water beneath and in a direction opposite to the surface current, esp. such a flow moving seaward beneath surf.

un·der·val·ue (un′dər·val′yōō) *v.t.* **·ued, ·u·ing** 1 To value or rate below the real worth. 2 To regard or esteem as of little worth. —**un′der·val′u·a′tion** *n.*

un·der·wa·ter (un′dər·wô′tər, -wot′ər) *adj.* 1 Being, occurring, used, etc., below the surface of a body of water: *underwater* research. 2 Below the water line of a ship. —*adv.* Below the surface of water.

under way 1 In progress: The meeting was already *under way.* 2 Into operation or motion: to get the fund drive *under way.*

un·der·wear (un′dər·wâr′) *n.* Garments worn underneath the ordinary outer garments.

un·der·weight (un′dər·wāt′) *adj.* Having less than the normal, desired, or permitted weight. —*n.* Weight less than normal, permitted, or desired.

un·der·went (un′dər·went′) *p.t.* of UNDERGO.

un·der·wood (un′dər·wōōd′) *n.* UNDERBRUSH.

un·der·world (un′dər·wûrld′) *n.* 1 The mythical abode of the dead; Hades. 2 The world of organized crime and vice.

un·der·write (un′dər·rīt′) *v.* **·wrote, ·writ·ten, ·writ·ing** *v.t.* 1 To write beneath or sign something, as a document. 2 To agree or subscribe to, esp. to agree to pay for (an enterprise, etc.). 3 In insurance: **a** To sign one's name to (an insurance policy), thereby assuming liability for certain designated losses or damage. **b** To insure. **c** To assume (a risk or a liability for a certain sum) by way of insurance. 4 To engage to buy, at a determined price and time, all or part of the stock in (a new enterprise or company) that is not subscribed for by the public. —*v.i.* 5 To act as an underwriter; esp., to issue a policy of insurance.

un·der·writ·er (un′dər·rī′tər) *n.* 1 A person or company in the insurance business; also, an insurance employee who determines the risks involved, the amount of the premiums, etc., for a specific applicant or policy. 2 One who underwrites something.

un·de·sir·a·ble (un′di·zīr′ə·bəl) *adj.* Not desirable; objectionable. —*n.* An undesirable person. —**un′de·sir′a·bil′i·ty** *n.* —**un′de·sir′a·bly** *adv.*

un·do (un·dōō′) *v.t.* **·did, ·done, ·do·ing** 1 To cause to be as if never done; reverse, annul, or cancel. 2 To loosen or untie. 3 To unfasten and open. 4 To bring to ruin; destroy. 5 To disturb emotionally. [< OE *undōn*] —**un·do′er** *n.*

un·do·ing (un·dōō′ing) *n.* 1 A reversal of what has been done. 2 Destruction; ruin; disgrace; also, the cause of such ruin or disgrace. 3 The action of unfastening, loosening, opening, etc.

un·done[1] (un·dun′) *adj.* 1 Untied; unfastened. 2 Ruined; disgraced. 3 Extremely disturbed or upset. [Orig. p.p. of UNDO]

un·done[2] (un·dun′) *adj.* Not done.

un·doubt·ed (un·dou′tid) *adj.* 1 Not doubted; assured; certain. 2 Not viewed with distrust; unsuspected. —**un·doubt′ed·ly** *adv.*

un·draw (un·drô′) *v.t. & v.i.* **·drew, ·drawn, ·draw·ing** To draw open, away, or aside.

un·dreamed-of (un·drēmd′uv′, -dremt′-) *adj.* Never imagined; wholly unforeseen: *undreamed-of* joy. Also **un·dreamt′-of′** (-dremt′-).

un·dress (un·dres′) *v.t.* 1 To divest of clothes; strip. 2 To remove the dressing or bandages from, as a wound. 3 To divest of special attire; disrobe. —*v.i.* 4 To remove one's clothing. —*n.* 1 The state of being nude or in only partial attire, as in undergarments, dressing robe, etc. 2 The military or naval uniform worn by officers when not in full dress.

un·due (un·dōō′) *adj.* 1 Excessive; immoderate. 2 Not justified by law; illegal. 3 Not yet due, as a bill. 4 Not appropriate; improper.

un·du·lant (un′dyə·lənt, -jə-) *adj.* Undulating; fluctuating.

undulant fever A persistent bacterial disease usu. transmitted to man by contact with infected cattle and characterized by recurrent fever, exhaustion, neuralgic pains, etc.

un·du·late (un′dyə·lāt, -jə-) *v.* **·lat·ed, ·lat·ing** *v.t.* 1 To cause to move like a wave or in waves. 2 To give a wavy appearance or surface to. —*v.i.* 3 To move like a wave or waves. 4 To have a wavy form or appearance. —*adj.* (-lit, -lāt) Having a wavelike appearance, surface, or markings: also **un′du·lat′ed.** [< L *unda* wave]

un·du·la·tion (un′dyə·lā′shən, -jə-) *n.* 1 A waving or sinuous motion. 2 An appearance as of waves; a gentle rise and fall. —**un′du·la·to′ry** (-lə·tôr′ē, -tō′rē) *adj.*

un·du·ly (un·dōō′lē) *adv.* 1 Excessively. 2 Improperly; unjustly.

un·dy·ing (un·dī′ing) *adj.* Immortal; eternal.

un·earned (un·ûrnd′) *adj.* 1 Not earned by labor, skill, etc. 2 Undeserved.

unearned increment An increase in the value of land or property independent of any efforts of the owner, as through an increase of population that creates demand.

un·earth (un·ûrth′) *v.t.* 1 To dig or root up from the earth. 2 To reveal; discover.

un·earth·ly (un·ûrth′lē) *adj.* 1 Not, or seemingly not, of this earth. 2 Supernatural; terrifying; weird; terrible. 3 *Informal* Ridiculous, absurd, preposterous, etc. —**un·earth′li·ness** *n.*

un·ease (un·ēz′) *n.* Mental or emotional discomfort, dissatisfaction, anxiety, etc.

un·eas·y (un·ē′zē) *adj.* **·eas·i·er, ·eas·i·est** 1 Deprived of ease; disturbed; unquiet. 2 Not comfortable; causing discomfort. 3 Showing embarrassment or constraint; strained. 4 Not stable or secure; precarious: an *uneasy* peace. —**un·eas′i·ly** *adv.* —**un·eas′i·ness** *n.*

un·em·ploy·a·ble (un′əm·ploi′ə·bəl) *adj.* Not employable because of illness, age, physical incapacity, etc. —*n.* An unemployable person.

un·em·ployed (un′əm·ploid′) *adj.* 1 Having no employment; out of work. 2 Not put to use or turned to account; idle. —**the unemployed** People who have no jobs. —**un′·em·ploy′ment** *n.*

un·e·qual (un·ē′kwəl) *adj.* 1 Not equal in size, importance, weight, ability, duration, etc. 2 Inadequate; insufficient: with *to.* 3 Not balanced or uniform; variable; irregular. 4 Involving poorly matched competitors or contestants: an *unequal* contest. —**un·e′qual·ly** *adv.*

un·e·qualed (un·ē′kwəld) *adj.* Not equaled or matched; unrivaled. Also **un·e′qualled.**

un·e·quiv·o·cal (un′i·kwiv′ə·kəl) *adj.* Understandable in only one way; not ambiguous; clear. —**un′e·quiv′o·cal·ly** *adv.* —**un′e·quiv′o·cal·ness** *n.*

un·err·ing (un·ûr′ing, -er′-) *adj.* 1 Making no mistakes. 2 Certain; accurate; infallible. —**un·err′ing·ly** *adv.*

UNESCO (yōō·nes′kō) United Nations Educational, Scientific, and Cultural Organization.

un·es·sen·tial (un′ə-sen′shəl) *adj.* Not essential; not needed. —*n.* Something not essential; an extra.

un·e·ven (un-ē′vən) *adj.* 1 Not even, smooth, or level; rough. 2 Not straight, parallel, or perfectly horizontal. 3 Not equal or even, as in length, width, etc. 4 Not balanced or matched equally. 5 Not uniform; variable; fluctuating. 6 Not fair or just. 7 Not divisible by two without remainder; odd: said of numbers. —**un·e′ven·ly** *adv.* —**un·e′ven·ness** *n.*

un·e·vent·ful (un′i-vent′fəl) *adj.* Devoid of any noteworthy or unusual events or incidents; quiet. —**un′e·vent′·ful·ly** *adv.* —**un′e·vent′ful·ness** *n.*

un·ex·am·pled (un′ig-zam′pəld) *adj.* Without a parallel example; unprecedented; unique.

un·ex·cep·tion·a·ble (un′ik-sep′shən-ə-bəl) *adj.* That cannot be objected to; without any flaw; irreproachable. —**un′ex·cep′tion·a·bly** *adv.*

un·ex·cep·tion·al (un′ik-sep′shən-əl) *adj.* 1 Not unusual or exceptional; ordinary. 2 Subject to no exception.

un·ex·pect·ed (un′ik-spek′tid) *adj.* Coming without warning; not expected; unforeseen. —**un′ex·pect′ed·ly** *adv.* —**un′ex·pect′ed·ness** *n.* —Syn. unanticipated, sudden.

un·fail·ing (un-fā′ling) *adj.* 1 Giving or constituting a supply that never fails; inexhaustible: an *unfailing* spring. 2 Always fulfilling requirements or expectation. 3 Sure; infallible. —**un·fail′ing·ly** *adv.* —**un·fail′ing·ness** *n.*

un·fair (un-fâr′) *adj.* 1 Marked by injustice, deception, or bias; not fair. 2 Not honest or ethical in business affairs. —**un·fair′ly** *adv.* —**un·fair′ness** *n.*

un·faith·ful (un-fāth′fəl) *adj.* 1 Not faithful to or abiding by a vow, agreement, duty, etc.; disloyal. 2 Not accurate or exact; unreliable. 3 Not true to marriage vows; adulterous. —**un·faith′ful·ly** *adv.* —**un·faith′ful·ness** *n.*

un·fa·mil·iar (un′fə-mil′yər) *adj.* 1 Not knowing well or at all: with *with*: *unfamiliar* with his plays. 2 Not familiarly known; strange: an *unfamiliar* face. —**un′fa·mil′i·ar′·i·ty** (-mil′ē·ar′ə·tē) *n.* —**un′fa·mil′iar·ly** *adv.*

un·fast·en (un-fas′ən, -fäs′-) *v.t.* To untie or undo; loosen or open.

un·fa·vor·a·ble (un-fā′vər-ə-bəl) *adj.* 1 Not favorable; adverse. 2 Not propitious. —**un·fa′vor·a·bly** *adv.*

un·feel·ing (un-fē′ling) *adj.* 1 Not sympathetic; hard; callous. 2 Having no feeling or sensation. —**un·feel′ing·ly** *adv.* —**un·feel′ing·ness** *n.*

un·feigned (un-fānd′) *adj.* Not feigned; sincere; genuine. —**un·feign′ed·ly** (-fān′id·lē) *adv.*

un·fit (un-fit′) *v.t.* **·fit·ted** or **·fit, ·fit·ting** To deprive of requisite fitness, skill, etc.; disqualify. —*adj.* 1 Not able to meet the requirements or needs; unsuitable. 2 Not physically or mentally sound or fit. 3 Not appropriate or proper for a given purpose. —**un·fit′ly** *adv.* —**un·fit′ness** *n.*

un·fix (un-fiks′) *v.t.* 1 To unfasten; loosen; detach. 2 To unsettle.

un·flag·ging (un-flag′ing) *adj.* Not diminishing or failing; tireless. —**un·flag′ging·ly** *adv.*

un·flap·pa·ble (un-flap′ə·bəl) *adj.* *Informal* Characterized by unshakable composure; imperturbable. —**un·flap′·pa·bil′i·ty** *n.*

un·fledged (un-flejd′) *adj.* 1 Not yet fledged, as a young bird. 2 Inexperienced or immature.

un·flinch·ing (un-flin′ching) *adj.* Done without shrinking; steadfast. —**un·flinch′ing·ly** *adv.*

un·fold (un-fōld′) *v.t.* 1 To open or spread out (something folded). 2 To unwrap. 3 To reveal or make clear, as by explaining or disclosing gradually. 4 To develop. —*v.i.* 5 To become opened; expand. 6 To become manifest or develop fully.

un·fore·seen (un′fôr·sēn′, -fōr-) *adj.* Unexpected.

un·for·get·ta·ble (un′fər·get′ə·bəl) *adj.* Difficult or impossible to forget; memorable. —**un′for·get′ta·bly** *adv.*

un·for·tu·nate (un-fôr′chə·nit) *adj.* 1 Not fortunate or lucky. 2 Causing, attended by, or resulting from misfortune; disastrous. 3 Not suitable or proper; bad; regrettable: an *unfortunate* thing to say. —*n.* One who is unfortunate. —**un′for′tu·nate·ly** *adv.* —**un′for′tu·nate·ness** *n.*

un·found·ed (un-foun′did) *adj.* 1 Not based on fact; groundless; baseless. 2 Not established.

un·fre·quent·ed (un′fri·kwent′id) *adj.* Rarely or never visited or frequented.

un·friend·ly (un-frend′lē) *adj.* 1 Not friendly or sympathetic. 2 Not favorable or propitious. —**un·friend′li·ness** *n.*

un·frock (un-frok′) *v.t.* 1 To remove a frock or gown from. 2 To depose, as a priest, from ecclesiastical rank.

un·furl (un-fûrl′) *v.t. & v.i.* 1 To unroll, as a flag; spread out. 2 To unfold. —**un·furled′** *adj.*

un·gain·ly (un-gān′lē) *adj.* 1 Awkward; clumsy. 2 Not attractive. —**un·gain′li·ness** *n.*

un·glued (un·glōōd′) *adj.* No longer glued together; separated. —**come unglued** *Slang* To become mentally or emotionally upset.

un·god·ly (un·god′lē) *adj.* 1 Without reverence for God; impious. 2 Unholy; sinful. 3 *Informal* Outrageous. —*adv.* *Informal* Outrageously. —**un·god′li·ness** *n.*

un·gov·ern·a·ble (un·guv′ər·nə·bəl) *adj.* That cannot be governed; wild; unruly. —**un·gov′ern·a·bly** *adv.*

un·gra·cious (un·grā′shəs) *adj.* 1 Lacking in graciousness of manner; unmannerly. 2 Not pleasing; offensive. —**un·gra′cious·ly** *adv.* —**un·gra′cious·ness** *n.* —Syn. 1 discourteous, rude, impolite, uncivil, ill-mannered, ill-bred.

un·grate·ful (un·grāt′fəl) *adj.* 1 Feeling or showing a lack of gratitude; not thankful. 2 Not pleasant; disagreeable. 3 Unrewarding; yielding no return. —**un·grate′ful·ly** *adv.* —**un·grate′ful·ness** *n.*

un·guard·ed (un·gär′did) *adj.* 1 Having no guard; unprotected. 2 Thoughtless; careless. 3 Without guile; direct; open. —**un·guard′ed·ly** *adv.*

un·guent (ung′gwənt) *n.* An ointment or salve. [< L *unguere* anoint] —**un·guen·ta·ry** (-gwən·ter′ē) *adj.*

un·guis (ung′gwis) *n. pl.* **·gues** (-gwēz) A hoof, claw, nail, or talon. [L, nail]

un·gu·late (ung′gyə·lit, -lāt) *adj.* Having hoofs. —*n.* A hoofed mammal. [< L *ungula* hoof]

un·hand (un·hand′) *v.t.* To remove one's hand from; release from the hand or hands; let go.

un·hand·y (un·han′dē) *adj.* **·di·er, ·di·est** 1 Hard to get to or use; inconvenient. 2 Clumsy; lacking in manual skill. —**un·hand′i·ly** *adv.*

un·hap·py (un·hap′ē) *adj.* **·pi·er, ·pi·est** 1 Sad; depressed. 2 Causing or constituting misery, unrest, or dissatisfaction: *unhappy* circumstances. 3 Unfortunate; unpropitious. 4 Exhibiting lack of tact or judgment; inappropriate. —**un·hap′pi·ly** *adv.* —**un·hap′pi·ness** *n.*

un·health·y (un·hel′thē) *adj.* **·health·i·er, ·health·i·est** 1 Lacking health, vigor, or wholesomeness; sickly. 2 Causing sickness; injurious to health. 3 Morally harmful. 4 Dangerous; risky. —**un·health′i·ly** *adv.* —**un·health′i·ness** *n.*

un·heard (un·hûrd′) *adj.* 1 Not perceived by the ear. 2 Not granted a hearing. 3 Obscure; unknown.

un·heard-of (un·hûrd′uv′, -ov′) *adj.* 1 Not known of before; unknown or unprecedented. 2 Outrageous; unbelievable.

un·hinge (un·hinj′) *v.t.* **·hinged, ·hing·ing** 1 To take from the hinges. 2 To remove the hinges of. 3 To detach; dislodge. 4 To throw into confusion; unsettle, as the mind.

un·hitch (un·hich′) *v.t.* To unfasten.

un·ho·ly (un·hō′lē) *adj.* **·ho·li·er, ·ho·li·est** 1 Not hallowed. 2 Wicked; sinful. 3 *Informal* Frightful; outrageous. —**un·ho′li·ly** *adv.* —**un·ho′li·ness** *n.*

uni- *combining form* One; single; one only: *unifoliate*. [< L *unus* one]

U·ni·ate (yōō′nē·at, -it) *n.* A member of any community of Eastern Christians that acknowledges the supremacy of the pope at Rome, but retains its own liturgy, ceremonies, and rites. —*adj.* Of the Uniates or their faith. Also **U′ni·at** (-it).

u·ni·cam·er·al (yōō′nə·kam′ər·əl) *adj.* Consisting of but one chamber, as a legislature.

UNICEF (yōō′nə·sef) United Nations Children's Fund. [< *U(nited) N(ations) I(nternational) C(hildren's) E(mergency) F(und),* its former name]

u·ni·cel·lu·lar (yōō′nə·sel′yə·lər) *adj.* Consisting of a single cell, as a protozoan.

u·ni·corn (yōō′nə·kôrn′) *n.* A mythical, horselike animal with

Unicorn

one horn growing from the middle of its forehead. [< L *unicornis* one-horned]

u·ni·cy·cle (yōō′nə·sī′kəl) *n.* A bicyclelike vehicle having only a single wheel propelled by pedals.

u·ni·form (yōō′nə·fôrm′) *adj.* 1 Being always the same or alike; not varying: *uniform* temperature. 2 Having the same form, color, character, etc. as others: a line of *uniform* battleships. 3 Being the same throughout in appearance, color, surface, etc.: a *uniform* texture. 4 Consistent in effect, action, etc.: a *uniform* law for all drivers. —*n.* A distinctive dress or suit worn, esp. when on duty, by members of the same organization, service, etc., as soldiers, sailors, postmen, etc. —*v.t.* To put into or clothe with a uniform. [< L *unus* one + *forma* form] —**u′ni·form·ly** *adv.*

u·ni·form·i·ty (yōō′nə·fôr′mə·tē) *n. pl.* **·ties** 1 The state or quality of being uniform. 2 An instance of it.

u·ni·fy (yōō′nə·fī) *v.t.* **·fied, ·fy·ing** To cause to be one; make uniform; unite. [< L *unus* one + *facere* make] —**u′ni·fi·ca′·tion** (-fə·kā′shən), **u′ni·fi′er** *n.*

u·ni·lat·er·al (yōō′nə·lat′ər·əl) *adj.* 1 Of, relating to, or affecting one side only; one-sided. 2 Made, undertaken, done, or signed by only one of two or more people or parties. 3 Growing on or turning toward one side only. —**u′ni·lat′er·al·ism** *n.* —**u′ni·lat′er·al·ly** *adv.*

un·im·peach·a·ble (un′im·pē′chə·bəl) *adj.* Not impeachable; beyond question as regards truth, honesty, etc.; faultless; blameless. —**un′im·peach′a·bly** *adv.*

un·im·proved (un′im·prōōvd′) *adj.* 1 Not improved; not bettered or advanced. 2 Having no improvements; not cleared, cultivated, or built upon. 3 Not made anything of; unused.

un·in·tel·li·gi·ble (un′in·tel′ə·jə·bəl) *adj.* Impossible to understand; incomprehensible. —**un′in·tel′li·gi·bil′i·ty** *n.* —**un′in·tel′li·gi·bly** *adv.*

un·in·ter·es·ted (un·in′tər·is·tid, -tris-) *adj.* Not interested; indifferent; unconcerned. • See DISINTERESTED.

un·ion (yōōn′yən) *n.* 1 The act or an instance of uniting two or more things into one, as: **a** A political joining together, as of states or nations. **b** Marriage; wedlock. 2 The condition of being united or joined; junction. 3 Something formed by uniting or combining parts, as: **a** A confederation, coalition, or league, as of nations, states, or individuals. **b** LABOR UNION. 4 A device for joining mechanical parts, esp. a coupling device for pipes or rods. 5 A college or university organization that provides facilities for recreation, meetings, light meals, etc.: also **student union**. 6 A device emblematic of union used in a flag or ensign, as the blue field with white stars in the flag of the U.S. —*adj.* Of, being, or relating to a union. —**the Union** The United States of America. [< L *unus* one]

un·ion·ism (yōōn′yən·iz′əm) *n.* 1 The principle of union. 2 Labor unions collectively; also, their principles and practices. —**un′ion·ist** *n.* —**un′ion·is′tic** *adj.*

Un·ion·ism (yōōn′yən·iz′əm) *n.* During the U.S. Civil War, the advocacy of political union between the States, as opposed to secession. —**Un′ion·ist** *n.*

un·ion·ize (yōōn′yən·īz) *v.* **·ized, ·iz·ing** *v.t.* To cause to join or to organize into a labor union. —*v.i.* To become a member of or organize a labor union. —**un′ion·i·za′tion** *n.*

Union Jack The British national flag.

Union of Soviet Socialist Republics A federal union of 15 republics in N Eurasia, 8,646,400 sq. mi., cap. Moscow.

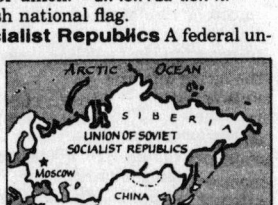

union shop A factory, office, hospital, etc., in which only members of a labor union are employed.

union suit A one-piece, man's or boy's undergarment consisting of shirt and drawers.

u·nique (yōō·nēk′) *adj.* 1 Being the only one of its kind; single; sole. 2 Being without equal; unparalleled. 3 Very

unusual or remarkable; exceptional, extraordinary, etc. [< L *unicus* < *unus* one] —**u·nique′ly** *adv.* —**u·nique′ness** *n.*

u·ni·sex (yōō′nə·seks′) *Informal adj.* For, appropriate to, or having characteristics of both sexes: *unisex* fashions. —*n.* The embodiment or integration of qualities, characteristics, etc., of both sexes, as in appearance, clothes, or activities.

u·ni·sex·u·al (yōō′nə·sek′shōō·əl) *adj.* 1 Of only one sex; dioecious: a *unisexual* plant. 2 *Informal* Of or having to do with unisex. —**u′ni·sex′u·al′i·ty** *n.* —**u′ni·sex′u·al·ly** *adv.*

u·ni·son (yōō′nə·sən, -zən) *n.* 1 A condition of perfect agreement and accord; harmony. 2 *Music* **a** The interval between tones of identical pitch. **b** The simultaneous sounding of the same tones by two or more parts. —**in unison** 1 So that identical tones are sounded simultaneously by two or more parts. 2 So that identical words or sounds are uttered simultaneously. 3 In perfect agreement. [< L *unisonus* having a single sound]

u·nit (yōō′nit) *n.* 1 A predetermined quantity, as of time, length, work, value, etc., used as a standard of measurement or comparison. 2 A fixed amount of work or classroom hours used in calculating a scholastic degree. 3 The quantity, as of a drug or antigen, required to produce a given effect or result. 4 A person or group considered both singly and as a constituent part of a whole: a military *unit*. 5 Something, as a mechanical part or device, having a specific function and serving as part of a whole: the electrical *unit* of a percolator. 6 *Math.* A quantity whose measure is represented by the number 1. —*adj.* Of or being a unit: the *unit* value of an article of merchandise. [Short for UNITY]

U·ni·tar·i·an (yōō′nə·târ′ē·ən) *n.* A member of a Protestant denomination which rejects the doctrine of the Trinity, but accepts the ethical teachings of Jesus and emphasizes complete freedom of religious opinion and the independence of each local congregation. —*adj.* Pertaining to the Unitarians, or to their teachings. —**U′ni·tar′i·an·ism** *n.*

u·ni·tar·y (yōō′nə·ter′ē) *adj.* 1 Of a unit or units. 2 Characterized by, based on, or pertaining to unity. 3 Having the nature of or used as a unit.

u·nite (yōō·nīt′) *v.* **u·nit·ed, u·nit·ing** *v.t.* 1 To join together so as to form a whole; combine. 2 To bring into close connection, as by legal, physical, marital, social, or other ties: to be *united* in marriage; allies *united* by a common interest. 3 To have or possess in combination: to *unite* courage with wisdom. 4 To cause to adhere; combine. —*v.i.* 5 To become or be merged into one; be consolidated by or as if by adhering. 6 To join together for action. [< L *unus* one]

u·nit·ed (yōō·nī′tid) *adj.* 1 Incorporated into one; combined. 2 Of or resulting from joint action. 3 Harmonious; in agreement. —**u·nit′ed·ly** *adv.* —**u·nit′ed·ness** *n.*

United Kingdom A constitutional monarchy located on several islands off the coast of N Europe, comprising Great Britain, Northern Ireland, and nearby islands, 94,284 sq. mi., cap. London.

United Kingdom

United Nations 1 A coalition to resist the military aggression of the Axis Powers in World War II, formed of 26 national states in January, 1942. 2 An international organization of sovereign states (originally called the **United Nations Organization**) created by the United Nations Charter adopted at San Francisco in 1945.

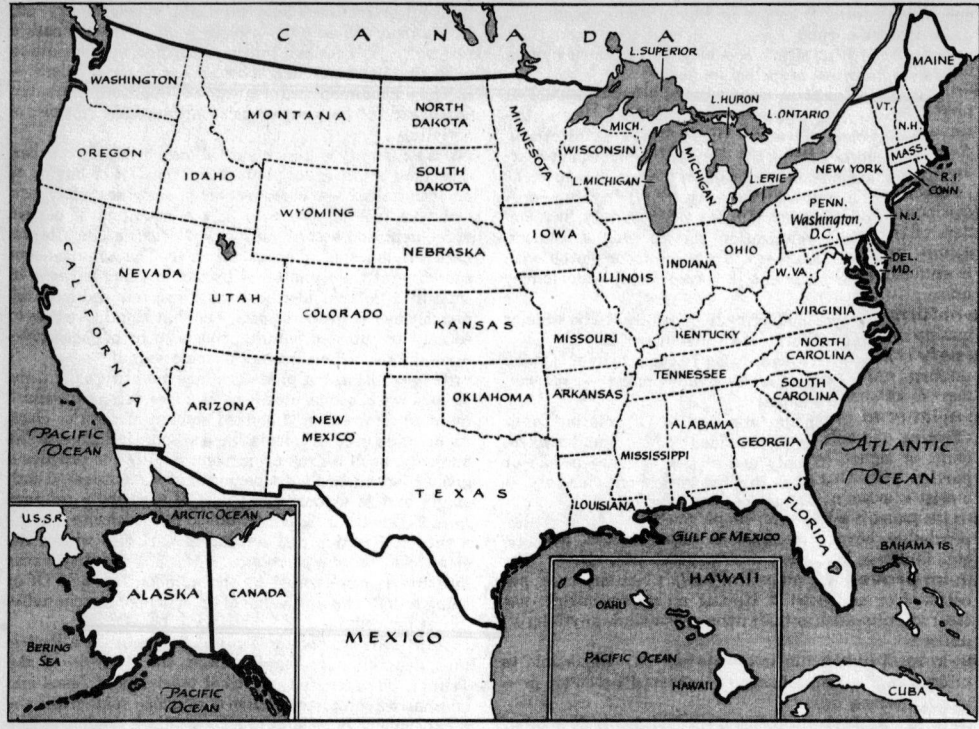

United States of America A federal republic including 50 states (49 in North America, and Hawaii, an archipelago in the Pacific Ocean), and the District of Columbia, 3,615,222 sq. mi., cap. Washington, D.C.

u·ni·ty (yōō′nə·tē) *n. pl.* **·ties 1** The state or quality of being one or united; oneness. **2** The product or result of being one or united. **3** Singleness of purpose or action. **4** A state of mutual understanding. **5** The quality or fact of being a whole through the unification of separate or individual parts. **6** In a literary or artistic production, a combination of parts that exhibits a prevailing oneness of purpose, thought, spirit, and style; also, the cohesive or harmonious effect so produced. **7** *Math.* **a** The number one. **b** The element of a number system that leaves any number unchanged under multiplication. [< L *unus* one]

Univ. Universalist; University.

univ. universal; universally; university.

u·ni·va·lent (yōō′nə·vā′lənt) *adj. Chem.* Having a valence or combining value of one; monovalent. —**u′ni·va′-lence, u′ni·va′len·cy** *n.*

u·ni·valve (yōō′nə·valv′) *adj.* Having the shell in one piece, as a snail. Also **u′ni·val′vate, u′ni·valved′.** —*n.* **1** A mollusk having a univalve shell; a gastropod. **2** A shell of a single piece. —**u′ni·val′vu·lar** (-val′vyə·lər) *adj.*

u·ni·ver·sal (yōō′nə·vûr′səl) *adj.* **1** Prevalent or common everywhere or among all things or persons. **2** Of, applicable to, for, or including all things, persons, cases, etc., without exception. **3** Accomplished or interested in a vast variety of subjects, activities, etc.: Leonardo da Vinci was a *universal* genius. **4** Adapted or adaptable to a great variety of uses, shapes, etc. **5** *Logic* Including or designating all the members of a class. —*n.* **1** *Logic* A universal proposition. **2** Any general or universal notion or idea. **3** A behavioral trait common to all men or cultures. —**u′ni·ver′sal·ly** *adv.* —**u′ni·ver·sal·ism, u′ni·ver·sal·ness** *n.*

u·ni·ver·sal·i·ty (yōō′nə·vər·sal′ə·tē) *n.* **1** The quality, condition, or an instance of being universal. **2** Limitlessness, as of range, occurrence, etc.

u·ni·ver·sal·ize (yōō′nə·vûr′səl·īz) *v.t.* **·ized, ·iz·ing** To make universal. —**u′ni·ver·sal·i·za′tion** *n.*

universal joint *Mech.* A coupling for connecting two shafts, etc., so as to permit angular motion in all directions. Also **universal coupling.**

u·ni·verse (yōō′nə·vûrs) *n.* **1** The aggregate of all existing things; the whole creation embracing all celestial bodies and all of space; the cosmos. **2** In restricted sense, the earth. **3** Something regarded as being a universe in its comprehensiveness, as a field of thought or activity. [< L *universus* turned, combined into one < *unus* one + *versus,* p.p. of *vertere* turn]

u·ni·ver·si·ty (yōō′nə·vûr′sə·tē) *n. pl.* **·ties 1** An educational institution for higher instruction, usu., in the U.S., an institution that includes an undergraduate college or colleges and professional schools granting advanced degrees in law, medicine, the sciences, academic subjects, etc. **2** The buildings, grounds, etc., of a university. **3** The students, faculty, and administration of a university.

un·just (un·just′) *adj.* Not legitimate, fair, or just; wrongful. —**un·just′ly** *adv.*

un·kempt (un·kempt′) *adj.* **1** Not combed: said of hair. **2** Not neat or tidy. **3** Without polish; rough. [< UN-¹ + *kempt* combed, p.p. of *kemb,* dial. var. of COMB]

un·kind (un·kīnd′) *adj.* Lacking kindness; unsympathetic; harsh; cruel. —**un·kind′ly** *adj.* **(·li·er, ·li·est)** & *adv.* —**un·kind′li·ness, un·kind′ness** *n.*

un·known (un·nōn′) *adj.* **1** Not known; not apprehended mentally; not recognized, as a fact or person. **2** Not determined or identified: an *unknown* substance. —*n.* An unknown person, thing, or quantity.

un·lace (un·lās′) *v.t.* **·laced, ·lac·ing** To loosen or unfasten the lacing of; untie.

un·law·ful (un·lô′fəl) *adj.* **1** Contrary to or in violation of law; illegal. **2** Not moral or ethical. —**un·law′ful·ly** *adv.* —**un·law′ful·ness** *n.*

un·learn (un·lûrn′) *v.t.* **·learned** or **·learnt, ·learn·ing 1** To dismiss from the mind (something learned); forget. **2** To attempt to abandon the habit of.

un·learn·ed (un·lûr′nid) *adj.* **1** Not possessed of or characterized by learning; illiterate; ignorant. **2** Characterized by lack of knowledge, professional skill, etc. **3** (un·lûrnd′) Not acquired by learning or study.

un·leash (un·lēsh′) *v.t.* To set free from or as from a leash: He *unleashed* his rage.

un·less (un·les′) *conj.* If it be not a fact that; except that: *Unless* we persevere, we shall lose. —*prep.* Save; except; excepting: with an implied verb: *Unless* a miracle, he'll not be back in time. [Earlier *onlesse (that)* in a less case < ON + LESS]

un·let·tered (un·let′ərd) *adj.* Not educated; not lettered; illiterate.

un·like (un·līk′) *adj.* Having little or no resemblance; different. —*prep.* **1** Not like; different from. **2** Not characteristic of: It's *unlike* her to complain. —**un·like′ness** *n.*

un·like·ly (un·līk′lē) *adj.* **1** Improbable. **2** Not inviting or promising success. —*adv.* Improbably. —**un·like′li·hood, un·like′li·ness** *n.*

un·lim·it·ed (un·lim′it·id) *adj.* **1** Having no limits in space, number, or time. **2** Not restricted or limited.

un·load (un·lōd′) *v.t.* **1** To remove the load or cargo from. **2** To take off or discharge (cargo, etc.). **3** To relieve of something burdensome or oppressive. **4** To withdraw the charge of ammunition from. **5** *Informal* To dispose of, esp. by selling in large quantities. —*v.i.* **6** To discharge freight, cargo, etc.

un·lock (un·lok′) *v.t.* **1** To unfasten (something locked). **2** To open; release. **3** To lay open; reveal or disclose. —*v.i.* **4** To become unlocked.

un·looked-for (un·lŏŏkt′fôr′) *adj.* Not anticipated; unexpected.

un·loose (un·lōōs′) *v.t.* **·loosed, ·loos·ing** To make loose; set free; undo, release, etc. Also **un·loos′en** (-lōō′sən).

un·luck·y (un·luk′ē) *adj.* **·luck·i·er, ·luck·i·est** **1** Not favored by luck; unfortunate. **2** Resulting in or attended by ill luck; disastrous. **3** Likely to prove unfortunate; inauspicious. —**un·luck′i·ly** *adv.* —**un·luck′i·ness** *n.*

un·make (un·māk′) *v.t.* **·made, ·mak·ing** **1** To reduce to the original condition or form. **2** To ruin; destroy. **3** To deprive of rank, power, etc.

un·man (un·man′) *v.t.* **·manned, ·man·ning** **1** To cause to lose courage; dishearten. **2** To deprive of manly qualities; make weak or timid. **3** To castrate; emasculate.

un·man·ly (un·man′lē) *adj.* Not manly; weak, cowardly, effeminate, etc. —**un·man′li·ness** *n.*

un·mask (un·mask′, -mäsk′) *v.t.* **1** To remove a mask from. **2** To expose the true nature of. —*v.i.* **3** To remove one's mask or disguise.

un·mean·ing (un·mē′ning) *adj.* **1** Having no meaning: an *unmeaning* speech. **2** Having no expression: an *unmeaning* stare. —**un·mean′ing·ly** *adv.* —**un·mean′ing·ness** *n.*

un·men·tion·a·ble (un·men′shən·ə·bəl) *adj.* Not fit to be mentioned or discussed; embarrassing. —*n.pl.* Things not ordinarily mentioned or discussed, esp. undergarments. —**un·men′tion·a·ble·ness** *n.* —**un·men′tion·a·bly** *adv.*

un·mer·ci·ful (un·mûr′sə·fəl) *adj.* **1** Showing no mercy; cruel; pitiless. **2** Extreme; exorbitant. —**un·mer′ci·ful·ly** *adv.* —**un·mer′ci·ful·ness** *n.*

un·mis·tak·a·ble (un′mis·tā′kə·bəl) *adj.* That cannot be mistaken for something else; evident; obvious. —**un′mis·tak′a·bly** *adv.*

un·mit·i·gat·ed (un·mit′ə·gā′tid) *adj.* **1** Not relieved or lessened: *unmitigated* sorrow. **2** Absolute; thoroughgoing: an *unmitigated* liar. —**un·mit′i·gat·ed·ly** *adv.*

un·mor·al (un·môr′əl, -mor′-) *adj.* **1** Incapable of distinguishing between right and wrong; not guided by moral considerations. **2** Outside the realm of morality or ethics. —**un·mo·ral·i·ty** (un′mə·ral′ə·tē) *n.* • *Unmoral, amoral,* and *immoral* are alike in meaning not moral. However, *unmoral* and *amoral* are synonymous in referring to objects or acts (or people involved with such objects or acts) which stand outside the realm of morality whereas *immoral* infers a conflict with accepted standards of morality.

un·nat·u·ral (un·nach′ər·əl, -nach′rəl, un′-) *adj.* **1** Contrary to the norm. **2** Contrary to the common laws of morality or decency; monstrous; inhuman. **3** Contrived; artificial. —**un·nat′u·ral·ly** *adv.* —**un·nat′u·ral·ness** *n.*

un·nec·es·sary (un·nes′ə·ser′ē, un′-) *adj.* Not required; not necessary. —**un·nec·es·sar·i·ly** (un′nes′ə·ser′ə·lē) *adv.*

un·nerve (un·nûrv′) *v.t.* **·nerved, ·nerv·ing** **1** To deprive of strength, firmness, courage, etc. **2** To make nervous.

un·num·bered (un·num′bərd) *adj.* **1** Not counted. **2** Innumerable. **3** Not numbered.

habited: an *unoccupied* house. **2** Idle; unemployed; at leisure.

un·of·fi·cial (un·ə·fish′əl) *adj.* **1** Not official; not authoritative. —**un·of·fi′cial·ly** *adv.*

un·or·gan·ized (un·ôr′gən·īzd) *adj.* **1** Not organized. **2** Without form or structure. **3** Not unionized.

un·pack (un·pak′) *v.t.* **1** To open and take out the contents of. **2** To take out of the container, as something packed. —*v.i.* **3** To take the contents out of a suitcase, etc.

un·par·al·leled (un·par′ə·leld) *adj.* Without parallel; unmatched; unprecedented.

un·peg (un·peg′) *v.t.* **·pegged, ·peg·ging** To unfasten by removing the peg or pegs from.

un·peo·ple (un·pē′pəl) *v.t.* **·pled, ·pling** To depopulate; deprive of inhabitants.

un·per·son (un′pûr′sən) *n.* One reduced to a state of oblivion, as by official action or the loss of position, after a period of fame or public importance.

un·pin (un·pin′) *v.t.* **·pinned, ·pin·ning** **1** To remove a pin or pins from. **2** To unfasten by removing pins.

un·pleas·ant (un·plez′ənt) *adj.* Disagreeable; objectionable. —**un·pleas′ant·ly** *adv.* —**un·pleas′ant·ness** *n.*

un·plug (un·plug′) *v.t.* **·plugged, ·plug·ging** **1** To remove a plug from. **2** To remove an obstruction from, as a drain. **3** To break an electrical connection by pulling out a plug.

un·plumbed (un·plumd′) *adj.* Not measured or explored fully; unfathomed; unknown.

un·polled (un·pōld′) *adj.* **1** Not cast or registered: said of a vote. **2** Not canvassed in a poll.

un·pop·u·lar (un·pop′yə·lər) *adj.* Generally disliked, unaccepted, etc. —**un·pop′u·lar·ly** *adv.* —**un·pop′u·lar′i·ty** (-lar′ə·tē) *n.*

un·prac·ticed (un·prak′tist) *adj.* **1** Not skilled; inexperienced. **2** Not used or tried.

un·prec·e·dent·ed (un·pres′ə·den′tid) *adj.* Being without precedent; preceded by no similar case; novel.

un·prej·u·diced (un·prej′ŏŏ·dist) *adj.* **1** Free from prejudice or bias; impartial. **2** Not impaired, as a right.

un·prin·ci·pled (un·prin′sə·pəld) *adj.* Without moral principles; unscrupulous.

un·print·a·ble (un·prin′tə·bəl) *adj.* Not fit for printing, esp. because of profanity, obscenity, etc.

un·pro·fes·sion·al (un′prə·fesh′ən·əl) *adj.* **1** Not pertaining to, characteristic of, or belonging to a particular profession. **2** Violating the standards, ethical code, etc., of a profession. —**un′pro·fes′sion·al·ly** *adv.*

un·qual·i·fied (un·kwol′ə·fīd) *adj.* **1** Being without the proper qualifications; unfit. **2** Without limitation or restrictions; absolute: *unqualified* approval.

un·ques·tion·a·ble (un·kwes′chən·ə·bəl) *adj.* Too certain or sure to be open to question, doubt, etc.; indisputable. —**un·ques′tion·a·bly** *adv.*

un·qui·et (un·kwī′ət) *adj.* **1** Turbulent; agitated; tumultuous. **2** Disturbed physically, mentally or emotionally; restless; uneasy. —**un·qui′et·ly** *adv.* —**un·qui′et·ness** *n.*

un·quote (un·kwōt′) *v.t. & v.i.* **·quot·ed, ·quot·ing** To close (a quotation).

un·rav·el (un·rav′əl) *v.* **·eled** or **·elled, ·el·ing** or **·el·ling** *v.t.* **1** To separate the threads of, as a tangled skein or knitted article. **2** To unfold; explain, as a mystery or a plot. —*v.i.* **3** To become unraveled.

un·read (un·red′) *adj.* **1** Having read very little; uninformed; unlearned. **2** Not yet read or examined.

un·read·y (un·red′ē) *adj.* Not ready; unprepared, as for speech, action, etc. —**un·read′i·ly** *adv.* —**un·read′i·ness** *n.*

un·re·al (un·rē′əl, -rēl′) *adj.* **1** Having no reality, actual existence, or substance. **2** Not true or sincere; false. **3** Fanciful; imaginary. —**un·re·al·i·ty** (un′rē·al′ə·tē) *n.*

un·rea·son·a·ble (un·rē′zən·ə·bəl, -rēz′nə-) *adj.* **1** Acting without or contrary to reason. **2** Immoderate; exorbitant. —**un·rea′son·a·ble·ness** *n.* —**un·rea′son·a·bly** *adv.*

un·rea·son·ing (un·rē′zən·ing) *adj.* Marked by the absence of reason; irrational. —**un·rea′son·ing·ly** *adv.*

un·reel (un·rēl′) *v.t. & v.i.* To unwind from a reel.

un·re·gen·er·ate (un′ri·jen′ər·it) *adj.* **1** Not changed spiritually by regeneration; unrepentant. **2** Not convinced by or converted to a particular doctrine, theology, cause, etc. **3** Stubborn; recalcitrant.

un·re·lent·ing (un'ri·lent'ing) *adj.* **1** Not relenting; inflexible. **2** Not diminishing in pace, effort, speed, etc. —**un're·lent'ing·ly** *adv.*

un·re·li·a·ble (un'ri·lī'ə·bəl) *adj.* Not to be relied upon; undependable. —**un're·li'a·bil'i·ty, un're·li'a·ble·ness** *n.* —**un're·li'a·bly** *adv.*

un·re·lig·ious (un'ri·lij'əs) *adj.* **1** IRRELIGIOUS. **2** Not related to or connected with religion.

un·re·mit·ting (un'ri·mit'ing) *adj.* Incessant; not stopping or relaxing. —**un're·mit'ting·ly** *adv.* —**un're·mit'ting·ness** *n.*

un·re·served (un'ri·zûrvd') *adj.* **1** Not qualified; unrestricted. **2** Not reticent; informal; open. **3** Not set aside, as seats. —**un·re·serv·ed·ly** (un'ri·zûr'vid·lē) *adv.* —**un're·serv'·ed·ness** *n.*

un·rest (un'rest', un·rest') *n.* **1** Restlessness, esp. of the mind. **2** Angry dissatisfaction, bordering on revolt.

un·rid·dle (un·rid'l) *v.t.* **·dled, ·dling** To solve, as a mystery.

un·right·eous (un·rī'chəs) *adj.* **1** Not righteous; wicked; sinful. **2** Unfair; inequitable. —**un·right'eous·ly** *adv.* —**un·right'eous·ness** *n.*

un·ripe (un·rīp') *adj.* **1** Not arrived at maturity; not ripe; immature. **2** Not ready; not prepared. —**un·ripe'ness** *n.*

un·ri·valed (un·rī'vəld) *adj.* Having no rival; peerless.

un·roll (un·rōl') *v.t.* **1** To spread or open (something rolled up). **2** To exhibit to view. —*v.i.* **3** To become unrolled.

un·ruf·fled (un·ruf'əld) *adj.* **1** Not disturbed or agitated; calm. **2** Not ruffled; smooth.

un·ru·ly (un·rōō'lē) *adj.* Disposed to resist rule or discipline; ungovernable. —**un·ru'li·ness** *n.*

un·sad·dle (un·sad'l) *v.* **·dled, ·dling** *v.t.* **1** To remove a saddle from. **2** To remove from the saddle. —*v.i.* **3** To take the saddle off a horse.

un·said (un·sed') *adj.* Not said; not spoken.

un·sat·u·rat·ed (un·sach'ə·rā'tid) *adj.* **1** Capable of dissolving more solute. **2** Having at least one free or multiple valence bond available for direct union with an atom or radical: said of organic compounds.

un·sa·vor·y (un·sā'vər·ē) *adj.* **1** Having a disagreeable taste or odor. **2** Having no savor; tasteless. **3** Disagreeable or offensive, esp. morally. —**un·sa'vor·i·ness** *n.*

un·say (un·sā') *v.t.* **·said, ·say·ing** To retract (something said).

un·scathed (un·skā*th*d') *adj.* Not injured.

un·scram·ble (un·skram'bəl) *v.t.* **·bled, ·bling** *Informal* To resolve the confused, scrambled, or disordered condition of.

un·screw (un·skrōō') *v.t.* **1** To remove the screw or screws from. **2** To remove or detach by withdrawing screws, or by turning. —*v.i.* **3** To become unscrewed or permit of being unscrewed.

un·scru·pu·lous (un·skrōō'pyə·ləs) *adj.* Not scrupulous; having no scruples; unprincipled. —**un·scru'pu·lous·ly** *adv.* —**un·scru'pu·lous·ness** *n.*

un·seal (un·sēl') *v.t.* **1** To break or remove the seal of. **2** To open (that which has been sealed or closed).

un·search·a·ble (un·sûr'chə·bəl) *adj.* That cannot be searched into or explored; mysterious. —**un·search'a·ble·ness** *n.* —**un·search'a·bly** *adv.*

un·sea·son·a·ble (un·sē'zən·ə·bəl) *adj.* **1** Not suitable to the season: *unseasonable* weather. **2** Untimely; inopportune. —**un·sea'son·a·ble·ness** *n.* —**un·sea'son·a·bly** *adv.*

un·seat (un·sēt') *v.t.* **1** To remove from a seat. **2** To throw (a rider) from a horse. **3** To deprive of office or rank; depose.

un·seem·ly (un·sēm'lē) *adj.* **·li·er, ·li·est** Unbecoming, indecent, unattractive, or inappropriate. —*adv.* In an unseemly fashion. —**un·seem'li·ness** *n.*

un·set·tle (un·set'l) *v.* **·tled, ·tling** *v.t.* **1** To move from a fixed or settled condition. **2** To confuse, upset, or disturb. —*v.i.* **3** To become unsettled. —**un·set'tling·ly** *adv.*

un·sex (un·seks') *v.t.* To deprive of sex, sexual power, or the distinctive qualities of one's sex.

un·shack·le (un·shak'əl) *v.t.* **·led, ·ling** **1** To unfetter; free from shackles. **2** To free, as from restraint.

un·sheathe (un·shē*th*') *v.t.* **·sheathed, ·sheath·ing** To take from or as from a scabbard or sheath; bare.

un·ship (un·ship') *v.t.* **·shipped, ·ship·ping** To unload from a ship or other vessel.

un·sight·ly (un·sīt'lē) *adj.* **·li·er, ·li·est** Offensive to the sight; ugly. —**un·sight'li·ness** *n.*

un·skilled (un·skild') *adj.* **1** Without special skill or training: an *unskilled* worker. **2** Requiring no special skill or training.

un·skill·ful (un·skil'fəl) *adj.* Lacking or not evincing skill; awkward; incompetent. Also **un·skil'ful.** —**un·skill'ful·ly** *adv.* —**un·skill'ful·ness** *n.*

un·snap (un·snap') *v.t.* **·snapped, ·snap·ping** To undo the snap or snaps of.

un·snarl (un·snärl') *v.t.* To undo snarls; disentangle.

un·so·cia·ble (un·sō'shə·bəl) *adj.* **1** Not sociable; not inclined to seek the society of others. **2** Lacking or not conducive to sociability. —**un·so·cia·bil'i·ty** (un·sō'shə·bil'ə·tē), **un·so'cia·ble·ness** *n.* —**un·so'cia·bly** *adv.*

un·sol·der (un·sod'ər) *v.t.* **1** To take apart (something soldered). **2** To separate; divide.

un·so·phis·ti·cat·ed (un'sə·fis'tə·kā'tid) *adj.* **1** Showing inexperience or naiveté; artless. **2** Genuine; pure. **3** Not complicated; simple. —**un'so·phis'ti·cat·ed·ly** *adv.* —**un'so·phis'ti·cat·ed·ness, un'so·phis'ti·ca'tion** *n.*

un·sound (un·sound') *adj.* **1** Not strong or solid: *unsound* construction. **2** Unhealthy in body or mind. **3** Untrue or logically invalid: *unsound* arguments. **4** Not deep; disturbed: said of sleep. —**un·sound'ly** *adv.* —**un·sound'ness** *n.*

un·spar·ing (un·spâr'ing) *adj.* **1** Not sparing or saving; lavish. **2** Showing no mercy. —**un·spar'ing·ly** *adv.* —**un·spar'ing·ness** *n.*

un·speak·a·ble (un·spē'kə·bəl) *adj.* **1** That cannot be expressed; unutterable: *unspeakable* joy. **2** Extremely bad or objectionable: an *unspeakable* crime. —**un·speak'a·ble·ness** *n.* —**un·speak'a·bly** *adv.*

un·sta·ble (un·stā'bəl) *adj.* **1** Lacking in stability or firmness; liable to move, sway, shake, etc. **2** Having no fixed purpose; easily influenced: an *unstable* character. **3** Emotionally unsteady. **4** Liable to change; fluctuating; variable: an *unstable* economy. **5** *Chem.* Easily decomposed, as certain compounds. —**un·sta'ble·ness** *n.* —**un·sta'bly** *adv.*

un·stead·y (un·sted'ē) *adj.* **·stead·i·er, ·stead·i·est** Not steady, as: **a** Not stable; liable to move or shake. **b** Variable; fluctuating. **c** Undependable or irregular. —**un·stead'i·ly** *adv.* —**un·stead'i·ness** *n.*

un·stop (un·stop') *v.t.* **·stopped, ·stop·ping** **1** To remove a stopper from. **2** To open by removing obstructions; clear.

un·stop·pa·ble (un·stop'ə·bəl) *adj.* Impossible to stop or check. —**un·stop'pa·bly** *adv.*

un·strap (un·strap') *v.t.* **·strapped, ·strap·ping** To undo or loosen the strap or straps of.

un·string (un·string') *v.t.* **·strung, ·string·ing** **1** To remove from a string, as pearls. **2** To take the string or strings from. **3** To loosen the string or strings of, as a bow or guitar. **4** To make unstable or nervous.

un·struc·tured (un·struk'chərd) *adj.* Not having a definite organization or plan.

un·strung (un·strung') *adj.* **1** Having the strings removed or loosened. **2** Emotionally upset.

un·stud·ied (un·stud'ēd) *adj.* **1** Not stiff or artificial; natural; unaffected. **2** Not acquainted through study.

un·sub·stan·tial (un'səb·stan'shəl) *adj.* **1** Lacking solidity or strength; unstable; weak. **2** Having no valid basis in fact. **3** Unreal; fanciful. —**un'sub·stan'tial·ly** *adv.* —**un'sub·stan'ti·al'i·ty** (-shē·al'ə·tē) *n.*

un·suit·a·ble (un·sōō'tə·bəl) *adj.* Not suitable; unfitting. —**un·suit·a·bil'i·ty** (un's*y*ōō·tə·bil'ə·tē), **un·suit'a·ble·ness** *n.* —**un·suit'a·bly** *adv.*

un·sung (un·sung') *adj.* **1** Not celebrated, as in song or poetry; obscure. **2** Not sung.

un·swerv·ing (un·swûr'ving) *adj.* **1** Not changing or wavering; consistent: *unswerving* loyalty. **2** Not swerving from a path or course. —**un·swerv'ing·ly** *adv.*

un·tan·gle (un·tang'gəl) *v.t.* **·gled, ·gling** **1** To free from tangles; disentangle. **2** To clear up or straighten out (a perplexing or confused situation, etc.).

un·taught (un·tôt') *adj.* **1** Not having been instructed; ignorant. **2** Known without having been taught; natural.

un·thank·ful (un·thangk'fəl) *adj.* **1** Not grateful. **2** Not appreciated. —**un·thank'ful·ly** *adv.* —**un·thank'ful·ness** *n.*

un·think·ing (un·thingk′ing) *adj.* Lacking thoughtfulness, care, or attention. —**un·think′ing·ly** *adv.* —**un·think′ing·ness** *n.*

un·thread (un·thred′) *v.t.* **1** To remove the thread from, as a needle. **2** To unravel; disentangle. **3** To find one's way out of, as a maze.

un·ti·dy (un·tī′dē) *adj.* ·**di·er**, ·**di·est** Not tidy; messy; disorderly. —**un·ti′di·ly** *adv.* —**un·ti′di·ness** *n.*

un·tie (un·tī′) *v.* ·**tied**, ·**ty·ing** *v.t.* **1** To loosen or undo, as a knot. **2** To free from that which binds or restrains. —*v.i.* **3** To become loosened or undone.

un·til (un·til′) *prep.* **1** Up to the time of; till: We will wait *until* midnight. **2** Before: used with a negative: The music doesn't begin *until* nine. —*conj.* **1** To the time when: *until* I die. **2** To the place or degree that: Walk east *until* you reach the river. **3** Before: with a negative: He couldn't leave *until* the car came for him. [< ME *und-* up to, as far as + TILL] • See TILL².

un·time·ly (un·tīm′lē) *adj.* Coming before time or not in proper time; premature or inopportune. —*adv.* Before time or not in the proper time; inopportunely.

un·to (un′tōō) *prep. Archaic* **1** To. **2** Until. [< ME *und-* up to, as far as + TO, on analogy with *until*]

un·told (un·tōld′) *adj.* **1** Not told, revealed, or described. **2** Of too great a number or extent to be counted or measured.

un·touch·a·ble (un·tuch′ə·bəl) *adj.* **1** Inaccessible to the touch; out of reach. **2** Forbidden to the touch. **3** Unpleasant, disgusting, or dangerous to touch. —*n.* In India, formerly, a member of the lowest caste.

un·to·ward (un·tôrd′, -tōrd′, -tə·wôrd′) *adj.* **1** Causing or characterized by difficulty or unhappiness; unfavorable. **2** Not easily managed; refractory. **3** Improper; unseemly. —**un·to·ward′ly** *adv.* —**un·to·ward′ness** *n.*

un·true (un·trōō′) *adj.* **1** Not true; false or incorrect. **2** Not conforming to rule or standard. **3** Disloyal; faithless. —**un·tru′ly** *adv.*

un·truth (un·trōōth′, un′trōōth′) *n. pl.* ·**truths** (-trōōths, -trōōthz) **1** The quality or character of being untrue. **2** Something that is not true; a falsehood; lie.

un·truth·ful (un·trōōth′fəl) *adj.* **1** Not truthful; not telling the truth. **2** Not consistent with the truth. —**un·truth′ful·ly** *adv.* —**un·truth′ful·ness** *n.*

un·tu·tored (un·t(y)ōō′tərd) *adj.* Not educated; untaught.

un·twine (un·twīn′) *v.* ·**twined**, ·**twin·ing** *v.t.* **1** To undo (something twined); unwind by disentangling. —*v.i.* **2** To become undone.

un·twist (un·twist′) *v.t.* **1** To separate by a movement the reverse of twisting; untwine. —*v.i.* **2** To become untwined.

un·used (un·yōōzd′) *adj.* **1** Not used. **2** Never having been used. **3** Not accustomed: with *to.*

un·u·su·al (un·yōō′zhōō·əl) *adj.* Not usual; odd, rare, or extraordinary. —**un·u′su·al·ly** *adv.* —**un·u′su·al·ness** *n.*

un·ut·ter·a·ble (un·ut′ər·ə·bəl) *adj.* Too great, deep, etc., to be expressed or described in words. —**un·ut′ter·a·ble·ness** *n.* —**un·ut′ter·a·bly** *adv.*

un·var·nished (un·vär′nisht) *adj.* **1** Not varnished. **2** Not embellished or adorned; simple: the *unvarnished* truth.

un·veil (un·vāl′) *v.t.* **1** To remove the veil or covering from; disclose to view; reveal. —*v.i.* **2** To remove one's veil; reveal oneself.

un·war·rant·a·ble (un·wôr′ən·tə·bəl, -wor′-) *adj.* That cannot be justified; inexcusable; indefensible. —**un·war′rant·a·bly** *adv.*

un·war·y (un·wâr′ē) *adj.* ·**war·i·er**, ·**war·i·est** Not careful; incautious. —**un·war′i·ly** *adv.* —**un·war′i·ness** *n.* —**Syn.** careless, heedless, reckless, unguarded.

un·well (un·wel′) *adj.* Sick; ailing.

un·wept (un·wept′) *adj.* **1** Not lamented or wept for. **2** Not shed, as tears.

un·whole·some (un·hōl′səm) *adj.* **1** Harmful to physical, mental, or moral health. **2** Sickly in health or in appearance. —**un·whole′some·ly** *adv.* —**un·whole′some·ness** *n.*

un·wield·y (un·wēl′dē) *adj.* ·**i·er**, ·**i·est** Difficult to move, manage, or control, as because of great size or awkward shape. —**un·wield′i·ly** *adv.* —**un·wield′i·ness** *n.*

un·will·ing (un·wil′ing) *adj.* **1** Not willing; reluctant; loath. **2** Done, said, granted, etc., with reluctance. —**un·will′ing·ly** *adv.* —**un·will′ing·ness** *n.*

un·wind (un·wīnd′) *v.* ·**wound**, ·**wind·ing** *v.t.* **1** To reverse the winding of; untwist or wind off. **2** To disentangle. —*v.i.* **3** To become disentangled or untwisted. **4** To free oneself from tension or anxieties; relax.

un·wise (un·wīz′) *adj.* Acting with, or showing, lack of wisdom or good sense. —**un·wise′ly** *adv.*

un·wit·ting (un·wit′ing) *adj.* **1** Having no knowledge or awareness; ignorant; unconscious. **2** Not intentional. —**un·wit′ting·ly** *adv.*

un·wont·ed (un·wôn′tid, -won′-) *adj.* Not ordinary or customary; unusual; uncommon. —**un·wont′ed·ly** *adv.* —**un·wont′ed·ness** *n.*

un·wor·thy (un·wûr′thē) *adj.* **1** Not worthy or deserving: often with *of.* **2** Not befitting or becoming: usu. with *of:* conduct *unworthy* of a gentleman. **3** Lacking worth or merit. **4** Not deserved or merited. —**un·wor′thi·ly** *adv.* —**un·wor′thi·ness** *n.*

un·wrap (un·rap′) *v.t.* ·**wrapped**, ·**wrap·ping** To take the wrapping from; open; undo.

un·writ·ten (un·rit′n) *adj.* **1** Not written down; traditional. **2** Having no writing upon it; blank.

unwritten law A law or rule of conduct, procedure, etc., whose authority stems from custom and tradition rather than from a written command, decree, or statute.

un·yoke (un·yōk′) *v.t.* ·**yoked**, ·**yok·ing** **1** To release from a yoke. **2** To separate; part.

up (up) *adv.* **1** Toward a higher place or level. **2** In or on a higher place. **3** To or at that which is literally or figuratively higher, as: **a** To or at a higher price: Barley is going *up.* **b** To or at a higher rank: people who have come *up* in the world. **c** To or at a greater size or amount: to swell *up.* **d** To or at a greater degree, intensity, volume, etc.: Turn *up* the radio. **e** To or at a place regarded as higher up: *up* north. **f** To a position above the horizon: when the sun comes *up.* **g** To a later point in time or life: from her childhood *up* to her teens. **4** In or into a vertical position; on one's feet. **5** Out of bed: to get *up.* **6** So as to be level or even (with) in time, degree, amount, etc.: *up* to the brim. **7** In or into commotion or activity: to be *up* in arms. **8** Into or in a place of safekeeping: to lay *up* provisions. **9** Completely; wholly: Houses were burned *up.* **10** In baseball, at bat. **11** In some sports: **a** In the lead. **b** Apiece; alike: said of a score. **12** So as to be compact, secure, etc.: Fold *up* the linen. **13** In or into view, existence, etc.: to bring *up* a subject; It will turn *up.* **14** *Naut.* Shifted to windward, as a tiller. **15** Into an aggregate number or quantity: Add *up* these figures. **16** To a source, conclusion, etc.: to follow *up* a rumor. —**be up against** *Informal* To meet with something to be dealt with. —**be up against it** *Informal* To be in trouble, usu. financial trouble. —**be up to 1** *Informal* To be doing or about to do: What is he *up to?* **2** To be equal to or capable of: I'm not *up* to playing golf today. **3** To be incumbent upon: It's *up* to her to help us. —*adj.* **1** Moving or directed upward. **2** In, at, or to a high level, condition, etc.: Is the river *up* today? **3** Above the ground or horizon: The jonquils are *up.* **4** In a raised or erect position or condition: The new school is finally *up.* **5** At an end: Your time is *up.* **6** *Informal* Going on; taking place: What's *up?* **7** *Informal* Informed; up-to-date: *up* on the newest movies. **8** Characterized by or showing agitation or excitement: Tempers are *up.* **9** In baseball, at bat. **10** *Informal* Alert; ready: to be *up* for a meeting. —**up and doing** Busy; bustling. —**up for 1** Being considered or presented for: *up for* reelection. **2** Charged with or on trial for: *up for* manslaughter. —*prep.* **1** To, toward, or at a higher point, position, etc., on or along: monkeys scampering *up* a tree; *up* the social ladder. **2** To or at a point farther above or along: The farm is *up* the road. **3** From the coast toward the interior of (a country). **4** From the mouth toward the source of (a river). —*n. Usu. pl.* **1** An ascent or upward movement. **2** A state of prosperity. —**on the up and up**

Slang Honest; genuine. **—ups and downs** Changes of fortune or circumstance. **—v. upped, up·ping** *Informal v.t.* 1 To increase; cause to rise: to *up* one's price. 2 To put, lift, or take up. **—vi.** 3 To rise. 4 To do quickly and abruptly: usu. followed by another verb: Then she *up* and left. [OE]

up·and·coming (up'ən·kum'ing) *adj.* Enterprising; energetic; promising.

u·pas (yōō'pəs) *n.* 1 A tall Asian and East Indian tree related to mulberry, with an acrid, milky, poisonous juice. 2 The sap of this tree, used to make arrow poison. [< Malay *(phon) upas* poison (tree)]

up·beat (up'bēt'; *for adj., also* up'bēt') *n. Music* An unaccented beat, esp. the last beat in a measure. **—adj.** Optimistic; confident.

up·braid (up·brād') *v.t* To reproach for some wrongdoing; scold. [< OE *up-* up + *bregdan* weave; twist] **—up·braid'er** *adj.* **—up·braid'ing·ly** *adv.* **—Syn.** admonish, chastise, rebuke, reprimand.

up·bring·ing (up'bring'ing) *n.* Rearing and training received during childhood.

up·chuck (up'chuk') *Informal v.t. & v.i.* To vomit. **—n.** Vomit.

up·coun·try (up'kun'trē) *Informal n.* Inland country. **—adj.** In, from, or characteristic of inland places. **—adv.** (up'kun'trē) In, into or toward the interior.

up·date (up'dāt') *v.t.* **·dat·ed, ·dat·ing** To bring up to date, as a textbook or manual.

up·end (up'end') *v.t. & v.i.* To stand on end.

up·front (up'frunt') *adj. Colloq.* Out in the open; unconcealed.

up·grade (up'grād'; *for v., also* up'grād') *n.* An upward incline or slope. **—vt.** **·grad·ed, ·grad·ing** To raise to a higher rank, responsibility, value, importance, etc., as an employee or job.

up·heav·al (up·hē'vəl) *n.* 1 The act of upheaving, or the state of being upheaved. 2 A violent change or disturbance, as of the established social order.

up·heave (up·hēv') *v.* **·heaved** *or* **·hove, ·heav·ing** *v.t.* 1 To heave or raise up. **—v.i.** 2 To be raised or lifted.

up·hill (up'hil') *adv.* Up or as up a hill or an ascent. **—adj.** 1 Going up hill or an ascent; sloping upward. 2 Attended with difficulty or exertion. 3 Situated on high ground. **—n.** (up'hil') An upward slope; rising ground; a steep rise.

up·hold (up·hōld') *v.t.* **·held, ·hold·ing** 1 To hold up; keep from falling or sinking. 2 To raise; lift up. 3 To aid, encourage, sustain, or confirm. **—up·hold'er** *n.*

up·hol·ster (up·hōl'stər) *v.t.* To fit, as furniture, with coverings, cushioning, springs, etc. [ult. < ME *upholder* tradesman] **—up·hol'ster·er** *n.*

up·hol·ster·y (up·hōl'stər·ē, ·strē) *n. pl.* **·ster·ies** 1 The materials used in upholstering. 2 The act, art, or business of upholstering.

UPI, U.P.I. United Press International.

up·keep (up'kēp') *n.* 1 The act of keeping in good condition. 2 The state of being kept in good condition. 3 The cost of keeping in good condition.

up·land (up'lənd, ·land') *n.* High land, esp. such land located far from the sea. **—adj.** Pertaining to or situated in an upland.

up·lift (up·lift') *v.t.* 1 To lift up, or raise aloft; elevate. 2 To put on a higher plane, mentally, morally, culturally, or socially. **—n.** (up'lift') 1 The act of lifting up raising. 2 An elevation to a higher mental, spiritual, moral, or social plane. 3 A social movement aiming to improve, esp. morally or culturally. 4 A brassiere designed to lift and support the breasts. **—up·lift'er** *n.*

up·most (up'mōst') *adj.,* UPPERMOST.

up·on (ə·pon', ə·pôn') *prep.* On: *upon* the throne. **—adv.** On: The paper has been written *upon.* • *Upon* no longer differs in meaning from *on,* but it is sometimes preferred for reasons of euphony. When *upon* has its original meaning of *up + on,* it is written and pronounced as two words: *Let's go up on the roof.*

up·per (up'ər) *adj.* 1 Higher, as in location or position.2 Higher in station, rank, authority, etc.: the *upper* house. 3 *Geol. Usu. cap.* Being a later division of a specified period or series. **—n.** 1 Something that is above another similar or related thing, part, etc., as an upper berth. 2 That part of a boot or shoe above the sole. 3 *Slang* Any of

various drugs that stimulate the central nervous system, as amphetamines. **—on one's uppers** *Informal* 1 Having worn out the soles of one's shoes. 2 At the end of one's resources; destitute. [ME, orig. compar. of UP]

up·per·case (up'ər·kās') *adj.* Of, in, or designating capital letters. **—v.t.** **·cased, ·cas·ing** To set in capital letters.

upper case 1 A case in which are kept capital letters and some auxiliary type for use in printing. 2 Capital letters.

upper class The socially or economically superior group in any society. **—up'per·class'** (·klas', ·kläs') *adj.*

up·per·class·man (up'ər·klas'mən, ·kläs'-) *n. pl.* **·men** (·mən) A junior or senior in a high school or college.

up·per·cut (up'ər·kut') *n.* In boxing, a swinging blow directed upward, as to an opponent's jaw. **—v.t & v.i.** **·cut, ·cut·ting** To strike with an uppercut.

upper hand The advantage; control.

Upper House The branch, in a bicameral legislature, where membership is more restricted, as the U.S. Senate.

up·per·most (up'ər·mōst') *adj.* Highest in place, rank, authority, importance, etc.; foremost. **—adv.** In the highest place, rank, importance, etc.

Upper Vol·ta (vol'tə) A republic of w Africa, 105,900 sq. mi., cap. Ouagadougou. • See map at AFRICA.

up·pish (up'ish) *adj. Informal* UPPITY. **—up'pish·ly** *adv.* **—up'pish·ness** *n.*

up·pi·ty (up'ə·tē) *adj. Informal* Arrogant; snobbish; haughty. **—up'pi·ti·ness** *n.*

up·raise (up·rāz') *v.t.* **·raised, ·rais·ing** To lift up; elevate.

up·right (up'rīt') *adj.* 1 Being in a vertical position; erect. 2 Righteous; just. **—n.** 1 The state of being upright: a post out of *upright.* 2 Something having an upright position, as a vertical timber. 3 An upright piano. 4 In a football, a goal post. **—adv.** In an upright position; vertically. [< OE *up-* up + *riht* right] **—up'right'ly** *adv.* **—up'right'ness** *n.*

upright piano A piano having the strings mounted vertically within a rectangular, upright case.

up·ris·ing (up'rī'zing) *n.* 1 The act of rising up; esp., a revolt or insurrection. 2 An ascent; upward slope; acclivity.

up·roar (up'rôr', ·rōr') *n.* 1 A state of confusion, disturbance, excitement, tumult, etc. 2 A loud, boisterous noise; din. [< Du. *op-* up + *roeren* stir]

up·roar·i·ous (up·rôr'ē·əs, ·rō'·rē-) *adj.* 1 Accompanied by or making uproar. 2 Very loud and boisterous. 3 Provoking loud laughter. **—up·roar'i·ous·ly** *adv.* **—up·roar'ous·ness** *n.*

up·root (up·rōōt', ·rŏŏt') *v.t.* 1 To tear up by the roots. 2 To destroy utterly; eradicate. **—up·root'er** *n.*

up·set (up·set') *v.* **·set, ·set·ting** *v.t.* 1 To overturn. 2 To throw into confusion or disorder. 3 To disconcert, derange, or disquiet. 4 To defeat (an opponent favored to win): The amateur team *upset* the professionals. **—v.i.** 5 To become overturned. **—adj.** (also up'set') 1 Overturned. 2 Physically ill or mentally disturbed. **—n.** (up'set') 1 The act of overturning. 2 A physical or emotional disorder. 3 A defeat of an opponent favored to win. **—up·set'ter** *n.*

up·shot (up'shot') *n.* The outcome; result.

up·side (up'sīd') *n.* The upper side or part.

upside down 1 So that the upper part is underneath: to turn a table *upside down.* 2 In or into disorder or confusion: to turn a room *upside down* looking for something.

up·si·lon (yōōp'sə·lon, up'sə·lon) *n.* The twentieth letter in the Greek alphabet (Y, υ). [< Gk. *u* u + *psilon* simple]

up·stage (up'stāj') *adj.* 1 Of or pertaining to the back half of a stage. 2 *Informal* Conceited; haughty; snobbish. **—adv.** Toward or at the back half of a stage. **—n.** That part of a stage farthest from the audience. **—v.** (up'stāj') **·staged, ·stag·ing** 1 To force (a fellow actor) to face away from the audience by moving or remaining upstage. 2 To try to outdo (someone), as in a professional or social encounter.

up·stairs (up'stârz') *adj.* Of or on an upper story. **—n.** The part of a building above the ground floor; an upper story or stories. **—adv.** To or on an upper story.

up·stand·ing (up·stan'ding) *adj.* 1 Standing up; erect. 2 Honest, straightforward, etc. **—up·stand'ing·ness** *n.*

up·start (up'stärt') *n.* A person who has suddenly risen from a humble position to one of consequence; esp., such a person who behaves in a way that is presumptuous, arrogant, etc.

up·state (up′stāt′) *adj.* Of, from, or designating that part of a state lying outside, usu. north, of a principal city. — *n.* The outlying, usu. northern, sections of a state. —*adv.* In or toward the outlying or northern sections of a state. —**up′stat′er** *n.*

up·stream (up′strēm′) *adv. & adj.* Toward or at the upper part or source of a stream.

up·sweep (up′swēp′) *n.* 1 A sweeping up or upward. 2 A hairdo in which the hair is piled on the top of the head and held there by pins or combs.

up·swing (up′swing′) *n.* 1 A swinging upward. 2 An increase or improvement.

up·take (up′tāk′) *n.* 1 The act of lifting or taking up. 2 Mental comprehension; understanding.

up·thrust (up′thrust′) *n.* 1 An upward thrust. 2 A sharp upward movement of rock in the earth's crust.

up·tight (up′tīt′) *adj. Slang* Uneasy, anxious, or nervous. Also **up′-tight′, up tight.** —**up′tight′ness** *n.*

up-to-date (up′tə-dāt′) *adj.* 1 Extending to the present; including the latest information, data, etc.: an *up-to-date* census report. 2 Abreast of the latest fashions, ideas, outlook, etc. —**up′-to-date′ness** *n.*

up·town (up′toun′) *adj. & adv.* Of, in, to, or toward the upper part of a town or city. —*n.* An uptown area.

up·turn (up′tûrn′, up′tûrn′) *v.t.* To turn up or over. —*n.* (up′tûrn′) A turn upward, as to improved business conditions.

up·ward (up′wərd) *adv.* 1 In or toward a higher place, position, or part. 2 Toward a source or interior part. 3 In the upper parts. 4 To or toward a higher, greater, or better condition. Also **up′wards.** —**upward** or **upwards** of Higher than or in excess of. —*adj.* Turned, directed toward, or located in a higher place. —**up′ward·ly** *adv.*

u·rae·mi·a (yŏŏ-rē′mē-ə) *n.* UREMIA.

U·ral-Al·ta·ic (yŏŏr′əl-al-tā′ik) *n.* A family of languages of Europe and N Asia, comprising the Uralic and Altaic subfamilies. —*adj.* Of or pertaining to these languages or the peoples speaking them.

U·ral·ic (yŏŏ-ral′ik) *n.* A family of languages comprising the Finno-Ugric and Samoyedic subfamilies. —*adj.* Of or pertaining to this linguistic family. Also **U·ra·li·an** (yŏŏ-rā′lē-ən).

U·ra·ni·a (yŏŏ-rā′nē-ə) *Gk. Myth.* The Muse of astronomy.

u·ra·ni·um (yŏŏ-rā′nē-əm) *n.* A heavy, radioactive, metallic element (symbol U), found only in combination and in association with radium, used in the generation of atomic energy. [< URANUS]

U·ra·nus (yŏŏr′ə-nəs, yŏŏr-ā′nəs) *Gk. Myth.* The son and husband of Gaea (Earth) and father of the Titans, Furies, and Cyclopes. —*n.* The planet of the solar system seventh in distance from the sun. • See PLANET. —**U·ra′ni·an** *adj.*

ur·ban (ûr′bən) *adj.* 1 Of, pertaining to, characteristic of, constituting, or including a city. 2 Living or located in a city or cities. [See URBANE.]

ur·bane (ûr-bān′) *adj.* Characterized by or having refinement, esp. in manner; polite; courteous; suave. [< L *urbs, urbis* a city] —**ur·bane′ly** *adv.* —**ur·bane′ness** *n.*

ur·ban·ism (ûr′bən-iz′əm) *n.* 1 Life in the cities. 2 The study of urban life. 3 The advocacy of living in a city. — **ur′ban·ist** *n.* —**ur′ban·is′tic** *adj.*

ur·ban·ite (ûr′bən-īt) *n.* One who lives in a city.

ur·ban·i·ty (ûr-ban′ə-tē) *n. pl.* **·ties** 1 The character or quality of being urbane. 2 *pl.* Urbane acts or behavior; courtesies, amenities, etc.

ur·ban·i·za·tion (ûr′bə-nə-zā′shən) *n.* 1 The act or process of urbanizing an area or a rural group of people. 2 The quality or state of being urbanized. *Brit. sp.* **·i·sa′tion.**

ur·ban·ize (ûr′bən-īz) *v.t.* **·ized, ·iz·ing** 1 To cause (an area) to assume the characteristics of a city. 2 To cause (people) to adopt an urban life style. *Brit. sp.* **·ise.**

ur·ban·ol·o·gy (ûr′bə-nol′ə-jē) *n.* The study of problems peculiar to cities. —**ur′ban·ol′o·gist** *n.*

urban renewal A program for rebuilding or replacing substandard housing and improving public facilities in distressed urban areas.

urban sprawl The uncontrolled spread of urban housing, shopping centers, etc., into rural or undeveloped areas close to a city.

ur·chin (ûr′chin) *n.* 1 A roguish, mischievous child. 2 A ragged street child. 3 HEDGEHOG. 4 SEA URCHIN. [< L *ericius* hedgehog]

Ur·du (ŏŏr′dŏŏ, ŏŏr-dŏŏ′, ûr′dŏŏ) *n.* An Indic language, a variety of Hindi that is the official language of Pakistan and is also spoken by some of the population of India.

-ure *suffix of nouns* 1 The act, process, or result of: *pressure.* 2 The condition of being: *exposure.* 3 The function, rank, or office of: *prefecture.* 4 The means or instrument of: *ligature.* [< L *-ura*]

u·re·a (yŏŏ-rē′ə) *n.* A soluble colorless crystalline compound excreted in urine and also made synthetically; used in the making of plastics. [< L *urina* urine] —**u·re′al** *adj.*

u·re·mi·a (yŏŏ-rē′mē-ə) *n.* A toxic condition of the blood due to the presence of substances ordinarily excreted by the kidneys. —**u·re′mic** *adj.*

u·re·ter (yŏŏr′ə-tər, yŏŏ-rē′-) *n.* The duct by which urine passes from the kidney to the bladder or the cloaca. [< Gk. *ourein* urinate] —**u·re·ter·al** (yŏŏ-rē′tə-rəl), **u·re·ter·ic** (yŏŏr′-ə-ter′ik) *adj.* • See KIDNEY.

u·re·thra (yŏŏ-rē′thrə) *n. pl.* **·thrae** (-thrē), **·thras** The duct by which urine is discharged from the bladder and which, in males, carries the seminal discharge. [< Gk. *ouron* urine] —**u·re′thral** *adj.*

urge (ûrj) *v.* **urged, urg·ing** *v.t.* 1 To drive or force forward. 2 To plead with or entreat earnestly: He *urged* them to accept the plan. 3 To advocate earnestly: to *urge* reform. 4 To move or force to some course or action. —*v.i.* 5 To present or press arguments, claims, etc. 6 To exert an impelling or prompting force. —*n.* 1 A strong impulse to perform a certain act. 2 The act of urging. [< L *urgere* to drive, urge] —Syn. *v.* 1 impel, press. 3 exhort, importune.

ur·gen·cy (ûr′jən-sē) *n. pl.* **·cies** 1 The quality of being urgent; insistence: the *urgency* of her plea. 2 Something urgent: to prepare for any possible *urgencies.*

ur·gent (ûr′jənt) *adj.* 1 Requiring prompt attention; pressing; imperative. 2 Eagerly importunate or insistent. [< L *urgere* drive] —**ur′gent·ly** *adv.*

-urgy *combining form* Development of or work with a (specified) material or product: *metallurgy.* [< Gk. *ergon* work]

u·ric (yŏŏr′ik) *adj.* Of, relating to, or derived from urine.

uric acid A white, odorless substance found in small quantity in urine.

u·ri·nal (yŏŏr′ə-nəl) *n.* 1 A fixture for men's use in urination; also, a place containing such a fixture or fixtures. 2 A receptacle for urine.

u·ri·nal·y·sis (yŏŏr′ə-nal′ə-sis) *n. pl.* **·ses** (-sēz) Chemical analysis of the urine.

u·ri·nar·y (yŏŏr′ə-ner′ē) *adj.* Of or pertaining to urine or to the organs concerned in its production and excretion.

u·ri·nate (yŏŏr′ə-nāt) *v.i.* **·nat·ed, ·nat·ing** To void or pass urine. —**u′ri·na′tion** *n.*

u·rine (yŏŏr′in) *n.* A usu. fluid substance secreted by the kidneys of vertebrates and some invertebrates and containing nitrogenous and saline wastes. [< L *urina*]

u·ri·no·gen·i·tal (yŏŏr′ə-nō·jen′ə-təl) *adj.* UROGENITAL.

urn (ûrn) *n.* 1 A vase, usu. having a foot or pedestal, variously used as a receptacle for the ashes of the dead, or ornament, etc. 2 A vase-shaped receptacle having a faucet, designed to make and serve tea, coffee, etc. [< L *urna*]

Urn

uro- *combining form* Urine; pertaining to urine or to the urinary tract: *urology.* [< Gk. *ouron* urine]

u·ro·gen·i·tal (yŏŏr′ō-jen′ə-təl) *adj.* Of or pertaining to the urinary and genital organs and their functions.

---

u·rol·o·gy (yŏŏ·rol'ə·jē) n. The branch of medicine relating to the urogenital or urinary system. —**u·ro·log·ic** (yŏŏr'·ə·loj'ik) or **·l·cal** adj. —**u·rol'o·gist** n.

u·ros·co·py (yŏŏ·ros'kə·pē) n. Examination of the urine, as for diagnosis. —**u·ro·scop·ic** (yŏŏr'ə·skop'ik) adj. —**u·ros'·co·pist** n.

Ur·sa Major (ûr'sə) Astron. The Great Bear, a large northern constellation containing seven conspicuous stars, including two which point to the polestar. [L]

Ursa Minor Astron. The Little Bear, a northern constellation including the polestar. [L]

Ursa Major and Ursa Minor
a. Ursa Major. b. Ursa Minor.
c. Polaris.

ur·sine (ûr'sīn, -sin) adj. Of, pertaining to, or like a bear. [<L ursus bear]

ur·ti·car·i·a (ûr'tə·kâr'ē·ə) n. A skin eruption of systemic origin characterized by evanescent wheals and itching; hives. [<L urtica nettle] —**ur'ti·car'i·al, ur'ti·car'i·ous** adj.

Uru. Uruguay.

U·ru·guay (yŏŏr'ə·gwā, Sp. ōō'rōō·gwī) n. A republic of SE South America, 72,172 sq. mi., cap. Montevideo. —**U'ru·guay'an** adj., n. • See map at ARGENTINA.

us (us) pron. The objective case of WE. [<OE ūs]

US, U.S. United States.

USA, U.S.A. United States of America; United States Army.

us·a·ble (yŏŏ'zə·bəl) adj. 1 Capable of being used. 2 That can be used conveniently. Also **use'a·ble.** —**us'a·ble·ness** n. —**us'a·bly** adv.

USAF, U.S.A.F. United States Air Force.

us·age (yŏŏ'sij, -zij) n. 1 The act or manner of using; treatment. 2 Customary or habitual practice; custom; habit. 3 The accepted and established way of using words, speech patterns, etc.

USCG, U.S.C.G. United States Coast Guard.

use (yŏŏz) v. used, us·ing v.t. 1 To put into service: to use a hammer. 2 To borrow; avail oneself of: May I use your pen? 3 To put into practice or employ habitually: to use diligence in business. 4 To conduct oneself toward; treat: to use one badly. 5 To partake of: He does not use tobacco. 6 To take advantage of; exploit: to use one's friends. 7 To expend, exhaust, or consume: usu. with up. —v.i. 8 To be accustomed: used in the past tense with an infinitive: We used to go to the theater regularly. —n. (yŏŏs) 1 The act of using, or the state of being used. 2 Function: He has lost the use of his legs. 3 Way or manner of using: to make good use of one's time. 4 Habitual practice or employment; custom; usage. 5 The ability or right to use, or the privilege of using. 6 Advantage; benefit; usefulness. 7 The purpose for which something is used. 8 Law The benefit or profit of property to which legal title is vested in another in trust for the beneficiary. —**have no use for** 1 To have no need of. 2 To have dislike or contempt for. —**in use** Being used or occupied. —**make use of** To have occasion to use; use. —**put to use** To utilize; employ. [<L usus, pp. of uti to use] —**us'er** n.

used (yŏŏzd) adj. 1 That has been employed in some way. 2 SECONDHAND. 3 Accustomed; experienced. —**used to** (yŏŏst) Accustomed to; habituated.

use·ful (yŏŏs'fəl) adj. Capable of being used; serviceable; helpful. —**use'ful·ly** adv. —**use'ful·ness** n.

use·less (yŏŏs'lis) adj. Being of or having no use; serving no function. —**use'less·ly** adv. —**use'less·ness** n.

us·er-friend·ly (yŏŏ'zər·frend'lē) adj. of a computer, program, software, etc., easy to use.

ush·er (ush'ər) n. 1 One who acts as doorkeeper, as of a court. 2 One who conducts persons to seats, etc., as in a church or theater. —v.t. 1 To act as an usher to; escort; conduct. 2 To precede as a harbinger; be a forerunner of. [<L ostiarius doorkeeper]

USM, U.S.M. United States Mail; United States Mint.

USMA, U.S.M.A. United States Military Academy.

USMC, U.S.M.C. United States Marine Corps; United States Maritime Commission.

USN, U.S.N. United States Navy.

USNA, U.S.N.A. United States Naval Academy.

USNG, U.S.N.G. United States National Guard.

USNR, U.S.N.R. United States Naval Reserve.

USO, U.S.O. United Service Organizations.

USS United States Ship, Steamer, or Steamship.

U.S.S. United States Senate.

USSR, U.S.S.R. Union of Soviet Socialist Republics.

usu. usual; usually.

u·su·al (yŏŏ'zhŏŏ·əl) adj. Such as occurs in the ordinary course of events; customary; common. [<L usus use] —**u'su·al·ly** adv. —**u'su·al·ness** n. —Syn. everyday, general, ordinary, prevalent.

u·su·fruct (yŏŏ'zə·frukt, yŏŏ'sə-) n. Law The right of using the fruits or profits of another's property. [<L usus et fructus use and fruit]

u·su·rer (yŏŏ'zhər·ər) n. One who practices usury. [<L usura use, usury]

u·su·ri·ous (yŏŏ·zhŏŏr'ē·əs) adj. 1 Practicing usury. 2 Of, relating to, or having the nature of usury. —**u·su'ri·ous·ly** adv. —**u·su'ri·ous·ness** n.

u·surp (yŏŏ·sûrp', -zûrp') v.t. To seize and hold (an office, rights, powers, etc.) without right or legal authority; take possesion of by force. [<L usurpare make use of, usurp]

u·sur·pa·tion (yŏŏ'sər·pā'shən, -zər-) n. The act of usurping, esp. the unlawful seizure of sovereign power.

u·su·ry (yŏŏ'zhər·ē) n. pl. **·ries** 1 The act or practice of lending money and charging interest that is excessive or unlawfully high. 2 Interest that is excessive or unlawfully high. [<L usura < usus, pp. of uti to use]

UT Utah (P.O. abbr.).

Ut. Utah.

u·ten·sil (yŏŏ·ten'səl) n. A vessel, tool, implement, etc., serving a useful purpose, esp. for domestic or farming use. [<L utensilis fit for use]

u·ter·ine (yŏŏ'tər·īn, -in) adj. 1 Of or pertaining to the uterus. 2 Born of the same mother, but having a different father. [<LL uterinus born of the same mother]

u·ter·us (yŏŏ'tər·əs) n. pl. **u·ter·i** (yŏŏ'tər·ī), **u·ter·us·es** The organ of a female mammal in which the fertilized ovum is deposited and develops until birth; womb. [L] • See OVARY.

u·til·i·tar·i·an (yŏŏ·til'ə·târ'ē·ən) adj. 1 Of or pertaining to utility; esp., placing utility above beauty, the amenities of life, etc. 2 Of, pertaining to, or advocating utilitarianism. —n. An advocate of utilitarianism.

u·til·i·tar·i·an·ism (yŏŏ·til'ə·târ'ē·ən·iz'əm) n. 1 The doctrine that holds usefulness to be the end and criterion of action. 2 The doctrine that the greatest happiness of the greatest number should be the sole end and criterion of all action.

u·til·i·ty (yŏŏ·til'ə·tē) n. pl. **·ties** 1 Fitness for some desirable, practical purpose; usefulness. 2 Fitness to supply the needs of people. 3 Something useful. 4 A public service, as a telephone system, gas, water, etc. 5 A company that provides such a service. [<L utilis useful < uti use]

u·til·ize (yŏŏ'təl·īz) v.t. **·ized, ·iz·ing** To make use of. Brit. sp. **u'til·ise.** —**u'til·i·za'tion, u'til·iz'er** n.

ut·most (ut'mōst) adj. 1 Of the highest or greatest degree. 2 Being at the farthest limit or most distant point; most remote; extreme. —n. The most possible. [<OE ūtmost]

U·to·Az·tec·an (yŏŏ'tō·az'tek·ən) n. One of the chief linguistic stocks of North American Indians formerly occupying NW and SW U.S., Mexico, and Central America. —adj. Of or pertaining to this linguistic stock.

u·to·pi·a (yŏŏ·tō'pē·ə) n. 1 Any state, condition, or place of ideal perfection. 2 A visionary, impractical scheme for social improvement. [<UTOPIA] —**u·to'pi·an** adj., n. —**u·to'pi·an·ism** n.

U·to·pi·a (yŏŏ·tō'pē·ə) n. An imaginary island described as the seat of a perfect social and political life in the book by Sir Thomas More, published in 1516. [<Gk. ou not + topos a place] —**U·to'pi·an** adj., n.

u·tri·cle (yŏŏ'tri·kəl) n. A small sac or cavity. [<L uter skin bag] —**u·tric·u·lar** (yŏŏ·trik'yə·lər) adj.

ut·ter[1] (ut'ər) v.t. 1 To say, express, give out, or send forth, as in words or sounds. **2** To put in circulation; esp., to deliver or offer (something forged or counterfeit). [< ME *out* say, speak out] —**ut′ter·er** *n.*

ut·ter² (ut′ər) *adj.* **1** Complete; absolute; total: *utter* misery. **2** Unqualified; final: an *utter* denial. [< OE *ūttra*, orig. compar. of *ūt* out] —**ut′ter·ly** *adv.*

ut·ter·ance (ut′ər·əns) *n.* **1** The act of uttering. **2** A manner of speaking. **3** A thing uttered.

ut·ter·most (ut′ər·mōst′) *adj. & n.* UTMOST.

U-turn (yōō′tûrn′) *n.* A complete turn which reverses the direction of movement, as of a vehicle on a road.

u·vu·la (yōō′vyə·lə) *n. pl.* **·las** or **·lae** (-lē) The pendent fleshy portion of the soft palate in the back of the mouth. [LL, dim. of *uva* grape] • See MOUTH.

u·vu·lar (yōō′vyə·lər) *adj.* **1** Pertaining to the uvula. **2** *Phonet.* Articulated with the back of the tongue near the uvula. —*n. Phonet.* A uvular sound.

ux. wife (L *uxor*).

ux·o·ri·ous (uk·sôr′ē·əs, -sō′rē-, ug·zôr′ē-, -zō′rē-) *adj.* Excessively devoted to or dominated by one's wife. [< L *uxor* wife] —**ux·o′ri·ous·ly** *adv.* —**ux·o′ri·ous·ness** *n.*

Uz·bek (ōōz′bek, uz′-) *n.* **1** A member of a Turkic people living in the Uzbek S.S.R. **2** The Turkic language of the Uzbeks.

V

V,v (vē) *n. pl.* **V's, v's, Vs, vs** (vēz) **1** The 22nd letter of the English alphabet. **2** Any spoken sound representing the letter *V* or *v.* **3** Something shaped like a V. **4** In Roman notation, the symbol for five. —*adj.* Shaped like a V.

V vanadium; vector; velocity; victory; volume.

V.,v. volt; volume.

v. valve; verb; verse; version; versus; vicar; village; vocative; voice; voltage; von.

VA Virginia (P.O. abbr.).

VA, V.A. Veterans Administration.

Va. Virginia.

va·can·cy (vā′kən·sē) *n. pl.* **·cies** **1** The state of being vacant; emptiness. **2** An apartment, room, etc., that is available for rent. **3** An unoccupied post, place, or office.

va·cant (vā′kənt) *adj.* **1** Containing or holding nothing; empty. **2** Not lived in or occupied. **3** Not being used; free: a *vacant* hour. **4** Being or appearing without intelligence: a *vacant* stare. **5** Having no incumbent, officer, or possessor. [< L *vacans* pr.p. of *vacare* be empty] —**va′cant·ly** *adv.* —**va′cant·ness** *n.* —Syn. **1** blank, void. **4** vapid, dull, vacuous, witless, obtuse, blank.

va·cate (vā′kāt′, vā·kāt′) *v.* **·cat·ed, ·cat·ing** *v.t.* **1** To make vacant, as a dwelling, position, etc. **2** To set aside; annul. —*v.i.* **3** To leave an office, dwelling, place, etc. **4** *Informal* To go away; leave. [< L *vacare* be empty]

va·ca·tion (vā·kā′shən) *n.* A time set aside from work, study, etc., for recreation or rest; a holiday. —*v.i.* To take a vacation. [See VACATE.] —**va·ca′tion·er, va·ca′tion·ist** *n.*

vac·ci·nate (vak′sə·nāt) *v.* **·nat·ed, ·nat·ing** *v.t.* **1** To inoculate with a vaccine as a preventive or therapeutic measure; esp., to inoculate against smallpox. —*v.i.* **2** To perform the act of vaccination. —**vac′ci·na′tor** *n.*

vac·ci·na·tion (vak′sə·nā′shən) *n.* **1** The act or process of vaccinating. **2** A scar produced at the site of inoculation with a vaccine.

vac·cine (vak·sēn′, vak′sēn) *n.* **1** The virus of cowpox, prepared for inoculation to produce immunity to smallpox. **2** Any modified virus or bacterium used to give immunity against a specific disease. [< L *vaccinus* pertaining to a cow] —**vac′ci·nal** (-sə·nəl) *adj.*

vac·il·late (vas′ə·lāt) *v.i.* **·lat·ed, ·lat·ing** **1** To move one way and the other; waver. **2** To waver in mind; be irresolute. [< L *vacillare* waver] —**vac′il·la′tion** *n.* —**vac′il·la·to′ry** (-ə·lə·tô′rē, -tō′rē) *adj.* —Syn. **1** fluctuate, oscillate, sway.

va·cu·i·ty (va·kyōō′ə·tē) *n. pl.* **·ties** **1** The state of being a vacuum; emptiness. **2** Vacant space; a void. **3** Lack of intelligence; stupidity. **4** An inane or stupid thing, statement, etc. [< L *vacuus* empty]

vac·u·ole (vak′yōō·ōl) *n.* A small cavity within a cell containing air or fluid or food particles. [< L *vacuus* empty]

vac·u·ous (vak′yōō-əs) *adj.* **1** Having no contents; empty. **2** Lacking intelligence; blank. [< L *vacuus*] —**vac′u·ous·ly** *adv.* —**vac′u·ous·ness** *n.*

vac·u·um (vak′yōō-əm, -yōōm) *n. pl.* **·u·ums** or **·u·a** (-yōō-ə) **1** *Physics* A space devoid, or nearly devoid, of matter. **2** A reduction of the pressure in a space below atmospheric pressure. **3** A void; an empty feeling. **4** *Informal* A vacuum cleaner. —*v.t. & v.i. Informal* To clean with a vacuum cleaner. [L, neut. of *vacuus* empty]

vacuum bottle THERMOS.

vacuum cleaner A machine for cleaning floors, carpets, etc., by means of suction.

vacuum pump A pump designed to remove gas or air from a sealed space.

vacuum tube *Electronics* An electron tube containing a negligible amount of gas.

va·de me·cum (vā′dē mē′kəm) Anything carried for constant use, as a guidebook, manual, etc. [L, go with me]

vag·a·bond (vag′ə·bond) *n.* **1** One who wanders from place to place without visible means of support; a tramp. **2** A shiftless, irresponsible person. —*adj.* **1** Wandering; nomadic. **2** Having no definite residence; irresponsible. **3** Driven to and fro; aimless. [< L *vagus* wandering] —**vag′a·bond′age, vag′a·bond′ism** *n.*

va·gar·y (vā′gə·rē, və·gâr′ē) *n. pl.* **·gar·ies** A wild fancy; extravagant notion. [< L *vagari* wander]

va·gi·na (və·jī′nə) *n. pl.* **·nas** or **·nae** (-nē) **1** The canal leading from the external genital orifice in female mammals to the uterus. **2** A sheath or sheathlike covering. [L, a sheath] —**vag·i·nal** (vaj′ə·nəl) *adj.*

va·gran·cy (vā′grən·sē) *n. pl.* **·cies** **1** The condition of being a vagrant. **2** The offense of being a vagrant: arrested for *vagrancy.*

va·grant (vā′grənt) *n.* A person who wanders from place to place without a settled home or job and who exists usu. by begging or stealing; a tramp. —*adj.* **1** Wandering about aimlessly; wayward. **2** Pertaining to or characteristic of a vagrant. [< OF *wacrer* to walk, wander] —**va′grant·ly** *adv.* —**va′grant·ness** *n.*

vague (vāg) *adj.* **vagu·er, vagu·est** **1** Lacking definiteness; not clearly stated: *vague* rumors; *vague* promises. **2** Indistinct; hard to perceive: *vague* shapes in the fog. **3** Not thinking or expressing oneself clearly. [< L *vagus* wandering] —**vague′ly** *adv.* —**vague′ness** *n.*

va·gus (vā′gəs) *n. pl.* **·gi** (-jī) *Anat.* Either of the pair of cranial nerves sending branches to the lungs, heart, stomach, and most of the abdominal viscera. Also **vagus nerve.** [L, wandering]

vain (vān) *adj.* **1** Having or showing excessive pride in oneself; conceited. **2** Unproductive; useless: *vain* efforts. **3** Without substantial foundation; unreal. —**in vain** **1** To no purpose; without effect. **2** Irreverently: to take the Lord's name *in vain.* [< L *vanus* empty] —**vain′ly** *adv.* —**vain′ness** *n.* —Syn. **1** boastful, egotistical, narcissistic.

vain·glo·ry (vān′glôr′ē, -glōr′-, vān·glôr′ē) *n.* **1** Excessive or groundless vanity; boastfulness. **2** Empty, showy pomp. [< Med. L *vana gloria* empty pomp, show] —**vain·glo′ri·ous** *adj.* —**vain·glo′ri·ous·ly** *adv.* —**vain·glo′ri·ous·ness** *n.*

val·ance (val′əns, vā′ləns) *n.* **1** A drapery hanging from the tester of a bedstead. **2** A short, full drapery across the top of a window. [Prob. < OF *avaler* descend] —**val′anced** *adj.* • See CANOPY.

---

add, āce, câre, pälm; end, ēven; it, īce; odd, ōpen, ôrder; tōōk, pōōl; up, bûrn; ə = a in *above, u* in *focus;* yōō = *u* in *fuse;* oil; pout; check; go; ring; thin; this; zh, *vision.* < derived from; ? origin uncertain or unknown.

vale[1] (vāl) n. VALLEY. [< L *vallis*]

va·le[2] (vä′lē) *interj.* Farewell. [L, lit., be in good health]

val·e·dic·tion (val′ə·dik′shən) n. **1** A bidding farewell. **2** VALEDICTORY. [< L *valedicere* say farewell]

val·e·dic·to·ri·an (val′ə·dik·tôr′ē·ən, -tō′rē-) n. A student, usu. the highest in scholastic rank, who delivers a valedictory at the graduating exercises of an educational institution.

val·e·dic·to·ry (val′ə·dik′tər·ē) *adj.* Pertaining to a leave-taking. —n. pl. **·ries** A parting address, as by a member (ordinarily the first in rank) of a graduating class.

va·lence (vā′ləns) n. *Chem.* The combining capacity of an atom or radical as measured by the number of electrons gained or lost or shared in forming a bond with another atom or radical. [< L *valens*, pr.p. of *valere* be well, be strong]

val·en·tine (val′ən·tīn) n. **1** A card or small gift sent as a token of affection on Valentine's Day. **2** A sweetheart.

Valentine's Day February 14, a day observed in honor of St. Valentine, and on which valentines are sent to sweethearts, etc.

va·le·ri·an (və·lir′ē·ən) n. **1** Any of various plants with small pink or white flowers and a strong odor. **2** A sedative derived from the roots of some of these plants. [< Med. L *valeriana*]

val·et (val′it, val′ā, val·ā′) n. **1** A man's personal servant. **2** A manservant in a hotel who cleans and presses clothes. —v.t. & v.i. To act as a valet. [F < OF *vaslet*, *varlet*, dim. of *vasal* vassal]

val·e·tu·di·nar·i·an (val′ə·t^yōō′də·nâr′ē·ən) n. **1** A chronic invalid. **2** A person unduly concerned about his health. —*adj.* **1** Infirm; ailing. **2** Unduly concerned about one's health. [< L *valetudo*, health, ill health < *valere* be well] —**val′e·tu′di·nar′i·an·ism** n.

Val·hal·la (val·hal′ə) n. *Norse Myth.* The great hall in which the souls of heroes, borne by the Valkyries, are received and feasted by Odin.

val·iant (val′yənt) *adj.* **1** Strong and intrepid; powerful and courageous. **2** Performed with valor; heroic. [< OF *valoir* be strong] —**val′iant·ly** adv. —**val′i·an·cy** or **val′i·ance**, **val′iant·ness** n.

val·id (val′id) *adj.* **1** Based on facts or evidence; sound: a *valid* argument. **2** Legally binding: a *valid* will. [< L *validus* powerful] —**val′id·ly** adv. —**va·lid·i·ty** (və·lid′ə·tē), **val′id·ness** n.

val·i·date (val′ə·dāt) v.t. **·dat·ed, ·dat·ing 1** To confirm by facts or authority. **2** To declare legally valid; legalize. —**val′i·da′tion** n.

va·lise (və·lēs′) n. A traveling bag; suitcase. [< Ital. *valigia*]

Val·kyr·ie (val·kir′ē, val′kir·ē) n. pl. **·ky·ries** or **·ky·rie** *Norse Myth.* One of the maidens who ride through the air and choose heroes from among those slain in battle, and carry them to Valhalla. Also **Val′kyr** (-kir). —**Val·kyr′i·an** adj.

val·ley (val′ē) n. **1** A long, wide area drained by a large river system: the Hudson *valley*. **2** Low land lying between mountains or hills. **3** Any hollow or depression shaped like a valley. [< L *vallis*]

val·or (val′ər) n. Marked courage; personal heroism; bravery. *Brit. sp.* **val′our.** [< L *valere* be strong] —**val′or·ous** adj. —**val′or·ous·ly** adv. —**val′or·ous·ness** n.

val·or·i·za·tion (val′ər·ə·zā′shən, -ī·zā′-) n. The maintenance by governmental action of an artificial price for any product. [< Pg. *valor* value] —**val′or·ize** (val′ə·rīz) v.t.

val·u·a·ble (val′yōō·ə·bəl, val′yə·bəl) *adj.* **1** Having financial worth, price, or value. **2** Very costly. **3** Worthy; estimable: a *valuable* friend. —n. Usu. pl. An article of value, as a piece of jewelry. —**val′u·a·ble·ness** n. —**val′u·a·bly** adv.

val·u·a·tion (val′yōō·ā′shən) n. **1** The act of estimating the value of something; evaluation. **2** Estimated value; appraisement. —**val′u·a′tion·al** adj.

val·ue (val′yōō) n. **1** The desirability or worth of a thing; merit: the *value* of self-discipline. **2** Something regarded as desirable, worthy, or right, as a belief or ideal. **3** Worth in money; market price. **4** A bargain. **5** Purchasing power: a decline in the *value* of money. **6** Exact meaning: the *value* of a word. **7** *Music* The relative length of a tone. **8** *Math.* The number assigned to or represented by a symbol or expression. **9** In art, the relative lightness or darkness of a color. **10** The relation, as of light and shade, of one part to another in a work of art. —v.t. **·ued, ·u·ing 1** To assess; appraise. **2** To regard highly; prize. **3** To place a relative estimate of value upon: to *value* health above all else. [< L *valere*] —**val′u·er** n.

val·ue-add·ed tax (val′yōō·ad′id) A tax levied on each stage of a product's manufacture and marketing, from the raw material to the final retailer, the ultimate burden being placed on the consumer in the form of higher prices.

val·ued (val′yōōd) *adj.* **1** Highly esteemed: a *valued* friend. **2** Having a specified value: *valued* at ten dollars.

val·ue·less (val′yōō·lis) *adj.* Having no value; worthless. —**val′ue·less·ness** n.

valve (valv) n. **1** *Mech.* Any device used to block, direct, or otherwise control motion of a fluid. **2** *Anat.* A membranous structure inside a vessel or other organ, allowing fluid to flow in one direction only. **3** *Zool.* One of the parts of a shell, as of a clam, etc. **4** *Bot.* One of the parts into which a seed capsule splits. —v.t. **valved, valv·ing** To control the flow by means of a valve. [< L *valva* leaf of a door]

val·vu·lar (val′vyə·lər) *adj.* **1** Pertaining to valves, as of the heart. **2** Having valves. **3** Having the form of a valve.

Gate valve in closed position (cross section)

va·moose (va·mōōs′) v.t. & v.i. **·moosed, ·moos·ing** *Slang* To leave or depart hastily. Also **va·mose′** (-mōs′) [< Sp. *vamos* let us go]

vamp[1] (vamp) n. **1** The piece of leather forming the upper front part of a boot or shoe. • See SHOE. **2** Something added to give an old thing a new appearance. —v.t. **1** To provide with a vamp. **2** To repair or patch. [< OF *avant* before + *pied* foot] —**vamp′er** n.

vamp[2] (vamp) *Slang* n. A seductive woman who entices and exploits men. —v.t. & v.i. To seduce (a man) by acting as a vamp. [Short for VAMPIRE]

vam·pire (vam′pīr) n. **1** In folklore, a reanimated corpse that rises from its grave at night to suck the blood of persons who are asleep. **2** A person who preys upon those of the opposite sex; esp. a woman who degrades or impoverishes her lover. **3** A bat of tropical America that drinks the blood of mammals: also **vampire bat. 4** An insect- or fruit-eating bat mistakenly thought to suck blood: also **false vampire.** [< Slavic] —**vam′pir·ism** n.

van[1] (van) n. **1** A large covered wagon or truck for transporting furniture, household goods, etc. **2** *Brit.* A closed railway car for luggage, etc. [Short for CARAVAN]

van[2] (van) n. VANGUARD. [Short for VANGUARD]

va·na·di·um (və·nā′dē·əm) n. A rare, silver-white metallic element (symbol V), used to produce **vanadium steel**, a tough, resilient alloy. [L < ON *Vanadis*, a name of the Norse goddess Freya]

Van Al·len belt (van al′ən) An extensive region of intense radiation consisting of charged atomic particles trapped by the earth's magnetic field and surrounding the earth in inner and outer belts. [< J. A. *Van Allen*, 1914–, U.S. physicist]

van·dal (van′dəl) n. One who engages in vandalism. [< VANDAL]

Van·dal (van′dəl) n. A member of a Germanic people that laid waste to Gaul, Spain, and North Africa in the fifth century and conquered Rome in 455.

van·dal·ism (van′dəl·iz′əm) n. Willful destruction or defacement of public or private property.

Van·dyke beard (van·dīk′) A small pointed beard. [< Anthony *Van Dyck*, 1599–1641, Flemish painter]

vane (vān) n. **1** A thin plate, pivoted on a vertical rod, to indicate the direction of the wind; a weathercock. **2** An arm or blade, as of a windmill, propeller, projectile, turbine, etc. **3** The web, or flat portion, of a feather. [< OE *fana* a flag] —**vaned** (vānd) adj.

Windmill vanes

van·guard (van'gärd) n. 1 The forward part of an advancing army. 2 The foremost position in a movement, trend, etc. 3 The leaders of a movement, trend, etc. [< OF *avant* before + *garde* guard]

va·nil·la (və·nil'ə) n. 1 Any of a genus of tall climbing orchids of tropical America. 2 The long seed capsule of one species: also vanilla bean. 3 A flavoring extracted from these capsules or made synthetically. [< Sp. *vaina* sheath, pod] —**va·nil'lic** adj.

va·nil·lin (və·nil'in) n. The organic compound which gives vanilla flavoring its distinct odor and taste.

van·ish (van'ish) v.i. 1 To disappear; fade away. 2 To pass out of existence. [< L *evanescere* fade away] —**van'ish·er** n.

Vanilla
a. flower. b. bean.
c. pod.

vanishing point 1 In perspective, the point at which receding parallel lines appear to meet. • See PERSPECTIVE. 2 The point at which something approaches an end.

van·i·ty (van'ə·tē) n. pl. ·ties 1 Excessive pride in one's talents, looks, possessions, etc. 2 Worthlessness; futility. 3 Something that is worthless or futile. 4 A low table with an attached mirror, for use while dressing the hair or putting on makeup. 5 VANITY CASE. [< L *vanus* empty, vain]

vanity case A small case holding face powder, rouge, puff, mirror, etc. Also vanity box.

van·quish (vang'kwish, van'-) v.t. 1 To defeat in battle; conquer. 2 To suppress or overcome (a feeling): to *vanquish* fear. 3 To defeat in any encounter. [< L *vincere*] — **van'quish·er van'quish·ment** n. —**Syn.** 1 beat, overcome, overpower, overwhelm, upset.

van·tage (van'tij) n. 1 Superiority, as over a competitor; advantage. 2 A position, place, situation, etc., that gives superiority or an advantage. [< OF *avantage* advantage]

vantage ground A position or condition which gives one an advantage.

van·ward (van'wərd) adj. & adv. Toward or in the front.

vap·id (vap'id, vā'pəd) adj. 1 Having lost sparkle and flavor. 2 Flat; insipid. [< L *vapidus* insipid] —**va·pid'i·ty** (və·pid'ə·tē), **vap'id·ness** n. —**vap'id·ly** adv.

va·por (vā'pər) n. 1 Moisture in the air; esp. visible floating moisture, as light mist. 2 Any cloudy substance in the air, as smoke. 3 The gaseous phase of any substance. 4 Something that is fleeting and unsubstantial. 5 A remedial agent applied by inhalation. —**the vapors** *Archaic* Depression of spirits. —v.t. 1 VAPORIZE. —v.i. 2 To emit vapor. 3 To pass off in vapor; evaporate. *Brit. sp.* va'pour. [< L *vapor* steam] —**va'por·er** n.

va·por·ize (vā'pə·rīz) v.t. & v.i. ·ized, ·iz·ing To convert or be converted into vapor. —**va'por·i·za'tion** n.

va·por·iz·er (vā'pə·rī'zər) n. 1 One who or that which vaporizes. 2 A device for boiling water or a medicated liquid to form a vapor for inhalation.

va·por·ous (vā'pər·əs) adj. 1 Of or like vapor; misty. 2 Emitting or forming vapor. 3 Whimsical; fanciful. —**va·por·os·i·ty** (vā'pə·ros'ə·tē), **va'por·ous·ness** n.

va·que·ro (vä·kā'rō) n. pl. ·ros (-rōz, *Sp.* -rōs) A herdsman; cowboy. [< Sp. *vaca* cow]

var. variant; variation; variety; various.

var·i·a·ble (vâr'ē·ə·bəl, var'-) adj. 1 Having the capacity of varying; alterable. 2 Having a tendency to change; not constant. 3 Having no definite value as regards quantity. 4 *Biol.* Prone to deviate from a type. —n. 1 That which is liable to change. 2 *Math.* a A quantity that may be equal to any one of a specified set of numbers. b A symbol representing such a quantity. 3 A shifting wind. —**var'i·a·bil'i·ty**, **var'i·a·ble·ness** n. —**var'i·a·bly** adv. —**Syn.** adj. 2 fluctuating, unstable, unsteady, wavering.

variable zone TEMPERATE ZONE.

var·i·ance (vâr'ē·əns, var'-) n. 1 The act of varying or the state of being varied. 2 Discrepancy; difference. 3 A dispute; quarrel. 4 A license or official permission to do something contrary to official regulations. —**at variance** Not in agreement; disagreeing.

var·i·ant (vâr'ē·ənt, var'-) adj. 1 Varying; differing, esp. differing from a standard or type. 2 *Archaic* Variable; changeable. —n. 1 A person or thing that differs from another in form only. 2 One of several different spellings, pronunciations, or forms of the same word.

var·i·a·tion (vâr'ē·ā'shən, var'-) n. 1 The act or process of varying; modification. 2 The extent to which a thing varies. 3 A thing changed in form from others of the same type. 4 *Music* A repetition of a theme or melody with changes in key, rhythm, harmony, etc. 5 *Biol.* Deviation from the typical structure or function. —**var'i·a'tion·al** adj.

var·i·col·ored (vâr'i·kul'ərd, var'-) adj. Variegated in color; parti-colored.

var·i·cose (var'ə·kōs) adj. 1 Abnormally dilated, as veins. 2 Having or resulting from varicose veins: *varicose* ulcer. [< L < *varix* a varicose vein] —**var'i·cos'i·ty** (-kos'ə·tē) n.

var·ied (vâr'ēd, var'-) adj. 1 Consisting of diverse sorts; assorted. 2 Altered; changed. —**var'ied·ly** adv.

var·i·e·gate (vâr'ē·ə·gāt', var'-) v.t. ·gat·ed, ·gat·ing 1 To mark with different colors; dapple; streak. 2 To make varied; diversify. —adj. VARIEGATED. [< L *varius* various + *agere* to drive, do] —**var'i·e·ga'tion** n.

var·i·e·gat·ed (vâr'ē·ə·gā'tid, var'-) adj. 1 Varied in color, as with streaks or blotches. 2 Having or exhibiting different forms, styles, or varieties.

va·ri·e·ty (və·rī'ə·tē) n. pl. ·ties 1 Absence of sameness or monotony; diversity; variation; difference. 2 Sort; kind: a sweet *variety* of pickle. 3 A collection of diverse kinds; assortment: a *variety* of flowers. 4 A subdivision of a species. 5 Vaudeville: also **variety show**. [< L *varius* various]

va·ri·o·la (ver'ē·ō'lə, və·rī'ə·lə) n. SMALLPOX. [< L *varius* speckled] —**va·ri'o·lar** adj.

var·i·o·rum (vâr'ē·ôr'əm, -ō'rəm, var'-) n. 1 An edition of a work containing various versions of the text. 2 An edition of a work with notes by different critics or editors. —adj. Of or pertaining to such an edition. [< L (*cum notis*) *variorum* (with the notes) of various persons]

var·i·ous (vâr'ē·əs, var'-) adj. 1 Characteristically different from one another; diverse: *various* customs. 2 Being more than one and easily distinguishable; several: *various* friends. 3 Separate; particular; identifiable: He shook hands with *various* people. 4 Differing in nature or appearance; dissimilar. 5 Versatile; multifaceted. [< L *varius*] —**var'i·ous·ly** adv. —**var'i·ous·ness** n.

var·let (vär'lit) n. *Archaic* A scoundrel. [OF, a groom] —**var'let·ry** n.

var·mint (vär'mənt) n. *Regional* Any person or animal considered as troublesome, esp. vermin. [Alter. of VERMIN]

var·nish (vär'nish) n. 1 A solution of certain gums or resins in alcohol, linseed oil, etc., used to produce a shining, transparent coat on a surface. 2 The glossy, hard finish made by this solution when dry. 3 Any substance or finish resembling varnish. 4 Outward show; deceptive appearance. —v.t. 1 To cover with varnish. 2 To give a glossy appearance to. 3 To hide by a deceptive appearance; gloss over. [< Med. L *vernicium*, a kind of resin] —**var'nish·er** n.

var·si·ty (vär'sə·tē) n. pl. ·ties *Informal* 1 *Brit.* UNIVERSITY. 2 The team that represents a university, college, or school in any competition. [Alter. of UNIVERSITY]

var·y (vâr'ē, var'-) v. var·ied, var·y·ing v.t. 1 To change the form, nature, substance, etc., of; modify. 2 To cause to be different from one another. 3 To diversify. 4 *Music* To systematically alter (a melody or other thematic element). —v.i. 5 To become changed in form, substance, etc. 6 To differ. 7 To deviate; depart: with *from*. 8 To alternate. 9 *Math.* To be subject to change. 10 *Biol.* To show variation. [< L *varius* various, diverse] —**var'y·ing·ly** adv.

vas (vas) n. pl. va·sa (vā'sə) *Biol.* A vessel or duct. [L, vessel, dish] —**va'sal** adj.

vas·cu·lar (vas'kyə·lər) adj. Of, pertaining to, or having vessels or ducts, as blood vessels, phloem tissue, etc. [< L *vasculum*, dim. of *vas* vessel] —**vas'cu·lar'i·ty** (-lar'ə·tē) n. —**vas'cu·lar·ly** adv.

---

vas def·er·ens (vas def′ər·ənz) The duct by which spermatozoa pass from the testicle to the penis. [<L *vas* vessel + *deferens* leading down]

vase (vās, vāz, väz) *n.* An urnlike vessel used as an ornament or for holding flowers. [<L *vas* vessel]

va·sec·to·my (və·sek′tə·mē) *n. pl.* **·to·mies** Surgical removal of a portion of the vas deferens, thus producing sterilization by preventing semen from reaching the seminal vesicles. [<VAS(O)- + -ECTOMY]

Vas·e·line (vas′ə·lēn, vas·ə·lēn′) *n.* PETROLATUM: a trade name.

vaso- *combining form* A vessel, esp. a blood vessel: *vasomotor.* [<L *vas* a vessel]

vas·o·mo·tor (vas′ō·mō′tər) *adj.* Producing contraction or dilation of blood vessels.

vas·sal (vas′əl) *n.* **1** In feudalism, a man who held land from a superior lord to whom he rendered, in return, military or other service. **2** A person who is in a position that is subordinate, lowly, servile, slavish, etc. —*adj.* Of or pertaining to a vassal. [<LL *vassus* a servant]

vas·sal·age (vas′əl·ij) *n.* **1** The condition, duties, and obligations of a vassal. **2** A position of servitude, dependence, or subjection.

vast (vast, väst) *adj.* **1** Of great extent; immense: a *vast* desert. **2** Very great in number, quantity, or amount. **3** Very great in degree, intensity, or importance. [<L, waste, empty, vast] —**vast′ly** *adv.* —**vast′ness** *n.* —Syn. 1, 2 enormous, extensive, huge, tremendous.

vat (vat) *n.* A large vessel, tub, or cistern, esp. for holding liquids during some process, as heating, fermenting, etc. —*v.t.* **vat·ted, vat·ting** To treat in a vat. [<OE *fæt*]

VAT value-added tax.

Vat. Vatican.

vat dye Any of a class of fast dyes in which the color develops, as by oxidation in air, subsequent to treatment of the fabric in a usu. colorless dye solution. —**vat′dyed′** *adj.*

Vat·i·can (vat′ə·kən) *n.* **1** The papal palace in Vatican City, Rome. **2** The papal government.

Vatican City A sovereign papal state included in Rome. 108.7 acres.

vau·de·ville (vô′də·vil, vōd′vil) *n.* A theatrical entertainment consisting of short dramatic sketches, songs, dances, acrobatic feats, etc.; a variety show. [<F *(chanson de) Vau de Vire* (song of) the valley of the Vire river (in Normandy)]

vault¹ (vôlt) *n.* **1** An arched roof or ceiling, usu. of masonry. **2** Any vaultlike covering, as the sky. **3** An arched passage or room. **4** An underground room or compartment for storage. **5** A place for keeping valuables: bank *vault.* **6** A burial chamber.—

Vaults
a. barrel. b. groined.

v.t. **1** To cover with or as with a vault. **2** To construct in the form of a vault. [<OF *volte, vaute*]

vault² (vôlt) *v.i.* **1** To leap, as over an object, by the use of one's hands on the object or by the use of a pole. —*v.t.* **2** To leap over. —*n.* **1** The act of vaulting. **2** A leap. [<OF *volter* to leap, gambol] —**vault′er** *n.*

vault·ing¹ (vôl′ting) *n.* The construction that forms a vault.

vault·ing² (vôl′ting) *adj.* **1** That leaps or leaps over. **2** Unduly confident or presumptuous. **3** Used for leaping and leaping over.

vaunt (vônt, vänt) *v.i.* **1** To boast. —*v.t.* **2** To boast of. —*n.* A brag or boast. [<LL *vanitare* brag<L *vanus* empty, vain]

vb. verb; verbal.

V.C. Victoria Cross; Vietcong.

VCR Videocassette recorder, a recorder utilizing videotape to record programs, movies, etc., for replay by means of a television set.

VD, V.D., v.d. venereal disease.

VDT Video (or visual) display terminal, a computer terminal with attached keyboard for the display of data; cathode-ray tube; terminal.

veal (vēl) *n.* **1** A calf, esp. one grown or suitable for food.

2 The flesh of a calf as food. [<L *vitellus,* dim. of *vitulus* calf]

vec·tor (vek′tər) *n.* **1** *Math.* A quantity defined by its magnitude and direction. **2** *Med.* An insect or other living carrier of pathogenic organisms from one host to another. [<L, carrier<*vehere* carry]

Ve·da (vā′də, vē′-) *n.* Any of four collections of ancient Hindu sacred writings. [Skt., knowledge] —**Ve·da·ic** (vi·dā′ik), **Ve′dic** *adj.* —**Ve·da·ism** (vā′də·iz′əm, vē′-) *n.*

V-E Day (vē′ē′) May 8, 1945, the official date of the Allied victory in Europe in World War II.

veep (vēp) *n. Slang* A vice president, esp. the vice president of the U.S. [<*V.P.,* abbr. of vice president]

veer (vir) *v.i.* **1** To shift or turn in position or direction: The wind *veered* to the east. **2** To shift from one opinion, belief, etc., to another. —*v.t.* **3** To change the direction of. —*n.* A change in direction. [<F *virer* to turn]

veer·y (vir′ē) *n. pl.* **veer·ies** A melodious tawny thrush that breeds in CEN. North America. [Prob. imit.]

veg. vegetable; vegetation.

Ve·ga (vē′gə, vā′-) *n.* A bright star in the constellation Lyra. [<Ar. *(al-Nasr) al-Waqi* the falling (vulture)]

veg·e·ta·ble (vej′ə·tə·bəl, vej′tə-) *n.* **1** A plant, esp. one cultivated for food. **2** The edible part of a plant, raw or cooked. **3** *Informal* A person who is mindless, apathetic, or passive. —*adj.* **1** Pertaining to plants, as distinct from animals: the *vegetable* kingdom. **2** Derived from, of the nature of, or resembling plants. **3** Made from or pertaining to edible vegetables: *vegetable* soup. **4** *Informal* Showing little mental activity; apathetic, passive, etc. [<L *vegetus* vigorous, lively<*vegere* be lively]

veg·e·tal (vej′ə·təl) *adj.* **1** Of or pertaining to plants or vegetables. **2** Pertaining to nonreproductive aspects of plant life.

veg·e·tar·i·an (vej′ə·târ′ē·ən) *n.* A person whose diet is made up of vegetables, fruits, grain, nuts, and sometimes animal products, as milk, eggs, etc. —*adj.* **1** Pertaining to or advocating the eating of only vegetable foods. **2** Made up exclusively of vegetables, fruits, grain, etc. —**veg′e·tar′i·an·ism** *n.*

veg·e·tate (vej′ə·tāt) *v.i.* **·tat·ed, ·tat·ing** **1** To grow, as a plant. **2** To live in a monotonous, passive way.

veg·e·ta·tion (vej′ə·tā′shən) *n.* **1** The process or condition of vegetating. **2** Plant life in the aggregate.

veg·e·ta·tive (vej′ə·tā′tiv) *adj.* **1** Of or pertaining to vegetation and plant growth. **2** Growing or capable of growing as plants; productive. **3** VEGETABLE (def. 4). **4** Concerned with nonreproductive life processes.

ve·he·ment (vē′ə·mənt) *adj.* **1** Arising from or marked by strong feeling or passing. **2** Acting with great force; violent. [<L *vehemens, -entis* impetuous, rash] —**ve′he·mence, ve′he·men·cy** *n.* —**ve′he·ment·ly** *adv.* —Syn. **1** ardent, fervent, zealous, fierce. **2** energetic, forceful, intense, powerful.

ve·hi·cle (vē′ə·kəl, vē′hi-) *n.* **1** Any device for carrying or transporting persons or things, as a car, spacecraft, etc. **2** A neutral medium for administering a medicine, etc. **3** The medium with which pigments are mixed in painting. **4** Any means by which thoughts or ideas are transmitted or communicated. [<L *vehiculum*<*vehere* to carry, ride] —**ve·hic·u·lar** (vi·hik′yə·lər) *adj.*

veil (vāl) *n.* **1** A piece of thin and light fabric, worn over the face or head for concealment, protection, or ornament. **2** A piece of cloth, as a curtain, that covers, conceals, etc. **3** Anything that conceals or covers. —**take the veil** To become a nun. —*v.t.* **1** To cover with a veil. **2** To conceal, cover, hide, disguise, etc. [<L *velum* piece of cloth, sail]

veil·ing (vā′ling) *n.* **1** The act of covering with a veil. **2** Material for veils. **3** A veil.

vein (vān) *n.* **1** Any of the tubular vessels that convey blood to the heart. **2** One of the radiating supports of an insect's wing. **3** One of the slender vascular bundles that form the framework of a leaf. **4** LODE. **5** A long, irregular, colored streak, as in wood, marble, etc. **6** A distinctive tendency or disposition. —*v.t.* **1** To furnish or fill with veins. **2** To streak or ornament with veins. **3** To extend over or throughout as veins. [<L *vena* blood vessel]

Veining of maple leaf

veined (vānd) *adj.* **1** Having veins, esp. many veins. **2** Marked with streaks of another color: *veined* marble.

vein·ing (vā′ning) *n.* **1** A vein or network of veins. **2** A streaked or veined surface.

vein·let (vān′lit) *n.* A small vein.

ve·lar (vē′lər) *adj.* **1** Of or pertaining to a velum, esp. the soft palate. **2** *Phonet.* Formed with the back of the tongue touching or near the soft palate, as (k) in *cool.* —*n. Phonet.* A velar sound. [< L *velum* sail, curtain]

veld (velt, felt) *n.* In South Africa, open country having few shrubs or trees. Also **veldt.** [< MDu. *velt* field]

vel·lum (vel′əm) *n.* **1** Fine parchment made from the skins of calves; used for expensive binding, printing, etc. **2** A manuscript written on vellum. **3** Paper or cloth made to resemble vellum. [< OF *veel, viel* calf]

ve·loc·i·pede (və·los′ə·pēd) *n.* **1** An early form of bicycle or tricycle. **2** A child's tricycle. [< L *velox* swift + -PEDE]

ve·loc·i·ty (və·los′ə·tē) *n. pl.* **·ties 1** Quickness of motion; speed; swiftness. **2** *Physics* A vector representing the rate of change of position of a body. [< L *velox* swift]

ve·lour (və·lŏŏr′) *n. pl.* **·lours 1** A soft, velvetlike, cotton or wool fabric having a short, thick pile. **2** A type of felt with a velvety nap, used esp. for hats. Also **ve·lours** (və·lŏŏr′. [See VELURE.]

ve·lum (vē′ləm) *n. pl.* **·la** (-lə) **1** SOFT PALATE. **2** A thin membranous covering or partition. [L, veil]

ve·lure (və·lyŏŏr′) *n. Archaic* A heavy fabric resembling velvet, formerly used for hangings, etc. [< F *velours* < L *villosus* shaggy]

vel·vet (vel′vit) *n.* **1** A fabric of silk, rayon, nylon, etc., having on one side a short, smooth pile. **2** Something resembling velvet. **3** *Slang* Unexpected profit or gain. —*adj.* **1** Made of velvet. **2** Smooth and soft to the touch like velvet. [Ult. < L *villus* shaggy hair] —**vel′vet·y** *adj.*

vel·vet·een (vel′və·tēn′) *n.* **1** A fabric, usu. of cotton, with a short, close pile like velvet. **2** Clothes, esp. slacks, made of velveteen.

Ven. Venerable; Venice; Venus.

ve·na ca·va (vē′nə kā′və) *pl.* **ve·nae ca·vae** (vē′nē kā′vē) Either of the two great veins that deliver blood to the right auricle of the heart. [L, hollow vein] • See HEART.

ve·nal (vē′nəl) *adj.* **1** Capable of being corrupted or bribed. **2** Characterized by corruption or bribery. [< L *venum* sale] —**ve·nal·i·ty** (vē·nal′ə·tē) *n.* —**ve′nal·ly** *adv.*

ve·na·tion (ve·nā′shən, vē-) *n.* **1** Veins collectively. **2** NERVATION. [< L *vena* a vein]

vend (vend) *v.t.* **1** To sell, as by peddling. **2** To sell by means of a vending machine. **3** To give expression to in public —*v.i.* **4** To sell merchandise. [< L *vendere*] —**Syn.** *v.t.* **1** dispense, hawk, market, peddle.

ven·dee (ven·dē′) *n.* The person or party to whom something is sold.

ven·det·ta (ven·det′ə) *n.* Private warfare or feud, as in revenge for a murder, injury, etc. [< L *vindicta* vengeance]

vend·i·ble (ven′də·bəl) *adj.* Salable; marketable. —*n.* A thing for sale. —**vend′i·bil′i·ty, vend′i·ble·ness** *n.* —**vend′i·bly** *adv.*

vending machine A machine that makes candy, stamps, etc., available when a coin is inserted.

ven·dor (ven′dər) *n.* **1** One who vends; seller. **2** VENDING MACHINE. Also **vender.**

ve·neer (və·nir′) *n.* **1** A thin layer, as of choice wood, upon a cheaper surface. **2** Mere surface or outside show: a *veneer* of politeness. —*v.t.* **1** To cover (a surface) with veneers. **2** To conceal, as something disagreeable or coarse, with an attractive and deceptive surface. [< G *furnieren* inlay < F *fournir* furnish] —**ve·neer′er** *n.*

ven·er·a·ble (ven′ər·ə·bəl) *adj.* Meriting or commanding veneration because of dignity, age, religious or historical associations, etc. [< L *venerari* revere] —**ven′er·a·bil′i·ty, ven′er·a·ble·ness** *n.* —**ven′er·a·bly** *adv.*

ven·er·ate (ven′ə·rāt) *v.t.* **·at·ed, ·at·ing** To regard with respect and deference; revere. [< L *venerari* revere]

ven·er·a·tion (ven′ə·rā′shən) *n.* **1** Profound respect combined with awe. **2** The act of worshiping; worship.

ve·ne·re·al (və·nir′ē·əl) *adj.* **1** Pertaining to or proceeding from sexual intercourse. **2** Communicated by sexual relations with an infected person: a *venereal* disease. **3** Pertaining to or curative of diseases so communicated. **4** Infected with syphilis, gonorrhea, or other venereal disease. [< L *Venus* goddess of love] —**ve·ne′re·al·ly** *adv.*

venereal disease Any of several diseases transmitted by sexual intercourse, as syphilis, gonorrhea, etc.

ven·er·y¹ (ven′ər·ē) *n.* The pursuit of sexual gratification. [< L *Venus*, goddess of love]

ven·er·y² (ven′ər·ē) *Archaic n. pl.* **·er·ies** The hunting of game; the chase. [< L *venari* to hunt]

Ve·ne·tian (və·nē′shən) *adj.* Pertaining to Venice or to its people. —*n.* A citizen or inhabitant of Venice.

Venetian blind A flexible window screen having movable, overlapping slats so fastened on webbing or tape as to exclude or admit light.

Ven·e·zue·la (ven′ə·zwā′lə, -zōō·ē′lə) *n.* A republic of N South America, 352,143 sq. mi, cap. Caracas. —**Ven′e·zue′lan** *adj., n.*

ven·geance (ven′jəns) *n.* The infliction of a deserved penalty; retributive punishment. —**with a vengeance 1** With great force or violence. **2** Extremely; to an unusual extent. [< L *vindicare* defend, avenge]

venge·ful (venj′fəl) *adj.* Seeking to inflict vengeance; vindictive. —**venge′ful·ly** *adv.* —**venge′ful·ness** *n.*

ve·ni·al (vē′nē·əl, vēn′yəl) *adj.* So slight or trivial as to be overlooked, as a fault. [< L *venia* forgiveness, mercy] —**ve′ni·al′i·ty** (-al′ə·tē), **ve′ni·al·ness** *n.* —**ve′ni·al·ly** *adv.* —**Syn.** excusable, forgivable, pardonable.

ve·ni·re (vi·nī′rē) *n. Law* A panel of people from which a jury is selected. [< L *venire facias* that you cause to come]

ve·ni·re·man (vi·nī′rē·mən) *n. pl.* **·men** (-mən) A member of a venire.

ven·i·son (ven′ə·zən, -sən) *n.* The flesh of a wild animal, esp. a deer, used for food. [< L *venari* to hunt]

ve·ni, vi·di, vi·ci (vā′nē, vē′dē, vē′chē; wā′nē, wē′dē, wē′kē) *Latin* I came, I saw, I conquered: Julius Caesar's report to the Roman Senate of a victory.

ven·om (ven′əm) *n.* **1** The poison secreted by certain reptiles, insects, etc., which is transferred to a victim by a bite or sting. **2** Ill will; spite. [< L *venenum* poison] —**Syn. 2** hate, malice, rancor, spitefulness.

ven·om·ous (ven′əm·əs) *adj.* **1** Able to give a poisonous sting. **2** Malicious; spiteful. —**ven′om·ous·ly** *adv.* —**ven′om·ous·ness** *n.*

ve·nous (vē′nəs) *adj.* **1** Of, pertaining to, contained, or carried in a vein or veins. **2** Designating the blood carried by the veins back to the heart and lungs. **3** Marked with or having veins: also **ve′nose.** [< L *vena* vein] —**ve′nous·ly** *adv.* —**ve·nos·i·ty** (vē·nos′ə·tē, və-), **ve′nous·ness** *n.*

vent (vent) *n.* **1** An outlet; means of escape. **2** An opening for the passage of liquids, gases, etc. **3** A slit in a garment, as a coat. **4** *Zool.* An opening through which wastes are eliminated. —**give vent to** To utter or express: to *give vent to* one's anger. —*v.t.* **1** To give expression to. **2** To permit to escape at a vent, as a gas. **3** To make a vent in. [< OF < *fendre* cleave < L *findere* split]

ven·ti·late (ven′tə·lāt) *v.t.* **·lat·ed, ·lat·ing 1** To produce a free circulation of air in, as by means of open windows, doors, etc. **2** To provide with a vent. **3** To expose to examination and discussion. **4** To oxygenate, as blood. [< L *ventus* wind] —**ven′ti·la′tion** *n.* —**ven′ti·la′tive** *adj.*

ven·ti·la·tor (ven′tə·lā′tər) *n.* **1** One who or that which ventilates. **2** A device or opening for replacing stale air with fresh air.

ven·tral (ven′trəl) *adj.* Toward, near, in, or on the abdomen. [< L *venter, ventris* belly] —**ven′tral·ly** *adv.*

ven·tri·cle (ven′tri·kəl) *n.* Any cavity in the body, esp. either of the two lower chambers of the heart, from which blood is forced into the arteries. [< L *venter, ventris* belly] —**ven·tric·u·lar** (-trik′yə·lər) *adj.* • See HEART.

---

add, āce, câre, pälm; end, ēven; it, īce; odd, ōpen, ôrder; tŏŏk, pōōl; up, bûrn; ə = a in *above, u* in *focus*; yōō = u in *fuse*; oil; pout; check; go; ring; thin; this; zh, *vision.* < derived from; ? origin uncertain or unknown.

ven·tril·o·quism (ven·tril′ə·kwiz′əm) *n.* The art of speaking in such a way that the sound seems to come from some source other than the person speaking. Also **ven·tril′·o·quy** (-kwē). [< L *venter* belly + *loqui* speak] —**ven·tril·o·qui·al** (ven′trə·lō′kwē·əl), **ven·tril′o·quis′tic** *adj.* —**ven′tri·lo′·qui·al·ly** *adv.* —**ven·tril′o·quist** *n.* —**ven·tril′o·quize′** (-kwīz) (·quized, ·qui·zing) *v.i.* & *v.t.*

ven·ture (ven′chər) *v.* ·**tured,** ·**tur·ing** *v.t.* **1** To expose to chance or risk; stake. **2** To run the risk of. **3** To express at the risk of denial or refutation: to *venture* a suggestion. **4** To place or send on a chance, as in a speculative investment. —*v.i.* **5** To take risk in going, coming, etc.: to *venture* into deep water. —*n.* **1** A risk; hazard. **2** An undertaking attended with risk. **3** That which is ventured, esp. property risk. —**at a venture** At random; haphazardly. [Alter. of ADVENTURE] —**ven′tur·er** *n.*

ven·ture·some (ven′chər·səm) *adj.* **1** Bold; daring. **2** Involving hazard; risky. —**ven′ture·some·ly** *adv.* —**ven′ture·some·ness** *n.*

ven·tur·ous (ven′chər·əs) *adj.* **1** Adventurous; bold. **2** Hazardous; risky; dangerous. —**ven′tur·ous·ly** *adv.* —**ven′·tur·ous·ness** *n.*

ven·ue (ven′yōō) *n. Law* **1** The place or neighborhood where a crime is committed or a cause of action arises. **2** The county or political division from which the jury must be summoned and in which the trial must be held. —**change of venue** The change of the place of trial, for good cause shown, from one county to another. [< OF *venir* come]

Ve·nus (vē′nəs) *Rom. Myth.* The goddess of love and beauty. —*n.* **1** A beautiful woman. **2** The planet of the solar system second in distance from the sun. • See PLANET.

Venus fly·trap (flī′trap′) An insectivorous plant of the SE U.S., with a basal rosette of leaves that entrap anything that touches certain sensitive hairs on their surface. Also **Ve′nus's-fly′trap** (vē′nəs·iz-).

ver. verse(s); version.

ve·ra·cious (və·rā′shəs) *adj.* **1** Speaking the truth; truthful. **2** True; accurate. [< L *verus* true] —**ve·ra′cious·ly** *adv.* —**ve·ra′cious·ness** *n.*

ve·rac·i·ty (və·ras′ə·tē) *n. pl.* ·**ties** **1** Honesty; truthfulness. **2** Accuracy; trueness. **3** That which is true; truth. [< L *verax*] —**Syn.** 1 candor, frankness, integrity.

Venus flytrap

ve·ran·da (və·ran′də) *n.* An open porch, usu. roofed, along one or more sides of a building. Also **ve·ran′dah.** [< Pg. *varanda* railing, balustrade]

verb (vûrb) *n. Gram.* **1** One of a class of words which express existence, action, or occurrence, or that function as a copula or an auxiliary. **2** Any word or construction functioning similarly. [< L *verbum* word]

ver·bal (vûr′bəl) *adj.* **1** Of, in, or pertaining to words: a *verbal* contract; a *verbal* image. **2** Of, pertaining to, or concerned with words rather than the ideas they convey. **3** Word for word; verbatim; literal: a *verbal* translation. **4** *Gram.* **a** Partaking of the nature of or derived from a verb: a *verbal* noun. **b** Used to form verbs: a *verbal* prefix. **5** *Informal* Adept at using words, as in choice or range of vocabulary: She's very *verbal* for her age. —*n. Gram.* A noun directly derived from a verb, in English often having the form of the present participle, as, "There shall be *weeping* and *wailing* and *gnashing* of teeth"; also, an infinitive used as a noun, as, *"To err* is human": also **verbal noun.** [< L *verbum* word] —**ver′bal·ly** *adv.* • See ORAL.

ver·bal·ism (vûr′bəl·iz′əm) *n.* **1** A verbal phrase or expression. **2** A meaningless form of words; verbiage.

ver·bal·ist (vûr′bəl·ist) *n.* **1** One who is skilled in the use and meanings of words. **2** A person overly concerned with words rather than facts or concepts.

ver·bal·ize (vûr′bəl·īz) *v.* ·**ized** ·**iz·ing** *v.t.* **1** *Gram.* To change (a noun, adj., etc.) into a verb. **2** To express in words. —*v.i.* **3** To speak or write verbosely. —**ver′bal·i·za′tion,** **ver′bal·iz′er** *n.*

ver·ba·tim (vər·bā′tim) *adj.* & *adv.* In the exact words; word for word. [< L *verbum* word]

ver·be·na (vər·bē′nə) *n.* Any of a genus of plants having

spikes of showy, often fragrant flowers. [< L, foliage, vervain]

ver·bi·age (vûr′bē·ij) *n.* **1** Use of too many words. **2** Manner of verbal expression. [< F *verbe* word]

ver·bose (vər·bōs′) *adj.* Using or containing an unnecessary number of words; wordy. [< L *verbum* word] —**ver·bose′ly** *adv.* —**ver·bose′ness, ver·bos′i·ty** (-bos′ə·tē) *n.* —**Syn.** garrulous, long-winded, prolix.

ver·bo·ten (vər·bōt′n, fər-) *adj. German* Forbidden.

ver·dant (vûr′dənt) *adj.* **1** Green with vegetation; fresh. **2** Immature in experience. [< F *verdoyer* grow green] —**ver′dan·cy** *n.* —**ver′dant·ly** *adv.*

ver·dict (vûr′dikt) *n.* **1** The decision of a jury in an action. **2** A conclusion expressed; an opinion. [< L *vere dictum* truly said]

ver·di·gris (vûr′də·grēs, -gris, -grē) *n.* **1** A green or greenish blue acetate of copper obtained by treating copper with acetic acid. **2** The blue-green crust formed by corrosion of copper, bronze, or brass in air, sea water, etc. [< OF *vert de Grece,* lit., green of Greece)

ver·dure (vûr′jər) *n.* **1** The fresh greenness of growing vegetation. **2** Green vegetation. [< F *verd* green]

verge[1] (vûrj) *n.* **1** The extreme edge; brink: on the *verge* of bankruptcy. **2** A bounding or enclosing line surrounding something. —*v.i.* **verged, verg·ing 1** To be contiguous or adjacent. **2** To form the limit or verge. [< L *virga* twig]

verge[2] (vûrj) *v.i.* **verged, verg·ing 1** To come near; approach: a remark *verging* on rudeness. **2** To tend; incline. [< L *vergere* to bend, turn]

ver·i·fi·ca·tion (ver′ə·fə·kā′shən) *n.* **1** The act of verifying, or the state of being verified. **2** A proof or confirmation, as by examination. —**ver′i·fi·ca′tive** *adj.*

ver·i·fy (ver′ə·fī) *v.t.* ·**fied,** ·**fy·ing 1** To prove to be true or accurate; confirm. **2** To test the accuracy or truth of. **3** *Law* To affirm under oath. [< L *verus* true + *facere* make] —**ver′i·fi′er** *n.* —**Syn.** 1 authenticate, corroborate, substantiate. 2 ascertain.

ver·i·ly (ver′ə·lē) *adv.* In truth; certainly. [< VERY]

ver·i·sim·i·lar (ver′ə·sim′ə·lər) *adj.* Appearing or seeming to be true; likely; probable. [< L *verus* true + *similis* like] —**ver′i·sim′i·lar·ly** *adv.*

ver·i·si·mil·i·tude (ver′ə·si·mil′ə·t'/ōōd) *n.* **1** Appearance of truth; likelihood. **2** That which resembles truth. [< L *verisimilitudo*]

ver·i·ta·ble (ver′ə·tə·bəl) *adj.* Genuine; true; real. [< F *vérité* truth] —**ver′i·ta·ble·ness** *n.* —**ver′i·ta·bly** *adv.*

ver·i·ty (ver′ə·tē) *n. pl.* ·**ties 1** Truth; correctness. **2** A true statement; a fact. [< L *veritas* truth < *verus* true]

vermi- *combining form* A worm; of or related to a worm: *vermicide.* [< L *vermis* a worm]

ver·mi·cel·li (vûr′mə·chel′ē, -sel′ē) *n.* A food paste made into slender wormlike cords thinner than spaghetti. [Ital., lit., little worms]

ver·mi·cide (vûr′mə·sīd) *n.* Any substance that kills worms, esp. a drug destructive of intestinal worms. —**ver′mi·cid′al** *adj.*

ver·mi·form (vûr′mə·fôrm) *adj.* Like a worm in shape.

vermiform appendix A slender, wormlike sac protruding from the large intestine. • See INTESTINE.

ver·mi·fuge (vûr′mə·fyōōj′) *n.* Any remedy that destroys intestinal worms. [< L *vermis* a worm + *fugare* expel]

ver·mil·ion (vər·mil′yən) *n.* **1** A brilliant, durable red pigment obtained from cinnabar or made synthetically. **2** An intense orange-red color. —*adj.* Of a bright orange-red color. —*v.t.* To color with vermilion. [< OF *vermeil*]

ver·min (vûr′min) *n. pl.* ·**min 1** Noxious small animals or parasitic insects, as lice, worms, mice, etc. **2** *Brit.* Certain animals injurious to game, as weasels, owls, etc. **3** A repulsive person or persons. [< L *vermis* a worm] —**ver′min·ous** *adj.* —**ver′min·ous·ly** *adv.* —**ver′min·ous·ness** *n.*

ver·mouth (vər·mōōth′) *n.* A fortified white wine flavored with aromatic herbs. [< G *Wermuth* wormwood]

ver·nac·u·lar (vər·nak′yə·lər) *n.* **1** The native language of a locality. **2** The common daily speech of any people. **3** The specialized vocabulary of a profession or trade. **4** An idiomatic word or phrase. —*adj.* **1** Belonging to one's native land; indigenous: said of a language, idiom, etc. **2** Using the colloquial native tongue: *vernacular* poets. **3** Written in the language indigenous to a people: a *vernacu-*

lar translation of the Bible. [< L *vernaculus* domestic, native] —**ver·nac′u·lar·ly** *adv.*

ver·nal (vûr′nəl) *adj.* 1 Belonging to, appearing in, or appropriate to spring. 2 Youthful; fresh. [< L *vernus* belonging to spring] —**ver′nal·ly** *adv.*

vernal equinox The equinox that occurs on or about March 21.

ver·ni·er (vûr′nē·ər) *n.* A small, movable, auxiliary scale for obtaining fractional parts of the subdivisions of a main scale. Also **vernier scale.** [< Pierre *Vernier,* 1580–1637, French mathematician]

Ver·o·nal (ver′ə·nəl) *n.* BARBITAL: a trade name.

ve·ron·i·ca (və·ron′i·kə) *n.* SPEEDWELL. [< St. *Veronica,* a legendary follower of Christ]

ver·sa·tile (vûr′sə·til, -tīl) *adj.* 1 Having many aptitudes or talents. 2 Having many uses: a *versatile* fabric. 3 Movable in more than one direction, as the toe of a bird. 4 *Bot.* Turning about freely on the support to which it is attached: said of an anther. [< L *versare,* freq. of *vertere* turn] —**ver′sa·tile·ly** *adv.* —**ver′sa·til′i·ty** (-til′ə·tē) *n.*

verse (vûrs) *n.* 1 A single line of a poem. 2 A group of lines in a poem; stanza. 3 Metrical composition as distinguished from prose; poetry. 4 A specified type of metrical composition: iambic *verse.* 5 One of the short divisions of a chapter of the Bible. [< L *versus* a turning, a verse]

versed (vûrst) *adj.* Having ready skill and knowledge; proficient. [< L *versari* occupy oneself] —**Syn.** experienced, practiced, seasoned, skillful.

ver·si·fy (vûr′sə·fī) *v.* **·fied, ·fy·ing** *v.t.* 1 To turn prose into verse. 2 To narrate or treat in verse. —*v.i.* 3 To write poetry. —**ver·si·fi·ca·tion** (vûr′sə·fə·kā′shən), **ver′si·fi′er** *n.*

ver·sion (vûr′zhən, -shən) *n.* 1 A translation or rendition from one language into another. 2 A description of an event, occurrence, etc., from a personal viewpoint. [< Med. L *versio* a turning < L *vertere* to turn] —**ver′sion·al** *adj.*

vers li·bre (ver lē′br′) *French* Free verse. —**vers li·brist** (lē′brist)

ver·so (vûr′sō) *n. pl.* **·sos** 1 A left-hand page of a book, leaflet, etc. 2 The reverse of a coin or medal. [< L *verso (folio)* a turned (leaf)]

verst (vûrst) *n.* A Russian measure of distance equal to about two thirds of a mile. [< Russ. *versta*]

ver·sus (vûr′səs) *prep.* 1 In law, sports, and contests, against. 2 Considered as the alternative of: free trade *versus* high tariffs. [L, toward, turned toward]

ver·te·bra (vûr′tə·brə) *n. pl* **·brae** (-brē, -brā) or **·bras** Any of the individual bones of the spinal column. [L, a joint, vertebra < *vertere* to turn] —**ver′te·bral** *adj.*

ver·te·brate (vûr′tə·brit, -brāt) *adj.* 1 Having a backbone or spinal column. 2 Pertaining to or characteristic of vertebrates. 3 Pertaining to, having, or composed of vertebrae. —*n.* Any of a division of animals characterized by a spinal column, as fishes, birds, and mammals. [< L *vertebratus* jointed] —**ver′te·brat′ed** *adj.*

ver·tex (vûr′teks) *n. pl.* **·tex·es** or **·ti·ces** (-tə·sēz′) 1 The highest point of anything; apex. 2 *Astron.* a ZENITH. b The point in the sky toward or from which a group of stars appears to be moving. 3 *Geom.* a The point of intersection of the sides of an angle. b The point farthest from the base. [L, the top < *vertere* to turn]

Human vertebrae
a. cervical.
b. thoracic. c. lumbar.

ver·ti·cal (vûr′ti·kəl) *adj.* 1 Perpendicular; upright. 2 Of or pertaining to the vertex. 3 Occupying a position directly overhead; at the highest point. 4 Of or pertaining to a business concern that undertakes a process from raw material to consumer: a *vertical* trust. —*n.* 1 A vertical line, plane, or circle. 2 An upright beam or rod in a truss. —**ver′ti·cal′i·ty** (-kal′ə·tē), **ver′ti·cal·ness** *n.* —**ver′ti·cal·ly** *adv.*

vertical angle Either one of two angles which lie on opposite sides of two intersecting lines.

ver·tig·i·nous (vər·tij′ə·nəs) *adj.* 1 Affected by vertigo; dizzy. 2 Turning round; whirling. 3 Liable to cause giddiness. —**ver·tig′i·nous·ly** *adv.* —**ver·tig′i·nous·ness** *n.*

ver·ti·go (vûr′tə·gō′) *n. pl.* **·goes** or **ver·tig·i·nes** (vər·tij′ə·nēz) A disorder in which a person or his surroundings seem to whirl about in such a way as to make the person dizzy and usu. sick. [L, lit., a turning around]

ver·vain (vûr′vān) *n.* A species of verbena supposedly having medicinal properties. [< L *verbena* verbena]

verve (vûrv) *n.* Enthusiasm or energy. [< L *verba,* pl. of *verbum* a word] —**Syn.** élan, liveliness, spirit, vigor.

ver·y (ver′ē) *adv.* 1 In a high degree; extremely: *very* generous. 2 Exactly: They both had the *very* same thought. —*adj.* **ver·i·er, ver·i·est** 1 Absolute; complete: the *very* truth. 2 Suitable; right: the *very* tool we need. 3 Unqualified; complete: a *very* scoundrel. 4 Selfsame; identical: my *very* words. 5 The (thing) itself: used as an intensive: The *very* stones cry out. [< L *verus* true]

very high frequency Any wave frequency from 30 to 300 megahertz.

very low frequency Any wave frequency from 3 to 30 kilohertz.

ves·i·cant (ves′i·kənt) *adj.* Blister-producing. —*n.* That which produces blisters, esp. a chemical warfare agent which attacks the skin on contact or lung tissue if inhaled. [< L *vesica* a blister, bladder]

ves·i·cate (ves′i·kāt) *v.* **·cat·ed, ·cat·ing** *v.t.* 1 To raise blisters on. —*v.i.* 2 To blister, as the skin. —**ves′i·ca′tion** *n.*

ves·i·ca·to·ry (ves′i·kə·tôr′ē, və·sik′ə·tôr′ē, -tō′rē) *adj., n. pl.* **·ries** VESICANT.

ves·i·cle (ves′i·kəl) *n.* Any small bladderlike cavity, cell, cyst, or blister. [< L *vesica* a bladder] —**ve·sic·u·lar** (və·sik′yə·lar) *adj.* —**ve·sic′u·lar·ly** *adv.*

ves·per (ves′pər) *n. Archaic* EVENING. —*adj.* Of or pertaining to evening. [L, the evening star]

Ves·per (ves′pər) *n.* EVENING STAR. [L]

ves·pers (ves′pərz) *n.pl. Often cap. Eccl.* 1 The sixth in order of the canonical hours. 2 A service of worship in the late afternoon or evening.

ves·sel (ves′əl) *n.* 1 A hollow receptacle capable of holding a liquid, as a pot, tub, pitcher, etc. 2 A ship or large boat. 3 Any of several aircraft. 4 *Biol.* A duct or canal for containing or transporting a fluid. [< L *vas* a vessel]

vest (vest) *n.* 1 A short sleeveless jacket worn, esp. under a suit coat, by men. 2 A similar garment worn by women. 3 A vestee. 4 *Chiefly Brit.* UNDERSHIRT. —*v.t.* 1 To confer (ownership, authority, etc.) upon some person or persons. 2 To place ownership, control, or authority with (a person or persons). 3 To clothe or robe, as with church vestments. —*v.i.* 4 To clothe oneself, as in vestments. 5 To be or become legally vested, as property. [< L *vestis* clothing, a garment]

Ves·ta (ves′tə) *Rom. Myth.* The goddess of the hearth and the hearth fire.

ves·tal (ves′təl) *n.* 1 One of the virgin priestesses of Vesta: also **vestal virgin.** 2 A chaste woman, esp. a virgin. —*adj.* 1 Of or relating to Vesta or her priestesses. 2 Chaste. [< L *Vesta* Vesta]

vest·ed (ves′tid) *adj.* 1 Wearing clothes, esp. church vestments. 2 Not dependent on any contingency; fixed; inalienable; absolute: a *vested* right.

vested interest 1 A special interest, as in an economic or political system or arrangement, often pursued by the holder at the expense of others. 2 A person or group that pursues such an interest.

vest·ee (ves·tē′) *n.* A garment worn by women to fill in the neckline of a jacket, blouse, etc. [Dim. of VEST]

ves·ti·bule (ves′tə·byōōl) *n.* 1 A small antechamber leading into a building or another room. 2 An enclosed passage from one railway passenger car to another. 3 *Anat.* Any cavity leading to another cavity: the *vestibule* of the ear. —*v.t.* **·buled, ·bul·ing** To provide with a vestibule or vestibules. [< L *vestibulum* an entrance hall] —**ves·tib·u·lar** (-tib′yə·lər) *adj.*

ves·tige (ves′tij) *n.* **1** A trace of something absent, lost, or gone. **2** *Biol.* A remnant of an organ that is no longer functional. [< F < L *vestigium* a footprint] —**Syn. 1** hint, remnant, tinge, touch.

ves·tig·i·al (ves·tij′ē·əl) *adj.* Of, or of the nature of a vestige; surviving in small or degenerate form. —**ves·tig′i·al·ly** *adv.*

vest·ment (vest′mənt) *n.* **1** An article of clothing. **2** Any of several ritual garments of the clergy. [< L *vestire* clothe] —**vest·ment·al** (vest·men′təl) *adj.*

vest-pock·et (vest′pok′it) *adj.* **1** Small enough to fit in a vest pocket. **2** Much smaller than standard or usual size: a *vest-pocket* battleship.

vest-pocket park A small urban park, often on a vacant lot.

ves·try (ves′trē) *n. pl.* **·tries 1** In a church, a room where vestments are put on or kept. **2** A room in a church used for Sunday school, meetings, etc. **3** In the Anglican and Episcopal churches, a body administering the affairs of a parish or congregation. [< L *vestis* a garment]

ves·try·man (ves′trē·mən) *n. pl.* **·men** (-mən) A member of a vestry.

ves·ture (ves′chər) *n. Archaic* **1** Garments; clothing. **2** A covering or envelope. —*v.t.* **·tured, ·tur·ing** To cover or clothe. [< L *vestire* clothe] —**ves′tur·al** *adj.*

vet[1] (vet) *Informal n.* VETERINARIAN. —*v.t. & v.i.* **vet·ted, vet·ting** To treat (animals) as a veterinarian does. [Short for VETERINARIAN]

vet[2] (vet) *n. Informal* A veteran.

vet. veteran; veterinarian; veterinary.

vetch (vech) *n.* Any of a genus of trailing, leguminous vines grown for fodder. [< L *vicia*]

vet·er·an (vet′ər·ən, vet′rən) *n.* **1** An experienced soldier or an ex-soldier. **2** A member of the armed forces who has been in active service. **3** A person with long experience in an occupation, calling, etc. —*adj.* **1** Having had long experience or practice. **2** Of, pertaining to, or for veterans. [< L *vetus, veteris* old]

Veterans Day The fourth Monday in October, a U.S. holiday honoring veterans of the armed forces, formerly celebrated November 11.

vet·er·i·nar·i·an (vet′ər·ə·nâr′ē·ən, vet′rə-) *n.* A practitioner of medical and surgical treatment of animals.

vet·er·i·nar·y (vet′ər·ə·ner′ē, vet′rə-) *adj.* Of, pertaining to, or designating the science or practice of preventing, curing, or alleviating the diseases and injuries of animals, esp. domestic animals. —*n. pl.* **·nar·ies** VETERINARIAN. [< L *veterinarius* pertaining to beasts of burden < *veterina* beasts of burden]

ve·to (vē′tō) *v.t.* **·toed, ·to·ing 1** To refuse approval of (a bill passed by a legislative body). **2** To forbid or refuse to consent to. —*n. pl.* **·toes 1** The right of one branch of government to cancel, prohibit, postpone, etc., the projects of another branch; esp., the right of a chief executive, as the president or a governor, to refuse to approve a legislative enactment by withholding his signature. **2** A message giving the reasons of a chief executive for refusing to approve a bill. **3** The exercise of the right to veto. **4** Any authoritative prohibition. [< L, I forbid] —**ve′to·er** *n.*

vex (veks) *v.t.* **1** To annoy by petty irritations. **2** To trouble or afflict. **3** To baffle, puzzle, or confuse. [< L *vexare* to shake] —**vex·ed·ly** (vek′sid·lē) *adv.* —**vex′ed·ness, vex′er** *n.* —**Syn. 1** chagrin, irritate, pester, pique.

vex·a·tion (vek·sā′shən) *n.* **1** The act of vexing, or the state of being vexed. **2** Trouble, annoyance, affliction, etc.

vex·a·tious (vek·sā′shəs) *adj.* Annoying; harassing. —**vex·a′tious·ly** *adv.* —**vex·a′tious·ness** *n.*

VFW, V.F.W. Veterans of Foreign Wars.

VHF, V.H.F., vhf, v.h.f. very high frequency.

VI Virgin Islands (P.O. abbr.).

V.I. Virgin Islands.

v.i. see below (L *vide infra*); verb intransitive.

vi·a (vī′ə, vē′ə) *prep.* **1** By way of; by a route passing through. **2** By means of. [< L *via* a way]

vi·a·ble (vī′ə·bəl) *adj.* **1** Capable of living and developing normally, as a newborn infant, a seed, etc. **2** Workable;

practicable: a *viable* plan. [< L *vita*] —**vi′a·bil′i·ty** *n.* —**vi′a·bly** *adv.*

vi·a·duct (vī′ə·dukt) *n.* A bridgelike structure, esp. a large one of arched masonry, to carry a road or railroad over a valley, section of a city, etc. [< L *via* a way + (AQUE)DUCT]

vi·al (vī′əl) *n.* A small bottle, usu. of glass, for medicines and other liquids. [< Gk. *phialē* a shallow cup]

vi·a me·di·a (vī′ə mē′dē·ə, vē′ə mä′-) *Latin* A middle way.

vi·and (vī′ənd) *n.* **1** An article of food, esp. meat. **2** *pl.* Provisions; food. [< OF *viande*]

Viaduct

vi·at·i·cum (vī·at′ə·kəm) *n. pl.* **·ca** (-kə) or **·cums 1** *Often cap.* The Eucharist, as given on *the verge of death.* **2** The provisions needed for a journey. [L, traveling money < *via* a way]

vibes (vībz) *n.pl.* (*usu. construed as sing. for def. 2*) *Slang* **1** Vibrations. See VIBRATION (def. 3). **2** VIBRAPHONE.

vi·brant (vī′brənt) *adj.* **1** Having, showing, or resulting from vibration; resonant. **2** Throbbing; pulsing: *vibrant* with enthusiasm. **3** Energetic; vigorous. **4** *Phonet.* VOICED (def. 3). —*n. Phonet.* A voiced sound. [< L *vibrare* to shake] —**vi′bran·cy** (-sē) *n.* (*pl.* **·cles**) —**vi′brant·ly** *adv.*

vi·bra·phone (vī′brə·fōn) *n.* A musical instrument like the marimba in which a vibrato is produced by rotating disks in electrically powered resonators.

vi·brate (vī′brāt) *v.* **·brat·ed, ·brat·ing** *v.i.* **1** To move back and forth, as a pendulum. **2** To move back and forth rapidly. **3** To resound: The note *vibrates* on the ear. **4** To be emotionally moved. —*v.t.* **5** To cause to move back and forth. **6** To cause to quiver. **7** To send forth (sound, etc.) by vibration. [< L *vibrare* to shake]

vi·bra·tile (vī′brə·til, -tīl) *adj.* **1** Pertaining to vibration. **2** Capable of vibration. **3** Having a vibratory motion. —**vi′bra·til′i·ty** (-til′ə·tē) *n.*

vi·bra·tion (vī·brā′shən) *n.* **1** The act of vibrating; oscillation. **2** *Physics* **a** A periodic, back-and-forth motion of a particle or body. **b** Any physical process characterized by cyclic changes in a variable, as wave motion. **c** A single cycle of such a process. **3** *pl. Slang* One's emotional response to an aura felt to surround a person or thing, esp. when considered in or out of harmony with oneself. —**vi·bra′tion·al** *adj.*

vi·bra·to (vē·brä′tō) *n. pl.* **·tos** *Music* A cyclic variation in the pitch of a tone. [Ital. < *vibrare* vibrate]

vi·bra·tor (vī′brā·tər) *n.* **1** One who or that which vibrates. **2** An electrically operated massaging apparatus.

vi·bra·to·ry (vī′brə·tôr′ē, -tō′rē) *adj.* **1** Pertaining to, causing, or characterized by vibration. **2** That vibrates or is capable of vibration.

vi·bur·num (vī·bûr′nəm) *n.* Any of a genus of shrubs or small trees related to honeysuckle. **2** The bark of several species, used medicinally. [L, the wayfaring tree]

Vic. Victoria.

vic. vicar; vicarage; vicinity.

vic·ar (vik′ər) *n.* **1** One who is authorized to perform functions in the stead of another; deputy. **2** In the Anglican Church, the priest of a parish of which the main revenues are appropriated by a layman, the priest himself receiving a salary. **3** In the Roman Catholic Church, a representative of a bishop or the pope. **4** In the Protestant Episcopal Church, the clergyman who is the head of a chapel. [< L *vicarius* a substitute < *vicis* a change]

vic·ar·age (vik′ər·ij) *n.* **1** The benefice, office, or duties of a vicar. **2** A vicar's residence.

vic·ar-gen·er·al (vik′ər·jen′ər·al, -jen′rəl) *n.* **1** In the Roman Catholic Church, a priest appointed by the bishop as assistant in administering a diocese. **2** In the Anglican church, an official assisting the bishop or archbishop.

vi·car·i·ous (vī·kâr′ē·əs, vi-) *adj.* **1** Suffered or done in place of another: a *vicarious* sacrifice. **2** Felt through identifying with another's experience: *vicarious* pleasure in his wife's talent. **3** Filling the office of or acting for another. **4** Delegated: *vicarious* authority. [< L *vicarius*] —**vi·car′i·ous·ly** *adv.* —**vi·car′i·ous·ness** *n.*

vice[1] (vīs) *n.* **1** Moral depravity; evil. **2** An immoral action, trait, etc. **3** A habitual, usu. trivial, failing or defect; short-coming. [<L *vitium* a fault] —**Syn. 1** corruption, dis-soluteness, profligacy.

vice[2] (vīs) *n. & v.t.* **viced, vic·ing** *Chiefly Brit.* VISE.

vice[3] (vī′sē) *prep.* Instead of; in place of. [<L *vicis* change]

vice- *prefix* One who acts for or takes the place of. [<L *vice*, abl. of *vicis* change]

vice admiral See GRADE. —**vice′-ad′mir·al·ty** (-mər·əl·tē) *n.*

vice-con·sul (vīs′kon′səl) *n.* A person who acts as a sub-stitute for or a subordinate to a consul. —**vice-con·su·lar** (vīs′kon′sə·lər) *adj.* **vice-con·su·late** (vīs′kon′sə·lit), **vice′-con′sul·ship** *n.*

vice-ge·rent (vīs·jir′ənt) *n.* One duly authorized to exer-cise the powers of another; a deputy. —*adj.* Acting in the place of another. [<L VICE + *gerere* carry, manage] —**vice-ge′ren·cy** (-sē) *n.* (*pl.* **·cies**)

vice president 1 An officer ranking next below a presi-dent, and acting, on occasion, in his place. **2** In the U.S. government, an officer of this rank designated by the Con-stitution to succeed the president if necessary. —**vice-pres′i-den·cy** (vīs′prez′·ə·dən·sē) (*pl.* **·cies**) *n.* —**vice′-pres′i·den′-tial** (-prez′ə·den′shəl) *adj.*

vice-re·gal (vīs·rē′gəl) *adj.* Of or relating to a viceroy. —**vice-re′gal·ly** *adv.*

vice-re·gent (vīs′rē′jənt) *n.* A person who acts in the place of a regent when necessary. —*adj.* Of or pertaining to a vice-regent. —**vice′-re′gen·cy** *n.*

vice·roy (vīs′roi) *n.* One who rules a country, colony, or province by the authority of his sovereign. [<VICE- + F *roi* a king] —**vice·roy′al** (-roi′əl) *adj.* —**vice′roy′al·ty** (*pl.* **·ties**), **vice′roy·ship′** *n.*

vice squad A police division charged with combating prostitution, gambling, and other vices.

vi·ce ver·sa (vī′sē vûr′sə, vī′sə vûr′sə, vīs′vûr′sə) With the relation of terms being reversed; conversely. [L]

vi·chy·ssoise (vē′shē·swäz′, vē′shē·swäz′, vish′-) *n.* A potato cream soup flavored with leeks, celery, etc., usu. served cold with a sprinkling of chives. [<*Vichy*, France]

Vi·chy water (vish′ē) **1** The effervescent mineral water from the springs at Vichy, France. **2** Any mineral water resembling it.

vi·cin·i·ty (vi·sin′ə·tē) *n. pl.* **·ties 1** A region adjacent or near; neighborhood. **2** Nearness; proximity. [<L *vicinus* nearby]

vi·cious (vish′əs) *adj.* **1** Corrupt in conduct or habits; de-praved; immoral. **2** Of the nature of vice: *vicious* acts. **3** Unruly or dangerous, as an animal: a *vicious* dog. **4** Marked by evil intent; malicious; spiteful: a *vicious* lie. **5** Worthless or invalidated because defective; full of errors or faults: *vicious* arguments. **6** *Informal* Unusually severe or punishing: a *vicious* blow. **7** *Informal* Savage; heinous: a *vicious* crime. [<OF<L *vitiosus*<*vitium* a fault] — **vi′cious·ly** *adv.* —**vi′cious·ness** *n.*

vicious circle 1 The predicament that arises when the solution of a problem creates a new problem, etc. **2** *Logic* A fallacy in reasoning created when a conclusion is based upon a premise which depends upon the conclusion.

vi·cis·si·tude (vi·sis′ə·t′ood) *n.* **1** *Usu. pl.* Irregular changes or variations, as of conditions or fortune: the *vi-cissitudes* of life. **2** A change or alteration; also, the condi-tion or quality of being changeable. [<L *vicis* a turn, change] —**vi·cis·si·tu·di·nary** (və·sis′ə·t′ōō′də·ner′ē), **vi·cis′·si·tu′di·nous** *adj.*

vic·tim (vik′tim) *n.* **1** A person injured or killed by circum-stances beyond his control: a *victim* of a flood. **2** A sufferer from any diseased condition: a *victim* of arthritis. **3** One who is swindled; a dupe. **4** A living creature killed as a sacrifice to a deity. [<L *victima* a beast for sacrifice]

vic·tim·ize (vik′tim·īz) *v.t.* **·ized, ·iz·ing 1** to make a victim of; cause suffering to. **2** To cheat; dupe: *victimized* by loan sharks. —**vic·tim·i·za·tion** (vik′tə·mə·zā′shən) *n.* —**vic′·tim·iz′er** *n.*

vic·tor (vik′tər) *n.* One who wins any struggle or contest. —*adj.* Victorious: the *victor* nation. [<L *victus*, p.p. of *vin-cere* conquer]

vic·to·ri·a (vik·tôr′ē·ə, ·tō′rē·ə) *n.* A low, light, four-wheeled carriage, with a folding top, a seat for two persons, and a raised driver's seat. [<*Victoria*, 1819–1901, Queen of England]

Victoria

Victoria Cross The highest British military decoration, awarded for outstanding valor.

Victoria Day In Canada, a na-tional holiday celebrated on the first Monday preceding May 25th.

Vic·to·ri·an (vik·tôr′ē·ən, ·tō′rē-) *adj.* **1** Of or relating to Queen Victoria of England, or to her reign. **2** Pertaining to or characteristic of the standards of morality and taste prevalent during that era. **3** Prudish; prim; priggish. —*n.* A person living during the time of Queen Victoria's reign; also, a person exhibiting the characteristic qualities, be-havior, etc., of her era. —**Vic·to′ri·an·ism** *n.*

vic·to·ri·ous (vik·tôr′ē·əs, ·tō′rē-) *adj.* **1** Having won vic-tory; triumphant. **2** Characterized by or relating to vic-tory. —**vic·to′ri·ous·ly** *adv.* —**vic·to′ri·ous·ness** *n.*

vic·to·ry (vik′tər·ē) *n. pl.* **·ries 1** The overcoming of an enemy or adversary; triumph, as in war. **2** An overcoming of any difficulty or obstacle, considered as an achievement earned through effort. [<L *victor* victor]

vict·ual (vit′l) *n.* **1** Food fit for consumption by man. **2** *pl.* Food prepared for consumption. **3** *pl.* A supply of food; pro-visions. [<L *victualis* of food<*victus* food]

vi·cu·ña (vi·kōōn′yə, -kyōō′nə, vī-) *n.* **1** A small llamalike ruminant of the Andes having fine wool. **2** A textile made from this wool or some substitute: also **vicuña cloth.** Also **vi·cu′na.** [<Que-chua]

Vicuña

vi·de (vī′dē, vē′dā′) *v.* See: used to direct attention to: *vide* p. 36. [L, imperative sing. of *videre* see]

vi·de in·fra (vī′dē in′frə) *Latin* See below.

vi·de·li·cet (vi·del′ə·sit, vī-, vi·dā′·li·ket′) *adv.* That is to say; namely. [L<*videre licet* it is per-mitted to see]

vid·e·o (vid′ē·ō) *adj.* **1** Of or pertaining to television, esp. to the picture. **2** Producing a signal convertible into a tele-vision picture: a *video* recording —*n.* **1** Television image or the electric signal corresponding to it. **2** Videotape. [L, I see]

vid·e·o·cas·sette (vid′ē·ō·kas·et′) *n.* A cassette that con-tains videotape for recording programs, movies, etc.

vid·e·o·disc (vid′ē·ō·disk′) *n.* A disc for recording both image and sound for replay through a television.

vid·e·o·tape (vid′ē·ō·tāp′) *n.* A recording of a television program on magnetic tape. —*v.t.* **taped, tap·ing** To make such a recording.

vi·de su·pra (vī′dē, sōō′prə) *Latin* See above.

vie (vī) *v.* **vied, vy·ing** *v.i.* To put forth effort to excel or outdo others. [<MF *envier* invite, challenge] —**vi′er** *n.*

Vi·en·nese (vē′ə·nēz′, ·nēs′) *adj.* Of or pertaining to Vi-enna, its inhabitants, culture, etc. —*n. pl.* **·ese 1** A native or inhabitant of Vienna. **2** The German dialect spoken in Vienna.

Vi·et·nam (vē·et·näm′) *n.* A country of SE Asia, cap. Hanoi; from 1954 to 1976 divided into: **Democratic Republic of Vietnam,** 63,344 sq. mi., cap. Hanoi: also **North Vietnam;** and **Republic of Vietnam,** 65,749 sq. mi., cap. Saigon: also **South Vietnam.** • See map at INDOCHINA.

Vi·et·nam·ese (vēet′nəm·ēz′, vyet′-, ·ēs′) *adj.* Of or per-taining to Vietnam, its people, or their language. —*n. pl.* **·ese 1** a native or citizen of Vietnam. **2** The language of Vietnam.

view (vyōō) *n.* **1** The act of seeing or examining; survey; examination; inspection. **2** Range of vision. **3** Something seen: a *view* of the harbor. **4** A representation of a scene, esp. a landscape. **5** Something regarded as the object of action; purpose. **6** Opinion; judgment; belief: What are your *views* on this subject? **7** The immediate or forseeable future: no end in *view*. —**in view of** In consideration of. —**on view** Set up for public inspection. —**with a view to** With the aim or purpose of. —*v.t.* **1** To look at; behold. **2** To scrutinize; examine. **3** To survey mentally; consider. **4** To regard in a certain way. [< OF *veoir* see < L *videre*]

view·er (vyōō′ər) *n.* **1** One who views; esp., one who watches television. **2** A device for viewing, esp. one for viewing photographic transparencies.

view·less (vyōō′lis) *adj.* **1** That cannot be viewed. **2** Having no opinions. —**view′less·ly** *adv.*

view·point (vyōō′point′) *n.* The position from which one views or evaluates something; point of view.

vi·ges·i·mal (vī·jes′ə·məl) *adj.* **1** Of, pertaining to, or based on the number 20. **2** Twentieth. [< L *vicesimus*]

vig·il (vij′əl) *n.* **1** An act or period of keeping awake. **2** An act or period of keeping watch. **3** *Eccl.* **a** The eve of a holy day. **b** *pl.* Religious devotions on such an eve. [< L *vigil* awake]

vig·i·lance (vij′ə·ləns) *n.* The quality of being vigilant; alertness to threat or danger.

vigilance committee A body of men self-organized and without official legal sanction, with the professed purpose of maintaining order and punishing crime.

vig·i·lant (vij′ə·lənt) *adj.* Alert to danger; wary. [< L *vigilare* keep awake < *vigil* awake] —**vig′i·lant·ly** *adv.* —**Syn.** cautious, circumspect, heedful, watchful.

vig·i·lan·te (vij′ə·lan′tē) *n.* A member of a vigilance committee. —**vig′i·lant·ism** *n.*

vi·gnette (vin·yet′) *n.* **1** A short, subtly wrought picture in words; sketch. **2** A decorative design before the title page of a book, at the end or beginning of a chapter, etc. **3** An engraving, photograph, etc., that shades off gradually into the background. —*v.t.* **·gnet·ted, ·gnet·ting** To finish, as an engraving or photograph, in the manner of a vignette. [< F *vigne* a vine]

vig·or (vig′ər) *n.* **1** Active bodily or mental strength; energy. **2** Vital or natural growth, as in a healthy plant. **3** Intensity or force. **4** Legal force; validity. *Brit. sp.* **vig′our.** [< L *vigere* be lively, thrive]

vig·or·ous (vig′ər·əs) *adj.* Possessing, characterized by, or done with vigor. —**vig′or·ous·ly** *adv.* —**vig′or·ous·ness** *n.*

vi·king (vī′king) *n. Often cap.* One of the Scandinavian sea rovers who harried the coasts of Europe from the eighth to the tenth centuries.

vil. village.

vile (vīl) *adj.* **vil·er, vil·est** **1** Morally base; corrupt. **2** Disgusting; loathsome. **3** Very bad: *vile* food. [< L *vilis* cheap] —**vile′ly** *adv.* —**vile′ness** *n.*

vil·i·fy (vil′ə·fī) *v.t.* **·fied, ·fy·ing** To speak of abusively or slanderously; defame. [< L *vilis* cheap + *facere* make] —**vil′i·fi·ca′tion** (-fə·kā′shən), **vil′i·fi′er** *n.* —**Syn.** denigrate, malign, revile, traduce.

vil·la (vil′ə) *n.* A house, usu. large and imposing, in the country or suburbs or at the seashore. [L, a country house, farm]

vil·lage (vil′ij) *n.* **1** A collection of houses in a rural district, smaller than a town but larger than a hamlet. **2** Such a settlement incorporated as a municipality. **3** The inhabitants of a village, collectively. [< L *villaticus* pertaining to a villa < *villa* a villa]

vil·lag·er (vil′ij·ər) *n.* One who lives in a village.

vil·lain (vil′ən) *n.* **1** One who has committed crimes or evil deeds; scoundrel: now often used humorously. **2** A character in a novel, play, etc., who is the opponent of the hero. **3** VILLEIN. [< OF *vilain* a farm servant]

vil·lain·ous (vil′ən·əs) *adj.* **1** Wicked; evil. **2** *Informal* Very bad; abominable. —**vil′lain·ous·ly** *adv.* —**vil′lain·ous·ness** *n.* —**Syn.** detestable, heinous, notorious, shameful.

vil·lain·y (vil′ən·ē) *n. pl.* **·lain·ies** **1** The quality or condition of being villainous. **2** A villainous act; crime.

vil·lein (vil′ən) *n.* In feudal England, a member of a class of serfs who, by the 13th century, were regarded as freemen in their legal relations with all persons except their lord. [< OF *vilain.* See VILLAIN.] —**vil′lein·age, vil′len·age** *n.*

vil·lus (vil′əs) *n. pl.* **vil·li** (vil′ī, -ē) **1** *Anat.* Any of numerous tiny projections from mucous membrane, as the absorp-

tive processes in the small intestine. **2** *Bot.* Any of the soft hairs on the surface of certain plants. [L, a tuft of hair, shaggy hair] —**vil′lous** *adj.*

vim (vim) *n.* Force or vigor; energy; spirit. [L, accusative of *vis* power]

vin (van) *n. French* Wine.

vi·na·ceous (vī·nā′shəs) *adj.* **1** Of or pertaining to wine or grapes. **2** Wine-colored; red. [< L *vinum* wine]

vin·ai·grette (vin′ə·gret′) *n.* **1** An ornamental box or bottle for holding vinegar, smelling salts, etc. **2** Vinaigrette sauce. [< F *vinaigre* vinegar]

vinaigrette sauce A sauce made of vinegar and oil with herbs, onions, parsley, etc., served usu. on cold meats or fish.

Vin·cent's infection (vin′sənts) TRENCH MOUTH. Also **Vincent's angina, Vincent's disease.** [< J. H. *Vincent,* 1862–1950, French physician]

vin·ci·ble (vin′sə·bəl) *adj.* That can be conquered or overcome; conquerable. [< L *vincere* conquer] —**vin′ci·bil′i·ty, vin′ci·ble·ness** *n.*

vin·di·ca·ble (vin′də·kə·bəl) *adj.* That can be vindicated; justifiable.

vin·di·cate (vin′də·kāt) *v.t.* **·cat·ed, ·cat·ing** **1** To clear of accusation, censure, suspicion, etc. **2** To defend or maintain, as a right or claim, against challenge or attack and show to be just, right, and reasonable. **3** To provide justification for; justify. [< L *vindicare* avenge, claim] —**vin·di·ca·tive** (vin·dik′ə·tiv, vin′də·kā′tiv), **vin′di·ca·to′ry** (-kə·tôr′ē, -tō′rē) *adj.* —**vin′di·ca′tor** *n.*

vin·di·ca·tion (vin′də·kā′shən) *n.* **1** The act of vindicating, or the state of being vindicated. **2** A justification; defense.

vin·dic·tive (vin·dik′tiv) *adj.* Having or characterized by a vengeful spirit. [< L *vindicta* a revenge] —**vin·dic′tive·ly** *adv.* —**vin·dic′tive·ness** *n.* —**Syn.** retaliatory, revengeful, spiteful.

vine (vīn) *n.* **1** Any climbing plant. **2** The flexible stem of such a plant. **3** GRAPEVINE (def. 1). [< L *vinum* wine]

vin·e·gar (vin′ə·gər) *n.* **1** A variously flavored solution of acetic acid obtained by the fermentation of cider, wine, etc., and used as a condiment and preservative. **2** Acerbity, as of speech. [< OF *vin* wine + *aigre* sour] —**vin′e·gar·y** *adj.*

vin·er·y (vī′nər·ē) *n. pl.* **·er·ies** A building or area where vines are grown.

vine·yard (vin′yərd) *n.* An area devoted to the growing of grapevines. [< OE *wingeard*] —**vine′yard·ist** *n.*

vingt-et-un (van·tā·œn′) *n.* BLACKJACK (def. 3). [F, twenty-one]

vin·i·cul·ture (vin′ə·kul′chər) *n.* The cultivation of grapes for making wine. [< L *vinum* wine] —**vin′i·cul′tur·al** *adj.*

vi·nous (vī′nəs) *adj.* **1** Pertaining to, characteristic of, or having the qualities of wine. **2** Caused by, affected by, or addicted to wine. [< L *vinum* wine] —**vi·nos·i·ty** (vī·nos′ə·tē) *n.*

vin·tage (vin′tij) *n.* **1** The yield of grapes or wine from a vineyard or wine-growing district for one season. **2** The harvesting of a vineyard and the making of wine; also, the season when these things are done. **3** Wine, esp. fine wine of a particular region and year. **4** The year or the region in which a particular wine is produced. **5** *Informal* The type or kind current at a particular time: a joke of ancient *vintage.* —*adj.* Of a fine vintage: *vintage* wines. [< OF *vendage* < L *vinum* wine + *demere* remove]

vint·ner (vint′nər) *n.* **1** A wine merchant. **2** A maker of wine. [< OF *vin* wine]

vin·y (vī′nē) *adj.* **·i·er, ·i·est** Pertaining to, like, of, full of, or yielding vines.

vi·nyl (vī′nəl) *n.* An organic radical derived from ethylene and entering into the composition of numerous plastics. [< L *vinum* wine + -YL]

vi·ol (vī′əl, -ōl) *n.* Any of a family of stringed musical instruments, predecessors of the violin family. [< Med. L *vidula, vitula*]

vi·o·la (vē·ō′lə, vī-) *n.* A four-stringed musical instrument of the violin family, somewhat larger than the violin, and tuned a fifth lower. [Ital., orig., a viol]

vi·o·la·ble (vī′ə·lə·bəl) *adj.* That can or is likely to be violated. —**vi'o·la·ble·ness, vi'o·la·bil'i·ty** n. —**vi'o·la·bly** adv.

vi·o·la da gam·ba (vē-ō'lə-də-gäm'bə) An early bass of the viol family, held between the legs, and having a range similar to that of the cello. [Ital., viola of the leg]

vi·o·late (vī'ə-lāt) v.t. **·lat·ed, ·lat·ing 1** To break or infringe, as a law, oath, agreement, etc. **2** To profane, as a holy place. **3** To break in on; interfere with: to *violate* one's privacy. **4** To ravish; rape. **5** To offend or treat contemptuously: to *violate* a person's beliefs. [< L *violare* use violence < *vis* force] —**vi'o·la'tion, vi'o·la'tor** n. —**vi'o·la'tive** adj. —**Syn. 2** desecrate, pollute. **3** disturb; interrupt.

vi·o·lence (vī'ə-ləns) n. **1** Physical force exercised to injure, damage, or destroy. **2** An instance of such exercise of physical force; an injurious or destructive act. **3** Intensity; severity; force: the *violence* of a tornado. **4** Injury or damage, as by irreverence, distortion, or alteration: editing that did *violence* to the original text.

vi·o·lent (vī'ə-lənt) adj. **1** Proceeding from or marked by great physical force or activity. **2** Caused by or exhibiting intense emotional or mental excitement; passionate: a *violent* rabble-rouser. **3** Characterized by intensity of any kind: *violent* heat. **4** Marked by the unjust or illegal exercise of force: to take *violent* measures. **5** Resulting from external force or injury; unnatural: a *violent* death. [< L *violentus* < *vis* force] —**vi'o·lent·ly** adv.

vi·o·let (vī'ə-lit) n. **1** Any of a widely distributed genus of perennial herbs, bearing irregular flowers usu. of a bluish purple color. **2** Any of several plants having violet-colored flowers. **3** A bluish purple color. —adj. Bluish purple. [< L *viola*]

vi·o·lin (vī'ə-lin') n. **1** A musical instrument having four strings and a sounding box of wood, and played by means of a bow. **2** A violinist, esp. in an orchestra. [< Ital. *viola* a viola]

vi·o·lin·ist (vī'ə-lin'ist) n. One who plays the violin.

vi·ol·ist (vī'əl-ist) n. **1** One who plays the viol. **2** (vē-ō'list) One who plays the viola.

vi·o·lon·cel·lo (vī'ə-lən-chel'ō, vē'ə-) n. pl. **·los** CELLO. [< Ital. *violone* a bass viol, aug. of *viola*] —**vi'o·lon·cel'list** n.

VIP, V.I.P. *Informal* very important person.

vi·per (vī'pər) n. **1** Any of a family of venomous Old World snakes, including the African puff adder. **2** Any of a family of typically American poisonous snakes, the **pit vipers,** including the rattlesnake, copperhead, etc., which are characterized by a small depression between the nostril and the eye. **3** Any poisonous or allegedly poisonous snake. **4** A malicious, treacherous, or spiteful person. [< L *vipera*] —**vi·per·ine** (vī'pə·rīn) adj.

vi·per·ous (vī'pər·əs) adj. **1** Of, pertaining to, or composed of vipers. **2** Malicious, treacherous, or spiteful. —**vi'per·ous·ly** adv.

vi·ra·go (vi·rä'gō, -rā'-, vī-) n. pl. **·goes** or **·gos** A loud, ill-tempered woman; shrew; scold. [L, manlike woman]

vi·ral (vī'rəl) adj. Of, pertaining to, or caused by a virus.

vir·e·o (vir'ē·ō) n. pl. **·os** Any of various inconspicuous, insectivorous songbirds of North America. [L, a kind of small bird]

vi·res·cent (vī·res'ənt) adj. Greenish or becoming green. [< L *virescere* grow green] —**vi·res'cence** n.

vir·gin (vûr'jin) n. **1** A person, esp. a young woman, who has never had sexual intercourse. **2** A maiden or unmarried woman. —adj. **1** Being a virgin. **2** Consisting of virgins: a *virgin* band. **3** Pertaining or suited to a virgin; chaste; maidenly. **4** Uncorrupted; pure; clean: *virgin* whiteness. **5** Not hitherto used, touched, tilled, or worked upon: *virgin* forest. **6** Not previously processed or manufactured; new: *virgin* wool. **7** Occurring for the first time; initial: a *virgin* effort. [< L *virgo* a maiden]

Vir·gin (vûr'jin) VIRGIN MARY. —n. VIRGO.

Violin
a. bridge.
b. chin rest.

vir·gin·al¹ (vûr'jin·əl) adj. **1** Of, pertaining to, like, or suited to a virgin; modest; maidenly. **2** Pure; pristine; unsullied. —**vir'gin·al·ly** adv.

vir·gin·al² (vûr'jin·əl) n. Often pl. A small, rectangular harpsichord with no legs. Also **pair of virginals.**

Virginal

virgin birth Usu. cap. Theol. The doctrine that Jesus Christ was conceived by divine agency and born without impairment of the virginity of his mother Mary.

Vir·gin·i·a cowslip (vər·jin'yə) A perennial herb of the E U.S. with clusters of blue or purple tubular flowers. Also **Virginia bluebell.**

Virginia creeper A woody vine of the grape family, with compound leaves, small green flowers, and inedible blue berries.

Virginia deer WHITE-TAILED DEER.

Virginia reel 1 A country dance performed by couples who stand initially in two parallel lines facing one another. **2** The music for such a dance.

vir·gin·i·ty (vər·jin'ə·tē) n. pl. **·ties 1** The state of being a virgin; maidenhood; virginal chastity. **2** The state of being fresh, untouched, etc.

Virgin Mary Mary, the mother of Jesus.

vir·gin's-bow·er (vûr'jinz·bou'ər) n. A species of clematis bearing white flowers in leafy clusters.

Vir·go (vûr'gō) n. A constellation and the sixth sign of the Zodiac; the Virgin. • See ZODIAC.

vir·gule (vûr'gyōōl) n. A slanting line (/) used to indicate a choice between two alternatives, as in the phrase *and/or*. [< L *virga* a rod]

vir·i·des·cent (vir'ə·des'ənt) adj. Greenish; turning green. [< L *viridis* green] —**vir'i·des'cence** n.

vir·ile (vir'əl, īl) adj. **1** Having the characteristics of manhood. **2** Having the vigor or strength of manhood. **3** Able to procreate. [< L *vir* a man] —**vi·ril·i·ty** (və·ril'ə·tē) n.

vi·rol·o·gy (vī·rol'ə·jē, vī-) n. The study of viruses, esp. in relation to disease. —**vi·rol'o·gist** n.

vir·tu (vər·tōō', vûr'tōō) n. **1** Rare, curious, or artistic quality: often in the phrase **objects** (or **articles**) **of virtu.** **2** A taste for or knowledge of such objects. **3** Such objects collectively. [< L *virtus*]

vir·tu·al (vûr'chōō·əl) adj. Being so in essence or effect, but not in form or fact. [< Med. L *virtualis* < L *virtus* strength] —**vir'tu·al'i·ty** (-al'ə·tē) n. —**vir'tu·al·ly** adv.

vir·tue (vûr'chōō) n. **1** General moral excellence; uprightness; goodness. **2** A particular moral excellence. **3** Any admirable quality or merit: Patience is a *virtue.* **4** Sexual purity; chastity. **5** Efficacy; potency, as of a medicine. —**by** (or **in**) **virtue of** By or through the force or authority of. —**make a virtue of necessity** To do willingly what one has to do anyhow. [< L *virtus* strength, bravery < *vir* man] —**Syn. 1** integrity, rectitude, righteousness, worthiness.

vir·tu·os·i·ty (vûr'chōō·os'ə·tē) n. pl. **·ties** The technical mastery of an art, as music.

vir·tu·o·so (vûr'chōō·ō'sō) n. pl. **·si** (-sē) or **·sos 1** A master of technique in some fine art, esp. in musical performance. **2** A knowledgeable collector or lover of curios or works of art. —adj. Of or characteristic of a virtuoso. [< LL *virtuosus* full of excellence]

vir·tu·ous (vûr'chōō·əs) adj. **1** Righteous; upright; dutiful. **2** Pure and chaste. —**vir'tu·ous·ly** adv. —**vir'tu·ous·ness** n.

vir·u·lent (vir'yə·lənt) adj. **1** Extremely harmful; noxious; deadly. **2** Severe and rapid in its progress: said of a disease. **3** Very infectious: said of a pathogenic microorganism. **4** Full of bitter hatred; hostile. [< L *virulentus* full of poison < *virus* a poison] —**vir'u·lence, vir'u·len·cy** n. —**vir'·u·lent·ly** adv.

vi·rus (vī'rəs) n. **1** Any of a class of ultramicroscopic filter-passing pathogens capable of reproduction only within specific living cells. **2** Venom, as of a snake. **3** Any evil influence: the *virus* of greed. [L, poison, slime]

vis (vis) *n. pl.* **vi·res** (vī′rēz) Force. [L]

Vis., Visc., Visct. Viscount; Viscountess.

vi·sa (vē′zə) *n.* An official endorsement on a passport certifying that it has been examined and that the bearer may enter or pass through the country which has granted the endorsement. —*v.t.* **·saed, ·sa·ing** 1 To put a visa on. 2 To give a visa to. [F< L <p.p. of *videre* see]

vis·age (viz′ij) *n.* **1** The face. **2** Appearance; aspect; look. [< L *visus* a look] —**vis′aged** *adj.*

vis-à-vis (vēz′ə·vē′, vēs-, -ä·vē′) *adj. & adv.* Face to face. —*prep.* **1** Opposite. **2** In relation to; toward. [F, face to face]

vis·cer·a (vis′ər·ə) *n.pl. sing.* **vis·cus** (vis′kəs) **1** The internal organs of the body, as the stomach, lungs, heart, etc. **2** Commonly, the intestines. [L, pl. of *viscus* an internal organ]

vis·cer·al (vis′ər·əl) *adj.* **1** Of or pertaining to the viscera. **2** Instinctive or emotional: a *visceral* reaction. —**vis′cer·al·ly** *adv.*

vis·cid (vis′id) *adj.* Glutinous in consistency; adhesive; syrupy; viscous. [< L *viscidum* birdlime]—**vis·cid·i·ty** (vi·sid′ə·tē), **vis′cid·ness** *n.* —**vis′cid·ly** *adv.*

vis·cose (vis′kōs) *n.* A viscid substance produced from cellulose as a step in the manufacture of rayon, cellophane, etc. —*adj.* **1** Viscous. **2** Of, pertaining to, containing, or made from viscose.

vis·cos·i·ty (vis·kos′ə·tē) *n. pl.* **·ties 1** The property of fluids by which they offer resistance to flow or to change in the arrangement of their molecules. **2** The measure of this property.

vis·count (vī′kount) *n.* A nobleman ranking below an earl or count and above a baron. [< OF *visconte*] —**vis′count·cy, vis′count·ship, vis′count·y** *n.*

vis·count·ess (vī′koun·tis) *n.* The wife of a viscount, or a peeress holding the title in her own right.

vis·cous (vis′kəs) *adj.* **1** Greatly resistant to flow; of high viscosity. **2** Viscid. [< L *viscum* birdlime] —**vis′cous·ly** *adv.* —**vis′cous·ness** *n.*

vise (vīs) *n.* A clamping device, usu. of two jaws made to be closed together with a screw, lever, or the like, for grasping and holding a piece of work. —*v.t.* **vised, vis·ing** To hold, force, or squeeze in or as in a vise. [< OF *vis* a screw < L *vitis* vine]

vi·sé (vē′zā) *n., v.t.* **vi·séed** or **vi·séd, vi·sé·ing** VISA.

Vish·nu (vish′nōō) In Hindu theology, the second god of the trinity (Brahma, Vishnu, and Siva), known as "the Preserver."

Machinist's vise (cross section)

vis·i·bil·i·ty (viz′ə·bil′ə·tē) *n. pl.* **·ties 1** The fact, condition, or degree of being visible. **2** *Meteorol.* The clearness of the atmosphere in terms of the distance at which objects can be seen distinctly.

vis·i·ble (viz′ə·bəl) *adj.* **1** Capable of being seen. **2** That can be perceived mentally; evident. [< L *visus,* p.p. of *videre* see] —**vis′i·ble·ness** *n.* —**vis′i·bly** *adv.* —**Syn. 1** perceptible. **2** clear, distinct, obvious, plain.

Vis·i·goth (viz′ə·goth) *n.* A member of the western Goths, a Teutonic people that invaded the Roman Empire in the late fourth century and established a monarchy in France and Spain. —**Vis′i·goth′ic** *adj.*

vi·sion (vizh′ən) *n.* **1** The act or power of seeing; sense of sight. **2** That which is seen. **3** A beautiful person, landscape, etc. **4** A mental representation of external objects or scenes, as in sleep. **5** A conception in the imagination; mental image: *visions* of power and wealth. **6** The ability to perceive, discern, and anticipate; foresight; imagination. —*v.t.* To see in or as in a vision. [< L *visus,* p.p. of *videre* see] —**vi′sion·al** *adj.* —**vi′sion·al·ly** *adv.*

vi·sion·ar·y (vizh′ən·er′ē) *adj.* **1** Not founded on fact; existing in the imagination; imaginary. **2** Able or disposed to see visions; affected by fantasies; dreamy. **3** Impractical, speculative, utopian. **4** Of, pertaining to, characterized by, or seen in a vision or visions. —*n. pl.* **·ar·ies 1** One who has visions. **2** One whose plans, projects, etc., are

unrealistic or impractical; dreamer. —**vi′sion·ar′i·ness** *n.*

vis·it (viz′it) *v.t.* **1** To go or come to see (a person) from friendship, courtesy, on business, etc. **2** To go or come to (a place, etc.), as for transacting business or for touring: to *visit* the Louvre. **3** To be a guest of; stay with temporarily: I *visited* them for several days. **4** To come upon or afflict. **5** To inflict upon. —*v.i.* **6** To pay a visit; call. **7** To stay with someone temporarily. **8** *Informal* To converse; chat. —*n.* **1** The act of visiting a person, place, or thing. **2** A social call or short stay. **3** *Informal* A friendly chat. **4** An official call, as for inspection, medical examination, etc. [< L *visare* < *visus,* p.p. of *videre* see]

vis·i·tant (viz′ə·tənt) *n.* **1** A visitor. **2** A migratory bird at a particular region for a limited period.

vis·i·ta·tion (viz′ə·tā′shən) *n.* **1** The act of visiting; esp., an official inspection, examination, etc. **2** A dispensation of punishment or reward, as by God. —**the Visitation 1** The visit of the Virgin Mary to her cousin, Elizabeth. *Luke* 1:39–56. **2** A church feast, observed on July 2, commemorating this event. —**vis′i·ta′tion·al** *adj.*

visiting card CALLING CARD.

vis·i·tor (viz′ə·tər) *n.* One who visits; guest.

vi·sor (vī′zər) *n.* **1** A projecting piece on a cap shielding the eyes. **2** In armor, the front piece of a helmet which protected the upper part of the face and could be raised or lowered. **3** A movable device over the inside of the windshield of a car, serving to reduce glare. [< OF *vis* face] —**vi′sored** (-zərd) *adj.*

vis·ta (vis′tə) *n.* **1** A view, esp. one seen through a long, narrow space, as along an avenue, between rows of trees, etc. **2** The space itself. **3** A mental view embracing a series of events. [Ital., sight < L *videre* see] —**vis′taed** (vis′təd) *adj.*

Visor *def. 2*

vis·u·al (vizh′ōō·əl) *adj.* **1** Of or pertaining to the sense of sight. **2** Perceptible by sight; visible. **3** Done or perceived by sight only. **4** Instructing through the sense of sight: *visual* aids. [< L *visus* a sight < *videre* see] —**vis′u·al·ly** *adv.*

visual aids Charts, diagrams, slides, motion pictures, etc., used as aids in teaching and lecturing.

vis·u·al·ize (vizh′ōō·əl·īz′, vizh′əl-) *v.* **·ized, ·iz·ing** *v.t.* **1** To form a mental image of; picture in the mind. —*v.i.* **2** To form mental images. *Brit. sp.* **vis·u·al·ise.** —**vis′u·al·i·za′tion, vis′u·al·iz′er** *n.*

vi·tal (vīt′l) *adj.* **1** Of or pertaining to life. **2** Essential to or supporting life. **3** Affecting life in a destructive way; fatal: a *vital* wound. **4** Of the utmost importance or interest. **5** Full of life; vigorous; energetic; dynamic. —*n.pl.* **1** The organs necessary to life, as the brain, heart, etc. **2** The necessary parts of anything. [< L *vitalis* < *vita* life] —**vi′tal·ly** *adv.*

vi·tal·ism (vīt′l·iz′əm) *n.* The doctrine that the life and functions of a living organism depend upon a vital force that differs in kind from all chemical and physical forces. —**vi′tal·ist** *n.* —**vi′tal·is′tic** *adj.*

vi·tal·i·ty (vī·tal′ə·tē) *n.* **1** The power to live and develop. **2** Power of continuing in force or effect. **3** Physical or mental energy; vigor; strength.

vi·tal·ize (vīt′l·īz) *v.t.* **·ized, ·iz·ing** To make vital; endow with life or energy; animate. —**vi′tal·i·za′tion, vi′tal·iz′er** *n.*

vital statistics Data relating to births, deaths, marriages, health, etc.

vi·ta·min (vī′tə·min) *n.* Any of a group of organic substances whose presence in the diet in minute quantities is essential for the maintenance of specific physiological functions. [< L *vita* life + AMINE] —**vi′ta·min′ic** *adj.*

vitamin A The fat-soluble vitamin essential to vision and occurring in all animal tissues and many vegetables.

vitamin B complex A varied group of water-soluble vitamins having distinct functions.

vitamin B$_1$ THIAMINE.

vitamin B$_2$ RIBOFLAVIN.

vitamin B$_6$ PYRIDOXINE.

vitamin B$_{12}$ A vitamin normally produced in the intestine and essential for the production of erythrocytes.

vitamin C ASCORBIC ACID.

vitamin D A substance essential in the formation of bone and the metabolism of calcium, occurring in fish-liver oils and formed from sterols in the skin when exposed to sunshine.

vitamin E An oily substance present in most foods and essential to fertility in experimental animals.

vitamin G RIBOFLAVIN.

vitamin H BIOTIN.

vitamin K₁ A vitamin, found in green leafy vegetables, which promotes the clotting of blood.

vitamin K₂ A form of vitamin K₁ prepared from fishmeal.

vitamin P A factor present in citrus juices that promotes the normal permeability of capillary walls.

vi·ti·ate (vish′ē·āt) v.t. ·at·ed, ·at·ing 1 To impair the use or value of; spoil. 2 To debase or corrupt. 3 To render weak, ineffective, legally invalid, etc.: Fraud *vitiates* a contract. [< L *vitium* a fault] —**vi′ti·a′tion, vi′ti·a′tor** n.

vit·i·cul·ture (vit′ə·kul′chər, vī′tə-) n. The science and art of grape-growing; cultivation of grapes. [< L *vitis* a vine + CULTURE] —**vit′i·cul′tur·al** adj. —**vit′i·cul′tur·er, vit′i·cul′tur·ist** n.

vit·i·li·go (vit′ə·lī′gō) n. A skin disorder characterized by partial loss of pigment resulting in white spots. [L, a vesicular skin disease]

vit·re·ous (vit′rē·əs) adj. 1 Of, pertaining to, or like glass; glassy. 2 Obtained from glass. 3 Of or pertaining to the vitreous humor. [< L *vitrum* glass] —**vit′re·os′i·ty** (-os′ə·tē), **vit′re·ous·ness** n.

vitreous humor The transparent jellylike tissue that fills the eyeball. Also **vitreous body.**

vit·ri·fy (vit′rə·fī) v.t. & v.i. ·fied, ·fy·ing To change into glass or a vitreous substance; make or become vitreous. [< L *vitrum* glass + *facere* make] —**vit′ri·fac′tion** (-fak′-shən), **vit′ri·fi·ca′tion** n.

vit·ri·ol (vit′rē·ol, -əl) n. 1 Any sulfate of a heavy metal, as green vitriol (iron); blue vitriol (copper); white vitriol (zinc). 2 Sulfuric acid: also **oil of vitriol.** 3 Anything sharp or caustic, as sarcasm. —v.t. ·oled or ·olled, ·ol·ing or ·ol·ling To subject (anything) to the agency of vitriol. [< L *vitrum* glass]

vit·ri·ol·ic (vit′rē·ol′ik) adj. 1 Of, like, or derived from vitriol. 2 Biting, sharp, or caustic: *vitriolic* remarks.

vit·tle (vit′l) n. VICTUAL.

vi·tu·per·ate (vī·t(y)ōō′pə·rāt, vi-) v.t. ·at·ed, ·at·ing To find fault with abusively; rail at; berate; scold. [< L *vituperare* blame, scold < *vitium* a fault + *parare* prepare] —**vi·tu′per·a′tion, vi·tu′per·a′tor** n. —**vi·tu′per·a′tive, vi·tu′per·a′tive·ly** adv.

viv. *Music* lively (It. *vivace*).

vi·va (vē′vä) *interj.* Live; long live (the person or thing specified): used in acclamation. [Ital. < *vivere* live < L]

vi·va·ce (vē·vä′chā) adv. *Music* Lively; quickly; briskly. [< L *vivax*]

vi·va·cious (vi·vā′shəs, vī-) adj. Full of life and spirits; lively; active. [< L *vivax* < *vivere* live] —**vi·va′cious·ly** adv. —**vi·va′cious·ness** n. —**Syn.** animated, brisk, cheerful, sparkling, spirited.

vi·vac·i·ty (vi·vas′ə·tē, vī-) n. pl. ·ties 1 The state or quality of being vivacious. 2 A vivacious act, expression, etc.

vi·var·i·um (vī·vâr′ē·əm) n. pl. ·var·i·a (-vâr′ē·ə) or ·var·i·ums A place for keeping or raising animals or plants for observation or research. Also **viv·a·ry** (viv′ər·ē). [< L *vivus* alive < *vivere* live]

vi·va vo·ce (vī′və vō′sē, vē′və vō′chā) By spoken word; orally or oral. [L]

vive (vēv) *interj.* French Live; long live (the person or thing specified): used in acclamation.

viv·id (viv′id) adj. 1 Having an appearance of vigorous life; lively; spirited. 2 Very strong; intense: said of colors. 3 Producing or suggesting lifelike images. 4 Producing a sharp impression on the senses: a *vivid* description. [< L *vividus* lively < *vivere* to live] —**viv′id·ly** adv. —**viv′id·ness** n.

viv·i·fy (viv′ə·fī) v.t. ·fied, ·fy·ing 1 To give life to; animate; vitalize. 2 To make more vivid or striking. [< L *vivus* alive + *facere* make] —**viv′i·fi·ca′tion** (-fə·kā′shən), **viv′i·fi′er** n.

vi·vip·a·rous (vī·vip′ər·əs) adj. Bringing forth young

that have developed from eggs within the mother's body. [< L *vivus* alive + *parere* bring forth] —**vi·vip′a·rous·ly** adv. —**vi·vip′a·rous·ness, viv·i·par·i·ty** (viv′ə·par′ə·tē) n.

viv·i·sect (viv′ə·sekt) v.t. 1 To perform vivisection on. —v.i. 2 To practice vivisection. —**viv′i·sec′tor** n.

viv·i·sec·tion (viv′ə·sek′shən) n. Cutting, dissection, or other operation on a living animal, esp. in experiments designed to promote knowledge of physiological and pathological processes. [< L *vivus* living, alive + *sectio* a cutting] —**viv′i·sec′tion·al** adj. —**viv′i·sec′tion·ist** n., adj.

vix·en (vik′sən) n. 1 A female fox. 2 A turbulent, quarrelsome woman; shrew. [< ME *fixen* a she-fox] —**vix′en·ish** adj. —**vix′en·ly** adj., adv.

viz, viz. namely (L *videlicet*).

viz·ard (viz′ərd) n. A mask or visor. [Alter. of VISOR]

vi·zier (vi·zir′) n. A high official of a Muslim country, as in the old Turkish Empire. Also **vi·zir′.** [< Ar. *wazīr* a counselor]

vi·zor (vī′zər) n. VISOR.

V-J Day (vē′jā′) Sept. 2, 1945, the official date of the Allied victory over Japan in World War II.

VL, V.L. Vulgar Latin.

VLF, V.L.F., vlf, v.l.f. very low frequency.

V-mail (vē′māl′) n. Mail transmitted overseas in World War II on microfilm, and enlarged at point of reception for final delivery. [< V(ICTORY) + MAIL¹]

V.M.D. Doctor of Veterinary Medicine (L *Veterinariae Medicinae Doctor*).

vo. verso.

voc. vocative.

vocab. vocabulary.

vo·ca·ble (vō′kə·bəl) n. A word viewed as a combination of sounds and letters apart from its meaning. [< L *vocabulum* a name, appellation < *vocare* to call]

vo·cab·u·lar·y (vō·kab′yə·ler′ē) n. pl. ·lar·ies 1 A list of words or of words and phrases, esp. one arranged in alphabetical order and defined or translated; a lexicon; glossary. 2 All the words of a language. 3 All the words used or understood by a particular person, class, profession, etc. 4 The range of expression at a person's disposal, esp. in art. [< L *vocabulum.* See VOCABLE.]

vo·cal (vō′kəl) adj. 1 Of or pertaining to the voice or the production of the voice. 2 Having voice; able to speak or utter sounds: *vocal* creatures. 3 Composed for, uttered by, or performed by the voice: a *vocal* score. 4 Full of voices or sounds; resounding: The air was *vocal* with their cries. 5 Freely expressing oneself in speech: the *vocal* segment of the populace. [< L *vocalis* speaking, sounding] —**vo·cal·i·ty** (vō·kal′ə·tē), **vo′cal·ness** n. —**vo′cal·ly** adv.

vocal cords Two ligaments extending across the larynx, which, when tense, are caused to vibrate by the passage of air, thereby producing voice.

vo·cal·ic (vō·kal′ik) adj. 1 Of, pertaining to, or like a vowel sound. 2 Characterized by or consisting of vowel sounds.

vo·cal·ist (vō′kəl·ist) n. A singer.

vo·cal·ize (vō′kəl·īz) v. ·ized, ·iz·ing v.t. 1 To make vocal; utter, say, or sing. 2 *Phonet.* a To change to or use as a vowel: to *vocalize* y. b To voice. —v.i. 3 To produce sounds with the voice, as in speaking or singing. 4 *Phonet.* To be changed to a vowel. —**vo′cal·i·za′tion, vo′cal·iz′er** n.

Vocal cords
a. open. b. closed.
c. voice. d. whisper.

vo·ca·tion (vō·kā′shən) n. 1 A stated or regular occupation. 2 A call to, or fitness for, a certain career. 3 The work or profession for which one has or believes one has a special fitness. [< L *vocare* to call] —**vo·ca′tion·al** adj. —**vo·ca′tion·al·ly** adv.

voc·a·tive (vok′ə·tiv) *Gram.* adj. In some inflected languages, denoting the case of a noun, pronoun, or adjective used in direct address. —n. 1 The vocative case. 2 A word in this case. [< L *vocare* to call]

vo·cif·er·ant (vō·sif′ər·ənt) adj. Vociferous; uttering loud cries. —**vo·cif′er·ance** n.

vo·cif·er·ate (vō·sif′ə·rāt) *v.t. & v.i.* **·at·ed, ·at·ing** To cry out with a loud voice; shout. [< L *vox* a voice + *ferre* carry] —**vo·cif′er·a′tion, vo·cif·er·a′tor** *n.* —**Syn.** bawl, bellow, clamor, scream, yell.

vo·cif·er·ous (vō·sif′ər·əs) *adj.* Making or characterized by a loud outcry; noisy; clamorous. —**vo·cif′er·ous·ly** *adv.* —**vo·cif′er·ous·ness** *n.*

vod·ka (vod′kə) *n.* A colorless alcoholic liquor originally made in Poland and Russia, distilled from a mash, as of rye, wheat, or potatoes. [< Russ. *voda* water]

vogue (vōg) *n.* **1** Fashion or style. **2** Popular favor; popularity. [F, fashion, orig., rowing] —**vogu′ish** *adj.*

voice (vois) *n.* **1** The sound produced by the vocal organs of a vertebrate, esp. by a human being in speaking, singing, etc. **2** The quality or character of such sound: a melodious *voice.* **3** The power or ability to make such a sound: to lose one's *voice.* **4** Something suggesting the sound of vocal utterance: the *voice* of the wind. **5** Expressed opinion, choice, etc. **6** The right to express an opinion, choice, etc. **7** A person or agency by which the thought, wish, or purpose of another is expressed: This journal is the *voice* of the teaching profession. **8** Expression: to give *voice* to one's ideals. **9** *Phonet.* The sound produced by vibration of the vocal cords, as heard in the utterance of vowels and certain consonants, as *b, d,* and *z.* **10** A singer: Caruso was a great *voice.* **11** In a musical composition, a part for a singer or an instrument. **12** *Gram.* A form of a verb which indicates whether its subject is active or passive. —**in voice** Having the voice in good condition for singing and speaking. —**lift up one's voice 1** To shout or sing loudly. **2** To protest. —**with one voice** With one accord; unanimously. —*v.t.* **voiced, voic·ing 1** To put into speech; give expression to; utter. **2** *Music* To regulate the tones of, as the pipes of an organ. **3** *Phonet.* To utter with voice. [< L *vox, vocis*] • When the subject of a verb performs the action, the verb is in the **active voice**: *My aunt baked a chocolate cake; Her father gave her a bicycle.* When the subject of a verb is acted upon, the verb is in the **passive voice**: *The chocolate cake was baked by my aunt; She was given a bicycle by her father.*

voiced (voist) *adj.* **1** Having a voice or a specified kind of voice: often used in combination: *high-voiced, soft-voiced.* **2** Expressed by voice. **3** *Phonet.* Uttered with vibration of the vocal cords, as (b), (d), (z).

voice·less (vois′lis) *adj.* **1** Having no voice, speech, or vote. **2** *Phonet.* Produced without voice, as (p), (t), (s). —**voice′less·ly** *adv.* —**voice′less·ness** *n.*

voice-o·ver (vois′ō′vər) *n.* In motion pictures and television programs, the voice of a narrator or announcer speaking off camera.

voice·print (vois′print′) *n.* A graphic representation of the sound of a person's voice, consisting of a complex pattern of wavy lines corresponding to the various pitches used in the utterance.

void (void) *adj.* **1** Containing nothing; without content; empty. **2** Having no legal force or validity; not binding. **3** Producing no effect; useless. —**void of** Lacking; without. —*n.* **1** An empty space; vacuum. **2** The quality or condition of feeling empty, lonely, lost, etc. —*v.t.* **1** To make void or of no effect; annul. **2** To empty or remove (contents); evacuate. —*v.i.* **3** To eliminate waste from the body; urinate or defecate. [< L *vacuus* empty] —**void′er, void′ness** *n.* —**void′ly** *adv.*

voi·là (vwá·lá′) *interj. French* There! behold! literally, see there.

voile (voil) *n.* A fine, sheer fabric, as of cotton, silk, wool, or rayon. [< OF *veile* veil]

vol. volcano; volume; volunteer.

vo·lant (vō′lənt) *adj.* **1** Flying, or capable of flying. **2** Agile; quick; nimble. **3** *Her.* Represented as flying, as a bird or bee. [< L *volare* to fly]

vol·a·tile (vol′ə·til; *chiefly Brit.* ·tīl) *adj.* **1** Evaporating rapidly; capable of being vaporized. **2** Inconstant; changeable. **3** Transient; fleeting. [< L *volatilis* < *volare* fly] —**vol′a·tile·ness, vol·a·til·i·ty** (vol′ə·til′ə·tē) *n.*

vol·a·til·ize (vol′ə·til·īz′) *v.t. & v.i.* **·ized, ·iz·ing** To pass off or cause to pass off in vapor. —**vol′a·til·i·za′tion** *n.*

vol·can·ic (vol·kan′ik) *adj.* **1** Of, pertaining to, produced by, or characterized by a volcano or volcanoes. **2** Like a

volcano; explosive; violent. —**vol·can′i·cal·ly** *adv.* —**vol·can·ic·i·ty** (vol′kə·nis′ə·tē) *n.*

vol·can·ism (vol′kən·iz′əm) *n.* The power or action of volcanoes.

vol·ca·no (vol·kā′nō) *n. pl.* **·noes** or **·nos** *Geol.* An opening in the earth's surface from which hot matter is or has been ejected, often surrounded by a hill or mountain of ejected material. [< L *Vulcanus* Vulcan]

vole (vōl) *n.* Any of various short-tailed, mouselike or rat-like rodents. [Short for earlier *vole mouse* field mouse]

vo·li·tion (və·lish′ən) *n.* **1** The act of willing; exercise of the will. **2** The power of willing; willpower. [< L *velle* to will] —**vo·li′tion·al, vo·li′tion·ar·y** (-ən·ər·ē), **vol·i·tive** (vol′ə·tiv) *adj.* —**vo·li′tion·al·ly** *adv.*

vol·ley (vol′ē) *n.* **1** A simultaneous discharge of many guns. **2** A discharge of many bullets, stones, arrows, etc. **3** Any discharge of many things at once: a *volley* of oaths. **4** In tennis, the flight of the ball before it touches the ground; also, a return of the ball before it touches the ground. —*v.t. & v.i.* **·leyed, ·ley·ing 1** To discharge or be discharged in a volley. **2** In tennis, to return (the ball) without allowing it to touch the ground. [< MF *voler* to fly] —**vol′ley·er** *n.*

vol·ley·ball (vol′ē·bôl′) *n.* **1** A game in which a number of players on both sides of a high net use their hands to hit a ball back and forth over the net without letting it drop. **2** The ball used in this game.

vol·plane (vol′plān) *v.i.* **·planed, ·plan·ing** To glide down in an airplane with the engine turned off. —*n.* An airplane glide. [< F *vol plané* gliding flight]

vols. volumes.

volt¹ (vōlt) *n.* A unit equal to the difference of electric potential which, when steadily applied to a conductor whose resistance is one ohm, will produce a current of one ampere. [< A. *Volta,* 1745–1827, Italian physicist]

volt² (vōlt) *n.* **1** In horse-training, a gait in which the horse moves sidewise round a center with the head turned out. **2** In fencing, a sudden leap to avoid a thrust. [< Ital. *volta,* p.p. fem. of *volvere* to turn]

volt·age (vōl′tij) *n.* Electromotive force expressed in volts.

vol·ta·ic (vol·tā′ik) *adj.* Pertaining to electricity developed through chemical action; galvanic.

voltaic battery A set of voltaic cells which operate as a unit.

voltaic cell A cell that generates electricity by a chemical reaction and that cannot be efficiently recharged.

volt·me·ter (vōlt′mē′tər) *n.* An instrument for measuring differences of electric potential.

vol·u·ble (vol′yə·bəl) *adj.* Having a flow of words or fluency in speaking; talkative. [< L *volubilis* easily turned < *volutus,* p.p. of *volvere* to turn] —**vol′u·bil′i·ty** (vol′yə·bil′ə·tē), **vol′u·ble·ness** *n.* —**vol′u·bly** *adv.*

vol·ume (vol′yŏŏm, -yəm) *n.* **1** A collection of sheets of paper bound together; a book. **2** A book that is part of a set. **3** A quantity or amount: a large *volume* of sales. **4** A measure of quantity in terms of space occupied, as cubic inch, cubic centimeter, liter, pint, etc. **5** *Acoustics* Fullness or quantity of sound or tone. —**speak volumes** To be full of meaning; express a great deal. [< L *volumen* a roll, scroll] —**vol′umed** *adj.*

vol·u·met·ric (vol′yə·met′rik) *adj.* Of, based on, or pertaining to measurement of substances by volume. Also **vol′u·met′ri·cal.** —**vol′u·met′ri·cal·ly** *adv.*

vo·lu·mi·nous (və·lōō′mə·nəs) *adj.* **1** Consisting of or capable of filling volumes: a *voluminous* correspondence. **2** Writing or speaking much. **3** Having great volume or bulk; large. [< L *volumen* a roll] —**vo·lu·mi·nos·i·ty** (və·lōō′mə·nos′ə·tē), **vo·lu′mi·nous·ness** *n.* —**vo·lu′mi·nous·ly** *adv.*

vol·un·tar·y (vol′ən·ter′ē) *adj.* **1** Done, made, or given by one's own free will or choice: a *voluntary* contribution. **2** Endowed with or exercising will or free choice. **3** Acting without constraint: a *voluntary* donor. **4** Subject to or directed by the will, as a muscle or movement. **5** Intentional; volitional: *voluntary* manslaughter. —*n. pl.* **·tar·ies 1** Voluntary action or work. **2** A solo, usu. on the organ, often improvised, played before, during, or after a church service. [< L *voluntas* will] —**vol·un·tar·i·ly** (vol′ən·ter′ə·lē, vol′ən·ter′-) *adv.* —**vol′un·tar′i·ness** *n.*

vol·un·teer (vol'ən·tir') n. 1 One who enters into any service of his own free will. 2 One who voluntarily enters military service. —adj. 1 Of, pertaining to, or composed of volunteers; voluntary. 2 Serving as a volunteer. —v.t. 1 To offer or give voluntarily: to *volunteer* one's services. —v.i. 2 To enter or offer to enter into some service or undertaking of one's free will. [< OF *voluntaire* voluntary]

vo·lup·tu·ar·y (və·lup'chŏo·er'ē) n. pl. ·ar·ies One addicted to luxury and sensual indulgence. [< L *voluptas* pleasure] —Syn. hedonist, sensualist, sybarite.

vo·lup·tu·ous (və·lup'chŏo·əs) adj. 1 Pertaining to, inclining to, producing, or produced by sensuous or sensual gratification. 2 Devoted to the enjoyment of pleasures or luxuries. 3 Suggesting the satisfaction of sensual desire. [< L *voluptas* pleasure] —vo·lup'tu·ous·ly adv. —vo·lup'tu·ous·ness n.

vo·lute (və·lōōt') n. 1 Archit. A spiral scroll-like ornament, as in Ionic capitals. 2 Zool. One of the whorls or turns of a spiral shell. 3 A spiral or twisted form. —adj. Having a spiral form; scroll-shaped. [< L *voluta* a scroll < p.p. of *volvere* to turn] —vo·lut'ed adj. —vo·lu'tion n.

Volute

vom·it (vom'it) v.i. 1 To disgorge the contents of the stomach; throw up. 2 To issue with violence from any hollow place; be ejected. —v.t. 3 To disgorge (the contents of the stomach). 4 To discharge or send forth copiously or forcibly: The volcano *vomited* smoke. —n. 1 The act of vomiting. 2 Matter ejected from the stomach in vomiting. [< L *vomere*] —vom'it·er n.

vom·i·tive (vom'ə·tiv) adj. Of, pertaining to, or causing vomiting. —n. EMETIC.

von (von; Ger. fôn, unstressed fən) prep. German Of; from: used in German and Austrian family names as an attribute of nobility.

voo·doo (vōō'dōō) n. 1 A primitive religion of African origin, found among Haitian and West Indian Negroes and the Negroes of the s U.S., characterized by belief in sorcery and the use of charms, fetishes, witchcraft, etc. 2 A person who practices voodoo. 3 A voodoo charm or fetish. —adj. Of or pertaining to the beliefs, ceremonies, etc., of voodoo. —v.t. To practice voodoo upon; bewitch. Also vou'dou. —voo'doo·ism, voo'doo·ist n. —voo'doo·is'tic adj.

vo·ra·cious (vô·rā'shəs, vō-, və-) adj. 1 Eating with greediness; ravenous. 2 Very eager, as in some desire; insatiable. 3 Immoderate: a *voracious* appetite. [< L *vorax* < *vorare* devour] —vo·ra'cious·ly adv. —vo·rac·i·ty (-ras'ə·tē), vo·ra'cious·ness n.

-vorous combining form Consuming; eating or feeding upon: *omnivorous, carnivorous*. [< L *vorare* devour]

vor·tex (vôr'teks) n. pl. ·tex·es or ·ti·ces (-tə·sēz) 1 A mass of rotating or whirling fluid, esp. one spiraling in toward a center; a whirlpool or whirlwind. 2 Something resembling a vortex, as an activity or situation from which it is difficult to escape. [< L, var. of *vertex* top, point] —vor'ti·cal (-ti·kəl) adj. —vor'ti·cal·ly adv.

vo·ta·ry (vō'tər·ē) n. pl. ·ries 1 One who is bound by vows, as a nun or priest. 2 One devoted to some particular worship, pursuit, study, etc. Also vo'ta·rist. —adj. 1 Of, pertaining to, or like a vow. 2 Consecrated by a vow. [< L *votus*, p.p. of *vovere* vow]

vote (vōt) n. 1 A formal expression of choice or opinion, as in electing officers, passing resolutions, etc. 2 That by which such choice or opinion is expressed, as the ballot, a show of hands, etc. 3 The number of ballots cast, hands raised, etc., to indicate such choice or opinion. 4 The votes of a specified group; also, the group itself. 5 The right to vote. 6 A voter. —v. vot·ed, vot·ing v.t. 1 To enact or determine by vote. 2 To cast one's vote for: to *vote* the Democratic ticket. 3 To elect or defeat by vote. 4 Informal To declare by general agreement: to *vote* a concert a success. —v.i. 5 To cast one's vote. —vote down To defeat or suppress by voting against. —vote in To elect. [< L *votum* a vow, wish, orig. p.p. neut. of *vovere* vow]

vot·er (vōt'ər) n. 1 A person who votes. 2 A person having the right to vote.

vo·tive (vō'tiv) adj. Performed, offered, lit, etc., as fulfillment of a vow, as an act of worship, in gratitude, etc. [< L *votum*. See VOTE.] —vo'tive·ly adv. —vo'tive·ness n.

vouch (vouch) v.i. 1 To give one's own assurance or guarantee: with *for*: I will *vouch* for their honesty. 2 To serve as assurance or proof: with *for*: The evidence *vouches* for his innocence. —v.t. 3 To bear witness to; attest or affirm. 4 To cite as support or justification, as a precedent, authority, etc. 5 To uphold by satisfactory proof or evidence; substantiate. [< L *vocare* call < *vox, vocis* a voice]

vouch·er (vou'chər) n. 1 A document that serves to vouch for the truth of something, or attest an alleged act, esp. the expenditure or receipt of money. 2 One who vouches for another; a witness.

vouch·safe (vouch'sāf') v. ·safed, ·saf·ing v.t. 1 To grant, as with condescension; permit; deign. —v.i. 2 To condescend; deign. [< VOUCH + SAFE] —vouch'safe'ment n.

vous·soir (vōō·swär') n. Archit. A wedge-shaped stone in an arch. [< OF *vausoir, volsoir* curvature of a vault]

vow (vou) n. 1 A solemn promise, as to God or a god. 2 A pledge of faithfulness: marriage *vows*. 3 A solemn and emphatic affirmation. —take vows To enter a religious order. —v.t. 1 To promise solemnly. 2 To declare with assurance or solemnity. 3 To make a solemn promise or threat to do, inflict, etc. —v.i. 4 To make a vow. [< L *votum*. See VOTE.] —vow'er n.

vow·el (vou'əl, voul) n. 1 Phonet. A voiced speech sound produced by the relatively unimpeded passage of air through the mouth. 2 A letter indicating such a sound, as *a, e, i, o,* or *u.* —adj. Of or pertaining to a vowel or vowels. [< L *vocalis* (*littera*) vocal (letter)]

vox pop. voice of the people (L *vox populi*).

vox po·pu·li (voks pop'yə·lī, -lē) The voice of the people; public sentiment. [L]

voy·age (voi'ij) n. 1 A journey by water, esp. by sea. 2 Any journey, as one by aircraft. —v. ·aged, ·ag·ing v.i. 1 To make a voyage; travel. —v.t. 2 To traverse. [< L *viaticum*] —voy'ag·er n. —Syn. n. 1 crossing, cruise, sail, trip.

vo·ya·geur (vwä·yȧ·zhœr') n. pl. ·geurs (-zhœr') Can. Formerly, a man engaged in a fur company to carry men, supplies, etc., between remote trading posts. [F]

vo·yeur (vwä·yûr') n. One who is sexually gratified by looking at sexual objects or acts. [< F *voir* see] —vo·yeur'·ism n.

V.P. Vice President.

vs. versus.

v.s. see above (L *vide supra*).

VSS versions.

VT Vermont (P.O. abbr.).

Vt. Vermont.

v.t. verb transitive.

VTOL vertical takeoff and landing.

Vul., Vulg. Vulgate.

Vul·can (vul'kən) Rom. Myth. The god of fire and of metallurgy. —Vul·ca·ni·an (-kā'nē·ən) adj.

vul·can·ite (vul'kən·īt) n. A dark-colored, hard, vulcanized rubber. [< VULCAN]

vul·can·ize (vul'kən·īz) v.t. & v.i. ·ized, ·iz·ing To heat (natural rubber) with sulfur in order to increase strength and elasticity. [< VULCAN] —vul'can·i·za'tion, vul'can·iz'er n.

vul·gar (vul'gər) adj. 1 Lacking good manners, taste, etc.; coarse; unrefined. 2 Offensive or obscene in expression: a *vulgar* usage. 3 Of or pertaining to the common people; general; popular. 4 Written in or translated into the common language or dialect; vernacular. [< L *vulgus* the common people] —vul'gar·ly adv. —Syn. 1 boorish, crude, tasteless. 2 indecent, taboo. 3 ordinary, plebeian.

vul·gar·i·an (vul·gâr'ē·ən) n. A person of vulgar tastes or manners; esp., a wealthy person with coarse habits.

vul·gar·ism (vul'gə·riz'əm) n. 1 A word, phrase, or expression generally considered to be incorrect or coarse and indicative of ignorance or ill breeding on the part of the user. 2 VULGARITY.

vul·gar·i·ty (vul·gar′ə·tē) n. pl. ·ties 1 The state, quality, or character of being vulgar. 2 Something vulgar, as an act or expression.

vul·gar·ize (vul′gə·rīz) v.t. ·ized, ·iz·ing To make vulgar. Brit. sp. **vul′gar·ise.** —**vul′gar·i·za′tion, vul′gar·iz′er** n.

Vulgar Latin The popular, informal speech of the ancient Romans, considered to be the chief source of the Romance languages.

vul·gate (vul′gāt) adj. Popular; accepted. —n. 1 Everyday speech. 2 A popularly accepted text. [< L vulgare make common < vulgus the common people]

Vul·gate (vul′gāt) n. A Latin version of the Bible, translated in the 4th century, since revised and used as the authorized version by Roman Catholics. —adj. Of or in the Vulgate.

vul·ner·a·ble (vul′nər·ə·bəl) adj. 1 That may be wounded; capable of being hurt. 2 Open to attack; assailable. 3 In contract bridge, having won one game of a rubber, and therefore subject to doubled penalities if contract is not fulfilled. [< L vulnerare to wound < vulnus a wound] —**vul′ner·a·bil′i·ty, vul′ner·a·ble·ness** n. —**vul′ner·a·bly** adv.

vul·pine (vul′pin, -pīn) adj. 1 Of or pertaining to a fox. 2 Like a fox; sly; crafty; cunning. [< L vulpes a fox]

vul·ture (vul′chər) n. 1 Any of various large birds related to hawks and falcons, having a naked head and dark plumage, and feeding on carrion. 2 Something or someone that preys upon others. [< L vultur] —**vul′tur·ous** adj.

Vulture

vul·va (vul′və) n. pl. ·vae (-vē) The external genital parts of the female. [L, a covering, womb] — **vul′val, vul′var, vul′vi·form** (-və·fôrm) adj.

vy·ing (vī′ing) pr.p. of VIE. —adj. That vies or competes. —**vy′ing·ly** adv.

W

W, w (dub′əl·yo͞o, -yo͞o) n. pl. **W's, w's, Ws, ws** (dub′əl·yo͞oz, -yo͞oz) 1 The 23rd letter of the English alphabet. 2 Any spoken sound representing the letter W or w. 3 Something shaped like a W. —adj. Shaped like a W.

W tungsten (G wolfram).

W., w., w, w watt; west; western.

w. warden; week(s); weight; wife; with; word; work.

WA Washington (P.O. abbr.).

wab·ble (wob′əl) n., v.t. & v.i. ·bled, ·bling WOBBLE. [Var. of WOBBLE] —**wab′bler** n. —**wab′bly** adj.

Wac (wak) n. A member of the WAC, the women's division of the U.S. Army. [< W(omen's) A(rmy) C(orps)]

wack·y (wak′ē) adj. wack·i·er, wack·i·est Slang Extremely irrational or erratic; crazy. Also **whack′y.** [Prob. < WHACK] —**wack′i·ly** adv. —**wack′i·ness** n.

wad (wod) n. 1 A small compact mass of any soft or flexible substance, esp. as used for stuffing, packing, or lining. 2 A lump; mass: a wad of tobacco. 3 A small plug used to hold in a charge of powder in a muzzleloading gun. 4 A pasteboard or paper disk to hold powder and shot in place in a shotgun shell. • See CARTRIDGE. 5 Fibrous material for stopping up breaks, leakages, etc.; wadding. 6 Informal A large amount, esp. of money. 7 Informal A roll of banknotes. —v. **wad·ded, wad·ding** v.t. 1 To press (fibrous substances, as cotton) into a mass or wad. 2 To roll or fold into a tight wad, as paper. 3 To pack or stuff with wadding for protection, as valuables. 4 To place a wad in (a gun, etc.). 5 To hold in place with a wad. —v.i. 6 To form into a wad. [?] —**wad′der** n.

wad·ding (wod′ing) n. 1 Wads collectively. 2 Any substance used as wads.

wad·dle (wod′l) v.i. ·dled, ·dling 1 To walk with short steps, swaying from side to side. 2 To move clumsily; totter. —n. A clumsy rocking walk, like that of a duck. [Freq. of WADE] —**wad′dler** n. —**wad′dly** adj.

wade (wād) v. wad·ed, wad·ing v.i. 1 To walk through water or any substance more resistant than air, as mud, sand, etc. 2 To proceed slowly or laboriously: to wade through a lengthy book. —v.t. 3 To pass or cross, as a river, by walking on the bottom; walk through; ford. —**wade in** (or **into**) Informal To attack or begin energetically or vigorously. —n. An act of wading. [< OE wadan go]

wad·er (wā′dər) n. 1 One who wades. 2 A long-legged wading bird, as a snipe, plover, or stork. 3 pl. High waterproof boots or pants, worn esp. by anglers.

wa·di (wä′dē) n. pl. ·dies 1 In Arabia and N Africa, a ravine containing the bed of a watercourse, usu. dry except in the rainy season. 2 The stream of water flowing through a wadi. Also **wa′dy.** [< Ar. wādī]

Waf (waf, wäf) n. A member of the WAF, the women's division of the U.S. Air Force. [< W(omen in the) A(ir) F(orce)]

wa·fer (wā′fər) n. 1 A very thin crisp biscuit, cooky, or cracker; also, a small disk of candy. 2 Eccl. A small flat disk of unleavened bread, used in the Eucharist in some churches. 3 A thin hardened disk of dried paste, gelatin, etc., used for sealing letters, attaching papers, or receiving the impression of a seal. —v.t. To attach, seal, or fasten with a wafer. [< AF wafre < MLG wafel]

waf·fle¹ (wof′əl, wô′fəl) n. A batter cake, crisper than a pancake, baked in a waffle iron. [< Du. wafel a wafer]

waf·fle² (wof′əl, wô′fəl) v.i. ·fled, ·fling 1 Chiefly Brit. Informal To speak or write nonsense. 2 Informal To avoid giving a direct answer; hedge. —n. Chiefly Brit. Informal Nonsense; twaddle. [< obs. woff, waff to yelp]

waffle iron A utensil for cooking waffles, consisting of two indented metal griddles, hinged together, between which the waffle is baked.

waft (waft, wäft) v.t. 1 To carry or bear gently or lightly over air or water; float. 2 To convey as if on air or water. —v.i. 3 To float, as on the wind. 4 To blow gently, as a breeze. —n. 1 The act of one who or that which wafts. 2 A breath or current of air. 3 A passing sound or odor. 4 A waving motion. [< Du. wachten to guard] —**waft′er** n.

wag (wag) v. **wagged, wag·ging** v.t. 1 To cause to move lightly and quickly from side to side or up and down, as a dog's tail. 2 To move (the tongue) in talking. —v.i. 3 To move lightly and quickly from side to side or up and down. 4 To move busily in animated talk or gossip: said of the tongue. —n. 1 The act or motion of wagging: a wag of the head. 2 A droll or humorous person; wit. [Prob. < Scand.]

wage (wāj) n. 1 Often pl. Payment for service rendered, esp. such payment calculated by the hour, day, or week, or for a certain amount of work. 2 Usu. pl. (construed as sing. or pl.) Reward: the wages of sin. —v.t. **waged, wag·ing** To engage in and maintain vigorously; carry on: to wage war. [< AF wagier pledge] —**Syn.** n. 1 compensation, earnings, pay, remuneration.

wage earner One who works for wages.

wa·ger (wā′jər) v.t. & v.i. To bet. —n. 1 A bet. 2 The thing bet on. [< AF wagier]

wage·work·er (wāj′wûr′kər) n. An employee receiving wages. —**wage′work′ing** n., adj.

wag·ger·y (wag′ər·ē) n. pl. ·ger·ies 1 Mischievous joking. 2 A practical joke. [< WAG]

wag·gish (wag′ish) adj. 1 Being or acting like a wag; humorous. 2 Said or done as a joke. —**wag′gish·ly** adv. —**wag′gish·ness** n. —**Syn.** 1 droll, facetious, funny, jocose.

wag·gle (wag′əl) v. ·gled, ·gling v.t. To wag; swing: The duck waggles its tail. —n. The act of waggling. [Freq. of WAG] —**wag′gling·ly** adv. —**wag′gly** adj. (·i·er, ·i·est)

Wag·ne·ri·an (väg·nir′ē·ən) adj. 1 Of or pertaining to Richard Wagner or to his music, style, or theories. 2 Specializing in the performance of Wagner's music. —n. One who admires the music or the theories of Richard Wagner.

wag·on (wag′ən) *n.* **1** Any of various four-wheeled, usu. horse-drawn vehicles for carrying heavy loads. **2** A child's open, four-wheeled cart, pulled and steered by a long handle. **3** PATROL WAGON. **4** STATION WAGON. **5** *Brit.* A railway freight car. **6** A stand on wheels or casters for serving food or drink: a tea *wagon.* —**on** (or **off**) **the (water) wagon** *Informal* Abstaining (or no longer abstaining) from alcoholic beverages. —**fix (someone's) wagon** *Slang* To even scores with; get revenge on. —*v.t.* To carry or transport in a wagon. *Brit. sp.* **wag′gon.** [< Du. *wagen*]

Wagon

wag·on·er (wag′ən·ər) *n.* One whose business is driving wagons. *Brit. sp.* **wag·gon·er.**

wag·on·load (wag′ən·lōd′) *n.* The amount that a wagon can carry. *Brit. sp.* **wag·gon·load.**

wagon train A line of wagons traveling together.

wag·tail (wag′tāl′) *n.* Any of various birds that habitually jerk the tail, as certain pipits.

Wa·ha·bi (wä·hä′bē) *n.* A member of a strict orthodox Muslim sect. Also **Wah·ha′bi.** —**Wa·ha′bism, Wah·ha′bism** (-biz·əm) *n.*

waif (wāf) *n.* **1** A homeless, neglected person, esp. a child. **2** A stray animal. [Prob. < Scand.]

wail (wāl) *v.i.* **1** To grieve with mournful cries; lament. **2** To make a mournful, crying sound, as the wind. —*v.t.* **3** To mourn; lament. **4** To cry out in sorrow. —*n.* **1** A prolonged, high-pitched sound of lamentation. **2** Any mournful sound, as of the wind. [< ON *vei* woe] —**wail′er** *n.* —**wail′ful** *adj.* —**wail′ful·ly, wail′ing·ly** *adv.*

Wailing Wall A high wall in Jerusalem reputedly containing fragments of Solomon's temple and traditionally a place for Jews to pray and mourn.

wain (wān) *n.* An open, four-wheeled wagon for hauling heavy loads. [< OE *wægn, wæn*]

wain·scot (wān′skət, -skŏt, -skot) *n.* **1** A facing for inner walls, usu. of paneled wood. **2** The lower part of an inner wall, when finished with material different from the rest of the wall. —*v.t.* **·scot·ed** or **·scot·ted, ·scot·ing** or **·scot·ting** To face or panel with wainscot. [< MLG *wagen* a wagon + *schot* a wooden partition]

wain·scot·ing (wān′skət·ing, -skot-) *n.* **1** WAINSCOT. **2** Material for a wainscot. Also **wain′scot·ting.**

wain·wright (wān′rīt) *n.* A maker of wagons.

waist (wāst) *n.* **1** The part of the body between the lower ribs and the hips. **2** The middle part of any object, esp. if narrower than the ends: the *waist* of a violin. **3** That part of a woman's dress covering the body from the waistline to the shoulders. **4** BLOUSE. **5** WAISTLINE (def. 2). [ME *wast*]

waist·band (wāst′band′) *n.* A band encircling the waist, esp. such a band inside a skirt or trousers.

waist·coat (wes′kit, wāst′kōt′) *n. Chiefly Brit.* VEST (def. 1).

waist·line (wāst′līn′) *n.* **1** The so-called line that encircles the middle of the waist. **2** That part of a garment covering this line or extending above or below it according to the dictates of fashion.

wait (wāt) *v.i.* **1** To stay in expectation, as of an anticipated action or event: with *for, until,* etc. **2** To be or remain in readiness. **3** To remain temporarily neglected or undone. **4** To perform duties of personal service; esp. to act as a waiter or waitress. —*v.t.* **5** To stay or remain in expectation of: to *wait* one's turn. **6** *Informal* To put off or postpone: Don't *wait* breakfast for me. —**wait on** (or **upon**) **1** To act as a clerk or attendant to. **2** To go to see; visit. **3** To attend as a result or consequence. —**wait up 1** To delay going to bed in anticipation of someone's arrival or

of something happening. **2** *Informal* To stop until someone catches up. —*n.* The act of waiting, or the time spent in waiting; delay. —**lie in wait** To remain hidden in order to make a surprise attack. [< AF *waitier*] —**Syn.** *v.* **1** abide, linger, remain, tarry.

wait·er (wā′tər) *n.* **1** A man employed to wait on table, as in a restaurant. **2** One who awaits something. **3** A tray for dishes, etc.

wait·ing (wā′ting) *n.* The act of one who waits. —**in waiting** In attendance, esp. at court.

waiting room A room for the use of persons waiting, as for a train, a doctor, etc.

wait·ress (wā′tris) *n.* A woman employed to wait on table, as in a restaurant.

waive (wāv) *v.t.* **waived, waiv·ing 1** To give up or relinquish a claim to. **2** To refrain from insisting upon or taking advantage of; forgo. **3** To put off; postpone; delay. [< OF *gaiver* abandon]

waiv·er (wā′vər) *n. Law* **1** The voluntary relinquishment of a right, privilege, or advantage. **2** The instrument which evidences such relinquishment. [< AF *weyver* abandon, waive]

wake¹ (wāk) *v.* **woke** or **waked, waked** (*Regional* **wok·en**), **wak·ing** *v.i.* **1** To emerge from sleep: often with *up.* **2** To be or remain awake. **3** To become aware or alert. **4** *Regional* To keep watch at night; esp., to hold a wake. —*v.t.* **5** To rouse from sleep or slumber; awake: often with *up.* **6** To rouse or stir up; excite. **7** To make aware; alert. **8** *Regional* To hold a wake over. —*n.* A vigil, esp. a watch over the body of a dead person through the night, just before the burial. [Fusion of OE *wacan* awaken and *wacian* be awake]

wake² (wāk) *n.* **1** The trail of turbulence left by a moving ship, aircraft, etc. **2** Any course passed over. —**in the wake of** Following close behind. [< ON *vök* an opening in ice]

wake·ful (wāk′fəl) *adj.* **1** Not sleeping or sleepy. **2** Watchful; alert. **3** Sleepless; restless: a *wakeful* time. —**wake′ful·ly** *adv.* —**wake′ful·ness** *n.* —**Syn.** **1** awake. **2** cautious, vigilant, wary.

wak·en (wā′kən) *v.t.* **1** To rouse from sleep; awake. **2** To rouse or urge to alertness or activity. —*v.i.* **3** To cease sleeping; wake up. [< OE *wacnian*] —**wak′en·er** *n.*

wake-rob·in (wāk′rob′in) *n.* **1** TRILLIUM. **2** JACK-IN-THE-PULPIT.

Wal·dorf salad (wôl′dôrf) A salad made of chopped celery, apples, walnuts, and mayonnaise. [< the first *Waldorf*-Astoria Hotel, New York City]

wale (wāl) *n.* **1** WELT (def. 1). **2** A ridge or rib on the surface of cloth, as on corduroy. **3** *Usu. pl.* One of several planks on the outer sides of a wooden ship. —*v.t.* **waled, wal·ing 1** To raise wales on by striking. **2** To manufacture (cloth) with ridges or ribs. [< OE *walu*]

walk (wôk) *v.i.* **1** To advance on foot in such a manner that one part of a foot is always on the ground, or, in quadrupeds, that two or more feet are always on the ground. **2** To go on foot for exercise or amusement. **3** To move in a manner suggestive of walking, as certain inanimate objects. **4** To act or live in some manner: to *walk* in peace. **5** In baseball, to advance to first base after being pitched four balls. —*v.t.* **6** To pass through, over, or across at a walk: to *walk* the floor. **7** To lead, ride, or drive at a walk: to *walk* a horse. **8** To force or help to walk. **9** To accompany on a walk: I'll *walk* you to school. **10** To bring to a specified condition by walking. **11** To cause to move with a motion resembling a walk: to *walk* a trunk on its corners. **12** In baseball, to allow to advance to first base by pitching four balls. —**walk away from 1** To outrun or outdo (someone). **2** To sustain little or no injury in an accident. —**walk off 1** To depart, esp. abruptly. **2** To get rid of (fat, etc.) by walking. —**walk off with 1** To win, esp. with little difficulty. **2** To steal. —**walk out** *Informal* **1** To go out on strike. **2** To depart suddenly. —**walk out on** *Informal* To forsake; desert. —**walk over 1** To defeat easily. **2** To treat with contempt. —*n.* **1** The act of walking, as for enjoyment. **2** Manner of walking; gait. **3** A place prepared for walking, as a sidewalk. **4** The distance covered or time spent in walking. **5** A piece of ground set apart for the feeding and exercise of domestic animals. **6** In baseball, the act of walking a batter; also, a being walked. —**walk of life** One's social or financial status. [< OE *wealcan* roll, toss] —**walk′er** *n.* —*Syn. v.* **1** saunter, step, stride, tread.

walk·a·way (wôk′ə·wā′) *n. Informal* A contest won without serious opposition. Also **walk′o′ver** (-ō′vər).

walk·ie-talk·ie (wô′kē·tô′kē) *n.* A portable radio transmitting and receiving set.

walking papers *Informal* Notice of dismissal from employment, office, etc.

walking stick 1 A staff or cane. **2** Any of various insects having legs and body resembling twigs.

walk-on (wôk′on′, -ôn′) *n.* A very small, usu. non-speaking role in a play, etc.

walk-out (wôk′out′) *n. Informal* A workmen's strike.

walk-up (wôk′up′) *Informal n.* **1** An apartment house or building of two or more stories having no elevator. **2** An apartment located higher than the ground floor in such an apartment house.

wall (wôl) *n.* **1** A continuous structure designed to enclose an area, to be the surrounding exterior of a building, or to be a partition between rooms or halls. **2** A fence of stone or brickwork, surrounding or separating yards, fields, etc. **3** *Usu. pl.* A barrier or rampart constructed for defense. **4** A sea wall; levee. **5** A barrier enclosing a cavity, vessel, or receptacle: the *wall* of the abdomen. **6** Something suggestive of a wall: a *wall* of bayonets. —**drive (push or thrust) to the wall** To force (one) to an extremity; crush. —**drive (or send) up the wall** *Informal* To make extremely nervous, tense, etc. —*v.t.* **1** To provide, surround, protect, etc., with or as with a wall or walls. **2** To fill or block with a wall: often with *up.* —*adj.* **1** Of or pertaining to a wall. **2** Hanging from, growing on, or built into a wall. [< OE *weall* < L *vallum* a rampart]

wal·la·by (wol′ə·bē) *n. pl.* **·bies** Any of various small to medium-sized kangaroos. [< Australian *wolaba*]

wall·board (wôl′bôrd′, -bōrd′) *n.* A material of varied composition pressed into sheets and used for walls, ceilings, etc.

wal·let (wol′it) *n.* A small, usu. folding case, as of leather, for holding paper money, cards, etc., and sometimes change, carried in a pocket or purse. [ME *walet*]

wall·eye (wôl′ī′) *n.* **1** An eye with a light-colored or white iris. **2** A kind of strabismus in which the eyes diverge. **3** Any of several walleyed fishes. [Back formation < WALL-EYED]

wall-eyed (wôl′īd′) *adj.* **1** Having a walleye or walleyes. **2** Having large, staring eyes, as certain fish. [< ON *vagl* a film on the eye + *auga* eye]

walleyed pike A large freshwater game fish of North America. Also **walleyed perch.**

wall·flow·er (wôl′flou′ər) *n.* **1** Any of various cultivated perennials related to mustard having fragrant yellow, orange, or red flowers. **2** *Informal* A person who because of unpopularity or shyness does not participate in some social activity, as a party or dance.

Wal·loon (wo·lōōn′) *n.* **1** One of a people of s Belgium and adjoining regions of France. **2** Their language, a dialect of French. —*adj.* Of or pertaining to the Walloons or their dialect.

wal·lop (wol′əp) *Informal v.t.* **1** To beat soundly; thrash. **2** To hit with a hard blow. —*n.* A hard blow. [< AF *waloper*] —**wal′lop·er** *n.*

wal·lop·ing (wol′əp·ing) *Informal adj.* Very large; whopping. —*n.* A beating; whipping or crushing defeat.

wal·low (wol′ō) *v.i.* **1** To roll about, as in mud, snow, etc. **2** To move with a heavy, rolling motion, as a ship in a storm. **3** To indulge oneself wantonly: to *wallow* in sensuality. —*n.* **1** The act of wallowing. **2** A depression or hollow made by wallowing. [< OE *wealwian*] —**wal′low·er** *n.*

wall·pa·per (wôl′pā′pər) *n.* Decorative paper for covering walls. —*v.t.* To cover with wallpaper.

Wall Street 1 A street in lower Manhattan, New York City, famous as the financial center of the U.S. **2** The U.S. financial world.

wall-to-wall (wôl′tə·wôl′) *adj.* Completely covering a floor: *wall-to-wall* carpeting.

wal·nut (wôl′nut′, -nət) *n.* **1** Any of various deciduous trees cultivated as ornamental shade trees and valued for their timber and their edible nuts. **2** The wood or nut of any of these trees. **3** The shagbark or its nut. **4** The color of the wood of any of these trees, esp. of the black walnut, a very dark brown: also **walnut brown.** [< OE *wealh* foreign + *hnutu* a nut]

Black walnut
a. shuck. b. nut.

Wal·pur·gis Night (väl·pŏŏr′gis) The night before May 1, thought to be the occasion of a gathering of witches for demonic rites and orgies. [< St. *Walpurga*, 8th-cent. English missionary in Germany]

wal·rus (wôl′rəs, wol′-) *n.* A very large, seallike mammal of arctic seas, with flexible hind limbs, projecting tusklike canines in the upper jaw, a bushy, bristly mustache on the muzzle, and a very tough hide. —*adj.* **1** Belonging or pertaining to a walrus. **2** Designating a type of bushy mustache drooping at the ends. [< Scand.]

waltz (wôlts) *n.* **1** A dance to music in triple time. **2** Music for or in the style of such a dance. —*v.i.* **1** To dance a waltz. **2** To move quickly: She *waltzed* out of the room. —*v.t.* **3** To cause to waltz. —*adj.* Pertaining to the waltz. [< G *walzen* to waltz, roll] —**waltz′er** *n.*

Walrus

wam·pum (wom′pəm, wôm′-) *n.* **1** Beads made of shells, formerly used as jewelry and currency among North American Indians. **2** *Informal* Money. [< Algon. *wampom(peag),* lit., a white (string of beads)]

wan (won) *adj.* **wan·ner, wan·nest 1** Pale, as from sickness; careworn. **2** Faint; feeble: a *wan* smile. [< OE *wann* dark, gloomy] —**wan′ly** *adv.* —**wan′ness** *n.* —*Syn.* **1** ashen, livid, pallid. **2** weak.

wand (wond) *n.* **1** A slender, flexible rod waved by a magician. **2** Any rod symbolizing authority, as a scepter. **3** A musician's baton. [< ON *vöndr*]

wan·der (won′dər) *v.i.* **1** To travel about without destination or purpose; roam. **2** To go casually or by an indirect route; stroll. **3** To twist or meander. **4** To stray. **5** To deviate in conduct or opinion; go astray. **6** To be delirious. —*v.t.* **7** To wander through or across. [< OE *wandrian*] —**wan′der·er** *n.* —**wan′der·ing·ly** *adv.* —*Syn.* **1** range, rove.

wan·der·lust (won′dər·lust′) *n.* An impulse to travel; restlessness. [< G *wandern* to travel + *Lust* joy]

wane (wān) *v.i.* **waned, wan·ing 1** To diminish in size and brilliance. **2** To decline or decrease gradually. **3** To draw to an end. —*n.* **1** A waning or decreasing. **2** The period of such decrease. —**on the wane** Decreasing; declining. [< OE *wanian* lessen]

wan·gle (wang′gəl) *v.* **·gled, ·gling** *Informal v.t.* **1** To obtain or make by indirect, manipulatory, or dishonest methods; finagle. —*v.i.* **2** To resort to indirect, irregular, or dishonest methods. [?] —**wan′gler** *n.*

Wan·kel engine (väng′kəl, wäng′-) A light, compact type of internal-combustion engine having combustion chambers bounded by the wall of a shallow cylinder and the sides of a triangular piston that rotates in one direction inside it. Also **Wan′kel.** [< F. *Wankel,* 1902–, German inventor]

want (wont, wônt) *v.t.* **1** To feel a desire or wish for. **2** To wish; desire: used with the infinitive: to *want* to help. **3** To be deficient in, esp. to a required or customary extent. **4** To desire to see, speak to, arrest, etc.: He *wants* you on the phone; *wanted* by the police. **5** *Chiefly Brit.* To need; require. —*v.i.* **6** To have need: usu. with *for.* **7** To be needy or destitute. —*n.* **1** Lack; scarcity; shortage. **2** Poverty; destitution. **3** Something lacking; a need or craving. [Prob. < ON *vanta* be lacking] —**want′er** *n.* —*Syn. n.* **1** dearth, deficiency, insufficiency. **2** indigence, privation.

want ad *Informal* A classified advertisement, as in a newspaper, for something wanted, as an employee, a job, a lodging, etc.

want·ing (won'ting, wôn'-) *adj.* 1 Missing; lacking: One juror is still *wanting.* 2 Not coming up to some standard, need, or expectation: He was found *wanting.* —**wanting in** Deficient in. —*prep.* 1 Lacking; without. 2 Less; minus.

wan·ton (won'tən) *adj.* 1 Licentious; lewd; lustful. 2 Heartless or unjust; malicious: *wanton* savagery. 3 Unprovoked; senseless: a *wanton* murder. 4 Extravagant; unrestrained: *wanton* speech. 5 Not bound or tied; loose: *wanton* curls. 6 Capricious; frolicsome. —*v.i.* 1 To act in a wanton manner; be wanton. —*v.t.* 2 To waste or squander carelessly. —*n.* A lewd or licentious person. [< OE *wan* deficient + *tēon* bring up, educate] —**wan'ton·ly** *adv.* —**wan'ton·ness** *n.*

wap·i·ti (wop'ə-tē) *n. pl.* **·tis** or **·ti** A large North American deer; the American elk. [< Algon.] • See ELK.

war (wôr) *n.* 1 Armed strife or conflict between nations or states, or between different parties in the same nation. 2 Any act or state of conflict, struggle, or strife: a *war* against poverty. 3 Military science or strategy. —*v.i.* **warred, war·ring** 1 To wage war; fight or take part in a war. 2 To be in any state of active opposition. —*adj.* Of, pertaining to, used in, or resulting from war. [< OHG *werra* strife, confusion]

War Between the States CIVIL WAR.

war·ble (wôr'bəl) *v.* **·bled, ·bling** *v.t.* 1 To sing (something) with trills and runs or with tremulous vibrations. —*v.i.* 2 To sing with trills, etc. 3 To make a liquid, murmuring sound, as a stream. 4 YODEL. —*n.* The act or sound of warbling. [< OF *werble* a warble]

war·bler (wôr'blər) *n.* 1 One who or that which warbles. 2 Any of a family of small, mostly Old World birds noted for their song. 3 Any of a large and varied family of small, migratory, New World birds, usu. having brilliant springtime plumage and distinctive songs.

war bonnet The ceremonial headdress of the North American Plains Indians.

war crime *Usu. pl.* Any of various crimes committed during or as a result of war, as maltreatment of prisoners, atrocities against civilians, genocide, etc. —**war criminal**

war cry A rallying cry or slogan used by combatants in a war, or by participants in any contest.

ward (wôrd) *n.* 1 In a hospital: **a** A large room for six or more patients. **b** A division for specific illnesses or groups of patients: the children's *ward.* 2 A division of a city for administrative or electoral purposes. 3 *Law* A person, as a minor, who is in the charge of a guardian or court. 4 The act of guarding or the state of being guarded. 5 A division or subdivision of a prison. 6 Any means of defense or protection. —*v.t.* To repel or turn aside, as a thrust or blow: usu. with *off.* [< OE *weardian* to watch, guard]

-ward *suffix* Toward; in the direction of: *upward, homeward.* Also **-wards.** [< OE *-weard*]

war dance A dance of certain tribes before going to war or in celebration of a victory.

war·den (wôr'dən) *n.* 1 A supervisor or custodian of something: a game *warden;* prison *warden.* 2 *Brit.* The head of certain colleges. 3 CHURCHWARDEN (def 1). [< AF *wardein*] —**war'den·ry** (*pl.* **·ries**), **war'den·ship** *n.*

ward·er (wôr'dər) *n.* 1 A guard or sentinel. 2 *Chiefly Brit.* A prison official; warden. [< OF *guarder* guard, keep]

ward heeler *Slang* A hanger-on of a political boss in a ward or other local area, who does minor tasks, canvasses votes, etc.

ward·robe (wôrd'rōb') *n.* 1 A large upright cabinet for wearing apparel. 2 All the garments belonging to any one person. 3 The clothes for a particular season: a spring *wardrobe.* 4 The costumes of a theater, theatrical troupe, motion-picture company, etc.; also, the place where such costumes are kept. [< AF *warder* keep + *robe* a robe]

ward·room (wôrd'rōōm', -rōōm') *n.* 1 On a warship, the eating or living quarters allotted to the commissioned officers, excepting the commander. 2 These officers regarded as a group.

ward·ship (wôrd'ship) *n.* 1 The state of being a ward of a guardian or court. 2 Custody; guardianship.

ware (wâr) *n.* 1 Articles of the same class: used collectively in compounds: *glassware.* 2 *pl.* Articles for sale; merchandise. 3 Pottery; earthenware. [< OE *waru*]

ware·house (wâr'hous') *n.* 1 A storehouse for goods or merchandise. 2 *Chiefly Brit.* A large wholesale shop. —*v.t.* **·housed** (-houzd'), **·hous·ing** (-hou'zing) To place or store in a warehouse.

ware·house·man (wâr'hous'mən) *n. pl.* **·men** (-mən) One who owns or works in a warehouse.

war·fare (wôr'fâr') *n.* 1 The waging or carrying on of war. 2 Struggle; strife.

war game 1 *pl.* Practice maneuvers imitating the conditions of actual warfare. 2 A simulated military conflict organized to test tactical procedures and concepts by discussion and analysis.

war·head (wôr'hed') *n.* The chamber in the nose of a bomb, guided missile, etc., containing an explosive, incendiary, or chemical charge.

war horse 1 A heavy horse used in warfare. 2 *Informal* A veteran of many struggles or contests, esp. political contests.

war·like (wôr'līk') *adj.* 1 Fond of or ready for war. 2 Relating to, used in, or suggesting war. 3 Threatening war. —**Syn.** 1 bellicose, belligerent. 2 martial, military.

war·lock (wôr'lok') *n.* 1 A male witch; sorcerer. 2 A magician or conjurer. [< OE *wær* a covenant + *lēogen* lie, deny]

warm (wôrm) *adj.* 1 Moderately hot; having heat somewhat greater than temperate: *warm* water; a *warm* climate. 2 Imparting heat: a *warm* fire. 3 Imparting or preserving warmth: a *warm* coat. 4 Having the natural temperature of most living persons or animals: *warm* blood. 5 Heated, as from exertion. 6 Ardent; enthusiastic; fervent: *warm* interest. 7 Lively; agitated: a *warm* argument. 8 Cordial; friendly: a *warm* welcome. 9 Amorous; loving: a *warm* glance. 10 Excitable; fiery: a *warm* temper. 11 Having predominating tones of red or yellow. 12 Recently made; fresh: a *warm* trail. 13 Near to finding a hidden object or fact, as in certain games. 14 *Informal* Uncomfortable by reason of annoyances or danger: They made the town *warm* for him. —*v.t.* 1 To make warm. 2 To make ardent or enthusiastic; interest. 3 To fill with kindly feeling. —*v.i.* 4 To become warm. 5 To become ardent or enthusiastic: often with *up* or *to.* 6 To become kindly disposed or friendly: with *to* or *toward.* —**warm up** 1 To warm. 2 To exercise the body, voice, etc., as before a game or performance. 3 To run an engine, etc., in order to attain correct operating temperature. —*n. Informal* A warming or being warm. [< OE *wearm*] —**warm'er, warm'ness** *n.* —**warm'ly** *adv.*

warm-blood·ed (wôrm'blud'id) *adj.* 1 Having a nearly uniform and warm body temperature, whatever the surrounding medium. 2 Enthusiastic; ardent; passionate.

warm-heart·ed (wôrm'här'tid) *adj.* Kind; affectionate.

warming pan A closed metal pan with a long handle, containing live coals or hot water, used for warming a bed.

war·mon·ger (wôr'mung'gər, -mong'-) *n.* One who favors or tries to incite war. —**war'mon·ger·ing** *adj., n.*

warmth (wôrmth) *n.* 1 The state, quality, or sensation of being warm. 2 Ardor or excitement of disposition or feeling. 3 Sympathetic friendliness, affection, or understanding. 4 The effect produced by warm colors.

warm-up (wôrm'up') *n.* The act or an instance of warming up.

warn (wôrn) *v.t.* 1 To make aware of possible harm; caution. 2 To advise; counsel. 3 To give notice in advance. 4 To notify (a person) to go or stay away. —*v.i.* 5 To give warning. [< OE *wearnian*] —**warn'er** *n.*

warn·ing (wôr'ning) *n.* 1 The act of one who warns or the state of being warned. 2 That which warns. —*adj.* Serving as a warning. —**warn'ing·ly** *adv.* —**Syn.** *n.* 2 admonition, advice, recommendation.

War of 1812 A war between the U.S. and Great Britain (1812–15).

War of Independence AMERICAN REVOLUTION.

---

add, āce, câre, pälm; end, ēven; it, īce; odd, ōpen, ôrder; tōōk, pōōl; up, bûrn; ə = a in *above*, u in *focus*; yōō = u in *fuse*; oil; pout; check; go; ring; thin; this; zh, *vision*. < derived from; ? origin uncertain or unknown.

warp (wôrp) *v.t.* **1** To turn or twist out of shape, as by shrinkage or heat. **2** To corrupt; pervert: a mind *warped* by bigotry. **3** *Naut.* To move (a vessel) by hauling on a rope or line fastened to something stationary. —*v.i.* **4** To become turned or twisted out of shape, as wood in drying. **5** To deviate from a correct or proper course: go astray. **6** *Naut.* To move by means of ropes fastened to a pier, anchor, etc. —*n.* **1** The state of being warped, twisted out of shape, or biased. **2** The threads that run the long way of a fabric, crossing the woof. **3** *Naut.* A rope or line used for warping. [< OE *weorpan* to throw] —**warp'er** *n.*

war paint 1 Paint applied to faces and bodies of primitive peoples as a sign of going to war. **2** *Informal* Cosmetics, as rouge, lipstick, etc. **3** *Informal* Official garb or regalia.

war·path (wôr′path′, -päth′) *n.* The route taken by an attacking party of American Indians. —**on the warpath 1** On a warlike expedition. **2** Ready for a fight; thoroughly angry.

war·plane (wôr′plān′) *n.* An airplane used in war.

war·rant (wôr′ənt, wor′-) *n.* **1** *Law* A judicial writ or order authorizing arrest, search, seizure, etc. **2** Something which assures or attests; guarantee. **3** That which gives authority for some course or act; sanction; justification. **4** A certificate of appointment given to a naval or military warrant officer. **5** A document giving a certain authority, esp. for the receipt or payment of money. —*v.t.* **1** To assure or guarantee the quality, accuracy, certainty, or sufficiency of: to *warrant* a title to property. **2** To guarantee the character or fidelity of; pledge oneself for. **3** To guarantee against injury, loss, etc. **4** To be sufficient grounds for; justify. **5** To give legal authority or power to; authorize. **6** *Informal* To say confidently; feel sure. [< AF *warant*] —**war'rant·er** *n.*

war·ran·tee (wôr′ən·tē′, wor′-) *n. Law* The person to whom a warranty is given.

warrant officer See GRADE.

war·rant·or (wôr′ən·tôr, wor′-) *n. Law* One who makes or gives a warranty to another.

war·ran·ty (wôr′ən·tē, wor′-) *n. pl.* **·ties 1** *Law* A guarantee by the seller of property, a product, etc., that whatever is sold is or shall be as represented. **2** An official authorization or warrant. [< AF *warant* a warrant]

war·ren (wôr′ən, wor′-) *n.* **1** A place where rabbits live and breed. **2** Any building or area overcrowded with people. [< AF *warenne* a game park, a rabbit warren]

war·ri·or (wôr′ē·ər, wôr′yər, wor′-) *n.* A man engaged in or experienced in warfare or conflict.

war·ship (wôr′ship′) *n.* Any vessel used in naval combat.

wart (wôrt) *n.* **1** A small, usu. hard, benign excrescence on the skin, caused by a virus. **2** Any of various natural protuberances on certain plants and animals. [< OE *wearte*] —**wart'y** *adj.* (**·i·er, ·i·est**)

wart hog An African wild hog having large tusks and warty excrescences on the face.

war whoop A yell, as made by American Indians, as a signal for attack, etc.

war·y (wâr′ē) *adj.* **war·i·er, war·i·est 1** Carefully watching and guarding. **2** Shrewd; wily. [< OE *wær*] —**war'i·ly** *adv.* —**war'i·ness** *n.*

Wart hog

was (woz, wuz, *unstressed* wəz) First and third person sing., past indicative of BE. [< OE *wæs*]

wash (wosh, wôsh) *v.t.* **1** To cleanse with water or other liquid, as by immersing, scrubbing, etc. **2** To wet or cover with water or other liquid. **3** To flow against or over: a beach *washed* by the ocean. **4** To remove or carry by the use or action of water: with *away, off, out,* etc. **5** To form or wear by erosion. **6** To purify, as gas, by passing through a liquid. **7** To coat with a thin layer of color. **8** To cover with a thin coat of metal. **9** *Mining* **a** To subject (gravel, earth, etc.) to the action of water so as to separate the ore, etc. **b** To separate (ore, etc.) thus. —*v.i.* **10** To wash oneself. **11** To wash clothes, etc., in water or other liquid. **12** To withstand the effects of washing: That calico will *wash.* **13** *Informal* To undergo testing successfully: That story won't *wash.* **14** To flow with a lapping sound, as waves. **15** To be carried away or removed by the use or action of

water: with *away, off, out,* etc. **16** To be eroded by the action of water. —**wash out** *Slang* To fail and be dropped from a course, esp. in military flight training. —*n.* **1** The act or an instance of washing. **2** A number of articles, as of clothing, set apart for washing. **3** Liquid or semiliquid refuse; swill. **4** Any preparation used in washing or coating, as a mouthwash. **5** A paint, as water color, spread lightly on a surface. **6** The breaking of a body of water upon the shore, or the sound made by this. **7** Erosion of soil or earth by the action of running water. **8** Material collected and deposited by water, as along a river bank. **9** Agitation or turbulence in water or air caused by something passing through it. **10** An area washed by a sea or river; a marsh; bog. **11** In the w U.S., the dry bed of a stream. —*adj.* Washable without injury: *wash* fabrics. [< OE *wascan*]

Wash. Washington.

wash·a·ble (wosh′ə·bəl, wôsh′-) *adj.* That can be washed without damage.

wash-and-wear (wosh′ən·wâr′, wôsh′-) *adj.* Designating a garment or fabric so treated as to require little or no ironing after washing.

wash·board (wosh′bôrd′, -bōrd′, wôsh′-) *n.* A board having a corrugated surface on which to rub clothes while washing them.

wash·bowl (wosh′bōl, wôsh′-) *n.* A basin or bowl used for washing the hands and face. Also **wash'ba·sin** (-bā′sən).

wash·cloth (wosh′klôth′, -kloth′, wôsh′-) *n.* A small cloth used for washing the body.

washed-out (wosht′out′, wôsht′-) *adj.* **1** Faded; pale. **2** *Informal* Exhausted; tired.

washed-up (wosht′up′, wôsht′-) *adj. Informal* **1** Finished; done with; through. **2** Exhausted.

wash·er (wosh′ər, wô′shər) *n.* **1** One who washes. **2** *Mech.* A small, flat, perforated disk of metal, rubber, etc., used to make a nut or joint tight. **3** WASHING MACHINE.

wash·er·wom·an (wosh′ər·wŏom′ən, wô′shər-) *n. pl.* **·wom·en** (-wim′in) LAUNDRESS.

wash·ing (wosh′ing, wô′shing) *n.* **1** The act of one who or that which washes. **2** Things (as clothing) washed or to be washed at one time. **3** A thin coating of metal: forks with only one *washing* of silver. **4** That which is obtained by washing: a *washing* of ore.

Washer *def 2*

washing machine A machine that washes and usu. rinses automatically, used to clean clothes, linens, etc.

washing soda SODIUM CARBONATE.

Washington's Birthday (wosh′ing·tənz, wô′shing-) The third Monday in February, a U.S. holiday observed in honor of the anniversary of George Washington's birth, February 22.

wash·out (wosh′out′, wôsh′-) *n.* **1** A considerable erosion of earth by the action of water; also, the excavation thus made. **2** *Slang* A hopeless or total failure.

wash·room (wosh′rŏom′, -rŏom′, wôsh′-) *n.* A restroom or lavatory.

wash·stand (wosh′stand′, wôsh′-) *n.* **1** A stand for washbowl, pitcher, etc. **2** A bathroom sink.

wash·tub (wosh′tub′, wôsh′-) *n.* A usu. stationary tub used for laundry.

wash·wom·an (wosh′wŏom′ən, wôsh′-) *n. pl.* **·wom·en** (-wim′in) LAUNDRESS.

wash·y (wosh′ē, wô′shē) *adj.* **wash·i·er, wash·i·est 1** Watery; diluted. **2** Weak; feeble.

was·n't (woz′ənt, wuz′-) Contraction of *was not.*

wasp (wosp, wôsp) *n.* Any of numerous insects related to bees, having membranous wings, biting mouth parts, and effective stings, and including both social and solitary species. [< OE *wæsp*]

WASP (wosp, wôsp) *n. Slang* A white Protestant American, esp. one of N European ancestry. Also **Wasp.** [< *w(hite) A(nglo)-S(axon) P(rotestant)*] —**WASP'ish, Wasp'ish** *adj.*

wasp·ish (wos′pish, wôs′-) *adj.* **1** Of or like a wasp. **2** Irritable; bad-tempered. —**wasp'ish·ly** *adv.* —**wasp'ish·ness** *n.*

wasp waist A very slim, narrow waist. **—wasp-waist-ed** (wosp′wās′tid, wôsp′-) *adj.*

was·sail (wos′əl, was′-, wo·sāl′) *n.* 1 An ancient toast, esp. to one's health. 2 The spiced drink, usu. ale and wine, prepared for a wassail. 3 An occasion of much drinking; a carousal. —*v.i.* 1 To take part in a wassail; carouse. —*v.t.* 2 To drink the health of; toast. [< ON *ves heill* be whole] **—was′sail·er** *n.*

Was·ser·mann test (wäs′ər·mən) A diagnostic test for syphilis, based on the detection of certain antibodies in the blood. Also **Wassermann reaction.** [< August von *Wassermann*, 1866–1925, German bacteriologist]

wast (wost, *unstressed* wəst) *Archaic* Were: used with THOU.

wast·age (wās′tij) *n.* That which is lost by leakage, waste, etc.

waste (wāst) *v.* **wast·ed, wast·ing** *v.t.* 1 To use or expend thoughtlessly; squander. 2 To make weak or feeble. 3 To use up; consume. 4 To fail to use or take advantage of, as an opportunity. 5 To lay waste; devastate. 6 *Slang* To kill; destroy. —*v.i.* 7 To lose strength, vigor, or bulk: often with *away.* 8 To diminish or dwindle gradually. 9 To pass gradually: said of time. —*n.* 1 Thoughtless or unnecessary expenditure, consumption, etc. 2 Failure to benefit or gain from something, as an opportunity. 3 A desolate or devastated place or region; wilderness; desert. 4 A continuous, gradual wearing away of strength, vigor, or substance. 5 Something discarded or rejected as worthless or unneeded, esp. tangled spun cotton thread. 6 Something that escapes without being used, as steam. 7 Garbage; rubbish; trash. 8 Something excreted from the body, as urine or excrement. **—lay waste** To destroy or devastate. —*adj.* 1 Cast aside as worthless; discarded. 2 Excreted from the body. 3 Not cultivated or inhabited; wild; barren. 4 Superfluous: *waste* energy. 5 Containing or conveying waste products. [< L *vastare* lay waste] **—wast′er** *n.* **—Syn.** *v.* 1 dissipate. 2 debilitate, enfeeble.

waste·bas·ket (wāst′bas′kit, -bäs′-) *n.* A container for paper scraps and other waste. Also **wastepaper basket.**

waste·ful (wāst′fəl) *adj.* 1 Prone to waste; extravagant. 2 Causing waste. **—waste′ful·ly** *adv.* **—waste′ful·ness** *n.*

waste·land (wāst′land′) *n.* A barren or desolate land.

waste·pa·per (wāst′pā′pər) *n.* Paper thrown away as worthless. Also **waste paper.**

waste pipe A pipe for carrying off waste water, etc.

wast·ing (wās′ting) *adj.* 1 Destructive; devastating. 2 Destructive to health; enfeebling.

wast·rel (wās′trəl) *n.* 1 A profligate; spendthrift. 2 An idler or loafer. [Dim. of *waster* one who wastes]

watch (woch, wôch) *v.i.* 1 To look attentively; observe closely. 2 To be on the alert. 3 To wait expectantly for something: with *for.* 4 To do duty as a guard or sentinel. 5 To keep vigil. —*v.t.* 6 To look at attentively; observe. 7 To keep informed concerning. 8 To be alert for; to *watch* one's opportunity. 9 To keep watch over; guard. **—watch out** To be careful. —*n.* 1 Close and continuous attention; careful observation. 2 Service as a guard or sentry. 3 The period of time during which a guard is on duty. 4 The person or persons set to guard or watch. 5 A small, portable timepiece worn on the wrist or carried in a pocket. 6 A vigil or wake. 7 *Naut.* a A spell of duty on board ship, usu. four hours. b The division of a crew on duty during such a period. [< OE *wæccan*] **—watch′er** *n.*

watch·case (woch′kās′, wôch′-) *n.* A metal covering for the mechanism of a watch.

watch·dog (woch′dôg′, -dog′, wôch′-) *n.* 1 A dog kept to guard a building or other property. 2 A person who keeps a vigilant lookout.

watch·ful (woch′fəl, wôch′-) *adj.* Watching carefully; vigilant; alert. **—watch′ful·ly** *adv.* **—watch′ful·ness** *n.*

watch·mak·er (woch′mā′kər, wôch′-) *n.* One who makes or repairs watches.

watch·man (woch′mən, wôch′-) *n. pl.* **·men** (-mən) A man employed to guard a building, etc., at night.

watch·tow·er (woch′tou′ər, wôch′-) *n.* A tower upon which a sentinel is stationed.

watch·word (woch′wûrd′, wôch′-) *n.* 1 PASSWORD. 2 A slogan or maxim.

wa·ter (wô′tər, wot′ər) *n.* 1 The colorless liquid that covers over 70 percent of the earth's surface, is capable of wetting and dissolving many different substances, and is an essential constituent of all organisms. 2 A chemical compound of hydrogen and oxygen which occurs as a solid, a liquid, or a vapor, depending upon its temperature. 3 *Often pl.* Any body of water, as a lake, river, or a sea. 4 Any liquid or liquid secretion of the body, as perspiration, tears, urine, etc. 5 Any preparation of water holding a substance in solution: mineral *water.* 6 An undulating sheen given to certain fabrics, as silk, etc. 7 In commerce and finance, stock issued without an increase of assets or earning power to back it. **—above water** Out of danger, debt, etc.; secure. **—hold water** To be logical, valid, or dependable. **—like water** Freely; prodigally. **—of the first water** Of the finest quality. —*v.t.* 1 To provide (land, plants, etc.) with water, as by sprinkling or irrigating. 2 To provide with water for drinking. 3 To dilute or weaken with water: often with *down.* 4 To give an undulating sheen to the surface of (silk, linen, etc.). 5 To enlarge the number of shares of (a stock company) without increasing the company assets in proportion. —*v.i.* 6 To secrete or discharge water, tears, etc. 7 To fill with saliva, as the mouth, from desire for food. 8 To drink water. [< OE *wæter*] **—wa′ter·er** *n.*

Water Bearer AQUARIUS.

wa·ter·bed (wô′tər·bed′, wot′ər-) *n.* A bed with a water-filled container serving as a mattress.

water bird Any bird living on or near water.

water bomber In Canada, an aircraft equipped to drop water on forest fires. Also **fire bomber.**

wa·ter·borne (wô′tər·bôrn′, -bōrn′, wot′ər-) *adj.* 1 Floating on water. 2 Transported in a ship, etc.

wa·ter·buck (wô′tər·buk′, wot′ər-) *n.* Either of two species of large African antelope, frequenting rivers, etc.

water buffalo A large, slow, oxlike animal of s Asia with curved horns, often domesticated as a draft animal.

water chestnut 1 The hard, nutlike, edible fruit of an aquatic plant native to Asia. 2 The plant itself: also **water cal·trop** (kal′trəp).

wa·ter·clock (wô′tər·klok′, wot′ər-) *n.* A device for measuring time by the fall or flow of water.

water closet TOILET (defs. 1 & 2).

wa·ter·col·or (wô′tər·kul′ər, wot′ər-) *n.* 1 A pigment or coloring matter prepared for painting with water as the medium. 2 A picture or painting done in watercolors. Also **water color.** —*adj.* Of or painted with watercolors.

wa·ter·cool (wô′tər·kōōl′, wot′ər-) *v.t.* To cool by means of water, as by a jacket or pipe.

water cooler A vessel or apparatus for cooling and dispensing drinking water.

wa·ter·course (wô′tər·kôrs′, -kōrs′, wot′ər-) *n.* 1 A stream of water, as a river or brook. 2 A channel for a stream of water.

wa·ter·craft (wô′tər·kraft′, -kräft′, wot′ər-) *n.* 1 Skill in sailing boats or in aquatic sports. 2 A boat or ship. 3 Boats and ships collectively.

wa·ter·cress (wô′tər·kres′, wot′ər-) *n.* An edible perennial herb of the mustard family, usu. growing in running water and cultivated for use as salad.

water cure HYDROPATHY.

wa·ter·fall (wô′tər·fôl′, wot′ər-) *n.* A fall of water over a precipice.

wa·ter·fowl (wô′tər·foul′, wot′ər-) *n. pl.* **·fowl** or **·fowls** A water bird, esp. a swimming game bird.

wa·ter·front (wô′tər·frunt′, wot′ər-) *n.* 1 Property abutting on or overlooking a natural body of water. 2 That part of a town which fronts on a body of water, usu. a commercial area of docks, warehouses, etc.

water gap A deep ravine in a mountain ridge giving passage to a stream.

water gas A poisonous fuel gas containing hydrogen and carbon monoxide produced by forcing steam over white-hot coke.

add, āce, cåre, pälm; end, ēven; it, īce; odd, ōpen, ôrder; tōōk, pōōl; up, bûrn; ə = *a* in *above, u* in *focus;* yōō = *u* in *fuse;* oil; pout; check; go; ring; thin; this; zh, *vision.* < derived from; ? origin uncertain or unknown.

wa·ter·gate (wô'tər·gāt', wot'ər-) n. FLOODGATE.

water gauge A gauge for indicating the level of water in a boiler, reservoir, etc.

wa·ter·glass (wô'tər·glas', -gläs', wot'ər-) n. 1 A drinking glass. 2 WATER GAUGE. 3 A glass-bottomed tube for examining objects lying under water. 4 A water-soluble silicate, as of sodium or potassium, used as an adhesive, for preserving eggs, etc. Also **water glass.**

water hole A pond or pool of water, esp. one used by animals for drinking.

water ice Chiefly Brit. SHERBET.

watering place 1 A place where water can be obtained, as a spring. 2 Chiefly Brit. A health resort having mineral springs; also, a pleasure resort near the water.

water jacket A casing containing water for cooling, as one surrounding a cylinder of an internal-combustion engine.

water level 1 The level of water in a body of water. 2 A ship's waterline.

wa·ter·lil·y (wô'tər·lil'ē, wot'ər-) n. pl. **·lil·ies** Any of various aquatic plants with large floating leaves and showy white or colored flowers.

wa·ter·line (wô'tər·līn', wot'ər-) n. 1 Naut. **a** A line on the hull of a ship which shows where the water surface reaches. **b** Short, horizontal lines on a ship's hull which correspond with the surface of the water when the ship is unloaded, partly loaded, or fully loaded. 2 Any line or mark showing to what level water has risen.

Waterlily

wa·ter·logged (wô'tər·lôgd', -logd', wot'ər-) adj. 1 So saturated or filled with water as to be unmanageable and barely able to float, as a ship, etc. 2 Soaked with water.

Wa·ter·loo (wô'tər·loo, wô'tər·loo') n. A decisive defeat, usu. in the phrase **meet one's Waterloo.** [< Waterloo, Belgium, scene of Napoleon's final defeat, 1815]

water main A main pipe in a system of pipes for carrying water, esp. one laid underground.

wa·ter·man (wô'tər·mən, wot'ər-) n. pl. **·men** (-mən) A boatman or oarsman.

wa·ter·mark (wô'tər·märk', wot'ər-) n. 1 WATERLINE (def. 2). 2 A mark or design made in paper by pressure while the paper is still in a pulpy state; also, the metal pattern which produces these markings. —v.t. 1 To impress (paper) with a watermark. 2 To impress (a mark or design) as a watermark.

wa·ter·mel·on (wô'tər·mel'ən, wot'ər-) n. 1 A gourd cultivated for its large edible fruit, having a juicy, sweet, red or pink pulp. 2 The fruit.

water mill A mill operated by waterpower.

water moccasin A venomous, brownish pit viper, found along rivers, etc., of the SE U.S.

water nymph Gk. & Rom. Myth. A nymph dwelling in a stream, lake, etc.

water of crystallization Water that combines with certain salts to form usu. unstable hydrates of distinct crystalline structure. Also **water of hydration.**

water ouzel Any of various small diving birds related to thrushes.

water pipe 1 A pipe for carrying water. 2 HOOKAH.

water polo A game in which two teams of swimmers attempt to take or throw an inflated ball across each other's goal line.

wa·ter·pow·er (wô'tər·pou'ər, wot'ər-) n. The power derived from the kinetic energy of flowing or falling water, used for driving machinery.

wa·ter·proof (wô'tər·proof', wot'ər-) adj. 1 WATERTIGHT. 2 Coated with some substance, as rubber, which prevents the passage of water. —n. 1 Waterproof fabric. 2 Brit. A raincoat or other waterproof garment. —v.t. To render waterproof.

water rat 1 MUSKRAT. 2 Any of various rodents that frequent lakes, streams, etc. 3 Slang A waterfront tough or thief.

wa·ter·shed (wô'tər·shed', wot'ər-) n. 1 A ridge of high land that divides two areas drained by different river sys-

tems. 2 The whole region from which a river receives its supply of water. 3 A decisive turning point affecting outlook, actions, etc.

wa·ter·side (wô'tər·sīd', wot'ər-) n. The shore of a body of water; the water's edge.

wa·ter·ski (wô'tər·skē', wot'ər-) v.i. **-skied, -ski·ing** To glide over water on skilike runners (**water skis**) while being towed by a motorboat. —**wa'ter·ski'er** n.

water snake 1 Any of various harmless North American snakes that live chiefly in water. 2 Any aquatic snake.

wa·ter·soak (wô'tər·sōk', wot'ər-) v.t. To saturate with water.

water softener A substance that removes dissolved minerals from water, as by precipitation, absorption, etc.

water spaniel A breed of spaniel having a water-resistant coat, used for retrieving waterfowl.

wa·ter·spout (wô'tər·spout', wot'ər-) n. 1 A moving, whirling column of spray and mist, resulting from a tornado at sea, on a lake, etc. 2 A pipe for the free discharge of water.

water sprite A nymph, sprite, etc., living in water.

water table The surface marking the upper level of a water-saturated subterranean zone of permeable rock.

wa·ter·tight (wô'tər·tīt', wot'ər-) adj. 1 So closely made that water cannot enter or leak through. 2 That cannot be misunderstood, found illegal or in error, etc.: a water tight contract. —**wat'er·tight'ness** n.

water tower 1 A tank or tower, used as a reservoir and to maintain pressure in a system of water distribution. 2 A vehicular towerlike structure from which water can be played on a burning building from a great height.

water vapor The vapor of water, esp. below the boiling point, as in the atmosphere.

wa·ter·way (wô'tər·wā', wot'ər-) n. A river, channel, or other stream of water, esp. when navigable by boats and ships.

water wheel A wheel designed to be turned by flowing water. • See UNDERSHOT.

water wings An inflatable device used to keep a beginning swimmer afloat.

wa·ter·works (wô'tər·wûrks', wot'ər-) n.pl. A system of buildings, pipes, pumps, etc. for furnishing a water supply, esp. for a city.

wa·ter·worn (wô'tər·wôrn', -wōrn', wot'ər-) adj. Worn smooth by running or falling water.

wa·ter·y (wô'tər·ē, wot'ər·ē) adj. 1 Of, containing, or like water. 2 Diluted. 3 Overly liquid; thin. 4 Tearful. 5 Weak; vapid; insipid. —**wa'ter·i·ness** n.

watt (wot) n. A unit of power equivalent to one joule per second, or about 1/746 of a horsepower. [< J. Watt, 1736–1819, Scottish engineer]

wat·tage (wot'ij) n. An amount of power, esp. electric power, expressed in watts.

watt·hour (wot'our') n. Energy equivalent to one watt acting for one hour.

watt-hr. watt-hour(s).

wat·tle (wot'l) n. 1 A framework of poles and twigs woven together, used for walls, fences, etc. 2 The poles and twigs used for this. 3 A fold of skin, often wrinkled and brightly colored, hanging from the throat of a bird or lizard. 4 Any one of various acacias of Australia, Tasmania, and South Africa. —v.t. **·tled, ·tling** 1 To weave or twist, as twigs, into a network. 2 To form,, as a fence, by intertwining flexible twigs. 3 To bind together with wattles. [< OE watul]

Wattle of turkey

watt·me·ter (wot'mē'tər) n. An instrument for measuring electric power in watts.

wave (wāv) v. **waved, wav·ing** v.i. 1 To move freely back and forth or up and down, as a flag in the wind. 2 To signal by moving something back and forth or up and down. 3 To have an undulating shape or form: Her hair waves. —v.t. 4 To cause to wave: to wave a banner. 5 To flourish, as a weapon. 6 To give a wavy appearance to or form into waves: to wave one's hair. 7 To signal by waving something: He waved me aside. 8 To express by waving something: to *wave* farewell. —*n.* **1** A ridge or undulation moving on the surface of a liquid. **2** A similar undulation on a freely moving surface: *waves* in the tall grass. **3** A curve or curl in the hair. **4** A curved pattern or shape, as on watered silk. **5** A back-and-forth or up-and-down motion, as with the hand. **6** A more or less prolonged meteorological condition: a heat *wave*. **7** An upsurge of something: a crime *wave;* a *wave* of emotion. **8** A surging movement, as of a mass or group: a *wave* of refugees. **9** *Usu. pl.* A large body of water. **10** *Physics* A periodic disturbance propagated through a medium, characterized by a function of time that defines its frequency, amplitude, phase, and velocity. [< OE *wafian*] —**wav'er** *n.*

Wave (wāv) *n.* A member of the **WAVES**, the women's division of the U.S. Navy. [< *W(omen) A(ppointed for) V(oluntary) E(mergency) S(ervice)*]

wave·form (wāv'fôrm') *n.* **1** The curve produced by recording, as on a graph, the varying dimensions of a wave through successive oscillations. **2** A mathematical formula for such a curve.

wave·length (wāv'length') *n. Physics* The distance, along the line of propagation, between two points of like phase in consecutive cycles of a wave.

wave·let (wāv'lit) *n.* A little wave.

wa·ver (wā'vər) *v.i.* **1** To move one way and the other; flutter. **2** To be uncertain; vacillate. **3** To show signs of falling back or giving way; falter. **4** To flicker; gleam. —*n.* A wavering. [< OE *wafian* to wave] —**wa'ver·er** *n.* —**wa'ver·ing·ly** *adv.* —**Syn. 1** oscillate, quiver, shake. **2** hesitate.

wav·y (wā'vē) *adj.* **wav·i·er, wav·i·est** Full of waves or curves, as hair, lines, etc. —**wav'i·ly** *adv.* —**wav'i·ness** *n.*

wax¹ (waks) *n.* **1** BEESWAX. **2** Any of various pliable plant and animal substances that are insoluble in water, that burn in air, or otherwise resemble beeswax. **3** A solid mineral substance resembling wax, as paraffin. **4** SEALING WAX. **5** A waxlike commercial product, used for polishing furniture, floors, etc. —*v.t.* To coat or polish with wax. —*adj.* Made of or pertaining to wax. [< OE *weax*]

wax² (waks) *v.i.* **waxed, waxed** (*Archaic* **wax·en**), **wax·ing 1** To increase in size: said esp. of the moon. **2** To become: to *wax* angry. [< OE *weaxan* grow]

wax bean A pale yellow variety of string bean.

wax·ber·ry (waks'ber'ē) *n. pl.* **·ries 1** The wax myrtle, or bayberry. **2** Its fruit.

wax·en (wak'sən) *adj.* **1** Consisting of or covered with wax. **2** Pale; pallid: a *waxen* complexion.

wax myrtle Any of various North American shrubs or small trees having fragrant leaves and small berries covered with white wax, often used in making candles.

wax palm Either of two South American palms yielding waxes widely used to make polishes, cosmetics, etc.

wax paper Paper coated with paraffin to render it moistureproof. Also **waxed paper.**

wax·wing (waks'wing') *n.* Any of various crested passerine birds having soft, mainly brown plumage, and red, waxy tips on the wings.

wax·work (waks'wûrk') *n.* **1** Work produced in wax; esp., life-size figures of notable persons. **2** *pl.* An exhibition of such figures. —**wax'work'er** *n.*

wax·y (wak'sē) *adj.* **wax·i·er, wax·i·est 1** Resembling wax in appearance, consistency, etc. **2** Pale; pallid, as wax. **3** Made of, abounding in, or polished with wax. —**wax'i·ness** *n.*

Cedar waxwing

way (wā) *n.* **1** Direction; route: Which *way* is the city? **2** A path, course, road, etc., leading from one place to another. **3** Space or room to advance or work: Make *way* for the king. **4** Distance in general: a little *way* off. **5** Direction in general: Look the other *way.* **6** Passage from one place to another: on our *way* to Europe. **7** A customary or habitual manner or style of acting or being: Do it her *way.* **8** A plan of action; procedure; method: In what *way* will you accomplish this? **9** Respect; point; particular: He erred in two

ways. **10** A course of life or experience: the *way* of sin. **11** Desire; wish: to get one's *way.* **12** *Informal* State or condition: to be in a bad *way.* **13** The range of one's experience or observation: An accident threw it in his *way.* **14** *Informal* Neighborhood or locality: out our *way.* **15** *Naut.* **a** Forward motion; headway. **b** *pl.* A tilted framework of timbers upon which a ship slides when launched. —**by the way** In passing; incidentally. —**by way of 1** With the object or purpose of; to serve as: *by way of* introduction. **2** Through; via. —**give way (to) 1** To yield or submit. **2** To collapse. —**go out of one's** (or **the**) **way** To inconvenience oneself. —**in the way** In a position that impedes or hinders. —**out of the way 1** In a position so as not to hinder or impede. **2** Out of the usual or convenient location or route. **3** Unusual. **4** Improper; wrong: Has he done anything *out of the way?* —**under way** In motion; making progress. —*adv. Informal* All the distance to: He went *way* to Denver. [< OE *weg*]

way·bill (wā'bil') *n.* A statement listing or giving instructions concerning the shipping of goods.

way·far·er (wā'fâr'ər) *n.* One who travels, esp. on foot. —**way'far'ing** *n., adj.*

way·lay (wā'lā') *v.t.* **·laid, ·lay·ing 1** To lie in ambush for and attack. **2** To accost on the way. —**way'lay'er** *n.*

way-out (wā'out') *adj. Slang* FAR-OUT.

-ways *suffix of adverbs* In a (specified) manner, direction, or position: *noways, sideways.*

ways and means 1 Means or methods of accomplishing an end or defraying expenses. **2** In legislation, methods of raising funds for the use of the government: also **Ways and Means.**

way·side (wā'sīd') *adj.* Pertaining to or near the side of a road. —*n.* The side or edge of the road or highway.

way station Any station between principal stations, esp. on a railroad.

way train A train stopping at way stations.

way·ward (wā'wərd) *adj.* **1** Willful; headstrong. **2** Not predictable; erratic. [< ME *awei* away + -WARD] —**way'ward·ly** *adv.* —**way'ward·ness** *n.* —**Syn. 1** disobedient, perverse, refractory, stubborn. **2** capricious.

WbN west by north.

WbS west by south.

w.c. water closet; without charge.

W.C.T.U. Women's Christian Temperance Union.

we (wē) *pron. pl.* **1** The persons speaking or writing, or a single person writing or speaking when referring to himself and one or more others. **2** A single person denoting himself, as a sovereign, editor, writer, or speaker, when wishing to give his words a formal or impersonal character. [< OE]

weak (wēk) *adj.* **1** Lacking in physical strength, energy, or vigor; feeble. **2** Incapable of resisting stress or supporting weight: a *weak* wall. **3** Lacking in strength of will or stability of character. **4** Not effective, forceful, or convincing: *weak* reasoning. **5** Lacking in power, intensity, etc.: a *weak* voice. **6** Lacking a specified component or components in the usual or proper amount: *weak* tea. **7** Lacking the power or ability to function properly: a *weak* heart. **8** Lacking mental or intellectual capability. **9** Lacking skill, experience, etc.: a *weak* player. **10** Lacking in power, influence, or authority: a *weak* state. **11** Deficient in some specified thing or quality: *weak* in languages. **12** *Gram.* Denoting a verb in English or other Germanic languages that forms its past tense and past participle by adding *d* or *t* rather than by vowel changes. **13** *Phonet.* Unstressed; unaccented, as a syllable or sound. **14** In prosody, indicating a verse ending in which the accent falls on a word or syllable otherwise without stress. **15** Characterized by declining prices: said of the stock market. [< ON *veikr*] —**Syn. 1** slight, puny, enfeebled, frail.

weak·en (wē'kən) *v.t. & v.i.* To make or become weak or weaker. —**weak'en·er** *n.* —**Syn.** debilitate, enervate, enfeeble, sap.

weak·fish (wēk'fish') *n. pl.* **·fish** or **·fish·es** Any of various marine food fishes, esp. several troutlike species of E U.S. coastal waters.

weak-kneed (wēk′nēd′) *adj.* **1** Weak in the knees. **2** Without resolution, strong purpose, or energy; spineless.

weak-ling (wēk′ling) *n.* A feeble person or animal. —*adj.* Weak.

weak-ly (wēk′lē) *adj.* **-li-er, -li-est** Sickly; feeble; weak. —*adv.* In a weak manner. —**weak′li-ness** *n.*

weak-mind-ed (wēk′mīn′did) *adj.* **1** Not resolute or firm; indecisive. **2** FEEBLE-MINDED. —**weak′mind′ed-ly** *adv.* —**weak′mind′ed-ness** *n.*

weak-ness (wēk′nis) *n.* **1** The state, condition, or quality of being weak. **2** A characteristic indicating feebleness. **3** A slight failing; a fault. **4** A strong liking or fondness; also, the object of such a liking.

weal[1] (wēl) *n.* *Archaic* A sound or prosperous condition. [< OE *wela*]

weal[2] (wēl) *n.* A welt, as from a blow. [Var. of WALE]

weald (wēld) *n.* *Chiefly Brit.* **1** A forest area. **2** An open region; down. [OE, a forest]

wealth (welth) *n.* **1** A large amount of money or property; riches. **2** The state of being rich. **3** Great abundance of anything: a *wealth* of learning. **4** *Econ.* **a** All material objects which have economic utility. **b** All property possessing a monetary value. [ME *welthe* < *wele* weal]

wealth-y (wel′thē) *adj.* **wealth-i-er, wealth-i-est 1** Possessing wealth; affluent. **2** More than sufficient; abounding. —**wealth′i-ly** *adv.* —**wealth′i-ness** *n.* —**Syn. 1** rich, prosperous, well-to-do, well-off.

wean (wēn) *v.t.* **1** To transfer (the young of any mammal) from dependence on its mother's milk to another form of nourishment. **2** To free from usu. undesirable habits or associations: usu. with *from.* [< OE *wenian* accustom] —**wean′er** *n.*

wean-ling (wēn′ling) *adj.* Freshly weaned. —*n.* A child or animal newly weaned.

weap-on (wep′ən) *n.* **1** Any implement of war or combat, as a sword, gun, etc. **2** Any means that may be used against an adversary. **3** Any defensive organ or part of an animal or plant, as a claw, tooth, thorn, etc. [< OE *wæpen*] —**weap′on-ry** (-rē) *n.*

wear (wâr) *v.* **wore, worn, wear-ing** *v.t.* **1** To have on the person as a garment, ornament, etc. **2** To have on the person habitually: He *wears* a derby. **3** To have in one's aspect; exhibit: He *wears* a scowl. **4** To have as a characteristic: She *wears* her hair short. **5** To display or fly: A ship *wears* its colors. **6** To impair or consume by use or constant action. **7** To cause by scraping, rubbing, etc.: to *wear* a hole in a coat. **8** To bring to a specified condition by wear: to *wear* a sleeve to tatters. **9** To exhaust; weary. —*v.i.* **10** To be impaired or diminished gradually by use, rubbing, etc. **11** To withstand the effects of use, handling, etc.: These shoes *wear* well. **12** To remain sound or interesting over a period of time: a friendship that *wore* well. **13** To become as specified from use or attrition: His patience is *wearing* thin. **14** To pass gradually: with *on* or *away.* **15** To have an unpleasant or exhausting effect. —**wear down 1** To make or become less through friction, use, etc. **2** To tire out; exhaust. **3** To overcome the resistance of by constant pressure, harassment, etc. —**wear off** To diminish gradually. —**wear out 1** To make or become worthless by use. **2** To waste or use up gradually. **3** To tire or exhaust. —*n.* **1** The act of wearing, or the state of being worn. **2** Material or articles of dress to be worn: often in combination: *footwear, underwear.* **3** Vogue; fashion. **4** Destruction or impairment from use or time. **5** Capacity to resist use or time; durability. —**wear and tear** Loss or damage from use over a period of time. [< OE *werian*] —**wear′er** *n.*

wear-ing (wâr′ing) *adj.* **1** Fatiguing; exhausting: a *wearing* day. **2** Capable of being, or designed to be, worn. —**wear′ing-ly** *adv.*

wearing apparel Clothing; garments.

wea-ri-some (wir′ē-səm) *adj.* Causing fatigue; tiresome. —**wea′ri-some-ly** *adv.* —**wea′ri-some-ness** *n.* —**Syn.** annoying, irksome, tedious, vexatious.

wea-ry (wir′ē) *adj.* **-ri-er, -ri-est 1** Worn out; tired; fatigued. **2** Discontented or bored: usu. with *of*: *weary* of life. **3** Indicating or characteristic of fatigue: a *weary* sigh. **4** Causing fatigue; wearisome. —*v.t.* & *v.i.* **-ried, -ry-ing** To make or become weary. [< OE *wērig*] —**wea′ri-ly** *adv.* —**wea′ri-ness** *n.*

wea-sel (wē′zəl) *n.* **1** Any of certain small, slender, usu. nocturnal carnivorous mammals. **2** A sly or treacherous person. —*v.i.* **-seled, -sel-ing** *Informal* **1** To fail to fulfill a promise, etc.; renege: with *out.* **2** To speak ambiguously; equivocate. [< OE *wesle*]

Weasel

weath-er (weth′ər) *n.* **1** The general atmospheric condition, as regards temperature, moisture, winds, or related phenomena. **2** Unpleasant atmospheric conditions. —**keep one's weather eye open** *Informal* To be alert. —**under the weather** *Informal* **1** Ailing; ill. **2** Suffering from a hangover. **3** Drunk. —*v.t.* **1** To expose to the action of the weather. **2** To discolor, crumble, or otherwise affect by action of the weather. **3** To pass through and survive, as a crisis. **4** *Naut.* To pass to windward of: to *weather* Cape Fear. —*v.i.* **5** To undergo changes from exposure to the weather. **6** To resist the action of the weather. —*adj.* Facing the wind. [< OE *weder*]

weath-er-beat-en (weth′ər-bēt′n) *adj.* **1** Bearing or showing the effects of exposure to weather. **2** Tanned, wrinkled, etc., by or as if by exposure to weather, as a face.

weath-er-board (weth′ər-bôrd′, -bōrd′) *n.* CLAPBOARD. —*v.t.* To fasten weatherboards on.

weath-er-bound (weth′ər-bound′) *adj.* Detained by unfavorable weather, as a ship.

weath-er-cock (weth′ər-kok′) *n.* **1** A weathervane, properly one in the form of a cock. **2** A fickle person or variable thing.

weath-er-glass (weth′ər-glas′, -gläs′) *n.* An instrument for indicating the weather, esp. a barometer.

weath-er-man (weth′ər-man′) *n. pl.* **-men** (-men′) *n.* A person who reports on daily weather conditions.

Weathercock

weather map *Meteorol.* A map or chart giving weather conditions for a given region and specified time.

weath-er-proof (weth′ər-prōōf′) *adj.* Capable of withstanding snow, rain, wind, etc., without appreciable deterioration. —*v.t.* To make weatherproof.

weather station A station or office where meteorological observations are made.

weath-er-strip (weth′ər-strip′) *n.* A narrow strip of material to be placed over or in crevices, as at doors and windows, to exclude drafts, rain, etc. Also **weath′er-strip′-ping.** —*v.t.* **-stripped, -strip-ping** To equip or fit with weatherstrips.

weath-er-vane (weth′ər-vān′) *n.* A vane that indicates the direction in which the wind is blowing.

weath-er-wise (weth′ər-wīz′) *adj.* Experienced in observing or predicting the weather, public opinion, etc.

weath-er-worn (weth′ər-wôrn′, -wōrn′) *adj.* Worn by exposure to the weather.

weave (wēv) *v.* **wove** or *esp. for defs. 7, 8, & 11* **weaved, wo-ven** or *esp. for defs. 7, 8, & 11* **weaved, weav-ing** *v.t.* **1** To make (a fabric) by interlacing threads or yarns, esp. on a loom. **2** To interlace (threads or yarns) into a fabric. **3** To form by interlacing strands, strips, twigs, etc.: to *weave* a basket. **4** To produce by combining details or elements: to *weave* a story. **5** To twist or introduce into: to *weave* ribbons through one's hair. **6** To spin (a web). **7** To make by going from one side to another: to *weave* one's way through a crowd. **8** To direct (a car, etc.) in this manner. —*v.i.* **9** To make cloth, etc., by weaving. **10** To become woven or interlaced. **11** To make one's way by moving from one side to another. —*n.* A particular method, style, or pattern of weaving. [< OE *wefan*]

weav-er (wē′vər) *n.* **1** One who weaves. **2** A person whose job is weaving. **3** WEAVERBIRD.

weav-er-bird (wē′vər-bûrd′) *n.* Any of various finchlike birds of Asia, Africa, and Australia, that weave intricate nests.

web (web) *n.* **1** Fabric being woven on a loom. **2** The network of delicate threads spun by a spider or by certain insect larvae. **3** An artfully contrived trap or snare. **4** Any complex network of interwoven parts, elements, etc.: a *web* of lies; a *web* of highways. **5** *Zool.* A membrane connecting the digits, as in aquatic birds, frogs, etc. **6** The vane of a feather. **7** *Anat.* A membrane or tissue. **8** A plate or sheet, as of metal, connecting the ribs, frames, etc., of a structure. **9** *Archit.* The part of a ribbed vault between the ribs. **10** A large roll of paper, as for use in a web press. —*v.t.* **webbed, web·bing 1** To provide with a web. **2** To cover or surround with a web; entangle. [< OE]

webbed (webd) *adj.* **1** Having a web. **2** Having the digits united by a membrane.

web·bing (web′ing) *n.* **1** A woven strip of strong fiber, used for safety belts, upholstery, etc. **2** Anything forming a web or weblike structure.

we·ber (vā′bər, wē′bər) *n.* A unit equal to the magnetic flux that, interacting with a single turn of wire, induces a potential difference of one volt as it is uniformly reduced to zero in one second. [< W. E. *Weber*, 1804–91, German physicist]

web·foot (web′fŏŏt′) *n.* **1** A foot with webbed toes. **2** A bird or animal having such feet. —**web′-foot′ed** *adj.*

web press A printing press which is fed from a continuous roll of paper instead of sheets.

wed (wed) *v.* **wed·ded, wed·ded** or **wed, wed·ding** *v.t.* **1** To take as one's husband or wife; marry. **2** To join in wedlock. **3** To unite or join closely: He is *wedded* to his job. —*v.i.* **4** To take a husband or wife; marry. [< OE *weddian* to pledge]

we'd (wēd) Contraction of *we had* or *we would*.

Wed. Wednesday.

wed·ding (wed′ing) *n.* **1** The ceremony of a marriage. **2** The anniversary of a marriage: golden *wedding*. [< OE *weddian* to pledge]

wedge (wej) *n.* **1** A V-shaped piece of metal, wood, etc., used for splitting wood, raising weights, etc. **2** Anything in the form of a wedge. **3** Any action which facilitates policy, entrance, intrusion, etc. **4** An iron golf club with the face at an angle for lofting the ball. —*v.* **wedged, wedg·ing** *v.t.* **1** To force apart with a wedge. **2** To fix in place with a wedge. **3** To crowd or squeeze (something). —*v.i.* **4** To force oneself or itself in like a wedge. [< OE *wecg*]

wedg·ie (wej′ē) *n.* A woman's shoe having a wedge-shaped piece making a solid, flat sole from heel to toe.

Wedg·wood (wej′wŏŏd′) *n.* A fine English pottery, characterized by small, white, classical figures in cameo relief against a tinted background. [< J. *Wedgwood*, 1730–95, English potter]

wed·lock (wed′lok) *n.* The state of being married. [< OE *wedd* a pledge + *-lāc*, suffix of nouns of action]

Wednes·day (wenz′dē, -dā) *n.* The fourth day of the week. [< OE *Wōdnesdæg* day of Woden]

wee (wē) *adj.* **we·er, we·est** Very small; tiny. [< OE *wēg* a quantity]

weed[1] (wēd) *n.* **1** Any unwanted or unsightly plant, esp. one that hinders the growth of cultivated plants. **2** *Informal* **a** Tobacco. **b** A cigarette or cigar. **c** Marihuana; also, a marihuana cigarette. **3** A thin, ungainly person. —*v.t.* **1** To pull up and remove weeds from. **2** To remove (a weed): often with *out.* **3** To remove (anything regarded as harmful or undesirable): with *out.* **4** To rid of anything harmful or undesirable. —*v.i.* **5** To remove weeds, etc. [< OE *wēod*] —**weed′er** *n.*

weed[2] (wēd) *n.* *Usu. pl.* Mourning garb, as that worn by widows. **2** A black band, as of crepe, worn by a man on his hat or sleeve as a token of mourning. [< OE *wǣd* garment]

weed·y (wē′dē) *adj.* **weed·i·er, weed·i·est 1** Abounding in weeds. **2** Of or pertaining to a weed or weeds. **3** Gawky; lanky: a *weedy* youth. —**weed′i·ly** *adv.* —**weed′i·ness** *n.*

week (wēk) *n.* **1** A period of seven successive days, esp. one beginning with Sunday. **2** The period within a week devoted to work: a 35-hour *week.* —**week in, week out** Every week. [< OE *wicu, wice*]

week·day (wēk′dā′) *n.* **1** Any day of the week except Sunday. **2** Any day other than those of the weekend.

week·end (wēk′end′) *n.* The time from Friday evening or Saturday to the following Monday morning. —*adj.* Of, for, or on a weekend. —*v.i.* To pass the weekend. —**week′end′er** *n.*

week·ly (wēk′lē) *adj.* **1** Of, pertaining to, or lasting a week. **2** Done or occurring once a week. **3** Reckoned by the week. —*adv.* **1** Once a week. **2** Every week. —*n. pl.* **·lies** A publication issued once a week.

ween (wēn) *v.t. & v.i. Archaic* To suppose; guess; fancy. [< OE *wēnan* think]

weep (wēp) *v.* **wept, weep·ing** *v.i.* **1** To manifest grief or other strong emotion by shedding tears. **2** To mourn; lament: with *for.* **3** To give out or shed liquid in drops. —*v.t.* **4** To weep for; mourn. **5** To shed (tears, or drops of other liquid). —*n.* **1** The act of weeping, or a fit of tears. **2** An exhudation of liquid; moisture. [< OE *wēpan*] —**weep′er** *n.* —**Syn.** *v.* **1** cry, sob. **2** bewail, grieve.

weep·ing (wē′ping) *adj.* **1** That weeps. **2** Having branches that curve downward.

weeping willow A willow, originally from China, noted for its long, drooping branches.

wee·vil (wē′vəl) *n.* Any of numerous small beetles with elongated snoutlike heads, often having larvae destructive to cotton, grain, fruit, etc. [< OE *wifel* a beetle] —**wee′vil·y, wee′vil·ly** *adj.*

Weeping willow

weft (weft) *n.* **1** The cross threads in a web of cloth; woof. **2** A woven fabric; web. [< OE]

weigh (wā) *v.t.* **1** To determine the weight of. **2** To balance or hold in the hand so as to estimate weight. **3** To measure (a quantity or quantities of something) according to weight: with *out.* **4** To consider or evaluate carefully: to *weigh* one's words. **5** To raise or hoist: now only in the phrase **weigh anchor.** —*v.i.* **6** To have a specified weight: She *weighs* ninety pounds. **7** To have influence or importance: The girl's testimony *weighed* heavily with the jury. **8** To be burdensome or oppressive: with *on* or *upon:* What *weighs* on your mind? **9** *Naut.* **a** To raise anchor. **b** To begin to sail. —**weigh down 1** To press or force down by weight or heaviness. **2** To burden or oppress. —**weigh in** To be weighed before a fight or other athletic contest. [< OE *wegan* weigh, carry, lift] —**weigh′er** *n.*

weight (wāt) *n.* **1** The quality of having heaviness. **2** The measure of this quality, expressed indefinitely or in standard units: Its *weight* is ten pounds. **3** A piece of something, usu. metal, used as a standard unit in weighing: a three-pound *weight.* **4** Any unit of heaviness, as a pound, ounce, etc.; also, a system of such units. **5** *Physics* The force of gravity exerted on any object, equal to the mass of the object multiplied by its acceleration due to gravity. **6** Any mass weighing a definite amount: a four-pound *weight* of flour. **7** Any object having heaviness and used to balance things, exert downward force, etc., as a paperweight, a counterbalance in a machine, a dumbbell for exercising, etc. **8** Burden; pressure: the *weight* of responsibility. **9** Influence; importance; consequence: the great *weight* of this decision. **10** The larger or most valuable part: the *weight* of the data is negative. **11** The comparative heaviness of clothes, as appropriate to the season: summer *weight.* —**carry weight** To be important, significant, influential, etc. —**pull one's weight** To do one's share. —**throw one's weight around** *Informal* To use one's importance or influence in an overbearing or improper manner. —*v.t.* **1** To add weight to; make heavy. **2** To oppress or burden. **3** To adulterate or treat (fabrics or other merchandise) with cheap foreign substances. [< OE *wiht, gewiht*]

weight·less (wāt′lis) *adj.* **1** Having little or no heaviness. **2** Subject to little or no gravitational force. —**weight′less·ly** *adv.* —**weight′less·ness** *n.*

weight·y (wā′tē) *adj.* **weight·i·er, weight·i·est 1** Having great importance; far-reaching; grave: a *weighty* decision.

2 Having power to move the mind; cogent; influential: a *weighty* argument. **3** Burdensome; onerous. **4** Having great weight; heavy. **—weight′i·ly** *adv.* **—weight′i·ness** *n.* —Syn. **1** momentous, serious, solemn.

weir (wir) *n.* **1** A dam placed in a stream to raise or divert the water. **2** A fence of twigs, rods, etc., in a stream, used to catch fish. [< OE *werian* dam up]

weird (wird) *adj.* **1** Manifesting or concerned with the supernatural; unearthly; uncanny. **2** Odd; bizarre; fantastic. [< OE *wyrd* fate] **—weird′ly** *adv.* **—weird′ness** *n.*

weird·o (wir′dō) *n. pl.* **·os** *Slang* A person who is strange or eccentric. Also **weird′ie, weird′y** (-dē) (*pl.* **·ies**).

welch (welch, welsh) *v.t. & v.i. Slang* WELSH. **—welch′er** *n.*

wel·come (wel′kəm) *adj.* **1** Admitted or received gladly and cordially. **2** Producing satisfaction or pleasure; pleasing: *welcome* tidings. **3** Made free to use or enjoy: She is *welcome* to our car. **—n.** The act of bidding or making welcome; a hearty greeting. **—wear out one's welcome** To come so often or to linger so long as no longer to be welcome. **—v.t. ·comed, ·com·ing 1** To greet gladly or hospitably. **2** To receive with pleasure: to *welcome* advice. [< OE *wilcuma*] **—wel′come·ly** *adv.* **—wel′come·ness, wel′·com·er** *n.*

weld (weld) *v.t.* **1** To unite, as two pieces of metal, by the application of heat along the area of contact. **2** To bring into close association or connection. **—v.i. 3** To be welded or capable of being welded. **—n.** The joining of pieces of metal by welding; also, the closed joint so formed. [Alter. of WELL¹] **—weld′a·ble** *adj.* **—weld′er** *n.*

wel·fare (wel′fâr) *n.* **1** The condition of being happy, healthy, prosperous, etc.; well-being. **2** WELFARE WORK. **3** Money given to those in need; relief. **—on welfare** Receiving welfare (def. 3) from the government. [< ME *wel* well + *fare* a going]

welfare state A state or social system in which the government assumes a large measure of responsibility for the welfare of its members, as regards employment, health insurance, social security, etc.

welfare work Organized efforts by a government or other organization to improve the economic condition of the needy. **—welfare worker**

wel·kin (wel′kin) *n. Archaic* **1** The vault of the sky; the heavens. **2** The air. [< OE *wolcn, wolcen* a cloud]

well¹ (wel) *n.* **1** A hole or shaft sunk into the earth to obtain a fluid, as water, oil, or natural gas. **2** A place where water issues naturally from the ground. **3** A source of continued supply; fount: a *well* of learning. **4** A depression, cavity, or vessel used to hold or collect a liquid: an *inkwell*. **5** A deep vertical opening descending through floors of a building, as for light, ventilation, stairs, etc. — *v.i.* **1** To pour forth or flow up, as water in a spring. **—v.t. 2** To gush: Her eyes *welled* tears. [< OE *weallan* boil, bubble up]

well² (wel) *adv.* **bet·ter, best 1** Satisfactorily; favorably: Everything goes *well*. **2** In a good or correct manner; expertly: to dance *well*. **3** Suitably; with propriety: I cannot *well* remain here. **4** Agreeably or luxuriously: He lives *well*. **5** Intimately: How *well* do you know him? **6** To a considerable extent or degree: *well* along in years. **7** Completely; thoroughly; fully: *well* aware. **8** Far: He lagged *well* behind us. **9** Kindly; graciously: to speak *well* of someone. **—as well 1** Also; in addition. **2** With equal effect or consequence: He might just *as well* have sold it. **—as well as 1** As satisfactorily as. **2** To the same degree as. **3** In addition to. **—adj. 1** Suitable, fortunate, right, etc.: It is *well* you called first. **2** In good health. **3** Prosperous; comfortable. **—interj.** An exclamation used to express surprise, expectation, indignation, etc., or to preface a remark. [< OE *wel*] **—Syn.** *adv.* **1** excellently. **3** befittingly, properly. **4** comfortably. • *Well* often appears in combination with participles to form modifiers. When used after a verb such as *be, seem,* etc., such a modifier is written as two words: to be *well satisfied*. When placed before a noun, it must be hyphenated: a *well-kept* secret.

we'll (wēl) Contraction of *we shall* or *we will*.

well-ap·point·ed (wel′ə·poin′tid) *adj.* Properly equipped; excellently furnished.

well-a·way (wel′ə·wā′) *interj. Archaic* Woe is me! [< OE *wei lā wei*]

well-bal·anced (wel′bal′ənst) *adj.* **1** Evenly balanced, adjusted, or proportioned. **2** Sound mentally; sensible.

well-be·ing (wel′bē′ing) *n.* A condition of health, happiness, or prosperity.

well-born (wel′bôrn′) *adj.* Of good family.

well-bred (wel′bred′) *adj.* **1** Well brought up; polite. **2** Of good or pure stock: said of animals.

well-dis·posed (wel′dis·pōzd′) *adj.* Favorably or kindly disposed or inclined, as to a person, idea, etc.

well-done (wel′dun′) *adj.* **1** Performed skillfully or satisfactorily. **2** Thoroughly cooked.

well-fa·vored (wel′fā′vərd) *adj.* Of attractive appearance; comely; handsome.

well-fed (wel′fed′) *adj.* **1** Plump; fat. **2** Properly fed.

well-fixed (wel′fikst′) *adj. Informal* Affluent; well-to-do.

well-found (wel′found′) *adj.* Well equipped.

well-found·ed (wel′foun′did) *adj.* Based on fact or sound thinking: *well-founded* suspicions.

well-groomed (wel′grōōmd′) *adj.* **1** Carefully dressed and scrupulously neat. **2** Carefully curried, as a horse.

well-ground·ed (wel′groun′did) *adj.* **1** Adequately schooled in the elements of a subject. **2** WELL-FOUNDED.

well-heeled (wel′hēld′) *adj. Slang* Plentifully supplied with money.

well-known (wel′nōn′) *adj.* **1** Widely known. **2** Famous. **3** Thoroughly known.

well-man·nered (wel′man′ərd) *adj.* Courteous; polite.

well-mean·ing (wel′mē′ning) *adj.* **1** Having good intentions. **2** Done with or showing good intentions: also **well′·meant′** (-ment′).

well-nigh (wel′nī′) *adv.* Very nearly; almost.

well-off (wel′ôf′, -of′) *adj.* **1** In comfortable circumstances; well-to-do. **2** Fortunate.

well-pre·served (wel′pri·zûrvd′) *adj.* Not showing many signs of age.

well-read (wel′red′) *adj.* Having a wide knowledge of literature or books; having read much.

well-round·ed (wel′roun′did) *adj.* **1** Having a good and balanced variety of elements: a *well-rounded* education. **2** Having many interests, abilities, etc.: a *well-rounded* person. **3** Fully formed: a *well-rounded* figure.

well-spo·ken (wel′spō′kən) *adj.* **1** Speaking fluently, suitably, or courteously. **2** Fitly or excellently said.

well-spring (wel′spring′) *n.* **1** The source of a stream, spring, etc. **2** A source of continual supply.

well-thought-of (wel′thôt′uv′, -ov′) *adj.* In good repute; esteemed; respected.

well-to-do (wel′tə·dōō′) *adj.* In prosperous or wealthy circumstances; affluent.

well-turned (wel′tûrnd′) *adj.* **1** Gracefully shaped; shapely. **2** Expressed in a graceful or felicitous manner: a *well-turned* phrase.

well-wish·er (wel′wish′ər) *n.* One who wishes well, as to another. **—well′·wish′ing** *adj., n.*

welsh (welsh, welch) *v.t. & v.i. Slang* To fail to pay a debt or fulfill an obligation. [?] **—welsh′er** *n.*

Welsh (welsh, welch) *adj.* Pertaining to Wales, its people, or their language. **—n. 1** The people of Wales. **2** The Celtic language of Wales.

Welsh·man (welsh′mən, welch′-) *n. pl.* **·men** (-mən) A native or citizen of Wales.

Welsh rabbit Melted cheese cooked with milk, ale, or beer and served hot on toast or crackers. • The form *rarebit* was a later development and is the result of mistaken etymology.

welt (welt) *n.* **1** A raised mark on the skin, resulting from a blow or lashing; wale. **2** A strip of material, covered cord, etc., applied to a seam to cover or strengthen it. **3** In shoemaking, a strip of leather set into the seam between the edges of the upper and the outer sole. **—v.t. 1** To sew a welt on or in; decorate with a welt. **2** *Informal* To flog severely, so as to raise welts. [ME *welte*]

wel·ter (wel′tər) *v.i.* **1** To roll about; wallow. **2** To lie or be soaked in some fluid, as blood. **—n. 1** A rolling movement, as of waves. **2** A turmoil; commotion. [< MDu. *welteren*]

wel·ter·weight (wel′tər·wāt′) *n.* A boxer or wrestler whose weight is between 136 and 147 pounds. [< earlier *welter* a heavyweight + WEIGHT]

Welt·schmerz (velt′shmerts) *n.* Weariness of life; melancholy. [G, lit., world pain]

wen (wen) *n.* A cyst containing sebaceous matter, occurring on the skin, esp. on the scalp. [< OE *wenn*]

wench (wench) *n.* *Archaic* 1 A young woman; girl: now a humorous usage. 2 A young peasant woman; also, a female servant. 3 A prostitute; strumpet. [< OE *wencel* a child, servant]

wend (wend) *v.* **wen·ded** (*Archaic* **went**), **wend·ing** *v.t.* 1 To go on (one's way); proceed. —*v.i.* 2 *Archaic* To proceed; go. [< OE *wendan*]

went (went) *p.t.* of GO.

wept (wept) *p.t. & p.p.* of WEEP.

were (wûr, *unstressed* wər) Plural and second person singular past indicative, and past subjunctive singular and plural of BE. [< OE *wære, wæron*]

we're (wir) Contraction of *we are.*

wer·en't (wûrnt, wûr′ənt) Contraction of *were not.*

were·wolf (wir′wŏŏlf′, wûr′-) *n. pl.* **·wolves** (-wŏŏlvz′) In European folklore, a person changed into a wolf or having power to assume wolf form at will. Also **wer′wolf′**. [< OE *werwulf* man-wolf]

wert (wûrt, *unstressed* wərt) *Archaic* Were: used with *thou.*

west (west) *n.* 1 The general direction in which the sun appears at sunset. 2 The point of the compass at 270°, directly opposite east. 3 Any region lying in this direction. —**the West** 1 The countries lying west of Asia and Asia Minor, including Europe and the Western Hemisphere; the Occident. 2 In the U.S.: **a** Formerly, the region west of the Allegheny Mountains. **b** The region west of the Mississippi, esp. the NW part of this region. 3 The noncommunist countries of Europe and the Western Hemisphere. —*adj.* 1 To, toward, facing, or in the west; western. 2 Coming from the west: the *west* wind. —*adv.* In or toward the west; in a westerly direction. [< OE]

west·er·ly (wes′tər·lē) *adj. & adv.* 1 In, toward, or of the west. 2 From the west. —**west′er·li·ness** *n.*

west·ern (wes′tərn) *adj.* 1 Of, in, directed toward, or facing the west. 2 From the west. —*n. Often cap.* A type of fiction or motion picture using cowboy and pioneer life in the western U.S. as its material.

West·ern (wes′tərn) *adj.* 1 Of, from, or characteristic of the West. 2 Belonging or pertaining to the Roman Catholic Church, as distinguished from the Eastern Orthodox Church.

west·ern·er (wes′tər·nər) *n.* 1 One who is native to or dwells in the west. 2 *Usu. cap.* One who is native to or dwells in the western U.S.

Western Hemisphere See HEMISPHERE.

west·ern·ize (wes′tər·nīz) *v.t.* **·ized**, **·iz·ing** To make western in characteristics, habits, etc. —**west′ern·i·za′tion** *n.*

Western Roman Empire The part of the Roman Empire w of the Adriatic, which existed as a separate empire from 395 until the fall of Rome in 476.

Western Sa·mo·a (sə·mō′ə) An independent state located in the w part of the islands of Samoa, 1,133 sq. mi., cap. Apia.

West Germany See GERMANY.

West·min·ster Abbey (west′min′stər) A Gothic church in Westminster, London, where English monarchs are crowned and many notable persons are buried.

west·north·west (west′nôrth′west′, *in nautical usage* west′nôr·west′) *n.* The direction midway between west and northwest. —*adj. & adv.* In, toward, or from this direction.

west·south·west (west′south′west′, *in nautical usage* west′sou·west′) *n.* The direction midway between west and southwest. —*adj. & adv.* In, toward, or from this direction.

west·ward (west′wərd) *adj. & adv.* Toward the west. —*n.* A westward direction or region.

west·wards (west′wərdz) *adv.* WESTWARD.

wet (wet) *adj.* **wet·ter, wet·test** 1 Moistened, saturated, or covered with water or other liquid. 2 Marked by showers or by heavy rainfall; rainy. 3 Not yet dry: *wet* varnish. 4 Permitting the manufacture and sale of alcoholic beverages: a *wet* county. 5 Preserved or bottled in a liquid. —**all wet** *Slang* Quite wrong; mistaken. —*n.* 1 Water; moisture; wetness. 2 Showery or rainy weather. 3 *Informal* One opposed to prohibition. —*v.t. & v.i.* **wet** or **wet·ted, wet·ting** To make or become wet. [< OE *wæt*] —**wet′ly** *adv.* —**wet′ness, wet′ter** *n.* —**Syn.** *v.* dampen, moisten, soak.

wet·back (wet′bak′) *n. Informal* A Mexican who enters the U.S. illegally, esp. by swimming or wading across the Rio Grande.

wet blanket One who or that which discourages any proceedings.

wet dream *Informal* A male's involuntary expulsion of semen during sleep, usu. accompanying an erotic dream.

weth·er (weth′ər) *n.* A castrated ram. [< OE]

wet·land (wet′land′) *n. Usu. pl.* Swamps, marshes, and other land areas with heavy soil moisture.

wet nurse A woman who is hired to suckle the child of another woman.

wet pack A therapeutic method consisting of wrapping the patient in wet sheets.

wet suit A skin-tight rubber garment worn by divers, surfers, etc., to retain body warmth in cold waters.

we've (wēv) Contraction of *we have.*

wf, w.f. wrong font (printing).

wh, wh., whr, whr., w.-hr. watt-hour(s).

whack (hwak) *v.t. & v.i. Informal* To strike sharply; beat; hit. —*n.* 1 *Informal* A sharp, resounding blow. 2 *Slang* A share; portion. —**have** (or **take**) **a whack at** *Slang* 1 To give a blow to. 2 To have a chance or turn at. —**out of whack** *Slang* Out of order. [?] —**whack′er** *n.*

whack·ing (hwak′ing) *adj. Chiefly Brit. Informal* Strikingly large; whopping.

whale[1] (hwāl) *n.* 1 Any of various very large, air-breathing marine mammals of fishlike form. 2 *Informal* Something extremely good or large: a *whale* of a party. —*v.i.* **whaled, whal·ing** To engage in the hunting of whales. [< OE *hwæl*]

Blue whale

whale[2] (hwāl) *v.t.* **whaled, whal·ing** *Informal* To beat; thrash; flog. [Prob. var. of WALE]

whale·back (hwāl′bak′) *n.* A freight steamer having a rounded bow and main deck, used on the Great Lakes.

whale·boat (hwāl′bōt′) *n.* A long, deep rowboat, sharp at both ends.

whale·bone (hwāl′bōn′) *n.* 1 The horny, pliable substance hanging in plates from the upper jaw of certain whales. 2 A strip of whalebone, used in stiffening corsets, etc.

whal·er (hwā′lər) *n.* A person or a ship engaged in whaling.

whal·ing (hwā′ling) *n.* The industry of capturing whales. —*adj. Slang* Huge; whopping.

wham·my (hwam′ē) *n. pl.* **·mies** *Slang* A jinx; hex: usu. in the phrase **put a** (or **the**) **whammy on.** [< *wham*, informal interjection imit. of the sound of a hard blow]

wharf (hwôrf) *n. pl.* **wharves** (hwôrvz) or **wharfs** 1 A structure of masonry or timber erected on the shore of a harbor, river, etc., alongside which vessels may lie to load or unload cargo, passengers, etc. 2 Any pier or dock. —*v.t.* 1 To moor to a wharf. 2 To deposit or store on a wharf. [< OE *hwearf* a dam]

wharf·age (hwôr′fij) *n.* 1 Charge for the use of a wharf. 2 Wharf accommodations for shipping.

wharf rat 1 A rat that inhabits wharves. 2 *Slang* One who loiters about wharves, esp. with criminal intent.

what (hwot, hwut) *pron.* 1 Which specific act, thing, name, value, etc.: *What* is going on? *What* is that? 2 That which: *What* followed is a mystery. 3 How much: *What* will it cost? —**and what not** And so forth. —**but what** But that. —**what have you** What is similar or need not be mentioned. —**what if** Suppose that. —**what's what** *Informal* The actual state of affairs. —**what with** Taking into consideration. —*adj.* 1 Which or which kind of: I know *what* things I want. **2** How surprising, great, etc.: *What* a genius! **3** How much: *What* cash has he? **4** Whatever: Take *what* books you may need. —*adv.* How or how much: *What* do you care? —*interj.* An expression of surprise, annoyance, etc.: *What!* They stole it! [< OE *hwæt*]

what·ev·er (ʰwot′ev′ər, ʰwut′-) *pron.* **1** Anything that: Say *whatever* you want to say. **2** No matter what: *Whatever* you cook will be good. **3** *Informal* What: usu. interrogative: *Whatever* are you doing? —*adj.* **1** No matter what or which: *Whatever* things are left, you can keep. **2** Of any kind, amount, etc.: He has no ability *whatever*.

what·not (ʰwot′not′, ʰwut′-) *n.* An ornamental set of shelves for holding bric-a-brac, etc.

what·so·ev·er (ʰwot′sō·ev′ər, ʰwut′-) *pron. & adj.* Whatever: a slightly more formal usage.

wheal (ʰwēl) *n.* A small raised area or pimple on the skin. [Alter. of WALE]

wheat (ʰwēt) *n.* **1** Any of a genus of cereal grasses, esp. cultivated species yielding spikes of edible grain. **2** Grains of these species collectively, constituting a staple food usu. ground into flour.

wheat·en (ʰwēt′n) *adj.* **1** Made of wheat. **2** Having the pale gold color of ripe wheat.

wheat germ The embryo of the wheat kernel, used as a vitamin source.

whee·dle (ʰwēd′l) *v.* **·dled, ·dling** *v.t.* **1** To persuade or try to persuade by flattery, cajolery, etc.; coax. **2** To obtain by cajoling or coaxing. —*v.i.* **3** To use flattery or cajolery. [?] —**whee′dler** *n.* —**whee′dling·ly** *adv.*

wheel (ʰwēl) *n.* **1** A solid disk or a circular rim connected to a hub by spokes or rays capable of rotating on a central axis and used to facilitate movement, as in vehicles, or to act with a rotary motion, as in machines. **2** Anything resembling or suggestive of a wheel. **3** An instrument or device having a wheel or wheels as its distinctive characteristic, as a steering wheel, a potter's wheel, a water wheel, etc. **4** *Informal* A bicycle. **5** An old instrument of torture or execution, consisting of a wheel to which the limbs of the victim were tied and then stretched or broken. **6** A turning or rotating movement; revolution. **7** *Usu. pl.* That which imparts or directs motion or controls activity: the *wheels* of democracy. **8** *Slang* A person of influence or authority: also **big wheel. 9** *pl. Slang* An automobile. —**at** (or **behind**) **the wheel 1** Steering a motor vehicle, motor boat, etc. **2** In charge or in control. —*v.t.* **1** To move or convey on wheels. **2** To cause to turn on or as on an axis; pivot or revolve. **3** To perform with a circular movement. **4** To provide with a wheel or wheels. —*v.i.* **5** To turn on or as on an axis; pivot. **6** To change one's course of action, attitudes, opinions, etc.: often with *about*. **7** To move in a circular or spiral course. **8** To move on wheels. —**wheel and deal** *Slang* To act freely, aggressively, and often unscrupulously, as in the arrangement of a business or political deal. [< OE *hwēol*]

wheel·bar·row (ʰwēl′bar′ō) *n.* A boxlike vehicle ordinarily with one wheel and two handles, for moving small loads. —*v.t.* To convey in a wheelbarrow.

wheel·base (ʰwēl′bās′) *n.* The distance separating the axles of the front and rear wheels, as an automobile, etc.

wheel·chair (ʰwēl′chār′) *n.* A mobile chair mounted between large wheels, for the use of invalids. Also **wheel chair.**

wheel·er (ʰwē′lər) *n.* **1** One who wheels. **2** WHEELHORSE (def. 1). **3** Something furnished with a wheel or wheels: a *side-wheeler.*

wheel·er-deal·er (ʰwē′lər·dē′lər) *n. Slang* One who wheels and deals. —**wheel′er-deal′er·ing** *n.*

wheel·horse (ʰwēl′hôrs′) *n.* **1** A horse harnessed next to the front wheels and behind other horses. **2** A person who works hard and dependably.

wheel·house (ʰwēl′hous′) *n.* PILOTHOUSE.

wheel·wright (ʰwēl′rīt′) *n.* A man whose business is making or repairing wheels.

wheeze (ʰwēz) *v.t. & v.i.* **wheezed, wheez·ing** To breathe or utter with a husky, whistling sound. —*n.* **1** A wheezing sound. **2** *Informal* A trite joke. [Prob. < ON *hvæsa* hiss] —**wheez′er, wheez′i·ness** *n.* —**wheez′i·ly, wheez′ing·ly** *adv.* —**wheez′y** *adj.* (**·i·er, ·i·est**)

whelk[1] (ʰwelk) *n.* Any of various large, spiral-shelled, marine snails, some of which are edible. [< OE *weoloc*]

whelk[2] (ʰwelk) *n.* A pimple or pustule. [< OE *hwelian* suppurate]

whelm (ʰwelm) *v.t.* **1** To submerge. **2** To overpower; overwhelm. [ME *whelmen*]

whelp (ʰwelp) *n.* **1** One of the young of a dog, wolf, lion, or certain other carnivores. **2** A dog. **3** A worthless young fellow. —*v.t. & v.i.* To give birth (to): said of certain carnivores. [< OE *hwelp*]

Common whelk

when (ʰwen) *adv.* **1** At what or which time: *When* did you arrive? **2** Under what circumstances: *When* do I apply the brake? **3** At an earlier time: I knew them *when.* —*conj.* **1** At which: the time *when* we went on the picnic. **2** At which or what time: They watched till midnight, *when* they fell asleep. **3** As soon as: He laughed *when* he heard it. **4** Although: He walks *when* he might ride. **5** At the time that; while: *when* we were young. **6** If it should happen that: An employee is fired *when* he is caught stealing. **7** After which; then: We had just awakened *when* you called. **8** Considering that: Why bother to ask me *when* you already know the answer? —*pron.* What or which time: since *when;* till *when.* —*n.* The time; date: to know the *when* and why of something. [< OE *hwanne, hwænne*]

whence (ʰwens) *adv.* From what place or source: *Whence* does he come? —*conj.* From what or out of which place, source, or cause: asked *whence* these sounds arise. [< OE *hwanne* when]

whence·so·ev·er (ʰwens′sō·ev′ər) *adv. & conj.* From whatever place, cause, or source.

when·ev·er (ʰwen′ev′ər) *adv. & conj.* At whatever time.

when·so·ev·er (ʰwen′sō·ev′ər) *adv. & conj.* WHENEVER.

where (ʰwâr) *adv.* **1** At or in what place, respect, or situation: *Where* is my book? *Where* am I at fault? **2** To what place or end: *Where* is this getting us? **3** From what place or source: *Where* did you get that hat? —*conj.* **1** At, in, or to which or what place: I know the hotel *where* they are. **2** At, in, or to the place, position, or situation in which: They are living *where* they are happiest. —*pron.* The place in which: from *where* we stood. —*n.* Place; locality. [< OE *hwǣr*]

where·a·bouts (ʰwâr′ə·bouts′) *adv.* Near or at what place; about where. —*n.pl. (construed as sing. or pl.)* The place in which a person or thing is.

where·as (ʰwâr·az′) *conj.* **1** Since the facts are such as they are; seeing that: often used in the preamble of a resolution, etc. **2** While on the contrary; when in truth. —*n. pl.* **·as·es** A clause or item beginning with the word "whereas."

where·at (ʰwâr·at′) *adv. Archaic* At what: *Whereat* are you angry? —*conj.* At which point.

where·by (ʰwâr·bī′) *adv. Archaic* By what; how. —*conj.* By which: a plan *whereby* we will win.

wher·e'er (ʰwâr·âr′) *adj. & conj.* WHEREVER.

where·fore (ʰwâr′fôr′, -fōr′) *adv. Archaic* For what reason; why: *Wherefore* didst thou doubt? —*conj.* **1** For which. **2** THEREFORE. —*n.* The cause; reason: the whys and *wherefores.* [< WHERE + FOR]

where·from (ʰwâr′frum′, -from′) *adv. & conj.* From which.

where·in (ʰwâr·in′) *adv.* In what way or regard: *Wherein* is the error? —*conj.* In which: a state *wherein* there is discord.

where·of (ʰwâr·uv′, -ov′) *adv. & conj.* Of which, whom, or what.

where·on (ʰwâr·on′, -ôn′) *adv. Archaic* On what or whom. —*conj.* On which: land *whereon* to build.

where·so·ev·er (ʰwâr′sō·ev′ər) *adv. & conj.* In, at, or to whatever place; wherever.

where·to (ʰwâr·tōō′) *Archaic adv.* To what place or end. —*conj.* To which or to whom. Also **where′un·to′.**

where·up·on (ʰwâr′ə·pon′, -ə·pôn′) *adv. Archaic* Upon

---

a|c|b
Wheat
a. bearded. b. beardless. c. grain: front and back of b.

what; whereon. —*conj.* Upon which or whom; in consequence of which; after which: *whereupon* they took in sail.

wher·ev·er (ʰwâr′ev′ər) *adv. & conj.* In, at, or to whatever place or situation.

where·with (ʰwâr′with′, -with′) *adv. Archaic* With what: *Wherewith* shall I do it? —*conj.* With which; by means of which: *wherewith* we abated hunger. —*pron.* That with or by which: used with an infinitive: I have not *wherewith* to do it.

where·with·al (ʰwâr′with·ôl′, -with-) *n.* The necessary means or resources, esp. money: used with *the*.

wher·ry (ʰwer′ē) *n. pl.* ·ries 1 A light, fast rowboat built for one person and used for racing or exercise. 2 *Brit.* A very broad, light barge. —*v.t. & v.i.* ·ried, ·ry·ing To transport in or use a wherry. [?]

whet (ʰwet) *v.t.* **whet·ted, whet·ting 1** To sharpen, as a knife, by friction. 2 To make more keen or eager; excite; stimulate, as the appetite. —*n.* 1 The act of whetting. 2 Something that whets. [< OE *hwettan*] —**whet′ter** *n.*

wheth·er (ʰweth′ər) *conj.* 1 If it be the case that: Tell us *whether* you are going or not. 2 In case; if: *whether* he lived or died, we never heard. 3 Either: He came in first, *whether* by luck or plan. —**whether or no** Regardless; in any case. [< OE *hwæther*]

whet·stone (ʰwet′stōn′) *n.* A fine-grained stone for whetting knives, axes, etc.

whew (ʰwyōō) *interj.* An exclamation of amazement, dismay, relief, etc.

whey (ʰwā) *n.* A clear liquid that separates from the curd when milk is curdled, as in making cheese. [< OE *hwæg*] —**whey′ey, whey′ish** *adj.*

whf. wharf.

which (ʰwich) *pron.* 1 What specific one or ones: *Which* are for sale? 2 The specific one or ones that: I know *which* I bought. 3 The thing, animal, or event designated earlier: used restrictively or nonrestrictively: The flood *which* wiped us out was last year; That car, *which* is not old, no longer runs. 4 *Archaic* The person or persons designated earlier: "Our Father, *which* art in heaven," 5 WHICHEVER: Use *which* you find most convenient. 6 A thing, situation, or fact that: He decided to go, *which* was lucky. —*adj.* 1 What specific one or ones: *Which* play did you see? 2 WHICHEVER: Take *which* one you want. 3 Being the one or ones designated earlier: The clock struck one, at *which* point he left. • See WHO. [< OE *hwelc, hwilc*]

which·ev·er (ʰwich′ev′ər) *pron. & adj.* 1 Any one (of two or of several): Select *whichever* (ring) you want. 2 No matter which: *Whichever* (song) you choose, sing it well. Also **which′so·ev′er.**

whiff (ʰwif) *n.* 1 A slight gust or puff of air. 2 A gust or puff of odor: a *whiff* of onions. 3 A sudden expulsion of breath or smoke from the mouth; a puff. —*v.t.* 1 To drive or blow with a whiff or puff. 2 To smoke, as a pipe. —*v.i.* 3 To blow or move in whiffs or puffs. 4 To exhale or inhale whiffs. [Imit.] —**whiff′er** *n.*

whif·fet (ʰwif′it) *n. Informal* 1 A trifling, useless person. 2 A small, snappish dog. [?]

whif·fle (ʰwif′əl) *v.* ·fled, ·fling *v.i.* 1 To blow with puffs or gusts, as the wind. 2 To vacillate; veer. —*v.t.* 3 To blow or dissipate with a puff. [Freq. of WHIFF] —**whif′fler** *n.*

whif·fle·tree (ʰwif′əl·trē′) *n.* A horizontal crossbar, to the ends of which the traces of a harness are attached. [Var. of WHIPPLETREE]

Whig (ʰwig) *n.* 1 An American colonist who supported the Revolutionary War in the 18th century. 2 A member of an American political party opposed to the Democratic and succeeded by the Republican party in 1856. 3 A member of a political party (later the Liberal party) in England in the 18th and 19th centuries. —*adj.* Belonging to, consisting of, or supported by the Whigs. [Prob. short for *Whiggamore*, one of a body of 17th cent. Scottish insurgents] — **Whig′ger·y, Whig′gism** *n.* —**Whig′gish** *adj.*

while (ʰwīl) *n.* A period of time: a brief *while*. —**between whiles** From time to time. —**the while** At the same time. —**worth (one's) while** Worth one's time, labor, trouble, etc. —*conj.* 1 During the time that. 2 At the same time

that; although: *While* he found fault, he also praised. 3 Whereas: This man is short, *while* that one is tall. —*v.t.* **whiled, whil·ing** To cause to pass pleasantly: usu. with *away*: to *while* away the time. [< OE *hwil*]

whiles (ʰwīlz) *Archaic* or *Regional adv.* Occasionally; at intervals. —*conj.* WHILE.

whi·lom (ʰwī′ləm) *Archaic adj.* FORMER. —*adv.* FORMERLY. [< OE *hwilum* at times < *hwil* a while]

whilst (ʰwīlst) *conj. Chiefly Brit.* WHILE.

whim (ʰwim) *n.* A sudden, capricious idea, notion, or desire; fancy. [Short for earlier *whim-wham* a trifle]

whim·per (ʰwim′pər) *v.i.* 1 To cry with plaintive broken sounds. —*v.t.* 2 To utter with or as if with a whimper. —*n.* A low, broken, whining cry. [Imit.] —**whim′per·er** *n.* —**whim′per·ing·ly** *adv.*

whim·si·cal (ʰwim′zi·kəl) *adj.* 1 Capricious; fanciful; unpredictable. 2 Odd; fantastic; quaint. —**whim·si·cal′i·ty** (-kal′ə·tē) (*pl.* ·ties), **whim′si·cal·ness** *n.* —**whim′si·cal·ly** *adv.*

whim·sy (ʰwim′zē) *n. pl.* ·sies 1 A whim; caprice. 2 Humor that is somewhat odd, fanciful, or quaint. Also **whim′sey.** [Prob. related to WHIM]

whine (ʰwīn) *v.* **whined, whin·ing** *v.i.* 1 To utter a high, plaintive, nasal sound expressive of grief or distress. 2 To complain in a fretful or childish way. 3 To make a steady, high-pitched sound, as a machine. —*v.t.* 4 To utter with a whine. —*n.* The act or sound of whining. [< OE *hwinan* whiz] —**whin′er** *n.* —**whin′ing·ly** *adv.* —**whin′y** *adj.*

whin·ny (ʰwin′ē) *v.* ·nied, ·ny·ing *v.i.* 1 To neigh, esp. in a low or gentle way. —*v.t.* 2 To express with a whinny. —*n. pl.* ·nies A low, gentle neigh. [< WHINE]

whip (ʰwip) *v.* **whipped, whip·ping** *v.t.* 1 To strike with a lash, rod, strap, etc. 2 To punish by striking thus; flog. 3 To drive or urge with lashes or blows: with *on, up, off,* etc. 4 To strike in the manner of a whip: The wind *whipped* the trees. 5 To beat, as eggs or cream, to a froth. 6 To seize, move, jerk, throw, etc., with a sudden motion: with *away, in, off, out,* etc. 7 In fishing, to make repeated casts upon the surface of (a stream, etc.). 8 To wrap or bind about something. 9 To sew, as a flat seam, with a loose overcast or overhand stitch. 10 *Informal* To defeat; overcome, as in a contest. —*v.i.* 11 To go, move, or turn suddenly and quickly: with *away, in, off, out,* etc. 12 To thrash about in the manner of a whip: pennants *whipping* in the wind. 13 In fishing, to make repeated casts with rod and line. — **whip up** 1 To excite; arouse. 2 *Informal* To prepare quickly, as a meal. —*n.* 1 An instrument consisting of a lash attached to a handle, used for discipline or punishment. 2 A whipping or thrashing motion. 3 A member of a legislative body, as congress or parliament, appointed unofficially to enforce discipline, attendance, etc.: also **party whip.** 4 A dessert containing whipped cream or beaten egg whites, flavoring, sometimes fruit, etc. [ME *wippen*] —**Syn.** *v.* 1 beat, scourge, switch, thrash.

whip·cord (ʰwip′kôrd′) *n.* 1 A strong, hard-twisted cord, used in making whiplashes. 2 A twill fabric with a pronounced diagonal rib.

whip hand 1 The hand in which a person holds the whip while driving. 2 A position or means of advantage.

whip·lash (ʰwip′lash′) *n.* 1 The flexible striking part of a whip. 2 An injury to the neck, due to a sudden snapping back and forth of the head, as in automobile accidents: also **whiplash injury.**

whip·per·snap·per (ʰwip′ər·snap′ər) *n.* A pretentious but insignificant person, esp. a young person. [?]

whip·pet (ʰwip′it) *n.* A swift dog resembling an English greyhound in miniature, used in racing, etc. [? < WHIP]

whip·ping (ʰwip′ing) *n.* 1 The act of one who or that which whips; esp. a punishment by flogging. 2 Material, as cord or twine, used to whip or bind.

Whippet

whipping boy Anyone who receives blame deserved by another; scapegoat.

whipping post The fixture to which those sentenced to flogging are secured.

whip·ple·tree (ʰwip′əl-trē′) n. WHIFFLETREE.

whip·poor·will (ʰwip′ər-wil) n. A small nocturnal bird, allied to the goatsuckers, common in E North America. [Imit.]

whip·saw (ʰwip′sô′) n. A thin, narrow, two-man ripsaw. —v.t. ·sawed, ·sawed or ·sawn, ·saw·ing 1 To saw with a whipsaw. 2 To beat (an opponent) in two ways at the same time.

whip·stitch (ʰwip′stich′) v.t. To sew or gather with overcast stitches. —n. An overcast stitch.

whip·stock (ʰwip′stok′) n. A whip handle.

whir (ʰwûr) v.t. & v.i. **whirred, whir·ring** To fly or move with a buzzing sound. —n. 1 A whizzing, swishing sound. 2 Confusion; bustle. Also **whirr.** [Prob. < Scand.]

whirl (ʰwûrl) v.i. 1 To turn or revolve rapidly, as about a center. 2 To turn away or aside quickly. 3 To move or go swiftly. 4 To have a sensation of spinning: My head whirls. —v.t. 5 To cause to turn or revolve rapidly. 6 To carry or bear along with a revolving motion. —n. 1 A swift rotating or revolving motion. 2 Something whirling. 3 A state of confusion. 4 A round of activities, social events, etc. 5 Informal A short drive. 6 Informal A try. [Prob. < ON hvirfla revolve] —**whirl′er** n.

whirl·i·gig (ʰwûr′lə-gig′) n. 1 Any toy that spins. 2 A merry-go-round. 3 Anything that moves in a cycle. 4 A whirling motion. 5 Any of certain water beetles that move on the water in swift circles: also **whirligig beetle.** [< WHIRL + GIG]

whirl·pool (ʰwûrl′po͞ol′) n. 1 An eddy or vortex where water moves in a rapid whirling motion, as from the meeting of two currents. 2 Anything resembling a whirlpool, esp. in movement.

whirl·wind (ʰwûrl′wind′) n. 1 A forward-moving column of air, with a rapid circular and upward spiral motion. 2 Anything resembling a whirlwind in movement, energy, or violence. —adj. Extremely swift or impetuous: a whirlwind courtship.

whish (ʰwish) v.i. To make or move with a whizzing sound. —n. Such a sound. [Imit.]

whisk (ʰwisk) v.t. 1 To brush or sweep off lightly: often with away or off. 2 To cause to move with a quick sweeping motion. 3 To beat with a quick movement, as eggs, cream, etc. —v.i. 4 To move quickly and lightly. —n. 1 A light sweeping or whipping movement. 2 A little bunch of straw, feathers, etc. for brushing. 3 A culinary instrument of wire loops for whipping (cream, etc.). [Prob. < Scand.]

whisk·broom (ʰwisk′bro͞om′, -bro͝om′) n. A small, short-handled broom for brushing clothing, etc.

whisk·er (ʰwis′kər) n. 1 pl. The hair of a man's beard, esp. the hair that grows on the cheeks. 2 A hair from the whiskers. 3 One of the long, bristly hairs near the mouth of some animals, as the cat, mouse, etc. [< WHISK] —**whisk′ered, whisk′er·y** adj.

whis·key (ʰwis′kē) n. pl. ·keys or ·kies 1 An alcoholic liquor obtained by the distillation of a fermented mash of grain, as rye, corn, barley, or wheat. 2 A drink of whiskey. —adj. Pertaining to or made of whiskey. Also **whis′ky.** [< Ir. uisce beathadh, lit., water of life] ● In the U.S. and Ireland, whiskey is usu. spelled with an e. Scotch and Canadian whisky, however, are traditionally spelled without the e.

whis·per (ʰwis′pər) n. 1 An act or instance of breathy speech with little or no vibration of the vocal chords. 2 An utterance made with such speech. 3 A secret communication; hint; insinuation. 4 Any low, rustling sound. —v.i. 1 To speak in a low, breathy way with little or no vibration of the vocal chords. 2 To talk cautiously or furtively; plot or gossip. 3 To make a low, rustling sound, as leaves. —v.t. 4 To utter in a whisper. 5 To speak to in a whisper. [< OE hwisprian] —**whis′per·er** n. —**whis′per·ing·ly** adv. —**whis′per·y** adj.

whispering campaign An organized effort to discredit a person, group, cause, etc., by rumors and gossip.

whist (ʰwist) n. A game of cards from which bridge developed, played by four persons with a full pack of 52 cards. [Alter. of earlier whisk]

whis·tle (ʰwis′əl) v. ·tled, ·tling v.i. 1 To make a sound by sending the breath through the teeth or through puckered lips. 2 To make a sharp, shrill sound by forcing air, steam, etc., through a small opening. 3 To make a similar sound by swift passage through the air, as bullets, the wind, etc. 4 To make a shrill cry, as certain animals or birds. 5 To blow or sound a whistle. —v.t. 6 To produce (a tune) by whistling. 7 To call, manage, or direct by whistling. —n. 1 An instrument for making whistling sounds: a train whistle; a toy whistle. 2 A whistling sound. 3 The act of whistling. —**wet one's whistle** Slang To take a drink. [< OE hwistlian a shrill pipe] —**whis′tler** n.

whis·tle-stop (ʰwis′əl-stop′) Informal v.i. ·stopped, ·stop·ping To make whistle stops, esp. as part of a political campaign.

whistle stop Informal 1 A small town, at which formerly a train stopped only on signal. 2 Any of a series of brief stops at small communities during a tour, esp. one made by a political candidate.

whit (ʰwit) n. The smallest particle; speck: usu. with a negative: not a whit abashed. [< OE (ænig) wiht a little amount] —**Syn.** bit, grain, iota, jot, shred.

white (ʰwīt) adj. **whit·er, whit·est** 1 Having the color produced by reflection of all the rays of the solar spectrum, as the color of pure snow. 2 Light or comparatively light in color: white wine. 3 Bloodless; ashen: white with rage. 4 Very fair; blond. 5 Silvery or gray, as with age. 6 Snowy. 7 Wearing white clothing: white nuns. 8 Not malicious or harmful: a white lie. 9 Innocent; pure. 10 Unmarked by ink or print; blank. 11 Having a light-colored skin; Caucasian. 12 Of, pertaining to, or controlled by Caucasians: the white power structure. 13 Informal Fair; straightforward; honest. 14 Music Of, pertaining to, or being a tonal quality having accuracy of pitch but lacking resonance, color, and warmth. —n. 1 A white color. 2 The state or condition of being white; whiteness. 3 The white or light-colored part of something; esp., the albumen of an egg, or the white part of the eyeball. 4 Anything that is white or nearly white, as cloth, white wine, etc. 5 pl. A white uniform or outfit: the summer whites of the Navy. 6 A Caucasian. —v.t. **whit·ed, whit·ing** To make white; whiten. [< OE hwīt] —**white′ly** adv. —**white′ness** n.

white ant TERMITE.

white·bait (ʰwīt′bāt′) n. The young of various fishes, esp. of sprat and herring, served as a delicacy.

white birch A North American birch with white bark that peels off in papery sheets.

white·cap (ʰwīt′kap′) n. A wave with foam on its crest.

white cedar 1 A strong-scented evergreen tree of the cypress family, having small, scalelike leaves and growing in moist places. 2 Its soft, easily worked wood.

white clover A common variety of clover, with white flowers.

white coal Water power.

white-col·lar (ʰwīt′kol′ər) adj. Of, pertaining to, or designating usu. salaried employees, as office personnel, whose work does not often expose their clothes to soil or stain, thus enabling them to wear garments, as white shirts, etc., that are easily stained.

white corpuscle LEUKOCYTE.

whited sepulcher A corrupt or evil person who pretends to be good; hypocrite.

white elephant 1 A rare pale-gray variety of Asian elephant held sacred in E Asia. 2 Anything that is a burden and an expense to maintain.

white feather A symbol of cowardice. —**show the white feather** To show cowardice.

white·fish (ʰwīt′fish′) n. pl. ·fish or ·fish·es 1 Any of various silvery North American food fishes, living mostly in lakes. 2 Any of various other whitish or silvery fishes.

white flag A white flag or banner used as a signal of surrender.

white gold Gold alloyed with a white metal, usu. nickel and zinc, sometimes palladium, which gives the gold a platinumlike appearance.

white heat 1 The temperature at which metal, etc., becomes white with heat. 2 A state of intense emotion, enthusiasm, etc.

white-hot (ʰwīt′hot′) adj. So hot as to glow with white light.

White House, The 1 The official residence of the president of the U.S., at Washington, D.C. 2 The executive branch of the U.S. government.

white lead A poisonous white pigment composed of lead carbonate and hydrated lead oxide.

white lie A harmless, trivial lie.

white matter The whitish portion of the brain and spinal cord that is composed mainly of nerve fibers.

white meat Any light-colored meat, as the breast of chicken, turkey, etc.

whit·en (ʰwīt′n) v.t. & v.i. To make or become white or nearly white. —**whit′en·er** n. —**Syn.** blanch, bleach.

white noise Noise in which the average intensity at any frequency between two stated limits is constant.

white oak 1 Any of numerous oaks having gray or whitish bark. 2 The wood of any white oak.

white pepper Pepper ground from the white seeds inside black peppercorns.

white pine 1 A pine of E North America, with soft, bluish-green leaves in clusters of five. 2 The light, soft wood of this tree. 3 Any of several related pines.

White oak
a. leaves. b. blossom. c. acorn.

white poplar A large, rapidly growing tree valued for its ornamental leaves, which are green above and silvery-white below.

white potato The common potato.

White Russian BYELORUSSIAN.

white sauce A cooked sauce of flour, butter, milk, etc.

white slave A woman forced into or held in prostitution. —**white-slave** (ʰwīt′slāv′) adj. —**white slaver** —**white slavery**

white-tailed deer (ʰwīt′tāld′) A common North American deer, having a tail white on the underside.

white tie 1 A white bow tie, worn with men's formal evening dress. 2 The formal evening dress of men.

white·wash (ʰwīt′wosh′, -wôsh′) n. 1 A mixture of slaked lime and water used for whitening walls, etc. 2 A suppressing or hiding of faults and defects. 3 Informal A defeat in which the loser fails to score. —v.t. 1 To coat with whitewash. 2 To gloss over; hide. 3 Informal In games or sports, to defeat without allowing one's opponent to score. —**white′wash′er** n.

whith·er (ʰwith′ər) adv. Archaic To what place, condition, end, etc.: Whither are we bound? —conj. 1 To which place, condition, end, etc.: the village whither we went. 2 To whatever place, condition, end, etc.: Go whither you will. [< OE hwider]

whith·er·so·ev·er (ʰwith′ər·sō·ev′ər) adv. Archaic To whatever place.

whit·ing[1] (ʰwī′ting) n. A powdered white chalk used as a pigment, for polishing, etc.

whit·ing[2] (ʰwī′ting) n. 1 A small European food fish related to cod. 2 A silvery-scaled hake. 3 Any of several silvery fishes, esp. the **Carolina whiting**, common on the coast of the S U.S. [< MDu. wit white]

Whiting[2]

whit·ish (ʰwī′tish) adj. Somewhat white or very light gray. —**whit′ish·ness** n.

whit·low (ʰwit′lō) n. An inflammatory, festering lesion at the edge of a fingernail. [< WHITE + FLAW]

Whit·sun (ʰwit′sən) adj. Of, pertaining to, or for Whitsunday or Whitsuntide.

Whit·sun·day (ʰwit′sun′dē, -dā) n. The seventh Sunday after Easter; Pentecost. [< OE Hwita Sunnandæg, lit., white Sunday < the white robes worn by recently baptized persons on that day]

Whit·sun·tide (ʰwit′sən·tīd′) n. The week that begins with Whitsunday. Also **Whitsun Tide.**

whit·tle (ʰwit′l) v. ·tled, ·tling v.t. 1 To cut or shave bits from (wood, a stick, etc.). 2 To make or shape by whittling. 3 To reduce or wear away a little at a time: with down, off, away, etc. —v.i. 4 To whittle wood. [< OE thwitan to cut] —**whit′tler** n. —**Syn.** v. 1 carve, trim, pare.

whiz (ʰwiz) v. **whizzed, whiz·zing** v.i. 1 To make a hissing and humming sound while passing rapidly through the air. 2 To move or pass with such a sound. —v.t. 3 To cause to whiz. —n. 1 The sound made by whizzing. 2 Slang Any person or thing of extraordinary excellence or ability. Also **whizz.** [Imit.] —**whiz′zer** n. —**whiz′zing·ly** adv.

whiz kid Slang A young person who is extraordinarily clever, talented, or successful. [Alter. of Quiz Kid, a panel member of a former quiz show made up of children]

who (hoo) pron. possessive case **whose**; objective case **whom** 1 Which or what person or persons: Who is she? They don't know who I am. 2 The person or persons that; whoever: Who insults my friends insults me. 3 That: used as a relative to introduce a clause: the man who mows our lawn. —**who's who** Who the most prominent people are. —**as who should say** As if one should say; so to speak. [< OE hwa, hwæ] • **who, which, that** Who as a relative is usu. applied only to persons, which only to animals or to inanimate objects, that to persons or things.

WHO World Health Organization.

whoa (ʰwō) interj. Stop! stand still! [Var. of HO]

who·dun·it (hoo·dun′it) n. Informal A mystery story, play, etc. [< WHO + DONE + IT]

who·ev·er (hoo·ev′ər) pron. 1 Any one without exception; any person who. 2 No matter who.

whole (hōl) adj. 1 Containing all the parts necessary to make up a total; entire; complete. 2 Not broken, injured, defective, etc.; sound; intact. 3 Being the full amount, number, duration, etc.: He failed the whole class. 4 In or having regained sound health; hale. 5 Having the same parents: a whole brother. 6 Math. Integral; not mixed or fractional. —**as a whole** Altogether. —**on the whole** Taking all into consideration; in general. —n. 1 All the parts or elements making up a thing. 2 A complete unity or system. [< OE hāl] —**whole′ness** n.

whole·heart·ed (hōl′här′tid) adj. Done or undertaken with all earnestness, energy, dedication, etc. —**whole′heart′ed·ly** adv. —**whole′heart′ed·ness** n.

whole note Music A note whose time value is the same as that of two half notes. • See NOTE.

whole number Any member of the set of numbers {. . . −3, −2, −1, 0, 1, 2, 3 . . .}; an integer.

whole·sale (hōl′sāl′) n. The sale of goods in large bulk or quantity, usu. for resale by retailers. —adj. 1 Pertaining to or engaged in such selling. 2 Made or done on a large scale or indiscriminately: wholesale murder. —adv. 1 In bulk or quantity. 2 Extensively or indiscriminately. —v.t. & v.i. ·saled, ·sal·ing To sell (something) in large quantity, usu. for resale by retailers. [< ME by hole sale in large quantities] —**whole′sal′er** n.

whole·some (hōl′səm) adj. 1 Tending to promote health: wholesome air or food. 2 Tending to promote mental or moral well-being: a wholesome play. 3 Healthy: wholesome red cheeks. [< WHOLE + -SOME] —**whole′some·ly** adv. —**whole′some·ness** n.

whole step An interval consisting of two semitones. Also **whole tone.**

whole-wheat (hōl′ʰwēt′) adj. 1 Made from the entire wheat kernel: whole-wheat flour. 2 Made from whole-wheat flour. Also **whole wheat.**

who'll (hool) Contraction of who will or who shall.

whol·ly (hō′lē, hōl′lē) adv. 1 Completely; totally. 2 Exclusively; only.

whom (hoom) pron. The objective case of WHO. [< OE hwam]

whom·ev·er (hoom·ev′ər) pron. The objective case of WHOEVER.

whom·so·ev·er (hoom′sō·ev′ər) pron. The objective case of WHOSOEVER.

whoop (hoop, ʰwoop, ʰwoop) v.i. 1 To utter loud cries, as of excitement, rage, or exultation. 2 To hoot, as an owl. 3 To make a loud, gasping intake of breath. —v.t. 4 To utter with a whoop or whoops. **5** To call, urge, chase, etc., with whoops. —**whoop it** (or **things**) **up** *Slang* **1** To celebrate in a noisy, riotous manner. **2** To arouse enthusiasm. — *n.* **1** A shout of excitement, joy, derision, etc. **2** A loud, convulsive intake of breath. **3** An owl's hoot. [Imit.]

whoop·ee (ʰwoo′pē, ʰwoop′ē) *Slang interj.* An exclamation of joy, excitement, etc. —**make whoopee** To have a noisy, festive time. [< WHOOP]

whooping cough A contagious respiratory disease of bacterial origin chiefly affecting children, marked in later stages by violent coughing.

whooping crane A large white North American crane having a whooplike cry.

whop·per (ʰwop′ər) *n. Informal* **1** Something large or remarkable. **2** An outrageous falsehood.

whop·ping (ʰwop′ing) *adj.* Unusually large, great, or remarkable.

whore (hôr, hōr) *n.* A woman who engages in sexual intercourse promiscuously; esp., a prostitute. —*v.i.* **whored, whor·ing 1** To have illicit sexual intercourse, esp. with a whore. **2** To be or act like a whore. [< OE *hōre*]

whorl (ʰwûrl, ʰwôrl) *n.* **1** The flywheel of a spindle. **2** *Bot.* A set of leaves, etc., distributed in a circle around a stem. **3** *Zool.* A turn of a spiral shell. **4** Any of the convoluted ridges of a fingerprint. [? < WHIRL] —**whorled** *adj.*

Whorl *def. 2*

whor·tle·ber·ry (ʰwûr′təl·ber′ē) *n. pl.* ·**ries 1** A European shrub with edible blueblack berries. **2** Its fruit. **3** HUCKLEBERRY. [< OE *horta whortleberry* + BERRY]

whose (hooz) The possessive case of WHO and often of WHICH. [< OE *hwæs*, genitive of *hwā* who]

who·so (hoo′sō) *pron. Archaic* WHOEVER.

who·so·ev·er (hoo′sō·ev′ər) *pron.* WHOEVER.

why (ʰwī) *adv.* For what cause, purpose, or reason: *Why did you go?* —*conj.* **1** The reason or cause for which: I don't know *why* he went. **2** For or because of which: I know the reason *why* he went. —*n. pl.* **whys** A cause; reason. —*interj.* An exclamation expressing surprise, doubt, etc. [< OE *hwī, hwȳ*]

WI Wisconsin (P.O. abbr.).

W.I. West Indian; West Indies.

wick (wik) *n.* A strand of loosely twisted or woven fibers, as in a candle or lamp, exerting by capillary attraction to convey fuel to a flame. [< OE *wēoca*] —**wick′ing** *n.*

wick·ed (wik′id) *adj.* **1** Evil; depraved. **2** Mischievous; roguish. **3** Troublesome; painful: a *wicked* headache. [< OE *wicca* a wizard] —**wick′ed·ly** *adv.* —**wick′ed·ness** *n.* —**Syn. 1** malevolent, sinful, wrong. **2** devilish.

wick·er (wik′ər) *adj.* Made of twigs, osiers, etc. —*n.* **1** A pliant young shoot or rod; twig; osier. **2** WICKERWORK. [Prob. < Scand.]

wick·er·work (wik′ər·wûrk′) *n.* A fabric or texture, as a basket, made of woven twigs, osiers, etc.

wick·et (wik′it) *n.* **1** A small door or gate often within a larger entrance. **2** A small opening in a door. **3** A small sluicegate at the end of a millrace. **4** In cricket: **a** Either of two arrangements of three upright rods set near together. **b** The level playing space between these. **c** A player's turn at bat. **5** In croquet, an arch, usu. of wire, through which one must hit the ball. [< AF *wiket*]

wick·et·keep·er (wik′it·kē′pər) *n.* In cricket, the fielder stationed right behind the wicket.

wide (wīd) *adj.* **wid·er, wid·est 1** Having relatively great extent between sides. **2** Extended far in every direction; spacious: a *wide* expanse. **3** Having a specified degree of width: an inch *wide*. **4** Distant from the desired or proper point, issue, etc.: *wide* of the mark. **5** Having great scope, range, inclusiveness, etc.: a *wide* variety. **6** Loose; ample; roomy: *wide* trousers. **7** Fully open; expanded or extended: *wide* eyes. **8** *Phonet.* Formed with a relatively relaxed tongue and jaw: said of certain vowels. —*n.* In cricket, a ball bowled so as not to be within the batsman's reach. —*adv.* **1** To a great distance; extensively. **2** Far from the mark, issue, etc. **3** To the greatest extent; fully open. [< OE *wīd*] —**wide′ly** *adv.* —**wide′ness** *n.* —**Syn.** *adj.* **2** ample, broad, extensive, vast.

wide-an·gle lens (wīd′ang′gəl) A type of camera lens

designed to permit an angle of view wider than that of the ordinary lens.

wide-a·wake (wīd′ə·wāk′) *adj.* **1** Totally awake. **2** Alert.

wide-eyed (wīd′īd′) *adj.* **1** With the eyes wide open. **2** Uninformed or unsophisticated.

wid·en (wīd′n) *v.t. & v.i.* To make or become wide or wider. —**wid′en·er** *n.*

wide-o·pen (wīd′ō′pən) *adj.* **1** Opened wide. **2** *Informal* Remiss in the enforcement of laws which regulate gambling, prostitution, etc.: a *wide-open* city.

wide·spread (wīd′spred′) *adj.* **1** Extending over a large space or territory. **2** Held, believed, indulged in, etc., by many people.

widg·eon (wij′ən) *n.* Any of various river ducks having a short bill and wedge-shaped tail. Also **wig·eon.** [?]

wid·get (wij′it) *n. Slang* **1** A product having a unique or ingenious feature; gadget. **2** Something unnamed and used as an example in a hypothetical situation. [Alter. of GADGET]

wid·ow (wid′ō) *n.* **1** A woman who has lost her husband by death and has not remarried. **2** In some card games, an additional hand dealt to the table. **3** *Printing* A short line of type ending a paragraph at the top of a page or column; also, such a line at the end of any paragraph. —*v.t.* To make a widow of. [< OE *widewe*]

wid·ow·er (wid′ō·ər) *n.* A man who has lost his wife by death and has not remarried.

widow's mite A contribution which, although small in amount, is all or even more than the giver can afford.

widow's peak A point of hair growing down from the hairline in the middle of the forehead.

width (width) *n.* **1** Dimension or measurement of an object taken from side to side, or at right angles to the length. **2** Something that has width: a *width* of cloth. [< WIDE]

width·wise (width′wīz) *adv.* In the direction of the width. Also **width′ways′.**

wield (wēld) *v.t.* **1** To use or handle, as a weapon or instrument. **2** To exercise (authority, power, influence, etc.). [Fusion of OE *wealdan* to cause and OE *wildan* to rule] —**wield′er** *n.*

wie·ner (wē′nər) *n.* A kind of smoked sausage, similar to a frankfurter, made of beef and pork. Also **wie·ner·wurst** (wē′nər·wûrst′). [Short for *wienerwurst* < G, Vienna sausage]

wife (wīf) *n. pl.* **wives** (wīvz) **1** A woman joined to a man in lawful wedlock. **2** *Archaic* A woman: now used in combination or in certain phrases: *housewife,* old *wives'* tales. —**take to wife** To marry (a woman). [< OE *wīf*] —**wife′dom, wife′hood** *n.*

wife·ly (wīf′lē) *adj.* ·**li·er, ·li·est 1** Of or like a wife. **2** Suitable to a wife.

wig (wig) *n.* A covering of real or artificial hair for the head. —*v.t.* **wigged, wig·ging 1** To furnish with a wig or wigs. **2** *Brit. Informal* To berate or scold. [Short for PERIWIG]

wig·gle (wig′əl) *v.t. & v.i.* ·**gled, ·gling** To move or cause to move quickly from side to side; wriggle. —*n.* The act of wiggling. [< MLG *wiggelen*] —**wig′gly** *adj.* (·**gli·er, ·gli·est)**

Barrister's wig

wig·gler (wig′lər) *n.* **1** One who or that which wiggles. **2** The larva of a mosquito.

wig·wag (wig′wag′) *v.t. & v.i.* ·**wagged, ·wag·ging 1** To move briskly back and forth; wag. **2** To send (a message) by hand flags, torches, etc. —*n.* **1** The act of wigwagging. **2** A message sent by wigwagging. [< dial. E *wig* wiggle + WAG¹] —**wig′wag′ger** *n.*

wig·wam (wig′wom, -wôm) *n.* A dwelling or lodge of certain North American Indians, commonly a rounded or conical framework of poles covered with bark, rush matting, or hides. [< Algon.]

Wigwam

wild (wīld) *adj.* **1** Living or growing in a natural state; not tamed, domesticated, or cultivated: *wild* animals; *wild* flowers. **2** Being in the natural state without civilized inhabitants or cultivation: *wild* prairies. **3** Uncivilized; primitive: the *wild* men of Borneo. **4** Undisciplined; unruly. **5** Morally dissolute; profligate. **6** Violent; turbulent: a *wild* night. **7** Reckless; imprudent: a *wild* speculation. **8** Unusually odd or strange; extravagant; bizarre: a *wild* imagination. **9** Eager and excited: *wild* with delight. **10** Frenzied; crazed: *wild* with fury. **11** Disorderly; disarranged: a *wild* mop of hair. **12** Far from the mark aimed at; erratic: a *wild* pitch. **13** In some card games, having its value arbitrarily determined by the dealer or holder. **14** *Slang* Terrific; great: The party was *wild*. **15** *Slang* Showy; jazzy: a *wild* necktie. —*n. Often pl.* An uninhabited or uncultivated place; wilderness: the *wilds* of Africa. —**the wild 1** The wilderness. **2** The free, natural, wild life. —*adv.* In a wild manner: to run *wild*. [< OE *wilde*] —**wild′ly** *adv.* —**wild′ness** *n.* —Syn. *adj.* **3** barbarous, savage. **7** irresponsible, rash. **8** fantastic.

wild boar An Old World hog often hunted as game.

wild carrot A weed from which the cultivated carrot is derived; Queen Anne's lace.

wild·cat (wīld′kat′) *n.* **1** Any of various undomesticated felines resembling the domestic cat, but larger and stronger, as the lynx, cougar, etc. **2** An aggressive, quick-tempered person. **3** An unattached locomotive, used on special work, as when sent out to haul a train, etc. **4** A successful oil well drilled in an area previously unproductive. **5** A tricky or unsound business venture, esp. a worthless mine. Also **wild cat.** —*adj.* **1** Unsound; risky; esp. financially. **2** Made, produced, or carried on without official sanction or authorization. **3** Not running on a schedule, as a locomotive. —*v.t. & v.i.* **·cat·ted, ·cat·ting** To drill for oil in (an area not known to be productive). —**wild′cat′-ter** *n.*

wildcat strike A strike unauthorized by regular union procedure.

wilde·beest (wīld′bēst, wil′də-) *n. pl.* **·beests** or **·beest** GNU. [< Du. *wild* wild + *beeste* a beast]

wil·der·ness (wil′dər·nis) *n.* **1** An uncultivated, uninhabited, or barren region. **2** A multitudinous and confusing collection of persons or things. [< OE *wilder* a wild beast + -NESS]

wild-fire (wīld′fīr′) *n.* A raging, destructive fire that is hard to extinguish. —**like wildfire** Very quickly; uncontrollably.

wild-flow·er (wīld′flou′ər) *n.* **1** Any uncultivated plant that bears flowers. **2** The flower of such a plant. Also **wild flower.**

wild-fowl (wīld′foul′) *n. pl.* **·fowl** or **·fowls** A wild bird, esp. wild duck, pheasant, etc., hunted as game. Also **wild fowl.**

wild-goose chase (wīld′gōōs′) Pursuit of the unknown or unattainable.

wild-life (wīld′līf′) *n.* Wild animals collectively.

wild oat 1 *Usu. pl.* Any of various uncultivated grasses. **2** *pl.* Indiscretions of youth, usu. in the phrase **sow one's wild oats.**

wild rice 1 A tall aquatic grass of North America. **2** The highly esteemed, edible grain of this plant.

Wild West The w U.S. in its early period of Indian fighting, lawlessness, etc. Also **wild West**

wild-wood (wīld′wŏŏd′) *n.* Natural forest land.

wile (wīl) *n.* **1** An act or a means of cunning deception. **2** Any trick or artifice. —*v.t.* **wiled, wil·ing** To lure, beguile, or mislead. —**wile away** To pass (time) pleasantly. [< OE *wil*] —Syn. *n.* **2** machination, maneuver, ruse, stratagem.

wil-ful (wil′fəl) *adj.* WILLFUL.

will¹ (wil) *n.* **1** The power to make conscious, deliberate choices or to control what one does. **2** The act or experience of exercising this power. **3** A specific desire, purpose, choice, etc.: the *will* of the people. **4** Strong determination or purpose: the *will* to succeed. **5** Self-control. **6** Attitude or inclination toward others: ill *will*. **7** *Law* The legal declaration of a person's intentions as to the disposition of his estate after his death. —**at will** As one pleases. —**with a will** Energetically. —*v.* **willed, will·ing 1** To decide upon; choose. **2** To resolve upon as an action or course. **3** *Law* To bequeath by a will. **4** To control, as a

hypnotized person, by the exercise of will. **5** To decree: The king *wills* it. —*v.i.* **6** To wish; desire: as you *will*. [< OE *willa*]

will² (wil) *v.* Present *sing. & pl.*: **will** (*Archaic* thou **wilt**); past: **would** (*Archaic* thou **would·est** or **wouldst**) As an auxiliary verb *will* is used with the infinitive without *to,* or elliptically without the infinitive, to express: **1** Futurity: They *will* arrive by dark. **2** Likelihood: You *will* be sorry. **3** Command; order: You *will* leave immediately. **4** Willingness or disposition: Why *will* you not tell the truth? **5** Capability or capacity: The ship *will* survive any storm. **6** Custom or habit: He *will* sit for hours and brood. **7** *Informal* Probability or inference: I expect this *will* be the main street. [< OE *willan*] • See SHALL.

willed (wild) *adj.* Having a will of a given character: used in combination: *weak-willed.*

will-ful (wil′fəl) *adj.* **1** Deliberate; intentional: *willful* disregard of the law. **2** Stubborn; headstrong: a *willful* child. —**will′ful·ly** *adv.* —**will′ful·ness** *n.*

wil-lies (wil′ēz) *n.pl. Slang* Nervousness; jitters: used with *the.* [?]

will-ing (wil′ing) *adj.* **1** Having the mind favorably inclined or disposed. **2** Readily and gladly acting, responding, doing, giving, etc. **3** Readily and gladly offered, done, given, etc. —**will′ing·ly** *adv.* —**will′ing·ness** *n.* —Syn. **3** accommodating, compliant, obliging.

will-o'-the-wisp (wil′ə-thə·wisp′) *n.* IGNIS FATUUS. [Earlier *Will with the wisp*]

wil-low (wil′ō) *n.* **1** Any of a large genus of shrubs and trees having usu. narrow leaves and flexible shoots often used in basketry. **2** The wood of a willow. **3** *Informal* Something made of willow wood, as a cricket bat. —*adj.* Made of willow wood. [< OE *wilige, welig*] • See WEEPING WILLOW.

wil-low-y (wil′ō-ē) *adj.* **·low·i·er, ·low·i·est 1** Tall and graceful. **2** Lithe; flexible; supple. **3** Abounding in willows. —**wil′low·i·ness** *n.*

will-pow·er (wil′pou′ər) *n.* Strength to direct or control one's actions or desires; determination.

wil-ly-nil-ly (wil′ē-nil′ē) *adj.* Being or happening whether one wants it or not. —*adv.* Willingly or unwillingly. [Earlier *will I, nill I* whether I will or not]

wilt¹ (wilt) *v.i.* **1** To lose freshness; droop or become limp. **2** To lose energy and vitality; become faint or languid. **3** To lose courage or spirit. —*v.t.* **4** To cause to wilt. —*n.* **1** The act of wilting or the state of being wilted. **2** A plant disease that causes wilting. [Prob. dial. var. of obs. *welk*]

wilt² (wilt) *Archaic* Will: used with *thou.*

Wil-ton (wil′tən) *n.* A kind of carpet having a velvety texture. Also **Wilton carpet, Wilton rug.** [< *Wilton,* England, where first made]

wi-ly (wī′lē) *adj.* **·li·er, ·li·est** Full of or characterized by wiles; sly; cunning. —**wi′li·ly** *adv.* —**wi′li·ness** *n.*

wim-ple (wim′pəl) *n.* A cloth wrapped in folds around the neck close under the chin and over the head, exposing only the face, worn by medieval women and still by certain nuns. —*v.* **·pled, ·pling** *v.t.* **1** To cover or clothe with a wimple. **2** To make or fold into pleats, as a veil. **3** To cause to move with slight undulations; ripple. —*v.i.* **4** To lie in plaits or folds. **5** To ripple. [< OE *wimpel*]

Wimple

win (win) *v.* **won, won, win·ning** *v.i.* **1** To gain a victory; be victorious in a contest, endeavor, etc. **2** To succeed in reaching or attaining a specified end or condition; get: often with *across, over, through,* etc. —*v.t.* **3** To be successful in; gain victory in: to *win* an argument. **4** To gain in competition or contest: to *win* the blue ribbon. **5** To gain by effort, persistence, etc.: to *win* fame. **6** To influence so as to obtain the good will or favor of: often with *over.* **7** To secure the love of; gain in marriage. **8** To succeed in reaching: to *win* the harbor. —**win out** *Informal* To succeed; triumph. —*n. Informal* A victory; success. [< OE *winnan* contend, labor] —Syn. *v.* **5** achieve, earn, secure.

wince (wins) *v.i.* **winced, winc·ing** To shrink back; flinch. —*n.* The act of wincing. [< AF *wenchier*] —**winc′er** *n.*

winch (winch) *n.* 1 A windlass, particularly one turned by a crank and used for hoisting. 2 A crank with a handle for transmitting motion. [<OE *wince*] — **winch′er** *n.*

Winch

Win·ches·ter rifle (win′ches·tər) A type of repeating rifle, first produced in 1866: a trade name. Also **Winchester.**

wind[1] (wind) *n.* 1 Any movement of air, esp. a natural horizontal movement. 2 Any powerful or destructive movement of air, as a tornado. 3 The direction from which a wind blows. 4 Air pervaded by a scent, as in hunting. 5 The power of breathing; breath: He lost his *wind*. 6 Idle chatter. 7 Bragging; vanity; conceit. 8 *pl.* The wind instruments of an orchestra; also, the players of these instruments. 9 The gaseous product of indigestion; flatulence. —**break wind** To expel gas through the anus. —**get wind of** To receive a hint or intimation of. —**how the wind blows** (or **lies,** etc.) What is taking place, being decided, etc. —**in the teeth of the wind** Directly against the wind: also **in the wind's eye.** —**in the wind** Impending; afoot. —*v.t.* 1 To follow by scent; to catch a scent of on the wind. 2 To exhaust the breath of, as by racing. 3 To allow to recover breath by resting. 4 To expose to the wind, as in ventilating. [<OE] —**Syn.** *n.* 1 blast, breeze, gale, gust, zephyr.

wind[2] (wīnd) *v.* **wound** or **wind·ed, wind·ing** *v.t.* 1 To coil (thread, rope, etc.) around some object or fixed core; twine. 2 To encircle or cover with something, as by coiling or wrapping: to *wind* a spool with thread. 3 To renew the motion of, as a clock, by turning a stem, key, etc. 4 To turn in a revolving motion: to *wind* a handle. 5 To cause to turn and twist. 6 To make (one's way) by a turning and twisting course. 7 To introduce carefully or deviously; insinuate: He *wound* himself into my confidence. 8 To raise or hoist, as by means of a capstan or windlass. —*v.i.* 9 To move in a turning, twisting course; meander. 10 To coil or twine about some central object or core. 11 To move in a circular or spiral course. 12 To proceed or gain an end carefully or deviously. —**wind down** To decrease or be decreased gradually; de-escalate: to *wind down* a war. —**wind up** 1 To coil or wind round and round. 2 To excite; arouse. 3 To bring to conclusion or settlement: He *wound up* his affairs. 4 In baseball, to swing the arm preparatory to pitching. 5 To hoist. —*n.* 1 The act of winding, or the condition of being wound. 2 A bend, turn, or twist. [<OE *windan*] —**wind′er** *n.*

wind[3] (wīnd, wind) *v.t.* **wind·ed** or **wound, wind·ing** 1 To blow, as a horn; sound. 2 To give (a call or signal), as with a horn. [<WIND[1]; infl. by WIND[2]]

wind·age (win′dij) *n.* 1 The rush of air caused by the rapid passage of an object, as a projectile. 2 Deflection of an object, as a bullet, from its natural course by wind. 3 *Naut.* The surface offered to the wind by a vessel.

wind·bag (wind′bag′) *n. Informal* An overly talkative person who says little of significance.

wind·blown (wind′blōn′) *adj.* 1 Tossed or blown by the wind. 2 Having a permanent direction of growth as determined by prevailing winds: said of plants and trees.

wind·borne (wind′bôrn′, -bōrn′) *adj.* Carried or transported by the wind.

wind·break (wind′brāk′) *n.* Anything, as a hedge, fence, etc., that protects from or breaks the force of the wind.

wind·break·er (wind′brā′kər) *n.* A sports jacket for outer wear, having a close-fitting or elastic waistband and cuffs. [<*Windbreaker*, a trade name]

wind·bro·ken (wind′brō′kən) *adj.* Having the heaves: said of a horse.

wind·chill factor (wind′chil′) 1 A measure of air temperature modified by the chilling effect of wind of a given velocity as felt on the surface of the skin. 2 The effect of wind in reducing perceived air temperature.

wind·ed (win′did) *adj.* 1 Out of breath. 2 Having a specified kind of wind or breath: used in combination: *short-winded.*

wind·fall (wind′fôl′) *n.* 1 Something, as ripening fruit, brought down by the wind. 2 A piece of unexpected good fortune.

wind·flow·er (wind′flou′ər) *n.* ANEMONE.

wind gauge An instrument for measuring the velocity of the wind; anemometer.

wind·hov·er (wind′huv′ər) *n. Brit.* KESTREL.

wind·ing (wīn′ding) *n.* 1 The act or condition of one who or that which winds; a turning or coiling. 2 A bend or turn, or a series of them. 3 Something that winds. —*adj.* 1 Turning spirally about an axis or core. 2 Having bends or lateral turns.

wind·ing sheet (wīn′ding) SHROUD (def. 1).

wind instrument (wind) A musical instrument whose sounds are produced by blowing air through it, esp. a portable one, as a flute, oboe, etc.

wind·jam·mer (wind′jam′ər) *n. Naut.* 1 A sailing vessel, as distinguished from a steamship. 2 A member of its crew.

wind·lass (wind′ləs) *n.* Any of several devices for hoisting or hauling, esp. one consisting of a drum turned by means of a crank so that the hoisting rope winds on the drum. [<ON *vinda* wind + *āss* a beam]

Differential windlass

wind·mill (wind′mil′) *n.* 1 A mill having at the top a system of adjustable slats, wings, or sails which, when turned by the wind, transmit power to a pump, millstone, or the like. 2 An imaginary wrong, evil, or foe: usu. in the phrase **tilt at windmills,** an allusion to Don Quixote's combat with windmills, which he mistook for giants. • See VANE.

win·dow (win′dō) *n.* 1 An opening in the wall of a building, etc., to admit light or air, usu. capable of being opened and closed, and including casements or sashes fitted with glass. 2 A windowpane or the sash or framework that encloses it. 3 Anything resembling or suggesting a window, as a transparent patch in certain envelopes. —*v.t.* To provide with a window or windows. [<ON *vindr* wind + *auga* an eye]

window box A box along a window ledge or sill, for growing plants.

window dressing 1 The act or art of arranging merchandise attractively in shop and store windows. 2 Any action, report, etc., designed to make something seem more attractive or plausible than it actually is.

win·dow·pane (win′dō·pān′) *n.* A pane of glass for a window.

window seat A seat in the recess of a window.

window shade A flexible covering for the inside of a window, used to regulate light.

win·dow·shop (win′dō·shop′) *v.i.* **-shopped, -shop·ping** To look at goods shown in store windows without buying them. —**win′dow·shop′per** *n.*

win·dow·sill (win′dō·sil′) *n.* The horizontal ledge at the bottom of a window opening.

wind·pipe (wind′pīp′) *n.* TRACHEA.

wind·row (wind′rō′) *n.* 1 A long row of hay or grain raked together preparatory to building into cocks. 2 A line of dust, surf, leaves, etc. swept together by wind. —*v.t.* To rake or shape into a windrow. —**wind′row′er** *n.*

wind·screen (wind′skrēn′) *n. Brit.* WINDSHIELD.

wind·shear (wind′shir′) *n.* A strong, rapid change in wind direction.

wind·shield (wind′shēld′) *n.* A transparent screen, as of glass, across and above the dashboard of motor vehicles, power boats, etc., providing protection from the wind.

wind·sock (wind′sok′) *n.* A large, conical bag, open at both ends, mounted on a pivot, and used to indicate the direction of the wind. Also **wind sock, wind sleeve.**

Wind·sor (win′zər) Name of the royal family of Great Britain since July 27, 1917.

Windsor chair A wooden chair, typically with a spindle back, slanting legs, and a flat or saddle seat.

Windsor knot A wide knot that can be used to tie a four-in-hand tie.

Windsor tie A wide, soft necktie tied in a loose bow.

wind·storm (wind′stôrm′) *n.* A violent wind, usu. with little or no precipitation.

wind·swept (wind′swept′) *adj.* Exposed to or propelled by the wind.

wind tunnel *Aeron.* A device in which the effects of artificially produced winds, as on airplane wings, can be studied.

wind·up (wīnd′up) *n.* 1 The act of concluding. 2 A conclusion or culmination; end. 3 In baseball, the swing of the arm preparatory to pitching the ball.

wind·ward (wind′wərd) *adj.* 1 Of or toward the direction from which the wind blows. 2 Being on the side exposed to the wind. —*n.* The direction from which the wind blows. —*adv.* In the direction from which the wind blows.

wind·y (win′dē) *adj.* **wind·i·er, wind·i·est** 1 Of or abounding in wind; stormy; tempestuous: *windy* weather. 2 Exposed to the wind. 3 Suggestive of wind; boisterous; violent. 4 Flatulent. 5 Boastful, talkative, or pompous. 6 Idle; empty: *windy* talk. —**wind′i·ly** *adv.* —**wind′i·ness** *n.*

wine (wīn) *n.* 1 The fermented juice of the grape, used as an alcoholic beverage and in cooking. 2 The fermented juice of any of several other fruits or vegetables: dandelion *wine.* 3 The color of red wine. —*v.* **wined, win·ing** *v.t.* 1 To entertain or treat with wine. —*v.i.* 2 To drink wine. [< OE *wīn*]

wine·bib·ber (wīn′bib′ər) *n.* A person given to excessive drinking of wine. —**wine′bib′bing** *adj., n.*

wine cellar A storage space for wines; also, the wines stored.

wine-col·ored (wīn′kul′ərd) *adj.* Having the color of red wine.

wine·glass (wīn′glas′, -gläs′) *n.* A small goblet, usu. stemmed, from which to drink wine.

wine·grow·er (wīn′grō′ər) *n.* One who cultivates a vineyard and makes wine. —**wine′grow′ing** *adj., n.*

wine·press (wīn′pres′) *n.* An apparatus or a place where the juice of grapes is expressed. —**wine′press′er** *n.*

win·er·y (wī′nər·ē) *n. pl.* **·er·ies** An establishment where wine is made.

Wine·sap (wīn′sap) *n.* An American variety of red winter apple.

wine·skin (wīn′skin′) *n.* A bag made of the entire skin of an animal, as a goat, used for containing wine.

wing (wing) *n.* 1 An organ of flight; esp. one of a pair of appendages of a bird or bat, adapted for flight. 2 An analogous organ in insects and some other animals. 3 Anything resembling or suggestive of a wing in form or function. 4 *Aeron.* The (or one of the) main supporting surface(s) of an airplane. 5 *Bot.* Any thin, winglike expansion of certain stems, seeds, etc. 6 A vane, as of a windmill. 7 Anything regarded as conferring the swift motion or rapture of flight: on *wings* of song. 8 Flight by or as by wings. 9 *Archit.* A part attached to a side, esp. a projection or extension of a building on the side of the main portion. 10 An annex or separate section of a large building: the surgical *wing* of a hospital. 11 Either of two sides, unseen by the audience, of a proscenium stage; also, a piece of scenery for the side of a stage. 12 Either of two sidepieces on the back of an armchair. 13 A side section of something that shuts or folds, as a screen. 14 A tactical and administrative unit of the U.S. Air Force, larger than a group. 15 *Mil.* Either division of a military force on either side of the center. 16 An analogous formation in certain outdoor games, as hockey or football. 17 Either of two extremist groups or factions in a political organization: the left *wing.* 18 A subsidiary group of a parent organization. 19 *Slang* An arm, esp., in baseball, a pitching or throwing arm. 20 *pl.* The insignia worn by certain qualified aircraft pilots, navigators, etc. —**on** (or **upon**) **the wing** 1 In flight. 2 Departing; also, journeying. —**take wing** To fly away. —**under one's wing** Under one's protection. —*v.t.* 1 To pass over or through in flight. 2 To accomplish by flying: the eagle *winged* its way. 3 To enable to fly. 4 To cause to go swiftly; speed. 5 To transport by flight. 6 To provide with wings for flight. 7 To supply with a side body or part. 8 To wound (a bird) in a wing. 9 To disable by a minor wound. —*v.i.* 10 To fly; soar. —**wing it** *Slang* To act, do, arrange, etc., without advance preparation; improvise. [< ON *vængr*]

wing chair A large, upholstered armchair with a high back and side pieces designed as protection from drafts.

winged (wingd, wing′id) *adj.* 1 Having wings. 2 Passing swiftly. 3 Sublime; lofty.

wing·spread (wing′spred′) *n.* The distance between the tips of the fully extended wings, as of a bird, insect, or airplane. Also **wing′span′.**

wink (wingk) *v.i.* 1 To close and open the eye or eyelids quickly. 2 To draw the eyelids of one eye together, as in making a sign. 3 To emit fitful gleams; twinkle. —*v.t.* 4 To close and open (the eye or eyelids) quickly. 5 To move, force, etc., by winking: with *away, off,* etc. 6 To signify or express by winking. —**wink at** To pretend not to see. —*n.* 1 The act of winking. 2 The time necessary for a wink. 3 A twinkle. 4 A hint conveyed by winking. 5 A brief bit (of sleep): I had a *wink* after lunch. —**forty winks** A short nap. [< OE *wincian* close the eyes]

Wing chair

wink·er (wing′kər) *n.* 1 One who winks. 2 *Slang* EYELASH.

win·ner (win′ər) *n.* 1 One who or that which wins. 2 *Informal* Someone or something likely to succeed.

win·ning (win′ing) *adj.* 1 Successful in achievement, esp. in competition. 2 Capable of charming; attractive; winsome. —*n.* 1 The act of one who wins. 2 *Usu. pl.* That which is won, as money in gambling. —**win′ning·ly** *adv.* —**win′ning·ness** *n.*

win·ning·est (win′ing·əst) *adj. Informal* Most often winning: the *winningest* team in baseball.

win·now (win′ō) *v.t.* 1 To separate (grain, etc.) from the chaff. 2 To blow away (the chaff) thus. 3 To separate (what is valuable) or to eliminate (what is valueless): to *winnow* out the good or the bad. 4 To blow upon; cause to flutter. 5 To beat or fan (the air) with the wings. 6 To scatter by blowing; disperse. —*v.i.* 7 To separate grain from chaff. 8 To fly; flap. —*n.* 1 Any device used in winnowing grain. 2 The act of winnowing. [< OE *windwian* < *wind* the wind] —**win′now·er** *n.*

win·o (wī′nō) *n. pl.* **·noes** or **·nos** *Slang* A drunkard who habitually drinks wine, esp. cheap wine. [< WINE]

win·some (win′səm) *adj.* Charming; attractive. [< OE *wyn* joy] —**win′some·ly** *adv.* —**win′some·ness** *n.* —**Syn.** amiable, appealing, engaging, pleasant, winning.

win·ter (win′tər) *n.* 1 The coldest season of the year, extending from the end of autumn to the beginning of spring. 2 A time marked by lack of life, warmth, and cheer. 3 A year as including the winter season: a man of ninety *winters.* —*v.i.* 1 To pass the winter. —*v.t.* 2 To care for, feed, or protect during the winter: to *winter* plants. —*adj.* Pertaining to, suitable for, or characteristic of winter. [< OE] —**win′ter·er** *n.*

win·ter·green (win′tər·grēn) *n.* 1 A small evergreen plant bearing aromatic oval leaves, white, bell-shaped flowers and edible red berries. 2 A colorless, volatile oil extracted from the leaves of this plant or made synthetically, used as a flavor.

win·ter·ize (win′tə·rīz) *v.t.* **·ized, ·iz·ing** To prepare or put in condition for winter, as a motor vehicle, etc.

win·ter·kill (win′tər·kil′) *v.t. & v.i.* To die or kill by exposure to extreme cold: said of plants. —*n.* The act, process, or an instance of winterkilling.

winter solstice See SOLSTICE.

winter wheat Wheat planted before snowfall and harvested the following summer.

win·try (win′trē) *adj.* **·tri·er, ·tri·est** Of or like winter; cold, bleak, cheerless, etc. Also **win′ter·y** (-tər·ē). —**win′tri·ly** *adv.* —**win′tri·ness** *n.*

win·y (wī′nē) *adj.* **win·i·er, win·i·est** Having the taste, color, smell, etc., of wine.

wipe (wīp) *v.t.* **wiped, wip·ing** 1 To subject to slight friction or rubbing, usu. with some soft, absorbent material. 2 To remove by rubbing lightly: usu. with *away* or *off.* 3 To move or draw for the purpose of wiping: He *wiped* his hand across his brow. **4** To apply by wiping. —**wipe out 1** To kill or murder. **2** To destroy utterly; annihilate. **3** In surfing, to be overturned by a wave. —*n.* The act of wiping. [< OE *wipian*] —**wip′er** *n.*

wire (wīr) *n.* **1** A slender rod, strand, or thread of metal. **2** Something made of wire, as a fence, a cord to conduct an electric current, etc. **3** WIREWORK. **4** A telephone or telegraph cable. **5** The telegraph system as a means of communication. **6** TELEGRAM. **7** The screen of a papermaking machine. **8** A line marking the finish of a race. —**get (in) under the wire** To conclude or achieve something at the very last moment. —**pull wires** *Informal* To use secret or private sources of influence to attain something. —*v.* **wired, wir·ing** *v.t.* **1** To fasten or bind with wire. **2** To furnish or equip with wiring. **3** To telegraph: to *wire* an order. **4** To place on wire, as beads. —*v.i.* **5** To telegraph. [< OE *wīr*] —**wir′er** *n.*

wire gauge 1 A gauge for measuring the diameter of wire. **2** A standard system of sizes for wire.

wire-haired terrier (wīr′hârd′) A fox terrier having a wiry coat. Also **wire′hair′** (-hâr′).

wire·less (wīr′lis) *adj.* **1** Without wire or wires; having no wires. **2** *Brit.* Radio. —*n.* **1** The wireless telegraph or telephone system, or a message transmitted by either. **2** *Brit.* Radio. —*v.t. & v.i. Brit.* To communicate (with) by radio.

Wire·pho·to (wīr′fō′tō) *n. pl.* **·tos** An apparatus and method for transmitting and receiving photographs by wire: a trade name.

wire-pull·er (wīr′pŏŏl′ər) *n.* **1** One who pulls wires, as of a puppet. **2** One who uses secret means to control others or gain his own ends; an intriguer. —**wire′pull′ing** *n.*

wire·tap (wīr′tap′) *n.* **1** A device used to make a connection with a telephone or telegraph wire to listen to or record the message transmitted. **2** The act of wiretapping. —*v.* **·tapped, ·tap·ping** *v.t.* **1** To connect a wiretap to. **2** To monitor by the use of a wiretap. —*v.i.* **3** To use a wiretap. —**wire′tap′per** *n.*

wire·work (wīr′wûrk′) *n.* A mesh or netting made of wire.

wir·ing (wīr′ing) *n.* An entire system of wire installed for the distribution of electric power, as for lighting, heating, sound, etc.

wir·y (wīr′ē) *adj.* **wir·i·er, wir·i·est 1** Lean, but tough and sinewy: said of persons. **2** Like wire; stiff; bristly. —**wir′i·ly** *adv.* —**wir′i·ness** *n.*

Wis., Wisc. Wisconsin.

wis·dom (wiz′dəm) *n.* **1** The ability to discern what is true or right and to make sound judgments based on such discernment. **2** Insight or intuition. **3** COMMON SENSE. **4** A high degree of knowledge; learning. **5** An accumulated body of knowledge, as in philosophy, science, etc. [< OE *wīs* wise] —**Syn. 1** sapience, sagacity. **4** enlightenment, erudition.

Wisdom of Solomon A book of the Old Testament Apocrypha, consisting of a hymn in praise of wisdom.

wisdom tooth The last tooth on either side of the upper and lower jaws in man. —**cut one's wisdom teeth** To acquire mature judgment. • See TOOTH.

wise¹ (wīz) *adj.* **wis·er, wis·est 1** Having or showing wisdom (def. 1). **2** Having or showing insight, intuition, common sense, or knowledge. **3** Shrewd; calculating; cunning. **4** *Informal* Aware of: *wise* to his motives. **5** *Slang* Arrogant; fresh: a *wise* guy. —**get wise** *Slang* **1** To learn the true facts about. **2** To become arrogant or fresh. —**wise up** *Slang* To make or become aware, informed, or sophisticated. [< OE *wīs*] —**wise′ly** *adv.* —**wise′ness** *n.*

wise² (wīz) *n.* Way of doing; manner; method: chiefly in the phrases **in any wise, in no wise,** etc. [< OE *wīse* manner]

-wise *suffix of adverbs & nouns* **1** In a (specified) way or manner: *nowise, likewise.* **2** In a (specified) direction or position: *lengthwise, clockwise:* often equivalent to *-ways.* **3** *Informal* With reference to: *Moneywise,* the job is worth considering. [< OE *wīse* manner, fashion]

wise·a·cre (wīz′ā′kər) *n.* A person who claims to know everything. [< MDu. *wijssegger* a soothsayer]

wise·crack (wīz′krak′) *Slang n.* A smart, insolent, or

supercilious remark. —*v.i.* To utter a wisecrack. —**wise′crack′er** *n.*

wish (wish) *n.* **1** A desire or longing, usu. for some definite thing. **2** An expression of such a desire; petition. **3** Something wished for. —*v.t.* **1** To have a desire or longing for; want: We *wish* to be sure. **2** To desire a specified condition or state for (a person or thing): I *wish* this day were over. **3** To invoke upon or for someone: I *wished* him good luck. **4** To bid: to *wish* someone good morning. **5** To request, command, or entreat: I *wish* you would stop yelling. —*v.i.* **6** To have or feel a desire; yearn; long: usu. with *for:* to *wish* for a friend's return. **7** To make or express a wish. —**wish on** *Informal* To impose (something unpleasant or unwanted) on a person. [< OE *wȳscan*] —**wish′er** *n.*

wish·bone (wish′bōn′) *n.* The forked bone situated in front of the sternum in most birds.

wish·ful (wish′fəl) *adj.* Having or indicating a wish or desire. —**wish′ful·ly** *adv.* —**wish′ful·ness** *n.*

wishful thinking A believing that what one wants to be true is true.

wish·y-wash·y (wish′ē-wosh′ē, -wôsh′ē) *adj. Informal* **1** Thin; diluted, as liquor. **2** Lacking in purpose, effectiveness, or strength.

wisp (wisp) *n.* **1** A small bunch, as of hay, straw, or hair. **2** A small bit; a mere indication: a *wisp* of vapor. **3** A slight, delicate thing: a *wisp* of a child. **4** WILL-O′-THE-WISP. [ME *wisp, wips*] —**wisp′y** *adj.* (**·i·er, ·i·est**)

wist (wist) *Archaic p.t. & p.p.* of WIT².

wis·te·ri·a (wis·tir′ē-ə, -târ′-) *n.* Any of a genus of woody twining shrubs of the bean family, with pinnate leaves, elongated pods, and showy clusters of blue, purple, or white flowers. Also **wis·tar·i·a** (wis·târ′ē-ə). [< C. *Wistar,* 1761–1818, U.S. anatomist]

wist·ful (wist′fəl) *adj.* **1** Wishful; yearning. **2** Musing; pensive. [Appar. < obs. *wistly* intently] —**wist′ful·ly** *adv.* —**wist′ful·ness** *n.*

Wisteria

wit¹ (wit) *n.* **1** The power of perceiving, reasoning, knowing, etc.; intelligence. **2** *pl.* **a** The mental faculties: to use one's *wits*. **b** Such faculties in relation to their state of balance: out of one's *wits*. **3** Practical intelligence; common sense. **4** The ability to perceive unexpected analogies or incongruities and to express them in an amusing or epigrammatic manner. **5** The ability to make jokes, amusing remarks, etc. **6** A person with wit (defs. 4 & 5). **7** Speech or writing characterized by wit (defs. 4 & 5). —**at one's wits′ end** At the limit of one's devices and resources. —**live by one's wits** To make a living by using one's practical intelligence and resourcefulness, often in unscrupulous or fraudulent ways. [< OE]

wit² (wit) *v.t. & v.i.* Present indicative: I **wot,** thou **wost,** he, she, it **wot,** we, ye, they **wite(n);** *p.t.* and *p.p.* **wist;** *pr.p.* **wit·ting** *Archaic* To be or become aware (of); learn; know. —**to wit** That is to say; namely. [< OE *witan* know]

witch (wich) *n.* **1** A woman who practices sorcery or has supernatural powers, esp. to work evil. **2** An ugly old woman; a hag. **3** A bewitching or fascinating woman or girl. —*v.t.* **1** To work an evil spell upon; effect by witchcraft. **2** To fascinate or charm. —*v.i.* **3** DOWSE². [< OE *wicce* a witch, fem. of *wicca* a wizard]

witch·craft (wich′kraft′, -kräft′) *n.* **1** Black magic; sorcery. **2** Extraordinary influence or fascination.

witch doctor Among certain primitive peoples, a man skilled in counteracting evil spells.

witch·er·y (wich′ər-ē) *n. pl.* **·er·ies 1** Witchcraft; black magic; sorcery. **2** Power to charm; fascination.

witch hazel 1 Any of a genus of shrubs and small trees with usu. yellow flowers. **2** An extract derived from the bark and dried leaves of a certain witch hazel, used as a mild astringent. [< OE *wice* wych-elm + HAZEL]

witch hunt *Slang* An investigation or harassment of dissenters, often for the undeclared purpose of weakening political opposition.

witch·ing (wich′ing) *adj.* Having the power to enchant; bewitching. —**witch′ing·ly** *adv.*

with (with, with) *prep.* **1** In the company of: Walk *with* me. **2** Having; bearing: a hat *with* a feather. **3** Characterized or marked by: a man *with* brains. **4** In a manner characterized by; exhibiting: to dance *with* grace. **5** Among, into, near to, etc.: counted *with* the others. **6** In the course of: We forget *with* time. **7** From: to part *with* the past. **8** Against: to struggle *with* an adversary. **9** In the opinion of: That is all right *with* me. **10** Because of: faint *with* hunger. **11** In or under the care, supervision, etc., of: Leave the key with the janitor. **12** By means or aid of: to write *with* a pencil. **13** By the use, addition, etc., of: trimmed *with* lace. **14** As an associate, member, etc., of: worked *with* her sister; played *with* an orchestra. **15** In spite of: *With* all his money, he could not buy health. **16** At the same time as: to go to bed *with* the chickens. **17** In the same direction as: to drift *with* the crowd. **18** In regard to; in the case of: I am angry *with* them. **19** Onto; to: Join this tube *with* that one. **20** In proportion to: His fame grew *with* his achievements. **21** In support of: He voted *with* the Left. **22** Of the same opinion as: I'm *with* you there! **23** Having received or been granted: *With* your consent I'll go now. [< OE]

with- *prefix* **1** Against: *withstand.* **2** Back; away: *withhold.* [< OE *with* against]

with·al (with·ôl′, with-) *adv.* **1** Besides; in addition. **2** Notwithstanding; nevertheless. —*prep. Archaic* With: used at the end of the clause: a bow to shoot *withal.* [ME *with* + *alle* all]

with·draw (with·drô′, with-) *v.* **·drew, ·drawn, ·draw·ing** *v.t.* **1** To draw or take away; remove. **2** To take back, as an assertion or a promise. **3** To keep from use, sale, etc. —*v.i.* **4** To draw back; retreat. **5** To remove oneself; leave, as from an activity.

with·draw·al (with·drô′əl, with-) *n.* **1** The act or process of withdrawing. **2** The act or process of overcoming one's addiction to a habit-forming drug.

withdrawal symptom Any of the symptoms caused by the withdrawal of a physically addictive drug from an addict, as tremors, sweating, chills, vomiting, and diarrhea.

with·drawn (with·drôn′, with-) *adj.* **1** Not responsive socially or emotionally; introverted. **2** Isolated; remote.

withe (with, with, with) *n.* A willowy, supple twig, used to bind or wrap. [< OE *withthe*]

with·er (with′ər) *v.i.* **1** To become limp or dry, as a plant when deprived of moisture. **2** To waste, as flesh. —*v.t.* **3** To cause to become limp or dry. **4** To abash, as by a scornful glance. [ME *widren*] —**Syn. 1** shrink, shrivel. **4** confuse, shame.

with·ers (with′ərz) *n.pl.* The highest part of the back of the horse, ox, etc., between the shoulder blades. [< OE *withre* resistance: so called because this part presses against the harness when a horse is pulling a load]

with·hold (with·hōld′, with-) *v.* **·held, ·hold·ing** *v.t.* **1** To hold back; restrain. **2** To refuse to grant, permit, etc. **3** To deduct (taxes, etc.) from a salary before payment. —*v.i.* **4** To refrain. —**with·hold′er** *n.*

withholding tax That part of an employee's wages or salary which is deducted as an installment on his income tax.

Withers

with·in (with·in′, with-) *adv.* **1** In the inner part; interiorly. **2** Inside the body, heart, or mind. **3** Indoors. —*prep.* **1** In the inner or interior part or parts of; inside: *within* the house. **2** In the limits, range, or compass of (a specified time, space, or distance): *within* a mile of here; *within* ten minutes' walk. **3** Not exceeding (a specified quantity): Live *within* your means. **4** In the reach, limit, or scope of: *within* my power. [< OE *with* with + *innan* in]

with-it (with′it) *adj. Slang* In touch with modern habits, fashions, trends, etc.; up-to-date.

with·out (with·out′, with-) *prep.* **1** Not having; lacking: *without* money. **2** In the absence of: We must manage *without* help. **3** Free from: *without* fear. **4** At, on, or to the outside of. **5** Outside of or beyond the limits of: living *without* the pale of civilization. **6** With avoidance of: He listened *without* paying attention. —*adv.* **1** In or on the

outer part; externally. **2** OUTDOORS. [< OE *with* with + *ūtan* out]

with·stand (with·stand′, with-) *v.* **·stood, ·stand·ing** *v.t. & v.i.* To resist, oppose, or endure, esp. successfully. [< OE *with-* against + *standan* stand]

with·y (with′ē, with′ē) *n. pl.* **with·ies** WITHE.

wit·less (wit′lis) *adj.* Lacking in wit; foolish. —**wit′less·ly** *adv.* —**wit′less·ness** *n.*

wit·ness (wit′nis) *n.* **1** A person who has seen or knows something and is therefore competent to give evidence concerning it. **2** That which serves as or furnishes evidence or proof. **3** *Law* **a** One who has knowledge of facts relating to a given cause and is subpoenaed to testify. **b** A person who has signed his name to a legal document in order that he may testify to its authenticity. **4** Evidence; testimony. —**bear witness 1** To give evidence; testify. **2** To be evidence. —*v.t.* **1** To see or know by personal experience. **2** To furnish or serve as evidence of. **3** To give testimony to. **4** To be the site or scene of: This spot has *witnessed* many heinous crimes. **5** *Law* To see the execution of (an instrument) and subscribe to its authenticity. —*v.i.* **6** To give evidence; testify. [< OE *witnes* knowledge, testimony] —**wit′ness·er** *n.*

witness stand The platform in a courtroom from which a witness gives evidence.

wit·ted (wit′id) *adj.* Having (a specified kind of) wit: used in combination: *quick-witted.*

wit·ti·cism (wit′ə·siz′əm) *n.* A witty or clever remark. [< WITTY]

wit·ting·ly (wit′ing·lē) *adv.* Designedly; knowingly. [< WIT²]

wit·ty (wit′ē) *adj.* **·ti·er, ·ti·est** Having, displaying, or full of wit. [< OE *wittig* wise] —**wit′ti·ly** *adv.* —**wit′ti·ness** *n.*

wive (wīv) *v.t. & v.i.* **wived, wiv·ing** *Archaic* To marry (a woman). [< OE *wīf* a wife, woman]

wives (wīvz) *n. pl.* of WIFE.

wiz·ard (wiz′ərd) *n.* **1** A magician or sorcerer. **2** *Informal* A very skillful or clever person. —*adj.* Of or pertaining to wizards. [< OE *wīs* wise]

wiz·ard·ry (wiz′ərd·rē) *n.* The practice or methods of a wizard.

wiz·ened (wiz′ənd) *adj.* Shriveled; dried up. [< OE *wisnian,* dry up, wither]

wk. weak; week; work.

wks. weeks; works.

WL, w.l. water line; wave length.

W. long. west longitude.

WNW, W.N.W., wnw, w.n.w. west-northwest.

WO, W.O. wait order; Warrant Officer.

woad (wōd) *n.* **1** An Old World herb related to mustard. **2** The blue dye obtained from its leaves. [< OE *wād*] —**woad′ed** *adj.*

wob·ble (wob′əl) *v.* **·bled, ·bling** *v.i.* **1** To move or sway unsteadily. **2** To show indecision or unsteadiness; vacillate. —*v.t.* **3** To cause to wobble. —*n.* A wobbling motion. [? < LG *wabbeln*] —**wob′bler** *n.* —**wob′bling·ly** *adv.* —**wob′bly** *adj.* **(·bli·er, ·bli·est)**

woe (wō) *n.* **1** Overwhelming sorrow; grief. **2** Heavy affliction or calamity; disaster; suffering. —*interj.* Alas! [< OE *wā* misery]

woe·be·gone (wō′bi·gôn′, -gon′) *adj.* Having or exhibiting woe; mournful; sorrowful. —**Syn.** dejected, depressed, lugubrious, melancholy.

woe·ful (wō′fəl) *adj.* **1** Accompanied by or causing woe; direful. **2** Expressive of sorrow; doleful. **3** Paltry; miserable; mean; sorry. —**woe′ful·ly** *adv.* —**woe′ful·ness** *n.*

wok (wok) *n.* A Chinese cooking pan, as of iron, aluminum, or copper, with handles and a rounded bottom, usu. equipped with a separate metal ring to prevent tipping. [< Chinese]

Wok

woke (wōk) *p.t.* of WAKE¹.

wok·en (wō′kən) *Regional & alternative Brit. p.p.* of WAKE¹.

wold (wōld) *n.* An undulating tract of treeless upland. [< OE *wald* a forest]

---

add, āce, câre, pälm; end, ēven; it, īce; odd, ōpen, ôrder; tŏŏk, pōōl; up, bûrn; ə = a in *above, u* in *focus;* yōō = u in *fuse;* oil; pout; check; go; ring; thin; this; zh, *vision.* < derived from; ? origin uncertain or unknown.

wolf (wŏŏlf) *n. pl.* **wolves** (wŏŏlvz) 1 Any of various wild, carnivorous mammals related to the dog. 2 Any ravenous, cruel, or rapacious person. 3 *Slang* A man who zealously and aggressively pursues women. —**cry wolf** To give a false alarm. —**keep the wolf from the door** To avert want or starvation. —*v.t.* To devour ravenously: often with *down*. [< OE *wulf*]

Timber wolf

wolf·ber·ry (wŏŏlf′ber′ē) *n. pl.* **·ries** A shrub of the honeysuckle family, with pinkish, bell-shaped flowers and spikes of white berries.

wolf·hound (wŏŏlf′hound′) *n.* Either of two breeds of large dogs, the **Russian wolfhound** and the **Irish wolfhound,** formerly trained to hunt wolves.

wolf·ish (wŏŏlf′ish) *adj.* Of or like a wolf; rapacious; savage. —**wolf′ish·ly** *adv.* —**wolf′ish·ness** *n.*

wolf·ram (wŏŏl′frəm) *n.* TUNGSTEN. [G]

wolf·ram·ite (wŏŏl′frəm·īt) *n.* A grayish black or brown mineral, an important source of tungsten. [< G *Wolfram* tungsten]

wolfs·bane (wŏŏlfs′bān′) *n.* A species of aconite, usu. with yellow flowers. Also **wolf′s-bane.**

wol·ver·ine (wŏŏl′və·rēn′) *n.* A rapacious carnivore related to weasels, with stout body and bushy tail. Also **wol′ver·ene′.** [< WOLF]

wolves (wŏŏlvz) *n. pl.* of WOLF.

wom·an (wŏŏm′ən) *n. pl.* **wom·en** (wim′in) 1 An adult human female. 2 The female part of the human race; women collectively. 3 Womanly character; femininity: usu. with *the*. 4 A female attendant or servant. 5 A paramour or mistress. 6 *Informal* A wife. —*adj.* 1 Of or characteristic of women. 2 Female: a *woman* lawyer. [< OE *wīf* a wife + *mann* a human being] • See LADY.

wom·an·hood (wŏŏm′ən·hŏŏd) *n.* 1 The state of a woman or of womankind. 2 Women collectively.

wom·an·ish (wŏŏm′ən·ish) *adj.* 1 For or characteristic of a woman; womanly. 2 Feminine or effeminate in nature, and according ill with the qualities associated with men. —**wom′an·ish·ly** *adv.* —**wom′an·ish·ness** *n.*

wom·an·ize (wŏŏm′ən·īz) *v.* **·ized, ·iz·ing** *v.t.* 1 To make effeminate or womanish. —*v.i.* 2 To have affairs with many women. —**wom′an·iz·er** *n.*

wom·an·kind (wŏŏm′ən·kīnd′) *n.* Women collectively.

wom·an·ly (wŏŏm′ən·lē) *adj.* Having the qualities natural, suited, or becoming to a woman; feminine. —**wom′an·li·ness** *n.*

womb (wŏŏm) *n.* 1 UTERUS. 2 A place where anything is engendered or brought into life. [< OE *wamb, womb* the belly]

wom·bat (wom′bat) *n.* Any of various burrowing Australian marsupials resembling a small bear. [< native Australian name]

wom·en (wim′in) *n. pl.* of WOMAN.

wom·en·folk (wim′in·fōk′) *n.pl.* Women collectively: also **wom′en·folks′.**

Wombat

won (wun) *p.t. & p.p.* of WIN.

won·der (wun′dər) *n.* 1 A feeling of mingled surprise, admiration, and astonishment. 2 One who or that which causes wonder. —*v.t.* 1 To have a feeling of curiosity or doubt in regard to. —*v.i.* 2 To be affected or filled with wonder; marvel. 3 To be curious or doubtful. —*adj.* Spectacularly successful: a *wonder* drug. [< OE *wundor*] —**won′der·er** *n.* —**won′der·ing·ly** *adv.*

won·der·ful (wun′dər·fəl) *adj.* 1 Of a nature to excite wonder; astonishing. 2 Very good; excellent. —**won′der·ful·ly** *adv.* —**won′der·ful·ness** *n.*

won·der·land (wun′dər·land′) *n.* 1 A realm of imaginary wonders. 2 Any place of unusual beauty, astonishing sights, etc.

won·der·ment (wun′dər·mənt) *n.* 1 The emotion of wonder; surprise. 2 Something wonderful; a marvel.

won·drous (wun′drəs) *adj.* Wonderful; marvelous. —*adv.* Surprisingly. —**won′drous·ly** *adv.* —**won′drous·ness** *n.*

wont (wônt, wōnt) *adj.* Accustomed: He is *wont* to eat

late. —*n.* Ordinary manner of doing or acting; habit. [< OE *gewunod,* p.p. of *gewunian* be accustomed]

won't (wōnt) Contraction of *will not.*

wont·ed (wun′tid, wōn′-) *adj.* 1 Commonly used or done; habitual. 2 Habituated; accustomed. —**wont′ed·ness** *n.*

woo (wŏŏ) *v.t.* 1 To make love to, esp. so as to marry. 2 To entreat earnestly; beg. 3 To seek. —*v.i.* 4 To pay court; make love. [< OE *wōgian*] —**woo′er** *n.*

wood (wŏŏd) *n.* 1 The hard, fibrous material between the pith and bark of a tree or shrub. 2 Trees or shrubs cut for use, as for building, fuel, etc. 3 *Usu. pl.* A large, dense growth of trees; forest. 4 Something made of wood, as a woodwind or certain golf clubs having a wooden head. —*adj.* 1 Made of wood; wooden. 2 Made for burning wood: a *wood* stove. 3 Living or growing in woods. —*v.t.* 1 To furnish with wood for fuel. 2 To plant with trees. —*v.i.* To take on a supply of wood. [< OE *widu, wiodu*]

wood alcohol Methanol, esp. if obtained from wood tar.

wood·bine (wŏŏd′bīn) *n.* 1 A climbing European honeysuckle. 2 VIRGINIA CREEPER. [< OE *wudu* wood + *bindan* bind]

wood·block (wŏŏd′blok′) *n.* 1 A block of wood. 2 WOODCUT. Also **wood block.**

wood·chuck (wŏŏd′chuk′) *n.* A hibernating marmot of North America; a groundhog. [Prob. < Algon.; infl. in form by WOOD and CHUCK]

wood·cock (wŏŏd′kok′) *n.* 1 A European game bird related to the snipe. 2 A smaller related North American bird.

Woodchuck

wood·craft (wŏŏd′kraft′, -kräft′) *n.* 1 Skill in knowing how to survive in the woods by making shelters, hunting game, etc. 2 The act or art of constructing articles of wood. —**wood′crafts′man** (*pl.* **·men**) *n.*

wood·cut (wŏŏd′kut′) *n.* 1 A block of wood engraved, as with a design, for making prints. 2 A print made from such a block.

wood·cut·ter (wŏŏd′kut′ər) *n.* One who cuts or chops wood. —**wood′cut′ting** *n.*

wood·ed (wŏŏd′id) *adj.* Abounding with trees.

wood·en (wŏŏd′n) *adj.* 1 Made of wood. 2 Stiff; awkward. 3 Dull; stupid. —**wood′en·ly** *adv.* —**wood′en·ness** *n.*

wood engraving 1 The art of cutting designs on wood for printing. 2 A block of wood with an engraving cut, as with a burin, into a surface that is perpendicular to the direction of the grain. 3 A print from such a block. —**wood engraver**

wood·en·head (wŏŏd′n·hed′) *n. Informal* A stupid person; blockhead. —**wood′en·head′ed** *adj.* —**wood′en·head′ed·ness** *n.*

wood·en·ware (wŏŏd′n·wâr′) *n.* Dishes, vessels, bowls, etc., made of wood.

wood·land (wŏŏd′lənd, -land′) *n.* Land covered with wood or trees; timberland. —*adj.* (-lənd) Belonging to or dwelling in the woods. —**wood′land′er** *n.*

wood louse Any of numerous small terrestrial flat-bodied crustaceans commonly found under old logs.

wood·note (wŏŏd′nōt′ *n.* A simple, artless, or natural song, call, etc., as of a woodland bird.

wood nymph A nymph of the forest.

wood·peck·er (wŏŏd′pek′ər) *n.* Any of a large family of birds having stiff tail feathers, strong claws, and a sharp bill for drilling holes in trees in search of wood-boring insects.

wood·pile (wŏŏd′pīl′) *n.* A pile of wood, esp. of wood cut in sizes for burning.

wood pulp Wood reduced to a pulp, used for making paper.

wood·shed (wŏŏd′shed′) *n.* A shed for storing firewood.

woods·man (wŏŏdz′mən) *n. pl.* **·men** (-mən) 1 A man who lives or works in the woods. 2 A man skilled in woodcraft.

wood sorrel A creeping perennial woodland plant with cloverlike leaves containing oxalic acid. • See SHAMROCK.

Red-headed woodpecker

woods·y (wŏŏd′zē) *adj.* **woods·i·er, woods·i·est** Of, pertaining to, or like the woods. —**woods′i·ness** *n.*

wood tar A tar produced by the dry distillation of wood.

wood thrush A large, common woodland thrush with reddish brown plumage, having a bell-like song. • See THRUSH[1].

wood turning The shaping of blocks of wood by means of a lathe. —**wood turner**

wood·wind (wŏŏd′wind′) n. **1** A musical wind instrument, as the flute, clarinet, bassoon, oboe, or saxophone. **2** pl. The woodwinds of an orchestra; also, the players of these instruments.

wood·work (wŏŏd′wûrk′) n. Things made of wood, esp. certain interior parts of a house, as moldings, doors, windowsills, etc. —**wood′work′er, wood′work′ing** n.

wood·worm (wŏŏd′wûrm′) n. A worm or larva dwelling in or that bores in wood.

wood·y (wŏŏd′ē) adj. **wood·i·er, wood·i·est 1** Made of or containing wood. **2** Resembling wood. **3** Wooded; abounding with trees. —**wood′i·ness** n.

woof[1] (wŏŏf, wōōf) n. **1** The threads that are carried back and forth across the warp in a loom. **2** The texture of a fabric. [<OE ōwef]

woof[2] (wŏŏf) n. A low barking sound or growl, esp. of a dog. —v.i. To make such a sound. [Imit.]

woof·er (wŏŏf′ər) n. A loudspeaker designed to reproduce sounds of low frequency. [<WOOF[2] + -ER]

wool (wŏŏl) n. **1** The soft, durable fiber obtained from the fleece of sheep and some allied animals, as goats, alpacas, etc. **2** Yarn or fabric made of such fibers. **3** Garments made of wool. **4** Something resembling or likened to wool. —**pull the wool over one's eyes** To delude or deceive one. —adj. Made of or pertaining to wool or woolen material. [<OE wull]

wool·en (wŏŏl′ən) adj. **1** Of or pertaining to wool. **2** Made of wool. —n. Usu. pl. Cloth or clothing made of wool. Also **wool′len.**

wool·gath·er·ing (wŏŏl′gath′ər·ing) n. Idle daydreaming; absent-mindedness. —**wool′gath′er·er** n.

wool·grow·er (wŏŏl′grō′ər) n. A person who raises sheep for the production of wool. —**wool′grow′ing** adj.

wool·ly (wŏŏl′ē) adj. **·li·er, ·li·est 1** Consisting of, covered with, or resembling wool. **2** Not clear or sharply detailed; fuzzy. **3** Resembling the roughness and excitement of the early American West, usu. in the phrase **wild and woolly.** —n. pl. **·lies** A garment made of wool, esp. woolen underwear. Also **wool′y. —wool′li·ness, wool′i·ness** n.

wooz·y (wŏŏ′zē) adj. **·i·er, ·i·est** Slang Befuddled, esp. with drink. [Prob. < wooze, var. of OOZE] —**wooz′i·ly** adv. —**wooz′i·ness** n.

word (wûrd) n. **1** A speech sound or combination of sounds which has come to signify and communicate a particular idea or thought, and which functions as the smallest meaningful unit of a language when used in isolation. **2** The letters or characters that stand for such a language unit. **3** Usu. pl. Speech; talk: hard to put into words. **4** A brief remark or comment. **5** A communication or message: Send him word. **6** A command, signal, or direction: Give the word to start. **7** A promise: a man of his word. **8** Rumor, gossip, or news: What's the latest word? **9** A watchword or password. **10** pl. The text of a song: words and music. **11** pl. Language used in anger, rebuke, etc.: They had words. —**in a word** In short; briefly. —**eat one's words** To retract what one has said. —**mince words** To be evasive or overly delicate in what one says. —**take one at his word** To believe literally in what another has said and act or respond accordingly. —**word for word** In exactly the same words; verbatim. —v.t. To express in a word or words; phrase. —**the Word 1** LOGOS (def. 2). **2** GOSPEL (def. 1). **3** The Scriptures; the Bible. [<OE]

word·age (wûr′dij) n. **1** Words collectively. **2** The number of words, as in a novel. **3** VERBIAGE. **4** WORDING.

word·book (wûrd′bŏŏk′) n. **1** A collection of words; vocabulary; lexicon; dictionary. **2** An opera libretto.

word·ing (wûr′ding) n. The style or arrangement of words; diction; phraseology.

word·less (wûrd′lis) adj. Having no words; dumb; silent.

word of mouth Spoken words; speech; oral communication. —**word-of-mouth** (wûrd′uv·mouth′) adj.

word order The sequence or arrangement of words in a sentence, phrase, or clause.

word·play (wûrd′plā′) n. **1** Clever repartee. **2** A play on words; pun.

word processing The computer-storage editing, transmittal, and reproduction of written information by means of a terminal, printer, memory, software, etc. —**word processor** n.

word·y (wûr′dē) adj. **word·i·er, word·i·est 1** Expressed in many or too many words; verbose. **2** Of or pertaining to words; verbal. —**word′i·ly** adv. —**word′i·ness** n. —Syn. **1** long-winded, prolix, roundabout, redundant.

wore (wôr, wōr) p.t. of WEAR.

work (wûrk) n. **1** Continued physical or mental exertion or activity directed to some purpose or end; labor; toil. **2** Employment; job: to be out of work. **3** One's profession, occupation, business, trade, etc.: What is your work? **4** The place where one is employed or occupied professionally: She is at work. **5** An undertaking or task, often a part of one's job or occupation: to take work home; also, the amount of this that is accomplished or required: a day's work. **6** pl. A place where something is made, undertaken, etc.: often used in combination: the oilworks. **7** The material used or processed in manufacturing something. **8** Something that has been made, created, accomplished, etc., esp.: **a** An engineering structure, as a bridge. **b** A feat or deed: remembered for her good works. **c** Needlework or embroidery. **d** A product of the mind and imagination: the works of Beethoven. **9** Manner, quality, or style of doing something; workmanship. **10** pl. Running gear or machinery: the works of a watch. **11** The action of natural forces or the result of such action: the work of a storm. **12** Physics A transfer of energy between physical systems. —**the works** Slang **1** Everything belonging, available, etc. **2** Drastic or vicious treatment: to give someone the works. —**shoot the works** Slang **1** To risk everything. **2** To make a final, supreme effort. —v. worked (Archaic wrought), work·ing v.i. **1** To perform work; labor; toil. **2** To be employed in some trade or business. **3** To perform a function; operate: The machine works well. **4** To prove effective or influential: His stratagem worked. **5** To move or progress gradually or with difficulty: He worked up in his profession. **6** To become as specified, as by gradual motion: The bolts worked loose. **7** To move from nervousness or agitation: His features worked with anger. **8** To undergo kneading, hammering, etc.; be shaped: Copper works easily. **9** To ferment. —v.t. **10** To cause or bring about: to work a miracle. **11** To direct the operation of: to work a machine. **12** To make or shape by toil or skill. **13** To prepare, as by manipulating, hammering, etc.: to work dough. **14** To decorate, as with embroidery or inlaid work. **15** To cause to be productive, as by toil: to work a mine. **16** To cause to do work: He works his employees too hard. **17** To cause to be as specified, usu. with effort: We worked the timber into position. **18** To make or achieve by effort: to work one's passage on a ship. **19** To carry on some activity in (an area, etc.); cover: to work a sales territory. **20** To solve, as a problem in arithmetic. **21** To cause to move from nervousness or excitement: to work one's jaws. **22** To excite; provoke: He worked himself into a passion. **23** To influence or manage, as by insidious means; lead. **24** To cause to ferment. **25** Informal To practice trickery upon; cheat; swindle. **26** Informal To make use of for one's own purposes; use. —**work in** To insert or be inserted. —**work off** To get rid of, as extra flesh by exercise. —**work on** (or **upon**) **1** To try to influence or persuade. **2** To influence or affect. —**work out 1** To make its way out or through. **2** To effect by work or effort; accomplish. **3** To exhaust, as a mine. **4** To discharge, as a debt, by labor rather than by payment of money. **5** To develop; form, as a plan. **6** To solve. **7 a** To prove effective or successful. **b** To result as specified. **8** To exercise, train, etc. —**work over 1** To repeat. **2** Slang To treat harshly or cruelly; beat up, torture, etc. —**work up 1** To excite; rouse, as rage or a person to rage. 2 To form or shape by working; develop: to *work up* a new advertising campaign. 3 To make one's or its way. 4 To cause or bring about. [< OE *weorc*]

-work *combining form* 1 A product made from a (specified) material: *brickwork*. 2 Work of a (given) kind: *piecework*. 3 Work performed in a (specified) place: *housework*.

work·a·ble (wûr′kə-bəl) *adj.* 1 Capable of being worked, developed, etc. 2 Practicable, as a plan. —**work′a·bil′i·ty, work′a·ble·ness** *n.*

work·a·day (wûrk′ə-dā′) *adj.* 1 Of, pertaining to, or suitable for working days; everyday. 2 Commonplace; prosaic.

work·bench (wûrk′bench′) *n.* A bench for work, esp. that of a carpenter, machinist, etc.

work·book (wûrk′book′) *n.* 1 A booklet based on a course of study and containing problems and exercises which a student works out directly on the pages. 2 A manual containing operating instructions. 3 A book for recording work performed or planned.

work·day (wûrk′dā′) *n.* 1 Any day, usu. not a Sunday or holiday, on which work is done. 2 The number of hours of one day spent in work. Also **working day.** —*adj.* WORKADAY.

work·er (wûk′kər) *n.* 1 One who or that which performs work. 2 A social insect, as a bee, ant, etc., that is sexually sterile and performs work for the colony. 3 A member of the working class.

work·fare (wûrk′fâr′) *n.* Welfare that is conditional upon assigned work or training by those receiving payments.

work·house (wûrk′hous′) *n.* 1 *Brit.* Formerly, a house for paupers able to work. 2 A prison in which petty offenders are put to work.

work·ing (wûr′king) *adj.* 1 Engaged actively in some employment. 2 That works, or performs its function: This is a *working* model. 3 Sufficient for use or action: They formed a *working* agreement. 4 Of, used in, or occupied by work: a *working* day. 5 Throbbing or twitching, as facial muscles. —*n.* 1 The act or operation of any person or thing that works. 2 *Usu. pl.* That part of a mine or quarry where excavation is going on or has gone on.

working capital That part of the finances of a business available for its operation or convertible into cash.

working class People who work for wages, esp. manual and industrial workers. —**work′ing-class′** *adj.*

work·man (wûrk′mən) *n. pl.* **·men** (-men′) 1 A male worker. 2 A man who earns his living by working with his hands or with machines. Also **work·ing·man** (wûr′king·man′).

work·man·like (wûrk′mən·līk) *adj.* Like or befitting a skilled workman; skillfully done. Also **work′man·ly.**

work·man·ship (wûrk′mən·ship) *n.* 1 The art or skill of a workman. 2 The quality of work. 3 The work produced.

work of art 1 A highly artistic product of the fine arts, esp. painting and sculpture. 2 Anything made or done with great beauty or skill.

work·out (wûrk′out′) *n.* 1 Any activity done to increase or maintain skill, physical fitness, etc. 2 Any instance of strenuous activity, disciplined work, etc.

work·room (wûrk′room, -room′) *n.* A room where work is performed.

work·shop (wûrk′shop′) *n.* 1 A building or room where any work is carried on; workroom. 2 A seminar or single session for training, discussion, etc., in a specialized field: a writers' *workshop.*

work·ta·ble (wûrk′tā′bəl) *n.* A table with drawers and other conveniences for use while working.

work·week (wûrk′wēk′) *n.* The total number of hours worked in a week; also, the number of required working hours in a week.

world (wûrld) *n.* 1 The earth. 2 The universe. 3 Any celestial body: Are there other inhabited *worlds?* 4 *Often cap.* A part of the earth: the *Old World.* 5 A specific time or period in history: the ancient *world.* 6 A division of existing or created things belonging to the earth; the animal *world.* 7 The human inhabitants of the earth: mankind. 8 A definite class of people having certain interests or activities in common: the scientific *world.* 9 Secular or worldly aims, pleasures, etc., as distinguished from religious or spiritual ones; also, those people who pursue such aims or pleasures. 10 Individual conditions or circum-

stances of a person's life: His *world* has changed. 11 A large quantity or amount: a *world* of trouble. —**come into the world** To be born. —**for all the world** 1 In every respect. 2 For any reason. —**on top of the world** *Informal* Elated. —**out of this world** *Informal* Exceptionally fine; wonderful. [< OE *weorold*]

world·ly (wûrld′lē) *adj.* **·li·er, ·li·est** 1 Pertaining to the world; mundane; earthly. 2 Devoted to secular, earthly things; not spiritual. 3 Sophisticated; worldly-wise. —*adv.* In a worldly manner. —**world′li·ness** *n.*

world·ly-mind·ed (wûrld′lē-mīn′did) *adj.* Absorbed in the things of this world. —**world′ly-mind′ed·ly** *adv.*

world·ly-wise (wûrld′lē-wīz) *adj.* Wise in the ways and affairs of the world; sophisticated.

world power A state or organization whose policies and actions have a worldwide influence.

World Series In baseball, the games played at the finish of the regular season between the champion teams of the two major U.S. leagues. Also **world series.**

World War I The war (1914–18) between the Allies and the Central Powers (Germany, Austria-Hungary, Turkey, and Bulgaria).

World War II The war (1939–45) between the United Nations and the Axis.

world-wea·ry (wûrld′wir′ē) *adj.* **·ri·er, ·ri·est** Weary of life and its conditions. —**world′-wea′ri·ness** *n.*

world·wide (wûrld′wīd′) *adj.* Extended throughout the world.

worm (wûrm) *n.* 1 *Zool.* Any of numerous limbless, elongated, soft-bodied invertebrate animals, including flatworms, roundworms, and annelids. 2 Any small animal resembling a worm, as a caterpillar, maggot, snake, shipworm, etc. 3 Something which suggests the inner, hidden gnawings of a worm: the *worm* of remorse. 4 A despicable or despised person. 5 Something conceived to be like a worm, as the thread of a screw. 6 *pl.* Any disorder due to parasitic worms in the intestines, etc. —*v.t.* 1 To move, proceed, insinuate, etc. (oneself or itself) in a wormlike manner: to *worm* one's way. 2 To draw forth by artful means, as a secret: with *out.* 3 To rid of intestinal worms. —*v.i.* 4 To move or progress slowly and stealthily. [< OE *wyrm*] —**worm′i·ness** *n.* —**worm′y** *adj.* **(·i·er, ·i·est)**

worm-eat·en (wûrm′ēt′n) *adj.* 1 Eaten or bored through by worms. 2 Worn-out or decayed.

worm gear A gear having teeth shaped so as to mesh with a threaded shaft.

worm·hole (wûrm′hōl′) *n.* The hole made by a worm or a wormlike animal. — **worm′holed′** *adj.*

worm·wood (wûrm′wood′) *n.* 1 Any of various European herbs or small shrubs related to the sagebrush, esp. a species yielding a bitter oil used in making absinthe. 2 Something that embitters or is unpleasant. [< OE *wermōd*]

Worm gear

worn (wôrn, wōrn) *p.p.* of WEAR. —*adj.* 1 Affected by wear, use, continuous action, etc.; frayed, damaged, etc. 2 Showing the effects of worry, anxiety, etc. 3 Hackneyed, as a phrase.

worn-out (wôrn′out′, wōrn′-) *adj.* 1 Used until without value or usefulness. 2 Thoroughly tired; exhausted.

wor·ri·some (wûr′i·səm) *adj.* Causing worry or anxiety.

wor·ry (wûr′ē) *v.* **·ried, ·ry·ing** *v.i.* 1 To be uneasy in the mind; feel anxiety. 2 To manage despite trials or difficulties; struggle: with *along* or *through.* —*v.t.* 3 To cause to feel uneasy in the mind; trouble. 4 To bother; pester. 5 To bite, pull at, or shake with the teeth. —*n. pl.* **·ries** 1 A state of anxiety or uneasiness. 2 Something causing such a state. [< OE *wrygan* strangle] —**wor′ri·er, wor′ri·ment** *n.*

worse (wûrs) Comparative of BAD and ILL. —*adj.* 1 Bad or ill in a great degree; inferior. 2 Physically ill in a greater degree. 3 Less favorable, as to conditions, circumstances, etc. 4 More evil, corrupt, etc. —*n.* Someone or something worse. —*adv.* 1 In a worse manner, way, etc. 2 With greater intensity, severity, etc. [< OE *wyrsa*]

wors·en (wûr′sən) *v.t. & v.i.* To make or become worse.

wor·ship (wûr′ship) *n.* 1 Adoration, homage, etc., given to a deity. 2 The rituals, prayers, etc., expressing such adoration or homage. 3 Excessive or ardent admiration or love. **4** The object of such love or admiration. **5** *Chiefly Brit.* A title of honor in addressing certain persons of station. —*v.* **·shiped** or **·shipped**, **·ship·ing** or **·ship·ping** *v.t.* **1** To pay an act of worship to; venerate. **2** To have intense or exaggerated admiration or love for. —*v.i.* **3** To perform acts or have sentiments of worship. [< OE *weorthscipe* < *weorth* worthy] —**wor'ship·er, wor'ship·per** *n.* —**Syn.** *v.* **1** exalt, praise. **2** adore, dote on, idolize.

wor·ship·ful (wûr'ship·fəl) *adj.* **1** Feeling or giving great reverence, love, etc. **2** *Chiefly Brit.* Worthy of respect by reason of character or position: applied to certain dignitaries. —**wor'ship·ful·ly** *adv.* —**wor'ship·ful·ness** *n.*

worst (wûrst) Superlative of BAD and ILL. —*adj.* **1** Bad or ill in the highest degree. **2** Least favorable, as to conditions, circumstances, etc. **3** Most evil, corrupt, etc. —**in the worst way** *Informal* Very much. —*n.* Someone or something that is worst. —**at worst** Under the worst possible circumstances or conditions. —**get the worst of it** To be defeated or put at a disadvantage. —*adv.* **1** To the greatest or most extreme degree. **2** To the greatest or most extreme degree of inferiority, badness, etc. —*v.t.* To defeat; vanquish. [< OE *wyrsta*]

wors·ted (wōōs'tid, wûr'stid) *n.* **1** Woolen yarn spun from long staple, with fibers combed parallel and twisted hard. **2** A tightly woven fabric made from such yarn. —*adj.* Consisting of or made from such yarn. [< *Worsted*, former name of a parish in Norfolk, England]

wort¹ (wûrt) *n.* A plant or herb: usu. in combination: *liverwort.* [< OE *wyrt* a root, a plant]

wort² (wûrt) *n.* The unfermented infusion of malt that becomes beer when fermented. [< OE *wyrt* a root, a plant]

worth (wûrth) *n.* **1** Value or excellence of any kind. **2** The market value of something. **3** The amount of something obtainable at a specific sum: two cents' *worth* of candy. **4** Wealth. —*adj.* **1** Equal in value (to); exchangable (for). **2** Deserving (of): not *worth* going. **3** Having wealth or possessions to the value of: He is *worth* a million. —**for all it is worth** To the utmost. —**for all one is worth** With every effort possible. [< OE *weorth*]

worth·less (wûrth'lis) *adj.* Having no worth, usefulness, virtue, etc. —**worth'less·ly** *adv.* —**worth'less·ness** *n.*

worth·while (wûrth'ʰwīl') *adj.* Sufficiently important to occupy the time; of enough value to repay the effort. —**worth'while·ness** *n.*

wor·thy (wûr'thē) *adj.* **·thi·er, ·thi·est 1** Possessing valuable or useful qualities. **2** Having such qualities as to deserve or merit some specified thing: *worthy* of the honor. —*n. pl.* **·thies** A person of eminent worth: sometimes used humorously. —**wor'thi·ly** *adv.* —**wor'thi·ness** *n.*

-worthy *combining form* **1** Meriting or deserving: *trustworthy.* **2** Valuable as; having worth as: *newsworthy.* **3** Fit for: *seaworthy.*

wot (wot) *p.t.*, first and third person singular, of WIT².

would (wŏŏd) *p.t.* of WILL, but used chiefly as an auxiliary to express: **1** Desire: They *would* like to go. **2** Condition: They *would* go if you asked them. **3** Futurity: He said he *would* bring it. **4** Determination: The dog *would* not let go. **5** Custom or habit: He *would* walk there every day. [< OE *wolde*, p.t. of *willan* will]

would-be (wŏŏd'bē') *adj.* Desiring, professing, or intended to be: a *would-be* actress.

would·n't (wŏŏd'nt) Contraction of *would not.*

wound¹ (wōōnd) *n.* **1** A hurt or injury, esp. one in which the skin is torn, cut, etc. **2** A cutting or scraping injury to a tree or plant. **3** Any cause of pain or grief, as to the feelings, honor, etc. —*v.t. & v.i.* **1** To inflict a wound or wounds (upon). **2** To injure the feelings or pride of. [< OE *wund*] —**Syn.** *v.* **2** affront, hurt, offend, pique.

wound² (wound) *p.t. & p.p.* of WIND².

wove (wōv) *p.t. & a p.p.* of WEAVE.

wo·ven (wō'vən) *p.p.* of WEAVE.

wow (wou) *interj. Informal* An exclamation of wonder, surprise, pleasure, etc. —*n. Slang* A person or thing that is extraordinary, successful, etc. —*v.t. Slang* To cause to feel excitement, admiration, etc.

WPA, W.P.A. Works Progress Administration.

wrack (rak) *n.* **1** Ruin; destruction: esp. in the phrase **wrack and ruin. 2** Marine vegetation cast ashore by the sea, as seaweed. **3** A wrecked vessel; wreckage. —*v.t. & v.i.* To wreck or be wrecked. [Fusion of OE *wræc* punishment, revenge and MDu. *wrak* a wreck]

wraith (rāth) *n.* **1** An apparition of a person seen shortly before or shortly after his or her death. **2** Any specter; ghost. [?]

wran·gle (rang'gəl) *v.* **·gled, ·gling** *v.i.* **1** To argue noisily and angrily. —*v.t.* **2** To argue; debate. **3** To get by stubborn arguing. **4** To herd or round up, as livestock. —*n.* An angry dispute. [ME *wranglen*] —**wran'gler** *n.*

wrap (rap) *v.* **wrapped** or **wrapt, wrap·ping** *v.t.* **1** To surround and cover by something folded or wound about. **2** To fold or wind (a covering) about something. **3** To surround so as to blot out or conceal: a mountain *wrapped* in clouds. **4** To fold or wind. —*v.i.* **5** To be or become twined, coiled, etc.: with *about, around,* etc. —**wrap up 1** To cover with paper, etc. **2** To put on warm garments. **3** *Informal* To conclude or finish. —**wrapped up in** Involved or absorbed in: *wrapped up in* his music. —*n.* **1** A garment folded about a person. **2** *pl.* Outer garments collectively. **3** A blanket. —**keep under wraps** To keep secret. [ME *wrappen*]

wrap·a·round (rap'ə·round') *adj.* **1** Made so as to be wrapped around the body and then fastened: a *wraparound* skirt. **2** Designed so as to curve back on each side: a *wraparound* windshield. —*n.* Anything that encircles or curves back on each side.

wrap·per (rap'ər) *n.* **1** A paper enclosing a newspaper, magazine, or similar packet for mailing or otherwise. **2** A woman's dressing gown. **3** One who or that which wraps.

wrap·ping (rap'ing) *n.* Often *pl.* A covering or something in which an object is wrapped.

wrap-up (rap'up') *n. Informal* **1** A summary or conclusion: a *wrap-up* of the news. **2** The final event, action, etc., in a connected series.

wrath (rath, räth; *Brit.* rôth) *n.* **1** Violent rage, anger, or fury. **2** An act done in violent rage. [< OE *wrǣth* wroth]

wrath·ful (rath'fəl, räth'-) *adj.* **1** Full of wrath; extremely angry. **2** Resulting from or expressing wrath. —**wrath'ful·ly** *adv.* —**wrath'ful·ness** *n.* —**Syn.** **1** furious, apoplectic, mad, raging.

wreak (rēk) *v.t.* **1** To inflict or exact, as vengeance. **2** To give free expression to, as a feeling or passion. [< OE *wrecan* drive, avenge]

wreath (rēth) *n. pl.* **wreaths** (rēthz, rēths) **1** A band, as of flowers or leaves, commonly circular, as for a crown, decoration, etc. **2** Any curled or spiral band, as of smoke, snow, etc. [< OE *writha*] —**wreath·y** (rē'thē, -thē) *adj.*

wreathe (rēth) *v.* **wreathed, wreath·ing** *v.t.* **1** To form into a wreath, as by twisting or twining. **2** To adorn or encircle with or as with wreaths. **3** To envelop; cover: His face was *wreathed* in smiles. —*v.i.* **4** To take the form of a wreath. **5** To twist, turn, or coil, as masses of cloud.

wreck (rek) *v.t.* **1** To cause the destruction of, as by a collision. **2** To bring ruin, damage, or destruction upon. **3** To tear down, as a building; dismantle. —*v.i.* **4** To suffer destruction; be ruined. **5** To engage in wrecking, as for plunder or salvage. —*n.* **1** The act of wrecking, or the condition of being wrecked. **2** That which has been wrecked or ruined by accident, collision, etc. **3** The broken remnants or remains of something wrecked. **4** SHIPWRECK. **5** The ruined, usu. stranded hulk of a ship that has been wrecked. **6** A person who is ill or under great strain. [< AF *wrec* < Scand.]

wreck·age (rek'ij) *n.* **1** The act of wrecking, or the condition of being wrecked. **2** Broken remnants or fragments from a wreck.

wreck·er (rek'ər) *n.* **1** One who causes destruction of any sort. **2** One employed in tearing down and removing old buildings. **3** A person, train, car, or machine that clears away wrecks. **4** One employed to recover disabled vessels or wrecked cargoes.

wren (ren) *n.* **1** Any of numerous small, active, usu. brown birds having short rounded wings and tail and a thin, curved bill. 2 Any one of numerous similar birds. [<OE *wrenna*]

wrench (rench) n. 1 A violent twist. 2 A sprain or violent twist or pull in a part of the body. 3 A sudden surge of emotion, as of sorrow, pity, etc. 4 Any of various gripping tools for turning or twisting bolts, nuts, pipes, etc. — *v.t.* 1 To twist violently; turn suddenly by force. 2 To twist forcibly so as to cause strain or injury; sprain. 3 To cause to suffer. 4 To twist from the proper meaning, intent, or use. —*v.i.* 5 To give a twist or wrench [<OE *wrencan* to wrench]

Wrenches *def. 4*
a. engineer's. b. offset. c. monkey.

wrest (rest) *v.t.* 1 To pull or force away by violent twisting or wringing; wrench. 2 To turn from the true meaning, intent, etc.; distort. 3 To seize forcibly. 4 To gain or extract by great effort. —*n.* 1 An act of wresting. 2 A key for tuning a piano, harp, etc. [<OE *wræstan*] —**wrest'er** n.

wres·tle (res'əl) *v.* **·tled, ·tling** *v.i.* 1 To engage in wrestling. 2 To struggle, as for mastery; contend. —*v.t.* 3 To contend with (someone) in wrestling. 4 To throw (a calf) and hold it down for branding. —*n.* 1 The act or an instance of wrestling. 2 A hard struggle. [<OE *wræstlian*] —**wres'tler** n.

wres·tling (res'ling) n. A sport or exercise in which each of two unarmed contestants endeavors to throw the other to the ground or force him into a certain fallen position.

wretch (rech) n. 1 A vile or contemptible person. 2 A miserable or unhappy person. [<OE *wrecca* an outcast]

wretch·ed (rech'id) adj. 1 Sunk in dejection; profoundly unhappy. 2 Causing or characterized by misery, poverty, etc. 3 Unsatisfactory in ability or quality. 4 Despicable; contemptible. —**wretch'ed·ly** adv. —**wretch'ed·ness** n. —**Syn.** 1 distressed, miserable. 3 bad, paltry, worthless.

wrig·gle (rig'əl) *v.* **·gled, ·gling** *v.i.* 1 To twist in a sinuous manner; squirm; writhe. 2 To proceed as by twisting or crawling. 3 To make one's way by evasive or indirect means. —*v.t.* 4 To cause to wriggle. 5 To make (one's way, etc.) by evasive or sly means. —*n.* The act or motion of one who or that which wriggles. [<MLG *wriggeln*] —**wrig'gly** adj.

wrig·gler (rig'lər) n. 1 Someone or something that wriggles. 2 A mosquito larva.

wright (rīt) n. One who builds or creates something: used in combination: *wheelwright; playwright*. [<OE *wyrhta*]

wring (ring) *v.* **wrung, wring·ing** *v.t.* 1 To squeeze or compress by twisting. 2 To squeeze or press out, as water, by twisting. 3 To acquire by forcible means. 4 To distress: Her plight *wrung* their hearts. 5 To twist violently: to *wring* his neck. —*v.i.* 6 To writhe or squirm with great effort. —*n.* A twisting or wringing. [<OE *wringan*]

wring·er (ring'ər) n. 1 One who or that which wrings. 2 A device used to press water out of fabrics after washing.

wrin·kle[1] (ring'kəl) n. 1 A small ridge, as on a smooth surface; a crease; fold. 2 A small fold or crease in the skin, usu. produced by age or by excessive exposure to the elements. —*v.* **·kled, ·kling** *v.t.* 1 To make wrinkles in. —*v.i.* 2 To become wrinkled. [<OE *wrincle*] —**wrin'kly** adj.

wrin·kle[2] (ring'kəl) n. *Informal* A new or ingenious method, device, etc. [Prob. dim. of OE *wrenc* a trick]

wrist (rist) n. 1 The part of the arm that lies between the hand and the forearm; the carpus. 2 The part of a glove or garment that covers the wrist. [<OE]

wrist·band (rist'band') n. 1 The band of a sleeve that covers the wrist. 2 A band for a wrist watch.

wrist·let (rist'lit) n. 1 A flexible band worn on the wrist for support or warmth. 2 A bracelet.

wrist pin *Mech.* A pin attaching a connecting rod to another part.

wrist watch A watch set in a band and worn at the wrist.

writ[1] (rit) n. 1 *Law* A written order, issued by a court, and commanding the person to do or not to do some act. 2 That which is written: now chiefly in the phrase **Holy Writ**, the Bible. [<OE *writan* write]

writ[2] (rit) *Archaic* or *Regional p.t.* & *p.p.* of WRITE.

write (rīt) *v.* **wrote** (or *Archaic* **writ**), **writ·ten·** (or *Archaic* **writ**), **writ·ing** *v.t.* 1 To trace or inscribe (letters, words, numbers, symbols, etc.) on a surface with pen or pencil. 2 To describe, set down, or signify in writing. 3 To communicate by letter. 4 To communicate with by letter. 5 To produce by writing; be the author or composer of. 6 To draw up; draft: to *write* a check. 7 To cover or fill with writing: to *write* two full pages. 8 To leave marks or evidence of: Anxiety is *written* on his face. 9 To underwrite: to *write* an insurance policy. 10 To store information in computer memory. —*v.i.* 11 To trace or inscribe letters, etc., on a surface, as of paper. 12 To communicate in writing. 13 To be engaged in the occupation of an author. —**write down** 1 To put into writing. 2 To injure or depreciate in writing. —**write in** 1 To insert in writing, as in a document. 2 To cast (a vote) for one not listed on a ballot by inserting his name in writing. —**write off** 1 To cancel or remove (claims, debts, etc.) from an open account. 2 To acknowledge the loss or failure of. —**write out** To write in full or complete form. —**write up** 1 To describe fully in writing. 2 To praise fully or too fully in writing. [<OE *writan*] • *Writ*, the archaic past participle of *write*, is now used chiefly in the phrase **writ large**, written or shown on a grand scale: *a name writ large in history*.

write-in (rīt'in') n. 1 The act of casting a vote for a candidate not listed on the ballot by writing in his name. 2 The name so written in. —*adj.* Of or pertaining to a write-in.

write-off (rīt'ôf, -of') n. 1 A cancellation. 2 An amount canceled or noted as a loss. 3 A person or thing acknowledged to be a failure or a loss.

writ·er (rī'tər) n. 1 One who writes. 2 One who engages in literary composition as a profession.

write-up (rīt'up') n. A written description or review.

writhe (rīth) *v.* **writhed, writh·ing** *v.t.* 1 To cause to twist or be distorted. —*v.i.* 2 To twist or distort the body, face, or limbs, as in pain. 3 To undergo suffering, as from embarrassment, sorrow, etc. —*n.* An act of writhing. [<OE *writhan*] —**writh'er** n.

writ·ing (rī'ting) n. 1 The act of one who writes. 2 HANDWRITING. 3 Anything written or expressed in letters, esp. a literary production. 4 A written form: put your request in *writing*. 5 The profession or occupation of a writer. —*adj.* 1 Used in or for writing: *writing* paper. 2 That writes.

writ·ten (rit'n) *p.p.* of WRITE.

wrong (rông) *adj.* 1 Not correct; mistaken. 2 Not appropriate: the *wrong* shoes for hiking. 3 Not morally or legally right. 4 Not in accordance with the correct or standard method: the *wrong* way to bake. 5 Not working or operating properly: What is *wrong* with the furnace? 6 Not meant to be seen, used, etc.: the *wrong* side of the fabric. 7 Not intended: a *wrong* turn. —**go wrong** 1 To behave immorally. 2 To turn out badly; fail. 3 To take a wrong direction, etc. —*adv.* In a wrong direction, place, or manner; erroneously. —*n.* 1 That which is morally or socially wrong or unacceptable. 2 An injury or injustice. —**in the wrong** In error; wrong. —*v.t.* 1 To violate the rights of; inflict injury or injustice upon. 2 To impute evil to unjustly: You *wrong* him. 3 To seduce (a woman). 4 To treat dishonorably. [<Scand.] —**wrong'er, wrong'ness** n. —**wrong·ly** adv.

wrong·do·er (rông'dōō'ər, rong'-) n. One who does wrong. —**wrong'do'ing** n.

wrong·ful (rông'fəl) adj. 1 Characterized by wrong or injustice; injurious; unjust. 2 Unlawful; illegal. —**wrong'·ful·ly** adv. —**wrong'ful·ness** n.

wrong-head·ed (rông'hed'id) adj. Stubbornly holding to a wrong judgment, opinion, etc. —**wrong'-head'ed·ly** adv. —**wrong'-head'ed·ness** n.

wrote (rōt) *p.t.* of WRITE.

wroth (rôth) adj. Filled with anger; angry. [<OE *wrāth*]

wrought (rôt) *Archaic p.t.* & *p.p.* of WORK. —*adj.* 1 Beaten or hammered into shape by tools: *wrought* gold. 2 Made delicately or elaborately. 3 Made; fashioned; formed. —**wrought up** Disturbed or excited; agitated. [ME *wrogt*, var. of *worht*, p.p. of *wirchen* work]

wrought iron Strong, malleable, commercially pure iron.

wrung (rung) *p.t.* & *p.p.* of WRING.

wry (rī) *adj.* **wri·er, wri·est 1** Bent to one side or out of position; contorted; askew. **2** Made by twisting or distorting the features: a *wry* smile. **3** Distorted or warped, as in interpretation or meaning. **4** Somewhat perverse or ironic: *wry* humor. —*v.t.* **wried, wry·ing** To twist; contort. [< OE *wrigian* move, tend] —**wry′ly** *adv.* —**wry′ness** *n.*
wry·neck (rī′nek′) *n.* **1** A bird allied to the woodpeckers, with the habit of twisting its head and neck. **2** A spasmodic twisting of the neck.
WSW, W.S.W., wsw, w.s.w. west-southwest.

wt, wt. weight.
WV West Virginia (P.O. abbr.).
W.Va. West Virginia.
WY Wyoming (P.O. abbr.).
wy·an·dotte (wī′ən·dot) *n.* One of an American breed of chicken. [< the *Wyandot* Indians, an Iroquoian tribe]
wych-elm (wich′elm′) *n.* **1** A wide-spreading elm with large, dull-green leaves, common in N Europe. **2** Its wood. Also **witch-elm.** [< OE *wice* wych-elm + ELM]
Wyo. Wyoming.

X

X, x (eks) *n. pl.* **X's, x's, Xs, xs** (ek′siz) **1** The 24th letter of the English alphabet. **2** Any spoken sound representing the letter *X* or *x*. **3** In Roman notation, the symbol for 10. **4** An unknown quantity, result, etc. **5** A mark shaped like an X, representing the signature of one who cannot write. **6** A mark used in diagrams, maps, etc., to indicate or point out something. **7** A mark indicating one's answer on a test, one's choice on a ballot, etc. **8** A mark used to indicate a kiss. **9** A mark indicating "times" in multiplication: $4 \times 2 = 8$. **10** A mark indicating "by" in dimensions: $8\frac{1}{2} \times 11$ inches. **11** Something shaped like an X. —*v.t.* **x-ed** or **x'd, x-ing** or **x'ing** **1** To mark with an *x*. **2** To cancel or obliterate with an *x*: usu. with *out*. —*adj.* Shaped like an X.
X Christ; Christian.
xan·thic (zan′thik) *adj.* **1** Having a yellow or yellowish color. **2** Of or pertaining to xanthin or xanthine. [< Gk. *xanthos* yellow]
xan·thin (zan′thin) *n.* A yellow pigment found in plants. Also **xan′tho·phyll** (-thə·fil). [< Gk. *xanthos* yellow]
xan·thine (zan′thēn, -thin) *n.* A white, crystalline, nitrogenous compound, contained in blood, urine, and other animal secretions. [< Gk. *xanthos* yellow]
Xan·thip·pe (zan·tip′ē) The wife of Socrates, renowned as a shrew. —*n.* A shrewish, ill-tempered woman.
xan·thous (zan′thəs) *adj.* Yellow. [< Gk. *xanthos*]
x-ax·is (eks′ak′sis) *n. Math.* A coordinate axis against which the variable *x* is plotted.
X chromosome The sex chromosome that occurs in pairs in the female and is coupled with a Y chromosome in the male of humans and most animals.
X.D., x.d., x-div. ex (without) dividend.
Xe xenon.
xe·bec (zē′bek) *n.* A small, three-masted Mediterranean vessel. [< Ar. *shabbāk*]
xe·non (zē′non) *n.* A heavy, colorless, gaseous element (symbol Xe) occurring in traces in the atmosphere and rarely forming compounds. [< Gk. *xenos* a stranger]
xen·o·pho·bi·a (zen′ə·fō′bē·ə, zē′nə-) *n.* Dislike or fear of strangers or foreigners. [< Gk. *xenos* a stranger + -PHOBIA] —**xen′o·phob′ic** *adj.*

xe·rog·ra·phy (zi·rog′rə·fē) *n.* A method of copying by which a colored powder is distributed by the action of light on an electrically charged plate to form a negative, which is then transferred thermally to a paper or other surface. [< Gk. *xēros* dry + -GRAPHY] —**xe·ro·graph·ic** (zir′ə·graf′ik) *adj.*
xe·roph·i·lous (zi·rof′ə·ləs) *adj.* Thriving under arid conditions: said of plants living in dry regions, as the cactus. [< Gk. *xēros* dry + *philos* loving]
xe·ro·phyte (zir′ə·fīt) *n. Bot.* A plant adapted to arid habitats. [< Gk. *xēros* dry + *phyton* plant] —**xe′ro·phyt′ic** (-fit′ik) *adj.*
Xer·ox (zir′oks) *n.* A xerographic copying process: a trade name. —*v.t.* To make or reproduce by Xerox. —*adj.* Of, for, or reproduced by Xeroxing. Also **xer′ox.**
xi (zī, sī; *Gk.* ksē) *n.* The fourteenth letter of the Greek alphabet (Ξ, ξ).
X.I., x.i., x-int. ex (without) interest.
Xmas (kris′məs, eks′məs) *n.* CHRISTMAS. [< *X*, abbr. for *Christ* < Gk. *X*, chi, the first letter of *Christos* Christ + -MAS(s)]
X-ray (eks′rā′) *n.* **1** An electromagnetic radiation having a wavelength shorter than that of ultraviolet light and longer than that of a gamma ray. **2** A photograph made with X-rays. —*adj.* Of, made by, or producing X-rays. —*v.t.* **1** To examine, diagnose, or treat with X-rays. —*v.i.* **2** To use X-rays. Also **X ray.**
x-ref. cross reference.
xy·lem (zī′ləm) *n.* The woody vascular bundles that serve as passageways for water in the roots, stems, and leaves of ferns and seed plants. [< Gk. *xylon* wood]
xy·lo·phone (zī′lə·fōn′) *n.* A musical instrument consisting of an array of wooden bars graduated in length to produce a scale, played by striking the bars with two small mallets. [< Gk. *xylon* wood + *phōnē* sound] —**xy′lo·phon′ist** *n.*

Xylophone

Y

Y, y (wī) *n. pl.* **Y's, y's, Ys, ys** (wīz) **1** The 25th letter of the English alphabet. **2** Any spoken sound representing the letter *Y* or *y*. **3** Something shaped like a Y. —*adj.* Shaped like a Y.
-y¹ *suffix* Being, possessing, or resembling what is expressed in the main element: *stony, rainy.* [< OE *-ig*]
-y² *suffix* **1** Quality; condition: *victory.* **2** The place or establishment where something specified happens or is made: *bakery.* **3** The entire group or body of: *soldiery.* [< L *-ia* or < Gk. *-ia, -eia*]
-y³ *suffix* Little; small: *kitty:* often used to express endearment. [ME *-ie*]

Y (wī) *n. pl.* **Y's** or **Ys 1** YMCA or YWCA. **2** YMHA or YWHA.
Y yttrium.
y. yard(s); year(s).
yacht (yot) *n.* Any of various relatively small sailing or motor-driven ships built or fitted for private pleasure excursions or racing. —*v.i.* To cruise, race, or sail in a yacht. [< Du. *jaghte,* short for *jaghtschip* a pursuit ship]
yacht·ing (yot′ing) *n.* The act, practice, or pastime of sailing in or managing a yacht.
yachts·man (yots′mən) *n. pl.* **-men** (-mən) One who owns or sails a yacht.

ya·hoo (yä′hōō, yā′-) *n.* An awkward or crude person; a bumpkin. [< *Yahoo,* one of a race of brutes in Swift's *Gulliver's Travels,* 1726]

Yah·weh (yä′we) In the Old Testament, a name for God. Also **Yah·ve, Yah·veh** (yä′ve). [< Heb. *YHWH*]

yak¹ (yak) *n.* A large, shaggy wild ox of CEN. Asia, often domesticated. [< Tibetan *gyag*]

yak² (yak) *Slang v.i.* **yakked, yak·king** To talk or chatter a great deal. —*n.* **1** Persistent chatter or talk. **2** A boisterous laugh. **3** Something, as a joke, causing such a laugh. Also (for *v.* and *n.* def. 1) **yak·e·ty-yak** (yak′ə·tē·yak′). [Imit.] —**yak′ker** *n.*

Yak

yam (yam) *n.* **1** The fleshy, edible, tuberous root of any of a genus of climbing tropical plants. **2** Any of the plants growing this root. **3** A variety of sweet potato. [< Pg. *inhame* < a native w African name]

yam·mer (yam′ər) *v.i. Informal* **1** To complain peevishly; whine; whimper. **2** To howl; roar; shout. —*v.t.* **3** To utter in a complaining or peevish manner. —*n.* The act of yammering. [< OE *geōmrian* to lament]

yang (yang) *n.* In Chinese philosophy, the male principle and element of the universe, source of life and heat and, with yin, co-creator of everything that is. [< Chin.]

yank (yangk) *v.t. & v.i.* To jerk or pull suddenly. —*n.* A sudden sharp pull; jerk. [?]

Yank (yangk) *n. & adj. Informal* YANKEE.

Yan·kee (yang′kē) *n.* **1** A native or citizen of the U.S. **2** A native or inhabitant of the northern U.S. **3** A native or inhabitant of New England. —*adj.* Of, like, or characteristic of Yankees. [?] —**Yan′kee·dom, Yan′kee·ism** *n.*

Yankee Doo·dle (dōōd′l) A song popular in the U.S. from pre-Revolutionary times.

yap (yap) *v.i.* **yapped, yap·ping 1** *Slang* To talk or jabber. **2** To bark or yelp, as a dog. —*n.* **1** A bark or yelp. **2** *Slang* Worthless talk; jabber. **3** *Slang* **a** A crude person. **b** The mouth. [Imit. of a dog's bark]

yard¹ (yärd) *n.* **1** A unit of length equal to 3 feet or 0.914 meter. **2** A long, slender spar set crosswise on a mast and used to support sails. [< OE *gierd* rod, yard measure]

yard² (yärd) *n.* **1** A plot of ground enclosed or set apart, as for some specific purpose: often in combination: *barnyard.* **2** The ground or lawn belonging and adjacent to a house, college, university, etc. **3** An enclosure used for building, selling, storing, etc.: often in combination: *shipyard; stockyard.* **4** An enclosure or piece of ground usu. adjacent to a railroad station, used for making up trains and for storage. —*v.t.* To put or collect into or as into a yard. [< OE *geard* an enclosure]

yard·age (yär′dij) *n.* The amount or length of something in yards.

yard·arm (yärd′ärm′) *n.* Either end of the yard of a square sail.

yard goods Fabric sold by the yard; piece goods.

yard·man (yärd′mən) *n. pl.* **-men** (-mən) A man employed in a yard, esp. in a railroad yard.

yard·mas·ter (yärd′mas′tər, -mäs′-) *n.* A railroad official having charge of a yard.

yard·stick (yärd′stik′) *n.* **1** A graduated measuring stick a yard in length. **2** Any measure or standard of comparison; criterion.

yar·mul·ke (yär′məl·kə) *n.* A skullcap traditionally worn by Jewish males in synagogues and often at school and in the home. Also **yar′mel·ke.** [Yiddish]

yarn (yärn) *n.* **1** Any spun fiber, as cotton, wool, or nylon, prepared for use in weaving, knitting, or crotcheting. **2** *Informal* A tale of adventure, often of doubtful truth. —*v.i. Informal* To tell a yarn or yarns. [< OE *gearn*]

yar·row (yar′ō) *n.* Any of a genus of perennial composite plants, esp. a common weed with finely divided, pungent leaves and clusters of small, usu. white flowers. [< OE *gearwe*]

yat·a·ghan (yat′ə·gan, -gən) *n.* A Turkish sword with a double-curved blade and without a handle guard. Also **yat′a·gan.**

Yataghan

yaw (yô) *v.i.* **1** To move wildly or out of its course, as a ship when struck by a heavy sea. **2** To deviate from a flight path by rotating about a vertical axis: said of spacecraft, projectiles, etc. — *v.t.* **3** To cause to yaw. —*n.* **1** The action of yawing. **2** The amount of deviation in yawing. [?]

yawl (yôl) *n.* **1** A small, fore-and-aft rigged, two-masted sailboat. **2** A ship's small boat; jolboat. [? < Du. *jol*]

yawn (yôn) *v.i.* **1** To open the mouth wide, usu. involuntarily, with a full inhalation, as the result of drowsiness, boredom, etc. **2** To stand wide open: A chasm *yawned* below. —*v.t.* **3** To express or utter with a yawn. —*n.* **1** An act of yawning. **2** A wide opening. [< OE *geonian*] —**yawn′er** *n.*

Yawl *def. 1*

yawp (yôp) *v.i.* **1** To bark or yelp. **2** *Informal* To talk or shout loudly. —*n.* The act or sound of yawping. [Imit.] — **yawp′er** *n.*

yaws (yôz) *n. pl.* A contagious tropical disease marked by skin lesions. [< Cariban *yáya*]

y-axis (wī′ak′sis) *n. Math.* A coordinate axis along which the variable *y* is plotted.

Yb ytterbium.

Y chromosome The smaller of the unmatched pair of sex chromosomes found in the male of humans and most animals.

y·clept (i·klept′) *adj. Archaic* Called; named. Also **y·cleped′.** [< OE *geclypod,* p.p. of *clypian* call]

yd. yard(s).

ye¹ (thē, yē) *definite article Archaic* The. [< an incorrect transliteration of the Old English thorn, properly transliterated as *th*]

ye² (yē) *pron. Archaic* The persons addressed; you. [< OE *gē*]

yea (yā) *adv.* **1** Yes: used in voting orally. **2** *Archaic* Not only so, but more so. **3** *Archaic* In reality; verily: a form of introduction in a sentence. —*n.* **1** An affirmative vote. **2** One who casts such a vote. [< OE *gēa*]

ye·ah (ye′ə) *adv. Informal* Yes.

yean (yēn) *v.t. & v.i.* To bring forth (young), as a goat or sheep. [< OE (assumed) *geēanian*]

yean·ling (yēn′ling) *n.* The young of a goat or sheep. — *adj.* Young; newly born.

year (yir) *n.* **1** The period of time in which the earth completes a revolution around the sun: about 365 days, 5 hours, 49 minutes, and, in the Gregorian calendar, divided into 12 months beginning January 1 and ending December 31. **2** Any period of 12 months. **3** The period of time during which a planet revolves around the sun. **4** Any part of a year devoted to some activity: the school *year.* **5** *pl.* Any extended or past period of time: the *years* before automobiles. **6** *pl.* Length or time of life; age: active for his *years.* [< OE *gēar*]

year·book (yir′bŏŏk′) *n.* A book published annually, usu. presenting information about the previous year.

year·ling (yir′ling) *n.* An animal between one and two years old. —*adj.* Being a year old.

year·long (yir′lông′, -long′) *adj.* Continuing through a year.

year·ly (yir′lē) *adj.* **1** Of a year. **2** Occurring once a year; annual. **3** Continuing for a year: a *yearly* subscription. — *adv.* Once a year; annually.

yearn (yûrn) *v.i.* **1** To desire something earnestly; long: with *for.* **2** To be deeply moved; feel sympathy. [< OE *giernan*] —**yearn′er** *n.* —**Syn.** **1** wish, want, covet, hunger, crave, pine for.

yearn·ing (yûr′ning) *n.* A strong emotion of longing or desire, esp. with tenderness.

year-round (yir′round′) *adj.* Continuing, operating, etc., throughout the entire year.

yeast (yēst) *n.* **1** Any of various single-celled fungi that produce ethyl alcohol and carbon dioxide in the process of fermenting carbohydrates. **2** A commercial preparation of certain yeasts, usu. in dry powdery form, used to leaven bread, make beer, etc. **3** Froth or spume. **4** Something causing mental or moral ferment. —*v.i.* To foam; froth. [< OE *gist*]

yeast·y (yēs′tē) *adj.* **yeast·i·er, yeast·i·est 1** Of or resembling yeast. **2** Causing fermentation. **3** Restless; unsettled. **4** Covered with froth or foam. **5** Light or unsubstantial. — **yeast′i·ness** *n.*

yegg (yeg) *n. Slang* A burglar, esp. one who cracks safes. Also **yegg′man.** [?]

yell (yel) *v.t.* & *v.i.* **1** To shout; scream. **2** To cheer. —*n.* **1** A sharp, loud cry, as of pain, terror, etc. **2** A rhythmic shout by a group, as in cheering an athletic team. [< OE *giellan*] —**yell′er** *n.*

yel·low (yel′ō) *adj.* **1** Of the color yellow. **2** Changed to a sallow color by age, sickness, etc.: a paper *yellow* with age. **3** Having a yellowish or light brown complexion. **4** Cheaply or offensively sensational: said of newspapers: *yellow* journalism. **5** *Informal* Cowardly; mean; dishonorable. —*n.* **1** The color of ripe lemons or, in the spectrum, the color between green and orange. **2** Any pigment or dyestuff having such a color. **3** The yolk of an egg. —*v.t.* & *v.i.* To make or become yellow. [< OE *geolu*] —**yel′low·ly** *adv.* —**yel′low·ness** *n.*

yel·low·bird (yel′ō-bûrd′) *n.* Any of various birds with yellow plumage, as the goldfinch.

yellow fever An acute tropical disease caused by a virus transmitted by a mosquito and characterized by jaundice and other symptoms.

yel·low·ham·mer (yel′ō-ham′ər) *n.* **1** A European bunting with bright yellow and black plumage. **2** The flicker or golden-winged woodpecker. [? < OE *geolo* yellow + *amore*, a kind of bird]

yel·low·ish (yel′ō-ish) *adj.* Somewhat yellow.

yellow jack 1 A yellow flag indicating quarantine. **2** YELLOW FEVER.

yellow jacket Any of various social wasps with bright yellow markings.

yellow peril The supposed threat to the West from the power of the peoples of E Asia.

yellow pine 1 Any of various American pines, as the loblolly. **2** Their tough, yellowish wood.

yel·low·wood (yel′ō-wōōd′) *n.* Any of various trees having yellow or yellowish wood or yielding a yellow dye.

yel·low·y (yel′ō-ē) *adj.* Yellowish.

yelp (yelp) *v.i.* To utter a sharp or shrill cry. —*v.t.* To express by a yelp or yelps. —*n.* A sharp, shrill cry, as of a dog in distress. [< OE *gielpan* boast] —**yelp′er** *n.*

Yem·en Arab Republic (yem′ən) A country of sw Arabia, 75,000 sq. mi., cap. San'a. —**Yem·e·ni** (yem′ə-nē), **Yem′e·nite** (-nīt) *adj., n.*

Yemen, People's Democratic Republic of A republic on the s coast of Arabia, 110,000 sq. mi., cap. Madinat ash Sha'b. Also **Southern Yemen.** —**Yem′e·ni, Yem′e·nite** *adj., n.*

yen¹ (yen) *Informal n.* An ardent longing or desire. —*v.i.* **yenned, yen·ning** To yearn; long. [< Chin., opium]

yen² (yen) *n.* The basic monetary unit of Japan.

yen·ta (yen′tə) *n.* A female gossip or meddler. Also **yen′·teh.** [Yiddish]

yeo·man (yō′mən) *n. pl.* **-men** (-mən) **1** A petty officer in the U.S. Navy or Coast Guard who performs clerical duties. **2** *Brit.* A farmer, esp. one who cultivates his own farm. **3** YEOMAN OF THE GUARD. **4** *Brit.* One of the attendants of a nobleman or of royalty. [? < OE *geong* young + *mann* a man]

yeo·man·ly (yō′mən-lē) *adj.* **1** Of or pertaining to a yeoman. **2** Brave; rugged. —*adv.* Like a yeoman; bravely.

Yeoman of the (Royal) Guard A member of the ceremonial bodyguard of the English royal household.

yeo·man·ry (yō′mən-rē) *n.* **1** Yeomen, as a group. **2** *Brit.* A home guard of volunteer cavalry, now part of the Territorial Army.

yeoman's service Faithful and useful support or service. Also **yeoman service.**

yep (yep) *adv. Informal* Yes.

yes (yes) *adv.* **1** As you say; truly; just so: a reply of affirmation or consent. **2** Moreover: She is willing, *yes* eager, to go. —*n. pl.* **yes·es** or **yes·ses** A reply in the affirmative. —*v.t.* & *v.i.* **yessed, yes·sing** To say "yes" (to). [< OE *gēa* yea + *sīe* it may be]

yes-man (yes′man′) *n. pl.* **-men** (men′) *Informal* A person who habitually agrees with the opinions or statements of others, esp. with those of his superiors.

yes·ter·day (yes′tər-dē, -dā′) *n.* **1** The day preceding today. **2** The near past. —*adv.* **1** On the day last past. **2** At a recent time. [< OE *geostran* yesterday + *dæg* day]

yes·ter·year (yes′tər-yir′) *n.* **1** Last year. **2** Recent years; recent past. **3** Time past; a past epoch: the peaceful days of *yesteryear*.

yet (yet) *adv.* **1** In addition; besides. **2** At some future time; eventually: he may *yet* succeed. **3** In continuance of a previous state or condition; still: I can hear him *yet*. **4** At the present time; now: Don't go *yet*. **5** After all the time that has or had elapsed: Are you not ready *yet*? **6** Up to the present time; heretofore: He has never *yet* lied to me. **7** Even: a *yet* hotter day. **8** Nevertheless: They are poor, *yet* happy. **9** As much as; even: He did not believe the reports, nor *yet* the evidence. —**as yet** Up to now. —*conj.* Nevertheless; but: I speak to you peaceably, *yet* you will not listen. [< OE *giet*]

yew (yōō) *n.* **1** Any of a genus of evergreen trees and shrubs, with narrow, flat, dark green, poisonous leaves and red berrylike cones containing a single seed. **2** The hard, tough wood of the yew. [< OE *ēow, īw*]

Yid·dish (yid′ish) *n.* A language derived from 13th- and 14th-century Middle High German, now spoken primarily by Eastern European Jews and their relatives or descendants in other countries. It contains elements of Hebrew and the Slavic languages. —*adj.* Of, written, or spoken in Yiddish. [< G *jüdisch* Jewish]

yield (yēld) *v.t.* **1** To give forth by a natural process, or as a result of labor or cultivation: The field will *yield* a good crop. **2** To give in return, as for investment; furnish: The bonds *yield* five percent interest. **3** To give up, as to superior power; surrender; relinquish: often with *up*: to *yield* oneself up to one's enemies. **4** To give up one's possession of: to *yield* the right of way. —*v.i.* **5** To provide a return; produce; bear. **6** To give up; submit; surrender. **7** To give way, as to pressure or force. **8** To assent or comply, as under compulsion; consent: We *yielded* to their persuasion. **9** To give place, as through inferiority or weakness: with *to*: We will *yield* to them in nothing. —*n.* The amount yielded; product; result, as of cultivation, investment, etc. [< OE *gieldan* pay] —**yield′er** *n.*

yield·ing (yēl′ding) *adj.* **1** Productive. **2** Flexible; easily bent. **3** Obedient. —**yield′ing·ly** *adv.* —**yield′ing·ness** *n.*

yin (yin) *n.* In Chinese philosophy, the female principle and element of the universe, standing for darkness, cold, and death. [< Chin.]

yip (yip) *n.* A yelp, as of a dog. —*v.i.* **yipped, yip·ping** To yelp. [Imit.]

-yl *suffix Chem.* Used to denote a radical: *ethyl.* [< Gk. *hylē* wood, matter]

YMCA, Y.M.C.A. Young Men's Christian Association. **YMHA, Y.M.H.A.** Young Men's Hebrew Association.

yock (yäk) *n. Slang* **1** A loud laugh or guffaw. **2** Something causing such a laugh. [Var. of YAK²]

yo·del (yōd′l) *v.t.* & *v.i.* **-deled** or **-delled, -del·ing** or **-del·ling** To sing by changing the voice quickly from its low register to a falsetto and back. —*n.* Something yodeled, as a melody or refrain. Also **yo′dle.** [< G *jodeln*, lit., utter the syllable *jo*] —**yo′del·er, yo′del·ler, yo′dler** *n.*

yo·ga (yō′gə) *n.* **1** A Hindu mystical and ascetic discipline, the ultimate purpose of which is to gain spiritual illumination by means of a prescribed series of mental and physical exercises. **2** The exercises, esp. certain physical exercises, based on yoga techniques. [Skt., lit., union] —**yo′gic** (-gik) *adj.*

yo·gi (yō′gē) *n. pl.* **-gis** A person who practices yoga. Also **yo′gin** (-gən, -gin).

yo·gurt (yō′gərt) *n.* A semifluid food made of milk curdled with cultures of bacteria and sometimes flavored with fruit. Also **yo′ghurt.** [<Turk. *yŏghurt*]

yoke (yōk) *n.* **1** A curved frame used for coupling draft animals, as oxen, usu. having a bow at each end to receive the neck of the animal. **2** Any of many similar contrivances, as a frame worn on the shoulder to balance pails of milk. **3** A pair of animals joined by a yoke. **4** Something that binds or connects; tie; bond: the *yoke* of marriage. **5** Any of various parts or pieces that connect or hold two things together. **6** Servitude; bondage. **7** A fitted part of a garment designed to support a plaited or gathered part, as at the hips or shoulders. —*v.* **yoked, yok·ing** *v.t.* **1** To attach by means of a yoke, as draft animals. **2** To join with or as with a yoke. —*v.i.* **3** To be joined or linked; unite. [<OE *geoc*]

Yoke *def. 1*

yoke·fel·low (yōk′fel′ō) *n.* A mate or companion, as in labor. Also **yoke′mate′** (-māt′).

yo·kel (yō′kəl) *n.* A country bumpkin.[?]

yolk (yōk, yōlk) *n.* **1** The yellow portion of an egg. **2** An oily exudation in unprocessed sheep's wool. [<OE *geolu* yellow] —**yolk′y** *adj.*

Yom Kip·pur (yom kip′ər, yōm, ki·pŏor′) The Jewish Day of Atonement, a holiday marked by prayer and fasting, celebrated in late September or in October.

yon (yon) *adj. & adv. Archaic & Regional* YONDER. [<OE *geon*]

yond (yond) *adj. & adv. Archaic & Regional* YONDER. [< OE *geond* across]

yon·der (yon′dər) *adj.* Being at a distance indicated or known. —*adv.* In that place; there. [<OE *geond*, yond]

yoo-hoo (yōō′hōō′) *interj.* A call used to attract the attention of someone

yore (yôr, yōr) *n.* Time long past: in days of *yore.* [<OE *geara* formerly]

York (yôrk) *n.* A royal house of England that reigned from 1461–85.

York·shire pudding (york′shir, -shər) A batter pudding baked in meat drippings.

you (yōō) *pron.* **1** The person or persons or the personified thing or things addressed: when used as a subject, always linked with a plural verb. **2** One; anyone: *You* learn by trying. [<OE *ēow*, dat. and acc. pl. of *ge* ye]

you'd (yōōd) Contraction of *you had* or *you would.*

you'll (yōōl) Contraction of *you will* or *you shall.*

young (yung) *adj.* **young·er** (yung′gər), **young·est** (yung′gist) **1** Being in the early period of life or growth; not old. **2** Not having progressed or developed far; newly formed: The day was *young.* **3** Pertaining to youth or early life. **4** Full of vigor or freshness. **5** Inexperienced; immature. **6** Denoting the younger of two persons having the same name or title; junior. **7** *Geol.* Having the characteristics of an early stage in the geological cycle: said of a river or of certain land forms. —*n.* **1** Young persons as a group. **2** Offspring, esp. of animals. —**with young** Pregnant. [< OE *geong*] —**young′ness** *n.* —**Syn. 4** lively, strong, active, spirited. **5** raw, green, unseasoned, uninitiated.

young·ber·ry (yung′ber′ē) *n. pl.* **·ries** A dark red berry resulting from crossing a blackberry and a dewberry. [< B. M. *Young*, U.S. horticulturist of late 19th c.]

young blood 1 Young people. **2** New, fresh ideas, attitudes, etc.

young·ish (yung′ish) *adj.* Rather young.

young·ling (yung′ling) *n.* **1** A young person, animal, or plant. **2** An inexperienced person. —*adj.* Young. [<OE *geongling*]

young·ster (yung′stər) *n.* A young person, esp. a child.

Young Turk One of a group bent on seizing control of or radically altering an organization, as a political party.

[Orig., a member of a 20th c. Turkish revolutionary party]

your (yôr, yŏŏr) *pronominal adj.* **1** Of, belonging to or pertaining to you: *your* fate. **2** Used before certain titles: *your* Majesty. [<OE *ēower*, genitive of *ge* ye]

you're (yŏŏr, yôr) Contraction of *you are.*

yours (yôrz, yŏŏrz) *pron.* (*construed as sing. or pl.*) The things or persons belonging or pertaining to you: a home as quiet as *yours.* —**of yours** Belonging or relating to you. [ME *youres*]

your·self (yôr·self′; yŏŏr-) *pron. pl.* **-selves** (-selvz′) **1** The one who is you: used as a reflexive or emphatic form: Try not to hurt *yourself.* **2** Your normal, healthy, etc., condition: You are not *yourself* today. **3** ONESELF: It's best to take care of it *yourself.*

youth (yōōth) *n. pl.* **youths** (yōōths, yōōthz) **1** The state or condition of being young. **2** The period when one is young; that part of life between childhood and adulthood. **3** The early period of being or development, as of a movement. **4** A young person, esp. a young man. **5** Young people as a group: the nation's *youth.* [<OE *geoguth*]

youth·ful (yōōth′fəl) *adj.* **1** Of, pertaining to, or characteristic of youth. **2** Buoyant; fresh; vigorous. **3** Having youth; being still young. **4** Not far advanced; early; new. **5** *Geol.* Young. —**youth′ful·ly** *adv.* —**youth′ful·ness** *n.*

you've (yōōv) Contraction of *you have.*

yowl (youl) *v.i.* To howl; yell. —*n.* A loud, prolonged, wailing cry; a howl. [ME *youlen*]

yo-yo (yō′yō′) *n. pl.* **-yos** A wheellike toy with a deep central groove around which is looped a string on which the wheel can be spun in a variety of movements.[?]

yr. year(s); younger; your.

yrs. years; yours.

Y.T. Yukon Territory.

yt·ter·bi·um (i·tûr′bē·əm) *n.* A rare metallic element (symbol Yb) of the lanthanide series. [<*Ytterby*, Sweden]

yt·tri·um (it′rē·əm) *n.* A rare metallic element (symbol Y) similar to and usu. found with ytterbium. [<*Ytterby*, Sweden]

yuc·ca (yuk′ə) *n.* **1** Any of a large genus of liliaceous American plants usu. found in dry, sandy places, having a woody stem which bears a large panicle of white flowers emerging from a crown of sword-shaped leaves. **2** The flower of this plant. [<Sp. *yuca*< Taino]

Yucca

yuck (yuk) *n. Slang* **1** A loud laugh or guffaw. **2** Something causing such a laugh. —*v.i.* To laugh uproariously. [Imit.]

Yu·go·slav (yōō′gō·släv′) *adj.* Of Yugoslavia or its people: also **Yu′go·slav′ic.** —*n.* A native or citizen of Yugoslavia.

Yu·go·sla·vi·a (yōō′gō·slä′vē·ə) *n.* A republic of SE Europe, 98,538 sq. mi., cap. Belgrade. —**Yu′go·sla′vi·an** *adj., n.* • See map at BALKAN STATES.

yuk (yuk) *Slang n. & v.i.* **yukked, yuk·king** YUCK.

Yule (yōōl) *n.* Christmas or Christmas time. [<OE *geōl*]

yule log Formerly, a large log, place on the hearth as the foundation of the traditional Christmas Eve fire.

Yule·tide (yōōl′tīd′) *n.* Christmas time.

yum·my (yum′ē) *Informal adj.* **·mi·er, ·mi·est** Agreeable to the senses, esp. to the taste; delicious. —*n.* Something delicious. [Imit. of the sound made when something is pleasurable to the taste]

yup·pie (yup′ē) *n.pl.* **yup·pies** A young, usually urban, middle-class professional person. [<Y(OUNG) U(RBAN) P(ROFESSIONAL) + -IE]

YWCA, Y.W.C.A. Young Women's Christian Association.

YWHA, Y.W.H.A. Young Women's Hebrew Association.

Z

Z, z (zē, *Brit. & Can.* zed) *n. pl.* **Z's, z's, Zs, zs** (zēz, zedz) **1** The 26th letter of the English alphabet. **2** Any spoken sound representing the letter *Z* or *z*. **3** Something shaped like a Z. —*adj.* Shaped like a Z.

Z., z. zero; zone.

zai·bat·su (zī′bat·sŏŏ′) *n. pl.* **zai·bat·su** The wealthy clique of Japan, representing four or five dominant families. [< Jap. *zai* property + *batsu* family]

Zaire (zīr′, zä·ir′) *n.* A republic of CEN. Africa, 904,754 sq. mi., cap. Kinshasa. • See map at AFRICA.

Zam·bi·a (zam′bē·ə) *n.* An independent member of the Commonwealth of Nations in CEN. Africa, 288,130 sq. mi., cap. Lusaka. • See map at AFRICA.

za·ny (zā′nē) *adj.* **·ni·er, ·ni·est** Absurdly funny; ludicrous. —*n. pl.* **·nies 1** In old comic plays, a clown who absurdly mimics the other performers. **2** Any ludicrous comic or buffoon. **3** A simpleton; fool. [< Ital. *zanni*] —**za′ni·ly** *adv.* —**za′ni·ness** *n.*

zap (zap) *Slang v.t.* **zapped, zap·ping 1** To kill. **2** To attack; hit; clobber. **3** To confront or impress suddenly and forcefully; astound; overwhelm. —*n.* **1** Vigorous effect; punch; vitality. **2** An attack or confrontation.

zeal (zēl) *n.* Ardor, as for a cause; fervor. [< Gk. *zēlos*] — **Syn.** enthusiasm, eagerness, devotion, passion, verve, spirit, heart.

zeal·ot (zel′ət) *n.* One who is zealous, esp. to an immoderate degree; partisan, fanatic, etc. —**zeal′ot·ry** *n.*

zeal·ous (zel′əs) *adj.* Filled with, marked by, or showing zeal; enthusiastic. —**zeal′ous·ly** *adv.* —**zeal′ous·ness** *n.*

ze·bec (zē′bek) *n.* XEBEC. Also **ze′beck.**

ze·bra (zē′brə, *Brit. & Can.* zeb′rə) *n.* Any of various African ponylike mammals having a whitish body with dark stripes. [Pg.] —**ze′brine** (-brēn, -brin), **ze′·broid** (-broid) *adj.*

Zebra

ze·bu (zē′byŏŏ) *n.* Any of various breeds of domesticated oxen of Asia and Africa, having a hump on the withers, a large dewlap, and short curved horns. [< Tibetan]

Zech. Zechariah.

zed (zed) *n. Brit. & Can.* The letter *z.* [< Gk. *zēta*]

zeit·geist (tsīt′gīst) *n. Often cap.* The intellectual, moral, and cultural tendencies that characterize any age or epoch. [< G < *Zeit* time + *Geist* spirit]

Zen (zen) *n.* A form of Buddhism that originated in China and became widespread in Japan, that lays particular stress on deep meditation as a means of achieving an abrupt, intuitive spiritual enlightenment. [< Jap. *zen* meditation]

Zend (zend) *n.* The ancient translation of and commentary on the Avesta. [< Pers., interpretation] —**Zend′ic** *adj.*

Zend-A·ves·ta (zend′ə·ves′tə) *n.* The sacred Zoroastrian writings including the Zend and the Avesta.

ze·nith (zē′nith) *n.* **1** The point of the celestial sphere that is exactly overhead. **2** The highest or culminating point; summit; acme. [< Ar. *samt (ar-rās)* the path (over the head)]

Zeph. Zephaniah.

zeph·yr (zef′ər) *n.* **1** The west wind. **2** Any soft, gentle wind. **3** Worsted or woolen yarn of very light weight: also **zephyr worsted.** [< Gk. *zephyros*]

zep·pe·lin (zep′ə·lin) *n.* A large, cigar-shaped dirigible. [< Count Ferdinand von *Zeppelin,* 1838–1917, German aircraft builder]

ze·ro (zir′ō, zē′rō) *n. pl.* **ze·ros** or **ze·roes 1** The numeral or symbol 0; a cipher. **2** *Math.* The element of a number

system that leaves any element unchanged under addition, esp. a real number *0* such that $a + 0 = 0 + a = a$ for any real number *a.* **3** The point on a scale, as of a thermometer, from which measures are counted. **4** The temperature registered at the zero mark on a thermometer. **5** Nothing. **6** The lowest point: Our hopes dropped to *zero.* —*v.t.* **ze·roed, ze·ro·ing** To adjust (instruments) to an arbitrary zero point for synchronized readings. —**zero in 1** To move or bring into a desired position, as an airplane. **2** To adjust the sight of (a gun) or direct (ammunition) toward (a target). —**zero in on 1** To direct gunfire, bombs, etc. toward (a specific target). **2** To concentrate or focus one's energy, attention, efforts, etc., on. —*adj.* **1** Of, at, or being zero. **2** That limits vertical visibility to 50 feet or less: said of a cloud ceiling. **3** That limits horizontal visibility to 165 feet or less: said of conditions on the ground. [< Ar. *ṣifr*] • In popular usage the symbol for zero (0) is often rendered orally as (ō), as if it were the letter O.

zero hour 1 The time set for an attack. **2** Any critical moment.

zest (zest) *n.* **1** Agreeable excitement and keen enjoyment. **2** A quality that imparts such excitement. **3** Any piquant flavoring. [< F *zeste* lemon or orange peel] —**zest′·ful, zest′y** (·i·er, ·i·est) —**zest′ful·ly** *adv.* —**zest′ful·ness** *n.* —**Syn.** **1** delight, gusto, relish, pleasure, gratification, savor, thrill, kick.

ze·ta (zā′tə, zē′-) *n.* The sixth letter of the Greek alphabet. (Z,ζ)

Zeus (zŏŏs) *Gk. Myth.* The supreme deity.

zig·gu·rat (zig′ŏŏ·rat) *n.* Among the Assyrians and Babylonians, a terraced temple tower pyramidal in form, each successive story being smaller than the one below. [< Assyrian *ziqquratu,* orig., a mountain top]

Ziggurat

zig·zag (zig′zag) *n.* **1** One of a series of sharp turns or angles. **2** A path or pattern characterized by such turns or angles going from side to side. —*adj.* Having a series of zigzags. —*adv.* In a zigzag manner. —*v.t. & v.i.* **·zagged, ·zag·ging** To move in zigzags. [< G *zickzack*]

zilch (zilch) *n. Slang* Nothing; zero. [Alter. of ZERO]

zil·lion (zil′yən) *n. Informal* A very large, indeterminate number: a *zillion* things to do before the plane left. [Imit. of *million, trillion,* etc.] —**zil′lionth** *adj.*

zinc (zingk) *n.* A bluish white metallic element (symbol Zn) occurring mostly in combination, extensively used in alloys, as bronze and brass, for galvanizing, and in electric batteries. —*v.t.* **zinced** or **zincked, zinc·ing** or **zinck·ing** To coat or cover with zinc; galvanize. [< G *zink*] —**zinc′ic** (-ik), **zinc′ous** (-əs), **zinck′y, zinc′y, zink′y** *adj.*

zinc ointment A medicated ointment containing zinc oxide.

zinc oxide A white powdery compound, used as a pigment and as a mild antiseptic.

zinc white Zinc oxide used as a pigment.

zing (zing) *Informal n.* **1** A high-pitched buzzing or humming sound. **2** Energy; vitality. —*v.i.* To make a shrill, humming sound.

zin·ni·a (zin′ē·ə, zin′yə) *n.* Any of various cultivated plants having opposite entire leaves and showy, composite flowers. [< J. G. *Zinn,* 1727–59, German botanist]

Zi·on (zī′ən) *n.* **1** A hill in Jerusalem, the site of the Temple of David and his successors. **2** The Jewish people. **3** Any place or community considered to be especially under God's rule, as ancient Israel. **4** The heavenly Jerusalem; heaven. [< Heb. *tsīyōn* a hill]

Zi·on·ism (zī'ən·iz'əm) *n.* A movement for a resettlement of the Jews in Palestine. —**Zi'on·ist** *adj. & n.*

zip (zip) *n.* 1 A sharp, hissing sound, as of a bullet passing through the air. 2 *Informal* Energy; vitality; vim. —*v.* **zipped, zip·ping** *v.t.* 1 To fasten with a zipper: often with *up:* to *zip* up a jacket. 2 To give speed and energy to. —*v.i.* 3 *Informal* To move or act with speed and energy. 4 To move with a sharp, hissing sound. [Imit.]

zip-code (zip'kōd') *v.t.* **-cod·ed, -cod·ing** *Sometimes cap.* To provide (mail) with a zip code.

zip code (zip) A numerical code devised to identify each postal delivery area in the U.S. Also **ZIP Code, Zip Code.** [< *z(one) i(mprovement) p(lan)*]

zip·per (zip'ər) *n.* A sliding fastener with two rows of interlocking teeth. [< *Zipper*, a trade name]

zip·py (zip'ē) *adj.* **-pi·er, -pi·est** *Informal* Brisk; energetic.

zir·con (zûr'kon) *n.* 1 An adamantine, variously colored zirconium silicate, used as a gem in certain varieties. 2 A variety of this mineral having an artificially produced lustrous blue appearance. [< Ar. *zarqūn* cinnabar < Pers. *zargūn* golden]

zir·co·ni·um (zûr·kō'nē·əm) *n.* A metallic element (symbol Zr), used in heat-resistant alloys. [< ZIRCON] —**zir·con'·ic** *adj.*

zith·er (zith'ər, zith'-) *n.* A stringed instrument having a flat sounding board and 30 to 40 strings that are played by plucking. Also **zith'ern** (-ərn). [< Gk. *kithara*]

zlo·ty (zlô'tē) *n. pl.* **·tys** or **·ty** The basic monetary unit of Poland.

Zn zinc.

zo·di·ac (zō'dē·ak) *n.* 1 An imaginary belt encircling the heavens and extending about 8° on each side of the ecliptic, within which are the orbits of the moon, sun, and larger planets. It is divided into twelve parts, called **signs of the zodiac,** which formerly corre-

Signs of the zodiac (reading clockwise):
A. Vernal equinox: Aries, Taurus, Gemini.
B. Summer solstice: Cancer, Leo, Virgo.
C. Autumnal equinox: Libra, Scorpio, Sagittarius.
D. Winter solstice: Capricorn, Aquarius, Pisces.

sponded to twelve constellations. 2 Any complete circuit; round. [< Gk. *(kyklos) zōdiakos* (circle) of animals] —**zo·di·a·cal** (zō·dī'ə·kəl) *adj.*

zom·bie (zom'bē) *n.* 1 In voodoo cults, a snake deity. 2 The supernatural power by which a dead body is believed to be reanimated. 3 A corpse reactivated by such power. 4 *Slang* A person who looks weird or behaves eccentrically, mechanically, etc. 5 A strong cocktail made of several kinds of rum, fruit juices, and liqueurs. Also, esp. for defs. 1, 2, & 3, **zom'bi.** [< West African]

Zither

zo·nal (zō'nəl) *adj.* Of, pertaining to, exhibiting, or marked by a zone or zones; having the form of a zone. Also **zo'na·ry** (-nər-ē). —**zon'al·ly** *adv.*

zone (zōn) *n.* 1 One of five divisions of the earth's surface, bounded by parallels of latitude and named for the prevailing climate. These are the **torrid zone,** extending on each side of the equator 23° 27'; the **temperate** or **variable zones,** included between the parallels 23° 27' and 66° 33' on both sides of the equator; and the **frigid zones,** within the parallels 66° 33' and the poles. 2 *Ecol.* A belt or area delimited from others by the character of its plant or animal life, its climate, geological formations, etc. 3 A region, area, belt, etc., distinguished or set off by some special characteristic: a demilitarized *zone;* a residential *zone;* a no-parking *zone.* 4 An area, usu. circular, within which a uniform rate is charged for delivery of goods, telephone calls, etc. 5 In the U.S. postal system: **a** Any of the areas within which a uniform rate is charged for parcel post. **b** Any of the numbered postal districts in a city. 6 *Geom.* A portion of the surface of a sphere enclosed between two parallel planes. —*v.t.* **zoned, zon·ing** 1 To divide into zones; esp., to divide (a city, etc.) into zones which are restricted as to types of construction and activity, as residential, industrial, etc. 2 To encircle with a zone or belt. 3 To mark with or as with zones or stripes. [< Gk. *zōnē* a girdle] —**zoned** *adj.*

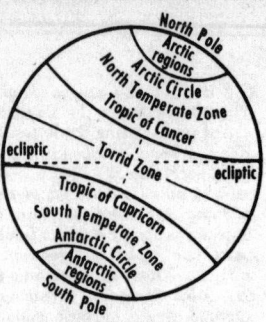

Terrestrial zones

zonk (zongk) *v.t. Slang* To hit, esp. on the head; clobber; brain.

zonked (zongkt) *adj. Slang* Highly intoxicated or stimulated, as by alcohol or a drug: often with *out.* [?]

zoo (zōō) *n. pl.* **zoos** A park or place where wild animals are kept for exhibition. [Short for *zoological garden*]

zoo- *combining form* Animal: *zoology.* [< Gk. *zōion* an animal]

zo·o·ge·o·graph·ic (zō'ə·jē'ə·graf'ik) *adj.* Of, pertaining to, or engaged in zoogeography. Also **zo'o·ge'o·graph'·i·cal.** —**zo'o·ge'o·graph'i·cal·ly** *adv.*

zo·o·ge·og·ra·phy (zō'ə·jē·og'rə·fē) *n.* 1 The systematic study of the distribution of animals and of the factors controlling it. 2 The study of the relations between special animal groups and the land or aquatic areas in which they predominate. —**zo'o·ge·og'ra·pher** *n.*

zo·og·ra·phy (zō·og'rə·fē) *n.* The branch of zoology that describes animals; descriptive zoology. —**zo·og'ra·pher** or **·phist** *n.* —**zo·o·graph·ic** (zō'ə·graf'ik) or **·i·cal** *adj.*

zo·oid (zō'oid) *n.* 1 An entity, usu. very small, capable of movement and independent existence, as a spermatozoon. 2 An individual member of a compound organism, as in a sponge. —*adj.* Having essentially the nature of an animal: also **zo·oi·dal** (zō·oid'l). [< zo(o)- + -OID]

zool. zoological; zoologist; zoology.

zo·o·log·i·cal (zō'ə·loj'i·kəl) *adj.* 1 Of, pertaining to, or occupied with zoology. 2 Relating to or characteristic of animals. Also **zo'o·log'ic.** —**zo'o·log'i·cal·ly** *adv.*

zoological garden zoo.

zo·ol·o·gy (zō·ol'ə·jē) *n.* 1 The science that treats of animals with reference to their structure, functions, development, nomenclature, and classification. 2 The animal life of a particular area. 3 A scientific treatise on animals. [< zoo- + -LOGY] —**zo·ol'o·gist** *n.*

zoom (zōōm) *v.i.* 1 To make a low-pitched but loud humming or buzzing sound, esp. when related to speed: The cars *zoomed* down the road. 2 To climb sharply upward, as an airplane. 3 To rise sharply, as prices. 4 To move a motion picture or TV camera rapidly or adjust the focus, as with a zoom lens, to make an image appear to come very close or become more distant: often with *in* or *out.* —*v.t.* 5 To cause to zoom. —*n.* The act of zooming. [Imit.]

zoom lens *Photog.* A lens, used chiefly on television and motion picture cameras, that permits the size of the image to be varied continuously without loss of focus.

zo·o·phyte (zō′ə-fīt) *n.* An invertebrate animal resembling a plant, as a coral or sea anemone. [< zoo- + Gk. *phyton* plant] —**zo′o·phyt′ic** (-fit′ik) or **-i·cal** *adj.*

zo·o·spore (zō′ə-spôr, -spōr) *n.* A motile, asexual spore of certain fungi and algae, usu. provided with cilia. [< zoo- + SPORE] —**zo′o·spor′ic** (-spôr′ik, -spor′ik), **zo·os·po·rous** (zō-os′pər-əs) *adj.*

zo·ri (zō′rē) *n.* A flat, thonged sandal of straw or rubber. [< Japanese]

Zo·ro·as·tri·an·ism (zō′rō-as′trē-ən-iz′əm) *n.* The religious system founded in ancient Persia by Zoroaster. It recognizes two creative powers, one good and the other evil, and teaches the final triumph of good over evil.

Zou·ave (zōō-äv′, zwäv) *n.* **1** A member of a unit of the French infantry wearing a brilliant Oriental uniform. **2** A member of any volunteer regiment wearing a similar uniform. [< Ar. *Zouaoua*, a tribal name]

zounds (zoundz) *interj.* An exclamation denoting astonishment. [Short for *God's wounds*]

Zr zirconium.

zuc·chet·to (tsōōk-ket′tō) *n. pl.* **·tos** A skullcap worn by ecclesiastics in the Roman Catholic Church, black for a priest, purple for a bishop, red for a cardinal, white for the pope. [Ital. < *zucchetta*, orig. a small gourd]

zuc·chi·ni (zōō-kē′nē) *n.* An elongated summer squash having a thin green skin. [< Ital. *zucca* a gourd, squash]

Zu·lu (zōō′lōō) *n. pl.* **Zu·lus** or **Zu·lu 1** A member of a Bantu nation of SE Africa. **2** The Bantu language of the Zulus. — *adj.* Of the Zulus or their language.

Zu·ñi (zōō′nyē) *n. pl.* **·ñi** or **·ñis 1** A member of a tribe of North American Indians, now living in New Mexico. **2** The language of this tribe.

zwie·back (zwī′bak, zwē′-, swī′-, swē′-, -bäk) *n.* A wheaten bread baked in a loaf and later sliced and toasted. [G, twice baked]

Zwing·li·an (zwing′lē-ən, tsving′-) *adj.* Of or pertaining to Huldreich Zwingli or his doctrines, esp. the doctrine that the Eucharist is simply a symbolic commemoration of the death of Christ. —*n.* A follower of Zwingli. —**Zwing′·li·an·ism** *n.*

zy·gote (zī′gōt, zig′ōt) *n.* **1** The product of the union of two gametes. **2** An individual developing from such a union. [< Gk *zygon* a yoke] —**zy·got·ic** (zī-got′ik) *adj.*

zy·mase (zī′mās) *n.* A mixture of enzymes that promotes fermentation by breaking down glucose and related carbohydrates into alcohol and carbon dioxide. [< Gk. *zymē* leaven]

zy·mol·o·gy (zī-mol′ə-jē) *n.* The science of fermentation. [< Gk. *zymē* leaven + -LOGY] —**zy·mo·log·ic** (zī′mə-loj′ik) or **-i·cal** *adj.* —**zy·mol′o·gist** *n.*

zy·mot·ic (zī-mot′ik) *adj.* Of, pertaining to, or caused by fermentation. [< Gk. *zymōtikos*]

zy·mur·gy (zī′mûr·jē) *n.* The chemistry of fermentation as applied to brewing, making of yeast, and wine making. [< Gk *zymē* leaven + -URGY]

ENCYCLOPEDIC SUPPLEMENTS
Table of Contents

Abbreviations

This list of abbreviations and meanings is a selection of those commonly in use in printed works. There are many forms of abbreviations—capital letters or lower-case letters, periods or no periods, spaces between letters or no spaces, and so on. In this list abbreviations are given without periods. Most are given without spaces and the majority are in lower-case letters unless usage dictates otherwise.

Most of the words that the abbreviations represent are spelled here in lower-case letters, although they may appear elsewhere with initial capital letters. Abbreviations such as *mt* for *mount* usually begin with a capital letter when used with proper nouns—as in *Mt Shasta*.

In abbreviations of foreign words or phrases, such as those from French or Latin, the English meaning always appears first, followed by the word or phrase in the language of origin.

A

a abbreviation, about, acre, alto, ampere, are (measure), argent, assists (baseball), before (Lat. *ante*), year (Lat. *anno*)
A absolute (temperature), angstrom (unit), argon
AA Alcoholics Anonymous, antiaircraft, author's alteration
AAA American Automobile Association
AAAL American Academy of Arts and Letters
AAAS American Academy of Arts and Sciences, American Association for the Advancement of Science
AAE American Association of Engineers
AAF Army Air Forces
A and M Agricultural and Mechanical (College)
Aar Aaron
AARP American Association of Retired Persons
AAU Amateur Athletic Union
ab able-bodied (seaman), (times) at bat

Ab alabamine
AB adapter booster, airborne, Bachelor of Arts (Lat. *Artium Baccalaureus*)
ABA American Bar Association, American Booksellers Association
a&b assault and battery
abbr, abbrev abbreviation
ABC the alphabet, American Broadcasting Company, Audit Bureau of Circulation, Australian Broadcasting Commission
ab ex from without (Lat. *ab extra*)
ab init from the beginning (Lat. *ab initio*)
abl ablative
ABM antiballistic missile
abp archbishop, arterial blood pressure
abr abridged, abridgment
abs absent, absolute (temperature), absolutely, abstract
abstr abstract, abstracted
ac before meals (Lat. *ante cibum*)
a/c account, account current, air conditioning
Ac actinium
AC after Christ, Air Corps, alternating current
acad academic, academy
acc acceptance, accompanied, account, accountant
acc, accus accusative
ACC Air Coordinating Committee
accel accelerando, accelerate
acct account, accountant
ack acknowledge, acknowledgment
ACLU American Civil Liberties Union
ACP American College of Physicians
acpt acceptance
ACS American Chemical Society
A/cs Pay accounts payable
A/cs Rec accounts receivable
act active
ACT American College Test
actg acting
ACTH adrenocorticotropic hormone
ad advertisement, before the day (Lat. *ante diem*)
AD year of our Lord (Lat. *anno domini*)

ADA American Dental Association, Americans for Democratic Action
adc aide-de-camp
ADC aid to families with dependent children
add addenda, addendum, addition, additional, address
ad fin at the end, to one end (Lat. *ad finem*)
ad inf to infinity (Lat. *ad infinitum*)
adj adjacent, adjective, adjourned, adjunct, adjustment
Adj, Adjt adjutant
ad lib to the amount desired (Lat. *ad libitum*)
adm administrative, administrator, admitted
Adm admiral, Admiralty
adv adverb, adverbial, advertisement
ad val according to value (Lat. *ad valorem*)
advt advertisement
ae, aet, aetat of age (Lat. *aetatis*)
AEA Actors' Equity Association
AE and P ambassador extraordinary and plenipotentiary
AEC Atomic Energy Commission
AEF American Expeditionary Force
aeron aeronautics
af audio frequency
Af Africa, African
AF Air Force
AFAM, AF & AM Ancient Free and Accepted Masons
AFB Air Force Base
AFC American Football Conference, automatic frequency control
AFDC aid to families with dependent children
Afg, Afgh Afghanistan
AFL, AF of L American Federation of Labor
AFL-CIO American Federation of Labor–Congress of Industrial Organizations
AFM American Federation of Musicians
Afr Africa, African
AFT American Federation of Teachers
AFTRA American Federation of Television and Radio Artists

Ag August, silver (Lat. *argentum*)
AG adjutant general, attorney general, corporation (Ger. *aktiengesellschaft*)
agcy agency
agr, agri, agric agricultural, agriculture, agriculturist
agt agent, agreement
AHQ Army Headquarters
AI artificial intelligence, in the year of the discovery (Lat. *anno inventionis*)
AIDS acquired immuno-deficiency syndrome
AIM American Indian Movement
AK Alaska
aka also known as
AKC American Kennel Club
al other things (persons) (Lat. *alia, alii*)
Al aluminum
AL Alabama, aviation electronicsman
Ala Alabama
ALA American Library Association
Alas Alaska
Alb Albania, Albanian, Albany, Alberta
Alba Alberta
Ald, Aldm alderman
alg algebra
Alg Algeria, Algerian
ALP American Labor Party, Australian Labor Party
alt alteration, alternate, altitude, alto
Alta Alberta
alum aluminum
am ammeter, before noon (Lat. *ante meridiem*)
Am alabamine, America, American, americium
AM air mail, amplitude modulation, in the year of the world (Lat. *anno mundi*), Master of Arts (Lat. *Artium Magister*)
AMA American Management Association, American Medical Association
Amb ambassador
AMDG to the greater glory of God (Lat. *ad majorem Dei gloriam*)
AME African Methodist Episcopal
Amer America, American
AMG Allied Military Government (of Occupied Territory)

Am Ind American Indian
amp ampere, amperage
amp-hr ampere-hour
amt amount
amu atomic mass unit
AMVETS American Veterans (of World War II and the Korean War)
an anonymous, before (Lat. *ante*)
anal analogous, analogy, analysis, analytic(al)
anat anatomical, anatomy
anc ancient, anciently
and moderately slow (It. *andante*)
And Andorra
Ang Anglican, Angola
Angl Anglican, Anglicized
anim animated (It. *animato*)
ann annals, annual, annuities, annuity, years (Lat. *anni*)
anon anonymous
ans answer, answered
ant antenna, antiquarian, antiquity, antonym
Ant Antarctic, Antarctica
anthrop, anthropol anthropological, anthropology
antilog antilogarithm
antiq antiquarian, antiquities
A/O account of
AOL absent over leave
ap apothecary
Ap apostle, April
AP Associated Press, antipersonnel
APB all points bulletin
apmt appointment
APO Army Post Office
Apoc Apocalypse, Apocrypha, Apocryphal
app apparatus, apparent, appended, appendix, apprentice
appar apparatus, apparent
approx approximate, approximately
Apr April
APR annual percentage rate
APS Army Postal Service
apt apartment
aq aqueous, water (Lat. *aqua*)
AQ Achievement Quotient
ar argent, aromatic, arrival, arrive, in the year of the reign (Lat. *anno regni*)
Ar argon, silver (Lat. *argentum*)
Ar, Arab Arabia, Arabian, Arabic
AR Arkansas
Aram Aramaic
ARC American Red Cross, AIDS-related complex
arch archaic, archaism, archery, archipelago, architect
Arch, Archbp archbishop
archaeol archaeology
Archd archdeacon, archduke
archeol archeology

archit architecture
archt architect
arg argent, silver (Lat. *argentum*)
Arg Argentina, Argyll
arith arithmetic, arithmetical
Ariz Arizona
Ark Arkansas
Arm Armenia, Armenian
ArM Master of Architecture (Lat. *Architecturae Magister*)
ARM adjustable-rate mortgage
arr arrange, arranged, arrangements, arrival, arrive, arrived
art article, artificial, artist
ARV American Revised (Standard) Version (of the Bible)
as, asym asymmetric
As arsenic
AS Anglo-Saxon, antisubmarine
ASA American Standards Association
asb asbestos
ASCAP American Society of Composers, Authors and Publishers
ASCII American Standard Code for Information Interchange
ASE American Stock Exchange
ASEAN Association of South-East Asian Nations
asgd assigned
ASPCA American Society for the Prevention of Cruelty to Animals
assd assigned
assn association
assoc associate, association
asst assistant
Assyr Assyria, Assyrian
astr, astron astronomer, astronomical, astronomy
astrol astrologer, astrological, astrology
ASVAB Armed Services Vocational Apptitude Battery
at atmosphere, atomic
At astatine
AT antitank
ATC Air Transport Command
athl athlete, athletic, athletics
Atl Atlantic
atm atmosphere, atmospheric
at no atomic number
ATS Army Transport Service, Auxiliary Territorial Service
att, attn, atten attention
att, atty attorney
Atty Gen attorney general
ATV all-terrain vehicle
at wt atomic weight
au angstrom unit
Au gold (Lat. *aurum*)
AUC from (the year of) the building of the city (of

Rome) (Lat. *ab urbe condita*)
aud audible, audit, auditor
Aug August, Augustan, Augustus
Aus, Aust Austria
Aus, Austl Australia
AUS Army of the United States
auth authentic, author, authority, authorized
Auth Ver Authorized Version (of the Bible)
auto automatic, automotive
aux, auxil auxiliary
av according to value (Lat. *ad valorem*)
av, avdp avoirdupois
av, avg average
Av avenue
AV Authorized Version (of the Bible)
avc automatic volume control
Ave avenue
avg average
avn aviation
avoir avoirdupois
A/W actual weight, all water
AWL absent with leave
AWOL absent without leave
AWVS American Women's Volunteer Services
ax axiom, axis
az azimuth, azure
AZ Arizona

B

b bachelor, balboa (coin), base, base hit, baseman, bass, basso, bat, battery, bay, bench, bicuspid, bolívar (coin), boliviano (coin), book, born, brass, breadth, brother
B bacillus, Bible, bishop (chess), boron, British, brotherhood
B/- bag, bale
Ba barium
BA Bachelor of Arts (Lat. *Baccalaureus Artium*), British Academy
bach bachelor
bact, bacteriol bacteriological, bacteriologist, bacteriology
BAE Bachelor of Aeronautical Engineering, Bachelor of Arts in Education
BAg, BAgr Bachelor of Agriculture
BAgSci Bachelor of Agricultural Science
bal balance, balancing
Balt Baltic
Bap, Bapt Baptist
bapt baptized
bar barometer, barometric, barrel, barrister
BAR Browning automatic rifle
BAr, BArch Bachelor of Architecture

barit baritone
Bart baronet
BAS, BASc Bachelor of Agricultural Science, Bachelor of Applied Science
BASIC Beginner's All-purpose Symbolic Instruction Code
bat, batt battalion, battery
bb base(s) on balls
BBA, BBusAd Bachelor of Business Administration
BBB Better Business Bureau
BBC British Broadcasting Corporation
bbl barrel
BC Bachelor of Chemistry, Bachelor of Commerce, before Christ, British Columbia
BCD binary coded decimal
BCE Bachelor of Chemical Engineering, Bachelor of Civil Engineering, before Christian era
bch bunch
BCL Bachelor of Civil Law
BCP Book of Common Prayer
BCS Bachelor of Chemical Science
bd board, bond, bound, bundle
BD Bachelor of Divinity
B/D bank draft, bills discounted, brought down
bd ft board foot
bdg binding
bdl, bdle bundle
bds bundles, (bound in) boards
BDS Bachelor of Dental Surgery
Be beryllium
BE Bachelor of Education, Bachelor of Engineering, Bank of England, Board of Education
B/E bills of exchange
BEE Bachelor of Electrical Engineering
bef before
BEF British Expeditionary Force(s)
Bel, Belg Belgian, Belgium
Beng Bengal, Bengali
B ès L Bachelor of Letters (Fr. *Bachelier ès Lettres*)
B ès S Bachelor of Sciences (Fr. *Bachelier ès Sciences*)
bet, betw between
bev billion electron volts
bf bold face
BF Bachelor of Finance, Bachelor of Forestry
B/F brought forward
BFA Bachelor of Fine Arts
bg bag
BG brigadier general
BHE Bureau of Higher Education
bhp brake horsepower
Bi bismuth

Bib Bible, Biblical
bibl biblical, bibliographical
bibliog bibliography
bicarb bicarbonate of soda
b i d twice a day (Lat. *bis in die*)
biochem biochemistry
biog biographer, biographical, biography
biol biological, biologist, biology
BIOS basic input-output system
BIS British Information Services
BJ Bachelor of Journalism
bk bank, block, book
Bk berkelium
bkg banking
bkkpg bookkeeping
bklr black letter
bkpt bankrupt
bks barracks, books
bkt basket, bracket
bl bale, barrel, black, blue
BL, BLL Bachelor of Laws
B/L bill of lading
BLA Bachelor of Liberal Arts
bld bold face
bldg, blg building
BLE Brotherhood of Locomotive Engineers
B Lit, B Litt Bachelor of Letters, Bachelor of Literature (Lat. *Baccallaureus Litterarum*)
blk black, block
bln balloon
bls bales, barrels
BLS Bachelor of Library Science, Bachelor of Library Service, Bureau of Labor Statistics
blvd boulevard
bm board measure
BM Bachelor of Medicine (Lat. *Baccalaureus Medicinae*), Bachelor of Music (Lat. *Baccalaureus Musicae*), Bureau of Mines
BME Bachelor of Mechanical Engineering, Bachelor of Mining Engineering
BMechE Bachelor of Mechanical Engineering
BMEWS Ballistic Missile Early Warning System
BMR basal metabolic rate
BMus Bachelor of Music
Bn battalion
BN bank note
BNA Basel Anatomical Nomenclature (Lat. *Basle Nomina Anatomica*), British North America Act
bo back order, body odor, box office, branch office, broker's order, buyer's option
BO Board of Ordnance
B/O brought over
Boh Bohemia, Bohemian

Bol Bolivia, Bolivian
bor borough
bot botanical, botanist, botany, bottle
BOT Board of Trade
bp below proof, birthplace, bishop, blood pressure, boiling point
BP Bachelor of Pharmacy
BP, BPh, BPhil Bachelor of Philosophy (Lat. *Baccalaureus Philosophiae*)
B/P bill of parcels, bills payable
BPd, BPe Bachelor of Pedagogy
BPE Bachelor of Physical Education
BPH Bachelor of Public Health
BPI Bureau of Public Inquiries
BPOE Benevolent and Protective Order of Elks
br branch, brand, bridge, brief, brig, bronze, brother
Br Breton, Britain, British, bromine
BR Bill of Rights
B/R bills receivable
Braz Brazil, Brazilian
Brazil Brazilian
BRCS British Red Cross Society
B Rec bills receivable
brev brevet, brevetted
Br Hond British Honduras
Brig brigade, brigadier
Brig Gen brigadier general
Brit Britain, Britannia, Britannica, British
bro brother
bros brothers
bs balance sheet
BS Bachelor of Surgery
B/S bags, bales, bill of sale
BS, BSc Bachelor of Science (Lat. *Baccalaureus Scientiae*)
BSA Bachelor of Scientific Agriculture, Bibliographical Society of America, Boy Scouts of America
BSEd Bachelor of Science in Education
bsh bushel
BSS, BSSc, BS in SS Bachelor of (Science in) Social Sciences
Bt baronet
BT, BTh Bachelor of Theology
BTU, Bthu, btu British thermal unit
Btry battery
bu bureau, bushel, bushels
buck buckram
bul, bull bulletin
Bulg Bulgaria, Bulgarian
BV Blessed Virgin (Lat. *Beata Virgo*), farewell (Lat. *bene vale*)

BVM Blessed Virgin Mary (Lat. *Beata Virgo Maria*)
bvt brevet, brevetted
bx box
Bz benzine

C

c about (Lat. *circa*), candle, capacity (electrical), carton, case, catcher (baseball), cathode, Celsius, cent, centigrade, centime, centimeter, chapter, chief, child, cost, cubic
C calends, capacity (electrical), cape, carbon, cathode, Catholic, Celtic, century, Chancellor, chapter, church, Congress, Conservative, constant, copyright, Court, current, Roman numeral for 100
ca about (Lat. *circa*), cathode, centiare, chief accountant, claim agent, commercial agent, consular agent, controller of accounts
Ca calcium
CA California, Catholic Action, Central America, chronological age, Coast Artillery, Confederate Army
C/A commercial account, credit account, current account
CAA Civil Aeronautics Administration
CAB Civil Aeronautics Board
CAD computer-aided design, computer-aided drafting
CAF cost and freight; cost, assurance, and freight
CAI computer-aided instruction
cal calendar, calends, caliber, calomel, small calorie
Cal caliber, large calorie
Cal, Calif California
Cam camouflage
CAM computer-aided manufacturing
can canon, canto
Can Canada, Canadian
Canad Canadian
canc cancel, cancellation, cancelled
cant canton, cantonment
Cant Canterbury, Canticles, Cantonese
Cantab Cambridge (Lat. *Cantabrigia*)
cap capital, capitalize, chapter (Lat. *caput*)
CAP Civil Air Patrol
caps capital letters
Capt Captain
car carat
CAR Civil Air Regulations
Card Cardinal
CARE Cooperative for American Remittances Everywhere

cat catalog, catechism
CAT computerized axial tomography
cath cathedral
Cath Catholic
CATV community antenna television
cav cavalier, cavalry
CAVU ceiling and visibility unlimited
cb center of buoyancy, confined to barracks
Cb columbium, cumulonimbus
CB citizens band (radio), Construction Battalion, Bachelor of Surgery (Lat. *Baccalaureus Chiurgiae*)
CBC Canadian Broadcasting Corporation
CBD cash before delivery
CBOE Chicago Board Options Exchange
CBOT Chicago Board of Trade
CBS Columbia Broadcasting System
cc carbon copy, cash credit, cashier's check, chapters, chief clerk, circuit court, city council, city councilor, civil court, common councilman, company clerk, company commander, consular clerk, contra credit, copy, county clerk, county commissioner, county council, county court, cubic centimeter, current account (Fr. *compte courant*)
Cc cirrocumulus
CC cyanogen chloride (poison gas)
CCA Chief Clerk of the Admiralty, circuit court of appeals
CCC Civilian Conservation Corps; Commodity Credit Corporation
CCF Cooperative Commonwealth Federation (of Canada)
CCS Combined Chiefs of Staff
cd candela, cash discount, cord
Cd cadmium
CD certificate of deposit, civil defense, compact disc
C/D carried down
cd ft cord foot (feet)
CDR, Cdr commander
CDT central daylight time
Ce cerium
CE chemical engineer, chief engineer, Church of England, civil engineer, Council of Europe, Corps of Engineers
CEA Council of Economic Advisers
CEEB College Entrance Examination Board
Celt Celtic

cen, cent central, century

cent centered, centigrade, centimeter, one hundred (Lat. *centum*)

CERN European Council for Nuclear Research (Fr. *Centre Européen des Recherches Nucléaires*)

cert certificate, certify

certif certificate, certificated

cet par other things being equal (Lat. *ceteris paribus*)

Cey Ceylon

cf center field, center fielder, compare (Lat. *confer*)

Cf californium

CF cost and freight

C/F carried forward

CFI cost, freight, and insurance

cfm cubic feet per minute

CFR Code of Federal Regulations

cfs cubic feet per second

cg center of gravity, consul general

cg, cgm centigram

CG Coast Guard, commanding general

CGH Cape of Good Hope

cgs centimeter-gram-second

ch chain, champion, chargé d'affaires, check (chess), chestnut, chevronets, chief, child, children, chirurgeon, church, clearinghouse, courthouse, customhouse, of surgery (Lat. *chiurgiae*)

c-h, c-hr candle-hour

ch chaplain, chapter

Ch Chaldean, Chaldee, China, Chinese

CH Companion of Honor

Chanc chancelor, chancery

chap chaplain, chapter

char character, charter

ChB Bachelor of Surgery (Lat. *Chiurgiae Baccalaureus*)

ChE, CheE chemical engineer

chem chemical, chemist, chemistry

chg charge

chgd charged

Chin Chinese

ChJ chief justice

ChM Master of Surgery (Lat. *Chiurgiae Magister*)

chm checkmate

chm, chmn chairman

Chr Christ, Christian

chron, chronol chronological, chronology

Chron Chronicles

chs chapters

Ci cirrus

Cia company (Sp. *Compania*)

CIA Central Intelligence Agency

CIC Counter-Intelligence Corps

CID Criminal Investigation · Division (Brit.)

Cie company (Fr. *compagnie*)

CIF cost, insurance, and freight

C in C, CINC, Cinc commander in chief

CIP cataloging in publication

CIO Congress of Industrial Organizations

cir, circ about (Lat. *circa, circiter, circum*), circular, circulation, circumference

cit citation, cited, citizen

civ civil, civilian

CJ body of law (Lat. *corpus juris*), chief judge, chief justice

ck cask, check, cook

cl carload, carload lots, center line, centiliter, civil law, claim, class, classification, clause, clearance, clergyman, clerk, cloth, craft loss (insurance)

Cl chlorine

clar clarinet

class classic, classical, classification, classified, classify

cler clerical

climatol climatological, climatology

clin clinic, clinical

clk clerk, clock

clm column

CLU chartered life underwriter

cm church missionary, circular mil, common meter, corresponding member

cm centimeter

Cm curium

CM court martial, Master of Surgery (Lat. *Chiurgiae Magister*)

Cmdr commander

CMG Companion (of the Order) of St. Michael and St. George

cml commercial

CMTC Citizens' Military Training Camp

Cn cumulonimbus

C/N circular note, credit note

CNN Cable News Network

CNO chief of naval operations

CNS central nervous system

c/o care of, carried over, cash order

Co cobalt, company, county

CO Colorado, commanding officer, conscientious objector

coad coadjutor

COBOL common business-oriented language

Cod codex

COD cash on delivery, collect on delivery

Codd codices

coef coefficient

C of C chamber of commerce

C of S chief of staff

cog, cogn cognate

col collected, collector, college, colonial, colony, color, colored, column

Col Colombia, colonel, Colorado, Colossians, Columbia

coll colleague, collect, collection, collective, collector, college, colloquial

collab collaborated, collaboration, collaborator

collat collateral

colloq colloquial, colloquialism, colloquially

Colo, Col Colorado

colog cologarithm

Coloss Colossians

com comedy, comic, comma, commentary, commerce, common, commonly, commune, communication, community

Com commission, commissioner, committee, commodore, communist

Com, Comdr commander, commodore

Com, Como commodore

comb combination

comdg commanding

Comdt Commandant

Com in Ch, Cominch Commander in Chief

coml commercial

comm commander, commentary, commerce, commercial, commissary, commission, committee, commonwealth, commutator

Como Commodore

comp companion, compare, compilation, compiled, complete, composition, compositor, compound, comprising

compar comparative

compt compartment, comptometer

Comr Commissioner

Com Ver Common Version (of the Bible)

con against (Lat. *contra*), concerto, conclusion, condense, conduct, connection, consols, consolidate, continued, wife (Lat. *conjunx*)

Con Conformist, Consul

conc concentrate, concentrated, concentration, concerning

Confed Confederate, Confederation

cong gallon (Lat. *congius*)

Cong Congregational, Congress, Congressional

conj conjugation, conjunction, conjunctive

Conn Connecticut

cons consecrated, conserve, consigned, consignment, consolidated, consonant, constable, constitution,

constitutional, construction, consul, consulting

consol consolidated

const constable, constant, constitution

constr construction, construed

cont containing, contents, continent, continue, contract, contraction, contrary, control

Cont Continental

contd continued

contemp contemporary

contg containing

contin continued, let it be continued (Lat. *continuetur*)

contr contract, contralto, control

contrib contribution, contributor

CONUS Continental United States

coop, co-op cooperative

cop copper, copyright, copyrighted

Cop Copernican, Coptic

cor corner, cornet, coroner, corpus, correct, corrected, correction, correlative, correspondence, correspondent, corresponding, corrupt

Cor Corinthians

corol, coroll corollary

corp, corpn corporation

Corp Corporal

corr correct, corrected, correspond, correspondence, correspondent, corresponding, corrupt, corrupted, corruption

correl correlative

corresp correspondence

cos companies, cosine, counties

COS cash on shipment

cosec cosecant

cosh hyperbolic cosine

cot cotangent

coth hyperbolic cotangent

covers coversed sine

cp candlepower, chemically pure, compare, court of probate

CP Canadian Press, Cape Province, center of pressure, Chief Patriarch, command post, Common Prayer, Communist Party

CPA certified public accountant

cpd compound

CPH Certificate in Public Health

Cpl corporal

cpm characters per minute, cost per million, cycles per minute

CPO chief petty officer

CPR cardiopulmonary resuscitation

cps characters per second, cycles per second

Abbreviations 869

cpt counterpoint
CQ charge of quarters
cr created, credit, creditor, crescendo, creek, crown
Cr chromium
CR carriage return, Costa Rica
craniol craniological, craniology
craniom craniometry
cres, cresc crescendo
crim con criminal conversation
crit critic, critical, criticism
CRLF carriage return and line feed
crs credits, creditors
CRT cathode-ray tube
cryst crystalline, crystallography, crystals
cs capital stock, civil service
Cs cesium, cirrostratus
CS Christian Science, Christian Scientist, Confederate States
C/S case
CSA Confederate States of America
csc cosecant
CSC Civil Service Commission, Conspicuous Service Cross
csch hyperbolic cosecant
CSigO chief signal officer
CSIRO Commonwealth Scientific and Industrial Research Organization (Australia)
CSO chief staff officer
CSS Commodity Stabilization Service
CST central standard time
ct cent, certificate, county, court
Ct Connecticut, Count
CT central time, communications technician, computed tomography, Connecticut
CTC Citizens' Training Camp
ctg cartridge
ctn carton, cotangent
ctnh hyperbolic cotangent
ctr center
cts centimes, cents, certificates
cu cubic
Cu copper (Lat. cuprum), cumulus
cu cm cubic centimeter
cu ft cubic foot
cu in cubic inch
cur currency, current
cu yd cubic yard
cv, cvt convertible
CV Common Version (of the Bible)
cw continuous wave
CWO cash with order, chief warrant officer, commissioned warrant officer
CWS Chemical Warfare Service

cwt hundredweight (Lat. centum weight)
cy capacity, currency, cycles
cyc cyclopedia, cyclopedic
cyl cylinder
CYO Catholic Youth Organization
CZ Canal Zone

D

d date, daughter, day, dead, decree, degree, delete, democrat, democratic, deputy, diameter, died, director, dividend, dollar, door, dose, dyne, give (Lat. da), penny, pence (Lat. denarius, denarii)
D December, department, deuterium, Dutch, God (Lat. Deus), Lord (Lat. Dominus), Roman numeral for 500
da daughter, day
DA delayed action, dental apprentice, district attorney
DAB Dictionary of American Biography
DAE Dictionary of American English
DAH Dictionary of American History
Dak Dakota
Dan Daniel, Danish
Danl Daniel
DAR Daughters of the American Revolution
DARE Dictionary of American Regional English
dat dative
DAT Dental Apptitude Test
dau daughter
Dav David
DAV Disabled American Veterans
db daybook
db,dB decibel, decibels
DB Domesday Book
dba doing business as
DBE Dame (Commander of the Order) of the British Empire
dbh diameter at breast height (forestry)
DBib Douai Bible
dbl double
DC Dental Corps, direct current, Disarmament Commission, District of Columbia, Doctor of Chiropractic, from the beginning (Ital. da capo)
DCL Doctor of Canon Law, Doctor of Civil Law
DCM Distinguished Conduct Medal (Brit.)
DCS deputy clerk of sessions, Doctor of Christian Science, Doctor of Commercial Science
dd days after date, days' date, delivered, demand draft

DD Department of Defense, developmentally disabled, Doctor of Divinity (Lat. Divinitatis Doctor)
DDS Doctor of Dental Science, Doctor of Dental Surgery
DDSc Doctor of Dental Science
DE Delaware, destroyer escort, Doctor of Engineering, Doctor of Entomology
deb, deben debenture
Deb Deborah
dec deceased, declaration, declension, declination, decrease, decrescendo
dec, decim decimeter
Dec December
decd deceased
decl declension
decoct decoction
decresc decrescendo
ded, dedic dedication
def defective, defendant, defense, deferred, defined, definite, definition
deg degree
del delegate, delete, deliver, he or she drew it (Lat. delineavit)
Del Delaware
deliq deliquescent
Dem Democrat, Democratic
demon demonstrative
Den Denmark
denom denomination
dent dental, dentist, dentistry
dep departs, departure, deposed, deposit, depot
dep, dept department, deponent, deputy
Dep dependency
der, deriv derivation, derivative, derive, derived
dermatol dermatological, dermatologist, dermatology
desc descendant
descr descriptive, description
D ès L Doctor of Letters (Fr. Docteur ès Lettres)
D ès S Doctor of Sciences (Fr. Docteur ès Sciences)
det detach, detachment, detail
Deu, Deut Deuteronomy
devel development
DF dean of the faculty, defender of the faith (Lat. Defensor Fidei), direction finding, Federal District (Port. Districto Federal; Sp. Distrito Federal)
DFC Distinguished Flying Cross
dg decigram
DG by the grace of God (Lat. Dei gratia)
dh deadhead, designated hitter (baseball), that is to say (Ger. das heisst)
DHQ division headquarters
di, dia diameter
Di didymium

diag, diagr diagram
dial dialect, dialectic, dialectical
diam diameter
dict dictation, dictator, dictionary
diet dietetics
diff difference, different, differential
dil dilute
dim dimension
dim, dimin diminuendo, diminutive
din dinar
dioc diocesan, diocese
dipl diplomat, diplomatic
dir director
dis distance, distant
disc discount, discover, discovered
disch discharged
diss dissertations
dist discount, distance, distant, distinguish, distinguished, district
Dist Atty district attorney
distr distribute, distributed, distribution, distributive, distributor
div divergence, diversion, divide, divided, dividend, divine, division, divisor, divorced
Div divinity
dk deck, dock
DK disbursing clerk
dkg dekagram
dkl dekaliter
dkm dekameter
dks dekastere
dl deciliter
D/L demand loan
D Lit, D Litt Doctor of Letters, Doctor of Literature (Lat. Doctor Litterarum)
dlr dealer
DLS Doctor of Library Science
dm decameter, decimeter
Dm Deutschmark
DM deputy master, draftsman
DMB defense mobilization board
DMD Doctor of Dental Medicine (Lat. Dentariae Medicinae Doctor)
D Mus Doctor of Music
DN our Lord (Lat. Dominus noster)
DNA deoxyribonucleic acid
DNB Dictionary of National Biography (Brit.)
do ditto
DO Doctor of Osteopathy
DOA dead on arrival
doc document
DOD Department of Defence
DOE Department of Education, Department of Energy
dol dolce, dollar
dols dollars
dom domestic, dominion

Dom Dominica, Dominican
Dor Dorian, Doric
DOS disk operating system
DOT Department of Transportation
dow dowager
doz dozen
DP data processing, degree of polymerization, diametrical pitch, displaced person
DPH Doctor of Public Health
DPHy Doctor of Public Hygiene
DPh, DPhil Doctor of Philosophy
dpt department, deponent
DPW Department of Public Works
dr debtor, dram
Dr doctor, drive
DR dead reckoning, deposit receipt
dram pers dramatis personae
ds daylight saving, days after sight, decistere, document signed, (repeat) from this sign (It. *dal segno*)
Ds dysprosium
DS, DSc Doctor of Science
DSC Distinguished Service Cross
DSIR Department of Scientific and Industrial Research
DSM Distinguished Service Medal
DSO Distinguished Service Order (Brit.), district staff officer
dsp died without issue (Lat. *decessit sine prole*)
DSRD Department of Scientific Research and Development
DST daylight saving time, Doctor of Sacred Theology
dt delerium tremens, double time
DT dental technician
DT, DTh, DTheol Doctor of Theology
dts delerium tremens
Du duke, Dutch
dup, dupl duplicate
Dv, DV God willing (Lat. *Deo volente*)
DV Douai Version (of the Bible)
DVM Doctor of Veterinary Medicine
DVMS Doctor of Veterinary Medicine and Surgery
D/W dock warrant
DWI driving while intoxicated, Dutch West Indies
DWS Department of Water Supply
dwt dead weight tons, pennyweight (Lat. *denarius* weight)
DX distance, distant
Dy dysprosium
dyn, dynam dynamics
dz dozen

E

e east, eastern, erg, error
E earl, Earth, east, eastern, English
ea each
e and o e errors and omissions excepted
Eb erbium
EBCDIC Extended Binary Coded Decimal Interchange Code
EbN east by north
EbS east by south
EC Engineering Corps, Established Church, European Community
ECA Economic Cooperation Administration
ECAFE Economic Commission for Asia and the Far East
eccl, eccles ecclesiastical
Ecc, Eccl, Eccles Ecclesiastes
Ecclus Ecclesiasticus
ECE Economic Commission for Europe
ECG electrocardiogram
ECLA Economic Commission for Latin America
ECME Economic Commission for the Middle East
ecol ecological, ecology
econ economic, economics, economy
ECOSOC Economic and Social Council (of the United Nations)
ECSC European Coal and Steel Community
Ecua Ecuador, Ecuadorian
ed edited, edition, editor
EdB Bachelor of Education
EdD Doctor of Education
edit edited, edition, editor
EdM Master of Education
EDT eastern daylight time
educ education, educational
ee errors excepted
EE Early English, electrical engineer, electrical engineering, envoy extraordinary
EEC European Economic Community
EE&MP envoy extraordinary and minister plenipotentiary
EEG electroencephalogram
EEOC Equal Employment Opportunity Commission
EER energy efficiency rating
eff efficiency
efflor efflorescent
EFTA European Free Trade Association
EFTS electronic funds transfer system
eg for example (Lat. *exempli gratia*)
Eg Egypt, Egyptian
Egyptol Egyptology
EHF extremely high frequency

EHFA electric home and farm authority
EHV extra high voltage
EI, EInd East Indian, East Indies
EKG electrocardiogram
el elevated, elevation
ELD electroluminescent display
elec, elect electric, electrical, electrician
elem elementary, elements
elev elevation
ellipt elliptical
e long east longitude
elong elongation
Em, eman emanation (chemistry)
EM electrician's mate, engineer of mines, enlisted man
emb, embryol embryology
emf electromotive force
EMH educable mentally handicapped
Emp emperor, empire, empress
emph emphasis, emphatic
EMT emergency medical technician
emu electromagnetic units
emul emulsion
enc, encl enclosed, enclosure
ency, encyc, encycl encyclopedia
ENE east-northeast
eng engine, engineer, engineering, engraved, engraver, engraving
Eng England, English
EngD Doctor of Engineering
engin engineering
engr engineer, engraved, engraver, engraving
enl enlarged, enlisted
Ens ensign
ENT ear, nose, throat (physician)
entom, entomol entomological, entomology
env envelope
eo from office (Lat. *ex officio*)
EOM end of month
ep en passant (chess)
Ep, Epis, Epist Epistle, Epistles
EP extended play
EPA Environmental Protection Agency
Eph, Ephes Ephesians
Epis Episcopal
epil epilogue
EPU European Payments Union
eq equal, equalizer, equation, equator, equivalent
EQ educational quotient
equiv equivalent
er earned run
Er erbium
ER emergency room, King Edward (Lat. *Eduardus*

Rex), Queen Elizabeth (Lat. *Elizabeth Regina*)
ERA earned run average, Educational Research Association, Emergency Relief Administration, Equal Rights Amendment
ERIC Educational Resources Information Center
ERISA Employee Retirement Income Security Act
ERP European Recovery Program
erron erroneous, erroneously
ERV English Revised Version (of the Bible)
Es einsteinium
ESA Economic Stabilization Administration
ESC Economic and Social Council (of the United Nations)
eschat eschatology
Esd Esdras
ESE east-southeast
Esk Eskimo
ESL English as a second language
ESOP employee stock option plan
esp especially
ESP extrasensory perception
espec especially
Esq, Esqr esquire
est estate, estimated, estuary
Est Estonia
EST eastern standard time
estab established
Esth Esther
esu electrostatic unit
ET electronics technician, extraterrestrial
eta estimated time of arrival
et al and others (Lat. *et alii*), and elsewhere (Lat. *et alibi*)
etc and so forth, and others (Lat. *et ceteri, ceterae,* or *cetera*)
eth ether, ethical, ethics
Eth Ethiopia, Ethiopian, Ethiopic
ethnog ethnographical, ethnography
ethnol ethnological, ethnology
ETO European Theater of Operations
et seq and the following, and what follows (Lat. *et sequens, sequentes,* or *sequentia*)
ety, etym, etymol etymological, etymology
Eu europium
euphem euphemism, euphemistic
Eur Europe, European
ev electron volt
EV English Version (of the Bible)
EVA extra-vehicular activity (in space)

evac evacuation

evan, evang evangelical, evangelist

Evang Evangelical

evap evaporation

ex examination, examine, examined, example, except, excepted, exception, exchange, excursion, executed, executive

Ex, Exod Exodus

exam examination, examined, examinee, examinor

exc excellent, except, excepted, exception, excursion

Exc excellency

exch exchange, exchequer

excl exclusive

excl, exclam exclamation

exec executive, executor

Ex-Im Export-Import Bank

ex int without interest

ex lib from the library (of) (Lat. *ex libris*)

ex off from office (Lat. *ex officio*)

exp expenses, expiration, expired, export, exportation, exported, exporter, express

exper experimental

expt experiment

exptl experimental

exr executor

ext extension, external, extinct, extra, extract

Ez, Ezr Ezra

Eze, Ezek Ezekiel

F

f activity coefficent, farad, farthing, fathom, feet, female, feminine, fine, fluid (ounce), folio, following, foot, formed, forte, foul, franc, frequency, from, function (of), let it be made (Lat. *fiat*), strong (Lat. *forte*)

f/ f number (photography)

F Fahrenheit, February, fellow, fluorine, France, French, Friday, son (Lat. *filius*)

fa fire alarm, freight agent

FA field artillery, fine arts, food administration

FAA Federal Aviation Administration

FAAAS Fellow of the American Association for the Advancement of Science

fac facsimile, factor, factory

FACD Fellow of the American College of Dentists

FACP Fellow of the American College of Physicians

FACS Fellow of the American College of Surgeons

FAF financial aid form

Fah, Fahr Fahrenheit

FAIA Fellow of the American Institute of Architects

fam familiar, family

FAM, F&AM Free and Accepted Masons

FAO Food and Agriculture Organization (of the United Nations)

fas free alongside ship

FASA Fellow of the Acoustical Society of America

fasc a bundle (Lat *fasiculus*)

fath fathom

fb freight bill, fullback

FBA Fellow of the British Academy

FBI Federal Bureau of Investigation

fbm feet board measure (board feet)

fc follow copy (printing)

Fc fractocumulus

FCA Farm Credit Administration

FCC Federal Communications Commission, Federal Council of Churches, first class certificate, Food Control Committee

FCDA Federal Civil Defense Administration

FCIC Federal Crop Insurance Corporation

fcp foolscap

FD defender of the faith (Lat. *Fidei Defensor*), fire department

FDA Food and Drug Administration, Food Distribution Administration

FDIC Federal Deposit Insurance Corporation

Fe iron (Lat. *ferrum*)

Feb, Febr February

FEB Fair Employment Board

fec he or she made it (Lat. *fecit*)

fed federal, federated, federation

fem female, feminine

FEPC Fair Employment Practices Commission

FERA Federal Emergency Relief Administration

feud feudal, feudalism

ff fixed focus, folios, following, fortissimo

ffa free foreign agent, free from alongside

FFA Future Farmers of America

FFS family financial statement

FFV First Families of Virginia

fg field goal

FGSA Fellow of the Geological Society of America

FHA Federal Housing Administration

FHLBB Federal Home Loan Bank Board

fhp friction horsepower

FICA Federal Insurance Contributions Act

fid fidelity, fiduciary

FIFO first in, first out

fig figuratively, figure

FIL Fellow of the Institute of Linguists

FILO first in, last out

fin finance, financial, finished

Fin Finland, Finnish

FIPS federal information processing standards

fl floor, florin, flower, fluid, flute

Fl Flanders, Flemish, fluorine

FL, Fla Florida

FLB Federal Land Bank

fl dr fluid dram

Flem Flemish

flex flexible

fl oz fluid ounce

fm fathom, from

Fm fermium

FM field manual, field marshal, frequency modulation

FMCS Federal Mediation and Conciliation Service

FmHA Farmers Home Administration

FNMA Federal National Mortgage Association ("Fannie Mae")

FO field officer, Foreign Office

fob free on board

FOE Fraternal Order of Eagles

fol folio, following

foll following

FOP Fraternal Order of Police

for foreign, forestry, free on rails

fort fortification, fortified

FORTRAN formula translator

fp fireplug, fire policy, floating policy, foolscap, footpound, forte piano (Ital.), forward pass, freezing point, fully paid

FPC Federal Power Commission

FPHA Federal Public Housing Administration

fpm feet per minute

FPO fleet post office

fps feet per second, footpound-second (system)

fr fragment, franc, from, right-hand page (Lat. *folio recto*)

Fr brother (Lat. *Frater*), father, France, francium, French, Friday, wife (Ger. *Frau*)

FRB Federal Reserve Bank, Federal Reserve Board

FRC Federal Radio Commission, Federal Relief Commission

FRCP Fellow of the Royal College of Physicians

FRCS Fellow of the Royal College of Surgeons

freq frequency, frequently, frequentitive

FRGS Fellow of the Royal Geographical Society

Fr Gui French Guiana

Fri Friday

Frl Miss (Ger. *Fräulein*)

FRS Federal Reserve System, Fellow of the Royal Society

FRSA Fellow of the Royal Society of Arts

frt freight

fs foot-second

Fs fractostratus

FS field service, fleet surgeon

FSA Farm Security Administration, Federal Security Agency

FSCC Federal Surplus Commodities Corporation

FSH follicle-stimulating hormone

FSLIC Federal Saving and Loan Insurance Corporation

FSP Food Stamp Program

FSR Field Service Regulations

ft feet, foot, fort, fortification, fortified

FT fire control technician

ft-c foot-candle

FTC Federal Trade Commission

FTE full-time equivalent

fth, fthm fathom

ft-l foot-lambert

ft-lb foot-pound

fur furlong

furl furlough

furn furnished, furniture

fut future

fv on the back of the page (Lat. *folio verso*)

FWA Federal Works Agency

fwd forward, front wheel drive

fwy freeway

FY fiscal year

FYI for your information

FZS Fellow of the Zoological Society

G

g conductance, gauge, gender, general, general intelligence, genitive, goal, goalie, goalkeeper, gold, gourde, grain, gram, grand, (specific) gravity, guide, guilder, guinea, gulf

G German, Germany, gram, (specific) gravity, gun

ga general average

Ga gallium, Georgia

GA Gamblers Anonymous, general agent, General Assembly, Georgia

Gael Gaelic

gal, gall gallon

Gal Galatians, Galen

galv galvanic, galvanism, galvanized

GAO General Accounting Office

GAR Grand Army of the Republic

GATT General Agreement on Tariffs and Trade

GAW guaranteed annual wage

gaz gazette, gazetteer

GB Great Britain

GBE (Knight or Dame) Grand (Cross) of the (Order of the) British Empire

GCA ground control approach (radar)

g-cal gram calorie

GCB (Knight) Grand Cross of the (Order of the) Bath

gcd greatest common divisor

gcf greatest common factor

GCI ground controlled interception (aircraft)

GCLH Grand Cross of the Legion of Honor

gcm greatest common measure

GCM general court martial

GCT Greenwich civil time

GCVO (Knight) Grand Cross of the (Royal) Victorian Order

Gd gadolinium

GD grand duchess, grand duchy, grand duke

gds goods

Ge germanium

geb born (Ger. *geboren*)

GED general equivalency diploma

gen gender, genera, general, generally, generator, generic, genitive, genus

Gen general, Genesis, Geneva, Genevan

geneal genealogical, genealogy

genit genitive

genl general

gent gentleman, gentlemen

geod geodesy, geodetic

geog geographer, geographic, geographical, geography

geol geologic, geological, geologist, geology

geom geometer, geometric, geometrical, geometry

ger gerund

Ger, Germ German, Germany

gest died (Ger. *gestorben*)

GFTU General Federation of Trade Unions

ggr great gross

GHA Greenwich hour angle

GHQ general headquarters

gi gastrointestinal, gill

GI general issue, government issue

Gib Gibralter

Gk Greek

gl glass, gloss

gld guilder

gloss glossary

gm gram

GM general manager, grand master, gunner's mate

Gmat Greenwich mean astronomical time

GmbH limited company (Ger. *Gesell-schaft mit beschränkter Haftung*)

Gmc Germanic

GMT Greenwich mean time

GNMA Government National Mortgage Association ("Ginnie Mae")

GNP gross national product

GO general orders

GOP Grand Old Party (Republican Party)

Goth gothic, Gothic

gov, govt government

Gov governor

GP general practitioner, Graduate in Pharmacy, general paresis

GPA grade point average

gpm gallons per minute

GPO General Post Office, Government Printing Office

gps gallons per second

GQ general quarters

gr grade, grain, gram, grammar, great, gross, group

Gr Grecian, Greece, Greek

GR King George (Lat. *Georgius Rex*)

grad graduate, graduated

gram grammar, grammarian, grammatical

GrBr, GrBrit Great Britain

GRE graduate record examination

gro gross

gr wt gross weight

GS general secretary, general staff, German silver, Girl Scouts

GSA General Services Administration, Girst Scouts of America

GSC General Staff Corps

GSO general staff officer

gt gilt, great

gtc good till canceled

gtd guaranteed

gtt a drop (Lat. *gutta*)

gu genitourinary

guar guaranteed

Guat Guatemala, Guatemalan

Guin Guinea

gun gunnery

guttat by drops (Lat. *guttatim*)

gv gravimetric volume

gym gymnasium, gymnastics

gyn, gynecol gynecological, gynecology

H

h harbor, hard, hardness, heavy sea, height, hence,

high, hit, horns (music), hour, hundred, husband

h, hy henry (electricity)

H hydrogen, intensity of magnetic field

ha hectare, this year (Lat. *hoc anno*)

Hab Habakkuk

hab corp have the body (Lat. *habeas corpus*)

Hag Haggai

Hal halogen

hb halfback

Hb hemoglobin

HBM his or her Britannic majesty

HC House of Commons

hcap, hcp handicap

hcf highest common factor

HCL high cost of living

hd hand, head

hdbk handbook

hdkf handkerchief

hdqrs headquarters

He helium

HE high explosive, his eminence, his or her excellency

Heb, Hebr Hebrew

her heraldic, heraldry

herp, herpetol herpetology

HEW (Department of) Health, Education, and Welfare

hex hexachord, hexagon, hexagonal

hf half

Hf hafnium

HF high frequency

hfbd half-bound (bookbinding)

hfmor half-morocco (bookbinding)

hg hectogram, heliogram

Hg mercury (Lat. *hydrargyrum*)

HG High German, his or her grace, Home Guard

hgt height

HH his or her highness, his holiness

hhd hogshead

HHFA Housing and Home Finance Agency

HHS (Department of) Health and Human Services

HI Hawaii

HIH his or her imperial highenss

HIM his or her imperial majesty

Hind Hindi, Hindu, Hindustan, Hindustani

hist histology, historian, historical, history

HJ here lies (Lat. *hic jacet*)

HJS here lies buried (Lat. *hic jacet sepultus*)

hkf handkerchief

hl hectoliter

HL House of Lords, mustard-lewisite (poison gas)

HLBB Home Loan Bank Board

hm hectometer, in this month (Lat. *hoc menses*)

HM his or her majesty

HMO health maintenance organization

HMS his or her majesty's service (or ship or steamer)

HN nitrogen mustard gas

ho house

Ho holmium

HO head office, Home Office

HOLC Home Owners' Loan Corporation

hon honorably, honorary

Hon honorable

Hond Honduras

hor horizon, horizontal

horol horology

hort, hortic horticultural, horticulture

Hos Hosea

hosp hospital

hp high pressure, horsepower

HP high power

hp-hr horsepower-hour

hq look for this (Lat. *hoc quaere*)

HQ headquarters

hr home run, hour

HR mister (Ger. *Herr*)

HR home rule, House of Representatives

HRE Holy Roman Empire

HRH his or her royal highness

HRIP here rest in peace (Lat. *hic requiescat in pace*)

hrs hours

HS here is buried (Lat. *hic sepultus*), here lies (Lat. *hic situ*), high school, Home Secretary (Brit.), in this sense (Lat. *hoc sensu*)

HSH his or her serene highness

HSM his or her serene majesty

ht at this time (Lat. *hoc tempore*), heat, height, in or under this title (Lat. *hoc titulo*)

Hts heights

HUD (Department of) Housing and Urban Development

Hun, Hung Hungarian, Hungary

HV high voltage

HVAC heating, ventilation, and air conditioning

hw high water

hwm high water mark

hwy highway

hyd, hydros hydrostatics

hydraul hydraulic, hydraulics

hyg hygiene, hygroscopic

hyp, hypoth hypotenuse, hypothesis, hypothetical

I

i incisor, interest, intransitive, island

I iodine, island or islands, isle or isles, Roman numeral for 1
Ia, IA Iowa
IADB Inter-American Defense Board
IAEA International Atomic Energy Agency (of the United Nations)
ib, ibid in the same place (Lat. *ibidem*)
IBEW International Brotherhood of Electrical Workers
IBRD International Bank for Reconstruction and Development
IBT International Brotherhood of Teamsters (Chauffeurs, Warehousemen, and Helpers of America)
ICA International Cooperation Administration
ICAO International Civil Aviation Organization (of the United Nations)
ICBM intercontinental ballistic missile
ICC Indian Claims Commission, Interstate Commerce Commission
Ice, Icel Iceland, Icelandic
ICES International Council for the Exploration of the Sea
ICFTU International Confederation of Free Trade Unions
icth ichthyology
ICJ International Court of Justice (of the United Nations)
ICNAF International Commission for Northwest Atlantic Fisheries
ICU intensive care unit
icw interrupted continuous wave
id the same (Lat. *idem*)
ID Idaho, identification, infantry division, intelligence department, inside diameter
Ida Idaho
ie that is (Lat. *id est*)
IE Indo-European
IEP individualized education program
if intermediate frequency
IFCTU International Federation of Christian Trade Unions
IFF identification friend or foe (British radar device)
IFO identified flying object
IG amalgamation (Ger. *Interessengemeinschaft*), Indo-Germanic, inspector general
ign ignites, ignition, unknown (Lat. *ignotus*)
ihp indicated horsepower
IHS Jesus. Often taken to mean Jesus Savior of Mankind (Lat. *Iesus hominum salvator*) or in this sign (Lat. *in hoc signo*).

Il illinium
IL Illinois
ILA International Longshoremen's Association
ILGWU International Ladies' Garment Workers' Union
ill, illus, illust illustrate, illustrated, illustration, illustrator
Ill Illinois
illit illiterate
ILO International Labor Organization (of the United Nations)
ILS instrument landing system
IMCO Intergovernmental Maritime Consultative Organization (of the United Nations)
IMF International Monetary Fund (of the United Nations)
imit imitation, imitative
immun immunology
imp imperative, imperfect, imperial, impersonal, import, important, imported, importer, imprimatur, improper
Imp emperor (Lat. *imperator*)
imper imperative
imperf imperfect, imperforate
impers impersonal
impf imperfect
imp gal imperial gallon
impv imperative
in inch
IN Indiana
inbd inboard, inbound
inc inclosure, including, inclusive, income, incorporated, increase
inch, incho inchoative
incl inclosure, including
incog incognito
incorp incorporated
incorr incorrect
incr increased, increasing
ind independence, independent, index, indicated, indicative, indigo, indirect, industrial
Ind India, Indian, Indiana, Indies
IND in the name of God (Lat. *in nomine Dei*)
indecl indeclinable
indef indefinite
inden, indent indention
indic indicating, indicative, indicator
individ individual
induc induction
ined unpublished
in ex at length (Lat. *in extenso*)
in f at the end (Lat. *in fine*)
inf below (Lat. *infra*), inferior, infinitive, information
Inf infantry
infin infinitive

infl influence, influenced
init initial, in the beginning (Lat. *initio*)
inj injection
in-lb inch-pound
in lim at the outset (on the threshold) (Lat. *in limine*)
in loc in its place (Lat. *in loco*)
in loc cit in the place cited (Lat. *in loco citato*)
inorg inorganic
INRI Jesus of Nazareth, King of the Jews (Lat. *Iesus Nazarenus Rex Iudaeorum*)
ins inches, inspector, insular, insulated, insulation, insurance
INS International News Service
insc, inscr inscribe, inscribed, inscription
insep inseparable
insol insoluble
insp inspected, inspector
inst instant, instantaneous, instrument
Inst institute, institution
instr instruction, instructor, instrument
insur insurance
int intelligence, interest, interior, interjection, internal, interval, intransitive
intens insensitive
inter intermediate
interj interjection
internat international
interp interpreted, interpreter
Interpol International Police Organization
interrog interrogative
intr, intrans intransitive
in trans on the way (Lat. *in transitu*)
Int Rev Internal Revenue
introd introduction, introductory
inv invented, invention, inventor, invitation, invoice
invert invertebrate
invt inventory
Io ionium
IOBB Independent Order of B'nai B'rith
IOOF Independent Order of Odd Fellows
IOU I owe you
ip in passing (chess), innings pitched (baseball)
IPA International Phonetic Alphabet (association)
IPI International Press Institute
IPPC International Penal and Penitentiary Commission
IPR Institute of Pacific Relations
ips inches per second
iq the same as (Lat. *idem quod*)
IQ intelligence quotient

iqed what was to be proved (Lat. *id quod erat demonstrandum*)
Ir Ireland, iridium, Irish
IRA individual retirement account, Irish Republican Army
Iran Iranian, Iranic
IRBM intermediate range ballistic missile
Ire Ireland
IRO International Refugee Organization (of the United Nations)
irreg irregular, irregularly
IRS Internal Revenue Service
is island or islands, isle or isles
Is, Isa Isaiah
ISBN international standard book number
isl island, islands
iso isotropic
isom isometric
isoth isothermal
Isr Israel
ISSN international standard serial number
isth isthmus
it, ital italic, italics
It, Ital Italian, Italy
ITA Initial Teaching Alphabet
itin itinerant, itinerary
ITO International Trade Organization
ITU International Telecommunication Union, International Typographical Union
IU international unit
IWW Industrial Workers of the World

J
J joule (physics), judge, justice
ja joint account
Ja January
JA judge advocate
JAG judge advocate general
Jam Jamaica, Jamaican
Jan January
Jap Japan, Japanese
Jas James
JCAH Joint Commission on Accreditation of Hospitals
JCD Doctor of Canon Law (Lat. *Juris Canonici Doctor*), Doctor of Civil Law (Lat. *Juris Civilis Doctor*)
JCS joint chiefs of staff
jct, jctn junction
JD Doctor of Laws (Lat. *Jurum Doctor*)
Je June
Jer Jeremiah
jg junior grade
Jl July
Jn John
Jon Jonah
Jos Joseph, Joshua, Josiah
jour journal, journalist, journeyman

JP jet propulsion, justice of the peace
jr junior
Ju Judges
JUD Doctor of Civil and Canon Law (Lat. *Juris Utriusque Doctor*)
Judg Judges
Jul July
jun junior
Jun June
junc, junct junction
JurD Doctor of Law (Lat. *Juris Doctor*)
jursp jurisprudence
jus, just justice
juv juvenile
jv junior varsity
jwlr jeweler
Jy July

K

k calends (Lat. *kalendae*), capacity, carat, constant, kilo, kilogram, king, king (chess), knot (naut.), kopeck (coin), koruna (coin), krone (coin)
K potassium (Lat. *kalium*), strikeout
ka kathode (cathode)
kal kalends (calends)
Kan, Kans, Kas Kansas
KB king's bench, king's bishop (chess), knight bachelor
KBP king's bishop's pawn (chess)
kc kilocycle
KC king's counsel, knight commander, Knights of Columbus
kcal kilocalorie
KCB Knight Commander of the (Order of the) Bath
KCVO Knight Commander of the (Royal) Victorian Order
Ken Kentucky
kg keg, kilogram
KG Knight of the (Order of the) Garter
KGB Commission of State Security (Russ. *Komitet Godsudarvstvennoi Bezopasnost'i*)
Ki Kings (book of the Bible)
kilo kilogram, kilometer
kilog kilogram
kilol kiloliter
kilom kilometer
kingd kingdom
KKK Ku Klux Klan
kl kiloliter
km kilometer
kn kronen (coin)
KN king's knight (chess)
KNP king's knight's pawn (chess)
ko knockout
K of C Knights of Columbus
K of P Knights of Pythias

kop kopeck (coin)
KP king's pawn (chess), kitchen police, Knight (of the Order of St.) Patrick, Knight of Pythias
kr krona (coin), krone (coin)
Kr krypton
KR king's rook (chess)
KRP king's rook's pawn (chess)
KS Kansas
kt karat (carat), knight
KT Knights Templar
kv kilovolt
kva kilovolt-ampere
kvar reactive kilovolt-ampere
kw kilowatt
kwh kilowatt-hour
Ky, KY Kentucky

L

l book (Lat. *liber*), (games) lost, lake, land, lat, latitude, law, leaf, league, left, lempira, length, leu, lev, lex, line, link, lira, lire, lit, liter, low, place (Lat. *locus*)
L coefficient of inductance, Latin, length, lewisite, licentiate, Linnaeus, longitude
La lanthanum, Louisiana
LA Legislative Assembly, Library Association, local agent, Los Angeles, Louisiana
lab laboratory
lam laminated
Lam Lamentations
LAM Master of Liberal Arts (Lat. *Liberalium Artium Magister*)
LAN local area network
lang language
laryngol laryngological, laryngology
lat latitude
Lat Latin, Latvia
Latv Latvia
lb pound (Lat. *libra*)
LB Bachelor of Letters (Lat. *Litterarum Baccalaureus*), local board
lb ap apothecary pound
lb av avoirdupois pound
LBO leveraged buyout
lbs pounds
lb t troy pound
lc in the place cited (Lat. *loco citato*), left center, lower case
l/c letter of credit
LC Library of Congress
LCD liquid crystal display, lowest common denominator
lcl less than carload lot
lcm least common multiple, lowest common multiple
ld lead (printing)
Ld lord

LD Low Dutch
ldg landing, leading, loading
LDiv Licentiate in Divinity
ld lmt load limit
ldry laundry
LDS Latter-day Saints, Latter Day Saints, Licentiate in Dental Surgery
le left end
lea league, leather, leave
led ledger
LED light-emitting diode
leg legal, legate, legato, legislation
legis legislation, legislative, legislature
LEM lunar excursion module
L ès S Licentiate in Sciences (Fr. *Licencié ès Sciences*)
Lev, Levit Leviticus
lex lexicon
lf left field, left fielder, left forward, lightface (printing), low frequency
lg left guard
LG Low German
lg, lge large
LGk Late Greek
lgth length
lh left halfback, left hand
LH luteinizing hormone
LHA local hour angle
LHD Doctor of Humanities (Lat. *Litterarum Humaniorum Doctor*)
Li lithium
LI lithographer, Long Island
lib book (Lat. *liber*), librarian, library
Lib Liberal, Liberia
Lieut lieutenant
LIFO last in, first out
LILO last in, last out
lin lineal, linear
ling linguistics
linim liniment
Linn Linnaeus, Linnean
lino linotype
liq liquid, liquor
li qts liquid quarts
lit liter, literal, literally, literary, literature
LitB, LittB Bachelor of Letters or Bachelor of Literature (Lat. *Litterarum Baccalaureus*)
LitD, LittD Doctor of Letters or Doctor of Literature (Lat. *Litterarum Doctor*)
lith, litho, lithog lithograph, lithography
Lith Lithuania, Lithuanian
Lk Luke
ll leaves, lines
LL Late Latin, Legal Latin, Low Latin, lower left
LLB Bachelor of Laws (Lat. *Legum Baccalaureus*)
LLD Doctor of Laws (Lat. *Legum Doctor*)
LLM Master of Laws (Lat. *Legum Magister*)

LM Legion of Merit, Licentiate in Medicine, Licentiate in Midwifery, lunar (excursion) module
LMT local mean time
ln lane
LNG liquefied natural gas
loc local, location
local localism
loc cit in the place cited (Lat. *loco citato*)
log logarithm
long longitude
loq he, she, or it speaks (Lat. *loquitur*)
lox liquid oxygen
lp large paper, long playing, long primer, low pressure
LPG liquified petroleum gas
LPS Lord Privy Seal
LR living room, long run, lower right
LS left side, library science, Licentiate in Surgery, place of the seal (Lat. *locus sigilli*), long shot
lsc in the place cited above (Lat. *loco supra citato*)
LSCA Library Services and Construction Act
LSD landing ship, dock; lysergic acid diethylamide
LSS lifesaving service
LST landing ship, tank
lt left tackle
lt long ton
Lt Lieutenant
LTA Lawn Tennis Association
ltd limited
ltn long ton
LTh Licentiate in Theology
LtInf light infantry
Ltjg lieutenant, junior grade
LTL less than truckload lot
LTS launch telemetry station, launch tracking system
Lu lutetium
lubric lubricate, lubrication
Luth Lutheran
Lux Luxemburg
lv leave, leaves
lw low water
Lw Lawrencium
lwl load waterline
lwm low water mark
LXX Septuagint
lyr lyric, lyrical

M

m majesty, male, manual, mark, married, masculine, mass, measure, medicine, medium, member, meridian, meter, mile, mill, minim, minute, month, moon, morning, mountain, noon (Lat. *meridies*)
M handful (Lat. *manipulus*), master, medieval, middle, monsieur, of medicine (Lat.

medicinae), Roman numeral for 1,000

Ma masurium

MA machine accountant, Maritime Administration, Massachusetts, Master of Arts (Lat. *Magister Artium*), mental age, military academy

Mac, Macc Maccabees

MAC mean aerodynamic chord

Maced Macedonia, Macedonian

mach machine, machinery, machinist

Mad Madam

MADD Mothers Against Drunk Driving

Madm Madam

mag magazine, magnet, magnetism, magnitude

MAgr, MAgric Master of Agriculture

maj majority

Maj major

Mal Malachi, Malay, Malayan, Malta

malac malacology

Man manila (paper), Manitoba

Manch Manchukuo, Manchuria, Manchurian

manuf manufacture, manufactured, manufacturer, manufacturing

mar marine, maritime, married

Mar March

March marchioness

marg margarine, margin, marginal

Marq marquess, marquis

mas, masc masculine

MASH mobile Army surgical hospital

Mass Massachusetts

mat matinee, matins, maturity

MAT Master of Arts in Teaching, Miller Analogy Test

MATS Military Air Transport Service

math mathematical, mathematician, mathematics

matr, matric matriculate, matriculation

Matt Matthew

max maximum

Max Maximilian

MB Bachelor of Medicine (Lat. *Medicinae Baccalaureus*)

MBA Master of Business Administration

MBS Mutual Broadcasting System

mc megacycle, millicurie

MC Maritime Commission, master commandant, master of ceremonies, Medical Corps, member of Congress

MCAT Medical College Admission Test

MCh Master of Surgery (Lat. *Magister Chiurgiae*)

MCL Master of Civil Law

m/d memorandum of deposit, months' date

Md Maryland, mendelevium

MD Doctor of Medicine (Lat. *Medicinae Doctor*), Maryland, medical department, mentally deficient, Middle Dutch

MDS Master of Dental Surgery

mdse merchandise

MDT Mountain Daylight Time

MDu Middle Dutch

me marbled edged (bookbinding)

Me Maine, methyl

ME Maine, mechanical engineer, Methodist Episcopal, Middle English, military engineer, mining engineer

meas measurable, measure

mech, mechan mechanical, mechanics, mechanism

med medical, medicine, medieval, medium

MEd Master of Education

MedGk Medieval Greek

Medit Mediterranean

MedL Medieval Latin

meg megabyte, megacycle, megohm

megs megabytes

mem member, memoir, memorandum, memorial

memo memorandum

mensur mensuration

mep mean effective pressure

mer meridian, meridional

merc mercantile, mercurial, mercury

Messrs messieurs

met metaphor, metaphysics, meteorological, metronome, metropolitan

metal, metall metallurgical, metallurgy

metaph metaphor, metaphorical, metaphysics

metath metathesis, metathetical

meteor, meteorol meteorological, meteorology

meth method, methylated

Meth Methodist

meton metonymy

metrol metrological, metrology

metrop metropolitan

mev million electron volts

Mex Mexican, Mexico

mf fairly loud (It. *mezzoforte*), millifarad

mf, mfd microfarad

MF medium frequency, Middle French

mfg manufacturing

MFlem Middle Flemish

mfr manufacture, manufacturer

mg milligram

Mg magnesium

MG military government

Mgr manager, monseigneur, monsignor

mgt management

mh millihenry

MH Medal of Honor

MHG Middle High German

mi mile

MI Michigan

Mic Micah

Mich Michigan

micro microcomputer

micros microscope, microscopic, microscopy

MICU mobile intensive care unit

mid middle, midshipman

MidDan Middle Danish

MidSw Middle Swedish

mil mileage, military, militia, million

milit military

mimeo mimeograph, mimeographed

min mineralogical, mineralogy, minim, minimum, mining, minor, minute

mineral mineralogy

Minn Minnesota

mip marine insurance policy, mean indicated pressure

MIPS million instructions per second

MIr Middle Irish

MIRV multiple independently targetable reentry vehicle

misc miscellaneous, miscellany

MISL Major Indoor Soccer League

Miss Mississippi

mkk mark, markka

Mk mark

mkd marked

MKS meter-kilogram-second (system)

mkt market

ml millileter

ML Medieval Latin, Middle Latin, molder

MLA member of the Legislative Assembly, Modern Language Association

MLD minimum lethal dose

MLG Middle Low German

Mlle Mademoiselle (Fr.)

Mlles Mesdemoiselles (Fr.)

MLS Master of Library Science

mm milimeter, thousands (Lat. *millia*), with the necessary changes (Lat. *mutatis mutandis*)

MM machinist's mate, messieurs (Fr.)

Mme Madame (Fr.)

Mmes Mesdames (Fr.)

mmf magnetomotive force

mmfd micromicrofarad

mn the name being changed (Lat. *mutato nomine*)

Mn manganese

MN Minnesota

mo month, monthly

Mo Missouri, molybdenum, Monday

MO mail order, medical officer, Missouri, money order

mod moderate, moderato, modern

ModGr Modern Greek

ModL Modern Latin

Moham Mohammedan

MOI Ministry of Information

mol molecular, molecule

mol wt molecular weight

mon monastery, monetary

Mon Monday, monsignor

Mong Mongolia, Mongolian

monocl monoclinic

monog, monogr monograph

Mons monsieur

Monsig monsignor

Mont Montana

mor morocco (bookbinding)

Mor Moroccan, Morocco

MOR middle of the road

morn morning

morph morpheme, morphological, morphology

mort mortuary

mos months

MOS military occupational specialty

mot motor, motorized

mp melting point, moderately soft (It. *mezzo piano*)

MP Member of Parliament, military police

MPd Master of Pedagogy

MPE Master of Physical Education

mpg miles per gallon

mph miles per hour

MPPDA Motion Picture Producers and Distributors of America (Inc.)

Mr Mister

MR machinery repairman, mentally retarded, motivational research

MRA Moral Re-Armament

MRI magentic resonance imaging

Mrs Mistress

ms manuscript, months after sight

MS Master of Science (Lat. *Magister Scientiae*), mine sweeper, Mississippi, multiple sclerosis, sacred to the memory of (Lat. *memoriae sacrum*)

MSA Mutual Security Agency

MSc Master of Science

msg message

MSG master sergeant, monosodium glutamate

Msgr monsignor

MSgt master sergeant

msl mean sea level

mss manuscripts

MST Mountain Standard Time

mt mean time, metric ton, motor transport, mount, mountain, mountain time

Mt Matthew

MT Montana

mtg meeting, mortgage

mtge mortgage

mtl material, mean tidal level

mtn mountain

MTO Mediterranean Theater of Operations

Mt Rev most reverend

mts mountains

MU musician

mun municipal, municipality

mus museum, music, musician

MusB Bachelor of Music (Lat. *Musicae Baccalaureus*)

MusD Doctor of Music (Lat. *Musicae Doctor*)

MusM Master of Music (Lat. *Musicae Magister*)

mut mutilated, mutual

mv millivolt, softly (It. *mezzo voce*)

Mv mendelevium

MVA Missouri Valley Authority

MVD Ministry of Internal Affairs (Rus. *Ministerstvo Vnutrennikh Del*)

MVP most valuable player

MW most worshipful, most worthy

MY May

mya myriare

mycol mycological, micology

myg myriagram

myl myrialiter

mym myriameter

myth, mythol mythological, mythology

N

n born (Lat. *natus*), name, net, neuter, neutron, new, nominative, noon, normal, note, noun, number, our (Lat. *noster*)

N knight (chess), nationalist, navy, nitrogen, Norse, north, northern, November

Na sodium (Lat. *natrium*)

NA national army, North America

NAACP National Association for the Advancement of Colored People

NAB New American Bible

NAD National Academy of Design

Nah Nahum

NAm North American

NAM National Association of Manufacturers

NAS National Academy of Sciences, naval air station

NASA National Aeronautics and Space Administration

NASCAR National Association of Stock Car Auto Racing

NASL North American Soccer League

nat national, native, natural, naturalist

nathist natural history

natl national

NATO North Atlantic Treaty Organization

NATS National Air Transport Service

naut nautical

nav naval, navigable, navigation

navig nagivation, navigator

nb note well (Lat. *nota bene*)

Nb niobium

NB New Brunswick

NBA National Basketball Association, National Boxing Association

NBC Natinal Broadcasting Company

NbE north by east

NBS National Bureau of Standards

NbW north by west

nc nitrocellulose

NC no charge, no credit, North Carolina, nurse corps

NCAA National Collegiate Athletic Association

NCar North Carolina

NCE New Catholic Edition (of the Bible)

NCO noncommissioned officer

nd no date

Nd neodymium

ND, NDak North Dakota

Ne neon

NE Nebraska, New England, northeast, northeastern

NEA National Education Association

NEB New English Bible

Neb, Nebr Nebraska

nec not elsewhere classified

NEC National Electrical Code

NED New English Dictionary (Oxford English Dictionary)

neg negative, negatively

Neh Nehemiah

nei not elsewhere indicated

neol neologism

NEP New Economic Policy

nes not elsewhere specified, not elsewhere stated

Neth Netherlands

neur, neurol neurological, neurologic

neut neuter, neutral

Nev Nevada

Newf Newfoundland

NewTest New Testament

nf noun feminine

NF National Formulary, Newfoundland, no funds, Norman French

NFC National Football Conference

NFL National Football League

ng no good

NG national guard, New Guinea

NGk New Greek

NH New Hampshire

NHG New High German

nhp nominal horsepower

NHS National Health Service (Brit.)

Ni nickel

NI Northern Ireland

Nic, Nicar Nicaragua, Nicaraguan

Nig Nigeria, Nigerian

NIH National Institutes of Health

NIMH National Institute of Mental Health

NIRA National Industrial Recovery Act

NIre Northern Ireland

NJ New Jersey

NKVD People's Commissariat of Internal Affairs (Rus. *Narodnyi Komissariat Vnutrennikh Del*)

nl new line (printing), north latitude, not clear (Lat. *non liquet*), not far (Lat. *non longe*), not lawful (Lat. *non licet*)

NL New Latin

Nlat north latitude

NLRB National Labor Relations Board

nm nautical mile, noun masculine

NM, NMex New Mexico

NMR nuclear magnetic resonsance

NMSQT National Merit Scholarship Qualifying Test

NMU National Maritime Union

NNE north-northeast

NNW north-northwest

no north, northern, number

No nobelium

NOAA National Oceanic and Atmospheric Administration

nob for our part or on our part (Lat. *nobis*)

nol pros unwilling to prosecute (Lat. *nolle prosequi*)

nom nomenclature, nominal, nominative

nomin nominative

noncom noncommissioned (officer)

non cul not guilty (Lat. *non culpabilis*)

non dest notwithstanding (Lat. *non destante*)

non obs, non obst notwithstanding (Lat. *non obstante*)

non pros he or she does not prosecute (Lat. *non prosequitur*)

non seq it does not follow (Lat. *non sequitur*)

nor north, northern

Nor Norman, Norway, Norwegian

NORAD North American Air Defense Command

norm normal

Norw Norway, Norwegian

nos numbers

nov novelist

Nov November

NOW National Organization for Women, negotiable order of withdrawal

np net proceeds, new paragraph, no paging, no place (of publication)

Np neptunium

NP knight's pawn, neuropsychiatrist, no protest, notary public, unless before (Lat. *nisi prius*)

NPN nonprotein nitrogen

np or d no place or date

NPR National Public Radio

npt normal pressure and temperature

nr near

NRA National Recovery Administration, National Rifle Association

NRC National Research Council, Nuclear Regulatory Commission

ns near side (shipping), new series, new style, not specified

Ns nimbostratus

NS new style, Nova Scotia

NSC National Security Council

NSF National Science Foundation, not sufficient funds

NSPCA National Society for the Prevention of Cruelty to Animals

NSPCC National Society for the Prevention of Cruelty to Children

NSW New South Wales

nt net

NT New Testament, Northern Territory (Australia)

ntp normal temperature and pressure

NTSB National Transportation Safety Board

nt wt net weight

num number, numeral

Num, Numb Numbers

numis numismatic, numismatics

ny nonvoting (stock)

NV Nevada

NW northwest, northwestern

NWT Northwest Territories (Canada)

NY New York

NYC New York City

NYSE New York Stock Exchange
NZ New Zealand

O

o octavo, off, ohm, old, only, order, pint (Lat. *octavius*)
o- ortho-
O ocean, October, Ohio, old, Ontario, Oregon, oxygen
OAPC Office of Alien Property Custodian
OAr Old Arabic
OAS Organization of American States
OAU Organization of African Unity
ob he or she died (Lat. *obit*), in passing (Lat. *obiter*), obstetrical, obstetrics
Ob, Obad Obadiah
obb obbligato
obdt obedient
OBE Officer of the (Order of the) British Empire
ob-gyn obstetrician gynecologist, obstetrics gynecology
obit obituary
obj object, objection, objective
obl oblique, oblong
obs obscure, observation, observatory, obsolete, obsolescence
obsol obsolescent
ob s p died without issue (Lat. *obit sine prole*)
obstet obstetrical, obstetrics
obt obedient
obv obverse
oc in the work cited (Lat. *opere citato*)
o/c old charter, overcharge
Oc ocean
OC office of censorship, officer commanding, original cover
OCAS Organization of Central American States
occ occasion, occasionally, occident, occidental
occult occultism
OCD Office of Civilian Defense
oceanog oceanography
OCR optical character reading, optical character recognition
OCS office of contract settlement, officer candidate school
oct octavo
Oct October
octupl octuplicate
od olive drab, on demand, outside diameter
OD Doctor of Optometry, officer of the day, Old Dutch, Ordnance Department, overdraft, overdrawn
ODan Old Danish

ODu Old Dutch
OE Old English
OECD Organization for Economic Cooperation and Development
OED Oxford English Dictionary
OEEC Organization for European Economic Cooperation
OEM original equipment manufacture
OES office of economic stabilization, Order of the Eastern Star
OF Old French
off offered, office, official, officinal
OFM Order of Friars Minor
OG officer of the guard, original gum (philately)
OH Ohio
OHG Old High German
OHMS on his or her majesty's service
OIAA office of inter-American affairs
OIC office of information and culture (of the State Department)
OIr Old Irish
OIT office of international trade
OK, Okla Oklahoma
OL Old Latin
Old Test Old Testament
oleo oleomargarine
OM Order of Merit (Brit.)
OMB Office of Management and Budget
ON Old Norse
ONI Office of Naval Intelligence
ONormFr Old Norman French
onomat onomatopoeia, onomatopoeic
ONR Office of Naval Research
Ont Ontario
OOD officer of the day, officer of the deck
op operation, opposite, out of print, overprint, overproof, work (Lat. *opus*), works (Lat. *opera*)
OP observation post, Order of Preachers
OPA office of price administration
op cit in the work cited (Lat. *opere citato*)
OPEC Organization of Petroleum Exporting Countries
OPer Old Persian
ophthal ophthalmology
opp oppose, opposed, opposite
opt optative, optical, optics
OR operating room, Oregon
orat oratorical, oratory
orch orchestra, orchestral

ord ordained, order, ordinal, ordinance, ordinary, ordnance
ordn ordnance
Ore, Oreg Oregon
org organic, organism, organized
orig origin, original, originally
Ork Orkney (Islands)
ornith, ornithol ornithological, ornithologist, ornithology
orth orthopedic, orthopedics
Orth orthodox
Os osmium
OS Old Saxon, old style, ordinary seaman
OSA Order of Saint Augustine
OSB Order of Saint Benedict
osc oscillating, oscillator
OSerb Old Serbian
OSF Order of Saint Francis
OSHA Occupational Safety and Health Administration
OSl Old Slavic
OSp Old Spanish
OSRD Office of Scientific Research and Development
OSS Office of Strategic Services
osteo osteopath, osteopathy
OT Old Testament, on truck, overtime
OTC Officer's Training Corps
otol otology
OTS Officer Training School
ott octave (It. *ottava*)
OW one-way
OWI Office of War Information
Oxon Oxford (Lat. *Oxonia*)
oz ounce
oz ap apothecary ounce
oz av avoirdupois ounce
ozs ounces
oz t troy ounce

P

p after (Lat. *post*), by (Lat. *per*), by weight (Lat. *pondere*), first (Lat. *primus*), for (Lat. *pro*), in part (Lat. *partim*), page, part, participle, past, penny, perch (measure), period, perishable, peseta, peso, pint, pipe, pitcher, pole (measure), population, post, power, pressure, softly (It. *piano*)
p- para- (chemistry)
P bishop (Lat. *pontifex*), father (Fr. *père*, Lat. *pater*), parental, pastor, pawn (chess), pengö, people (Lat. *populus*), peso, phosphorus, piaster, pope (Lat. *papa*), president, pressure, priest, prince, prisoner, prompter (theater)

P- pursuit (military)
pa for the year (Lat. *pro anno*), paper, participial adjective, particular average (insurance), public address, yearly (Lat. *per annum*)
Pa Pennsylvania, protactinium
PA passenger agent, Pennsylvania, personal assistant, physician's assistant, power of attorney, press agent, private account, public address (system), purchasing agent
PABA para-aminobenzoic acid
Pac, Pacif Pacific
PAC Pan-American Congress, political action committee
p ae equal parts (Lat. *partes aequales*)
Pal Palestine
paleob paleobotany
paleog paleography
paleontol paleontology
palm palmistry
pam, pamph pamphlet
Pan Panama
p and h postage and handling
P and L profit and loss
pap paper
par paragraph, parallel, parenthesis
Par, Para Paraguay
paren parenthesis
parens parentheses
parl parliamentary
part participle, particular
pass everywhere (Lat. *passim*), passage, passenger, passive
pat patent, patented, patrol, pattern
PAT point after touchdown
patd patented
path, pathol pathology
Pat Off Patent Office
pat pend patent pending
PAU Pan American Union
PAYE pay as you earn, pay as you enter
payt payment
PB Pharmacopoeia Britannica, prayer book
PBA Public Buildings Administration
PBS Public Broadcasting Service, Public Buildings Service
PBX private branch (telephone) exchange
pc after meals (Lat. *post cibos*), percent, percentage, piece, postcard, price
p/c petty cash, price current
PC personal computer, police constable, post commander, Privy Council, professional corporation
PCA Progressive Citizens of America
PCB polychlorinated biphenyl

Pcs preconscious
pct percent
pd by the day (Lat. *per diem*), paid, potential difference
Pd palladium
PD per diem, phenyl dichloride, police department, postal district
PdB Bachelor of Pedagogy (Lat. *Pedagogiae Baccalaureus*)
PdD Doctor of Pedagogy (Lat. *Pedagogiae Doctor*)
PdM Master of Pedagogy (Lat. *Pedagogiae Magister*)
PDT Pacific Daylight Time
p/e price-earnings ratio
PE petroleum engineer, presiding elder, printer's error, probable error, Protestant Episcopal
ped pedal, pedestal, pedestrian
PEI Prince Edward Island
pen peninsula, penitent, penitentiary
PEN (International Association of) Poets, Playwrights, Editors, Essayists, and Novelists
Penn, Penna Pennsylvania
penol penology
per period, person
per an, per ann by the year (Lat. *per annum*)
perd, perden dying away (It. *perdendo*)
perf perfect, perforated, performer
perh perhaps
perm permanent
perp perpendicular, perpetual
pers person, personal
Pers Persia, Persian
persp perspective
pert pertaining
Peru, Peruv Peruvian
pet petroleum
petn petition
petrog petrography
petrol petrology
pf louder (It. *più forte*), pfennig (coin), power factor
pg page
PFC private first class
pfd preferred
pfg pfennig (coin)
Pg Portugal, Portuguese
PG past grand (master), paying guest, postgraduate
PGA Professional Golfers' Association
ph phrase
Ph phenyl
PH Purple Heart
phar, pharm pharmaceutical, pharmacist, pharmacy
PharB Bachelor of Pharmacy (Lat. *Pharmaciae Baccalaureus*)
PharD Doctor of Pharmacy (Lat. *Pharmaciae Doctor*)

PharM Master of Pharmacy (Lat. *Pharmaciae Magister*)
pharmacol pharmacology
PhB Bachelor of Philosophy (Lat. *Philosophiae Baccalaureus*)
PhC pharmaceutical chemist
PhD Doctor of Philosophy (Lat. *Philosophiae Doctor*)
phil philosopher, philosophical, philosophy
Phil Philippians, Philippines
Phila Philadelphia
philol philology
philos philosopher, philosophical, philosophy
phon phonetic, phonetics, phonology
phonet phonetic, phonetics
phot, photo, photog photograph, photographer, photographic, photography
photom photometrical, photometry
phr phrase
phren, phrenol phrenological, phrenology
PHS Public Health Service
phys physical, physician, physicist, physics
physiol physiological, physiology
Pi, pias piaster
pict pictorial, picture
pil pill (Lat. *pilla*)
pinx he or she painted (Lat. *pinxit*)
PIO public information officer
pizz plucked (music) (It. *pizzicato*)
pk pack, park, peak, peck
pkg package
pkt packet
PKU phenylketonuria
pl place, plate, plural
plat plateau, platform, platoon
plen plenipotentiary
plf, plff plaintiff
plu plural
plup, plupf pluperfect
plur plural, plurality
pm after death (Lat. *post mortem*), afternoon (Lat. *post meridiem*), postmortem
Pm promethium
PM pacific mail, past master, paymaster, police magistrate, postmaster, prime minister, provost marshall
pmk postmark
pmkd postmarked
pn promissory note
pneum pneumatic, pneumatics
png a person who is not acceptable (Lat. *persona non grata*)
PNG Papua New Guinea
pnxt he or she painted (Lat. *pinxit*)

po personnel officer, petty officer, postal order, post office, put-out
Po polonium
PO post office
POC port of call
pod pay on delivery
PoD Doctor of Podiatry
POD Post Office Department
POE port of embarkation, port of entry
poet poetic, poetical, poetry
pol, polit political, politics
Pol Poland, Polish
pol econ, polit econ political economy
pop popular, population
POP point of purchase
por pay on return
port portrait
Port Portugal, Portuguese
pos, posit position, positive
poss possession, possessive, possible, possibly
post postal
pot potential
POW prisoner of war
pp pages, parcel post, parish priest, past participle, postpaid, privately printed, very softly (It. *pianissimo*)
PP pellagra preventive (factor)
ppc to take leave (Fr. *pour prendre congé*)
ppd postpaid, prepaid
pph pamphlet
ppi policy proof of interest
PPI plan position indicator (radar)
ppl participle, past participle
ppm parts per million
ppp pianissimo
ppr present participle
pps additional postscript (Lat. *post postscriptum*), Parliamentary private secretary
ppv pay per view (television)
pq previous questions
PQ Province of Quebec
pr pair, pairs, paper, power, preferred, preposition, present, price, priest, prince, printing, pronoun
Pr praseodymium
PR proportional representation, public relations, Puerto Rico
preb prebend, prebendary
prec preceding
pred predicate, predication, predicative, prediction
pref preface, prefatory, preference, preferred, prefix
prelim preliminary
prem premium
prep preparation, preparatory, prepare, preposition
pres present, presidency, president, presumptive
Presb, Presbyt presbyter, Presbyterian

pret preterit
prev previous, previously
prim primary, primitive
prin principal, principally, principle
print printer, printing
priv private, privately, privative
prn whenever necessary (Lat. *pro re nata*)
pro professional
PRO Professional Review Organization, public relations officer
prob probable, probably, problem
proc proceedings, process, proclamation
prod produce, produced, product
prof professor
prog program, progress, progressive
prom promenade, promontory
pron pronoun, pronounced, pronunciation
pronom pronominal
prop proper, properly, property, proposition, proprietary, proprietor
propr proprietary, proprietor
pros prosody
Prot protectorate, Protestant
pro tem for the time being (Lat. *pro tempore*)
prov proverbial, providence, provident, province, provincial, provision, provost
Prov Proverbs
prox next (month) (Lat. *proximo*)
prs pairs
prtd printed
prtg printing
Prus, Pruss Prussia, Prussian
prv to return a call (Fr. *pour rendre visite*)
ps passenger steamer, permanent secretary, pieces, postscript, private secretary, prompt side (theater), pseudonym, public sale
Ps Psalms
PS police sergeant, Privy Seal, public school
PSAT Preliminary Scholastic Aptitude Test
pseud pseudonym
psf pounds per square foot
psi pounds per square inch
PSRO Professional Standards Review Organization
pss postscripts
PSS Psalms
PST Pacific Standard Time
psych, psychol psychological, psychologist, psychology
psychoanal psychoanalysis
pt for the time being (Lat. *pro tempore*), part, part time, payment, pint, point, port, post town, postal telegraph, preterit

Pt platinum

PT part time, physical training

pta peseta

PTA Parent-Teachers' Association

ptbl portable

ptg printing

pts parts, payments, pints

PTSA Parent-Teacher-Student Association

pty proprietary

Pu plutonium

pub public, publication, published, publisher

publ publication, published, publisher

pulv pulverized

punct punctuation

pur, purch purchaser, purchasing

pv par value, post village, priest vicar

PVC polyvinyl chloride

Pvt private

PW prisoner of war

PWA Public Works Administration

PWP Parents Without Partners

pwr power

pwt pennyweight

PX post exchange

pymt payment

Q

q quart, quarter, quarterly, quarto, query, question, queen

Q quarto, Quebec, queen (chess)

qb quarterback

QB Queen's Bench, queen's bishop (chess)

QBP queen's bishop's pawn (chess)

QC Quartermaster Corps, Queen's Counsel

qd as if he or she had said (Lat. *quasi dixisset*), as if one should say (Lat. *quasi dicat*), as if said (Lat. *quasi dictum*)

qe which is (Lat. *quod est*)

QED which was to be demonstrated (Lat. *quod erat demonstrandum*)

QEF which was to be done (Lat. *quod erat faciendum*)

QEI which was to be found out (Lat. *quod erat inveniendum*)

QID four times a day (Lat. *quater in die*)

ql as much as you please (Lat. *quantum libet*), quintal

Qld Queensland

qlty quality

QM quartermaster

QMC Quartermaster Corps

QMG quartermaster general

qn question

QN queen's knight (chess)

QNP queen's knight's pawn (chess)

QP queen's pawn (chess)

q pl, QP as much as you wish (Lat. *quantum placeat*)

Qq quartos

qqv which see (plural) (Lat. *quos vide*)

qr quarter, quarterly, quire

QR queen's rook (chess)

QRP queen's rook's pawn (chess)

qrs farthings (Lat. *quadrantes*), quarters, quires

qrtly quarterly

qs as much as suffices (Lat. *quantum sufficit*), quarter section

qt quantity, quart, quiet

qto quarto

qts quarts

qu quart, queen, query, question

quad quadrangle, quadrant, quadrat, quadrilateral, quadruple, quadruplet

quar, quart quarter, quarterly

Que Quebec

ques question

quin, quint quintuple, quintuplet

quor quorum

quot quotation, quoted

qv as much as you will (Lat. *quantum vis*), which see (Lat. *quod vide*)

qy query

R

r range, rare, received, recipe, residence, resides, retired, right, right-hand page (Lat. *recto*), rises, river, road, rod, roentgen, royal, rubber, ruble, run

R commonwealth (Lat. *res publica*), gas constant (chemistry), king (Lat. *rex*), queen (Lat. *regina*), rabbi, radical (chemistry), radius, railroad, railway, ratio, Réaumur, rector, redactor, Republican, resistance (electrical), respond or response (ecclesiastical), ring (chemistry), rook (chess), ruble, rupee, take (Lat. *recipe*)

Ra radium

RA rear admiral, regular army, right ascension, Royal Academy

rad radical, radio, radius, root (Lat. *radix*)

RAF Royal Air Force

ral, rall gradually slower (It. *rallentando*)

RAM random-access memory

R&D research and development

RAR radio acoustic ranging

Rb rubidium

rbi run batted in

RC Red Cross, reserve corps, Roman Catholic

RCAF Royal Canadian Air Force

RCCh Roman Catholic Church

rcd received

RCMP Royal Canadian Mounted Police

RCP Royal College of Physicians

rcpt receipt

RCS Royal College of Surgeons

Rct recruit

rd reduce, rix-dollar, road, rod, round

Rd Radium, road

RD research and development, rural delivery

re right end

Re rhenium, rupee

RE real estate, Reformed Episcopal, right excellent, Royal Engineers

REA Rural Electrification Administration

react reactance (electricity)

rec receipt, received, recipe, record, recorded, recorder, recording

recd received

recip reciprocal, reciprocity

recit recitative

rec sec recording secretary

rect receipt, rectified, rector, rectory

red reduced, reduction

redisc rediscount

redup, redupl reduplicated, reduplication

ref referee, reference, referred, refining, reformation, reformed

Ref Ch Reformed Church

refl reflection, reflective, reflectively, reflex, reflexive

refrig refrigeration

reg regent, regiment, region, register, registered, registrar, registry, regular, regularly, regulation, regulator

Reg queen (Lat. *regina*)

regt regent, regiment

REIT real estate investment trust

rel relating, relative, relatively, released, religion, religious

rel pron relative pronoun

rem remittance

REM rapid eye movement

rep repair, repeat, report, reporter, representative, reprint, republic

Rep representative, republic, Republican

repr representing, reprinted

Repub Republican

req required, requisition

res research, reserve, residence, resides, residue, resigned, resistance, resistor, resolution

resp respective, respiration, respondent

rest restaurant

Resurr Resurrection

ret retain, retired, returned

retd retained, returned

retrog retrogressive

rev revenue, reverse, reversed, review, revise, revised, revision, revolution, revolving

Rev Revelation, reverend

Rev Ver Revised Version (of the Bible)

rf radio frequency, range finder, rapid fire, right field, right fielder, right forward

RFA Royal Field Artillery

RFC Reconstruction Finance Corporation, Royal Flying Corps

RFD rural free delivery

rg right guard

RGB red-blue-green television tube

rh relative humidity, right halfback, right hand

Rh Rhesus (blood factor), rhodium

RH Royal highness

rhap rhapsody

rhbdr rhombohedral

rhet rhetoric, rhetorical

rhin, rhinol rhinology

rhomb rhombic

rhp rated horsepower

RI king and emperor (Lat. *rex et imperator*), queen and empress (Lat. *regina et imperatrix*), Rhode Island

rip supplementary (music) (It. *ripieno*)

RIP may he, she, or they rest in peace (Lat. *requiescat* or *requiescant in pace*)

RISC reduced instruction set computer

rit slow (It. *ritardando*)

riv river

rkva reactive kilovolt-ampere

rm ream, room

Rm Reichsmark

rms reams, rooms, root mean square

Rn radon

RN Royal Navy

RNA ribonucleic acid

RNR Royal Naval Reserve

RNWMP Royal Northwest Mounted Police

ro recto, rood

ROK Republic of Korea

rom roman (type)

Rom Roman, Romance, Romania, Romanian, Romans

ROM read-only memory

ROP record of production, run of press

rot rotating, rotation
ROTC Reserve Officers' Training Corps
roul roulette (philately)
roy royal
RP Reformed Presbyterian, Regius Professor
RPD Doctor of Political Science (Lat. *Rerum Politicarum Doctor*)
rpm revolutions per minute
RPO railway post office
rps revolutions per second
rpt report
rr very rarely (Lat. *rarissime*)
RR railroad, right reverend
RRB Railroad Retirement Board
rs reis, rupees
RS recording secretary, reformed spelling, revised statutes
RSFSR Russian Soviet Federated Socialist Republic
RSV Revised Standard Version (of the Bible)
rsvp please reply (Fr. *répondez s'il vous plait*)
RSVP Retired Seniors Volunteer Program
rt right, right tackle
Rt Hon right honorable
Rt Rev right reverend
Rts rights
Ru Ruth, ruthenium
rub ruble
Rus, Russ Russia, Russian
RV recreational vehicle, Revised Version (of the Bible)
rva reactive volt-ampere
RW right worshipful, right worthy
ry railway

S

s buried (Lat. *sepultus*), fellow (Lat. *socius* or *sodalis*), lies (Lat. *situs*), sacral, saint, school, scribe, second, secondary, section, see, semi-, senate, series, set, shilling (Lat. *solidus*), sign, signed, silver, singular, sire, socialist, society, solo, son, soprano, southern, steel, stem, stere, stock, substantive, sun, surplus
s- symmetrical (chemistry)
S knight (chess) (Ger. *Springer*), sabbath, Saturday, Saxon, seaman, Senate, September, signature, Signor, south, southern, sulfur, Sunday
Sa samarium, Samuel
SA corporation (Fr. *société anonyme*), Salvation Army, seaman apprentice, sex appeal, South Africa, South America, South Australia
Sab sabbath

SAC Strategic Air Command
SADD Students Against Driving Drunk
SAE Society of Automotive Engineers
SAfr South Africa, South African
SALT strategic arms limitation talks
SAm, SAmer South America, South American
SAM surface-to-air missile
Sans, Sansk Sanskrit
S ap apothecary's scruple
SAR Sons of the American Revolution
Sask Saskatchewan
sat saturated, saturation
Sat Saturday, Saturn
SAT Scholastic Aptitude Test
sav savings
sb stolen base, substantive
Sb antimony (Lat. *stibium*)
SB Bachelor of Science (Lat. *Scientiae Baccalaureus*)
SBA Small Business Administration
SbE south by east
SbW south by west
sc he or she carved or engraved it (Lat. *sculpsit*), namely (Lat. *scilicet*), salvage charges, scale, scene, science, screw, scruple (weight), sized and calendered, small capitals (printing), supercalendered
Sc scandium, stratocumulus
SC Security Council (of the United Nations), Signal Corps, South Carolina, Supreme Court
Scan, Scand Scandinavia, Scandinavian
s caps small capitals (printing)
ScB Bachelor of Science (Lat. *Scientiae Baccalaureus*)
ScD Doctor of Science (Lat. *Scientiae Doctor*)
sch school, schooner
sched schedule
schol scholar, scholastic
sci science, scientific
sci fa show cause (Lat. *scire facias*)
scil namely (Lat. *scilicet*)
ScM Master of Science (Lat. *Scientiae Magister*)
Scot Scotland, Scots, Scottish
scr scrip, script, scruple (weight)
Script scriptural, scriptures
sculpt he or she carved it (Lat. *sculpsit*), sculptor
sd indefinitely (without date) (Lat. *sine die*), standard deviation
SD Doctor of Science (Lat. *Scientiae Doctor*), South Dakota, steward
SDR special drawing rights

SDS Students for a Democratic Society
Se selenium
SE southeast, southeastern
SEATO Southest Asia Treaty Organization
sec according to (Lat. *secundum*), secant, second, secondary, secretary, section, sector
SEC Securities and Exchange Commission
sec-ft second-foot
sech hyperbolic secant
sec leg according to law (Lat. *secundum legem*)
sec reg according to rule (Lat. *secundum regulam*)
secs seconds, sections
sect section, sectional
secy secretary
seg segment
seismol seismology
sel selected, selection
Sem seminary, Semitic
sen senate, senator, senior
sent sentence
sep sepal, separate
Sep, Sept September, Septuagint
seq sequel
seq, seqq the following (Lat. *sequens, sequentia*)
ser serial, series, sermon
serv servant, service
sess session
sf, sforz with emphasis (It. *sforzando, sforzato*)
SFSR Soviet Federated Socialist Republic
sfz with emphasis (It. *sforzando, sforzato*)
sg senior grade, specific gravity
sgd signed
Sgt sergeant
sh share, sheet, shilling, shunt
SHAEF Supreme Headquarters, Allied Expeditionary Forces
Shak Shakespeare
SHAPE Supreme Headquarters Allied Powers (Europe)
SHF super-high frequency
shipt, shpt shipment
shtg shortage
sh tn short ton
Si silicon
SI international system of weights and measures (Fr. *Système International*), Staten Island
Sib Siberia, Siberian
SIDS sudden infant death syndrome
sig signal, signature, signor, signore, signori
sigill seal (Lat. *sigillum*)
sim simile
sin sine
sing singular

sinh hyperbolic sine
SIPC Securities Investment Protection Corporation
sist sister
sj under consideration (Lat. *sub judice*)
SJ Society of Jesus (Lat. *Societas Jesu*)
SJD Doctor of Juridical Science (Lat. *Scientiae Juridicae Doctor*)
sk sack
Skr, Skt Sanskrit
sl without place (Lat. *sine loco*)
slan without place, date, or name (Lat. *sine loco, anno, vel nomine*)
S lat south latitude
Slav Slavic, Slavonian
sld sailed, sealed
slp without lawful issue (Lat. *sine legitima prole*)
SLR single-lens reflex (camera)
sm small
Sm samarium
SM Master of Science (Lat. *Scientiae Magister*), sergeant major, state militia
sm c, sm caps small capitals
smorz dying away (It. *smorzando*)
smp without male issue (Lat. *sine mascula prole*)
SMSA standard metropolitan statistical area
sn without name (Lat. *sine nomine*)
Sn tin (Lat. *stannum*)
so seller's option, strike out
So south, southern
soc socialist, society
sociol sociologist, sociology
sol solicitor, soluble, solution
Sol Solomon
soln solution
Som Somalia
son sonata
sop soprano
SOP standard operating procedure
SOPA senior officer present afloat
sos, sost, sosten sustained (It. *sostenuto*)
sp single phase, single pole, special, species, specific, specimen, spelling, spirit, without issue (Lat. *sine prole*)
Sp Spain, Spaniard, Spanish
SP shore patrol, shore police
SPAS Fellow of the American Philosophical Society (Lat. *Societatis Philosophiae Americanae Socius*)
SPCA Society for the Prevention of Cruelty to Animals
SPCC Society for the Prevention of Cruelty to Children
spec special, specification, speculation

specif specifically

spg spring

sp gr specific gravity

sp ht specific heat

sph spherical

spp species (plural)

SPQR government and people of Rome (Lat. *Senatus populusque Romanus*)

SPR Society for Psychical Research

spt seaport

sq sequence, square, the following (Lat. *sequentia*)

Sq squadron, Square (street)

sq ft square foot

sq in square inch

sq mi square mile

sq rd square rod

sq yd square yard

sr steradian

Sr senior, señor, sir, sister, strontium

Sra señora

SRO standing room only

Srta señorita

ss namely (in law) (Lat. *scilicet*), shortstop

SS saints, Silver Star, steamship, storm troopers (Ger. *Schutz-staffeln*), Sunday school, written above (Lat. *supra scriptum*)

SSA Social Security Act (Administration)

SSB Social Security Board

SSE south-southeast

SSgt staff sergeant

SSR Soviet Socialist Republic

SSS Selective Service System

SST supersonic transport

SSW south-southwest

st short ton, stand, stanza, statute, stet, stitch, stone (weight), street, strophe

St saint, straight, strait, stratus, street

sta station, stationary, stator

Sta saint (Sp. *Santa*), station

stac, stacc staccato

stan stanchion

Staph staphylococcus

stat immediately (Lat. *statim*), static, stationary, statistics, statuary, statute

STB Bachelor of Sacred Theology (Lat. *Sacrae Theologiae Baccalaureus*)

stbd starboard

std standard

STD Doctor of Sacred Theology (Lat. *Sacrae Theologiae Doctor*), sexually transmitted disease

Ste saint (Fr. *Sainte*)

steno, stenog stenographer, stenography

ster, stg sterling

St Ex stock exchange

stge storage

stip stipend, stipendiary, stipulation

Stir Stirling, Stirlingshire

stk stock

STOL short take-off and landing

stor storage

stp stamped

STP standard temperature and pressure

str steamer, strait, string

Strep streptococcus

stud student

sub subaltern, submarine, subscription, substitute, suburb, suburban, understand (or supply) (Lat. *subaudi*)

subd subdivision

subj subject, subjective, subjunctive

subs subscription, subsidiary

subseq subsequent, subsequently

subst substantive, substitute

succ successor

suf, suff suffix

sug, sugg suggested, suggestion

Sun, Sund Sunday

sup above (Lat. *supra*), superfine, superior, superlative, supplement, supplementary, supply, supreme

super superfine, superintendent, superior, supernumerary

superl superlative

supp, suppl supplement, supplementary

supr supreme

supt superintendent

sur surcharged, surplus

surg surgeon, surgery, surgical

surr surrender, surrendered

surv survey, surveying, surveyor, surviving

susp suspended

sv sailing vessle, under this word (Lat. *sub verbo*)

SV Holy Virgin (Lat. *Sancta Virgo*)

SW southwest, southwestern

Sw Sweden, Swedish

SWA, SWAfr South-West Africa

SWAT special weapons and tactics (team)

Swe, Swed Sweden, Swedish

Swit, Switz, Swtz Switzerland

syl, syll syllable

sym symbol, symmetrical, symphony

syn synchronize, synonym, synonymous, synonymy

syr syrup (pharmacy)

Syr Syria, Syriac, Syrian

syst system, systematic

T

t in the time of (Lat. *tempore*), tare, target, tea-

spoon, telephone, temperature, tempo, tenor, tense (grammar), terminal, territory, time, tome, ton, town, township, transit, transitive, troy (weight), volume (Lat. *tomus*)

T tablespoon, tantalum, technician, temperature (absolute), tension (surface), testament, time, trinity, Tuesday, Turkish

Ta tantalum

tab table, tablet

TAC Tactical Air Command, Technical Assistance Committee

tal qual as they come (or average quality) (Lat. *talis qualis*)

tan tangent

tanh hyperbolic tangent

TAP Technical Assistance Program

tart tartaric

taut tautological, tautology

tb trial balance

Tb terbium

TB tubercule bacillus, tuberculosis

tba to be announced

tbs, tbsp tablespoon, tablespoonful

tc tierce

Tc technetium

TC Trusteeship Council (of the United Nations)

tchr teacher

td touchdown

TD tank destroyer, tradesman, traffic director, Treasury Department

tdn total digestible nutrients

Te tellurium

tech technical, technological, techonology

technol technology

TEFL teaching English as a foreign language

tel telegram, telegraph, telegraphic, telephone

telecom telecommunication

teleg telegram, telegraph, telegraphic, telegraphy

temp in the time of (Lat. *tempore*), temperature, temporary

ten hold (It. *tenuto*), tenement, tenor

Tenn Tennessee

terr terrace, territorial, territory

term terminal, termination, terminology

test testamentary, testator

Test testament

tetr, tetrag tetragonal

Teut Teuton, Teutonic

Tex Texas, Texan

tfr transfer

tg type genus

TGIF thank God it's Friday

tgt target

Th thorium

Th Thursday

ThB Bachelor of Theology (Lat. *Theologiae Baccalaureus*)

ThD Doctor of Theology (Lat. *Theologiae Doctor*)

Th-Em thoron (thorium emanation)

theol theologian, theological, theology

theor theorem

theos theosophical, theosophist, theosophy

therm thermometer

thermochem thermochemical, thermochemistry

thermodynam thermodynamics

Thess Thessalonians, Thessaly

THI temperature-humidity index

Thu, Thurs Thursday

Ti titanium

t i d three times daily (Lat. *ter in die*)

tinct tincture

tit title

Tit Titus

tk truck

TKO technical knock-out

Tl thallium

TL trade last

T/L time loan

TLC tender loving care

tm true mean

Tm thulium

TMH trainable mentally handicapped

tn ton, train

Tn thoron

TN Tennessee

tng training

TNT trinitrotoluene, trinitrotoluol

to turn over, turnover

tonn tonnage

top, topog topographical, topography

tp title page, township, troop

tpke turnpike

tpr temperature, pulse, respiration

tps townships

tr tare, tincture, trace, train, transitive, translated, translation, translator, transpose, treasurer, trust

Tr terbium, troop

trag tragedy, tragic

trans transactions, transfer, transferred, transitive, translated, translation, translator, transportation, transpose, transverse

transf transfer, transference, transferred

transl translated, translation

transp transparent, transportation

trav traveler, travels

treas treasurer, treasury
trf transfer, tuned radio frequency
trfd transferred
tricl triclinic (crystal)
trig trigonometric, trigonomy
trim trimetric (crystal)
triple triplicate
trit triturate
trl trail
trop tropic, tropical, tropics
ts tensile strength
TSgt technical sergeant
tsp teaspoon, teaspoonful
Tu thulium
Tu Tuesday
TU trade union, training unit
TUC Trades Union Congress (Brit.)
Tue, Tues Tuesday
Turk Turkey, Turkish
TV television, terminal velocity
TVA Tennessee Valley Authority
twp township
TX Texas
Ty territory
typ, typo, typog typographer, typographic, typographer
typo typographic error
typw typewriter, typewritten

U

u and (Ger. *und*), uncle, university, upper
U uranium
UAW United Automobile (Aircraft, and Agricultural Implement) Workers (of America)
uc upper case (printing)
UCMJ Uniform Code of Military Justice
UFO unidentified flying object
UHF ultra-high frequency
UJD Doctor of Civil and Canon Law (Lat. *Utriusque Juris Doctor*)
UK United Kingdom
Ukr Ukraine
ult ultimate, ultimately
ult, ulto last month (Lat. *ultimo*)
UMT universal military training
UMW United Mine Workers
UN United Nations
unabr unabridged
unb, unbd unbound (bookbinding)
undsgd undersigned
undtkr undertaker
UNEDA United Nations Economic Development Administration
Unesco, UNESCO United Nations Educational, Scientific, and Cultural Organization

ung ointment (Lat. *unguentum*)
UNICEF United Nations Children's Fund (originally United Nations International Children's Emergency Fund)
Unit Unitarian, Unitarianism
univ universal, universally, university
Univ Universalist
unl unlimited
unm unmarried
unof unofficial
unp unpaged
unpub unpublished
UNREF United Nations Refugee Emergency Fund
UNRRA United Nations Relief and Rehabilitation Administration
UNRWA United Nations Relief and Works Agency
UNSCOB United Nations Special Committee on the Balkans
UP Union Pacific (railroad), United Press
UPC universal product code
UPI United Press International
UPS United Parcel Service
UPU Universal Postal Union (of the United Nations)
Ur uranium
urol urology
Uru Uruguay, Uruguayan
us as above (Lat. *ut supra*), in the place mentioned above (Lat. *ubi supra*)
US United States
USA United States Army, United States of America
USAF United States Air Force
USC&GS United States Coast and Geodetic Survey
USCG United States Coast Guard
USDA United States Department of Agriculture
USES United States Employment Service
USIA United States Information Agency
USM United States Mail, United States Marines, United States Mint
USMA United States Military Academy
USMC United States Marine Corps, United States Maritime Commission
USN United States Navy
USNA United States Naval Academy
USNG United States National Guard
USNR United States Naval Reserve
USO United Service Organizations
USOE United States Office of Education

USP United States patent, United States Pharmacopoeia
US Pharm United States Pharmacopoeia
USPHS United States Public Health Service
USPS United States Postal Service
USS United States Senate, United States Ship
USSCt United States Supreme Court
USSR Union of Soviet Socialist Republics
usu usual, usually
usw and so forth (Ger. *und so weiter*)
USW United Steel Workers
ut universal time, utility
Ut, UT Utah
UTC universal time coordinate
ut dict as directed (Lat. *ut dictum*)
ut sup as above (Lat. *ut supra*)
UTWA United Textile Workers of America
ux wife (Lat. *uxor*)

V

v against (Lat. *versus*), of (Ger. *von*), see (Lat. *vide*), valve, ventral, verb, verse, version, versus, vicar, vice-, village, vision, vocative, voice, volt, voltage, volume, volunteer, von
V vanadium, vector, velocity, venerable, victory, viscount, volume
va active verb, verbal adjective, volt-ampere
Va Virginia
VA Veterans Administration, Vicar apostolic, vice admiral, (Order of) Victoria and Albert, Virginia
vac vacuum
val valentine, valuation, value
var reactive volt-ampere, variant, variation, variety, various
Vat Vatican
VAT value-added tax
v aux auxiliary verb
vb verb, verbal
vb n verbal noun
VC Veterinary Corps, vice chairman, vice chancellor, vice consul, Victoria Cross
vd vapor density, various dates
Vd vanadium
VD venereal disease
VDT video display terminal
VDU video display unit
veg vegetable, vegetation
vel vellum (bookbinding)
Ven venerable, Venice, Venus
Venez Venezuela, Venezuelan

vent ventilating, ventilation, ventilator
ver verse, version
vers versed sine, versine
vert vertebra, vertebrate, vertical
ves vessel, vestry, vesicle, vesicular
vet veteran, veterinarian, veterinary
veter veterinary
VFD volunteer fire department
VFR visual flight rules
VFW Veterans of Foreign Wars (of the United States)
vg for example (Lat. *verbi gratia*)
VG vicar general
VHF very high frequency
vi see below (Lat. *vide infra*), intransitive verb
Vi virginium
VI Virgin Islands
vic vicar, vicarage
Vic, Vict Victoria, Victorian
vil village
v imp impersonal verb
VIP very important person
v irr irregular verb
vis visibility, visual
Vis, Visc, Visct viscount, viscountess
VISTA Volunteers in Service to America
viv lively (music) (Lat. *vivace*)
viz namely (Lat. *videlicet*)
VL Vulgar Latin
VLF very low frequency
vm voltmeter
VMD Doctor of Veterinary Medicine (Lat. *Veterinariae Medicinae Doctor*)
vn, v neut neuter verb
vo verso
vocab vocabulary
vol volcano, volume, volunteer
volc volcanic, volcano
vols volumes
vox pop voice of the people (Lat. *vox populi*)
voy voyage
vp passive verb, various pagings, various places, voting pool (stocks)
VP vice president
vr reflexive verb
VR Queen Victoria (Lat. *Victoria Regina*)
V Rev very reverend
vs see above (Lat. *vide supra*), versus, vibration seconds (sound), volumetric solution
VS veterinary surgeon
VSS versions
vt transitive verb
Vt, VT Vermont
VTOL vertical take-off and landing

Abbreviations

883

Vul, Vulg Vulgate
vulg vulgar, vulgarity
vv verses, vice versa, violins

W

w wanting, warden, warehousing, watt, week, weight, west, western, wide, width, wife, with, won, word, work
W tungsten (Ger. *wolfram*), Wales, Washington, watt, Wednesday, Welsh, west, western
WA Washington (state)
WAC Women's Army Corps
wae when actually employed
WAF Women in the Air Force
war warrant
WASP Women's Air Force Service Pilots
watt-hr watt-hour
WAVES Women Appointed for Voluntary Emergency Service
wb warehouse book, water ballast, westbound
W/B waybill
WbN west by north
WbS west by south
wc water closet, without charge
WCTU Women's Christian Temperance Union
Wed Wednesday
wf wrong font (printing)
WFlem West Flemish

WFTU World Federation of Trade Unions
WGmc, WGer West Germanic
wh, whr watt-hour
whf wharf
WHO World Health Organization (of the United Nations)
wi when issued (stocks), wrought iron
WI West Indies, West Indian, Wisconsin
WInd West Indies
Wis, Wisc Wisconsin
wk weak, week, work
wkly weekly
wks weeks, works
wl water line, wavelength
wldr welder
W long west longitude
wm wattmeter
wmk watermark
WMO World Meteorological Organization (of the United Nations)
WNW west-northwest
WO wait order, warrant officer
wp weather permitting, wire payment, word processing
WPA Work Projects Administration, Works Progress Administration
wpm words per minute
WRAC Women's Royal Army Corps
WRAF Women's Royal Air Force

WREN, WRNS Women's Royal Naval Service
wrnt warrant
WSW west-southwest
wt weight
WV, WVa West Virginia
WVS Women's Volunteer Service
WY, Wyo Wyoming

X

x symbol for an unknown quantity
X Christ, Christian, a ten-dollar bill, xenon
xc ex-coupon
xd unlisted (ex-directory), ex-dividend
Xe xenon
x-int ex-interest
Xmas Christmas
Xn Christian
Xnt Christianity
x ref cross-reference
x-rts ex-rights
Xtian Christian
Xty Christianity
xyl xylograph

Y

y yard, year, younger, youngest
Y Young Men's Christian Association, Young Men's Hebrew Association, Young Women's Christian Associ-

ation, Young Women's Hebrew Association, yttrium
Yb ytterbium
yd yard
yds yards
Yid Yiddish
YM, YMCA Young Men's Christian Association
YM, YMHA Young Men's Hebrew Association
YPSCE Young People's Society of Christian Endeavor
yr year, younger, your
yrs years, yours
YSL Young Socialists' League
Yt yttrium
YT Yukon Territory
YW Young Women's Christian Association, Young Women's Hebrew Association
YWCA Young Women's Christian Association
YWHA Young Women's Hebrew Association

Z

z zone
Z zenith distance, zone
Zec, Zech Zechariah
Zep, Zeph Zephaniah
Z/F zone of fire
Zn zinc
zool zoological, zoologist, zoology
ZPG zero population growth
Zr zirconium

Gazetteer

This section lists all of the more important political divisions and geographical features of the world, and all the urban localities in the United States and Canada having a population of 15,000 or more. The population figures given for places in the United States are from the census of 1990; those for Canada are from the census of 1976. All other population figures are from the latest available official censuses or official estimates, usually 1990. Maps of virtually all countries and of other important geographical features may be found in the main section of this dictionary at the appropriate alphabetic place of entry.

Postal ZIP codes are included for places in the United States. These were not, however, available in all cases. The asterisk (*) following some ZIP codes indicates that the city is further divided into postal zones and that the number given does not adequately identify a post office. In such cases further information is available from local postal authorities.

In the table below the authorized post office abbreviations of U.S. states are listed.

Alabama	AL	Kentucky	KY	Ohio	OH
Alaska	AK	Louisiana	LA	Oklahoma	OK
Arizona	AZ	Maine	ME	Oregon	OR
Arkansas	AR	Maryland	MD	Pennsylvania	PA
California	CA	Massachusetts	MA	Puerto Rico	PR
Colorado	CO	Michigan	MI	Rhode Island	RI
Connecticut	CT	Minnesota	MN	South Carolina	SC
Delaware	DE	Mississippi	MS	South Dakota	SD
District of		Missouri	MO	Tennessee	TN
Columbia	DC	Montana	MT	Texas	TX
Florida	FL	Nebraska	NE	Utah	UT
Georgia	GA	Nevada	NV	Vermont	VA
Hawaii	HI	New Hampshire	NH	Virginia	VA
Idaho	ID	New Jersey	NJ	Virgin Islands	VI
Illinois	IL	New Mexico	NM	Washington	WA
Indiana	IN	New York	NY	West Virginia	WV
Iowa	IA	North Carolina	NC	Wisconsin	WI
Kansas	KS	North Dakota	ND	Wyoming	WY

The following abbreviations have been used throughout this section:

ab.	about	pop.	population
adm.	administrative	poss.	possession
ASSR	Autonomous Soviet	prot.	protectorate
n	Socialist Republic	prov.	province
betw.	between	reg.	region
boro.	borough	RSFSR	Russian Soviet
caps(s).	capital(s)	m	Federated Social-
CEN.	central	m	ist Republic
co.	county	s	south(ern)
col.	colony	SE	southeast(ern)
ctr.	center	sq. mi.	square mile(s)
dept.	department	SSR	Soviet Socialist
dist.	district	m	Republic
div.	division	sw	southwest(ern)
E	east(ern)	terr.	territory
ft.	feet	twp.	township
isl(s).	island(s)	uninc.	unincorporated
mi.	mile(s)	urb.	urban
mtn(s).	mountain(s)	USSR	Union of Soviet So-
N	north(ern)	m	cialist Republics
NE	northeaster(ern)	vill.	village
NW	northwest(ern)	w	west(ern)
penin.	Peninsula	m	m

Aachen city, w Germany; pop. 242,971.
Aarhus co., E Denmark; 310 sq. mi.; pop. 534,000.
— city, E Aarhus co.; cap.; pop. 244,839.
Aberdeen co., NE Scotland; 1,972 sq. mi.; pop. 324,574.
— city, SE Aberdeen co.; cap.; pop. 209,189.
— city, NE South Dakota 57401*; pop. 24,927.
— city, w Washington 98520; pop. 16,565.
Abidjan city, SE Ivory Coast; cap.; pop. 1,100,000.
Abilene city, CEN. Texas 79604*; pop. 106,654.
Acapulco city, sw Mexico; pop. 421,100.
Accra city, s Ghana; cap.; pop. 633,880.
Achaea dept., N Peloponessus, Greece; 1,146 sq. mi.; pop. 229,000; cap. Patras.
Aconcagua extinct volcano, CEN. Argentina; 22,831 ft.
Acre city, NE Israel; pop. 37,900.
Addis Ababa city, CEN. Ethiopia; cap.; pop. 1,125,340.
Addison vill. NE Illinois 60101; pop. 32,058.
Adelaide city, SE South Australia; cap.; pop. 933,350.
Aden former British col.; now part of Yemen.
— city, Yemen; pop. 318,000.
Aden, Gulf of inlet of Arabian Sea betw. Yemen and Somalia.
Aden Protectorate former group of Arab tribal districts comprising a British protectorate; now part of Yemen.
Adirondack Mountains mtn. range, NE New York.
Adrian city, SE Michigan 49221; pop. 22,097.
Adriatic Sea inlet of the Mediterranean Sea, E of Italy.
Aegean Sea inlet of the Mediterranean Sea betw. Greece and Asia Minor.
Afghanistan republic, sw Asia; 251,825 sq. mi.; pop. 15,592,000; cap. Kabul.
Africa second largest continent, s of Europe and w of Asia; 11,710,000 sq. mi.
Affton uninc. place, NE Missouri 63123; pop. 21,106.
Agaña city, w Guam 96910; cap.; pop. 896.
Agawam town, w Massachusetts 01001; pop. 27,323.
Agra city, N India; site of Taj Mahal; pop. 591,917.
Aguadilla town, NW Puerto Rico 00603*; pop. 20,879.
Aguascalientes state, CEN. Mexico; 2,499 sq. mi.; pop. 430,000.
— city, CEN. Aguascalientes state; cap.; pop. 247,800.
Agulhas, Cape cape, s South Africa; southernmost point of Africa.
Ahmedabad city, w India; former cap. of Gujarat; pop. 1,585,544.
Aisne river, N France; 175 mi. long.
Ajaccio city, w Corsica; cap.; birthplace of Napoleon; pop. 41,000.
Akron city, NE Ohio 44309*; pop. 223,019.
Alabama state, SE United States; 51,705 sq. mi.; pop. 4,062,608; cap. Montgomery.
Alameda city, w California 94501*; pop. 76,459.
Alamogordo town, s New Mexico 88310; site of the first atom bomb test; pop. 27,596.
Alaska state of the United States, NW North America; 591,004 sq. mi.; pop. 551,947; cap. Juneau.
Alaska, Gulf of inlet of the Pacific on the s coast of Alaska.
Alaska Highway road joining Dawson Creek, British Columbia and Fairbanks, Alaska; 1,527 mi.
Alaska Peninsula promontory of sw Alaska; ab. 400 mi. long.
Alaska Range mtn. range, CEN. Alaska.
Albania Balkan republic s of Yugoslavia; 11,100 sq. mi.; pop. 3,262,000; cap. Tirana.
Albany city sw Georgia 31701*; pop. 78,122.
— city, E New York 12207*; cap.; pop. 101,082.

— city, w Oregon 97321; pop. 29,462.

Albemarle Sound inlet of the Atlantic, NE North Carolina.

Alberta prov., w Canada; 255,290 sq. mi.; pop. 1,838,037; cap. Edmonton.

Albert Lea city, s Minnesota 56007; pop. 18,310.

Albuquerque city, NW New Mexico 87101*; pop. 384,736.

Alcan Highway *unofficial name of* Alaska Highway.

Alderney island, N Channel Islands; 3 sq. mi.

Aleppo city, NE Syria; pop. 878,000.

Aleutian Islands isl. group, sw of Alaska Peninsula.

Alexandria N Egypt; summer cap., pop. 2,409,000.

— city, CEN. Louisiana 71301*; pop. 49,188.

— city, NE Virginia 22313*; pop. 111,183.

Algeria republic, NW Africa; 919,595 sq. mi.; pop. 23,039,000; cap. Algiers.

Algiers city, N Algeria; cap.; pop. 1,507,241.

Alhambra city, sw California 91802*; pop. 82,106.

Alicante prov., E Spain; 2,264 sq. mi.; pop. 920,000.

— city, E Alicante prov.; cap.; pop. 235,868.

Alice city, s Texas, 78332; pop. 19,788.

Aliquippa boro., w Pennsylvania 15001; pop. 13,374.

Allahabad city N India; pop. 490,622.

Allegheny Mountains mtn. range of Appalachian system; extends from Pennsylvania through Virginia.

Allegheny River river, w New York and Pennsylvania; 325 mi. long.

Allen Park vill., SE Michigan 48101; pop. 31,092.

Allentown city, E Pennsylvania 18101*; pop. 105,090.

Alliance city, NE Ohio 44601; pop. 23,376.

Alma city, s Quebec, Canada; pop. 25,638.

Alma-Ata city, SE Kazakh SSR; cap.; pop. 928,000.

Alps mtn. system, s Europe; extends from s coast of France to w coast of Yugoslavia.

Alsace reg. and former prov., NE France.

Alsace-Lorraine oft-disputed border reg., NE France; adjoins sw Germany

Altadena uninc. place, sw California 91001; pop. 42,658.

Altai Mountains mtn. system, CEN. Asia.

Altamont uninc. place, s Oregon 97601; pop. 18,591.

Altamonte Springs city, CEN Florida 32715*; pop. 34,879.

Alton city, sw Illinois 62002; pop. 32,905.

Altoona city, CEN. Pennsylvania 16603*; pop. 51,881.

Altus city, sw Oklahoma 73521*; pop. 21,910.

Alum Rock uninc. place, sw California 95116; pop. 16,890.

Amarillo city, NW Texas 79105*; pop. 157,615.

Amazon river, N South America; 3,910 mi. long; carries the largest volume of water of all rivers.

America 1 The United States of America. 2 North and South America; the western Hemisphere.

American Samoa See Samoa.

Americus city, CEN. Georgia 31709; pop. 16,512.

Ames city, CEN. Iowa 50010*; pop. 47,198.

Amherst uninc. place, CEN. Massachusetts 01002*; pop. 17,824.

Amiens city, N France; pop. 131,476.

Amman city, CEN. Jordan; cap.; pop. 648,587.

Amoy isl. of China, Formosa Strait.

— city, Amoy isl.; pop. 224,000.

Amritsar city, w Punjab, India; pop. 407,628.

Amsterdam city, w Netherlands; cap.; pop. 694,680.

— city, CEN. New York 12010; pop. 20,714.

Amur river, E Asia; 2,700 mi. long.

Anaheim city, sw California 92803*; pop. 266,406.

Anatolia penin. at w end of Asia; comprises most of Turkey.

Anchorage city, s Alaska 99510*; pop. 226,338.

Andalusia reg., s Spain.

Anderson city, CEN. Indiana 46011*; pop. 59,459.

— city, NW South Carolina 29621*; pop. 26,184.

Andes mtn. range, w South America; connects with the Rockies; more than 4,000 mi. long.

Andorra Co-principality betw. France and Spain; 181 sq. mi.; pop. 51,000.

— city, CEN. Andorra; cap.; pop. 2,000.

Andover town, NE Massachusetts 01810; pop. 29,152.

Angel Falls waterfall, SE Venezuela; more than 3,300 ft.

Angola republic, w Africa; 481,354; sq. mi.; pop. 10,002,000; cap. Luanda.

Anjou town, s Quebec, Canada; pop. 36,596.

Ankara city, CEN. Turkey; cap.; pop. 2,553,209.

Annandale uninc. place, NE Virginia 22003*; pop. 50,975.

Annapolis city, CEN. Maryland 21401*; cap.; site of U.S. Naval Academy; pop. 33,187.

Ann Arbor city, SE Michigan 48106*; pop. 109,592.

Anniston city, NE Alabama 36201*; pop. 26,623.

Ansonia city, sw Connecticut 06401; pop. 18,403.

Antarctica continent surrounding the South Pole; 5,405,000 sq. mi. Also **Antarctic Continent.**

Antarctic Circle parallel of latitude at 66° 33′ s; the boundary of the South Frigid Zone.

Antarctic Ocean parts of Atlantic, Pacific, and Indian oceans bordering on Antarctica.

Antarctic Zone region enclosed by the Antarctic Circle.

Antigua and Barbuda monarchy, island group of the West Indies; 171 sq. mi.; pop. 80,600; cap. St. John's.

Antilles islands of the West Indies excluding the Bahamas; comprises Greater Antilles: Cuba, Hispaniola, Jamaica, and Puerto Rico; and Lesser Antilles: Trinidad, the Windward Islands, the Leeward Islands, and other small islands.

Antioch city, s Turkey; pop. 91,511.

— city, w California 94509; pop. 62,195.

Antwerp city, N Belgium; pop. 1,105,000.

Apennines mtn. range of Italy s of Po valley.

Appalachian Mountains E North America.

Appleton city, E Wisconsin 54911*; pop. 65,695.

Aquitaine reg., sw France.

Arabia penin., sw Asia, betw. the Red Sea and Persian Gulf.

Arabian Gulf See **Persian Gulf.**

Arabian Sea part of the Indian Ocean betw. Arabia and India.

Arab Republic of Egypt See **Egypt.**

Aragon reg., NE Spain.

Aral Sea salt inland sea, CEN. USSR.

Ararat, Mount mtn., E Turkey; 17,011 ft.; traditional landing place of Noah's ark.

Arcadia dept., CEN. Peloponnesus, Greece; 1,168 sq. mi.; pop. 112,000; cap. Tripolis.

— city, sw California 91006*; pop. 48,290.

Arctic Circle parallel of latitude at 66° 33′ N; the boundary of the North Frigid Zone.

Arctic Ocean sea, N of Arctic Circle, surrounding North Pole.

Arden-Arcade uninc. place, CEN. California 95825; pop. 92,040.

Ardmore city, s Oklahoma 73401; pop. 23,079.

Arecibo town, N Puerto Rico 00612*; pop. 48,586.

Argentina republic, s South America; 1,073,399 sq. mi.; pop. 23,364,431; cap. Buenos Aires.

Argonne ridge, N France; site of battles in World Wars I and II.

Arizona state, sw United States; 114,000 sq. mi.; pop. 3,677,985; cap. Phoenix.

Arkansas state, CEN. United States; 53,187 sq. mi.; pop. 2,362,239; cap. Little Rock.

Arkhangelsk city, NW RSFSR; pop. 387,000.

Arlington town, E Massachusetts 02174; pop. 44,630;

— city, N Texas 76010*; pop. 261,721.

— city, NE Virginia 22210*; pop. 170,936.

— urb. co., NE Virginia; site of **Arlington National Cemetery,** containing tomb of the Unknown Soldier.

Arlington Heights vill., NE Illinois 60004*; pop. 75,460.

Armenia 1 former country, sw Asia. 2 the Armenian SSR.

Armenian SSR republic, s USSR; 11,500 sq. mi.; pop. 3,074,000, cap. Yerevan.

Arnhem city, E Netherlands; pop. 127,846.

Aruba island member of the Netherlands, N of Venezuala; 75 sq. mi.; pop. 62,900; cap. Oranjestad.

Arvada town, CEN. Colorado 80001*; pop. 89,235.

Arvida city, CEN. Quebec, Canada; pop. 18,448.

Asbury Park city, E New Jersey 07712; pop. 16,799.

Ascension isl. poss. of Great Britain, South Atlantic; 34 sq. mi.; pop. 750.

Asheville city, w North Carolina 28801*; pop. 61,607.

Ashland city, NE Kentucky 41101; pop. 23,622.

— city, CEN. Ohio 44805; pop. 20,079.

Ashtabula city, NE Ohio 44004; pop. 21,633.

Asia, E part of Eurasian land mass; largest of the continents; 17,240,000 sq. mi.

Asia Minor penin. of extreme w Asia, comprising most of Turkey.

Aspen Hill uninc. place, NW Maryland 20906; pop. 44,494.
Astrakhan city, SE RSFSR; pop. 465,000.
Asunción city, SW Paraguay; cap.; pop. 607,706.
Aswan city, S Egypt; site of **Aswan Dam,** 1¼ mi. long; pop. 144, 377.
Athens city, SE Greece; cap.; pop. 2,885,737.
— city, CEN. Georgia, 30603*; pop. 45,734.
— city, SE Ohio 45701; pop. 21,265.
Atlanta city, CEN. Georgia 30301*; cap.; pop. 394,017.
Atlantic City city, SE New Jersey 08401*; pop. 37,986.
Atlantic Ocean ocean, extending from the Arctic to the Antarctic between the Americas and Europe and Africa.
Atlas Mountains mtn. range, NW Africa.
Attleboro city, SE Massachusetts 02703; pop. 38,383.
Auburn city, CEN. Alabama 36830*; pop. 33,830.
— city, SW Maine 04210; pop. 24,309.
— town, CEN. Massachusetts 01501; pop. 15,005.
— city, CEN. New York 13021; pop. 31,258.
— city, CEN. Washington, 98002*; pop. 33,102.
Auckland city, N North Island, New Zealand; pop. 775,000.
Augsburg city, S Germany; pop. 245,940.
Augusta city, E Georgia 30901*; pop. 44,639.
— city, S Maine 04330; cap.; pop. 21,325.
Aurora city, CEN. Colorado 80010*; pop. 222,103.
— city, NE Illinois 60507*; pop. 99,581.
Auschwitz, German name for Oświecim, city, SW Poland; site of Nazi extermination camp in World War II; pop. 44,200.
Austin city, SE Minnesota 55912; pop. 21,907.
— city, CEN. Texas 78710*; cap.; pop. 465,622.
Austintown uninc. place, NE Ohio 44515; pop. 32,371.
Australasia isls. of the South Pacific, including Australia, New Zealand, and New Guinea.
Australia federal state, situated on an isl. continent in South Pacific; 2,966,200 sq. mi.; pop. 17,073,000; cap. Canberra.
Australia Capital Territory reg., SE Australia; 900 sq. mi.; contains Canberra, the capital; pop. 241.500.
Austria republic, CEN. Europe; 32,376 sq. mi.; pop. 7,623,000.
Austronesia isls. of the South Pacific, including Indonesia, Melanesia, Micronesia, and Polynesia.
Avignon city, SE France; pop. 90,786.
Avon river, CEN. England; 96 mi. long.
Azerbaijan prov., NW Iran: **Eastern Azerbaijan:** 25,908 sq. mi.; pop. 4,097,000; cap. Tabriz; **Western Azerbaijan:** 15,000 sq. mi.; pop. 1,915,000; cap. Orumiyeh.
Azerbaijan SSR republic, SW USSR; 33,400 sq. mi.; pop. 6,112,000; cap. Baku.
Azores three isl. groups of Portugal, E Atlantic; 922 sq mi.; pop. 335,000.
Azov, Sea of inlet of the Black Sea, S USSR.
Azusa city, S California 91702; pop. 41,333.
Baden-Baden city, SW Germany; site of famous mineral springs; pop. 49,399.
Bad Lands arid plateau, South Dakota and Nebraska. also **Badlands.**
Baghdad city, CEN. Iraq; cap.; pop. 5,348,117.
Baguio city, Luzon, N Philippines; pop. 97,449.
Bahamas isl. republic SE of Florida; 5,382 sq. mi.; pop. 253,000; cap. Nassau.
Bahrain isl. monarchy, Persian Gulf near Saudi Arabia; 267 sq. mi.; pop. 503,000; cap. Manama.
Baikal freshwater lake, S USSR; 12,150 sq. mi.
Baker, Mount mtn., Cascade range, N Washington; 10,750 ft.
Bakersfield city, S California 93302*; pop. 105,611.
Baku city, SE Azerbaijan SRR; cap.; pop. 1,800,000.
Balboa Heights adm. ctr. of Canal Zone, near Balboa; pop. 232.
Baldwin uninc. place, SE New York 11510; pop. 22,719.
— boro., SW Pennsylvania 15234; pop. 21,923.
Baldwin Park city, SW California 91706; pop. 69,330.
Balearic Islands isl. group, W Mediterranean; prov. of Spain; 1,936 sq. mi.; pop. 642,702; cap. Palma.
Bali isl. of Indonesia, E of Java; 2,243 sq. mi.
Balkan Mountains, mtn. range, Balkan penin.
Balkan Peninsula large penin. of SE Europe.
Balkan States countries of Balkan penin.: Albania, Bulgaria, Greece, Rumania, Yugoslavia, and part of Turkey.
Baltic Sea inlet of the Atlantic in NW Europe.
Baltimore city, N Maryland 21233*; pop. 736,014.

Bamako city, CEN. Mali; cap.; pop. 646,163.
Banaras Hindu sacred city, NE India; pop. 553,000. Also **Benares.**
Bandar Seri Begawan city, N Brunei; cap.; pop. 37,000.
Bandung city, W Java, Indonesia; pop. 1,201,730.
Bangalore city, E Mysore, India; cap.; pop. 1,540,741.
Bangkok city, SW Thailand; cap.; pop. 3,133,834.
Bangladesh republic, S Asia; 55,598 sq. mi.; pop. 113,005,000; cap. Dacca.
Bangor city, CEN. Maine 04401; pop. 33,181.
Bangui city, SW Central African Republic; cap.; pop. 596,776.
Banjul city, W Gambia; cap.; pop. 45,600.
Barbados isl. monarchy, E Caribbean; 166 sq. mi.; pop. 267,000; cap. Bridgetown.
Barberton city, NE Ohio 44203; pop. 27,623.
Barcelona prov., NE Spain; 2,985 sq. mi.; pop. 3,975,000.
— city, S Barcelona prov.; cap.; pop. 1,902,713.
Barnstable town, SE Massachusetts 02630; pop. 30,898.
Barranquilla city, N Colombia; pop. 859,000.
Barrie city, S Ontario, Canada; pop. 34,389.
Barrington town, E Rhode Island 02806; pop. 15,849.
Barrow, Point extreme N point of Alaska.
Barstow city, E California 92311; pop. 21,472.
Bartlesville city, NE Oklahoma 74003*; pop. 34,256.
Basel city, N Switzerland; pop. 180,900.
Bataan prov. S Luzon, Philippines; 517 sq. mi.; pop. 116,000; cap. Balanga; occupies **Bataan Peninsula,** scene of World War II surrender of U.S. forces to the Japanese.
Batavia city, W New York 14020; pop. 16,310.
Bath co. boro., SW England; pop. 83,900.
Bathurst town, NE New Brunswick, Canada; pop. 16,301.
— Banjul; *the former name of.*
Baton Rouge city, CEN. Louisiana 70821*; cap.; pop. 219,531.
Battle Creek city, S Michigan 49016*; pop. 53,540.
Bavaria state, SE Germany; 27,241 sq. mi.; pop. 10,870,968; cap. Munich.
Bayamon town, N Puerto Rico 00619; pop. 184,854.
Bay City city, CEN. Michigan 48706*; pop. 38,936.
Bayonne city, NE New Jersey 07002; pop. 61,144.
Baytown city, S Texas 77520*; pop. 63,850.
Bay Village city, NE Ohio 44140; pop. 17,000.
Beaconsfield town, S Quebec, Canada; pop. 20,417.
Beaumont city, SE Texas 77701*; pop. 114,323.
Beaverton city, NW Oregon 97005*; pop. 53,310.
Beckley city, S West Virginia 25801*; pop. 18,296.
Bedford city, NE Ohio 44146; pop. 14,822.
Beijing. See Peking.
Beirut city, W Lebanon; cap.; pop. 200,000.
Belém city, N Brazil; pop. 565,097.
Belfast co. boro., and port, SE N. Ireland; cap.; pop. 354,400.
Belgium monarchy, NW Europe; 11,783 sq. mi.; pop. 9,958,000; cap. Brussels.
Belgrade city E Yugoslavia; cap.; pop. 770,140.
Belize monarchy, NE Central America; 8,867 sq. mi.; pop. 189,000; cap. Belmopan.
Bell city, S California 90201; pop. 34,365.
Bellaire city, S Texas 77401; pop. 13,842.
Belle Glade city, SE Florida 33430; pop. 16,177.
Belleville city, SW Illinois 62220*; pop. 42,785.
— town, NE New Jersey 07109; pop. 34,213.
— city, SE Ontario, Canada; pop. 35,311.
Bellevue city, E Nebraska 68005; pop. 30,982.
— city, CEN. Washington 98009*; pop. 86,874.
Bellflower city, SW California 90706; pop. 61,815.
Bell Gardens city, SW California 90201; pop. 42,355.
Bellingham city, NW Washington 98225*; pop. 52,179.
Bellmawr boro., SW New Jersey 08031; pop. 12,603.
Bellmore uninc. place, SE New York 11710; pop. 16,438.
Bellwood vill., NE Illinois 60104; pop. 20,241.
Belmont city, CEN. California 94002; pop. 24,127.
— town, E Massachusetts 02178; pop. 24,720.
Beloit city, S Wisconsin 53511; pop. 35,573.
Bengal former prov., NE British India; divided (1947) into; East Bengal, now part of Bangladesh, and **West Bengal,** a state of India; 34,200 sq. mi.; pop. 49,788,000; cap. Calcutta.
Benghazi city, N Libya; pop. 170,000.
Benin republic, W Africa; 43,450 sq. mi.; pop. 4,741,000.
Benton city, CEN. Arkansas 72015; pop. 17,177.

Benton Harbor city, sw Michigan 49022; pop. 12,818.
Berea city, NE Ohio 44017; pop. 19,051.
Bergen city, sw Norway; pop. 209,000.
Bergenfield boro., NE New Jersey 07621; pop. 24,458.
Bering Sea part of the North Pacific betw. Alaska and the USSR, joined to the Arctic by Bering Strait.
Berkeley city, w California 94701*; pop. 102,724.
— city, CEN. Missouri 63134; pop. 12,450.
Berkley city, SE Michigan 48072; pop. 16.960.
Berlin city, CEN. Germany; cap. prior to 1945 when divided into the British, French, Soviet, and US sectors. In 1949 the Soviet sector, East Berlin, was designated capital of East Germany. The remaining sectors formed West Berlin, associated with West Germany; when Germany was reunited in 1990, Berlin became the capital again in 1991; pop. 3,352,848.
— city, N New Hampshire 03570; pop. 11,824.
Bermuda isl. group, w Atlantic; British col.; 21 sq. mi. pop. 59,330, cap. Hamilton.
Bern city, CEN. Switzerland; cap.; pop. 141,300. Also Berne.
Berwyn city, NE Illinois 60402; pop. 45,426.
Bessemer city, CEN. Alabama 35020*; pop. 33,497.
Bethany city, CEN. Oklahoma 73008; pop. 20,075.
Bethel Park boro., sw Pennsylvania 15102; pop. 33,823.
Bethesda uninc. area, w Maryland 20814*; pop. 62,936.
Bethlehem ancient town, w Jordan; birthplace of Jesus; pop. 25,000.
— city, E Pennsylvania 18016*; pop. 71,428.
Bettendorf city, CEN. Iowa 52722; pop. 28,132.
Beverly city, NE Massachusetts 01915; pop. 38,195.
Beverly Hills city, sw California, 90210*; pop. 31,971.
Bhutan monarchy, s Asia, between NE India and Tibet; 18,150 sq. mi.; pop. 1,442,000; cap. Thimphu.
Biddeford city, sw Maine 04005; pop. 20,710.
Big Spring city, w Texas 79720*; pop. 23,093.
Bikini atoll, Marshall Islands; 2 sq. mi.; site of US nuclear tests, July 1946.
Billerica town, NE Massachusetts 01821; pop. 37,609.
Billings city, CEN. Montana 59011*; pop. 81,151.
Biloxi city, SE Mississippi 39530*; pop. 46,319.
Binghamton city, CEN. New York 13902*; pop. 53,008.
Birkenhead co. boro., NW England; pop. 342,300.
Birmingham co. boro., CEN. England; pop. 1,033,900.
— city, CEN. Alabama 35203*; pop. 268,968.
— city, SE Michigan 48012*; pop. 19,997.
Biscay, Bay of inlet, of the Atlantic betw. w and sw France and N and NW Spain.
Bismarck city, CEN. North Dakota 58501*; cap.; pop. 49,256.
Bismarck Archipelago isl. group, Trust Territory of New Guinea; 19,200 sq. mi.
Bizerte city, N Tunisia; pop. 62,856.
Black Forest wooded mtn. reg., sw Germany.
Black Hills mtn. reg., sw South Dakota and NE Wyoming.
Black Sea inland sea betw. Europe and Asia, connects with the Aegean via the Bosporus, the Sea of Marmara, and the Dardanelles.
Blaine vill., E Minnesota 55433; pop. 38,975.
Bloomfield town, CEN. Connecticut 06002; pop. 19,483.
— city, NE New Jersey 07003; pop. 45,061.
Bloomington city, CEN. Illinois 61701; pop. 51,972.
— city, CEN. Indiana 47401*; pop. 60,633.
— city, CEN. Minnesota 55420; pop. 86,335.
Bluefield city, s West Virginia 24701; pop. 12,756.
Blue Island city, NE Illinois 60406; pop. 21,203.
Blue Ridge Mountains, sw part of the Appalachians.
Blytheville city, NE Arkansas 72315*; pop. 22,906.
Boardman uninc. place, NE Ohio 44512; pop. 38,596.
Boca Raton city, SE Florida 33432*; pop. 61,492.
Bogalusa city, SE Louisiana 70427; pop. 14,280.
Bogotá city, CEN. Colombia; cap.; pop. 4,067,000.
Bohemia former prov., w Czechoslovakia.
Boise city, sw Idaho 83707*; cap.; pop. 102,160.
Bolivia republic, CEN. South America; 424,164 sq. mi.; pop. 7,332,000; caps. Sucre (judicial), La Paz (admin).
Bologna prov., CEN. Italy; 1,429 sq. mi.; pop. 925,113.
— city, cap. of Bologna prov.; pop. 422,204.
Bombay city, w India; pop. 5,970,575.
Bonn city, w Germany; was cap. of West Germany; pop. 286,184.

Bordeaux city, sw France; pop. 201,000.
Borneo (Kalimantan) isl., betw. Java and South China seas; comprising North Borneo, Sarawak, Brunei, and Indonesian Borneo; 286,969 sq. mi.
Bosnia and Herzegovina constituent republic, CEN. Yugoslavia; 19,741 sq. mi.; pop. 4,029,000; cap. Sarajevo.
Bosporus strait, betw. the Black Sea and the Sea of Marmara.
Bossier City city, NW Louisiana 71111*; pop. 52,721.
Boston city, E Massachusetts 02205*; cap.; pop. 574,283.
Botany Bay inlet of the Pacific, s of Sydney, Australia.
Botswana republic, s Africa; 224,607 sq. mi.; pop. 1,295,000; cap. Gaborone.
Boucherville town, s Quebec, Canada; pop. 25,530.
Boulder city, CEN. Colorado 80302*; pop. 83,312.
Boulder Dam the former name of Hoover Dam.
Bountiful city, CEN. Utah 84010; pop. 36,659.
Bowie city, CEN. Maryland 20715; pop. 37,589.
Bowling Green city, s Kentucky 42101*; pop. 40,641.
— city, NW Ohio 43402*; pop. 28,176.
Boynton Beach city, SE Florida 33435*; pop. 46,194.
Bozeman city, sw Montana 59715*; pop. 22,660.
Bradenton city, w Florida 33506*; pop. 43,779.
Braintree town, E Massachusetts 02184; pop. 33,836.
Brampton town, SE Ontario, Canada; pop. 103,459.
Brandon city, sw Manitoba, Canada; pop. 34,901.
Branford town, CEN. Connecticut 06405; pop. 27,603.
Brantford city, SE Ontario, Canada; pop. 66,950.
Brasilia city, CEN. Brazil; cap.; pop. 750,000.
Brazil republic, NE and CEN. South America; 3,286,500 sq. mi.; pop. 150,368,000; cap. Brasilia.
Brazzaville city, SE Congo; cap.; pop. 596,200.
Brea city, sw California 92621; pop. 32,873.
Breed's Hill hill, near Bunker Hill. See Bunker Hill.
Bremen state, NW Germany, 156 sq. mi.; pop. 695,115;
— city, cap. of Bremen state; pop. 556,128.
Bremerhaven city, part of Bremen state, NW Germany; pop. 138,987.
Bremerton city, w Washington 98310*; pop. 38,142.
Brenner Pass Alpine pass, Austrian–Italian border.
Brentwood uninc. place, SE New York 11717; pop. 45,218.
Breslau Wroclaw: German name of city in Poland.
Brest city, NW France; pop. 166,826.
— city, sw Byelorussian SSR; pop. 186,000.
Bridgeport city, sw Connecticut 06601*; pop. 141,686.
Bridgeton town, E Missouri 63044; pop. 17,779.
— city, sw New Jersey 08302; pop. 18,942.
Brighton co. boro. and resort, sw England; pop. 166,000.
Brisbane city, SE Queensland, Australia; cap.; pop. 1,240,300.
Bristol co. boro., sw England; pop. 408,000.
— city, CEN. Connecticut 06010; pop. 60,640.
— urb. twp., SE Pennsylvania 19007; pop. 10,405.
— town, E Rhode Island 02809; pop. 21,625.
— city, NE Tennessee 37620*; pop. 23,421.
Bristol Channel inlet of the Atlantic betw. Wales and sw England.
Britain see Great Britain.
British Columbia prov., w Canada; 358,971 sq. mi.; pop. 2,466,608; cap. Victoria.
British Guiana former British col., NE South America. See Guyana.
British Virgin Islands British col., E Greater Antilles; 59 sq. mi.; pop. 10,484; cap. Road Town.
British West Indies See WEST INDIES.
Brittany reg., w France; former prov.
Brno city, CEN. Czechoslovakia; pop. 372,793.
Brockton city, E Massachusetts 02403*; pop. 92,788.
Brockville town, SE Ontario, Canada; pop. 19,903.
Bronx borough, N New York City, New York 10400*; pop. 1,203,789. Also the Bronx.
Brookfield vill., NE Illinois 60513; pop. 18,876.
— city, SE Wisconsin 53005; pop. 35,184.
Brookline town, E Massachusetts 02146; pop. 54,718.
Brooklyn (Kings) borough, SE New York City, New York 11200*; pop. 2,300,664.
Brooklyn Center vill., SE Minnesota 55429; pop. 28,887.
Brooklyn Park vill., SE Minnesota 55007; pop. 56,381.
Brook Park vill., N Ohio 44142; pop. 22,865.
Brossard city, s Quebec, Canada; pop. 37,641.

Browardale uninc. place, SE Florida 33311; pop. 6,257.

Brownsville uninc. place, NW Florida 33142; pop. 18,058.

— city, S Texas 78520*; pop. 98,962.

Brownwood city, CEN. Texas 76801*; pop. 18,387.

Brunei sultanate, NW Borneo; 2,226 sq. mi.; pop. 259,000; cap. Bandar Sari Begawan.

Brunswick city, NE Germany; pop. 261,669.

— city, SE Georgia 31520*; pop. 16,433.

— uninc. place, S Maine 04011; pop. 14,683.

— vill., N Ohio 44212; pop. 28,230.

Brussels city, CEN. Belgium; cap.; pop. 2,400,000.

Bryan city, CEN. Texas 77801*; pop. 55,002.

Bucharest city, S Rumania; cap.; pop. 1,858,418.

Budapest city, CEN. Hungary; cap.; pop. 2,060,000.

Buena Park city, SW California 90622*; pop. 68,784.

Buenos Aires city, E Argentina; cap.; pop. 10,300,000.

Buffalo city, W New York 14240*; pop. 328,123.

Bulgaria republic, SE Europe; 42,855 sq. mi.; pop. 8,997,400; cap. Sofia.

Bull Run small stream, NE Virginia; site of Union defeats in the Civil War, 1861 and 1862.

Bunker Hill hill, Charlestown, Massachusetts, near which (on Breed's Hill) occurred the first organized engagement of the American Revolution, June 17, 1775.

Burbank city, SW California 91505*; pop. 93,643.

Burgundy reg., CEN. France.

Burkina Faso republic, W Africa; 105,869 sq. mi.; pop. 9,012,000; cap. Ouagadougou.

Burlingame city, CEN. California 94010*; pop. 26,801.

Burlington city, SE Iowa 52601*; pop. 27,208.

— town, NE Massachusetts 01803; pop. 23,302.

— city, CEN. North Carolina 27215*; pop. 39,498.

— city, NW Vermont 05401*; pop. 39,127.

— town, SE Ontario, Canada; pop. 104,314.

Burma See Myanmar.

Burma Road road betw. N Burma and SW China; a World War II supply route.

Burnsville city, SE Minnesota 55337; pop. 51,288.

Burundi military régime, CEN. Africa; *formerly part of* Ruanda-Urundi; 10,747 sq. mi.; pop. 5,451,000; cap. Bujumbura.

Butler city, W Pennsylvania 16001*; pop. 15,714.

Butte city, SW Montana 59701*; pop. 33,336.

Byelorussian SSR constituent republic, USSR; 80,200 sq. mi.; pop. 9,611,000; cap. Minsk.

Cádiz city, SW Spain; pop. 156,328.

Caguas town, CEN. Puerto Rico 00625*; pop. 87,218.

Cahokia vill. SW Illinois 62206; pop. 17,550.

Cairo city, NE Egypt; cap.; pop. 6,052,836.

Calais city, N France; pop. 78,820.

Calcutta city, NE India; pop. 3,148,746.

Calgary city, S Alberta, Canada; pop. 469,917.

Caticut *an alternate name of* Kozhikode.

California state, W United States; 158,706 sq. mi.; pop. 29,839,250; cap. Sacramento.

California, Gulf of inlet of the Pacific, W Mexico, betw. Lower California and the rest of Mexico.

Calumet City city, NE Illinois 60409; pop. 37,840.

Camarillo city, SW California 93010; pop. 52,303.

Cambodia (State of Kampuchia), republic, 70,238 sq. mi.; pop. 8,592,000; cap. Phnom Penh.

Cambridge city, SE England; site of Cambridge University; pop. 101,600.

— city, E Massachusetts 02138*; pop. 95,802.

Camden city, S Arkansas 71701; pop. 14,380.

— city, SW New Jersey 08101*; pop. 87,492.

Cameroon republic, W equatorial Africa; 179,714 sq. mi.; pop. 7,663,246; cap. Yaounde. Also **Cameroun.**

Campbell city, W California 95008; pop. 36,048.

Camp Springs uninc. place, SW Maryland 20748; pop. 16,392.

Canada independent member of the Commonwealth of Nations, N North America; 3,849,675 sq. mi.; pop. 22,992,604; cap. Ottawa.

Canal Zone US leased terr., CEN. Panama; extending five miles on either side of the Panama Canal.

Canary Islands isl. group of Spain near NW coast of Africa; 2,796 sq. mi.; pop. 1,410,655.

Canaveral, Cape, cape, E Florida 32920; pop. 8,014; site of the **John F. Kennedy Space Center,** a space research and missiles installation.

Canberra city, SE Australia; cap.; pop. 277,300.

Canea city, NW Crete; pop. 40,564. Also **Khania.**

Cannes city, SE France; pop. 70,527.

Canterbury co. boro., SE England; site of famous cathedral; pop. 34,512.

Canton city, S China; pop. 1,296,000.

— town, E Massachusetts 02021; pop. 18,503.

— city, NE Ohio 44701*; pop. 84,161.

Cap-de-la-Madeleine city, S Quebec, Canada; pop. 31,126.

Cape Girardeau city, SE Missouri 63701; pop. 34,438.

Cape Town city, S South Africa; legislative cap.; pop. 776,617. Also **Capetown.**

Cape Verde Islands republic in the CEN. Atlantic Ocean, W of Cape Verde; 1,557 sq. mi.; pop. 339,000; cap. Praia.

Capri isl. near the W coast of Italy; 4 sq. mi.

Caracas city, N Venezuela; cap.; pop. 1,658,500.

Carbondale city, S Illinois 62901; pop. 27,033.

Cardiff co. boro., SE Wales; pop. 282,000.

Caribbean Sea part of the Atlantic betw. the West Indies and Central and South America.

Carlisle boro., S Pennsylvania 17013; pop. 18,419.

Carlsbad city, SE New Mexico 88220; pop. 24,952.

Carlsbad Caverns National Park area, SE New Mexico; contains **Carlsbad Caverns,** a series of limestone caves.

Carmichael uninc. place, CEN. California 95608; pop. 48,702.

Carnegie boro., SW Pennsylvania 15106; pop. 9,278.

Carol City uninc place, SE Florida, 33055*; pop. 53,331.

Caroline Islands isl. group in the Pacific, E of the Philippines; 463 sq. mi.

Carpathian Mountains mtn. range, CEN. and E Europe.

Carpentersville vill., NE Illinois 60110; pop. 23,049.

Carrara city, CEN. Italy; site of white marble quarries; pop. 70,227.

Carson city, SW California 90744; pop. 40,443.

Carson City city, W Nevada 89701*; cap.; pop. 40,443.

Carteret boro., NE New Jersey 07009; pop. 19,025.

Casablanca city, NW Morocco; pop. 1,506,373.

Cascade Range mtn. range in Oregon, Washington, and British Columbia.

Cashmere See Kashmir.

Casper city, CEN. Wyoming 82601; pop. 46,742.

Caspian Sea saltwater lake in the S USSR and N Iran; 163,800 sq. mi.

Castile reg., N and CEN. Spain.

Castro Valley uninc. place, W California 94546; pop. 48,619.

Catalina Island *an alternate name of* Santa Catalina.

Catalonia reg. NE Spain.

Catania prov., E Sicily; 1,371 sq. mi.; pop. 1,029,515.

— city, Catania prov.; cap.; pop. 370,679.

Cataño town, N Puerto Rico 00638; pop. 26,318.

Catonsville uninc. place, CEN. Maryland 21228; pop. 35,233.

Catskill Mountains range of the Appalachians in SE New York.

Caucasus mtn. range betw. the Black and Caspian Seas.

— reg., SW USSR, betw. the Black and Caspian Seas. Also **Caucasia.**

Cayey town, CEN. Puerto Rico 00633; pop. 40,927.

Cedar Falls city, CEN. Iowa 50613; pop. 36,322.

Cedar Grove twp., NE New Jersey 07009; pop. 12,053.

Cedar Rapids city, E Iowa 52401; pop. 108,751.

Celebes *the former name of* Sulawesi.

Center Point uninc. place, CEN. Alabama 35215; pop. 23,317.

Central African Republic , republic, CEN. Africa; 240,324 sq. mi.; pop. 2,875,000; cap. Bangui.

Central America S part of North America, betw. Mexico and Colombia.

Central Falls city, NE Rhode Island 02863; pop. 17,637.

Centralia city, S Illinois 62801*; pop. 14,274.

Central Islip uninc. place, SE New York 11722; pop. 26,028.

Cerritos city, S California 90701; pop. 53,020.

Ceylon See Sri Lanka.

Chad, Lake lake, CEN. Africa; 8,000 sq. mi.

Chad, Republic of republic, CEN. Africa; 495,752 sq. mi.; pop. 5,678,000; cap. N'Djamena.

Chambersburg boro., S Pennsylvania 17201; pop. 16,647.

Champaign city, CEN. Illinois 61820; pop. 63,502.

Champlain, Lake lake, betw. New York and Vermont, extending into Canada; 600 sq. mi.

Changchun city, NE China; pop. 1,309,000.
Channel Islands British isl. group, English Channel near Normandy; includes Jersey, Guernsey, Alderney, and Sark; 75 sq. mi.
Chapel Hill town, CEN. North Carolina 27514*; pop. 38,719.
Charlesbourg city, S Quebec, Canada; pop. 63,147.
Charleston city, E Illinois 61920; pop. 20,398.
— city, SE South Carolina 29401*; pop. 80,414.
— city, CEN. West Virginia 25301*; cap.; pop. 57,287.
Charlotte city, CEN. North Carolina 28202*; pop. 395,934.
Charlotte Amalie city, S St. Thomas, U.S. Virgin Islands 00801*; cap.; pop. 12,220.
Charlottesville city, CEN. Virginia 22906*; pop. 40,341.
Charlottetown city, CEN. Prince Edward Island, Canada; cap.; pop. 17,063.
Chateauguay town, S Quebec, Canada; pop. 36,329.
Chatham city, S Ontario, Canada; pop. 38,685.
Chattanooga city, SE Tennessee 37401*; pop. 152,466.
Cheektowaga uninc. place, W New York 14225; pop. 84,387.
Chelmsford town, NE Massachusetts 01824; pop. 32,388.
Chelsea metropolitan boro., SW London, England; pop. 47,000.
— city, E Massachusetts 02150; pop. 25,431.
Cheltenham urb. twp., SE Pennsylvania 19012; pop. 35,509.
Cherbourg city, N France; pop. 32,536.
Chesapeake city, SE Virginia 23320*; pop. 151,976.
Chesapeake Bay inlet of the Atlantic in Virginia and Maryland.
Cheshire town, CEN. Connecticut 06410; pop. 25,684.
Chester co. boro., W Cheshire, England; cap.; pop. 61,370.
— city, SE Pennsylvania 19013*; pop. 41,856.
Cheviot Hills mtn. range, on the border betw. England and Scotland.
Cheyenne city, SE Wyoming 82001*; cap.; pop. 50,008.
Chicago city, NE Illinois 60607*; third largest city in the United States; pop. 2,783,726.
Chicago Heights city, NE Illinois 60411; pop. 33,072.
Chico city, CEN. California 95926*; pop. 40,079.
Chicopee city, SW Massachusetts 01021*; pop. 56,632.
Chicoutimi city, S Quebec, Canada; pop. 57,737.
Chihuahua state, N Mexico; 94,830 sq. mi.; pop. 2,000,000.
Chihuahua city, Chihuahua state, Mexico; cap.; pop. 369,500.
Chile republic, W South America; 292,153 sq. mi.; pop. 13,173,000; cap. Santiago.
Chillicothe city, CEN. Ohio 45601; pop. 21,923.
Chillum uninc. place, SW Maryland 20783; pop. 31,309.
China, People's Republic of republic, E and CEN. Asia; 3,696,100 sq. mi.; pop. 1,133,683,000; cap. Peking (Beijing).
China, Republic of (Taiwan) republic on Taiwan and several smaller isls.; 13,900 sq. mi.; pop. 20,221,000; cap. Taipei.
China Sea part of the Pacific bordering on China. See **East China Sea, South China Sea.**
Chino city, SW California 91710; pop. 59,682.
Chula Vista city, SW California 92010*; pop. 135,163.
Chungking city, CEN. China; cap. during World War II; pop. 1,900,000.
Cicero city, NE Illinois 60650; pop. 67,436.
Cincinnati city, SW Ohio 45234*; pop. 364,040.
Circassia reg., NW Caucasus, RSFSR.
Citrus Heights uninc. place, NE California 95610; pop. 107,439.
Clairton city, SW Pennsylvania 15025; pop. 9,656.
Claremont city, SW California 91711*; pop. 32,503.
Clark twp., N New Jersey 07066; pop. 14,629.
Clarksburg city, N West Virginia 26301*; pop. 18,059.
Clarksdale city, NW Mississippi 38614; pop. 19,717.
Clarksville city, N Tennessee 37041*; pop. 75,494.
Clawson city, SE Michigan 48017; pop. 13,874.
Clayton city, E Missouri 63105; pop. 13,874.
Clearwater city, W Florida 33515*; pop. 98,784.
Cleburne city, CEN. Texas 76031; pop. 22,205.
Cleveland city, N Ohio 44101*; pop. 505,616.
— city, SE Tennessee 37311*; pop. 30,354.
Cleveland Heights city, N Ohio 44118; pop. 54,052.
Clifton city, NE New Jersey 07015*; pop. 71,742.
Clinton city, E Iowa 52732; pop. 29,201.
Clovis city, E New Mexico 88101; pop. 30,954.
Cocoa city, E Florida 32922*; pop. 17,722.
Cod, Cape penin, SE Massachusetts.
Coeur d'Alene city, N Idaho 83814; pop. 24,563.

Coffeyville city, SE Kansas 67337; pop. 12,917.
Cohoes city, E New York 12047; pop. 16,825.
College Park city, W Georgia 30337; pop. 20,457.
— city, W Maryland 20740*; pop. 21,927.
College Station city, CEN. Texas 77840*; pop. 52,456.
Collingswood boro., W New Jersey 08108; pop. 15,289.
Collinsville city, SW Illinois 62234; pop. 22,446.
Cologne city, W Germany; pop. 976,136.
Colombia republic, NW South America; 440,831 sq. mi.; pop. 32,978,000; cap. Bogotá.
Colombo city, W Sri Lanka; cap.; pop. 609,000.
Colón city, Caribbean end of the Canal Zone; an enclave of Panama; pop. 73,600.
Colonial Heights city, CEN. Virginia, 23834; pop. 16,064.
Colorado state, CEN. United States; 104,091 sq. mi.; pop. 3,307,912; cap. Denver.
Colorado River river flowing through Colorado, Utah, Arizona, California, and Mexico to the Gulf of California; length ab. 1,400 mi.
Colorado Springs city, CEN. Colorado 80901*; site of U.S. Air Force Academy; pop. 281,140.
Colton city, S California, 92324; pop. 40,213.
Columbia city, CEN. Missouri 65201*; pop. 69,101.
— city, CEN. South Carolina 29201*; cap.; pop. 98,052.
— city, CEN. Tennessee 38401*; pop. 28,583.
Columbia Heights city, E Minnesota 55421; pop. 18,910.
Columbia River river, SW Canada and NW United States; 1,200 mi. long.
Columbus, city, W Georgia 31902*; pop. 179,278.
— city, CEN. Indiana 47201*; pop. 31,80230,614.
— city, E Mississippi 39701*; pop. 23,799.
— city, E Nebraska 68601; pop. 19,480.
— city, CEN. Ohio 43216*; cap.; pop. 632,910.
Commerce City town, CEN. Colorado 80022; pop. 16,466.
Comoros Islands isl. republic in the Indian Ocean, NW of Madagascar; 719 sq. mi.; pop. 463,000; cap. Moroni.
Compton city, SW California 90220*; pop. 90,454.
Conakry city, W Guinea; cap.; pop. 197,267.
Concord city, W California 94520*; pop. 111,348.
— town, NE Massachusetts 01742; pop. 17,076.
— uninc. place, NE Missouri 63128; pop. 19,859.
— city, CEN. New Hampshire 03301*; cap.; pop. 36,006.
— city, CEN. North Carolina 28025; pop. 27,347.
Congo republic, CEN. Africa; 132,047 sq. mi.; pop. 2,326,000; cap. Brazzaville.
Congo River river, CEN. Africa; 2,720 mi. long.
Connecticut state, NE United States; 5,018 sq. mi.; pop. 3,295,669; cap. Hartford.
Connersville city, E Indiana 47331; pop. 15,55017,023.
Continental Divide ridge of the Rockies separating westflowing and east-flowing streams in North America.
Conway city, CEN. Arkansas 72032; pop. 26,481.
Coon Rapids vill., E Minnesota 55433; pop. 52,978.
Copenhagen city, E Denmark; cap.; pop. 1,343,916.
Copiague uninc. place, SE New York 11726; pop. 20,769.
Coral Gables city, SE Florida 33134; pop. 40,091.
Coral Sea part of the Pacific, E of Australia and New Guinea.
Cork co., SW Ireland; 2,880 sq. mi.; pop. 402,465.
— co. boro., Cork co.; cap.; pop. 138,267.
Corner Brook city, W Newfoundland, Canada; pop. 25,198.
Corning city, W New York 14830; pop. 11,938.
Cornwall city, SE Ontario, Canada; pop. 46,121.
Corona city, S California 91720; pop. 76,095.
Coronado city, S California 92118; pop. 26,540.
Corpus Christi city, S Texas 78408*; pop. 257,453.
Corsica isl., N Mediterranean; a dept. of France; 3,352. sq. mi.; pop. 244,600; cap. Ajaccio.
Corsicana city, CEN. Texas 75110; pop. 22,911.
Cortland city, CEN. New York 13045; pop. 19,801.
Corvallis city, W Oregon 97333*; pop. 44,757.
Costa Mesa city, SW California 92626*; pop. 96,357.
Costa Rica republic, Central America; 19,730 sq. mi.; pop. 3,015,000; cap. San José.
Côte d'Ivoire See **Ivory Coast.**
Côte-St.-Luc city, S Quebec, Canada; pop. 25,721.
Council Bluffs city, SW Iowa 51501*; pop. 54,315.
Coventry city and co. boro., CEN. England; pop. 339,300.
— town, CEN. Rhode Island 02816; pop. 31,083.

Covina city, sw California 91722*; pop. 43,207.
Covington city, N Kentucky 41011*; pop. 43,264.
Cranford urb. twp., E New Jersey 07106. pop. 22,624.
Cranston city, E Rhode Island 02910; pop. 76,060.
Crestwood city, E Missouri 63126; pop. 11,234.
Crete isl., E Mediterranean; adm. div. of Greece; 3,219 sq. mi.; pop. 502,165.
Crimea penin., SE Ukrainian SSR.
Croatia constituent republic, w Yugoslavia; 21,829 sq. mi.; pop. 4,648,000; cap. Zagreb.
Crowley city, s Louisiana 70526; pop. 13,983.
Crystal vill., SE Minnesota 55428; pop. 23,788.
Cuba isl. republic, Caribbean Sea; 42,804 sq. mi. (with the Isle of Pines); pop. 10,603,000; cap. Havana.
Cudahy city, sw California 90201; pop. 22,817.
— city, SE Wisconsin 53110; pop. 18,659.
Culver City city, sw California 90230*; pop. 38,793.
Cumberland city, NW Maryland 21502*; pop. 23,706.
Cumberland Gap passage through Cumberland Mountains, betw. Tennessee and Virginia.
Cumberland River river, Kentucky and Tennessee; flows to Ohio River.
Cupertino city, w California 95014; pop. 40,263.
Curaçao isl., w Netherlands Antilles; 171 sq. mi.; pop. 147,388; cap. Willemstad.
Cutler Ridge uninc. place, SE Florida 33157; pop. 21,268.
Cuyahoga Falls city, NE Ohio 44222*; pop. 48,950.
Cyclades isl. group, s Aegean; a dept. of Greece; 1,023 sq. mi.; pop. 86,000; cap. Hermoupolis.
Cypress city, sw California 90630; pop. 42,655.
Cyprus isl. republic, E Mediterranean; 2,276 sq. mi.; pop. 568,000; cap. Nicosia.
Czechoslovakia republic, CEN. Europe; 49,381 sq. mi.; pop. 15,664,000; cap. Prague.
Dacca city, CEN. Bangladesh; cap.; pop. 5,300,000.
Dachau town, SE Germany; site of a Nazi concentration camp; pop. 34,162.
Dakar city, w Senegal; cap.; pop. 1,382,000.
Dallas city, N Texas 75260*; pop. 1,006,877.
Dalmatia reg., Croatia, w Yugoslavia; 4,954 sq. mi. pop. 750,000; cap. Split.
Dalton city, NW Georgia 30720; pop. 21,761.
Daly City city, w California 94017*; pop. 92,311.
Damascus city, sw Syria; cap.; pop. 1,156,000.
Danbury city, sw Connecticut 06810*; pop. 65,585.
Danube river, CEN. and E Europe; 1,770 mi. long.
Danvers town, NE Massachusetts 01923; pop. 24,174.
Danville city, E Illinois 61832; pop. 33,828.
— city, s Virginia 24541*; pop. 53,056.
Danzig the former name of Gdańsk.
Dardanelles strait, NW Turkey; connects Sea of Marmara with the Aegean.
Darien town, sw Connecticut 06820; pop. 18,196.
Darien, Gulf of inlet of the Caribbean, E coast of Panama.
Dartmouth town, SE Massachusetts 02714; pop. 27,244.
— city, s Nova Scotia, Canada; pop. 65,341.
Davenport city, E Iowa 52802*; pop. 95,333.
Davis city, CEN. California 95616; pop. 46,209.
Dayton city, sw Ohio 45401*; pop. 182,044.
Daytona Beach city, E Florida 32015*; pop. 61,921.
Dead Sea large salt lake on Israel–Jordan border; 1,292 ft. below sea level.
Dearborn city, SE Michigan 48120*; pop. 89,286.
Dearborn Heights city, SE Michigan 48127; pop. 60,838.
Death Valley desert basin, SE California; maximum depth 280 ft. below sea level.
Decatur city, N Alabama 35601*; pop. 48,761.
— city, CEN. Georgia 30030*; pop. 17,336.
— city, CEN. Illinois 62521*; pop. 83,885.
Deccan Plateau triangular tableland covering most of the penin. of India.
Dedham town, E Massachusetts 02026; pop. 23,782.
Deerfield vill., NE Illinois 60015; pop. 17,327.
Deerfield Beach town, SE Florida 33441; pop. 46,325.
Deer Park uninc. place, SE New York 11729; pop. 28,840.
Defiance city, NW Ohio 43512; pop. 16,768.
De Kalb city, N Illinois 60115; pop. 34,925.
Delaware state, E United States; 2,044 sq. mi.; pop. 668,696;

cap. Dover.
— city, CEN. Ohio 43015; pop. 20,030.
Delaware River river separating Pennsylvania and Delaware from New York and New Jersey; 315 mi. long.
Del City city, CEN. Oklahoma 73115; pop. 23,928.
Delhi terr., CEN. India; 573 sq. mi.; pop. 5,116,000; contains New Delhi.
— city; Delhi terr.; cap.; pop. 3,706,558.
Delray Beach city, SE Florida 33444; pop. 47,181.
Del Rio city, sw Texas 78840; pop. 30,705.
Denison city, N Texas 75020; pop. 21,505.
Denmark monarchy, NW Europe; 16,633 sq. mi.; pop. 5,139,000; cap. Copenhagen.
Denton city, N Texas 76201; pop. 66,270.
Denver city, CEN. Colorado 80202*; cap.; pop. 467,610.
Depew vill., w New York 14043; pop. 17,673.
Des Moines city, CEN. Iowa 50318*; cap.; pop. 193,187.
Des Plaines city, NE Illinois 60016*; pop. 53,223.
Detroit city, SE Michigan 48233*; pop. 1,027,974.
Devil's Island rocky isl. off the coast of French Guiana; formerly a penal colony.
District of Columbia federal dist., E United States; coextensive with Washington, the capital; pop. 606,900.
Dixon city, N Illinois 61021; pop. 15,144.
Djibouti republic, E Africa; 8,950 sq. mi.; pop. 530,000; cap. Djibouti.
Dnepropetrovsk city, sw Ukrainian SSR; pop. 1,083,000. Also Dnipropetrovsk.
Dnieper river, sw USSR; 1,420 mi. long. Also Dnepr.
Dniester river, sw USSR; 876 mi. long. Also Dnestr.
Dodecanese isl. group, Aegean Sea; a dept. of Greece; 1,036 sq. mi.; pop. 120,000; cap. Rhodes.
Dolomite Alps E div. of the Alps, N Italy.
Dolton vill., NE Illinois 60419; pop. 23,930.
Dominican Republic republic, E Hispaniola; 18,704 sq. mi.; pop. 7,170,000; cap. Santo Domingo.
Don river, sw RSFSR; 1,222 mi. long.
Donets river sw USSR; 631 mi. long.
Dorval city, s Quebec, Canada; pop. 19,131.
Dothan city, SE Alabama 36301*; 53,589.
Douai town, N France; pop. 45,239.
Dover municipal boro., SE England; pop. 34,160.
— city, CEN. Delaware 19901; cap.; pop. 27,630.
— city, SE New Hampshire 03820; pop. 25,042.
Dover, Strait of strait at the E end of the English Channel; 21 mi. wide.
Downers Grove vill., NE Illinois 60515; pop. 46,858.
Downey city, sw California 90241*; pop. 91,444.
Dracut town, NE Massachusetts 01826; pop. 25,594.
Drayton Plains city, SE Michigan 48020; pop. 18,000.
Dresden city, s Germany; pop. 514,508.
Drummondville city, s Quebec, Canada; pop. 29,286.
Dublin city, E Ireland; cap.; pop. 544,586.
— city, CEN. Georgia 31021; pop. 16,312.
Dubuque city, E Iowa 52001*; pop. 57,546.
Duisburg city, w Germany; pop. 559,066.
Duluth city, NE Minnesota 55806*; pop. 85,493.
Dumont boro., NE New Jersey 07628; pop. 17,187.
Duncan city, s Oklahoma 73533; pop. 21,732.
Dundalk uninc. place, CEN. Maryland 21222; pop. 65,800.
Dundas town, s Ontario, Canada; pop. 19,179.
Dundee burgh, E Scotland; pop. 190,793.
Dunedin city, w Florida 33528; pop. 34,012.
Dunkerque town, N France; scene of evacuation of British forces in World War II, May–June 1940; pop. 83,163.
Dunkirk city, w New York 14048; pop. 13,989.
Dunmore boro., NE Pennsylvania 18512; pop. 15,403.
Durban city, SE South Africa; pop. 634,301.
Durham city, CEN. North Carolina 27701*; pop. 131,611.
Düsseldorf city, w Germany; pop. 594,770.
Dutch Guiana See Surinam.
Eagle Pass city, sw Texas 78852; pop. 20,651.
East Berlin See Berlin.
Eastchester uninc. place, SE New York 10709; pop. 18,537.
East Chicago city, NW Indiana 46312*; pop. 33,892.
East China Sea NE part of the China Sea.
East Cleveland city, NE Ohio 44112; pop. 33,096.
East Detroit city, SE Michigan 48021; pop. 35,283.

Easter Island isl. of Chile, South Pacific; known for stone monuments found there; 45 sq. mi.

East Germany See **Germany.**

East Hartford town, CEN. Connecticut 06108; pop. 50,452.

East Haven town, s Connecticut 06512; pop. 26,144.

East Indies **1** The isls. of the Malay Archipelago. **2** SE Asia. **3** Formerly, India. Also **East India.**

Eastlake city, NE Ohio 44094; pop. 21,161.

East Lansing city, CEN. Michigan 48823*; pop. 50,677.

East Liverpool city, E Ohio 43920; pop. 13,654.

East Los Angeles uninc. place, SW California 90022; pop. 126,379.

East Meadow uninc. place, SE New York 11554; pop. 36,909.

East Millcreek uninc. place, NE Utah 84101; pop. 21,184.

East Moline city, NW Illinois 61244; pop. 20,147.

Easton city, s Pennsylvania 18042; pop. 26,276.

East Orange city, NE New Jersey 07019*; pop. 73,552.

East Peoria city, CEN. Illinois 61611; pop. 21,378.

East Point city, CEN. Georgia 30044; pop. 34,402.

East Providence town, E Rhode Island 02914; pop. 50,380.

East Prussia former prov. of Prussia, NE Germany.

East Ridge town, SE Tennessee 37412; pop. 21,101.

East Saint Louis city, SW Illinois 62201*; pop. 40,944.

Eau Claire city, CEN. Wisconsin 54703*; pop. 56,856.

Ecuador republic, NW South America; 103,930 sq. mi.; pop. 10,782,000; cap. Quito.

Eden city, CEN. North Carolina 27288; pop. 15,238.

Edina city, SE Minnesota 55424; pop. 46,070.

Edinburg city, s Texas 78539; pop. 29,885.

Edinburgh city, E Scotland; cap.; pop. 420,169.

Edmond city, CEN. Oklahoma 73034; pop. 52,315.

Edmonds city, NW Washington 98020; pop. 30,744.

Edmonton city, CEN. Alberta, Canada; cap.; pop. 573,982.

Egypt republic, NE Africa; 385,229 sq. mi.; pop. 53,170,000; cap. Cairo: official name **Arab Republic of Egypt.**

Eire the Irish Gaelic name of Ireland.

Elba isl. betw. Italy and Corsica; sovereign under the exiled Napolean Bonaparte, 1814N15.

Elbe river, CEN. Europe; 725 mi. long.

Elbrus, Mount mtn., NW Georgian SSR; 18,603 ft.

Elburz Mountains mtn. range N Iran.

El Cajon city, SW California 92020*; pop. 88,693.

El Centro city, s California 92243*; pop. 31,384.

El Cerrito city, W California 94530; pop. 4,490.

El Dorado city, s Arkansas 71730; pop. 23,146.

Elgin city, NE Illinois 60120; pop. 77,010.

Elizabeth city, NE New Jersey 07201*; pop. 110,002.

Elk Grove Village vill., NE Illinois 60007; pop. 33,429.

Elkhart city, N Indiana 46515*; pop. 43,627.

Ellis Island isl., upper New York Bay; former site of US immigration station, now a museum about immigration.

Elmhurst city, NE Illinois 60126; pop. 42,029.

Elmira city, s New York 14901*; pop. 33,724.

Elmont uninc. place, SE New York 11003; pop. 28,612.

El Monte city, SW California 91734*; pop. 106,209.

Elmwood Park vill., NE Illinois 60635; pop. 23,206.

El Paso city, W Texas 79940*; pop. 515,342.

El Salvador republic, W Central America; 8,124 sq. mi.; pop. 5,221,000; cap. San Salvador.

Elyria city, N Ohio 44035*; pop. 56,746.

Emporia city, CEN. Kansas 66801; pop. 25,512.

Enfield town, N Connecticut 06082; pop. 45,532.

England s part and largest political division of Great Britain; 50,363 sq. mi.; pop. 47,536,300; cap. London.

Englewood city, CEN. Colorado 80110; pop. 28,387.

— city, NE New Jersey 07631*; pop. 24,850.

English Channel strait, betw. England and France; 20–100 mi. wide.

Enid city, N Oklahoma 73701*; pop. 45,309.

Eniwetok atoll, Marshall Islands; U.S. nuclear weapons testing area.

Enterprise city, SE Alabama 36330*; pop. 20,123.

Epsom town, SE England; site of famous racecourse; pop. 72,000.

Equatorial Guinea republic, W Africa; 10,831 sq. mi.; pop. 350,000; cap. Malabo.

Erie city, NW Pennsylvania 16501*; pop. 108,718.

Erie, Lake southernmost of the Great Lakes; 9,940 sq. mi.

Erie Canal waterway betw. Albany and Buffalo, New York; integrated with New York State Barge Canal.

Eritrea state E Africa; federated with Ethiopia; 45,300 sq. mi.; pop. 2,704,000; cap. Asmara.

Erivan see YEREVAN.

Escondido city, SW California 92025*; pop. 108,635.

Essen city, W Germany; pop. 652,501.

Essex uninc. place, N Maryland 21221; pop. 40,872.

Estonia republic, E Europe; 17,400 sq. mi.; pop. 1,573,000; cap. Tallinn. Formerly **Estonian SSR.**

Ethiopia republic, E Africa; 472,400 sq. mi.; pop. 50,341,000; cap. Addis Ababa.

Etna, Mount volcano, E Sicily, Italy; 10,868 ft.

Euboea isl. of Greece in the Aegean; 1,457 sq. mi.

Euclid city, NE Ohio 44117; pop. 54,875.

Eugene city, W Oregon 97401*; pop. 112,669.

Euphrates river, SW Asia; 1,740 mi. long.

Eurasia large land mass comprising Europe and Asia.

Eureka city, NW California 95501*; pop. 27,025.

Europe continent comprising the W part of the Eurasian land mass; about 4,063,000 sq. mi.

Evanston city, NE Illinois 60204*; pop. 73,233.

Evansville city, SW Indiana 47708*; pop. 126,272.

Everest mtn., E Nepal; highest point of the earth's surface; 29,028 ft.

Everett city, E Massachusetts 02149; pop. 35,701.

— city, w Washington 98201*; pop. 69,961.

Everglades large swampy reg., s Florida.

Evergreen Park vill., NE Illinois 60642; pop. 20,874.

Exeter co. boro., CEN. Devonshire, England; cap; pop. 95,600.

Faeroe Islands isl. group of Denmark, North Atlantic; 540 sq. mi.; pop. 48,400; cap. Tórshavn.

Fairborn city, SW Ohio 45324; pop. 31,300.

Fairfax town, N Virginia 22030; pop. 19,622.

Fairfield city, CEN. California 94533; pop. 58,099.

— town, SW Connecticut 06430; pop. 53,418.

Fairhaven town, SE Massachusetts 02719; pop. 16,132.

Fair Lawn boro., NE New Jersey 07410; pop. 30,548.

Fairmont city, N West Virginia 26554*; pop. 20,210.

Fairview Park city, NE Ohio 44126; pop. 18,028.

Falkland Islands British col., South Atlantic; 4,618 sq. mi.; pop. 1,081; cap. Stanley.

Fall River city, SE Massachusetts 02722*; pop. 92,703.

Falls urb. twp., NE Pennsylvania 18615; pop. 36,083.

Falmouth town, E Massachusetts 02540; pop. 27,960.

Fargo city, SE North Dakota 58102*; pop. 74,111.

Faribault city, SE Minnesota 55021; pop. 17,085.

Farmers Branch city, N Texas 75234; pop. 24,250.

Farmington town, NW New Mexico 87401; pop. 33,997.

Fayetteville city, NW Arkansas 72701*; pop. 42,099.

— city, CEN. North Carolina 28302*; pop. 75,695.

Federal Republic of Germany See **Germany.**

Ferguson city, E Missouri 63135; pop. 22,286.

Ferndale city, SE Michigan 48220; pop. 25,084.

Fiji republic, South Pacific; comprises **Fiji Islands** (7,039 sq. mi.) and **Rotuma** (18 sq. mi.); pop. 740,000; cap. Suva.

Findlay city, CEN. Ohio 45840*; pop. 35,703.

Finland republic, N Europe; 130,559 sq. mi.; pop. 4,978,000; cap. Helsinki.

Finland, Gulf of part of the Baltic Sea betw. Finland and the USSR.

Fitchburg city, N Massachusetts 01420*; pop. 41,194.

Flagstaff city, CEN. Arizona 86001*; pop. 45,857.

Flanders reg., N France and s Belgium.

Flint city, CEN. Michigan 48502*; pop. 140,761.

Floral Park vill., SE New York 11001*; pop. 15,947.

Florence city, CEN. Tuscany, Italy; cap.; pop. 417,487.

— city, NW Alabama 35630*; pop. 36,426.

— city, E South Carolina 29501; pop. 29,813.

Florence-Graham uninc. place, SW California 90001; pop. 48,662.

Florida state, SE United States; 58,664 sq. mi.; pop. 13,003,362; cap. Tallahassee.

Florida Keys isl. group SW of Florida.

Florissant city, E Missouri 63033*; pop. 51,206.

Fond du Lac town, N Wisconsin 54935; pop. 37,757.

Fontainebleau town, N France; site of a former royal residence; pop. 16,778.

Fontana city, CEN. California 92335; pop. 87,535.
Forest Park town, CEN. Georgia 30050; pop. 16,925.
— vill., NE Illinois 60130; pop. 14,918.
— city, SW Ohio 45405; pop. 18,609.
Forestville uninc. place, SW Maryland 20747; pop. 16,731.
Formosa *a former name of* Taiwan.
Fort Benning South uninc. place, W Georgia 31905; pop. 15,074.
Fort Collins city, N Colorado 80521*; pop. 87,758.
Fort Dodge city, CEN. Iowa 50501; pop. 25,894.
Forth, Firth of estuary of the Forth River; 51 mi. long.
Forth River river, SE Scotland; 65 mi. long.
Fort Knox military reservation, N Kentucky 40120*; site of the Federal gold bullion depository.
Fort-Lamy *the former name of* N'Djamena.
Fort Lauderdale city, SE Florida 33301*; pop. 149,377.
Fort Lee boro., NE New Jersey 07024; pop. 31,997.
Fort Myers city, SW Florida 33920*; pop. 45,206.
Fort Pierce city, E Florida 33454*; pop. 36,830.
Fort Smith city, W Arkansas 72901*; pop. 72,798.
Fort Thomas city, N Kentucky 41075; pop. 16,032.
Fort Walton Beach city, NW Florida 32548; pop. 21,471.
Fort Wayne city, NE Indiana 46802*; pop. 173,072.
Fort Worth city, N Texas 76101*; pop. 447,619.
Fostoria city, N Ohio 44830; pop. 14,983.
Fountain Valley city, SW California 92708; pop. 53,691.
Framingham town, E Massachusetts 01701; pop. 64,994.
France republic, W Europe; 210,026 sq. mi.; pop. 56,647,000; cap. Paris.
Frankfort city, CEN. Kentucky 40601; cap.; pop. 25,968.
Frankfurt am Main city, CEN. Germany; pop. 628,203.
Frankfurt an der Oder city, E Germany; pop. 77,175.
Franklin town, E Massachusetts 02038; pop. 22,095.
Franklin Park vill., NE Illinois 60131; pop. 18,485.
Franklin Square uninc. place, SE New York 11010; pop. 28,205.
Frederick city, NW Maryland 21701; pop. 40,148.
Fredericton city, CEN. New Brunswick, Canada; pop. 45,248.
Freeport city, NW Bahamas, on Grand Bahama Island; pop. 25,423.
— city, N Illinois 61032; pop. 25,840.
— vill., SE New York 11520; pop. 39,894.
Fremont city, N California 94536; pop. 173,339.
— city, E Nebraska 68025; pop. 23,680.
— city, N Ohio 43420; pop. 17,648.
French Guiana French overseas dept. NE South America; 33,399 sq. mi.; pop. 117,000; cap. Cayenne.
French Polynesia French overseas terr., South Pacific; comprises the Society, Marquesas, Gambier, and other islands; 1,550 sq. mi.; pop. 197,000; cap. Papeete.
French West Indies isls. comprising Guadaloupe and Martinique.
Fresno city, CEN. California 93706*; pop. 354,202.
Fridley city, E Minnesota 55421; pop. 28,335.
Friesland prov., N Netherlands; 1,295 sq. mi.; pop. 597,600; cap. Leeuwarden.
Frigid Zone See **North Frigid Zone, South Frigid Zone.**
Frisian Islands isl. group, North Sea near Germany, Denmark, and the Netherlands.
Fuji extinct volcano, Honshu, Japan; 12,389 ft.
Fullerton city, SW California 92631*; pop. 114,144.
Fundy, Bay of inlet of the Atlantic betw. Nova Scotia and New Brunswick and NE Maine.
Fuzhou city, SE China; pop. 710,000.
Gabon republic, W equatorial Africa; 103,347 sq. mi.; pop. 1,171,000; cap. Libreville.
Gadsden city, NE Alabama 35901*; pop. 42,523.
Gainesville city, N Florida 32601*; pop. 84,770.
— city, CEN. Georgia 30501*; pop. 17,885.
Galápagos Islands isl. group of Ecuador, South Pacific.
Galesburg city, W Illinois 61401; pop. 33,530.
Galicia reg., SE Poland and NW Ukrainian SSR.
— reg., NW Spain.
Galilee reg., N Israel.
Galilee, Sea of freshwater lake; betw. NE Israel, SW Syria, and NW Jordan; 64 sq. mi.
Gallipoli Peninsula penin., NW Turkey.
Galveston city, SE Texas 77550*; pop. 59,070.

Gambia, Republic of the, republic, W Africa; 4,127 sq. mi.; pop. 860,000; cap. Banjul.
Ganges river, N India and Bangladesh, sacred to Hindus; 1,560 mi. long.
Gardena city, SW California 90247*; pop. 49,847.
Garden City city, SE Michigan 48135; pop. 31,846.
— vill., SE New York 11530; pop. 21,686.
Garden Grove city, SW California 92640*; pop. 143,050.
Gardner city, N Massachusetts 01440; pop. 20,125.
Garfield city, NE New Jersey 07026; pop. 26,727.
Garfield Heights city, NE Ohio 44125; pop. 31,739.
Garland city, N Texas 75040*; pop. 180,650.
Gary city, NW Indiana 46401*; pop. 116,646.
Gascony reg., SW France.
Gastonia city, SW North Carolina 28052*; pop. 54,732.
Gatineau town, SW Quebec, Canada; pop. 73,479.
Gaza city, SW Israel; the **Gaza Strip,** the surrounding area; pop. 356,261.
Gdańsk port city, N Poland: formerly, as **Danzig,** cap. of the territory of the Free City of Danzig; pop. 449,200.
Gdynia city, NW Poland; pop. 232,500.
Geneva city, SW Switzerland; pop. 389,000.
— city, CEN. New York 14456; pop. 14,143.
Geneva, Lake of lake, SW Switzerland; 224 sq. mi.
Genoa city, NW Italy; pop. 714,641.
Georgetown city, N Guyana; cap.; pop. 187,056.
Georgia state, SE United States; 58,910 sq. mi.; pop. 6,508,419.
Georgian SSR constituent republic, SW USSR; 26,900 sq. mi.; pop. 5,171,000; cap. Tbilisi.
German Democratic Republic See **Germany.**
Germany republic, CEN. Europe; divided 1949–90, into the **Federal Republic of Germany** (West Germany), cap. Bonn; and the **German Democratic Republic** (East Germany), cap. East Berlin. 137,820 sq. mi.; pop. 79,082,000; cap. Berlin.
Ghana republic W Africa; 92,098 sq. mi.; pop. 12,815,000; cap. Accra.
Ghent city, NW Belgium; pop. 241,695.
Gibraltar British col. on the Rock of Gibraltar; 2.25 sq. mi.; pop. 29,760.
Gibraltar, Rock of penin., s Spain; dominates the Strait of Gibraltar.
Gibraltar, Strait of strait, betw. Spain and Africa, W Mediterranean.
Gilbert Islands See **Kiribati.**
Glace Bay town, NE Nova Scotia, Canada; pop. 21,836.
Gladstone city, W Missouri 64118; pop. 26,243.
Glasgow burgh, SW Scotland; pop. 794,316.
Glastonbury city, CEN. Connecticut 06033; pop. 27,901.
Glen Burnie uninc. place, N Maryland 21061; pop. 37,305.
Glen Cove city, SE New York 11542; pop. 24,149.
Glendale city, CEN. Arizona 85301*; pop. 148,134.
— city, SW California 91209*; pop. 180,038.
Glendora city, SW California 91740; pop. 47,828.
Glen Ellyn vill., NE Illinois 60137*; pop. 24,944.
Glens Falls city, E New York 12801; pop. 15,023.
Glenview vill., NE Illinois 60025; pop. 37,093.
Gloucester co. boro., CEN. Gloucestershire, England; cap.; pop. 91,300.
— city, NE Massachusetts 01930*; pop. 28,716.
Gloversville city, CEN. New York 12078; pop. 16,656.
Goa former Portuguese terr., W India; annexed by India in 1961; 1,394 sq. mi., pop. 954,000; cap. New Goa.
Gobi Desert desert, CEN. Asia; 500,000 sq. mi.
Golden Gate strait betw. San Francisco Bay and the Pacific.
Golden Valley vill., SE Minnesota 55427; pop. 20,971.
Goldsboro city, CEN. North Carolina 27530; pop. 40,709.
Good Hope, Cape of promontory, SW South Africa.
Gorki city, CEN. RSFSR; pop. 1,358,000. Also **Gorkiy, Gorky.**
Goshen city, N Indiana 46526; pop. 23,797.
Göteborg city, SW Sweden; pop. 434,699.
Gotland isl. of SE Sweden, Baltic Sea; 1,167 sq. mi.
Granada city, s Spain; pop. 229,108.
Granby city, s Quebec, Canada; pop. 37,132.
Grand Banks submarine shoal, North Atlantic; near Newfoundland.
Grand Canyon gorge of the Colorado River, NW Arizona; ab.

250 mi. long.

Grand Forks uninc. place, E North Dakota 58201*; pop. 49,425.

Grand Island city, CEN. Nebraska 68801; pop. 39,386.

Grand Junction city, W Colorado; 81501*; pop. 29,034.

Grand' Mère city, CEN. Quebec, Canada; pop. 15,999.

Grand Prairie city, N Texas 75051*; pop. 99,616.

Grand Rapids city, W Michigan 49501*; pop. 189,126.

Grandview city, W Missouri 64030; pop. 24,967.

Granite City city, SW Illinois 62040; pop. 32,862.

Great Barrier Reef coral reef off the coast of Queensland, Australia.

Great Bend city, CEN. Kansas 67530; pop. 15,423.

Great Britain principal isl. of the United Kingdom; comprises England, Scotland, and Wales; 94,248 sq. mi.; pop. 56,518,000; cap. London.

Great Divide See **Continental Divide.**

Greater Antilles See **Antilles.**

Great Falls city, CEN. Montana 59401*; pop. 55,097.

Great Lakes chain of five lakes, CEN. North America; on Canada–United States border; comprises Lakes Superior, Michigan, Huron, Ontario, and Erie; total 94,710 sq. mi.

Great Plains plateau, W North America; E of the Rockies.

Great Russia CEN. and NW reg. of the USSR.

Great Salt Lake salt lake, NW Utah; ab. 2,000 sq. mi.

Great Slave Lake lake, S Northwest Territories, Canada; 11,170 sq. mi.

Great Smoky Mountains mtn. range, North Carolina and Tennessee.

Greece republic, SE Europe; 50,949 sq. mi.; pop. 10,038,000; cap. Athens.

Greeley city, N Colorado 80631*; pop. 60,536.

Green Bay city, E Wisconsin 54305*; pop. 96,466.

Greenbelt city, CEN. Maryland 20770; pop. 21,096.

Greendale vill., SE Wisconsin 53129; pop. 15,128.

Greenfield uninc. place, NW Massachusetts 01301*; pop. 18,666.

— town, SE Wisconsin 53220; pop. 33,403.

Greenfield Park town, S Quebec, Canada; pop. 18,430.

Greenland isl. territory of Denmark near NE North America; 840,000 sq. mi.; pop. 55,900.

Green Mountains mtn. range, CEN. Vermont.

Greensboro city, CEN. North Carolina 27420*; pop. 183,521.

Greensburg city, SW Pennsylvania 15601*; pop. 16,318.

Greenville city, W Mississippi 38701*; pop. 45,226.

— city, E North Carolina 27834*; pop. 44,972.

— city, NW South Carolina 29602*; pop. 58,282.

— city, NE Texas 75401; pop. 23,071.

Greenwich boro., SE London; former site of the Royal Observatory; location of prime meridian; pop. 218,000.

— town, SW Connecticut 06830*; pop. 58,441.

Greenwood city, CEN. Mississippi 38930; pop. 18,906.

— city, W South Carolina 29646*; pop. 20,807.

Grenada republic in the West Indies; 133 sq. mi.; pop. 101,000; cap. St. George's.

Gretna city, SE Louisiana 70053; pop. 17,208.

Griffin city, CEN. Georgia 30223; pop. 21,347.

Griffith town, NW Indiana 46319; pop. 17,916.

Grimsby town, S Ontario, Canada; pop. 15,567.

Grosse Pointe city, SE Michigan 48236; pop. 17,715.

Groves city, SE Texas 77619; pop. 16,513.

Guadalajara city, CEN. Mexico; pop. 1,813,100.

Guadalcanal isl., British Solomons; scene of an Allied invasion in World War II, 1943.

Guadeloupe French overseas dept., Lesser Antilles; 687 sq. mi.; pop. 380,000; cap. Basse-Terre.

Guam uninc. terr. of the United States, an isl. in the Marianas; 209 sq. mi. pop. 134,000; cap. Agaña.

Guantánamo city, SE Cuba, near, **Guantánamo Bay;** pop. 155,217.

Guatemala republic, N Central America; 42,042 sq. mi.; pop. 9,197,000.

— **City,** CEN. Guatemala; cap.; pop. 1,057,210.

Guayama town, SE Puerto Rico 00654; pop. 21,044.

Guayaquil city, W Ecuador; pop. 1,022,010.

Guelph city, S Ontario, Canada; pop. 67,538.

Guernica town, N Spain; object of a German bombing, 1937; pop. 11,704.

Guernsey one of the Channel Islands; 25 sq. mi.

Guiana coastal reg., NE South America. See **British Guiana, French Guiana, Guyana, Surinam.**

Guinea republic, W Africa; 94,900 sq. mi.; pop. 5,429,000; cap. Conakry.

Guinea, Gulf of large bay of the Atlantic off W Africa.

Guinea-Bissau republic, W Africa; 13,948 sq. mi.; pop. 973,000; cap. Bissau.

Gulfport city, SE Mississippi 39501*; pop. 40,775.

Gulf Stream A warm ocean current flowing from the Gulf of Mexico northeastward toward Europe.

Guyana republic, NE South America, 83,044 sq. mi.; pop. 756,000; cap. Georgetown.

Harlem city, W Netherlands; pop. 158,291.

Hackensack city, NE New Jersey 07602*; pop. 37,049.

Haddonfield city, SW New Jersey 08033; pop. 11,628.

Hagerstown city, W Maryland 21740; pop. 35,445.

Hague, The city, W Netherlands; seat of government; pop. 443,845. Also **s'Gravenhage.**

Haifa city, NW Israel; pop. 229,300.

Haiti republic, W Hispaniola; 10,579 sq. mi.; pop. 5,862,000; cap. Port-au-Prince.

Halifax city, S Nova Scotia; Canada; cap.; pop. 117,882.

Hallandale city, SE Florida 33009; pop. 30,996.

Halle city, SW Germany; pop. 232,543.

Haltom City vill., N Texas 76117; pop. 32,856.

Hamburg state and city, N Germany; 288 sq. mi.; pop. 1,653,043.

Hamden town, S Connecticut 06514; pop. 52,434.

Hamilton city, CEN. Bermuda; cap.; pop. 2,060.

— city, SW Ohio 45012*; pop. 61,368.

— city, S Ontario, Canada; pop. 312,003.

Hammond city, NW Indiana 46320*; pop. 84,236.

Hampton city, SE Virginia 23660*; pop. 133,793.

Hampton Roads channel, SE Virginia; connects several rivers with Chesapeake Bay; scene of the engagement of the "Monitor" and the "Merrimack," 1862.

Hamtramck city, SE Michigan 48212; pop. 18,372.

Hanford city, CEN. California 93230*; pop. 30,897.

Hangzhou city, E China; pop. 933,000.

Hannibal city, NE Missouri 63401*; pop. 18,004.

Hannover city, CEN. Germany; pop. 535,834.

Hanoi city, CEN. Vietnam; cap; pop. 1,600,000.

Harbin city, NE China; pop. 2,094,000.

Harlingen city, S Texas 78551*; pop. 48,735.

Harper Woods city, SE Michigan 48236; pop. 14,903.

Harrisburg city, CEN. Pennsylvania 17105*; cap; pop. 52,376.

Hartford city, CEN. Connecticut 06101*; cap.; pop. 139,739.

Harvey city, NE Illinois 60426; pop. 29,771.

Hastings city, S Nebraska 68901; pop. 22,837.

Hattiesburg city, SE Mississippi 39401*; pop. 41,882.

Havana city, W Cuba; cap.; pop. 1,961,674.

Haverford urb. twp., SE Pennsylvania 19083; pop. 52,371.

Haverhill city, NE Massachusetts 01831*; pop. 51,418.

Hawaii state of the United States, North Pacific; coextensive with the Hawaiian Islands; 6,471 sq. mi.; pop. 1,115,274; cap. Honolulu.

— largest of the Hawaiian Islands; 4,020 sq. mi.

Hawthorne city, SW California 90250; pop. 71,349.

— boro., NE New Jersey 07007; pop. 17,084.

Hays city, CEN. Kansas 67601; pop. 17,767.

Hayward city, W California 94544*; pop. 111,498.

Hazel Park city, SE Michigan 48030; pop. 20,051.

Hazleton city, E Pennsylvania 18201; pop. 24,730.

Hebrides isl. group off W coast of Scotland, ab. 3,000 sq. mi.

Heidelberg city, SW Germany; pop. 128,773.

Hejaz div., W Saudi Arabia; 150,000 sq. mi.; pop. 1,754,000; cap. Mecca.

Helena city, CEN. Montana 59601*; cap.; pop. 24,569.

Helicon mtn. range, CEN. Greece.

Helsinki city, S Finland; cap.; pop. 490,693.

Hempstead vill., SE New York 11551*; pop. 49,453.

Henderson city, NW Kentucky 42420; pop. 25,945.

— city, S Nevada 89015*; pop. 69,942.

Hermosa Beach city, SW California 90254; pop. 18,219.

Herzegovina See **Bosnia and Herzegovina.**

Hesse state, W Germany; 8,152 sq. mi.; pop. 5,576,085; cap. Wiesbaden.

Hialeah city, SE Florida 33010*; site of a famous racetrack; pop. 188,004.

Hibbing vill., NE Minnesota 55746; pop. 18,046.

Hickory city, CEN. North Carolina 28601*; pop. 28,301.

Hicksville uninc. place, SE New York 11802*; pop. 40,174.

Highland town, NW Indiana 46322; pop. 23,696.

Highland Park city, NE Illinois 60035*; pop. 30,575.

— city, SE Michigan 48203; pop. 20,121.

High Point city, CEN. North Carolina 27260*; pop. 69,496.

Hillcrest Heights city, S Maryland; pop. 17,136.

Hillside urb. twp., NE New Jersey 07205; pop. 21,044.

Hilo city, E Hawaii island, Hawaii 96720; pop. 37,808.

Himalayas mtn. range. CEN. Asia.

Hindustan 1 loosely, the reg. of the Ganges where Hindi is spoken. 2 loosely, India.

Hingham town, E Massachusetts 02043; pop. 19,821.

Hinsdale vill., NE Illinois 60521*; pop. 16,029.

Hiroshima city, SW Honshu isl., Japan; devastated by the first atom bomb used in war, Aug. 6, 1945; pop. 899,394.

Hispaniola isl., West Indies; ab. 30,000 sq. mi.; divided into Haiti and the Dominican Republic.

Hobart city, SE Tasmania, Australia; cap; pop. 170,200.

— city, NW Indiana 46342; pop. 21,822.

Hobbs city, SE New Mexico 88240; pop. 29,115.

Hoboken city, NE New Jersey 07030; pop. 33,397.

Ho Chi Minh City See Saigon.

Hoffman Estates city, NE Illinois 60172; pop. 46,561.

Hokkaido isl. of N Japan; ab. 29,000 sq. mi.

Holladay uninc. place, NW Utah 84117; pop. 22,189.

Holland See **Netherlands.**

— city, SW Michigan 49423*; pop. 30,745.

Hollywood area, NW Los Angeles, California; ctr. of US motion-picture industry.

— city, SE Florida 33022*; pop. 121,697.

Holyoke city, CEN. Massachusetts 01040*; pop. 43,704.

Homewood city, CEN. Alabama 35209; pop. 22,922.

— vill., NE Illinois 60430; pop. 19,278.

Honduras republic, NE Central America; 43,277 sq. mi.; pop. 4,674,000; cap. Tegucigalpa.

Hong Kong British col., SE China; includes **Hong Kong Island**; 415 sq. mi.; pop. 5,841,000; cap. Victoria.

Honolulu city, SE Oahu, Hawaii 96815*; cap.; pop. 365,272.

Honshu isl. of GEN. Japan; 88,745 sq. mi.

Hood, Mount volcanic peak, Cascade Range, NW Oregon 11,245 ft.

Hoover Dam dam, Colorado River at the Arizona–Nevada border; 727 ft. high; 1,282 ft. long.

Hopewell city, SE Virginia 23860; pop. 23,101.

Hopkinsville city, SW Kentucky 42240; pop. 29,809.

Horn, Cape S extremity of South America.

Hot Springs city, CEN. Arkansas 71901; pop. 32,462.

Houma city, SE Louisiana 70360*; pop. 30,495.

Houston city, SE Texas 77013*; pop. 1,630,533.

Huber Heights city, SW Ohio 45424; pop. 38,696.

Hudson Center uninc. place, CEN. Massachusetts 01749; pop. 14,247.

Hudson Bay inland sea, N Canada; connected with the Atlantic by **Hudson Strait;** ab. 475,000 sq. mi.

Hudson River river, E New York; 306 mi. long.

Hull city, SW Quebec, Canada; pop. 61,039.

Hungary republic, CEN. Europe; 35,920 sq. mi.; pop. 10,437,000; cap. Budapest.

Huntington city, NE Indiana 46750; pop. 16,389.

— city, W West Virginia 25701*; pop. 54,844.

Huntington Beach city, SW California 92647*; pop. 181,519.

Huntington Park city, SW California 90255*; pop. 56,065.

Huntington Station uninc. place, SE New York 11746*; pop. 28,247.

Huntsville city, N Alabama 35804*; pop. 159,789.

— city, E Texas 77340*; pop. 27,925.

Huron, Lake one of the Great Lakes; betw. Michigan and Ontario; 23,010 sq. mi.

Hurst city, N Texas 76053; pop. 33,574.

Hutchinson city, CEN. Kansas 67501; pop. 39,308.

Hwang Ho river, N China; 2,900 mi. long.

Hyde Park public park, London, England.

Hyderabad city, CEN. India; pop. 1,607,396.

— city, SE Pakistan; pop. 600,796.

Iberia part of SW Europe containing Spain and Portugal.

Iceland isl. republic, North Atlantic; 39,699 sq. mi.; pop. 256,000; cap. Reykjavik.

Idaho state, NW United States; 83,564 sq. mi.; pop. 1,011,986; cap. Boise.

Idaho Falls city, SE Idaho 83402*; pop. 43,929.

Ijssel, Lake freshwater lake, CEN. Netherlands.

Illinois state, CEN. United States; 56,345 sq. mi.; pop. 11,466,682; cap. Springfield.

Imperial Beach city, SW California 92032; pop. 25,512.

Imperial Valley agricultural reg., SE California.

Independence city, W Missouri 64051*; pop. 112,301.

India republic, S Asia; 1,222,559 sq. mi.; pop. 853,373,000; cap. New Delhi.

Indiana state, CEN. United States; 36,185 sq. mi.; pop. 5,564,228; cap. Indianapolis.

— boro., CEN. Pennsylvania 15701; pop. 15,174.

Indianapolis city, CEN. Indiana 46206*; cap.; pop. 741,952.

Indian Ocean ocean betw. Africa, Asia, Australia, and Antarctica.

Indies See **East Indies, West Indies.**

Indochina 1 SE penin. of Asia. 2 Cambodia, Laos, Vietnam.

Indonesia republic, SE Asia; comprises over 100 isls. of the Malay Archipelago; 752,409 sq. mi.; pop. 180,763,000; cap. Jakarta.

Indus river, Tibet, Kashmir, and Pakistan; 1,800 mi. long.

Inglewood city, SW California 90306*; pop. 109,602.

Inkster vill. SE Michigan 48141; pop. 30,772.

Ionian Sea part of the Mediterranean betw. Greece and Sicily.

Iowa state, CEN. United States; 56,275 sq. mi.; pop. 2,787,424; cap. Des. Moines.

Iowa City city, E Iowa 52240*; pop. 59,738.

Iraklion city, N CEN. Crete; pop. 78,000. Also **Candia, Heraklion.**

Iran republic, SW Asia; ab. 636,372 sq. mi.; pop. 56,293,000; cap. Tehran.

Iraq republic, SW Asia; 169,975 sq. mi.; pop. 17,754,000; cap. Baghdad.

Ireland westernmost of the British Isles; 31,838 sq. mi.

— republic, S Ireland; 27,137 sq. mi.; pop. 3,614,000; cap. Dublin. See also **Northern Ireland.**

Irish Sea part of the Atlantic betw. Great Britain and Ireland.

Irkutsk city, S USSR; pop. 561,000.

Irondequoit uninc. place, W New York 14617; pop. 52,322.

Irrawaddy river, Tibet and Myanmar; 1,200 mi. long.

Irving city, N Texas 75061*; pop. 155,037.

Irvington town, NE New Jersey 07111; pop. 59,774.

Islamabad city, NE Pakistan; cap.; pop. 204,364.

Israel republic, E end of the Mediterranean; 7,992 sq. mi.; pop. 4,666,000; cap. Jerusalem.

Istanbul city, NE Turkey; pop. 6,748,435.

Italy republic, S Europe; 116,324 sq. mi.; pop. 57,512,000; cap. Rome.

Ithaca isl. of Greece, Ionian Sea; 36 sq. mi.

— city, CEN. New York 14850; pop. 29,541.

Ivory Coast (Côte d'Ivoire) republic, W Africa; 123,847 sq. mi.; pop. 12,657,000; cap. Abidjan.

Izmir city, W Turkey; pop. 1,762,849. Also **Smyrna.**

Jackson city, S Michigan 49201*; pop. 37,446.

— city, CEN. Mississippi 39205*; cap.; pop. 196,637.

— city, W Tennessee 38301*; pop. 48,949.

Jacksonville city, CEN. Arkansas 72076*; pop. 29,101.

— city, NE Florida 32201*; pop. 672,971.

— city, CEN. Illinois 62650*; pop. 19,324.

— city, E North Carolina 28540*; pop. 30,013.

Jakarta city, NW Java; cap. of Indonesia; pop. 7,829,000.

Jamaica isl. monarchy of the Greater Antilles; 4,244 sq. mi.; pop. 2,391,000; cap. Kingston.

Jamestown town, NW St. Helena; cap.; pop. 1,516.

— city, SW New York 14701; pop. 34,681.

— city, CEN. North Dakota 58401; pop. 15,571.

— restored vill., E Virginia 23081; site of the first English settlement in the present limits of the United States, 1607.

Jammu and Kashmir state, N India; subject of a territorial dispute with Pakistan; 85,806 sq. mi.; pop. 5,120,000; caps. Sringar and Jammu.

Janesville city, S Wisconsin 53545*; pop. 52,133.

Japan constitutional monarchy; E Asia; situated on a chain of

isls.; 145,862 sq. mi.; pop. 123,692,000; cap. Tokyo.
Japan, Sea of part of the Pacific betw. Japan and the Asian mainland.
Java isl. of Indonesia; SE of Sumatra; 48,842 sq. mi.
Jefferson uninc. place, NE Virginia 22042; pop. 25,782.
Jefferson City city, CEN. Missouri 65101*; cap.; pop. 35,481.
Jefferson uninc. place, SE Louisiana 70121; pop. 14,521.
Jeffersonville city, SE Indiana 47130*; pop. 21,220.
Jennings city, E Missouri 63136; pop. 15,905.
Jericho vill., W Jordan; on the site of the ancient city.
Jersey one of the Channel Islands; 45 sq. mi.
Jersey City city, NE New Jersey 07303*; pop. 228,537.
Jerusalem city, E Israel; cap., pop. 493,500.
Jidda city, W Saudi Arabia; pop. 561,104.
Johannesburg city, NE South Africa; cap.; pop. 632,369.
Johnson City vill., S New York 13790; pop. 16,890.
— city, NE Tennessee 37601; pop. 49,381.
Johnstown city, CEN. Pennsylvania 15901*; pop. 28,134.
Joliet city, NE Illinois 60431*; pop. 76,836.
Joliette city, S Quebec, Canada; pop. 18,118.
Jonesboro city, NE Arkansas 72401; pop. 46,535.
Jonquière city, CEN. Quebec, Canada; pop. 60,691.
Joplin city, SW Missouri 64801*; pop. 40,961.
Jordan constitutional monarchy, W Asia; 34,443 sq. mi.; pop. 3,169,000; cap. Amman.
Jordan River river, CEN. Palestine; more than 200 mi. long.
Junction City city, CEN. Kansas 66441; pop. 20,604.
Juneau city, SE Alaska 99801; cap.; pop. 26,751.
Jungfrau mtn. peak, CEN. Switzerland; 13,653 ft.
Jura Mountains mtn. range, E France and W Switzerland.
Jutland penin., N Europe; comprises continental Denmark and part of Germany.
Kabul city, CEN. Afghanistan; cap.; pop. 1,424,400.
Kailua uninc. place, E Oahu, Hawaii 96734*; pop. 36,818.
Kalamazoo city, SW Michigan 49001*; pop. 80,277.
Kalimantan *the Indonesian name of* Borneo.
Kaliningrad city, extreme W USSR; pop. 361,000.
Kamchatka penin, E USSR, betw. The Bering and Okhotsk Seas.
Kampuchea, Roat (Cambodia) republic, SW Indochina peninsula, formerly **Khmer Republic**; 69,698 sq. mi.; pop. 8,592,000; cap. Phnom Penh.
Kaneohe uninc. place, E Oahu, Hawaii 96744; pop. 35,448.
Kankakee city, NE Illinois 60901; pop. 27,575.
Kannapolis uninc. place, CEN. North Carolina 28081; pop. 29,696.
Kansas state, CEN. United States; 82,277 sq. mi.; pop. 2,485,600; cap. Topeka.
Kansas City city, NE Kansas 66110*; pop. 149,767.
— city, W Missouri 64108*; pop. 435,146.
Karachi city, S Pakistan; former cap.; pop. 5,208,132.
Karelian ASSR adm. div., NW RSFSR; 66,560 sq. mi.; pop. 711,000; cap. Petrozavodsk.
Karnak vill., S Egypt; near the site of ancient Thebes.
Kashmir See **Jammu and Kashmir.**
Kathmandu city, CEN. Nepal; cap.; pop. 150,402.
Kauai one of the Hawaiian Islands; 551 sq. mi.
Kaunas city, CEN. Lithuanian SSR; pop. 377,000.
Kazakh SSR constituent republic, CEN. USSR; 1,049,200 sq. mi.; pop. 15,654,000; cap. Alma-Ata.
Kazan city, NW Tatar ASSR; cap.; pop. 1,002,000.
Kearney city, CEN. Nebraska 68847; pop. 24,396.
Kearns uninc. place, N Utah 84118; pop. 28,374.
Kearny town, NE New Jersey 07032; pop. 34,874.
Keene city, SW New Hampshire 03431; pop. 22,430.
Kelowna city, S British Columbia, Canada; pop. 51,955.
Kendall uninc. place, SE Florida 33156; pop. 87,271.
Kenmore vill., W New York 14217; pop. 17,180.
Kennedy, Cape *the former name of* Cape Canaveral.
Kenner city, SE Louisiana 70062; pop. 72,033.
Kennewick city, S Washington 99336; pop. 42,155.
Kenosha city, SE Wisconsin 53141*; pop. 80,352.
Kent city, NE Ohio 44240*; pop. 28,835.
— city, CEN. Washington 98031; pop. 37,960.
Kentucky state, CEN. United States; 40,409 sq. mi.; pop. 3,698,969; cap. Frankfort.
Kentucky River river, N Kentucky; 259 mi. long.
Kentwood city, SW Michigan 49508; pop. 37,826.

Kenya republic, E Africa; 224,961 sq. mi.; pop. 24,872,000; cap. Nairobi.
Kenya, Mount extinct volcano, CEN. Kenya; 17,058 ft.
Kettering city, SW Ohio 45429; pop. 60,569.
Key West southwesternmost of the Florida Keys.
— city, Key West Island, Florida 33040; pop. 24,832.
Kharkov city, NE Ukrainian SSR; pop. 1,464,000.
Khartoum city, CEN. Sudan; cap.; pop. 790,000.
Khmer Republic *the former name of* Cambodia.
Khyber Pass mtn. pass betw. Afghanistan and Pakistan; ab. 30 mi. long.
Kiel city, N Germany; pop. 250,750.
Kiel Canal ship canal betw. Kiel and the mouth of the Elbe; ab. 61 mi. long.
Kiev city, CEN. Ukrainian SSR; cap.; pop. 2,192,000.
Kilauea active crater, Mauna Loa volcano, Hawaii.
Kilimanjaro, Mount mtn., NE Tanzania; highest in Africa; 19,565 ft.
Killeen city, CEN. Texas 76540*; pop. 63,535.
Kimberley city, CEN. South Africa; pop. 105,258.
Kings borough Brooklyn, SE New York City, New York 11200*; pop. 2,300,664.
Kingsport city, NE Tennessee 37662*; pop. 36,365.
Kingston city, SE Jamaica; cap.; pop. 524,638.
— city, SE New York 12401; pop. 23,095.
— boro., CEN. Pennsylvania 18704; pop. 14,507.
— city, SE Ontario, Canada; pop. 56,032.
Kingsville city, S Texas 78363*; pop. 25,276.
Kinshasa city, W Zaire; cap.; pop. 3,562,122.
Kinston city, CEN. North Carolina 28501; pop. 25,295.
Kirghiz SSR constituent republic, S USSR; 76,600; sq. mi.; pop. 3,875,000; cap. Frunze.
Kiribati, republic including 3 isl. groups SW Pacific, comprising the Gilbert, Line, Phoenix Islands, and Banaba Island; 328 sq. mi.; pop. 71,000; cap. Bairiki.
Kirkland city, CEN. Washington 98033; pop. 40,052.
Kirksville city, N Missouri 63501; pop. 17,152.
Kirkwood city, E Missouri 63122; pop. 27,291.
Kitchener city, S Ontario, Canada; pop. 131,870.
Kitty Hawk vill., NE North Carolina; site of the first sustained airplane flight, by Wilbur and Orville Wright, 1903.
Klamath Falls city, S Oregon 97601*; pop. 17,737.
Klondike reg., NW Canada in the basin of the **Klondike River.**
Knoxville city, E Tennessee 37901*; pop. 165,121.
Kobe city, S Japan; pop. 1,367,392.
Kodiak Island isl., S Alaska; pop. 6,365.
Kokomo city, CEN. Indiana 46902*; pop. 44,962.
Kolonia city, cap. Micronesia; pop. 6,000.
Königsberg *the former German name of* Kaliningrad.
Korea penin., E Asia; 85,509 sq. mi.; divided into the **Democratic People's Republic of Korea** (North Korea) single-party republic; 47,250 sq. mi.; pop. 22,937,000; cap. Pyongyang; and the **Republic of Korea** (South Korea) multi-party republic; 38,259 sq. mi.; pop. 42,793,000; cap. Seoul.
Korea Strait strait, betw. the Sea of Japan and the East China Sea.
Kozhikode city, S India; pop. 333,979. Also **Calicut.**
Krakatoa isl. volcano betw. Sumatra and Java, Indonesia; site of most violent volcanic eruption of modern times, 1883.
Kraków city, S Poland; pop. 743,700.
Krasnodar city, SW USSR; pop. 620,000.
Kronshtadt city, W USSR; pop. 39,477.
Kuala Lumpur city, CEN. Malaysia; cap.; pop. 1,103,200.
Kunming city, SW China; pop. 1,085,100.
Kurdistan reg., NW Iran, NE Iraq, and SE Turkey; peopled largely by Kurds.
Kure city, SW Japan; pop. 234,550.
Kurile Island isl. group, SE USSR; 5,700 sq. mi.
Kuwait monarchy, NE Arabia; 6,880 sq. mi.; pop. 2,143,000.
— City, E Kuwait; cap.; pop. 44,224.
Kyoto city, SW Japan; pop. 1,470,564.
Kyushu isl., S Japan; 16,247 sq. mi.; pop. 1,034,328.
Labrador terr., Newfoundland, Canada; ab. 110,000 sq. mi.; pop. 21,157.
— the penin. of North America betw. the St. Lawrence River and Hudson Bay.
La Canada-Flintridge uninc. place, SW California 91011; pop. 19,378.

Lachine city, s Quebec, Canada; pop. 41,503.
Lackawanna city, w New York 14218; pop. 20,585.
La Crosse city, w Wisconsin 54601*; pop. 51,003.
Ladoga, Lake lake, nw RSFSR; 7,100 sq. mi.
Lafayette uninc. place, w California 94549; pop. 23,501.
— city, cen. Indiana 47901*; pop. 43,764.
— city, s Louisiana 70509*; pop. 94,440.
Lagos city, sw Nigeria; cap.; pop. 1,274,000.
La Grange city, w Georgia 30240; pop. 25,597.
— vill., ne Illinois 60525; pop. 15,362.
La Habra city, sw California 90631*; pop. 51,266.
Lahore city, e Pakistan; pop. 2,952,689.
Lake Charles city, sw Louisiana 70601*; pop. 70,580.
Lake District reg., nw England; contains 15 lakes.
Lake Forest city, ne Illinois 60045; pop. 17,836.
Lakeland city, cen. Florida 33082*; pop. 70,576.
Lakewood city, sw California 90714*; pop. 73,557.
— city, cen. Colorado 80215; pop. 126,481.
— uninc. place, e New Jersey 08701; pop. 26,095.
— city, n Ohio 44107, pop. 59,718.
Lake Worth city, se Florida 33460; pop. 28,564.
La Marque city, se Texas 77568; pop. 14,120.
La Mesa city, sw California 92041*; pop. 52,931.
La Mirada city, sw California 90638; pop. 40,452.
Lancaster city, sw California 93534*; pop. 97,291.
— city, cen. Ohio 43130; pop. 34,507.
— city, se Pennsylvania 17604*; pop. 55,551.
Lanzhou city, nw China; pop. 1,151,700.
Lansdale boro., se Pennsylvania 19446; pop. 16,362.
Lansdowne–Baltimore Highlands uninc. place, cen. Mary-
land 21227; pop. 15,509.
Lansing vill., ne Illinois 60438; pop. 28,086.
— city, cen. Michigan 48924*; cap.; pop. 127,321.
Laos republic, nw Indochina; 91,430 sq. mi.; pop. 4,024,000.
La Paz city, w Bolivia; admin. cap.; pop. 1,049,800.
Lapland reg., n Norway, Sweden, and Finland, and the ne
USSR; inhabited by Lapps.
La Plata city, e Argentina; pop. 454,884.
LaPorte city, nw Indiana 46350; pop. 21,507.
La Puente city, sw California 91747*; pop. 36,955.
Laramie city, se Wyoming 82070; pop. 26,687.
Laredo city, s Texas 78040*; pop. 122,899.
Largo city, w Florida 33540*; pop. 65,674.
La Salle city, s Quebec, Canada; pop. 76,713.
Las Cruces city, s New Mexico 88001*; pop. 62,126.
Las Vegas city, se Nevada 89114*; pop. 258,295.
Latvia republic, ne Europe; 24,900 sq. mi.; pop. 2,680,000;
cap. Riga. Formerly Latvian SSR.
Laurel city, se Mississippi 39440*; pop. 18,827.
Lurentian Mountains mtn. range, e Canada.
Lausanne city, w Switzerland; pop. 128,800.
Laval town, s Quebec, Canada; pop. 284,164.
Lawndale city, sw California 90260; pop. 27,331.
Lawrence town, cen. Indiana 46226; pop. 26,763.
— city, e Kansas 66044*; pop. 65,608.
— city, ne Massachusetts 08142*; pop. 70,207.
Lawton city, sw Oklahoma 73501*; pop. 80,561.
Leavenworth city, ne Kansas 66048; pop. 38,495.
Lebanon republic, sw Asia; 3,950 sq. mi.; pop. 2,965,000;
cap. Beirut.
— city, se Pennsylvania 17042; pop. 24,800.
Leeds city and co. boro., cen. England; pop. 451,845.
Lee's Summit city, w Missouri 64063; pop. 46,418.
Leeward Islands n isl. group, Lesser Antilles.
Leghorn city, nw Italy; pop. 176,757. Also Livorno.
Le Havre city, n France; pop. 196,000.
Leicester co. boro., cen. England; pop. 328,835.
Leiden city, w Netherlands; pop. 109,254.
Leipzig city, cen. Germany; pop. 545,307.
Lemon Grove city, sw California 92045; pop. 23,984.
Leningrad city, nw RSFSR; pop. 4,456,000; also called St.
Petersburg.
Leominster city, cen. Massachusetts 01453; pop. 38,145.
Leopoldville the former name of Kinshasa.
Lesbos isl. of Greece off nw Turkey; 623 sq. mi.
Lesotho independent member of the Commonwealth of Nations;
enclave in e South Africa; 11,720 sq. mi.; pop. 1,760,000;
cap. Maseru.

Lesser Antilles See Antilles.
Lethbridge city, s Alberta, Canada; pop. 46,752.
Lévis city, s Quebec, Canada; pop. 17,819.
Levittown uninc. place, se New York 11756; pop. 53,286.
Lewiston city, w Idaho 83501; pop. 28,082.
— city, sw Maine 04240; pop. 39,757.
Lexington city, cen. Kentucky 40511*; pop. 204,165.
— town, ne Massachusetts 02173; pop. 28,974.
— city, cen. North Carolina 27292; pop. 16,581.
Leyden See Leiden.
Leyte isl., e Philippines, 2,875 sq. mi.
Lhasa city, s Tibet, cap.; pop. 80,000.
Liberia republic, w Africa; 38,250 sq. mi.; pop. 2,595,000;
cap. Monrovia.
Libreville city, w Gabon; cap.; pop. 352,000.
Libya socialist state, n Africa; 685,524 sq. mi.; pop.
4,206,000; cap. Tripoli.
Liechtenstein monarchy, cen. Europe; 62 sq. mi.; pop. 28,000;
cap. Vaduz.
Liège city, e Belgium pop. 196,825.
Lille city, n France; pop. 167,791.
Lilongwe city, cen. Malawi; cap.; pop. 220,300.
Lima city, w Peru; cap.; pop. 5,659,200.
— city, w Ohio; 45802*; pop. 45,549.
Limerick co. boro., w Ireland; pop. 60,665.
Limoges city, cen. France; pop. 133,000.
Lincoln city, cen. Illinois 62656; pop. 15,418.
— city, se Nebraska 68501*; cap.; pop. 191,972.
Lincoln Park city, se Michigan 48146; pop. 41,832.
Linden city, ne New Jersey36,701; pop. 37,836.
Lindenhurst vill., se New York 11757; pop. 26,879.
Lisbon city, w Portugal; cap; pop. 829,600.
Lithuania republic, e Europe; 25,200 sq. mi.; pop. 3,690,000;
cap. Vilnius. Formerly Lithuanian SSR.
Little Rock city, cen. Arkansas 72201*; cap.; pop. 175,795.
Littleton town, cen. Colorado 80120*; pop. 33,685.
Livermore city, w California 94550*; pop. 56,741.
Liverpool co. boro., w England; pop. 544,861.
Livingston urb. twp., ne New Jersey 07039; pop. 26,609.
Livonia city, se Michigan 48150*; pop. 100,850.
Lockport city, nw New York 14094; pop. 24,426.
Lodi city, cen. California 95240*; pop. 51,874.
— boro., ne New Jersey 07644; pop. 22,355.
Lódz city, cen. Poland; pop. 851,500.
Logan city, n Utah 84321; pop. 32,764.
Logan, Mount peak, sw Yukon Territory, Canada; 19,850 ft.
Logansport city, cen. Indiana 46947; pop. 17,731.
Loire river, se France; 620 mi. long.
Lombard vill., ne Illinois 60148; pop. 39,408.
Lomé city, s Togo; cap.; pop. 366,476.
Lomita city, sw California 90717; pop. 19,382.
Lompoc city, sw California 93436*; pop. 37,649.
London city and co., se England; cap.; 1 sq. mil.; pop. 5,000
(the city proper): 117 sq. mi.; pop. 3,195,000 (the co.): 610 sq.
mi.; pop. 6,677,928 (Greater London).
— city, Ontario, Canada; pop. 240,392.
Long Beach city, sw California 90801*; pop. 429,433.
— city, se New York 11561*; pop. 33,510.
Long Branch city, e New Jersey 07740*; pop. 28,658.
Long Island isl., se New York; 1,723 sq. mi.
Long Island Sound inlet of the Atlantic betw. Long Island and
Connecticut.
Longmeadow town, s Massachusetts 01106; pop. 15,467.
Longmont city, n Colorado 80501; pop. 42,942.
Loungueuil city, sw Quebec, Canada; pop. 122,429.
Longview city, ne Texas 75601*; pop. 70,311.
— city, sw Washington 98632; pop. 31,499.
Lorain city, n Ohio 44052*; pop. 71,245.
Lorraine reg., e France.
Los Alamos uninc. place, cen. New Mexico 87544; site of the
development of the atom bomb; pop. 11,455.
Los Altos city, w California 94022; pop. 26,303.
Los Angeles city, sw California 90052*; pop. 3,485,398.
Los Gatos city, w California 95030*; pop. 27,357.
Louisiana state, s United States; 47,752 sq. mi.; pop.
4,238,216; cap. Baton Rouge.
Louisville city, n Kentucky 40201*; pop. 269,063.
Lourdes town, sw France; famous shrine; pop. 17,870.

Loveland city, N Colorado 80537; pop. 37,352.
Lowell city, NE Massachusetts 01853*; pop. 103,439.
Lower California penin., NW Mexico; betw. the Gulf of California and the Pacific. Also **Baja California.**
Lowlands areas of low elevation, E and S Scotland.
Luanda city, NW Angola; cap.; pop. 475,328.
Lubbock city, NW Texas 79408*; pop. 186,206.
Lübeck city, NE Germany; pop. 210,681.
Lucerne, Lake of lake, CEN. Switzerland; 44 sq. mi.
Lucknow city, CEN. Uttar Predesh, India; cap.; pop. 895,721.
Lüda city, NE China; pop. 1,185,000.
Ludlow town, S Massachusetts 01056; pop. 18,820.
Lufkin city, E Texas 75901*; pop. 30,206.
Lumberton city, S North Carolina 28358; pop. 18,601.
Lusaka city, CEN Zambia; cap.; pop. 870,030.
Lutherville-Timonium uninc. place, NE Maryland 21093; pop. 16,442.
Luxembourg, Grand Duchy of, monarchy; betw. Belgium, France, and Germany; 999 sq. mi.; pop. 379,000.
— city, CEN. Luxembourg; cap.; pop. 76,640. Also **Luxemburg.**
Luxor city, E Egypt; near the site of ancient Thebes; pop. 30,000.
Luzon isl., N Philippines; 40,420 sq. mi.
Lvov city, W Ukrainian SSR; pop. 790,000.
Lynbrook vill., SE New York 11563; pop. 19,208.
Lynchburg city, CEN. Virginia 24505*; pop. 66,049.
Lyndhurst urb. twp., NE New Jersey 07071; pop. 18,262.
— city, N Ohio 44124; pop. 15,982.
Lynn city, NE Massachusetts 01901*; pop. 81,245.
Lynnwood city, CEN. Washington 98036; pop. 28,695.
Lynwood city, SW California 90262*; pop. 61,945.
Lyon city, CEN. France; pop. 415,000.
Macao isl., Canton river delta, China.
— Portuguese special terr. comprising a penin. of Macao isl. and two small isls.; 6 sq. mi.; pop. 461,000.
— city; cap of Macao; pop. 461,000.
Macedonia reg., SE Europe; divided among Bulgaria, Greece, and Yugoslavia; 25,636 sq. mi.
Mackenzie river, NW Canada; 2,640 mi. long.
Mackinac, Straits of channel betw. Lakes Michigan and Huron; ab. 5 mi. wide and 40 mi. long.
Mackinac Island isl., Straits of Mackinac.
Macomb city, W Illinois 61455; pop. 19,952.
Macon city, CEN. Georgia 31201*; pop. 106,612.
Madagascar isl. republic, Indian Ocean off SE Africa; 226,662 sq. mi.; pop. 11,980,000; cap. Antananarivo: also called **Malagasy Republic.**
Madeira isl. group W of Morocco; an adm. dist. of Portugal; 306 sq. mi.; pop. 264,787; cap. Funchal.
Madera city, CEN. California 93637; pop. 29,281.
Madison boro., N New Jersey 07940; pop. 15,850.
— city, CEN. Wisconsin 53701*; cap.; pop. 191,262.
Madison Heights city, SE Michigan 48071; pop. 32,196.
Madisonville city, W Kentucky 42431; pop. 16,200.
Madras city, S India; pop. 3,276,622.
Madrid city, CEN. Spain; cap.; pop. 3,100,507.
Madura isl. of Indonesia E of Java; 1,762 sq. mi.
Magdeburg city, CEN. Germany; pop. 290,579.
Magellan, Strait of channel betw. the Atlantic and Pacific, separating the South American mainland from Tierra del Fuego.
Magnitogorsk city, S RSFSR; pop. 410,000.
Maine state, NE United States; 33,265 sq. mi.; pop. 1,233,223; cap. Augusta.
Main River river, CEN. Germany; 305 mi. long.
Majorca largest of the Balearic Islands; 1,405 sq. mi.
Malabar coastal reg., SW India. Also **Malabar Coast.**
Malacca city, W Malaysia; pop. 86,357.
Malacca, Strait of strait betw. Sumatra and the Malay Peninsula.
Málaga city, S Spain; pop. 566,330.
Malagasy Republic See Madagascar.
Malawi republic, SE Africa; 45,747 sq. mi.; pop. 8,831,000; cap. Lilongwe.
Malay Archipelago isl. group off SE Asia; includes isls. of Indonesia, Malaysia, and the Philippines.
Malay Peninsula S penin. of Asia; includes Malaya, Singapore, and part of Thailand.

Malaysia island monarchy including Malaya, Sarawak, and Sabah (North Borneo); 127,581 sq. mi.; pop. 17,886,000; cap. Kuala Lumpur.
Malden city, NE Massachusetts 02148; pop. 53,884.
Maldives isl. republic, Indian Ocean S of India; 115 sq. mi.; pop. 214,000; cap. Male.
Mali republic, W Africa; 478,841 sq. mi.; pop. 8,151,000; cap. Bamako.
Mallorca *the Spanish name of* Majorca.
Malta republic, CEN. Mediterranean; comprises the islands of Malta, Gozo, Comino, and two islets; 122 sq. mi.; pop. 353,000; cap. Valletta.
Mamaroneck vill., SE New York 10543; pop. 17,325.
Man, Isle of one of the British Isles, CEN. Irish Sea; 227 sq. mi.; pop. 61,723; cap. Douglas.
Managua city, SW Nicaragua; cap.; pop. 552,900.
Managua, Lake lake, SW Nicaragua; 390 sq. mi.
Manchester co. boro. and city, SE Lancashire, England; pop. 448,604.
— town, N Connecticut 06040*; pop. 51,618.
— city, S New Hampshire 03101*; pop. 99,567.
Manchuria former div., NE China.
Mandalay city, CEN. Myanmar; pop. 533,000.
Manhattan city, NE Kansas 66502*; pop. 37,712.
— borough (New York), isl., New York City, New York 10001*; pop. 1,487,536.
Manhattan Beach city, SW California 90266; pop. 32,063.
Manila city, SW Luzon, Philippines; pop. 1,879,000.
Manitoba prov., CEN. Canada; 246,512 sq. mi.; pop. 1,021,506; cap. Winnipeg.
Manitoba, Lake lake, SW Manitoba; 1,817 sq. mi.
Manitowoc city, E Wisconsin 54220*; pop. 32,520.
Mankato city, S Minnesota 56001*; pop. 31,477.
Mansfield city, NE Connecticut 06250; pop. 21,103.
— city, CEN. Ohio 44901*; pop. 50,627.
Maple Heights city, NE Ohio 44137; pop. 27,089.
Maple Shade urb. twp., SW New Jersey 08052; pop. 19,211.
Maplewood vill., E Minnesota 55109; pop. 30,954.
— urb. twp. NE New Jersey 07040; pop. 21,756.
Maracaibo city, NW Venezuela; pop. 1,206,726.
Maracaibo, Lake lake, NW Venezuela; ab. 5,000 sq. mi.
Marblehead town, NE Massachusetts 01945*; pop. 19,971.
Marietta city, NW Georgia; 30060*; pop. 44,129.
— city, SE Ohio 45750; pop. 15,026.
Marion city, CEN. Indiana 46952*; pop. 32,618.
— city, E Iowa 52302; pop. 20,403.
— city, CEN Ohio 43302; pop. 34,075.
Markham vill., NE Illinois 60426; pop. 13,136.
Marlborough city, CEN. Massachusetts 01752; pop. 31,813.
Marmara, Sea of sea betw. Europe and Asia, connecting the Bosporus and the Dardanelles. Also **Marmora.**
Marne river, NE France; 325 mi. long.
Marquesas Islands isl. group, French Polynesia; 492 sq. mi.
Marquette city, NW Michigan 49855; pop. 21,977.
Marrakech city, SW Morocco; provincial cap.; pop. 1,455,000.
Marrero uninc. place; SW Louisiana 70072; pop. 36,671.
Marseille city, SE France; pop. 801,000. Also **Marseilles.**
Marshall city, NE Texas 75670*; pop. 23,682.
Marshall Islands isl. group in Pacific; an adm. dist. of the Trust Terr. of the Pacific Islands; 66 sq. mi.; pop. 25,000; cap. Jaluit.
Marshalltown city, CEN. Iowa 50158; pop. 25,178.
Marshfield city, E Massachusetts 02050; pop. 21,531.
Marshfield city, CEN. Wisconsin 54449; pop. 19,291.
Martinez city, W California 94553*; pop. 31,808.
Martinique isl. Lesser Antilles; French overseas dept.; 421 sq. mi.; pop. 360,000; cap. Fort-de-France.
Martinsville city, S Virginia 24112*; pop. 16,162.
Maryland state, E United States; 10,460 sq. mi.; pop. 4,798,622; cap. Annapolis.
Mason City city, N Iowa 50401*; pop. 29,040.
Mason-Dixon Line boundary betw. Pennsylvania and Maryland, surveyed by Charles Mason and Jeremiah Dixon in 1763; regarded as the division line for the North and the South, United States.
Massachusetts state, NE United States; 8,284 sq. mi.; pop. 6,029,051; cap. Boston.
Massapequa uninc. place, SE New York; 11758*; pop. 22,018.

Massapequa Park vill., SE New York 11762; pop. 18,044.

Massillon city, NE Ohio 44646; pop. 31,007.

Matsu isl. of the Republic of China, Formosa Strait; 4 sq. mi.

Matterhorn mtn. in the Alps on the Swiss-Italian border; 14,701 ft.

Mattoon city, CEN. Illinois 61938; pop. 18,441.

Maui isl. of the Hawaiian Islands; 728 sq. mi.

Maumee city, NW Ohio 43537; pop. 15,561.

Mauna Loa active volcano, CEN. Hawaii (isl.); 13,675 ft.

Mauritania, Islamic Republic of republic, w Africa; 397,700 sq. mi.; pop. 2,000,000; cap. Nouakchott.

Mauritius island monarchy in the Indian Ocean, 788 sq. mi., pop. 1,080,000; cap. Port Louis.

Mayagüez city, w Puerto Rico 00708; pop. 82,703.

Mayfield Heights city, N Ohio 44124; pop. 19,847.

Mayotte dependency of France, isl. in the Mozambique Channel, off Madagascar, 144 sq. mi.; pop. 82,300; cap. Dzaoudzi.

Maywood city, SW California 90270; pop. 27,850.

— vill., NE Illinois 60153*; pop. 27,139.

McAlester city, CEN. Oklahoma 74501*; pop. 16,370.

McAllen city, S Texas 78501*; pop. 84,021.

McKeesport city, SW Pennsylvania 15134*; pop. 26,016.

McKinley, Mount peak, CEN. Alaska, highest in North America; 20,300 ft.

McKinney city N Texas 75069; pop. 21,283.

McLean uninc. place, NE Virginia 22101; pop. 38,168.

Mead, Lake reservoir formed by Hoover Dam in the Colorado River, Arizona and Nevada; 246 sq. mi.

Meadville city, NW Pennsylvania 16335; pop. 14,318.

Mecca city, w Saudi Arabia; birthplace of Mohammed and holy city to which Muslims make pilgrimages; pop. 550,000.

Medford NE Massachusetts 02155; pop. 57,407.

— city, SW Oregon 97501*; pop. 49,951.

Medicine Hat city, SE Alberta, Canada; pop. 32,811.

Medina city, w Saudi Arabia; a Muslim holy city and site of Mohammed's tomb; pop. 90,000.

Mediterranean Sea sea betw. Europe, Asia, and Africa; 965,000 sq. mi.

Mekong river, SE Asia; 2,500 mi. long.

Melanesia isls. of the w Pacific s of the Equator; ab. 60,000 sq. mi.

Melbourne city, s Victoria, Australia; cap.; pop. 3,002,300.

— city, E Florida 32901*; pop. 59,646.

Melrose city, NE Massachusetts 02176; pop. 28,150.

Melrose Park vill., NE Illinois 60160*; pop. 20,859.

Memphis city, SW Tennessee 38101*; pop. 610,337.·

— ancient city, cap. of Egypt during the Old Kingdom, s of the Nile Delta.

Menlo Park city, w California 94025*; pop. 28,040.

Menomonee Falls vill., SE Wisconsin 53051*; pop. 26,840.

Mentor city, NE Ohio 44060; pop. 47,358.

Merced city, CEN. California 95340*; pop. 56,216.

Mercerville-Hamilton Square uninc. place, CEN. New Jersey 08619*; pop. 26,873.

Meriden city, CEN. Connecticut 06450; pop. 59,479.

Meridian city, E Mississippi 39301*; pop. 41,036.

Merrick uninc. place, SE New York 11566; pop. 23,042.

Merrillville city, NW Indiana 46410; pop. 27,257.

Merritt Island uninc. place, CEN. Florida 32952; pop. 32,886.

Mesa city, CEN. Arizona 85201*; pop. 288,091.

Mesabi Range range of hills, NE Minnesota; site of iron ore deposits.

Mesquite city, N Texas 75149; pop. 101,484.

Messina city, NE Sicily; pop. 272,119.

Metairie city, SW Louisiana 70004*; pop. 149,428.

Methuen city, NE Massachusetts 01844; pop. 39,990.

Meuse river, w Europe; 580 mi. long.

Mexico republic s North America; 756,066 sq. mi., 81,883,000.

— **City**, CEN Mexico; cap.; pop. 8,236,960.

Mexico, Gulf of inlet of the Atlantic, among the United States, Mexico, and Cuba; 700,000 sq. mi.

Miami city, SE Florida 33152*; pop. 358,548.

Miami Beach city SE Florida 33139; pop. 92,639.

Michigan state, N United States; 58,527 sq. mi.; pop. 9,328,784; cap. Lansing.

Michigan, Lake one of the Great Lakes; betw. Michigan and Wisconsin; 22,400 sq. mi.

Michigan City city, N Indiana 46360; pop. 33,822.

Micronesia, Federated States of, isl. republic of the w Pacific, N of the equator; 271 sq. mi.; pop. 108,000; cap. Kolonia.

Middle River uninc. place, N Maryland 21220; pop. 24,616.

Middletown city, CEN Connecticut; 06457; pop. 42,762.

— urb. twp., E New Jersey 07748; pop. 62,298.

— city, SE New York 10940; pop. 24,160.

— city, SW Ohio 45042; pop. 46,022.

— town, SE Rhode Island 02840; pop. 19,460.

Midi s reg. of France.

Midland city, CEN. Michigan 48640*; pop. 38,053.

— city, w Texas 79701*; pop. 89,443.

Midlands counties of CEN. England.

Midway Islands 2 isls. NW of Honolulu, under control of the U.S. Navy; 2 sq. mi.; scene of an important battle of World War II, June 1942.

Midwest City city, CEN. Oklahoma 73110; pop. 52,267.

Milan city, N Italy; pop. 1,464,127.

Milford city, SW Connecticut 06460; pop. 48,168.

— uninc. place, CEN. Massachusetts 01757; pop. 25,355.

Millbrae city, w California 94030; pop. 20,412.

Millburn urb. twp., NE New Jersey 07041; pop. 18,630.

Millington town, SW Tennessee 38053; pop. 17,866.

Millville city, s New Jersey 08332; pop. 25,992.

Milpitas city, w California 95035; pop. 50,686.

Milton town, E Massachusetts 02186; pop. 25,725.

Milwaukee city, SE Wisconsin 53203*; pop. 628,088.

Milwaukie city, NW Oregon 97222; pop. 18,692.

Mindanao isl. s Philippines; 36,537 sq. mi.

Mindoro isl., CEN. Philippines; 3,759 sq. mi.

Mineola vill., SE New York 11501*; pop. 18,994.

Minneapolis city, E Minnesota 55401*; pop. 368,383.

Minnesota state, N United States; 84,402 sq. mi.; pop. 4,387,029; cap. St. Paul.

Minnetonka vill., E Minnesota 55343; pop. 48,370.

Minorca one of the Balearic islands; 271 sq. mi.

Minot city, N North Dakota 58701*; pop. 34,544.

Minsk city, CEN. Byelorussian SSR; cap.; pop. 1,295,000.

Miramar city, SE Florida 33023; pop. 40,663.

Mishawaka city, N Indiana 46544; pop. 42,608.

• **Mississippi** state s United States; 47,689 sq. mi.; pop. 2,586,443; cap. Jackson.

Mississippi River river, CEN. United States; 2,350 mi. long.

Missoula city, w Montana 59801; pop. 33,351.

Missouri state, CEN. United States; 69,697 sq. mi.; pop. 5,137,804; cap. Jefferson City.

Missouri River river, CEN. United States; 2,470 mi. long.

Mobile city, SW Alabama 36601*; pop. 196,278.

Mobile Bay inlet of the Gulf of Mexico, SW Alabama.

Modesto city, CEN. California 95350*; pop. 164,730.

Mojave Desert arid reg. s California; ab. 15,000 sq. mi.

Moldavian SSR constituent republic, SW USSR; 13,000 sq. mi.; pop. 4,338,000; cap. Kishinev. Also **Moldavia.**

Moline city, NW Illinois 61265; pop. 43,202.

Molokai isl., CEN. Hawaiian Islands; 259 sq. mi.

Molucca Islands isl. group of Indonesia, betw. Sulawesi and New Guines; 33,315 sq. mi.

Monaco monarchy, SE France; 368 acres: pop. 29,000.

Moncton city, SE New Brunswick, Canada; pop. 55,934.

Mongolia republic (**Mongolian People's Republic**, formerly **Outer Mongolia**). CEN Asia; 604,000 sq. mi.; pop. 2,116,000; cap. Ulan Bator

— **Inner Mongolia** reg. N China, 454,600 sq. mi.; pop. 21,456,798; cap. Hohhot.

Monongahela River river, West Virginia and w Pennsylvania; 128 mi. long.

Monroe city, N Louisiana 71201*; pop. 54,909.

— city, SE Michigan 48161; pop. 22,902.

Monroeville boro., SW Pennsylvania 15145; pop. 29,169.

Monrovia city, E Liberia; cap.; pop. 421,000.

— city, SW California 91016; pop. 35,761.

Montana state, NW United States; 147,046 sq. mi.; pop. 803,655; cap. Helena.

Mont Blanc highest mountain of the Alps, on the French-Italian border; 15,781 ft.; site of tunnel, 7½ mi. long, connecting France and Italy.

Montclair city, SW California 91763; pop. 28,434.

— town, NE New Jersey 07042*; pop. 37,729.

Gazetteer   899

Montebello city, sw California 90640; pop. 59,564.
Monte Carlo city, Monaco; pop. 10,000.
Montenegro constituent republic, s Yugoslavia; 5333 sq. mi.; pop. 633,000; cap. Titograd.
Monterey city, w California 93940*; pop. 31,954.
Monterey Park city, sw California 91754; pop. 60,738.
Monterrey city, NE Mexico; pop. 1,090,000.
Montevideo city, s Uruguay; cap.; pop. 1,311,976.
Montgomery city, CEN. Alabama 36104*; cap.; pop. 187,106.
Monticello estate and residence of Thomas Jefferson, near Charlottesville, Virginia.
Montmartre dist., N Paris; former artists' quarter.
Montpelier city, CEN. Vermont 05602*; cap.; pop. 8,247.
Montreal city, s Quebec, Canada; pop. 1,080,546.
Montreal-Nord city, s Quebec, Canada; pop. 97,250. Also Montreal-North.
Mont-Royal town, s Quebec, Canada; pop. 20,514.
Mont Saint Michel isl. off NW France; site of an ancient fortress and abbey.
Montville city, SE Connecticut 06353; pop. 16,673.
Moorhead city, w Minnesota 56560; pop. 32,295.
Mooreland city, CEN. Oklahoma 73852; pop. 18,761.
Moose Jaw city, s Saskatchewan, Canada; pop. 32,581.
Moravia reg., CEN. Czechoslovakia.
Morgan City city, s Louisiana 70380; pop. 14,531.
Morgantown city, N West Virginia 26505*; pop. 25,879.
Morocco monarchy, NW Africa; ab. 177,117 sq. mi.; pop. 25,113,000; cap. Rabat.
Morristown town, CEN. New Jersey 07960; pop. 16,189.
— city, NE Tennessee 37814*; pop. 21,385.
Morton Grove vill., NE Illinois 60053; pop. 22,408.
Moscow city, w USSR; cap. USSR and RSFSR; pop. 7,915,000.
Moselle river, NE France, Luxembourg, and w Germany; 320 mi. long.
Moss Point city, SE Mississippi 39563; pop. 18,998.
Mosul city, N Iraq; pop. 293,100.
Mountain Brook city, CEN. Alabama 35223; pop. 18,810.
Mountain View city, w California 94042*; pop. 67,460.
Mount Clemens city, SE Michigan 48046*; pop. 18,405.
Mountlake Terrace city, CEN. Washington 98043; pop. 19,320.
Mount Lebanon uninc. urb. twp., sw Pennsylvania 15228; pop. 33,362.
Mount Pleasant city, CEN. Michigan 48858; pop. 23,285.
Mount Prospect vill., NE Illinois 60056*; pop. 53,170.
Mount Vernon home and burial place of George Washington, near Washington, D.C.
— city, s Illinois 62864; pop. 16,988.
— city, SE New York 10551*; pop. 67,153.
Mozambique republic SE Africa; 313,661 sq. mi.; pop. 15,696,000; cap. Maputo.
Muncie city, E Indiana 47302; pop. 71,035.
Mundelein vill., NE Illinois 60060; pop. 21,215.
Munich city, SE Germany; pop. 1,211,617.
Munster town, NW Indiana 46321; pop. 19,949.
Murfreesboro city, CEN. Tennessee; 37130*; pop. 44,922.
Murmansk city, NW USSR; pop. 388,000.
Murray city, CEN. Utah 84107; pop. 31,282.
Murray River river, SE Australia; 1,600 mi. long.
Muscat and Oman: the former name of Oman.
Muscatine city, E Iowa 52761; pop. 22,881.
Muskegon city, w Michigan 49440*; pop. 40,283.
Muskogee city, E Oklahoma 74401*; pop. 37,708.
Myanmar military govt., formerly Burma, SE Asia; 261,228 sq. mi.; pop. 41,675,000; cap. Yangôn (Rangoon).
Mysore city, s India; pop. 355,685.
Nacogdoches city E Texas 75961*; pop. 30,872.
Nagasaki city, NW Kyushu island, Japan; largely destroyed by a U.S. atomic bomb, Aug. 9, 1945; pop. 445,854.
Nagoya city, CEN. Honshu isl., Japan; pop. 2,149,517.
Nagpur city, CEN. India; pop. 1,219,461.
Nairobi city, sw Kenya; cap.; pop. 1,103,600.
Namibia republic, sw Africa; 317,818 sq. mi.; pop. 1,302,000; cap. Windhoek.
Nampa city, sw Idaho 83651; pop. 28,365.
Nanjing city, E China; cap. 1928N37; pop. 2,022,500.
Nantes city, w France; pop. 245,000.

Nantucket isl. off SE Massachusetts; 57 sq. mi.; pop. 6,012.
Napa city, w California 94558*; pop. 61,842.
Naperville city, NE Illinois 60540; pop. 85,351.
Naples city, sw Italy; pop. 1,202,582.
Narragansett Bay inlet of the Atlantic, SE Rhode Island.
Nashua city, s New Hampshire 03060; pop. 67,865.
Nashville city, CEN. Tennessee 37202*; cap.; pop. 488,374.
Nassau city, New Providence, Bahamas Islands; cap.; pop. 101,503.
Natal prov., E South Africa; 21,344 sq. mi.; pop. 2,145,018; cap. Pietermaritzburg.
Natchez city, sw Mississippi 39120*; pop. 19,460.
Natchitoches city, CEN. Louisiana 71457; pop. 16,609.
Natick town, NE Massachusetts 01760*; pop. 30,510.
National City city, sw California 92050; pop. 54,249.
Naugatuck town, CEN. Connecticut 06770; pop. 30,625.
Nauru Republic, isl. W-CENT. Pacific just south of Equator (Oceania); 8 sq. mi., pop. 9,000; cap. Yaren.
Navarre reg. and former kingdom, N Spain and sw France.
Nazareth town, N Israel; scene of Christ's childhood; pop. 40,400.
Nebraska state, CEN. United States; 77,355 sq. mi.; pop. 1,584,617; cap. Lincoln.
Nederland city, SE Texas 77627; pop. 16,192.
Needham town, NE Massachusetts 02192; pop. 27,557.
Neenah city, CEN. Wisconsin 54956; pop. 23,219.
Negev desert reg., s Israel; 4,700 sq. mi. Also Negeb.
Nejd prov., CEN. Saudi Arabia; ab. 450,000 sq. mi.; cap. Riyadh.
Nepal republic betw. Tibet and India; 56,827 sq. mi.; pop. 19,000,000; cap. Kathmandu.
Netherlands monarchy, NW Europe; 16,026 sq. mi.; pop. 14,472,000; cap. Amsterdam; seat of government, The Hague.
Netherlands Antilles 3 isls. N of Venezuela and 3 in the Leeward Islands group; 308 sq. mi.; pop. 196,000; cap. Willemstad.
Netherlands Guiana See Suriname.
Nevada state, w United States; 110,561 sq. mi.; pop. 1,206,152 cap. Carson city.
New Albany city, s Indiana 47150; pop. 36,322.
Newark city, w California 94560; pop. 37,861.
— city, NW Delaware 19715*; pop. 25,098.
— city, NE New Jersey 07102*; pop. 275,221.
— city, CEN. Ohio 43055*; pop. 44,389.
New Bedford city, SE Massachusetts 02741*; pop. 99,922.
New Berlin city, SE Wisconsin 53151; pop. 33,592.
New Braunfels city, CEN. Texas 78130*; pop. 27,334.
New Brighton vill., E Minnesota 55112; pop. 22,207.
New Britain city, CEN. Connecticut 06050*; pop. 75,491.
New Brunswick city, CEN. New Jersey 08901*; pop. 41,711.
— prov., SE Canada; 27,834 sq. mi.; pop. 718,400; cap. Fredericton.
Newburgh city, SE New York 12550*; pop. 26,454.
Newburyport city, NE Massachusetts 01950; pop. 16,317.
New Caledonia isl. E of Australia; comprising with adjacent isls. a French overseas terr.; 7,233 sq. mi.; pop. 168,000; cap. Nouméa.
New Canaan city, sw Connecticut 06840; pop. 17,864.
New Castle city, E Indiana 47362; pop. 17,753.
— city, w Pennsylvania 16101*; pop. 28,334.
Newcastle upon Tyne city, NE England; pop. 203,591. Also Newcastle, Newcastle on Tyne.
New City uninc. place, SE New York, 10956; pop. 33,673.
New Delhi city, Delhi terr., India; cap. of India; pop. 273,036.
New England NE section of the United States, including Maine, New Hampshire, Vermont, Massachusetts, Rhode Island, and Connecticut.
Newfoundland prov., E Canada; comprising the island of Newfoundland (43,359 sq. mi.) and Labrador on the mainland; 143,510 sq. mi.; pop. 579,700; cap. St. John's.
New Georgia isl. group, British Solomon Islands; ab. 2,000 sq. mi.
New Guinea isl., N of Australia; 304,200 sq. mi. See Papua New Guinea, West New Guinea.
New Hampshire state, NE United States; 9,279 sq. mi.; pop. 1,113,915 cap. Concord.
New Haven city, s Connecticut 06510*; pop. 130,474.
New Hebride See Vanuatu.

New Hope city, SE Minnesota 55428; pop. 21,853.

New Iberia city, S Louisiana 70560*; pop. 31,828.

New Ireland volcanic isl. of the Bismarck Archipelago, S Pacific; 3,700 sq. mi.; pop. 70,800; part of Papua New Guinea.

Newington city, CEN. Connecticut 06111; pop. 29,208.

New Jersey state, E United States; 7,787 sq. mi.; pop. 7,748,634; cap. Trenton.

New Kensington city, W Pennsylvania 15068*; pop. 15,894.

New London city, SE Connecticut 06320; pop. 28,540.

Newmarket town S Ontario, Canada; pop. 24,795.

New Mexico state, SW United States; 121,593 sq. mi.; pop. 1,512,779; cap. Santa Fe.

New Milford boro., NE New Jersey 07646; pop. 15,990.

New Orleans city, SE Louisiana 70113*; pop. 496,938.

New Philadelphia city, CEN. Ohio 44663; pop. 15,698.

Newport city, N Kentucky 41071*; pop. 18,871.

— city, SE Rhode Island 02840*; pop. 28,227.

Newport Beach city, SW California 92660*; pop. 66,643.

Newport News city, SE Virginia 23607*; pop. 170,045.

New Rochelle city, SE New York 10802*; pop. 67,265.

New South Wales state, SE Australia; 309,500 sq. mi.; pop. 5,771,900; cap. Sydney.

Newton city, CEN. Iowa 50208; pop. 14,789.

— city, CEN. Kansas 67114; pop. 16,700.

— city, E Massachusetts 02158; pop. 85,585.

Newtown city, SW Connecticut 06470; pop. 20,779.

New Westminster city, SW British Columbia, Canada; pop. 36,393.

New York state, NE United States; 49,108 sq. mi.; pop. 18,044,505; cap. Albany.

— City, SE New York 10001*; divided into the five boroughs of the Bronx, Kings (Brooklyn), New York (Manhattan), Queens, and Richmond (Staten Island); 365 sq. mi.; pop. 7,322,564.

— borough (Manhattan), CEN. New York City, New York 10001*; pop. 1,487,536.

New York State Barge Canal waterway system, New York; connects the Hudson River with Lakes Erie, Champlain, and Ontario, 525 mi. long.

New Zealand monarchy, comprising a group of isle SE of Australia; 104,454 sq. mi.; pop. 3,389,000; cap. Wellington.

Niagara Falls city, W New York 14302*; pop. 61,840.

— city, S Ontario, Canada; pop. 69,423.

Niagara River river betw. Ontario, Canada, and New York State, connecting Lakes Erie and Ontario; in its course occurs **Niagara Falls**, a cataract divided by Goat Island into the American Falls, ab. 167 ft. high and 1,000 ft. wide, and Horseshoe Falls on the Canadian side, ab. 160 ft. high and 2,500 ft. wide.

Nicaragua republic, Central America; 49,291 sq. mi.; pop. 3,871,000; cap. Managua.

Nicaragua, Lake lake, SW Nicaragua; 3,100 sq. mi.

Nice city, SE France; pop. 342,000.

Nicobar Islands isl. terr. of India; 19 isls. in the Bay of Bengal; 754 sq. mi.; pop. 22,000.

Nicosia city, CEN. Cyprus; cap.; pop. 166,900.

Niger river, W Africa; ab. 2,600 mi. long.

Niger, Republic of republic, CEN. Africa, 458,074 sq. mi.; pop. 7,800,000; cap. Niamey.

Nigeria, Federation of republic, W Africa; 356,669 sq. mi.; pop. 119,812,000; cap. Lagos.

Nile river, E Africa; 4,130 mi. long; the longest river in the world.

Niles vill., NE Illinois 60648; pop. 28,284.

— city, NE Ohio 44446; pop. 21,128.

Norfolk city, NE Nebraska 68701; pop. 21,476.

— city, SE Virginia 23501*; pop. 261,229.

Normal town, CEN. Illinois 61761; pop. 40,023.

Norman city, CEN. Oklahoma 73070*; pop. 80,071.

Normandy reg. and former prov., NW France.

Norridge vill., NE Illinois 60655*; pop. 14,459.

Norristown boro., SE Pennsylvania 19401*; pop. 30,749.

North Adams city, NW Massachusetts 01247*; pop. 16,797.

North America N continent of the Western Hemisphere; 9,410,000 sq. mi. (including adjacent islands).

Northampton city, W Massachusetts 01060*; pop. 29,289.

North Andover town, NE Massachusetts 01845; pop. 22,792.

North Arlington boro., NE New Jersey 07032; pop. 13,790.

North Attleborough town, E Massachusetts 02760*; pop. 16,178.

North Bay city, CEN. Ontario, Canada; pop. 51,639.

North Bergen urb. twp., NE New Jersey 07047; pop. 48,414.

North Borneo See **Sabah.**

Northbrook vill., NE Illinois 60062*; pop. 32,308.

North Cape promontory, N Norway.

North Carolina state, SE United States; 52,669 sq. mi.; pop. 6,657,630; cap. Raleigh.

North Chicago city, NE Illinois 60064; pop. 34,978.

North Dakota state, N United States; 70,702 sq. mi.; pop. 641,364; cap. Bismarck.

Northern Ireland part of the United Kingdom in N reg. of Ireland; 5,452 sq. mi.; pop. 1,578,100; cap. Belfast.

Northern Territory reg., N Australia; 519,800 sq. mi.; pop. 156,500; cap. Darwin.

Northglenn city, CEN. Colorado 80233; pop. 27,195.

North Haven city, S Connecticut 06473; pop. 22,249.

North Highlands uninc. place, CEN. California 95660; pop. 42,105.

North Island isl., N New Zealand; 44,281 sq. mi.

North Kingston town, S Rhode Island 02852; pop. 23,786.

North Korea See **Korea.**

North Las Vegas city, SE Nevada 89030; pop. 47,707.

North Little Rock city, CEN. Arkansas 72114*; pop. 61,741.

North Miami city, SE Florida 33161; pop. 49,998.

North Miami Beach city, SE Florida 33160; pop. 35,359.

North Olmsted city, N Ohio 44070; pop. 34,204.

North Plainfield boro., NE New Jersey 07060; pop. 18,820.

North Platte city, CEN. Nebraska 69101*; pop. 22,605.

North Pole N extremity of the earth's axis.

North Providence town, NE Rhode Island 02908; pop. 32,090.

North Richland Hills town, N Texas 76118; pop. 45,895.

North Sea part of the Atlantic betw. Great Britain and Europe.

North Tonawanda city, SW New York 14120; pop. 34,989.

North Vancouver city, SW British Columbia, Canada; pop. 31,934.

Northwest Territories adm. div., N Canada; 1,271,442 sq. mi.; pop. 42,609.

Northwest Territory reg. awarded to the United States by Britain in 1783, extending from the Great Lakes S to the Ohio River and from Pennsylvania W to the Mississippi.

Norton Shores city, SW Michigan 49441; pop. 21,755.

Norwalk city, SW California 90650; pop. 94,279.

— city, SW Connecticut 06856*; pop. 78,331.

Norway monarchy, N Europe; 125,050 sq. mi.; pop. 4,246,000; cap. Oslo.

Norwich co. boro., E England; pop. 119,300.

— city, SE Connecticut 06360; pop. 37,391.

Nottingham co. boro., CEN. England; pop. 278,600.

Nova Scotia prov., E Canada; 20,402 sq. mi.; pop. 828,571; cap. Halifax.

Novato city, W California 94947; pop. 47,585.

Novaya Zemlya two isls., Arctic Ocean, NE RSFSR; ab. 35,000 sq. mi.

Novosibirsk city, SW Asian Russian SFSR, ab. 1,700 mi. E of Moscow; pop. 1,328,000.

Nürnberg city, CEN. Germany; pop. 484,184.

Nutley town, NE New Jersey 07110; pop. 27,099.

Oahu isl., CEN. Hawaiian Islands; 589 sq. mi.

Oak Forest city, NE Illinois 60452; pop. 26,203.

Oakland city, W California 94615*; pop. 372,242.

Oakland Park city, SE Florida 33308; pop. 1,743.

Oak Lawn vill., NE Illinois 60454*; pop. 56,182.

Oak Park vill., NE Illinois 60301*; pop. 53,648.

— city, SE Michigan 48237; pop. 30,462.

Oak Ridge city, E Tennessee 37830*; pop. 27,310.

Oakville town, S Ontario, Canada; pop. 68,950.

Ocala city, CEN. Florida 32670; pop. 42,045.

Oceania isls. of Melanesia, Micronesia, and Polynesia, and sometimes the Malay Archipelago and Australasia.

Oceanside city, SW California 92054*; pop. 128,398.

— uninc. place, SE New York 11572; pop. 32,423.

Oder river, CEN. Europe; 563 mi. long.

Odessa city, S Ukrainian SSR; pop. 1,115,000.

— city, W Texas 79760*; pop. 89,699.

Ogden city, N Utah 84401*; pop. 63,909.

Ohio state, CEN. United States; 41,330 sq. mi.; pop.

10,887,325; cap. Columbus.

Ohio River river, CEN. United States; 981 mi. long.

Oildale uninc. place, CEN. California 93308; pop. 26,553.

Okhotsk, Sea of inlet of the Pacific w of Kamchatka and the Kurile Islands.

Okinawa Japanese isl., largest of the Ryukyu Islands; 870 sq. mi.; pop. 1,161,000; cap. Naha.

Oklahoma state, CEN. United States; 69,956 sq. mi.; pop. 3,157,604; cap. Oklahoma City.

Oklahoma City city, CEN. Oklahoma 73100*; cap.; pop. 444,719.

Okmulgee city, CEN. Oklahoma 74447; pop. 13,441.

Okolona uninc. place, NW Kentucky 40219; pop. 18,902.

Olathe city, E Kansas 66061; pop. 63,352.

Old Bridge city, CEN. New Jersey 08857; pop. 22,151.

Olean city, SW New York 14760; pop. 16,946.

Olympia city, W Washington 98501*; cap.; pop. 33,840.

Olympus, Mount mtn., N Greece; regarded in Greek mythology as the home of the gods; 9,570 ft.

Omaha city, E Nebraska 68108; pop. 335,795.

Oman independent sultanate, SE Arabia; 120,000 sq. mi.; pop. 1,400,000; cap. Muscat.

Omsk city, S RSFSR; pop. 1,028,000.

Ontario city, SW California 91760*; pop. 133,179.

— prov., SE Canada; 344,090 sq. mi.; pop. 8,264,465; cap. Toronto.

Ontario, Lake easternmost of the Great Lakes; 7,540 sq. mi.

Opelika city, E Alabama 36801; pop. 22,122.

Opelousas city, CEN. Louisiana 70570; pop. 18,151.

Oporto city, W Portugal; pop. 335,700.

Opportunity uninc. place, E Washington 99214; pop. 22,326.

Orange former principality, now part of SE France.

— city, SW California 92667*; pop. 91,450.

— city, NE New Jersey 07050*; pop. 29,925.

— city, E Texas 77630*; pop. 19,381.

Orange River river, S Africa; 1,300 mi. long.

Oregon state, NW United States; 97,073 sq. mi.; pop. 2,853,733; cap. Salem.

— city, N Ohio 43616; pop. 18,334.

Orem city, CEN. Utah 84057; pop. 63,909.

Orillia town, S Ontario, Canada; pop. 24,412.

Orinoco river, Venezuela; ab. 1,700 mi. long.

Orkney Islands isl. group, N of Scotland, comprising **Orkney**, a co. of Scotland; 376 sq. mi.; pop. 18,134; cap. Kirkwall.

Orlando city, CEN. Florida 32802*; pop. 164,693.

Orléans city, CEN. France; pop. 106,246.

Osaka city, S Honshu, Japan; pop. 2,635,156.

Oshawa city, S Ontario, Canada; pop. 107,023.

Oshkosh city, E Wisconsin 54901*; pop. 55,006.

Oslo city, SE Norway; cap.; pop. 457,819.

Ossa mtn., E Greece; 6,490 ft. See **Pelion.**

Ossining vill., SE New York 10562; pop. 22,5826.

Ostend city, NW Belgium; pop. 70,125.

Oswego city, N New York 13216; pop. 19,195.

Otranto, Strait of strait betw. the Adriatic and Ionian seas; ab. 43 mi. wide.

Ottawa city, N Illinois 61350; pop. 17,451.

— city, SE Ontario, Canada; cap. of Canada; pop. 304,462.

Ottumwa city, SE Iowa 52501; pop. 24,488.

Ouagadougou city, CEN. Burkina Faso; cap.; pop. 441,500.

Outremont city, S Quebec, Canada; pop. 27,089.

Overland city, E Missouri 63114; pop. 17,987.

Overland Park uninc. place, NE Kansas 66204; pop. 111,790.

Owatonna city, S Minnesota 55060; pop. 19,384.

Owensboro city, NW Kentucky 42301*; pop. 53,549.

Owen Sound city, S Ontario, Canada; pop. 19,525.

Owosso city, CEN. Michigan 48867; pop. 16,322.

Oxford co. boro., CEN. England; pop. 119,909.

— city, SW Ohio 45056; pop. 18,937.

Oxnard city, SW California 93030*; pop. 142,216.

Ozark Mountains hilly uplands, SW Missouri, NW Arkansas, and NE Oklahoma.

Pacifica city, W California 94044; pop. 37,670.

Pacific Ocean ocean betw. the American continents and Asia and Australia; extending betw. the Arctic and Antarctic regions; ab. 70 million sq. mi.

Padua city, NE Italy; pop. 222,163.

Paducah city, W Kentucky 42001*; pop. 27,256.

Pago Pago town, SE Tutuila, American Samoa 96920; pop. 2,450.

Painesville city, NE Ohio 44077; pop. 15,699.

Pakistan republic, S Asia; 307,374 sq. mi.; pop. 122,666,000; cap. Islamabad.

Palatine vill., NE Illinois 60067; pop. 39,253.

Palau Islands isl. group, W Caroline Island; 188 sq. mi.

Palermo city, NW Sicily, Italy; cap.; pop. 731,483.

Palestine terr., E Mediterranean; 10,434 sq. mi.; divided (1947) by the United Nations into Israel and a terr. that became part of Jordan.

Palma city, W Majorca; cap. of the Balearic Islands, pop. 287,389.

Palm Springs city, S California 92263*; pop. 40,181.

Palo Alto city, W California 94303*; pop. 55,900.

Palomar, Mount mtn., S California; 6,126 ft.; site of **Mount Palomar Observatory.**

Pampa city, N Texas 79065; pop. 19,959.

Panama republic, Central America; 29,157 sq. mi. (excluding Canal Zone); pop. 2,418,000.

— City, near the Pacific end of the Panama Canal; cap of Panama; pop. 411,500.

Panama, Isthmus of isthmus connecting North and South America.

Panama Canal ship canal connecting the Atlantic and the Pacific across Panama; completed (1914) by the United States on the leased Canal Zone; 40 mi. long.

Panama Canal Zone See **Canal Zone.**

Panama City city, NW Florida 32401*; pop. 34,378.

Panay isl., CEN. Philippines; 4,446 sq. mi.

Papal States region in CEN. and NE Italy over which the Roman Catholic Church formerly had temporal power.

Papua New Guinea independent monarchy in the Commonwealth of Nations, S Pacific, consisting of the E half of New Guinea; the isls. of the Bismarck Archipelago; Bougainville and Buka in the Solomon Isls.; and a number of smaller isls.; 178,704 sq. mi.; pop. 3,671,000; cap. Port Moresby.

Paradise uninc. place, SE Nevada 89109; pop. 84,818.

Paraguay republic, CEN. South America; 157,048 sq. mi.; pop. 4,279,000; cap. Asunción.

Paraguay River river, CEN. South America; ab. 1,300 mi. long.

Paramaribo city, N Surinam; cap.; pop. 175,000.

Paramount city, SW California 90723; pop. 47,669.

Paramus boro., NE New Jersey 07652; pop. 25,067.

Paraná river, CEN. South America; ab. 1,827 mi. long.

Paris city, N France; cap.; pop. 2,150,500.

— city, NE Texas 75460; pop. 24,699.

Parkersburg city, W West Virginia 26101*; pop. 33,862.

Park Forest vill., NE Illinois 60466; pop. 24,656.

Parkland uninc. place, CEN. Washington 98444; pop. 20,882.

Park Ridge city, NE Illinois 60068; pop. 36,175.

Parkville-Carney uninc. place N Maryland 21234; pop. 31,617.

Parma city, CEN. Italy; pop. 174,827.

— city, N Ohio 44129; pop. 87,876.

Parma Heights city, NE Ohio 44130; pop. 21,448.

Parnassus, Mount mtn., CEN. Greece; anciently regarded as sacred to Apollo and the Muses; 8,062 ft.

Parsippany-Troy Hills city, N New Jersey 07054; pop. 48,478.

Pasadena city, SW California 91109*; pop. 131,591.

— city, SE Texas 77501*; pop. 119,363.

Pascagoula city, SE Mississippi 39567; pop. 25,899.

Passaic city, NE New Jersey 07055*; pop. 58,041.

Patagonia reg. at the S tip of South America.

Paterson city, NE New Jersey 07510*; pop. 140,891.

Pawtucket city, NE Rhode Island 02860*; pop. 72,644.

Peabody city, NE Massachusetts 01960*; pop. 47,039.

Pearl City city, S Oahu, Hawaii 96782; pop. 30,993.

Pearl Harbor inlet, S Oahu, Hawaii; site of a U.S. naval base, bombed by Japanese, December 7, 1941.

Pearl River uninc. place, SE New York 10965; pop. 15,314.

Peekskill city, SE New York 10566; pop. 19,536.

Pekin city, CEN. Illinois 61554*; pop. 32,254.

Peking city, N China; cap.; pop. 9,540,000; Also **Beijing.**

Pelion mtn. range, SE Thessaly, Greece, In Greek mythology, the Titans attempted to reach heaven by piling Pelion on Ossa and both on Olympus.

Peloponnesus penin. betw. Aegean and Ionian Seas; one of the main divisions of s Greece; 8,603 sq. mi.; pop. 986,000.

Pembroke town, SE Ontario, Canada; pop. 14,927.

Pembroke Pines city, SE Florida 33023; pop. 65,452.

Penn Hills uninc. place; sw Pennsylvania 15235; pop. 51,430.

Pennine Alps sw div. of the Alps on the Swiss–Italian border.

Pennsauken urb. twp., w New Jersey 08110; pop. 34,733.

Pennsylvania state, E United States, 45,308 sp. mi.; pop. 11,924,710; cap. Harrisburg.

Pensacola city, NW Florida 32502*; pop. 58,165.

Penticton city, s British Columbia, Canada; pop. 21,344.

Peoria city, CEN, Illinois 61601*; pop. 113,504.

Persia *the former name of* Iran.

Persian Gulf inlet of the Arabian Sea betw. Iran and Arabia; also the **Arabian Gulf.**

Perth city, sw Western Australia; cap. pop. 1,118,800.

Perth Amboy city, E New Jersey 08861*; pop. 41,067.

Peru republic, w South America; 496,225 sq. mi.; pop. 22,332,000; cap. Lima.

Petaluma city, w California 94952*; pop. 43,184.

Peterborough city, s Ontario, Canada; pop. 59,683.

Petersburg city, SE Virginia 23803*; pop. 38,386.

Pharr city, s Texas 78577; pop. 32,921.

Phenix City city, E Alabama 36867; pop. 25,312.

Philadelphia city, SE Pennsylvania 19104*; pop. 1,585,577.

Philippines, Republic of the republic occupying the **Philippine Islands,** a Pacific archipelago SE of China; 115,800 sq. mi.; pop. 61,480,000; cap. Manila.

Phillipsburg city, w New Jersey 08865*; pop. 15,757.

Phnom Penh city, s CEN. Cambodia; cap.; pop. 564,000.

Phoenix city CEN. Arizona 85026*; cap.; pop. 983,403.

Picardy reg. and former prov., N France.

Pico Rivera city, sw California 90660; pop. 59,177.

Piedmont reg., E United States; extends from New Jersey to Alabama E of the Appalachians; ab. 80,000 sq. mi.

Pierre city, CEN. South Dakota 57501; cap.; pop. 12,906.

Pierrefonds town, s Quebec, Canada; pop. 35,402.

Pike's Peak mtn., CEN. Colorado; 14,110 ft.

Pikesville uninc. place, w Maryland 21208; pop. 24,815.

Pine Bluff city, CEN. Arkansas 71601*; pop. 57,140.

Pinellas Park city, w Florida 33565; pop. 43,426.

Piqua city, w Ohio 45356; pop. 20,612.

Piraeus city, s Greece; pop. 187,362.

Pisa city, NW Italy; noted for its leaning tower; pop. 102,908.

Pittsburg city, w California 94565; pop. 47,564.

— city, SE Kansas 66762; pop. 17,775.

Pittsburgh city, w Pennsylvania 15200*; pop. 369,879.

Pittsfield city, w Massachusetts 01201; pop. 48,622.

Placentia city, sw California 92670; pop. 41,259.

Plainfield city, NE New Jersey 07061*; pop. 46,567.

Plainview uninc. place, SE New York 11803; pop. 26,207.

— city, NW Texas 79072*; pop. 21,700.

Plainville city, CEN. Connecticut 06062; pop. 17,392.

Plano city, CEN. Texas 75074*; pop. 128,713.

Plantation city, NE Florida 33314; pop. 1,885.

Plant City city w Florida 33566; pop. 22,754.

Platte River river, s Nebraska; 310 mi. long.

Plattsburgh city, NE New York 12901; pop. 21,255.

Pleasant Hill uninc. place, w California 94523; pop. 31,585.

Pleasanton city, w California 94566; pop. 50,553.

Pleasure Ridge Park uninc. place, N Kentucky 40258; pop. 25,131.

Plum boro., sw Pennsylvania 15239; pop. 25,609.

Plymouth co. boro. and port, sw England; pop. 255,500.

Plymouth town, E Massachusetts 02360*; site of the first settlement in New England; pop. 45,608.

— vill., E Minnesota 55427; pop. 50,889.

Plymouth Colony colony of the shore of Massachusetts Bay founded by the Pilgrim Fathers in 1620.

Plymouth Rock rock at Plymouth, Massachusetts, on which the Pilgrim Fathers are said to have landed in 1620.

Pocatello city, Idaho 83201*; pop. 46,080.

Pointe-aux-Trembles city, s Quebec, Canada; pop. 55,618.

Pointe-Claire city, s Quebec, Canada; pop. 25,917.

Point Pleasant boro., E New Jersey 08742; pop. 18,177.

Poland republic, CEN. Europe; 120,727 sq. mi.; pop. 38,064,000; cap. Warsaw.

Polynesia isls. of Oceania, CEN. and SE Pacific; E of Melanesia and Micronesia.

Pomerania former province of Prussia, N Germany; now divided between Germany and Poland.

Pomona city, sw California 91766*; pop. 131,723.

Pompano Beach city, SE Florida 33060*; pop. 72,411.

Pompeii ancient city, s Italy; buried in the eruption of Mount Vesuvius, A.D. 79, now excavated.

Ponca City city N Oklahoma 74601*; pop. 26,359.

Ponce city, s Puerto Rico 00731; pop. 161,260.

Pontiac city, SE Michigan 48053*; pop. 71,166.

Poona city, w India; pop. 356,105.

Poplar Bluff city, SE Missouri 63901; pop. 16,996.

Popocatepetl dormant volcano, CEN. Mexico; 17,887 ft.

Po River river, N Italy; 405 mi. long.

Portage town, NW Indiana 46368; pop. 29,060.

— city, sw Michigan 49081; pop. 41,042.

Port Angeles city, NW Washington 98362; pop. 17,710.

Port Arthur city, SE Texas 77640*; pop. 58,724.

Port-au-Prince city, s Haiti; cap.; pop. 514,438.

Port Chester vill., SE New York 10573*; pop. 24,728.

Port Colborne town, s Ontario, Canada; pop. 20,536.

Port Huron city, E Michigan 48060*; pop. 33,694.

Portland city, sw Maine 04101*; pop. 64,358.

— city, NW Oregon 97208*; pop. 437,319.

Port-of-Spain city, NW Trinidad; cap. of Trinidad and Tobago; pop. 58,300. Also **Port of Spain.**

Porto-Novo city, s Benin; cap.; pop. 104,000.

Port Said city, NE Egypt; at the Mediterranean end of the Suez Canal; pop. 400,000.

Portsmouth co. boro., s England; site of the chief British naval station; pop. 191,000.

— city, SE New Hampshire 03801*; pop. 25,925.

— city, s Ohio 45662; pop. 22,676.

— city, SE Virginia 23705*; pop. 103,907.

Portugal republic, sw Europe; 35,672 sq. mi.; pop. 10,388,000; cap. Lisbon.

Potomac River river through Maryland, West Virginia, and Virginia; 287 mi. long.

Potsdam city, CEN. Germany; scene of meeting of Allied leaders, 1945; pop. 126,262.

Pottstown boro., SE Pennsylvania 19464; pop. 21,831.

Pottsville city, CEN. Pennsylvania 17901; pop. 18,195.

Poughkeepsie city, SE New York 12601*; pop. 28,844.

Poznan city, w Poland; pop. 586,600.

Prague city, w Czechoslovakia; cap.; pop. 1,213,792.

Prairie Village city, NE Kansas 66208; pop. 23,186.

Pretoria city, CEN. South Africa; adm. cap.; pop. 443,059.

Prichard city, sw Alabama 36610; pop. 34,311.

Prince Albert city, CEN. Saskatchewan, Canada; pop. 28,631.

Prince Edward Island prov., NE Canada; 2,185 sq. mi.; pop. 118,229; cap. Charlottetown.

Prince George city, CEN. British Columbia, Canada; pop. 59,929.

Prince Rupert city, w British Columbia, Canada; pop. 14,754.

Provence reg. and former prov., SE France.

Providence city, NE Rhode Island 02904*; cap.; pop. 160,728.

Provo city, CEN. Utah 84601; pop. 86,835.

Prussia former state, N Germany; dissolved 1947.

Pueblo city, CEN. Colorado 81003*; pop. 98,640.

Puerto Rico isl., Greater Antilles; a Commonwealth of the United States 3,515 sq. mi.; pop. 3,187,570; cap. San Juan.

Puget Sound inlet of the Pacific, NW Washington.

Pullman city, SE Washington 99163*; pop. 23,478.

Punjab reg., NW India and E Pakistan.

P'yongyang city, w North Korea; cap.; pop. 2,000,000.

Pyrenees mtn. chain betw. France and Spain.

Qatar monarchy, E Arabia, w coast of the Persian Gulf; 4,400 sq. mi.; pop. 444,000; cap. Doha.

Quebec prov., E Canada; 523,859 sq. mi.; pop. 6,572,300.

— city, s Quebec prov., cap.; pop. 164,580.

Queens borough, E New York City, New York 11300*; pop. 1,951,598.

Queensland state, NE Australia; 666,900 sq. mi.; pop. 2,505,100; cap. Brisbane.

Quemoy Islands 2 isls. of the Republic of China in Formosa Strait; 54 sq. mi.

Quezon City city, CEN. Philippines; cap.; pop. 1,587,140.

Quincy city, w Illinois 62301*; pop. 39,681.

— city, E Massachusetts 02169; pop. 84,985.

Quito city, CEN. Ecuador; cap.; pop. 1,233,865.
Rabat city, N Morocco; cap.; pop. 518,616.
Racine city, SE Wisconsin 53401*; pop. 84,298.
Rahway city, NE New Jersey 07065*; pop. 25,325.
Rainier, Mount extinct volcano, Cascade Range, SW Washington; 14,408 ft.
Raleigh city, CEN. North Carolina 27611*; cap.; pop. 207,951.
Rancho Cordova uninc. place, CEN. California 95670; pop. 48,731.
Randallstown uninc. place, NE Maryland 21133; pop. 26,277.
Randolph town, E Massachusetts 02368; pop. 30,093.
Rangoon (Yangôn) city, S Myanmar; cap.; pop. 2,500,000.
Rantoul vill., CEN. Illinois 61866; pop. 17,212.
Rapid City city, SW South Dakota 57701*; pop. 54,523.
Ravenna city, N Italy, famous for its art treasures and architecture; pop. 136,306.
Rawalpindi city, N Pakistan; pop. 794,843.
Raytown city, W Missouri 64133; pop. 30,601.
Reading town, NE Massachusetts 01867; pop. 22,539.
— city, SE Pennsylvania 19603*; pop. 78,380.
Recife city, NE Brazil; pop. 1,184,215.
Red Deer city, CEN. Alberta, Canada; pop. 32,184.
Redding city, N California 96001*; pop. 66,462.
Redlands city, SW California 92373*; pop. 60,394.
Redondo Beach city, SW California 90277*; pop. 57,102.
Red River river in Texas, Arkansas, and Louisiana; ab. 1,300 mi. long.
— river in N United States and S Canada; 540 mi. long.
Red Sea sea betw. Egypt and Arabia; 1,450 mi. long; ab. 170,000 sq. mi.
Redwood City city, W California 94064*; pop. 66,072.
Regina city, S Saskatchewan, Canada; cap.; pop. 149,593.
Reims NE France; site of a famous cathedral; pop. 181,000.
Reno city, W Nevada 89501*; pop. 133,850.
Renton city, CEN. Washington 98055; pop. 41,688.
Repentigny town, S Quebec, Canada; pop. 26,698.
Réunion French overseas dept.; isl. E of Madagascar; 970 sq. mi.; pop. 600,000; cap. Saint-Denis.
Revere city, E Massachusetts 02151; pop. 42,786.
Reykjavik city, SW Iceland; cap.; pop. 96,708.
Rheims an alternate name of Reims.
Rhine river, CEN. Europe; 810 mi. long.
Rhode Island state, NE United States; 1,212 sq. mi.; pop. 1,005,984; cap. Providence.
Rhodes isl. of the Dodecanese groups; 545 sq. mi.
Rhodesia See Zimbabwe.
Rhône river, Switzerland and SE France; 504 mi. long. Also Rhone.
Rialto city, S California 92376; pop. 72,388.
Richardson city, N Texas 75080*; pop. 74,840.
Richfield vill., E Minnesota 55423; pop. 35,710.
Richland city, S Washington 99352; pop. 32,315.
Richmond borough (Staten Island), SW New York City, New York 10300*; pop. 378,977.
— city, W California 94802*; pop. 87,425.
— city, E Indiana 47374; pop. 38,705.
— city, CEN. Kentucky 40475; pop. 21,155.
— city, CEN. Virginia 23232*; cap.; cap. of the Confederacy 1861–65; pop. 203,056.
Richmond Hill town, S Ontario, Canada; pop. 34,716.
Ridgewood urb. twp., NE New Jersey 07451*; pop. 24,142.
Rif mtn. range, N Morocco. Also Riff.
Riga city, CEN. Latvia; cap.; pop. 915,000.
Rijeka City, NW Yugoslavia; including its SE suburb and officially called Rijeka-Susak; pop. 132,933.
Rimouski town, E Quebec, Canada; pop. 27,897.
Rio de Janeiro city, SE Brazil; former cap.; pop. 5,603,388. Also Rio.
Rio de la Plata estuary of the Paraná and Uruguay rivers betw. Argentina and Uruguay; 170 mi. long.
Rio Grande river betw. Texas and Mexico; 1,890 mi. long.
Riverside city, SW California 92502*; pop. 226,505.
Riviera coastal strip on the Mediterranean from Hyeres, France to La Spezia, Italy.
Riviera Beach town, SE Florida 33404; pop. 27,639.
Roanoke city, W Virginia 24001*; pop. 96,39700,427.
Roanoke Island isl. off North Carolina; 12 mi. long, 3 mi.

wide.
Rochester city, SE Minnesota 55901; pop. 70,745.
— city, SE New Hampshire 03867; pop. 26,630.
— city, W New York 14603*; pop. 231,636.
Rockford city, N Illinois 61125*; pop. 139,426.
Rock Hill city, N South Carolina 29730*; pop. 41,643.
Rock Island city, NW Illinois 61201*; pop. 40,552.
Rockland town, E Massachusetts 02370; pop. 16,123.
Rockville city, CEN. Maryland 20850*; pop. 44,835.
Rockville Centre vill., SE New York 11570*; pop. 24,727.
Rocky Mount city, CEN. North Carolina 27801*; pop. 48,997.
Rocky Mountains mtn. system, W North America; extends from the Arctic to Mexico.
Rocky River city, N Ohio 44116; pop. 20,410.
Rolling Meadows city, NE Illinois 60008; pop. 22,591.
Romania an alternate form of Rumania.
Rome city, W Italy; cap.; site of the Vatican City; cap. of the former Roman republic, the Roman Empire, and the States of the Church; pop. 2,816,474.
— city, NW Georgia 30161*; pop. 30,362.
— city, CEN. New York 13440*; pop. 44,350.
Rosario city, CEN. Argentina; pop. 810,000.
Rosedale uninc. place, NW Maryland 21237; pop. 18,703.
Roselle boro., NE New Jersey 07203 pop. 20,314.
Rosemead city, SW California 91770; pop. 51,638.
Roseville city, CEN. California 95678; pop. 44,685.
— city SE Michigan 48066; pop. 51,412.
— vill., SE Minnesota 55113; pop. 33,485.
Rostov-on-Don city, SW RSFSR; pop. 934,000.
Roswell city, SE New Mexico 88201*; pop. 44,654.
Rotterdam city, W Netherlands; pop. 1,576,232.
Rouen city, N France; site of a famous cathedral; scene of the burning of Joan of Arc; pop. 114,927.
Roumania an alternate form of Rumania.
Rouyn city, W Quebec, Canada; pop. 17,678.
Royal Oak city, SE Michigan 48068*; pop. 65,410.
Rugby municipal boro., CEN. England; site of a boys' school; pop. 60,380.
Ruhr river, W Germany; 142 mi. long.
— reg. S of the Ruhr, an industrial and coal-mining district. 1,770 sq. mi.
Rumania republic, SE Europe; 91,700 sq. mi.; pop. 22,265,000; cap. Bucharest.
Russia before 1917, an empire, E Europe and N Asia; cap. Saint Petersburg (Petrograd); now part of the Union of Soviet Socialist Republics.
Russian Soviet Federated Socialist Republic constituent republic, N USSR; 6,592,800 sq. mi.; pop. 147,400,000; cap. Moscow.
Ruston city, N Louisiana 71270*; pop. 20,027.
Rutherford boro., NE New Jersey 07070*; pop. 17,790.
Rutland city, CEN. Vermont 05701; pop. 18,230.
Rwanda republic, CEN. Africa; 10,169 sq. mi.; pop. 7,232,000; cap. Kigali.
Rye city, SE New York, 10580; pop. 14,936.
Ryukyu Islands isl. group betw. Kyushu and Taiwan; 870 sq. mi.; pop. 1,161,000; chief isl. Okinawa; adm. by Japan.
Saar river, NE France and Germany; 152 mi. long.
Saar, The state, W Germany; 993 sq. mi.; pop. 1,051,000; cap. Saarbrücken.
Sabah part of Malaysia in N Borneo; 28,460 sq. mi.; pop. 1,176,400; cap. Kota Kinabalu.
Sacramento city, CEN. California; 95813*; cap.; pop. 369,365.
Sacramento River river, CEN. California; 382 mi. long.
Saginaw city, CEN. Michigan 48605*; pop. 69,512.
Sahara desert area, N Africa; ab. 3 million sq. mi. Also Sahara Desert.
Saigon city, S Vietnam; formerly cap. of South Vietnam; pop. 3,169,135; also called Ho Chi Minh City.
Saipan one of the Mariana isls.; 47 sq. mi.; captured from Japan by U.S. forces in World War II, 1944.
Saint, Sainte See entries beginning ST., STE.
Sakhalin isl. SE RSFSR; 29,700 sq. mi.; pop. 649,000; adm. ctr. Yuzhno-Sakhalinsk.
Salem city, NE Massachusetts 01970*; pop. 38,091.
— city, SE New Hampshire 03079; pop. 25,746.
— city, NW Oregon 97301*; cap.; pop. 107,786.
— town, CEN. Virginia 24153; pop. 23,756.

Salerno city, sw Italy; scene of a battle in World War II betw. Germans and Allied landing forces, 1943; pop. 153,091.
Salina city, CEN Kansas 67401*; pop. 42,303.
Salinas city, w California 93901*; pop. 108,777.
Salisbury city, SE Maryland 21801; pop. 20,592.
— city, CEN. North Carolina 28144; pop. 23,087.
— city, N Zimbabwe; cap.; pop. 633,000: Now called **Harare**.
Salonika city, NE Greece; pop. 345,799.
Salt Lake City city, CEN. Utah 84101*; cap.; pop. 159,936.
Salvador city, E Brazil; pop. 1,506,602.
— See **El Salvador**.
Salzburg city, w Austria; birthplace of Mozart; pop. 139,000.
Samar one of the Visayan isls., Philippines; 5,050 sq. mi.
Samarkand city, E Uzbek SSR; pop. 481,000.
Samoa isl. group, sw Pacific; 1,173 sq. mi.; divided into **American (or Eastern) Samoa**, an uninc. terr. of the United States; 76 sq. mi.; pop. 27,159; cap. Pago Pago; and **Western Samoa**, an independent monarchy; 1,093 sq. mi.; pop. 165,000; cap. Apia.
Samos isl. of Greece, E Aegean; 184 sq. mi.
Samothrace isl. of Greece, NE Aegean; 71 sq. mi.
San Angelo city, CEN. Texas 76902*; pop. 84,474.
San Antonio city, CEN. Texas 78284*; site of the Alamo; pop. 935,933.
San Benito city, s Texas 78586; pop. 20,125.
San Bernardino city, sw California 92403*; pop. 164,164.
San Bruno city, w California 94066; pop. 38,961.
San Carlos city, w California 94070; pop. 26,167.
San Clemente city, s California 92672; pop. 41,100.
San Diego city, sw California 92109*; pop. 1,110,549.
San Dimas city, sw California 91773; pop. 32,397.
Sandusky city, N Ohio 44870*; pop. 29,764.
San Fernando city, sw California 91340*; pop. 22,580.
Sanford city, Florida 32771; pop. 32,387.
— city, sw Maine 04073; pop. 10,296.
San Francisco city, w California 94101*; pop. 723,959.
San Francisco Bay inlet of the Pacific, w California.
San Gabriel city, sw California 91776*; pop. 37,120.
San Joaquin River river, CEN. California; 317 mi. long.
San José city, CEN. Costa Rica; cap.; pop. 239,800.
San Jose city, w California 95101*; pop. 782,248.
San Juan city, NE Puerto Rico 00936*; cap.; pop. 431,227.
San Leandro city, w California 94577*; pop. 68,223.
San Lorenzo uninc. place, w California 94580; pop. 19,987.
San Luis Obispo city, w California 93401*; pop. 41,958.
San Marcos city, CEN. Texas 78666; pop. 28,743.
San Marino republic, an enclave in NE Italy; 24 sq. mi.; pop. 23,000.
— city, San Marino; cap.; pop. 2,343.
San Mateo city, w California 94402*; pop. 85,486.
San Pablo city, w California 94806; pop. 25,158.
San Rafael city, w California 94901*; pop. 48,404.
San Salvador city, s El Salvador; cap.; pop. 459,902.
— isl. CEN. Bahamas; site of Columbus' first landing in the western hemisphere, 1492.
Santa Ana city, sw California 92711*; pop. 293,742.
Santa Barbara city, sw California 93102*; pop. 85,571.
Santa Catalina isl. off sw California; 70 sq. mi.
Santa Clara city, w California 95050*; pop. 93,613.
Santa Cruz city, w California 95060*; pop. 49,040.
Santa Fe city, N New Mexico 87501*; cap.; pop. 55,859.
Santa Fe Trail trade route, important from 1821N80, betw. Independence, Missouri, and Santa Fe, New Mexico.
Santa Maria city, sw California 93454*; pop. 61,284.
Santa Monica city, sw California 90406*; pop. 86,905.
Santa Paula city, sw California 93060; pop. 25,062.
Santa Rosa city, w California 95402*; pop. 113,313.
Santee uninc. place, sw California 92071; pop. 52,902.
Santiago city, CEN. Chile; cap.; pop. 5,133,700. Also **Santiago de Chile**.
Santo Domingo city, s Dominican Republic; cap.; pop. 1,600,000.
São Paulo city, SE Brazil; pop. 10,063,000.
São Tomé and Principe republic, isls. off w Africa; 366 sq. mi.; pop. 121,000; cap. São Tomé.
— São Tomé city; cap. São Tomé isl.; 34,997.
Sapulpa city, CEN. Oklahoma 74066; pop. 18,074.
Sarajevo city, CEN. Yugoslavia; scene of the assassination of

Archduke Franz Ferdinand, June 28, 1914; pop. 244,045.
Sarasota city sw Florida 33578*; pop. 50,961.
Saratoga city, w California 95070; pop. 28,061.
Saratoga Springs city, CEN. New York 12866; pop. 25,001.
Sarawak part of Malaysia on NW Borneo; 48,050 sq. mi.; pop. 1,591,100; cap. Kuching.
Sardinia isl., CEN. Mediterranean; with adjacent isls. a reg. of Italy; 9,301 sq. mi.; pop. 1,617,215; cap. Cagliari.
Sarnia city, s Ontario, Canada; pop. 55,576.
Saskatchewan prov., CEN. Canada; 251,866 sq. mi.; pop. 1,000,300; cap. Regina.
Saskatoon city, CEN. Saskatchewan, Canada; pop. 177,641.
Saudi Arabia monarchy, N and CEN. Arabia; 865,000 sq. mi.; pop. 14,131,000; cap. Riyadh.
Saugus town, NE Massachusetts 01906; pop. 25,549.
Sault Ste. Marie city, CEN. Ontario, Canada; pop. 81,044.
Sault Sainte Marie Canals 3 canals that circumvent the rapids in the St. Marys River betw. Lakes Superior and Huron.
Savannah city, E Georgia 31401*; pop. 137,560.
Saxony reg. and former duchy, electorate, kingdom, and prov., CEN. Germany.
Sayreville boro., E New Jersey 08872; pop. 34,986.
Scandinavia reg. NW Europe; includes Sweden, Norway, and Denmark and sometimes Finland, Iceland, and the Faeroe Islands.
Scapa Flow sea basin and British naval base in the Orkney Islands, Scotland; 50 sq. mi.
Scarsdale town, SE New York 10583; pop. 16,987.
Schaumburg city, NE Illinois 60172; pop. 68,586.
Scheldt river, N France, Belgium and the Netherlands; 270 mi. long.
Schenectady city, E New York 12301*; pop. 65,566.
Schleswig-Holstein state, NE Germany; 6,069 sq. mi.; pop. 2,614,000; cap. Kiel.
Schuylkill River river, SE Pennsylvania; 130 mi. long.
Scituate city, NE Massachusetts 02066; pop. 16,786.
Scotch Plains urb. twp., NE New Jersey 07076; pop. 21,160.
Scotland a political div. and the N part of Great Britain; a separate kingdom until 1707; 30,418 sq. mi.; pop. 5,094,000; cap. Edinburgh.
Scottsdale city, CEN. Arizona 85251*; pop. 130,069.
Scranton city, NE Pennsylvania 18503*; pop. 81,805.
Seaford uninc. place, SE New York 11783; pop. 15,597.
Seal Beach city, sw California 90740; pop. 25,098.
Seaside city, w California 93955; pop. 38,901.
Seattle city, CEN. Washington 98109*; pop. 516,259.
Sebastopol See Sevastopol.
Security unic. place, CEN. Colorado 80911; pop. 18,768.
Sedalia city, CEN. Missouri 65301*; pop. 19,800.
Seguin city, CEN. Texas 78155; pop. 18,853.
Seine river, NE France; 482 mi. long.
Selma city, CEN. Alabama 36701*; pop. 23,755.
Semarang city, N Java, Indonesia; pop. 646,590.
Senegal river, NW Africa; ab. 1,000 mi. long.
Senegal, Republic of republic, NW Africa; 75,955 sq. mi.; pop. 7,277,000; cap. Dakar.
Seoul city, NW South Korea; cap.; pop. 8,114,000.
Sept-Iles city, E Quebec, Canada; pop. 30,617.
Serbia constituent republic, E Yugoslavia; 21,609 sq. mi.; pop. 5,627,000; cap. Belgrade.
Sevastopol city, s Crimea, USSR; pop. 308,000.
Severn river, N Wales and w England; 210 mi. long.
Severna Park city, NE Maryland 21146; pop. 25,879.
Seville city, sw Spain; pop. 655,435.
Sèvres city, N France; pop. 21,149.
Seychelles isl. republic off E Africa; 175 sq. mi.; pop. 68,700; cap. Victoria.
Shaker Heights city, N Ohio 44120; pop. 30,831.
Shanghai city, E China; pop. 7,228,600.
Shannon river, CEN. Ireland; 224 mi. long.
Sharon city, w Pennsylvania 16146; pop. 17,493.
Shasta, Mount extinct volcano, Cascade Range, N California; 14,162 ft.
Shawinigan city, s Quebec, Canada; pop. 24,921.
Shawnee city, NE Kansas 66203*; pop. 29,653.
— city, CEN. Oklahoma 74801*; pop. 26,017.
Sheboygan city, E Wisconsin 53081; pop. 49,676.
Sheffield co. boro., CEN. England; pop. 544,200.

Shelby city, sw North Carolina 28150; pop. 14,669.
Shelton city, sw Connecticut 06484; pop. 35,418.
Shenandoah river, N Virginia and NE West Virginia; 170 mi. long.
Shenyang city, NE China; pop. 3,700,000; formerly called Mukden.
Sherbrooke city, s Quebec, Canada; pop. 76,804.
Sherman city, N Texas 75090; pop. 31,601.
Shetland Islands isl. group NE of the Orkney Islands, comprising **Shetland**, a co. of Scotland; 551 mi.; pop. 17,000; cap. Lerwick.
Shikoku isl., sw Japan; 7,248 sq. mi.
Shiloh national military park, sw Tennessee; scene of a Union victory in the Civil War, 1862; 6 sq. mi.
Shively city, N Kentucky 40216; pop. 15,535.
Shreveport city, NW Louisiana 71102*; pop. 198,525.
Shrewsbury city, CEN. Massachusetts 01545; pop. 24,146.
Siam *the former name of* Thailand.
Siam, Gulf of part of the South China Sea betw. the Malay Peninsula and Indochina.
Siberia reg., E RSFSR; ab. 5 million sq. mi.
Sicily isl. of Italy, CEN. Mediterranean; comprises with neighboring islands a reg. of 9,926 sq. mi.; pop. 5,006,684; cap. Palermo.
Sidney city, w Ohio 45365; pop. 18,710.
Sierra Leone republic, w Africa; 27,699 sq. mi.; pop. 4,151,000; cap. Freetown.
Sierra Nevada mtn. range, E California.
Silesia reg., CEN. Europe; divided betw. Czechoslovakia and Poland.
Silver Spring uninc. place, w Maryland 20907*; pop. 76,046.
Simi Valley city, sw California 93065; pop. 100,217.
Simla city, N India; pop. 55,368.
Simsbury city, CEN. Connecticut 06070; pop. 22,023.
Sinai penin., E Egypt, betw. the Mediterranean and the Red Sea.
Singapore isl. republic off the tip of the Malay Peninsula; 239 sq. mi.; pop. 2,718,000.
— city, s Singapore; cap.; pop. 2,390,800.
Sinkiang-Uigur Autonomous Region div. w China; 635,900 sq. mi.; pop. ab. 15,155,000; cap. Urumchi (Tihwa). Also formerly **Sinkiang**.
Sioux City city, w Iowa 51101*; pop. 80,505.
Sioux Falls city, SE South Dakota 57101*; pop. 100,814.
Skokie vill., NE Illinois 60076*; pop. 59,432.
Slidell town, E Louisiana 70458; pop. 24,124.
Slovakia reg. and former prov., E Czechoslovakia.
Slovenia constituent republic, NW Yugoslavia; 7,819 sq. mi.; pop. 1,866,000; cap. Ljubljana.
Smyrna town, CEN. Georgia 30080; pop. 30,981.
— *an alternate name of* Izmir, Turkey.
Society Islands isl. group, French Polynesia; ab. 650 sq. mi.
Sofia city, w Bulgaria; cap.; pop. 1,047,920.
Solomon Islands isl. monarchy, sw Pacific; ab. 10,954 sq. mi.; pop. 319,000; cap. Honiara.
Somalia republic, E Africa; 246,000 sq. mi.; pop. 7,555,000; cap. Mogadishu. Also **Somali Democratic Republic.**
Somerset town, SE Massachusetts 02725; pop. 17,665.
Somerville city, E Massachusetts 02143, pop. 76,210.
Somme river, N France; 150 mi. long.
Soo Canals *informal name of* Sault Sainte Marie Canals.
Sorel city, s Quebec, Canada; pop. 19,666.
South Africa, Republic of republic, s Africa; 433,680 sq. mi.; pop. 30,797,000; seat of government Pretoria; seat of legislature Cape Town.
South America s continent of the Western Hemisphere; ab. 6,860,000 sq. mi.
Southampton co. boro., s England; pop. 207,800.
South Australia state, s Australia; 379,900 sq. mi.; pop. 1,425,000; cap. Adelaide.
South Bend city, N Indiana 46624*; pop. 105,511.
Southbridge uninc. place s Massachusetts 01550*; pop. 17,816.
South Carolina state, SE United States; 31,113 sq. mi.; pop. 3,505,707; cap. Columbia.
South Charleston city, CEN. West Virginia 25303; pop. 13,645.
South China Sea part of the Pacific betw. SE Asia and the Malay Archipelago.

South Dakota state, CEN. United States; 77,116 sq. mi.; pop. 699,999; cap. Pierre.
Southern Yemen See Yemen.
South Euclid city, NE Ohio 44121; pop. 23,866.
Southfield city, SE Michigan 48075*; pop. 75,728.
Southgate city, SE Michigan 48198; pop. 30,771.
South Gate city, sw California 90280; pop. 86,284.
South Hadley town, CEN. Massachusetts 01075; pop. 16,685.
South Holland vill., SE Illinois 60473; pop. 22,105.
Southington city, CEN. Connecticut 06489; pop. 38,518.
South Island one of the two main isls. of New Zealand; 58,093 sq. mi.
South Korea See Korea.
South Milwaukee city SE Wisconsin 53172; pop. 20,958.
South Orange vill., NE New Jersey 07079; pop. 16,390.
South Pasadena city, sw California 91030; pop. 23,936.
South Plainfield boro., NE New Jersey 07080; pop. 20,489.
South Pole s extremity of the earth's axis.
South Portland city, sw Maine 04106; pop. 23,163.
South St. Paul city, E Minnesota 55075; pop. 20,197.
South San Francisco city, w California 94080*; pop. 54,312.
South Sea Islands isls. of the South Pacific.
South Seas waters of the Southern Hemisphere, esp. the **South Pacific Ocean.**
South-West Africa formerly mandated terr., sw Africa; administered by the Republic of South Africa; now **Namibia.**
South Windsor city, CEN. Connecticut 06074; pop. 22,090.
Soviet Russia 1 Russian Soviet Federated Socialist Republic. 2 Union of Soviet Socialist Republics.
Soviet Union *an alternate name of* Union of Soviet Socialist Republics.
Spain monarchy, sw Europe; 194,885 sq. mi.; pop. 39,618,000; cap. Madrid.
Spanish America parts of the w hemisphere where Spanish is the predominant language.
Spanish Lake uninc. place, NE Missouri 63138; pop. 20,322.
Sparks city, w Nevada 89431; pop. 53,367.
Sparta city-state of ancient Greece, famous for its military power: sometimes called **Lacedaemon.**
Spartanburg city, NW South Carolina 29301*; pop. 43,467.
Spitsbergen See Svalbard.
Spokane city E Washington 99210*; pop. 177,196.
Springdale city, NW Arkansas 72764; pop. 29,941.
Springfield city, CEN. Illinois 62703*; cap.; pop. 105,227.
— city, sw Massachusetts 01101*; pop. 156,983.
— city, sw Missouri 63801*; pop. 140,494.
— city, CEN. Ohio 45501*; pop. 70,487.
— city, w Oregon 97477; pop. 44,683.
— uninc. place, SE Pennsylvania 19063; pop. 24,160.
Spring Valley vill., SE New York 10977; pop. 21,802.
Sri Lanka isl. republic s of India, formerly called Ceylon; 25,332 sq. mi.; pop. 16,109,000; cap. Colombo.
Stalingrad *the former name of* Volgograd.
Stamford city, sw Connecticut 06904*; pop. 108,056.
St. Ann city, E Missouri 63074; pop. 14,489.
Stanton city, sw California 90680; pop. 30,491.
State College boro., CEN. Pennsylvania 16801*; pop. 38,923.
Staten Island isl., SE New York City, at the entrance to New York Harbor.
— Richmond borough, sw New York City, New York 10300*; pop. 378,977.
Statesville city, CEN North Carolina 28677; pop. 17,567.
Staunton city, CEN. Virginia 24401; pop. 24,461.
St.-Bruno-de-Montarville town, CEN. Quebec, Canada; pop. 21,272.
St. Catharines city, s Ontario, Canada; pop. 123,351.
St. Charles city, E Missouri 63301*; pop. 54,555.
St. Clair, Lake lake betw. s Ontario and SE Michigan; 460 sq. mi.
St. Clair Shores vill., SE Michigan 48083*; pop. 68,107.
St. Cloud city, CEN. Minnesota 56301*; pop. 48,812.
St. Croix one of the Virgin Islands of the United States; 82 sq. mi.
Ste.-Foy city, s Quebec, Canada; pop. 71,237.
Sterling city, NW Illinois 61081; pop. 15,132.
Sterling Heights city, SE Michigan 48078*; pop. 117,810.
Ste.-Thérèse city, s Quebec, Canada; pop. 17,479.

Stettin *the German name for* Szczecin.
Steubenville city, E Ohio 43952; pop. 22,125.
Stevens Point city, CEN. Wisconsin 54481; pop. 23,006.
St. Helena isl., South Atlantic; British colony with Ascension Island and the Tristan da Cunha group as dependencies; 133 sq. mi.; pop. 5,147; cap. Jamestown; site of Napoleon's exile, 1815 to 21.
St. Hubert town, S Quebec, Canada; pop. 49,706.
St. Hyacinthe city, S Quebec, Canada; pop. 37,500.
Stillwater city, CEN. Oklahoma 74074*; pop. 36,676.
St. Jean city, S Quebec, Canada; pop. 34,363.
St. Jérôme city, S Quebec, Canada; pop. 25,175.
St. John one of the Virgin Islands of the United States; 19 sq. mi.
— city, S New Brunswick, Canada; pop. 85,976.
St. John's city, SE Newfoundland, Canada; cap.; pop. 86,576.
St. Joseph city, NW Missouri 64501*; pop. 71,852.
St. Kitts and Nevis monarchy isls. in the Lesser Antilles; 104 sq. mi.; pop. 44,100; cap. Basseterre.
St. Lambert city, S Quebec, Canada; pop. 20,318.
St. Laurent city, S Quebec, Canada; pop. 64,404.
St. Lawrence, Gulf of inlet of the Atlantic E Canada.
St. Lawrence River river, SE Canada; the outlet of the Great Lakes system; 1,900 mi. long.
St. Lawrence Seaway system of ship canals extending 114 miles along the St. Lawrence River from Montreal to Lake Ontario.
St. Leonard city, CEN. Quebec, Canada; pop. 78,452.
St. Louis city, E Missouri 63155*; pop. 396,685.
St. Louis Park vill., E Minnesota 55426; pop. 43,787.
Stockholm city, SE Sweden; cap.; pop. 1,629,631.
Stockton city, CEN. California 95204*; pop. 210,943.
Stoneham town, NE Massachusetts 02180; pop. 22,203.
Stonington city, NE Connecticut 06378; pop. 16,919.
Stoughton town, E Massachusetts 02072; pop. 26,777.
Stow vill., CEN. Ohio 44224; pop. 27,702.
St. Paul city, SE Minnesota 55101*; cap.; pop. 272,235.
St. Petersburg city, W Florida 33730*; pop. 893,629.
— *the former name of* Leningrad.
Strasbourg city, NE France; pop. 253,834.
Stratford town, SE Connecticut 06497; pop. 49,389.
— city, S Ontario, Canada; pop. 25,657.
Stratford-on-Avon town, CEN. England; birthplace and burial place of Shakespeare; pop. 20,080.
Streamwood city, NE Illinois 60103; pop. 30,987.
Strongsville vill., N Ohio 44136; pop. 35,308.
St. Thomas one of the Virgin Islands of the United States; 28 sq. mi.; pop. 16,201.
— city, S Ontario, Canada; pop. 27,206.
Stuttgart city, SW Germany; pop. 581,989.
St. Vincent and the Grenadines monarchy isls. in the Windward Islands; 150 sq. mi.; pop. 115,000; cap. Kingstown.
Sucre city, CEN. Bolivia; judicial cap.; pop. 105,800.
Sudan reg., N Africa S of the Sahara.
Sudan, Republic of the republic, NE Africa; 966,757 sq. mi.; pop. 28,311,000; cap. Khartoum.
Sudbury city, CEN. Ontario, Canada; pop. 97,604.
Sudetenland border dists., W Czechoslovakia.
Suez city, NE Egypt; pop. 204,000.
Suez, Gulf of inlet of the Red Sea, NE Egypt.
Suez, Isthmus of strip of land joining Asia and Africa, betw. the Gulf of Suez and the Mediterranean.
Suez Canal ship canal across the Isthmus of Suez; 107 mi.
Suitland-Silver Hills uninc. place, CEN. Maryland 20023; pop. 35,111.
Sulawesi isl. of Indonesia, E of Borneo; 73,057 sq. mi.; pop. 11,341,000.
Sulu Archipelago isl. group, SW Philippines; 1,086 sq. mi.
Sumatra isl. of Indonesia S of the Malay Peninsula; 208,948 sq. mi.; pop. 22,934,000.
Summit city, NE New Jersey 07901; pop. 19,757.
Sumter city, CEN. South Carolina 29150*; pop. 41,943.
Sunnyvale city, W California 94086*; pop. 117,229.
Superior city, NW Wisconsin 54880*; pop. 27,134.
Superior, Lake largest of the Great Lakes; 31,820 sq. mi.
Surabaya city, NE Java, Indonesia; pop. 2,027,913.
Suriname republic, former Dutch colony NE coast of S. America; 63,251 sq. mi.; pop. 411,000; cap. Paramaribo.

Susquehanna river, New York, Pennsylvania, and Maryland; 444 mi. long.
Suwannee River river, Georgia and Florida; 250 mi. long.
Svalbard isl. group of Norway, Arctic Ocean; 23,958 sq. mi.: sometimes called Spitsbergen.
Swaziland republic, SE Africa; 6,704 sq. mi.; pop. 770,000; caps. Mbabane (admin.) and Lobamba (legislat.).
Sweden monarchy, NW Europe; 173,732 sq. mi.; pop. 8,529,000; cap. Stockholm.
Sweetwater Creek city, NW Florida 33601; pop. 13,909.
Swift Current city, SW Saskatchewan, Canada; pop. 14,264.
Switzerland federal state, CEN. Europe; 15,943 sq. mi.; pop. 6,756,000; cap. Bern.
Sydney city, NE Nova Scotia, Canada; pop. 30,645.
— city, E New South Wales, Australia; cap.; pop. 3,596,000.
Syracuse city, CEN. New York 13201*; pop. 163,860.
Syria republic, SW Asia; 71,498 sq. mi.; pop. 12,116,000; cap. Damascus.
Szczecin city, NW Poland; pop. 409,500. German name Stettin.
Tabriz city, NW Iran; pop. 971,482.
Tacoma city, W Washington 98402*; pop. 176,664.
Tadzhik SSR constituent republic, S USSR; 55,300 sq. mi.; pop. 5,109,000; cap. Dushanbe.
Tahiti isl., Society group; 402 sq. mi.; pop. 85,000.
Tahoe, Lake lake E California and W Nevada; ab. 195 sq. mi.
Taipei N Taiwan; cap.; pop. 2,681,857.
Taiwan isl. off SE China; comprises with the Pescadores, the Republic of China; 13,900 sq. mi.; pop. 20,221,000; cap. Taipei; *formerly called* Formosa.
Takoma Park city W Maryland 20912; pop. 16,700.
Talledaga city, CEN. Alabama 35160; pop. 18,175.
Tallahassee city, N Florida 32303*; cap.; pop. 124,773.
Tallinn city, N Estonia; cap.; pop. 482,000.
Tallmadge city, NE Ohio 44278; pop. 14,870.
Tampa city, W Florida 33602*; pop. 280,015.
Tampico city, E Mexico; pop. 240,000.
Tanganyika, Lake lake, CEN. Africa; 12,700 sq. mi.
Tangier city, N Morocco; pop. 187,894.
Tanzania republic, E Africa, includes Tanganyika and Zanzibar; 364,217 sq. mi.; pop. 24,403,000; cap. Dar es Salaam.
Taranto city, SE Italy; pop. 247,681.
Tashkent city, E Uzbek SSR; cap.; pop. 1,816,000.
Tasmania isl., SE Australia; comprises a state; 26,200 sq. mi.; pop. 437,300; cap. Hobart.
Taunton city, SE Massachusetts 02780*; pop. 49,832.
Taylor city, SE Michigan 48180; pop. 70,811.
Tbilisi city, SE Georgian SSR; cap.; pop. 1,260,000.
Teaneck urb. twp., NE New Jersey 07666; pop. 37,825.
Tegucigalpa city, CEN. Honduras; cap.; pop. 551,606.
Tehran city, CEN. Iran; cap.; pop. 6,042,584.
Tel Aviv city, W Israel; includes Jaffa; pop. 317,800.
Tempe city, CEN. Arizona 85282*; pop. 141,865.
Temple CEN. Texas 76501; pop. 46,109.
Tennessee state, CEN. United States; 42,144 sq. mi.; pop. 4,896,641; cap. Nashville.
Tennessee River river, flowing through E Tennessee, N Alabama, W Tennessee, and SW Kentucky; 652 mi. long.
Terre Haute city, W Indiana 47808*; pop. 57,483.
Tewksbury city, NE Massachusetts 01876; pop. 27,266.
Texarkana city, SW Arkansas at the Arkansas-Texas line 75501; pop. 22,631.
— city, NE Texas; adjacent to and integrated with Texarkana, Arkansas 75501*; pop. 31,656.
Texas N state S United States; 266,807 sq. mi.; pop. 17,059,805; cap. Austin.
Texas City city, SE Texas 77590*; pop. 40,822.
Thailand monarchy, SE Asia; 198,115 sq. mi.; pop. 56,217,000; cap. Bangkok; *formerly called* Siam.
Thames river, S England; 209 mi. long.
Thessaly div., CEN. Greece; 5,399 sq. mi.
Thetford Mines city S Quebec, Canada; pop. 20,784.
Thomasville city, S Georgia 31792; pop. 17,457.
Thorold town, S Ontario, Canada; pop. 14,944.
Thousand Islands group of ab. 1,500 isls. in the St. Lawrence River.
Thousand Oaks city, SE California 91360*; pop. 104,352
Thrace reg., E Balkan Peninsula.
Thunder Bay city, W Ontario, Canada; pop. 111,476.

Tiber river, CEN. Italy; 245 mi. long.
Tibet adm. div., w China; 471,700 sq. mi.; pop. 1,930,000; cap. Lhasa; formerly independent.
Tientsin city, NE China; pop. 4,300,000.
Tierra del Fuego isl. group, s South America, included in Chile and Argentina; 7,996 sq. mi. (Argentina), 19,480 sq. mi. (Chile).
Tiffin city, CEN. Ohio 44883; pop. 18,604.
Tigris river, sw Asia, ab. 1,150 mi. long.
Tijuana city, NW Lower California, Mexico; pop. 535,000.
Timbuktu town, CEN. Mali; pop. 11,900.
Timmins town, CEN. Ontario, Canada; pop. 44,747.
Timonium-Lutherville uninc. place, CEN. Maryland 21093; pop. 17,845.
Timor isl., SE Malay Archipelago; 11,965 sq. mi.; pop. 1,356,000; w Timor has been part of Indonesia since 1949; E Timor, formerly a Portuguese overseas province, was annexed by Indonesia in 1976.
Tirana city, CEN. Albania; cap.; pop. 238,100.
Tirol See Tyrol.
Titicaca, Lake lake betw. SE Peru and w Bolivia; 3,200 sq. mi.; elevation 12,500 ft.
Titusville city, E Florida 32870; pop. 39,394.
Tobago See **Trinidad and Tobago.**
Togo republic, w Africa; 21,925 sq. mi.; pop. 3,764,000; cap. Lomé.
Tokyo city, E Japan; cap.; pop. 8,278,116.
Toledo city, CEN. Spain; pop. 56,414.
— city, NW Ohio 43601*; pop. 332,943.
Tomsk city, s RSFSR; pop. 431,000.
Tonawanda city, w New York 14150*; pop. 17,284.
Tonga monarchy; isl. group, SE of Fiji; 301 sq. mi.; pop. 96,300; cap. Nuku'alofa.
Topeka city, NE Kansas 66603*; cap.; pop. 119,883.
Toronto city, s Ontario, Canada; pop. 633,318.
Torrance city, sw California 90510*; pop. 133,107.
Torrington city, sw Connecticut 06790*; pop. 33,687.
Toulon city, s France; pop. 168,000.
Toulouse city, s France; pop. 359,000.
Towson uninc. place, CEN. Maryland 21204; pop. 49,445.
Trafalgar, Cape headland, sw Spain; scene of a naval victory of Nelson over the French and Spanish, 1805.
Transcaucasia reg., SE USSR; betw. the Caucasus mountains and Iran and Turkey.
Transvaal province, NE South Africa; 101,352 sq. mi.; pop. 8,950,000; cap. Pretoria.
Traverse City city, NW Michigan 49684; pop. 15,155.
Trenton city, SE Michigan 48183; pop. 20,586.
— city, w New Jersey 08608*; cap.; pop. 88,675.
Trieste city, NE Italy; pop. 235,014.
Trinidad and Tobago isl republic off N Venezuela; comprises isls. of **Trinidad;** 1,864 sq. mi., and **Tobago;** 116 sq. mi.; pop. 1,233,000; cap. Port-of-Spain.
Tripoli city, NW Lebanon; pop. 500,000.
— city, NW Libya; cap.; pop. 591,062.
Trois-Rivieres city, s Quebec, Canada; pop. 52,518.
Troy city, SE Michigan 48084; pop. 72,884.
— city, E New York 12180*; pop. 54,269.
— city, w Ohio 45373; pop. 19,478.
Trumbull city, SE Connecticut 06611; pop. 32,016.
Tucson city, SE Arizona 85726*; pop. 405,390.
Tulare city, CEN. California 93274; pop. 33,249.
Tullahoma city, CEN. Tennessee 37388; pop. 16,761.
Tulsa city, NE Oklahoma 74101*; pop. 367,302.
Tunis city, NE Tunisia; cap.; pop. 596,654.
Tunisia republic, N Africa; 59,664 sq. mi.; pop. 8,182,000; cap. Tunis.
Tupelo city, NE Mississippi 38801*; pop. 30,685.
Turin city, NW Italy; pop. 1,160,162.
Turkestan reg., CEN. Asia; extends from the Caspian Sea to the Gobi Desert.
Turkey republic, sw Asia; 300,948 sq. mi.; pop. 56,941,000; cap. Ankara. See **Anatolia.**
Turkmen SSR constituent republic, s USSR; 188,500 sq. mi.; pop. 3,534,000; cap. Ashkhabad.
Tuscaloosa city, CEN. Alabama 35403*; pop. 77,759.
Tustin city, sw California 92680; pop. 50,689.
Tutuila chief isl., American Samoa; 53 sq. mi.

Twin Falls city, s Idaho 83301*; pop. 27,591.
Tyler city, E Texas 75702*; pop. 75,450.
Tyrol reg., w Austria and N Italy.
Ubangi river, CEN. Africa; 1,400 mi. long.
Uganda military republic, CEN. Africa; 93,100 sq. mi.; pop. 16,928,000; cap. Kampala.
Ukrainian SSR constituent republic sw USSR; 233,100 sq. mi.; pop. 51,707,000; cap. Kiev. Also **Ukraine.**
Ulan Bator city, CEN. Mongolia; cap.; pop. 548,400.
Ulster former prov., N Ireland, of which the N part became Northern Ireland, 1925.
— prov., N Republic of Ireland; comprises the part of Ulster that remained after 1925; 3,093 sq. mi.; pop. 230,159.
Union urb. twp., NE New Jersey 07083*; pop. 50,024.
Union City city, NE New Jersey 07087; pop. 58,012.
Uniondale uninc. place, SE New York 11553; pop. 20,328.
Union of Soviet Socialist Republics federal union of 12 constituent republics occupying most of N Eurasia; 8,649,800 sq. mi.; pop. 290,122,000; cap. Moscow.
United Arab Emirates monarchy, E Arabia, composed of 7 emirates (*formerly* **Trucial States**); 30,000 sq. mi.; pop. 1,903,000; cap. Abu Dhabi.
United Arab Republic *the former name of* Egypt.
United Kingdom constitutional monarchy comprising Great Britain (England, Scotland, and Wales), Northern Ireland, the Isle of Man, and the Channel Islands; 94,248 sq. mi.; pop. 57,384,000; cap. London: officially **United Kingdom of Great Britain and Northern Ireland.**
United States of America federal republic, including 50 states (49 in North America, and Hawaii, an archipelago in the Pacific Ocean), and the District of Columbia (3,679,192 sq. mi.; pop. 248,709,873), and the Canal Zone, Puerto Rico, the Virgin Islands of the United States, American Samoa, and Guam, Wake, and other Pacific isls.; cap. Washington, coextensive with the District of Columbia.
University City city, E Missouri 63130; pop. 40,087.
University Heights city, N Ohio 44118; pop. 14,790.
University Park city, N Texas 76308; pop. 22,259.
Upland city, sw California 91786; pop. 63,374.
Upper Arlington city, CEN. Ohio 43221; pop. 34,128.
Upper Darby uninc. place, SE Pennsylvania 19082; pop. 84,054.
Upper Volta *the former name of* Burkina Faso.
Ural Mountains mtn. system in the RSFSR, extending from the Arctic Ocean to the Kasakh SSR.
Ural River river s RSFSR and w Kazakh SSR; 1,574 mi. long.
Urbana city, E Illinois 61801*; pop. 36,344.
Uruguay republic, SE South America; 68,037 sq. mi.; pop. 3,033,000; cap. Montevideo.
Uruguay River river, SE South America; 1,000 mi. long.
Utah state, CEN. United States; 84,899 sq. mi.; pop. 1,727,784; cap. Salt Lake City.
Utica city, CEN. New York 13503*; pop. 68,637.
Utrecht city, CEN. Netherlands; pop. 230,634.
Uzbek SSR constituent republic s USSR; 172,700 sq. mi.; pop. 19,905,000; cap. Tashkent.
Vacaville city, CEN. California 95688; pop. 71,479.
Val-d'Or town, w Quebec, Canada; pop. 19,915.
Valdosta city, s Georgia 31603*; pop. 39,806.
Valencia city, E Spain; pop. 732,491.
Vallejo city, w California 94590*; pop. 109,199.
Valleyfield city, s Quebec, Canada; pop. 29,716. Also **Salaberry de Valleyfield.**
Valley Forge locality, SE Pennsylvania, scene of Washington's winter encampment 1777–78.
Valley Station uninc. place, N Kentucky 40272; pop. 22,840.
Valley Stream vill., SE New York 11580*; pop. 33,946.
Valparaiso city, CEN. Chile; pop. 288,294.
— city, NW Indiana 46383; pop. 24,414.
Vancouver city, sw Washington 98660*; pop. 46,380.
— city, sw British Columbia, Canada; pop. 431,137.
Vancouver Island isl., off sw British Columbia, Canada; 12,408 sq. mi.
Vanuatu republic, isl. group member of the Commonwealth, sw Pacific, formerly **New Hebrides;** 4,707 sq. mi.; pop. 147,000; cap. Vila.
Vatican City sovereign papal state within Rome; includes the Vatican and St. Peter's Church; established June 10, 1929;

108.7 acres; pop. 1,000.

Venezuela republic, N South America; 352,144 sq. mi.; pop. 19,735,000; cap. Caracas.

Venice city, NE Italy; pop. 324,294.

Venice, Gulf of N part of the Adriatic.

Ventura city, S California 93002*; pop. 92,575.

Veracruz state, SE Mexico; 27,683 sq. mi.; pop. 6,171,000; cap. Jalapa; largest city Veracruz.

Verde, Cape westernmost point of Africa; a penin.; ab. 20 mi. long.

Verdun town, NE France; scene of several battles of World War I; pop. 23,621.

— city, S Quebec, Canada; pop. 68,013.

Vermont state, NE United States; 9,279 sq. mi.; pop. 564,964; cap. Montpelier.

Vernon city, NE Connecticut 06060; pop. 29,841.

Verona city, NE Italy; pop. 258,724.

Versailles city, N France; site of the palace of Louis XIV; scene of the signing of a treaty (1919) betw. the Allies and Germany after World War I; pop. 94,145.

Vesuvius active volcano, W Italy; 3,891 ft.

Vichy city, CEN. France; provisional cap. during German occupation, World War II; pop. 32,117.

Vicksburg city, W Mississippi 39180; pop. 20,908; besieged and taken by the Union Army in the Civil War, 1863.

Victoria state, SE Australia; 87,900 sq. mi.; pop. 4,321,500; cap. Melbourne.

— city, SW British Columbia; cap.; pop. 62,551.

— city, S Texas 77901*; pop. 55,076.

Victoria, Lake lake betw. Uganda, Tanganyika, and Kenya; 26,828 sq. mi. Also **Victoria Nyanza.**

Victoria Falls cataract on the Zambesi River betw. Northern and Southern Rhodesia; 343 ft. high; over a mile wide.

Victoriaville town, S Quebec, Canada; pop. 21,825.

Vienna city, NE Austria; cap.; pop. 1,482,825.

— town, NE Virginia 22180; pop. 14,852.

Vientiane city, CEN. Laos; adm cap.; pop. 377,409.

Vietnam republic, SW Indochina; 127,246 sq. mi.; pop. 66,128,000; cap. Hanoi; from 1954 to 1976 divided into **North Vietnam** and **South Vietnam**, with caps. at Hanoi and Saigon, respectively.

Villa Park vill., NE Illinois 60181; pop. 22,253.

Vilnius city, SE Lithuania; cap.; pop. 582,000. Also **Vilna, Vilnyus.**

Vincennes city, SW Indiana 47591; pop. 19,859.

Vineland boro., S New Jersey 08360; pop. 54,780.

Virginia state, E United States; 40,767 sq. mi.; pop. 6,216,568; cap. Richmond.

Virginia Beach city, SE Virginia 23458*; pop. 393,069.

Virgin Islands isl. group, West Indies E of Puerto Rico. See **British Virgin Islands.**

Virgin Islands of the United States uninc. terr., Virgin Islands; 136 sq. mi.; pop. 107,000; cap. Charlotte Amalie.

Visalia city, CEN. California 93279*; pop. 75,636.

Visayan Islands isl. group, CEN. Philippines; 23,621 sq. mi.

Vista city, SW California 92083; pop. 71,872.

Vistula river, CEN. and N Poland; 678 mi. long.

Vladivostok city, SE RSFSR; pop. 558,000.

Volga river, W RSFSR; 2,290 mi. long.

Volgograd city, W RSFSR; scene of a Russian victory over German forces in World War II, Sept. 1942 to Jan. 1943; pop. 999,000: from 1925–61 **Stalingrad.**

Volta river, E Ghana; 800 mi. long.

Vosges Mountains mtn., chain, E France.

Wabash river, W Ohio and Indiana; 475 mi. long.

Waco city, CEN. Texas 76701*; pop. 103,590.

Wade-Hampton uninc. place, NW South Carolina 29607; pop. 20,014.

Wahiawa city, CEN. Oahu, Hawaii 96786; pop. 17,386.

Waikiki beach on Honolulu harbor, SE Oahu, Hawaii.

Waipio city, Oahu, Hawaii 96786; pop. 11,812.

Wakefield town, E Massachusetts 01880*; pop. 24,825.

Wake Island coral atoll in the North Pacific; 4 sq. mi.; site of a U.S. naval and air base.

Wales penin., SW Britain; a principality of England; 8,019 sq. mi.; pop. 2,857,000.

Walla Walla city, SE Washington 99362; pop. 26,478.

Wallingford town, CEN. Connecticut 06492; pop. 40,822.

Walnut Creek city, W California 94596*; pop. 60,569.

Walpole town, E Massachusetts 02081; pop. 20,212.

Waltham city, E Massachusetts 02154; pop. 57,878.

Wantagh uninc. place, SE New York 11793; pop. 18,567.

Warminster uninc. place, SE Pennsylvania 18974; pop. 35,543.

Warner Robins city, CEN. Georgia 31093*; pop. 43,726.

Warren city, SE Michigan 48089*; pop. 144,864.

— city, NE Ohio 44481*; pop. 50,793.

Warrensville Heights vill., N Ohio 44122; pop. 15,745.

Warrington uninc. place, NW Florida 32507; pop. 16,040.

Warsaw city, N Poland; cap.; pop. 1,651,200.

Warwick city, CEN. Rhode Island 02887*; pop. 85,427.

Washington state, NW United States; 68,139 sq. mi.; pop. 4,887,941; cap. Olympia.

— city, E United States; coextensive with the District of Columbia 20013*; pop. 606,900.

— city, SW Pennsylvania 15301; pop. 15,864.

Waterbury city, W Connecticut 06701*; pop. 108,961.

Waterford city, NE Connecticut 06385; pop. 17,930.

Waterloo vill., CEN. Belgium; scene of Napoleon's final defeat, June 18, 1815; pop. 24,536.

— city, CEN. Iowa 50701*; pop. 66,467.

— city, S Ontario, Canada; pop. 46,623.

Watertown city, SW Connecticut 06795; pop. 20,456.

— town, E Massachusetts 02172; pop. 33,284.

— city, N New York 13601; pop. 29,429.

— city, SE Wisconsin 53094; pop. 19,142.

Waterville city, CEN. Maine 04901*; pop. 17,173.

Waukegan city, NE Illinois 60085*; pop. 69,392.

Waukesha city, SE Wisconsin 53186*; pop. 56,958.

Wausau city, CEN. Wisconsin 54401*; pop. 37,060.

Wauwatosa city, SE Wisconsin 53213; pop. 49,366.

Waycross city, SE Georgia 31501; pop. 16,410.

Wayne vill., SE Michigan 48184; pop. 19,899.

— urb. twp., N New Jersey 07470*; pop. 47,025.

Waynesboro city, CEN. Virginia 22980; pop. 18,549.

Webster Groves city, E Missouri 63119; pop. 22,987.

Weimar city, SW Germany; pop. 62,803.

Weirton city, NW West Virginia 26062; pop. 22,124.

Welland city, S Ontario, Canada; pop. 45,047.

Welland Canal waterway betw. Lakes Erie and Ontario.

Wellesley town. E Massachusetts 02181; pop. 26,615.

Wellington city, CEN. New Zealand; cap.; pop. 135,400.

Wenatchee city, CEN. Washington 98801; pop. 21,756.

Weslaco city, S Texas 78596; pop. 21,877.

West Allis city, SE Wisconsin 53214; pop. 63,221.

West Bend city, SE Wisconsin 53095; pop. 23,916.

West Berlin See **Berlin.**

Westchester vill., NE Illinois 60153; pop. 17,701.

West Chester boro., SE Pennsylvania 19380; pop. 18,041.

West Covina city, SW California 91793*; pop. 96,086.

West Des Moines city, CEN. Iowa 50265; pop. 31,702.

Westerly city, SW Rhode Island 02891; pop. 21,605.

Western Australia state, W Australia; 975,100 sq. mi.; pop. 1,549,700; cap. Perth.

Western Sahara area on the W coast of Africa, claimed by Mauritania and Morocco; 102,703 sq. mi.; pop. 152,000.

Western Samoa See **Samoa.**

Westfield city, SW Massachusetts 01085; pop. 38,372.

— town, E New Jersey 07091*; pop. 28,870.

West Germany See **Germany.**

West Hartford town, CEN. Connecticut 06107; pop. 60,110.

West Haven town, S Connecticut 06516; pop. 54,021.

West Hollywood city, SW California 90069; pop. 36,118.

West Indies series of isl. groups separating the North Atlantic from the Caribbean, including Cuba, Jamaica, Hispaniola, Puerto Rico, the Bahamas, Trinidad and Tobago, and the Leeward and Windward Islands.

West Indies, the group of British cols. in the Caribbean, including the Leeward Islands (Antigua, St. Kitts-Nevis-Anguilla, Montserrat, and the British Virgin Islands) and the Windward Islands (St. Vincent, St. Lucia and Dominica).

West Lafayette city, CEN. Indiana 47906; pop. 25,907.

Westlake city, N Ohio 44145; pop. 27,018.

Westland city, SE Michigan 48185; pop. 84,724.

West Memphis city, E Arkansas 72301; pop. 28,259.

West Mifflin boro., SW Pennsylvania 15122; pop. 23,644.

Westminster city and metropolitan boro., London, England;

site of the Houses of Parliament and Buckingham Palace; pop. 85,000.
— city, sw California 92863; pop. 78,118.
— city, CEN. Colorado 80030; pop. 74,625.
Westmont city, SE California 90047; pop. 31,044.
Westmount city, S Quebec, Canada; pop. 22,153.
West Orange town, NE New Jersey 07052; pop. 39,103.
West Palm Beach city, SE Florida 33401*; pop. 67,643.
West Pensacola uninc. place, sw Florida 32505; pop. 22,107.
West Point U.S. military reservation, SE New York 10996; seat of the U.S. Military Academy.
Westport city, sw Connecticut 06880; pop. 24,410.
West Saint Paul city, E Minnesota 55118; pop. 19,248.
West Seneca uninc. place, w New York 14224; pop. 47,866.
West Springfield town, S Massachusetts 01089; pop. 27,537.
West Virginia state, E United States; 24,231 sq. mi.; pop. 1,801,625; cap. Charleston.
West Warwick town, CEN. Rhode Island 02893; pop. 29,268.
Wethersfield town, CEN. Connecticut 06109; pop. 25,651.
Weymouth town, E Massachusetts 02188; pop. 54,063.
Wheaton city, NE Illinois 60187*; pop. 51,464.
Wheaton Glenmont uninc. place, CEN. Maryland 20902; pop. 53,720.
Wheat Ridge uninc. place, CEN. Colorado 80033; pop. 29,419.
Wheeling city, NW West Virginia 26003*; pop. 34,882.
Whitby Whitby town, s Ontario, Canada; pop. 28,173.
White Bear Lake city, E Minnesota 55110; pop. 24,704.
Whitehall city, CEN. Ohio 43213; pop. 20,572.
— boro, sw Pennsylvania 18052; pop. 14,451.
White Mountains range of the Appalachians, CEN. New Hampshire.
White Plains city, SE New York 10602*; pop. 48,718.
Whitney, Mount peak, E California; 14,496 ft.
Whittier city, sw California 90605*; pop. 77,671.
Wichita city CEN. Kansas 67202*; pop. 304,011.
Wichita Falls city, N Texas 76307*; pop. 96,259.
Wickliffe city, NE Ohio 44092; pop. 14,558.
Wight, Isle of isl. off the S coast of England; 147 sq. mi.
Wilkes-Barre city, NE Pennsylvania 18701*; pop. 47,523.
Wilkinsburg boro., sw Pennsylvania 15221; pop. 21,080.
Williamsburg city, E Virginia 23185; capital of Virginia (1699–1779); restored to colonial condition; pop. 11,530.
Williamsport city, CEN. Pennsylvania 17701; pop. 31,933.
Willoughby city, NE Ohio 44094; pop. 20,510.
Willowick city, NE Ohio 44094; pop. 15,269.
Wilmette vill., NE Illinois 60091; pop. 26,690.
Wilmington city, N Delaware; 19899*; pop. 71,529.
— city, NE Massachusetts 01887; pop. 17,654.
— city, SE North Carolina 28401*; pop. 55,530.
Wilson town, CEN. North Carolina 27893; pop. 36,930.
Wilson, Mount peak, sw California; 5,710 ft; site of a famous observatory.
Wilson Dam power dam in the Tennessee River at Muscle Shoals, NW Alabama; 137 ft. high, 4,862 ft. long.
Wimbledon town and municipal boro., S England; scene of international tennis matches; pop. 20,000.
Winchester town, E Massachusetts 01890; pop. 20,267.
Windham town, NE Connecticut 06280; pop. 22,039.
Windhoek city, CEN. Namibia; cap.; pop. 114,000.
Windsor municipal boro., S England; site of **Windsor Castle**, a residence of the English sovereigns; pop. 29,660: officially **New Windsor.**
— city, SE Ontario, Canada; pop. 196,526.
Windward Islands isl. group, S Lesser Antilles.
Winnipeg city, SE Manitoba, Canada; cap.; pop. 560,874.
Winnipeg, Lake lake, S Manitoba, Canada; 9,398 sq. mi.
Winona city, SE Minnesota 55987*; pop. 25,399.
Winston-Salem city, CEN. North Carolina 27102*; pop. 143,485.
Winter Haven city, CEN. Florida 33880*; pop. 24,725.
Winter Park city, CEN. Florida 32708; pop. 22,242.
Winthrop town, E Massachusetts 02152; pop. 18.127.
Wisconsin state, N United States; 56,153 sq. mi.; pop. 4,906,745.
Wisconsin Rapids city, CEN. Wisconsin 54494; pop. 18,245.
Woburn city, E Massachusetts 01808*; pop. 35,943.
Woodbridge urb. twp., NE New Jersey 07095; pop. 90,074.
Woodbridge city, NE Virginia 22193; pop. 26,401.
Woodland city, CEN. California 95695*; pop. 39,802.

Woodmere uninc. place, SE New York 11598; pop. 15,578.
Woodstock city, S Ontario, Canada; pop. 26,779.
Woonsocket city, NE Rhode Island 02895; pop. 43,877.
Wooster city, CEN. Ohio 44691*; pop. 22,191.
Worcester city, CEN. Massachusetts 01613*; pop. 169,759.
Worms city, sw Germany; pop. 73,505.
Worthington city, CEN. Ohio 43085; pop. 14,869.
Wroclaw city, sw Poland; pop. 637,400: *formerly called* **Breslau.**
Wuhan collective name for the cities of Hankow, Hanyang, and Wuchang, CEN. China; pop. 4,250,000.
Wuppertal city, w Germany; pop. 371,283.
Würzburg city, CEN. Germany; pop. 125,589.
Wyandotte city, SE Michigan 48192*; pop. 30,938.
Wyckoff urb. twp., NE New Jersey 07481; pop. 15,372.
Wyoming state, NW United States; 97,809 sq. mi.; pop. 455,975; cap. Cheyenne.
— city, w Michigan 49509; pop. 63,891.
Xenia city, CEN. Ohio 45385; pop. 24,664.
Yakima city, S Washington 98901*; pop. 54,827.
Yalta city, S Crimea; scene of a conference of Roosevelt, Churchill, and Stalin in February, 1945; pop. 81,000.
Yalu river forming part of the boundary betw. NE China and Korea; 500 mi. long.
Yangôn See **Rangoon.**
Yangtze river flowing from Tibet to the East China Sea; 3,600 mi. long.
Yellow River *an alternate name of* Hwang Ho.
Yellow Sea inlet of the Pacific betw. Korea and China; 400 mi. long, 400 mi. wide.
Yellowstone Falls 2 waterfalls of the Yellowstone River in Yellowstone National Park: **Upper Yellowstone Falls,** 109 ft.; **Lower Yellowstone Falls,** 308 ft.
Yellowstone National Park largest and oldest of the US national parks, largely in NW Wyoming; 3,458 sq. mi.; established 1872.
Yellowstone River river, NW Wyoming, SE Montana, and NW North Dakota; 671 mi. long.
Yemen, Republic of, republic, sw Arabia, formed by the joining of the former **People's Democratic Republic of Yemen (South Yemen)** and **The Yemen Arab Republic (North Yemen)** on May 22, 1990; 531,869 sq. mi.; pop. 11,546,000; cap. San'a.
Yerevan city, w Armenian SSR; cap.; pop. 1,199,000.
Yokohama city, CEN. Honshu, Japan; pop. 2,773,322.
Yonkers city, SE New York 10701*; pop. 188,082.
York co. boro., CEN. Yorkshire, England; cap.; pop. 126,377.
— city, S Pennsylvania 17405*; pop. 42,192.
Yosemite Valley gorge in **Yosemite National Park** (1,183 sq. mi., established 1890), CEN. California; 7 mi. long, 1 mi. wide; traversed by the Merced River that forms **Yosemite Falls:** Upper Fall, 1,430 ft.; Lower Fall, 320 ft.; with intermediate cascades, 2,425 ft.
Youngstown city, NE Ohio 44501*; pop. 95,732.
Ypres town, NW Belgium; site of three major battles of World War I, 1914, 1915, 1917; pop. 21,000.
Ypsilanti city, SE Michigan 48197; pop. 24,846.
Yucaipa uninc. place, sw California 92399; pop. 32,824 .
Yucatán penin., SE Mexico and NE Central America; 70,000 sq. mi.
Yugoslavia, Socialist Federal Republic of republic, SE Europe; 98,766 sq. mi.; pop. 23,861,000; cap. Belgrade.
Yukon terr., NW Canada; 186,661 sq. mi.; pop. 26,000; cap. Whitehorse.
Yukon River river, NW Canada and CEN. Alaska; 1,770 mi. long.
Yuma city, sw Arizona 85364; pop. 54,923.
Zagreb city, CEN. Croatia, Yugoslavia; cap.; pop. 649,586.
Zaire republic, CEN. Africa; 905,446 sq. mi.; pop. 34,138,000; cap Kinshasa.
Zambezi river, S Africa; 1,700 mi. long.
Zambia republic, CEN. Africa; 290,586 sq. mi.; pop. 8,456,000; cap. Lusaka.
Zanesville city, CEN. Ohio 43701*; pop. 26,778.
Zanzibar reg. of Tanzaniatoff the coast of E Africa; comprises isls. of Zanzibar (640 sq. mi.) and **Pemba** (380 sq. mi.); pop. 354,000.
— city, w Zanzibar; cap.; pop.110,506.
Zealand isl. of Denmark betw. the Kattegat and the Baltic Sea;

2,709 sq. mi.

Zimbabwe republic, s Africa; 150,873 sq. mi.; pop. 9,369,000; cap. Harare.

Zion city, NE Illinois 60099; pop. 19,755.

Zululand dist., NE Natal, South Africa; formerly a native monarchy; 10,362 sq. mi.; pop. 570,000.

Zurich city, NE Switzerland; pop. 345,159.

Zuyder Zee former shallow inlet of the North Sea, NW Netherlands; drainage projects have reclaimed much of the land and formed Lake Ijssel. Also **Zuider Zee.**

Grammar and Usage Handbook

Word Usage and Word Relationships

Agreement of Subject and Verb

It may seem needless to say that a singular subject takes a singular verb, while a plural subject takes a plural verb; however, when phrases or other elements come between the subject and the verb, the agreement may not be clear.

The small table around which the children play *was* in the hall.

The small tables owned by the church *were* in the hall.

The men, as well as the policeman, *were* aghast at the sight.

The following words are generally considered singular and take singular verbs: *each, either, neither, one, someone, anyone, everybody, nobody, somebody, much, anybody, everyone.*

The following words are plural and take plural verbs: *both, few, many, several.*

The following pronouns may be singular or plural depending on the meaning intended: *all, most, some, every, none, any, half, more.*

When one is referring to two or more persons who are of different sexes, or to a group of people whose gender one has no way of determining, the pronouns *they, them,* and *their* are often used to refer to *anyone, each, everybody,* etc., in order to avoid the awkward *he or she, him or her, his or her.*

Either—Or; Neither—Nor

Neither always takes *nor; either* takes *or.*

When a subject is compounded with *neither . . . nor* or *either . . . or,* the verb is normally singular if the nouns joined are singular, and plural if they are plural. If, however, one noun is singular and one plural, the verb agrees with the second or nearer subject.

Either Bill or Ralph *is* lying.

Neither she nor her sisters *skate* well.

Collective Nouns

A collective noun, such as *class, company, club, crew, jury, committee,* takes a singular verb when the whole is considered as a unit, and a plural verb when members of the whole are being considered separately.

The jury *has* deliberated for six hours.

The crew *were* near exhaustion after their many hours of exposure.

Some collective nouns, as *police* and *cattle,* are used only in the plural form; others, as *mankind* and *wildlife,* are generally used in the singular form.

The cattle *were* almost destroyed by the severe storm.

The New England wildlife *has* been protected.

Agreement of Pronoun with Its Antecedent

If the antecedent is singular, the pronoun is singular, if the antecedent is plural, the pronoun is likewise plural.

The *boy* did *his* best in the contest.

The *boys* in the school did *their* best.

The *boy* and the *girl* did *their* best.

Neither one of the boys did *his* best.

Capitalization

Conventions governing the use of capital letters are quite clear.

Capitalize the first word of every sentence.

The first person singular pronoun *I* and the vocative *O* are generally capitalized.

Unless style requires a different form, *a.m.* and *p.m.* are set in small letters without a space between them. Capital letters are used for B.C. and A.D. but, again, there is no space between them.

9:30 a.m.   10:30 p.m.

A.D. 1760 *or* 1760 A.D.

76 B.C.

Note: Although A.D. should technically precede the number of the year, popular usage permits it to follow the date. In printed matter B.C., A.D., a.m., and p.m. usually appear in small capitals (B.C., A.D., A.M., P.M.).

The first letter of a line of conventional poetry is capitalized. Much modern poetry, however, ignores this convention.

Hickory, dickory, dock
The mouse ran up the clock.

The first word after a colon should be capitalized only when it begins a complete sentence.

The candidate made only one promise: If elected, he would fight for better conditions.

The list contained these items: five pounds of flour, two dozen eggs, and a pound of butter.

Every direct quotation should begin with a capital,

except where the quoted passage is grammatically woven into the text preceding it.

> The announcer shouted, "There it goes, over the back wall for a home run!"
> The announcer shouted that the ball was going "over the back wall for a home run."

Capitalize the first letters of all important words in the titles of books, newspapers, magazines, chapters, poems, articles. Short conjunctions and prepositions are generally not capitalized.

> How to Win Friends and Influence People

Geographical divisions and regions require capitals.

Arctic Circle	the Atlantic Seaboard
the Orient	the Great Plains

Compass points are capitalized when they are part of a generally accepted name, but not when they denote direction or locality.

Middle East	eastern New York
Old South	Head west for twenty-five miles.

Capitalize names of streets, parks, buildings, but not the general categories into which they fall.

> Fifth Avenue
> Which avenue is widest?
> General Post Office
> We went to the post office.

Religions, religious leaders, the various appellations for God and the Christian Trinity require capitalization, as do all names for the Bible and its parts.

> the Father, the Son, and the Holy Ghost
> Virgin Mary, the Immaculate Virgin
> Yahweh, Jehovah, Saviour, Messiah
> Buddhism, Shintoism, Taoism
> New Testament
> Exodus
> Sermon on the Mount
> Ten Commandments

Capitalize the names of political parties, classes, clubs, organizations, movements, and their adherents. Use small letters for the terms that refer generally to ideology (bolshevism, fascism, socialism).

> Democratic Party
> the Right Wing
> Farm bloc
> Boy Scouts of America

Political Divisions are capitalized.

Holy Roman Empire	the Colonies
French Republic	Suffolk County
the Dominion	Eighth Election District

Government bodies, departments, bureaus, and courts are capitalized.

the Supreme Court	the Cabinet
House of Representatives	Census Bureau
Department of Labor	British Parliament

Capitalize the titles of all high-ranking government officials, and all appellations of the President of the United States. Many publishers, it should be pointed out, prefer small letters for titles that are not accompanied by the name of the official.

President	Commander-in-Chief
Secretary of State	Chief Justice
Undersecretary	Prime Minister
Ambassador to India	Minister of War

Capitalize the names of treaties, documents, and important events.

Second World War	Declaration of Independence
Treaty of Versailles	Boston Tea Party

Family designations, when used without a possessive pronoun, take a capital letter.

> I sent Mother home by taxi.
> I sent my mother home by taxi.

Capitalize seasons only when they are personified. All personifications require capitals.

> The frosty breath of Winter settled on the land.
> The voice of Envy whispered in her ear.
> Necessity is the mother of Invention.
> When Headquarters commands, we jump.
> He saw Mother Nature's grim visage.

Names and epithets of peoples, races, and tribes are capitalized.

Caucasian	Sioux
Negro	Cliff Dwellers

Articles and prepositions are generally capitalized in the names of Englishmen and Americans, and are not capitalized in French, Italian, Spanish, German, and Dutch names, unless otherwise specified by family usage.

Thomas De Quincey	Ludwig van Beethoven
Martin Van Buren	Leonardo da Vinci
Fiorello La Guardia	San Juan de la Cruz

Capitalize the names of holidays and festivals.

Christmas	Shrove Tuesday
Yom Kippur	New Year's Day

Capitalize such parts of a book as Glossary, Contents, Index, and Preface.

Capitalize the first and last words in the salutation in business letters, and all titles.

My dear Sir	Dear Doctor Brown
My dear Reverend Lothrop	Dear Reverend Father

Capitalize only the first word of the complimentary close of a letter.

Very truly yours   Sincerely yours

Spelling

General Suggestions

When in doubt as to the correct spelling of a word, consult the dictionary; do not take anything for granted.

Keep a list of your spelling errors and study them.

Learn the most commonly misspelled words in the lists below.

Learn to spell by syllables, carefully pronouncing each syllable. Faulty spelling is often due to faulty pronunciation.

Use newly acquired words and make them part of your oral and written vocabulary.

Do not use the simplified or modern forms of spelling in business correspondence, as *thru* for *through*.

Learn some basic spelling rules such as the following.

cede, ceed, and sede endings According to the Government Style Manual, there is only one word which ends in *sede—supersede,* and three that end in *ceed—proceed, exceed, succeed.* All other words having this sound end in *cede—precede, secede, recede,* etc.

ie and ei a. After *c,* when the sound is long *e* (ē), the *e* usually precedes the *i: receive, deceive, ceiling, receipt.*

b. After most other letters, the *i* precedes the *e: thief, grief, believe, achieve, lien.*

c. When the sound is *not* long *e* (ē); and especially if the sound is long *a* (ā), the *e* precedes the *i: sleigh, veil.*

The exceptions must be learned, since they follow no rule: *neither, leisure, weird, seize.*

Beginnings and Endings of Words (Prefixes and Suffixes)

a. As a general rule, drop the final *e* in the base word when a suffix beginning with a vowel is added.

decide—deciding; write—writing; type—typist

b. As a rule, retain the final *e* in the base word when a suffix beginning with a consonant is added.

remote—remotely; care—carefully; infringe—infringement

c. In applying the rule for adding *ed* or *ing,* the accent (or lack of it) may serve as a guide. Words of one syllable (and most words of more than one syllable) that end in a single consonant (except *f, h,* or *x*), preceded by a single vowel, double the final consonant *if the accent falls on the last syllable.*

plan—planned, planning; whet—whetted, whetting

transfer—transferred, transferring; control—controlled, controlling

When the word is *not* accented on the last syllable, the consonant is usually not doubled.

travel—traveled, traveler; profit—profited, profiteer

d. When the endings *ness* and *ly* are added to a word not ending in *y,* the base word rarely changes. In most words ending in *y,* the *y* changes to *i* when *ly* is added.

natural—naturally; similar—similarly; genuine—genuineness; blessed—blessedness; hazy—hazily; body—bodily

If the base word ends in *n* and the suffix *ness* is added, the *n* is doubled.

sudden—suddenness; mean—meanness; vain—vainness

e. In regard to the word endings *ise, ize, yze,* the most common form is *ize,* but here the dictionary should be consulted if there is doubt.

legalize, fraternize, criticize, jeopardize

advertise, merchandise, surmise, enterprise

paralyze, analyze

In British English *ise* is sometimes used for *ize,* as *realise* for *realize.*

f. When adding the suffix *ful,* the *l* is single except when *ly* is also added (*fully*).

care—careful—carefully;   hope—hopeful—hopefully

g. When the word beginnings (prefixes) *in, en, im, em, un, dis, mis, be, de, re, il,* and *over* are added to a word, the spelling of the word is not changed.

inactive, enjoy, impending, embrace, uneasy, dismiss, mistrust, beguile, degrade, retreat, illegal, overhaul

Forming the Plurals of Nouns

a. Most nouns form the plural by simply adding *s.*

table—tables; house—houses

b. Some nouns, especially those ending in *s,* form the plural by adding *es.*

class—classes; fox—foxes

c. Words ending in *y* preceded by a consonant form the plural by changing the *y* to *i* and adding *es.*

candy—candies; study—studies; secretary—secretaries

d. Words ending in *y* preceded by a vowel form the plural by adding *s* but without any other change in the word.

key—keys; boy—boys

e. Nouns ending in *o* preceded by a vowel form the plural by adding *s.*

rodeo—rodeos; radio—radios

When the *o* is preceded by a consonant, the plural is formed by adding *es.*

hero—heroes; torpedo—torpedoes

f. Nouns referring to music which end in *o* preceded by a consonant form the plural by simply adding *s*.

piano—pianos; oratorio—oratorios; contralto—contraltos; soprano—sopranos

g. Some few nouns follow none of the above rules but form the plural in an unusual way.

child—children; tooth—teeth; mouse—mice; ox—oxen

h. Compound nouns (more than one word) form the plural from the main word.

trade union—trade unions; father-in-law—fathers-in-law

i. When a solid compound ends in *ful*, the plural is formed at the end of the solid compound and not within the word.

basketful—basketfuls; pocketful—pocketfuls

j. When the words in compounds are of almost equal importance, both parts of the compound are pluralized.

head of department—heads of departments; woman operator—women operators

k. Words taken from another language sometimes form the plural as they would in the original language.

stratum—strata; addendum—addenda; datum—data

Summary of Spelling Rules

Problem	Rule	Examples	Exceptions

IE and **EI**	I before E, except after C.	ach*ie*ve, but ce*i*ling	1. Use *EI* when:
			  a. Sounded as *ā*: n*ei*ghbor, w*ei*gh
			  b. Sounded as *ī*: counterf*ei*t
			  c. Sounded as *ī*: h*ei*ght
			2. Use *IE* for almost all other sounds: friend, lieutenant.
			3. If *i* and *e* do not form a digraph, rules do not apply: f*ie*ry, de*i*ty.

Final Silent **E**	1. **Drop** before suffix beginning with a vowel. 2. **Retain** before suffix beginning with a consonant.	grieve—grievance absolute—absolutely	1. Retain *e* after soft *c* and soft *g* before suffixes beginning with *a* or *o*: peaceable, manageable.
Final **Y**	1. **Change** final *y* to *i* if *y* is **preceded** by a **consonant** and **followed** by any **suffix** except one beginning with *i*. 2. **Retain** final *y* if it is **preceded** by a **vowel.**	beauty—beautiful BUT carry—carrying boy—boys; valley—valleys	dry—dryness; sly—slyness. day—daily; pay—paid
Final Consonants	**Double** final consonants when: 1. Preceded by a single vowel 2. Followed by a suffix beginning with a vowel. 3. The consonant terminates a monosyllabic word. 4. The consonant terminates a polysyllabic word accented on the last syllable.	1. drop—dropped; beg—beggar 2. quit—quitting; swim—swimmer 3. hit—hitter; run—running 4. omit—omitted; transfer—transferred	Final consonant is not doubled if: 1. Accent shifts to preceding syllable when suffix is added: confer′—confer′ring BUT con′ference. 2. Final consonant is preceded by a consonant: start—started. 3. Final consonant is preceded by two vowels: beat—beating; boil—boiling.
k added to words ending in **c**	**Add** *k* to words ending in *c* before a suffix beginning with *e*, *i*, *y*.	frolic—frolicking—frolicked; picnic—picnicking—picnicked	
-cede **-ceed** **-sede**	Except for super*sede*, ex*ceed*, pro*ceed*, suc*ceed*, all words having this sound end in *-cede*.	accede, precede, recede, concede	

Plurals	1. Regular noun plurals add *-s* to the singular.
	2. Irregular plurals:
	  a. Add *-es* if noun ends in *o* preceded by consonant.
	  b. Change *y* to *i* and add *-es* if noun ends in *y* preceded by consonant.
	  c. Add *-s* if noun ends in *y* preceded by vowel.
		boy—boys; book—books
		
		a. echo—echoes; Negro—Negroes
		b. sky—skies; enemy—enemies
		c. play—plays; day—days
			a. piano—pianos; zero—zeros; solo—solos.

Possessives	1. Don't confuse contractions with possessive pronouns.
	
	2. Use no apostrophes with possessive or relative pronouns.
	3. If singular or plural noun **does not** end in *s*, add **apostrophe** and *s*.
	4. If singular or plural noun **does** end in *s*, add **apostrophe**
		Contraction Possessive
		1. it's (it is) its
		    they're their
		    (they are)
		2. his, hers, ours, yours, theirs, whose
		3. child's (Sing.), children's (Plur.)
		
		4. hostess' (Sing.), hostesses' (Plur.), princes' (Plur.)	

From *Business Letter Writing Made Simple*, revised ed., by Irving Rosenthal and Harry W. Rudman, Copyright © 1955, 1968 by Doubleday & Co., Inc.

Spelling Lists

List of Words Most Frequently Misspelled by High School Seniors

The list of words below* contains 149 words most frequently misspelled by high school seniors. These words and word-groups (those which are variants of the same word, as *acquaint* and *acquaintance*), were compiled by Dean Thomas Clark Pollock of New York University from 14,651 examples of misspelling submitted by 297 teachers in the United States, Canada and Hawaii. Each of the words represented was misspelled twenty times or more, and yet these words, comprising fewer than three per cent of the original list of 3,811 words, account for thirty per cent of the total misspellings.

NOTE: The trouble spots in each word are italicized. [Nu]mbers beside the words indicate how frequently each [word] is misspelled.

accom*mo*date	25	*to*gether	23	mea*n*t	21
excel*l*ent	25	de*sc*end	13	whe*r*e	21
op*p*ortunity	25	de*sc*end*a*nt	9	chie*f*	20
mar*r*y	4	du*r*ing	22	her*o*	10
mar*r*ies	6	fo*r*ty	22	her*oe*s	9
mar*r*iage	15	wo*m*an	22	her*o*ine	1
		cer*t*ain	21		
				lon*e*ly	20
chara*c*ter	24	com*mit*	4	op*i*nion	20
comple*t*e	24	com*mit*ted	12	parl*i*ament	20
frien*d*	24	com*mit*ting	5	poss*e*ss	20
tru*l*y	24	criti*c*ism	21	prof*e*ssor	20
acciden*t*ally	23	di*s*appear	21	rest*au*rant	20
doesn*'*t	23	ex*agg*erate	21	villa*in*	20

179	all *r*ight	91	*its*	52
163	separa*t*e	91	*it's*	22
152	unti*l*	88		
	privi*le*ge	82	*occur*	9
11	defini*t*e	78	*occur*red	52
81	the*r*e	78	*occur*rence	10
13	belie*v*e	77	*occur*ring	2
28	stu*d*y	1	prob*ab*ly	33
38	stu*d*ied	3	spee*ch*	33
	stu*d*ies	3	argu*m*ent	32
64	stu*d*ying	34		
48	conv*e*nience	5	*image*	3
15	conv*e*nient	33	*imag*ine	7
			*imag*inary	5
54	di*ff*erence	15	*imag*ination	17
8	di*ff*erent	23		
			qui*e*t	32
25	tha*n*	38	the*n*	32
22	a*t*hletic	37		
12	*to*	37	pre*j*udice	30
	busine*ss*	36	*sense*	30
56			simil*ar*	30
55	equip*p*ed	21		
	equip*m*ent	14	*your*	2
3			*you're*	28
51	princi*pal*	18		
	princi*ple*	18	appea*r*ance	29
53			con*sc*ious	29
48	pro*ph*ecy	35	pleas*a*nt	29
47	pro*ph*esy	35		
	*benefi*t	16	*stop*	1
2	*benefi*cial	5	*stop*ped	24
45	*benefi*ted	11	*stop*ping	4
	*benefi*ting	1		
3			sur*p*rise	29
43	develo*p*	34		
	envi*r*onment	34	*exci*te	1
28	recom*m*end	34	*exci*ted	7
15	fas*c*inate	33	*exci*tement	13
	final*l*y	33	*exci*ting	7
42				
41	nece*ss*ary	24	exp*er*ience	28
	nece*ss*ity	9	gover*n*ment	27
17			lab*o*ratory	27
9	for*ei*gn	14	tr*i*ed	27
	for*ei*gners	9		
26			famili*ar*	21
25	perfor*m*ance	23	esc*a*pe	21

*...ompiled by Dr. Pollock appears in the *Teachers' Service* ...nglish (Macmillan, November, 1952).

List of 100 Words Most Frequently Misspelled by College Freshmen

absence	effect	o'clock
accidentally	eighth	omitted
across	embarrassed	parallel
aggravate	environment	perhaps
all right	exercise	principal
amateur	February	principles
argument	forth	privilege
around	forty	proceed
athletic	fourth	pronunciation
believed	friend	quiet
benefited	government	quite
business	grammar	received
busy	grievance	recommend
capital	hadn't	referred
cemetery	height	relieve
choose	indispensable	rhythm
chosen	interested	schedule
coming	its	seize
committee	it's	separate
competition	knowledge	shining
conscientious	laboratory	stationery
conscious	latter	strength
coolly	literature	succeed
council	loose	superintendent
counsel	lose	supersede
criticism	losing	tragedy
deceive	maintenance	tries
definite	marriage	truly
desert	mischievous	villain
dessert	noticeable	Wednesday
dining	occasion	weird
disappointed	occurred	whether
doesn't	occurrence	woman
don't		

List of Words Frequently Misspelled on Civil Service Examinations

accident	municipal	society
all right	principal	simplified
auxiliary	principle	technicality
athletic	promotional	tendency
buoyant	president	their
catalogue		thousandth
career	precede	transferred

comptroller	proceed	transient
criticise	promissory	truly
dividend	recommend	villain
	personnel	
embarrass	purchasable	Wednesday
expedient	responsibility	writ
government	received	whether
inveigle	regrettable	yield
monetary	supersede	

Confusing Words

accept See EXCEPT.

addition, edition *Addition* means the process of joining together or finding the sum of. *Edition* refers to the form in which a book, magazine, or other literary work is published: first *edition*.

advice, advise *Advice* is the noun: to give *advice*. *Advise* is the verb: to *advise* a person.

affect See EFFECT.

all ready See ALREADY.

all right, alright *All right* is the only spelling to be used: It is *all right* to do so. The spelling *alright* is not yet considered acceptable and should not be used.

allude, elude *Allude* means to make indirect or casual reference: He *alluded* to one of Shakespeare's sonnets. *Elude* means to avoid or escape: The meaning *eludes* me.

already, all ready *Already* means before or by this time or the time mentioned: The group has *already* gone. *All ready* (two words) means that everyone is ready to do a given thing. We are *all ready* to go.

among, between *Among* is used when referring to more than two persons or things. *Between* is usually preferable when referring to only two persons or things.

appraise, apprise *Appraise* means to make an official valuation of. *Apprise* means to notify or inform.

ascent, assent *Ascent* means rising, soaring, or climbing: the *ascent* of the mountain. *Assent* means agreement, consent, sanction: *assent* to a course of action.

between See AMONG.

can See MAY.

capital, capitol *Capital* means a city that is important in some special way: Albany is the *capital* of New York. *Capitol* means a building in which a State legislature meets: The *capitol* is on Chamber Street.

censor, censure *Censor* means (n.) an official examiner of manuscripts, plays, etc.; (v.) to act as a censor; delete; suppress. *Censure* means (v.) to express disapproval of; (n.) the expression of disapproval or blame.

census See SENSES.

cite, sight, site *Cite* means to mention or bring forward: to *cite* an incident. *Sight* (n.) means a view, a vision: a beautiful *sight*. *Site* means a place or location: the *site* of the church.

compliment, complement *Compliment* (n.) means praise or congratulation. *Complement* (n.) means one of two parts that mutually complete each other.

consul See COUNCIL.

council, counsel, consul *Council* (n.) means an assembly convened for consultation. *Counsel* (n.) means guidance, advice; also, a lawyer. *Consul* (n.) means an officer residing in a foreign country to protect his own country's interests.

creditable, credible *Creditable* means deserving credit or esteem; praiseworthy: a *creditable* project for reducing poverty. *Credible* means capable of being believed; reliable: a *credible* alibi.

decent, descent, dissent *Decent* means proper; respectable. *Descent* means the act of descending or going downward. *Dissent* means (v.) to disagree; (n.) a disagreement.

devise, device *Devise* (v.) means to invent, contrive, or plan. *Device* (n.) is something devised; invention; contrivance.

dissent See DECENT.

edition See ADDITION.

effect, affect *Effect*, common as both a noun and a verb, means (v.) to bring about; to cause or achieve: The treatments will *effect* an early cure; and (n.) result, outcome. *Affect*, in common use a verb only, means to influence or act upon: Fear *affects* the mind.

effective, effectual *Effective* means producing a desired result: *Effective* action averted the strike. *Effectual* means having the power to produce a desired result: *effectual* legal steps.

elicit, illicit *Elicit* means to bring to light: to *elicit* th truth. *Illicit* means unlawful or unauthorized.

elude See ALLUDE.

eminent, imminent *Eminent* means high in station; tinguished; prominent: an *eminent* statesman. *Imm* means about to happen (said especially of dang *imminent* calamity.

except, accept *Except* (v.) means to take or le to *except* no one from the restrictions. *Acce* to receive or agree to; acknowledge: to *acce* vitation.

formerly, formally *Formerly* means some t once: He was *formerly* a judge. *Formally* me formality or with regard to form: *formally* dr

illicit See ELICIT.

imminent See EMINENT.

lay, lie See not under LAY[1] in the body of this di

learn See TEACH.

lesson, lessen *Lesson* refers to instructive or co example. *Lessen* means to make less; decrease.

loose, lose *Loose* means not fastened or attached means to mislay or be deprived of.

may, can *May* expresses permission: The child *m* in the yard. *Can* expresses ability to do: The chi do better than he is doing at present.

past, passed *Past* means (adj.) ended or finishe hopes are *past;* and (n.) time gone by: He drea the *past*. *Passed*, the past tense and past parti *pass*, means went (or gone) beyond or farther The car, which was going at high speed, *passe* easily.

persecute, prosecute *Persecute* means to maltreat press; to harass. *Prosecute*, generally used in a sense, means to bring suit against.

personal, personnel *Personal* pertains to a perso *sonal* matters, *personal* opinions. *Personnel* to a body or group of persons: *personnel* proble *sonnel* department.

practical, practicable *Practical* pertains to ac and experience. *Practicable* means feasible o

prosecute See PERSECUTE.

senses, census *Senses, the plural of sense,* awareness and rationality or to the faculty of s to come to one's *senses;* Her *senses* were the accident. *Census* refers to an official cou people of a country or district, etc.

shall, will See note under SHALL in the body of tionary.

sight See CITE.

site See CITE.

stationery, stationary *Stationery* refers to wr plies. *Stationary* means remaining in one pl

sweet, suite *Sweet* means having a taste like sugar. *Suite* refers to a set or series of things intended to be used together: *suite* of rooms, *suite* of furniture.

teach, learn *Teach* means to impart knowledge; *learn*

means to acquire knowledge. The teacher *teaches;* the student *learns*.

will, shall See note under SHALL in the body of this dictionary.

Sample Business Letters

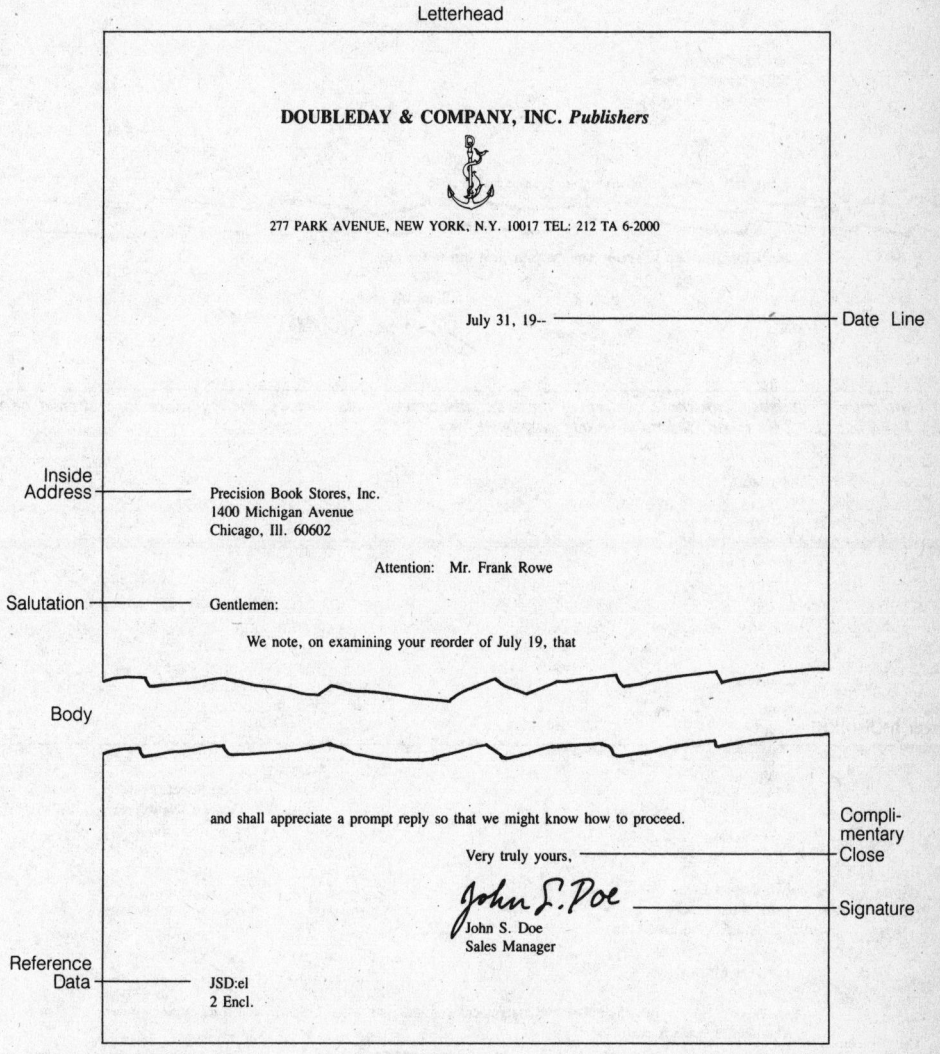

Letterhead

DOUBLEDAY & COMPANY, INC. *Publishers*

277 PARK AVENUE, NEW YORK, N.Y. 10017 TEL: 212 TA 6-2000

July 31, 19-- —————————————— Date Line

Inside Address ———
Precision Book Stores, Inc.
1400 Michigan Avenue
Chicago, Ill. 60602

Attention: Mr. Frank Rowe

Salutation ———
Gentlemen:

We note, on examining your reorder of July 19, that

Body

and shall appreciate a prompt reply so that we might know how to proceed.

Very truly yours, ————— Complimentary Close

John S. Doe ————— Signature
John S. Doe
Sales Manager

Reference Data ———
JSD:el
2 Encl.

This model letter includes in standard form all *the elements normally employed in the* business letter.

From *Business Letter Writing Made Simple,* revised ed., by Irving Rosenthal and Harry W. Rudman, Copyright © 1955, 1968 by Doubleday & Co., Inc.

The "Modified Block" Form

February 28, 19

Mr. John Jones
1492 Columbus Avenue
Louisville 3, Kentucky

Dear Mr. Jones:

I was very pleased to receive your prompt response to

and I look forward to seeing you on your next trip to the city.

Sincerely yours,

George Sabrin
George Sabrin

All the letter's contents, with the exception of the date, the complimentary close, the signature, are aligned on the left hand margin. This is still the most widely employed form.

Full Indention

19 Elm Street
Oswego, New York
April 5, 19

Mr. Gilbert Kahn
67 Wren Road
Miami, Florida 33138

My dear Mr. Kahn:

       In undertaking the assignment you gave me when I was in your office last
Thursday, I made it clear

nevertheless intend to do the best job I can.

Sincerely yours,

Lucille Graham
Lucille Graham

This form is all but obsolete, and there seems little doubt that in time it will cease entirely to be used.

Additional Sheets

Mr. John Jones—page 2—January 14, 19

therefore feel that we cannot accept the return of the merchandise at this late date. We like to cooperate

with all our accounts. . . .

It was necessary, because of its length, to continue this letter on an additional sheet. The additional sheet is headed by the addressee's name, the page number, and the date. There is the requisite minimum of three lines of text, in addition to complimentary close and signature.

The "Full Block" Form

February 28, 19

Mr. John Jones
1492 Columbus Avenue
Louisville 3, Kentucky

Dear Mr. Jones:

I was very pleased to receive your prompt response to my

and I look forward to seeing you on your next trip to the city.

Sincerely yours,

George Sabrin
George Sabrin

In the "full block" form all the letter's contents are aligned on the left hand margin.

Forms of Address

President of the United States

Address: Business: The President
                The White House
                Washington, D.C.
       Social: The President
                and Mrs. Roberts
                The White House
                Washington, D.C.
Salutation: Formal: Mr. President:
       Informal: Dear Mr. President:
Closing: Formal: Most respectfully yours,
       Informal: Sincerely yours,
In Conversation: Mr. President *or* Sir
Title of Introduction: The President *or* Mr. Roberts

Vice President of the United States

Address: Business: The Vice President
                United States Senate
                Washington, D.C.
       Social: The Vice President
                and Mrs. Hope
                Home Address
Salutation: Formal: Mr. Vice President:
       Informal: Dear Mr. Vice President:
Closing: Formal: Very truly yours,
       Informal: Sincerely yours,
In Conversation: Mr. Vice President *or* Sir
Title of Introduction: The Vice President *or* Mr. Hope

Chief Justice of the United States

Address: Business: The Chief Justice
                The Supreme Court
                Washington, D.C.
       Social: The Chief Justice
                and Mrs. Page
                Home Address
Salutation: Formal: Sir:
       Informal: Dear Mr. Chief Justice:
Closing: Formal: Very truly yours,
       Informal: Sincerely yours,
In Conversation: Mr. Chief Justice *or* Sir
Title of Introduction: The Chief Justice

Associate Justice of the Supreme Court

Address: Business: Mr. Justice Katsaros
                The Supreme Court
                Washington, D.C.
       Social: Mr. Justice Katsaros
                and Mrs. Katsaros
                Home Address
Salutation: Formal: Sir:
       Informal: Dear Mr. Justice Katsaros:
Closing: Formal: Very truly yours,
       Informal: Sincerely yours,
In Conversation: Mr. Justice *or* Mr. Justice
                Katsaros *or* Sir
Title of Introduction: Mr. Justice Katsaros

Cabinet Officer

Address: Business: The Honorable Gary George
                Gussin
                Secretary of the Treasury *or*
                Attorney General of the United
                States
                Washington, D.C.
       Social: The Secretary of the Treasury
                and Mrs. Gussin
                Home Address
                or (for a woman cabinet member)
                The Honorable Beatrice Schwartz
                or (if she is married)
                Mr. and Mrs. Henry Leo Woods
Salutation: Formal: Sir: *or* Dear Sir: *or* Madam:
       Informal: Dear Mr. Secretary: *or*
                Dear Madam Secretary:
Closing: Formal: Very truly yours,
       Informal: Sincerely yours,
In Conversation: Mr. Secretary *or* Madam Secretary
                or Mr. Attorney General *or*
                Mr. (*or* Miss *or* Mrs.) Smith
Title of Introduction: The Secretary of the Treasury,
                Mr. Smith *or*
                The Attorney General of the
                United States, Mr. Smith

Former President

Address: Business: The Honorable Alfred Edward
                Work
                Office Address
       Social: The Honorable and Mrs. Alfred
                Edward Work
                Home Address
Salutation: Formal: Sir:
       Informal: Dear Mr. Work:
Closing: Formal: Very truly yours,
       Informal: Sincerely yours,
In Conversation: Mr. Work *or* Sir
Title of Introduction: The Honorable Alfred Edward
                Work

United States Senator

Address: Business: The Honorable John Wandzilak
                United States Senate
                Washington, D.C.
       Social: The Honorable and Mrs. John
                Wandzilak
                Home Address
                or (for a woman senator)
                The Honorable Marguerite
                Sanders
                or (if she is married)
                Mr. and Mrs. John Row Doe
Salutation: Formal: Sir: *or* Madam:
       Informal: Dear Senator Wandzilak:
Closing: Formal: Very truly yours,
       Informal: Sincerely yours,
In Conversation: Senator *or* Senator Wandzilak *or*
                Sir
Title of Introduction: Senator Wandzilak

Speaker of the House of Representatives

Address: Business: The Honorable Walter Fry
                The Speaker of the House of
                Representatives
                Washington, D.C.
       Social: The Speaker of the House of
                Representatives and Mrs. Fry
                Home Address
Salutation: Formal: Sir:
       Informal: Dear Mr. Speaker:
Closing: Formal: Very truly yours,

Informal: Sincerely yours,
In Conversation: Mr. Speaker *or* Sir
Title of Introduction: The Speaker of the House of
Representatives *or*
The Speaker, Mr. Fry

Member of the House of Representatives

Address: Business: The Honorable Henry Cobb
Wellcome
United States House of
Representatives
Washington, D.C.
Social: The Honorable and Mrs. Henry
Cobb Wellcome
Home Address
or (for a woman member)
The Honorable Ann Davenport
or (if she is married)
Mr. and Mrs. John Knox Jones
Salutation: Formal: Sir: *or* Madam:
Informal: Dear Mr. Wellcome:
Closing: Formal: Very truly yours,
Informal: Sincerely yours,
In Conversation: Mr. Wellcome *or* Miss Davenport *or*
Mrs. Jones *or* Sir *or* Madam
Title of Introduction: Representative Wellcome

Ambassador of the United States

Address: Business: The Honorable John Wilson
Smith
The Ambassador of the United
States
American Embassy
London, England
Social: The Honorable and Mrs. John
Wilson Smith
Home Address
or (for a woman ambassador)
The Honorable Janet Lund
or (if she is married)
Mr. and Mrs. Joseph Leeds
Walker
Salutation: Formal: Sir: *or* Madam:
Informal: Dear Mr. Ambassador: *or* Dear
Madam Ambassador:
Closing: Formal: Very truly yours,
Informal: Sincerely yours,
In Conversation: Mr. Ambassador *or* Madam
Ambassador *or* Sir *or* Madam
Title of Introduction: The American Ambassador *or*
The Ambassador of the
United States

Minister Plenipotentiary of the United States

Address: Business: The Honorable James Lee Row
The Minister of the United States
American Legation
Oslo, Norway
Social: The Honorable and Mrs. James
Lee Row
Home Address
or (for a woman minister)
The Honorable Eugenia Carlucci
or (if she is married)
Mr. and Mrs. Arthur Johnson
Salutation: Formal: Sir: *or* Madam:

Informal: Dear Mr. Minister *or* Dear
Madam Minister:
Closing: Formal: Very truly yours,
Informal: Sincerely yours,
In Conversation: Mr. Row *or* Miss Carlucci *or*
Mrs. Johnson
Title of Introduction: Mr. Row, the American
Minister

Consul of the United States

Address: Business: Mr. John Smith
American Consul
Rue de Quelque Chose
Paris, France
Social: Mr. and Mrs. John Smith
Home Address
Salutation: Formal: Sir: *or* Dear Sir:
Informal: Dear Mr. Smith:
Closing: Formal: Very truly yours,
Informal: Sincerely yours,
In Conversation: Mr. Smith
Title of Introduction: Mr. Smith

Ambassador of a Foreign Country

Address: Business: His Excellency, Juan Luis Ortega
The Ambassador of Mexico
Washington, D.C.
Social: His Excellency
The Ambassador of Mexico and
Señora Ortega
Home Address
Salutation: Formal: Excellency:
Informal: Dear Mr. Ambassador:
Closing: Formal: Very truly yours,
Informal: Sincerely yours,
In Conversation: Mr. Ambassador *or* Sir
Title of Introduction: The Ambassador of Mexico

Minister of a Foreign Country

Address: Business: The Honorable
Carluh Matti
The Minister of Kezeah
Washington, D.C.
Social: The Honorable and Mrs. Carluh
Matti
Home Address
Salutation: Formal: Sir:
Informal: Dear Mr. Minister:
Closing: Formal: Very truly yours,
Informal: Sincerely yours,
In Conversation: Mr. Minister *or* Sir
Title of Introduction: The Minister of Kezeah

Governor of a State

Address: Business: The Honorable Joseph L. Marvin
Governor of Idaho
Boise, Idaho
Social: The Honorable and Mrs. Joseph L.
Marvin
Home Address
or (for a woman governor)
The Honorable Katherine Marvin
or (if she is married)
Mr. and Mrs. Walter O'Reilly
Salutation: Formal: Sir:
Informal: Dear Governor Marvin:

Closing: Formal: Very truly yours,
     Informal: Sincerely yours,
In Conversation: Governor Marvin *or* Sir *or* Madam
Title of Introduction: The Governor *or* The
               Governor of Idaho

State Senators and Representatives are addressed

in the same manner as U.S. Senators and Representatives.

Mayor

Address: Business: Honorable Roger Shute
               Mayor of Easton
               City Hall
               Easton, Maryland
     Social: The Honorable
               and Mrs. Roger Shute
               Home Address
               or (for a woman mayor)
               The Honorable Martha Wayne
               or (if she is married)
               Mr. and Mrs. Walter Snow
Salutation: Formal: Sir: *or* Madam:
     Informal: Dear Mayor Shute:
Closing: Formal: Very truly yours,
     Informal: Sincerely yours,
In Conversation: Mr. Mayor *or* Madam Mayor
Title of Introduction: Mayor Shute

Judge

Address: Business: The Honorable Carson Little
               Justice, Appellate Division
               Supreme Court of the State of
               New York
               Albany, New York
     Social: The Honorable and Mrs. Carson
               Little
               Home Address
               or (for a woman judge)
               The Honorable Josefina Gonzalez
               or (if she is married)
               Mr. and Mrs. Rafael Montoya
Salutation: Formal: Sir:
     Informal: Dear Judge Little:
Closing: Formal: Very truly yours,
     Informal: Sincerely yours,
In Conversation: Mr. Justice *or* Madam Justice
Title of Introduction: Justice Little

Protestant Bishop

Address: Business: The Right Reverend John S.
               Bowman
               Bishop of Rhode Island
               Providence, Rhode Island
     Social: The Right Reverend and
               Mrs. John S. Bowman
Salutation: Formal: Right Reverend Sir:
     Informal: Dear Bishop Bowman:
Closing: Formal: Respectfully yours,
     Informal: Sincerely yours,
In Conversation: Bishop Bowman
Title of Introduction: Bishop Bowman

Protestant Clergyman

Address: Business: The Reverend David Dekker
               or (if he holds the degree)
               The Reverend David Dekker,
               D.D.
               Address of his church
     Social: The Reverend and Mrs. David
               Dekker
               Home Address
Salutation: Formal: Dear Sir:
     Informal: Dear Mr. (*or* Dr.) Dekker:
Closing: Formal: Sincerely yours,
     Informal: Sincerely yours,
In Conversation: Mr. (*or* Dr.) Dekker
Title of Introduction: Mr. (*or* Dr.) Dekker

Rabbi

Address: Business: Rabbi Paul Aaron Fine
               or (if he holds the degree)
               Dr. Paul Aaron Fine, D.D.
               Address of his synagogue
     Social: Rabbi (*or* Dr.) and Mrs. Paul
               Aaron Fine
               Home Address
Salutation: Formal: Dear Sir:
     Informal: Dear Rabbi (*or* Dr.) Fine:
Closing: Formal: Sincerely yours,
     Informal: Sincerely yours,
In Conversation: Rabbi (*or* Dr.) Fine
Title of Introduction: Rabbi (*or* Dr.) Fine

The Pope

Address: His Holiness Pope Paul VI
     or His Holiness the Pope
     Vatican City
Salutation: Your Holiness:
Closing: Your Holiness' most humble servant,
In Conversation: Your Holiness
Title of Introduction: *One is presented to:* His
               Holiness *or* The Holy Father

Cardinal

Address: His Eminence Alberto Cardinal Vezzetti
     Archbishop of Baltimore
     Baltimore, Maryland
Salutation: Formal: Your Eminence:
     Informal: Dear Cardinal Vezzetti:
Closing: Your Eminence's humble servant,
In Conversation: Your Eminence
Title of Introduction: *One is presented to:* His
               Eminence, Cardinal Vezzetti

Roman Catholic Archbishop

Address: The Most Reverend Preston Lowen
     Archbishop of Philadelphia
     Philadelphia, Pennsylvania
Salutation: Formal: Your Excellency: *or* Most
               Reverend Sir:
     Informal: Dear Archbishop Lowen:
Closing: Your Excellency's humble servant,
In Conversation: Your Excellency
Title of Introduction: *One is presented to:* The Most
               Reverend
               The Archbishop of Philadelphia

Roman Catholic Bishop

Address: The Most Reverend Matthew S. Borden
        Address of his church
Salutation: Formal: Your Excellency: *or* Most
          Reverend Sir:
          Informal: Dear Bishop Borden:
Closing: Formal: Your obedient servant,
        Informal: Sincerely yours,
In Conversation: Your Excellency
Title of Introduction: Bishop Borden

Monsignor

Address: The Right Reverend Monsignor Ryan
        Address of his church
Salutation: Formal: Right Reverend Monsignor:
          Informal: Dear Monsignor Ryan:
Closing: Formal: I remain, Right Reverend
              Monsignor, yours faithfully,
        Informal: Faithfully yours,
In Conversation: Monsignor Ryan
Title of Introduction: Monsignor Ryan

Priest

Address: The Reverend John Matthews (and the
        initials of his order)
        Address of his church
Salutation: Formal: Reverend Father:
          Informal: Dear Father Matthews:
Closing: Formal: I remain, Reverend Father, yours
              faithfully,
        Informal: Faithfully yours,
In Conversation: Father *or* Father Matthews
Title of Introduction: The Reverend Father
                     Matthews

Member of Religious Order

Address: Sister Angelica (and initials of order) *or*
        Brother James (and initials)
        Address
Salutation: Formal: Dear Sister: *or* Dear Brother:
          Informal: Dear Sister Angelica: *or* Dear
              Brother James
Closing: Formal: Respectfully yours,
        Informal: Faithfully yours,
In Conversation: Sister Angelica *or* Brother James
Title of Introduction: Sister Angelica *or* Brother
                     James

University Professor

Address: Business: Professor Robert Knowles
                  Office Address
        Social: Professor *or* Mr.
              or (if he holds the degree)
              Dr. and Mrs. Robert Knowles
              Home Address
              or (for a woman professor)
              Professor or Miss (*or* Dr.)
                  Catherine Stone
              or (if she is married)
              Mr. and Mrs. Wallace Bryant
Salutation: Formal: Dear Professor (*or* Dr.) Knowles:
          Informal: Dear Mr. (*or* Miss *or* Mrs. *or*
              Ms.) Knowles:
Closing: Formal: Very truly yours,

Informal: Sincerely yours,
In Conversation: Professor (*or* Dr. *or* Mr. *or* Miss
              or Mrs.) Knowles
Title of Introduction: Professor (*or* Dr.) Knowles

Physician

Address: Business: William L. Barnes, M.D. *or*
                  Dr. William L. Barnes
                  Office Address
        Social: Dr. and Mrs. William L. Barnes
                  Home Address
Salutation: Dear Dr. Barnes:
Closing: Formal: Very truly yours,
        Informal: Sincerely yours,
In Conversation: Dr. Barnes
Title of Introduction: Dr. Barnes

Canada

Prime Minister

Address: Business: The Right Hon. John Smith,
                  P.C., M.P.
                  Prime Minister of Canada
                  Parliament Building
                  Ottawa, Ontario
        Social: The Hon. and Mrs. John Smith
                  Home Address
Salutation: Formal: Sir: *or* Dear Sir:
          Informal: Dear Mr. Prime Minister: *or*
              Dear Mr. Smith:
Closing: Formal: Yours very truly,
        Informal: Yours very sincerely,
In Conversation: Mr. Prime Minister *or* Mr. Smith
              or Sir

Governor General—The Commonwealth

Address: Business: His Excellency
                  John Smith (or his personal title)
                  Government House
                  Ottawa, Ontario
        Social: Their Excellencies
                  The Governor General and
                  Mrs. John Smith
                  Home Address
Salutation: Formal: Sir: *or* Dear Sir:
          Informal: Dear Mr. Smith:
Closing: Formal: Your Excellency's obedient servant,
        Informal: Yours very sincerely,
In Conversation: Your Excellency

Former Prime Minister

Address: The Honourable (*or* Right Honourable)
        John Smith
        Home Address (*or* Office Address)

Cabinet Officer

Address: Business: The Hon. John Smith, P.C., M.P.
                  Minister of Forestry
                  Ottawa, Ontario
        Social: The Hon. and Mrs. John Smith
                  Home Address
                  or (for a woman cabinet member)
                  The Hon. Mary Jones
                  (or, if she is married)
                  Mr. and Mrs. John Smith

Salutation: Formal: Sir: *or* Dear Sir: *or* Madam:
　　　　　　or Dear Madam:
Informal: Dear Mr. Smith; *or* Dear
　　　　　　Mrs. Smith:
Closing: Formal: Yours very truly,
　　Informal: Yours very sincerely,
In Conversation: Sir *or* Madam (*formally*); Mr. *or*
　　　　　　Mrs. Smith *or* Mr. Minister
　　　　　　(*informally*)

Judges

　　Judges of the following federal and provincial courts have the title The Honourable.
　　Supreme Court of Canada, Exchequer Court of Canada, Courts of appeal of the provinces of British Columbia, Manitoba, and Saskatchewan, Court of Chancery of the province of Prince Edward Island, Courts of Queen's Bench of the Provinces of Manitoba, Quebec, and Saskatchewan, Superior Court of the province of Quebec, Supreme courts of the provinces of Alberta, British Columbia, New Brunswick, Nova Scotia, Ontario, Prince Edward Island, and Newfoundland; and the territorial courts.
Address: Business: The Hon. Mr. Justice John Smith
　　　　Social: The Hon. Mr. Justice John Smith
　　　　　　and Mrs. Smith
Salutation: Formal: Sir:

Informal: Dear Mr. Justice Smith:
Closing: Formal: Yours very truly,
　　Informal: Yours very sincerely,
In Conversation: Sir (*formally*); Mr. Justice
　　　　　　(*informally*)

Mayor

Address: His Worship
　　　　The Mayor of St. Lazare
Salutation: Formal: Dear Sir:
　　　　Informal: Dear Mr. Mayor:
Closing: Formal: Yours very truly,
　　Informal: Yours very sincerely,
In Conversation: Sir (*formally*): Mr. Mayor
　　　　　　(*informally*)

Member of Parliament

Address: John Smith, Esq., M.P.
　　　　House of Commons
　　　　Ottawa, Ontario
Salutation: Formal: Dear Sir: *or* Dear Madam:
　　　　Informal: Dear Mr. (*or* Miss *or* Mrs.) Smith
Closing: Formal: Yours very truly,
　　Informal: Yours very sincerely,
In Conversation: Sir *or* Madam (*formally*): Mr. (*or*
　　　　　　Miss *or* Mrs.) Smith (*informally*)

The Library Research Paper

by William W. Watt

What is research? In recent years the word has filtered out of the ivory tower and spread like an epidemic in the marketplace. Loose popular usage has worn the sharp edges from its meaning and threatened to deface its value. To many people *research* refers loosely to the act of looking up or checking up on anything, anywhere, in any way. Political polls, television ratings, the detection of factual errors in unpublished magazine articles, traffic counts at intersections, questionnaires on consumer habits, comparison shopping to price silk stockings—all are called *research*. The transitive verb ("I'll research it for you") appears to be catching up with the noun in popularity, and the well-drilled team is crowding out the lonely adventurer.

Though the weakening of a noble word may be disturbing, it is a useful reminder that the natural human passion for discovering, recording, and evaluating data is not—and never was—the special province of the academic expert in the library, laboratory, museum, geological quarry, or archaeological digging. The scholar's methods may be more systematic and his conclusions more profound. He may have a more sincere faith in the freedom that lies in the pursuit of truth for its own sake—in "pure" research. But he has no monopoly on the activity of research.

Of the infinite varieties, none is more generally useful than the experience that begins as a hunting expedition in a library and ends when the last period is typed on the finished paper. The library research paper is an inevitable academic assignment. Commonly known as the *term paper,* it regularly serves as a sort of commencement exercise at the end of the course or year. For the secondary school student who goes on to college, or for the college undergraduate who proceeds to graduate professional school, there is always another commencement, another beginning of a new research paper. But though the project may become increasingly ambitious and the process more complex, the essential discipline does not change with academic advancement. The basic rules remain the same. The student who forms scholarly habits of research in school will find them invaluable later, whether under the discipline of further formal education or the self-discipline of his vocation, his avocation, or a civic activity. Because the responsible adult is a student all his life, the word *student* will have no chronological limits in this article.

The experience of writing even a single research paper pays educational dividends to any serious student. It encourages him to develop a personal interest in a subject of his own choice. It offers an opportunity for genuine independent study. It introduces him to the resources of whatever library he is privileged to use. It shows him the excitement of tracking down knowledge that is not neatly packaged in a textbook or on a blackboard. It offers him the satisfaction of completing a task more thorough than any routine writing assignment. (The word *re-search* suggests thoroughness: a *searching again,* checking *and* double-checking.)

The task demands discriminating reading at various speeds and levels, accurate note-taking, intelligent summarizing, honest and systematic acknowledgement of intellectual indebtedness, and a more intricate organization than is ever required on a short composition. The process of separating truth from error and facts from judgments, of compiling and selecting evidence to support a credible conclusion, is a general application of *scientific* method; the problem of organizing the results on paper so that they will instruct and even intrigue a reader belongs to the province of *art.* In first-rate research the "two cultures" meet.

Ideally, then, the library research paper is the product of both critical thinking and creative writing. It should reflect the enthusiasm of an alert mind, not the methodological digging of a reluctant mole. But the most talented and enthusiastic student cannot even approach the ideal unless he is aware from the start that rigorous scholarly method (not pedantic methodology) is the foundation of success. To present an elementary understanding of that method is the purpose of this article.

Finding and Limiting a Subject

Unless the student has a specific assignment thrust upon him by a teacher, his first problem is to choose a subject for investigation. (He is luckier, of course, if the subject has chosen him.) Selecting a suitable subject should not be a haphazard process like rolling dice at random until the right combination pays off. As soon as the writer knows that he is faced with a research deadline—usually a comfortable number of weeks away—he should do some preliminary prowling in the library, along the open stacks if that is permitted, to see what, if anything, it contains within his spheres of general interest. If a teacher has restricted the choice to the limits of a single course, he should be on the alert for clues in the unfinished business of the required reading or class discussion. A good discussion in class is full of loose ends that need to be tied together or of questions that require more time and information to answer. A good teacher will always start more game than he can bring to earth; few mortals irritate him more than the student who, after weeks of classroom suggestions, both explicit and implicit ("This would make a good subject for a research paper") comes staggering toward the deadline still fumbling around for "something to write about."

The first rule for finding a subject is hallowed by age. Two thousand years ago the Roman poet Horace put it this way: "Choose a subject, ye who write, suited to your strength." This does not mean that a student should regard a research assignment only as another chance to ride a familiar hobby. It means that the beginner's reach should not so far exceed his grasp that he will quickly become bogged down in learned technicalities that defy translation.

The second rule is that even a subject well suited to the writer's taste and talent should be strictly limited in accordance with the proposed or required length of the paper. Overly ambitious intentions usually lead to unsuccessful research papers because the student cannot possibly treat his subject adequately within the allotted space and time.

The tentative choice of a subject may be nothing more than a general idea of the territory to be explored, but before the student has ventured far he should become aware of the boundaries so that he won't waste precious hours wandering off limits. Sometimes during the early stages of research a large, nebulous subject will rapdily assume a clearly defined shape, if only because of the limitations of a particular library. More often the reverse is true: a general topic divides and subdivides and the student, who thought he had focused on a subject, finds himself helplessly confused. It is best to limit the subject in advance and avoid this predicament, especially when there is a deadline to meet.

The problem of limiting a subject for research is no different in kind from the routine dilemma of channeling an ambitious idea into a short composition. The same writer who struggles to capture the significance of "Love" or "Ambition" or "The Beat Generation" in 500 words is just as likely to propose a research paper of 3,000 on "The Poetry of Robert Browning" or "The History of Television." Certainly "Browning's Dramatic Monologues" or "Educational Television" would be preferable. Making the necessary allowances for the experience of the writer and the resources of the library, "Browning's Dramatic Monologues on Renaissance Painters" or "Closed Circuit Television in the High School Science Class" would be even better. Nothing more quickly betrays the limitations of a writer's knowledge than his inability to limit his subject.

A more specific way of limiting is to begin with a definite *thesis*—a proposition to prove, perhaps even a side to defend in a hypothetical pro and con debate: to presume to show, for example, that Browning's failure to achieve success in the theater was largely the fault of the Victorian audience, or that classroom television costs more money than it's worth. Such a proposition gives direction to the research and provides a convenient mold for the paper. But the pre-fabricated thesis has caused many dangerous detours from the truth. When a writer has flown effortlessly to a conclusion, it is hard for him to persuade himself that he ought to go back and trudge over the land on foot. It is a human weakness, even among scholars, to warp the truth to accommodate a foregone conclusion, casually ignoring the stubborn facts that won't conform. Moreover, many useful subjects for research do not lend themselves to a thesis statement: they involve explanation, narrative, analysis, or revelation—but not necessarily proof. On the whole, unless a writer is already something of an expert on his subject at the start, he should postpone the choice of a thesis until he has done most of the digging.

He might, like a scientist, begin with a *working hypothesis*, a tentative proposition to serve as a guidepost. But he should always be careful not to mistake a hunch for a fact, or a prejudice for an opinion. Objectivity is at the heart of genuine scholarship. Any researcher would do well to remember Thomas Henry Huxley's definition of a tragedy: "the slaying of a beautiful hypothesis by an ugly fact."

Whatever the subject, there should be no misconceptions about the requirements of the job. Though no two subjects require identical treatment, *the final paper should make it clear that the writer has reflected on the material and marshaled it as evidence to support one or more convincing conclusions*. Many beginners honestly believe that research is only an exercise in genteel plagiarism: tracking down information and transferring it—in great chunks or little snippets—from print to typescript by way of hastily jotted notes—producing a result that could have been achieved more efficiently with a Gillette blade and a roll of Scotch tape. Many failing papers are little more than anthologies of unfamiliar quotations or patchwork quilts of paraphrase. To be sure, the novice is not required to aim at the goal of the ideal Ph.D. dissertation: "an original contribution to knowledge." He is not expected to be an authority on his subject and should not presume to be. Most of his material will have been carefully sifted by more experienced hands, but this does not exempt him from the duty of critical thinking. If he understands this from the start, he will not arbitrarily divide his labor into a physical act of compilation and a mental act of composition. From the first visit to the library he will be reflecting carefully upon the material, not just thoughtlessly jotting down notes. The final product will be a transfusion, not a series of transplants.

Using the Library

Because no two libraries are identical, no general instruction on "how to use the library" is custom-tailored to the individual in Azusa or Zanesville. The best way for a reader to get familiar with the machinery of a particular library is to make himself at home there. He should not stride directly to the delivery desk and say to whoever is in charge: "Do you have any books on closed circuit television?" Though the librarian—especially a trained reference librarian—may provide indispensable help at a later stage of the investigation, the student should begin with a declaration of independence. Given the run of the stacks in a small or middle-sized library, he can get off to a good start by going at once to the general territory of his subject (he can find *English Literature* or *American History* on a chart without memorizing the Dewey Decimal System). Wandering up and down the aisles from A to Z, he can get a preliminary view of the land by merely scanning the backbones of books.

But such freedom is not usually permitted in a large library, where the student may have to spend many minutes at the delivery desk waiting to receive the books he has requested. Moreover, a good research paper is not the end-product of aimless browsing. The student will save both himself and the librarian time and trouble by learning the names of the standard reference guides, where to find them, and how to use them. To do this is to practice one of the fundamental principles of research: *Always take pains in the present to avoid panic in the future*.

Regardless of the subject, three reference guides will probably prove indispensable: (1) the card catalogue; (2) a comprehensive encyclopedia; and (3) the *Reader's Guide to Periodical Literature*.

The Card Catalogue

The proper use of a card catalogue requires both imagination and persistence. (Serendipity—the ability to discover treasures that you are not looking for—is probably more of a reward for alertness and patience than a native gift.) In a complete catalogue any book in the library may be listed alphabetically on at least three cards:

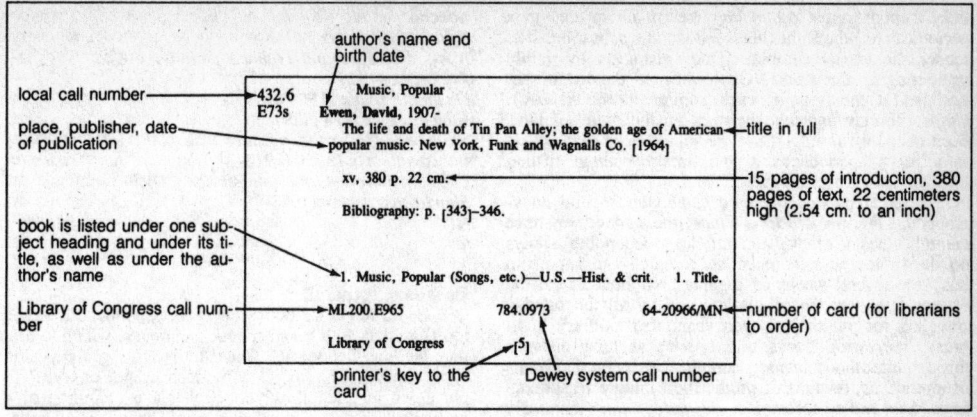

by subject, author (last name first), and title. Other cards serve as cross-references.

For example, a student planning a paper on "Closed Circuit Television in the High School Science Class" might begin by looking up "Television." He should find a number of subject cards with this label at the top (probably typed in red), each alphabetically arranged by author. As he shuffles further, he should find other cards with more specific subject labels. "Television—apparatus and supplies" may interest him; "Television—law and legislation" may not. A group of books catalogued under "Television in education" certainly will. The student is on his way.

A single card, like a single dictionary entry, contains a wealth of information, some of which is essential for a bibliography. Consider the scope of the data on a typical subject card of the kind disseminated throughout the country by the Library of Congress (*above*).

A Comprehensive Encyclopedia

The reader digging for a research paper should ordinarily regard a complete encyclopedia as an indispensable guide, not an ultimate goal. The writer whose footnotes and bibliography show that he has quarried his material from a half dozen competing encyclopedias—however reputable—is easily identified as an explorer who has never left his safe home in the reference room.

For the conscientious student a good encyclopedia article has two main virtues: (1) it provides an authoritative and comprehensive view of a general subject, probably one in which he has staked out a more restricted claim; (2) it supplies bibliographical references which the student may not have discovered in the card catalogue. Let us take one possible example. The 1963 printing of the *Encyclopaedia Britannica* has an article on "Television" that runs to 19 large double-column pages, complete with photographs and diagrams. As the key to the contributors' initials reveals in the index volume, it is an authoritative article written by the Director of the Research Division of the Philco Corporation. But less than half a column is devoted to the applications of closed circuit TV in education. On the other hand, the article is followed by a list of six more extensive treatments of the general subject, any one of which might find a place in the student's final bibliography. Moreover, if the reader turns to "television" in the index volume, he will find

other references to "educational television" that do not appear in the general entry. By consulting several good encyclopedias on a subject the student may choose one which he feels will best help him construct a firm foundation for a research paper.

The *Reader's Guide*

Neither the card catalogue nor the most complete encyclopedia can pretend to give a comprehensive listing of magazine articles that have not been corralled in a book. Even in these days of prolific publishing, many interesting subjects of limited appeal have never been fully treated in book form. New developments, especially in science, are arriving and changing with such speed that even an encyclopedia publishing an annual supplement can never be completely up-to-date. On almost any subject of general interest the first place to hunt for magazine articles is the *Reader's Guide to Periodical Literature*.

The *Reader's Guide* has been indexing current contributions to the best-known American magazines since 1901 and now includes references to more than 125 publications. The semi-monthly issues (monthly in July and August) are conveniently bound in volumes that cover periods of one to four years. Articles are listed by author and subject. If a student's chosen subject relates to a specific event since 1901 ("The Hamlet of John Barrymore," "The Attack on Pearl Harbor"), he can begin at that date and work toward the present. If not, especially if he has no clues to authors, he should start with the subject entries in the most recent issues and hunt backward through the bound volumes. On looking up "Television," for example, in the volume for March 1963–February 1964, he would find three articles listed under "TELEVISION, Closed circuit" and twenty-one under "TELEVISION in education." (Any abbreviations in the entries can be understood easily by referring to a key at the front of the volume.) And these would be only a selection of the articles for one year in popular magazines: a glance at the *Education Index* (see below) would uncover many more in professional journals. It is no wonder that teachers turn gray when students report that they "can't find any material" on an obvious subject in an adequate library.

The reader with limited time and facilities cannot expect to locate every one of these articles. It is one of the inevitable frustrations of research to find that the article with the most promising title of all appears in a periodical to which the library does not subscribe. The reader should not compound the frustration by vainly wandering in the stacks. On turning to the list of periodicals at the front of each volume in the *Reader's Guide*, he may find that the ones on the premises have been ticked off in ink. If not, he should have easy access to a list of periodicals in the library without riffling through the card catalogue.

After consulting the card catalogue, several encyclopedias, and the *Reader's Guide*, the student may have enough clues to books and articles—depending always on the subject and scope of his research—to keep him busy for several weeks of digging. No amateur can be expected to play the scholar's game by all the rules—traveling for months, or even years, from library to library, borrowing books and articles at long distance through interlibrary loans, examining others on photostats or microfilms, tracking down the most infinitesimal detail to its final hiding place. But any reader can vicariously experience the excitement of such sleuthing on a smaller scale. Even the beginner should be familiar with more than three guides to research. Some of these tools can prove indispensable to him for detecting clues to possible sources of information on his topic.

Of the unnumerable research tools in a great library—including reference guides to reference books and bibliographies of bibliography—the following list contains only a generous sample.

Catalogues and Bibliographies

Books in Print (1948–   ). An annual author and title index to the *Publisher's Trade List Annual*. Lists the books still available from more than 1,100 American publishers. *Subject Guide to Books in Print* (1957–   ) lists them annually by subject.

Library of Congress Catalog (1942–   ). A complete catalogue by authors, showing facsimiles of the cards in the great library in Washington, D.C. A similar catalogue arranges books by subject.

Periodical Indexes

General

Book Review Digest (1905–   ). A monthly collection of excerpts from current book reviews indexed by author, subject, and title. It helps the reader to get a quick general picture of whether the first greetings were favorable, unfavorable, or lukewarm. More important, it directs him to reviews that he may want to read *in toto*.

International Index to Periodicals (1907–   ). A key to articles in scholarly journals that are not indexed in the *Reader's Guide*, which is limited to more popular magazines.

New York Times Index (1913–   ). A detailed index (now published twice a month) to a distinguished newspaper. Indispensable for a writer whose subject is related to any newsworthy event since the year before World War I. Even if the library does not have the complete file of the *Times* (now available in microfilm), he can make extensive use of the index to pin down exact dates, establish the chronological order of events, and find leads to news in any paper that may be available.

Poole's Index to Periodical Literature (1802–1906). Though much less thorough than the *Reader's Guide*, this annual subject index is a useful key to articles in English and American magazines in the nineteenth century.

Special

Agricultural Index (1916–   ).
Applied Science and Technology Index (1858–   ).
Art Index (1929–   ).
Dramatic Index (1909–   ).
Education Index (1929–   ).
Essay and General Literature Index (1900–   ).
Industrial Arts Index (1913–1957).
Public Affairs Information Service (1915–   ).
Short Story Index (1953–   ).

Dictionaries

Language (general)

Of all reference books, the general reader should be most familiar with his own desk dictionary, which to him may be "the dictionary." But if he is writing a paper on some aspect of English or American usage, or trying to pin down an accurate or comprehensive definition of a particular term at a particular time, he will find more complete or specialized information in the following works:

Dictionary of American English on Historical Principles. 4 vols. Chicago, 1936–1944. Supplemented by *A Dictionary of Americanisms*, 1951.

New "Standard" Dictionary. rev. ed. New York, 1959. A revision of an unabridged dictionary published by Funk and Wagnalls since 1913.

Oxford English Dictionary. 12 vols. and supplement. London and New York, 1933. When a writer is summoning up remembrance of things past, few records are more suggestive than the changing history of a word's meaning through the years. The great OED supplies such a record by citing the use of words in passages of prose and poetry, arranged in chronological order from the earliest occurrences. Once published as the *New English Dictionary* (NED).

Webster's Third New International Dictionary. Springfield, Mass., 1961. "Webster's Third" contains many new words and meanings not included in the second edition of the 1934 and illustrates them profusely in actual contexts. Based on recent linguistic theory, it records—often without restrictive labels—many usages that are widely frowned on.

Language (special)

Evans, Bergen and Cornelia. *A Dictionary of Contemporary American Usage*. New York, 1957.

Fowler, H. W. *A Dictionary of Modern English Usage*. London, 1926.

Nicholson, Margaret. *A Dictionary of American-English Usage*. New York, 1957. Based on Fowler.

Roget's International Thesaurus. 3rd ed., New York, 1962.

Webster's Dictionary of Synonyms. Springfield, Mass., 1942.

Biography

Dictionary of American Biography. 20 vols. and supplements. New York, 1928–   . The DAB contains lives of dead Americans.

Dictionary of National Biography. 22 vols. and supplements. London, 1885–   . The DNB has lives of dead Britons.

International Who's Who. London, 1936–   . Annual.

Kunitz, Stanley J. and Howard Haycraft. *Twentieth Century Authors*. New York, 1942. Supplement, 1945.

Webster's Biographical Dictionary. Springfield, Mass., 1943.

Who's Who. London, 1849– . An annual dictionary of living Britons.

Who's Who in America. Chicago, 1899– . A biennial dictionary of living Americans.

Encyclopedias and Surveys

General

There are many good, comprehensive encyclopedias which are following an editorial program of constant revision. Any good library should have several such encyclopedias of recent copyright. These encyclopedia publishers also supply yearbooks or supplemental material to make the most recent information promptly available to the researcher.

Special

Bailey, Liberty Hyde, ed. Cyclopedia of American Agriculture. 4 vols. New York, 1908–1909.

Baldwin, James M., and B. Rand, eds. Dictionary of Philosophy and Psychology. new ed. 3 vols. New York, 1949.

Bartlett's Familiar Quotations. 13th ed. Boston, 1955.

Blom, Eric., ed. Grove's Dictionary of Music and Musicians. 5th ed. 10 vols. London, 1954. Supplement, 1961.

Cambridge Ancient History. 17 vols., including plates. Cambridge, 1928–1939.

Cambridge Medieval History. 16 vols., including maps and plates. Cambridge, 1911–1936.

Cambridge Modern History. 2nd ed. 13 vols. and atlas. Cambridge, 1902–1926.

Cambridge Bibliography of English Literature. 5 vols. Cambridge, 1941. Supplement 1957.

Cambridge History of American Literature. 4 vols. New York, 1917–1921.

Cambridge History of English Literature. 15 vols. Cambridge, 1907–1927.

Catholic Encyclopedia. rev. ed. 17 vols. New York, 1936– .

Dictionary of American History. rev. ed. 5 vols. and index. New York, 1946.

Encyclopedia of World Art. New York, 1958– . In progress.

Feather, Leonard. Encyclopedia of Jazz. rev. ed. New York, 1960.

Fletcher, Sir Banister. A History of Architecture. 17th ed. New York, 1961.

Good, C. V. Dictionary of Education. 2nd ed. New York, 1959.

Harper's Encyclopedia of Art. 2 vols. New York, 1937. Re-issued as New Standard Encyclopedia of Art, 1939.

Hart, James D. Oxford Companion to American Literature. 3rd ed. New York, 1956.

Harvey, Sir Paul, ed. Oxford Companion to Classical Literature. 3rd ed. New York, 1956. Oxford Companion to English Literature. 3rd ed. New York, 1946.

Hastings, James, ed. Encyclopedia of Religion and Ethics. new ed. 13 vols. New York, 1951.

Kirk, Raymond E., and Donald F. Othmer. Encyclopedia of Chemical Technology. 15 vols. and supplements. New York, 1947– .

Langer, William L., ed. Encyclopedia of World History. rev. ed. Boston, 1952.

McGraw-Hill Encyclopedia of Science and Technology. 15 vols. New York, 1960.

McLaughlin, Andrew C., and A. B. Hart, eds. Cyclopedia of American Government. 3 vols. New York, 1914.

Monroe, Walter S., ed. Encyclopedia of Educational Research. 3rd ed. by Chester Harris, New York, 1960.

Munn, Glenn G. Encyclopedia of Banking and Finance. rev. ed. L. Garcia. Boston, 1962.

Oxford History of English Literature. 12 vols. projected. Oxford, 1947–

Sarton, George. Introduction to the History of Science. 3 vols. Baltimore, 1927–1948.

Seligman, Edwin R. A., and A. Johnson, eds. Encyclopedia of the Social Sciences. 15 vols. New York, 1930–1935. Reissued in 8 vols., 1948.

Singer, Charles, ed. History of Technology. 5 vols. New York, 1956–1958.

Smith, Horatio, ed. Columbia Dictionary of Modern European Literature. New York, 1947.

Spiller, Robert E., ed. A Literary History of the United States. 3 vols. New York, 1948. rev. ed. 1 vol. 1953. Supplement by R. M. Ludwig, 1959.

Stevenson, Burton. The Home Book of Quotations. 9th ed. New York, 1959. Organized by subjects.

Thompson, Oscar, and N. Slonimsky, eds. International Cyclopedia of Music and Musicians. new ed. 3 vols. New York, 1940.

Tweney, C. F., and L. E. C. Hughes, eds. Chamber's Technical Dictionary. 3rd rev. ed. New York, 1958.

Universal Jewish Encyclopedia. 10 vols. and index. New York, 1939–1944.

Van Nostrand's Scientific Encyclopedia. 3rd ed. New York, 1958.

Yearbooks

In addition to the yearbooks made available by encyclopedia publishers, the following may be found useful.

American Year Book (1910–).
The New International Year Book (1907–).
Statesman's Year Book (1864–).
World Almanac and Book of Facts (1868–).

The Working Bibliography

At the very beginning of his search for materials the reader should be armed with a dependable pen and a supply of 3 x 5 index cards. (Pencils may smudge and encourage illegible scribbling; items jotted in notebooks or on miscellaneous scraps of paper are harder to organize and easier to overlook.) Though the search through the reference guides will turn up some material that will later prove unavailable or useless, it will pay at this stage to make a written record of every title that may conceivably bear on the chosen subject. When arranged in alphabetical form—with no more than one title on a card—these entries will form a tentative list of sources: a working bibliography. When the actual reading of sources begins, some of the cards will be jettisoned, and—as new references turn up in the reading—others will be added. The final bibliography, compiled after the paper is written, may have only a general family resemblance to its pioneering ancestor. But it is far less trouble to tear up a card that has not proved useful than to remember an unrecorded title or to return repeatedly to the reference guides.

To avoid trouble later on, the student should write down the same facts in the same form that will be required in the final bibliography. Authorities differ about the formal details, but if every researcher were permitted to follow his own fancy, whether through careless indifference or conscious resistance to tradition, the useful shorthand of scholarship would soon degenerate into chaos. The forms illustrated here for both bibliography and footnotes (pp. 1024–1026) are those recommended in *The MLA Style Sheet* (revised edition), compiled by William Riley Parker for the Modern Language Association after consulting with the editors of 109 journals and 34 university presses. No prudent beginner would ignore such an expert jury to accommodate his own whims. Accurate scholarly form demands *the right facts in the right order with the right punctuation*. Though the standard may seem pedantic to the novice, even the substitution of a semicolon for a colon is not acceptable.

Here are some sample entries for bibliography cards.

For a book with one author:

Galbraith, John K. *The Affluent Society*. Boston, 1958.

Notice that the entry contains four parts in the following order: (1) Author's name, last name first—for alphabetizing; (2) full title—underlined (italicized); (3) place of publication; (4) date of publication. Periods separate the parts except for the comma between place and date. A period also comes at the end of the entry. Unless a different form of an author's name is well known (Eliot T. S. or Maugham, W. Somerset), give the first name and any initials. Nobody wants to search through a large catalogue for Brown, J.

Some authorities insist on including the name of the publisher. It comes after the place of publication and is preceded by a colon and followed by a comma:

Galbraith, John K. *The Affluent Society*. Boston: Houghton Mifflin, 1958.

For a book with more than one author:

Sledd, James H., and Gwin J. Kolb. *Dr. Johnson's Dictionary*. Chicago, 1955.

Because the second name does not determine the alphabetical placing of the entry, it follows the normal order. If a book has more than two authors, it is sufficient to give the name of the first and add "and others."

For a periodical article:

Lippmann, Walter. "Cuba and the Nuclear Risk," *Atlantic*, CCXI (February 1963), 55–58.

The standard form has five parts in this order: (1) Author's name, last name first (the title comes first if the author is not known); (2) full title of article—in quotes; (3) name of periodical—underlined (italicized); (4) volume—in Roman numerals—and date—in parentheses; (5) page numbers. Except for the period after the author's name, the parts are separated by commas. Notice that this form differs from that of the *Reader's Guide*, where the entry reads:

Cuba and the nuclear risk. Atlan 211:55–8 F '63.

Such an abbreviated form should not be copied onto bibliography cards.

For a newspaper article:

New York *Times*, December 28, 1964, p. 6.

The place of publication is not ordinarily underlined, and the page number is preceded by the standard abbre-

viation for *page* (lower case p.). If a newspaper has two or more sections with separate paging, the section number is included after the date:

New York *Times*, January 3, 1965, sec. 4, p. 7.

For an encyclopedia article:

Fink, Donald G. "Television," *Encyclopaedia Britannica* (1963), XXI, 910A–913.

In addition to this minimum of information, the student should allow room in the upper left-hand corner of the card for the call number. This will save unnecessary trips to the card catalogue. If the library is large and unfamiliar and the stacks are open, it is helpful to add a further note about the location:

613.84   Neuberger, Maurine B. *Smoke Screen:*
N478s   *Tobacco and the Public Welfare*. En-
(2nd floor,   glewood Cliffs, N.J., 1963.
north stack)

Evaluating Sources

As soon as the student turns from the cards of his working bibliography to the actual pages of the sources, he can begin to evaluate the material. Often a quick glance at a book or article will assure him that it is not appropriate; the card, in this case, may be torn up at once. Though other sources will require more careful attention, the researcher should always be ready to change his reading pace, slowing down when the material is complicated or difficult, and speeding up when it is readily comprehensible. The independent reading for research will give him an incomparable opportunity to practice whatever he knows about the difference between skimming and thorough reading. Bacon's proverbial wisdom will become a practical reality: "Some books are to be tasted, others to be swallowed, and some few to be chewed and digested. . . ." "A man," said Samuel Johnson, "will turn over half a library to make one book." But not, the Doctor might have added, if the man plods through all the reading at the same unchanging pace.

Only a seasoned expert in a field can know for certain what authors to respect as authorities or disregard as quacks. But even the beginner can show some intelligent discrimination. The inexperienced reader can learn to evaluate sources just as the scholar does, by asking a few questions based on *external* and *internal* evidence. For example:

External Evidence
Who wrote the book or article? What's in a name? To a conscientious scholar, a great deal. If a name turns up again and again during the investigation—especially if others explicitly refer to the owner as an authority—it is a reasonable, though not a foolproof, assumption that he is more dependable than an obscure author. If the author has a pedigree in one or more standard biographical dictionaries, so much the better, though it must not be forgotten that the elect compile their own pedigrees. A Civil War historian in a great university probably knows more about the battle of Gettysburg than a feature writer commemorating the anniversary for a small town newspaper. A professional folklorist should have a more accurate knowledge of the history of the popular ballad than an itinerant guitar strummer.

Who published it? Though it is risky to make odious comparisons in the mushrooming world of publishing, a reader with some experience will be safer in trusting a reputable imprint of long standing than a new and untested brand name. A scholarly book published by a university press is probably a safer, if duller, guide to a specialized subject than a popular best-seller concocted for the trade. A sober account in the New York *Times* should be fitter to quote than a sensational exposé in a cheap tabloid.

When was it written? Is the material first-hand, second or third? A newspaper extra printed on December 8, 1941 might capture the confused excitement of the attack on Pearl Harbor, but an unbiased study published ten years later would probably be a more reliable source for the facts. An estimate of Winston Churchill published in 1919 would lack the perspective of a book written after the Battle of Britain. A student writing on a subject that is changing as swiftly as "Space Travel" or "Jet Propulsion" will naturally look for the latest word; a scholar delving into the past will be eager to uncover the earliest. The investigator with limited time and experience will lack the scholar's opportunities for tracking down a subject to its *primary sources*—burrowing beyond the printed page to the original manuscript. But he can share the scholar's desire for getting as near as possible to the first-hand truth of an event, the actual wording of a text or document. If he is writing about Shakespeare's treatment of the theme of mercy, he doesn't have to summarize a paraphrase of Portia's speech from a student cram book when a reputable text of *The Merchant of Venice* is close at hand. Nor should he quote a critic from the *Book Review Digest* when the original review is on a nearby shelf.

Internal Evidence

What does the actual text of the book or article reveal about the reliability of the author? The experienced reader will find it easier to answer such a question than the novices but it does not take much sophistication to distinguish between critical thinking and slanted writing (is the author's manner analytical or emotional, are the words neutral or loaded?); or between a distintersted search on all sides of the truth and an argument that is mere propaganda; or between a thorough investigation leading to conclusions founded on facts and a superficial survey resulting in unsupported conjectures.

Considering the amount of piffle on paper, no experienced reader has an ingenuous faith in the sanctity of print for its own sake. But many a reader who ought to know better, eager to accumulate evidence to support a thesis, will gather material at random without the slightest attention to the quality or reliability of his sources. The true scholar does not snap up ill-considered trifles; he is a discriminating reader and a natural skeptic. He not only wants to be shown, he insists on being convinced.

Taking Notes

It is sometimes convenient to jot down a general note about a book or article on one of the 3 x 5 bibliography cards. "A comprehensive survey with no recent evidence on the subject." "A jazzy sketch to amuse the reader, not inform him." But more specific or extensive notes should be on separate cards. Because they will not be shuffled in the same deck with the bibliography, these note cards need not be of the same size. Most scholars recommend 4 x 6 note cards (or slips of paper); some prefer half sheets (5½ x 8). Here convenience is more important than tradition. Note cards should be small enough to sort handily, large enough to allow room for legible notes, but not so large as to invite wholesale transcribing.

Note taking is a useful art, whether in routine reading, lectures, class discussions, or meetings of clubs and

---

II.2.a   'Social Balance'   Galbraith, 251-269

We ignore need for balance between private production and public services. Inadequate services in cities, blighted and polluted countryside, neglected education and recreation inadequate housing -- vs. more and more cars, T.V. sets, comic books, switchblade knives, gimmicks and gadgets. "Social balance," which would bring greater enjoyment to life, hindered by power of private advertising, "the truce on inequality," tendency to inflation.

[This published in 1958. How much progress since?]

committees. In research it assumes some of the dimensions of an exact science. The individual may eventually derive a personal method that suits him best. The following are some hints and warnings:

Do not take too many notes. Note-taking should be an aid to discriminating reading, not an opportunity for voluminous writing. The reader who postpones all his mental sorting until he begins to go through his note cards to write the paper is making his task unnecessarily difficult.

Restrict each note to one point on one side of the card. The definition of *point* is always arbitrary. It may be a sharp point like a brief direct quotation or a broad point like a short summary of a paragraph or a whole article. But do not clutter up a note with a miscellaneous scattering of quotations and reactions scribbled at random on both sides. The careful assignment of points to cards is another step in the winnowing process that accompanies research from start to finish. Organizing a research paper is not unlike playing a hand of bridge. If aces could not be quickly distinguished from deuces, or face-up cards from face-down, the game would be impossible.

Identify each card accurately at the top with a brief caption for the note and a key to the source, including the exact page number or numbers. If the complete information on that source appears as it should, on a bibliography card, all that is necessary on a note card is the author's name and the page—or, if he is responsible for more than one source, a short title: Muir, p. 61 or *The Present Age*, pp. 158–159. If a direct quotation extends from one page to another, carefully indicate the division with a slant line (/) at the appropriate point.

Taking notes with meticulous care. Note-taking is not jotting. Even when reading rapidly, come to a full stop at any important intersection. If necessary, look back and ahead to avoid the common distortion that comes from ripping a passage hastily out of its context. Remember that a careless glance may change *psychology* to *physiology*, and a single illegible word in a key quotation may later require an emergency trip to the library to revisit a book that somebody else has since withdrawn. Get it right the first time.

Take pains to distinguish between direct quotations and paraphrase and between the author's ideas and your own reactions to them. (The word *paraphrase* is used here in its general sense to mean any rewriting of another's material in your own words, whether it expands, contracts (summarizes), or keeps to the scale of the original.)

Nothing is more confusing and annoying to the reader of a research paper than the writer's failure to make these distinctions clear. Wholesale transgressions of this kind may represent conscious plagiarism. More often they result from ignorance of the meaning of research or of the rules of literary ethics. Because the problem sometimes arises at the writing stage, it is discussed in more detail on page 1024. But often a bad research paper—like a failing examination—can be traced back to poor or carelessly taken notes. Any passage taken word-for-word from the text, even a clause or unusual phrase, should appear in the notes in bold quotation marks. The student who "forgot to put in the quotes" is either dishonest, naive, or inexcusably careless. If the note-taker temporarily abandons direct quotations for paraphrase, he should carefully close the quotes and open them again when the paraphrase is finished. If he makes an independent comment of his own in the middle of a quotation or paraphrase, he should enclose it in square brackets [thus], not parentheses (thus). He might even go so far as to identify it with his own initials.

Take particular pains to copy quotations precisely.

Any scholar will quote much more than he finally uses, but even at the note-taking stage, it is wise to limit direct quotations to short passages *precisely* transcribed. Precisely means word for word, spelling for spelling (except for obvious typographical errors), punctuation mark for punctuation mark. Any omission from a quotation should be carefully identified with three spaced periods (. . .) followed by the period at the end of the sentence where appropriate. Every theater-lover is familiar with the way a press agent can play fast and loose with a critic's review. The reviewer may write: "My final judgment is that, except for the acting, the play is brilliant." With the dots carefully omitted, the advertisement reads: "My final judgment is that the play is brilliant." The scholar's rule is not pedantry, but simple honesty.

Examine each of the sample note cards carefully. The first note, conceivably for a paper on "The Economics of American Poverty," presents a brief summary of an entire chapter in John Kenneth Galbraith's *The Affluent Society.* (The code number in the upper left-hand corner has presumably been supplied later when the cards were organized to match an outline for the paper.) Because the phrases "Social Balance" and "the truce on inequality" are, at least in this context, Galbraith's own, they are put in quotation marks. The reader's reaction is carefully segregated in square brackets.

A passage of direct quotation has been sandwiched between two short pieces of paraphrase in the second note. Notice the slant line marking the transition from page 258 to 259, the parentheses (Galbraith's, not the note-taker's), the line under *minimum* to represent Galbraith's italics, and the three spaced periods to mark an omission from the quotation. Were the omission at the end of a sentence, a fourth spaced period would follow (. . . .).

The Outline

When a student has made the last of his notes and carefully read them all through to get a bird's eye view of the land, he is finally ready to plan the actual writing of the paper. Teachers of writing differ about the value of a formal outline for a short composition, but for a research paper of 2,000 words or more, some sort of blueprint is indispensable. Even the liveliest argument can't move ahead in a straight line without a well-articulated skeleton.

Though the traditional outline form can at times become a strait jacket for a writer, it has a number of virtues: (1) It tells the writer where he has been, where he is, and where he is going; (2) It reminds the writer that the reader demands the same information, suggesting the need for topic sentences (expressed or implied) and adequate transitions; (3) It avoids unnecessary repetition; (4) It emphasizes the importance of symmetry and proportion; (5) It requires the writer to coordinate his main points, subordinate his subpoints, and relegate trivia to limbo.

A formal outline should follow the accepted method of subordination:

I.
  A.
    1.
    2.
      a.
      b.
  B.

11.3.4   Services   Galbraith, pp. 258-259

Residential housing can't be limited to private sector. "It is improbable that the housing industry is greatly more incompetent or inefficient in the United States than in those countries--Scandinavia, Holland, or (for the most part) England-- where slums have been largely eliminated and where minimum standards of cleanliness and comfort are well above our own. As the experience of these countries shows ... the housing industry functions well only in combination with a large, complex, and costly array of public services." Land purchase, clearance, city planning, zoning, research and architectural services, public assistance for poor.

The writer should use either a *topic outline* (limited to words or phrases) or a *sentence outline* (with complete sentences). According to strict rule, the two types should not be mixed. The sentence outline has the advantage of requiring specific assertions (which may turn into topic sentences) instead of ambiguous catchall topics. But with many kinds of material, sustaining a sentence outline is an artificial struggle.

Common errors in outlining should be strictly avoided; examples of these are given below.

The meaningless category

"Introduction," "Body," and "Conclusion," for example, are often too general to be useful. Oftentimes a writer can do better by ignoring the introduction entirely and plunging his pen right into the body.

Illogical coordination

I. Athletics
  A. Football
  B. Baseball
  C. Basketball
  D. Team sports

Improper subordination

Placing a topic under the wrong heading:

I. Athletics
  A. Football
  B. Baseball
    1. Good sportsmanship
Or putting a main point in a subordinate position:

I. School life
  A. Athletics

    1. Major sports
    2. Minor sports
  B. Classroom activities
    1. Discussion
    2. Learning

Single subdivision

If *I* is divided at all, it should have at least two subheads, A and B. If A is divided, it should have at least two subheads, 1 and 2. And so forth. The temptation to use a single subhead can be resisted by following a heading with a colon and a qualifying phrase. A. Athletics: a cause of student failure.

Here is a topic outline displaying the organization of this article: (Because details can be tucked in place as the writing progresses, a practical working outline might be simpler than this. The small bones are supplied here to help the reader in studying and reviewing the article.)

The Library Research Paper

I. The meaning of research
  A. A fashionable word
  B. A popular human activity
  C. The value of the research paper

II. Choosing and limiting a subject
  A. How and where to look
  B. Over-sized subjects
  C. Ways of reducing
    1. From general to specific
    2. The thesis: use and abuse
    3. The working hypothesis
  D. Keeping the end in view

III. Using the library
  A. Browsing in the stacks
  B. Consulting reference works

1. Three indispensable guides
   a. The card catalogue
   b. A comprehensive encyclopedia
   c. The *Reader's Guide*
2. Other research tools
   a. Catalogues and bibliographies
   b. Periodical indexes
   c. Dictionaries
   d. Encyclopedias and surveys
   e. Yearbooks

IV. The working bibliography
   A. The value of cards and completeness
   B. The proper forms
      1. For a book
      2. For a periodical article
      3. For a newspaper article
      4. For an encyclopedia article
   C. Evaluating sources
      1. Shifting reading speed
      2. External evidence
         a. Who wrote it?
         b. Who published it?
         c. When was it written?
      3. Internal evidence: the necessity for skepticism

V. Taking notes
   A. Hints and warnings
      1. Taking too many
      2. One to a card
      3. Identifying cards
      4. Meticulous care
      5. Quotation, paraphrase, comment
      6. Precise copying
   B. Samples

VI. The outline
   A. The uses of outlining
   B. The accepted form
      1. Proper subordination
      2. Topic and sentence outlines
   C. Common errors
      1. The meaningless category
      2. Illogical coordination
      3. Improper subordination
      4. Single subdivision
   D. A sample

VII. Writing the paper
   A. Style: English vs. Academese
   B. Tone
   C. Quotation and paraphrase revisited
      1. Short quotation
      2. Long quotation
      3. Partial paraphrase
      4. Complete paraphrase
      5. Half-baked paraphrase
   D. Footnotes
      1. For a book
      2. For a periodical article
      3. For a newspaper article
      4. For an encyclopedia article
      5. Shortened footnotes
   E. Abbreviations
   F. The final bibliography
   G. The final draft

Writing the Paper

Except for the greater complexity of organization and the special problems of quotation, paraphrase, and proper acknowledgment, "writing up" the results of research is not essentially different from writing any other kind of paper. Whatever laws govern grammar and diction, spelling and punctuation, sentence and paragraph structure, none of them is suspended for research. The freedom to experiment with language may be more limited; the premium on clarity and accuracy is even higher. There is less room for the infinite riches of rhetoric: the drama and poetry of narrative and description are usually replaced by the humbler virtues of clear exposition. But good writing is good writing regardless of its habitat.

Illusions about research die hard. Even students who are convinced that the paper should be composed, not compiled, often assume that the art of composition requires a special style—freighted with *Academese*—and a special tone—impersonal, stuffy, and deadly dull.

Academese is only one kind of jargon. There is also *Pedagese*, the jargon of educationists, and *Scientese*, the jargon of would-be scientists, *Legalese, Commercialese,* and *Officialese.* All these dialects share the traits of jargon: involved sentence structure; unnecessary repetition and interminable circumlocution; a pseudotechnical vocabulary. Such writing has been called *gobbledygook* or—suggesting that it is often contrived to impress or even confuse—*bafflegab.* It might be better to revive the old-fashioned word *crabbed*—pronounced slowly with two syllables. A crabbed style suggests an animal that can move its imposing armaments forward only by slow, sideways slithering.

An expert talking to other experts will inevitably use the technical terms of his trade. Nobody writing on a technical subject, whether the propulsion of a rocket or the scansion of a poem, can entirely avoid technical language. But the problem is to explain it, not exploit it, to understand it, not merely parrot it. Genuine technical language is concise, concrete, and clear; it serves to identify and limit a phenomenon—a *paramecium*, not a *wiggly beasty, iambic pentameter*, not *words with a regular beat*. Pseudotechnical language is pulpy, abstract, and cryptic—*the intellectual confrontation in an interpersonal situation* instead of *the meeting of human minds*. The proliferation of such jargon by scholars does not make it scholarly.

The style and tone appropriate to a research paper will vary, of course, with the subject, the writer, and the intended reader. A style can be formal without being involved, or informal without being casual and careless. For the general writer who does not pretend to expert knowledge, the best advice on style is simply this: Relax but don't be lax; say simple things simply in your own language; do not write anything, even a quotation or a borrowed idea, in words that you do not understand yourself; be as concrete as possible; remember that, of all the virtues of good writing, the greatest is *clarity*.

The tone of a research paper can be serious without solemnity, dignified without stuffiness. The goal is not a charming personal essay; the reader is presumably interested in the subject, not the personality of the middle man. But the studied effort to be impersonal—and therefore ostensibly disinterested—often results in writing without either personality or interest. Though practice varies, it is better for a writer to use the first person, *I*, than to get tangled in the circumlocutions—the passive voice, for example—of the impersonal manner. Humor and irony may be useful if they grow naturally out of the subject instead of being thrust upon it. Irrelevant wisecracking is taboo. Jokes will not improve stale prose. The essential rule for tone is that all good writing more nearly reflects the living sound of a human voice, than the metallic chatter of a computer.

Quotation and Paraphrase Revisited

One special writing problem—anticipated in the discussion of note-taking—requires expansion here: the proper use of quotation and paraphrase. Make a careful comparison of the following samples:

(1) Short quotation

Leo Stein once said this about composition: "Every personal letter one writes, every personal statement one makes, may be creative writing if one's interest is to make it such."

(A short quotation in a research paper, as in any other paper, is introduced by a colon, or a comma, and carefully enclosed in quotation marks.)

(2) Long quotation

Talking about how to teach the proper use of language, Leo Stein said:

There is no difficulty in teaching them the routine of expression . . . but it is good to make them realize that there is no essential difference between them and those who write, except interest, use and purpose—that creativity in writing means nothing more than fitting words accurately and specifically to what one specifically and accurately intends. Shakespeare certainly intended more than most and had exceptional gifts, but anyone who has anything to say and wants to interest the receiver has a like object. Every personal letter one writes, every personal statement one makes, may be creative writing if one's interest is to make it such. Most people do not have this interest; what they write in ordinary communications is as dull as they can make it. They have never been taught to think of all writing as in its degree *writing* and all speaking *speaking*, and so they write in rubber stamps [clichés] and speak in the current routine of slang, as though writing and speaking were something reserved for the elect.

(Because the quotation is long—meaning, according to a common rule, five lines or more of typescript—it is set off in a separate paragraph, indented, and typed single-space without quotation marks. The student has represented Stein's italics (*writing, speaking*) by underlining. The three spaced periods in the first sentence stand for a deletion by the writer of the paper, and the bracketed word [clichés] in his addition.)

(3) Partial paraphase

Leo Stein maintains that creative writing is "nothing more than fitting words accurately and specifically to what one specifically and accurately intends." That Shakespeare had greater intentions and gifts does not, he insists, alter the rule. "Every personal letter one writers, every personal statement one makes, may be creative writing if one's interest is to make it such." A person who has no interest in writing or speaking, who mistakenly assumes that they are "reserved for the elect," will inevitably settle for dullness couched in clichés.

(To compress Stein's passage while preserving some of the original flavor, the writer of the paper uses an acceptable blend of paraphrase and direct quotation. Restricting the paraphrase to his own words and carefully setting off Stein's exact words in quotation marks, he weaves the two into a single tapestry.)

(4) Complete paraphrase

Leo Stein argues that creativity is not a special gift awarded to writers and speakers and denied to ordinary mortals. If he has something to say and is interested in saying it well, anyone, even in a personal letter, can be a creative writer.

(The summary, entirely in the student's own words, reproduces Stein's essential meaning but loses some of the flavor. It has the advantage of brevity.)

All four techniques are acceptable, depending on the purpose and scope of the paper. One *unacceptable* technique is far too common: a confusing mixture of the words of the source and the words of the student without proper distinction between them. It has been called *half-baked paraphrase*.

(5) Half-baked paraphrase

Stein says that students ought to be taught that people in general just don't bother to take advantage of their creativity, which only means in writing fitting words accurately and specifically to what one specifically and accurately intends. Shakespeare intended more than most and had exceptional gifts, but anyone who has anything to say and wants to interest the receiver has a like object. People in general are dull with words because they couldn't care less. They don't bother to think of all writing as in its degree writing and all speaking speaking, and so they use rubber stamps and slang.

(Though they are mixed clumsily with some comment of his own, the student has appropriated appreciable amounts of Stein's own wording without identifying it in quotation marks. A footnote or a bibliographical entry does not excuse this common practice. Whether it results from carelessness, laziness, or dishonesty, it is plagiarism.)

To quote or not to quote? No sacred formula answers the question. A historian working with original documents will resort to frequent quotation. A literary scholar cannot adequately analyze the work of a poet without reproducing excerpts from the poems, line by line, exactly as they appear in the original. But many inexperienced students quote too much: their research papers are merely collections of quotes loosely tethered by incidental interruptions. Generally speaking, direct quotation is useful to clinch an important point, to preserve some of the authentic flavor of the source, or to reproduce a passage that is particularly well written or peculiarly inept. A student should never quote at length unless the passage is especially important for his purpose.

Footnotes

Footnotes should be carefully supplied during the writing process, not superimposed later as an afterthought. In the first draft they can be included temporarily in the text itself. Even in the final draft, short notes may be conveniently inserted in the text in parentheses (*Hamlet* III, ii. 61–64) if the source is clearly identified and they do not clutter up the page with too many interruptions. Otherwise, footnotes are usually placed at the bottom of the page, not at the end of the paper. They are keyed to the text with Arabic numerals—not asterisks or other symbols—and should be numbered consecutively throughout the paper. The number in the text should be raised slightly above the line, and placed after any mark of punctuation and at the end—not the beginning—of any quotation, long or short. The number should not be enclosed in parentheses or followed by a period, either in the text or at the bottom of the page. At the foot of the page each note should begin with a capital letter on a new line—with the number raised and indented—and end with a period.

Occasionally a footnote is useful to supply an interesting detail or incidental comment that does not fit conveniently into the text. But in a research paper most footnotes are supplied to acknowledge specific borrowings from sources. Unlike the bibliography, which is a general listing of sources, they usually provide exact page references. With that exception, a complete footnote furnishes the same essential information as a bibliographical entry, but with a different system of punctuation and in a slightly different order.

A footnote is always used to acknowledge a direct quotation unless its exact source is made clear in the text or is familiar (like the Gettysburg Address) to any educated reader. But in spite of a common illusion, the student's responsibility does not end there. He should also use a footnote (1) to acknowledge the use of another writer's idea or opinion *even if it is completely paraphrased,* and (2) as a receipt for the loan of any facts, statistics, or other illustrative material that he has not acquired by original observation.

Here is a representative group of complete footnotes: (Compare them with the bibliographical entries on page 7, observing the differences in punctuation and order of their parts.)

For a book with one author:

[1]John K. Galbraith, *The Affluent Society* (Boston, 1958), p. 23.

For a book with more than one author:

[2]James H. Sledd and Gwin J. Kolb, *Dr. Johnson's Dictionary* (Chicago, 1955), pp. 49–50.

For a periodical article:

[3]Walter Lippman, "Cuba and the Nuclear Risk," *Atlantic,* CCXI (February 1963), 57.

For a newspaper article:

[4]New York *Times,* December 28, 1964, p. 6.

[4]New York *Times,* January 3, 1965, sec. 4, p. 7.

For an encyclopedia article:

[5]Donald G. Fink, "Television," *Encyclopaedia Britannica* (1963), XXI, 912.

Whenever a source is used for the first time, the student should give a complete footnote even though most of the information will be repeated in the bibliography. If, however, some of the details appear in the text—the author's name, for example, or the title—it is unnecessary to repeat them at the foot of the page. After the first footnote, an abbreviated form may be used if the complete note is not buried too far back. The easiest short form is the author's last name:

[6]Galbraith, p. 29.

If previous notes refer to more than one work by the same author, a shortened title should be added:

[7]Galbraith, *Affluent Society,* p. 29.

The popularity of the following Latin abbreviations is on the wane, partly because they have led to widespread misunderstanding. Though the writer may never be required to use them, he should understand their meaning in the footnotes of others: (They are sometimes italicized because of their foreign origin.)

Ibid.	short for *ibidem,* meaning "in the same place." Refers to the same page of the same source cited in the footnote *immediately preceding.*
Ibid., p. 57.	another page of the same source cited in the footnote *immediately preceding.*
Galbraith, *op. cit.,* p. 59.	short for *opere citato,* meaning "in the work cited." Refers here to page 59 of the opus by Galbraith cited in a recent footnote. Obviously has no advantage over the use of the author's name alone or author and short title.
Op. cit., p. 59.	may be used if the author's name is made clear in the text.
Loc. cit.	short for *loco citato,* meaning "in the place cited"—that is, the same passage as in a recent footnote. Never used with a page number. Not used at all by many modern scholars.

Because documentation is intended to help the reader, not impress or confuse him, discretion is the better part of valor. If, for example, a number of short quotations from the same source appear in one paragraph of the paper, or if the writer is indebted to one authority for a tissue of small facts, it is unnecessary to present the reader with a whole flock of ibids. On occasion a single covering note may be sufficient:

[1]My main authority for the facts about the charge of the Light Brigade is Cecil Woodham-Smith, *The Reason Why* (New York, 1953), pp. 207–257.

As Frank Sullivan once observed, if you give a footnote an inch it will take a foot.

The student may find the following abbreviations useful in either footnotes or bibliography:

Abbreviations Commonly Used in Footnotes and Bibliographies

anon.—anonymous

c. or ca.—from Latin *circa,* meaning "about." Used with approximate dates (c. 1340).

cf.—compare (cf. p. 47). Should not be used interchangeably with *see* (see p. 79).

ch., chs., chap., chaps.—chapter(s)

col., cols.—column(s)

ed., eds.—editor(s), edition(s)

f., ff.—and the following page(s) or line(s). 76f. or 76ff. 76–78 and 76–87 are more exact.

l., ll.—line(s)

n., nn.—note(s). For example, p. 69, n. 3 refers to the third footnote on page 69. Also p. 69*n* (italicized without the period).

n.d.—no date. Inserted in square brackets when date of publication is not given.

no., nos.—number(s)

par., pars.—paragraph(s)

passim—here and there throughout the work

pseud.—pseudonym

rev.—review, reviewed (by), revised (by), revision

sc.—scene in a play. Unnecessary in short notes if acts are put in large Roman numerals, scenes in small Roman numerals, lines in Arabic (IV.iii.27–46).

sic—Latin for "thus" or "so." Inserted in square brackets to make a succinct comment on something in a quotation such as an error in logic or spelling [sic].

vol., vols.—volume(s)

The Final Bibliography

If exact indebtedness to sources is carefully acknowledged throughout the footnotes, a final bibliography may not be required. In scholarly publishing, a full-length book is usually supplied with one, an article is not. A teacher will often insist on a bibliography as an exercise in formal acknowledgment and a convenient map of the ground actually covered in preparing the paper. Ordinarily it should be no more than a *selected bibliography*. A complete inventory of all the discoverable sources may be useful to a specialist, but only an ingenuous student would expect extra credit for his ability to transcribe the card catalogue and the *Reader's Guide*. A selected bibliography contains only those items on the bibliography cards that have proved useful in writing the paper. The length of the list is roughly proportionate to the paper's scope. In a long list it may be convenient to have two or more groupings, separating books from articles, or sources of special importance from sources of general interest. For most research papers a single alphabetical listing is sufficient. Note that each entry in the following specimen contains the same information in the same order as on a bibliography card. If a book or article does not have an author, it is usually listed alphabetically under the first important word of the title.

Selected Bibliography

Ashworth, John. "Olivier, Freud, and Hamlet," *Atlantic,* CLXXXIII (May 1949), 30–33.

Brown, John R., "Theatrical Research and the Criticism of Shakespeare and His Contemporaries," *Shakespeare Quarterly,* XIII (1962), 451–461.

Hankins, John E. "Caliban the Bestial Man," PMLA, LXII (September 1947), 793–801.

Knight, G. Wilson. "The Embassy of Death: An Essay on Hamlet," *The Wheel of Fire* (London, 1949), 17–30.

Littleton, Taylor, and Robert R. Rea, eds. *To Prove a Villain: The Case of King Richard III.* New York, 1964.

Raysor, Thomas M., ed. *Coleridge's Shakespearean Criticism.* 2 vols. Cambridge, Mass. 1930.

"Shakespeare at 400," *Life,* LVI (April 24, 1964), 58–99.

Shakespeare, William. *The Complete Works,* ed. George Lyman Kittredge. Boston, 1936.

Tillyard, E. M. W. *The Elizabethan World Picture.* London, 1943.

Traversi, D. A. *An Approach to Shakespeare,* 2nd rev. ed. New York, 1956.

The Final Draft

The final draft of the research paper should be typed—double-spaced—on one side of heavy white paper (not onion skin) 8½ x 11 inches and unlined. Footnotes and long indented quotations should be single-spaced. Two spaces should appear between footnotes and three between the text and the first note. The pages should be numbered with Arabic numerals, either centered at the top or in the upper right-hand corner. Whether held in a binder or merely with a paper clip, the pages should be kept flat, not folded as in a shorter composition. Margins should be at least an inch wide all around. The title should appear on both the first page (about two inches from the top) and on a separate title page, which should also include the author's name, the date, and the name of the course, if any. Corrections in the final draft should be strictly limited, preferably made by neat erasing and retyping. A sloppy paper inevitably suggests a sloppy mind. Besides, it is absurd for the writer to stumble in haste over the final barrier after he has taken so long to come so far.

Greek and Latin Elements in English

Combining Forms

Greek/Latin	English	Example(s)
acantho-, Gk	spiny	acanthoid
acid-, acri-, acer-, acu-, L	keen, sharp, point	acrid, acerbic, acute
acme, Gk	culmination	acme
acous-, Gk	to hear	acoustic
acro-, Gk	tip, top	acrophobia
act-, -action, L	lead, drive, carry	interaction
actino-, Gk	light ray, radiate	actinoid
adeno-, Gk	gland	adenoid
adip-, L	fat	adipose
aeri-, L	air	aerie
aero-,Gk	air, aircraft, gas	aerobic, aerodrome
agit-, ag-, ig-, -act, L	to drive	agitate, agent, exigency, counteract
-agog, -agogue, Gk	leading	demagog, pedagogue
agon-, -agonist, Gk	contest, struggle	agony, antagonist
agri-, agro-, Gk	agriculture, field	agriculture, agronomy
alb-, L	white	albino, albumin
-algia, Gk	pain	neuralgia
alien-, alia-, alter-, L	foreign, strange, other	alienation, alternative
allo-, Gk	other	allotropy
alti, alto-, L	high, height	altimeter
amat-, ami-, amo-, -amour, L	love	amatory, amicable, paramour
ambi-, L	both	ambiguous
ambul-, L	to walk	ambulatory
amphi-, Gk	both	amphibian
amylo-, Gk	starch	amylopectin
andro-, -androus, anthropo-, Gk	man	android, polyandrous, anthropology
anemo-, Gk	wind	anemometer
angi-, angu-, anx-, L	choking	angina, anguish, anxiety
angio-, Gk	vessel	angiosperm
Anglo-, L	English	Anglo-American
anima, L	breath, mind	animal, animate
ankylo-, Gk	bent	ankylosis
ann-, L	year	annual
antho-, Gk	flower	anthophore, anthology
aqua-, aque-, L	water	aquatic, aqueous
arbor-, L	tree, beam	arboretum
arch-, archi-, Gk	chief, primitive	architect
archeo-, Gk	ancient	archeology
-archy, Gk	govern	monarchy
arterio-, Gk	artery	arteriosclerosis
arthro-, arthri-, Gk	joint	arthropod, arthritis
articul-, L	joint	articulate

Greek/Latin	English	Example(s)
asco-, Gk	bag	ascospore
atmo-, Gk	air, breath, wind	atmosphere
audio-, L	hear	audiovisual
aug-, L	increase	augment
auto-, Gk	self	automatic
auro-, auriculo-, L	ear	auroventricular, auricle
aux-, Gk	strengthen	auxiliary
avi-, L	bird	aviation
bacci-, L	berry	baccivorous
bacteri-, Gk & L	bacterium	bacteriophage
ball-, Gk	to throw	ballistic
barb-, barbar-, L	beard	barber, barbarian
baro-, bari-, Gk	atmospheric pressure, weight	barometer, bariatrics
-base, bass-, L	low	abase, bassoon
basis, basi-, Gk	a step, foot	basic, basidium
bat-, L	to beat	battle
batho-, bathy-, Gk	deep, depth	bathos, bathysphere
bi-, bin-, L	two, double	bisect, binary
bibl-, biblio-, Gk	book	bible, bibliography
bio-, -biosis, Gk	life	biography, symbiosis
blasto-, -blast, Gk	bud, shoot	blastocele
blephar-, blepharo-, Gk	eyelid	blepharitis
bovi-, L	cattle	bovine
brachio-, -brace, Gk	arm	brachial
brachy-, Gk	short	brachycephaly
brady-, Gk	slow	bradycardia
branch-, Gk	fin, paw, limb	branching
branchio-, -branch, Gk	gills	branchiopod
brevi-, L	short	brevity
bronch-, broncho-, Gk	windpipe	bronchoscopy
bull-, L	bubble	bullet, ebullient
burs-, L	purse	bursar, bursitis
caco-, Gk	bad	cacophany
cad-, cid-, L	case, casualty, to fall	decadent, incident
cal-, chal-, L	to be hot	calorie, chaldron
calcul-, L	pebble, stone	calculate
calli-, Gk	fair, beautiful	calligraphy
camer-, L	chamber	bicameral
camp-, champ-, L	a plain	campus, champion
canal-, channel-, L	canal	canalization
cani-, L	dog	canine
cap-, capt-, cept-, L	to seize, take hold of	capable, capture, concept
capit-, cipit-, L	head	capital, occipital
carbo-, carboni-, -carbon, L	carbon	carboniferous, fluorocarbon
cardio-, Gk	heart	cardiovascular, cardiac
carn-, L	flesh	carnivorous
carpo-, -carpous, Gk	fruit	carpogonium, syncarpous
caus-, cus-, L	cause	causation, excuse
-cele, Gk	cavity, tumor, hernia, swelling	blastocele
-cene, Gk	recent	eocene
ceno-, Gk	common	cenocyte
centi-, cent-, L	hundred	centimeter, century
centr-, Gk & L	center	central
cephalo-, -cephalic, -cephalous, Gk	head, brain	microcephalic

Greek/Latin	English	Example(s)
cer-, cero-, Gk & L	wax	cerumin
cerebro-, L	brain	cerebrospinal
cervic-, cervico-, L	neck	cervical
chalc-, chalco-, Gk	copper	chalcedony
chemo-, Gk	chemical	chemotherapy
chilo-, Gk	lip	chiloplasty
chiro-, Gk	hand	chiropody
chloro-, Gk	green, chlorine	chlorophyll, chloromethane
chole-, cholo-, Gk	bile	cholesterol
chondro-, Gk	cartilage	chondritis
choreo-, choro-, Gk	dance	choreography, chorus
chromato-, chromo-, -chrome, Gk	color	chromatography
chron-, chrono-, Gk	time	chroni, chronograph
chryso-, Gk	gold	chrysolite
-cidal, -cide, L	to kill	suicidal, genocide
cine-, Gk	motion pictures	cinema
circ-, L	ring	circle, circus
cirri-, cirro-, L	curly	cirrostratus
cit-, L	incite	cite, solicit
clar-, L	clear	clarify, declare
claud-, claus-, clud-, clus-, L	to shut	claustrophobia, occlude
climato-, Gk	climate	climatology
clino, -cline, Gk & L	slope	clinometer, incline
cocci-, -coccus, Gk & L	berry-shaped, bacterium	streptococci
col-, cult-, L	to till	colony, culture
colo-, Gk	colon	colorectal
colori-, L	color	colorimeter
cono-, Gk	cone	conoid
contra-, counter-, L	against	contrast
copro-, Gk	dung	coprophagous
corn-, cornu-, L	horn	cornea, cornucopia
cosmo-, Gk	world, universe	cosmology
cost-, costo-, L	rib	costal
-cracy, -crat, Gk	govern	democracy
cred-, L	believe	credible, credit
cruci-, L	cross	crucial
cryo-, Gk	cold	cryogenic
crypto-, Gk	hidden	cryptogram
crystallo-, Gk	crystal	crystallography
cteno-, Gk	comb	ctenoid
cupri-, cupro-, L	copper	cupric, cuprous
curr-, curs-, cour-, L	to run	current, excursion, course
curvi-, curva-, L	curved	curvilinear, curvaceous
cyano-, cyani-, Gk	bluish, cyanogen	cyanotic, cyanide
cyclo-, -cyclic, -cycle, Gk	circle	cyclopentane, tricycle
cymo-, Gk	wave	cymoscope
cyst-, cysto-, Gk	bladder, cyst	cystic, cystotomy
cyto-, Gk	cell	cytoplasm
dactylo-, -dactyl, Gk	finger	pterodactyl
deca-, Gk	ten	decameron
deci-, L	a tenth	decile
demi-, L	half	demimonde

Greek/Latin	English	Example(s)
demn-, dam-, L	loss	condemn, indemnity, damn
demo-, Gk	people	democrat
dendro-, -dendron, Gk	tree	rhododendron
denti-, L	tooth	dentition
dermato-, derm-, dermo-, Gk	skin	dermatologist
deuter-, deutero-, Gk	second (adj.)	deuterium
dextro-, L	right	ambidextrous
di-, Gk	double	dimer
di-, dis-, L	apart	digress
digit-, digiti-, digito-, L	finger	digitigrade
dino-, Gk	terrible	dinosaur
diplo-, Gk	double	diploma, diplomacy
dodeca-, Gk	twelve	dodecahedron
dors-, dorsi-, dorso-, L	back	dorsoventral
-drome, -dromous, Gk	run	hippodrome
duo-, du-, L	two	dualism
duoden-, duodeno-, L	duodenum	duodenal
dyna-, dynamo-, Gk	power	dynamic, dynamometer
dys-, Gk	bad, difficult	dyslexia
echino-, Gk	spiny	echinoderm
ecto-, exo-, Gk	external, outside	ectomorphy, exogenous
electro-, Gk & L	electric	electromechanical
embryo-, Gk	embryo	embryology
-emia, Gk	blood condition or disease	septicemia
endo-, ento-, Gk	interior	endogenous
ennea-, Gk	nine	ennead
enter-, entero-, Gk	intestine	enteritis
eo-, Gk	early, earliest	eocene
equ-, equi-, L	equal, like, same	equate
erg-, Gk	work	ergon
erythro-, Gk	red	erythrocyte
ethn-, ethno-, Gk	nation	ethnocentric
eu-, Gk	good	euphoria
eury-, Gk	broad	eurycephalic
extra-, extro-, L	external	extraneous, extrovert
fac-, fec-, fic-, fact-, fect-, fict-, L	to do	fact, perfect, deficit
febri-, L	fever	febrile
-fend, -fense, L	to strike	defend
-fer, -ferous, L	bearing	transfer
ferro-, ferri-, L	iron	ferric
fibro-, L	fibrous	fibroid
fid-, L	faith	confidence
fin-, L	end	final, finance
fissi-, -fid, L	split	fission
-fix, L	to fix	prefix
flagr-, L	to burn	conflagration
flexi-, L	bent	flexible
flig-, -flict, L	to strike	profligate, inflict
fluo-, fluoro-, fluor-, L	fluorescence, fluorine	fluoride
flor-, flour-, L	flower	florist, flourish

Greek/Latin	English	Example(s)
fluv-, fluvi-, fluvio-, L	river	fluvial
foli-, folia-, folio-, L	leaf, leafy	foliation
form-, -form, L	form	formal, conform
fort-, forti-, L	strong	fortify
fract-, frang-, frag-, L	to break	fraction, frangible, fragment
fru-, fruit-, L	to enjoy	fruition
fug-, fuge-, -fugal, L	to flee	refugee, centrifugal
fund-, found-, L	bottom	fundament, profound
fungi-, L	fungus	fungicide
galacto-, Gk	milk	galactose
Gallo-, Gall-, L	French	Gallic
gameto-, Gk	gamete	gametophyte
gamo-, -gamy, Gk	union, sexual union	gamogenesis, oogamy
ganglio-, gangli-, Gk	ganglion	gangliated
gastro-, gastero-, Gk	stomach, abdomen	gastroenterology
gemm-, L	bud	gemmule
gen-, L	kin	genus
-gen, -genous, -geny, -gony, Gk	producing	oxygen, cosmogony
genito-, L	genital	genitourinary
geo-, Gk	earth	geography
geri-, geronto-, Gk	old age	geriatric, gerontology
-gerous, L	bearing	crystalligerous
giganto-, Gk	gigantic	gigantomachy
glauco-, Gk	light or blue-gray	glaucoma
glosso-, gloss-, Gk	tongue	glossary
glyco-, Gk	sweet	glycolysis
glypto-, -glyph, Gk	carved, carving	glyptodont, hieroglyphics
gnatho-, -gnathous, Gk	jaw	prognathous
-gon, gonio-, Gk	angle	polygon, goniometer
-gonium, Gk	seed	syngonium
gono-, Gk	reproduction	gonorrhea
-grade, -gress, L	walking, step	plantigrade, congress
grani-, L	grain	graniform
grapho-, -graph, -graphy, -gram, Gk	to write	polygraph
grat-, grate-, grati-, L	pleasing	gratitude
Greco-, L	Greek	Greco-Roman
greg-, L	a flock	aggregate, gregarious
gust-, gusta-, L	a tasting	disgust, gustatory
gymno-, gymn-, Gk	naked	gymnosophist, gymnast
gyneco-, gyneo- gyno-, Gk	woman, ovary	gynecology
gyro-, gyr-, Gk	circle	gyrate
hab-, hib-, L	to have	habit, inhibit
hagio-, hagi, Gk	sacred	hagiography
halo-, Gk	salt, sea	halogen, halophyte
haplo-, Gk	simple, single	haploid
hect-, hecto-, Gk	hundred	hectare
-hedral, -hedron, Gk	side	polyhedron
heli-, helico-, Gk	spiral	helicopter
helio-, Gk	sun	heliocentric
hema-, hemato-, hemo-, Gk	blood	hematocrit

Greek/Latin	English	Example(s)
hemi-, Gk	half	hemisphere
hepa-, hepat-, hepato-, Gk	liver	heparin
hepta-, Gk	seven	heptad
her-, L	heir	heredity
hernio-, L	hernia	herniotomy
hetero-, Gk	different	heteronym
hexa-, Gk	six	hexagon
hiero-, Gk	sacred	hieroglyph
hippo-, Gk	horse	hippocampus
histo-, Gk	tissue	histopathology
holo-, hol-, Gk	whole	hologram, holism
homo-, homeo-, homoio-, Gk	like, same	homoiothermy
horr-, -hor, L	to bristle	horrible, abhor
hum-, L	the ground	humus, humble
hyalo-, Gk	glass, glassy	hyaloid
hydro-, Gk	water	hydrotherapy
hygro-, Gk	wet	hygrometer
hylo-, Gk	matter, material	hylozoism
hymeno-, Gk	membrane	hymenopterous
hypno-, Gk	sleep	hypnosis
hystero-, hyster-, Gk	hysteria, uterus	hysterotomy, hysterical
i-, -it, L	to go	exit, itinerary
-iasis, Gk	disease	schistosomiasis
iatro-, -iatrics, -iatry, Gk	medicine	iatrogenic, psychiatry
ichth-, ichthyo-, Gk	fish	ichthyosaur
icono-, Gk	image	iconoclast
ideo-, Gk	idea	ideology
idio-, Gk	individual	idiosyncrasy
igni-, L	fire	ignition
ileo-, -ileac, L	ileum (small intestine)	ileocecal
ilio-, -iliac, L	ilium	sacroiliac
inguin-, inguino-, L	groin	inguinal
int-, L	within	intestine, internal
intra-, intro-, L	interior, inward	introduce
iodo-, Gk	iodine	iodoform
iso-, Gk	equal, like, same	isometric
-itis, Gk	inflammation	chondritis
jac-, -ject, L	to throw	adjacent, eject
jug-, junct-, -join, L	to join, yoke	conjugal, conjunction
jur-, jus-, L	to swear	jury, justify
juxta-, L	near	juxtaposition
kerato-, Gk	cornea, horn	keratin
kinesi-, kineto-, -kinesis, Gk	movement	psychokinesis
labi-, labio-, L	lip	labium
labor-, L	labor	elaborate
lac-, lec-, lic-, L	to entice	delectable
lacto-, L	milk	lactose
laryngo-, Gk	larynx	laryngoscope
lati-, L	broad	latitude
leg-, lect-, L	to collect, read	legible, recollect
lepid-, lepido-, Gk	scale, scaly	lepidopterous
-lepsy, -leptic, Gk	seizure	epilepsy

Greek/Latin	English	Example(s)
lept-, lepto-, Gk	small, think	leptophyllous
leuko-, Gk	white	leukocyte
levo-, L	left, left-sided	levotartaric
liber-, L	free	liberty
lig-, L	to bind	ligament, oblige
ligni-, lign-, L	wood	lignite
lin-, L	a line	delineate
lip-, lipo-, Gk	fat	lipoma
litera-, L	a letter	literature
litho-, -lith, Gk	stone	monolith
loc-, L	a place	local, locomotion
logo-, log-, Gk	speech, word	logic
-logy, -logical, Gk	science of	ecology
longi-, L	long	longitude
luci-, L	light	lucid
lumin-, lumini-, L	light	illuminate
lun-, luni-, L	moon	lunar
lympho-, lymphat-, lymphato-, L	lymph	lymphoma
lyo-, -lysis, -lyte, Gk	dissolving	electrolyte
-machy, Gk	fight	tauromachy
macro-, Gk	large	macrocosm
magneto-, L	magnet	magnetosphere
magni-, L	great, large	magnificent
mal-, L	bad	maladjustment
man-, main-, L	hand	manner, maintain
-mancy, -mantic, Gk	divining	chiromancy
-mania, -maniac, Gk	craving	monomania
mast-, masto-, Gk	breast	mastectomy
matri-, L	mother	matrilineal
medi-, medio-, L	middle	mediocre
medico-, L	medicine	medicolegal
mega-, megalo-, Gk	great	megalomania
melan-, melano-, Gk	black, dark	melanin
mem-, L	remembering	memoir
ment-, mon-, L	mind	mental, demonstrate
mero-, -mere, -merous, Gk	part, of parts	blastomere, trimerous
meso-, mes-, Gk	middle	mesozoic
metro-, -meter, -metry, Gk	measure	metrology, centimeter, telemetry
micro-, Gk	small	micron
milli-, L	thousand, thousandth	millipede
mir-, mar-, L	wonderful	miracle, marvel
miso-, mis-, Gk	hate	misanthrope
-mit, -miss, L	to send	emit, mission
mod-, L	manner	model, modify
mono-, Gk	one	monocle
mor-, mori-, mort-, L	to die	morgue, mortal
-morph, morpho-, -morphic, -morphous, Gk	form	endomorph, amorphous
mot-, mov-, L	to move	emotion, remove
moun-, L	hill	mound, mountain
muco-, muci-, L	mucus, slimy	mucilage
multi-, L	many	multifaceted
myco-, -mycete, Gk	fungus	ascomycete

Greek/Latin	English	Example(s)
myel-, myelo-, Gk	spinal cord	myelin
myo-, Gk	muscle	myocardial
myria-, Gk	very many	myriad
mytho-, Gk	myth	mythology
myxo-, Gk	slime	myxophobia
narco-, Gk	torpor	narcolepsy
nas-, naso-, L	nose	nasal
nati-, L	birth	nativity
necro-, Gk	corpse	necromancy
-nect, -nex, L	to bind	connect, annex
nemato-, Gk	thread	nematode
neo-, Gk	new	neo-Freudian
nephro-, Gk	kidney	nephron
neuro-, Gk	nerve	neuroanatomy
nitro-, nitr-, L	nitrogen	nitrate
noct-, nocti-, L	night	nocturnal
nomen-, nomin-, -noun, L	name	nomenclature, pronoun
nomo-, Gk	custom, law	nomothetic
noso-, -nose, -nosis, Gk	disease	diagnosis
not-, nit-, nis-, L	to get to know	notice, cognition
nota-, L	a mark	notary, notation
noto-, Gk	a back	notochord
nucleo-, L	nucleus	nucleotide
nudi-, L	bare	nudity
numer-, L	number	enumerate
nutr-, nur-, L	to nourish	nutrition, nurse
nycti-, nycto-, nyct-, Gk	night	nyctalopic
octa-, octo-, Gk & L	eight	octopus
oculo-, ocul-, L	eye	oculist
odonto-, -odont, Gk	tooth	odontology
odyno-, -odynia, Gk	pain	odynometer
-oid, -ode, Gk	like	spheroid
oleo-, L	oil	oleomargarine
oligo-, olig-, Gk	few	oligarchy
-oma, Gk	tumor	lymphoma
omni-, L	all	omnipotent
oneiro-, Gk	dream	oneiromancy
onto-, Gk	existence	ontology
oo-, Gk	egg	oogonium
ophio-, Gk	snake	ophiophobia
ophthalmo-, Gk	eye	ophthalmologist
-opia, Gk	vision defect	myopia
-opsis, Gk	appearance, sight	synopsis
orb-, L	a circle	orbit
orchido-, Gk	orchid	orchid
orchio-, orchi-, Gk	testicle	orchialgia
ord-, ordin-, L	order	ordain, subordinate
organo-, Gk	organ, organic	organometallic
ornitho-, Gk	bird	ornithology
oro-, L	mouth	oronasal
ortho-, Gk	correct, upright	orthopedic
-osis, Gk	disease	neurosis
ossi-, L	bone	ossify
oste-, osteo-, Gk	bone	osteoarthritis

Greek/Latin	English	Example(s)
pneumat-, pneumato-, Gk	breath	pneumatic
pneumo-, Gk	lung	pneumothorax
-pod, -podous, Gk	foot	arthropod
-poietic, Gk	making	hematopoietic
polio-, Gk	gray matter	poliomyelitis
poly-, Gk	many	polygyny
pon-, pos-, L	to place	opponent, position
popul-, pub-, L	people	popular, public
port-, L	to carry	portable
-prehend, L	to seize	apprehend
primi-, prim-, L	first	prime
procto-, Gk	rectum	proctoscope
proto-, Gk	first	prototype
pseudo-, Gk	false	pseudonym
psycho-, psych-, Gk	mind; spirit	psychology; psychic
psychro-, Gk	cold	psychrometer
ptero-, -pterous, -pter, Gk	wing	pterodactyl, helicopter
pulmo-, L	lung	pulmonary
punct-, pung-, L	to prick	puncture, pungent
pur-, L	pure	purity, puritan
-pute, L	clear	compute
py-, pye-, Gk	pus	pyorrhea
pyelo, Gk	pelvis	pyelogram
pyro-, pyr-, Gk	fire	pyromania, pyre
quadri-, quadru-, L	four	quadrilateral
quasi-, L	like, as if	quasi-serious
-quer, -quire, -quest, L	to seek	conquer, acquire, inquest
quin-, quinque-, quinqua-, L	five	quintuplet
radic-, L	root	radical
radio-, L	radiant energy, radio, radioactive	radioactivity, radioisotope
rat-, rati-, L	to suppose	ratio, ratify
recti-, L	straight	rectitude
recto-, L	rectum	rectoabdominal
reg-, res-, L	to rule	regal, resource
ren-, reni-, L	kidney	renal, reniform
rheo-, Gk	current	rheostat
rhino-, Gk	nose	rhinoceros
rhizo-, Gk	root	rhizome
rot-, rotat-, L	a wheel	rotor, rotate
-rrhea, -rrhagia, -rrhagic, -rrhage, Gk	flow	hemorrhage
-rupt, L	to break	interrupt
acchar-, saccharo-, Gk	sugar	saccharin
sacro-, L	sacrum	sacroiliac
sangui-, L	blood	sanguine
sapro-, Gk	decompose	saprophyte
sarco-, Gk	flesh	sarcophagus
scato-, Gk	dung	scatological
-scend, L	to climb	condescend
schisto-, Gk	to divide	schistosome
schizo-, Gk	to split	schizophrenia
sclero-, Gk	hard	sclerosis
-scope, -scopy, Gk	observation	microscope

Greek/Latin	English	Example(s)
oto-, Gk	ear	otology
ovi-, ovo-, ov-, L	egg	ovate
oxy-, Gk	oxygen; sharp	oxyacid; oxytone
pachy-, Gk	thick	pachyderm
paleo-, Gk	ancient	paleolithic
palmi-, palm-, L	palm	palmitic
pan-, panto-, Gk	all	pandemic, pantothenic
par-, per-, L	to prepare	apparatus, imperative
para-, Gk	near	paragraph
pari-, L	equal, like	par, disparity
-parous, L	bearing	viviparous
part-, -part, L	part	depart, partake
-pathy, patho-, Gk	disease, suffering	neuropathy, pathos
patri-, L	father	patrician
-ped, -pede, pedi-, L	foot	impede
peda-, pedo-, Gk	child	pedagogue
-pel, L	to drive	compel
pelvi-, L	pelvis	pelvic
-pend, -pond, L	to weigh	depend, ponder
penta-, Gk	five	pentagon
petro-, Gk	stone	petroglyph
-phage, phago-, -phagous, -phagy, Gk	eat	phagocyte
pharmaco-, Gk	drug	pharmacology
pharyngo-, Gk	pharynx	pharyngoscope
-phasia, Gk	speech defect	aphasia
pheno-, phanero-, -phany, Gk	visible	phenomenon
-philia, -phily, Gk	morbid love	pedophilia
philo-, -phile, Gk	love	philosophy, bibliophile
phleb-, phlebo-, Gk	vein	phlebitis
-phobia, Gk	fear	agoraphobia
-phone, phono-, -phony, Gk	sound	phonograph
photo-, Gk	light	photograph
phren-, phreno-, Gk	brain, mind	schizophrenic, phrenology
phyl-, phylo-, Gk	species	phylum, phylogeny
phyllo-, -phyllous, -phyll, Gk	leaf, leafy	chlorophyll
physio-, Gk	nature	physiocrat
-phyte, phyto-, Gk	plant (bot.)	phytoplankton
picr-, picro-, Gk	bitter	picric
piezo-, Gk	pressure	piezochemistry
pinna-, pinni-, L	fin, web, leaf	pinnate, pinniped
pisci-, L	fish	pisciculture
plano-, L	flat	planoconvex
-plasia, -plasis, Gk	growth	hyperplasia
-plasm, Gk	material, matter	cytoplasm
-plast, Gk	cell	chloroplast
-plastic, -plasty, Gk	making, forming	rhinoplasty
platy-, Gk	flat	platypus
-plegia, Gk	paralysis	quadriplegia
plen-, L	to fill	plenty
pleur-, pleuro-, Gk	pleura, side	pleurisy
plic-, -plex, L	to fold	implicate, complex
plumb-, plumbo-, L	lead (metal)	plumbing

Greek/Latin	English	Example(s)
scoto-, Gk	darkness	scotoma
-scribe, scrip-, L	to write	describe, scripture
scyph-, Gk & L	cup	scyphiform
seb-, sebi-, sebo-, L	fat, fatty	sebaceous
-sect, -section, L	cut	bisect
sed-, sid-, -sess, siz-, L	to sit	sediment, residue, possess, size
seismo-, Gk	earthquake	seismograph
semi-, L	half	semiconductor
-sent, sent-, L	to feel	assent, sentiment
sept-, septi-, L	seven	septet
sequ-, sec-, L	to follow	sequence, second
sero-, L	serum	serous
serv-, -serve, L	a slave	servant, conserve
sex-, L	six	sexagenarian
sider-, sidero-, Gk	star	sidereal
-sign, L	a sign	assign, signal
silico-, L	silicon	silicosis
simil-, sem-, L	same	similar, resemble
simplici-, L	simple	simplicity
Sino-, L	Chinese	Sino-Soviet
sito-, -site, Gk	food, eat	parasite
socio-, L	society	socioeconomic
sol-, solit-, L	alone	sole, solitary
solu-, -solve, L	to loosen	solution, resolve
somato-, -soma, -some, Gk	body	chromosome
somn-, somni-, L	sleep	insomnia
-son, son-, L	sound	sonata
-sophy, -sopher, Gk	knowledge of	philosopher
spec-, -spect, L	to look	specimen, inspect
spectro-, L	spectrum	spectrogram
speleo-, spel-, Gk & L	cave	spelunker
spermo-, spermato-, -spermous, Gk	seed, spermatozoa	spermatozoid
-sphere, Gk	sphere	hemisphere
sphygmo-, Gk	pulse	sphygmomanometer
spiro-, spir-, Gk	spiral	spirogyra, spiral
spiro-, -spire, spir-, L	breath	spirometer, inspire, spirit
-stant, -sist, -stitute, -stance, L	to stand	constant, desist, institute, substance
-stat, Gk	to stop	thermostat, static
stato-, stat-, Gk	position	status
stell-, stelli-, L	star	stellar
steno-, Gk	narrow	stenosis
stereo-, Gk	solid	stereophonic
stetho-, Gk	chest	stethoscope
-stomy, Gk	surgical opening	ileostomy
-strict, -strain, L	to draw tight	constrict, restrain
-struct, L	to build	construct
sulfa-, sulfo-, L	sulfur	sulfonamide
sup-, sum-, L	above	superior, summit
tachy-, Gk	swift	tachyon
-tain, tang-, L	to touch	attain, tangible
tauro-, Gk	cattle	tauromachy
tauto-, Gk	same	tautology

Greek/Latin	English	Example(s)
taxo-, -taxis, -taxy, Gk	order	taxonomy
techno-, Gk	art, technical	technology
teg-, -tect, L	to cover	tegument, detect
tele-, teleo-, telo-, Gk	far, final	television, teleology
temp-, L	time	temporary
ten-, -tain, L	to hold	tenacity, contain
ter-, tre-, tri-, L	three	tercentenary
terato-, Gk	monster	teratology
termin-, L	end	exterminator
terr-, -ter, L	to scare	terror, deter
terri-, L	earth	territory
test-, -test, L	witness	testament, contest
tetra-, Gk	four	tetrad
-text, text-, L	to weave	context, textile
thanato-, Gk	death	thanatology
theo-, Gk	god	theology
thermo-, Gk	heat	thermometer
thio-, Gk	sulfur	Thiokol
thorac-, thoraco-, Gk	thorax	thoracic
thyro-, Gk	thyroid	thyroxin
tom-, -tome, tomo-, Gk	knife, cutting	tome, epitome, tomograph
tono-, Gk	tone	tonometer
topo-, Gk	place	topology
tot-, toti-, L	whole	totalitarian
toxico-, Gk	poison	toxicology
tracheo-, Gk	trachea	tracheotomy
-tract, treat-, L	to draw	extract, treatise
trib-, L	tribe	contribute
tricho-, Gk	hair	trichomonad
trop-, -troupous, -tropy, Gk	turned	tropism
tropho-, -trophy, Gk	nourishment	dystrophy
typhlo-, Gk	blind	typhlosis
typo-, Gk	type	typology
ultima-, ultra-, L	beyond	ultimate
uni-, L	one	unite
urethr-, urethro-, Gk	urethra	urethral
urin-, urino-, L	urine	urinary
uro-, -uria, Gk	urine	glycosuria
uter-, utero-, L	uterus	uterology
vagin-, vagino-, L	vagina	vaginectomy
val-, -vail, L	to be strong	valid, prevail
vari-, vario-, L	different	various
vaso-, L	vessel	vasodilation
vei-, -vey, veh-, L	to carry	vein, convey, vehicle
ven-, veni-, L	vein	venous
ven-, -vent, -vene, L	to turn	avenue, adventure, convene
ventr-, ventro-, L	abdomen	ventral
ver-, verit-, L	true	verdict, very, verity
vermi-, L	worm	vermiculite
-verse, -vert, vert-, L	to turn	adverse, revert, vertigo
via-, vio-, -vey, -voy, L	way	viaduct, obvious, convey, convoy

Greek/Latin	English	Example(s)
vic-, -vid, vis-, -view, -vise, L	to see	evident, visage, review, supervise
vice-, L	substitute	vice-president
vin-, vini-, L	wine, grapes	vineyard, viniculture
-vince, -vict, L	to conquer	convince, evict
vitr-, vitri-, L	glass	vitreous, vitriform
viv-, -vive, L	to live	vivacity, survive
voc-, -voke, L	voice	vocal, evoke
-volve, -volt, L	to roll	evolve, revolt
vor-, -vorous, L	eat	voracious, omnivorous
xeno-, Gk	foreign	xenophobia
xero-, Gk	dry	xerography
xylo-, Gk	wood	xylophone
zoo-, Gk	animal	zoology
zygo-, Gk	pair, yoke	zygote
-zyme, zymo-, Gk	fermentation	enzyme

Prefixes

Greek/Latin	English	Example(s)
a-, an-, Gk	not	amoral, anesthesia
ab-, a-, abs-, L	from, away, off, away from, down	abject, absent
ad-, a-, ac-, af-, ag-, al-, an-, ap-, ar-, as-, at-, L	to, toward	admit, align, accept, affinity, aggregate, alleviate, annex, appear, arrest, assimilate, attend
ana-, Gk	again	anadiplosis
ana-, Gk	according to, similar to	analog
ana-, Gk	thoroughly	anaphylaxis
ana-, Gk	up	analysis, anabolism
ana-, Gk	upon	anaclitic
ante-, Gk & L	before	antediluvian
anti-, Gk	against	antiaircraft
apo-, Gk	away from, off	apogee
cata-, cath-, cat-, Gk	down, away, in accordance with, against, very, completely	catacomb, catalog, catharsis, catabolism
cis-, L	on this side of	cisalpine
com-, co-, col-, con-, cor-, L	with, together, very, thoroughly	combat, collect, connect, correspond
contra-, L	against	contradict
de-, L	not	decentralize
de-, L	down	decline
dia-, Gk	through	diameter
dis-, di-, L	apart, not	disperse, disapprove, digress
en-, el-, em-, L	in, into	encounter, embed
endo-, Gk	within	endogenous
epi-, eph-, Gk	on, beside, among, outside, over, before	epilog, epitome, epiphenomenon
ex-, e-, ec-, ef-, Gk & L	out, off, from, beyond, not, thoroughly	exhale, exclude, exceed, efface
exo-, Gk	outside	exogenous
extra-, L	outside	extracurricular
hyper-, Gk	over, above, beyond	hyperactive
hypo-, Gk	under, beneath, less than	hypokinesis
in-, il-, im-, ir-, L	in, into, on	invade, induce
in-, il-, im-, ir-, L	not, against	inimical
inter-, L	between, among, together, mutual	intermix, interdependent
intra-, L	within	intramural
juxta-, L	next to	juxtapose

Greek/Latin	English	Example(s)
mal-, L	badly, evil	malcontent, maltreat
meta-, met-, Gk	after, beyond, changed, along with	metaphysics, metamorphosis
mis-, L	badly	misadventure
non-, L	not	nonchalant
ob-, oc-, of-, op-, L	against	obverse, oppress
para-, Gk	beside, beyond	parallel
per-, L	through, very, thoroughly	percussion
peri-, Gk	around, about, round, near	perimeter, perigee
post-, L	after	postpartum, postwar
pre-, L	before	premarital
preter-, L	beyond	preternatural
pro-, Gk	before	progestin
pro-, L	for	proslavery
pro-, Gk & L	forward	progress
pro-, L	substitute	pronoun
re-, L	again, back	rerun, return
retro-, L	back, backward	retrograde
sub-, suc-, suf-, sug-, sum-, sup-, sur-, sus-, L	under, less, subordinate, division	substance, subcategory, suffer
subter-, L	under, beneath, less than	subterfuge
super-, supra-, L	over, above, exceeding	superpose, suprarational
sym-, sy-, syl-, syn-, Gk	with, associated, simultaneous	symmetry, syllogism, synthesis
trans-, L	on that side of, across	transpose
ultra-, L	beyond, exceeding	ultraconservative

Suffixes of Adjectives

Greek/Latin	English	Example(s)
-able, -ive, L	tending to	irritable, restive
-able, -ile, -il, L	able to, able to be	teachable, ductile
-ac, L & Gk	affected by	maniac
-ac, -ic, Gk & L	pertaining to	iliac, manic
-aceous, -al, -ar, -ary, -ile, -il, -ine, -ory, Gk & L	pertaining to	curvaceous, dorsal, temporary, puerile, promissory
-al, -ate, -id, L	characterized by	jovial, ornate, flaccid
-an, L	coming from, originating in	European
-an, L	adhering to or following	Republican
-an, L	belonging to (in biology)	crustacean
-ant, -ent, L	doing, agency	errant, decadent
-escent, L	beginning to	obsolescent
-fic, -ficent, L	causing, making	terrific, magnificent
-ine, -in, -ing, -ive, -ory, L	like, of the nature of	bovine, charming, desultory
-ose, -ous, L	full of	verbose, aqueous

Suffixes of Nouns

Greek/Latin	English	Example(s)
-al, L	instance, nouns formed from adjs.	oval, signal
-al, L	act, action	recital
-ana, L	collection	Americana
-ance, -ence, -ancy, -ency, L	act, condition, concrete thing	assistance, violence, eminence

Greek/Latin	English	Example(s)
-arium, -ary, -orium, -ory, L	place	aquarium, apiary, auditorium, dormitory
-ary, L	practitioner	notary
-ate, L	office	episcopate
-ate, L	result	mandate
-cion, -sion, -ion, -tion, L	action, result, condition	ascension, demolition, condition
-ese, -ic, -ics, Gk	native art, system	Chinese, chiropractic, phonics
-ist, L	practitioner	psychiatrist
-ist, -ite, Gk	advocate, adherent	separatist, Jacobite
-ite, Gk	descendent of	Israelite
-ite, Gk	native	Canaanite
-ity, L	condition	acidity
-ium, L	chemical element	uranium
-ment, L	act, condition, instrument, result	movement, predicament, instrument
-mony, L	result	alimony
-or, L	practitioner	elector
-ory, L	instrument	depilatory
-trix, L	female practitioner	aviatrix
-tude, L	condition	negritude
-ure, L	action, office, result, instrument	divestiture, suture

Suffixes of Verbs

Greek/Latin	English	Example(s)
-ate, L	combine, combine with, treat with	associate, medicate
-esce, L	begin	coalesce
-fy, L	become, make	solidify, codify
-ize, Gk	become, make, practice, treat with	realize, canonize, idolize, simonize

Foreign Words and Phrases

A

à bas [Fr.], down, down with.

à beau jeu, beau retour [Fr.], one good turn deserves another; tit for tat.

ab extra [L.], from without.

ab imo pectore [L.], from the bottom of the heart.

ab incunabulis [L.], from the cradle.

ab initio [L.], from the beginning.

ab intra [L.], from within.

a bisogni si conoscono gli amici [It.], a friend in need is a friend indeed.

à bon chat, bon rat [Fr.], to a good cat, a good rat; tit for tat.

à bon marché [Fr.], cheap; a good bargain.

ab origine [L.], from the origin.

ab ovo [L.], from the egg; from the beginning.

ab ovo usque ad mala [L.], from the egg to the apples (as in Roman banquets); from beginning to end.

à bras ouverts [Fr.], with open arms.

abrégé [Fr.], an abridgment.

absens hæres non erit [L.], the absent one will not be heir; out of sight, out of mind.

absente reo [L.], the accused being absent.

absit invidia [L.], let there be no ill-will; envy apart.

absit omen [L.], may this not prove of (evil) omen.

ab uno disce omnes [L.], from one specimen judge of all the rest.

a buon vino non bisogna frasca [It.], good wine needs no bush.

ab urbe condita [L.], from the founding of the city, i.e. Rome (753 B.C.).

a capite ad calcem [L.], from head to heel.

à chaque saint sa chandelle [Fr.], to each saint his candle; honor to whom honor is due.

à cheval [Fr.], on horseback.

a che vuole, non mancano modi [It.], where there's a will there's a way.

à compte [Fr.], on account.

à corps perdu [Fr.], with breakneck speed.

à coup sûr [Fr.], of a certainty; without fail.

à couvert [Fr.], under cover.

a cruce salus [L.], salvation by the cross.

actionnaire [Fr.], shareholder in a company.

ad aperturam (libri) [L.], at the opening of the book; wherever the book opens.

ad arbitrium [L.], at will.

ad astra per aspera [L.], to the stars through hardship.

ad calendas Græcas [L.], at the Greek calends; i.e. never, as the Greeks had no calends in their mode of reckoning.

ad captandum vulgus [L.], to attract or please the rabble.

a Deo et rege [L.], from God and the king.

à dessein [Fr.], on purpose; intentionally.

à deux mains [Fr.], for two hands; two-handed; having a double office.

ad extremum [L.], to the last, or extremity.

ad finem [L.], to the end; at or near the end.

ad gustum [L.], to one's taste.

ad hominem [L.], to the man; to an individual's interests or passions.

adhuc sub judice lis est [L.], the case is still before the judge; the controversy is not yet settled.

a die [L.], from that day.

ad infinitum [L.], to infinity.

ad instar [L.], after the fashion of.

ad interim [L.], in the meanwhile.

ad internecionem [L.], to extermination.

à discrétion [Fr.], at discretion; without restriction.

ad libitum [L.], at pleasure.

ad majorem Dei gloriam [L.], for the greater glory of God.

ad modum [L.], in the manner of.

ad multos annos [L.], for many years.

ad nauseam [L.], to disgust or satiety.

adorer le veau d'or [Fr.], to worship the golden calf.

ad patres [L.], gathered to his fathers.

ad referendum [L.], for further consideration.

ad rem [L.], to the purpose; to the point.

à droite [Fr.], to the right.

adscriptus glebæ [L.], attached to the soil.

adsum [L.], I am present; here!

ad summum [L.], to the highest point.

ad unguem [L.], to the nail; to a nicety; exactly; perfectly.

ad unum omnes [L.], all to a man.

ad utrumque paratus [L.], prepared for either case or alternative.

ad valorem [L.], according to the value.

ad vitam aut culpam [L.], for life or fault; i.e. till some misconduct be proved.

ad vivum [L.], to the life; portrayed in a lifelike manner.

ægrescit medendo [L.], he becomes worse by the remedies used.

æquabiliter et diligenter [L.], equably and diligently.

æquo animo [L.], with an equal mind; with equanimity.

ære perennius [L.], more lasting than brass.

æs triplex [L.], triple brass; armor of adamant.

ætatis suæ [L.], of his (or her) age.

affaire d'amour [Fr.], a love affair.

affaire d'honneur [Fr.], an affair of honor; a duel.

affaire du cœur [Fr.], an affair of the heart.

affreux [Fr.], frightful; shocking.

à fleur d'eau [Fr.], on a level with the water.

à fond [Fr.], to the bottom; thoroughly; heartily.

a fortiori [L.], with stronger reason. See in Dict.

à gauche [Fr.], to the left.

à genoux [Fr.], on the knees.

age quod agis [L.], attend to what you are about.

à grands frais [Fr.], at great expense.

à haute voix [Fr.], aloud.

à huis clos [Fr.], with closed doors; secretly.

aide toi, et le ciel t'aidera [Fr.], help yourself, and Heaven will help you.

à la belle étoile [Fr.], under the stars; in the open air.

à la bonne heure [Fr.], in good time; very well, all right, as you please.

à l'abri [Fr.], under shelter.

à la campagne [Fr.], in the country.

à la carte [Fr.], according to the bill of fare at table.

à la dérobée [Fr.], by stealth.

à la française [Fr.], after the French mode.

à la mode [Fr.], according to the custom or fashion.

à la Tartuffe [Fr.], like Tartuffe, i.e. hypocritically.

al bisogno si conoscono gli amici [It.], friends are known in time of need.

à l'envi [Fr.], emulously; so as to vie.

alere flammam [L.], to feed the flame.

al fresco [It.], in the open air; cool.

alieni appetens, sui profusus [L.], greedy of other people's possessions, lavish of his own.

à l'improviste [Fr.], on the sudden.

alla vostra salute [It.], to your health.

allez-vous-en! [Fr.], away with you!

allons [Fr.], let us go; come on; come.

al piu [It.], at most.

alter ego [L.], another self.

alter idem [L.], another exactly similar.

alter ipse amicus [L.], a friend is the counterpart of oneself.

alterum tantum [L.], as much more.

à main armée [Fr.], by force of arms.

amantium iræ amoris integratio [L.], the quarrels of lovers are the renewal of love.

à ma puissance [Fr.], to the best of my power.

amar y saber no puede ser [Sp.], no one can love and also be wise.

a maximis ad minima [L.], from the greatest to the least.

âme de boue [Fr.], a soul of mud.

amende honorable [Fr.], satisfactory apology; reparation.

à merveille [Fr.], to a wonder; marvellously.

amici probantur rebus adversis [L.], friends are tested in adversity.

amicus humani generis [L.], a friend of the human race.

amicus Plato, sed magis amica veritas [L.], Plato is my friend, but truth is still more a friend to me.

amicus usque ad aras [L.], a friend even to the sacrificial altar, i.e. to the utmost extremity.

ami de cour [Fr.], a court friend; a false or unreliable friend.

à mon avis [Fr.], in my opinion.

amor patriæ [L.], love of country.

amour propre [Fr.], self-love; vanity.

ancient régime [Fr.], the ancient or former order of things.

anglicé [Fr.], in English; in the English language.

anguis in herba [L.], a snake in the grass; an unsuspected danger; a false friend.

animo et fide [L.], with courage and confidence.

anno ætatis suæ [L.], in the year of his or her age.

anno Christi [L.], in the year of Christ.

anno Domini [L.], in the year of our Lord.

anno humanæ salutis [L.], in the year of man's redemption.

anno mundi [L.], in the year of the world.

anno urbis conditæ [L.], in the year from the time the city (Rome) was founded (753 B.C.).

annuit cœptis [L.], He (God) has smiled on our

undertakings: motto, adapted from Virgil, on the reverse of the great seal of the United States.

annus mirabilis [L.], year of wonders; especially used in reference to the year 1666, in which occurred the great plague, and the great fire of London.

ante lucem [L.], before the dawn.

ante meridiem [L.], before noon.

à outrance [Fr.], to extremities.

à pas de géant [Fr.], with a giant's stride; with gigantic steps.

à peindre [Fr.], to be painted; worthy of the painter's art.

aperçu [Fr.], a general sketch or survey.

à perte de vue [Fr.], till beyond one's view.

à peu près [Fr.], nearly.

à pied [Fr.], on foot.

à point [Fr.], to a point; just in time; perfectly right.

a posse ad esse [L.], from possibility to reality.

appartement [Fr.], set of rooms on the same floor.

aprés moi le déluge [Fr.], after me the deluge.

a prima vista [It.], at first sight.

à propos de bottes [Fr.], apropos of boots; in an irrelevant manner; without rhyme or reason.

à propos de rien [Fr.], apropos of nothing; without reference to anything in particular; without a motive.

aquila non capit muscas [L.], an eagle does not catch flies.

arbiter bibendi [L.], ruler of the symposium; toastmaster.

arbiter elegantiarum [L.], a judge or supreme authority in matters of taste.

arcades ambo [L.], Arcadians both; fellows of the same stamp.

arcana cælestia [L.], celestial mysteries.

arcana imperii [L.], state secrets.

ardentia verba [L.], glowing language.

argent comptant [Fr.], ready money.

argumentum ad crumenam [L.], an argument to the purse, i.e. to one's interests.

argumentum ad hominem [L.], an argument to the individual man, i.e. to his interests and prejudices.

argumentum ad ignorantiam [L.], an argument intended to work on a person's ignorance.

argumentum ad judicium [L.], argument appealing to the judgment.

argumentum ad verecundiam [L.], argument appealing to modesty.

argumentum baculinum [L.], the argument of the cudgel; brute force.

ariston metron [Gr.], moderation is best.

arrectis auribus [L.], with ears pricked up; all attention.

arrière pensée [Fr.], mental reservation.

ars est celare artem [L.], it is true art to conceal art.

ars longa, vita brevis [L.], art is long, life is short.

Artium Magister [L.], Master of Arts.

asinus ad lyram [L.], an ass at the lyre; a stupid awkward fellow.

Athanasius contra mundum [L.], Athanasius against the world.

à tort et à travers [Fr.], at random; without consideration.

à toute force [Fr.], with all one's might.

à tout hasard [Fr.], at all hazards.

à tout prix [Fr.], at any price; at all costs.

at spes non fracta [L.], but hope is not crushed.

au bout de son Latin [Fr.], at the end of his Latin, at his wit's end; in a fix or quandary.

au contraire [Fr.], on the contrary.

au courant [Fr.], fully acquainted with matters; up to date.

audaces (or audentes) fortuna juvat [L.], fortune aids the bold.

au désespoir [Fr.], in despair.

audi alteram partem [L.], hear the other side.

audiatur et altera pars [L.], let the other side also be heard.

au fait [Fr.], well acquainted with; expert.

au fond [Fr.], at bottom; in reality.

auf Wiedersehen [G.], till we meet again; **au revoir.**

au grand sérieux [Fr.], in all seriousness.

au jour le jour [Fr.], from day to day; without thought of tomorrow; from hand to mouth.

au naturel [Fr.], in the natural state.

au pis aller [Fr.], at the worst.

aurea mediocritas [L.], the golden or happy mean.

au reste [Fr.], as for the rest.

au revoir [Fr.], adieu; until we meet again.

auri sacra fames [L.], the accursed craving for gold.

au sérieux [Fr.], seriously.

auspicium melioris ævi [L.], an auspice (or augury) of a better age (to come).

aussitôt dit, aussitôt fait [Fr.], no sooner said than done.

autant d'hommes, autant d'avis [Fr.], so many men, so many minds.

aut Cæsar aut nullus [L.], either Cæsar or nobody.

aut inveniam viam aut faciam [L.], I shall either find a way or make one.

autrefois acquit [Fr.], formerly acquitted; previously tried for the same offense and acquitted.

autre temps, autres mœurs [Fr.], other times, other manners.

au troisième [Fr.], on the third story.

aut vincere aut mori [L.], either to conquer or to die; victory or death.

aux armes! [Fr.], to arms!

auxilium ab alto [L.], help from on high.

avant-propos [Fr.], preliminary matter; preface.

avec permission [Fr.], with permission.

ave, Imperator! morituri te salutant [L.], hail, Emperor! those about to die (gladiators) salute thee.

a verbis ad verbera [L.], from words to blows.

avito viret honore [L.], flourishes on his ancestral honors.

à volonté [Fr.], at pleasure.

a vostra salute [It.] }
à votre santé [Fr.] } to your health.
a vuestra salud [Sp.] }

B

badaud [Fr.], a lounger in the streets; an idler.

badinage [Fr.], jocularity; chaff.

ballon d'essai [Fr.], a balloon sent up to ascertain the direction of the air-currents; hence, a device to test public opinion on any subject.

bas bleu [Fr.], a blue-stocking; a literary woman.

beatæ memoriæ [L.], of blessed memory.

beau idéal [Fr.], the ideal of perfection.

beauté du diable [Fr.], the devil's good looks; youthful freshness.

beaux esprits [Fr.], men of wit.

beaux yeux [Fr.], fine eyes; good looks.

bel esprit [Fr.], a person of wit or genius; a brilliant mind.

bella! horrida bella! [L.], wars! horrid wars!

bella matribus detestata [L.], wars hated by mothers.

bellum internecinum [L.], a war of extermination.

benedetto è quel male che vien solo [It.], blessed the misfortune that comes singly.

bene orasse est bene studuisse [L.], to have prayed well is to have striven well.

ben trovato [It.], well invented; cleverly fabricated or concocted.

bête noire [Fr.], a black beast; a bugbear.

bêtise [Fr.], a piece of stupidity; stupidity.

billet d'amour [Fr.], a love-letter.

bis dat qui cito dat [L.], he gives twice who gives quickly.

bis peccare in bello non licet [L.], it is not permissible to blunder twice in war.

bis pueri sens [L.], old men are twice boys.

bona bleu [L.], in good faith.

bona fides [L.], good faith.

bon ami [Fr.], good friend.

bon avocat, mauvais voisin [Fr.], a good lawyer is a bad neighbor.

bon diable [Fr.], a good-natured fellow.

bon gré, mal gré [Fr.], with good or ill grace; willing or unwilling.

bon jour [Fr.], good day; good morning.

bon jour, bonne œuvre [Fr.], a good day, a good work; i.e. the better the day, the better the deed.

bonne bouche [Fr.], a delicate morsel, tidbit.

bonne et belle [Fr.], good and handsome.

bonne foi [Fr.], good faith.

bon soir [Fr.], good evening.

bon vivant [Fr.], one fond of luxury and good living; a gourmet.

bon voyage! [Fr.], a good voyage (or journey) to you!

Borgen macht Sorgen [G.], borrowing makes sorrowing; who goes a-borrowing goes a-sorrowing.

breveté [Fr.], patented.

brevi manu [L.], with a short hand; extemporaneously.

brevis esse laboro obscurus fio [L.], if I labor to be brief, I become obscure.

brutum fulmen [L.], a senseless thunderbolt; striking blindly.

C

cadit quæstio [L.], the question falls; there is no further discussion.

cæca est invidia [L.], envy is blind.

cælum non animum mutant qui trans mare currunt [L.], they who cross the sea change their sky but not their feelings.

cætera desunt [L.], the rest is wanting.

cæteris paribus [L.], other things being equal.

campo santo [It.], a burying-ground—lit. "holy field."

candida Pax [L.], white-robed Peace.

cantabit vacuus coram latrone viator [L.], the penniless traveler will sing in the presence of the highwayman; i.e. a penniless man has nothing to lose.

cantate Domino [L.], sing unto the Lord.

cap à pié [Fr.], from head to foot.

caput mortuum [L.], lit. "dead head"; worthless residue.

cara sposa [It.], dear wife.

carent quia vate sacro [L.], because they have no sacred bard (to celebrate their praise).

carpe diem [L.], enjoy the present day; improve the time.

castello che dà orecchia si vuol rendere [It.], the fortress that parleys speedily surrenders.

casus belli [L.], that which causes or justifies war.

catalogue raisonné [Fr.], a catalogue arranged according to the subjects.

causa sine qua non [L.], an indispensable cause or condition.

cause célèbre [Fr.], a celebrated law case or trial.

caveat emptor [L.], let the buyer beware.

cave canem [L.], beware of the dog.

cavendo tutus [L.], safe by using caution.

cedant arma togæ [L.], let arms yield to the gown, that is, military authority to the civil power.

cela va sans dire [Fr.], that goes without saying; needless to say; that is a matter of course.

cela viendra [Fr.], that will come.

ce n'est pas être bien aise que de rire [Fr.], laughing is not always a sign that the mind is at ease.

ce n'est que le premier pas qui coute [Fr.], it is only the first step that is difficult.

censor morum [L.], a censor of morals.

c'est à dire [Fr.], that is to say.

c'est le commencement de la fin [Fr.], it is the beginning of the end.

c'est magnifique, mais ce n'est pas la guerre [Fr.], it is magnificent, but it is not war; said by a French officer as he watched the Charge of the Light Brigade at Balaklava.

c'est selon [Fr.], that is according to circumstances; that is as may be.

c'est un autre chose [Fr.], that's quite another thing.

cetera desunt [L.], the rest is wanting; here there is a break.

ceteris paribus [L.], see cæteris.

chacun à son goût [Fr.], every one to his taste.

chacun tire de son coté [Fr.], every one inclines to his own side.

chapeau bras [Fr.], a cocked hat.

chapelle ardente [Fr.], the chamber in which a dead body lies in state.

chemin de fer [Fr.], iron road; a railway.

cherchez la femme [Fr.], look for the woman (to find where she has had a hand in the matter).

chère amie [Fr.], a dear (female) friend.

che sarà, sarà [It.], what will be, will be.

cheval de bataille [Fr.], a war-horse; what one chiefly relies on.

chevalier d'industrie [Fr.], lit. a knight of industry; a swindling or cheating rogue; one who lives by his wits.

chi tace confessa [It.], he who keeps silence confesses.

ci git [Fr.], here lies.

clarior e tenebris [L.], brighter from darkness or obscurity.

clarum et venerabile nomen [L.], an illustrious and venerable name.

cogito, ergo sum [L.], I think, therefore I exist.

comitas inter gentes [L.], politeness between nations.

comme il faut [Fr.], as it should be.

commune bonum [L.], a common good.

commune periculum concordiam parit [L.], common danger begets concord.

communibus annis [L.], on the annual average.

communi consensu [L.], by common consent.

compagnon de voyage [Fr.], a traveling companion.

componere lites [L.], to settle disputes.

compos voti [L.], having obtained one's wish.

compte rendu [Fr.], an account rendered; a report.

con amore [It.], with love; very earnestly.

conciergerie [Fr.], a doorkeeper's lodge; also name of an ancient prison at Paris.

concio ad clerum [L.], a discourse to the clergy.

concordia discors [L.], discordant concord.

concours [Fr.], a competition, as for a prize.

con diligenza [It.], with diligence.

conditio sine qua non [L.], a necessary condition.

con dolore [It.], with grief; sorrowfully.

confido et conquiesco [L.], I trust and am at peace.

conjunctis viribus [L.], with united powers.

conseil d'état [Fr.], a council of state; a privy-council.

consensus facit legem [L.], consent makes the law.

consilio et animis [L.], by wisdom and courage.

consilio et prudentia [L.], by wisdom and prudence.

constantia et virtute [L.], by constancy and virtue (or bravery).

consuetudo pro lege servatur [L.], custom or usage is held as law.

consule Planco [L.], when Plancus was consul; when I was a young fellow.

contra bonos mores [L.], against good manners or morals.

copia verborum [L.], rich supply of words.

coram nobis [L.], before us; in our presence.

coram non judice [L.], before one who is not a proper judge.

coram populo [L.], in presence of the people.

cordon bleu [Fr.], blue-ribbon; a cook of the highest excellence.

cordon sanitaire [Fr.], a line of guards to prevent the spreading of contagion or pestilence; a quarantine.

corps d'armée [Fr.], the body of an army; an army corps.

corps de garde [Fr.], a body of men in a guardroom; the room itself.

corps diplomatique [Fr.], a diplomatic body; a body of ambassadors and similar representatives.

corrigenda [L.], things to be corrected; a list of errors or imperfections.

corruptio optimi pessima [L.], a corruption of what is best is worst.

cos ingeniorum [L.], a whetstone for wits.

couleur de rose [Fr.], rose-color; an alluring aspect of circumstances.

coup [Fr.], a stroke.

coup de grâce [Fr.], a finishing stroke.

coup de main [Fr.], a sudden attack of enterprise.

coup de maître [Fr.], a master stroke.

coup de pied [Fr.], a kick.

coup de soleil [Fr.], sunstroke.

coup d'essai [Fr.], a first attempt.

coup d'état [Fr.], a sudden decisive blow in politics; a stroke of policy.

coup de théâtre [Fr.], a theatrical effect.

coup d'œil [Fr.], a rapid glance of the eye.

courage sans peur [Fr.], fearless courage.

coûte que coûte [Fr.], cost what it may.

crambe repetita [L.], cabbage warmed up a second time; i.e. the repetition of an old joke, a truism, etc.

credat Judæus Apella [L.], let Apella, the superstitious Jew, believe it, I won't; "tell that to the marines."

crede quod habes, et habes [L.], believe that you have it, and you have it.

credo quia absurdum [L.], I believe because it is absurd.

credo quia impossibele est [L.], I believe it because it is impossible.

crème de la crème [Fr.], cream of the cream; the very best or most select.

crescit amor nummi, quantum ipsa pecunia crescit [L.], the love of money increases as wealth grows.

crescit eundo [L.], it increases as it goes.

crescit sub pondere virtus [L.], virtue increases beneath oppression.

crimen falsi [L.], the crime of perjury.

crimen læsæ majestatis [L.], the crime of high treason; lese-majesty.

Croix rouge [Fr.], Red Cross.

crux [L.], a cross; puzzle; difficulty.

crux criticorum [L.], the puzzle of critics.

crux medicorum [L.], the puzzle of the doctors.

cucullus non facit monachum [L.], the cowl does not make the friar; i.e. don't trust to appearances.

cui bono? [L.], for whose advantage? to what end?

cui Fortuna ipsa cedit [L.], to whom Fortune herself yields.

cuilibet in arte sua credendum est [L.], everyone is to be trusted in his own special art.

culpam pœna premit comes [L.], punishment follows hard on crime.

cum bona venia [L.], with your good leave.

cum grano salis [L.], with a grain of salt; with some allowance.

cum multis aliis [L.], with many others.

cum notis variorum [L.], with the notes of various commentators.

cum privilegio [L.], with privilege or license from the authorities.

curiosa felicitas [L.], nice felicity of expression.

currente calamo [L.], with a running or rapid pen.

custus morum [L.], guardian of manners (or morals).

D

d'accord [Fr.], in agreement.

da locum melioribus [L.], give place to your betters.

dame d'honneur [Fr.], matron of honor.

dames de la halle [Fr.], women who sell articles in a market; market-women.

damnant quod non intelligunt [L.], they condemn what they do not understand.

dare pondus fumo [L.], to give weight to smoke; i.e. attach importance to matters of no consequence.

das Beste ist gut genug [G.], the best is good enough.

das Ewig-Weibliche zieht uns hinan [G.], the eternal-feminine draws us upwards.

data et accepta [L.], expenses and receipts.

data obolum Belisario [L.], give an obolus to Belisarius (a general of Justinian, said to have been neglected in his old age by that emperor and compelled to beg).

Davus sum non Œdipus [L.], I am Davus not Œdipus (who solved the riddle of the Sphinx); I am a bad hand at riddles.

de bon augure [Fr.], of good augury or omen.

de bonne grâce [Fr.], with good grace; willingly.

deceptio visus [L.], an optical illusion.

decet verecundum esse adolescentem [L.], it becomes a young man to be modest.

decies repetita placebit [L.], when ten times repeated it will still please.

decipimur specie recti [L.], we are deceived by the show of rectitude.

decori decus addit avito [L.], he adds distinction to his ancestral honors.

de die in diem [L.], from day to day.

de facto [L.], in point of fact; actual; actually.

dégagé [Fr.], free; easy; unconstrained.

de gustibus non est disputandum [L.], there is no disputing about tastes.

de haut en bas [Fr.], in a contemptuous or supercilious manner.

dei gratia [L.], by the grace of God.

de integro [L.], anew; over again from beginning to end.

déjeuner à la fourchette [Fr.], breakfast with a fork; a breakfast or luncheon with meat.

de jure [L.], from the law; by right.

de l'audace, encore de l'audace, et toujours de l'audace [Fr.], audacity, more audacity, and always audacity.

delenda est Carthago [L.], Carthage must be blotted out, or destroyed.

de luxe [Fr.], of luxury; made with unusual elegance.

de mal en pis [Fr.], from bad to worse.

de minimis non curat lex [L.], the law does not concern itself with trifles.

de mortuis nil nisi bonum [L.], (say) nothing but good of the dead.

de nihilo nihil fit [L.], from nothing nothing is made.

dénouement [Fr.], issue; solution.

de novo [L.], anew.

Deo adjuvante [L.], God assisting.

Deo duce [L.], God being the leader.

Deo favente [L.], God favoring.

Deo gratias [L.], thanks to God.

Deo juvante [L.], with God's help.

de omnibus rebus et quibusdam aliis [L.], concerning all things and certain others.

Deo non fortuna [L.], from God, not by chance.

Deo volente [L.], God willing.

de pis en pis [Fr.], from worse to worse.

de profundis [L.], out of the depths.

de retour [Fr.], having come back; returned.

de rigueur [Fr.], imperatively necessary; not to be dispensed with.

dernier ressort [Fr.], a last resource.

désagrément [Fr.], something disagreeable.

desipere in loco [L.], to jest or be jolly at the proper time.

désorienté [Fr.], having lost one's way; not knowing where to turn.

desunt cætera [L.], the remainder is wanting.

de trop [Fr.], too much; more than is wanted.

detur digniori [L.], let it be given to the more worthy.

detur pulchriori [L.], let it be given to the more (or most) beautiful.

Deus avertat! [L.], God forbid!

deus ex machina [L.], a god out of the machine; a deity introduced to bring about the dénouement of a drama; referring to the machinery and practice of the Greek and Roman stage.

Deus vobiscum! [L.], God be with you!

Deus vult [L.], God wills it.

di buona volontà sta pieno l'inferno [It.], hell is full of good intentions.

Dichtung und Wahrheit [G.], fiction and fact; poetry and truth.

dictum factum [L.], no sooner said than done.

dies non [L.], a day on which a law-court is not held.

Dieu est toujours pour les plus gros bataillons [Fr.], God is always on the side of the largest battalions; the leader with the largest army has the best chance of victory.

Dieu et mon droit [Fr.], God and my right.

Dieu vous garde [Fr.], God protect you.

digito monstrari [L.], to be pointed out with the finger (as a person of note).

dignus vindice nodus [L.], a difficulty worthy of powerful intervention.

dii majorum gentium [L.], gods of the superior class; the twelve higher gods of the Romans.

dii penates [L.], household gods.

diis aliter visum [L.], the gods decided otherwise; fate willed differently.

Dios me libre de hombre de un libro [Sp.], God deliver me from a man of one book.

di salto [It.], by leaps.

diseur de bons mots [Fr.], a sayer of good things; one noted for witty sayings.

disjecta membra [L.], scattered remains.

divide et impera [L.], divide and rule.

docendo discimus [L.], we learn by teaching.

dolce far niente [It.], sweet doing-nothing; sweet idleness.

Dominus vobiscum [L.], the Lord be with you.

domus et placens uxor [L.], home and a pleasing wife.

dorer la pilule [Fr.], to gild the pill.

double entendre [Fr.], incorrect for next.

double entente [Fr.], a double or equivocal meaning; a play on words.

do ut des [L.], I give that you may give; reciprocity.

doux yeux [Fr.], soft glances.

dramatis personæ [L.], the characters in the play.

droit au travail [Fr.], the right to live by labor.

droit des gens [Fr.], the law of nations.

drôle [Fr.], funny; a comic actor.

ducit amor patriæ [L.], love of country draws me.

dulce domum [L.], sweet home (or rather homeward).

dulce est desipere in loco [L.], it is pleasant to play the fool at times.

dulce et decorum est pro patria mori [L.], it is sweet and glorious to die for one's country.

dum spiro, spero [L.], while I breathe, I hope.

dum vivimus, vivamus [L.], while we live, let us live.

duomo [It.], a cathedral.

durante bene placito [L.], during good pleasure.

durante vita [L.], during life.

E

eau sucrée [Fr.], sweetened water: a French beverage.

ébauche [Fr.], a preliminary sketch; a rough outline.

ecce homo! [L.], behold the man!

ecce signum! [L.], behold the sign!

école [Fr.], a school.

e contra [L.], on the other hand.

édition de luxe [Fr.], a splendid and expensive edition of a book.

editio princeps [L.], the first printed edition of a book.

égarement [Fr.], bewilderment, mental confusion.

ego et rex meus [L.], I and my king.

eheu! fugaces labuntur anni [L.], alas! the fleeting years glide by.

elapso tempore [L.], the time having elapsed.

élève [Fr.], a pupil or student.

embarras de richesses [Fr.], an embarrassment of riches; an over-supply.

emeritus [L.], retired or superannuated after long service.

empressement [Fr.], promptitude; eagerness.

en ami [Fr.], as a friend.

en arrière [Fr.], in the rear; behind; back.

en attendant [Fr.], in the meantime.

en avant [Fr.], forward.

en badinant [Fr.], in sport; jestingly.

en cueros [Sp.], naked; unclothed.

en déshabillé [Fr.], in undress.

en Dieu est ma fiance [Fr.], my trust is in God.

en Dieu est tout [Fr.], in God are all things.

en effet [Fr.], in effect; substantially; really.

en famille [Fr.], with one's family; in a domestic state.

enfant gâté [Fr.], a spoiled child.

enfants perdus [Fr.], lost children; the soldiers forming a forlorn hope.

enfant terrible [Fr.], a terrible child, or one that makes disconcerting remarks.

enfant trouvé [Fr.], a foundling.

enfin [Fr.], in short; at last; finally.

en grand seigneur [Fr.], like a grandee or magnate.

en grande tenue [Fr.], in full dress, either official or evening.

en masse [Fr.], in a mass.

en passant [Fr.], in passing.

en pension [Fr.], in a boarding-house.

en plein jour [Fr.], in broad day.

en queue [Fr.], standing one behind another.

en rapport [Fr.], in harmony; in agreement.

en règle [Fr.], according to rules; in order.

en revanche [Fr.], in requital; in return.

en route [Fr.], on the way.

en suite [Fr.], in company; in a set.

entente cordiale [Fr.], cordial understanding, especially between two states.

entêté [Fr.], obstinate; self-willed.

entourage [Fr.], surroundings; adjuncts.

entr'acte [Fr.], the interval between the acts of a play.

entre deux feux [Fr.], between two fires.

entre deux vins [Fr.], between two wines; half-drunk.

entremets [Fr.], side dishes of dainties to be eaten between the serving of the joints.

entre nous [Fr.], between ourselves.

en vérité [Fr.], in truth; verily.

en vieillissant on devient plus fou et plus sage [Fr.], in growing old, men become more foolish and more wise.

eo animo [L.], with that mind or design.

eo nomine [L.], by that name.

epea pteroenta [Gr.], winged words.

Epicuri de grege porcus [L.], a swine from the herd of Epicurus; an Epicurean.

e pluribus unum [L.], one out of many; one composed of many.

epulis accumbere divum [L.], to sit down at the banquets of the gods.

e re nata [L.], according to the exigency.

errare humanum est [L.], to err is human.

esprit borné [Fr.], a narrow or contracted spirit.

esprit de corps [Fr.], the animating spirit of a collective body, as a regiment.

essayez [Fr.], try; make the attempt.

esse quam videri [L.], to be, rather than to seem.

est modus in rebus [L.], there is a method in all things.

esto quod esse videris [L.], be what you seem to be.

et cætera (or et cetera) [L.], and the rest.

et hoc genus omne [L.], and everything of the sort.

et id genus omne [L.], and everything of the kind.

et sequentes or **et sequentia** [L.], and those that follow.

et sic de cæteris [L.], and so of the rest.

et sic de similibus [L.], and so of the like.

et tu, Brute! [L.], thou also, Brutus!

eureka [Gr.], I have found it.

événement [Fr.], an event.

eventus stultorum magister [L.], fools must be taught by the result.

Ewigkeit [G.], eternity.

ex abrupto [L.], suddenly.

ex abundantia [L.], out of the abundance.

ex adverso [L.], on the opposite side; over against.

exæquo et bono [L.], agreeably to what is good and right.

ex animo [L.], heartily; sincerely.

ex auctoritate mihi commissa [L.], by virtue of the authority intrusted to me.

ex capite [L.], from the head; from memory.

ex cathedra [L.], from the chair or seat of authority; with high authority.

excelsior [L.], higher; that is, loftier or taller; not correctly used as an adverb.

exceptio probat regulam [L.], the exception proves (or tests) the rule.

exceptis excipiendis [L.], the due exceptions being made.

excerpta [L.], extracts.

ex concesso [L.], from what has been conceded or granted in argument.

ex curia [L.], out of court.

ex delicto [L.], from the crime.

ex dono [L.], by the gift.

exegi monumentum ære perennius [L.], I have reared a monument more lasting than brass.

exempla sunt odiosa [L.], examples are offensive.

exempli gratia [L.], by way of example.

ex facto jus oritur [L.], the law springs from the fact.

excitus acta probat [L.], the event justifies the deed.

ex mera gratia [L.], through mere favor.

ex mero motu [L.], from his own impulse; from his own free-will.

ex more [L.], according to custom.

ex necessitate rei [L.], from the necessity of the case.

ex nihilo nihil fit [L.], from, or out of, nothing, nothing comes; nothing produces nothing.

ex officio [L.], by virtue of office.

ex opere operato [L.], by outward acts.

ex pede Herculem [L.], from the foot (we recognize) a Hercules; we judge of the whole from the specimen.

experientia docet stultos [L.], experience instructs fools.

experimentum crucis [L.], the trial or experiment of the cross; an experiment of a most searching nature.

experto crede [L.], trust one who has had experience.

expertus metuit [L.], having experience, he fears it.

exposé [Fr.], statement; showing up.

ex post facto [L.], after the deed is done; retrospective.

expressis verbis [L.], in express terms.

ex professo [L.], professedly.

ex propriis [L.], from one's own resources.

ex quocunque capite [L.], for whatever reason.

ex tacito [L.], tacitly.

extinctus amabitur idem [L.], the same man when dead will be loved.

extrait [Fr.], extract.

extra muros [L.], beyond the walls.

ex ungue leonem [L.], from a claw (we may know) the lion.

ex uno disce omnes [L.], from one learn all; from this specimen judge of the rest.

ex usu [L.], by use.

ex vi termini [L.], by the force or meaning of the term or word.

ex voto [L.], according to one's prayer or vow.

F

faber suæ fortunæ [L.], the architect of his own fortune, a self-made man.

fâcheux [Fr.], vexatious; annoying; troublesome.

facies non omnibus una [L.], all have not the same face or features.

facile est inventis addere [L.], it is easy to add to things already invented.

facile princeps [L.], easily preëminent; indisputably the first; the admitted chief.

facilis descensus Averni [L.], the descent to the lower world is easy; the road to evil is easy.

facit indignatio versum [L.], indignation instigates the verse.

façon [Fr.], manner, style.

façon de parler [Fr.], manner of speaking.

facta non verba [L.], deeds not words.

fade [Fr.], insipid; tasteless.

fænum habet in cornu, longe fuge [L.], he has hay upon his horn (of old the sign of a dangerous bull), beware of him.

fæx populi [L.], the dregs of the people.

faire bonne mine [Fr.], to put a good face upon the matter.

faire l'homme d'importance [Fr.], to assume an air of importance.

faire mon devoir [Fr.], to do my duty.

faire sans dire [Fr.], to do, not to say; to act without ostentation.

fait accompli [Fr.], a thing already done.

falsi crimen [L.], the crime of forgery.

falsus in uno, falsus in omnibus [L.], false in one thing, false in all.

fama clamosa [L.], a current scandal; a prevailing report.

fama nihil est celerius [L.], nothing travels swifter than scandal.

fama semper vivat [L.], may his fame endure forever.

far niente [It.], the doing of nothing.

fas est et ab hoste doceri [L.], it is right to be taught even by an enemy.

Fata obstant [L.], the Fates oppose it.

Fata viam invenient [L.], the Fates will find a way.

faux pas [Fr.], a false step; a slip in behavior; a lapse from virtue.

fax mentis incendium gloriæ [L.], the passion for glory is the torch of the mind.

felicitas multos habet amicos [L.], prosperity has many friends.

femme couverte [Fr.], a married woman.

femme de chambre [Fr.], a chambermaid.

femme galante [Fr.], a gay woman; a courtesan.

femme seule (as a law term, **femme sole**) [Fr.], an unmarried woman.

fendre un cheveu en quatre [Fr.], to split a hair in four; to make a very subtle distinction.

festina lente [L.], hasten slowly.

fête champêtre [Fr.], an open-air festival or entertainment; a rural festival.

feu de joie [Fr.], a fire of joy; a bonfire; a fusillade as a sign of rejoicing.

feuilleton [Fr.], a fly-sheet; a novel or a story appearing in a newspaper.

fiat experimentum in corpore vili [L.], let the trial (or experiment) be made on a worthless subject.

fiat justitia, ruat cælum [L.], let justice be done though the heavens should fall.

fiat lux [L.], let there be light.

fide et amore [L.], by faith and love.

fide et fiducia [L.], by fidelity and confidence.

fide et fortitudine [L.], with faith and fortitude.

fidei coticula crux [L.], the cross is the touchstone of faith.

fidei defensor [L.], defender of the faith.

fideli certa merces [L.], to the faithful one reward is certain.

fide non armis [L.], by faith, not by arms.

fide, sed cui vide [L.], trust, but see whom.

fides et justitia [L.], fidelity and justice.

fides Punica [L.], Punic faith; treachery.

fidus Achates [L.], faithful Achates; i.e. a true friend.

fidus et audax [L.], faithful and bold.

filius nullius [L.], a son of nobody.

filius populi [L.], a son of the people.

filius terræ [L.], a son of the earth; one of low birth.

fille de chambre [Fr.], a chambermaid.

fille de joie [Fr.], a woman of licentious pleasure; a prostitute.

fille d'honneur [Fr.], a maid of honor.

fin de siècle [Fr.], end of the (nineteenth) century.

finem respice [L.], look to the end.

finis coronat opus [L.], the end crowns the work.

flagrante bello [L.], during hostilities.

flagrante delicto [L.], in the actual commission of the crime.

flamma fumo est proxima [L.], flame is akin to smoke; where there is smoke there is fire.

flâneur [Fr.], a lounger.

flecti, non frangi [L.], to be bent, not broken.

flosculi sententiarum [L.], flowers of fine thoughts.

flux de bouche [Fr.], an inordinate flow of words; garrulity.

foi en tout [Fr.], faith in everything.

foi pour devoir [Fr.], faith for duty.

fons et origo [L.], the source and origin.

forensis strepitus [L.], the clamor of the forum.

forte scutum salus ducum [L.], a strong shield is the safety of leaders.

fortes fortuna juvat [L.], fortune helps the brave.

forti et fideli nihil difficile [L.], nothing is difficult to the brave and faithful.

fortiter et recte [L.], with fortitude and rectitude.

fortiter, fideliter, feliciter [L.], boldly, faithfully, successfully.

fortiter in re [L.], with firmness or resolution in acting.

fortunæ filius [L.], a spoiled child of fortune.

fortuna favet fortibus [L.], fortune favors the bold.

frangas, non flectes [L.], you may break but not bend (me).

fraus pia [L.], a pious fraud.

fripon [Fr.], a rogue; a knave; a cheat.

froides mains, chaud amour [Fr.], cold hands, warm heart.

front à front [Fr.], face to face.

fronti nulla fides [L.], there is no trusting to appearances.

fruges consumere nati [L.], born to consume fruits; born only to eat.

fugit irreparabile tempus [L.], irrecoverable time flies on.

fuimus Troes [L.], we were once Trojans (but Troy has been overthrown).

fuit Ilium [L.], Troy has been (but is now no more).

fulmen brutum [L.], a senseless thunderbolt; striking blindly.

fumum et opes, strepitumque Romæ [L.], the smoke, the show, and the noise of Rome.

functus officio [L.], having performed one's office or duty; hence, out of office.

furor arma ministrat [L.], rage provides arms.

furor loquendi [L.], a rage for speaking.

furor poeticus [L.], poetic fire.

furor scribendi [L.], a rage for writing.

fuyez les dangers de loisir [Fr.], avoid the dangers of leisure.

G

gage d'amour [Fr.], a pledge of love.

gaieté de cœur [Fr.], gaiety of heart.

Gallice [L.], in French.

garçon [Fr.], a boy; a waiter.

garde à cheval [Fr.], a mounted guard.

garde du corps [Fr.], a body-guard.

garde mobile [Fr.], a guard liable to general service.

gardez [Fr.], be on your guard; take care.

gardez bien [Fr.], take good care.

garde la foi [Fr.], keep the faith.

gaudeamus igitur [L.], therefore let us be joyful.

gaudet tentamine virtus [L.], virtue rejoices in temptation.

gaudium certaminis [L.], the joy of conflict.

genius loci [L.], the presiding spirit or genius of the place.

gens d'armes [Fr.], men at arms.

gens de condition [Fr.], people of standing.

gens d'église [Fr.], churchmen.

gens de guerre [Fr.], military men.

gens de lettres [Fr.], literary men.

gens de loi [Fr.], lawyers.

gens de même famille [Fr.], persons of the same family; birds of a feather.

gens de peu [Fr.], the meaner class of people.

gens togata [L.], civilians.

gentilhomme [Fr.], a gentleman.

genus irritabile vatum [L.], the irritable race of poets.

Germanice [L.], in German.

gibier de potence [Fr.], a gallowsbird.

giovine santo, diavolo vecchio [It.], a young saint, an old devil.

gitano [Sp.], a gypsy.

gli assenti hanno torto [It.], the absent are in the wrong.

gloria in excelsis [L.], glory to God in the highest.

gloria Patri [L.], glory be to the Father.

glückliche Reise! [G.], a pleasant journey!

gnothi seauton [Gr.], know thyself.

gobe-mouche [Fr.], a person who has no ideas of his own; a ninny; a trifler.

goût [Fr.], taste; relish.

goutte à goutte [Fr.], drop by drop.

grâce à Dieu [Fr.], thanks to God.

gradu diverso, via una [L.], the same road by different steps.

gradus ad Parnassum [L.], a step to Parnassus; aid in writing Greek or Latin verse.

grande chère et beau feu [Fr.], good cheer and a good fire; comfortable quarters.

grande fortune, grande servitude [Fr.], a great fortune is a great slavery.

grande parure ⎱ [Fr.], full
grande toilette ⎰ dress.

grand merci [Fr.], many thanks.

gratia placendi [L.], the delight of pleasing.

gratis dictum [L.], mere assertion.

graviora manent [L.], greater afflictions await us, more serious matters remain.

graviora quædam sunt remedia periculis [L.], some remedies are worse than the disease.

grex venalium [L.], a venal rabble.

grosse tête et peu de sens [Fr.], a large head and little sense.

grossièreté [Fr.], coarseness; vulgarity in conversation.

guerra al cuchillo [Sp.], war to the knife.

guerra cominciata, inferno scatenato [It.], war begun, hell unchained.

guerre à mort [Fr.], war to the death.

guerre à outrance [Fr.], war to the uttermost.

gutta cavat lapidem non vi, sed sæpe cadendo [L.], the drop hollows the stone by frequent falling, not by force.

H

habitué [Fr.], one who is in the habit of frequenting a place.

hac lege [L.], on this condition; with this restriction.

hæc olim meminisse juvabit [L.], it will delight us to remember this some day.

Hannibal ad portas [L.], Hannibal before the gates; the enemy close at hand.

hapax legomenon [Gr.], a word or expression occurring once only.

hardi comme un coq sur son fumier [Fr.], bold as a cock on his own dunghill.

haud longis intervallis [L.], at intervals of no great length.

haud passibus æquis [L.], not with equal steps.

haut goût [Fr.], high flavor; elegant taste.

helluo librorum [L.], a devourer of books; a bookworm.

heu pietas! heu prisca fides! [L.], alas for piety! alas for the ancient faith!

hiatus valde deflendus [L.], a hiatus or deficiency much to be regretted.

hic et nunc [L.], here and now.

hic et ubique [L.], here and everywhere.

hic jacet [L.], here lies.

hic labor, hoc opus est [L.], this is a laborious task; this is a toil.

hic sepultus [L.], here buried.

hinc illæ lacrimæ [L.], hence these tears.

hoc opus, hic labor est [L.], same as **hic labor, hoc opus est**.

hodie mihi, cras tibi [L.], mine today, yours tomorrow.

hoi polloi [Gr.], the many; the vulgar; the rabble.

hombre de un libro [Sp.], a man of one book.

hominis est errare [L.], to err is human.

homme d'affaires [Fr.], a businessman.

homme de bien [Fr.], a good man.

homme de lettres [Fr.], a man of letters.

homme d'épée [Fr.], a man of the sword; a soldier.

homme de robe [Fr.], a man in civil office; magistrate.

homme d'esprit [Fr.], a man of wit or genius.

homme d'état [Fr.], a statesman.

homo factus ad unguem [L.], a highly polished man; one finished to the highest degree.

homo homini lupus [L.], man is a wolf to man.

homo multarum litterarum [L.], a man of great learning.

homo sui juris [L.], a man who is his own master.

homo sum; humani nihil a me alienum puto [L.], I am a man; I count nothing that is human indifferent to me.

honi soit qui mal y pense [O. Fr.], shame to him who thinks evil of it; evil to him who evil thinks.

honores mutant mores [L.], honors change men's manners or characters.

honos habet onus [L.], honor brings responsibility.

horæ canonicæ [L.], prescribed hours for prayer; canonical hours.

horas non numero nisi serenas [L.], I number only hours of sunshine. (Motto for a sun dial.)

horresco referens [L.], I shudder as I relate.

horribile dictu [L.], horrible to relate.

hors de combat [Fr.], rendered unable any longer to fight.

hors de concours [Fr.], out of the competition.

hors de la loi [Fr.], in the condition of an outlaw.

hors de propos [Fr.], not to the point or purpose.

hors de saison [Fr.], out of season.

hors d'œuvre [Fr.], out of course; out of order.

hos ego versiculos feci, tulit alter honores [L.], I wrote these lines, another has borne away the honor.

hôtel de ville [Fr.], a townhall; municipal building of a town.

hôtel Dieu [Fr.], a hospital.

hôtel garni [Fr.], a furnished lodging.

humanum est errare [L.], to err is human.

hunc tu Romane caveto [L.], Roman, beware of that man.

hurtar para dar por Dios [Sp.], to steal for the purpose of giving to God (in alms).

I

ich dien [G.], I serve.

ici on parle Français [Fr.], French is spoken here.

idée fixe [Fr.], a fixed idea.

id genus omne [L.], all of that sort or description.

ignorantia legis neminem excusat [L.], ignorance of the law excuses no one.

ignorantio elenchi [L.], ignorance of the point in question; the logical fallacy of arguing to the wrong point.

ignoscito sæpe alteri, nunquam tibi [L.], forgive others often, yourself never.

ignoti nulla cupido [L.], no desire is felt for a thing unknown.

ignotum per ignotius [L.], the unknown (explained) by the still more unknown.

i gran dolori sono muti [It.], great griefs are silent.

il aboie après tout le monde [Fr.], he snarls at everybody.

il a la mer à boire [Fr.], he has the sea to drink up; i.e. all his powers will be taxed to succeed.

il a le diable au corps [Fr.], the devil is in him.

il conduit bien sa barque [Fr.], he steers his boat well; he knows how to get on.

il est plus aisé d'être sage pour les autres, que pour soi-même [Fr.], it is easier to be wise for others than for oneself.

il est plus honteux de se défier de ses amis, que d'en être trompé [Fr.], it is more disgraceful to suspect one's friends than to be deceived by them.

il faut attendre le boiteux [Fr.], it is necessary to wait for the lame man; we must wait for the truth.

il faut de l'argent [Fr.], money is needful.

Ilias malorum [L.], an Iliad of ills; a host of evils.

il n'a ni bouche ni éperon [Fr.], he has neither mouth nor spur; neither wit nor courage.

il n'appartient qu'aux grands hommes d'avoir de grands défauts [Fr.], only great men may have great faults.

il ne faut jamais défier un fou [Fr.], never defy a fool.

il ne faut pas éveiller le chat qui dort [Fr.], it is not wise to awake the cat that sleeps; let sleeping dogs lie.

il n'y a pas de héros pour son valet de chambre [Fr.], no man is a hero in the eyes of his valet.

il penseroso [It.], the pensive man.

il rit bien qui rit le dernier [Fr.], he laughs best who laughs last.

il sent le fagot [Fr.], he smells of the faggot; he is suspected of heresy.

il vaut mieux tâcher d'oublier ses malheurs, que d'en parler [Fr.], it is better to try to forget one's misfortunes, than to talk of them.

imitatores, servum pecus [L.], imitators, a servile herd.

immedicabile vulnus [L.], an incurable wound; irreparable injury.

imo pectore [L.], from the bottom of the breast.

impari Marte [L.], with unequal military strength.

impedimenta [L.], travelers' luggage; the baggage of an army.

imperium in imperio [L.], a state within a state, a government within another.

implicite [Fr.], by implication.

impos animi [L.], of weak mind.

in actu [L.], in act or reality.

in æternum [L.], forever.

in ambiguo [L.], in doubt.

in articulo mortis [L.], at the point of death; in the last struggle.

in bianco [It.], in blank; in white.

in camera [L.], in the chamber of the judge; in secret.

in capite [L.], in chief.

in cælo quies [L.], there is rest in heaven.

incredulus odi [L.], being incredulous I cannot endure it.

in curia [L.], in court.

inde iræ [L.], hence these resentments.

Index Expurgatorius [L.], a list of expurgated books (compiled by the Roman Catholic authorities).

Index Prohibitorius [L.], a list of prohibited books (prohibited to Roman Catholics).

in dubio [L.], in doubt.

in equilibrio [L.], in equilibrium; equally balanced.

in esse [L.], in being; in actuality.

in extenso [L.], at full length.

in extremis [L.], at the point of death.

infandum renovare dolorem [L.], to revive unspeakable grief.

in forma pauperis [L.], as a poor man or pauper.

in foro conscientiæ [L.], before the tribunal of conscience.

infra dignitatem [L.], below one's dignity.

in futuro [L.], in future; henceforth.

in hoc signo spes mea [L.], in this sign is my hope.

in hoc signo vinces [L.], under this sign or standard thou shalt conquer.

in limine [L.], at the threshold.

in loco [L.], in the place; in the passage mentioned; in the natural or proper place.

in loco parentis [L.], in the place of a parent.

in medias res [L.], into the midst of things.

in medio tutissimus ibis [L.], you will go safest in a middle course.

in memoriam [L.], to the memory of; in memory.

in necessariis unitas, in dubiis libertas, in omnibus caritas [L.], in things essential unity, in things doubtful liberty, in all things charity.

in nomine [L.], in the name of.

in nubibus [L.], in the clouds.

in nuce [L.], in a nutshell.

in omnia paratus [L.], prepared for all things.

inopem copia fecit [L.], abundance made him poor.

in ovo [L.], in the egg.

in pace [L.], in peace.

in partibus infidelium [L.], in parts belonging to infidels, or countries not adhering to the Roman Catholic faith.

in perpetuam rei memoriam [L.], in perpetual memory of the thing.

in perpetuum [L.], forever.

in petto [It.], within the breast; in reserve.

in pleno [L.], in full.

in posse [L.], in possible existence; in possibility.

in præsenti [L.], at the present moment.

in propria persona [L.], in one's own person.

in puris naturalibus [L.], purely in a state of nature; quite naked.

in re [L.], in the matter of.

in rerum natura [L.], in the nature of things.

in sæcula sæculorum [L.], for ages on ages.

in sano sensu [L.], in a proper sense.

in situ [L.], in its original situation.

in solo Deo salus [L.], in God alone is safety.

insouciance [Fr.], unconcern; careless indifference.

insouciant [Fr.], unconcerned; indifferent.

instar omnium [L.], equivalent to them all.

in statu quo [L.], in the former state; in the same state as before (some event).

in te, Domine, speravi [L.], in thee, Lord, have I put my trust.

inter alia [L.], among other things.

inter arma silent leges [L.], laws are silent in the midst of arms.

inter canem et lupum [L.], between dog and wolf; at twilight.

interdum vulgus rectum videt [L.], the rabble sometimes see what is right.

inter nos [L.], between ourselves.

inter pocula [L.], at one's cups.

in terrorem [L.], as a means of terrifying; by way of warning.

inter se [L.], among themselves.

inter spem et metum [L.], between hope and fear.

in totidem verbis [L.], in so many words.

in toto [L.], in whole; entirely.

intra muros [L.], within the walls.

in transitu [L.], in course of transit or passage.

intra parietes [L.], within walls; in private.

in usum Delphini [L.], for the use of the Dauphin; applied to editions of the classical authors.

in utramque fortunam paratus [L.], prepared for either fortune (or result).

in utroque fidelis [L.], faithful in both or each (of two).

in vacuo [L.], in empty space; in a vacuum.

inverso ordine [L.], in an inverse order.

in vino veritas [L.], there is truth in wine; truth is told under the influence of intoxicants.

invita Minerva [L.], against the will of Minerva; at variance with one's mental capacity; without genius.

ipse dixit [L.], he himself said it; a dogmatic saying or assertion.

ipsissima verba [L.], the very words.

ipso facto [L.], by the fact itself.

ipso jure [L.], by the law itself.

ira furor brevis est [L.], anger is a short madness.

ir por lana y volver trasquilado [Sp.], to go for wool, and come back shorn.

ita est [L.], it is so.

ita lex scripta [L.], thus the law stands written.

Italice [L.], in the Italian language.

J–K

Jacquerie [Fr.], French peasantry; a revolt of peasants.

jacta est alea [L.], the die is cast.

j'ai bonne cause [Fr.], I have a good cause.

jamais arrière [Fr.], never behind.

jamais bon coureur ne fut pris [Fr.], a good runner is never caught; an old bird is not to be caught with chaff.

januis clausis [L.], with closed doors.

je maintiendrai le droit [Fr.], I will maintain the right.

je me fie en Dieu [Fr.], I trust in God.

je ne sais quoi [Fr.], I know not what; a something or other.

je n'oublierai jamais [Fr.], I shall never forget.

je suis prêt [Fr.], I am ready.

jet d'eau [Fr.], a jet of water; a fountain.

jeu de main [Fr.], horseplay, practical joke.

jeu de mots [Fr.], a play on words; a pun.

jeu d'esprit [Fr.], a display of wit; a witticism.

jeu de théâtre [Fr.], stage-trick; clap-trap.

jeunesse dorée [Fr.], gilded youth; rich young fellows.

je vis en espoir [Fr.], I live in hope.

joci causa [L.], for the sake of a joke.

joli [Fr.], pretty; fine.

jour de fête [Fr.], a feast day.

jour de l'an [Fr.], New Year's day.

jubilate Deo [L.], rejoice in God; be joyful in the Lord.

jucundi acti labores [L.], accomplished labors are pleasant.

judex damnatur cum nocens absolvitur [L.], the judge is condemned when the offender is acquitted.

judicium Dei [L.], the judgment of God.

judicium parium, aut leges terræ [L.], the judgment of our peers or the laws of the land.

juge de paix [Fr.], a justice of peace.

juniores ad labores [L.], the younger men (are fittest) for labors.

jurare in verba magistri [L.], to swear to the words of a master.

jure divino [L.], by divine law.

jure humano [L.], by human law.

juris peritus [L.], skilled in the law; one who is learned in the law.

juris utriusque doctor [L.], doctor of both the civil and canon law.

jus canonicum [L.], the canon law.

jus civile [L.], the civil law.

jus divinum [L.], the divine law.

jus et norma loquendi [L.], the law and rule of speech.

jus gentium [L.], the law of nations.

jus gladii [L.], the right of the sword.

jus possessionis [L.], right of possession.

jus proprietatis [L.], the right of property.

jus summum sæpe summa malitia est [L.], law carried to extremes is often extreme wrong.

juste milieu [Fr.], the golden mean.

justum et tenacem propositi virum [L.], a man upright and tenacious of purpose.

kein Kreuzer, kein Schweizer [G.], no money no Swiss; a proverb of the time when the Swiss were common as mercenaries.

ktema es aei [Gr.], a possession for all time.

L

la beauté sans vertu est une fleur sans parfum [Fr.], beauty without virtue is like a flower without perfume.

labitur et labetur in omne volubilis ævum [L.], it glides on, and will glide on forever. See Rusticus expectat.

laborare est orare [L.], to work is to pray.

labore et honore [L.], by labor and honor.

labor ipse voluptas [L.], labor itself is a pleasure.

labor omnia vincit [L.], labor conquers everything.

laborum dulce lenimen [L.], the sweet solace of our labors.

la bride sur le cou [Fr.], with rein on neck; at full speed.

la critique est aisée, et l'art est difficile [Fr.], criticism is easy, and art is difficult.

l'affaire s'achemine [Fr.], the business is progressing.

la fortune passe partout [Fr.], fortune passes everywhere; all suffer change or vicissitude.

l'allegro [It.], the merry man.

l'amour et la fumée ne peuvent se cacher [Fr.], love and smoke cannot conceal themselves.

lana caprina [L.], goat's wool; hence, a thing of little worth.

langage des halles [Fr.], the language of the markets, profane or foul.

la patience est amère, mais son fruit est doux [Fr.], patience is bitter, but its fruit is sweet.

lapis philosophorum [L.], the philosophers' stone.

la poverta è la madre di tutte le arti [It.], poverty is the mother of all the arts.

la propriété c'est le vol [Fr.], property is robbery.

lapsus calami [L.], a slip of the pen.

lapsus linguæ [L.], a slip of the tongue.

lapsus memoriæ [L.], a slip of the memory.

lares et penates [L.], household gods.

la reyne (or le roy) le veult [Norm. Fr.], the queen (or the king) wills it; the formula expressing the sovereign's assent to a bill.

l'argent [Fr.], money.

lasciate ogni speranza, voi ch'entrate [It.], abandon hope all ye who enter here.

lateat scintillula forsan [L.], perhaps a small spark may lie hid.

latet anguis in herba [L.], a snake lies hid in the grass.

Latine dictum [L.], spoken in Latin.

lauda la moglie e tieni donzello [It.], praise a wife and remain a bachelor.

laudari a viro laudato [L.], praised by one who is himself praised.

laudationes eorum qui sunt ab Homero laudati [L.], praises from those who were themselves praised by Homer.

laudator temporis acti [L.], one who praises time past.

laudum immensa cupido [L.], insatiable desire for praise.

laus Deo [L.], praise to God.

l'avenir [Fr.], the future.

la vertu est la seule noblesse [Fr.], virtue is the only nobility.

le beau monde [Fr.], the fashionable world.

le bon temps viendra [Fr.], the good time will come.

le coût ôte le goût [Fr.], the cost takes away the taste.

lector benevole [L.], kind or gentle reader.

le dessous des cartes [Fr.], the underside of the cards.

le diable boiteux [Fr.], the devil on two sticks or with crutches.

legalis homo [L.], a lawful person, i.e. one not outlawed, infamous, or excommunicated.

legatus a latere [L.], a papal ambassador.

le génie c'est la patience [Fr.], genius is patience.

le grand monarque [Fr.], the great monarch; a name applied to Louis XIV of France.

le grand œuvre [Fr.], the great work; the philosophers' stone.

le jeu ne vaut pas la chandelle [Fr.], the game is not worth the candle; the object is not worth the trouble.

le jour viendra [Fr.], the day will come.

le mieux est l'ennemi du bien [Fr.], the better is the enemy of the good.

le monde est le livre des femmes [Fr.], the world is woman's book.

le monde savant [Fr.], the learned world.

le mot de l'énigme [Fr.], the key to the mystery.

l'empire des lettres [Fr.], the republic (lit. empire) of letters.

leonina societas [L.], partnership with a lion.

le pas [Fr.], precedence in place or rank.

le point du jour [Fr.], daybreak.

le roi est mort, vive le roi! [Fr.], the king is dead, long live the king (his successor)!

le roi et l'état [Fr.], the king and the state.

le roi le veut [Fr.], the king wills it.

le roi s'avisera [Fr.], the king will consider or deliberate.

les absents ont toujours tort [Fr.], the absent are always in the wrong.

les affaires font les hommes [Fr.], business makes men.

les bras croisés [Fr.], with folded arms; idle.

les doux yeux [Fr.], tender glances.

lèse majesté [Fr.], high treason.

les extrèmes se touchent [Fr.], extremes meet.

les murailles ont des oreilles [Fr.], walls have ears.

les plus sages ne le sont pas toujours [Fr.], the wisest are not so always.

le style, c'est l'homme [Fr.], the style is the man.

l'état, c'est moi [Fr.], it is I who am the state.

l'étoile du nord [Fr.], the star of the north.

le tout ensemble [Fr.], the whole together.

lettre de cachet [Fr.], a sealed letter containing private orders; a royal warrant.

lettre de change [Fr.], bill of exchange.

lettre de créance [Fr.], letter of credit.

lettre de marque [Fr.], a letter of marque or reprisal.

levamen probationis [L.], relief from proving.

leve fit quod bene fertur onus [L.], the burden which is well borne becomes light.

le vrai n'est pas toujours vraisemblable [Fr.], the truth is not always probable; truth is stranger than fiction.

lex loci [L.], the law or custom of the place.

lex non scripta [L.], unwritten law; common law.

lex scripta [L.], statute (or written) law.

lex talionis [L.], the law of retaliation.

lex terræ [L.], the law of the land.

l'homme propose, et Dieu dispose [Fr.], man proposes, and God disposes.

libertas et natale solum [L.], liberty and one's native land.

liberum arbitrium [L.], free will.

libraire [Fr.], a bookseller.

licentia vatum [L.], the license of the poets; poetic license.

limæ labor et mora [L.], the labor and delay of the file; the slow and laborious polishing of a literary composition.

l'inconnu [Fr.], the unknown.

l'incroyable [Fr.], the incredible.

lingua franca [It.], the mixed language used between Europeans and Orientals in the Levant.

lis litem generat [L.], strife begets strife.

lit de justice [Fr.], a bed of justice; the throne of the king in the parliament of Paris; the sitting of that parliament when the king was present.

litem lite resolvere [L.], to settle strife by strife, to remove one difficulty by introducing another.

lite pendente [L.], during the trial.

littera scripta manet [L.], the written letter remains.

l'occasion fait le larron [Fr.], opportunity makes the thief.

loci communes [L.], common places.

loco citato [L.], in the place or passage cited.

locos y niños dicen la verdad [Sp.], fools and children speak the truth.

locum tenens [L.], one occupying the place of another; a substitute.

locus classicus [L.], a classical passage.

locus criminis [L.], place of the crime.

locus in quo [L.], the place in which.

locus pænitentiæ [L.], place for repentance.

locus sigilli [L.], the place of the seal on a document.

longe aberrat scopo [L.], he goes far from the mark.

longo intervallo [L.], by or with a long interval.

loyal devoir [L.], loyal duty.

loyal en tout [Fr.], loyal in everything.

loyauté m'oblige [Fr.], loyalty binds me.

loyauté n'a honte [Fr.], loyalty has no shame.

lucidus ordo [L.], a lucid arrangement.

lucri causa [L.], for the sake of gain.

lucus a non lucendo [L.], used as typical of an absurd derivation or explanation— *lucus,* meaning *grove,* is wrongly implied to be another form of *lucere,* meaning to *shine.*

ludere cum sacris [L.], to trifle with sacred things.

lupum auribus teneo [L.], I hold a wolf by the ears, i.e. I have caught a tartar.

lupus in fabula [L.], the wolf in the fable.

lupus pilum mutat, non mentem [L.], the wolf changes his coat, not his disposition.

lusus naturæ [L.], a sport or freak of nature.

M

ma chère [Fr.], my dear (fem.).

macte virtute [L.], go on or persevere in virtue.

ma foi [Fr.], upon my faith.

maggiore fretta, minore atto [It.], the more haste the less speed.

magister cæremoniarum [L.], master of the ceremonies.

magna civitas, magna solitudo [L.], a great city is a great solitude.

magnæ spes altera Romæ [L.], another hope of great Rome.

magna est veritas et prevalebit [L.], truth is mighty and will prevail.

magna est vis consuetudinis [L.], great is the force of habit.

magnanimiter crucem sustine [L.], bear the cross nobly.

magnas inter opes inops [L.], poor in the midst of great wealth.

magni nominis umbra [L.], the shadow of a great name.

magnum bonum [L.], a great good.

magnum vectigal est parsimonia [L.], economy is itself a great income.

magnum opus [L.], a great work.

magnus Apollo [L.], great Apollo, i.e. one of great authority.

maigre [Fr.], fasting. See in Dict.

main de justice [Fr.], the hand of justice; the sceptre.

maintien le droit [Fr.], maintain the right.

maison de campagne [Fr.], a country house.

maison de santé [Fr.], a private asylum or hospital.

maison de ville [Fr.], a town-house.

maître des basses œuvres [Fr.], literally, "master of low works"; i.e. a sewer-cleaner.

maître des hautes œuvres [Fr.], an executioner; a hangman.

maître d'hôtel [Fr.], a house-steward.

maladie du pays [Fr.], home-sickness.

mala fide [L.], with bad faith; treacherously.

mal à propos [Fr.], ill-timed. See in Dict.

mal de dents [Fr.], toothache.

mal de mer [Fr.], sea-sickness.

mal de tête [Fr.], headache.

malentendu [Fr.], a misunderstanding; a mistake.

male parta, male dilabuntur [L.], things ill gotten are consumed without doing any good.

malgré nous [Fr.], in spite of us.

malgré soi [Fr.], in spite of himself.

malheur ne vient jamais seul [Fr.], misfortunes never come singly.

mali exempli [L.], of a bad example.

mali principii malus finis [L.], bad beginnings have bad endings.

malis avibus [L.], with unlucky birds; with bad omens.

malo modo [L.], in a bad manner.

malo mori quam fœdari [L.], I would rather die than be debased.

malpropre [Fr.], slovenly; not neat and clean.

malum in se [L.], evil or an evil in itself.

malum prohibitum [L.], an evil prohibited; evil because prohibited.

malus pudor [L.], false shame.

manet alta mente repostum [L.], it remains deeply fixed in the mind.

manibus pedibusque [L.], with hands and feet.

manu forti [L.], with a strong hand.

manu propria [L.], with one's own hand.

Mardi gras [Fr.], Shrove Tuesday.

mare clausum [L.], a closed sea; a bay.

mariage de conscience [Fr.], a private marriage.

mariage de convenance [Fr.], marriage from motives of material interest rather than of love.

mariage de la main gauche [Fr.], left-handed marriage; a morganatic marriage.

Mars gravior sub pace latet [L.], a severer war lies hidden under peace.

más vale saber que haber [Sp.], better to be wise than to be rich.

más vale ser necio que porfiado [Sp.], better to be a fool than obstinate.

más vale tarde que nunca [Sp.], better late than never.

materfamilias [L.], the mother of a family.

materiam superabit opus [L.], the workmanship will prove superior to the material.

matre pulchra filia pulchrior [L.], a daughter more beautiful than her beautiful mother.

mauvaise honte [Fr.], false modesty.

mauvais goût [Fr.], bad taste.

mauvais sujet [Fr.], a bad subject; a worthless scamp.

maxima debetur puero reverentia [L.], the greatest reverence is due to a boy.

maximus in minimis [L.], very great in trifles.

mea culpa [L.], by my fault.

médecin, guéris-toi toi-même [Fr.], physician, heal thyself.

mediocria firma [L.], moderate or middle things are surest.

medio tutissimus ibis [L.], in a medium course you will be safest.

medium tenuere beati [L.], happy are they who have held the middle course.

mega biblion, mega kakon [Gr.], a great book is a great evil.

me judice [L.], I being judge; in my opinion.

memento mori [L.], remember death.

memor et fidelis [L.], mindful and faithful.

memoria in æterna [L.], in eternal remembrance.

mendacem memorem esse oportet [L.], a liar should have a good memory.

mens agitat molem [L.], mind moves matter.

mens legis [L.], the spirit of the law.

mens sana in corpore sano [L.], a sound mind in a sound body.

mens sibi conscia recti [L.], a mind conscious of its own rectitude.

meo periculo [L.], at my own risk.

meo voto [L.], according to my wish.

merum sal [L.], pure or genuine wit.

mésalliance [Fr.], marriage with one of a lower rank.

meum et tuum [L.], mine and thine.

mihi cura futuri [L.], my care is for the future.

mirabile dictu [L.], wonderful to relate.

mirabile visu [L.], wonderful to see.

mirabilia [L.], wonders.

mirum in modum [L.], in a wonderful manner.

mise en scène [Fr.], the getting up for the stage, or the putting on the stage.

miserabile vulgus [L.], a wretched crew.

miseris succurere disco [L.], I learn to succor the wretched.

mittimus [L.], we send; name of a writ in law. See in Dict.

mobile perpetuum [L.], perpetual motion.

modo et forma [L.], in manner and form.

modus operandi [L.], manner of working.

mole ruit sua [L.], it falls in ruins by its own weight.

mollia tempora fandi [L.], times favorable for speaking.

mon ami [Fr.], my friend.

mon cher [Fr.], my dear (masc.).

montani semper liberi [L.], mountaineers are always free men.

monumentum ære perennius [L.], a monument more lasting than brass.

more Hibernico [L.], after the Irish fashion.

more majorum [L.], after the manner of our ancestors.

more suo [L.], in his own way.

mors janua vitæ [L.], death is the gate of eternal life.

mors omnibus communis [L.], death is common to all.

mos pro lege [L.], custom or usage for law.

mot du guet [Fr.], a watchword.

mots d'usage [Fr.], words in common use.

motu proprio [L.], of his own accord.

mucho en el suelo, poco en el cielo [Sp.], much on earth, little in heaven.

muet comme un poisson [Fr.], dumb as a fish.

multa gemens [L.], with many a groan.

multum in parvo [L.], much in little.

mundus vult decipi [L.], the world wishes to be deceived.

munus Apolline dignum [L.], a gift worthy of Apollo.

muraglia bianca, carta di matto [It.], a white wall is the fool's paper.

murus aeneus conscientia sana [L.], a clear conscience is a firm wall.

mutare vel timere sperno [L.], I scorn to change or to fear.

mutatis mutandis [L.], with the necessary changes.

mutato nomine de te fabula narratur [L.], the name being changed the story is true of yourself.

muta est pictura poema [L.], a picture is a silent poem.

mutuus consensus [L.], mutual consent.

N

naissance [Fr.], birth.

natale solum [L.], native soil.

natura lo fece, e poi ruppe la stampa [It.], nature made him, and then broke the mould.

naturam expellas furca tamen usque recurret [L.], though you drive out Nature with a pitchfork, yet will she ever return.

natura non facit saltum [L.], nature does not make a leap; i.e. nature proceeds slowly.

naviget Anticyram [L.], let him sail to Anticyra (where he will get hellebore to cure him of madness).

nec cupias, nec metuas [L.], neither desire nor fear.

ne cede malis [L.], yield not to misfortune.

necessitas non habet legem [L.], necessity has no law.

nec mora, nec requies [L.], neither delay nor repose.

nec pluribus impar [L.], not an unequal match for numbers.

nec prece, nec pretio [L.], neither by entreaty nor by bribe.

nec quærere, nec spernere honorem [L.], neither to seek nor to contemn honors.

nec scire fas est omnia [L.], it is not permitted to know all things.

nec temere, nec timide [L.], neither rashly nor timidly.

née [Fr.], born; having as her maiden name.

nefasti dies [L.], days on which judgment could not be pronounced, nor assemblies of the people be held; hence, unlucky-days.

ne fronti crede [L.], trust not to appearances.

négligé [Fr.], morning dress; an easy loose dress.

ne Jupiter quidem omnibus placet [L.], not even Jupiter pleases everybody.

nel bisogno si conoscono gli amici [It.], a friend in need is a friend indeed.

nemine contradicente [L.], no one speaking in opposition; without opposition.

nemine dissentiente [L.], no one dissenting; without a dissenting voice.

nemo bis punitur pro eodem delicto [L.], no one is twice punished for the same offence.

nemo me impune lacessit [L.], no one assails me with impunity.

nemo mortalium omnibus horis sapit [L.], no one is wise at all times.

nemo repente fuit turpissimus [L.], no one ever became a villain in an instant.

nemo solus sapit [L.], no one is wise alone (with no person to consult).

ne nimium [L.], avoid excess.

ne plus ultra [L.], nothing further; the uttermost point, perfection.

ne puero gladium [L.], intrust not a boy with a sword.

ne quid detrimenti respublica capiat [L.], lest the state receive any detriment.

ne quid nimis [L.], in nothing go too far.

nervi belli pecunia [L.], money is the sinews of war.

nervus probandi [L.], the sinews of the argument.

n'est-ce pas? [Fr.], is it not so?

ne sutor supra crepidam [L.], let not the shoemaker go beyond his last (properly sandal); let no one meddle with what lies beyond his range.

ne tentes, aut perfice [L.], either attempt it not or succeed.

netteté [Fr.], neatness.

ne vile fano [L.], let nothing vile be in the temple.

niaiserie [Fr.], silliness; simplicity.

nicht wahr? [G.], is it not so? am I not right?

ni firmes carta que no leas, ni bebas agua que no veas [Sp.], never sign a paper you have not read, nor drink water you have not examined.

nihil ad rem [L.], nothing to the point.

nihil (properly nullum) quod tetigit non ornavit [L.], he touched nothing without embellishing it.

nil admirari [L.], to be astonished at nothing.

nil conscire sibi nulla pallescere culpa [L.], to be conscious of no fault, and to turn pale at no accusation.

nil desperandum [L.], there is no reason for despair.

nil nisi cruce [L.], no dependence but on the cross.

ni l'un ni l'autre [Fr.], neither the one nor the other.

nimium ne crede colori [L.], trust not too much to looks (or externals).

n'importe [Fr.], it matters not.

nisi Dominus frustra [L.], unless God be with us all is in vain.

nitor in adversum [L.], I strive against opposition.

nobilitas sola atque unica virtus [L.], virtue is the true and only nobility.

noblesse oblige [Fr.], rank imposes obligations; much is expected from one in good position.

no es oro todo lo quo reluce [Sp.], all is not gold that glistens.

no hay cerradura si es de oro la ganzúa [Sp.], there is no lock that a golden key will not open.

nolens volens [L.], willing or unwilling.

noli irritare leones [L.], do not irritate lions.

noli me tangere [L.], touch me not.

nolle prosequi [L.], to be unwilling to proceed. See in Dict.

nolo episcopari [L.], I do not wish to be made a bishop.

nom de guerre [Fr.], a war name; an assumed traveling name; pen name.

nom de plume [Fr.], an assumed name of a writer: an English expression formed from the French.

nomina stultorum parietibus hærent [L.], fools' names are stuck upon the walls.

non compos mentis [L.], not of sound mind.

non cuivis homini contingit adire Corinthum [L.], every man has not the fortune to go to Corinth.

non datur tertium [L.], there is not given a third one or a third chance.

non deficiente crumena [L.], the purse not failing; if the money holds out.

non est [L.], it is not; it is wanting or absent.

non est inventus [L.], he has not been found.

non est vivere sed valere vita [L.], life is not merely to live, but to be strong.

non far mai il medico tuo erede [It.], never make your physician your heir.

non ignara mali, miseris succurere disco [L.], not unacquainted with misfortune I learn to succor the wretched.

non libet [L.], it does not please me.

non liquet [L.], the case is not clear or proved.

non mi ricordo [It.], I do not remember.

non multa, sed multum [L.], not many things but much.

non nobis solum [L.], not to ourselves alone.

non nostrum est tantas componere lites [L.], it is not for us to settle such weighty disputes.

nonobstant clameur de haro [Fr.], notwithstanding the hue and cry.

non ogni fiore fa buon odore [It.], not every flower has a sweet perfume.

non omne licitum honestum [L.], not every lawful thing is honorable.

non omnia possumus omnes [L.], we cannot, all of us, do everything.

non omnis moriar [L.], I shall not wholly die.

non quis, sed quid [L.], not who but what, not the person but the deed.

non quo, sed quomodo [L.], not by whom, but in what manner.

non sequitur [L.], it does not follow.

non sibi, sed omnibus [L.], not for self, but for all.

non sibi, sed patriæ [L.], not for himself but for his country.

non sine numine [L.], not without divine aid.

non sum qualis eram [L.], I am not what I once was.

non tali auxilio [L.], not with such aid or help.

nonum prematur in annum [L.], let it be kept back (from publication) till the ninth year.

nosce te ipsum [L.], know thyself.

noscitur a (or **e**) **sociis** [L.], he is known by his companions.

nostro periculo [L.], at our risk.

nota bene [L.], mark well.

Notre Dame [Fr.], Our Lady.

n'oubliez pas [Fr.], don't forget.

nous avons changé tout cela [Fr.], we have changed all that.

nous verrons [Fr.], we shall see.

novus homo [L.], a new man; one who has raised himself from obscurity.

nuance [Fr.], shade; subtle variation.

nudis verbis [L.], in plain words.

nudum pactum [L.], a mere agreement, unconfirmed by writing.

nugæ canoræ [L.], melodious trifles.

nul bien sans peine [Fr.], no pains, no gains.

nulla dies sine linea [L.], not a day without a line; no day without something done.

nulla nuova, buona nuova [It.], no news is good news.

nulli secundus [L.], second to none.

nullius addictus jurare in verba magistri [L.], not bound to swear to the opinions of any master.

nullius filius [L.], a son of nobody; an illegitimate son.

nunc aut nunquam [L.], now or never.

nunquam minus solus, quam cum solus [L.], never less alone than when alone.

nunquam non paratus [L.], never unprepared; always ready.

nuptiæ [L.], nuptials; wedding.

O

obiit [L.], he, or she, died.

obiter dictum [L.], a thing said by the way.

obra de común, obra de ningún [Sp.], everybody's business is nobody's business.

obscurum per obscurius [L.], explaining an obscurity by something more obscure still.

observanda [L.], things to be observed.

obsta principiis [L.], resist the beginnings.

obstupui steteruntque comæ [L.], I was astonished and my hair stood on end.

occasio facit furem [L.], opportunity makes the thief.

occurrent nubes [L.], clouds will intervene.

oderint dum metuant [L.], let them hate provided they fear.

odi profanum vulgus [L.], I loathe the profane rabble.

odium medicum [L.], the hatred of physicians.

odium in longum jacens [L.], hatred long cherished.

odium theologicum [L.], the hatred of theologians.

œil de bœuf [Fr.], a bull's-eye.

œuvres [Fr.], works.

officina gentium [L.], the workshop of the world.

O fortunatos nimium sua si bona norint agricolas [L.], O too happy husbandmen if only they knew their own blessings.

ofrecer mucho especie es de negar [Sp.], to offer much is a kind of denial.

ogni bottega ha la sua malizia [It.], every shop has its tricks; tricks in all trades.

ogni medaglia ha il suo riverso [It.], every medal has its reverse side.

ogniuno per se, e Dio per tutti [It.], every one for himself, and God for all.

ohe! jam satis [L.], hold! enough.

ohne Hast, aber ohne Rast [G.], without haste, but without rest.

olet lucernam [L.], it smells of the lamp ("the midnight oil"); it is a labored production.

omen faustum [L.], a favorable omen.

omne ignotum pro magnifico [L.], whatever is unknown is held to be magnificent.

omnem movere lapidem [L.], to turn every stone; to leave no stone unturned; to make every exertion.

omne solum forti patria [L.], every soil is a brave man's country.

omne trinum perfectum [L.], every perfect thing is threefold.

omne tulit punctum qui miscuit utile dulci [L.], he gains the approval of all who mixes the useful with the agreeable.

omne vivum ex ovo [L.], every living thing comes from an egg (or germ).

omnia ad Dei gloriam [L.], all things for the glory of God.

omnia bona bonis [L.], all things are good to the good.

omnia mutantur, nos et mutamur in illis [L.], all things change, and we change with them.

omnia vincit amor [L.], love conquers all things.

omnia vincit labor [L.], labor overcomes all things.

omnis amans amens [L.], every lover is demented.

on commence par être dupe, on finit par être fripon [Fr.], one begins by being a fool, and ends in becoming a knave.

on connaît l'ami au besoin [Fr.], a friend is known in time of need.

operæ pretium est [L.], it is worthwhile.

opprobrium medicorum [L.], the reproach of the doctors.

optimates [L.], men of the first rank. See in Dict.

opus operatum [L.], an effective work or operation. See **Opus**, in Dict.

ora et labora [L.], pray and work.

ora pro nobis [L.], pray for us.

orator fit, poeta nascitur [L.], an orator is made, a poet is born.

ore rotundo [L.], with round full voice.

ore tenus [L.], from the mouth merely.

origo mali [L.], origin of the evil.

oro è che oro vale [It.], that is gold that is worth gold; all is not gold that glitters.

O! si sic omnia [L.], O! if all things were so; O! if he had always so spoken or acted.

O tempora! O mores! [L.], O the times! O the manners!

otia dant vitia [L.], idleness occasions vice.

otiosa sedulitas [L.], idle industry; laborious trifling.

otium cum dignitate [L.], ease with dignity; dignified leisure.

otium sine litteris est mors [L.], leisure without literature is death.

oublier je ne puis [Fr.], I can never forget.

oui-dire [Fr.], hearsay.

ou la chèvre est attachée, il faut qu'elle broute [Fr.], where the goat is tethered, there it must browse.

ouvrage de longue haleine [Fr.], a work of long breath; a work long in being accomplished; a long-winded or tedious business.

ouvrier [Fr.], a workman; an operative.

P

pabulum Acherontis [L.], food for Acheron, or the tomb.

pace [L.], by leave of; not to give offence to.

pace tua [L.], by your leave; with your consent.

pacta conventa [L.], the conditions agreed on.

pactum illicitum [L.], an illegal agreement.

padrone [It.], a master; a landlord.

pallida mors [L.], pale death.

palmam qui meruit ferat [L.], let him who has won the palm wear it.

palma non sine pulvere [L.], the palm is not won without dust; i.e. no success without exertion.

par accès [Fr.], by fits and starts.

par accident [Fr.], by accident or chance.

par accord [Fr.], by agreement; in harmony.

par avion [Fr], by airplane: French label for air mail.

par ci par là [Fr.], here and there.

par complaisance [Fr.], by complaisance.

par dépit [Fr.], out of spite.

pardonnez-moi [Fr.], pardon me; excuse me.

parem non fert [L.], he suffers no equal.

par excellence [Fr.], by way of eminence.

par exemple [Fr.], by example; for instance.

parfaitement bien [Fr.], perfectly well.

par faveur [Fr.], by favor; with the countenance of.

par force [Fr.], by force.

par hasard [Fr.], by chance.

pari passu [L.], with equal step; together.

paritur pax bello [L.], peace is produced by war.

par le droit du plus fort [Fr.], by the right of the strongest.

par les mêmes voies on ne va pas toujours aux mêmes fins [Fr.], by the same methods we do not always attain the same ends.

parlez du loup, et vous en verrez sa queue [Fr.], speak of the wolf, and you will see his tail; talk of the devil and he will appear.

parlez peu et bien si vous voulez qu'on vous regarde comme un homme de mérite [Fr.], speak little and well if you would be esteemed as a man of merit.

par manière d'acquit [Fr.], by way of acquittal; for form's sake.

par negotiis, neque supra [L.], neither above nor below his business.

par nobile fratrum [L.], a noble pair of brothers; two just alike; the one as good or as bad as the other.

parole d'honneur [Fr.], word of honor.

par oneri [L.], equal to the burden.

par parenthèse [Fr.], by way of parenthesis.

par pari refero [L.], I return like for like; tit for tat.

par précaution [Fr.], by way of precaution.

par privilège [Fr.], by privilege; license.

par rapport [Fr.], by reason of.

pars adversa [L.], the opposite party.

par signe de mépris [Fr.], as a token of contempt.

pars pro toto [L.], part for the whole.

parti [Fr.], a party; person.

particeps criminis [L.], an accomplice in a crime.

particulier [Fr.], a private person.—**en particulier**, in private.

partout [Fr.], everywhere; in all directions.

parturiunt montes, nascetur ridiculus mus [L.], the

mountains are in travail, a ridiculous mouse will be brought forth.

parva componere magnis [L.], to compare small things with great.

parva leves capiunt animas [L.], trifles captivate small minds.

parvenu [Fr.], a person of low origin who has risen suddenly to wealth or position.

parvum parva decent [L.], trifles become a little person.

pas [Fr.], a step.

pas à pas on va bien loin [Fr.], step by step one goes a long way.

passé [Fr.], past; out of date.

passe-partout [Fr.], a master-key, passport.

pas seul [Fr.], a dance performed by one person.

passim [L.], everywhere; throughout the book or writing referred to.

pasticcio [It.], patchwork.

paté de foie gras [Fr.], goose-liver paste.

pater patriæ [L.], father of his country.

patience passe science [Fr.], patience surpasses knowledge.

pâtisserie [Fr.], pastry; pastry shop.

patois [Fr.], a provincial dialect; the language of the lower classes.

patres conscripti [L.], the conscript fathers; Roman senators.

patriis virtutibus [L.], by ancestral virtues.

paucis verbis [L.], in a few words.

paulo majora canamus [L.], let us sing of somewhat higher themes.

pax in bello [L.], peace in war.

pax vobiscum [L.], peace be with you.

peccavi [L.], I have sinned.

peine forte et dure [Fr.], strong and severe punishment; a kind of judicial torture.

penchant [Fr.], a strong liking.

pensée [Fr.], a thought.

penetralia [L.], secret or inmost recesses.

per [L.], by; by means of; through.

per [It.], for; through; by.

per ambages [L.], by circuitous ways; hence, by allegory; figuratively; metaphorically.

per angusta ad augusta [L.], through trials to triumphs.

per annum [L.], by the year; annually.

per aspera ad astra [L.], through rough ways to the stars; through suffering to renown.

per baroniam [L.], by right of barony.

per capita [L.], by the head or poll.

per centum [L.], by the hundred.

per contante [It.], for cash.

per conto [It.], upon account.

per contra [L.], contrariwise.

per curiam [L.], by the court.

per diem [L.], by the day; daily.

perdu [Fr.], lost.

pereant qui ante nos nostra dixerunt [L.], deuce take

those who said our good things before us.

père de famille [Fr.], the father of a family.

pereunt et imputantur [L.], they (the hours) pass away and are laid to our charge.

per fas et nefas [L.], through right and wrong.

perfervidum ingenium Scotorum [L.], the intense earnestness of Scotsmen.

per gradus [L.], step by step.

periculum in mora [L.], there is danger in delay.

per interim [L.], in the meantime.

perjuria ridet amantium Jupiter [L.], at lovers' perjuries Jove laughs.

per mare per terras [L.], through sea and land.

per mese [It.], by the month.

permitte divis cetæra [L.], leave the rest to the gods.

per pares [L.], by one's peers.

per più strade si va a Roma [It.], there are many roads to Rome.

per saltum [L.], by a leap or jump.

per se [L.], by, or in, itself.

per stirpes [L.], by stocks.

per troppo dibatter la verità si perde [It.], truth is lost by too much controversy.

per viam [L.], by the way of.

petit chaudron, grandes oreilles [Fr.], little pitchers (have) big ears.

petitio principii [L.], a begging of the question.

petit-maître [Fr.], a fop.

peu-à-peu [Fr.], little by little; by degrees.

peu de chose [Fr.], a little thing; a trifle.

peu de gens savent être vieux [Fr.], few people know how to be old.

pezzo [It.], a piece; an Italian coin.

piccolo [It.], small.

pièce de résistance [Fr.], the chief dish of a meal; something substantial by way of entertainment; a substantial joint of meat.

pied-à-terre [Fr.], a resting-place; a temporary lodging.

pietra mossa non fa muschio [It.], a rolling stone gathers no moss.

pinxit [L.], he, or she, painted it.

pis aller [Fr.], the worst or last shift.

piuttosto mendicante che ignorante [It.], better be a beggar than be ignorant.

place aux dames [Fr.], make way for the ladies.

plebs [L.], common people; the multitude.

plein de soi-même [Fr.], full of himself.

plein pouvoir [Fr.], full power or authority.

pleno jure [L.], with full power or authority.

plus aloes quam mellis habet [L.], he has more gall than honey; sarcastic wit.

plus on est de fous, plus on rit [Fr.], the more fools, the more fun.

plus sage que les sages [Fr.], wiser than the wise.

poca barba, poca verguenza [Sp.], little beard, little shame.

poca roba, poco pensiero [It.], little wealth, little care.

poco a poco [It.], little by little.

poeta nascitur, non fit [L.], the poet is born, not made; nature, not study, must form the poet.

point d'appui [Fr.], point of support; prop.

poisson d'avril [Fr.], April fool (lit. April fish).

pondere, non numero [L.], by weight not by number.

pons asinorum [L.], an ass's bridge; a name given to the fifth proposition of the first book of Euclid.

populus vult decipi [L.], the populace wishes to be deceived.

possunt quia posse videntur [L.], they are able because they think they are.

post bellum auxilium [L.], aid after the war.

post cineres gloria venit [L.], after death comes glory.

post equitem sedet atra cura [L.], behind the rider sits black care.

poste restante [Fr.], to be left at the post office till called for: applied to letters.

post hoc ergo propter hoc [L.], after this, therefore on account of this; a non sequitur in argument.

post nubila jubila [L.], after sorrow joy.

post nubila Phœbus [L.], after clouds comes Phœbus, or the sun.

post obitum [L.], after death.

pour acquit [Fr.], received payment; paid; written at the bottom of a discharged account.

pour comble de bonheur [Fr.], as the height of happiness.

pour couper court [Fr.], to cut the matter short.

pour encourager les autres [Fr.], to encourage the others.

pour faire rire [Fr.], to excite laughter.

pour faire visite [Fr.], to pay a visit.

pour passer le temps [Fr.], to pass away the time.

pour prendre congé [Fr.], to take leave: often abbreviated p.p.c. on visiting-cards.

pour se faire valoir [Fr.], to make himself of value.

pour tout potage [Fr.], all that one gets; all that a person is allotted.

pour y parvenir [Fr.], to attain the object.

præcognita [L.], things previously known.

præmonitus, præmunitus [L.], forewarned, forearmed.

præscriptum [L.], a thing prescribed.

prendre la balle au bond [Fr.], to catch the ball as it bounds.

prendre la lune avec les dents [Fr.], to take the moon by the teeth; to aim at impossibilities.

prends moi tel que je suis [Fr.], take me just as I am.

prenez garde [Fr.], beware; look out.

presto maturo, presto marcio [It.], soon ripe, soon rotten.

prêt d'accomplir [Fr.], ready to accomplish.

prêt pour mon pays [Fr.], ready for my country.

preux chevalier [Fr.], a brave knight.

prima donna [It.], the chief female vocalist. See in Dict.

primæ viæ [L.], the first passages; the chief canals of the body.

prima facie [L.], on first sight. See in Dict.

primo [L.], in the first place.

primo uomo [It.], the chief actor or vocalist.

primum mobile [L.], the souce of motion, the mainspring.

primus inter pares [L.], first among his peers.

principia, non homines [L.], principles, not men.

principiis obsta [L.], resist the beginnings.

prior tempore, prior jure [L.], first in time, first by right; first come, first served.

pro aris et focis [L.], for our altars and our hearths; for civil and religious liberty.

probatum est [L.], it is proved.

probitas laudatur, et alget [L.], honesty is praised, and is left to starve.

pro bono publico [L.], for the good of the public.

pro confesso [L.], as if conceded.

procul, O procul este, profani [L.], far, far hence, O ye profane!

pro Deo et ecclesia [L.], for God and the church.

pro et contra [L.], for and against.

profanum vulgus [L.], the profane rabble.

pro forma [L.], for the sake of form.

pro hac vice [L.], for this occasion.

proh pudor! [L.], for shame!

projet de loi [Fr.], a legislative bill.

prolétaire [Fr.], member of the lower classes; workingman.

pro memoria [L.], for a memorial.

pro nunc [L.], for the present.

propaganda [L.], the propagation of principles or views. See in Dict.

pro patria [L.], for our country.

propria quæ maribus [L.], things appropriate to males, men, or husbands (a fragment of a rule in old Latin grammars).

propriétaire [Fr.], an owner or proprietor.

pro rata [L.], according to rate or proportion.

pro rege, lege, et grege [L.], for the king, the law, and the people.

pro re nata [L.], for a particular emergency arising.

pro salute animæ [L.], for the health of the soul.

prosit! [L.], a health to you!

pro tanto [L.], for so much; for as far as it goes.

protégé [Fr.], one under the protection of another.

pro virili parte [L.], according to one's power; with all one's might.

prudens futuri [L.], thoughtful of the future.

publice [L.], publicly.

publiciste [Fr.], one who writes on national laws and customs; a publicist.

pugnis et calcibus [L.], with fists and heels; with all one's might.

punctum saliens [L.], a salient or prominent point.

Punica fides [L.], Punic or Carthaginian faith; treachery.

Q

quæ fuerunt vitia, mores sunt [L.], what were once vices are now customs.

quæ nocent, docent [L.], things which injure, instruct; we learn by what we suffer.

qualis ab incepto [L.], the same as at the beginning.

qualis rex, talis grez [L.], like king, like people.

qualis vita, finis ita [L.], as life is, so is its end.

quam diu se bene gesserit [L.], during good behavior.

quand même [Fr.], even though; nevertheless.

quand on ne trouve pas son repos en soi-même, il est inutile de le chercher ailleurs [Fr.], when a man finds no repose in himself, it is futile for him to seek it elsewhere.

quand on voit la chose, on la croit [Fr.], that which one sees he gives credit to.

quandoque bonus dormitat Homerus [L.], even good Homer sometimes nods; the wisest make mistakes.

quanti est sapere [L.], how desirable is wisdom or knowledge.

quantum libet [L.], as much as you please.

quantum meruit [L], as much as he deserved.

quantum mutatus ab illo! [L.], how changed from what he once was!

quantum sufficit [L.], as much as suffices; a sufficient quantity.

quantum vis [L.], as much as you wish.

que la nuit paraît longue à la douleur qui veille! [Fr.], to sleepless grief how long must night appear.

quelque chose [Fr.], something; a trifle.

quelqu'un [Fr.], somebody.

quem deus vult perdere prius dementat [L.], whom a god would destroy he first drives mad.

quem di diligunt adolescens moritur [L.], he whom the gods love dies young.

querelle d'Allemand [Fr.], a German quarrel; a drunken affray.

qui a bu boira [Fr.], the tippler will go on tippling.

quid faciendum? [L.], what is to be done?

qui docet discit [L.], he who teaches learns.

quid pro quo [L.], one thing for another; tit for tat; value received.

quid rides? [L.], why do you laugh?

quién sabe? [Sp.] who knows?

quieta non movere [L.], not to disturb things at rest.

qui facit per alium facit per se [L.], he who acts by another acts by himself.

qu'il soit comme il est desiré [Fr.], let it be as desired.

qui m'aime, aime mon chien [Fr.], love me, love my dog.

qui n'a point de sens à trente ans, n'en aura jamais [Fr.], he who has no sense when thirty years old, will never have any.

qui n'a santé n'a rien [Fr.], he who lacks health lacks everything.

qui nimium probat, nihil probat [L.], he proves nothing who proves too much.

qui non proficit, deficit [L.], he who does not advance goes backward.

qui perd, péche [Fr.], he who loses, offends; an unsuccessful man is always deemed to be wrong.

quis custodiet ipsos custodes? [L.], who shall keep the keepers themselves?

qui s'excuse s'accuse [Fr.], he who excuses himself accuses himself.

qui tacet consentit [L.], he who is silent gives consent.

qui timide rogat, docet negare [L.], he who asks timidly invites denial.

qui transtulit sustinet [L.], he who transports, supports.

qui va là? [Fr.], who goes there?

qui vive? [Fr.], a challenge: "Who goes there?"

quoad hoc [L.], to this extent.

quo animo? [L.], with what intention?

quocunque jeceris stabit [L.], where-ever you throw it, it will stand.

quocunque modo [L.], in whatever manner.

quocunque nomine [L.], under whatever name.

quod avertat Deus! [L.], which may God avert!

quod bene notandum [L.], which may be especially noticed.

quod bonum, felix, faustumque sit! [L.], and may it be advantageous, fortunate, and favorable!

quod erat demonstrandum [L.], which was to be proved or demonstrated.

quod erat faciendum [L.], which was to be done.

quod non opus est, asse carum est [L.], what is not wanted (or is of no use to a person) is dear at a copper.

quod semper, quod ubique, quod ab omnibus [L.], what (has been believed) always, everywhere, by all.

quod vide [L.], which see; see that reference.

quo Fata vocant [L.], whither the Fates call.

quo jure [L.], by what right?

quo pax et gloria ducunt [L.], where peace and glory lead.

quorum pars magna fui [L.], of whom, or which, I was an important part.

quot homines, tot sententiæ [L.], many men, many minds.

R

raconteur [Fr.], a teller of stories.

railleur [Fr.], a jester; one addicted to raillery.

raison d'état [Fr.], a reason of state.

raison d'être [Fr.], the reason for a thing's existence.

rappel [Fr.], a recall.

rapprochement [Fr.], the act of bringing together.

rara avis in terris, nigroque simillima cygno [L.], a rare bird on earth, and very like a black swan (formerly believed to be nonexistent).

rari nantes in gurgite vasto [L.], swimming here and there on the vast sea.

Rathaus [G.], a townhall.

ratione soli [L.], as regards the soil.

re [L.], in the matter of; in reference to the question of.

Realschule [G.], a real school; a secondary German school giving an education more in modern subjects than in classics.

réchauffé [Fr.], lit. something warmed up; hence old literary material worked up into a new form.

recoje tu heno mientras que el sol luziere [Sp.], make hay while the sun shines.

reconnaissance [Fr.], survey. See Dict.

recte et suaviter [L.], justly and agreeably.

rectus in curia [L.], upright in court; with clean hands.

reçu [Fr.], received; a receipt.

recueil [Fr.], a collection.

reculer pour mieux sauter [Fr.], to go back in order to leap the better.

rédacteur [Fr.], an editor; one who edits or gives literary form to something.

redolet lucerna [L.], it smells of the lamp; it is a labored production.

reductio ad absurdum [L.], the reducing of a supposition or hypothesis to an absurdity.

regium donum [L.], a royal gift; the former annual grant of public money to the Presbyterian ministers of Ireland. See in Dict.

re infecta [L.], the business being unfinished.

relâche [Fr.], intermission; relaxation; respite.

relata refero [L.], I repeat the story as it was given me.

religieux [Fr], a monk or friar. See in Dict.

religio loci [L.], the religious spirit of the place.

rem acu tetigisti [L.], you have touched the matter with a needle; you have hit the thing exactly.

rem facias, rem; recte si possis, si non quocumque modo rem [L.], make money, money; honestly if you can, if not, make it anyhow.

remisso animo [L.], with mind remiss or listless.

remis velisque [L.], with oars and sails; using every endeavor.

remuda de pasturaje haze bizerros gordos [Sp.], change of pasture makes fat calves.

renascentur [L.], they will be born again.

rencontre [Fr.], an encounter; a hostile meeting.

renommée [Fr.], renown; celebrity.

renovate animos [L.], renew your courage.

renovato nomine [L.], by a revived name.

rentes [Fr.], funds; stocks.

répertoire [Fr.], a list; a stock of songs, dramas, etc., already prepared. See in Dict.

répondez s'il vous plait [Fr.], send an answer if you please.

répondre en Normand [Fr.], to give an evasive answer.

requiescat in pace [L.], may he (or she) rest in peace; **requiescant,** may they.

rerum primordia [L.], the first elements of things.

res angusta domi [L.], narrow circumstances at home.

res est sacra miser [L.], a sufferer is a sacred thing.

res gestæ [L.], things done; exploits.

res judicata [L.], a case or suit already settled.

respice finem [L.], look to the end.

respublica [L.], the commonwealth.

résumé [Fr.], a summary or abstract. See in Dict.

resurgam [L.], I shall rise again.

revanche [Fr.], revenge.

revenons à nos moutons [Fr.], let us return to our sheep; let us return to our subject.

re vera [L.], in truth; in actual fact.

revoir [Fr.], a meeting again; **au revoir,** good-bye until we meet again.

rez-de-chaussée [Fr.], the ground-floor.

rideau d'entr'acte [Fr.], the scene let down between the acts of a play.

ridere in stomacho [L.], to laugh secretly; to laugh in one's sleeve.

ride si sapis [L.], laugh, if you are wise.

rien n'arrive pour rien [Fr.], nothing comes for nothing.

rien n'est beau que le vrai [Fr.], there is nothing beautiful except the truth.

rifacimento [It.], a remaking. See Dict.

rigueur [Fr.], strictness; strict etiquette.

rira bien, qui rira le dernier [Fr.], he laughs well who laughs last.

rire entre cuir et chair [Fr.] } to laugh in one's
rire sous cape [Fr.] } sleeve.

risum teneatis, amici? [L], could you keep from laughing, friends?

rixatur de lana caprina [L.], he contends about goat's wool; he quarrels about trifles.

robe de chambre [Fr.], a morning-gown or dressing-gown.

robe de nuit [Fr.], a nightgown.

rôle [Fr.], a character represented on the stage. See in Dict.

rôle d'équipage [Fr.], the list of a ship's crew.

roué [Fr.], a man of fashion devoted to sensual pleasure. See in Dict.

rouge et noir [Fr.], red and black, a game of chance. See in Dict.

ruat cælum [L.], let the heavens fall.

rudis indigestaque moles [L.], a rude and undigested mass.

ruit mole sua [L.], it falls to ruin by its own weight.

ruse contre ruse [Fr.], trick against trick; diamond cut diamond.

ruse de guerre [Fr.], a stratagem of war.

rus in urbe [L.], the country in town.

rusticus expectat dum defluat amnis at ille labitur et labetur in omne volubilis ævum [L.], the rustic waits till the river flows past (and ceases to flow), but it glides on and will glide for all time.

S

sa boule est demeurée [Fr.], his bowl has stopped short of the mark; he has failed in his object.

sabreur [Fr.], a brave soldier distinguished for his use of his sabre.

sæpe stylum vertas [L.], often turn the style or pen (and make erasures with the blunt end on the waxen tablets); correct freely (if you wish to produce good literature).

saggio fanciullo è chi conosce il suo vero padre [It.], he is a wise child who knows his own father.

sal Atticum [L.], Attic salt; i.e. wit.

salle [Fr.], a hall; **salle à manger**, a dining-room; **salle de batailles**, a gallery or room decorated with pictures of martial subjects; **salle de réception**, a room in which visitors are received.

salon [Fr.], a saloon or drawing-room; a picture gallery.

salus populi suprema lex est [L.], the welfare of the people is the supreme law.

salve! [L.], hail!

salvo jure [L.], the right being safe; without prejudice to one's rights.

salvo pudore [L.], without offence to modesty.

salvo sensu [L.], the sense being preserved.

sang-froid [Fr.], coolness; indifference. See in Dict.

sang pur [Fr.], pure blood; of aristocratic birth.

sans cérémonie [Fr.], without ceremony or formality.

sans-culotte [Fr.], without breeches. See in Dict.

sans Dieu rien [Fr.], nothing without God.

sans façon [Fr.], without ceremony.

sans pain, sans vin, amour n'est rien [Fr.], without bread, without wine, love is naught.

sans pareil [Fr.], without equal.

sans peine [Fr.], without difficulty.

sans peur et sans reproche [Fr.], without fear and without reproach.

sans rime et sans raison [Fr.], without rhyme or reason.

sans souci [Fr.], without care.

sans tache [Fr.], without spot, stainless.

santé [Fr.], health; **en bonne santé**, in good health; **maison de santé**, a private hospital.

sapere aude [L.], dare to be wise.

sartor resartus [L.], the botcher repatched; the tailor re-tailored or mended.

sat cito, si sat bene [L.], soon enough done, if well enough done.

satis dotata si bene morata [L.], well enough dowered, if well principled.

satis eloquentiæ, sapientiæ parum [L.], eloquence enough, but little wisdom.

satis superque [L.], enough, and more than enough.

satis verborum [L.], enough of words; no more need be said.

sat pulchra, si sat bona [L.], she is handsome enough, if good enough.

sauce piquante [Fr.], a pungent sauce; a relish.

sauf et sain [Fr.], safe and sound.

sauve qui peut [Fr.], let him save himself who can.

savoir faire [Fr.], the knowing how to act; tact.

savoir vivre [Fr.], good-breeding; refined manners.

scandalum magnatum [L.], speech or writing defamatory to dignitaries.

scire facias [L.], cause it to be known. See in Dict.

scribendi recte sapere est et principium et fons [L.], the principle and source of good writing is to possess good sense.

scribimus indocti doctique [L.], learned and unlearned, we all write.

sdegno d'amante poco dura [It.], a lover's anger is short-lived.

séance [Fr.], See in Dict.

secrétaire [Fr.], a secretary; **secrétaire d'état**, a secretary of state.

secret et hardi [Fr.], secret and bold.

secundum artem [L.], according to art or rule; scientifically.

secundum naturam [L.], according to nature.

secundum ordinem [L.], in due order.

secundum usum [L.], according to practice.

sed hæc hactenus [L.], but so far, this will suffice.

seigneur [Fr.], a lord, nobleman; a seignior (which see in Dict.).

se jeter dans l'eau de peur de la pluie [Fr.], to cast oneself into the water out of fear of rain.

selon les règles [Fr.], according to rule.

selon lui [Fr.], according to him.

semel abbas, semper abbas [L.], once an abbot, always an abbot.

semel et simul [L.], once and together.

semel insanivimus omnes [L.], we have all, at some time, been mad.

semel pro semper [L.], once for all.

semper avarus eget [L.], the avaricious is always in want.

semper fidelis [L.], always faithful.

semper idem [L.], always the same.

semper paratus [L.], always ready.

semper timidum scelus [L.], guilt is always timid.

semper vivit in armis [L.], he lives always in arms.

sempre il mal non vien per nuocere [It.], misfortune does not always come to injure.

senatus consultum [L.], a decree of the senate.

senex bis puer [L.], the old man is twice a child.

se non è vero, è ben trovato [It.], if not true, it is cleverly invented (or fabricated).

sensu bono [L.], in a good sense.

sensu malo [L.], in a bad sense.

sequiturque patrem non passibus æquis [L.], he follows his father, but not with equal steps.

sero sed serio [L.], late, but seriously.

sero venientibus ossa [L.], those who come late shall have the bones.

serus in cælum redeas [L.], late may you return to heaven; may you live long.

servabo fidem [L.], I will keep faith.

servare modum [L.], to keep within bounds.

servus servorum Dei [L.], a servant of the servants of God.

sesquipedalia verba [L.], words a foot and a half long.

sic eunt fata hominum [L.], thus go the fates of men.

sic itur ad astra [L.], such is the way to the stars, or to immortality.

sic passim [L.], so here and there throughout; so everywhere.

sic semper tyrannis [L.], ever so to tyrants.

sic transit gloria mundi [L.], thus passes away the glory of this world.

sicut ante [L.], as before.

sicut patribus, sit Deus nobis [L.], as with our fathers, so may God be with us.

sic volo sic jubeo; stat pro ratione voluntas [L.], thus I will, thus I command; let my will stand for a reason.

sic vos non vobis [L.], thus you labor but not for yourselves.

si Deus nobiscum, quis contra nos? [L.], if God be with us, who shall stand against us?

si Dieu n'existait pas, il faudrait l'inventer [Fr.], if God did not exist, it would be necessary to invent him.

si diis placet [L.], if it pleases the gods.

siècle [Fr.], an age; **siècle d'or**, the golden age; **siècles des ténèbres**, the dark ages.

siesta [Sp.], a short nap during the heat of the day.

sile et philosophus esto [L.], be silent and pass for a philosopher.

silentium altum [L.], deep silence.

silent leges inter arma [L.], amidst arms, or in war, laws are silent, or disregarded.

similia similibus curantur [L.], like things are cured by like.

similis simili gaudet [L.], like is pleased with like.

si monumentum quæris circumspice [L.], if you seek his monument, look around you.

simplex munditiis [L.], elegant in simplicity.

sine cura [L.], without charge or care.

sine die [L.], without a day being appointed.

sine dubio [L.], without doubt.

sine mora [L.], without delay.

sine præjudicio [L.], without prejudice.

sine qua non [L.], without which, not.

si nous n'avions point de défauts, nous ne prendrions pas tant de plaisir à en remarquer dans les autres [Fr.], if we had no faults we should not take so much pleasure in remarking those of others.

si parva licet componere magnis [L.], if small things may be compared with great.

siste viator [L.], stop, traveler!

sit tibi terra levis [L.], light lie the earth upon thee.

sit ut est aut non sit [L.], let it be as it is, or not at all.

sit venia verbis [L.], may the words be excused.

si vis pacem, para bellum [L.], if you wish for peace, prepare for war.

sobriquet [Fr.], a nickname. See in Dict.

sœurs de charité [Fr.], sisters of charity.

soi-disant [Fr.], self-styled.

soi-même [Fr.], oneself.

sola nobilitas virtus [L.], virtue the only nobility.

solitudinem faciunt, pacem appellant [L.], they make a wilderness and call it peace.

sottise [Fr.], absurdity; foolishness.

sotto voce [It.], in an undertone.

soubrette [Fr.], a waiting-maid; an actress who plays the part of a waiting-maid, etc.

souffler le chaud et le froid [Fr.], to blow hot and cold.

sous tous les rapports [Fr.], in all respects or relations.

soyez ferme [Fr.], be firm; persevere.

spero meliora [L.], I hope for better things.

spes sibi quisque [L.], let every one hope in himself.

spirituel [Fr.], intellectual; witty.

splendide mendax [L.], nobly untruthful; untrue for a good object.

spolia optima [L.], the choicest of the spoils.

sponte sua [L.], of one's (or its) own accord.

spretæ injuria formæ [L.], the insult of despising her beauty.

stat magni nominis umbra [L.], he stands in the shadow of a mighty name.

stat pro ratione voluntas [L.], will stands in place of reason.

statu quo ante bellum [L.], in the state in which things were before the war.

status quo [L.], the state in which.

sta viator, heroem calcas [L.], halt, traveler, thou standest on a hero's dust.

stemmata quid faciunt? [L.], of what value are pedigrees?

sternitur alieno vulnere [L.], he is slain by a blow aimed at another.

stratum super stratum [L.], layer above layer.

studium immane loquendi [L.], an insatiable desire for talking.

Sturm und Drang [G.], storm and stress.

sua cuique voluptas [L.], every man has his own pleasures.

suaviter in modo, fortiter in re [L.], gentle in manner, resolute in execution (or action).

sub colore juris [L.], under color of law.

sub hoc signo vinces [L.], under this standard you will conquer.

sub judice [L.], still before the judge; under consideration.

sublata causa, tollitur effectus [L.], the cause being removed, the effect ceases.

sub pœna [L.], under a penalty.

sub prætexto juris [L.], under the pretext of justice.

sub rosa [L.], under the rose; secretly.

sub silentio [L.], in silence.

sub specie [L.], under the appearance of.

sub voce [L.], under such or such a word.

succès d'estime [Fr.], success of esteem; success with more prestige than profit.

sufre por saber y trabaja por tener [Sp.], suffer in order to be wise, and labor in order to have.

suggestio falsi [L.], suggestion of falsehood.

sui generis [L.], of its own or of a peculiar kind.

suivez raison [Fr.], follow reason.

summa summarum [L.], the sum total.

summum bonum [L.], the chief good.

summum jus, summa injuria [L.], the rigor of the law is the height of oppression.

sumptibus publicis [L.], at the public expense.

sum quod eris; fui quod es [L.], I am what you will be (dead), I was what you are (alive): inscription on tombstones.

sunt lacrimæ rerum [L.], there are tears for misfortune.

suo Marte [L.], by his own prowess.

suppressio veri, suggestio falsi [L.], a suppression of the truth

is the suggestion of a falsehood.

surgit amari aliquid [L.], something bitter arises.

sursum corda! [L.], lift up your hearts!

surtout pas de zèle! [Fr.], above all, no zeal!

suum cuique [L.], to each his own.

suus cuique mos [L.], every one has his particular habit.

T

tabagie [Fr.], a smoking-room.

table à manger [Fr.], a dining-table.

tableau vivant [Fr.], a living picture; the representation of some scene by groups of persons.

table d'hôte [Fr.], a public dinner at a hotel; a meal at a fixed price.

tabula rasa [L.], a smooth or blank tablet.

tâche sans tache [Fr.], a work (or task) without a stain.

tædium vitæ [L.], weariness of life.

taisez-vous [Fr.], be quiet; hold your tongue.

tam Marte quam Minerva [L.], as much by Mars as by Minerva; as much by courage as by skill.

tangere vulnus [L.], to touch the wound.

tantæne animis cælestibus iræ? [L.], can such anger dwell in heavenly minds?

tant mieux [Fr.], so much the better.

tanto buon che val niente [It.], so good as to be good for nothing.

tant pis [Fr.], so much the worse.

tant s'en faut [Fr.], far from it.

tantum vidit Virgilium [L.], he merely saw Virgil; he only looked on the great man.

Te, Deum, laudamus [L.], we praise Thee, O God (or rather, as God).

te judice [L.], you being the judge.

tel brille au second rang qui s'éclipse au premier [Fr.], a man may shine in the second rank, who would be eclipsed in the first.

tel est notre plaisir [Fr.], such is our pleasure.

tel maître, tel valet [Fr.], like master, like man.

tel père, tel fils [Fr.], like father, like son.

telum imbelle, sine ictu [L.], a feeble weapon thrown without effect.

tempora mutantur, nos et mutamur in illis [L.], the times are changing and we with them.

tempori parendum [L.], we must yield to the times.

tempus edax rerum [L.], time the devourer of all things.

tempus fugit [L.], time flies.

tempus ludendi [L.], the time for play.

tempus omnia revelat [L.], time reveals all things.

tenax propositi [L.], tenacious of his purpose.

tenez [Fr.], take it; hold; hark; look here.

tentanda via est [L.], a way must be attempted.

teres atque rotundus [L.], smooth and round; polished and complete.

terminus ad quem [L.], the term or limit to which.

terminus a quo [L.], the term or limit from which.

terræ filius [L.], a son of the earth.

terra firma [L.], solid earth; a secure foothold.

terra incognita [L.], an unknown or unexplored region.

tertium quid [L.], a third something; a nondescript.

tête de famille [Fr.], the head of the house; paterfamilias.

tête de fou ne blanchit jamais [Fr.], the head of a fool never becomes white.

tibi seris, tibi metis [L.], you sow for yourself, you reap for yourself.

tiens à la vérité [Fr.], maintain the truth.

tiens ta foi [Fr.], keep thy faith.

tiers-état [Fr.], the third estate. See in Dict.

timeo Danaos et dona ferentes [L.], I fear the Greeks even when they bring gifts.

tirailleur [Fr.], a sharpshooter; skirmisher. See in Dict.

toga virilis [L.], the manly toga; the dress of manhood.

to kalon [Gr.], the beautiful; the chief good.

tomava la por rosa mas devenia cardo [Sp.], I took her for a rose but she proved to be a thistle.

tombé des nues [Fr.], fallen from the clouds.

ton [Fr.], taste; fashion; high life.

to prepon [Gr.], the becoming (or proper).

tôt gagné, tôt gaspillé [Fr.], soon gained, soon spent.

tot homines, quot sententiæ [L.], so many men, so many opinions.

totidem verbis [L.], in just so many words.

toties quoties [L.], as often as.

totis viribus [L.], with all his might.

toto cælo [L.], by the whole heavens; diametrically opposite.

tôt ou tard [Fr.], sooner or later.

totus, teres, atque rotundus [L.], complete, polished, and rounded.

toujours perdrix [Fr.], always partridges; always the same thing over again.

toujours prêt [Fr.], always ready.

tour de force [Fr.], a feat of strength or skill.

tourner casaque [Fr.], to turn one's coat; to change sides.

tous frais faits [Fr.], all expenses paid.

tout-à-fait [Fr.], wholly; entirely.

tout-à-l'heure [Fr.], instantly.

tout au contraire [Fr.], on the contrary.

tout à vous [Fr.], wholly yours.

tout bien ou rien [Fr.], the whole or nothing.

tout comprendre est tout pardonner [Fr.], to understand all is to forgive all.

tout court [Fr.], quite short; abruptly.

tout de même [Fr.], quite the same.

tout de suite [Fr.], immediately.

tout ensemble [Fr.], the whole together. See in Dict.

tout frais fait [Fr.], all expenses paid.

tout le monde est sage après le coup [Fr.], everybody is wise after the event.

tout mon possible [Fr.], everything in my power.

tout vient de Dieu [Fr.], all things come from God.

traducteur [Fr.], a translator.

traduction [Fr.], a translation.

traduttori traditori [It.], translators are traitors.

trahit sua quemque voluptas [L.], every one is attracted by his own liking.

transeat in exemplum [L.], may it pass into an example or precedent.

travaux forcés [Fr.], hard labor.

tria juncta in uno [L.], three joined in one.

tristesse [Fr.], depression of spirits.

Troja fuit [L.], Troy was; Troy is no more.

Tros Tyriusque mihi nullo discrimine agetur [L.], Trojan and Tyrian—there shall be no distinction so far as I am concerned.

trottoir [Fr.], the pavement; the footway on the side of a street or road.

trouvaille [Fr.], sudden good fortune; a godsend.

truditur dies die [L.], one day is pressed onward by another.

tu ne cede malis [L.], do not thou yield to evils.

tu quoque [L.], thou also; you're another.

tu quoque, Brute! [L.], thou also, Brutus!

tutor et ultor [L.], protector and avenger.

tutte le strade conducono a Roma [It.], all roads lead to Rome.

tuum est [L.], it is your own.

U

uberrima fides [L.], superabounding faith.

ubi bene, ibi patria [L.], where it is well, there is one's country.

ubi jus incertum, ibi jus nullum [L.], where the law is uncertain, there is no law.

ubi lapsus? [L.], where have I fallen?

ubi libertas, ibi patria [L.], where liberty is, there is my country.

ubi mel, ibi apes [L.], where honey is, there are the bees.

ubique [L.], everywhere.

ubique patriam reminisci [L.], to remember our country everywhere.

ubi supra [L.], where above mentioned.

Übung macht den Meister [G.], practice makes the master; practice makes perfect.

ultima ratio regum [L.], the last argument of kings; war.

ultima Thule [L.], remotest Thule; some far distant region.

ultimus Romanorum [L.], the last of the Romans.

ultra licitum [L.], beyond what is allowable.

ultra vires [L.], transcending authority.

una scopa nuova spazza bene [It.], a new broom sweeps clean.

una voce [L.], with one voice, unanimously.

una volta furfante e sempre furfante [It.], once a knave, always a knave.

un bienfait n'est jamais perdu [Fr.], an act of kindness is never lost.

un cabello hace sombra [Sp.], a single hair makes a shadow.

und so weiter [G.], and so forth.

une affaire flambée [Fr.], a gone case.

une fois n'est pas coutume [Fr.], one act does not constitute a habit.

un fait accompli [Fr.], an accomplished fact.

unguibus et rostro [L.], with claws and beak; tooth and nail.

unguis in ulcere [L.], a claw in the wound.

un je servirai [Fr.], one I will serve.

uno animo [L.], with one mind; unanimously.

un sot a triple étage [Fr.], an egregious fool.

un sot trouve toujours un plus sot qui l'admire [Fr.], a fool always finds a greater fool to admire him.

unter vier Augen [G.], under four eyes; between ourselves.

urbem lateritiam invenit, marmoream reliquit [L.], he (Augustus) found the city (Rome) brick, and left it marble.

urbi et orbi [L.], to the city (Rome) and the world.

usque ad aras [L.], to the very altars; to the last extremity.

usque ad nauseam [L.], so as to induce disgust.

usus loquendi [L.], usage in speaking.

ut ameris, amabilis esto [L.], that you may be loved, be lovable.

ut apes geometriam [L.], as bees practice geometry.

utcunque placuerit Deo [L.], as it shall please God.

utile dulci [L.], the useful with the pleasant.

utinam noster esset [L.], would that he were of our party.

ut infra [L.], as below.

uti possidetis [L.], as you now possess; each retaining what he at present holds.

ut pignus amicitiæ [L.], as a pledge of friendship.

ut prosim [L.], that I may do good.

ut quocunque paratus [L.], prepared for every event.

ut supra [L.], as above stated.

V—W—Z

vacuus cantat coram latrone viator [L.], the traveler with an empty purse sings in presence of the highwayman.

vade in pace [L.], go in peace.

væ victis [L.], woe to the vanquished.

vale (sing), valete (pl.) [L.], farewell.

valeat quantum valere potest [L.], let it pass for what it is worth.

valet anchora virtus [L.], virtue serves as an anchor.

valet de chambre [Fr.], a personal attendant; a body-servant.

valet de place [Fr.], a guide for visitors to a place.

valete et plaudite [L.], good-by and applaud us; said by Roman actors at the end of a piece.

variæ lectiones [L.], various readings.

variorum notæ [L.], the notes of various commentators.

varium et mutabile semper femina [L.], woman is ever a changeful and capricious thing.

vaudeville [Fr.], a ballad; a comic opera. See in Dict.

vaurien [Fr.], a worthless fellow.

vedi Napoli e poi muori [It.], see Naples and then die.

vehimur in altum [L.], we are carried out into the deep.

velis et remis [L.], with sails and oars; by every possible means.

vel prece, vel pretio [L.], with either entreaty or payment; for love or money.

veluti in speculum [L.], even as in a mirror.

venalis populus, venalis curia patrum [L.], the people are venal, and the senate is equally venal.

venenum in auro bibitur [L.], poison is drunk from golden vessels.

venia necessitati datur [L.], indulgence is granted to necessity; necessity has no law.

venienti occurrite morbo [L.], meet the coming of the disease; prevention is better than cure.

venit summa dies et ineluctabile tempus [L.], the last day has come, and the inevitable doom.

veni, vidi, vici [L.], I came, I saw, I conquered.

ventis secundis [L.], with favoring winds.

ventre à terre [Fr.], with belly to the ground; at full speed.

vera incessu patuit dea [L.], the real goddess was made manifest by her walk.

vera pro gratiis [L.], truth before favor.

vera prosperità è non necessità [It.], it is true prosperity to have no want.

verbatim et litteratim [L.], word for word and letter for letter.

verbum sat sapienti [L.], a word is enough for a wise man.

verdad es verde [Sp.], truth is green.

veritas odium parit [L.], truth begets hatred.

veritas prevalebit [L.], truth will prevail.

veritas vincit [L.], truth conquers.

veritatis simplex oratio est [L.], the language of truth is simple.

vérité sans peur [Fr.], truth without fear.

ver non semper viret [L.], spring is not always green; as a punning motto of the Vernons, Vernon always flourishes.

vestigia nulla retrorsum [L.], no returning footsteps; no traces backward.

vexata quæstio [L.], a disputed question.

via [L.], by way of. See in Dict.

via crucis, via lucis [L.], the way of the cross, the way of light.

via media [L.], a middle course.

via militaris [L.], a military road.

via trita, via tuta [L.], the beaten path is the safe path.

vice [L.], in the place of. Vice versa. See in Dict.

vide et crede [L.], see and believe.

videlicet [L.], namely.

video meliora proboque deteriora sequor [L.], I see and approve the better things, I follow the worse.

videtur [L.], it appears.

vide ut supra [L.], see what is stated above.

vidi tantum [L.], I merely saw him.

vi et armis [L.], by force and arms; by main force; by violence.

vigilate et orate [L.], watch and pray.

vigueur de dessus [Fr.], strength from on high.

vilius argentum est auro, virtutibus aurum [L.], silver is less valuable than gold, and gold than virtue.

vincit amor patriæ [L.], the love of our country prevails.

vincit omnia veritas [L.], truth conquers all things.

vincit qui patitur [L.], he who endures conquers.

vincit qui se vincit [L.], he conquers who conquers himself.

vinculum matrimonii [L.], the bond of marriage.

vindex injuriæ [L.], an avenger of injury.

vino dentro, senno fuori [It.], when the wine is in, the wit is out.

vin ordinaire [Fr.], a cheap wine commonly used in wine-growing countries.

vires acquirit eundo [L.], as it goes it acquires strength (originally said of rumor).

Virgilium vidi tantum [L.], Virgil (or some great man) I merely saw.

virginibus puerisque [L.], for girls and boys.

vir sapit qui pauca loquitur [L.], he is a wise man who says but little.

virtus in actione consistit [L.], virtue consists in action.

virtus in arduis [L.], virtue or courage in difficulties.

virtus incendit vires [L.], virtue kindles strength.

virtus laudatur, et alget [L.], virtue is praised, and suffers from cold.

virtus millia scuta [L.], virtue (or valor) is a thousand shields.

virtus semper viridis [L.], virtue is always green.

virtus sola nobilitat [L.], virtue alone ennobles.

virtus vincit invidiam [L.], virtue overcomes envy or hatred.

virtute et fide [L.], by or with virtue and faith.

virtute et labore [L.], by or with virtue and labor.

virtute non astutia [L.], by virtue (or valor), not by craft.

virtute non verbis [L.], by virtue, not by words.

virtute officii [L.], by virtue of office.

virtute quies [L.], rest or quietude in virtue.

virtute securus [L.], secure through virtue.

virtuti, non armis, fido [L.], I trust to virtue, not to weapons.

virtutis amore [L.], from love of virtue.

virtutis fortuna comes [L.], fortune is the companion of valor or virtue.

virum volitare per ora [L.], to hover on men's lips; to be in everybody's mouth.

vis-à-vis [Fr.], opposite; face to face.

vis comica [L.], comic power or talent.

vis conservatrix naturæ [L.], the preservative power of nature.

vis consili expers mole rui sua [L.], strength without judgment falls by its own might.

vis inertiæ [L.], the power of inertia; dead resistance to force applied.

vis medicatrix naturæ [L.], the healing power of nature.

vis unita fortior [L.], united power is stronger.

vis vitæ [L.], the vigor of life.

vita brevis, ars longa [L.], life is short, art is long.

vitæ via virtus [L.], virtue, the way of life.

vitam impendere vero [L.], to stake one's life for the truth.

vita sine litteris mors est [L.], life without literature is death.

vivat regina! [L.], long live the queen!

vivat respublica! [L.], long live the republic!

vivat rex! [L.], long live the king!

viva voce [L.], by the living voice; orally.

vive la bagatelle! [Fr.], long live folly!

vive le roi! [Fr.], long live the king!

vive memor leti [L.], live ever mindful of death.

vivere est cogitare [L.], to live is to think.

vive ut vivas [L.], live that you may live.

vive, vale [L.], farewell, be happy.

vivida vis animi [L.], the living force of the mind.

vivit post funera virtus [L.], virtue survives the grave.

vivre ce n'est pas respirer, c'est agir [Fr.], life consists not in breathing, but in doing.

vix ea nostra voco [L.], I scarcely call these things our own.

vixere fortes ante Agamemnona [L.], brave men lived before Agamemnon; great men lived in previous ages.

vogue la galère! [Fr.], let come what may!

voilà! [Fr.], behold! there is; there are.

voilà tout [Fr.], that's all.

voilà une autre chose [Fr.], that's another thing; that is quite a different matter.

voir le dessous des cartes [Fr.], to see the under side of the cards; to be in the secret.

volens et potens [L.], willing and able.

volenti non fit injuria [L.], no injustice is done to the consenting person.

volo, non valeo [L.], I am willing, but unable.

volventibus annis [L.], as the years roll by.

vota vita mea [L.], my life is devoted.

vous y perdrez vos pas [Fr.], you will there lose your steps or labor.

vox et præterea nihil [L.], a voice and nothing more; sound but no sense.

vox faucibus hæsit [L.], his voice, or words, stuck in his throat; he was dumb from astonishment.

vox populi, vox Dei [L.], the voice of the people is the voice of God.

vraisemblance [Fr.], probability; apparent truth.

vulgo [L.], commonly.

vulnus immedicabile [L.], an irreparable injury.

vultus animi janua et tabula [L.], the countenance is the portal and picture of the mind.

vultus est index animi [L.], the countenance is the index of the mind.

Wahrheit gegen Freund und Feind [G.], truth in spite of friend and foe.

Wahrheit und Dichtung. See **Dichtung.**

Zeitgeist [G.], the spirit of the age.

zonam perdidit [L.], he has lost his purse; he is in straitened circumstances.

zum Beispiel [G.], for example.

Given Names

Masculine Names

Aar·on (âr′ən, ar′ən) ? Enlightener. [< Hebrew]

A·bel (ā′bəl) Breath. [< Hebrew]

A·bi·el ā′bē·el, ə·bī′əl) Strong father. [< Hebrew]

Ab·ner (ab′nər) Father of light. [< Hebrew]

A·bra·ham (ā′brə·ham; *Fr.* à·brà·àm′; *Ger.* ä′brä·häm) Exalted father of multitudes. [< Hebrew] Also *Sp.* **A·bra·hán** (ä′brä·än′). Dims. **Abe, A′bie.**

A·bram (ā′brəm; *Fr.* à·bräň′; *Sp.* ä· bräm′) Exalted Father. [< Hebrew]

Ab·sa·lom (ab′sə·ləm) The father is peace. [< Hebrew]

Ad·am (ad′əm) Red; man of red earth. [< Hebrew]

Ad·el·bert (ad′l·bûrt, ə·del′bûrt) Var. of ALBERT.

Ad·olph (ad′olf, ā′dolf) Noble wolf. [< Gmc.] Also *Dan., Du., Ger.* **A·dolf** (ä′dôlf; *Fr.* **A·dolphe** (à·dôlf′), *Ital., Sp.* **A·dol·fo** (*Ital.* ä·dôl′fō; *Sp.* ä·thôl′fō), *Lat.* **A·dol·phus** (ə·dol′fəs), *Pg.* **A·dol·pho** (ə·thôl′fŏŏ).

A·dri·an (ā′drē·ən) Of Adria: from the name of two Italian cities, or the Adriatic Sea. [< L] Also *Fr.* **A·dri·en** (à·drē·aň′), *Ital.* **A·dri·a·no** (ä′drē·ä′nō), *Lat.* **A·dri·a·nus** (ä′drē·ä′nəs).

Af·fon·so (ə·fôn′sŏŏ) Pg. form of ALPHONSO.

Al·an (al′ən) Handsome [< Celtic] Also **Al′lan, Al′len.** Dim. **Al.**

Al·a·ric (al′ə·rik) All-ruler. [< Gmc.]

Al·as·tair (al′əs·tər) Scot. contr. of ALEXANDER. Also **Al′·is·ter.**

Al·ban (ôl′bən, al′-) White; of Alba: from the name of several Italian cities. [< L] Also **Al′bin.**

Al·bert (al′bûrt; *Fr.* àl·bâr′; *Ger., Sw.* äl′bert) Nobly bright. [< F < Gmc.] Also *Ital., Sp.* **Al·ber·to** (äl·ber′tō), *Lat.* **Al·ber·tus** (al·bûr′təs). Dims. **Al, Alb, Bert.**

Al·den (ôl′dən) Old friend. [OE]

Al·do (al′dō) Meaning uncertain. [< Gmc. or Hebrew]

Al·dous (ôl′dəs, al′-) From the old place. [OE] Also **Al′·dis, Al′dus.**

Al·ex·an·der (al′ig·zan′dər, -zän′-; *Du., Ger.* ä′lek·sän′dər) **Defender of men.** [< Gk.] Also *Fr.* **A·lex·an·dre** (à·lek·säň′dr′), *Modern Gk.* **A·le·xan·dros** (ä·lâ′ksän·drôs), *Ital.* **A·les·san·dro** (ä′läs·sän′drō), *Pg.* **A·le·xan·dre** (ə·lē·shaňn′·drə), *Russ.* **A·le·ksandr** (ə·lyi·ksän′dər), *Sp.* **A·le·jan·dro** (ä′lä·hän′drō). Dims. **Al′ec, Al′eck, Al′ex, San′der, San′dy.**

A·lex·is (ə·lek′sis) Defender. [< Gk.]

Al·fon·so (äl·fôn′sō) Ital. and Sp. form of ALPHONSO. Also *Dan., Ger.* **Al·fons** (äl′fôns).

Al·fred (al′frid; *Fr.* àl·frät; *Fr.* àl·fred′) Elf counselor; hence, wise. [OE] Also *Ital., Sp.* **Al·fre·do** (*Ital.* äl·frä′dō; *Sp.* äl·frä′thō), *Lat.* **Al·fre·dus** (al·frē′dəs) or **Al·u·re·dus** (al′yŏŏ·rē′dəs). Dims **Al, Alf, Fred.**

Al·ger (al′jər) Noble spear. [< Gmc.]

Al·ger·non (al′jər·nən) Mustached. [< OF] Dims. **Al·gie, Al·gy** (al′jē).

Al·len (al′ən) Var. of ALAN. Also **Al′lan.**

A·lon·zo (ə·lon′zō) Var. of ALPHONSO. Also *Ital., Sp.* **A·lon·so** (ä·lôn′sō).

Al·o·y·sius (al′ō·ish′əs) Lat. form of LOUIS. Also **A·lois** (ə·lois′).

Al·phon·so (al·fon′zō, -sō) Nobly ready. [< Sp. < Gmc.] Also *Fr.* **Al·phonse** (àl·fôns′). Dims. **Al, Alph, Al′phy.**

Al·va (al′və; *Sp.* äl′vä) White. [< L]

Al·vin (al′vin) Noble friend. [< Gmc.] Also **Al·win** (al′·win; *Ger.* äl′vēn), **Al′van,** *Fr.* **A·luin** (à·lwaň′), *Ital.* **Al·vi·no** (äl·vē′nō), *Sp.* **A·lui·no** (ä·lwē′nō).

Am·brose (am′brōz) Divine; immortal. [< Gk.] Also *Fr.* **Am·broise** (äň·brwàz′), *Lat.* **Am·bro·si·us** (am·brō′zhē·əs, -zē·əs).

A·me·ri·go (ä′mä·rē′gō) Ital. form of EMERY.

A·mos (ā′məs) Burden. [< Hebrew]

An·a·tole (an′ə·tōl; *Fr.* à·nà·tôl′) Sunrise. [< Gk.]

An·drew (an′drŏŏ) Manly. [< Gk.] Also **An·dre·as** (an′·drē·əs, an·drē′əs; *Dan.* än·dres′; *Du., Ger.* än·drä′äs; *Lat.* an′drē·əs), *Fr.* **An·dré** (äň·drā′), *Ital.* **An·dre·a** (än·drā′ä), *Russ.* **An·drei** (än·drā′), *Sp.* **An·drés** (än·drās′). Dims. **An′·dy, Drew.**

An·gus (ang′gəs) Singular. [< Celtic]

An·selm (an′selm; *Ger.* än′zelm) Divine helmet. [< Gmc.] Also **An·sel** (an′səl), *Fr.* **An·selme** (äň·selm′), *Ital., Sp.* **An·sel·mo** (än·sel′mō), *Lat.* **An·sel·mus** (an·sel′məs).

An·tho·ny (an′thə·nē,-tə-) Inestimable: from the name of a Roman clan. Also **An·to·ny** (an′tə·nē). *Fr.* **An·toine** (äň·twàn′) *Ger., Lat.* **An·to·ni·us** (*Ger.* än·tō′nē·ŏŏs; *Lat.* an·tō′nē·əs), *Ital., Sp.* **An·to·nio** (än·tō′nyō). Dim. **To′ny.**

An·ton (än′tōn) Dan., Du., Ger. and Sw. form of ANTHONY.

Ar·chi·bald (är′chə·bôld) Nobly bold. [< Gmc.] Dims. **Ar′chie, Ar′chy.**

Ar·mand (är′mänd; *Fr.* àr·mäň′) Fr. form of HERMAN.

Ar·min·i·us (är·min′ē·əs) Lat. form of HERMAN.

Ar·nold (är′nəld; *Ger.* är′nôlt) Eagle power. [< Gmc.] Also *Fr.* **Ar·naud** (àr·nō′), *Ital.* **Ar·nol·do** (är·nôl′dō), *Sp.* **Ar·nal·do** (är·näl′tho). Dims. **Arn, Ar′nie.**

Ae·te·mas (är′tə·məs) He of Artemis. [< Gk.] Also **Ar′·te·mus.**

Ar·thur (är′thər; *Fr.* àr·tŏŏr′) He-bear; from a totemic or royal title suggesting valor, strength, and nobility. [< Celtic] Also *Ital.* **Ar·tu·ro** (är·tŏŏ′rō). Dims. **Art, Art′ie.**

A·sa (ā′sə) Healer. [< Hebrew]

Ash·ley (ash′lē) Dweller among ash trees: from a surname. [< Gmc.]

Ath·el·stan (ath′əl·stan) Noble stone or jewel. [OE] Also **Ath′el·stane** (-stän).

Au·brey (ô′brē) Elf ruler. [< F < Gmc.]

Au·gus·tine (ô′gəs·tēn, ô·gus′tin) Dim. of AUGUSTUS. Also **Au·gus·tin** (ô·gus′tən; *Fr.* ō·güs·taň′; *Ger.* ou′gŏŏs·tēn′), *Ital.* **A·go·sti·no** (ä′gō·stē′nō), *Lat.* **Au·gus·ti·nus** (ô′gəs·tī′nəs), *Pg.* **A·gos·ti·nho** (ə·gŏŏsh·tē′nyŏŏ), *Sp.* **A·gus·tin** (ä′gŏŏs·tēn′).

Au·gus·tus (ô·gus′təs) Venerable. [< L] Also **Au·gust** (ô′gəst; *Ger.* ou′gŏŏst), *Fr.* **Au·guste** (ō·güst′).

Au·re·li·us (ô·rē′lē·əs, ô·rēl′yəs) The golden one. [< L]

Aus·tin (ôs′tən) Contr. of AUGUSTINE.

A·ver·y (ā′vər·ē, ā′vrē) Courageous. [< Gmc.] Also **A·ver·il, A·ver·ill** (ā′vər·əl, ā′vrəl).

Bald·win (bôld′win) Bold friend. [< Gmc.] Also *Fr.* **Bau·doin** (bō·dwaň′).

Bal·tha·zar (bäl·thä′zər, -thaz′ər) Bel's or Baal's prince [< Chaldean], or splendid prince [< Persian]. Also **Bal·tha′sar** (-zər).

Bap·tist (bap′tist) Baptizer. [< Gk.] Also *Fr.* **Bap·tiste** (bà·tēst′).

Bar·na·bas (bär′nə·bəs) Son of consolation [< Hebrew], or prophetic son [< Aramaic]. Also **Bar·na·by** (bär′nə·bē). Dim. **Bar′ney.**

Bar·nard (bär′nərd) Var. of BERNARD.

Bar·ney (bär′nē) Dim. of BARNABAS or BERNARD.

Bar·ry (bar′ē) Spear; hence, straightforward. [< Celtic]

Bar·thol·o·mew (bär·thol′ə·myōō)　Son of furrows. [< Hebrew]　Also *Fr.* **Bar·thé·le·my** (bár·tãl·mē′), *Ger.* **Bar·tho·lo·mä·us** (bär′tō·lō·mä′ŏŏs), *Ital.* **Bar·to·lo·me·o** (bär·tō′lō·mä′ō), *Lat.* **Bar·thol·o·mae·us** (bär·tol′ə·mē′əs), *Sp.* **Bar·to·lo·mé** (bär·tō′lō·mã′). Dims. **Bart, Bat.**

Bas·il (baz′əl, bã′zəl)　Kingly. [< Gk.]

Bax·ter (bak′stər)　Baker. [< Gmc.]

Bay·ard (bã′ərd, bĭ′-, -ärd)　From a surname. [< OF]

Ben·e·dict (ben′ə·dikt)　Blessed. [< L]　Also **Ben′e·dick,** *Fr.* **Be·noît** (bə·nwä′), *Ger.* **Be·ne·dikt** (bã′nä·dikt), *Ital.* **Be·ne·det·to** (bã′nä·dāt′tō) or **Be·ni·to** (bã·nē′tō), *Lat.* **Ben·e·dic·tus** (ben′ə·dik′təs), *Sp.* **Be·ni·to** (bã·nē′tō).

Ben·ja·min (ben′jə·mən; *Fr.* bań·zhá·mań′; *Ger.* ben′yä·mēn)　Son of the right hand; hence, favorite son. [< Hebrew]　Also *Ital.* **Ben·ia·mi·no** (ben′yä·mē′nō), *Sp.* **Ben·ja·mín** (ben′hä·mēn′). Dims. **Ben, Ben′jy, Ben′ny.**

Ben·net (ben′it)　Var. of BENEDICT.　Also **Ben′nett.**

Ber·nard (bûr′nərd, bər·närd′; *Fr.* ber·nár′)　Bear-brave: probably from a totemic title. [< Gmc.]　Also *Ger.* **Bern·hard** (bern′härt), *Ital.,* *Sp.* **Ber·nar·do** (*Ital.* Bär·när′dō; *Sp.* (ber·när′thō), *Lat.* **Ber·nar·dus** (bər·när′dəs). Dims. **Bar′·ney, Ber′ney, Ber′nie.**

Bert (bûrt)　Dim. of ALBERT, BERTRAM, GILBERT, HERBERT, and HUBERT.　Also **Ber·tie** (bûr′tē).

Ber·tram (bûr′trəm)　Bright raven. [< Gmc.]　Also **Ber·trand** (bûr′trənd; *Fr.* ber·trän′).　Dim. **Bert.**

Bill (bil)　Dim. of WILLIAM.　Also **Bil′ly.**

Bob (bob)　Dim. of ROBERT.　Also **Bob′bie, Bob′by.**

Bo·ris (bôr′is, bō′ris; *Russ.* bə·ryēs′)　Warrior. [< Russ.]

Boyd (boid)　Yellow-haired. [< Celtic]

Bri·an (brī′ən)　Strong. [< Celtic]　Also **Bry′an, Bry·ant** (brī′ənt).

Brice (brīs)　Meaning uncertain. [? < Celtic]　Also **Bryce.**

Bruce (brōōs)　From a Norman Fr. surname; orig. a place name.

Bru·no (brōō′nō)　The brown one. [< Gmc.]

Bur·gess (bûr′jis)　Citizen. [< Gmc.]

By·ron (bī′rən)　From a Fr. surname; orig. a place name. Also **Bi′ron.**

Cad·wal·la·der (kad·wol′ə·dər)　Battle arranger. [< Welsh] Also **Cad·wal′a·der.**

Cae·sar (sē′zər)　Long-haired: ? symbolic title suggesting royalty or holiness. [< L]　Also **Ce′sar,** *Fr.* **Cé·sar** (sã·zàr′), *Ital.* **Ce·sa·re** (chã′zä·rä).

Ca·leb (kã′ləb)　Dog; hence, loyal. [< Hebrew]

Cal·vin (kal′vin)　Bald: from a Roman name. [< L]　Dim. **Cal.**

Carl (kärl)　English form of KARL.

Car·ol (kar′əl)　English form of CAROLUS.

Car·o·lus (kar′ə·ləs)　Lat. form of CHARLES.

Car·y (kâr′ē)　? Dim. of CAROL.　Also **Car′ey.**

Cas·per (kas′pər)　English form of KASPAR.　Also **Cas′par** (-pər).

Ce·cil (sē′səl, ses′əl)　Blind: from the name of a Roman clan.

Ced·ric (sed′rik, sē′drik)　War chief. [< Celtic]

Charles (chärlz; *Fr.* shárl)　Manly. [< F < Gmc.]　Also *Ital.* **Car·lo** (kär′lō), *Lat.* **Car·o·lus** (kar′ə·ləs), *Sp.* **Car·los** (kär′lōs). Dims. **Char′ley, Char′lie, Chuck.**

Chaun·cey (chôn′sē, chän′-)　Chancellor. [< OF]

Ches·ter (ches′tər)　Dweller in camp; hence, soldier: from a surname. [< L]　Dims. **Ches, Chet.**

Chris·tian (kris′chən; *Ger.* kris′tē·än)　Christian. [< L < Gk.]　Also *Fr.* **Chré·tien** (krã·tyań′).　Dim. **Chris.**

Chris·to·pher (kris′tə·fər)　Bearer of Christ. [< Gk.]　Also *Fr.* **Chris·tophe** (krēs·tôf′), *Ger.* **Chris·toph** (kris′tōf), *Ital.* **Chri·sto·fo·ro** (krēs·tō′fō·rō), *Sp.* **Cris·tó·bal** (krēs·tō′·väl). Dims. **Chris, Kit.**

Clar·ence (klar′əns)　From the name of an English dukedom.

Claude (klôd; *Fr.* klôd)　Lame: from the name of a Roman clan.　Also *Ital.,* *Sp.* **Clau·di·o** (*Ital.* klou′dyō; *Sp.* klou′·thyō), *Lat.* **Clau·di·us** (klō′dē·əs).

Clay·ton (klãtən)　From an English surname; orig. a place name.

Clem·ent (klem′ənt)　Merciful. [< L]　Dim. **Clem.**

Clif·ford (klif′ərd)　From an English surname; orig. a place name.　Dim. **Cliff.**

Clif·ton (klif′tən)　From an English surname; orig. a place name.

Clin·ton (klin′tən)　From an English surname; orig. a place name.　Dim. **Clint.**

Clive (klīv)　Cliff; cliff-dweller: from an English surname.

Clyde (klīd)　From a Scot. surname; orig. the river *Clyde.*

Col·in (kol′ən, kō′lən)　Dove. [< Scot. < L]

Con·rad (kon′rad)　Bold counsel. [< Gmc.]

Con·stant (kon′stənt; *Fr.* kôn·stän′)　Var. of CONSTANTINE.

Con·stan·tine (kon′stən·tīn, -tēn)　Constant; firm. [< L]

Cor·nel·ius (kôr·nēl′yəs; *Ger.* kôr·nä′lē·ŏŏs)　? Horn: from the name of a Roman clan.　Dims. **Con, Con′nie, Neil.**

Craig (krãg)　Crag; crag-dweller: from a Scot. surname.

Cris·pin (kris′pin)　Curly-headed. [< L]　Also *Lat.* **Cris·pi·nus** (kris·pī′nəs) or **Cris·pus** (kris′pəs).

Cur·tis (kûr′tis)　Courteous. [< OF]

Cuth·bert (kuth′bərt)　Notably brilliant. [OE]

Cyr·il (sir′əl)　Lordly [< Gk.]

Cy·rus (sī′rəs)　The sun. [< Persian]　Dim. **Cy.**

Dan (dan)　Judge. [< Hebrew]

Dan·iel (dan′yəl; *Fr.* dà·nyel′; *Ger.* dä′nē·el)　God is my judge. [< Hebrew]　Dims. **Dan, Dan′ny.**

Da·ri·us (də·rī′əs)　Wealthy. [< Persian]

Da·vid (dã′vid; *Fr.* dä·vēd′; *Ger.* dä′vēt)　Beloved. [< Hebrew]　Dims. **Dave, Da′vey, Da′vie, Da′vy.**

Dean (dēn)　From an ancient religious or military title. [< OF < LL]　Also **Deane.**

De·me·tri·us (di·mē′trē·əs)　He of Demeter. [< Gk.]　Also *Russ.* **Dmi·tri** (dmyē′trē).

Den·nis (den′is)　Var. of DIONYSIUS.　Also **Den′is,** *Fr.* **De·nis** or **De·nys** (də·nē′).　Dim. **Den′ny.**

Der·ek (der′ik)　Du. dim. of THEODORIC.　Also **Der′rick, Dirck** (dûrk; *Du.* dirk), **Dirk.**

DeWitt (də·wit′)　From a surname.　Also **De Witt.**

Dex·ter (dek′stər)　Right; right-handed; hence, fortunate or skillful. [< L]

Dick (dik)　Dim. of RICHARD.

Dolph (dolf)　Dim. of ADOLPH or RUDOLPH.　Also **Dolf.**

Dom·i·nic (dom′ə·nik)　Of the Lord. [< L]　Also **Dom′i·nick.**　Dim. **Dom.**

Don·ald (don′əld)　World chief. [< Celtic]　Dims. **Don, Don′nie.**

Doug·las (dug′ləs)　Dark. [< Celtic]　Dims. **Doug, Doug′ie.**

Drew (drōō)　Skilled one [< Gmc.], or dim. of ANDREW.

Duane (dwän, dōō·än′)　Poem. [< Celtic]

Dud·ley (dud′lē)　From an English surname; orig. a place name.

Duke (dōōk, dyōōk)　From the title. [< OF]

Dun·can (dung′kən)　Brown warrior. [< Celtic]

Dun·stan (dun′stən)　From an English place name.

Dwight (dwīt)　Meaning uncertain. [< Gmc.]

Earl (ûrl)　From the title. [OE]　Also **Earle.**

Eb·en·e·zer (eb′ə·nē′zər)　Stone of help. [< Hebrew]　Dim. **Eb·en** (eb′ən).

Ed·gar (ed′gər)　Rich spear; hence, fortunate warrior. [OE]　Dims. **Ed, Ed′die, Ned.**

Ed·mund (ed′mənd; *Ger.* et′mŏŏnt)　Rich protector. [OE]　Also **Ed·mond** (ed′mənd; *Fr.* ed·môń′).　Dims. **Ed, Ed′die, Ned.**

Ed·ward (ed′wərd)　Rich guardian. [OE]　Also *Fr.* **É·dou·ard** (ã·dwàr′), *Ger.* **E·du·ard** (ã′dŏŏ·ärt), *Sp.* **E·duar·do** (ã·thwär′thō).　Dims. **Ed, Ed′die, Ned, Ted, Ted′dy.**

Ed·win (ed′win)　Rich friend. [OE]　Dims. **Ed, Ed′die.**

Eg·bert (eg′bərt)　Bright sword; hence, skilled swordsman. [OE]　Dims. **Bert, Bert′ie.**

El·bert (el′bərt)　Var. of ALBERT.

El·dred (el′drid)　Mature counsel. [OE]

El·e·a·zar (el′ē·ã′zər)　God has helped. [< Hebrew]　Also **El′e·a′zer.**

E·li (ē′lī)　The highest one. [< Hebrew]

E·li·as (i·lī′əs)　Var. of ELIJAH.

El·i·hu (el′ə·hyōō)　Var. of ELIJAH.

E·li·jah (i·lī′jə)　Jehovah is God. [< Hebrew]

El·i·ot (el'ē·ət) God's gift. [< Hebrew] Also El'li·ot, El'li·ott.

E·li·sha (i·lī'shə) God is salvation. [< Hebrew]

El·lis (el'is) Var. of ELIAS.

El·mer (el'mər) Nobly famous. [OE]

El·ton (el'tən) From an English surname; orig. a place name.

El·vin (el'vin) Of the elves. [OE] Also El·win (el'win).

E·man·u·el (i·man'yōō·əl) Var. of IMMANUEL. Also Em·man'u·el.

Em·er·y (em'ər·ē) Work ruler. [< Gmc.] Also Em·er·ic (em'ər·ik), Em'o·ry.

E·mile (ā·mēl') From the name of a Roman clan. Also Fr. É·mile (ā·mēl'), Ger. E·mil (ā'mēl), Ital. E·mi·lio (ā·mē'lyō).

Em·mett (em'it) Ant; hence, industrious. [OE] Also Em'met.

E·ne·as (i·nē'əs) Praiseworthy. [< Gk.]

E·noch (ē'nək) Dedicated. [< Hebrew]

E·nos (ē'nəs) Man. [< Hebrew]

En·ri·co (än·rē'kō) Ital. form of HENRY.

E·phra·im (ē'frē·əm, ē'frəm) Doubly fruitful. [< Hebrew]

E·ras·mus (i·raz'məs) Lovable. [< Gk.]

E·ras·tus (i·ras'təs) Lovable. [< Gk.] Dim. Ras·tus (ras'·təs).

Er·ic (er'ik) Honorable king. [< Scand.] Also Er'ich, Er'ik.

Er·man·no (er·män'nō) Ital. form of HERMAN.

Er·nest (ûr'nist) Earnest. [< Gmc.] Also Ger. Ernst (ernst). Dims. Ern, Er'nie.

Er·win (ûr'win) Var. of IRVING.

Es·te·ban (äs·tä'bän) Sp. form of STEPHEN.

E·than (ē'thən) Firmness. [< Hebrew]

Eth·el·bert (eth'əl·bûrt) Nobly bright. [OE]

Eth·el·red (eth'əl·red) Noble council. [< Gmc.]

É·tienne (ā·tyen') Fr. form of STEPHEN.

Eu·gene (yōō·jēn') Well-born. [< Gk.] dim. Gene.

Eus·tace (yōōs'tis) Good harvest. [< Gk]

Ev·an (eva'n) Welsh form of JOHN.

Eve·e·lyn (ēv'lin, ev'ə·lin) Ancestor. [< OF < Gmc]

Ev·er·ard (ev'ər·ärd) Strong as a boar. [< Gmc.] Also Ev·er·art (ev'ər·ärt).

Ev·er·ett (ev'ər·it) Var. of EVERARD. Also Ev'er·et.

E·ze·ki·el (i·zē'kē·əl, -kyəl) God gives strength. [< Hebrew] Dim. Zeke (zēk).

Ez·ra (ez'rə) Helper. [< Hebrew]

Fë·dor (fyô'dər) Russ. form of THEODORE. Also Fe·o·dor (fyi·ô'dər).

Fe·li·pe (fā·lē'pā) Sp. form of PHILIP.

Fe·lix (fē'liks) Happy; fortunate. [< L]

Fer·di·nand (fûr'də·nand; Fr. fer·dē·nän'; Ger. fer'dē·nänt) Peaceful courage. [< Gmc.] Also Fr. Fer·nan·do (fer·nän'dō), Her·nan·do (her·nän'dō). Dim. Fer'die.

Floyd (floid) Var. of LLOYD.

Fran·cis (fran'sis, frän'-) Free. [< Gmc.] Also Fr. Fran·çois (frän·swä'), Ger. Franz (fränts), Ital. Fran·ce·sco (frän·chā'skō), Sp. Fran·cis·co (frän·thēs'kō). Dim. Frank, Frank'ie.

Frank (frangk) Dim. of FRANCIS or FRANKLIN. Also Frank'ie.

Frank·lin (frangk'lin) Freeman. [ME] Dims. Frank, Frank'ie.

Fred (fred) Dim. of ALFRED, FREDERICK, or WILFRED. Also Fred'die, Fred'dy.

Fred·er·ick (fred'ər·ik, fred'rik) Peace ruler. [< Gmc.] Also Fred'er·ic, Fred'ric, Fred'rick, Fr. Fré·dé·ric (frā·dā·rēk'), Ger. Frie·drich (frē'driҟh), Sp. Fe·de·ri·co (fā'dā·rē'·kō). Dims. Fred, Fred'die, Fred'dy, Fritz.

Fritz (frits) Ger. dim. of FREDERICK.

Ga·bri·el (gā'brē·əl; Fr. gȧ·brē·el'; Ger. gä'brē·el) Man of God. [< Hebrew] Dim. Gabe (gāb).

Ga·ma·li·el (gə·mā'lē·əl, -māl'yəl) Reward of God. [< Hebrew]

Gar·di·ner (gärd'nər, gär'də·nər) From an English surname. Also Gar'de·ner, Gard'ner.

Gar·ret (gar'it) Var. of GERARD. Also Gar'rett.

Gar·y (gâr'ē) Dim. of GARRET.

Gas·par (gas'pər) Var. of CASPER. Also Fr. Gas·pard (gás·pär').

Gas·ton (gas'tən; Fr. gȧs·tôn') Meaning uncertain.

Gau·tier (gō·tyā') Fr. form of WALTER.

Gene (jēn) Dim. of EUGENE.

Geof·frey (jef'rē) English form of Fr. Geoffroi; var. of GODFREY. Dim. Jeff.

George (jôrj) Earthworker; farmer. [< Gk.] Also Fr. Georges (zhôrzh), Ger. Ge·org (gä·ôrҟh'), Ital. Gior·gio (jôr'·jō), Russ. Ge·or·gi (gyi·ôr'gyi). Dim. Georg'ie, Geor'die.

Ger·ald (jer'əld) Spear ruler. [< Gmc.] Also Fr. Gé·raud (zhā·rō') or Gi·raud (zhē·rō'). Dims. Ger'ry, Jer'ry.

Ge·rard (ji·rärd'; Brit. jer'ärd) Hard spear. [< Gmc.] Also Fr. Gé·rard (zhā·rär'), Ger. Ger·hard (gär'härt). Dims. Ger'ry, Jer'ry.

Ge·ro·ni·mo (jä·rô'nē·mō) Ital. form of JEROME.

Gia·co·mo (jä'kô·mō) Ital. form of JAMES.

Gid·e·on (gid'ē·ən) Hewer. [< Hebrew]

Gi·e·ron·y·mus (jē'ə·ron'i·məs) Lat. form of JEROME.

Gif·ford (gif'ərd, jif'-) Meaning uncertain. [< Gmc.]

Gil·bert (gil'bərt; Fr. zhēl·bâr') Bright wish. [< Gmc.] Dims. Bert, Gil.

Giles (jīlz) From the name of the goddess Athena's shield; hence, shield or protection. [< OF < Gk.]

Gio·van·ni (jō·vän'nē) Ital. form of JOHN.

Giu·lio (jōō'lyō) Ital. form of JULIUS.

Giu·sep·pe (jōō·zep'pā) Ital. form of JOSEPH.

Glenn (glen) From a Celtic surname; orig. a place name. Also Glen.

God·dard (god'ərd) Divine resoluteness. [< Gmc.]

God·frey (god'frē) Peace of God. [< Gmc.] Also Ger. Gott·fried (gôt'frēt).

God·win (god'win) Friend of God. [OE]

Gor·don (gôr'dən) From a Scot. surname.

Gra·ham (grā'əm) From an English surname; orig. a place name.

Grant (grant) From a Norman Fr. surname.

Greg·o·ry (greg'ər·ē) Vigilant. [< Gk.] Dim. Greg.

Grif·fin (grif'in) Var. of GRIFFITH.

Grif·fith (grif'ith) Red-haired. [< Celtic]

Gro·ver (grō'vər) Grove-dweller. [< Gmc.]

Gual·te·ri·o (gwäl·tä'rē·ō) Sp. form of WALTER.

Gu·gliel·mo (gōō·lyel'mō) Ital. form of WILLIAM.

Guil·laume (gē·yōm') Fr. form of WILLIAM.

Guil·ler·mo (gē·lyer'mō, gē·yer'mō) Sp. form of WILLIAM.

Gus (gus) Dim. of AUGUSTUS or GUSTAVUS.

Guy (gī; Fr. gē) Leader [< F < Gmc.] Also Ital. Gui·do (gwē'dō).

Hal (hal) Dim. of HAROLD or HENRY.

Ham·il·ton (ham'əl·tən) From a surname.

Hank (hangk) Dim. of HENRY.

Han·ni·bal (han'ə·bəl) Grace of Baal. [< Phoenician]

Hans (häns) Ger. dim. of JOHANNES. See JOHN.

Har·ley (här'lē) From an English surname; orig. a place name.

Har·old (har'əld) Chief of the army. [OE < Scand.] Dim. Hal.

Har·ry (har'ē) Dim. of HAROLD or var. of HENRY.

Har·vey (här'vē) Army battle. [< F < Gmc.]

Hec·tor (hek'tər) He who holds fast; defender. [< Gk.]

Hen·ry (hen'rē) Home ruler. [< F < Gmc.] Also Du. Hen·drick (hen'drik), Fr. Hen·ri (än·rē'), Ger. Hein·rich (hīn'riҟh). Dims. Hal, Hank, Har'ry, Hen.

Her·bert (hûr'bərt) Glory of the army. [OE] Dims. Bert, Bert'ie, Herb.

Her·man (hûr'mən) Man of the army. [< Gmc.] Also Ger. Her·mann (her'män).

Her·mes (hûr'mēz) Of the earth. [< Gk.]

Her·nan·do (er·nän'dō) Sp. form of FERDINAND.

Hez·e·ki·ah (hez'ə·kī'ə) God strengthens. [< Hebrew]

Hil·a·ry (hil'ər·ē) Joyful. [< L] Also Fr. Hi·laire (ē·lâr').

Hi·ram (hī'rəm) Honored brother. [< Hebrew] Dims. Hi, Hy.

Ho·bart (hō'bərt, -bärt) Var. of HUBERT.

Hodge (hoj) Dim. of ROGER. Also **Hodg'kin.**
Ho·mer (hō'mər) Pledge, or blind one. [< Gk.]
Ho·no·ré (ô·nô·rā') Honored. [< F < L]
Hor·ace (hôr'is, hor'-) Var. of HORATIO.
Ho·ra·ti·o (hə·rā'shē·ō) From the name of a Roman clan.
Ho·se·a (hō·zē'ə, -zā'ə) Salvation. [< Hebrew]
How·ard (hou'ərd) From an English surname. Dim.
How'ie.
Hu·bert (hyōō'bərt) Bright spirit or mind. [< F < Gmc.]
Hugh (hyōō) Mind; intelligence. [< OF < Gmc.] Also
Hu·go (hyōō'gō), *Fr.* **Hugues** (üg) Dim. **Hugh'ie.**
Hum·bert (hum'bərt) Bright support. [< OF < Gmc.]
Hum·phrey (hum'frē) Peaceful stake or support. [< OF < Gmc.] Also **Hum'frey, Hum'phry.**

I·an (ē'ən, ī'ən) Scot. form of JOHN.
Ich·a·bod (ik'ə·bod) ? Inglorious. [< Hebrew]
Ig·na·ti·us (ig·nā'shē·əs, -shəs) Fiery. [< Gk.] Also *Fr.* **I·gnace** (ē·nyäs'), *Ger.* **Ig·naz** (ig'näts), *Ital.* **I·gna·zio** (ē·nyä'tsyō).
Im·man·u·el (i·man'yōō·əl) God with us. [< Hebrew]
I·ra (ī'rə) Vigilant. [< Hebrew]
Ir·ving (ûr'ving) From a Scot. surname; orig. a place name. Also **Ir·vin** (ûr'vin).
Ir·win (ûr'win) Var. of IRVING.
I·saac (ī'zək) Laughter. [< Hebrew] Dim. **Ike** (īk).
I·sa·iah (ī·zā'ə, ī·zī'ə) Salvation of God. [< Hebrew]
Is·i·dore (iz'ə·dôr, -dōr) Gift of Isis. [< Gk.] Also **Is'a·dore, Is'a·dor, Is'i·dor.** Dim. **Iz·zy** (iz'ē).
Is·ra·el (iz'rē·əl) Contender with God. [< Hebrew]
I·van (ī'vən; *Russ.* i·vän') Russ. form of JOHN.

Ja·bez (jā'biz) Sorrow. [< Hebrew]
Jack (jak) English form of Fr. **Jacques;** dim. of JOHN.
Ja·cob (jā'kəb) He who seizes by the heel; hence, successor. [< LL < Hebrew] Also *Ger.* **Ja·kob** (yä'kôb). Dims. **Jack, Jake** (jāk), **Jock** (jok).
Jacques (zhák) Fr. form of JACOB. Or [< OF < LL]
James (jāmz) English form of Sp. **Jaime;** var. of JACOB. [< Sp. < LL] Also *Sp.* **Jai·me** (hī'mā). Dims. **Jam·ie** (jā'mē), **Jem, Jem'my, Jim, Jim'mie, Jim'my.**
Jan (yän)Du., Ger., and Pol. form of JOHN.
Já·nos (yä'nōsh) Hung. form of JOHN.
Ja·pheth (jā'fith) Enlarged; hence, powerful or honored. [< Hebrew] Also **Ja'phet** (-fit).
Jar·ed (jâr'id) Descent. [< Hebrew]
Jar·vis (jär'vis) From a Norman Fr. surname. Also **Jer·vis** (jûr'vis; *Brit.* Jär'vis).
Ja·son (jā'sən) Healer. [< Gk.]
Jas·per (jas'pər) Treasury lord [< OF, ? < Persian], or from the name of the jewel.
Jay (jā) ? Jay bird. [? < OF]
Jean (jēn; *Fr.* zhän) French form of JOHN.
Jef·frey (jef'rē) Var. of GEOFFREY. Dim. **Jeff.**
Je·hu (jē'hyōō) Jehovah is he. [< Hebrew]
Jeph·thah (jef'thə) Opposer. [< Hebrew]
Jer·e·mi·ah (jer'ə·mī'ə) God's chosen. [< Hebrew] Also **Jer·e·my** (jer'ə·mē). Dim. **Jer'ry.**
Je·rome (jə·rōm'; *Brit.* jer'əm) Holy name. [< Gk.] Also *Fr.* **Jé·rôme** (zhā·rôm'), *Sp.* **Je·ró·ni·mo** (hā·rō'nē·mō).
Jer·ry (jer'ē) Dim. of GERALD, GERARD, JEREMIAH, or JEROME.
Jes·se (jes'ē) Meaning uncertain. [< Hebrew] Also **Jess.**
Je·sus (jē'zəs) English form of Lat. *Josua;* var. of JOSHUA.
Jeth·ro (jeth'rō) Abundant or excellent. [< Hebrew]
Jim (jim) Dim. of JAMES. Also **Jim'mie, Jim'my.**
Jo·ab (jō'ab) Jehovah is father. [< Hebrew]
Jo·a·chim (jō'ə·kim) Jehovah will judge. [< Hebrew] Also *Sp.* **Joa·quín** (hwä·kēn')
João (hwouñ) Pg. form of JOHN.
Job (jōb) Persecuted. [< Hebrew]
Jock (jok) Scot. form of JACK.
Joe (jō) Dim. of JOSEPH. Also **Jo'ey.**
Jo·el (jō'əl) Jehovah is God. [< Hebrew]
John (jon) God is good. [< Hebrew] Also *Ger.* **Jo·hann** (yō'hän) or **Jo·han·nes** (yō·hän'əs). Dims. **Jack, Jack'ie, Jack'y, Jock, John'nie, John'ny.**

Jon (jon) Var. of JOHN, or dim. of JONATHAN.
Jo·nah (jō'nə) Dove. [< Hebrew] Also **Jo·nas** (jō'nəs).
Jon·a·than (jon'ə·thən) God has given. [< Hebrew] Dims. **Jon, Jon'nie, Jon'ny.**
Jor·ge (*Pg.* zhôr'zhə; *Sp.* hôr'hā) Pg. and Sp. form of GEORGE.
Jo·seph (jō'zəf; *Fr.* zhō·zef'; *Ger.* yō'zef) God shall give (a son). [< Hebrew] Also *Lat.* **Jo·se·phus** (jō·sē'fəs), *Pg., Sp.* **Jo·sé** (*Pg.* zhōō·ze'; *Sp.* hō·sā'). Dims. **Jo, Joe, Jo'ey.**
Josh·u·a (josh'ōō·ə) God is salvation. [< Hebrew] Also *Fr.* **Jo·sué** (zhō·zwā'), *Lat.* **Jos·u·a** (jos'ōō·ə). Dim. **Josh.**
Jo·si·ah (jō·sī'ə) God supports. [< Hebrew] Also *Lat.* **Jo·si·as** (jō·sī'əs).
Jo·tham (jō'thəm) God is perfection. [< Hebrew]
Juan (hwän) Sp. form of JOHN.
Ju·dah (jōō'də) Praised. [< Hebrew] Also **Jude** (jōōd; *Fr.* zhüd), *Lat.* **Ju·das** (jōō'dəs).
Jules (jōōlz; *Fr.* zhül) Fr. form of JULIUS.
Jul·ian (jōōl'yən) Var. of JULIUS.
Jul·ius (jōōl'yəs) Downy-beared; youthful: from the name of a Roman clan. Also *Sp.* **Ju·lio** (hōō'lyō). Dims. **Jule** (jōōl), **Jul·ie** (jōō'lē).
Jun·ius (jōōn'yəs, jōō'nē·əs) Youthful: from the name of a Roman clan.
Jus·tin (jus'tin) Just. [< L] Also **Jus·tus** (jus'təs).

Karl (kärl) Ger. form of CHARLES.
Kas·par (käs'pär) Ger. form of JASPER.
Keith (kēth) From a Scot. surname; orig. a place name.
Kel·vin (kel'vin) From a Celtic surname.
Ken·neth (ken'ith) Handsome. [< Celtic] Dims. **Ken, Ken'nie, Ken'ny.**
Kent (kent) From an English surname; orig. a place name.
Kev·in (kev'ən) Handsome birth. [< Celtic]
Kit (kit) Dim. of CHRISTOPHER.
Kon·rad (kôn'rät) Ger. form of CONRAD.

La·ban (lā'bən) White. [< Hebrew]
La·fay·ette (lä'fē·et', laf'ē·et'; *Fr.* à·fà·yet') From a Fr. surname. Dim. **Lafe** (läf).
Lam·bert (lam'bərt) The land's brightness. [< F < Gmc.]
Lance (lans, läns) Of the land. [< Gmc.]
Lan·ce·lot (lan'sə·lot, län'-; *Fr.* läñ·slō') Fr. dim. of LANCE. Also **Laun·ce·lot** (lôn'sə·lot, lan'-, län'-).
Lars (lärz; *Fr.* lärs) Sw. form of LAURENCE.
Lau·rence (lôr'əns, lor'-) Laureled; hence, prophetic or poetic. [< L] Also **Law'rence,** *Fr.* **Lau·rent** (lō·räñ'), *Ger.* **Lo·renz** (lō'rents). Dims. **Lar·ry** (lar'ē), **Lau·rie** or **Law·rie** (lôr'ē)
Laz·a·rus (laz'ə·rəs) God has helped. [< Hebrew] Also *Fr.* **La·zare** (lä·zàr'), *Ital.* **Laz·za·ro** (läd'dzä·rō).
Le·an·der (lē·an'dər) Lion man. [< Gk.]
Lee (lē) From an English surname.
Leif (lēf) Loved one. [< Scand.]
Leigh (lē) From an English surname.
Lem·u·el (lem'yōō·əl) Belonging to God. [< Hebrew] Dim. **Lem.**
Le·o (lē'ō) Lion. [< L < Gk.]
Le·on (lē'on, -ən) Lion. [< L < Gk.] Also *Fr.* **Lé·on** (lā·ôñ').
Leon·ard (len'ərd) Lion-strong. [< Gmc.] Also *Fr.* **Lé·o·nard** (lā·ō·nár'), *Ger.* **Le·on·hard** (lā'ōn·härt), *Ital.* **Le·o·nar·do** (lā'ō·när'dō). Dims. **Len, Len'ny.**
Le·on·i·das (lē·on'ə·dəs) Lionlike. [< Gk.]
Le·o·pold (lē'ə·pōld; *Ger.* lā'ō·pōlt) The people's strong one. [< Gmc.]
Le·roy (lə·roi', lē'roi) Royal. [< OF]
Les·lie (les'lē, lez'-) From an English surname. Dim. **Les.**
Les·ter (les'tər) From an English surname; orig. the place name *Leicester.* Dim. **Les.**
Le·vi (lē'vī) He who unites. [< Hebrew]
Lew·is (lōō'is) Var. of LOUIS. Dims. **Lew, Lew'ie.**
Lin·coln (ling'kən) From an English surname.
Li·nus (lī'nəs) Meaning uncertain. [< Gk]
Li·o·nel (lī'ə·nəl, -nel) Young lion. [< F < L]
Lisle (līl) Var. of LYLE.
Llew·el·lyn (lōō·el'ən) Meaning uncertain. [< Welsh]
Lloyd (loid) Gray. [< Welsh]

Lo·ren·zo (lə·ren′zō; *Ital.* lô·ren′tsō; *Sp.* lō·rän′thō) Var. of LAURENCE.

Lot (lot) Veiled. [< Hebrew] Also **Lott.**

Lou·is (lōō′is, lōō′ē; *Fr.* lwē) War famous. [< OF < Gmc.] Also **Lew′is,** *Du.* **Lo·de·wijk** (lō′də·vīk), *Ger.* **Lud·wig** (lōōt′·viRh), *Ital.* **Lu·i·gi** (lōō·ē′jē), or **Lo·do·vi·co** (lō′dō·vē′kō), *Pg.* **Lu·iz** (lōō·ēsh′), *Sp.* **Lu·is** (lōō·ēs′). Dims. **Lew, Lou.**

Low·ell (lō′əl) Beloved. [OE] Also **Lov·ell** (luv′əl).

Lu·cas (lōō′kəs) Light. [< L]

Lu·cian (lōō′shən) Var. of LUCIUS. [< L *Lucianus*] Also **Lu·cien** (lōō′shən; *Fr.* lü·syań′).

Lu·ci·fer (lōō′sə·fər) Light-bearer. [< L]

Lu·cius (lōō′shəs) Light. [< L]

Lu·cre·tius (lōō·krē′shəs, -shē·əs) Shining or wealthy. [< L]

Luke (lōōk) English form of LUCAS.

Lu·ther (lōō′thər) Famous warrior. [< Gmc.] Also *Fr.* **Lo·thaire** (lô·târ′), *Ital.* **Lo·ta·rio** (lo·tä′ryō).

Mac (mak) Son. [< Celtic] Also **Mack.**

Mal·a·chi (mal′ə·ki) Messenger. [< Hebrew]

Mal·colm (mal′kəm) Servant of (St.) Columbia. [< Celtic]

Ma·nu·el (mä·nwel′) Sp. form of IMMANUEL.

Mar·cel·lus (mär·sel′əs) Dim. of MARCUS. Also *Fr.* **Mar·cel** (mår·sel′), *Ital.* **Mar·cel·lo** (mär·chel′lō).

Mar·cus (mär′kəs) Of Mars. [< L]

Mar·i·on (mar′ē·ən, mâr′-) Of Mary. [< F]

Mark (märk) English form of MARCUS. Also *Fr.* **Marc** (márk), *Ital.* **Mar·co** (mär′kō).

Mar·ma·duke (mär′mə·dōōk, -dyōōk) Meaning uncertain. [? < Celtic]

Mar·shal (mär′shəl) From the title. [< Gmc.] Also **Mar′shall.**

Mar·tin (mär′tən; *Fr.* mår·tań; *Ger.* mär′tēn) Of Mars. [< L] Dims. **Mart, Mar′ty.**

Mar·vin (mär′vin) Sea friend. [< Gmc.]

Ma·son (mä′sən) Stoneworker. [< Gmc.]

Mat·thew (mat′yōō) Gift of God. [< Hebrew] *Fr.* **Ma·thieu** (må·tyœ′), *Ital.* **Mat·te·o** (mät·tä′ō), *Sp.* **Ma·te·o** (mä·tä′ō). Dims. **Mat, Matt.**

Mat·thi·as (mə·thī′əs) Var. of MATTHEW. [< Gk.]

Mau·rice (mə·rēs′, môr′is, mor′is; *Fr.* mô·rēs′) Moorish; dark. [< F < L]

Max (maks; *Ger.* mäks) Dim. of MAXIMILIAN.

Max·i·mil·ian (mak′sə·mil′yən; *Ger.* mäk′sē·mē′lē·än) Prob. coined by Frederick III from the Roman names *Maximus* and *Aemilianus.* Dim. **Max.**

May·nard (mā′nərd, -närd) Powerful strength. [< Gmc.]

Mel·vin (mel′vin) High protector. [OE] Dim. **Mel.**

Mer·e·dith (mer′ə·dith) Sea protector. [< Welsh]

Mer·vin (mû′vin) Var. of MARVIN.

Mi·cah (mī′kə) Who is like God? [< Hebrew]

Mi·chael (mī′kəl; *Ger.* mi′Rhä·el) Who is like God? [< Hebrew] Also *Fr.* **Mi·chel** (mē·shel′), *Ital.* **Mi·che·le** (mē·kâ′lā), *Sp.,* *Pg.* **Mi·guel** (mē·gel′). Dims. **Mike** (mīk), **Mick·ey** or **Mick·y** (mik′ē), **Mik·ey** (mī′kē).

Mi·klós (mi′klōsh) Hung. form of NICHOLAS.

Miles (mīlz) Meaning uncertain. [< Gmc.] Also **Myles.**

Mi·lo (mī′lō; *Ital.* mē′lō) Ital. var. of MILES.

Mil·ton (mil′tən) From an English surname; orig. a place name. [< Gmc.] Dim. **Milt.**

Mitch·ell (mich′əl) Var. of MICHAEL. Dim. **Mitch.**

Mon·roe (mən·rō′, *Brit.* mun′rō) From a Celtic surname; orig. a place name.

Mon·ta·gue (mon′tə·gyōō) From a Norman Fr. surname; orig. a place name. Dim. **Mon′ty.**

Mont·gom·er·y (mont·gum′ər·ē) From a Norman Fr. surname; orig. a place name. Dim. **Mon′ty.**

Mor·gan (môr′gən) Sea-dweller. [< Welsh]

Mor·ris (môr′is, mor′-) Var. of MAURICE.

Mor·ti·mer (môr′tə·mər) From a Norman Fr. surname; orig. a place name. Dims. **Mort, Mor′ty.**

Mor·ton (môr′tən) From an English surname; orig. a place name. Dim. **Mort, Mor′ty.**

Mo·ses (mō′zis, -ziz) ? Son. [< Hebrew, ? < Egyptian] Dim. **Moe** (mō), **Moi·she** (moi′shə), **Mose** (mōz).

Moss (môs, mos) Var. of MOSES.

Mur·dock (mûr′dok) Seaman. [< Celtic] Also **Mur′doch.**

Mur·ray (mûr′ē) From a Scot. surname, or var. of MAURICE.

Myles (Mīlz) Var. of MILES.

Na·hum (nä′əm) Consolation. [< Hebrew]

Na·po·le·on (nə·pō′lē·ən) Of the new city. [< F < Gk.] Also *Fr.* **Na·po·lé·on** (nà·pô·lā·ôń′), *Ital.* **Na·po·le·o·ne** (nä·pō′lā·ō′nä).

Na·than (nä′thən) Gift. [< Hebrew] Dims. **Nat.** (nat), **Nate** (nāt).

Na·than·iel (nə·than′yəl) Gift of God. [< Hebrew] Also **Na·than′a·el.** Dims. **Nat, Nate.**

Ned (ned) Dim. of EDGAR, EDMUND, or EDWARD. Also **Ned′dy.**

Ne·he·mi·ah (nē′hə·mī′ə) Comfort of God. [< Hebrew]

Neil (nēl) Champion. [< Celtic] Also **Neal.**

Nel·son (nel′sən) Neal's son: from an English surname.

Ne·ro (nir′ō) Strong: from the name of a Roman clan.

Nev·ille (nev′il, -əl) From a Norman Fr. surname; orig. a place name. Also **Nev′il, Nev′ile, Nev′ill.**

New·ton (nōōt′n, nyōōt′n) From an English surname; orig. a place name.

Nich·o·las (nik′ə·ləs) The people's victory. [< Gk.] Also **Nic′o·las,** *Fr.* **Ni·co·las** (nē·kô·lä′), *Ital.* **Nic·co·lò** (nēk′kō·lô′), *Lat.* **Ni·co·la·us** (nik′ō·lā′əs), *Russ.* **Ni·ko·lai** (nyi·kɐ·lī′), *Sp.* **ni·co·lás** (nē′kō·läs′). Dims. **Nick, Nick′y.**

Ni·gel (nī′jəl) Noble. [< Celtic]

No·ah (nō′ə) Comfort. [< Hebrew]

No·el (nō′əl) Christmas. [< OF < L] Also *Fr.* **No·ël** (nō·el′).

Nor·bert (nôr′bərt) Brightness of Njord. [< Gmc.]

Nor·man (nôr′mən) Northman. [< Scand.] Dim. **Norm.**

O·ba·di·ah (ō′bə·dī′ə) Servant of God. [< Hebrew]

Oc·ta·vi·us (ok·tā′vē·əs) The eighth (born). [< L]

O·laf (ō′laf; *Dan., Norw.* ō′läf; *Sw.* ōō′läf) Ancestor's heirloom. Also **O′lav** [< Scand.]

Ol·i·ver (ol′ə·vər) Of the olive tree. [< F < L] Dims. **Ol′lie, Ol′ly.**

Or·lan·do (ôr·lan′dō; *Ital.* ôr·län′dō) Ital. form of ROLAND.

Os·bert (ôz′bərt) Divine brilliance. [OE]

Os·car (os′kər) Divine spear. [OE]

Os·wald (oz′wəld, -wôld) Divine power. [OE] Also **Os′·wold.**

Ot·to (ot′ō; *Ger.* ôt′ō) Rich. [< Gmc.]

O·wen (ō′ən) Young warrior [< Welsh]

Pat·rick (pat′rik) Patrician; aristocratic. [< L] Dims. **Pad′dy, Pat, Patsy.**

Paul (pôl; *Fr.* pôl; *Ger.* poul) Little: from a given name of the Aemiliani, a Roman clan. Also *Ital.* **Pa·o·lo** (pä′ō·lò), *Lat.* **Pau·li·nus** (pô·lī′nəs) or **Pau·lus** (pô′ləs), *Pg.* **Pau·lo** (pou′lōō), *Sp.* **Pa·blo** (pä′vlō).

Per·ci·val (pûr′sə·vəl) Meaning uncertain. [< OF] Also **Per′ce·val.**

Per·cy (pûr′sē) From a Norman Fr. surname; orig. a place name.

Per·ry (per′ē) Of the pear tree: from an English surname.

Pe·ter (pē′tər; *Du., Ger., Norw., Sw.* pā′tər) A rock. [< Gk.] Also *Dan.* **Pe·der** (pā′thər), *Du.* **Pie·ter** (pē′tər), *Fr.* **Pierre** (pyâr), *Modern Gk.* **Pe·tros** (pâ′trôs), *Ital.* **Pie·tro** (pyä′trō), *Pg., Sp.* **Pe·dro** (*Pg.* pä′ṭhrōō; *Sp.* pä′ṭhrō), *Russ.* **Pëtr** (pyô′tər). Dim. **Pete.**

Phi·lan·der (fi·lan′dər) Lover of men. [< Gk.]

Phi·le·mon (fi·lē′mən) Loving. [< Gk.]

Phil·ip (fil′ip) Lover of horses. [< Gk.] Also *Fr.* **Phi·lippe** (fē·lēp′), *Ger.* **Phi·lipp** (fē′lip). Dims. **Phil, Pip.**

Phin·e·as (fin′ē·əs) Mouth of brass: prob. an oracular priest's title. [< Hebrew]

Quen·tin (kwen′tin) The fifth (born). [< L] Also **Quin·tin** (kwin′tən).

Quin·cy (kwin′sē) ? var. of QUENTIN. [< OF]

Ralph (ralf; *Brit.* räf) Wolf-wise. [< Gmc.] *Fr.* **Ra·oul** (rå·ōōl′).

Ran·dal (ran'dəl) Shield wolf. [OE] Also **Ran'dall.**
Ran·dolph (ran'dolf) Shield wolf. [OE] Dim. **Ran'dy.**
Ra·pha·el (rā'fē·əl, raf'ē·əl) God has healed. [< Hebrew]
Ray (rā) Dim. of RAYMOND.
Ray·mond (rā'mənd; *Fr.* rä·môn') Wise protection. [< Gmc.] Also **Ray'mund,** *Sp.* **Rai·mun·do** (rī·mōōn'dō) or **Ra·món** (rä·môn'). Dim. **Ray.**
Reg·i·nald (rej'ə·nəld) Judicial ruler. [< Gmc.] Also *Fr.* **Re·gnault** (rə·nyō') or **Re·naud** (rə·nō'), *Ital.* **Ri·nal·do** (rē·näl'dō), *Sp.* **Rey·nal·do** (rā·näl'tħō). Dims. **Reg** (rej), **Reg'gie, Rex.**
Re·né (rə·nā') Reborn. [< F < L]
Reu·ben (rōō'bin) Behold, a son! [< Hebrew] Dim. **Rube.**
Rex (reks) King [< L], or dim. of REGINALD.
Rey·nard (rā'nərd, ren'ərd) Brave judgment. [< Gmc.]
Reyn·old (ren'əld) Var. of REGINALD. [< OF]
Rich·ard (rich'ərd; *Fr.* rē·shàr'; *Ger.* riħħ'ärt) Strong king. [< OF < Gmc.] Also *Ital.* **Ric·car·do** (rēk·kär'dō), *Sp.* **Ri·car·do** (rē·kär'tħō). Dims. **Dick, Dick'ie, Dick'y, Rich, Rich'ie, Rick, Rick'y.**
Ro·ald (rō'äl) Famous power. [< Norw. < Gmc.]
Rob·ert (rob'ərt; *Fr.* rô·bâr') Bright fame. [< Gmc.] Also *Ital., Sp.* **Ro·ber·to** (rō·ber'tō). Dims. **Bob, Bob'by, Dob, Dob'bin, Rob, Rob'bie, Rob'in.**
Rod·er·ick (rod'ər·ik) Famous king. [< Gmc.] Also **Rod'·er·ic, Rod·rick** (rod'rik), *Fr.* **Ro·drigue** (rô·drēg'), *Ital., Sp.* **Ro·dri·go** (*Ital.* rō·drē'gō; *Sp.* rō·tħrē'gō). Dims. **Rod, Rod'dy.**
Rod·ney (rod'nē) From an English surname; orig. a place name. Dim. **Rod.**
Ro·dolph (rō'dolf) Var. of RUDOLPH. Also **Ro·dol·phus** (rō·dol'fəs).
Rog·er (roj'ər; *Fr.* rô·zhä') Famous spear. [< OF < Gmc.] Dims. **Hodge, Hodg'kin, Rodge.**
Ro·land (rō'lənd; *Fr.* rô·län') Country's fame. [< Celtic < Gmc.] Also **Row'land.**
Rolf (rolf) Dim. of RUDOLPH. Also **Rolph.**
Rol·lo (rol'ō) Dim. of RUDOLPH.
Ron·ald (ron'əld; *Norw.* rō'näl') Old Norse form of REGINALD.
Ro·ry (rôr'ē, rō'rē) Red. [< Celtic]
Ros·coe (ros'kō) From an English surname; orig. a place name.
Ross (rôs) From an English surname; orig. a place name.
Roy (roi) King. [< OF]
Ru·dolph (rōō'dolf) Famous wolf. [< Gmc.] Also **Ru'·dolf, Ru·dol·phus** (rōō·dol'fəs), *Fr.* **Ro·dolphe** (rô·dôlf'), *Ital.* **Ro·dol·pho** (rō·dôl'fō), *Sp.* **Ro·dol·fo** (rō·tħôl'fō). Dims. **Rol'lo, Ru'dy.**
Ru·fus (rōō'fəs) Red-haired. [< L] Dim. **Rufe.**
Ru·pert (rōō'pərt) Var. of ROBERT. [< G] Also *Ger.* **Ru·precht** (rōō'preħħt).
Rus·sell (rus'əl) Red: from an English surname. [OE < OF] Dim. **Russ.**

Sal·o·mon (sal'ə·mən) Var. of SOLOMON.
Sam·son (sam'sən) The sun. [< Hebrew] Also **Samp'·son** (samp'sən, sam'-).
Sam·u·el (sam'yōō·əl) Name of God. [< Hebrew] Dims. **Sam, Sam'my.**
San·dy (san'dē) Dim. of ALEXANDER. Also **San·der** (san'·dər, sän'-).
Saul (sôl) Asked (of God). [< Hebrew]
Schuy·ler (skī'lər) Shelter. [< Du.]
Scott (skot) The Scot: from an English surname.
Seam·us (shā'məs) Irish form of JAMES.
Sean (shôn, shan) Irish form of JOHN.
Se·bas·tian (si·bas'chən) Venerable. [< Gk.]
Seth (seth) Appointed. [< Hebrew]
Sew·ard (sōō'ərd) ? Sow-herder: from an English surname.
Sey·mour (sē'môr, -mōr) From an English surname; orig. a place name. Dims. **Cy, Sy.**
Shawn (shôn) Irish form of JOHN. Also **Shaun.**
Shel·don (shel'dən) From an English surname; orig. a place name.

Shir·ley (shûr'lē) From an English surname; orig. a place name.
Sid·ney (sid'nē) St. Denis: from an English surname. Dim. **Sid.**
Sieg·fried (sēg'frēd; *Ger.* zēk'frēt) Victorious peace. [< Gmc.]
Sig·is·mund (sij'ə s·mənd, sig'-) Victorious protection. [< Gmc.]
Sig·mund (sig'mənd; *Ger.* zeħħ'mōōnt) Var. of SIGISMUND.
Si·las (sī'ləs) Meaning uncertain. [< Gk.] Dim. **Si** (sī).
Sil·va·nus (sil·vā'nəs) From the name of the Roman god of woods and crops.
Sil·ves·ter (sil·ves'tər) Of the woods; rustic. [< L]
Sim·e·on (sim'ē·ən) He who is heard (widely); hence, famous. [< Hebrew] Dim. **Sim** (sim).
Si·mon (sī'mən) Var. of SIMEON.
Sin·clair (sin·klâr', sin'klâr) St. Clair: from a Norman Fr. surname.
Sol·o·mon (sol'ə·mən) Peaceful. [< Hebrew] Dim. **Sol.**
Stan·ley (stan'lē) From an English surname; orig. a place name. Dim. **Stan.**
Ste·phen (stē'vən) Crown. [< Gk.] Also **Ste'ven,** *Ger.* **Ste·phan** or **Ste·fan** (shte'fän), *Ital.* **Ste·fa·no** (stā'fä·nō), *Russ.* **Ste·pan** (styi·pän'). Dims. **Steve, Ste'vie.**
Stew·art (stooərt, styōō'-) Steward: from an English surname. Also **Stu'art.** Dims. **Stew, Stu.**
Sum·ner (sum'nər) Summoner: from an English surname.
Syd·ney (sid'nē) Var. of SIDNEY.
Syl·va·nus (sil·vā'nəs) Var. of SILVANUS.
Syl·ves·ter (sil·ves'tər) Var. of SILVESTER.

Taf·fy (taf'ē) Welsh dim. of DAVID.
Tad (tad) Dim. of THEODORE or THADDEUS.
Ted (ted) Dim. of EDWARD or THEODORE. Also **Ted'dy.**
Ter·ence (ter'əns) From the name of a Roman clan. Also **Ter'rence.** Dim. **Ter'ry.**
Thad·de·us (thad'ē·əs) Praised. [< Aramaic] Dims. **Tad, Thad, Tha'dy, Thad'dy.**
The·o·bald (thē'ə·bôld, tib'əld) The people's brave one. [< Gmc.]
The·o·dore (thē'ə·dôr, -dōr) Gift of God. [< Gk.] Also *Fr.* **Thé·o·dore** (tā·ô·dôr'), *Ger.* **The·o·dor** (tā'ō·dôr), *Modern Gk.* **The·o·do·ros** (thä·ô'tħô·rôs), *Ital., Sp.* **Te·o·do·ro** (*Ital.* tä'ō·dô'rō; *Sp.* tä'ō·tħô'rō). Dims. **Tad, Ted, Ted'dy, Dode** (dōd).
Thom·as (tom'əs; *Fr.* tô·mä'; *Ger.* tō'mäs) Twin. [< Aramaic] Also *Ital.* **Tom·ma·so** (tōm·mä'zō), *Sp.* **To·más** (tō·mäs'). Dims. **Tom, Tom'my.**
Thurs·ton (thûrs'tən) Thor's stone. [< Scand.]
Tim·o·thy (tim'ə·thē) Honor of God. [< Gk.] Also *Fr.* **Ti·mo·thée** (tē·mô·tā'), *Ital.* **Tim·mo·te·o** (tē·mô'tä·ō). Dims. **Tim, Tim'my.**
Ti·tus (tī'təs) Meaning uncertain. [< L]
To·bi·as (tō·bī'əs) God is good. [< Hebrew] Also **To·bi·ah** (tō·bī'ə). Dim. **To·by** (tō'bē).
Tod (tod) Fox: from an English surname. Also **Todd.**
To·ny (tō'nē) Dim. of ANTHONY.
Tris·tan (tris'tän; -tən) Confusion. [< Celtic] Also **Tris·tram** (tris'trəm). Dim. **Tris.**
Tyb·alt (tib'əlt) Var. of THEOBALD.

U·lys·ses (yōō·lis'ēz) ? Hater: Lat. form of Gk. *Odysseus.*
Um·ber·to (ōōm·ber'tō) Ital. form of HUMBERT.
Ur·ban (ûr'bən) Of the city. [< L]
U·ri·ah (yōō·rī'ə) God is light. [< Hebrew] Also **U·ri·as** (yōō·rī'əs).
U·ri·el (yōōr'ē·əl) Light of God. [< Hebrew]

Val·en·tine (val'ən·tīn) Strong; healthy. [< L] Dim. **Val.**
Van (van) From an English surname, or from the Ger. or Du. name element *von, van,* indicating residence or origin.
Va·si·li (və·syē'lyē) Russ. var. of BASIL.
Ver·gil (vûr'jəl) Var. of VIRGIL.
Ver·non (vûr'nən) Meaning uncertain. [< L or F] Dim. **Vern.**
Vic·tor (vik'tər; *Fr.* vēk·tôr') Conqueror. [< L] Also *Ital.* **Vit·to·rio** (vit·tô'ryō). Dims. **Vic, Vick.**

Vin·cent (vin'sənt; *Fr.* vaṅ·säṅ') Conquering. [< L] Also *Ger.* Vin·cenz (vin'tsents), *Ital.* Vin·cen·zo (vēn·chen'tsō), *Sp.* Vi·cen·te (vē·thän'tā). Dims. Vin, Vince, Vin'ny.

Vir·gil (vûr'jəl) Flourishing: from the name of a Roman clan. Also Ver'gil. Dims. Virge, Vir'gie.

Viv·i·an (viv'ē·ən, viv'yən) Lively. [< F] Also Viv·i·en (viv'ē·ən; *Fr.* vē·vyäṅ').

Wal·do (wôl'dō, wol'-) Ruler. [< Gmc.]

Wal·lace (wol'is) Welsh(man): from a Scot. surname. Also Wal'lis. Dim. Wal'ly.

Wal·ter (wôl'tər; *Ger.* väl'tər) Ruler of the Army. [< Gmc.] Also *Ger.* Wal·ther (väl'tər). Dims. Walt, Wal'ly.

Ward (wôrd) Guard: from an English surname.

War·ren (wôr'ən, wor'-) From an English surname.

Wayne (wān) From an English surname. [? < Celtic]

Wes·ley (wes'lē; *Brit.* wez'lē) From an English surname; orig. a place name. Dim. Wes.

Wil·bur (wil'bər) Bright will. [< Gmc.] Also Wil'ber.

Wil·fred (wil'frid) Resolute peace. [< Gmc.] Also Wil'frid. Dim. Fred.

Wil·lard (wil'ərd) From an English surname.

Wil·liam (wil'yəm) Resolute protection. [< Gmc.] Also *Du.* Wil·lem (vil'əm), *Ger.* Wil·helm (vil'helm). Dims. Bill, Bil'ly, Will, Wil'lie, Wil'ly.

Wil·lis (wil'is) Willie's son: from an English surname.

Win·fred (win'frid) Friend of peace. [OE] Also Win'frid. Dims. Win, Win'nie.

Win·ston (win'stən) From an English surname; orig. a place name.

Wy·att (wī'ət) Dim. of GUY. [< OF]

Wys·tan (wis'tən) Battle stone. [OE]

Zach·a·riah (zak'ə·rī'ə) Remembrance of God. [< Hebrew] Also Zach·a·ri·as (zak'ə·rī'əs). Dims. Zach (zak), Zack.

Zach·a·ry (zak'ər·ē) Var. of ZACHARIAH.

Zeb·a·di·ah (zeb'ə·dī'ə) Gift of God. [< Hebrew]

Zeb·e·dee (zeb'ə·dē) Contr. of ZEBADIAH.

Zech·a·ri·ah (Zek'ə·rī'ə) Var. of ZACHARIAH.

Zeke (zēk) Dim. of EZEKIEL.

Zeph·a·ni·ah (zef'ə·nī'ə) Protected by God. [< Hebrew] Dim. Zeph.

Feminine Names

Ab·i·gail (ab'ə·gāl) Father's joy. [< Hebrew] Dims. Ab'by, Ab'bie.

A·da (ā'də) Joyful; flourishing. [< Gmc.]

A·dah (ā'də) Beauty. [< Hebrew] Also A'da.

Ad·e·la (ad'ə·lə; *Sp.* ä·thä'lä) Noble. [< Gmc.] Also A·dele (ə·del'). *Fr.* A·dèle (à·del'), *Ger.* A·de·le (ä·dā'lə).

Ad·e·laide (ad'ə·lād) Nobility. [< Gmc.] Also *Fr.* A·dé·la·ide (à·dā·lä·ēd'), *Ger.* A·del·heid (ä'dəl·hīt), *Ital.* A·de·la·i·de (ä'd·lä'ē·dä). Dims. Ad'die, Ad'dy.

Ad·e·line (ad'ə·līn; *Fr.* äd·lēn') Of noble birth. [< Gmc.] Also Ad'a·line, Ad·e·li·cia (ad'ə·lish'ə), Ad·e·li·na (ad'ə·lī'nə). Dims. Ad'die, Ad'dy.

A·dri·enne (ā'drē·en; *Fr.* à·drē·en') Fem. of ADRIAN. [< F]

Ag·a·tha (ag'ə·thə) Good; kind. [< Gk.] Also *Fr.* A·gathe (à·gàt'), *Ger.* A·ga·the (ä·gä'tə). Dim. Ag'gie.

Ag·nes (ag'nis; *Ger.* äg'nes) Pure; sacred. [< Gk.] Also *Fr.* A·gnès (à·nyâs'). Dim. Ag'gie.

A·i·da (ä·ē'dä, ä'ē·dä) From the heroine of Verdi's opera.

Ai·leen (ā·lēn'; *Irish* ī·lēn') Var. of EILEEN.

Ai·mée (ā·mā') French form of AMY.

Al·ber·ta (al·bûr'tə) Fem. of ALBERT. Also Al·ber·ti·na (al'bər·tē'nə), Al·ber·tine (al'bər·tēn).

Al·e·the·a (al'ə·thē'ə, ə·lē'thē·ə) Truth. [< Gk.]

Al·ex·an·dra (al'ig·zan'drə, -zän'-) Fem. of ALEXANDER. Also Al·ex·an·dri·na (al'ig·zan·drē'nə, -zän-), *Fr.* A·lex·an·drine (à·lek·sän·drēn'), *Ital.* A·les·san·dra (ä'läs·sän'drä), *Sp.* A·le·jan·dra (ä'lä·hän'drä) or A·le·jan·dri·na (ä'lä·hän·drē'nä). Dims. A·lex·a (ə·lek'sə), Al·ex·in·a (al'ig·zē'nə), Al·ix (al'iks), San·dra (san'drə).

A·lex·is (ə·lek'sis) Fem. of ALEX. Also A·lex·i·a (ə·lek'sē·ə).

Al·fre·da (al·frē'də) Fem. of ALFRED.

Al·ice (al'is; *Fr.* à·lēs'; *Ger.* ä·lē'sə; *Ital.* ä·lē'chä) Truth. [< OF < Gmc.] Also Al'lis, Al'yce, Al'ys. Dim. Al'lie.

A·li·cia (ə·lish'ə, ə·lish'ē·ə) Var. of ALICE. [< L]

A·line (ə·lēn', al'ēn) Var. of ADELINE.

Al·i·son (al'ə·sən) Of sacred memory. [< Gmc.] Also Al'li·son.

Al·ix (al'iks) Dim. of ALEXANDRIA.

Al·le·gra (ə·lā'grə) Spirited. [< Ital. < L]

Al·ma (al'mə) Providing; gracious. [< L]

Al·mi·ra (al·mī'rə) Lofty; princess. [< Arabic]

Al·the·a (al·thē'ə) Healer. [< Gk.]

Al·vi·na (al·vī'nə, al·vē'nə) Fem. of ALVIN.

Am·a·bel (am'ə·bel) Lovable. [< L] also Am'a·belle. Dim. Mab (mab).

A·man·da (ə·man'də) Lovable. [< L] Also *Fr.* A·man·dine (à·män·dēn'). Dim. Man'dy.

Am·a·ran·tha (am'ə·ran'thə) Immortal. [< Gk.]

Am·a·ryl·lis (am'ə·ril'əs) Country sweetheart. [< L]

A·mel·ia (ə·mēl'yə, ə·mēl'ē·ə; *Ital.* ä·mâ'lyä; *Sp.* ä·mä'lyä) Industrious. [< Gmc.] Also *Fr.* A·mé·lie (à·mä·lē'). Dim. Mil'lie, Mil'ly.

Am·i·ty (am'ə·tē) From the abstract noun.

A·my (ā'mē) Beloved. [< L]

An·as·ta·sia (an'ə·stā'zhə, -shə) Able to live again. [< L]

An·dre·a (an'drē·ə; *Ital.* än·drā'ä) Fem. of ANDREW.

An·ge·la (an'jə·lə) Angel. [< Gk.] Also An·ge·li·na (an'·jə·lē'nə, -lī'-), *Fr.* An·gèle (äṅ·zhel').

An·gel·i·ca (an·jel'i·kə; *Ital.* än·jâ'lē·kä) Angelic. [< Gk.] Also *Fr.* An·gé·lique (äṅ·zhä·lēk').

A·ni·ta (ə·nē'tə) Dim. of ANNA. [< Sp.] Also A·ni·tra (ə·nē'trə).

Ann (an) Grace. [< Hebrew] Also *Sp.* A·na (ä'nä). Dims. An'nie, Nan, Nan'cy, Ni'na.

An·na (an'ə; *Ger.* ä'nä) Var. of HANNAH. Dim. An'nie.

An·na·bel (an'ə·bel) Gracefully fair. [< Hebrew] Also An·na·bel·la (an'ə·bel'ə), An'na·belle.

Anne (an) Var. of ANN.

An·nette (ə·net'; *Fr.* à·net') Dim. of ANNE. [< F]

An·the·a (an·thē'ə) Flowery. [< Gk.]

An·toi·nette (an'twə·net'; *Fr.* äṅ·twä·net') Fr. form of ANTONIA. Also *Ital.* An·to·niet·ta (än'tō·nyet'tä). Dims. Net'tie, Net'ty, To'ni.

An·to·ni·a (an·tō'nē·ə, an·tō'·nē'a) Fem. of ANTHONY. [< L] Also *Ital., Sp.* An·to·ni·na (än'tō·nē'nä).

A·pril (ā'prəl) From the name of the month.

Ar·i·ad·ne (ar'ē·ad'nē) Most pure. [< Gk.]

Ar·lene (är·lēn') Meaning and origin uncertain. Also Ar·leen (är·lēn'), Ar·line (är·lēn')

As·pa·sia (as·pā'zhə, -zhē·ə) Welcome. [< L < Gk.]

As·trid (as'trid) God's power. (< Scand.]

A·the·na (ə·thē'nə) From the name of the greek goddess of wisdom. Also A·the·ne (ə·thē·nē).

Au·drey (ô'drē) Noble might. [< OF < Gmc.]

Au·gus·ta (ô·gus'tə; *Ger.* ou·gōōs'tä; *Ital.* ou·gōōs'tä) Fem. of AUGUSTUS. Also Au·gus·ti·na (ô'gəs·tē'nə), Au·gus·tine (ô'gəs·tēn). Dims. Gus'sie, Gus'ta.

Au·re·lia (ô·rēl'yə) Golden. [< L]

Au·ro·ra (ô·rôr'ə, ô·rō'rə) From the name of the Roman goddess of the dawn.

A·va (ā'və) Meaning and origin uncertain.

Av·e·line (av'ə·lēn, -līn) Hazel. [< F]

A·vis (ā'vis) Bird. [< L]

Ba·bette (ba·bet') Fr. dim. of ELIZABETH.

Bap·tis·ta (bap·tis'tə) Fem of BAPTIST. Also *Ital.* Bat·tis·ta (bät·tēs'tä).

Bar·ba·ra (bär′bər·ə, -brə) Foreign; strange. [< Gk.] Dims. **Bab, Bab′bie, Babs, Barb, Bar′bie, Bob′bie.**

Bath·she·ba (bath·shē′bə, bath′shi·bə) Daughter of the promise. [< Hebrew]

Be·a·ta (bē·ä′tə) Blessed. [< L]

Be·a·trice (bē′ə·tris; *Ital.* bä′ä·trē′chä) She who makes happy. [< L] Also **Be·a·trix** (bē′ə·triks; *Ger.* bä·ä′triks), *Fr.* **Bé·a·trice** or **Bé·a·trix** (bä·ä·trēs′). Dims. **Bea, Bee, Trix, Trix′ie, Trix′y.**

Beck·y (bek′ē) Dim. of REBECCA.

Be·lin·da (bə·lin′də) Serpent: title of an oracular priestess. [< Gmc.] Dim. **Lin′da.**

Bel·la (bel′ə) Dim. of ARABELLA or ISABELLA. Also **Bell.**

Belle (bel) Beautiful. [< F]

Ben·e·dic·ta (ben′ə·dik′tə) Fem. of BENEDICT. Also *Ital.* **Be·ne·det·ta** (bā′nā·dāt′tä), *Sp.* **Be·ni·ta** (bä·nē′tä).

Ber·e·ni·ce (ber′ə·nī′sē) Victorious. [< Gk.]

Ber·na·dette (bûr′nə·det′, *Fr.* ber·nà·det′) Fem. of BERNARD. [< F]

Ber·nar·dine (bûr′nər·dēn) Fem. of BERNARD. [< F] Also **Ber·nar·di·na** (bûr′nər·dē′nə).

Ber·nice (bər·nēs′, bûr′nis) Var. of BERENICE.

Ber·tha (bûr′thə; *Du., Ger., Sw.* ber′tä) Bright; famous. [< Gmc.] Also *Fr.* **Berthe** (bert), *Ital., Sp.* **Ber·ta** (ber′tä). Dims. **Ber′tie, Ber′ty.**

Ber·yl (ber′əl) From the name of the jewel.

Bess (bes) Dim. of ELIZABETH. Also **Bes′sie, Bes′sy.**

Beth (beth) Dim. of ELIZABETH.

Beth·el (beth′əl) House of God. [< Hebrew]

Bet·sy (bet′sē) Dim. of ELIZABETH.

Bet·ti·na (bə·tē′nə) Dim. of ELIZABETH. [< Ital.]

Bet·ty (bet′ē) Dim. of ELIZABETH. Also **Bet′te** (bet′ē, bet).

Beu·lah (byōō′lə) Married. [< Hebrew] Also **Beu′la.**

Bev·er·ly (bev′ər·lē) From an English surname; orig. a place name. Also **Bev′er·ley.** Dim. **Bev.**

Bid·dy (bid′ē) Dim. of BRIDGET.

Blanche (blanch, blänch; *Fr.* blänsh) White; shining. [< F < Gmc.] Also **Blanch,** *Ital.* **Bian·ca** (byäng′kä), *Sp.* **Blan·ca** (bläng′kä).

Bon·ny (bon′ē) Good. [< F] Also **Bon′nie.**

Bren·da (bren′də) Sword or torch. [< Gmc.]

Bridg·et (brij′it) High; august. [< Celtic] Also **Brig·id** (brij′id, brē′id). Dims. **Bid′dy, Bri·die** (brī′dē).

Ca·mel·lia (kə·mēl′yə) From the name of the flower.

Ca·mil·ia (kə·mil′ə; *Ital.* kä·mēl′lä) Attendant at a sacrifice. [< L] Also *Fr.* **Ca·mille** (kà·mēl′), *Sp.* **Ca·mi·la** (kä·mē′lä).

Can·dice (kan′dis) Radiant. [< L] Also **Can·da·ce** (kan′·də·sē, kan′dā′sē).

Can·di·da (kan′di·də) White; pure. [< L]

Ca·ra (kär′ə) Loved one. [< L]

Car·la (kär′lə) Fem. of CARLO.

Car·lot·ta (kär·lot′ə; *Ital.* kär·lôt′tä) Ital. form of CHARLOTTE. Also *Sp.* **Car·lo·ta** (kär·lō′tä). Dims. **Lot′ta, Lot′tie, Lot′ty.**

Car·mel (kär′məl) Garden. [< Hebrew] Also **Car·mel·a** (kär·mel′ə). Dim. **Car·me·li·ta** (kär′mə·lē′tə).

Car·men (kär′mən) Song. [< L]

Car·ol (kar′əl) From CAROL, masc., var. of CHARLES. Also **Car·o·la** (kar′ə·lə), **Car′ole, Kar′ol.**

Car·o·line (kar′ə·līn, -lin; *Fr.* kà·rô·lēn′) Fem. of CHARLES. Also **Car·o·lyn,** (kar′ə·lin), **Car·o·li·na** (kar′ə·lī′nə; *Ital., Sp.* kä′rō·lē′nä). Dim. **Car′rie.**

Cas·san·dra (kə·san′drə) From the name of the Trojan prophetess in the *Iliad.* [< Gk.] Dims. **Cass, Cas′sie.**

Cath·er·ine (kath′ər·in, kàth′rin, *Fr.* ka·trēn′) Purity. [< L] Also **Kath′er·ine, Cath′a·rine, Cath·a·ri·na** (kath′ə·rē′nə), *Ital.*, *Sp.* **Ca·ta·ri·na** (kä′tä·rē′nä), or **Ca·te·ri·na** (kä′·tä·rē′nä). Dims. **Cath′y, Kate, Kath′y, Kath′ie, Ka′tie, Kay, Kit, Kit′ty.**

Cath·leen (kath′lēn, kàth·lēn′) Var. of KATHLEEN.

Ce·cil·ia (si·sil′yə, -sēl′yə) Fem. of CECIL. Also **Ce·cel′ia, Ce·cile** (si·sēl′), **Cec·i·ly** (ses′ə·lē), *Fr.* **Cé·cile** (sā·sēl′). Dims. **Cis, Cis′sie, Cis′sy.**

Ce·leste (si·lest′) Heavenly. [< F < L] Also **Ce·les·tine** (si·les′tin, sel′is·tīn), *Fr.* **Cé·les·tine** (sā·les·tēn′).

Cel·ia (sēl′yə, sē′lē·ə; *Ital.* chä′lyä) From the name of a Roman clan. Also *Fr.* **Cé·lie** (sā·lē′).

Cha·ris·sa (kə·ris′ə) Love; grace. [< Gk.]

Char·i·ty (char′ə·tē) From the abstract noun. Dim. **Cher′ry.**

Char·lene (shär·lēn′) Fem. of CHARLES.

Char·lotte (shär·lət; *Fr.* shär·lôt′; *Ger.* shär·lôt′ə) Fem. of CHARLES. [< F] Dims. **Car′ry, Lot′ta, Lot′tie, Lot′ty.**

Cher·yl (cher′əl) Meaning and origin uncertain.

Chlo·e (klō′ē) Bud; sprout. [< Gk.]

Chris·ta·bel (kris′tə·bel) The fair anointed. [< L] Also **Chris′ta·bel′la, Chris′ta·belle.**

Chris·ti·an·a (kris′tē·an′ə) Fem. of CHRISTIAN. Also *Ger.* **Chri·sti·a·ne** (kris′tē·ä′nə)

Chris·ti·na (kris·tē′nə) Var. of CHRISTIANA. Also **Chris·tine** (kris·tēn′; *Fr.* krēs·tēn′; *Ger.* kris·tē′nə). Dims. **Chris, Chris′sie, Chris′ta, Chris′tie, Ti′na.**

Cic·e·ly (sis′ə·lē) Var. of CECILIA.

Cin·dy (sin′dē) Dim. of LUCINDA.

Claire (klâr) Var. of CLARA. [< F] Also **Clare.**

Clar·a (klar′ə, klâr′ə; *Ger., Sp.* klä′rä) Bright; illustrious. [< L]

Clar·i·bel (klar′ə·bel) Brightly fair. [< L] Also **Clar′a·belle.**

Cla·rice (klə·rēs′, klar′is) Derived from CLARA. Also **Cla·ris·sa** (klə·ris′ə), **Cla·risse** (klə·rēs′).

Cla·rin·da (klə·rin′də) Derived from CLARA.

Clau·dette (klô·det′; *Fr.* klō·det′) Fem. of CLAUDE. [< F]

Clau·di·a (klô′dē·ə) Fem. of *Claudius,* Lat. form of CLAUDE.

Clem·en·tine (klem′ən·tēn, -tīn) Fem. of CLEMENT. [< F]

Cle·o·pat·ra (klē′ə·pat′rə, -pä′trə, -pä′trə) Celebrated of her country. [< Gk.] Dim. **Cle·o** (klē′ō).

Cli·o (klī′ō, klē′ō) From the name of the Greek muse of history.

Clo·til·da (klō·til′də) Famous in war. [< Gmc.] Also **Clo·thil′da, Clo·thil′de,** *Fr.* **Clo·tilde** (klô·tēld′).

Co·lette (kō·let′; *Fr.* kô·let′) Fem. dim. of NICHOLAS. [< F]

Col·leen (kol′ēn, ko·lēn′) Girl. [< Irish]

Con·stance (kon′stəns, *Fr.* kôn·stäns′) Constant; firm. [< L] Dims. **Con′nie, Con′ny.**

Con·sue·lo (kən·swä′lō; *Sp.* kōn·swä′lō) Consolation. [< Sp.]

Co·ra (kôr′ə, kō′rə) Maiden. [< Gk.]

Cor·del·ia (kôr·dēl′yə, -dē′lē·ə) Meaning uncertain. [< L]

Co·rin·na (kə·rin′ə) Maiden. [< Gk.] Also **Co·rinne** (kə·rin′, -rēn′; *Fr.* kô·rēn′).

Cor·nel·ia (kôr·nēl′yə, -nē′lē·ə) Fem. of CORNELIUS. [< L]

Cris·ti·na (krēs·tē′nä) Ital. and Sp. form of CHRISTINA.

Crys·tal (kris′təl) From the common noun.

Cyn·thi·a (sin′thē·ə) Of Mount Cynthiuis: an epithet of the Greek goddess Artemis; poetically ,the moon.

Dag·mar (dag′mär) Bright day. [< Dan.]

Dai·sy (dā′zē) From the name of the flower.

Dale (dāl) From the common noun.

Daph·ne (daf′nē) Laurel. [< Gk.]

Dar·leen (därl·lēn′) Beloved. [OE] Also **Dar·lene′, Dar·line′.**

Dawn (dôn) From the common noun.

Deb·o·rah (deb′ər·ə, deb′rə) Queen bee. [< Hebrew] Dims. **Deb, Deb′by.**

Deir·dre (dir′drə) From the name of a heroine of Irish myth.

Del·ia (dēl′yə) Of Delos: an epithet of the Greek goddess Artemis. [< Gk.]

De·li·lah (di·lī′lə) Delicate; languid. [< Hebrew]

Del·la (del′ə) Var. of ADELA.

Del·phin·i·a (del·fin′ē·ə) Of Delphi. [< Gk.] Also *Fr.* **Del·phine** (del·fēn′).

De·nise (də·nēz′, -nēs′) Fem. of *Denis.* Fr. form of DENNIS.

Des·i·ree (dez′ə·rē) Desired. [< F] Also *Fr.* **Dé·si·rée** (dā·zē·rā′).

Di·an·a (dī·an′ə) From the name of the Roman goddess of the moon. Also **Di·ane** (dī·an′; *Fr.* dyàn). Dim. **Di** (dī).

Di·nah (dī′nə) Judged. [< Hebrew]

Do·lo·res (də·lôr′is, -lō′ris; *Sp.* dō·lō′räs) Our Lady of

Sorrows: a title of the Virgin Mary. [< Sp.] Dim. **Lo·la** (lō′lə).

Dom·i·nique (dom′ə·nēk; *Fr.* dô·mē·nēk′) Fr. fem. of DOMINIC. Also **Dom·i·ni·ca** (dom′ə·nē′kə, də·min′ə·kə).

Don·na (don′ə) Lady. [< Ital.]

Do·ra (dôr′ə, dō′rə) Dim. of DOROTHY, EUDORA, or THEODORA.

Dor·cas (dôr′kəs) Gazelle. [< Gk.]

Do·reen (dô·rēn′, dôr′ēn, dō-) Irish dim. of DORA.

Do·rin·da (də·rin′də) Gift. [< Gk.]

Do·ris (dôr′is, dor′-) Dorian woman. [< Gk.]

Dor·o·thy (dôr′ə·thē, dor′-) Gift of God. [< Gk.] Also **Dor·o·the·a** (dôr′ə·thē′ə, dor′-; *Ger.* dō′rō·tä′ä), *Fr.* **Do·ro·thée** (dô·rō·tā′). Dims. **Doll, Dol′lie, Dol′ly, Do′ra, Dot, Dot′ty.**

Dru·sil·la (drōō·sil′ə) She who strengthens. [< L] Also **Dru·cil′la.**

E·dith (ē′dith) Prosperous in war. [OE] Also *Lat.* **Ed·i·tha** (ed′i·thə, ē′di·thə). Dim. **E·die** or **Ea·die** (ē′dē).

Ed·na (ed′nə) Rejuvenation. [< Hebrew]

Ed·wi·na (ed·wē′nə, -win′ə) Fem. of EDWIN.

Ef·fie (ef′ē) Dim. of EUPHEMIA.

Ei·leen (ī·lēn′) Irish form of HELEN.

E·ka·te·ri·na (yə·kə·tyi·ryē′nə) Russ. form of CATHERINE.

E·laine (i·lān′, ē·lān′) Var. of HELEN. [< OF] Also **E·layne′.**

El·ber·ta (el·bûr′tə) Fem. of ELBERT.

El·ea·nor (el′ə·nər, -nôr) Var. of HELEN. [< F] Also **El′i·nor, El·ea·no·ra** (el′ə·nôr′ə, -nō′rə, el′ē·ə-), *Fr.* **É·lé·o·nore** (ā·lā·ô·nôr′), *Ger.* **E·le·o·no·re** (ā′lā·ō·nō′rə), *Ital.* **E·le·o·no·ra** (ā′lā·ō·nō′rä). Dims. **El′la, El′lie, Nell, Nel′lie, Nel′ly.**

E·lec·tra (i·lek′trə) Shining; golden-haired. [< Gk.] Also **E·lek′tra.**

El·e·na (el′ə·nə, ə·lē′nə; *Ital.* â′lā·nä) Var. of HELEN. [< Ital.]

E·li·za (i·lī′zə) Dim. of ELIZABETH. Also *Fr.* **É·lise** (ā·lēz′)

E·liz·a·beth (i·liz′ə·bəth) Consecrated to God. [< Hebrew] Also **E·lis·a·beth** (i·liz′ə·bəth; *Ger.* ā·lē′zä·bet), *Fr.* **É·lis·a·beth** (ā·lē·zà·bet′), *Ital.* **E·li·sa·bet·ta** (ā·lē′zä·bāt′tä). Dims. **Bess, Bes′sie, Beth, Bet′sy, Bet′te, Bet′ty, El′sa, El′sie, Lib′by, Li′sa, Liz, Liz′beth, Liz′zie, Liz′zy.**

El·la (el′ə) Dim. of ELEANOR. Also **El′lie.**

El·len (el′ən) Var. of HELEN.

E·lo·i·sa (ā′lō·ē′zä) Ital. form of LOUISE.

El·o·ise (el′ō·ēz′, el′ō·ēz) Var. of LOUISE. [< F]

El·sa (el′sə; *Ger.* el′zä) Dim. of ELIZABETH. Also **El·sie** (el′-sē).

El·speth (el′spəth) Scot. form of ELIZABETH.

El·va (el′və) Elf. [< Gmc.]

El·vi·ra (el·vī′rä, -vir′ə) Elf ruler. [< Sp. < Gmc.]

Em·e·line (em′ə·līn, -lēn) Derived from EMILY. Also **Em′·me·line.**

Em·i·ly (em′ə·lē) Fem. of EMIL. Also **Em′i·lie,** *Fr.* **É·mi·lie** (ā·mē·lē′), *Ger.* **E·mi·li·e** (e·mē′lē·ə), *Ital., Sp.* **E·mi·lia** (ā·mē′lyä). Dim. **Em.**

Em·ma (em′ə) Grandmother. [< Gmc.] Dims. **Em, Em′·mie.**

E·nid (ē′nid) Chastity; purity. [< Celtic]

Er·i·ca (er′i·kə) Fem. of ERIC. Also **Er′i·ka.**

Er·ma (ûr′mə) Dim. of ERMENGARDE.

Er·men·garde (ûr′mən·gärd) Great guardian. [< Gmc.]

Er·men·trude (ûr′mən·trōōd) Great strength. [< Gmc.]

Er·nes·tine (ûr′nəs·tēn) Fem. of ERNEST.

Es·me·ral·da (es′mə·ral′də) Emerald. [< Sp.]

Es·telle (es·tel′) Star. [< L] Also **Es·tel·la** (es·tel′ə).

Es·ther (es′tər) Star. [< Pers.] Dims. **Es′sie, Het′ty.**

Eth·el (eth′əl) Noble. [< Gmc.]

Et·ta (et′ə) Dim. of HENRIETTA.

Eu·do·ra (yōō·dôr′ə, -dō′rə) Good gift. [< Gk.]

Eu·ge·nia (yōō·jē′nē·ə, -jēn′yə) Fem. of EUGENE. Also **Eu·ge·nie** (yōō·jē′nē), *Fr.* **Eu·gé·nie** (œ·zhā·nē′). Dims. **Gene, Ge′nie.**

Eu·la·li·a (yōō·lā′lē·ə, -lāl′yə) Fair speech. [< Gk.] Also **Eu·la·lie** (yōō′lə·lē; *Fr.* œ·là·lē′).

Eu·nice (yōō′nis; *Lat.* yōō·nī′sē) Good victory. [< Gk.]

Eu·phe·mi·a (yōō·fē′mē·ə) Of good repute. [< Gk.] Also *Fr.* **Eu·phé·mie** (œ·fā·mē′). Dims. **Ef·fie** (ef′ē), **Phe′mie.**

E·va (ē′və; *Ger., Ital., Sp.* ā′vä) Var. of EVE. [< L]

E·van·ge·line (i·van′jə·lin, -līn, -lēn) Bearer of glad tidings. [< Gk.]

Eve (ēv; *Fr.* ev) Life. [< Hebrew]

Eve·lyn (ev′ə·lin; *Brit.* ēv′lin) Hazelnut. [< L] Also **Ev·e·li·na** (ev′ə·lī′nə, -lē′-).

E·vi·ta (ā·vē′tä) Sp. dim. of EVA.

Faith (fāth) From the abstract noun. Dim. **Fay.**

Fan·ny (fan′ē) Dim. of FRANCES. Also **Fan′nie.**

Faus·ti·na (fôs·tī′nə, -tē′-) Lucky. [< L] Also **Faus·tine** (fôs·tēn′; *Fr.* fôs·tēn′)

Fawn (fôn) From the name of the animal.

Fay (fā) Fairy or faith. [OF] Also **Fae, Faye.**

Fe·li·cia (fə·lish′ə, -lish′ē·ə, -lē′shə) Happy. [< L] Also **Fe·lice** (fə·lēs′), **Fe·lic′i·ty** (-lis′ə·tē)

Fern (fûrn) From the common noun.

Fer·nan·da (fer·nän′dä) Fem. of *Fernando,* Sp. form of FERDINAND.

Fi·del·ia (fi·dēl′yə, -dē′lē·ə) Faithful. [< L]

Fi·o·na (fē·ō′nə) Fair or white. [< Celtic]

Fla·vi·a (flā′vē·ə) Blonde. [<]

Flo·ra (flôr′ə, flō′rə) Flower. [< L]

Flor·ence (flôr′əns, flor′-; *Fr.* flô·räns′) Blooming. [< L] Dims. **Flo** (flō), **Flor·rie** (flôr′ē, flor′ē), **Flos·sie** (flos′ē).

Fran·ces (fran′sis, frän′-) Fem. of FRANCIS. Also *Fr.* **Fran·çoise** (frän·swàz′) or **Fran·cisque** (frän·sēsk′), *Ital.* **Fran·ces·ca** (frän·chäs′kä). Dims. **Fan′nie, Fan′ny, Fran, Fran′cie, Frank, Fran′nie.**

Fran·cine (fran·sēn′) Derived from FRANCES. Also **Fran·cene′.**

Fred·er·i·ca (fred′ə·rē′kə, fred·rē′kə) Fem. of FREDERICK. Dim. **Fred′die.**

Frie·da (frē′də) Peace. [< G] Also **Fre′da.**

Ga·bri·elle (gä′brē·el′, gab′rē-; *Fr.* gà·brē·el′) Fem. of GABRIEL. Also **Ga·bri·el·la** (gä′brē·el′ə) Dim. **Ga·by** (gä·bē′).

Gail (gāl) Short for ABIGAIL. Also **Gale.**

Gay (gā) From the adjective.

Gen·e·vieve (jen′ə·vēv, jen′ə·vēv′) White wave. [< F < Celtic] Also *Fr.* **Ge·ne·viève** (zhen·vyev′).

Ge·nev·ra (ji·nev′rə) Var. of GUINEVERE. [< Ital.] Also **Ge·ne·va** (ji·nē′və).

Geor·gia (jôr′jə) Fem. of GEORGE.

Geor·gi·an·a (jôr′jē·an′ə) Fem. of GEORGE. Also **Geor·gi·na** (jôr·jē′nə), *Fr.* **Geor·gine** (zhôr·zhēn′) or **Geor·gette** (zhôr·zhet′).

Ger·al·dine (jer′əl·dēn) Fem. of GERALD. Dims. **Ger′ry, Jer′ry.**

Ger·maine (jər·mān′) German. [< F < L]

Ger·trude (gûr′trōōd, *Fr.* zher·trüd′) Spear maid. [< Gmc.] Also *Ger.* **Ger·trud** (ger′trōōt). Dims. **Ger′tie, Ger′·ty, Tru′da, Tru′dy.**

Gil·ber·ta (gil·bûr′tə) Fem. of GILBERT. Also **Gil·ber·tine** (gil′bər·tēn), *Fr.* **Gil·berte** (zhēl·bert′)

Gil·da (gil′də) Servant of God. [< Celtic]

Gil·li·an (gil′ēl·ən, jil′yən) Var. of JULIANA.

Gi·nev·ra (ji·nev′rə) Var. of GUINEVERE. [< Ital.]

Gin·ger (jin′jer) From the plant name.

Gio·van·na (jō·vän′nä) Fem. of *Giovanni,* Ital. form of JOHN.

Gi·sele (zhē·zel′) Pledge or hostage. [< F < Gmc.] Also **Gi·selle′.**

Giu·lia (jōō′lyä) Ital. form of JULIA.

Glad·ys (glad′is) Welsh fem. form of CLAUDIUS.

Glen·na (glen′ə) Fem. of GLENN. Also **Glen·nis** (glen′is), **Gly·nis** (glin′is).

Glo·ri·a (glôr′ē·ə, glō′rē·ə) Glory. [< L]

Grace (grās) Grace; favor. [< L] Also **Gra·ci·a** or **Gra·ti′a** (grā′shē·ə, -shə).

Gret·a (gret′ə, grēt′ə; *Ger.* grä′tə) Dim. of MARGARET. [< G] Also **Gre·tel** or **Gre·thel** (grā′təl).

Gretch·en (grech′ən; *Ger.* grät′Ҝhən) Dim. of MARGARET. [< G]

Gri·sel·da (gri·zel′də) Stony or unbeatable heroine. [< Gmc.] Also **Gris·sel** (gris′əl), **Griz·el** (griz′əl).

Gus·sie (gus′ē) Dim. of AUGUSTA. Also **Gus·ta** (gus′tə)

Gwen·do·lyn (gwen′də·lin) White-browed. [< Celtic] Also **Gwen′do·len, Gwen′do·line** (-lin, -lēn). Dims. **Gwen, Gwenᴀ, Wen·dy** (wen′dē).

Gwen·eth (gwen′ith) Fair or blessed. [< Celtic] Also **Gwen′ith, Gwyn·eth** (gwin′ith), **Gyn·eth** (gin′ith).

Gwyn (gwin) Fair or White. [< Celtic] Also **Gwynne.**

Han·nah (han′ə) Grace. [< Hebrew] Also **Han′na.**

Har·ri·et (har′ē·ət) Fem. of HARRY. Dims. **Hat′tie, Hat′ty.**

Ha·zel (hā′zəl) From the plant name.

Heath·er (heth′ər) From the plant name.

Hed·da (hed′ə) War. [< Gmc.]

Hed·wig (hed′wig) War. [< Gmc.]

Hel·en (hel′ən) Light; a torch. [< Gk.] Also *Fr.* **Hé·lène** (ā·len′). Dims. **Nell, Nel′lie, Nel′ly.**

Hel·e·na (hel′ə·nə) Var. of HELEN. Dim. **Le·na** (lē′nə).

Hel·ga (hel′gə) Holy. [< Gmc.]

Hé·lo·ïse (ā·lō·ēz′) Fr. form of ELOISE.

Hen·ri·et·ta (hen′rē·et′ə) Fem. of HENRY. Also *Fr.* **Hen·ri·ette** (äṅ·ryet′). Dims. **Et′ta, Et′tie, Hat′tie, Hat′ty, Het′·ty, Net′tie, Ret′ta.**

Heph·zi·bah (hep′zə·bə) She who is my delight. [< Hebrew].

Her·mi·o·ne (hər·mī′ə·nē) Fem. of HERMES.

Hes·ter (hes′tər) Var. of ESTHER. Also **Hes′ther.** Dim. **Het′ty.**

Het·ty (het′ē) Dim. of ESTHER, HENRIETTA, or HESTER.

Hil·a·ry (hil′ər·ē) Joyful. [< L]

Hil·da (hil′də) Battle maiden. [OE]

Hil·de·garde (hil′də·gärd) Guardian battle maiden. [< Gmc.] Also **Hil′de·gard.**

Hol·ly (hol′ē) From the plant name.

Ho·no·ra (hō·nôr′ə, -nō′rə) Honor. [< L] Also **Ho·no·ri·a** (hō·nôr′ē·ə, -nō′rē·ə) Dims. **No′ra, No′rah.**

Hope (hōp) From the abstract noun.

Hor·tense (hôr′tens; *Fr.* ôr·täṅs′) Gardener: from the name of a Roman clan. [< F < L] Also *Lat.* **Hor·ten·si·a** (hôr·ten′shē·ə).

I·da (ī′də) Happy; godlike. [< Gmc.]

I·lo·na (i·lō′nə) Radiantly beautiful. [< Hung. < Gk.]

Il·se (il′sə; *Ger.* il′zə) Dim. of ELIZABETH. [< G]

Im·o·gene (im′ə·jēn) Meaning and origin uncertain. Also **Im·o·gen** (im′ə·jən).

I·na (ī′nə) From the Lat. suffix for fem. names.

I·nez (ī′nez, ē′nez; *Sp.* ē·näth′) Var. of AGNES. [< Sp. & Pg.]

In·grid (ing′grid) Daughter of Ing (a god in Gmc. mythology). [< Gmc.] Also **In·ga** (ing′gə).

I·rene (ī·rēn′) Peace. [< Gk.]

I·ris (ī′ris) Rainbow. [< Gk.], or from the name of the flower.

Ir·ma (ûr′mə) Var. of ERMA.

Is·a·bel (iz′ə·bel; *Sp.* ē′sä·bel′) Oath of Baal. [< Hebrew] Also **Is·a·bel·la** (iz′ə·bel′ə; *Ital.* ē′zä·bel′lä), **Is·a·belle** (iz′ə·bel; *Fr.* ē·zà·bel′), **Is′o·bel**, *Fr.* **I·sa·beau** (ē·zà·bō′). Dims. **Bell, Bel′la, Belle.**

Is·a·do·ra (iz′ə·dôr′ə, -dō′rə) Fem. of ISIDORE.

I·vy (ī′vē) From the plant name.

Jac·que·line (jak′wə·lin, -lēn, jak′ə-; *Fr.* zhä·klēn′) Fem. of *Jacques*, Fr. form of JACOB. Dim. **Jac′kie.**

Jane (jān) Var. of JOAN. [< OF]

Jan·et (jan′it, jə·net′) Dim. of JANE.

Jan·ice (jan′is) Var. of JANE.

Jas·mine (jaz′min, jas′-) From the name of the flower.

Jean (jēn) Var. of JOAN. [< F]

Jeanne (jēn, *Fr.* zhän) Fr. form of JOAN.

Jean·nette (jə·net′) Dim. of JEANNE.

Je·mi·ma (jə·mī′mə) Dove. [< Hebrew]

Jen·ni·fer (jen′ə·fər) Var. of GUINEVERE. Dims. **Jen′ny, Jin′ny.**

Jer·ry (jer′ē) Dim. of GERALDINE.

Jes·si·ca (jes′i·kə) Fem. of JESSE. Dims. **Jess, Jes′sie, Jes′sy.**

Jew·el (jōō′əl) From the common noun.

Jill (jil) Short for JULIA.

Jo (jō) Dim. of JOSEPHINE.

Joan (jōn, jō·an′) Fem. of JOHN. Also **Jo·an·na** (jō·an′ə), **Jo·anne** (jō·an′)

Joc·e·lyn (jos′ə·lin) Playful; merry. [< L] Also **Joc′e·lin, Joc′e·line** (-lin).

Jo·han·na (jō·han′ə; *Ger.* yō·hän′ä) Ger. form of JOAN.

Jo·se·pha (jō·sē′fə) Var. of JOSEPHINE.

Jo·se·phine (jō′sə·fēn, -zə) Fem. of JOSEPH. [< F] Dims. **Jo, Jo′sie, Jo′zy.**

Joy (joi) From the abstract noun.

Joyce (jois) Joyful. [< L]

Jua·na (wä′nə; *Sp.* hwä′nä) Fem. of *Juan*, Sp. form of JOHN.

Jua·ni·ta (wä·nē′tə; *Sp.* hwä·nē′tä) Sp. dim. of JUANA.

Ju·dith (jōō′dith) Praised. [< Hebrew] Dim. **Ju′dy.**

Jul·ia (jōōl′yə) Fem. of JULIUS. Also **Ju·lie** (jōō′lē; *Fr.* zhü·lē′).

Ju·li·an·a (jōō′lē·an′ə, -ä′nə) Fem. of JULIAN. Also *Fr.* **Ju·li·enne** (zhü·lyen′).

Ju·li·et (jōō′lē·et, jōō′lē·et′) Dim. of JULIA.

June (jōōn) From the name of the mouth.

Jus·ti·na (jus·tī′nə, -tē′-) Fem. of JUSTIN. Also **Jus·tine** (jus·tēn′; *Fr.* zhüs·tēn′).

Kar·en (kâr′ən; *Dan., Norw.* kä′rən) Var. of CATHERINE. [< Dan. & Norw.]

Kate (kāt) Dim. of CATHERINE. Also **Ka′tie.**

Kath·a·rine (kath′ə·rin, kath′rin) Var. of CATHERINE. Also **Kath′er·ine, Kath′ryn.**

Kath·leen (kath′lēn, kath·lēn′) Irish form of CATHERINE.

Kath·y (kath′ē) Dim. of CATHERINE.

Ka·tri·na (kə·trē′nə) Var. of CATHERINE. Also **Kat·rine** (kat′rin, -rēn). Dim. **Tri·na** (trē′nə).

Kay (kā) Dim. of CATHERINE.

Kir·sten (kûr′stən; *Norw.* ʀhish′tən, ʀhir′stən) Norw. form of CHRISTINE.

Kit·ty (kit′ē) Dim. of CATHERINE. Also **Kit.**

Kla·ra (klä′rä) Ger. form of CLARA.

Lau·ra (lôr′ə) Laurel. [< L] Also *Fr.* **Laure** (lôr). Dims. **Lau′rie, Lol′ly.**

Lau·ret·ta (lô·ret′ə) Dim. of LAURA. Also **Lau·rette′.**

Lau·rin·da (lô·rin′də) Derived from LAURA.

La·verne (lə·vûrn′) From the name of the Roman goddess of spring and grain.

La·vin·i·a (lə·vin′ē·ə) Purified. [< L]

Le·ah (lē′ə) Gazelle. [< Hebrew] Also **Le′a.**

Lei·la (lē′lä) Dark night or dark beauty. [< Arabic]

Le·na (lē′nə) Dim. of HELENA or MAGDALENE.

Le·no·ra (lə·nôr′ə, -nō′rə) Var. of ELEANOR. Also **Le·nore** (lə·nôr′).

Le·o·na (lē·ō′nə) Fem. of LEO and LEON. Also *Fr.* **Lé·o·nie** (lā·ō·nē′).

Le·or·a (lē·ôr′ə, -ō′rə) Var. of LEONORA.

Les·lie (les′lē, les′-) From LESLIE. masc. Also **Les′ley.**

Le·ti·tia (li·tish′ə) Joy. [< L] Dim. **Let′ty** (let′ē).

Lib·by (lib′ē) Dim. of ELIZABETH.

Li·la (lī′lə, lē′-) Var. of LILLIAN.

Lil·i·an (lil′ē·ən, lil′yən) Lily. [< L] Also **Lil′li·an.** Dims. **Lil, Lil′ly, Lil′y.**

Lil·y (lil′ē) From the name of the flower; also, dim. of LILIAN.

Lin·da (lin′də) Pretty [< Sp.], or short for BELINDA or MELINDA.

Li·sa (lī′zə, lē′) Dim. of ELIZABETH. Also **Li′za**, *Ger.* **Li·se** (lē′zə).

Li·sette (lē·zet′) Fr. dim. of ELIZABETH. Also **Li·zette′.**

Liz·beth (liz′bəth) Dim. of ELIZABETH.

Liz′zie (liz′ē) Dim. of ELIZABETH. Also **Liz′zy, Liz. Lo·is** (lō′is) Desirable. [< Gk.]

Lo·la (lō′lə, *Sp.* lō′lä) Dim. of DOLORES. [< Sp.] Dim. **Lo·li·ta** (lō·lē′tə; *Sp.* lōl·lē′tä).

Lor·ene (lō·rēn′) Var. of LAURA. Also **Laur·een′, Laur·ene′, Lor·een′.**

Lor·et·ta (lô·ret′ə, lō-) Dim. of LAURA. Also Lor·ette (lô·ret′).

Lo·rin·da (lô·rin′də, lə-) Var. of LAURINDA.

Lor·na (lôr′nə) Lost. [OE]

Lor·raine (lə·rān′) Var. of LAURA.

Lot·tie (lot′ē) Dim. of CHARLOTTE. Also Lot′ta, Lot′ty.

Lou·el·la (loo·el′ə) Var. of LUELLA.

Lou·ise (loo·ēz′) Fem. of LOUIS. [< F] Also Lou·i·sa (loo·ē′zə). Dims. Lou, Lou′ie, Lu, Lu′lu.

Lu·cia (loo′shə; Ital. loo·chē′ä) Fem. of LUCIUS.

Lu·cille (loo·sēl′) Var. of LUCIA [< F] Also Lu·cile′.

Lu·cin·da (loo·sin′də) Derived from LUCY. Dim. Cin·dy (sin′dē).

Lu·cre·tia (loo·krē′shə, -shē-ə) Fem. of LUCRETIUS. Also Fr. Lu·crèce (lü·kres′), Ital. Lu·cre·zia (loo·krä′tsyä).

Lu·cy (loo′sē) Var. of LUCIA. Also Fr. Lu·cie (lü·sē′).

Lu·el·la (loo·el′ə) Meaning and origin uncertain. Also Lou·el′la.

Lu·i·sa (loo·ē′zä) Ital. form of LOUISA. Also Ger. Lu·i·se (loo·ē′zə).

Lu·lu (loo′loo) Dim. of LOUISE.

Lyd·i·a (lid′ē·ə) She of Lydia. [< Gk.]

Ma·bel (mā′bəl) Short for AMABEL. Dim. Mab (mab).

Mad·e·leine (mad′ə·lin, -lān, Fr. má·dlen′) Var. of MAGDALENE. [< F] Also Mad·e·line (mad′ə·lin, -līn).

Madge (madj) Dim. of MARGARET.

Mae (mā) Var. of MAY.

Mag (mag) Dim. of MARGARET. Also Mag′gie.

Mag·da·lene (mag′də·lēn, mag′də·lē′nē) Woman of Magdala. [< Hebrew] Also Mag·da·len (mag′də·lən), Mag·da·le·na (mag′də·lē′nə; Sp. mäg ′thä·lā′nä). Dims. Le·na (lē′nə), Mag·da (mag′də).

Mai·sie (mā′zē) Dim. of MARGARET. [< Scot.]

Mal·vi·na (mal·vī′nə, -vē′-) Meaning and origin uncertain.

Ma·mie (mā′mē) Dim. of MARGARET.

Man·dy (man′dē) Dim. of AMANDA.

Mar·cel·la (mär·sel′ə) Fem. of MARCELLUS. Also Fr. Mar·celle (mär·sel′).

Mar·cia (mär′shə) Fem. of Marcius, var. of MARCUS.

Mar·ga·ret (mär′gə·rit, mär′grit) Pearl. [< Gk.] Also Ger. Mar·ga·re·te (mär′gä·rā′tə), Ital. Mar·ghe·ri·ta (mär′·gä·rē′tä), Ital., Sp. Mar·ga·ri·ta (mär′gä·rē′tä). Dims. Gret′a, Gretch′en, Madge, Mag, Mag′gie, Ma′mie, Meg, Me′ta, Peg, Peg′gy, Ri′ta.

Marge (märj) Dim. of MARJORIE. Also Mar′gie, Marj.

Mar·ger·y (mär′jər·ē) Var. of MARGARET.

Mar·got (mär′gō; Fr. mȧr·gō′) Var. of MARGARET. [< F] Also Mar′go.

Mar·gue·rite (mär′gə·rēt′; Fr. mȧr·gə·rēt′) Var. of MARGARET. [< F]

Ma·ri·a (mə·rī′ə, -rē′ə; Ger., Ital. mä·rē′ä) Var. of MARY. [< L] Also Sp. Ma·rí·a (mä·rē′ä).

Mar·i·an (mar′ē·ən, mâr′-) Var. of MARION.

Mar·i·anne (mâr′ē·an′) From MARY and ANNE. Also Mar·i·an·na (mâr′ē·an′ə).

Ma·rie (mə·rē′; Fr. mȧ·rē′) Var. of MARY. [< F]

Mar·i·et·ta (mâr′ē·et′ə, mar′-) Dim. of MARIA.

Mar·i·gold (mar′ə·gōld, mâr′-) From the name of the flower.

Mar·i·lyn (mar′ə·lin, mâr′-) Var. of MARY.

Mar·i·on (mar′ē·ən, mâr′-) Var. of MARY.

Mar·jo·rie (mär′jər·ē) Var. of MARGARET. Also Mar′jo·ry. Dims. Marge, Mar′gie, Marj.

Mar·lene (mär·lēn′; Ger. mär·lā′nə) Var. of MAGDALENE.

Mar·sha (mär′shə) Var. of MARCIA.

Mar·tha (mär′thə) Lady. [< Aramaic] Also Fr. Marthe (mȧrt), Ital., Sp. Mar·ta (mär′tä). Dims. Mar′ty, Mat′tie, Mat′ty.

Mar·y (mâr′ē) Meaning uncertain. [< Hebrew] Dims. May, Min′nie, Mol′ly, Pol′ly.

Ma·til·da (mə·til′də) Mighty battle maiden. [< Gmc.] Also Ma·thil·da (mə·til′də), Ger. Ma·thil·de (mä·til′də). Dims. Mat′tie, Mat′ty, Pat′ty, Til′da, Til′lie, Til′ly.

Maud (môd) Contr. of MAGDALENE. Also Maude.

Mau·ra (môr′ə) Irish form of MARY. Also Maur·ya (môr′·yə).

Mau·reen (mô·rēn′) Dim. of MAURA.

Ma·vis (mā′vis) From the name of the bird, or the Irish fairy queen Maeve or Mab.

Max·ine (mak·sēn′, mak′sēn) Fem. of MAX. [< F]

May (mā) Dim. of MARY.

Meg (meg) Dim. of MARGARET.

Mel·a·nie (mel′ə·nē) Black. [< Gk.]

Me·lin·da (mə·lin′də) Var. of BELINDA.

Me·lis·sa (mə·lis′ə) Bee. [< Gk.]

Mer·ce·des (mər·sā′dēz, -sē′-, mûr′sə·dēz; Sp. mer·thä′thäs) Mercies. [< Sp.]

Mer·cy (mûr′sē) From the abstract noun.

Me·ta (mā′tə, mē′-) Dim. of MARGARET. [< G]

Mi·gnon (min′yon, Fr. mē·nyôn′) Dainty. [< F]

Mil·dred (mil′drid) Moderate power. [OE] Dims. Mil′·lie, Mil′ly.

Mil·li·cent (mil′ə·sənt) Power to work. [< Gmc.] Also Mil′i·cent.

Mi·mi (mē′mē) Fr. dim. of WILHELMINA.

Mi·na (mē′nə) Dim. of WILHELMINA.

Mi·ner·va (mi·nûr′və) From the name of the Roman goddess of wisdom.

Min·na (min′ə) Dim. of WILHELMINA.

Min·nie (min′ē) Memory or love [< Gmc.]; also, dim. of MARY.

Mi·ran·da (mi·ran′də) Admirable. [< L]

Mir·i·am (mir′ē·əm) Var. of MARY. [< Hebrew]

Moi·ra (moi′rə) Var. of MAURA.

Mol·ly (mol′ē) Dim. of MARY. Also Moll.

Mo·na (mō′nə) Noble. [< Irish]

Mon·i·ca (mon′ə·kə) Adviser. [< L]

Mu·ri·el (myoŏr′ē·əl) Myrrh. [< Gk.]

Myr·na (mûr′nə) Meaning and origin uncertain.

Myr·tle (mûrt′l) From the plant name.

Na·dine (nā·dēn′, nə-; Fr. nȧ·dēn′) Hope. [< F < Russ.]

Nan (nan) Dim. of ANN.

Nan·cy (nan′sē) Dim. of ANN.

Nan·nette (na·net′) Dim. of ANN. [< F] Also Na·nette′.

Na·o·mi (nā·ō′mē, nā′ō·mē) Pleasant. [< Hebrew]

Nat·a·lie (nat′ə·lē) Christmas child. [< L] Also Russ. Nat·ta·sha (nä·tä′shə).

Nell (nel) Dim. of ELEANOR, ELLEN, or HELEN. Also Nel′·lie, Nel′ly.

Net·tie (net′ē) Dim. of ANTOINETTE, HENRIETTA, or JEANNETTE. Also Net′ty.

Ni·cole (ni·kōl′; Fr. Nē·kôl′) Fem. of Nicolas, Fr. form of NICHOLAS.

Ni·na (nī′nə, nē′-) Dim. of ANN. [< Russ.]

Ni·ta (nē′tə; Sp. nē′tä) Dim. of JUANITA. [< Sp]

No·na (nō′nə) Ninth. [< L]

No·ra (nôr′ə, nō′rə) Dim. of ELEANOR, HONORA, LEONORA. Also No′rah.

No·reen (nôr′ēn, nô·rēn′) Irish dim. of NORA.

Nor·ma (nôr′mə) Pattern. [< L]

Oc·ta·vi·a (ok·tā′vē·ə) Fem. of OCTAVIUS.

Ol·ga (ol′gə) Holy. [< Russ. < Scand.]

O·live (ol′iv) Var. of OLIVIA.

O·liv·i·a (ō·liv′ē·ə) She of the olive tree: prob. an epithet of the goddess Athena. [< L] Dims. Liv′i·a, Liv′ie.

O·lym·pi·a (ō·lim′pē·ə) She of Olympus. [< L < Gk.]

O·pal (ō′pəl) From the name of the gem.

O·phel·ia (ō·fēl′yə) Help. [< Gk.]

Ot·ti·lie (ot′ə·lē) Fem. of OTTO. [< Ger.]

Pam·e·la (pam′ə·lə) ? Invented by Sir Philip Sidney Dim. Pam.

Pan·sy (pan′zē) From the name of the flower.

Pa·tience (pā′shəns) From the abstract noun.

Pa·tri·cia (pə·trish′ə) Fem. of PATRICK. Dims. Pat, Pat′sy, Pat′ty.

Paul·a (pô′lə) Fem. of PAUL.

Pau·lette (pô·let′) Fr. fem. dim. of PAUL.

Pau·line (pô·lēn′) Fem. of PAUL. [< F] Also Lat. Pau·li·na (pô·lī′nə).

Pearl (pûrl) From the name of the jewel.

Peg (peg) Dim. of MARGARET. Also Peg′gy.

Pe·nel·o·pe (pə·nel′ə·pē)　Weaver.　[< Gk.]　Dim. **Pen′ny.**

Per·sis (pûr′sis)　She of Persia.　[< Gk.]

Phi·lip·pa (fi·lip′ə, fil′ə·pə)　Fem. of PHILIP.

Phoe·be (fē′bē)　Bright; shining: an epithet of Artemis. [< Gk.]　Also **Phe′be.**

Phyl·lis (fil′is)　Green bough or leaf.　[< Gk.]　Also **Phil′lis.**

Pol·ly (pol′ē)　Dim. of MARY.

Pop·py (pop′ē)　From the name of the flower.

Por·tia (pôr′shə, pōr′-)　Fem. of *Porcius,* name of a Roman clan.　[< L]

Pris·cil·la (pri·sil′ə)　Ancient.　[< L]

Pru·dence (prōōd′ns)　From the abstract noun.　Dim. **Prue.**

Queen·ie (kwē′nē)　Derived from QUEEN, used as dim. of REGINA.

Ra·chel (rā′chəl; *Fr.* rȧ·shel′)　Ewe or lamb.　[< Hebrew]　Dims. **Rae, Ray.**

Ra·mo·na (rə·mō′nə)　Fem. of *Ramón,* Sp. form of RAYMOND.

Re·ba (rē′bə)　Short for REBECCA.

Re·bec·ca (ri·bek′ə)　Ensnarer.　[< Hebrew]　Dim. **Beck′y.**

Re·gi·na (ri·jē′nə, -jī′-)　Queen.　[< L]

Re·née (rə·nā′, rā′nē, rē′nē)　Reborn.　[< F]

Rhe·a (rē′ə)　From the name of the Greek goddess.

Rho·da (rō′də)　Rose.　[< Gk.]

Ri·ta (rē′tə)　Dim. of *Margarita,* Ital. and Sp. form of MARGARET.

Ro·ber·ta (rə·bûr′tə)　Fem. of ROBERT.　Dims. **Bert, Bob′·bie, Bob′by.**

Rob·in (rob′in)　From the name of the bird, or from the masc. name.

Ro·chelle (rə·shel′)　Stone or small rock.　[< F]

Ron·ny (ron′ē)　Dim. of VERONICA.　Also **Ron′nie.**

Ro·sa (rō′zə)　Var. of ROSE.　[< L]

Ro·sa·bel (rō′zə·bel)　Beautiful rose.　[< L]

Ro·sa·lie (rō′zə·lē)　Little rose.　[< L]　Also **Ro·sal·ia** (rō·zāl′yə, -zā′lē·ə).

Ros·a·lind (roz′ə·lind)　Fair rose.　[< Sp.]　Also **Ros·a·lin·da** (roz′ə·lin′də).

Ros·a·line (roz′ə·lin, -līn, -lēn, rō′zə-)　Var. of ROSALIND.　Also **Ros′a·lyn** (-lin).

Ros·a·mond (roz′ə·mənd, rō′zə-)　Famous protector. [< Gmc.]　Also **Ros′a·mund, Ro·sa·mun·da** (rō′zə·mun′də).

Ros·anne (rōz·an′)　From ROSE and ANNE.　Also **Ros·an·na** (rōz·an′ə), **Rose·anne′, Rose·an′na.**

Rose (rōz)　From the name of the flower.　Also **Ro·sa** (rō′zə; *Fr.* rō·zȧ′; *Ger.* rō′zä; *Ital.* rō′zä; *Sp.* rō′sä).

Rose·mar·y (rōz′mâr′ē, -mə·rē)　From the plant name.　Also **Rose·ma·rie** (rōz′mə·rē).

Row·e·na (rō·ē′nə)　? From the name of an ancient Celtic goddess.

Rox·an·a (rok·san′ə)　Dawn of day.　[< Persian]　Also **Rox·an′na,** *Fr.* **Rox·ane** (rôk·san′).　Dim. **Rox′y.**

Ru·by (rōō′bē)　From the name of the jewel.

Ruth (rōōth)　Companion.　[< Hebrew]

Sa·bi·na (sə·bī′nə)　A Sabine woman.　[< L]

Sa·die (sā′dē)　Dim. of SARAH.

Sal·ly (sal′ē)　Dim. of SARAH.

Sa·lo·me (sə·lō′mē)　Peace.　[< Hebrew]

San·dra (san′drə, sän′-)　Dim. of ALEXANDRA.

Sar·ah (sâr′ə)　Princess.　[< Hebrew]　Also **Sar·a** (sâr′ə). Dims. **Sa′die, Sal′ly.**

Sel·ma (sel′mə)　Fair　[< Celtic], or a fem. dim. of ANSELM.

Se·re·na (sə·rē′nə)　Serene.　[< L]

Shar·on (shar′ən, shâr′-)　Of Sharon.　[< Hebrew]

Shei·la (shē′lə)　Irish form of CECILIA.

Shir·ley (shûr′lē)　From an English surname; orig. a place name.

Sib·yl (sib′əl)　Prophetess.　[< Gk.]　Also **Syb′il.**

Sid·ney (sid′nē)　From an English surname.　Also **Syd′ney.**

Sig·rid (sig′rid; *Ger.* zē′grit; *Norw.* sē′grē)　Conquering counsel.　[< Gmc.]

Sil·vi·a (sil′vē·ə)　Var. of SYLVIA.

Si·mone (sē·mōn′)　Fr. fem. of SIMON.

So·fi·a (sō·fē′ä)　Ger., Ital., and Sw. form of SOPHIA.

Son·ia (sōn′yə)　Russ. dim. of SOPHIA.　Also **Son′ya.**

So·phi·a (sō·fī′ə, -fē′ə)　Wise.　[< Gk.]　Also **So·phie** (sō′·fē; *Fr.* sô·fē′)　Dims. **So′phie, So′phy.**

So·phro·ni·a (sə·frō′nē·ə)　Prudent.　[< Gk.]

Sta·cie (stā′sē)　Orig. dim. of ANASTASIA.　Also **Sta′cy.**

Stel·la (stel′ə)　Star.　[< L]

Steph·a·nie (stef′ə·nē)　Fem. of STEPHEN.　Also **Steph·a·na** (stef′ə·nə), *Fr.* **Sté·pha·nie** (stā·fä·nē′).

Su·san (sōō′zən)　Var. of SUSANNAH.　Dims. **Sue, Su′sie, Su′zy.**

Su·san·nah (sōō·zan′ə)　Lily.　[< Hebrew]　Also **Su·san′·na, Su·zanne** (sōō·zan′; *Fr.* sü·zaṅ′).　Dims. **Sue, Su·ky** (sōō′kē), **Su′sie, Su′zy.**

Syb·il (sib′əl)　Var. of SYBIL.

Syl·vi·a (sil′vē·ə)　Of the forest.　[< L]　Also **Sil′vi·a.**

Tab·i·tha (tab′ə·thə)　Gazelle.　[< Aramaic]

Te·re·sa (tə·rē′sə, -zə); *Ital.* tā·rā′zä; *Sp.* tä·rā′sä)　Var. of THERESA.　[< Ital. & Sp.]　Dims. **Ter′ry, Tess, Tes′sie.**

Thal·ia (thăl′yə, thal′-)　Flourishing; blooming.　[< Gk.]

The·a (thē′ə)　Goddess.　[< Gk.]

Thel·ma (thel′mə)　? Var. of SELMA.

The·o·do·ra (thē′ə·dôr′ə, -dō′rə)　Fem. of THEODORE. Dims. **Do′ra, The′da, The′o.**

The·o·do·sia (thē′ə·dō′shə)　Gift of God.　[< Gk.]

The·re·sa (tə·rē′sə, -zə)　She who reaps.　[< Gk.]　Also *Fr.* **Thé·rèse** (tā·râz′)　Dims. **Ter′ry, Tess, Tes′sie.**

Til·da (til′də)　Dim. of MATILDA.

Til·ly (til′ē)　Dim. of MATILDA.　Also **Til′lie.**

Ti·na (tē′nə)　Dim. of CHRISTINA.

Tri·na (trē′nə)　Dim. of KATRINA.

Trix·ie (trik′sē)　Dim. of BEATRICE or BEATRIX.　Also **Trix, Trix′y.**

Tru·dy (trōō′dē)　Dim. of GERTRUDE.

U·na (yōō′nə)　One.　[< L]

Un·dine (un·dēn′, un′dēn)　She of the waves.　[< L]

U·ra·ni·a (yōō·rā′nē·ə)　From the name of the Greek goddess of heaven, the muse of astronomy.

Ur·su·la (ûr′syə·lə, -sə-)　Little she-bear.　[< L]

Va·le·ri·a (və·lir′ē·ə)　Fem. of *Valerius,* name of a Roman clan.　Also **Val·er·ie** or **Val·er·y** (val′ər·ē), *Fr.* **Va·lé·rie** (vȧ·lā·rē′).　Dim. **Val.**

Va·nes·sa (və·nes′ə)　Butterfly.　[< Gk.]

Ve·ra (vir′ə)　Faith　[< Slavic], or truth　[< L].

Ver·na (vûr′nə)　Short for *Laverna,* var. of LAVERNE.

Ve·ron·i·ca (və·ron′i·kə)　True image.　[< LL]　Also *Fr.* **Vé·ro·nique** (vā·rô·nēk′).　Dim. **Ron′nie, Ron′ny.**

Vic·to·ri·a (vik·tôr′ē·ə, -tō′rē·ə)　Victory.　[< L]　Also *Fr.* **Vic·toire** (vēk·twár′).　Dim. **Vick′y.**

Vi·o·la (vī′ō·lə, vī·ō′lə, vē-)　Violet.　[< L]

Vi·o·let (vī′ə·lit)　From the name of the flower.

Vir·gin·ia (vər·jin′yə)　Fem. of *Virginius,* name of a Roman clan.　Also *Fr.* **Vir·gi·nie** (vēr·zhē·nē′).　Dim. **Gin′ny.**

Viv·i·an (viv′ē·ən, viv′yən)　Lively.　[< L]　also **Viv′i·en,** *Fr.* **Vi·vienne** (vē·vyen′).

Wan·da (wän′də)　Shepherdess or roamer.　[< Gmc.]

Wen·dy (wen′dē)　Dim. of GWENDOLYN.

Wil·hel·mi·na (wil′hel·mē′nə, wil′ə-; *Ger.* vil′hel·mē′nä)　Fem. of *Wilhelm,* Ger. form of WILLIAM.　Dims. **Mi′na, Min′na, Wil′la, Wil′ma.**

Wil·la (wil′ə)　Dim. of WILHELMINA.

Wil·ma (wil′mə)　Dim. of WILHELMINA.

Win·i·fred (win′ə·frid, -fred)　White wave or stream. [< Welsh]　Dim. **Win′nie.**

Yo·lan·a (yō·lan′də)　Meaning uncertain.　[? < OF]　Also **Yo·lan′de** (-də).

Y·vonne (i·von′, ē-)　Meaning uncertain.　[< F]

Ze·no·bi·a (zi·nō′bē·ə)　She who was given life by Zeus. [< Gk.]

Zo·e (zō′ē)　Life.　[< Gk.]

Business
Law

Business law deals with legal rules and principles of primary interest to the business community. Because of the complexity of modern business, the laws affecting businesses necessarily reach into diverse areas. Many of the laws are difficult and technical. Nevertheless, the person going into business or already in business should gain at least some familiarity with basic regulations and principles.

Although not a substitute for legal advice, such basic knowledge of the law allows the business person to make intelligent decisions and to foresee problems that may actually require legal advice or assistance. The following material provides an introduction to key concepts of business law.

Establishing a Business: Formats

Typically, the person going into business wants to be the sole owner of a particular enterprise. The simplicity of sole ownership, or *sole proprietorship*, is attractive. Whether the owner plans to add partners or employees later, it is usually possible simply to "set up shop."

The two main alternatives to sole proprietorship are the *partnership* and the *corporation*. In the former, two or more persons work together in a business enterprise, often on the basis of a partnership agreement. With a corporation (a separate legal entity) one or more persons can conduct business operations without taking responsibility for the debts of the business. Both the partnership and the corporation can take variant forms while maintaining a basic organizational pattern.

The Sole Proprietorship

The person operating a sole proprietorship owns the business in his or her own name. But the business can operate under the owner's name or a trade or business name: for example, "Mary Jones DBA ("doing business as") Jones Dress Shoppe."

Many states require that the person going into business as a sole proprietor register an assumed or fictitious business name under state and county laws. Typically, such a law is called an Assumed Names Act. Specific information is usually required, including the business name and the names and addresses of all persons who have an interest in the business.

There are many advantages to creating a sole proprietorship. The owner can keep track of the business' progress from month to month or year to year. He or she can control operating costs and can often avoid much of the paperwork required by other business arrangements. The sole proprietor remains the boss. If the business stays small, fulltime employees may not be needed.

Partnerships

A partnership is somewhat more complicated than the sole proprietorship but is less complex than the corporation. Formed, by two or more persons, the partnership is considered a business entity but not a tax entity. In other words, each partner must pay taxes on all partnership income.

Some other factors identify the partnership. Each partner, for example, is responsible for the debts and credit arrangements contracted by any other partner. Thus, any member of the partnership can bind the business and all its partners to business contracts and transactions. Professional partnerships were once common, but today, because most state laws allow doctors, lawyers, accountants, and other professional people to incorporate, the professional corporation has become a more standard form of business association. All members of such corporations share in the tax benefits.

The partnership agreement is sometimes informal—even oral. But ideally, partners should decide the terms of their agreement with the aid of a lawyer (see below).

A partnership has many of the advantages of a sole proprietorship but may also face similar strictures or regulations. An assumed or fictitious name must be registered. Generally, the various states levy no taxes on the right to function as a partnership or franchise. In addition, the partnership does not have to keep the general records required of a corporation. Unlike a corporation, which can stay in business indefinitely, a partnership usually dissolves on the death, retirement, or withdrawal of a partner.

The four main types of partnerships, each of which is used in specific circumstances, are the limited partnership, the joint venture, syndication, and the joint stock company.

Limited Partnership

In a limited partnership some or most of the partners can avoid the unlimited liability that characterizes the general partnership. Usually, the limited partnership has one general partner and a number of limited partners. The general partner is liable for the debts of the partnership and often for supervising all operations; the limited partners are liable only to the extent that they have invested in the partnership.

In those states that have Uniform Limited Partnership acts, the persons establishing a limited partnership must file a certificate of registration, usually with the secretary of state. The certificate gives the name of the business, its location, the names of the limited partners, and the partners' liabilities, powers, privileges, and duties.

A typical limited partnership may buy, manage, and sell apartment houses, hotels, and other kinds of real estate. The partners invest capital in the business and receive shares of the profits according to the amounts invested. A hybrid between the general partnership and the corporation, the limited partnership does not have to file articles of incorporation. Nor is it required to keep min-

982 Business Law

utes or other records of operations. The limited partnership must, however, file partnership tax returns.

The Joint Venture

When two or more persons agree to join in a single transaction or project their partnership is called a joint venture. The partners in a joint venture agree to control and manage the business together. They must also agree to share profits and losses, usually on the basis of each partner's ownership interest in the property or project.

Thus, for example, should two or more persons jointly buy and own property but for some reason do not share its profits or losses, this would not be considered a joint venture. A joint venture occurs only when the parties intend to do business as a *partnership*.

Syndication

A joint venture that involves a large number of individuals is usually known as a *syndicate*. As with all true joint ventures, syndication requires tax filing as a partnership.

A public offering to sell a syndicate share or interest in a property or business requires special legal handling. The Securities and Exchange Commission (SEC) has ruled that such sales to the public fall under securities laws.

Joint Stock Company or Association

Some partnerships operate under articles of association that provide for the issuance of a share or certificate to each partner. The certificates represent each partner's interest. In such a joint stock company or association, the articles of association also provide that a group of partners, called the board of directors, will control the business. Individual partners cannot bind the other partners by entering into separate transactions in the name of the company or association. But participants in the association are responsible for all the legal debts and obligations incurred by the association as a whole.

Federal and state securities laws apply to sales of joint stock company shares or certificates. But, under the typical articles of association, individual partners can transfer their certificates without the consent of other participants. The articles normally specify how long the association will exist and provide that the death or withdrawal of any member will not affect the association.

The Corporation

Many consider the corporation the ideal way to organize a business. By law, the person or persons who own and operate the corporation are separate from it.

The corporation may be small or large. A small corporation is usually referred to as a *close*, or *closely held*, *corporation*. An individual may own all the stock in such a corporation and manage it alone or jointly with a few others.

But many corporations have hundreds or thousands of shareholders or stockholders. In either case the corporation files its own tax returns and pays its own taxes. Corporate meetings must be held and minutes kept for each meeting. To do business under an assumed name, the corporation—like the sole proprietorship or the partnership—must register according to state law.

The corporation, as a flexible form of business organization, generally has the following advantages:

• The persons who invest in the corporation have no liability for corporate debts or obligations beyond the amounts each has invested.

• By selling stock and securities the corporation can raise substantial sums to finance business programs and projects.

• By corporate charter, the corporation can exist "in perpetuity"—in effect, forever.

• Because the typical corporation of any size has a manager or board of directors who run day-to-day operations, the individual shareholders need not bother with the details of such operations.

The corporate format does have some disadvantages. For example, the corporation must pay taxes on its earnings. Later, when these earnings are distributed to shareholders as *dividends,* the shareholders must claim them in their own tax returns and pay additional taxes on them. Careful planning, however, can reduce or eliminate the hazards of such "double taxation." And many corporations find ways to enjoy other major tax advantages.

Another disadvantage of the corporation is that, as a separate legal entity, it must operate in accordance with specific laws and keep certain records. Some expense is involved in incorporating, and an application for a corporate charter must be accompanied by initial tax statements and other documentation in addition to the necessary filing fees.

Two other kinds of corporations or corporation-like business structures should be noted: the Subchapter S corporation and the business trust.

Subchapter S Corporations

The unique advantage of the Subchapter S structure is that such a business may operate as a corporation while following partnership tax regulations. This type of business organization, permitted under federal and most state laws, thus avoids corporate taxes while operating in corporate form.

All the income or losses of a Subchapter S corporation are taxed individually according to the amount invested by each shareholder. The shareholders have immunity from personal liability for the debts and obligations of the firm. At the same time they avoid double taxation. But a "Sub-S" corporation can have no more than 35 shareholders.

The Business Trust

The business trust is taxed as a corporation and enjoys many of the advantages of a corporation. It can be formed and operated under federal and most state tax laws. The death or withdrawal of a shareholder does not terminate the trust, nor do the shareholders have personal liability for the trust's debts and obligations.

Also known as a Massachusetts business trust or a common trust, the business trust has been defined as an unincorporated business organization. The trust document specifies that property is to be held and managed by the trustee for the benefit of beneficiaries who hold transferable certificates. The beneficiaries receive the profits from management of the property. The states that provide for the legal creation of business trusts generally require that a declaration of trust be filed before beneficiaries' shares can be sold or distributed. Transfers or sales of trust shares must take place in accordance with the securities laws of the various states.

Launching a Business: Documents and Procedures

"I'm forming a partnership with a close friend. Do I need an agreement in writing?"

This is a question that lawyers hear frequently. In nearly all cases the answer is Yes, definitely. Prospective partners may be members of the same family, old friends, or business associates, but the written agreement is nonetheless appropriate.

The reasons for drawing up such a partnership agreement are much the same as for preparation of a pre-incorporation agreement. Both help to build a foundation for the enterprise and to reduce the possibility of later misunderstandings and disagreements.

The Partnership Agreement

Most states have adopted what is called the Uniform Partnership Act to guide partners as they set up and conduct their businesses. Such an act has some common-sense provisions. For example, it may provide that if *no* partnership agreement exists, the partners will share equally in the business' profits. The law may also specify that each partner will, in the absence of an agreement, have an equal voice in the operation of the business.

An agreement in writing takes precedence over such legal provisions. The partners may specify in the agreement the percentage of profits each will receive or who will supervise which aspects of the business. For instance, Partner A may receive 60% of the profits and Partner B may supervise the business' sales force. Someone who brings special knowledge or expertise to the business, or who will have to work unusually long hours, may receive advance recognition. The agreement might also specify special compensation arrangements.

Other Terms of the Agreement

In general, the terms of a partnership should deal with basics as well as with the finer points of the business relationship. The basics include the name chosen for the business, the rights and duties of each partner, and the objectives of the business. The agreement can also make note of the investments or other assets contributed by each partner, such as real estate, vehicles, or office equipment.

The business name deserves some thought. Do not choose a name that could be confused with another company name already in use. It is important to select a name that will characterize the business, give it stature, or make it sound attractive or impressive. Some partnerships have names formed from partners' initials or names.

The agreement should typically indicate how long the partnership will last. If all partners feel it is appropriate, the partnership may be of indefinite duration. In such a case, the partnership will continue until it is dissolved by one or more of the partners or until one of them dies or withdraws.

Many partnership agreements state that the partnership will continue for ten or ten years. At the end of the specified period the agreement can be renewed if desired. Other clauses typically appear in partnership agreements. For example, the agreement gives the starting and ending dates of the partnership's fiscal year. Specific provisions may indicate how any partner can exercise the right to examine the partnership's books, make specific banking arrangements, and lay out procedures for hiring employees, with special attention in many cases to employment contracts.

Contribution of Capital

It is important that the partnership agreement indicate how much capital or other assets each partner has contributed. Insofar as possible, all such assets should be

listed. They can include not only those items mentioned but leases, patent rights, and special equipment of one kind or another. All such items rank as *capital*.

In any partnership one partner may contribute one kind of capital whereas another may contribute another kind. The agreement should specify clearly what is being contributed and what its value is. Some evaluations may have to be made by rough estimate; in other cases an appraiser should be hired to place a value on a partner's noncash contribution.

The terms of the agreement should spell out, with dates or target times if possible, when partners' contributions are due. One partner may invest cash at the time the partnership comes into being; another may contribute funds a year later; a third may make working premises available from the time the partnership goes into business. A partner may agree to invest in the business the first $10,000 of his share of the partnership's profits. Another may loan money to the partnership under specified conditions of repayment. The conditions should include the interest rate to be charged.

Partners' Responsibilities and Powers

In most partnerships, the various partners perform different but complementary jobs. The roles to be played by the partners should be described in the agreement as clearly as possible.

Making such terms clear beyond the possibility of misunderstanding may be impossible. But the effort should be made. The management responsibilities and the amount of time to be devoted to each can obviously vary widely. Insofar as a determination of such details can be made, it should be.

Court cases involving partners frequently hinge on the question of whether one partner is devoting enough time and effort to the business. That fact alone suggests the importance of the advance thinking put into this part of the agreement. A number of related questions should receive attention. Is each partner to be allowed to engage in other business activities while also working for the partnership? To what extent? What other business activities? Will the partners be allowed to take part only in other activities that are completely different from the partnership business?

The answers to such questions may call for thought—in particular where the question of partners' participation in other businesses is concerned. Will a partner investing in and operating a business identical to that of the partnership be in competition with his or her partners? Such questions lie at the heart of many court decisions.

Profits and Losses

The most basic method of providing for equitable distribution of profits and losses is simple. The partners simply agree to distribute profits according to the investment of each partner in the business. A partner who contributes 25% of the funding for the partnership, receives 25% of the profits. He or she also bears 25% of the losses, if any.

That formula need not control in any given case. For any group of partners, another approach may be more appropriate. The important thing is that the partners work the formula out in advance and include it in the agreement. A special formula may work best. In one case three partners establishing a real estate management business agreed that in the first year Partner A would receive half of the first $50,000 in profits while partners B and C would receive $12,500 each. From that point on the partners would divide the profits equally.

Among other important financial questions, salaries and expense accounts rank high. Unless the agreement contains provisions on salaries, for example, no partner would be entitled to anything more than a share of the profits. Yet a salary might be appropriate if one partner is to spend more time on partnership business than the others. As for expense accounts, is any partner to have unlimited privileges? Will any partner receive advances from company funds to cover business travel and entertainment?

Dissolution of the Partnership

The terms of the partnership agreement should specify under what conditions dissolution may take place. Some examples suggest possibilities. In one case a partnership agreement provided that the business would continue if any of the four partners died or had to withdraw for health or other reasons. Thus, the agreement, in effect, ensured that a new partnership would take the place of the original one. The agreement also specified how the partner leaving the business, or that partner's family, would be compensated in case of death or withdrawal. The partnership share could, of course, have substantial value.

In another case a partnership agreement contained a buy–sell clause. That provision, common to most partnership agreements, specified the conditions under which the remaining partners could buy the share of a partner who was withdrawing for any reason. A method of establishing the value of a partnership share was also specified; an arbitrator familiar with business appraisals would be named to conduct an evaluation.

Such terms, in a sense, help to resolve legal problems in advance. They can, however, be even more specific. Some buy–sell provisions provide for a departing partner's right to select an arbitrator. The remaining partner or partners have the same right. After the two arbitrators have selected a third person to assist in the arbitration, the three jointly decide on the value of a partnership share. The decision is then final and binding.

A recommended way to make sure that surviving partners will be able to buy the share of a deceased or ailing partner is to buy life insurance on the lives of all the partners. The insurance provides the cash needed for the surviving partners to buy the deceased's share.

Corporate Agreements

Three friends have decided to go into business and incorporate. What now?

First, remember that state law controls the establishment of corporations. But different laws refer to the basic documents of incorporation in different ways. The *articles of incorporation* may, for example, be called the *articles of agreement* or *charter,* or the *certificate of incorporation.*

Second, in forming their corporation they will be making decisions regarding the ownership of the business, issuance of stock shares, contributions of the various owners, and other matters. As in the case of partnership agreements, the more thorough the answers to such questions are, the better the chance that the business will succeed.

There will be four directors. Because the state in which this corporation is formed requires a minimum of three directors, they have fulfilled a basic requirement. Many other states, as noted, would allow an individual to incorporate alone. But either way, as a group or singly, the procedures are essentially the same from state to state,

with one exception. An individual incorporating as a one-person firm would not prepare a preincorporation agreement, but for four persons incorporating together, such an agreement is a good idea even though it is not required by law.

The Preincorporation Agreement

The agreement serves as an opportunity for each of the associates to make all the key decisions in advance. They can focus on areas of agreement and areas of potential disagreement and can make sure they are thinking alike. In this way they build for future business success.

The preincorporation agreement contains much that can be found in the typical partnership agreement: the corporate name, the purposes of the business, and so on. But the preincorporation agreement should address other questions as well, such as the stock to be issued, the number of shares to be authorized, the price per share, and the number of shares each associate will buy. The agreement should also specify any restrictions on transfers of shares and the procedures under which the corporation would buy the shares of an associate who dies or decides to sell out.

If such procedures are listed, the method of funding the purchases of associates' shares should be noted. Life insurance offers one effective method of funding in case of death.

Information as to how the corporation will be managed and controlled should appear in the agreement. It is important to specify the number of directors, to agree on what work each associate will perform in the corporation, and to establish salary schedules.

The name of the corporation has legal status. Most states require that the name be different enough from others already in use to avoid confusion. Because a name that is identical or very similar to any existing one may be rejected by state authorities, it is advisable to check with the governmental agency responsible for the registry of names to make sure the desired choice is available. If the name is already being used, it may nevertheless be possible to use it or a variation of it anyway, by obtaining permission from the owner of the name. Such permission should be in writing.

Most states require that the business name include a word or abbreviation indicating that the business is incorporated. The words that appear most often are *Incorporated, Corporation, Company, Limited,* or their abbreviated forms: *Inc., Corp., Co.,* and *Ltd.*

The Articles of Incorporation

With the preincorporation agreement on paper, the articles of incorporation can follow. This is the document that actually establishes the corporation: the corporate charter, filed with a state agency and usually in a standard form according to instructions issued by the agency itself. The agency may be the office of the secretary of state. In some states the articles of incorporation have to be filed with the local county clerk as well.

Other information in the articles of incorporation parallels that of the preincorporation agreement to some extent. The corporate name appears, followed by a statement of corporate purposes. Whereas some states require only a statement that the new firm will engage exclusively in lawful activities, others need specific information. The statement should be worded broadly so that the corporation has reasonable latitude in its later selection of business activities.

The business purposes of many young corporations change with time. In such cases the corporations simply file an amendment to the articles of incorporation to broaden the range of corporate purposes.

The articles of incorporation state how many shares of stock will be issued, where the firm's main office will be, and who in the corporation can be served with lawsuit papers. Most states do not require that all the shares of stock be issued at once. For that reason many corporations issue only enough shares to cover immediate and foreseeable needs. In some states lawsuit papers have to be filed with the secretary of state, who then serves the corporate officer designated in the articles of incorporation.

Finally, the articles of incorporation should note the names and addresses of the incorporators. The period for which the corporation is formed should be given if it is not perpetual. The state collects a filing fee when the incorporators register the articles.

Normally, the beginning corporation faces five other basic challenges.

1. To draw up bylaws. Much more complete than the articles of incorporation, the bylaws detail the rights and powers of the corporate officers, shareholders, and directors. The bylaws also give a time and place for the annual meetings, specify how notices of meetings will be sent out, indicate what constitutes a quorum, make provision for special meetings, and state how shareholders can act without formal meetings.

The bylaws touch on other subjects as well. They note how many directors the corporation has—usually a president, secretary, and treasurer; who the directors are and how they are elected; and what their powers and responsibilities are. In other provisions the bylaws describe the stock certificates, name the person or persons authorized to sign contracts and insert the corporate books and records, and specify how the bylaws can be amended.

2. To adopt the bylaws and elect the first board of directors. This task falls to the shareholders of the new corporation, the persons holding ultimate power. In a meeting held after the state has approved the articles of incorporation, the shareholders adopt the bylaws and elect the corporation's first board of directors.

In a small corporation, the same people may be officers, directors, and shareholders. When they set the ground-rules under which the business will operate, they are in effect making rules for themselves. In a larger corporation, the shareholders set policy but do not take part in day-to-day operations. They meet at least annually—and more frequently if the need arises. The annual meetings provide opportunities to review the corporation's annual report, elect new directors or reelect incumbents, and vote on policy changes.

3. To hold the first directors' meeting. The directors of the new corporation usually meet for the first time after the incorporators' meeting. Among other items of business, the directors elect the corporate officers, consider and ratify contracts, and approve all management plans. The board of directors may also confirm corporate banking arrangements and authorize the issuance of stock.

4. To issue corporate stock. Once the stock has been paid for, the corporation issues certificates that show the name of the corporation, the number of shares that each certificate represents, the type of share, and the name of the individual shareholder. Usually, the corporate president and secretary sign the certificates. If the stock sale is restricted, this information generally appears on the back of each certificate.

5. To make a Subchapter S election. In this step the business founders decide whether they want to be treated, for federal tax purposes, as a Subchapter S corporation. To be eligible to make such an election, the firm cannot have more than 35 shareholders. It must also have only one class of stock. The election must be made during the first 75 days of the tax year. All the shareholders must agree that the election of Subchapter S status should be made.

The Factor of Control

Whether a new business starts as a partnership or corporation, the founders should carefully consider the question of control: of ways and means of maintaining the authority of the founders and protecting their interests in the business.

A number of considerations are involved, such as those framed in the following questions: Who will be allowed to buy, inherit, or otherwise gain ownership of partners' or other shares? How do the controlling parties ensure that they retain management and supervisory responsibility? Who might be admitted to the inner circle in the future?

Retention of control involves complex legal questions. These reinforce the contention that a lawyer should help prepare all the basic business documents. The type of business, the methods by which interests may be transferred to others, possible restrictions on such transfers, employment contracts—all are important. Particular questions may hinge on interpretations of state laws dealing with restrictions on transfers of shares, on transfers of business control, and on other questions.

Some widely used methods of retaining control include the following:

1. Restrictions on transfers of interest. In general, the law frowns on restraints on sales or on assignments of business or property rights. But shareholders in a corporation can, for example, agree on a stock transfer restriction. Under such an agreement, the other partners or shareholders have the right of first refusal before a business share or stock can be sold to a third party outside the business. Where multiple shares are for sale, the other shareholders can usually buy in proportion to the total number of shares each owns.

Stock transfer restrictions generally appear in corporate bylaws. They are also printed on share certificates. The printed restriction puts a prospective purchaser on legal notice that resale restrictions exist.

2. Employment Contracts. An employment contract, or a series of them, between a partnership and its partners or between a corporation and its officers ranks as another way to retain control of a business. The contract spells out the rights, duties, and obligations of both parties—company and individual. The contract may restrict the individuals' ownership rights.

An employment contract may have other purposes. It may, for example, help the owner of a business protect patents or inventions with which the employee becomes acquainted. The contract may also provide details on a complicated compensation plan, or protect against competition from the employee should he or she leave the firm's employment.

3. Voting Rights. As businesses grow and add employees, shareholders, and others, voting rights become extremely important. A majority of shareholders might, in a given case, try to assume control by changing the business' purpose, design, or basic direction. Various kinds of voting restrictions can be used to protect the business operation, among them these:

• A corporation may provide for voting and non-voting stock, for voting rules that ensure that the minority group is represented on the board of directors, and for elections of different directors in specified years.

• Shareholder agreements may require that shareholders vote their stock in a certain way. Shareholders might, for example, be able to vote only for other shareholders for the board of directors. "Outsiders" would be excluded. It should be noted, however, that such restrictions on voting or transfers of shares could inhibit many investors from buying the company's stock.

• Using a voting trust agreement, a number of shareholders may join together to give a lesser number, called the trustees, the right to vote on all the shares. The trustees themselves can agree on how the votes will be cast.

• Where state laws permit, the charter and bylaws of a corporation may provide for special requirements on quorums and shareholder votes. For example, a two-thirds majority might be needed to change the business' bylaws.

• A corporation's bylaws, a partnership agreement, or a shareholder agreement might make arbitration an alternative where disagreements arise. The arbitration option would be invoked in case of a voting deadlock.

4. Buy–Sell Agreements. A buy–sell agreement among the shareholders of a corporation ensures that the corporation can buy the stock of a deceased stockholder. The estate of the deceased has to sell the stock; the corporation has an obligation to buy. To ensure the corporation's ability to repurchase such shares, the firm must have a *stock retirement program*. Under an alternative program, called a *cross-purchase plan*, other stockholders can buy the shares of the deceased.

Establishing a price for stock to be purchased from the estate of a deceased shareholder may or may not be a problem. If the shares are traded on a regional or national stock exchange, the price quotation for a given day determines the price. In a close corporation, however, the problem of evaluation becomes critical. A mandatory buy–sell agreement always outlines an effective method of determining the price of a share of stock. The methods include the appraisal, the book value, and various other methods.

5. Partnership Buy–Sell Agreement. Under a partnership buy–sell agreement, the estate of a deceased partner has an obligation to offer the decedent's partnership interest for sale to the surviving partner or partners. The agreement should specify the terms of the sale. Both the partners and their spouses should sign the agreement. In many cases, life insurance offers the best method of purchasing the partnership interest of a deceased partner.

Business Contracts

You decide to have your office painted. You sit down with Tom Johnson, a painter, to discuss cost. Tom says he can do the job for $550. He would have the work completed in exactly two weeks. You say, "It's a deal." With those words you have a legally binding contract. All the necessary elements are present:

• Parties competent to contract.
• An offer (Tom's indication that he can do the work at a certain price by a certain date).
• Acceptance (your agreement to pay the $550).
• Consideration. The two of you are exchanging things of value. You have promised to pay $550 and Tom has promised to paint your office.

The Four Elements

Obviously, business contracts are rarely as simple and straightforward as the above example. But all contracts have to share the basic elements or they will not be regarded as contracts under the law.

The requirement that the parties to the contract be competent has special meaning. The contracting parties cannot be minors, for example, under the laws of the state in which the contract is made. Also, the parties must be sane. They must be capable of handling their own affairs.

At the offer stage of contract formulation, the law presumes that one party to the arrangement can provide something of value. In the example, Tom the painter *offered* to paint your office. He told you what the work would cost. He did not say he could *probably* do the work for $550, or that he would need half of that sum down, with the rest to follow on completion of the job; he stated his price.

Your acceptance followed when you said, "It's a deal." Where the second element involves *mutuality of obligation*, the acceptance phase involves *legal consideration:* in this case, what you agree to pay. The legal consideration can be many things besides money or property. An exchange can involve services.

Another type of consideration is known as *detrimental reliance*. You would have created the possibility of such a consideration if you had said to five painters, "I will pay $500 if one of you will paint my office." A painter relies on your promise, paints your office, and can sue you for breach of contract if you do not pay the $500.

Legality of purpose has equally broad legal meanings. No contract is enforceable if its purpose is illegal. But what does illegal mean? If the contract calls for the performance of an immoral or statutorily illegal act, it is unenforceable. The same applies if it goes contrary to a state's public policy. Examples of the latter include contracts to restrain trade, to evade or oppose revenue laws, and to corrupt legislative or judicial bodies.

Breach of Contract

Whether written or oral, a contract that has the four basic elements is enforceable at law. Enforcement becomes an alternative in the case of a *breach of contract* by one party or the other. A lawsuit in such a case seeks to recover whatever damages are suffered because of the breach.

The Uniform Commercial Code (UCC), valid in all states except Louisiana, sets the standards of some key aspects of contract law. The UCC, for example, provides that a written agreement be produced in a breach-of-contract case involving the sale of goods for $500 or more. The agreement need not be extremely detailed. It has only to indicate that the parties agreed on the sale and that such-and-such a quantity was involved. The UCC requires inclusion of such other factors as price, time and place of delivery, and quality of the goods.

Article Two of the UCC deals with the sale or transfer of goods or personal property. It specifies that a "merchant" (a person with special knowledge, skills, and familiarity with a business) has special rights and obligations. He or she has a kind of professional status. Three principal rules apply:

• Between merchants, the law usually requires a written contract where goods valued at more than $500 are sold.
• A merchant's offer to buy or sell goods, made in

writing and signed by the merchant, must be held open for a "reasonable" or specified length of time—and is not revocable during that time.

• A definite, written, and timely expression of acceptance creates a contract between merchants.

Violation of any of the stated UCC rules creates a cause of action—a reason to sue. A successful plaintiff generally receives *compensatory damages*. Insofar as possible, these compensate the plaintiff for damages ensuing from the broken contract. But there are other kinds of damages:

• *Consequential damages*, awarded where a plaintiff proves that a breach of contract had secondary negative effects.

• *Liquidated damages*, awarded when, for example, delay in the delivery of services or goods resulted in day-by-day losses for a plaintiff.

• *Equitable relief* may be invoked by a court to compel a delinquent defendant to deliver on a promise in a contract. A defendant may be required to deliver, for example, a work of art or an item of jewelry as promised in a legal contract.

Required Written Contracts

Under the statutes of frauds enacted by all states, some contracts have to be in writing. Typically, a statute of frauds would require that contracts be written when:

• the ownership of real estate is changing hands;
• real estate is being leased for more than a year;
• someone promises to pay the debt of someone else;
• performance under the contract will take more than a year;
• someone is agreeing to pay a commission for the sale of real estate; or
• a sale of goods, or tangible personal property, is being transacted.

Ordinarily, a contract need not be a formal legal document. A memorandum may be enough. But it should give the names of the parties, information on the subject matter, and the important terms and conditions. The signatures of the contracting parties should appear on the memorandum even though both may not be required legally.

What happens when a statute of frauds states that a contract is required but the parties have proceeded under an oral agreement? A lawsuit may be possible anyway. A suit may be justified, for example, where the oral agreement has been partially performed.

Defenses in a Breach-of-Contract Suit

A defendant in a breach-of-contract suit can utilize any of a variety of defenses. He or she may, depending on the circumstances, claim any of the following:

• That no breach took place.
• That the plaintiff suffered no damages.
• That the contract is invalid because a basic element is missing.
• That the statute of frauds requires a written contract and none exists.
• That the contract is illegal or against public policy and is therefore illegal.
• That the other contracting party misrepresented the facts to induce the defendant to sign the contract.
• That the contracting parties made a mutual mistake that resulted in a misunderstanding of what was to be sold or done.

The Business and the Consumer

Currently, the consumer protection movement is gathering momentum. Based on the concept that the consumer needs the protection of the law, the movement tries to prevent companies from exerting pressure on the consumer, or from taking advantage of him or her. Because the consumer is in fact vulnerable when buying goods, borrowing funds, or investing for financial gain, a business owner should know some basics of consumer law.

Consumers have protection today in a number of areas, including the following:

• methods by which goods are presented, including during sales and in advertising;
  • packaging and labeling of goods;
  • methods used in selling goods;
  • credit sales; and
  • protection of consumer defenses.

Many more such areas could be listed. But these are among the most important. Each can be discussed separately.

Deceptive Practices in Sales

Various government agencies have passed statutes, rules, and regulations that forbid or restrict deceptive practices in the sale of consumer goods. Endorsements by persons with high public exposure, for example, may not be false or misleading. In a typical case an athlete or movie star will state publicly (perhaps on television or radio) that a specific product is safe or of outstanding quality. If the product does not meet the described standards, the endorser has taken part in deception. A lawsuit may be the consumer's best remedy.

Even if not intended to do so, a company's advertising may in effect deceive potential buyers. The deception need not involve an intentionally fraudulent act; the only test today is whether the buyer was misled.

The Federal Trade Commission (FTC) repeatedly challenges advertisers regarding misleading or deceptive advertising. The FTC also tries to protect consumers in other ways. The Public Health Cigarette Smoking Act, for example, requires that a health warning appear on each package of cigarettes sold. Radio and TV can no longer carry cigarette advertising. Other forms of cigarette advertising have to display the health warning prominently.

In advertising goods for sale at retail, store owners and others once used various forms of deception. One, called the "bait and switch," involved ads for "specials" that were not in stock in sufficient quantity to meet anticipated demand—or that were not in stock at all. The advertiser counted on "baiting" the customer into the shop or store and then selling him or her some other item or items, usually at higher prices.

The laws of many states outlaw such practices. Such laws may also prohibit "going out of business" advertising when the business is not really being discontinued, "fire sales" when there has been no fire, or "lost our lease" sales when no lease has been lost.

Packaging and Labeling

Many federal laws have dealt in recent years with deception in labeling and packaging. Among the laws are the Fair Packaging and Labeling Act; the Fair Products

Labeling Act; and the Food, Drug, and Cosmetics Act. In addition, various state and federal laws have outlawed the use of such terms as "full," "jumbo size," and "giant size."

Legislation in existence also requires specifics on labels. Under the Fair Products Labeling Act, a product label must identify the type of product, the name and place of business of the manufacturer, the packer or distributor, the net quantity of all the contents, and the net quantity of one serving if the label also gives the number of servings. Both the FTC and the U.S. Department of Health and Human Services have authority to require additional information or disclosures on a label.

Other legislation establishes standards and protects consumers in various ways. Food, drugs, and cosmetics receive special attention. The federal Food and Drug Administration (FDA) regulates labeling and packaging of all such items. The FDA also has authority to prevent "quackery" in medicine and drugs and to investigate "miracle drug" claims.

Approval and Testing of Goods

Many products are sold with a guarantee, tag, or other indication that the products have been tested and approved by some agency or organization. The "seal of approval" or tag means that the product has been tested and approved for normal consumer use. The seller has violated a warranty made to the consumer and may be liable for fraud if the product has not actually been tested and approved.

Tests and approvals, or tests alone, may precede the sale of some products. Products involving fire and electrical safety features may undergo tests by manufacturers' associations or testing companies for insurance purposes. Successful testing means a product meets industry safety standards. Some private and industry testing agencies, including consumer organizations that publish test results in their own magazines, simply report what their tests have revealed. No conclusions are drawn.

Some magazines also accept product advertising that includes "money back" guarantees. The guarantee requires only that the price of a product be refunded or that it be replaced if the product is defective. If a consumer is injured by the defective item, the magazine or organization giving its approval may be liable under the expanding concept of *product liability*.

Controls on Methods of Selling Goods

Many laws today regulate the ways in which merchants can sell their goods. The goal is always the same: to prevent violations of consumer rights. But some laws also provide for means of punishing the fraudulent or unlawful merchant. In two areas in particular, fair disclosure of contract terms and sales by mail, legislative action has created a network of protections for buyers or consumers.

Fair Disclosure of Contract Terms

The Consumer Credit Protection Act, better known as the "Truth in Lending Act," was designed to let the consumer know exactly what the credit offered by a lender will cost. Knowing what one lender's rates are, the consumer can "comparison shop" for a better "deal." This is true whether the individual is taking out a mortgage loan to buy a house, buying furniture or an auto-

mobile, paying for home improvements on the installment plan, or charging meals, gasoline, or repair costs.

The Truth in Lending Act does not apply if no interest or other charges are added to the basic cost of a given item. The Act does ensure the availability of information on the two key factors in the cost of credit—the finance charge, or the amount paid to obtain credit, and the annual percentage rate (APR), the percentage of interest paid over a year's time. The finance charge includes not only the interest to be paid but also any service, carrying, or other charges. The APR must be computed for the consumer on the total cost of credit.

The Truth in Lending Act deals also with advertising. Where an ad mentions one feature of credit, such as the amount of the down payment, it must also mention all the other important terms.

Mail-Order Sales

More and more businesses are offering goods and services through the mail. Federal laws protect the consumer from mail fraud. State statutes may also prohibit mail-order fraud or deceit. Because most mail-order sales involve small amounts, the consumer may find it difficult or impossible to recover losses.

In mail-order sales the consumer has the following rights:
• to know when shipment of the merchandise can be expected;
• to have the merchandise shipped within 30 days;
• to cancel an order when merchandise is not shipped within 30 days;
• to be notified of delays and to have a free means of replying, such as a postage-free postcard;
• to agree to a new shipping date; and
• to have any payment returned if 30 days elapse and the merchandise is not shipped.

Where a person receives free samples or items mailed by charitable organizations seeking contributions, the recipient can, as he or she wishes, regard the merchandise as a gift.

Control of Methods of Payment

Protective laws regulate the methods by which payments may be made or demanded by a creditor on a consumer sale. Some state laws provide that if a creditor accepts payment in a form other than cash or check, the creditor takes a chance. State laws may also provide that installment payments have to be applied to the oldest unpaid portions of a debt. The payment sent by a debtor who is three months delinquent on an open credit account must go toward payment of the oldest monthly charge.

Both federal and state laws regulate accelerated and "balloon" final payments. At one time unscrupulous creditors or lenders could make the last payment in a monthly series larger than the debtor could pay. The lender could then repossess the merchandise when the debtor defaulted. Most laws now specify that if the final payment is double the average of the earlier scheduled payments, the debtor has the right to refinance the final payment on terms similar to those of the original transaction.

Other Financial Areas

In many other money areas the laws protect the consumer without prejudicing the rights of the businessperson. Credit cards, for example, the symbols of the so-called "cashless society," can no longer be issued to persons who have not applied for them. Also, in case of loss of a credit card, the owner cannot be held liable for more than $50 for purchases made illegally by the finder. But such purchases must have been made before the owner has notified the company issuing the card. If they are made after that time, the card holder cannot be held liable at all.

In contract sales, the "fine print" on the reverse sides of some agreements once provided that the buyer waived some legal protections. Under some recent consumer statutes, however, the buyer cannot inadvertently waive all such defenses. Where a household appliance is defective, for example, under the consumer protection statutes of many states the buyer has the right to withdraw from the contract.

Wages and salaries make up another sensitive area.

In general, the laws provide that the right to earn a living and support one's family takes precedence over any right to garnish or attach a person's earnings.

Federal and state laws contain many other provisions designed to protect the consumer. For example, the methods by which debts may be collected are strictly controlled. Credit reporting, which affects the individual's credit rating and, often, his or her ability to get a job and to purchase needed items, falls under the provisions of the Fair Credit Reporting Act of 1970. The Act applies only to personal, household, and family credit, and not to business or commercial credit. Very importantly, the Act gives the person whose credit-worthiness is in question the right to find out the name and address of the reporting agency. The individual then has the right to have any errors in the report corrected.

Business Math

Business Math is, as the term implies, the math that meets the needs of business. It differs from the math used in our daily lives only in the respect that its methods have been adapted to the special requirements of business. The businessman wants to know at what price to sell an article in order to make a certain profit, how much he may deduct from a bill if he pays for an order in cash, whether it is to his advantage to invest his money in one kind of stock or another. These and other practical problems that the businessman faces constitute the bulk of our Business Math section. In addition, we present at the outset some helpful hints that will save time in performing the mathematical computation that is required in solving the business problems later in the section.

It is suggested that the steps given here in solving problems be followed exactly, and that all information required be written down and clearly labeled. Only later, when the methods of solution can be readily applied, should short cuts be taken and steps be performed without indicating them on paper.

Easy Methods of Calculation

Short Cuts in Addition

In adding a column of figures, speed and rapidity will be attained by following these suggestions:

1. Take a combination of numbers which adds to 10 and add them as 10.

Example

Add:

$$\begin{matrix} 8 & 7 & 5 \\ 2 & 8 & 6 \\ 2 & 8 & 4 \\ 2 & 8 & 3 \\ 2 & 2 & 2 \\ 8 & 9 & 5 \\ \hline 2 \; 8 & 4 & 5 \end{matrix}$$

Add the right-hand column from the top down as follows: 5, 15, 25, carry 2.

Add the second column from the top down as follows: 2, 9, 17, 25, 35, 44, carry 4.

Add the third column from the top down as follows: 4, 14, 16, 18, 28.

2. Take any combination of numbers which total 10 or less and add them as that total. For example, add 2, 3, 4 as 9; add 2, 2, 3 as 7; add 1, 2, 3 as 6; add 2, 4, 2 as 8.

3. Add 9 as 10 and then subtract 1. For example, $65 + 9 = 75 - 1 = 74$.

Short Cuts in Multiplication

1. To multiply an integer (whole number) by 10 or a power of 10. **Rule:** Add one zero to the number to be multiplied for each zero in the multiplier.

Example

65×10	$= 650$	Add 1 zero.
301×100	$= 30,100$	Add 2 zeros.
750×1000	$= 750,000$	Add 3 zeros.
$236 \times 10,000$	$= 2,360,000$	Add 4 zeros.
$185 \times 100,000$	$= 18,500,000$	Add 5 zeros.

2. To multiply an integer by 5. **Rule:** Multiply by 10; take ½ of the answer.

Example

$$650 \times 5$$
$$650 \times 10 = 6500$$
$$\tfrac{1}{2} \text{ of } 6500 = 3250, \textit{Answer}$$

3. To multiply an integer by 15. **Rule:** Multiply by 10; take ½ the answer and add both.

Example

$$786 \times 15$$
$$786 \times 10 = \quad 7860$$
$$\tfrac{1}{2} \text{ of } 7860 = \quad \underline{3930}$$
$$11,790, \textit{Answer}$$

4. To multiply an integer by 11. **Rule:** Multiply by 10; add the original number.

Example

$$295 \times 11$$
$$295 \times 10 = 2950$$
$$295$$
(original
number) $\quad \underline{295}$
$$3245, \textit{Answer}$$

5. To multiply an integer by 9. **Rule:** Multiply by 10; subtract the original number.

Example

$$293 \times 9$$
$$293 \times 10 = 2930$$
$$293$$
(original
number) $- \underline{293}$
$$2637, \textit{Answer}$$

6. To multiply an integer by 50, 25, 12½. **Rule:** Multiply by 100; then multiply the answer by ½, ¼, or ⅛ as the case may be because 50, 25, and 12½ are ½, ¼, and ⅛ of 100 respectively.

Example 1

$$275 \times 50$$
$$275 \times 100 = 27,500$$
½ of $27,500 = 13,750, \textit{Answer}$

Example 2

$$326 \times 25$$
$$326 \times 100 = 32,600$$
¼ of $32,600 = 8150, \textit{Answer}$

Short Cuts in Division

1. To divide an integer by 10 or a power of 10. **Rule:** Move the decimal point in the number to be divided as many places to the left as there are zeros in the divisor.

Example 1

$$875 \div 10$$
$$875 \div 10 = 87.50, \textit{Answer}$$

Example 2

$$\$975.85 \div 1000$$
$$\$975.85 \div 1000 = \$.97585, \textit{Answer}$$

Exercise

1. $800 \times 10 =$ **9.** $285 \times 5 =$
2. $900 \times 50 =$ **10.** $88 \times 11 =$
3. $1756 \times 100 =$ **11.** $99 \times 9 =$
4. $288 \times 25 =$ **12.** $1725 \times 15 =$
5. $300 \times 15 =$ **13.** $836 \times 1000 =$
6. $756 \div 10 =$ **14.** $19.5 \div 10 =$
7. $97.8 \div 100 =$ **15.** $28.65 \div 100 =$
8. $42.6 \div 1000 =$

Answers:
1. 8000   **9.** 1425
2. 45,000   **10.** 968
3. 175,600   **11.** 891
4. 7200   **12.** 25,875
5. 4500   **13.** 836,000
6. 75.6   **14.** 1.95
7. .978   **15.** .2865
8. .0426

Devices for Checking the Four Fundamental Operations

Addition

Add the column from top to bottom. Write the answer. Check by adding the column from bottom to top.

Subtraction

Add the answer or remainder to the subtrahend. The result should equal the minuend.

Operation	Check
86 minuend	68 remainder
− 18 subtrahend	+ 18 subtrahend
68 remainder	86 minuend

Multiplication

Multiply the multiplicand by the multiplier. Then make the multiplicand the multiplier and the multiplier the multiplicand, and multiply.

Operation	Check
85 multiplicand	15 multiplicand
× 15 multiplier	× 85 multiplier
425	75
85	120
1275 product	1275 product

A second check is to divide the product by the multiplier. The answer should be the multiplicand. Or divide the product by the multiplicand and the answer should be the multiplier.

Check

$$\begin{array}{r} 85 \text{ multiplicand} \\ \text{multiplier } 15 \overline{)\ 1275} \text{ product} \\ 120 \\ \hline 75 \end{array}$$

$$\begin{array}{r} 15 \text{ multiplier} \\ \text{multiplicand } 85 \overline{)\ 1275} \text{ product} \\ 85 \\ \hline 425 \\ 425 \end{array}$$

Division

Multiply the answer or quotient by the divisor. The product should equal the dividend.

Operation

$$\begin{array}{r} 416\frac{2}{3} \text{ quotient} \\ \text{divisor } 18 \overline{)\ 7500} \text{ dividend} \\ 72 \\ \hline 30 \\ 18 \\ \hline 120 \\ 108 \\ \hline 12 \\ 18 \end{array} = \frac{2}{3}$$

Check

$$\begin{array}{r} 416\frac{2}{3} \text{ quotient} \\ 18 \text{ divisor} \\ \hline 3\overline{)\ 36} \\ 12 \\ 3328 \\ 416 \\ \hline 7500 \text{ dividend} \end{array}$$

Percentage

The term "per cent" is derived from the Latin. It means "by the hundred." To illustrate, take the number 1 and divide it into 100 parts. Each part is $\frac{1}{100}$ of 1 and may be expressed in three ways, as follows:

1. Common fraction—$\frac{1}{100}$.
2. Decimal fraction—.01.
3. Per cent—1%.

The value of percentage lies in its use as a basis of comparison in various business transactions. It acts as a common denominator to which everything may be reduced, thus enabling the comparison to be made.

Per Cent, Fractions, and Decimals

1. To change a decimal to per cent. **Rule:** Move the decimal point two places to the right and then write a per cent sign.

Example 1

Change .15 to per cent.
.15 = 15%

Example 2

Change .075 to per cent.
.075 = 7.5%

Example 3

Change 6 to per cent.
6.00 = 600%

2. To change a common fraction to per cent. **Rule:** Change the common fraction to a decimal; then change the decimal to a per cent.

Example 1

Change $\frac{3}{8}$ to a per cent.

$$\frac{3}{8} = 8\overline{)3.000}$$
$$.375$$
$$.375 = 37.5\% \text{ or } 37\frac{1}{2}\%$$

Example 2

Change $\frac{17}{19}$ to a per cent.

$$\frac{.89\frac{9}{19}}{\frac{17}{19} = 19\overline{)17.00}}$$
$$\frac{15\ 2}{18\ 0}$$
$$\frac{17\ 1}{\frac{9}{19}}$$
$$.89\frac{9}{19} = 89\frac{9}{19}\%$$

Exercise

Express the following as per cent:

1. $\frac{1}{2}$ 6. .0075
2. $\frac{4}{3}$ 7. .02½
3. $\frac{5}{6}$ 8. .3
4. $\frac{11}{20}$ 9. $\frac{15}{28}$
5. .08   10. .006

Answers:
1. 50%   6. .75% or $\frac{3}{4}$%
2. 133⅓%   7. 2½%
3. 83⅓%   8. $\frac{3}{10}$% or 30%
4. 55%   9. 53$\frac{4}{7}$%
5. 8%   10. $\frac{3}{5}$% or .6%

3. To change a per cent to a decimal. **Rule:** Move the decimal point two places to the left and take away the per cent sign.

Example 1

Express 17% as a decimal.
17% = .17

Example 2

Express 8.5% as a decimal.
08.5% = .085

Example 3

Express 525% as a decimal.
525% = 5.25

Example 4

Express .75% as a decimal.
75% = .0075

Exercise

Express the following per cents as decimals:

1. 2½%   6. .5%
2. 37½%   7. .05%
3. 650%   8. .25%
4. 7.5%   9. 16.75%
5. 18.8%   10. 123%

Answers:
1. .025   6. .005
2. .375   7. .0005
3. 6.50   8. .0025
4. .075   9. .1675
5. .188   10. 1.23

4. To change a per cent to a common fraction. **Rule:** Change the common fraction to a decimal; then to a per cent.

Example 1

Change 25% to a common fraction.
$$25\% = .25$$
$$.25 = \frac{25}{100} = \frac{1}{4}, \text{ Answer}$$

Example 2

Change 150% to a common fraction.
$$150\% = 1.50$$
$$1.50 = 1\frac{1}{2} \text{ or } \frac{3}{2}, \text{ Answer}$$

Exercise

Change the following to common fractions:

1. 50%   6. 75%
2. 20%   7. 80%
3. 40%   8. 62½%
4. 33⅓%   9. 87½%
5. 16⅔%   10. 12½%

Answers:
1. ½   6. ¾
2. ⅕   7. ⅘
3. ⅖   8. ⅝
4. ⅓   9. ⅞
5. ⅙   10. ⅛

Problems in Percentage

In computing a problem in percentage, the number or quantity upon which the per cent is to be computed is called the *base,* the per cent is called the *rate,* and the product of the base and the rate is called the *percentage.* All problems in percentage fall into three groups or cases.

Case I. Given the base and the rate, to find the percentage. **Rule:** Base × Rate = Percentage.

Example 1

Find 25% of 7800.

Change 25% to .25; then multiply:
7800 × .25 = 1950, *Answer*

Example 2

Find 250% of 19,600.

19,600 × 2½ = 49,000, *Answer*

Exercise

Find the percentage:

1. 15% of 980
2. 12½% of 640
3. 33⅓% of 999
4. 125% of 260
5. 18% of 480

6. ¾% of 1200
7. .75% of 1600
8. 2½% of 1640
9. 10% of 968
10. 19% of 200

Answers:

1. 147
2. 80
3. 333
4. 325
5. 86.4

6. 9
7. 12
8. 41
9. 96.8
10. 38

Case II. Given the base and the percentage, to find the rate. **Rule:** Divide the percentage by the base.

Example

17 is what per cent of 29?
$^{17}/_{29}$ = .58$^{18}/_{29}$ = 58$^{18}/_{29}$%

Exercise

1. 25 is what per cent of 800?
2. 16 is what per cent of 280?
3. 180 is what per cent of 36,000?
4. 17.5 is what per cent of 85.6?
5. 18.4 is what per cent of 2.86?

Answers:

1. 3⅛%
2. 5$^5/_7$%

3. ½% or .5%
4. 20$^9/_{214}$%

5. 643$^{51}/_{143}$%

Case III. Given the percentage and rate, to find the base. This is called the indirect case. **Rule:** Percentage divided by rate equals the base.

Example

18 is 3% of what number?
18 ÷ .03 = 600, *Answer*

Exercise

1. 25 is 20% of what number?
2. 180 is 50% of what number?
3. 27 is 75% of what number?
4. 260 is 80% of what number?
5. 1704 is 12% of what number?

Answers:

1. 125
2. 360

3. 36
4. 325

5. 14,200

Aliquot Parts

Arithmetical calculations may be made much easier if the aliquot parts of 100% are used. By an aliquot part is meant a number which can be divided into another number so that the answer will be a whole number. Thus 25% is an aliquot part of 100% because 100% divided by 25% equals 4. It would be well to memorize the aliquot parts of 100%, and multiples of these aliquot parts for greater ease and speed in performing problems.

Aliquot Parts of 100%

50% = ½	87½% = ⅞	70% = $^7/_{10}$
25% = ¼	1% = $^1/_{100}$	80% = ⅘
75% = ¾	10% = $^1/_{10}$	33⅓% = ⅓
6¼% = $^1/_{16}$	20% = ⅕	66⅔% = ⅔
12½% = ⅛	30% = $^3/_{10}$	16⅔% = ⅙
37½% = ⅜	40% = ⅖	8⅓% = $^1/_{12}$
62½% = ⅝	60% = ⅗	83⅓% = ⅚

Example

Find 37½% of 800.
⅜ of 800 = 300, *Answer*

Exercise

Compute the following, using aliquot parts:

1. 20% of 850
2. 87½% of 864
3. 12½% of 960
4. 75% of 1200
5. 33⅓% of 963
6. 10% of 786
7. 16⅔% of 282
8. 66⅔% of 1296

9. 80% of 9000
10. 8⅓% of 2460
11. 83⅓% of 288
12. 62½% of 1200
13. 6¼% of 3200
14. 5% of 870
15. 50% of 1900

Answers:

1. 170
2. 756
3. 120
4. 900
5. 321
6. 78.6
7. 47
8. 864

9. 7200
10. 205
11. 240
12. 750
13. 200
14. 43½
15. 950

Aliquot Parts of $1.00

It will be noticed that the aliquot parts of $1.00 are the same as those of 100%. Therefore the same fractional equivalents may be used at all times.

Example

Find cost of 840 yards of silks @ 62½¢ per yd.
62½ = ⅝
⅝ of 840 = 525, *Answer*

Exercise

Compute the following, using aliquot parts:

1. 160 yds. @ 50¢
2. 980 yds. @ 10¢
3. 750 yds. @ 40¢
4. 138 lbs. @ 33⅓¢
5. 280 lbs. @ 62½¢
6. 1780 lbs. @ 60¢
7. 66⅔ lbs. @ 90¢
8. 16⅔ lbs. @ 48¢

9. 75 yds. @ 88¢
10. 40 yds. @ $2.50
11. 270 lbs. @ 66⅔¢
12. 726 ft. @ 16⅔¢
13. 6480 yds. @ 62½¢
14. 22½ lbs. @ 40¢
15. 256 ft. @ 6¼¢

In problems 7 to 10, the base and the rate may be interchanged so that problem 7 will read 90 lbs. @ 66⅔¢ and will be done in the same manner as problems 1 to 6.

Business Uses of Math

Discounts on Invoices

Invoices and Terms

After a sale is made, the seller sends an *invoice* to the buyer. On it is listed the date, terms, goods and quantity sold, the price of each item, the extensions, and the total. The terms are most important because they are the conditions of payment. Some examples of terms are:

C.O.D.—Collect or cash on delivery.
Cash—Cash is to be paid on the date of the sale.
On account—Payment to be made within a reasonable time after the end of the month.
E.O.M.—End of the month.
n/30—Net 30 days after the date of the invoice (net means no discounts).
2/10 n/30—2% discount if paid within 10 days after the date of the invoice, net after 10 days and within 30 days.
2/5 1/15 n/30—2% discount if paid within 5 days, 1% discount if paid after 5 days but within 15 days; net if paid after 15 days and within 30 days.

Trade and Cash Discounts

Discounts on invoices are of two kinds, cash discounts and trade discounts. Cash discounts are those mentioned under terms, an inducement to the customer to pay his bill ahead of time. The customer is the one who decides whether he will take advantage of the discount. Trade discounts differ from cash discounts because they are deducted, not by the customer, but by the seller.

Manufacturers and wholesalers print catalogues once or twice a year. They are expensive. In order to bring the catalogue price down to the market price, they send their customers discount sheets, on which they list discounts given on the catalogue price to bring it down to the market price. If the price drops, two or more trade discounts may be given.

Problem 1: The Rowe Co. offers to sell a dining room suite for $250 less 20%, 10%, and 10%. The Wilson Co. offers a similar suite for $260 less 40%. Which is the better offer and by how much?

Rowe Co.

$250	List Price or Catalogue Price
50	Trade Discount 20%
$200	Balance
20	Trade Discount 10%
$180	Balance
18	Trade Discount 10%
$162	Net Cost

Wilson Co.

$260	List Price
140	Trade Discount 40%
$156	Net Cost

$162	Net Cost—Rowe Co.
156	Net Cost—Wilson Co.
$6	Wilson Co. offer better.

Problem 2: The Domestic Rug Co. received an invoice on November 10 amounting to $1280 less 20%, and 5%, terms 3/10 n/60. The invoice was paid November 20. Find the amount of the payment.

$1280.00	List Price
256.00	Trade Discount 20%
$1024.00	Balance
51.20	Trade Discount 5% (½ of 10%)
$ 972.80	Balance
29.18	Cash Discount 3%
$ 943.62	Net Cost

Problem 3: A dealer purchased a bicycle for $32.40 less 33⅓%, terms 2/10 n/30, plus a freight charge of 90¢. The invoice was dated March 15 and paid March 25. Find the amount of the payment.

$32.40	List Price
10.80	Trade Discount 33⅓%
$21.60	Balance
.43	Cash Discount 2%
$21.17	Net Cost
.90	Freight Charge
$22.07	Total Cost

Note: The discounts are taken only on the invoice; they cannot be taken on the freight charge or any other buying expense.

Exercise

1. Find net cost of invoice of $1375 less 20% and 10%.
2. Find total cost of invoice of $45 less 20% and buying expense of $2.10.
3. Find net cost of invoice dated April 16, terms 2/10 n/30, amounting to $1500 less 20% and 10% and paid on April 26.
4. A dealer offeres a rug for $60 less 30% and 10%. Another offers the same quality for $60 less 40%. Which offer is better and how much?

Answers:
| 1. $990 | 3. $1058.40 |
| 2. $38.10 | 4. Second offer by $1.80 |

Single Discount Equivalent to a Series of Trade Discounts

For ease in computation and for purposes of comparison, it is often desirable to find one discount that is equivalent to a series. The procedure is as follows: Consider the catalogue price as 100%. Multiply this by the first discount and subtract from 100%. Multiply this difference or balance by the second discount and subtract the answer from the balance. Continue this multiplication and subtraction until all the discounts have been taken. The answer will be the net cost. To find the single discount, subtract the net cost from 100%.

Problem: Find one discount equivalent to a series of 30%, 20% and 10%.

100%	List Price
30	Trade Discount 30%
70%	Balance
14	Trade Discount 20% (20% of 70%)
56.0%	Balance
5.6	Trade Discount 10% (10% of 56%)
50.4	Net Cost

100% List Price − 50.4% Net Cost = 49.6%, *Ans.*
Proof: 30% + 14% + 5.6% = 49.6%, *Answer*

Exercise

Find one discount equivalent to the following series:

1. 20% and 10%
2. 30% and 10%
3. 50% and 20%
4. 25% and 20%
5. 37½% and 24%

6. 20%, 10%, and 5%
7. 20%, 10%, and 10%
8. 50%, 25%, and 20%
9. 40%, 30%, 20%, and 10%
10. 50%, 25%, and 10%

Answers:
1. 28%
2. 37%
3. 60%
4. 40%
5. 52½%

6. 31.6%
7. 35.2%
8. 70%
9. 69.76%
10. 66.25%

Commissions

Salesmen are usually paid a percentage of their sales as compensation for their work. This percentage is called *commission*. Commissions are generally paid on the amount of the sales, although in some cases they are calculated on the quantity of merchandise sold. When a salesman is paid commission only, he is on a straight commission basis. If he receives a drawing account, the amount of the drawings is deducted from his total commission at the end of the accounting period, and the balance paid him at that time.

To encourage salesmen to greater efforts, commission may be paid on a graduated basis; that is for example, 10% commission on the first $20,000 of sales and 15% on all sales over $20,000. Inside salesmen are usually paid on a commission and salary basis. Very often, no commission is paid until a stated amount or quota has been sold; commission is then paid on sales over the

quota. The problems that follow deal with each of these phases of selling.

Straight Commission

Problem 1: A salesman sells 2500 yards of silk at $2 per yard. His rate of commission is 2½%. Find his commission.

$$2500 \times \$2 = \$5000, \text{ Sales}$$
$$2\tfrac{1}{2}\% \text{ of } \$5000 = \$125, \text{ Commission}$$

Problem 2: A salesman sells 2500 yards of silk at $2 per yard. His rate of commission is 5¢ per yard. Find his commission.

$$2500 \text{ yards} \times 5¢ = \$125, \text{ Commission}$$

Note that in the first problem the commission was based on price whereas in the second problem it was based on quantity.

Salary and Commission

Problem: A salesman is offered a salary of $50 per week and a commission of 5% on all sales. His sales for the year are $36,000. Find his yearly earnings.

Time	Sales	5% Commission	Salary	Total
1 year	$36,000	$1800	$2600 (52 × $50)	$4400 Answer

Salary, Commission, and Quota

Problem: A salesman is offered a salary of $110 per month and a 6% commission on all sales over $2000 per month. In April, his sales were $1950; in May, $3250; in June, $3375. Find his total earnings.

Time	Salary	Sales	Quota Over $2000	6% Commission	Totals
April	$110	$1950	$ 0	$ 0	$110.00
May	110	3250	1250	75.00	185.00
June	110	3375	1375	82.50	192.50
Totals	$330	$8575	$2625	$157.50	$487.50 Answer

To check the answer, add the vertical totals, then the horizontal totals. The grand total must be the same.
Thus, vertically, 110 + 185 + 192.50 = 487.50
horizontally, 330 + 157.50 = 487.50

Salary, Graduated Commission, and Quota

Problem: Noll, a salesman, receives a salary of $200 per month, 1% commission on all sales, and 2% commission on all monthly sales over $3000. In January his sales were $6000; in February, $4500; in March, $7400. Find his total income for the three months.

Salary, Graduated Commission, and Quota Problem Table

Time	Salary	Sales	On All Sales Com. 1%	Quota Over $3000	Over $3000 Com. 2%	Totals
January	$200	$ 6000	$ 60	$3000	$ 60	$320
February	200	4500	45	1500	30	275
March	200	7400	74	4400	88	362
Totals	$600	$17,900	$179	$8900	$178	$957 Answer

To check the answer of the problem just solved, add the horizontal totals:

$$600 + 179 + 178 = 957.$$

Exercise

In doing these problems use the diagram method of the previous problems. The headings can be found very easily by reading the problem carefully and then heading each column as the problem indicates.

1. Find the commission a salesman receives if his sales are $6500 and the commission is 7%.
2. John Miller, a salesman, receives a monthly salary of $90 and 5% commission on all sales. In addition, he receives 2% on sales over $3000 in any single month. His sales in April were $3850 and in May $2700. Find his total earnings.
3. A salesman has offers of employment from two firms. Kolapep offers him a salary of $100 per month, a commission of 5% in total monthly sales and 2% additional commission on monthly sales in excess of $2000. Cocapep offers him a commission of 8% on the first $1000 of monthly sales, 10% on the next $1000 of monthly sales and 12% on all monthly sales in excess of $2000. If his average sales are $3500 a month, where would he earn more and how much more?
4. The Electric Supply Co. has an agency for the sale of vacuum cleaners. Their commission is $12.50 each for the first 50 cleaners; $15 each for the second 50 cleaners or part thereof; $17.50 each for all over 100 cleaners sold each month. In May, they sold 76 cleaners; in June, they sold 105 cleaners. Find their commission.

Answers:
1. $455
2. $524.50
3. Cocapep is better by $55
4. $2477.50

Commission Merchants

For those people who cannot do their own buying or selling, agents known as commission merchants will attend to all such transactions. They charge a commission for their services, in the same manner as do salesmen. After selling the merchandise, they submit a statement called an *account sales*. After buying the merchandise, they submit a statement called an *account purchase*.

Problem 1: Williams has 860 bushels of potatoes to sell. He can sell them at $2.10 a bushel, with no expense. However, he sends them to a commission merchant who sells 450 bushels at $2.60 and the remainder at $2.25 a bushel. The merchant charges 3¢ a bushel for storage, $36.80 for freight, 1% for insurance, and 3% commission.

A. Find the amount of the net proceeds remitted to Williams.

B. How much does Williams gain or lose by having the merchant sell the potatoes?

A.   **Income**

450 bu. @ $2.60 .... $1170.00
410 bu. @ $2.25 .... 922.50
     Total Proceeds $2092.50

Charges

Storage (3¢ per bu., 860 bu.) .. $25.80
Freight 36.80
Insurance (1% of $2092.50) 20.93
Commission (3% of $2092.50) .   62.78
     Total Charges .... $ 146.31
     Net Proceeds $1946.19

B.   860 bu. @ $2.10 = $1806, Total Proceeds

$1946.19, Net Proceeds—Commission Merchant
1806.00, Total Proceeds
$ 140.19, Gain by sending to commission merchant

Note: All charges or expenses must be subtracted on a sale.

Problem 2: Benton, a sugar broker, purchases 35,000 pounds of sugar for a candy manufacturer at 5.5¢ per pound. Benton's expenses and charges are: handling $23.40, freight 36¢ per hundredweight, commission 5%. Find the total cost of the sugar to the candy manufacturer.

35,000 lbs. sugar @ 5.5¢ per lb. = $1925, Cost

Charges

Handling .... $ 23.40
Freight (36¢ per cwt.—35,000
    lbs. 126.00
Commission (5% of $1925) 96.25
     Total Charges .... $ 245.65
     Total Cost $2170.65

Note: All charges and expenses must be added on a purchase.

Exercise

1. Wilson, a commission merchant, receives 1500 bushels of potatoes to sell. He sold 635 bushels at $1.50; 475 bushels at $1.40; and the remainder at $1.30 a bushel. He charged a commission of 5%. His expenses were: freight charges $84.50, sorting and weighing $38.40, and storage charges of 3¢ per bushel. Find the net proceeds.
2. Harris purchased 50,000 feet of lumber for a builder at $60 per 1000 feet. Freight charges were $150, insurance 1%, trucking $75 and commission 4%. Find the total cost of the lumber to the builder.

3. A fruit farm shipped 100 crates (32 boxes per crate) of strawberries to a commission merchant. He sold 1280 boxes at $.20, 960 boxes at $.15 and the remainder at $.12 per box. Freight charges were $24, storage $22.66, cartage $15.60, commission 5%. Find the net proceeds.

Answers:
1. $1850.37   **2.** $3375   **3.** $427.18

Payrolls

Time Basis

Employees other than salesmen are usually paid on a time basis. So-called white-collar workers such as clerks, bookkeepers, and the like are paid on an annual, monthly, or weekly salary basis. Other workers, especially those who do manual labor, are paid on an hourly basis, with forty hours per week generally regarded as regular time, and everything over forty hours as overtime. In many organizations each employee has a time card on which an accurate record of his time may be kept.

Problem 1: Below is the time card of a worker showing the time he has worked for one week. His regular wage is $1.10 per hour for a 40 hour week.

Day	In	Out	In	Out
Monday	7:00	12:00	1:00	4:00
Tuesday	7:00	12:00	1:00	4:00
Wednesday	7:00	12:00	1:00	4:00
Thursday	7:00	12:00	1:00	4:00
Friday	7:00	12:00	1:00	4:00

A. Find his total wages for the week.
B. His employer deducts 3% for social security and $6.38 for withholding tax. What is his take-home pay?

A.

Day	Hours
Monday	8
Tuesday	8
Wednesday	8
Thursday	8
Friday	8
Total	40
	× 1.10
	$44.00, Total Wages

B. Total wages $44.00

Deductions
Social Security (3%) $1.32
Withholding Tax 6.38
                                       7.70
Take-home pay $36.30

Problem 2: A mechanic is working in a factory where his regular time is 40 hours a week. He is paid time and a half (1½ times) for overtime. His regular wages are $1.50 per hour. Deductions are 3% for social security and $14.25 for withholding tax. Last week he worked 57 hours.

A. Find his total earnings.
B. Find his take-home pay.

A.

Total Time (Hours)	Regular Time (Hours)	1½ Over-Time (Hours)*
57	40	17
		× 1½
		8½
		17
		25½

*(One hour of overtime equals 1½ hours of regular time. Convert overtime to regular time by multiplying by the overtime rate.)

      40   Regular Allowance
      25½   Overtime Allowance
      65½   Total Hours
 × $1.50   Rate
   $98.25, Total Wages

B. Total wages $98.25

Deductions
Social Security (3%) .... $ 2.95
Withholding Tax 14.25
                                17.20
Take-home pay $81.05

Exercise

1. William Randall, a machinist, worked last week as follows: Monday 8 hours, Tuesday 10 hours, Wednesday 11 hours, Thursday 9 hours, Friday 10 hours and Saturday 5 hours. His regular time is 40 hours per week, with time and a half for overtime. His hourly rate is $1.60 per hour. Deductions of 3% for social security taxes and $13.81 for withholding taxes are made.
a. Find his total wages.
b. Find his take-home pay.

2. Hawkins, a mechanic, worked 47 hours last week. His regular time is 40 hours with time and a half for overtime. His hourly rate is $1.40 per hour. Social security tax deduction was 3% and withholding tax was $11.67.
a. Find his total wages.
b. Find his take-home pay.

Answers:
1. a. $95.20   **2.** a. $70.70
    b. $78.53   b. $56.91

Piecework Wages

Another method of compensation depends not on the time worked but on the quantity or pieces which the worker produces. The wage is computed by multiplying the number of pieces by the rate per piece.

Problem: Harris, a dress operator, produces 108 pieces of work during the week. His rate per piece is 35¢. Find his total wages.

      108 × .35 = $37.80, Total Wages

Deductions for social security and withholding tax are computed in the same manner as in time wages.

Averages

By an average is meant a figure which is typical of a group of numbers. Averages are useful in comparing groups of numbers. To find an average, add all the items and divide the total by the number of items.

Problem 1: A salesman's sales per week are $1500, $2000, $3000, $6000, and $2500. Find his average sales for the five weeks.

$$\begin{array}{r} \$1500 \\ 2000 \\ 3000 \\ 6000 \\ 2500 \\ \hline \$15,000 \end{array}$$

$15,000 ÷ 5 = $3000, Average Sales per Week

Problem 2: Clark's average sales for the last 8 weeks of the year were $362.15 a week. For the first 3 weeks of the new year, his sales per week were $415.16, $523.25, and $392.35. Find his average sales per week for the 11 weeks.

$362.15 × 8 = $2897.20, Total sales for 8 weeks

$$\begin{array}{r} 415.16 \\ 523.25 \\ 392.35 \\ \hline \$4227.96, \end{array} \text{ Total sales for 11 weeks}$$

$4227.96 ÷ 11 = $384.36, Average sales per week for 11 weeks

Exercise

1. The Acme Sales Co. had a contest for its salesmen. Potter's average sales for the last 8 weeks of the year were $340. For the first 4 weeks of the new year, his weekly sales were $376, $625, $429, and $374. Find his average weekly sales for the 12 weeks.
2. In the same contest, Wolcott's sales for the last 6 weeks averaged $425. For the first 4 weeks of the new year, his weekly sales were $500, $735, $658, and $695. Find his average weekly sales for the 10 weeks.

Answers:
1. $377   2. $513.80

Simple Interest

Basic Method of Calculation

Interest is the charge made for the use of money for a specified time. The money used is called the *principal*. The per cent is called the *rate*. The rule for calculating interest is:

Principal × Rate × Time = Interest

Problem 1: Find the interest on $600 for 1 year at 6%.

$600 × $\frac{6}{100}$ × 1 = $36, Interest

Problem 2: Find the interest on $1200 for 90 days at 4%.

$1200 × $\frac{4}{100}$ × $\frac{90}{360}$ = $12, Interest

Note that for purposes of easier and faster computation the year is considered to have 360 days, and each month, regardless of how many days it actually has, is considered to have only 30 days.

Exercise

Find the interest:

	Principal	Time	Rate %	Rate %	Rate %
1.	$1600	6 months	6	4	3
2.	1200	3 months	6	3	2
3.	2400	2 months	6	5	3
4.	720	60 days	6	1	4
5.	840	80 days	6	1	2
6.	480	40 days	6	5	4
7.	220	120 days	6	3	2
8.	180	9 months	6	8	4½
9.	2800	8 months	6	2	3
10.	960	30 days	6	4	3

Answers:

1.	$ 48	$32	$24
2.	18	9	6
3.	24	20	12
4.	7.20	1.20	4.80
5.	11.20	1.87	3.73
6.	3.20	2.67	2.13
7.	4.40	2.20	1.47
8.	8.10	10.80	6.08
9.	112	37.33	56
10.	4.80	3.20	2.40

The Sixty-Day Method

To find interest on sums of money when the time is less than a year, the *sixty-day method* is used. This method is based upon the fact that 60 days (2 months) are ⅙ of one year. Therefore, if the annual interest rate is 6%, the interest charge for 60 days is ⅙ of 6% or 1%. **Rule:** To find the interest on any sum of money for 60 days (2 months) take 1% of that amount.

Problem 1: Find the interest on $1200 for 60 days at 6%.

1% of $1200 = $12.00, Interest for 60 days
Proof: $1200 × $\frac{6}{100}$ × $\frac{60}{360}$ = $12.

Finding the interest for 60 days is the basis for computing interest for other periods of time. For example, the interest for 30 days is half of that for 60 days; for 15 days, a quarter; for 10 days, a sixth, etc.

Problem 2: Find the interest on $1200 at 6% for the days shown below:

Interest on $1200 for 60 days at 6%	=	$12.00
Interest for 30 days (½ of 60)	=	6.00
Interest for 20 days (⅓ of 60)	=	4.00
Interest for 15 days (¼ of 60)	=	3.00
Interest for 12 days (⅕ of 60)	=	2.40
Interest for 10 days (⅙ of 60)	=	2.00
Interest for 6 days (¹⁄₁₀ of 60)	=	1.20

From this point, it is easy to find the interest for any number of days. Always find the interest for 60 days first. That is the base. Then, break up the days for which the interest is to be calculated into aliquot parts of 60 and add the interest for those days. The following illustrations will show just what is to be done:

Problem 3: Find the interest on $1800 for 90 days at 6%.

90 = 60 + 30.

Interest on $1800 for 60 days at 6% =	$18
Interest on $1800 for 30 days at 6% =	9
Interest on $1800 for 90 days at 6% =	$27

Problem 4: Find the interest on $1500 for 47 days at 6%.

A. 47 = 20 + 20 + 6 + 1

or

B. 47 = 30 + 15 + 2.

A.

Interest on $1500 for 60 days at 6% = $15.00	
Interest on $1500 for 20 days at 6% =	$5.00
Interest on $1500 for 20 days at 6% =	5.00
Interest on $1500 for 6 days at 6% =	1.50
Interest on $1500 for 1 day at 6% =	.25
Interest on $1500 for 47 days at 6% =	$11.75

B.

Interest on $1500 for 60 days at 6% = $15.00	
Interest on $1500 for 30 days at 6% =	$7.50
Interest on $1500 for 15 days at 6% =	3.75
Interest on $1500 for 2 days at 6% =	.50
Interest on $1500 for 47 days at 6% =	$11.75

Problem 5: Find the interest on $270 for 56 days at 6%.

A. 56 = 30 + 20 + 6.

or

B. 56 = 20 + 20 + 12 + 4.

or

C. 56 = 60 − 4.

A.

Interest on $270 for 60 days at 6% = $2.70	
Interest on $270 for 30 days at 6% =	$1.35
Interest on $270 for 20 days at 6% =	.90
Interest on $270 for 6 days at 6% =	.27
Interest on $270 for 56 days at 6% =	$2.52

B.

Interest on $270 for 60 days at 6% = $2.70	
Interest on $270 for 20 days at 6% =	$ .90
Interest on $270 for 20 days at 6% =	.90
Interest on $270 for 12 days at 6% =	.54
Interest on $270 for 4 days at 6% =	.18
Interest on $270 for 56 days at 6% =	$2.52

C.

Interest on $270 for 60 days at 6% = $2.70	
Interest on $270 for 4 days at 6% =	.18
Interest on $270 for 56 days at 6% = $2.52	

Note that it is also possible to use aliquot parts of the other numbers besides 60 as well. Thus in Problem 4a, 1 day is ⅙ of 6 days. Therefore ⅙ of $1.50 = $.25. In Problem 5b, 4 days are ⅓ of 20 days or ⅓ of 12 days. The interest can be computed by taking ⅓ of $.90 or ⅓ of $.54, the answer in each case being $.18.

Exercise

Find the interest:

	Principal	Time	Rate %
1.	$1600	80 days	6
2.	1800	3 months	6
3.	1200	75 days	6
4.	4000	46 days	6
5.	280	23 days	6
6.	970	38 days	6
7.	250.68	14 days	6
8.	168.95	4 months	6
9.	1280	53 days	6
10.	560.80	44 days	6

Answers:

1.	$21.33	5.	$1.07	9.	$11.31
2.	27.00	6.	6.14	10.	4.11
3.	15.00	7.	.58		
4.	30.67	8.	3.38		

To Find the Interest at 6% for Any Time in Days

Frequently the number of days in an interest problem cannot easily be divided into aliquot parts of 60, such as 29 days, 71 days, etc. In such cases another method may be used, as follows:

Rule:

1. Divide the principal by 1000.
2. Multiply the result by the number of days.
3. Divide the product by 6.

Problem: Find the interest on $150 for 29 days at 6%.

$$\frac{\$150}{1000} = \$.150$$

```
    $.150
      29
    1350
    300
 6 ) 4350
    .725  Answer
```

The answer arrived at by this method may be checked by the first method:

Interest on $150 for 60 days at 6% = $1.50	
Interest on $150 for 30 days at 6% =	$.75
Interest on $150 for 1 day at 6% =	$.025
Interest on $150 for 31 days at 6% =	.775
Interest on $150 for 29 days at 6% = $ .725 or $.73	

Exercise

Do the examples in the preceding exercise, but use the above method.

To Find the Interest at Rates Other Than 6%

Rule:

1. Find the interest at 6%.
2. Multiply the answer by the desired rate.
3. Divide by 6.

Problem: Find the interest on $800 for 37 days at 4½%.

A.

Interest on $800 for 60 days at 6% = $8.00	
Interest on $800 for 30 days at 6% =	$4.00
Interest on $800 for 6 days at 6% =	.80
Interest on $800 for 1 day at 6% =	.133
Interest on $800 for 37 days at 6% =	$4.933

B.

```
    $4.933
       4½
   $22.1985
```

C.

```
 6 ) 22.1985
    3.6997½ or $3.70,  Answer
```

Another method may also be used. For 5% take ⅚ of the answer; for 4%, ⅔ (or 4/6); for 3%, ½ (or 3/6); for 2%, ⅓ (or 2/6) and for 1%, ⅙. Whichever method is used is a matter of one's own preference.

Exercise

Find the interest.

	Principal	Time	Rate %	Rate %	Rate %
1.	$1836	60 days	5	4	3
2.	680	26 days	4	3	2
3.	275	3 months	3	2	1
4.	368	6 months	2	1	5
5.	212.50	72 days	1	5	4
6.	505.80	90 days	5	4	3
7.	906	36 days	4	3	2
8.	412.76	45 days	3	2	1
9.	1300	18 days	2	1	5
10.	1560	52 days	1	5	4

Answers:

1.	$15.30	$12.24	$9.18
2.	1.97	1.48	.98
3.	2.06	1.38	.69
4.	3.68	1.84	9.20
5.	.43	2.13	1.70
6.	6.32	5.06	3.79
7.	3.62	2.72	1.81
8.	1.55	1.03	.52
9.	1.30	.65	3.25
10.	2.25	11.27	9.01

Bank Discount

Discounting One's Own Notes

When a businessman needs money, he borrows it at the bank. In return he will give the bank his written promise to repay the money at a certain time. This written promise is called a *promissory note*. The bank will charge interest on the loan which it will deduct in advance, giving the borrower the difference between the value of the note at maturity and the interest. This difference is called the *net proceeds*. When interest is deducted in advance, it is called *bank discount*, and the rate is called the *rate of bank discount*.

In order to find how much a borrower will actually receive on a loan, calculate the interest and subtract the amount from the principal.

Problem: A businessman borrows $1500 from a bank on his 60-day note at a discount rate of 6%. Find the net proceeds.

> Interest on $1500
> for 60 days at 6% = $15, Bank Discount
>
> $1500 Maturity Value
>   15 Bank Discount
> $1485 Net Proceeds

Exercise

Find the net proceeds of the following notes:

	Note	Time of Discount	Rate of Discount %
1.	$1200	90 days	6
2.	680	45 days	6
3.	420	120 days	6
4.	1100	60 days	6
5.	975	30 days	6

Answers:

1.	$1182	3. $ 411.60	5. $970.12
2.	674.90	4. 1089	

Discounting Others' Notes

Frequently, a businessman who is in need of money has customers' notes and acceptances on hand. He may borrow on these.

Problem 1: Harry Williams has received a note of $600 from a customer. It is dated April 15 and runs for 90 days. On May 12, he needs money. He sells it to the bank or, to use the correct business term, he *discounts* the note. What are the net proceeds?

To do this problem, four steps must be performed.

1. Find the day the note is due (date of maturity).
2. Find how long the bank must wait for payment (term of discount).
3. Find the bank discount.
4. Find the net proceeds.

Date of Maturity

> Apr. 30
>   − 15
> Apr. 15
> May 31
> June 30
> July 14 Date of Maturity
> 90 days

Term of Discount

> May 31
>   − 12
> May 19
> June 30
> July 14
>   63 days, Term of Discount

Bank Discount

$6.30 for 63 days (By previously indicated method)

Net Proceeds

> $600.00 Maturity Value
>   6.30 Bank Discount
> $593.70 Net Proceeds

Note that in finding the date of maturity and the term of discount, the actual number of days is used.

Explanation of the Solution:

1. *Date of Maturity.* The date of maturity is 90 days from April 15. There are 30 days in April; 15 days have already passed, so we have 15 days left in April. In May there are 31, in June, 30 days. This gives us 76 days, leaving 14 more to make up the 90. We reach, then, July 14.
2. *Term of Discount.* Counting from the date the note was discounted, May 12, to the date of maturity, July 14, there are 63 days.
3. *Bank Discount.* The bank discount is found by finding the interest for the term of discount, 63 days.
4. *Net Proceeds.* Net proceeds are found by deducting the bank discount from the value at maturity.

When the time of the note is not in days, but in months, the date of maturity is found by counting months, and not days.

Problem 2: Find the net proceeds of a note of $1500, dated July 16, time 3 months, and discounted August 31.

<table>
<tr><td colspan="2">

Date of Maturity

July 16
Aug.
Sept.
Oct. 16 Date of Maturity
        3 months

Term of Discount

Aug. 31
 − 31
Aug. 0
Sept. 30
Oct. 16
     46 days, Term of Discount

Bank Discount

$11.50, for 46 days (By previously indicated method)

Net Proceeds

$1500.00 Maturity Value
  11.50 Bank Discount
$1488.50 Net Proceeds

</td><td colspan="2">

Term of Discount

Feb. 28
     − 13
Feb. 15
Mar. 19
     34 days, Time of Discount

Interest and Maturity Value

$1200.00 Face
    9.00 Interest
$1209.00 Maturity Value

Bank Discount

$6.85 for 34 days (By previously indicated method)

Net Proceeds

$1209.00 Maturity Value
   6.85 Bank Discount
$1202.15 Net Proceeds

Note that there is a new step in this solution; namely, finding the maturity value. Otherwise the solution is the same as in the non-interest-bearing notes.

</td></tr>
</table>

Exercise

Find the net proceeds:

	Face Value	Date	Time	Rate %	Date of Discount
1.	$1200	Mar. 2	60 days	6	Apr. 7
2.	1800	Apr. 30	90 days	6	June 3
3.	240	Sept. 16	30 days	6	Sept. 25
4.	550	Jan. 20	1 mo.	6	Jan. 31
5.	728	Feb. 17	3 mo.	6	Apr. 12
6.	2800	May 4	2 mo.	6	June 6

Answers:
1. $1195.20   3. $239.16   5. $ 723.75
2. 1783.20   4. 548.17   6. 2786.93

Discounting Interest-Bearing Notes

The face value and the maturity value of a non-interest-bearing note are the same. In the case of an interest-bearing note, the face value and maturity value differ, because the interest must be added to the face value to arrive at the maturity value.

Problem 1: Find the maturity value of a 60-day note of $800 bearing interest at 3%.

Interest = $4

$800 Face Value
   4 Interest
$804 Maturity Value

To discount an interest-bearing note, the maturity value must be found, because the bank discount is computed on the maturity value, not the face value.

Problem 2: Find the net proceeds of a 60-day note of $1200, bearing interest at 4%, dated January 18 and discounted February 13.

Date of Maturity

Jan. 31
     − 18
Jan. 13
Feb. 28
Mar. 19, Date of Maturity
     60 days

Exercise

Find the net proceeds:

	Face Value	Date	Time	Interest Rate %	Rate of Discount %	Date of Discount
1.	$ 900	Mar. 12	60 da.	6	6	Mar. 30
2.	1200	Dec. 28	3 mo.	6	6	Feb. 6
3.	2600	July 6	1 mo.	3	6	July 25
4.	750	Nov. 19	90 da.	4	6	Jan. 20
5.	960	Aug. 27	120 da.	2	6	Oct. 14

Answers:
1. $ 902.64   3. $2601.29   5. $954.80
2. 1207.85   4.   753.96

Borrowing Money to Pay a Bill

A firm may buy goods and the discount for cash may be so great that it will be worthwhile borrowing the money to be able to take advantage of the discount. It is important, then, to be able to figure out how much can be gained by borrowing to pay for cash, and, also, whether it is actually worthwhile to do so.

Problem: On April 3, F. B. Clark bought goods for $1500, terms 2/10, n/30. He did not have the money to pay the invoice on April 13, so that he could take advantage of the discount. He therefore borrowed sufficient money to pay the bill on his 20-day interest-bearing note. Did he gain or lose and how much?

$1500 Amount of Invoice
  30 Cash discount 2%
$1470 Net Cost
     Interest on $1470 for 20 days
        at 6% = $4.90
$30.00 Cash Discount
 4.90 Interest
$25.10 Gain by borrowing

Note that he must borrow the amount of the *net cost*.

Exercise

1. A merchant bought goods for $3640, terms 3/10, n/90. To take advantage of the cash discount, he borrowed the money for 80 days at 6% and paid the bill. How much was gained by borrowing the money?
2. A merchant purchased goods for $1500 less 20% and 10%, terms 2/10, n/30. To take advantage of the cash discount, he borrowed the money for 20 days at 6% and paid the bill. How much was gained by borrowing?
3. The Hudson Co. bought goods for $2480 less 25%, terms 2/10, n/60. To take advantage of the cash discount, they borrowed the money at 6% for 50 days. How much was gained by borrowing?

Answers:
1. $62.12   **2.** $18.07   **3.** $22.01

Borrowing Money for Loan Companies

Small-loan companies are permitted by law to lend money, usually up to $300, and charge a stated rate per cent of interest on the unpaid balance. Payments on such loans are generally made in monthly installments.

Problem: A man borrows $300 from a finance company. The company charges 2% interest per month on the unpaid balance. Payments of $50 are to be made monthly. The loan is for 6 months. Find the total amount of interest paid.

Interest Period	Unpaid Balance	Interest at 2%	Payment
End of first month	$300	$6.00	$50
End of second month	250	5.00	50
End of third month	200	4.00	50
End of fourth month	150	3.00	50
End of fifth month	100	2.00	50
End of sixth month	50	1.00	50
Total Interest		$21.00	

Note that the interest is computed on the amount due at the end of each month. The unpaid balance at the end of the first month is $300 so the interest at 2% of $300 is $6. At the end of the next month the unpaid balance, reduced by $50, is $250, and the interest is $5, etc.

Problem: A man borrows $200 for 4 months. The interest charges are 2½% on the first $100, 2% on the balance. Find the interest charges.

Interest Period	Unpaid Balance	Interest Charges	Payment
End of first month	$200	$4.50	$50
End of second month	150	3.50	50
End of third month	100	2.50	50
End of fourth month	50	1.25	50
Total Interest		$11.75	

Computation:
2½% of $100 = $2.50; 2% of $100 = $2.00; Total $4.50
2½% of $100 = $2.50; 2% of $ 50 = $1.00; Total $3.50
2½% of $100 = $2.50
2½% of $ 50 = $1.25

Exercise

1. Gates borrows $240 from a credit union for 5 months. He repays the loan in five monthly installments of $48 each, plus interest charges of ¾% per month on the unpaid balance. Find the interest charges.

2. Brown borrows $150 from a finance company and will repay it in 5 monthly installments of $30 each. The company charges 2½% on the first $100, 2% on the balance. Find the interest charges.
3. Aarons borrows $150 from a finance company and will repay it in 6 monthly installments of $25 each. The company charges 2% on the unpaid balance. Find the interest charges.

Answers:
1. $5.40   **2.** $10.90   **3.** $10.50

Compound Interest

Compound interest is interest which has been added to the principal, to form a part of the new principal. For example, if Brown deposits $100 in a savings bank and at the end of the year he is credited with 2% interest, his new principal is $102. At the end of the next year, the bank will compute the interest upon $102. If this is done each year, the interest is compounded annually. Banks add interest at stated periods, such as at the end of a month, quarter year, half year, or year, and interest is said to be compounded monthly, quarterly, semi-annually, or annually. Banks use compound-interest tables to compute the compound interest. Below, it will be computed arithmetically. Interest is not computed on cents, but on dollars only.

Problem: On January 2, 1943, Clark deposited $500 in a savings bank. Interest at the rate of 2% per annum was compounded semi-annually. On January 2, 1944, Clark deposited an additional $400. Find how much he had on deposit July 1, 1944.

$500.00	Principal Jan. 2, 1943
5.00	Interest July 1, 1943 (2% per year, 1% for ½ year)
$505.00	Principal July 1, 1943
5.05	Interest Jan. 2, 1944
$510.05	Principal Jan. 2, 1944
400.00	Deposit Jan. 2, 1944
$910.05	Principal Jan. 2, 1944
9.10	Interest July 1, 1944
$919.15	Principal July 1, 1944

Note that interest is computed and added before deposits are added or withdrawals deducted.

Exercise

1. A savings bank pays 2% interest on its deposits and adds the interest on June 1 and December 1 of each year. On June 1, 1944 H. Williams deposits $600. If he makes no deposits or withdrawals, how much will he have on deposit December 1, 1945?
2. A savings bank pays 1½% interest on its deposits and adds the interest on January 2 and July 1 of each year. On January 2, 1943 W. Harris deposits $600. He deposits $400 on July 1, 1943 and withdraws $100 on January 2, 1944. How much will he have on deposit July 1, 1944?

Answers:
1. $618.18   **2.** $918.87

Profits and Pricing

Per Cent of Profit

Businessmen, in order to stay in business, must operate at a profit. To do so, it is imperative that they have certain information on their operations. This information will be considered here.

Per Cent of Profit on Cost

The selling price of goods less the cost of goods is the entire or gross profit. The gross profit less the overhead is the net profit. By overhead is meant the expenses or cost of doing business, such as rent, salaries, supplies, etc. What the businessman wants to know very often is whether he is making a big enough profit in comparison to his cost.

Problem: Goods costing $500 are sold for $800. The overhead is $100. Find *A.* rate of gross profit on cost; *B.* rate of net profit on cost.

$800 Selling Price
$500 Cost
$300 Gross Profit
$100 Overhead
$200 Net Profit

A. $300/500$ = 60%, Rate of Gross Profit on Cost
B. $200/500$ = 40%, Rate of Net Profit on Cost

Per Cent of Profit on Sales

Many businessmen prefer to base their profit on sales and not on cost. The reasons are that the sales price is known at once whereas the cost must be looked up and because expenses and profits are compared with sales.

Problem: Goods costing $500 are sold for $800. The overhead is $100. Find *A.* rate of gross profit on sales; *B.* rate of net profit on sales.

$800 Selling Price
$500 Cost
$300 Gross Profit
$100 Overhead
$200 Net Profit

A. $300/800$ = 37½%, Rate of Gross Profit on Sales
B. $200/800$ = 25%, Rate of Net Profit on Sales

Exercise

	Selling Price	Cost	Gain	Rate of Gain on Cost	Rate of Gain on Sales
1.	$ 75	$ 60			
2.	48	32			
3.	25	15			
4.	60	30			
5.	150	100			

Answers:

		Gain	Rate of Gain on Cost %	Rate of Gain on Sales %
1.		$15	25	20
2.		16	50	33⅓
3.		10	66⅔	40
4.		30	100	50
5.		50	50	33⅓

Selling Prices

Find the Selling Price, Given the Cost and Percent of Profit on Cost

Having determined the rate of gain on cost, it will be easy to compute the selling price of similar articles with the same rate of profit or mark-up.

Problem: Goods cost $50. The rate of profit on cost is 20%. Find the sales price.

$50 Cost
$10 20% Rate of Profit on Cost 20%
$60 Sales Price

Exercise

Find the sales price.

	Cost	Rate of Gross Profit on Cost %
1.	$120	50
2.	264	16⅔
3.	180	33⅓
4.	290	40
5.	175	100

Answers:
1. $180   3. $240   5. $350
2.   308   4.   406

Finding the Selling Price, Given the Cost and Per Cent of Profit on Sales

Here the rate of profit is figured on sales and not on cost. The procedure in finding the sales price differs because an indirect method is used.

Problem: A refrigerator is billed to a dealer at $75 less 20% and 10%. At what price should he sell the refrigerator to gain 20% of the sales price?

$75 List Price
$15 Trade Discount 20%
$60 Balance
$6 Trade Discount 10%
$54 Net Cost

Sales Price	100%	
Profit	20%	
Cost		$54

Sales Price	100%	$67.50
Profit	20%	$13.50
Cost	80%	$54.00

$54 ÷ .8 = $67.50 or $54 ÷ ⅘ =
$54 × ⁵⁄₄ = $67.50, *Answer*

To prove, take 20% of the sales, $67.50. The profit is $13.50. Sales, $67.50, minus Profit, $13.50, equal $54, Cost.

In this type of problem, the unknown is the sales price. This is 100%. The profit on sales is known to be 20% of 100%, or 20%. The cost is known to be $54. Now, subtract 20% from 100% to get the cost: 80%. The cost also equals $54. The problem now is: $54 is 80% of what number? As done in Percentage, Percentage ÷ Rate = Base or 54 ÷ .8.

Finding the Selling Price, Given the Cost, the Per Cent of Profit and Overhead Based on Selling Price

Problem: A refrigerator is billed to a dealer at $75 less 20% and 10%. At what price should he sell the refrigerator to gain 20% on sales, if he gives his salesman a commission of 8% on sales and his overhead is 12% of sales?

$75 List Price
 15 Trade Discount 20%
$60 Balance
  6 Trade Discount 10%
$54 Net Cost

Sales Price		100%	
Commission	8%		
Overhead	12%		
Profit	20%	40%	
Cost			$54

Sales Price		100%	$90
Commission	8%		
Overhead	12%		
Profit	20%	40%	$36
Cost		60%	$54

$54 ÷ .6 = 90 or
$54 ÷ ⅗ = 54 × ⁵⁄₃ = $90, *Answer*

The procedure followed is as in the previous problem. Everything based on sales is placed in the middle of the diagram, totaled, and subtracted from the sales, 100%. The difference is the cost. The problem is the same as before: the net cost is a certain percentage of what number? Prove as before.

Exercise

1. A merchant bought rugs at $27 less 25%. At what price must he sell them to make a profit of 16⅔% on sales?
2. A druggist buys face powder at 50¢ per box. The wholesaler offers the druggist a discount of 10% and 5%, if he will buy a carton (36 boxes). The druggist accepts. At what price must he mark each box to make a profit of 33⅓% on cost?
3. A dealer buys radios at $150 less 20% and 10%. He has an expense of $6 per radio for delivery and installation. (This is a selling expense and must be added to sales price to get total sales price.)
   a. At what price must he sell each radio to gain 25% on the purchase price?
   b. At what price must he sell each radio to gain 25% on the sales price?
4. A dealer buys fountain pens at $36 per dozen less 25% and 20%. The overhead is 25% of sales. At what price must he sell each pen to gain 15% on the sales price?
5. In 1944 the Brown Rug Co. determined its sales price by basing the gross profit of 40% on cost. In 1945, the company decided to base the 40% gross profit on sales price.
   a. If a rug cost $6, what was the sales price in 1944?
   b. If the cost of the rug was $6 in 1945, what was the sales price in 1945?
   c. By what per cent was the gross profit decreased or increased in 1945 as compared with 1944.
6. A dealer ordered 24 thermometers at $45 a dozen, less

20%. He found 6 defective items and returned them. The buying expenses on the purchase were $2.16. (Add buying expenses to find total cost.) If he wished to make a profit of 30% on sales, and if the overhead was 10%, at what price was each thermometer sold?
7. A dealer purchased bicycles at $32.50 less 20% and 5%, plus a freight charge of 90¢ on each bicycle. If his overhead is 24% of sales, at what price must he sell each bicycle to make a profit of 12% of the sales price?

Answers:
1. $24.30   4. $3   6. $ 5.20
2. 57   5. a. 8.40   7. 40
3. a. 141   b. 10
   b. 150   c. 19½₁% Increase

Find the List or Marked Price, Given the Selling Price and the Trade Discount

Wholesalers who sell their goods subject to a trade discount must be able to compute the list or catalogue price so that they will receive the market price they desire. The procedure is the same as in the preceding problem.

Problem: A radio cost $150 and it is to be sold at a profit of 33⅓% on cost. At what price should it be listed in the catalogue, if there is a trade discount of 60% to be given?

First Step.—To Find the Sales Price:
$150 Cost
  50 Profit 33⅓% on cost
$200 Selling Price

Second Step.—To Find the List Price:

List Price	100%	$500
Trade Discount	60%	$300
Selling Price	40%	$200

$200 ÷ .40 = $500, List Price or
$200 ÷ ⅖ = $200 × ⁵⁄₂ = $500, List Price

Problem: A shoe store owner buys shoes at $7 a pair. He wants to make a profit of 20% on the sales price, after offering a discount of 12½% on the marked or list price. Find the marked price.

*First Step–*To Find the Sales Price:

Sales Price	100%	$8.75
Profit	20%	$1.75
Cost	80%	$7.00

$7 ÷ .80 = $8.75, Sales Price or
$7 ÷ ⅘ = $7 × ⁵⁄₄ = ³⁵⁄₄ = $8.75, Sales Price

*Second Step–*To Find the List Price:

List Price	100%	$10.00
Trade Discount	12½%	$1.25
Sales Price	87½%	$8.75

$8.75 ÷ .875 = $10, List Price or
$8.75 ÷ ⅞ = $8.75 × ⁸⁄₇ = $10, List Price

Exercise

1. A haberdasher buys hats at $40 per dozen less 25% and 20%. He wants to make a profit of 25% on the cost and to offer a trade discount of 16⅔% off the list price. Find the marked or list price.
2. A merchant buys gloves at $18 per dozen pairs. He wants to make a profit of 33⅓% on cost and offer a trade discount of 20% off the list price. Find the list price.
3. A dealer pays $60 less 30%, and 10% for a rug. Selling expenses are 7½% of the selling price. He sells the rug to gain 25% on the sales price, after allowing a trade discount of 20% off the marked price. Find the marked price.
4. It cost a manufacturer $17 to make a rug. At what price should he list the rug in his catalogue to make a profit of 15% on the sales price after allowing a trade discount of 33⅓% on the catalogue price?
5. A merchant buy rugs at $28 less 25%. What is the marked price if he wishes to make a profit of 20% on the selling price after allowing a discount of 40% on the marked price?
6. A merchant buys a desk for $80. He wants to make a profit of 25% on cost. At what price must he mark it to allow a discount of 20% off the marked price?
7. A dealer buys suits at $40 less 10%. He wants to make a profit of 25% on the selling price and allow a special discount of 16⅔% off the marked price. Find the marked price.
8. A merchant buys stoves for $40 less 20% and 10%. He wants to make a profit on 33⅓% on the selling price after allowing a 10% discount on the marked price. Find the marked price.

Answers:
1. $36   4. $ 30   7. $57.60
2. 30   5. 43.75   8. 48
3. 70   6. 125

Comparison of Profits

Very often a merchant will have a special sale on certain goods. He then wishes to make a comparison between the profit realized on the goods sold at the old price and the profit at the sale price.

Problem: During November a hardware dealer sold 24 coal stoves at $125 each. The net cost of each stove was $87.50. The overhead expense was $17.50 per stove. In December, he ran a special sale and reduced the sales price to $117.50 per stove, and sold 32 stoves. The overhead in December was $17.25 per stove.

A. How much profit did the dealer make in November?
B. How much profit did he make in December?
C. What was the rate of increase or decrease?

This problem may be calculated by two methods: on the basis of one stove or the total number of stoves.

Calculation on 1 Stove

A.   *November*

1 stove @ $125.00 each = $125.00 Sales Price
1 stove @ $ 87.50 each =   87.50 Cost
                         $ 37.50 Gross Profit
                           17.50 Overhead
                         $ 20.00 Net Profit
24 stoves @ $20.00 profit on ea. = $480, Total Profit
                                        Answer

B.   *December*

1 stove @ $117.50 each = $117.50 Sales Price
1 stove @ $ 87.50 each =   87.50 Cost
                         $ 30.00 Gross Profit
                           17.25 Overhead
                         $ 12.75 Net Profit
32 stoves @ $12.75 profit on ea. = $408, Total Profit
                                        Answer

C. $480 Net Profit, November
        408 Net Profit, December
       $ 72 Decrease in Profit

       $ 72 Decrease
       $480 Net Profit, November = $\frac{72}{480}$ =

       15% Rate of Decrease, *Answer*

Calculation on Total Number of Stoves

A.   *November*

24 stoves @ $125.00 each = $3000 Sales Price
24 stoves @ $ 87.50 each = 2100 Cost
                           $ 900 Gross Profit
24 stoves @ $ 17.50 each =   420 Overhead
                           $ 480 Net Profit,
                                 Answer

B.   *December*

32 stoves @ $117.50 each = $3760 Sales Price
32 stoves @ $ 87.50 each = 2800 Cost
                           $ 960 Gross Profit
32 stoves @ $ 17.25 each =   552 Overhead
                           $ 408 Net Profit,
                                 Answer

C. $480 Net Profit, November
        408 Net Profit, December
       $ 72 Decrease in Profit

       $ 72 Decrease
       $480 Net Profit, November = $\frac{72}{480}$ =

       15% Decrease, *Answer*

Exercise

1. A merchant bought chairs at $15 each. He sold them at $25 each. During October his sales were 150 chairs. In November, he ran a special sale, reducing the sales price to $20 per chair. The sales increased to 400 chairs.
   a. How much was the profit in October?
   b. How much was the profit in November?
   c. What was the rate of increase or decrease in the profit?
2. The Home Appliance Co. bought washing machines at $130 less 30% each. During April, 15 machines were sold at $129 each. During May, each machine was sold at $117.50 each. As a result 30 machines were sold.
   a. During which month did the company make more profit and how much?
   b. What was the rate of increase or decrease in the profit?

Distribution of Partnership Profits

Profits are distributed among partners according to the arrangements set forth in the partnership contract. If no mention is made, the profits or losses are distributed equally.

There are three usual methods of division of profits. They are:

1. According to an agreed-upon ratio.
2. According to partnership investment ratio.
3. Allowing interest on investment, and then dividing the balance equally.

Problem: Vincent, Dugan, and Carver have invested $6000, $8000, and 12,000 respectively in their wholesale business. The first year their profit was $7800.

A. How much will each receive if they agree to divide their profits equally?
B. How much will each receive if they agree to divide their profits in proportion to their investments (capital ratio)?
C. How much will they receive if each partner is allowed 6% on his investment, and then the remaining profit is divided equally?

A. There are three partners.
⅓ of $7800 = $2600, each partner's share

B.

Partner	Invest-ment	Share according to Capital Ratio	Computation of Share	Share
Vincent	$ 6000	6000/2600	³⁄₁₃ of $7800	$1800
Dugan	8000	8000/26000	⁴⁄₁₃ of $7800	2400
Carver	12000	12000/26000	⁶⁄₁₃ of $7800	3600
Totals	$26000	26000/26000	¹³⁄₁₃ of $7800	$7800

C.

Partner	Invest-ment	6% Interest on Captial	⅓ of Remaining Profit	Share
Vincent	$6000	$360	$2080	$2440
Dugan	8000	480	2080	2560
Carver	12000	720	2080	2800
Totals	$26000	$1560	$6240	$7800 Total Profit

$$\begin{array}{r} \$7800 \text{ Total Profit} \\ 1560 \text{ Interest} \\ \hline 3\overline{)6240} \\ \$2080 \end{array}$$

Exercise

1. Todd invested $12,000 and Olsen $15,000 in their business. They agreed to allow interest on their investments of 8% and divide the remaining profit equally.
   a. How much must the business earn in one year to cover the 8% interest?
   b. If the profit at the end of the year was $5380, how much did each receive?
2. Abbot invested $12,000, Johnson $16,000, and Moore his services. Out of the first year's profit of $9675, Abbot and Johnson were allowed 12½% interest on their investments, and Moore $1600 as salary. The remaining profit was divided equally. Find each partner's income for the year.
3. Davis and Lee invested $8000 and $4000 respectively in their business. At the end of the year their sales were $18,525, cost of goods sold was $12,200 and overhead expenses were $1522. If the profit was to be divided according to their capital ratio, find each partner's share of the profit.
4. Young and Harrington invested $6000 and $12,000 respectively in their business. The sales for the year 1944 were $28,440; cost of goods sold, $15,460; overhead, $3200.
   a. Find the net profit.
   b. The profits are to be shared in capital ratio. Find each partner's share.
   c. If each partner is allowed 6% on his investment and the profit which remains is to be shared equally, how much will each partner receive?

Corporation Stock

Definitions and Terms

Corporations issue stock as evidence of ownership in the corporation. When a corporation makes a profit, its directors distribute a part or all of this profit among the stockholders. This distribution of profit is called a *dividend*. All undistributed profit is called *surplus*.

The value imprinted on the face of the stock certificate is called its par value. The par value of the stock is usually $100, although stock may be issued at other par values, such as $50 or $25. Some corporations issue stock with no par value. The market price of stock is the price at which the stock is sold in the various stock markets.

In this section we take up some of the problems of computing dividends and buying and selling stock.

Computing Dividends on Stock

Problem: A corporation has a capital stock of $500,000, each share having a par value of $100. It declares a dividend of 9%. If the net profits for the year are $75,000, find the amount of the dividend and how much is left in surplus.

$500,000 \div \$100 = 5000$ shares
9% of $100 = \$9$, Dividend on 1 share
5000 shares $\times \$9 = \$45,000$, Dividend declared
$75,000 - \$45,000 = \$30,000$, Amount left in surplus

Problem: A corporation has a capital stock of $400,000 each share having par value of $100. Its net profit for the year is $60,000. The directors declare a dividend of 4%. Find *A.* the amount of the dividend; *B.* the amount added to surplus; *C.* the dividend received by a stockholder who owns 60 shares of stock.

A. $400,000 \div 100$ = 4000 shares
    4% of 100   = $4, dividend on 1 share

    4000×4 = $16,000, amount of dividend

B. $60,000 - \$16,000$ = $44,000 amount added to surplus

C. 60 shares @ $4 per share = $240, dividend received by stockholder

Exercise

(Where no par value is stated, assume it is $100.)

1. A corporation declares a semi-annual dividend of 5%. Find Mr. Jones' dividend if he owns 100 shares.
2. A corporation's capital stock is $600,000. It declares a dividend of 5%. Find the amount of the dividend declared.
3. The Lincoln Radio Co. has capital stock of $500,000. Its profit is $80,000. Its directors declare an annual dividend of 6%.
   a. What does the total annual dividend amount to?
   b. How much will go to surplus?
   c. If Harry Wells has 75 shares, how much dividend will he receive?
4. The Ocean Hardware Corp. has a capital stock of $200,000. It declares semi-annual dividends of 3%.
   a. Find the total annual dividend.
   b. Find how much Max Morse, who owns 50 shares, will receive annually.
5. Anthony Lamb has 50 shares of common stock and 12 shares of 8% preferred stock in a certain corporation. A quarterly dividend of 60¢ per share is paid on the common stock and the regular 8% dividend on the preferred. How much income annually will Mr. Lamb receive from his stock holdings?

Answers:
1. $500   3. *a.* $30,000   4. *a.* $12,000
2. $30,000   *b.* $50,000   *b.* $300
                  c. $450   5. $216

Finding the Rate of Dividend

Problem: A corporation which has a capital stock of $400,000 has a net profit of $80,000 for the year. It decides to keep $20,000 in surplus and distribute the rest of the profits as dividends. Find the annual rate of dividend.

    $80,000 Total Profit
     20,000 Surplus
    $60,000 Dividend declared

$$\frac{60,000 \text{ Dividend declared}}{400,000 \text{ Capital stock}} = 15\%, \text{ Rate of dividend, } Answer$$

Exercise

1. A corporation with capital stock of $300,000 has a net profit of $50,000. The directors declare a dividend of $30,000. Find the rate of dividend.
2. A corporation is capitalized at $200,000. It makes a profit of $45,000. If $15,000 is set aside for surplus, what will be the rate of dividend?
3. The Borax Corp, is capitalized at $500,000. At the end of the year it will pay $60,000 in dividends.
   a. Find the annual dividend rate.
   b. Find how much a person who has 50 shares will receive in dividends.
4. The Lastelle Corp., with capital stock of $1,000,000, earns $180,000 for the year. The directors declare a dividend of $120,000.
   a. Find the amount left in surplus.
   b. Find the annual rate of dividend on the stock.
   c. Find how much a stockholder who has 100 shares receives.

Answers:
1. 10%   3. *a.* 12%   4. *a.* $60,000
2. 15%   *b.* $600   *b.* 12%
                                   c. $1200

Buying and Selling Stock

Stock may be bought and sold at any stock exchange through the medium of a broker who is a member of that exchange. The broker charges a fee, called *brokerage*, for his services. In addition a state and a federal tax must be paid on all stock sold.

Problem: Harry Wilson bought 300 shares of stock at 56½ (i.e., $56.50) and sold it at 65. Brokerage each way was 25¢ a share and the total taxes were 4¢ per share. Find his net profit on the transaction.

Sale

300 shares @ $65 each   = $19,500 Sales Price
300 shares
  @ 25¢ each = $75 brokerage
300 shares
  @ 4¢ each = $12 tax   87
                           $19,413 Net Proceeds

Purchase

300 shares @ $56.50 each = $16,950 Cost
300 shares @   25¢ each =   75 Brokerage
                         $17,025 Total Cost

    $19,413 Net Proceeds of Sale
     17,025 Total Cost
    $ 2,388 Net Profit

Exercise

1. Stock costing $50 per share was sold for $58 per share. Brokerage each way was 24¢ per share and the taxes on the sale amounted to 4¢ per share. Find the net profit.
2. Warren bought 100 shares of stock at 90 and sold them for 105. Brokerage each way was 24¢ per share and the taxes on the sale were 4½¢ per share. Find the net profit.

3. Harris bought 300 shares of stock at 98½¢ and sold them at 112½. If brokerage is 25¢ per share each way and the taxes on the sale were 4¢ per share, find the amount of the net profit.

Answers:
1. $7.48   **2.** $1447.50   **3.** $4038

Finding Profit on Sale of Stock, Dividends Having Been Received

Problem: Morris bought 300 shares of stock at 98 and sold them at 110, after holding them a year. During this time, he received 2 semi-annual dividends of 4%. Brokerage was 25¢ per share each way and taxes on the sale were 4¢. Find his total profit.

Sale

300 shares @ $110 each	=	$33,000 Sales Price
300 shares @ 25¢ each	=	$75 brokerage
300 shares @ 4¢ each	=	$12 tax

$\underline{87}$
$32,913 Net Proceeds

Purchase

300 shares @ $98 each	=	$29,400 Cost
300 shares @ 25¢ each	=	$\underline{75}$ Brokerage

$29,475 Total Cost

$32,913 Net Proceeds of Sale
$\underline{28,475}$ Total Cost
$ 3,438 Net Profit on Sale

Dividends

4% of 100	=	$4 per share, dividend for ½ year
300 shares @ $4	=	1200, Dividend for ½ year
1200 × 2	=	2400, Dividend for 1 year

$ 3,438 Net Profit on Sale
$\underline{2,400}$ Dividends
$ 5,838 Total Profit, *Answer*

Exercise

1. Harvey bought 50 shares of stock at 32, brokerage 24¢ per share. The stock pays a quarterly dividend of 1%. At the end of a year, he sold the stock at 40, brokerage 25¢ per share, tax 4¢ per share. Find his total profit on the transaction.
2. On February 1, M. King bought 70 shares of stock at 98½, brokerage 22¢ a share. On April 1 and again on October 1, he received a cash dividend of $2.50 a share. On November 1 he sold the stock at 112, brokerage 24¢ a share, tax 4¢ a share. What was King's profit?
3. Mr. Carson bought 10 shares of 7% preferred stock at $140 a share. He received dividends for one year and then sold the stock at $142 per share. Brokerage was 26¢ per share on the purchase, 27¢ per share on the sale, and there was a tax of 10¢ per share on the sale. Find his total gain on the transaction.

Answers:
1. $573.50   **2.** $1260   **3.** $83.70

Finding the Rate of Return on Investment
Problem: A share of stock, par value $100, is bought for $81. A dividend of 9% is declared on the stock. Find the rate of return.

9% of $100 = $9, Dividend on 1 share

$$\frac{\$\ 9\ \text{Dividend}}{\$81\ \text{Cost of Stock}} = \frac{1}{9} = 11\frac{1}{9}\%, \text{Rate of return}$$

Exercise

1. On January 2, 1945 J. Martin invested $3400 in aircraft stock at 42½ (including brokerage). During 1945 he received 4 quarterly dividends of 60¢ each on each share of stock. (To find the number of shares, divide the investment by the cost of 1 share.) Find the rate of return on his investment.
2. An industrial stock, which yields an annual dividend of 3%, sells at $60. A public utility stock is quoted at 90 and yields a dividend of 5%. (No brokerage charges.)
   a. Find the rate of return on each.
   b. Which is the better investment and by how much?
3. H. G. Lee purchases 50 shares of American Telephone & Telegraph at 190, paying a dividend of 9% per year. (Disregard brokerage.) Find the rate of return.

Answers:
1. 5¹¹/₁₇%
2. a. Industrial 5%, utility 5⁵/₉%
    b. Utility by ⁵/₉%
3. 4¹⁴/₁₉%

Bonds

Definitions and Interest

A bond is an indebtedness of a corporation. As a rule, the par value of bonds is $1000, unless otherwise stated. Bonds with a par value of less than $1000 are called baby bonds. Since bonds are evidence of debt, the corporation which issues the bonds pays interest on the bonds, usually semi-annually. The interest is called the *income* or *yield*.

Bonds are bought and sold through brokers on the stock exchanges. The price of bonds is shown in two figures, for example, 98½; however the price actually represents three figures, namely $985. Brokers charge a commission on the purchase and sale of each bond.

Bond problems, as a rule, follow the procedures set forth in the solution of stock problems, with one exception which will be shown below.

Purchase of Bonds with Accrued Interest

Since interest on bonds is usually paid semi-annually, it follows that when bonds are bought on a day which is not a day on which interest is due and payable, the buyer will have to refund to the seller the interest which has accumulated or accrued up to the date of the purchase.

Problem: Find the cost of 10 bonds, par value $1000, bought at 96 on February 1. The interest rate is 6%. Interest is payable on January 1 and July 1. Brokerage, $2.50 per bond.

Accrued interest on $1000 for 31 days from January 1 to February 1 at 6% ....$	5.17
Brokerage	2.50
Price of 1 bond	960.00
Cost of 1 bond :.....................$	967.67
Cost of 10 bonds—$967.67 × 10	$9676.70, *Answer*

Exercise

1. Find the cost of 4 bonds, par value $1000, bought at 110 on March 28, interest rate 4%, interest due March 1 and September 1, brokerage $2.50 per bond.
2. Find the cost of 20 bonds, par value $1000, bought at 98 on February 18, interest rate 6%, interest due January 1 and July 1, brokerage $2.50 per bond.

Answers:
1. $4422   2. $19,810

Sale of Bonds with Accrued Interest

The procedure in the sale of bonds is the opposite of that in computing the purchase of bonds. The accrued interest is given to the seller because it is his. Therefore, the accrued interest is added on to the selling price and the commission deducted.

Problem: A man sold 10 bonds, par value $1000, for 98 on November 30. Interest on the bonds was at the rate of 6%; the interest was due on April 1 and October 1. Brokerage was $2.50 per bond.

Accrued interest on $1000 at 6% from
  October 1 to November 30; 60
  days ....$ 10.00
Price of 1 bond 980.00
Gross Proceeds ....$ 990.00
Brokerage, $2.50 ....2.50
Net Proceeds for 1 bond ....$ 987.50
Net Proceeds for 10 bonds—
  $987.50 × 10 ....$9875.00, *Answer*

Exercise

1. Find the net proceeds of 5 bonds, par value $1000, sold for 105 on September 19. Interest at the rate of 6% is due on January 1 and July 1. Brokerage $2.50 per bond.
2. Find the net proceeds of 15 bonds, par value $1000, sold for 97½ on October 30. Interest at the rate of 4%, payable on February 1 and August 1. Brokerage is $2.50 per bond.

Answers:
1. $5304.15   2. $14,737.50

Fire Insurance

Computation of Premiums

Insurance is the protection of the insured against any money loss arising from destruction or damage to the insured property.

Problem: Conroy's place of business, valued at $7500, was insured for 60% of its value for one year. The 1-year rate was 15¢ per C (per hundred dollars). Find the amount of the premium.

60% of $7500   = $4500, Value of Policy
$4500 @ 15¢ per C = $6.75, Premium for 1 year

Suppose that in the above problem the insurance company offers Conroy a 3-year rate which is 2½ times the annual rate. Find the premium for the 3 years and the average annual premium on a 3-year policy.

$6.75, Premium for 1 year
$6.75 × 2½ = $16.88, Premium for 3 years
$1688 ÷ 3 = $5.62⅔ or $5.63, Average annual
          premium

Exercise

1. George Allen owns a building valued at $18,000. He insures it for 80% of its value at $1.65 per $100 for 3 years. He has a stock of goods worth $5250. He insures the stock at its inventory value at $1.20 per $100 for 1 year.
   a. Find the premium on the building.
   b. Find the premium on the stock.
   c. Find the total yearly cost of insurance.
2. Personal property valued at $5000 was insured for 80% of its value at the 3-year rate of $5.00 per M ($1000). Find the average yearly cost of insurance.
3. On January 1 a man received a bill for insurance as follows: car insurance for 1 year, $48.50; fire insurance for $6000 on his home at a 3-year rate of $8 per M, and insurance for $3000 on the contents at the 3-year rate of 50¢ per C.
   a. Find the total cost of the premiums to be paid.
   b. Find the average yearly cost of the insurance.

Answers:
1. a. $237.60   2. $6.66⅔ or $6.67
   b. $ 63.00   3. a. $111.50
   c. $142.20   b. $ 69.50

Eighty Per Cent Co-Insurance Clause

Experience has shown that a fire will seldom destroy a piece of property completely. Consequently, many people insure themselves only for a fraction of the value of the property. To encourage people to take greater precautions, the insurance companies have a clause in the policy which states that the insured will not be paid in full for a fire loss, unless he has insured himself for at least 80% of the value of the property. If he has insured himself for less than the stipulated 80%, he becomes a co-insurer with the insurance company and bears part of the loss.

Problem: A factory building valued at $24,000 was insured for $12,800 under an 80% co-insurance clause. A fire caused a loss of $6600. How much did the insurance company pay and how much of the loss did the insured bear?

The formula for determining the loss is:

$$\frac{\text{Policy}}{80\% \text{ of value of property}} \times \text{Loss}$$

Substituting:

$$\frac{\$12,800}{80\% \text{ of } \$24,000} = \frac{\$12,800}{\$19,200} = \frac{2}{3} \times \$6600$$
$$= \$4400 \text{ Company pays}$$

$6600 Loss
 4400 Company pays
$2200 Loss suffered by insured

Exercise

1. A house valued at $7500 was insured for $5000. The policy contained an 80% co-insurance clause. A fire caused a loss of $4200.
   a. How much did the insurance company pay?
   b. How much loss did the insured suffer?

2. Martin's house is valued at $6000. He insures it for $4800 under a policy containing an 80% co-insurance clause. A fire caused a loss of $3000.
  a. How much did Martin receive under his policy?
  b. How much loss did he suffer?

3. A residence valued at $9000 was insured for $6000 under a policy containing an 80% clause. A fire caused a loss of $3600.
  a. How much did the insurance company pay?
  b. What per cent of the fire loss was borne by the owner?

Answers:
1. *a.* $3500   **2.** *a.* $3000   **3.** *a.* $3000
    b. $700   *b.* 0   *b.* 16⅔%

Reinsurance and Contributing Insurance

If a policy calls for a very large amount, the insurance company may share the risk with other companies by reinsuring the property with other companies. Thus, if a policy of $600,000 is issued, the company will reinsure the property with other companies for, say, $500,000. Thus, by reinsuring the company assumes a risk of only $100,000. Another method of sharing the risk is to have the owner of the property take policies with a number of companies. Then, when a loss occurs, each company will pay a pro-rata share.

Problem: A building is insured for $50,000 as follows: Phoenix Insurance Co., $10,000; Globe Insurance Co., $20,000; World Insurance Co., $20,000. There is a loss of $20,000. How much will each company pay?

Com-pany	Policy	Pro-rata Share	Calcula-tion of Share	Share
Phoenix	$10,000	$\frac{10,000}{50,000}=\frac{1}{5}$	⅕ of $20,000	$ 4000
Globe	20,000	$\frac{20,000}{50,000}=\frac{2}{5}$	⅖ of 20,000	8000
World	20,000	$\frac{20,000}{50,000}=\frac{2}{5}$	⅖ of 20,000	8000
Total	$50,000	$\frac{50,000}{50,000}=\frac{5}{5}$	5/5 of $20,000	$20,000

Note that this problem is solved in the same way as the partnership problem which involved pro-rata share of profits according to capital ratio.

Exercise

1. The Atlas Co. insured its building for $10,000 in three companies as follows: Star Insurance Co., $4500; Western Insurance Co., $3500, and United Insurance Co., $2000. A fire caused a partial loss of $2000. For how much is each company liable?

2. A building was insured in three companies as follows: National Co., $8000; Standard Co., $9000; Mutual Co., $3000. If a loss of $1620 occurred, for how much is each company liable?

3. A factory valued at $20,000 was insured in two companies, each policy having an 80% co-insurance clause. The policy in the Arrow Co. was for $4000 and in the Bow Co. for $10,000. There is a fire loss of $3200. How much must each company pay? (Note: The first step is to find the loss under the 80% clause; then distribute the loss between the two companies.)

Answers:
1. Star $900   **3.** Arrow $800
    Western $700   Bow $2000
    United $400
2. National $648
    Standard $729
    Mutual $243

Real Estate

Rent

People who wish to buy real estate are confronted by a number of problems. Among them are:

1. Is it cheaper to rent or to buy?
2. If the house is rented to a tenant, what will be the per cent of return on the investment?
3. If the house is rented to a tenant, how much rent should be charged?

Renting vs. Buying

Problem: Henry Clark is paying $35 a month rent for a cottage. He can buy it for $4900 by paying 10% of the purchase price in cash and giving a mortgage bearing 5% interest on the balance. His estimated annual expenses are: taxes $125, water charges $25, repairs $50, and insurance $2. If he can earn 2% interest on his cash investment in the bank, will it be cheaper to rent or to buy?

Rental

12 months @ $35 per mo. = $420 Rental per year

Purchase

    $4900 Cost of House
      490 Cash Payment 10%
    $4410 Mortgage

Expenses

Interest on mortgage (5% of $4410)	$220.50
Taxes	125.00
Water charges	25.00
Repairs	50.00
Insurance	2.00
Interest on investment (2% of $490)	9.80
Total Expense	$432.30

    $432.30 Total Expense
    420.00 Rental
    $ 12.30 Cheaper to Rent

Rate of Return on Investment

Problem: Vinson bought a house for $6700, giving $1200 cash as a down payment and a 5% mortgage for the balance. In addition to the mortgage interest, other annual expenses were: taxes $143, insurance $9, repairs $75, depreciation 2% of cost of house. He rented the house to a tenant for $60 per month. Find the rate of return on his cash investment.

Rental to Tenant

12 months @ $60 per mo. = $720, Rental

Annual Expense

    $6700 Cost of House
    1200 Cash Payment
    $5500 Mortgage

Expenses

Interest on mortgage (5% of $5500)	$275.00
Taxes	143.00
Insurance	9.00
Repairs	75.00
Depreciation (2% of $6700)	134.00
Total Expenses	$636.00

$720 Rental
636 Expenses
$ 84 Net Income

$$\frac{84}{1200} = 7\% \text{ Return}, Answer$$

Note that the actual cash investment is the down payment of $1200.

How Much Rent to Charge a Tenant

Problem: Harris owns a house that cost $8500. His yearly taxes are $225, repairs $100, insurance $26, and water bill $20. What monthly rental, to the nearest dollar, must he charge to realize 6% on his investment?

Desired Income

6% of $8500 = $510 Desired Annual Income

Expenses

Taxes	$225
Repairs	100
Insurance	26
Water bill	20
Total expenses	$371

$510 Desired Income
371 Expenses
$881 Annual Rent to be charged

$881 ÷ 12 = $73.41⅔ or $74.00
per month (to the nearest dollar)

Since the expenses must be borne by the tenant, they are added to the desired income to calculate the rental to be paid by the tenant.

Exercise

1. Brown buys a house for $5500, paying $1000 cash and giving a 5% mortgage for the balance. He insures the house for $4500 at the rate 50¢ per C. Taxes amount to $85 and depreciation and repairs are estimated at 3% of the cost. Brown desires a 6% return on his cash investment. What monthly rent, to the nearest dollar, must he charge a tenant?
2. Bernard bought a house for $10,000, paying $3500 cash and giving a 5% mortgage for the balance. Besides the interest on the mortgage, his annual expenses were: Taxes $300, water $80, oil $250, insurance $110, depreciation $490. He rented the house to a tenant for $150 per month. Find the rate of return on his cash investment.
3. Altman is paying $4800 a year rent for the first floor of a building. He can buy the building for $60,000. He would then receive $3000 yearly in rent from the other two floors. His annual expenses would amount to: taxes $950, insurance $240, repairs and janitor service $1700. If money is worth 6% to him in his business (6% of $60,000 would be lost and therefore is considered an expense), how much would he gain or lose by buying the building?

Answers:
1. $47   2. 7%   3. $1310 saved

Real Estate Taxes

Finding the Tax Rate

A government, to maintain itself, must impose taxes. Chief among taxes are those imposed on real estate. To levy the tax equitably and fairly, a value is given each piece of real estate. This value is called the *assessed value* and the tax is levied on the *assessed valuation*. To find out the tax rate the rule to follow is:

$$\frac{\text{Money Needed or Expenses}}{\text{Assessed Valuation}} = \text{Tax Rate}$$

The tax rate may be expressed as a per cent, or mills per dollar (a mill is .001 cent) or dollars per C ($100) or M ($1000).

Problem: Property in the city of Newcastle is assessed at $9,850,000. The expenses for the year are estimated to be: street improvements, $18,600; salaries, $46,300; schools, $102,500; sewers, $7250; buildings, $13,750; interest on bonded debt, $1300. It is estimated that $1500 will be received from special licenses and $5000 from the state as aid for schools.

A. Find the tax rate correct to the nearest hundred thousandth (5 places).
B. Express this rate per $1000.

A.   **Money Needed or Expenses**

$ 18,600	Street improvements
46,300	Salaries
102,500	Schools
7,250	Sewers
13,750	Buildings
1,300	Interest on debt
$189,700	Total expense
6,500	Total income
$183,200	Net expense to be raised by taxes

Income

$1500	Special licenses
5000	State school aid
$6500	Total income

$189,700	Total expense
6,500	Total income
$183,200	Net expense to be raised by taxes

$$\frac{\$183,200}{\$9,850,000} = \$.01859 \text{ per dollar}, Answer$$

B. $.01859 × 1000 = $18.59 per M ($1000), *Answer*

Finding the Tax Rate

When an owner of real estate knows his assessed valuation and the tax rate, he can find how much tax he must pay by multiplying the assessed valuation by the tax rate.

Problem: In the above problem, how much will Jones pay if his house, worth $10,000, is assessed at 80% of its value?

80% of $10,000 = $8000, Assessed valuation
$8000 × .01859 (tax rate) or
$8000 × 18.59 per M ($1000) = $148.72 Tax

Exercise

1. Taxable property in a certain town is assessed at
   $4,540,000. It is estimated that $2500 will be received from special licenses and $75,300 in state aid
   for schools. The estimated yearly expenses are:
   wages, $55,000; schools, $52,800; buildings,
   $20,000; improvements, $8000; interest on bonds,
   $12,000.
   a. Find the tax rate (correct to 5 places) to yield income to pay the budget (expenses).
   b. Express this rate as a tax per M ($1000).
   c. Mr. Johnson's property is valued at $7500 and is
   assessed at 80% of its value. How much tax will
   Mr. Johnson pay?
2. The assessed valuation of taxable property in a school
   district is $9,450,000. The gross cost of operating the
   schools is $300,669.21. Income from state aid and
   non-resident tuition fees is $126,623.97.
   a. Find the tax rate (carry the decimal to five places).
   b. Express this rate as tax rate per M ($1000).
   c. John Sperry's house is valued at $12,000 and as-
   sesssed for 75% of its value. Find the amount of
   Mr. Sperry's school tax.
3. In a certain city, the assessed valuation of taxable
   property is $63,143,000. The city's total budget to
   meet expenses is $1,896,190. Receipts from other
   sources will amount to $736,240.
   a. Find the tax rate (carry the decimal to five places).
   b. Express the rate as a tax rate per M ($1000).
   c. H. Groves' property, valued at $16,000, is as-
   sessed at 75% of its value. Find the amount of his
   tax.

Answers:
1. a. .01541   2. a. .01841   3. a. .01837
   b. $15.41   b. $18.41   b. $18.37
   c. $92.46   c. $165.69   c. $220.44

Business Letter Writing

by Irving Rosenthal
and Harry W. Rudman

Appearance and Structure of the Business Letter

In your letters, just as in your clothes, a good appearance is vital to making a favorable first impression. And the first is usually the lasting impression. Therefore it pays to take pains with the looks of your business letters. Use good paper; see that the typing is neat, well spaced and free from erasures; and let no error slip through that you can possibly catch.

Paper

Use good stationery. A secretary, sorting her employer's mail, may put your letter into the heap for "second" instead of "first reading" if it is on recognizably cheap paper. Why run that risk?

Showy, expensive stationery should also be avoided. Certainly the reader may take notice of parchment textures, deckle edges, and other ostentation; but it may not be with the reactions you desire. Such paper may arouse suspicion or contempt. A paper stock suitable for diplomatic correspondence, ceremonial invitations, or graduation certificates is obviously out of place in business correspondence.

Moreover, the most expensive paper is not always the best for correspondence. It may take ink poorly and prevent even and legible typing.

Sizes

Use standard 8½ by 11 inch sheets for longer letters and half sheets, 5½ by 8½ inches, for shorter letters. A brief message on a half sheet will look better than the same message lost on a full-size sheet.

Sometimes the so-called "Baronial" size, 10½ by 7¼ inches, is used. But this is generally reserved for correspondence by executives, with their names and titles engraved and embossed on the letterheads.

Color

White will probably remain the favored color of business letters. But the trend to other colors, especially in sales correspondence, has been increasing. It has been found that the bright colors, such as yellow and red, are "attention getters." These are being used increasingly for just that purpose. Color may also be used for associative value. An air travel company may select sky blue for its stationery; a vacation resort, green.

The Letterhead

Your letterhead has two purposes. Because it is your identification, you want it to be attractive and impressive.

And because it supplies the reader with essential information about your company—name, address, telephone number, etc., you want it to be clear and readable.

Fussy lettering and fancy symbols, mistakenly intended to impress the reader, unfortunately produce a different effect. Like pretentiously expensive stationery they may evoke annoyance and ill will instead. In any case, if they serve to a make a letterhead hard to read at first glance, they may be considered unsatisfactory.

Below are some letterheads showing attractive lettering and symbols that are impressive and in good taste without sacrifice of clarity.

Bottom and Side-Margin Messages

Business stationery sometimes carries printed matter at the foot of the sheet or down the side margins. The foot-line (it is seldom longer than a line) is usually the motto or slogan of the firm or a special sales message. Such messages may also be printed on the side margins, usually the left-hand margin. Most marginal matter, however, consists of lists of officers, sponsors, or branches of the organization.

Additional Sheets

Whenever a letter is longer than one page, the extra sheets should be of the same paper stock but without the letterhead imprint. A continuation line carrying the name of the addressee (the person to whom the letter is addressed), the page number, and the date should be typed at the top of each additional page. See that a minimum of three lines of text, besides the complimentary close and the signature, appear on the final page of the letter. For the sake of appearance it will be worth retyping the preceding page, if necessary, to make that possible.

Framing

Good typography requires proper placement of type on the page so that it sits in its margins like a well-framed picture. Since typewriting is a form of typography, accordingly it follows the same rules. The typewriting on a letter should be so arranged that, within its margins, in the spacing of dateline, salutation, and closing lines, and in its paragraphing, it resembles a well-composed and well-framed picture.

To achieve this pleasing effect the typist does not have to be an artist. She need only follow her own orderly habits of care in her margins (which should be larger in a brief letter), in her paragraph spacing, and in her indentations.

From *Business Letter Writing Made Simple*, revised ed., by Irving Rosenthal and Harry W. Rudman, Copyright © 1955, 1968 by Doubleday & Co., Inc.

Indentations

When letters were hand-written, paragraph indentations were necessary for visual clarity. The universal use of the typewriter has tended to make indentations encumbrances instead of conveniences. Many business letters, today, dispense with them. It is becoming general practice to use line space separations instead. This device speeds up stenographic work and improves the appearance as well. But whichever practice is used, it should be employed uniformly throughout the letter.

Nevertheless, the change from indentations to line spaces for paragraph indications and other purposes has not been complete. Today four forms are in use: The "full block" form; a kind of transitional form called "modified block"; the old "full indentation" form; and a type used for special effects, called "hanging indentation."

Additional Sheets

Mr. John Jones—page 2—January 14, 19

therefore feel that we cannot accept the return of the

merchandise at this late date. We like to cooperate

with all our accounts. . . .

It was necessary, because of its length, to continue this letter on an additional sheet. The additional sheet is headed by the addressee's name, the page number, and the date. There is the requisite minimum of three lines of text, in addition to complimentary close and signature.

The "Full Block" Form

February 28, 19

Mr. John Jones
1492 Columbus Avenue
Louisville 3, Kentucky

Dear Mr. Jones:

I was very pleased to receive your prompt response to my

and I look forward to seeing you on your next trip to the city.

Sincerely yours,

George Sabrin
George Sabrin

In the "full block" form all the letter's contents are aligned on the left hand margin.

The "Modified Block" Form

February 28, 19

Mr. John Jones
1492 Columbus Avenue
Louisville 3, Kentucky

Dear Mr. Jones:

I was very pleased to receive your prompt response to

and I look forward to seeing you on your next trip to the city.

Sincerely yours,

George Sabrin
George Sabrin

All the letter's contents, with the exception of the date, the complimentary close, and the signature are aligned on the left hand margin. This is still the most widely employed form.

Full Indention

19 Elm Street
Oswego, New York
April 5, 19

Mr. Gilber Kahn
67 Wren Road
Miami, Florida 33138

My dear Mr. Kahn:

In undertaking the assignment you gave me when I was in your office last
Thursday, I made it clear

nevertheless intend to do the best job I can.

Sincerely yours,

Lucille Graham
Lucille Graham

This form is all but obsoleté, and there seems little doubt that in time it will cease entirely to be used.

The "Full Block" Form

The "full block" form is gaining in usage because of its simplicity. In the full block form everything under the letterhead—dateline, inside address, salutation, body of the letter, complimentary close and signature—is aligned along the left-hand margin.

The "Modified Block" Form

The "modified block" form is the style in widest use. Here certain parts of the letter, such as the date line, the complimentary close, and the signature, are aligned to the right to help balance the rest of the letter, which has a left-hand alignment.

Some companies use the full block form for short letters (where it makes a better appearance) and the modified block form for longer letters.

Full Indentation

As mentioned before, the fully indented letter is a survival of the period when letters were hand-written. The typewriter has rendered this form obsolete. Today only a small proportion of business correspondence is typed in the full indentation form.

In the full indentation form not only paragraphs are indented but also the separate lines in the inside address and other sequences of lines in salutations and complimentary closings.

Hanging Indentation

"Hanging indentation" is seldom seen in business correspondence other than sales-promotion letters. There, it is used to focus attention or attain a repetitive, "hammering-home" effect.

Punctuation and
Abbreviations

Along with the dropping of indentations there has been a tendency to do without unessential punctuation and to avoid abbreviations, especially in the inside address where these would necessitate punctuation. This economy is for improvement of appearance—lines without terminal punctuation marks look less fussy—and for speed and convenience. The typist, freed of the bother of punctuating and figuring out abbreviations, can turn out more letters a day.

A stark, attractive simplicity, characteristic of the full block form of business letter, is increasingly to be noticed in the modified block letter as well. Periods are being omitted from the end of the dateline and after ordinal numbers such as 43rd and 44th; and commas, from the ends of the inside address lines. It is now also allowable to omit the colon from the salutation and the comma from the complimentary close. Most letters, however, still retain these marks of punctuation.

Abbreviations of cities and states are being avoided. Such abbreviations as Mr. or initials for first names are being retained and are followed by periods.

The new, unpunctuated form, where all punctuation is omitted, is called "open punctuation." The practice of using some punctuation is termed "mixed punctuation." The old form is called "closed punctuation." See the examples below:

Open Punctuation
Mr. Ferdinand L. Shorey
12 West 44 Street
New York, N.Y. 10036
Dear Mr. Shorey
         Yours sincerely

Mixed Punctuation
Mr. Ferdinand L. Shorey,
12 West 44 Street,
New York, N.Y. 10036.
Dear Mr. Shorey:
         Yours sincerely,

Closed Punctuation
Mr. Ferdinand L. Shorey
12 West 44 Street
New York, N.Y. 10036
Dear Mr. Shorey:
         Yours sincerely,

Hanging Indention

Dear Sir:

If you've been reading COSMOS for years, I hope you'll forgive me for sending you a letter

you don't need—But you'll understand why I jumped at the chance to write a special

letter to a list (on which your name appears) of successful executives who have been

appointed to even more responsible posts.

For readers of COSMOS know that the busier a man is the more rewarding COSMOS can be.

And if you haven't yet discovered the added advantage of reading COSMOS for every

week's news, then I hope you'll look into it now.

It's a quick, reliable short-cut to information you'll use a dozen times a day. A readable, reli-

able report on the

It is to be noted that this form is not appropriate for normal business correspondence, but is widely used in the sales letter for the apparent reason that it readily strikes the eye, arrests attention.

Even in the past the use in the salutation of the semicolon or the colon and dash was incorrect. Such practices today are grossly illiterate. Do not use **Dear Mr. Shorey;** or **Dear Mr. Shorey:—**

Elements of the Letter

Business letters should have at least the following elements: the letterhead, dateline, inside address, salutation, body, complimentary close, two signatures (the name of the company typed out and the written signature of the writer), and the dictator's and typist's initials, the former, usually in capitals and the latter in small letters. In addition, depending upon the operating procedure of the writer's company, there may be a file number, an order number, or a subject line for the purpose of future reference; an "attention" line where the letter is directed to a particular person or department; notice of an enclosure; and a postscript.

The Dateline

Usually the dateline is typed at the right. In full block letters it may be typed flush with the left margin. Sometimes it is centered under the letterhead.

The customary sequence is month, day, and year: as April 5, 1971. Some logical persons have been advocating a usage, now standard in Great Britain and in our armed forces, of a progressive time-interval sequence—the shortest interval, the day, first, followed by the month, and then the year: as 5 April 1971. Although not common, this form is acceptable.

The Inside Address

Inside addresses are included in business letters for several practical purposes. The inside address serves as a ready identification since envelopes are usually thrown away; it helps in filing correspondence; and it can be used with window envelopes. It is also useful to the post office when checking misdirected letters or letters with no return address on the envelope.

The inside address usually consists of three lines: the name of the person or the firm, the street address, and the line carrying city, state, and zip code. In foreign mail a fourth line carries the name of the country. If the addressee is associated with a company, its name may appear under his as the second line.

Examples: Mr. Thomas Smith
24 West 98 Street
New York, N.Y. 10025

Mr. Alan May
16 Charing Cross
London, N.W. (Zone No.)
England

Mr. Thomas Smith
West Side Riding Academy
24 West 98 Street
New York, N.Y. 10025

The Salutation

Present-day usage for the normal salutation is the word **Dear** and the title and the name of the addressee: as **Dear Mr. Doe** or **Dear Mr. Roe**. In personal friendships between businessmen it is permissible for them to use first names or nicknames in salutations: as **Dear John**

or **Dear Hank.** In formal address the expression, **My Dear Mr. Doe,** is often used.

Sales letters addressed to regular patrons may use terms like **Dear Customer, Dear Madam, Dear Subscriber,** etc. In mass mailings any general terms such as **Dear Sir, Dear Madam, Dear Friend, Dear Fellow Citizen, Dear Reader** or any other salutation considered appropriate may be used—or none at all.

Whenever open punctuation is used, the colon may be omitted after the salutation. But, as we have mentioned before, it is more customary to retain it. The colon-dash and the semicolon, however, are never correct.

There are special forms of address for persons of high rank in government, the armed forces, the church, and the professions. These will be found in Appendix D.

Body

The body of the letter is, of course, its most important part. In appearance it should be clearly typed, neatly spaced, and uniform in typographical construction.

Long paragraphs should be avoided. The paragraphs should not be so short, however, as to give any impression of talking down to the addressee. But in sales letters short paragraphs are almost always the rule, in order to sustain interest.

Underlining to indicate italics or to give emphasis is being displaced by capitalizing. Capitals are regarded as more readable, more emphatic, and more pleasing in appearance. Moreover, capitalizing makes for easier and more rapid typing. Titles of books and names of periodicals, however, should continue to be underlined or placed in quotation marks.

The contents of the body will be dealt with at greater length in the separate sections discussing the different types of business letters. Here we may generalize as follows:

The opening paragraph should be short and, unless there is a compelling negative reason, it should immediately introduce the subject of the letter or connect it with a previous development in the correspondence. The middle paragraphs should do the main job of the letter—expand on the subject in such a way as to persuade the addressee to act upon it in the manner you desire. Let it convince him that it will be proper for or advantageous to him to conclude the purchase or the agreement, or to make the postponement, the payment, or the adjustment you are seeking.

The closing paragraph should summarize your message and make clear the action you desire. Avoid wavering words like **hoping, wishing, trusting,** etc. Be positive. Say something like "We feel certain that you will agree that this is the most satisfactory solution." Avoid dangling participial endings, such as "Hoping we hear from you."

The Complimentary Close

Just as you open your letter with a word of friendly greeting, so you close it with a cordial expression—what is called the complimentary close. Some people propose dispensing with both, and recommended plunging into the letter without salutation and closing abruptly with the signature. But the convention is so firmly entrenched as to render it unlikely that this suggested procedure will take hold.

The customary forms are "Yours truly," "Yours sincerely," or "Yours very truly" where the relationship is formal. The terms "Yours sincerely," "Sincerely yours," "Faithfully yours," and "Cordially yours" express rising degrees of intimacy. "Respectfully yours" has gone out of fashion and is now generally restricted to correspondence with dignitaries or official superiors in formal situations.

The Signature

It is considered a discourtesy not to sign a letter personally. If this becomes an impossibility and a rubber stamp has to be used, it should be inked and imprinted in such a way as to resemble the true signature as closely as possible. If the writer's secretary signs for him, she should put her initials under the signature to make that fact clear.

New attitudes regarding the position of women do not seem to have penetrated into business correspondence, at least as regards their marital status. That has to be indicated in the signature. A married woman who wishes to use her maiden name in business should add her married name (Mrs._____) in parentheses. A widow retains her married name unless she takes legal steps to resume her maiden name. A divorcee retains her former husband's surname but may not use his initials or his first name.

Where the company name is included in the signature, it is typed one or two lines below the complimentary close. Four spaces should be left for the writer's signature, and his name and company position should follow:

Yours sincerely,

Thomas Smith

THE JOHN JONES COMPANY
Sales Manager

To make sure that the signature is not misread, the name is often typed above or below it.

Yours sincerely,
THE JOHN JONES COMPANY

Thomas Smith

Thomas Smith
Sales Manager

Special Parts of the Business
Letter: File Numbers

In addition to the standard parts of the letter special requirements may call for additional lines or items. On traffic or mail order correspondence file or other reference numbers may appear, usually at the left of the dateline or under it.

Attention Line

When a letter is addressed to an individual in a firm but is not intended for him exclusively, or if it is intended to be routed to a certain department, a line is added to that effect. Letters are often addressed to the **attention** of an individual instead of to him directly so that, if he should be away, the letter will not be held up but will be acted upon by the person temporarily taking his place.

The attention line is usually put between the inside address and the salutation, and may be placed either at the left, as in the example below, or in the center of the line.

The John Jones Company
710 West 10 Street
New York, N.Y. 10011

Attention Mr. Thomas Smith, Sales Manager

Gentlemen:

Note that where the attention line is used, the salutation is **Gentlemen,** not **Dear Mr. Smith.**

Enclosure Line

The enclosure line in the letter is not for the addressee, who will be informed about the enclosure in the text of the letter. It is for the mailing clerk or the stenographer herself as a reminder to include the enclosure in the mailing. It should therefore be in an inconspicuous position. It is usually typed under the stenographer's initials, as an abbreviation: Encl.

Postscripts

Postscripts in business letters differ from those in personal letters, which are afterthoughts set down after the letters have been finished. In business correspondence, postscripts have a definite, planned function. They may emphasize a point made elsewhere in the letter, or they may make a special offer. They are more customary in sales letters than in other business correspondence, and are designed to draw special attention. Examples will be found in the section on sales letters.

Envelopes

As much care should be observed with the envelope as with the letter itself. It is the first part of the letter to be seen, and, as we have already observed, the first impression is important. It should, of course, be of the same paper stock as the letter. The address should be typed in such a way as to be in pleasing balance with the imprint on the top left-hand corner, if there is such an imprint; or it should be well framed on the front of the envelope if the return address is imprinted on the flap in back.

The two standard envelope sizes are the number 6¾ and the number 10. The latter is also called the "official size" envelope. It is long enough to hold the full standard letterhead width of 8½ inches. The number 6¾ size averages that number of inches in width. Envelopes used for Baronial size stationery average 7½ inches in width, enough to permit enclosure folded the full width of the sheet.

Folding the Letter and
Inserting Enclosures

Part of the appearance of the letter depends, of course, on the way it is folded and placed in the envelope. Here the convenience of the addressee also receives consideration. The letter should be folded so that he can open it with ease and read it with comfort.

For the number 10 or the long "official size" envelope, the letter should be folded from the bottom to a little over a third of the page. Crease the fold down firmly. Then fold the top third down over the bottom fold and crease firmly again. Then slip the folded letter into the envelope.

For the number 6¾ envelope, fold the letter from

Sample Business Letter

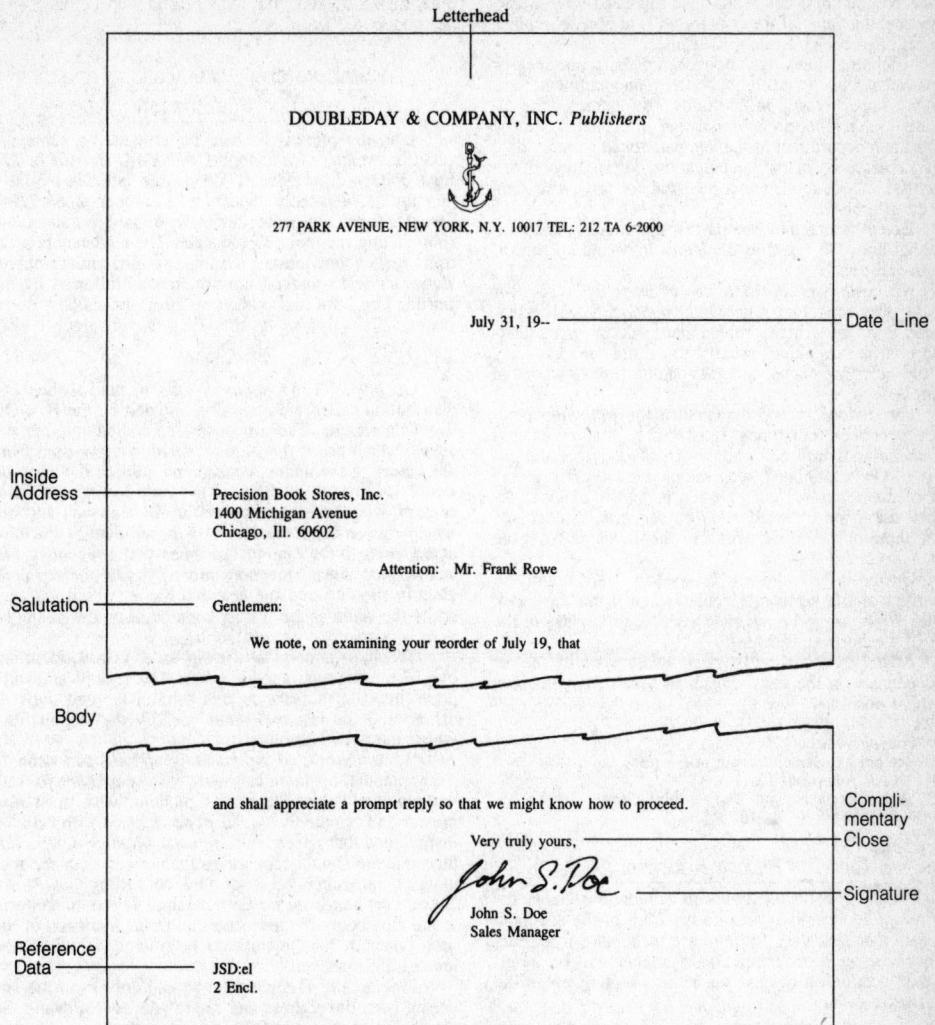

Letterhead

DOUBLEDAY & COMPANY, INC. *Publishers*

277 PARK AVENUE, NEW YORK, N.Y. 10017 TEL: 212 TA 6-2000

July 31, 19-- ——————————————— Date Line

Inside
Address ——— Precision Book Stores, Inc.
1400 Michigan Avenue
Chicago, Ill. 60602

Attention: Mr. Frank Rowe

Salutation ——— Gentlemen:

We note, on examining your reorder of July 19, that

Body

and shall appreciate a prompt reply so that we might know how to proceed.

Compli-
mentary
Very truly yours, ——————————— Close

John S. Doe ———————————— Signature

John S. Doe
Sales Manager

Reference
Data ——— JSD:el
2 Encl.

This model letter includes in standard form all *the elements normally employed in the business letter.*

the bottom to about a quarter of an inch from the top. See that the sides are even when creasing. Now fold from the sides, first from right to left about a third of the way and then from left to right, creasing firmly after each of the two folds. Then enclose the letter with the last fold toward you. This will insure that when it is received the letter can be removed with the open end on top.

Checks, receipts, or other small enclosures should be placed inside the folds. If placed outside the folds, in the envelope, such vital items may be torn or cut when the envelope is opened; or they may be overlooked by the recipient and thrown away with the discarded envelope.

Letters mailed in window envelopes must be folded in a special way.

The Outside Address

Each year, according to post office records, some thirty million pieces of mail end up in the dead letter office. The chief reason is careless addressing.

The customary address form consists of four lines: the name and title of the addressee, street address or post office box number, city, state, and zip code. On all foreign mail the name of the country will, of course, replace the state, or be added as a fifth line.

Additional lines may be required for a province or department name in a foreign address, an apartment number, a company name in addition to the name of the individual addressee, an attention line if the letter is to be routed to a department of the company or to an individual in a department, or the specification, **Personal** or **Confidential**, where the letter is intended for private reading by the addressee.

Except where they are part of the address, such additional lines are typed in the lower left-hand corners of the envelopes.

No customary position has been settled upon for postal directions like **Air Mail** or % **S.S. America.** These may be written, rubber-stamped, or typed anywhere on the envelope, usually above the address. They should be conspicuous, but they should not obscure the address.

For readability and appearance the following positions have been found most satisfactory. In all cases start the address slightly below the vertical center of the envelope. On a number 6¾ envelope start slightly to the left of the horizontal center when using the block style. When using the indented style on this size of envelope start about one third the width of the envelope from the left.

On the larger number 10 envelope start slightly to the right of the horizontal center when using the block style. When using the indented style, start slightly to the left of the horizontal center.

Addresses of unusual size or envelopes with the return address on the flap in back may call for variations of these positions.

Professor Michael T. Kellogg
Bernard M. Baruch School of Business and
  Civil Administration
Lexington Avenue and Twenty-third Street
New York, N.Y. 10010

The Return Address

It is more convenient as well as more customary for the return address to appear on the front of the envelope than on the back flap. In any case make sure it appears somewhere on the envelope. This practice will be an additional precaution against the letter's ending up in the dead letter office.

Titles of Respect

It is customary to include certain titles of respect in the address. This courtesy extends to physicians after whose name M.D. usually appears, and to engineers (C.E., M.E., or E.E.). These abbreviations are professional as well as academic designations. Purely scholastic

titles like M.A. or non-professional titles like B.S. or Ph.B., etc., are omitted. In formal correspondence, however, higher degrees like D.D., LL.D., Ph.D., etc., may be used in the address.

Numbers and Abbreviations and Their Punctuation

It is the preferred usage to write out a numbered street or avenue—for example, **500 Fifth Avenue** or **223 East Thirty-third Street.** Where the number is above ninety-nine, it usually appears as a number: **2204 220th Street.** Do not abbreviate the name of the city, and avoid abbreviating the name of the state. The tendency is away from such abbreviations. Ordinal number-ending abbreviations like **th** and **rd** are not, today, followed by the period. Use 33rd and 34th, not 33rd. and 34th.

Zip Codes

On July 1, 1963, a new system of mail sorting and distribution called zip code was initiated by the Post Office Department. The zip code is a 5-digit number designed to cut down the steps required to move mail from the sender to the addressee, thereby holding down postal costs. The first three digits of the code identify sectional centers, which are main points of air, highway, and rail transportation, and the last two digits identify the post office or delivery station. In cities that previously had local postal zones, the first three digits of the zip code identify the city and the last two digits (which are generally the same as the former zone number) designate the branch post office or substation.

The first numeral of the zip code, 0 to 9, identifies one of ten national service areas. The second and third digits indicate the service area subdivision and the post office, and the last two digits identify the station from which the mail is delivered.

While the use of zip codes is optional but strongly recommended for first-class mail, it is *mandatory* for second-class and third-class bulk mailers, who must also presort and bundle their mail in accordance with detailed instructions that appear in the *Postal Manual.* Large-volume mailers should familiarize themselves with the regulations regarding zip codes by consulting the *Postal Manual* or their local post office, since failure to conform to the zip coding requirements can result in refusal of the post office to handle improperly zip-coded mail at the lower bulk rates.

Placement. The zip code should appear on the last line of both the address and return address following the city and state. There should be not less than two nor more than six spaces between the last letter of the state and the zip code, and no characters of any kind should follow the zip code:

Mr. Harold Jones
3025 Theresa Street
Arlington, Va.   22207

The Sales Letter

The concern of all business is to sell goods or services. Consequently all business letters are, directly or indirectly, sales letters.

Your best collection letter, for example, is one that does more than induce a delinquent customer to pay up.

It is the one that leaves him convinced, after the payment, that he has been dealing with a fair and considerate house with which he is glad to continue doing business.

Sales letters, as such, are distinguished from other business letters by the fact that their sales objective is not indirect but direct and, more or less, immediate. The qualifying phrase, "more or less," is used because some varieties of sales letters are not intended to make an immediate sale but rather to lead **gradually** to sales. And others are intended to pave the way for sales by other means.

Certain sales letters, for example, may be written to help a salesman make the sale. Others may be written to bring customers for your products to one of your dealers.

The most common and largest variety of sales letter is used in direct mail selling. Devices employed in that type of sales letter are presented in a later section; here we shall deal with the more general aspects of sales letters, and take up types of sales correspondence that are part of regular business operations.

Your Satisfied Customer

No selling job is ever over. The alert businessman keeps analyzing his accounts. Can A's volume be increased? B's orders show a slight decline over last year's; does that mean a decline in his business? Or is he sampling the ware of a competitor? Whatever his conclusion, the alert businessman sends off the appropriate letter.

In An Effort to Increase
Sales

Dear Mr. Martin:

I have been very pleased to note the steady increase in the frequency and size of your orders since we started doing business together. It is gratifying to know that our product is being well received in your area and that you are making money with it.

My reason for writing is twofold—to thank you for your patronage and to offer our cooperation in any way that will build your sales of our product even further. Under separate cover I am sending you some advertising aids that can be used in window and counter displays; mats for newspaper ads; and suggested spot announcements for your local radio station. Frank Moss, our representative in your territory, will drop in on you next Thursday to help you set up these displays and to offer his assitance in every way. If there is anything special you may need, don't hesitate to get in touch with me.

I look forward to the continuance of our pleasant, and I hope, mutually profitable relationship. With all good wishes, I am,

Sincerely yours,
Robert Johns

In An Effort to Retain
Good Will

Dear Mr. Burke:

Somewhere or other we read: "There are many good excuses for losing an order—but no excuse whatever for losing good will!"

That's why we're writing to you—not to ask why you preferred to place your recent order with somebody else, but to make sure it wasn't because of something which has lost us your good will as well.

If it was the latter, we'd be most grateful if you'd write us about it.

But regardless, we sincerely hope your new equipment gives you the kind of performance you expect of it—and that you won't hesitate to make use of
our nationwide service facilities should the need arise.

Next time, perhaps, it will be our good fortune to take care of your requirements.

Sincerely,
William H. Wolcott

The alert businessman never feels smug about his satisfied customers. He does not leave the initiative to them, content merely to take orders. He bears in mind those two business adages: "It costs less to keep a customer than to get one," and "Your customer is your competitor's prospect."

If he starts a new line, if he makes an improvement in one of his staples, if he has a plan for reducing the price to a customer by quantity shipping of combined orders, the alert businessman lets his satisfied customer know about it. He does not wait for the word to get around; he sees to it that it gets around. Keeping the satisfied customer posted is a good way of keeping them satisfied.

Dear Larry:

I hope this finds you well and your business booming. I think I have something that you ought to be able to go to town on.

I've just picked up a special lot of piece goods off-price that I'm going to cut tomorrow in Style 637, with which you have done so well. I plan to bring out the number at two dollars less than you have been paying, and I know it will fit in well with your January sale.

I can get a limited number of garments out of the lot, so I'd like to know how many you can use before I offer it to anyone else. We'll be able to ship within ten days.

All good wishes.

Sincerely yours,
Phil Nelson

Dear Mr. Forman:

When you were in the city several weeks ago, you mentioned the difficulties you were having in getting fast deliveries of merchandise shipped to you by us and by other manufacturers. I think I've come across something that can help you.

I have just had a conversation with Jack Bell of Vanguard Trucking, 247 Terhune Place, Jersey City, N.J., who runs a fleet of trucks through your territory. He told me that if you can work out an arrangement with a few other merchants near you to consolidate shipments, he will be glad to set aside one of his trucks to serve your group. If the amount of freight warrants it, he can provide daily overnight deliveries, and is confident he can cut your present transportation costs by forty per cent. I think its worth looking into, and I suggest you get in touch with Mr. Bell for more particulars.

Sincerely yours,
Robert Glass

Frequent Communication

Keep the contacts with your customers unbroken and, so far as you can, make the contacts personal. Some firms regard communication with their customers, once a month, a minimum requirement for good customer relations. They do not limit the correspondence to invoices and routine acknowledgments of orders and payments. To the routine mail they add interesting enclosures. And they take advantage of every suitable occasion to extend the contact. They avoid formalities and try to set up a personal relationship. For signatures they do not use only the firm name but rather the name of an officer of the firm, the head of a department, or a salesman.

Some concerns go about unobtrusively getting personal items about their customers and keep the data current. Birthdays are remembered. If a buyer gets married or has an addition to the family, the event is observed.

Many service firms such as laundries and cleaning establishments find it profitable to send their customers and prospective customers blotters bearing calenders and reminders of seasonal cleaning needs.

Department stores keep in touch with their charge-customers by sending them advance notices of sales, seasonal announcements, and letters about special services. Whatever your business is, there are sure to be occasions for getting in touch with your customers other than through routine notices and acknowledgments.

Special Customers

In every business there are customers who rate or demand special attention. Some should get it merely because the large volume of their business calls for every possible special and even personal consideration. Special and personal letters, if feasible, will be in order.

Others may have special needs. For example, dealers located in hot, moist regions may require special packaging or other measures to keep the wares they receive in good condition. Letters dealing with such special needs are in order.

Others may be merely fussy or eccentric. These may be hard to do business with and require special sales correspondence. If you decide that the volume of their business justifies it, carry on that additional correspondence with good grace.

Letters to Help
Your Salesmen

The salesman may be assisted, through letters, in two general ways. One type of letter prepares the ground for him—introduces him, mentions the new line he will demonstrate, some special offer he will explain in detail, etc.

Such help to a salesman may be needed for several reasons. One is the lingering effect of the fictional presentation of the salesman as an intrusive, high-pressure man with his toes wedged in the door sill, launched on a non-stop spiel. Even dealers who have good relations with salesmen and have found them helpful may think of those they know as exceptions and look for the obnoxious type in a new man. A letter can help the new man by presenting him in a friendly light, stressing the useful service he is to perform—the demonstration he will make or the plan he will explain, etc.

In such letters, however, take care not to tell the customer too much. Remember that the purpose is to introduce the salesman, not to substitute for his call. The letter should stimulate the customer's curiosity and leave it to the salesman to satisfy it. Similar letters can serve to bring customers to your show rooms, to exhibition booths, to dealers handling your products or services.

Letters sent between sales calls can strengthen the salesman-customer relationship. The seasonal nature of certain kinds of merchandise or the fact that salesmen will make only a few trips a year in the ordinary course, gives rise to considerable correspondence about reorders, substitutions, cancellations, returns, complaints, and the acknowledgments and adjustments these call for. As much of this correspondence as is practical should go out under the salesman's signature.

In addition it is frequently advisable to send out, also under the salesman's signature, letters advising the customer of new developments, new lines, new policies, etc.

Even in business the strongest bonds are personal, and a good salesman-customer relationship means a good relationship with the customer for the firm.

Testimonials

When enough time has elapsed for a new account to have tested your products and your business procedures, it is a good plan to write to the customer and ask whether he is satisfied and whether he has any suggestions or comments to make. This kind of inquiry should be the first step in the continuous keeping-your-customer-sold campaign that was mentioned earlier.

Such letters may evoke testimonials that will prove valuable in your promotion. And the letters will probably have the additional value of providing a running check on your business methods by revealing from time to time the need for changes.

Build up a testimonial file from the favorable letters your inquiries bring you. You can draw upon such a file when approaching prospects in the same area or in the same general line as the writers of the testimonials. The signer of the testimonial can say more for you than almost anything you can say for yourself.

Dear Mr. Seaman:

It is now eight months since we first started doing business together, and I note with satisfaction that the volume each month has been increasing nicely. At first, we were skeptical about the possibility of developing sales in your territory, because our product has been sold mainly in colder sections of the country. Your experience, therefore, has been gratifying.

My purpose in writing is to find out whether you have any thoughts about how we can increase our volume to mutual advantage even further. As you can see, we're trying to work with you the best way we know how, and we'd appreciate hearing from you with any comments you may wish to make about our service and product. We like to receive brickbats as well as pats on the back. We can correct our faults—to the advantage of all concerned—only when they're pointed out.

                        Sincerely yours,
                        John Thomas

The Inquiry Letter

Answers to inquiries are a major part of business correspondence, and can be the most important type of sales letter. Those that are part of a direct-mail sales campaign will be dealt with in the next section. Here we touch upon the type of inquiry that originates in other ways.

Someone in the market for your sort of goods or services has looked up your firm in a trade directory; or has had it recommended to him by one of your customers with whom he is acquainted; or has heard of you in some other way. He writes to you for information. His inquiry to you may be the only one he is making. But the chances are that he is simultaneously asking for similar information from your competitors.

It is wise to assume that that is the case, and that your answer must stand the test of competition. Do your best to make your reply a sales letter that wins the inquirer's business.

Promptness is of the first importance. Your prospect will be quite as much sold by evidence of your alertness and efficiency as by what you may say.

Directness is also important. Give specific answers to the questions. If the questions are vague, don't follow that bad example; be specific about what you have to sell and thus you will probably answer effectively the questions your prospect has not been able to express.

Being specific does not mean being detailed. Leave the details to the catalogue or the other enclosures you send. A good sales letter is organized to have a certain impact. It cannot have that impact if it interrupts itself to go into minutiae.

Enclosures

Your postage outlay pays for an ounce per unit of reading matter. That ounce gives you leeway for several sheets besides your letter which—barring necessary exceptions—will usually be less than a page in length. Businessmen have found it profitable to take advantage of the full permissible weight by adding enclosures that reinforce the sales punch.

The enclosures can be particularly useful in supplying details which, if put into the body of the letter, might blunt its impact. If the prospect had to pause, while reading the letter, to take in details of measurement, construction, delivery schedules, etc., his interest would be too diffused for him to react as you would like him to.

Your letter should do two things. It should put the prospect into the buying mood and whet his interest so that he will want to look up the details. These can be furnished in an effective enclosure.

However, avoid a clutter of accompanying "literature." Some mailers believe in the more-the-better principle. But experience has shown that beyond a certain point **more** can become **too much.** Then, no matter how colorful and clever the enclosures are, they begin to clash with one another. They distract attention from the letter. They even become a nuisance to the recipient—and the letter may lose its effectiveness.

Moreover, the enclosures should not overshadow the letter. The letter itself should be attractive to look at, but above all its copy should be so carefully, sensibly, and effectively prepared that it produces the results desired.

It is generally advisable, when dealing with a smaller enclosure, to fold it into the letter so that it comes out along with the letter when the envelope is opened.

Dear Mr. Merton:
  I am going to make this letter brief. I feel the enclosed brochure speaks for itself. But I am writing merely to let you know that the sales potential of the lamp described has been tested carefully in thirty selected stores similar to yours. Every one of them has come back with quick reorders. So we know WE HAVE SOMETHING YOU CAN DO WELL WITH.
  We developed this item with a view to shooting for volume. We've brought it out at the lowest price possible, and we have complete confidence in its sales potential.
  We all get a steady stream of mail across our desks, but I hope you will take a few minutes to study the brochure carefully, and to try out a sample order of the lamp. We'll let the selling talk for itself.
                              Sincerely yours,
                                    Ivan Hubbell

Form Letters

Whatever the special function of the sales letter you write, make it personal if possible. If the volume of the correspondence makes this impractical, use forms and methods that will make it appear like a personal letter.

There are two main kinds of form letters—**complete** and **paragraph.** The complete form, even when it is individually typed and signed, is prepared in advance to cover certain standard needs.

Usually **complete form letters** are produced on a word processor or xeroxed, depending on the purpose they serve. Word processing is useful in letters where spaces can be provided to fill in dates, individual salutations, addresses, etc. In virtually all cases, the name of an individual, even in rubber stamp or stencil reproductions, is preferable in the signature to simply the name of the firm.

Complete form letters are usually identified by some combination of letters or initials under which they can be filed. Thus there may be a series of form letters with which catalogues are to be enclosed. These are keyed with the letter C and their numbers in the series. Then the secretary can be instructed to send out Form Letter C-4.

The greater flexibility of the **paragraph form letter** makes it possible to meet a larger number of calculable special situations. Such a letter is assembled from designated prepared passages kept on file in a "paragraph book." Some firms have several paragraph books with hundreds of paragraphs in each.

For illustration let us take a paragraph book containing ninety passages. Of these, one to ten may be devoted to letter openings; eleven to forty may consist of second paragraphs; forty-one to seventy may consist of third paragraphs; and the remaining twenty entries may be closings. Thus a typist may be instructed to use 7: 24: 51: 82, and will construct the letter from corresponding paragraphs in the paragraph book.

Structure of
the Sales Letter

In **sales letters** the same general principles of structure apply as in all business letters. But greater latitude is allowed in sales letters, just as greater latitude is allowed in the sales approach in general. You can be more unconventional and use more color and typographic tricks; and you will be pardoned a certain amount of puffing. Of course, if any one of these is carried to excess, it will prove self-defeating.

The salutation: One of the liberties that may be taken is with the salutation. In mass-mailings, where fill-in salutations and inside addresses are impossible, anonymous salutations such as **Dear Friend, Dear Sir** or **Dear Madame** may be used; or, if the list is a selected one permitting such specifications, **Dear Doctor, Dear Business Executive, Dear Fellow-Angler,** etc.

In some cases the salutation may be dispensed with and a flattering introductory phrase substituted for it, such as "To a Forward-Looking and Ambitious Young Businessman" or "To a Young Lady Who Keeps in Step with the Times." Or just a catchy headline like "Play Ball!" may be employed. However, these devices should be shunned in ordinary correspondence, and might be resorted to only where the multitude of identical letters is so great that individual salutations are impractical.

The opening: The opening is more crucial in a sales letter than in any other business correspondence. It is the sender's bid for attention; if it fails, the whole effort is wasted.

Some firms go to considerable trouble and expense in striving for attention-getting openings. In a conspicuous position on the letter they may have—stapled, glued on, or affixed in some other way—a small metal, cloth, or plastic object that pictorially symbolizes the opening line.

For example, one firm used a cord lasso, fastened to an upper corner of a letter so that the rope end touched the first line, to give animation to this opening: "Yes, we want to rope you in—and you'll be glad of it. . . ." Similarly a small aluminum bat glued to another letter helped to fix attention on this opening: "This is the season to go to bat for . . ."

Devices like these must be used with care for they are novelties that may appeal to some readers and by their "cuteness" irritate others. You may not be able to afford such expensive attention-getters; but still less can you afford a dull or lifeless opening. You can always attract attention with an imaginative thought and vivid words.

The question opening: One sure method is to put your opening in the form of a question. In that way you can take advantage of a quirk of human nature. We always react to a question as a challenge, and it is a rare person who does not feel the compulsion to make some response.

Of course the question should be provocative and relevant personally to the prospect, and should bring in the article or service being promoted.

This question opening was used by a home development company: "Are you over thirty, married, and a churchgoer?" Since the mailing list had been selected to concentrate on mature, married, churchgoing people, the reader was bound to answer "yes" and was thereby put in a receptive frame of mind to the rest of the proposition.

The striking statement: Another good type of opening is the **striking statement**. A good example is the one used, some twenty-five years ago, by the New York *Daily News* when it introduced itself and tabloid journalism to the metropolis. To its advertising prospects it sent a letter advising them to "Tell it to the Sweeneys" (through its pages) because "the Vanderbilts don't care." This was followed of course, with interesting material on the advantages of the mass market and its lower sales resistance.

Another example of the striking statement as an opening was the following, used in a letter to advertisers by a large woman's magazine: "Yes, men still carry on most of the nation's business—but their wives do still more of the buying!"

A proverb, too, can provide a good opening, especially when it is given an arresting new twist: "The early bird catches the worm—but was it wise for the worm to be early?"

Body of the letter: Having gained attention by your opening, you must next sustain interest while making sales points in the body of the letter.

The anecdote: Some writers have recourse to a story or anecdote for this purpose. An organization arranging outdoor exercise and entertainment for businessmen used this anecdote in a sales letter to its prospects:

"A vigorous man in his nineties was asked the secret of his longevity. 'Wal,' he replied, 'when my wife and I got married we agreed to do something to spare our nerves. If I was the grumpy one she'd go into the other room and take up her knittin'. And if she started to pick on me I'd put on my hat and go out for a walk. . . . So you see I been outdoors most of my life.'

"Being outdoors, that tried and true recipe for a long life and a healthy one, can be made easy for you by joining the _____Outdoors Club. (And equally easy for your wife as well, who won't be so inclined to pick on you if you include her.) Drive out in your own car or one of the Club's limousines will pick you up outside your office and bring you to the club grounds. Then you can swim, golf, swing a racket, walk or do anything else you like in clear sunlight and unpolluted country air."

Enclosures gave further details.

Facts and figures: Other writers rely on facts and figures. They support tempting descriptions of the article or service they are marketing with data giving the results of laboratory tests, consumption statistics, testimonials, guarantees, and other inducements.

Incidentally, experienced sales-letter writers advise that the core of the sales message should appear about two-fifths of the way down the letter.

The closing: In earlier business correspondence, in the days when businessmen dressed in frock coats and striped trousers like diplomats, it was considered proper to close sales letters with polite wishes like "hoping" or "trusting we shall hear from you." Such expressions tend to linger on. Usually they are left in mid-air as dangling participles. If you find them in your correspondence, pull out the blue pencil!

Sales letters now end with forceful suggestions for immediate action. They ask for the order; and they enforce it with all sorts of inducements, bargain offers, samples, free examination privileges, and a wide variety of other appeals.

Here is an example of the appeal of **exclusiveness:** "There are many more than three thousand discriminating readers who will want this book, but only three thousand copies were printed. As this letter is being mailed, the day's orders reduce the number still available to 422. Better make sure of getting **your** free-examination copy by filling out and mailing the enclosed card **today.**"

The "You" Attitude again: Among the numerous factors that contribute to effective correspondence, the "you" attitude, referred to earlier, is paramount. The seller takes care not to show his anxiety to make a sale. What he stresses is the buyer's interests. The buyer will get a bargain; he will be guaranteed against dissatisfaction by the privilege of returning the merchandise; payment will be made easy for him by special terms, etc. In sales letters as much as in any other form of business correspondence be sure to consider the reader at all times.

The postscript: In that same frock-coat-and-striped-pants business era alluded to above, the postscript was frowned upon. It was considered unkempt—allowable, perhaps, in private correspondence, but distinctly incorrect in well-dressed business correspondence.

Today, however, few sales letters are without postscripts. As a typographical device, the postscript has won general adoption because of the special services it can perform. It can remove from the body of the letter, whose unity it might impair, some special matter which should be brought to the reader's attention. Or it can give a needed emphasis to something as no other method can.

"P.S. Special discount terms can be arranged" stands out in a postscript, yet does not interfere with other persuasions as it might if set in the body of the letter. And if you have already mentioned your booth at a convention, a postscript reminder can do a lot to draw visits there: for example, "P.S. We're looking forward to seeing you at booth 16. Ask for Mr. Elkin."

"Letters You Don't Have To Write"

A recent speech by Maxwell C. Ross, a well known sales promotion expert, listed **sixteen** ways letters can be used to create good will—and, eventually, sales. "There's just one prerequisite," he said; "the person using them has to be a nice guy, courteous, friendly, and above all, sincere."

Each is simply a friendly, personal letter that you send on some occasion when nobody would have thought very much about it if you hadn't sent the letter at all. They don't *have* to be written, but they create a tremendously favorable impression because they *are* written.

1. *You can use a letter to follow up a salesman's call.* You don't need to, for it isn't expected, but you'll be surprised at the reception it gets. You could start something like this: "John Smith told me today of the pleasant visit he had with you about your insurance program. I know that John will do a fine job for you." Then finish off in your own words.

2. *You can use letters to make appointments.* You say, "It's about time for me to sit down with you, Jim, and go over your insurance in the light of the new tax changes. I want to do this when you have the time for it, but it should be soon. I suggest that we get together late Friday afternoon. How would 4 o'clock be?" You don't need to say much more, but you'll be surprised at the nice reception you get.

3. *Whenever a customer or client has been promoted or changed jobs,* it's a nice gesture to send a letter like this—"Congratulations on your appointment to District Sales Manager. This is fine news, and I know you'll do a great job. If I can ever be of any help to you, please let me know."

4. *When a customer is ill,* there's no more appreciated time to get mail. All you need to say is—"I'm certainly sorry to hear that you are laid up for an operation. I hope it won't be many days before you're back at your desk." Add to that a book, or the loan of one, a magazine, or a box of candy, and the good will you build is far above the effort you take in doing it.

5. *When there is a death in the family.* If it's tactfully done a short message of sympathy can mean much.

6. *When a daughter or son gets married,* or *a new baby arrives.* These letters make no tangible effort to sell; they're simply good-will builders—the kind that some day will bring something nice to you because you went out of your way to do something nice for somebody else.

7. *When people buy a home,* write to them. You letter doesn't need to be long or fancy. Perhaps: "I hope you are enjoying your new home, and that you have recovered from the trials of moving." If you have somethinag to sell, go ahead and mention it. Tell these folks you'd appreciate a chance to call when things are squared away. In some cases, an inexpensive gift like a small rosebush or a young tree creates far more good will than the cost.

8. *When a customer has a birthday.* Quite a few successful salesmen make a practice of keeping birthday lists and sending cards or letters. A personal letter is best, but if you use a card, write something in longhand on it.

9. *When people move to your town* a letter of welcome is an excellent source of new business. They don't know where to go for dry cleaning, laundry, milk—what service station to trade with, where to do their banking, or the nicer places to eat. So you write: "Welcome to Omaha. We know you'll like it here. If there is any way we can help you get settled, please let us know."

10. *When people move from your town,* it may seem a futile gesture to seem sorry—but the intangible good will you create may come back to you in unsuspected ways. And sometimes people *do* return. So you write: "I am sorry you are moving away from Lincoln. We will miss you as a customer, but should you ever return we'll be waiting to serve you again."

11. *When you read about a customer in the newspaper,* send him a letter. Clip the article, send it to him, and say: "I don't know whether your children keep a scrapbook of the nice things that happen to you, but just in case they do, here's an extra copy I clipped for you to give them." And if congratulations are deserved, give them!

12. *When a customer is elected to some office,* or honored in any other way, perhaps you would say: "I've heard some nice things about the work you've done for the Chamber of Commerce, so I was not surprised to see that you have been elected vice president for the coming year."

13. *When someone has done you a favor* he will appreciate a note from you. "Those two extra tickets got me off a rough spot. I hope I can repay the favor soon."

14. *When some product or service pleases you,* take time to write about it. "Quite often people write to you only with their complaints, but I wanted you to know how pleased I am with our new floor furnace, and with the courteous and efficient way your men installed it."

15. *When a serviceman comes home write to him* or to his parents if he lives at home. That's a small way to show your appreciation for all he has done for you and his country. Never again in his life will he so much *want* to be welcomed back; or want to feel that all he went through was not in vain.

16. *You can use letters to thank new and old customers for their orders.* Perhaps you do, but many don't. In Des Moines, a filling station operator sends a post card to new customers. All the card says is, "It was nice of you to stop at our station. I hope you'll come back often." That's all it needs to say.

Talent scout, G. L. Fultz, St. Louis' best dressed credit man, and staunch enemy of Whiskers and Goozle, says of the following assembled hogwash: "I know you will want to read this letter, for it's a dandy."

> "Thank you very kindly (who was kind?) for your letter of November 12th, just received. I am sorry that our bookkeeping department (mass production) erroneiously (new spelling) billed you for storage on the car that we handled for you. I am attaching corrected bill for which (?) I am sure you will find in order. Thanking you very kindly, we remain, very truly yours."

Miscellaneous Business Letters

Inquiries and Replies; Orders and Acknowledgments; Introduction and Recommendation;
Social Correspondence in Business, Inter-Office; Good Will; Payments By Mail.

Routine Letters

In terms of quantity the largest part of business correspondence consists of routine letters—inquiries, replies to inquiries, orders and remittances, acknowledgments, bills, etc. In these letters the writer needs little art; the basic requirements are to be clear and accurate.

Inquiry Letters

Inquiry letters and replies to inquiries should be concise, simple, and direct, except in cases that call for sensitivity, judgment, or tact. An inquiry about the price of an article need do no more than ask the price. But an inquiry about credit standing or about a job opportunity, and the answers to such inquiries, require care and tact. Similarly answers to inquiries in mail-order campaigns, where the objective is to produce sales, call for thought and skill.

In ordinary inquiries, however, the important thing, on the part of the inquirer, is to phrase his question simply, precisely, and inclusively so that he can be told just what he wants to know, without extraneous matter; and also all that he wants to know so that he does not have to send further letters to fill out details. Similarly, the important thing on the part of the correspondent in answering such inquiries is to make the reply full and precise so that the inquirer does not have to come back to him to have matters cleared up or filled out.

If the information sought is adequately covered in a catalogue or booklet, enclose it in your reply and use the letter to refer to the paragraphs or pages dealing explicitly with the matter inquired about.

To facilitate quick comprehension both of the inquiry and the reply it is advisable to present them as separate items, allowing an individual paragraph for each.

If either the question or the answer is to be kept confidential, do not rely on the other person to guess it. Say so. Examles:

Gentlemen:

We are organizing a summer camp for boys and are in the market for 24 two-occupant portable tents for camping out. We are undecided whether to use conventional canvas tents, with which we are familiar, or your new nylon tents. Would you be good enough:

To send us whatever literature you have available on the construction of your nylon tents, accessory equipment, etc.

To inform us of their suitability to the summer climate of the Catskill Mountains, where the camp is located.

To furnish comparative weights and costs between canvas and nylon.

To give us an idea of the durability of your product with estimates of how many years of service may be expected in ordinary use.

We shall appreciate your referring us to customers who have had experience with your tents in conditions approximating those of the boys' camp in the Catskills.

Sincerely yours,
Arthur Ives

Gentlemen:

We are in the market for a line of work pants. We should like to know—

What fabrics you make up.

What colors.

Minimum orders accepted per size.

Terms (including discount for cash).

Please send us a swatch catalogue with your reply.

Sincerely yours,
Bruce Samuelson

Gentlemen:

My wife and I will be in New York for the Christmas week vacation. We are people of modest means—I am an associate professor at the University here. We should like good (not lavish) hotel accommodations in Manhattan, but a little out of the immediate railroad-terminal district. We would like to take in the theater (dramas, not musicals). We enjoy good cooking, preferably without noisy entertainment.

Would your bureau book reservations such as we describe and provide information about restaurants?

Could you send us a selected list of hotels that would come within our description, listing locations and price ranges for rooms for two?

Could you list the well-reviewed plays and the price range for seats in medium locations. Fortunately our vision and hearing are good.

If you can provide such services, we will send you, by return mail, our first and alternate choices of hotel and theater reservations and a check for whatever sum you may require for deposit.

Sincerely yours,
Howard Carver

Answers to Inquiries

Dear Mr. Alexander:

We thank you for your letter of August 16 about our line of women's belts.

We wish to call your attention to the perforated pages in the back of the enclosed catalogue containing information on terms and convenient order forms.

Ours is a quality line. It is used for accessories by manufacturers serving exclusive shops, and is stocked by the New York Fifth Avenue stores.

We hope to have the pleasure of serving you.

Sincerely yours,
A. S. Cantor

Dear Mr. Jones:

Because of the decline in demand we have discontinued manufacture of the "union suit" type of men's underwear.

As the enclosed catalogue illustrates, we carry a full line of the currently popular types of men's underwear in a wide range of styles, colors, and prices.

We will be happy to serve you.

Sincerely yours,
V. A. Miles

Dear Mr. Hector:

Since your letter does not make clear what your speech defect is, we are unable to furnish a specific answer.

Our public speaking course has been designed to help shy people who are not sure of themselves to speak readily and effectively in public. If your defect is among those associated with shyness, we are confident that the course will help you overcome it.

But if the defect is organic, that may require surgical treatment. If it is a long-standing problem, such as chronic stuttering, that may call for pyschiatric treatment. We recommend that you try to determine the cause with the aid of a physician or professionally qualified person.

But common difficulties in speaking—such as inability to face an audience, lack of practice of organizing a speech, unfamiliarity with the techniques of preparing material, groping for words, difficulties over parliamentary rules, etc.,—can be overcome by our course of study.

If you do not find the answer you require, please try us again with the questions put in more specific terms.

Sincerely yours,
Marc Rafferty

A final note: Though answers to inquiries need not be elaborate, they should avoid stuffy over-formality. For example, instead of "Acknowledging yours of the 20th requesting a copy of our booklet, *Paint It Yourself,* we wish to advise you that the booklet is being mailed to you forthwith," write something like: "We are pleased to send you our booklet, *Paint It Yourself,* which you requested on May 20. Its suggestions have been useful to people of good taste who must keep within a modest budget." Or, instead of "Yours of September 10 received and contents noted. Be advised that the matter has been put into the hands of our Sales Department from whom you should hear shortly," write something like, "Our Sales Department has your inquiry of September 10 and is assembling material which should be helpful in answering your questions."

Orders

Many firms use printed order forms. If for some reason a letter is needed to accompany or precede the order to add some specific instructions about the order, make the letter concise and unmistakably clear.

Where the letter itself constitutes the order, care should be taken to make it direct, clear, and accurate. To facilitate this it is advisable to arrange the items in tabular form, giving a separate line to each. Details of color, size, material, price, identifying mark or number, etc., should be precisely stated. Manner of shipment should be specified—whether by mail, express, freight, etc.

If the goods are needed by a certain date, if method of payment is, in any way, to differ from the customary procedure, if delivery is to be made to an address other than the regular mailing address, anything requiring specific instructions should be made clear, and should be given a separate paragraph to prevent its being misunderstood or ignored.

Where remittance is enclosed, attention should be drawn to it and its nature specified—whether it is by check, money-order, express-order, draft, cash, or stamps.

Even in letters transmitting orders for goods, ordinary courtesy and tact should be observed. In his book *"Effective Letters in Business,"* Robert L. Shurter gives an example of a tactless order letter that drew a deservedly caustic reply: The letter—"Gents. Please send me one of them gasoline engines you show on page 785 and if it's any good I'll send you a check for it."

The reply—"Dear Mr. . . . Please send us the check and if it's any good we'll send you the engine."

Variations from ordinary punctuation are frequently used in orders. To compress items into single lines or a minimum number of lines, customary punctuation may be omitted and every possible abbreviation used. Names of separate articles are capitalized and also words that help to distinguish them from other kinds of goods of the same order. Thus Red will be capitalized to distinguish it from other colors an article may be manufactured in; or Wool to distinguish a garment in that fabric from garments in other fabrics. The objectives are conciseness and clarity and any typographic or grammatical means that promote these ends is justified.

Order Letters— Some Examples

Gentlemen:
Please rush to us to reach our stockroom next Thursday: 10 doz. Yo-yos, 50 checker sets, 50 anagram sets. This is for a special sales week which is going well. Our stock on these items is running out.

Our regular purchase order is being made out in the routine way and should reach you in a day or two; but please do not hold up delivery of this special order. A delay of even a few hours may mean lost sales.

Sincerely yours,
Kenneth Miller

Dear Mr. Bates:
The enclosed purchase order is in confirmation of the order we placed with you over the phone this morning. The order was phoned in to avoid delays. I must emphasize again that the shipment must reach us before October 4, when our sales will start.

Sincerely yours,
Seth Bellows

Gentlemen:
Please send us, for earliest possible delivery, the following goods selected from your latest catalogue. Charge my account.

3	doz.	Men's Nylon Hose, Black, asst. sizes @ $4.00	$12.00
3	doz.	Men's Nylon Hose, Blue, asst. sizes @ $4.00	12.00
3	doz.	Men's Nylon Hose, Brown, asst. sizes @ $4.00	12.00
1½	doz.	Men's Nylon Hose, Green, asst. sizes @ $4.00	6.00
4	doz.	Men's Cotton Hose, Black, Triangle Clocks @ $4.50	18.00
2	doz.	#61 Work Shirts, asst. sizes @ $9.00	18.00
2	doz.	Men's White Broadcloth Cotton Shirts, asst. sizes @ $16.00	32.00

$110.00

Ship freight.

Sincerely yours,
Charles Bloom

Acknowledgments

Dear Mr. Thayer:
Thank you for your order of October 5. As you instructed, it will be shipped freight, via the D & W. The order is being made up today and will be at the yards tomorrow. It should reach you well within the time you specified.

Sincerely yours,
J. H. Hudson

Dear Mr. Jones:
We have just telegraphed you the following: "Cannot ship your order May 10. Goods not available." The telegram was sent to minimize any incon-

venience this may cause you. We can supply the cheaper grade, #43, on the date required. The earliest we can supply the #41 grade specified in your order would be June 11. If the #43 grade is all right, please wire collect and we will ship immediately.

Sincerely yours,
Adam Pierce

Dear Mr. Poynter:
Thank you for your order of August 14.
Unfortunately your letter did not specify which color or colors, and which weight or weights, you wish. In our Queen's Taste stationery line the colors are Rose, Fern, Mauve, Beige, Robin's Egg, Canary, Russet, Shell White, and Alpine Snow. The weights are Tissue, Regular and Baronial. Probably our catalogue was not at hand when you made out your order. We are enclosing another giving samples of each color and weight.
A prompt reply will be to our mutual advantage.

Yours sincerely,
Eric Hunter

Dear Mr. Magnes:
Thank you for your order for Clover Danish Blue Cheese. It is being shipped out to you today.
We enclose a catalogue of our other products. Please note that with orders of $10.00 or more, customers may receive, free, their choice of a jar of Lingonberry or Currant preserves.

Yours sincerely,
Einar Toksvig

Follow-Ups on Orders

Sometimes orders are poorly attended to and it is necessary, strange as it may seem, to jog the attention of the supplier. Here, again, as emphasized in the section on **Complaints and Adjustments,** an irritable tone is inadvisable, even where loss or inconvenience has been caused by the delay. A calm letter will get quicker and more favorable attention and will enhance the writer's status as a considerate customer whose patronage is worth retaining. It is seldom necessary to write more than one reminder; but when that becomes necessary, a sharper tone is not always politic, especially where the writer has reasons of his own for maintaining business relations with the ineffecient firm. Examples:

Gentlemen:
Although our order #216 was acknowledged on June 2, and it is now near the end of the month, the air conditioners have not yet arrived. We have already undergone a hot spell and soon July will be upon us. I cannot understand the delay or your leaving us without an explanation for your delay in delivery of such a seasonal article. Up to now your deliveries have been prompt; and expecting delivery any day, I did not write to you. There is no question now that I shall lose some sales and I expect you to make up for the lost time, not to speak of the lost business, by shipping the goods by express at your expense. Please wire what you plan to do in the matter.

Sincerely yours,
Edward Hines

Answers to follow-ups on orders should be prompt, and they should be tactful even where the tone of the complaining letter is disagreeable. Give the reason for the delay, assure the customer that care will taken to avoid such delays in the future, and specify the date and the manner of the planned shipment.

Dear Mr. Osgood:
We regret the delay in shippping out your order #644, dated February 10.
You probably have read of the recent labor troubles in the lumber industry. These made it difficult for us to secure proper crating materials for the goods. Rather than risk damage in transit we held up the shipment until satisfactory crates were available. We have now managed to get some from another source of supply. Even though our shipping costs have risen, we feel the added expense, like the delay, is preferable to having the machinery arrive in poor condition.
Your order was shipped out today, express. We hope it reaches you in good time as, we are confident now, it will reach you in good order.

Sincerely yours,
Mark Lyons

Letters with Enclosures

When remittance such as checks, etc., or when invoices or special notices are enclosed, the number of enclosures should be stated in the letter. This is customarily done in a separate line, at the left margin, under the signature.

Gentlemen:
The enclosed check for $146.00 is in settlement of our account to date. We also enclose your bill. Please receipt and return it.

Sincerely yours,
Joseph Evans

2 enclosures

Gentlemen:
Thank you for your order #324 for a dozen Pop-Up Toasters. They were shipped today. The invoice is enclosed. We also enclose the catalogue on waffle irons requested in your letter.

Sincerely yours
Morton James

2 enclosures

Letters of Introduction

Letters of introduction should not be given thoughtlessly. Avoid them unless you can feel that it would actually be in the interest of both parties to get acquainted. Good-natured people often do harm when they mean to do good, by writing letters of introduction indiscriminately. The tenth "promising" young chap sent to glean advice in the field of his ambition from a busy executive is likely to get a discouraging brushoff.

Therefore, the first consideration in writing a letter of introduction is whether to write it at all. Having decided that the letter should be written, you might well consider several other elements. Since the best way to present letters of introduction is in person, the envelope containing the introduction should be unsealed and should bear the name of the person to whom it is addressed and, in the lower left-hand corner, the line "Introducing Mr. . . ." This enables the recipient to welcome the caller by name and facilitates the relationship.

The letter should be brief and restrained. A long letter might impose an embarrassingly long wait on the caller while the letter is read. And extravagant statements about the caller, if they do not predispose the reader to skepticism, may evoke embarrassing comments of other sorts.

Sometimes there is a reason to mail the letter to the person addressed; for example, to allow him to appoint a time for the meeting. In that case a copy should be sent to the person being introduced so that he will be familiar with what has been said about him. Examples:

Dear Mr. Clements:

I hope you will have the time to see Mr. Wilbur, who was a student in my class this semester. You have several times expressed an interest in seeing "the cream of the crop" in each graduating class. It is because I can unreservedly place Mr. Wilbur in that category that I have suggested that he call on you.

Yours sincerely,
Roger Hessian

Dear Mr. Canning:

It gives me great pleasure to introduce to you Mr. Harvey Wright, who operates a large bottling plant in our city.

Mr. Wright is contemplating opening a branch in your city, and I could think of no one better for him to see than you for a quick survey of local conditions and prospects. My business association with Mr. Wright is now in its twelfth year and has led to a friendship which has enabled me to discover and appreciate his personal qualities.

I feel certain that any association this introduction may result in will be valued on both sides.

Yours sincerely,
Hiram Godkin

Letters of Recommendation

There are two main types of recommendation—the general recommendation "to whom it may concern," and the individual recommendation addressed to a specific person. The latter obviously is preferable, since the writer's personal acquaintance with the person addressed generally means that the letter will be given more attention than might otherwise be the case.

The best kind of recommendation is the one that performs a mutual service to the recommended person and the one to whom he is sent. So far as possible, therefore, it will be well to find out beforehand whether and how the person about whom you are writing can be of service to the individual you are addressing.

Vital to any letter of recommendation is truthfulness and restraint. False statements are almost inevitably found out. In time they create handicaps that outweigh any temporary advantage that they gain for the person recommended. And exaggerated claims usually predispose the reader to skepticism and suspicion, and thus are often more injurious than helpful. Examples:

To Whom It May Concern:

Mr. Clarence Loman has been on our sales staff for the past eight years and has compiled an excellent sales record. He is a friendly person by nature and has won the friendship as well as the business patronage of his customers. We have convincing evidence of that from the letters we have received in response to the announcement of his retirement from traveling.

For reasons of health he cannot continue traveling, but he can serve in an inside position. We regret there is nothing of this kind available in our organization. He would make a crackerjack inside salesman and we can unreservedly recommend him to anyone in need of a person with real selling talents. It would take him no time to get a feeling of your stock and your methods; and to establish really friendly relations with customers. We are confident that he would be an asset to any firm that can use his services.

Very truly yours,
Martin Ullmann

Dear Mr. Carter:

I am taking the liberty of writing to you because

I know that you sometimes give out manuscripts for first readings, and accepted manuscripts for preparations for the printer, to qualified young people, on a free-lance basis. I have heard that you do this, as a means of testing or training candidates for anticipated future openings in your editorial staff.

If that is the case, I feel that you will appreciate my sending Miss Ethel Willison to you. You have already become acquainted with her work and have even complimented her, without knowing it, when you complimented me on the excellent shape of the manuscript I turned in, and again, when I sent back corrected proofs. Miss Willison assisted me through all the stages of my book, and it is to her that I owe the smoothness and ease with which it went through all its stages.

Miss Willison has taken all the courses given here in preparation for a career in publishing and has applied what she learned, first on the college paper and, later, in helping other faculty members, as she has helped me, in preparing articles and books.

I am confident that she is just the kind of person you will look for when you are considering taking on a new editorial assistant. I take great pleasure in recommending her to you.

Sincerely yours,
David Proctor

Social Correspondence in Business

Though the phrase "strictly business" symbolizes freedom from emotional involvements in or out of business, the words connote an attitude or a goal, rather than the reality of business itself. It would be unnatural to expect that human beings, who spend most of their waking hours in business, would not form personal relationships of varying degrees of closeness in the course of their business. The truth is that most of the friendships men form in their mature years arise out of business contacts. And friendly qualities are recognized as assets in business.

This is so generally understood that trade associations of businessmen have the fostering of friendly cooperation as their major aim. Generally, too, a business relationship would hardly be accounted good or secure if it failed to develop some measure of personal regard between heads or representatives of the two firms.

Consequently, there are many occassions for letters that should not be "strictly business," although they are essential to the conduct of business. Examples are given in the following pages:

Letters of Congratulations

Dear Mr. Leonard:

What a pleasure it was to see the item in *The Times* business section this morning about your promotion to the position of Sales-Manager. Actually I think I ought to write to the President of your concern, Mr. Tate, to congratulate him. He had the good sense to recognize a good man. From what I know about people in the field he couldn't have picked a better man. Congratulations on a well-deserved promotion.

Dear Mr. Slocum:

I don't know how others are reacting to the news in this morning's real-estate section, but I want to congratulate you on taking such a far-sighted and enterprising step. I have already heard some say that the site is too remote for such a development, but I put them with those who once thought Forty-second Street was too far outside the city. I think you have judged correctly that the site is directly in the path of the city's future growth.

Again, my congratulations and my best wishes for the success of a project which should serve the community as well as bring you well-deserved returns.

Admiringly yours,
Edmund Gates

Letters of Sympathy and Condolence

Dear Walter:

When your secretary called this morning to tell me that you wouldn't be able to keep our appointment because of your sudden illness, I was deeply disturbed. She told me that you were to spend some days in the hospital, under observation, to determine whether an operation will be necessary. I hope the tests indicate no such necessity and that you will be back in your office very soon and in condition to renew our postponed engagement.

Cordially yours,
Arthur Reinhardt

Dear Mrs. Rodd:

It was a hard blow to us, too, to hear of your husband's death. We missed him here, very much, two years ago, when he retired. During our association with him over the twelve years that he was with us, all of us developed the highest regard for his wonderful qualities. We can fully understand how deeply you must feel his loss. But it must be a consolation to you that his last years were serene. We and his other friends feel grateful to you for having contributed so much to making him so happy.

Sincerely yours,
Charles U. Clifford

Dear George:

I was very sorry to receive the sad news of your great loss. I know that nothing anyone may say at a time like this can assuage your deep grief, but I hope that you will soon find abiding comfort in the high regard everyone had for your father's accomplishments, and in the good health, happiness, and achievements of those dear to you. I hope you will have no more sorrow for many years to come.

Sincerely yours,
Frank

Dear Mr. Cass:

I have just learned of the emergency appendicitis operation you have had to undergo. I had Miss Hale phone the hospital immediately and was reassured to hear that there were no complications and that you are getting along nicely.

That's fine and we want to keep it so. Therefore, I want it understood that no matter how good your recovery is, you are not to come back to the office until the doctor, on his most conservative estimate, tells you you may. And don't think of the office. This is an order!

In the meanwhile, to help you pass the time, there will be a package of books at the hospital. The well-read Miss Hale did the choosing and I think she has a good idea of your taste.

With all best wishes,
Robert E. Griffin

Accepting Invitations

Dear Mr. Canby:

It will be a pleasure to see you when I visit New York next month. Thank you for suggesting it. Indeed one of the prospects that made the trip so pleasing to

me was the opportunity it might give me to become acquainted with you personally.

Sincerely yours,
Elmer Robinson

Dear Sir:

I consider it a great honor to be asked to speak at the Credit Men's Luncheon next month. Thank you very much.

I hope the enclosed data are what you need for the newspaper release. And I will be on hand an hour before the start of the luncheon, as you suggest, to talk over the details of the program.

Yours very truly,
Leon Hart

Declining Invitations

Dear Mr. Hopkins:

Unfortunately I will be out of town during the week of March 10 and will not be able, therefore, to be present at the reception celebrating the opening of your new store. Since I will not be there to offer my congratulations to you in person, permit me to do so here. And I wish to add my sincere best wishes for the success of the new store and the continued growth of your business.

Sincerely yours,
Anthony Asch

Dear Mr. Mann:

It is with deep regret that I must decline the great honor of organizing and heading the committee to arrange a reception for the Vice-President, who is to be one of the speakers at our coming convention. As you may have heard, Mr. Bixby, head of our Foreign Department, died suddenly last week. I have had to take over his duties temporarily, which for the present rules out any other activities for me. I will let you know as soon as I am free again for any service to the organization.

Sincerely yours,
Horace Seton

Resignations

Dear Sir:

I have just been appointed Coordinator of Sales for our firm. This will mean extensive traveling in order to keep in continual contact with our stores throughout the country. It will, therefore, be impossible for me to continue to serve as secretary of the club. And, so, with deep regret, I must tender my resignation from that office.

It has been a pleasure to serve the club during the past four years, and I have enjoyed and profited from the association with its able officers and members. Needless to say, I will be on hand for every get-together my new duties will permit.

Sincerely yours,
Edwin Robbins

Dear Sir:

I have agreed to serve on the Mayor's Committee for Emergency Housing. Since it may prejudice the value of the work I can do for the committee, if I continue as a member of the firm, I am submitting my resignation to take effect immediately.

This is a step I take not without regret, for the years I have been privileged to spend with the firm have been happy ones. But I feel that the opportunity afforded me by the Mayor to serve the community in so important a sphere of activity is one that I cannot pass up.

Sincerely yours,
Alan W. Furness

Inter-Office Correspondence

In concerns of any size a good many memos pass between departments, between the management and the staff, between individuals in different departments, etc. Thus the Stock Department may inform the Sales Department of the arrival of certain needed goods; or the management will send memoranda to department heads about certain changes of policy; or it may send a memo to the entire staff about price changes, the announcement of a special holiday, etc.; or a salesman may send a note to Shipping giving special instructions regarding the shipment of an order; or Promotion may send a memo to Sales and other departments concerned, reminding them of the start of a national advertising campaign so that they can prepare for the anticipated inquiries and orders.

Most firms provide printed forms and restrict inter-office correspondence to one subject only in order to encourage conciseness and clarity and to facilitate filing and reference. The printed forms also assure that the date, the department, the person, and the subject are clearly indicated. This makes salutations and signatures superfluous and they are omitted except, in memoranda with a deliberately personal touch.

Although such notes are "stripped for action," the tone should nevertheless always be courteous. Inter-departmental feuds have often begun over tactless expression in such memoranda. And office morale has sometimes been damaged by an unintended curt note by management. Certain indispensible formalities of respect should be observed in inter-office correspondence as in other forms. Examples:

Form G-14	One Subject Only
Inter-Office Memo-	Made Simple Books
randum	Inc.
To:	From:
Department:	Department:
Subject:	Date:

To: Staffs	From: J. B. Wolcott
Department: Sales,	Department: Man-
Correspondence	agement
Subject: New Price	Date: April 10, 1954
List	

On May 1, our new price-list goes into effect. Copies should be in the hands of all our salesmen before the end of the week and in the hands of our dealers by April 28. Copies can be obtained from Miss Andrews.

To: Staffs	From: G. E. Ander-
Department: All	son
departments	Department: Per-
Subject: July 4	sonnel
Holiday	Date: July 1, 1954

Since July 4, this year, falls on a Sunday, the office will be closed Monday, July 5, to allow a full holiday weekend.

To: Mr. Taylor, Mr.	From: Edward
Green, Mr. Johns,	Earnshaw
Mr. Maxfield	Department: Promo-
Department: Sales,	tion
Shipping, Personnel,	Date: February 10,
Accounting	1954
Subject: Advertising	
campaign	

This weekend our special advertising campaign on our new Infra-Red cooker opens with full pages in the magazine supplements of metropolitan newspapers. There will be page ads in leading national magazines, along with other promotion: Most of the advertising will carry keyed coupons. Your departments should be prepared for the special load of mail that will come in. Just a reminder.

To: E. Dirksen	From: J. Meyers
Department:	Department: Sales
Shipping	Date: January 11,
Subject: Johnson	1954
Brothers order	

Dear Ed:

When Billing sends down the Johnson Brothers' order, please put a note on it to double wrap the shipment. Old Mr. Johnson complains that our wrapping paper isn't thick enough. The trouble is in his storeroom, which is a filthy damp place. So it'll be best to double wrap his stuff, or he'll come back at us with claims for spoilage. Hope it's not too much bother. Thanks.

Joe

Other types of memo forms frequently used are:

From the Desk of Frank Gannon

To:_____ Date:_____
To:_____ Date:_____

From:_____

It might be noted, in passing, that in large corporations or organizations, intra-company mail is frequently placed in heavy-stock envelopes that can be used over and over again. These envelopes have ruled lines on the outside, and the sender need merely place on the first free line the name and department of the person to whom the communication is addressed. That person in turn can use the same envelope by doing similarly the next time he wishes to dispatch a memo or some papers to another person in the organization.

Good-Will Letters

It should be enough, of course, to service customers promptly and efficiently. Yet it is human for them to want to be appreciated as well and to be given personal attention. If thanking a customer for his order has been overlooked, write him a special note of appreciation for his business.

Letting customers feel that they are "in" on your operations is another way of building their good will. If you are expanding your business, or promoting a man on your staff with whom your customers may have had occasion to become acquainted, or if you are making any operational change of interest to them, let your customers know about it.

If you are making gifts—calendars, personal memopads, initialed pencils, etc.,—to new customers, don't leave the old customers out. Give it to them, also.

There are also occasions and circumstances that might be used for the promotion of good will by drawing attention to them. We have already mentioned letters of congratulation and letters of sympathy and condolence. Watch significant dates in the lives or careers of customers, when it is possible or advisable—anniversaries of the concern, birthdays of the officers, marriages in their families, and send congratulations and appropriate gifts.

Send Christmas greetings to all customers, and mail them well in advance of the rush period, so that they don't come so late as to seem like afterthoughts.

Unusual occurrences may be made the occasion for a good-will note. Thus when Lever Brothers were constructing their striking New York building, they sent letters to all in the neighborhood within range of the sounds of construction, private families in nearby residential blocks as well as business neighbors, apologizing for the noise. They gave assurance that everything was being done to finish the building as soon as possible and that all avoidable construction sounds were being eliminated.

During the recent period of rapid and successive price boosts some firms notified their customers that they were not raising their prices though raw-material costs had risen; and others explained what they were doing to absorb part of the necessary price advances in operational economies.

Good will within an organization is as important as the good will of outside customers and neighbors. Well run concerns make use of their inter-office correspondence to keep up office morale through informational memoranda that make the staff feel they are part of what is happening: through announcements that will please the staff; and through personal notes of congratulation from management on pleasant occasions, such as the birth of children, the graduation of sons, etc.; and condolences in bereavements. Examples:

Dear Mr. Smythe:
     The enclosed is the latest issue of our house organ, *Cuttings*. I am sure you will be interested in the piece on page twelve, on the old Smythe Tool Works which, I believe, were founded by your great-grandfather.
     Would you like to get *Cuttings* regularly? I'd have it sent without asking if it weren't for my own experience. I groan at the amount of unsolicited mail I get from people who send it with the best of intentions; there aren't enough hours in the day to read everything that comes through the mail. So for that reason I have made it a policy to send *Cuttings* only if customers let us know that they want it. Incidentally, I shall be happy to send you as many copies of this issue as you may require.
                          Sincerely yours,
                          Gabriel Harcourt

Dear Mr. Connor:
     It occurred to me, recently, that it was just about ten years ago that I entered your first order with our company in our order book. I was not then sales manager, of course—that came as the result of the good orders you and other friendly customers favored me with.
     To make sure, I had my secretary look it up, and it turned out, sure enough, that our business connections did begin ten years ago, this month! That first order, incidentally, was for an assortment of our fans. Your latest order is for air conditioners! Time does move.
     If we could get together, we'd be celebrating the glad occasion properly at Ludlow's or Keen's. But since that's not possible, here's the next best thing. Please join me in a glass of champagne of a kind I've found particularly palatable. A case of it should be in your office this morning if American Express is on its toes.
     Your health and best wishes for ten more good years of business together.
                          Cordially,
                          Ed Schacht

Dear Mr. Alter:
     We prepared a map for use by our office staff of the new city postal zones. It proved to be such a convenience that we decided to print up copies for our customers. Here's your copy and we hope you'll find it useful.
                          Sincerely yours,
                          Conrad Dietrichstein

Dear Mr. Freud:
     As a customer of the Hooker Hat Company you will be interested to know that we have just completed negotiations which bring this fine firm into our organization. It was our desire to fill out our line of men's furnishings with a quality hat line, and Hooker was our choice.
     We were glad, of course, that with so fine a product we could make the acquaintance of new customers appreciative of fine quality apparel for men.
     We want to assure you that you will continue to receive the efficient service you have become accustomed to from the Hooker staff (which is being preserved intact), plus, we venture to add, special services made possible by the facilities of our larger organization.
     On his next call your Hooker salesman will have our other lines of quality goods to offer you. We are mailing you our catalogue so that you may become acquainted with them. Any orders you wish to place from the catalogue will be credited to the salesman's account, and you will be billed on the same terms as in your account with Hooker.
     Please let us know if there is any way that we can be of service to you. I look forward to the continuance of what I hope will be a pleasant and profitable relationship for us both.
                          Sincerely yours,
                          A. E. Handley

Dear Mr. Gates:
     Thank you for your order number 112, which arrived this morning. It will be shipped today; the invoice is enclosed.
     The same company is making a new line of waffle irons, and the introductory offer is so attractive we decided to call it to the attention of all our customers. We have tested the device and found it sturdy and efficient. We are enclosing a circular giving the details. Perhaps you'll want to take advantage of this offer.
                          Sincerely yours,
                          Morton James
2 enclosures

Dear Mr. Magnus:
     Thank you for your order of Clover Danish Blue Cheese. It is being shipped to you today.
     I think you will be interested in seeing a copy of a periodical we issue, *Good Cheer*, which contains recipes and notes about new European delicacies being introduced to American lovers of good foods. If you would like to receive it regularly, we shall be glad to put you on our mailing list.
                          Sincerely yours,
                          Gail Longinetti
1 enclosure

Requests for Charity

Although the solicitation of contributions for charity is a highly specialized, professional activity these days, businessmen frequently have occasion to sell theater tickets or to ask for donations for a pet organization. In such cases make your letter brief; leave the "selling" to the professional fund-raiser. You will get a check because the person you are writing to knows you, and values your friendship or patronage. Some examples:

Dear Mr. Adams:

I am taking the liberty of sending you the enclosed advertising blank in behalf of the United Orphans League. I am very much interested in the organization and know of its good work and great need. I shall appreciate your check to the best of your ability. With many thanks and good wishes, I am,

Sincerely yours,
Sam Laury

Dear Ben:

Enclosed are a couple of tickets for "Ah, Take the Cash." The seats are not so good, and I don't know anything about the show, but the cause is good. So I'd appreciate your taking the tickets and letting me have your check for $20 made out to the Community Chest. I hope you will enjoy the show and have the double satisfaction of knowing you've aided a worthy cause.

Sincerely yours,
Norman Rich

Although it is desirable to keep letters of this type short, they can vary in tone, length, and appeal if in the judgement of the writer, the nature of his relationship with the person to whom he is writing requires more than the semi-formal approach illustrated above.

Example of an Acceptance Letter

Dear Mr. Bingham:

I am happy to send you the enclosed check for the theater tickets you sent me. I know the cause is a good one, and I hope the project is a success. Keep up the good work.

Sincerely yours,
David K. Nelson

Words and Expressions to Avoid

Superfluous, Overformal, Flabby, Tactless, Hackneyed Language

According to our records—Often superfluous and can be omitted.

Acknowledge receipt of your letter—Overformal. Better, **We thank you for your letter.**

(Please) advise—Better **inform** or **tell** unless actually soliciting advice.

Agreeable to your letter—Old fashioned.

Along these lines—Better, **the gist of his remarks** or simply **like.**

Amount of, preceded by **in the, to the, for the**—Better say **check** or **remittance** for $_____.

(Please) arrange to return—Sufficient to say, **please return.**

As per your letter—**As per** is a legal term, therefore out of place in an ordinary letter. Better, **according to** or **as mentioned in.**

As stated above—Better to repeat what you stated, or **as I have mentioned.**

As yet—For **yet.**

Assuring you of—Old fashioned.

As to—Awkward.

At all times, at this time—Usually superfluous.

At hand—Usually superfluous.

Attached you will find—Overformal. Better, **we are attaching** or **we are enclosing.**

At the present time—**Now** is preferable.

At this writing—Formal. Better **now.**

At your earliest convenience, at an early date, at the earliest possible moment—Overformal. Better say **soon.**

Awaiting your favor—Better, **please let us hear from you soon.**

Beg—Relic of old-fashioned courtesy, now abandoned in business correspondence.

Claim—Avoid in the sense of **to assert** or **assertion**; might antagonize.

Communication—Formal. Better, **message, letter, report, inquiry,** etc.

Complaint—Aggressive sound. Usually better to say **request for adjustment.**

In compliance with your request—Overformal.

Contents noted—Superfluous.

(To) date—Overformal. "To date we have not received"—better, **we have not yet received.**

Deal—Improperly used for **transaction.**

It is desired that we receive—Inactive, weak, and long-winded. Better, **we want to receive** or **we'd appreciate receiving.**

We have duly investigated—**Duly** is superfluous.

Each and every—**Each** or **every** is sufficient by itself.

Early date—May mean two or three days or two or three weeks. Better be specific.

Enclosed please find—Better **here is** or **I enclose.**

Esteemed—Old-fashioned.

Even date—(meaning today). Better be specific. Say **your letter of this morning** or **of December _____ 19 _____.**

Event—Avoid "in the event that." **If** is preferable.

Favor—In sense of letter—old-fashioned, better say **your letter of _____.** Only proper, nowadays, when referring to a specific act of kindness.

For the reason that—**Because** is preferable.

Forward—**Send** or **ship** are preferable.

For your information—Superfluous. Omit.

Hand you—**Send out check** or **enclose our check** preferable.

Have for acknowledgement—Simpler to say "thanks."

Herewith—Superfluous.

Hoping—Weak and usually superfluous. Avoid, especially as dangling particple before complimentary close of letter.

Inasmuch as—Just say, **because.**

(We are) in receipt of—Overformal. Better, **we have received** or **thank you for.**

In order to—Just say **to.**

In reference to—Overformal, avoid. Better, **about.**

In regard to—Just say **about.**

In reply would wish to—Overformal, avoid.

Instant—Abbreviated as Inst., meaning the current month. A legal term, out of place in ordinary correspondence. Better name the month—instead of "the 5th Inst." say **October 5.**

In the nature of—Long-winded. Just say **like.**

It is the hope of the undersigned—for **I hope.**

Kindly let us know—Kindly is old fashioned. **Please let us know** is preferable.

Liberty (May we take the liberty to . . .)—Usually no

liberty involved. Preferable to be direct and say **may we.**

Line—Sometimes inaccurately used in sense of a business.

(To) lineup—Vague. Better say **try to interest, try to sell,** etc.

Lot—Often inaccurately used to indicate quantity. Watch it.

Miss—Avoid using alone. Always use with a name.

Must say—Avoid. Just say it.

Oblige—Antiquated.

Our Mr. . . .—Pretentious. If name does not sufficiently identify him, describe him as **Mr. . . . , our representative,** or **our Chicago manager,** etc.

Passive constructions—Avoid them. Recast when convenient into active construction. Instead of **The goods ordered by you have been shipped,** say **We have shipped the goods you ordered.**

Permit me to say—No permission needed; just say it.

Pertaining to—**About** is better.

Pleasure (We take pleasure in)—Overformal. Better, **We are sending** or **are glad to send.**

Posted—In sense of informed, is a poor usage. Better say **informed** or **well informed.**

Prior to—**Before** is better.

Pronoun—Should not be omitted because of risk of sounding curt. Avoid, "Goods received. Sending check today." Better say, "We have received the goods and are sending you our check today."

Proposition—Avoid using the term in the sense of task. "To ship this order during the Christmas rush will be a difficult proposition" is not as good as "To ship this order during the Christmas rush will be difficult."

Proximo—(Abbreviated as prox.) Meaning next month. Legal term, out of place in ordinary business correspondence. Say **next month.**

Pursuant to your order—Overformal. Better say **following your directions.**

Recent date—your letter of—Preferable, **your letter** or **your order of . . .** (give date).

Regret—When used the following way: **we regret very deeply,** or **most sincerely,** overformal. Better, **I'm sorry,** or **I regret.**

Replying, Regarding, Referring—Weak. Avoid hanging participles. The simple straight statement is usually more direct and forceful.

Return mail—Shopworn. Better, **this week.**

Same—Stilted. Instead of "We received the goods and found same satisfactory," "We received the goods and found them satisfactory."

State—Not as good as simple word **say** or some other expression. For example: Instead of as **stated above,** use **as we have said** or merely repeat the statement.

Thanking you in advance—A trite device; may antagonize as unwarranted.

Thank you again—Once is enough.

Trust—**Hope, believe, think,** etc. preferable.

Ultimo—(Abbreviation ult.) Meaning last month. A legal term, out of place in business correspondence. Better say, **last month.**

Under separate cover—Use sparingly. Better specify means of shipment, **we are sending you by parcel post.**

(The) Undersigned—Overformal. Preferable to say **I.**

Valued—Formal word. Avoid expressions like **your valued patronage.**

We—In place of **I,** is right only when emphasis is on action by the firm. Otherwise it is preferable to say **I.**

Wish to say—Say it.

Would say—Say it.

(The) Writer—Overformal. Don't hesitate to say **I.**

Glossary of Terms Commonly
Used in Business and Formal
Correspondence

Abstract of Title—Record summarizing deeds, mortgages, and other documents and transactions affecting title to a piece of real estate.

Accessory after the Fact—One who knowingly aids the criminal after a criminal act.

Accessory before the Fact—One who instigates or aids in a crime but takes no part in its commission.

Accommodation Paper—Negotiable paper bearing the endorsement of a person who thereby lends his credit to the maker of the paper.

Account—Right to transact business in a bank by depositing money or its equivalent therein; a salesman's customers; business transacted with a firm or an individual; right to conduct business with a firm by establishing credit; record of business transactions with a firm or an individual.

Accountant—One skilled in keeping the accounts of a firm and responsible for their accuracy. Certified Public Accountants (abbrev. CPA), corresponding to a Chartered Accountant in England, is one who has qualified for a certificate from the state and is consequently engaged to check on and certify the accuracy of a firm's books.

Account Sales—Record delivered by a broker or commission merchant to the owner of a consignment of goods, showing the amount and sale prices of goods sold and deductions for commissions and freight and other expenses.

Actuary—One whose profession is to calculate insurance risks and premiums.

Adjust (in insurance)—To determine the sum to be paid in settlement of a loss covered by a policy. **Adjustor, Adjuster**—one who makes the settlement in claims arising out of losses or complaints with the purpose of avoiding possible litigation.

Administrator, Administratrix—A person appointed by a court to settle an estate.

Advertising—Promotion of business through notices in the public prints, on posters, by radio, television, or other media. **Classified Advertising**—small advertisements listed alphabetically. **Display Advertising**—large advertisements usually using illustrations and type arrangements for effect. **Poster Advertising**—advertising on large cards posted in public places. **Outdoor Advertising**—very large advertising posted on roadside structures, on top of buildings, on sides of wall, etc. **Car Card Advertising**—small poster inserted in panels on cars, buses, railroad cars, etc. **Radio Advertising**—advertising over the radio with an "advertiser" paying the cost of programs as "sponsor." **Television Advertising**—advertising over television with an "advertiser" paying the cost of programs as "sponsor." **Mail Order Advertising**—advertising by mail or periodical advertisements, leading to purchases transacted by mail.

Affiant—A signer of an affidavit.

Affidavit—An attestation of the truth of a written statement.

Affiliate—A company in financial association with another.

Agent—Person or company acting for another person or company.

Agreement—Mutual consent to terms of trade or employment, usually in written form.

Allocation—Apportionment of goods in short supply so that all companies, when the government is the allocator, or all customers, when a company is the allocator, may secure a share assigned according to their regular consumption or their comparative immediate needs.

Allowance—A customary deduction from the gross weight of goods; in law, a sum in addition to regular taxable costs awarded by the court; a reduction in cost allowed the purchaser by the seller.

Amortization—Gradual liquidation of a mortgage or other debt by periodic payments in addition to interest.

Announcer—A person hired by a radio station or commercial sponsor to introduce radio programs and performers.

Annuity (in insurance)—Annual or periodic income to the insured for life or for a specified long term.

Appeal—Resort to a higher court for review of a lower court's decision in the hope of having it reversed, or the case retried.

Appraise—To set a value on goods, land, the estate of a deceased person; to estimate loss as by fire, etc.; **Appraisal**—act of appraising or the stated result of appraising; **Appraiser**—one designated by court or appointed by agreement to set a value on property.

Appreciate—To increase in value; **Appreciation**—a rise in value.

Arbitrage—Purchase of stock in one market for profitable resale in another.

Arbitration—Submission of a dispute to judgment by a third party agreed on by both parties to the dispute.

Arraignment—Formal summoning of accused into court where indictment is read to him and he is called upon to plead "guilty" or "not guilty."

Arrival Notice—Announcement by transportation company to consignee when shipment reaches destination.

Arson—Deliberate burning of a house (in some states, of any property); a statutory crime.

Assess—To set a value for taxation; to impose a fine; to impose a contribution as a "lodge assessment." **Assessment**—a valuation of property; a fine; an imposed contribution; **Assessor**—one appointed or elected to value property for taxation.

Asset Currency (in banking)—Currency secured exclusively by the general assets of the issuing bank as distinguished from that secured by special deposit of government bonds, commercial paper, etc.

Assets (Property)—In accounting, items on balance sheet of business showing book values of its resources as at a given date; **Fixed or Permanent Assets**—land, building, machinery, capital stock of another company which can be used repeatedly; **Current, Liquid or Floating Assets**—cash or materials which can be used only at one time; **Quick Assets**—cash or goods which can be immediately disposed of without loss.

Association—Organization of a large number of people

to transact business; if not incorporated, members are liable for its debts as in a partnership.

Attachment—Court order authorizing seizure of property, usually pending outcome of trial.

Auction—Public sale of property by competitive bidding of prospective buyers.

Auctioneer—A person whose job it is to conduct auction sales.

Audit—A verification of accounts; to make an audit.

Auditor—A person authorized to examine accounts.

Backlog—Amount of orders remaining to be filled.

Balance (in bookkeeping)—To prepare an accounting of assets and liabilities; the money in a bank account left after current withdrawals.

Balance Sheet—Statement of financial condition showing current assets and liabilities.

Bank—Institution where money or other property is deposited A **National Bank** is one organized under the National Bank Act; it functions as a commercial bank but may have trust and savings departments, depending on the laws of the state in which it operates. A **State Bank** is organized under state laws; it operates as a commercial bank, but may have trust and savings departments. A **Commercial Bank** does business primarily in short-term and seasonal loans to business organizations. A **Savings Bank** does business primarily in savings and their investment, but may also do commercial banking where state law permits. A **Trust Company** acts as fiduciary agent for trust funds of individuals or corporations; if part of commercial bank, trust funds are separate from bank funds. The **Federal Reserve Bank** is a banker's bank acting under the Federal Reserve Act as agent for the government in relations with other banks. The **Land Bank** lends money on real estate mortgages under terms of the Federal Farm Loan Act.

Bank Discount—Interest deducted in advance.

Banker—Officer of a bank. **Investment Banker** is one who supplies capital in securities, and finances transactions or advises on investments. **Private Banker** generally lends money to finance international projects, may also engage in commercial banking.

Bankruptcy—Condition of a company unable to meet its debts. In **Voluntary Bankruptcy**, the company petitions to be declared bankrupt; in **Involuntary Bankruptcy**, a creditor or group of creditors is the petitioner.

Bargain—Agreement or terms of a sale; purchase of material at an advantage.

Barter—Direct exchange of commodities without use of money.

Bear—One with a pessimistic attitude toward business; one who anticipates downswings in the market, as opposed to Bull.

Beneficiary—One in whose benefit a gift, trust fund income, or insurance money, is drawn.

Bequeath—To will personal property (property other than realty).

Bid—A possible offer at which goods will be supplied or work performed.

Big Board—A term for the New York Stock Exchange.

Bill—Account of or invoice for goods sold or work done. Abbreviations for "bill or exhcange," now chiefly designating piece of paper money.

Bill of Lading—Certificate drawn up and signed by transportation company, enumerating articles being shipped; acts as contract and receipt for shipment.

Binder—A sum of money or other valuable consideration binding parties to a contract.

Black Market—Trading that violates legal restrictions such as price ceilings, etc.

Blanket—Covering everything, rather than a specified item, such as blanket insurance, etc.

Block (in currency)—Legal prohibition or restriction of foreign credit, currency, securities or other property, usually during war; e.g., blocked currency.

Blue Chip—A stock regarded as an especially good investment.

Board of Directors—Group of persons directing affairs of a company, corporation, or association.

Board Room—Room in which Board of Directors meets; room in brokerage office containing board on which is posted records of transactions, prices, etc.

Board of Trade—Organization for advancement of business, usually of an industry or geographical area such as a town or state.

Bourse—The Paris Stock Exchange

Bond—An interest-bearing certificate of indebtedness; a bond differs from stock in not representing ownership. In actuality, bonds are long-term interest-bearing notes representing loans; or goods being manufactured, stored, or transported under care of bonded agencies.

Bonded Debt—Bond issue representing indebtedness.

Bonus—Extra goods shipped without charge on an order; sum given to employee in addition to contracted wages or salary.

Bookkeeper—One who keeps "books" or accounts of a company; generally distinguished from an accountant in having less formal training and lower status.

Book Value—Value given to assets on the books of owner, may be above or below current market value.

Boycott—Organized effort to prevent purchases of goods produced by a certain firm or industry and usually arising out of labor trouble.

Brand Name—Name of manufactured article registered to prevent copying.

Breach of Contract—Refusal to carry out terms of a contract in whole or in part.

Brief—Lawyer's statement of his client's case, containing legal citations supporting it.

Broker—Agent; one who buys or sells for another on commission.

Bucket Shop—A dishonest brokerage house where the customer's money is gambled with, against the customer's interest.

Budget—Plan for the expenditure of income.

Building and Loan Association—Association of investors whose savings are used to finance home construction and make loans on improved real estate.

Bull—One with optimistic attitude toward business; one who anticipates upswings in the market; opposite of Bear.

Bullion—Bars of gold and silver intended for coinage.

Business—Commercial transaction; organization conducting commercial transactions.

Business cycle—Recurrent succession of business fluctuations loosely divided into prosperity, crisis, liquidation, depression, recovery.

Call—Purchased rights to demand a certain amount of goods at a fixed price or within a fixed time; demand for payment of money as on a stock-holder, member of a mutual insurance company, etc., to pay installment of subscription to capital, or a contribution to meet losses.

Call Loan—One which may be terminated by either party at any time.

Call Money—Money that must be returned when demanded.

Cancel—To annul an order for goods or services.

Capacity—Calculated space of any form of container from warehouse or ship to carton.

Capital—A stock of accumulated wealth; amount of property and funds as distinguished from income.

Capitalism—An economic system in which capital plays a leading part in production and distribution.

Capitalist—One who uses capital for investment.

Capital Stock—Shares of a corporation considered as an aggregate.

Capital Surplus—Profits, such as from sale of stock above par value, other than earned surplus.

Carrier—A company transporting passengers or freight, e.g., railroad, airlines, bus or trucking company, etc.

Cartel—International combination allocating markets and supplies, and fixing prices in order to eliminate competitive buying and selling.

Catalogue—A list, usually with illustrations and textual description, of items for sale at announced prices.

Ceiling—Maximum wage, rent, etc., fixed by the government.

Certified Check—Bearing the signature or stamp of the cashier of the bank on which it is drawn. Its significance is that the sum has been withdrawn from the account of the drawer and the bank assumes responsibility for payment.

Chain Store—Branch of a large system of stores belonging to a single ownership.

Chamber of Commerce—A board of trade; an association to promote the commerce of a community, state or nation.

Charter—Certificate from the state approving the organization of a company and authorizing it to do business in the approved form.

Check—A standard form of written order to a bank to make a designated payment out of a depositor's balance.

Circulation—In a periodical, the number of purchasers by subscription or individual sales; in a store, movement of customers in and out.

Clearing House—Organization maintained by a banking group to exchange checks and adjust accounts among its members.

Closed Corporation—One in which all stock is privately held in a few hands; it usually may not be disposed of by holders without the consent of the other holders.

C.O.D.—Abbreviation for "cash on delivery." In C.O.D. transactions, goods must be paid for at the time of delivery.

Code—An arrangement of words, letters or other symbols to achieve secrecy or brevity in communication; a set of rules governing the conduct of a business.

Codicil—Addition to a will, modifying some provision in it.

Collateral—Property used as security for a loan.

Collective Bargaining—Negotiations between employers and a committee of their workers and/or representatives of the union.

Co-Maker—One who shares obligations of another by endorsing a contract.

Commercial Paper—Promissory notes of a large, reputable firm; dealt in by note brokers and sold to banks which discount them and, in that way, realize interest on them.

Commission—Percentage or allowance made to broker or agent for transacting business for another, e.g., salesman's commission.

Company—Association of persons for carrying on commercial or industrial enterprise; may be partnership, corporation or other joint enterprise.

Complaint (in law)—Statement of the cause of an action; the person initiating the complaint is called the complainant. In commerce, customer's charge of faulty goods, delivery or other service.

Comptroller—Auditor with the rank of executive.

Consign—To send or address goods by bill of lading, etc., to an agent in another place to be stored, sold or otherwise cared for.

Consignee—One to whom goods are shipped.

Consignment—Transaction in which purchase is not final; unsold goods may be returned to consignor.

Consumer—Ultimate purchaser or user of merchandise.

Contingent Order (in advertising)—Space in small circulation media to be paid for by returns from the advertisement.

Contract—Witnessed agreement, usually in writing, the terms of which are legally enforceable.

Contractor—One who specializes in a certain type of work; e.g., building contractor. **Sub-contractor**—one who performs part of a piece of work; e.g., plumbing sub-contractor.

Convenience Merchandise—Goods kept in a store for the convenience of certain customers.

Cooperative—A business enterprise or association with the object of producing, purchasing, selling, or occupying quarters at common savings to members by eliminating middle-man fees and profits.

Copy—Text of advertising; duplicate of an original letter or of an article of commerce. Ordinarily, carbon copy duplication for typing.

Copyright—Exclusive publication rights, now extended to cover plays, movie scenarios and movie films and radio and television scripts; other pieces of creative work are copyrighted **after** publication. Application must be made to Register of Copyrights, Library of Congress, Washington, D.C.

Corner—To secure such control of stock or commodities as to be able to dictate quotation prices.

Corporation—A business association operating on a state franchise and with liability limited to the amount of the investment.

Co-Sign—To assume joint responsibility in indebtedness by adding one's signature to the note of another.

Cottage Industry—One where operations are performed by workers at home.

Countermand—To reverse a personal order.

Courts—Where cases involving offenses against the law or claims protected by the law are tried. Courts where large claim cases are tried include Superior, Circuit, certain District, Chancery or County courts. Courts where small claim cases are tried are Justice courts, presided over by a Justice of the peace, and include Magistrate's court and certain District courts.

Covenant—Promise of some future action, made in contracts and other legal papers.

Coverage—The amount and type of protection against risks agreed on in an insurance policy.

Credit—Financial standing influencing sales to a concern on deferred payment; permission to defer payment for a certain period.

Creditor—One who extends credit; lender.

Credit Line—Amount of credit extended; e.g., "X's credit line is $2,000." Also, reproduction of signature, symbol or other acknowledgment in print to signify the originator or owner of writing, photographs or illustrations.

Credit Rating—Summary of credit line as published in Dun & Bradstreet or other credit house ratings and reports.

Cum Div—With dividend declared or pending.

Curb Market—The usual reference is to the American

Stock Exchange (formerly New York Curb Exchange), formerly conducted out-of-doors but now housed in a building of its own; it is the second largest stock market in the United States.

Custom—Generally accepted practice, company practice; customer's account.

Customer—Person or concern purchasing goods.

Cut—In printing, zinc etching, or copper or zinc half-tone, usually reproducing a picture or hand-lettering.

Cutback—Reduction in production schedule; reduction in salary or other compensation.

Damage—Loss in merchandise, machinery, service, productive capacity or trade standing. Compensation for such damage may be claimed depending on the circumstances, in a court of law.

Dead Spot—Store location at point of little traffic.

Dead Stock—Unsaleable merchandise.

Debenture—Synonym for debt; documentary evidence of debt.

Debit and Credit Memoranda—Issued by companies to effect necessary adjustments in the course of business transactions.

Decontrol—Removal of government restrictions on prices, rents, etc.

Deduction—Sum or money subtracted from amount to be paid for goods or services.

Deed—Contract by which real estate is conveyed by one party to another; **Warranty Deed** contains a guarantee to clear title ownership; **Quick Claim Deed** relinquishes rights of former owner without guaranteeing clear title to purchaser; **Joint Tenancy Deed** transfers property to two or more owners with the provision that the survivor will own the entire property; **Trust Deed** is given as security for a debt and is a form of mortgage; **Tax Deed** is received by purchaser at a tax sale.

Defalcation—Misappropriation of money placed in trust; the sum misappropriated.

Default—To fail in fulfilling a contract or other financial obligation.

Deficit—Amount by which expenses exceed income, liabilities exceed assets, production falls below expectation.

Deflation—Decline in prices, volume of production, etc., usually accompanied by unemployment.

Delaware Corporation—A corporation chartered in Delaware to take advantage of low incorporation fees and tax rates.

Demand—Desire to purchase commodity together with capacity to pay for it.

Demand Bill or Draft—A bill payable at sight, or on demand.

Demand Item—Article in constant demand, which must be carried in stock constantly.

Demand Loan—Loan payable on demand.

Demand Note—Note payable on demand.

Demurrage—Charge by transportation company for detention of carriers beyond allotted time.

Deposit—Money or equivalent entrusted for safe-keeping with another, as in a bank; money given as partial payment in a transaction or as a binder in a contract.

Deposition—Testimony given by witness unable to appear in court.

Depreciation—Decline in value, usually as a result of loss through wear, neglect, exposure, etc. Machinery is usually calculated to suffer an annual depreciation of 10% in value through wear.

Depression—Deep and prolonged deline of industrial and general business activity.

Deteriorate—To spoil or lose quality with time, e.g.,

food and certain manufactured articles such as photographic film.

Detriment—Damage by intangible cause, such as injury to a firm's reputation through rumors.

Devise—To will property in real estate.

Director—Person entrusted with determining policies and decisions of a firm.

Disbursements—Payments to meet bills.

Discount—Allowance for cash or quick payment; **Trade Discounts** are discounts from wholesale prices allowed to customers and scaled according to amount of purchases and other considerations.

Distributor—Person or company through whom goods reach the consuming public; **Wholesale Distributors** supply **Retail Distributors** who serve the public directly.

Dividend—Money paid to shareholders or depositors as share of profits.

Dock Receipt—Signed by steamship company for freight delivered to dock.

Draft—Papers by which one party, usually the seller, orders another party, usually the buyer, to deliver to a third party, usually a bank, a sum to be credited to the account of the first party. Used to assure payment and to secure settlement of unpaid accounts, since rejection of a draft when presented by the bank is recorded and affects credit standing.

Drawee—Bank on which check or draft is drawn.

Drawer—Person who draws money from his bank account by check.

Dry Goods—Commodities made from fabrics.

Due Bill—In brokerage business, a type of IOU by broker, promising to deliver certain stocks not available at time of sale; also used for promised future delivery of dividends, etc.

Dummy—Sample of proposed book, magazine, or booklet to show size, format, and sample pages.

Dummy Corporation—One organized solely for intermediate purposes, and not for open business activity.

Duplicate—Copy or identical likeness, e.g., duplicate of bill.

Duty—Payment imposed by the government on goods imported, exported, or consumed, such as customs duties, excises, etc.

Earned Income—Income derived from wages, salary, or fees in return for labor, advice or management services.

Earned Surplus—Balance of profits and income remaining after deducting losses, dividends, and transfers to capital stock, etc.

Earnest Money—Deposit or binder; a sum of money paid to seal a bargain and to be deducted from purchase payment.

Economy—Organization of the production, distribution, and consumption of goods in a community.

Efficiency Engineer—A person whose profession it is to plan or change production methods to secure greater economy and efficiency.

Embezzle—To fraudulently appropriate to one's own use property entrusted to him.

Endorse (also Indorse)—To sign one's name as a payee or to indicate co-responsibility for payment on a check, bill, note, or other document.

Enterprise—In association with the word "free" or "private" has come to replace "capitalism" to differentiate the non-socialist from the socialist type of economy.

Entrepreneur—One who takes commercial risks; enterpriser.

Entry—Item in a business record.

Equity—In real estate, difference between value of property and owner's debt on it. In margin buying difference between market value of a stock and customer's indebtedness for its purchase.

Escrow—Papers or money in keeping of responsible third party such as a bank, held until certain conditions are fulfilled.

Estate—Property in lands or tenements, sometimes inaccurately used for property other than lands or tenements; total property left by a deceased person.

Estimate—Statement of amount of goods to be produced or stored or of sum for which certain work will be done.

Ex-Bonus
Ex-Coupon
Ex-Dividend ⎫ Earnings or privileges not in-
Ex-Interest ⎬ cluded in the purchase of partic-
Ex-Privileges ⎭ ular shares.
Ex-Rights

Exchange—Transfer of goods; place where business interests of a certain sort meet for transaction, e.g., stock exchange, cotton exchange, etc.

Executor (Executrix)—One designated to carry out terms of a will.

Execution—Carrying out a term of a will or a court order.

Expedite—To accelerate production or distribution of goods or rendering of service.

Expediter—One whose job it is to expedite or facilitate business and other transactions.

Export-Import Bank of Washington—Organized by the government in 1934 to facilitate foreign trade.

Express—Shipment by fast or unobstructed transportation; via Railway Express Agency.

Facsimile—Exact copy not necessarily of same size; photostat can serve as satisfactory facsimile.

Factor—Commercial agent who sells or buys goods for others on commission; commission agent.

Factor—Building where manufacture of goods is carried on.

Fail—To become insolvent.

Fee—Compensation for professional or special services; fixed charge for services of a public officer, e.g., sheriff's fee.

Feeder—Branch line in railroad, bus, or air transport that connects with trunkline.

Fee Simple—Unrestricted title to property.

Felony—Crime whose penalty is death or prison sentence.

Fiduciary—In trust; a fiduciary is a trustee.

Finance—Management of money matters.

Financial Rating—Financial information carried in directory such as *Moody's Manual.*

Firm—Correct meaning is partnership; in common usage, any business organization.

Fiscal—Relating to finance, e.g., U.S. fiscal year, period in which annual taxes are collected.

Fixtures—Fixed equipment in business or professional premises.

Foreclosure—Transfer of property to mortgagee when mortgagor defaults on interest payment.

Franchise—Special commercial rights granted by a city to operator of a public conveyance, e.g., a bus line; special rights granted by a manufacturer to a dealer.

Freight Bill—Prepared by transportation company and rendered to receiver or sender, depending on who is paying the freight charges.

Freight Claim—Also called "Loss and Damage Claim" or "Overcharge Claim," claim on transportation company for loss, damage or overcharge.

Fund—Cash or specified assets set aside for a specific purpose.

Funded Debt—Fund set up for payment of long-term indebtedness.

Funded Reserve—A reserve for which a fund has been invested to earn income.

Futures—In commodity exchange, contracts for subsequent delivery, as of a crop not yet harvested.

Garnishee—To take over property or money to satisfy a debt or a claim. A claimant may "garnishee" a defendant's wages.

Gold Standard—Rating of currency in terms of supposed value in gold.

Good will—Intangible asset resting on a special earning power gained through advertising, reputation, good business methods, favorable location, business standing, etc.

Gray Market—Trading by undercover methods, in between black market and regular market methods.

Gross—As a number, 12 dozen or 144; as an adjective, indicating a complete sum before deductions have been made, e.g., gross income before deductions of taxes, expenses, etc.

Handbill—Printed announcement handed out to passers-by.

Handicrafts—Goods produced by hand, e.g., certain pottery, woven goods, embroidery, basket work, etc.

Hedging—Stock trading in which sales or purchases are made to offset or "hedge" against possible loss in other transactions. "Puts and calls" are a form of hedging.

Heir—Person entitled by law or terms of a will to an inheritance.

High Pressure—To make sales of goods not actually needed or desired.

Holding Company—One organized to buy and hold stock of another company.

Holographic Will—One entirely in the handwriting of the testator, not valid in some states.

Huckster—One who prepares radio or television advertising, usually with methods of exaggerated showmanship.

Hypothecation—Pledging of collateral. Governments may "hypothecate" tax revenues as security for a loan. Property may be "hypothecated" for payment of a debt. Its earnings may be so used and the property remain with the debtor; but if payment is defaulted, the creditor may demand sale of the property to secure payment of the debt.

Identification—Driver's license, social security card or other document required as identification in check payments at stores, hotels, or other public places.

Implement—To find means to carry out an agreement.

Impulse Item—Something marketed to appeal to spontaneous decision of customer, usually novelties and luxuries as opposed to staples or necessities.

Income Group—Classification of people according to earnings.

Incorporate—To secure a charter of incorporation from a state, and to organize operations under its provisions.

Indemnify—To make secure against loss or damage; to make good a loss or damage.

Indenture—Sealed agreement of which each party concerned holds a signed copy.

Index—Stock market term referring to listed price quotations of securities traded on the market and analyzed for trends.

Indictment—Formal grand jury charge against a person accused of a major crime.

Industry—Collectively, manufacturing as contrasted to

agriculture; any branch of production, e.g., shoe industry, paper industry, etc.

Inflation—Rise in prices where income advance fails to keep up with prices.

Injunction—Court order restraining certain action.

Insert—Something added in a document; an enclosure in a mailing.

Insolvency—Inability to meet current financial obligations.

Installment—Periodic payment on a time-payment purchase. The British equivalent is "hire-purchase."

Institutional Advertising—Directed not at immediate sales but at increasing prestige leading to consideration of a company as an established institution.

Instrument—Person or document useful in accomplishing a stated purpose.

Interest—Payment by borrower for use of borrowed money measured in percentages and units of time; **simple** interest is payment on principal alone; **compound** interest is payment of accrued interest added to capital; **penal** interest is payment of special interest by defaulting debtor.

Interstate Commerce—Commerce across state boundaries.

Intestate—Descriptive of a property holder who dies without leaving a will. Division of property will then be made according to state inheritance laws.

Intrastate Commerce—Commerce within a state.

Inventory—Record of merchandise on hand and in stock rooms; **perpetual** inventory is one maintained by recording every sale and receipt of goods on an inventory card. Usually inventories are made at periodic intervals.

Investment—Money or other property risked with expectations of profit.

Investment Trust—Company whose business is investment in securities and bond issue, and which markets its own securities on the basis of these investments.

Invoice—A bill itemizing goods shipped and their prices.

IOU—Document bearing the letters "IOU" and a notation of a sum of money. If signed, an IOU has legal status as a debit account.

Island Counter—Table displaying or carrying goods for sale in such a position in a store that customers may walk around it.

Joint Stock Company—Large partnership with some of the features of a corporation.

Journal—Bookkeeping record in which transactions are first entered.

Judgment—Court decision; in a civil trial for damages, the sum awarded to the plaintiff.

Jury—Of two kinds. The **grand** jury consists of 12 to 23 persons who serve as an investigating body and dismiss or indict a suspect, depending on the evidence at hearings. Functions only in cases involving major crimes. **Petit** jury, an ordinary jury, usually consisting of 12 persons who hear civil suits and cases of minor law-breaking.

Kickback—Unauthorized payment out of wages, prices, or fees as extortion or bribery.

Know-How—Technical skill gained through training and experience.

Kraft—Strong brown paper used in packing for shipping.

Landlord—Owner of real estate; usually reference is to owner of specified building.

Layout—Sketch of a proposed advertisement, booklet, etc., in store merchandising, arrangement of merchandise.

Lease—A contract for the temporary conveyance of property, usually in consideration of rent.

Ledger—Account book. In larger sense, accounting in general.

Legacy—Inheritance through a will.

Legal Standard—Measure of value in gold or silver established by a government for the rating of its currency.

Legal Tender—Money that may lawfully be used in settlement of debts.

Lessee—Tenant under a lease.

Lessor—One who grants a lease.

Letters Patent—Document transferring title to public lands or rights to inventions (see Patent).

Liability—Indebtedness; **current** liabilities are short term debts such as taxes, accounts payable, etc., to be met within the year; **fixed** liabilities are long term debts such as mortgages, bonds, etc.; **deferred** liabilities are advance payments such as rent or interest before they come due.

Libel—Written statement held to be damaging to person or business about which it is made. To be distinguished from **slander,** which is a damaging statement made orally.

License—Legal permission to sell certain goods, e.g., a liquor license; or to practice a profession; or to sell goods on the street, e.g., a peddler's license, etc.

Lien—Legal right to property in payment of debt; usually has priority over other claims, e.g., tax lien, mechanics lien, etc.

Limit Order—Order to buy or sell stock at or above or below a specified price.

Line—Type of merchandise offered for sale, e.g., line of pearl buttons.

Liquid—Convertible into cash, e.g., liquid assets.

Liquidate—To convert assets into cash, generally in reference to business in financial difficulty and in need of ready cash.

List Price—Selling price as listed in catalogue.

Loan—Money lent on interest.

Lockout—Shutting out of employees during a labor dispute. Now illegal.

Logotype—Trademark or symbol used by a firm in its advertising.

Long and Short—To be **long** is to hold stock in expectation of a rise; to be **short** is to sell stocks one does not own, in a falling market, in expectation of buying them in at a still lower quotation and profiting from the difference.

Lots—In real estate, specified arrangement of ground; in the stock market, number of shares traded in. **Round** lots are those taken in round numbers, such as 100 shares; **odd** lots are transactions in lots under 100.

Maintenance of Membership—Clause in labor contract making it obligatory upon workers to keep in good standing in the union in order to retain jobs.

Malfeasance—Wrongful action: To be distinguished from **nonfeasance,** failure to perform an action agreed upon; and **misfeasance,** performance of an agreed action in such a way as to violate the rights of others.

Malice Aforethought—Intentional or planned injury.

Manifest—Invoice of a ship's cargo, for evidence at customs house.

Manufacture—Conversion of raw materials into a finished product, e.g., converting iron ore into steel plate.

Margin—Money deposited with a broker as security on stock purchases; thus margin may be forfeited if stock quotations take an adverse turn.

Markdown—Lowering of prices, usually to make sales for slow-moving goods.

Market—In general, the range for buying and selling; in particular, the range for buying and selling in a particular field, e.g., the stock market, the cotton market, etc.

Market Order—Order to sell at the market price of the day on which the order is issued.

Mark-Up—Amount added, in selling price, to wholesale price to cover overhead and profit.

Marshall Plan—Plan to extend economic aid abroad, initiated by George C. Marshall as United States Secretary of State in 1947.

Mass Market—The general public considered as potential consumers.

Mass Production—Large scale, mechanized production designed to lower production costs to permit purchase by the majority of potential consumers.

Maximum Hours—Limit of time workers may be employed without overtime payment.

Mediation—Resort to third party in disputes between employer and worker; not as conclusive as arbitration.

Melon—Extra dividend on stock, distributing surplus earnings or profits.

Merger—Consolidation of two or more companies into one.

Metes and Bounds—Dimensions and boundaries of a parcel of real estate.

Mill—A machine for grinding, pressing, stamping, or almost every repetitive process; a building or group of buildings containing manufacturing machinery.

Minimum Wage—Lowest limit of wages that may be paid to workers.

Minor—Person under legal age to assume certain responsibilities. The age varies—it is different for marriage, for business transaction, or for liability to criminal charges.

Model Change-Over—Reorganization of manufacturing process for the manufacture of a new model (sometimes called **mark**) of an article.

Monopoly—Exclusive control of an industry or some form of trade.

Morris Plan Company—Makes small personal loans for repayment in installments.

Mortgage—Transfer of rights in property as security for a loan or for other considerations. **Real estate** mortgages are on land and improvements upon it; **chattel** mortgages cover other forms of property; **crop** mortgage is a chattel mortgage on crops; a **first** mortgage is one which has priority in any claims on the property over subsequent mortgages (**second** and **third** mortgages, etc.)

Mortgage Certificates—Certificates for small shares of large first mortgages or first mortgage bonds. Issued by mortgage customers to investors.

National Advertising—Advertising in periodicals or over radio and television, nationwide in scope.

Negotiable—Salable or transferable as payment for debts.

Net—Sum, after deductions have been made, e.g., net income after expenses, taxes, etc. have been taken out.

Nonfeasance—see Malfeasance.

Notary Public—A person authorized by state law to witness and certify to the authenticity of signatures affixed to documents or statements in his presence.

Number—Item of manufacture; usually refers to item in a catalogue.

O.K.—With signature, constitutes endorsement or approval of something presented in writing. According to popular belief, from Old Kinderhook, birthplace of Martin van Buren, and used by his supporters in his campaign for the presidency.

Omnibus Clause—Section in a contract covering several items not specifically covered elsewhere in the document.

One Day Order—Order for stock transaction on a certain day, and cancelled if not executed on that day.

Open Order—Order for a stock transaction to be executed at any time and to hold good until notice of withdrawal is received. Also called GTC (Good till cancelled) order.

Option—First choice or right to obtain goods or services without competition for a specified period, e.g., ten days' option.

Order—Customer's itemized descripton of goods desired for purchase.

Overhead—Fixed expenses, such as rent, salaries, maintenance costs, etc.

Overstock—Goods in excess of current demand.

Over-the-Counter Trading—Trading by private dealers in securities not listed on the stock exchange.

Package—Combined merchandise and/or services, offered as a unit, in a "package deal," e.g., radio or television program in which script, actors, announcer, etc., are all provided as a unit in a "package program."

Pamphlet—Paper-covered booklet used as advertising or to convey information about a business.

Panic—Sudden widespread fright over financial situation causing artifical depression through sales of securities and other property.

Paper—Documents of any sort, negotiable notes, bills, etc.

Par—Normal or face value of securities.

Parcel—Package of goods; piece of property; to apportion merchandise in small lots to provide some supply to all accounts.

Parity—Rate of exchange at which different currencies acquire equal purchasing power.

Partnership—Defined in Uniform Partnership Act: "An association of two or more persons to carry on as co-owners of a business for profit"; except in "limited partnership" in which liability of certain partners is restricted to the amount of capital contributed, partners are individually liable for debts contracted by the business.

Passbook—A book borne by customer, containing records of credit purchases; also bankbook.

Passing a Dividend—Failure to declare an expected dividend.

Patent—Right granted by the government for a term of seventeen years, for the exclusive production of an invented article or for an improvement of an article, not renewable.

Patent Attorney—One specializing in the preparation of patent applications and in the search to determine that the invention is new and does not infringe on previous patents.

Patent Office—Government bureau that registers patent applications and issues "letters patent," granting patent rights.

Patron—Customer.

Patronage—Business given by a customer.

Pattern (in industry)—A model made for duplication as in metal casting, dress manufacture, etc.

Pattern-Maker—One who makes patterns needed in industry.

Pay—to make an acceptable return, usually in money, for property delivered, or services rendered; remuneration such as wages or salaries.

Payee—Person to whom money has been, or is to be, paid.

Paymaster—One under whose management wage or salary payments are made.

Payroll—Paymaster's list of those entitled to wages or salary.

Peculation—Embezzlement.

Peg—To hold market prices at a set value by manipulating purchases or sales.

Pension—Payment made through grant, insurance, or other arrangement to person retired from employment, business, or public office.

"Percents"—Investments such as bonds or other securities, described by their interest rate, e.g., 3%.

Perpetual Trust—Trust estate with no prescribed duration.

Personal Property or Personal Estate—Property other than real estate.

Personnel—Employed staff.

Petition—Written application to a court instituting an action or requesting action upon a matter before it.

Petition in Bankruptcy—Written application by a debtor or his creditors that he be declared bankrupt.

Petty Cash—Cash fund used to make small payments.

Photo Engraving—Process of reproducing pictures through photography, where printing surface is in relief in contrast to lithography or gravure.

Photostat—Photographic process for reproducing documents, drawings, etc.; a document or drawing so reproduced.

Pica—12-point type, usually used on typewriters and in other print where readability is desired.

Picket—Person, during a strike, standing or walking back and forth before entrance of business to discourage non-striking employees or customers from entering.

Piece-Goods—Fabrics sold by pieces or fixed lengths.

Pilot Plant—A business operated to determine rates to be charged in its industry.

Pipeline—Piping over long distances used in the transportation of oil or gas.

Piracy—Infringement on copyrighted or patent property rights.

Pit—Section of Chicago Board of Trade where a specific commodity is traded; e.g., wheat pit.

Pivotal—A stock whose quotations influence the course of the market.

Planned Economy—Economical organization, usually of a state, in which production is arranged to prevent or reduce fluctuation and waste.

Plant—The building, machinery, etc., taken together that are used in a unit of industrial production.

Plantation—Large scale farming operation, carried on by hired labor; e.g., rubber plantation.

Plastics (in industry)—Synthetic materials mainly produced by molding process.

Pledge—Piece of property given as security for a loan.

Point—Unit used in quoting prices on stocks. In the United States, one point usually stands for $1 a share.

Point System—Method of wage payment by time units of work performed. Also called the "Bedaux System," from its originator.

Policy—Contract of insurance; guiding principles of a concern, usually determined or governed by a Board of Directors.

Pool—Merger of property or financial interests of a group, usually with the expectation of manipulating the market in its favor.

Portal-to-Portal Pay—Payment for time spent, as in mines, in passing to and from the entrance of the actual place of work.

Position—On produce exchanges, undertaking to make delivery in a given month; e.g., October position.

Possession—Such control of property as to give exclusive legal enjoyment of it.

Posthumous—Taking effect after death.

Power of Attorney—Legal authority to act for another, not as a lawyer, but to carry out transactions.

Practice—Professional service; e.g., legal practice; customary procedure of a firm.

Pre-Fab—A prefabricated article, usually a house or small industrial building, to facilitate speedy erection.

Preference Shop—One where, by agreement between union and management, preference is given to union members in employment, promotion, and tenure, but management may employ non-union workers if union cannot supply qualified personnel.

Preferred Stock—Issue which receives preference over common stock in dividends or distribution of assets.

Premium (in insurance)—Money or other consideration paid by the insured according to terms of contract. (In economics)—Greater value of one currency over another; additional payment for loan of money. (On the stock market)—Amount above par that securities are being quoted at; sum paid for an option.

Prepaid—Paid in advance.

Price—Value at which goods are exchanged or services rendered.

Pricing—Setting a price on goods.

Primary Markets—Markets in farm produce such as foods or fibers.

Principal—Actual party to transaction as distinguished from agent; money or other property on which interest is earned.

Priority—Precedence as in transportation, goods production, delivery of order, etc.

Privilege—Option on the sale or purchase of securities on specified items.

Probate—Proof established by legal procedures; e.g., probate of a will.

Process—A method of manufacture or of rendering services.

Production—Creation of goods having value to purchasers; e.g., agricultural production, industrial production.

Profit—What remains after production and sales costs have been deducted.

Profit and Loss—Accounting, after a given period, to determine condition of a business.

Promissory Note—Note undertaking payment of a debt at a specified time or occasion.

Promoter—One who initiates organization of a company, floating of securities, or other business undertaking.

Property—Things owned; real property is property in real estate, while personal property or personal estate refers to all other possessions of value.

Proprietor—Owner; one with legal right to possession.

Proxy—To act for another; one whose voting rights are entrusted to another, the usual reference being to voting of stock holders.

Public Domain—The field of property rights belonging to the public at large, such as manufacturing processes or literary properties not, or no longer, covered by patents and copyrights.

Public Utility—Company servicing the general public, such as a railroad, supplier of electricity, etc.

Put and Call—To "put" is to deliver, according to agreement, specified stock at a specified price to a buyer who receives a payment for this service. The privilege of "putting" may be sold to a third party. To "call" is to receive on demand specified stock at a specified price from a seller who is paid for this service. The privilege of "calling" may be sold to a third party.

Pyramid—To engage in transactions in banking or stock market, using gains as "margin" for further purchases or sales, in order to take continuous advantage of a market trend.

Qualified—Fit to do required work.

Quantity—Used relatively, usually in reference to goods in bulk, e.g., "These castings can be supplied in any reasonable quantity."

Quantity Theory of Money—Economic theory that changes in quantity of money in circulation affect price levels and currency values.

Query—To recheck a shipment, a shipper or an account; may refer to goods, invoices, personnel, etc. e.g., "Please query Hobson, rubber tape shipment overdue at warehouse."

Quit Claim—Document in legal form relinquishing some property right.

Quotations—Statements, oral or written, of market prices of stocks, bonds or commodities.

Quotation Board—Board in brokerage office on which market quotations are displayed.

Rebate—Repayment of a percentage of sum received in payment for goods or services. Rebate may be allowed for damage, delay, or savings in shipping costs, etc.

Receipt—Signed paper in evidence that goods or money has been received.

Receipts—Earnings of a business for a given period; e.g., "today's receipts."

Receiver—Person, firm, or bank appointed by courts to conduct a business declared bankrupt.

Recession—Decline in industrial activity, not so drastic as a depression.

Redemption—Payment of outstanding loans; e.g., redemption of a bond issue.

Referee—Appointed by court to hear evidence and render decision in business disputes.

Refund—Return of entire amount paid for goods or services, usually because of their unsatisfactory nature.

Reimburse—Repay money expended by another. An agent will be reimbursed for costs incurred during his operation.

Reorganization—Reestablishment of insolvent business with the consent of creditors and under court supervision, with the aim of avoiding receivership costs and forced sale losses.

Requisition—Order for supplies, materials, etc.

Rescued—Withdrawal of order or instructions.

Restrictive—Limiting. A restrictive covenant is a clause in a document setting certain conditions, as in real estate contracts restricting residence to certain races.

Retail Trade—Trade with consumers.

Retirement—Withdrawal from circulation, e.g., retirement of a currency.

Revenue—Source of income, usually referring to government income from taxation.

Revenue Bond—Short-term issue in anticipation of revenue payments.

Rigged Market—Subject to manipulation so that it does not reflect real values.

Rollback—Price reduction to previous levels, usually by government action.

Royalty—Share of profits paid by manufacturer to inventor (or owner of an invention), author, etc. or to his heirs.

Runaway—Removal of business to a region of low labor costs as an employer measure in labor trouble.

Sabotage—Obstruction, malicious waste of materials, or spoilage of product by workers during labor trouble.

Sales Engineering—Computing and adjusting installation and production costs from plans, as a means of promoting sales of equipment and machinery to a specific industry or factory.

Salvage—Goods rescued from shipwreck or other disaster.

Sample—A representative piece of an article offered for sale; e.g., swatch of cloth.

Scab—Opprobrious term, used in labor relations for person employed in place of strikers or refusing to strike with his fellow workers.

Schedule—Systematic listing of time for production or other performance in manufacturing, transportation, distribution, etc.

Search—To verify status of a property; e.g., mortgage title search, patent search, etc.

Seat—Membership in the Stock Exchange entitling one to share in its assets and privilege of trading there.

Security—(Chiefly used in the plural.) Stock certificates, bonds, or other documentary evidence of indebtedness giving the possessor the right to claim property secured by the document; listed security is one which, by meeting certain requirements, is listed for trading on the Stock Exchange.

Self-Mailer—Advertising message that can be sent by mail without enclosure in an envelope. A sticker or stamp is affixed to hold pages or folded edges together.

Shakeout—Minor decline in industrial activity in course of adjustment after inflation.

Shape-up—Hiring of dockworkers by selection of applicants at piers, usually arbitrarily, at the discretion of labor supervisor.

Shortage—Something missing from inventory or from cash, due to theft, loss, or error.

Silver Standard—Rating of currency in terms of a specified value in silver.

Sinking Fund—Fund continually added to and invested toward the payment of bonds or other maturing debts.

Sitdown Strike—One where striking employees stay in or at their places of work to prevent operation of machinery by others.

Slander—Oral statement held to be damaging to person or business about whom it is made. To be distinguished from libel, which is a damaging written statement.

Sleeper—Film, book, novel, or other property or article of trade that gains unexpected commercial success, doing better business than other items for which greater sales were anticipated.

Slowdown—Slowing down of work operations without actual walkout, as a worker tactic in labor dispute.

Smog—Saturation of air with smoke or other industrial exhausts leading to fog conditions.

Social Security—System and fund set up, under the Social Security Act, to insure security in old age. The fund is made up of compulsory contributions by employers and employees

Solicit—To seek business accounts.

Solvency—Capacity to meet financial obligations.

Specie—Metal (hard) money as distinguished from paper currency.

Specimen—Sample of minerals, ores, plants, or other things that are complete units of their kind.

Speculation—Buying or selling with chance of high profits and risk of considerable loss.

Spot Announcement (in radio advertising)—A commercial not part of a sponsored program.

Spot Delivery—In stock market, immediate delivery of stock.

Staple—An established product; e.g., oil is a staple of Texas.

Statement—List of unpaid items in a business account; a financial statement is a listing of assets and liabilities.

Statute of Limitations—Law setting time limit for legal action.

Stipulation—Condition specified in agreement or contract, usually something undertaken by buyer to bolster his credit.

Stock—Share of ownership in an incorporated business; supply of merchandise for sale; **common** stock is ordinary stock as distinguished from **preferred** stock, which takes precedence over it in distribution of assets or dividends; **guaranteed** stock is one whose dividends are guaranteed by another company.

Stockpile—Reserve supply of essential material.

Strike—Refusal by employees to work unless demands, generally for pay increases, vacations, and other benefits are met. Usually accompanied by picketing of the premises of the business affected.

Strike-Breaking—Coercive action with the intention of defeating strike action.

Sublease—To lease all or part of premises one has leased.

Sublet—To rent all or part of premises one has rented.

Subpoena—Court order served on witnesses summoning them to give testimony.

Subsidiary—A company, control of whose stock is held by another company.

Subsidy—Agreed sum paid, over and above market charges, to assure supply or service that would otherwise be unavailable because of lack of profit.

Substandard—Below standard quality.

Supermarket—Departmentalized branch in chain store system, where some departments may be rented as concessions, and doing a gross annual business of a specified figure, usually $100,000.

Supply—Amount of goods for sale at a given price.

Surplus—Oversupply; amount by which assets exceed liabilities and capital; amount of goods on hand above current demand.

Swindle—To defraud; dishonest business transaction.

Swindler—One who defrauds.

Swindle Sheet—Expense account, when padding or the possibility of padding is implied.

Syndicate—Group organized for special financing, such as purchase and resale of certain securities or underwriting of a stock issue, purchasing it at a discount.

Take-Home Pay—What is left of earnings after withholding tax and other deductions have been made.

Tariff—Schedule of duties imposed on importers and exporters.

Tax—To exact payment, usually payment exacted by government to provide revenue for its operations.

Tax Sale—Sale of a property to recover unpaid taxes.

Technological—Referring to technical processes or changes in industry; e.g., technological unemployment.

Tenant—Occupant of premises, generally one who pays rent for the occupancy.

Tenders—Sealed bids or offers for securities.

Terms—Terms of payment; prearranged conditions for payment of a debt; e.g., cash in 30 days, $5 down and $1 a week, etc.

Testator—One who makes a will.

Ticker—Machine in which messages are stamped on paper tape, used in reporting market quotations.

Tie-in Sale—Where additional product must be purchased to effect purchase of a certain article.

Title—All factors combined which accord right to exclusive possession of property.

Tool Engineering—New branch of engineering concerned with perfecting new machinery processes, equipment and use of raw material in preparation for production of a new product or a new model.

Tracer—Investigation designed to trace article undelivered by post office or transportation company; one who makes such an investigation.

Trade Acceptance—Bill of exchange governing purchase price, drawn by seller upon buyer whose endorsement constitutes "acceptance."

Trade Agreement—Agreement between employer and union, fixing wages, hours, working conditions.

Trade Edition or Trade Book—Edition designed for general public as distinguished from educational and professional use.

Trademark—Coined name, monogram, logotype, signature, picture, distinctively designed words or name, symbol, emblem or device, which may be registered in the Government Patent Office for exclusive use by the applicant. Registration term is 20 years and may be renewed.

Trade Name—Name or other symbol under which a firm does business and protected by common law against attempt to deceive customers by use of a similar name by a competing firm.

Trade Paper—Endorsed notes (two or more names) given in payment for merchandise; a periodical published in the interest of a certain branch of business.

Transcript—Letter-perfect copy of a document, which does not seek to reproduce exact appearance of original.

Travelers Checks—Issued by banks, travel agencies, American Express, and Western Union for the convenience of travelers.

Treasury Bills—Short-term government offerings, bearing no interest, but sold at a discount to buyers.

Treasury Certificates—Interest-bearing certificates of indebtedness issued in place of short-term bonds.

Trust—Holding of property by a responsible person or bank (trustee) for the good of another person (beneficiary).

Turnover—Number of times, within a specified period such as a year, in which a given commodity is sold out.

Upgrade—To advance an employee, a work process or a product in rank, earnings, price or quality.

Venue—Place where case is tried. **A change of venue** may be granted with the object of securing a fairer trial.

Volume—Amount of business done.

Voucher—A receipt or other proof of money paid, vouches for the accuracy of the terms of a transaction.

Wages—Payment for labor.

Waive—To voluntarily forego a right.

Warrant—Order for the payment of money or delivery of goods or documents; in banking, primarily written order for the payment of money.

Wash Sale—Fictitious trading to give an appearance of activity to inactive stocks.

Wharfage—Fee for use of piers.

Wholesale—Sale of goods to dealers for resale to retail merchants.

Will—Testament of a property-holder directing the distribution of his property after his death.

Window Dressing—Manipulations in financial statement to give it a more favorable appearance than is due.

Withholding Tax—Income tax payment deducted at source, as from wages, dividends, etc.

Without Prejudice—A contract term signifying that the agreement will not injure any prior or subsequent rights.

Zoning—Laws governing real estate, setting off special areas for special types of occupation; e.g., residence, business, hospitals, etc.

Wills and
Estate Planning

Everyone should have an up-to-date will that reflects an estate plan adapted to individual needs and circumstances. The estate plan is a thoughtfully designed arrangement for the distribution of one's assets in such a way as to achieve maximum realization of the planner's objectives. These can include keeping taxes at a minimum; providing financial management for the benefit of a surviving widow and children; selection of a trusted relative, friend, or advisor as executor or guardian; and so on. An estate plan can be simple and inexpensive to draw up; for a larger estate or one with special problems the plan may be extremely complex.

Most persons or couples of reasonable means should have an estate plan—and a will or wills as integral parts of that plan. But whether it is part of an estate plan or not the will is ordinarily a written document that takes effect on the death of the testator, the legal term for the person making out a will. The will's purpose is to distribute one's worldly assets to those whom the testator desires or "wills" to have them.

The estate plan may deal with broader categories of assets than the will. The estate plan may, for example, have provisions covering gifts, insurance, and annuities, special types of contracts such as those providing for the purchase of a business by surviving associates, trusteeship arrangements, and other devices designed to accomplish the testator's purposes. The estate plan may also provide for changes in the estate to be made before the planner's death. The will generally takes effect only on the testator's death.

Estate Planning:
Four Main Tools

You can make a beginning toward estate planning by considering the four main tools a planner can use. The four are trusts, lifetime gifts, joint ownership, and wills. Other tools are, of course, available, and each has a valid purpose. Under specific arrangements, for example, death benefits may be paid to named beneficiaries under pension plans, profit-sharing programs, IRAs, tax-sheltered annuities, and deferred compensation arrangements. Some estates use irrevocable living trusts or buy-sell agreements dealing with businesses.

Adding It Up. In general, property is anything you can own. Everything you own belongs in your estate. That includes both real property, or real estate, meaning both land and all the things that are permanently attached to the land, and personal property. The latter includes tangibles, those items that have bulk or substance, and intangibles, things without physical substance. Among common tangibles are furniture, an automobile, cameras, clothing, a boat, and so on. Intangibles are such items as stocks, bonds, life insurance policies, and bank deposits.

A first step in estate planning involves inventorying all your property of whatever kind. With each item you should note the value or estimated value. You should also indicate how the property is owned—outright, in joint tenancy, or otherwise.

Objectives. What do you want to accomplish when you plan your estate? Your objectives should be clear; they often determine what methods you will use to transfer your property, or specific parts of it, to your spouse, relatives, friends, charities, or other beneficiaries. At the least you will want to know who your heirs will be and what each heir will receive.

Some specific objectives help to shape estate plans. A property owner may want to provide financial support for dependents, including both money to live on and funds that would be available in emergencies. Nearly all estate planners hope to reduce such estate transfer costs as federal estate and state inheritance taxes, the expenses of administering the estate, and others. Very basically, a valid objective is to ensure that the estate will have sufficient assets to meet its obligations.

Other objectives may seem obvious. As noted, you will want to name the person or persons who will administer or settle your estate after your death—and under what terms. The disposition of closely held business interests should be provided for. Finally, property distribution should make up parts of the estate plan.

Tool 1: Trusts

As one of the key tools of estate planning, trusts play unique roles. Whatever the type of trust, and there are many kinds for persons in many economic categories, the typical trust instrument places *legal* title in one person, called the *trustee,* and *equitable* title in another person, the *beneficiary.* In each case the "person" may be an individual, a corporation, group, or organization. The *grantor* (or creator or settlor) who establishes the trust gives the trustee the right to hold and administer the trust *corpus,* or principle, for the benefit of the other person or entity.

Three main kinds of trusts are used by the estate planner: living, or *inter vivos* ("between the living"), trusts; testamentary trusts established by will; and insurance trusts. Living trusts are set up while the grantor is alive, and take effect at once. Testamentary trusts take effect on the grantor's death. The corpus of the insurance trust consists of funds from an insurance policy—or funds to be paid out under an insurance policy or policies—and, possibly, other property as well.

Why a trust? To some extent the reasons parallel those that justify estate planning itself. Among the reasons:

• To protect spendthrift heirs or other beneficiaries who may be mentally, physically, or emotionally unable to manage property. The trustee can have total management responsibility.
• To enable the trustee to use discretion and, often, expert knowledge in managing trust property for the benefit of heirs, the grantor, and family members or others.

• To have a device for giving or leaving property to minors with the assurance that the trustee will manage the property until the beneficiaries are old enough to handle the property themselves.

• To take all or part of your estate property out of probate and in that way to save your heirs the costs and delays of going through the probate process.

• To set up a useful tax-saving plan.

Tax Savings

Depending on your financial status and the complexity of the trust you want to set up, you could pay from $100 to $10,000 or more to an attorney to prepare your trust agreement. On average, you would pay about $300 to $500.

Such an expense could definitely be worth it. Remember that the federal government has provided that estates of $500,000 or less were to escape estate taxes in 1986. That figure was to rise to $600,000 in 1987 and subsequent years. In one case a couple had property worth $800,000, all in the husband's name. Assuming that the husband dies first, in 1987 or later, the entire estate passes to the wife. The so-called *marital deduction* allows whole estates of whatever kind to pass to a surviving spouse tax-free. But when the wife dies a different rule applies.

On the wife's death in 1987 or later, the federal exemption would apply only to the first $600,000 of the $800,000 estate. At rates in effect in 1986 the couple's heirs would pay $52,000 in estate taxes on the remaining $200,000.

This couple could have saved all $52,000 in federal taxes by establishing a trust. The couple would have had several choices, including these:

• A *bypass trust* that would set aside $600,000 of the husband's estate as the trust principle, with income from the trust and part of its principle going to the wife during her lifetime. The other $200,000 in the husband's estate would go directly, on his death, to the wife for her unrestricted use. On the wife's death the trust would dissolve and the entire estate would be distributed to the beneficiaries free of federal taxes.

• A *marital deduction trust,* with either of two kinds available: a general power of appointment trust or a so-called QTIP (qualified terminable interest property) trust. Again the couple's beneficiaries would pay no federal estate taxes on the death of the second spouse.

Under the general power of appointment trust, your spouse can decide after you die who will receive the trust's assets after he or she dies. The QTIP, by contrast, makes it possible for you to select the ultimate trust beneficiaries. With the QTIP you can make sure, if desired, that your spouse will not cut off your children by an earlier marriage. Otherwise the general power of appointment and the QTIP trust are virtually identical. Both, for example, qualify for the marital deduction and are included in the surviving spouse's estate. Both also produce income that must go to the surviving spouse.

• A *generation-skipping trust,* under which trust income goes to a grantor's children rather than to the wife and the principle goes to the grantor's grandchildren.

In many cases a grantor can use an *irrevocable life insurance trust* under which the proceeds from insurance policies are removed from the grantor's estate, to be distributed after the second spouse's death to the named beneficiaries. The spouse receives income from the trust until he or she dies.

Selecting the Trustee

The problem of selecting a trustee usually resolves into a choice between an individual and a corporation. The individual, whether the creator of the trust or someone else, might be closer to the trust beneficiaries than a corporate trustee—and might therefore be more responsive to the beneficiaries' needs. The individual might not even charge a fee. Under any circumstances, the person or persons serving as trustees could, as needed, obtain legal, investment, accounting, and other advice from experts.

The corporate trustee could offer different advantages. Such trustees are professional money and property managers. Unlike the individual trustee, they do not, usually, die or become incapacitated; personnel changes do not interrupt their services. Beyond that, they remain unbiased, independent of family pressures, and able to answer to charges of mismanagement. By comparison with the individual trustee who is also a trust beneficiary, the corporate trustee cannot incur personal income tax liabilities in administering trust property. A corporate trustee can, of course, act as cotrustee with an individual or individuals.

Tool 2: Gifts

Lifetime gifts function much like trusts. Essentially, they reduce the value of your estate and thus help to avoid estate taxes. An important difference, however, is that your surviving spouse has no access to the money you have given away. Thus most persons make certain that the surviving spouse will have enough income to live on after the first spouse's death.

In the 1980s the federal government liberalized the laws regulating gifts of property or money. In 1986 individuals could give up to $10,000 each to as many persons as they chose. For couples, the law allowed joint gifts of as much as $20,000 each to any number of donees. You need not report gifts of less than $10,000 to the Internal Revenue Service, but must (whether individual or couple) report all gifts exceeding that sum. After your death, the IRS will add up all the taxable gifts—those exceeding $10,000 per year per person—that you made during your lifetime and (if applicable) subtract the total from your $600,000 (1987) estate tax exemption.

Kinds of Gifts

You can give gifts in many different ways. A *charitable remainder trust* is actually a way to give assets to a charity while ensuring that you or your beneficiaries will receive the income from the gift property for a specified period. At the end of the period the trust dissolves and the charity receives the principle. Very wealthy persons may use a *GRIT* (grantor retained income trust) that sets aside part of the grantor's estate as a gift to a family member or friend. The grantor receives the income from the gift property for a specified period, whereupon it passes out of his or her estate and into the ownership of the beneficiary.

A third method of giving away assets operates on a principle opposite to that of the remainder trust. This *charitable lead trust* provides that a charity will receive the income from the specified property—but not the principle. When the trust ends, your heirs receive the principle. You arrange for a charitable lead trust in your will. Often, your estate enjoys even larger tax deductions than it would under a remainder trust.

Tool 3: Joint Ownership

Joint ownership of property offers both advantages and disadvantages that should be considered in estate planning. Joint ownership (a legal device that exists when two or more persons have ownership rights in property) allows that property to pass automatically to the other joint owner or owners *outside the probate estate* of the first owner to die. The device thus saves the time and expenses often involved in the probate process.

Other advantages may be noted. Some states levy lower inheritance taxes, or no taxes, where property is held jointly. Usually, too, the survivor receives jointly held property free of the claims of the creditors of a deceased joint owner.

Joint, Outright, and Community Property Ownership

Joint ownership is one of four basic ways in which real or personal property may be owned. The other three are outright ownership, community property ownership or rights, and tenancy in common. The three types of joint ownership or tenancy include:

Joint Tenancy with Right of Survivorship. Under joint tenancy with right of survivorship (WROS), the property interest of a descedant passes with his or her death to the surviving joint owner or owners. A married couple typically own their home jointly. When one dies, the property interest of that deceased passes to the survivor, who then owns the property outright in his or her own name.

A joint tenant can destroy the survivorship aspect of a joint tenancy. For example, if one joint tenant sells his or her share in property to a third party, that person and the remaining joint tenant own the property as tenants in common (see below).

Tenancy by the Entirety. A second form of joint tenancy is tenancy by the entirety. Some states provide for this special kind of joint ownership when a wife and husband own property jointly and exclusively. Tenancy by the entirety differs from joint tenancy with right of survivorship in three key ways: the former can only exist between husband and wife; in many states the survivorship rights can be terminated only with the consent of both parties; and, again depending on the laws of the particular state, the husband may have control over the property (and the right to any income from it) during their lifetimes.

Other Joint Interests. Where joint bank accounts or jointly owned government savings bonds are concerned, the owners may again have rights of survivorship. Thus family members commonly hold both types of property under this joint ownership arrangement. With a bank account, either party can make deposits or withdraw funds. On the death of one, the survivor becomes sole owner of the account by operation of law.

With savings bonds, a similar rule applies. Both joint owners have survivorship rights even though the bonds may be registered in co-ownership form and held in the name of "A" or "B." Either A or B could cash the bonds during the lifetime of the other.

Tenancy in Common

Under tenancy in common arrangements, no co-owner has survivorship rights: none acquires the interest of another in case of the other's death. Rather, the interest of a decedent goes to the decedent's heirs as if the interest had been owned outright. The survivor retains his or her share. Tenants in common can own proportionate interests in property—for example, 75 percent and 25 percent respectively.

In outright ownership, one person owns property exclusively in his or her name. Community property is discussed below.

Not a Will

Despite some advantages, joint ownership does not take the place of a will. In cases on record, couples owning property jointly, but having no wills, were involved in serious accidents. One spouse died instantly. The other survived by a few hours or days. The survivor could not make out a will. By law, the property passed to the surviving spouse on the death of the other. On the death of the second spouse, the property typically passed entirely to the second spouse's relatives.

Joint ownership may also produce results contrary to those intended, may save few or no taxes and other expenses, and may even increase taxes dramatically. The effects depend on state laws. But in many states lawyers cannot say for certain what the effects of joint tenancy may be. It may nonetheless be advisable to hold checking accounts and small savings accounts in joint ownership to provide the survivor with ready cash on the death of one joint owner; even if the account is frozen for a time it will normally become available well before the assets of the deceased's estate.

For sentimental or other reasons, a husband and wife usually own the family home jointly. Ownership of other assets should be based on sound legal advice—which also applies to the overall estate plan, including the will.

Joint Ownership—How Much?

No simple rules are available to indicate how much property should be held in joint tenancy. If the federal estate tax is not an important factor, a couple may hold all property jointly. But even if the couple's estate is large enough to be federally taxable, some joint ownership may be appropriate for the reasons noted.

The Economic Recovery Tax Act (ERTA) of 1981 produced some new rules on joint tenancies held by married couples. In particular, the act provided that only one-half of the value of the property held in a taxable joint tenancy is includable in the gross estate of the first spouse to die. This "fractional interest" applies regardless of whether the surviving spouse contributed to the purchase of the property.

As a caveat, joint ownership may actually result in a gift. This occurs where one joint owner has contributed all or a disproportionate share of the cost of purchasing property. If Mrs. Jones, for example, uses her own funds to buy corporate stock in her own and Daughter Joanne's name, and if the ownership is irrevocable, Mrs. Jones has made a gift, for federal tax purposes, to her daughter of one-half the value of the stocks. Her daughter has also gained some control over the stocks.

Different from Community Property

Property owned jointly should not be confused with community property. The latter exists in some western and southwestern states that follow Roman law rather than the English common law where property relationships between husbands and wives are concerned. In common-law states marriage gives husbands and wives certain rights in each other's property that often cannot be changed by a will. This is also true in community property states, but the rights are somewhat different.

In these states one-half the income earned during the marriage by either spouse belongs to the other. All property owned by the couple is presumably community property, of which each owns half. But property owned by either spouse before marriage and kept separate, with the income from such property also kept separate, and property acquired by one spouse individually, without contributions from the other spouse—for example, by gift or inheritance—are the separate properties of each spouse owning it.

In community property states married couples' wills cannot touch the separate property of either spouse or either spouse's share of the community property. But a couple can by contract agree on what is community property and what is the separate property of either. Such contracts take effect when written and signed. They are an essential tool of estate planning in community property states. But they do not obviate the need for a will any more than joint tenancy does.

The nine community property states are Arizona, California, Idaho, Louisiana, Nevada, New Mexico, Texas, Washington, and Wisconsin. In these states estate planners should be wary of making a person other than the spouse a joint owner of community property. As a rule, half the wife's or husband's share of the community property passes to the surviving spouse and the other half goes to the heirs named in the descendant's will. The surviving spouse may or may not be named as an heir.

Tool 4: Wills

As the fourth and most important tool used in estate planning, wills need always to be individualized to the creator's (or testator's) situation, estate, and desires. The written will is signed by the testator in the presence of witnesses; it operates at his or her death to distribute property according to specifications in the document itself. The law imposes certain obligations, including the primary duty to pay tax liabilities, debts, funeral expenses, and the costs of administration. The law also provides for a surviving spouse's legal rights in a decedent's estate and refuses to recognize, on public policy grounds, provisions discouraging marriage, wasting assets, or tying up wealth for unreasonable periods of time.

Wills may be short and simple or long and complex. But in all cases certain essential requirements must be met. The will must, for example, be signed and witnessed to be valid. For his or her own peace of mind, a testator should have a lawyer prepare the "last will and testament." "Do-it-yourself" wills, and wills written on standard forms, are generally inadvisable, largely because so many of them lead to legal problems later.

Advantages

A will allows you to dispose of your property to the persons you select, at the time you choose, in the amounts and proportions you specify. You can also indicate how your property will be protected and who will be responsible for its protection. Anyone who is 21 years of age and mentally capable of understanding the nature of a will can have one drawn up. In some states or under some conditions the age requirement is reduced or waived.

The cases of husbands and wives who sustained fatal injuries in a common disaster point up the importance of wills. Usually, the husband and wife have left their estates to each other. The deaths of both in the same accident could create difficulty, especially where the order in which the two died cannot be determined. For that reason most wills contain a common disaster clause providing for the distribution of family assets in the event of simultaneous deaths or deaths resulting from the same accident.

Selecting an Executor

Selecting the person who will oversee the distribution of your estate according to your will is as important as choosing a trustee. Many of the same principles apply.

The loyalty and ability of the executor may be the single most critical factor in ensuring effective and fair administration of your assets after your death: particularly in preventing losses and protecting the property you have left under your will.

Subject to the supervision of an appropriate court, the executor takes possession of the assets specified in the will, manages the estate as the deceased would have, pays debts, taxes, and expenses, retains legal counsel as required, and through counsel handles all the legal obligations and procedures incident to the "execution" of the will. The executor also accounts to the court and heirs for his or her stewardship and distributes the estate's assets according to the provisions of the will and applicable legal strictures. Business skill and judgment, diligence, and the capacity to attend to details and maintain proper records are essential qualities of the good executor.

As a testator, you can nominate the executor of your choice, and can also name alternates if desired. Often a testator appoints a surviving widow or trusted friend or relative. Testators often name their legal counsel as executor or co-executor. At your discretion as testator, you can name a corporate executor or trustee—usually the trust department of a bank. Such a selection means that your executor will have complete institutional facilities available, will enjoy permanence and freedom from personal and business distractions, and will be able to call on the staff and professional skills necessary to do the work properly. The widow, a relative, or a lawyer may be named coexecutor as a means of combining the close personal relationship of a trusted individual with the skills and facilities of the corporate executor.

Obviously, where a will establishes a trust, the bank trust officer or some equally qualified person is a logical choice as executor/trustee. The executor or trustee must be compensated for his or her services—except in the case of a relative or friend who serves out of a sense of duty or because he or she is a principal heir. Executors' fees are based on the size of the estate, but typically range from 1 or 1.5 percent to about 2.5 percent of the gross estate.

Preparation and Execution

Some statutory formalities govern the preparation of all wills. For example, as noted, wills must be in writing, must demonstrate the testator's intent to pass property to heirs, and may as a rule incorporate another document or other documents if the other documents exist when the will is drawn and if the will adequately identifies the additions. The only exceptions to the rule that wills must be written are *nuncupative*, or oral, wills. All wills have also to be signed, or given some visible mark intended as a signature—at the end of the will in some states and in other places in other jurisdictions.

Most states require that two witnesses *attest to*, or witness, the will's signature; some others require three witnesses. Where statutes require it, wills have to be published, with the testator stating that the will is his or her own. Witnesses generally sign in the presence of the testator and each other. No witness should be a beneficiary under the will. An attestation clause appearing before the witnesses' signatures states that all formalities have been complied with, but is not mandatory; the clause merely serves as evidence of proper execution.

Alteration, Revocation

A will can be either changed or revoked. But alteration or revocation has to take place before the death of the testator. The latter must sign any amendment, or codicil, in the presence of witnesses—exactly as when the original was executed.

Revocation may take place in a number of ways. Marking with intent to revoke, tearing up, or burning, or otherwise destroying a will effects revocation; so may the operation of law in given cases, or the testator's preparation and execution of a new will containing a specific clause of revocation or provisions that nullify or clash with provisions in an earlier document. Legal invalidation of a will may take place when a testator remarries, obtains a divorce along with agreement to a property settlement, or becomes a parent. State laws generally govern such invalidations.

Depending on the jurisdiction, destruction or revocation of a later will may revive an earlier one. But some states recognize revival only through republication—unless the intent appears otherwise.

Instructions and Disposition

A letter of instructions may provide a lawyer or executor with essential information and simplify the task of carrying out a testator's desires. Such a letter is not part of the will, and need not comply with any formal requirements. Its purpose is to furnish a detailed inventory of the estate's assets, give instructions regarding the locations of all needed documents—including birth, marriage, and military discharge records; social security card; insurance policies; a list of bank accounts and safe deposit boxes; title deeds; pension papers; and so on—and summarize instructions regarding liquidation of business affairs.

Other portions of the letter may indicate where the will is kept, detail funeral instructions, and state the testator's wishes concerning investment of the proceeds of the estate, the education of children or grandchildren, future plans for the widow or widower, and similar subjects. The will becomes a public record; the letter remains private, and can thus express hopes or suggestions on very private, personal matters.

Where to keep the will? The safe deposit box is the most appropriate place if it can be opened without undue delay after the testator's death. Alternatively, the will may be delivered to the executor or to the testator's lawyer, or kept in a safe place with personal papers at home. In no event should it be accessible to a "disappointed heir."

Intestacy

The person who dies *intestate*—without having made out a will—already has a kind of will: state laws governing intestacy. These laws comprise a "standard" will reflecting the legislature's conception of the deceased's probable objectives. Under intestacy laws, property left by a decedent passes to survivors according to rules fixed by the deceased's state of residence.

Such rules never operate as would an individual will made out according to a person's wishes. The rules frequently lead to serious shrinkage of the estate—and often to a distribution of assets quite different from what the deceased probably wanted. If the estate is large, long and costly litigation may follow the person's death. If the estate is small, it may be divided among various survivors in portions too small to help anyone. If the deceased leaves minor children, they will inherit part of the estate along with his widow.

The laws of intestacy provide in other ways for minor children. A guardian is usually appointed for the children, a process that involves expensive and time-consuming court proceedings. The guardian has to post a bond, renewable annually at a substantial premium. The guardian is supervised by the court and must account to it annually, resulting in more expense and loss of time. All of these procedures are designed to protect the children—and none takes into consideration the fact that the guardian may be the children's mother and the deceased's widow.

Intestacy laws have other effects. They make it impossible for all assets to go to the widow if there are children too. Nor do the laws consider the needs of the deceased's parents if a widow or child survives. Children are treated equally even though their needs may be quite unequal. Under the laws, faithful, loving spouses and mere legal mates are treated exactly alike; so are helpless widows and surviving spouses who are capable in business affairs.

In brief, the time and expense involved in making out a will is infinitesimal in comparison with the problems that may come with intestacy. The "will you already have" is always inferior to the will you ought to have—even though the laws represent the state's best efforts to protect and provide for survivors.

Common Provisions

Intestacy laws work in parallel ways in specific situations. For example, where a husband leaves a widow but no children or parents, the widow inherits the entire estate—after deductions for various expenses that a proper will could have avoided. Where only the decedent's parents survive, the parents usually receive the whole estate—though in some states brothers and sisters also receive shares. As indicated, where a deceased leaves as survivors both wife and parents, the wife usually receives everything even if she is financially independent and the parents are aged and destitute. In a few states, however, the parents receive up to half of their son's estate regardless of the widow's needs.

If the wife and one child survive, each, usually, takes half the estate—but in some jurisdictions the child may take two-thirds or even virtually the entire estate under certain circumstances. Where the wife and two or more children survive, one-third of the estate generally goes to the wife and the remaining two-thirds are divided equally among the children.

The various state laws may, obviously, work great hardship or injustice. Further, the laws are subject to change without notification. A will, by contrast, can be changed only by the person making it out or under the circumstances already noted. A will should be reviewed from time to time, for example when a testator moves to another state; but the will remains the best available means of disposing of property after death.

What Law Governs?

The laws of the testator's state of legal residence determine the validity (or nonvalidity) of a will where personal property is involved. But because each state reserves the right to fix title to land situated within its boundaries, the law of the state where real property is located governs the validity and effect of the will respect to real estate.

All of this may affect the estate plan. A sound plan may call for avoidance of unnecessary ownership of real estate in states where the testator is a nonresident, particularly if there is any possibility that two or more states may claim a descendant as a resident and try to tax the entire estate rather than just the local real property. Most states, and indeed most countries of the world, cooperate with one another by recognizing as valid a will that is valid in the jurisdiction in which the will was made, the jurisdiction in which the testator was a resident, or—as regards real estate—the jurisdiction in which the property is located.

The extent of this cooperation may vary in given situations. The protocols governing such cooperation may, also, change. Thus it is desirable that the will be consistent with the requirements of the state of residence. Some unusual types of wills are recognized in only a few states; but a proper will drawn by legal counsel will be prepared in such a way as to meet the requirements of most if not all states.

Perpetual Calendar

Directions: Choose year you want in key below. Number opposite year is number of calendar to use for that year.

1776....9	1793....3	1810....2	1827....2	1844....9	1861....3	1878....3	1895....3	1912....9	1929....3	1946....3	1963....3	1980...10	1997....4
1777....4	1794....4	1811....3	1828...10	1845....4	1862....4	1879....4	1896..11	1913....4	1930....4	1947....4	1964..11	1981....5	1998....5
1778....5	1795....5	1812..11	1829....5	1846....5	1863....5	1880..12	1897....6	1914....5	1931....5	1948..12	1965....6	1982....6	1999....6
1779....6	1796..13	1813....6	1830....6	1847....6	1864..13	1881....7	1898....7	1915....6	1932..13	1949....7	1966....7	1983....7	2000...14
1780..14	1797....1	1814....7	1831....7	1848..14	1865....1	1882....1	1899....1	1916..14	1933....1	1950....1	1967....1	1984....8	2001....2
1781....2	1798....2	1815....1	1832....8	1849....2	1866....2	1883....2	1900....1	1917....2	1934....2	1951....2	1968....9	1985....3	2002....3
1782....3	1799....3	1816....9	1833....3	1850....3	1867....3	1884..10	1901....3	1918....3	1935....3	1952..10	1969....4	1986....4	2003....4
1783....4	1800....4	1817....4	1834....4	1851....4	1868..11	1885....5	1902....4	1919....4	1936..11	1953....5	1970....5	1987....5	2004..12
1784..12	1801....5	1818....5	1835....5	1852..12	1869....6	1886....6	1903....5	1920..12	1937....6	1954....6	1971....6	1988..13	2005....7
1785....7	1802....6	1819....6	1836..13	1853....7	1870....7	1887....7	1904..13	1921....7	1938....7	1955....7	1972..14	1989....1	2006....1
1786....1	1803....7	1820..14	1837....1	1854....1	1871....1	1888....8	1905....1	1922....1	1939....1	1956....8	1973....2	1990....2	2007....2
1787....2	1804....8	1821....2	1838....2	1855....2	1872....8	1889....3	1906....2	1923....2	1940....9	1957....3	1974....3	1991....3	2008...10
1788..10	1805....3	1822....3	1839....3	1856..10	1873....4	1890....4	1907....3	1924..10	1941....4	1958....4	1975....4	1992..11	2009....5
1789....5	1806....4	1823....4	1840..11	1857....5	1874....5	1891....5	1908..11	1925....5	1942....5	1959....5	1976..12	1993....6	2010....6
1790....6	1807....5	1824..12	1841....6	1858....6	1875....6	1892..13	1909....6	1926....6	1943....6	1960..13	1977....7	1994....7	2011....7
1791....7	1808..13	1825....7	1842....7	1859....7	1876..14	1893....1	1910....7	1927....7	1944..14	1961....1	1978....1	1995....1	2012....8
1792....8	1809....1	1826....1	1843....1	1860....8	1877....2	1894....2	1911....1	1928....2	1945....2	1962....2	1979....2	1996....9	2013....3

5

JANUARY
S M T W T F S
1 2 3
4 5 6 7 8 9 10
11 12 13 14 15 16 17
18 19 20 21 22 23 24
25 26 27 28 29 30 31

FEBRUARY
S M T W T F S
1 2 3 4 5 6 7
8 9 10 11 12 13 14
15 16 17 18 19 20 21
22 23 24 25 26 27 28

MARCH
S M T W T F S
1 2 3 4 5 6 7
8 9 10 11 12 13 14
15 16 17 18 19 20 21
22 23 24 25 26 27 28
29 30 31

APRIL
S M T W T F S
1 2 3 4
5 6 7 8 9 10 11
12 13 14 15 16 17 18
19 20 21 22 23 24 25
26 27 28 29 30

MAY
S M T W T F S
1 2
3 4 5 6 7 8 9
10 11 12 13 14 15 16
17 18 19 20 21 22 23
24 25 26 27 28 29 30
31

JUNE
S M T W T F S
1 2 3 4 5 6
7 8 9 10 11 12 13
14 15 16 17 18 19 20
21 22 23 24 25 26 27
28 29 30

JULY
S M T W T F S
1 2 3 4
5 6 7 8 9 10 11
12 13 14 15 16 17 18
19 20 21 22 23 24 25
26 27 28 29 30 31

AUGUST
S M T W T F S
1
2 3 4 5 6 7 8
9 10 11 12 13 14 15
16 17 18 19 20 21 22
23 24 25 26 27 28 29
30 31

SEPTEMBER
S M T W T F S
1 2 3 4 5
6 7 8 9 10 11 12
13 14 15 16 17 18 19
20 21 22 23 24 25 26
27 28 29 30

OCTOBER
S M T W T F S
1 2 3
4 5 6 7 8 9 10
11 12 13 14 15 16 17
18 19 20 21 22 23 24
25 26 27 28 29 30 31

NOVEMBER
S M T W T F S
1 2 3 4 5 6 7
8 9 10 11 12 13 14
15 16 17 18 19 20 21
22 23 24 25 26 27 28
29 30

DECEMBER
S M T W T F S
1 2 3 4 5
6 7 8 9 10 11 12
13 14 15 16 17 18 19
20 21 22 23 24 25 26
27 28 29 30 31

6

JANUARY
S M T W T F S
1 2
3 4 5 6 7 8 9
10 11 12 13 14 15 16
17 18 19 20 21 22 23
24 25 26 27 28 29 30
31

FEBRUARY
S M T W T F S
1 2 3 4 5 6
7 8 9 10 11 12 13
14 15 16 17 18 19 20
21 22 23 24 25 26 27
28

MARCH
S M T W T F S
1 2 3 4 5 6
7 8 9 10 11 12 13
14 15 16 17 18 19 20
21 22 23 24 25 26 27
28 29 30 31

APRIL
S M T W T F S
1 2 3
4 5 6 7 8 9 10
11 12 13 14 15 16 17
18 19 20 21 22 23 24
25 26 27 28 29 30

MAY
S M T W T F S
1
2 3 4 5 6 7 8
9 10 11 12 13 14 15
16 17 18 19 20 21 22
23 24 25 26 27 28 29
30 31

JUNE
S M T W T F S
1 2 3 4 5
6 7 8 9 10 11 12
13 14 15 16 17 18 19
20 21 22 23 24 25 26
27 28 29 30

JULY
S M T W T F S
1 2 3
4 5 6 7 8 9 10
11 12 13 14 15 16 17
18 19 20 21 22 23 24
25 26 27 28 29 30 31

AUGUST
S M T W T F S
1 2 3 4 5 6 7
8 9 10 11 12 13 14
15 16 17 18 19 20 21
22 23 24 25 26 27 28
29 30 31

SEPTEMBER
S M T W T F S
1 2 3 4
5 6 7 8 9 10 11
12 13 14 15 16 17 18
19 20 21 22 23 24 25
26 27 28 29 30

OCTOBER
S M T W T F S
1 2
3 4 5 6 7 8 9
10 11 12 13 14 15 16
17 18 19 20 21 22 23
24 25 26 27 28 29 30
31

NOVEMBER
S M T W T F S
1 2 3 4 5 6
7 8 9 10 11 12 13
14 15 16 17 18 19 20
21 22 23 24 25 26 27
28 29 30

DECEMBER
S M T W T F S
1 2 3 4
5 6 7 8 9 10 11
12 13 14 15 16 17 18
19 20 21 22 23 24 25
26 27 28 29 30 31

7

JANUARY
S M T W T F S
1
2 3 4 5 6 7 8
9 10 11 12 13 14 15
16 17 18 19 20 21 22
23 24 25 26 27 28 29
30 31

FEBRUARY
S M T W T F S
1 2 3 4 5
6 7 8 9 10 11 12
13 14 15 16 17 18 19
20 21 22 23 24 25 26
27 28

MARCH
S M T W T F S
1 2 3 4 5
6 7 8 9 10 11 12
13 14 15 16 17 18 19
20 21 22 23 24 25 26
27 28 29 30 31

APRIL
S M T W T F S
1 2
3 4 5 6 7 8 9
10 11 12 13 14 15 16
17 18 19 20 21 22 23
24 25 26 27 28 29 30

MAY
S M T W T F S
1 2 3 4 5 6 7
8 9 10 11 12 13 14
15 16 17 18 19 20 21
22 23 24 25 26 27 28
29 30 31

JUNE
S M T W T F S
1 2 3 4
5 6 7 8 9 10 11
12 13 14 15 16 17 18
19 20 21 22 23 24 25
26 27 28 29 30

JULY
S M T W T F S
1 2
3 4 5 6 7 8 9
10 11 12 13 14 15 16
17 18 19 20 21 22 23
24 25 26 27 28 29 30
31

AUGUST
S M T W T F S
1 2 3 4 5 6
7 8 9 10 11 12 13
14 15 16 17 18 19 20
21 22 23 24 25 26 27
28 29 30 31

SEPTEMBER
S M T W T F S
1 2 3
4 5 6 7 8 9 10
11 12 13 14 15 16 17
18 19 20 21 22 23 24
25 26 27 28 29 30

OCTOBER
S M T W T F S
1
2 3 4 5 6 7 8
9 10 11 12 13 14 15
16 17 18 19 20 21 22
23 24 25 26 27 28 29
30 31

NOVEMBER
S M T W T F S
1 2 3 4 5
6 7 8 9 10 11 12
13 14 15 16 17 18 19
20 21 22 23 24 25 26
27 28 29 30

DECEMBER
S M T W T F S
1 2 3
4 5 6 7 8 9 10
11 12 13 14 15 16 17
18 19 20 21 22 23 24
25 26 27 28 29 30 31

8 (Leap Year)

JANUARY
S M T W T F S
1 2 3 4 5 6 7
8 9 10 11 12 13 14
15 16 17 18 19 20 21
22 23 24 25 26 27 28
29 30 31

FEBRUARY
S M T W T F S
1 2 3 4
5 6 7 8 9 10 11
12 13 14 15 16 17 18
19 20 21 22 23 24 25
26 27 28 29

MARCH
S M T W T F S
1 2 3
4 5 6 7 8 9 10
11 12 13 14 15 16 17
18 19 20 21 22 23 24
25 26 27 28 29 30 31

APRIL
S M T W T F S
1 2 3 4 5 6 7
8 9 10 11 12 13 14
15 16 17 18 19 20 21
22 23 24 25 26 27 28
29 30

MAY
S M T W T F S
1 2 3 4 5
6 7 8 9 10 11 12
13 14 15 16 17 18 19
20 21 22 23 24 25 26
27 28 29 30 31

JUNE
S M T W T F S
1 2
3 4 5 6 7 8 9
10 11 12 13 14 15 16
17 18 19 20 21 22 23
24 25 26 27 28 29 30

JULY
S M T W T F S
1 2 3 4 5 6 7
8 9 10 11 12 13 14
15 16 17 18 19 20 21
22 23 24 25 26 27 28
29 30 31

AUGUST
S M T W T F S
1 2 3 4
5 6 7 8 9 10 11
12 13 14 15 16 17 18
19 20 21 22 23 24 25
26 27 28 29 30 31

SEPTEMBER
S M T W T F S
1
2 3 4 5 6 7 8
9 10 11 12 13 14 15
16 17 18 19 20 21 22
23 24 25 26 27 28 29
30

OCTOBER
S M T W T F S
1 2 3 4 5 6
7 8 9 10 11 12 13
14 15 16 17 18 19 20
21 22 23 24 25 26 27
28 29 30 31

NOVEMBER
S M T W T F S
1 2 3
4 5 6 7 8 9 10
11 12 13 14 15 16 17
18 19 20 21 22 23 24
25 26 27 28 29 30

DECEMBER
S M T W T F S
1
2 3 4 5 6 7 8
9 10 11 12 13 14 15
16 17 18 19 20 21 22
23 24 25 26 27 28 29
30 31

9 (Leap Year)

JANUARY
S M T W T F S
1 2 3 4 5 6
7 8 9 10 11 12 13
14 15 16 17 18 19 20
21 22 23 24 25 26 27
28 29 30 31

FEBRUARY
S M T W T F S
1 2 3
4 5 6 7 8 9 10
11 12 13 14 15 16 17
18 19 20 21 22 23 24
25 26 27 28 29

MARCH
S M T W T F S
1 2
3 4 5 6 7 8 9
10 11 12 13 14 15 16
17 18 19 20 21 22 23
24 25 26 27 28 29 30
31

APRIL
S M T W T F S
1 2 3 4 5 6
7 8 9 10 11 12 13
14 15 16 17 18 19 20
21 22 23 24 25 26 27
28 29 30

MAY
S M T W T F S
1 2 3 4
5 6 7 8 9 10 11
12 13 14 15 16 17 18
19 20 21 22 23 24 25
26 27 28 29 30 31

JUNE
S M T W T F S
1
2 3 4 5 6 7 8
9 10 11 12 13 14 15
16 17 18 19 20 21 22
23 24 25 26 27 28 29
30

JULY
S M T W T F S
1 2 3 4 5 6
7 8 9 10 11 12 13
14 15 16 17 18 19 20
21 22 23 24 25 26 27
28 29 30 31

AUGUST
S M T W T F S
1 2 3
4 5 6 7 8 9 10
11 12 13 14 15 16 17
18 19 20 21 22 23 24
25 26 27 28 29 30 31

SEPTEMBER
S M T W T F S
1 2 3 4 5 6 7
8 9 10 11 12 13 14
15 16 17 18 19 20 21
22 23 24 25 26 27 28
29 30

OCTOBER
S M T W T F S
1 2 3 4 5
6 7 8 9 10 11 12
13 14 15 16 17 18 19
20 21 22 23 24 25 26
27 28 29 30 31

NOVEMBER
S M T W T F S
1 2
3 4 5 6 7 8 9
10 11 12 13 14 15 16
17 18 19 20 21 22 23
24 25 26 27 28 29 30

DECEMBER
S M T W T F S
1 2 3 4 5 6 7
8 9 10 11 12 13 14
15 16 17 18 19 20 21
22 23 24 25 26 27 28
29 30 31

10 (Leap Year)

JANUARY
S M T W T F S
1 2 3 4 5
6 7 8 9 10 11 12
13 14 15 16 17 18 19
20 21 22 23 24 25 26
27 28 29 30 31

FEBRUARY
S M T W T F S
1 2
3 4 5 6 7 8 9
10 11 12 13 14 15 16
17 18 19 20 21 22 23
24 25 26 27 28 29

MARCH
S M T W T F S
1
2 3 4 5 6 7 8
9 10 11 12 13 14 15
16 17 18 19 20 21 22
23 24 25 26 27 28 29
30 31

APRIL
S M T W T F S
1 2 3 4 5
6 7 8 9 10 11 12
13 14 15 16 17 18 19
20 21 22 23 24 25 26
27 28 29 30

MAY
S M T W T F S
1 2 3
4 5 6 7 8 9 10
11 12 13 14 15 16 17
18 19 20 21 22 23 24
25 26 27 28 29 30 31

JUNE
S M T W T F S
1 2 3 4 5 6 7
8 9 10 11 12 13 14
15 16 17 18 19 20 21
22 23 24 25 26 27 28
29 30

JULY
S M T W T F S
1 2 3 4 5
6 7 8 9 10 11 12
13 14 15 16 17 18 19
20 21 22 23 24 25 26
27 28 29 30 31

AUGUST
S M T W T F S
1 2
3 4 5 6 7 8 9
10 11 12 13 14 15 16
17 18 19 20 21 22 23
24 25 26 27 28 29 30
31

SEPTEMBER
S M T W T F S
1 2 3 4 5 6
7 8 9 10 11 12 13
14 15 16 17 18 19 20
21 22 23 24 25 26 27
28 29 30

OCTOBER
S M T W T F S
1 2 3 4
5 6 7 8 9 10 11
12 13 14 15 16 17 18
19 20 21 22 23 24 25
26 27 28 29 30 31

NOVEMBER
S M T W T F S
1
2 3 4 5 6 7 8
9 10 11 12 13 14 15
16 17 18 19 20 21 22
23 24 25 26 27 28 29
30

DECEMBER
S M T W T F S
1 2 3 4 5 6
7 8 9 10 11 12 13
14 15 16 17 18 19 20
21 22 23 24 25 26 27
28 29 30 31

11 (Leap Year)

JANUARY
S M T W T F S
1 2 3 4
5 6 7 8 9 10 11
12 13 14 15 16 17 18
19 20 21 22 23 24 25
26 27 28 29 30 31

FEBRUARY
S M T W T F S
1
2 3 4 5 6 7 8
9 10 11 12 13 14 15
16 17 18 19 20 21 22
23 24 25 26 27 28 29

MARCH
S M T W T F S
1 2 3 4 5 6 7
8 9 10 11 12 13 14
15 16 17 18 19 20 21
22 23 24 25 26 27 28
29 30 31

APRIL
S M T W T F S
1 2 3 4
5 6 7 8 9 10 11
12 13 14 15 16 17 18
19 20 21 22 23 24 25
26 27 28 29 30

MAY
S M T W T F S
1 2
3 4 5 6 7 8 9
10 11 12 13 14 15 16
17 18 19 20 21 22 23
24 25 26 27 28 29 30
31

JUNE
S M T W T F S
1 2 3 4 5 6
7 8 9 10 11 12 13
14 15 16 17 18 19 20
21 22 23 24 25 26 27
28 29 30

JULY
S M T W T F S
1 2 3 4
5 6 7 8 9 10 11
12 13 14 15 16 17 18
19 20 21 22 23 24 25
26 27 28 29 30 31

AUGUST
S M T W T F S
1
2 3 4 5 6 7 8
9 10 11 12 13 14 15
16 17 18 19 20 21 22
23 24 25 26 27 28 29
30 31

SEPTEMBER
S M T W T F S
1 2 3 4 5
6 7 8 9 10 11 12
13 14 15 16 17 18 19
20 21 22 23 24 25 26
27 28 29 30

OCTOBER
S M T W T F S
1 2 3
4 5 6 7 8 9 10
11 12 13 14 15 16 17
18 19 20 21 22 23 24
25 26 27 28 29 30 31

NOVEMBER
S M T W T F S
1 2 3 4 5 6 7
8 9 10 11 12 13 14
15 16 17 18 19 20 21
22 23 24 25 26 27 28
29 30

DECEMBER
S M T W T F S
1 2 3 4 5
6 7 8 9 10 11 12
13 14 15 16 17 18 19
20 21 22 23 24 25 26
27 28 29 30 31

12 (Leap Year)

JANUARY
S M T W T F S
1 2 3
4 5 6 7 8 9 10
11 12 13 14 15 16 17
18 19 20 21 22 23 24
25 26 27 28 29 30 31

FEBRUARY
S M T W T F S
1 2 3 4 5 6 7
8 9 10 11 12 13 14
15 16 17 18 19 20 21
22 23 24 25 26 27 28
29

MARCH
S M T W T F S
1 2 3 4 5 6
7 8 9 10 11 12 13
14 15 16 17 18 19 20
21 22 23 24 25 26 27
28 29 30 31

APRIL
S M T W T F S
1 2 3
4 5 6 7 8 9 10
11 12 13 14 15 16 17
18 19 20 21 22 23 24
25 26 27 28 29 30

MAY
S M T W T F S
1
2 3 4 5 6 7 8
9 10 11 12 13 14 15
16 17 18 19 20 21 22
23 24 25 26 27 28 29
30 31

JUNE
S M T W T F S
1 2 3 4 5
6 7 8 9 10 11 12
13 14 15 16 17 18 19
20 21 22 23 24 25 26
27 28 29 30

JULY
S M T W T F S
1 2 3
4 5 6 7 8 9 10
11 12 13 14 15 16 17
18 19 20 21 22 23 24
25 26 27 28 29 30 31

AUGUST
S M T W T F S
1 2 3 4 5 6 7
8 9 10 11 12 13 14
15 16 17 18 19 20 21
22 23 24 25 26 27 28
29 30 31

SEPTEMBER
S M T W T F S
1 2 3 4
5 6 7 8 9 10 11
12 13 14 15 16 17 18
19 20 21 22 23 24 25
26 27 28 29 30

OCTOBER
S M T W T F S
1 2
3 4 5 6 7 8 9
10 11 12 13 14 15 16
17 18 19 20 21 22 23
24 25 26 27 28 29 30
31

NOVEMBER
S M T W T F S
1 2 3 4 5 6
7 8 9 10 11 12 13
14 15 16 17 18 19 20
21 22 23 24 25 26 27
28 29 30

DECEMBER
S M T W T F S
1 2 3 4
5 6 7 8 9 10 11
12 13 14 15 16 17 18
19 20 21 22 23 24 25
26 27 28 29 30 31

13 (Leap Year)

JANUARY

S	M	T	W	T	F	S
					1	2
3	4	5	6	7	8	9
10	11	12	13	14	15	16
17	18	19	20	21	22	23
24	25	26	27	28	29	30
31						

FEBRUARY

S	M	T	W	T	F	S
	1	2	3	4	5	6
7	8	9	10	11	12	13
14	15	16	17	18	19	20
21	22	23	24	25	26	27
28	29					

MARCH

S	M	T	W	T	F	S
	1	2	3	4	5	
6	7	8	9	10	11	12
13	14	15	16	17	18	19
20	21	22	23	24	25	26
27	28	29	30	31		

APRIL

S	M	T	W	T	F	S
					1	2
3	4	5	6	7	8	9
10	11	12	13	14	15	16
17	18	19	20	21	22	23
24	25	26	27	28	29	30

MAY

S	M	T	W	T	F	S
1	2	3	4	5	6	7
8	9	10	11	12	13	14
15	16	17	18	19	20	21
22	23	24	25	26	27	28
29	30	31				

JUNE

S	M	T	W	T	F	S
			1	2	3	4
5	6	7	8	9	10	11
12	13	14	15	16	17	18
19	20	21	22	23	24	25
26	27	28	29	30		

JULY

S	M	T	W	T	F	S
					1	2
3	4	5	6	7	8	9
10	11	12	13	14	15	16
17	18	19	20	21	22	23
24	25	26	27	28	29	30
31						

AUGUST

S	M	T	W	T	F	S
	1	2	3	4	5	6
7	8	9	10	11	12	13
14	15	16	17	18	19	20
21	22	23	24	25	26	27
28	29	30	31			

SEPTEMBER

S	M	T	W	T	F	S
				1	2	3
4	5	6	7	8	9	10
11	12	13	14	15	16	17
18	19	20	21	22	23	24
25	26	27	28	29	30	

OCTOBER

S	M	T	W	T	F	S
						1
2	3	4	5	6	7	8
9	10	11	12	13	14	15
16	17	18	19	20	21	22
23	24	25	26	27	28	29
30	31					

NOVEMBER

S	M	T	W	T	F	S
		1	2	3	4	5
6	7	8	9	10	11	12
13	14	15	16	17	18	19
20	21	22	23	24	25	26
27	28	29	30			

DECEMBER

S	M	T	W	T	F	S
				1	2	3
4	5	6	7	8	9	10
11	12	13	14	15	16	17
18	19	20	21	22	23	24
25	26	27	28	29	30	31

14 (Leap Year)

JANUARY

S	M	T	W	T	F	S
						1
2	3	4	5	6	7	8
9	10	11	12	13	14	15
16	17	18	19	20	21	22
23	24	25	26	27	28	29
30	31					

FEBRUARY

S	M	T	W	T	F	S
		1	2	3	4	5
6	7	8	9	10	11	12
13	14	15	16	17	18	19
20	21	22	23	24	25	26
27	28	29				

MARCH

S	M	T	W	T	F	S
			1	2	3	4
5	6	7	8	9	10	11
12	13	14	15	16	17	18
19	20	21	22	23	24	25
26	27	28	29	30	31	

APRIL

S	M	T	W	T	F	S
						1
2	3	4	5	6	7	8
9	10	11	12	13	14	15
16	17	18	19	20	21	22
23	24	25	26	27	28	29
30						

MAY

S	M	T	W	T	F	S
	1	2	3	4	5	6
7	8	9	10	11	12	13
14	15	16	17	18	19	20
21	22	23	24	25	26	27
28	29	30	31			

JUNE

S	M	T	W	T	F	S
				1	2	3
4	5	6	7	8	9	10
11	12	13	14	15	16	17
18	19	20	21	22	23	24
25	26	27	28	29	30	

JULY

S	M	T	W	T	F	S
						1
2	3	4	5	6	7	8
9	10	11	12	13	14	15
16	17	18	19	20	21	22
23	24	25	26	27	28	29
30	31					

AUGUST

S	M	T	W	T	F	S
	1	2	3	4	5	
6	7	8	9	10	11	12
13	14	15	16	17	18	19
20	21	22	23	24	25	26
27	28	29	30	31		

SEPTEMBER

S	M	T	W	T	F	S
					1	2
3	4	5	6	7	8	9
10	11	12	13	14	15	16
17	18	19	20	21	22	23
24	25	26	27	28	29	30

OCTOBER

S	M	T	W	T	F	S
1	2	3	4	5	6	7
8	9	10	11	12	13	14
15	16	17	18	19	20	21
22	23	24	25	26	27	28
29	30	31				

NOVEMBER

S	M	T	W	T	F	S
			1	2	3	4
5	6	7	8	9	10	11
12	13	14	15	16	17	18
19	20	21	22	23	24	25
26	27	28	29	30		

DECEMBER

S	M	T	W	T	F	S
					1	2
3	4	5	6	7	8	9
10	11	12	13	14	15	16
17	18	19	20	21	22	23
24	25	26	27	28	29	30
31						

Word Processing Glossary

abbreviation document A document on which words or phrases are stored; each one is identified by a short code or abbreviation and can be called out and inserted into your main document by using that code or abbreviation only, rather than having to re-enter the entire word or phrase. For complicated words that are used often, use of an abbreviation document saves both time and typographical errors.

access To make something available to use; to access a document means to call it out for revision or printing.

application A specific task that your system can perform; you can "apply" the software/hardware parts of your system to achieve a desired result. Copying a document from one disk to another is a concrete application of one of your system's many possibilities.

automatic A function your system will perform repeatedly for you without specific prompting each time. An "automatic sheet feeder" feeds a new sheet of paper for each new page without your having to put the sheet into the system manually; "automatic page numbering" prints the proper page number on each sheet on a large job without your having to enter each page number separately.

automatic sheet feeder An optional piece of hardware that feeds single sheets of paper automatically to the printer. Most automatic sheet feeders have two trays and can feed the first sheet of a document from one tray, with all the rest of the sheets needed for that document being fed from the second tray. This feature permits the use of letterhead for the first page and blank sheets for all the following pages. Every automatic sheet feeder system has a manual feed option, so you can slip in a single job that bypasses the automatic feature.

backspace A key that moves the cursor backward one space at a time; in some systems the use of this key will delete the character the cursor backs over.

back up To move the cursor backward through the document without deleting copy.

backup copy A copy of an entire disk or documents on a disk that is made for safekeeping. Backup copies can also be made of program (systems or software) disks.

batch printing Lining up jobs in a queue (a waiting line) to print automatically one right after another. The creation or revision of other documents that are not in the printing queue can take place while the printing is going on.

bidirectional Pertaining to the ability to move in both directions. Most daisy wheel and thimble printwheels used on letter-quality printers and most matrix printheads move and print in both right-to-left and left-to-right directions. If your system can print superscripts and subscripts, the paper moves bidirectionally—first up and then down or first down and then up—when printing these characters.

block A storage space on a diskette that holds a certain number of characters. Each block holds the same number of characters. Your manufacturer can tell you how many characters are contained in the blocks in your system. Knowing this information is helpful in determining the total size of any document.

boilerplate Standard paragraphs used in your work. They can be filed by name or number and stored in a paragraph document to be called up for inclusion in a document whenever needed.

bold To overprint the same text with the same characters in order to make them appear slightly darker. Not all systems have the capability of printing each character twice.

breaking hyphen A hyphen that joins compound words ("long-standing") and will break if the first half of the compound word is at the end of a line ("long-"; "standing"). Entering a breaking hyphen may require a supershift, depending on the software program in your system.

brightness control The device on your system that allows you to lighten or darken the text that appears on your screen. It is especially useful if you work in a natural light setting in which the room's light varies from strong sunlight to early winter darkness.

carbon ribbon A better-quality printer ribbon. It normally is used only once, with each character striking at an unused spot on the ribbon, in contrast to a cloth ribbon that is used several times in a continuous loop. The carbon ribbon produces a darker, cleaner image.

carriage The mechanism in your printer that holds the printwheel or printhead and moves the printwheel (printhead) back and forth across the paper while printing is taking place. (Sometimes called a "carrier.")

carriage return (carrier return) *See* **return.**

center To position a word or phrase at the center of a line or centered on a tab stop. Once the centering location is determined and the centering commands are executed, the word or phrase will automatically center as it is entered.

character Any letter, number, space, command, or instruction that you enter into the system. You will normally see only the letters, punctuation marks, numbers, and spaces on the screen. If you enter a display or view mode, you will see all the other special characters you have entered that control the format of your document, such as hard returns, superscripts, tab stops, format changes, and so on. These normally invisible characters will not print out, but they do take up space on your disk.

cloth ribbon A printer ribbon that is on a continuous loop and can be reused until you decide it is printing too light to use any longer. A carbon ribbon is used only once and has to be replaced when it has run once through the printer.

code In some systems the supershift key is called "code." It needs to be pressed at the same time (or on some systems, just before) a coded character key is pressed to make the key perform its coded function. For example, the "u" key pressed alone results in a lowercase "u" being entered; shift + "u" results in an uppercase "U" being entered; and supershift (or code) + "u" results in the word last entered being underlined (if underlining a word is the function of the supershift + "u" key in your system).

column Vertically arranged blocks of text, usually found in tables or in newsletters or bulletins. Some systems will adjust the space between the columns automatically; some require you to tab to the space manually. Most systems will center columns around a center point, around a decimal, around a comma, or will print a column flush right or flush left.

communications The transferring of data to and from your word processing system to another computer system (word processor, data processor, intelligent copier, and so on) by cable or telephone. Communications requires special hardware (cable and/or modem) and software.

composite character A character that is produced by two or more characters one on top of the other.

continuous-form paper A long piece of paper that can go continuously through your printer. The paper is perforated at regular intervals so pages can be separated. This paper is pulled through the printer by a form-feed tractor.

copy (1) The content of your document; (2) to duplicate your document or disk on another disk, or to duplicate your document elsewhere on the same disk; (3) the duplicate of your document or disk.

create To start a new document. The first step is to give this new document a name, so you can later go back to it for revision or call it up for printing, or even instruct the system to erase it.

CRT An abbreviation of "cathode ray tube," another name for your screen (sometimes more technically called "video display" or VD).

cursor The indicator that shows where the next character to be entered will enter the system (sometimes a blinking underline or rectangle, sometimes a solid highlight).

cursor keys Some systems have keys with arrows that move the cursor up or down, right or left, depending on which key is pressed. If the key is held down, the cursor will continue to move in a given direction until the key is released. Other systems have keys with names that move the cursor forward or backward by character, by word, by sentence, by paragraph, or by page. Most systems have supershift combinations that enable you to move the cursor directly to a particular page in a long document, or to the start (top) or the end (bottom) of the document. By using "find" or "search" commands, you can move the cursor to particular words in your document.

cut To remove or copy part of a document (sometimes called "move"). In some systems you have to "paste" this part of the document elsewhere in the document; in other systems you have an option of "forgetting it," and thus deleting a sizable portion of the document at once rather than word by word or line by line.

date and time A time clock in the system. It must be set with the current date and time each time the system is turned on. Some systems can print the date and time from the clock onto a document, thus providing an automatic "stamp" as to when work was begun and/or ended. A system with a date and time feature will automatically keep track of the time spent working on each document.

decimal alignment The ability of the system to line up numbers in a column on a decimal point.

default The settings that are preassigned and will format and control the system unless you specifically enter different settings. The software manufacturer initially preassigns these settings, on the basis of the most widespread expected usage. You may enter new settings for a particular document: these will thereafter apply to that document unless you change the settings later. In some systems, you can enter new settings on the program diskette—creating your own default settings to which the system will automatically revert when not specifically told otherwise.

delete To remove (erase) characters, words, pages, documents, or entire disks. Deleted parts of a document normally cannot be retrieved (only if they are placed in the system's temporary memory can they be retrieved).

directory Another name for index: the system's list of documents that are stored on a disk.

disk A thin, flexible magnetic disk, enclosed in a rather stiff protective jacket. Depending on your system, it will be 5¼ inches in diameter or 8 inches in diameter. Some newer minisystems are appearing with disks that are 3 inches in diam-

eter. Documents and software programs are stored on disks. The amount of data that can be placed on a disk is not directly related to its diameter, but rather to the density of its formatting. (Often disks are called "diskettes.")

disk drives The recording and reading devices that are located on your screen console or in a separate disk drive unit. You place the disks into the slots in the disk drive, close the slot door or gate, and the system will automatically load the contents of the disks into the system for work. (In some systems, you need to instruct the system to load, or "boot," the program disk into the system.

disk name The name you assign a disk. It may be an actual name, an abbreviation, or an alphanumeric code. This name will thereafter be used in the system to gain access to the contents of the disk. You can change a disk name at any time.

display To show the contents of a disk on the screen. In a display mode, the hidden or invisible characters are also shown.

document A body of text of any length that you create, name, and store on a document disk.

document comment Some systems allow you to enter a comment about the document. This comment will serve as a reminder of some work function, deadline, or routing you need to remember. This comment will appear only on your screen: it will not be printed out, nor will it affect the formatting of the document. The document comment is a kind of electronic memo slip you can attach to your document, if you wish.

document name The name you give a document when you create it. That name is the means you have thereafter to gain access to the document for revision, copying, printing, or deletion.

document number Some systems will assign each document on a disk a number. That number does not change as you add or delete other documents on the disk.

double-density disk A disk that is initialized in such a way as to take considerably more data than a single-density disk. The amount varies from nearly double to over three times as much, depending on your system.

draft printer A high-speed matrix printer that prints out documents on continuous-form paper. You can use this printer for initial proofing and revision; its output is not as attractive as the output of a letter-quality printer.

duplicate To copy a document or disk elsewhere, but still leave the original intact.

edit To revise the text of a document.

edit keys The functional keys that allow you to instruct the system directly to perform functions relating to editing. Moving the cursor, going to a page or word, searching or finding, replacing, filing or ending, inserting required page ends, calling up view mode, are all typical functions performed directly by pressing edit keys.

elite Another name for a 12-pitch typeface; a 10-pitch typeface is sometimes called "pica."

end A term used in some systems for filing a document onto the document disk. Some systems require using a page end key to file each page as you proceed through the document, without having to file the entire document and then recall it again to continue work.

enter To put text and instructions into the system by pressing on keys. Some systems use the term "enter" to refer to their execute-an-instruction command.

erase To remove or delete text from a disk, making that space available for receiving new text. A system will normally have several methods of erasing text, ranging from single characters to documents to entire disks.

error message A brief message that may appear on your screen to tell you that you cannot perform a function the way you are trying to perform it. The message will usually prompt you to help you perform the function in a way that works in the system.

execute A command to the system to perform a function. You usually need to set the function up; when you execute the command, the function occurs. Some systems have a special "execute" or "enter" key; others use the return key as the execute key.

feature A function that your system is capable of performing. A spelling-hyphenation dictionary is an example of a feature.

field A distinctly identifiable part of your document that can be recalled and used by reference to its identity. For example, a list of addresses may include the state as a separate identifiable part or field. "State" is the field name, and "Iowa" or "IA" is a part of the field. When the field name is called up for use, the system will use "Iowa" or "IA."

file To store a document on a disk for future use. Also, "file" is another name for the document itself.

file name The name or alphanumeric code you have given the system to identify a particular document.

find A term used in some systems to define the search feature.

footer Text placed automatically at the bottom of each page, such as a document name, page number, date, or author's name.

format The layout of the page, using such specific instructions as margin width, tabs, number of lines, and line spacing.

global search and replace A feature that automatically searches out every instance of a string of characters in a document and replaces them with a different string of characters. You have told the system which word or phrase to search and which word or phrase to use as the replacement. The word "global" indicates this process occurs throughout the entire document without stopping, rather than moving from one instance to the next individually on your command.

go-to A feature that enables you to move quickly to a specific page (by page number) in a document.

hard copy A printout on paper of a document from your system.

hard return A return caused by pressing the return key rather than an automatic return (soft return) created by the system when a line turns over. The hard return will function wherever it appears, even though the document rearranges itself when text is added or deleted.

hard space A space made in combination with a supershift key; this space holds letters together as though it were a character itself. It is useful in ensuring that initials that are part of a person's name do not separate over two different lines.

hardware The physical equipment parts of a word processing system. Printers and keyboards are hardware.

header Text placed automatically at the top of each page, such as a document name, page number, date, or author's name.

highlight A feature that makes some text stand out on the screen. Highlighting may be by underlining, by brighter appearance of certain characters, or by lighting up the background behind characters, words, or blocks of text.

hyphenation Use of the character - at the end of a line to divide a word into syllables or between parts of compound words. Some systems can use a hyphenation dictionary to divide words automatically (though not always correctly). All systems differentiate between a hard hypen, which always appears and holds characters on either side together; a breaking hyphen, which always appears but will allow the characters that follow it to drop down to the next line if a line turnover is required: and an invisible hyphen, which is used in word division and will appear if at the end of a line but will not be printed if the word is elsewhere in the text.

index The list of documents on a document disk. The index can be viewed on the screen and printed out on paper.

initialize To prepare a disk to receive data. The data may be a software program or documents. The preparation may be for single- or double-density use, depending on your needs and the capabilities of your system.

insert To place text into a document between characters that are already in the document. The system will rearrange existing text around the new, inserted text.

justify To print a document with even right and left margins. Some systems have a "half-justify" option that makes the right-hand margin somewhat more even than a regular ragged right but not exactly even as in a justified right-hand margin. The system will require hyphenating when printing a justified right-hand margin, since the lines will spread so open as to be unattractive if there are too few characters on a line.

keyboard The hardware part that has keys for entering characters and commands. It is either part of the terminal or is connected to the terminal by a flexible cable.

keystroke One press of any key on the keyboard, including spaces, returns, and any command keys.

keystroke save A feature on some systems that allows you to put a certain number of characters into a temporary memory and play them back on command for any number of times until you replace them with a new set of characters. On other systems, this feature can be used with the cut-and-paste feature.

left justify A tab stop on which the first character of any entry in a column always lines up; the words or figures build toward the right.

left margin The place where all left-hand lines normally start to print. The placement of your left-hand margin on the paper is related to how you set up your margins when you format the page. You should learn how far in from the edge of the paper your left-hand margin should be for letterhead correspondence and use that setting routinely for correspondence work.

letter-quality printer Often referred to as an LQP. This printer uses an impact printing method with printwheels or thimbles to produce a quality of printing equal to or better than that produced by a good typewriter.

library A feature that enables you to store words, phrases, and even paragraphs elsewhere on a disk (in a library document) and to call them up for reproduction in the document you are working on by using a shorthand code of letters or numbers.

line counter Some systems show you which line you are working on at any given time. They normally count from the top of the page, so you have to calculate the number of top margin lines to figure out how far down the page you are at any line number.

line spacing The spacing between lines of print when your document prints out. Systems vary in their capability of ranging from single-line spacing (normally six lines to an inch) to increments of a single line or triple-line spacing. Half-line spacing or less is useful in printing superscripts and subscripts: if you can control your system to produce less than half-line spacing, your superscripts will not overlap the descenders on the line above when you are printing them in a single-spaced document.

list processing The feature that allows you to combine lists with a form (or shell) document in order to produce an original, personalized document that combines the individual features in the list with the copy in the form document.

load The term used in some systems to describe the function of placing your software program into the system's computer after you have turned the machine on.

lowercase The uncapitalized form of letters. The term is taken from earlier printing times when these letters were manually taken by typesetters one by one from a large compartmentalized drawer (called a "case") in which the uncapitalized letters were stored in the compartments located at the lower two-thirds of the case.

margin The space between any of the four edges of the paper and the place where your printing begins or ends. There are top, right, left, and bottom margins to each job.

math A feature that allows you to enter numbers together with numeric commands (addition, subtraction, multiplication, division, percentage) that will function in your job. Most often this feature is used in list processing and sorting work.

matrix printer A high-speed printer that prints dots instead of entire letters. The dots fit into a matrix, or pattern, to form the general shape of a letter or number. The more dots and the tighter the matrix, the more the matrix-produced letter looks like an impact-produced letter.

menu Choices listed on the screen from which you can select on option. You need to go to the proper menu to select a particular feature you want to make happen. Your manual illustrates all the possible menus you can call up and tells you how to call them up.

merge The act of combining elements from lists with a form document when list processing.

message Information, questions, or warnings that appear on your screen as a result of some condition that calls for a response from you. This condition may be due to the fact that you have asked the machine to do something it cannot do, or do it out of its own sequence, or it may be due to the printer running out of paper or ribbon, or needing a printwheel change.

module A piece of hardware that can be combined with other hardware pieces to form a working computer or word processing unit. Some modules are changeable; for instance, you can use more than one kind of printing module (printer) with a word processor. Or you can use more than one kind of keyboard (for instance, if you have a French-language software program, you could use a French-language keyboard without having to change any other elements in your system except to secure a French-language printwheel).

numeric keyboard Some systems use a special ten-key (0–9) section for numbers, configured in the same style as most calculators. Other systems use the 1–0 sequence of keys on an upper row in the main keyboard section.

operator A person who makes a word processing system function by entering characters and commands.

option Any one of the choices that can be selected by an operator from a menu.

originator A person who writes or dictates a document for word processing by a word processing operator.

overstrike To place a character over another character. If the same character overstrikes a character, the result is a slightly bolder appearance; if a different character overstrikes, the result is a combined character or a character with an accent mark. In legal work, many words are overstruck with a hyphen (as in "effective immediately") to show words that are proposed to be deleted from a legal document. Many word processing systems are able to actually delete those overstruck words in a revision after both parties have agreed to their deletion and the final document is being prepared.

page A section in a document marked off by a page end mark. This mark may be placed there automatically during pagination or it may be placed there manually. The system registers this area in the document as a page in its numbering system. The page may be full of type, partially full, or even completely empty.

page mark (page end mark) A character that instructs the system to end a page and to begin a new page with the next character. The page end mark may be placed automatically or manually. This mark is sometimes called a "new page" mark.

pagination The feature that divides a document into pages. You determine how many lines should be on a page when you enter the automatic pagination instructions, or you do so by entering a required page end mark at the place of your choice.

paper jam Paper has become wedged into the printer or feeder and needs to be manually removed.

paragraph Text of one or more lines that is separated from other text in the document by a paragraph marker (if your system has one and if you use it) or by two hard returns. In some systems, a number of printed paragraphs that you separate by a single hard return followed by a tab indent will be understood by the system's logic to be a single long paragraph if you try to move forward or backward by paragraphs. The system only recognizes the paragraph mark or two hard returns in sequence for its paragraph functioning.

paragraph document Copy—from a single word to an entire paragraph in length—that is stored in an alternate location, that is, not in the document you are working on, but can be inserted into your document either by a couple of manual keystrokes or by including a format command in your shell document.

paste To insert data that has been temporarily stored in a "paste" area or "keystroke save" area. The content of the data in the paste area does not change (and so can be used many times) until new data are stored in that area.

pica An often-used name for 10-pitch characters.

pitch The number of characters per horizontal inch. The pitches normally used in word processing are 10-pitch (sometimes called "pica"), 12-pitch (sometimes called "elite"), and 15-pitch. You need to instruct your system about which pitch you are using and make sure that you have the proper printwheel in the printer for that pitch setting.

platen The cylinder against which the printhead strikes to produce an impression.

printer The hardware unit that produces a paper copy of your document.

printhead The hardware device in the printer that produces matrix characters or that strikes a printwheel to produce impact characters.

printwheel A circular printing element, sometimes called a "daisy wheel" or a "thimble," depending on its shape.

program A software set of instructions that enables your system to perform word processing functions. You load your program into the system each time you turn the system on. Your manual explains how to enter commands into the system to make it perform functions that the program enables it to do. Most word processing programs are "packaged"; that is, they are prepared by the manufacturer and are licensed property. Generally, you are not able to change the content of a word processing program.

prompt A message that appears on your screen and requires a response from you.

proportional spacing Spacing between characters that is somewhat proportional to the amount of space taken up by each character (for instance, in proportional spacing, or PS, an "m" uses more space than an "I"). To use proportional spacing, your system must be able to use a PS print setting and you must have PS printwheels that are compatible with your system.

queue A waiting line. Sometimes you can have a queue of documents to be printed one after the other automatically, while you are editing yet a different document.

ragged right An uneven right-hand margin. Unless you justify a document, it will print out as you see it on the screen.

replace A feature of putting in new characters in the place of previously entered characters that now are deleted.

return Use of the return key ends a line at that point where it is pressed. The return key is also used in many systems to execute commands.

revision The work you do to change the contents of a document or the commands that control its appearance.

ribbon A narrow strip of carbon or cloth used in the printer against which the printwheel or printhead strikes to create an impression on the paper. In word processors, ribbons come in self-contained cartridges. Some ribbons made of cloth are in continuous-loop cartridges and can be used several times over; other ribbons can be used only once.

right justify A tab setting for the rightmost character in a column. All the other characters or numbers in the column will build out toward the left from the tab setting.

right margin The setting that controls the placing of rightmost characters on the page. If your document is ragged right, no character will extend beyond the right margin setting; if it is justified, all lines will end on the right margin setting (except possibly the last line of each paragraph).

screen The video screen on which your document and various menus, messages, and other information are displayed.

scroll To move the cursor forward or backward through a document, often resulting in the text of the document moving up or down the screen.

search To instruct the system to look for (find) a particular string of characters (a word or phrase), most often with a view to replacing those characters with others.

sentence The part of a document ending with a period, a question mark, or an exclamation mark. If your system advances or backs up by sentences, it will move from period to period (or the other sentence end marks). If there are several periods after initials (as in "F.D.R."), your system will read the text between each period as a sentence.

setting A location (margin setting) or command (typeface setting) you have put into a document or a program. Settings can be changed through appropriate menus.

shadow printing Some systems have the capability of overstriking characters with the same character moved slightly to one side of the original character, giving an impression of very bold printing.

shared printer A feature whereby more than one terminal can use the same printer.

shell A form document that permits the inclusion of variables taken from a list.

single density A method of formatting a disk to receive information that permits the storage of much less information per disk than double-density formatting. Systems that have double-density capability can normally read single-density diskettes, but single-density systems can read only single-density diskettes.

software Instructions on a program disk that tell the hardware (the physical equipment) what functions to perform and lead you through a series of menus to give the appropriate commands to make the system perform the functions you want. Software that works on your system to perform a wide variety of tasks can be purchased directly from your manufacturer or from companies that write software programs for your brand of equipment.

sort A feature that enables your system to organize lists in a wide variety of alphanumeric combinations. Each alphanumeric element in your sort is organized in either an ascending or a descending order (A to Z, 1 to 10000; or reverse).

spelling A feature that loads a spelling dictionary into the system to check the spelling of words in a document. The size of these dictionaries varies from 10,000 to 150,000 words, depending on the complexity of the software and the hardware. The larger the dictionary, the larger the working memory the system requires.

store To place (file) information on a disk, where it is available for recall and adjustment later. Depending on your system, print settings, lists, rulers or margins, paragraphs, phrases, and words can be stored in various ways for recall and inclusion in the content or formatting of a document.

subscript and superscript Characters printed off the main line of the text. Subscripts are generally printed half a line below the main line (H_2); superscripts above the main line (for footnote reference[5]).

swap Some systems have a special key function that exchanges a character with the character to its right. This is useful when correcting transpositions ("teh" instead of "the").

system The entire word processing unit, including all its hardware and software parts.

system page number The page number in a document assigned by the system for a given page. Each document begins with a system number of "1." If your document is the second one of a long work that is consecutively numbered, you may instruct the system to number the pages of the document beginning with another number, such as "38." In such a case, book or report page 38 will be system page 1, 39 will be 2, and so on. Depending on your system, you will need to use the system page number to "go to" or "print" a particular page (although some systems renumber all the pages in a document based on the initial page number you enter for the document).

systems disk The disk that holds the software program.

tab To enter a tab mark or to press the tab key to move the cursor over to the next tab mark.

temporary marker Markers that are automatically erased by the system when they are no longer needed. Some are entered by the system, such as a word-wrap return—as opposed to a hard return—that the system places at the end of each line when it drops down to the text line. If you rearrange the text, old word-wrap returns will be erased automatically, and new word-wrap returns entered automatically for the new lines, if line endings have been changed. The same happens to soft page end markers when lines are added or deleted.

text The part of a document that is normally displayed on the screen and printed out as the desired output. All the commands—both hard and soft—are considered not part of the text, even though they are essential to the word processing operation. The characters that show which commands have been entered can usually be seen only on the view (display) mode.

thousands separator On some systems a comma can be used in columnar work as a point on which numbers line up. The comma, in this case, separates the thousands position from the hundreds in large numbers.

top margin The number of lines between the top of the sheet of paper and the first line of printing.

typeface or typestyle The characters of a particular design of type appearance and size. A printwheel will contain characters of a single typestyle or typeface and of a single pitch. Light Italic is an example of a typeface, as are Boldface and Prestige.

underline To print with a line under the text for emphasis or as a substitute for italics. Each system has special function keys to make underlining easy.

update To revise text and bring the information on a disk to current status. It is especially important to update backup copies of disks, so you don't inadvertently use disks that are unlike the most recently revised printout.

uppercase The capitalized form of letters. The term is taken from earlier printing times when these letters were manually taken one by one by typesetters from a large compartmentalized drawer (called a "case") in which the capitalized letters were stored in compartments located at the upper third of the case.

variable Information, usually in a list or in a stored paragraph, that can be inserted automatically into a standardized form (shell) document.

view mode A special display of the document that shows all the commands as well as the text.

word A group of characters separated from adjoining groups by space. A punctuation mark is considered by the system to be part of the word it is attached to. The space following a word is also usually read by the system as being part of that word. When deleting the characters that make up a word, it is also necessary to delete the appropriate space, since the system does not do so automatically.

word processing The use of a computer system to create, edit, store, and print text. Dedicated word processors are computers in which many word processing functions are built into the construction of the hardware and the nature of the program in the software to perform the required tasks as rapidly and efficiently as possible.

word wrap A feature wherein a word that is entered and passes over the right-hand margin drops down to form the first word of the next line. This feature is performed automatically on word processors. Word wraps will be automatically readjusted by the system when line endings are changed due to text editing.

work station The screen/disk drive/computer/keyboard parts of your word processor considered as the place where you perform your word processing. The printer is not automatically a part of your work station, since you can share a printer with another work station.

Metrics
Glossary

Ampere A unit for measuring the flow of electricity. Symbol: amp.

Area Amount of surface, measured in square units.

Are A metric surface measure, equal to 100 m². Symbol: a.

Atto- A prefix indicating one quintillionth of a given unit.

Barrel The amount contained in a barrel; especially the amount (as 31 gallons of fermented beverage or 42 gallons of petroleum) fixed for a certain commodity and used as a unit of measure for that particular commodity. Symbol: bbl.

Boardfoot A unit of quantity for lumber equal to the volume of a board 12 × 12 × 1 inches. Symbol: fbm.

Bushel A unit of dry capacity equal to 4 pecks (2150.42 in³) or 35.238 liters

Candela A unit for measuring the luminous intensity (amount) of a light produced by a light source.

Capacity See Volume.

Celsius The name of the scale for temperature commonly used in conjunction with the metric system. Also known as the Centigrade scale. In the Celsius scale, water boils at 100° C and freezes at 0° C, as opposed to 212° F and 32° F, respectively, in the Fahrenheit scale. Symbol: ° C.

Centare A metric surface measure equal to 1 m². Symbol: ca.

Centi- A prefix indicating one hundredth of a given unit.

Centigram One hundredth of a gram. Symbol: cg.

Centiliter One hundredth of a liter. Symbol: cl.

Centimeter One hundredth of a meter. One centimeter equals .3937 inch. Symbol: cm.

Chain A unit of measure equal to 66 feet (20.1168 meters). Symbol: ch.

Cubic unit symbols Examples: mm³, cm³, m³, etc., used to denote volume.

Customary unit Units of weights and measures currently in use in the United States, known also as English units. These include: inches, feet, yards, and miles for length; ounces, pounds, and tons for weight; pints, quarts, and gallons.

Deci- A prefix indicating one tenth of a given unit.

Decigram One tenth of a gram. Symbol: dg.

Deciliter One tenth of a liter. Roughly equal to .21 pint. Symbol: dl.

Decimeter Ten centimeters or one tenth of a meter. Symbol: dm.

Deka- A prefix indicating ten times a given unit.

Dekagram Ten grams. Symbol: dag.

Dekaliter Ten liters, roughly equivalent to 2.64 gallons. Symbol: dal.

Dekameter Ten meters. One dekameter roughly equals 10.91 yards. Symbol: dam.

Density The weight of any sample of a substance divided by the volume measure of that sample.

Dram A unit of avoirdupois weight equal to 27.343 grains or .0625 ounce (1.771 grams). Symbol: dr.

Fathom A unit of length equal to 6 feet (1.8288 meters) used for measuring the depth of water. Symbol: fath.

Femto- A prefix indicating one quadrillionth of a given unit.

Furlong A unit of distance equal to 220 yards (201.168 meters). No symbol.

Giga- A prefix indicating a billion times a given unit.

Gill A unit of liquid measure equal to .25 pint or 118.291 milliliters.

Grain A unit of weight equal to .002083 ounce (.0648 gram), originally based on the weight of a grain of wheat. Symbol: gr.

Gram A common metric unit of weight equal to one thousandth of a kilogram. Symbol: g.

Hectare The common unit of land measure in the metric system, equal to 100 acres or 10,000 square meters and equivalent to 2.471 acres. Symbol: ha.

Hecto- A prefix indicating one hundred times a given unit.

Hectogram One hundred grams. Symbol: hg.

Hectoliter One hundred liters. Symbol: hl.

Hectometer One hundred meters. Symbol: hm.

Hogshead A U.S. unit of capacity equal to 63 gallons (238.4809 liters). Symbol: hka.

Hundredweight A unit of weight (avoirdupois) commonly equivalent to 100 lbs. (45.359 kilograms) in the United States and 112 lbs (50.803 kilograms) in England. The former is known as the short hundredweight and the latter as the long hundredweight. Symbol: cwt.

Kelvin scale A temperature scale often used with the metric system and developed by the British physicist Lord Kelvin. The starting or zero point on the Kelvin scale is absolute zero (—273.15° C, —459.67° F)—the lowest theoretical temperature that a can reach. On this scale, water freezes at 273.15° K and boils at 373.15° K.

Kilo- A prefix indicating one thousand times a given unit.

Kilogram The standard unit of mass in the metric system. The kilogram is a cylinder of platinum-iridium alloy kept by the International Bureau of Weights and Measures near Paris. A duplicate kilogram is kept by the National Bureau of Standards in Washington and serves as the mass standard for the United States. One kilogram is approximately equal to 2.2 pounds. Symbol: kg.

Kiloliter One thousand liters. Symbol: kl.

Kilometer One thousand meters, equivalent to 3,280.8 feet or .621 mile. Symbol: km.

Link One of the standardized divisions of a surveyor's chain that is 7.92 inches (201.168 millimeters) long and serves as a measure of length. No symbol.

Liter The basic metric unit of liquid measure, equal to the volume of one kilogram of water at 4° C or one cubic decimeter. A liter is equivalent to 1.057 quarts. Symbol: l.

Lumen A unit for measuring the brightness of light when it reaches the surface of an object.

Mass The amount of material in an object, measured in kilograms (q.v.).

Mega- A prefix indicating one million times a given unit.

Meter The basic unit of length in the metric system. It is defined in terms of the wavelength of orange-red light emitted by a krypton-86 atom (1,650,763.73 such wavelengths to the meter). One meter equals 39.37 inches. Symbol: m.

Metric system A decimal system of weights and measures, adopted first in France and now in common use worldwide.

Metric ton One thousand kilograms, roughly equivalent to 2,200 pounds. Symbol: t.

Micron The millionth part of a meter. Symbol: μ.

Mile, International Nautical A unit of distance in sea and air navigation equal to 1.852 kilometers or 6,076.1033 feet.

Mill A unit of money (but not an actual coin) used primarily in accounting.

Milli- A prefix indicating one thousandth of a given unit.

Milligram One thousandth of a gram. Symbol: mg.

Milliliter One thousandth of a liter. Symbol: ml.

Millimeter One tenth of a centimeter or one thousandth of a meter. Symbol: mm.

Minim The smallest unit of liquid measure, the sixtieth part of a fluid dram, roughly equivalent to one drop.

Nano- A prefix indicating one billionth of a given unit.

Ounce, avoirdupois A unit of weight equal to 437.5 grains or .625 pound avoirdupois (28.349 grams). Symbol: oz. avdp.

Ounce, troy A unit of weight equal to 480 grains or .833 pound troy (31.103 grams). Symbol: oz. tr.

Peck A dry measure of 8 quarts or the fourth part of a bushel (8.89 liters).

Perimeter The measure of the distance around a figure.

Pico- A prefix indicating one trillionth of a given unit.

Pound, avoirdupois A unit of weight and mass equal to 7,000 grains (.453 kilogram) divided into 16 ounces, used for ordinary commercial purposes. Symbol: lb. avdp.

Pound, troy A unit of weight equal to 5,760 grains (.373 kilogram) divided into 12 ounces troy, used for gold, silver, and other precious metals. Symbol: lb. tr.

Radian An arc of a circle equal in length to the radius of that circle. An angle emanating from the center of a circle that subtends (cuts off) such an arc is said to measure one radian. Measuring angles in radians is preferred with the metric system.

Rod A unit of linear, 5.5 yards or 16.5 feet (5.0292 meters). A unit of surface measure 30.25 yd^2 (25.2901 m^2). No symbol.

Second The sixtieth part of a minute of a degree, often represented by the sign " as in 13 15' 45", read as 13 degrees, 15 minutes, 45 seconds.

Specific gravity The ratio of the density of a substance to the density of water at 4° C.

Square unit symbol Example: mm^2, cm^2, m^2, etc.

Stere A cubic measure equivalent to 35.315 cubic feet or 1.3080 cubic yards (1.001 m^3). Used to measure cordwood. No symbol.

Tera- A prefix indicating a trillion times a given unit.

Ton, metric See Metric ton.

Volume The measure in cubic units of the amount of space inside any given container; also the measure of the amount such a container will hold. The latter is known as the *capacity* of the container and can be given in either units of liquid measure (see Liter, also Milliliter) or in cubic units.

Weight The force of the earth's pull on an object. Weight, in the Metric system, is commonly measured in grams.

Units of Measurement–
Conversion Factors*

Units of Length

To Convert from **Centimeters**

To	Multiply by
Inches	0.393 700 8
Feet	0.032 808 40
Yards	0.010 936 13
Meters	**0.01**

To Convert from **Meters**

To	Multiply by
Inches	39.370 08
Feet	3.280 840
Yards	1.093 613
Miles	0.000 621 37
Millimeters	**1,000**
Centimeters	**100**
Kilometers	**0.001**

To Convert from **Inches**

To	Multiply by
Feet	0.083 333 33
Yards	0.027 777 78
Centimeters	**2.54**
Meters	**0.025 4**

To Convert from **Feet**

To	Multiply by
Inches	**12**
Yards	0.333 333 3
Miles	0.000 189 39
Centimeters	**30.48**
Meters	**0.304 8**
Kilometers	**0.000 304 8**

To Convert from **Yards**

To	Multiply by
Inches	**36**
Feet	**3**
Miles	0.000 568 18
Centimeters	**91.44**
Meters	**0.914 4**

To Convert from **Miles**

To	Multiply by
Inches	**63,360**
Feet	**5,280**
Yards	**1,760**
Centimeters	**160,934.4**
Meters	**1,609.344**
Kilometers	**1.609 344**

Units of Mass

To Convert from **Grams**

To	Multiply by
Grains	15.432 36
Avoirdupois drams	0.564 383 4
Avoirdupois ounces	0.035 273 96
Troy ounces	0.032 150 75
Troy pounds	0.002 679 23
Avoirdupois pounds	0.002 204 62
Milligrams	**1,000**
Kilograms	**0.001**

To Convert from **Avoirdupois Pounds**

To	Multiply by
Grains	**7,000**
Avoirdupois drams	**256**
Avoirdupois ounces	**16**
Troy ounces	14.583 33
Troy pounds	1.215 278
Grams	**453.592 37**
Kilograms	**0.453 592 37**
Short hundredweights	**0.01**
Short tons	**0.000 5**
Long tons	0.000 446 428 6
Metric tons	**0.000 453 592 37**

*All boldface figures are exact; the others generally are given to seven signficant figures.

In using conversion factors, it is possible to perform division as well as the multiplication process shown here. Division may be particularly advantageous where more than the significant figures published here are required. Division may be performed in lieu of multiplication by using the reciprocal of any indicated multiplier as divisor. For example, to convert from centimeters to inches by division, refer to the table headed "To Convert from *Inches*" and use the factor listed at "centimeters" (*2.54*) as divisor.

To Convert from **Kilograms**

To	Multiply by
Grains	15,432.36
Avoirdupois drams	564.383 4
Avoirdupois ounces	35.273 96
Troy ounces	32.150 75
Troy pounds	2.679 229
Avoirdupois pounds	2.204 623
Grams	**1,000**
Short hundredweights	0.022 046 23
Short tons	0.001 102 31
Long tons	0.000 984 2
Metric tons	**0.001**

To Convert from **Metric Tons**

To	Multiply by
Avoirdupois pounds	2,204.623
Short hundredweights	22.046 23
Short tons	1.102 311 3
Long tons	0.984 206 5
Kilograms	**1,000**

To Convert from **Grains**

To	Multiply by
Avoirdupois drams	0.036 571 43
Avoirdupois ounces	0.002 285 71
Troy ounces	0.002 083 33
Troy pounds	0.000 173 61
Avoirdupois pounds	0.000 142 86
Milligrams	**64.798 91**
Grams	**0.064 798 91**
Kilograms	**0.000 064 798 91**

To Convert from **Troy Ounces**

To	Multiply by
Grains	**480**
Avoirdupois drams	17.554 29
Avoirdupois ounces	1.097 143
Troy pounds	0.083 333 3
Avoirdupois pounds	0.068 571 43
Grams	**31.103 476 8**

To Convert from **Long Tons**

To	Multiply by
Avoirdupois ounces	**35,840**
Avoirdupois pounds	**2,240**
Short hundredweights	**22.4**
Short tons	**1.12**
Kilograms	**1,016.046 908 8**
Metric tons	**1.016 046 908 8**

To Convert from **Avoirdupois Ounces**

To	Multiply by
Grains	**437.5**
Avoirdupois drams	**16**
Troy ounces	0.911 458 3
Troy pounds	0.075 954 86
Avoirdupois pounds	**0.062 5**
Grams	**28.349 523 125**
Kilograms	**0.028 349 523 125**

To Convert from **Short Hundredweights**

To	Multiply by
Avoirdupois pounds	**100**
Short tons	**0.05**
Long tons	0.044 642 86
Kilograms	**45.359 237**
Metric tons	**0.045 359 237**

To Convert from **Short Tons**

To	Multiply by
Avoirdupois pounds	**2,000**
Short hundredweights	**20**
Long tons	0.892 857 1
Kilograms	**907.184 74**
Metric tons	**0.907 184 74**

To convert from **Troy Pounds**

To	Multiply by
Grains	**5,760**
Avoirdupois drams	210.651 4
Avoirdupois ounces	13.165 71
Troy ounces	**12**
Avoirdupois pounds	0.822 857 1
Grams	**373.241 721 6**

Units of Capacity, or Volume, Liquid Measure

To Convert from **Milliliters**

To	Multiply by
Minims	16.230 73
Liquid ounces	0.033 814 02
Gills	0.008 453 5
Liquid pints	0.002 113 4
Liquid quarts	0.001 056 7
Gallons	0.000 264 17
Cubic inches	0.061 023 74
Liters	**0.001**

To Convert from **Cubit Meters**

To	Multiply by
Gallons	264.172 05
Cubic inches	61,023.74
Cubic feet	35.314 67
Liters	**1,000**
Cubic yards	1.307 950 6

To Convert from **Liters**

To	Multiply by
Liquid ounces	33.814 02
Gills	8.453 506
Liquid pints	2.113 376
Liquid quarts	1.056 688
Gallons	0.264 172 05
Cubic inches	61.023 74
Cubic feet	0.035 314 67
Milliliters	**1,000**
Cubic meters	**0.001**
Cubic yards	0.001 307 95

To Convert from **Minims**

To	Multiply by
Liquid ounces	0.002 083 33
Gills	0.000 520 83
Milliliters	0.061 611 52
Cubic inches	0.003 759 77

To Convert from **Liquid Pints**

To	Multiply by
Minims	**7,680**
Liquid ounces	**16**
Gills	**4**
Liquid quarts	**0.5**
Gallons	**0.125**
Cubic inches	**28.875**
Cubic feet	0.016 710 07
Milliliters	**473.176 473**
Liters	**0.473 176 473**

To Convert from **Gills**

To	Multiply by
Minims	**1,920**
Liquid ounces	**4**
Liquid pints	**0.25**
Liquid quarts	**0.125**
Gallons	**0.031 25**
Cubic inches	**7.218 75**
Cubic feet	0.004 177 517
Milliliters	**118.294 118 25**
Liters	**0.118 294 118 25**

To Convert from **Liquid Ounces**

To	Multiply by
Minims	**480**
Gills	**0.25**
Liquid pints	**0.062 5**
Liquid quarts	**0.031 25**
Gallons	**0.007 812 5**
Cubic inches	1.804 687 5
Cubic feet	0.001 044 38
Milliliters	29.573 53
Liters	0.029 573 53

To Convert from **Cubic Inches**

To	Multiply by
Minims	265.974 0
Liquid ounces	0.554 112 6
Gills	0.138 528 1
Liquid pints	0.034 632 03
Liquid quarts	0.017 316 02
Gallons	0.004 329 0
Cubic feet	0.000 578 7
Milliliters	**16.387 064**
Liters	**0.016 387 064**
Cubic meters	**0.000 016 387 064**
Cubic yards	0.000 021 43

To Convert from **Liquid Quarts**

To	Multiply by
Minims	**15,360**
Liquid ounces	**32**
Gills	**8**
Liquid pints	**2**
Gallons	**0.25**
Cubic inches	**57.75**
Cubic feet	0.033 420 14
Milliliters	**946.352 946**
Liters	**0.946 352 946**

To Convert from **Cubic Feet**

To	Multiply by
Liquid ounces	957.506 5
Gills	239.376 6
Liquid pints	59.844 16
Liquid quarts	29.922 08
Gallons	7.480 519
Cubic inches	**1,728**
Liters	**28.316 846 592**
Cubic meters	**0.028 316 846 592**
Cubic yards	0.037 037 04

To convert from **Cubic Yards**

To	Multiply by
Callons	201.974 0
Cubic inches	**46,656**
Cubic feet	**27**
Liters	**764.554 857 984**
Cubic meters	**0.764 554 857 984**

To Convert from **Gallons**

To	Multiply by
Minims	**61,440**
Liquid ounces	**128**
Gills	**32**
Liquid pints	**8**
Liquid quarts	**4**
Cubic inches	**231**
Cubic feet	0.133 680 6
Milliliters	**3,785.411 784**
Liters	**3.785 411 784**
Cubic meters	**0.003 785 411 784**
Cubic yards	0.004 951 13

Units of Capacity, or Volume, Dry Measure

To Convert from **Liters**

To	Multiply by
Dry pints	1.816 166
Dry quarts	0.908 082 98
Pecks	0.113 510 4
Bushels	0.028 377 59
Dekaliters	**0.1**

To Convert from **Dekaliters**

To	Multiply by
Dry pints	18.161 66
Dry quarts	9.080 829 8
Pecks	1.135 104
Bushels	0.283 775 9
Cubic inches	610.237 4
Cubic feet	0.353 146 7
Liters	**10**

To Convert from **Cubic Meters**

To	Multiply by
Pecks	113.510 4
Bushels	28.377 59

To Convert from **Dry Pints**

To	Multiply by
Dry quarts	**0.5**
Pecks	**0.062 5**
Bushels	**0.015 625**
Cubic inches	**33.600 312 5**
Cubic feet	0.019 444 63
Liters	0.550 610 47
Dekaliters	0.055 061 05

To Convert from **Dry Quarts**

To	Multiply by
Dry pints	**2**
Pecks	**0.125**
Bushels	**0.031 25**
Cubic inches	**67.200 625**
Cubic feet	0.038 889 25
Liters	1.101 221
Dekaliters	0.110 122 1

To Convert from **Pecks**

To	Multiply by
Dry pints	**16**
Dry quarts	**8**
Bushels	**0.25**
Cubic inches	**537.605**
Cubic feet	0.311 114
Liters	8.809 767 5
Dekaliters	0.880 976 75
Cubic meters	0.008 809 77
Cubic yards	0.011 522 74

To Convert from **Bushels**

To	Multiply by
Dry pints	**64**
Dry quarts	**32**
Pecks	**4**
Cubic inches	**2,150.42**
Cubic feet	1.244 456
Liters	35.239 07
Dekaliters	3.523 907
Cubic meters	0.035 239 07
Cubic yards	0.046 090 96

To Convert from **Cubic Inches**

To	Multiply by
Dry pints	0.029 761 6
Dry quarts	0.014 880 8
Pecks	0.001 860 10
Bushels	0.000 465 025

To Convert from **Cubic Yards**

To	Multiply by
Pecks	86.784 91
Bushels	21.696 227

To Convert from **Cubit Feet**

To	Multiply by
Dry pints	51.428 09
Dry quarts	25.714 05
Pecks	3.214 256
Bushels	0.803 563 95

Units of Area

To Convert from **Square Centimeters**

To	Multiply by
Square inches	0.155 000 3
Square feet	0.001 076 39
Square yards	0.000 119 599
Square meters	**0.000 1**

To Convert from **Square Feet**

To	Multiply by
Square inches	**144**
Square yards	0.111 111 1
Acres	0.000 022 957
Square centimeters	**929.030 4**
Square meters	**0.092 903 04**

To Convert from **Square Meters**

To	Multiply by
Square inches	1,550.003
Square feet	10.763 91
Square yards	1.195 990
Acres	0.000 247 105
Square centimeters	**10,000**
Hectares	**0.000 1**

To Convert from **Square Yards**

To	Multiply by
Square inches	**1,296**
Square feet	**9**
Acres	0.000 206 611 6
Square miles	0.000 000 322 830 6
Square centimeters	**8,361.273 6**
Square meters	**0.836 127 36**
Hectares	**0.000 083 612 736**

To Convert from **Hectares**

To	Multiply by
Square feet	107,639.1
Square yards	11,959.90
Acres	2.471 054
Square miles	0.003 861 02
Square meters	**10,000**

To Convert from **Acres**

To	Multiply by
Square feet	**43,560**
Square yards	**4,840**
Square miles	**0.001 562 5**
Square meters	**4,046.856 422 4**
Hectares	**0.404 685 642 24**

To Convert from **Square Inches**

To	Multiply by
Square feet	0.006 944 44
Square yards	0.000 771 605
Square centimeters	**6.451 6**
Square meters	**0.000 645 16**

To Convert from **Square Miles**

To	Multiply by
Square feet	**27,878,400**
Square yards	**3,097,600**
Acres	**640**
Square meters	**2,589,988.110 336**
Hectares	**258.998 811 033 6**

Tables of Weights and Measures

Linear Measure

Measure		Equivalents
1 inch		2.54 centimeters
12 inches	1 foot	0.3048 meter
3 feet	1 yard	0.9144 meter
5½ yards	1 rod	5.029 meters
16½ feet	(or pole or perch)	
40 rods	1 furlong	201.17 meters
8 furlongs		
1,760 yards	1 (statute) mile	1,609.3 meters
5,280 feet		
3 miles	1 (land) league	4.83 kilometers

Square Measure

Measure	Equivalents	
1 square inch		6.452 square centimeters
144 square inches	1 square foot	929 square centimeters
9 square feet	1 square yard	0.8361 square meter
30¼ square yards	1 square rod (or square pole or square perch)	25.29 square meters
160 square rods or 4,840 square yards or 43,560 square feet	1 acre	0.4047 hectare
640 acres	1 square mile	259 hectares 2.59 square kilometers

Cubic Measure

Measure	Equivalents	
1 cubic inch		16.387 cubic centimeters
1,728 cubic inches	1 cubic foot	0.0283 cubic meter
27 cubic feet	1 cubic yard (in units for cordwood, etc.)	0.7646 cubic meter
16 cubic feet	1 cord foot	
8 cord feet	1 cord	3.625 cubic meters

Chain Measure (for Gunter's, or surveyor's, chain)

Measure	Equivalents	
7.92 inches	1 link	20.12 centimeters
100 links	1 chain	20.12 meters
66 feet		
10 chains	1 furlong	201.17 meters
80 chains	1 mile (for engineer's chain)	1,609.3 meters
1 foot	1 link	0.3048 meter
100 feet	1 chain	30.48 meters
52.8 chains	1 mile	1,609.3 meters

Surveyor's (Square) Measure

Measure	Equivalents	
625 square links	1 square pole	25.29 square meters
16 square poles	1 square chain	404.7 square meters
10 square chains	1 acre	0.4047 hectare
640 acres	1 square mile	259 hectares
	1 section	2.59 square kilometers
36 square miles	1 township	9,324.0 hectares
		93.24 square kilometers

Nautical Measure

Measure	Equivalents	
6 feet	1 fathom	1.829 meters
100 fathoms	1 cable's length (ordinary)[1]	
10 cables' lengths	1 nautical mile	1.852 kilometers[2]
	6,076.10333 feet	
1 nautical mile	1.1508 statute miles[3]	
3 nautical miles	1 marine league	5.56 kilometers
	3.45 statute miles	
60 nautical miles	1 degree of a great circle of the earth	

Dry Measure

Measure	Equivalents		
1 pint		33.60 cubic inches	0.5505 liter
2 pints	1 quart	67.20 cubic inches	1.1012 liters
8 quarts	1 peck	537.61 cubic inches	8.8096 liters
4 pecks	1 bushel	2,150.42 cubic inches	35.2383 liters
1 British dry quart	1.032 U.S. dry quarts		

According to United States government standards, the following are the weights avoirdupois for single bushels of the specified grains: for wheat, 60 pounds; for barley, 48 pounds; for oats, 32 pounds; for rye, 56 pounds; for corn, 56 pounds. Some states have specifications varying from these.

Liquid Measure

Measure	Equivalents		
1 gill	4 fluid ounces (see next table)	7.219 cubic inches	0.1183 liter
4 gills	1 pint	28.875 cubic inches	0.4732 liter
2 pints	1 quart	57.75 cubic inches	0.9463 liter
4 quarts	1 gallon	231 cubic inches	3.7853 liters
4 British imperial quarts	1 imperial gallon	277.42 cubic inches	4.546 liters

The barrel in Great Britain equals 36 imperial gallons, in the United States, usually 31½ gallons.

Apothecaries' Fluid Measure

Measure	Equivalents		
1 minim		0.0038 cubic inch	0.0616 milliliter
60 minims	1 fluid dram	0.2256 cubic inch	3.6966 milliliters
8 fluid drams	1 fluid ounce	1.8047 cubic inches	0.0296 liter
16 fluid ounces	1 pint	28.875 cubic inches	0.4732 liter
1 British pint	20 fluid ounces		

See table immediately preceding for quart and gallon equivalents.

[1]In the U.S. Navy 120 fathoms or 720 feet equals 1 cable's length; in the British Navy, 608 feet equals 1 cable's length.
[2]By international agreement, 1954
[3]The length of a minute of longitude at the equator. Also called geographical, sea, or air mile, and, in Great Britain, Admiralty mile.

Circular (or Angular) Measure

Measure	Equivalent
60 seconds (″)	1 minute (′)
60 minutes	1 degree (°)
90 degrees	1 quadrant
	1 right angle
4 quadrants	1 circle
360 degrees	

Avoirdupois Weight

Measure	Equivalents	
1 grain		0.0648 gram[1]
1 dram		1.772 grams
27.34 grains		
16 drams	1 ounce	28.3495 grams
437.5 grains		
16 ounces	1 pound[2]	453.59 grams
7,000 grains		
100 pounds	1 hundredweight	45.36 kilograms
2,000 pounds	1 ton	907.18 kilograms

Troy Weight

Measure	Equivalents	
1 grain		0.0648 gram[1]
3.086 grains	1 carat	200 milligrams
24 grains	1 pennyweight	1.5552 grams
20 pennyweights	1 ounce	31.1035 grams
480 grains		
12 ounces	1 pound	373.24 grams
5,760 grains		

Apothecaries' Weight

Measure	Equivalents	
1 grain		0.0648 gram[1]
20 grains	1 scruple	1.296 grams
3 scruples	1 dram	3.888 grams
8 drams	1 ounce	31.1035 grams
480 grains		
12 ounces	1 pound	373.24 grams
5,760 grains		

[1]The grain is the same in all three tables of weight.
[2]In Great Britain, 14 pounds (6.35 kilograms) equals 1 stone, 112 pounds (50.80 kilograms) equals 1 hundredweight, and 2,240 pounds (1,016.05 kilograms) equal 1 long ton.

CCNP ROUTE 642-902

Official Certification Guide

Wendell Odom, CCIE No. 1624

Cisco Press

800 East 96th Street

Indianapolis, IN 46240

CCNP ROUTE 642-902 Official Certification Guide

Wendell Odom

Copyright© 2010 Pearson Education, Inc.

Published by:
Cisco Press
800 East 96th Street
Indianapolis, IN 46240 USA

Printed in the United States of America

First Printing   January 2010

Odom, Wendell.
   CCNP Route 642-902 official certification guide / Wendell Odom.
     p. cm.
   ISBN 978-1-58720-253-7 (hardback w/cd)
  1. Routers (Computer networks)--Examinations--Study guides. 2.
Routing protocols (Computer network protocols)--Examinations--Study
guides. 3. Internetworking (Telecommunication)--Examinations--Study
guides. 4. Telecommunications
engineers--Certification--Examinations--Study guides. I. Title.
   TK5105.543.O36 2010
   004.6'2--dc22
2009049908

ISBN-13: 978-1-58720-253-7

ISBN-10: 1-58720-253-0

Warning and Disclaimer

This book is designed to provide information about the Cisco ROUTE exam (642-902). Every effort has been made to make this book as complete and as accurate as possible, but no warranty or fitness is implied.

The information is provided on an "as is" basis. The authors, Cisco Press, and Cisco Systems, Inc. shall have neither liability nor responsibility to any person or entity with respect to any loss or damages arising from the information contained in this book or from the use of the discs or programs that may accompany it.

The opinions expressed in this book belong to the author and are not necessarily those of Cisco Systems, Inc.

Trademark Acknowledgments

All terms mentioned in this book that are known to be trademarks or service marks have been appropriately capitalized. Cisco Press or Cisco Systems, Inc., cannot attest to the accuracy of this information. Use of a term in this book should not be regarded as affecting the validity of any trademark or service mark.

Corporate and Government Sales

The publisher offers excellent discounts on this book when ordered in quantity for bulk purchases or special sales, which may include electronic versions and/or custom covers and content particular to your business, training goals, marketing focus, and branding interests. For more information, please contact: U.S. Corporate and Government Sales   1-800-382-3419   corpsales@pearsontechgroup.com

For sales outside the United States please contact: International Sales   international@pearsoned.com

Feedback Information

At Cisco Press, our goal is to create in-depth technical books of the highest quality and value. Each book is crafted with care and precision, undergoing rigorous development that involves the unique expertise of members from the professional technical community.

Readers' feedback is a natural continuation of this process. If you have any comments regarding how we could improve the quality of this book, or otherwise alter it to better suit your needs, you can contact us through email at feedback@ciscopress.com. Please make sure to include the book title and ISBN in your message.

We greatly appreciate your assistance.

Publisher: Paul Boger	**Business Operation Manager, Cisco Press:** Anand Sundaram
Associate Publisher: Dave Dusthimer	**Manager Global Certification:** Erik Ullanderson
Executive Editor: Brett Bartow	**Technical Editors:** Michelle Plumb, Jerold Swan, Rick Graziani
Managing Editor: Patrick Kanouse	**Copy Editor:** Apostrophe Editing Services
Development Editor: Dayna Isley	**Proofreader:** Barbara Hacha
Project Editor: Mandie Frank	**Editorial Assistant:** Vanessa Evans
Book Designer: Louisa Adair	
Composition: Mark Shirar	
Indexer: Ken Johnson	

Americas Headquarters	Asia Pacific Headquarters	Europe Headquarters
Cisco Systems, Inc.	Cisco Systems (USA) Pte. Ltd.	Cisco Systems International BV
San Jose, CA	Singapore	Amsterdam, The Netherlands

Cisco has more than 200 offices worldwide. Addresses, phone numbers, and fax numbers are listed on the Cisco Website at **www.cisco.com/go/offices.**

CCDE, CCENT, Cisco Eos, Cisco HealthPresence, the Cisco logo, Cisco Lumin, Cisco Nexus, Cisco StadiumVision, Cisco TelePresence, Cisco WebEx, DCE, and Welcome to the Human Network are trademarks; Changing the Way We Work, Live, Play, and Learn and Cisco Store are service marks; and Access Registrar, Aironet, AsyncOS, Bringing the Meeting To You, Catalyst, CCDA, CCDP, CCIE, CCIP, CCNA, CCNP, CCSP, CCVP, Cisco, the Cisco Certified Internetwork Expert logo, Cisco IOS, Cisco Press, Cisco Systems, Cisco Systems Capital, the Cisco Systems logo, Cisco Unity, Collaboration Without Limitation, EtherFast, EtherSwitch, Event Center, Fast Step, Follow Me Browsing, FormShare, GigaDrive, HomeLink, Internet Quotient, IOS, iPhone, iQuick Study, IronPort, the IronPort logo, LightStream, Linksys, MediaTone, MeetingPlace, MeetingPlace Chime Sound, MGX, Networkers, Networking Academy, Network Registrar, PCNow, PIX, PowerPanels, ProConnect, ScriptShare, SenderBase, SMARTnet, Spectrum Expert, StackWise, The Fastest Way to Increase Your Internet Quotient, TransPath, WebEx, and the WebEx logo are registered trademarks of Cisco Systems, Inc. and/or its affiliates in the United States and certain other countries.

All other trademarks mentioned in this document or website are the property of their respective owners. The use of the word partner does not imply a partnership relationship between Cisco and any other company. (0812R)

About the Author

Wendell Odom, CCIE No. 1624, is a 28-year veteran of the networking industry. He currently works as an independent author of Cisco certification resources and occasional instructor of Cisco authorized training for Skyline ATS. He has worked as a network engineer, consultant, systems engineer, instructor, and course developer. Wendell is the author of several best-selling Cisco certification titles. He maintains lists of current titles, links to Wendell's blogs, and other certification resources at www.thecertzone.com.

About the Technical Reviewers

Michelle Plumb is a full-time Cisco certified instructor for Skillsoft. Michelle has more than 19 years experience in the field as an IT professional and telephony specialist. She maintains a high level of Cisco and Microsoft certifications. Michelle has been a technical reviewer for numerous books related to the Cisco CCNP and CCVP course material track. Michelle currently lives in Scottsdale, Arizona, with her husband and two dogs.

Jerold Swan, CCIE No. 17783, CCSP, works as a senior network engineer for the Southern Ute Indian Tribe Growth Fund in southwest Colorado. Prior to that he was a Cisco instructor for Global Knowledge. He has also worked in IT in the service provider and higher education sectors. His areas of interest include routing protocols, security, and network monitoring. He is a graduate of Stanford University. His other interests include trail running, mountain biking, and volunteer search and rescue.

Rick Graziani teaches computer science and computer networking courses at Cabrillo College in Aptos, California. Rick has worked and taught in the computer networking and information technology field for almost 30 years. Prior to teaching Rick worked in IT for various companies including Santa Cruz Operation, Tandem Computers, and Lockheed Missiles and Space Corporation. He holds an M.A. degree in computer science and systems theory from California State University Monterey Bay. Rick also does consulting work for Cisco and other companies. When Rick is not working he is most likely surfing. Rick is an avid surfer who enjoys surfing at his favorite Santa Cruz breaks.

Dedications

For Jeffrey Lanier Odom. My favorite brother. Gentle soul. Lover of stupid jokes ("baby bigger," "tankety-tankety-tank," "supplies"...) Nice guy. Good friend. Miss you, bro. 10/7/1959–6/15/2009.

Acknowledgments

As usual, Brett Bartow, executive editor, deserves thanks for allowing me to be involved with this book. Brett continually keeps an eye on the horizon for the right projects for me, essentially completing a run of books from the basics, to CCENT, CCNA, now CCNP, and CCIE. My work life wouldn't be possible without Brett keeping me pointed in the right direction. Thanks, Brett!

Jay Swan and Michelle Plumb did a nice job for us with technical edits of the book. Jay was particularly helpful with both ends of the tech edit spectrum, noticing specific and easy-to-overlook errors, while keeping an eye out for the big picture of how the text in one section impacted other sections. Michelle's diligent work helped us uncover several specific issues and make this a better book. Thanks to you both for helping make this book much better!

Rick Graziani deserves thanks with this book for several reasons. First, Rick wrote the questions on the CD with this book, a task that can be laborious–but Rick did a great job and with a positive outlook. Additionally, Rick gave us an additional set of experienced and thoughtful technical editor eyes on the BGP chapters. And while he was working on the CD questions, Rick gladly went the extra mile to point out technical edits to the other book chapters as well. Rick's great attitude toward helping with the book was very impressive.

Dayna Isley worked as the development editor for this book. Dayna and I have worked very well together for a long time, and having such a trusted editor look over every word on this new book has helped quite a bit. Dayna's attention to detail helps keep me on the authoring straight-and-narrow, this time while navigating a sometimes fluid set of processes. Dayna, thanks for sifting through this process and making me look good on paper!

Patrick Kanouse, managing editor, led us through many new production tools (WriteRAP) and processes. Additionally, Patrick happily agreed to continue several additional production tasks at my request (translated: more work for him and his team), while allowing me to manage the entire illustration process for the first time on one of my books–none of which he had to do. Patrick, thanks for your great attitude and willingness to work with me on so many extras.

The folks on Patrick's production team probably had the biggest challenge with this book compared to my other books. Mandie Frank worked as project editor, guiding the book through the various back-end processes to complete the book. Mandie got to sift though all the changing processes, help figure out when we were doing which tasks, and keep us all on track. Thanks, Mandie! San Dee Phillips retired last year so she could work even more, coming back to do the copyedit work–thanks for jumping in again, San Dee! And for Mark Shirar, Ken Johnson, and Barbara Hacha, doing the composition, indexing, and proofreading, thanks so much for handling these details–I do see the difference with having professionals working on every step of the book creation process, and I do appreciate the results.

Thanks to Rich Bennett, good friend and part-time do-everything guy for my books and other projects. Thanks for doing all the Illustrator drawings and editing them all so many times!

The old expression "my better half" is lived out every day here at the Odom house in the person of my wife Kris. Many thanks to Kris, who listens when I need to talk through something in the book, and lets me go hide in the basement for a few weeks to meet the latest writing deadline. Thanks, doll!

Finally and foremost, many thanks to Jesus Christ, for demonstrating your love, and for helping me and my family learn better each day how to not be a clanging symbol, but instead to show others your love.

Contents at a Glance

Contents

Icons Used in This Book

Router Workgroup Switch Multilayer Switch Firewall Server

Network Cloud Serial Cable Line: Ethernet VPN Tunnel PC

Standing Man Scroll

Command Syntax Conventions

The conventions used to present command syntax in this book are the same conventions used in the IOS Command Reference. The Command Reference describes these conventions as follows:

- **Boldface** indicates commands and keywords that are entered literally as shown. In actual configuration examples and output (not general command syntax), boldface indicates commands that are manually input by the user (such as a **show** command).

- *Italic* indicates arguments for which you supply actual values.

- Vertical bars (|) separate alternative, mutually exclusive elements.

- Square brackets ([ ]) indicate an optional element.

- Braces ({ }) indicate a required choice.

- Braces within brackets ([{ }]) indicate a required choice within an optional element.

Foreword

CCNP ROUTE 642-902 Official Certification Guide is an excellent self-study resource for the CCNP ROUTE exam. Passing this exam is a crucial step to attaining the valued CCNP Routing and Switching certification.

Gaining certification in Cisco technology is key to the continuing educational development of today's networking professional. Through certification programs, Cisco validates the skills and expertise required to effectively manage the modern enterprise network.

Cisco Press Certification Guides and preparation materials offer exceptional—and flexible—access to the knowledge and information required to stay current in your field of expertise or to gain new skills. Whether used as a supplement to more traditional training or as a primary source of learning, these materials offer users the information and knowledge validation required to gain new understanding and proficiencies.

Developed in conjunction with the Cisco certifications and training team, Cisco Press books are the only self-study books authorized by Cisco and offer students a series of exam practice tools and resource materials to help ensure that learners fully grasp the concepts and information presented.

Additional authorized Cisco instructor-led courses, e-learning, labs, and simulations are available exclusively from Cisco Learning Solutions Partners worldwide. To learn more, visit http://www.cisco.com/go/training.

I hope that you find these materials to be an enriching and useful part of your exam preparation.

Erik Ullanderson
Manager, Global Certifications
Learning@Cisco
January 2010

Introduction

This book focuses on one major goal: to help you prepare to pass the ROUTE exam (642-902). To help you prepare, this book achieves other useful goals as well: It explains a wide range of networking topics, shows how to configure those features on Cisco routers, and explains how to determine if the feature is working. As a result, you also can use this book as a general reference for IP routing and IP routing protocols. However, the motivation for this book, and the reason it sits within the Cisco Press Certification Guide series, is that its primary goal is to help you pass the ROUTE exam.

The rest of this introduction focuses on two topics: the ROUTE exam and a description of this book.

The CCNP ROUTE Exam

Cisco announced the ROUTE (642-902) exam in January 2010. The term ROUTE does not act as an acronym; instead, the name describes the content of the exam, which focuses on IP routing. Generally, the exam includes detailed coverage of the EIGRP, OSPF, and BGP IP routing protocols, IPv6, and a few other smaller topics related to IP routing.

Cisco first announced its initial Professional level certifications in 1998 with the CCNP Routing and Switching certification. CCNP Routing and Switching certification from its inception has included the same kinds of IP routing topics found in today's ROUTE exam, but the exam names changed over the years. The exam names have tracked the names of the associated Cisco authorized courses for the same topics: Advanced Cisco Router Configuration (ACRC) in the early days, Building Scalable Cisco Internetworks (BSCI) for much of the last 10 years, and now ROUTE, because the newly revised (in 2010) Cisco authorized course also goes by the name ROUTE.

Like its ancestors, the ROUTE exam is a part of the certification requirements for several Cisco certifications, as follows:

- Cisco Certified Networking Professional (CCNP)

- Cisco Certified Internetworking Professional (CCIP)

- Cisco Certified Design Professional (CCDP)

Each of these certifications emphasizes different perspectives on some similar topics. CCNP focuses on the skills needed by a network engineer working for an Enterprise–that is, a company that deploys networking gear for its own purposes. CCIP focuses on the skills required by network engineers deploying gear at a service provider, with the service provider then offering network services to customers. Finally, CCDP focuses more on design–but good design requires solid knowledge of the technology and configuration. So, although this book frequently refers to the most popular certification of these three–CCNP–the ROUTE exam does apply to several certifications.

Contents of the ROUTE Exam

Every student who ever takes an exam wants to know what's on the exam. As with all their exams, Cisco publishes a set of exam topics. These exam topics give general guidance as to what's on the exam.

You can find the exam topics at the Cisco website. The most memorable way to navigate is to go to www.cisco.com/go/ccnp, and look for the ROUTE exam. Also, you can go to the Cisco Learning Network website (www.cisco.com/go/learnnetspace)–a less memorable URL, but a great Cisco certification site. The Cisco Learning Network site hosts exam information, learning tools, and forums in which you can communicate with others and learn more about this and other Cisco exams.

Table I-1 lists the ROUTE exam topics, with a reference to the part of the book that covers the topic.

Table I-1 ROUTE Exam Topics

Book Part	Exam Topic
Implement an EIGRP based solution, given a network design and a set of requirements	
II	Determine network resources needed for implementing EIGRP on a network
II	Create an EIGRP implementation plan
II	Create an EIGRP verification plan
II	Configure EIGRP routing
II	Verify EIGRP solution was implemented properly using **show** and **debug** commands
II	Document results of EIGRP implementation and verification
Implement a multi-area OSPF Network, given a network design and a set of requirements	
III	Determine network resources needed for implementing OSPF on a network
III	Create an OSPF implementation plan
III	Create an OSPF verification plan
III	Configure OSPF routing
III	Verify OSPF solution was implemented properly using show and debug commands
III	Document results of OSPF implementation and verification plan
Implement an eBGP based solution, given a network design and a set of requirements	
V	Determine network resources needed for implementing eBGP on a network
V	Create an eBGP implementation plan
V	Create an eBGP verification plan
V	Configure eBGP routing
V	Verify eBGP solution was implemented properly using show and debug commands
V	Document results of eBGP implementation and verification plan

Table I-1 ROUTE Exam Topics

Book Part	Exam Topic
Implement an IPv6 based solution, given a network design and a set of requirements	
VI	Determine network resources needed for implementing IPv6 on a network
VI	Create an IPv6 implementation plan
VI	Create an IPv6 verification plan
VI	Configure IPv6 routing
VI	Configure IPv6 interoperation with IPv4
VI	Verify IPv6 solution was implemented properly using show and debug commands
VI	Document results of IPv6 implementation and verification plan
Implement an IPv4 or IPv6 based redistribution solution, given a network design and a set of requirements	
IV, VI	Create a redistribution implementation plan based upon the results of the redistribution analysis.
IV, VI	Create a redistribution verification plan
IV, VI	Configure a redistribution solution
IV, VI	Verify that a redistribution was implemented
IV, VI	Document results of a redistribution implementation and verification plan
IV, VI	Identify the differences between implementing an IPv4 and IPv6 redistribution solution
Implement Layer 3 Path Control Solution	
IV	Create a Layer 3 path control implementation plan based upon the results of the redistribution analysis.
IV	Create a Layer 3 path control verification plan
IV	Configure Layer 3 path control
IV	Verify that a Layer 3 path control was implemented
IV	Document results of a Layer 3 path control implementation and verification plan
Implement basic teleworker and branch services	
VII	Describe broadband technologies
VII	Configure basic broadband connections
VII	Describe basic VPN technologies
VII	Configure GRE
VII	Describe branch access technologies

How to Take the ROUTE Exam

As of the publication of this book, Cisco exclusively uses testing vendor Pearson Vue (www.vue.com) for delivery of all Cisco career certification exams. To register, go to www.vue.com, establish a login, and register for the 642-902 ROUTE exam. You also need to choose a testing center near to your home.

Who Should Take This Exam and Read This Book?

This book has one primary audience, with several secondary audiences. First, this book is intended for anyone wanting to prepare for the ROUTE 642-902 exam. The audience includes self-study readers–people who pass the test by studying 100 percent on their own. It includes Cisco Networking Academy students taking the CCNP curriculum, who use this book to round out their preparation as they get close to the end of the Academy curriculum.

The broader question about the audience may well be why you should take the ROUTE exam. First, the exam is required for the aforementioned CCNP, CCIP, and CCDP certifications from Cisco. These certifications exist at the midpoint of the Cisco certification hierarchy. These certifications have broader and deeper technology requirements as compared to the Cisco Certified Entry Network Technician (CCENT) and Cisco Certified Network Associate (CCNA) certifications.

The real question then about audience for this book–at least the intended audience–is whether you have motivation to get one of these Professional-level Cisco certifications. CCNP in particular happens to be a popular, well-respected certification. CCIP, although less popular in numbers, focuses on topics more important to service providers, so it gives you a good way to distinguish yourself from others looking for jobs at SP companies. CCDP has been a solid certification for a long time, particularly for engineers who spend a lot of time designing networks with customers, rather than troubleshooting.

Format of the CCNP ROUTE Exam

The ROUTE exam follows the same general format as the other Cisco exams. When you get to the testing center and check in, the proctor will give you some general instructions and then take you into a quiet room with a PC. When you're at the PC, you have a few things to do before the timer starts on your exam—for instance, you can take a sample quiz, just to get accustomed to the PC and to the testing engine. Anyone who has user-level skills in getting around a PC should have no problems with the testing environment.

When you start the exam, you will be asked a series of questions. You answer the question and then move on to the next question. *The exam engine does not let you go back and change your answer.* Yes, that's true—when you move on to the next question, that's it for the earlier question.

The exam questions can be in one of the following formats:

■ Multiple choice (MC)

■ Testlet

■ Drag-and-drop (DND)

■ Simulated lab (Sim)

■ Simlet

The first three types of questions are relatively common in many testing environments. The multiple choice format simply requires that you point-and-click on a circle beside the correct answer(s). Cisco traditionally tells you how many answers you need to choose, and the testing software prevents you from choosing too many answers. Testlets are questions with one general scenario, with multiple MC questions about the overall scenario. Drag-and-drop questions require you to left-click and hold, move a button or icon to another area, and release the clicker to place the object somewhere else—typically into a list. So, for some questions, to get the question correct, you might need to put a list of five things into the proper order.

The last two types both use a network simulator to ask questions. Interestingly, the two types actually allow Cisco to assess two very different skills. First, Sim questions generally describe a problem, and your task is to configure one or more routers and switches to fix the problem. The exam then grades the question based on the configuration you changed or added. Interestingly, Sim questions are the only questions that Cisco (to date) has openly confirmed that partial credit is given.

The Simlet questions may well be the most difficult style of question on the exams. Simlet questions also use a network simulator, but instead of answering the question by changing the configuration, the question includes one or more MC questions. The questions require that you use the simulator to examine the current behavior of a network, interpreting the output of any **show** commands that you can remember to answer the question. Although Sim questions require you to troubleshoot problems related to a configuration, Simlets require you to both analyze working networks and networks with problems, correlating **show** command output with your knowledge of networking theory and configuration commands.

The Cisco Learn Network (www.cisco.com/go/learnnetspace) website has tools that let you experience the environment and see how each of these question types work. The environment should be the same as when you passed CCNA (a prerequisite for CCNP, CCIP, and CCDP).

CCNP ROUTE 642-902 Official Certification Guide

This section lists a general description of the contents of this book. The description includes an overview of each chapter, and a list of book features seen throughout the book.

Book Features and Exam Preparation Methods

This book uses several key methodologies to help you discover the exam topics on which you need more review, to help you fully understand and remember those details, and to help you prove to yourself that you have retained your knowledge of those topics. So, this book does not try to help you pass the exams only by memorization, but by truly learning and understanding the topics.

The book includes many features that provide different ways to study to be ready for the test. If you understand a topic when you read it, but do not study it any further, you probably will not be ready to pass the test with confidence. The book features included in this book give you tools that help you determine what you know, review what you know, better learn what you don't know, and be well prepared for the exam. These tools include

- **"Do I Know This Already?" Quizzes:** Each chapter begins with a quiz that helps you determine the amount of time you need to spend studying that chapter.

- **Foundation Topics:** These are the core sections of each chapter. They explain the protocols, concepts, and configuration for the topics in that chapter.

- **Exam Preparation Tasks:** The Exam Preparation Tasks section lists a series of study activities that should be done after reading the Foundation Topics section. Each chapter includes the activities that make the most sense for studying the topics in that chapter. The activities include

  — **Planning Tables:** The ROUTE exam topics includes some perspectives on how an engineer plans for various tasks. The idea is that the CCNP-level engineer in particular takes the design from another engineer, plans the implementation, and plans the verification steps–handing off the actual tasks to engineers working during change-window hours. Because the engineer plans the tasks, but may not be at the keyboard when implementing a feature, that engineer must master the configuration and verification commands so that the planned commands work for the engineer making the changes off-shift. The planning tables at the end of the chapter give you the chance to take the details in the Foundation Topics core of the chapter and think about them as if you were writing the planning documents.

  — **Key Topics Review:** The Key Topics icon is shown next to the most important items in the Foundation Topics section of the chapter. The Key Topics Review activity lists the Key Topics from the chapter, and page number. Although the contents of the entire chapter could be on the exam, you should definitely know the information listed in each key topic. Review these topics carefully.

  — **Memory Tables:** To help you exercise your memory and memorize some lists of facts, many of the more important lists and tables from the chapter are included in a document on the CD. This document lists only partial information, allowing you to complete the table or list. CD-only Appendix D holds the incomplete tables, and Appendix E includes the completed tables from which you can check your work.

  — **Definition of Key Terms:** Although the exams may be unlikely to ask a question such as "Define this term," the ROUTE exam requires that you learn and know a lot of networking terminology. This section lists the most important terms from the chapter, asking you to write a short definition and compare your answer to the glossary at the end of the book.

- **CD-based practice exam:** The companion CD contains an exam engine (from Boson software, www.boson.com), which includes 100 unique multiple-choice questions. Chapter 20 gives two suggestions on how to use these questions: either as study questions, or to simulate the ROUTE exam.

■ **Companion website:** The website http://www.ciscopress.com/title/9781587202537 posts up-to-the-minute materials that further clarify complex exam topics. Check this site regularly for new and updated postings written by the author that provide further insight into the more troublesome topics on the exam.

Book Organization

This book contains 20 chapters, plus appendixes. The topics all focus in some way on IP routing and IP routing protocols, making the topics somewhat focused, but with deep coverage on those topics.

The book organizes the topics into seven major parts. Parts 1 and 7 include topics with less technical depth, and Parts 2 through 6 include the major technical topics in the book. The following list outlines the major part organization of this book:

Part I: "Perspectives on Network Planning": This part includes a single chapter:

■ **Chapter 1: "Planning Tasks for the CCNP Exams":** This chapter discusses the CCNP ROUTE exam's perspectives on the planning process, including network design, implementation plans, and verification plans.

Part II: "EIGRP": This part starts with a CCNA-level EIGRP review and moves through EIGRP theory, configuration, authentication, route summarization, and more in the following chapters:

■ **Chapter 2: "EIGRP Overview and Neighbor Relationships":** This chapter reviews CCNA-level EIGRP topics and then closely examines the concepts, configuration, and verification of EIGRP neighbor relationships.

■ **Chapter 3: "EIGRP Topology, Routes, and Convergence":** This chapter examines the EIGRP topology database and the processes by which EIGRP processes this data to choose routes. It also examines the convergence process using feasible successors and with the Query process.

■ **Chapter 4: "EIGRP Route Summarization and Filtering":** This chapter discusses the theory behind route summarization and route filtering. It also shows how to configure and verify both features for EIGRP.

Part III: "OSPF": Similar to Part II, this part starts with a CCNA-level OSPF review and moves through OSPF theory, configuration, authentication, metric tuning, default routing, route filtering, and route summarization, plus OSPF multiarea issues and different stubby area types, as follows:

■ **Chapter 5: "OSPF Overview and Neighbor Relationships":** This chapter reviews CCNA-level OSPF topics and then closely examines the concepts, configuration, and verification of OSPF neighbor relationships.

■ **Chapter 6: "OSPF Topology, Routes, and Convergence":** This chapter examines the OSPF topology database for routes internal to OSPF. The chapter also discusses how OSPF routers choose the best internal OSPF routes and how OSPF converges when a change occurs.

- **Chapter 7: "OSPF Route Summarization, Filtering, and Default Routing":** This chapter discusses the design, configuration, and verification of OSPF route summarization and route filtering. It also discusses default routes and how to manage the size of the OSPF database and IP routing tables by using stubby areas.

- **Chapter 8: "OSPF Miscellany":** This chapter discusses two additional OSPF topics: OSPF virtual links and OSPF issues when using NBMA networks (such as Frame Relay).

Part IV: "Path Control": The term path control refers to a wide variety of topics related to IP routing and IP routing protocols. This part examines the path control topics not specifically included in the other parts of the book:

- **Chapter 9: "Basic IGP Redistribution":** This chapter examines the concepts, configuration, and verification of IGP route redistribution. In particular, this chapter looks at the mechanics of redistribution without the use of route maps for any purpose.

- **Chapter 10: "Advanced IGP Redistribution":** This chapter essentially continues Chapter 9, in this case focusing on the more complex configuration and issues. In particular, this chapter shows how to manipulate and filter routes at the redistribution function by using route maps, and how to avoid routing loops and inefficient routes when multiple redistribution points exist.

- **Chapter 11: "Policy Routing and IP Service Level Agreement":** This chapter picks up two small path control topics that simply do not fit into any other broader chapter in this book: Policy Based Routing (PBR) and IP Service Level Agreement (IP SLA).

Part V: "BGP": This part assumes no prior knowledge of BGP. It first examines BGP design issues, to give perspective on why BGP works differently than its IGP cousins OSPF and EIGRP. This part examines basic BGP concepts, configuration, and verification, including the path control functions of incluencing both inbound and outbound BGP routes:

- **Chapter 12: "Internet Connectivity and BGP":** This chapter introduces BGP. It begins with a review of Internet connectivity from a Layer 3 perspective. It then looks at the basics of how BGP works. It also examines some Internet access design issues, discussing the cases in which BGP can be helpful and the cases in which BGP has no practical use.

- **Chapter 13: "External BGP":** This chapter examines the configuration and verification of BGP between an Enterprise and its ISP(s).

- **Chapter 14: "Internal BGP and BGP Route Filtering":** This chapter examines the cases in which routers in the same ASN need to become BGP peers, creating an Internet BGP connection. It also discusses the need for BGP filtering and the mechanics of configuring BGP filtering.

- **Chapter 15: "BGP Path Control":** This chapter discusses the concept of the BGP Best Path Algorithm to choose the best BGP routes and how to influence those choices. In particular, this chapter shows the basic configuration for BGP weight, Local Preference, AS_Path length, and Multi-Exit Discriminator (MED).

Part VI: "IPv6": This part assumes no prior knowledge of IPv6. The chapters in this part work through IPv6 addressing and IGP configuration (RIPng, EIGRP for IPv6, and OSPFv3). It also discusses route redistribution for IPv6 and IPv6/IPv4 coexistence mechanisms:

- **Chapter 16: "IP Version 6 Addressing":** This chapter begins with an overview of IP Version 6 (IPv6). It then dives into IPv6 addressing concepts, plus the related protocols, including address assignment options and neighbor discovery. The chapter shows how to configure and verify IPv6 addresses on Cisco routers.

- **Chapter 17: "IPv6 Routing Protocols and Redistribution":** This chapter introduces three IPv6 IGPs: RIP Next Generation (RIPng), EIGRP for IPv6, and OSPF Version 3 (OSPFv3). The chapter focuses on basic configuration and verification. It also discusses IPv6 redistribution in comparison with IPv4 IGP redistribution.

- **Chapter 18: "IPv4 and IPv6 Coexistence":** This chapter discusses the many options to use during the potentially long migration from a purely IPv4 network to a future purely IPv6 network.

Part VII: "Branch Office Networking": This short part includes one chapter that addresses a few small topics related to branch offices that connect to their Enterprise networks using the Internet:

- **Chapter 19: "Routing over Branch Internet Connections":** Branch office routers can be configured to use the Internet as a WAN connection path back to the rest of an Enterprise network. This chapter takes a wide look at the surprisingly large number of networking functions that must occur on a branch router in such cases. It also gives examples of configurations for IPsec and GRE tunnels, DHCP server, NAT, and DSL.

Part VIII: "Final Preparation": This short part includes one chapter as well. This chapter does not include any new technical topics:

- **Chapter 20: "Final Preparation":** This chapter suggests some study strategies for your final preparation before the ROUTE exam.

In addition to the core chapters of the book, the book has several appendixes as well. Some appendixes exist in the printed book, whereas others exist in softcopy form on the CD included with the book.

Printed Appendixes

Appendixes printed in the book include

- **Appendix A, "Answers to the "Do I Know This Already?" Quizzes":** Includes the answers to all the questions from Chapters 2 through 19.

- **Appendix B, "Conversion Tables":** Lists a decimal-to-binary conversion table, decimal values 0 through 255, along with the binary equivalents. It also lists a hex-to-decimal conversion table as well.

- **Appendix C, "CCNP ROUTE Exam Updates:** Version 1.0": Covers a variety of short topics that either clarify or expand upon topics covered earlier in the book. This appendix is updated from time to time, and posted at http://www.ciscopress.com/title/9781587202537, with the most recent version available at the time of printing included here as Appendix C. (The first page of the appendix includes instructions on how to check to see if a later version of Appendix C is available online.)

CD Appendixes

The appendixes included on the CD-ROM are

- **Appendix D, "Memory Tables":** This appendix holds the key tables and lists from each chapter with some of the content removed. You can print this appendix, and as a memory exercise, complete the tables and lists. The goal is to help you memorize facts that can be useful on the exams.

- **Appendix E, "Memory Tables Answer Key":** This appendix contains the answer key for the exercises in Appendix D.

- **Appendix F, "Completed Planning Practice Tables":** The end of Chapters 2 through 19 list planning tables that you can complete to help learn the content more deeply. If you use these tables, refer to this appendix for the suggested answers.

- **Glossary:** The glossary contains definitions for all the terms listed in the "Define Key Terms" section at the conclusion of Chapters 2 through 19.

For More Information

If you have any comments about the book, you can submit those via the www.ciscopress.com. Just go to the website, select Contact Us, and type in your message.

Cisco might make changes that affect the ROUTE exam from time to time. You should always check www.cisco.com/go/ccnp for the latest details.

This chapter covers the following subjects:

Perspectives on CCNP Exam Topics Related to Planning:
This section outlines the goals of the CCNP certification.

How to Prepare for the Planning Topics on the Exams: This
section explains what you should know generally about planning in order to be prepared for the exam.

**Background Information on Implementation and Verifica-
tion Plans:** This short section discusses specific plans, and
why there is no one specific plan used for the exam.

Planning Tasks for the CCNP Exams

The predecessor exam to the ROUTE exam—the Building Scalable Cisco Internetworks (BSCI) exam—required mastery of the most typically used features of many routing and routing protocol technologies. The ROUTE exam requires that same mastery, but the ROUTE exam also includes many exam topics that use the words "plan" and "document." The predecessor BSCI exam did not include such wording in the exam topics, so presumably the new ROUTE exam adds this as a new requirement.

This opening chapter examines the meaning, purpose, and some perspectives on these planning and documentation tasks as they relate to preparing for and passing the ROUTE 642-902 exam.

Perspectives on CCNP Exam Topics Related to Planning

Cisco introduced the Cisco Certified Networking Professional (CCNP) certification in 1998. Since that time, Cisco has revised the exams and related courses on several occasions. Each major revision adjusted the scope of topics by expanding and adding some topics while shrinking or removing other topics. At the same time, the depth of coverage has changed over time as well, with the depth of coverage for each topic either becoming deeper or shallower.

The version of CCNP announced by Cisco in January 2010, including the 642-902 exam about which this book is written, narrows the breadth of topics included in CCNP compared to the previous version of CCNP. Cisco removed several sizable topics from CCNP—notably Quality of Service (QoS), Wireless LANs (WLANs), and many security topics. The new CCNP squarely focuses on routing and switching, but with a deeper troubleshooting requirement, with a new TSHOOT (642-832) exam. These changes also reflect that CCNP now requires only three exams instead of the four exams formerly required.

However, although the smaller number of CCNP topics may make CCNP easier, two other factors balance the CCNP so it is still a challenging, difficult, and respected certification. First, the exams appear to require a higher level of mastery for most topics. Second, that mastery is more than just technical knowledge; it requires the ability to plan the implementation and verification of a network engineering project.

Many CCNP ROUTE Exam Topics list the word "plan," collectively meaning that the CCNP candidate must approach problems in the same manner as a network engineer in a medium- to large-sized business. The skills related to these exam topics can be built as a side-effect of doing many network engineering jobs, for instance

■   The ability to analyze a network design document, extrapolate that design into the complete detailed implementation plan, including completed configurations for each router and switch.

■   The ability to analyze a design document and discover the missing items—questions that must be answered before a detailed implementation plan (including configurations) can be completed.

■   The ability to perform a peer review on another engineer's implementation plan, to discover weaknesses and omissions in the planned configurations, and to update the implementation plan.

■   The ability to build a verification plan that lists the specific **show** commands and command options that list key pieces of information—information that directly either confirms or denies whether each planned feature has been implemented correctly.

■   The ability to write a verification plan that can be understood and used by a less-experienced worker, allowing that worker to implement the change and to verify the changes worked, off-shift, when you are not on-site.

■   The ability to perform a peer review on another engineer's verification plan, to discover which key design features are not verified by that plan, and to discover inaccuracies in the plan.

This chapter discusses the whole area of implementation and verification planning for the CCNP ROUTE exam, including how you should prepare for these exam topics. By considering the ideas in this chapter first, you should have the right perspectives to know how to use the tools that help you add the planning skills and perspectives needed for the exam.

CCNP Route Exam Topics That Do Not Require the CLI

Cisco lists a set of Exam Topics for each Cisco exam. These Exam Topics follow a general type of phrasing, typically starting with an action word that defines what action or skill you must do for the exam. (Unfortunately, this style seldom gives much insight into the breadth or depth of coverage of a given topic.)

For example, consider the six Exam Topics for the CCNP ROUTE exam specifically related to EIGRP:

■   Determine network resources needed for implementing EIGRP on a network.

■   Create an EIGRP implementation plan.

■   Create an EIGRP verification plan.

■   Configure EIGRP routing.

■   Verify EIGRP solution was implemented properly using **show** and **debug** commands.

■   Document results of EIGRP implementation and verification.

The two gray-highlighted exam topics focus on the commands available from the CLI, specifically that you need to configure EIGRP, and to use both **show** and **debug** commands to verify (confirm) whether EIGRP is working correctly. The unhighlighted topics in the list require knowledge of the commands, but the tasks do not require any hands-on activities from the CLI. Instead, when doing these tasks in real life, you would more likely be using a word processor rather than a terminal emulator.

Besides this list of the EIGRP exam topics, the entire list of CCNP ROUTE Exam Topics includes many more items that use words like "document" and "plan." Of the roughly 40 CCNP ROUTE Exam Topics, approximately half of the exam topics refer to the various types of plans and documentation. In particular, the phase "Create a _____ verification plan" occurs six times in the CCNP ROUTE list of Exam Topics—one each for EIGRP, OSPF, eBGP, IPv6, redistribution, and Layer 3 path control.

Impressions on the Planning Exam Topics

After a first glance through the CCNP ROUTE Exam Topics, you might think that the new CCNP certification has been changed significantly—and you therefore need to significantly change how you prepare for CCNP. However, it turns out that by focusing on the following aspects of your study, you should be well prepared for the CCNP exams in general and the CCNP ROUTE exam in particular:

■   As with any other Cisco career certification exam, understand the concepts, configuration, and verification commands (**show** and **debug** commands).

■   As with any other Cisco career certification exam, master the configuration and verification tasks and commands.

■   Unlike most other Cisco career certification exams, spend some time thinking about the concepts, configuration, and verification tasks as if you were writing or reviewing a network design document, a network project implementation plan, or a verification plan.

In this list, the first two tasks are simply what most people normally do when preparing for a Cisco exam. The third item represents the new type of preparation task, in which you simply think about the same concepts, commands, and features, but from a planning perspective.

At this point in this brief first chapter, you can choose whether to keep reading the topics in order, or whether to skip to the section "How to Prepare for the Planning Topics on the Exam" later in this chapter. Those of you who have a pretty good idea of the planning tasks done by most IT shops can consider skipping ahead. For those of you with little or no experience in reading network design documents, building or using network implementation and verification plans, the next section can give you some useful perspectives before you dive into studying the technologies in CCNP ROUTE.

Relating the Exam Topics to a Typical Network Engineer's Job

The need to plan, and the need to document those plans, increases as the size of the organization increases. Even if only one person at a company cares about the router and switch infrastructure, that engineer probably does not want to be writing configurations at 2 a.m. Sunday morning when the change window begins. So, even in a small IT shop, some planning occurs when the engineer creates the configurations in a text editor before the weekend change window. When the staff grows to 3 to 4 people, particularly when some of those people work different shifts, the need to document the design, implementation, and verification/operational procedures becomes more important.

For perspective, this section examines a medium- to large-sized company, along with some of the planning tasks done in the real world—the same kinds of tasks listed as part of the CCNP Exam Topics.

A Fictitious Company and Networking Staff

Imagine if you will a medium to large company, one large enough to have several network engineers on staff. For the sake of discussion, this company has roughly 50,000 employees, with 1000 smallish remote sites, four large sites with at least 2000 employees on each large campus, and maybe a smattering of other sites with 500 or so employees. Of course, the company has a few data centers, has plans for a companywide IP telephony deployment, is adding video over IP, already has the usual security needs, and has a growing teleworker community, several network connections to partner companies, and Internet connections. Oh yeah, and there's always the growing need for smart buildings to reduce energy consumption, all hooked into the IP network.

With a company of this size, the job roles for this fictitious company includes IT customer support (Help Desk, manned 24x7), an operations team that covers most hours of the day, network engineering, and a design team.

Next, consider the various roles in the network and the type of work done by the people in those roles:

■ Help desk personnel may perform diagnosis of network health, taking a general problem statement from a customer down to a specific issue, for example, that a user's device is not pingable.

■ Operations staff may be the second level of support for problems, both reacting to calls from the Help Desk and monitoring the network proactively. The operations staff also often implements changes on behalf of the engineering team during off-shift hours.

■ The network engineering team may be the third level of support for problems but typically focuses on project work, including the detailed planning for new configurations to support new sites, new network features, and new sites in the network.

■ The network designers may actually log in to the network devices far less than the operations and engineering teams, instead focusing on gathering requirements from internal and external customers, translating those requirements into a network design, and even doing proof-of-concept testing—but leaving the details of how to deploy the design for all required sites to the network engineering team.

The number of individuals in each role varies in different organizations, of course. Maybe only a single network designer and single network engineer are required, with maybe 2 to 3 people as network operations specialists—not enough for 24x7 coverage with a specialist, but close. The Help Desk position may simply require most people to have the same fundamental networking skill set, depending on the size of the shop. On the other end of the scale, in the largest companies, the engineering staff might include several departments of network engineers.

The Design Step

Next, consider the basic workflow when a new network project happens, new sites are added, or any noticeable change occurs. The network designer begins the process by determining the requirements and creating a plan. That plan typically lists the following:

- The requirements for the project

- The sites affected

- Sample configurations

- Results from proof-of-concept testing

- Dependencies and assumptions

- Business requirements, financials, and management commitments

Many other items might be included as well.

After creating the design document, the network designer often uses a peer review process to refine and confirm the design. The designer cannot simply work in a vacuum, define the design, and then toss the design document to network engineering to be deployed. In smaller shops, a peer review may simply be 2 to 3 people standing around a dry erase board discussing the project. In larger shops, the design peer review probably requires a thorough written document be distributed before the meeting, with attendance from network engineering, operations, and the Help Desk, and with formal sign-off required.

Implementation Planning Step

The next step in the life of the project occurs when a network engineer takes the approved design document from the design team and begins planning the implementation of the project. To do this task, the network engineer must interpret the examples and general cases described in the design document and develop a very specific implementation plan that lists all significant tasks and actions by each group and on each device. The design document, for instance, may show example cases of typical branch offices—a typical one-router branch, a typical two-router larger branch, a typical district (medium-sized) site, and so on. The network engineer must then determine what must be done on every device to implement the project and document those details in an implementation plan.

For example, imagine this fictitious company plans to deploy IP telephony to the 1000 remote sites. The design document lists the following requirements:

■ Switches with Power over Ethernet (PoE) at each remote office (switch models listed in the design doc).

■ The convention of placing all phones at a site in one VLAN/subnet and all PCs in a second VLAN/subnet.

■ VLAN trunking between the switch and the 1 or 2 routers at each remote site.

■ A particular version and feature set of router IOS on the remote site routers to support Survivable Remote Site Telephony (SRST).

■ More aggressive tuning of EIGRP to improve convergence time, particularly by ensuring both routes from a remote site back into the network core are in the routing table at the same time.

The design document certainly contains more details than the preceding list, but the list gives you an idea of the starting point when the network engineer first work on his implementation plan by reviewing the design document.

After a thorough review of the design, the network engineer then develops an implementation plan that includes items like the following:

■ A list of all remote offices, with notations of which require a switch hardware upgrade (for PoE support) and which do not

■ Total numbers of switches to be ordered, prices, and delivery schedules

■ A table that lists the specific VLAN and subnet numbers used at each site for the phone VLAN/subnet and PC VLAN/subnet

■ The IP address ranges from each remote site subnet that needs to be added to the DHCP servers configurations for dynamic assignment

■ A list of the remote site routers that require a router hardware upgrade to support either trunking or the required IOS, including pricing and delivery schedules

■ A list of remote site routers that do not require a replacement router but do require a memory upgrade to support the needed IOS

■ Annotated sample configurations for typical sites, including VLAN trunking to the switch, SRST, and EIGRP convergence tuning

■ A reference to the location of the switch and router configuration for every device that will be configured as part of the project

The preceding list represents the types of items that would be documented in the implementation plan for this project. The list is certainly not exhaustive but represents a smattering of what might end up in such a plan.

The implementation plan probably has many informal reviews as the network engineer works through the plan. Additionally, larger shops often have a peer review after the plan is more fully developed, with network designers, operations, and fellow network engineers typically included in the review.

Verification Planning Step

The design step tells us "this is what we want to accomplish," whereas the implementation planning step tells us "this is exactly what we will do, and when, to accomplish this design." With that in mind, the verification plan tells whoever will actually perform the actions to implement a project how to answer this question:

"Did the actions we took per the implementation plan work?"

The verification plan is used with the actual implementation of the changes in the network. The larger the network, the less likely that the network engineer does any of the implementation work, instead planning the implementation. More often than not, the operations staff follows the implementation plan, or more specific instructions for each individual change window, taking the appropriate actions (copying in configurations, for instance). The engineer that implements the changes then uses the verification plan to determine if the changes met the requirements.

The most important part of the verification plan, at least for being ready to pass the CCNP exams, identifies what commands confirm whether each key design point was implemented correctly. For example, the section "Implementation Planning Step" earlier in this chapter briefly describes a project to deploy IP telephony to all remote sites. For that same project, the following list describes some of the actions listed in the verification plan:

■   After copy/pasting a remote site's new router configuration, use the **show ip interface brief** command, confirm an up/up state on the two subinterfaces of Fa0/0, and confirm the IP addresses match the planning chart in IP address repository.

■   For each remote site router, use the **show ip route** command to confirm two routes exist for each Data Center subnet. See "Data Center Subnet Reference" in the IP address repository.

■   From the WAN edge routers, use the **show ip eigrp neighbors detail** command, and find neighbors listed as stub routers. For the routers configured in tonight's change window, compare this output to the Stub Router planning table in the implementation plan, and confirm that the correct remote site routers have been configured as EIGRP stubs.

Note: The "IP address repository" mentioned in the list does not exist in this chapter; it just represents the idea that an implementation plan would include some reference to the location of all subnet/address reference information.

The important part of the verification plan lists the specific commands used, at what point in the implementation process, and what output should be seen. In practice, this plan should also include samples of output, spelling out what should be seen when correct, and what output would tell the operations staff that the change did not work correctly.

Documenting the Results of the Implementation

Continuing the story of the typical but fictitious company, when a set of changes is attempted during a change window, some documentation must be changed based on the results. If a different final configuration is used, the implementation documents must be changed.

> **Note:** This particular step is mentioned mainly because several CCNP ROUTE Exam Topics refer to the task of documenting the results of the implementation and verification.

Summary of the Role of Network Engineer

The CCNP certification focuses on skills required to do the job of network engineer as generally described in this chapter. For perspective, then, consider the following list, which compares and contrasts some of the expectations for CCNP network engineers by interpreting the CCNP ROUTE Exam Topics:

■ Does not create the design document

■ Does participate in design peer reviews, finding oversights, asking further questions that impact the eventual implementation, and confirming the portions of the design that appear complete and valid

■ Does not deploy the configurations off-shift

■ Does plan and document the specific configurations for each device, documenting those configurations in the implementation plan so that others can add the configuration to various devices

■ Does participate in peer reviews of the implementation plans written by fellow network engineers, finding omissions, caveats, and problems

■ Does not verify that the changes worked as planned when implemented off-shift

■ Does create the verification plan that others use to verify that the changes worked as planned when implemented off-shift

■ Does perform peer reviews of other engineers' verification plans

Now that you've had a chance to think generally about the role of the network engineer, the next section brings the discussion back around to the CCNP ROUTE exam, and how you should prepare for the exam.

How to Prepare for the Planning Topics on the Exams

Can you create a networking implementation plan for each technology area on the CCNP exams? Can you create a verification plan for those same technologies? According to the CCNP Exam Topics, these skills now fall into the scope of topics on the CCNP exams. However, Cisco can't reasonably ask you a question as open-ended as "Create an entire EIGRP implementation plan based on the following design document." Such a question would take too much time relative to the typical 1 minute 15 seconds or so average question time for a typical Cisco exam.

Even though the exam may not ask you to literally create a plan, you do need the skills to perform those same tasks. As with any other exam topic, expect the exam to ask questions that zero in on a small subset of the required skill.

To prepare for the planning-oriented topics, you do NOT need to learn any more facts about the technology or commands. The CCNP Exam Topics already cover the technology, particularly the configuration, verification, and troubleshooting of the listed technologies. For the planning-related Exam Topics, however, you do need to think about those technologies with a slightly different perspective. The question is whether you could, with only pencil, paper, and a word processor—but definitely without a router or switch CLI—do the following:

Step 1.   Read design goals extracted from a design document, develop a configuration that meets those goals, and discover missing information that needs to be gathered before you can complete the configuration.

Step 2.   Read an extract from the design and implementation plans to determine what is wrong or missing.

Step 3.   Read a configuration and design goal as stated in an implementation plan, and create the verification steps that would confirm whether the feature was working.

Step 4.   Analyze a portion of a verification plan, along with the stated configuration and design goals, and determine any problems or missing elements in the verification plan.

Figure 1-1 shows the same concepts, with numbers referencing the preceding steps.

After you have a solid understanding of the configuration and verification commands for a topic, to prepare for the planning-related Exam Topics, you simply need to take the time to think about those same topics, but from the perspective of the tasks shown in Figure 1-1. To that end, this book adds some tools to the end of each chapter. These tools should help organize your thinking and remind you to take some time to ponder the topics in a chapter from a design perspective.

The end of most chapters in this book include a new section titled "Planning Preparation" as part of the broader "Foundation Summary" review section. The "Planning Preparation" guides you through various aspects of the planning process, focused on the technologies included in that chapter. All the Planning Preparation tables list some information and give you the opportunity to complete the tables as an exercise. Appendix F, "Completed Planning Practice Tables," found on the CD included with this book, lists completed versions of the tables for reference. This section uses four different types of tables that mimic some of the planning and analysis tasks, as described under the next four headings.

Note: You may want to glance at the Planning Preparation tables at the end of Chapter 2, "EIGRP Overview and Neighbor Relationships," for perspective as you read through this chapter.

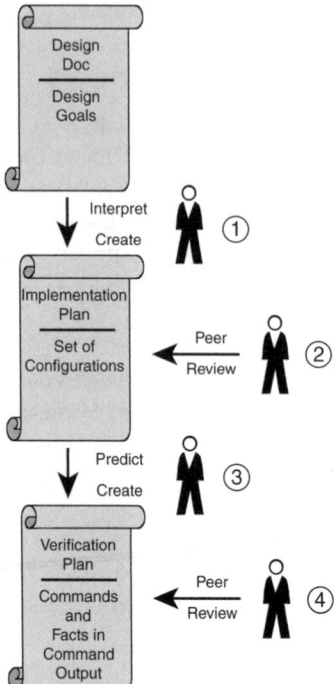

Figure 1-1   *Planning Tasks for the CCNP Candidate*

Planning Preparation: Design Review Table

When in a real design review, a network engineer must look at the requirements and decide what configuration options might be used. The Design Review table in the Planning
Preparation section of most chapters lists design goals that you might see in a design document. Your job is to interpret each design goal, think about what features might be used
to reach the goal, and then list those features.

This tool is designed to help you think about the broader view of a network that is typically seen in design documents.

Planning Preparation: Implementation Plan Peer Review Table

When you attend a real implementation plan peer review, you and other engineers can see
the plan and immediately think of different questions. Those questions may be questions
about the technology—some fact you used to know but forgot, some confusion about
how a command would work given the specific design, or some question about the design
goal that led to the listed configuration.

The Implementation Plan Peer Review table predicts some of the questions that might
come to mind when performing a peer review. Your job with this table is to then answer
the questions. Some questions may be basic, and really meant more for review, whereas
others strive to force you to think about some of the subtleties of the topics in the chapter.

Create an Implementation Plan Table

The Implementation Plan table is a pure memory aid, but the task fits directly into the Exam Topics that read "Create a _____ implementation plan." This tool uses a table that simply lists the configuration topics from the chapter and asks that you write all related configuration commands from memory. Although you may not need to memorize every command and parameter for the exam, this exercise can help you mentally group commands together, which may aid in questions directed at building implementation plans.

Choose Commands for a Verification Plan Table

This final tool helps you think about verification commands by first thinking of the fact you need to discover and then choosing the command that lists the fact. Many resources—including Cisco documents, many Cisco authorized courses, and many books (mine included)—begin with the **show** commands and then explain the information displayed by the command. The reverse order of thinking is required to be prepared to create a verification plan. You must first decide what facts must be discovered to confirm a feature is working and then remember which commands supply that information.

This final planning preparation tool lists many of the key individual pieces of information that matter to the technologies included in that chapter. Your job is to list the commands that display the requested piece of information.

Background Information on Implementation and Verification Plans

The last major section of this chapter also discusses the topics of implementation and verification planning, but with a different twist. So far, this chapter has been focused on how you might prepare for CCNP exams. This section instead focuses on implementation and verification planning as an end to themselves.

No Single Plan Style

Upon reading the CCNP ROUTE Exam Topics, and seeing the references to "implementation plan" and "verification plan," you might be at least slightly curious to see examples of such plans. However, no such example implementation plan or verification plan exists in this book because no one specific type of plan matters to the exam. In fact, the Cisco authorized course for this exam, also called ROUTE, also does not offer a specific type or style of implementation or verification plan.

Several reasons exist as to why no one type of implementation or verification plan is suggested as the model for preparing for the exams, including the following:

- Every company does something different, from completely ad-hoc discussions around a white board to formal reviews and processes.

- Several standards exist for methodologies that include implementation and verification planning, but each uses different terminology, so a single suggested plan format would implicitly recommend one method or another.

■   Creating a pseudo-standard example plan for the sake of CCNP was not actually nec-
    essary to assess the test-taker's planning skills.

Typical Elements in an Implementation Plan

Although no one style of plan matters, the types of items inside a plan have some interest
for the exam. It is also useful to know a few terms regarding some of the formalized methods for implementation planning.

When an IT organization takes the time to require and review a written implementation
plan for a project, those plans still vary in terms of depth and detail. The plan may include
many details about the existing network, or it may rely on other documentation, ignoring
those details in the implementation plan. The plan may list financials, particularly when
hardware and software must be purchased, or it may leave those details out of the planning document, instead leaving those details for the management team to handle.

Just for perspective, Table 1-1 outlines some of the types of items you might see in a
network implementation plan:

Table 1-1

The existing network:	Router and switch hardware
	IOS versions and feature sets
	RAM and flash in each device
	Existing configurations
	IP Subnet and Addressing Plan, Assignments, and Conventions
Management:	Personnel and roles, contact information
	Assumptions and dependencies
	Required management sign-offs
	New tools, reporting, status update process
New project details:	Design goals (reference to design doc possibly)
	Hardware upgrades
	Software upgrades
	Timelines to make changes
	Specific configurations for each device
	Migration issues (assuming a subset of sites are implemented in any one change window)
	Network diagrams, possibly for each interim step during a migration
Project completion:	Final sign-off requirements
	Definitions of success
	Submission of revised site documentation, operational procedures, and any other permanent documentation

Focus for Implementation Plans for CCNP

Although this sample includes typical elements, the three highlighted elements have some particular interest in the context of the CCNP exams. The Exam Topics do not state a general "Create a network project implementation plan," but rather focuses on a technology area. Specifically for CCNP ROUTE, the Exam Topics that mention an implementation plan specifically focus on EIGRP, OSPF, eBGP, redistribution, path control, and IPv6, respectively.

For the exam, the highlighted elements in the sample plan represent the most likely items to be within the scope of the Exam Topics. An EIGRP implementation plan in real life—say for a migration from RIP-2 to EIGRP—probably includes all the elements listed in the sample plan. However, because EIGRP is a Cisco IOS Software feature, the likely implementation plan topics relate to EIGRP configuration, verification, and issues about migrating from one design to another.

Structured Implementation Planning Methodologies

The Cisco authorized courses for the CCNP track mention a few structured methodologies that can be used to manage network projects. These methodologies include steps, terminology, and conventions that include the implementation planning, the actual implementation, and in some cases, specific items for verification planning. (In some cases, the verification plan is part of the implementation plan or change management process.) Table 1-2 lists these methodologies, and a few facts about each, for perspective.

Table 1-2 *Project Planning Methodologies*

Key Topic

Method	Owner	Comment
FCAPS	ISO	Fault, Configuration, Accounting, Performance, and Security: This standard focuses on network and systems management. Implementation planning falls into the change management category.
ITIL	Great Britain	Information Technology Infrastructure Library: A set of best practices for systems management that has been widely used in the IT industry. It is managed by the government of Great Britain. www.itil-official-site.com.
TMN	ITU-T	Telecommunications Management Network: Created by the ITU-T's Study Group 4, this ongoing effort defines system management practices from the ITU. Originally based on FCAPS. www.itu.int.
Cisco Lifecycle Services	Cisco	Quoting the Cisco website: "The Cisco Lifecycle Services approach defines the activities needed to help you successfully deploy and operate Cisco technologies and optimize their performance throughout the lifecycle of your network."
PPDIOO	Cisco	Prepare, Plan, Design, Implement, Operate, Optimize: The popular acronym for the steps defined by Cisco Lifestyle Services.

Typical Verification Plan Components

A typical verification plan is much smaller than the implementation plan. The verification plan often focuses on a specific change made on a specific day, or on a type a change made repeatedly at different sites over a longer migration period. The following list outlines the more common items in a verification plan:

■ The specific **show** and **debug** commands to be used

■ The specific facts in the output that must be confirmed

■ Explanations of why a particular command's output confirms that a feature is or is not working

■ Sample command output

■ Any data that should be gathered when the output is not correct

Conclusions

The various CCNP ROUTE Exam Topics that require planning and documentation do not require more technical knowledge, but they do require you to be more comfortable with the technical topics. The best way to become more comfortable is to have a job in which you use the features but that you can become very comfortable with the technology through study as well. For those of you with little experience with the technologies included in this book, please take the time to do the exercises in the "Planning Practice" sections near the end of each chapter—we believe such practice can help you prepare for the planning perspectives expected to be on the exams.

This chapter covers the following subjects:

EIGRP CCNA Review: This section reviews the EIGRP concepts, configuration, and verification commands assumed as prerequisites, specifically those details included in the CCNA Exam's coverage of EIGRP.

EIGRP Neighborships: This section discusses a variety of features that impact when a router attempts to form EIGRP neighbor relationships (neighborships), what must be true for those neighborships to work, and what might prevent those neighborships.

Neighborships over WANs: This short section examines the typical usage of EIGRP neighborships over various types of WAN technologies.

CHAPTER 2

EIGRP Overview and Neighbor Relationships

Enhanced Interior Gateway Routing Protocol (EIGRP) is configured with a few relatively simple commands. In fact, for most any size network, you could go to every router, configure the **router eigrp 1** command, followed by one or more **network** *net-id* subcommands (one for each classful network to which the router is connected), and EIGRP would likely work, and work very well, with no other configuration.

In spite of that apparent simplicity, here you sit beginning the first of three chapters of EIGRP coverage in this book. Many reasons exist for the amount of EIGRP material included here. First, EIGRP includes many optional configuration features that you need to both understand and master for the CCNP ROUTE exam. Many of these features require a solid understanding of EIGRP internals as well—a topic that can be conveniently ignored if you just do the minimal configuration, but something very important to planning, implementing, and optimizing a medium/large Enterprise network.

Another reason for the depth of EIGRP coverage in this book is due to a fundamental change in the philosophy of the CCNP exams, as compared with earlier CCNP exam versions. Cisco has increased the focus on planning for the implementation and verification of new network designs. The bar has been raised, and in a way that is consistent with typical engineering jobs. Not only do you need to understand all the EIGRP features, but you also need to be able to look at a set of design requirements, and from that decide which EIGRP configuration settings could be useful—and which are not useful. You also must be able to direct others as to what verification steps would tell them if the implementation worked or not, rather than just relying on typing a **?** and looking around for that little piece of information you know exists somewhere.

Part II of this book contains three chapters. This chapter briefly reviews the basics of EIGRP, and delves into all topics related to how EIGRP routers form neighbor relationships. Chapter 3, "EIGRP Topology, Routes, and Convergence," then examines many topics related to how EIGRP chooses routes. Chapter 4, "EIGRP Route Summarization and Filtering," then moves on to examine route filtering and route summarization, which closes the discussion of specific EIGRP features.

This chapter in particular begins with the "EIGRP Basics" section, which is a review of the core prerequisite facts about EIGRP. Following the review, the chapter examines EIGRP neighbor relationships, including a variety of configuration commands that impact neighbor relationships, and the verification commands that you can use to confirm how well EIGRP neighbors work.

"Do I Know This Already?" Quiz

The "Do I Know This Already?" quiz allows you to assess if you should read the entire chapter. If you miss no more than one of these eight self-assessment questions, you might want to move ahead to the "Exam Preparation Tasks." Table 2-1 lists the major headings in this chapter and the "Do I Know This Already?" quiz questions covering the material in those headings so that you can assess your knowledge of these specific areas. The answers to the "Do I Know This Already?" quiz appear in Appendix A.

Table 2-1   *"Do I Know This Already?" Foundation Topics Section-to-Question Mapping*

Foundation Topics Section	Questions
EIGRP CCNA Review	1, 2
EIGRP Neighborships	3–7
Neighborships over WANs	8

1. A router has been configured with the commands **router eigrp 9** and **network 172.16.1.0 0.0.0.255**. No other EIGRP-related commands have been configured. The answers list the IP addresses that could be assigned to this router's Fa0/0 interface. Which answers list an IP address/prefix length that would cause the router to enable EIGRP on Fa0/0?

    a.   172.16.0.1/23

    b.   172.16.1.1/26

    c.   172.16.1.1/24

    d.   172.16.0.255/23

    e.   None of the other answers is correct.

2. Router R1 has working interfaces S0/0, S0/1, and S0/2, with IP address/prefix combinations of 10.10.10.1/24, 10.10.11.2/24, and 10.10.12.3/22. R1's configuration includes the commands **router eigrp 9** and **network 10.0.0.0**. The **show ip eigrp interfaces** command lists S0/0 and S0/1 in the command output, but not S0/2. Which answer gives the reason for the omission? (Choose two answers.)

    a.   R1 has EIGRP neighbors reachable via S0/0 and S0/1, but not via S0/2, so it is not included.

    b.   S0/2 may currently be in a state other than up/up.

    c.   The **network 10.0.0.0** command requires the use of mask 255.0.0.0 due to EIGRP being classful by default.

    d.   S0/2 may be configured as a passive interface.

3. Routers R1 and R2 are EIGRP neighbors using their Fa0/0 interfaces, respectively. An engineer adds the **ip hello-interval eigrp 9 6** command to R1's Fa0/0 configuration. Which of the following is true regarding the results from this change?

    a. The **show ip eigrp neighbors** command on R1 lists the revised Hello timer.

    b. The **show ip eigrp interfaces** command on R1 lists the revised Hello timer.

    c. The R1-R2 neighborship fails due to Hello timer mismatch.

    d. The **show ip eigrp interfaces detail** command on R1 lists the revised Hello timer.

4. Routers R1 and R2, currently EIGRP neighbors over their Fa0/0 interfaces (respectively), both use EIGRP authentication. Tuesday at 8 p.m. the neighborship fails. Which of the following would *not* be useful when investigating whether authentication had anything to do with the failure?

    a. debug eigrp packet

    b. show key chain

    c. show ip eigrp neighbor failure

    d. show clock

5. Router R1 has been configured with the commands **router eigrp 9** and **network 172.16.2.0 0.0.0.255**, with no other current EIGRP configuration. R1's (working) Fa0/0 interface has been configured with IP address 172.16.2.2/26. R1 has found three EIGRP neighbors reachable via interface Fa0/0, including the router with IP address 172.16.2.20. When the engineer attempts to add the **neighbor 172.16.2.20 fa0/0** command in EIGRP configuration mode, which of the following occurs?

    a. Fa0/0 fails.

    b. The command is rejected.

    c. The existing three neighbors fail.

    d. The neighborship with 172.16.2.20 fails and then reestablishes.

    e. None of the other answers is correct.

6. Which of the following settings could prevent two potential EIGRP neighbors from becoming neighbors? (Choose two answers.)

    a. The interface used by one router to connect to the other router is passive in the EIGRP process.

    b. Duplicate EIGRP router IDs.

    c. Mismatched Hold Timers.

    d. IP addresses of 10.1.1.1/24 and 10.2.2.2/24, respectively.

7. An engineer has added the following configuration snippet to an implementation planning document. The configuration will be added to Router R1, whose Fa0/0 interface connects to a LAN to which Routers R2 and R3 also connect. R2 and R3 are already EIGRP neighbors with each other. Assuming the snippet shows all commands on R1 related to EIGRP authentication, which answer lists an appropriate comment to be made during the implementation plan peer review?

key chain fred
 key 3
  key-string whehew
 interface fa0/0
  ip authentication key-chain eigrp 9 fred

    a. The configuration is missing one authentication-related configuration command.

    b. The configuration is missing two authentication-related configuration commands.

    c. Authentication type 9 is not supported; type 5 should be used instead.

    d. The key numbers must begin with key 1, so change the **key 3** command to **key 1**.

8. A company has a Frame Relay WAN with one central-site router and 100 branch office routers. A partial mesh of PVCs exists: one PVC between the central site and each of the 100 branch routers. Which of the following could be true about the number of EIGRP neighborships?

    a. A partial mesh totaling 100: one between the central-site router and each of the 100 branches.

    b. A full mesh – (101 * 100) / 2 = 5050–One neighborship between each pair of routers.

    c. 101–One between each router (including the central site) and its nearby PE router.

    d. None of the answers is correct.

Foundation Topics

EIGRP CCNA Review

All the CCNP exams consider CCNA materials as prerequisites, so the Cisco Press CCNP Exam Certification Guide series of books also assumes the reader is already familiar with CCNA topics. However, the CCNP exams do test on features that overlap with CCNA. Additionally, most people forget some details along the way, so this section reviews the CCNA level topics as a brief refresher.

To that end, this section begins with a review of EIGRP configuration using only the **router eigrp** and **network** commands. Following that, the next section details the key fields used to verify that EIGRP is working. Finally, the last part of this introduction summarizes the basic EIGRP internals behind this initial simple example.

Configuration Review

Cisco IOS uses the **router eigrp** *asn* command, plus one or more **network** *net-id wild-card-mask* subcommands, to enable EIGRP on the router and on router interfaces. The rules for these commands are as follows:

Key Topic

1. Neighboring routers' **router eigrp** *asn* commands must be configured with the same ASN parameter to become neighbors.

2. IOS enables only EIGRP on interfaces matched by an EIGRP **network** command. When enabled, the router does the following:
   a. Attempts to discover EIGRP neighbors on that interface by sending multicast EIGRP Hello messages
   b. Advertises to other neighbors about the subnet connected to the interface

3. If no wildcard-mask is configured on the EIGRP **network** command, the command's single parameter should be a classful network number (in other words, a class A, B, or C network number).

4. If no wildcard-mask is configured on the EIGRP **network** command, the command enables EIGRP on all of that router's interfaces directly connected to the configured classful network.

5. If the **network** command includes a wildcard-mask, the router performs access control list (ACL) logic when comparing the net-id configured in the **network** command with each interface's IP address, using the configured wildcard-mask as an ACL wildcard mask.

Example 2-1 shows a sample configuration for each router in Figure 2-1, with several variations in the **network** commands to make the details in the preceding list more obvious.

Note: All IP addresses begin with 10.1 unless otherwise noted.

Figure 2-1 *Three Router Internetwork*

Example 2-1 *EIGRP Configuration on Routers R1, R2, and R3*

```
! On Router R1: !!!!!!!!!!!!!!!!!!!!!!!!!!!!!!!!!!!!!!!!!!!!!!!
router eigrp 1
 network 10.0.0.0
 network 192.168.9.0
! On Router R2: !!!!!!!!!!!!!!!!!!!!!!!!!!!!!!!!!!!!!!!!!!!!!!
router eigrp 1
 network 10.1.0.0 0.0.31.255
 network 10.1.2.2 0.0.0.0
! On Router R3: !!!!!!!!!!!!!!!!!!!!!!!!!!!!!!!!!!!!!!!!!!!!!!!
router eigrp 1
 network 10.1.0.0 0.0.255.255
```

First, note that all three routers use the **router eigrp 1** command, so all three routers' ASN values match.

Next, consider the two **network** commands on R1. The **network 10.0.0.0** command, without a *wildcard-mask* parameter, means that R1 matches all interface in class A network 10.0.0.0—which in this case means R1's Fa0/0, S0/0/0, and S0/0/1 interfaces. The **network 192.168.9.0** command, again without a wildcard, matches interface Fa0/1.

On R2, the **network 10.1.0.0 0.0.31.255** command requires a little more thought. The router uses the 0.0.31.255 value—the wildcard (WC) mask—just like an ACL WC mask.

IOS compares the 10.1.0.0 value with each interface IP address, but only for the bit positions for which the WC mask lists a binary 0. For example, 0.0.31.255 represents 19 binary 0s, followed by 13 binary 1s, so R2 would compare the first 19 bits of 10.1.0.0 with the first 19 bits of each interface's IP address. (Note that Appendix B lists a binary/decimal conversion table.)

Two features of the mechanics of the **network** command require a little extra attention. First, IOS may convert the *address* portion of the **network** *address wc-mask* command before putting the command into the running-config. Just as IOS does for the address/WC mask combinations for the **access-list** command, IOS inverts the WC mask and then performs a Boolean AND of the address and mask. For example, if you type the **network 10.1.1.1 0.0.255.255** command, IOS inverts the WC mask (to 255.255.0.0), ANDs this value with 10.1.1.1, resulting in 10.1.0.0. As a result, IOS stores the command **network 10.1.0.0 0.0.255.255**.

The second feature is that when you know for sure the values in the **network** command, you can easily find the range of interface addresses that match the address/WC mask combination in the **network** command. The low end of the range is the address as listed in the **network** command. To find the high end of the range, just add the address and WC mask together. For example, the **network 10.1.0.0 0.0.31.255** command has a range of 10.1.0.0 through 10.1.31.255. (Note that the math suggested in this paragraph does not work when the wildcard mask does not have a single string of consecutive binary 0s followed by a single string of consecutive binary 1s.)

Finally, on R3, the **network 10.1.0.0 0.0.255.255** command tells R3 to enable EIGRP on all interfaces whose IP addresses begin with 10.1, which includes all three interfaces on R3, as shown in Figure 2-1.

Taking a step back from the details, this config has enabled EIGRP, with ASN 1, on all three routers, and on all interfaces shown in Figure 2-1—except one interface. R2's Fa0/1 interface is not matched by any **network** commands on R2, so EIGRP is not enabled on that interface. The next section reviews the commands that can be used to confirm that EIGRP is enabled, the interfaces on which it is enabled, the neighbor relationships that have been formed, and which EIGRP routes have been advertised and learned.

Verification Review

Even before starting to configure the routers, an engineer first considers all requirements. Those requirements lead to a design, which in turn leads to a chosen set of configuration commands. Then, the verification process that follows must consider the design requirements. The goal of verification is to determine that the internetwork works as designed, not just that some EIGRP routes have been learned.

For the purposes of this section, assume that the only design goal for the internetwork in Figure 2-1 is that EIGRP be used so that all routers have routes to reach all subnets shown in the figure.

To verify such a simple design, an engineer should start by confirming on which interfaces EIGRP has been enabled on each router. The next step should be to determine if the EIGRP neighbor relationships that should occur are indeed up and working. Then, the

EIGRP topology table should be examined to confirm that there is at least one entry for each subnet or network in the design. Finally, the IP routes on each router should be examined, confirming that all routes are known. To that end, Table 2-2 summarizes five key **show** commands that provide the information to answer these questions:

Note: The table mentions some information that is covered later in this chapter (passive interfaces) or in other chapters (successor/feasible successors).

Example 2-2 shows samples of each command listed in Table 2-2. Note that the output highlights various samples of items that should be verified: the interfaces on which EIGRP is enabled, the known neighbors, the subnets in the topology table, and the EIGRP routes.

Table 2-2   *Key EIGRP Verification Commands*

Command	Key Information
show ip eigrp interfaces	Lists the working interfaces on which EIGRP is enabled (based on the **network** commands); it omits passive interfaces.
show ip protocols	Lists the contents of the **network** configuration commands for each routing process, and a list of neighbor IP addresses.
show ip eigrp neighbors	Lists known neighbors; does not list neighbors for which some mismatched parameter is preventing a valid EIGP neighbor relationship.
show ip eigrp topology	Lists all successor and feasible successor routes known to this router. It does not list all known topology details. (See Chapter 3 for more detail on successors and feasible successors.)
show ip route	Lists the contents of the IP routing table, listing EIGRP-learned routes with a code of D on the left side of the output.

Example 2-2   *EIGRP Verification on Routers R1, R2, and R3*

```
! On Router R1: !!!!!!!!!!!!!!!!!!!!!!!!!!!!!!!!!!!!!!!!!!!!!
R1#show ip eigrp interfaces
IP-EIGRP interfaces for process 1


                         Xmit Queue    Mean   Pacing Time   Multicast    Pending
Interface       Peers    Un/Reliable   SRTT   Un/Reliable   Flow Timer   Routes
Fa0/0           0        0/0           0      0/1           0            0
Se0/0/0         1        0/0           25     0/15          123          0
Se0/0/1         1        0/0           23     0/15          111          0
Fa0/1           0        0/0           0      0/1           0            0
```

```
! On Router R2: !!!!!!!!!!!!!!!!!!!!!!!!!!!!!!!!!!!!!!!!!!!!!!!!
R2#show ip protocols
Routing Protocol is "eigrp 1"
  Outgoing update filter list for all interfaces is not set
  Incoming update filter list for all interfaces is not set
  Default networks flagged in outgoing updates
  Default networks accepted from incoming updates
  EIGRP metric weight K1=1, K2=0, K3=1, K4=0, K5=0
  EIGRP maximum hopcount 100
  EIGRP maximum metric variance 1
  Redistributing: eigrp 1
  EIGRP NSF-aware route hold timer is 240s
  Automatic network summarization is in effect
  Maximum path: 4
  Routing for Networks:
     10.1.2.2/32
     10.1.0.0/19
  Routing Information Sources:
    Gateway          Distance       Last Update
    10.1.12.1            90          00:19:36
    10.1.23.1            90          00:19:36
  Distance: internal 90 external 170
! On Router R3: !!!!!!!!!!!!!!!!!!!!!!!!!!!!!!!!!!!!!!!!!!!!!!!!
R3#show ip eigrp neighbors
IP-EIGRP neighbors for process 1
H   Address                 Interface      Hold Uptime   SRTT   RTO  Q  Seq
                                           (sec)         (ms)        Cnt Num
1   10.1.23.2               Se0/0/1        11 00:19:53    31    200  0  6
0   10.1.13.1               Se0/0/0        10 00:19:53    32    200  0  6
! On Router R2: !!!!!!!!!!!!!!!!!!!!!!!!!!!!!!!!!!!!!!!!!!!!!!!!
R2#show ip eigrp topology
IP-EIGRP Topology Table for AS(1)/ID(10.1.222.2)


Codes: P - Passive, A - Active, U - Update, Q - Query, R - Reply,
       r - reply Status, s - sia Status


P 10.1.13.0/30, 2 successors, FD is 2681856
        via 10.1.23.1 (2681856/2169856), Serial0/0/0
        via 10.1.12.1 (2681856/2169856), Serial0/0/1
P 10.1.12.0/30, 1 successors, FD is 2169856
        via Connected, Serial0/0/1
P 10.1.3.0/26, 1 successors, FD is 2172416
        via 10.1.23.1 (2172416/28160), Serial0/0/0
P 10.1.2.0/25, 1 successors, FD is 28160
        via Connected, FastEthernet0/0
```

```
P 10.1.1.0/24, 1 successors, FD is 2172416
         via 10.1.12.1 (2172416/28160), Serial0/0/1
P 10.1.23.0/30, 1 successors, FD is 2169856
         via Connected, Serial0/0/0
P 192.168.9.0/24, 1 successors, FD is 2172416
         via 10.1.12.1 (2172416/28160), Serial0/0/1
! On Router R3: !!!!!!!!!!!!!!!!!!!!!!!!!!!!!!!!!!!!!!!!!!!!!
R3#show ip route
Codes: C - connected, S - static, R - RIP, M - mobile, B - BGP
       D - EIGRP, EX - EIGRP external, O - OSPF, IA - OSPF inter area
       N1 - OSPF NSSA external type 1, N2 - OSPF NSSA external type 2
       E1 - OSPF external type 1, E2 - OSPF external type 2
       i - IS-IS, su - IS-IS summary, L1 - IS-IS level-1, L2 - IS-IS level-2
       ia - IS-IS inter area, * - candidate default, U - per-user static route
       o - ODR, P - periodic downloaded static route


Gateway of last resort is not set


D    192.168.9.0/24 [90/2172416] via 10.1.13.1, 00:19:55, Serial0/0/0
     10.0.0.0/8 is variably subnetted, 6 subnets, 4 masks
C        10.1.13.0/30 is directly connected, Serial0/0/0
D        10.1.12.0/30 [90/2681856] via 10.1.23.2, 00:19:55, Serial0/0/1
                      [90/2681856] via 10.1.13.1, 00:19:55, Serial0/0/0
C        10.1.3.0/26 is directly connected, FastEthernet0/0
D        10.1.2.0/25 [90/2172416] via 10.1.23.2, 00:19:55, Serial0/0/1
D        10.1.1.0/24 [90/2172416] via 10.1.13.1, 00:19:55, Serial0/0/0
C        10.1.23.0/30 is directly connected, Serial0/0/1
```

To verify the interfaces on which EIGRP is enabled, both the **show ip eigrp interfaces** command (shown on R1), and the **show ip protocols** command (shown on R2) list the information. Later in this chapter, in the "Preventing Unwanted Neighbors Using Passive Interfaces" section, the discussion around the **passive-interface** EIGRP configuration subcommand shows an example of how one command lists passive EIGRP interfaces, and the other does not. For this example, look at the list of interfaces in R2's **show ip protocols** command output: S0/0/0, S0/0/1, and FA0/0 are listed, but Fa0/1—unmatched by any of R2's **network** commands—is not.

In this design, each router should form a neighbor relationship with the other two routers, in each case over a point-to-point serial link. The **show ip eigrp neighbors** command (on R3) confirms R3's neighbors.

Finally, one design goal was for all routers to have routes for all subnets/networks. You could move on to the **show ip route** command or first look for all prefixes in the **show ip eigrp topology** command. With relatively general requirements, just looking at the IP routing table is fine. The example highlights R3's topology data and IP route for subnet 10.1.1.0/24. Of more interest might be the fact that the **show ip route** command output on

R3 lists all subnet/network numbers except one: subnet 10.1.22.0/27. This subnet exists off R2's Fa0/1 interface, which is the interface on which EIGRP has not yet been enabled.

Internals Review

To complete the review of prerequisite CCNA-level EIGRP knowledge, this section looks at a few of the internals of EIGRP. Some of the facts listed here simply need to be memorized, whereas other topics will be discussed in more detail in the next several chapters.

EIGRP follows three general steps to add routes to the IP routing table, as follows:

Step 1. **Neighbor discovery:** EIGRP routers send Hello messages to discover potential neighboring EIGRP routers and perform basic parameter checks to determine which routers should become neighbors.

Step 2. **Topology Exchange:** Neighbors exchange full topology updates when the neighbor relationship comes up, and then only partial updates as needed based on changes to the network topology.

Step 3. **Choosing Routes:** Each router analyzes their respective EIGRP topology tables, choosing the lowest-metric route to reach each subnet.

Because the majority of the rest of this chapter examines EIGRP neighborships, this review section skips any discussion of EIGRP neighbors, instead focusing on the second and third items in the preceding list.

Exchanging Topology Information

Each of these steps may cause a router to update one of three key tables used by EIGRP. First, the EIGRP neighbor table lists the neighboring routers. Second, the EIGRP topology table holds all the topology information learned from EIGRP neighbors. Finally, EIGRP chooses the best IP routes and places those into the IP routing table. (Table 2-2 earlier in this chapter lists the **show** commands that can be used to examine these tables.) EIGRP routers follow the process shown in Figure 2-2 to build the necessary information in these tables, with the end goal of populating the IP routing table.

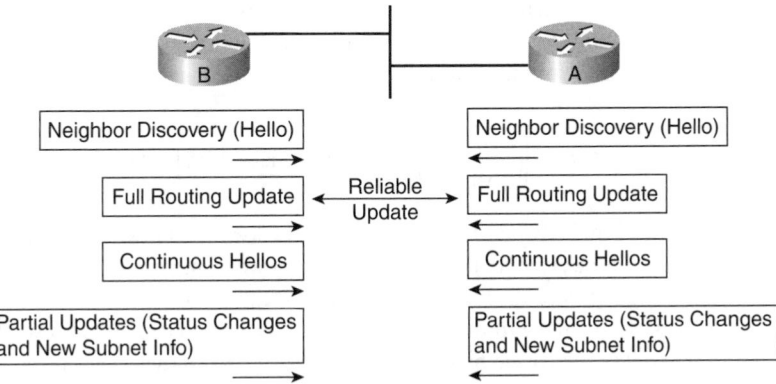

Figure 2-2 *EIGRP Discovery and Update Process*

EIGRP uses *Update messages* to send topology information to neighbors. These Update messages can be sent to multicast IP address 224.0.0.10 if the sending router needs to update multiple routers on the same subnet. Unlike OSPF, there is no concept of a designated router (DR) or backup designated router (BDR), but the use of multicast packets on LANs allows EIGRP to exchange routing information with all neighbors on the LAN efficiently.

The update messages are sent using the *Reliable Transport Protocol (RTP)*. The significance of RTP is that, like OSPF, EIGRP resends routing updates that are lost in transit. By using RTP to guarantee delivery of the EIGRP messages, EIGRP can better avoid loops.

Note: The acronym RTP also refers to a different protocol, Real-time Transport Protocol (RTP), which is used to transmit voice and video IP packets.

Neighbors use both full routing updates and partial updates as depicted in Figure 2-2. A full update means that a router sends information about all known routes, whereas a partial update includes only information about recently changed routes. Full updates occur when neighbors first come up. After that, the neighbors send only partial updates in reaction to changes to a route.

Calculating the Best Routes for the Routing Table

EIGRP topology information includes the subnet number and mask, along with the components of the EIGRP composite metric. Each router then calculates an integer metric for each route, using the individual values of the EIGRP metric components listed in the EIGRP topology database. By default, EIGRP only uses the bandwidth and delay settings when calculating the metric. Optionally, the calculation can also include interface load and interface reliability, although Cisco recommends against using either.

Note: Past documents and books often stated that EIGRP, and its predecessor IGRP, also could use MTU as a part of the metric, but MTU cannot be used and was never considered as part of the calculation. However, the MTU is listed in the EIGRP Update messages.

EIGRP calculates the metric for each possible route by inserting the values of the composite metric into a formula. If the choice is made to just use the default parameters of bandwidth and delay the formula is as follows:

$$\text{Metric} = \left(\left(\frac{10^7}{\text{least-bandwidth}} \right) + \text{cumulative-delay} \right) * 256$$

In this formula, the term *least-bandwidth* represents the lowest-bandwidth link in the route, using a unit of kilobits per second. For instance, if the slowest link in a route is a 10 Mbps Ethernet link, the first part of the formula is $10^7 / 10^4$, because 10 Mbps equals 10,000 Kbps, or 10^4 Kbps. You use 10^4 in the formula because 10 Mbps is equal to 10,000 kbps (10^4 kbps). The *cumulative-delay* value used by the formula is the sum of all the delay values for all links in the route, with a unit of "tens of microseconds." You can set both bandwidth and delay for each link, using the **bandwidth** and **delay** interface subcommands.

Table 2-3 summarizes some of the key facts about EIGRP.

This completes the CCNA-level EIGRP review. The rest of this chapter now examines EIGRP neighbor relationships.

Key Topic

Table 2-3   *EIGRP Feature Summary*

Feature	Description
Transport	IP, protocol type 88 (does not use UDP or TCP).
Metric	Based on constrained bandwidth and cumulative delay by default, and optionally load and reliability.
Hello interval	Interval at which a router sends EIGRP Hello messages on an interface.
Hold Timer	Timer used to determine when a neighboring router has failed, based on a router not receiving any EIGRP messages, including Hellos, in this timer period.
Update destination address	Normally sent to 224.0.0.10, with retransmissions being sent to each neighbor's unicast IP address. Can also be sent to the neighbor's unicast IP address.
Full or partial updates	Full updates are used when new neighbors are discovered; otherwise, partial updates are used.
Authentication	Supports MD5 authentication only.
VLSM/classless	EIGRP includes the mask with each route, also allowing it to support discontiguous networks and VLSM.
Route Tags	Allows EIGRP to tag routes as they are redistributed into EIGRP.
Next-hop field	Supports the advertisement of routes with a different next-hop router than the advertising router.
Manual route summarization	Allows route summarization at any point in the EIGRP network.
Automatic Summarization	EIGRP supports, and defaults to use, automatic route summarization at classful network boundaries.
Multiprotocol	Supports the advertisement of IPX and AppleTalk routes, and IP Version 6, which is discussed in Chapter 17 of this book.

EIGRP Neighborships

Like OSPF, EIGRP uses three major steps to achieve its goal of learning the best available loop-free routes:

Step 1. Establish EIGRP neighbor relationships—*neighborships*—with other routers that share a common subnet.

Step 2. Exchange EIGRP topology data with those neighbors.

Step 3. Calculate the currently best IP route for each subnet, based on the known EIGRP topology data, and add those best routes to the IP routing table.

This three-step process hinges on the first step—the successful creation of neighbor relationships between EIGRP routers. The basic EIGRP configuration described earlier in this chapter, particularly the **network** command, most directly tells EIGRP on which interfaces to dynamically discover neighbors. After EIGRP neighborships have been formed with neighboring routers that are reachable through those interfaces, the final two steps occur without any additional direct configuration.

EIGRP dynamically discovers neighbors by sending EIGRP Hello messages on each EIGRP-enabled interface. When two routers hear EIGRP Hello messages from each other, they check the EIGRP parameters listed in those messages and decide whether the two routers should or should not become neighbors.

The rest of this section focuses on topics related to EIGRP neighborship, specifically:

- Manipulating EIGRP Hello and Hold Timers

- Controlling whether routers become neighbors by using either passive interfaces or statically defined neighbors

- Authenticating EIGRP neighbors

- Examining configuration settings that can prevent EIGRP neighborships

Manipulating EIGRP Hello and Hold Timers

The word *convergence* defines the overall process by which routers notice internetwork topology changes, communicate about those changes, and change their routing tables to contain only the best currently working routes. EIGRP converges very quickly even with all default settings.

One of the slower components of the EIGRP convergence process relates to the timers EIGRP neighbors use to recognize that the neighborship has failed. If the interface over which the neighbor is reachable fails, and IOS changes the interface state to anything other than "up/up", then a router immediately knows that the neighborship should fail. However, in some cases, the interface state may stay "up/up" during times when the link may not be usable. In such cases, EIGRP convergence relies on the Hold Timer to expire, which by default on LANs means a 15-second wait. (The default EIGRP hold time with interfaces/subinterfaces with a bandwidth of T1 or slower, with encapsulation of Frame Relay, is 60 seconds.)

The basic operation of these two timers is relatively simple. EIGRP uses the Hello messages in part as a confirmation that the link between the neighbors still works. If a router does not receive a Hello from a neighbor for one entire Hold time, that router considers the neighbor to have failed. For example, with a default LAN setting of Hello of 5, and Hold of 15, the local router sends Hellos every 5 seconds. The neighbor resets its downward-counting Hold Timer to 15 upon receiving a Hello from that neighbor. Under normal operation on a LAN, with defaults, the Hold Timer for a neighbor would vary from 15, down to 10, and then be reset to 15. However, if the Hellos were no longer received for 15 seconds, the neighborship would fail, driving convergence.

To optimize convergence, an engineer could simply reduce the Hello and Hold Timers, accepting insignificant additional overhead, in return for shorter convergence times. These settings can be made per interface/subinterface, and per EIGRP process.

Note: Although expected to be outside the scope of CCNP, EIGRP can also use the Bidirectional Forwarding Detection (BFD) feature that provides a means for subsecond detection of a failure in IP connectivity between two neighboring routers.

Configuring the Hello/Hold Timers

Most design engineers would normally choose Hello/Hold Timers that match on all router interfaces on a subnet. However, these settings do not have to match. More interestingly, by setting the Hello and Hold Timers to nondefault values, you can see some oddities with the configuration of these values.

For example, consider four WAN distribution routers, as shown in Figure 2-3. These routers may each have a number of Frame Relay PVCs to remote branches, or multiple MPLS VPN connections to branches. However, to communicate with each other and with data centers at the home office, these four routers connect via a core VLAN/subnet. Note that the design shows routers, rather than Layer 3 switches, but the concept applies the same in either case.

Note: All IP addresses begin with 172.16.1

Figure 2-3 *Four WAN Distribution Routers on the Same VLAN/Subnet*

A design that hoped to speed EIGRP convergence might call for setting the Hello and Hold Timers to 2 and 6, respectively. (The Hold Timer does not have to be three times the Hello timer, but the 3:1 ratio is a reasonable guideline.) However, to make an important point about operation of the configuration commands, Example 2-3 sets only R1's Fa0/1 timers to the new values. Note that in this case, EIGRP has already been configured on all four routers, using ASN 9.

Example 2-3   *EIGRP Hello and Hold Timer Configuration—R1*

```
interface Fastethernet0/1
 ip hello-interval eigrp 9 2
 ip hold-time eigrp 9 6
```

A couple of interesting points can be made about the operation of these seemingly simple commands. First, these two settings can be made per interface/subinterface, but not per neighbor. In Figure 2-3, the Example 2-3 configuration then applies on R1 for all three neighbors reachable on interface Fa0/1.

The second interesting point about these commands is that one parameter (the Hello interval) tells R1 what to do, whereas the other (the Hold Timer) actually tells the neighboring routers what to do. As shown in Figure 2-4, **ip hello-interval eigrp 9 2** interface subcommand tells R1 to send Hellos every 2 seconds. However, the **ip hold-time eigrp 9 6** interface subcommand tells R1, again for the EIGRP process with ASN 9, to tell its neighbors to use a Hold Timer of 6 for their respective neighbor relationships with R1. In short, the EIGRP Hello message sent by R1 announces the Hold Timer that other routers should use in the neighbor relationship with R1. Figure 2-4 shows the same idea in graphical form.

Note: IOS does not prevent you from making the unfortunate configuration choice of setting the Hold timer to a value smaller than the Hello interval. In such a case, the neighborship repeatedly fails and recovers, flapping routes in and out of the routing table.

Verifying the Hello/Hold Timers

Interestingly, finding the settings for the Hello interval and Hold time requires more effort than simply using a **show** command. A router's Hello timer can be seen with the **show ip eigrp interface** *type number* **detail** command, but this command does not display a router's Hold Timer on the interface. You can of course look at a router's configuration, but the **show running-config** command may not be available to you on some question types on the ROUTE exam. However, if you have access to only user mode, you can typically make a good guess as to the settings by repeatedly using the **show ip eigrp neighbors** command. This command shows the current value of the Hold Timer for each neighbor. By repeating the command during times when everything is working, and observing the range of values, you should be able to infer each router's Hello and Hold Timer settings.

Example 2-4 shows examples of the command output on R1, R2, and R3. Note that the Hello and Hold Timer settings on R1 are all between 10—15 seconds, because the timers

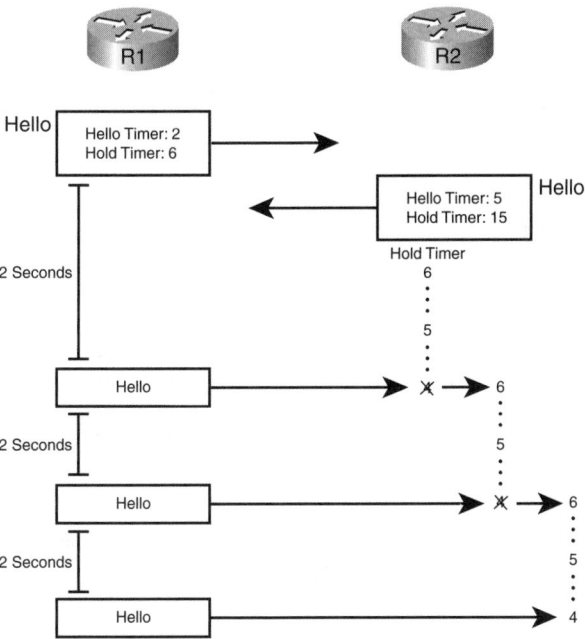

Figure 2-4 *R1 Announcing New Hello and Hold Timers*

on R2, R3, and R4 all still default to 5 and 15 seconds, respectively. R2's neighborship with R1 lists a Hold Timer of 4, which is within the expected range from 6 to 4 seconds remaining.

Example 2-4 *Demonstration that R2 and R3 Use R1's Configured Hold Timer*

```
! On Router R1: !!!!!!!!!!!!!!!!!!!!!!!!!!!!!!!!!!!!!!!!!!!!!!
R1#show ip eigrp interfaces detail fa0/1
IP-EIGRP interfaces for process 9

                       Xmit Queue   Mean   Pacing Time   Multicast    Pending
Interface      Peers  Un/Reliable   SRTT   Un/Reliable  Flow Timer    Routes
Fa0/1            3       0/0        535       0/1           50           0
  Hello interval is 2 sec
  Next xmit serial <none>
  Un/reliable mcasts: 0/1  Un/reliable ucasts: 4/9
  Mcast exceptions: 1  CR packets: 1  ACKs suppressed: 1
  Retransmissions sent: 2  Out-of-sequence rcvd: 0
  Authentication mode is not set
  Use multicast


R1#show ip eigrp neighbors
IP-EIGRP neighbors for process 9
```

```
H   Address                 Interface        Hold Uptime   SRTT   RTO  Q  Seq
                                             (sec)         (ms)      Cnt Num
2   172.16.1.4              Fa0/1            11 00:03:17  1596   5000  0  7
1   172.16.1.3              Fa0/1            11 00:05:21     1    200  0  5
0   172.16.1.2              Fa0/1            13 00:09:04     4    200  0  2
! On Router R2: !!!!!!!!!!!!!!!!!!!!!!!!!!!!!!!!!!!!!!!!!!!!
R2#show ip eigrp neighbors
IP-EIGRP neighbors for process 9
H   Address                 Interface        Hold Uptime   SRTT   RTO  Q  Seq
                                             (sec)         (ms)      Cnt Num
2   172.16.1.4              Fa0/1            11 00:03:36     4    200  0  6
1   172.16.1.3              Fa0/1            11 00:05:40    12    200  0  4
0   172.16.1.1              Fa0/1             4 00:09:22     1    200  0  2
! On Router R3: !!!!!!!!!!!!!!!!!!!!!!!!!!!!!!!!!!!!!!!!!!!!
R3#show ip eigrp neighbors
IP-EIGRP neighbors for process 9
H   Address                 Interface        Hold Uptime   SRTT   RTO  Q  Seq
                                             (sec)         (ms)      Cnt Num
2   172.16.1.4              Fa0/1            11 00:03:40     4    200  0  5
1   172.16.1.1              Fa0/1             5 00:05:44  1278   5000  0  4
0   172.16.1.2              Fa0/1            13 00:05:44  1277   5000  0  4
```

Preventing Unwanted Neighbors Using Passive Interfaces

When an EIGRP **network** configuration subcommand matches an interface, EIGRP on that router does two things:

Step 1. Attempts to find potential EIGRP neighbors by sending Hellos to the 224.0.0.10 multicast address

Step 2. Advertises about the subnet connected to that interface

In some cases, however, no legitimate EIGRP neighbors may exist off an interface. For example, consider the small internetwork of Figure 2-5, with three routers, and with only one router connected to each LAN interface. Each router needs to advertise about the subnets connected to their various FastEthernet interfaces, but at the same time, there is no benefit to multicast EIGRP Hellos on those interfaces because only one router connects to each LAN.

The network designer may reasonably choose to limit EIGRP on those interfaces that have no legitimate EIGRP neighbors. However, the subnets connected to those same interfaces also typically need to be advertised by EIGRP. For example, subnet 10.1.1.0/24, off R1's Fa0/0 interface, still needs to be advertised by EIGRP, even though R1 should never find an EIGRP neighbor on that interface.

Note: All IP addresses begin with 10.1 unless otherwise noted.

Figure 2-5   *LAN Interfaces That Benefit from the Passive Interface Feature*

Given such a requirement—to advertise about the subnet, but disallow EIGRP neighbor-ships on the interface—an engineer has two main configuration options to add to the implementation plan:

Step 1.   Enable EIGRP on the interface using the EIGRP **network** command, but tell the router to not send any EIGRP messages on the interface by making the interface passive (using the **passive-interface** command).

Step 2.   Do not enable EIGRP on the interface, and advertise about the connected route using route redistribution (and the **redistribute connected** configuration command).

The first option relies on the passive interface feature—a feature specifically created with this design requirement in mind. When an interface is passive, EIGRP does not send any EIGRP messages on the interface—multicasts or EIGRP unicasts—and the router ignores any EIGRP messages received on the interface. However, EIGRP still advertises about the connected subnets if matched with an EIGRP **network** command. As a result, the first option in the preceding list directly meets all design requirements. It has the added advantage of being very secure in that no EIGRP neighborships are possible on the interface.

The second option—redistributing connected subnets—also works, but frankly it is the less preferred option in this case. The passive interface option clearly meets the requirement, plus the redistribution process means that EIGRP advertises the connected route as an external EIGRP route, which could cause problems in some cases with multiple redistribution points between routing domains (as discussed in Chapter 10, "Advanced IGP Redistribution").

The configuration of passive-interface itself is somewhat straightforward. To configure the **passive-interface** option, these three routers could be configured as follows in Example 2-5.

Example 2-5 *Configuration of* **passive-interface** *Commands on R1, R2, and R3*

```
! On Router R1: !!!!!!!!!!!!!!!!!!!!!!!!!!!!!!!!!!!!!!!!!!!!
router eigrp 1
 passive-interface fastethernet0/0
 passive-interface fastethernet0/1
 network 10.0.0.0
 network 192.168.9.0
! On Router R2: !!!!!!!!!!!!!!!!!!!!!!!!!!!!!!!!!!!!!!!!!!!!
router eigrp 1
 passive-interface default
 no Passive-interface serial0/0/0
 no Passive-interface serial0/0/0
 network 10.0.0.0
! On Router R3: !!!!!!!!!!!!!!!!!!!!!!!!!!!!!!!!!!!!!!!!!!!!
router eigrp 1
 passive-interface fastethernet0/0
 network 10.0.0.0
```

R1's configuration lists two **passive-interface** commands, one per LAN interface. As a result, R1 no longer sends EIGRP messages at all on these two interfaces, including the multicast EIGRP Hellos used to discover neighbors.

R2's configuration uses a slightly different option: the **passive-interface default** command. This command essentially changes the default for an interface from not being passive to instead being passive. Then, to make an interface not passive, you have to use a **no** version of the **passive-interface** command for those interfaces.

Two commands help to verify that the passive interface design is working properly. First, the **show ip eigrp interfaces** command omits passive interfaces, listing the nonpassive interfaces matched by a **network** command. Alternatively, the **show ip protocols** command explicitly lists all passive interfaces. Example 2-6 shows samples of both commands on R2.

Example 2-6   *Verifying the Results of* **passive-interface** *on R2*

```
R2#show ip eigrp interfaces
IP-EIGRP interfaces for process 1


                        Xmit Queue   Mean   Pacing Time   Multicast   Pending
Interface       Peers   Un/Reliable  SRTT   Un/Reliable   Flow Timer  Routes
Se0/0/0           1        0/0         32       0/15          159        0
Se0/0/1           1        0/0        1290      0/15         6443        0
R2#show ip protocols
Routing Protocol is "eigrp 1"
  Outgoing update filter list for all interfaces is not set
  Incoming update filter list for all interfaces is not set
  Default networks flagged in outgoing updates
  Default networks accepted from incoming updates
  EIGRP metric weight K1=1, K2=0, K3=1, K4=0, K5=0
  EIGRP maximum hopcount 100
  EIGRP maximum metric variance 1
  Redistributing: eigrp 1
  EIGRP NSF-aware route hold timer is 240s
  Automatic network summarization is in effect
  Maximum path: 4
  Routing for Networks:
    10.0.0.0
  Passive Interface(s):
    FastEthernet0/0
    FastEthernet0/1
  Routing Information Sources:
    Gateway         Distance      Last Update
    10.1.12.1            90       00:00:39
    10.1.23.1            90       00:00:39
  Distance: internal 90 external 170
```

Controlling Neighborships Using EIGRP Authentication

EIGRP authentication causes routers to authenticate every EIGRP message. To do so, the routers should use the same preshared key (PSK), generating an MD5 digest for each EIGRP message based on that shared PSK. If a router configured for EIGRP authentication receives an EIGRP message, and the message's MD5 digest does not pass the authentication checking based on the local copy of the key, the router silently discards the message. As a result, when authentication fails, two routers cannot become EIGRP neighbors, because they ignore the EIGRP Hello messages.

From a design perspective, EIGRP authentication helps prevent denial of service (DoS) attacks, but it does not provide any privacy. The EIGRP messages can be read by the device that physically receives the bits. Note that on LANs, the updates flow to the 224.0.0.10 multicast IP address, so any attacker could join the 224.0.0.10 multicast group and read the packets. However, authentication prevents attackers from forming neighborships with legitimate routers, preventing the advertisement of incorrect routing information.

Next, this section examines EIGRP authentication configuration generically, followed by a deeper look at the time-based authentication configuration settings, and finally showing an example of EIGRP authentication configuration.

EIGRP Authentication Configuration Checklist

The EIGRP authentication configuration process requires several commands, which are summarized as follows:

Key Topic

Step 1. Create an (authentication) key chain:

Create the chain and give it a name with the **key chain** *name* global command (also puts the user into key chain config mode). The name does not have to match on the neighboring routers.

Create one or more key numbers using the **key** *number* command in key chain configuration mode. The key numbers do not have to match on the neighboring routers.

Define the authentication key's value using the **key-string** *value* command in key configuration mode. The key strings must match on the neighboring routers.

(Optional) Define the lifetime (time period) for both sending and accepting each key string.

Step 2. Enable EIGRP MD5 authentication on an interface, for a particular EIGRP ASN, using the **ip authentication mode eigrp** *asn* **md5** interface subcommand.

Step 3. Refer to the correct key chain to be used on an interface using the **ip authentication key-chain eigrp** *asn name-of-chain* interface subcommand.

The configuration at Step 1 is fairly detailed, but Steps 2 and 3 are relatively simple. Essentially, IOS configures the key values separately (Step 1) and then requires an interface subcommand to refer to the key values. To support the ability to have multiple keys, and even multiple sets of keys, the configuration includes the concept of a key chain and multiple keys on each key chain.

Key Chain Time-Based Logic

The key chain configuration concept, as outlined in Step 1, allows the engineer to migrate from one key value to another over time. Just like a real key chain that has multiple keys, the IOS key chain concept allows the configuration of multiple keys—each identified with a number. If no lifetime has been configured for a key, it is considered to be valid during all time frames. However, when a key has been defined with a lifetime, the key is valid only during the valid lifetime.

The existence of multiple keys in a key chain, and the existence of valid lifetimes for each key, can cause some confusion about when the keys are used. The rules can be summarized as follows:

- **Sending EIGRP messages:** Use the lowest key number among all currently valid keys.

- **Receiving EIGRP message:** Check the MD5 digest using ALL currently valid keys.

For example, consider the case shown in Figure 2-6. The figure represents the logic in a single router, Router R1, both when receiving and sending EIGRP messages on the right. The figure shows a key chain with four keys. All the keys have lifetimes configured. Key 1's lifetime has passed, making it invalid. Key 4's lifetime has yet to begin, making it invalid. However, keys 2 and 3 are both currently valid.

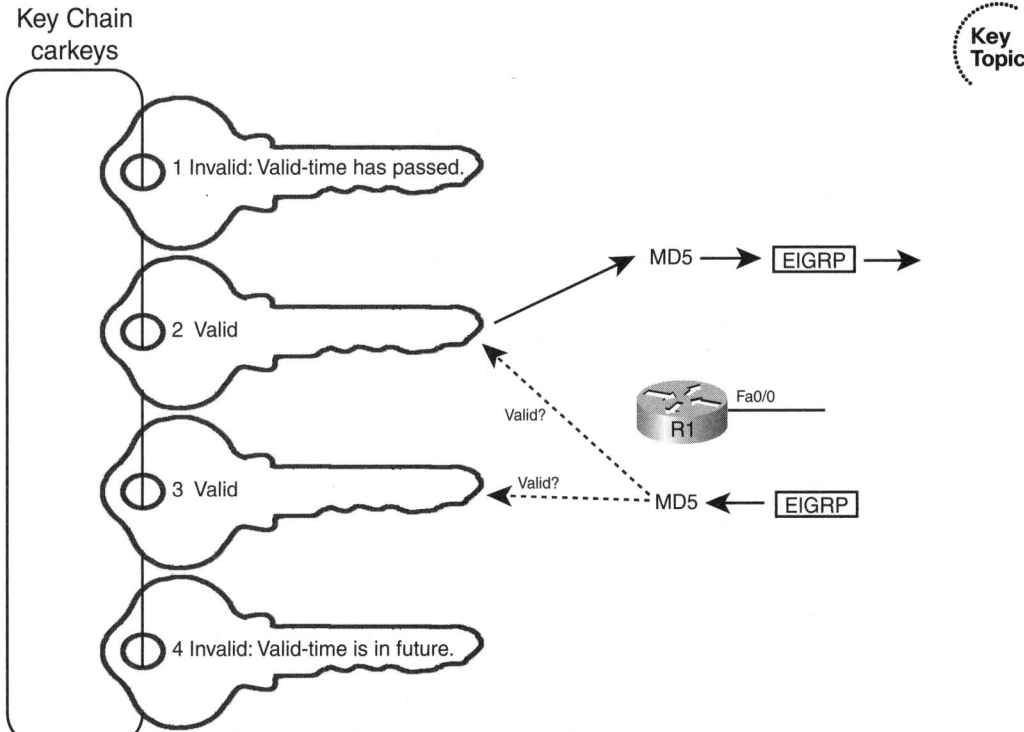

Figure 2-6   *EIGRP's Usage of Authentication Keys*

Figure 2-6 shows that the EIGRP message sent by Router R1 uses key 2, and key 2 only. Keys 1 and 4 are ignored because they are currently invalid; R1 then simply chooses the lowest-numbered key among the two valid keys. The figure also shows that R1 processes the received EIGRP message using both key 2 and key 3, because both are currently valid.

Note: Neighboring EIGRP routers that use authentication should be configured to use NTP to synchronize their time-of-day clocks. For quick tests in a lab, you can just set the time using the **clock set** exec command.

EIGRP Authentication Configuration and Verification Example

Example 2-7 shows a sample configuration, based on the network topology shown back in Figure 2-3 (the figure with four routers connected to a single LAN subnet). Key chain "carkeys" has two keys, each with different lifetimes, so that the router will use new keys automatically over time. The example shows the configuration on a single router, but similar configuration would be required on the other routers as well.

Example 2-7 *EIGRP Authentication Configuration on R1*

```
! Chain "carkeys" will be used on R1's Fa0/1 interface. R1 will use key "fred" for
! about a month, and then start using "wilma."
key chain carkeys
 key 1
  key-string fred
  accept-lifetime 08:00:00 Feb 11 2009 08:00:00 Mar 11 2009
  send-lifetime 08:00:00 Feb 11 2009 08:00:00 Mar 11 2009
 key 2
  key-string wilma
  accept-lifetime 08:00:00 Mar 11 2009 08:00:00 Apr 11 2009
  send-lifetime 08:00:00 Mar 11 2009 08:00:00 Apr 11 2009

! Next, R1's interface subcommands are shown. First, the key chain is referenced
! using the ip authentication key-chain command, and the ip authentication mode
eigrp
! command causes the router to use an MD5 digest of the key string.
interface FastEthernet0/1
 ip address 172.16.1.1 255.255.255.0
 ip authentication mode eigrp 9 md5
 ip authentication key-chain eigrp 9 carkeys
```

The best method to confirm the authentication worked is to verify that the neighbors remain up using the **show ip eigrp neighbors** command. However, if some neighbors do not remain active, and a problem exists, two commands in particular can be helpful: **show key chain** and **debug eigrp packet**. The first of these commands lists the key chain configuration and also lists which keys are valid right now—a key consideration when troubleshooting EIGRP authentication. The **debug** command lists a message regarding why neighboring routers have failed the authentication process.

Example 2-8 shows a sample output from each of these two commands. Note that in this case, again from Figure 2-3:

■ R1 and R2 have been configured to use MD5 authentication, but a typo exists in R2's key string.

■ R3 and R4 have not yet been configured for MD5 authentication.

Example 2-8 *EIGRP Authentication Verification on R1*

```
R1#show key chain
Key-chain carkeys:
    key 1 — text "fred"
```

```
        accept lifetime (08:00:00 UTC Feb 11 2009) - (08:00:00 UTC Mar 11 2009)
        send lifetime (08:00:00 UTC Feb 11 2009) - (08:00:00 UTC Mar 11 2009)
    key 2 - text "wilma"
        accept lifetime (08:00:00 UTC Mar 11 2009) - (08:00:00 UTC Apr 11 2009)
[valid now]
        send lifetime (08:00:00 UTC Mar 11 2009) - (08:00:00 UTC Apr 11 2009)
[valid now]
R1#debug eigrp packet
EIGRP Packets debugging is on
    (UPDATE, REQUEST, QUERY, REPLY, HELLO, IPXSAP, PROBE, ACK, STUB, SIAQUERY,
SIAREPLY)
R1#
Apr  1 08:09:01.951: EIGRP: Sending HELLO on FastEthernet0/1
Apr  1 08:09:01.951:    AS 9, Flags 0x0, Seq 0/0 idbQ 0/0 iidbQ un/rely 0/0
Apr  1 08:09:01.967: EIGRP: pkt key id = 2, authentication mismatch
Apr  1 08:09:01.967: EIGRP: FastEthernet0/1: ignored packet from 172.16.1.2,
opcode = 5 (invalid authentication)
Apr  1 08:09:02.287: EIGRP: FastEthernet0/1: ignored packet from 172.16.1.4,
opcode = 5 (missing authentication)
Apr  1 08:09:03.187: EIGRP: FastEthernet0/1: ignored packet from 172.16.1.3, opcode
= 5 (missing authentication)
```

In particular, note that the different highlighted phrasing in the debug output implies different problems. From 172.16.1.2 (R2), the message "invalid authentication" implies that the MD5 digest existed in the message, but was invalid. With the message "missing authentication," the meaning is that the message did not include an MD5 digest.

Also, when troubleshooting EIGRP authentication, keep the following in mind:

Key
Topic

■   Examine the configuration and the current time (**show clock**) on both routers.

■   The key chain name and key number used on the two routers do not have to match.

■   The key string on each of the two potential neighbors must match.

■   Check which keys are currently valid using the **show key chain** command.

■   Both the **ip authentication mode eigrp** *asn* **md5** interface subcommand and the **ip authentication key-chain eigrp** *asn name-of-chain* interface subcommand must be configured on the interface; if one is omitted, authentication fails.

Controlling Neighborships with Static Configuration

EIGRP supports the ability to statically define neighbors instead of dynamically discovering neighbors.

Although seldom used, you can use this feature to reduce the overhead associated with EIGRP multicast messages. Frame Relay WANs in particular may benefit from the static neighbor definitions because to support multicasts and broadcasts over Frame Relay, a router must replicate the frame and send a copy over every PVC associated with the interface or subinterface. For example, if a multicast subinterface has 10 PVCs associated with it, but only two of the remote routers used EIGRP, without static neighbors, all 10 routers would be sent a copy of the EIGRP multicast Hello packets. With static neighbor definitions for the two routers, EIGRP messages would be sent as unicasts to each of the two neighbors, with no EIGRP messages sent to the eight non-EIGRP routers, reducing overhead.

The configuration seems simple, but it has a few subtle caveats. This section examines the straightforward configuration first and then examines the caveats.

Configuring Static EIGRP Neighbors

To define a neighbor, both routers must configure the **neighbor** *ip-address outgoing-interface* EIGRP router subcommand. The IP address is the interface IP address of the neighboring router. Also, the configured IP address must be from the subnet connected to the interface listed in the **neighbor** command; otherwise, the command is rejected. Also, note that the EIGRP configuration does not have to include a **network** command that matches the interface; EIGRP will still advertise about the subnet connected to the interface.

For example, consider Figure 2-7, which adds a new router (R5) to the internetwork of Figure 2-3. R1 and R5 have a PVC connecting them, with IP addresses and subinterface numbers shown.

Figure 2-7 *Adding a Branch, with a Static EIGRP Neighbor*

Example 2-9 shows the configuration on both R1 and R5 to use static neighbor definitions. Of note, R1's **neighbor** command refers to R5's IP address on their common subnet (10.10.15.5), with R1's local interface (S0/0/0.5). R5 lists the reverse, with R1's 10.10.15.1 IP address, and R5's local S0/0.1 interface. Also note that neither router has a **network** command that references network 10.0.0.0, but they do advertise about subnet 10.10.15.0/29.

Example 2-9 *Static EIGRP Neighborship Between R1 and R5*

```
! New configuration on router R1
R1#show running-config
! lines omitted
router eigrp 9
 network 172.16.0.0
 no auto-summary
 Neighbor 10.10.15.5 Serial0/0/0.5
! R5's new config added to support the neighbor
R5#show running-config
! lines omitted
router eigrp 9
 no auto-summary
 neighbor 10.10.15.1 Serial0/0.1
! Back to R1
R1#show ip eigrp neighbors detail
IP-EIGRP neighbors for process 9
H   Address                   Interface      Hold Uptime    SRTT   RTO  Q  Seq
                                             (sec)          (ms)      Cnt Num
3   10.10.15.5                Se0/0/0.5      10 00:00:51    15    200  0  2
    Static neighbor
    Version 12.4/1.2, Retrans: 0, Retries: 0
2   172.16.1.2                Fa0/1          11 00:02:57    3     200  0  25
    Version 12.4/1.2, Retrans: 1, Retries: 0
1   172.16.1.3                Fa0/1          10 00:03:45    5     200  0  21
    Version 12.4/1.2, Retrans: 0, Retries: 0
0   172.16.1.4                Fa0/1          13 00:03:45    5    200  0  18
```

The **show ip eigrp neighbors** command does not identify a neighbor as static, but the **show ip eigrp neighbors detail** command does. Example 2-9 shows the more detailed output near the end, with the designation of 10.10.15.5 (R5) as a static neighbor.

Caveat When Using EIGRP Static Neighbors

IOS changes how it processes EIGRP packets on any interface referenced by an EIGRP **neighbor** command. Keeping in mind the design goal for this feature—to reduce multicasts—IOS disables all EIGRP multicast packet processing on an interface when an EIGRP **neighbor** command has been configured. For example, in Example 2-9, R1's S0/0/0.5 subinterface will not process EIGRP multicast packets any more as a result of R1's **neighbor 10.10.5.5 Serial0/0/0.5** EIGRP subcommand.

Because of the operation of the EIGRP **neighbor** command, if at least one EIGRP static neighbor is defined on an interface, no dynamic neighbors can be either discovered or continue to work if already discovered. For example, again in Figure 2-7 and Example 2-9, if R1 added a **neighbor 172.16.1.5 FastEthernet0/1** EIGRP subcommand, R1 would lose its current neighborships with Routers R2, R3, and R4.

Configuration Settings That Could Prevent Neighbor Relationships

Some of the configuration settings already mentioned in this chapter, when configured incorrectly, may prevent EIGRP neighborships. This section summarizes those settings, and introduces a few other configuration settings that can prevent neighbor relationships. The list of items that must match—and that do not have to match—can be a useful place to start troubleshooting neighbor initialization problems in real life, and to troubleshoot neighborship problems for Sim questions on the CCNP ROUTE exam.

Table 2-4 lists the neighbor requirements for both EIGRP and OSPF. (OSPF is included here just as a frame of reference for those more familiar with OSPF; this information will be repeated in Chapter 5, "OSPF Overview and Neighbor Relationships," which discusses OSPF neighborship requirements.) Following the table, the next few pages examine some of these settings for EIGRP.

Key Topic

Table 2-4 *Neighbor Requirements for EIGRP and OSPF*

Requirement	EIGRP	OSPF
The routers must be able to send/receive IP packets to one another.	Yes	Yes
Interfaces' primary IP addresses must be in same subnet.	Yes	Yes
Must not be passive on the connected interface.	Yes	Yes
Must use the same ASN (EIGRP) or process-ID (OSPF) on the **router** configuration command.	Yes	No
Hello interval/timer, plus either the Hold (EIGRP) or Dead (OSPF) timer, must match.	No	Yes
Must pass neighbor authentication (if configured).	Yes	Yes
Must be in same area.	N/A	Yes
IP MTU must match.	No	Yes
K-values (used in metric calculation) must match.	Yes	N/A
Router IDs must be unique.	No[1]	Yes

[1]Duplicate EIGRP RIDs do not prevent routers from becoming neighbors, but it can cause problems when adding external EIGRP routes to the routing table.

Going through Table 2-4 sequentially, the first two items (highlighted) relate to IP connectivity. Two routers must be able to send and receive IP packets with each other. Additionally, the primary IP address on the interfaces—in other words, the IP address configured *without* the secondary keyword on the **ip address** command—must be in the same subnet.

Note: It should not matter for CCNP ROUTE, but possibly for CCIE: EIGRP's rules about neighbor IP addresses being in the same subnet are less exact than OSPF. OSPF requires matching subnet numbers and masks. EIGRP just asks the question of whether the neighbor's IP address is in the range of addresses for the subnet as known to the local router. For example, two routers with addresses of 10.1.1.1/24 (range 10.1.1.1–10.1.1.254) and 10.1.1.2/30 (range 10.1.1.1–10.1.1.2) would actually allow EIGRP neighborship, because each router believes the neighbor's IP address to be in the same subnet as the local router.

The next four items in Table 2-4 (unhighlighted)—passive interfaces, matching the EIGRP ASN number, allowing mismatching Hello/Hold Timers, and authentication—have already been covered in this chapter, and do not require any further discussion.

The next two (highlighted) items in the table—matching the IP MTU and matching OSPF areas—do not prevent EIGRP neighborships. These topics, are requirements for OSPF neighborship and will be discussed in Chapter 5.

Finally, the last two items (unhighlighted) in the table (K-values and router-id) each require more than a cursory discussion for EIGRP and will be explained in the upcoming pages.

Configuring EIGRP Metric Components (K-values)

EIGRP calculates its integer metric, by default, using a formula that uses constraining bandwidth and cumulative delay. You can change the formula to use link reliability, link load, and even disable the use of bandwidth and/or delay. To change the formula, an engineer can configure five weighting constants, called *k-values*, which are represented in the metric calculation formula as constants k1, k2, k3, k4, and k5.

From a design perspective, Cisco strongly recommends against using link load and link reliability in the EIGRP metric calculation. Most shops that use EIGRP never touch the k-values at all. However, in labs, it can be useful to disable the use of bandwidth from the metric calculation, because that simplifies the metric math, and makes it easier to learn the concepts behind EIGRP.

The mechanics of setting these values (with the **metric weights** EIGRP subcommand) is covered in Chapter 3, in the "Metric Weights (K-values)" section. This command sets 5 variables (k1 through k5), each of which weights the metric calculation formula more or less heavily for various parts of the formula.

Mismatched k-value settings prevent two routers from becoming neighbors. Thankfully, determining if such a mismatch exists is easy. When a router receives an EIGRP Hello with mismatched K-values (as compared to itself), the router issues a log message stating that a k-value mismatch exists. You can also examine the values either by looking at running configuration, or look for the k-values listed in the output of the **show ip protocols** command, as shown in Example 2-10.

Example 2-10   *Mismatched K-values*

```
R2(config)#router eigrp 1
R2(config-router)#metric weights 0 1 0 1 1 0
R2(config-router)#end
Feb 23 18:48:21.599: %DUAL-5-NBRCHANGE: IP-EIGRP(0) 1: Neighbor 10.1.12.1
(Serial0/0/1) is down: metric changed
R2#
Feb 23 18:48:24.907: %DUAL-5-NBRCHANGE: IP-EIGRP(0) 1: Neighbor 10.1.12.1
(Serial0/0/1) is down: K-value mismatch
R2#show ip protocols
Routing Protocol is "eigrp 1"
  Outgoing update filter list for all interfaces is not set
  Incoming update filter list for all interfaces is not set
  Default networks flagged in outgoing updates
  Default networks accepted from incoming updates
  EIGRP metric weight K1=1, K2=0, K3=1, K4=1, K5=0

! lines omitted for brevity
```

EIGRP Router-ID

EIGRP uses a concept of a representing each router with a router ID (RID). The EIGRP RID is a 32-bit number, represented in dotted decimal. Each router determines its RID when the EIGRP process starts, using the same general rules as does OSPF for determining the OSPF RID, as follows:

Step 1.   Use the configured value (using the **eigrp router-id** *a.b.c.d* EIGRP subcommand).

Step 2.   Use the highest IPv4 address on an up/up loopback interface.

Step 3.   Use the highest IPv4 address on an up/up non-loopback interface.

Although EIGRP does require each router to have an RID, the actual value is of little practical importance. The EIGRP **show** commands seldom list the RID value, and unlike for the OSPF RID, engineers do not need to know each router's EIGRP RID to interpret the EIGRP topology database. Additionally, although it is best to make EIGRP RIDs unique, duplicate RIDs do not prevent routers from becoming neighbors.

The only time the value of EIGRP RIDs matters is when injecting external routes into EIGRP. In that case, the routers injecting the external routes must have unique RIDs to avoid confusion.

Neighborship over WANs

EIGRP configuration and neighborship rules do not differ when comparing typical LAN and typical WAN technologies. However, some design and operational differences exist, particularly regarding which routers become neighbors with which other routers. This short section closes the EIGRP neighbor discussion with a brief look at Frame Relay, MPLS VPNs, and Metro Ethernet as implemented with Virtual Private LAN Service (VPLS).

Neighborship on Frame Relay

Frame Relay provides a Layer 2 WAN service. Each router connects to the service using a physical serial link, called a Frame Relay access link. The provider then creates logical connection, called *permanent virtual circuits (PVCs)*, which is a logical path between a pair of routers connected to the Frame Relay service. Any pair of routers that connect to the ends of a Frame Relay PVC can send Frame Relay frames to each other, IP packets, and they can become EIGRP neighbors. Figure 2-8 shows a typical case, with R1 as a central-site router, and R2, R3, and R4 acting as branch routers.

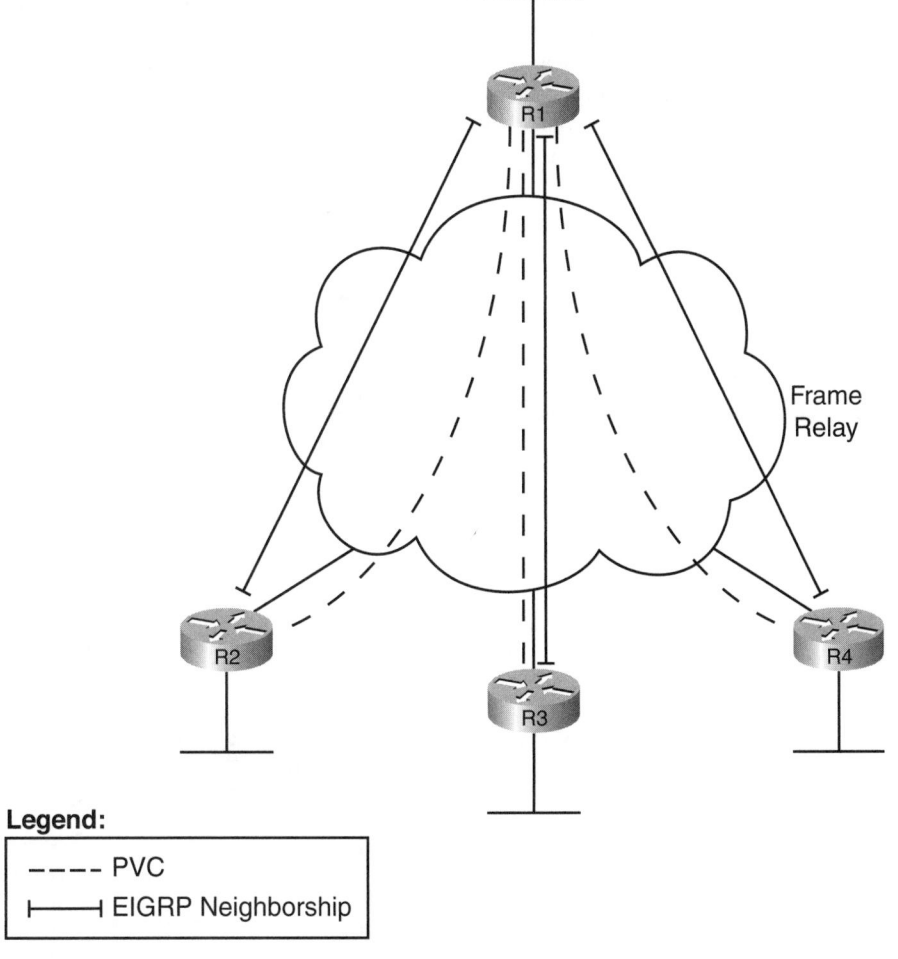

Figure 2-8 *EIGRP Neighborships over Frame Relay*

Figure 2-8 shows EIGRP neighborships, but note that all routers can learn all routes in the internetwork, even though not all routers become neighbors. The neighborships can only form when a PVC exists between the two routers.

Neighborship on MPLS VPN

Multiprotocol Label Switching (MPLS) Virtual Private Networks (VPNs) create a WAN service that has some similarities but many differences when compared to Frame Relay. The customer routers connect to the service, often times with serial links, but other times with Frame Relay PVCs or with Ethernet. The service itself is a Layer 3 service, forwarding IP packets through the cloud. As a result, no pre-defined PVCs need exist between the customer routers. Additionally, the service uses routers at the edge of the service provider cloud—generically called provider edge (PE) routers—and these routers are Layer 3 aware.

That Layer 3 awareness means that the customer edge (CE) routers form an EIGRP neighborship with the PE router on the other end of their local access link, as shown in Figure 2-9. The PE routers exchange their routes, typically using Multiprotocol BGP (MP-BGP), a topic outside the scope of this book. However, all the CE routers then learn routes from each other, although each CE router has only one EIGRP neighborship for each of its connections into the MPLS VPN cloud.

Figure 2-9 *EIGRP Neighborships over MPLS VPN*

Neighborship on Metro Ethernet

The term *Metropolitan Ethernet (MetroE)* represents a range of Layer 2 WAN services in which the CE device connects to the WAN service using some form of Ethernet. Because MetroE provides a Layer 2 Ethernet service, the service delivers an Ethernet frame sent by one customer router to one other customer router (for unitcast frames), or to many other routers (for multicast or broadcast frames).

MetroE encompasses several underlying technologies to create the service. Of note for the purposes of this book are the Virtual Private Wire Service (VPWS) and the Virtual Private LAN Service (VPLS). Both technical specifications allow for connections using Ethernet links, with the service forwarding Ethernet frames. VPWS focuses on point-to-point topologies, whereas VPLS supports multipoint, approximating the concept of the entire WAN service acting like one large Ethernet switch. Because it is a Layer 2 service, MetroE does not have any Layer 3 awareness, and the customer routers (typically referenced as with the more general service provider term *customer premise equipment*, or CPE) see the MetroE service as a VLAN. Because the customer routers connect to the service as a VLAN, all the routers connected to the service can become EIGRP neighbors, as shown in Figure 2-10.

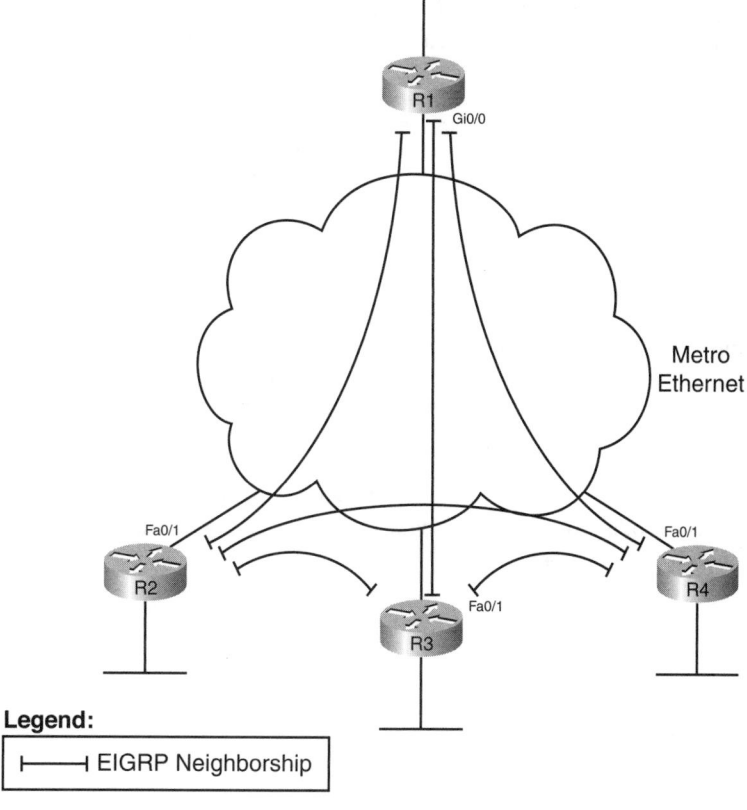

Figure 2-10   *EIGRP Neighborships over Metro Ethernet*

Exam Preparation Tasks

Planning Practice

The CCNP ROUTE exam expects test takers to be able to review design documents, create implementation plans, and create verification plans. This section provides some exercises that may help you to take a step back from the minute details of the topics in this chapter so that you can think about the same technical topics from the planning perspective.

For each planning practice table, simply complete the table. Note that any numbers in parentheses represent the number of options listed for each item in the solutions in Appendix F, "Completed Planning Practice Tables," which you can find on the CD-ROM accompanying this book.

Design Review Table

Table 2-5 lists several design goals related to this chapter. If these design goals were listed in a design document, and you had to take that document and develop an implementation plan, what implementation options come to mind? For any configuration items, a general description can be used, without concern about the specific parameters.

Table 2-5 *Design Review*

Design Goal	Possible Implementation Choices Covered in This Chapter
Improve EIGRP convergence.	
Implement EIGRP on each router so that neighbor-ships are formed (2).	
Limit neighborship formation on interfaces matched with an EIGRP network command (3).	

Implementation Plan Peer Review Table

Table 2-6 shows a list of questions that others might ask, or that you might think about, during a peer review of another network engineer's implementation plan. Complete the table by answering the questions.

Table 2-6 *Notable Questions from This Chapter to Consider During an Implementation Plan Peer Review*

Question	Answer
What happens on a router interface on which an **EIGRP network** command matches the interface? (2)	
What configuration settings prevent EIGRP neighbor discovery on an EIGRP-enabled interface? (2)	
What configuration settings prevent any neighborships on an EIGRP-enabled interface?	
What settings do potential neighbors check before becoming EIGRP neighbors? (5)	
What settings that you might think would impact EIGRP neighbor relationships actually do not prevent neighborship? (3)	
What issues typically arise when the design calls for the use of EIGRP authentication key chains with lifetime settings? (2)	

Create an Implementation Plan Table

To practice skills useful when creating your own EIGRP implementation plan, list in Table 2-7 configuration commands related to the configuration of the following features. You may want to record your answers outside the book, and set a goal to complete this table (and others like it) from memory during your final reviews before taking the exam.

Table 2-7 *Implementation Plan Configuration Memory Drill*

Feature	Configuration Commands/Notes
Enabling EIGRP on interfaces	
Setting Hello and Hold Timers	
EIGRP authentication	
Passive interfaces	
Static EIGRP neighbors	
K-values	
EIGRP router ID	

Choose Commands for a Verification Plan Table

To practice skills useful when creating your own EIGRP verification plan, list in Table 2-8 all commands that supply the requested information. You may want to record your answers outside the book, and set a goal to complete this table (and others like it) from memory during your final reviews before taking the exam.

Table 2-8   *Verification Plan Memory Drill*

Information Needed	Command
Which routes have been added to the IP routing table by EIGRP?	
All routes in a router's routing table.	
The specific route for a single destination address or subnet.	
A list of all (both static and dynamically discovered) EIGRP neighbors.	
Notation of whether a neighbor was dynamically discovered or statically configured.	
Lists statistics regarding the numbers of EIGRP messages sent and received by a router.	
List interfaces on which EIGRP has been enabled (by virtue of the EIGRP **network** command).	
List the number of EIGRP peers known via a particular interface.	
The elapsed time since a neighborship was formed.	
The parameters of any EIGRP **network** commands.	
The configured Hello timer for an interface.	
The configured Hold Timer for an interface.	
The current actual Hold Timer for a neighbor.	
A router's EIGRP ASN.	
A list of EIGRP passive interfaces.	
A list of nonpassive EIGRP interfaces.	
The currently used EIGRP authentication key, when sending EIGRP packets.	
The currently used EIGRP authentication key, when receiving EIGRP packets.	
Lists EIGRP K-values.	
Lists traffic statistics about EIGRP.	
A router's EIGRP Router ID.	

Review All the Key Topics

Key Topic

Review the most important topics from inside the chapter, noted with the key topics icon in the outer margin of the page. Table 2-9 lists a reference of these key topics and the page numbers on which each is found.

Table 2-9 *Key Topics for Chapter 2*

Key Topic Element	Description	Page Number
List	Configuration step review for basic EIGRP configuration	23
Table 2-2	Key EIGRP verification commands	26
Table 2-3	Summary of EIGRP features and facts	31
List	Methods of disallowing EIGRP neighborships on an interface, while still advertising the connected subnet	37
Step list	Configuration checklist for EIGRP authentication	40
Figure 2-6	Conceptual view of which keys are used by EIGRP authentication based on timeframe	41
List	EIGRP authentication troubleshooting hints	43
Table 2-4	List of items that may impact the formation of EIGRP neighborships	46
List	Rules for choosing an EIGRP Router ID	48

Complete the Tables and Lists from Memory

Print a copy of Appendix D, "Memory Tables," (found on the CD), or at least the section for this chapter, and complete the tables and lists from memory. Appendix E, "Memory Tables Answer Key," also on the CD, includes completed tables and lists to check your work.

Define Key Terms

Define the following key terms from this chapter, and check your answers in the glossary.

K-value, neighborship, Hello interval, Hold Timer, passive interface

This chapter covers the following subjects:

Building the EIGRP Topology Table: This section discusses how a router seeds its local EIGRP topology table, and how neighboring EIGRP routers exchange topology information.

Building the IP Routing Table: This section explains how routers use EIGRP topology data to choose the best routes to add to their local routing tables.

Optimizing EIGRP Convergence: This section examines the items that have an impact on how fast EIGRP converges for a given route.

CHAPTER 3

EIGRP Topology, Routes, and Convergence

EIGRP, like OSPF, uses three major branches of logic, each of which populates a different table. EIGRP begins by forming neighbor relationships and listing those relationships in the EIGRP neighbor table (as described in Chapter 2, "EIGRP Overview and Neighbor Relationships"). EIGRP then exchanges topology information with these same neighbors, with newly learned information being added to the router's EIGRP topology table. Finally, each router processes the EIGRP topology table to choose the currently best IP routes, adding those IP routes to the IP routing table.

This chapter moves from the first major branch (neighborships, as covered in Chapter 2) to the second and third branches: EIGRP topology and EIGRP routes. To that end, the first major section of this chapter describes the protocol used by EIGRP to exchange the topology information and details exactly what information EIGRP puts in its messages between routers. The next major section shows how EIGRP examines the topology data to then choose the currently best route for each prefix. The final section of this chapter examines how to optimize the EIGRP convergence processes so that when the topology does change, the routers in the internetwork quickly converge to the then-best routes.

"Do I Know This Already?" Quiz

The "Do I Know This Already?" quiz allows you to assess if you should read the entire chapter. If you miss no more than one of these nine self-assessment questions, you might want to move ahead to the "Exam Preparation Tasks." Table 3-1 lists the major headings in this chapter and the "Do I Know This Already?" quiz questions covering the material in those headings, so you can assess your knowledge of these specific areas. The answers to the "Do I Know This Already?" quiz appear in Appendix A.

Table 3-1 *"Do I Know This Already?" Foundation Topics Section-to-Question Mapping*

Foundations Topics Section	Questions
Building the EIGRP Topology Table	1-3
Building the IP Routing Table	4–7
Optimizing EIGRP Convergence	8, 9

1. Which of the following are methods EIGRP uses to initially populate (seed) its EIGRP topology table, before learning topology data from neighbors? (Choose two.)

   a. By adding all subnets listed by the **show ip route connected** command

   b. By adding the subnets of working interfaces over which static neighbors have been defined

   c. By adding subnets redistributed on the local router from another routing source

   d. By adding all subnets listed by the **show ip route static** command

2. Which of the following are both advertised by EIGRP in the Update message and included in the formula for calculating the integer EIGRP metric? (Choose two.)

   a. Jitter

   b. Delay

   c. MTU

   d. Reliability

3. Router R1 uses S0/0 to connect via a T/1 to the Frame Relay service. Five PVCs terminate on the serial link. Three PVCs (101, 102, and 103) are configured on subinterface S0/0.1, and one each (104 and 105) are on S0/0.2 and S0/0.3. The configuration shows no configuration related to EIGRP WAN bandwidth control, and the **bandwidth** command is not configured at all. Which of the following is true about how IOS tries to limit EIGRP's use of bandwidth on S0/0?

   a. R1 limits EIGRP to around 250Kbps on DLCI 102.

   b. R1 limits EIGRP to around 250Kbps on DLCI 104.

   c. R1 limits EIGRP to around 150Kbps on every DLCI.

   d. R1 does not limit EIGRP because no WAN bandwidth control has been configured.

4. The output of **show ip eigrp topology** on Router R1 shows the following output, which is all the output related to subnet 10.11.1.0/24. How many feasible successor routes does R1 have for 10.11.1.0/24?

   ```
   P 10.11.1.0/24, 2 successors, FD is 2172419
           via 10.1.1.2 (2172423/28167), Serial0/0/0.1
           via 10.1.1.6 (2172423/28167), Serial0/0/0.2
   ```

   a. 0

   b. 1

   c. 2

   d. 3

5. A network design shows that R1 has four different possible paths from itself to the Data Center subnets. Which of the following can influence which of those routes become feasible successor routes, assuming that you follow the Cisco recommended practice of not changing metric weights? (Choose two.)

   a. The configuration of EIGRP offset lists

   b. Current link loads

    c.   Changing interface delay settings

    d.   Configuration of variance

6. Router R1 is three router hops away from subnet 10.1.1.0/24. According to various **show interfaces** commands, all three links between R1 and 10.1.1.0/24 use the following settings: bandwidth: 1000, 500, 100000 and delay: 12000, 8000, 100. Which of the following answers correctly identifies a value that feeds into the EIGRP metric calculation? (Choose two correct answers.)

    a.   Bandwidth of 101,500

    b.   Bandwidth of about 34,000

    c.   Bandwidth of 500

    d.   Delay of 1200

    e.   Delay of 2010

    f.   Delay of 20100

7. Routers R1 and R2 are EIGRP neighbors. R1 has been configured with the **eigrp stub connected** command. Which of the following is true as a result? (Choose two correct answers.)

    a.   R1 can learn EIGRP routes from R2, but R2 cannot learn EIGRP routes from R1.

    b.   R1 can send IP packets to R2, but R2 cannot send IP packets to R1.

    c.   R2 no longer learns EIGRP routes from R1 for routes not connected to R1.

    d.   R1 no longer replies to R2's Query messages.

    e.   R2 no longer sends to R1 Query messages.

8. A network design shows that R1 has four different possible paths from itself to the Data Center subnets. Which one of the following commands is most likely to show you all the possible next-hop IP addresses for these four possible routes?

    a.   **show ip eigrp topology**

    b.   **show ip eigrp topology all-links**

    c.   **show ip route eigrp**

    d.   **show ip route eigrp all-links**

    e.   **show ip eigrp topology all-learned**

9. Router R1 lists 4 routes for subnet 10.1.1.0/24 in the output of the **show ip eigrp topology all-links** command. The **variance 200** command is configured, but no other related commands are configured. Which of the following rules are true regarding R1's decision of what routes to add to the IP routing table? Note that RD refers to reported distance and FD to feasible distance.

    a.   Adds all routes for which the metric is <= 200 * the best metric among all routes

    b.   Adds all routes because of the ridiculously high **variance** setting

    c.   Adds all successor and feasible successor routes

    d.   Adds all successor and feasible successor routes for which the metric is <= 200 * the best metric among all routes

Foundation Topics

Building the EIGRP Topology Table

The overall process of building the EIGRP topology table is relatively straightforward. EIGRP defines some basic topology information about each route for each unique prefix/length (subnet). This basic information includes the prefix, prefix length, metric information, and a few other details. EIGRP neighbors exchange topology information, with each router storing the learned topology information in their respective EIGRP topology table. EIGRP on a given router can then analyze the topology table, or topology database, and choose the best route for each unique prefix/length.

EIGRP uses much simpler topology data than does OSPF, which is a link state protocol that must describe the entire topology of a portion of a network with its topology database. EIGRP, essentially an advanced distance vector protocol, does not need to define nearly as much topology data, nor do EIGRP routers need to run the complex Shortest Path First (SPF) algorithm. This first major section examines the EIGRP topology database, how routers create and flood topology data, and some specific issues related to WAN links.

Seeding the EIGRP Topology Table

Before a router can send EIGRP topology information to a neighbor, that router must have some topology data in its topology table. Routers can, of course, learn about subnets and the associated topology data from neighboring routers. However to get the process started, each EIGRP router needs to adds topology data for some prefixes, so it can then advertise these routes to its EIGRP neighbors. A router's EIGRP process adds subnets to its local topology table, without learning the topology data from an EIGRP neighbor, from three sources:

- Prefixes of connected subnets for interfaces on which EIGRP has been enabled on that router using the **network** command

- Prefixes of connected subnets for interfaces referenced in an EIGRP **neighbor** command

- Prefixes learned by the redistribution of routes into EIGRP from other routing protocols or routing information sources

After a router adds such prefixes to its local EIGRP topology database, that router can then advertise the prefix information, along with other topology information associated with each prefix, to each working EIGRP neighbor. Each router adds any learned prefix information to their topology table, and then that router advertises the new information to other neighbors. Eventually, all routers in the EIGRP domain learn about all prefixes—unless some other feature, such as route summarization or route filtering, alters the flow of topology information.

The Content of EIGRP Update Message

EIGRP uses five basic protocol messages to do its work:

- Hello

- Update

- Query

- Reply

- ACK (acknowledgment)

EIGRP uses two messages as part of the topology data exchange process: Update and Ack. The Update message contains the topology information, whereas the ACK acknowledges receipt of the update packet.

The EIGRP Update message contains the following information:

- Prefix

- Prefix length

- Metric components: bandwidth, delay, reliability, and load

- Nonmetric items: MTU and hop count

Note: Many courses and books over the years have stated that MTU is part of the EIGRP metric. In practice, the MTU has never been part of the metric calculation, although it is included in the topology data for each prefix.

To examine this whole process in more detail, see Figure 3-1 and Figure 3-2. Figure 3-1 shows a portion of an Enterprise network that will be used in several examples in this chapter. Routers B1 and B2 represent typical branch office routers, each with two Frame Relay PVCs connected back to the main site. WAN1 and WAN2 are WAN distribution routers, each of which would normally have dozens or hundreds of PVCs.

The routers in Figure 3-1 have been configured and work. For EIGRP, all routers have been configured with as many defaults as possible, with the only configuration related to EIGRP being the **router eigrp 1** and **network 10.0.0.0** commands on each router.

Next, consider what Router B1 does for its connected route for subnet 10.11.1.0/24, which is located on B1's LAN. B1 matches its Fa0/0 interface IP address (10.11.1.1) due to its **network 10.0.0.0** configuration command. So as mentioned earlier, B1 seeds its own topology table with an entry for this prefix. This topology table entry also lists the interface bandwidth of the associated interface and delay of the associated interface. Using default settings for FastEthernet interfaces, B1 uses a bandwidth of 100,000 Kbps (the same as 100 Mbps) and a delay of 10, meaning 10 tens-of-microseconds. Router B1 also includes a default setting for the load (1) and reliability (255), even though the router, using the default K-value settings, will not use these values in its metric calculations. Finally, B1 adds to the topology database the MTU of the local interface and a hop count of zero because the subnet is connected.

Note: All WAN IP addresses begin with 10.1.

Figure 3-1 *Typical WAN Distribution and Branch Office Design*

Figure 3-2 *Contents of EIGRP Update Messages*

Now that B1 has added some topology information to its EIGRP topology database, Figure 3-2 shows how B1 propagates the topology information to router WAN1 and beyond.

The steps in Figure 3-2 can be explained as follows:

Step 1.   B1 advertises the prefix (10.11.1.0/24) using an EIGRP Update message. The message includes the four metric components, plus MTU and hop count– essentially the information in B1's EIGRP topology table entry for this prefix.

Step 2.   WAN1 receives the Update message and adds the topology information for 10.11.1.0/24 to its own EIGRP topology table, with these changes:

WAN1 considers the interface on which it received the Update (S0/0/0.1) to be the outgoing interface of a potential route to reach 10.11.1.0/24.

WAN1 adds the delay of S0/0/0.1 (2000 tens-of-microseconds per Figure 3-2) to the delay listed in the Update message.

WAN1 compares the bandwidth of S0/0/0.1 (1544 Kbps per Figure 3-2) to the bandwidth listed in the Update message (100,000 Kbps) and chooses the lower value (1544) as the bandwidth for this route.

WAN1 also updates load (highest value), reliability (lowest value), and MTU (lowest value) based on similar comparisons, and adds 1 to the hop count.

Step 3.   WAN1 then sends an Update to its neighbors, with the metric components listed in its own topology table.

This example provides a good backdrop to understand how EIGRP uses cumulative delay and minimum bandwidth in its metric calculation. Note that at Step 2, router WAN1 adds to the delay value but does not add the bandwidth. For bandwidth, WAN1 simply chooses the lowest bandwidth, comparing the bandwidth of its own interface (S0/0/0.1) with the bandwidth listed in the received EIGRP update.

Next, consider this logic on other routers—not shown in the figure—as WAN1 floods this routing information throughout the Enterprise. WAN1 then sends this topology information to another neighbor, and that router sends the topology data to another, and so on. If bandwidth of those links was 1544 or higher, the bandwidth setting used by those routers would remain the same, because each router would see that the routing update's bandwidth (1544 Kbps) was lower than the link's bandwidth. However, each router would add something to the delay.

As a final confirmation of the contents of this Update process, Example 2-1 shows the details of the EIGRP topology database for prefix 10.11.1.0/24 on both B1 and WAN1.

Example 3-1   *Topology Database Contents for 10.11.1.0/24, on B1 and WAN1*

```
! On Router B1: !!!!!!!!!!!!!!!!!!!!!!!!!!!!!!!!!!!!!!!!!!!
B1#show ip eigrp topology 10.11.1.0/24
IP-EIGRP (AS 1): Topology entry for 10.11.1.0/24
  State is Passive, Query origin flag is 1, 1 Successor(s), FD is 28160
  Routing Descriptor Blocks:
  0.0.0.0 (FastEthernet0/0), from Connected, Send flag is 0x0
      Composite metric is (28160/0), Route is Internal
      Vector metric:
        Minimum bandwidth is 100000 Kbit
        Total delay is 100 microseconds
        Reliability is 255/255
        Load is 1/255
        Minimum MTU is 1500
        Hop count is 0
! On Router WAN1: !!!!!!!!!!!!!!!!!!!!!!!!!!!!!!!!!!!!!!!!!!!!
WAN1#show ip eigrp topology 10.11.1.0/24
IP-EIGRP (AS 1): Topology entry for 10.11.1.0/24
  State is Passive, Query origin flag is 1, 1 Successor(s), FD is 2172416
  Routing Descriptor Blocks:
  10.1.1.2 (Serial0/0/0.1), from 10.1.1.2, Send flag is 0x0
      Composite metric is (2172416/28160), Route is Internal
      Vector metric:
        Minimum bandwidth is 1544 Kbit
        Total delay is 20100 microseconds
```

```
Reliability is 255/255
Load is 1/255
Minimum MTU is 1500
Hop count is 1
```

The highlighted portions of output match the details shown in Figure 3-2, but with one twist relating to the units on the delay setting. The IOS **delay** command, which lets you set the delay, along with the data stored in the EIGRP topology database, use a unit of tens-of-microsecond. However, the **show interfaces** and **show ip eigrp topology** commands list delay in a unit of microseconds. For example, WAN1's listing of "20100 microseconds" matches the "2010 tens-on-microseconds" shown in Figure 3-2.

The EIGRP Update Process

So far, this chapter has focused on the detailed information EIGRP exchanges with a neighbor about each prefix. This section takes a broader look at the process.

When EIGRP neighbors first become neighbors, they begin exchanging topology information using Update messages using these rules:

Key Topic

- When a neighbor first comes up, the routers exchange full updates, meaning the routers exchange all topology information.

- After all prefixes have been exchanged with a neighbor, the updates cease with that neighbor if no changes occur in the network. There is no periodic reflooding of topology data.

- If something changes—for example, one of the metric components change, links fail, links recover, new neighbors advertise additional topology information—the routers send partial updates about only the prefixes whose status or metric components have changed.

- If neighbors fail and then recover, or new neighbor adjacencies are formed, full updates occur over these adjacencies.

- EIGRP uses Split Horizon rules on most interfaces by default, which impacts exactly which topology data EIGRP sends during both full and partial updates.

Split Horizon, the last item in the list, needs a little more explanation. Split Horizon limits the prefixes that EIGRP advertises out an interface. Specifically, if the currently best route for a prefix lists a particular outgoing interface, Split Horizon means that EIGRP will not include that prefix in the Update sent out that same interface. For example, router WAN1 uses S0/0/0.1 as its outgoing interface for subnet 10.11.1.0/24, so WAN1 would not advertise prefix 10.11.1.0/24 in its Update messages sent out S0/0/0.1.

Note: Route summarization and route filtering, as explained in Chapter 4, "EIGRP Route Summarization and Filtering," also affect which subsets of the topology table are flooded.

To send the Updates, EIGRP uses the *Reliable Transport Protocol (RTP)* to send the EIGRP updates and confirm their receipt. On point-to-point topologies such as serial links, MPLS VPN, and Frame Relay when using point-to-point subinterfaces, the EIGRP Update and ACK messages use a simple process of acknowledging each Update with an ACK. On multiaccess data links, EIGRP typically sends Update messages to multicast address 224.0.0.10 and expects a unicast EIGRP ACK message from each neighbor in reply. RTP manages that process, setting timers so that the sender of an Update waits a reasonable time, but not too long, before deciding whether all neighbors received the Update or whether one or more neighbors did not reply with an ACK.

Although EIGRP relies on the RTP process, network engineers cannot manipulate how it works.

WAN Issues for EIGRP Topology Exchange

With all default settings, after you enable EIGRP on all the interfaces in an internetwork, the topology exchange process typically does not pose any problems. However, a few scenarios exist, particularly on Frame Relay, which can cause problems. This section summarizes two issues and shows the solution.

Split Horizon Default on Frame Relay Multipoint Subinterfaces

IOS support for Frame Relay allows the configuration of IP addresses on the physical serial interface, multipoint subinterfaces, and point-to-point subinterfaces. Additionally, IP packets can be forwarded over a PVC even when the routers on the opposite ends do not have to use the same interface or subinterface type. As a result, many small intricacies exist in the operation of IP and IP routing protocols over Frame Relay, particularly related to default settings on different interface types.

Frame Relay supports several reasonable configuration options using different interfaces and subinterfaces, each meeting different design goals. For instance, if the design includes a few centralized WAN distribution routers, with PVCs connecting each branch router to each distribution router, both distribution and branch routers might use point-to-point subinterface. Such a choice makes the Layer 3 topology simple, with all links acting like point-to-point links from a Layer 3 perspective. This choice also removes issues such as Split Horizon.

In some cases, a design might include a small set of routers that have a full mesh of PVCs connecting each. In this case, multipoint subinterfaces might be used, consuming a single subnet, reducing the consumption of the IP address space. This choice also reduces the number of subinterfaces.

Both options–using point-to-point subinterfaces or using multipoint subinterfaces–have legitimate reasons for being used. However, when using the multipoint subinterface option, a particular EIGRP issue can occur when the following are true:

■   Three or more routers, over Frame Relay, are configured as part of a single subnet.

■   The routers use multipoint interfaces.

■   Either permanently or for a time, a full mesh of PVCs between the routers does not exist.

For example, consider Router WAN1 shown earlier in Figure 3-1 and referenced again in Figure 3-3. In the earlier configurations, the WAN distribution routers and branch routers all used point-to-point subinterfaces and a single subnet per VC. To see the problem raised in this section, consider that same internetwork, but now the engineer has chosen to configure WAN1 to use a multipoint subinterface and a single subnet for WAN1, B1, and B2, as shown in Figure 3-3.

Figure 3-3   *Partial Mesh, Central Sites (WAN1) Uses Multipoint Subinterface*

The first issue to consider in this design is that B1 and B2 will not become EIGRP neighbors with each other, as noted with Step 1 in the figure. EIGRP routers must be reachable using Layer 2 frames before they can exchange EIGRP Hello messages and become EIGRP neighbors. In this case, there is no PVC between B1 and B2. B1 exchanges Hellos with WAN1, and become neighbors, as will B2 with WAN1. However, routers do not forward received EIGRP Hellos, so WAN1 will not receive a Hello from B1 and forward it to B2 or vice versa. In short, although in the same subnet (10.1.1.0/29), B1 and B2 will not become EIGRP neighbors.

The second problem occurs due to Split Horizon logic on Router WAN1, as noted with Step 2 in the figure. As shown with Step 2 in the figure, B1 could advertise its routes to WAN1, and WAN1 could advertise those routes to B2–and vice versa. However, with default settings, WAN1 will not advertise those routes due to its default setting of Split Horizon (a default interface subcommand setting of **ip split-horizon eigrp** *asn*.) As a result, WAN1 receives the Update from B1 on its S0/0/0.9 subinterface, but Split Horizon prevents WAN1 from advertising that topology data to B2 in Updates sent out interface S0/0/0.9, and vice versa.

The solution is somewhat simple–just configure the **no ip split-horizon eigrp** *asn* command on the multipoint subinterface on WAN1. The remote routers, B1 and B2 in this case, still do not become neighbors, but that does not cause a problem by itself. With Split Horizon disabled on WAN1, B1 and B2 learn routes to the other branch's subnets. Example 3-2 lists the complete configuration and the command to disable Split Horizon:

Note: Frame Relay configuration is considered a prerequisite because it is part of the CCNA exam and courses. Example 3-2 uses **frame-relay interface-dlci** commands and relies on Inverse ARP. However, if **frame-relay map** commands were used instead, disabling Inverse ARP, the EIGRP details discussed in this example would remain unchanged.

Example 3-2 *Frame Relay Multipoint Configuration on WAN1*

```
! On Router WAN1: !!!!!!!!!!!!!!!!!!!!!!!!!!!!!!!!!!!!!!!!!!!!!!!
interface Serial0/0/0
 no ip address
 encapsulation frame-relay

interface Serial0/0/0.9 multipoint
 ip address 10.1.1.1 255.255.255.248
 no ip split-horizon eigrp 1
 frame-relay interface-dlci 103
 frame-relay interface-dlci 104
!
router eigrp 1
 network 10.0.0.0
```

Note: The [no] **ip split-horizon** command controls Split Horizon behavior for RIP; the [no] **ip split-horizon eigrp** *asn* command controls Split Horizon behavior for EIGRP.

Displaying the EIGRP Split Horizon state of an interface is an unusually difficult piece of information to find without simply displaying the configuration. By default, IOS enables EIGRP Split Horizon. To find the setting for an interface, look for the presence or absence of the **no ip split-horizon eigrp** command on the configuration. Also, the **debug ip eigrp** command output displays messages stating when prefixes are not advertised out an interface due to split horizon.

EIGRP WAN Bandwidth Control

In a multiaccess WAN, one physical link passes traffic for multiple data link layer destinations. For example, a WAN distribution router connected to many branches using Frame Relay might literally terminate hundreds, or even thousands, of Frame Relay PVCs.

In a nonbroadcast multiaccess (NBMA) medium such as Frame Relay, when a router needs to send EIGRP updates, the Updates cannot be multicasted at Layer 2. So, the router must send a copy of the Update to each reachable neighbor. For a WAN distribution router with many Frame Relay PVCs, the sheer amount of traffic sent over the Frame Relay access link might overload the link.

The EIGRP WAN bandwidth control allows the engineer to protect a multiaccess Frame Relay interface from being overrun with too much EIGRP message traffic. By default, a router sends EIGRP messages out an interface but only up to 50 percent of the bandwidth defined on the interface with the **bandwidth** command. The engineer can adjust this percentage using the **ip bandwidth-percent eigrp** *asn percent* interface/subinterface subcommand. Regardless of the percentage, IOS then limits the rate of sending the EIGRP messages so that the rate is not exceeded. To accomplish this, IOS queues the EIGRP messages in memory, delaying them briefly.

The command to set the bandwidth percentage is simple, but there are a few caveats to keep in mind when trying to limit the bandwidth consumed by EIGRP:

- The IOS default for bandwidth serial interfaces and subinterfaces is 1544 (Kbps).

- EIGRP limits the consumed bandwidth based on the percentage of interface/ subinterface bandwidth.

- This feature keys on the bandwidth of the interface or subinterface through which the neighbor is reachable, so don't set only the physical interface bandwidth and forget the subinterfaces.

- Recommendation: Set the bandwidth of point-to-point links to the speed of the Committed Information Rate (CIR) of the single PVC on the subinterface.

- General recommendation: Set the bandwidth of multipoint subinterfaces to around the total CIR for all VCs assigned to the subinterface.

- Note that for multipoint subinterfaces, IOS WAN bandwidth control first *divides the subinterface bandwidth by the number of configured PVCs* and then determines the EIGRP percentage based on that number.

For example, consider Figure 3-4, which shows a router with one multipoint subinterface and one point-to-point subinterface. With the configuration shown in Example 3-3, WAN1 uses the following bandwidth, at most, with each neighbor:

- B1, B2, and B3: 20 Kbps (20% of 300Kbps / 3 VCs)

- B4: 30 Kbps (30% of 100 Kbps)

Example 3-3   *Configuration of WAN1, One Multipoint, One Point-to-Point*

```
! On Router WAN1: !!!!!!!!!!!!!!!!!!!!!!!!!!!!!!!!!!!!!!!!!!!!!!
interface Serial0/0/0.20 multipoint
 ip address 172.16.1.1 255.255.255.240
 frame-relay interface-dlci 201
 frame-relay interface-dlci 202
 frame-relay interface-dlci 203
```

```
   bandwidth 300
     ip bandwidth-percent eigrp 1 20
 !
interface Serial0/0/0.21 point-to-point
  ip address 172.16.1.17 255.255.255.252
  frame-relay interface-dlci 221
    bandwidth 100
    ip bandwidth-percent eigrp 1 30
```

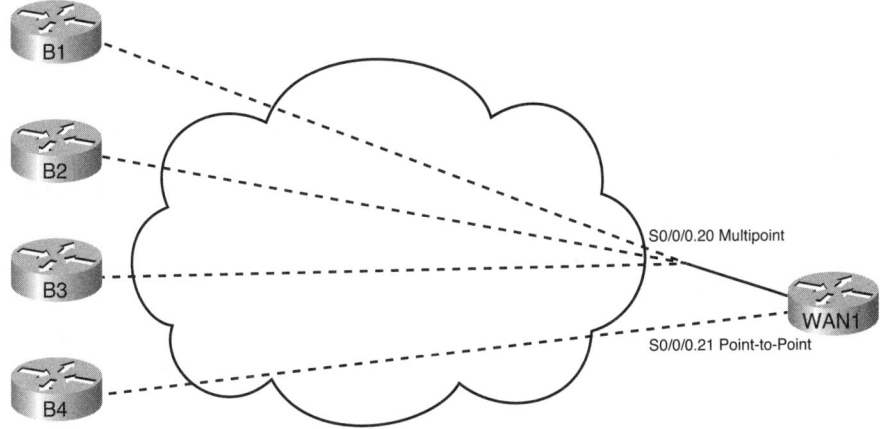

Figure 3-4   *WAN1, One Multipoint, One Point-to-Point*

Building the IP Routing Table

An EIGRP router builds IP routing table entries by processing the data in the topology table. Unlike OSPF, which uses a computationally complex SPF process, EIGRP uses a computationally simple process to determine which, if any, routes to add to the IP routing table for each unique prefix/length. This part of the chapter examines how EIGRP chooses the best route for each prefix/length and then examines several optional tools that can influence the choice of routes to add to the IP routing table.

Calculating the Metrics: Feasible Distance and Reported Distance

The EIGRP topology table entry, for a single prefix/length, lists one or more possible routes. Each possible route lists the various component metric values—bandwidth, delay, and so on. Additionally, for connected subnets, the database entry lists an outgoing interface. For routes not connected to the local router, in addition to an outgoing interface, the database entry also lists the IP address of the EIGRP neighbor that advertised the route.

EIGRP routers calculate an integer metric based on the metric components. Interesting, an EIGRP router does this calculation both from its own perspective and from the perspective of the next-hop router of the route. The two calculated values are

- **Feasible Distance (FD):** Integer metric for the route, from the local router's perspective, used by the local router to choose the best route for that prefix.

- **Reported Distance (RD):** Integer metric for the route, from the neighboring router's perspective (the neighbor that told the local router about the route). Used by the local router when converging to new routes.

Note: Some texts use the term *Advertised Distance (AD)* instead of Reported Distance (RD) as used in this book. Be ready for either term on the CCNP ROUTE exam. However, this book uses RD exclusively.

Routers use the FD to determine the best route, based on the lowest metric, and use the RD when falling back to an alternative route when the best route fails. (EIGRP's use of the RD is explained in the upcoming section "Successor and Feasible Successor Concepts.") Focusing on the FD, when a router has calculated the integer FD for each possible route to reach a single prefix/length, that router can then consider adding the lowest-metric route to the IP routing table.

As a reminder, the following formula shows how EIGRP calculates the metric, assuming default settings of the EIGRP metric weights (K-values). The metric calculation grows when the slowest bandwidth in the end-to-end route decreases (the slower the bandwidth, the worse the metric), and its metric grows (gets worse) when the cumulative delay grows:

$$\text{Metric} = 256 * ((10^7 / \text{slowest-bandwidth}) + \text{cumulative-delay})$$

An example certainly helps in this case. Figure 3-5 repeats some information about the topology exchange process between Routers B1 and WAN1 (refer to Figure 3-1), essentially showing the metric components as sent by B1 to WAN1 (Step 1) and the metric components from WAN1's perspective (Step 2).

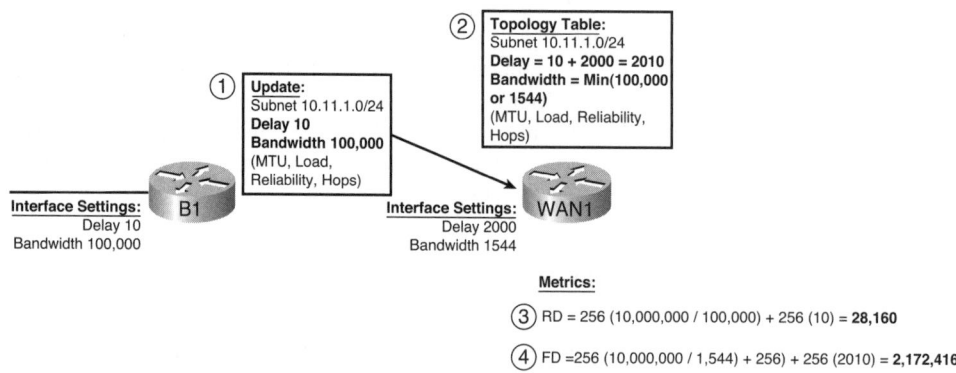

Figure 3-5 *Example Calculation of RD and FD on Router WAN1*

Steps 3 and 4 in Figure 3-5 show WAN1's calculation of the RD and FD for 10.11.1.0/24, respectively. Router WAN1 takes the metric components as received from B1, and plugs them into the formula, to calculate the RD, which is the same integer metric that Router

B1 would have calculated as its FD. Step 4 shows the same formula but with the metric components as listed at Step 2–after the adjustments made on WAN1. Step 4 shows WAN1's FD calculation, which is much larger due to the much lower constraining bandwidth plus the much larger cumulative delay.

WAN1 chooses its best route to reach 10.11.1.0/24 based on the lowest FD among all possible routes. Looking back to the much more detailed Figure 3-1, presumably a couple of other routes might have been possible, but WAN1 happens to choose the route shown in Figure 3-5 as its best route. As a result, WAN1's **show ip route** command lists the FD calculated in Figure 3-5 as the metric for this route, as shown in Example 3-4.

Example 3-4 *Router WAN1's EIGRP Topology and IP Route Information for 10.11.1.0/24*

```
! Below, note that WAN1's EIGRP topology table lists two possible next-hop
! routers: 10.1.1.2 (B1) and 10.9.1.2 (WAN2). The metric for each route,
! the first number in parenthesis, shows that the lower metric route is the one
! through 10.1.1.2 as next-hop. Also note that the metric components
! match Figure 3-5.
!
WAN1#show ip eigrp topo 10.11.1.0/24
IP-EIGRP (AS 1): Topology entry for 10.11.1.0/24
  State is Passive, Query origin flag is 1, 1 Successor(s), FD is 2172416
  Routing Descriptor Blocks:
  10.1.1.2 (Serial0/0/0.1), from 10.1.1.2, Send flag is 0x0
      Composite metric is (2172416/28160), Route is Internal
      Vector metric:
        Minimum bandwidth is 1544 Kbit
        Total delay is 20100 microseconds
        Reliability is 255/255
        Load is 1/255
        Minimum MTU is 1500
        Hop count is 1
  10.9.1.2 (FastEthernet0/0), from 10.9.1.2, Send flag is 0x0
      Composite metric is (2174976/2172416), Route is Internal
      Vector metric:
        Minimum bandwidth is 1544 Kbit
        Total delay is 20200 microseconds
        Reliability is 255/255
        Load is 1/255
        Minimum MTU is 1500
        Hop count is 2
!
! The next command not only lists the IP routing table entry for 10.11.1.0/24,
! it also lists the metric (FD), and components of the metric.
!
WAN1#show ip route 10.11.1.0
Routing entry for 10.11.1.0/24
```

```
     Known via "eigrp 1", distance 90, metric 2172416, type internal
     Redistributing via eigrp 1
     Last update from 10.1.1.2 on Serial0/0/0.1, 00:02:42 ago
     Routing Descriptor Blocks:
     * 10.1.1.2, from 10.1.1.2, 00:02:42 ago, via Serial0/0/0.1
         Route metric is 2172416, traffic share count is 1
         Total delay is 20100 microseconds, minimum bandwidth is 1544 Kbit
         Reliability 255/255, minimum MTU 1500 bytes
         Loading 1/255, Hops 1
 !
 ! Below, the route for 10.11.1.0/24 is again listed, with the metric (FD), and
 ! the same next-hop and outgoing interface information.
 !
WAN1#show ip route eigrp
     10.0.0.0/8 is variably subnetted, 7 subnets, 2 masks
D       10.11.1.0/24 [90/2172416] via 10.1.1.2, 00:10:40, Serial0/0/0.1
D       10.12.1.0/24 [90/2172416] via 10.1.1.6, 00:10:40, Serial0/0/0.2
D       10.1.2.0/30 [90/2172416] via 10.9.1.2, 00:10:40, FastEthernet0/0
D       10.1.2.4/30 [90/2172416] via 10.9.1.2, 00:10:40, FastEthernet0/0
```

EIGRP Metric Tuning

EIGRP metrics can be changed using several methods: setting interface bandwidth, setting interface delay, changing the metric calculation formula by configuring k-values, and even by adding to the calculated metric using offset-lists. In practice, the most reasonable and commonly used methods are to set the interface delay and the interface bandwidth. This section examines all the methods, in part so you will know which useful tools exist, and in part to make you aware of some other design issues that then might impact the routes chosen by EIGRP.

Configuring Bandwidth and Delay

The **bandwidth** and **delay** interface subcommands set the bandwidth and delay associated with the interface. The commands themselves require little thought, other than keeping the units straight. The unit for the **bandwidth** command is Kilobits/second, and the **delay** command uses a unit of tens-of-microseconds.

If a design requires that you influence the choice of route by changing bandwidth or delay, setting the delay value is typically the better choice. IOS uses the bandwidth setting of an interface for many other reasons: calculating interface utilization, as the basis for several QoS parameters, and for SNMP statistics reporting. However, the delay setting has little influence on other IOS features besides EIGRP, so the better choice when influencing EIGRP metrics is to tune the delay.

Table 3-2 lists some of the common default values for both bandwidth and delay. As a reminder, **show** commands list the bandwidth in Kbps, which matches the **bandwidth** command, but lists the delay in microseconds, which does not match the tens-of-microseconds unit of the **delay** command.

Table 3-2 *Common Defaults for Bandwidth and Delay*

Interface Type	Bandwidth (Kbps)	Delay (Microseconds)
Serial	1544	2000
GigE	1,000,000	10
FastE	100,000	100
Ethernet	10,000	1000

Note that on LAN interfaces that can run at different speeds, the bandwidth and delay settings default based on the current actual speed of the interface.

Choosing Bandwidth Settings on WAN Subinterfaces

Frame Relay and Metro Ethernet installations often use an access link with a particular physical sending rate–clock rate if you will–but with the contracted speed, over time, being more or less than the speed of the link. For example, with Frame Relay, the provider may supply a full T1 access link, so configuring **bandwidth 1544** for such an interface is reasonable. However, the subinterfaces have one or more PVCs associated with them, and those PVCs each have Committed Information Rates (CIR) that are typically less than the access link's clock speed. However, the cumulative CIRs for all PVC often exceeds the clock rate of the physical interface. Conversely, MetroE designs use Ethernet access links of 10 Mbps, 100 Mbps, or 1 Gbps actual link speed, but often the business contract limits the amount of traffic to some number below that link speed.

Choosing a useful interface **bandwidth** setting on the subinterfaces in a Frame Relay or MetroE design requires some thought, with most of the motivations for choosing one number or another being unrelated to EIGRP. For example, imagine the network shown in Figure 3-6. Router WAN1 has a single T1 (1.544 Mbps) access link. That interface has one multipoint subinterface, with three PVCs assigned to it. It also has nine other point-to-point subinterfaces, each with a single PVC assigned.

For the sake of discussion, the design in Figure 3-6 oversubscribes the T1 access link off Router WAN1 by a 2:1 factor. Assume all 12 PVCs have a CIR of 256 Kbps, making the total bandwidth for the 12 PVCs roughly 3 Mbps. The design choice to oversubscribe the access link may be reasonable given the statistical chance of all sites sending at the same time.

Now imagine that Router WAN1 has been configured with subinterfaces as shown in the figure:

■ S0/0/0.20 - multipoint, 3 PVCs

■ S0/0/0.21 through S0/0/0.29 – point-to-point, 1 PVC each

Next, consider the options for setting the **bandwidth** command's value on these 10 subinterfaces. The point-to-point subinterfaces could be set to match the CIR of each PVC (256 Kbps in this example). You could choose to set the bandwidth based on the CIR of all combined PVCs on the multipoint subinterface–in this case, setting **bandwidth 768** on multipoint subinterface s0/0/0.20. However, these bandwidths would total about 3

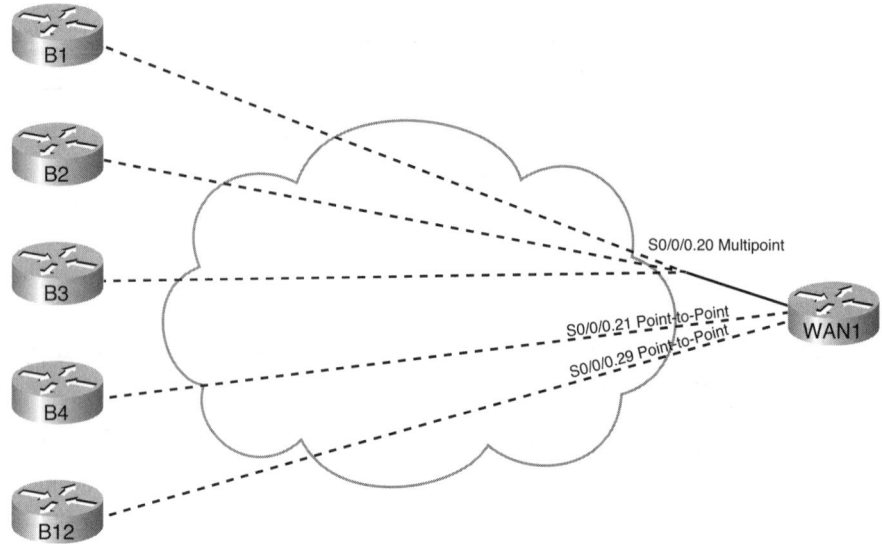

Figure 3-6 *One Multipoint and Nine Point-to-Point Subinterfaces*

Mbps–twice the actual speed of WAN1's access link. Alternatively, you could set the various bandwidths so that the total matches the 1.5 Mbps of the access link. Or you could split the difference, knowing that during times of low activity to most sites that the sites with active traffic get more than their CIR's worth of capacity anyway.

As mentioned earlier, these bandwidth settings impact much more than EIGRP. The settings impact interface statistics, both in **show** commands and in SNMP reporting. They impact QoS features to some extent as well. Given that the better option for setting EIGRP metrics is to set the interface delay, EIGRP metric tuning may not be the driving force behind the decision as to what bandwidth values to use. However, some installations may change these values over time while trying to find the right compromise numbers for features other than EIGRP. So, you need to be aware that changing those values may result in different EIGRP metrics and impact the choices of best routes.

Similar issues exist on the more modern Layer 2 WAN services like MetroE, particularly with the multipoint design of VPLS. Figure 3-7 shows a design that might exist after migrating the internetwork of Figure 3-6 to VPLS. Router WAN1 has been replaced by a Layer 3 switch, using a Gigabit interface to connect to the VPLS service. The remote sites might use the same routers as before, using a FastEthernet interface, or might be replaced with Layer 3 switch hardware as well.

Concentrating on the mechanics of what happens at the central site, WAN1 might use 802.1Q trunking. With 12 remote sites, WAN1 configures 12 VLAN interfaces, one per VLAN, with a different subnet used for the connection to each remote branch. Such a design, from a Layer 3 perspective, looks like the age-old Frame Relay design with a point-to-point link from the main site to each remote branch.

Additionally, the VPLS business contract might specify that WAN1 cannot send more than 200 Mbps of traffic into the VPLS cloud, with the excess being discarded by the

Figure 3-7 *VPLS Service–Issues in Choosing Bandwidth*

VPLS service. To prevent unnecessary discards, the engineer likely configures a feature called *shaping*, which slows down the traffic leaving the Gi0/1 interface of WAN1 (regardless of VLAN). To meet the goal of 200 Mbps, WAN1 would send only part of the time–in this case averaging a sending rate of 1/5th of the time–so that the average rate is 1/5th of 1 Gbps, or 200 Mbps.

Of note with the shaping function, the shaping feature typically limits the cumulative traffic on the interface, not per VLAN (branch). As a result, if the only traffic waiting to be sent by WAN1 happens to be destined for branch B1, WAN1 sends 200 MBps of traffic to just branch B1.

Pulling the discussion back around to EIGRP, as with Frame Relay, other design and implementation needs may drive the decision to set or change the bandwidth on the associated interfaces. In this case, Layer 3 switch WAN1 probably has 12 VLAN interfaces. Each VLAN interface can be set with a bandwidth that influences EIGRP route choices. Should this setting be 1/12th of 1 Gbps, which is the speed at which the bits are actually sent? 1/12th of 200 Mbps, the shaping rate? Or knowing that a site might get most or all of that 200 Mbps for some short period of time, should the bandwidth be set somewhere in between? As with Frame Relay, there is no set answer; for the sake of EIGRP, be aware that changes to the bandwidth settings impact the EIGRP metrics.

Metric Weights (K-values)

Engineers can change the EIGRP metric calculation by configuring the weightings (also called k-values) applied to the EIGRP metric calculation. To configure new values, use the **metric weights** *tos k1 k2 k3 k4 k5* command in EIGRP configuration mode. To configure this command, configure any integer 0–255 inclusive for the five k-values. By default, k1 = k3 = 1, and the others default to 0. The **tos** parameter has only one valid value, 0, and can be otherwise ignored.

The full EIGRP metric formula is as follows. Note that some items reduce to 0 if the corresponding k-values are also set to 0.

EIGRP requires that two routers' k-values match before those routers can become neighbors. Also note that Cisco recommends again using k-values k2, k4, and k5, because a nonzero value for these parameters causes the metric calculation to include interface load and reliability. The load and reliability change over time, which causes EIGRP to reflood topology data, and may cause routers to continually choose different routes (route flapping).

Offset Lists

EIGRP Offset Lists, the final tool for manipulating the EIGRP metrics listed in this chapter, allow an engineer to simply add a value–an offset, if you will–to the calculated integer metric for a given prefix. To do so, an engineer can create and enable an EIGRP Offset List that defines the value to add to the metric, plus some rules regarding which routes should be matched and therefore have the value added to their computed FD.

An Offset List can perform the following functions:

- Match prefixes/prefix lengths using an IP ACL, so that the offset is applied only to routes matched by the ACL with a permit clause

- Match the direction of the Update message, either sent (out) or received (in)

- Match int interface on which the Update is sent or received

- Set the integer metric added to the calculation for both the FD and RD calculations for the route

The configuration itself uses the following command in EIGRP configuration mode, in addition to any referenced IP ACLs:

offset-list {*access-list-number* ¦ *access-list-name*} {**in** ¦ **out**} **offset** [*interface-type interface-number*]

For example, consider again branch office Router B1 in Figure 3-1, with its connection to both WAN1 and WAN2 over a Frame Relay network. Formerly, WAN1 calculated a metric of 2,172,416 for its route, through B1, to subnet 10.11.1.0/24. (Refer to Figure 3-5 for the math behind WAN1's calculation of its route to 10.11.1.0/24.) Router WAN1 also calculated a value of 28,160 for the RD of that same direct route. Example 3-5 shows the addition of an offset on WAN1, for received updates from Router B1.

Example 3-5   *Inbound Offset of 3 on WAN1, for Updates Received on S0/0/0.1*

```
WAN1(config)#access-list 11 permit 10.11.1.0
WAN1(config)#router eigrp 1
WAN1(config-router)#offset-list 11 in 3 Serial0/0/0.1
WAN1(config-router)#end

Mar  2 11:34:36.667: %DUAL-5-NBRCHANGE: IP-EIGRP(0) 1: Neighbor 10.1.1.2
(Serial0/0/0.1) is resync: peer graceful-restart
WAN1#show ip eigrp topo 10.11.1.0/24
IP-EIGRP (AS 1): Topology entry for 10.11.1.0/24
  State is Passive, Query origin flag is 1, 1 Successor(s), FD is 2172416
```

```
    Routing Descriptor Blocks:
    10.1.1.2 (Serial0/0/0.1), from 10.1.1.2, Send flag is 0x0
        Composite metric is (2172419/28163), Route is Internal
        Vector metric:
            Minimum bandwidth is 1544 Kbit
            Total delay is 20100 microseconds
            Reliability is 255/255
            Load is 1/255
            Minimum MTU is 1500
            Hop count is 1
! output omitted for brevity
```

The configuration has two key elements: ACL 11 and the **offset-list** command. ACL 11 matches prefix 10.11.1.0, and that prefix only, with a permit clause. The **offset-list 11 in 3 s0/0/0.1** command tells Router WAN1 to examine all EIGRP Updates received on S0/0/0.1, and if prefix 10.11.1.0 is found, add 3 to the computed FD and RD for that prefix.

Note: Standard ACL 11 matches prefix 10.11.1.0 in this case, regardless of prefix length. To match the exact prefix and prefix length, use an extended ACL. When doing so, use the destination address field to match the prefix length. For example, **access-list 111 permit ip host 10.11.1.0 host 255.255.255.0** matches 10.11.1.0/24 exactly, including the prefix length.

The **show ip eigrp topology 10.11.1.0/24** command in Example 3-4 shows that the FD and RD, highlighted in parentheses, are now each three larger as compared with the earlier metrics.

Next, continuing this same example, Router B1 has now been configured to add an offset (4) in its sent updates to all routers, but for prefix 10.11.1.0/24 only.

Example 3-6 *Outbound Offset of 4 on B1, for Updates Sent to All Neighbors, 10.11.1.0/24*

```
B1(config)#access-list 12 permit 10.11.1.0
B1(config)#router eigrp 1
B1(config-router)#offset-list 12 out 4
B1(config-router)#end
B1#
! Back to router WAN1
WAN1#show ip eigrp topology
IP-EIGRP Topology Table for AS(1)/ID(10.9.1.1)

Codes: P - Passive, A - Active, U - Update, Q - Query, R - Reply,
       r - reply Status, s - sia Status
```

```
P 10.11.1.0/24, 1 successors, FD is 2172419
        via 10.1.1.2 (2172423/28167), Serial0/0/0.1
! lines omitted for brevity
```

Note that the metrics, both FD and RD, are now four larger than in Example 3-4.

Optimizing EIGRP Convergence

The previous major section of this chapter focused on how EIGRP calculates metrics and how to change that metric calculation. However, that section discussed only one motivation for changing the metric: to make a router pick one route instead of another. This section, which focuses on optimizing the EIGRP convergence process, discusses another reason for choosing to manipulate the EIGRP metric calculations: faster convergence.

EIGRP converges very quickly, but EIGRP does not achieve the most optimal fast convergence times in all conditions. One design goal might be to tune EIGRP configuration settings so that EIGRP uses the faster convergence methods for as many routes as possible, and when not possible, that EIGRP converge as quickly as it can without introducing routing loops. As a result, routers might converge in some cases in a second instead of tens of seconds (from the point of a router realizing that a route has failed).

For those of you who have not thought about EIGRP convergence before now, you must first get a comfortable understanding of the concept of EIGRP Feasible Successors–the first topic in this section. Following that, the text examines the EIGRP query process. This section ends with EIGRP load balancing, which both allows spreading the load across multiple routes in addition to improving EIGRP convergence.

Fast Convergence to Feasible Successors

Earlier in this chapter, under the heading "Calculating the Metrics: Feasible Distance and Reported Distance," the text explains how a router, for each possible route, calculates two metric values. One value is the *feasible distance* (FD), which is the metric from that router's perspective. The other metic is the *reported distance* (RD), which is the integer metric from the perspective of the next-hop router.

EIGRP routers use the RD value when determining if a possible route can be considered to be a loop-free backup route called a *feasible successor*. This section explains the concepts and shows how to confirm the existence or nonexistence of such routes.

Successor and Feasible Successor Concepts

For each prefix/prefix length, when multiple possible routes exist, the router chooses the route with the smallest integer metric (smallest FD). EIGRP defines each such route as the *successor route* for that prefix, and EIGRP defines the next-hop router in such a route as the *successor*. EIGRP then creates an IP route for this prefix, with the successor as the next-hop router, and places that route into the IP routing table.

If more than one possible route exists for a given prefix/prefix length, the router examines these other (non-successor) routes and asks this question: Can any of these routes be used immediately if the currently best route fails, without causing a routing loop? EIGRP runs a simple algorithm to identify which routes could be used without causing a routing loop, and EIGRP keeps these loop-free backup routes in its topology table. Then, if the successor route (the best route) fails, EIGRP then immediately uses the best of these alternate loop-free routes for that prefix.

EIGRP calls these alternative, immediately usable, loop-free routes *feasible* successor routes, because they can feasibly be used as a new successor route when the current successor route fails. The next-hop router of such a route is called the *feasible successor*.

Note: In general conversation, the term *successor* may refer to the route or specifically to the next-hop router. Likewise, the term *feasible successor* may refer to the route, or the next-hop router, of an alternative route.

A router determines if a route is a feasible successor based on the *feasibility condition*, defined as follows:

Key Topic

> If a non-successor route's RD is less than the FD, the route is a feasible successor route.

Although technically correct, the preceding definition is much more understandable with an example as shown in Figure 3-8. The figure illustrates how EIGRP figures out which routes are feasible successors for Subnet 1.

Figure 3-8   *Successors and Feasible Successors with EIGRP*

In Figure 3-8, Router E learns three routes to Subnet 1, from Routers B, C, and D. After calculating each route's metric, Router E finds that the route through Router D has the lowest metric. Router E adds this successor route for Subnet 1 to its routing table, as shown. The FD in this case for this successor route is 14,000.

EIGRP decides if a route can be a feasible successor if the reported distance for that route (the metric as calculated on that neighbor) is less than its own best computed metric (the FD). When that neighbor has a lower metric for its route to the subnet in question, that route is said to have met the *feasibility condition*.

For example, Router E computes a metric (FD) of 14,000 on its successor route (through Router D). Router C's computed metric–E's RD for this alternate router through Router C–is 13,000, which is lower than E's FD (14,000). As a result, E knows that C's best route for this subnet could not possible point toward router E, so Router E believes that its route, to Subnet 1, through Router C, would not cause a loop. As a result, Router E marks its topology table entry for the route through Router C as a feasible successor route.

Conversely, E's RD for the route through Router B, to Subnet 1, is 15,000, which is larger than Router E's FD of 14,000. So, this alternative route does not meet the feasibility condition, so Router E does not consider the route through Router B a feasible successor route.

If the route to Subnet 1 through Router D fails, Router E can immediately put the route through Router C into the routing table without fear of creating a loop. Convergence occurs almost instantly in this case. However, if both C and D fail, E would not have a feasible successor route, and would have to do additional work, as described later in the section "Converging by Going Active," before using the route through Router B.

By tuning EIGRP metrics, an engineer can create feasible successor routes in cases where none existed, improving convergence.

Verification of Feasible Successors

Determining which prefixes have both successor and feasible successor routes is somewhat simple if you keep the following in mind:

Key Topic

- The **show ip eigrp topology** command does not list all known EIGRP routes, but instead lists only successor and feasible successor routes.

- The **show ip eigrp topology all-links** command lists all possible routes, including those that are neither successor nor feasible successor routes.

For example, consider Figure 3-9, which again focuses on Router WAN1's route to Router B1's LAN subnet, 10.11.1.0/24. The configuration on all routers has reverted back to defaults for all settings that impact the metric: default bandwidth and delay, no offset lists, and all interfaces are up.

Figure 3-9 shows the three topologically possible routes to reach 10.11.1.0/24, labeled 1, 2, and 3. Route 1, direct to Router B1, is the current successor. Route 3, which goes to another branch router, back to the main site, and then to Router B1, is probably a route you would not want to use anyway. However, route 2, through WAN2, would be a reasonable back-up route.

If the PVC between WAN1 and B1 failed, WAN1 would converge to route 2 from the figure. However, with all default settings, route 2 is not an FS route, as demonstrated in Example 3-7.

Example 3-7   *Only a Successor Route on WAN1 for 10.11.1.0/24*

```
WAN1#show ip eigrp topology
IP-EIGRP Topology Table for AS(1)/ID(10.9.1.1)
```

```
Codes: P - Passive, A - Active, U - Update, Q - Query, R - Reply,
       r - reply Status, s - sia Status


P 10.11.1.0/24, 1 successors, FD is 2172416
        via 10.1.1.2 (2172416/28160), Serial0/0/0.1
! lines omitted for brevity; no other lines of output pertain to 10.11.1.0/24.

WAN1#show ip eigrp topology all-links
IP-EIGRP Topology Table for AS(1)/ID(10.9.1.1)


Codes: P - Passive, A - Active, U - Update, Q - Query, R - Reply,
       r - reply Status, s - sia Status


P 10.11.1.0/24, 1 successors, FD is 2172416, serno 45
        via 10.1.1.2 (2172416/28160), Serial0/0/0.1
        via 10.9.1.2 (2174976/2172416), FastEthernet0/0
! lines omitted for brevity; no other lines of output pertain to 10.11.1.0/24.
```

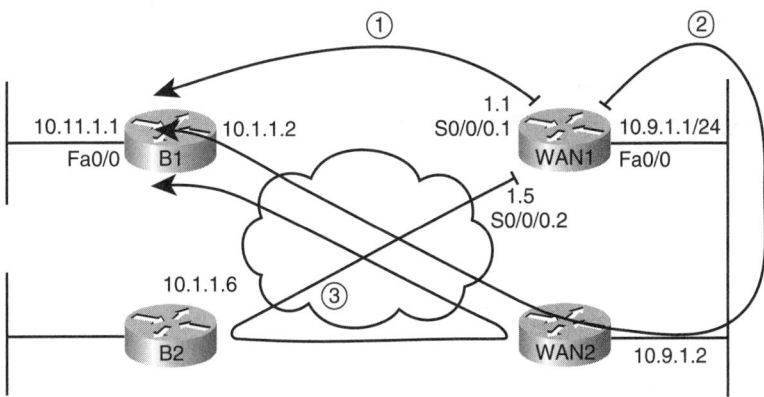

Note: All WAN IP addresses begin with 10.1

Figure 3-9   *Three Possible Routes from WAN1 to 10.11.1.0/24*

A quick comparison of the two commands show that the **show ip eigrp topology** command shows only one next-hop address (10.1.1.2), whereas the **show ip eigrp topology all-links** command shows two (10.1.1.2 and 10.9.1.2). The first command lists only successor and feasible successor routes, so in this case, only one such route for 10.1.1.0/24 exists—the successor route, direct to B1 (10.1.1.2).

The output of the **show ip eigrp topology all-links** command is particularly interesting in this case. It lists two possible next-hop routers: 10.1.1.2 (B1) and 10.9.1.2 (WAN2). It does not list the route through Router B2 (10.1.1.6) at all, because B2's current successor route for 10.11.1.0/24 is through WAN1. EIGRP Split Horizon rules tell B2 to not advertise 10.11.1.0/24 to WAN1.

Next, focus on the route labeled as option 2 in Figure 3-9, the route from WAN1, to WAN2, then to B1. Per the **show ip eigrp topology all-links** command, this route has an RD of 2,172,416–the second number in parenthesis as highlighted toward the end of Example 3-6. WAN1's successor route has an FD of that exact same value. So, this one possible alternate route for 10.11.1.0/24, through WAN2, does not meet the feasibility condition–but just barely. To be an FS route, the route's RD must be less than the FD, and in this example, the two are equal.

To meet the design requirement for quickest convergence, you could use any method to manipulate the metrics such that either WAN2's metric for 10.11.1.0 is lower, or WAN1's metric for its successor route is higher. Example 3-8 shows the results of simply adding back the offset-list on WAN1, as seen in Example 3-5, which increases WAN1's metric by 3.

Example 3-8   *Increasing WAN1's Metric for 10.11.1.0/24, Creating an FS Route*

```
WAN1#configure terminal
Enter configuration commands, one per line.  End with CNTL/Z.
WAN1(config)#access-list 11 permit 10.11.1.0
WAN1(config)#router eigrp 1
WAN1(config-router)#offset-list 11 in 3 s0/0/0.1
WAN1(config-router)#^Z
WAN1#show ip eigrp topology
IP-EIGRP Topology Table for AS(1)/ID(10.9.1.1)


Codes: P - Passive, A - Active, U - Update, Q - Query, R - Reply,
       r - reply Status, s - sia Status


P 10.11.1.0/24, 1 successors, FD is 2172419
        via 10.1.1.2 (2172419/28163), Serial0/0/0.1
        via 10.9.1.2 (2174976/2172416), FastEthernet0/0
! lines omitted for brevity; no other lines of output pertain to 10.11.1.0/24.
```

Note that now WAN1's successor route FD is 2,172,419, which is higher than WAN2's (10.9.1.2's) RD of 2,172,416. As a result, WAN1's route through WAN2 (10.9.1.2) now meets the feasibility condition. Also, the **show ip eigrp topology** command, which lists only successor and feasible successor routes, now lists this new feasible successor route. Also note that the output still states "1 successor," so this counter indeed counts successor routes and does not include FS routes.

When EIGRP on a router notices that a successor route has been lost, if a feasible successor exists in the EIGRP topology database, EIGRP places that feasible successor route into the routing table. The elapsed time from noticing that the route failed, until the route is replaced, is typically less than 1 second. (A Cisco Live conference presentation asserts this convergence approaches 200 milliseconds.) With well-tuned EIGRP Hold Timers and with feasible successor routes, convergence time can be held low.

Converging by Going Active

When EIGRP removes a successor route and no FS route exists, the router begins a process by which the router discovers if any loop-free alternative routes each reach that prefix. This process is called *going active* on a route. Routes for which the router has a successor route, and no failure has yet occurred, remain in a passive state. Routes for which the successor route fails, with no feasible successor routes, move to an active state, as follows:

- Change the state, as listed in the **show ip eigrp topology** command, from passive (p) to active (a).

- Send EIGRP *Query* messages to every neighbor except the neighbor in the failed route. The Query asks a neighbor whether that neighbor has a loop-free route for the listed prefix/length.

- The neighbor considers itself to have a loop-free route if that neighbor is passive for that prefix/length. If so, the neighbor 1) sends an EIGRP Reply message, telling the original router that it does indeed have a loop-free route and 2) does not forward the Query.

- If the neighbor itself is active on this route, that neighbor 1) floods EIGRP Query messages to its neighbors and 2) does not immediately send an EIGRP Reply back to the original router–instead waiting on replies to its own set of Query messages.

- When a router has received Reply messages from all neighbors to which it sent any Query messages, that router can then send a Reply message to any of its neighbors as necessary.

- When a router has received a Reply for all its Query messages, that router may safely use the best of the routes confirmed to be loop free.

Key Topic

Note: The EIGRP convergence process when going active on a route is sometimes also referenced by the name of the underlying algorithm, named Diffusing Update Algorithm (DUAL).

The process can and does work well in many cases, often converging to a new route in less than 10 seconds. However, in internetworks with many remote sites, with much redundancy, and with a large number of routers in a single end-to-end route, convergence when going active can be inefficient. For example, consider the internetwork in Figure 3-10. The figure shows five branch routers as an example, but the internetwork has 300 branch routers, each with a PVC connected to two WAN routers, WAN1 and WAN2. When Router WAN1 loses its route for the LAN subnet at branch B1, without an FS route, the Query process can get out of hand.

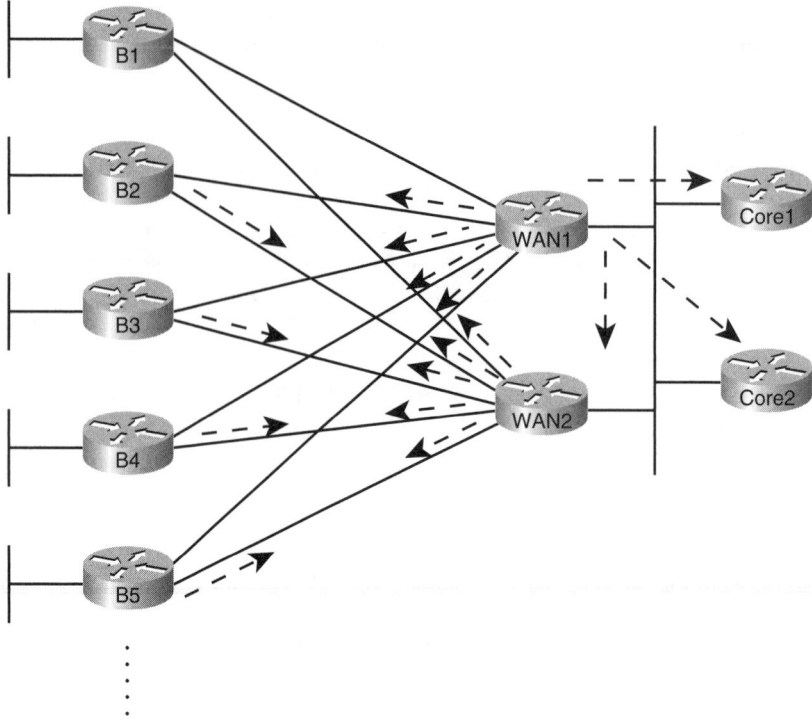

Figure 3-10   *Issues with Query Scope*

The arrowed lines show WAN1's Query messages and the reaction by several other routers to forward the Query messages. Although only 5 branch routers are shown, WAN1 would forward Query messages to 299 branch routers. WAN2 would do the same, assuming its route to B1's LAN also failed. These branch routers would then send Query messages back to the WAN routers. The network would converge, but more slowly than if an FS route existed.

> **Note:**   EIGRP sends every Query and Reply message using RTP, so every message is acknowledged using an EIGRP ACK message.

By configuring EIGRP so that a router has FS routes for most routes, the whole Query process can be avoided. However, in some cases, creating FS routes for all routes on all routers is impossible, so engineers should take action to limit the scope of queries. The next two sections discuss two tools—stub routers and route summarization—that help reduce the work performed by the DUAL algorithm and the scope of Query messages.

The Impact of Stub Routers on Query Scope

Some routers, by design, should not be responsible for forwarding traffic between different sites. For example, consider the familiar internetwork shown throughout this chapter, most recently in Figure 3-10, and focus on the branch routers. If WAN2's LAN interface failed, and WAN1's PVC to B1 failed, then a route still exists from the core to branch B1's 10.11.1.0/24 subnet: WAN1–B2–WAN2–B1. (This is the same long route shown as route 3 in Figure 3-9.) However, this long route consumes the link bandwidth between the core and branch B2, and the traffic to/from B1 will be slower. Users at both branches will suffer, and these conditions may well be worse than just not using this long route.

Route filtering could be used to prevent WAN1 from learning such a route. However, using route filtering would require a lot of configuration on all the branch routers, with specifics for the subnets–and it would have to change over time. A better solution exists, which is to make the branch routers stub routers. EIGRP defines *stub routers* as follows:

A router that should not forward traffic between two remote EIGRP-learned subnets.

Key Topic

To accomplish this goal, the engineer configures the stub routers using the **eigrp stub** command. Stub routers do not advertise EIGRP-learned routes from one neighbor to other EIGRP neighbors. Additionally, and possibly more significantly, nonstub routers note which EIGRP neighbors are stub routers, and the nonstub routers do not send Query messages to the stub routers. This action greatly reduces the scope of Query messages when a route goes active, in addition to preventing the long, circuitous, and possibly harmful route.

The **eigrp stub** command has several options. When issued simply as **eigrp stub**, the router uses default parameters, which are the **connected** and **summary** options. (Note that IOS adds these two parameters onto the command as added to the running-config.) Table 3-3 lists the **eigrp stub** command options and explains some of the logic behind using them.

Table 3-3 *Parameters on the eigrp stub Command*

Key Topic

Option	This router is allowed to...
Connected	Advertise connected routes but only for interfaces matched with a **network** command.
Summary	Advertise auto-summarized or statically configured summary routes.
Static	Advertises static routes, assuming the **redistribute static** command is configured.
Redistributed	Advertises redistributed routes, assuming redistribution is configured.
Receive-only	Does not advertise any routes. This option cannot be used with any other option.

Note that stub routers still form neighborships, even in receive-only mode. The stub router simply performs less work and reduces the Query Scope because neighbors will not send these routes any Query messages.

For example, Example 3-9 shows the **eigrp stub connected** command on Router B2, with the results being noticable on WAN1 (**show ip eigrp neighbors detail**).

Example 3-9   *Evidence of Router B2 as an EIGRP Stub Router*

```
B2#configure terminal
B2(config)#router eigrp 1
B2(config-router)#eigrp stub connected
B2(config-router)#
Mar  2 21:21:52.361: %DUAL-5-NBRCHANGE: IP-EIGRP(0) 1: Neighbor 10.9.1.14
(FastEthernet0/0.12) is down: peer info changed
! A message like the above occurs for each neighbor.
! Moving to router WAN1 next
WAN1#show ip eigrp neighbors detail
IP-EIGRP neighbors for process 1
H   Address                  Interface        Hold Uptime   SRTT   RTO  Q  Seq
                                              (sec)         (ms)         Cnt Num
1   10.9.1.2                 Fa0/0            11 00:00:04    7     200  0  588
    Version 12.4/1.2, Retrans: 0, Retries: 0, Prefixes: 8
2   10.1.1.6                 Se0/0/0.2        13 00:21:23    1     200  0  408
    Version 12.4/1.2, Retrans: 2, Retries: 0, Prefixes: 2
    Stub Peer Advertising ( CONNECTED ) Routes
    Suppressing queries
0   10.9.1.6                 Fa0/0.4          12 00:21:28    1     200  0  175
    Version 12.2/1.2, Retrans: 3, Retries: 0, Prefixes: 6
```

The Impact of Summary Routes on Query Scope

In addition to EIGRP stub routers, route summarization also limits EIGRP Query scope and therefore improves convergence time. The reduction in Query scope occurs due to the following rule:

Key Topic

If a router receives an EIGRP Query for a prefix/prefix length, does not have an exactly matching (both prefix and prefix length) route, but does have a summary route that includes the prefix/prefix length, that router immediately sends an EIGRP Reply and does not flood the Query to its own neighbors.

For example, consider Figure 3-11. Multilayer Switches C1 and C2 sit in the core of the network shown in various other figures in this chapter, and both C1 and C2 run EIGRP. The IP subnetting design assigns all branch office LAN subnets from the range 10.11.0.0/16 and 10.12.0.0/16. As such, Routers WAN1 and WAN2 advertise summary routes for these ranges, rather than for individual subnets. So, under normal operation, ignoring the whole Query scope issue, C1 and C2 would never have routes for individual branch subnets like 10.11.1.0/24 but would have routes for 10.11.0.0/16 and 10.12.0.0/16.

The figure highlights three steps:

Step 1.   WAN1 and WAN2 advertise summary routes, so that C1, C2, and all other routers in the core have a route for 10.11.0.0/16 but not a route for 10.11.1.0/24.

Step 2.   Some time in the future, WAN1 loses its route for 10.11.1.0/24, so WAN1 sends a Query for 10.11.1.0/24 to C1 and C2.

Figure 3-11   *Route Summaries Limiting Query Scope*

Step 3.   C1 and C2 send an EIGRP Reply immediately afterward, because both do not
have a route for that specific prefix/length (10.11.1.0/24), but both do have a
summary route (10.11.0.0/16) that includes that range of addresses.

Chapter 4, "EIGRP Route Summarization and Filtering," explains the configuration of
EIGRP route summarization as an end to itself.

Stuck in Active

When a router notices a route failure and moves a route from passive to active state, that
router sends Query messages to its neighbors. With a sufficiently large network, particularly when routers exist several router hops away, the number of Queries may not only be
large, but there also may be a string of routers that all must wait on multiple Reply messages before they can, in turn, issue a Reply. For example, in Figure 3-12, Router R1 must
wait on routers R11, R12, and R13 to send a Reply. R11 must wait on routers R21, R22,
and R23. R21 must wait on three other routers, and so on–meaning that R1 may have to
wait quite a while before getting a response.

Although the design shown in Figure 3-12 is admittedly contrived, the point is that a
router may wait awhile before getting a Reply message in response to each Query message
for an Active route. A router cannot use any alternative paths for that route until all such
Reply messages have been received.

To deal with this potentially long time, IOS first sets a limit on how long it should take to
receive all such replies. That timer, called the *active timer*, is set to 3 minutes by default.
(The timer can be configured for an entire EIGRP process using the **timers active-time**
time EIGRP subcommand, with a units of a number of minutes.) Routes for which a
router does not receive a Reply within the active timer are considered to be Stuck-in-
Active (SIA) routes.

IOS has two major branches of logic when reacting to SIA routes. Earlier versions of IOS
took a rather drastic action, bringing down the uncooperative neighbors that had yet to
send back an EIGRP Reply for that route. For example, in Figure 3-12, if R1 received Reply
messages from R11 and R12, but not R13, and the active timer expired, R1 would bring

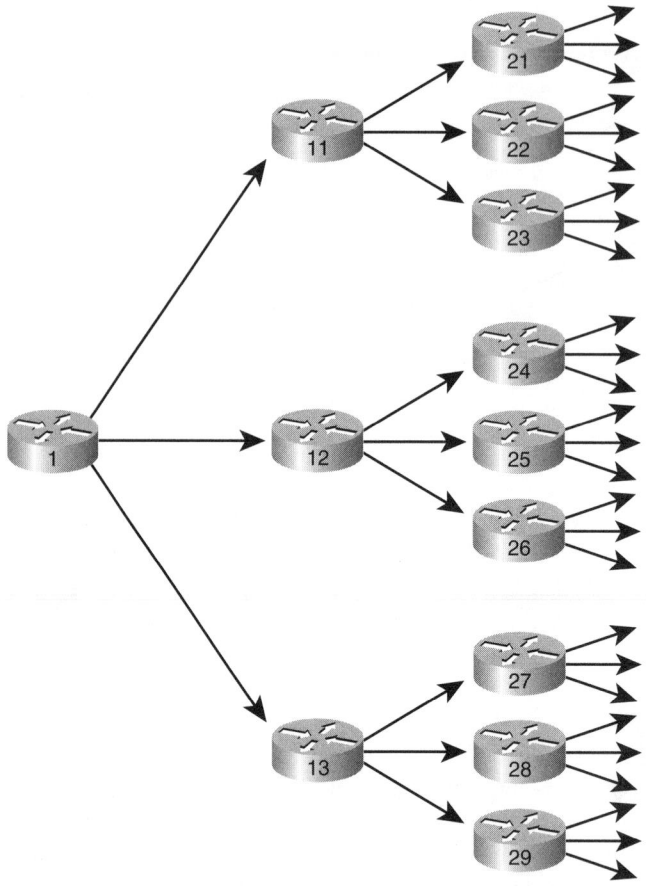

Figure 3-12   *Network Design That Causes Unreasonably Long Convergence*

down the neighborship with R13. The active route would be considered to have failed, and all routes known through the failed neighbor would also be considered to have failed–possibly generating more Query messages for other routes.

Later IOS versions (beginning in the 12.2 mainline) make an attempt to avoid failing the neighborship. At the halfway point through the Active timer–a seemingly long 90 seconds by default–a router sends an SIA-Query (Stuck-in-Active query) EIGRP message to each neighbor that has yet to send back a Reply. The purpose of the message is to either get an SIA-Reply back, meaning that the neighbor really is still waiting for replies to its own queries, or to get nothing in reply. In the first case, because the neighbor is alive and still working, there is no need to kill the neighborship. In the second case, the neighbor was not able to reply, so the action of failing the neighborship is reasonable.

Unequal Metric Route Load Sharing

Convergence to a feasible successor route should happen within a second after a router re-alizes the successor route has failed. Even in large well-designed networks, particularly with features like stub routers and route summarization in use, convergence can still happen in a reasonable amount of time even when going active. The next feature, load sharing, takes convergence to another level, giving instantaneous convergence, while reaching other goals as well.

IOS allows routing protocols to place multiple routes into the routing table for an individual prefix/length. IOS then balances traffic across those routes, by default balancing traffic on a per-destination IP address basis.

Load balancing, sometimes called load sharing, provides a primary benefit of making use of the available bandwidth, rather than using some links as simply backup links. For example, with the two-PVC designs repeatedly shown in this chapter (Figures 3-1, 3-9, and 3-10), without load sharing, a branch router would send traffic over one PVC, but not both. With load sharing, some traffic would flow over each PVC.

A useful secondary benefit–faster convergence–occurs when using load balancing. By placing multiple routes into the routing table for a single prefix, convergence happens essentially instantly. For example, if a branch router has two routes for each data center subnet—one using each PVC that connects the branch to the core—and one of the routes fails, the other route is already in the routing table. In this case, the router does not need to look for FS routes nor go active on the route. The router uses the usual EIGRP convergence tools only when all such routes are removed from the routing table.

The load balancing configuration requires two commands, one of which already defaults to a reasonable setting. First, you need to define the number of allowed routes for each prefix/prefix length using the **maximum-paths** *number* EIGRP subcommand. The default setting of 4 is often big enough, because most internetworks do not have enough redundancy to have more than four possible routes.

Note: The maximum number of paths varies based on IOS version and router platform. However, for the much older IOS versions, the maximum was 6 routes, with later versions typically supporting 16 or more.

The second part of the load balancing configuration overcomes a challenge introduced by EIGRP's metric calculation. The EIGRP integer metric calculation often results in 8-to-10-digit integer metrics, so the metrics of competing routes are seldom the exact same value. Calculating the exact same metric for different routes for the same prefix is statistically unlikely.

IOS includes the concept of EIGRP *variance* to overcome this problem. Variance lets you tell IOS that the EIGRP metrics can be close in value and still be considered worthy of being added to the routing table—and you can define how close.

The **variance** *multiplier* EIGRP router subcommand defines an integer between 1 and 128. The router then multiplies the variance times the successor route's FD–the metric of the best route to reach that subnet. Any FS routes whose metric is less than the product of the variance times the FD are considered to be equal routes and may be placed into the routing table, up to the number of routes defined by the **maximum-paths** command.

For example, consider the example as shown in Figure 3-13 and Table 3-4. In this example, to keep the focus on the concepts, the metrics are small easy-to-compare numbers, rather than the usual large EIGRP metrics. The example focuses on R4's three possible routes to reach Subnet 1. The figure shows the RD of each route next to Routers R1, R2, and R3, respectively.

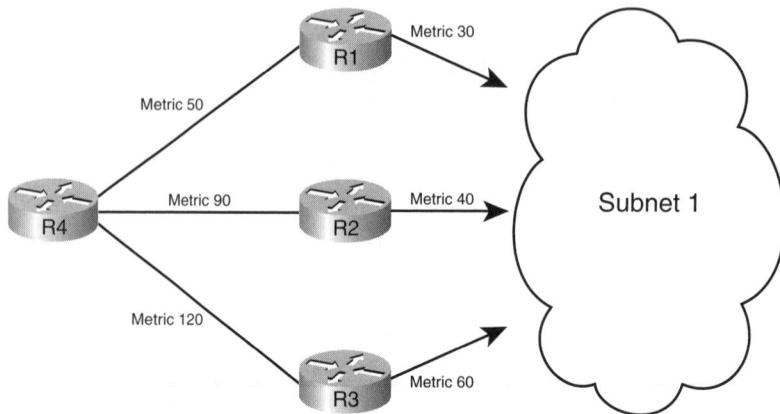

Figure 3-13   *Example of the Use of Variance*

Table 3-4   *Example of Routes Chosen as Equal Due to Variance*

Next-hop	Metric	RD	Added to Routing Table at Variance 1?	Added to Routing Table at Variance 2?	Added to Routing Table at Variance 3?
R1	50	30	Yes	Yes	Yes
R2	90	40	No	Yes	Yes
R3	120	60	No	No	No

Before considering the variance, note that in this case the route through R1 is the successor route because it has the lowest metric. This also means that the FD is 50. The route through R2 is an FS route because its RD of 40 is less than the FD of 50. The route through R3 is not an FS route, because R3's RD of 60 is more than the FD of 50.

At a default variance setting of 1, the metrics must be exactly equal to be considered equal, so only the successor route is added to the routing table (the route through R1). With variance 2, the FD (50) is multiplied by the variance (2) for a product of 100. The route through R2, with FD 90, is less than 100, so R4 will add the route through R2 to the routing table as well. The router can then load balance traffic across these two routes. Table 3-4 summarizes these cases, plus one other, which is described after the table.

In the third case, with variance 3, the product of the FD (50) times 3 results equals 150. All three routes' calculated metrics (their FD values) are less than 150. However, the route through R3 is not an FS route, so it cannot be added to the routing table for fear of causing a routing loop. So, R4 adds only the routes through R1 and R2 to its IP routing table. (Note that the variance and maximum-paths settings can be verified by using the **show ip protocols** command.)

The following list summarizes the key points about variance:

- The variance is multiplied by the current FD (the metric of the best route to reach the subnet).

- Any FS routes whose calculated metric is less than or equal to the product of variance times FD are added to the IP routing table, assuming the **maximum-paths** setting allows more routes.

- Routes that are neither successor nor feasible successor can never be added to the IP routing table, regardless of the variance setting.

When the routes have been added to the routing table, the router supports a couple of methods for how to load balance traffic across the routes. The router can balance the traffic proportionally with the metrics, meaning that lower metric routes send more packets. Also, the router can send all traffic over the lowest-metric route, with the other routes just being in the routing table for faster convergence in case the best route fails.

Key Topic

Exam Preparation Tasks

Planning Practice

The CCNP ROUTE exam expects test takers to review design documents, create implementation plans, and create verification plans. This section provides exercises that may help you to take a step back from the minute details of the topics in this chapter so that you can think about the same technical topics from the planning perspective.

For each planning practice table, simply complete the table. Note that any numbers in parentheses represent the number of options listed for each item in the solutions in Appendix F, "Completed Planning Practice Tables."

Design Review Table

Table 3-5 lists several design goals related to this chapter. If these design goals were listed in a design document, and you had to take that document and develop an implementation plan, what implementation options come to mind? For any configuration items, a general description can be used, without concern about the specific parameters.

Table 3-5 *Design Review*

Design Goal	Possible Implementation Choices Covered in This Chapter
Limit consumption of IP subnets in Frame Relay WAN design.	
In a relatively slow Frame Relay WAN, protect against consuming too much bandwidth with overhead EIGRP traffic.	
Plan to change bandwidth from 1X CIR to 2X CIR on all Frame Relay subinterfaces.	
Plan to set bandwidth to values other than actual interface speeds to manipulate EIGRP metrics.	
A goal of ensuring all remote routers' secondary EIGRP routes does not require Queries for convergence.	
What tools can we use to meet the design goal of fast convergence? (four items)	

Implementation Plan Peer Review Table

Table 3-6 shows a list of questions that others might ask, or that you might think about, during a peer review of another network engineer's implementation plan. Complete the table by answering the questions.

Table 3-6   *Notable Questions from This Chapter to Consider During an Implementation Plan Peer Review*

Question	Answer
A Frame Relay multipoint interface, with 20 PVCs attached, has a configuration for 10% of the bandwidth to be used for EIGRP. How much is allocated per PVC?	
A configuration lists the **no ip split-horizon** command–when would that matter?	
The plan calls for setting all EIGRP K-values to 1. What negative effect could this have on routes in the IP routing table?	
The configuration uses offset lists. Will that impact the calculation of FD and/or RD?	
The plan lists a sample configuration migrating an interface from **delay 20** to **delay 200**. How much will the metric go up?	
The plan shows the use of the **variance 4** command. What must be configured to add other routes to a routing table? (two items)	

Create an Implementation Plan Table

To practice skills useful when creating your own EIGRP implementation plan, list in Table 3-7 configuration commands related to the configuration of the following features. You may want to record your answers outside the book and set a goal to complete this table (and others like it) from memory during your final reviews before taking the exam.

Table 3-7   *Implementation Plan Configuration Memory Drill*

Feature	Configuration Commands/Notes
Enabling EIGRP on interfaces	
Enabling or disabling Split Horizon for EIGRP	
Setting the Bandwidth consumed by EIGRP on an interface	
Setting an interface's logical bandwidth	
Setting an interface's logical delay	
K-values	
Configuring an EIGRP offset list that matches a prefix	
Configuring an EIGRP offset list that matches a prefix and prefix length	
Configuring unequal cost load balancing	
Configure an EIGRP stub router	

Choose Commands for a Verification Plan Table

To practice skills useful when creating your own EIGRP verification plan, list in Table 3-8 all commands that supply the requested information. You may want to record your answers outside the book, and set a goal to complete this table (and others like it) from memory during your final reviews before taking the exam.

Table 3-8 *Verification Plan Memory Drill*

Information Needed	Command
The composite metric values for all EIGRP prefixes.	
Display EIGRP Split Horizon settings.	
Calculate the maximum bandwidth EIGRP will consume on a physical or point-to-point subinterface.	
Calculate the maximum bandwidth EIGRP will consume per PVC on a multipoint Frame Relay subinterface.	
Display the increase in RD after implementing an EIGRP offset list.	
Display interface bandwidth and delay settings.	
Lists EIGRP K-values.	
Find the number of successor and feasible successor routes.	
Find all routes, including non-successors.	
Determine if the local router is a stub router.	
Determine if a neighboring router is a stub router.	
Find the current setting of variance and maximum-paths.	
Display messages each time EIGRP suppresses a prefix advertisement due to Split Horizon.	

Review all the Key Topics

Review the most important topics from the chapter, noted with the key topics icon in the outer margin of the page. Table 3-9 lists a reference of these key topics and the page numbers on which each is found.

Table 3-9   *Key Topics for Chapter 3*

Key Topic Element	Description	Page Number
List	Three sources for seeding a local router's EIGRP topology table	60
List	EIGRP message types (5)	61
List	Rules for EIGRP topology exchange	64
Definitions	Feasible Distance, Reported Distance	70
Definition	Feasibility Condition	79
Figure 3-8	Conceptual view of successors and feasible successors	79
List	Two commands to find all EIGRP routes versus all successor/feasible successor routes	80
List	EIGRP process of finding routes when going active	83
Definition	EIGRP stub router	85
Table 3-3	List of options on the **eigrp stub** command	85
Definition	Rule by which summary routes reduce Query scope	86
List	Rules for unequal-cost multipath	91

Complete the Tables and Lists from Memory

Print a copy of Appendix D, "Memory Tables," (found on the CD) or at least the section for this chapter, and complete the tables and lists from memory. Appendix E, "Memory Tables Answer Key," also on the CD, includes completed tables and lists to check your work.

Define Key Terms

Define the following key terms from this chapter, and check your answers in the glossary.

feasibility condition, feasible distance, feasible successor, full update, partial update, reported distance, advertised distance, successor, Split Horizon, bandwidth, delay, K-value, offset list, going active, DUAL, Query scope, EIGRP stub router, unequal-cost load balancing, variance

This chapter covers the following subjects:

Route Filtering: This section examines how to filter prefixes from being sent in EIGRP Updates or filter them from being processed when received in an EIGRP Update.

Route Summarization: This section discusses the concepts and configuration of EIGRP route summarization.

Default Routes: This section examines the benefits of using default routes, and the mechanics of two methods for configuring default routes with EIGRP.

EIGRP Route Summarization and Filtering

Engineers can choose to implement routing protocols such that all routers know routes to all prefixes in an internetwork. By allowing all routers to share all known prefixes, every router in an Enterprise has the potential ability to forward packets to all subnets in the Enterprise, assuming the internetwork is working correctly.

However, a reasonable network design may not need nor want the unfettered flow of routing information in an Enterprise. The design should consider the flow of data in the network, in particular, the fact that most data applications do not send packets directly between end user hosts. Most often, the packets go from one host to a server, and then the server communicates directly with the other end user host. So the design may require or desire that some routes are filtered so that routers in one part of the internetwork cannot forward packets to another part.

Additionally, the design may call for a general goal to reduce the size of the typical router's IP routing table. Although routers consume only a small amount of CPU to forward each packet, the amount of CPU required does increase slightly based on the number of routes. Additionally, a smaller routing table may be simpler and require less time when troubleshooting problems.

This chapter explains three categories of tools that you can use to limit the number of routes in the routing table: route filtering, route summarization, and default routes.

"Do I Know This Already?" Quiz

The "Do I Know This Already?" quiz allows you to assess if you should read the entire chapter. If you miss no more than one of these nine self-assessment questions, you might want to move ahead to the "Exam Preparation Tasks." Table 4-1 lists the major headings in this chapter and the "Do I Know This Already?" quiz questions covering the material in those headings so that you can assess your knowledge of these specific areas. The answers to the "Do I Know This Already?" quiz appear in Appendix A.

Table 4-1 *"Do I Know This Already?" Foundation Topics Section-to-Question Mapping*

Foundations Topics Section	Questions
Route Filtering	1–4
Route Summarization	5–7
Default Routes	8, 9

1. Router R1 has been configured for EIGRP. The configuration also includes an ACL with one line–**access-list 1 permit 10.100.32.0 0.0.15.255**–and the EIGRP configuration includes the **distribute-list 1 in** command. Which of the following routes could not be displayed in the output of the **show ip eigrp topology** command as a result?

   a. 10.10.32.0/19

   b. 10.10.44.0/22

   c. 10.10.40.96/27

   d. 10.10.48.0/23

   e. 10.10.60.0/30

2. The command output that follows was gathered from router R1. If correctly referenced by an EIGRP distribution list that filters outbound Updates, which of the following statements is true about the filtering of various prefixes by this Prefix list?

```
R1#sh ip prefix-list
ip prefix-list question: 4 entries
    seq 5 deny 10.1.2.0/24 ge 25 le 27
    seq 15 deny 10.2.0.0/16 ge 30 le 30
    seq 20 permit 0.0.0.0/0
```

   a. Prefix 10.1.2.0/24 will be filtered due to clause 5.

   b. Prefix 10.1.2.224/26 will be filtered due to clause 5.

   c. Prefix 10.2.2.4/30 will be filtered due to clause 15.

   d. Prefix 10.0.0.0/8 will be permitted.

   e. Prefix 0.0.0.0/0 will be permitted.

3. R1 has correctly configured EIGRP to filter routes using a route map named *question*. The configuration that follows shows the entire route map and related configuration. Which of the following is true regarding the filtering action on prefix 10.10.10.0/24 in this case?

```
route-map question deny 10
 match ip address 1
route-map question permit 20
 match ip address prefix-list fred
!
access-list 1 deny 10.10.10.0 0.0.0.255
ip prefix-list fred permit 10.10.10.0/23 le 25
```

   a. It will be filtered due to the deny action in route map clause 10.

   b. It will be allowed because of the double negative (two deny references) in clause 10.

   c. It will be permitted due to matching clause 20's reference to prefix-list fred.

   d. It will be filtered due to matching the implied deny all route map clause at the end of the route map.

4. An engineer has typed four different single-line prefix lists in a word processor. The four answers show the four different single-line prefix lists. The engineer then does a copy/paste of the configuration into a router. Which of the lists could match a subnet whose prefix length is 27?

    a.   **ip prefix-list fred permit 10.0.0.0/24 ge 16 le 28**

    b.   **ip prefix-list barney permit 10.0.0.0/24 le 28**

    c.   **ip prefix-list wilma permit 10.0.0.0/24 ge 25**

    d.   **ip prefix-list betty permit 10.0.0.0/24 ge 28**

5. An engineer plans to configure summary routes with the **ip summary-address eigrp** *asn prefix mask* command. Which of the following, when added to such a command, would create a summary that includes all four of the following subnets: 10.1.100.0/25, 10.1.101.96/27, 10.1.101.224/28, and 10.1.100.128.25?

    a.   10.1.0.0 255.255.192.0

    b.   10.1.64.0 255.255.192.0

    c.   10.1.100.0 255.255.255.0

    d.   10.1.98.0 255.255.252.0

6. R1 has 5 working interfaces, with EIGRP neighbors existing off each interface. R1 has routes for subnets 10.1.1.0/24, 10.1.2.0/24, and 10.1.3.0/24, with EIGRP integer metrics of roughly 1 million, 2 million, and 3 million, respectively. An engineer then adds the **ip summary-address eigrp 1 10.1.0.0 255.255.0.0** command to interface Fa0/0. Which of the following is true?

    a.   R1 loses and then reestablishes neighborships with all neighbors.

    b.   R1 no longer advertises 10.1.1.0/24 to neighbors connected to Fa0/0.

    c.   1 advertises a 10.1.0.0/16 route out Fa0/0, with metric of around 3 million (largest metric of component subnets).

    d.   R1 advertises a 10.1.0.0/16 route out Fa0/0, with metric of around 2 million (median metric of component subnets).

7. In a lab, R1 connects to R2, which connects to R3. R1 and R2 each have several working interfaces, all assigned addresses in class A network 10.0.0.0. Router R3 has some working interfaces in class A network 10.0.0.0, and others in class B network 172.16.0.0. The engineer experiments with the **auto-summary** command on R2 and R3, enabling and disabling the command in various combinations. Which of the following combinations will result in R1 seeing a route for 172.16.0.0/16, instead of the individual subnets of class B network 172.16.0.0?

    a.   **auto-summary** on R2 and **no auto-summary** on R3

    b.   **auto-summary** on R2 and **auto-summary** on R3

    c.   **no auto-summary** on R2 and **no auto-summary** on R3

    d.   **no auto-summary** on R2 and **auto-summary** on R3

8. Router R1 exists in an Enterprise that uses EIGRP as its routing protocol. The **show ip route** command output on router R1 lists the following phrase: "Gateway of last resort is 1.1.1.1 to network 2.0.0.0". Which of the following is most likely to have caused this output to occur on R1?

   a. R1 has been configured with an **ip default-network 2.0.0.0** command.

   b. R1 has been configured with an **ip route 0.0.0.0 0.0.0.0 1.1.1.1** command.

   c. R1 has been configured with an **ip route 2.0.0.0 255.0.0.0 1.1.1.1** command.

   d. Another router has been configured with an **ip default-network 2.0.0.0** command.

   e. Another router has been configured with an **ip route 2.0.0.0 255.0.0.0 1.1.1.1** command.

9. Enterprise Router R1 connects an Enterprise to the Internet. R1 needs to create and advertise a default route into the Enterprise using EIGRP. The engineer creating the implementation plan has chosen to base this default route on the **ip route** command, rather than using **ip default-network**. Which of the following is not a useful step with this style of default route configuration?

   a. Create the default route on R1 using the **ip route 0.0.0.0 0.0.0.0** *outgoing-interface* command.

   b. Redistribute the statically configured default route.

   c. Disable auto-summary.

   d. Configure the **network 0.0.0.0** command.

   e. Ensure R1 has no manually configured summary routes using the **ip summary-address eigrp** command.

Foundation Topics

Route Filtering

Does a router in a branch office need to be able to forward packets to hosts in another branch office? Does a router in the sales division need to be able to forward packets to hosts in the manufacturing division? These questions are just a sampling of design questions for which route filtering can be part of the solution.

Route filtering allows the engineer to filter which routes are advertised in an EIGRP update. If routers in a branch do not need to learn routes about subnets in other branches, routers can filter that routing information. This filtering reduces the size of routing tables, saving memory, possibly improving routing performance, and makes the internetwork more secure by limiting the flow of packets.

EIGRP enables route filtering using the **distribute-list** router subcommand. The concept is relatively straightforward: The distribute list refers to either an access control list (ACL), prefix list, or route map. These three tools classify whether a route should be permitted to be sent/received in an EIGRP Update or be denied (filtered). The **distribute-list** command also specifies the direction–outbound updates or inbound updates–and optionally, the specific interface on which to filter updates.

For example, Figure 4-1 shows an expanded version of the internetwork used frequently in the previous two chapters. The figure adds several links between the WAN routers and some core Layer 3 switches. It also notes the address ranges for all data centers (10.16.0.0/16) and the range of addresses used for subnets in the manufacturing division (10.17.32.0/19).

The design engineer could make many choices about what routes to filter, for example:

- Filter routes to WAN subnets so that the core and manufacturing do not learn those routes, because these subnets should not be the destination of any user traffic.

- Filter manufacturing routes from being advertised to the branches, because the branches are in the sales division.

- Filter routes for the subnets sitting between the Layer 3 switches in the core, preventing them from being advertised to either manufacturing or the sales branches, because no users in these divisions should be sending packets to these subnets.

The examples in this chapter focus on the first of these design options.

Filtering the subnets that exist between Layer 3 devices, as is suggested in the second and third items in the list, have both pros and cons. For example, the second design goal filters the WAN subnets, because no end users need to be able to send packets to those subnets. This meets the goal of having smaller routing tables. However, operations personnel may have a larger challenge when monitoring and troubleshooting, because when a **ping** or **traceroute** fails, they also need to figure out whether the command failed by design due to the purposefully filtered routes, or whether a problem has occurred.

Note: All WAN IP addresses begin with 10.1.
       All LAN Core IP addresses begin with 10.9.1.

Figure 4-1   *Expanded Design with a Range of Addresses in Manufacturing*

This section next examines how to filter EIGRP routes using ACLs, prefix lists, and then route maps. All three of these tools will be used throughout this book, so this chapter lays the foundation for understanding these tools, in addition to showing how to use these tools when filtering EIGRP routes.

Filtering by Referencing ACLs

To filter EIGRP routes by matching them using ACLs, the ACL must match a route with a **permit** clause to then allow the route to be advertised, and match the route with a **deny** clause to filter the route. Before getting into how an ACL matches a route, first it is important to review what can be examined based on the configuration of an IP ACL.

EIGRP distribute lists support the use of standard IP ACLs. The syntax of both numbered and named standard ACLs allows a configuration of one dotted decimal number and its corresponding wildcard (WC) mask. When used for packet filtering, this number is compared to the source IP address of the packet. When referenced by the **distribute-list** command for the purpose of EIGRP route filtering, EIGRP compares the standard ACL source-address field to the subnet number (prefix) of each EIGRP route.

The best way to learn the specifics is to consider several examples. Figure 4-2 shows the specific size subnets being advertised from the manufacturing division into the core. The design calls for the WAN routers to filter these routes from being advertised toward the Sales division's branch offices.

Figure 4-2 shows the **distribute-list 2 out s0/0/0.1** command on Router WAN1 as one sample of the syntax. A command like this would need to be included in WAN1's configuration for each interface connected to a branch. ACL number 2 would then be configured

Routes from Manufacturing:
10.17.32.0/23
10.17.34.0/24
10.17.35.0/25
10.17.35.128/25
10.17.36.0/26
10.17.36.64/26

Figure 4-2   *Specific Manufacturing Routes to Be Filtered*

to match the manufacturing routes with a deny clause, and all other routes with a permit clause, filtering the routes.

If WAN1 has hundreds of serial subinterfaces for its WAN connections, then following the sample in the previous paragraph, WAN1 would have hundreds of **distribute-list 2 out se-rial** *number* commands, one per WAN interface/subinterface. Alternatively, the engineer could configure a single **distribute-list 2 out** command on Router WAN1, not specifying an interface. In this case, Router WAN1 would not advertise these routes to any neighbors, greatly reducing WAN1's configuration.

Given that this section represents the first use of ACLs in this book, at your option, take the time to try the following exercise as a review of ACLs. Consider the following **access-list** commands. Imagine that each command in this list is the first of two commands in a single access-list. The second and only other command is a command that permits all other routes—for example, **access-list 2 permit any**. Then, ask yourself—if used by a **distribute-list** on WAN1 to filter the manufacturing routes (as seen in Figure 4-2), and you want that ACL to filter only manufacturing routes, which of these 2-line ACLs meet the requirements?

```
access-list 3 deny 10.17.32.0
access-list 4 deny 10.17.32.0 0.0.0.255
access-list 5 deny 10.17.32.0 0.0.3.255
access-list 6 deny 10.16.0.0 0.1.255.255
```

To keep from giving away the answers, Table 4-2, which supplies the answers and explanation, is located on the next page.

Table 4-2 *Analysis of the Sample ACLs Used with the distribute-list Command*

ACL	Routes Filtered	Explanation
3	10.17.32.0/23	The ACL matches exactly prefix 10.17.32.0, so it matches a single manufacturing route.
4	10.17.32.0/23	The ACL matches all prefixes that begin with 10.17.32 because of the WC mask, again matching a single route.
5	10.17.32.0/23 10.17.34.0/24 10.17.35.0/25 10.17.35.128/25	The ACL matches all prefixes in the range 10.17.32.0–10.17.35.255, which includes four manufacturing routes.
6	All manufacturing and data center routes	The ACL matches all prefixes in the range 10.16.0.0–10.17.255.255, which includes the data center routes.

Note: To find the range of numbers matched by an ACL's address and wildcard mask values, use the address field as the low end of the range, and simply add the address and wildcard mask to find the high end of the range.

Example 4-1 shows the configuration on router WAN1 to filter the manufacturing routes, with distribute lists enabled on its two WAN subinterfaces. The ACL matches (with a deny action) all manufacturing routes, and matches all other routes with a permit clause.

Example 4-1 *WAN1's distribute-list to Filter Manufacturing Routes*

```
! On Router B1, before the filtering is applied:
B1#show ip route | include 10.17
D       10.17.35.0/25 [90/2300416] via 10.1.1.1, 00:00:18, Serial0/0/0.1
D       10.17.34.0/24 [90/2300416] via 10.1.1.1, 00:00:18, Serial0/0/0.1
D       10.17.32.0/23 [90/2300416] via 10.1.1.1, 00:00:18, Serial0/0/0.1
D       10.17.36.0/26 [90/2300416] via 10.1.1.1, 00:00:18, Serial0/0/0.1
D       10.17.36.64/26 [90/2300416] via 10.1.1.1, 00:00:18, Serial0/0/0.1
D       10.17.35.128/25 [90/2300416] via 10.1.1.1, 00:00:18, Serial0/0/0.1
! On Router WAN1:

WAN1#configure terminal
Enter configuration commands, one per line.  End with CNTL/Z.
WAN1(config)#access-list 2 deny 10.17.32.0 0.0.31.255
WAN1(config)#access-list 2 permit any
WAN1(config)#router eigrp 1
WAN1(config-router)#distribute-list 2 out
WAN1(config-router)#^Z
WAN1#
```

```
! On Router B1, after the filtering is applied
B1#show ip route ¦ include 10.17
B1#
```

Note: The same configuration added to Router WAN1 was also added to Router WAN2; however, the commands were not repeated in Example 4-1.

The ACL in this case, ACL 2, matches all subnets with a value between 10.17.32.0–10.17.63.255, inclusive, based on the IP address value of 10.17.32.0 and WC mask of 0.0.31.255. By matching these routes with a **deny** clause, the ACL, used as a distribute list, filters the routes. The **access-list 2 permit any** command matches all other routes, allowing them to be advertised.

Table 4-2 lists the answers to the exercise listed a few pages back.

Filtering by Referencing IP Prefix Lists

The IOS IP **prefix-list** feature gives the network engineer another tool for matching routes when performing route filtering. IP prefix lists can examine both the prefix and the prefix length, and a range of prefixes or a range of prefix lengths. The command then sets either a deny or permit action for each matched prefix/length. To use the prefix-list, the configuration simply refers to the **prefix-list** with the same **distribute-list** command seen earlier.

Using IP prefix lists for route filtering has several advantages. First, IP prefix lists allow matching of the prefix length, whereas the ACLs used by the EIGRP **distribute-list** command cannot. (Some other route filtering configurations can match both the prefix and prefix length using extended ACLs.) Many people find IP prefix lists more intuitive for configuring route filtering. Finally, the internal processing of the IP prefix lists uses an internal tree structure that results in faster matching of routes as compared with ACLs.

This section begins by examining IP prefix lists as an end to itself, followed by an example of filtering EIGRP routes using a prefix list.

IP Prefix List Concepts

IP prefix lists provide mechanisms to match two components of an IP route:

■ The route prefix (the subnet number)

■ The prefix length (the subnet mask)

Each single IP prefix list has similar characteristics to a single ACL, with subtle similarities to both numbered and named ACLs. The IP prefix list consists of one or more global configuration commands (like numbered ACLs), with commands using the same name being in the same list (like named ACLs). As with named ACLs, each **ip prefix-list** command has a sequence number to allow later deletion of individual commands and insertion of commands into a particular sequence position. Each command has a **permit** or **deny** action—but because it is used only for matching routes, and not for packet filtering, the **permit** or **deny** keyword just implies whether a route is matched (**permit**) or not (**deny**).

The generic command syntax is as follows:

```
ip prefix-list list-name [seq seq-value] {deny ¦ permit prefix/prefix-
length}[ge ge-value] [le le-value]
```

The following statements summarize the logic:

Step 1.   The route's prefix must be within the range of addresses implied by the **prefix-list** command's *prefix/prefix-length* parameters.

Step 2.   The *route's prefix length* must match the *range of prefixes* implied by the **prefix-list** command's prefix-*length*, **ge**, and **le** parameters.

The matching of the prefix works much like the ACL matching logic. The configured prefix/prefix-length implies a range of IP addresses. For example, an **ip prefix-list barney deny 10.0.0.0/8...** implies any number whose first 8 bits (per the /8) match 10.0.0.0–in other words, all IPv4 addresses that begin with 10. Any route whose prefix is in this range–for example, 10.0.0.0, 10.1.1.0, and 10.5.255.128—would be considered to match this part of the logic.

However, IP prefix lists always examine the prefix length as well. To perform the logic of matching a route's prefix length, IOS considers the following parts of the **ip prefix-list** command:

■   The required *prefix-length* parameter

■   The optional *ge-value*, which stand for *greater-than-or-equal-to*

■   The optional *le-value, which stand for less-than-or-equal-to*

For a given **ip prefix-list** command, one of four configuration combinations affect the logic of matching prefix lengths, as listed in Table 4-3. The text following the table provides a more detailed explanation as compared with the summarized information in the table.

Table 4-3   *LE and GE Parameters on IP Prefix List, and the Implied Range of Prefix Lengths*

Prefix List Parameter	Range of Prefix Length
Neither	*conf-length must = route-length*
Both ge and le	*ge-value <= route-length <= le-value*
Only le	*conf-length <= route-length <= le-value*
Only ge	*ge-value <= route-length <= 32*

The first case in the table occurs when neither **ge** nor **le** is configured. In that case, an exact match of prefix-length must occur between the configured prefix length and a route's prefix length. For example, the command **ip prefix-list fred deny 10.0.0.0/8** matches route 10.0.0.0/8, but not 10.0.0.0/20.

The second case in the table occurs when both **ge** and **le** are configured. In that case, the route's prefix length must be between the configured **ge** and **le** values, inclusive. For instance, **ip prefix-list fred deny 10.0.0.0/8 ge 20 le 22** matches route 10.0.0.0/20, but not 10.0.0.0/8, because the prefix length must either be 20, 21, or 22.

The cases in which either **ge** or **le** is configured, but not both, requires a little more thought. A visual representation can help, as shown in Figure 4-3.

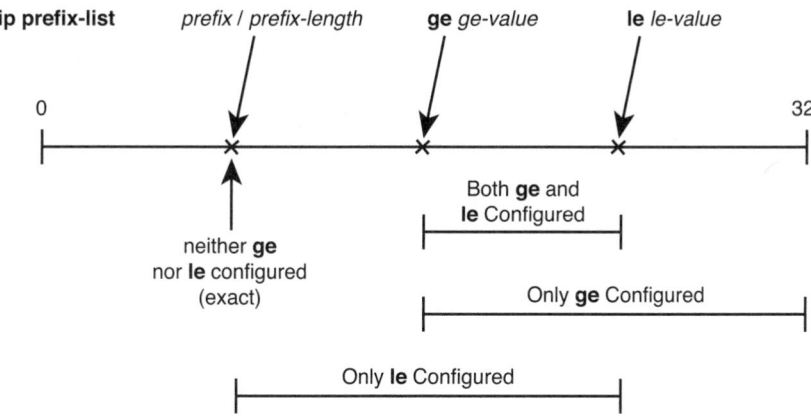

Figure 4-3   *Representation of Prefix Length Ranges for ip prefix-list Command*

In short, with only **ge** configured, the command matches prefix-length ranges from the *ge-value* up to 32 (the longest IPv4 prefix length), inclusive. With only **le** configured, the command matches prefix-length ranges between the *prefix-length* parameter and the *le-value*, inclusive.

Note: IOS requires that the configured prefix-length, ge-value, and le-value meet the following requirement: prefix-length <= ge-value <= le-value. Otherwise, IOS rejects the **ip prefix-list** command.

Samples of Prefix List Matching

Several examples can really help nail down prefix list logic. The following routes will be examined by a variety of prefix lists, with the routes numbered for easier reference:

Step 1.   10.0.0.0/8

Step 2.   10.128.0.0/9

Step 3.   10.1.1.0/24

Step 4.   10.1.2.0/24

Step 5.   10.128.10.4/30

Step 6.   10.128.10.8/30

Next, Table 4-4 shows the results of seven different one-line prefix lists applied to these six example routes. The table lists the matching parameters in the **prefix-list** commands, omitting the first part of the commands. The table explains which of the six routes would match the listed prefix list, and why.

Table 4-4   *Example Prefix Lists Applied to the List of Routes*

prefix-list Command Parameter	Routes Matched from previous list of prefixes	Result
10.0.0.0/8	1	Without **ge** or **le** configured, both the prefix (10.0.0.0) and length (8) must be an exact match.
10.128.0.0/9	2	Without **ge** or **le** configured, the prefix (10.128.0.0) and length (9) must be an exact match.
10.0.0.0/8 ge 9	2–6	The 10.0.0.0/8 means "all routes whose first octet is 10." The prefix length must be between 9 and 32, inclusive.
10.0.0.0/8 ge 24 le 24	3, 4	The 10.0.0.0/8 means "all routes whose first octet is 10," and the prefix range is 24 to 24—meaning only routes with prefix length 24.
10.0.0.0/8 le 28	1–4	The prefix length needs to be between 8 and 28, inclusive.
0.0.0.0/0	None	0.0.0.0/0 means "match all prefixes." However, because no le nor ge parameter is configured, the /0 also means that the prefix length must be 0. So, it would match all routes' prefixes, but none of their prefix lengths. Only a default route would match this prefix list.
0.0.0.0/0 le 32	All	The range implied by 0.0.0.0/0 is all IPv4 addresses. The **le 32** combined with prefix length 0 implies any prefix length between 0 and 32, inclusive. This is the syntax for "match all" prefix list logic.

Note: Pay particular attention to the match all logic of the final entry in the table.

Using IP Prefix Lists to Filter EIGRP Routes

After you master the logic behind IP prefix lists, using them with the **distribute-list** command requires minimal extra effort. For example, to refer to a prefix list name Fred, you could configure the **distribute-list prefix Fred...** command, instead of **distribute-list 2...** to refer to ACL 2. (Note that the prefix list names are case-sensitive.)

For example, using the internetwork of Figure 4-1 and Figure 4-2 again, consider the following revised design requirements for route filtering:

- Of the routes from manufacturing, filter only those routes that begin with 10.17.35 and 10.17.36.

- Of the routes for subnets on the WAN link, filter routes to prevent the core routers and branch routers from learning routes whose prefix length is /30.

Although the first of the preceding two requirements mainly exists to demonstrate the **ip prefix-list** command, the second goal may be more useful for real networks. Often, routes with a /30 prefix length are routes used between two routers, either on WAN links or over LANs between Layer 3-enabled devices. Users should not need to send packets to addresses in these subnets. So, the only need to have routes to these subnets is for network management (ping tests, for instance).

Example 4-2 shows the configuration on WAN1; the equivalent configuration has been added on WAN2 as well.

Example 4-2 *Filtering All Routes with a /30 Prefix Length*

```
! On Router WAN1: !!!!!!!!!!!!!!!!!!!!!!!!!!!!!!!!!!!!!!!!!!!!!!
WAN1#show running-config
! lines omitted for brevity
router eigrp 1
 network 10.0.0.0
 distribute-list prefix fred out
auto-summary
!
ip prefix-list fred seq 5 deny 10.17.35.0/24 ge 25 le 25
ip prefix-list fred seq 10 deny 10.17.36.0/24 ge 26 le 26
ip prefix-list fred seq 15 deny 0.0.0.0/0 ge 30 le 30
ip prefix-list fred seq 20 permit 0.0.0.0/0 le 32
! On Router B1:
B1#show ip route
Codes: C - connected, S - static, R - RIP, M - mobile, B - BGP
       D - EIGRP, EX - EIGRP external, O - OSPF, IA - OSPF inter area
       N1 - OSPF NSSA external type 1, N2 - OSPF NSSA external type 2
       E1 - OSPF external type 1, E2 - OSPF external type 2
       i - IS-IS, su - IS-IS summary, L1 - IS-IS level-1, L2 - IS-IS level-2
       ia - IS-IS inter area, * - candidate default, U - per-user static route
       o - ODR, P - periodic downloaded static route
```

```
Gateway of last resort is not set


     10.0.0.0/8 is variably subnetted, 7 subnets, 3 masks
C        10.11.1.0/24 is directly connected, FastEthernet0/0
D        10.12.1.0/24 [90/2684416] via 10.1.2.1, 00:06:15, Serial0/0/0.2
                       [90/2684416] via 10.1.1.1, 00:06:15, Serial0/0/0.1
C        10.1.2.0/30 is directly connected, Serial0/0/0.2
C        10.1.1.0/30 is directly connected, Serial0/0/0.1
D        10.16.1.0/24 [90/2172672] via 10.1.2.1, 00:00:32, Serial0/0/0.2
                       [90/2172672] via 10.1.1.1, 00:00:32, Serial0/0/0.1
D        10.17.34.0/24 [90/2300416] via 10.1.2.1, 00:06:15, Serial0/0/0.2
                       [90/2300416] via 10.1.1.1, 00:06:15, Serial0/0/0.1
D        10.17.32.0/23 [90/2300416] via 10.1.2.1, 00:06:15, Serial0/0/0.2
                       [90/2300416] via 10.1.1.1, 00:06:15, Serial0/0/0.1


B1#show ip route 10.17.32.0 255.255.248.0 longer-prefixes
! The legend is normally displayed; omitted here for brevity


     10.0.0.0/8 is variably subnetted, 7 subnets, 3 masks
D        10.17.34.0/24 [90/2300416] via 10.1.2.1, 00:04:12, Serial0/0/0.2
                       [90/2300416] via 10.1.1.1, 00:04:12, Serial0/0/0.1
D        10.17.32.0/23 [90/2300416] via 10.1.2.1, 00:04:12, Serial0/0/0.2
                       [90/2300416] via 10.1.1.1, 00:04:12, Serial0/0/0.1
```

The configuration on WAN1 includes a four-line prefix list. The first line (sequence number 5) matches 10.17.35.0/25 and 10.17.35.128/25, in part because it asks for a range of prefix lengths from 25 to 25–meaning an exact length of 25. Similarly, the second statement (sequence number 10) matches routes 10.17.36.0/26 and 10.17.36.64/26. The third statement (sequence number 15) uses wildcard logic (**0.0.0.0/0**) to match all prefixes, but only those with prefix length 30 (**ge 30 le 30**). The last command matches all prefixes, with prefix lengths from 0 to 32 (all prefix lengths).

The resulting IP routing table on branch Router B1 shows only a small number of routes. B1 has a route to the other example branch's subnet (10.12.1.0), and another in the range of addresses for the data centers (10.16.1.0/24). It has the two routes leaked from manufacturing. Note that the only two /30 routes known on B1 are two connected routes, so the **distribute-list** is filtering all the /30 routes.

Filtering by Using Route Maps

Route maps, the third EIGRP route filtering tool that can be referenced with the **distribute-list** command, provides programming logic similar to the If/Then/Else logic seen in programming languages. A single route map has one or more **route-map** commands in it, and routers process **route-map** commands in sequential order based on sequence numbers. Each **route-map** command has underlying matching parameters, configured with the aptly named **match** command. (To match all packets, the **route-map** clause simply omits the **match** command.)

Route maps can be used for many functions besides being used to filter routes for a single routing protocol like EIGRP. Route maps can be used to filter routes during the route redistribution process, and to set BGP Path Attributes (PAs) for the purpose of influencing the choice of the best routes in an internetwork.

When used for filtering EIGRP routes, route maps do provide a few additional features beyond what can be configured using ACLs and prefix lists. However, route maps can be tricky to understand and sometimes counterintuitive. This section begins with an examination of the concepts behind IOS route maps, followed by some examples of their use for filtering EIGRP routes.

Route Map Concepts

Route maps have many similarities when compared to ACLs and prefix lists. A single route map has several **route-map** commands, with the commands in the same route map all having the same text name. When referenced by the **distribute-list** command, IOS processes the commands in the route map sequentially, based on the sequence numbers in the commands. Like ACLs and prefix lists, IOS adds the sequence numbers automatically if omitted when configuring the **route-map** commands. And once a particular route has been matched and determined to be either filtered (deny) or allowed to pass (permit), even if more **route-map** commands exist later in the list, IOS stops processing the route-map for that route.

Each **route-map** command includes the name of the route map, an action (**permit** or **deny**), and possibly a sequence number (optional). After typing this command, the CLI user is in **route-map** configuration mode for that route-map clause. Any **match** commands configured in that mode apply to that single **route-map** command. For instance, Example 4-3 shows the configuration of a sample route map on router WAN1.

Example 4-3   *Pseudocode for Route Map Used as EIGRP Route Filter*

```
route-map sample-rm deny 8
 match (1st set of criteria)
route-map sample-rm permit 17
 match (2nd set of criteria)
route-map sample-rm deny 30
 match (3rd set of criteria)
route-map sample-rm permit 35
!
router eigrp 1
 distribute-list route-map sample-rm out
```

Example 4-3 shows pseudocode, ignoring the specifics of what is matched with the **match** commands. Focus on the actions in the **route-map** command (permit or deny), and the overall logic, as listed here:

■   **Seq #8:** The action is **deny**, so discard or filter all routes matched by the **match** command (1st set of criteria).

- **Seq #17:** The action is **permit**, so allow through all routes matched by the **match** command (2nd set of criteria).

- **Seq #30:** The action is **deny**, so discard or filter all routes matched by the **match** command (3rd set of criteria).

- **Seq #35:** The action is **permit**. The absence of a **match** command means "match all," so allow through all remaining routes.

The **match** command can reference an ACL or prefix list, but doing so does introduce the possibility of confusion. The confusing part is that the decision to filter a route or allow the route through is based on the **deny** or **permit** in the **route-map** command, and *not the deny or permit in the ACL or prefix list*. When referencing an ACL or prefix list from a route map, the ACL or prefix list simply matches all routes permitted by the ACL or prefix list. Routes that are denied by the ACL or prefix list simply do not match that **match** command's logic, making IOS then consider the next **route-map** command.

The following list summarizes the key points about route map logic when used for redistribution:

Key Topic

- **route-map** commands with the **permit** option either cause a route to be allowed through (if matched by the **match** command) or remain in the list of routes to be examined by the next **route-map** clause.

- **route-map** commands with the **deny** option either filter the route (if matched by the **match** command) or remain in the list of routes to be examined by the next **route-map** clause.

- If a clause's **match** commands refer to an ACL or prefix list, and the ACL or prefix list matches a route with the **deny** action, the route is not necessarily filtered. Instead, it just means that route does not match that particular **match** command and can then be considered by the next **route-map** clause.

- The **route-map** command includes an implied deny all clause at the end; to configure a permit all, use the **route-map** command, with a **permit** action, but without a **match** command.

Route maps have several more options on the **match command** as compared to what can be examined by ACLs and IP prefix lists. However, for the purposes of EIGRP route filtering, the items that may be matched do not provide significant help in filtering routes. However, when redistributing routes from other routing protocols, as is covered in Chapter 9, "Basic IGP Redistribution," and Chapter 10, "Advanced IGP Redistribution," some of the **match** command's other options can be very helpful.

Using Route Maps to Filter EIGRP Routes

The mechanics of the configuration works much like the other two filtering features. The **distribute-list** command refers to the feature that matches the packets, in this case a **route-map** command option. The **distribute-list** command again lists a direction (in or out), and optionally an interface.

Example 4-4 shows the configuration results in an excerpt from the **show running-config** command, along with the output of the **show route-map** command. The configuration implements the same logic as used in Example 4-2 earlier in this chapter, under the heading "Using IP Prefix Lists to Filter EIGRP Routes." The design criteria are the same as with that earlier example:

■   Of the routes from manufacturing, filter only those routes that begin with 10.17.35 and 10.17.36.

■   Filter WAN routers from advertising any /30 routes in the Layer 3 core.

Example 4-4   *Filtering All Routes with a /30 Prefix Length, Plus Some Routes from Manufacturing*

```
! On Router WAN1: !!!!!!!!!!!!!!!!!!!!!!!!!!!!!!!!!!!!!!!!!!!!
WAN2#show running-config
! lines omitted for brevity
router eigrp 1
 network 10.0.0.0
 distribute-list route-map filter-man-slash30 out
 auto-summary
!
ip prefix-list manufacturing seq 5 permit 10.17.35.0/24 ge 25 le 25
ip prefix-list manufacturing seq 10 permit 10.17.36.0/24 ge 26 le 26
!
ip prefix-list slash30 seq 5 permit 0.0.0.0/0 ge 30 le 30
!
route-map filter-man-slash30 deny 8
 match ip address prefix-list manufacturing
!
route-map filter-man-slash30 deny 15
 match ip address prefix-list slash30
!
route-map filter-man-slash30 permit 23

! Notice - no match commands, so the above clause matches all remaining routes
!
! lines omitted for brevity
WAN2#show route-map
route-map filter-man-slash30, deny, sequence 8
  Match clauses:
    ip address prefix-lists: manufacturing
  Set clauses:
  Policy routing matches: 0 packets, 0 bytes
route-map filter-man-slash30, deny, sequence 15
  Match clauses:
    ip address prefix-lists: slash30
  Set clauses:
  Policy routing matches: 0 packets, 0 bytes
route-map filter-man-slash30, permit, sequence 23
```

```
Match clauses:
Set clauses:
Policy routing matches: 0 packets, 0 bytes
```

In particular, note that the first two **route-map** commands list a **deny** action, meaning that all routes matched in these two clauses will be filtered. The IP prefix lists referenced in the **match** commands, called **manufacturing** and **slash30**, respectively, each match (permit) the routes listed in one of the two design goals. Note that the logic of both prefix lists could have easily been configured into a single prefix list, reducing the length of the **route-map** command as well. Finally, note that the last **route-map** command has a **permit** action, with no **match** command, meaning that the default action is to allow the route to be advertised.

Also, it can be useful to take a moment and review Example 4-2 as a point of comparison for the use of the IP prefix lists in each case. In the **route-map** of Example 4-4, the prefix list needs to match the routes with a permit clause so that the route-map **deny** action causes the routes to be filtered. Earlier, Example 4-2 shows the same basic logic in the prefix list, but with an action of deny. The reasoning is that when the **distribute-list prefix-list...** command refers directly to an IP prefix list, IOS then filters routes denied by the prefix list.

Route Summarization

As mentioned in the introduction to this chapter, keeping routing tables small helps conserve memory and may improve the time required by a router to forward packets. Route filtering allows an engineer to reduce the size of the routing table, but with the side effect of limiting the destinations reachable by each router. That effect may or may not be acceptable, given the other design goals of a particular internetwork, and given the need to operate the network.

Route summarization allows an engineer to keep the routing tables more manageable, without limiting reachability. Instead of advertising routes for every subnet, a router advertises a single route that represents the same range of IP addresses as more than one subnet. Each router can forward packets to the same set of destinations, but the routing table is smaller. For example, instead of advertising routes 10.11.0.0/24, 10.11.1.0/24, 10.11.2.0/24, and so on–all subnets up through 10.11.255.0/24–a router could advertise a single route for 10.11.0.0/16, which includes the exact same range of addresses.

This section begins by examining some design issues related to route summarization. Then the text moves on to explain how to explicitly configure EIGRP summary routes, finishing with a discussion of automatically created summaries based on the **auto-summary** command and feature.

Route Summarization Design

Route summarization works best when the subnet planning process considers route summarization. To accommodate summarization, the engineer assigning subnets can assign larger address blocks to one part of the topology. The engineers working with that part of the internetwork can break the address blocks into individual subnets as needed. At the edge of that part of the network, the engineers can configure route summaries to be advertised to the other parts of the internetwork. In short, when possible, plan the route summaries before deploying the new parts of an internetwork, and then assign addresses to different parts of the internetwork within their assigned address blocks.

For example, consider Figure 4-4, which shows a variation on the same internetwork shown earlier in this chapter, with the address blocks planned before deployment.

Figure 4-4   *Address Blocks Planned for Example Enterprise Internetwork*

Figure 4-4 shows the address blocks planned for various parts of the internetwork, as follows:

■   Assign branch subnets come from two consecutive ranges–10.11.0.0/16 and 10.12.0.0/16.

■   Assign WAN router-to-router subnets from the range 10.1.0.0/16.

■   Assign core LAN router-to-router subnets from the range 10.9.0.0/16.

■   Assign Data Center subnets from the range 10.16.0.0/16.

■   Give the manufacturing division, which has a separate IT staff, address block 10.17.32.0/19.

Inside each of the circles in Figure 4-4, the engineering staff can assign subnets as the need arises. As long as addresses are not taken from one range and used in another part of the internetwork, the routers at the boundary between the regions (circles) in Figure 4-4 can configure EIGRP route summarization to both create one large summary route and prevent the advertisement of the smaller individual routes.

Calculating Summary Routes

Note that the examples in this chapter generally use simpler examples of summary routes, using prefix lengths like /24 and /16 most often. However, for the exam, you need to be comfortable interpreting prefix/prefix length pairs, and subnet/mask pairs, whether they represent an actual subnet or a summary route.

The math to analyze a subnet/mask pair, or prefix/length pair, is identical to the math included as part of the CCNA certification. As such, this book does not attempt to explain those same concepts, other than this brief review of one useful shortcut when working with potential summary routes.

If you can trust that the subnet/mask or prefix/length is a valid subnet or summary, then the following method can tell you the range of numbers represented. For example, consider 10.11.0.0/16. Written in subnet/mask form, it is 10.11.0.0/255.255.0.0. Then, invert the mask by subtracting the mask from 255.255.255.255, yielding 0.0.255.255 in this case. Add this inverted mask to the subnet number (10.11.0.0 in this case), and you have the high end of the range (10.11.255.255). So, summary 10.11.0.0/16 represents all numbers from 10.11.0.0–10.11.255.255.

When using less obvious masks, the process works the same. For example, consider 10.10.16.0/20. Converting to mask format, you have 10.10.16.0/255.255.240.0. Inverting the mask gives you 0.0.15.255. Adding the inverted mask to the subnet number gives you 10.10.31.255, and a range of 10.10.16.0–10.10.31.255.

Before closing this short section about calculating summary routes, note that the the the process of adding the inveretd subnet mask assumes that the prefix/length or subnet/mask is a valid subnet number or valid summary route. If it is not, then you can still do the math, but neither the low end nor high end of the range is valid. For example, 10.10.16.0/19, similar to the previous example, is not actually a subnet number. 10.10.16.0 would be an IP address in subnet 10.10.0.0/19, with range of addresses 10.10.0.0–10.10.31.255.

Choosing Where to Summarize Routes

EIGRP supports route summarization at any router, unlike OSPF, which requires that summarization be performed only at area border routers (ABR) or autonomous system border routers (ASBR). EIGRP's flexibility helps when designing the internetwork, but it also poses some questions as to where to summarize EIGRP routes.

In some cases, the options are relatively obvious. For example, consider the 10.17.32.0/19 address block in manufacturing in Figure 4-4. The manufacturing division's router could summarize all its routes as a single 10.17.32.0/19 route when advertising to Core1. Alternately, Core1 could summarize all those same routes, advertising a summary for 10.17.32.0/19. In either case, packets from the rest of the internetwork shown in Figure 4-4 will flow toward Core1 and then to the Manufacturing division.

Next, consider the 10.16.0.0/16 address block in the Data Center. Because all these subnets reside to the right of Layer 3 switches Core1 and Core2, these two devices could summarize 10.16.0.0/16. However, these routes could also be summarized on WAN1/WAN2 for advertisement to the branches on the left. Summarizing on Core1/Core2 helps reduce the size of the routing tables on WAN1 and WAN2. However, the sheer number of subnets in a Data Center is typically small compared to the number of small remote sites, so the savings of routing table space may be small.

One advantage of summarizing 10.16.0.0/16 on WAN1/WAN2 instead of Core1/Core2 in this case is to avoid routing inefficiencies in the core of the internetwork. The later section "Suboptimal Forwarding with Summarization" discussed the concept with a different example.

Influencing the Choice of Best Route for Summary Routes

Often, engineers plan route summarization for the same address block on multiple routers. Such a design takes advantage of redundancy and can be used to perform basic load balancing of traffic across the various paths through the internetwork. Figure 4-5 shows one such example, with Routers WAN1 and WAN2 summarizing routes for the two address blocks located on the branch office LANs: 10.11.0.0/16 and 10.12.0.0/16.

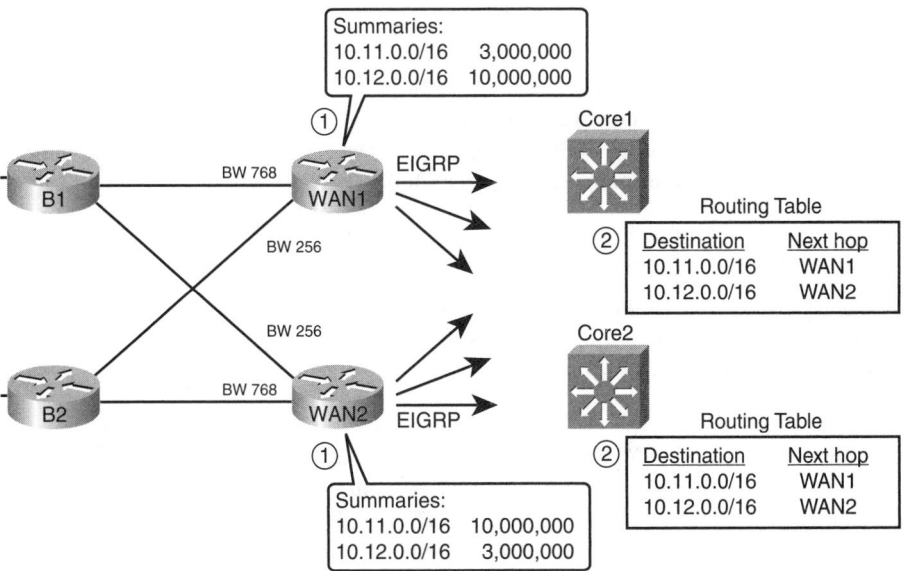

Figure 4-5   *Choosing Locations for Route Summarization*

The figure shows the advertisements of the summary routes. WAN1 and WAN2 both advertise the same summarizes: 10.11.0.0/16 for some branches and 10.12.0.0/16 for the others. Note that by advertising the WAN routes, instead of filtering, the operations staff might have an easier time monitoring and troubleshooting the internetwork, while still meeting the design goal of reducing the size of the routing table. (Also, note that Router WAN1 summarizes Manufacturing's routes of 10.17.32.0/19.)

In some cases, the network designer has no preference for which of the two or more routers should be used to reach hosts within the summary route range. For example, for most Data

Center designs, as shown earlier in Figure 4-4, the routes from the left of the figure toward the Data Center, through Core1 and Core2, would typically be considered equal.

However, in some cases, as in the design shown in Figure 4-5, the network designer wants to improve the metric of one of the summary routes for a single address block to make that route the preferred route. Using 10.11.0.0/16 as an example, consider this more detailed description of the design:

■ Use two PVCs to each branch—one faster PVC with 768 Kbps CIR and one slower PVC (either 128 Kbps or 256 Kbps CIR).

■ Roughly half the branches should have a faster PVC connecting to Router WAN1, and the other half of the branches should have a faster PVC connecting to Router WAN2.

■ Assign user subnets from the range 10.11.0.0/16 for branches that use WAN1 as the primary WAN access point, and from 10.12.0.0/16 for the branches that use WAN2 as primary.

■ Routing should be influenced such that packets flow in both directions over the faster WAN link, assuming that link is working.

This design requires that both directions of packets flow over the faster PVC to each branch. Focusing in the outbound (core-toward-branch) direction for now, by following the design, and setting the interface bandwidth settings to match the PVC speeds, the outbound routes will send packets over the faster PVCs. The main reason for the route choices is the following fact about summary routes with IOS:

> Set the summary route's metric components based on the lowest metric route upon which the summary route is based.

By setting the interface bandwidth settings to match the design, the two WAN routers should summarize and advertise routes for 10.11.0.0/16 and 10.12.0.0/16, advertising these routes toward the core—but with different metrics.

WAN1 advertises its 10.11.0.0/16 route with a lower metric than WAN2's summary for 10.12.0.0/16 because all of WAN1's routes for subnets that begin 10.11 are reachable over links set to use 768 Kbps of bandwidth. All WAN1's links to branches whose subnets begin 10.12 are reachable over links of speed 128 KBps or 256 Kbps, so WAN1's metric is higher that WAN2's metric for the 10.12.0.0/16 summary. WAN2 follows the same logic but with the lower metric route for 10.12.0.0/16.

As a result of the advertisements on WAN1 and WAN2, the core routers both have routing table entries that drive traffic meant for the faster-through-WAN1 branches to WAN1, and traffic for the faster-through-WAN2 branches to WAN2.

Suboptimal Forwarding with Summarization

The final concept to consider when summarizing routes is that the packets may take a longer path than if summarization is not used. The idea works a little like this story. Say you were travelling to Europe from the USA. You knew nothing of European geography, other than that you wanted to go to Paris. So, you look around and find hundreds of flights to Europe and just pick the cheapest one. When you get to Europe, you worry about how to get the rest of the way to Paris–be it a Taxi ride from the Paris airport, or whether it takes a day of train travel. Although you do eventually get to Paris, if you had chosen to know more about European geography before you left, you could have saved yourself some travel time in Europe.

Similarly, routers that learn a summary route do not know about the details of the subnets inside the summary. Instead, like the person who just picked the cheapest flight to Europe, the routers pick the lowest metric summary route for a prefix. That router forwards packets based on the summary route. Later, when these packets arrive at routers that do know all the subnets inside the summary, those routers can then use the best route–be it a short route or long route.

For example, Figure 4-6 shows the less efficient routing of packets to host 10.11.1.1, a host off Router B1, assuming that the route summarization shown in Figure 4-5 still exists. When R1's 768 Kbps CIR PVC to Router B1 fails, WAN1 does not change its route advertisement for its 10.11.0.0/16 summary route. When EIGRP advertises a summary route, the advertising router considers the summary route to be up and working unless all subordinate routes fail. Unless all of WAN1's specific routes in the 10.11.0.0/16 range failed, R1 would not notify routers on the right about any problem. So, when the example shown in Figure 4-6 begins, the 10.11.0.0/16 summary advertised by WAN1, as seen earlier in Figure 4-5, is still working, and both Core1 and Core2 use WAN1 as their next-hop router for their routes to 10.11.0.0/16.

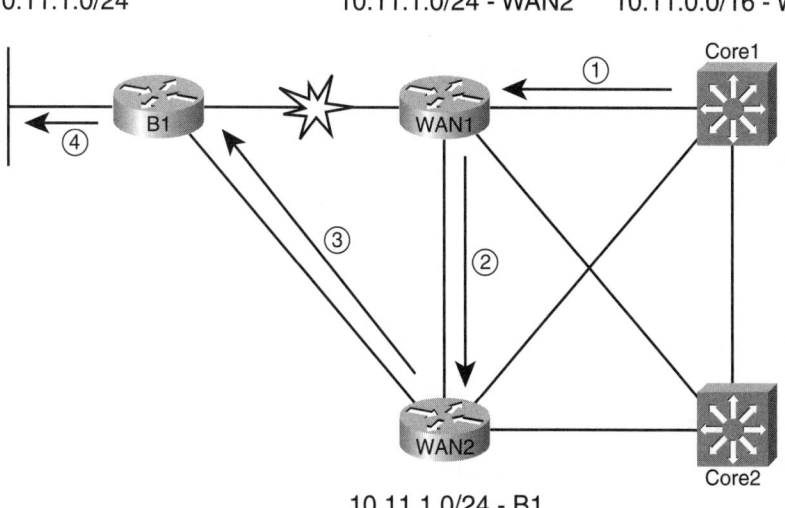

Figure 4-6 *Suboptimal Forwarding Path when Primary PVC Fails*

Following the steps in the figure:

Step 1.   Core 1 sends a packet to 10.11.1.1, using its route for 10.16.0.0/16, to WAN1.

Step 2.   WAN1, which has routes for all the subnets that begin 10.11, has a route for
10.11.1.0/24 with WAN2 as the next hop (because WAN1's link to B1 has
failed).

Step 3.   WAN2 has a route for 10.11.1.0/24, with B1 as the next hop, so WAN2 forwards the packet.

Step 4.   B1 forwards the packet to host 10.11.1.1.

Route Summarization Benefits and Trade-Offs

The previous section showed details of a classic trade-off with route summarization: the
benefits of the summary route versus the possibility of inefficient routing. For easier
study, the benefits and trade-offs for route summarization are listed here:

Benefits:

- Smaller routing tables, while all destinations still reachable.

- Reduces Query scope: EIGRP Query stops at a router that has a summary route that
  includes the subnet listed in the Query but not the specific route listed in the Query.

- EIGRP supports summarization at any location in the internetwork.

- The summary has the metric of the best of the subnets being summarized.

Trade-offs:

- Can cause suboptimal routing.

- Packets destined for inaccessible destinations will flow to the summarizing router before being discarded.

Configuring EIGRP Route Summarization

The more difficult part of EIGRP route summarization relates to the planning, design, and
analysis of trade-offs as covered in the preceding section. After you have made those design choices, configuring route summarization requires the addition of a few instances of
the following interface subcommand:

`ip summary-address eigrp` *asn prefix subnet-mask*

When configured on an interface, the router changes its logic for the EIGRP Update messages sent out the interface, as follows:

- The router brings down, and then back up, all EIGRP neighbors reachable on that interface, effectively causing neighbors to forget previous topology information, and
  listen to new information (when the neighborships recover).

- When the neighborships recover, the router advertises the summary route, per the **ip
  summary-address** command, assuming the router has at least one route whose address range is inside the range of the summary route.

- The router does *not* advertise the subordinate routes. (The term *subordinate route
  refers to the routes whose address ranges are inside the range of addresses are defined by the summary route.*)

■   The router adds a route to its own routing table, for the summary prefix/prefix-length, with an outgoing interface of null0.

In Figure 4-7, WAN1 and WAN2 summarize the routes for the Data Center in the range 10.16.0.0/16, instead of sending individual routes for this range to the branch offices. Example 4-5 shows the results of summarization on both routers.

Figure 4-7   *Summary for 10.16.0.0/16 on WAN1, WAN2*

Example 4-5   *Summarizing Routes for Data Center (10.16.0.0/16) on WAN1/WAN2*

```
! On Router WAN2: !!!!!!!!!!!!!!!!!!!!!!!!!!!!!!!!!!!!!!!!!!!!!!
WAN2#show running-config
! lines omitted for brevity
!
interface Serial0/0/0.1 point-to-point
 bandwidth 256
 ip address 10.1.2.1 255.255.255.252
 ip summary-address eigrp 1 10.16.0.0 255.255.0.0 5
 frame-relay interface-dlci 103
!
interface Serial0/0/0.2 point-to-point
 bandwidth 768
 ip address 10.1.2.5 255.255.255.252
 ip summary-address eigrp 1 10.16.0.0 255.255.0.0 5
 frame-relay interface-dlci 104
!
WAN2#show ip eigrp topology 10.16.0.0/16
IP-EIGRP (AS 1): Topology entry for 10.16.0.0/16
  State is Passive, Query origin flag is 1, 1 Successor(s), FD is 28416
```

```
        Routing Descriptor Blocks:
        0.0.0.0 (Null0), from 0.0.0.0, Send flag is 0x0
            Composite metric is (28416/0), Route is Internal
            Vector metric:
              Minimum bandwidth is 100000 Kbit
              Total delay is 110 microseconds
              Reliability is 255/255
              Load is 1/255
              Minimum MTU is 1500
              Hop count is 1
        10.1.2.2 (Serial0/0/0.1), from 10.1.2.2, Send flag is 0x0
            Composite metric is (11026688/3847936), Route is Internal
            Vector metric:
              Minimum bandwidth is 256 Kbit
              Total delay is 40110 microseconds
              Reliability is 255/255
              Load is 1/255
              Minimum MTU is 1500
              Hop count is 3


! Note that the following command lists only routes in the range
! of the summary - 10.16.0.0 - 10.16.255.255.
WAN2#show ip route 10.16.0.0 255.255.0.0 longer-prefixes
Codes: C - connected, S - static, R - RIP, M - mobile, B - BGP
       D - EIGRP, EX - EIGRP external, O - OSPF, IA - OSPF inter area
       N1 - OSPF NSSA external type 1, N2 - OSPF NSSA external type 2
       E1 - OSPF external type 1, E2 - OSPF external type 2
       i - IS-IS, su - IS-IS summary, L1 - IS-IS level-1, L2 - IS-IS level-2
       ia - IS-IS inter area, * - candidate default, U - per-user static route
       o - ODR, P - periodic downloaded static route


Gateway of last resort is not set


     10.0.0.0/8 is variably subnetted, 23 subnets, 6 masks
D       10.16.2.0/24 [90/156160] via 10.9.1.14, 00:19:06, FastEthernet0/0.12
D       10.16.3.0/24 [90/156160] via 10.9.1.14, 00:19:06, FastEthernet0/0.12
D       10.16.0.0/16 is a summary, 00:14:07, Null0
D       10.16.1.0/24 [90/28416] via 10.9.1.18, 00:19:06, FastEthernet0/1.16
                     [90/28416] via 10.9.1.14, 00:19:06, FastEthernet0/0.12
D       10.16.4.0/24 [90/156160] via 10.9.1.14, 00:19:06, FastEthernet0/0.12
WAN2#show ip route 10.16.0.0 255.255.0.0
Routing entry for 10.16.0.0/16
  Known via "eigrp 1", distance 5, metric 28416, type internal
  Redistributing via eigrp 1
```

```
Routing Descriptor Blocks:
* directly connected, via Null0
      Route metric is 28416, traffic share count is 1
      Total delay is 110 microseconds, minimum bandwidth is 100000 Kbit
      Reliability 255/255, minimum MTU 1500 bytes
      Loading 1/255, Hops 0
```

Example 4-5 shows the results only on Router WAN2, but WAN1 will be identically configured with the **ip summary-address** command. With only two branch office routers actually implemented in my lab, WAN2 needs only two **ip summary-address** commands: one for the subinterface connected to Router B1, and another for the subinterface connected to B2. With a full implementation, this same command would be needed on each subinterface connected to a branch router.

The example also shows how a router like WAN2 uses a summary route to null0. This route–10.16.0.0/16 with an outgoing interface of null0–causes the router (WAN2) to discard packets matched by this route. However, as you can see from the end of Example 4-5, WAN2 also has routes for all the known specific subnets. Pulling all these thoughts together, when the summarizing router receives a packet within the summary route's range

- If the packet matches a more specific route than the summary route, the packet is forwarded based on that route.

- When the packet does not match a more specific route, it matches the summary route and is discarded.

To ensure that the router adds this local summary route, the router uses the administrative distance (AD) setting of 5. The user may have typed the **ip summary-address eigrp 1 10.16.0.0 255.255.0.0** command, without the 5 at the end. Even so, IOS will add this default AD value as seen in Example 4-5. With an AD of 5, WAN2 will ignore any EIGRP-advertised summary routes for 10.16.0.0/16–for example, the summary created by neighbor WAN1—because EIGRP's default AD for internal routes is 90. In fact, the output of WAN2's **show ip eigrp topology 10.16.0.0/16** command lists two known routes for 10.16.0.0/16: one to null0 and the other to branch router WAN1 (outgoing interface S0/0/0.1). WAN1 uses the lower-AD route to null0, which prevents a routing loop. (Note that this summary route with outgoing interface null0 is often called a *discard route.)*

Next, consider the results on the branch routers. The following might be reasonable design requirements that should be verified on the branch routers:

- Each branch router's route for 10.16.0.0/16 should use the primary (faster) PVC (see Figure 4-7).

- Each branch router should be able to converge quickly to the other 10.16.0.0/16 summary route without using EIGRP Queries (in other words, there should be an FS route).

Example 4-6 confirms that both requirements are met.

Example 4-6   *Results of the 10.16.0.0/16 Summary on Routers B1, B2*

```
! Router B1 first !!!!!!!!!!!!!!!!!!!!!!!
B1#show ip route 10.16.0.0 255.255.0.0 longer-prefixes
! lines omitted for brevity

     10.0.0.0/8 is variably subnetted, 5 subnets, 3 masks
D        10.16.0.0/16 [90/3847936] via 10.1.1.1, 00:16:53, Serial0/0/0.1

B1#show ip eigrp topology
! lines omitted for brevity
P 10.16.0.0/16, 1 successors, FD is 3847936
        via 10.1.1.1 (3847936/28416), Serial0/0/0.1
        via 10.1.2.1 (10514688/28416), Serial0/0/0.2
! Router B2 Next !!!!!!!!!!!!!!!!!!!!!!
B2#show ip route 10.16.0.0 255.255.0.0 longer-prefixes
! lines omitted for brevity

     10.0.0.0/8 is variably subnetted, 5 subnets, 3 masks
D        10.16.0.0/16 [90/3847936] via 10.1.2.5, 00:16:44, Serial0/0/0.2
```

First, on Router B1, the router has an IP route for 10.16.0.0/16, with outgoing interface S0/0/0.1. Per Figure 4-7, this subinterface indeed connects to the primary PVC. Per the **show ip eigrp topology** command, two possible routes for 10.16.0.0/16 are listed; this command only lists successor and feasible successor routes. Also, note that the FS route's RD (28,416) is less than the successor route's FD (3,847,936), which means the secondary route indeed meets the feasibility condition.

The reverse is true on Router B2. B2's best route for 10.16.0.0/16 uses its S0/0/0.2, which connects to B2's primary (faster) PVC through WAN2. Although not shown, it also lists its backup route over the slower PVC as a feasible successor.

The route summarization feature discussed in this section is sometimes referred to as *manual* route summarization to contrast it with the term *auto* summarization. EIGRP auto summarization is explained next.

Auto-summary

Automatic summarization, also called auto-summary, causes a router to automatically advertise a summary route under certain conditions, without the use of the **ip summary-address** command. When using auto-summary, if a router has interfaces in more than one Class A, B, or C network, then that router will advertise a single summary route for an entire Class A, B, or C network into the other classful network, rather than advertise routes for the individual subnets. The following is a more formal definition:

Key Topic

When a router has multiple working interfaces, and those interfaces use IP addresses in different classful networks, the router advertises a summary route for each classful network on interfaces attached to a different classful network.

The auto-summary feature first existed as a required feature of *classful routing protocols*. By definition, classful routing protocols (RIPv1 and IGRP) do not advertise subnet mask information. The omission of the subnet mask in routing updates causes several design problems—in particular, these protocols cannot support variable length subnet masks (VLSM), route summarization, or discontiguous network designs.

The newer IGPs—EIGRP, OSPF, and RIP-2—are classless routing protocols because they advertise the subnet mask and support VLSM. However, with auto-summary enabled, EIGRP acts like classful routing protocols in one specific way: they do not support discontiguous networks. To support discontiguous networks with EIGRP, simply disable auto-summary. The rest of this section further defines the terms and the problem, and shows the solution of disabling auto-summary.

To better understand discontiguous networks, consider this analogy. U.S. residents can appreciate the concept of a discontiguous network based on the common term *contiguous 48*, referring to the 48 U.S. states other than Alaska and Hawaii. To drive to Alaska from the contiguous 48 U.S. states, for example, you must drive through another country (Canada, for the geographically impaired), so Alaska is not contiguous with the 48 states. In other words, it is discontiguous.

More formally:

- **Contiguous network:** A single classful network in which packets sent between every pair of subnets will pass only through subnets of that same classful network, without having to pass through subnets of any other classful network.

- **Discontiguous network:** A single classful network in which packets sent between at least one pair of subnets must pass through subnets of a different classful network.

Figure 4-8 shows a classic example of a discontiguous network 10.0.0.0. Subnets of class A network 10.0.0.0 exist on the left and the right, with subnets of class B network 172.16.0.0 in the middle of the internetwork. Following the figure, the problem created by the auto-summary feature is described.

Figure 4-8   *Discontiguous Network 10.0.0.0*

The problem is that when EIGRP auto-summarizes routes at the boundary between classful networks, then routers in other classful networks cannot route packets to all the destinations. For example, because both Yosemite and Seville use auto-summary, they both advertise a route for 10.0.0.0/8 to Albuquerque. Albuquerque may choose one of the two as the better route–for example, it may choose the route to the left, through Yosemite. However, in that case, then Albuquerque cannot forward packets to the network 10.0.0.0 hosts on the right. Even if Albuquerque decided to add both routes to its routing table, the load sharing typically occurs per destination IP address, not per subnet. So, some packets might be delivered to the correct host, and others not.

For EIGRP, two solutions exist. First, you could design the network to not use a discontiguous network. Alternatively, you can just disable auto-summary using the **no auto-summary** subcommand inside EIGRP configuration mode. This command affects the behavior of the router on which it is configured only and tells that router to not advertise a summary route for the entire classful network. Instead, that router advertises all the subnets, as if the auto-summary feature did not exist.

Note: The **auto-summary** and **no auto-summary** commands have no effect on routers that connect to a single classful network.

For classful routing protocols, the only solution is to not use discontiguous classful networks.

Note: Some confusion exists related to EIGRP's default for auto-summary. Some IOS documentation claims that EIGRP defaults to use **no auto-summary** at later IOS releases, including 12.4T, but experiments show the opposite. You can confirm the actual setting by looking at the output of the **show ip protocols** command.

Default Routes

A router's default route matches the destination of all packets that are not matched by any other route in the IP routing table. In fact, a default route can be thought of as the ultimate summary route–a route for the prefix that includes all IPv4 addresses, as represented by prefix/length 0.0.0.0/0.

This section first examines the most common use of default routes inside an Enterprise: to draw Internet traffic toward the Internet-connected routers without having to put routes for all Internet destinations into the Enterprise routers' routing tables. Following that, this section examines two methods for EIGRP to advertise the default route.

Default Routing to the Internet Router

Consider an Enterprise network and its connection to the Internet, as shown in Figure 4-9. For now, the design shows a single Internet-facing router (I1). As is often the case, the entire Enterprise in this figure uses private IP addresses. In this case, all Enterprise subnets are part of private class A network 10.0.0.0.

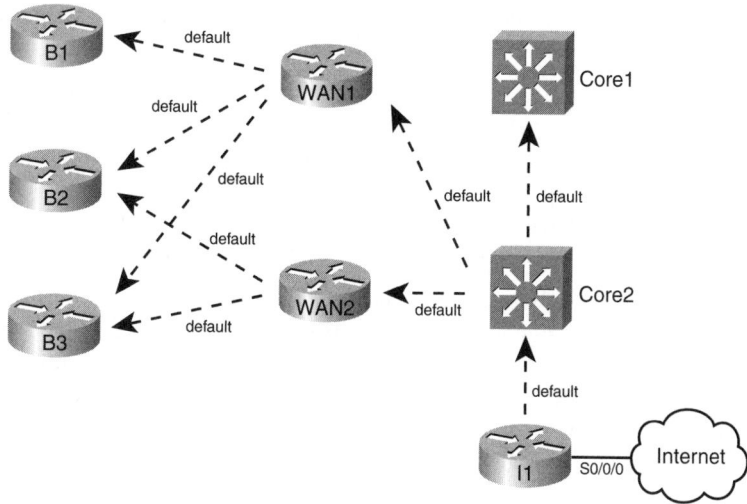

Figure 4-9   *Pulling Packets to the Internet Router (I1)*

From a design perspective, the entire Enterprise can use a default route to forward packets to the Internet. To accomplish this design, the Internet-facing router advertises a default route. All routers flood this default prefix throughout the EIGRP domain, building
their own default routes.

When converged, all routers have a default route, plus the usual Enterprise routes. Packets
destined for addresses inside the Enterprise use the same old routes, ignoring the default
route. Packets destined outside the Enterprise use each router's respective default route because no other routes match the destination. Eventually, these packets arrive at Router I1.
When I1 receives these packets, it can forward toward the Internet, either based on a default route or on routes learned using BGP.

Figure 4-9 shows a case with just one Internet-facing router, but with multiple, the same
concepts can be used. The multiple Internet-facing routers can each advertise a default
route, and each Enterprise router will think one of the available defaults is best–causing
the packets to arrive at the nearest Internet access point.

Default Routing Configuration with EIGRP

This section examines the two main options for EIGRP to advertise default routes: to define a static default route and advertise it with EIGRP and to flag an existing route to be
used also as a default route.

Advertising Static Default Routes with EIGRP

To cause the advertisement of the default routes shown in Figure 4-9, Router I1 can follow
these steps:

Step 1.   Create a static route default route using the **ip route 0.0.0.0 0.0.0.0 S0/0/0**
command.

Key
Topic

Step 2. Inject this route into the EIGRP topology database, either using the **network 0.0.0.0** command or by redistributing the static route.

First, examine the command listed for Step 1: **ip route 0.0.0.0 0.0.0.0 S0/0/0**. The prefix and mask together represent all IPv4 addresses. The reasoning is that if a mask of 255.255.0.0 means "the last two octets can be any value," and 255.0.0.0 means "the last three octets can be any value," then a subnet mask of 0.0.0.0 means that all four octets can be any value. The outgoing interface, S0/0/0 in this case, tells I1 to send packets for otherwise unknown destinations over the link to the Internet, as intended.

After Step 1, Router I1 has a route in its routing table, but EIGRP does not yet advertise the route. I1 could be configured to perform route redistribution for this static route. (Refer to Chapter 9 for more information on route redistribution.) The other option is to use the **network 0.0.0.0** EIGRP subcommand. Oddly enough, this command does not actually match interface IP addresses of interfaces, but is a special case in which IOS thinks "if my routing table has a default route in it, put a default route (0.0.0.0/0) into the EIGRP table." (If the route leaves the routing table, then the router will notify neighbors that the route has failed.)

Configuring a Default Network

The second option for creating a default route is to flag a route for a classful network—for a prefix that will be advertised into the EIGRP domain—as a route that can be used as a default route. Then each router can use the forwarding details in that route—the outgoing interface and next-hop router—as its default route.

Configuring this feature requires a couple of steps. The concepts require the most thought, with the configuration commands that follow being relatively simple:

Step 1. On the router to which all traffic should be directed, identify a classful network that can be advertised into the EIGRP domain, and ensure that network is being advertised into EIGRP (typically using the EIGRP **network** command).

Step 2. Configure that network as a default network using the global command **ip default-network** *network-number*.

Step 1 requires a class A, B, or C network, known in the routing table of the router that will generate the default route (Router I1 in Figure 4-9). Most often, that route is either created off a loopback interface for the purpose of making this process work, or an existing route on the Internet side of the router is used.

Figure 4-10 shows two examples. First, class C network 198.133.219.0/24 exists off I1's S0/0/0 interface, so I1 has a connected route for this class C network in its routing table. Alternatively, the engineer could configure a loopback interface, such as loopback 9, so that I1 would have a connected route for 192.31.7.0/24. In both cases, the routes would need to be advertised into EIGRP, by matching the address using the **network** command.

If the configuration stopped at Step 1, then the Enterprise routers simply know yet another route. By adding the **ip default-network** command to refer to one of these networks, EIGRP then flags this route as a candidate default route. As a result, each EIGRP router treats their route for this particular network also as if it were a default route.

Figure 4-10 *Example Default Networks*

Example 4-7 shows an example of the configuration on Router I1, along with some of the **show** commands on Router I1.

Example 4-7 *Configuring a Default Network on Router I1*

```
I1#configure terminal
Enter configuration commands, one per line.  End with CNTL/Z.
I1(config)#interface loopback 8
I1(config-if)#ip address 192.31.7.1 255.255.255.0
I1(config-if)#router eigrp 1
I1(config-router)#network 192.31.7.0
I1(config-router)#exit
I1(config)#ip default-network 192.31.7.0
I1(config-router)#^Z


I1#show ip route
Codes: C - connected, S - static, R - RIP, M - mobile, B - BGP
       D - EIGRP, EX - EIGRP external, O - OSPF, IA - OSPF inter area
       N1 - OSPF NSSA external type 1, N2 - OSPF NSSA external type 2
       E1 - OSPF external type 1, E2 - OSPF external type 2
       i - IS-IS, su - IS-IS summary, L1 - IS-IS level-1, L2 - IS-IS level-2
       ia - IS-IS inter area, * - candidate default, U - per-user static route
       o - ODR, P - periodic downloaded static route

Gateway of last resort is not set

     10.0.0.0/8 is variably subnetted, 15 subnets, 3 masks
```

```
! lines omitted for brevity
C*    192.31.7.0/24 is directly connected, Loopback8


I1#show ip eigrp topology 192.31.7.0/24
IP-EIGRP (AS 1): Topology entry for 192.31.7.0/24
  State is Passive, Query origin flag is 1, 1 Successor(s), FD is 128256
  Routing Descriptor Blocks:
  0.0.0.0 (Loopback8), from Connected, Send flag is 0x0
      Composite metric is (128256/0), Route is Internal
      Vector metric:
        Minimum bandwidth is 10000000 Kbit
        Total delay is 5000 microseconds
        Reliability is 255/255
        Load is 1/255
        Minimum MTU is 1514
        Hop count is 0
      Exterior flag is set
```

The configuration has several results, as seen in the example:

- A connected route for 192.31.7.0/24, a class C network

- The advertisement of that network into EIGRP due to the **network 192.31.7.0** command

- The setting of the exterior flag on the route

Because of the **ip default-network 192.31.7.0** command, the routing table lists the route as a candidate default route, as denoted by an asterisk.

Interestingly, the router with the **ip default-network** command configured–I1 in this case–does not use that route as a default route, as indicated by the highlighted phrase "Gateway of last resort not set." (*Gateway of last resort* refers to the next-hop router of a router's current default route.) Although I1 flags the route as a candidate default route, I1 itself does not use that route as its default, because I1 is actually the original advertiser of the default.

Moving on to another Enterprise router, in this case B1, you can see in Example 4-8 that not only does the remote router learn the candidate default route, but that the B1 uses this same information as B1's default route.

Example 4-8   *Gateway of Last Resort on Router B1*

```
B1#show ip route
Codes: C - connected, S - static, R - RIP, M - mobile, B - BGP
       D - EIGRP, EX - EIGRP external, O - OSPF, IA - OSPF inter area
       N1 - OSPF NSSA external type 1, N2 - OSPF NSSA external type 2
       E1 - OSPF external type 1, E2 - OSPF external type 2
       i - IS-IS, su - IS-IS summary, L1 - IS-IS level-1, L2 - IS-IS level-2
```

```
        ia - IS-IS inter area, * - candidate default, U - per-user static route
        o - ODR, P - periodic downloaded static route

Gateway of last resort is 10.1.1.1 to network 192.31.7.0


     10.0.0.0/8 is variably subnetted, 15 subnets, 3 masks
Lines omitted for brevity
D*    192.31.7.0/24 [90/2297856] via 10.1.1.1, 00:05:10, Serial0/0/0.1
```

In this case, B1 has indeed learned an EIGRP route for 192.31.7.0/24, a route flagged as exterior. Because this happens to be the only candidate default route learned by B1 at this point, it is the best default route. So, B1 sets its gateway of last resort to 10.1.1.1–the next-hop IP address of B1's route to 192.31.7.0/24. If B1 knew of multiple candidate default routes, it would have chosen the best route based on administrative distance and then metric, and used that route as the basis for the gateway of last resort.

Exam Preparation Tasks

Planning Practice

The CCNP ROUTE exam expects test takers to review design documents, create implementation plans, and create verification plans. This section provides some exercises that may help you to take a step back from the minute details of the topics in this chapter so that you can think about the same technical topics from the planning perspective.

For each planning practice table, simply complete the table. Note that any numbers in parentheses represent the number of options listed for each item in the solutions in Appendix F, "Completed Planning Practice Tables."

Design Review Table

Table 4-5 lists several design goals related to this chapter. If these design goals were listed in a design document, and you had to take that document and develop an implementation plan, what implementation options come to mind? For any configuration items, a general description can be used, without concern about the specific parameters.

Table 4-5 *Design Review*

Design Goal	Possible Implementation Choices Covered in This Chapter
Prevent the edge routers in sites for one division of the company from knowing routes for subnets in another division.	
The design shows the use of class B networks 172.16.0.0, 172.17.0.0, and 172.18.0.0 throughout the Enterprise, with a goal to reduce routing table sizes when possible. (3 options)	
R1 and R2 will advertise the same summary route; ensure that R1 is the preferred EIGRP path for that summary.	
Always ensure that the shortest path is taken with each route.	

Implementation Plan Peer Review Table

Table 4-6 shows a list of questions that others might ask, or that you might think about, during a peer review of another network engineer's implementation plan. Complete the table by answering the questions.

Table 4-6 *Notable Questions from This Chapter to Consider During an Implementation Plan Peer Review*

Question	Answer
The plan calls for filtering 10.10.10.0/26 and 10.10.12.0/26, but not 10.10.11.0/24. What tools can be used?	
A plan lists a configuration of an EIGRP distribution list, referring to route-map *one*. The route-maps clauses use only the deny option. However, it refers to prefix lists that use some deny and permit actions. Can any routes pass through the filter?	
A plan lists a configuration of an EIGRP distribution list, with a route-map with two clauses, each with a permit action. Both clauses refer to a different prefix list, each of which has some permit and deny actions. Characterize which routes will be filtered, and which will not, based on matching deny and permit clauses in each prefix list.	
The plan shows extensive use of class C private networks inside a large Enterprise. What effect might EIGRP auto-summary have?	
The plan shows a sample configuration of the **ip summary-address eigrp 1 10.10.0.0 255.255.252.0** command on Router R1. What routes should I see on R1? What will their administrative distance be?	

Create an Implementation Plan Table

To practice skills useful when creating your own EIGRP implementation plan, list in Table 4-7 configuration commands related to the configuration of the following features. You may want to record your answers outside the book and set a goal to complete this table (and others like it) from memory during your final reviews before taking the exam.

Table 4-7 *Implementation Plan Configuration Memory Drill*

Feature	Configuration Command/Notes
Filtering EIGRP routes using numbered ACLs	
Filtering EIGRP routes using prefix lists	
Enabling filtering EIGRP routes using route-maps	
Commands to create a route-map clause, and match based on a standard numbered ACL, a standard named ACL, and a prefix-list	
Configuring a summary route	
Enable/disable auto-summary	
Configure a default route using ip default-network	
Configure a default route using static routes	

Choose Commands for a Verification Plan Table

To practice skills that are useful when creating your own EIGRP verification plan, list in Table 4-8 all commands that supply the requested information. You may want to record your answers outside the book and set a goal to complete this table (and others like it) from memory during your final reviews before taking the exam.

Table 4-8   *Verification Plan Memory Drill*

Information Needed	Command
Display access lists.	
Display prefix lists.	
Display route maps.	
Verify whether a filter worked by displaying all known routes in a range of addresses.	
Display a summary IP route.	
On summarizing router, display EIGRP topology info on a summary route.	
On summarizing router, display IP routes for a summary route and it subordinate routes.	
On summarizing router, display the administrative distance of the null route.	
Display the current auto-summary setting.	
Determine if a prefix in the EIGRP topology table has been flagged as a candidate default route.	
Determine if an IP route has been flagged as a candidate default route.	
Display a router's preferred default route.	

Review all the Key Topics

Key Topic

Review the most important topics from this chapter, noted with the key topics icon in the outer margin of the page. Table 4-9 lists a reference of these key topics and the page numbers on which each is found.

Table 4-9   *Key Topics for Chapter 4*

Key Topic Element	Description	Page Number
List	Summary of matching logic for prefix lists	106
Table 4-3	Summary of comparisons of prefix length for IP prefix lists	106
List	Summary of matching logic for route maps	112
List	Benefits and negatives regarding the use of route summarization	120
List	A summary of what occurs when configuring an EIGRP summary route	120
Definition	auto-summary	124
List	Steps to advertise static default routes	127
List	Steps to configure a default network	128

Complete the Tables and Lists from Memory

Print a copy of Appendix D, "Memory Tables," (found on the CD), or at least the section for this chapter, and complete the tables and lists from memory. Appendix E, "Memory Tables Answer Key," also on the CD, includes completed tables and lists to check your work.

Define Key Terms

Define the following key terms from this chapter, and check your answers in the glossary.

Prefix list, route map, distribute list, address block, subordinate route, auto summary, default network, static default route, gateway of last resort

This chapter covers the following subjects:

OSPF Review: This section reviews the OSPF concepts, configuration, and verification commands assumed as prerequisites, specifically those details included in the CCNA Exam's coverage of OSPF.

OSPF Neighbors and Adjacencies on LANs: This section discusses a variety of features that impact when a router attempts to form OSPF neighbor relationships (neighborships), what must be true for those neighborships to work, and what might prevent those neighborships.

OSPF Neighbors and Adjacencies on WANs: This short section examines the typical usage of OSPF neighborships over various types of WAN technologies.

CHAPTER 5

OSPF Overview and Neighbor Relationships

Open Shortest Path First (OSPF) requires only a few relatively simple commands when using it in a small- to medium-sized internetwork. However, behind those commands resides a fairly complex routing protocol, with internals that can intimidate those new to OSPF. When compared to the less-complex EIGRP, OSPF requires more thought when planning and a few more configuration commands than does EIGRP. Additionally, the underlying complexity of OSPF makes operating and verifying an OSPF internetwork more challenging.

Part III of this book contains four chapters. This chapter briefly reviews the basics of OSPF and delves into all topics related to how OSPF routers form neighbor relationships. Chapter 6, "OSPF Topology, Routes, and Convergence," then examines how OSPF exchanges topology data, as stored in its Link State Database (LSDB), for internal OSPF routes. Chapter 6 also discusses how OSPF then chooses the best internal OSPF routes. Chapter 7, "OSPF Route Summarization, Filtering, and Default Routing," moves examine several tools that optimize the operation of OSPF, including route filtering, route summarization, and special OSPF area types. Finally, Chapter 8, "OSPF Virtual Links and Frame Relay Operations," discusses a few miscellaneous topics.

"Do I Know This Already?" Quiz

The "Do I Know This Already?" quiz allows you to assess if you should read the entire chapter. If you miss no more than one of these eight self-assessment questions, you might want to move ahead to the "Exam Preparation Tasks." Table 5-1 lists the major headings in this chapter and the "Do I Know This Already?" quiz questions covering the material in those headings so that you can assess your knowledge of these specific areas. The answers to the "Do I Know This Already?" quiz appear in Appendix A, "Answers to the 'Do I Know This Already?' Quiz."

Table 5-1 *"Do I Know This Already?" Foundation Topics Section-to-Question Mapping*

Foundations Topics Section	Question
OSPF Review	1–3
OSPF Neighbors and Adjacencies on LANs	4–7
OSPF Neighbors and Adjacencies on WANs	8

1. A router has been configured with the commands **router ospf 9, network 172.16.1.0 0.0.0.255 area 8**, and **network 172.16.0.0 0.0.255.255 area 9**, in that order. No other OSPF-related commands have been configured. The answers list the IP addresses that could be assigned to this router's Fa0/0 interface. Which answers list an IP address/prefix length that would cause the router to put Fa0/0 into area 9? (Choose two.)

   a. 172.16.0.1/23

   b. 172.16.1.1/26

   c. 172.16.1.1/24

   d. 172.16.0.255/23

   e. None of the other answers is correct.

2. Which of the following is true about an OSPF area border router (ABR)?

   a. The ABR must have multiple interfaces connected to the backbone area.

   b. An ABR is a router with two interfaces, each connected to a different non-backbone area.

   c. The only requirement to be considered an ABR is at least one interface connected to the backbone area.

   d. An ABR must have at least one interface in the backbone area plus at least one other interface in a nonbackbone area.

3. Which of the following can either directly or indirectly identify all the interfaces for which both 1) OSPF has been enabled and 2) OSPF is not passive? (Choose two.)

   a. **show ip ospf database**

   b. **show ip ospf interface brief**

   c. **show ip protocols**

   d. **show ip route ospf**

   e. **show ip ospf neighbors**

4. Router R1 directly connects to subnet 10.1.1.0/24 with its Fa0/0 interface. R1 can ping four other working OSPF routers in that subnet. R1 is neither the designated router (DR) nor backup DR (BDR). OSPF is working correctly on all five routers. Which of the following is true on R1? (Choose two.)

   a. The **show ip ospf neighbors** command lists two neighbors off Fa0/0.

   b. The **show ip ospf neighbors** command lists four neighbors off Fa0/0.

   c. The **show ip ospf neighbors** command lists two neighbors off Fa0/0 in the FULL state.

   d. The **show ip ospf neighbors** command lists two neighbors off Fa0/0 in the DISCO state.

5. Routers R1 and R2 are OSPF neighbors using their Fa0/0 interfaces, respectively, using default settings for all timers. An engineer adds the **ip ospf hello-interval 6** command to R1's Fa0/0 configuration. Which of the following is true regarding the results
from this change? (Choose 2)

   a. The **show ip ospf neighbor** command on R1 lists the revised Hello timer.

   b. The **show ip ospf interface brief** command on R1 lists the revised Hello
   timer.

   c. The R1-R2 neighborship fails due to Hello timer mismatch.

   d. The **show ip ospf interface** command on R1 lists the revised Hello timer.

6. Routers R1 and R2, OSPF neighbors in area 0 over their Fa0/0 interfaces (respectively), currently both successfully use OSPF MD5 authentication. The OSPF configuration includes the **area 0 authentication** command under the **router ospf 1**
command. Which of the following commands must have been configured on R1's
Fa0/0 interface? (Choose two.)

   a. ip ospf authentication null

   b. ip ospf authentication message-digest

   c. ip ospf authentication-key whatever-it-is

   d. ip ospf message-digest-key 1 md5 whatever-it-is

   e. ip ospf md5 1 key whatever-it-is

7. Which of the following settings do not prevent two potential OSPF neighbors from
becoming neighbors?

   a. The interface used to connect to that neighbor being passive in the OSPF
   process

   b. Duplicate OSPF router IDs

   c. Mismatched dead timers

   d. IP addresses of 10.1.1.1/24 and 10.2.2.2/24

   e. Mismatched OSPF process IDs

8. A company has a Frame Relay WAN with one central-site router and 100 branch office routers. A partial mesh of PVCs exists: one PVC between the central site and
each of the 100 branch routers. All routers use point-to-point subinterfaces and one
subnet per PVC. Which of the following is true about OSPF in this design?

   a. The central site router has 100 fully adjacent neighborships with the 100
   branches.

   b. The central site router has neighborships with all branch routers, but fully
   adjacent neighbors with only two branches.

   c. The central site router has a neighborship with the Frame Relay switch.

   d. None of the other answers is correct.

Foundation Topics

OSPF Review

All the CCNP exams consider CCNA materials as prerequisites, so the Cisco Press CCNP Exam Certification Guide series of books also assumes the reader is already familiar with CCNA topics. However, the CCNP exams do include features that overlap with CCNA. Additionally, most people forget some details about CCNA topics along the way. This section is intended as a quick reminder of the basics from your earlier CCNA studies related to OSPF, with the addition of a few related details you may not have seen suring your CCNA study.

Note that this section does not cover every detail of CCNA-level OSPF topics–the main goal is a quick refamiliarization. Following this review, throughout this and the next three chapters, the rest of the CCNA-level OSPF features, plus many new OSPF-features, will be detailed.

To that end, this section begins with a review of OSPF terminology and link state theory, followed by a configuration and verification sample.

OSPF Link State Concepts

OPSF uses link state (LS) logic, which can be broken into three major branches. The first step, neighbor discovery, has the same overall goal as EIGRP's neighbor discovery process: to find the neighboring routers, and exchange enough information so that the two routers know whether they should exchange topology data. (Like EIGRP, OSPF keeps a list of neighbors in its neighbor table.)

The second step, topology database exchange, requires each OSPF router to cooperate by sending messages so that all routers learn topology information–information that is the equivalent of the kinds of information a human would draw and write in a diagram of the internetwork. Each router stores this topology information in its topology database, sometimes called its link state database (LSDB). The information communicated by OSPF routers and held in their LSDBs includes:

- The existence of, and an identifier for, each router (router ID)

- Each router interface, IP address, mask, and subnet

- The list of routers reachable by each router on each interface

The third major step, route computation, means that each router independently analyzes the topology data to choose the best routes from their perspective. In particular, LS algorithms such as OSPF use a Shortest Path First (SPF) algorithm to analyze the data, choose the shortest (best) route for each reachable subnet, and add the correct next-hop/outgoing interface information for those routes to the IP routing table.

OSPF requires more planning than does EIGRP, particularly with regard to the necessity for a hierarchical design using OSPF areas. Each router interface exists in a single area, with some special routers, called area border routers (ABR), being the boundary between areas. Inside an area, routers exchange detailed topology information. However, the detailed topology information does not flow between areas. Instead, the ABRs advertise briefer information between areas, including information about subnets/masks, but the information advertised into one area does not include details about the topology of the other area. For perspective on the OSPF design issues, consider Figure 5-1, which shows a typical hierarchical design.

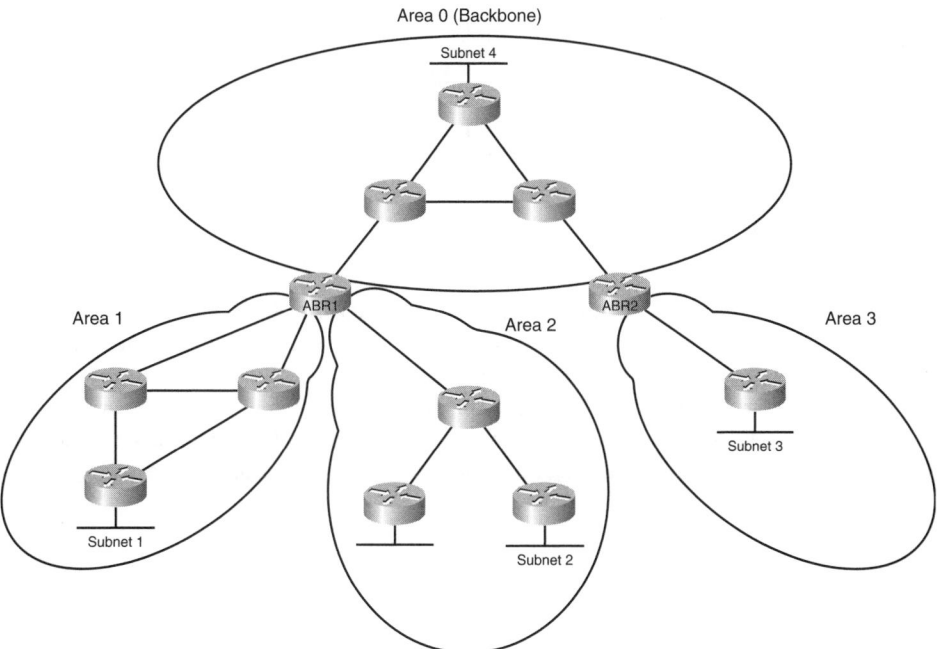

Figure 5-1   *Typical Hierarchical OSPF Design*

One area, called the backbone area, must connect to all other areas. Packets that need to pass between two nonbackbone areas must pass through (at least) one backbone router. The ABRs must keep a copy of the LSDB for each area to which they attach; for example, ABR1 has LSDBs for area 0, area 1, and area 2. However, the ABRs do not forward all the topology details between areas; instead, they simply advertise the subnets (prefix/length) between the areas.

Because of the sparse information advertised into one area about another area, topologically, routers inside one area know only about the subnets in another area. They do not know about the details of the topology in the other area; instead, from a topology perspective, it appears as if the subnets from another area connect to the ABR. Figure 5-2 shows the concept with the two routers in area 3 from Figure 5-1.

Figure 5-2 essentially shows the contents of area 3's LSDB in graphical form. Two routers exist, with a link between them, and one LAN subnet (Subnet 3) internal to the area. However, the other three sample subnets shown in Figure 5-1 (Subnets 1, 2, and 3) appear

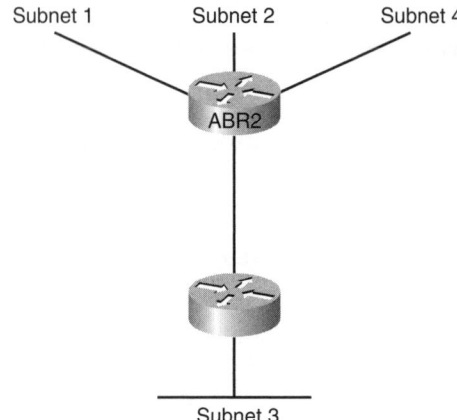

Figure 5-2 *Area 3 LSDB Concept*

connected to ABR2. (Other subnets exist outside area 3 as well; the figure just shows a few as examples.) The routers inside area 3 can calculate and add routes to their routing tables, but without needing all the topology shown in Figure 5-1. By using areas as a design as in Figure 5-1, network engineers can group routers and interfaces into areas, which results of smaller topology databases on those routers, as shown in Figure 5-2. As a result, each router reduces the processing time, memory consumption, and effort to calculate the best routes.

OSPF does have a fairly large number of terms. Table 5-2 lists some of the more common OSPF terms as an early reference as you read through the chapter.

Key
Topic

Table 5-2 *Commonly Used OSPF Terms*

Term	Definition
Link state database	The data structure held by an OSPF router for the purpose of storing topology data.
Shortest Path First (SPF)	The name of the algorithm OSPF uses to analyze the LSDB. The analysis determines the best (lowest cost) route for each prefix/length.
Link State Update (LSU)	The name of the OSPF packet that holds the detailed topology information, specifically LSAs

Table 5-2 *Commonly Used OSPF Terms*

Term	Definition
Link State Advertisement (LSA)	The name of a class of OSPF data structures that hold topology information. LSAs are held in memory in the LSDB and communicated over the network in LSU messages.
Area	A contiguous grouping of routers and router interfaces. Routers in an area strive to learn all topology information about the area, but they do not learn topology information about areas to which they do not connect.
Area Border Router (ABR)	A router that has interfaces connected to at least two different OSPF areas, including the backbone area. ABRs hold topology data for each area, and calculate routes for each area, and advertise about those routes between areas.
Backbone router	Any router that has at least one interface connected to the backbone area.
Internal routers	A router that has interfaces connected to only one area, making the router completely internal to that one area.
Designated Router (DR)	On multiaccess data links like LANs, an OSPF router elected by the routers on that data link to perform special functions. These functions include the generation of LSAs representing the subnet, and playing a key role in the database exchange process.
Backup Designated Router (BDR)	A router on a multiaccess data link that monitors the DR and becomes prepared to take over for the DR, should the DR fail.

OSPF Configuration Review

Other than the configuration of the OSPF areas, the configuration of OSPF basics looks similar to a simple EIGRP configuration. IOS uses the **router ospf** *process-id* command, plus one or more **network** *net-id wildcard-mask* **area** *area-id* subcommands, to enable OSPF on the router and on router interfaces. The rules for these commands are as follows:

Key Topic

Step 1. Neighboring routers' **router ospf** *process-id* commands do not have to be configured with the same *process-id* parameter to become neighbors.

Step 2. IOS only enables OSPF on interfaces matched by an OSPF **network** command. When enabled, the router does the following:

Attempts to discover OSPF neighbors on that interface by sending multicast OSPF Hello messages

Includes the connected subnet in future topology database exchanges

Step 3. To match an interface with the **network** command, IOS compares the *net-id* configured in the **network** command with each interface's IP address, while using the configured wildcard-mask as an ACL wildcard mask.

Step 4. Regardless of the order in which the **network** commands are added to the configuration, IOS puts these commands into the configuration file with the most specific (most binary 0s) wildcard mask first. IOS lists the **network** commands in this sorted order in the configuration.

Step 5. The first **network** command that matches an interface, per the order shown in the output of the **show running-config** command, determines the OSPF area number associated with the interface.

Example 5-1 shows a sample configuration for each router in Figure 5-3.

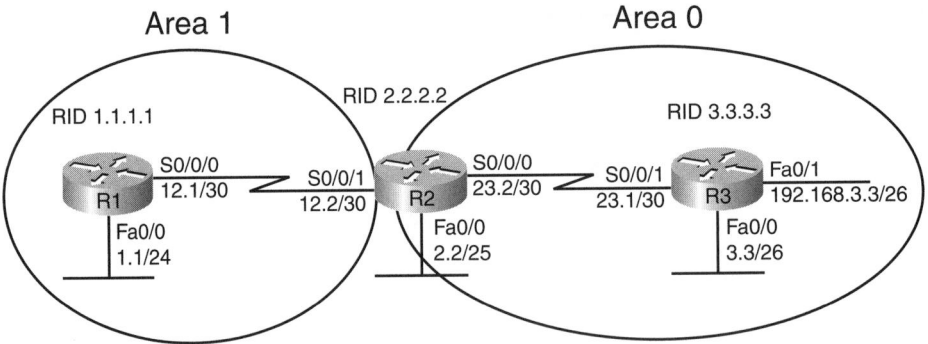

Figure 5-3 *Three Router Internetwork with Two OSPF Areas*

Example 5-1   *OSPF Configuration on Routers R1, R2, and R3*

```
! On Router R1: !!!!!!!!!!!!!!!!!!!!!!!!!!!!!!!!!!!!!!!!!!!!!!
interface loopback 1
 ip address 1.1.1.1 255.255.255.255
router ospf 1
 network 10.0.0.0 0.255.255.255 area 1
! On Router R2: !!!!!!!!!!!!!!!!!!!!!!!!!!!!!!!!!!!!!!!!!!!!!!
interface loopback 1
 ip address 2.2.2.2 255.255.255.255

router ospf 2
 network 10.1.12.2 0.0.0.0 area 1
 network 10.1.0.0 0.0.255.255 area 0
! On Router R3: !!!!!!!!!!!!!!!!!!!!!!!!!!!!!!!!!!!!!!!!!!!!!!
interface loopback 1
 ip address 3.3.3.3 255.255.255.255

router ospf 3
 network 10.1.0.0 0.0.255.255 area 0
 network 192.168.3.3 0.0.0.0 area 0
```

First, note that all three routers use a different process ID on their respective **router ospf** *process-id* commands; these mismatches do not prevent neighborship.

Next, consider the requirement that R1's S0/0/0 and R2's S0/0/1 must be in the same area. Typically, all routers on the same subnet need to be in the same area; the routers themselves are the boundary between areas. In this case, R1's **network 10.0.0.0 0.255.255.255 area 1** command matches all interfaces whose addresses begin with 10 in the first octet and assigns those interfaces (Fa0/0 and S0/0/0) to area 1. Similarly, R2's **network 10.1.12.2 0.0.0.0 area 1** command matches only one IP address–R2's S0/0/1 IP address–and places it in area 1. Looking further at R2's OSPF configuration, note that both **network** commands actually match the 10.1.12.2 S0/0/1 IP address: one with area 0, and one with area 1. However, R2 orders these two **network** commands with the most-specific wildcard mask first, placing the command with wildcard mask 0.0.0.0 first, and the one with wildcard 0.0.255.255 second. Then, R2 compares the commands to the interface IP addresses in order, so R2 places S0/0/1 into area 1. (Note that in real internetworks, choosing wildcard masks such that it is clear which **network** command should match each interface is the better choice.)

On R3, the **network 10.1.0.0 0.0.255.255 area 0** command matches interfaces Fa0/0 and S0/0/0, adding them to area 0. R3 then needs an additional **network** command to enable OSPF on R3's Fa0/1 interface with all three interfaces in area 0.

Finally, note that the addition of the loopback interfaces causes each router to choose an obvious OSPF router ID (RID). OSPF uses the same logic as does EIGRP to choose a router ID on each router, at the time the OSPF process is initialized, as follows, in the listed order of precedence:

Step 1.   Use the router ID defined in the **router-id** *x.x.x.x* OSPF router subcommand.

Step 2.   Use the highest IP address of any up/up loopback interface.

Step 3.   Use the highest IP address of any up/up non-loopback interface.

Note that for the second and third choices, the interface does not need to have OSPF enabled.

OSPF Verification Review

The verification process, whether it uses a formal verification plan, must have some knowledge of the intended design and function of the network. The design and implementation documents dictate what the network should do, and the verification plan should confirm whether the network is meeting those goals.

For the purposes of this OSPF review section, assume that the only design goal for the internetwork in Figure 5-3 is that OSPF be used so that all routers have routes to reach all subnets shown in the figure, within the constraints of the area design.

To verify such a simple design, an engineer should start by confirming on which interfaces OSPF has been enabled on each router. The next step should be to determine if the OSPF neighbor relationships that should occur are indeed up and working. Then, the OSPF topology table should be examined to confirm that non-ABRs have only topology information for their respective areas. Finally, the IP routes on each router should be examined, confirming that all routes are known. To that end, Table 5-3 summarizes five key **show** commands that provide the information to answer these questions:

Table 5-3   *Most Commonly Used OSPF show Commands*

Command	Key Information
show ip ospf interface brief	Lists the interfaces on which OSPF is enabled (based on the **network** commands); it omits passive interfaces.
show ip protocols	Lists the contents of the **network** configuration commands for each routing process, and a list of enabled but passive interfaces.
show ip ospf neighbors	Lists known neighbors, including neighbor state; does not list neighbors for which some mismatched parameter is preventing a valid OSPF neighbor relationship.
show ip ospf database	Lists all LSAs for all connected areas. (See Chapter 6 for more detail on the LSA types seen in the database.)
show ip route	Lists the contents of the IP routing table, listing OSPF-learned routes with a code of O on the left side of the output.

Example 5-2 shows samples of each command listed in Table 5-3. Note that the output highlights various samples of items that should be verified, including the interfaces on which OSPF is enabled, the known neighbors, the neighbors' state, the LSAs in the topology table, and the OSPF routes.

Example 5-2   *OSPF Verification on Routers R1, R2, and R3*

```
! On Router R2: !!!!!!!!!!!!!!!!!!!!!!!!!!!!!!!!!!!!!!!!!!!!
! Note that S0/0/1 is shown as in area 1, while the other 3 interfaces are all in
! Area 0.


R2#show ip ospf interface brief
Interface    PID   Area             IP Address/Mask    Cost  State Nbrs F/C
Se0/0/0      2     0                10.1.23.2/30       64    P2P   1/1
Fa0/0        2     0                10.1.2.2/25        1     DR    0/0
Se0/0/1      2     1                10.1.12.2/30       64    P2P   1/1


! Next, note that R2 lists two "Routing Information Sources", 1.1.1.1 (R1) and
! 3.3.3.3 (R3). These routers, listed by RID, should mirror those listed
! in the output of the show ip ospf neighbors command that follows.


R2#show ip protocols
Routing Protocol is "ospf 2"
  Outgoing update filter list for all interfaces is not set
  Incoming update filter list for all interfaces is not set
  Router ID 2.2.2.2
  It is an area border router
  Number of areas in this router is 2. 2 normal 0 stub 0 nssa
  Maximum path: 4
  Routing for Networks:
    10.1.12.2 0.0.0.0 area 1
    10.1.0.0 0.0.255.255 area 0

 Reference bandwidth unit is 100 mbps
  Routing Information Sources:
    Gateway         Distance      Last Update
    3.3.3.3              110      00:01:08
    1.1.1.1              110      00:01:08
  Distance: (default is 110)


! Note that the Full state means that the database exchange process is
```

```
! fully completed between these two neighbors.
R2#show ip ospf neighbors

Neighbor ID     Pri   State        Dead Time   Address      Interface
3.3.3.3           0   FULL/  -     00:00:34    10.1.23.1    Serial0/0/0
1.1.1.1           0   FULL/  -     00:00:34    10.1.12.1    Serial0/0/1
! On Router R1: !!!!!!!!!!!!!!!!!!!!!!!!!!!!!!!!!!!!!!!!!!!!
! Note that R1's LSDB includes a "Router Link State" for RID 1.1.1.1 (R1)
! and R2 (2.2.2.2), but not 3.3.3.3 (R3), because R3 is not attached  to area
1.


R1#show ip ospf database

               OSPF Router with ID (1.1.1.1) (Process ID 1)

                   Router Link States (Area 1)

Link ID         ADV Router       Age         Seq#        Checksum Link count
1.1.1.1         1.1.1.1          210         0x80000004 0x001533 3
2.2.2.2         2.2.2.2          195         0x80000002 0x0085DB 2

                   Summary Net Link States (Area 1)

Link ID         ADV Router       Age         Seq#        Checksum
10.1.2.0        2.2.2.2          190         0x80000001 0x00B5F0
10.1.3.0        2.2.2.2          190         0x80000001 0x00AE76
10.1.23.0       2.2.2.2          190         0x80000001 0x0031A4
192.168.3.0     2.2.2.2          191         0x80000001 0x008B3B

! Below, note that R1 has routes for all remote subnets, including R3's
! LAN subnets, even though R1 does not list R3 in its LSDB.


R1#show ip route ospf
     10.0.0.0/8 is variably subnetted, 5 subnets, 4 masks
O IA    10.1.3.0/26 [110/129] via 10.1.12.2, 00:04:13, Serial0/0/0
O IA    10.1.2.0/25 [110/65] via 10.1.12.2, 00:04:13, Serial0/0/0
O IA    10.1.23.0/30 [110/128] via 10.1.12.2, 00:04:13, Serial0/0/0
     192.168.3.0/26 is subnetted, 1 subnets
O IA    192.168.3.0 [110/129] via 10.1.12.2, 00:04:13, Serial0/0/0
```

OSPF Feature Summary

Table 5-4 summarizes some of the key facts about OSPF. The table includes some review items from the CCNA level OSPF topics, plus some topics that will be developed in chapters 5 through 8. The items that are not CCNA topics are included just for convenience when reviewing for final preparation before taking the exam.

Table 5-4 *OSPF Feature Summary*

Key Topic

Feature	Description
Transport	IP, protocol type 89 (does not use UDP or TCP).
Metric	Based on cumulative cost of all outgoing interfaces in a route. The interface cost defaults to a function of interface bandwidth but can be set explicitly.
Hello interval	Interval at which a router sends OSPF Hello messages on an interface.
Dead interval	Timer used to determine when a neighboring router has failed, based on a router not receiving any OSPF messages, including Hellos, in this timer period.
Update destination address	Normally sent to 224.0.0.5 (All SPF Routers) and 225.0.0.6 (All Designated Routers).
Full or partial updates	Full updates are used when new neighbors are discovered; otherwise, partial updates are used.
Authentication	Supports MD5 and clear-text authentication.
VLSM/classless	OSPF includes the mask with each route, also allowing it to support discontiguous networks and VLSM.
Route Tags	Allows OSPF to tag routes as they are redistributed into OSPF.
Next-hop field	Supports the advertisement of routes with a different next-hop router than the advertising router.
Manual route summarization	Allows route summarization at ABR routers only.

This concludes the review of OSPF topics. The rest of this chapter focuses on OSPF topics related to the formation of OSPF neighbor relationships.

OSPF Neighbors and Adjacencies on LANs

With EIGRP, neighborship is relatively simple. If two EIGRP routers discover each other (using Hellos) and meet several requirements (like being in the same subnet), the two routers become neighbors. After becoming neighbors, the two EIGRP routers exchange topology information.

Comparing OSPF and EIGRP, OSPF neighborship is more complex. First, with EIGRP, two routers either become neighbors or they do not. With OSPF, even after all the neighbor parameter checks pass, two classes of neighborships exist: neighbors and fully adjacent neighbors. The OSPF neighbor discovery process has many pitfalls when the internetwork uses Frame Relay, with a class of issues that simply do not exist with EIGRP. Finally, OSPF uses an underlying Finite State Machine (FSM) with eight neighbor states used to describe the current state of each OSPF neighbor, adding another layer of complexity compared to EIGRP.

This section breaks down the OSPF neighbor relationship, the logic, and the OSPF configuration settings–anything that impacts OSPF neighborship on LAN interfaces. In particular, this section examines the following questions:

■ On what interfaces will this router attempt to discover neighbors by sending multicast OSPF Hello messages?

■ When a potential neighbor is discovered, do they meet all requirements to become neighbors at all?

This section examines these topics, in sequence.

Enabling OSPF Neighbor Discovery on LANs

OSPF sends multicast OSPF Hello messages on LAN interfaces, attempting to discover OSPF neighbors, when two requirements are met:

■ OSPF has been enabled on the interface, either through the **network** router subcommand or the **ip ospf area** interface subcommand.

■ The interface has not been made passive by the **passive-interface** router subcommand.

When both requirements are met, OSPF sends Hellos to the 224.0.0.5 multicast address, an address reserved for all OSPF-speaking routers. The Hello itself contains several parameters that must be checked, including the OSPF RID of the router sending the Hello, and the OSPF area that router has assigned to that LAN subnet.

Of the three configuration commands that might impact whether a router attempts to discover potential neighbors on an interface, one is commonly understood (**network**) and was already covered in this chapter's "OSPF Configuration Review" section. The second configuration command that impacts whether potential neighbors discover each other, **passive-interface**, works just like it does with EIGRP. In short, when a router configures an interface as passive to OSPF, OSPF quits sending OSPF Hellos, so the router will not discover neighbors. The router will still advertise about the interface's connected subnet if OSPF is enabled on the interface, but all other OSPF processing on the interface is stopped.

The third configuration command that impacts whether a router discovers potential neighbors using Hellos is the **ip ospf** *process-id* **area** *area-id* interface subcommand. This command acts as a replacement for the OSPF **network** command. Simply put, this command enables OSPF directly on the interface and assigns the area number.

To demonstrate the **ip ospf area** and **passive-interface** commands, Example 5-3 shows a revised configuration on Router R3 as seen originally back in Example 5-1. In this new example configuration, R3 has made two interfaces passive, because no other OSPF routers exist on its LAN subnets–making any attempt to discover OSPF neighbors have no benefit. Additionally, R3 has migrated its configuration away from the older **network** commands, instead using the **ip ospf area** interface subcommand.

Example 5-3   *Configuring passive-interface and ip ospf area*

```
Interface loopback 1
 Ip address 3.3.3.3 255.255.255.255

router ospf 3
 passive-interface FastEthernet0/0
 passive-interface FastEthernet0/1

interface FastEthernet0/0
 ip ospf 3 area 0
interface FastEthernet0/1
 ip ospf 3 area 0
interface Serial0/0/1
 ip ospf 3 area 0

R3#show ip protocols
Routing Protocol is "ospf 3"
  Outgoing update filter list for all interfaces is not set
  Incoming update filter list for all interfaces is not set
  Router ID 3.3.3.3
  Number of areas in this router is 1. 1 normal 0 stub 0 nssa
  Maximum path: 4
  Routing for Networks:
  Routing on Interfaces Configured Explicitly (Area 0):
    Serial0/0/1
    FastEthernet0/1
    FastEthernet0/0
  Reference bandwidth unit is 100 mbps
  Passive Interface(s):
    FastEthernet0/0
    FastEthernet0/1
  Routing Information Sources:
    Gateway         Distance      Last Update
  Distance: (default is 110)
```

Note that in the second half of Example 5-3 the **show ip protocols** command now lists the interfaces as matched with the **ip ospf area** commands, and it lists the passive interfaces. You can take the list of explicitly configured interfaces, remove the passive interfaces, and know which interfaces on which R3 will attempt to discover OSPF neighbors. Also, take a moment to compare this output with the same command's output in Example 5-2, with the earlier example listing the parameters of the configured **network** commands.

Settings That Must Match for OSPF Neighborship

After an OSPF router has discovered a potential neighbor by receiving a Hello from the other router, the local router considers the router that sent the Hello as a potential neighbor. The local router must examine the contents of the received Hello, plus a few other factors, compare those settings to its own, check for agreement, and only then may that other router be considered an OSPF neighbor.

For reference, the following list details the items seen in OSPF Hello messages. Note that some fields might not be present in a Hello, depending on the conditions in the network.

- OSPF Router ID
- Stub area flag
- Plus the following interface-specific settings:
    - Hello interval
    - Dead Interval
    - Subnet mask
    - List of neighbors reachable on the interface
    - Area ID
    - Router priority
    - Designated Router (DR) IP address
    - Backup DR (BDR) IP address
    - Authentication digest

Table 5-5 summarizes the items that two routers will compare when deciding whether they can become OSPF neighbors. For study purposes, the table also lists some items that one might think prevent OSPF neighborship but do not, with comparisons to EIGRP.

Table 5-5   *Neighbor Requirements for EIGRP and OSPF*

Requirement	OSPF	EIGRP
Interfaces' primary IP addresses must be in same subnet.	Yes	Yes
Must not be passive on the connected interface.	Yes	Yes
Must be in same area.	Yes	N/A
Hello interval/timer, plus either the Hold (EIGRP) or Dead (OSPF) timer, must match.	Yes	No
Router IDs must be unique.	Yes	No
IP MTU must match.	Yes[1]	No

Must pass neighbor authentication (if configured).	Yes	Yes
K-values (used in metric calculation) must match.	N/A	Yes
Must use the same ASN (EIGRP) or process-ID (OSPF) on the **router** configuration command.	No	Yes

[1]May allow the other router to be listed in the `show ip ospf neighbor` command, but the MTU mismatch will prevent proper operation of the topology exchange.

Note: Table 5-5 repeats most of the information listed in Chapter 2, Table 2-4, but in an order that focuses on OSPF issues.

The first few items in Table 5-5 require only a minor amount of discussion. First, OSPF checks the IP address (found as the source address of the Hello message) and mask (listed in the Hello message) of the potential neighbor, calculates the subnet number, and compares the subnet number and mask to its own interface IP address. Both the subnet number and mask must match. Additionally, the OSPF Hello messages include the area number on the subnet, as defined by that router. The receiving router compares the received Hello with its own configuration and rejects the potential neighbor if the area numbers do not match.

The next several headings inside this section examine the other three settings that can prevent OSPF neighborship: Hello and Dead intervals, OSPF Router ID, IP MTU, and authentication.

Optimizing Convergence Using Hello and Dead Timers

Using the same concept as EIGRP, but with different terminology, OSPF uses two timers to monitor the reachability of neighbors. With OSPF, the Hello interval defines how often the router sends a Hello on the interface. The Dead interval defines how long a router should wait, without hearing any Hello messages from that neighbor, before deciding that the neighbor failed. For example, with a default LAN interface setting of Hello of 10, and Dead of 40, the local router sends Hello messages every 10 seconds. The neighbor resets its downward-counting Hold timer to 40 upon receiving a Hello from that neighbor. Under normal operation on a LAN, with defaults, the Dead timer for a neighbor would vary from 40, down to 30, and then be reset to 40 upon receipt of the next Hello. However, if the Hello messages were no longer received for 40 seconds, the neighborship would fail, driving convergence.

To tune for faster convergence, you can configure OSPF to set a lower Hello and Dead timer. It speeds convergence in some cases; note that if the interface fails, OSPF will immediately realize that all neighbors reached through that interface have also failed and not wait on the Dead timer to count down to zero. For example, consider the internetwork in Figure 5-4. This internetwork has four routers connected to the same VLAN, with the interfaces, IP addresses, masks, and OSPF areas as shown.

Figure 5-4 *Four OSPFs Routers on the Same Subnet, with Two OSPF Areas*

Example 5-4 verifies some of the facts about the routers in Figure 5-4, showing the changes to the Hello interval and the resulting failed neighborships. Each router has been assigned an obvious RID: 1.1.1.1 for R1, 2.2.2.2 for R2, and so on.

Example 5-4 *The Effect of Configuring a Different OSPF Hello Interval*

```
R4#show ip ospf neighbors


Neighbor ID     Pri   State          Dead Time   Address          Interface
1.1.1.1          1    2WAY/DROTHER   00:00:35    10.5.5.1
FastEthernet0/0
2.2.2.2          1    FULL/BDR       00:00:39    10.5.5.2
FastEthernet0/0
3.3.3.3          1    FULL/DR        00:00:38    10.5.5.3
FastEthernet0/0
R4#conf t
Enter configuration commands, one per line.  End with CNTL/Z.
R4(config)#interface fastethernet0/0
R4(config-if)#ip ospf hello-interval 9
R4(config-if)#^Z
*Apr 28 00:06:20.271: %SYS-5-CONFIG_I: Configured from console by console
R4#show ip ospf interface fa0/0
FastEthernet0/0 is up, line protocol is up
```

```
     Internet Address 10.5.5.4/28, Area 0
     Process ID 4, Router ID 4.4.4.4, Network Type BROADCAST, Cost: 1
     Enabled by interface config, including secondary ip addresses
     Transmit Delay is 1 sec, State DROTHER, Priority 1
     Designated Router (ID) 3.3.3.3, Interface address 10.5.5.3
     Backup Designated router (ID) 2.2.2.2, Interface address 10.5.5.2
     Timer intervals configured, Hello 9, Dead 36, Wait 36, Retransmit 5
       oob-resync timeout 40
       Hello due in 00:00:01
     Supports Link-local Signaling (LLS)
     Index 1/1, flood queue length 0
     Next 0x0(0)/0x0(0)
     Last flood scan length is 0, maximum is 3
     Last flood scan time is 0 msec, maximum is 4 msec
     Neighbor Count is 3, Adjacent neighbor count is 2
       Adjacent with neighbor 2.2.2.2  (Backup Designated Router)
       Adjacent with neighbor 3.3.3.3  (Designated Router)
     Suppress hello for 0 neighbor(s)
R4#
*Apr 28 00:06:51.559: %OSPF-5-ADJCHG: Process 4, Nbr 1.1.1.1 on FastEthernet0/0
from 2WAY to DOWN, Neighbor Down: Dead timer expired
*Apr 28 00:06:57.183: %OSPF-5-ADJCHG: Process 4, Nbr 3.3.3.3 on FastEthernet0/0
from FULL to DOWN, Neighbor Down: Dead timer expired
*Apr 28 00:06:58.495: %OSPF-5-ADJCHG: Process 4, Nbr 2.2.2.2 on FastEthernet0/0
from FULL to DOWN, Neighbor Down: Dead timer expired
```

This example demonstrates several interesting facts. First, note that upon configuring the **ip ospf hello-interval 9** command under Fa0/0, the **show ip ospf interface fa0/0** command shows that not only did the Hello interval change, but the Dead timer was set to 4X the Hello interval, or 36. To directly set the Dead timer on the interface, use the **ip ospf dead-interval** *value* interface subcommand. Then, at the end of the example, note that all three of R4's neighbor relationships failed, because those routers now have mismatched Hello and Dead timers. However, the neighbor relationships failed only after the dead timers expired, as noted in the messages, and as confirmed by the timestamps on the messages.

Example 5-4 also shows the two normal, stable, and working neighbor states. Look to the heading "state" in the output of the **show ip ospf neighbors** command at the top of the example. The first word (before the /) lists the state or status of each neighbor. FULL refers to a fully adjacent neighbor, meaning the OSPF topology has been fully exchanged with that neighbor. The other state listed there, 2WAY, is a normal, stable, working state for neighbors with which topology data was not exchanged directly. As described in Chapter 6, in some cases OSPF routers exchange their topology information to one specific router on a LAN, called the designated router (DR), but they do not exchange their database directly with other routers. In the preceding example, taken from R4, R4 lists its relationship with R1 as 2WAY, which happens to be the status for a working neighbor that does not become fully adjacent.

Chapter 6's section "Exchange with a Designated Router" discusses the database exchange process when using a DR.

Note: OSPF has two methods to tune the Hello and Dead intervals to subsecond values. Like EIGRP, OSPF supports Bidirectional Forwarding Detection (BFD). Additionally, OSPF supports command **ip ospf dead-interval minimal hello-multiplier** *multiplier*, which sets the dead interval to one second, and the Hello interval to a fraction of a second based on the multiplier. For example, the command **ip ospf dead-interval minimal hello-multiplier 4** sets the dead interval to one second, with Hellos occurring four times (the multiple) per second, for an effective Hello interval of ¼ seconds.

Using a Unique OSPF Router-ID

As mentioned earlier in the "OSPF CCNA Review" section, each OSPF router assigns itself a router ID, based on the same rules as EIGRP. In OSPF's case, that means a router first looks for the OSPF **router-id** *rid-value* OSPF subcommand; next, to the highest IP address of any up/up loopback interface; and finally, to the highest IP address of any up/up non-loopback interface.

An OSPF RID mismatch makes for unpredictable results because OSPF routers base their view of the topology on the topology database, and the database identifies routers based on their RIDs. By design, all OSPF RIDs in a domain should be unique; to avoid such issues, OSPF prevents neighborships between routers with duplicate RIDs.

The next example shows what happens when two routers discover each other as potential neighbors, but notice a duplicate RID. Using the same network as in Figure 5-4, each router has been assigned an obvious RID: 1.1.1.1 for R1, 2.2.2.2 for R2, and so on. Unfortunately, R4 has been mistakenly configured with RID 1.1.1.1, duplicating R1's RID. R4 is powered on after all three other routers have established neighbor relationships. Example 5-5 shows some of the results.

Example 5-5 *OSPF RID Mismatch – R1 and R4, R4 Connects after R1*

```
! On R1... the following output occurs AFTER R4 powers on. R1, RID 1.1.1.1,
! does not form a neighbor relationship with R4.


R1#show ip ospf neighbors

Neighbor ID     Pri    State        Dead Time    Address       Interface
2.2.2.2          1     FULL/BDR     00:00:35     10.5.5.2
FastEthernet0/0
3.3.3.3          1     FULL/DR      00:00:33     10.5.5.3
FastEthernet0/0
! On R3
! R3 does form a neighbor relationship, but does not learn routes from the
! R4. Note that R3 does not have a route for R4's 10.4.4.0/27 subnet.
```

```
R3#show ip ospf neighbors

Neighbor ID      Pri   State          Dead Time   Address        Interface
1.1.1.1            1   FULL/DROTHER   00:00:38    10.5.5.1
FastEthernet0/0
1.1.1.1            1   FULL/DROTHER   00:00:37    10.5.5.4
FastEthernet0/0
2.2.2.2            1   FULL/BDR       00:00:35    10.5.5.2
FastEthernet0/0
R3#show ip route ospf
     10.0.0.0/8 is variably subnetted, 4 subnets, 4 masks
O       10.2.2.0/25 [110/2] via 10.5.5.2, 00:06:56, FastEthernet0/0
O       10.1.1.0/24 [110/2] via 10.5.5.1, 00:01:34, FastEthernet0/0
```

As you can see from the output on R1, whose RID is duplicated with R4, the routers with duplicate RIDs do not form a neighbor relationship. Additionally, other routers, such as R3 as shown in the example, do form a neighbor relationship with the two routers, but the duplication confuses the topology flooding process. Because R3 formed its neighborship with R1 before R4, R3 does learn a route for R1's 10.1.1.0/24 subnet, but does not for R4's 10.4.4.0/27 subnet. However, with the same configuration, but a different sequence and timing of neighbors coming up, R3 might learn about 10.4.4.0/27 instead of 10.1.1.0/24.

Note: Note that the OSPF process will not start without an RID.

Using the Same IP MTU

The maximum transmission unit (MTU) of an interface tells IOS the largest IP packet that can be forwarded out the interface. This setting protects the packet from being discarded on data links whose Layer 2 features will not pass a frame over a certain size. For example, routers typically default to an IP MTU of 1500 bytes to accommodate Ethernet's rules about frames not exceeding 1526 bytes.

From a data plane perspective, when a router needs to forward a packet larger than the outgoing interface's MTU, the router either fragments the packet or discards it. If the IP header's don't fragment (DF) bit is set, the router discards the packet. If the DF bit is not set, the router can perform Layer 3 fragmentation on the packet, creating two (or more) IP packets with mostly identical IP headers, spreading the data that follows the original IP packet header out among the fragments. The fragments can then be forwarded, with the reassembly process being performed by the receiving host.

From a design perspective, the MTU used by all devices attached to the same data link ought to be the same value. However, routers have no dynamic mechanism to prevent the misconfiguration of MTU on neighboring routers.

When an MTU mismatch occurs between two OSPF neighbors, one router will attempt to become neighbors with the other router whose MTU differs. The other router will be listed in the list of neighbors (**show ip ospf neighbor**). However, the two routers will not exchange topology information, and the two routers will not calculate routes that use this neighbor as the next-hop router.

The IP MTU can be set on an interface using the **ip mtu** *value* interface subcommand and for all Layer 3 protocols with the **mtu** *value* interface subcommand. Example 5-6 shows an example, with R4 again configured so that it has problems.

Example 5-6   *Setting IP MTU and Failing the OSPF Database Exchange Process*

```
R4#configure terminal
Enter configuration commands, one per line.  End with CNTL/Z.
R4(config)#int fastethernet0/0
R4(config-if)#ip mtu 1498
R4(config-if)#^Z
R4#
R4#show ip interface fa0/0
FastEthernet0/0 is up, line protocol is up
  Internet address is 10.5.5.4/28
  Broadcast address is 255.255.255.255
  Address determined by non-volatile memory
  MTU is 1498 bytes
! lines omitted for brevity
R4#show ip ospf neighbors

Neighbor ID     Pri   State           Dead Time   Address      Interface
1.1.1.1           1   EXSTART/DROTHER 00:00:39    10.5.5.1
FastEthernet0/0
2.2.2.2           1   EXSTART/DROTHER 00:00:37    10.5.5.2
FastEthernet0/0
3.3.3.3           1   EXSTART/BDR     00:00:39    10.5.5.3
FastEthernet0/0

*Apr 28 12:36:00.231: %OSPF-5-ADJCHG: Process 4, Nbr 2.2.2.2 on FastEthernet0/0
from EXSTART to DOWN, Neighbor Down: Too many retransmissions
R4#show ip ospf neighbors

Neighbor ID     Pri   State           Dead Time   Address      Interface
1.1.1.1           1   INIT/DROTHER    00:00:39    10.5.5.1
FastEthernet0/0
2.2.2.2           1   DOWN/DROTHER        -       10.5.5.2
FastEthernet0/0
3.3.3.3           1   INIT/DROTHER    00:00:39    10.5.5.3      FastEthernet0/0
```

Note that you could argue that the mismatched MTU does not prevent routers from becoming neighbors, but it does prevent them from successfully exchanging topology data. When the mismatch occurs, a pair of routers tries to become neighbors, and they list each other in the output of **show ip ospf neighbors**, as seen in Example 5-6. However, the neighbor state (listed before the /, under heading "State") moves from EXSTART (which means the database exchange process is starting), but it fails as implied by the highlighted message in the example. Then, the state changes to DOWN, and later one router tries again, moving to INIT (initializing) state. So, the neighbor is listed in the output of **show ip ospf neighbors** command, but never succeeds at exchanging the topology data.

Chapter 6 discusses the database exchange process, making reference to neighbor states. Table 6-5, in Chapter 6s section "OSPF Message and Neighbor State Reference," summarizes the neighbor state values and their meaning.

OSPF Authentication

OSPF authentication causes routers to authenticate every OSPF message. To do so, the routers use the same preshared key value, generating an MD5 digest for each OSPF message and sending that digest as part of each OSPF message. If a router configured for OSPF authentication receives an OSPF message, and the received message's MD5 digest does not pass the authentication checking based on the local key value, the router silently discards the message. As a result, when authentication fails, two routers cannot become OSPF neighbors, because they ignore the inauthentic OSPF Hello messages.

OSPF authentication uses one of three types: type 0 (no authentication), type 1 (clear text), and type 2 (MD5), with MD5 being the only reasonable option in production networks. To configure to have no authentication, do nothing, because IOS defaults to not attempt OSPF authentication. However, for either of the other two OSPF authentication options, you need to follow two configuration steps, as follows:

Step 1.   Authentication must be enabled, plus the authentication type must be selected, through one of two means:

Enabling per interface using the ip ospf authentication [message-digest] interface subcommand

Enabling on all interfaces in an area by changing the area-wide authentication setting using the area area-no authentication [message-digest] subcommand under router ospf

Step 2.   The authentication keys must be configured per interface.

Table 5-6 lists the three OSPF authentication types, along with the *interface* commands to both enable authentication and to define the authentication keys. Note that the three authentication types can be seen in the messages generated by the **debug ip ospf adjacency** command.

Table 5-6   *OSPF Authentication Types*

Type	Meaning	Enabling Interface Subcommand	Authentication Key Configuration Interface Subcommand
0	None	ip ospf authentication null	—
1	Clear text	ip ospf authentication	ip ospf authentication-key *key-value*
2	MD5	ip ospf authentication message-digest	ip ospf message-digest-key *key-number* md5 *key-value*

Note: The maximum length of the key is 16 characters.

Although IOS defaults to use type 0 authentication (no authentication), you can override this default using the **area authentication** command in OSPF configuration mode. For example, on a router with 12 interfaces, you plan to use type 2 (MD5) authentication on all interfaces. Rather than add the **ip ospf authentication message-digest** command to all 12 interfaces, you could override the default that applies to all interface on that router, in a given area. Table 5-7 lists the commands to set the default values.

Table 5-7   *Effect of the area authentication Command on OSPF Interface Authentication Settings*

area authentication Command	Interfaces in That Area Default to Use...
default; no configuration required	Type 0
area *num* authentication	Type 1
area *num* authentication message-digest	Type 2

Note that if the area-wide default and the interface subcommand have both been configured, the interface setting takes precedence. For example, if the interface has been configured with the **ip ospf authentication** subcommand (type 1, clear text), and the **area authentication** command sets MD5 authentication, that particular interface uses clear text authentication.

Example 5-7 shows the authentication configuration on Router R3 from Figure 5-4. In this case, all four routers use MD5 authentication on their common subnet, with key number 1, and key value *really-a-secret*. R3 also configures simple password authentication on its Fa0/1 interface, just to demonstrate the various commands. Also for the purposes of demonstrating the commands, R3 overrides the default authentication, setting the default area 0 authentication to MD5.

Example 5-7   *OSPF Authentication Using Only Interface Subcommands*

```
! First, overriding the default in area 0 so that it uses MD5 authentication,
! meaning Fa0/0, in area 0, will use MD5.

R3#conf t
Enter configuration commands, one per line.  End with CNTL/Z.
R3(config)#router ospf 3
R3(config-router)# area 0 authentication message-digest
R3(config-router)#interface fastethernet0/0
R3(config-if)# ip ospf message-digest-key 1 md5 really-a-secret
!
```

```
! Next, two interface subcommands to enable simple password authentication
! on Fa0/1, which is in area 3.

R3(config-if)#interface fastethernet0/1
R3(config-if)#ip ospf authentication
R3(config-if)#ip ospf authentication-key secret
R3(config-if)# ctl-z
R3#
R3#show ip ospf interface fastethernet0/0
! Lines omitted for brevity - the last few lines list authentication information
  Message digest authentication enabled
    Youngest key id is 1


R3#show ip ospf interface fastethernet0/1
! Lines omitted for brevity - the last few lines list authentication information
  Simple password authentication enabled
```

Note that to verify whether OSPF authentication is enabled, and the authentication type, use the **show ip ospf interface** command, and look to the very end of the output, as shown at the end of Example 5-7. Note that these messages identify the configuration setting and do nothing to confirm whether authentication passed. To confirm whether it worked, look for the neighbor in the output of **show ip ospf neighbor**: A neighbor with whom authentication fails will not be listed. The reason is that the Hello will be rejected due to authentication, and the Hello contains several parameters that must be checked before a router will choose to become an OSPF neighbor with that router. You can also use the **debug ip ospf adj** command, whose output explicitly states that a mismatch exists with the authentication key.

Unlike EIGRP authentication, OSPF authentication does not allow the configuration of a key chain with time-based authentication keys. However, multiple keys can be configured on an interface, each with a different key number. To migrate to a new key, you would first configure a new key value on all routers in a subnet and then delete the configuration of the old keys.

To avoid having network failures during this cutover, OSPF actually sends and accepts messages that use all the currently configured authentication keys on the interface. For example, if the four routers in Figure 5-4 had been configured with key numbers 1 and 2, every OSPF message would be sent twice—once with each key.

This concludes the discussion of OSPF neighborships on LANs. The final brief section examines some issues with OSPF neighborship on WANs.

OSPF Neighbors and Adjacencies on WANs

To form OSPF neighbor relationships on WAN connections, OSPF still must meet the same requirements as on LANs. The area number must match with each neighbor; the IP subnet number and mask of each router must match; authentication must pass; and so on. In short, the items in Table 5-5 earlier in this chapter must be true.

However, the operation of OSPF on WAN links of various types requires some additional thought, particularly when developing an implementation and verification plan. In particular, depending on the WAN technology and configuration, the following additional questions may matter for proper OSPF operation over WAN connections:

■ Will the routers discover each other using multicast OSPF Hello messages, or do the neighbors require predefinition?

■ Will the routers try to elect a DR, and if so, which router should be allowed to be the DR?

■ With which other routers should each router become an OSPF neighbor?

The first two of these items depend in part on the setting of the OSPF *network type*, and the third question depends on the WAN service. This section first examines the concept of OSPF network types and then examines the use of OSPF over common WAN technologies included in the CCNP ROUTE exam.

OSPF Network Types

The OSPF network type–a per-interface setting–directs OSPF in regard to three important facts:

■ Whether the router can expect to discover neighbors using multicast Hello messages

■ Whether only two or more than two OSPF routers can exist in the subnet attached to the interface

■ Whether the router should attempt to elect an OSPF DR on that interface

For instance, LAN interfaces require a DR because of the default OSPF network type of *broadcast*. OSPF defines this interface network type to use multicast Hellos to dynamically discover neighbors, allows more than two routers to be in the same subnet, and to attempt to elect a DR. Conversely, point-to-point links and point-to-point WAN subinterfaces default to use a network type of *point-to-point*, meaning that only two OSPF routers can exist in the subnet, neighbors can be dynamically discovered through Hellos, and that the routers do not elect a DR.

Note: The discussion of the motivation for using OSPF DRs occurs in Chapter 6 section "Background of Designated Routers." For now, note that DRs become useful but are not always required, when a subnet supports more than two OSPF routers (for example, on a LAN subnet).

In production networks, the network type is often ignored, because there is no motivation to change this setting–you pick a combination that works, and most everyone ignores it. For the sake of CCNP ROUTE, you need to be aware of the setting and know a few of the caveats found in some Frame Relay configurations. To keep the discussion focused on the core topics, Chapters 6 and 7 avoid the Frame Relay configurations that require more consideration of the OSPF network type setting. Chapter 8's section "OSPF over Multipoint Frame Relay" discusses the OSPF network types in more depth.

Table 5-8 summarizes the OSPF network types and their meanings. Note that this per-interface or per-subinterface setting is configured with the **ip ospf network** *type* interface subcommand; the first column in the table lists the exact keyword according to this command. Note that the gray highlighted rows will be discussed in Chapter 8.

Table 5-8 *OSPF Network Types*

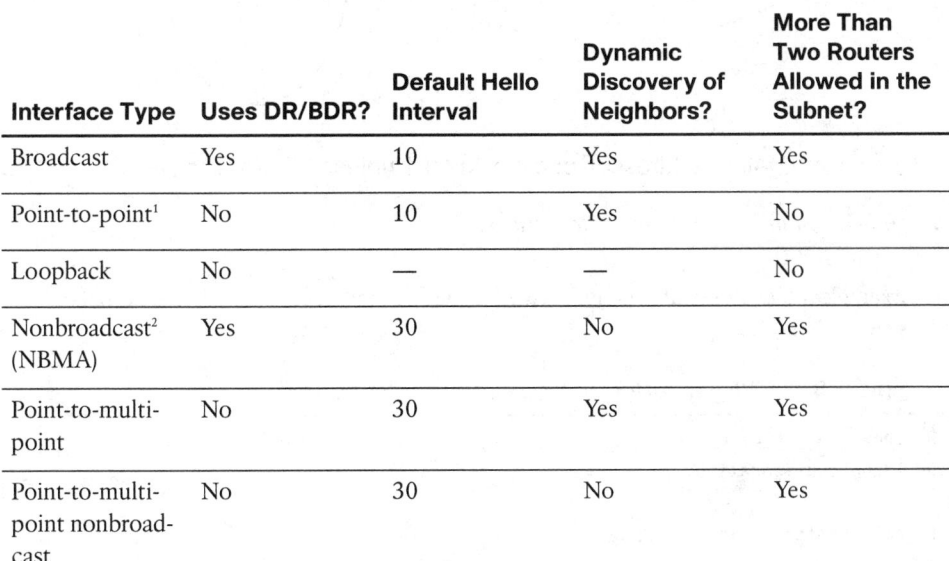

Interface Type	Uses DR/BDR?	Default Hello Interval	Dynamic Discovery of Neighbors?	More Than Two Routers Allowed in the Subnet?
Broadcast	Yes	10	Yes	Yes
Point-to-point[1]	No	10	Yes	No
Loopback	No	—	—	No
Nonbroadcast[2] (NBMA)	Yes	30	No	Yes
Point-to-multipoint	No	30	Yes	Yes
Point-to-multipoint nonbroadcast	No	30	No	Yes

[1]Default on Frame Relay point-to-point subinterfaces.
[2]Default on Frame Relay physical and multipoint subinterfaces.

OSPF Neighborship over Point-to-Point Links

Point-to-point serial links can be a bit boring. You configure IP addresses on either end, configure the **clock rate** if using a back-to-back serial cable in a lab, and **no shutdown** the interfaces. When enabling OSPF on the interfaces, no extra effort is required compared to LANs–just enable OSPF on the interface, and rely on the default OSPF network type of *point-to-point*.

However, serial links can provide a convenient and uncluttered place to experiment with OSPF network types. As such, Figure 5-5 shows a small network with two routers, with

Example 5-8 that follows showing several examples of the OSPF network type. (This small network matches a portion of the network shown in Figure 5-1 earlier in this chapter.)

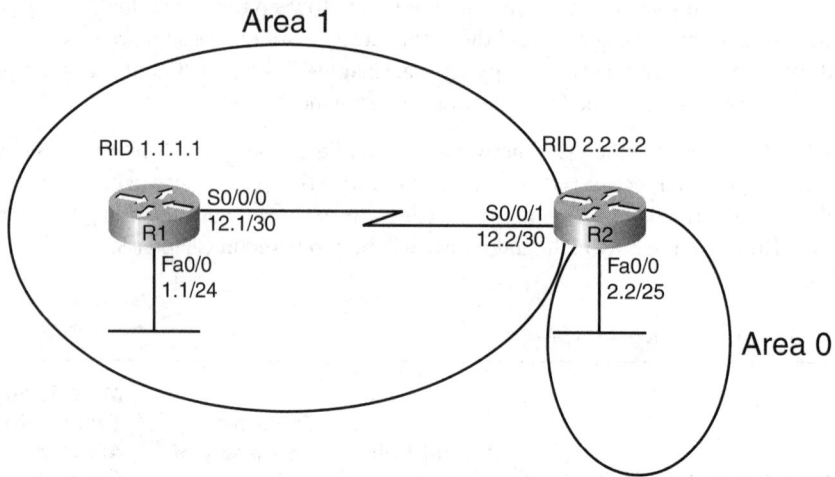

Note: All IP addresses begin with 10.1 unless otherwise noted.

Figure 5-5   *Simple Two Router Internetwork*

Example 5-8 demonstrates OSPF network types with all defaults on the HDLC link between R1 and R2.

Example 5-8   *OSPF Network Types, Default, on an HDLC Link*

```
R1#show run int s0/0/0
Building configuration...

Current configuration : 102 bytes
!
interface Serial0/0/0
 ip address 10.1.12.1 255.255.255.252
 no fair-queue
 clock rate 1536000
!
router ospf 1
 network 10.0.0.0 0.255.255.255 area 0
!
end


R1#show ip ospf interface s0/0/0
Serial0/0/0 is up, line protocol is up
  Internet Address 10.1.12.1/30, Area 1
```

```
    Process ID 1, Router ID 1.1.1.1, Network Type POINT_TO_POINT, Cost: 64
! lines omitted for brevity

R1#show ip ospf neighbor

Neighbor ID      Pri    State         Dead Time    Address       Interface
2.2.2.2           0    FULL/   -      00:00:31     10.1.12.2     Serial0/0/0
```

Example 5-6 begins listing R1's configuration on the serial link, mainly to make the point that the OSPF network type has not been explicitly configured. The **show ip ospf interface** command then lists the network type (point-to-point). Based on Table 5-7, this type should dynamically discover neighbors, and it does, with neighbor 2.2.2.2 (R2) being listed at the end of the example. In particular, note that under the state heading in the **show ip ospf neighbor** command output, after the /, only a dash is listed. This notation means that no attempt was made to elect a DR. If the network type had implied a DR should be elected, then some text would be listed after the /, for example, "/DR" meaning that the neighbor was the DR. (Refer back to the end of Example 5-4 for an example of the output of **show ip ospf neighbor** in which a DR has been elected.)

Example 5-9 shows an alternative where both routers change their OSPF network type on the serial link to nonbroadcast. This change is nonsensical in real designs and is only done for the purposes of showing the results: that the neighbors are not discovered dynamically, but once defined, a DR is elected.

Note: R2 has been preconfigured to match the configuration on R1 in Example 5-9, namely, the OSPF network type has been changed (**ip ospf network non-broadcast**), and R2 has been configured with a **neighbor 10.1.12.1** OSPF router subcommand.

Example 5-9 *Configuring OSPF Network Type Nonbroadcast on an HDLC Link*

```
R1#configure terminal
Enter configuration commands, one per line.  End with CNTL/Z.
R1(config)#interface s0/0/0
R1(config-if)#ip ospf network ?
  broadcast              Specify OSPF broadcast multi-access network
  non-broadcast          Specify OSPF NBMA network
  point-to-multipoint    Specify OSPF point-to-multipoint network
  point-to-point         Specify OSPF point-to-point network
R1(config-if)#ip ospf network non-broadcast
R1(config-if)#^Z

R1#show ip ospf neighbor

R1#configure terminal
Enter configuration commands, one per line.  End with CNTL/Z.
R1(config)#router ospf 1
```

```
R1(config-router)#neighbor 10.1.12.2
R1(config-router)#^Z
R1#


*Apr 28 20:10:15.755: %OSPF-5-ADJCHG: Process 1, Nbr 2.2.2.2 on Serial0/0/0 from
LOADING to FULL, Loading Done
R1#show ip ospf neighbor


Neighbor ID     Pri   State          Dead Time   Address        Interface
2.2.2.2           1   FULL/DR        00:01:58    10.1.12.2      Serial0/0/0
```

The example begins with R2 already configured, so the neighbor relationship has already
failed. When the OSPF network type changes on R1's S0/0/0, the routers do not dynamically discover each other, based on the network type (nonbroadcast). However, by completing the configuration in the example by adding R1's **neighbor 10.1.12.2** command, the
neighbor relationship is formed. Also, note that the final **show ip ospf neighbor** command
lists a state of FULL, then a /, and then DR, meaning that a DR was indeed elected, as required by this OSPF network type.

Neighborship over Frame Relay Point-to-Point Subinterfaces

Frame Relay design allows several options for IP addressing and subnetting. One option
treats each pair of routers on the ends of each PVC as a point-to-point topology, with one
subnet assigned to each pair of routers. Another option treats more than two routers as a
group, whether connected with a full mesh or partial mesh of PVCs, with a single subnet
assigned to that group.

Many Frame Relay designs use the first option, treating each pair of routers on the ends
of a PVC as a single subnet, as shown in Figure 5-6. In such cases, it makes sense to treat
each PVC as a separate point-to-point connection, assigning a single subnet (at Layer 3) to
each Layer 2 PVC.

With this design, if all the routers use point-to-point subinterfaces as shown in R1's configuration in the figure, you can ignore the OSPF network (interface) type, and OSPF
works fine. IOS point-to-point subinterfaces unsurprisingly default to use OSPF network
type point-to-point. The two routers discover each other using multicast OSPF Hellos,
they do not bother to elect a DR, and everything works well.

Chapter 8 discusses alternative Frame Relay configurations.

Neighborship on MPLS VPN

Multiprotocol Label Switching (MPLS) virtual private networks (VPN) create a WAN
service that has some similarities but many differences when compared to Frame Relay.
The customer routers connect to the service, often times with serial links, but other times
with Frame Relay PVCs or with Ethernet. The service itself is a Layer 3 service, forwarding
IP packets through the cloud. As a result, no predefined PVCs need exist between the customer routers. Additionally, the service uses routers at the edge of the service provider
cloud—generically called provider edge (PE) routers—and these routers are Layer 3-aware.

interface S0/0.0.1 point-to-point
ip address 10.1.1.1 255.255.255.252
frame-relay interface-dlci 101

interface S0/0.0.2 point-to-point
ip address 10.1.1.5 255.255.255.252
frame-relay interface-dlci 102

interface s0/0.0.3 point-to-point
ip address 10.1.1.9 255.255.255.252
frame-relay interface-dlci 103

10.1.1.0/30

10.1.1.8/30

Frame
Relay

10.1.1.4/30

⊢———⊣ OSPF Neighborship

Figure 5-6 *Partial Meshed Frame Relay Network*

That Layer 3 awareness means that the customer edge (CE) routers form an OSPF neighborship with the PE router on the other end of their local access link, as shown in Figure 5-7. The PE routers exchange their routes, typically using Multiprotocol BGP (MP-BGP), a topic outside the scope of this book. So, unlike the design seen previously in Figure 5-6, the central site router will not have an OSPF neighborship with each branch office router but will have a neighborship with the MPLS VPN provider's PE router.

MPLS VPN does impact the data seen in the LSDB in the Enterprise routers and requires some different thinking in regard to area design. However, these details remain outside the scope of this book.

Neighborship on Metro Ethernet

In the like-named section "Neighborship on Metro Ethernet" in Chapter 2, that chapter explained the basic terminology with Metro Ethernet, including of VPWS, a point-to-point service, and VPLS, a multipoint service. In both cases, however, if the customer connects to the service using a router, the configuration typically uses VLAN trunking with subinterfaces off the FastEthernet or Gigabit Ethernet interface. If connecting with a Layer 3 switch, the configuration again often uses VLAN trunking, with the Layer 3 configuration being made on various VLAN interfaces inside the switch configuration.

Figure 5-7   *OSPF Neighborships over MPLS VPN*

Because MetroE services provide Layer 2 connectivity, customer routers do not form OSPF neighborships with routers inside the service provider's network. Instead, the OSPF neighborships forms between customer routers, essentially as if the service were a large WAN. Figure 5-8 shows the basic idea, with four routers connected to the service.

Figure 5-8 shows four routers with any-to-any connectivity, typical of a VPWS service. However, from an OSPF design perspective, each pair of routers could communicate over a different VLAN, using a different Layer 3 subnet. Each Layer 3 subnet could be in a different area. Although (like MPLS VPN area design) beyond the scope of this book, these options give the network designer many options on how to define areas.

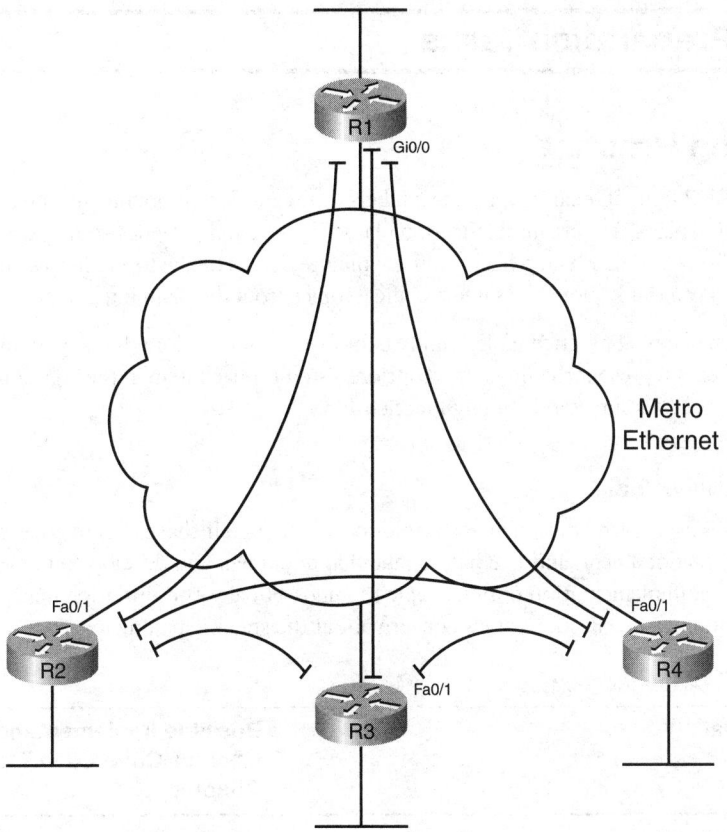

Figure 5-8 *OSPF Neighborships over Metro Ethernet*

Exam Preparation Tasks

Planning Practice

The CCNP ROUTE exam expects test takers to review design documents, create implementation plans, and create verification plans. This section provides some exercises that may help you to take a step back from the minute details of the topics in this chapter so that you can think about the same technical topics from the planning perspective.

For each planning practice table, simply complete the table. Note that any numbers in parentheses represent the number of options listed for each item in the solutions in Appendix F, "Completed Planning Practice Table."

Design Review Table

Table 5-9 lists several design goals related to this chapter. If these design goals were listed in a design document, and you had to take that document and develop an implementation plan, what implementation options come to mind? For any configuration items, a general description can be used, without concern about the specific parameters.

Table 5-9 *Design Review*

Design Goal	Possible Implementation Choices Covered in This Chapter
Improve OSPF convergence.	
Implement OSPF on each router so that neighborships are formed (2).	
Limit neighborship formation on OSPF-enabled interfaces (2).	
The design shows branch routers with WAN interfaces in area 0 and LAN interfaces in different areas for each branch. What LSDB information do you expect to see in the branch routers?	

Implementation Plan Peer Review Table

Table 5-10 shows a list of questions that others might ask, or that you might think about, during a peer review of another network engineer's implementation plan. Complete the table by answering the questions.

Table 5-10   *Notable Questions from This Chapter to Consider During an Implementation Plan Peer Review*

Question	Answers
What happens on a router interface on which an OSPF **network** command matches the interface? (2)	
What configuration settings prevent OSPF neighbor discovery on an OSPF-enabled interface?	
What settings do potential neighbors check before becoming OSPF neighbors? (7)	
What settings that you might think would impact OSPF neighbor relationships actually do not prevent neighborship?	
A design shows one main site and 100 branches, with OSPF, and MPLS VPNs. How many OSPF neighborships over the WAN do you expect to see on the central site router?	
A design shows one main site and 100 branches, with one Frame Relay PVC between the main site and each branch. How many OSPF neighborships over the WAN do you expect to see on the central site router?	
A design shows six routers connected to the same VLAN and subnet. How many OSPF fully adjacent neighborships over this subnet do you expect each router to have?	
A design shows one main site and 100 branches, each connected with a VPWS service. The configuration shows that the central site router uses a separate VLAN subinterface to connect to each branch, but the branch routers do not have a VLAN connecting to other branches. How many OSPF fully adjacent neighborships over the WAN do you expect to see on the central site router?	

Create an Implementation Plan Table

To practice skills useful when creating your own OSPF implementation plan, list in Table 5-11 configuration commands related to the configuration of the following features. You may want to record your answers outside the book and set a goal to complete this table (and others like it) from memory during your final reviews before taking the exam.

Table 5-11   *Implementation Plan Configuration Memory Drill*

Feature	Configuration Commands/Notes
Enabling OSPF on interfaces–traditional method	
Enabling OSPF on interfaces–using interface subcommands	
Setting Hello and Dead intervals	

Table 5-11   *Implementation Plan Configuration Memory Drill*

Feature	Configuration Commands/Notes
MD5 authentication, with no **router** subcommands	
MD5 authentication, with **router** subcommands	
Passive interfaces, with router subcommands	
OSPF router ID	

Choose Commands for a Verification Plan Table

To practice skills useful when creating your own OSPF verification plan, list in Table 5-12 all commands that supply the requested information. You may want to record your answers outside the book and set a goal to complete this table (and others like it) from memory during your final reviews before taking the exam.

Table 5-12   *Verification Plan Memory Drill*

Information Needed	Command
Which routes have been added to the IP routing table by OSPF	
All routes in a router's routing table	
The specific route for a single destination address or subnet	
A list of all (both static and dynamically discovered) OSPF neighbors	
List interfaces on which OSPF has been enabled	
List the number of OSPF neighbors and fully adjacent neighbors known via a particular interface	
The elapsed time since a neighborship was formed	
The configured Hello timer for an interface	
The configured Dead Interval timer for an interface	
The current actual dead timer for a neighbor	
A router's RID	
A list of OSPF passive interfaces	
The currently used OSPF authentication type	
The smallest-numbered OSPF authentication key number	
Lists traffic statistics about OSPF	

Note: Some of the entries in this table may not have been specifically mentioned in this chapter but are listed in this table for review and reference.

Review All the Key Topics

Review the most important topics from inside the chapter, noted with the key topics icon in the outer margin of the page. Table 5-13 lists a reference of these key topics and the page numbers on which each is found.

Key Topic

Table 5-13   *Key Topics for Chapter 5*

Key Topic Element	Description	Page Number
Table 5-2	Common OSPF terminology	142
List	Base OSPF configuration steps	144
List	Rules for choosing the OSPF Router ID	146
Table 5-3	Five most commonly used OSPF **show** commands	146
Table 5-4	Summary table of OSPF features	149
List	Requirements before OSPF will attempt to dynamically discover neighbors	150
Table 5-5	Requirements for neighbor formation–OSPF and EIGRP	152
List	Rules for enabling OSPF authentication on an interface	159
Table 5-6	OSPF Authentication command summary	159
Table 5-7	Commands to set the default OSPF authentication type	160
Table 5-8	OSPF network types	163

Complete the Tables and Lists from Memory

Print a copy of Appendix D, "Memory Tables," (found on the CD), or at least the section for this chapter, and complete the tables and lists from memory. Appendix E, "Memory Tables Answer Key," also on the CD, includes completed tables and lists to check your work.

Define Key Terms

Define the following key terms from this chapter, and check your answers in the glossary:

Area, Area Border Router (ABR), Backbone router, Router ID, Hello Interval, Dead Interval, Fully adjacent, OSPF network type

This chapter covers the following subjects:

LSAs and the OSPF Link State Database: This section examines LSA Types 1, 2, and 3, and how they allow OSPF routers to model the topology and choose the best routes for each known subnet.

The Database Exchange Process: This section details how neighboring routers use OSPF messages to exchange their LSAs.

Choosing the Best Internal OSPF Routes: This section examines how OSPF routers calculate the cost for each possible route to each subnet.

CHAPTER 6

OSPF Topology, Routes, and Convergence

OSPF and EIGRP both use three major branches of logic, each of which populates a different table: the neighbor table, the topology table, and the IP routing table. This chapter examines topics related to the OSPF topology table–the contents, and the processes by which routers exchange this information–and how OSPF routers choose the best routes in the topology table to be added to the IP routing table.

In particular, this chapter begins by looking at the building blocks of OSPF topology, namely the OSPF link state advertisement (LSA). Following that, the chapter examines the process by which OSPF routers exchange LSAs with each other. Finally, the last major section of the chapter discusses how OSPF chooses the best route among many when running the Shortest Path First (SPF) algorithm.

Note that this chapter focuses on OSPF Version 2, the long-available version of OSPF that supports IPv4 routes. Chapter 17, "IPv6 Routing Protocols and Redistribution," discusses OSPF Version 3, which applies to IPv6.

"Do I Know This Already?" Quiz

The "Do I Know This Already?" quiz allows you to assess if you should read the entire chapter. If you miss no more than one of these nine self-assessment questions, you might want to move ahead to the "Exam Preparation Tasks." Table 6-1 lists the major headings in this chapter and the "Do I Know This Already?" quiz questions covering the material in those headings so that you can assess your knowledge of these specific areas. The answers to the "Do I Know This Already?" quiz appear in Appendix A.

Table 6-1 *"Do I Know This Already?" Foundation Topics Section-to-Question Mapping*

Foundations Topics Section	Questions
LSAs and the OSPF Link State Database	1–3
The Database Exchange Process	4, 5
Choosing the Best OSPF Routes	6–9

1. A network design shows area 1 with three internal routers, area 0 with four internal routers, and area 2 with five internal routers. Additionally, one ABR (ABR1) connects areas 0 and 1, plus a different ABR (ABR2) connects areas 0 and 2. How many Type 1 LSAs would be listed in ABR2's LSDB?

   a. 6

   b. 7

   c. 15

   d. 12

   e. None of the other answers is correct.

2. A network planning diagram shows a large internetwork with many routers. The configurations show that OSPF has been enabled on all interfaces, IP addresses correctly configured, and OSPF working. For which of the following cases would you expect a router to create and flood a Type 2 LSA?

   a. When OSPF is enabled on a LAN interface, and the router is the only router connected to the subnet.

   b. When OSPF is enabled on a point-to-point serial link, and that router has both the higher router ID and higher interface IP address on the link.

   c. When OSPF is enabled on a Frame Relay point-to-point subinterface, has the lower RID and lower subinterface IP address, and otherwise uses default OSPF configuration on the interface.

   d. When OSPF is enabled on a working LAN interface on a router, and the router has been elected BDR.

   e. None of the other answers is correct.

3. A verification plan shows a network diagram with branch office Routers B1 through B100, plus two ABRs, ABR1, and ABR2, all in area 100. The branches connect to the ABRs using Frame Relay point-to-point subinterfaces. The verification plan lists the output of the **show ip ospf database summary 10.100.0.0** command on a router B1, one of the branches. Which of the following is true regarding the output that could be listed for this command?

   a. The output lists nothing unless 10.100.0.0 has been configured as a summary route using the **area range** command.

   b. If 10.100.0.0 is a subnet in area 0, the output lists one Type 3 LSA, specifically the LSA with the lower metric when comparing ABR1's and ABR2's LSA for 10.100.0.0.

   c. If 10.100.0.0 is a subnet in area 0, the output lists two Type 3 LSAs, one each created by ABR1 and ABR2.

   d. None, because the Type 3 LSAs would exist only in the ABR's LSDBs.

4. Which of the following OSPF messages contains entire complete LSAs used during the database exchange process?

    a. LSR

    b. LSAck

    c. LSU

    d. DD

    e. Hello

5. Routers R1, R2, R3, and R4 connect to the same 10.10.10.0/24 LAN-based subnet. OSPF is fully working in the subnet. Later, R5, whose OSPF priority is higher than the other four routers, joins the subnet. Which of the following are true about the OSPF database exchange process over this subnet at this point? (Choose two.)

    a. R5 will send its DD, LSR, and LSU packets to the 224.0.0.5 all-DR-routers multicast address.

    b. R5 will send its DD, LSR, and LSU packets to the 224.0.0.6 all-DR-routers multicast address.

    c. The DR will inform R5 about LSAs by sending its DD, LSR, and LSU packets to the 224.0.0.6 all-SPF-routers multicast address.

    d. The DR will inform R5 about LSAs by sending its DD, LSR, and LSU packets to the 224.0.0.5 all-SPF-routers multicast address.

6. R1 is internal to area 1, and R2 is internal to area 2. Subnet 10.1.1.0/24 exists in area 2 as a connected subnet off R2. ABR ABR1 connects area 1 to backbone area 0, and ABR2 connects area 0 to area 2. Which of the following LSAs must R1 use when calculating R1's best route for 10.1.1.0/24?

    a. R2's Type 1 LSA

    b. Subnet 10.1.1.0/24's Type 2 LSA

    c. ABR1's Type 1 LSA in area 0

    d. Subnet 10.1.1.0/24's Type 3 LSA in Area 0

    e. Subnet 10.1.1.0/24's Type 3 LSA in Area 1

7. Which of the following LSA types describes topology information that, when changed, requires a router in the same area to perform an SPF calculation? (Choose two.)

    a. 1

    b. 2

    c. 3

    d. 4

    e. 5

    f. 7

8. The following output was taken from Router R3. A scan of R3's configuration shows that no **bandwidth** commands have been configured in this router. Which of the following answers lists configuration settings could be a part of a configuration that results in the following output? (Choose two.)

```
R3#show ip ospf interface brief
Interface    PID   Area          IP Address/Mask      Cost   State Nbrs F/C
Se0/0/0.2    3     34            10.10.23.3/29        647    P2P   1/1
Se0/0/0.1    3     34            10.10.13.3/29        1000   P2P   1/1
Fa0/0        3     34            10.10.34.3/24        20     BDR   1/1
```

    a. An auto-cost reference-bandwidth 1000 command in router ospf mode

    b. An auto-cost reference-bandwidth 2000 command in router ospf mode

    c. An ip ospf cost 1000 interface S0/0/0.1 command in router ospf mode

    d. An auto-cost reference-bandwidth 64700 command in router ospf mode

9. Which of the following LSA types describe information related to topology or subnets useful for calculating routes for subnets inside the OSPF domain? (Choose three.)

    a. 1

    b. 2

    c. 3

    d. 4

    e. 5

    f. 7

Foundation Topics

LSAs and the OSPF Link State Database

Every router that connects to a given OSPF area should learn the exact same topology data. Each router stores the data, composed of individual link state advertisements (LSA), in their own copy of the link state database (LSDB). Then, the router applies the Shortest Path First (SPF) algorithm to the LSDB to determine the best (lowest cost) route for each reachable subnet (prefix/length).

When a router uses SPF to analyze the LSDB, the SPF process has some similarities to how humans put a jigsaw puzzle together–but without a picture of what the puzzle looks like. Humans faced with such a challenge might first look for the obvious puzzle pieces, such as the corner and edge pieces, because they are easily recognized. You might then group puzzle pieces together if they have the same color or look for straight lines that might span multiple puzzle pieces. And of course, you would be looking at the shapes of the puzzle pieces to see which ones fit together.

Similarly, a router's SPF process must examine the individual LSAs and see how they fit together, based on their characteristics. To better appreciate the SPF process, the first section of this chapter examines the three LSA types OSPF uses to describe an Enterprise OSPF topology inside the OSPF domain. By understanding the types of LSAs, you can get a better understanding of what a router might look for to take the LSAs–the pieces of a network topology puzzle if you will–and build the equivalent of a network diagram.

For reference, Table 6-2 lists the various OSPF LSA types. Note that Chapter 9 explains three other LSA types, all used when redistributing routes into the OSPF domain.

Table 6-2   *OSPF LSA Types*

Key Topic

LSA Type	Common Name	Description
1	Router	Each router creates its own Type 1 LSA to represent itself for each area to which it connects. The LSDB for one area contains one Type 1 LSA per router per area, listing the RID and all interface IP addresses on that router that are in that area. Represents stub networks as well.
2	Network	One per transit network. Created by the DR on the subnet, and represents the subnet and the router interfaces connected to the subnet.
3	Net Summary	Created by ABRs to represent subnets listed in one area's type 1 and 2 LSAs when being advertised into another area. Defines the links (subnets) in the origin area, and cost, but no topology data.
4	ASBR Summary	Like a type 3 LSA, except it advertises a host route used to reach an ASBR.

Table 6-2 *OSPF LSA Types*

LSA Type	Common Name	Description
5	AS External	Created by ASBRs for external routes injected into OSPF.
6	Group Membership	Defined for MOSPF; not supported by Cisco IOS.
7	NSSA External	Created by ASBRs inside an NSSA area, instead of a type 5 LSA.
8	External Attributes	Not implemented in Cisco routers.
9–11	Opaque	Used as generic LSAs to allow for easy future extension of OSPF; for example, type 10 has been adapted for MPLS traffic engineering.

LSA Type 1: Router LSA

An LSA type 1, called a *router LSA*, identifies an OSPF router based on its OSPF router ID (RID). Each router creates a Type 1 LSA for itself and floods the LSA throughout the same area. To flood the LSA, the originating router sends the Type 1 LSA to its neighbors inside the same area, who in turn send it to their other neighbors inside the same area, until all routers in the area have a copy of the LSA.

Besides the RID of the router, this LSA also lists information about the attached links. In particular, the Type 1 LSA lists:

■   For each interface on which no DR has been elected, it lists the router's interface subnet number/mask and interface OSPF cost. (OSPF refers to these subnets as *stub networks.*)

■   For each interface on which a DR has been elected, it lists the IP address of the DR and a notation that the link attaches to a *transit network* (meaning a type 2 LSA exists for that network).

■   For each interface with no DR, but for which a neighbor is reachable, it lists the neighbor's RID.

As with all OSPF LSAs, OSPF identifies a Type 1 LSA using a 32-bit *link state identifier* (LSID). When creating its own Type 1 LSA, each router uses its own OSPF RID value as the LSID.

Internal routers each create a single Type 1 LSA for themselves, but ABRs create multiple Type 1 LSAs for themselves: one per area. The Type 1 LSA in one area will list only interfaces in that area and only neighbors in that area. However, the router still has only a single RID, so all its Type 1 LSAs for a single router list the same RID. The ABR then floods each of its Type 1 LSAs into the appropriate area.

To provide a better backdrop for the upcoming LSA discussions, Figure 6-1 shows a sample internetwork, which will be used in most of the examples in this chapter.

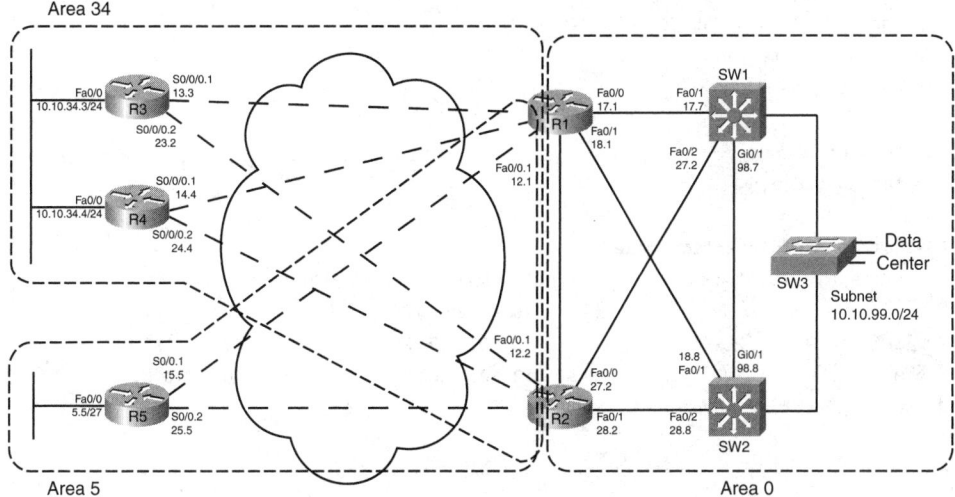

Figure 6-1 *Sample OSPF Multi-Area Design*

All routers that participate in an area, be they internal routers or ABRs, create and flood a Type 1 LSA inside the area. For example, in Figure 6-1, area 5 has one internal router (R5, RID 5.5.5.5), and two ABRs: R1 with RID 1.1.1.1 and R2 with RID 2.2.2.2. Each of these three routers create and flood their own Type 1 LSA inside area 5 so that all three routers know the same three Type 1 LSAs.

Next, to further understand the details inside a Type 1 LSA, first consider the OSPF configuration of R5 as an example. R5 has three IP-enabled interfaces: Fa0/0, S0/0/0.1, and S0/0.2. R5 uses point-to-point subinterfaces, so R5 should form neighbor relationships with both R1 and R2 with no extra configuration beyond enabling OSPF, in area 5, on all three interfaces. Example 6-1 shows this baseline configuration on R5.

Example 6-1 *R5 Configuration–IP Addresses and OSPF*

```
interface Fastethernet0/0
 ip address 10.10.5.5 255.255.255.224
 ip ospf 5 area 5
!
interface s0/0.1 point-to-point
 ip addr 10.10.15.5 255.255.255.248
 frame-relay interface-dlci 101
 ip ospf 5 area 5
!
interface s0/0.2 point-to-point
```

```
 ip addr 10.10.25.5 255.255.255.248
 frame-relay interface-dlci 102
 ip ospf 5 area 5
!
router ospf 5
 router-id 5.5.5.5
!
R5#show ip ospf interface brief
Interface     PID   Area          IP Address/Mask    Cost   State  Nbrs F/C
se0/0.2       5     5             10.10.25.5/29      64     P2P    1/1
se0/0.1       5     5             10.10.15.5/29      64     P2P    1/1
fa0/0         5     5             10.10.5.5/27       1      DR     0/0
R5#show ip ospf neighbor

Neighbor ID   Pri   State         Dead Time  Address     Interface
2.2.2.2       0     FULL/  -      00:00:30   10.10.25.2  Serial0/0.2
1.1.1.1       0     FULL/  -      00:00:38   10.10.15.1  Serial0/0.1
```

R5's OSPF configuration enables OSPF, for process ID 5, placing three interfaces in area 5. As a result, R5's type 1 LSA will list at least these three interfaces as links, plus it will refer to the two working neighbors. Example 6-2 displays the contents of R5's area 5 LSDB, including the detailed information in R5's Type 1 LSA, including the following:

■   The LSID of R5's Type 1 LSA (5.5.5.5)

■   Three links that connect to a stub network, each listing the subnet/mask

■   Two links that state a connection to another router, one listing R1 (RID 1.1.1.1) and one listing R2 (RID 2.2.2.2)

Example 6-2   *R5 Configuration–IP Addresses and OSPF*

```
R5#show ip ospf database


            OSPF Router with ID (5.5.5.5) (Process ID 5)


                Router Link States (Area 5)


Link ID         ADV Router      Age         Seq#        Checksum Link count
1.1.1.1         1.1.1.1         835         0x80000002 0x006BDA 2
2.2.2.2         2.2.2.2         788         0x80000002 0x0082A6 2
5.5.5.5         5.5.5.5         787         0x80000004 0x0063C3 5


                Summary Net Link States (Area 5)
```

```
Link ID           ADV Router         Age        Seq#        Checksum
10.10.12.0        1.1.1.1            835        0x80000001  0x00F522
10.10.12.0        2.2.2.2            787        0x80000001  0x00D73C
! lines omitted for brevity

R5#show ip ospf database router 5.5.5.5

                OSPF Router with ID (5.5.5.5) (Process ID 5)

                    Router Link States (Area 5)


  LS age: 796
  Options: (No TOS-capability, DC)
  LS Type: Router Links
  Link State ID: 5.5.5.5
  Advertising Router: 5.5.5.5
  LS Seq Number: 80000004
  Checksum: 0x63C3
  Length: 84
  Number of Links: 5

    Link connected to: another Router (point-to-point)
     (Link ID) Neighboring Router ID: 2.2.2.2
     (Link Data) Router Interface address: 10.10.25.5
      Number of TOS metrics: 0
       TOS 0 Metrics: 64

    Link connected to: a Stub Network
     (Link ID) Network/subnet number: 10.10.25.0
     (Link Data) Network Mask: 255.255.255.248
      Number of TOS metrics: 0
       TOS 0 Metrics: 64

    Link connected to: another Router (point-to-point)
     (Link ID) Neighboring Router ID: 1.1.1.1
     (Link Data) Router Interface address: 10.10.15.5
      Number of TOS metrics: 0
       TOS 0 Metrics: 64

    Link connected to: a Stub Network
     (Link ID) Network/subnet number: 10.10.15.0
     (Link Data) Network Mask: 255.255.255.248
      Number of TOS metrics: 0
       TOS 0 Metrics: 64
```

```
Link connected to: a Stub Network
  (Link ID) Network/subnet number: 10.10.5.0
  (Link Data) Network Mask: 255.255.255.224
  Number of TOS metrics: 0
   TOS 0 Metrics: 1
```

The first command, **show ip ospf database**, displays a summary of the LSAs known to R5. The output mainly consists of a single line per LSA, listed by LSA ID. The three high-lighted lines of this command, in Example 6-2, highlight the RID of the three router (Type 1) LSAs, namely 1.1.1.1 (R1), 2.2.2.2 (R2), and 5.5.5.5 (R5).

The output of the **show ip ospf database router 5.5.5.5** command displays the detailed information in R5's router LSA. Looking at the highlighted portions, you see three stub networks–three interfaces on which no DR has been elected–and the associated subnet numbers. The LSA also lists the neighbor IDs of two neighbors (1.1.1.1 and 2.2.2.2) and the interfaces on which these neighbors can be reached.

Armed with the same kind of information in R1's and R2's Type 1 LSAs, a router has enough information to determine which routers connect, over which stub links, and then use the interface IP address configuration to figure out the interfaces that connect to the other routers. Figure 6-2 shows a diagram of area 5 that could be built just based on the detailed information held in the router LSAs for R1, R2, and R5.

Figure 6-2   *Three Type 1 LSAs in Area 5*

Note that Figure 6-2 displays only information that could be learned from the Type 1 router LSAs inside area 5. Each Type 1 router LSA lists information about a router but only the details related to a specific area. As a result, Figure 6-2 shows R1's interface in area 5 but none of the interfaces in area 34 nor in area 0. To complete the explanation surrounding Figure 6-2, Example 6-3 lists R1's Type 1 router LSA for area 5.

Example 6-3 *R1's Type 1 LSA in Area 5*

```
R5#show ip ospf database router 1.1.1.1


            OSPF Router with ID (5.5.5.5) (Process ID 5)

                Router Link States (Area 5)


Routing Bit Set on this LSA
LS age: 1306
Options: (No TOS-capability, DC)
LS Type: Router Links
Link State ID: 1.1.1.1
Advertising Router: 1.1.1.1
LS Seq Number: 80000002
Checksum: 0x6BDA
Length: 48
Area Border Router
Number of Links: 2

  Link connected to: another Router (point-to-point)
   (Link ID) Neighboring Router ID: 5.5.5.5
   (Link Data) Router Interface address: 10.10.15.1
    Number of TOS metrics: 0
     TOS 0 Metrics: 64

  Link connected to: a Stub Network
   (Link ID) Network/subnet number: 10.10.15.0
   (Link Data) Network Mask: 255.255.255.248
    Number of TOS metrics: 0
     TOS 0 Metrics: 64
```

Note: Because the OSPF uses the RID for many purposes inside different LSAs–for instance, as the LSID of a type 1 LSA–Cisco recommends setting the RID to a stable, predictable value. To do this, use the OSPF **router-id** *value* OSPF subcommand, or define a loopback interface with an IP address, as discussed in Chapter 5's section "Using a Unique OSPF Router ID."

LSA Type 2: Network LSA

SPF requires that the LSDB model the topology with nodes (routers) and connections between nodes (links). In particular, each link must be between a pair of nodes. When a multiaccess data link exists—for instance, a LAN—OSPF must somehow model that LAN so that the topology represents nodes and links between only a pair of nodes. To do so, OSPF uses the concept of a Type 2 Network LSA.

OSPF routers actually choose whether to use a Type 2 LSA for a multiaccess network based on whether a designated router (DR) has or has not been elected on an interface. So, before discussing the details of the Type 2 network LSA, a few more facts about the concept of a DR need to be discussed.

Background on Designated Routers

As discussed in Chapter 5's section "OSPF Network Types," the OSPF network type assigned to a router interface tells that router whether to attempt to elect a DR on that interface. Then, when a router has heard a Hello from at least one other router, the routers elect a DR and BDR.

OSPF uses a DR in a particular subnet for two main purposes:

- To create and flood a Type 2 network LSA for that subnet

- To aid in the detailed process of database exchange over that subnet

Routers elect a DR, and a backup DR (BDR), based on information in the OSPF Hello. The Hello message lists each router's RID and a priority value. When no DR exists at the time, routers use the following election rules when neither a DR nor BDR yet exists:

- Choose the router with the highest priority (default 1, max 255, set with **ip ospf priority** *value* interface subcommand).

- If tied on priority, choose the router with highest RID.

- Choose a BDR, based on next-best priority, or if a tie, next-best (highest) RID.

Although the preceding describes the election when no DR currently exists, the rules differ a bit when a DR and BDR already exist. After a DR and BDR are elected, no election is held until either the DR or BDR fails. If the DR fails, the BDR becomes the DR——regardless of whether a higher priority router has joined the subnet—and a new election is held to choose a new BDR. If the BDR fails, a new election is held for BDR, and the DR remains unchanged.

On LANs, the choice of DR matters little from a design perspective, but does matter from an operational perspective. Throughout this chapter, note the cases in which output of **show** commands identify the DR and its role. Now, back to the topic of Type 2 LSAs.

Note: On Frame Relay WAN links, the choice of DR may impact whether OSPF functions at all. This topic is covered in Chapter 8, "OSPF Virtual Links and Frame Relay Operations."

Type 2 Network LSA Concepts

OSPF uses the concept of a Type 2 LSA to model a multiaccess network–a network with more than two routers connected to the same subnet–while still conforming to the "a link connects only two nodes" rule for the topology. For example, consider the network in Figure 6-3 (also shown as Figure 5-4 in the previous chapter). As seen in Chapter 5, all four routers form neighbor relationships inside area 0, with the DR and BDR becoming fully adjacent with the other routers.

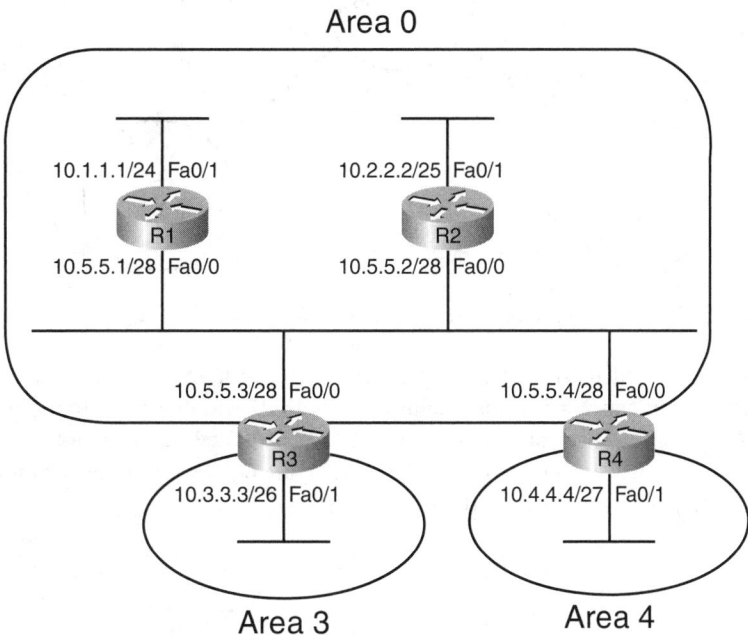

Figure 6-3   *Small Network, Four Routers, on a LAN*

OSPF cannot represent the idea of four routers connected via a single subnet by using a link connected to all four routers. Instead, OSPF defines the Type 2 network LSA, used as a *pseudonode*. Each router's Type 1 router LSA lists a connection this pseudonode, often called a *transit network*, which is then modeled by a Type 2 network LSA. The Type 2 network LSA itself then lists references back to each Type 1 router LSA connected to it–four in this example, as shown in Figure 6-4.

The elected DR in a subnet creates the Type 2 LSA for that subnet. The DR identifies the LSA by assigning an LSID of the DR's interface IP address in that subnet. The type 2 LSA also lists the DR's RID as the router advertising the LSA.

Type 2 LSA show Commands

To see these concepts in the form of OSPF **show** commands, next consider area 34 back in Figure 6-1. This design shows that R3 and R4 connect to the same LAN, which means that

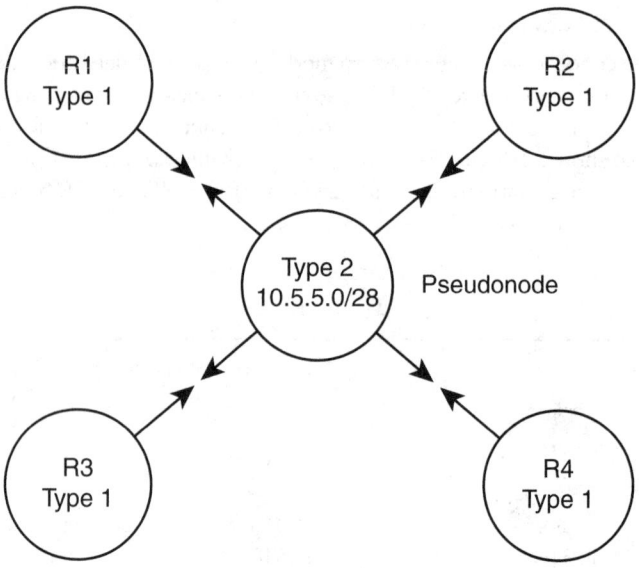

Figure 6-4   *OSPF Topology when Using a Type 2 Network LSA*

a DR will be elected. (OSPF elects a DR on LANs when at least two routers pass the neighbor requirements and can become neighbors.) If both R3 and R4 default to use priority 1, then R4 wins the election, due to its 4.4.4.4 RID (versus R3's 3.3.3.3). So, R4 creates the Type 2 LSA for that subnet and floods the LSA. Figure 6-5 depicts the area 34 topology, and Example 6-4 shows the related LSDB entries.

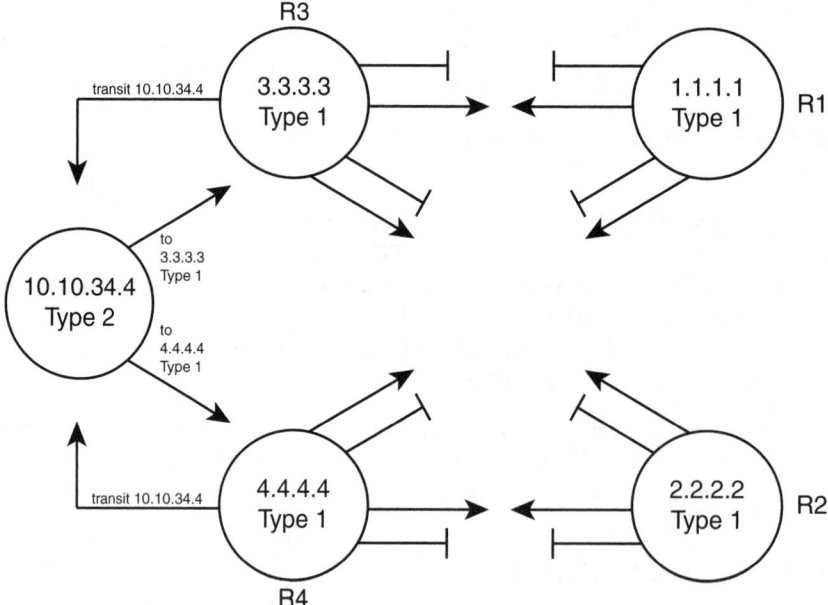

Figure 6-5   *Area 34 Topology with Four Type 1 LSAs and One Type 2 LSA*

Example 6-4   *Area 34 LSAs for R4, Network 10.10.34.0/24*

```
R5#show ip ospf database


                OSPF Router with ID (3.3.3.3) (Process ID 3)

                    Router Link States (Area 34)

Link ID         ADV Router       Age        Seq#        Checksum Link count
1.1.1.1         1.1.1.1          1061       0x80000002 0x00EA7A 4
2.2.2.2         2.2.2.2          1067       0x80000001 0x0061D2 4
3.3.3.3         3.3.3.3          1066       0x80000003 0x00E2E8 5
4.4.4.4         4.4.4.4          1067       0x80000003 0x007D3F 5

                    Net Link States (Area 34)


Link ID         ADV Router       Age        Seq#        Checksum
10.10.34.4      4.4.4.4          1104       0x80000001 0x00AB28

                    Summary Net Link States (Area 34)

Link ID         ADV Router       Age        Seq#        Checksum
10.10.5.0       1.1.1.1          1023       0x80000001 0x000BF2
10.10.5.0       2.2.2.2          1022       0x80000001 0x00EC0D
! lines omitted for brevity

R3#show ip ospf database router 4.4.4.4

                OSPF Router with ID (3.3.3.3) (Process ID 3)

                    Router Link States (Area 34)

  LS age: 1078
  Options: (No TOS-capability, DC)
  LS Type: Router Links
  Link State ID: 4.4.4.4
  Advertising Router: 4.4.4.4
  LS Seq Number: 80000003
  Checksum: 0x7D3F
  Length: 84
```

```
    Number of Links: 5

      Link connected to: another Router (point-to-point)
       (Link ID) Neighboring Router ID: 2.2.2.2
       (Link Data) Router Interface address: 10.10.24.4
        Number of TOS metrics: 0
         TOS 0 Metrics: 64

      Link connected to: a Stub Network
       (Link ID) Network/subnet number: 10.10.24.0
       (Link Data) Network Mask: 255.255.255.248
        Number of TOS metrics: 0
         TOS 0 Metrics: 64

      Link connected to: another Router (point-to-point)
       (Link ID) Neighboring Router ID: 1.1.1.1
       (Link Data) Router Interface address: 10.10.14.4
        Number of TOS metrics: 0
         TOS 0 Metrics: 64

      Link connected to: a Stub Network
       (Link ID) Network/subnet number: 10.10.14.0
       (Link Data) Network Mask: 255.255.255.248
        Number of TOS metrics: 0
         TOS 0 Metrics: 64

      Link connected to: a Transit Network
       (Link ID) Designated Router address: 10.10.34.4
       (Link Data) Router Interface address: 10.10.34.4
        Number of TOS metrics: 0
         TOS 0 Metrics: 1

R3#show ip ospf database network 10.10.34.4

             OSPF Router with ID (3.3.3.3) (Process ID 3)

                 Net Link States (Area 34)

   Routing Bit Set on this LSA
   LS age: 1161
   Options: (No TOS-capability, DC)
   LS Type: Network Links
   Link State ID: 10.10.34.4 (address of Designated Router)
   Advertising Router: 4.4.4.4
```

```
LS Seq Number: 80000001
Checksum: 0xAB28
Length: 32
Network Mask: /24
       Attached Router: 4.4.4.4
       Attached Router: 3.3.3.3
```

The **show ip ospf database** command lists a single line for each LSA. Note that the (highlighted) heading for network LSAs lists one entry, with LSID 10.10.34.4, which is R4's Fa0/0 IP address. The LSID for Type 2 Network LSAs is the interface IP address of the DR that creates the LSA.

The **show ip ospf database router 4.4.4.4** command shows the new style of entry for the reference to a *Transit Network*, which again refers to a connection to a Type 2 LSA. The output lists a LSID of 10.10.34.4, which again is the LSID of the Type 2 LSA.

Finally, the **show ip ospf database network 10.10.34.4** command shows the details of the Type 2 LSA, based on its LSID of 10.10.34.4. Near the bottom, the output lists the attached routers, based on RID. The SPF process can then use the cross-referenced information, as shown in Figure 6-5, to determine which routers connect to this transit network (pseudonode). The SPF process has information in both the Type 1 LSAs that refer to the transit network link to a Type 2 LSA, and the Type 2 LSA has a list of RIDs of Type 1 LSAs that connect to the Type 2 LSA, making the process of modeling the network possible.

OSPF can model all the topology inside a single area using Type 1 and 2 LSAs. When a router uses its SPF process to build a model of the topology, it can then calculate the best (lowest cost) route for each subnet in the area. The next topic completes the LSA picture for internal OSPF routes by looking at Type 3 LSAs, which are used to model interarea routes.

LSA Type 3: Summary LSA

OSPF areas exist in part so that engineers can reduce the consumption of memory and compute resources in routers. Instead of having all routers, regardless of area, know all Type 1 and Type 2 LSAs inside an OSPF domain, ABRs do not forward Type 1 and Type 2 LSAs from one area into another area, and vice versa. This convention results in smaller per-area LSDBs, saving memory and reducing complexity for each run of the SPF algorithm, which saves CPU and improves convergence time.

However, even though ABRs do not flood Type 1 and Type 2 LSAs into other areas, routers still need to learn about subnets in other areas. OSPF advertises these interarea routes using the Type 3 summary LSA. ABRs generate a Type 3 LSA for each subnet in one area, and advertises each Type 3 LSA into the other areas.

For example, if subnet A exists in area 3, then the routers in area 3 learn of that subnet as part of Type 1 and Type 2 LSAs. However, an ABR connected to area 3 will not forward the Type 1 and Type 2 LSAs into other areas, instead creating a Type 3 LSA for each subnet (including subnet A). The routers inside the other areas can then calculate a route for the subnets (like subnet A) that exist inside another area.

Type 3 summary LSAs do not contain all the detailed topology information, so in comparison to Types 1 and 2, these LSAs summarize the information–hence the name *summary LSA*. Conceptually, a Type 3 LSA appears to be another subnet connected to the ABR that created and advertised the Type 3 LSA. The routers inside that area can calculate their best route to reach the ABR, which gives the router a good loop-free route to reach the subnet listed in a Type 3 LSA.

An example can certainly help in this case. First, consider the comparison shown in the top and bottom of Figure 6-6. The top depicts the topology shown back in Figure 6-1 if that design had used a single area. In that case, every router would have a copy of each Type 1 LSA (shown as a router name in the figure), and each Type 2 (abbreviated as T2 in the figure). The bottom of Figure 6-6 shows the area 5 topology, when holding to the three area design shown in Figure 6-1.

Figure 6-6   *Comparing a Single Area LSDB to a Three Area LSDB*

The ABR creates and floods each Type 3 LSA into the next area. The ABR assigns an LSID of the subnet number being advertised. It also adds its own RID to the LSA as well, so that routers know which ABR advertised the route. It also includes the subnet mask. The correlation between the advertising router's RID and the LSID (subnet number) allows the OSPF processes to create the part of the topology as shown with Type 3 LSAs at the bottom of Figure 6-6.

Example 6-5 focuses on the Type 3 LSAs in Area 34 of the network shown in Figure 6-1. Ten subnets exist outside area 34. As ABRs, both R1 and R2 create and flood a Type 3 LSA for each of these 10 subnets, resulting in 20 Type 3 LSAs listed in the output of the **show ip ospf database** command inside area 34. Then, the example focuses specifically on the Type 3 LSA for subnet 10.10.99.0/24.

Example 6-5 *Type 3 LSAs in Area 34*

```
R3#show ip ospf database


              OSPF Router with ID (3.3.3.3) (Process ID 3)

                Router Link States (Area 34)

Link ID         ADV Router      Age         Seq#        Checksum Link count
1.1.1.1         1.1.1.1         943         0x80000003 0x00E87B 4
2.2.2.2         2.2.2.2         991         0x80000002 0x005FD3 4
3.3.3.3         3.3.3.3         966         0x80000004 0x00E0E9 5
4.4.4.4         4.4.4.4         977         0x80000004 0x007B40 5


                Net Link States (Area 34)

Link ID         ADV Router      Age         Seq#        Checksum
10.10.34.4      4.4.4.4         977         0x80000002 0x00A929


              Summary Net Link States (Area 34)

Link ID         ADV Router      Age         Seq#        Checksum
10.10.5.0       1.1.1.1         943         0x80000002 0x0009F3
10.10.5.0       2.2.2.2         991         0x80000002 0x00EA0E
10.10.12.0      1.1.1.1         943         0x80000002 0x00F323
10.10.12.0      2.2.2.2         991         0x80000002 0x00D53D
10.10.15.0      1.1.1.1         943         0x80000002 0x0021BA
10.10.15.0      2.2.2.2         993         0x80000003 0x008313
10.10.17.0      1.1.1.1         946         0x80000002 0x00BC55
10.10.17.0      2.2.2.2         993         0x80000002 0x00A864
10.10.18.0      1.1.1.1         946         0x80000002 0x00B15F
10.10.18.0      2.2.2.2         994         0x80000002 0x009D6E
```

```
10.10.25.0      1.1.1.1      946      0x80000002 0x00355C
10.10.25.0      2.2.2.2      993      0x80000002 0x009439
10.10.27.0      1.1.1.1      946      0x80000002 0x0058AE
10.10.27.0      2.2.2.2      993      0x80000002 0x0030D3
10.10.28.0      1.1.1.1      947      0x80000002 0x004DB8
10.10.28.0      2.2.2.2      993      0x80000002 0x0025DD
10.10.98.0      1.1.1.1      946      0x80000002 0x004877
10.10.98.0      2.2.2.2      993      0x80000002 0x002A91
10.10.99.0      1.1.1.1      946      0x80000002 0x003D81
10.10.99.0      2.2.2.2      993      0x80000002 0x001F9B

R3#show ip ospf database summary 10.10.99.0

              OSPF Router with ID (3.3.3.3) (Process ID 3)


              Summary Net Link States (Area 34)


  Routing Bit Set on this LSA
  LS age: 1062
  Options: (No TOS-capability, DC, Upward)
  LS Type: Summary Links(Network)
  Link State ID: 10.10.99.0 (summary Network Number)
  Advertising Router: 1.1.1.1
  LS Seq Number: 80000002
  Checksum: 0x3D81
  Length: 28
  Network Mask: /24
        TOS: 0  Metric: 2


  Routing Bit Set on this LSA
  LS age: 1109
  Options: (No TOS-capability, DC, Upward)
  LS Type: Summary Links(Network)
  Link State ID: 10.10.99.0 (summary Network Number)
  Advertising Router: 2.2.2.2
  LS Seq Number: 80000002
  Checksum: 0x1F9B
  Length: 28
  Network Mask: /24
        TOS: 0  Metric: 2
```

Note: The Type 3 Summary LSA is not used for the purpose of route summarization. OSPF does support route summarization, and Type 3 LSAs may indeed advertise such a summary, but the Type 3 LSA does not inherently represent a summary route. The term summary reflects the idea that the information is sparse compared to the detail inside Type 1 and Type 2 LSAs.

The upcoming section "Calculating the Cost of Inter-area Routes" discusses how a router determines the available routes to reach subnets listed in a Type 3 LSA and how a router chooses which route is best.

Limiting the Number of LSAs

By default, Cisco IOS does not limit the number of LSAs a router can learn. However, it may be useful to protect a router from learning too many LSAs to protect router memory. Also, with a large number of LSAs, the router may be unable to process the LSDB with SPF well enough to converge in a reasonable amount of time.

The maximum number of LSAs learned from other routers can be limited by a router using the **max-lsa** *number* OSPF subcommand. When configured, if the router learns more than the configured number of LSAs from other routers (ignoring those created by the router itself), the router reacts. The first reaction is to issue log messages. The router ignores the event for a time period, after which the router repeats the warning message. This ignore-and-wait strategy can proceed through several iterations, ending when the router closes all neighborships, discards its LSDB, and then starts adding neighbors again. (The ignore time, and the number of times to ignore the event, can be configured with the **max-lsa** command.)

Summary of Internal LSA Types

OSPF uses Type 1, 2, and 3 LSAs to calculate the best routes for all routes inside the OSPF routing domain. Later, Chapter 9 explains Types 4, 5, and 7, which OSPF uses to calculate routes for external routes–routes redistributed into OSPF.

Table 6-3 summarizes some of the key points regarding OSPF Type 1, 2, and 3 LSAs. In particular for the ROUTE exam, the ability to sift through the output of various **show ip ospf database** commands can be important. Knowing what the OSPF LSID represents can help you interpret the output, and knowing the keywords used with the **show ip ospf database** *lsa-type lsid* commands can also be very useful. Table 6-3 summarizes these details.

Table 6-3 *Facts about LSA Types 1, 2, and 3*

Key Topic

LSA Type (Number)	LSA Type (Name)	This Type Represents	Display Using show ip ospf database *keyword...*	LSID Is Equal To	Created By
1	Router	A router	**router**	RID of router	Each router creates its own

Table 6-3 *Facts about LSA Types 1, 2, and 3*

LSA Type (Number)	LSA Type (Name)	This Type Represents	Display Using show ip ospf database keyword...	LSID Is Equal To	Created By
2	Network	A subnet in which a DR exists	**network**	DR's IP address in the subnet	The DR in that subnet
3	Summary	Subnet in another area	**summary**	Subnet number	An ABR

The Database Exchange Process

Every router in an area, when OSPF stabilizes after topology changes occur, should have an identical LSDB for that area. Internal routers (routers inside a single area) have only that area's LSAs, but an ABR's LSDB will contain LSAs for each area to which it connects. The ABR does, however, know which LSAs exist in each area.

OSPF routers flood both the LSAs they create, and the LSAs they learn from their neighbors, until all routers in the area have a copy of each of the most recent LSAs for that area. To manage and control this process, OSPF defines several messages, processes, and neighbor states that indicate the progress when flooding LSAs to each neighbor. This section begins by listing reference information for the OSPF messages and neighbor states. Next, the text describes the flooding process between two neighbors when a DR does not exist, followed by a description of the similar process used when a DR does exist. This section ends with a few items related to how the routers avoid looping the LSA advertisements and how they periodically reflood the information.

OSPF Message and Neighbor State Reference

For reference, Table 6-4 lists the OSPF message types that will be mentioned in the next few pages. Additionally, Table 6-5 lists the various neighbor states as well. Although useful for study, when you first learning this topic, feel free to skip these tables for now.

Key Topic

Table 6-4 *OSPF Message Types and Functions*

Message Name/number	Description
Hello (1)	Used to discover neighbors, supply information used to confirm two routers should be allowed to become neighbors, to bring a neighbor relationship to a 2-way state, and to monitor a neighbor's responsiveness in case it fails
Database Description (DD or DBD) (2)	Used to exchange brief versions of each LSA, typically on initial topology exchange, so that a router knows a list of that neighbor's known LSAs

Table 6-4   *OSPF Message Types and Functions*

Message Name/number	Description
Link-State Request (LSR) (3)	A packet that lists the LSIDs of LSAs the sender of the LSR would like the receiver of the LSR to supply during database exchange
Link-State Update (LSU) (4)	A packet that contains fully detailed LSAs, typically sent in response to an LSR message
Link-State Acknowledgment (LSAck) (5)	Sent to confirm receipt of an LSU message

Table 6-5   *OSPF Neighbor State Reference*

State	Meaning
Down	No Hellos have been received from this neighbor for more than the dead interval.
Attempt	Used when the neighbor is defined with the **neighbor** command, after sending a Hello, but before receiving a Hello from that neighbor.
Init	A Hello has been received from the neighbor, but it did not have the local router's RID in it or lists parameters that do not pass the neighbor verification checks. This is a permanent state when Hello parameters do not match.
2Way	A Hello has been received from the neighbor, it has the router's RID in it, and all neighbor verification checks passed.
ExStart	Currently negotiating the DD sequence numbers and master/slave logic used for DD packets.
Exchange	Finished negotiating the DD process particulars, and currently exchanging DD packets.
Loading	All DD packets are exchanged, and the routers are currently sending LSR, LSU, and LSAck packets to exchange full LSAs.
Full	Neighbors are fully adjacent, meaning they believe that their LSDBs for that area are identical. Routing table (re)calculations can begin.

Exchange Without a Designated Router

As discussed in Chapter 5, the OSPF interface network type tells that router whether to attempt to elect a DR on that interface. The most common case for which routers do not elect a DR occur on point-to-point topologies, such as true point-to-point serial links and point-to-point subinterfaces. This section examines the database exchange process on such interfaces, in preparation for the slightly more complex process when using a DR on an OSPF broadcast network type, like a LAN.

Every OSPF neighborship begins by exchanging Hellos until the neighbors (hopefully) reach the 2-Way state. During these early stages, the routers discover each other by sending multicast Hellos and then check each other's parameters to make sure all items match (as listed in Chapter 5's Table 5-5). Figure 6-7 shows the details, with the various neighbor states listed on the outside of the figure and the messages listed in the middle.

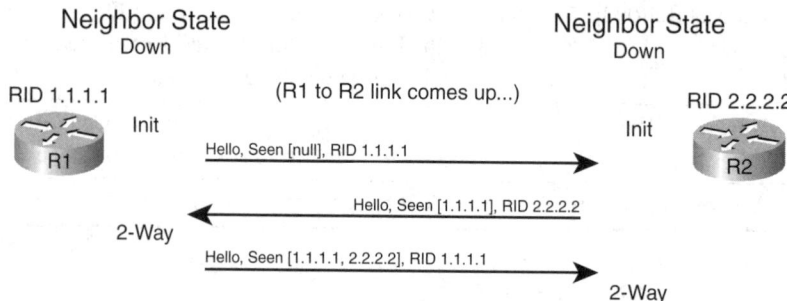

Figure 6-7 *Neighbor Initialization–Early Stages*

Figure 6-7 shows an example that begins with a failed neighborship, so the neighborship is in a down state. When a router tries to reestablish the neighborship, each router sends a multicast Hello and moves to an INIT state. After a router has both received a Hello and verified that all the required parameters agree, the router lists the other router's RID in the Hello as being seen, as shown in the bottom two Hello messages in the figure. When a router receives a Hello that lists its own RID as having been seen by the other router, the router can transition to 2-Way state.

When a router has reached the 2-Way state with a neighbor, as shown at the end of Figure 6-7, the router then decides whether it should exchange its LSDB entries. When no DR exists, the answer is always "yes." Each router next follows this general process:

Step 1. Discover the LSAs known to the neighbor but unknown to me.

Step 2. Discover the LSAs known by both routers, but the neighbor's LSA is more up to date.

Step 3. Ask the neighbor for a copy of all the LSAs identified in the first two steps.

Figure 6-8 details the messages and neighbor states used to exchange the LSAs between two neighbors.

Figure 6-8 shows many details. As with Figure 6-7, Figure 6-8 shows neighbor states on the outer edges of the flows (refer to Table 6-5 for reference). Routers display these neighbor states (in the **show ip ospf neighbor** command variants), so a particular state may be useful in determining how far two neighbors have gotten in the database exchange process. The more important neighbor states will be mentioned throughout the chapter.

The inner portions of Figure 6-8 represent the OSPF message flows, with Table 6-2 earlier in the chapter listing the messages for reference. The next several pages examine the process shown in Figure 6-8 in more detail.

Discovering a Description of the Neighbor's LSDB

After a router has decided to move forward from 2-Way state and exchange its LSDB with a neighbor, the routers use the sequence shown in Figure 6-8. The next step in that process

RID 1.1.1.1

RID 2.2.2.2

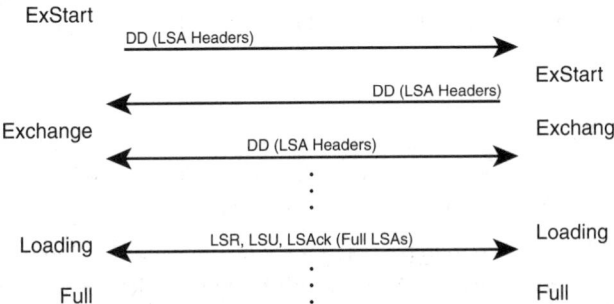

Figure 6-8 *Overview of the Database Exchange Process Between Two Neighbors*

requires both routers to tell each other the LSIDs of all their known LSAs in that area. The primary goal is for each neighbor to realize which LSAs it does not know, so it can then ask for those full LSAs to be sent. To learn the list of LSAs known by the neighbor, the neighboring routers follow these steps:

Step 1. Multicast database description packets (abbreviated as both DD and DBD, depending on the reference) to 224.0.0.5, which is the all SPF routers multicast address.

Step 2. When sending the first DD message, transition to the *ExStart* state until one router, the one with the higher RID, becomes master in a master/slave relationship.

Step 3. After electing a master, transition the neighbor to the *Exchange* state.

Step 4. Continue multicasting DD messages to each other until both routers have the same shared view of the LSIDs known collectively by both routers, in that area.

Note that the DD messages themselves do not list the entire LSAs, but rather LSA headers. These headers include the LSIDs of the LSAs and the LSA sequence number. The LS sequence number for an LSA begins at value 0x80000001 (hex) when initially created; the router creating the LSA increments the sequence number, and refloods the LSA, whenever the LSA changes. For example, if an interface moves from up to down state, that router changes its Type 1 LSA to list that interface state as down, increments the LSA sequence number, and refloods the LSA.

The master router for each exchange controls the flow of DD messages, with the slave responding to the master's DD messages. The master keeps sending DD messages until it lists all its known LSIDs in that area. The slave responds by placing LSA headers in its DD messages. Some of those LSA headers simply repeat what the slave heard from the master, for the purpose of acknowledging to the master that the slave learned that LSA header from the master. Additionally, the slave also includes the LSA headers for any LSAs that the master did not list.

This exchange of DD messages ends with each router knowing a list of LSAs that it does not have in its LSDB, but that the other router does have those LSAs. Additionally, each router also ends this process with a list of LSAs that the local router already knows, but for which the other router has a more recent copy (based on the sequence number).

Exchanging the LSAs

When the two neighbors realize that they have a shared view of the list of LSIDs, they transition to the Loading state and start exchanging the full LSAs–but only those that they do not yet know about or those that have changed.

For example, when the two routers in Figure 6-8 first become neighbors, neither router will have a copy of the Type 1 LSA for the other router. So, R1 will request that R2 send its LSA with LSID 2.2.2.2; R2 will send its Type 1 LSA; and R1 will acknowledge receipt. The mechanics work like this:

Step 1.   Transition the neighbor state to Loading.

Step 2.   For any missing LSAs, send a *Link State Request* (LSR) message, listing the LSID of the requested LSA.

Step 3.   Respond to any LSR messages with an *Link State Update* (LSU), listing one or more LSAs in each message.

Step 4.   Acknowledge receipt by either sending a *Link State Acknowledgment* (LSAck) message (called explicit acknowledgment), or by sending the same LSA that was received back to the other router in an LSU message (implicit acknowledgment).

Step 5.   When all LSAs have been sent, received, and acknowledged, transition the neighborship to the FULL state (fully adjacent).

Note: Because this section examines the case without a DR, all these messages flow as multicasts to 224.0.0.5, the all SPF routers multicast address, unless the neighbors have been defined with an OSPF **neighbor** command.

By the end of this process, both routers should have an identical LSDB for the area to which the link has been assigned. At that point, the two routers can run the SPF algorithm to choose the currently best routes for each subnet.

Exchange with a Designated Router

Database exchange with a DR differs slightly than database exchange when no DR exists. The majority of the process is similar, with the same messages, meanings, and neighbor states. The big difference is the overriding choice of with whom each router chooses to perform database exchange.

Non-DR routers do not exchange their databases directly with all neighbors on a subnet. Instead, they exchange their database with the DR. Then, the DR exchanges any new/changed LSAs with the rest of the OSPF routers in the subnet.

The concept actually follows along with the idea of a Type 2 LSA as seen earlier in Figure 6-4. Figure 6-9 represents four Type 1 LSAs, for four real routers on the same LAN, plus a single Type 2 LSA that represents the multiaccess subnet. The DR created the Type 2 LSA as part of its role in life.

Figure 6-9 *Conceptual View–Exchanging the Database with a Pseudonode*

Figure 6-9 shows two conceptual steps for database exchange. The non-DR router (R3) first exchanges its database with the pseudonode, and then the type 2 pseudonode exchanges its database with the other routers. However, the pseudonode is a concept, not a router; to make the process depicted in Figure 6-9 work, the DR takes on the role of the Type 2 pseudonode. The messages differ slightly as well, as follows:

- The non-DR performs database exchange with the same messages, as shown in Figure 6-9, but sends these messages to the 224.0.0.6 All-DR-routers multicast address.

- The DR performs database exchange with the same messages but sends the messages to the 224.0.0.5 all-SPF-routers multicast address.

Consider these two conventions one at a time. First, the messages sent to 224.0.0.6 are processed by the DR and the BDR only. The DR actively participates, replying to the messages, with the BDR acting as a silent bystander. In effect, this allows the non-DR router to exchange their database directly with the DR and BDR, but with none of the other routers in the subnet.

Key Topic

Next, consider the multicast messages from the DR to the 224.0.0.5 all-SPF-router multicast address. All OSPF routers process these messages, so the rest of the routers—the DROthers to use the IOS term—also learn the newly exchanged LSAs. This process completes the second step shown in the conceptual Figure 6-9, where the DR, acting like the pseudonode, floods the LSAs to the other OSPF routers in the subnet.

The process occurs in the background and can be generally ignored. However, for operating an OSPF network, an important distinction must be made. With a DR in existence, a DROther router performs the database exchange process (as seen in Figure 6-9) with the DR/BDR only and not any other DROther routers in the subnet. For example, in Figure 6-9, R1 acts as DR, R2 acts as BDR, and R3/R4 act as DROther routers. Because the underlying process does not make R3 and R4 perform database exchange with each other, the routers do not reach the FULL neighbor state, remaining in 2-Way state.

Example 6-6 shows the resulting output for the LAN shown in Figure 6-9, with four routers. The output, taken from DROther R3, shows a 2-Way state with R4, the other DROther. It also shows on interface Fa0/0 that its own priority is 1. This output also shows a neighbor count (all neighbors) of 3 and an adjacent neighbor count (all fully adjacent neighbors) of 2, again because the neighborship between DROthers R3 and R4 is not a full adjacency.

Example 6-6   *Demonstrating OSPF FULL and 2-Way Adjacencies*

```
R3#show ip ospf interface fa0/0
FastEthernet0/0 is up, line protocol is up
  Internet Address 172.16.1.3/24, Area 0
  Process ID 75, Router ID 3.3.3.3, Network Type BROADCAST, Cost: 1
  Transmit Delay is 1 sec, State DROTHER, Priority 2
  Designated Router (ID) 1.1.1.1, Interface address 172.16.1.1
  Backup Designated router (ID) 2.2.2.2, Interface address 172.16.1.2
  Timer intervals configured, Hello 10, Dead 40, Wait 40, Retransmit 5
    oob-resync timeout 40
    Hello due in 00:00:02
  Supports Link-local Signaling (LLS)
  Cisco NSF helper support enabled
  IETF NSF helper support enabled
  Index 1/1, flood queue length 0
  Next 0x0(0)/0x0(0)
  Last flood scan length is 0, maximum is 4
  Last flood scan time is 0 msec, maximum is 0 msec
  Neighbor Count is 3, Adjacent neighbor count is 2
    Adjacent with neighbor 1.1.1.1  (Designated Router)
    Adjacent with neighbor 2.2.2.2  (Backup Designated Router)
  Suppress hello for 0 neighbor(s)
```

```
R3#show ip ospf neighbor fa0/0

Neighbor ID     Pri    State            Dead Time    Address       Interface
1.1.1.1           4    FULL/DR          00:00:37     172.16.1.1
FastEthernet0/0
2.2.2.2           3    FULL/BDR         00:00:37     172.16.1.2
FastEthernet0/0
44.44.44.44       1    2WAY/DROTHER     00:00:36     172.16.1.4    FastEthernet0/0
```

Flooding Throughout the Area

So far in this section, the database exchange process has focused on exchanging the database between neighbors. However, LSAs need to be flooded throughout an area. To do so, when a router learns new LSAs from one neighbor, that router then knows that its other neighbors in that same area may not know of that LSA. Similarly, when an LSA changes, for example, when an interface changes state, a router may learn the same old LSA but with a new sequence number, and again need to flood the changed LSA to other neighbors in that area.

Figure 6-10 shows a basic example of the process. In this case, R2, R3, and R4 have established neighbor relationships, with four LSAs in their LSDB in this area. R1 is again the new router added to the internetwork.

Figure 6-10 *Flooding Throughout an Area*

First, consider what happens as the new R1-R2 neighborship comes up and goes through database exchange. When R1 loads, and the link comes up, R1 and R2 reach a full state and have a shared view of the Area 1 LSDB. R2 has learned all R1's new LSAs (should only be R1's Type 1 router LSA), and R1 has learned all the area 1 LSAs known to R2, including the Type 1 LSAs for R3 and R4.

Next, think about the LSDBs of R3 and R4 at this point. The database exchange between R1-R2 did not inform R3 nor R4 about any of the new LSAs known by R1. So, R2, when it learns of R1's Type 1 LSA, sends DD packets to the DR on the R2/R3/R4 LAN. LSR/LSU packets follow, resulting in R3 and R4 learning about the new LSA for R1. If more routers existed in area 1, the flooding process would continue throughout the entire area, until all routers know of the best (highest sequence number) copy of each LSA.

The flooding process prevents the looping of LSAs as a side-effect of the database exchange process. Neighbors use DD messages to learn the LSA headers known by the neighbor, and then only request the LSAs known by the neighbor but not known by the local router. By requesting only unknown LSAs or new versions of old LSAs, routers prevent the LSAs advertisements from looping.

Periodic Flooding

Although OSPF does not send routing updates on a periodic interval, as do distance vector protocols, OSPF does reflood each LSA every 30 minutes based on each LSA's age variable. The router that creates the LSA sets this age to 0 (seconds). Each router then increments the age of its copy of each LSA over time. If 30 minutes pass with no changes to an LSA–meaning no other reason existed in that 30 minutes to cause a reflooding of the LSA–the owning router increments the sequence number, resets the timer to 0, and refloods the LSA.

Because the owning router increments the sequence number and resets the LSAge every 1800 seconds (30 minutes), the output of various **show ip ospf database** commands should also show an age of less than 1800 seconds. For example, referring back to Example 6-5, the Type 1 LSA for R1 (RID 1.1.1.1) shows an age of 943 seconds and a sequence number of 0x80000003. Over time the sequence number should increment once per every 30 minutes, with the LSAge cycle upward toward 1800 and then back to 0 when the LSA is reflooded.

Note also that when a router realizes it needs to flush an LSA from the LSDB for an area, it actually sets the age of the LSA to the MaxAge setting (3600) and refloods the LSA. All the other routers receive the LSA, see the age is already at the maximum, causing those routers to also remove the LSA from their LSDBs.

Choosing the Best OSPF Routes

All this effort to define LSA types, create areas, and fully flood the LSAs has one goal in mind: to allow all routers in that area to calculate the best, loop-free routes for all known subnets. Although the database exchange process may seem laborious, the process by which SPF calculates the best routes requires a little less thought, at least to the level required for the CCNP ROUTE exam. In fact, the choice of the best route for a given subnet, and calculated by a particular router, can be summarized as follows:

- Analyze the LSDB to find all possible routes to reach the subnet.

- For each possible route, add the OSPF interface cost for all outgoing interfaces in that route.

- Pick the route with the lowest total cost.

Key Topic

For humans, if you build a network diagram, note the OSPF cost for each interface (as shown with **show ip ospf interface**), you can easily add up the costs for each router's possible routes to each subnet and tell which route OSPF will choose. The routers must use a more complex SPF algorithm to derive a mathematical model of the topology based on the LSAs. This section examines both the simpler human view of metric calculation and folds in some of the basics of what SPF must do on a router to calculate the best routes. It also goes through the options for tuning the metric calculation to influence the choice of routes.

OSPF Metric Calculation for Internal OSPF Routes

The process of calculating the cost from a router to each subnet may be intuitive to most people. However, spending a few minutes considering the details is worthwhile, in part to link the concepts with the LSAs, and to be better prepared for questions on the ROUTE exam. This section breaks the discussion into three sections: intra-area routes, interarea routes, a short discussion about cases when both intra-area and interarea routes exist for the same subnet, and an explanation of SPF calculations.

Calculating the Cost of Intra-Area Routes

When a router analyzes the LSDB to calculate the best route to each subnet, it does the following:

Step 1.   Finds all subnets inside the area, based on the stub interfaces listed in the Type 1 LSAs and based on any Type 2 network LSAs

Step 2.   Runs SPF to find all possible paths through the area's topology, from itself to each subnet

Key Topic

Step 3.   Calculates the OSPF interface costs for all outgoing interfaces in each route, picking the lowest total cost route for each subnet as the best route

For example, Figure 6-11 shows the routers and links inside area 34, as a subset of the internetwork also shown in Figure 6-1. Figure 6-11 shows the interface numbers and OSPF costs.

Following the basic three-step process, at Step 1, R1 can determine that subnet 10.10.34.0/24 exists in area 34 because of the Type 2 LSA created by the DR in that subnet. For Step 2, R1 can then run SPF and determine four possible routes, two of which are clearly more reasonable to humans: R1-R3 and R1-R4. (The two other possible routes, R1-R3-R2-R4 and R1-R4-R2-R3, are possible and would be considered by OSPF but would clearly be higher cost.) For Step 3, R1 does the simple math of adding the costs of the outgoing interfaces in each route, as follows:

- R1-R3: Add R1's S0/0/0.3 cost (647) and R3's Fa0/0 cost (10), total 657

- R1-R4: Add R1's S0/0/0.4 cost (647) and R4's Fa0/0 cost (10), total 657

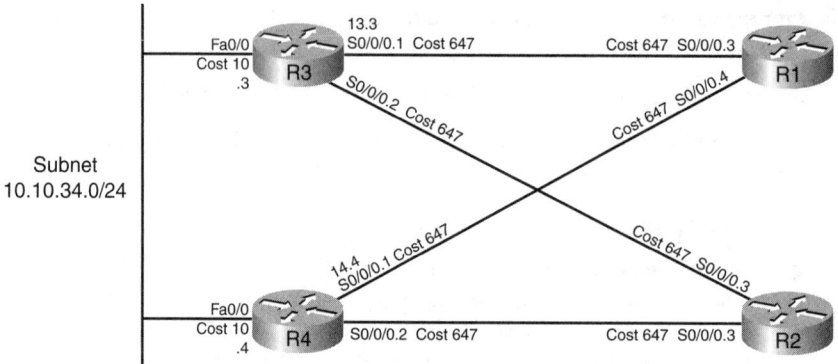

Figure 6-11   *Area 34 Portion of Figure 6-1*

The metrics tie, so with a default setting of **maximum-paths 4**, R1 adds both routes to its routing table. In particular, the routes list the metric of 657, and the next-hop IP address on the other end of the respectively links: 10.10.13.3 (R3's S0/0/0.1) and 10.10.14.4 (R4's S0/0/0.1).

Note that OSPF supports equal-cost load balancing, but it does not support unequal-cost load balancing. The **maximum-paths** OSPF subcommand can be set as low as 1, with the maximum being dependent on router platform and IOS version. Modern IOS versions typically support 16 or 32 concurrent routes to one destination (maximum).

Calculating the Cost of Interarea Routes

From a human perspective, the cost for interarea routes can be calculated just like for intra-area routes if we have the full network diagram, subnet numbers, and OSPF interface costs. To do so, just find all possible routes from a router to the destination subnet, add up the costs of the outgoing interfaces, and choose the router with the lowest total cost.

However, OSPF routers cannot do the equivalent for interarea routes, because routers internal to one area do not have topological data—LSA Types 1 and 2—for other areas. Instead, ABRs create and flood Type 3 summary LSAs into an area, listing the subnet number and mask, but not listing details about routers and links in the other areas. For example, Figure 6-12 shows both Areas 34 and 0 from Figure 6-1, including interface costs. Then consider how OSPF determines the lowest-cost route from router R3 for subnet 10.10.99.0/24, the Data Center subnet on the right.

R3 has a large number of possible routes to reach subnet 10.10.99.0/24. For example, just to get from R3 to R1, there are several possibilities: R3-R1, R3-R4-R1, and R3-R2-R1. From R1 the rest of the way to subnet 10.10.99.0/24, many more possibilities exist. The SPF algorithm has to calculate all possible routes inside an area to the ABR, so with more redundancy, SPF's run time goes up. And SPF has to consider all the options, whereas we humans can rule out some routes quickly because they appear to be somewhat ridiculous.

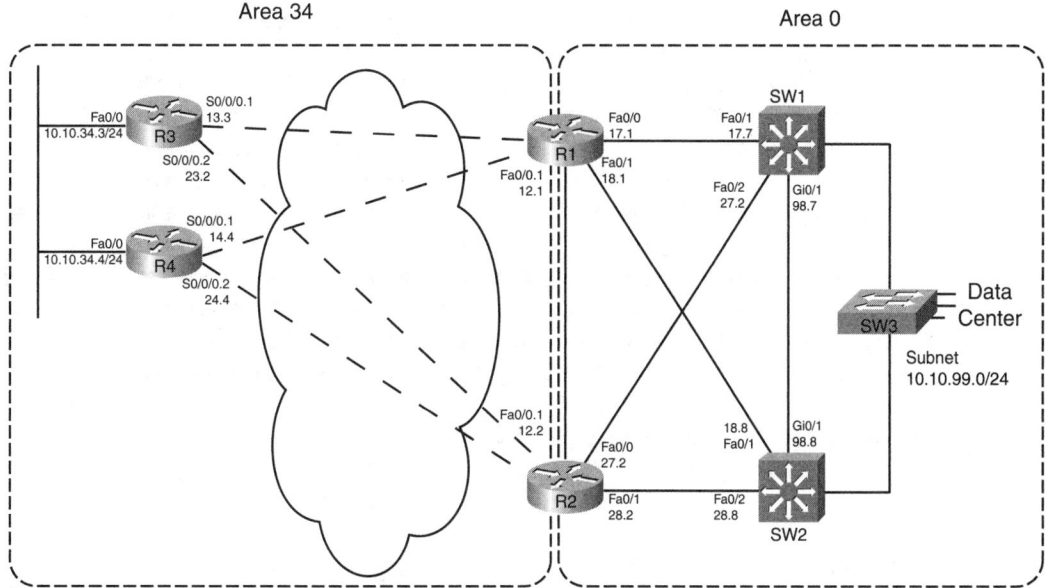

Figure 6-12   *Area 34 and Area 0 Portion of Figure 6-1*

Because of the area design, with R1 and R2 acting as ABRs, R3 does not process all the topology shown in Figure 6-12. Instead, R3 relies on the Type 3 Summary LSAs created by the ABRs, which have the following information:

■   The subnet number/mask represented by the LSA

■   The cost of the ABR's lowest-cost route to reach the subnet

■   The RID of the ABR

Example 6-7 begins to examine the information R3 will use to calculate its best route for subnet 10.10.99.0/24, on the right side of Figure 6-12. To see these details, Example 6-7 lists several commands taken from R1. It lists R1's best route (actually two that tie) for subnet 10.10.99.0/24, with cost 11. It also lists the Type 3 LSA R1 generated by R1 for 10.10.99.0/24, again listing cost 11, and listing the Type 3 LSA created by ABR R2 and flooded into area 34.

Example 6-7   *Route and Type 3 LSA on R1 for 10.10.99.0/24*

```
R1#show ip route ospf
     10.0.0.0/8 is variably subnetted, 15 subnets, 3 masks
O       10.10.5.0/27 [110/648] via 10.10.15.5, 00:04:19, Serial0/0/0.5
O       10.10.23.0/29 [110/711] via 10.10.13.3, 00:04:19, Serial0/0/0.3
```

```
O         10.10.24.0/29 [110/711] via 10.10.14.4, 00:04:19, Serial0/0/0.4
O         10.10.25.0/29 [110/711] via 10.10.15.5, 00:04:19, Serial0/0/0.5
O         10.10.27.0/24 [110/11] via 10.10.17.7, 00:04:19, FastEthernet0/0
                        [110/11] via 10.10.12.2, 00:04:19, FastEthernet0/0.1
O         10.10.28.0/24 [110/11] via 10.10.18.8, 00:04:19, FastEthernet0/1
                        [110/11] via 10.10.12.2, 00:04:19, FastEthernet0/0.1
O         10.10.34.0/24 [110/648] via 10.10.14.4, 00:04:19, Serial0/0/0.4
                        [110/648] via 10.10.13.3, 00:04:19, Serial0/0/0.3
O         10.10.98.0/24 [110/11] via 10.10.18.8, 00:04:19, FastEthernet0/1
                        [110/11] via 10.10.17.7, 00:04:19, FastEthernet0/0
O         10.10.99.0/24 [110/11] via 10.10.18.8, 00:04:19, FastEthernet0/1
                        [110/11] via 10.10.17.7, 00:04:19, FastEthernet0/0


R1#show ip ospf database summary 10.10.99.0

            OSPF Router with ID (1.1.1.1) (Process ID 1)


! omitting output for area 5...
                Summary Net Link States (Area 34)

  LS age: 216
  Options: (No TOS-capability, DC, Upward)
  LS Type: Summary Links(Network)
  Link State ID: 10.10.99.0 (summary Network Number)
  Advertising Router: 1.1.1.1

  LS Seq Number: 80000003
  Checksum: 0x951F
  Length: 28
  Network Mask: /24
        TOS: 0   Metric: 11



  LS age: 87
  Options: (No TOS-capability, DC, Upward)
  LS Type: Summary Links(Network)
  Link State ID: 10.10.99.0 (summary Network Number)
  Advertising Router: 2.2.2.2

  LS Seq Number: 80000002
  Checksum: 0x7938
  Length: 28
  Network Mask: /24
        TOS: 0   Metric: 11
```

Note: The examples use default bandwidth settings, but with all routers configured with the **auto-cost reference-bandwidth 1000** command. This command is explained in the upcoming section "Reference Bandwidth."

For routers in one area to calculate the cost of an interarea route, the process is simple when you realize that the Type 3 LSA lists the ABR's best cost to reach that interarea subnet. To calculate the cost:

Step 1.   Calculate the intra-area cost from that router to the ABR listed in the type 3 LSA.

Step 2.   Add the cost value listed in the Type 3 LSA. (This cost represents the cost from the ABR to the destination subnet.)

A router applies these two steps for each possible route to reach the ABR. Following the example of router R3 and subnet 10.10.99.0/24, Figure 6-13 shows the components of the calculation.

Figure 6-13   *R3's Calculation of Cost for 10.10.99.0/24*

Figure 6-13 shows the calculation of both routes, with intra-area cost to reach R1 either 647 or 657 in this case. For both routes, the cost listed in the Type 3 LSA sourced by R1, cost 11, is added.

When more than one ABR exists, as is the case as shown in Figure 6-12, each ABR should have created a Type 3 LSA for the subnet. In fact, the output in Example 6-7 showed the Type 3 LSA for 10.10.99.0/24 created by both R1 and another created by R2. For instance, in the internetwork used throughout this chapter, ABRs R1 and R2 would create a Type 3 LSA for 10.10.99.0/24. So, in this particular example, R3 would also have to calculate the best route to reach 10.10.99.0/24 through ABR R2. Then, R3 would choose the best route among all routes for 10.10.99.0/24.

Each router repeats this process for all known routes to reach the ABR, considering the Type 3 LSAs from each ABR. In this case, R3 ties on metrics for one route through R1 and one through R2, so R3 adds both routes to its routing table, as shown in Example 6-8.

Example 6-8   *Route and Type 3 LSA on R1 for 10.10.99.0/24*

```
R3#show ip route 10.10.99.0 255.255.255.0
Routing entry for 10.10.99.0/24
  Known via "ospf 3", distance 110, metric 658, type inter area
  Last update from 10.10.13.1 on Serial0/0/0.1, 00:08:06 ago
  Routing Descriptor Blocks:
  * 10.10.23.2, from 2.2.2.2, 00:08:06 ago, via Serial0/0/0.2
      Route metric is 658, traffic share count is 1
    10.10.13.1, from 1.1.1.1, 00:08:06 ago, via Serial0/0/0.1
      Route metric is 658, traffic share count is 1


R3#show ip route ospf
      10.0.0.0/8 is variably subnetted, 15 subnets, 3 masks
O IA    10.10.5.0/27 [110/1304] via 10.10.23.2, 00:07:57, Serial0/0/0.2
                     [110/1304] via 10.10.13.1, 00:07:57, Serial0/0/0.1
O IA    10.10.12.0/24 [110/657] via 10.10.23.2, 00:08:17, Serial0/0/0.2
                      [110/657] via 10.10.13.1, 00:08:17, Serial0/0/0.1
! lines omitted for brevity
O IA    10.10.99.0/24 [110/658] via 10.10.23.2, 00:08:17, Serial0/0/0.2
                      [110/658] via 10.10.13.1, 00:08:17, Serial0/0/0.1
```

Besides the information that matches the expected outgoing interfaces per the figures, the output also flags these routes as interarea routes. The first command lists "type inter area" explicitly, and the **show ip route ospf** command lists the same information with the code "O IA," meaning OSPF, interarea. Simply put, interarea routes are routes for which the subnet is known from a Type 3 summary LSA.

Special Rules Concerning Intra-area and Interarea Routes on ABRs

OSPF has a couple of rules concerning intra-area and interarea routes that take precedence over the simple comparison of the cost calculated for the various routes. The issue exists when more than one ABR connects to the same two areas. Many designs use two routers between the backbone and each nonbackbone area for redundancy, so this design occurs in many OSPF networks.

The issue relates to the fact that with two or more ABRs, the ABRsthemselves, when calculating their own routing tables, can calculate both an intra-area route and interarea route for subnets in the backbone area. For example, consider the perspective of Router R1 from the last several examples, as depicted in Figure 6-14.

Conceptually, R1 could calculate both the intra-area route and interarea route to 10.10.99.0/24. However, the OSPF cost settings could be set so that the lower cost route

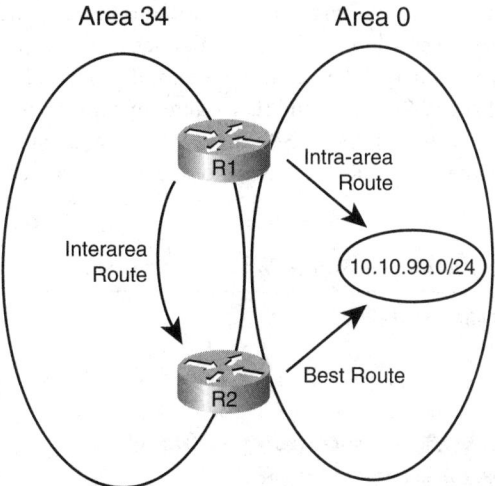

Figure 6-14 *R1's Choice: Intra-Area or Interarea Route to 10.10.99.0/24*

for R1 actually goes through area 34, to ABR R2, and then on through Area 0 to
10.10.99.0/24. However, two OSPF rules prevent such a choice by R1:

Step 1.   When choosing the best route, an intra-area route is always better than a competing interarea route, regardless of metric.

Step 2.   If an ABR learns a Type 3 LSA inside a nonbackbone area, the ABR ignores
that LSA when calculating its own routes.

Because of the first rule, R1 would never choose the interarea route if the intra-area
route were available. The second rule goes further, stating that R1 could never choose the
interarea route at all–R1 simply ignores that LSA for the purposes of choosing its own
best IP routes.

Metric and SPF Calculations

Before moving on to discuss how to influence route choices by changing the OSPF interface costs, first take a moment to consider the CPU-intensive SPF work done by a router.
SPF does the work to piece together topology information to find all possible routes to a
destination. As a result, SPF must execute when the intra-area topology changes, because
changes in topology impact the choice of best route. However, changes to Type 3 LSAs
do not drive a recalculation of the SPF algorithm, because the Type 3 LSAs do not actually describe the topology.

To take the analysis a little deeper, remember that an internal router, when finding the best
interarea route for a subnet, uses the intra-area topology to calculate the cost to reach the
ABR. When each route is identified, the internal router adds the intra-area cost to the
ABR, plus the corresponding Type 3 LSA's cost. A change to the Type 3 LSA–it fails,
comes back up, or the metric changes–does impact the choice of best route, so the
changed Type 3 LSA must be flooded. However, no matter the change, the change does
not affect the topology between a router and the ABR—and SPF focuses on processing
that topology data. So, only changes to Type 1 and 2 LSAs require an SPF calculation.

You can see the number of SPF runs, and the elapsed time since the last SPF run, using several variations on the **show ip ospf** command. Each time a Type 3 LSA changes and is flooded, SPF does not run, and the counter does not increment. However, each time a Type 1 or 2 LSA changes, SPF runs, and the counter increments. Example 6-9 highlights the counter that shows the number of SPF runs on that router, in that area, and the time since the last run. Note that ABRs list a group of messages per area, showing the number of runs per area.

Example 6-9   *Example with New Route Choices but No SPF Run*

```
R3#show ip ospf  ¦ begin Area 34
    Area 34
        Number of interfaces in this area is 3
        Area has no authentication
        SPF algorithm last executed 00:41:02.812 ago
        SPF algorithm executed 15 times
        Area ranges are
        Number of LSA 25. Checksum Sum 0x0BAC6B
        Number of opaque link LSA 0. Checksum Sum 0x000000
        Number of DCbitless LSA 0
        Number of indication LSA 0
        Number of DoNotAge LSA 0
        Flood list length 0
```

Metric Tuning

Engineers have a couple of commands available that allow them to tune the values of the OSPF interface cost, thereby influencing the choice of best OSPF route. This section discusses the three methods: changing the reference bandwidth, setting the interface bandwidth, and setting the OSPF cost directly.

Changing the Reference Bandwidth

OSPF calculates the default OSPF cost for an interface based on the following formula:

$$\frac{Reference-brandwidth}{interface-bandwidth}$$

The reference-bandwidth, which you can set using the **auto-cost reference-bandwidth** *bandwidth* router subcommand, sets the numerator of the formula for that one router, with a unit of Mbps. This setting may be different on different routers, but Cisco recommends using the same setting on all routers in an OSPF routing domain.

For example, serial interfaces default to a bandwidth setting of 1544, meaning 1544 Kbps. The reference bandwidth defaults to 100, meaning 100 Mbps. After converting the reference bandwidth units to Kbps to match the bandwidth, the cost, calculated per the defaults, for serial links would be

$$\frac{100,000}{1544} = 64$$

Note: OSPF always rounds down when the calculation results in a fraction.

The primary motivation for changing the reference bandwidth is to accommodate good defaults for higher-speed links. With a default of 100 Mbps, the cost of FastEthernet interfaces calculates to cost 1. However, the minimum OSPF cost is 1, so Gigabit Ethernet and 10 Gigabit interfaces also then default to OSPF cost 1. By setting the OSPF reference bandwidth so that there is some difference in cost between the higher speed links, OSPF can then choose routes that use those higher speed interfaces.

Note: Although Cisco recommends that all routers use the same reference bandwidth, the setting is local to each router.

Note that in the examples earlier in this chapter, the bandwidth settings used default settings, but the **auto-cost reference-bandwidth 1000** command was used on each router to allow different costs for FastEthernet and Gigabit interfaces.

Setting Bandwidth

You can indirectly set the OSPF cost by configuring the **bandwidth** *speed* interface subcommand. In such cases, the formula shown in the previous section is used, just with the configured bandwidth value.

While on the topic of the interface bandwidth subcommand, a couple of seemingly trivial facts may matter to your choice of how to tune the OSPF cost. First, on serial links, the bandwidth defaults to 1544. On subinterfaces of those serial interfaces, the same bandwidth default is used.

On Ethernet interfaces, if not configured with the **bandwidth** command, the interface bandwidth matches the actual speed. For example, on an interface that supports autonegotiation for 10/100, the bandwidth is either 100,000 (kbps, or 100 Mbps) or 10,000 (Kbps, or 10 Mbps) depending on whether the link currently runs at 100 or 10 Mbps, respectively.

Configuring Cost Directly

The most controllable method to configure OSPF costs, but the most laborious, is to configure the interface cost directly. To do so, use the **ip ospf cost** *value* interface subcommand, substituting your chosen value as the last parameter.

Verifying OSPF Cost Settings

Several commands can be used to display the OSPF cost settings of various interfaces. Example 6-10 shows several, along with the configuration of all three methods for changing the OSPF cost. In this example, the following has been configured:

- The reference bandwidth is set to 1000.

- Interface S0/0/0.1 has its bandwidth set to 1000 Kbps.

- Interface Fa0/0 has its cost set directly to 17.

Example 6-10   *R3 with OSPF Cost Values Set*

```
router ospf 3
 auto-cost reference-bandwidth 1000
interface S0/0/0.1
 bandwidth 1000
interface fa0/0
 ip ospf cost 17


R3#show ip ospf interface brief
Interface     PID    Area              IP Address/Mask    Cost   State Nbrs F/C
Se0/0/0.2     3      34                10.10.23.3/29      647    P2P   1/1
Se0/0/0.1     3      34                10.10.13.3/29      1000   P2P   1/1
Fa0/0         3      34                10.10.34.3/24      17     BDR   1/1


R3#show ip ospf interface fa0/0
FastEthernet0/0 is up, line protocol is up
  Internet Address 10.10.34.3/24, Area 34
  Process ID 3, Router ID 3.3.3.3, Network Type BROADCAST, Cost: 17
  Enabled by interface config, including secondary ip addresses
  Transmit Delay is 1 sec, State BDR, Priority 1
  Designated Router (ID) 4.4.4.4, Interface address 10.10.34.4
  Backup Designated router (ID) 3.3.3.3, Interface address 10.10.34.3
! lines omitted for brevity
```

Exam Preparation Tasks

Planning Practice

The CCNP ROUTE exam expects test takers to review design documents, create implementation plans, and create verification plans. This section provides some exercises that may help you to take a step back from the minute details of the topics in this chapter so that you can think about the same technical topics from the planning perspective.

For each planning practice table, simply complete the table. Note that any numbers in parentheses represent the number of options listed for each item in the solutions in Appendix F, "Completed Planning Practice Tables."

Design Review Table

Table 6-6 lists several design goals related to this chapter. If these design goals were listed in a design document, and you had to take that document and develop an implementation plan, what implementation options come to mind? For any configuration items, a general description can be used, without concern about the specific parameters.

Table 6-6 *Design Review*

Design Goal	Possible Implementation Choices Covered in This Chapter
The design sets specific limits to the number of Type 1 and 2 LSAs in each area. Describe how to predict the number of each type of LSA.	
How could you tune OSPF metrics to favor 10 Gbps links over 1 Gbps and 1 Gig over 100 Mbps (2)?	
The design shows one physical path from ABR1 to core subnet 1 inside area 0, and one longer area 1 path to the same subnet. What can be done to ensure both paths can be used?	

Implementation Plan Peer Review Table

Table 6-7 shows a list of questions that others might ask, or that you might think about, during a peer review of another network engineer's implementation plan. Complete the table by answering the questions.

Table 6-7 *Notable Questions from This Chapter to Consider During an Implementation Plan Peer Review*

Question	Answers
What conditions must be true for a router to create/flood a Type 2 LSA? (2)	
The plan shows Frame Relay with all point-to-point subinterfaces. By default, will a DR/BDR be elected?	
The plan shows a reference bandwidth change planned for all routers with high speed links, but not all other routers. What is the impact? (2)	
The plan shows many different WAN links speeds but with the interface bandwidths not matching the actual speed. tAll OSPF cost changes are made explicitly with the **ip ospf cost** interface subcommand. Do the incorrect bandwidths cause any OSPF problems?	

Create an Implementation Plan Table

To practice skills useful when creating your own OSPF implementation plan, list in Table 6-8 configuration commands related to the configuration of the following features. You may want to record your answers outside the book and set a goal to complete this table (and others like it) from memory during your final reviews before taking the exam.

Table 6-8 *Implementation Plan Configuration Memory Drill*

Feature	Configuration Commands/Notes
Tune metrics by changing the formula for calculating OSPF cost based on interface bandwidth.	
Tune metrics by changing interface bandwidth.	
Change metrics by setting cost directly.	
Set the number of equal-cost OSPF routes allowed in a router's routing table.	
Influence the choice of DR on a LAN. (2)	

Choose Commands for a Verification Plan Table

To practice skills useful when creating your own OSPF verification plan, list in Table 6-9 all commands that supply the requested information. You may want to record your answers outside the book and set a goal to complete this table (and others like it) from memory during your final reviews before taking the exam.

Table 6-9 *Verification Plan Memory Drill*

Information Needed	Command(s)
Display a summary of the OSPF database.	
Display all Type 1 router LSAs known to a router.	
Display the details of a particular Type 1 router LSA.	
Display all Type 2 network LSAs known to a router.	
Display the details of a particular Type 2 router LSA.	
Display all Type 3 summary LSAs known to a router.	
Display the details of a particular Type 3 router LSA.	
Display a list of OSPF-enabled interfaces on a router.	
Determine on which interfaces a router has formed at least one OSPF neighborship.	
Determine the number of fully adjacent neighbors on an interface.	
Determine which transit networks connect to a Type 1 LSA.	
Determine the router that created and flooded a Type 3 LSA.	
Determine the router that created and flooded a Type 2 LSA.	
Determine the router that created and flooded a Type 1 LSA.	
Display the IP address of the current DR and BDR on a LAN.	
Display the OSPF interface cost (metric).	
Display all OSPF-learned routes.	
Display statistics about the number of SPF algorithm runs.	

Note: Some of the entries in this table may not have been specifically mentioned in this chapter but are listed in this table for review and reference.

Review All the Key Topics

Key Topic

Review the most important topics from inside the chapter, noted with the Key Topics icon in the outer margin of the page. Table 6-10 lists a reference of these key topics and the page numbers on which each is found.

Table 6-10   *Key Topics for Chapter 6*

Key Topic Element	Description	Page Number
Table 6-2	OSPF LSA types	179
List	Two main functions of a DR	186
Table 6-3	Facts about LSA Types 1, 2, and 3	195
Table 6-4	OSPF Message Types	196
Table 6-5	OSPF neighbor states	197
List	Key differences between database exchange with and without a DR	201
List	Three steps a router considers when choosing the best OSPF IP routes	205
List	Three steps to calculate OSPF costs for intra-area routes	205
List	Two steps for calculating OSPF costs for interarea routes	209

Complete the Tables and Lists from Memory

Print a copy of Appendix D, "Memory Tables," (found on the CD), or at least the section for this chapter, and complete the tables and lists from memory. Appendix E, "Memory Tables Answer Key," also on the CD, includes completed tables and lists to check your work.

Define Key Terms

Define the following key terms from this chapter, and check your answers in the glossary.

Link State Identifier (LSID), Designated Router (DR), Backup Designated Router (BDR), Internal Router, Area Border Router (ABR), All SPF Routers multicast, All DR multicast, Link State Advertisement, Database Description (DD) packet, Link State Request (LSR) packet, Link State Acknowledgement (LSA) packet, Link State Update (LSU) packet, Router LSA, Network LSA, Summary LSA, Type 1 LSA, Type 2 LSA, Type 3 LSA, Reference bandwidth, SPF calculation

This chapter covers the following subjects:

Route Filtering: This section introduces three separate methods of route filtering with OSPF and discusses the commands to configure two of these methods.

Route Summarization: This section examines how OSPF can summarize routes at ABRs and at ASBRs.

Default Routes and Stub Areas: This section examines the two main reasons an Enterprise might use default routes and then shows OSPF's solution to each need: flooding a domain-wide default route and using OSPF stub areas.

CHAPTER 7

OSPF Route Summarization, Filtering, and Default Routing

This chapter discusses several features that optimize OSPF operations: route filtering, route summarization, default routing, plus OSPF stub areas.

Of these topics, the chapter focuses most on route filtering and route summarization, both of which have the same reasoning and motivation as the same features in EIGRP, as discussed throughout Chapter 4, "EIGRP Route Summarization and Filtering." Route filtering can be used to purposefully prevent hosts in one part of an internetwork from sending packets to another part. It can also reduce the size of the topology table and IP routing table, reducing both OSPF memory and CPU consumption, plus make the packet forwarding process run slightly better. Route summarization can also reduce routing protocol and packet forwarding overhead, but with a potential negative effect of creating less-efficient paths through the internetwork.

Additionally, this chapter briefly covers default routing, again the same motivations as the equivalent EIGRP feature, as discussed in Chapter 4. Finally, an OSPF-unique feature, OSPF stub routers, can also be used to limit the amount of topology data in an area, again reducing overhead.

"Do I Know This Already?" Quiz

The "Do I Know This Already?" quiz allows you to assess if you should read the entire chapter. If you miss no more than one of these eight self-assessment questions, you might want to move ahead to the "Exam Preparation Tasks." Table 7-1 lists the major headings in this chapter and the "Do I Know This Already?" quiz questions covering the material in those headings so that you can assess your knowledge of these specific areas. The answers to the "Do I Know This Already?" quiz appear in Appendix A.

Table 7-1 *"Do I Know This Already?" Foundation Topics Section-to-Question Mapping*

Foundations Topics Section	Questions
Route Filtering	1–3
Route Summarization	4, 5
Default Routing and Stub Areas	6–8

1. Router B1, an internal router in area 1, displays the following output. The only two ABRs connected to area 1 are performing Type 3 LSA filtering. Which of the following answers is true based on the information in the output from B1?

```
R1# show ip route 10.1.0.0 255.255.0.0 longer-prefixes
! Legend lines omitted for brevity

      10.0.0.0/8 is variably subnetted, 17 subnets, 3 masks
O        10.1.2.0/24 [110/658] via 10.10.13.1, 00:00:32, Serial0/0/0.1
O IA     10.1.1.0/24 [110/658] via 10.10.23.2, 00:41:39, Serial0/0/0.2
O IA     10.1.3.0/24 [110/658] via 10.10.23.2, 00:41:39, Serial0/0/0.2
```

   a. A Type 3 LSA for 10.2.2.0/24 was filtered by both ABRs.

   b. A Type 3 LSA for 10.1.2.0/24 was not filtered by both ABRs.

   c. A Type 3 LSA for 10.1.3.0/24 was not filtered by at least one ABR.

   d. A Type 3 LSA for 10.1.1.0/24 filtered by both ABRs.

2. The following command output was gathered from Router R1, an ABR between areas 0 (backbone) and area 1. In this internetwork, area 0 contains all the subnets of class A network 10.0.0.0. R1's OSPF process has a **distribute-list prefix question in** command configured. Assuming the subnets listed in the answers actually exist in area 0, which of the following occurs on router R1?

```
R1#sh ip prefix-list
ip prefix-list question: 4 entries
    seq 5 deny 10.1.2.0/24 ge 25 le 27
    seq 15 deny 10.2.0.0/16 ge 30 le 30
    seq 20 permit 0.0.0.0/0 le 32
```

   a. R1 will not create/flood a type 3 LSA for subnet 10.1.2.0/26 into area 1.

   b. R1 will not create/flood a Type 3 LSA for subnet 10.1.2.0/24 into area 1.

   c. R1 will not have an OSPF route for subnet 10.1.2.0/26 in its IP routing table.

   d. R1 will not have an OSPF route for subnet 10.1.2.0/24 in its IP routing table.

3. Use the same scenario as the previous question, with one change. Instead of the **distribute-list prefix question in** command configured on R1, R1's OSPF process has an **area 1 filter-list prefix question in** command configured. Again assuming that the subnets listed in the answers actually exist in area 0, which of the following occurs on router R1?

```
R1#sh ip prefix-list
ip prefix-list question: 4 entries
    seq 5 deny 10.1.2.0/24 ge 25 le 27
    seq 15 deny 10.2.0.0/16 ge 30 le 30
    seq 20 permit 0.0.0.0/0 le 32
```

   a. R1 will not create/flood a type 3 LSA for subnet 10.1.2.0/26 into area 1.

   b. R1 will not create/flood a Type 3 LSA for subnet 10.1.2.0/24 into area 1.

   c. R1 will not have an OSPF route for subnet 10.1.2.0/26 in its IP routing table.

   d. R1 will not have an OSPF route for subnet 10.1.2.0/24 in its IP routing table.

4. R1, an ABR between backbone area 0 and area 1, has intra-area routes in area 0 for 10.1.1.0/24, 10.1.2.0/24, and 10.1.3.0/24. These routes have metrics of 21, 22, and 23, respectively. An engineer then adds the **area 0 range 10.1.0.0 255.255.0.0** command under the OSPF process of R1. Which of the following is true? (Choose two.)

    a. R1 loses and then re-establishes neighborships with all neighbors.

    b. R1 no longer advertises 10.1.1.0/24 to neighbors into area 1.

    c. R1 advertises a 10.1.0.0/16 route into area 1 with a metric of 23 (largest metric).

    d. R1 advertises a 10.1.0.0/16 route into area 1 with metric of 21 (lowest metric).

5. The following output exists on Router R1, a router internal to area 1. What can you determine as true from the output of the **show ip ospf database summary** command?

```
Routing Bit Set on this LSA
LS age: 124
Options: (No TOS-capability, DC, Upward)
LS Type: Summary Links (Network)
Link State ID: 10.1.0.0 (summary Network Number)
Advertising Router: 1.1.1.1
LS Seq Number: 80000001
Checksum: 0x878F
Length: 28
Network Mask: /22
      TOS: 0   Metric: 11
```

    a. The LSA was created by an ABR due to an **area range** command.

    b. The LSA was created by an ASBR due to a **summary-address** command.

    c. If created by an **area range** command, the best metric for a subordinate subnet on that ABR must have been 11.

    d. None of the other answers is correct.

6. Router R1, an ASBR connected to the Internet and to backbone area 0, has been configured with a **default-information originate** command. Which of the following is true about the effects of this configuration command?

    a. R1 will always create and flood a default route into the OSPF domain.

    b. R1 will create and flood an LSA for prefix/length 0.0.0.0/0 into the OSPF domain if R1's IP routing table has a route to 0.0.0.0/0.

    c. R1 will set a flag on the LSA for the subnet between itself and one of the ISPs, noting this subnet as a default network, regardless of whether R1 has a default route.

    d. R1 will set a flag on the LSA for the subnet between itself and one of the ISPs, noting this subnet as a default network, but only if R1 has a route to 0.0.0.0/0.

7. Which of the following is true about routers internal to a totally NSSA area? (Choose two.)

    a. Routers cannot redistribute external routes into the area.

    b. Routers should have zero Type 3 LSAs in their LSDBs.

    c. Routers should have zero Type 5 LSAs in their LSDBs.

    d. Routers should learn default routes from the ABRs attached to the area.

8. ABR R1 has been configured with an **area 1 stub no-summary** command. Which stubby area type is area 1?

    a. Stub

    b. Totally stubby

    c. NSSA

    d. Totally NSSA

Foundation Topics

Route Filtering

OSPF supports several methods to filter routes. However, the OSPF's internal logic restricts most filtering, requiring that the filtering be done either on an ABR or ASBR. This same internal logic dictates what each type of filtering can do and what it cannot do. So, when thinking about OSPF route filtering, you need to go beyond the concept of matching IP prefix/length information and consider OSPF internals as well. This first major section begins with a discussion of the OSPF internals that impact OSPF route filtering, followed by information about two of OSPF's route filtering tools.

First, consider the difference in how OSPF chooses intra-area versus interarea routes. For intra-area routes, OSPF uses pure link state logic, with full topology information about the area, piecing together the topology map from the Type 1 and Type 2 LSAs. This logic relies on all routers inside the area having an identical copy of the LSDB for that area. With the full topology, the SPF algorithm can be run, finding all possible routes to each subnet.

For interarea routes, OSPF uses distance vector logic. The intra-area SPF calculation includes the calculation of the metric of the best route to reach each ABR in the area. To choose the best interarea route, a router uses distance vector logic of taking its known metric to reach the ABR and adds the metric for that subnet as advertised by the ABR. In particular, no additional SPF calculation is required to find all interarea routes for a given prefix/length, making this logic more like distance vector logic.

Keeping these thoughts in mind, next consider the concept of route filtering inside one area. First, OSPF routers do not advertise routes; instead, they advertise LSAs. Any filtering applied to OSPF messages would need to filter the transmission of LSAs. However, inside one area, all routers must know all LSAs, or the whole SPF concept fails, and routing loops could occur. As a result, OSPF cannot and does not allow the filtering of LSAs inside an area, specifically the Type 1 and Type 2 LSAs that describe the intra-area topology.

OSPF does allow some route filtering, however, taking advantage that OSPF uses distance vector logic with Type 3 LSAs (and the Type 5 LSAs used for external routes). Because of the underlying distance vector logic, an OSPF ABR can be configured to filter Type 3 LSAs, with no risk of creating routing loops. (The same applies for autonomous system border routers [ASBRs] filtering the Type 5 LSAs created for external routes.) As a result of these related concepts, IOS limits OSPF route filtering to the following:

- Filtering Type 3 LSAs on ABRs

- Filtering Type 5 LSAs on ASBRs

- Filtering the routes OSPF would normally add to the IP routing table on a single router

Of these, the second option occurs as an option of the route redistribution process as explained in Chapter 9, "Basic IGP Redistribution," so it will not be covered further in this chapter. The other two topics will be examined next.

Type 3 LSA Filtering

ABRs, by definition, connect to the backbone area and at least one other area. ABRs, as a fundamental part of their role as ABR, create and flood Type 3 Summary LSAs into one area to represent the subnets in the other areas connected to that ABR. Type 3 LSA filtering tells the ABR to filter the advertisement of these Type 3 LSAs.

For example, consider Figure 7-1, which shows a generalized design with two ABR routers. The figure focuses on three subnets in area 0 for which each ABR would normally create and flood a Type 3 Summary LSA into area 1. However, in this case, the engineer has made the following choices:

- On ABR1, filter subnet 3 from being advertised.

- On ABR2, filter both subnet 2 and 3 from being advertised.

The goal of such a filtering plan could be to prevent all area 1 users from reaching subnet 3 and to allow access to subnet 2–but only through ABR1. If ABR1 were to fail, none of the area 1 routers could calculate a route for subnet 2 through ABR2, because ABR2 has not created and flooded a Type 3 LSA for that subnet. The goal for subnet 1 would be to allow each area 1 router to choose the best route through either ABR, while having a redundant route in case one route failed.

To configure type 3 LSA filtering, you use the **area** *number* **filter-list prefix** *name* **in | out** command under **router ospf**. The referenced **prefix-list** matches subnets, with subnets matched by a deny action being filtered, and subnets match with a permit action allowed through as normal. Then OSPF performs the filtering by not flooding the Type 3 LSAs into the appropriate areas. (See Chapter 4's section "IP Prefix List Concepts" for a review of IP prefix lists.)

Figure 7-1 *Generic View of Type 3 LSA Filtering*

The trickiest part of the configuration relates to the **in** and **out** parameters at the end of the **area filter-list** router subcommand. These parameters define the direction relative to the area listed in the command, as follows:

■ When **in** is configured, IOS filters prefixes being created and flooded *into the configured area.*

■ When **out** is configured, IOS filters prefixes coming *out of the configured area.*

The need for the **in** and **out** parameters makes more sense when you consider an ABR connected to at least three areas. Figure 7-2 shows just such a sample, with both the in and out directions represented.

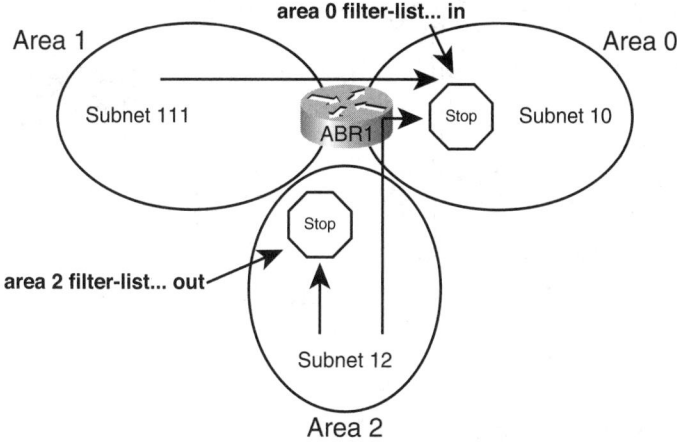

Figure 7-2   *Generic View of Type 3 LSA Filtering*

The **area 0 filter-list... in** command in the figure shows the ABR considers filtering routes from all other areas (area 1 and 2 in this case) when creating and flooding Type 3 LSAs into area 0. The **area 2 filter-list... out** command in the figure shows how the ABR only considers prefixes that exist in area 2. However, in this case, the ABR filters LSAs regardless of the area into which the Type 3 LSA would be advertised.

For example, consider the case of subnet 111, in area 1. Assume that all prefix lists happen to match subnet 111 so that subnet 111 should be filtered. The following list summarizes what happens on ABR1 regarding the potential advertisement of a Type 3 LSA for this subnet being flooded into areas 0 and 2.

■ ABR1 filters the subnet 111 LSA from being sent into area 0 due to the **area 0 filter-list... in** command.

■ ABR1 does not filter the subnet 111 LSA from being sent into area 2, because there is no **area 1 filter-list... out** command nor **area 2 filter-list... in** command.

As another example, Figure 7-3 shows an example internetwork with three candidate routes to be filtered by ABRs R1 and R2. ABRs R1 and R2 will play the roles of ABR1 and

ABR2 in Figure 7-1, with R1 filtering one of the three subnets, and R2 filtering two of the subnets. Note that R1 and R2 will each use different **in** and **out** keywords as well.

Figure 7-3   *Type 3 LSA Filtering Example*

Example 7-1 shows the configuration on both R1 and R2.

Example 7-1   *WAN1's distribute-list to Filter Manufacturing Routes*

```
! On Router R1:
ip prefix-list filter-into-area-34 seq 5 deny 10.16.3.0/24
ip prefix-list filter-into-area-34 seq 10 permit 0.0.0.0/0 le 32
!
router ospf 1
 area 34 filter-list prefix filter-into-area-34 in
```

```
! On Router R2:
ip prefix-list filter-out-of-area-0 seq 5 deny 10.16.2.0/23 ge 24 le 24
ip prefix-list filter-out-of-area-0 seq 10 permit 0.0.0.0/0 le 32
!
router ospf 2
 area 0 filter-list prefix filter-out-of-area-0 out
```

First, take a closer look at the specifics of the R1 configuration commands. The prefix list on R1 matches exactly route 10.16.3.0/24, with a **deny** action. The second prefix-list command matches all subnets, because the **0.0.0.0/0** parameter matches all subnet numbers, and the **le 32** parameter, combined with the original /0 prefix length, matches all prefix lengths from /0 to /32. The **area 34... in** command tells R1 to apply this filtering to all Type 3 LSAs that R1 creates and would otherwise flood into area 34. As a result, the area 34 LSDB will not contain a Type 3 LSA for 10.16.3.0/24, as injected by R1.

R2's configuration uses a slightly different prefix list. The filter examines all Type 3 LSAs for subnets in area 0. The first **prefix-list** command matches all prefixes in range 10.16.2.0–10.16.3.255 (per the **10.16.2.0/23** parameter) but specifically for a prefix length of exactly 24. With a deny action, these routes are filtered. The second **prefix-list** command matches all other subnets with the same match all logic seen earlier on R1, using a permit action. R2's **area 0... out** command tells R2 to filter the subnets that R2 learns in area 0 and for which R2 would normally create Type 3 LSAs to flood into all other areas. So, neither area 34 nor area 5 will learn these two filtered subnets (10.16.2.0/24 and 10.16.3.0/24) in Type 3 LSAs from R2.

The end result of this added configuration results in the following Type 3 LSAs for the three subnets shown on the right side of Figure 7-3:

- Two Type 3 LSAs for 10.16.1.0/24 (created by R1 and R2, respectively)

- One Type 3 LSA for 10.16.2.0/24 (created by R1)

- None for 10.16.3.0/24

Example 7-2 confirms the contents of the LSDB in area 34, on Router R3.

Example 7-2 *Area 34 LSDB, as Seen on R3*

```
! On Router R3: gather show ip ospf database, and highlight all the Type 3's.
R3# show ip route 10.16.0.0 255.255.0.0 longer-prefixes
! Legend lines omitted for brevity

      10.0.0.0/8 is variably subnetted, 17 subnets, 3 masks
O IA    10.16.2.0/24 [110/658] via 10.10.13.1, 00:00:32, Serial0/0/0.1
O IA    10.16.1.0/24 [110/658] via 10.10.23.2, 00:41:39, Serial0/0/0.2
                     [110/658] via 10.10.13.1, 00:00:32, Serial0/0/0.1


R3#show ip ospf database | include 10.16
10.16.1.0        1.1.1.1         759         0x80000002 0x008988
10.16.1.0        2.2.2.2         745         0x80000002 0x006BA2
10.16.2.0        1.1.1.1         759         0x80000002 0x007E92
```

The first command in the example lists R3's routes for all subnets whose first two octets are 10.16. Note that R3 has no route to 10.16.3.0/24, because both R1 and R2 filtered the Type 3 LSA. R3 happens to have equal-cost routes for 10.16.1.0/24, which is possible because both R1 and R2 permitted the advertisement of the Type 3 LSA for that subnet. R3 has only one route for 10.16.2.0/24, through R1, because R2 filtered its Type 3 LSA for that prefix.

The second command in Example 7-2 lists all LSAs that include "10.16," which includes the two Type 3 LSAs for 10.16.1.0/24, and the single Type 3 LSA for 10.16.2.0/24.

Finally, note that although the configuration in Example 7-1 showed **area filter-list** commands with both **in** and **out** parameters for variety, the result of R2's **area filter-list... out** command is that does not flood the filtered LSAs to either area 34 or area 5. If the design goals specifically meant to filter only LSAs from being advertised from Area 0 into Area 34, the **area 34 filter-list... in** command should have been used on both routers.

Filtering OSPF Routes Added to the Routing Table

In some cases, an engineer may need to filter a route, but the area design does not work well compared to the filtering goals. For instance, if an area has 20 routers, and the engineer wants to filter the route so that five of the routers do not learn the route, Type 3 LSA filtering cannot be used. Type 3 LSA filtering can only filter the LSA from being flooded throughout the entire area.

The next feature discussed in this section, referenced as *filtering with distribute lists* (based the configuration command it uses), allows individual routers to filter OSPF routes from getting into their respective IP routing tables. This type of filtering injects logic between the SPF algorithm on a router and that same router's IP routing table. This feature does not change the LSDB flooding process, does not change the LSAs added by ABRs or ASBRs, and does not change the SPF algorithm's choice of best route. However, when SPF chooses routes to add to the IP routing table, if a router has been configured with a **distribute-list in** OSPF router subcommand, enabling this feature, that router then filters the routes before adding them to that router's IP routing table. Figure 7-4 shows the general idea.

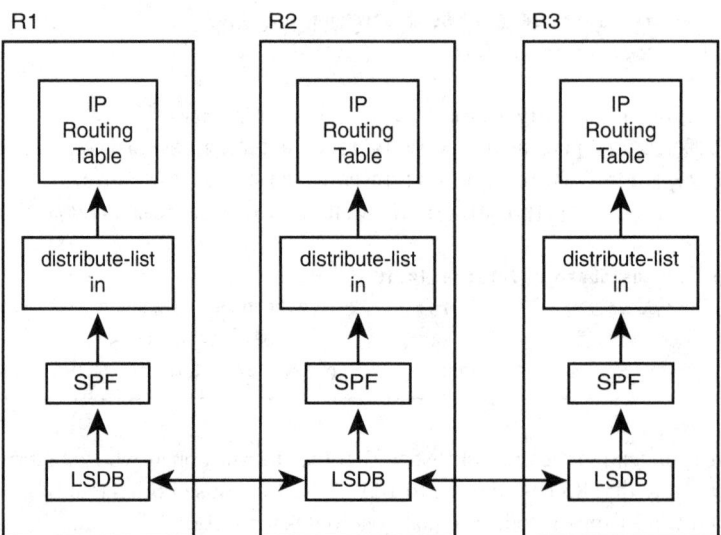

Figure 7-4 *OSPF Filtering with Distribute Lists*

In effect, you could prevent an OSPF route from being added to one or more routers' routing tables, but without risking causing routing loops, because the intra-area LSDB topology remains intact. By filtering routes from being added to the IP routing table, you prevent the routers from forwarding packets to the filtered subnets, but presumably that's the intended goal of route filtering.

The mechanics of the **distribute-list** router subcommand has a few surprises, which are summarized in this list:

- The command requires either an **in** or **out** direction. Only the **in** direction works for filtering routes as described in this section.

- The command must refer to either a numbered ACL, named ACL, prefix list, or route map. Regardless, routes matched with a **permit** action are allowed into the routing table, and routes matched with a **deny** action are filtered.

- Optionally, the command can include the **interface** *interface-name-and-number* parameters. The router compares these parameters to the route's outgoing interface.

Example 7-3 shows a sample configuration on Router R3 from Figure 7-3. In this case, all filtering listed in Examples 7-1 and 7-2 has been removed, so no routes or LSAs have been filtered. Then, the engineer adds the **distribute-list** command on R3 to filter the route for 10.16.1.0/24, based on prefix-list filter-1.

Example 7-3 *R3's distribute-list to Filter 10.16.1.0/24*

```
! On Router R3:
ip prefix-list filter-1 seq 5 deny 10.16.1.0/24
ip prefix-list filter-1 seq 10 permit 0.0.0.0/0 le 32
!
router ospf 3
 distribute-list prefix filter-1 in
!
R3#show ip route ospf | include 10.16.1
R3#
R3#show ip ospf database | include 10.16.1.0
10.16.1.0       1.1.1.1         1143        0x80000007 0x007F8D
10.16.1.0       2.2.2.2         1538        0x80000007 0x0061A7
```

Note that the configuration matches only prefix 10.16.1.0/24 with a deny clause and permits all other routes. As a result, OSPF on R3 does not add a route for subnet 10.16.1.0/24 to the IP routing table, as implied by the null output of the **show ip route ospf | include 10.16.1** command. The **show ip ospf database | include 10.16.1** command lists all LSAs that have 10.16.1 in the text output, showing the two Type 3 LSAs for the subnet.

Route Summarization

OSPF allows summarization at both ABRs and ASBRs but not on other OSPF routers. The main reason is again that the LSDB must be the same for all routers in a single area. So, if summarization is needed, the summary prefixes should be created at the edge of an area (ABR or ASBR) and flooded throughout that area. However, the idea of summarizing on a router internal to an area, hoping that some routers in the area use the summary route, and others in the same area do not, cannot be done with OSPF.

Good planning of route summaries can overcome the restriction of performing the summarization only on ABRs and ASBRs. A good OSPF area design includes consideration of future address summaries, and a good OSPF route summarization design considers the ABR locations. Although it is rare to design a large internetwork from scratch, an addressing plan that assigns all or most subnets in an area from one large address block does make address summarization easier.

OSPF summarization differs slightly on ABRs versus ASBRs. This section first examines route summarizations on ABRs and then ASBRs.

Manual Summarization at ABRs

The more difficult task with OSPF route summarization occurs when planning the design of IP address blocks and OSPF areas. When the IP addressing plan and OSPF design have been completed, if the subnet numbers inside an area happen to be from the same general range, and none of the subnet in that range exist in other OSPF areas, then a reasonable summary route can be created at the ABRs connected to that area. Without first having such a reasonable block of addresses, route summarization may not be a useful option.

After a range of subnets has been chosen for summarization, the parameters in the **area range** command must be planned. This command defines the parameters for the summary route, most notably the origin area from which the subnets exist, and the subnet number/mask that defines the summary route that should be advertised. The generic version of the command is listed next, followed by some notes about the various parameters:

```
area area-id range ip-address mask [cost cost]
```

- The configured area number refers to the area where the subnets exist; the summary will be advertised into all other areas connected to the ABR.

- The ABR compares the summary route's range of addresses with all intra-area OSPF routes, in the origin area, for which the ABR is creating Type 3 LSAs. If at least one subordinate subnet exists (subnets that sit inside the range), then the ABR advertises the summary route as a Type 3 LSA.

- The ABR does not advertise the subordinate subnet's Type 3 LSAs.

- The ABR assigns a metric for the summary route's Type 3 LSA, by default, to match the best metric among all subordinate subnets.

- The **area range** command can also explicitly set the cost of the summary.

- If no subordinate subnets exist, the ABR does not advertise the summary.

For example, Figure 7-3 (earlier in this chapter) lists three subnets on the right side of the figure, noted as Data Center subnets: 10.16.1.0/24, 10.16.2.0/24, and 10.16.3.0/24. ABR R1 could be configured to summarize these routes as 10.16.0.0/22, which includes all three subnets. (10.16.0.0/22 implies a range from 10.16.0.0–10.16.3.255.) The ABRs (R1 and R2) could be configured to advertise a summary route using the **area 0 range 10.16.0.0 255.255.252.0** router subcommand.

Behind the scenes, ABR route summarization causes the ABR to no longer advertise the subordinate routes' Type 3 LSAs, but to instead advertise one Type 3 LSA for the summary prefix. Figure 7-5 shows this concept on ABR R1, assuming the **area 0 range 10.16.0.0 255.255.252.0** router subcommand has been configured. The three Type 3 LSAs that would normally have been advertised are shown above the ABR, and the one Type 3 LSA for the summary route, which replaces the upper LSAs, is shown under the ABR.

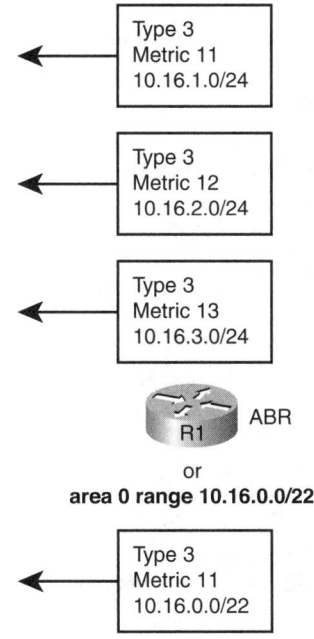

Figure 7-5   *OSPF Area Summarization–Consolidating Type 3 LSAs*

Example 7-4 shows some **show** command output related to this example. All route filtering in earlier examples has been removed, and both R1 and R2 have configured OSPF to summarize 10.16.0.0/22 with the **area 0 range 10.16.0.0 255.255.252.0** router OSPF subcommand. However, in R2's case, the **metric 12** parameter was used.

Example 7-4   *R3's distribute-list to Filter 10.16.1.0/24*

```
! On Router R1, before the summarization:
R1#sh ip route ospf | incl 10.16
O        10.16.2.0/24 [110/12] via 10.10.17.7, 00:00:24, FastEthernet0/0
O        10.16.3.0/24 [110/13] via 10.10.17.7, 00:00:24, FastEthernet0/0
O        10.16.1.0/24 [110/11] via 10.10.17.7, 00:00:34, FastEthernet0/0
```

```
! Next, configuring the summarization:
router ospf 1
 area 0 range 10.16.0.0 255.255.252.0
```

```
! Next, on R2, configuring the same summary
router ospf 2
 area 0 range 10.16.0.0 255.255.252.0 cost 12
```

```
! Next, from R3
R3#show ip ospf database summary 10.16.0.0

               OSPF Router with ID (3.3.3.3) (Process ID 3)


               Summary Net Link States (Area 34)


   Routing Bit Set on this LSA
   LS age: 124
   Options: (No TOS-capability, DC, Upward)
   LS Type: Summary Links(Network)
   Link State ID: 10.16.0.0 (summary Network Number)
   Advertising Router: 1.1.1.1
   LS Seq Number: 80000001
   Checksum: 0x878F
   Length: 28
   Network Mask: /22
         TOS: 0  Metric: 11


   LS age: 103
   Options: (No TOS-capability, DC, Upward)
   LS Type: Summary Links(Network)
   Link State ID: 10.16.0.0 (summary Network Number)
   Advertising Router: 2.2.2.2
   LS Seq Number: 80000001
   Checksum: 0x739E
   Length: 28
   Network Mask: /22
         TOS: 0  Metric: 12


R3#show ip route 10.16.0.0 255.255.0.0 longer-prefixes
! legend omitted for brevity


     10.0.0.0/8 is variably subnetted, 16 subnets, 4 masks
O IA    10.16.0.0/22 [110/658] via 10.10.13.1, 00:03:46, Serial0/0/0.1
```

The example demonstrates the theory of what happens behind the scenes. R3 lists only two Type 3 LSAs related to the 10.16.1.0/24, 10.16.2.0/24, and 10.16.3.0/24 subnets: the Type 3 LSAs created by R1 and R2 for 10.16.0.0/22. However, the output does not denote that this LSA represents a summarized route–it simply looks like yet another Type 3 LSA.

(Any mention of the word "summary" in the output refers to the fact that Type 3 LSAs are called summary LSAs.) In this case, R3's path to reach both R1 and R2 ties, but the LSA for R1's 10.16.0.0/22 summary was injected with metric 11, based on the lowest metric subordinate route on R1, whereas R2's uses the explicitly configured metric 12. As a result, R3's best route for 10.16.0.0/22 uses R1, as shown in the route at the end of the example.

The first **show** command in the example shows R1's metrics for the three subordinate subnets, specifically metrics 11, 12, and 13. As such, R1's summary for 10.16.0.0/22, as shown in R3's **show ip ospf database summary 10.16.0.0** command, confirms that by default R1 gave the summary route's Type 3 LSA the best metric among the component subnets.

Note: Although not discussed in depth here, the optional **not-advertise** option on the **area range** command tells the ABR to not advertise the Type 3 LSA for the summary route, making it possible to do the equivalent of Type 3 LSA filtering with the **area range** command.

Manual Summarization at ASBRs

OSPF defines an ASBR as a router that redistributes routes into OSPF from some other routing source. When redistributing the routes, the ASBR creates a Type 5 External LSA for each redistributed subnet, listing the subnet number as the LSID and listing the mask as one of the fields in the LSA. The LSA also lists the ASBR's RID as the advertising router and a cost metric for the route. For the purposes of route summarization, you can think of a Type 5 LSA as working much like a Type 3 LSA, except for routes learned externally.

Chapter 9 discusses external OSPF routes in more depth, including some additional background on Type 5 LSAs. However, to keep the discussion of OSPF route summarization together, this section describes ASBR route summarization, which has many similarities to summarization by an ABR.

If you add the **summary-address** *prefix mask* OSPF subcommand, OSPF will then attempt to summarize the external routes by creating a Type 5 LSA for the summary route, and by no longer advertising the Type 5 LSAs for the subordinate subnets. When looking for potential subordinate subnets inside the summary, the ASBR looks at all routes being redistributed into OSPF from all outside route sources, and if any subordinate subnets exist, the ASBR performs the route summarization.

Notably, this command works very much like the **area range** command on ABRs, with the main exception being that the **summary-address** command cannot explicitly set the metric of the summary route. The list of features is as follows:

- The ASBR compares the summary route's range of addresses with all routes redistributed into OSPF on that ASBR to find any subordinate subnets (subnets that sit inside the summary route range). If at least one subordinate subnet exists, the ASBR advertises the summary route.

- The ASBR does not advertise the subordinate subnets.

- To create the summary, the ASBR actually creates a Type 5 LSA for the summary route.

- The ASBR assigns the summary route the same metric as the lowest metric route amongst all subordinate subnets.

- If no subordinate subnets exist, the ASBR does not advertise the summary.

- Unlike the **area range** command, the **summary-address** command cannot be used to directly set the metric of the summary route.

The **summary-address** OSPF subcommand defines the summary route on the ASBR, with similar syntax and parameters as compared to the **area range** command seen on ABRs. Table 7-2 lists the two commands for comparison and study.

Table 7-2   *OSPF Route Summarization Commands*

Where Used	Command
ASBR	**summary-address** {{*ip-address mask*} | {*prefix mask*}} [**not-advertise**]
ABR	**area** *area-id* **range** *ip-address mask* [**advertise** | **not-advertise**] [**cost** *cost*]

Default Routes and Stub Areas

Enterprises typically use default routes in two different cases:

- To direct remote-site routers at the edge of the Enterprise network to send all packets toward the core of the Enterprise, with the core routers knowing all the more specific routes to Enterprise destination addresses.

- To direct traffic on all Enterprise routers toward an Internet-facing router so that all traffic destined for the Internet eventually arrives at the Enterprise's Internet-connected routers.

Engineers could achieve both of these goals by using route summarization with the **area range** and **summary-address** commands. For example, consider a case in which the goal is to drive all packets destined for Internet hosts to one of two equal Internet routers for an Enterprise, as shown in Figure 7-6. The design shows two ASBRs connected to the Internet. Both ASBRs could learn routes with BGP. Rather than redistribute all BGP routes into the Enterprise, the ASBRs summarize to the ultimate summary, 0.0.0.0/0. The two OSPF ASBRs flood the Type 5 LSA for a summary route–one from ASBR1 and one from ASBR2–throughout the Enterprise. As a result, all OSPF routers choose a default route, with the packets destined for locations in the Internet eventually reaching one of the two ASBRs, which then forwards the packets into the Internet.

To meet the other design goal for using defaults–to get the routers in an area to use default routing to deliver packets to the ABR–the ABR could use the **area range** command to flood a default route into a single area. Again in Figure 7-6, if the design called for the routers in area 1 to use a default route to reach other destinations in the Enterprise, the ABRs connected to area 1, like ABR1, could use the **area 0 range 0.0.0.0 0.0.0.0** com-

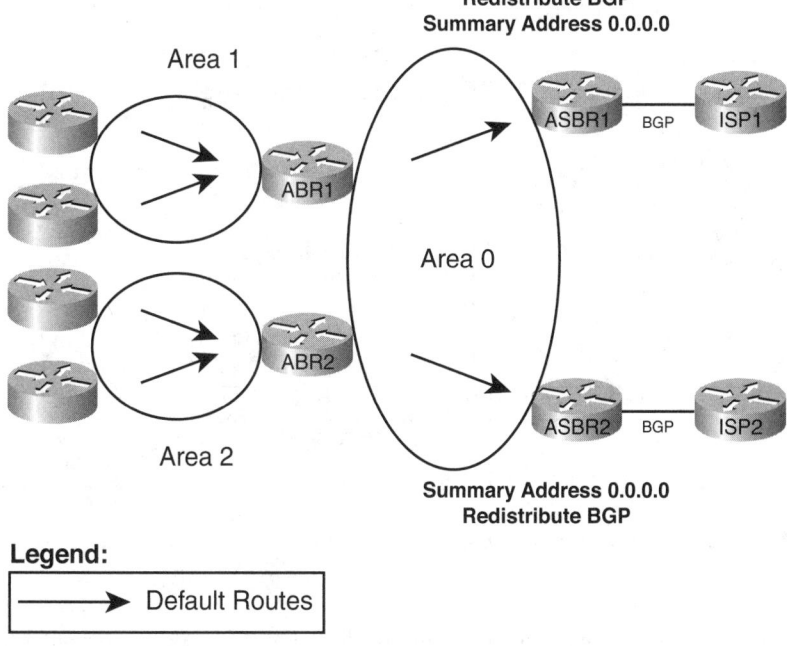

Figure 7-6 *Using ASBR Route Summarization to Advertise Summary Routes*

mand. ABR1 would then advertise a default route into the area, as an LSA type 3, and not advertise any of the other Type 3 LSAs known from area 0. The routers internal to area 1 would use their default route for packets destined to unknown destination addresses, but the ABRs would have full knowledge of the routes inside the Enterprise and know how to forward the packets at that point.

Even though you can use the **summary-address** and **area range** commands, most engineers use other methods to introduce and control default routes inside the OSPF domain. The first tool, the **default-information originate** OSPF subcommand, introduces a default route to be flooded throughout the OSPF domain. As a result, it is most useful for default routing to draw packets toward ASBRs connected to external networks. The other tool, stub areas, focuses on the other common use of default routes, controlling when ABRs flood default routes into a given area. This section examines both topics.

Domain-wide Defaults Using the default-information originate Command

The OSPF subcommand **default-information originate** tells OSPF to create a Type 5 LSA (used for external routes) for a default route–0.0.0.0/0–and flood it like any other Type 5 LSA. In other words, it tells the router to create and flood information about a default route throughout the OSPF domain.

For example, consider a typical dual-homed Internet design, as shown in Figure 7-7. In this case, the Enterprise has two Internet-connected routers, and the engineer wants to use default routing inside the Enterprise to cause all the Enterprise routers to send packets toward either ASBR1 or ASBR2.

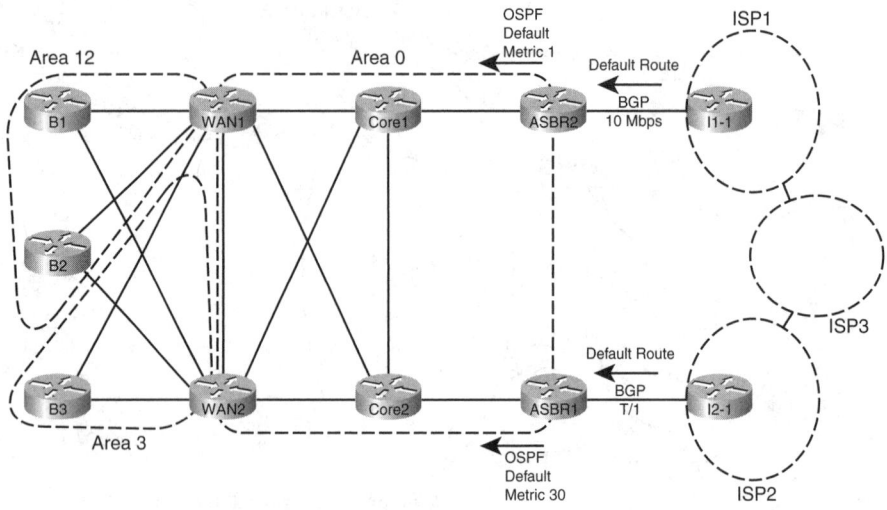

Figure 7-7   *Dual-Homed Internet Design Using Default Routes*

The **default-information originate** command tells the ASBRs to flood a default route into OSPF, but only if the ASBR itself has a default route in its IP routing table. This logic relies on the fact that the ASBRs typically either have a static default route pointing to the connected ISP router, or they learn a default route from the ISP using BGP. (Figure 7-7 each ISP advertising a default route in this case.) All the routers then learn a default route, based on the Type 5 LSAs for 0.0.0.0/0 as flooded by the ASBRs.

Because a router withdraws its OSPF default route when its own IP route to 0.0.0.0/0 fails, OSPF allows the design in Figure 7-7 to fail over to the other default route. When all is well, both ISP1 and ISP2 advertise a default route to the Enterprise using BGP, so both ASBR1 and ASBR2 have a route to 0.0.0.0/0. As shown in the figure, ASBR2 has been configured to advertise its OSPF default with a lower metric (1) than does ASBR1 (metric 30), so the Enterprise routers will forward traffic to the Internet through ASBR2. However, if ISP1 quits advertising that default with BGP, or BGP fails between ASBR2 and ISP1's I1-1 router, ASBR2 will withdraw its OSPF default route. The only remaining OSPF default route will be the one that leads to ASBR1, making use of the backup default route.

The full command syntax, as shown here, provides several optional parameters that impact its operation:

```
default-information originate [always] [metric metric-value] [metric-type type-
value] [route-map map-name]
```

The following list summarizes the features of the **default-information originate** OSPF subcommand:

- With all default parameters, it injects a default route into OSPF, as an External Type 2 route, using a Type 5 LSA, with metric 1, but only if a default route exists in that router's routing table.

- With the **always** parameter, the default route is advertised even if there is no default route in the router's routing table.

- The **metric** keyword defines the metric listed for the default route (default 1).

- The **metric-type** keyword defines whether the LSA is listed as external type 1 or external type 2 (default). (Chapter 9's section "Redistribution into OSPF" discusses OSPF external route types.)

- The decision of when to advertise, and when to withdraw, the default route is based on matching the referenced **route-map** with a permit action.

When configured, OSPF will flood the default route throughout the OSPF routing domain, drawing traffic to each ASBR, as shown earlier in Figure 7-6.

Note: The type of external OSPF route (Type 1 or Type 2) is explained more fully in Chapter 9.

Stubby Areas

As mentioned earlier, the two most common reasons to consider using default routes are to drive all Internet-destined traffic toward the Internet-connected routers in the Enterprise and to drive traffic inside an area toward one of the ABRs in that area. This second design choice allows the routers in an area to use default routes for forwarding packets to ABRs, rather than more specific routes. Using default routes inside an area reduces memory consumption and CPU processing time on the routers inside the area, because the routers in that area can have fewer LSAs in their LSDBs.

The OSPF stub router feature provides engineers a very simple way to enable the function of flooding default routes inside an area, with those default routes driving IP packets back toward the ABRs attached to that area. ABRs in stub areas advertise a default route into the stub area. At the same time, the ABR chooses to not advertise external routes (5 LSAs) into the area, or even instead to no longer advertise interarea routes (in Type 3 LSAs) into the area. As a result, all routers in the stub area can still route to the destinations (based on the default route), but the routers require less memory and processing.

The following list summarizes these features of stub areas for easier study and review:

- ABRs create a default route, using a Type 3 LSA, listing subnet 0.0.0.0 and mask 0.0.0.0, and flood that into the stub area.

- ABRs do not flood Type 5 LSAs into the stub area.

- ABRs may not flood other Type 3 LSAs into the area.

- The default route has a metric of 1 unless otherwise configured using the OSPF subcommand **area** *area-num* **default-cost** *cost*.

- Routers inside stub areas cannot redistribute external routes into the stubby area, because that would require a Type 5 LSA in the area.

■ All routers in the area must be configured to be stubby; if not, neighbor relationships cannot form between potential neighbors based on this mismatched configuration.

Figure 7-8 shows a familiar design in which area 34 will become a stub area. The design shows three external routes and lists three of many internal routes inside area 0. The figure shows ABRs R1 and R2 advertising defaults into area 34.

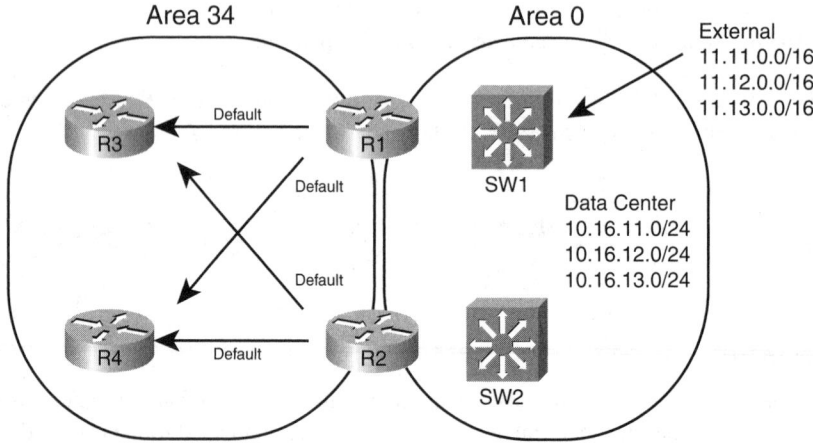

Figure 7-8   *Stubby Area Design*

Figure 7-8 demonstrates the core feature common to all types of stub areas: the ABRs flood a default route into the area. The routers inside the area can then calculate their best default route. Next, the text examines the different types of OSPF areas, before moving on to the details of configuration and verification.

Introducing Stubby Area Types

Even within the realm of stubby areas, four types of stubby areas exist: stub, totally stubby, not-so-stubby areas (NSSA), and totally NSSA.

Two types of stubby areas have the word "totally" as part of the name, and two do not. The differences between those with the word "totally" and those without have to do with whether Type 3 LSAs are flooded into the area. The rules are

■ For all types of stubby areas, the ABR always filters Type 5 (external) LSAs.

■ For totally stubby and totally NSSA areas, the ABR also filters Type 3 LSAs.

■ For stubby and NSSA areas–those without the word "totally" in the name–the ABRs do not filter Type 3 LSAs, advertising Type 3 LSAs as normal.

For example, consider the diagram in Figure 7-8, with area 34 as simply a stub area. As for all types, the ABRs each advertise a default route into area 34. As for all stubby area types, the ABRs filter all Type 5 LSAs, which means that the three Type 5 LSAs for

11.11.0.0/16, 11.12.0.0/16, and 11.13.0.0/16 would not exist in the LSDBs for area 34. Finally, because the area is not a totally stubby area, the ABRs do create and flood Type 3 LSAs for interarea routes as usual, so they flood LSAs for the 10.16.11.0/24, 10.16.12.0/24, and 10.16.13.0/24 subnets listed in the figure.

Next, consider a similar scenario but with a totally stubby area for area 5. As for all stubby area types, the ABRs each advertise a default route into area 5. As for all stubby area types, the ABRs filter all Type 5 LSAs, which means that the three Type 5 LSAs for 11.11.0.0/16, 11.12.0.0/16, and 11.13.0.0/16 would not exist in the LSDBs for area 5. The key difference exists in that the ABRs also would not create and flood Type 3 LSAs for interarea routes as usual, so they would not advertise Type 3 LSAs for the 10.16.11.0/24, 10.16.12.0/24, and 10.16.13.0/24 subnets listed in the figure into area 5.

The other difference in stubby area types relates to whether the name uses NSSA (NSSA or totally NSSA) or not (stubby, totally stubby). Stubby area types that use the NSSA name can redistribute external routes into the area; stubby area types without NSSA in the name cannot.

Configuring and Verifying Stubby Areas

Configuring stub and totally stubby areas requires only three commands, but with at least one command on each router, as listed in Table 7-3:

Note: For totally stubby areas, only the ABR must have the **no-summary** keyword on the **area** *area-id* **stub no-summary** command. However, including this keyword on internal routers does not cause a problem.

Figure 7-9 shows a more detailed view of area 34 from Figure 7-8, so by making area 34 a stub area, ABRs R1 and R2 will not flood Type 3 LSAs into area 34–other than the Type 3 LSA for the default routes. Example 7-4 shows the configuration on Routers R1, R2, and R3 from Figure 7-9.

Table 7-3 *Stub Area Configuration Options*

Action	Configuration Steps
Stubby	Configure **area** *area-id* **stub** on each router in the area
Totally stubby	Configure **area** *area-id* **stub no-summary** command on the ABRs
	Configure **area** *area-id* **stub**, without the **no-summary** keyword, on all other routers in the area
Set the metric of the default route	Configure **area** *area-id* **default-metric** *metric* on an ABR; can differ from ABR to ABR. Default value is 1.

Area 34 (Stubby)

Figure 7-9   *Detailed View of Area 34*

Example 7-4   *Stub Area Configuration*

```
! On Router R1:
router ospf 1
 area 34 stub
 auto-cost reference-bandwidth 1000
 !
interface s0/0/0.3 point-to-point
 ip ospf area 34
 !
interface s0/0/0.4 point-to-point
  ip ospf area 34
! On Router R2:
router ospf 2
 area 34 stub
 auto-cost reference-bandwidth 1000
 !
interface s0/0/0.3 point-to-point
 ip ospf area 34
 !
interface s0/0/0.4 point-to-point
 iip ospf area 34
```

```
! On Router R3:
router ospf 3
 area 34 stub
 auto-cost reference-bandwidth 1000
!
interface s0/0/0.1 point-to-point
 ip ospf area 34
 ip ospf cost 500
!
interface s0/0/0.2 point-to-point
 ip ospf area 34
!
interface fa0/0
 ip ospf area 34
```

With the configuration as shown, both R1 and R2 will inject a default route, represented as a Type 3 LSA, with default metric 1. They will also not flood the Type 5 LSAs into area 34. Example 7-5 confirms these facts, showing the Type 3 LSA for the summary, and the absence of Type 5 LSAs in the output of the **show ip ospf database** command on router R3.

Example 7-5   *Evidence of Type 5's Existing, Disappearing, and Defaults Appearing*

```
! Before making Area 34 stubby:


R3#show ip ospf database | begin AS External
                Type-5 AS External Link States

Link ID         ADV Router      Age        Seq#        Checksum Tag
11.11.0.0       7.7.7.7         929        0x80000001 0x00016D 0
12.12.0.0       7.7.7.7         845        0x80000001 0x00E784 0
13.13.0.0       7.7.7.7         835        0x80000001 0x00CE9B 0


! After making area 34 stubby - no output from the next command.


R3#show ip ospf database | begin AS External
R3#

! The database for area 34 now has two Type 3 LSAs for default routes.
R3#show ip ospf database

                OSPF Router with ID (3.3.3.3) (Process ID 3)


                    Router Link States (Area 34)
```

```
! Lines omitted for brevity - skipped to "Summary Net" (Type 3) section


                  Summary Net Link States (Area 34)


Link ID          ADV Router       Age         Seq#         Checksum
0.0.0.0          1.1.1.1          692         0x80000001 0x0093A6
0.0.0.0          2.2.2.2          686         0x80000001 0x0075C0
10.10.5.0        1.1.1.1          692         0x8000000E 0x00445C
10.10.5.0        2.2.2.2          686         0x8000000F 0x002477
10.10.12.0       1.1.1.1          692         0x8000000E 0x0054AF
10.10.12.0       2.2.2.2          686         0x8000000E 0x0036C9
! Many Type 3 LSA's omitted for brevity's sake
```

Example 7-5 shows the existence of the Type 5 external LSAs before area 34 became a stubby area, and the disappearance of those same LSAs once it was made a stubby area. The **show ip ospf database** command then shows two LSAs that list default routes, one learned from RID 1.1.1.1 (R1), and one learned from RID 2.2.2.2 (R2).

Example 7-6 continues the verification of how stub areas work with three more commands.

Example 7-6 *Three External Routes Before and None Afterward Changing to Stubby*

```
! Next, R3 confirms it thinks area 34 is a stub area
R3#show ip ospf
 Routing Process "ospf 3" with ID 3.3.3.3
 Start time: 00:00:38.756, Time elapsed: 07:51:19.720
! lines omitted for brevity
   Area 34
        Number of interfaces in this area is 3
        It is a stub area
        Area has no authentication
        SPF algorithm last executed 00:11:21.640 ago
        SPF algorithm executed 18 times
        Area ranges are
        Number of LSA 29. Checksum Sum 0x0D3E01
        Number of opaque link LSA 0. Checksum Sum 0x000000
        Number of DCbitless LSA 0
        Number of indication LSA 0
        Number of DoNotAge LSA 0
        Flood list length 0


! The next command shows all Type 3 (summary) LSAs of prefix 0.0.0.0


R3#show ip ospf database summary 0.0.0.0


                OSPF Router with ID (3.3.3.3) (Process ID 3)
```

```
                    Summary Net Link States (Area 34)


  Routing Bit Set on this LSA
  LS age: 879
  Options: (No TOS-capability, DC, Upward)
  LS Type: Summary Links(Network)
  Link State ID: 0.0.0.0 (summary Network Number)
  Advertising Router: 1.1.1.1
  LS Seq Number: 80000001
  Checksum: 0x93A6
  Length: 28
  Network Mask: /0
        TOS: 0   Metric: 1


  LS age: 873
  Options: (No TOS-capability, DC, Upward)
  LS Type: Summary Links(Network)
  Link State ID: 0.0.0.0 (summary Network Number)
  Advertising Router: 2.2.2.2
  LS Seq Number: 80000001
  Checksum: 0x75C0
  Length: 28
  Network Mask: /0
        TOS: 0   Metric: 1

! The next command lists statistics of the number of LSAs of each type -
! note a total of 0 Type 5 LSAs, but many Type 3

R3#show ip ospf database database-summary

            OSPF Router with ID (3.3.3.3) (Process ID 3)


Area 34 database summary
  LSA Type        Count    Delete    Maxage
  Router          4        0         0
  Network         1        0         0
  Summary Net     24       0         0
  Summary ASBR    0        0         0
  Type-7 Ext      0        0         0
     Prefixes redistributed in Type-7   0
  Opaque Link     0        0         0
  Opaque Area     0        0         0
  Subtotal        29       0         0
```

```
Process 3 database summary
   LSA Type      Count    Delete    Maxage
   Router        4        0         0
   Network       1        0         0
   Summary Net   24       0         0
   Summary ASBR  0        0         0
   Type-7 Ext    0        0         0
   Opaque Link   0        0         0
   Opaque Area   0        0         0
   Type-5 Ext    0        0         0
        Prefixes redistributed in Type-5  0
   Opaque AS     0        0         0
   Non-self      28
   Total         29       0         0
```

Following are the three commands in Example 7-6 in order:

- **show ip ospf**–Confirms with one (highlighted) line that the router believes that the area is a stub area.

- **show ip ospf database summary 0.0.0.0**–By definition, this command lists all summary (Type 3) LSAs with prefix 0.0.0.0. It lists two such LSAs, created by R1 and R2 (RIDs 1.1.1.1 and 2.2.2.2, respectively), both with metric 1 (the default setting).

- **show ip ospf database database-summary**–This command lists statistics about the numbers of and types of LSAs in the database. The counters show 0 Type 5 LSAs, and a few dozen Type 3s–confirming that the area, while stubby, is not totally stubby.

Configuring and Verifying Totally Stubby Areas

Configuring totally stubby areas requires almost no additional effort as compared with stubby areas. As listed earlier in Table 7-3, the only difference for totally stubby configuration versus stubby configuration is that the ABR's include the **no-summary** keyword on the **area stub** command. (**no-summary** refers to the fact that ABRs in totally stubby areas do not create/flood Type 3 summary LSAs.)

Example 7-7 shows another example configuration, this time with area 34 as a totally stubby area. Additionally, the default routes' metrics have been set so that both R3 and R4 will use R1 as their preferred ABR, by setting R2's advertised summary to a relatively high metric (500). Example 7-7 just shows the changes to the configuration shown in Example 7-4.

Example 7-7 *Totally Stubby Area Configuration*

```
! On Router R1:
router ospf 1
 area 34 stub no-summary
 auto-cost reference-bandwidth 1000
```

```
! On Router R2:
router ospf 2
 area 34 stub no-summary
 area 34 default-cost 500
 auto-cost reference-bandwidth 1000
```

The configuration of a totally stubby area reduces the size of the LSDB in area 34, because the ABRs no longer flood Type 3 LSAs into area 34, as shown in Example 7-8. R3 displays its LSDB, listing only two Summary (Type 3) LSAs–the two default routes advertised by the two ABRs, respectively. No other Type 3 LSAs exist, nor do any external (Type 5) or ASBR summary (Type 4) LSAs.

Also, note that the example lists the OSPF routes known to R3. Interestingly, in the topology shown for area 34, R3 learns only three OSPF routes: the two intra-area routes for the subnets between R4 and the two ABRs, plus the best default route. The default route has a metric of 501, based on R3's S0/0/0.1 interface cost plus the cost 1 listed for R1's Type 3 LSA for the default route.

Example 7-8   *Confirmation of the Effects of a Totally Stubby Area*

```
! On Router R3: show ip ospf database, show ip route ospf, get show ip ospf
database database-summary –
R3#show ip route
Codes: C - connected, S - static, R - RIP, M - mobile, B - BGP
       D - EIGRP, EX - EIGRP external, O - OSPF, IA - OSPF inter area
       N1 - OSPF NSSA external type 1, N2 - OSPF NSSA external type 2
       E1 - OSPF external type 1, E2 - OSPF external type 2
       i - IS-IS, su - IS-IS summary, L1 - IS-IS level-1, L2 - IS-IS level-2
       ia - IS-IS inter area, * - candidate default, U - per-user static route
       o - ODR, P - periodic downloaded static route

Gateway of last resort is 10.10.13.1 to network 0.0.0.0


     10.0.0.0/8 is variably subnetted, 5 subnets, 2 masks
C       10.10.13.0/29 is directly connected, Serial0/0/0.1
O       10.10.14.0/29 [110/657] via 10.10.34.4, 00:57:37, FastEthernet0/0
C       10.10.23.0/29 is directly connected, Serial0/0/0.2
O       10.10.24.0/29 [110/657] via 10.10.34.4, 00:57:37, FastEthernet0/0
C       10.10.34.0/24 is directly connected, FastEthernet0/0
O*IA 0.0.0.0/0 [110/501] via 10.10.13.1, 00:24:35, Serial0/0/0.1


R3#show ip ospf database database-summary

             OSPF Router with ID (3.3.3.3) (Process ID 3)
```

```
! lines omitted for brevity

Process 3 database summary
   LSA Type        Count    Delete    Maxage
   Router          4        0         0
   Network         1        0         0
   Summary Net     2        0         0
   Summary ASBR    0        0         0
   Type-7 Ext      0        0         0
   Opaque Link     0        0         0
   Opaque Area     0        0         0
   Type-5 Ext      0        0         0
       Prefixes redistributed in Type-5   0
   Opaque AS       0        0         0
   Non-self        6
   Total           7        0         0


R3#show ip ospf database ¦ begin Summary
              Summary Net Link States (Area 34)


Link ID         ADV Router       Age        Seq#        Checksum
0.0.0.0         1.1.1.1          1407        0x80000003 0x008FA8
0.0.0.0         2.2.2.2          1506        0x80000004 0x00FF3E
```

Following are the three commands in Example 7-8 in order:

- **show ip route–**It lists a single interarea route–a default route, with destination 0.0.0.0/0. The output also lists this same next-hop information as the gateway of last resort.

- **show ip ospf database database-summary–**The statistics still show no External Type 5 LSAs, just as when the area was stubby, but now shows only 2 Type 3 LSAs, whereas before a few dozen existed.

- **show ip ospf database | begin Summary–**This command shows the output beginning with the Type 3 Summary LSAs. It lists two default route LSAs: one from R1 and one from R2.

Examples 7-6 and 7-8 demonstrate the key differences between stub (they do see Type 3 LSAs) and totally stubby areas (which do not see Type 3 LSAs). Next, this section looks at the different types of not-so-stubby areas.

The Not-So-Stubby Area (NSSA)

Stub and totally stubby areas do not allow external routes to be injected into a stubby area–a feature that originally caused some problems. The problem is based on the fact that stub areas by definition should never learn a Type 5 LSA, and OSPF injects external routes into OSPF as Type 5 LSAs. These two facts together mean that a stubby area could not normally have an ASBR that was injecting external routes into the stub area.

The not-so-stubby area (NSSA) option for stubby areas overcomes the restriction on external routes. The solution itself is simple: Because stubby areas can have no Type 5 LSAs, later OSPF RFCs defined a newer LSA type (Type 7) that serves the same purpose as the Type 5 LSA, but only for external routes in stubby areas. So, an NSSA area can act just like a stub area, except that routers can inject external routes into the area.

Figure 7-10 shows an example, with four steps. The same stubby area 34 from the last few figures still exists; it does not matter at this point whether area 34 is totally stubby or simply stubby.

Figure 7-10   *External Routes in an NSSA Area (34)*

The steps labeled in the figure are as follows:

Step 1.   ASBR R3 learns routes from some external source of routing information, in this case, EIGRP from R9.

Step 2.   An engineer configures route redistribution using the **redistribute** command, taking the routes learned with EIGRP, and injecting them into OSPF.

Step 3.   R3 floods Type 7 LSAs throughout stub area 34.

Step 4.   ABRs R1 and R2 then create Type 5 LSAs for the subnets listed in the Type 7 LSAs, and flood these Type 5 LSAs into other areas, like area 0.

The configuration of an NSSA area requires only a little effort compared to configuring stubby and totally stubby areas: Just use the **area nssa** command instead of the **area stub** command, with no differences in other parameters. NSSA areas can be simply stubby, filtering only external routes from getting into the area, or totally stubby. The NSSA designation just defines whether routers in that area can redistribute external routes into OSPF.

Example 7-9 shows a sample with the configuration of a totally NSSA area 34 from the network represented in the last four figures. Note that as with the **area stub** command, the **area nssa** command's **no-summary** option is required only on the ABRs.

Example 7-9 *Totally NSSA Area Configuration and Verification*

```
! On Router R1:
router ospf 1
 area 34 nssa no-summary
! On Router R2:
router ospf 2
 area 34 nssa no-summary
 area 34 default-cost 500
! On Router R3:
router ospf 3
 area 34 nssa
! On Router R4:
router ospf 4
 area 34 nssa
```

The same verification steps and commands can be used for NSSA areas as were shown in the earlier examples for stub areas. In particular, the **show ip ospf** command states that the area is an NSSA area. You can also see Type 7 LSAs in the OSPF LSDB after redistribution has been configured, as shown in Chapter 9.

Stubby Area Summary

Table 7-4 summarizes the key points regarding stubby areas.

Table 7-4 *OSPF Stubby Area Types*

Area Type	ABRs flood Type 5 External LSAs into the area?	ABRs flood Type 3 Summary LSAs into the area?	Allows redistribution of external LSAs into the stubby area?
Stub	No	Yes	No
Totally stubby	No	No	No
NSSA	No	Yes	Yes
Totally NSSA	No	No	Yes

Note: Both types of totally stubby areas (totally stubby, totally NSSA) are Cisco proprietary.

Exam Preparation Tasks

Planning Practice

The CCNP ROUTE exam expects test takers to review design documents, create implementation plans, and create verification plans. This section provides some exercises that may help you to take a step back from the minute details of the topics in this chapter so that you can think about the same technical topics from the planning perspective.

For each planning practice table, simply complete the table. Note that any numbers in parentheses represent the number of options listed for each item in the solutions in Appendix F, "Completed Planning Practice Tables."

Design Review Table

Table 7-5 lists several design goals related to this chapter. If these design goals were listed in a design document, and you had to take that document and develop an implementation plan, what implementation options come to mind? For any configuration items, a general description can be used, without concern about the specific parameters.

Table 7-5 *Design Review*

Design Goal	Possible Implementation Choices Covered in This Chapter
When using OSPF, prevent the routers in sites for one division of the company from knowing IP routes for subnets in another division. (3)	
The design shows an Enterprise that uses only OSPF. It lists a goal of keeping the LSDBs and routing tables in each area small. (3)	
The design lists a goal of extremely small LSDBs and IP routing tables on branch office routers–which stub area types work best? (2)	
The design calls for the flooding of a domain-wide default route to draw traffic toward the Internet-connected routers.	

Implementation Plan Peer Review Table

Table 7-6 shows a list of questions that others might ask, or that you might think about, during a peer review of another network engineer's implementation plan. Complete the table by answering the questions.

Table 7-6 *Notable Questions from This Chapter to Consider During an Implementation Plan Peer Review*

Question	Answers
The plan shows a design with area 0, with different ABRs connecting area 0 to areas 1, 2, and 3. The configurations show Type 3 LSA filtering into the nonbackbone areas but not in the opposite direction. Could this configuration filter subnets in area 1 from being seen in area 2?	
The design shows the configuration of Type 3 LSA filtering on an internal router in area 1. Could the filter have any effect?	
The plan shows the configuration of the **area range** command on an ABR. What is the metric for the summary route? And in what conditions will the ABR advertise the summary?	
The plan shows the configuration of the **area 1 stub** command for an area mostly located on the west coast of the USA. The company just bought another company whose sites are also on the west coast. What issues exist if you add links from the acquired company into area 1?	
The plan shows the configuration of the **default-information originate always** command on the one router to which the Internet links connect. What happens to default route when Internet link fails? What happens to packets destined for the Internet during this time?	

Create an Implementation Plan Table

To practice skills useful when creating your own OSPF implementation plan, list in Table 7-7 configuration commands related to the configuration of the following features. You may want to record your answers outside the book, and set a goal to complete this table (and others like it) from memory during your final reviews before taking the exam.

Table 7-7 *Implementation Plan Configuration Memory Drill*

Feature	Configuration Commands/Notes
Filter Type 3 LSAs from being sent into an area.	
Filter the OSPF routes calculated on one router from being added to that one router's routing table.	
Configure route summarization on ABRs.	
Configure route summarization on ASBRs.	
Configure the OSPF domain-wide advertisement of a default route.	
Configure stubby or totally stubby areas.	
Configure NSSA or totally NSSA areas.	

Choose Commands for a Verification Plan Table

To practice skills useful when creating your own OSPF verification plan, list in Table 7-8 all commands that supply the requested information. You may want to record your answers outside the book, and set a goal to complete this table (and others like it) from memory during your final reviews before taking the exam.

Table 7-8 *Verification Plan Memory Drill*

Information Needed	Command(s)
Display all IP routes for subnets in a range, regardless of prefix length.	
Display the contents of an IP prefix list.	
Display details of all Type 3 LSAs known to a router.	
Display details of all Type 5 external LSAs known to a router.	
Display the metric advertised in a summary route created by the **area range** command.	
Display the metric advertised in a summary route created by the **summary-address** command.	
Discover whether a router resides in a stubby area, and if so, which kind.	
Confirm stubby area concepts by looking at the numbers of Type 3 and Type 5 LSAs known to a router.	

Note: Some of the entries in this table may not have been specifically mentioned in this chapter but are listed in this table for review and reference.

Review All the Key Topics

Review the most important topics from inside the chapter, noted with the key topics icon in the outer margin of the page. Table 7-9 lists a reference of these key topics and the page numbers on which each is found.

Key Topic

Table 7-9 *Key Topics for Chapter 7*

Key Topic Element	Description	Page Number
List	Explanations of the features of the **area range** command	232
List	Explanations of the features of the **summary-address** command	235

Complete the Tables and Lists from Memory

Print a copy of Appendix D, "Memory Tables," (found on the CD), or at least the section for this chapter, and complete the tables and lists from memory. Appendix E, "Memory Tables Answer Key," also on the CD, includes completed tables and lists to check your work.

Define Key Terms

Define the following key terms from this chapter, and check your answers in the glossary.

Type 3 LSA Filtering, Stub area, Totally stubby area, Not-so-stubby area, Type 5 External LSA

This chapter covers the following subjects:

Virtual Links: This section examines how engineers can use virtual links to connect separate parts of an area through another area to maintain the requirement that OSPF areas be contiguous.

OSPF over Frame Relay: This section examines the issues related to multipoint Frame Relay designs and configurations, in particular issues related to neighbor discovery or definition, whether the routers use a DR, and issues related to Frame Relay mapping.

CHAPTER 8

OSPF Virtual Links and Frame Relay Operations

This chapter contains two topics that at first glance seem to have little in common. The first topic, OSPF virtual links, gives network designers a tool to overcome an area design issue that occurs from time to time. The second topic, making OSPF work over Frame Relay multipoint interfaces, focuses on the implementation choices with different IOS commands when using OSPF with Frame Relay.

Although unrelated from a technology perspective, these two OSPF topics share that both provide a solution to specific types of problems–problems that occur in a small percentage of OSPF internetworks. Because these features solve particular (but different) problems, rather than include these topics in Chapters 5, 6, or 7–which cover the most central and common OSPF features–we decided to put these less-commonly seen features here in Chapter 8. Hopefully, this separation allowed a little more focus in the other OSPF chapters, while still including these two topics in the book.

"Do I Know This Already?" Quiz

The "Do I Know This Already?" quiz allows you to assess if you should read the entire chapter. If you miss no more than one of these five self-assessment questions, you might want to move ahead to the "Exam Preparation Tasks." Table 8-1 lists the major headings in this chapter and the "Do I Know This Already?" quiz questions covering the material in those headings so that you can assess your knowledge of these specific areas. The answers to the "Do I Know This Already?" quiz appear in Appendix A.

Table 8-1 *"Do I Know This Already?" Foundation Topics Section-to-Question Mapping*

Foundations Topics Section	Questions
Virtual Links	1, 2
OSPF over Frame Relay	3–5

1. Which of the following answers can be verified as true based on the following command output from Router R1?

```
R1#show ip ospf virtual-links
Virtual Link OSPF_VL0 to router 4.4.4.4 is up
  Run as demand circuit
  DoNotAge LSA allowed.
```

```
Transit area 1, via interface FastEthernet0/1, Cost of using 3
```

    a. R1 is configured with an **area 0 virtual-link 4.4.4.4 cost** 3 command.

    b. The **ping 4.4.4.4** command on R1 must currently be successful.

    c. R1's Fa0/0 OSPF cost is 3.

    d. 4.4.4.4 is known to R1 based on a Type 1 LSA in area 1.

2. Several links have been broken so that for the next day or two, what was formerly a contiguous area 0 has been broken into two parts. However, both parts of area 0 have working links into area 1 using routers with RID 1.1.1.1 and 2.2.2.2. Which answers list the command on the router with RID 1.1.1.1 to create a virtual link to help solve this temporary problem?

    a. area 0 virtual-link 2.2.2.2

    b. area 1 virtual-link 2.2.2.2

    c. area 0 source-rid 1.1.1.1 dest-rid 2.2.2.2

    d. virtual-link transit-area 1 RID 2.2.2.2

3. Router R1 connects to a Frame Relay cloud using a multipoint subinterface, with ten PVCs associated with the subinterface. What command would make this router not use a DR and require static OSPF neighbor definition?

    a. ip ospf network broadcast

    b. ip ospf network non-broadcast

    c. ip ospf network point-to-multipoint

    d. ip ospf network point-to-multipoint non-broadcast

4. Router R1 connects to a Frame Relay cloud using a multipoint subinterface, with ten PVCs associated with the subinterface. What command would make this router not use a DR, and dynamically discover OSPF neighbors?

    a. ip ospf network broadcast

    b. ip ospf network non-broadcast

    c. ip ospf network point-to-multipoint

    d. ip ospf network point-to-multipoint non-broadcast

5. Ten routers, R1 through R10, connect in a partial mesh over Frame Relay. For the mesh, R1 and R2 have PVCs connected to all other routers, but Routers R3 through R10 act as branch routers, with only two PVCs–one to R1 and one to R2. The routers use IP subnet 10.1.1.0/24, with addresses 10.1.1.1, 10.1.1.2, and so on, through 10.1.1.10, respectively. The routers all use Inverse ARP to learn Frame Relay mapping information. All routers use a multipoint subinterface with network type point-to-multipoint nonbroadcast. A co-worker's implementation plan lists lots of configuration commands related to this design. The design states that all hosts should be able to ping all other hosts. Which commands are required for proper functioning of OSPF in this case? (Choose two.)

   a. **frame-relay map** commands on R3–R10 referencing the other routers in this group.

   b. Nine OSPF **neighbor** commands on each router.

   c. Nine OSPF **neighbor** commands on R1 and R2, with only two such commands on R3–R10.

   d. R1 and R2 with **ip ospf priority 1** commands to ensure they become DR and BDR.

   e. R3–R10 with **ip ospf priority 0** commands to ensure they do not become DR or BDR.

Foundation Topics

Virtual Links

OSPF area design requires the use of a backbone area, area 0, with each area connecting to area 0 through an ABR. However, in some cases two backbone areas exist; in other cases, a nonbackbone area may not have a convenient point of connection to the backbone area, for example:

Case 1. An existing internetwork needs to add a new area, with a convenient, low-cost connection point with another nonbackbone area. However, that connection does not give the new area any connection to area 0.

Case 2. Even with a well-designed area 0, a combination of link failures might result in a discontiguous backbone area, essentially creating two backbone areas.

Case 3. Two companies could merge, each using OSPF. To merge the OSPF domains, one backbone area must exist. It may be more convenient to connect the two networks using links through an existing nonbackbone area, but that design means two backbone areas, which is not allowed.

Figure 8-1 shows an example of each of the first two cases.

The problems in each case have different symptoms, but the problems all stem from the area design requirements: Each area should be contiguous, and each nonbackbone area should connect to the backbone area through an ABR. When the network does not meet these requirements, engineers could simply redesign the areas. However, OSPF provides an alternative tool called an OSPF virtual link.

Understanding OSPF Virtual Link Concepts

An OSPF virtual link allows two ABRs that connect to the same nonbackbone area to form a neighbor relationship through that nonbackbone area, even when separated by many other routers and subnets. This virtual link acts like a virtual point-to-point connection between the two routers, with that link inside area 0. The routers form a neighbor relationship, inside area 0, and flood LSAs over that link.

For example, consider the topology in Figure 8-2, which shows an example of the third of the three cases described in the beginning of this section. In this case, two companies merged. Both companies had a small office in the same city, so for expediency's sake, they connected the two former Enterprise internetworks through a newly combined local sales office in area 1.

Although adding the link between branch offices may be a cost-effective temporary choice, it creates a design problem: Two backbone areas now exist, and OSPF requires that the backbone area be contiguous. To solve this problem, the engineer configures a virtual link between ABRs C1 and C2. The virtual link exists inside area 0, making area 0 contiguous.

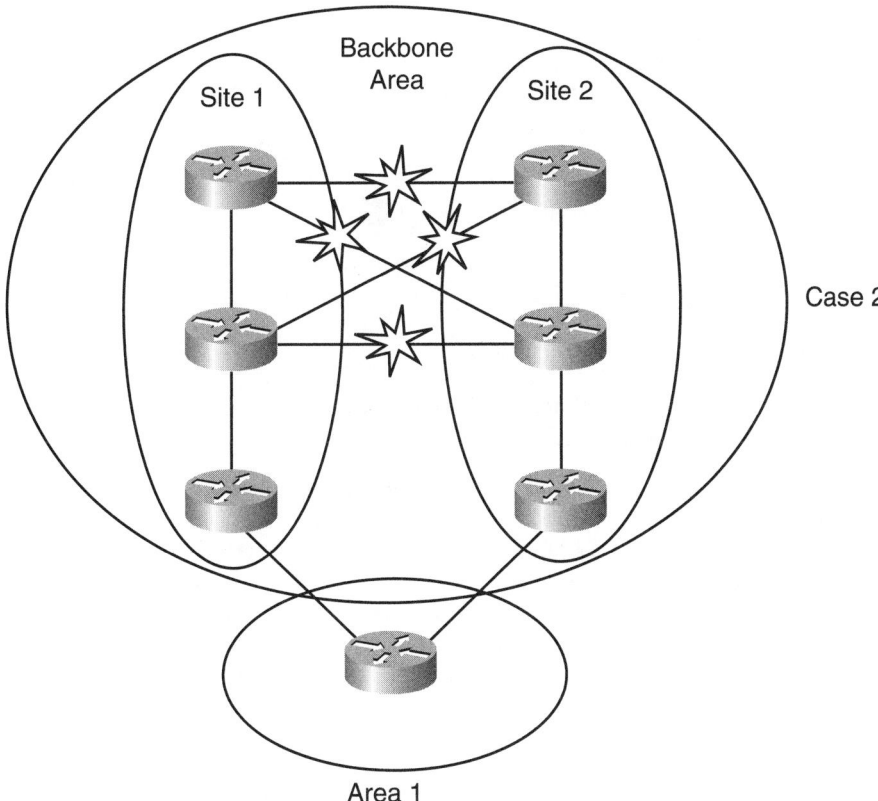

Figure 8-1   *Examples of Area Design Issues*

To define the virtual link, each router configures the other router's RID and a reference to
the area through which the virtual link passes (area 1 in this case). The two routers send
the usual OSPF message types, encapsulated inside unicast IP packets, with a destination
IP address of the router on the other end of the virtual link. Any routers between the two
routers that create the virtual link—for instance, the two branch routers in Figure 8-2—
just forward these OSPF packets like any other packet. The neighbors on the ends of the
virtual link flood their LSDBs to each other so that all routers in both parts of area 0 learn
the routes from the other area 0.

Figure 8-2   *Connecting Two Area 0s with a Virtual Link*

The ABRs connected over a virtual link act mostly like any other ABR, with a couple of differences. The first difference is that ABRs send all OSPF messages as unicasts to the IP address of the router on the other end of the link. Second, the routers also mark the *Do Not Age (DNA)* bit in the LSAs, meaning that all routers on the other side of the virtual link will not expect the LSAs to be reflooded over the virtual link on the usual 30-minute refresh interval. This helps reduce overhead over the virtual link, which often runs over slower links and less-powerful routers. The router also assigns an OSPF cost to the virtual link, just as it would for an interface.

After the virtual link is up, the ABRs' SPF processes can calculate their best routes just like before, using the virtual link as another point-to-point link in area 0. For packets destined to pass from one part of the backbone over the virtual link to the other part of the backbone, the chosen best routes eventually lead the packets to the router with the virtual link. That router, connected to the transit nonbackbone area, has already calculated its next hop based on the LSDB in the transit area (Router C1 and transit area 1 in the example of Figure 8-2). The routers in the transit area choose routes that eventually deliver the packet to the router on the other end of the virtual link (Router C2 in Figure 8-2).

Configuring OSPF Virtual Links with No Authentication

Configuring an OSPF virtual link requires a minor amount of configuration just to get the link working, with several optional configuration items. Most of the optional configuration settings relate to features that would normally be configured on the interface connecting two neighboring routers, but with a virtual link, there is no such interface, so the parameters must be added to the **area virtual-link** command. The following list summarizes the key configuration options on the **area virtual-link** router subcommand:

- The *remote-RID* in the **area** *area-num* **virtual-link** *remote-RID* command refers to the other router's RID.

- The *area-num* in the **area** *area-num* **virtual-link** *remote-RID* command refers to the transit area over which the packets flow between the two routers.

- The transit area over which the two routers communicate must not be a stubby area.

- The optional configuration of OSPF neighbor authentication parameters, normally configured as interface subcommands, must be configured as additional parameters on the **area virtual-link** command.

- The optional configuration of Hello and Dead intervals, normally configured as interface subcommands, must be configured as additional parameters on the **area virtual-link** command.

- The router assigns the virtual link an OSPF cost as if it were a point-to-point link. The router calculates the cost as the cost to reach the router on the other end of the link, as calculated using the transit area's LSDB.

Key Topic

Example 8-1 shows the configuration of a virtual link on Router C1 and Router C2 shown in Figure 8-2. The configuration shows the virtual link, referencing area 1 as the transit area, with each router referring to the other router's RIDs. The configuration also shows the loopback IP addresses on which the ABR's RIDs are based being advertised into OSPF.

Example 8-1   *OSPF Virtual Link Configuration on Routers C1 and C2*

```
! On Router C1:
router ospf 1
 area 1 virtual-link 4.4.4.4
!
interface fastethernet0/0
 ip address 10.1.1.1 255.255.255.0
 ip ospf 1 area 0
!
interface fastethernet0/1
 ip address 10.21.1.1 255.255.255.0
 ip ospf 1 area 1
!
interface loopback 1
 ip address 1.1.1.1 255.255.255.0
 ip ospf 1 area 1

! On Router C2:
router ospf 4
 area 1 virtual-link 1.1.1.1
```

```
!
interface fastethernet0/0
 ip address 10.1.1.1 255.255.255.0
 ip ospf 4 area 0
!
interface fastethernet0/1
 ip address 10.21.1.1 255.255.255.0
 ip ospf 4 area 1
!
interface loopback 1
 ip address 4.4.4.4 255.255.255.0
 ip ospf 4 area 1
```

Verifying the OSPF Virtual Link

To prove whether the virtual link works, a neighbor relationship between C1 and C2 must reach FULL state, resulting in all routers in both parts of area 0 having the same area 0 LSDB. Example 8-2 shows the working neighbor relationship, plus status information for the virtual link with the **show ip ospf virtual-link** command.

Example 8-2 *OSPF Virtual Link Configuration on Routers C1 and C2*

```
C1#show ip ospf virtual-links
Virtual Link OSPF_VL0 to router 4.4.4.4 is up
  Run as demand circuit
  DoNotAge LSA allowed.
  Transit area 1, via interface FastEthernet0/1, Cost of using 3
  Transmit Delay is 1 sec, State POINT_TO_POINT,
  Timer intervals configured, Hello 10, Dead 40, Wait 40, Retransmit 5
    Hello due in 00:00:02
    Adjacency State FULL (Hello suppressed)
    Index 1/2, retransmission queue length 0, number of retransmission 0
    First 0x0(0)/0x0(0) Next 0x0(0)/0x0(0)
    Last retransmission scan length is 0, maximum is 0
    Last retransmission scan time is 0 msec, maximum is 0 msec
!
! next, note that the neighbor reaches FULL state, with no DR elected.

C1#show ip ospf neighbor

Neighbor ID     Pri   State          Dead Time   Address         Interface
4.4.4.4           0   FULL/  -           -        10.24.1.1       OSPF_VL0
2.2.2.2           1   FULL/DR        00:00:35     10.21.1.2
FastEthernet0/1
```

```
C1#show ip ospf neighbor detail 4.4.4.4
 Neighbor 4.4.4.4, interface address 10.24.1.1
    In the area 0 via interface OSPF_VL0
    Neighbor priority is 0, State is FULL, 6 state changes
    DR is 0.0.0.0 BDR is 0.0.0.0
    Options is 0x32 in Hello (E-bit, L-bit, DC-bit)
    Options is 0x72 in DBD (E-bit, L-bit, DC-bit, O-bit)
    LLS Options is 0x1 (LR)
    Neighbor is up for 00:00:21
    Index 1/2, retransmission queue length 0, number of retransmission 0
    First 0x0(0)/0x0(0) Next 0x0(0)/0x0(0)
    Last retransmission scan length is 0, maximum is 0
   Last retransmission scan time is 0 msec, maximum is 0 msec
```

The only new command in the example, **show ip ospf virtual-links**, details some items unique to virtual links. In particular, the first highlighted portion shows the assignment of a name to the link (VL0); if multiple were configured, each would have a different number. This virtual link name/number is then referenced inside the LSDB. It also shows that the routers both allow the use of the Do Not Age (DNA) bit, so periodic reflooding will not occur over this virtual link. It lists a cost of 3; as it turns out, each of the three interfaces between Router C1 and C2 have an OSPF cost of 1, so C1's area 1 cost to reach C4 is 3. The output also confirms that the routers have reached a fully adjacent state and is suppressing the periodic Hello messages.

The familiar **show ip ospf neighbor** command lists a few new items as well. Note that the interface refers to the virtual link "OSPF VL0" instead of the interface, because there is no interface between the neighbors. It also lists no dead timer, because the neighbors choose to not use the usual Hello/Dead interval process over a virtual link. (Instead, if all the transit area's routes to reach the router on the other router of the link fail, the virtual link fails.) Finally, the **show ip ospf neighbor detail 4.4.4.4** command shows the interesting phrase "In the area 0 via interface OSPF VL0," confirming that the neighborship does indeed exist in area 0.

Note: OSPF does not require that the RID IP address range be advertised as a route in OSPF. As a result, the RID listed in the **area virtual-link** command may not be pingable, but the virtual link still work.

Configuring Virtual Link Authentication

Because virtual links have no underlying interface on which to configure authentication, authentication is configured on the **area virtual-link** command itself. Table 8-2 shows the variations of the command options for configuring authentication on virtual links. Note that the configuration shown in Table 8-2 may be typed in one longer **area virtual-link** command, as shown in the table, or the authentication type and key can be configured on separate **area virtual-link** commands. Regardless, IOS stores two different **area virtual-link** commands into the running-config: one command that enables the type of authentication, and one that lists the authentication key, as shown in upcoming Example 8-3.

Key
Topic

Table 8-2   *Configuring OSPF Authentication on Virtual Links*

Type (Name)	Type (Number)	Command Syntax for Virtual Links
none	0	**area** *num* **virtual-link** *router-id* **authentication null**
clear text	1	**area** *num* **virtual-link** *router-id* **authentication authentication-key** *key-value*
MD5	2	**area** *num* **virtual-link** *router-id* **authentication message-digest message-digest-key** *key-num* **md5** *key-value*

Example 8-3 shows a modified version of the configuration shown in Example 8-2, now with MD5 authentication configured on both C1 and C2.

Example 8-3   *OSPF Virtual Link Configuration on Routers C1 and C2*

```
! On Router C1 - configuring the authentication type and key
Router ospf 1
 Area 1 virtual-link 4.4.4.4 authentication message-digest message-digest-key 1
md5 fred
! On Router C2 - configuring the authentication type and key
router ospf 4
 Area 1 virtual-link 1.1.1.1 authentication message-digest message-digest-key 1
md5 fred
!
! The router separated the authentication type and authentication key
! into two separate commands.
C2#show running-config
! line omitted for brevity
router ospf 4
 area 1 virtual-link 1.1.1.1 authentication message-digest
 area 1 virtual-link 1.1.1.1 message-digest-key 1 md5 fred

C2#show ip ospf virtual-links
Virtual Link OSPF_VL0 to router 1.1.1.1 is up
! lines omitted for brevity
 Message digest authentication enabled
   Youngest key id is 1
```

This concludes the discussion of OSPF virtual links. As mentioned in the introduction of this chapter, the chapter now changes focus completely to discuss OSPF issues when using Frame Relay.

OSPF over Multipoint Frame Relay

To form OSPF neighbor relationships on LANs and point-to-point WAN interfaces, OSPF simply needs to be enabled on the interface, and the neighboring routers must agree to a set of parameters (as summarized in Chapter 5, Table 5-5.) However, when using Frame Relay in certain configurations, engineers must do more implementation planning and use additional configuration commands to make OSPF work. Additionally, the people monitoring and operating the network must also understand several differences in how OSPF works in such cases and be ready to interpret the output of **show** commands.

The issues described in this section of the chapter arise when the IP subnetting and Frame Relay design places more than two WAN routers into a single subnet. Such a design requires multipoint logic, either configured on the physical serial interface or on a multipoint subinterface.

This section begins by reviewing the IP subnetting design issues that can lead to the broader OSPF issues over Frame Relay. Next, this section examines the issues of running OSPF over Frame Relay, concentrating on the concepts. This final part of this section ends with several OSPF configuration examples using multipoint Frame Relay.

IP Subnetting Design over Frame Relay

When planning the subnets to use over a Frame Relay WAN, the design engineer has several options. The simplest and most obvious choice uses a single subnet for every PVC (as seen throughout the examples in Chapters 5, 6, and 7), with all routers using point-to-point subinterfaces associated with each single PVC. Most companies who still use Frame Relay today still use such a subnetting design.

In some cases, a shortage of IP addresses may make a design engineer choose to use fewer WAN subnets, with less waste. Many companies use private IP addresses inside their Enterprise internetwork–often times specifically class A network 10.0.0.0–and most companies do not have a shortage of IP addresses and subnets available. However, using one subnet per PVC does consume more IP addresses than the alternative–to put more than two routers into a Frame Relay WAN subnet. You get the advantage of fewer IP addresses consumed in the WAN but the penalty of more configuration and complexity with the OSPF implementation.

For example, consider the two internetworks shown in Figure 8-3. On the left, four routers connect in a full mesh of PVCs, whereas on the right, the four routers use a partial mesh. In each case, assume each router uses their s0/0/0 interface to connect to the cloud.

First, consider the differences in IP addressing for the one-subnet-per-PVC choice and the single-subnet choice. The single-subnet design could use just one subnet–for instance, subnet 10.1.1.0/29, with usable address 10.1.1.1–10.1.1.6 (subnet broadcast 10.1.1.7). With four routers, the subnet contains enough IP addresses for each router, plus two additional addresses. Conversely, with a single-subnet-per-PVC, the design would require six subnets,

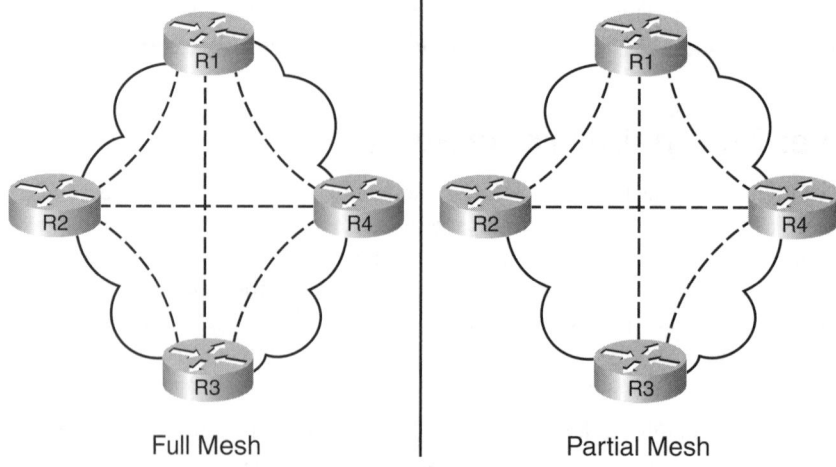

Full Mesh   Partial Mesh

Figure 8-3   *Sample Full and Partial Mesh Frame Relay*

each of which consumes four numbers: subnet number, two usable IP addresses, and a
subnet broadcast address. For example, the design could use subnets 10.1.1.0/30,
10.1.1.4/30, 10.1.1.8/30, 10.1.1.12/30, 10.1.1.16/30, and 10.1.1.20.0/30 for a range of consumed numbers of 10.1.1.0–10.1.1.23.

Sample Configuration Using Physical Interfaces

Ignoring OSPF for now, to implement such a design on the internetwork shown in Figure
8-3, a somewhat short configuration could be used on each router. Example 8-4 shows the
configuration, with the IP addresses being defined on the physical serial interfaces on
each router.

Example 8-4   *OSPF over Point-to-Point Frame Relay Subinterfaces*

```
! Router R1
interface S0/0/0
 encapsulation frame-relay
 ip address 10.2.123.1 255.255.255.248
! Router R2
interface S0/0/0
 encapsulation frame-relay
 ip address 10.2.123.2 255.255.255.248
! Router R3
interface S0/0/0
 encapsulation frame-relay
 ip address 10.2.123.3 255.255.255.248
! Router R4
interface S0/0/0
 encapsulation frame-relay
 ip address 10.2.123.4 255.255.255.248
```

This brief configuration works in part because of many default settings. IOS enables Frame Relay Inverse ARP (InARP) by default, so all four routers learn of the other routers' IP address/DLCI mappings dynamically. All PVCs learned on the interface will be associated with the physical interface.

As a result, after creating this configuration, with a working Frame Relay network, the four routers can **ping** each other in every case for which a PVC exists between the two routers. In other words, in the full mesh case, all four routers should ping the other three routers' IP addresses in the 10.1.1.0/29 subnet. In the partial mesh case, the R1/R3 pair cannot ping each other.

The ping problem between R1 and R3 demonstrates some key concepts related to how Frame Relay mapping works. InARP allows the routers to learn the IP address of any router on the other end of a PVC, but R1/R3 do not have a PVC connecting them in the partial mesh side of Figure 8-3, so InARP does not learn the mapping. Then, when R1 (10.2.123.1) wants to send a packet to 10.2.123.3 (R3), R1 looks at its Frame Relay mapping information and does not find 10.2.123.3. As a result, R1 discards the packet because it does not know what DLCI to use to forward the packet.

Sample Configuration Using Multipoint Subinterfaces

The same effects occur with a valid alternate configuration using a multipoint subinterface, both in the full and partial mesh cases. When using subinterfaces, IOS needs a command under a Frame Relay subinterface that associates each PVC with that subinterface: either a **frame-relay interface-dlci** command or **frame-relay map** command. The **frame-relay interface-dlci** command just associates the DLCI with the subinterface, relying on Frame Relay InARP to discover mappings. The second command (**frame-relay map**) statically configures that mapping, while also associating the DLCI with the subinterface.

Example 8-5 shows an alternative configuration on Router R1, using a multipoint subinterface. All four routers could mimic the same configuration, but that configuration is not shown in the example.

Example 8-5   *OSPF over Multipoint Frame Relay Subinterfaces*

```
! Router R1
interface S0/0/0
 encapsulation frame-relay
!
interface S0/0/0.1 multipoint
 ip address 10.1.123.1 255.255.255.248
 frame-relay interface-dlci 102
 frame-relay interface-dlci 103
 frame-relay interface-dlci 104
```

This configuration on R1, with similar configuration on the other three routers, has the same results as those with Example 8-4. When a full mesh exists, all routers should be pingable. With a partial mesh, all routers should be pingable, except those with no PVC between the two routers (R1/R3 in this case).

With those background details in mind, the chapter now examines the challenges that arise when trying to use multipoint.

OSPF Challenges When Using Multipoint

Next, consider OSPF over both the full and partial meshes as described in the last few pages. As it turns out, if you enabled OSPF on the interfaces, but do not add OSPF configuration, OSPF does not form neighborships in either case.

Note: Rather than repeat the long phrase "on physical interfaces or on multipoint interfaces" many times in the coming pages, the rest of this chapter simply refers to both as "multipoint interfaces," because more than one destination may be reachable through these types of interfaces.

The default OSPF network type on multipoint interfaces–the nonbroadcast network type–prevents OSPF from working without further configuration. Additionally, depending on the configuration you add to make OSPF work, the network may appear to be working in that the correct routes are learned, but packets cannot be forwarded. Worse yet, packet forwarding could work when testing, but later, when the DR in that subnet failed, packet forwarding could fail, even though paths exist over different PVCs.

To avoid such pitfalls, this section examines the issues. To understand the issues, an engineer needs to know the answer to three questions related to OSPF over Frame Relay multipoint interfaces:

■   Do the routers attempt to discover neighbors by sending and receiving multicast OSPF Hello messages, or do the neighbors require static definition?

■   Do the routers attempt to elect a DR/BDR?

■   Does a partial mesh exist or full mesh?

The next few pages examine these topics one at a time.

Neighbor Discovery or Static Neighbor Definition

The OSPF network type–a per-interface setting–defines whether a router attempts to discover OSPF neighbors on an interface. When the router attempts discovery, it sends multicast (224.0.0.5) OSPF Hello messages out the interface.

The first potential problem occurs when a Frame Relay configuration oversight causes the dynamic OSPF neighbor discovery process to fail. When a router needs to send a broadcast or multicast over Frame Relay, the router must actually send a copy of the packet over each PVC instead, because the Frame Relay network does not have the ability to replicate the broadcast or multicast packet. Routers do send the multicast OSPF Hellos for any PVCs listed in **frame-relay interface-dlci** commands, and for any DLCIs listed in **frame-relay map** commands if the **broadcast** keyword was included. However, if the **frame-relay map** command omits the **broadcast** keyword, that router will not replicate the OSPF multicasts, or any other broadcast or multicast frames for that DLCI.

Alternatively, some OSPF network types tell a router to not attempt automatic discovery of neighbors. In such a case, the router should be configured with the **neighbor** *ip-address* OSPF router subcommand. This command overcomes the issue with neighbor discovery.

The actions to take for the issues related to neighbor discover are somewhat straightforward:

■ If the configured network type allows for neighbor discovery using Hellos, and you use InARP, the neighbors should be discovered.

Key
Topic

■ If the configured network type allows for neighbor discovery, and you use **frame-relay map**, ensure that the **broadcast** keyword is included.

■ If the configured network type does not allow for neighbor discovery, statically configure neighbors.

The upcoming samples show cases of using network types that dynamically discover neighbors and cases that show static definition of neighbors.

To Use a Designated Router, or Not

IOS has several available OSPF network types for Frame Relay, some of which tell the router to try to elect a DR/BDR. The reasoning is that when choosing a subnet design like those shown in Figure 8-3, with a single subnet that includes more than two Frame Relay routers, the design looks like a LAN from a Layer 3 perspective. Other options for OSPF network types tell the routers to not elect a DR/BDR.

A potential issue exists when using a DR over Frame Relay. The issue relates to whether the Frame Relay partial mesh includes the right PVCs to support the OSPF messages that flow in the presence of a DR/BDR. As you may recall from Chapter 6, "OSPF Topology, Routes, and Convergence," when a DR exists, all OSPF routers must send and receive OSPF messages with the DR, with messages to the DR being sent to the 224.0.0.6 all-DR's multicast address. Additionally, the DR sends messages to the 224.0.0.5 all-SPF router's multicast address, with these messages intended for all OSPF routers in the subnet. For the same reason, all routers should send and receive messages with the BDR, in case it takes over for the DR. However, two DROther routers do not need to send each other OSPF messages.

For a Frame Relay partial mesh to work when also using an OSPF DR, a PVC must exist between any two routers that need to perform database exchange directly with each other. In short, the following PVCs must exist:

■ Between the DR and every other router in the subnet

■ Between the BDR and every other router in the subnet

For example, consider the partial mesh shown in Figure 8-4, which mirrors the partial mesh seen on the right side of Figure 8-3. In this case, R1 acts as DR, and R2 as BDR. OSPF actually works fine in this design, until the fated day when R1's serial link fails. When it fails, R2 takes over as DR, but R3 has no way to send and receive OSPF messages with R2. As a result, R3 will no longer learn routes that pass over the WAN.

Figure 8-4 *Poor Choices of BDR in a Partial Mesh*

To deal with this particular issue with a partial mesh, either avoid using a DR at all by changing the OSPF network type on all routers in the subnet, or restrict the role of DR/BDR to routers with PVCs connected to all other routers in a subnet. For example, R1 and R4 in Figure 8-4 have three PVCs, one each to the other three routers. By configuring the routers so that R2 and R3 refuse to become DR or BDR, you can avoid the case of a poor choice of DR/BDR.

Summarizing the key points about the issues in this section:

Key Topic

■   If using a network type that requires a DR/BDR, restrict the role of DR and BDR to routers that have a PVC connecting to all other routers.

■   Configure the OSPF network type to avoid using a DR/BDR.

Mapping Issues with a Partial Mesh

The last issue with OSPF over multipoint Frame Relay topologies relates to the Layer 2 mapping, either created by InARP or statically configured with **frame-relay map** commands. This mapping on a router lists each neighbor's IP address, and that router's DLCI used to reach that router. InARP learns this mapping for each router on the other end of a PVC, but not for other routers where no PVC exists. For example, in Figure 8-4, R2 and R3 would not learn mapping for each other with InARP. Similarly, when configuring the **frame-relay map** command, many engineers think only of statically creating mappings for neighboring routers on the other end of each PVC. In short, the mapping in both cases matches the partial mesh.

OSPFmultipoint interfaces have problems when the Frame Relay mapping matches the partial mesh but does not include mapping to every other router in the subnet—even those routers where no PVC exists. The best way to describe the problem is to start with an example, as seen in Figure 8-5. The figure shows the same old partial mesh, with some IP addresses and DLCIs shown.

R2's IP Routing Table

Subnet	Next-hop
10.3.3.0/26	10.2.14.3

Frame Relay Mapping

IP	DLCI
10.2.14.2	101
10.2.14.3	101
10.2.14.4	104

Figure 8-5 *Frame Relay Mapping Issues*

When OSPF works over this Frame Relay WAN, the next-hop address of the learned routes will list the IP address of a router in that WAN subnet–*even if no PVC connects to that next-hop router*. In this case, R2's route for 10.3.3.0/26 lists R3, 10.2.14.3, as next hop. When R2 attempts to add a Frame Relay header to the packet, and assign a DLCI, R2 must have a mapping between that next-hop address (10.2.14.3) and the DLCI to use to reach that next hop. However, no such Frame Relay mapping exists on R2, because R2 was relying on InARP–and InARP works only directly over a PVC and not indirectly.

To solve the problem, R2 needs a mapping for next hop 10.2.14.3 to use a DLCI to another router, allowing that other router to use IP routing to forward the packet to R3. For example, R2 could use DLCI 101, the PVC connecting R2 to R1. By doing so, R2 will encapsulate forwarded packets inside a frame with DLCI 101, sending the packet to R1. R1 will then use IP routing to forward the packet on to R3. Similarly, R3 could use a command that statically mapped 10.2.14.2, R2's IP address, to DLCI 101, which is R3's DLCI used for its PVC to R1.

Summarizing the issue and the solution to this problem:

For any routers without a direct PVC, statically configure a IP-address-to-DLCI mapping with the other router's next-hop IP address, and a DLCI that does connect to a router that has PVCs with each of the two routers

Key Topic

Configuring and Verifying OSPF Operations on Frame Relay

The concepts related to the issues of running OSPF over Frame Relay can require a bit of thought about things that many of us can ignore when working with a typical OSPF network. Thankfully, the implementation choices are a little more straightforward. When the design dictates more than two routers per subnet over Frame Relay, you need to configure Frame Relay to use either physical interfaces or multipoint subinterfaces. In those cases, only four OSPF network types exist. Then, the choice of OSPF network type answers two big questions: Will the routers try and elect a DR, and will they try to discover neighbors? From there, the rest of the implementation plan flows from the issues already discussed in this chapter.

For reference, Table 8-3 summarizes the four OSPF network types available on serial interfaces that use Frame Relay, either the physical interface or a multipoint subinterface. Note that the setting is per interface and can be set with the **ip ospf network** *type* interface subcommand; the first column in the table lists the exact keyword according to this command.

Key Topic

Table 8-3 *OSPF Network Types*

Interface Type	Uses DR/BDR?	Dynamic Discovery of Neighbors?	Default Hello Interval	Cisco Proprietary?
broadcast	Yes	Yes	10	Yes
nonbroadcast	Yes	No	30	No
point-to-multi-point	No	Yes	30	Yes
point-to-multi-point nonbroadcast	No	No	30	No

All the upcoming examples use the same network diagram as shown in Figure 8-6. After the figure, the text moves on to the examples showing this internetwork configured with three options for network type on Frame Relay serial and multipoint subinterfaces: nonbroadcast, point-to-multipoint, and point-to-multipoint nonbroadcast. (This chapter does not include a sample of using network type broadcast, because the LAN-based examples in Chapter 5 all use a default of network type broadcast.)

Note: The following samples all use multipoint subinterfaces. Also, for each example, all four routers use the same OSPF network type. However, note that IOS has no mechanism to prevent routers from using different interface types or different OSPF network types, but such inconsistency can cause problems and be very difficult to operate. Configurations that mix OSPF network types in the same subnet are outside the scope of this book.

Figure 8-6 *Sample Partial Mesh for Frame Relay Configuration*

Using Network Type Nonbroadcast (NBMA)

By using the (default) network type setting of nonbroadcast, all four routers will elect a DR and BDR. They also will not attempt to multicast Hellos to discover each other, so they need to configure each other in an OSPF **neighbor** commands, as follows:

```
neighbor next-hop-IP [cost cost-value] [priority priority-value]
```

To statically configure an OSPF neighbor, simply use the **neighbor** command in OSPF configuration mode, one command per neighbor. The command references the IP address of the neighbor, specifically the IP address in the subnet to which both the local and neighboring router connect. Also, OSPF requires only this command for two routers connected to the same PVC; routers not connected with a PVC cannot become OSPF neighbors, so no **neighbor** command is required. So, in the design shown in Figure 8-6, router pairs R2-R3, R3-R4, and R2-R4 will not define each other as neighbors with the **neighbor** command.

Next, consider the issue of election of a DR/BDR. The section "To Use a Designated Router, or Not" earlier in this chapter discussed that if a DR is indeed elected, you need to restrict routers so that only routers with PVCs to all other routers are allowed to become DR or BDR. In Figure 8-6, only R1 meets the requirement, so the configuration must limit on R1 to become the DR and simply not use a BDR. (Given the design, a failure of R1 would prevent any further communication on the WAN anyway, so the lack of a BDR does not make the problem worse.)

The OSPF priority defines the priority when choosing a DR and BDR. Configured with the **ip ospf priority** *value* interface subcommand, the higher number (ranges from 0–255) wins. Also, a priority of 0 has special meaning: it prevents that router from becoming the DR or BDR. By configuring OSPF priority of 0 on routers that do not have a PVC connected to each other router (such as R2, R3, and R4 in this case), the other routers (R1 in this case) will be the only routers eligible to become the DR.

Example 8-6 begins by showing the required configuration, defining neighbors and setting the OSPF priority on R2, R3, and R4 to 0. The example shows just R1 and R2; R3's and R4's configuration mirror R2's, other than the IP address settings.

Example 8-6 *OSPF over Multipoint Frame Relay Subinterfaces–Default Configuration*

```
! First, R1's configuration
R1#show running-config int s0/0/0.1
Building configuration...

Current configuration : 169 bytes
!
interface Serial0/0/0.1 multipoint
 ip address 10.2.123.1 255.255.255.248
 frame-relay interface-dlci 102
 frame-relay interface-dlci 103
 frame-relay interface-dlci 104
end


R1#show running-config ¦ begin router ospf
router ospf 1
 network 10.0.0.0 0.255.255.255 area 0
 router-id 1.1.1.1
 neighbor 10.2.123.2
 neighbor 10.2.123.3
 neighbor 10.2.123.4
! Next, R2's configuration
R2#show running-config interface s0/0/0.1
Building configuration...

Current configuration : 113 bytes
!
interface Serial0/0/0.1 multipoint
 ip address 10.2.123.2 255.255.255.248
 frame-relay interface-dlci 101
 ip ospf priority 0
end
```

```
R2#show running-config ¦ begin router ospf
router ospf 2
 network 10.0.0.0 0.255.255.255 area 0
 router-id 2.2.2.2
 neighbor 10.2.123.1

R2#show ip ospf interface s0/0/0.1
Serial0/0/0.1 is up, line protocol is up
  Internet Address 10.2.123.2/29, Area 0
  Process ID 2, Router ID 2.2.2.2, Network Type NON_BROADCAST, Cost: 64
  Transmit Delay is 1 sec, State DROTHER, Priority 0
  Designated Router (ID) 1.1.1.1, Interface address 10.2.123.1
  No backup designated router on this network
  Timer intervals configured, Hello 30, Dead 120, Wait 120, Retransmit 5
```

Example 8-6 shows the configuration of three neighbors on router R1 (R2, R3, and R4), plus one neighbor on R2 (R1). It does not show the explicit configuration of the OSPF network type because each router uses the default for multipoint subinterfaces of non-broadcast. However, the **show ip ospf interface** command at the end of the output confirms the network type on the multipoint subinterface of R2.

The priority configuration results in R1 becoming DR, and none of the other routers being willing to even become BDR. R1 omits an **ip ospf priority** command, defaulting to 1, while R2 shows an **ip ospf priority 0** command, removing itself from consideration as DR or BDR. The output at the bottom of the page again confirms the result on R2, with its own priority of 0, the result of RID 1.1.1.1 (R1) as DR, but with no BDR elected.

Note: You can also attempt to configure a neighboring router's OSPF priority with the **neighbor** *address* **priority** *priority-value* command.

Although the configuration shown in Example 8-6 takes care of the particulars of defining neighbors and of influencing the choice of DR/BDR, it does not, however, include the configuration for the Frame Relay mapping issue with a partial mesh. All four routers need mapping to the other three router's IP addresses in their common Frame Relay subnet. In this particular case, R1 learns all the mappings with InARP, because it has a PVC connected to all the other routers. However, R2, R3, and R4 have learned all OSPF routes but cannot forward traffic to each other because they have not learned the mappings.

Example 8-7 shows the background regarding this issue, along with an example solution on R2 using **frame-relay map** commands. Note that comments inside the example show the progression of proof and changes to solve the problem.

Example 8-7   *The Need for frame-relay map Commands*

```
! First, R2 has routes for the LAN subnets off R1, R3, and R4, each referring
! to their respective routers as the next-hop IP address
R2#show ip route ospf
     10.0.0.0/8 is variably subnetted, 5 subnets, 5 masks
O      10.4.4.0/27 [110/65] via 10.2.123.4, 00:03:52, Serial0/0/0.1
O      10.3.3.0/26 [110/65] via 10.2.123.3, 00:06:02, Serial0/0/0.1
O      10.1.1.0/24 [110/65] via 10.2.123.1, 00:06:12, Serial0/0/0.1


! Next, R2 successfully pings R1's LAN IP address


R2#ping 10.1.1.1


Type escape sequence to abort.
Sending 5, 100-byte ICMP Echos to 10.1.1.1, timeout is 2 seconds:
!!!!!
Success rate is 100 percent (5/5), round-trip min/avg/max = 4/4/4 ms


! Next, R2 fails when pinging R3's LAN IP address


R2#ping 10.3.3.3


Type escape sequence to abort.
Sending 5, 100-byte ICMP Echos to 10.3.3.3, timeout is 2 seconds:
.....
Success rate is 0 percent (0/5)


! R2 has mapping only for 10.2.123.1 in the Frame Relay subnet
R2#show frame-relay map
Serial0/0/0.1 (up): ip 10.2.123.1 dlci 101(0x65,0x1850), dynamic,
                broadcast,
                CISCO, status defined, active


! Next, the engineer adds the mapping for R3 and R4, with DLCI 101 as the
! PVC, which connects to R1


R2#configure terminal
Enter configuration commands, one per line.  End with CNTL/Z.
R2(config)#int s0/0/0.1
R2(config-subif)#frame-relay map ip 10.2.123.3 101 broadcast
R2(config-subif)#frame-relay map ip 10.2.123.4 101 broadcast
R2(config-subif)#^Z
!
! Not shown, similar mapping configured on R3 and R4
```

```
! R2 now has the necessary mappings
R2#show frame-relay map
Serial0/0/0.1 (up): ip 10.2.123.4 dlci 101(0x65,0x1850), static,
            broadcast,
            CISCO, status defined, active
Serial0/0/0.1 (up): ip 10.2.123.3 dlci 101(0x65,0x1850), static,
            broadcast,
            CISCO, status defined, active
Serial0/0/0.1 (up): ip 10.2.123.1 dlci 101(0x65,0x1850), dynamic,
            broadcast,
            CISCO, status defined, active


! Same ping now works

R2#ping 10.3.3.3

Type escape sequence to abort.
Sending 5, 100-byte ICMP Echos to 10.3.3.3, timeout is 2 seconds:
!!!!!
Success rate is 100 percent (5/5), round-trip min/avg/max = 8/8/8 ms
```

Although the example demonstrates the original problem and then the solution, it does also demonstrate a particularly difficult challenge for a verification plan. Before adding the mapping, OSPF appeared to be working on R2, because R2 had learned all the routes it should have learned. However, packet forwarding failed due to the lack of the correct Frame Relay mappings. When reviewing verification plans for the exam, take extra care when using Frame Relay, and do not rely solely on seeing OSPF routes as proof that connectivity exists between two routers.

Using Network Type Point-to-Multipoint

Network type *point-to-multipoint* tells routers to act oppositely compared to the non-broadcast type: to not elect a DR/BDR and to dynamically discover neighbors. Both options allow the routers to simply not configure additional commands. As a result, the only configuration requirement, beyond enabling OSPF on the multipoint subinterface or physical serial interface, is to configure any static Frame Relay mappings if a partial mesh exists.

Example 8-8 shows a completed OSPF configuration on Routers R1 and R2 in Figure 8-6. All the routers change their network type using the **ip ospf network point-to-multipoint** interface subcommand. The other big change as compared to using the nonbroadcast network type (as seen in Examples 8-6 and 8-7) is the absence of configuration. (Example 8-8 does show all OSPF-related configuration on R1 and R2.) As with Example 8-6, the example omits the R3 and R4 configuration, but the configuration follows the same conventions as on R2. Also, note that the routers without PVCs to each other router still require the **frame-relay map** commands (included in the example) for the same reasons as shown in Example 8-7.

Example 8-8 *Configuring Multipoint OSPF Using Network Type Point-to-Multipoint*

```
! First, R1's configuration
R1#show run int s0/0/0.1
Building configuration...

Current configuration : 169 bytes
!
interface Serial0/0/0.1 multipoint
 ip address 10.2.123.1 255.255.255.248
 frame-relay interface-dlci 102
 frame-relay interface-dlci 103
 frame-relay interface-dlci 104
 ip ospf network point-to-multipoint
end
R1#show run | begin router ospf
router ospf 1
 network 10.0.0.0 0.255.255.255 area 0
 router-id 1.1.1.1
```

```
! Next, on R2:
R2#show run int s0/0/0.1
Building configuration...

Current configuration : 169 bytes
!
interface Serial0/0/0.1 multipoint
 ip address 10.2.123.2 255.255.255.248
 frame-relay interface-dlci 101
 frame-relay map ip 10.2.123.3 101 broadcast
 frame-relay map ip 10.2.123.4 101 broadcast
 ip ospf network point-to-multipoint
end
R2#show run | begin router ospf
router ospf 1
 network 10.0.0.0 0.255.255.255 area 0
 router-id 2.2.2.2
```

Example 8-9 confirms a few details about the operation with the point-to-multipoint network type. Taken from R1, the **show ip ospf interfaces S0/0/0.1** command confirms the network type, and it also confirms full adjacency with the other three routers. Also, compared to the same command on Router R2 near the end of Example 8-6, note that this command does not even mention the concept of a DR nor BDR, because this network type does not expect to use a DR/BDR.

Example 8-9   *Confirming the Operation of Network Type Point-to-Multipoint*

```
! First, R1's configuration
R1#show ip ospf interface s0/0/0.1
Serial0/0/0.1 is up, line protocol is up
  Internet Address 10.2.123.1/29, Area 0
  Process ID 1, Router ID 1.1.1.1, Network Type POINT_TO_MULTIPOINT, Cost: 64
  Transmit Delay is 1 sec, State POINT_TO_MULTIPOINT
  Timer intervals configured, Hello 30, Dead 120, Wait 120, Retransmit 5
    oob-resync timeout 120
    Hello due in 00:00:23
  Supports Link-local Signaling (LLS)
  Cisco NSF helper support enabled
  IETF NSF helper support enabled
  Index 4/4, flood queue length 0
  Next 0x0(0)/0x0(0)
  Last flood scan length is 1, maximum is 1
  Last flood scan time is 0 msec, maximum is 0 msec
  Neighbor Count is 3, Adjacent neighbor count is 3
    Adjacent with neighbor 2.2.2.2
    Adjacent with neighbor 4.4.4.4
    Adjacent with neighbor 3.3.3.3
  Suppress hello for 0 neighbor(s)
```

Using Network Type Point-to-Multipoint Nonbroadcast

OSPF network type *point-to-multipoint nonbroadcast* tells routers to act like the similarly named point-to-multipoint type by not electing a DR/BDR. However, the difference lies in neighbor discovery–the keyword "nonbroadcast" implies that the routers cannot broadcast (or multicast) to discover neighbors.

The configuration uses a mix of the commands seen for the nonbroadcast and point-to-multipoint network types. Essentially, the configuration of priority for the purpose of influencing the DR/BDR election can be ignored, because no DR/BDR will be elected. However, the routers need **neighbor** commands to predefine neighbors. Also, regardless of network type, for those routers without direct PVCs, Frame Relay mapping must be added.

This particular OSPF network type does have some design advantages if the design also uses multipoint subinterfaces. The required **neighbor** commands also have an optional **cost** parameter so that the cost associated with each neighbor can be different. With point-to-multipoint, the router considers the dynamically discovered neighbors to be reachable with a cost equal to the cost of the associated multipoint subinterface, so the cost cannot be set per neighbor.

Example 8-10 shows the configurations on R1 and R2 for this case, with the configuration of R3 and R4 mirroring R2s.

Example 8-10 *Configuring Multipoint OSPF Using Network Type Point-to-Multipoint Nonbroadcast*

```
! First, R1's configuration
R1#show run int s0/0/0.1
Building configuration...

Current configuration : 169 bytes
!
interface Serial0/0/0.1 multipoint
 ip address 10.2.123.1 255.255.255.248
 frame-relay interface-dlci 102
 frame-relay interface-dlci 103
 frame-relay interface-dlci 104
 ip ospf network point-to-multipoint non-broadcast

end
R1#show run ¦ begin router ospf
router ospf 1
 network 10.0.0.0 0.255.255.255 area 0
 router-id 1.1.1.1
 neighbor 10.2.123.2
 neighbor 10.2.123.3
 neighbor 10.2.123.4
```

```
! Next, on R2:
R2#show run int s0/0/0.1
Building configuration...

Current configuration : 169 bytes
!
interface Serial0/0/0.1 multipoint
 ip address 10.2.123.2 255.255.255.248
 frame-relay interface-dlci 101
 frame-relay map ip 10.2.123.3 101 broadcast
 frame-relay map ip 10.2.123.4 101 broadcast
 ip ospf network point-to-multipoint non-broadcast

end
R2#show run ¦ begin router ospf
router ospf 1
 network 10.0.0.0 0.255.255.255 area 0
 router-id 2.2.2.2
 neighbor 10.2.123.1
```

Exam Preparation Tasks

Planning Practice

The CCNP ROUTE exam expects test takers to review design documents, create implementation plans, and create verification plans. This section provides some exercises that may help you to take a step back from the minute details of the topics in this chapter so that you can think about the same technical topics from the planning perspective.

For each planning practice table, simply complete the table. Note that any numbers in parentheses represent the number of options listed for each item in the solutions in Appendix F, "Completed Planning Practice Tables."

Design Review Table

Table 8-4 lists several design goals related to this chapter. If these design goals were listed in a design document, and you had to take that document and develop an implementation plan, what implementation options come to mind? For any configuration items, a general description can be used, without concern about the specific parameters.

Table 8-4 *Design Review*

Design Goal	Possible Implementation Choices Covered in This Chapter
A merger design plan shows two companies with OSPF backbone areas. How can the two areas 0 be connected? (2)	
The subnetting design over Frame Relay calls for a set of 20 routers to use a single WAN subnet. What Frame Relay interface types make sense?	
The design shows 20 routers connected to Frame Relay, in a partial mesh, with one subnet. What OSPF network type would avoid the use of DR/BDR?	
The design shows 20 routers connected to Frame Relay, in a full mesh, with one subnet. What OSPF network type would allow dynamic neighbor discovery?	

Implementation Plan Peer Review Table

Table 8-5 shows a list of questions that others might ask, or that you might think about, during a peer review of another network engineer's implementation plan. Complete the table by answering the questions.

Table 8-5 *Notable Questions from This Chapter to Consider During an Implementation Plan Peer Review*

Question	Answers
The subnetting design over Frame Relay calls for a set of 20 routers to use a single WAN subnet. What three general issues exist that requires extra configuration?	
The plan shows a virtual link between R1 and R2, through area 99, with the connection using R1's Fa0/0 interface. The configuration shows MD5 authentication configuration as interface subcommands on Fa0/0. Will those commands apply to the virtual link?	
The plan shows a sample OSPF configuration with five routers, Frame Relay connected, with one subnet, each using multipoint subinterfaces. A full mesh exists. The configuration shows network type point-to-multipoint nonbroadcast. What OSPF configuration is needed beyond the enabling of OSPF on the interfaces?	
Using the same scenario as the previous row but with network type nonbroadcast, and a partial mesh, answer the same questions.	

Create an Implementation Plan Table

To practice skills useful when creating your own OSPF implementation plan, list in Table 8-6 configuration commands related to the configuration of the following features. You may want to record your answers outside the book and set a goal to complete this table (and others like it) from memory during your final reviews before taking the exam.

Table 8-6 *Implementation Plan Configuration Memory Drill*

Feature	Configuration Commands/Notes
Create a virtual link through transit area X.	
Configure MD5 authentication on a virtual link.	
Configure clear-text authentication on a virtual link.	
Configure null authentication on a virtual link.	
Configure the OSPF network type on a Frame Relay multipoint interface.	
Statically configure OSPF neighbors.	
Influence OSPF priority of the local router.	
Influence OSPF priority of a neighboring router.	
Add static Frame Relay mappings.	

Choosing Commands for a Verification Plan Table

To practice skills useful when creating your own OSPF verification plan, list in Table 8-7 all commands that supply the requested information. You may want to record your answers outside the book and set a goal to complete this table (and others like it) from memory during your final reviews before taking the exam.

Table 8-7   *Verification Plan Memory Drill*

Information Needed	Command(s)
Display the name and status of a virtual link.	
Display the RID of a neighbor on a virtual link.	
Display the OSPF authentication type and youngest key for MD5 authentication on a Virtual Link.	
Display the OSPF network type for an interface.	
Display a router's own OSPF priority.	
Display the mapping of neighbor IP address and Frame Relay DLCI.	
Display neighbors known on an interface.	

Author's note: Some of the entries in this table may not have been specifically mentioned in this chapter but are listed in this table for review and reference.

Review All the Key Topics

Review the most important topics from inside the chapter, noted with the key topics icon in the outer margin of the page. Table 8-8 lists a reference of these key topics and the page numbers on which each is found.

Key
Topic

Table 8-8   *Key Topics for Chapter 8*

Key Topic Element	Description	Page Number
List	Summary of options on the **area virtual-link** command	263
Table 8-2	Summary of OSPF authentication methods and commands for virtual links	266
List	Recommendations related to multipoint Frame Relay and either neighbor discovery or neighbor definition	271
List	Recommendations related to multipoint Frame Relay when a DR is elected	272
Paragraph	Recommendation with a partial mesh in multipoint Frame Relay regarding static Frame Relay mapping	273
Table 8-3	List of OSPF network types used for Frame Relay physical interfaces and multipoint subinterfaces	274

Complete the Tables and Lists from Memory

Print a copy of Appendix D, "Memory Tables," (found on the CD), or at least the section for this chapter, and complete the tables and lists from memory. Appendix E, "Memory Tables Answer Key," also on the CD, includes completed tables and lists to check your work.

Define Key Terms

Define the following key terms from this chapter, and check your answers in the glossary.

Virtual Link, OSPF network type, Full mesh, Partial mesh, Frame Relay mapping, Frame Relay Inverse ARP (InARP), Multipoint subinterface

This chapter covers the following subjects:

Route Redistribution Basics: This section discusses the reasons why designers might choose to use route redistribution, and how routing protocols redistribute routes from the IP routing table.

Redistribution in EIGRP: This section discusses the mechanics of how IOS redistributes routes from other sources into EIGRP.

Redistribution in OSPF: This section discusses the mechanics of how IOS redistributes routes from other sources into OSPF.

CHAPTER 9

Basic IGP Redistribution

This chapter begins Part 4 of this book: "Path Control." Path control refers to a general class of tools and protocols that Layer 3 devices use to learn, manipulate, and use IP routes. EIGRP and OSPF certainly fit into that category.

The three chapters in Part 4 examine path control features that go beyond the base function of learning IP routes. In particular, Chapter 9, "Basic IGP Redistribution," and Chapter 10, "Advanced IGP Redistribution," examine how routers can exchange routes between routing protocols through route redistribution. Chapter 9 begins by discussing the mechanics of what happens when the routes are redistributed. Chapter 10 then goes further to discuss how to also filter and summarize routes when redistributing–yet another path control function–and discusses some issues and solutions when multiple routers redistribute the same routes. Finally, Chapter 11, "Policy-Based Routing and IP Service Level Agreement," discusses a few smaller path control topics, including IP Service-Level Agreement (SLA) and Policy-Based Routing (PBR).

"Do I Know This Already?" Quiz

The "Do I Know This Already?" quiz allows you to assess if you should read the entire chapter. If you miss no more than one of these eight self-assessment questions, you might want to move ahead to the "Exam Preparation Tasks." Table 9-1 lists the major headings in this chapter and the "Do I Know This Already?" quiz questions covering the material in those headings so that you can assess your knowledge of these specific areas. The answers to the "Do I Know This Already?" quiz appear in Appendix A.

Table 9-1 *"Do I Know This Already?" Foundation Topics Section-to-Question Mapping*

Foundations Topics Section	Questions
Route Redistribution Basics	1–2
Redistribution into EIGRP	3–5
Redistribution into OSPF	6–8

1. Which of the following answers is the least likely reason for an engineer to choose to use route redistribution?

    a. To exchange routes between merged companies

    b.   To give separate control over routing to different parts of one company

    c.   To support multiple router vendors

    d.   To knit together an OSPF area if the area becomes discontiguous

2. For a router to successfully redistribute routes between OSPF and EIGRP, which of the following are true? (Choose two.)

    a.   The router must have one routing protocol configured, but configuration for both routing protocols is not necessary.

    b.   The router must have at least one working link connected to each routing domain.

    c.   The **redistribute** command must be configured under EIGRP to send the routes to OSPF.

    d.   The **redistribute** command should be configured under OSPF to take routes from EIGRP into OSPF.

3. Process EIGRP 1 is redistributing routes from process OSPF 2. Which two of the following methods may be used to set the metrics of the redistributed routes? (Choose 2)

    a.   Let the metrics default.

    b.   Set the metric components using the **redistribute** command's **metric** keyword.

    c.   Set the metric components using the **default-metric** router subcommand.

    d.   Set the integer (composite) metric using the **redistribute** command's **metric** keyword.

4. Examine the following excerpt from the **show ip eigrp topology 10.2.2.0/24** command on router R1. Which answer can be verified as definitely true based on this output?

```
External data:
  Originating router is 10.1.1.1
  AS number of route is 1
  External protocol is OSPF, external metric is 64
  Administrator tag is 0 (0x00000000)
```

    a.   R1 is the router that redistributed the route.

    b.   R1's metric to reach subnet 10.2.2.0/24 is 64.

    c.   The route was redistributed on a router that has a **router ospf 1** command configured.

    d.   R1 is redistributing a route to prefix 10.2.2.0/24 into OSPF.

5. Router R1 has a connected route for 10.1.1.0/24 off interface Fa0/0. Interface Fa0/0 has been enabled for OSPF due to a **router ospf 1** and **network 10.0.0.0 0.0.0.255 area 0** command. R1 also has EIGRP configured, with the **redistribute ospf 1 metric 1000 100 10 1 1500** command configured under EIGRP. Which one of the following is true?

    a. R1 will not redistribute 10.1.1.0/24 into EIGRP, because R1 knows it as a connected route and not as an OSPF route.

    b. For any OSPF routes redistributed into EIGRP, the metric components include a value equivalent to 1 Mbps of bandwidth.

    c. For any OSPF routes redistributed into EIGRP, the metric components include a value equivalent to 100 microseconds of delay.

    d. No subnets of network 10.0.0.0 will be redistributed due to the omission of the **subnets** parameter.

6. Process OSPF 1 is redistributing routes from process OSPF 2. Which of the following methods may be used to set the metrics of the redistributed routes? (Choose two.)

    a. Let the metrics default.

    b. Use each redistributed route's OSPF metric using the **redistribute** command's **metric transparent** keywords.

    c. Set the metric using the **default-metric** router subcommand.

    d. Redistribution is not allowed between two OSPF processes.

7. Examine the following excerpt from the **show ip ospf database asbr-summary** command on router R1 (RID 1.1.1.1). Which answer can be verified as definitely true based on this output?

```
LS Type: Summary Links (AS Boundary Router)
Link State ID: 9.9.9.9 (AS Boundary Router address)
Advertising Router: 3.3.3.3
LS Seq Number: 8000000D
Checksum: 0xE43A
Length: 28
Network Mask: /0
      TOS: 0  Metric: 100
```

    a. The output describes the contents of a Type 5 LSA.

    b. 3.3.3.3 identifies a router as being the router performing redistribution.

    c. R1's metric for its best route to reach the router with RID 9.9.9.9 is 100.

    d. The router with RID 3.3.3.3's metric for its best route to reach the router with RID 9.9.9.9 is 100.

8. Router R1 sits inside OSPF area 1. Router R2 redistributes an E1 route into OSPF for prefix 2.2.2.0/24, with external metric 20. Router R22 redistributes an E2 route for the same prefix/length, external metric 10. Under what conditions will R1 choose as its best route the route through R22?

    a. R1 will always choose the route through R22.

    b. As long as R1's best internal OSPF cost to reach R22 is less than 10.

    c. As long as R1's best internal OSPF cost to reach R22 is less than 20.

    d. R1 will never choose the route through R22 if the E1 route through R2 is available.

Foundation Topics

Route Redistribution Basics

Most internetworks use a single IGP to advertise and learn IP routes. However, in some cases, more than one routing protocol exists inside a single enterprise. Also, in some cases, the routes learned with an IGP must then be advertised with BGP, and vice versa. In such cases, engineers often need to take routing information learned by one routing protocol and advertise those routes into the other routing protocol–a function provided by the IOS route redistribution feature.

This section examines the basics of route redistribution.

The Need for Route Redistribution

The potential need for route redistribution exists when a route learned through one source of routing information, most typically one routing protocol, needs to be distributed into a second routing protocol domain. For example, two companies might merge, with one company using EIGRP and the other using OSPF. The engineers could choose to immediately migrate away from OSPF to instead use EIGRP exclusively, but that migration would take time and potentially cause outages. Route redistribution allows those engineers to connect a couple of routers to both routing domains, and exchange routes between the two routing domains, with a minimal amount of configuration and with little disruption to the existing networks.

Figure 9-1 shows just such a case, with R1 performing redistribution by using its knowledge of subnet 1 from the EIGRP domain and advertising a route for subnet 1 into the OSPF domain. Note that the opposite should also occur, with the OSPF domain's subnet 2 being redistributed into the EIGRP domain.

Figure 9-1   *Typical Use of Redistribution*

The main technical reason for needing redistribution is straightforward: An internetwork uses more than one routing protocol, and the routes need to be exchanged between those routing domains, at least temporarily. The business reasons vary widely but include the following:

■   Mergers when different IGPs are used.

■   Mergers when the same IGP is used.

■   Momentum (The Enterprise has been using multiple routing protocols a long time.)

■   Different company divisions under separate control for business or political reasons.

■   Connections between partners.

■   To allow multivendor interoperability (OSPF on non-Cisco, EIGRP on Cisco, for instance).

■   Between IGPs and BGP when BGP is used between large segments of a multinational company.

■   Layer 3 WAN (MPLS).

The list begins with two entries for mergers just to make the point that even if both merging companies use the same IGP, redistribution may still be useful. Even if both companies use EIGRP, they probably use a different AS number in their EIGRP configuration (with the **router eigrp** asn command). In such a case, to have all routers exchange routing information with EIGRP, all the former company's routers would need to migrate to use the same ASN as the first company. Such a migration may be simple, but it still requires disruptive configuration changes in a potentially large number of routers. Redistribution could be used until a migration could be completed.

Although useful as an interim solution, many permanent designs use redistribution as well. For example, it could be that a company has used different routing protocols (or different instances of the same routing protocol) in different divisions of a company. The network engineering groups may remain autonomous, and manage their own routing protocol domains, using redistribution to exchange routes at a few key connecting points between the divisions. Similarly, partner companies have separate engineering staffs, and want autonomy for managing routing, but also need to exchange routes for key subnets to allow the partnership's key applications to function. Figure 9-2 depicts both of these cases.

The last two cases in the previous list each relate to BGP in some way. First, some large corporations actually use BGP internal to the company's internetwork, redistributing routes from IGPs. Each large autonomous division of the company can design and configure their respective routing protocol instance, redistribute into BGP, and then redistribute out of BGP into other divisions. Also, when an Enterprise uses an MPLS VPN service, the MPLS provider's provider edge (PE) router typically redistributes customer routes with BGP inside the MPLS provider's MPLS network. Figure 9-3 shows samples of both these cases. In each of these cases, a given prefix/length (subnet/mask) is typically distributed into BGP at one location, advertised over a BGP domain, and redistributed back into some IGP.

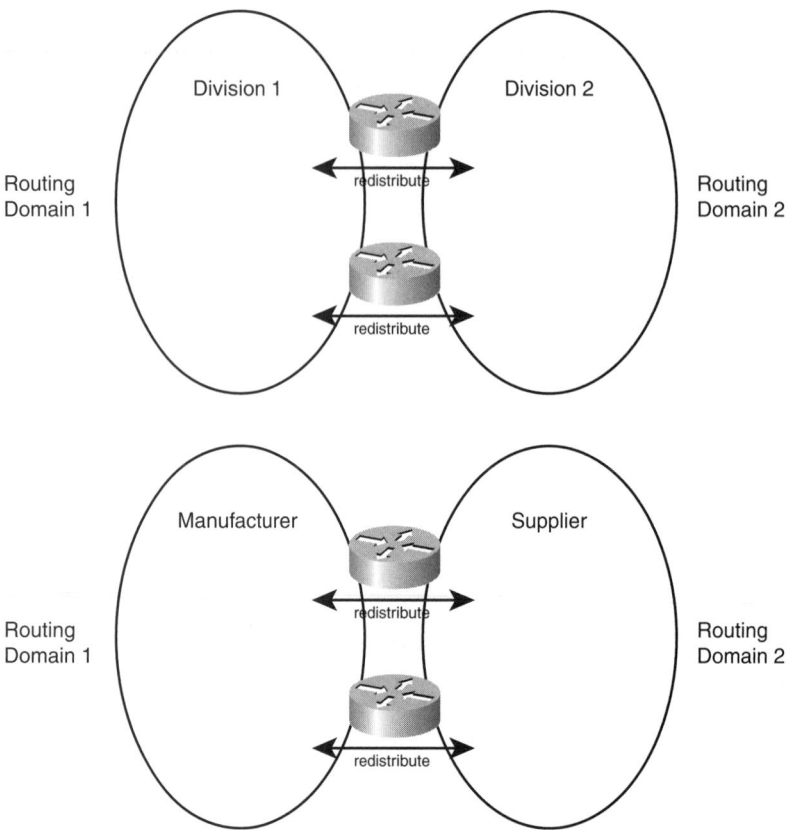

Figure 9-2   *Permanent Uses for Route Redistribution*

Note: Although Enterprises often use BGP to exchange routes with ISPs, redistribution is often not used. Chapter 13, "External BGP," discusses the issues and alternatives for how to advertise Enterprise routes into BGP.

Redistribution Concepts and Processes

Route redistribution requires at least one router to do the following:

Key Topic

Step 1.   Use at least one working physical link with each routing domain.

Step 2.   A working routing protocol configuration for each routing domain.

Step 3.   Additional redistribution configuration for each routing protocol, specifically the **redistribute** command, which tells the routing protocol to take the routes learned by another source of routing information and to then advertise those routes.

The first two steps do not require any new knowledge or commands, but the third step represents the core of the redistribution logic and requires some additional background

Figure 9-3   *Using Redistribution to Pass Routes Using BGP*

information. To appreciate the third step, Figure 9-4 shows an example router, RD1, that has completed Steps 1 and 2. RD1 uses EIGRP on the left, OSPF on the right, and has learned some routes with each routing protocol (Steps 1 and 2). However, no redistribution has been configured yet.

The goal for redistribution in this case is to have EIGRP advertise about subnets 11, 12, and 13, which exist inside the OSPF domain, and have OSPF advertise about subnets 1, 2, and 3, which exist inside the EIGRP domain. To do that, EIGRP must put topology information about subnets 11, 12 and 13 into its EIGRP topology table, and OSPF must put topology information about subnets 1, 2, and 3 into its topology table. However, OSPF's topology table has a lot of different information in it compared to EIGRP's topology table. OSPF has LSAs, and EIGRP does not. EIGRP lists the components of the composite metric and the neighbor's reported distance (RD)–but OSPF does not. In short, EIGRP and OSPF differ significantly for the contents of their topology tables.

Because the details of various routing protocols' topology tables differ, the redistribution process does not use the topology tables when redistributing routes. Instead, redistribution uses the one table that both routing protocols understand: the IP routing table. Specifically, the IOS **redistribute** command takes routes from the IP routing table and passes those routes to a routing protocol for redistribution. The **redistribute** command, configured inside a routing protocol configuration mode, redistributes routes into that routing protocol from some other source. Figure 9-5 spells it out with an example, which focuses on the internal logic of Router RD1 as shown in Figure 9-4.

Starting on the left of the figure, RD1's EIGRP 1 process configuration lists the **redistribute ospf 2** command. This command tells RD1 to look in the IP routing table, take all OSPF routes added to the IP routing table by the OSPF 2 process on RD1, and put those routes into EIGRP's topology table. Conversely, the **redistribute eigrp 1** command

Figure 9-4   *Routing Protocol Tables on a Router Doing Redistribution*

Figure 9-5   *Mutual Redistribution Between OSPF and EIGRP on Router RD1*

configured on the OSPF process tells RD1 to take IP routes from the IP routing table, if learned by EIGRP process 1, and add those routes to OSPF 2's topology table.

The process works as shown in Figure 9-5, but the figure leaves out some important details regarding the type of routes and the metrics used. For EIGRP, the EIGRP topology table needs more than the integer metric value held by the IP routing table–it needs values for the components of the EIGRP composite metric. EIGRP can use default settings that define the metric components for all routes redistributed into EIGRP, or the engineer can set the metric components in a variety of ways, as covered in several locations later in this chapter.

Like EIGRP, OSPF treats the redistributed routes as external routes. OSPF creates an LSA to represent each redistributed subnet–normally a Type 5 LSA, but when redistributed into an NSSA area, the router instead creates a Type 7 LSA. In both cases, OSPF needs an integer metric to assign to the external route's LSA; the redistribution configuration should include the OSPF cost setting, which may or may not match the metric listed for the route in the redistributing router's IP routing table.

The last concept before moving on to the configuration options is that the **redistribute** command tells the router to take not only routes learned by the source routing protocol, but also connected routes on interfaces enabled with that routing protocol–including passive interfaces. Example 9-1 later in this chapter demonstrates this concept.

Redistribution into EIGRP

This section looks at the specifics of how EIGRP performs redistribution–that is, how EIGRP takes routes from other routing sources, such as OSPF, and advertises them into EIGRP. Before moving into the specifics, however, note that the redistribution as discussed in this chapter does not include any filtering or summarization. In real life, engineers often use both route filtering and route summarization at the redistribution point on a router. For the sake of making the underlying concepts clear, this chapter focuses on the mechanics of redistribution, without filtering, or summarization, or any other changes to the redistributed routes. Chapter 10 then looks at the fun options for manipulating routes at the redistribution point.

This section begins with a couple of short discussions of reference information. The first topic summarizes the parameters of the main configuration command, the EIGRP **redistribute** command, and its parameters. Next, the baseline configuration used in the upcoming samples is listed, including all EIGRP and OSPF configuration, but no redistribution configuration. With those details listed for reference, the rest of this section examines the configuration of redistribution into EIGRP.

EIGRP **redistribute** Command Reference

First, for reference, the following lines show the generic syntax of the **redistribute** command when used as a **router eigrp** subcommand. Note that the syntax differs slightly depending on the routing protocol into which routes will be redistributed. Following that, Table 9-2 lists the options on the command with a brief description.

```
redistribute protocol [process-id ¦ as-number] [metric bw delay reliability load
mtu ] [match {internal ¦ nssa-external ¦ external 1 ¦ external 2}]  [tag tag-
value] [route-map name]
```

Table 9-2 *Commonly Used OSPF Terms*

Option	Description
protocol	The source of routing information. Includes **RIP, OSPF, EIGRP, IS-IS, BGP**, connected, and static.
process-id, as-number	If redistributing a routing protocol that uses a process ID or ASN on the **router** global config command, use this parameter to refer to that process or ASN value.
metric	A keyword after which follows the four metric components (bandwidth, delay, reliability, link load), plus the MTU associated with the route.
match	If redistributing from OSPF, this keyword lets you match internal OSPF routes, external (by type), and NSSA external routes, essentially filtering which routes are redistributed.
tag	Assigns a unitless integer value to the routes redistributed by this command—tags which can be later matched by other routers using a route-map.
route-map	Apply the logic in the referenced route-map to filter routes, set metrics, and set route tags.

Baseline Configuration for EIGRP Redistribution Examples

The best method to see the results of redistribution is to use examples, so this section explains the sample internetwork used in the upcoming EIGRP redistribution examples. Figure 9-6 shows the sample internetwork. In this case, the EIGRP domain on the left uses subnets of class B network 172.30.0.0, and the OSPF domain on the right uses subnets of class B network 172.16.0.0. Note that all OSPF subnets reside in area 0 in this example internetwork, although that is not a requirement.

The internetwork uses a single router (RD1) to perform redistribution, just to avoid some interesting issues that occur when multiple routers redistribute the same routes. (Chapter 10 discusses these issues in some depth.) Example 9-1 shows the configuration on RD1, listing the IP addresses of the four active serial interfaces shown in Figure 9-6, plus the complete but basic EIGRP and OSPF configuration—but without any redistribution configured yet.

EIGRP

OSPF

Area 0

Subnet 172.30.7.0/23

Subnet 172.16.8.0/25

Fa0/1
7.7/23

Fa0/1
8.8/25

R7   S0/0
17.2/30

S0/0
18.2/30   R8

Fa0/0
27.7/23

Fa0/0
48.8/25

Subnet
172.30.26.0/23

S0/1/1
17.1/30

S0/0/1
18.1/30

Subnet
172.16.48.0/25

RD1

Fa0/0
27.2/23

S0/0/0
12.1/30

S0/1/0
14.1/30

Fa0/0
48.4/25

R2   S0/0/1
12.2/30

S0/0/0
14.2/30   R4

Fa0/1
2.2/23

Fa0/1
4.4/25

Subnet 172.30.2.0/23

Subnet 172.16.4.0/25

All addresses begin 172.30

All addresses begin 172.16

Figure 9-6 *Sample Internetwork Used for Redistribution Examples*

Example 9-1 *Configuration on Router RD1 Before Adding Redistribution Configuration*

```
interface Serial0/0/0
 ip address 172.30.12.1 255.255.255.252
 clock rate 1536000
!
interface Serial0/0/1
 ip address 172.16.18.1 255.255.255.252
 clock rate 1536000
!
interface Serial0/1/0
 ip address 172.16.14.1 255.255.255.252
 clock rate 1536000
!
interface Serial0/1/1
 ip address 172.30.17.1 255.255.255.252
 clock rate 1536000
!
router eigrp 1
 network 172.30.0.0
 no auto-summary
```

```
!
router ospf 2
 router-id 1.1.1.1
 network 172.16.0.0 0.0.255.255 area 0
```

Configuring EIGRP Redistribution with Default Metric Components

For the internetwork of Figure 9-6, a reasonable design goal would be to redistribute EIGRP routes into OSPF, and OSPF routes into EIGRP. This section examines the case of redistributing the routes into EIGRP from OSPF.

First, consider the EIGRP **redistribute** command. For those unfamiliar with the command, it may not be obvious of the direction of redistribution. A better command name might have been "take-routes-from," because the first parameter after the command tells IOS from where to get the routes.

For example, consider the configuration in Example 9-2, which was added to RD1's existing configuration in Example 9-1. The configuration uses only required parameters, namely a reference to the source from which routes should be redistributed. Because the configuration places this command in EIGRP configuration mode, the command tells IOS to redistribute the routes into EIGRP 1, from OSPF 2 in this case.

Example 9-2 *Minimal Configuration for Redistribution from OSPF into EIGRP*

```
RD1#configure terminal
Enter configuration commands, one per line.  End with CNTL/Z.
RD1(config)#router eigrp 1
RD1(config-router)#redistribute ospf 2
RD1(config-router)#^Z
```

IOS does accept the configuration; unfortunately, IOS does not actually redistribute routes from OSPF into EIGRP in this case. EIGRP does not have a default setting for the metric components to use when redistributing into EIGRP from OSPF. To confirm these results, examine the output in Example 9-3, which lists **show** command output from RD1 when configured as shown in the previous example. Note that that RD1's EIGRP topology table lists only routes for class B network 172.30.0.0, which all sit inside the EIGRP domain; none of the routes from class B network 172.16.0.0, which exist inside the OSPF domain, have been added to RD1's EIGRP topology table.

Example 9-3 *Redistribution Did Not Work on RD1*

```
RD1#show ip eigrp topology
IP-EIGRP Topology Table for AS(1)/ID(172.30.17.1)

Codes: P - Passive, A - Active, U - Update, Q - Query, R - Reply,
       r - reply Status, s - sia Status

P 172.30.17.0/30, 1 successors, FD is 2169856
         via Connected, Serial0/1/1
P 172.30.26.0/23, 2 successors, FD is 2172416
         via 172.30.12.2 (2172416/28160), Serial0/0/0
```

```
             via 172.30.17.2 (2172416/28160), Serial0/1/1
P 172.30.2.0/23, 1 successors, FD is 2172416
             via 172.30.12.2 (2172416/28160), Serial0/0/0
             via 172.30.17.2 (2174976/30720), Serial0/1/1
P 172.30.6.0/23, 1 successors, FD is 2172416
             via 172.30.17.2 (2172416/28160), Serial0/1/1
             via 172.30.12.2 (2174976/30720), Serial0/0/0
P 172.30.12.0/30, 1 successors, FD is 2169856
             via Connected, Serial0/0/0
```

To complete the configuration of redistribution into EIGRP, Router RD1 needs to set the metric values. EIGRP can set the metrics for redistributed routes in three ways, as summarized in Table 9-3.

Table 9-3 *Methods of Setting EIGRP Metrics When Redistributing into EIGRP*

Key
Topic

Function	Command
Setting the default for all **redistribute** commands	The **default-metric** bw delay reliability load mtu EIGRP subcommand
Setting the component metrics applied to all routes redistributed by a single **redistribute** command	The **metric** bw delay reliability load mtu parameters on the **redistribute** command
Setting different component metrics to different routes from a single route source	Use the **route-map** parameter on the **redistribute** command, matching routes and setting metric components.

Note: EIGRP does have a default metric when redistributing from another EIGRP process, in which case it takes the metric from the source of the routing information. In all other cases, the metric must be set using one of the methods in Table 9-3.

If the metrics do not matter to the design, which is likely when only a single redistribution point exists as in Figure 9-6, either of the first two methods listed in Table 9-3 is reasonable. The first method, using the **default-metric** command in EIGRP configuration mode, sets the metric for all routes redistributed into EIGRP, unless set by one of the other methods. Alternatively, the second method, which uses additional parameters on the **redistribute** command, sets the metric for all routes redistributed because of that one **redistribute** command. Finally, if the **redistribute** command also refers to a route map, the route map can use the set metric command to set the metric components for routes matched by the route map clause, overriding the metric settings in the **default-metric** command or with the **metric** keyword on the **redistribute** command.

Example 9-4 shows the addition of the **default-metric 1000 33 255 1 1500** command to RD1's configuration. This command sets the bandwidth to 1000 (Kbps), the delay to 33 (tens-of-microseconds, or 330 microseconds), reliability to 255 (a value between 1–255,

255 is best), load to 1 (a value between 1–255, 1 is best), and MTU of 1500. Note that even though EIGRP ignores the last three parameters by default when calculating integer metrics, you still must configure these settings for the commands to be accepted.

Example 9-4 *Redistributed Routes in RD1*

```
RD1#configure terminal
Enter configuration commands, one per line.  End with CNTL/Z.
RD1(config)#router eigrp 1
RD1(config-router)#default-metric 1000 33 255 1 1500
RD1(config-router)#^Z
```

Because this example uses a single **redistribute** command for the EIGRP 1 process, you could have used the **redistribute ospf 2 metric 1000 33 255 1 1500** command and ignored the **default-metric** command to achieve the same goal.

Verifying EIGRP Redistribution

As shown earlier in Figure 9-5, redistribution takes routes from the routing table and places the correct information for those subnets into the redistributing router's topology table. The redistributing router then advertises the routes from its topology table as it would for other routes. To verify that redistribution works, Example 9-5 shows the proof that RD1 indeed created entries in its EIGRP topology table for the five subnets in the OSPF domain.

Example 9-5 *Verifying RD1 Added EIGRP Topology Data for Five OSPF Subnets*

```
RD1#show ip eigrp topology
IP-EIGRP Topology Table for AS(1)/ID(172.30.17.1)

Codes: P - Passive, A - Active, U - Update, Q - Query, R - Reply,
       r - reply Status, s - sia Status

! Note - all lines for class B network 172.30.0.0 have been omitted for brevity
P 172.16.48.0/25, 1 successors, FD is 2568448
        via Redistributed (2568448/0)
P 172.16.18.0/30, 1 successors, FD is 2568448
        via Redistributed (2568448/0)
P 172.16.14.0/30, 1 successors, FD is 2568448
        via Redistributed (2568448/0)
P 172.16.8.0/25, 1 successors, FD is 2568448
        via Redistributed (2568448/0)
P 172.16.4.0/25, 1 successors, FD is 2568448
        via Redistributed (2568448/0)
RD1#show ip eigrp topology 172.16.48.0/25
IP-EIGRP (AS 1): Topology entry for 172.16.48.0/25
  State is Passive, Query origin flag is 1, 1 Successor(s), FD is 2568448
```

```
Routing Descriptor Blocks:
172.16.18.2, from Redistributed, Send flag is 0x0
    Composite metric is (2568448/0), Route is External
    Vector metric:
      Minimum bandwidth is 1000 Kbit
      Total delay is 330 microseconds
      Reliability is 255/255
      Load is 1/255
      Minimum MTU is 1500
      Hop count is 0
    External data:
      Originating router is 172.30.17.1 (this system)
      AS number of route is 2
      External protocol is OSPF, external metric is 65
      Administrator tag is 0 (0x00000000)
```

The **show** command output lists several interesting facts, including

■ On Router RD1, which performed the redistribution, the EIGRP topology table lists the outgoing interface as "via redistributed."

■ All the redistributed routes have the same feasible distance (FD) calculation (2568448), because all use the same component metrics per the configured **default-metric** command.

■ RD1's two connected subnets in the OSPF 2 domain–subnets 172.16.14.0/30 and 172.16.18.0/30–were also redistributed, even though these routes are connected routes in RD1's routing table.

■ The output of the **show ip eigrp topology 172.16.48.0/25** command confirms the component metrics match the values configured on the **default-metric** command.

■ The bottom of the output of the **show ip eigrp topology 172.16.48.0/25** command lists information about the external source of the route, including the routing source (OSPF) and that source's metric for the route (65). It also lists the phrase "(this system)," meaning that the router on which the command was issued (RD1 in this case) redistributed the route.

The third item in the list–the fact that RD1 redistributed some connected routes–bears further consideration. The **redistribute ospf 2** command tells EIGRP to redistribute routes learned by the OSPF 2 process. However, it also tells the router to redistribute connected routes for interfaces on which process OSPF 2 has been enabled. Back in Example 9-1, the configuration on RD1 lists a **network 172.16.0.0 0.0.255.255 area 0** command, enabling OSPF 2 on RD1's S0/0/1 and S0/1/0 interfaces. As such, the redistribution process also redistributed those routes.

Stated more generally, when the **redistribute** command refers to another IGP as the routing source, it tells the router to redistribute the following:

■ All routes in the routing table learned by that routing protocol

■ All connected routes of interfaces on which that routing protocol is enabled

Although Example 9-5 shows the evidence that Router RD1 added the topology data to its EIGRP topology database, it did not show any routes. Example 9-6 shows the IP routing tables on both RD1 and Router R2, a router internal to the EIGRP domain. R2's routes forward the packets toward the redistributing router, which in turn has routes from the OSPF domain with which to forward the packet to the destination subnet.

Example 9-6 *Verification of IP Routes on RD1 and R2*

```
! First, on RD1
RD1#show ip route 172.16.0.0
Routing entry for 172.16.0.0/16, 5 known subnets
  Attached (2 connections)
  Variably subnetted with 2 masks
  Redistributing via eigrp 1


O        172.16.48.0/25 [110/65] via 172.16.18.2, 00:36:25, Serial0/0/1
                        [110/65] via 172.16.14.2, 00:36:25, Serial0/1/0
C        172.16.18.0/30 is directly connected, Serial0/0/1
C        172.16.14.0/30 is directly connected, Serial0/1/0
O        172.16.8.0/25 [110/65] via 172.16.18.2, 00:36:25, Serial0/0/1
O        172.16.4.0/25 [110/65] via 172.16.14.2, 00:36:25, Serial0/1/0
! Next, on Router R2
R2#show ip route
Codes: C - connected, S - static, R - RIP, M - mobile, B - BGP
       D - EIGRP, EX - EIGRP external, O - OSPF, IA - OSPF inter area
       N1 - OSPF NSSA external type 1, N2 - OSPF NSSA external type 2
       E1 - OSPF external type 1, E2 - OSPF external type 2
       i - IS-IS, su - IS-IS summary, L1 - IS-IS level-1, L2 - IS-IS level-2
       ia - IS-IS inter area, * - candidate default, U - per-user static route
       o - ODR, P - periodic downloaded static route

Gateway of last resort is not set

     172.16.0.0/16 is variably subnetted, 5 subnets, 2 masks
D EX    172.16.48.0/25 [170/3080448] via 172.30.12.1, 00:25:15, Serial0/0/1
D EX    172.16.18.0/30 [170/3080448] via 172.30.12.1, 00:25:15, Serial0/0/1
D EX    172.16.14.0/30 [170/3080448] via 172.30.12.1, 00:25:15, Serial0/0/1
D EX    172.16.8.0/25 [170/3080448] via 172.30.12.1, 00:25:15, Serial0/0/1
D EX    172.16.4.0/25 [170/3080448] via 172.30.12.1, 00:25:15, Serial0/0/1
     172.30.0.0/16 is variably subnetted, 5 subnets, 2 masks
D       172.30.17.0/30 [90/2172416] via 172.30.27.7, 00:25:15, FastEthernet0/0
```

```
C       172.30.26.0/23 is directly connected, FastEthernet0/0
C       172.30.2.0/23 is directly connected, FastEthernet0/1
D       172.30.6.0/23 [90/30720] via 172.30.27.7, 00:25:15, FastEthernet0/0
C       172.30.12.0/30 is directly connected, Serial0/0/1
```

Beginning with the output for R2, in the second half of the example, R2 knows routes for all five subnets in class B network 172.16.0.0, listing all as external EIGRP routes. The routes all use R2's link connected to RD1. Also, note that the administrative distance (AD) is set to 170, rather than the usual 90 for EIGRP routes. EIGRP defaults to use AD 90 for internal routes and AD 170 for external routes. Chapter 10 shows cases in which this default helps prevent routing loops when multiple redistribution points exist.

RD1 has routes for all routes in the OSPF domain as well, but as either connected or OSPF-learned routes.

Redistribution into OSPF

As you might expect, OSPF redistribution has several similarities and differences as compared to redistribution into EIGRP. Unlike EIGRP, OSPF does have useful default metrics for redistributed routes, but OSPF does use the same general methods to configure metrics for redistributed routes. Like EIGRP, OSPF flags redistributed routes as being external. Unlike EIGRP, OSPF creates LSAs to represent each external route, and OSPF must then apply some much different logic than EIGRP to calculate the best route to each external subnet.

This section examines the OSPF redistribution process and configuration. It also discusses background on three OSPF LSA Types—Types 4, 5, and 7—all created to help OSPF distribute information so that routers can calculate the best route to each external subnet.

OSPF **redistribute** Command Reference

First, for reference, the following lines show the generic syntax of the **redistribute** command when used as a **router ospf** subcommand. Note that the syntax differs slightly depending on the routing protocol into which routes will be redistributed. Following that, Table 9-4 lists the options on the command with a brief description:

```
redistribute protocol [process-id ¦ as-number] [metric metric-value] [metric-type
type-value] [match {internal ¦ external 1 ¦ external 2 ¦ nssa-external}] [tag
tag-value] [route-map map-tag] [subnets]
```

Table 9-4 *Parameters on the OSPF* redistribute *Command*

Option	Description
protocol	The source of routing information. Includes **RIP, OSPF, EIGRP, IS-IS, BGP, connected,** and **static.**
process-id, as-number	If redistributing a routing protocol that uses a process-id or ASN on the **router** global config command, use this parameter to refer to that process or ASN value.

Table 9-4 *Parameters on the OSPF* **redistribute** *Command*

Option	Description
metric	Defines the cost metric assigned to routes redistributed by this command, unless overridden by a referenced route map.
metric-type {1 | 2}	Defines the external metric type for the routes redistributed by this command: **1** (E1 routes) or **2** (E2 routes).
match	If redistributing from another OSPF process, this keyword lets you match internal OSPF routes, external (by type), and NSSA external routes, essentially filtering which routes are redistributed.
tag	Assigns a unitless integer value to the routes redistributed by this command—a tag that can be later matched by other routers using a route-map.
route-map	Apply the logic in the referenced route-map to filter routes, set metrics, and set route tags.
subnets	Redistribute subnets of classful networks. Without this parameter, only routes for classful networks are redistributed. (This behavior is unique to the OSPF **redistribute** command.)

Configuring OSPF Redistribution with Minimal Parameters

The **redistribute** subcommand under **router ospf** has many optional settings. To better appreciate some of these settings, this section first examines the results when using all defaults, using as few parameters as possible. Following the discussion of the behavior with defaults, the next examples add the parameters that complete the redistribution configuration.

Redistribution into OSPF uses the following defaults:

- When taking from BGP, use a default metric of 1.

- When taking from another OSPF process, take the source route's metric.

- When taking from all other sources, use a default metric of 20.

- Create a Type 5 LSA for each redistributed route (external) if not inside an NSSA area; create a Type 7 LSA if inside an NSSA area.

- Use external metric type 2.

- Redistribute only routes of classful (class A, B, and C) networks, and not routes for subnets.

To demonstrate OSPF redistribution, this section uses an example that uses the same inter-network shown in Figure 9-6, including the baseline configuration shown in Example 9-1, and the EIGRP redistribution configuration shown in Examples 9-2 and 9-4. Essentially, the upcoming OSPF examples begin with Router RD1 including all the configurations seen in all the earlier examples in this chapter. According to those examples, OSPF has been correctly configured on the routers on the right side of Figure 9-6, EIGRP has been con-figured on the left, and the configuration of redistribution of OSPF routes into EIGRP has been completed. However, no redistribution into OSPF has been configured yet.

For perspective, before showing the redistribution into OSPF, Example 9-7 reviews the OSPF configuration before adding the redistribution configuration, along with **show** com-mands listing RD1's IP routing table entries and its OSPF LSDB.

Example 9-7 *Router RD1 Routing Protocol Configuration, Before Redistribution into OSPF*

```
RD1#show run
! lines omitted for brevity
router eigrp 1
 redistribute ospf 2
 network 172.30.0.0
 default-metric 1000 33 255 1 1500
 no auto-summary
!
router ospf 2
 router-id 1.1.1.1
 log-adjacency-changes
 network 172.16.0.0 0.0.255.255 area 0

RD1#show ip route 172.30.0.0
Routing entry for 172.30.0.0/16, 5 known subnets
  Attached (2 connections)
  Variably subnetted with 2 masks
  Redistributing via eigrp 1

C       172.30.17.0/30 is directly connected, Serial0/1/1
D       172.30.26.0/23 [90/2172416] via 172.30.17.2, 01:08:50, Serial0/1/1
                       [90/2172416] via 172.30.12.2, 01:08:50, Serial0/0/0
D       172.30.2.0/23 [90/2172416] via 172.30.12.2, 01:08:50, Serial0/0/0
D       172.30.6.0/23 [90/2172416] via 172.30.17.2, 01:08:50, Serial0/1/1
C       172.30.12.0/30 is directly connected, Serial0/0/0
RD1#show ip ospf database

            OSPF Router with ID (1.1.1.1) (Process ID 2)

                Router Link States (Area 0)
```

```
Link ID         ADV Router      Age       Seq#        Checksum Link count
1.1.1.1         1.1.1.1         1425      0x80000007 0x007622 4
4.4.4.4         4.4.4.4         1442      0x8000000D 0x00B1E9 4
8.8.8.8         8.8.8.8         1466      0x80000006 0x00640E 4

                Net Link States (Area 0)

Link ID         ADV Router      Age       Seq#        Checksum
172.16.48.4     4.4.4.4         1442      0x80000004 0x007E07
! The following occurs on OSPF internal router R4

R4#show ip route 172.30.0.0
% Network not in table
```

The output in Example 9-7 shows several important points relative to the upcoming redistribution configuration. First, by design, the EIGRP domain contains subnets of network 172.30.0.0; router RD1 knows routes for five subnets in this range. RD1 has four LSAs: three Type 1 Router LSAs (one each for routers RD1, R4, and R8), plus one Type 2 network LSAs (because only one subnet, 172.16.48.0/25, has elected a DR). Because the design for this internetwork puts all OSPF routers in area 0, no Type 3 summary LSAs exist in RD1's LSDB. Also, because no routers have redistributed external routes into OSPF yet, no Type 5 external nor Type 7 NSSA external routes are listed, either.

By adding the **redistribute eigrp 1** command in OSPF configuration mode, OSPF tries to redistribute routes from EIGRP–but with no success. The reason is that by omitting the **subnets** parameter, OSPF will only redistribute routes for entire classful subnets, and only if such a route is listed in the IP routing table. Example 9-8 shows the results.

Example 9-8   *Redistributing into OSPF from EIGRP 1, all Default Settings*

```
RD1#configure terminal
Enter configuration commands, one per line.  End with CNTL/Z.
RD1(config)#router ospf 2
RD1(config-router)#redistribute eigrp 1
% Only classful networks will be redistributed
RD1(config-router)#^Z
RD1#
RD1#show ip ospf database

            OSPF Router with ID (1.1.1.1) (Process ID 2)

                Router Link States (Area 0)

Link ID         ADV Router      Age       Seq#        Checksum Link count
1.1.1.1         1.1.1.1         6         0x80000008 0x007A1B 4
```

```
4.4.4.4          4.4.4.4          1782        0x8000000D 0x00B1E9  4
8.8.8.8          8.8.8.8          1806        0x80000006 0x00640E  4


                 Net Link States (Area 0)


Link ID          ADV Router       Age         Seq#       Checksum
172.16.48.4      4.4.4.4          1782        0x80000004 0x007E07
```

IOS even mentions that only classful routes will be redistributed. As seen in Example 9-7, no route exists for the exact class B network prefix of 172.30.0.0/16, and by default, OSPF does not redistribute any subnets inside that range, as noted in the informational message in Example 9-8. So, the OSPF database on Router RD1 remains unchanged.

By changing the configuration to use the **redistribute eigrp 1 subnets** command, OSPF indeed redistributes the routes, as shown in Example 9-9.

Example 9-9   *Redistributing from EIGRP into OSPF, with Subnets*

```
RD1#configure terminal
Enter configuration commands, one per line.  End with CNTL/Z.
RD1(config)#router ospf 2
RD1(config-router)#redistribute eigrp 1 subnets
RD1(config-router)#^Z
RD1#
May 12 12:49:48.735: %SYS-5-CONFIG_I: Configured from console by console
RD1#show ip ospf database
! omitting the Type 1 and 2 LSA output for brevity


              Type-5 AS External Link States


Link ID          ADV Router       Age         Seq#       Checksum Tag
172.30.2.0       1.1.1.1          3           0x80000001 0x008050  0
172.30.6.0       1.1.1.1          3           0x80000001 0x005478  0
172.30.12.0      1.1.1.1          3           0x80000001 0x0005C3  0
172.30.17.0      1.1.1.1          3           0x80000001 0x00CDF5  0
172.30.26.0      1.1.1.1          3           0x80000001 0x007741  0
! The following occurs on router R4
R4#show ip route 172.30.0.0
Routing entry for 172.30.0.0/16, 5 known subnets
  Variably subnetted with 2 masks

O E2    172.30.17.0/30 [110/20] via 172.16.14.1, 00:01:10, Serial0/0/0
O E2    172.30.26.0/23 [110/20] via 172.16.14.1, 00:01:11, Serial0/0/0
O E2    172.30.2.0/23 [110/20] via 172.16.14.1, 00:01:11, Serial0/0/0
O E2    172.30.6.0/23 [110/20] via 172.16.14.1, 00:01:11, Serial0/0/0
O E2    172.30.12.0/30 [110/20] via 172.16.14.1, 00:01:11, Serial0/0/0
```

After adding the **subnets** option, router RD1 redistributes the five routes from the EIGRP domain. Of particular interest:

- If you look back to Example 9-7's **show ip route** command output from Router RD1, you see three EIGRP-learned routes, plus two connected routes, inside the EIGRP domain. Example 9-9's two **show** commands in Example 9-9 confirm that OSPF redistributes the three EIGRP-learned routes, plus the two connected subnets on which EIGRP is enabled (172.30.12.0/30 and 172.30.17.0/30).

- The **show ip ospf database** command in Example 9-9 lists R1 (RID 1.1.1.1) as the advertising router of the five new Type 5 LSAs, because RD1 (with RID 1.1.1.1) created each Type 5 LSA.

- Per OSPF internal router R4's **show ip route 172.30.0.0** command at the end of Example 9-9, the external metric type is indeed E2, meaning external type 2.

- Per that same command on router R4, the metric for each route is 20. The reasoning is that the default metric is 20 when redistributing from EIGRP into OSPF, and with an E2 route, internal OSPF costs are not added to the cost of the route.

That last point regarding the external route type requires a little more discussion. OSPF defines external routes as either an external type 1 (E1) or external type 2 (E2) route. By default, the OSPF **redistribute** command creates Type 2 routes, noting this external route type in the Type 5 LSA. The difference between the two lies in how OSPF calculates the metrics for E1 and E2 routes.

The next section completes the discussion of how OSPF can set the metrics when redistributing routes–or more specifically, the metric as listed in the Type 5 LSA created for that subnet. Following that, the text takes a detailed look at how OSPF calculates the best route for E2 routes. Later, a different section titled "Redistributing into OSPF as E1 Routes" discusses the same subject, but for E1 routes.

Setting OSPF Metrics on Redistributed Routes

As mentioned earlier, no matter the source of the redistributed route, OSPF has a default metric to use. However, OSPF can set the metrics for redistributed routes using the same options used for EIGRP. Table 9-5 summarizes the defaults and metric setting options for redistribution into OSPF.

Table 9-5   *Summary of Metric Values When Redistributing into OSPF*

Function	Command or Metric Values
Default if no metric configuration exists	Cost 1 for routes learned from BGP.
	If redistributed from another OSPF process, use the source route's OSPF cost.
	Cost 20 for all other route sources.
Setting the default for all **redistribute** commands	The **default-metric** cost OSPF subcommand.

Table 9-5 *Summary of Metric Values When Redistributing into OSPF*

Function	Command or Metric Values
Setting the metric for one route source	The **metric** cost parameters on the **redistribute** command.
Setting different metrics for routes learned from a single source	Use the **route-map** parameter on the **redistribute** command.

LSAs and Metrics for External Type 2 Routes

To appreciate how OSPF calculates the possible routes for each E2 route, you need to take a moment to think about the Type 5 LSA in more detail. First, by definition, the router that performs the redistribution into OSPF becomes an autonomous system border router (ASBR) because it injects external routes into OSPF. For each such route, that ASBR creates a Type 5 LSA for that subnet. The Type 5 LSA includes the following fields:

- **LSID:** The subnet number

- **Mask:** The subnet mask

- **Advertising router:** The RID of the ASBR injecting the route

- **Metric:** The metric as set by the ASBR

- **External Metric Type:** The external metric type, either 1 or 2

When created, the ASBR floods the Type 5 LSA throughout the area. Then, if any ABRs exist, the ABRs flood the Type 5 LSAs into any normal (nonstubby) areas. (Note that ABRs must not forward Type 5 LSAs into any type of stubby area, instead relying on default routes.) Figure 9-7 shows a sample flooding of the Type 5 LSA for EIGRP subnet 172.30.27.0/23 as an E2 route.

When flooded, OSPF has little work to do to calculate the metric for an E2 route, because by definition, the E2 route's metric is simply the metric listed in the Type 5 LSA. In other words, the OSPF routers do not add any internal OSPF cost to the metric for an E2 route.

Because routers ignore internal cost when calculating E2 external route metrics, whenever an alternative route can be calculated, the metrics tie. For example, in Figure 9-7, Router R4 has two possible physical routes to ASBR RD1–one directly to RD1, and one through R8. The cost for both routes to external subnet 172.30.26.0/23 will be 20, because that is the cost RD1 assigned to the route (actually, the Type 5 LSA) when redistributing the route.

To avoid loops, OSPF routers use a tiebreaker system to allow a router to choose a best external route. The logic differs slightly depending on whether the router in question resides in the same area as the ASBR (intra-area), or in a different area (interarea), as discussed in under the next two headings.

Determining the Next-Hop for Type 2 External Routes–Intra-area

When a router finds multiple routes for the same E2 destination subnet, it chooses the best route based on the lowest cost to reach any ASBR(s) that advertised the lowest E2 metric. For example, if five ASBRs all advertised the same subnet as an E2 route, and two ASBRs

Figure 9-7   *Flooding of Type 5 LSAs*

advertised a metric of 10, and the other three advertised a metric of 20, either of the first two ASBRs could be used. Then, the router calculates its lowest cost route to reach the ASBR and uses the next-hop IP address and outgoing interface listed in that route.

The following list spells out the mechanics of the calculation used to break the tie when multiple equal-cost E2 routes exist for a particular subnet:

Step 1.   Find the advertising ASBR(s) as listed in the Type 5 LSA(s) for Type 5 LSAs.

Step 2.   Calculate the lowest cost route to reach any of the ASBR(s) based on the intra-area LSDB topology.

Step 3.   Use the outgoing interface and next hop based on the best route to reach the ASBR (as chosen at Step 2).

Step 4.   The route's metric is unchanged–it is still simply the value listed in the Type 5 LSA.

For example, use Router R4 in Figure 9-7 as an example and the E2 route for 172.30.26.0/23. Before using these four steps, R4 calculated two possible routes for 172.16.26.0/23: an E2 route directly to RD1, and another route through R8. Both routes use metric 20 in this case, so the routes tie. Because of the tie, R4 proceeds with these steps as follows:

Step 1.   R4 looks in the Type 5 LSA, and sees RID 1.1.1.1 (RD1) is the advertising ASBR.

Step 2. R4 then looks at its area 0 LSDB entries, including the Type 1 LSA for RID 1.1.1.1, and calculates all possible area 0 routes to reach 1.1.1.1.

Step 3. R4's best route to reach RID 1.1.1.1 happens to be through its S0/0/0 interface, to next-hop RD1 (172.16.14.1), so R4's route to 172.16.26.0/23 uses these details.

Step 4. The route lists metric 20, as listed in the Type 5 LSA.

Figure 9-8 shows the interface costs Router R4 will use, based on its LSDB, to calculate the cost for two possible routes to reach ASBR RD1. Again using subnet 172.30.26.0/23 as an example, RD1 first looks at the Type 5 external LSA and sees RID 1.1.1.1 as the advertising ASBR. R4 then calculates the costs based on its intra-area LSDB–but we can perform the equivalent by adding the interface costs seen in Figure 9-8. Example 9-10 lists the external Type 5 LSAs, highlighting subnet 172.30.26.0/23, and the interface costs on both R4 and R8 as seen in the figure.

Figure 9-8   *R4's Cost to Reach ASBR RD1*

Example 9-10   *Verifying OSPF External Routes–Intra-area*

```
R4#show ip ospf database | begin Ext
                    Type-5 AS External Link States


Link ID          ADV Router      Age        Seq#        Checksum Tag
172.30.2.0       1.1.1.1         189        0x80000002 0x007E51 0
172.30.6.0       1.1.1.1         189        0x80000002 0x005279 0
172.30.12.0      1.1.1.1         189        0x80000002 0x0003C4 0
172.30.17.0      1.1.1.1         189        0x80000002 0x00CBF6 0
172.30.26.0      1.1.1.1         189        0x80000002 0x007542 0


R4#show ip ospf database external 172.30.26.0
```

```
            OSPF Router with ID (4.4.4.4) (Process ID 4)


               Type-5 AS External Link States


Routing Bit Set on this LSA
LS age: 175
Options: (No TOS-capability, DC)
LS Type: AS External Link
Link State ID: 172.30.26.0 (External Network Number )
Advertising Router: 1.1.1.1
LS Seq Number: 80000001
Checksum: 0x7741
Length: 36
Network Mask: /23
        Metric Type: 2 (Larger than any link state path)
        TOS: 0
        Metric: 20
        Forward Address: 0.0.0.0
        External Route Tag: 0

R4#show ip ospf interface brief
Interface    PID    Area           IP Address/Mask    Cost   State  Nbrs F/C
Se0/0/0       4      0             172.16.14.2/30      64     P2P    1/1
Fa0/1         4      0             172.16.4.4/25        1     DR     0/0
Fa0/0         4      0             172.16.48.4/25       1     DR     1/1
Se0/0/1       4      1             172.16.45.4/25      64     P2P    1/1
! Next output occurs on R8

R8#show ip ospf interface brief
Interface    PID    Area           IP Address/Mask    Cost   State  Nbrs F/C
Fa0/1         8      0             172.16.8.8/25        1     DR     0/0
Se0/0         8      0             172.16.18.2/30      64     P2P    1/1
Fa0/0         8      0             172.16.48.8/25       1     BDR    1/1
```

Determining the Next-hop for Type 2 External Routes–Interarea

When a router exists in a different area than the ASBR, the issues remain the same, but the tie-breaker calculation of choosing the least cost route to reach the ASBR changes. If a router finds multiple routes to reach a single E2 subnet, some or all may tie based on metric, because the metric is based solely on the external cost as defined by the ASBR. (If multiple ASBRs redistribute routes for the same prefix, each ASBR can assign a different metric.) A router then chooses the best route based on the least-cost route to reach an ASBR that has advertised the lowest E2 cost for the subnet.

When the ASBR is in a different area, the calculation of the cost to reach the ASBR requires more information, and even an additional LSA type, as compared with the intra-area calculation. To calculate their best route to reach the ASBR, a router in another area adds the cost to reach an ABR between the areas, plus that ABR's cost to reach the ASBR. To make more sense of that concept, Figure 9-9 shows a portion of Figure 9-7, with costs highlighted, assuming the OSPF reference bandwidth is also using default settings.

Figure 9-9 *R5's Cost to Reach ASBR RD1*

R5 has two possible routes shown in Figure 9-9 to reach ASBR RD1. On the left, the path through R3 has a total cost of 65. To the right, the router through ABR R4 has a total cost of 128. R5 then chooses the route through R3 as the best route based on the least cost to reach the ASBR.

For humans, when you have a figure and know all costs, the calculation of the costs of the two routes is simple. However, for routers, the calculation occurs in two parts:

Step 1. Calculate the cost to reach the ABR, based on the local area's topology database.

Step 2. Add the cost from the ABR to the ASBR, as listed in a Type 4 LSA.

ABRs create this new type of LSA—the Type 4 Summary ASBR LSA—to support the logic mentioned at Step 2. The Type 4 ASBR LSA lists the RID of the ASBR, and the RID of the ABR that created and flooded the Type 4 LSA. Most importantly, the Type 4 LSA lists that ABR's cost to reach the ASBR. In effect, the LSA makes an announcement like this: "I am ABR X, I can reach ASBR Y, and my cost to reach that ASBR is Z." In short, it allows the second part of the computation.

ABRs create Type 4 LSAs in reaction to receiving an external LSA from some ASBR. When an ABR forwards a Type 5 LSA into an area, the ABR looks at the RID of the ASBR that created the Type 5 LSA. The ABR then creates a Type 4 LSA listing that ASBR, and the cost to reach that ASBR, flooding that Type 4 LSA into the neighboring areas.

For example, using Figure 9-9 again, R3 would create and flood a Type 4 Summary ASBR LSA into area 1. R3's Type 4 LSA lists ASBR 1.1.1.1 (RD1), ABR 3.3.3.3 (itself), and cost 1 (R3's cost to reach 1.1.1.1). Similarly, in that same example, ABR R4 would create another Type 4 ASBR Summary LSA. This LSA also lists ASBR 1.1.1.1 (RD1), but with advertising ABR 4.4.4.4 (R4), and lists cost 64 (R4's cost to reach 1.1.1.1).

R5, internal to area 1, then calculates the cost for each competing route by adding R5's intra-area cost to reach the respective ABRs (Step 1 in the previous list), to the cost listed in the corresponding Type 4 LSAs (Step 2 in the previous list). When R5 calculates two possible routes to reach external subnet 172.30.26.0/23, R5 finds routes both have a metric of 20, so R5 tries to break the tie by looking at the cost to reach the ASBR over each route. To do so, R5 examines each route, adding its intra-area cost to reach the ABR to the ABR's cost to reach the ASBR (as listed in the Type 4 LSA). In this case, R5 finds the route through R3 has the lower cost (65), so R5 uses outgoing interface s0/0 for its route to 172.30.26.0/23.

Example 9-11 lists the **show** command output that demonstrates the same example. Again focusing on R5's route for 172.30.26.0/23, the example first shows R5's LSDB, beginning with the Summary ASBR LSAs. More discussion follows the example.

Example 9-11   *Redistributing from EIGRP into OSPF, with Subnets*

```
R5#show ip ospf database | begin ASB
                Summary ASB Link States (Area 1)


Link ID          ADV Router       Age       Seq#        Checksum
1.1.1.1          3.3.3.3          956       0x8000000D 0x00E43A
1.1.1.1          4.4.4.4          1044      0x8000000B 0x00439A


                Type-5 AS External Link States


Link ID          ADV Router       Age       Seq#        Checksum Tag
172.30.2.0       1.1.1.1          1185      0x8000000B 0x006C5A 0
172.30.6.0       1.1.1.1          1185      0x8000000B 0x004082 0
172.30.12.0      1.1.1.1          1185      0x8000000B 0x00F0CD 0
172.30.17.0      1.1.1.1          1185      0x8000000B 0x00B9FF 0
172.30.26.0      1.1.1.1          1185      0x8000000B 0x00634B 0


R5#show ip ospf database asbr-summary


               OSPF Router with ID (5.5.5.5) (Process ID 5)


                Summary ASB Link States (Area 1)


  Routing Bit Set on this LSA
```

```
      LS age: 984
      Options: (No TOS-capability, DC, Upward)
      LS Type: Summary Links(AS Boundary Router)
      Link State ID: 1.1.1.1 (AS Boundary Router address)
      Advertising Router: 3.3.3.3
      LS Seq Number: 8000000D
      Checksum: 0xE43A
      Length: 28
      Network Mask: /0
            TOS: 0  Metric: 1


      LS age: 1072
      Options: (No TOS-capability, DC, Upward)
      LS Type: Summary Links(AS Boundary Router)
      Link State ID: 1.1.1.1 (AS Boundary Router address)
      Advertising Router: 4.4.4.4
      LS Seq Number: 8000000B
      Checksum: 0x439A
      Length: 28
      Network Mask: /0
            TOS: 0  Metric: 64

R5#show ip ospf border-routers
OSPF Process 5 internal Routing Table
Codes: i - Intra-area route, I - Inter-area route

i 4.4.4.4 [64] via 172.16.45.4, Serial0/1, ABR, Area 1, SPF 6
I 1.1.1.1 [65] via 172.16.35.3, Serial0/0, ASBR, Area 1, SPF 6
i 3.3.3.3 [64] via 172.16.35.3, Serial0/0, ABR, Area 1, SPF 6

R5#show ip route 172.30.0.0
Routing entry for 172.30.0.0/16, 5 known subnets
  Variably subnetted with 2 masks

O E2    172.30.17.0/30 [110/20] via 172.16.35.3, 05:48:42, Serial0/0
O E2    172.30.26.0/23 [110/20] via 172.16.35.3, 05:48:42, Serial0/0
O E2    172.30.2.0/23 [110/20] via 172.16.35.3, 05:48:42, Serial0/0
O E2    172.30.6.0/23 [110/20] via 172.16.35.3, 05:48:42, Serial0/0
O E2    172.30.12.0/30 [110/20] via 172.16.35.3, 05:48:42, Serial0/0
```

The **show ip ospf database | begin ASB** command's output lists two Type 4 LSAs. (The command itself lists the summary of R5's OSPF LSDB, beginning with the section that lists Type 4 LSAs.) Both Type 4 LSAs list ASBR RD1's RID of 1.1.1.1 as the LSID, but they each list difference advertising routers: 3.3.3.3 (R3) and 4.4.4.4 (R4). In that same command, the output lists five Type 5 LSAs for the five subnets in the EIGRP domain, each with advertising router 1.1.1.1 (RD1).

The next command, **show ip ospf database asbr-summary**, lists the same two Type 4 LSAs seen in the previous command, but in detail. The first lists ASBR 1.1.1.1 (RD1), with ABR 3.3.3.3 (R3), and a cost of 1. The second lists ASBR 1.1.1.1, but with ABR 4.4.4.4 (R4), and a cost of 64. The costs list the respective ABR's cost to reach ASBR 1.1.1.1.

The third command, **show ip ospf border-routers**, lists a line for every ABR and ASBR known to the local router. It lists whether the router is inside the same area or in another area, the RID of the ABR or ASBR, and this router's best route to reach each ABR and ASBR. This command essentially shows the answer to the question "which route to ASBR 1.1.1.1 is best." Finally, the last command lists R5's IP route for 172.30.26.0, with the same next-hop and outgoing interface information as seen in the entry for RID 1.1.1.1 in the output of the **show ip ospf border-routers** command.

Redistributing into OSPF as E1 Routes

OSPF's external metric type feature allows engineers a design tool for influencing the choice of best route. E2 routes work well when the design needs to choose the best route based on the external metric–in other words, the metric as perceived outside the OSPF domain. E2 routes ignore the internal OSPF cost (except when breaking ties for best route), so when OSPF compares two E2 routes for the same subnet, that first choice to pick the lowest-metric route is based on the external metric only.

OSPF routers calculate the metrics of E1 routes by adding the internal cost to reach the ASBR to the external cost defined on the redistributing ASBR. As a result, engineer can influence the choice of routes based on the combination of the external and internal OSPF cost simply by redistributing a route as an E1 route instead of as an E2 route. To take advantage of this feature, the **redistribute** command simply needs to set the metric type.

Example 9-12 shows the simple change to the redistribution configuration on RD1 (as shown earlier in Example 9-9) to make all routes redistributed from EIGRP into OSPF be E1 routes. The example also lists output from R4 demonstrating the metric, which is based on the (default) external metric (20) plus R4's best internal metric to reach ASBR 1.1.1.1 (64).

Example 9-12   *Redistributing from EIGRP into OSPF, with Subnets*

```
RD1#conf t
Enter configuration commands, one per line.  End with CNTL/Z.
RD1(config)#router ospf 2
RD1(config-router)#redistribute eigrp 1 subnets metric-type 1
RD1(config-router)#^Z
RD1#
! Moving to router R4
R4#show ip route 172.30.0.0
Routing entry for 172.30.0.0/16, 5 known subnets
  Variably subnetted with 2 masks

O E1    172.30.17.0/30 [110/84] via 172.16.14.1, 00:00:06, Serial0/0/0
O E1    172.30.26.0/23 [110/84] via 172.16.14.1, 00:00:06, Serial0/0/0
```

```
O E1    172.30.2.0/23 [110/84] via 172.16.14.1, 00:00:06, Serial0/0/0
O E1    172.30.6.0/23 [110/84] via 172.16.14.1, 00:00:06, Serial0/0/0
O E1    172.30.12.0/30 [110/84] via 172.16.14.1, 00:00:06, Serial0/0/0


R4#show ip ospf border-routers

OSPF Process 4 internal Routing Table        .
Codes: i - Intra-area route, I - Inter-area route


i 1.1.1.1 [64] via 172.16.14.1, Serial0/0/0, ASBR, Area 0, SPF 16
i 3.3.3.3 [65] via 172.16.14.1, Serial0/0/0, ABR, Area 0, SPF 16
i 3.3.3.3 [128] via 172.16.45.5, Serial0/0/1, ABR, Area 1, SPF 8
```

Note that for routers in a different area than the ASBR, the calculation of metric follows the same general logic used when breaking ties for E2 routes. Generally, the computation adds three items:

■ The best intra-area cost to reach the ABR (per that area's LSDB)

■ The cost from that ABR to the ASBR (per Type 4 LSA)

■ The external cost for the route (per Type 5 LSA)

For example, Figure 9-9 shows that R5's best cost to reach ASBR RD1 was out S0/0, to R3 next, with cost 65. Adding the external cost of 20, R5's best route will have a metric of 85. R5 calculates that cost by adding the following:

■ The intra-area cost to ABR R3 (64), by analyzing the area 1 LSDB entries

■ R3's cost to reach ASBR 1.1.1.1, as listed in its Type 4 LSA (1)

■ The external cost as listed in the Type 5 LSA (20)

A Brief Comparison of E1 and E2 Routes

OSPF defines two types of external routes to give network designers two slightly different tools with which to calculate the best route to reach destination external to OSPF. For E1 routes, both the external cost and internal OSPF cost matters to the choice of best route. For E2 routes, only the external cost matters to the choice of best route (unless a tie needs to be broken.)

The benefits of the different external route types apply mostly to when multiple ASBRs advertise the same subnet. For example, imagine two ASBRs, ASBR1 and ASBR2, between OSPF and another routing domain. If the goal is to always send traffic through ASBR1, you could use E2 routes and set the metric for ASBR1's redistributed routes to a lower metric than ASBR2. Because routers ignore the internal metrics when calculating the E2 metrics, then every router will choose ASBR1 as the better ASBR. Conversely, if the goal were to balance the traffic, and make each router pick the closest ASBR, both ASBRs could set the same metric to their redistributed routes, but make the routers Type E1. As a result, routers closer to each ASBR choose best routes based on the lower OSPF internal costs.

Also, note that for a given prefix/length, OSPF always prefers an E1 route over an E2 route.

External Routes in NSSA Areas

Routes may be redistributed into OSPF on any OSPF router, with a few exceptions. The router may be internal to Area 0, like router RD1 in the many examples earlier in this chapter. It can also be an ABR connected to several areas. It can be a router internal to a non-backbone area as well.

Of the four types of stubby areas, two do not allow redistribution into the area, and two do allow redistribution–even though none of the stubby area types allow Type 5 LSAs. OSPF does not allow routers in stubby and totally stubby areas to inject external routes. However, routers in not-so-stubby areas–NSSA areas–can redistribute routes, while still holding to the restriction of having no Type 5 LSAs.

OSPF supports the injection of external routes into NSSA areas by defining the Type 7 AS External LSA. This LSA type essentially replaces the Type 5 LSA's role, but only inside the NSSA area. Figure 9-10 shows a conceptual view.

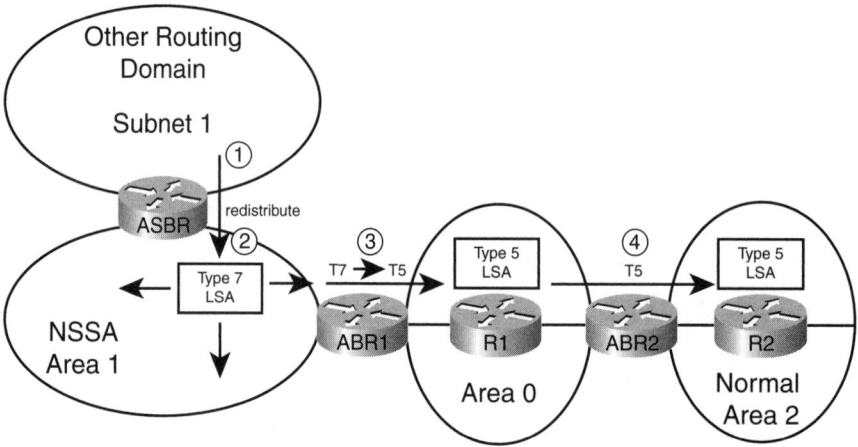

Figure 9-10 *Process of Adding and Converting Type 7 LSAs*

Following the steps in the figure:

Step 1. The ASBR attached to NSSA area 1 redistributes a route for subnet 1, creating a Type 7 LSA.

Step 2. The ASBR floods the Type 7 LSA throughout NSSA area 1.

Step 3. ABR1 converts the Type 7 LSA to a Type 5 LSA when forwarding into other areas (area 0 in this case).

Step 4.   ABR2, connected to another normal area, forwards the Type 5 LSA for subnet 1 into normal area 2.

Example 9-13 demonstrates the concept using area 1 from Figures 9-7 and 9-9. Area 1 has been converted to be an NSSA area. R5 has been configured to redistribute connected routes. This feature allows a router to inject connect routes into a routing domain without having to enable the routing protocol on the corresponding interfaces. In this case, R5 will redistribute subnet 10.1.1.0/24, a connected route added by R5 using interface loopback0.

Example 9-13   *Redistributing from EIGRP into OSPF, with Subnets*

```
! R5's new configuration here:
interface loopback0
 ip address 10.1.1.1 255.255.255.0
router ospf 5
 redistribute connected subnets


R5#show ip ospf database | begin Type-7
                Type-7 AS External Link States (Area 1)


Link ID          ADV Router       Age        Seq#         Checksum Tag
10.1.1.0         5.5.5.5          26         0x80000001 0x00E0A6 0


R5#show ip ospf database nssa-external


            OSPF Router with ID (5.5.5.5) (Process ID 5)


                Type-7 AS External Link States (Area 1)


  LS age: 69
  Options: (No TOS-capability, Type 7/5 translation, DC)
  LS Type: AS External Link
  Link State ID: 10.1.1.0 (External Network Number )
  Advertising Router: 5.5.5.5
  LS Seq Number: 80000001
  Checksum: 0xE0A6
  Length: 36
  Network Mask: /24
        Metric Type: 2 (Larger than any link state path)
        TOS: 0
        Metric: 20
        Forward Address: 172.16.45.5
        External Route Tag: 0
! Moving to router R8
R8#show ip ospf database | begin Type-7


R8#show ip ospf database | begin External
```

```
                Type-5 AS External Link States

Link ID          ADV Router        Age         Seq#        Checksum Tag
10.1.1.0         4.4.4.4           263         0x80000001 0x009302 0
172.30.2.0       1.1.1.1           1655        0x8000000E 0x00665D 0
172.30.6.0       1.1.1.1           1655        0x8000000E 0x003A85 0
172.30.12.0      1.1.1.1           1655        0x8000000E 0x00EAD0 0
172.30.17.0      1.1.1.1           1655        0x8000000E 0x00B303 0
172.30.26.0      1.1.1.1           1655        0x8000000E 0x005D4E 0
```

The example begins with configuration on R5, followed by **show** commands on both Router R5 and R4. In particular, the **show ip ospf database | begin Type-7** command on R5 skips output until the heading for Type 7 LSAs, listing one such LSA. The LSA lists the subnet number (10.1.1.0) as the LSID, and the ASBR's RID (5.5.5.5, or R5). The next command, show detailed output from the **show ip ospf database nssa-external** command on R5 shows the details in the Type 7 LSA, including the LSA cost of 20–the same default used when injecting routes as Type 5 LSAs.

The second half of the output, on Router R8, starts with another **show ip ospf database | begin Type-7** command—the same exact command seen earlier in the example on R5. The null output in this command confirms that R8 has no Type 7 LSAs. However, the final command in the example confirms that R8 does have a Type 5 external LSA for subnet 10.1.1.0, with a listing of R4 (4.4.4.4) as the advertising router. This LSA does not list R5's RID of 5.5.5.5 as the advertising router, because R5 did not create this Type 5 LSA. Instead, R4 created this Type 5 LSA when R4 reacted to learning the Type 7 LSA inside area 1.

Finally, Example 9-14 shows a few interesting items about the IP routing table with NSSA areas. Routers inside the NSSA area use a different code in the output of **show ip route** to denote NSSA external routes as compared with normal external routes. The example shows R4's IP routing table, which lists an N2 route. This means that it is external Type 2, but inside an NSSA area, and using a Type 7 AS external LSA. The second part of the example shows R8's route for the same subnet. Because R8 is inside a non-NSSA area, R8 knows of subnet 10.1.1.0/24 because of a type 5 LSA, so R8 lists the route as an E2 route.

Example 9-14 *Redistributing from EIGRP into OSPF, with Subnets*

```
! R4's output here:
R4#show ip route
Codes: C - connected, S - static, R - RIP, M - mobile, B - BGP
       D - EIGRP, EX - EIGRP external, O - OSPF, IA - OSPF inter area
       N1 - OSPF NSSA external type 1, N2 - OSPF NSSA external type 2
       E1 - OSPF external type 1, E2 - OSPF external type 2
       i - IS-IS, su - IS-IS summary, L1 - IS-IS level-1, L2 - IS-IS level-2
       ia - IS-IS inter area, * - candidate default, U - per-user static route
       o - ODR, P - periodic downloaded static route

Gateway of last resort is not set
```

```
! lines omitted for brevity

     10.0.0.0/24 is subnetted, 1 subnets
O N2     10.1.1.0 [110/20] via 172.16.45.5, 00:10:54, Serial0/0/1
! R8, in area 0, next
R8#show ip route | begin 10.0.0.0
     10.0.0.0/24 is subnetted, 1 subnets
O E2     10.1.1.0 [110/20] via 172.16.48.4, 00:10:24, FastEthernet0/0
```

Exam Preparation Tasks

Planning Practice

The CCNP ROUTE exam expects test takers to review design documents, create implementation plans, and create verification plans. This section provides some exercises that may help you to take a step back from the minute details of the topics in this chapter so that you can think about the same technical topics from the planning perspective.

For each planning practice table, simply complete the table. Note that any numbers in parentheses represent the number of options listed for each item in the solutions in Appendix F, "Completed Planning Practice Tables."

Design Review Table

Table 9-6 lists several design goals related to this chapter. If these design goals were listed in a design document, and you had to take that document and develop an implementation plan, what implementation options come to mind? For any configuration items, a general description can be used, without concern about the specific parameters.

Table 9-6 *Design Review*

Design Goal	Possible Implementation Choices Covered in This Chapter
A design shows Router R1 as being connected to both an EIGRP and OSPF routing domain, with all external EIGRP routes using a particular set of component EIGRP metrics. How can these metrics be set? (3)	
A design shows Router R1 as being connected to two different EIGRP domains, with redistribution planned. Can the design cause the routers to calculate metrics based on both the metric assigned when redistributing and the internal EIGRP topology?	
The same design as in the previous row is shown, except describe whether or not the design can cause the routers to calculate metrics based solely on the metric components assigned when redistributing.	

Table 9-6 *Design Review*

Design Goal	Possible Implementation Choices Covered in This Chapter
A design shows Router R1 as being connected to two different OSPF domains, with redistribution planned, and all routes calculated by including internal and external OSPF distance.	
The same design as in the previous row is shown, except that all external route metrics are based solely on external metrics.	

Implementation Plan Peer Review Table

Table 9-7 shows a list of questions that others might ask, or that you might think about, during a peer review of another network engineer's implementation plan. Complete the table by answering the questions.

Table 9-7 *Notable Questions from This Chapter to Consider During an Implementation Plan Peer Review*

Question	Answer
A design shows Router R1 as being connected to both an EIGRP and OSPF routing domain. What default metrics will be used by the **redistribute** command for each routing protocol, if not set in R1's configuration?	
A plan shows redistribution between two EIGRP domains. What must be done to use the source route's original component metrics?	
A plan shows redistribution between two OSPF domains. What must be done to use the source route's original component metrics?	
The plan shows the **redistribute eigrp 2** command to redistribute from EIGRP 2 into OSPF. What other optional parameters are required to ensure redistribution of 10.1.1.0/24 from EIGRP?	
R1 has two connected interfaces in the EIGRP 2 domain and knows dozens of EIGRP routes. The plan shows the **redistribute eigrp 2 subnets** under an OSPF process. What else must be done to redistribute the two connected subnets inside the EIGRP domain?	

Create an Implementation Plan Table

To practice skills useful when creating your own implementation plan, list in Table 9-8 configuration commands related to the configuration of the following features. You may want to record your answers outside the book and set a goal to complete this table (and others like it) from memory during your final reviews before taking the exam.

Table 9-8 *Implementation Plan Configuration Memory Drill*

Feature	Configuration Commands/Notes
Configuring redistribution into EIGRP from OSPF. (List all parameters you can recall.)	
Configuring redistribution into EIGRP from OSPF. (List all parameters you can recall.)	
Setting default metrics for all **redistribute** commands, redistributing into EIGRP.	
Setting default metrics for all redistribute commands, redistributing into OSPF.	

Choosing Commands for a Verification Plan Table

To practice skills useful when creating your own verification plan, list in Table 9-9 all commands that supply the requested information. You may want to record your answers outside the book and set a goal to complete this table (and others like it) from memory during your final reviews before taking the exam.

Table 9-9 *Verification Plan Memory Drill*

Information Needed	Command(s)
Display a brief version of the EIGRP topology table, listing external routes.	
Display the EIGRP topology table, including notations identifying external routes.	
For external EIGRP routes, display the source of the route, external metric, and IP address of the router that redistributed the route.	
Identify external EIGRP-learned IP routes.	
Display a brief version of the OSPF topology table, listing Type 5 External LSAs.	
Display all OSPF Type 4 LSAs.	
Display all OSPF Type 5 LSAs.	
Display all OSPF Type 7 LSAs.	
Display the external route type for an OSPF external route.	
Display OSPF cost for each interface, briefly.	

On an internal router, display any same-area ABRs' costs to reach any ASBRs.

On an internal router, display that router's best cost to reach an ASBR.

Display the metric for all currently best external OSPF routes.

Note: Some of the entries in this table may not have been specifically mentioned in this chapter but are listed in this table for review and reference.

Review all the Key Topics

Review the most important topics from inside the chapter, noted with the key topics icon in the outer margin of the page. Table 9-10 lists a reference of these key topics and the page numbers on which each is found.

Key Topic

Table 9-10 *Key Topics for Chapter 9*

Key Topic Element	Description	Page Number
List	Requirements for redistribution in a router	294
Table 9-2	Parameters on the EIGRP **redistribute** command	298
Table 9-3	Commands and options to set metrics when redistributing into EIGRP	301
List	Rules from what is redistributed from an IGP	304
Table 9-4	Parameters on the OSPF **redistribute** command	305
List	Defaults of the OSPF **redistribute** command	306
Table 9-5	Commands and options to set metrics when redistributing into OSPF	310
List	Tiebreaker rules for choosing the best E2 routes	312
List	Rules for calculating the metric of an interarea E1 route	319

Complete the Tables and Lists from Memory

Print a copy of Appendix D, "Memory Tables," (found on the CD), or at least the section for this chapter, and complete the tables and lists from memory. Appendix E, "Memory Tables Answer Key," also on the CD, includes completed tables and lists to check your work.

Define Key Terms

Define the following key terms from this chapter, and check your answers in the glossary.

Redistribution, External route, Type 4 Summary ASBR LSA, Type 5 External LSA, Type 7 AS External LSA, External Type 1, External Type 2

This chapter covers the following subjects:

Redistribution with Route Maps and Distribution Lists: This section focuses on the functions available using route maps and distribute lists on the same router that performs redistribution into either EIGRP or OSPF.

Issues with Multiple Redistribution Points: This section examines the domain loop problem that can occur when multiple routers redistribute routes between the same two routing domains. This section also examines various solutions, including the setting of large metrics, setting the administrative distance, and using route tags.

CHAPTER 10

Advanced IGP Redistribution

This chapter progresses past the basic mechanics of route redistribution (Chapter 9, "Basic IGP Redistribution") to examine two major topics. The first part of this chapter looks at the methods by which a router can manipulate the routes being redistributed beyond the settings of the metrics. This manipulation includes the filtering of routes and the setting of other values that can be associated with a route during the redistribution process.

The second part of the chapter examines a variety of design issues that occur when multiple redistribution points exist between routing domains. Many designs use multiple redistribution points for redundancy and even for load sharing. This redundancy creates some additional complexity. (This complexity has long been a favorite topic for the CCIE Routing lab exam.) This chapter also shows methods of dealing with the design issues, including the manipulation of metrics, administrative distance, and route tags.

"Do I Know This Already?" Quiz

The "Do I Know This Already?" quiz allows you to assess if you should read the entire chapter. If you miss no more than one of these eight self-assessment questions, you might want to move ahead to the "Exam Preparation Tasks." Table 10-1 lists the major headings in this chapter and the "Do I Know This Already?" quiz questions covering the material in those headings so that you can assess your knowledge of these specific areas. The answers to the "Do I Know This Already?" quiz appear in Appendix A.

Table 10-1 *"Do I Know This Already?" Foundation Topics Section-to-Question Mapping*

Foundations Topics Section	Questions
Redistribution with route maps and distribute lists	1-4
Issues with multiple redistribution points	5-8

1. Router R1 has been configured with the **redistribute ospf 1 route-map fred** command under **router eigrp 1**. The route map named fred needs to be configured to match routes to determine which routes are redistributed into EIGRP. Which of the following answers lists an item that cannot be matched by route map fred?

   a. Subnet number

   b. Next-hop router IP address of the route

   c. Whether the route is an E1 or E2 route

   d. The route's tag

   e. The number of router hops between the router and the subnet

2. Router R1 refers to route-map fred when redistributing from EIGRP into OSPF. The entire route-map is listed next. Which of the following answers must be true based on the configuration as shown?

```
route-map fred deny 10
 match ip address one
route-map fred deny 20
 match ip address two
route-map fred permit 100
```

   a. The third route map clause will allow any routes not already filtered by the first two clauses.

   b. Routes permitted by ACL "two" will be redistributed.

   c. Routes denied by ACL "one" will be redistributed.

   d. All routes will be filtered.

3. On Router R1, process EIGRP 1 is redistributing routes from process OSPF 2, calling route-map fred with the **redistribute ospf 2** command. R1 has learned intra-area routes for 10.1.1.0/24 and 10.1.2.0/24 in part due to the Type 2 LSAs known for each subnet. The route map filters route 10.1.1.0/24 and allows 10.1.2.0/24 through. Which of the following commands on router R1 list subnet 10.1.1.0/24? (Choose two.)

   a. show ip route

   b. show ip eigrp topology

   c. show ip ospf topology

   d. show ip eigrp topology 10.1.1.0/24

4. Router R1 is redistributing between two OSPF processes. Given the configuration shown, which includes all commands in the route map named fred, which of the following answers is true regarding the redistribution into OSPF process 1?

```
router ospf 1
 redistribute ospf 2 external 2 route-map fred
!
route-map fred permit 10
 match ip address 1
 set metric-type type-1
```

   a. No routes are redistributed because a route cannot be both E1 and E2.

   b. Only OSPF E2 routes in the OSPF 2 domain will be considered for redistribution.

   c. Inside the OSPF 2 domain, any formerly E2 routes will become E1 routes.

   d. Routes permitted by ACL 1 will be redistributed, regardless of whether the routes are E1 or E2 routes.

5. Which of the following is not true regarding IOS default settings for administrative distance?

    a. EIGRP internal: 90

    b. OSPF external: 110

    c. EIGRP external: 90

    d. RIP: 120

    e. OSPF internal: 110

6. A network includes a RIPv2 domain, an EIGRP domain, and an OSPF domain. Each pair of routing domains has multiple routers redistributing routes between the pair of domains. The design requires that the redistribution configuration avoid matching based on prefix/length because of the trouble in maintaining such configurations. Which one of the following tools can be used in all three routing domains to attempt to prevent domain loops? (This book uses the term *domain loop* to refer to the long routes that might be chosen for routes when redistribution exists–for example, a route may forward packets from the EIGRP domain, to the OSPF domain, back to EIGRP, and then to subnet X in the RIP domain.)

    a. Setting route tags

    b. Setting the default administrative distance differently for internal and external routes

    c. Setting administrative distance differently per route

    d. Setting metrics much higher for all external routes than for all internal routes

7. A co-worker is developing an implementation plan for a design that uses OSPF 2 and RIPv2 routing domains, with two routers redistributing between the two domains. The co-worker asks your help in choosing how to prevent domain loops by setting administrative distance. (This chapter uses the term *domain loop* to refer to the long routes that might be chosen for routes when redistribution exists–for example, a route may forward packets from the EIGRP 1 domain, to OSPF2, back to EIGRP 1, and then to subnet X in the RIP domain.) Assuming all other related settings use defaults, which of the following would solve the domain loop problem?

    a. The **distance ospf intra-area 80 inter-area 80** OSPF subcommand

    b. The **distance ospf external 80** OSPF subcommand

    c. The **distance ospf intra-area 180 inter-area 180** OSPF subcommand

    d. The **distance ospf external 180** OSPF subcommand

8. Router R1 sets a route tag for subnet 10.1.1.0/24 when redistributing from OSPF into EIGRP. Which of the following unit is assigned to the route tag?

    a. Kilobits/second.

    b. Tens of microseconds.

    c. Cost.

    d. Hop count.

    e. No unit is assigned.

Foundation Topics

Redistribution with Route Maps and Distribute Lists

In some cases, a redistribution design calls for all routes to be redistributed, all with the same metric, and all with the same external route type (if applicable). However, in other cases, the metrics may need to be set differently for different routes. Additionally, some designs require that only a subset of the routes should be redistributed, for instance, when only a few key subnets need to be exposed for connections from a partner. And with routing protocols that have different types of external routes, such as OSPF and IS-IS, the design may or may not allow all redistributed routes to be of the same external route type.

All these features require a tool by which IOS can identify the routes that need to be treated differently, whether given different metrics, filtered, and assigned a different external route type. IOS provides such a feature by allowing a reference to a **route-map** from the **redistribute** command. In particular, the route-map can perform the following:

**Key
Topic**

- Identify the subset of the routes to filter or change based on the route's prefix/length, plus many other factors.

- Make filtering choices about which routes are redistributed, and which are not.

- Set the metric to different values based on information matchable by the route-map.

- Set the type of External route for different redistributed routes, for example, OSPF Type 1 for some routes, Type 2 for others.

- Set a route tag, a unitless integer value that can later be matched with a **route-map** at another redistribution point.

This section examines the mechanics of using the **redistribute... route-map** command option to filter routes and set the metrics, along with a few other small features.

> **Note:** Chapter 4's section "Filtering by Using route-maps" describes the logic behind the **route-map** command, so this chapter simply reviews the logic as needed. Refer to Chapter 4, "EIGRP Route Summarization and Filtering," for more detail on route maps.

Overview of Using route-maps with Redistribution

The **redistribute** command has two mechanisms that allow filtering of routes:

- The **match {internal | external 1 | external 2 | nssa-external}** parameters

- The **route-map** *map-name* option

Of these two options, the first applies only when redistributing from OSPF, and matches routes solely based on the types of routes listed here. However, the **route-map** referenced by the **redistribute** command has many options for identifying routes by matching various facts about the route.

To identify the routes, route-maps use the **match** subcommand. The **match** command can refer to ACLs and prefix-lists to match anything matchable by those tools, plus match other facts more directly. Table 10-2 lists the **match** command options that matter when using route-maps for IGP redistribution.

Table 10-2 *match Command Options for Redistribution*

Key
Topic

match Command	Description
match interface *interface-type interface-number* [*... interface-type interface-number*]	Looks at outgoing interface of routes
˙**match ip address** {[*access-list-number* | *access-list-name*] | **prefix-list** *prefix-list-name*}	Examines route destination prefix and prefix length
˙**match ip next-hop** {*access-list-number* | *access-list-name*}	Examines route's next-hop address
˙**match ip route-source** {*access-list-number* | *access-list-name*}	Matches advertising router's IP address
match metric *metric-value* [**+-** deviation]	Matches route's metric, or a range (plus/minus the configured deviation)
match route-type {**internal** | **external** [**type–1** | **type–2**] | **level–1** | **level–2**}	Matches route type
match tag *tag-value* [*...tag-value*]	Matches the route tag, which requires that another router has earlier set the tag

* Can reference multiple numbered and named ACLs on a single `match` command.

A route-map referenced by the **redistribute** command always attempts to filter routes. If the route-map matches a particular route with a particular route-map clause, and the action in that clause is **permit**, then the route is redistributed. However, if the first route-map clause matched by a packet has a **deny** action, the packet is filtered–in other words, not redistributed. In short, the logic matches the same logic as described in Chapter 4 for route-maps referenced by the **distribute-list** command. (Chapter 4 shows how to filter routes inside EIGRP, without redistributing.)

Additionally, for routes not filtered by the route-map, the route-map can set other values (like the route's metric) using the aptly-named **set** command. Table 10-3 lists the various route-map **set** subcommands that can be used to set the values used for routes redistributed into IGPs.

Table 10-3   *set Command Options for Redistribution into IGPs*

set Command	Description
set metric *metric-value*	Sets the route's metric for OSPF, RIP, and IS-IS
set metric *bandwidth delay reliability loading mtu*	Sets the EIGRP route's metric values
set metric-type {**type–1** | **type–2**}	Sets type of route for OSPF
set tag *tag-value*	Sets the unitless tag value in the route

Filtering Redistributed Routes with Route Maps

As usual, the best way to understand the configuration, and the methods to verify the re-sults, is to use an example. In this case, the same internetwork used throughout Chapter 9 is used, but with some more routes added. Figure 10-1 shows some of the detail of the internetwork.

Figure 10-1   *Sample Internetwork Used for Redistribution Route Map Examples*

The internetwork has been preconfigured with mainly defaults, as follows:

■   EIGRP works well on the left side of Figure 10-1.

■   OSPF works well on the right side.

■   Mutual redistribution has been configured on router RD1, with no filtering.

■   All routes use these metric settings: EIGRP (1500 10 255 1 1500), OSPF (20).

Example 10-1 shows the routing protocol configuration on Router RD1 at the beginning of the example.

Example 10-1   *Initial Configuration–Mutual Redistribution, No Filtering*

```
RD1#show run
! lines omitted for brevity
router eigrp 1
 redistribute ospf 2
 network 172.30.0.0
 default-metric 1500 10 255 1 1500
 auto-summary
!
router ospf 2
 router-id 1.1.1.1
 log-adjacency-changes
 redistribute eigrp 1 subnets
 network 172.16.0.0 0.0.255.255 area 0
```

Configuring Route Filtering with Redistribution

The configuration shown in Example 10-1 shows mutual redistribution with no filtering. The next example extends that same configuration to now use a **route-map** that should filter routes being redistributed from OSPF process 2 into EIGRP AS 1. Any routes not mentioned in Table 10-4, but shown in Figure 10-1, should be redistributed.

Table 10-4   *Parameters Used in Route Filtering Example*

Prefixes	Action
172.16.101.0/24	deny
172.16.102.0/25	permit
172.16.103.0/26	
172.16.104.0/27	deny
172.16.105.0/28	
172.16.106.0/29	permit
172.16.107.0/30	

The route-map simply needs to match the routes to be filtered with a route-map clause that has a **deny** action and match the routes to not be filtered with a clause with a **permit** action. Example 10-2 shows two such potential solutions, with **route-map** names option1 and option2. The general style of the two options, both of which work, is as follows:

■ **Option 1:** Begin with a match of the routes to be filtered, using extended IP ACLs, with a **deny** action so the routes are filtered. Then use a **permit** clause with no **match** command at all, matching and allowing through all remaining routes.

■ **Option 2:** Begin with a match of the routes to be allowed, matching with prefix lists, with a **permit** action. Then use the implicit deny all at the end of the route-map to filter unwanted routes.

Example 10-2 *Redistribution Filtering Configuration Example*

```
! This ACL matches subnet 172.16.101.0, with mask 255.255.255.0
ip access-list extended match-101
 permit ip host 172.16.101.0 host 255.255.255.0


! This ACL matches subnets 172.16.104.0 and 172.16.105.0, with masks
! 255.255.255.224 and 255.255.255.240, respectively.
ip access-list extended match-104-105
 permit ip host 172.16.104.0 host 255.255.255.224
 permit ip host 172.16.105.0 host 255.255.255.240
!
! This prefix list matches the five subnets in area 0
ip prefix-list match-area0-permit seq 5 permit 172.16.14.0/30
ip prefix-list match-area0-permit seq 10 permit 172.16.18.0/30
ip prefix-list match-area0-permit seq 15 permit 172.16.8.0/25
ip prefix-list match-area0-permit seq 20 permit 172.16.4.0/25
ip prefix-list match-area0-permit seq 25 permit 172.16.48.0/25
!
! This prefix list matches the two sets of two area 3 subnets that will
! be permitted to be redistributed
ip prefix-list match-area3-permit seq 5 permit 172.16.102.0/23 ge 25 le 26
ip prefix-list match-area3-permit seq 10 permit 172.16.106.0/23 ge 29 le 30


! The first alternative route-map:
route-map option1 deny 10
 match ip address match-101
!
```

```
route-map option1 deny 20
 match ip address match-104-105
!
route-map option1 permit 100
```

```
! The second alternative route-map:
route-map option2 permit 10
 match ip address prefix-list match-area3-permit
!
route-map option2 permit 20
 match ip address prefix-list match-area0-permit
```

```
! Finally, the configuration shows the enablement of option 1.
Router eigrp 1
 Redistribute ospf 2 route-map option1
```

Route-map option1 takes the approach of denying the redistribution of some routes, and then allowing the rest through. The last clause in this route map, with sequence number 100, does not have a **match** command at all, meaning that it will match any and all routes. The **permit** action on this last clause overrides the implied deny all at the end of the route-map.

The ACLs referenced by **route-map option1** show some particular interesting features for matching routes. With an extended ACL, IOS compares the source IP address parameter to the subnet number of the route and the destination IP address to the subnet mask of the route. For example, the **permit ip host 172.16.1.0 host 255.255.255.0** command matches the specific route for subnet 172.16.101.0, specifically with mask 255.255.255.0.

Route-map option2 takes the opposite approach compared to option1, for no other reason than to just show an alternative. It uses two different prefix lists to match the routes—one for subnets in area 0, all of which are redistributed, another for subnets in area 3 that should be allowed through the redistribution process. Alternatively, all routes could have been matched with a single prefix list, with a single **permit** clause in the option2 route-map.

Finally, the very end of the example shows the syntax of the **redistribute** command, with **route-map option1** enabled.

Verifying Redistribution Filtering Operations

The redistribution process takes routes from the IP routing table of a router and adds the appropriate entries to the destination routing protocol's topology table. The filtering process prevents some of the routes from being added to the topology table, so an examination of the destination routing protocol's topology table shows whether the filtering worked correctly. Additionally, the routing tables of other routers in the destination routing domain can be checked.

A good redistribution verification plan should check that the correct routes are filtered and confirm that no extra routes are filtered. In a production environment, that work might be laborious. With the example shown in Figure 10-1 and Example 10-2, verification takes a little less time due to the relatively small number of routes and that the subnets in the OSPF domain all begin with 172.16.

Example 10-3 shows an abbreviated version of the EIGRP topology table on Router RD1. The **show ip route 172.16.0.0** command lists the 12 OSPF subnets that currently exist in the OSPF domain (as shown in Figure 10-1). The **show ip eigrp topology | include 172[.]16** command lists only routes that include text "172.16," listing only nine subnets–and omitting the three subnets that should have been filtered, which confirms that the filtering worked.

Note: The brackets in the **show ip eigrp topology | include 172[.]16** command tell IOS to treat the period as a literal, searching for the text "172.16" in the command output, instead of treating the period as a wildcard in an IOS regular expression.

Example 10-3   *Verifying Redistribution Filtering*

```
RD1#show ip route 172.16.0.0
Routing entry for 172.16.0.0/16, 12 known subnets
  Attached (2 connections)
  Variably subnetted with 7 masks
  Redistributing via eigrp 1

O       172.16.48.0/25 [110/65] via 172.16.18.2, 03:25:56, Serial0/0/1
                       [110/65] via 172.16.14.2, 03:24:09, Serial0/1/0
C       172.16.18.0/30 is directly connected, Serial0/0/1
C       172.16.14.0/30 is directly connected, Serial0/1/0
O       172.16.8.0/25 [110/65] via 172.16.18.2, 03:25:56, Serial0/0/1
O       172.16.4.0/25 [110/65] via 172.16.14.2, 03:24:49, Serial0/1/0
O IA    172.16.104.0/27 [110/65] via 172.16.14.2, 03:24:44, Serial0/1/0
O IA    172.16.105.0/28 [110/65] via 172.16.14.2, 03:24:44, Serial0/1/0
O IA    172.16.106.0/29 [110/65] via 172.16.14.2, 03:24:44, Serial0/1/0
O IA    172.16.107.0/30 [110/65] via 172.16.14.2, 03:24:44, Serial0/1/0
O IA    172.16.101.0/24 [110/65] via 172.16.14.2, 03:24:44, Serial0/1/0
O IA    172.16.102.0/25 [110/65] via 172.16.14.2, 03:24:44, Serial0/1/0
O IA    172.16.103.0/26 [110/65] via 172.16.14.2, 03:24:44, Serial0/1/0

RD1#show ip eigrp topology | include 172[.]16
P 172.16.48.0/25, 1 successors, FD is 1709056
P 172.16.18.0/30, 1 successors, FD is 1709056
P 172.16.14.0/30, 1 successors, FD is 1709056
```

```
P 172.16.8.0/25, 1 successors, FD is 1709056
P 172.16.4.0/25, 1 successors, FD is 1709056
P 172.16.106.0/29, 1 successors, FD is 1709056
P 172.16.107.0/30, 1 successors, FD is 1709056
P 172.16.102.0/25, 1 successors, FD is 1709056
P 172.16.103.0/26, 1 successors, FD is 1709056
```

Besides examining the topology tables on the router doing the redistribution, a **show ip route** command on other routers inside the EIGRP domain, like R2, could be used to confirm the presence and absence of the routes according to the plan. However, the routing table on the redistributing router will list the routes as learned from the original routing domain.

Any ACLs or prefix lists used to match packets can also be used as a gauge to tell if the correct statements matched routes. The **show ip access-list** *[number|name]* and **show ip prefix-list detail** *[name]* commands list counters that increment each time IOS matches a route for redistribution. Particularly when first using the ACL or prefix list, these commands can confirm which statements have been matched. The counters do increment each time the router considers whether to redistribute a route. In particular, when a route fails, and the redistributing router removes the route from the routing table, and then later adds the route to the routing table again, the counters for matching the ACL or prefix list will increment. Example 10-4 shows an example of each command, and the appropriate counters.

Example 10-4   *Verifying Redistribution Filtering*

```
RD1#show access-list
Extended IP access list match-101
    10 permit ip host 172.16.101.0 host 255.255.255.0 (1 match)
Extended IP access list match-104-105
    10 permit ip host 172.16.104.0 host 255.255.255.224 (1 match)
    20 permit ip host 172.16.105.0 host 255.255.255.240 (1 match)
RD1#show ip prefix-list detail match-area-0-permit
ip prefix-list match-area0-permit:
   count: 5, range entries: 0, sequences: 5 - 25, refcount: 3
   seq 5 permit 172.16.14.0/30 (hit count: 6, refcount: 1)
   seq 10 permit 172.16.18.0/30 (hit count: 5, refcount: 1)
   seq 15 permit 172.16.8.0/25 (hit count: 4, refcount: 2)
   seq 20 permit 172.16.4.0/25 (hit count: 3, refcount: 3)
   seq 25 permit 172.16.48.0/25 (hit count: 2, refcount: 2)
```

Setting Metrics when Redistributing

Setting a different metric for different redistributed routes requires only a minor amount of additional configuration. The redistributing router still needs a route-map and still needs to match the routes. Additionally, to set the metric for routes matched by a particular clause, the route-map needs the **set metric** route-map subcommand. When redistributing into EIGRP, this command has five parameters (bandwidth, delay, reliability, load, and MTU). When redistributing into OSPF or RIP, a single integer metric is used.

Configuring the Metric Settings

Continuing with the same internetwork shown in Figure 10-1, and with the same filtering goals summarized earlier in Table 10-4, Table 10-5 further defines the goals from redistribution from OSPF into EIGRP in this internetwork. The same routes will be filtered, but now the metrics of the allowed routes will be set differently as listed in the table.

Table 10-5   *Parameters Used in Metric and Tag Setting Example*

Prefix	Action	Metric (Bandwidth, delay, reliability, load, MTU)
172.16.101.0	deny	N/A
172.16.102.0	permit	1000 44 255 1 1500
172.16.103.0		
172.16.104.0	deny	N/A
172.16.105.0		
172.16.106.0	permit	100 4444 255 1 1500
172.16.107.0		
All others	permit	1500 10 255 1 1500

The requirements in Table 10-5 list three different sets of metrics for the redistributed routes. To implement this design, the route-map needs at least three clauses: one for each set of routes for which the metric should differ. The example route-maps listed earlier in Example 10-2 do not happen to separate the three groups of allowed routes into different route-map clauses, so a new route-map will be used. Example 10-5 shows the new configuration. Note that it does make use of one of the old IP prefix-lists, namely **match-area0-permit**.

Example 10-5   *Route-map to Set Metrics According to Table 10-5*

```
! First, two new prefix lists are added - one to match subnets 102 and 103,
! and another to match subnets 106 and 107.


ip prefix-list match-102-103 seq 5 permit 172.16.102.0/23 ge 25 le 26
!
ip prefix-list match-106-107 seq 5 permit 172.16.106.0/23 ge 29 le 30

! The following is a repeat of the prefix list that matches the five routes
! in area 0
ip prefix-list match-area0-permit seq 5 permit 172.16.14.0/30
ip prefix-list match-area0-permit seq 10 permit 172.16.18.0/30
```

```
ip prefix-list match-area0-permit seq 15 permit 172.16.8.0/25
ip prefix-list match-area0-permit seq 20 permit 172.16.4.0/25
ip prefix-list match-area0-permit seq 25 permit 172.16.48.0/25

! A new route map to filter and set metrics, with three clauses


route-map set-metric permit 10
 match ip address prefix-list match-area0-permit
!
route-map set-metric permit 20
 match ip address prefix-list match-102-103
 set metric 1000 44 255 1 1500
!
route-map set-metric permit 30
 match ip address prefix-list match-106-107
 set metric 100 4444 255 1 1500


!
router eigrp 1
 default-metric 1500 10 255 1 1500
 redistribute ospf 2 route-map set-metric
```

The new route-map has three explicitly configured clauses, two of which explicitly set the metric values using the **set metric** command. However, the first clause (sequence number 10), which matches routes for the five subnets inside area 0, does not use a **set metric** command to set the metric. Instead, because this route map clauseomits the **set metric** command, routes that match this clause use the **metric** keyword on the **redistribute** command, or if not listed, the metrics as defined by the **default-metric** EIGRP subcommand. In this case, because the **redistribute** command does not list a **metric** keyword, routes matched by this clause (sequence number 30) use the metric values listed in the **default-metric** command.

Verifying the Metric Settings

Verifying the metrics again requires an examination of the EIGRP topology table. In this case, Example 10-6 displays a couple of views of RD1's EIGRP topology table, focusing on routes to 172.16.102.0/25 and 172.16.106.0/29. The configuration in Example 10-5 earlier set the metrics to different values, and next the output in Example 10-6 shows the differences:

Example 10-6 *Verifying Metrics as Set During Redistribution*

```
RD1#show ip eigrp topology 172.16.102.0/25
IP-EIGRP (AS 1): Topology entry for 172.16.102.0/25
  State is Passive, Query origin flag is 1, 1 Successor(s), FD is 1709056
```

```
      Routing Descriptor Blocks:
      172.16.14.2, from Redistributed, Send flag is 0x0
          Composite metric is (2571264/0), Route is External
          Vector metric:
            Minimum bandwidth is 1000 Kbit
            Total delay is 440 microseconds
            Reliability is 255/255
            Load is 1/255
            Minimum MTU is 1500
            Hop count is 0
          External data:
            Originating router is 172.30.17.1 (this system)
            AS number of route is 2
            External protocol is OSPF, external metric is 65
            Administrator tag is 0 (0x00000000)

RD1#show ip eigrp topology 172.16.104.0/25
% IP-EIGRP (AS 1): Route not in topology table

RD1#show ip eigrp topo 172.16.106.0/29
IP-EIGRP (AS 1): Topology entry for 172.16.106.0/29
  State is Passive, Query origin flag is 1, 1 Successor(s), FD is 1709056
  Routing Descriptor Blocks:
  172.16.14.2, from Redistributed, Send flag is 0x0
      Composite metric is (26737664/0), Route is External
      Vector metric:
        Minimum bandwidth is 100 Kbit
        Total delay is 44440 microseconds
        Reliability is 255/255
        Load is 1/255
        Minimum MTU is 1500
        Hop count is 0
      External data:
        Originating router is 172.30.17.1 (this system)
        AS number of route is 2
        External protocol is OSPF, external metric is 65
        Administrator tag is 0 (0x00000000)
!
RD1#show ip prefix-list detail match-102-103
ip prefix-list match-102-103:
   count: 1, range entries: 1, sequences: 5 - 5, refcount: 2
   seq 5 permit 172.16.102.0/23 ge 25 le 26 (hit count: 14, refcount: 1)
```

Although you could use variations of the **show ip route** command to verify the new metrics, because the redistribution process sets the EIGRP component metrics, the **show ip eigrp topology** command displays much more useful verification information.

Setting the External Route Type

When redistributing into OSPF, IOS automatically sets the external route type to external Type 2 (E2). When redistributing into OSPF, IOS can set the type to E1 or E2 by using the **set metric-type {type-1 | type-2}** route-map subcommand. When a **redistribute** OSPF subcommand references such a route-map, the routes matched by the route-map clause with the **set metric-type** command will be designated as that external type in the Type 5 LSA created for that subnet.

Note that the **redistribute** command also allows the **match {internal | external 1 | external 2 | nssa-external}** parameters, but these parameters do not set the type or route. Instead, these parameters match existing routes as part of the process of deciding which routes to redistribute.

Redistribution Filtering with the **distribute-list** Command

Using a route-map as referenced on the **redistribute** command provides many features. You can filter routes, assign different metrics for different routes, and assign external route types. You can even assign route tags as discussed later in the section "Preventing Domain Loops by Filtering on Route-tag Using Distribute Lists." However, if the plan calls for route filtering only when redistributing, but none of the other functions supplied by a route-map are needed, and you can match all the routes with a single ACL or prefix list, then IOS supports a second style of route filtering configuration using the **distribute-list** command.

This book has reviewed two uses of the **distribute-list** command in earlier chapters (Chapters 4 and 8), both of which show how to filter routes inside a single routing domain. For example, Chapter 4 shows how to filter EIGRP routes using the **distribute-list** command, both for routing updates received in and for routing updates sent out by a router. The **distribute-list** command refers to the direction, and to either an ACL or IP prefix-list, allowing the routes matched with a permit and filtering routes matched with a deny action.

The **distribute-list** command can be configured to refer to the routing process from which routes are redistributed and cause the router to filter routes taken from that process. To do so, the command must use the **out** direction, and it must refer to the routing process from which routes are redistributed. For example, **distribute-list 1 out ospf 2**, configured under an EIGRP process, tells EIGRP to apply ACL 1 to routes redistributed from the OSPF 2 process. For another example, under an OSPF process, the **distribute-list prefix fred out eigrp 1** command tells OSPF to apply IP prefix list fred to routes redistributed from the EIGRP 1 process.

Finally, one note about internals of how this command works. The filtering takes place as the routes are redistributed. As a result, routes filtered by the **distribute-list** command prevent the routes from being added to the topology table of the destination routing protocol. So, the same verification commands seen in earlier examples, with focus on the topology tables, can be used to show whether the filtering worked. Also, the counters in the **show ip access-list** and **show ip prefix-list detail** commands also increment to show whether the filtering worked.

Issues with Multiple Redistribution Points

The use of a single router to redistribute routes means that a single failure could cause hosts in different routing domains to fail. The redistributing router could simply fail, or interfaces or links on that router could fail. To avoid that single point of failure, most redistribution designs call for a minimum of two routers performing redistribution, particularly in cases where the redistribution function will be somewhat permanent.

The existence of two or more redistribution points between the same two routing domains introduces some complexity and caveats. The issues revolve around the concept that a route in one domain can be advertised into another domain, and then back into the original routing domain. In fact, the CCIE Routing and Switching exam has included such tricky redistribution issues as a central part of the exam for many years.

Figure 10-2 shows one of the issues when using multiple redistribution points. In this case, the arrowed lines show the best route from a router in domain 2 to reach a subnet also in domain 2. However, the route actually passes through domain 1.

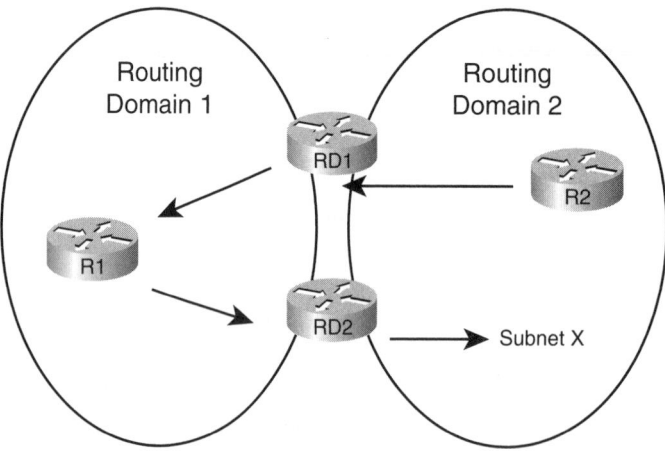

Figure 10-2   *A Domain Loop*

Figure 10-2 shows the long route that goes from R2, through RD1, to R1, back into routing domain 2 through RD2. This long route occurs because of the routing advertisements that flow in the opposite direction: advertised by RD2 into routing domain 1 and then by RD1 back into routing domain 2. The problem occurs when the twice-redistributed route for subnet X is redistributed back into the original domain with a relatively low metric. The twice-redistributed route then has a better metric than the route that was advertised only internal to that routing domain.

This section examines how to prevent this "domain loop" problem when using multiple redistribution points. Interesting, this problem does not occur, at least with default settings, when EIGRP is one of the two routing protocols. So this section begins with examples of RIP and OSPF redistribution, showing how to prevent this domain looping problem, and then showing why EIGRP accomplishes this same feat with default settings.

Note: I know of no industry standard name for the problem shown in Figure 10-2. For the duration of this chapter, I refer to it simply as the *domain loop* problem.

Preventing Routing Domain Loops with Higher Metrics

One easy method of preventing the domain loop problem is to assign purposefully high metric values when redistributing routes. For example, consider the case shown in Figure 10-3, with a RIP domain on the left, and OSPF on the right. In this case, the two routers doing the redistribution (RD1 and RD2) assign OSPF metric 500 when redistributing routes into OSPF, and metric 5 when redistributing routes into RIP.

Figure 10-3   *Defeating Domain Loops by Using Very Large Metrics*

First, focus on routes inside the RIP domain. This design prevents the domain loop problem–routes that send packets from the RIP domain, into OSPF, and back again–if the normal intra-domain RIP routes never exceed a hop count of 4. Then, all routes redistributed from RIP into OSPF, and then back into RIP, will at least have a metric of 5. As a result, the route advertisements that looped back into the RIP domain will always have less desirable metrics than the RIP advertisements from within the RIP domain.

The same concept applies to OSPF. For routes completely internal to the OSPF domain, if the highest cost is 499, then the redistribution of external routes as metric 500 makes prevents the domain loop. For example, a subnet that exists in the OSPF domain could be advertised into RIP by RD1, and then re-advertised by RD2 back into the OSPF domain–but with a metric that begins at 500. Again, assuming all the normal OSPF routes that were not reintroduced as external routes have a cost of less than 500, the domain loop problem is defeated.

Note that OSPF actually defeats the domain loop problem without using the higher metrics. OSPF always prefers internal routes over E1 routes, and E1 routes over E2 routes, before even considering the metrics.

Preventing Routing Domain Loops with Administrative Distance

Each router associates an *administrative distance* (AD) with every route it considers to be added to the routing table. When a router must consider multiple routes from different sources for the exact same prefix/length, the first item considered by the router is not the metric, but rather the AD. The lower the AD, the better the route.

Note that the AD is a local setting on a router and cannot be advertised to neighboring routers.

Each routing source has a default AD according to IOS. In some cases, a given routing source has different defaults for different types of routes inside that routing source. For example, EIGRP has a separate setting for EIGRP internal routes (AD 90) than EIGRP external routes (AD 170). Table 10-6 lists the default settings.

Key Topic

Table 10-6 *Default Administrative Distances*

Route Type	Administrative Distance
Connected	0
Static	1
EIGRP summary route	5
eBGP	20
EIGRP (internal)	90
IGRP	100
OSPF	110
IS-IS	115
RIP	120
On-Demand Routing (ODR)	160
EIGRP (external)	170
iBGP	200
Unreachable	255

EIGRP Default AD Defeats Loop from EIGRP to OSPF to EIGRP

The default AD settings for EIGRP takes care of the domain loop problem when redistributing between EIGRP and OSPF. First, consider an EIGRP and OSPF domain with two redistribution points (Routers RD1 and RD2), as shown in Figure 10-4. The figure shows a general idea of route advertisements for subnet X, which exists in the EIGRP domain. (Note: to reduce clutter, the figure shows only route advertisements that affect router RD2's logic; the same issue exists on both redistributing routers.)

Figure 10-4   *Subnet X: Internal EIGRP, External OSPF, on Router RD2*

Router RD2 hears about a route for subnet X as an internal EIGRP route (default AD 90) on the left. RD2 also hears about the subnet as an external OSPF route on the right (default AD 110). As a result, RD2 will do a couple of things that are important to this discussion:

■ RD2 considers the internal EIGRP route as the best route, because of the lower AD, and places that route in its own IP routing table.

■ RD2 does not redistribute a route for subnet X, from OSPF back to EIGRP, because RD2 does not have an OSPF route for subnet X.

The second point is particularly important but easily missed. Remember that routers use the IP routing table as the basis for route redistribution. Both RD1 and RD2 redistribute routes in both directions between both domains. However, a route must be in the routing table before it can be redistributed. Because RD2's route for subnet X will list its EIGRP route, RD2's redistribution from OSPF into EIGRP will not redistribute a route for subnet X. Because RD2 will not advertise a route for subnet X from OSPF back into EIGRP, the domain loop has been prevented.

EIGRP Default AD Defeats Loop from OSPF to EIGRP to OSPF

The reverse case–routes taken from OSPF, advertised into EIGRP, and then advertised back into OSPF–is the more interesting possible domain loop case. However, the default EIGRP AD settings still defeat the domain loop issue. Figure 10-5 shows an example similar to Figure 10-4, but this time with subnet Y in the OSPF domain. As before, the focus of the figure is on the routing advertisements that reach Router RD2, with other details omitted to reduce clutter.

In this case, Router RD2 hears about a route for subnet Y as an external EIGRP route (default AD 170) and an internal OSPF route (default AD 110). As a result, RD2 chooses the OSPF internal route as the best route and adds that to RD2's routing table. Because RD2 does not have an EIGRP route for subnet Y, RD2 will not redistribute a route for subnet Y from EIGRP into OSPF, again defeating the domain loop problem.

Figure 10-5   *Avoiding Domain Loops from OSPF to EIGRP to OSPF*

Setting AD per Route Source for Internal and External Routes

The reason that the default EIGRP AD settings work well can be summarized generically as follows:

> For each of the two routing protocols, the AD used for internal routes for one routing protocol is better than the AD used for external routes by the other routing protocol.

When comparing EIGRP's and OSPF's defaults, both of the generic criteria are met:

- EIGRP internal AD 90 < OSPF external AD 110

- OSPF internal AD 110 < EIGRP external AD 170

Likewise, when redistributing between EIGRP and RIP:

- EIGRP internal AD 90 < RIP external AD 120

- RIP internal AD 120 < EIGRP external AD 170

Note: RIP does not have a concept of internal and external routes; the preceding references refer to internal routes as routes that exist inside the RIP domain, and external as routes that exist outside the RIP domain.

When redistributing between OSPF and RIP, the default AD settings do not defeat the domain loop problem. However, IOS supports the definition of different AD settings for all routing protocols. With EIGRP, the internal and external AD settings can be overridden, although the defaults work well for the preventing of domain loops. OSPF can be configured to use a different AD for external routes, intra-area routes, and interarea routes. RIP, which does not have a concept of internal and external routes, can only be set with a single AD value. Table 10-7 shows the router subcommands to set the AD values, per route category.

Table 10-7 *Setting AD Values with the **distance** Command*

Routing Protocol	Command
RIP	distance *ad-value*
EIGRP	distance **eigrp** *internal-ad external-ad*
OSPF	distance **ospf** {**external** *ad-value*} {**intra-area** *ad-value*} {**inter-area** *ad-value*}

To defeat the OSPF-RIP domain loop problem by setting AD, just configure the AD for OSPF external routes using the **distance ospf external** *ad-value* command in OSPF configuration mode. The actual AD value does not matter much, but it should be higher than RIP's AD on that same router. For example, the **distance ospf external 130** command in OSPF configuration mode results in the following, assuming all other AD values default:

- RIP internal AD 120 < OSPF external AD 130

- OSPF internal AD 110 < RIP external AD 120

Domain Loop Problems with More than Two Routing Domains

With only two routing domains, the domain loop solutions seen so far–setting higher metrics and setting AD—can deal with the domain loop problems. However, with three or more routing domains, setting metrics and AD values does not always solve the domain loop problem. In particular, problems can occur when three or more routing domains connect in sequence, as shown in Figure 10-6.

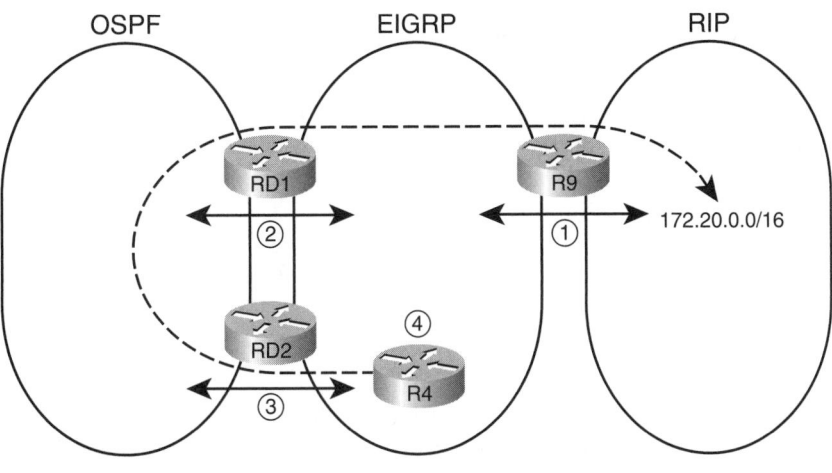

Figure 10-6 *Inefficient Routing with Looped Routing Advertisements*

The steps noted in the figure are as follows:

Step 1.   Router R9 advertises a route for network 172.20.0.0/16 from the RIP domain into the EIGRP domain where the route is treated with (default) AD 170 as an external route.

Step 2.   Router RD1 redistributes this EIGRP external route into OSPF where it is treated as an E2 route, AD 110, by default.

Step 3.   Router RD2 uses the AD 110 E2 route, rather than the AD 170 EIGRP external route, as its best route for 172.20.0.0/16. As a result, RD2 can then redistribute that OSPF route back into EIGRP as an external route.

Step 4.   Router R4 learns of two external routes for 172.20.0.0/16, and the routes tie based on AD (170). R4 may have a better EIGRP metric through RD2, depending on the metrics used at redistribution, preferring this long route through the OSPF domain as shown.

This is just one example case for such problems, but the problem exists because the obviously better route and the longer domain loop route are both external routes. The two competing routes tie on AD as a result. In the earlier cases, with only two routing domains, this problem does not occur.

Several solutions exist for such problems. None of the solutions require a lot of extra configuration, other than that some of the solutions require ACLs or prefix lists that match the prefixes from the various routing domains. The next three sections address each option, namely: using per-route AD settings, filtering routes based on prefix/length, and using route tags.

Using Per-route Administrative Distance Settings

As seen in Table 10-7, you can use the **distance** router subcommand to set the AD value per routing protocol, per type (internal and external). The **distance** command also supports another syntax in which the router sets the AD for individual routes based on the following criteria:

■   The router that advertised the routing information

■   Optionally, for the prefixes/lengths of the routes as matched by a referenced ACL

The syntax of the command in this case is

```
distance distance ip-adv-router wc-mask [acl-number-or-name]
```

In this command, the required parameters match the neighboring router that advertises a route. The router with the **distance** command configured compares the advertising router's IP address to the range of addresses implied by the *ip-adv-router* and *wc-mask* parameters of the command, as if these were parameters in an ACL. For routes advertised by a matching neighbor, that router then applies the AD listed in the command.

Optionally, the **distance** command can also refer to an ACL. If included, that router compares the ACL to the prefix/length of each route learned from any matched neighbors and uses the listed AD only for routes permitted by the ACL.

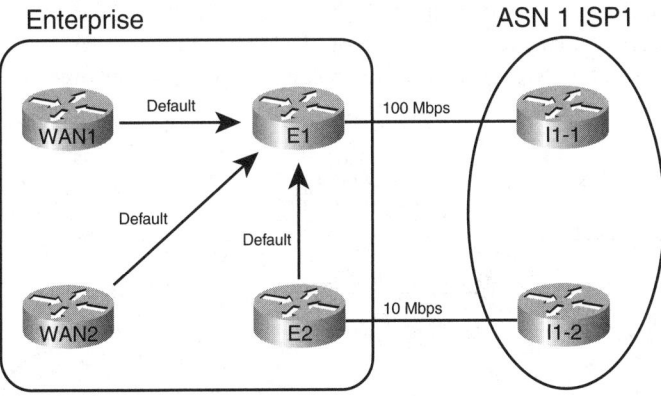

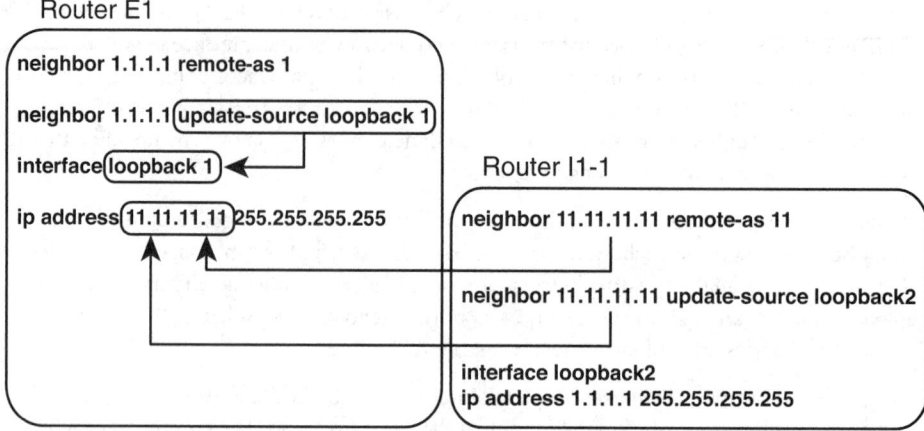

Step 4.   Similarly, Router I1-1, inside ASN 1, advertises the route to ASN3. Because ASN 3 is a different ASN, I1-1 adds its own ASN (1) to the AS_Path PA so that the AS_Path lists ASNs 12, 2, and 1.

Figure 12-5   *Advertisement of NLRI to Demonstrate AS_Path*

Now, step back from the details, and consider the two alternative routes learned collectively by the routers in ASN 1:

■   192.31.7.32/29, AS_Path (12,2)

■   192.31.7.32/29, AS_Path (12,2,3)

Because the BGP path selection algorithm uses the shortest AS_Path, assuming no other PAs have been manipulated, the routers in ASN 1 use the first of the two paths, sending packets to ASN 2 next, and not using the path through ASN 3. Also, as a result, note the advertisement from ASN 1 into ASN 11 lists an AS_Path that reflects the best path selection of the routers inside ASN 1, with the addition of ASN 1 to the end of the AS_Path of the best route (12,2,1).

BGP routers also prevent routing loops using the ASNs listed in the AS_Path. When a BGP router receives an update, and a route advertisement lists an AS_Path with its own ASN, the router ignores that route. The reason is that because the route has already been advertised through the local ASN, to believe the route and then advertise it further might cause routing loops.

Internal and External BGP

BGP defines two classes of neighbors (peers): internal BGP (iBGP) and external BGP (eBGP). These terms use the perspective of a single router, with the terms referring to whether a BGP neighbor is in the same ASN (iBGP) or a different ASN (eBGP).

A BGP router behaves differently in several ways depending on whether the peer (neighbor) is an iBGP or eBGP peer. The differences include different rules about what must be true before the two routers can become neighbors, different rules about which routes the BGP best path algorithm chooses as best, and even some different rules about how the routers update the BGP AS_Path PA. These differences will be highlighted in the context of other features throughout this chapter and in Chapters 13, 14, and 15, but for now, it is interesting to examine the differences related to AS_Path.

When advertising to an eBGP peer, a BGP router updates the AS_Path PA, but it does not do so when advertising to an iBGP peer. For example, Figure 12-6 shows the same design, with the same route advertisement, as in Figure 12-5. However, in this case, all the BGP connections have been listed as either iBGP or eBGP.

Figure 12-6 *iBGP, eBGP, and Updating AS_Path for eBGP Peers*

The figure highlights the route advertisement from ASN 12, over the lower path through ASN 2 and 3. Note that at Step 1, Router I2, advertising to an eBGP peer, adds its own ASN to the AS_Path. At Step 2, Router I2-1 is advertising to an iBGP peer (I2-2), so it does not add its own ASN (2) to the AS_Path. Then, at Step 3, Router I2-2 adds its own ASN (2) to the AS_Path before sending an update to eBGP peer I3-2, and so on.

Public and Private ASNs

For the Internet to work well using BGP, IANA administers the assignment of ASNs much like it does with IP address prefixes. One key reason why ASNs must be assigned as unique values is that if ASNs are duplicated, the BGP loop prevention process can actually prevent parts of the Internet from learning about a route. For example, consider Figure 12-7, with the same design as in the last few figures–but this time with a duplicate ASN.

In this figure, both ISP1 and Company 1 use ASN 12. The example BGP updates begin as in Figures 12-5 and 12-6, with Company 1 advertising its prefix. Routers inside ISP1 re-

Figure 12-7 *Duplicate ASN (12) Preventing Route Advertisement*

ceive BGP updates that list the same prefix used by Company 1, but both Updates list an AS_Path that includes ASN 12. Because ISP1 thinks it uses ASN 12, ISP1 thinks that these BGP Updates should be ignored as part of the BGP loop prevention process. As a result, customers of ISP1 cannot reach the prefixes advertised by routers in Company 1.

To prevent such issues, IANA controls the ASN numbering space. Using the same general process as for IPv4 addresses, ASNs can be assigned to different organizations. The 16-bit BGP ASN implies a decimal range of 0 through 65,535. Table 12-5 shows some of the details of IANA's current ASN assignment conventions.

Table 12-5 *16-Bit ASN Assignment Categories from IANA*

Value or Range	Purpose
0	Reserved
1 through 64,495	Assignable by IANA for public use
64,496 through 65,511	Reserved for use in documentation
64,512 through 65,534	Private use
65,535	Reserved

Like the public IPv4 address space has suffered with the potential for complete depletion of available addresses, the public BGP ASN space has similar issues. To help overcome this issue, the ASN assignment process requires that each AS justify whether it truly needs a publicly unique ASN or whether it can just as easily use a private ASN. Additionally, RFC

5398 reserves a small range of ASNs for use in documentation so that the documents can avoid the use of ASNs assigned to specific organizations.

Private ASNs allow the routers inside an AS to participate with BGP, while using the same ASN as many other organizations. Most often, an AS can use a private AS in cases where the AS connects to only one other ASN. (Private ASNs can be used in some cases of connecting to multiple ASNs as well.) The reason is that with only one connection point to another ASN, loops cannot occur at that point in the BGP topology, so the need for unique ASNs in that part of the network no longer exists. (The loops cannot occur due to the logic behind the BGP best path algorithm, coupled with that BGP only advertises the best path for a given prefix.)

Outbound Routing Toward the Internet

The single biggest reason to consider using BGP between an Enterprise and an ISP is to influence the choice of best path (best route). The idea of choosing the best path sounds appealing at first. However, because the majority of the end-to-end route exists inside the Internet, particularly if the destination is 12 routers and a continent away, it can be a challenge to determine which exit point from the Enterprise is actually a better route.

As a result, Enterprises typically have two major classes of options for outbound routing toward the Internet: default routing and BGP. Using default routes is perfectly reasonable, depending on the objectives. This section examines the use of default routes toward the Internet, and some of the typical Enterprise BGP designs and how they can be used to influence outbound routes toward the Internet.

Comparing BGP and Default Routing for Enterprises

Chapter 4, "EIGRP Route Summarization and Filtering," section "Default Routing to the Internet Router," introduced the concept of using default routes on branch office routers, with static routes and redistribution on the WAN edge routers. With this design, the branch router could use a default static route pointing toward the core of the network. The WAN edge routers then needed static routes for the subnets at each branch, with the WAN edge routers advertising these branch subnets into the core using an IGP.

The branch office default routing design results in less processing on the routers, less memory consumption, and no IGP overhead on the link between the branch and WAN distribution routers. In particular, the branch routers can have a single or a few default routes, instead of potentially hundreds of routes for specific prefixes, all with the same next-hop information.

The same general concept of using defaults and static routes at Enterprise branches can be applied to the Enterprise network and its connections to one or a few ISPs. Similar to a branch router, an entire Enterprise often has only a few connections to the Internet. If one of those connections is considered better than the others, then all packets sent from the Enterprise toward the Internet would normally follow that one Internet link, for all Internet destinations. Likewise, the ISPs, similar to WAN distribution routers in this analogy, could configure static routes for the Enterprise's public IP address prefix and then use BGP in the Internet to advertise those routes. Figure 12-8 shows the general idea.

Company 1 Enterprise Network -
Public Addresses: 128.107.0.0/16

ip route 0.0.0.0 0.0.0.0 ISP-1

ip route
128.107.0.0 255.255.0.0 E1

Figure 12-8 *Use of Static Default into the Internet*

Although the Enterprise could choose to use BGP in this case, such a decision is not automatic. First, the alternative of using static routes, as shown in the figure, does not require a lot of work. The Enterprise network engineer just needs to configure a default route and advertise it throughout the Enterprise; the dashed lines in the figure represent the advertisement of the default route with the Enterprise's IGP. (See Chapter 4's section "Default Routing to the Internet Router," and Chapter 7, "OSPF Route Summarization, Filtering, and Default Routing," section "Domain-wide Defaults Using the **default-information originate** Command," for a review of how to flood the static route inside an EIGRP or OSPF domain, respectively.)

In addition to the configuration on the Enterprise router (E1), the ISP network engineer has to configure static routes for that Enterprise's public IP address range, and redistributing those routes into BGP and advertising throughout the Internet. The figure shows a static route for Company 1's 128.107.0.0/16 public address range. Additionally, this prefix would need to be injected into BGP for advertising into the rest of the Internet.

Instead of using static default routes, you could enable BGP between E1 and ISP-1. Running BGP could mean that the Enterprise router requires significant memory and more processing power on the router. The design may also require other Enterprise routers besides the Internet-connected routers to know the BGP routes, requiring additional routers to have significant CPU and memory. Finally, although you can configure BGP to choose one route over another using PAs, the advantage of choosing one path over another may not be significant. Alternatively, you could ask the ISP to advertise only a default route with BGP.

Now that you have seen a few of the reasons why you may be fine using static routes instead of BGP, consider why you might want to use BGP. First, it makes most sense to use BGP when you have at least two Internet connections. Second, BGP becomes most useful when you want to choose one outbound path over another path for particular destinations in the Internet. In short, when you have multiple Internet connections, and you want to influence some packets to take one path and some packets to take another, consider BGP.

The rest of this chapter examines different cases of Internet connectivity and weighs the reasons why you might choose to use BGP. For this discussion, the perspective of the Enterprise network engineer will be used. As such, outbound routing is considered to be routes that direct packets from the Enterprise toward the Internet, and inbound routing refers to routes that direct packets into the Enterprise from the Internet.

To aid in the discussion, this section examines four separate cases:

- Single homed (1 link per ISP, 1 ISP)

- Dual homed (2+ links per ISP, 1 ISP)

- Single multihomed (1 link per ISP, 2+ ISPs)

- Dual multihomed (2+ links per ISP, 2+ ISPs)

> **Note:** The terms in the preceding list may be used differently depending on what book or document you read. For consistency, this book uses these terms in the same way as the Cisco authorized ROUTE course associated with the ROUTE exam.

Single Homed

The single-homed Internet design uses a single ISP, with a single link between the Enterprise and the ISP. With single-homed designs, only one possible next-hop router exists for any and all routes for destinations in the Internet. As a result, no matter what you do with BGP, all learned routes would list the same outgoing interface for every route, which minimizes the benefits of using BGP.

Single-homed designs often use one of two options for routing to and from the Internet:

- Use static routes (default in the Enterprise, and a static for the Enterprise's public address range at the ISP).

- Use BGP, but only to exchange a default (ISP to Enterprise) and a route for the Enterprise's public prefix (Enterprise to ISP).

The previous section, "Comparing BGP and Defaults for Enterprises," already showed the main concepts for the first option. For the second option, the concept still uses the IGP's mechanisms to flood a default throughout the Enterprise, causing all packets to go toward the Internet facing router. Instead of static routes, however, the following must happen:

- The ISP router uses BGP to advertise a default route to the Enterprise.

- You must configure the IGP on the Enterprise's Internet-facing router to flood a default route (typically only if the default route exists in that router's routing table).

- You must configure BGP on the Enterprise router and advertise the Enterprise's public prefix toward the ISP.

Both options–using static defaults and BGP learned defaults–have some negatives. Some packets for truly nonexistent destinations flow through the Enterprise to the Internet-facing router (E1 in the example of Figure 12-8), and over the link to the Internet, before being discarded for lack of a matching route. For example, if the Enterprise used private network 10.0.0.0/8 internally, packets destined for addresses in network 10.0.0.0/8 that have not yet been deployed will match the default route and be routed to the Internet.

To avoid wasting this bandwidth by sending packets unnecessarily, a static route for 10.0.0.0/8, destination null0, could be added to the Internet-facing router but not advertised into the rest of the Enterprise. (This type of route is sometimes called a *discard route*.) This route would prevent the Internet-facing router from forwarding packets destined for network 10.0.0.0/8 into the Internet.

Dual Homed

The dual-homed design has two (or more) links to the Internet, but with all links connecting to a single ISP. This type of design can use a pair of routers, two pairs, or a combination, as shown in the three cases in Figure 12-9.

Comparing the dual-homed case to the single-homed design, the second link gives the Enterprise a choice. The Enterprise router(s) could choose between one of two links, and in the case with two Enterprise routers, the choice of a different link also means the choice of sending packets to a different router.

Each of the cases shown in Figure 12-9 is interesting, but the case with two Enterprise routers provides the most ideas to consider. When considering whether to use BGP in this case, and if so, how to use it, first think about whether you want to influence the choice of outbound route. The common cases when using defaults works well, ignoring BGP, are:

- To prefer one Internet connection over another for all destinations, but when the better ISP connection fails, all traffic re-routes over the secondary connection.

- To treat both Internet connections as equal, sending packets for some destinations out each path. However, when one fails, all traffic re-routes over the one still-working path.

The text now examines each option, in order, including a discussion of how to choose the best outbound routing using both partial and full BGP updates.

Preferring One Path over Another for All Destinations

When the design calls for one of the two Internet connections to always be preferred, regardless of destination, BGP can be used, but it is not required. With a goal of preferring one path over another, the routers can use default routes into the Internet.

To demonstrate the concept, Figure 12-10 shows a dual-homed design, this time with two routers (E1 and E2) connected to the Internet. Each router has a single link into the single ISP. (Using the terminology from the ROUTE class, dual homed means two or more links

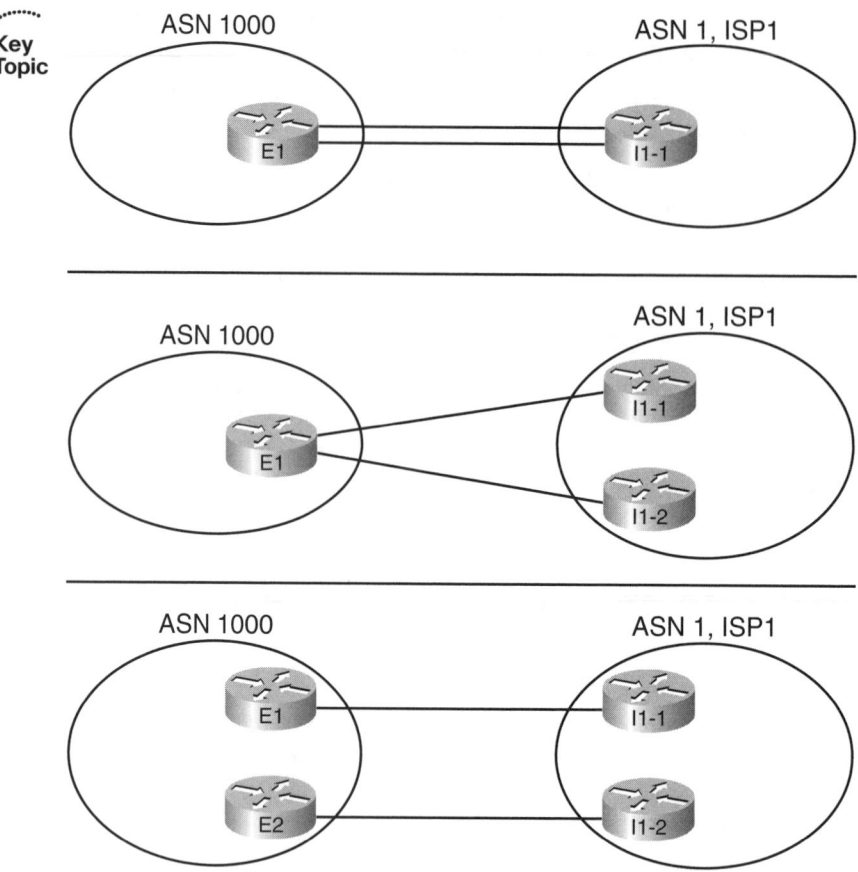

Figure 12-9   *Dual-Homed Design Options*

but to a single ISP; dual multihomed means two or more links each to two or more differ-ent ISPs.) Figure 12-10 shows the routes that result from using default routes to forward all traffic toward Router E1.

Figure 12-10 shows that all routers forward the Internet-destined packets toward Router E1, because this router has the faster Internet connection to ISP1 (100 Mbps in this case). Again in this example, the other connection from Router E2 to ISP3 uses a 10 Mbps link.

To make this design work, with failover, both E1 and E2 need to advertise a default route into the Enterprise, but the route advertised by the primary router (E1) needs to have met-rics set so that it is always the better of the two routes. For example, with EIGRP, E1 can configure a static default route with Router I1-1 as the next hop, but with very high band-width and very low delay upon redistribution into EIGRP. Conversely, E2 can create a de-fault for Router I1-2 as the next-hop router, but with a low bandwidth but high delay. Example 12-1 shows the configuration of the static default route on both E1 and E2, with the **redistribute** command setting the metrics.

Figure 12-10   *Dual-Homed Design, Using Defaults to Favor One Link*

Example 12-1   *Default Routing on Router E1*

```
! Configuration on router E1 - note that the configuration uses
! a hostname instead of I1-1's IP address
ip route 0.0.0.0 0.0.0.0 I1-1
router eigrp 1
 redistribute static metric 100000 1 255 1 1500
! Configuration on router E2 - note that the configuration uses
! a hostname instead of I2-1's IP address
ip route 0.0.0.0 0.0.0.0 I2-1
router eigrp 1
 redistribute static metric 10000 100000 255 1 1500
```

Note: With EIGRP as the IGP, do not forget that the delay setting must be set higher to avoid cases where some routers forward packets toward the secondary Internet router (E2). The reason is that EIGRP uses constraining bandwidth, so a high setting of bandwidth at the redistribution point on E1 may or may not cause more remote routers to use that route.

A slightly different approach can be taken in other variations of the dual-homed design, as seen back in Figure 12-9. The first two example topologies in that figure show a single router with two links to the same ISP. If the design called to using one link as the preferred link, and the engineer decided to use default routes, that one router would need two default routes. To make one route be preferred, that static default route would be assigned a better administrative distance (AD) than the other route. For example, the commands **ip route 0.0.0.0 0.0.0.0 I1-1 3** and **ip route 0.0.0.0 0.0.0.0 I1-2 4** could be used on Router E1 in Figure 12-9, giving the route through I1-1 a lower AD (3), preferring that route. If the link to I1-1 failed, the other static default route, through I1-2, would be used.

Choosing One Path over Another Using BGP

The big motivation to use BGP occurs when you want to influence which link is used for certain destinations in the Internet. To see such a case, consider Figure 12-11, which adds

Company 3 to the design. In this case, Company 3 uses prefix 192.135.250.0/28 as its public address range. Company 3 may be located closer to I1-2 inside ISP1 than to Router I1-1, and in such cases, the BGP design calls for making the packets flow over the route as shown.

Figure 12-11   *Preferring One Outbound Link over Another*

Two notable actions must take place for this design to work, beyond the basic configuration of the eBGP peers as shown. First, the engineers at the Enterprise and ISP must agree as to how to make BGP specify a prefix as being best reached through a particular link. In this particular case, the routes advertised by I1-2 for prefix for 192.135.250.0/28 must have BGP PA settings that appear better than those learned from I1-1. In this case, you cannot just rely on the default of checking the AS_Path length, because the AS_Path length should tie, because I1-1 and I1-2 are in the same ASN. So when planning with the engineers of ISP1, the Enterprise network engineer must discuss what kinds of prefixes that might work better through I1-1, which would be better through I1-2, and how the ISP might set PA values to which the Enterprise routers (E1 and E2) can react. (Chapter 15 discusses some of the options to influence the outbound routes.)

The second big consideration occurs inside the Enterprise network with a need to run BGP between multiple routers. So far in this chapter, the Enterprise routers all used default routes to send packets to the Internet-facing routers, and only those routers knew Internet routes. However, for the design of Figure 12-11 to work, E1 and E2 must communicate BGP routes using an iBGP connection. And because packet forwarding between E1 and E2 goes through other routers (such as Core1 and Core2), those routers typically also need to run BGP. You might even decide to run BGP on the WAN routers as well. By doing so, the core routers know the best BGP routes; for instance, they all know that the better route for Company 3's 192.135.250.0/28 public address space is through E2, so the packet is forwarded to E2. The following list outlines the logic matching Figure 12-11:

Step 1.   A host at Branch B1 sends a packet to 192.135.250.1.

Step 2.   Router B1 matches its default route, forwarding the packet to Router WAN2.

Step 3.   WAN2 matches its iBGP-learned route for 192.135.250.0/28, forwarding to Core2.

Step 4.   Core2 matches its iBGP-learned route for 192.135.250.0/28, forwarding to E2.

Step 5.   E2 matches its eBGP-learned route for 192.135.250.0/28, forwarding to I1-2.

Step 6.   The routers in ISP1 forward the packet to Router I3, in Company 3.

The routers in the core of the Enterprise need to run BGP because without it, routing loops can occur. For example, if WAN1, WAN2, Core1, and Core2 did not use BGP, and relied on default routes, their default would drive packets to either E1 or E2. Then, E1 or E2 might send the packets right back to Core1 or Core2. (Note that there is no direct link between E1 and E2.) Figure 12-12 shows just such a case.

Figure 12-12   *A Routing Loop Without BGP in the Enterprise Core*

In this case, both E1 and E2 know that E2 is the best exit point for packets destined to 192.135.250.0/28 (from Figure 12-11). However, the core routers use default routes, with WAN1 and Core1 using defaults that send packets to E1. Following the numbers in the figure

Step 1.   WAN1 gets a packet destined for 192.135.250.1 and forwards the packet to Core1 based on its default route.

Step 2.   Core1 gets the packet and has no specific route, so it forwards the packet to E1 based on its default route.

Step 3.   E1's BGP route tells it that E2 is the better exit point for this destination. To send the packet to E2, E1 forwards the packet to Core1.

Step 4.   Core1, with no knowledge of the BGP route for 192.135.250.0/28, uses its default route to forward the packet to E1, so the packet is now looping.

A mesh of iBGP peerings between at least E1, E2, Core1, and Core2 would prevent this problem.

Partial and Full BGP Updates

Unfortunately, Enterprise routers must pay a relatively large price for the ability to choose between competing BGP routes to reach Internet destinations. As previously mentioned, the BGP table in the Internet core is at approximately 300,000 routes as of the writing of this chapter in 2009. To make a decision to use one path instead of another, an Enterprise router must know about at least some of those routes. Exchanging BGP information for such a large number of routes consumes bandwidth. It also consumes memory in the routers and requires some processing to choose the best routes. Some samples at Cisco.com show BGP using approximately 70 MB of RAM for the BGP table on a router with 100,000 BGP-learned routes.

To make matters a bit worse, in some cases, several Enterprise routers may also need to use BGP, as shown in the previous section. Those routers also need more memory to hold the BGP table, and they consume bandwidth exchanging the BGP table.

To help reduce the memory requirements of receiving full BGP updates (BGP updates that include all routes), ISPs give you three basic options for what routes the ISP advertises:

- **Default route only:** The ISP advertises a default route with BGP, but no other routes.

- **Full updates:** The ISP sends you the entire BGP table.

- **Partial updates:** The ISP sends you routes for prefixes that might be better reached through that ISP, but not all routes, plus a default route (to use instead of the purposefully omitted routes as needed).

If all you want to do with a BGP connection is use it by default, then you can have the ISP send just a default route. If you are willing to take on the overhead of getting all BGP routes, then asking for full updates is reasonable. However, if you want something in between, the partial updates option is useful.

BGP partial updates give you the benefit of choosing the best routes for some destinations, while limiting the bandwidth and memory consumption. With partial updates, the ISP advertises routes for prefixes that truly are better reached through a particular link. However, for prefixes that may not be any better through that link, the ISP does not advertise those prefixes with BGP. Then the Enterprise routers can use the better path based on the routes learned with BGP, and use a default route for the prefixes not learned with BGP. For example, previously in Figure 12-11, Router I1-2 could be configured to only advertise routes for those such as 192.135.250.0/28, from Company 3 in that figure–in other words, only routes for which Router I1-2 had a clearly better route than the other ISP1 routers.

Single Multihomed

A single-multihomed topology means a single link per ISP, but multiple (at least 2) ISPs. Figure 12-13 shows a couple of single-multihomed designs, each with two ISPs:

The single-multihomed design has some similarities with both the single-homed and dual-homed designs previously seen in this section. The single-multihomed design on the top of the figure, which uses a single router, acts like the single-homed design for default routes in the Enterprise. This design can flood a default route throughout the Enterprise, drawing traffic to that one router, because only one router connects to the Internet. With the two-router design on the lower half of Figure 12-13, defaults can still be used in the

Figure 12-13   *Single-Multihomed Designs*

Enterprise to draw traffic to the preferred Internet connection (if one is preferred) or to balance traffic across both.

The single-multihomed design works like the dual-homed design in some ways because two (or more) links connect the Enterprise to the Internet. With two links, the Internet design might call for the use of defaults, always preferring one of the links. The design engineer might also choose to use BGP, learn either full or partial updates, and then favor one connection over another for some of the routes.

Figure 12-14 shows these concepts with a single-multihomed design, with default routes in the Enterprise to the one Internet router (E1).

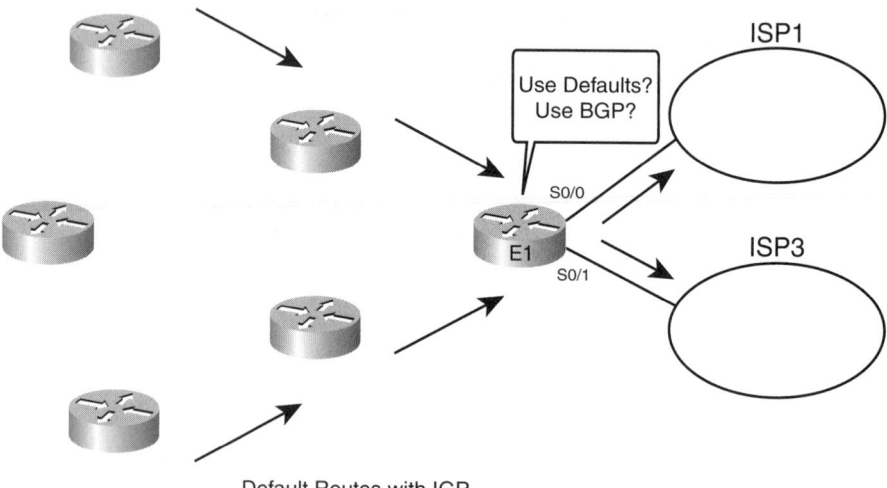

Figure 12-14 *Outbound Routing with a Single-Multihomed Design*

Dual Multihomed

The last general category of Internet access topologies is called dual multihomed. With this design, two or more ISPs are used, with two or more connections to each. A number of different routers can be used. Figure 12-15 shows several examples.

Figure 12-15 does not show all design options, but because at least two ISPs exist, and at least two connections per ISP, much redundancy exists. That redundancy can be used for backup, but most often, BGP is used to make some decisions about the best path to reach various destinations.

Figure 12-15 *Dual-Multihomed Options*

Exam Preparation Tasks

Planning Practice

The CCNP ROUTE exam expects test takers to review design documents, create implementation plans, and create verification plans. This section provides some exercises that may help you to take a step back from the minute details of the topics in this chapter so that you can think about the same technical topics from the planning perspective.

For each planning practice table, simply complete the table. Note that any numbers in parentheses represent the number of options listed for each item in the solutions in Appendix F, "Completed Planning Practice Tables."

Design Review Table

Table 12-5 lists several design goals related to this chapter. If these design goals were listed in a design document, and you had to take that document and develop an implementation plan, what implementation options come to mind? You should write a general description; specific configuration commands are not required.

Table 12-5 *Design Review*

Design Goal	Possible Implementation Choices Covered in This Chapter
A design shows a single router connected to the Internet as part of a single-homed Internet design. It lists sections for Enterprise routing toward the Internet-facing router(s) in the Enterprise, and another section for choosing routes on the Internet-facing router into the Internet. List the reasonable options.	
Use the same criteria as the previous item in this table, except the single Enterprise router connected to the Internet now has two links to the same ISP (dual homed).	
Use the same criteria as the previous item, except use two routers with one link each to the same ISP (dual homed).	
Same criteria as previous row, but with a single multihomed with two routers.	

Implementation Plan Peer Review Table

Table 12-6 shows a list of questions that others might ask, or that you might think about, during a peer review of another network engineer's implementation plan. Complete the table by answering the questions.

Table 12-6 *Notable Questions from This Chapter to Consider During an Implementation Plan Peer Review*

Question	Answers
The plan shows a single router in a dual-homed Internet design, with the router using BGP over each link to that same ISP. What criteria would impact your choice of accepting only default routes, or partial updates, or full updates, using BGP in this case? (3)	
The plan shows four Enterprise routers with BGP configuration, with two of those routers with links to two different ISPs. Which connections are eBGP? iBGP?	

Create an Implementation Plan Table

This chapter does not focus on implementation or verification, but it did review one concept about static routes, as listed in Table 12-7.

Table 12-7 *Implementation Plan Configuration Memory Drill*

Feature	Configuration Commands/Notes
Configuring multiple static default routes, each with different administrative distance settings	

Review all the Key Topics

Review the most important topics from inside the chapter, noted with the Key Topics icon in the outer margin of the page. Table 12-8 lists a reference of these key topics and the page numbers on which each is found.

Key Topic

Table 12-8 *Key Topics for Chapter 12*

Key Topic Element	Description	Page Number
Figure 12-1	Public IP Address Assignment model	391
Table 12-4	Comparisons of OSPF and EIGRP to BGP	396
List	Two key functions for BGP AS_Path	397
Figure 12-5	BGP process to update AS_Path when advertising NLRI	399
Figure 12-7	Demonstration of how AS_Path can be used to prevent loops	401
Table 12-5	16-bit BGP ASN assignment ranges	401

Complete the Tables and Lists from Memory

Print a copy of Appendix D, "Memory Tables," (found on the CD), or at least the section for this chapter, and complete the tables and lists from memory. Appendix E, "Memory Tables Answer Key," also on the CD, includes completed tables and lists to check your work.

Define Key Terms

Define the following key terms from this chapter, and check your answers in the glossary.

public IP address, private IP address, Network Address Translation (NAT), Port Address Translation (PAT), AS Sequence, Path Attribute (PA), AS path, public ASN, private ASN, default route, single homed, dual homed, single multihomed, dual multihomed, Autonomous System Number (ASN)

This chapter covers the following subjects:

External BGP for Enterprises: This section examines the required configuration for external BGP connections, plus a few optional but commonly used configuration settings. It also examines the commands used to verify that eBGP works.

Verifying the BGP Table: This section discusses the contents of the BGP table, particularly the routes learned using eBGP connections.

Injecting Routes into BGP for Advertisement to the ISPs: This section shows how you can configure an eBGP router to advertise the public IP address range used by an Enterprise.

External BGP

BGP configuration differs slightly when comparing the configuration of an External BGP (eBGP) peer and an Internal BGP (iBGP) peer. Many small differences in operation exist as well.

This chapter focuses on external BGP configuration and verification. The chapter begins with a discussion of the fundamentals of BGP configuration that applies to both internal and external peers. It then discusses the reasons why eBGP peers may or may not benefit from additional optional configuration settings.

After the eBGP neighborships have been established, the BGP routers exchange routes. The chapter examines the verification commands used to see the BGP routes learned from eBGP neighbors by examining the BGP table. The chapter closes with a discussion of how to configure the **network** command and to configure route redistribution to make a BGP router advertise an Enterprise's public IP prefix to its eBGP peers.

Chapter 14, "Internal BGP and BGP Route Filtering," discusses the particulars of iBGP configuration and verification, plus BGP route filtering (for both iBGP and eBGP).

"Do I Know This Already?" Quiz

The "Do I Know This Already?" quiz allows you to assess if you should read the entire chapter. If you miss no more than one of these eight self-assessment questions, you might want to move ahead to the "Exam Preparation Tasks." Table 13-1 lists the major headings in this chapter and the "Do I Know This Already?" quiz questions covering the material in those headings so you can assess your knowledge of these specific areas. The answers to the "Do I Know This Already?" quiz appear in Appendix A.

Table 13-1 *"Do I Know This Already?" Foundation Topics Section-to-Question Mapping*

Foundations Topics Section	Questions
External BGP for Enterprises	1–4
Verifying the BGP Table	5–7
Injecting Routes into BGP for Advertisement to the ISPs	8

1. Enterprise Router R1, in ASN 1, connects to ISP Router I1, ASN 2, using eBGP. The single serial link between the two routers uses IP addresses 10.1.1.1 and 10.1.1.2, respectively. Both routers use their S0/0 interfaces for this link. Which of the following commands would be needed on R1 to configure eBGP? (Choose two.)

    a. router bgp 2

    b. router bgp 1

    c. neighbor 10.1.1.2 remote-as 2

    d. neighbor 10.1.1.2 Update-source 10.1.1.1

    e. neighbor 10.1.1.2 Update-source S0/0

2. Enterprise Router R1, in ASN 1, connects to ISP Router I1, ASN 2, using eBGP. There are two parallel serial links between the two routers. The implementation plan calls for each router to base their BGP TCP connection on their respective loopback1 interfaces, with IP addresses 1.1.1.1 and 2.2.2.2, respectively. Which of the following commands would not be part of a working eBGP configuration on Router R1?

    a. router bgp 1

    b. neighbor 2.2.2.2 remote-as 2

    c. neighbor 2.2.2.2 update-source loopback1

    d. neighbor 2.2.2.2 multihop 2

3. The following output, taken from a **show ip bgp** command on Router R1, lists two neighbors. In what BGP neighbor state is neighbor 1.1.1.1?

```
Neighbor        V     AS MsgRcvd MsgSent   TblVer  InQ OutQ Up/Down
State/PfxRcd
1.1.1.1         4      1     60      61       26    0    0 00:45:01
0
2.2.2.2         4      3    153     159       26    0    0 00:38:13
1
```

    a. Idle

    b. Opensent

    c. Active

    d. Established

4. The following output was taken from the **show ip bgp** command on Router R2. In this
case, which of the following commands are most likely to already be configured on
R2? (Choose two.)

```
BGP router identifier 11.11.11.11, local AS number 11
...
Neighbor        V    AS MsgRcvd MsgSent   TblVer  InQ OutQ Up/Down
State/PfxRcd
1.1.1.1         4     1    87      87         0    0    0 00:00:06 Idle
(Admin)
2.2.2.2         4     3   173     183        41    0    0 00:58:47
2
```

    a. router bgp 11

    b. neighbor 1.1.1.1 remote-as 11

    c. neighbor 2.2.2.2 prefix-limit 1

    d. neighbor 1.1.1.1 shutdown

5. Which of the following answers is most true about the BGP Update message?

    a. It lists a set of path attributes, along with a list of prefixes that use those PAs.

    b. It lists a prefix/length, plus the PA settings for that prefix.

    c. It lists withdrawn routes, but never in the same Update message as newly advertised routes.

    d. A single Update message lists at most a single prefix/length.

6. The following output occurs on Router R1. Which of the following cannot be determined from this output?

```
R1# show ip route 180.1.1.0 255.255.255.240
Routing entry for 180.1.1.0/28
  Known via "bgp 2", distance 20, metric 0
  Tag 3, type external
  Last update from 192.168.1.2 00:10:27 ago
  Routing Descriptor Blocks:
  * 192.168.1.2, from 192.168.1.2, 00:10:27 ago
      Route metric is 0, traffic share count is 1
      AS Hops 2
      Route tag 3
```

    a. The type of BGP peer (iBGP or eBGP) that advertised this route to R1

    b. R1's ASN

    c. The next-hop router's ASN

    d. The AS_Path length

7. The following line of output was extracted from the output of the **show ip bgp** command on Router R1. Which of the following can be determined from this output?

```
Network             Next Hop            Metric LocPrf Weight Path
*   130.1.1.0/28        1.1.1.1                            0 1 2 3 4 i
```

    a. The route is learned from an eBGP peer.

    b. The route has no more than three ASNs in the AS_Path.

    c. The route is the best route for this prefix.

    d. None of these facts can be positively determined by this output.

8. Router R1 has eBGP connections to I1 and I2, routers at the same ISP. The company that owns R1 can use public address range 130.1.16.0/20. The following output lists all the IP routes in R1's routing table within this range. Which of the following answers would cause R1 to advertise the 130.1.16.0/20 prefix to its eBGP peers? (You should assume default settings for any parameters not mentioned in this question.)

```
R1# show ip route 130.1.16.0 255.255.240.0 longer-prefixes
! lines omitted...
O        130.1.16.0/24 [110/3] via 10.5.1.1, 00:14:36, FastEthernet0/1
O        130.1.17.0/24 [110/3] via 10.5.1.1, 00:14:36, FastEthernet0/1
O        130.1.18.0/24 [110/3] via 10.5.1.1, 00:14:36, FastEthernet0/1
```

    a. Configure R1 with the **network 130.1.16.0 mask 255.255.240.0** command.

    b. Configure R1 with the **network 130.1.16.0 mask 255.255.240.0 summary-only** command.

    c. Redistribute from OSPF into BGP, filtering so that only routes in the 130.1.16.0/20 range are redistributed.

    d. Redistribute from OSPF into BGP, filtering so that only routes in the 130.1.16.0/20 range are redistributed, and create a BGP summary for 130.1.16.0/20.

Foundation Topics

External BGP for Enterprises

Some of the core operational concepts of BGP mirror those of EIGRP and OSPF. BGP first forms a neighbor relationship with peers. BGP then learns information from its neighbors, placing that information in a table–the BGP table. Finally, BGP analyzes the BGP table to choose the best working route for each prefix in the BGP table, placing those routes into the IP routing table.

This section discusses external BGP (eBGP), focusing on two of the three aspects of how a routing protocol learns routes: forming neighborships and exchanging the reachability or topology information that is stored in the BGP table. First, this section examines the baseline configuration of eBGP peers (also called neighbors), along with several optional settings that may be needed specifically for eBGP connections. This configuration should result in working BGP neighborships. Then, this section examines the BGP table, listing the prefix/length and path attributes (PA) learned from the Internet, and the IP routing table.

eBGP Neighbor Configuration

At a minimum, a router participating in BGP needs to configure the following settings:

■   The router's own ASN (**router bgp** *asn* global command)

Key Topic

■   The IP address of each neighbor and that neighbor's ASN (**neighbor** *ip-address* **remote-as** *remote-asn* BGP subcommand)

For example, consider a typical multihomed Enterprise Internet design, as shown in Figure 13-1. In this case, the following design requirements have already been decided, but you must then determine the configuration, knowing the information in the following list and the figure:

■   The Enterprise uses ASN 11.

■   The connection to ISP1 (two T-1's) is considered the primary connection, with the connection to ISP3 (one T-1) being secondary.

■   ISP1 advertises a default route, plus full updates.

■   ISP1 uses ASN 1.

■   ISP3 advertises a default route, plus partial updates that includes only ISP3's local customers.

■   ISP3 uses ASN 3.

■   Each ISP uses the IP address of its lowest-numbered interface for its peer relationships.

For Router E1, the BGP configuration requires only three commands, at least to configure BGP to the point where E1 will form neighborships with the two other routers. (Note that this chapter continues to change and add to this configuration when introducing new concepts.) The example also shows the configuration on Routers I1-1 and I3-1 added

Figure 13-1   *Sample Single Multihomed Design*

solely to support the neighbor connections to E1; other BGP configuration on these
routers is not shown.

Example 13-1   *BGP Configuration on E1: Neighborships Configured*

```
! Configuration on router E1
router bgp 11
 neighbor 10.1.1.2 remote-as 1
 neighbor 192.168.1.2 remote-as 3
! Next commands are on I1-1
router bgp 1
 neighbor 10.1.1.1 remote-as 11
! Next commands are on I3-1
router bgp 3
 neighbor 192.168.1.1 remote-as 11
```

The gray portions of the output highlight the configuration of the local ASN and the
neighbors' ASNs – parameters that must match for the neighborships to form. First, E1
configures its own ASN as 11 by using the **router bgp 11** command. The other routers
must refer to ASN 11 on the **neighbor** commands that refer to E1; in this case I1-1 refers to
ASN 11 with its **neighbor 10.1.1.1 remote-as 11** command. Conversely, I1-1's local ASN
(1) on its **router bgp 1** global command must match what E1 configures in a **neighbor**
command, in this case with E1's **neighbor 10.1.1.2 remote-as 1** command.

Requirements for Forming eBGP Neighborships

Routers must meet several requirements to become BGP neighbors:

- A local router's ASN (on the **router bgp** *asn* command) must match the neighboring router's reference to that ASN with its **neighbor remote-as** *asn* command.

- The BGP router IDs of the two routers must not be the same.

- If configured, MD5 authentication must pass.

- Each router must be part of a TCP connection with the other router, with the remote router's IP address used in that TCP connection matching what the local router configures in a BGP **neighbor remote-as** command.

Consider the first two items in this list. First, the highlights in Example 13-1 demonstrate the first of the four requirements. Next, the second requirement in the list requires only a little thought if you recall the similar details about router IDs (RID) with EIGRP and OSPF. Like EIGRP and OSPF, BGP defines a 32-bit router ID, written in dotted-decimal notation. And like EIGRP and OSPF, BGP on a router chooses its RID the same general way, by using the following steps, in order, until a BGP RID has been chosen:

- **Configured:** Use the setting of the **bgp router-id** *rid* router subcommand.

- **Highest Loopback:** Choose the highest numeric IP address of any up/up loopback interface, at the time the BGP process initializes.

- **Highest other interface:** Choose the highest numeric IP address of any up/up non-loopback interface, at the time the BGP process initializes.

The third requirement in the list, the MD5 authentication check, occurs only if authentication has been configured on at least one of the two routers, using the **neighbor** *neighbor-ip* **password** *key* command. If two BGP neighbors configure this command, referring to the other routers' IP address, while configuring a matching MD5 authentication key value, the authentication passes. If both omit this command, then no authentication occurs, and the neighbor can still work. However, if the keys do not match, or if only one router configures authentication, then authentication fails.

The fourth neighbor requirement–that the IP addresses used for the neighbor TCP connection match–requires a more detailed discussion. BGP neighbors first form a TCP connection; later, BGP messages flow over that connection, which allows BGP routers to know when the messages arrived at the neighbor, and when they did not.

A BGP router creates the TCP connection by trying to establish a TCP connection to the address configured in the **neighbor** *neighbor-ip* **remote-as** command. However, IOS does not require the BGP configuration to explicitly state the source address that router uses when establishing this TCP connection, and if not explicitly configured, IOS picks an IP address on the local router. By default, IOS chooses its BGP source IP address for a given neighbor as the interface IP address of the outgoing interface of the route used to forward packets to that neighbor. That's a lot of words to fight through, and much more easily seen with a figure, such as Figure 13-2, which focuses on the eBGP connection between E1 and I1-1 shown in Figure 13-1.

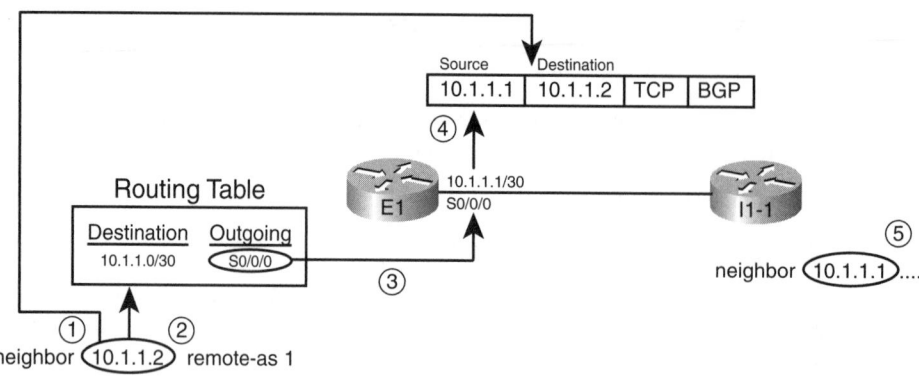

Figure 13-2 *A Default Choice for Update Source*

A description of the steps in logic shown in the figure follows:

Step 1. E1 finds the **neighbor 10.1.1.2** command, so E1 sends the BGP messages for this neighbor inside packets with destination IP address 10.1.1.2.

Step 2. E1 looks in the IP routing table for the route that matches destination 10.1.1.2.

Step 3. The route matched in Step 2 lists S0/0/0 as outgoing interface.

Step 4. E1's interface IP address for S0/0/0 is 10.1.1.1, so E1 uses 10.1.1.1 as its source IP address for this BGP peer.

Step 5. The **neighbor** command on the other router, I1-1, must refer to E1's source IP address (10.1.1.1 in this case).

Now, consider again the last of the four requirements to become neighbors. Restated, for proper operation, the BGP update source on one router must match the IP address configured on the other router's **neighbor** command, and vice versa. As shown in Figure 13-2, E1 uses update source 10.1.1.1, with I1-1 configuring the **neighbor 10.1.1.1...** command. Conversely, I1-1 uses 10.1.1.2 as its update source for this neighbor relationship, with E1 configuring a matching **neighbor 10.1.1.2** command.

Note: The update source concept applies per neighbor.

Issues When Redundancy Exists Between eBGP Neighbors

In many cases, a single Layer 3 path exists between eBGP neighbors. For example, a single T1, or single T3, or maybe a single MetroE Virtual Private Wire Service (VPWS) path exists between the two routers. In such cases, the eBGP configuration can simply use the interface IP addresses on that particular link. For example, in Figure 13-1, a single serial link exists between Routers E1 and I3-1, and they can reasonably use the serial link's IP addresses, as shown in Example 13-1.

However, when redundant Layer 3 paths exist between two eBGP neighbors, the use of interface IP addresses for the underlying TCP connection can result in an outage when only one of the two links fails. BGP neighborships fail when the underlying TCP connection fails. TCP uses a concept called a *socket*, which consists of a local TCP port number and an IP address. That IP address must be associated with a working interface (an interface whose state is line status up, line protocol up, per the **show interfaces** command). If the interface whose IP address is used by BGP were to fail, then the TCP socket would fail, closing the TCP connection. As a result, the BGP neighborship can only be up when the associated interfaces also happens to be up.

Two alternative solutions exist in this case. One option would be to configure two **neighbor** commands on each router, one for each of the neighbor's interface IP addresses. This solves the availability issue, because if one link fails, the other neighborship can remain up and working. However, in this case, both neighborships exchange BGP routes, consuming bandwidth and more memory in the BGP table.

The preferred option, which uses loopback interfaces as the TCP connection endpoints, solves the availability problem while avoiding the extra overhead. The two routers each configure a loopback interface and IP address, and use those loopback IP addresses as the source of their single BGP TCP connection. If one of the multiple links fails, the loopback interface does not fail. As long as the two routers have working routes to reach each other's loopback IP addresses, the TCP connection does not fail.

Configuring eBGP peers to use a loopback interface IP address with BGP requires several steps, as follows:

Key
Topic

Step 1.   Configure an IP address on a loopback interface on each router.

Step 2.   Tell BGP on each router to use the loopback IP address as the source IP address using the **neighbor... update-source** *ip-address* command.

Step 3.   Configure the BGP **neighbor** command on each router to refer to the other router's loopback IP address at the neighbor IP address in the **neighbor** *neighbor-ip* **remote-as** command.

Step 4.   Make sure each router has IP routes so that they can forward packets to the loopback interface IP address of the other router.

Step 5.   Configure eBGP multihop using the **neighbor... ebgp-multihop** *hops* command.

The first three steps in the list require configuration on both the routers. Figure 13-3 shows the details related to the first three steps, focusing on Router E1's use of its loopback1 interface (based on Figure 13-1).

The fourth step in the list is an overt reminder that for TCP to work, both routers must be able to deliver packets to the IP address listed in the **neighbor** commands. Because the **neighbor** commands now refer to loopback IP addresses, the routers cannot rely on connected routes for forwarding the packets. To give each router a route to the other router's loopback, you can run an instance of an IGP to learn the routes, or just configure static routes. If using static routes, make sure to configure the routes so that all redundant paths would be used (as seen in upcoming Example 13-2). If using an IGP, make sure the configuration allows the two routers to become IGP neighbors over all redundant links as well.

Figure 13-3   *Using Loopbacks with Update Source for eBGP*

eBGP Multihop Concepts

The fifth configuration step for using loopback IP addresses with eBGP peers refers to a feature called *eBGP multihop*. By default, when building packets to send to an eBGP peer, IOS sets the IP Time-To-Live (TTL) field in the IP header to a value of 1. With this default action, the eBGP neighborship fails to complete when using loopback interface IP addresses. The reason is that when the packet with TTL=1 arrives at the neighbor, the neighbor discards the packet.

The logic of discarding the BGP packets may be a bit surprising, so an example can help. For this example, assume the default action of TTL=1 is used and that eBGP multihop is not configured yet. Router E1 from Figure 13-1 is trying to establish a BGP connection to I1-1, using I1-1's loopback IP address 1.1.1.1, as shown in Figure 13-3. The following occurs with the IP packets sent by E1 when attempting to form a TCP connection for BGP to use:

Step 1.   E1 sends a packet to destination address 1.1.1.1, TTL=1.

Step 2.   I1-1 receives the packet. Seeing that the packet is not destined for the receiving interface's IP address, I1-1 passes the packet off to its own IP forwarding (IP routing) logic.

Step 3.   I1-1's IP routing logic matches the destination (1.1.1.1) with the routing table and finds interface loopback 2 as the outgoing interface.

Step 4.   I1-1's IP forwarding logic decrements TTL by 1, decreasing TTL to 0, and as a result, I1-1 discards the packet.

In short, the internal IOS packet forwarding logic decrements the TTL before giving the packet to the loopback interface, meaning that the normal IP forwarding logic discards the packet.

Configuring the routers with the **neighbor ebgp-multihop 2** command, as seen in upcoming Example 13-2, solves the problem. This command defines the TTL that the router will use when creating the BGP packets (2 in this case). As a result, the receiving router will decrement the TTL to 1, so the packet will not be discarded.

Configuring for eBGP Redundancy and Authentication

To pull these optional configuration steps together, Example 13-2 shows a new configuration for E1 and I1-1 (as compared with Example 13-1). In this case:

- Both routers use BGP authentication, with authentication key **fred**.

- Two Layer 3 paths exist between E1 and I1-1, so the configuration uses all the steps required to make both routers use the loopback interfaces listed in Figure 13-3.

- Both routers use eBGP multihop. (Otherwise, the neighborships would fail.)

- Both routers use static routes to provide reachability to the loopback interfaces, with two routes each, one using each redundant path.

Example 13-2 *Broader eBGP Configuration Example*

```
! Configuration on router E1
interface loopback 1
 ip address 11.11.11.11 255.255.255.255
!
ip route 1.1.1.1 255.255.255.255 s0/0/0
ip route 1.1.1.1 255.255.255.255 s0/0/1
!
router bgp 11
 neighbor 1.1.1.1 remote-as 1
 neighbor 1.1.1.1 update-source loopback 1
 neighbor 1.1.1.1 ebgp-multihop 2
 neighbor 1.1.1.1 password fred
! Next commands are on I1-1
interface loopback 2
 ip address 1.1.1.1 255.255.255.255
!
ip route 11.11.11.11 255.255.255.255 s0/0/0
ip route 11.11.11.11 255.255.255.255 s0/0/1
!
router bgp 1
 neighbor 11.11.11.11 remote-as 11
 neighbor 11.11.11.11 update-source loopback 2
 neighbor 11.11.11.11 ebgp-multihop 2
 neighbor 11.11.11.11 password fred
```

Besides listing the various configuration commands, this example is also the first in this chapter that demonstrates how to configure multiple settings for a single BGP neighbor. The IOS BGP **neighbor** command has many options. To set those options for a single neighbor, the command begins with **neighbor** *neighbor-ip-address*, followed by the parameters. So, instead of one **neighbor** command with a large number of parameters, the configuration includes several **neighbor** commands, each listing the IP address of the same neighbor, but each listing a different set of parameters. In this case, each router now uses four **neighbor** commands: one to define the remote ASN, one for the update source, one to enable eBGP multihop, and one for the authentication key.

BGP Internals and Verifying eBGP Neighbors

Similar to OSPF, the BGP neighbor relationship goes through a series of states over time. Although the Finite State Machine (FSM) for BGP neighbor states has many twists and turns, particularly for handling exceptions, retries, and failures, the overall process works as follows:

Step 1. A router tries to establish a TCP connection with the IP address listed on a **neighbor** command, using well-known destination port 179.

Step 2. When the three-way TCP connection completes, the router sends its first BGP message, the BGP *Open* message, which generally performs the same function as the EIGRP and OSPF Hello messages. The Open message contains several BGP parameters, including those that must be verified before allowing the routers to become neighbors.

Step 3. After an Open message has been sent and received and the neighbor parameters match, the neighbor relationship is formed, and the neighbors reach *established* state.

Table 13-2 lists the various BGP states. If all works well, the neighborship reaches the final state: *established*. When the neighbor relationship (also called a BGP peer or BGP peer connection) reaches the established state, the neighbors can send BGP Update messages, which list PAs and prefixes. However, if neighbor relationship fails for any reason, then the neighbor relationship can cycle through all the states listed in Table 13-2 while the routers periodically attempt to bring up the neighborship.

Key Topic

Table 13-2 *BGP Neighbor States*

State	Typical Reasons
Idle	The BGP process is either administratively down or awaiting the next retry attempt.
Connect	The BGP process is waiting for the TCP connection to be completed. You cannot determine from this state information whether the TCP connection can complete.
Active	The TCP connection has been completed, but no BGP messages have been sent to the peer yet.
Opensent	The TCP connection exists, and a BGP Open message has been sent to the peer, but the matching Open message has not yet been received from the other router.
Openconfirm	An Open message has been both sent to and received from the other router. The next step is to receive a BGP Keepalive message (to confirm all neighbor-related parameters matched) or BGP Notification message (to learn there is some mismatch in neighbor parameters).

Table 13-2 *BGP Neighbor States*

State	Typical Reasons
Established	All neighbor parameters match, the neighbor relationship works, and the peers can now exchange Update messages.

Verifying eBGP Neighbor Status

The two most common commands to display a BGP neighbor's status are **show ip bgp summary** and **show ip bgp neighbors** [*neighbor-id*]. Interestingly, most people use the first of these commands because it supplies a similar amount of information, 1 line per neighbor, as do the familiar **show ip eigrp neighbors** and **show ip ospf neighbor** commands. The **show ip bgp neighbors** command lists a large volume of output per neighbor, which, although useful, usually contains far too much information for the verification of the current neighbor state. Examples 13-3 and 13-4 show samples of the output of each of these two commands on Router E1, respectively, based on the configuration shown in Example 13-2, with some description following each example.

Example 13-3 *Summary Information with the* **show ip bgp summary** *Command*

```
E1# show ip bgp summary
BGP router identifier 11.11.11.11, local AS number 11
BGP table version is 26, main routing table version 26
6 network entries using 792 bytes of memory
7 path entries using 364 bytes of memory
6/4 BGP path/bestpath attribute entries using 888 bytes of memory
5 BGP AS-PATH entries using 120 bytes of memory
0 BGP route-map cache entries using 0 bytes of memory
0 BGP filter-list cache entries using 0 bytes of memory
Bitfield cache entries: current 1 (at peak 2) using 32 bytes of memory
BGP using 2196 total bytes of memory
BGP activity 12/6 prefixes, 38/31 paths, scan interval 60 secs


Neighbor        V    AS  MsgRcvd  MsgSent  TblVer  InQ OutQ  Up/Down  State/PfxRcd
1.1.1.1         4     1       60       61      26    0    0  00:45:01             6
192.168.1.2     4     3      153      159      26    0    0  00:38:13             1
```

The first line in the summary lists the local router's BGP RID (11.11.11.11), along with the local router's ASN (11). The rest of the summary focuses on statistics for the BGP table entries. The bottom of the output lists a heading line (highlighted in the output), plus one line per neighbor, with two neighbors in this case. The Neighbor column lists the IP address as defined on the local router's **neighbor** command and not the neighbor's BGP RID. Other notable information includes the neighbor's ASN (as configured on the local router's **neighbor remote-as** command), the time spent in the current state, and an interesting heading: State/PfxRcd.

This final heading, State/PfxRcd, either lists the BGP neighbor state, as summarized in Table 13-2, or the number of prefixes received (PfxRcd) from that neighbor. A numeric value under this heading implies a neighbor state of established, because the peers must be in established state before Updates can be sent. If the peer is not in an established state, the value in this heading lists the text name of the current BGP state.

Example 13-4 shows a sample of the **show ip bgp neighbors 1.1.1.1** command on router E1, which displays information about the connection to Router I1-1 in Figure 13-1. This command lists several facts not seen in the shorter **show ip bgp summary** command output in Example 13-3. The example highlights some of those key items, with the following comments referring to those highlighted items, in order:

- The neighbor is an eBGP neighbor (external link).

- The neighbor's BGP RID (1.1.1.1).

- The current state (Established) is explicitly listed.

- Route refresh is enabled (as referenced in Chapter 14's section titled "Clearing BGP Neighbors").

- The eBGP multihop setting (2 hops).

- Local and remote TCP socket information (IP addresses and port numbers).

Example 13-4 *Detailed Information with the* **show ip bgp neighbors** *Command*

```
E1# show ip bgp neighbors 1.1.1.1
BGP neighbor is 1.1.1.1,  remote AS 1, external link
  BGP version 4, remote router ID 1.1.1.1
  BGP state = Established, up for 00:45:08
  Last read 00:00:02, last write 00:00:38, hold time is 180, keepalive interval
is 60 seconds
  Neighbor capabilities:
    Route refresh: advertised and received(new)
    Address family IPv4 Unicast: advertised and received
  Message statistics:
    InQ depth is 0
    OutQ depth is 0

                         Sent       Rcvd
    Opens:                 2          2
    Notifications:         0          0
    Updates:              16         12
    Keepalives:           43         47
    Route Refresh:         0          0
    Total:                61         61
  Default minimum time between advertisement runs is 30 seconds
```

```
 For address family: IPv4 Unicast
  BGP table version 26, neighbor version 26/0
  Output queue size : 0
  Index 1, Offset 0, Mask 0x2
  1 update-group member
                                        Sent        Rcvd
  Prefix activity:                      — —         — —
     Prefixes Current:                   6           6 (Consumes 312 bytes)
     Prefixes Total:                     19          7
     Implicit Withdraw:                  11          0
     Explicit Withdraw:                   2          1
     Used as bestpath:                  n/a          5
     Used as multipath:                 n/a          0

                                      Outbound    Inbound
   Local Policy Denied Prefixes:       — — —       — — —·
     AS_PATH loop:                       n/a          2
     Total:                               0           2
   Number of NLRIs in the update sent: max 3, min 1


   Address tracking is enabled, the RIB does have a route to 1.1.1.1
   Connections established 2; dropped 1
   Last reset 00:45:10, due to Peer closed the session
   External BGP neighbor may be up to 2 hops away.
   Transport(tcp) path-mtu-discovery is enabled
 Connection state is ESTAB, I/O status: 1, unread input bytes: 0
 Connection is ECN Disabled, Minimum incoming TTL 0, Outgoing TTL 2
 Local host: 11.11.11.11, Local port: 179
 Foreign host: 1.1.1.1, Foreign port: 28995
 Connection tableid (VRF): 0


 Enqueued packets for retransmit: 0, input: 0  mis-ordered: 0 (0 bytes)


 Event Timers (current time is 0x8217A0):
 Timer           Starts      Wakeups          Next
 Retrans            49           0             0x0
 TimeWait            0           0             0x0
 AckHold            49          46             0x0
 SendWnd             0           0             0x0
 KeepAlive           0           0             0x0
 GiveUp              0           0             0x0
 PmtuAger            0           0             0x0
 DeadWait            0           0             0x0
 Linger              0           0             0x0
 ProcessQ            0           0             0x0
```

```
iss: 2070882650   snduna: 2070884280   sndnxt: 2070884280      sndwnd:  15890
irs: 3327995414   rcvnxt: 3327996693   rcvwnd:      16156  delrcvwnd:    228


SRTT: 300 ms, RTTO: 306 ms, RTV: 6 ms, KRTT: 0 ms
minRTT: 0 ms, maxRTT: 300 ms, ACK hold: 200 ms
Status Flags: passive open, gen tcbs
Option Flags: nagle, path mtu capable, md5
IP Precedence value : 6


Datagrams (max data segment is 516 bytes):
Rcvd: 98 (out of order: 0), with data: 50, total data bytes: 1278
Sent: 99 (retransmit: 0, fastretransmit: 0, partialack: 0, Second Congestion: 0),
with data: 50, tot
al data bytes: 1629
 Packets received in fast path: 0, fast processed: 0, slow path: 0
 fast lock acquisition failures: 0, slow path: 0
E1# show tcp brief
TCB         Local Address          Foreign Address        (state)
66D27FE0    192.168.1.1.179        192.168.1.2.16489      ESTAB
66D27378    11.11.11.11.179        1.1.1.1.28995          ESTAB
```

Note that the end of the example shows another command that you can use to confirm the TCP socket details of the underlying TCP connection: **show tcp brief**.

Administratively Controlling Neighbor Status

Interestingly, Cisco IOS provides a means by which network operations personnel can administratively disable any BGP neighbor. To do so, the operator would enter BGP configuration mode and issue the **neighbor** *neighbor-ip* **shutdown** command. This command brings down the current neighbor to an idle state. Later, when the BGP connection should be brought up, the operator should repeat the process, but with the **no** version of the command (**no neighbor** *neighbor-ip* **shutdown**).

These commands can be particularly useful to try in lab when learning BGP. Teamed with the **debug ip bgp** command, you can bring down neighbors and see the somewhat-readable BGP messages. These messages list the BGP states from Table 13-2. It also shows the information inside the Open messages. Example 13-5 shows a sample, with the debug messages that note a state transition highlighted. The output also lists the **show ip bgp summary** command, with the administratively idle state created by the **neighbor 1.1.1.1 shutdown** BGP configuration command on Router E1.

Example 13-5 *BGP Shutdown and BGP Neighbor State Transitions*

```
E1# debug ip bgp
BGP debugging is on for address family: IPv4 Unicast
E1# conf t
```

```
Enter configuration commands, one per line.  End with CNTL/Z.
E1(config)# router bgp 11
E1(config-router)# neighbor 1.1.1.1 shutdown
E1(config-router)#


*Aug 11 20:23:01.335: BGPNSF state: 1.1.1.1 went from nsf_not_active to
nsf_not_active
*Aug 11 20:23:01.335: BGP: 1.1.1.1 went from Established to Idle
*Aug 11 20:23:01.335: %BGP-5-ADJCHANGE: neighbor 1.1.1.1 Down Admin. Shutdown


E1(config-router)# do show ip bgp summary
! lines omitted for brevity


Neighbor        V    AS MsgRcvd MsgSent   TblVer  InQ OutQ Up/Down  State/PfxRcd
1.1.1.1         4     1      87      87        0    0    0 00:00:06 Idle (Admin)
192.168.1.2     4     3     173     183       41    0    0 00:58:47            1


E1(config-router)# no neighbor 1.1.1.1 shutdown
E1(config-router)#
*Aug 11 20:23:26.571: BGP: 1.1.1.1 went from Idle to Active
*Aug 11 20:23:26.571: BGP: 1.1.1.1 open active, local address 11.11.11.11
*Aug 11 20:23:26.575: BGP: 1.1.1.1 read request no-op
*Aug 11 20:23:26.575: BGP: 1.1.1.1 went from Active to OpenSent
*Aug 11 20:23:26.575: BGP: 1.1.1.1 sending OPEN, version 4, my as: 11, holdtime
180 seconds
*Aug 11 20:23:26.579: BGP: 1.1.1.1 send message type 1, length (incl. header) 45
*Aug 11 20:23:26.583: BGP: 1.1.1.1 rcv message type 1, length (excl. header) 26
*Aug 11 20:23:26.587: BGP: 1.1.1.1 rcv OPEN, version 4, holdtime 180 seconds
*Aug 11 20:23:26.587: BGP: 1.1.1.1 rcv OPEN w/ OPTION parameter len: 16
*Aug 11 20:23:26.587: BGP: 1.1.1.1 rcvd OPEN w/ optional parameter type 2
(Capability) len 6
*Aug 11 20:23:26.587: BGP: 1.1.1.1 OPEN has CAPABILITY code: 1, length 4
*Aug 11 20:23:26.587: BGP: 1.1.1.1 OPEN has MP_EXT CAP for afi/safi: 1/1
*Aug 11 20:23:26.587: BGP: 1.1.1.1 rcvd OPEN w/ optional parameter type 2
(Capability) len 2
*Aug 11 20:23:26.587: BGP: 1.1.1.1 OPEN has CAPABILITY code: 128, length 0
*Aug 11 20:23:26.587: BGP: 1.1.1.1 OPEN has ROUTE-REFRESH capability(old) for all
address-families
*Aug 11 20:23:26.587: BGP: 1.1.1.1 rcvd OPEN w/ optional parameter type 2
(Capability) len 2
*Aug 11 20:23:26.587: BGP: 1.1.1.1 OPEN has CAPABILITY code: 2, length 0
*Aug 11 20:23:26.587: BGP: 1.1.1.1 OPEN has ROUTE-REFRESH capability(new) for all
address-families
BGP: 1.1.1.1 rcvd OPEN w/ remote AS 1
*Aug 11 20:23:26.587: BGP: 1.1.1.1 went from OpenSent to OpenConfirm
*Aug 11 20:23:26.591: BGP: 1.1.1.1 went from OpenConfirm to Established
*Aug 11 20:23:26.591: %BGP-5-ADJCHANGE: neighbor 1.1.1.1 Up
*Aug 11 20:23:26.603: BGP_Router: unhandled major event code 128, minor 0
```

BGP Message Summary

So far, this chapter has mentioned three of the four BGP messages. For reference, Table 13-3 lists the four BGP messages, with comparisons to EIGRP messages for perspective.

Table 13-3 *BGP Message Types*

Message	Purpose	Similarity with EIGRP
Open	Used to establish a neighbor relationship and exchange basic parameters, including ASN and MD5 authentication values.	Hello
Keepalive	Sent on a periodic basis to maintain the neighbor relationship. The lack of receipt of a Keepalive message within the negotiated Hold timer causes BGP to bring down the neighbor connection.	Hello
Update	Used to exchange PAs and the associated prefix/length (NLRI) that use those attributes.	Update
Notification	Used to signal a BGP error; typically results in a reset to the neighbor relationship.	No direct equivalent

Verifying the BGP Table

When an Enterprise router has established its eBGP neighbor relationships, that router can advertise and learn routes using BGP. To learn routes, an Enterprise BGP router does not need additional configuration beyond the configuration of eBGP neighbors as discussed in the first section of this chapter. To advertise routes to eBGP peers, particularly the public IP address prefix(es) used by that Enterprise, the Enterprise BGP router needs some additional configuration, as discussed in the upcoming section "Injecting Routes into BGP for Advertisement to the ISPs."

The BGP table plays a key role in the process of learning and using routing information with BGP. A router stores all learned BGP prefixes and PAs in its BGP table. The router will later choose which route for each prefix is the best BGP route. The router can then advertise its BGP table to its neighbors, advertising only the best route for each prefix.

This section begins with a brief examination of the BGP Update process by which BGP neighbors exchange routing information. Next, the text looks at the various **show** commands that can be used to examine and confirm the contents of the BGP table.

The BGP Update Message

When a BGP neighborship reaches the established state, those neighbors begin sending BGP Update messages to each other. The router receiving an Update places those learned prefixes into its BGP table, regardless of whether the route appears to be the best route. Like EIGRP and OSPF, BGP puts all learned routing information into its table, and then BGP processes all such potential routes to choose the best route for each prefix.

The BGP Update message itself can be revealing about the motivations behind BGP. Figure 13-4 shows the format of the Update message.

Figure 13-4   *Format of the BGP Update Message*

Interestingly, the format of the Update message tells us something about the nature of BGP as a *Path Vector* algorithm. The message lists a set of PAs and then a potentially long list of prefixes that use that set of PAs. So, you might view the BGP Update message as focusing on advertising paths, or a set of PAs, along with the associated list of prefixes that use the advertised path. (Both are important, of course.) Then, because BGP uses the information in the combined set of PAs to make a decision of which path is best, its underlying logic is called *path vector*.

Note: BGP also uses the term Network Layer Reachability Information (NLRI) to describe the IP prefix and length. This book uses the more familiar term *prefix*.

BGP uses the Update message to both announce and withdraw routes. For example, when a router realizes that a route in the router's BGP table has failed, that router withdraws that route by sending a BGP Update to its neighbors, listing the prefix in the list of withdrawn routes. When a router receives an Update that lists a prefix as withdrawn, that router knows that the route has failed. (Note the field near the top of the Update message that lists withdrawn routes.) That same Update message may contain other announced prefixes later in the Update message.

Examining the BGP Table

One of the key tasks in a BGP verification plan should be to examine the prefixes in the BGP table and confirm that the right prefixes have been learned from the expected neighbors. The BGP table should hold all learned prefixes, from each neighbor, except for any prefixes filtered by an inbound BGP filter. For example, in a router configured a **neighbor route-map in** command, the local router would first filter the routes and then add the allowed routes into the BGP table. (Chapter 14's section "Route Filtering and Clearing BGP Peers" discusses the filtering and its impact on the BGP table.)

As an example, consider Figure 13-5, which shows the same basic topology as Figure 13-1 but with only the information pertinent to the upcoming discussions listed in the figure. In this case, five prefixes exist somewhere in the Internet, with ISP1 and ISP3 learning these prefixes from ISP2. An additional prefix exists at the site of a customer of ISP3. The design calls for the following actions by ISP1 and ISP3 in their eBGP advertisements to the Enterprise:

■ ISP1 should supply a default route plus full BGP updates.

■ ISP3 should supply a default route plus partial BGP updates that include only ISP3's customers' prefixes (for example, 192.135.250.0/28).

Figure 13-5 *Three Prefixes to be Advertised to E1*

The **show ip bgp** lists the entirety of the BGP routing table. Example 13-6 shows a sample from Router E1. Note that the configuration of this network is based on Example 13-2, with Routers E1 and I1-1 still using their loopback interfaces in their **neighbor** commands.

Example 13-6 *E1's BGP Table with Routes Learned from the ISPs*

```
E1# show ip bgp
BGP table version is 78, local router ID is 11.11.11.11
Status codes: s suppressed, d damped, h history, * valid, > best, i - internal,
              r RIB-failure, S Stale
Origin codes: i - IGP, e - EGP, ? - incomplete

   Network          Next Hop         Metric LocPrf Weight Path
*  0.0.0.0          192.168.1.2           0          0 3 i
*>                  1.1.1.1               0          0 1 i
*> 181.0.0.0/8      1.1.1.1                          0 1 2 111 111 i
*> 182.0.0.0/8      1.1.1.1                          0 1 2 222 i
*> 183.0.0.0/8      1.1.1.1                          0 1 2 i
*> 184.0.0.0/8      1.1.1.1                          0 1 2 i
*> 185.0.0.0/8      1.1.1.1                          0 1 2 i
*  192.135.250.0/28 1.1.1.1                          0 1 2 3 4 i
*>                  192.168.1.2                      0 3 4 i
```

First, examine the overall format and the headings in the output of the **show ip bgp** command. The Network column lists the prefix/length (NLRI). The Next Hop heading lists the next-hop IP address that would be used for the route. Then, skipping over to the far right, the Path heading lists the AS_Path PA. (Note that it is difficult to see the beginning of the AS_Path, but the weight [another PA] for each route is 0 in this case, so the next number after the 0, in this case, is the beginning of the AS_Path.)

Next, focus on the last two lines of output from the **show ip bgp** command. Each of the last two lines describes a different route to reach 192.135.250.0/28–one with next-hop 1.1.1.1 (router I1-1) and one with next-hop 192.168.1.2 (router I3-1). Because the second of these two lines does not list a prefix (under the heading "Network"), the output implies that this line is just another route for the prefix listed on the previous line. Next, examine the highlighted AS_Path values at the end of each of these lines. For the route through I1-1 (1.1.1.1), the AS_Path lists ASNs 1, 2, 3, and 4. Similarly, the AS_Path for the other route lists only ASNs 3 and 4.

Note: BGP **show** commands list the AS_Path with the first-added ASN on the right and the last-added ASN on the left. BGP uses this convention because when BGP adds an ASN to the AS_Path, BGP prepends the ASN to the list, causing the new ASN to show up as the leftmost ASN in the AS_Path.

Continuing to focus on the final two lines of the **show ip bgp** output, examine the far left part of the output, and note that the second of these two lines has a > highlighted. Per the legend at the top of the command output, the > denotes the chosen best route. In this case, none of the routers inside the various ISPs set PAs for the purpose of influencing the best path choice, so the first used BGP best path decision is the shortest AS_Path. As a result, the path through ISP3, ASN 3, is best, having only 2 ASNs, compared to the path through ISP1, ASN 1, with four ASNs.

You can confirm that all E1's BGP table entries were learned using eBGP, rather than iBGP, by the absence of the letter "i" in the third column. Immediately after the *>, a space appears in the output. If a route was learned with iBGP, an "i" would appear in this third character position. By implication, all the routes in Example 13-6 are eBGP routes due to the absence of the letter i in the third character of possible output.

Finally, taking a broader view of the output of the **show ip bgp** command, consider which prefixes have two known routes and which have only one. Then, consider the design requirements listed before Example 13-6: I1-1 would advertise all prefixes, plus a default, but I3-1 would advertise only partial updates plus a default. As such, I3-1 did not advertise the prefixes that begin 181 through 185, by design, resulting in Router E1 only learning one route for each of these prefixes.

E1 chose the route through I3-1 as the best route for prefix 192.135.250.0/28. Example 13-7 shows the details of the IP routing table entry for this route.

Example 13-7 *E1's IP Route for 192.135.250.0/28*

```
E1# show ip route 192.135.250.0 255.255.255.240
Routing entry for 192.135.250.0/28
  Known via "bgp 11", distance 20, metric 0
  Tag 3, type external
  Last update from 192.168.1.2 00:10:27 ago
  Routing Descriptor Blocks:
  * 192.168.1.2, from 192.168.1.2, 00:10:27 ago
      Route metric is 0, traffic share count is 1
      AS Hops 2
      Route tag 3
```

The output of the **show ip route 192.135.250.0 255.255.255.240** command lists the source of the route (BGP process 11), the next-hop router (192.168.1.2), and the AS Path length (AS Hops 2). The output also confirms that the route is an external (eBGP) route.

Most of the remaining details in the BGP table relate to BGP PAs, which are discussed in more detail in Chapter 15, "BGP Path Control."

Viewing Subsets of the BGP Table

When accepting full or partial BGP updates, the sheer number of BGP table entries can be much too large for the **show ip bgp** command to be useful. The command could list thousands, or even hundreds of thousands, of prefixes. In practice, you need to be comfortable with a variety of options on the **show ip bgp** command, each listing a different part of the BGP table.

For example, you will likely want to look at BGP table entries for specific prefixes, including the default route prefix of 0.0.0.0/0. Additionally, you may want to see routes per neighbor, and see which routes were heard from that neighbor—and which of those routes passed through any inbound route filters to make it into the BGP table. Finally, to verify whether neighboring ISPs sent full or partial updates, you can look at counters for the number of prefixes learned from each neighbor. Although you probably will never know the exact number of prefixes to expect, you should see a significant difference in the number of prefixes learned from a neighbor sending full updates as compared to a neighbor sending partial updates.

Table 13-4 summarizes some of the key command options that can supply these subsets of information.

Table 13-4 *Verification Commands for eBGP-Learned Routes*

Verification Step	Command
List possible default routes.	**show ip bgp 0.0.0.0 0.0.0.0**
List possible routes, per prefix.	**show ip bgp** *prefix [subnet-mask]*
List routes learned from one neighbor, before any inbound filtering is applied.	**show ip bgp neighbors** *ip-address* **received-routes**
List routes learned from a specific neighbor that passed any inbound filters.	**show ip bgp neighbors** *ip-address* **routes**
Lists routes advertised to a neighbor after applying outbound filtering.	**show ip bgp neighbors** *ip-address* **advertised-routes**
List the number of prefixes learned per neighbor.	**show ip bgp summary**

Example 13-8 shows a few samples of these commands on Router E1 from Figures 13-1 and 13-5. The configuration remains unchanged since Example 13-2.

Example 13-8 *Command Samples from Table 13-4*

```
E1# show ip bgp 0.0.0.0 0.0.0.0
BGP routing table entry for 0.0.0.0/0, version 75
Paths: (2 available, best #2, table Default-IP-Routing-Table)
  Advertised to update-groups:
        1
  3
    192.168.1.2 from 192.168.1.2 (3.3.3.3)
      Origin IGP, metric 0, localpref 100, valid, external
```

```
  1
      1.1.1.1 from 1.1.1.1 (1.1.1.1)
        Origin IGP, metric 0, localpref 100, valid, external, best


E1# show ip bgp 192.135.250.0
BGP routing table entry for 192.135.250.0/28, version 78
Paths: (2 available, best #2, table Default-IP-Routing-Table)
  Advertised to update-groups:
        1
  1 2 3 4
    1.1.1.1 from 1.1.1.1 (1.1.1.1)
      Origin IGP, localpref 100, valid, external
  3 4
    192.168.1.2 from 192.168.1.2 (3.3.3.3)
      Origin IGP, localpref 100, valid, external, best


E1# show ip bgp summary
BGP router identifier 11.11.11.11, local AS number 11
BGP table version is 78, main routing table version 78
7 network entries using 924 bytes of memory
9 path entries using 468 bytes of memory
8/5 BGP path/bestpath attribute entries using 1184 bytes of memory
7 BGP AS-PATH entries using 168 bytes of memory
0 BGP route-map cache entries using 0 bytes of memory
0 BGP filter-list cache entries using 0 bytes of memory
Bitfield cache entries: current 1 (at peak 2) using 32 bytes of memory
BGP using 2776 total bytes of memory
BGP activity 7/0 prefixes, 53/44 paths, scan interval 60 secs

Neighbor        V    AS MsgRcvd MsgSent   TblVer  InQ OutQ Up/Down  State/PfxRcd
1.1.1.1         4     1     186     189       78    0    0 00:53:33            7
192.168.1.2     4     3     161     199       78    0    0 00:51:48            2
```

The first command, **show ip bgp 0.0.0.0 0.0.0.0**, displays details about the default routes in the BGP table. The output lists three lines per route, with the AS_Path on the first line. Working through the highlighted portions of the output, in this case, the AS_Path is either 3 or 1, because the ISP routers each originated the route, and those neighboring ASNs are ASN 1 and ASN 3. The output also lists the next-hop address of the route (192.168.1.2 and 1.1.1.1) and the neighbor's BGP RID (I1-1's is 1.1.1.1 and I3-1's is 3.3.3.3). Finally, instead of the > seen in the output of **show ip bgp**, this command simply lists the term "best" for the best route.

The next command, **show ip bgp 192.135.250.0**, looks much like the first. In this case, with no subnet mask listed in the command, IOS displays information for any prefix 192.135.250.0 regardless of prefix length. The output again lists three lines per route beginning with the AS_Path values (as highlighted).

The final command listed earlier in Table 13-4, **show ip bgp summary**, lists the number of prefixes received from each neighbor on the far right side. Also, you can see the amount of memory used for the prefixes (listed as network entries) and for different PAs.

The rest of the commands from Table 13-4 focus on displaying information relative to whether BGP filtering has yet occurred. The first, **show ip bgp neighbors** *neighbor-ip* **received-routes**, lists routes received from the neighbor before inbound BGP filtering. The second, **show ip bgp neighbors** *neighbor-ip* **routes**, lists routes received from that neighbor that passed through any inbound filtering. These commands are particularly useful when verifying the results of any configured BGP filters or route maps. The section "Displaying the Results of BGP Filtering" in Chapter 14 discusses the information in these commands and an extra configuration requirement to use the **received-routes** option.

Injecting Routes into BGP for Advertisement to the ISPs

So far, this chapter has focused on configuring eBGP peers and the routes learned by Enterprise routers from eBGP peers at ISPs. These outbound routes let the Enterprise routers forward packets toward the Internet.

At the same time, the ISPs need to learn routes for the Enterprise's public IP address space. This chapter assumes that the choice to use BGP has already been made, so using BGP to advertise the Enterprise's public IP address range makes good sense. This short final major section of this chapter examines the options for advertising these routes. In particular, this section looks at two options:

- BGP **network** command
- Redistribution from an IGP

Injecting Routes Using the network Command

The BGP **network** router subcommand differs significantly from the **network** command used by IGPs. For OSPF and EIGRP, the **network** command lists parameters that the router then compares to all its interface IP addresses. If matched, the router enables the IGP routing protocol on those interfaces. BGP does not use the **network** command to enable BGP on interfaces–in fact, BGP has no concept of being enabled on interfaces at all. For a point of comparison, note that the **show ip ospf interface** and **show ip eigrp interfaces** commands identify the enabled interfaces for OSPF and EIGRP, respectively, but no such equivalent BGP command even exists.

The BGP **network** command does cause a comparison to occur, but the comparison occurs between the **network** command's parameters and the *contents of that router's IP routing table*, as follows:

> Look for a route in the router's current IP routing table that exactly matches the parameters of the **network** command; if a route for that exact prefix/length exists, put the equivalent prefix/length into the local BGP table.

Note: The preceding statement, and the remaining logic in this section, assumes a BGP default setting of **no auto-summary**. The effect of reversing this setting to **auto-summary** is described in the upcoming section "The Effect of **auto-summary** on the BGP **network** Command."

For example, the Enterprise shown earlier on the left side of both Figures 13-1 and 13-5 might use a private address range and use NAT to translate to use public addresses. For example, the Enterprise might use private Class A network 10.0.0.0 for all private address needs and public address block 128.107.0.0/19 for public addresses. Enterprise Router E1 would then need to advertise the public prefix (128.107.0.0/19) to its ISPs, but not the private address range. Example 13-9 shows an example.

Example 13-9 *E1's Configuration of a* **network** *Command to Advertise Prefixes with eBGP*

```
router bgp 11
 network 128.107.0.0 mask 255.255.224.0
E1# sh ip bgp
BGP table version is 9, local router ID is 11.11.11.11
Status codes: s suppressed, d damped, h history, * valid, > best, i - internal,
              r RIB-failure, S Stale
Origin codes: i - IGP, e - EGP, ? - incomplete

   Network          Next Hop          Metric LocPrf Weight Path
*  0.0.0.0          192.168.1.2            0           0 3 i
*>                  1.1.1.1                0           0 1 i
*> 128.107.0.0/19   10.1.1.66              3       32768 i

*> 181.0.0.0/8      1.1.1.1                        0 1 2 111 111 i
*> 182.0.0.0/8      1.1.1.1                        0 1 2 222 i
*> 183.0.0.0/8      1.1.1.1                        0 1 2 i
*> 184.0.0.0/8      1.1.1.1                        0 1 2 i
*> 185.0.0.0/8      1.1.1.1                        0 1 2 i
*  192.135.250.0/28 1.1.1.1                        0 1 2 3 4 i
*>                  192.168.1.2                    0 3 4 i
```

The **network 128.107.0.0 mask 255.255.224.0** command lists both the subnet number and mask. It adds this prefix to the BGP table only if the exact prefix with that same mask exists in Router E1's routing table. In this case, such a route existed, so the **show ip bgp** command output that follows now lists 128.107.0.0/19 in the BGP table.

In some cases, the Internet-connected router may not have a single route for the entire public prefix. For example, with such a large range of public addresses as 128.107.0.0/19, the Enterprise will most likely have broken that range into subnets, and the Enterprise router may not have a route for the entire range. For example, Router E1 might see routes for 128.107.1.0/24, 128.107.2.0/24, and so on but no route for 128.107.0.0/19.

When a router knows routes only for subsets of the prefix that needs to be advertised, an additional step is needed when using the **network** command. For instance, the **network 128.107.0.0 mask 255.255.224.0** command will not add this prefix to the BGP table even if routes for subsets of this range exist, such as 128.107.1.0/24. So, either configure a static route for the entire range, with outgoing interface null0, on the Internet facing router, or use IGP route summarization to create a summary route for the entire prefix with IGP.

Note: The static route for 128.107.0.0/19 to null0—a discard route—is not meant to be advertised to other routers. It's only purpose is to enable the operation of the **network** command. This discard route should not cause routing problems on the local router, because of the more specific routes for subnets inside the same range of addresses.

Finally, the **network** command examples in this section use the **mask** parameter, but if omitted, IOS assumes a classful network mask. For example, a **network 9.0.0.0** command assumes a Class A default mask of 255.0.0.0, and the **network 128.1.0.0** command assumes a Class B default mask of 255.255.0.0.

The Effect of auto-summary on the BGP network Command

As of Cisco IOS version 12.3 mainline, BGP defaults to a setting of **no auto-summary**, and the previous section's discussion of the **network** command assumed this default setting. However, if the configuration is changed to **auto-summary**, then IOS makes a small change in how it interprets the **network** command.

The change in logic occurs only when the **network** command omits its **mask** parameter; there is no difference in logic if the mask parameter is explicitly configured. When the **network** command refers to a Class A, B, or C network, with no **mask** parameter configured, and with **auto-summary** configured, the router adds a route for that classful network to the BGP table:

■   If the exact classful route is in the IP routing table

or

■   If any subset routes of that classful network are in the routing table

In summary, of the two actions in the list, the first occurs regardless of the **auto-summary** setting, and the second occurs only if **auto-summary** is configured.

For example, with **network 9.0.0.0** configured, regardless of the **auto-summary** setting, if a route to 9.0.0.0/8 exists, the router adds 9.0.0.0/8 to the BGP table. However, if the **network 9.0.0.0** (without the mask parameter) and the **auto-summary** commands were both configured, and if only a subset route exists (for example, 9.1.1.0/24), but no route for exactly 9.0.0.0/8 exists, then the router still adds a route for the classful network (9.0.0.0/8) to the BGP table. This second example demonstrates the additional logic that occurs with the **auto-summary** command configured.

Injecting Routes Using Redistribution

Instead of using a BGP **network** command to add routes to the BGP table, the Enterprise BGP routers can instead redistribute routes from an IGP into BGP. The end goals are the same:

■   Inject the public address range, but not the private IP address range, into the BGP table.

■   Advertise one route for the public address range, instead of any individual subnets of the range.

The Enterprise routers that run BGP often already run the IGP as well and have learned routes for either the entire public range as one route or with subset routes. If a single route exists for the entire public range, for example the 128.107.0.0/19 range used in the last several examples, then the engineer simply needs to add a **redistribute** command to the BGP configuration to redistribute that route, and only that route, into BGP. If only subset routes exist, one of several additional steps need to be taken to meet the design goal to inject one route for the entire public address range.

Example 13-10 shows the majority of the work in a case for which Router E1 has three subset routes in the 128.107.0.0/19 range: 128.107.1.0/24, 128.107.2.0/24, and 128.107.3.0/24. However, E1 does not have a single route for the entire 128.107.0.0/19 public prefix. The example shows the redistribution configuration, all of which uses the same familiar redistribution commands shown in Chapters 9 and 10. The configuration matches prefixes in the public range and redistributes them into BGP.

Example 13-10   *Redistributing OSPF into BGP, but for Public Range Only*

```
router bgp 11
 redistribute ospf 1 route-map only-128-107
!
route-map only-128-107 permit
 match ip address prefix 128-107
!
ip prefix-list 128-107 permit 128.107.0.0/19 le 32

E1# show ip route 128.107.0.0 255.255.224.0 longer-prefixes
! Legend omitted for brevity

Gateway of last resort is 1.1.1.1 to network 0.0.0.0


     128.107.0.0/24 is subnetted, 3 subnets
O       128.107.3.0 [110/3] via 10.1.1.66, 00:05:26, FastEthernet0/0
O       128.107.2.0 [110/3] via 10.1.1.66, 00:05:26, FastEthernet0/0
O       128.107.1.0 [110/3] via 10.1.1.66, 00:05:36, FastEthernet0/0

E1# show ip bgp 128.107.0.0/19 longer-prefixes
BGP table version is 11, local router ID is 11.11.11.11
Status codes: s suppressed, d damped, h history, * valid, > best, i - internal,
```

```
              r RIB-failure, S Stale
Origin codes: i - IGP, e - EGP, ? - incomplete

   Network          Next Hop         Metric LocPrf Weight Path
*> 128.107.1.0/24   10.1.1.66            3          32768 ?
*> 128.107.2.0/24   10.1.1.66            3          32768 ?
*> 128.107.3.0/24   10.1.1.66            3          32768 ?
```

The two **show** commands following the configuration list the IP routes that should match the redistribution configuration, and the resulting BGP table entries. The **show ip route 128.107.0.0 255.255.224.0 longer-prefixes** command lists all three IP routes in the public address range in this case. The **show ip bgp 128.107.0.0/19 longer-prefixes** command shows the same range, listing the three BGP table entries created by the **redistribute ospf** command. These BGP table entries list the same next-hop IP addresses listed in the OSPF routes in the IP routing table, with the same metrics.

Left as is, this configuration results in Router E1 advertising all three BGP routes to the ISPs. However, to reach the goal of advertising only a single route for the entire public prefix 128.107.0.0/19, another step must be taken, typically one of the following:

■ Use IGP route summarization to create the route for the entire prefix.

■ Configure a null static route (a discard route) for the entire prefix on the Internet-connected router.

■ Configure BGP route summarization to make BGP advertise only the entire prefix.

The first two would cause E1 to list a route for the entire public prefix–128.107.0.0/19 in this case–in its IP routing table. The redistribution configuration could then be changed so that only that exact prefix would be redistributed. (For example, removing the **le 32** parameter from the **ip prefix-list 128-107 permit 128.107.0.0/19 le 32** command would make this command match only the exact route.)

The third option would be to use BGP route summarization, telling Router E1 that when any subnet routes of 128.107.0.0/19 exists in the BGP table, advertise only 128.107.0.0/19 but none of the subset routes. Example 13-11 shows this last option.

Example 13-11 *The BGP* **aggregate-address** *Command to Advertise the Entire Public IP Address Prefix*

```
E1# conf t
Enter configuration commands, one per line.  End with CNTL/Z.
E1(config)# router bgp 11
E1(config-router)#aggregate-address 128.107.0.0 255.255.224.0 summary-only
E1(config-router)#^Z

E1# show ip bgp 128.107.0.0/19 longer-prefixes
BGP table version is 15, local router ID is 11.11.11.11
```

```
Status codes: s suppressed, d damped, h history, * valid, > best, i - internal,

              r RIB-failure, S Stale
Origin codes: i - IGP, e - EGP, ? - incomplete

     Network          Next Hop          Metric LocPrf Weight Path
*>  128.107.0.0/19    0.0.0.0                         32768 i
s>  128.107.1.0/24    10.1.1.66            3           32768 ?

s>  128.107.2.0/24    10.1.1.66            3           32768 ?
s>  128.107.3.0/24    10.1.1.66            3           32768 ?
```

Note that with the addition of the **aggregate-address** command, the BGP table now also has a route for 128.107.0.0/19, which will be advertised to E1's neighbors at the two ISPs. Also, the **summary-only** keyword in the **aggregate-address** command tells IOS to suppress the advertisement the subset routes, as noted by the code "s" beside the other three routes listed at the end of the example.

Exam Preparation Tasks

Planning Practice

The CCNP ROUTE exam expects test takers to review design documents, create implementation plans, and create verification plans. This section provides some exercises that may help you to take a step back from the minute details of the topics in this chapter so that you can think about the same technical topics from the planning perspective.

For each planning practice table, simply complete the table. Note that any numbers in parentheses represent the number of options listed for each item in the solutions in Appendix F, "Completed Planning Practice Tables."

Design Review Table

Table 13-5 lists several design goals related to this chapter. If these design goals were listed in a design document, and you had to take that document and develop an implementation plan, what implementation options come to mind? You should write a general description; specific configuration commands are not required.

Table 13-5 *Design Review*

Design Goal	Possible Implementation Choices Covered in This Chapter
The plan shows the use of public prefix 200.1.1.0/26 by an Enterprise. What methods should I consider adding to my implementation plan for advertising that prefix to my ISPs using BGP? (2)	

Implementation Plan Peer Review Table

Table 13-6 shows a list of questions that others might ask, or that you might think about, during a peer review of another network engineer's implementation plan. Complete the table by answering the questions.

Table 13-6 *Notable Questions from This Chapter to Consider During an Implementation Plan Peer Review*

Question	Answers
The plan shows Enterprise Router R1, with two parallel Layer 3 paths to ISP Router R2, with a need for BGP. What options exist for high availability eBGP peering? (2) Which is better?	

Table 13-6 *Notable Questions from This Chapter to Consider During an Implementation Plan Peer Review*

Question	Answers
The implementation plan shows an Enterprise router with an eBGP connection to an ISP router, using a loopback interface as Update source. What other feature must be configured to make the eBGP connection work?	
Router R1 connects via eBGP to Router I1 at ISP1. R1 has routes for 130.1.1.0/24 and 130.1.2.0/24 in its routing table. The design claims the company uses 130.1.0.0/21 as its public range. What methods can be used to advertise one route for the entire range to the eBGP peer? (2)	

Create an Implementation Plan Table

This chapter does not focus on implementation or verification, but it did review one concept about static routes, as listed in Table 13-7.

Table 13-7 *Implementation Plan Configuration Memory Drill*

Feature	Configuration Commands/Notes
Configure an eBGP connection as follows: local AS 1, remote AS 2, remote router uses 1.1.1.1 for BGP peering, with 1.1.1.1 being an IP address on a common link between the routers.	
Configure an eBGP connection as follows: local AS 1, remote AS 2, local uses loopback1 (1.1.1.1), remote uses loopback2 (2.2.2.2).	
Add to the previous row the configuration to use MD5 authentication, key "barney."	
Administratively disable the neighbor configured in the previous two items in this table	
Re-enable the neighbor that was disabled in the previous row of this table.	
Cause the advertisement of IGP-learned prefix 130.1.1.0/24 to the neighbor configured in this table, without redistribution.	
Repeat the task in the previous row of this table, but this time with route redistribution, assuming OSPF process 1 is used for the IGP.	

Choose Commands for a Verification Plan Table

To practice skills useful when creating your own verification plan, list in Table 13-8 all commands that supply the requested information. You may want to record your answers outside the book and set a goal to complete this table (and others like it) from memory during your final reviews before taking the exam.

Table 13-8 *Verification Plan Memory Drill*

Information Needed	Commands
Display a single-line neighbor status for each iBGP neighbors.	
Display the number of prefixes learned from a neighbor. (List where the information is located.)	
Display the number of prefixes advertised to a neighbor. (List where the information is located.)	
Display the local and neighbor ASN.	
Display the number of eBGP hops allowed.	
List the current TCP ports used for BGP connections.	
List all prefixes in the BGP table.	
List all the best routes in the BGP table.	
Find the AS_Path for each BGP Table entry. (Describe how.)	
Determine if a particular BGP table entry is iBGP-learned. (Describe how.)	
Display one-line entries for all BGP table entries with a given prefix/length, plus any subnets inside that ranges.	
List possible default routes.	
List possible routes per prefix.	
List routes learned from one neighbor, which passed any inbound filters.	
List routes learned from one neighbor before any inbound filtering is applied.	
Display routes suppressed and added to the BGP table due to BGP route summarization (aggregation).	

Note: Some of the entries in this table may not have been specifically mentioned in this chapter but are listed in this table for review and reference.

Review all the Key Topics

Review the most important topics from inside the chapter, noted with the Key Topics icon in the outer margin of the page. Table 13-9 lists a reference of these key topics and the page numbers on which each is found.

Key Topic

Table 13-9 *Key Topics for Chapter 13*

Key Topic Element	Description	Page Number
List	Minimal eBGP configuration checklist	423
List	Required plus commonly used optional eBGP configuration command checklist	425
List	Rules for how a router chooses its BGP Router ID	425
Figure 13-2	Diagram of how the **router bgp** and **neighbor remote-as** commands on neighboring routers refer to ASNs	426
List	eBGP Configuration checklist including use of loopbacks as Update source and eBGP Multihop	427
Figure 13-3	Diagram of how the configuration matches on two BGP neighbors when using loopbacks	428
Table 13-2	BGP neighbor states	430
Table 13-3	BGP Messages	436
Table 13-4	Commonly used **show** commands to display eBGP-learned routes	441

Complete the Tables and Lists from Memory

Print a copy of Appendix D, "Memory Tables," (found on the CD), or at least the section for this chapter, and complete the tables and lists from memory. Appendix E, "Memory Tables Answer Key," also on the CD, includes completed tables and lists to check your work.

Define Key Terms

Define the following key terms from this chapter, and check your answers in the glossary.

eBGP multihop, Update Source (BGP), Established (BGP State), Open, Update, Active (BGP state), BGP Table

This chapter covers the following subjects:

Internal BGP Between Internet-Connected Routers: This section examines the need for iBGP peering inside an Enterprise, and the required commonly used optional configuration settings.

Avoiding Routing Loops When Forwarding Toward the Internet: This section discusses the issues that occur when the Internet-connected routers may forward packets to each other through routers that do not use BGP, and how such a design requires some means to supply BGP-learned routes to the internal Enterprise routers.

Route Filtering and Clearing BGP Peers: This section gives a brief description of the options for filtering the contents of BGP Updates, along with explaining some operational issue related to the BGP **clear** command.

Internal BGP and BGP Route Filtering

Outbound routing is simple with a single Internet-connected router. The Enterprise IGP could flood a default route throughout the Enterprise funneling all Internet traffic toward the one Internet-connected router. That router could then choose the best route to any and all Internet destinations it learned with eBGP.

With two (or more) Internet-connected routers in a single Enterprise, additional issues arise, in particular, issues related to outbound routing. These issues require the use of BGP between Enterprise routers; in some cases, the design may require BGP even on Enterprise routers that do not peer with routers at the various ISPs. This chapter examines the scenarios in which using iBGP makes sense, and shows the related configuration and verification commands.

Chapter 14 begins focusing on the issues that occur when an Enterprise uses a pair of Internet-connected routers. In particular, the examples use the sample network shown in Figure 14-1. This design uses the same ISPs and ISP routers as in Chapter 13, "External BGP," with familiar IP address ranges but with a few different links. The design now also shows two of the core routers (actually Layer 3 switches) inside the Enterprise—routers that do not directly connect to any ISP. Figure 14-1 shows the design that will be referenced throughout the chapter.

Note: Figure 14-1 shows the IP addresses as just the last octet of the address; in these cases, the first three octets are 10.1.1.

The first section of this chapter focuses on concepts, configuration, and verification of the iBGP connection between E1 and E2 in the figure. The second major section of this chapter, "Avoiding Routing Loops when Forwarding Toward the Internet," examines the need for iBGP on routers internal to the Enterprise, such as Routers Core1 and Core2 in the figure. The final section of this chapter examines the process of filtering both iBGP and eBGP routing updates.

"Do I Know This Already?" Quiz

The "Do I Know This Already?" quiz allows you to assess if you should read the entire chapter. If you miss no more than one of these eight self-assessment questions, you might want to move ahead to the "Exam Preparation Tasks." Table 14-1 lists the major headings in this chapter and the "Do I Know This Already?" quiz questions covering the material in

Figure 14-1   *Dual Internet Router Design Used Throughout Chapter 14*

those headings so that you can assess your knowledge of these specific areas. The answers to the "Do I Know This Already?" quiz appear in Appendix A.

Table 14-1   *"Do I Know This Already?" Foundation Topics Section-to-Question Mapping*

Foundations Topics Section	Questions
Internal BGP Between Internet-Connected Routers	1–4
BGP Synchronization and iBGP Meshes	5
Route Filtering and Clearing BGP Peers	6–8

1. R1 in ASN 1 with loopback1 address 1.1.1.1 needs to be configured with an iBGP connection to R2 with loopback2 IP address 2.2.2.2. The connection should use the loopbacks. Which of the following commands is required on R1?

   a. neighbor 1.1.1.1 remote-as 1

   b. neighbor 2.2.2.2 remote-as 2

   c. neighbor 2.2.2.2 update-source loopback1

   d. neighbor 2.2.2.2 ibgp-multihop 2

   e. neighbor 2.2.2.2 ibgp-mode

2. The following output occurred as a result of the **show ip bgp** command on Router R1. The output shows all BGP table entries on R1. How many iBGP-learned routes exist on this router?

```
*>i181.0.0.0/8      10.100.1.1          0    100      0 1 2 111 112 i
*>i182.0.0.0/8      10.100.1.1          0    100      0 1 2 222 i
*>i183.0.0.0/8      10.100.1.1          0    100      0 1 2 i
*>i184.0.0.0/8      10.100.1.1          0    100      0 1 2 i
*> 192.135.250.0/28 192.168.1.6                       0 3 4 i
```

   a. 1

   b. 2

   c. 3

   d. 4

   e. 5

3. The following output on Router R1 lists details of a BGP route for 190.1.0.0/16. Which of the following is true based on this output? (Choose 2)

```
R1# show ip bgp 190.1.0.0/16
BGP routing table entry for 190.1.0.0/16, version 121
Paths: (1 available, best #1, table Default-IP-Routing-Table)
  Advertised to update-groups:
        1
  1 2 3 4
    1.1.1.1 from 2.2.2.2 (3.3.3.3)
      Origin IGP, metric 0, localpref 100, valid, internal, best
```

   a. R1 has a **neighbor 1.1.1.1** command configured.

   b. R1 has a **neighbor 2.2.2.2** command configured.

   c. The **show ip bgp** command lists a line for 190.1.0.0/16 with both an > and an i on the left.

   d. R1 is in ASN 1.

4. A company uses Routers R1 and R2 to connect to ISP1 and ISP2, respectively, with Routers I1 and I2 used at the ISPs. R1 peers with I1 and R2; R2 peers with I2 and R1. Assuming as many default settings as possible are used on all four routers, which of the following is true about the next-hop IP address for routes R1 learns over its iBGP connection to R2?

   a. The next hop is I2's BGP RID.

   b. The next hop is I2's IP address used on the R2-I2 neighbor relationship.

   c. The next hop is R2's BGP RID.

   d. The next hop is R2's IP address used on the R1–R2 neighbor relationship.

5. A company uses Routers R1 and R2 to connect to ISP1 and ISP2, respectively, with Routers I1 and I2 used at the ISPs. R1 peers with I1 and R2; R2 peers with I2 and R1. R1 and R2 do not share a common subnet, relying on other routers internal to the Enterprise for IP connectivity between the two routers. Which of the following could be used to prevent potential routing loops in this design? (Choose 2)

    a. Using an iBGP mesh inside the Enterprise core

    b. Configuring default routes in the Enterprise pointing to both R1 and R2

    c. Redistributing BGP routes into the Enterprise IGP

    d. Tunneling the packets for the iBGP connection between R1 and R2

6. R1 is currently advertising prefixes 1.0.0.0/8, 2.0.0.0/8, and 3.0.0.0/8 over its eBGP connection to neighbor 2.2.2.2 (R2). An engineer configures a prefix list (fred) on R1 that permits only 2.0.0.0/8 and then enables the filter with the **neighbor R2 prefix-list fred out** command. Upon exiting configuration mode, the engineer uses some **show** commands on R1, but no other commands. Which of the following is true in this case?

    a. The **show ip bgp neighbor 2.2.2.2 received-routes** command lists the three original prefixes.

    b. The **show ip bgp neighbor 2.2.2.2 advertised-routes** command lists the three original prefixes.

    c. The **show ip bgp neighbor 2.2.2.2 routes** command lists the three original prefixes.

    d. The **show ip bgp neighbor 2.2.2.2 routes** command lists only 2.0.0.0/8.

    e. The **show ip bgp neighbor 2.2.2.2 advertised-routes** command lists only 2.0.0.0/8.

7. Which of the following three BGP filtering methods enabled with the **neighbor** command will filter BGP prefixes based on the prefix and prefix length? (Choose 3)

    a. A **neighbor distribute-list out** command, referencing a standard ACL

    b. A **neighbor prefix-list out** command

    c. A **neighbor filter-list out** command

    d. A **neighbor distribute-list out** command, referencing an extended ACL

    e. A **neighbor route-map out** command

8. Which of the following commands causes a router to bring down BGP neighbor relationships?

    a. clear ip bgp *

    b. clear ip bgp 1.1.1.1

    c. clear ip bgp * soft

    d. clear ip bgp 1.1.1.1 out

Foundation Topics

Internal BGP Between Internet-Connected Routers

When an Enterprise uses more than one router to connect to the Internet, and those routers use BGP to exchange routing information with their ISPs, those same routers need to exchange BGP routes with each other as well. The BGP neighbor relationships occur inside that Enterprise–inside a single AS–making these routers iBGP peers.

This first major section of Chapter 14 begins with a look at why two Internet-connected routers need to have an iBGP neighbor relationship. Then, the text looks at various iBGP configuration and verification commands. Finally, discussion turns to a common issue that occurs with next-hop reachability between iBGP peers, with an examination of the options to overcome the problem.

Establishing the Need for iBGP with Two Internet-Connected Routers

Two Internet-connected routers in an Enterprise need to communicate BGP routes to each other because these routers may want to forward IP packets to the other Internet-connected router, which in turn would forward the packet into the Internet. With an iBGP peer connection, each Internet-connected router can learn routes from the other router and decide if that other router has a better route to reach some destinations in the Internet. Without that iBGP connection, the routers have no way to know if the other router has a better BGP path.

For example, consider Figure 14-2, which shows two such cases. The figure shows a topology that uses the following design options, as agreed upon with ISP1 and ISP3:

Figure 14-2 *Choosing the Best Routes from ASN 11 to 181.0.0.0/8 and 192.135.250.0/28*

- ISP1 sends full routing updates and a default route.

- ISP3 sends partial updates and a default route.

First, consider the eBGP routing updates, particularly for the two prefixes highlighted in the figure. Both ISP1 and ISP3 know routes for 181.0.0.0/8, but ISP3's agreement with the Enterprise is that ISP3 sends partial updates. This usually means ISP3 sends updates for prefixes in its own ASN plus prefixes for customers attached to its ASN, such as 192.135.250.0/28 in this case. ISP1, however, sends full updates, so E1 learns an eBGP route for both 181.0.0.0/8 and 192.135.250.0/28, but Router E2 only learns an eBGP route for 192.135.250.0/28.

Next, take a closer look at the routes for 181.0.0.0/8, both on E1 and E2. Only E1 learns an eBGP route for 181.0.0.0/8; E2 does not, because of ISP3's partial updates. If E1 and E2 did not use iBGP between each other, E2 would never know that E1 had a good route for 181.0.0.0/8. So, without an iBGP connection, packets destined to hosts in 182.0.0.0/8 if they arrived at E2 would be sent to ISP3 because of E2's default route learned from ISP3. However, if E1 and E2 form an iBGP neighbor relationship, E2 would know a route for 181.0.0.0/8 through E1 and would choose this route as its best route and would forward such packets to E1. Then E1 would forward the packets to ISP1, as shown in the figure.

Finally, take a closer look at the routes for 192.135.250.0/28 on both E1 and E2. If none of the ISPs changed the default PA settings for these routes, both E1 and E2 would choose the route through E2 as the better route, due to the shorter AS_Path length (two ASNs away through ISP3 versus four ASNs away through ISP1). Without iBGP between E1 and E2, E1 would not learn of this better route through E2, so any packets destined to 192.135.250.0/28 that reach E1 would be forwarded to ISP1. With iBGP, E1 would know of E2's better route and forward the packets toward E2, as shown in the figure.

For both prefixes, iBGP allowed both routers in the same ASN to reach the same conclusion about the better router through which to send packets for each Internet destination.

Configuring iBGP

The most basic iBGP configuration differs only slightly compared to eBGP configuration. The configuration does not explicitly identify an eBGP versus an iBGP peer. Instead, for iBGP, the neighbor's ASN listed on the **neighbor... remote-as** *neighbor-asn* command lists the same ASN as the local router's **router bgp** command. eBGP **neighbor remote-as** commands list a different ASN.

When two iBGP peers share a common physical link, such as E1 and E2 in Figure 14-1, the iBGP configuration simply requires a single **neighbor remote-as** command on each router. Example 14-1 shows the BGP configuration on both Router E1 and E2 with this single **neighbor** command highlighted. The rest of the configuration lists the commands used to configure other BGP settings (as described after the example). Note that Figure 14-1 in the introduction to this chapter shows more detail about the eBGP peers as well.

Example 14-1 *BGP Configuration on E1: Neighborships Configured*

```
! Configuration on router E1
router bgp 11
 no synchronization
 bgp log-neighbor-changes
 aggregate-address 128.107.0.0 255.255.224.0 summary-only
 redistribute ospf 1 route-map only-128-107
 neighbor 1.1.1.1 remote-as 1
 neighbor 1.1.1.1 password fred
 neighbor 1.1.1.1 ebgp-multihop 2
 neighbor 1.1.1.1 update-source Loopback1
 neighbor 10.1.1.10 remote-as 11
 no auto-summary
!
! Next, static routes so that the eBGP neighbor packets can reach
! I1-1's loopback interface address 1.1.1.1
ip route 1.1.1.1 255.255.255.255 Serial0/0/0
ip route 1.1.1.1 255.255.255.255 Serial0/0/1
!
ip prefix-list 128-107 seq 5 permit 128.107.0.0/19 le 32
!
route-map only-128-107 permit 10
 match ip address prefix-list 128-107 Neighbor 192.168.1.2 remote-as 3
! Now, on router E2
router bgp 11
 no synchronization
 bgp log-neighbor-changes
 network 128.107.32.0
 aggregate-address 128.107.0.0 255.255.224.0 summary-only
 redistribute ospf 1 route-map only-128-107
 neighbor 10.1.1.9 remote-as 11
 neighbor 192.168.1.6 remote-as 3
 neighbor 192.168.1.6 password barney
 no auto-summary
!
ip prefix-list 128-107 seq 5 permit 128.107.0.0/19 le 32
!
route-map only-128-107 permit 10
 match ip address prefix-list 128-107 Neighbor 192.168.1.2 remote-as 3
```

Only the four highlighted configuration commands are required for the E1-E2 iBGP peering. Both refer to the other router's IP address on the FastEthernet link between the two routers, and both refer to ASN 11. The two routers then realize the neighbor is an iBGP neighbor because the neighbor's ASN (11) matches the local router's ASN, as seen on the **router bgp 11** command.

The example also lists the rest of the BGP configuration. Focusing on Router E1, the configuration basically matches the configuration of Router E1 from the end of Chapter 13, except that E1 has only one eBGP peer (I1-1) in this case instead of two eBGP peers. The configuration includes the eBGP peer connection to I1-1, using loopback interfaces (1.1.1.1 on I1-1 and 11.11.11.11 on E1). The eBGP peers need to use eBGP multihop because of the use of the loopbacks, and they use MD5 authentication as well. Finally, the configuration shows the redistribution of the Enterprise's public address range of 128.107.0.0/19 by redistributing from OSPF and summarizing with the **aggregate-address** BGP subcommand.

E2's configuration lists the same basic parameters, but with a few differences. E2 does not use a loopback for its peer connection to I3-1, because only a single link exists between the two routers. As a result, E2 also does not need to use eBGP multihop.

Refocusing on the iBGP configuration, Example 14-1 uses the interface IP addresses of the links between Routers E1 and E2. However, often the Internet-connected routers in an Enterprise do not share a common subnet. For example, the two routers may be in separate buildings in a campus for the sake of redundancy. The two routers may actually be in different cities, or even different continents. In such cases, it makes sense to configure the iBGP peers using a loopback IP address for the TCP connection so that a single link failure does not cause the iBGP peer connection to fail. For example, in Figure 14-1, if the FastEthernet link between E1 and E2 fail, the iBGP connection defined in Example 14-1, which uses the interface IP addresses of that link, would fail even though a redundant IP path exists between E1 and E2.

The configuration to use loopback interfaces as the update source mirrors that same configuration for eBGP peers, except that iBGP peers do not need to configure the **neighbor... ebgp-multihop** command. One difference between iBGP and eBGP is that IOS uses the low TTL of 1 for eBGP connections by default but does not for iBGP connections. So, for iBGP connections, only the following steps are required to make two iBGP peers use a loopback interface:

Key Topic

Step 1. Configure an IP address on a loopback interface on each router.

Step 2. Configure each router to use the loopback IP address as the source IP address, for the neighborship with the other router, using the **neighbor... update-source** *ip-address* command.

Step 3. Configure the BGP **neighbor** command on each router to refer to the other router's loopback IP address as the neighbor IP address in the **neighbor** *neighbor-ip* **remote-as** command.

Step 4. Make sure each router has IP routes so that they can forward packets to the loopback interface IP address of the other router.

Example 14-2 shows an updated iBGP configuration for Routers E1 and E2 to migrate to use a loopback interface. In this case, E1 uses loopback IP address 10.100.1.1/32 and E2 uses 10.100.1.2/32. OSPF on each router has already been configured with a **network 10.0.0.0 0.255.255.255 area 0** command (not shown), which then causes OSPF to advertise routes to reach the respective loopback interface IP addresses.

Example 14-2   *iBGP Configuration to Use Loopbacks as the Update Source*

```
! Configuration on router E1
interface loopback 0
 ip address 10.100.1.1 255.255.255.255
router bgp 11
 neighbor 10.100.1.2 remote-as 11
 neighbor 10.100.1.2 update-source loopback0
! Configuration on router E2
interface loopback 1
 ip address 10.100.1.2 255.255.255.255
router bgp 11
 neighbor 10.100.1.1 remote-as 11
 neighbor 10.100.1.1 update-source loopback1
```

The highlighted portions of the output link the key values together for the E1's definition of its loopback as the update source and E2's reference of that same IP address on its **neighbor** command. The **neighbor 10.100.1.2 update-source loopback0** command on E1 tells E1 to look to interface loopback0 for its update source IP address. Loopback0's IP address on E1 has IP address 10.100.1.1. Then, E2's **neighbor** commands for Router E1 all refer to that same 10.100.1.1 IP address, meeting the requirement that the update source on one router matches the IP address listed on the other router's **neighbor** command.

Verifying iBGP

iBGP neighbors use the same messages and neighbor states as eBGP peers. As a result, the same commands in Chapter 13 for BGP neighbor verification can be used for iBGP peers. Example 14-3 shows a couple of examples, using Router E1's iBGP neighbor relationship with E2 (10.100.1.2) based on the configuration in Example 14-2.

Example 14-3   *Verifying iBGP Neighbors*

```
E1# show ip bgp summary
BGP router identifier 11.11.11.11, local AS number 11
BGP table version is 190, main routing table version 190
11 network entries using 1452 bytes of memory
14 path entries using 728 bytes of memory
11/7 BGP path/bestpath attribute entries using 1628 bytes of memory
7 BGP AS-PATH entries using 168 bytes of memory
0 BGP route-map cache entries using 0 bytes of memory
0 BGP filter-list cache entries using 0 bytes of memory
Bitfield cache entries: current 3 (at peak 4) using 96 bytes of memory
BGP using 4072 total bytes of memory
BGP activity 31/20 prefixes, 100/86 paths, scan interval 60 secs

Neighbor        V     AS MsgRcvd MsgSent   TblVer  InQ OutQ Up/Down   State/PfxRcd
1.1.1.1         4      1     339     344      190    0    0 00:28:41             7
10.100.1.2      4     11      92     132      190    0    0 01:02:04             3
```

```
E1# show ip bgp neighbors 10.100.1.2
BGP neighbor is 10.100.1.2,  remote AS 11, internal link
  BGP version 4, remote router ID 10.100.1.2
  BGP state = Established, up for 01:02:10
  Last read 00:00:37, last write 00:00:59, hold time is 180, keepalive interval
is 60 seconds
  Neighbor capabilities:
    Route refresh: advertised and received(new)
    Address family IPv4 Unicast: advertised and received
! lines omitted for brevity
```

Key Topic

The **show ip bgp summary** command lists E1's two neighbors. As with eBGP peers, if the last column (the State/PfxRcd column) lists a number, then the neighbor has reached established state, and BGP Update messages can be sent. The output can distinguish between an iBGP or eBGP neighbor but only by comparing the local router's ASN (in the first line of output) to the ASN listed in each line at the bottom of the output.

The **show ip bgp neighbors 10.100.1.2** command lists many details specifically for the neighbor. In particular, it states that the neighbor is an iBGP neighbor with the phrase "internal link," as highlighted in the output.

Examining iBGP BGP Table Entries

To better understand the BGP table with two (or more) Internet-connected routers inside the same company, start with one prefix, and compare the BGP table entries on the two routers for that one prefix. By examining several such examples, you can appreciate more about the benefits and effects of these iBGP neighborships.

This section examines the BGP tables on Routers E1 and E2, focusing on the prefixes highlighted in Figure 14-2–namely, prefixes 181.0.0.0/8 and 192.135.250.0/28. To make reading the output of the **show** commands a little more obvious, Figure 14-3 collects some key pieces of information into a single figure. This figure shows the two BGP neighbor relationships on each router, showing the update source and neighbor IP address of each BGP neighbor relationship. It also lists the BGP RID of the routers.

Examples 14-4 and 14-5 compare the output on Routers E2 and E1 for prefix 181.0.0.0/8. Example 14-4 lists output on Router E2, listing the BGP table entries for prefix 181.0.0.0/8. Remember, the design calls for ISP3 to only send partial updates, so E2 has not received an eBGP route for 181.0.0.0/8 from I3-1. However, E1 has indeed learned of that prefix from I1-1 (ISP1), and E1 has already advertised prefix 181.0.0.0/8 to E2.

Note: Several BGP routes seen in the examples in this chapter originate in ASNs not shown in the figure. The figure shows enough of the topology to understand the first few ASNs in the AS_Path for these routes.

Figure 14-3   *Reference Information for BGP Table Verification*

Example 14-4   *Notations of iBGP Learned Routes in the* **show ip bgp** *Command*

```
E2# show ip bgp 181.0.0.0/8 longer-prefixes
BGP table version is 125, local router ID is 10.100.1.2
Status codes: s suppressed, d damped, h history, * valid, > best, i - internal,
              r RIB-failure, S Stale
Origin codes: i - IGP, e - EGP, ? - incomplete

   Network          Next Hop            Metric LocPrf Weight Path
*>i181.0.0.0/8      1.1.1.1                  0    100      0 1 2 111 112 i

E2# show ip bgp 181.0.0.0/8
BGP routing table entry for 181.0.0.0/8, version 121
Paths: (1 available, best #1, table Default-IP-Routing-Table)
  Advertised to update-groups:
        1
  1 2 111 111
    1.1.1.1 from 10.100.1.1 (11.11.11.11)
      Origin IGP, metric 0, localpref 100, valid, internal, best
```

The first command, **show ip bgp 181.0.0.0/8 longer-prefixes**, lists output with the same general format as the **show ip bgp** command, but it limits the output to the prefixes in the listed range. Only one such route exists in this case. The legend information at the top of the output, plus the headings and meanings of the different fields, is the same as with the **show ip bgp** command.

Next, the first command's output denotes this route as an iBGP-learned route with code "i" in the third character. The second command in the example, **show ip bgp 181.0.0.0/8**, which displays a more detailed view of the BGP table entry and denotes this route as iBGP-learned with the word "internal." Similarly, the briefer **show ip bgp 181.0.0.0/8** command output lists this one route as E2's best route by displaying a > in the second column, whereas the more verbose output in the second command simply lists this route as "best."

Next, consider these same commands on Router E1, as shown in Example 14-5. Comparing the highlighted fields as matched in each of the examples:

- Both list the same AS_Path (1, 2, 111, 112) because iBGP peers do not add ASNs to the AS_Path when advertising to each other. So, both E1 and E2 have the same perspective on the AS_Path and AS_Path length.

- Both list the one route for 181.0.0.0/8 as the best path in part because each has learned only one such path.

- Both list a next_hop (a BGP PA) as 1.1.1.1, which is I1-1's loopback interface used in the E1 to I1-1 BGP neighbor relationship (also called the BGP neighbor ID).

- E2 lists the route as an internal (iBGP-learned) route, whereas E1 lists it as an external route.

Example 14-5   *Router E1's **show** Commands for BGP Routes for 181.0.0.0/8*

```
E1# show ip bgp 181.0.0.0/8 longer-prefixes
BGP table version is 190, local router ID is 11.11.11.11
Status codes: s suppressed, d damped, h history, * valid, > best, i - internal,
              r RIB-failure, S Stale
Origin codes: i - IGP, e - EGP, ? - incomplete


   Network          Next Hop            Metric LocPrf Weight Path
*> 181.0.0.0/8      1.1.1.1                            0 1 2 111 112 i

E1# show ip bgp 181.0.0.0/8
BGP routing table entry for 181.0.0.0/8, version 181
Paths: (1 available, best #1, table Default-IP-Routing-Table)
  Advertised to update-groups:
        2
  1 2 111 111, (received & used)
    1.1.1.1 from 1.1.1.1 (1.1.1.1)
      Origin IGP, localpref 100, valid, external, best
```

The output from these examples confirms that E1 learned the eBGP route for 181.0.0.0/8, advertised it to E2, and E2 chose to use that iBGP learned route as its best route to reach 181.0.0.0/8.

Next, consider the route for 192.135.250.0/28, a route learned in the full BGP updates from ISP1's Router I1-1 and in the partial BGP updates from ISP3's Router I3-1. After exchanging this route using their iBGP peering, both E1 and E2 should see two possible routes: an eBGP route learned from their one connected ISP and the iBGP route learned from each other. Again assuming that the ISPs have not made any attempt to set PA values to influence the best path choice, and knowing the neither E1 nor E2 have configured BGP to influence the best path choice, the route through E2 should be best because of the shorter AS_Path.

Example 14-6 shows the output of the **show ip bgp** command on both E1 and E2, again for comparison. Note that the command used in the examples, **show ip bgp 192.135.250.0/28 longer-prefixes**, is used because it lists only the routes for that prefix, rather than the full BGP table displayed by **show ip bgp**, but the format of the output is almost identical.

Example 14-6   *Comparing BGP Routes for 192.135.250.0/28 on E1 and E2*

```
! First, on E1:
E1# show ip bgp 192.135.250.0/28 longer-prefixes
BGP table version is 26, local router ID is 128.107.9.1
Status codes: s suppressed, d damped, h history, * valid, > best, i - internal,
              r RIB-failure, S Stale
Origin codes: i - IGP, e - EGP, ? - incomplete


   Network          Next Hop          Metric LocPrf Weight Path
*  192.135.250.0/28 1.1.1.1                               0 1 2 3 4 i
*>i                 192.168.1.6            0    100       0 3 4 i
! Next, on E2:
E2# show ip bgp 192.135.250.0/28 longer-prefixes
BGP table version is 25, local router ID is 10.100.1.2
Status codes: s suppressed, d damped, h history, * valid, > best, i - internal,
              r RIB-failure, S Stale
Origin codes: i - IGP, e - EGP, ? - incomplete


   Network          Next Hop          Metric LocPrf Weight Path
*> 192.135.250.0/28 192.168.1.6                           0 3 4 i
```

First, E1 lists two routes for this prefix, one external and one internal. The output identifies external routes by the absence of an "i" in the third character, whereas the output lists an "i" in the third character for internal routes. In this case, E1's internal route, with next_hop 192.168.1.6, is E1's best route, as was shown back in Figure 14-2. E1 chose this iBGP route because of the shorter AS_Path length; the AS_Path is highlighted at the end of each line.

E2's output in the second half of Example 14-6 lists only a single route–its eBGP route for 192.135.250.0/28. That only one route appears, rather than two, is a good example of the effect of two rules about how BGP operates:

■   Only advertise the best route in any BGP Update.

■   Do not advertise iBGP-learned routes to iBGP peers.

E2's output lists a single route for 192.135.250.0/28—its external route learned from ISP3—because E1 chooses not to advertise a route for 192.135.250.0/28 over the iBGP connection. If you look back at E1's output, E1's best route for this prefix is its internal route; so, if E1 were to advertise any route for this prefix to E2, E1 would advertise this internal route, because it is E1's best BGP route for that prefix. However, the second rule–do not advertise iBGP-learned routes to iBGP peers–prevents E1 from advertising this route back to E2. (Logically speaking, it makes no sense for E1 to tell E2 about a route when E2 is the router that originally advertised the route to E1 in the first place—a concept much like Split Horizon, although technically the term does not apply to BGP.) As a result, E2 lists a single route for 192.135.250.0/28.

Note that if the route for 192.135.250.0/28 through ISP3 failed, then E1 would start using the route through ISP1 as its best route. E1 would then advertise that best route to E2 that could then forward traffic through E1 for destinations in 192.135.250.0/28.

Understanding Next-Hop Reachability Issues with iBGP

With IGPs, the IP routes added to the IP routing table list a next-hop IP address. With few exceptions, the next-hop IP address routes exist in a connected subnet. For example, the E1-E2 iBGP connection uses loopback interfaces 10.100.1.1 (E1) and 10.100.1.2 (E2). E1's OSPF-learned route to reach 10.100.1.2 lists outgoing interface Fa0/1, next-hop 10.1.1.10–an address in the LAN subnet that connects E1 and E2. (See Figure 14-3 a few pages back for reference.)

Examples 14-5 and 14-6 also happened to show two examples of iBGP-learned routes and their next-hop addresses. The next-hop addresses were not in connected subnets; the next-hop addresses were not even IP addresses on a neighboring router. The two examples were as follows; again, it may be helpful to refer to the notations in Figure 14-3:

■   Example 14-4: E2's route for 181.0.0.0/8 lists next-hop address 1.1.1.1, a loopback interface IP address on I1-1.

■   Example 14-6: E1's route for 192.135.250.0/28 lists next-hop address 192.168.1.6, which is I3-1's interface IP address on the link between E2 and I3-1.

In fact, in the case of Example 14-4, the output of the **show ip bgp 181.0.0.0/8** command on E2 listed the phrase "1.1.1.1 from 10.100.1.1 (11.11.11.11)". This phrase lists the next hop (1.1.1.1) of the route, the neighbor from which the route was learned (10.100.1.1 or E1) and the neighbor's BGP RID (11.11.11.11, as listed in Figure 14-3).

BGP advertises these particular IP addresses as the next-hop IP addresses because of a default behavior for BGP. By default, when a router advertises a route using eBGP, the advertising router lists its own update-source IP address as the next-hop address of the route. In other words, the next-hop IP address is the IP address of the eBGP neighbor, as listed on the **neighbor remote-as** command. However, when advertising a route to an iBGP peer, the advertising router (by default) does not change the next-hop address. For example, when I1-1 advertises 181.0.0.0/8 to E1, because it is an eBGP connection, I1-1 sets its own IP address (1.1.1.1)–specifically the IP address I1-1 uses on its eBGP peer connection to E1—as the next-hop. When E1 advertises that same route to iBGP peer E2, E1 does not change the next-hop address of 1.1.1.1, so router E2's iBGP-learned route lists 1.1.1.1 as the next-hop address.

The IP routing process can use routes whose next-hop addresses are not in connected subnets as long as each router has an IP route that matches the next-hop IP address. So, engineers must understand these rules about how BGP sets the next-hop address and ensure each router can reach the next-hop address listed in the BGP routes. Two main options exist to ensure reachability to these next-hop addresses:

■   Create IP routes so that each router can reach these next-hop addresses that exist in other ASNs.

■   Change the default iBGP behavior with the **neighbor next-hop-self** command.

The text now examines each of these two options in more detail.

Ensuring Routes Exist to the Next-Hop Address

Routers can still forward packets using routes whose next-hop addresses are not in connected subnets. To do so, when forwarding packets, the router performs a recursive route table lookup. For example, for packets arriving at E2 with a destination of 181.0.0.1, the following would occur:

Step 1.   E2 would match the routing table for destination address 181.0.0.1, matching the route for 181.0.0.0/8, with next hop 1.1.1.1.

Step 2.   E2 would next look for its route matching destination 1.1.1.1–the next-hop of the first route–and forward the packet based on that route.

So, no matter the next-hop IP address listed in the routing table, as long as a working route exists to reach that next-hop IP address, the packet can be forwarded. Figure 14-4 shows the necessary routes in diagram form using two examples. E1 has a route to 192.135.250.0/28 with next hop 192.168.1.6; two arrowed lines show the required routes on Routers E1 and E2 for forwarding packets to this next-hop address. Similarly, the dashed lines also show the necessary routes on E2 and E1 for next-hop address 1.1.1.1, the next-hop IP address for their routes to reach 181.0.0.0/8.

Two easily implemented solutions exist to add routes for these nonconnected next-hop IP addresses: Either add static routes or use an IGP between the Enterprise and the ISPs for the sole purpose of advertising these next-hop addresses.

Using neighbor... next-hop-self to Change the Next-Hop Address

The second option for dealing with these nonconnected next-hop IP addresses changes the iBGP configuration so that a router changes the next-hop IP address on iBGP-advertised routes. This option simply requires the **neighbor** *neighbor-ip* **next-hop-self** com-

Figure 14-4 *Ensuring Routes Exist for Next-Hop Addresses in Other ASNs*

mand to be configured for the iBGP neighbor relationship. A router with this command
configured advertises iBGP routes with its own update-source IP address as the next-hop
IP address. And because the iBGP neighborship already relies on a working route for these
update source IP addresses, if the neighborship is up, then IP routes already exist for these
next-hop addresses.

For example, on the iBGP connection from E1 to E2, E1 would add the **neighbor
10.100.1.2 next-hop-self** command, and E2 would add the **neighbor 10.100.1.1 next-hop-
self** command. When configured, E1 advertises iBGP routes with its update source IP address (10.100.1.1) as the next-hop address. E2 likewise advertises routes with a next-hop
address of 10.100.1.2. Example 14-7 shows E2's BGP table, with a few such examples highlighted, after the addition of these two configuration commands on the respective routers.

Example 14-7 *Seeing the Effects of* **next-hop-self** *from Router E2*

```
E2#show ip bgp
BGP table version is 76, local router ID is 10.100.1.2
Status codes: s suppressed, d damped, h history, * valid, > best, i - internal,
              r RIB-failure, S Stale
Origin codes: i - IGP, e - EGP, ? - incomplete

   Network          Next Hop          Metric LocPrf Weight Path
*> 0.0.0.0          192.168.1.6            0               0 3 i
*  i                10.100.1.1             0      100      0 1 i
*  i128.107.0.0/19  10.100.1.1             0      100      0 i
*>                  0.0.0.0                             32768 i
```

```
s> 128.107.1.0/24    10.1.1.77            2         32768 ?
s> 128.107.2.0/24    10.1.1.77            2         32768 ?
s> 128.107.3.0/24    10.1.1.77            2         32768 ?
*>i181.0.0.0/8       10.100.1.1           0    100     0 1 2 111 112 i
*>i182.0.0.0/8       10.100.1.1           0    100     0 1 2 222 i
*>i183.0.0.0/8       10.100.1.1           0    100     0 1 2 i
*>i184.0.0.0/8       10.100.1.1           0    100     0 1 2 i
*>i185.0.0.0/8       10.100.1.1           0    100     0 1 2 i
*> 192.135.250.0/28 192.168.1.6                      0 3 4 i
```

This completes the discussion of iBGP configuration and operation as related to the routers actually connected to the Internet. The next section continues the discussion of iBGP but with a focus on some particular issues with routing that may require iBGP on routers other than the Internet-connected routers.

Avoiding Routing Loops when Forwarding Toward the Internet

A typical Enterprise network design uses default routes inside the Enterprise, as advertised by the IGP, to draw all Internet traffic toward one or more Internet-connected routers. The Internet-connected routers then forward the traffic into the Internet.

However, as discussed in Chapter 12, "Internet Connectivity and BGP," in the section "Choosing One Path over Another Using BGP," routing loops can occur when the Internet-connected routers do not have a direct connection to each other. For example, if the Internet-connected routers sit on opposite sides of the country, the two routers may be separated by several other internal routers in the Enterprise because they do not have a direct link.

To show a simple example, the same Enterprise network design shown in all previous figures in this chapter can be changed slightly by just disabling the FastEthernet link between the two routers, as shown in Figure 14-5.

Figure 14-5 shows an example of the looping problem. The figure uses the same general criteria as the other examples in this chapter, so that E1's best route for 192.135.250.0/28 points to Router E2 as the next hop. E1's best route for the next-hop IP address for its route to 192.135.250.0/28–regardless of whether using **next-hop self** or not–sends the packet back toward the Enterprise core. However, some (or possibly all) of the Enterprise routers internal to the Enterprise, such as WAN1 and Core1, use a default that sends all packets toward Router E1. Per the steps in the figure, the following happens for a packet destined to 192.135.250.1:

Step 1. WAN1 sends the packet using its default route to Core1.

Step 2. Core1 sends the packet using its default route to E1.

Step 3. E1 matches its BGP route for 192.135.250.0/28, with next hop E2 (10.100.1.2); the recursive lookup on E1 matches a route for 10.100.1.2 with next hop Core1, so E1 sends the packet back to Core1.

Figure 14-5 *Routing Loop for Packets Destined to 192.135.250.1*

At this point, Steps 2 and 3 repeat until the packet's TTL mechanism causes one of the routers to discard the packet.

The lack of knowledge about the best route for subnet 192.135.250.0/28, particularly on the routers internal to the Enterprise, causes this routing loop. To avoid this problem, internal routers, such as Core1 and Core2, need to know the best BGP routes. Two solutions exist to help these internal routers learn the routes:

■   Run BGP on at least some of the routers internal to the Enterprise (such as Core1 and Core2 in Figure 14-5).

■   Redistribute BGP routes into the IGP (not recommended).

Both solutions solve the problem by giving some of the internal routers the same best-path information already known to the Internet-connected routers–for example, if Core1 knew a route for 192.135.250.0/28, and that route caused the packets to go to Core2 next and then on to Router E2, the loop could be avoided. This section examines both solutions briefly.

Note: Other BGP features, namely BGP Confederations and BGP Route Reflectors, exist as well. However, these more advanced features are outside the scope of this book.

Using an iBGP Mesh

To let the internal routers in the Enterprise learn the best BGP routes, one obvious solution is to just run BGP on these routers as well. The not so obvious part relates to the implementation choice of what routers need to be iBGP peers with each other. Based on the topology shown in Figure 14-5, at first glance, the temptation might be to run BGP on E1, E2, Core1, and Core2, but use iBGP peers as shown in Figure 14-6.

Figure 14-6 *Partial Mesh of iBGP Peers*

The iBGP peers shown in the figure actually match the kinds of IGP neighbor relationships you might expect to see with a similar design. With an IGP routing protocol, each router would learn routes and tell its neighbor so that all routers would learn all routes. Unfortunately, with this design, not all the routers learn all the routes because of the following feature of iBGP:

> When a router learns routes from an iBGP peer, that router does not advertise the same routes to another iBGP peer.

Key
Topic

Note: This particular iBGP behavior helps prevent BGP routing loops.

Because of this feature, to ensure that all four routers in ASN 11 learn the same BGP routes, a full mesh of iBGP peers must be created. By creating an iBGP peering between all routers inside ASN 11, they can all exchange routes directly and overcome the restriction. In this case, six such neighborships exist: one between each pair of routers.

The configuration itself does not require any new commands that have not already been explained in this book. However, for completeness, Example 14-8 shows the configuration on both E1 and Core1. Note that all configuration related to iBGP has been included, and the routers use the loopback interfaces shown in Figure 14-6.

Example 14-8 *iBGP Configuration for the Full Mesh Between E1, E2, Core, and Core2–E1 and Core1 Only*

```
! First, E1's configuration
router bgp 11
 neighbor 10.100.1.2 remote-as 11
 neighbor 10.100.1.2 update-source loopback0
```

```
  neighbor 10.100.1.2 next-hop-self
!
  neighbor 10.100.1.3 remote-as 11
  neighbor 10.100.1.3 update-source loopback0
  neighbor 10.100.1.3 next-hop-self
!
  neighbor 10.100.1.4 remote-as 11
  neighbor 10.100.1.4 update-source loopback0
  neighbor 10.100.1.4 next-hop-self
! Next, Core1's configuration
interface loopback0
 ip address 10.100.1.3 255.255.255.255
 !
router bgp 11
 neighbor 10.100.1.1 remote-as 11
 neighbor 10.100.1.1 update-source loopback0
 !
 neighbor 10.100.1.2 remote-as 11
 neighbor 10.100.1.2 update-source loopback0
 !
 neighbor 10.100.1.4 remote-as 11
 neighbor 10.100.1.4 update-source loopback0
```

The configurations on E1 and Core1 mostly match. The commonly used commands simply define the neighbor's ASN (**neighbor... remote-as**) and list the local router's BGP update source interface (**neighbor... update-source**). However, note that the engineer also configured E1–the Internet-connected router–with the **neighbor... next-hop-self** command. In this case, the Internet-connected routers want to set their own update-source IP addresses as the next hop for any routes. However, the engineer purposefully chose not to use this command on the two internal routers (Core1 and Core2) because the eventual destination of these packets will be to make it to either E1 or E2 and then out to the Internet. By making the next-hop router for all iBGP-learned routes an address on one of the Internet-connected routers, the packets will be correctly forwarded.

For perspective, Example 14-9 shows Core1's BGP table after adding the configuration shown in Example 14-8, plus the equivalent configuration in E2 and Core2. Focusing on the routes for 181.0.0.0/8 and 192.135.250.0/28 again, note that E1 and E2 had already agreed that E1's route for 181.0.0.0/8 was best and that E2's route for 192.135.250.0/28 was best. As a result, Core1 knows only one route for each of these destinations, as shown in the example. Also, the next-hop addresses for each route refer to the correct of the two Internet-connected routers: 10.100.1.1 (E1) for the route to 181.0.0.0/8 and 10.100.1.2 (E2) for the route to 192.135.250.0/28.

Example 14-9 *BGP Table on Router Core1*

```
Core-1# show ip bgp
BGP table version is 10, local router ID is 10.100.1.3
Status codes: s suppressed, d damped, h history, * valid, > best, i - internal,
              r RIB-failure, S Stale
Origin codes: i - IGP, e - EGP, ? - incomplete

   Network          Next Hop          Metric LocPrf Weight Path
r  i0.0.0.0         10.100.1.2             0    100      0 3 i
r>i                 10.100.1.1             0    100      0 1 i
*  i128.107.0.0/19  10.100.1.2             0    100      0 i
*>i                 10.100.1.1             0    100      0 i
*>i181.0.0.0/8      10.100.1.1             0    100      0 1 2 111 112 i
*>i182.0.0.0/8      10.100.1.1             0    100      0 1 2 222 i
*>i183.0.0.0/8      10.100.1.1             0    100      0 1 2 i
*>i184.0.0.0/8      10.100.1.1             0    100      0 1 2 i
*>i185.0.0.0/8      10.100.1.1             0    100      0 1 2 i
*>i192.135.250.0/28 10.100.1.2            0    100      0 3 4 i
```

IGP Redistribution and BGP Synchronization

You can also redistribute BGP routes into the IGP to solve the routing loop problem. This solution prevents the routing loop by giving the internal Enterprise routers knowledge of the best exit point for each known Internet destination.

Although it solves the problem, particularly when just learning with lab gear at home, re-distribution of BGP routes into an IGP is generally not recommended. This redistribution requires a relatively large amount of memory and a relatively large amount of processing by the IGP with the much larger number of routes to process. Redistributing the number of routes in the full Internet BGP table could crash the IGP routing protocols.

Note: BGP consumes less memory and uses less CPU for a large number of routes as compared to the equivalent number of routes advertised by an IGP, particularly when com-pared to OSPF. So using the iBGP mesh may cause internal routers to learn all the same routes but without risk to the IGP.

Although not recommended, the idea of redistributing eBGP-learned Internet routes into the Enterprise IGP needs to be discussed as a backdrop to discuss a related BGP feature called *synchronization* or *sync*. The term refers to the idea that the iBGP-learned routes must be synchronized with IGP-learned routes for the same prefix before they can be used. In other words, if an iBGP-learned route is to be considered to be a usable route, then that same prefix must be in the IP routing table and learned using some IGP protocol such as EIGRP or OSPF. More formally, the synchronization features tells a BGP router the following:

Do not consider an iBGP-learned route as "best" unless the exact prefix was learned via an IGP and is currently in the IP routing table.

For companies, such as the Enterprise shown in Figure 14-5, the combination of redistributing eBGP routes into an IGP, and configuring synchronization on the two routers that run BGP (E1 and E2), prevents the routing loop shown in that figure. Again using prefix 192.135.250.0/28 as an example (see Figure 14-5), E2 again learned this prefix with eBGP. E1 learns this same prefix through its iBGP neighborship with E2, and both agree that E2's BGP route is best.

When E2 has successfully redistributed prefix 192.135.250.0/28 into the Enterprise's IGP (OSPF in the examples in this chapter), E1, with sync enabled, thinks like this:

> I see an IGP route for 192.135.250.0/28 in my IP routing table, so my iBGP route for that same prefix is safe to use.

However, if for some reason the redistribution does not result in an IGP route for 192.135.250.0/28, then E1 thinks as follows:

> I do not see an IGP-learned route for 192.135.250.0/28 in my IP routing table, so I will not consider the iBGP route through E2 to be usable.

In this second case, E1 uses its eBGP-learned route through I1-1, which defeats the routing loop caused at Step 3 of Figure 14-5.

Later IOS versions default to disable synchronization because most sites avoid redistributing routes from BGP into an IGP when using BGP for Internet routes, instead preferring iBGP meshes (or alternatives) to avoid these routing black holes. The setting is applied to the entire BGP process, with the **synchronization** command enabling synchronization and the **no synchronization** command (default) disabling it.

Note: The suggestion to avoid redistribution from BGP into an IGP generally applies to cases in which BGP is used to exchange Internet routes. However, BGP can be used for other purposes as well, including the implementation of Multiprotocol Label Switching (MPLS). Redistribution from BGP into an IGP when using BGP for MPLS is reasonable and commonly done.

Route Filtering and Clearing BGP Peers

BGP allows the filtering of BGP Update messages on any BGP router. The router can filter updates per neighbor for both inbound and outbound Updates on any BGP router.

After adding a new BGP filter to a router's configuration, the BGP neighbor relationships must be reset or cleared to cause the filter to take effect. The IOS BGP **clear** command tells the router specifically how to reset the neighborship. This section also examines the variations on the BGP **clear** command, including the more disruptive hard reset options and the less disruptive soft reset options.

BGP Filtering Overview

BGP filtering works generally like IGP filtering, particularly like EIGRP. Similar to EIGRP, BGP Updates can be filtered on any router, without the restrictions that exist for OSPF with various area design issues. The filtering can examine the prefix information about each router and both the prefix and prefix length information, in either direction (in or out), on any BGP router.

The biggest conceptual differences between BGP and IGP filtering relate to what BGP can match about a prefix to make a choice of whether to filter the route. EIGRP focuses on matching the prefix/length. BGP can also match the prefix/length but can also match the large set of BGP Path Attributes (PA). For example, a filter could compare a BGP route's AS_Path PA and check to see if the first ASN is 4, that at least three ASNs exist, and that the AS_Path does not end with 567. The matching of routes based on their PA settings has no equivalent with any of the IGPs.

The biggest configuration difference between BGP and IGP filtering, beside the details of matching BGP PAs, has to do with the fact that the filters must apply to specific neighbors with BGP. With EIGRP, the filters can be applied to all outbound updates from EIGRP, or all inbound updates into EIGRP, using a single EIGRP **distribute-list** command. BGP configuration does not allow filtering of all inbound or outbound updates. Instead, the BGP filtering configuration enables filters per neighbor (using a **neighbor** command), referencing the type of BGP filter, the filter number or name, and the direction (in or out). So, a router could literally use the same filter for all BGP Updates sent by a router, but the configuration would require a **neighbor** command for each neighbor that enabled the same filter.

The ROUTE course and exam focus on Enterprise routing topics, whereas BGP filtering—especially the more detailed filtering with BGP PAs—is used most frequently by ISP network engineers. As a result, CCNP ROUTE appears to cover BGP filtering very lightly, at least compared to IGP filtering.

This section does briefly describe the BGP filtering commands, showing a few samples just for perspective. Table 14-2 summarizes the BGP filtering options and commands, along with the fields in the BGP Update message that can be matched with each type. Following the table, the text shows an example of how an Enterprise might apply an outbound and inbound filter based on prefix/length.

Table 14-2 *BGP Filtering Tools*

BGP Subcommand	Commands Referenced by neighbor Command	What Can Be Matched
neighbor distribute-list (standard ACL)	**access-list, ip access-list**	Prefix, with WC mask
neighbor distribute-list (extended ACL)	**access-list, ip access-list**	Prefix and prefix length, with WC mask for each
neighbor prefix-list	**ip prefix-list**	Exact or "first *N*" bits of prefix, plus range of prefix lengths

| neighbor filter-list | ip as-path access-list | AS_PATH contents; all NLRI whose AS_PATHs are matched considered to be a match |
| neighbor route-map | route-map | Prefix, prefix length, AS_PATH, and/or any other PA matchable within a BGP route map |

Inbound and Outbound BGP Filtering on Prefix/Length

Enterprises that choose to use BGP benefit from both learning routes from the connected ISPs and advertising the Enterprise's public prefix to the same ISPs. However, when the eBGP connections to the various ISPs come up, the Enterprise BGP routers advertise all the best routes in each router's BGP table over the eBGP connection. As a result, the ISPs could learn a best route that causes one ISP to send packets to the Enterprise, with the Enterprise then forwarding the packet out to another ISP. In such a case, the Enterprise AS would be acting as a *transit AS*; in other words, an AS through which packets go through, rather than being the destination or source of the packet.

The Enterprise engineers can, and probably should, make an effort to filter inappropriate routes sent to the ISP over the eBGP peer connections with the goal of preventing the Enterprise AS from becoming a transit AS. Additionally, the Enterprise can filter all private IP address ranges, in case any such address ranges get into the Enterprise BGP router's BGP table.

As an example, consider Figure 14-7, with the now-familiar prefix 192.135.250.0/28. As seen in earlier examples, both E1 and E2 learn this prefix, and both agree that the best route from ASN 11 (the Enterprise) toward this prefix is through E2. The figure shows the BGP routing updates as dashed lines.

E1's best route for 192.135.250.0/28 lists E2 as the next-hop router, so without any filtering in place, E1 then advertises prefix 192.135.250.0/28 to Router I1-1 in ISP1. I1-1 may be configured to filter this prefix. (In the examples throughout Chapters 13 and 14, router I1-1 was indeed configured to filter such prefixes.) However, if the Enterprise did not filter this prefix when advertising to ISP1, and ISP1 did not filter it, then ISP1 might choose the route through ASN 11 as its best route, making ASN 11 a transit AS for this prefix and consuming the Enterprise's Internet bandwidth.

Typically, an Enterprise would use outbound filtering on its eBGP neighborships, filtering all routes except for the known public prefixes that need to be advertised into the Internet. Example 14-10 shows just such a case, using the **neighbor prefix-list** command. The example also highlights a particularly useful command, **show ip bgp neighbor** *neighbor-id* **advertised-routes**, which shows the post-filter BGP update sent to the listed neighbor. The example shows the BGP Update before adding the filter, after adding the filter, and then after clearing the peer connection to router I1-1.

Figure 14-7   *The Need for Enterprise BGP Filtering*

Example 14-10   *Filtering to Allow Only Public Prefix 128.107.0.0/19 Outbound*

```
! The next command occurs before filtering is added.
E1# show ip bgp neighbor 1.1.1.1 advertised-routes
BGP table version is 16, local router ID is 128.107.9.1
Status codes: s suppressed, d damped, h history, * valid, > best, i - internal,
              r RIB-failure, S Stale
Origin codes: i - IGP, e - EGP, ? - incomplete


   Network          Next Hop         Metric LocPrf Weight Path
*>  128.107.0.0/19   0.0.0.0                          32768 i
*>i192.135.250.0/28 10.100.1.2          0     100      0 3 4 i


Total number of prefixes 2


! Next, the filtering is configured.
E1# configure terminal
Enter configuration commands, one per line.  End with CNTL/Z.

E1(config)#ip prefix-list only-public permit 128.107.0.0/19
E1(config)#router bgp 11
```

```
E1(config-router)#neighbor 1.1.1.1 prefix-list only-public out
E1(config-router)#^Z
E1#


! Next, the Update sent to I1-1 is displayed.
E1# show ip bgp neighbor 1.1.1.1 advertised-routes
BGP table version is 16, local router ID is 128.107.9.1
Status codes: s suppressed, d damped, h history, * valid, > best, i - internal,
              r RIB-failure, S Stale
Origin codes: i - IGP, e - EGP, ? - incomplete

   Network          Next Hop          Metric LocPrf Weight Path
*> 128.107.0.0/19   0.0.0.0                          32768 i
*>i192.135.250.0/28 10.100.1.2             0    100      0 3 4 i


Total number of prefixes 2

! Next, the peer connection is cleared, causing the filter to take effect.
E1# clear ip bgp 1.1.1.1
E1#
*Aug 17 20:19:51.763: %BGP-5-ADJCHANGE: neighbor 1.1.1.1 Down User reset
*Aug 17 20:19:52.763: %BGP-5-ADJCHANGE: neighbor 1.1.1.1 Up

! Finally, the Update is displayed with the filter now working.
E1# show ip bgp neighbor 1.1.1.1 advertised-routes
BGP table version is 31, local router ID is 128.107.9.1
Status codes: s suppressed, d damped, h history, * valid, > best, i - internal,
              r RIB-failure, S Stale
Origin codes: i - IGP, e - EGP, ? - incomplete


   Network          Next Hop          Metric LocPrf Weight Path
*> 128.107.0.0/19   0.0.0.0                          32768 i

Total number of prefixes 1
```

Example 14-10 shows an interesting progression if you just read through the example start
to finish. To begin, the **show ip bgp 1.1.1.1 advertised-routes** command lists the routes
that E1 has advertised to neighbor 1.1.1.1 (Router I1-1) in the past. Then, the configuration
shows a prefix-list that matches only 128.107.0.0/19, with a permit action; all other prefixes
will be denied by the implied deny all at the end of each prefix list. Then, the **neighbor
1.1.1.1 prefix-list only-public out** BGP subcommand tells BGP to apply the prefix list to
filter outbound routes sent to I1-1.

The second part of the output shows an example of how BGP operates on a Cisco router,
particularly how BGP requires that the neighbor be cleared before the newly configured
filter takes effect. Router E1 has already advertised two prefixes to this neighbor:

128.107.0.0/19 and 192.135.250.0/28, as seen at the beginning of the example. To make the filtering action take effect, the router must be told to clear the neighborship with router I1-1. The **clear ip bgp 1.1.1.1** command tells E1 to perform a hard reset of that neighbor connection, which brings down the TCP connection, and removes all BGP table entries associated with that neighbor. The neighbor (I1-1, using address 1.1.1.1) also removes its BGP table entries associated with Router E1. After the neighborship recovers, E1 resends its BGP Update to Router I1-1–but this time with one less prefix, as noted at the end of the example with the output of the **show ip bgp neighbor 1.1.1.1 advertised-routes** command.

This same filtering action could have been performed with several other configuration options: using the **neighbor distribute-list** or **neighbor route-map** commands. The **neighbor distribute-list** command refers to an IP ACL, which tells IOS to filter routes based on matching the prefix (standard ACL) or prefix/length (extended ACL). The **neighbor route-map** command refers to a route-map that can use several matching options to filter routes, keeping routes matched with a route-map permit clause and filtering routes matched with a route-map deny clause. Example 14-11 shows two such options just for comparison's sake.

Example 14-11   *Alternatives to the Configuration in Example 14-10*

```
! First option – ACL 101 as a distribute-list
access-list 101 permit ip host 128.107.0.0 host 255.255.224.0
router bgp 11
 neighbor 1.1.1.1 distribute-list 101 out

! Second option: Same prefix list as Example 12-10, referenced by a route map
ip prefix-list only-public seq 5 permit 128.107.0.0/19
!
route-map only-public-rmap permit 10
 match ip address prefix-list only-public
!
router bgp 11
 neighbor 1.1.1.1 route-map only-public-rmap out
```

Clearing BGP Neighbors

As noted in Example 14-10 and the related explanations, IOS does not cause a newly configured BGP filter to take effect until the neighbor relationship is cleared. The neighborship can be cleared in several ways, including reloading the router and by administratively disabling and re-enabling the BGP neighborship using the **neighbor shutdown** and **no neighbor shutdown** configuration commands. However, IOS supports several options on the **clear ip bgp** exec command for the specific purpose of resetting BGP connections. This section examines the differences in these options.

Each variation on the **clear ip bgp...** command either performs a hard reset or soft reset of one or more BGP neighborships. When a hard reset occurs, the local router brings down the neighborship, brings down the underlying TCP connection, and removes all BGP table entries learned from that neighbor. Both the local and neighboring router reacts just like it does for any failed BGP neighborship by removing its BGP table entries learned over that neighborship. With a soft reset, the router does not bring down the BGP neighborship or the underlying TCP connection. However, the local router re-sends outgoing Updates, adjusted per the outbound filter and reprocesses incoming Updates per the inbound filter, which adjusts the BGP tables based on the then-current configuration.

Table 14-3 lists many of the variations on the **clear ip bgp** command, with a reference as to whether it uses hard or soft reset.

Key Topic

Table 14-3 *BGP clear Command Options*

Command	Hard or Soft	One or All Neighbors	Direction (in or out)
clear ip bgp *	Hard	all	both
clear ip bgp *neighbor-id*	Hard	one	both
clear ip bgp *neighbor-id* out	Soft	one	out
clear ip bgp *neighbor-id* soft out	Soft	one	out
clear ip bgp *neighbor-id* in	Soft	one	in
clear ip bgp *neighbor-id* soft in	Soft	one	in
clear ip bgp * soft	Soft	all	both
clear ip bgp *neighbor-id* soft	Soft	one	both

The commands listed in the table should be considered as pairs. In the first pair, both commands perform a hard reset. The first command uses a * instead of the neighbor IP address, causing a hard reset of all BGP neighbors, while the second command resets that particular neighbor.

The second pair of commands performs soft resets for a particular neighbor but only for outgoing updates, making these commands useful when a router changes its outbound BGP filters. Both commands do the same function; two such commands exist in part because of the history of the BGP implementation in the IOS. When issued, these two commands cause the router to reevaluate its existing BGP table and create a new BGP Update for that neighbor. The router builds that new Update based on the existing configuration, so any new or changed outbound filters affect the contents of the Update. The router sends the new BGP Update, and the neighboring router receives the new Update and adjusts its BGP table as a result.

The third pair of commands performs soft resets for a particular neighbor, but only for incoming updates, making these commands useful when a router changes its inbound BGP filters. However, unlike the two previous commands in the table, these two commands do have slightly different behavior and need a little more description.

The **clear ip bgp** *neighbor-id* **soft in** command, the older command of the two, works only if the configuration includes the **neighbor** *neighbor-id* **soft-reconfiguration inbound** BGP configuration command for this same neighbor. This configuration command causes the router to retain the received BGP Updates from that neighbor. This consumes extra memory on the router, but it gives the router a copy of the original pre-filter Update received from that neighbor. Using that information, the **clear ip bgp** *neighbor-id* **soft in** tells IOS to reapply the inbound filter to the cached received Update, updating the local router's BGP table.

The newer version of the **clear ip bgp** command, namely the **clear ip bgp** *neighbor-id* **in** command (without the **soft** keyword), removes the requirement for the **neighbor** *neighbor-id* **soft-reconfiguration inbound** configuration command. Instead, the router uses a newer BGP feature, the *route refresh* feature, which essentially allows a BGP router to ask its neighbor to re-send its full BGP Update. The **clear ip bgp** *neighbor-id* **in** command tells the local router to use route refresh feature to ask the neighbor to re-send its BGP Update, and then the local router can apply its current inbound BGP filters, updating its BGP table.

Example 14-12 shows a sample of how to confirm whether a router has the route refresh capability. In this case, both the local router (E1 from Figure 14-5) and the neighbor (I1-1 from Figure 14-5) have route refresh capability. As a result, E1 can perform a soft reset inbound without the need to consume the extra memory with the **neighbor soft-reconfiguration inbound** configuration command.

Example 14-12 *Alternatives to the Configuration in Example 14-10*

```
E1# show ip bgp neighbor 1.1.1.1
BGP neighbor is 1.1.1.1,  remote AS 1, external link
  BGP version 4, remote router ID 1.1.1.1
  BGP state = Established, up for 00:04:21
  Last read 00:00:20, last write 00:00:48, hold time is 180, keepalive interval
is 60 seconds
  Neighbor capabilities:
    Route refresh: advertised and received(new)
! Lines omitted for brevity
```

The last pair of commands in Table 14-3 do a soft reset both inbound and outbound at the same time, either for all neighbors (the * option) or for the single neighbor listed in the **clear** command.

Displaying the Results of BGP Filtering

To verify and troubleshoot filtering configurations, you need to see both the before and after results of the filter. IOS provides several **show** commands that allow you to do exactly that. For instance, Example 14-10 shows several cases of the **show ip bgp neighbor advertised-routes** command that shows the post-filter BGP Updates sent by a router. Figure 14-8 summarizes these commands, showing how they can be used to display the pre- and post-filter BGP table contents. The figure shows Router E1, with inbound filtering for Updates received from Router I3-1 and outbound filtering of BGP Updates sent to Router I1-1.

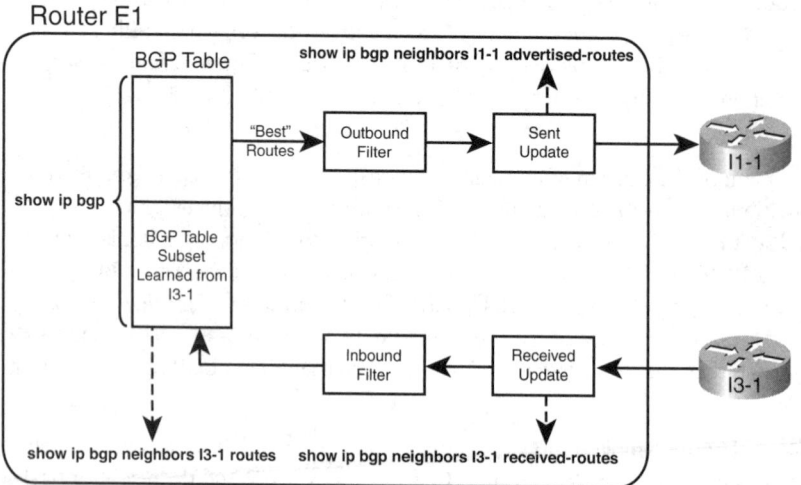

Router E1

Figure 14-8   show *Commands Related to BGP Filtering*

The commands for displaying inbound updates, at the bottom of the figure, display output in the same format as the **show ip bgp** command. These commands restrict the contents to either exactly what has been received from that one neighbor (the **show ip bgp neighbor received-routes** command) or what has been received and passed through any inbound filter (the **show ip bgp neighbor routes** command).

One of the two commands helpful for the inbound direction, namely the **show ip bgp neighbor received-routes** command, requires the configuration of the BGP subcommand **neighbor soft-reconfiguration inbound.** As a result, to see the pre-filter BGP Update received from a neighbor, a router must configure this extra command, which causes the router to use more memory to store the inbound Update. (A router cannot use the BGP route refresh option just to get another copy of the incoming Update to list in this command.) However, when learning in a lab, the extra memory should not pose a problem.

Of the two commands for outbound filtering, the post-filter command is somewhat obvious, but there is no command to specifically display a pre-filter view of the BGP Update sent to a neighbor. However, BGP advertises the best route for each prefix in the BGP table, within certain restrictions. Those restrictions include that BGP will not advertise iBGP-learned routes to an iBGP peer, and a router will not advertise the best route back to the same neighbor that advertised that route. So, to see the pre-filter BGP table entries, use the **show ip bgp** command, look for all the best routes, and then consider the additional rules. Use the **show ip bgp neighbor advertised-routes** to display the post-filter BGP Update for a given neighbor.

Example 14-13 shows the output of these commands on E1. In this case, E1 has been already been configured with an inbound filter that filters inbound prefixes 184.0.0.0/8 and

185.0.0.0/8. (The filter configuration is not shown.) As a result, the post-filter output lists five prefixes, and the pre-filter output lists seven prefixes. The example also shows the error message when soft-reconfiguration is not configured.

Example 14-13 *Displaying the BGP Table Pre- and Post-Inbound Filter*

```
E1# show ip bgp neighbors 1.1.1.1 routes
BGP table version is 78, local router ID is 11.11.11.11
Status codes: s suppressed, d damped, h history, * valid, > best, i - internal,
              r RIB-failure, S Stale
Origin codes: i - IGP, e - EGP, ? - incomplete

   Network          Next Hop           Metric LocPrf Weight Path
*> 0.0.0.0          1.1.1.1                 0            0 1 i
*> 181.0.0.0/8      1.1.1.1                              0 1 2 111 111 i
*> 182.0.0.0/8      1.1.1.1                              0 1 2 222 i
*> 183.0.0.0/8      1.1.1.1                              0 1 2 i
*  192.135.250.0/28 1.1.1.1                              0 1 2 3 4 i

Total number of prefixes 5
E1# show ip bgp neighbors 1.1.1.1 received-routes
% Inbound soft reconfiguration not enabled on 1.1.1.1

E1# configure terminal
Enter configuration commands, one per line.  End with CNTL/Z.
E1(config)#router bgp 11
E1(config-router)#neighbor 1.1.1.1 soft-reconfiguration inbound
E1(config-router)#^Z
E1#
E1# show ip bgp neighbors 1.1.1.1 received-routes
BGP table version is 78, local router ID is 11.11.11.11
Status codes: s suppressed, d damped, h history, * valid, > best, i - internal,
              r RIB-failure, S Stale
Origin codes: i - IGP, e - EGP, ? - incomplete

   Network          Next Hop           Metric LocPrf Weight Path
*> 0.0.0.0          1.1.1.1                 0            0 1 i
*> 181.0.0.0/8      1.1.1.1                              0 1 2 111 111 i
*> 182.0.0.0/8      1.1.1.1                              0 1 2 222 i
*> 183.0.0.0/8      1.1.1.1                              0 1 2 i
*> 184.0.0.0/8      1.1.1.1                              0 1 2 i
*> 185.0.0.0/8      1.1.1.1                              0 1 2 i
*  192.135.250.0/28 1.1.1.1                              0 1 2 3 4 i

Total number of prefixes 7
```

Exam Preparation Tasks

Planning Practice

The CCNP ROUTE exam expects test takers to review design documents, create implementation plans, and create verification plans. This section provides some exercises that may help you to take a step back from the minute details of the topics in this chapter so that you can think about the same technical topics from the planning perspective.

For each planning practice table, simply complete the table. Note that any numbers in parentheses represent the number of options listed for each item in the solutions in Appendix F, "Completed Planning Practice Tables."

Design Review Table

Table 14-4 lists several design goals related to this chapter. If these design goals were listed in a design document, and you had to take that document and develop an implementation plan, what implementation options come to mind? You should write a general description; specific configuration commands are not required.

Table 14-4 *Design Review*

Design Goal	Possible Implementation Choices Covered in This Chapter
The plan shows a typical single-multihomed design with two routers connected to 2 ISPs. How will you ensure next-hop reachability? (2)	
The plan shows the same design as the last item. The two Enterprise Internet-connected routers do not have a direct link between each other. What methods discussed in this chapter can be used to prevent packet loops in the Enterprise core? (2)	
The plan shows the same design as the previous items but with public range 200.1.1.0/24 being the only public address range used by the Enterprise. How can the Enterprise avoid becoming a transit AS?	

Implementation Plan Peer Review Table

Table 14-5 shows a list of questions that others might ask, or that you might think about, during a peer review of another network engineer's implementation plan. Complete the table by answering the questions.

Table 14-5 *Notable Questions from This Chapter to Consider During an Implementation Plan Peer Review*

Question	Answers
The plan shows a typical single-multihomed design with two routers (R1 and R2) connected to 2 ISPs. Will R1 and R2 be BGP neighbors? Why?	
The plan shows the same design as the previous item. What configuration setting must be used to ensure the routers are iBGP rather than eBGP peers?	
The plan calls for filtering all prefixes except the 200.1.1.0/24 public address range when advertising the any eBGP peers. Which **neighbor** command options exist for filtering based on the prefix/length? (3)	

Create an Implementation Plan Table

This chapter does not focus on implementation or verification, but it did review one concept about static routes, as listed in Table 14-6.

Table 14-6 *Implementation Plan Configuration Memory Drill*

Feature	Configuration Commands/Notes
Configure an iBGP peer.	
Advertise the local router's Update source IP address as the next-hop address to iBGP peers.	
Configure an iBGP mesh with peers 1.1.1.1, 2.2.2.2, 3.3.3.3.	
Enable BGP synchronization.	
Configure filtering of routes sent to eBGP peer 9.9.9.9, using a prefix list to allow only 200.1.1.0/24.	
Configure filtering of routes sent to eBGP peer 9.9.9.9, using an ACL to allow only 200.1.1.0/24.	

Choosing Commands for a Verification Plan Table

To practice skills useful when creating your own verification plan, list in Table 14-7 all commands that supply the requested information. You may want to record your answers outside the book and set a goal to complete this table (and others like it) from memory during your final reviews before taking the exam.

Table 14-7 *Verification Plan Memory Drill*

Information Needed	Commands
Display a single-line neighbor status for all iBGP neighbors.	
Determine if a particular BGP table entry is iBGP-learned.	
Determine the next-hop IP address of an iBGP learned route.	
Identify the neighbor from which a BGP route was learned.	
Display one-line entries for all BGP table entries with a given prefix/length, plus any subnets inside that ranges.	
Display BGP routes learned from a neighbor, before being processed by an inbound filter.	
The same as the previous item, but after applying the inbound filter.	
Display BGP routes sent to a neighbor but after applying the outbound filter.	
Display whether a neighbor can perform BGP route refresh.	

Note: Some of the entries in this table may not have been specifically mentioned in this chapter but are listed in this table for review and reference.

Review all the Key Topics

Review the most important topics from inside the chapter, noted with the Key Topics icon in the outer margin of the page. Table 14-8 lists a reference of these key topics and the page numbers on which each is found.

Table 14-8   *Key Topics for Chapter 14*

Key Topic Element	Description	Page Number
List	Configuration steps for iBGP peer using a loopback as Update source.	462
Text	Paragraph about the default behavior of eBGP and iBGP peers regarding the setting of the next-hop IP address.	464
Figure 14-4	eBGP next-hop default behavior.	470
Text	iBGP behavior regarding not forwarding iBGP learned routes.	473
Figure 14-7	Preventing an Enterprise from becoming a Transit AS.	479
Table 14-3	Options on the BGP **clear** command.	482
Figure 14-8	Reference for BGP filtering verification commands.	484

Complete the Tables and Lists from Memory

Print a copy of Appendix D, "Memory Tables," (found on the CD), or at least the section for this chapter, and complete the tables and lists from memory. Appendix E, "Memory Tables Answer Key," also on the CD, includes completed tables and lists to check your work.

Definitions of Key Terms

Define the following key terms from this chapter, and check your answers in the glossary.

BGP synchronization, iBGP Mesh, Next-hop self, BGP soft reset, BGP hard reset

This chapter covers the following subjects:

BGP Path Attributes and Best Path Algorithm: This section describes the BGP Path Attributes that have an impact on the BGP best path algorithm–the algorithm BGP uses to choose the best BGP route for each destination prefix.

Influencing an Enterprise's Outbound Routes: This section shows how to use the BGP features that influence the BGP best path algorithm.

Influencing an Enterprise's Inbound Routes with MED: This section shows how to use the MultiExit Discriminator BGP feature that influences the BGP best path algorithm for inbound routes.

BGP Path Control

IGPs choose the best route based on some very straightforward concepts. RIP uses the least number of router hops between a router and the destination subnet. EIGRP uses a formula based on a combination of the fastest bandwidth and least delay. And OSPF uses lowest cost but with that cost typically calculated based on bandwidth.

BGP uses a much more detailed process to choose the best BGP route. BGP does not consider router hops, bandwidth, or delay when choosing the best route to reach each subnet. Instead, BGP defines several items to compare about the competing routes, in a particular order. Some of these comparisons use BGP features that can be set based on the router configuration, allowing network engineers to then influence which path BGP chooses as the best path.

BGP's broader set of tools allow much more flexibility when influencing the choice of best route. This BGP best path process also requires only simple comparisons by the router to choose the best route for a prefix. Although the detail of the BGP best path selection process requires more work to understand, that complexity gives engineers additional design and implementation options, and gives engineers many options to achieve their goals when working with the large interconnected networks that comprise the Internet.

Chapter 15 completes the BGP coverage in this book by examining the topic of BGP Path Control, including BGP Path Attributes (PA), the BGP Best Path selection process, along with a discussion of how to use four different features to influence the choice of best path by setting BGP PA values.

"Do I Know This Already?" Quiz

The "Do I Know This Already?" quiz allows you to assess if you should read the entire chapter. If you miss no more than one of these eight self-assessment questions, you might want to move ahead to the "Exam Preparation Tasks." Table 15-1 lists the major headings in this chapter and the "Do I Know This Already?" quiz questions covering the material in those headings so you can assess your knowledge of these specific areas. The answers to the "Do I Know This Already?" quiz appear in Appendix A.

Table 15-1 *"Do I Know This Already?" Foundation Topics Section-to-Question Mapping*

Foundations Topics Section	Questions
BGP Path Attributes and Best Path Algorithm	1–3

1. An engineer is preparing an implementation plan in which the configuration needs to influence BGP's choice of best path. Which of the following is least likely to be used by the configuration in this implementation plan?

   a. Weight

   b. Origin code

   c. AS_Path

   d. Local_Pref

2. Router R1 learns two routes with BGP for prefix 200.1.0.0/16. Comparing the two routes, route 1 has a longer AS_Path Length, bigger MED, bigger Weight, and smaller Local Preference. Which of the following is true about Router R1's choice of best path for this prefix?

   a. Route 1 is the best route.

   b. Route 2 is the best route.

   c. The routes tie as best, but one will be picked to be placed in the routing table based on tiebreakers.

   d. Neither route is considered best.

3. Router R1 learns two routes with BGP for prefix 200.1.0.0/16. Comparing the two routes, route 1 has a shorter AS_Path Length, smaller MED, the same Weight, and smaller Local Preference. Which of the following is true about Router R1's choice of best path for this prefix?

   a. Route 1 is the best route.

   b. Route 2 is the best route.

   c. The routes tie as best, but one will be picked to be placed in the routing table based on tiebreakers.

   d. Neither route is considered best.

4. An engineer has been told to create an implementation plan to influence the choice of best BGP route on a single router using the Weight feature. The sole Enterprise Internet-connected router, Ent1, has neighbor relationships with Routers ISP1 and ISP2, which reside inside two different ISPs. The goal is to prefer all routes learned from ISP1 over ISP2 using Weight. Which of the following answers lists a configuration step that would not be useful for achieving these goals? (Choose two.)

   a. Configuring the **neighbor weight** command on Ent1.

   b. Having the ISPs configure the **neighbor route-map out** command on ISP1 and ISP2, with the route map setting weight.

   c. Configuring the **set weight** command inside a route map on Router Ent1.

    d.   Configuring a prefix list to match all class C networks.

5. The following output on Router R1 lists details of a BGP route for 190.1.0.0/16. Which of the following is true based on this output? (Choose two.)

```
R1# show ip bgp 190.1.0.0/16
BGP routing table entry for 190.1.0.0/16, version 121
Paths: (1 available, best #1, table Default-IP-Routing-Table)
  Advertised to update-groups:
        1
  1 2 3 4
    1.1.1.1 from 2.2.2.2 (3.3.3.3)
      Origin IGP, metric 0, localpref 100, valid, internal, best
```

    a.   R1 has a **neighbor 1.1.1.1** command configured.

    b.   R1 has a **neighbor 2.2.2.2** command configured.

    c.   The **show ip bgp** command lists a line for 190.1.0.0/16 with both an ">" and an "i" on the left.

    d.   R1 is in ASN 1.

6. An Enterprise router, Ent1, displays the following excerpt from the **show ip bgp** command. ENT1 has an eBGP connection to an ISP router with address 3.3.3.3 and an iBGP connection to a router with address 4.4.4.4. Which of the following is most likely to be true?

```
   Network          Next Hop            Metric LocPrf Weight Path
*>                   3.3.3.3                  0           0 1 1 1 1 2
18 i
```

    a.   The Enterprise likely uses ASN 1.

    b.   The neighboring ISP likely uses ASN 1.

    c.   The route has been advertised through ASN 1 multiple times.

    d.   Router Ent1 will add another ASN to the AS_Path before advertising this route to its iBGP peer (4.4.4.4).

7. The following line of output was gathered on Enterprise Router Ent1 using the command **show ip route**. Which of the following answers is most likely to be true, based on this output?

```
B      128.107.0.0 [20/10] via 11.11.11.11, 00:02:18
```

    a.   This router has set the Weight of this route to 10.

    b.   This router's BGP table lists this route as an iBGP route.

    c.   This router's MED has been set to 10.

    d.   This router's BGP table lists an AS_Path length of 10 for this route.

Foundation Topics

BGP Path Attributes and Best Path Algorithm

BGP supports a wide variety of Path Attributes. Some of the PAs exist solely to be used as part of the litany of options in the BGP best path algorithm, some have nothing to do with the BGP best path algorithm, and some impact the best path algorithm as well as being used for other purposes. For example, the Local Preference PA exists to give control to a single AS regarding their outbound routes from an AS-wide perspective. Conversely, the BGP Next_Hop PA provides BGP a place to list the next-hop IP address for a path, but it does not provide a useful means for engineers to set different values for the purpose of influencing the best path choice.

The term *BGP best path algorithm* refers to the process by which BGP on a single router examines the competing BGP paths (routes) in its BGP table, for a single prefix, choosing one route as the best route. The best path algorithm has many steps, but it eventually results in the choice of a single route for each prefix as that router's best BGP path.

The initial major section of this chapter examines the BGP PAs used by the BGP best path algorithm, the BGP best path algorithm itself, and some related topics.

BGP Path Attributes

BGP Path Attributes define facts about a particular route or path through a network. Each PA defines something different about the path, so to truly understand BGP PAs, you need to examine each PA. This section begins by reviewing a few PAs that should now be familiar to you if you have read the preceding BGP chapters, and then this section introduces a few new PAs.

BGP uses the *Autonomous System Path* (AS_Path) PA for several purposes, as already seen in Chapters 12, 13, and 14. This particular PA lists the ASNs in the end-to-end path. BGP uses the AS_Path PA as its primary loop-prevention tool: When an eBGP peer receives an Update, if its own ASN is already in the received AS_Path, then that route has already been advertised into the local ASN and should be ignored. In addition to loop prevention, the BGP best path algorithm uses the AS_Path PA to calculate the AS_Path length, which the algorithm considers as one of its many steps.

BGP also defines the *next-hop IP address* (Next_Hop) of a route as a PA. BGP may advertise one of several different IP addresses as a route's Next_Hop, depending on several factors. To support such features, BGP needs to list the Next_Hop IP address for each path (route), and BGP defines this concept in the Next_Hop PA. The best path algorithm includes a check related to the Next_Hop IP address of the route.

Table 15-2 lists these two PAs, plus a few more PAs, and a related BGP feature (Weight) that is not a PA but is used by Cisco BGP best path implementation. The table lists the PAs in the same order that they will be considered by the BGP best path algorithm. The table also describes each feature listed in the table, relative to whether it is most useful to influence outbound routes (away from the Enterprise) and inbound routes (toward the Enterprise).

Table 15-2   *BGP Path Attributes That Affect the BGP Best Path Algorithm*

Key
Topic

PA	Description	Enterprise Route Direction (Typical)
NEXT_HOP	Lists the next-hop IP address used to reach a prefix.	N/A
Weight[1]	A numeric value, range 0 through $2^{16} - 1$, set by a router when receiving Updates, influencing that one router's route for a prefix. Not advertised to any BGP peers.	Outbound
Local Preference (LO-CAL_PREF)	A numeric value, range 0 through $2^{32} - 1$, set and communicated throughout a single AS for the purpose of influencing the choice of best route for all routers in that AS.	Outbound
AS_PATH (length)	The number of ASNs in the AS_Path PA.	Outbound, Inbound
ORIGIN	Value implying the route was injected into BGP; I (IGP), E (EGP), or ? (incomplete information).	Outbound
Multi Exit Discriminator (MED)	Set and advertised by routers in one AS, impacting the BGP decision of routers in the other AS. Smaller is better.	Inbound

[1]Weight is not a BGP PA; it is a Cisco-proprietary feature that acts somewhat like a PA.

The short descriptions in the table can be helpful for review when doing your final preparation study, but the table does not hold enough information to truly appreciate how an engineer might use these PAs effectively. The second and third major sections of this chapter examine most of these PAs and how to influence the best path choice with each.

To find the current settings of the features in Table 15-2, you can use commands like **show ip bgp** and **show ip bgp** *prefix/length*. However, picking the values out of the clutter in the output of the **show ip bgp** command can be a challenge. Figure 15-1 shows a sample of this command's output and some notations on where to find the various PA settings.

The examples throughout this chapter include examples of these commands, along with the PA settings as changed by various route maps.

Overview of the BGP Best Path Algorithm

The BGP best path algorithm follows the steps shown in shorthand form in Table 15-3. The table lists steps 0 through 8, a short descriptive phrase, and a notation about the criteria for one value to be better than another.

R3 #show ip bgp
BGP table version is 12, local router ID is 3.3.3.3
Status codes: s suppressed, d damped, h history, * valid, > best, i - internal,
　　　　　r RIB-failure, S stale
Origin codes: i - IGP, e - EGP, ? - incomplete

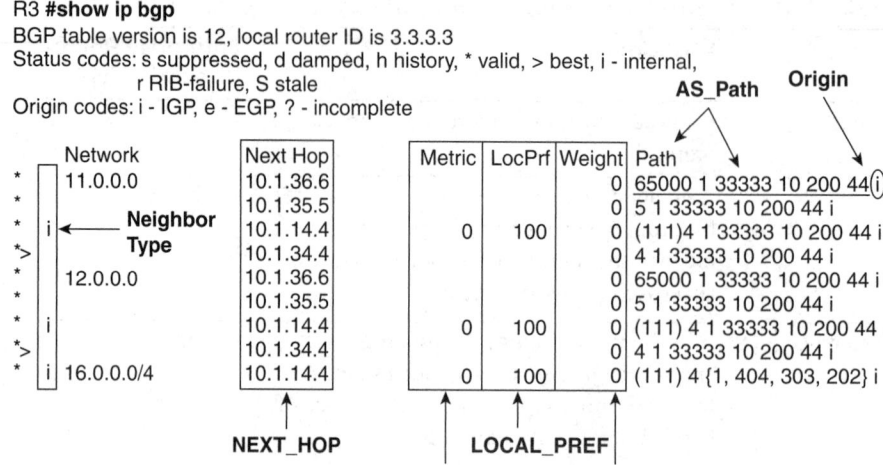

Comments: To Discover Other Details...
Neighbor Type: No Letter Means "EBGP"
IGP Metric: **show ip route** *next-hop-address*
RID: **show ip bgp** *n/ri*

Key Topic

Figure 15-1　*Finding PA Settings in the Output of the* **show ip bgp** *Command*

Key Topic

Table 15-3　*BGP Decision Process Plus Mnemonic: N WLLA OMNI*

Step	Mnemonic Letter	Short Phrase	Which Is Better?
0	N	Next hop: reachable?	If no route to reach Next_Hop, router cannot use this route.
1	W	Weight	Bigger.
2	L	LOCAL_PREF	Bigger.
3	L	Locally injected routes	Locally injected is better than iBGP/eBGP learned.
4	A	AS_PATH length	Smaller.
5	O	ORIGIN	Prefer I over E. Prefer E over ?
6	M	MED	Smaller.
7	N	Neighbor Type	Prefer eBGP over iBGP.
8	I	IGP metric to Next_Hop	Smaller.

Note:　The step numbering of the BGP best path steps does not exist in the BGP RFCs. The steps are numbered in this book for easier reference. Because the RFCs do not dictate a particular step numbering, other references likely use different step numbers; do not be concerned about memorizing the step numbers.

Starting with a Step 0 may seem odd, but it helps make an important point about the logic listed at this step. Some BGP best path references include the logic in this step as a best path step, and some just list this same information as a side note. Regardless, the step 0 concept is important. For step 0, a router looks at the BGP route and compares the Next_Hop IP address to the IP routing table.

If that router does not have a matching IP route for the BGP route's Next_Hop IP address, then that router will not know how to forward packets for that particular prefix, using that particular route. To avoid using such a route, at Step 0, the BGP best path algorithm removes such routes from consideration.BGP then uses the following eight steps, in order, until one best route is chosen for a given prefix.

If a router still did not determine a best route when finishing Step 8, the router takes several other small steps to break the tie. At this point, the competing routes are considered to be just as good as each other. However, unlike IGPs, BGP needs to choose one and only one route as best, in part because BGP advertises only the best routes to its neighbors. In such cases, BGP breaks the tie with these additional steps, which would be considered Steps 9-11:

Step 9.   Oldest (longest-known) eBGP route

Step 10.   Lowest neighbor BGP RID

Step 11.   Lowest neighbor IP address

Taking a more detailed view of the entire best path algorithm, BGP begins by choosing the oldest known route for a given prefix as the best route. It then takes the next longest-known route for that same prefix and compares the two routes using the best path algorithm. The router eventually chooses one of the two BGP routes as the best path (route). If another route exists for the same prefix, the router repeats the process, using the winner of the previous comparisons and the new route, choosing one of those as the better route. The process continues until all routes have been considered, with one route being listed as best in the BGP table.

For example, if Router R1 were considering two routes for prefix 181.0.0.0/8, it would first make sure that both routes had reachable Next_Hop IP addresses. The router would then compare the weight settings, choosing the route with the bigger weight. If they tied on weight, the router would prefer the route with a bigger Local_Pref. If again a tie, the router would prefer the one route that was injected into BGP locally (using the **network** command or using route redistribution). If neither or both routes were locally injected, the router moves on to AS_Path length, and so on, until the router chooses one of the two as the better route.

As soon as one of the steps determines a best route, the comparison of those two routes stops.

Perspectives on the Core 8 Best Path Steps

Some of the BGP best path steps purposefully give the engineer a tool for influencing the choice of best path, whereas other steps have a different purpose, often simply being a side effect of some BGP feature. So, when an engineer starts building a BGP implementation plan, only a subset of the core 8 BGP best path steps need be considered, as follows:

- Weight (Step 1)

- Local_Pref (Step 2)

- AS_Path Length (Step 4)

- MED (often called metric) (Step 6)

Because the ROUTE exam focuses on the more practical aspects of BGP for Enterprises, it gives much more attention to these four features and less attention to the other BGP best path steps. This chapter describes each of these four features to some depth in the context of best path selection. However, before focusing on these four items, it can be helpful to see a small glimpse into the meaning of the other steps, which can be helpful as you work to memorize the steps in the BGP best path algorithm.

Step 3 compares the source from which the routes were added to the BGP table. When the BGP best path algorithm compares two routes at this step, if one were injected into BGP locally, and the other were not (it was learned from a BGP peer), the router chooses the route that was injected locally. Chapter 13, "External BGP," section "Injecting Routes into BGP for Advertisement to the ISPs," describes the two ways to locally inject these routes, the **network** command and redistribution from an IGP.

Step 5 refers to the BGP Origin PA. The Origin PA attempts to identify the source from *outside BGP* from which the route was injected into BGP. The three Origin code values are

- **I:** Injected from an IGP (for example, redistribution from EIGRP)

- **E:** Injected from Exterior Gateway Protocol (EGP)

- **?:** Undetermined

Although the original intent of the Origin PA is to identify the source from which BGP learned the route, routers can also set the Origin PA as part of a strategy to influence the BGP best path.

Step 7 refers to the Neighbor type: iBGP or eBGP. Remembering that BGP compares two routes at a time, if one is learned with eBGP, and the other with iBGP, the router chooses the eBGP route as best. Using this feature to influence the best path choice would be difficult, because the ASN in which a router resides is fixed by the BGP design.

Finally, Step 8 refers to the IGP metric to the Next_Hop address. At this step, the router compares the metrics of the IP routes for each Next_Hop IP address and chooses the BGP route with the lower IGP metric to its Next_Hop. (If an IGP-learned route is not used, for example, if both use connected routes, BGP considers the metrics to tie.) It is conceivable that an engineer might tune the IGP to manipulate BGP's best path choice, but this step is so far into the algorithm that the earlier and more flexible settings would be much better options.

Memorization Tips for BGP Best Path

This short section suggests a mnemonic tool to help you memorize Steps 0 through 8 of the BGP best path algorithm. Feel free to skim this section for now, or ignore it entirely–there is no requirement that you memorize the best path algorithm using the mnemonics in this section. (However, you may want to at least review upcoming Figure 15-2, which gives a good visual reference for some of the information summarized in Table 15-3.) But you should plan on memorizing the list at some point before the exam, even if you ignore the mnemonic device.

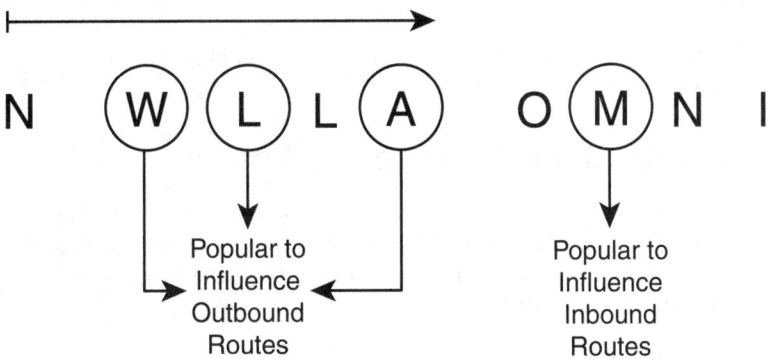

Figure 15-2 *BGP Best Path Mnemonics*

First, if you refer back to the BGP best path algorithm as listed in table 15-3, you see that the second column lists a single-letter mnemonic letter. These letters match the first letter of the description in the third column of that table. Then, take these initial letters and group them as follows:

- N

- WLLA

- OMNI

The N is listed separately because it represents the "is the next-hop reachable" logic of Step 0 and is somewhat separate from the other steps.

The mnemonic groups the eight main steps as two sets of four letters for a couple of reasons. Both sets can be pronounced, even if they don't spell words. It should be easier to memorize as two sets of four. And maybe most important, the first set of four letters, representing Steps 1 through 4, include all the features that engineers typically use to influence outbound routes from the Enterprise:

- **WLLA:** Refers to the three steps that an engineer might use to influence outbound routes: Weight, Local_Pref, and AS_Path length. (Additionally, the second L, in WLLA for Step 3, represents the "Locally injected routes" choice.)

■ **OMNI:** As listed in Table 15-3, the letters represent Origin (I or ?), MED, neighbor type (eBGP over iBGP), and IGP metric to Next-hop.

So, if you can memorize N WLLA OMNI, by the time you've read this chapter you can probably pick out which of those correlate to the four bigger topics later in this chapter: Weight, Local_Pref, AS_Path length, and MED. Hopefully with a little more study, you can memorize the rest of the list.

Figure 15-2 shows the mnemonic letters in graphical form just as another aid in memorizing the steps. It also shows a reminder of which features are most likely to be used to influence outbound routes from the Enterprise, and the one setting (MED) most likely to be used to influence inbound routes into the Enterprise.

The rest of this chapter focuses on a deeper explanation of the four best path steps that engineers typically use to influence the choice of best path.

Influencing an Enterprise's Outbound Routes

This section examines three different features that can influence the outbound routes from an Enterprise: Weight, the Local_Pref PA, and AS_Path length. The topics are listed in the order used by the BGP best path algorithm (Steps 1, 2, and 4). It also introduces the concept of a Routing Table Manager (RTM) function on a router.

Influencing BGP Weight

A Cisco router can use the BGP Weight, on that single router, to influence that one router's choice of outbound route. To do so, when a router receives a BGP Update, that router can set the Weight either selectively, per route, using a route map, or for all routes learned from a single neighbor. The router's best path algorithm then examines the Weight of competing routes, choosing the route with the bigger Weight.

The Cisco-proprietary Weight settings configured on a single router can influence only that one router because the Weight cannot be communicated to other neighboring BGP routers. So, to use the Weight, a router must be configured to examine incoming Updates to set the Weight. The Weight cannot simply be learned in a received Update because that Update message does not support a field in which to communicate the Weight setting.

Table 15-4 summarizes some of the key facts about BGP administrative Weight. Following the table, the text first explains a sample internetwork and its existing configuration, a configuration that begins with configurations that do not set any values that influence the choice of best paths. The next section shows how to set the Weight using the **neighbor route-map in** command, which allows a router to set different Weights for different routes. The second example shows how to set the Weight for all routes learned from a neighbor, using the **neighbor weight** command.

Table 15-4 *Key Features of Administrative Weight*

Feature	Description
Is it a PA?	No; Cisco proprietary feature

Table 15-4 *Key Features of Administrative Weight*

Feature	Description
Purpose	Identifies a single router's best route
Scope	Set on inbound route Updates; influences only that one router's choice
Range	0 through 65,535 ($2^{16} - 1$)
Which is best?	Bigger values are better
Default	0 for learned routes, 32,768 for locally injected routes
Defining a new default	Not supported
Configuration	**neighbor route-map** (per prefix) **neighbor weight** (all routes learned from this neighbor)

Note: For those of you memorizing using the N WLLA OMNI mnemonic, Weight is the W in WLLA.

Sample Internetwork Used in the Weight Examples

Figure 15-3 shows a sample Internetwork used to demonstrate setting the Weight. The figure shows a single Enterprise and a single Enterprise router. The following design requirements have already been met by the configuration in Router E1 and in the ISP routers:

- E1 and I1-1 uses loopback IP addresses (11.11.11.11 and 1.1.1.1) for their neighborship.

- E1 and I3-1 use interface IP addresses for their neighborship.

- None of the routers have attempted to change any settings that can impact the choice of best path.

Next, to have some routes to manipulate with the upcoming examples, the ISP routers each advertise BGP routes for the same five prefixes. Figure 15-4 shows five such prefixes that both ISPs advertise to E1.

Just to get a little deeper understanding of the best path algorithm before getting into the Weight configuration, consider the original configuration state of the sample internetwork, with no attempt to influence E1's choice of best path. The best path for four of the five prefixes will be obvious. Prefixes 181.0.0.0/8 and 182.0.0.0/8 have a shorter AS_Path through ISP1, and 184.0.0.0/8 and 185.0.0.08 have a shorter AS_Path through ISP3. Only 183.0.0.0/8 is in question because its AS_Path length for the competing routes is equal. Example 15-1 shows the output of the **show ip bgp 176.0.0.0/4 longer-prefixes** command, which lists all five of the BGP prefixes listed in Figure 15-4, confirming the results. (Prefix 176.0.0.0/4 implies a range of values whose first octets are in the range 176 through 191, which includes the routes listed in Example 15-1.)

Figure 15-3 *Sample Internetwork for BGP Weight Examples*

Figure 15-4 *Prefixes and AS_Path Lengths Used in Upcoming Examples*

Example 15-1   *BGP Configuration on E1: Neighborships Configured*

```
E1# show ip bgp 176.0.0.0/4 longer-prefixes
BGP table version is 41, local router ID is 128.107.9.1
Status codes: s suppressed, d damped, h history, * valid, > best, i - internal,
              r RIB-failure, S Stale
Origin codes: i - IGP, e - EGP, ? - incomplete

     Network          Next Hop          Metric LocPrf Weight Path
*    181.0.0.0/8      192.168.1.2            0             0 3 2 50 51 52 1811 i
*>                    1.1.1.1                0             0 1 1811 i
*    182.0.0.0/8      192.168.1.2            0             0 3 2 50 51 1822 i
*>                    1.1.1.1                0             0 1 2 1822 i
*    183.0.0.0/8      192.168.1.2            0             0 3 2 50 1833 i
*>                    1.1.1.1                0             0 1 2 50 1833 i
*>   184.0.0.0/8      192.168.1.2            0             0 3 2 1844 i
*                     1.1.1.1                0             0 1 2 50 51 1844 i
*>   185.0.0.0/8      192.168.1.2            0             0 3 1855 i
*                     1.1.1.1                0             0 1 2 50 51 52 1855 i
```

First, consider the best path algorithm on Router E1 for 181.0.0.0/8. E1 knows two BGP routes for 181.0.0.0/8, as expected. The one listed as the best path has 1.1.1.1 (I1-1) as Next_Hop. The following list outlines the best path logic:

Step 0.   The Next_Hop of each is reachable. (Otherwise the neighbors would not be up.)

Step 1.   The Weight ties (both 0).

Step 2.   The Local_Pref ties (unset, so no value is listed; defaults to 100).

Step 3.   Neither route is locally injected; both are learned using BGP, so neither is better at this step.

Step 4.   AS_Path length is shorter for the route through I1-1 (1.1.1.1).

Next, consider the example of the route to 183.0.0.0/8. E1 currently lists the path through I1-1 (1.1.1.1) as best, but the best path decision actually falls all the way to Step 9. For completeness' sake, E1's best path logic runs as follows:

Step 0.   The Next_Hop of each is reachable (otherwise the neighbors would not be up)

Step 1.   The Weight ties (both 0).

Step 2.   The Local_Pref ties (unset, defaults to 100).

Step 3.   Neither route is locally injected.

Step 4.   AS_Path length is 4 in both cases.

Step 5.   Both Origin codes are i.

Step 6.   MED, listed under the Metric column, ties (0).

Step 7.   Neighbor type for each neighbor is eBGP.

Step 8. IGP metric does not apply, because neither uses IGP routes. (The routes from E1 to 1.1.1.1 are static routes.)

Step 9. The route learned from 1.1.1.1 is the oldest route.

Although you may believe the claims at Step 9, the output in Example 15-1 does not explicitly state that fact. However, when IOS lists output in the variations of the **show ip bgp** command, the oldest route for each prefix is listed last, and the newest (most recently learned) is listed first. Example 15-2 confirms this logic, and confirming how Step 9 works in this case. Example 15-2 clears peer 1.1.1.1 (I1-1), making E1's route through 192.168.1.2 (I3-1) become the oldest known route for 183.0.0.0/8:

Example 15-2 *Clearing Neighbors to Force a* **New Route**

```
E1# clear ip bgp 1.1.1.1
E1#
*Aug 24 11:30:41.775: %BGP-5-ADJCHANGE: neighbor 1.1.1.1 Down User reset
*Aug 24 11:30:43.231: %BGP-5-ADJCHANGE: neighbor 1.1.1.1 Up
E1# show ip bgp 176.0.0.0/4 longer-prefixes
BGP table version is 47, local router ID is 128.107.9.1
Status codes: s suppressed, d damped, h history, * valid, > best, i - internal,
              r RIB-failure, S Stale
Origin codes: i - IGP, e - EGP, ? - incomplete

    Network          Next Hop          Metric LocPrf Weight Path
*>  181.0.0.0/8      1.1.1.1                0             0 1 1811 i
*                    192.168.1.2            0             0 3 2 50 51 52 1811 i
*>  182.0.0.0/8      1.1.1.1                0             0 1 2 1822 i
*                    192.168.1.2            0             0 3 2 50 51 1822 i
*   183.0.0.0/8      1.1.1.1                0             0 1 2 50 1833 i
*>                   192.168.1.2            0             0 3 2 50 1833 i
*   184.0.0.0/8      1.1.1.1                0             0 1 2 50 51 1844 i
*>                   192.168.1.2            0             0 3 2 1844 i
*   185.0.0.0/8      1.1.1.1                0             0 1 2 50 51 52 1855 i
*>                   192.168.1.2            0             0 3 1855 i
```

After the hard reset of peer 1.1.1.1, E1's oldest-known route for 183.0.0.0/8 is the route through 192.168.1.2, listed second (last). That E1 now chooses this route as best is another confirmation that E1's best path decision fell to Step 9.

Setting the BGP Administrative Weight Using a Route Map

The **neighbor** *neighbor-ip* **route-map in** BGP subcommand tells a router to apply the route map to all BGP Updates received from the listed neighbor. Such route maps *always attempt to filter routes*. The router allows routes first matched in a permit clause and filters (discards) routes first matched with a deny clause.

BGP route maps can also be used to change the PAs of routes by using the **set** command. For example, a router could use a **neighbor 1.1.1.1 route-map fred in** command. The route map could contain permit clauses that cause some routes to not be filtered. In those same route map clauses, the inclusion of commands such as **set weight 100** and **set local-pref- erence 200** can be used to set items such as the Weight or Local_Pref of a route. (Al- though you can configure a **set** command in a route map deny clause, the set has no effect because the deny clause filters the route.)

Example 15-3 shows a sample configuration that sets the Weight for prefix 181.0.0.0/8 as learned from I3-1 (neighbor ID 192.168.1.2). As shown in Examples 15-1, E1's original best route for this prefix is through I1-1 (1.1.1.1), due to the shorter AS_Path length at Step 4 of the best path algorithm. By setting the Weight higher on the route learned from I3-1, E1 now chooses the route through I3-1.

Example 15-3 *Setting the Weight to 50 for 181/8, as Learned from I3-1*

```
E1# conf t
Enter configuration commands, one per line.  End with CNTL/Z.
E1(config)# ip prefix-list match-181 permit 181.0.0.0/8
E1(config)# route-map set-weight-50 permit 10
E1(config-route-map)# match ip address prefix-list match-181
E1(config-route-map)# set weight 50
E1(config-route-map)# route-map set-weight-50 permit 20
E1(config-route-map)# router bgp 11
E1(config-router)# neighbor 192.168.1.2 route-map set-weight-50 in
E1(config-router)# ^Z
E1#
E1# clear ip bgp 192.168.1.2 soft
E1# show ip bgp 176.0.0.0/4 longer-prefixes
BGP table version is 48, local router ID is 128.107.9.1
Status codes: s suppressed, d damped, h history, * valid, > best, i - internal,
              r RIB-failure, S Stale
Origin codes: i - IGP, e - EGP, ? - incomplete


   Network          Next Hop          Metric LocPrf Weight Path
*  181.0.0.0/8      1.1.1.1                0          0 1 1811 i
*>                  192.168.1.2            0         50 3 2 50 51 52 1811 i
*> 182.0.0.0/8      1.1.1.1                0          0 1 2 1822 i
*                   192.168.1.2            0          0 3 2 50 51 1822 i
*  183.0.0.0/8      1.1.1.1                0          0 1 2 50 1833 i
*>                  192.168.1.2            0          0 3 2 50 1833 i
*  184.0.0.0/8      1.1.1.1                0          0 1 2 50 51 1844 i
*>                  192.168.1.2            0          0 3 2 1844 i
*  185.0.0.0/8      1.1.1.1                0          0 1 2 50 51 52 1855 i
*>                  192.168.1.2            0          0 3 1855 i


! The next command lists the pre-route-map received Update
E1# show ip bgp neigh 192.168.1.2 received-routes ¦ include 181
*  181.0.0.0/8      192.168.1.2            0          0 3 2 50 51 52 1811 i
```

```
! The next command shows the post-route-map received Update
E1# show ip bgp neigh 192.168.1.2 routes ¦ incl 181
*> 181.0.0.0/8      192.168.1.2            0          50 3 2 50 51 52 1811 i
```

The configuration uses a single-line IP prefix list that matches exactly prefix 181.0.0.0/8, and a 2-clause route map. The first route-map clause, a permit clause, matches 181.0.0.0/8. The permit action allows the route through the filter. The **set weight 50** command then sets the weight.

The second **route-map** clause, also with a permit action, matches the rest of the prefixes in the Update because there is no **match** command. The permit action allows these routes through the filter. Without clause 20, this route map would have matched all other routes with the route map's implied deny clause at the end of every route map, filtering all other routes learned from 192.168.1.2 except 181.0.0.0/8.

The configuration also includes a **neighbor 192.168.1.2 route-map set-weight-50 in** command to enable the route map for incoming updates from Router I3-1. The example also shows that the neighbor must be cleared, in this case with a soft reset of the **clear ip bgp 192.168.1.2 soft** command because the route map logic takes effect.

Examining the results of this change, note that E1 now thinks the better route is through I3-1 (192.168.1.2). The output lists the new weight of 50, with the route through I1-1 (1.1.1.1) using the default weight of 0. With weight, bigger is better.

Finally, the last two commands in the example show the pre-route-map received update (with the **received-routes** option) and the post-route-map results of the received update (with the **routes** option). The received Update does not include Weight because it is Cisco-proprietary, so E1 initially assigned the Weight to its default value (0). After applying the route map, E1 now lists a Weight of 50.

Setting Weight Using the **neighbor weight** Command

Alternatively, the weight can be set for all routes learned from a neighbor using the **neighbor weight** command. Example 15-4 shows this configuration added to E1, setting the Weight for all routes learned from I1-1 (1.1.1.1) to 60. As a result, E1's route for 181.0.0.0/8 switches back to using the route through 1.1.1.1 (I1-1).

Example 15-4   *Setting the Weight to 60 for All Routes Learned from I1-1*

```
E1# conf t
Enter configuration commands, one per line.  End with CNTL/Z.
E1(config)# router bgp 11
E1(config-router)# neighbor 1.1.1.1 weight 60
E1(config-router)#^Z
E1# clear ip bgp 1.1.1.1 soft
```

```
E1# show ip bgp 176.0.0.0/4 longer-prefixes
BGP table version is 54, local router ID is 128.107.9.1
Status codes: s suppressed, d damped, h history, * valid, > best, i - internal,
              r RIB-failure, S Stale
Origin codes: i - IGP, e - EGP, ? - incomplete

    Network           Next Hop          Metric LocPrf Weight Path
*> 181.0.0.0/8        1.1.1.1                0           60 1 1811 i
*                     192.168.1.2            0           50 3 2 50 51 52 1811 i
*> 182.0.0.0/8        1.1.1.1                0           60 1 2 1822 i
*                     192.168.1.2            0            0 3 2 50 51 1822 i
*> 183.0.0.0/8        1.1.1.1                0           60 1 2 50 1833 i
*                     192.168.1.2            0            0 3 2 50 1833 i
*> 184.0.0.0/8        1.1.1.1                0           60 1 2 50 51 1844 i
*                     192.168.1.2            0            0 3 2 1844 i
*> 185.0.0.0/8        1.1.1.1                0           60 1 2 50 51 52 1855 i
*                     192.168.1.2            0            0 3 1855 i
```

The **neighbor weight** command does not use an in or out direction because Weight can only be set on input. The configuration results in all routes learned from 1.1.1.1 (I1-1) having a Weight of 60, as noted in the Weight column of the **show ip bgp** output.

Setting the Local Preference

The BGP Local Preference (Local_Pref) PA gives the routers inside a single AS a value that they can set per-route, advertise to all iBGP routers inside the AS, so that all routers in the AS agree about which router is the best exit point for packets destined for that prefix. By design, the Local_Pref can be set by routers as they receive eBGP routes by using an inbound route map. The routers then advertise the Local_Pref in iBGP updates. As a result, all the routers in the same AS can then make the same choice of which route is best, agreeing as to which router to use to exit the AS for each prefix.

As with the discussion of Weight, this section begins with a description of a sample scenario. Following that, a sample Local_Pref configuration is shown, using a route-map to set Local_Pref for routes advertised into an Enterprise. Table 15-5 summarizes some of the key features of Local_Pref as demonstrated in the upcoming pages.

Table 15-5 *Key Features of Local_Pref*

Key Topic

Feature	Description
PA?	Yes
Purpose	Identifies the best exit point from the AS to reach a given prefix
Scope	Throughout the AS in which it was set; not advertised to eBGP peers
Range	0 through 4,294,967,295 ($2^{32} - 1$)
Which is best?	Higher values are better

Default	100
Changing the default	Using the **bgp default local-preference <0-4294967295>** BGP sub-command
Configuration	Via **neighbor route-map** command; **in** option is required for updates from an **eBGP** peer

Note: For those of you memorizing using the N WLLA OMNI mnemonic, Local_Pref is the first L in WLLA.

Sample Internetwork Used in the Local_Pref and AS_Path Length Examples

Figure 15-5 shows a sample Internetwork used to demonstrate setting both Local_Pref, and later, AS_Path Length. The figure shows a single Enterprise with two Internet-connected routers. A full iBGP mesh exists with these two routers plus two routers internal to the Enterprise. Two eBGP neighborships exist, one with ISP1, and one with ISP3. (Note in particular that unlike Figure 15-3, E1 does not have a neighborship with router I3-1 in this case.) The following design requirements have already been met by the initial configuration in all routers shown in the figure:

■   E1 and I1-1 uses loopback IP addresses (11.11.11.11 and 1.1.1.1) for their neighborship.

■   E2 and I3-1 use interface IP addresses for their neighborship.

■   None of the routers have attempted to change any settings that can impact the choice of best path, and Weight settings in the previous examples have been removed.

Figure 15-5 *Sample Internetwork for BGP Local_Pref and AS_Path Length Examples*

As with the Weight example, both ISPs advertise the same five prefixes, with different AS_Paths so that the routers have some prefixes to manipulate. Figure 15-6 shows five such prefixes that both ISPs advertise to E1 and E2. Note that this example network uses the same five prefixes, prefix lengths, and As_Path values as the previous Weight examples in this chapter.

Figure 15-6 *Prefixes and AS_Path Lengths Used in Upcoming Examples*

Before showing the example of how to set the Local_Pref and how it impacts the routes, it is helpful to look at the best BGP routes on the Enterprise routers before any PAs have been changed. Example 15-6 shows the relevant BGP table entries on E1, E2, and Core1 with no attempt to influence E1's choice of best path. The best path for four of the five prefixes will be obvious, but the output listed in the commands requires some review. Prefixes 181.0.0.0/8 and 182.0.0.0/8 have a shorter AS_Path through ISP1, so E1 and E2 will agree that E1's path, through ISP1, is best. Similarly, 184.0.0.0/8 and 185.0.00.08 have a shorter AS_Path through ISP3, so both E1 and E2 agree that E2's path is best for these prefixes. Again, 183.0.0.0/8 ties on AS_Path length.

Example 15-5 *BGP Tables on E1, E2, and Core1, with No Changes to Settings That Affect Best Path*

```
! First, on router E1
E1# show ip bgp 176.0.0.0/4 longer-prefixes
BGP table version is 15, local router ID is 128.107.9.1
Status codes: s suppressed, d damped, h history, * valid, > best, i - internal,
```

```
                    r RIB-failure, S Stale
Origin codes: i - IGP, e - EGP, ? - incomplete


   Network          Next Hop          Metric LocPrf Weight Path
*> 181.0.0.0/8      1.1.1.1               0           0 1 1811 i
*> 182.0.0.0/8      1.1.1.1               0           0 1 2 1822 i
*  i183.0.0.0/8     10.100.1.2            0    100    0 3 2 50 1833 i
*>                  1.1.1.1               0           0 1 2 50 1833 i
*>i184.0.0.0/8      10.100.1.2            0    100    0 3 2 1844 i
*                   1.1.1.1               0           0 1 2 50 51 1844 i
*>i185.0.0.0/8      10.100.1.2            0    100    0 3 1855 i
*                   1.1.1.1               0           0 1 2 50 51 52 1855 i
```

```
! Next, on router E2
E2# show ip bgp 176.0.0.0/4 longer-prefixes
! legend omitted for brevity


   Network          Next Hop          Metric LocPrf Weight Path
*>i181.0.0.0/8      10.100.1.1            0    100    0 1 1811 i
*                   192.168.1.6           0           0 3 2 50 51 52 1811 i
*>i182.0.0.0/8      10.100.1.1            0    100    0 1 2 1822 i
*                   192.168.1.6           0           0 3 2 50 51 1822 i
*  i183.0.0.0/8     10.100.1.1            0    100    0 1 2 50 1833 i
*>                  192.168.1.6           0           0 3 2 50 1833 i
*> 184.0.0.0/8      192.168.1.6           0           0 3 2 1844 i
*> 185.0.0.0/8      192.168.1.6           0           0 3 1855 i
```

```
! Next, on router Core1
Core1# show ip bgp 176.0.0.0/4 longer-prefixes
! legend omitted for brevity


   Network          Next Hop          Metric LocPrf Weight Path
*>i181.0.0.0/8      10.100.1.1            0    100    0 1 1811 i
*>i182.0.0.0/8      10.100.1.1            0    100    0 1 2 1822 i
*>i183.0.0.0/8      10.100.1.1            0    100    0 1 2 50 1833 i
*  i                10.100.1.2            0    100    0 3 2 50 1833 i
*>i184.0.0.0/8      10.100.1.2            0    100    0 3 2 1844 i
*>i185.0.0.0/8      10.100.1.2            0    100    0 3 1855 i
```

First, pay close attention to the LocPrf column of output in the example. This column lists the Local_Pref settings of each route. Some list a (default) value of 100, and some list nothing. As it turns out, because Updates received from eBGP peers do not include the Local_Pref PA, IOS lists a null value for Local_Pref for eBGP-learned routes by default. However, Updates from iBGP peers do include the Local_Pref. Because this network does not have any configuration that attempts to set Local_Pref yet, the routers advertise their default Local_Pref value of 100 over the iBGP connections.

Also note that when comparing the output on both E1 and E2, the output lists a single eBGP route, but not the alternative iBGP route through the other Internet-connected router in the Enterprise. For example, E2 lists a single route for 184.0.0.0/8 and 185.0.0.0/8, through I3-1 (192.168.1.6). The reason that E2 does not list an alternative route through E1 is that E1's best route for these prefixes, as seen near the top of the example, is E1's iBGP-learned route through E2 (10.100.1.2). BGP does not allow a router to advertise iBGP-learned routes to iBGP peers, so E1 will not advertise routes for 184.0.0.0/8 or 185.0.0.0/8 to router E2.

Finally, For prefix 183.0.0.0/8, both E1 and E2 tie on the As_Path length. In this case, all best path choices tie until Step 7, which prefers eBGP routes over iBGP routes. E1 prefers its eBGP route for 183.0.0.0/8 through ISP1's Router I1-1, and E2 prefers its eBGP route through ISP3's Router I3-1.

Setting the BGP Local_Pref Using a Route Map

To set the Local_Pref, a router can use the **neighbor** *neighbor-ip* **route-map in** BGP sub-command. Typically, a router uses this command with the inbound direction for routes received from eBGP peers. Then, with no additional configuration required, the router then advertises the Local_Pref to any iBGP peers.

To show the Local_Pref configuration and results, start with the sample network shown in the previous section. The configuration will now be changed to set the Local_Pref for two different prefixes for Updates received on E1 from I1-1, as shown in Figure 15-7. Note that the figure reinforces the idea that BGP does not include the Local_Pref PA in eBGP Updates but will in iBGP Updates.

Figure 15-7   *Example Local_Pref Settings for the Upcoming Example*

The figure shows a series of steps, as follows:

Step 1.   I1-1 and I3-1 advertise the prefixes into the Enterprise but with no Local_Pref set because the connections are eBGP peers.

Step 2.   E1 sets the Local_Pref for routes learned from I1-1: 184.0.0.0/8 (50) and 185.0.0.0/8 (150).

Step 3.   E1 includes the Local_Pref settings in its iBGP Updates to Core1, Core2, and E2.

Step 4.   E2 realizes that E1's route for 185.0.0.0/8, Local_Pref 150, is better than E2's eBGP route for this prefix, which E2 assigned default Local_Pref 100. Conversely, E1's advertised route for 184.0.0.0/8, Local_Pref 50, is worse than E2's eBGP route for that same prefix, with assigned default Local_Pref 100.

Example 15-6 shows the configuration on router E1 to assign the Local_Pref values shown in Figure 15-7. The example also shows the results on E1 and E2. Note that the configuration differs only slightly as compared with the configuration for administrative Weight as shown in Example 15-3, the only substantive difference being the **set local-preference** route map command rather than the **set weight** command.

Example 15-6   *Configuring Local_Pref on Router E1 (Step 2 per Figure 15-7)*

```
E1# show running-config
! only pertinent portions shown
ip prefix-list match-184 seq 5 permit 184.0.0.0/8
!
ip prefix-list match-185 seq 5 permit 185.0.0.0/8
!
route-map set-LP-150 permit 10
 match ip address prefix-list match-185
 set local-preference 150
!
route-map set-LP-150 permit 15
 match ip address prefix-list match-184
 set local-preference 50
!
route-map set-LP-150 permit 20
!
router bgp 11
 neighbor 1.1.1.1 route-map set-LP-150 in
! The clearing of BGP neighbor I1-1 is done next, but not shown.
! Next, E1's Updated BGP Table

E1# show ip bgp 176.0.0.0/4 longer-prefixes
BGP table version is 29, local router ID is 128.107.9.1
Status codes: s suppressed, d damped, h history, * valid, > best, i - internal,
              r RIB-failure, S Stale
Origin codes: i - IGP, e - EGP, ? - incomplete

   Network          Next Hop            Metric LocPrf Weight Path
*> 181.0.0.0/8      1.1.1.1                  0             0 1 1811 i
*> 182.0.0.0/8      1.1.1.1                  0             0 1 2 1822 i
```

```
 *  i183.0.0.0/8      10.100.1.2           0     100     0 3 2 50 1833 i
 *>                   1.1.1.1              0             0 1 2 50 1833 i
 *>i184.0.0.0/8       10.100.1.2           0     100     0 3 2 1844 i
 *                    1.1.1.1              0      50     0 1 2 50 51 1844 i
 *>  185.0.0.0/8      1.1.1.1              0     150     0 1 2 50 51 52 1855 i


E1# show ip bgp 185.0.0.0/8
BGP routing table entry for 185.0.0.0/8, version 7
Paths: (1 available, best #1, table Default-IP-Routing-Table)
  Advertised to update-groups:
       1
  1 2 50 51 52 1855, (received & used)
    1.1.1.1 from 1.1.1.1 (1.1.1.1)
      Origin IGP, metric 0, localpref 150, valid, external, best


! The next output occurs on router E2
E2# show ip bgp 185.0.0.0/8 longer-prefixes
! heading lines omitted


  Network          Next Hop          Metric LocPrf Weight Path
 *>i185.0.0.0/8     10.100.1.1            0    150     0 1 2 50 51 52 1855 i
 *                  192.168.1.6           0            0 3 1855 i
```

Example 15-6's output shows E1's BGP table entries, now with updated Local_Pref values as compared with Example 15-5. E1 now uses its eBGP route, Next_Hop 1.1.1.1, for prefix 185.0.0.0/8 because of the higher Local_Pref.

The end of the example shows E2 with two possible routes for 185.0.0.0/8. The following list outlines E2's BGP best path logic in this case:

Step 0.   The two routes both have reachable Next_Hop IP addresses.

Step 1.   Both have Weight 0 (tie).

Step 2.   The iBGP route through 10.100.1.1 (E1) has a bigger (better) Local_Pref (150 versus 100) that the route through 192.168.1.6 (I3-1), so it is the better route.

Also, note that both the **show ip bgp longer-prefixes** command's briefer output, and the **show ip bgp 185.0.0.0/8** commands more verbose output, both identify the Local_Pref value. However, the longer command output does not list the Weight value.

IP Routes Based on BGP Best Paths

Some of the complexity related to BGP occurs around the BGP functions created by BGP PAs, including their use by the best path algorithm. When the BGP best path algorithm has gotten through this complexity and chosen a best route for a prefix, the router then tries to add that route to the IP routing table. However, rather than add the BGP route to the IP routing table directly, BGP actually gives that best BGP route to another process for consideration: The IOS *Routing Table Manager (RTM)*.

The IOS RTM chooses the best route among many competing sources. For example, routes may be learned by an IGP, BGP, or even as connected or static routes. IOS collects the best such route for each prefix and feeds those into the RTM function. The RTM then chooses the best route. Figure 15-8 shows the general idea:

Among its tasks, RTM uses the concept of Administrative Distance (AD) to choose the best route among these different sources. Table 15-6 repeats the list of default AD values as shown earlier in Table 10-6 from Chapter 10, "Advanced IGP Redistribution," but with highlights for the two BGP-related default values:

For the most part, an Enterprise router should not see cases in which a prefix learned with BGP has also been learned as a connected or IGP-learned route. (Conversely, these issues

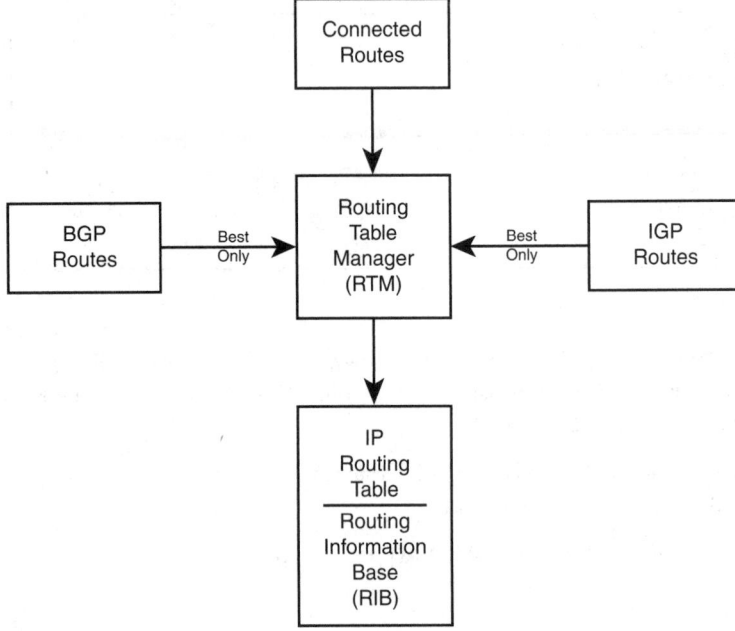

Figure 15-8 *Routing Table Manager Concept*

Table 15-6 *Default Administrative Distances*

Route Type	Administrative Distance
Connected	0
Static	1
EIGRP summary route	5
eBGP	20
EIGRP (internal)	90

Table 15-6   *Default Administrative Distances*

Route Type	Administrative Distance
IGRP	100
OSPF	110
IS-IS	115
RIP	120
On-Demand Routing (ODR)	160
EIGRP (external)	170
iBGP	200
Unreachable	255

occur more often when implementing MPLS VPNs with BGP/IGP redistribution.) However, it can happen, and when it does, the **show ip bgp rib-failures** command can be helpful. This command lists routes for which BGP has chosen the route as best, but the RTM function has not placed the route into the Routing Information Base (RIB), which is simply another name for the IP routing table.

Example of a BGP RIB Failure

To show an example of a RIB failure, imagine that an Enterprise engineer needed to do some testing, so the engineer just picked an IP address range to use. The engineer tries to avoid problems by not using network 10.0.0.0, which is used throughout the Enterprise. So rather than choosing another private network, the engineer then chooses public range 185.0.0.0/8. After changing the lab configuration a few hundred times, a route for 185.0.0.0/8 leaks into the OSPF topology database.

Keep in mind that at the end of the previous example, E1 had chosen its eBGP route for 185.0.0.0/8 as its best route, and E2 had chosen its iBGP route as its best route for 185.0.0.0/8. Example 15-7 shows the results, based on RTM's comparisons of the AD values.

Example 15-7   *Example with the RTM and RIB Failures*

```
! First, E1's IP Routing table for 185.0.0.0/8
E1# show ip route 185.0.0.0 255.0.0.0 longer-prefixes
Codes: C - connected, S - static, R - RIP, M - mobile, B - BGP
       D - EIGRP, EX - EIGRP external, O - OSPF, IA - OSPF inter area
       N1 - OSPF NSSA external type 1, N2 - OSPF NSSA external type 2
       E1 - OSPF external type 1, E2 - OSPF external type 2
       i - IS-IS, su - IS-IS summary, L1 - IS-IS level-1, L2 - IS-IS level-2
       ia - IS-IS inter area, * - candidate default, U - per-user static route
       o - ODR, P - periodic downloaded static route
```

```
Gateway of last resort is 1.1.1.1 to network 0.0.0.0

B     185.0.0.0/8 [20/0] via 1.1.1.1, 00:25:11
! Next, E2's IP Routing table
E2# show ip route 185.0.0.0 255.0.0.0 longer-prefixes
! Legend omitted for brevity

Gateway of last resort is 192.168.1.6 to network 0.0.0.0

O     185.0.0.0/8 [110/2] via 10.1.1.77, 00:15:44, FastEthernet0/0

E2# show ip bgp rib-failure
Network              Next Hop                      RIB-failure      RIB-NH Matches
185.0.0.0/8          10.100.1.1            Higher admin distance          n/a
```

The first command shows that E1, with an eBGP route, actually adds its route to the IP routing table. The route lists a code of B, meaning BGP. The output lists the eBGP default AD of 20, which is a better default AD than OSPF's 110. RTM added this BGP route to the IP routing table on E1 because of eBGP's better AD.

E2 currently lists its iBGP route through E1 as its current best BGP route for 185.0.0.0/8 because of the higher Local_Pref configured in Example 15-6. However, after giving this route to the RTM, RTM instead choose the lower-AD OSPF route (AD 110) rather than the higher-AD iBGP route (AD 200).

Finally, the **show ip bgp rib-failure** command lists one line for each best BGP route that the RTM does not place into the IP routing table. In this case, this command on Router E2 lists the route for 185.0.0.0/8, with the reason listed.

BGP and the maximum-paths Command

Like the IGP protocols, BGP supports the **maximum-paths** *number-of-paths* subcommand, but BGP uses significantly different logic than the IGPs. Unlike the IGP routing protocols, BGP truly needs to pick one route, and only one route, as the best path for a given prefix/length. In effect, the BGP best path algorithm already breaks the ties for "best" route for each prefix, so from BGP's perspective, one route for each prefix is always best.

BGP does allow multiple BGP routes for a prefix to be considered to tie, at least for the purpose of adding multiple routes to the IP routing table. The conditions are as follows:

> If the BGP best path algorithm does not choose a best path by Step 8 (per the numbering in this book), the routes which still tie for being best path through Step 8 will be allowed into the IP routing table, up to the number defined by the BGP **maximum-paths** *number-of-paths* router subcommand.

The section "Overview of the BGP Best Path Algorithm" earlier in this chapter lists the best path steps, including the tiebreaker steps that allow routes to be considered by the **maximum-paths** command.

Increasing the Length of the AS_Path Using AS_Path Prepend

Step 4 of the BGP best path algorithm examines the length of the AS_Path PA. The length of the AS_Path may appear to be obvious: Just add the number of ASNs listed in the AS_Path. However, some BGP features outside the scope of this book actually impact the AS_Path length calculation as well. However, for the purposes of this book, AS_Path length is simply the number of ASNs listed in the AS_Path.

The AS_Path prepend tool gives engineers a means to increase the length of an AS_Path by adding ASNs to the AS_Path, while not impacting the loop prevention role of the AS_Path PA. By increasing the length of an AS_Path, a route is less likely to become the best route. By adding ASNs that already exist inside a particular route's AS_Path, the feature does not inadvertently prevent a route from being ignored due to AS_Path loop prevention.

For example, using the design shown most recently in Figures 15-5, 15-6, and 15-7, imagine that the Enterprise considers ISP1 to be the better ISP, but they do not want to send all traffic through ISP1. So, the Enterprise network engineers could make the following type of implementation choice:

Make the AS_Paths received from ISP3 be 2 ASNs longer.

By making such a choice, when an AS_Path through ISP1 is better, or when it's a tie on AS_Path between ISP1 and ISP3, or when the AS_Path through ISP1 is even slightly longer than through ISP3, the routers can still choose their routes through ISP1. Only when the AS_Path (before prepending) is at least 2 ASNs shorter through ISP3 can the ISP3 path be chosen.

Note: For those of you memorizing using the N WLLA OMNI mnemonic, AS_Path Length is the A in WLLA.

Figure 15-9 shows the mechanics of how an Enterprise route would prepend the AS_Path for routes received by Router E2 from ISP3, namely Router I3-1. Looking specifically at the route for 185.0.0.0/8, in this case, I3-1 has not changed the AS_Path and advertised the route with AS_Path (3, 1855). At Step 2, Router E2 prepends ASN 3–twice–making the AS_Path length 4. At Step 3, E2 advertises the route to its iBGP peers–peers that may now prefer to the other route for this prefix through Router E1.

The configuration itself requires only a little additional work compared to the other examples. As shown in Figure 15-9, Router E1 could use an inbound route map, using the **set as-path prepend 3 3** command to add the two ASNs. (The router sending the Update, ISP3's Router I3-1 in this case, could instead use an outbound route map.) Example 15-8 shows the configuration on E2 to add the ASNs at ingress into E2. (Note that all configuration for changing the Weight and Local_Pref, and the extra OSPF route for 185.0.0.0/8 shown in Example 15-6, have been removed before gathering the output in this example.)

Figure 15-9   *Prepending Two ASNs to an AS_Path*

Example 15-8   *Prepending Additional ASNs to the AS_Path*

```
! First, E2's new configuration
route-map add-two-asns permit 10
 set as-path prepend 3 3
router bgp 11
 neighbor 192.168.1.6 route-map add-two-asns in
!
! Next, note the AS_Path values all start with 3, 3, 3
E2# show ip bgp 176.0.0.0/4 longer-prefixes
BGP table version is 41, local router ID is 10.100.1.2
Status codes: s suppressed, d damped, h history, * valid, > best, i - internal,
              r RIB-failure, S Stale
Origin codes: i - IGP, e - EGP, ? - incomplete


   Network          Next Hop          Metric LocPrf Weight Path
*>i181.0.0.0/8      10.100.1.1             0    100      0 1 1811 i
*                   192.168.1.6            0             0 3 3 3 2 50 51 52 1811 i
*>i182.0.0.0/8      10.100.1.1             0    100      0 1 2 1822 i
*                   192.168.1.6            0             0 3 3 3 2 50 51 1822 i
*>i183.0.0.0/8      10.100.1.1             0    100      0 1 2 50 1833 i
*                   192.168.1.6            0             0 3 3 3 2 50 1833 i
*  i184.0.0.0/8     10.100.1.1             0    100      0 1 2 50 51 1844 i
*>                  192.168.1.6            0             0 3 3 3 2 1844 i
*> 185.0.0.0/8      192.168.1.6            0             0 3 3 3 1855 i
```

Note: When using AS_Path prepending, do not prepend just any ASN. BGP still uses the AS_Path for loop avoidance, so using an ASN already in the AS_Path, like the ASN of the most recently added ASN (for example, ASN 3 in this case), or the local ASN (for example, ASN 11 in this case), makes the most sense.

Although presented here as a tool for influencing outbound routes, As_Path prepending can also be used to influence the inbound routes as well.

Influencing an Enterprise's Inbound Routes with MED

An Enterprise has reasonably good control over its outbound IP routes. The engineers can configure BGP to set and react to Weight, Local_Pref, and AS_Path length, manipulating each to choose a different outgoing link or different router through which to forward packets to the Internet.

An Enterprise has much less control over inbound routes: routes for packets coming back toward the Enterprise. First, these inbound routes exist on routers that the Enterprise does not own. Even if an ISP or set of ISPs can be convinced by engineers at the Enterprise to make their routes toward an Enterprise take a particular path, technical issues may prevent the design from being implemented. In particular, if the Enterprise's public IP address range is summarized, the companies that use addresses in that range may have competing goals, so no policy can be applied to influence the best route.

However, several tools exist that allow some control over the last ASN hop between an ISP and their Enterprise customer. This book examines one such tool, called Multi-Exit Discriminator (MED), originally worked for a dual-homed design—that is, with a single ISP but with multiple links to that ISP. MED was later expanded to support dual-multihomed designs (2+ ASNs, 2+ links), relying on the concept that ISPs would work together. This section examines the dual-homed case, with a single ISP.

MED Concepts

The name Multi Exit Discriminator actually describes its function to a great degree. With a dual-homed design, at least two links exist between the Enterprise and the ISP. The Enterprise can announce to the ISP a value (MED) that tells the ISP which path into the Enterprise is best. As a result, the ISP can discriminate between the multiple exit points from that ISP to the Enterprise.

Because MED lets the Enterprise ASN tell just the neighboring ASN which link into the Enterprise to use, engineers typically use MED when advertising an Enterprise's public IP address space. Those inbound routes into the Enterprise from the ISP typically consist of either one, or a few, public IP address ranges.

For example, consider a new network design as shown in Figure 15-10. In this case, the Enterprise uses the same 128.107.0.0/19 public address range used in Chapters 13 and 14. The Enterprise connects only to ASN 1 with a total of four physical links and three BGP neighbors.

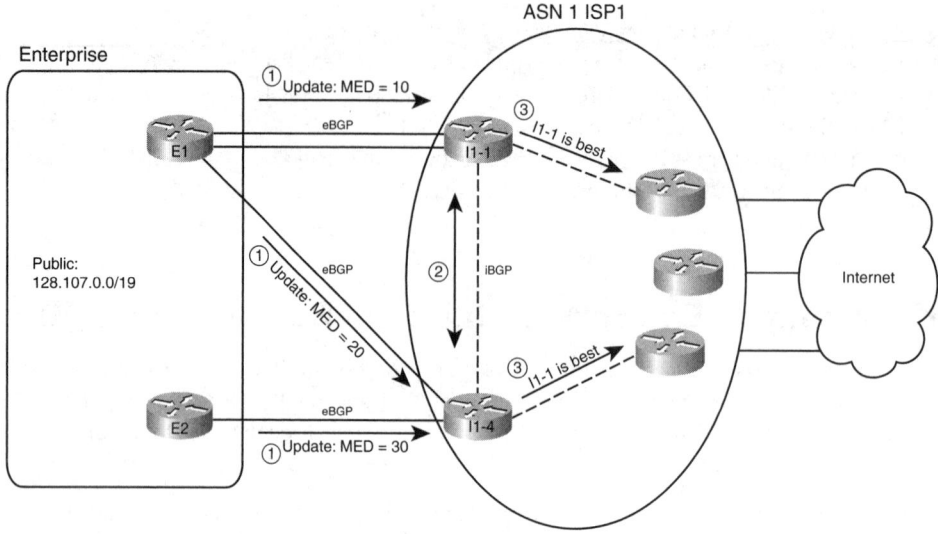

Figure 15-10 *Example of Using MED*

MED uses smallest-is-best logic. As a result, the figure shows a design in which the Enterprise engineer prefers the top BGP neighborship as the best path to use for inbound routes (MED 10), the middle link next (Med 20), and the bottom connection last (MED 30). Following the steps in the figure:

Step 1. E1 and E2 advertise 128.107.0.0/19, setting MED with an outbound route map, to various settings: MED 10 sent by E1 to I1-1, MED 20 sent by E1 to I1-4, and MED 30 sent by E2 to I1-4.

Step 2. I1-1 and I1-4 have an iBGP connection, so they learn each other's routes and agree as to which route wins based on MED.

Step 3. I1-1 and I4-1 also tell the other routers inside ISP1, causing all inbound traffic to funnel toward router I1-1.

Note that Routers I1-1 and I4-1 in this example could have chosen a better route based on all the earlier best path steps. However, a brief analysis of the steps tells us that unless someone makes an effort to override the effects of MED, these routers' best path algorithms will use MED. Assuming the Enterprise and ISP agree to rely on MED, the earlier Best Path steps should not matter. Here's why:

Step 1. **Weight:** Needs to be set locally, so if relying on MED, the ISP simply chooses to not set the Weight for received Updates from the Enterprise.

Step 2. **Local_Pref:** Again, this takes overt effort to match and set the Local_Pref, so if relying on MED, the ISP simply chooses to not set the Local_Pref.

Step 3. **Locally injected?** All these public routes from the Enterprise will be learned with eBGP and not locally injected.

Step 4. **AS_Path length:** All such routes on the ISP routers should list one ASN—the Enterprise's ASN—so all should tie on this point.

Step 5.   Origin: Whatever the Origin is (I or ?), it should tie.

Step 6.   MED: None of the other steps determined the best route, so now MED takes effect.

Table 15-7 summarizes the key points about MED.

Table 15-7   *Key Features of MED*

Key
Topic

Feature	Description
Is it a PA?	Yes.
Purpose	Allows an AS to tell a neighboring AS the best way to forward packets into the first AS.
Scope	Advertised by one AS into another, propagated inside the AS, but not sent to any other autonomous systems.
Range	0 through 4,294,967,295 ($2^{32} - 1$).
Which is best?	Smaller is better.
Default	0
Configuration	Via **neighbor route-map out** command, using the **set metric** command inside the route map.

Note: For those of you memorizing using the N WLLA OMNI mnemonic, MED is the M in OMNI.

MED Configuration

MED configuration usually occurs on the routers in the AS that wants to control inbound routes from the neighboring AS. As such, in the example design shown in Figure 15-10, Routers E1 and E2 would configure MED. Example 15-9 shows E1's configuration.

Example 15-9   *MED Configuration on Router E1*

```
route-map set-med-to-I1-1 permit 10
 match ip address prefix only-public
 set metric 10
!
route-map set-med-to-I1-4 permit 10
 match ip address prefix only-public
 set metric 20
!
ip prefix-list only-public permit 128.107.0.0/19
!
```

```
router bgp 11
  neighbor 1.1.1.1 route-map set-med-I1-1 out
  neighbor 192.168.1.2 route-map set-med-I1-4 out
```

Both the configuration and the **show ip bgp** command output refers to MED as metric. Note that the route map in Example 15-8 uses the **set metric** command, rather than **set med** (which does not exist). And as shown in I1-1's output for the **show ip bgp** command in Example 15-10, the output lists MED under the heading metric. In particular, note that even the **show ip route** command lists the MED value in brackets as the metric for the BGP route.

Example 15-10   *BGP Table and IP Routing Table on Router I1-1*

```
I1-1# show ip bgp 128.107.0.0/19
BGP routing table entry for 128.107.0.0/19, version 13
Paths: (1 available, best #1, table Default-IP-Routing-Table)
Flag: 0x820
  Not advertised to any peer
  11, (aggregated by 11 128.107.9.1), (received & used)
    11.11.11.11 from 11.11.11.11 (128.107.9.1)
      Origin IGP, metric 10, localpref 100, valid, external, atomic-aggregate, best


I1-1# sh ip bgp 128.107.0.0/19 longer-prefixes
BGP table version is 13, local router ID is 1.1.1.1
Status codes: s suppressed, d damped, h history, * valid, > best, i - internal,
              r RIB-failure, S Stale
Origin codes: i - IGP, e - EGP, ? - incomplete


   Network          Next Hop            Metric LocPrf Weight Path
*> 128.107.0.0/19   11.11.11.11             10           0 11 i


I1-1# show ip route 128.107.0.0 255.255.224.0 longer-prefixes
! Legend omitted for brevity

Gateway of last resort is not set

     128.107.0.0/19 is subnetted, 1 subnets
B      128.107.0.0 [20/10] via 11.11.11.11, 00:02:18
```

Exam Preparation Tasks

Planning Practice

The CCNP ROUTE exam expects test takers to review design documents, create implementation plans, and create verification plans. This section provides some exercises that may help you to take a step back from the minute details of the topics in this chapter so that you can think about the same technical topics from the planning perspective.

For each planning practice table, simply complete the table. Note that any numbers in parentheses represent the number of options listed for each item in the solutions in Appendix F.

Design Review Table

Table 15-8 lists several design goals related to this chapter. If these design goals were listed in a design document, and you had to take that document and develop an implementation plan, what implementation options come to mind? You should write a general description; specific configuration commands are not required.

Table 15-8 *Design Review*

Design Goal	Possible Implementation Choices Covered in This Chapter
Influence outbound route from an Enterprise toward prefixes in the Internet (3).	
Influence outbound route from an Enterprise toward prefixes in the Internet so that multiple Internet-connected Enterprise routers make the same choice based on the same information (2).	
Influence inbound routes into the Enterprise from the neighboring AS (2).	

Implementation Plan Peer Review Table

Table 15-9 shows a list of questions that others might ask, or that you might think about, during a peer review of another network engineer's implementation plan. Complete the table by answering the questions.

Table 15-9   *Notable Questions from This Chapter to Consider During an Implementation Plan Peer Review*

Question	Answers
A plan shows two Enterprise routers, R1 and R2, connected to two different ISPs, with iBGP between R1 and R2. The plan shows R1 setting Weight for routes learned from an ISP. Will R2 react to those settings? Why or why not?	
A plan shows two Enterprise routers, R1 and R2, connected to two different ISPs, with iBGP between R1 and R2. The plan shows R1 setting Local_Pref for routes learned from an ISP. Will R2 react to those settings? Why or why not?	
The Plan calls for the use of BGP Weight, but the incomplete plan lists no configuration yet. What configuration alternatives exist? (2)	
The Plan calls for the use of BGP Local Preference, but the incomplete plan lists no configuration yet. What configuration alternatives exist?	
A plan shows two Enterprise routers, R1 and R2, connected to different ISPs. The plan calls for using MED to influence inbound routes. Which configuration options exist?	
A plan shows the use of BGP Weight, Local Preference, AS_Path prepending, and MED to influence the best path algorithm. Which of these can be set and advertised to eBGP peers?	

Create an Implementation Plan Table

This chapter does not focus on implementation or verification, but it did review one concept about static routes, as listed in Table 15-10.

Table 15-10   *Implementation Plan Configuration Memory Drill*

Feature	Configuration Commands/Notes
Configure a route map that sets Weight.	
Enable a route map to set BGP weight.	
Enable a router to set BGP weight for all routes received from a neighbor.	
Configure a route map that sets BGP Local Preference.	
Enable a route map to set BGP Local Preference.	
Configure a route map that prepends ASNs to an AS_Path.	
Enable a route map to perform AS_Path prepending.	
Configure a route map that sets MED.	
Enable a route map to set MED.	

Choose Commands for a Verification Plan Table

To practice skills useful when creating your own BGP verification plan, list in Table 15-11 all commands that supply the requested information. You may want to record your answers outside the book and set a goal to complete this table (and others like it) from memory during your final reviews before taking the exam.

Table 15-11   *Verification Plan Memory Drill*

Information Needed	Commands
Display the BGP table, including the chosen best path for each prefix. (State how to identify the best paths.)	
List 1 line per BGP route but for the prefixes within a range.	
Identify a BGP table entry's BGP Weight. (Specify where to find output.)	
Identify a BGP table entry's BGP Local Preference. (Specify where to find output.)	
Identify a BGP table entry's AS_Path length. (Specify where to find output.)	
Identify a BGP table entry's MED. (Specify where to find output.) (4 methods)	
Display routes received from a neighbor before being processed by an inbound filter.	
The same as the previous item but after applying the inbound filter.	
Display BGP routes sent to a neighbor but after applying the inbound filter.	
Display BGP best paths that were not added to the IP routing table.	

Note: Some of the entries in this table may not have been specifically mentioned in this chapter but are listed in this table for review and reference.

Review all the Key Topics

Review the most important topics from inside the chapter, noted with the Key Topics icon in the outer margin of the page. Table 15-12 lists a reference of these key topics and the page numbers on which each is found.

Table 15-12 *Key Topics for Chapter 15*

Key Topic Element	Description	Page Number
Table 15-2	BGP path attributes that affect the BGP Best Path algorithm	495
Figure 15-1	Figure showing the location of BGP PA information in the output of **show ip bgp**	496
Table 15-3	Summary of BGP Best Path algorithm	496
List	Four items commonly set for the purpose of influencing the BGP best path decision	498
Table 15-4	Reference Table for BGP Weight	500
Table 15-5	Reference Table for BGP Local_Pref	507
Figure 15-7	Example of how Local_Pref influences best path choice	511
Figure 15-9	Example of how AS_Path Prepending works	518
Table 15-7	Reference Table for BGP MED	521

Complete the Tables and Lists from Memory

Print a copy of Appendix D, "Memory Tables," (found on the CD), or at least the section for this chapter, and complete the tables and lists from memory. Appendix E, "Memory Tables Answer Key," also on the CD, includes completed tables and lists to check your work.

Define Key Terms

Define the following key terms from this chapter, and check your answers in the glossary.

BGP Weight, Local Preference, AS_Path Prepending, Multi Exit Discriminator, Best Path algorithm, Routing Table Manager, RIB Failure, path attribute

This chapter covers the following subjects:

Global Unicast Addressing, Routing, and Subnetting: This section introduces the concepts behind unicast IPv6 addresses, IPv6 routing, and how to subnet using IPv6, all in comparison to IPv4.

IPv6 Global Unicast Address Assignment: This section examines how global unicast addresses can be assigned to hosts and other devices.

Survey of IPv6 Addressing: This section examines all types of IPv6 addresses.

Configuring IPv6 Addresses on Cisco Routers: This section shows how to configure and verify static IPv6 addresses on Cisco routers.

CHAPTER 16

IP Version 6 Addressing

IP Version 6 (IPv6), the replacement protocol for IPv4, is well known for a couple of reasons. IPv6 provides the ultimate solution for the problem of running out of IPv4 addresses in the global Internet by using a 128-bit address–approximately 10^{38} total addresses, versus the mere (approximate) $4* 10^9$ total addresses in IPv4. However, many articles over the years have discussed when, if ever, would a mass migration to IPv6 take place. IPv6 has been the ultimate long-term solution for more than 10 years, in part because the interim IPv4 solutions, including NAT/PAT, have thankfully delayed the day in which we truly run out of public unicast IP addresses.

As more IPv6 deployments continue to emerge, Cisco has steadily added more and more IPv6 content to its certification exams. CCNA now includes basic IPv6 concepts and configuration, with this version of the CCNP ROUTE exam examining IPv6 to greater depth than its predecessor BSCI exam. In particular, ROUTE includes the basic concepts, configuration, and verification of most of the router-based tools needed to deploy IPv6 in the Enterprise. As with most of the other topics, ROUTE's coverage of IPv6 does not include all skills and knowledge to plan an Enterprise IPv6 deployment, but it does include enough to take an IPv6 design plan and make a good start on developing an IPv6 implementation and verification plan.

Part VI of this book includes three chapters. This chapter examines the concepts around IPv6 addressing, and how to configure and verify those addresses on Cisco routers. Chapter 17, "IPv6 Routing Protocols and Redistribution," looks at IPv6 routing protocols, as well as route redistribution and static routing. Both these chapters focus on pure IPv6, essentially ignoring issues related to migration from IPv4 and coexistence with IPv4. The final chapter in this part, Chapter 18, "IPv4 and IPv6 Coexistence," looks at the migration and coexistence issues.

"Do I Know This Already?" Quiz

The "Do I Know This Already?" quiz allows you to assess if you should read the entire chapter. If you miss no more than one of these eight self-assessment questions, you might want to move ahead to the "Exam Preparation Tasks." Table 16-1 lists the major headings in this chapter and the "Do I Know This Already?" quiz questions covering the material in those headings so you can assess your knowledge of these specific areas. The answers to the "Do I Know This Already?" quiz appear in Appendix A.

Table 16-1   *"Do I Know This Already?" Foundation Topics Section-to-Question Mapping*

Foundations Topics Section	Questions
Global Unicast Addressing, Routing, and Subnetting	1–2
IPv6 Global Unicast Address Assignment	3–4
Survey of IPv6 Addressing	5–6
Configuring IPv6 Addresses on Cisco Routers	7–8

1. Which of the following is the shortest valid abbreviation for FE80:0000:0000:0000:0010:0000:0000:0123?

   a. FE80::10::123

   b. FE8::1::123

   c. FE80:0:0:0:10::123

   d. FE80::10:0:0:123

2. An ISP has assigned prefix 3000:1234:5678::/48 to Company1. Which of the following terms would typically be used to describe this type of public IPv6 prefix?

   a. Subnet prefix

   b. ISP prefix

   c. Global routing prefix

   d. Registry prefix

3. Which of the following answers lists either a protocol or function that can be used by a host to dynamically learn its own IPv6 address? (Choose two.)

   a. Stateful DHCP

   b. Stateless DHCP

   c. Stateless autoconfiguration

   d. Neighbor Discovery Protocol

4. Which of the following is helpful to allow an IPv6 host to learn the IP address of a default gateway on its subnet?

   a. Stateful DHCP

   b. Stateless RS

   c. Stateless autoconfiguration

   d. Neighbor Discovery Protocol

5. Which of the following answers lists a multicast IPv6 address?

   a. 2000::1:1234:5678:9ABC

   b. FD80::1:1234:5678:9ABC

    c. FE80::1:1234:5678:9ABC

    d. FF80::1:1234:5678:9ABC

6. Router R1 has two LAN interfaces and three serial interfaces enabled for IPv6. All the interfaces use link local addresses automatically generated by the router. Which of the following could be the link local address of R1's interface S0/0?

    a. FEA0::200:FF:FE11:0

    b. FE80::200:FF:FE11:1111

    c. FE80::0213:19FF:FE7B:0:1

    d. FEB0::211:11FF:FE11:1111

7. Router R1 has the following configuration. Assuming R1's F0/0 interface has a MAC address of 0200.0011.1111, what IPv6 addresses will R1 list for interface F0/0 in the output of the **show ipv6 interface brief** command?

```
interface f0/0
 ipv6 address 2345:0:0:8::1/64
```

    a. 2345:0:0:8::1

    b. 2345:0:0:8:0:FF:FE11:1111

    c. FE80::8:0:FF:FE11:1111

    d. FE80:0:0:8::1

8. Router R1 lists the following output from a **show** command. Which of the following is true about R1?

```
R1# show ipv6 interface f0/0
FastEthernet0/0 is up, line protocol is up
  IPv6 is enabled, link-local address is FE80::213:19FF:FE12:3456
  No Virtual link-local address(es):
  Global unicast address(es):
    2000::4:213:19FF:FE12:3456, subnet is 2000:0:0:4::/64 [EUI]
  Joined group address(es):
    FF02::1
    FF02::2
    FF02::1:FF:12:3456
```

    a. R1's solicited node multicast address is FF02::1:FF:12:3456.

    b. R1's 2000::4:213:19FF:FE12:3456 address is a global unicast with all 128 bits statically configured.

    c. Address FF02::2 is R1's solicited node multicast.

    d. R1's solicited node multicast, not listed in this output, would be FF02::213:19FF:FE12:3456.

Foundation Topics

The world has changed tremendously over the last 10–20 years as a result of the growth and maturation of the Internet and networking technologies in general. As recently as 1990, a majority of the general public did not know about nor use global networks to communicate, and when businesses needed to communicate, those communications mostly flowed over private networks. During the 1990s, the public Internet grew to the point where people in most parts of the world could connect to the Internet; many companies connected to the Internet for a variety of applications, with the predominate applications being email and web. During the first decade of the 21st century, the Internet has grown further to billions of addressable devices with the majority of people on the planet having some form of Internet access. With that pervasive access came a wide range of applications and uses, including voice, video, collaboration, and social networking, with a generation that has grown up with this easily accessed global network.

The eventual migration to IPv6 will likely be driven by the need for more and more IP addresses. Practically every mobile phone supports Internet traffic, requiring the use of an IP address. Most new cars have the capability to acquire and use an IP address, along with wireless communications, allowing the car dealer to contact the customer when the car's diagnostics detect a problem with the car. Some manufacturers have embraced the idea that all their appliances need to be IP-enabled.

Although the two biggest reasons why networks might migrate from IPv4 to IPv6 are the need for more addresses and mandates from government organizations, at least IPv6 includes some attractive features and migration tools. Some of those advantages are

- **Address assignment features:** IPv6 supports a couple of methods for dynamic address assignment, including DHCP and Stateless Autoconfiguration.

- **Built-in support for address renumbering:** IPv6 supports the ability to change the public IPv6 prefix used for all addresses in an Enterprise, using the capability to advertise the current prefix with a short timeout and the new prefix with a longer lease life.

- **Built-in support for mobility:** IPv6 supports mobility such that IPv6 hosts can move around the Internetwork and retain their IPv6 address without losing current application sessions.

- **Provider independent and dependent public address space:** ISPs can assign public IPv6 address ranges (dependent), or companies can register their own public address space (independent).

- **Aggregation:** IPv6's huge address space makes for much easier aggregation of blocks of addresses in the Internet, making routing in the Internet more efficient.

- **No need for NAT/PAT:** The huge public IPv6 address space removes the need for NAT/PAT, which avoids some NAT-induced application problems and makes for more efficient routing.

- **IPsec:** Unlike IPv4, IPv6 requires that every IPv6 implementation support IPsec. IPv6 does not require that each device use IPsec, but any device that implements IPv6 must also have the ability to implement IPsec.

- **Header improvements:** Although it might seem like a small issue, the IPv6 header actually improves several things compared to IPv4. In particular, routers do not need to recalculate a header checksum for every packet, reducing per-packet overhead. Additionally, the header includes a flow label that allows for easy identification of packets sent over the same single TCP or UDP connection.

- **No broadcasts:** IPv6 does not use Layer 3 broadcast addresses, instead relying on multicasts to reach multiple hosts with a single packet.

- **Transition tools:** As covered in Chapter 18, the IPv6 has many rich tools to help with the transition from IPv4 to IPv6.

This list includes many legitimate advantages of IPv6 over IPv4, but the core difference, and the main topic of this chapter, is IPv6 addressing. The first two section of this chapter examine one particular type of IPv6 addresses, global unicast addresses, which have many similarities to IPv4 addresses–particularly public IPv4 addresses. The third section broadens the discussion to include all types of IPv6 addresses, and protocols related to IPv6 address assignment, default router discovery, and neighbor discovery. The final section looks at the router configuration commands for IPv6 addressing.

Global Unicast Addressing, Routing, and Subnetting

The original Internet design called for all organizations to register and be assigned one or more public IP networks (Class A, B, or C). By registering to use a particular public network number, the company or organization using that network was assured by the numbering authorities that no other company or organization in the world would be using the same addresses. As a result, all hosts in the world would have globally unique IP addresses.

From the perspective of the Internet infrastructure, in particular the goal of keeping Internet routers' routing tables from getting too large, assigning an entire network to each organization helped to some degree. The Internet routers could ignore all subnets as defined inside an Enterprise, instead having a route for each classful network. For instance, if a company registered and was assigned Class B network 128.107.0.0/16, the Internet routers just needed one route for that whole network.

Over time, the Internet grew tremendously. It became clear by the early 1990s that something had to be done, or the growth of the Internet would grind to a halt when all the public IP networks were assigned, and no more existed. Additionally, the IP routing tables in Internet routers were becoming too large for the router technology of that day. So, the Internet community worked together to come up with both some short-term and long-term solutions to two problems: the shortage of public addresses and the size of the routing tables.

The short-term solutions included a much smarter public address assignment policy, in which public addresses were not assigned as only Class A, B, and C networks, but as smaller subdivisions (prefixes), reducing waste. Additionally, the growth of the Internet routing tables was reduced by smarter assignment of the actual address ranges based on geography. For example, assigning the class C networks that begin with 198 to only a particular ISP in a particular part of the world allowed other ISPs to use one route for 198.0.0.0/8–in other words, all addresses that begin with 198–rather than a route for each of the 65,536 different Class C networks that begin with 198. Finally, NAT/PAT achieved amazing results by allowing a typical home or small office to consume only one public IPv4 address, greatly reducing the need for public IPv4 addresses.

IPv6 provides the long-term solution to both problems (address exhaustion and Internet routing table size). The sheer size of IPv6 addresses takes care of the address exhaustion issue. The address assignment policies already used with IPv4 have been refined and applied to IPv6, with good results for keeping the size of IPv6 routing tables smaller in Internet routers. This section provides a general discussion of both issues, in particular how *global unicast* addresses, along with good administrative choices for how to assign IPv6 address prefixes, aid in routing in the global Internet. This section concludes with a discussion of subnetting in IPv6.

Global Route Aggregation for Efficient Routing

By the time the Internet community started serious work to find a solution to the growth problems in the Internet, many people already agreed that a more thoughtful public address assignment policy for the public IPv4 address space could help keep Internet routing tables much smaller and more manageable. IPv6 public address assignment follows these same well-earned lessons.

Note: The descriptions of IPv6 global address assignment in this section provides a general idea about the process. The process may vary from one RIR to another, and one ISP to another, based on many other factors.

The address assignment strategy for IPv6 is elegant, but simple, and can be roughly summarized as follows:

- Public IPv6 addresses are grouped (numerically) by major geographic region.

- Inside each region, the address space is further subdivided by ISPs inside that region.

- Inside each ISP in a region, the address space is further subdivided for each customer.

The same organizations handle this address assignment for IPv6 as for IPv4. The Internet Corporation for Assigned Network Numbers (ICANN, www.icann.org) owns the process, with the Internet Assigned Numbers Authority (IANA) managing the process. IANA assigns one or more IPv6 address ranges to each Regional Internet Registries (RIR), of which there are five at the time of publication, roughly covering North America, Central/South America, Europe, Asia/Pacific, and Africa. These RIRs then subdivide their assigned address space into smaller portions, assigning prefixes to different ISPs and other smaller registries, with the ISPs then assigning even smaller ranges of addresses to their customers.

The IPv6 global address assignment plan results in more efficient routing, as shown in Figure 16-1. The figure shows a fictitious company (Company1) which has been assigned an IPv6 prefix by a fictitious ISP, NA-ISP1 (meaning for North American ISP number 1). The figure lists the American Registry for Internet Numbers (ARIN), which is the RIR for North America.

Figure 16-1   *Conceptual View of IPv6 Global Routes*

Key
Topic

As shown in the figure, the routers installed by ISPs in other major geographies of the world can have a single route that matches all IPv6 addresses in North America. Although there might be hundreds of ISPs operating in north America, and hundreds of thousands of Enterprise customers of those ISPs, and tens of millions of individual customers of those ISPs, all the public IPv6 addresses can be from one (or a few) very large address blocks–requiring only one (or a few) routes on the Internet routers in other parts of the world. Similarly, routers inside other ISPs in North America (for example, NA-ISP2, meaning North American ISP number 2 in the figure), can have one route that matches all address ranges assigned to NA-ISP2. And the routers inside NA-ISP1 just need to have one route that matches the entire address range assigned to Company1, rather than needing to know about all the subnets inside Company1.

Besides keeping the routers' routing table much smaller, this process also results in fewer changes to Internet routing tables. For example, if NA-ISP1 signed a service contract with another Enterprise customer, NA-ISP1 could assign another prefix inside the range of addresses already assigned to NA-ISP1 by ARIN. The routers outside NA-ISP1's network–the majority of the Internet–do not need to know any new routes, because their existing routes already match the address range assigned to the new customer. The NA-ISP2 routers (another ISP) already have a route that matches the entire address range assigned to NA-ISP1, so they do not need any more routes. Likewise, the routers in ISPs in Europe and South America already have a route that works as well.

Conventions for Representing IPv6 Addresses

IPv6 conventions use 32 hexadecimal numbers, organized into 8 quartets of 4 hex digits separated by a colon, to represent a 128-bit IPv6 address, for example:

2340:1111:AAAA:0001:1234:5678:9ABC

Each hex digit represents 4 bits, so if you want to examine the address in binary, the conversion is relatively easy if you memorize the values shown in Table 16-2.

Table 16-2 *Hexadecimal/Binary Conversion Chart*

Hex	Binary	Hex	Binary
0	0000	8	1000
1	0001	9	1001
2	0010	10	1010
3	0011	11	1011
4	0100	12	1100
5	0101	13	1101
6	0110	14	1110
7	0111	15	1111

Writing or typing 32 hexadecimal digits, although more convenient writing or typing 128 binary digits, can still be a pain. To make things a little easier, two conventions allow you to shorten what must be typed for an IPv6 address:

- Omit the leading 0s in any given quartet.

- Represent one or more consecutive quartets of all hex 0s with "::" but only for one such occurrence in a given address.

Note: For IPv6, a quartet is one set of 4 hex digits in an IPv6 address. There are 8 quartets in each IPv6 address.

For example, consider the following address. The bold digits represent digits in which the address could be abbreviated.

FE00:**0000:0000:0001:0000:0000:0000:00**56

This address has two different locations in which one or more quartets have 4 hex 0s, so two main options exist for abbreviating this address–using the :: abbreviation in one or the other location. The following two options show the two briefest valid abbreviations:

FE00::1:0:0:0:56

FE00:0:0:1::56

In particular, note that the "::" abbreviation, meaning "one or more quartets of all 0s," cannot be used twice because that would be ambiguous. So, the abbreviation FE00::1::56 would not be valid.

Conventions for Writing IPv6 Prefixes

IPv6 prefixes represent a range or block of consecutive IPv6 addresses. Just like routers use IPv4 subnets in IPv4 routing tables to represent ranges of consecutive addresses, routers use IPv6 prefixes to represent ranges of consecutive IPv6 addresses as well. The concepts mirror those of IPv4 addressing when using a classless view of the IPv4 address. Figure 16-2 reviews both the classful and classless view of IPv4 addresses, compared to the IPv6 view of addressing and prefixes.

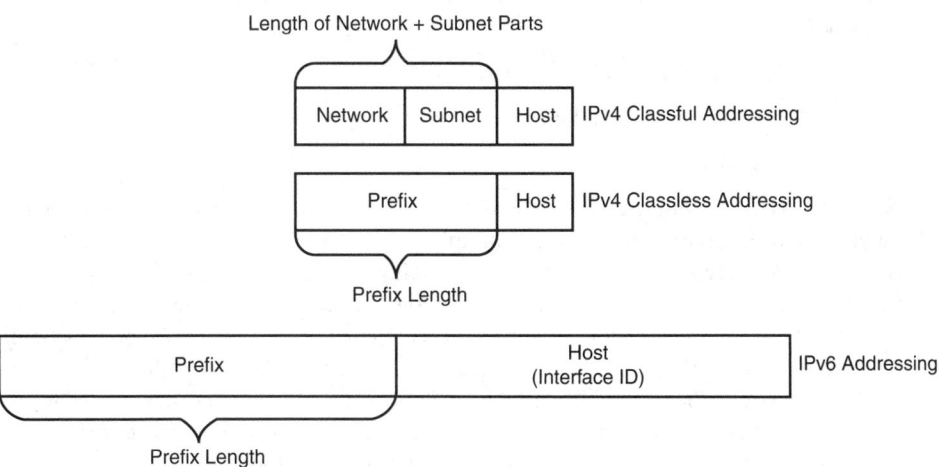

Figure 16-2 *IPv4 Classless and Classful Addressing, IPv6 Addressing*

First, for perspective, compare the classful and classless view of IPv4 addresses. Classful IPv4 addressing means that the class rules always identify part of the address as the network part. For example, the written value 128.107.3.0/24 (or 128.107.3.0 255.255.255.0) means 16 network bits (because the address is in a class B network), 8 host bits (because the mask has 8 binary 0s), leaving 8 subnet bits. The same value, interpreted with classless rules, means prefix 128.107.3.0, prefix length 24. Classless addressing and classful addressing just give slightly different meaning to the same numbers.

IPv6 uses a classless view of addressing, with no concept of classful addressing. Like IPv4, IPv6 prefixes list some prefix value, a slash, and then a numeric prefix length. Like IPv4 prefixes, the last part of the number, beyond the length of the prefix, will be represented by binary 0's. And finally, IPv6 prefix numbers can be abbreviated with the same rules as IPv4 addresses.

Note: IPv6 prefixes are often called IPv6 subnets as well. This book uses these terms interchangeably.

For example, consider the following IPv6 address that is assigned to a host on a LAN:

2000:1234:5678:9ABC:1234:5678:9ABC:1111/64

This value represents the full 128-bit IP address–there are no opportunities to even abbreviate this address. However, the /64 means that the prefix (subnet) in which this address resides is the subnet that includes all addresses that begin with the same first 64 bits as the address. Conceptually, it is the same logic as an IPv4 address, for example, address 128.107.3.1/24 is in the prefix (subnet) whose first 24 bits are the same values as address 128.107.3.1.

As with IPv4, when writing or typing a prefix, the bits past the end of the prefix length are all binary 0s. In the IPv6 address previously shown, the prefix in which the address resides would be

2000:1234:5678:9ABC:0000:0000:0000:0000/64

Which, when abbreviated, would be

2000:1234:5678:9ABC::/64

Next, one last fact about the rules for writing prefixes before seeing some examples and moving on. If the prefix length is not a multiple of 16, then the boundary between the prefix and the interface ID (host) part of the address is inside a quartet. In such cases, the prefix value should list all the values in the last octet in the prefix part of the value. For example, if the address just shown with a /64 prefix length instead had a /56 prefix length, the prefix would include all of the first 3 quartets (a total of 48 bits), plus the first 8 bits of the fourth quartet. The next 8 bits (last 2 hex digits) of the fourth octet should now be binary 0s, as part of the host portion of the address. So, by convention, the rest of the fourth octet should be written, after being set to binary 0s, as follows:

2000:1234:5678:9A00::/56

The following list summarizes some key points about how to write IPv6 prefixes.

- The prefix has the same value as the IP addresses in the group for the number of bits in the prefix length.

- Any bits after the prefix length number of bits are binary 0s.

- The prefix can be abbreviated with the same rules as IPv6 addresses.

- If the prefix length is not on a quartet boundary, write down the value for the entire quartet.

Examples can certainly help in this case. Table 16-3 shows several sample prefixes, their format, and a brief explanation.

Table 16-3   *Example IPv6 Prefixes and Their Meanings*

Prefix	Explanation	Incorrect Alternative
2000::/3	All addresses whose first 3 bits are equal to the first 3 bits of hex number 2000 (bits are 001).	2000/3 (omits ::) 2::/3 (omits the trailing 0s in the first quartet)
2340:1140::/26	All addresses whose first 26 bits match the listed hex number.	2340:114::/26 (omits trailing 0 in the second quartet)
2340:1111::/32	All addresses whose first 32 bits match the listed hex number.	2340:1111/32 (omits ::)

Note which options are not allowed. For example, 2::/3 is not allowed instead of 2000::/3, because it omits the rest of the octet, and a device could not tell if 2::/3 means "hex 0002" or "hex 2000".

Now that you understand a few of the conventions about how to represent IPv6 addresses and prefixes, a specific example can show how IANA's IPv6 global unicast IP address assignment strategy can allow the easy and efficient routing shown in Figure 16-1.

Global Unicast Prefix Assignment Example

IPv6 standards reserve the range of addresses inside the 2000::/3 prefix as global unicast addresses. This address range includes all IPv6 addresses that begin with binary 001, or as more easily recognized, all IPv6 addresses that begin with a 2 or 3. IANA assigns global unicast IPv6 addresses as public and globally unique IPv6 addresses, as discussed using the example previously shown in Figure 16-1, allowing hosts using those addresses to communicate through the Internet without the need for NAT. In other words, these addresses fit the purest design for how to implement IPv6 for the global Internet.

Figure 16-3 shows an example set of prefixes that could result in a company (Company1) being assigned a prefix of 2340:1111:AAAA::/48.

The process starts with IANA, who owns the entire IPv6 address space and assigns the rights to *registry prefix* to one of the RIRs (ARIN in this case, in North America). For the purposes of this chapter, assume that IANA assigns prefix 2340::/12 to ARIN. This assignment means that ARIN has the rights to assign any IPv6 addresses that begin with the first 12 bits of hex 2340 (binary value 0010 0011 0100). For perspective, that's a large group of addresses: 2^{116} to be exact.

Next, NA-ISP1 asks ARIN for a prefix assignment. After ARIN ensures that NA-ISP1 meets some requirements, ARIN might assign *site prefix* 2340:1111::/32 to NA-ISP1. This too is a large group: 2^{96} addresses to be exact. For perspective, this one address block may

Company1 Owns
2340:1111:AAAA/48

Assigns
2340:1111:AAAA/48

NA-ISP1Owns
2340:1111/32

Assigns
2340:1111/32

Assigns 2340::/12

ARIN (RIR)
Owns 2340::/12

IANA

Key Topic

Figure 16-3 *Example IPv6 Prefix Assignment in the Internet*

well be enough public IPv6 addresses for even the largest ISPs, without that ISP ever needing another IPv6 prefix.

Finally, Company1 asks its ISP, NA-ISP1, for the assignment of an IPv6 prefix. NA-ISP1 assigns Company1 the site prefix 2340:1111:AAAA::/48, which is again a large range of addresses: 2^{80} in this case. A little later in this section the text shows what Company1 could do with that prefix, but first, examine Figure 16-4, which presents the same concepts as in Figure 16-1, but now with the actual prefixes shown.

The figure shows the perspectives of routers outside North America, routers from another ISP in North America, and other routers in the same ISP. Routers outside North America can use a route for prefix 2340::/12, knowing the IANA assigned this prefix to be used only by ARIN. This one route could match all IPv6 addresses assigned in North America. Routers in NA-ISP2, an example alternative ISP in North America, need one route for 2340:1111::/32, the prefix assigned to NA-ISP1. This one route could match all packets destined for all customers of NA-ISP1. Inside NA-ISP1, its routers need to know to which NA-ISP1 router to forward packets to for that particular customer (named ISP-1 in this case), so the routes inside NA-ISP1's routers lists a prefix of 2340:1111:AAAA::/48.

Figure 16-4 *IPv6 Global Routing Concepts*

Note: The /48 prefix assigned to a single company is called either a *global routing prefix* or a *site prefix*.

Subnetting Global Unicast IPv6 Addresses Inside an Enterprise

The original IPv4 Internet design called for each organization to be assigned a classful network number, with the Enterprise subdividing the network into smaller address ranges by subnetting the classful network. This same concept of subnetting carries over from IPv4 to IPv6, with the Enterprise subnetting its assigned global unicast prefix into smaller prefixes.

To better understand the IPv6 subnetting, you can draw on either classful or classless IPv4 addressing concepts, whichever you find most comfortable. From a classless perspective, you can view the IPv6 addresses as follows:

■ The prefix assigned to the Enterprise by the ISP (the global routing prefix) acts like the prefix assigned for IPv4.

Key
Topic

■ The Enterprise engineer extends the prefix length, borrowing host bits, to create a subnet part of the address with which to identify individual subnets.

■ The remaining part of the addresses on the right, called either the interface ID or host part, works just like the IPv4 host part, uniquely identifying a host inside a subnet.

For example, Figure 16-5 shows a more detailed view of the Company1 Enterprise network shown in several of the previous figures in this chapter. The design concepts behind how many subnets are needed with IPv6 are identical as with IPv4–a subnet is needed for each VLAN, and for each serial link, with the same options for subnets with Frame Relay. In this case, two LANs and two serial links exist, so Company1 needs four subnets.

Figure 16-5 *Company1–Needs Four Subnets*

The figure also shows how the Enterprise engineer extended the length of the prefix as assigned by the ISP (/48) to /64, thereby creating a 16-bit subnet part of the address structure. To create this extra 16-bit subnet field, the engineer uses the same concept as with IPv4 when choosing a subnet mask by borrowing bits from the host field of an IPv4 address. In this case, think of the original host field (before subnetting) as having 80 bits, because the site prefix is 48-bits long, leaving 80 bits. The design in Figure 16-5 borrows 16 bits for the subnet field, leaving a measly 64 bits for the host field.

A bit of math about the design choices can help provide some perspective on the scale of IPv6. The 16-bit subnet field allows for 2^{16}, or 65,536, subnets–overkill for all but the very largest organizations or companies. (There are no worries about a zero or broadcast subnet in IPv6!) The host field is seemingly even more overkill: 2^{64} hosts per subnet, which is more than 1,000,000,000,000,000,000 addresses per subnet. However, there is a good reason for this large host or interface ID part of the address because it allows one of the automatic IPv6 address assignment features to work well, as covered later in the section "Assigning IPv6 Global Unicast IP Addresses."

Figure 16-6 takes the concept to the conclusion, assigning the specific four subnets to be used inside Company1. Note that the figure shows the subnet fields and prefix lengths (64 in this case) in bold.

Note: The subnet numbers in Figure 16-6 could be abbreviated slightly, removing the three leading 0s from the last shown quartets. The figure includes the leading 0s to show the entire subnet part of the prefixes.

Figure 16-6 *Company1–4 Subnets Assigned*

Figure 16-6 just shows one option for subnetting the prefix assigned to Company1. However, any number of subnet bits could be chosen if the host field retained enough bits to number all hosts in a subnet. For example, a /112 prefix length could be used, extending the /48 prefix by 64 bits (4 hex quartets). Then, for the design in Figure 16-6, you could choose the following four subnets:

2340:1111:AAAA::0001:0000/112

2340:1111:AAAA::0002:0000/112

2340:1111:AAAA::0003:0000/112

2340:1111:AAAA::0004:0000/112

By using global unicast IPv6 addresses, Internet routing can be very efficient; Enterprises can have plenty of IP addresses and plenty of subnets with no requirement for NAT functions to conserve the address space.

Prefix Terminology

Before wrapping up this section, a few new terms need to be introduced. The process of global unicast IPv6 address assignment examines many different prefixes with many different prefix lengths. The text scatters a couple of more specific terms, but for easier study, Table 16-4 summarizes the four key terms with some reminders of what each means.

Table 16-4 *Example IPv6 Prefixes and Their Meanings*

Term	Assignment	Example from Chapter 16
Registry prefix	By IANA to an RIR	2340::/12
ISP prefix	By an RIR to an ISP[1]	2340:1111/32
Site prefix or global routing prefix	By an ISP or registry to a customer (site)	2340:1111:AAAA/48
Subnet prefix	By an Enterprise engineer for each individual link	2340:1111:AAAA:0001/64

[1]Although an RIR can assign a prefix to an ISP, an RIR may also assign a prefix to other Internet registries, which might subdivide and assign additional prefixes, until eventually an ISP and then their customers are assigned some unique prefix.

Assigning IPv6 Global Unicast Addresses

This section still focuses on global unicast IPv6 addresses but now examines the topic of how a host, router interface, or other device knows what global unicast IPv6 address to use. Also, hosts (and sometimes routers) also need to know a few other facts that can be learned at the same time as learning their IPv6 address. So, this section also discusses how hosts can get all the following relevant information that lets them use their global unicast addresses:

- IP address

- IP subnet mask (prefix length)

- Default router IP address

- DNS IP address(es)

IPv6 actually has four major options for IPv6 global unicast address assignment. This section looks at these options in the same order as listed in Table 16-5. Each method can use dynamic processes or static configuration, and each method can differ in terms of how a host or router gathers the other pertinent information (such as DNS IP addresses). Table 16-5 summarizes these main methods for easier review.

Table 16-5 *Summary of IPv6 Address Assignment for Global Unicast Addresses*

Method	Dynamic or static	Prefix and length learned from...	Host learned from...	Default router learned from...	DNS addresses learned from...
Stateful DHCP	Dynamic	DHCP Server	DHCP Server	Router, using NDP	(Stateful) DHCP Server
Stateless autoconfig	Dynamic	Router, using NDP	Derived from MAC	Router, using NDP	Stateless DHCP
Static configuration	Static	Local config	Local config	Router, using NDP	Stateless DHCP
Static config with EUI-64	Static	Local config	Derived from MAC	Router, using NDP	Stateless DHCP

The rest of this section develops more detail about the topics in the table. Some of the processes work much like IPv4, and some do not. Regardless, as you work through the material, keep in mind one key fact about how IPv6 protocols approach the address assignment process:

IPv6 address assignment processes may split the IPv6 address assignment into two parts: the prefix/length assignment and the host (interface ID) assignment.

Stateful DHCP for IPv6

IPv6 hosts can use stateful DHCP to learn and lease an IP address and corresponding prefix length (mask), the IP address of the default router, and the DNS IP address(es). The concept works basically like DHCP for IPv4; the host sends a (multicast) packet searching for the DHCP server. When a server replies, the DHCP client sends a message asking for a lease of an IP address, and the server replies, listing an IPv6 address, prefix length, and DNS IP addresses. (Note that Stateful DHCPv6 does not supply the default router information, instead relying on Neighbor Discovery Protocol between the client and local routers.) The names and formats of the actual DHCP messages have changed quite a bit from IPv4 to IPv6, so DHCPv4 and DHCPv6 actually differ in detail, but the basic process remains the same. (The term DHCPv4 refers to the version of DHCP used for IPv4, and the term DHCPv6 refers to the version of DHCP used for IPv6.)

DHCPv4 servers retain *state information* about each client, such as the IP address leased to that client, and the length of time for which the lease is valid. In other words, DHCPv4 tracks the current state of DHCP clients. DHCPv6 servers happen to have two operational modes: stateful, in which the server does track state information, and stateless, in which the server does not track any state information. Stateful DHCPv6 servers fill the same role as the older DHCPv4 servers, whereas stateless DHCPv6 servers fill a different purpose as one part of the stateless autoconfiguration process. (Stateless DHCP, and its purpose, is covered in the upcoming section "Finding the DNS IP Addresses Using Stateless DHCP.")

One difference between DHCPv4 and stateful DHCPv6 is that IPv4 hosts send IP broadcasts to find DHCP servers, whereas IPv6 hosts send IPv6 multicasts. IPv6 multicast addresses have a prefix of FF00::/8, meaning that if the first 8 bits of an address are binary 11111111, or FF in hex. The multicast address FF02::1:2 (longhand FF02:0000:0000:0000:0000:0000:0001:0002) has been reserved in IPv6 to be used by hosts to send packets to an unknown DHCP server, with the routers working to forward these packets to the appropriate DHCP server.

Stateless Autoconfiguration

The second of the two options for dynamic IPv6 address assignment uses a built-in IPv6 feature called *stateless autoconfiguration* as the core tool. Stateless autoconfiguration allows a host to automatically learn the key pieces of addressing information–prefix, host, and prefix length–plus the default router IP address and DNS IP addresses. To learn or derive all these pieces of information, stateless autoconfiguration actually uses the following functions:

Step 1.   IPv6 Neighbor Discovery Protocol (NDP), particularly the router solicitation and router advertisement messages, to learn the prefix, prefix length, and default router

Step 2.   Some math to derive the interface ID (host ID) portion of the IPv6 address, using a format called EUI-64

Step 3.   Stateless DHCP to learn the DNS IPv6 addresses

This section examines all three topics in order.

Learning the Prefix/Length and Default Router with NDP Router Advertisements

The IPv6 Neighbor Discovery Protocol (NDP) has many functions. One function allows IPv6 hosts to multicast a message that asks all routers on the link to announce two key pieces of information: the IPv6 addresses of routers willing to act as a default gateway and all known IPv6 prefixes on the link. This process uses ICMPv6 messages called a Router Solicitation (RS) and a Router Advertisement (RA).

For this process to work, before a host sends an RS message on a LAN, some router connected to that same LAN must already be configured for IPv6. The router must have an IPv6 address configured, and it must be configured to route IPv6 traffic. At that point, the router knows it can be useful as a default gateway, and it knows at least one prefix that can be useful to any clients on the LAN.

For example, Figure 16-7 shows a subset of the internetwork seen in Figures 16-5 and 16-6, with the same IPv6 addresses and subnets used. Router R1's Fa0/0 has already been configured with an IPv6 address (2340:1111:AAAA:1:213:19FF:FE7B:5004/64) and has been configured to route IPv6 with the **ipv6 unicast-routing** global command.

Figure 16-7   *Example NDP RS/RA Process to Find the Default Routers*

In the figure, host PC1, using stateless autoconfig, sends the RS message as an IPv6 multicast message destined to all IPv6 routers on the local link. The RS asks all routers to respond to the questions "What IPv6 prefix(s) is used on this subnet?" and "What is the IPv6 address(s) of any default routers on this subnet?" The figure also shows R1's response (RS), listing the prefix (2340:1111:AAAA:1::/64), and with R1's own IPv6 address as a potential default router.

Note: IPv6 allows for multiple prefixes and multiple default routers to be listed in the RA message; Figure 16-7 just shows one of each for simplicity's sake. One router's RA would include IPv6 addresses and prefixes advertised by other routers on the link as well.

IPv6 does not use broadcasts. In fact, there is no such thing as a subnet broadcast address, a networkwide broadcast address, or an equivalent of the all-hosts 255.255.255.255 broadcast IPv4 address. Instead, IPv6 makes use of multicast addresses. By defining a different multicast IPv6 address for different functions, an IPv6 host that has no need to participate in a particular function can simply ignore those particular multicasts, reducing the impact to the host.

For example, the RS message needs to be received and processed only by routers, so the RS message's destination IP address is FF02::2, which IPv6 reserves for use only by IPv6 routers. IPv6 defines that routers send RA messages to a multicast address intended for use by all IPv6 hosts on the link (FF02::1); routers do not forward these messages to other links. As a result, not only does the host that sent the RS message learn the information, all other hosts on the link learn the details as well. Table 16-6 summarizes some of the key details about the RS/RA messages.

Table 16-6   *Details of the RS/RA Process*

Message	RS	RA
Multicast destination	FF02::2	FF02::1
Meaning of Multicast address	All routers on this link	All IPv6 nodes on this link

Calculating the Interface ID Using EUI-64

Earlier in the chapter, Figure 16-5 shows the format of an IPv6 global unicast address with the second half of the address called the host ID or interface ID. The value of the interface ID portion of a global unicast address can be set to any value if no other host in the same subnet attempts to use the same value.

To automatically create a guaranteed-unique interface ID, IPv6 defines a method to calculate a 64-bit interface ID derived from that host's MAC address. Because the burned-in MAC address should be literally globally unique, the derived interface ID should also be globally unique as well.

The EUI-64 process takes the 6-byte (48-bit) MAC address and expands it into a 64-bit value. To do so, IPv6 fills in 2 more bytes into the middle of the MAC address. IPv6 separates the original MAC address into two 3-byte halves and inserts hex FFFE in between the halves to form the Interface ID field of the IPv6 address. The conversion also requires flipping the seventh bit inside the IPv6 address, resulting in a 64-bit number that conforms to a convention called the EUI-64 format. The process is shown in Figure 16-8.

Although it may seem a bit convoluted, it works. Also, with a little practice, you can look at an IPv6 address and quickly notice the FFFE late in the address and then easily find the two halves of the corresponding interface's MAC address.

Figure 16-8 *IPv6 Address Format with Interface ID and EUI-64*

For example, the following two lines list a host's MAC address, and corresponding EUI-64 format Interface ID, assuming the use of an address configuration option that uses the EUI-64 format:

0034:5678:9ABC

0234:56FF:FE78:9ABC

Note: To change the seventh bit (left-to-right) in the example, hex 00 converts to binary 00000000, change the seventh bit to 1 (00000010), convert back to hex, for hex 02 as the first two digits.

At this point in the stateless autoconfig process, a host knows its full IPv6 address and prefix length, plus a local router to use as default gateway. The next section discusses how to complete the process using stateless DHCP.

Finding the DNS IP Addresses Using Stateless DHCP

Although the DHCP server function for IPv4 does not explicitly use the word "stateful" in its name, IPv4 DHCP servers keep state information about DHCP clients. The server keeps a record of the leased IP addresses, and when the lease expires. The server typically re-leases the addresses to the same client before the lease expires, and if no response is heard from a DHCP client in time to renew the lease, the server releases that IP address back into the pool of usable IP addresses–again keeping that state information. The server also has configuration of the subnets in uses and a pool of addresses in most subnets from which the server can assign IP addresses. It also serves other information, such as the default router IP addresses in each subnet, and the DNS server IP addresses.

The IPv6 stateful DHCP server, as previously discussed in the section "Stateful DHCP for IPv6", follows the same general idea. However, for IPv6, this server's name includes the word stateful, to contrast it with the stateless DHCP server function in IPv6.

The stateless DHCP server function in IPv6 solves one particular problem: It supplies the DNS server IPv6 address(es) to clients. Because all hosts typically use the same small number of DNS servers, the stateless DHCP server does not need to keep track of any state information. An engineer simply configures the stateless DHCP server to know the IPv6 addresses of the DNS servers, and the servers tells any host or other device that asks, keeping no record of the process.

Hosts that use stateless autoconfig also use stateless DHCP to learn the DNS server IPv6 addresses.

Table 16-7 summarizes some of the key features of stateful and stateless DHCPv6.

Table 16-7 *Comparing Stateless and Stateful DHCPv6 Services*

Key Topic

Feature	Stateful DHCP	Stateless DHCP
Remembers IPv6 address (state information) of clients that make requests	Yes	No
Assigns IPv6 address to client	Yes	No
Supplies useful information, such as DNS server IP addresses	Yes	Yes
Most useful in conjunction with stateless autoconfiguration	No	Yes

Static IPv6 Address Configuration

Two options exist for static configuration of IPv6 addresses. For one option, you configure the entire 128-bit IPv6 address, and for the other, you just configure the 64-bit prefix and tell the device to use an EUI-64 calculation for the interface ID portion of the address. Both options result in the host or router interface knowing its full 128-bit IPv6 address and prefix length.

When a host uses either form of static IPv6 address configuration, the host does not need to statically configure the other key pieces of information (default router and DNS IP addresses). The host can use the usual NDP process to discover any default routers and stateless DHCP to discover the DNS IPv6 addresses.

When a router uses static IPv6 address configuration, it may still use stateless DHCP to learn the DNS IP addresses. The upcoming section "Configuring IPv6 Addresses on Cisco Routers" shows several examples of this configuration.

Survey of IPv6 Addressing

So far, this chapter has focused on the IPv6 addresses that most closely match the concept of IPv4 addresses: the global unicast IPv6 address. This section now takes a broader look at IPv6 addressing, including some concepts that can be tied to older IPv4 concepts, and some that are unique to IPv6.

This section begins with a brief overview of IPv6 addressing. It then looks at unicast IPv6 addresses, along with a brief look at some of the commonly used multicast addresses. This section ends with a discussion of a couple of related protocols, namely Neighbor Discovery Protocol (NDP) and Duplicate Address Detection (DAD).

Overview of IPv6 Addressing

The whole concept of global unicast addressing does have many similarities as compared with IPv4. If viewing IPv4 addresses from a classless perspective, both IPv4 and IPv6 global unicast addresses have two parts: subnet plus host for IPv4 and prefix plus interface ID for IPv6. The format of the addresses commonly list a slash followed by the prefix length–a convention sometimes referred to as *CIDR notation*, and other times as *prefix notation*. Subnetting works much the same, with a public prefix assigned by some numbering authority, and the Enterprise choosing subnet numbers, extending the length of the prefix to make room to number the subnets.

IPv6 addressing, however, includes several other types of unicast IPv6 addresses beside the global unicast address. Additionally, IPv6 defines other general categories of addresses, as summarized in this list.

- **Unicast:** Like IPv4, hosts and routers assign these IP addresses to a single interface for the purpose of allowing that one host or interface to send and receive IP packets.

- **Multicast:** Like IPv4, these addresses represent a dynamic group of hosts, allowing a host to send one packet that is then delivered to every host in the multicast group. IPv6 defines some special-purpose multicast addresses for overhead functions (such as NDP). IPv6 also defines ranges of multicast addresses for application use.

- **Anycast:** This address type allows the implementation of a nearest server among duplicate servers concept. This design choice allows servers that support the exact same function to use the exact same unicast IP address. The routers then forward a packet destined for such an address to the nearest server that is using the address.

Two big differences exist when comparing general address categories for IPv4 and IPv6. First, IPv6 adds the formal concept of Anycast IPv6 addresses as shown in the preceding list. IPv4 does not formally define an Anycast IP address concept, although a similar concept may be implemented in practice. Second, IPv6 simply has no Layer 3 broadcast addresses. For example, all IPv6 routing protocols send Updates either to Unicast or Multicast IPv6 addresses, and overhead protocols such as NDP make use of multicasts as well. In IPv4, ARP still uses broadcasts, and older routing protocols such as RIP-1 also used broadcasts. With IPv6, there is no need to calculate a subnet broadcast address (hoorah!) and no need to make hosts process overhead broadcast packets meant only for a few devices in a subnet.

Finally, note that IPv6 hosts and router interfaces typically have at least two IPv6 addresses and may well have more. Hosts and routers typically have a Link Local type of IPv6 address (as described in the upcoming section "Link Local Unicast Addresses"). A router may or may not have a global unicast address, and may well have multiple. IPv6 simply allows the configuration of multiple IPv6 addresses with no need for or concept of secondary IP addressing.

Unicast IPv6 Addresses

IPv6 supports three main types of unicast addresses: link local, global unicast, and unique local. This section takes a brief look at link local and unique local addresses.

Unique Local IPv6 Addresses

Unique local unicast IPv6 addresses have the same function as IPv4 RFC 1918 private addresses. RFC 4193 states that these addresses should be used inside a private organization, and should not be advertised into the Internet. Unique local unicast addresses begin with hex FD (FD00::/8), with the format shown in Figure 16-9.

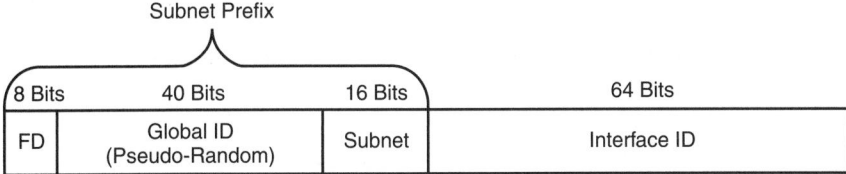

Figure 16-9 *Unique Local Address Format*

To use these addresses, an Enterprise engineer would choose a 40-bit global ID in a pseudo-random manner rather than asking for a registered public prefix from an ISP or other registry. To form the complete prefix, the chosen 40 bits would be combined with the initial required 8 bits (hex FD) to form a 48-bit site prefix. The engineer can then use a 16-bit subnet field to create subnets, leaving a 64-bit Interface ID. The interface ID could be created by static configuration or by the EUI-64 calculation.

This type of unicast address gives the engineer the ability to create the equivalent of an IPv4 private address structure, but given the huge number of available public IPv6 addresses, it may be more likely that engineers plan to use global unicast IP addresses throughout an Enterprise.

Link Local Unicast Addresses

IPv6 uses link local addresses for sending and receiving IPv6 packets on a single subnet. Many such uses exist; here's just a small sample:

- Used as the source address for RS and RA messages for router discovery (as previously shown in Figure 16-7)

- Used by Neighbor discovery (the equivalent of ARP for IPv6)

- As the next-hop IPv6 address for IP routes

By definition, routers use a link local scope for packets sent to a link local IPv6 address. The term *link local* scope means exactly that–the packet should not leave the local link, or local subnet if you will. When a router receives a packet destined for such a destination address, the router does not forward the packet.

The link local IPv6 addresses also help solve some chicken-and-egg problems because each host, router interface, or other device can calculate its own link local IPv6 address without needing to communicate with any other device. So, before sending the first packets, the host can calculate its own link local address, so the host has an IPv6 address to use when doing its first overhead messages. For example, before a host sends an NDP RS (router solicitation) message, the host will have already calculated its link local address, which can be used as the source IPv6 address on the RS message.

Link local addresses come from the FE80::/10 range, meaning the first 10 bits must be 1111 1110 10. An easier range to remember is that all hex link local addresses begin FE8, FE9, FEA, or FEB. However, practically speaking, for link local addresses formed automatically by a host (rather than through static configuration), the address always starts FE80, because the automatic process sets bits 11-64 to binary 0s. Figure 16-10 shows the format of the link local address format under the assumption that the host or router is deriving its own link local address, therefore using 54 binary 0s after the FE80::/10 prefix.

10 Bits	54 Bits	64 Bits
FE80/10 1111111010	All 0s	Interface ID

Figure 16-10 *Link Local Address Format*

IPv6 Unicast Address Summary

You may come across a few other types of IPv6 addresses in other reading. For example, earlier IPv6 RFCs defined the Site Local address type, which was meant to be used like IPv4 private addresses. However, this address type has been deprecated (RFC 3879). Also, the IPv6 migration and coexistence tools discussed in Chapter 18 use some conventions for IPv6 unicast addresses such that IPv4 addresses are imbedded in the IPv6 address.

Additionally, it is helpful to know about other special unicast addresses. An address of all hex 0s, written ::/128, represents an unknown address. This can be used as a source IPv6 address in packets when a host has no suitable IPv6 address to use. The address ::1/128, representing an address of all hex 0s except a final hex digit 1, is a loopback address. Packets sent to this address will be looped back up the TCP/IP stack, allowing for easier software testing. (This is the equivalent of IPv4's 127.0.0.1 loopback address.)

Table 16-8 summarizes the IPv6 unicast address types for easier study.

Table 16-8 *Common Link-Local Multicast Addresses*

Type of Address	Purpose	Prefix	Easily Seen Hex Prefix(es)
Global unicast	Unicast packets sent through the public Internet	2000::/3	2 or 3
Unique local	Unicast packets inside one organization	FD00::/8	FD

Table 16-8 *Common Link-Local Multicast Addresses*

Type of Address	Purpose	Prefix	Easily Seen Hex Prefix(es)
Link local	Packets sent in the local subnet	FE80::/10	FE8
Site local	Deprecated; originally meant to be used like private IPv4 addresses	FECO::/10	FEC, FED, FEE, FEF
Unspecified	An address used when a host has no usable IPv6 address	::/128	N/A
Loopback	Used for software testing, like IPv4's 127.0.0.1	::1/128	N/A

IPv6 RFCs define the FE80::/10 prefix, which technically means that the first three hex digits could be FE8, FE9, FEA, or FEB. However, bit positions 11-64 of link local addresses should be 0, so in practice, link local addresses should always begin with FE80.

Multicast and Other Special IPv6 Addresses

IPv6 supports multicasts on behalf of applications and multicasts to support the inner workings of IPv6. To aid this process, IPv6 defines ranges of IPv6 addresses and an associated scope, with the scope defining how far away from the source of the packet that the network should forward a multicast.

All IPv6 multicast addresses begin with FF::/8 – in other words, with FF as the first two digits. Multicasts with a link local scope, like most of the multicast addresses referenced in this chapter, begin with FF02::/16; the 2 in the fourth hex digit identifies the scope as link local. A fourth digit of hex 5 identifies the broadcast as site local scope, with those multicasts beginning with FF05::/16.

For reference, Table 16-9 lists some of the more commonly seen IPv6 multicast addresses. Of particular interest are the addresses chosen for use by RIP, OSPF, and EIGRP, which somewhat mirror the multicast addresses each protocol uses for IPv4. Note also that all but the last two entries have link local scope.

Table 16-9 *Common Multicast Addresses*

Purpose	IPv6 Address	IPv4 Equivalent
All IPv6 nodes on the link	FF02::1	subnet broadcast address

All IPv6 routers on the link	FF02::2	N/A
OSPF messages	FF02::5, FF02::6	224.0.0.5, 224.0.0.6
RIP-2 messages	FF02::9	224.0.0.9
EIGRP messages	FF02::A	224.0.0.10
DHCP relay agents (routers that forward to the DHCP server)	FF02:1:2	N/A
DHCP servers (site scope)	FF05::1:3	N/A
All NTP servers (site scope)	FF05::101	N/A

Layer 2 Addressing Mapping and Duplicate Address Detection

As with IPv4, any device running IPv6 needs to determine the data link layer address used by devices on the same link. IPv4 uses Address Resolution Protocol (ARP) on LANs and Inverse ARP (InARP) on Frame Relay. IPv6 defines a couple of new protocols that perform the same function. These new functions use ICMPv6 messages and avoid the use of broadcasts, in keeping with IPv6's avoidance of broadcasts. This section gives a brief explanation of each protocol.

Neighbor Discovery Protocol for Layer 2 Mapping

When an IPv6 host or router needs to send a packet to another host or router on the same LAN, the host/router first looks in its neighbor database. This database contains a list of all neighboring IPv6 addresses (addresses in connected links) and their corresponding MAC addresses. If not found, the host or router uses the Neighbor Discovery Protocol (NDP) to dynamically discover the MAC address.

Figure 16-11 shows a sample of such a process, using the same host and router seen earlier in Figure 16-8.

The process acts like the IPv4 ARP process, just with different details. In this case, PC1 sends a multicast message called a Neighbor Solicitation (NS) ICMP message, asking R1 to reply with R1's MAC address. R1 sends a Neighbor Advertisement (NA) ICMP message, unicast back to PC1, listing B's MAC address. Now PC1 can build a data link frame with R1's MAC listed as the destination address and send encapsulated packets to R1.

The NS message uses a special multicast destination address called a *solicited node multicast* address. On any given link, the solicited node multicast address represents all hosts with the same last 24 bits of their IPv6 addresses. By sending packets to the solicited node multicast address, the packet reaches the correct host, but it may also reach a few other hosts–which is fine. (Note that packets sent to a solicited node multicast address have a link local scope.)

The solicited node multicast address begins with FF02::1:FF:0/104. The final 24 bits (6 hex digits) of the address is formed by adding the last 24 bits of the IPv6 address to which the message is being sent. This convention allows convenient use of LAN multicast addresses, which begin with hex 01005E hex, followed by one additional binary 0, and then an addi-

Figure 16-11 *Neighbor Discovery Protocol*

tional 23 bits–in this case taken from the low order 23 bits of the IPv6 address. All IPv6 listen for frames sent to their own solicited node multicast address, so that when a host or router receives such a multicast, the host can realize that it should reply. For example, in this case, based on R1's IPv6 address previously seen in Figure 16-8:

■ R1's IPv6 address: 2340:1111:AAAA:1:213:19FF:FE7B:5004

■ R1's solicited node address: FF02::1:FF:7B:5004

Note: The corresponding Ethernet multicast MAC address would be 0100.5E7B.5004.

Duplicate Address Detection (DAD)

When an IPv6 interface first learns an IPv6 address, or when the interface begins working after being down for any reason, the interface performs duplicate address detection (DAD). The purpose of this check is to prevent hosts from creating problems by trying to use the same IPv6 address already used by some other host on the link.

To perform such a function, the interface uses the same NS message shown in Figure 16-11 but with small changes. To check its own IPv6 address, a host sends the NS message to the solicited node multicast address based on its own IPv6 address. If some host sends a reply, listing the same IPv6 address as the source address, the original host has found that a duplicate address exists.

Inverse Neighbor Discovery

The ND protocol discussed in this section starts with a known neighbor's IPv6 address and seeks to discover the link layer address used by that IPv6 address. On Frame Relay networks, and with some other WAN data link protocols, the order of discovery is reversed. A router begins with knowledge of the neighbor's link layer address and instead needs to dynamically learn the IPv6 address used by that neighbor.

IPv4 solves this discovery problem on LANs using ARP, and the reverse problem over Frame Relay using Inverse ARP (InARP). IPv6 solves the problem on LANs using ND, and now for Frame Relay, IPv6 solves this problem using Inverse Neighbor Discovery (IND). IND, also part of the ICMPv6 protocol suite, defines an Inverse NS (INS) and Inverse NA (INA) message. The INS message lists the known neighbor link layer address (DLCI for Frame Relay), and the INS asks for that neighboring device's IPv6 addresses. The details inside the INS message include the following:

■   Source IPv6: IPv6 unicast of sender

■   Destination IPv6: FF02::1 (all IPv6 hosts multicast)

■   Link layer addresses

■   Request: Please reply with your IPv6 address(es)

The IND reply lists all the IPv6 addresses. As with IPv4, the **show frame-relay map** command lists the mapping learned from this process.

Configuring IPv6 Addresses on Cisco Routers

Most IPv6 implementation plans make use of both static IPv6 address configuration and dynamic configuration options. As is the case with IPv4, the plan assigns infrastructure devices with static addresses, with client hosts using one of the two dynamic methods for address assignment.

IPv6 addressing includes many more options than IPv4, and as a result, many more configuration options exist. A router interface can be configured with a static global unicast IPv6 address, either with or without using the EUI-64 option. Although less likely, a router could be configured to dynamically learn its IPv6 address with either stateful DHCP or stateless autoconfig. The router interface could be configured to either not use a global unicast address, instead relying solely on its link local address, or to borrow another interface's address using the IPv6 unnumbered feature.

This section summarizes the address configuration commands and shows several examples of configuration and verification commands for IPv6. To that end, Table 16-10 summarizes the IPv6 configuration commands and their meanings.

Table 16-10   *Router IOS IPv6 Configuration Command Reference*

Command	Description
ipv6 address *address/length*	Static configuration of the entire IPv6 unicast address.
ipv6 address *prefix/length* **eui-64**	Static configuration of the first 64 address bits; the router derives the last 64 bits with EUI-64.

ipv6 address autoconfig	Router uses stateless autoconfig to find address.
ipv6 address dhcp	Router uses stateful DHCP to find address.
ipv6 unnumbered *interface-type number*	Uses the same IPv6 unicast address as the referenced interface.
ipv6 enable	Enables IPv6 on the interface, but results in only a link local address.
ipv6 address *address* link-local	Overrides the automatically created link local address. The configured value must conform to the FE80::/10 prefix.
ipv6 address *address/length* anycast	Designates that the unicast address is an anycast.

Note: All the interface subcommands in Table 16-10 enable IPv6 on the interface, which means the router derives an IPv6 link local address for the interface. The description shows what the command does in addition to enabling IPv6.

Configuring Static IPv6 Addresses on Routers

The configuration examples in this section use the internetwork shown in Figure 16-12. The figure shows a diagram you might see in an implementation plan, with the five IPv6 subnet numbers shown over the five links. The interface ID of each interface is then abbreviated, or shown as eui-64, as a reminder of whether to configure the whole 128-bit address or to rely on the EUI-64 feature.

Figure 16-12 *Sample IPv6 Address Planning Diagram*

Example 16-1 shows the configuration process on Router R2, which uses EUI-64 on two interfaces, and a complete IPv6 address on another. Also, note that the configuration includes the **ipv6 unicast-routing** global configuration command, which enables the router to route IPv6 traffic. (The addresses can be configured without also configuring **ipv6 unicast-routing**, but without this command, the router acts more like an IPv6 host, and it will not forward IPv6 packets until this command has been configured.)

Example 16-1   *R2's IPv6 Configuration*

```
R2# show running-config
! lines omitted for brevity

interface FastEthernet0/0
 ipv6 address 2000:0:0:4::/64 eui-64
!
interface FastEthernet0/1
 ipv6 address 2000:0:0:2::2/64
!
interface Serial0/0/1
 ipv6 address 2000:0:0:1::/64 eui-64
!
!
R2# show ipv6 interface brief
FastEthernet0/0            [up/up]
    FE80::213:19FF:FE7B:5004
    2000::4:213:19FF:FE7B:5004
FastEthernet0/1            [up/up]
    FE80::213:19FF:FE7B:5005
    2000:0:0:2::2
Serial0/0/0               [administratively down/down]
    unassigned
Serial0/0/1               [up/up]
    FE80::213:19FF:FE7B:5004
    2000::1:213:19FF:FE7B:5004
Serial0/1/0               [administratively down/down]
    unassigned
Serial0/1/1               [administratively down/down]
    unassigned

R2# show interfaces fa0/0

FastEthernet0/0 is up, line protocol is up
  Hardware is Gt96k FE, address is 0013.197b.5004 (bia 0013.197b.5004)
  MTU 1500 bytes, BW 100000 Kbit/sec, DLY 100 usec,
     reliability 255/255, txload 1/255, rxload 1/255
! lines omitted for brevity
```

The **ipv6 address** commands both enable IPv6 on the associated interfaces and define either the prefix (with the **eui-64** option) or the entire address. The **show** commands listed after the configuration confirm the IPv6 addresses. Of particular note

■   All three interfaces now have link local addresses that begin FE80.

■   F0/1 has the address exactly as configured.

- S0/0/1 and F0/0 have the configured prefixes (2000:0:0:1 and 2000:0:0:4, respectively), but with EUI-64 derived interface-IDs.

- S0/0/1 uses Fa0/0's MAC address (as shown in the **show interfaces f0/0** command) when forming its EUI-64.

On this last point, whenever IOS needs a MAC address for an interface, and that interface does not have a built-in MAC address, the router uses the MAC address of the lowest-numbered LAN interface on the router–in this case, F0/0. The following list shows the derivation of the last 64 bits (16 digits) of R2's IPv6 interface IDs for its global unicast IPv6 addresses on F0/0 and S0/0/1:

Step 1.   Use F0/0's MAC Address: 0013.197B.5004.

Step 2.   Split and insert FFFE: 0013:19FF:FE7B:5004.

Step 3.   Invert bit 7: Hex 00 = 00000000 binary, flip for 00000010, and convert back to hex 02, resulting in 0213:19FF:FE7B:5004.

Multicast Groups Joined by IPv6 Router Interfaces

Next, consider the deeper information held in the **show ipv6 interface f0/0** command on Router R2, as shown in Example 16-2. Not only does it list the same link local and global unicast addresses, but it lists other special addresses as well.

Example 16-2   *All IPv6 Addresses on an Interface*

```
R2# show ipv6 interface f0/0
FastEthernet0/0 is up, line protocol is up
  IPv6 is enabled, link-local address is FE80::213:19FF:FE7B:5004
  No Virtual link-local address(es):
  Global unicast address(es):
    2000::4:213:19FF:FE7B:5004, subnet is 2000:0:0:4::/64 [EUI]
  Joined group address(es):
    FF02::1
    FF02::2
    FF02::1:FF7B:5004
  MTU is 1500 bytes
  ICMP error messages limited to one every 100 milliseconds
  ICMP redirects are enabled
  ICMP unreachables are sent
  ND DAD is enabled, number of DAD attempts: 1
  ND reachable time is 30000 milliseconds (using 22807)
  ND advertised reachable time is 0 (unspecified)
  ND advertised retransmit interval is 0 (unspecified)
  ND router advertisements are sent every 200 seconds
  ND router advertisements live for 1800 seconds
  ND advertised default router preference is Medium
  Hosts use stateless autoconfig for addresses.
```

The three joined multicast groups should be somewhat familiar after reading this chapter. The first multicast, FF02::1, represents all IPv6 devices, so router interfaces must listen for packets sent to this address. FF02::2 represents all IPv6 routers, so again, R2 must listen for packets sent to this address. Finally, the FF02::1:FF beginning value is the range for an address' solicited node multicast address, used by several functions, including the duplicate address detection (DAD) and neighbor discovery (ND).

Connected Routes and Neighbors

The third example shows some new concepts with the IP routing table. Example 16-3 shows R2's current IPv6 routing table that results from the configuration shown in Example 16-1. Note that no IPv6 routing protocols have been configured, and no static routes have been configured.

Example 16-3   *Connected and Local IPv6 Routes*

```
R2# show ipv6 route
IPv6 Routing Table - Default - 7 entries
Codes: C - Connected, L - Local, S - Static, U - Per-user Static route
       B - BGP, M - MIPv6, R - RIP, I1 - ISIS L1
       I2 - ISIS L2, IA - ISIS interarea, IS - ISIS summary, D - EIGRP
       EX - EIGRP external
       O - OSPF Intra, OI - OSPF Inter, OE1 - OSPF ext 1, OE2 - OSPF ext 2
       ON1 - OSPF NSSA ext 1, ON2 - OSPF NSSA ext 2
C   2000:0:0:1::/64 [0/0]
      via Serial0/0/1, directly connected
L   2000::1:213:19FF:FE7B:5004/128 [0/0]
      via Serial0/0/1, receive
C   2000:0:0:2::/64 [0/0]
      via FastEthernet0/1, directly connected
L   2000:0:0:2::2/128 [0/0]
      via FastEthernet0/1, receive
C   2000:0:0:4::/64 [0/0]
      via FastEthernet0/0, directly connected
L   2000::4:213:19FF:FE7B:5004/128 [0/0]
      via FastEthernet0/0, receive
L   FF00::/8 [0/0]
      via Null0, receive
```

First, the IPv6 routing table lists the expected connected routes, but a new type of route–a "local" route–designated by an L in the output of the **show ipv6 route** command. The connected routes occur for any unicast IPv6 addresses on the interface that happen to have more than link local scope. So, R2 has routes for subnets 2000:0:0:1::/64, 2000:0:0:2::/64, and 2000:0:0:4::/64, but no connected subnets related to R2's link local addresses. The Local routes, all /128 routes, are essentially host routes for the router's unicast IPv6 addresses. These local routes allow the router to more efficiently process packets directed to the router itself, rather than for packets directed toward connected subnets.

The IPv6 Neighbor Table

The IPv6 neighbor table replaces the IPv4 ARP table, listing the MAC address of other devices that share the same link. Example 16-4 shows a **debug** that lists messages during the NDP process, a ping to R3's F0/0 IPv6 address, and the resulting neighbor table entries on R2.

Example 16-4   *Creating Entries and Displaying the Contents of R2's IPv6 Neighbor Table*

```
R2# debug ipv6 nd
  ICMP Neighbor Discovery events debugging is on
R2# ping 2000:0:0:2::3

Type escape sequence to abort.
Sending 5, 100-byte ICMP Echos to 2000:0:0:2::3, timeout is 2 seconds:
!!!!!
Success rate is 100 percent (5/5), round-trip min/avg/max = 0/0/4 ms
R2#
*Sep  2 17:07:25.807: ICMPv6-ND: DELETE -> INCMP: 2000:0:0:2::3
*Sep  2 17:07:25.807: ICMPv6-ND: Sending NS for 2000:0:0:2::3 on FastEthernet0/1
*Sep  2 17:07:25.807: ICMPv6-ND: Resolving next hop 2000:0:0:2::3 on interface
FastEthernet0/1
*Sep  2 17:07:25.811: ICMPv6-ND: Received NA for 2000:0:0:2::3 on FastEthernet0/1
from 2000:0:0:2::3
*Sep  2 17:07:25.811: ICMPv6-ND: Neighbour 2000:0:0:2::3 on FastEthernet0/1 : LLA
0013.197b.6588

R2# undebug all
All possible debugging has been turned off

R2# show ipv6 neighbors
IPv6 Address                          Age Link-layer Addr State Interface
2000:0:0:2::3                           0 0013.197b.6588  REACH Fa0/1
FE80::213:19FF:FE7B:6588              0 0013.197b.6588  REACH Fa0/1
```

The example shows the entire NDP process by which R2 discovers R3's Fa0/0 MAC address. The example begins with a **debug ipv6 nd** command, which tells R2 to issue messages related to NDP messages. The **ping 2000:0:0:2::3** command that follows tells IOS to use IPv6 ping R3's F0/0 address–but R2 does not know the corresponding MAC address. The debug output that follows shows R2 sending an NS, with R3 replying with an NA message, listing R3's MAC address.

The example ends with the output of the **show ipv6 neighbor** command, which lists the neighbor table entries for both R3's IPv6 addresses.

Stateless Autoconfiguration

The final example in this section demonstrates stateless autoconfiguration using two routers, R2 and R3. In Example 16-5, R2's F0/1 configuration will be changed, using the ipv6 address autoconfig subcommand on that interface. This tells R2 to use stateless autoconfig process, with R2 learning its prefix from Router R3. R2 then builds the rest of its IPv6 address using EUI-64.

Example 16-5 *Using Stateless Autoconfig on Router R2*

```
R2# conf t
Enter configuration commands, one per line.  End with CNTL/Z.
R2(config)# interface fa0/1
R2(config-if)# no ipv6 address
R2(config-if)# ipv6 address autoconfig
R2(config-if)#^Z

R2# show ipv6 interface brief
FastEthernet0/0              [up/up]
    FE80::213:19FF:FE7B:5004
    2000::4:213:19FF:FE7B:5004
FastEthernet0/1              [up/up]
    FE80::213:19FF:FE7B:5005
    2000::2:213:19FF:FE7B:5005
Serial0/0/0                  [administratively down/down]
    unassigned
Serial0/0/1                  [up/up]
    FE80::213:19FF:FE7B:5004
    2000::1:213:19FF:FE7B:5004
Serial0/1/0                  [administratively down/down]
    unassigned
Serial0/1/1                  [administratively down/down]
    unassigned

R2# show ipv6 router
Router FE80::213:19FF:FE7B:6588 on FastEthernet0/1, last update 0 min
  Hops 64, Lifetime 1800 sec, AddrFlag=0, OtherFlag=0, MTU=1500
  HomeAgentFlag=0, Preference=Medium
  Reachable time 0 (unspecified), Retransmit time 0 (unspecified)
  Prefix 2000:0:0:2::/64 onlink autoconfig
    Valid lifetime 2592000, preferred lifetime 604800
```

Starting with the configuration, the **no ipv6 address** command actually removes all configured IPv6 addresses from the interface and also disables IPv6 on interface F0/1. Then, the **ipv6 address autoconfig** command again enables IPv6 on F0/1 and tells R2 to use stateless autoconfig.

The **show** commands confirm that R2 does indeed learn its IPv6 address: 2000:0:0:2:0213:19FF:FE7B:5005. The **show ipv6 router** command, which lists the cached contents of any received RA messages, lists the information received from R3's RA message, including R3's link local address (used to identify the routers) and R3's advertised prefix (2000:0:0:2::/64).

Exam Preparation Tasks

Planning Practice

The CCNP ROUTE exam expects test takers to review design documents, create implementation plans, and create verification plans. This section provides some exercises that may help you to take a step back from the minute details of the topics in this chapter so that you can think about the same technical topics from the planning perspective.

For each planning practice table, simply complete the table. Note that any numbers in parentheses represent the number of options listed for each item in the solutions in Appendix F.

Design Review Table

Table 16-11 lists several design goals related to this chapter. If these design goals were listed in a design document, and you had to take that document and develop an implementation plan, what implementation options come to mind? You should write a general description; specific configuration commands are not required.

Table 16-11   *Design Review*

Design Goal	Possible Implementation Choices Covered in This Chapter
An IPv6 design suggests that all client hosts should dynamically learn their IPv6 addresses. Which tools can be used? (2)	
A plan shows the use of stateless autoconfiguration. What functions should we expect the IPv6 DHCP server to perform?	

Implementation Plan Peer Review Table

Table 16-12 shows a list of questions that others might ask, or that you might think about, during a peer review of another network engineer's implementation plan. Complete the table by answering the questions.

Table 16-12 *Notable Questions from This Chapter to Consider During an Implementation Plan Peer Review*

Question	Answers
An implementation plan states that router IPv6 address should be assigned as obvious values, using the lowest numbers in the range per each assigned prefix. What configuration methods could be used to configure these low address values?	
A plan calls for the use of stateless autoconfig for client hosts. What must be configured on the routers to support this process?	

Create an Implementation Plan Table

To practice skills useful when creating your own implementation plan, list in Table 16-13 all configuration commands related to the configuration of the following features. You may want to record your answers outside the book, and set a goal to complete this table (and others like it) from memory during your final reviews before taking the exam.

Table 16-13 *Implementation Plan Configuration Memory Drill*

Feature	Configuration Commands/Notes
Configure the full global unicast address on an interface.	
Configure the unicast IPv6 prefix on an interface, and let the router add the interface ID.	
Configure an interface to find its unicast IPv6 address using stateless autoconfig.	
Configure an interface to enable IPv6 and use another interface's IPv6 address as needed.	
Enable IPv6 on an interface and do not configure a unicast IPv6 address.	
Configure the link local address of an interface.	

Choose Commands for a Verification Plan Table

To practice skills useful when creating your own verification plan, list in Table 16-14 all commands that supply the requested information. You may want to record your answers outside the book, and set a goal to be able to complete this table (and others like it) from memory during your final reviews before taking the exam.

Note: Some of the entries in this table may not have been specifically mentioned in this chapter but are listed in this table for review and reference.

Table 16-14 *Verification Plan Memory Drill*

Information Needed	Commands
All IPv6 routes	
A single line per IPv6 address	
Detailed information about IPv6 on an interface, including multicast addresses	
The MAC address used by an interface	
The MAC addresses of neighboring IPv6 hosts	
The information learned from another router in an RA message	

Review all the Key Topics

Review the most important topics from inside the chapter, noted with the Key Topics icon in the outer margin of the page. Table 16-15 lists a reference of these key topics and the page numbers on which each is found.

Table 16-15 *Key Topics for Chapter 16*

Key Topic Element	Description	Page Number
Figure 16-1	Conceptual view of IPv6 global routes	535
List	Rules for abbreviating IPv6 addresses	536
List	Rules about how to write IPv6 prefixes	538
Figure 16-3	IPv6 public prefix assignment concepts	540
List	IPv6 subnetting process	541
Figure 16-5	IPv6 subnetting concepts	542
List	Three steps used by the stateless autoconfig feature	545
Figure 16-8	IPv6 Address format when using EUI-64	548
Table 16-7	Comparisons of Stateful and Stateless DHCP	549
List	IPv6 address types (unicast, multicast, and anycast)	550
Figure 16-10	Link local address format	552
Table 16-9	Address types and prefixes	552
Figure 16-11	NDP concepts	555

Complete the Tables and Lists from Memory

Print a copy of Appendix D, "Memory Tables," (found on the CD), or at least the section for this chapter, and complete the tables and lists from memory. Appendix E, "Memory Tables Answer Key," also on the CD, includes completed tables and lists to check your work.

Define Key Terms

Define the following key terms from this chapter, and check your answers in the glossary.

global unicast address, link local address, unique local address, stateful DHCP, stateless DHCP, stateless autoconfig, Neighbor Discovery Protocol (NDP), Neighbor Solicitation (NS), Neighbor Advertisement (NA), Router Solicitation (RS), Router Advertisement (RA), solicited node multicast address, duplicate address detection (DAD), inverse neighbor discovery

This chapter covers the following subjects:

RIP Next Generation (RIPng): This section compares and contrasts IPv4's RIPv2 and IPv6's RIPng routing protocols and shows how to configure RIPng.

EIGRP for IPv6: This section compares and contrasts EIGRP for IPv4 and for IPv6 and shows how to configure EIGRP for IPv6.

OSPF Version 3: This section compares and contrasts OSPFv2, which applies to IPv4, and OSPFv3, which applies to IPv6, along with how to configure OSPFv3.

IPv6 IGP Redistribution: This section compares and contrasts IPv4 and IPv6 IGP redistribution concepts and configuration.

IPv6 Static Routes: This short section shows the syntax of the **ipv6 route** command and how you can use it to configure static IPv6 routes.

CHAPTER 17

IPv6 Routing Protocols and Redistribution

IPv6 uses an updated version of the three popular IGPs (RIP, EIGRP, and OSPF) to exchange routes inside an Enterprise. Additionally, updates to the BGP Version 4 standard, called multiprotocol extensions for BGP-4 (RFC 4760), allow the exchange of IPv6 routing information in the Internet.

As you might imagine, these updated routing protocols have many features in common with their IPv4 cousins. This chapter examines each of the three IPv6 IGPs, with an eye toward the similarities and differences between the IPv4 and IPv6 versions of each IGP protocol. This chapter also examines IPv6 route redistribution between IPv6 IGPs and static IPv6 routes.

Note that as in Chapter 16, "IP Version 6 Addressing," this chapter also discusses the issues of native support of IPv6, ignoring the transition and translation features discussed in Chapter 18, "IPv4 and IPv6 Coexistence."

"Do I Know This Already?" Quiz

The "Do I Know This Already?" quiz allows you to assess if you should read the entire chapter. If you miss no more than one of these eight self-assessment questions, you might want to move ahead to the "Exam Preparation Tasks." Table 17-1 lists the major headings in this chapter and the "Do I Know This Already?" quiz questions covering the material in those headings so that you can assess your knowledge of these specific areas. The answers to the "Do I Know This Already?" quiz appear in Appendix A.

Table 17-1 *"Do I Know This Already?" Foundation Topics Section-to-Question Mapping*

Foundations Topics Section	Questions
RIP Next Generation (RIPng)	1–2
EIGRP for IPv6	3–4
OSPF Version 3	5–6
IPv6 IGP Redistribution	7
IPv6 Static Routes	8

1. Which of the following features work the same in both RIP-2 and RIPng? (Choose three.)

   a. Distance Vector Logic

   b. Uses UDP

   c. Uses RIP-specific authentication

   d. Maximum useful metric of 15

   e. Automatic route summarization

2. Router R1 currently has no configuration related to IPv6 or IPv4. The following configuration exists in a planning document, intended to be used to copy/paste into Router R1 to enable RIPng and IPv6 on interfaces F0/0 and S0/0/0. No other related configuration exists. Which of the following is true about RIPng on R1 after this configuration has been pasted into R1?

   ```
   ipv6 unicast-routing
   interface f0/0
   ipv6 rip one enable
   ipv6 address 2000::1/64
   interface s0/0/0
   ipv6 address 2001::/64 eui-64
   ipv6 rip one enable
   ```

   a. RIPng will be enabled on no interfaces.

   b. RIPng will be enabled on one interface.

   c. RIPng will be enabled on two interfaces.

   d. RIPng will advertise about prefixes connected to S0/0/0 and F0/0, but only send Updates on one interface.

3. Router R1 currently has no configuration related to IPv6 or IPv4. The following configuration exists in a planning document intended to be used to copy/paste into Router R1 to enable EIGRP for IPv6 on interfaces F0/0 and S0/0/0. No other related configuration exists. Assuming F0/0 and S0/0/0 reach an up/up state, which of the following is true about EIGRP for IPv6 on R1 after this configuration has been pasted into R1?

```
ipv6 router eigrp 1
ipv6 unicast-routing
interface f0/0
ipv6 address 2000::1/64
ipv6 eigrp 1
interface s0/0/0
ipv6 address 2001::/64 eui-64
ipv6 eigrp 1
```

    a. EIGRP works on F0/0 and S0/0/0 without further configuration.

    b. EIGRP works with the addition of one command: a **no shutdown** command in EIGRP router configuration mode.

    c. EIGRP works with the addition of one command: an **eigrp router-id** command in EIGRP router configuration mode.

    d. EIGRP for IPv6 needs at least two more configuration commands before it works on R1.

4. Router R1 connects to Router R2 over an Ethernet LAN with both routers using their F0/0 interfaces. R1 learns a route from R2 using EIGRP for IPv6. That route lists F0/0 as the outgoing interface with R2 as the next hop. The configuration excerpt shows all relevant configuration on R2's F0/0 interface. Which of the following is true about R1's route?

```
interface f0/0
mac-address 1111.1111.1111
ipv6 address 2000::/64 eui-64
ipv6 address 2001::1/64
```

    a. The next hop is 2000::1311:11FF:FE11:1111

    b. The next hop is FE80::1311:11FF:FE11:1111

    c. The next hop is FE80::5111:11FF:FE11:1111

    d. The next hop is 2001::1

5. Which of the following are true of both OSPFv2 and OSPFv3? (Choose two.)

    a. The method of choosing an OSPF router ID

    b. Verification checks that must be validated before two routers can become OSPF neighbors

    c. Support for route tags

    d. Support for multiple instances per interface

6. Router R1 currently has no configuration related to IPv6 or IPv4. The following configuration exists in a planning document, intended to be used to copy/paste into Router R1 to enable OSPFv3 on interfaces F0/0 and S0/0/0. No other related configuration exists. Assuming F0/0 and S0/0/0 reach an up/up state, which of the following is true about OSPFv3 on R1 after this configuration has been pasted into R1?

```
ipv6 router ospf 1
ipv6 unicast-routing
interface f0/0
ipv6 address 2000::1/64
ipv6 ospf 1 area 1
interface s0/0/0
ipv6 address 2001::/64 eui-64
ipv6 ospf 1 area 0
```

   a. OSPF works on F0/0 and S0/0/0 without further configuration.

   b. OSPF works with the addition of one command: a **no shutdown** command in OSPF router configuration mode.

   c. OSPF works with the addition of one command: an **router-id** command in OSPF router configuration mode.

   d. OSPFv3 needs at least two more configuration commands before it works on R1.

7. The following output occurs on Router R1, which runs both EIGRP for IPv6 and OSPFv3, with redistribution from EIGRP into OSPF configured with the **redistribute eigrp 1 metric 25** command. Interface S0/0/1 has been enabled for EIGRP ASN 1. Which of the following should be true of redistribution in this case?

```
D    2000::/64 [90/1422516]
        via FE80::213:19FF:FE7B:5026, Serial0/0/1
C    2000:0:0:1::/64 [0/0]
        via Serial0/0/1, directly connected
L    2000::1:213:19FF:FE7B:5004/128 [0/0]
        via Serial0/0/1, receive
```

   a. Route 2000::/64 will be redistributed.

   b. Route 2000:0:0:1::/64 will be redistributed.

   c. Route 2000:1:213:19FF:FE7B:5004/128 will be redistributed.

   d. No routes will be redistributed because of the omission of the **subnets** parameter of the **redistribute** command.

8. Router R1 has been configured with an **ipv6 route 2000::/64 S0/0/0 64** command. Which of the following does the 64 at the end of the command represent?

   a. Metric

   b. Administrative distance

   c. Timeout (seconds)

   d. Prefix length

   e. Interface ID

Foundation Topics

To support IPv6, all the IPv4 routing protocols had to go through varying degrees of changes, with the most obvious being that each had to be changed to support longer addresses and prefixes. The actual messages used to send and receive routing information have changed in some cases, using IPv6 headers instead of IPv4 headers, and using IPv6 addresses in those headers. In particular, like their IPv4 versions, each IPv6 IGP uses IPv6 multicast addresses—for example, RIPng sends routing updates to the IPv6 destination address FF02::9 instead of the old RIP-2 IPv4 224.0.0.9 address. Also, the routing protocols typically advertise their link-local IP address as the next hop in a route.

Even with these changes, each IPv6 IGP has more similarities than differences compared to their respective IPv4 cousins. For example, RIPng, based on RIP-2, is still a Distance Vector protocol, with hop count as the metric and 15 hops as the longest valid route (16 is infinity). OSPF Version 3 (OSPFv3), created specifically to support IPv6, uses Link State logic like OSPFv2, uses cost as the metric, and retains the LSA types—but there are some changes to how the LSAs work. However, most of the core OSPF operational concepts remain the same.

Table 17-2 lists the IPv6 routing protocols and their new RFCs (as appropriate).

Table 17-2   *Updates to Routing Protocols for IPv6*

Routing Protocol	Full Name	RFC
RIPng	RIP Next Generation	2080
OSPFv3	OSPF Version 3	5340
MP-BGP4	Multiprotocol BGP-4	4760
EIGRP for IPv6	EIGRP for IPv6	Proprietary

This chapter examines the three IGPs, the redistribution between the IGPs, and static IPv6 routes.

RIP Next Generation (RIPng)

Routing Information Protocol (RIP) began life as one of the earliest efforts in the field of dynamic IP routing protocols. It eventually became the first dynamic routing protocol for the emerging IP protocol back in the 1970s. Later, in the mid-1990s, the RIP Version 2 (RIP-2) specifications enhanced RIP, with the original version becoming known as RIP Version 1, or simply RIP-1.

Also in the mid-1990s, the process of defining IPv6 was drawing toward completion, at least for the original IPv6 standards. To support IPv6, the IETF committees defined a new version of RIP to support IPv6. But rather than number this updated flavor of RIP as RIP Version 3, the creators chose to number this new protocol as version 1, treating it like a new protocol. However, no one bothered to put "version 1" in the name, simply calling it

RIP Next Generation (RIPng), or even simply RIP. To date, no new version of RIPng has been defined, making the original RIPng still the most recent version of the protocol.

Note: For you Star Trek TV show fans, yes, the name in part came from "Star Trek: The Next Generation."

RIPng–Theory and Comparisons to RIP-2

The RIPng RFC states that the protocol uses many of the same concepts and conventions as the original RIP-1 specification, also drawing on some RIP-2 concepts. However, knowing that many of you might not remember a lot of details about RIP-2, particularly because RIP-2 is included in the CCNA certification rather than CCNP, Table 17-3 lists a variety of facts about RIP-2 and RIPng.

Table 17-3 *Comparing RIP-2 to RIPng*

Feature	RIP-2	RIPng
Advertises routes for...	IPv4	IPv6
RIP messages use these Layer 3/4 protocols	IPv4, UDP	IPv6, UDP
UDP Port	520	521
Use Distance Vector	Yes	Yes
Default Administrative distance	120	120
Supports VLSM	Yes	Yes
Can perform automatic summarization	Yes	N/A
Uses Split Horizon	Yes	Yes
Uses Poison Reverse	Yes	Yes
30 second periodic full updates	Yes	Yes
Uses triggered updates	Yes	Yes
Uses Hop Count metric	Yes	Yes
Metric meaning infinity	16	16
Supports route tags	Yes	Yes
Multicast Update destination	224.0.0.9	FF02::9
Authentication	RIP-specific	uses IPv6 AH/ESP

The overall operation of RIPng closely matches RIP-2. In both, routers send periodic full updates with all routes, except for routes omitted due to Split Horizon rules. No neighbor relationships occur; the continuing periodic Updates, on a slightly-variable 30 second period, also serve the purpose of confirming that the neighboring router still works. The metrics work exactly the same. When a router ceases to see a route in received updates, ceases to receive updates, or receives a poisoned (metric 16) route, it reacts to converge, but relatively slowly compared to EIGRP and OSPF.

Some differences relate specifically to IPv6. First, the messages themselves list IPv6 prefixes/lengths, rather than subnet/mask. In RIP-1 and RIP-2, RIP encapsulated RIP Update messages inside an IPv4 and UDP header; with IPv6, the encapsulation uses IPv6 packets, again with a UDP header. Some small differences in the Update message format exist as well, with the most obvious difference being that the updates list IPv6 prefixes and prefix lengths.

The last difference of note is that because IPv6 supports authentication using the IPsec Authentication Header (AH), RIPng does not natively support authentication, instead relying on IPsec.

Configuring RIPng

RIPng uses a new command style for the basic configuration, but most of the optional features and verification commands look much like the commands used for RIP for IPv4. This section first takes a look at the basic RIPng configuration, accepting as many defaults as possible.

The big difference between RIP-2 and RIPng configuration is that RIPng discards the age-old RIP **network** command in deference to the **ipv6 rip** *name* **enable** interface subcommand, which enables RIPng on the interface. Another difference relates to the routing of IPv4 and IPv6: IOS routes IPv4 by default (due to a default global configuration command of **ip routing**), but IOS does not route IPv6 by default (a default of **no ipv6 unicast routing**). Finally, RIPng allows multiple RIPng processes on a single router, so IOS requires that each RIPng process is given a text name that identifies each RIPng process for that one router–another difference compared to RIP-2.

The following list shows the basic configuration steps for RIPng, including steps to enable IPv6 routing and enabling IPv6 on the interfaces.

Step 1. Enable IPv6 routing with the **ipv6 unicast-routing** global command.

Step 2. Enable RIPng using the **ipv6 router rip** *name* global configuration command. The name must be unique on a router but does not need to match neighboring routers.

Step 3. Enable IPv6 on the interface, typically with one of these two methods:
Configure an IPv6 unicast address on each interface using the **ipv6 address** *address/prefix-length* [**eui-64**] interface command.
Configure the **ipv6 enable** command, which enables IPv6 and causes the router to derive its link local address.

Step 4. Enable RIP on the interface with the **ipv6 rip** *name* **enable** interface subcommand (where the name matches the **ipv6 router rip** *name* global configuration command).

> Key
> Topic

Note: For a complete discussion of options for enabling IPv6 on an interface, as mentioned at Step 3, refer to Chapter 16's Table 16-11.

The list includes just a few straightforward configuration commands, but a few subtle interactions also exist. The list shows steps related directly to RIPng (Steps 2 and 4), plus other steps related to making IPv6 itself work (Steps 1 and 3). The list also pairs two sets of dependent steps with each other, as follows:

■ Step 2 relies on Step 1 because IOS rejects the command at Step 2 (**ipv6 router rip** *name*) if the command at Step 1 (**ipv6 unicast-routing**) has been omitted.

■ Step 4 relies on Step 3 because IOS rejects the command at Step 4 if IPv6 has yet been enabled on the interface, either statically as mentioned at Step 3 or with one of the other methods listed in Chapter 16's Table 16-11.

Finally, note that although the **ipv6 rip** *process-name* **enable** interface subcommand (Step 4) refers to the process name configured at Step 2 (the **ipv6 router rip** *process-name* command), IOS creates the RIP process in reaction to the **ipv6 rip** *process-name* **enable** interface subcommand if that RIPng process name does not yet exist. In other words, if you followed the previous steps in order, but forgot to do Step 2, the command at Step 4 causes IOS to automatically create the command at Step 2.

As with RIP-1 and RIP-2, for any interface on which RIPng has been enabled, the RIP process does three main actions. First, it starts sending RIP updates on that interface. It also starts processing any RIP updates received on that interface. Finally, it advertises about the connected routes on that interface. In particular, because IPv6 allows the configuration of multiple IPv6 unicast addresses on an interface, RIP advertises about most IPv6 unicast prefixes associated with the interface. The notable exceptions are that RIP does not advertise about any link local addresses, nor does RIP advertise about the local host routes–routes with a /128 prefix length–created for each interface IPv6 address. In short, RIP advertises all routable subnets associated with the interface.

Figure 17-1 shows a sample internetwork with IPv6 global unicast IPv6 subnets shown. The sample internetwork uses addressing values that are both memorable and make for shorter IPv6 addresses when abbreviated. All the subnets use /64 prefix length, with quartets 2, 3, and 4 composed of all 0 values. The interface ID portion of each address uses all hex 0's in the first three quartets (quartets 5, 6, and 7 in the overall address), with the final digit in the final quartet used to identify each router. This last digit matches the name of each router in most cases.

For example, all R1's IPv6 addresses' last four octets are 0000:0000:0000:0001. R1's S0/0/0.3 subinterface, which connects with a PVC to Router R3, uses a prefix of 2003:0000:0000:0000::/64, making the entire IPv6 address on this interface, when abbreviated, 2003::1/64–a convenient value for sifting through all the output in the upcoming examples.

Example 17-1 shows the RIPng configuration on Router R1 in this design. The RIP process name is fred.

Subnet 2034::/64

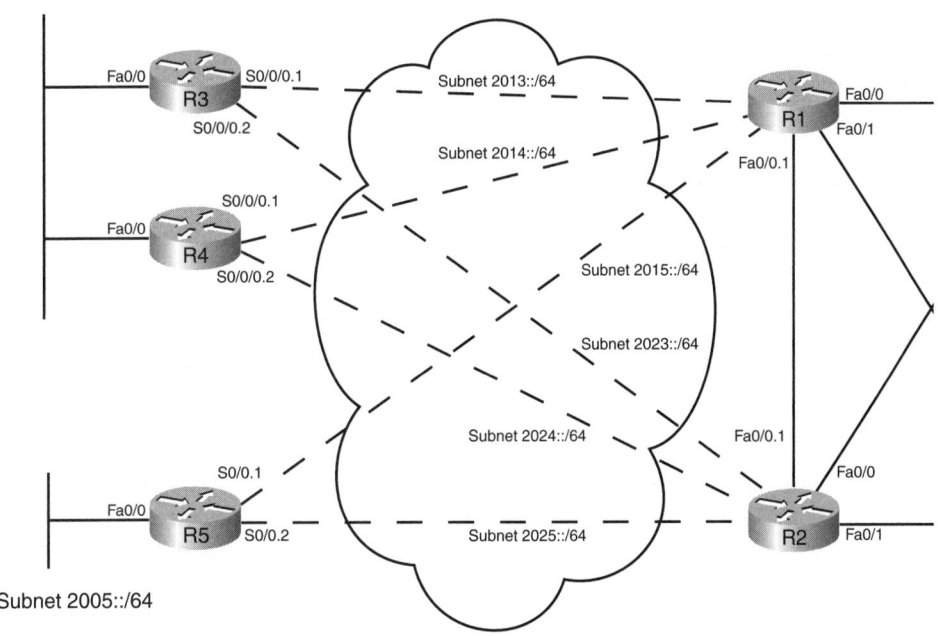

Figure 17-1   *Sample Internetwork for IPv6 Routing Protocol Configuration*

Example 17-1   *Configuring IPv6 Routing and Routing Protocols on R1*

```
R1# show running-config
! The output is edited to remove lines not pertinent to this example.
! Next, step 1's task: enable IPv6 routing
ipv6 unicast-routing
!
! Next, on 5 interfaces, steps 3 and 4: configuring an IPv6 address,
! and enable RIPng, process "fred".
interface FastEthernet0/0.1
 ipv6 address 2012::1/64
 ipv6 rip fred enable
!
interface FastEthernet0/0.2
 ipv6 address 2017::1/64
 ipv6 rip fred enable
!
interface FastEthernet0/1.18
 ipv6 address 2018::1/64
 ipv6 rip fred enable
!
interface Serial0/0/0.3
 ipv6 address 2013::1/64
```

```
 ipv6 rip fred enable
!
interface Serial0/0/0.4
 ipv6 address 2014::1/64
 ipv6 rip fred enable
!
interface Serial0/0/0.5
 ipv6 address 2015::1/64
 ipv6 rip fred enable
!
! Next, step 2's task, creating the RIPng process named "fred"
ipv6 router rip fred
```

Verifying RIPng

The **show** commands related to RIPng have the same general kinds of information as seen with RIP-2. However, some of the commands used to get to the same piece of information differ, and of course, some obvious differences exist due to the different IPv6 address structure. Table 17-4 lists a cross-reference comparing all commands related to RIP that begin either **show ip** or **show ipv6**. It also lists the similar **debug** commands used to display RIP routing information.

Table 17-4   *Comparing Verification Commands:* **show ip** *and* **show ipv6**

Function	IPv4	IPv6
All routes	... route	... route
All RIP learned routes	... route rip	... route rip
Details on the routes for a specific prefix	... route *subnet mask*	... route *prefix/length*
Interfaces on which RIP is enabled	... protocols	... protocols
List of routing information sources	... protocols	... rip next-hops
Debug that displays sent and received Updates	debug ip rip	debug ipv6 rip

The most notable differences occur with the information seen with IPv4 in the **show ip protocols** command. The **show ip protocols** command displays a wide variety of information for IPv4 RIP, whereas the IPv6 commands spread the information over a couple of different commands, as listed in Table 17-4. Example 17-2 shows a sampling of the commands, taken from Router R3 in Figure 17-1. The explanatory comments are listed within the example in this case. Note that Router R3 used a RIPng process name of barney.

Example 17-2   *IPv6 RIPng* show *Commands*

```
! On R3, process name "barney" has two current routes to reach the
! datacenter prefix 2099::/64.

R3# show ipv6 route 2099::/64
Routing entry for 2099::/64
  Known via "rip barney", distance 120, metric 3
  Route count is 2/2, share count 0
  Routing paths:
    FE80::22FF:FE22:2222, Serial0/0/0.2
      Last updated 00:27:12 ago
    FE80::11FF:FE11:1111, Serial0/0/0.1
      Last updated 00:27:10 ago


! Note that the next command lists only RIP-learned routes. It lists
! two next-hops for 2099::64. Note the next-hop information lists
! link-local addresses.
R3# show ipv6 route rip
IPv6 Routing Table - Default - 19 entries
Codes: C - Connected, L - Local, S - Static, U - Per-user Static route
       B - BGP, M - MIPv6, R - RIP, I1 - ISIS L1
       I2 - ISIS L2, IA - ISIS interarea, IS - ISIS summary, D - EIGRP
       EX - EIGRP external
       O - OSPF Intra, OI - OSPF Inter, OE1 - OSPF ext 1, OE2 - OSPF ext 2
       ON1 - OSPF NSSA ext 1, ON2 - OSPF NSSA ext 2
R   2005::/64 [120/3]
     via FE80::11FF:FE11:1111, Serial0/0/0.1
     via FE80::22FF:FE22:2222, Serial0/0/0.2
R   2012::/64 [120/2]
     via FE80::11FF:FE11:1111, Serial0/0/0.1
     via FE80::22FF:FE22:2222, Serial0/0/0.2


! lines omitted for brevity...
R   2099::/64 [120/3]
     via FE80::22FF:FE22:2222, Serial0/0/0.2
     via FE80::11FF:FE11:1111, Serial0/0/0.1


! Unlike show ip protocols, show ipv6 protocols displays little info.
R3# show ipv6 protocols
IPv6 Routing Protocol is "connected"
IPv6 Routing Protocol is "rip barney"
  Interfaces:
    Serial0/0/0.2
    Serial0/0/0.1
    FastEthernet0/0
```

```
        Redistribution:
          None


! This command lists the timers displayed for RIP-2 with show ip protocols.
R3# show ipv6 rip
RIP process "barney", port 521, multicast-group FF02::9, pid 258
       Administrative distance is 120. Maximum paths is 16
       Updates every 30 seconds, expire after 180
       Holddown lasts 0 seconds, garbage collect after 120
       Split horizon is on; poison reverse is off
       Default routes are not generated
       Periodic updates 57, trigger updates 10
    Interfaces:
       Serial0/0/0.2
       Serial0/0/0.1
       FastEthernet0/0
    Redistribution:
       None


! This command lists the equivalent of the information in the
! show ip protocols commands' "Routing Information Sources" heading.
! Note the link local addresses are listed.
R3# show ipv6 rip next-hops
 RIP process "barney", Next Hops
    FE80::11FF:FE11:1111/Serial0/0/0.1 [9 paths]
    FE80::44FF:FE44:4444/FastEthernet0/0 [3 paths]
    FE80::22FF:FE22:2222/Serial0/0/0.2 [9 paths]
```

Beyond the information emphasized in the comments inside the example, the next-hop IPv6 addresses in the example need to be scrutinized. RIPng uses the link local IPv6 address as the next-hop IP address. (Reminder: link local addresses begin with FE80.) The **show ipv6 route 2099::/64** and **show ipv6 route** commands early in the example, and the **show ipv6 rip next-hops** command at the end of the example, all show next-hop IP addresses that begin with FE80, confirming that RIP indeed uses link local addresses as next-hop addresses.

To discover which routers use which link local addresses, and make it easier to work with link local addresses, you have a couple of options. First, you can set the MAC address of each LAN interface to something noticeable. For Example 17-2, the routers each used a recognizable MAC: R1 used 0200.1111.1111, R2 used 0200.2222.2222, and so on. Alternatively, you can just configure the link local address with the **ipv6 address** command, using the **link-local** keyword at the end, and make each link local address be more recognizable. Regardless, to find the router whose link local address is listed in the IPv6 routing table, the **show cdp entry** *name* command can be useful because it lists both the IPv4 and IPv6 addresses, including the neighbor's link local address.

EIGRP for IPv6

Cisco originally created EIGRP to advertise routes for IPv4, IPX, and AppleTalk. This original EIGRP architecture easily allowed for yet another Layer 3 protocol, IPv6, to be added. As a result, Cisco did not have to change EIGRP significantly to support IPv6, so many similarities exist between the IPv4 and IPv6 versions of EIGRP.

Note: Many documents, including this chapter, refer to the IPv6 version of EIGRP as EIGRP for IPv6. However, some documents at www.cisco.com also refer to this protocol as EIGRPv6, not because it is the sixth version of the protocol, but because it implies a relationship with IPv6.

As with the previous section "RIP Next Generation (RIPng)," this section begins with a discussion of the similarities and differences between the IPv4 and IPv6 versions of EIGRP. The remaining coverage of EIGRP focuses on the changes to EIGRP configuration and verification in support of IPv6.

EIGRP for IPv4 and IPv6–Theory and Comparisons

For the most part, EIGRP for IPv4 and for IPv6 have many similarities. The following list outlines some of the key differences:

■   EIGRP for IPv6 advertises IPv6 prefixes/lengths, rather than IPv4 subnet/mask information.

■   EIGRP for IPv6 uses the neighbor's link local address as the next-hop IP address; EIGRP for IPv4 has no equivalent concept.

■   EIGRP for IPv6 encapsulates its messages in IPv6 packets, rather than IPv4 packets.

■   Like RIPng and OSPFv3, EIGRP for IPv6 authentication relies on IPv6's built-in authentication and privacy features.

■   EIGRP for IPv4 defaults to use automatic route summarization at the boundaries of classful IPv4 networks; IPv6 has no concept of classful networks, so EIGRP for IPv6 cannot perform any automatic summarization.

■   EIGRP for IPv6 does not require neighbors to be in the same IPv6 subnet as a requirement to become neighbors.

Other than these differences, most of the details of EIGRP for IPv6 works like EIGRP for IPv4. For reference, Table 17-5 compares the features of each.

Table 17-5 *Comparing EIGRP for IPv4 and IPv6*

Key Topic

Feature	EIGRP for IPv4	EIGRP for IPv6
Advertises routes for...	IPv4	IPv6
Layer 3 protocol for EIGRP messages	IPv4	IPv6

Table 17-5   *Comparing EIGRP for IPv4 and IPv6*

Feature	EIGRP for IPv4	EIGRP for IPv6
Layer 3 header protocol type	88	88
UDP Port	N/A	N/A
Uses Successor, Feasible Successor logic	Yes	Yes
Uses Dual	Yes	Yes
Supports VLSM	Yes	Yes
Can perform automatic summarization	Yes	N/A
Uses triggered updates	Yes	Yes
Uses composite metric, default using bandwidth and delay	Yes	Yes
Metric meaning infinity	$2^{32} - 1$	$2^{32} - 1$
Supports route tags	Yes	Yes
Multicast Update destination	224.0.0.10	FF02::10
Authentication	EIGRP-specific	Uses IPv6 AH/ESP

Configuring EIGRP for IPv6

EIGRP for IPv6 follows the same basic configuration style as for RIPng, plus a few additional steps, as follows:

Step 1.   Enable IPv6 routing with the **ipv6 unicast-routing** global command.

Step 2.   Enable EIGRP using the **ipv6 router eigrp** *{1 – 65535}* global configuration command.

Step 3.   Enable IPv6 on the interface, typically with one of these two methods:
Configure an IPv6 unicast address on each interface, using the `ipv6 address address/prefix-length [eui-64]` interface command.
Configure the `ipv6 enable` command, which enables IPv6 and causes the router to derive its link local address.

Step 4.   Enable EIGRP on the interface with the **ipv6 eigrp** *asn* interface subcommand (where the name matches the **ipv6 router eigrp** *asn* global configuration command).

Step 5.   Enable EIGRP for IPv6 with a **no shutdown** command while in EIGRP configuration mode.

Step 6.   If no EIGRP router ID has been automatically chosen, due to not having at least one working interface with an *IPv4* address, configure an EIGRP router ID with the **eigrp router-id** *rid* command in EIGRP configuration mode.

Note: For a complete discussion of options for enabling IPv6 on an interface, as mentioned at Step 3, refer to Chapter 16's Table 16-11.

The first four steps essentially mirror the four steps in the RIPng configuration process previously listed in this chapter. The same interdependencies exist for EIGRP for IPv6 as well; in particular, the command at Step 2 works only if Step 1's command has been configured, and the command at Step 4 fails if the command at Step 3 has not yet been completed.

EIGRP for IPv6 requires Steps 5 and 6, whereas RIPng does not need equivalent steps. First, at Step 5, IOS supports the ability to stop and start the EIGRP process with the **shutdown** and **no shutdown** router mode subcommands. After initial configuration, the EIGRP for IPv6 process starts in shutdown mode, so to make the process start, IOS requires a **no shutdown** command.

Step 6 shows the other difference as compared to RIPng configuration, but this step may or may not be needed. The EIGRP for IPv6 process must have a router ID (RID) before the process works. EIGRP for IPv6 uses the same process as EIGRP for IPv4 for choosing the RID. The EIGRP for IPv6 RID is indeed a 32-bit number, with two of the EIGRP RID decision steps based on IPv4 configuration. The following list defines how EIGRP for IPv6 picks its RID, listed in the order of preference:

Step 1.   Use the configured value (using the **eigrp router-id** *a.b.c.d* EIGRP subcommand under the **ipv6 router eigrp** command).

Key
Topic

Step 2.   Use the highest IPv4 address on an up/up loopback interface.

Step 3.   Use the highest IPv4 address on an up/up nonloopback interface.

Note that although most installations already have IPv4 addresses configured, it is possible that the EIGRP for IPv6 process cannot derive a RID value. If the router has no working interfaces that have IPv4 addresses, and the EIGRP for IPv6 RID is not explicitly configured, then the EIGRP for IPv6 process simply does not work. So, the six-step configuration process includes a mention of the EIGRP RID; more generally, it may be prudent to configure a RID explicitly as a matter of habit.

After being enabled on an interface, EIGRP for IPv6 performs the same two basic tasks as it does with EIGRP for IPv4: it discovers neighbors and advertises about connected subnets. EIGRP for IPv6 uses the same set of neighbor checks as do routers using EIGRP for IPv4, except that EIGRP for IPv6 does not require that neighboring IPv6 routers have IPv6 addresses in the same subnet. (See Table 2-4 in Chapter 2, "EIGRP Overview and Neighbor Relationships," for the list of neighbor validations performed by EIGRP for IPv4). Also, as with EIGRP for IPv4, EIGRP for IPv6 advertises about any and all connected subnets on the interface, with the exception of the link local addresses and the local routes (the host routes for a router's own interface IPv6 addresses).

Example 17-3 shows a sample configuration on Router R1 from Figure 17-1. All neighboring routers must use the same ASN; ASN 9 will be used in this case.

Example 17-3   *Configuring EIGRP for IPv6 Routing and Routing Protocols on R1*

```
R1# show running-config
! output is edited to remove lines not pertinent to this example
! Configuration step 1: enabling IPv6 routing
ipv6 unicast-routing

! Next, configuration steps 3 and 4, on 5 different interfaces
interface FastEthernet0/0.1
 ipv6 address 2012::1/64
 ipv6 eigrp 9
!
interface FastEthernet0/0.2
 ipv6 address 2017::1/64
 ipv6 eigrp 9
!
interface FastEthernet0/1.18
 ipv6 address 2018::1/64
 ipv6 eigrp 9
!
interface Serial0/0/0.3
 ipv6 address 2013::1/64
 ipv6 eigrp 9
!
interface Serial0/0/0.4
 ipv6 address 2014::1/64
 ipv6 eigrp 9
!
interface Serial0/0/0.5
 ipv6 address 2015::1/64
 ipv6 eigrp 9
!
! Configuration steps 2, 5, and 6
ipv6 router eigrp 9
 no shutdown
 router eigrp 10.10.34.3
```

Verifying EIGRP for IPv6

The EIGRP for IPv6 **show** commands generally list the same kinds of information as the equivalent commands for EIGRP for IPv4, even more so than RIPng. In most cases, simply use the same **show ip...** commands applicable with IPv4 and EIGRP, and substitute **ipv6** instead of **ip**. Table 17-6 lists a cross-reference comparing the most popular EIGRP-related commands for both versions. Note that the table assumes that the commands begin either **show ip** or **show ipv6** in all but the last row of the table.

Table 17-6 *Comparing EIGRP Verification Commands:* **show ip** *and* **show ipv6**...

Function	show ip...	show ipv6...
All routes	... route	... route
All EIGRP learned routes	... route eigrp	... route eigrp
Details on the routes for a specific prefix	... route *subnet mask*	... route *prefix/length*
Interfaces on which EIGRP is enabled, plus metric weights, variance, redistribution, maxpaths, admin distance	... protocols	... protocols
List of routing information sources	... protocols ... eigrp neighbors	... eigrp neighbors
Hello interval	... eigrp interfaces detail	... eigrp interfaces detail
EIGRP database	... eigrp topology [all-links]	... eigrp topology [all-links]
Debug that displays sent and received Updates	debug ip eigrp notifications	debug ipv6 eigrp notifications

Example 17-4 shows a few sample **show** commands taken from Router R3 in the internetwork shown in Figure 17-1. The explanatory comments are listed within the example in this case.

Example 17-4 *IPv6 EIGRP* **show** *Commands*

```
! On R3, as when using RIPng, the next-hop address is the
! link-local address of the next router.

R3# show ipv6 route 2099::/64
Routing entry for 2099::/64
  Known via "eigrp 9", distance 90, metric 2174976, type internal
  Route count is 2/2, share count 0
  Routing paths:
    FE80::22FF:FE22:2222, Serial0/0/0.2
      Last updated 00:24:32 ago
    FE80::11FF:FE11:1111, Serial0/0/0.1
      Last updated 00:07:51 ago

! Note that the next command lists only EIGRP-learned routes. It lists
! two next-hops for 2099::64. Note the next-hop information lists
! link-local addresses.
R3# show ipv6 route eigrp
IPv6 Routing Table - Default - 19 entries
```

```
Codes: C - Connected, L - Local, S - Static, U - Per-user Static route
       B - BGP, M - MIPv6, R - RIP, I1 - ISIS L1
       I2 - ISIS L2, IA - ISIS interarea, IS - ISIS summary, D - EIGRP
       EX - EIGRP external
       O - OSPF Intra, OI - OSPF Inter, OE1 - OSPF ext 1, OE2 - OSPF ext 2
       ON1 - OSPF NSSA ext 1, ON2 - OSPF NSSA ext 2
D   2005::/64 [90/2684416]
       via FE80::11FF:FE11:1111, Serial0/0/0.1
       via FE80::22FF:FE22:2222, Serial0/0/0.2
D   2012::/64 [90/2172416]
       via FE80::22FF:FE22:2222, Serial0/0/0.2
       via FE80::11FF:FE11:1111, Serial0/0/0.1
D   2014::/64 [90/2681856]
       via FE80::11FF:FE11:1111, Serial0/0/0.1
D   2015::/64 [90/2681856]
       via FE80::11FF:FE11:1111, Serial0/0/0.1

! lines omitted for brevity...
D   2099::/64 [90/2174976]
       via FE80::22FF:FE22:2222, Serial0/0/0.2
       via FE80::11FF:FE11:1111, Serial0/0/0.1


! show ipv6 protocols displays less info than its IPv4 cousin.
R3# show ipv6 protocols
IPv6 Routing Protocol is "eigrp 9"
  EIGRP metric weight K1=1, K2=0, K3=1, K4=0, K5=0
  EIGRP maximum hopcount 100
  EIGRP maximum metric variance 1
  Interfaces:
    FastEthernet0/0
    Serial0/0/0.1
    Serial0/0/0.2
  Redistribution:
    None
  Maximum path: 16
  Distance: internal 90 external 170


! This command lists the equivalent of the information in the
! show ip protocols commands' "Routing Information Sources" heading.
! Note the link local addresses are listed.
R3# show ipv6 eigrp neighbors
IPv6-EIGRP neighbors for process 9
H   Address                 Interface      Hold Uptime    SRTT    RTO  Q  Seq
                                           (sec)          (ms)       Cnt Num
1   Link-local address:     Se0/0/0.2      14 01:50:51     3      200  0  82
```

```
          FE80::22FF:FE22:2222
0    Link-local address:     Se0/0/0.1        13 01:50:52   14   200  0   90
          FE80::11FF:FE11:1111


! The next command lists the EIGRP topology database, including
! feasible distance calculations, reported distance, and listing
! all successor and feasible successor routes.
R3# show ipv6 eigrp topology
IPv6-EIGRP Topology Table for AS(9)/ID(10.10.34.3)


Codes: P - Passive, A - Active, U - Update, Q - Query, R - Reply,
       r - reply Status, s - sia Status


P 2005::/64, 2 successors, FD is 2684416
        via FE80::11FF:FE11:1111 (2684416/2172416), Serial0/0/0.1
        via FE80::22FF:FE22:2222 (2684416/2172416), Serial0/0/0.2
P 2012::/64, 2 successors, FD is 2172416
        via FE80::11FF:FE11:1111 (2172416/28160), Serial0/0/0.1
        via FE80::22FF:FE22:2222 (2172416/28160), Serial0/0/0.2
P 2013::/64, 1 successors, FD is 2169856
        via Connected, Serial0/0/0.1


! lines omitted for brevity
P 2099::/64, 2 successors, FD is 2174976
        via FE80::11FF:FE11:1111 (2174976/30720), Serial0/0/0.1
        via FE80::22FF:FE22:2222 (2174976/30720), Serial0/0/0.2


! Finally, the link-local address of neighbor R1 is identified.
R3# show cdp entry R1
— — — — — — — — — — —.
Device ID: R1
Entry address(es):
   IP address: 10.10.13.1
   IPv6 address: 2013::1   (global unicast)
   IPv6 address: FE80::11FF:FE11:1111   (link-local)
Platform: Cisco 1841,  Capabilities: Router Switch IGMP
Interface: Serial0/0/0.1,  Port ID (outgoing port): Serial0/0/0.3
! lines omitted for brevity
```

The most notable fact listed in the example is that the output confirms that little difference exists with the **show** commands for EIGRP for IPv4 versus IPv6. The main differences relate to the **show ip protocols/show ipv6 protocols** commands and that EIGRP for IPv6 uses a link-local IP address for the next hop of each route.

OSPF Version 3

The original OSPF, created to exchange routing information for IPv4, began life as Version 1 and was later enhanced as Version 2. The original OSPFv2 RFC (1247) made draft standard status in 1991. Although some changes and additions have occurred in OSPFv2 over the years, the OSPF many companies have used for a long time is OSPFv2.

To support IPv6, an IETF working group took the OSPFv2 standard and made changes to the protocol to support IPv6, resulting in the new protocol named OSPF Version 3 (OSPFv3). OSPFv3 does advertises IPv6 prefixes, but it does not advertise IPv4 prefixes, so in most OSPF shops that begin migration to IPv6, the routers run OSPFv2 for IPv4 support and OSPFv3 for IPv6 support, just like a network running EIGRP for IPv4 would then add configuration for EIGRP for IPv6.

As with the earlier sections about RIPng and EIGRP for IPv6, this section first examines the similarities and differences between the IPv6 version of OSPF and the earlier IPv4 version. It then looks at the OSPFv3 configuration and finally OSPFv3 verification.

Comparing OSPFv2 and OSPFv3

Because OSPFv2 should already be somewhat familiar to you after reading Part 3 of this book, this section summarizes the similarities and differences, and then explains some of the differences briefly. To that end, Table 17-7 summarizes a wide variety of OSPF features, comparing OSPFv2 and OSPFv3.

Table 17-7   *Comparing OSPFv2 and OSPFv3*

Feature	OSPFv2	OSPFv3
Advertises routes for...	IPv4	IPv6
OSPF messages use this layer 3 protocol	IPv4	IPv6
IP Protocol Type	89	89
Uses Link State logic	Yes	yes
Supports VLSM	Yes	Yes
Process to choose RID, compared to OSPFv2	Same	Same
LSA flooding and aging compared to OSPFv2	Same	Same
Area structure compared to OSPFv2	Same	Same
Packet types and uses compared to OSPFv3 (Table 6-4)	Same	Same
LSA flooding and aging compared to OSPFv2	Same	Same
RID based on highest up/up loopback IPv4 address, or highest other IPv4 interface address?	Yes	Yes
32-bit LSID	Yes	Yes

Table 17-7 *Comparing OSPFv2 and OSPFv3*

Feature	OSPFv2	OSPFv3
Uses interface cost metric, derived from interface bandwidth	Yes	Yes
Metric meaning infinity	$2^{16} - 1$	$2^{16} - 1$
Supports route tags	Yes	Yes
Elects DR based on highest priority, then highest RID	Yes	Yes
Periodic reflooding every...	30 minutes	30 minutes
Multicast–all SPF routers	224.0.0.5	FF02::5
Multicast–All Designated routers	224.0.0.6	FF02::6
Authentication	OSPF-specific	Uses IPv6 AH/ESP
Neighbor checks compared to OSPFv2 (table 5-5)	Same	Same, except no "same subnet" check
Multiple instances per interface	No	Yes

Some of the comparisons in the table require further explanation:

Key Topic

■ The multicast addresses used by OSPFv3 of course differ, but they keep similar numbers compared to OSPFv2.

■ OSPF uses IPv6's inherent IPsec capabilities, rather than defining a separate authentication process.

■ As with RIPng and EIGRP for IPv6, OSPFv3 does not require neighboring routers to be in the same subnet as a requirement for becoming neighbors. However, OSPFv3 does follow all other neighbor verification checks as compared with OSPFv2, as summarized in Table 5-5 in Chapter 5, "OSPF Overview and Neighbor Relationships."

■ Support for multiple *instances* of OSPF on a single link, whereas OSPFv2 supports only a single instance per link.

■ OSPF uses the neighbor's link local IPv6 address as the next-hop IP address.

■ The RID is still based on IPv4 addresses, not IPv6 addresses. Like EIGRP for IPv6, a router must have a RID before OSPFv3 will work.

Other differences exist as well, particularly when examining the details listed in the OSPFv3 LSDB. However, keeping to a scope that includes general concepts, configuration, and verification, this chapter does not get into those details.

Configuring OSPFv3

OSPFv3 configuration requires no new steps and few changes syntactically when compared to the newer style of OSPFv2 configuration discussed in Chapter 5's section "Enabling OSPF Neighbor Discovery on LANs." That section explained how to configure OSPF using the interface **ip ospf area** interface subcommand to enable OSPF on an interface, rather than relying on the indirect reference made by OSPFv2's **network** router subcommand. With OSPFv3, only one configuration style is supported, using the similar **ipv6 ospf area** command to enable OSPFv3 on an interface. IOS does not support a **network** command for OSPFv3.

The basic OSPFv3 configuration matches the newer style of OSPFv2 configuration, except for substituting **ipv6** instead of **ip** in the configuration commands. The following list shows the basic configuration steps, including the assignment of an IPv6 address to the interface.

Key Topic

Step 1.   Enable IPv6 routing with the **ipv6 unicast-routing** global command.

Step 2.   Create an OSPFv3 routing process using the **ipv6 router ospf** *process-id* global configuration command.

Step 3.   Enable IPv6 on the interface, typically by configuring static IPv6 addresses as follows:
Configure an IPv6 unicast address on each interface, using the `ipv6 address` `address`/`prefix-length` [`eui-64`] interface command.
Configure the `ipv6 enable` command, which enables IPv6 and causes the router to derive its link local address.

Step 4.   Enable OSPFv3 on the interface with the **ipv6 ospf** *process-id* **area** *area-number* interface subcommand.

Step 5.   If no OSPF router ID has been automatically chosen, due to not having at least one working interface with a IPv4 address, configure an OSPF router ID with the **router-id** *rid* command in OSPFv3 configuration mode.

Note: for a complete discussion of options for enabling IPv6 on an interface, as mentioned at Step 3, refer to Chapter 16's Table 16-11.

Note: Unlike a new EIGRP for IPv6 routing process, a newly created OSPFv3 routing process defaults to an administratively enabled state. As a result, the previous configuration checklist does not include the **no shutdown** OSPFv3 subcommand. However, the router mode subcommands **shutdown** and **no shutdown** can be used to disable and re-enable the OSPFv3 routing process.

To be complete, Example 17-5 lists the OSPFv3 configuration on Router R1 from Figure 17-. Figure 17-2 shows the area design used for the configuration.

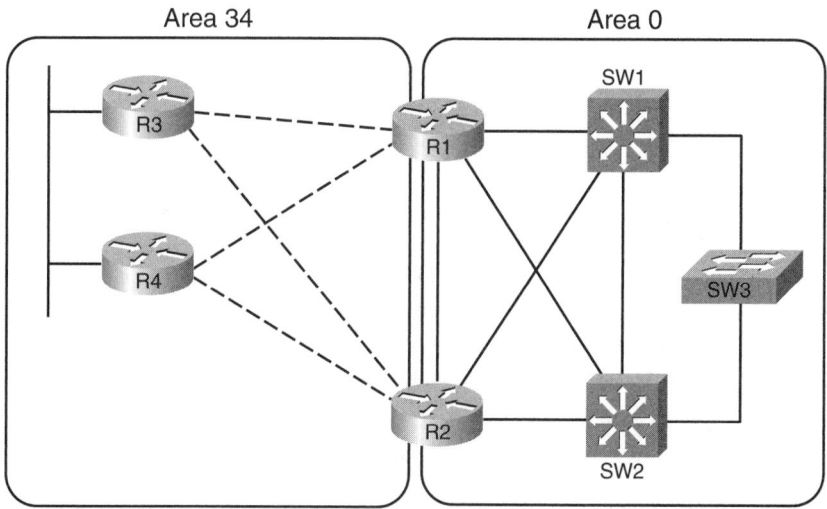

Figure 17-2   *Area Design Used for Example 17-5*

Example 17-5   *Configuring IPv6 Routing and Routing Protocols on R1*

```
R1# show running-config
! output is edited to remove lines not pertinent to this example
! Step 1: Enable IPv6 routing
ipv6 unicast-routing
!
! On five interfaces, do steps 3 and 4: configure static IPv6 addresses,
! and enable OSPFv3 process 5, in the appropriate areas
interface FastEthernet0/0.1
 ipv6 address 2012::1/64
 ipv6 ospf 5 area 0
!
interface FastEthernet0/0.2
 ipv6 address 2017::1/64
 ipv6 ospf 5 area 0
!
interface FastEthernet0/1.18
 ipv6 address 2018::1/64
 ipv6 ospf 5 area 0
!
interface Serial0/0/0.3
 ipv6 address 2013::1/64
 ipv6 ospf 5 area 34
!
interface Serial0/0/0.4
 ipv6 address 2014::1/64
 ipv6 ospf 5 area 34
```

```
! Steps 2 and 5 - creating the OSPFv3 process, and defining the RID
ipv6 router ospf 5
 router-id 1.1.1.1
```

The configuration example shows two interface subcommands on each interface: an **ipv6 address** command that defines a global unicast IPv6 address, plus the **ipv6 ospf area** command to enable OSPFv3 on the interface. The interface subcommands place each interface into the correct area. But these interface subcommands have no effect unless the configuration also includes a matching **ipv6 router ospf 5** global command, with the 5 in this case matching the **ipv6 ospf 5 area** commands on the interfaces.

Beyond this basic OSPFv3 configuration, many of the optional OSPF features match when comparing the OSPFv2 and OSPFv3 configuration as well, for example:

■   The concept and commands related to OSPF stub areas are literally identical, using commands such as **area 34 stub**. (See Table 7-3 for a reminder of the commands for OSPFv2.)

■   Like OSPFv2, OSPFv3 can only summarize routes on ABRs and ASBRs, using the similar command **area** *x* **range** *ipv6-prefix/length* router subcommand, with the only difference being that the command lists an IPv6 prefix rather than an IPv4 subnet and mask.

■   Like OSPFv2, OSPFv3 uses the concept of OSPF interface types as configured with the **ipv6 ospf network** *type* interface subcommand. These types dictate whether OSPFv3 attempts to elect a DR, and whether routers need to configure neighbors with the **ipv6 ospf neighbor** interface subcommand, with the same issues seen with OSPFv2.

Verifying OSPFv3

Most of the **show** commands for OSPFv3 have similar output compared to the OSPFv2 versions of the commands. The biggest differences exist in the output related to the OSPF database, both due to the changes in LSA terminology, the addition of new LSA types, and that some LSDB information is located with a different LSA type when comparing OSPFv2 and OSPFv3. Table 17-8 lists a cross-reference comparing the key commands related to both OSPFv2 and OSPFv3, with the second column listing the parameters after **show ip**, and the third column listing parameters after **show ipv6**.

Table 17-8   *Comparing OSPF Verification Commands:* show ip *and* show ipv6...

Function	show ipv4...	show ipv6...
All OSPF-learned routes	... route ospf	... route ospf
Router ID, Timers, ABR, SPF statistics	... ospf	... ospf
List of routing information sources	... protocols ... ospf neighbor	... ospf neighbor

Interfaces assigned to each area	... protocols ... ospf interface brief	... protocols ... ospf interface brief
OSPF interfaces–costs, state, area, number of neighbors	... interface brief	... interface brief
Detailed information about OSPF interfaces	... ospf interface	... ospf interface
Displays summary of OSPF database	... ospf database	... ospf database

The first verification example focuses on some of the differences between OSPFv2 and OSPFv3 for the display of neighbor status. Example 17-6 shows output from Router R3, as shown in Figures 17-1 and 17-2. The output highlights the only noticeable difference between the output of the **show ip ospf neighbor** and **show ipv6 ospf neighbor** commands: OSPFv2 displays the interface IP address of neighbors, but OSPFv3 displays an interface ID. OSPFv3 routers create a locally significant interface ID, using that in LSAs that describe the intra-area topology, rather than using neighbor IPv4 addresses to describe the topology. OSPFv3 separates the topology information from the Layer 3 addressing information, so OSPFv3 uses the interface ID concept to identify how a router reaches a particular neighbor.

Example 17-6   *IPv6 OSPFv3 Interface IDs on Router R3*

```
! On R3, IPv4 OSPFv2 neighbors are listed, with interface IPv4 addresses.
R3# show ip ospf neighbor

Neighbor ID     Pri   State      Dead Time    Address        Interface
2.2.2.2          0    FULL/  -   00:00:31     10.10.23.2     Serial0/0/0.2
1.1.1.1          0    FULL/  -   00:00:31     10.10.13.1     Serial0/0/0.1
4.4.4.4          1    FULL/DR    00:00:39     10.10.34.4
FastEthernet0/0

! On R3, IPv6 OSPFv3 neighbors are listed, with interface IDs.
R3# show ipv6 ospf neighbor

Neighbor ID     Pri   State      Dead Time    Interface ID   Interface
2.2.2.2          1    FULL/  -   00:00:36     19             Serial0/0/0.2
1.1.1.1          1    FULL/  -   00:00:35     19             Serial0/0/0.1
4.4.4.4          1    FULL/DR    00:00:34     3
FastEthernet0/0

! Next, the LSA for R3 (RID 3.3.3.3) lists its own interface ID and
! the neighbor interface ID, for each link.
R3# show ipv6 ospf database router adv-router 3.3.3.3

            OSPFv3 Router with ID (3.3.3.3) (Process ID 5)
```

```
                  Router Link States (Area 34)


    LS age: 996
    Options: (V6-Bit, E-Bit, R-bit, DC-Bit)
    LS Type: Router Links
    Link State ID: 0
    Advertising Router: 3.3.3.3
    LS Seq Number: 80000007
    Checksum: 0xDC04
    Length: 72
    Number of Links: 3

      Link connected to: another Router (point-to-point)
        Link Metric: 64
        Local Interface ID: 17
        Neighbor Interface ID: 19
        Neighbor Router ID: 2.2.2.2

      Link connected to: another Router (point-to-point)
        Link Metric: 64
        Local Interface ID: 16
        Neighbor Interface ID: 19
        Neighbor Router ID: 1.1.1.1

      Link connected to: a Transit Network
        Link Metric: 1
        Local Interface ID: 3
        Neighbor (DR) Interface ID: 3
        Neighbor (DR) Router ID: 4.4.4.4
```

Example 17-7 displays the output of a few other IPv6 **show** command, just for perspective. The **show ipv6 ospf interface brief** command lists the same kind of information
shown in the similar **show ip ospf interface brief** command, but again listing the interface
ID as new information. The **show ipv6 protocols** command lists much sparser information
as compared to the similar **show ip protocols** command. Note that both commands identify which OSPFv3 interfaces have been assigned to each area.

Example 17-7 *Finding Interfaces and Areas for OSPFv3, on Router R3*

```
R1# show ipv6 protocols
IPv6 Routing Protocol is "connected"
IPv6 Routing Protocol is "ospf 1"
  Interfaces (Area 34):
    Serial0/0/0.1
    Serial0/0/0.2
```

```
    FastEthernet0/0
  Redistribution:
    None
R1# show ipv6 ospf interface brief
Interface    PID   Area            Intf ID    Cost   State  Nbrs F/C
Se0/0/0.1    1     34              19         64     P2P    1/1
Se0/0/0.2    1     34              19         64     P2P    1/1
Fa0/0        1     34              3          1      BDR    1/1
```

IPv6 IGP Redistribution

IPv6 routing protocols can perform route redistribution, much like IPv4 route redistribution (as detailed in Chapter 9, "Basic IGP Redistribution," and Chapter 10, "Advanced IGP Redistribution"). This section shows a few examples to confirm those similarities and compares IPv4 and IPv6 route redistribution.

The following list summarizes some of those key similarities between both IPv4 and IPv6 route redistribution:

Key Topic

- Redistribution takes routes from the IP routing table, not from the topology tables and databases controlled by the source routing protocol.

- Route maps can be applied when redistributing for the purpose of filtering routes, setting metrics, and setting route tags.

- IPv6 routing protocols use the same default administrative distances, with the same basic mechanisms to override those defaults.

- The same basic mechanisms exist in IPv6 to defeat routing loop problems: administrative distance, route tags, and filtering.

- The routing protocols use the same default administrative distance (AD) settings for internal and external routes.

- The redistribution configuration uses practically the same syntax with the same commands.

Some differences do exist, both in configuration and in concept, as follows:

- Any matching done with distribution lists or route maps would use IPv6 prefix lists and IPv6 ACLs, which match based on IPv6 prefix and length.

- The IPv6 version of the **redistribute** command takes only routes learned from an IGP but by default does not take connected routes on interfaces enabled for that IGP. To also redistribute those connected routes, the **redistribute** command must include the **include-connected** parameter. When an IPv4 routing protocol redistributes from an IGP, it always attempts to take both the IGP-learned routes and the connected routes for interfaces enabled for that IGP.

- Unlike OSPFv2, OSPFv3 does not require a **subnets** parameter on the **redistribute** command, because IPv6 does not maintain the IPv4 concept of classful networks and the subnets inside those classful networks.

■   IPv6 redistribution ignores the "local" routes in the IPv6 routing table (the /128 host
    routes for a router's own interface IPv6 addresses). IPv4 has no equivalent concept.

Redistributing without Route Maps

As with IPv4 redistribution, IPv6 redistribution can be done without applying a route
map. The first redistribution example shows such a case, with router R2 performing the redistribution. In this case, R2 redistributes routes learned from an OSPF domain on the
right, into a RIP domain on the left, without applying a route map. Figure 17-3 shows the
two routing domains and the IPv6 subnets used.

Figure 17-3   *Redistribution Plan*

Example 17-8 shows the redistribution configuration on Router R2, which takes routes
from OSPF process number 5 and redistributes them into RIP process "left." The example
begins with a **show ipv6 route** command on R2 to list the routes that could be redistributed, and ends with those routes being seen on Router R1.

Example 17-8   *Redistributing from OSPF into RIP, with Default Metrics*

```
R2# show ipv6 ospf interface brief
Interface    PID    Area             Intf ID    Cost   State Nbrs F/C
Fa0/1         5     0                4          1      BDR    1/1


R2# show ipv6 route
IPv6 Routing Table - Default - 9 entries
Codes: C - Connected, L - Local, S - Static, U - Per-user Static route
       B - BGP, M - MIPv6, R - RIP, I1 - ISIS L1
       I2 - ISIS L2, IA - ISIS interarea, IS - ISIS summary, D - EIGRP
       EX - EIGRP external
       O - OSPF Intra, OI - OSPF Inter, OE1 - OSPF ext 1, OE2 - OSPF ext 2
       ON1 - OSPF NSSA ext 1, ON2 - OSPF NSSA ext 2
R    2000::/64 [120/2]
      via FE80::213:19FF:FE7B:5026, Serial0/0/1
C    2000:0:0:1::/64 [0/0]
```

```
          via Serial0/0/1, directly connected
L    2000::1:213:19FF:FE7B:5004/128 [0/0]
          via Serial0/0/1, receive
C    2000:0:0:2::/64 [0/0]
          via FastEthernet0/1, directly connected
L    2000:0:0:2::2/128 [0/0]
          via FastEthernet0/1, receive
O    2000:0:0:3::/64 [110/2]
          via FE80::213:19FF:FE7B:6588, FastEthernet0/1
C    2000:0:0:4::/64 [0/0]
          via FastEthernet0/0, directly connected
L    2000::4:213:19FF:FE7B:5004/128 [0/0]
          via FastEthernet0/0, receive
L    FF00::/8 [0/0]
          via Null0, receive


R2# configure terminal
Enter configuration commands, one per line.  End with CNTL/Z.
R2(config)# ipv6 router rip left
R2(config-rtr)# redistribute ospf 5 include-connected
R2(config-rtr)# ^Z
R2#
```

```
! The next command is executed on router R1
R1# show ipv6 route rip
IPv6 Routing Table - Default - 8 entries
Codes: C - Connected, L - Local, S - Static, U - Per-user Static route
        B - BGP, M - MIPv6, R - RIP, I1 - ISIS L1
        I2 - ISIS L2, IA - ISIS interarea, IS - ISIS summary, D - EIGRP
        EX - EIGRP external
        O - OSPF Intra, OI - OSPF Inter, OE1 - OSPF ext 1, OE2 - OSPF ext 2
        ON1 - OSPF NSSA ext 1, ON2 - OSPF NSSA ext 2
R    2000:0:0:2::/64 [120/2]
        via FE80::213:19FF:FE7B:5004, Serial0/0/0
R    2000:0:0:3::/64 [120/3]
        via FE80::213:19FF:FE7B:5004, Serial0/0/0
R    2000:0:0:4::/64 [120/2]
        via FE80::213:19FF:FE7B:5004, Serial0/0/0
```

The brief configuration shows both the simplicity and one difference in the IPv4 and IPv6 redistribution configuration. First, the redistribution function works with only the **redistribute ospf 5** command, which takes routes from R2's OSPF 5 process. However, the **redistribute** command has the **include-connected** keyword, which tells RIP to not only take the OSPF-learned routes for 2000:0:0:3::/64, but also the connected route for 2000:0:0:2::/64, the connected route off R2's F0/1 interface. The beginning of the example lists a **show ipv6 ospf interface brief** command, which lists that only F0/1 has been enabled for OSPF.

The **show ipv6 route rip** command on R1, at the end of the example, shows that R2 indeed redistributed the two routes from the OSPF side of Figure 17-3.

Redistribution into RIPng uses a metric as taken from the IPv6 routing table by default. In this case, the output from R1 at the end of the example lists the two redistributed routes with metrics 2 and 3. You can see from the earlier output in the example that R2's metric for its OSPF route to 2000:0:0:3::/64 was 2, so R3's metric is now listed as 3.

Using RIPng's default action to take the integer metric from the source IGP worked in this case, but in most cases, the metric should be set via configuration. OSPF metrics will often be more than the maximum usable RIP metric of 15, making these routes instantly unusable in RIP. Redistributing from EIGRP into RIP would not work either, given the relatively large integer metrics calculated by EIGRP. So when redistributing into RIP, change the configuration to set the metric. For instance, using the command **redistribute ospf 5 include-connected metric 3** would have set the default metric for all redistributed routes and avoided such problems.

Redistributing with Route Maps

IPv6 redistribution can also call route maps, for all the usual reasons: setting metrics for different routes, filtering routes, and setting route tags, to name a few. To demonstrate the configuration, Example 17-9 shows another example, using the same design in Figure 17-3. In this case, Router R2 redistributes RIP routes into OSPF, with the following criteria:

■ Redistribute only LAN subnets, with OSPF metric 200.

■ Filter all other subnets.

Example 17-9 shows the configuration on R2 and the resulting OSPF routes on R3.

Example 17-9 *Redistributing from RIP into OSPF, Using a Route Map*

```
R2# show run
! unrelated lines omitted
ipv6 router ospf 5
 router-id 2.2.2.2
 redistribute rip left route-map only-RIP-lan include-connected
!
ipv6 router rip left
 redistribute ospf 5 metric 3 include-connected
!
ipv6 prefix-list rip-to-ospf seq 5 permit 2000::/64
ipv6 prefix-list rip-to-ospf seq 10 permit 2000:0:0:4::/64
!
route-map only-RIP-lan permit 10
 match ipv6 address prefix-list rip-to-ospf
 set metric 200
R3# show ipv6 route ospf
IPv6 Routing Table - Default - 7 entries
Codes: C - Connected, L - Local, S - Static, U - Per-user Static route
```

```
    B - BGP, M - MIPv6, R - RIP, I1 - ISIS L1
    I2 - ISIS L2, IA - ISIS interarea, IS - ISIS summary, D - EIGRP
    EX - EIGRP external
    O - OSPF Intra, OI - OSPF Inter, OE1 - OSPF ext 1, OE2 - OSPF ext 2
    ON1 - OSPF NSSA ext 1, ON2 - OSPF NSSA ext 2
OE2 2000::/64 [110/200]
    via FE80::213:19FF:FE7B:5005, FastEthernet0/0
OE2 2000:0:0:4::/64 [110/200]
    via FE80::213:19FF:FE7B:5005, FastEthernet0/0
```

First, the configuration shows an IPv6 prefix list and a route map that uses a **match ipv6** command that refers to the prefix list. The prefix list works just like an IPv4 prefix list, other than matching with the IPv6 prefix format rather than IPv4. The route map works with the same logic as well, in this case referencing the IPv6 prefix list with the **match ipv6 address prefix rip-to-ospf** command. The route map matches the two LAN subnets in the RIP domain with the first route map clause and sets the metric to 200. The implied deny clause at the end of the route map matches all other routes, which makes R2 filter all other routes from being redistributed into OSPF. As a result, the serial IPv6 subnet, 2000:0:0:1::/64, is filtered by the redistribution process.

The **show ipv6 route ospf** command on R3 at the end of the example confirms that R3 learned routes for both LAN subnets in the RIP domain but no other routes. Of particular interest, note that OSPFv3 lists the route as OSPF external Type 2, because just like OSPFv2, OSPFv3 defaults to redistribute routes as external Type 2 routes. Note also that the output lists metrics for each route as 200, because R2 set the metric to 200, and OSPF does not add anything to the metric of E2 routes.

Static IPv6 Routes

IPv6 supports the configuration of static routes with similar syntax compared to the **ip route** command used to configured IPv4 static routes. The syntax of the **ipv6 route** command matches the **ip route** command, other than that the IPv6 destination is represented as prefix/length, and any next-hop IP address is an IPv6 address, of course. The generic syntax is

ipv6 route *prefix/length* {*outgoing-interface* [*next-hop-address*] ¦ *next-hop-address*} [*admin-distance*] [**tag** *tag-value*]

The parameters use the same concepts as the same parameters used for IPv4. However, with IPv6, a few interesting differences exist. First, when using the next-hop IP address, you can use any address on the neighboring router, including the neighbor's link local IPv6 address. Second, if using a link local address as the next-hop address, then you must configure both the outgoing interface and the link local address.

Example 17-10 shows such a case, with a static route configured on Router R3 in Figure 17-4. R3 adds a static route for R1's LAN prefix, 2000::/64, using R2 as next hop, specifically R2's F0/1 link local address as next hop.

Figure 17-4   *Static IPv6 Route on Router R3*

Example 17-10   *Static Route on R3, with Link Local Next-Hop Address*

```
R3# conf t
Enter configuration commands, one per line.  End with CNTL/Z.
R3(config)# ipv6 route 2000::/64 FE80::213:19FF:FE7B:5005
% Interface has to be specified for a link-local nexthop

R3(config)# ipv6 route 2000::/64 f0/0 FE80::213:19FF:FE7B:5005
R3(config)# ^Z
R3# show ipv6 route
IPv6 Routing Table - Default - 7 entries
Codes: C - Connected, L - Local, S - Static, U - Per-user Static route
       B - BGP, M - MIPv6, R - RIP, I1 - ISIS L1
       I2 - ISIS L2, IA - ISIS interarea, IS - ISIS summary, D - EIGRP
       EX - EIGRP external
       O - OSPF Intra, OI - OSPF Inter, OE1 - OSPF ext 1, OE2 - OSPF ext 2
       ON1 - OSPF NSSA ext 1, ON2 - OSPF NSSA ext 2
S   2000::/64 [1/0]
     via FE80::213:19FF:FE7B:5005, FastEthernet0/0
C   2000:0:0:2::/64 [0/0]
     via FastEthernet0/0, directly connected
L   2000:0:0:2::3/128 [0/0]
     via FastEthernet0/0, receive
C   2000:0:0:3::/64 [0/0]
     via FastEthernet0/1, directly connected
L   2000::3:213:19FF:FE7B:6589/128 [0/0]
     via FastEthernet0/1, receive
OE2 2000:0:0:4::/64 [110/200]
     via FE80::213:19FF:FE7B:5005, FastEthernet0/0
L   FF00::/8 [0/0]
     via Null0, receive
R3# show ipv6 route 2000::/64
Routing entry for 2000::/64
  Known via "static", distance 1, metric 0
```

```
Backup from "ospf 1 [110]"
Route count is 1/1, share count 0
Routing paths:
  FE80::213:19FF:FE7B:5005, FastEthernet0/0
    Last updated 00:11:50 ago
```

The example shows a static route that uses a multiaccess interface as the outgoing interface, so using both the outgoing interface (F0/0) and the next-hop address in the **ipv6 route** command prevents ambiguity. Also, note that IPv6 routers do not actually have a route that matches the neighbor's link local address. As a result, the **ipv6 route** command must supply the outgoing interface as well, so the local router (R3 in this case) knows on which interface to use NDP to discover how to reach this neighboring IPv6 address. The example shows an attempt to configure the **ipv6 route** command with only R2's next-hop link local address, but R3 rejects the command. When both the outgoing interface (F0/0) has been listed, plus R2's link local address as next hop, R3 accepts the command and adds this static route to its IPv6 routing table.

Finally, the output of the **show ipv6 route 2000::/64** command at the end of the example lists some information not seen in the equivalent IPv4 command. The output reveals some insight into the operation of the routing table manager (RTM), which chooses the best route for a prefix among many sources. In this case, the static route for 2000::/64 used a default administrative distance of 1. The routers in this design were also still configured as they were at the end of Example 17-9, with RIP on the left of the figure, OSPF on the right, and redistribution between the two. So, R3 still has an OSPF route for 2000::/64, with default administrative distance 110. The output of this command lists not only the static route, but also the backup route, with a worse administrative distance, in this case the OSPF-learned route. When configuring a floating static route–a static route with a high administrative distance so that the route will not be used until the IGP routes have all failed–this command can be useful to confirm that this backup route is known to IOS.

Exam Preparation Tasks

Planning Practice

The CCNP ROUTE exam expects test takers to review design documents, create implementation plans, and create verification plans. This section provides some exercises that may help you to take a step back from the minute details of the topics in this chapter so that you can think about the same technical topics from the planning perspective.

For each planning practice table, simply complete the table. Note that any numbers in parentheses represent the number of options listed for each item in the solutions in Appendix F, "Completed Practice Planning Tables."

Implementation Plan Peer Review Table

Table 17-9 shows a list of questions that others might ask, or that you might think about, during a peer review of another network engineer's implementation plan. Complete the table by answering the questions.

Table 17-9   *Notable Questions from This Chapter to Consider During an Implementation Plan Peer Review*

Question	Answers
A RIPng implementation plan lists two neighboring routers with unicast IPv6 addresses 2000::1/64 and 2001::2/64, respectively. Will this cause a neighborship issue?	
Same issues as in the previous row, but the plan uses EIGRP for IPv6.	
A plan shows a planned config for a new router, with no IPv4 addresses, IPv6 addresses on all interfaces, and EIGRP for IPv6 configuration. What potential issues should you look for in the configuration? (3)	
Same scenario as the previous row, but with OSPFv3.	
The plan shows an EIGRP for IPv6 and OSPFv3 domain with mutual redistribution. The configuration shows a **redistribute eigrp 1** command under the OSPF process. What kinds of routes should be redistributed? Which kinds will not?	

Create an Implementation Plan Table

To practice skills useful when creating your own implementation plan, list in Table 17-10 all configuration commands related to the configuration of the following features. You may want to record your answers outside the book, and set a goal to complete this table (and others like it) from memory during your final reviews before taking the exam.

Table 17-10 *Implementation Plan Configuration Memory Drill*

Feature	Configuration Commands/Notes
Assuming IPv6 routing and IPv6 addresses have already been configured, configure RIPng.	
Assuming IPv6 routing and IPv6 addresses have already been configured and no IPv4 addresses exist on the router, configure EIGRP for IPv6.	
Assuming IPv6 routing and IPv6 addresses have already been configured and no IPv4 addresses exist on the router, configure OSPFv3.	
Configure RIPng to redistribute routes from OSPF process 1 including subnets, and connected interfaces.	

Choose Commands for a Verification Plan Table

To practice skills useful when creating your own EIGRP verification plan, list in Table 17-11 all commands that supply the requested information. You may want to record your answers outside the book, and set a goal to complete this table (and others like it) from memory during your final reviews before taking the exam.

Table 17-11 *Verification Plan Memory Drill*

Information Needed	Commands
All IPv6 routes	
Details about a given IPv6 prefix	
All routes within a given range of IPv6 addresses	
All RIP-learned IPv6 routes	
All next-hop IPv6 addresses used by RIP routes	
The interfaces on which RIP is enabled	
All EIGRP-learned IPv6 routes	
All EIGRP neighbors	
Summary of the EIGRP topology table	
OSPF router ID and SPF statistics	
List of OSPF neighbors	
All OSPF-learned IPv6 routes	
Interfaces enabled for OSPF and their assigned areas	
OSPF costs per interface	
Summary of the OSPF database	

> **Note:** Some of the entries in this table may not have been specifically mentioned in this chapter but are listed in this table for review and reference.

Review all the Key Topics

Review the most important topics from inside the chapter, noted with the Key Topics icon in the outer margin of the page. Table 17-12 lists a reference of these key topics and the page numbers on which each is found.

Key
Topic

Table 17-12   *Key Topics for Chapter 17*

Key Topic Element	Description	Page Number
Table 17-3	Comparisons between RIP-2 and RIPng	574
List	Configuration steps for RIPng	575
Table 17-5	Comparisons between EIGRP for IPv4 and EIGRP for IPv6	581
List	Configuration steps for EIGRP for IPv6	582
List	Decision process for choosing an EIGRP for IPv6 router ID	583
Table 17-7	Comparisons between EIGRP for IPv4 and EIGRP for IPv6	588
List	Additional explanations of key differences between OSPFv3 and OSPFv2	589
List	Configuration steps for OSPFv3	590
List	Similarities and differences with IPv4 and IPv6 redistribution	595

Complete the Tables and Lists from Memory

Print a copy of Appendix D, "Memory Tables," (found on the CD), or at least the section for this chapter, and complete the tables and lists from memory. Appendix E, "Memory Tables Answer Key," also on the CD, includes completed tables and lists to check your work.

Define Key Terms

Define the following key terms from this chapter, and check your answers in the glossary.

RIP Next Generation, OSPF Version 3, EIGRP for IPv6

This chapter covers the following subjects:

IPv4 and IPv6 Migration and Coexistence Concepts: This section introduces the three main branches of coexistence tools: dual stacks, tunnels, and protocol translation.

Static Point-to-Point IPv6 Tunnels: This section explains the concepts behind IPv6 point-to-point tunnels, their differences, and the configuration of each.

Dynamic Multipoint IPv6 Tunnels: This section explains the concepts behind IPv6 multipoint tunnels, their differences, and the configuration of each.

CHAPTER 18

IPv4 and IPv6 Coexistence

Most of the barriers for a migration to IPv6 have been removed. The IPv6 protocol set has been complete for more than a decade. Many products, including the most common client and server operating systems, support IPv6. Cisco routers have supported IPv6 long enough that IPv6 support exists in the most commonly deployed IOS versions. The product support means that IPv6 deployment should not be inhibited by the availability of IPv6 in commonly used software. Additionally, the Internet's support for IPv6 is growing. Barriers do still exist, but IPv6 adoption may have finally reached the point of gathering momentum worldwide.

Although the tools exist, the process of migrating billions of IPv4-based computers and devices to IPv6–devices under the control of millions of organizations and maybe billions of individual people–will not happen overnight. In the real world, the migration from IPv4 to IPv6 will probably take a generation to complete–arguably, it has been in progress for a decade already. Knowing that the migration would take years, the creators of IPv6 wisely planned for coexistence tools that allow both a single Enterprise, and the Internet, to use both IPv4 and IPv6 at the same time, coexisting peacefully.

This chapter discusses the three major categories of migration and coexistence tools for IPv6: dual stacks, tunneling, and protocol translation. However, the majority of the chapter examines four different options for tunneling IPv6 over IPv4 networks.

"Do I Know This Already?" Quiz

The "Do I Know This Already?" quiz allows you to assess if you should read the entire chapter. If you miss no more than one of these nine self-assessment questions, you might want to move ahead to the "Exam Preparation Tasks." Table 18-1 lists the major headings in this chapter and the "Do I Know This Already?" quiz questions covering the material in those headings so that you can assess your knowledge of these specific areas. The answers to the "Do I Know This Already?" quiz appear in Appendix A.

Table 18-1 *"Do I Know This Already?" Foundation Topics Section-to-Question Mapping*

Foundations Topics Section	Questions
IPv4 and IPv6 Migration and Coexistence Concepts	1–3
Static Point-to-Point IPv6 Tunnels	4–6
Dynamic Multipoint IPv6 Tunnels	7–9

1. An enterprise has plans to start adding IPv6 support. For the first year, the IPv6 will be in small pockets spread around the existing large IPv4 network, with occasional IPv6 traffic while applications teams test IPv6-enabled servers and applications. Which of the following tools would be most appropriate?

   a. Native IPv6

   b. Point-to-point tunnels

   c. Multipoint tunnels

   d. NAT-PT

2. An enterprise has plans to start adding IPv6 support. The initial deployment requires support from some IPv6-only devices that need to access servers that support only IPv4. Which of the following tools would be most appropriate?

   a. Native IPv6

   b. Point-to-point tunnels

   c. Multipoint tunnels

   d. NAT-PT

3. A client host uses IPv4 to communicate with one server and IPv6 to communicate with another. Which of the following IPv6 coexistence features is likely at work on the host?

   a. Native IPv6

   b. Point-to-point tunnels

   c. Multipoint tunnels

   d. NAT-PT

   e. Dual stacks

4. The following configuration exists on a router on one end of an IPv6 tunnel. Which type of tunnel is created by this configuration?

   ```
   interface loopback 1
    ip address 1.1.1.1 255.255.255.255
   interface tunnel 2
    ipv6 address 2000::1::/64
    tunnel source loopback 1
    tunnel destination 2.2.2.2
    tunnel mode ipv6ip
    ipv6 eigrp 1
   ```

   a. Automatic 6to4

   b. Manually configured tunnel

   c. ISATAP

   d. GRE

5. An engineer is reviewing another engineer's sample configuration for a GRE tunnel used to pass IPv6 traffic. The tunnel has not yet been configured on the router. Which of the following commands is not required for the configuration to pass IPv6 traffic?

    a. tunnel source

    b. tunnel destination

    c. tunnel mode

    d. All these commands are required.

6. Which of the following IPv6 tunneling mechanisms support IPv6 IGP routing protocols? (Choose two.)

    a. Automatic 6to4

    b. Manually configured tunnel

    c. ISATAP

    d. GRE

7. The following configuration exists on a router on one end of an IPv6 tunnel. Although the configuration added so far is correct, the configuration is incomplete. Which type of tunnel is most likely to be intended by the network engineer?

```
interface loopback 1
 ip address 192.168.1.1 255.255.255.255
interface tunnel 2
 ipv6 address 2002:C0A8:101::1/64
 tunnel source loopback 1
```

    a. Automatic 6to4

    b. Manually configured tunnel

    c. ISATAP

    d. GRE

8. The answers each list a tunnel method and two consecutive IPv6 address quartets. Which answers identify a tunneling method that relies on an IPv4 address to be embedded into an IPv6 address, within the correct quartets listed? (Choose two.)

    a. Automatic 6to4, quartets 2 and 3

    b. Automatic 6to4, quartets 7 and 8

    c. ISATAP, quartets 2 and 3

    d. ISATAP, quartets 7 and 8

9. Router R1 uses MAC address 1111.1111.1111 for its Fa0/0 interface. An engineer sees the following configuration in the output of a **show running-config** command. Then, the engineer issues a **show ipv6 interface brief** command. What global unicast IPv6 address does this command display for interface tunnel 1?

```
interface loopback 1
 ip address 192.168.1.1 255.255.255.255
interface tunnel 1
 tunnel source loopback 1
 tunnel destination 192.168.1.2
 tunnel mode ipv6ip isatap
 ipv6 address 2000::/64 eui-64
```

    a.   2000::1311:11FF:FE11:1111

    b.   2000::C0A5:101

    c.   2000:C0A5:101::

    d.   2000::5EFE:C0A5:101

Foundation Topics

IPv4 and IPv6 Migration and Coexistence Concepts

Most Enterprises do not move from having no formal IPv6 support to creating a full native IPv6 implementation on all routers, hosts, servers, and other devices. In the real world, some Enterprise networks will begin with several locations that need consistent and working IPv6 support. Other companies may begin with a small set of people who want to experiment with IPv6 in anticipation of the day in which IT will take advantage of IPv6. Eventually, IPv6 may well become the predominate traffic in the Enterprise, and one day, IPv4 may go away altogether, but that day may be decades away. As a result, IPv4 and IPv6 will likely coexist in a given internetwork for a very long time.

During this possibly long migration, three main classes of tools may be used to allow IPv4 to continue to work well, while supporting IPv6:

■ Dual IPv4/IPv6 stacks (*dual stacks*)

■ Tunneling

■ NAT Protocol Translator (NAT-PT)

This section looks at each type of tool in succession.

IPv4/IPv6 Dual Stacks

The term *dual stacks* means that the host or router uses both IPv4 and IPv6 at the same time. For hosts, this means that the host has both an IPv4 and IPv6 address associated with each NIC, that the host can send IPv4 packets to other IPv4 hosts, and that the host can send IPv6 packets to other IPv6 hosts. For routers, it means that in addition to the usual IPv4 IP addresses and routing protocols, the routers would also have IPv6 addresses and routing protocols configured as discussed in Chapters 16, "IP Version 6 Addressing," and 17, "IPv6 Routing Protocols and Redistribution." To support both IPv4 and IPv6 hosts, the router could then receive and forward both IPv4 packets and IPv6 packets.

Note: Although not used as often today, the general term *protocol stack* refers to the layers in a protocol suite, with a protocol stack referring to the implementation of all layers of that protocol on a computer. Historical examples include Novell Netware, AppleTalk, and IBM SNA protocol stacks.

The hosts using dual stacks follow the same general process of using DNS to resolve a name into an IP address. The DNS requests can return either an IPv4 address or an IPv6 address. The dual stack host can then choose to use IPv4 to communicate with an IPv4 host or IPv6 to communicate with an IPv6 host.

To support dual stack hosts, routers need to forward both IPv4 and IPv6 packets. To forward IPv6 packets to the various destinations, the design engineer can use one of two general approaches:

■ **Native IPv6:** Configure IPv6 on most or all routers, on most or all production interfaces, making all routers use a dual stack.

■ **IPv6 tunnels:** Configure some routers with IPv6, others without IPv6, and tunnel the IPv6 packets over the IPv4 network by encapsulating IPv6 packets inside IPv4 packets.

Configuring native IPv6 simply means that you configure IPv6 as discussed in detail in Chapters 16 and 17, giving each interface one or more IPv6 addresses, enabling IPv6 routing protocols, and so on. Assuming an IPv4 network already exists, the engineer could build and execute an implementation plan to configure native IPv6 by enabling IPv6 on the same interfaces as IPv4, configuring an IPv6 routing protocol, and the routers would be ready to forward both types of packets.

A router that has been configured to forward both IPv4 and IPv6 is a dual stack router. This works well, but it does require the implementation of IPv6 on all routers that might one day receive an IPv6 packet that needs to be forwarded. Alternatively, using tunnels may be more reasonable to support smaller pockets of IPv6 hosts, because tunnels require fewer routers to be configured with IPv6 at all.

From a practical exam-preparation perspective for the CCNP ROUTE exam, the implementation of dual stacks means that you need to configure IPv6 as detailed in Chapters 16 and 17, while leaving the existing IPv4 configuration in place. Therefore, this chapter does not discuss the dual stack option's configuration, instead relying on the detail in Chapters 16 and 17.

Tunneling

Tunneling refers to a process by which one router or host encapsulates the IPv6 packet inside an IPv4 packet. The networking devices forward the IPv4 packet, ignoring the fact that the packet's payload is an IPv6 packet. Some later device or host decapsulates the original IPv6 packet, forwarding it on to the final destination.

From a network design perspective, tunneling IPv6 over IPv4 results in fewer routers needing any IPv6 configuration at all. As such, it allows a quicker migration from no IPv6 support to enough support to get IPv6 packets between two sites. Fewer routers need new configuration, the smaller number of changes means less operational risk, and the end hosts can still forward IPv6 traffic to each other.

This section begins by examining the concepts behind IPv6 tunneling. Then the text more closely examines the two main categories of tunnels: point-to-point tunnels and multipoint tunnels.

General Tunneling Concepts

To appreciate the configuration of the many types of IPv6 tunnels discussed in this chapter, you need a solid understanding of the basics. Throughout this chapter, most examples will be built on a small internetwork that represents a pre-existing IPv4-only Enterprise network. The IPv6 tunneling discussed in this chapter will be built on this simple network, as shown in Figure 18-1.

Figure 18-1   *Simple IPv4 Enterprise Network*

Next, consider the case in which an engineer must create an implementation plan to allow PC1 and server S1 to communicate using IPv6. They both may use IPv6 exclusively, or maybe one or both use a dual stack. In either case, for this example, the engineer's task is to ensure delivery of IPv6 packets sent between these two hosts. Additionally, the native mode option–in other words, configuring IPv6 on all three routers and all interface on each router–has been rejected, so IPv6 tunneling will be used.

To configure an IPv6 tunnel, the engineer could enable IPv6 on R1 and R3, and not at all on R2. The configuration on R1 and R3 would not need to enable IPv6 on the inner interfaces at all. Additionally, R1 and R3 would need the configuration related to a point-to-point tunnel. Figure 18-2 shows some of the concepts behind this point-to-point tunnel between R1 and R3.

Figure 18-2   *IPv6 Tunneling Encapsulation and De-encapsulation*

Following the steps in Figure 18-2

Step 1.   PC1, acting as an IPv6 host, sends an IPv6 packet to S1, IPv6 address 2222::2. (PC1 would have likely used a DNS process to find S1's IPv6 address at some point prior to this step to find S1's IPv6 address.)

Step 2.   R1 encapsulates the IPv6 packet into an IPv4 packet, with R1's IPv4 address as source IPv4 address, and R3's IPv4 address as the destination IPv4 address.

Step 3.   R2 forwards the IPv4 packet to R3, with no knowledge of IPv6.

Step 4.   R3 decapsulates the original IPv6 packet, forwarding the IPv6 packet on its IPv6-enabled F0/1 interface, to server S1.

Although the figure and steps show the mechanics of the IPv6 tunnel, with such a small sample network, it may be easier to just natively configure IPv6 on all three routers. However, imagine that the Enterprise has 500 branches, hundreds of servers, and only 10 branches and two servers need IPv6 support. Additionally, the distribution and core layers were rightfully designed with redundancy, so to support 10 branches, 30-40 routers may need IPv6 support added to support IPv6 natively just to cover all possible cases of links or routers failing. Alternatively, a tunnel could be created from each branch router to the new IPv6 server subnet. In such cases, the use of tunneling can give you a much quicker and easier start to the journey toward IPv6.

Point-to-Point IPv6 Tunnels

Some tunnels use a point-to-point concept, whereas others use a multipoint concept. For point-to-point, two devices (and only two) sit at the ends of the tunnel, as did routers R1 and R3 in Figure 18-2. These point-to-point tunnels work like a virtual point-to-point serial link. Figure 18-3 shows these concepts, plus a few other details, using the same underlying network as shown in Figures 18-1 and 18-2.

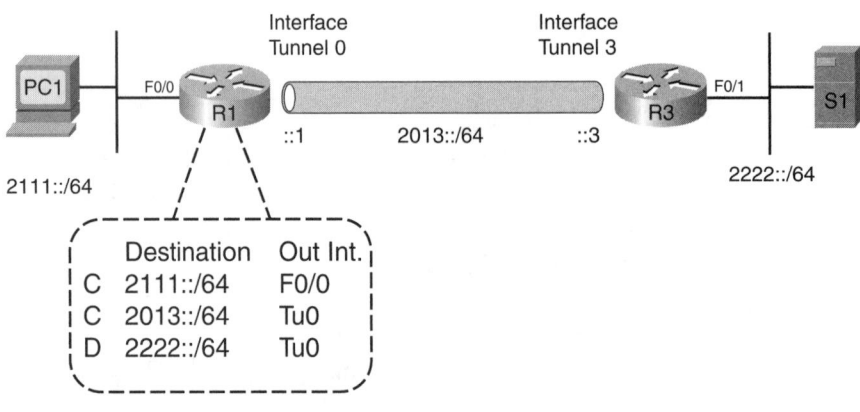

Figure 18-3   *IPv6 Point-to-Point Tunnel Concept*

To create the tunnel shown in the figure, each router configures a type of virtual interface called a *tunnel* interface. The configuration associated with the tunnel interfaces tells IOS the encapsulation details as previously shown in Figure 18-2. In the example of Figure 18-3, R1 uses tunnel interface 0, and R3 uses tunnel interface 3. The tunnel interface numbers can be any integer (up into the low billions), much like choosing loopback interface numbers, with no advantage or disadvantage of using any particular interface number.

The two routers on the ends of the tunnel treat the tunnel interfaces like serial interfaces on a point-to-point serial link, at least from a Layer 3 forwarding perspective. For example, to support IPv6, the engineer would actually enable IPv6 on the tunnel interfaces with the same commands shown in Chapter 16 and configure a routing protocol so that it runs over the tunnel interfaces, as shown in Chapter 17. In this case, Figure 18-3 shows IPv6 addresses assigned to the tunnel interfaces from within the 2013::/64 subnet.

When the configuration is complete, R1 and R2 exchange IPv6 routes and route IPv6 packets over the tunnel interface, which then triggers the encapsulation seen back in Figure 18-2.

Point-to-Multipoint IPv6 Tunnels

Multipoint IPv6 tunnels allow the sending router–the "point" if you will–to use a single tunnel interface to send packets to multiple remote routers. In some ways, a multipoint tunnel works much like a LAN, or even more like a Non-Broadcast Multi-Access (NBMA) network like Frame Relay. Multipoint tunnels still encapsulate the IPv6 packets, but they need additional logic so that the sending router (the "point") knows to which of several remote routers (the "multipoints") to send the encapsulating IPv4 packet.

The biggest leap in logic from point-to-point tunnels to point-to-multipoint tunnels is the logic in how a router chooses which of the many remote tunnel endpoints should receive a particular packet. Multipoint tunnels rely on either the IPv6 packet's destination address, or next-hop information in the IPv6 routing table, to determine which of the multiple remote devices should receive a given packet. This decision happens dynamically on the sending router. In some cases, this dynamic decision process can result in less configuration when adding a new member of the multipoint group. In other cases, the dynamic decision just happen to be how it works, but with no real advantage over point-to-point tunnels.

In all types of multipoint IPv6 tunnels, the tunneling process starts when the router receives an IPv6 packet and then tries to route that packet out the multipoint tunnel interface. This action triggers the logic by which the source router determines how to forward the IPv6 packet, inside an IPv4 packet, to the correct router. Figure 18-4 shows the general idea of how the logic works. In this case, R1 acts as the point–the encapsulating router that must dynamically decide to what IPv4 address to encapsulate and send the IPv6 packet. The figure shows one example of how R1 reacts when it receives an incoming IPv6 packet from the left.

Figure 18-4 illustrates the following steps:

Step 1.   R1 receives an IPv6 packet in its LAN interface and decides that the packet should be forwarded out its multipoint tunnel interface.

Step 2.   R1 analyzes the destination IPv6 address (listed as Y in the figure), deriving the tunnel endpoint's IPv4 address (in this case, R9's IPv4 address).

Step 3.   R1 builds an IPv4 packet header, with its own address as source address and using R9's IPv4 address as the destination (as derived at Step 2).

Step 4.   R1 puts the original IPv6 packet into the new IPv4 packet.

Step 5.   The IPv4 routers forward the IPv4 packet to R9.

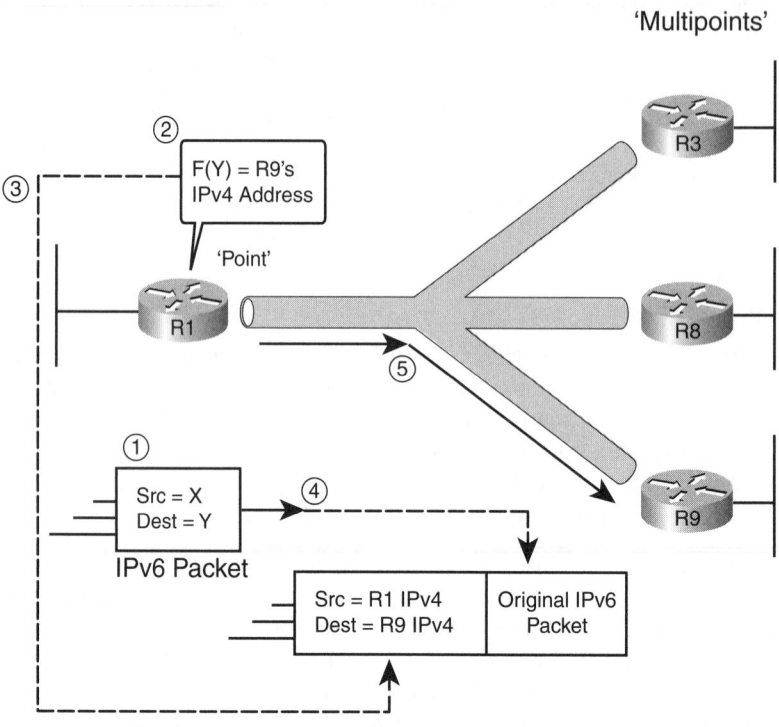

Figure 18-4   *Dynamic Multipoint IPv6 Tunnel Concepts*

The particularly interesting part of this process relates to how the encapsulating router (R1 in this case) determines to what IPv4 address to send the IPv4 packet, shown as Step 2 in the figure. Two general options for these dynamic tunnels exist: automatic 6to4 tunnels and ISATAP tunnels. In both cases, the 32-bit IPv4 address of the destination is embedded in the destination IPv6 address. To make the whole process work, the network engineer must plan the IPv6 and IPv4 addresses so that they conform to various rules, so that the sending router can derive the correct destination IPv4 address.

Summary of IPv6 Tunneling Methods

Tunneling IPv6 over IPv4 gives engineers a tool with which to avoid a full native migration to IPv6 on all routers. However, all tunneling methods add more overhead to the routers that perform the tunneling encapsulation and decapsulation. The engineer designing each network needs to weigh the benefits of a full native IPv6 implementation versus a more gradual migration using IPv6 tunnels.

The tunnels themselves also have many pros and cons. Generally, the point-to-point tunnels work best when the IPv6 occurs regularly. In such cases, it should be worth the effort to run an IPv6 IGP over the tunnel. Multipoint tunnels generally work best when the IPv6 traffic occurs infrequently, or even in cases where the traffic volumes are less predictable. Also, the dynamic capabilities of multipoint tunnels allow hosts to form dynamic tunnels with routers, without requiring any additional router configuration.

The more detailed discussion of tunneling in the rest of this chapter more fully develops these pros and cons. For now, Table 18-2 lists the tunneling techniques discussed in more detail inside this chapter, along with some notes that will make more sense as you work through the chapter.

Table 18-2   *Summary of IPv6 Tunneling Options in This Chapter*

Key Topic

Method	Static or Dynamic	Topology	Advantages and Other Notes
Manually Configured	Static	Pt-pt	Acts like a virtual point-to-point link, supporting IPv6 IGPs. Good for more permanent tunnels. Supports IPv6 IGPs. Slightly less overhead than GRE.
GRE	Static	pt-pt	Generic Routing Encapsulation. Same advantages as previous row, plus it can support other Layer 3 protocols over the same tunnel.
6to4	Dynamic	Mpt	It may require less configuration than all other types when adding a new site. Supports global unicasts, with some extra configuration. Uses second and third quartets to store IPv4 address.
ISATAP	Dynamic	Mpt	It easily supports global unicast addresses for all prefixes. Uses seventh and eighth quartets to store IPv4 address.

NAT Protocol Translation

The migration toward IPv6 typically begins with no IPv6 installed but with pervasive IPv4 support on hosts, routers, and other devices. Next, engineers start adding IPv6 support, typically making hosts dual stacked. To support those hosts, network engineers either configure IPv6 natively in the network, or use some form of tunneling. Eventually, some devices migrate fully to IPv6. Those devices may be new devices that speak only to IPv6 servers. They may be traditional end-user clients that need to communicate only with IPv6-capable servers.

In all these cases, when any pair of hosts communicate, they both support the same protocol, whether IPv4 and IPv6. Because they send and receive either IPv4 packets, or both send and receive IPv6 packets, the network simply needs to deliver those packets. The packets may be encapsulated at some point in its journey, but if the packet left one host as a particular version of IP, the packet received by the other host is the same version.

However, at some time during the migration toward IPv6, the network may need to support the ability for an IPv4-only host to communicate with an IPv6-only host. The IPv6 migration and coexistence RFCs actually make allowance for such a feature, but to do so, something between the two hosts must translate between the two different protocols (IPv4 and IPv6). The solution is the *Network Address Translation–Protocol Translation* (NAT-PT) feature.

NAT-PT gets the first part of its name from the old IPv4 Network Address Translation (NAT) feature. The venerable IPv4 NAT translates the IP addresses inside an IPv4 header, most often changing the Enterprise host's private IPv4 address into a public, Internet-routable IPv4 address. NAT-PT translates both the source and destination IP address, translating between an IPv4 and IPv6 address for both. Not only does NAT-PT translate IP addresses, but also it translates the entire IPv4 and IPv6 header, plus other headers as well, such as TCP, UDP, and ICMP. Figure 18-5 shows an example of the results of NAT-PT on Router R1, with PC1 sending a packet to Server S1, and S1 returning the packet.

Key Topic

Figure 18-5 *NAT-PT Translation on Router R1*

Following the steps in the figure

Step 1. PC1, an IPv6-only host, sends an IPv6 packet to destination 2333::1, source 2111::1. And 2333::1 actually resides on R1, so the IPv6 network forwards the packet to R1.

Step 2. R1, with NAT-PT configured, listens for packets sent to 2333::1. R1 converts the IPv6 header and other packet headers to IPv4 standards.

Step 3. The IPv4 network forwards the packet to IPv4 host Server S1.

Step 4. S1 sends an IPv4 packet back to what it thinks of as PC1, source IPv4 address 10.2.2.2, destination IPv4 address 10.9.9.1. 10.9.9.1 actually resides on Router R1, so the IPv4 network forwards the IPv4 packet to R1.

Step 5. R1, with NAT-PT configured, listens for IPv4 packets sent to 10.9.9.1. R1 converts the IPv4 header and other packet headers to IPv6 standards.

Step 6.   R1 forwards the IPv6 packet through the IPv6 side of the network to PC1, the IPv6-onlt host.

For the process in Figure 18-5 to work, NAT-PT must also be heavily involved in DNS flows as well. For example, before the flow in Figure 18-5, PC1 will have sent a DNSv6 request to resolve the name of the server (www.example.com in this case). The router performing NAT-PT must convert the requests between DNSv4 and DNSv6, keeping track of the names and address bindings so that the NAT-PT translation process converts to the correct addresses.

Note: NAT-PT, while interesting, has actually been moved to historic status (RFC 2766). IOS still supports NAT-PT, and the ROUTE course's e-learning component still includes coverage of NAT-PT. However, NAT-PT will likely fade away over time. Protocols meant to replace the function of NAT-PT are under development as of the writing of this book.

This completes the overview of IPv6 coexistence tools. The final two major sections of this chapter examine the various IPv6 tunneling methods in depth.

Static Point-to-Point IPv6 Tunnels

This section examines the configuration and some basic verification for two different types of IPv6 point-to-point tunnels:

■   Manually configured tunnels (MCT)

■   Generic Routing Encapsulation (GRE) tunnels

Note: The phrase *manually configured tunnels* refers to an RFC standard encapsulation of IPv6 inside IPv4 packets. There is no formal name for this feature, so most documents refer to it as "manually configured tunnels," "manual tunnels," or "configured tunnels." This chapter uses the term manually configured tunnels (MCT) for consistency and easier reference.

MCT and GRE tunnels have many similarities, including the configuration. They both create a virtual point-to-point link between two IPv4 routers for the purpose of supporting the forwarding of IPv6 packets. IPv6 IGP routing protocols can run over these virtual links. To support the IGPs, plus other features, the routers will assign link local addresses on these links and allow the forwarding of IPv6 multicast traffic. Both types allow the configuration of additional security features over the tunnel interfaces. Finally, both require static configuration of both the tunnel source and the tunnel destination IPv4 addresses.

To the depth used for these topics in this book, these two tunneling options have only minor differences. Manually configured tunnels simply conform to the rules about generic IPv6 tunnels outlined in RFC 4213, which defines how to encapsulate IPv6 inside an IPv4 packet, without additional headers. GRE tunnels use a generic encapsulation originally defined by Cisco and later standardized in RFC 2784. GRE uses an additional stub header between the IPv4 and IPv6 header; this extra header includes a protocol type field, which allows a GRE tunnel to carry many passenger protocols. (The passenger protocol is the protocol encapsulated inside another protocol's header.) GRE also supports several transport protocols (transport protocols encapsulate the passenger protocol), although IPv4 typically is the only transport protocol used for tunneling IPv6. GRE's flexibility allows a single GRE tunnel to carry IPv6 plus other traffic as well, whereas manually configured tunnels cannot.

This section examines manually configured tunnels in detail and then compares GRE tunnels to manually configured tunnels.

Manually Configured Tunnels

The main planning task for an implementation plan that includes manually configured tunnels requires a little thought about the tunnel source and destination IPv4 addresses. Other than that, the configuration uses straightforward commands that refer to the key elements in the conceptual drawings in Figures 18-2 and 18-3. However, even though the individual commands are straightforward, the configuration requires several steps. So, this section breaks the configuration into two sections: tunnel configuration steps and IPv6 configuration steps.

Configuring and Verifying a Manually Configured Tunnel

To configure the tunnel, first you need to choose what IPv4 addresses will be used when encapsulating packets (as shown in Figure 18-2). A router's tunnel interface borrows the IPv4 address on some other interface; the router then uses that IPv4 address as the source address when encapsulating packets. Comparing the configuration on the two routers on either end of the tunnel, the two routers must agree to the correct IPv4 addresses: the source address used by one router should match the other router's tunnel destination IPv4 address and vice versa. Finally, for better availability, if any IPv4 redundancy exists between the two routers, the engineer should choose to use loopback interface IPv4 addresses, because the tunnel interface fails if the interface associated with the source IP address fails.

The configuration centers around the configuration of a virtual interface called a tunnel interface. The tunnel interface creates an object that can be configured like an interface, so that additional commands can set parameters for a given tunnel. For instance, the engineer configures the source and destination IPv4 addresses (two different interface subcommands), with another command to configure the tunnel encapsulation (GRE or manually configured tunnel). The following list outlines the steps to configure the tunnel.

Key Topic

Step 1.   Find the tunnel IPv4 addresses planned for the tunnel, and ensure that each router can forward IPv4 packets between the addresses. If using a new loopback interface, create the loopback using the **interface loopback** *number* command, assign it an IPv4 address with the **ip address** command, and confirm that routes for this interface will be advertised by IPv4.

Step 2.   Create a tunnel interface using the **interface tunnel** *number* command, selecting a locally significant integer as the tunnel interface number.

Step 3.   Define the source IPv4 address of the tunnel using the **tunnel source** {*interface-type interface-number* | *ipv4-address*} interface subcommand. (This address must be an IPv4 address configured on the local router.)

Step 4.   Define the destination IPv4 address for the encapsulation using the **tunnel destination** *ipv4-address* interface subcommand; the address must match the **tunnel source** command on the other router.

Step 5.   Define the tunnel as a manually configured tunnel (not GRE), as defined in RFC 4213, using the **tunnel mode ipv6ip** interface subcommand.

For example, consider Figure 18-6, which shows an updated representation of the Enterprise network shown in Figures 18-1, 18-2, and 18-3. In this case, even though no redundancy exists, the engineer plans to use loopback addresses (10.9.9.1 on R1 and 10.9.9.3 on R3). Example 18-1 that follows shows the tunnel configuration on R1 and R3.

Figure 18-6   *Figure Showing Configuration Items in Example 18-1*

Example 18-1   *Configuring an IPv6IP Tunnel on R1 and R3*

```
R1# conf t
Enter configuration commands, one per line.  End with CNTL/Z.
R1(config)# interface loopback 1
R1(config-if)# ip address 10.9.9.1 255.255.255.255
R1(config-if)# interface tunnel 0
R1(config-if)# tunnel source loopback 1
R1(config-if)# tunnel destination 10.9.9.3
R1(config-if)# tunnel mode ipv6ip
! Next, on router R3
R3# conf t
Enter configuration commands, one per line.  End with CNTL/Z.
R3(config)# interface loopback 3
R3(config-if)# ip address 10.9.9.3 255.255.255.255
R3(config-if)# interface tunnel 3
R3(config-if)# tunnel source loopback 3
R3(config-if)# tunnel destination 10.9.9.1
R3(config-if)# tunnel mode ipv6ip
```

At this point, assuming IPv4 connectivity exists between the two tunnel endpoints, the tunnel interfaces should be up. A quick **show** command, as shown in Example 18-2, confirms the tunnel interface's status on R1, plus a few other interesting tidbits. Beside the tunnel interface being up, the output confirms the source and destination IPv4 addresses.

It also confirms that the tunnel mode uses IPv6 over IP (the word "IP" implying IPv4) to match the **tunnel mode ipv6ip** configuration command.

Example 18-2   *Verification of the Tunnel*

```
R1# show interfaces tunnel0
Tunnel0 is up, line protocol is up
  Hardware is Tunnel
  MTU 17920 bytes, BW 100 Kbit/sec, DLY 50000 usec,
      reliability 255/255, txload 1/255, rxload 1/255
  Encapsulation TUNNEL, loopback not set
  Keepalive not set
  Tunnel source 10.9.9.1 (Loopback1), destination 10.9.9.3
  Tunnel protocol/transport IPv6/IP
  Tunnel TTL 255
  Tunnel transport MTU 1480 bytes
  Tunnel transmit bandwidth 8000 (kbps)
  Tunnel receive bandwidth 8000 (kbps)
! the rest of the output is the typical counter information
```

Configuring and Verifying the Manually Configured Tunnel

The configuration shown in the previous section prepares the tunnel to encapsulate traffic inside IPv4 packets, but it does complete the configuration. The configuration also needs to enable IPv6 on the routers that create the tunnel, treating the tunnel interfaces just like you would for serial interfaces connected with a leased line.

The configuration steps mirror those discussed at some length in Chapters 16 and 17, so the specific commands will not be discussed here. However, Example 18-3 shows the configuration of both the tunnel and the IPv6 details on R1, with the newly added IPv6 commands highlighted.

Example 18-3   *Completed Tunnel and IPv6 Configuration on Router R1*

```
R1# show running-config
! Only pertinent portions retained
ipv6 unicast-routing
!
interface Loopback1
 ip address 10.9.9.1 255.255.255.255
!
interface Tunnel0
 no ip address
 ipv6 address 2013::1/64
 ipv6 eigrp 1
 tunnel source Loopback1
 tunnel destination 10.9.9.3
 tunnel mode ipv6ip
```

```
!
interface FastEthernet0/0
 ip address 10.1.1.1 255.255.255.0
 ipv6 address 2111::1/64
 ipv6 eigrp 1
!
ipv6 router eigrp 1
 eigrp router-id 1.1.1.1
 no shutdown
```

The new configuration should be somewhat familiar from the last few chapters, but a few items could use some emphasis. First, note that the tunnel interface does indeed have an IPv6 address configured, and EIGRP enabled, just as if it were a physical interface. However, the tunnel interface does not have, nor does not need, an IPv4 address. The tunnel interface needs only a Layer 3 address for the passenger protocols – in other words, the protocols carried as data inside the encapsulating packets. So, only an IPv6 address is needed on the interface. The rest of the highlighted IPv6 configuration uses the same logic discussed in Chapters 16 and 17.

The same verification commands seen in Chapters 16 and 17 can confirm the IPv6 details on the tunnel. Example 18-4 lists the output from a few of these commands, highlighting some of the key details.

Example 18-4   *Verifying IPv6 Works over the Tunnel*

```
R1# show ipv6 interface brief
FastEthernet0/0                [up/up]
    FE80::213:19FF:FE7B:5026
    2111::1
! irrelevant lines omitted for brevity
Loopback1                      [up/up]
    unassigned
Tunnel0                        [up/up]
    FE80::A09:901
    2013::1
R1# show ipv6 interface tunnel0
Tunnel0 is up, line protocol is up
  IPv6 is enabled, link-local address is FE80::A09:901
  No Virtual link-local address(es):
  Global unicast address(es):
    2013::1, subnet is 2013::/64
  Joined group address(es):
    FF02::1
    FF02::2
    FF02::A
    FF02::1:FF00:1
```

```
    FF02::1:FF09:901
  MTU is 1480 bytes
  ICMP error messages limited to one every 100 milliseconds
  ICMP redirects are enabled
  ICMP unreachables are sent
  ND DAD is enabled, number of DAD attempts: 1
  ND reachable time is 30000 milliseconds (using 42194)
  Hosts use stateless autoconfig for addresses.
R1# traceroute ipv6 2222::3

Type escape sequence to abort.
Tracing the route to 2222::3
  1 2013::3 0 msec 4 msec 4 msec
```

The first two commands show how routers create the link local IPv6 addresses for manually configured tunnel interfaces. Routers normally form a serial interface's link local IPv6
address using EUI-64 rules based on the MAC address of the first LAN interface on the
router. In this case, the router forms the link local address with a FE80::/96 prefix and then
adds the 32-bit tunnel source IPv4 address as the last 32 bits. For example, the first two
show commands in Example 18-4 list R1's link local address on its tunnel interface:
FE80::A90:901. Adding back the leading 0s in the last two quartets, the last two quartets
look like this:

    0A09:0901

Converting each pair of hex characters to decimal, you can find the IPv4 address of
10.9.9.1. (Appendix B, "Conversion Tables," includes a hex/decimal conversion table.)

The **show ipv6 interface tunnel0** command lists the usual IPv6 addresses. It lists the link
local address, along with the statically configured global unicast address (2013::1). It lists
multicast addresses, including EIGRP's FF02::A, and the (highlighted) solicited node multicast address associated with both the link local and the global unicast address on the interface. (When a multicast needs to be sent out a manually configured tunnel's interface,
the router encapsulates the IPv6 multicast and forwards it inside a unicast IPv4 packet to
the other end of the tunnel.)

The **traceroute ipv6 2222::3** command at the end of the example confirms that IPv6 traffic can pass over the tunnel.

GRE Tunnels

Only one difference exists in the configuration between manually configured tunnels and
point-to-point GRE tunnels: the tunnel mode. IOS uses the **tunnel mode ipv6ip** command
for manually configured tunnels, which also tells IOS to use the encapsulation as defined
in RFC 4213. IOS uses the **tunnel mode gre ip** command to instead configure a GRE tunnel, meaning that IOS uses the RFC 2784 GRE encapsulation. This encapsulation adds the
GRE header to the encapsulation. (Also, because IOS defaults to use GRE over IP, you can
alternatively just omit the **tunnel mode** command as well.)

The configurations are indeed almost identical. For example, to migrate from the configuration shown in Example 18-3, which shows all of R1's configuration for both the tunnel and IPv6 with a manually configured tunnel, simply use one of the following two options:

- Issue the **tunnel mode gre ip** command on both routers' tunnel interfaces.

- Issue the **no tunnel mode ipv6ip** command on both routers' tunnel interfaces, which reverts to the default of GRE over IP.

Key
Topic

Note: If the two routers' tunnel modes do not match, the tunnel interfaces can stay up/up, but the routers cannot forward IPv6 packets because of the mismatched encapsulations.

The verification command output looks almost identical as well, but with just a few differences to note. IOS uses a different convention for the link local address created for a GRE tunnel interface. It works as if the tunnel interface is a serial interface, deriving the interface ID using EUI-64 rules and the MAC address of the first LAN interface on the router. The second difference relates to how IOS automatically sets the MTU of the passenger protocols (IPv6 in this case) to 1476 for GRE tunnels; with manually configured tunnels, the passenger MTU was set to 1480. These settings allow space in both modes for the 20-byte additional IPv4 header that encapsulates the packet, plus in the case of GRE, the additional 4-byte GRE header. Example 18-5 highlights some of these minor differences.

Example 18-5 *Verifying GRE over IP Tunnels That Support IPv6*

```
R1# show interfaces tunnel 0
Tunnel0 is up, line protocol is up
Hardware is Tunnel
MTU 17916 bytes, BW 100 Kbit/sec, DLY 50000 usec,
reliability 255/255, txload 1/255, rxload 1/255
Encapsulation TUNNEL, loopback not set
Keepalive not set
Tunnel source 10.9.9.1 (Loopback1), destination 10.9.9.3
Tunnel protocol/transport GRE/IP
Key disabled, sequencing disabled
Checksumming of packets disabled
Tunnel TTL 255
Fast tunneling enabled
Tunnel transport MTU 1476 bytes
Tunnel transmit bandwidth 8000 (kbps)
Tunnel receive bandwidth 8000 (kbps)
! the remaining omitted lines list interface counters
```

Point-to-Point IPv6 Tunnel Summary

Point-to-point IPv6 tunnels give engineers a means to implement IPv6 connectivity without requiring extensive deployment of native IPv6. At the same time, these tunnels act like native IPv6 links, running IPv6 IGPs, using link local addresses, and requiring no static route configuration. The two options in this category have almost no practical difference. Table 18-3 summarizes the key features, with the small differences highlighted in the table.

Table 18-3   *Comparing Manual and GRE IPv6-over-IP Tunnels*

	Manual Tunnels	GRE
RFC	4213	2784
Tunnel mode command	tunnel mode ipv6ip	tunnel mode gre ip
Passenger MTU default	1480	1476
Supports IPv6 IGPs?	Yes	Yes
Forwards IPv6 multicasts?	Yes	Yes
Uses static configuration of tunnel destination?	Yes	Yes
Supports multiple passenger protocols?	No	Yes
Link local based on...	FE80::/96, plus 32 bits from tunnel source IPv4 address	IPv6 EUI-64, using lowest numbered interface's MAC address

Dynamic Multipoint IPv6 Tunnels

Multipoint tunnels give engineers a convenient tool to use when irregular or infrequent IPv6 traffic occurs between sites. The multipoint topology creates the possibility that new sites can join into the tunnel without requiring additional configuration on the existing routers. Additionally, these multipoint tunnels in some cases allow IPv6 hosts to act as tunnel endpoints, allowing a host at a remote site to connect into the Enterprise IPv6 network even if the local router has no knowledge of IPv6. This flexibility and ability to add routers and hosts with potentially no extra configuration makes multipoint IPv6 tunnels a very useful migration tool.

Multipoint tunnels also have some disadvantages. To take advantage of the possibility to limit future configuration changes, IPv6 address planning must follow some additional rules and constraints. These tunnels also do not support IPv6 IGPs, requiring the use of either static routes or multiprotocol BGP. The dynamic forwarding logic requires more work per packet as compared with point-to-point tunnels, which is one of the main reasons multipoint tunnels are best used for less frequent traffic, with point-to-point tunnels best used for more frequent traffic. Finally, the additional addressing rules and considerations require a bit more of a learning curve to become comfortable with these tools, at least as compared with point-to-point tunnels.

This section examines the configuration of two types of multipoint tunnels: automatic 6to4 tunnels, as defined in RFC 3056, and ISATAP tunnels, as defined in RFC 4214.

Automatic 6to4 Tunnels

As previously described in the section "Point-to-Multipoint IPv6 Tunnels," a multipoint tunnel does not explicitly define the tunnel endpoint IPv4 addresses. Instead, the incoming IPv6 packet's destination IPv6 address implies the IPv4 address that a router should use when encapsulating and forwarding the packet. Because the tunnels rely on the IPv6 address to determine the destination IPv4 address for these tunnels, network engineers must spend more time initially planning IPv6 and IPv4 addresses used to deploy IPv6.

The first big planning and design choice when using automatic 6to4 tunnels relates to whether to use global unicast addresses for the end user subnets, or whether to use a special reserved range of addresses (2002::/16). If the Enterprise expects all Internet traffic to/from the Enterprise to remain IPv4-only for the foreseeable future, then the IPv6 addresses used in the Enterprise do not matter much, and the network engineer can take advantage of the 2002::/16 reserved range. Using this range allows new sites to be added to the multipoint tunnel at a later time, without requiring new configuration on the existing routers in a multipoint tunnel. However, if the Enterprise needs to use its registered global unicast site prefix, automatic 6to4 tunnels can still be used, just with a little more configuration effort over time.

This section first examines the case where the Enterprise needs no IPv6 Internet connectivity, using the 2002::/16 reserved range of addresses. Following that, this section examines the same tool, this time using a registered global unicast site prefix.

Using the Automatic 6to4 Prefix for All Devices

RFC 3056 defines a reserved range of IPv6 addresses for use with automatic 6to4 tunnels: 2002::/16. Even though this range appears to come from the range of global unicast IPv6 addresses (2000::/3), IANA reserves the 2002::/16 prefix as a set of addresses that will never be assigned as global unicast addresses.

By starting with the 2002::/16 prefix, a network engineer can then create a /48 prefix:

- The network engineer can assign each tunnel endpoint (router or host) its own /48 prefix, used for all prefixes connected to that local router, by adding the hex version of the router's IPv4 address as bits 17 through 48 (quartets 2 and 3).

- The engineer can allocate /64 prefixes for each required subnet connected to each router by allocating a unique subnet number in the fourth quartet (much like when an Enterprise receives a /48 site prefix from an IPv6 registrar).

Figure 18-7 shows the format of the automatic 6to4 tunnel IPv6 addresses.

2002 : AABB : CCDD : Subnet : : /64
Prefix   4 Octet IPv4 Address

Figure 18-7 *Reserved Automatic 6to4 IPv6 Addresses*

The first half of the address has three major parts, with the second half of the address structure used for the host ID as with most implementations of global unicast addresses. The addresses always begin with a first quartet of 2002. The second and third quartet list the hex version of the IPv4 address for that site–usually the IPv4 address of a loopback interface on a router. (In this case, the hex value AABBCCDD represents 170.187.204.221, found by converting each pair of hex digits to the decimal equivalent.) The fourth quartet can be conveniently used as a subnet field so that the engineer can assign the various subnets connected to each router. The /48 prefix chosen for each router works much like when a registrar gives a company a /48 global unicast prefix, leaving 16 bits for the company to use for subnetting.

For example, consider the case with a multipoint tunnel with three routers, R1, R3, and R4, as shown in Figure 18-8. The figure depicts the planning steps taken by the engineer when using the 2002::/16 prefix for all IPv6 addresses.

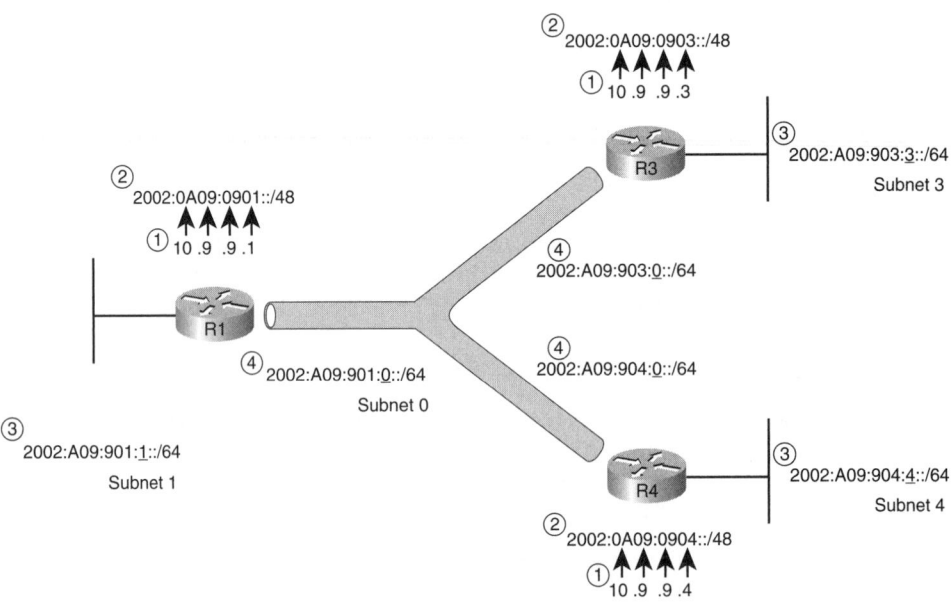

Key Topic

Figure 18-8   *Example Planning Diagram for 2002::/16 Prefixes*

Following the steps in Figure 18-8

Step 1.   The engineer chooses an IPv4 address on each router to use as the tunnel endpoints. In this case, he chose loopback IPv4 addresses, which is typical.

Step 2.   The engineer then derived the /48 prefix used for allocating subnets off each router by converting each octet of the IPv4 addresses to hex to form the /48 prefix used on each router.

Step 3.   The engineer then allocates the first /64 prefixes, one for each router's LAN subnet. The IPv6 hosts on these LANs uses IPv6 addresses from these prefixes.

Step 4.   The engineer picks an IPv6 address to use on each tunnel interface. With automatic 6to4 tunnels, these IPv6 addresses typically come from each router's own prefix, so each router's tunnel IPv6 address will actually be in different IPv6 subnets.

That completes an example of the address planning, but the underlying logic is not yet complete. Multipoint IPv6 tunnels do not support IGP routing protocols, but to trigger the dynamic encapsulation process for the tunnel, the routers must route IPv6 traffic out the tunnel interface. The solution is actually simple: because all the IPv6 addresses start with 2002::/16 (by implementation choice), the engineer plans a static route for prefix 2002::/16, forwarding all packets destined for these special 2002::/16 addresses out the multipoint tunnel interface. This process triggers the tunnel as previously discussed for Figure 18-4.

So, what happens when an IPv6 packet now arrives at one of these routers? With these well-chosen IPv6 address, the following occurs:

Step 1.   The packet's IPv6 destination address begins with 2002, so the router tries to forward the packet out its tunnel interface, triggering the process.

Step 2.   The router notices the tunnel type (automatic 6to4), which tells IOS to encapsulate and send the IPv6 packet to the destination IPv4 address found in quartets 2 and 3.

Configuring the Automatic 6to4 Tunnel

The configuration of the automatic 6to4 tunnel has some similarities and some differences compared to point-to-point tunnels. For the tunnel itself, unlike point-to-point tunnels, the multipoint tunnel configuration does not need a configured **tunnel destination** command, because the destination IPv4 address is instead embedded in the destination IPv6 address. Also, the setting of the **tunnel mode** command differs. Otherwise, the tunnel configuration details remain the same.

Some differences also exist for the IPv6-specific configuration related to the tunnel. An IPv6 IGP is not needed, because the router finds the destination IPv4 address on the other end of the tunnel embedded in the destination IPv6 address in the received packet. Although IPv6 IGPs cannot be configured on the automatic 6to4 tunnel, static IPv6 routes and multiprotocol BGP (for IPv6) can be configured. And even though the tunnel interface must be enabled for IPv6, as with point-to-point tunnels, the IPv6 addresses are not in the same subnet as the other routers' tunnel interfaces.

The following list outlines the steps to configure the automatic 6to4 tunnel and to enable IPv6 forwarding across the tunnel. Note that the steps list the use of a loopback interface because most sites use a loopback, but any interface's IPv4 address may be used.

Step 1.   Configure the planned loopback interface (**interface loopback** *number* global command), and assign the planned IPv4 address. (Ensure that the IPv4 IGP advertises a route for this address.)

Key Topic

Step 2. Create a tunnel interface using the **interface tunnel** *number* command, selecting a locally significant integer as the tunnel interface number.

Step 3. Define the source IPv4 address of the tunnel using the **tunnel source** {*interface-type interface-number* | *ipv4-address*} interface subcommand using the loopback IP address from Step 1.

Step 4. Do NOT define a tunnel destination with the **tunnel destination** interface subcommand.

Step 5. Identify the tunnel as an automatic 6to4 tunnel using the **tunnel mode ipv6ip 6to4** interface subcommand.

Step 6. Enable IPv6 on the tunnel interface, typically with the **ipv6 address** interface subcommand.

Step 7. Complete the normal IPv6 configuration, include defining the LAN interface IPv6 addresses per the planning chart, and enable IPv6 routing with the **ipv6 unicast-routing** command.

Step 8. Define a static route for 2002::16, with outgoing interface of the tunnel interface, using the **ipv6 route 2002::/16 tunnel** *number* global command.

Example 18-6 shows the configuration on Router R1 from Figure 18-8. Note that although not shown, the routers in the figure do exchange IPv4 routes for their respective loopback addresses so that all IPv4 loopbacks in Figure 18-7 are pingable. The routers also use IPv6 addresses on their interfaces, rather than just having IPv6 enabled with the **ipv6 enable** command: 2002:A09:901::1 on R1, 2002:A09:903::3 on R3, and 2002:A09:904::4 on R4.

Example 18-6 *R1 Configuration for an Automatic 6to4 Tunnel*

```
ipv6 unicast-routing
!
interface Loopback1
 ip address 10.9.9.1 255.255.255.255
!
interface Tunnel0
 no ip address
 ipv6 address 2002:a09:901::/128
 tunnel source Loopback1
 tunnel mode ipv6ip 6to4
!
interface FastEthernet0/0
 ip address 10.1.1.1 255.255.255.0
 ipv6 address 2002:A09:901:1::1/64
!
ipv6 route 2002::/16 Tunnel0
```

This configuration defines all the small pieces listed in the configuration checklist, but the configuration does not spell out the underlying logic. Looking at the configuration, along with the design and the knowledge of how automatic 6to4 tunnels work, the following logic occurs in the background:

Step 1.   R1 will have two connected IPv6 routes (F0/0's and tunnel0's) in the 2002::/16 range, plus a static route for the entire 2002::/16 range.

Step 2.   When R1 receives an IPv6 packet, destination in the 2002::/16 range, and the destination is not in one of the connected subnets, R1 will try to forward the packet out tunnel0.

Step 3.   The **tunnel mode ipv6ip 6to4** command tells R1 to look to the $2^{nd}/3^{rd}$ octets to find the destination IPv4 address, and perform the tunneling.

Also, take another moment to review the configuration in Example 18-6, looking specifically for any configuration on R1 that references anything specific about either R3 or R4 in Figure 18-8. No such specifics exist. R1's logic works without any preconfigured addressing information about R3, and to R4, and to hundreds of future routers, if the engineer plans the IPv6 addresses correctly. So, if this Enterprise decided to enable the automatic tunnel on yet another router, only the configuration in that one new router would need to be changed, but the configuration on R1, R3, and R4 would be unchanged. The rest of the routers would not need any more configuration because the static route for 2002::/16 triggers the routing of IPv6 packets, tunneled in IPv4, to the correct remote routers.

Example 18-7 lists the **show** commands that confirm some of these facts.

Example 18-7   *R1's State When Using the Automatic 6to4 Tunnel*

```
R1# show ipv6 route
IPv6 Routing Table - Default - 5 entries
Codes: C - Connected, L - Local, S - Static, U - Per-user Static route
       B - BGP, M - MIPv6, R - RIP, I1 - ISIS L1
       I2 - ISIS L2, IA - ISIS interarea, IS - ISIS summary, D - EIGRP
       EX - EIGRP external
       O - OSPF Intra, OI - OSPF Inter, OE1 - OSPF ext 1, OE2 - OSPF ext 2
       ON1 - OSPF NSSA ext 1, ON2 - OSPF NSSA ext 2
S    2002::/16 [1/0]
     via Tunnel0, directly connected
LC   2002:A09:901::/128 [0/0]
     via Tunnel0, receive
C    2002:A09:901:1::/64 [0/0]
     via FastEthernet0/0, directly connected
L    2002:A09:901:1::1/128 [0/0]
     via FastEthernet0/0, receive
L    FF00::/8 [0/0]
     via Null0, receive

R1# show ipv6 interface brief
FastEthernet0/0          [up/up]
```

```
    FE80::213:19FF:FE7B:5026
    2002:A09:901:1::1
FastEthernet0/1                 [administratively down/down]
    unassigned
! unrelated lines omitted
Tunnel0                         [up/up]
    FE80::A09:901
    2002:A09:901::


R1# trace 2002:a09:903:3::3


Type escape sequence to abort.
Tracing the route to 2002:A09:903:3::3

  1 2002:A09:903::3 4 msec 4 msec 4 msec
```

The **show ipv6 route** command lists the static route and both connected routes. Note that in this case, the configuration used a /128 prefix length for Tunnel0's IPv6 address, so the connected route shows up on the same line as the local route, both of which have a /128 prefix length. The **show ipv6 interface brief** command confirms the configured IPv6 address from the 2002::/16 range, plus the link local address derived for the Tunnel0 interface. Note that link local address uses an unusual convention–instead of using the usual EUI-64 logic, the link local address starts with FE80::/96, with the last two quartets the same as the tunnel's IPv4 source address. Finally, the **traceroute** command at the end of the example proves the tunnel works.

Using Global Unicasts with Automatic Tunnels

The previous example of automatic 6to4 tunnels assumed that the engineer chose all IPv6 addresses from the reserved 2002::/16 range because no need existed for IPv6 Internet connectivity. This section looks at the same automatic 6to4 concepts but with global unicasts used for the LAN subnets.

The big conceptual difference that occurs when using global unicast addresses relates to when using an assigned global unicast prefix, the second and third quartets are set, are the same for all subnets in the Enterprise, and can no longer be used to store the tunnel destination's IPv4 address. For example, if an Enterprise were assigned 2000:0:1::/48 as a site prefix, then all the subnets at the Enterprise would need to begin 2000:0:1, instead of encoding the IPv4 address of the site in the second and third quartets.

The problem can be overcome, however, through a piece of logic used when the router forwards packets out the tunnel interface after doing a recursive route lookup:

> When the router matches a route with an outgoing 6to4 tunnel interface, but with no next-hop IPv6 address, AND this route was matched due to route recursion, then derive the tunnel's destination IPv4 address based on the previously matched route's next-hop IPv6 address.

Although true, the formal definition is a bit much to work through. So, consider Figure 18-9, which shows a revised version of Figure 18-8. The figure uses the same three routers, same IPv4 loopback addresses, and same IPv6 addresses on the tunnel interfaces. However, for the three LANs, the engineer chose IPv6 prefixes from within the site's 2000:0:1::/48 prefix, essentially making R1's LAN Subnet 1, R3's LAN Subnet 3, and R4's LAN Subnet 4.

Figure 18-9   *Automatic Tunnels, Using Global Unicast IPv6 Addresses*

The underlying logic hinges on the two static routes in R1's IPv6 routing table, as shown in Figure 18-9. One route is the old route for 2002::/16, whereas the other route, added because of the use of global unicast addresses, matches the prefix for R3's LAN. Following the numbered sequence in the figure

Step 1.   PC1 sends an IPv6 packet to PC3, destination address 2000:0:1:3::33.

Step 2.   R1 compares the destination IPv6 address, matching the first route (destination 2000:0:1:3::/64) with outgoing interface Tunnel0 and next-hop router 2002:A09:903:: (R3's tunnel IPv6 address).

Step 3.   R1 needs to decide how to forward packets to 2002:A09:903::, so R1 performs route recursion to find the matching route for this destination. R1 matches the static route for 2002::/16 with outgoing interface tunnel0 and with no next-hop address listed.

At this point, the usual automatic 6to4 tunnel logic kicks in but based on the first route's next-hop address of 2002:a09:903::.

Summarizing, the differences in planning and configuration for using global unicasts with automatic 6to4 tunnels are

Step 1. Plan the prefixes and addresses for the LANs using the global unicast range assigned to the Enterprise.

Step 2. Configure an additional static route for each remote subnet, configuring the tunnel as outgoing interface and configuring the next-hop IPv6 address. That next-hop must be the remote router's tunnel IPv6 address, which embeds the destination IPv4 address as the second and third octets.

Note: You also can use BGP for IPv6 to learn the route listed in Step 2.

For R1 to forward traffic to the IPv6 hosts PC3 and PC4 in Figure 18-9, R1 would need the following two additional routes:

■ **ipv6 route 2000:0:1:3::/64 tunnel0 2002:a09:903::**

■ **ipv6 route 2000:0:1:4::/64 tunnel0 2002:a09:904::**

Finally, the introduction to this section mentioned that the use of global unicast addresses required more configuration changes. When a new router is added to the multipoint tunnel, each router already on the tunnel needs to add additional static routes or the alternative additional BGP configuration.

IPv6 ISATAP Tunnels

You can use ISATAP–the Intra-site Automatic Tunnel Addressing Protocol–to identify the IPv4 address of the remote site for the purposes of tunneling IPv6 packets. As a result, you can create dynamic multipoint tunnels using ISATAP, in general a concept much like the multipoint tunnels created using automatic 6to4 tunnels.

Comparing ISATAP and Automatic 6to4 Concepts

ISATAP tunnels differ in some ways with automatic 6to4 tunnels. However, ISATAP IPv6 tunnels use concepts that closely match those used by automatic 6to4 tunnels when using global unicast addresses (as previously shown in Figure 18-9). The following list makes some important comparisons between these two options with the items that differ between ISATAP tunnels and automatic 6to4 tunnels highlighted in gray:

Step 1. ISATAP tunnels use global unicast prefixes for user subnets.

Step 2. ISATAP tunnel interfaces use IPv6 addresses that embed the tunnel's destination IPv4 address inside the IPv6 address.

Step 3. The routers need static routes for the destination end-user IPv6 prefixes; the route must list a next-hop IPv6 address, which in turn embeds the tunnel destination IPv4 address.

Step 4. ISATAP tunnel interface IPv6 addresses embed the IPv4 address in the last two quartets.

Step 5. ISATAP tunnels do not use a special reserved range of IPv6 addresses at all, instead using just normal IPv6 unicast prefixes.

Step 6. ISATAP tunnels typically use a single prefix to which all tunnel interfaces connect, so all routers have a connected IPv6 route to that same subnet.

Step 7. ISATAP tunnels can automatically derive the tunnel interface's interface ID by using modified EUI-64 rules.

As usual, an example can help sift through some of the details; Figure 18-10 shows just such an example. The figure is the same as Figure 18-9's automatic 6to4 tunnel example with the same user IPv6 prefixes from the global unicast range. However, the design and configuration has been changed to work with ISATAP tunnels, as follows:

- The three tunnel interfaces now have IPv6 addresses in common IPv6 subnet 2000:0:1:9::/64. (The actual subnet number is not important; just choose a currently unused IPv6 subnet.)

- The tunnel interfaces' IPv6 addresses conform to *modified* EUI-64 rules (explained following the figure) embedding the IPv4 address in the last two quartets.

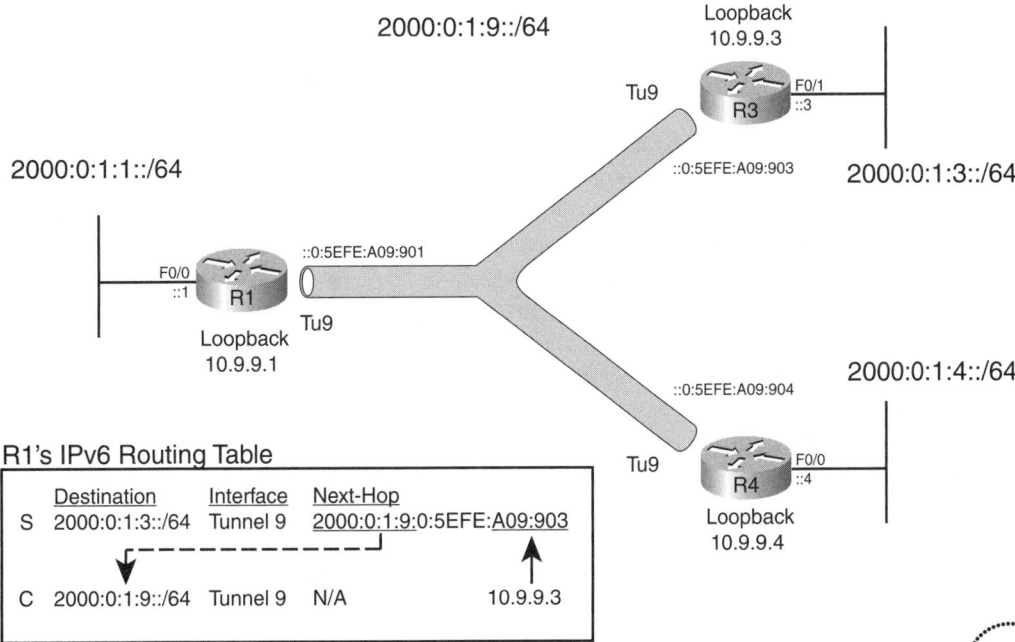

Figure 18-10 *ISATAP Tunnel Example, with Minimal Changes Compared to Figure 18-9*

- The routers no longer need a route for 2002::/16, instead relying on the connected route created for subnet 2000:0:1:9::/64.

First, examine the four IPv6 global unicast prefixes in the figure. The three LAN-based prefixes match the same ones used in the example of Figure 18-9. The fourth prefix includes all three routers' tunnel interfaces, much like a typical LAN. All three router's tunnel interfaces use an IPv6 address from this same prefix (2000:0:1:9::/64), and each will configure their address using a /64 prefix length.

Next, consider R1's routing logic when it receives an IPv6 packet destined for R3's LAN IPv6 prefix. R1's routing table lists a static route for R3's LAN subnet (2000:0:1:3::/64), with R3's tunnel IPv6 address listed as next hop (2000:0:1:9:0:5EFE:A09:903). When R1 receives an IPv6 packet destined for R3's LAN IPv6 subnet, R1 matches this static route. R1 also notices that the outgoing interface is not only a tunnel, but also an ISATAP tunnel, so R1 derives the tunnel's destination IPv4 address from the last two quartets of the next-hop address of the route (A09:903). (These values convert to 10.9.9.3.) R1 can then encapsulate and send the IPv4 transport packet to 10.9.9.3.

Beyond the detail in Figure 18-10, the only other item that needs some explanation is the format of the ISATAP-defined IPv6 address. The addresses can be configured manually but can also be derived by the router using *modified EUI-64 rules*. The rules work as follows:

Key Topic

- Configure a 64-bit prefix on the tunnel interface, and use the **eui-64** parameter, telling the router to derive the second half (interface ID) of the address.

- The router adds 0000:5EFE as quartets 5 and 6.

- The router finds the tunnel's source IPv4 address, converts it to hex, and adds that as quartets 7 and 8.

Configuring ISATAP IPv6 Tunnels

The overall configuration includes many steps, as usual, but most of the steps mirror the steps seen in the automatic 6to4 tunnel configurations. The following list outlines the steps. It also highlights in gray the steps not used when configuring automatic 6to4 tunnels for the case that used addresses in the 2002::/16 range exclusively.

Key Topic

Step 1. Configure the planned loopback interface and its IPv4 address, ensuring the IPv4 IGP advertises a route for this address.

Step 2. Create a tunnel interface using the **interface tunnel** *number* command.

Step 3. Define the tunnel source (**tunnel source** {*interface-type interface-number* | *ipv4-address*}) using the loopback IP address from Step 1.

Step 4. Do NOT define a tunnel destination with the **tunnel destination** interface subcommand.

Step 5. Identify the tunnel as an ISATAP tunnel using the **tunnel mode ipv6ip isatap** interface subcommand.

Step 6. Configure an IPv6 prefix with EUI-64 option using the e **ipv6 address**prefix/length**eui-64** interface subcommand.

Step 7.   Complete the normal IPv6 configuration, include defining the LAN interface
IPv6 addresses per the planning chart and enabling IPv6 routing with the **ipv6
unicast-routing** command.

Step 8.   Define static IPv6 routes (using the **ipv6 route** global command) for each destination IPv6 prefix, with an outgoing interface and next-hop address. (The
next-hop should be the destination router's IPv6 address that embeds the IPv4
address as the last two octets.)

Example 18-8 shows the configuration on Routers R1 and R3 from Figure 18-10 with the
tunnel details highlighted.

Example 18-8   *Configuring R1 and R3 for an ISATAP Tunnel per Figure 18-10*

```
! First, on router R1:
R1# show running-config
! only relevant portions shown
ipv6 unicast-routing
!
interface Loopback1
 ip address 10.9.9.1 255.255.255.255
!
interface Tunnel9
 no ip address
 ipv6 address 2000:0:1:9::/64 eui-64
 tunnel source Loopback1
 tunnel mode ipv6ip isatap
!
interface FastEthernet0/0
 ip address 10.1.1.1 255.255.255.0
 ipv6 address 2000:0:1:1::1/64
!
ipv6 route 2000:0:1:3::/64 2000:0:1:9:0:5EFE:A09:903
ipv6 route 2000:0:1:4::/64 2000:0:1:9:0:5EFE:A09:904
! Next, on router R3:

R3# show running-config
! only relevant portions shown
ipv6 unicast-routing
!
interface Loopback3
 ip address 10.9.9.3 255.255.255.255
!
interface Tunnel9
 no ip address
 ipv6 address 2000:0:1:9::/64 eui-64
 tunnel source Loopback3
 tunnel mode ipv6ip isatap
```

```
!
interface FastEthernet0/1
 ip address 10.1.3.3 255.255.255.0
 ipv6 address 2000:0:1:3::3/64
!
ipv6 route 2000:0:1:1::/64 2000:0:1:9:0:5EFE:A09:901
ipv6 route 2000:0:1:4::/64 2000:0:1:9:0:5EFE:A09:904
```

The most important parts of the configurations are the tunnel configuration and the static routes. First, on R1's new tunnel interface (Tunnel 9), the configuration sets the mode to ISATAP (**tunnel mode ipv6ip isatap**). This command, in combination with the **ipv6 address 2000:0:1:9::/64 eui-64** command, tells R1 to use the modified EUI-64 rules to give R1's Tunnel 9 interface an IPv6 address of 2000:0:1:9:0:5EFE:A09:901. R1 derives the last two octets based on the indirect reference made in the **tunnel source loopback 1** command, using loopback 1's IPv4 address (10.9.9.1) to complete Tunnel 9's IPv6 address.

The two static routes on R1 simply define routes to the LAN subnet on each remote router with the important part being the next-hop IPv6 address. The listed addresses exist on R3 and R4, generated by the modified EUI-64 process on those routers.

Example 18-9 shows some supporting verification commands on Router R1.

Example 18-9   *Verifying Tunnel Operation on R1*

```
R1# show ipv6 interface brief
FastEthernet0/0              [up/up]
    FE80::213:19FF:FE7B:5026
    2000:0:1:1::1
! irrelevant interfaces removed
Loopback1                    [up/up]
    unassigned
Tunnel9                      [up/up]
    FE80::5EFE:A09:901
    2000:0:1:9:0:5EFE:A09:901

R1# show ipv6 route
IPv6 Routing Table - Default - 7 entries
Codes: C - Connected, L - Local, S - Static, U - Per-user Static route
       B - BGP, M - MIPv6, R - RIP, I1 - ISIS L1
       I2 - ISIS L2, IA - ISIS interarea, IS - ISIS summary, D - EIGRP
       EX - EIGRP external
       O - OSPF Intra, OI - OSPF Inter, OE1 - OSPF ext 1, OE2 - OSPF ext 2
       ON1 - OSPF NSSA ext 1, ON2 - OSPF NSSA ext 2
C    2000:0:1:1::/64 [0/0]
     via FastEthernet0/0, directly connected
L    2000:0:1:1::1/128 [0/0]
     via FastEthernet0/0, receive
```

```
S   2000:0:1:3::/64 [1/0]
      via 2000:0:1:9:0:5EFE:A09:903
S   2000:0:1:4::/64 [1/0]
      via 2000:0:1:9:0:5EFE:A09:904
C   2000:0:1:9::/64 [0/0]
      via Tunnel9, directly connected
L   2000:0:1:9:0:5EFE:A09:901/128 [0/0]
      via Tunnel9, receive
L   FF00::/8 [0/0]
      via Null0, receive


R1# traceroute
Protocol [ip]: ipv6
Target IPv6 address: 2000:0:1:3::3
Source address: 2000:0:1:1::1
Insert source routing header? [no]:
Numeric display? [no]:
Timeout in seconds [3]:
Probe count [3]:
Minimum Time to Live [1]:
Maximum Time to Live [30]:
Priority [0]:
Port Number [0]:
Type escape sequence to abort.
Tracing the route to 2000:0:1:3::3

  1 2000:0:1:9:0:5EFE:A09:903 0 msec 0 msec 4 msec
```

The example begins with the **show ipv6 interfaces brief** command, which shows the two IPv6 addresses R1 derives. It lists the 2000:0:1:9::5EFE:A09:901 address, derived using the modified EUI-64 rules. It also lists a link local address on the interface, formed not with traditional EUI-64 rules but instead with the same modified EUI-64 rules used for the global unicast address.

The **show ipv6 route** command output highlights the same routes shown in Figure 18-10. It lists the static route for R3's LAN subnet, a route to 2000:0:1:3::/64, with R3's modified EUI-64 IPv6 address as the next hop. The output also shows R1's connected route for the tunnel subnet (2000:0:1:9::/64). Finally, the **traceroute** command at the end confirms that R1 can send packets to R3's LAN IPv6 address (2000:0:1:3::3) from R1's LAN IPv6 address (2000:0:1:1::1).

Multipoint IPv6 Tunnel Summary

Multipoint IPv6 tunnels give engineers a good means to implement IPv6 connectivity for short periods of time. The tunnels can allow easier addition of new sites, with less config- uration on existing routers. These tunnels also support tunneling with IPv6 hosts. How- ever, these tunnels do not support IPv6 IGPs. Also, the extra processing required to forward each IPv6 packet makes this solution most useful as a short-term temporary solution, with native IPv6 and point-to-point tunnels more reasonable for more extended periods of time. Table 18-4 summarizes the key features with the small differences highlighted in the table.

Key Topic

Table 18-4   *Comparing IPv6 Multipoint Tunnels*

	Automatic 6to4	ISATAP
RFC	3056	4214
Uses a reserved IPv6 address prefix.	Yes (2002::/16)	No
Supports the use of global unicast addresses?	Yes	Yes
Quartets holding the IPv4 destination address.	2/3	7/8
End-user host addresses embed the IPv4 destination?	Sometimes	No
Tunnel endpoints IPv6 addresses embed IPv4 destination.	Sometimes	Yes
Uses modified EUI-64 to form tunnel IPv6 addresses?	No	Yes

Exam Preparation Tasks

Planning Practice

The CCNP ROUTE exam expects test takers to review design documents, create implementation plans, and create verification plans. This section provides some exercises that may help you to take a step back from the minute details of the topics in this chapter so that you can think about the same technical topics from the planning perspective.

For each planning practice table, simply complete the table. Note that any numbers in parentheses represent the number of options listed for each item in the solutions in Appendix F, "Completed Practice Planning Tables."

Design Review Table

Table 18-5 lists several design goals related to this chapter. If these design goals were listed in a design document, and you had to take that document and develop an implementation plan, what implementation options come to mind? You should write a general description; specific configuration commands are not required.

Table 18-5   *Design Review*

Design Goal	Possible Implementation Choices Covered in This Chapter
The design states that an Enterprise needs IPv6 support for most LANs, with a regular high-volume of IPv6 traffic. Would native IPv6, point-to-point tunnels, or multipoint tunnels seem most appropriate?	
The design states that an Enterprise needs IPv6 support for a set small subset of LANs but that their traffic will be regular. Would native IPv6, point-to-point tunnels, or multipoint tunnels seem most appropriate?	
The design states that an Enterprise needs IPv6 support for a set small subset of LANs but that their traffic will be irregular and occasional. Would native IPv6, point-to-point tunnels, or multipoint tunnels seem most appropriate?	
The plan calls for IPv6 tunneling so that new routers, when added to the tunnel, do not require additional configuration on existing routers. What type tunnel would you choose, and what IPv6 address ranges?	

Implementation Plan Peer Review Table

Table 18-6 shows a list of questions that others might ask, or that you might think about, during a peer review of another network engineer's implementation plan. Complete the table by answering the questions.

Table 18-6   *Notable Questions from This Chapter to Consider During an Implementation Plan Peer Review*

Question	Answers
The plan calls for the use of OSPFv3 along with the implementation of IPv6 tunnels. What tunnel types do you expect to find the sample configurations? (2)	
The planning diagrams show multipoint tunnels, with IPv6 addresses that embed an IPv4 address in the last two quartets. What type of tunneling do you expect to see in the sample configurations?	
The plan lists a sample configuration with the command **tunnel mode ipv6ip** under a tunnel interface. What type of tunneling is used in this case?	
Same question as the previous row, but the command listed is **tunnel mode ipv6ip isatap**.	
Same question as the previous row, but the command listed is **tunnel mode gre ip**.	
Same question as the previous row, but the command listed is **tunnel mode ipv6ip 6to4**.	
A plan shows the use of a manually configured tunnel and an ISATAP tunnel. What tunnel sub-command would you expect to see for the point-to-point tunnel, but not the multipoint tunnel?	

Create an Implementation Plan Table

To practice skills useful when creating your own implementation plan, list in Table 18-7 all configuration commands related to the configuration of the following features. You may want to record your answers outside the book and set a goal to complete this table (and others like it) from memory during your final reviews before taking the exam.

Table 18-7 *Implementation Plan Configuration Memory Drill*

Feature	Configuration Commands/Notes
Configure an IPv6 manually configured tunnel using a loopback IPv4 address. Ignore IPv6 addressing and routing configuration.	
Add IPv6 addressing and routing configuration to the previous row's list. Assume EIGRP for IPv6 ASN 1 is preconfigured.	
Configure an IPv6 GRE tunnel using a loopback IPv4 address. Ignore IPv6 addressing and routing configuration.	
Configure an IPv6 automatic 6to4 tunnel using a loopback IPv4 address. Include only IPv6 configuration required for the tunnel to pass IPv6 traffic. Assume all hosts use addresses in the 2002::/16 range.	
List steps to migrate from the automatic 6to4 tunnel from the previous row to a comparable ISATAP tunnel	

Choose Commands for a Verification Plan Table

To practice skills useful when creating your own verification plan, list in Table 18-8 all commands that supply the requested information. You may want to record your answers outside the book and set a goal to complete this table (and others like it) from memory during your final reviews before taking the exam.

Note: Some of the entries in this table may not have been specifically mentioned in this chapter but are listed in this table for review and reference.

Table 18-8 *Verification Plan Memory Drill*

Information Needed	Commands
Tunnel interface status for IPv6.	
Tunnel interface's IPv6 address(es).	
Connected routes related to the tunnel.	
The tunnel source and destination IPv4 addresses.	
Test the tunnel to see if it can pass traffic.	

Review all the Key Topics

Review the most important topics from inside the chapter noted with the Key Topics icon in the outer margin of the page. Table 18-9 lists a reference of these key topics and the page numbers on which each is found.

Table 18-9 *Key Topics for Chapter 10*

Key Topic Element	Description	Page Number
Figure 18-3	Point-to-point IPv6 tunnel concept	614
Figure 18-4	Multipoint IPv6 tunnel concept	616
Table 18-2	Comparisons of four IPv6 tunnel types	617
Figure 18-5	NAT-PT concepts	618
List	Manually configured tunnel configuration checklist	620
List	Configuration differences between GRE and manually configured IPv6 tunnels	625
Table 18-3	Comparisons of manually configured tunnels and GRE tunnels	626
Figure 18-8	Address planning for automatic 6to4 tunnels	628
List	Configuration checklist for automatic 6to4 tunnels	629
List	Comparisons of automatic 6to4 and ISATAP tunnels	634
Figure 18-10	ISATAP tunnel logic	635
List	Modified EUI-64 rules for forming ISATAP IPv6 addresses	636
List	ISATAP tunnel configuration checklist	636
Table 18-4	Comparisons of Automatic 6to4 and ISATAP tunnels	640

Complete the Tables and Lists from Memory

Print a copy of Appendix D, "Memory Tables," (found on the CD), or at least the section for this chapter, and complete the tables and lists from memory. Appendix E, "Memory Tables Answer Key," also on the CD, includes completed tables and lists to check your work.

Define Key Terms

Define the following key terms from this chapter, and check your answers in the glossary.

Dual stacks, Network Address Translation–Protocol Translation (NAT-PT), tunneling, tunnel, tunnel interface, point-to-point tunnel, multipoint tunnel, ISATAP tunnel, ISATAP, automatic 6to4 tunnel, manually configured tunnel, GRE tunnel, Modified EUI-64

This chapter covers the following subjects:

Branch Office Broadband Internet Access: This section introduces some of the issues related to using the Internet as a WAN connectivity option for an Enterprise network.

Broadband Branch Access Configuration: This section generally discusses the configuration of a DSL connection on a router, along with the associated NAT and DHCP configuration.

VPN Configuration: This section generally discusses IPSec VPN and GRE tunnel configuration, particularly the routing aspects as they apply to branch office routers.

CHAPTER 19

Routing over Branch Internet Connections

This chapter discusses routing from the Enterprise branch office perspective, specifically for cases in which the branch uses the Internet for its connectivity back to the rest of the Enterprise network. Such a branch router needs to supply many functions: NAT, DHCP services, firewall, and even dynamic routing when multiple connections exist to the Enterprise. This chapter examines each of these and some basics regarding Internet access technologies as well.

From an exam preparation perspective, this chapter differs from the other 17 technology-focused chapters (Chapters 2 through 18) in this book. For the most part, the other chapters not only introduce some networking topics, the descriptions, figures, and examples go quite deep into the subject. This chapter, however, discusses more generalized concepts and some configuration samples without getting into every command option. Some topics mentioned in this chapter are actually part of the prerequisite CCNA topics, and some fit into other Cisco certifications, such as CCNA Security and CCSP. This chapter attempts to maintain the intended depth and breadth of the exam for this small set of remaining topics.

"Do I Know This Already?" Quiz

The "Do I Know This Already?" quiz allows you to assess if you should read the entire chapter. If you miss no more than one of these six self-assessment questions, you might want to move ahead to the "Exam Preparation Tasks." Table 19-1 lists the major headings in this chapter and the "Do I Know This Already?" quiz questions covering the material in those headings so that you can assess your knowledge of these specific areas. The answers to the "Do I Know This Already?" quiz appear in Appendix A.

Table 19-1 *"Do I Know This Already?" Foundation Topics Section-to-Question Mapping*

Foundations Topics Section	Questions
Branch Office Broadband Internet Access	1-2
Branch Router Configuration for Broadband Access	3-4
VPN Configuration	5

1. Router R1 sits at an Enterprise branch office, using the Internet for its only connectivity back to the rest of the Enterprise. Which of the following is not a benefit of using an IPsec tunnel for packets sent through the Internet, between R1 and the rest of the Enterprise?

    a. Privacy

    b. Authentication

    c. Allows using an IGP between R1 and the Enterprise

    d. Secure communications

2. Router R1 sits at an Enterprise branch office, using both the Internet and a leased line to another Enterprise router for its two connectivity options back into the rest of the Enterprise network. The engineer planning for this branch decided to use the leased line for all Enterprise traffic, unless it fails, in which case the Internet connection should be used to pass traffic to the Enterprise. Which of the following is most likely to be useful on the branch router? (Choose two.)

    a. IPsec tunnel

    b. GRE tunnel

    c. Floating static route

    d. An IGP

3. Router R1, a branch router, connects to the Internet using DSL. The engineer plans to use a configuration with a dialer interface. The answers list a feature and interface on which the feature could be configured. Which combinations accurately describe the interface under which a feature will be configured?

    a. PPP on the ATM interface

    b. VPI/VCI on the dialer interface

    c. IP address on the ATM interface

    d. CHAP on the dialer interface

4. Router R1, a branch router, connects to the Internet using DSL. Some traffic flows through a GRE and IPsec tunnel, over the DSL connection, and into the core of an Enterprise network. The branch also allows local hosts to communicate directly with public sites in the Internet over this same DSL connection. Which of the following answers defines how the branch NAT config avoids performing NAT for the Enterprise-directed traffic but does perform NAT for the Internet-directed traffic?

    a. By not enabling NAT on the IPsec tunnel interface

    b. By not enabling NAT on the GRE tunnel interface

    c. By configuring the NAT-referenced ACL to not permit the Enterprise traffic

    d. By asking the ISP to perform NAT in the cloud

5. Router R1, a branch router, connects to the Internet using DSL. Some traffic flows through a GRE and IPsec tunnel, over the DSL connection, destined for an Enterprise network. Which of the following answers best describes the router's logic that tells the router, for a given packet, to apply GRE encapsulation to the packet?

    a. When the packet received on the LAN interface is permitted by the ACL listed on the **tunnel gre** *acl* command under the incoming interface

    b. When routing the packet, matching a route whose outgoing interface is the GRE tunnel interface

    c. When routing the packet, matching a route whose outgoing interface is the IPsec tunnel interface

    d. When permitted by an ACL that was referenced in the associated crypto map

Foundation Topics

Branch Office Broadband Internet Access

Many options exist today for private connectivity between an Enterprise branch office and the core of an Enterprise network. These options include leased lines, Frame Relay, MPLS VPNs, and Metro Ethernet. Although each differs in some way, they all share an important characteristic: They provide an inherently private path over which two Enterprise routers can send packets to each other.

Several other public options exist for branch office connectivity. All these options use the Internet for connectivity between the branch office and the core of the Enterprise network. Regardless of the particular physical Internet access technology–typically digital subscriber line (DSL), cable, or wireless broadband–all these options use a public Internet to forward the packets.

The differences between the public Internet and private connectivity mean that the branches need to use several additional functions just to make the connectivity work, plus the branches need to add other functions to make the connection secure. This chapter focuses on the functions required, and how they impact routing between the branch and the rest of the Enterprise.

The branch routing for the Internet-connected branch differs in part depending on the design. Figure 19-1 shows three examples of branch offices of different sizes. The figure labels these branches as small, medium, and large, but frankly, those descriptions are a bit subjective. For the purposes of this chapter, as the size increases, the number of connections or routers increases, and with that, the number of issues to consider also increases.

For the small branch design, most of the implementation challenges fall into two main categories: features needed for communication with hosts in the public Internet, and features needed to support secure communications with hosts in the Enterprise. The first category includes the Internet access details–how to make DSL, cable, and so on work–plus services likely to be required to learn, allocate, and translate the public IP addresses learned from the ISP, such as NAT and DHCP. The second category focuses on virtual private network (VPN) options that allow the Enterprise to trust that a packet comes from a legitimate branch office, and to prevent attackers from reading the contents of the packet as it crosses the Internet.

The rest of this first section of the chapter gives an overview of the various pieces of the puzzle of supporting private Enterprise traffic, over the public Internet, between the branch and the rest of the Enterprise.

Broadband Internet Access Basics

The term *broadband* has been around in the world of networking for a long time. The original meaning related to the frequency bands used by some Layer 1 standards that used a wider (broader) range of frequencies to achieve a higher bit rate. Today, the term broadband has grown to become synonymous with *high speed*.

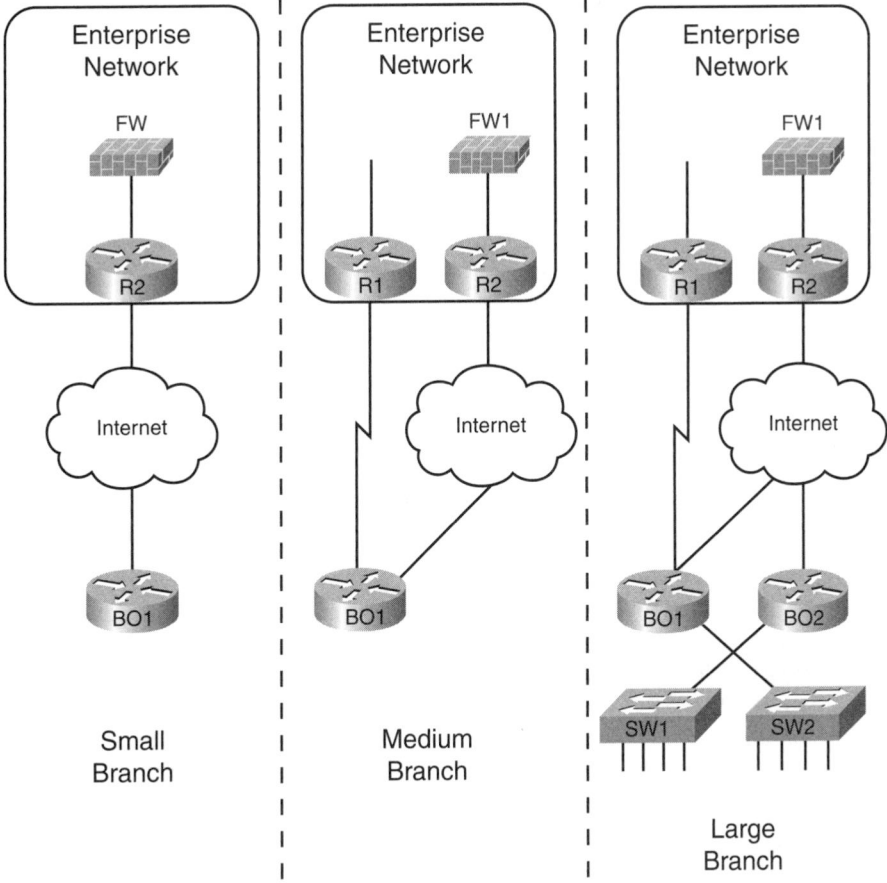

Figure 19-1   *Example Small, Medium, and Large Branch Designs*

The term *broadband Internet access technology* simply refers to a class of high-speed (a relative term) communications methods that allows a device to access some ISP, and in turn the Internet. Today, this term generally refers to (high-speed) cable Internet access, (high-speed) DSL Internet access, and (high-speed) wireless Internet access, with DSL and cable as the most commonly used options.

The hardware used at the branch office for each of these access technologies varies. However, whether a single piece of hardware does all the work, or whether several pieces of hardware combine to do the work, the hardware typically includes an IP router and either a cable modem or DSL modem. Again, like the term broadband, the term *modem* has taken new meaning over the years compared to its original historic use. However, a cable modem or DSL modem sits in the same location as a traditional analog modem, so the term has grown to a broader meaning. For example, Figure19-2 shows a typical branch office LAN with a router and a cable modem.

Figure 19-2 shows a typical connection at a small office/home office (SOHO) site, with a separate router and cable modem. The router in this case uses two LAN interfaces, routing

Figure 19-2 *Typical Cabling with Cable Modem at a Small Office/Home Office (SOHO)*

over those interfaces. However, on the LAN interface connected toward the ISP, the router uses a slightly different convention on the Ethernet called *PPP over Ethernet (PPPoE)*. The frames sent by the router still use an Ethernet header, but then include a PPP header, and then an IP header.

The PPP header gives the router and ISP the capability to use PPP features such as the Challenge Handshake Authentication Protocol (CHAP). CHAP allows the ISP to perform authentication, which allows the ISP to confirm the identity of the router that sent the packet. This allows the ISP to check the user's account, make accounting records of the access, and confirm that the customer is not late in paying their high-speed cable bill. (DSL uses a similar protocol, PPP over ATM (PPPoA), also in part to support PPP CHAP.)

Branch Router as DHCP Server and Client

When planning the permanent connection from an Enterprise to the Internet, as discussed at some length in Chapter 12, "Internet Connectivity and BGP," the ISP uses a range of registered public IP addresses. The ISP often assigns this range, or the Enterprise may register a prefix directly. Most Enterprises then use RFC 1918 private IPv4 addresses for most hosts inside the Enterprise. To make the whole package work, the Enterprise must also configure NAT, typically with the port address translation (PAT) feature, to translate between the private and public addresses.

Each Internet-connected branch follows the same public IP addressing model in general, but with some differences. First, the ISP typically assigns one and only one public IP address for the branch site, expecting the branch to use PAT. That public IP address may change over time; even though most broadband Internet access technologies use "always on" logic, the underlying protocols act more like a dial connection that never stops. So, the ISP dynamically assigns the public IP address so that if the subscriber stops using the connection, fails to pay the bill, or cancels the account, the public IP address can be easily and automatically reclaimed into the pool of available addresses.

The IP address assignment process differs slightly for the branch LAN as well. Hosts still learn their IP address, mask, default gateway, and DNS server addresses, but rather than require a separate host at each branch to act as DHCP server, the branch router may act as

DHCP server. Figure 19-3 shows the idea of the branch router learning its public address, plus acting as DHCP server for local LAN hosts.

Figure 19-3   *Branch Office Router Acting as DHCP Client and DHCP Server*

As you can see, the two branch hosts both received the appropriate addressing information for private network 192.168.1.0/24. R1 itself learns similar information from the ISP's DHCP server. R1 will use this learned IP address on the interface it uses to connect to the ISP. R1 also adds a default route to its IP routing table, using the ISP1's IP address as next hop–in this case, 64.100.1.2.

Finally, R1 must enable NAT/PAT. As a reminder, the term NAT today refers to all NAT functions, including the port address translation feature. PAT allows a little more than 65,000 concurrent flows to use a single public IP address by using a different TCP or UDP port number for each flow. As a result, this single public IP address should be more than enough for a typical branch office.

Note: Consumer-class products enable by default most of the features described in this section, such as DHCP client, server, and NAT/PAT. Enterprise-class routers typically rely on explicit configuration by a network engineer for these same features.

Branch Office Security

With a permanent Internet connection near the core of the Enterprise network, the Enterprise typically uses one or more border security products. These products include stateful firewalls such as the ASA appliance from Cisco, plus Intrusion Prevention Systems (IPS).

Now that a branch has a connection to the Internet, most Enterprises implement similar features at the branch. Again, for economic reasons, it makes more sense to implement those features on the same router platform already needed for so many other reasons. So, Cisco includes firewall and IPS features in IOS. These features include the older Context

Based Access Control (CBAC) and newer IOS Zone-Based Firewall. Cisco also supplies the IOS IPS feature as well.

Although it may seem that running such features on a branch router might overload the router, Cisco designed its Integrated Services Routers (ISR) to have the power to concurrently run many services for exactly this type of application. ISRs include the older model series 800, 1800, 2800, and 3800 ISR families, plus model series 1900, 2900, and 3900, introduced in 2009.

Using IPsec Tunnels

The technologies reviewed up to this point, when implemented at the branch, give hosts at the branch the capability to access hosts in the Internet, and to do so securely. However, the hosts at the branch typically cannot access applications inside the Enterprise at this point.

Several problems prevent the branch hosts from accessing hosts with private IP addresses inside the Enterprise core. One problem is that packets from branch hosts at this point look like packets from any other Internet-based hosts, and the Enterprise firewall could (and should) discard such packets. For example, if a branch host tries to send a packet to a host inside the Enterprise core, the branch would NAT the packet to use the branch's public IP address. When that packet arrives at the Enterprise's firewall at the company's main Internet connection, the firewall would have no way to know whether the packet came from a legitimate host at the branch. One solution would be to allow packets past the firewall, making the server available to the Internet, and rely on host security to prevent access, but that may be too risky.

To solve this problem, typically the engineer configures a tunnel between the branch and the Enterprise core. Then the branch router directs traffic destined for the Enterprise through the tunnel. For such packets, the branch router will not translate the IP address of the original packet using NAT. Instead, the branch router will encrypt the IP packet and encapsulate the encrypted packet inside another IPv4 header, using public source and destination addresses in this new packet. Then, the branch router can forward this packet through the public Internet, with a device in the Enterprise core receiving and decrypting the packet. That device can tell from additional security headers in the encrypted packet whether it comes from a trusted branch router. Figure 19-4 shows an example of the process.

Following the steps in Figure 19-4:

Step 1.   PC1 creates a packet, with its own 10.99.1.1 address as source, and server S1's 10.1.1.1 IP address as destination. PC1 sends the packet to its default gateway (BO1).

Step 2.   When Router BO1 tries to route the packet toward the Internet, the router's logic tells it to check an ACL. All packets permitted by the ACL go through the tunnel—in this case, all packets destined for 10.0.0.0/8, the private network used by this Enterprise.

Step 3.   Router BO1 encrypts the original packet so that no one in the Internet can read the data.

Figure 19-4 *IPsec Tunnel Concept*

Step 4.   Router BO1 adds a security header (IPsec header), which helps the receiver de-crypt the packet, and know that it came from a trusted router.

Step 5.   Router BO1 adds a new IPv4 header, this time with BO1's public IP address as source, and the tunnel destination's public IPv4 address as destination. In this case, the destination is a public IPv4 address used by Firewall FW1.

Step 6.   Router BO1 sends the packet into the Internet, with the various routers for-warding the packet to FW1's public IP address.

Step 7.   Firewall FW1 de-encapsulates and decrypts the original packet, leaving the original packet as described at Step 1. FW1 forwards the packet toward Server S1.

The process of tunneling the packet gives the branch office the logical equivalent of a point-to-point link between the branch router and the firewall. The tunnel logic works like the point-to-point tunnel logic discussed throughout Chapter 18, "IPv4 and IPv6 Coexis-tence," except for two key differences. First, this tunnel uses IPv4 as both the transport protocol and passenger protocol, rather than using IPv4 to transport IPv6 as the passenger protocol. Also, this tunnel uses additional security features, like the encryption shown in Figure 19-4.

IP Security (IPsec) defines the details of how this particular tunnel works. IPsec defines which security standards may be used to encrypt the packet–for example, IPsec allows the use of triple DES (3DES) and Advanced Encryption Standard (AES). IPsec also allows the use of authentication protocols and headers as well, which the firewall can use to ver-ify that the packet came from a legitimate branch office and not some attacker.

Although the security protocols may be interesting, this book does not delve into the de-tails, other than to say that the protocols ensure that the data in the tunnel is private (through encryption) and comes from a legitimate branch (through authentication).

Branch Routing for the Small Branch

Figure 19-1 shows a sample small branch whose only WAN connectivity is to the Internet. It may seem that such a router has no need to be concerned about routing. However, with the addition of an IPsec tunnel from the branch to the Enterprise core, the branch does have a kind of routing decision to make: to send a packet through the tunnel, or to send it to the local ISP after performing NAT. Both actions result in the packet flowing toward the ISP, but one option results in the original packet successfully arriving at the Enterprise, with private IP addresses. The other routing choice results in the packet being changed with NAT and forwarded to an address somewhere in the public Internet.

Figure 19-5 shows an example of such a routing decision, again using branch Router BO1. Host PC1 has two windows open—one using a web-based application with a server inside the Enterprise core, with another web browser window open and connected to the user's favorite public website.

Figure 19-5   *Routing over the IPsec Tunnel or Through the Public Internet*

Following the steps in the Figure 19-5

Step 1.   PC1 sends a packet destined to the Enterprise server's 10.x.x.x IP address.

Step 2.   Router BO1 uses logic that matches destination addresses in the 10.0.0.0/8 range and directs the packet over the IPsec tunnel. This action results in the encapsulation shown in Figure 19-4 and in the original packet being forwarded into the Enterprise core.

Step 3.   PC1 sends another packet; this one is destined for the public web server's public IP address.

Step 4.   Router BO1 does not match the packet with its IPsec ACL, so BO1 just routes the packet out its Internet connection, after using NAT.

Routing in Medium and Large Branches

The final concept in this broad overview section has to do with routing in medium and large branches, after the branch has a working Internet connection plus an IPsec tunnel. In the medium- and large-branch examples, another private WAN connection exists between the branch and the Enterprise core. So, the branch needs to make choices about when to use routes that use the private connection and when to use routes that use the public connection. Likewise, the routers in the Enterprise need to make good routing choices about how to route packets back to the branch.

Focusing on the branch router's logic, two main options exist: using static routes and using an IGP. Static routes can be used to forward traffic over the private connection and over the IPsec tunnel. However, IPsec does not directly support IGP protocols, because the IPsec tunnel cannot natively forward IPv4 multicasts. To overcome this restriction, you can use a GRE tunnel that actually runs over the IPsec tunnel. GRE supports multicasts by encapsulating them in unicast packets, so GRE supports IGPs. Summarizing, by using GRE, you get the following features:

■   A GRE tunnel acts like a point-to-point link from a Layer 3 perspective.

■   A GRE tunnel supports many passenger protocols, including IPv4.

■   A GRE tunnel encapsulates/forwards broadcasts and multicasts, therefore supporting IPv4 IGPs.

■   Although not mentioned in Chapter 18, GRE tunnels can run through IPsec tunnels.

After configuring a GRE tunnel to run over the IPsec tunnel on a medium or large branch, from a routing perspective, the branch now has two Layer 3 paths to the rest of the Enterprise network: out the GRE tunnel interface and out the private WAN interface. Then you can run an IGP on each, and the branch can choose which path is best using the usual IGP criteria. Figure 19-6 shows an example with a single branch router, a leased line, and a GRE tunnel running through the Internet.

For the network in the figure, branch Router BO1 has two possible outgoing interface choices for any static or IGP-learned route: interface S0/0 (the leased line) or tunnel0 (the GRE tunnel). When a packet arrives at BO1, if the route forwards the packet over tunnel0, the next step in the logic triggers the GRE tunnel logic, encapsulating the packet. Then, that packet matches the IPsec ACL for all packets destined for network 10.0.0.0/8 (in this case) and causes the IPsec process to occur. The IPsec-generated packet can then be routed through the public Internet.

Note: Figure 19-12, in the section "Summary–Branch Routing from PC1 to Enterprise Server S1," shows the encapsulation used to support the design shown in Figure 19-6.

Figure 19-6   *Competing Routes–Private Link and GRE Tunnel*

Next, the text examines the static routing option at the branch, followed by the option to use IGPs and GRE tunnels.

Routing Using Floating Static Routes

A floating static route occurs when the **ip route** command configures a static route in which the command overrides the default AD value of 1. With a higher AD for the static route, the router may consider some other routes for that same prefix as being better. For example, if the IGP learns a route for the same prefix as defined in the static route, the router does not use the static route with the higher AD, instead uses the dynamically learned route with the lower AD. Should the dynamically learned route fail, the router adds the static route back to the IP routing table. The term *floating static* refers to that the route may float in and out of the routing table.

A branch router can use a floating static route directing Enterprise traffic over the Internet, but only using that route when the IGP-learned route over the private link fails. Often, the branch design uses the Internet connection just as a backup for the private link into the Enterprise. To implement such a design, a branch router can use a floating static route for the route over the Internet, only using that route when the IGP-learned route over the private link fails. For example, in Figure 19-6, Router BO1 could use EIGRP over the leased line and configure a floating static route for 10.0.0.0/8 that routes traffic over the Internet connection. Router BO1 would prefer an EIGRP learned, AD 90 route for 10.0.0.0/8 instead, until that route through S0/0 failed.

Note that to use the floating static route option, a GRE tunnel would not be required, because the routers do not need to use an IGP through the Internet.

Dynamic Routing over the GRE Tunnel

If the design engineer decides that the branch router should use both paths into the Enterprise, a somewhat simple solution exists. Simply configure an IGP to run as normal, over both the private WAN connection and over a GRE tunnel. For example, with Figure 19-6, enable EIGRP on the branch Router BO1 on both interface S0/0 and Tu0. The design can then use all the usual tools to manipulate the choice of routes, including tuning the metrics and configuring variance to influence load sharing.

This concludes the overview of branch office routing. The next two major sections of this chapter examine broadband access and IPsec VPNs. These sections go a little deeper on the concepts and show sample configurations for perspective.

Branch Router Configuration for Broadband Access

This section focuses on a branch office router configuration using DSL and the services that must be configured to support Internet traffic. The discussion starts with a little more background about DSL concepts, followed by some sample configurations.

Understanding DSL Concepts

DSL uses the Telco local loop: the phone line that runs between the phone company's nearby facility (called the central office, or CO) and the customer site. In other words, DSL uses the same phone line that runs to most people's homes and to most office buildings. The phone company has used these types of lines for the better part of a century to carry analog electrical signals for voice traffic, but DSL uses other frequency ranges to carry a digital signal for the purpose of sending data.

From the customer premise perspective, the customer can still use the same old analog phones, which still use frequencies below 4000 Hz. The DSL router connects to another RJ-11 socket in the wall, just as if it were just another analog telephone. However, the router sends digital signals at frequencies above 4000 Hz, which does not interfere with the voice traffic. So, both the voice and DSL electrical signals flow over the same cable, at the same time, just at different frequencies.

Note: Although the human voice generates frequencies below 4000 Hz, the human ear can hear some higher frequencies, so some DSL installations require the use of filters on the lines connected to the phones. These filters prevent humans from hearing some of the higher frequency DSL tones.

From the telco perspective, the Telco has to separate the voice and DSL signals. To do so, the Telco uses a device called a DSL Access Multiplexor (DSLAM). It splits the analog signal off to the switch that handles traditional analog voice calls and splits the digital traffic to a router. Figure 19-7 shows these ideas, both for the customer premise and central office.

At Layer 1, the DSL uses digital signals that use some encoding that does not matter to the discussions in this book. However, at Layer 2, DSL uses two different data link protocols: Asynchronous Transfer Mode (ATM) and Point-to-Point Protocol (PPP).

DSL uses ATM in the traditional role of a data link protocol, and PPP for several reasons, but particularly for its CHAP authentication. For DSL, ATM controls the use of the Layer 1 medium so that data can be successfully sent over the link and to the right device. ATM defines the headers used on the link, the data link addresses, and the rules for passing Layer 3 data up and down the protocol stack. For instance, the ATM cell headers enable the DSLAM to know where to send the data received from a customer over a DSL link.

Figure 19-7   *DSL at the Home and the Telco Local Loop*

ATM uses a PVC concept similar to a Frame Relay PVC. With DSL, an ATM PVC would exist between the DSL router at the branch and the ISP router in Figure 19-7. Similar to Frame Relay, an ATM address identifies the PVC, but the address value is local, so the value used by one endpoint may be different than the address used on the other end of the PVC. Frame Relay uses the DLCI as the identifier of a PVC, whereas ATM uses a two-part address, called the Virtual Path Identifier/Virtual Connection Identifier (VPI/VCI).

Frame Relay and ATM differ quite a bit in relation to Layer 2 encapsulation. Frame Relay uses simpler conventions than ATM: When a packet needs to be sent out a Frame Relay interface, the router adds a Frame Relay header and trailer and sends the frame. ATM adds a short extra header to the packet and then performs *segmentation*. The segmentation process breaks the data into 48-byte segments and adds a 5-byte header to each to create ATM *cells*. The cell header holds the VPI/VCI pair, which allows the network to forward the cells to the correct destination end of the PVC. Figure 19-8 shows an example of the encapsulation.

Follow the steps in Figure 19-8:

Step 1.   The router wants to send a packet out the DSL ATM interface. (This logic occurs after any tunneling logic and NAT, and works the same whether using IPSec, GRE over IPSec, or the packet is just destined for a public host in the Internet.)

Step 2.   The router, using PPPoA concepts, adds a PPP header.

Step 3.   The router adds another short header (details unimportant here).

Figure 19-8   *ATM Encapsulation and Segmentation*

Step 4.   The router's segmentation and reassembly (SAR) chip segments the frame from the previous step into 48-byte segments.

Step 5.   The SAR chip encapsulates these segments inside 5-byte cell headers and sends the cells over the DSL link.

The DSLAM then receives the cells and forwards them on to the router. The router at the other end of the PVC reassembles the cells–the finishing touch on the ATM SAR process. The receiving router can then begin interpreting the various headers and de-encapsulate the packet.

Briefly, note that the encapsulation process also adds a PPP header to the IP packet before sending the data over the DSL link. The routers use the PPP header for several reasons, including PPP authentication with CHAP, and for dynamic address assignment and discovery. This convention to use both PPP and ATM protocols together is called PPP over ATM (PPPoA).

Configuring DSL

DSL configuration–even ignoring related services like DHCP and NAT–requires several steps. The goal of this section is to give you a general idea of the configuration by showing one example, just to give you a sense of the configuration pieces.

To appreciate the sample configuration, first consider that DSL is a switched connection. Most people think DSL (and cable) provide an *always on* or leased Internet connection, because typically the user does not need to do anything to start and stop the connection. However, a router can start and stop the DSL connection–or using the traditional terms, the router can dial and hang-up the connection. The idea that DSL routers do something to dial the connection means that the connection is actually switched.

Because cable and DSL connections use switched logic, IOS implements DSL configuration using some older switched network commands, including dialer interfaces and virtual templates. The option used in this section's example, the dialer interface, has been around IOS for a long time as a place to configure the logic and features related to a dialed connection.

The main pieces of the DSL configuration as shown in this section are as follows:

- The configuration creates a dialer interface.

- The Layer 3 and PPP configuration related to DSL is applied to the dialer interface.

- The ATM configuration is applied to the physical ATM interface.

- The ATM interface is linked to the dialer interface.

- An IP route forwards traffic out the dialer interface, which triggers the DSL encapsulation process, as shown in Figure 19-8.

Figure 19-9 shows the configuration, with some notes about the interactions of the various pieces of the configuration.

Figure 19-9 *DSL Configuration on Router BO1*

First examine the ATM interface. The configuration defines the VPI/VCI as 0/42; the ISP needs to match this value, or more likely, dictates the value to the customer. The **encapsulation** command defines that PPP will also be used (as shown in Step 2 of Figure 19-8's encapsulation), and it defines the style of ATM header added at Step 3 of that same figure (AAL5MUX). The **encapsulation aal5mux ppp dialer** command's **dialer** parameter defines that this PVC will use the logic of a dialer interface. Finally, the **dialer pool-member 1** command associates the ATM interface with the dialer interface as noted in the figure.

The dialer interface has five subcommands in this case, including three related to PPP. One command tells the router to use PPP to learn its IP address from the ISP (**ip address negotiated**). The **dialer pool 1** command tells the dialer interface that when it needs to signal a new connection, look for interfaces with **dialer pool-member 1** configured, such as interface ATM 0/0.

Finally, the static default route sends traffic out the dialer interface. Packets forwarded out this DSL connection will match this route, causing IOS to try to forward the packet using the dialer interface, triggering the encapsulation and logic described in Figure 19-8.

Configuring NAT

When the branch router receives a packet over the LAN interface, it has several options of how to process the packet. For instance, using the medium-sized branch from Figure 19-1, which has a leased line into the Enterprise plus a DSL Internet connection, the router could do the following:

■ Forward the packet out the serial interface, unchanged, to the rest of the Enterprise network.

■ Forward the packet out the tunnel, changed somewhat (encrypted, encapsulated, and so on), to the rest of the Enterprise network.

■ Forward the packet over the Internet link (the DSL dialer interface), after using NAT to change the source private address to a public address, to some public IP destination address.

Only the third option requires NAT. Thankfully, NAT configuration easily supports the concept of performing NAT for traffic going to Internet destinations and not performing NAT for traffic in the tunnel. Example 19-1 shows a sample configuration, again using Router BO1. This configuration assumes that BO1 was already configured, as shown in Figure 19-9.

Example 19-1 *NAT Configuration for Router BO1*

```
interface fastethernet 0/0
 ip address 10.99.1.9 255.255.255.0
 ip nat inside

interface dialer 2
 ip nat outside
ip nat inside source list local-lan interface dialer2 overload
ip access-list extended local-lan
 permit ip 10.99.1.0 0.0.0.255 any
```

The configuration shows NAT overload, using a single public IP address–namely, dialer2's dynamically learned IP address. ACL local-lan matches all packets whose source IP address is from the branch's local LAN subnet (10.99.1.0/24). The ACL, referenced by the **ip nat inside** global command, tells the router to NAT traffic permitted by this ACL. The traffic going through the tunnel will already be encapsulated in a new IP header, and no longer have a source address from the LAN subnet, so only traffic destined for Internet destinations will have NAT applied. Finally, the interface subcommands **ip nat inside** and **ip nat outside** tell the interfaces on which to attempt the translation.

Configuring DHCP Server

The branch router also may need to act as the DHCP server. If so, the router needs to have a pool of IP addresses appropriate for the local branch LAN. It needs to know the IP addresses of the DNS servers–both inside the Enterprise and the ISP's DNS server. It also needs to assign a default gateway, typically that same branch router's LAN IP address. Example 19-2 continues the same configuration.

Example 19-2   *DHCP Configuration for Router BO1*

```
ip dhcp pool fred
 network 10.99.1.0 255.255.255.0
 default-router 10.99.1.9
 ip dhcp exclude-address 10.99.1.9
 dns-server 10.2.2.2 128.107.2.1
```

Note that no interface configuration is needed on the LAN interface–the router notices the incoming interface of the DHCP request, compares the connected subnets to the pool, and picks a pool that matches the correct address range.

VPN Configuration

Earlier, this chapter introduced the concept of an IPsec VPN between the branch router and another device in the Enterprise core. This VPN, sometimes called a *VPN tunnel*, gives the Enterprise engineer a way to send a packet native to the Enterprise, with private IP addresses, through the Internet. Additionally, the VPN provides privacy (through encryption) and verification that the sender is legitimate (through authentication).

Although extremely useful, the IPsec tunnel unfortunately does not allow IGP traffic to flow directly over the IPsec VPN tunnel. One solution is to also use a GRE tunnel, which does support IGPs because it can encapsulate the IGP's multicasts inside a unicast IP packet. As previously shown in Figure 19-6, GRE solves the problem by routing over the GRE tunnel interface, whose traffic is, in turn, processed by the IPSsec tunnel.

Other alternatives exist for supporting routing over an IPsec tunnel. These options include

- **Virtual Tunnel Interfaces:** Similar in concept to GRE tunnels but it uses an encapsulation that does not add and extra 4-byte header. (GRE adds such a header.)

- **Dynamic Multipoint VPN (DMVPN):** Creates a multipoint VPN concept, allowing less configuration to add new sites.

■ **Group Encrypted Transport (GET) VPN:** A more recent addition to IOS, also supporting multipoint VPNs with less configuration to add new sites.

This section shows a sample configuration for both IPsec and GRE tunnels, just to complete the perspectives on the Internet-connected branch router.

Configuring an IPsec VPN

To fully understand the IPsec configuration, you need a deeper understanding of the security protocols than the detail included in this book. However, if you ignore the particulars about security protocols, a sample configuration can reveal some interesting facts about branch routing, which is the focus of this chapter.

Figure 19-10 shows a sample IPsec configuration for Router BO1. Again, this configuration assumes the configuration in the previous examples, plus Figure 19-9, have already occurred.

Figure 19-10   *IPsec Configuration*

Focus first on the crypto map (named branchmap) and the dialer interface. The dialer interface enables IPsec with the **crypto map branchmap** command, causing IOS to consider applying IPsec to packets *exiting* Dialer 2. The crypto map causes IOS to only encrypt and tunnel the packets that are matched by ACL 101 in this case. (See the arrows in the figures as to how the crypto map is linked to using ACL 101.) The crypto map also identifies the destination IP address used when the encapsulation takes place (128.107.9.9). This address is the public IP address of the device on the other end of the tunnel; the earlier figures showed that as Router Ent1.

Next, think about a packet received by BO1 over the LAN, in light of ACL 101, and in light of the crypto map processing outbound traffic on interface Dialer 2. The packet arrives in BO1's F0/0 interface. The packet may be processed by a GRE tunnel first, or it may not. Then, some route must route the packet out Dialer 2. At that point, the logic of the commands in Figure 19-10 finally begins.

Continuing with this same packet, the ACL matches packets that were tunneled by GRE, or other packets that come from the LAN and are going toward the rest of the Enterprise. The first line in the ACL matches the packets from the local LAN (10.99.1.0/8) going to another destination in the Enterprise. The second line in the ACL matches all GRE packets. Note that packets destined to some public IP address in the Internet would not match the ACL with a permit action. So, only packets destined for the Enterprise network match ACL 101; only the packets permitted by ACL 101 will be processed by the IPsec tunnel logic.

Configuring GRE Tunnels

The GRE tunnel configuration on the branch router does not require any additional commands as compared with the GRE tunnels discussed in Chapter 18, which showed how to tunnel IPv6 (the passenger protocol) over IPv4 (the transport protocol). In this case, the GRE tunnel carries IPv4 as the passenger protocol, inside an IPv4 packet.

The fact that an IPSec tunnel exists, plus the issues related to the public and private addresses used over the Internet connection, does make the application of the tunnel a bit more challenging. First, to make more sense of what will be configured, Figure 19-11 shows the concepts and parameters related to configuring a GRE tunnel in this case.

Loop 1
10.12.1.1

Loop 1
10.12.1.9

BO1

Tu 9
10.99.2.1/24

Tu 9
10.99.2.2/24

Ent1

Figure 19-11 *GRE Tunnel Topology and Addresses*

The link that appears as a tunnel between the branch router (BO1) and central site Enterprise router (Ent1) acts like a point-to-point serial link. In the many examples in Chapter 18, this link would have had IPv6 addresses because IPv6 was the passenger protocol. In this case, the tunnel interfaces have IPv4 addresses because IPv4 is the passenger protocol, with the addresses in a new subnet allocated just for this tunnel.

The configuration also uses loopback interfaces, with those interfaces and their IP addresses used as the tunnel endpoints. This configuration means that the new IP packet header created by GRE will use addresses 10.12.1.1 and 10.12.1.9. Finally, any routes learned over the tunnel will list tunnel 9 as an outgoing interface, with next-hop address 10.99.2.2.

Example 19-3 shows a sample configuration, again on Router BO1.

Example 19-3   *GRE Tunnel Configuration*

```
interface tunnel 9
ip address 10.99.2.1 255.255.255.255
 tunnel source loopback 1
 tunnel destination 10.12.1.9

interface loopback 1
 ip address 10.12.1.1 255.255.255.0

router eigrp 1
 network 10.12.1.1 0.0.0.0
 network 10.99.2.1 0.0.0.0

ip route 10.12.1.9 255.255.255.255 dialer2
```

The tunnel configuration just uses three subcommands: one to define the source IP address (indirectly, as loopback 1's 10.12.1.1), the tunnel destination (10.12.1.9), and the interface's passenger protocol address (IP address 10.99.2.1). The **tunnel mode** command is not needed, because IOS defaults to use IPv4 as the transport protocol, which then allows any of the supported passenger protocols.

The configuration also requires two main branches of logic for routing to work correctly. First, for the tunnel to function, the tunnel destination must be reachable; in this example, a static route was added for this purpose. Additionally, the routers need to exchange routes that will list the tunnel interface as the outgoing interface, which in turn directs packets through the tunnel. The example includes the EIGRP configuration that enables EIGRP on tunnel 9 just as a reminder that one of the primary motivations for bothering with the GRE tunnel is to support IGP routing protocols.

Summary–Branch Routing from PC1 to Enterprise Server S1

To complete the chapter, this section works through an example where a host at the branch sends a packet to a server inside the Enterprise. For the sake of argument, the branch prefers to send this packet over the Internet. It is immaterial whether the branch does not have a private link into the Enterprise, or if the engineer chose to implement routing so that the path through the Internet is currently preferred. The example then gives us a chance to work through the logic when the packet is sent through a GRE tunnel, and an IPsec tunnel, and then out the DSL ATM interface.

Figure 19-12 shows the example. The example begins with the arrival of a packet from PC1, destined from servers S1, 10.1.1.1. The packet has arrived at Router BO1, which has removed the incoming frame's data link header/trailer. The figure picks up the story as BO1 makes its first routing decision about this packet.

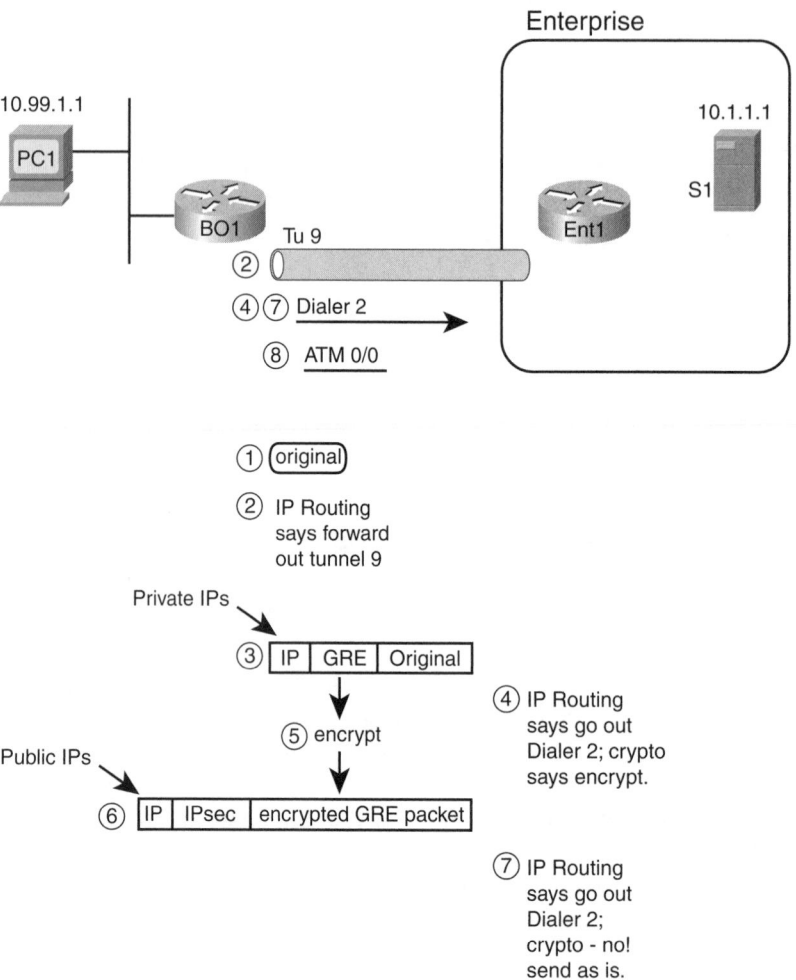

Figure 19-12   *Example of Routing and Encapsulation with GRE over IPsec*

Following are the steps in Figure 19-12:

Step 1.   R1 has the original packet in memory, source 10.99.1.1 (PC1), destination 10.1.1.1 (S1).

Step 2.   BO1's best route for destination 10.1.1.1 uses outgoing interface tunnel 9. This route may have been learned by an IGP running over this GRE tunnel.

Step 3.   BO1 adds a new IPv4 header and GRE header to the original packet. This new packet as a destination based on BO1's tunnel 9 subcommand **tunnel destination,** per the previous Example 19-3, is address 10.12.1.9.

Step 4.   BO1 routes the packet formed in the previous step. This best route for 10.12.1.9 lists Dialer 2 as the outgoing interface. The crypto map on interface Dialer 2 refers to an ACL, and ACL matches this packet with a permit action. This combination of logic tells BO1 to use IPsec to encrypt this packet for transmission over the IPsec tunnel.

Step 5.   BO1 encrypts the packet that was created in Step 3–in other words, it encrypts the GRE-created packet.

Step 6.   BO1 encapsulates the encrypted data, adding several IPsec headers, plus a new IPv4 header. The new IPv4 header uses BO1's public IPv4 address as source and the configured public IPv4 address of the other end of the IPsec tunnel as destination. Per the example in Figure 19-10, the destination IP address would be 128.107.9.9.

Step 7.   BO1 routes this latest packet, with its destination IP address of 128.107.9.9, matching a route (probably a default route) that lists Dialer 2 (again) as the outgoing interface. However, the crypto map's ACL does not match the packet with a permit action, so BO1 bypasses any further IPsec functions and simply tries to forward the packet.

Step 8.   Forwarding out the dialer interface then causes this DSL-connected router to forward the packet out the underlying ATM interface, which performs the encapsulation and segmentation previously shown in Figure 19-8.

Interestingly, this process drives the branch router to make comparisons to the routing table three separate times when forwarding this data. The most important thing to remember from this example is to get a sense for how the pieces work together and how the steps add additional headers.

Exam Preparation Tasks

Planning Practice

The CCNP ROUTE exam expects test takers to review design documents, create implementation plans, and create verification plans for most topics. However, the CCNP ROUTE exam topics require less depth for the topics in this chapter. For example, the exam topics do not specifically mention the verification task for any of the topics in this chapter, so the chapter does not examine **show** command output.

Because of this key difference, the typical tables at the end of each chapter are not as useful for this chapter. However, some review can be helpful. Table 19-2 lists a series of questions for the purpose of reviewing the content in this chapter. Refer to the same appendix you have been using throughout this book for the suggested answers.

Table 19-2   *Design Review*

Question	Answer
When a branch uses its broadband Internet connection to communicate into the rest of an Enterprise network, what benefits does an IPsec tunnel provide? (3)	
To make the basic broadband connection work, and to support flows from the branch office hosts to/from public websites, what features discussed in this chapter might the router need to configure? (5)	
What method allows a branch to statically route over the IPsec tunnel to the rest of the Enterprise, but only when routes through the private WAN connection fail?	
For what reasons might a network engineer consider also using a GRE tunnel when connecting a branch router, over the Internet, with the rest of the Enterprise network?	
When configuring DSL using dialer interfaces, in what configuration mode are the ATM details configured? PPP details? Layer 3 details?	
A branch router has configured its one LAN interface as a NAT inside interface and its DSL dialer interface as an outside interface. What prevents packets in the IPsec tunnel from being NATted?	
When configuring an IPsec tunnel on a branch router, identify the three main configuration components that link the interface to the matching logic that determines which packets the router processes into the tunnel.	

Note that all the questions assume that a branch office router exists and that it uses some form of broadband access to the Internet.

Review all the Key Topics

Review the most important topics from inside the chapter, noted with the key topics icon in the outer margin of the page. Table 19-3 lists a reference of these key topics and the page numbers on which each is found.

Table 19-3 *Key Topics for Chapter 10*

Key Topic Element	Description	Page Number
Figure 19-3	Branch router's role as DHCP server and client	653
Figure 19-4	IPsec tunnel concepts	655
Figure 19-6	Comparing the competing routes–private and tunnel	658
Figure 19-10	IPsec configuration	665

Define Key Terms

Define the following key terms from this chapter, and check your answers in the glossary.

IPsec, IPsec tunnel, GRE tunnel, Floating static route, Digital Subscriber Line (DSL), Cable, PPP over ATM (PPPoA), PPP over Ethernet (PPPoE), Challenge Handshake Authentication Protocol (CHAP)

CHAPTER 20

Final Preparation

The first 19 chapters of this book cover the technologies, protocols, commands, and features required to be prepared to pass the ROUTE exam. Although these chapters supply the detailed information, most people need more preparation than simply reading the first 19 chapters of this book. This chapter details a set of tools and a study plan to help you complete your preparation for the exams.

This short chapter has two main sections. The first section lists the exam preparation tools useful at this point in the study process. The second section lists a suggested study plan now that you have completed all the preceding chapters in this book.

Note: Appendixes D, E, and F exist as soft-copy appendixes on the CD included in the back of this book.

Tools for Final Preparation

This section lists some information about the available tools and how to access the tools.

Exam Engine and Questions on the CD

The CD in the back of the book includes the Boson Exam Environment (BEE). The BEE is the exam-engine software that delivers and grades a set of free practice questions written by Cisco Press. The BEE supports multiple-choice questions, drag-and-drop questions, and many scenario-based questions that require the same level of analysis as the questions on the ROUTE exam. The installation process has two major steps. The first step is installing the BEE software; the CD in the back of this book has a recent copy of the BEE software, supplied by Boson Software (http://www.boson.com). The second step is activating and downloading the free practice questions. The practice questions written by Cisco Press for the ROUTE exam are not on the CD. Instead, the practice questions must be downloaded from www.boson.com.

Note: The CD case in the back of this book includes the CD and a piece of paper. The paper contains the activation key for the practice questions associated with this book. Do not lose this activation key.

Install the Software from the CD

Following are the steps you should perform to install the software:

Step 1.   Insert the CD into your computer.

Step 2.   From the main menu, click the option to install the Boson Exam Environment (BEE). The software that automatically runs is the Cisco Press software needed to access and use all CD-based features, including the BEE, a PDF of this book, and the CD-only appendixes.

Step 3.   Respond to the prompt windows as you would with any typical software installation process.

The installation process might give you the option to register the software. This process requires that you establish a login at the www.boson.com website. You need this login to activate the exam; therefore, you should register when prompted.

Activate and Download the Practice Exam

After the Boson Exam Environment (BEE) is installed, you should activate the exam associated with this book.

Step 1.   Launch the BEE from the Start menu.

Step 2.   The first time you run the software, you should be asked to either log in or register an account. If you do not already have an account with Boson, select the option to register a new account. You must register to download and use the exam.

Step 3.   After you register or log in, the software might prompt you to download the latest version of the software, which you should do. Note that this process updates the BEE, not the practice exam.

Step 4.   From the Boson Exam Environment main window, click the Exam Wizard button to activate and download the exam associated with this book.

Step 5.   From the Exam Wizard dialog box, select Activate a purchased exam and click the Next button. Although you did not purchase the exam directly, you purchased it indirectly when you bought the book.

Step 6.   In the EULA Agreement window, click Yes to accept the terms of the license agreement and click the Next button. If you do not accept the terms of the license agreement, you cannot install or use the software.

Step 7.   In the Activate Exam Wizard dialog box, enter the activation key from the paper inside the CD holder in the back of the book, and click the Next button.

Step 8.   Wait while the activation process downloads the practice questions. When the exam has been downloaded, the main BEE menu should list a new exam. If you do not see the exam, click the My Exams tab on the menu. You might also need to click the plus sign icon (+) to expand the menu and see the exam.

At this point, the software and practice questions are ready to use.

Activating Other Exams

You need to install the exam software and register only once. Then, for each new exam, you need to complete only a few additional steps. For instance, if you bought this book along with *CCNP SWITCH 642-813 Official Certification Guide* or *CCNP TSHOOT 642-832 Official Certification Guide*, you would need to perform the following steps:

Step 1. Launch the BEE (if it is not already open).

Step 2. Perform the preceding Steps 4 through 7 under Activate and Download the Practice Exam.

Step 3. Repeat Steps 1 and 2 for any exams in other Cisco Press books.

You can also purchase Boson ExSim-Max practice exams that are written and developed by Boson Software's subject-matter experts at www.boson.com. The ExSim-Max practice exams simulate the content on the actual certification exams allowing you to gauge whether you are ready to pass the real exam. When you purchase an ExSim-Max practice exam, you receive an activation key; you can then activate and download the exam by performing the preceding Steps 1 and 2.

The Cisco Learning Network

Cisco provides a wide variety of CCNP preparation tools at a Cisco website called the Cisco Learning Network. This site includes a large variety of exam preparation tools, including sample questions, forums on each Cisco exam, learning video games, and information about each exam.

To reach the Cisco Learning Network, go to www.cisco.com/go/learnnetspace, or just search for "Cisco Learning Network." You need to use the login you created at www.cisco.com. If you don't have such a login, you can register for free. To register, simply go to www.cisco.com, click Register at the top of the page, and supply some information.

Memory Tables

Like most Certification Guides from Cisco Press, this book purposefully organizes information into tables and lists for easier study and review. Re-reading these tables can be very useful before the exam. However, it is easy to skim over the tables without paying attention to every detail, especially when you remember having seen the table's contents when reading the chapter.

Instead of simply reading the tables in the various chapters, this book's Appendixes D and E give you another review tool. Appendix D, "Memory Tables," lists partially completed versions of many of the tables from the book. You can open Appendix D (a PDF on the CD that comes with this book) and print the appendix. For review, you can attempt to complete the tables. This exercise can help you focus on the review. It also exercises the memory connectors in your brain; plus it makes you think about the information without as much information, which forces a little more contemplation about the facts.

Appendix E, "Memory Tables Answer Key," also a PDF located on the CD, lists the completed tables to check yourself. You can also just refer to the tables as printed in the book.

Chapter-Ending Review Tools

Chapters 2 through 19 each have several features in the Exam Preparation Tasks section at the end of the chapter. You may have used some of or all these tools at the end of each chapter. It can also be useful to use these tools again as you make your final preparations for the exam.

Suggested Plan for Final Review/Study

This section lists a suggested study plan from the point at which you finish reading through Chapter 19 until you take the ROUTE exam. Certainly, you can ignore this plan, use it as is, or just take suggestions from it.

The plan uses six steps. If following the plan verbatim, you should proceed by part through the steps as previously listed. That is, starting with Part 2 (EIGRP), do the following six steps. Then, for Part 3 (OSPF), do the following six steps, and so on. The steps are as follows:

Step 1.   **Review key topics and DIKTA questions:** You can use the table that lists the key topics in each chapter, or just flip the pages looking for the Key Topics icons. Also, reviewing the DIKTA questions from the beginning of the chapter can be helpful for review.

Step 2.   **Complete memory tables:** Open Appendix D on the CD, and print the entire appendix, or print the tables by major part. Then complete the tables and check your answers in Appendix E, which also appears on the CD.

Step 3.   **Hands-on practice:** Most people practice CCNP configuration and verification before the exam. Whether you use real gear, a simulator, or an emulator, practice the configuration and verification commands.

Step 4.   **Build configuration checklists:** Glance through the Table of Contents, looking for major configuration tasks. Then from memory create your own configuration checklists for the various configuration commands.

Step 5.   **Planning practice:** Even if you use the "Planning Practice" tables when you initially read each chapter, repeat the process, particularly the tables related to interpreting a design and reviewing another engineer's implementation plan.

Step 6.   **Subnetting practice:** If you can no longer do subnetting well and quickly without a subnetting calculator, take some time to get better and faster before going to take the ROUTE exam.

Step 7.   **Use the exam engine to practice:** The exam engine on the CD can be used to study using a bank of 100 unique exam-realistic multiple-choice questions available only with this book.

The rest of this section describes Steps 1, 3, 6, and 7 for which a little more explanation may be helpful.

Step 1: Review Key Topics and DIKTA Questions

This review step focuses on the core facts related to the ROUTE exam. The exam certainly covers other topics as well, but the DIKTA questions and the Key Topics items attempt to focus attention on the more important topics in each chapter.

As a reminder, if you follow this plan after reading the first 19 chapters, working a major part at a time (EIGRP, Chapters 2 through 4, for example) helps you pull each major topic together.

Step 3: Hands-On Practice

Although this book gives you many configuration checklists, specific configuration examples, examples of output, and explanations for the meaning of that output, there is no substitute for hands-on practice. This short section provides a couple of suggestions regarding your efforts at practice from the CLI.

First, most people use one or more of the following options for hands-on skills:

■ **Real gear:** Either purchased (often used), borrowed, or rented

■ **Simulators:** Software that acts like real gear

■ **Emulators:** Software that acts like router hardware, with IOS running inside that environment

First, a few words about finding these tools. For real gear, this book makes no attempt at suggesting how to go about getting, borrowing, or renting gear. However, the topic of what gear to buy for a home Cisco certification lab tends to be a popular topic from time-to-time on my (the author's) blog. Because the blog makes a good place for discussion, but a poor place for reference material, some of the base information about used gear, IOS versions/feature sets, relative to CCNP ROUTE (and other exams) is listed at www.thecert-zone.com. The site also lists a link to the blog as well.

As for emulators, two exist of note. For the general public, a group of three free software offerings cooperate to allow you to run multiple instances of IOS on a PC: Dynagen and Dynamips (see www.dynagen.org) for the emulation, and GNS3 for the graphical interface (see www.gns3.net). Many websites devote attention to how to best use these tools; this book simply mentions the tools and their websites to get you started if interested.

Step 6: Subnetting Practice

This book assumes that you have mastered subnetting and the related math. However, many people who progress through CCNA, and move on to CCNP, follow a path like this:

Step 1.   Learn subnetting conceptually.

Step 2.   Get really good at doing the math quickly.

Step 3.   Pass CCNA.

Step 4.   Don't practice regularly and therefore become a lot slower at doing the subnetting math.

Step 5.   Study for CCNP ROUTE.

Although subnetting should not be assessed as an end to itself on CCNP ROUTE, many questions require that you understand subnetting math and can do that math just as quickly as you did when you passed CCNA. If you are a little slow on doing subnetting math, before you go to the ROUTE exam, try some of the following exercises:

■   Practice finding the subnet number, broadcast address, and range of addresses in a subnet. To do so, pick a number and mask, calculate the values, and use your favorite subnet calculator to check your work. Look at the Cisco Learning Network for a calculator if you don't have one.

■   Use the Cisco Subnetting Game, also at the Cisco Learning Network.

■   Practice choosing the best summary route for a range of subnets. Pick three to four addresses/masks. Calculate the subnet number and range. Then, try to choose the summary (subnet number/mask) that includes those three to four subnets, without including any more subnets than what is required. You can check your math with a subnet calculator as well.

If you like using binary/decimal conversions when you work through these problems, but just need to go faster, check out the Cisco Binary game, also at the Cisco Learning Network.

Step 7: Use the Exam Engine

The Boson Exam Engine (BEE) software on the CD includes a 100-question database of questions created specifically for this book. You can use the BEE software either in study mode or simulation mode, as follows:

■   **Study mode:** Study mode is most useful when you want to use the questions to learn and practice. In study mode, you can select options such as whether you want to randomize the order of the questions, randomize the order of the answers, automatically see answers to the questions, refer to specific sections of the text that resides on the CD, and many other options.

■   **Simulation mode:** Simulation mode presents questions in a timed environment, providing you with a more exam realistic experience. It also restricts your ability to see your score as you progress through the exam, view answers to questions as you take the exam, and refer to sections of the text. These timed exams not only allow you to study for the actual ROUTE exam, but they also help you simulate the time pressure that can occur on the actual exam.

When doing your final preparation, you can use study mode, simulation mode, or both. However, after you have seen each question a couple of times, you will likely start to remember the questions, and the usefulness of the exam database may go down. So, consider the following options when using the exam engine:

■ Use this question database for review. Use study mode, and study the questions by major book part, just as with the other final review steps listed in this chapter. Plan on getting another exam (possibly from Boson, who supplies the BEE software–www. boson.com) if you want to take simulated exams.

■ Save the question database, not using it for review during your review of each book part. Save it until the end, so you will not have seen the questions before. Then, use simulation mode to simulate the exam.

Picking the correct mode from the exam engine's user interface is quite obvious. The following steps show how to move to the screen from which to select study or simulation mode:

Step 1. Click the Choose Exam button, which should list the exam under the title ROUTE/Cisco Press CCNP Route.

Step 2. Click the name of the exam once, which should highlight the exam name.

Step 3. Click the Load Exam button.

By taking these actions, the engine should display a window from which you can choose Simulation Mode or Study Mode with a radio button on the right side of the window and the exam bank in the left side of the window. When selecting Custom Exam, you can further choose the book chapters by using the Modify Settings button, limiting the questions to those explained in the specified chapters of the book.

Summary

The tools and suggestions listed in this chapter have been designed with one goal in mind: to help you develop the skills required to pass the ROUTE exam. This book has been developed from the beginning to not just tell you the facts, but also help you learn how to apply the facts. No matter what your experience level is leading up when you take the exams, it is our hope that the broad range of preparation tools, and even the structure of the books, can help you pass the exams with ease. I hope you do well on the exam.

Answers to "Do I Know This Already?" Quizzes

Chapter 2

1. B and C. The **network 172.16.1.0 0.0.0.255** command tells IOS to match the first three octets when comparing the interface IP addresses to the configured "172.16.1.0" value. Only two answers match in the first three octets. The other two answers have a 0 in the 3rd octet, making the addresses not match the **network** command.

2. B. The **show ip eigrp interfaces** command displays working (up/up) interfaces on which EIGRP has been enabled but omits passive interfaces. A failure of the interface, or making the interface passive, would omit the interface from the output of this command.

3. D. The **show ip eigrp interfaces detail** command does display a router's EIGRP Hello timer setting for each enabled interface. The other listed commands do not display the timer. Also, EIGRP routers do not have to have matching Hello timers to become neighbors.

4. C. The **show ip eigrp neighbors failure** command is not a valid IOS command. The debug displays messages that state when a neighborship fails due to authentication each time Hellos are exchanged. The **show key chain** command lists the specific keys that are currently valid, allowing you to determine if both routers use the same key values in currently valid keys. The **show clock** command displays the current time-of-day clock setting on a router, allowing you to check the valid times of the various keys versus the two router's clocks.

5. C. The **neighbor 172.16.2.20 fa0/0** command would only be rejected if the IP address (172.16.2.20) is not inside the range of addresses in the subnet (172.16.2.0/26, range 172.16.2.0–172.16.2.63). This command does not impact interface state. The command does disable all EIGRP multicasts, and because the three dynamically discovered neighbors require the EIGRP multicasts, all three neighbors fail. Although 172.16.2.20 is a valid potential neighbor, both routers must be configured with static **neighbor** commands, and we know that 172.16.2.20 was not previously configured with a static **neighbor** command; otherwise, it could not have been a neighbor with R1.

6. A and D. Table 2-4 lists the issues. For EIGRP, Router IDs do not have to be unique for EIGRP routers to become neighbors, and the hold timer does not have to match between the two neighbors. However, making an interface passive disables the processing of all EIGRP messages on the interface, preventing all neighborships. Mismatched IP subnets also prevent neighborships from forming.

7. A. The configuration requires the **ip authentication mode eigrp** *asn* **md5** command, which is currently missing. This command enables MD5-style authentication, rather than the default of no authentication. Adding this one command completes the configuration. Any valid key numbers can be used. Also, the 9 in the **ip authentication key-chain eigrp 9 fred** command refers to the EIGRP ASN, not an authentication type.

8. A. EIGRP forms neighborships only when two routers can communicate directly over a data link. As a result, with Frame Relay, EIGRP neighborships occur only between routers on the ends of a PVC, so in this case, 100 neighborships exist.

Chapter 3

1. B and C. Other than the two listed correct answers, the local router also adds connected routes for which the **network** command matches the corresponding interfaces, so it may not add all connected routes. Also, EIGRP does not add static routes to the EIGRP topology table, unless those routes are redistributed, as discussed in Chapter 9, "Basic IGP Redistribution."

2. B and D. EIGRP sends bandwidth, delay, reliability, load, MTU, and hop-count in the message. The formula to calculate the metric includes bandwidth, delay, reliability, and load.

3. A. EIGRP performs WAN bandwidth control without any explicit configuration, using default settings. Because no **bandwidth** commands have been configured, each subinterface uses the default 1544 Kbps setting. For S0/0.1, WAN bandwidth control divides the 1544 by 3 (515 Kbps), and then takes the (default) WAN bandwidth of 50 percent, meaning about 250 Kbps for each of the three DLCIs. For the two subinterfaces with one PVC, the default 1544 is multiplied by the 50 percent default WAN bandwidth, meaning that each could use about 750 Kbps.

4. A. This command lists all successor and feasible successor routes. The output states that two successors exist, and only two routes (listed with the "via..." text) exist. So, no feasible successor routes exist.

5. A and C. By default, the metric weights cause EIGRP to consider bandwidth and delay in the metric calculation, so changing either bandwidth or delay impacts the calculation of the feasible distance and reported distance, and impacts choice of feasible successor routes. Offset lists also change the metric, which in turn can change whether a route is an FS route. Link loading would impact the metrics, but not without changing the metric weights to nonrecommended values. Finally, variance impacts which routes end up in the IP routing table, but it is not considered by EIGRP when determining which routes are FS routes.

6. C and E. The EIGRP metric calculation treats bandwidth and delay differently. For bandwidth, EIGRP takes the lowest bandwidth, in Kbps, which is in this case 500 Kbps. For delay, EIGRP takes the cumulative delay, which is 20100 per the various **show interfaces** commands. However, the **show interfaces** command uses a unit of microseconds, and the interface **delay** command, and the EIGRP metric formula uses a unit of tens-of-microseconds, making the delay that feeds into the formula be 2010.

7. C and E. R1, as a stub router with the **connected** option, still advertises routes, but only routes for connected subnets. R1 announces its stub attribute to R2, so R2 chooses to not send Query messages to R1, knowing that R1 cannot be a transit router for other subnets anyway.

8. B. Of the five options, the **show ip route eigrp all-links** and **show ip eigrp topology all-learned** are not valid commands. Both **show ip eigrp topology** and **show ip route eigrp** can show at most successor and feasible successor routes. However, **show ip eigrp topology all-links** shows also nonfeasible successor routes, making it more likely to show all possible neighbors.

9. D. EIGRP considers only successor and feasible successor routes. Each of those routes must have metrics such that variance * metric is less than the best route's metric; the best route's metric is called the feasible distance (FD).

Chapter 4

1. D and E. The two listed commands correctly configure EIGRP route filtering such that prefixes matched by the ACL's permit clause will be allowed. All other prefixes will be filtered due to the implied deny all at the end of the ACL. The ACL permits numbers in the range 10.10.32.0–10.10.47.255, which leaves 10.10.48.0 and 10.10.60.0 unmatched by the permit clause.

2. B, C, and E. Sequence number 5 matches prefixes from 10.1.2.0–10.1.2.255, with prefix lengths between 25–27, and denies (filters) those prefixes. This results in answer A being incorrect, because the prefix length (/24) is not in the correct range. Clause 15 matches prefixes from 10.2.0.0–10.2.255.255, with prefix length exactly 30, matching answer C. Clause 20 matches only prefix 0.0.0.0 with length /0, so only a default route would match this entry. As a result, 10.0.0.0/8 does not match any of the three clauses.

3. C. When used for route filtering, the route map action (permit or deny) defines the filtering action, and any referenced **match** commands' permit or deny action just defines whether the prefix is matched. By not matching ACL 1 with a permit action, EIGRP does not consider a match to have occurred with clause 10, so it moves to clause 20. The prefix list referenced in clause 20 has a permit action, matching prefixes from 10.10.10.0–10.10.11.255, with prefix lengths from 23–25. Both criteria match the prefix in question, making answer C correct.

4. B and C. Answer A is invalid–the **ge** value must be larger than /24 in this case, so the command is rejected. Answer B implies a prefix length range from 24–28, inclusive. Answer C implies a range from 25–32 inclusive, because no **le** parameter exists to limit the prefix length lower than the full length of an IPv4 subnet mask. The same logic applies with answer D, but with a range from 28–32, so this final list could not match prefix lengths of /27.

5. B. 10.1.0.0/18 implies a range from 10.1.0.0–10.1.63.255, which includes none of the four subnets. 10.1.64.0/18 implies a range from 10.1.64.0–10.1.127.255, which includes all subnets. 10.1.100.0/24 implies range 10.1.100.0–10.1.100.255, which leaves out two of the subnets. Finally, 10.1.98.0/22 does not actually represent a summary–instead, 10.1.96.0/22 represents range 10.1.96.0–10.1.99.255, with 10.1.98.0 as listed in answer D being an IP address in that range. As such, IOS would actually accept the command, and change the parameter from 10.1.98.0 to 10.1.96.0, and would not include the four listed subnets.

6. B. The **ip summary-address** command does reset neighborships, but only on the interface under which it is configured. After those neighborships come up, R1 will advertise the summary route, but none of the subordinate routes inside that summary. The summary route will us a metric equal to the metric of the lowest metric subordinate route, approximately 1,000,000 in this case.

7. B and D. R2 has interfaces only in class A network 10.0.0.0, so the auto-summary setting has no effect. R3 has interfaces in both class A network 10.0.0.0 and class B network 172.16.0.0, so auto-summary causes R3 to summarize all subnets of 172.16.0.0/16 as a summary route when advertising to R2.

8. D. The phrase quoted in the question means that R1 is using its route for class A network 2.0.0.0 to decide where to send packets by default. R1's route for network 2.0.0.0 must have 1.1.1.1 as its next-hop router. This phrase occurs when EIGRP has learned a route for class A network 2.0.0.0 that has been flagged as a candidate default route by another router. The router flagging a route as a candidate default route, using the **ip default-network** command, does not actually use the route as its default route.

9. C and E. With the suggested configuration style, the static route must first be configured statically, as shown in answer A. Then, either this route must be redistributed as a static route into EIGRP (answer B), or pulled into EIGRP by virtue of the **network 0.0.0.0** EIGRP subcommand (answer D). The other two options have no effect on default route creation and advertisement.

Chapter 5

1. A and D. The wildcard mask is used for matching the prefix only, and not the prefix length. As such, 172.16.1.0 0.0.0.255 matches all addresses that begin with 172.16.1, and 172.16.0.0 0.0.255.255 matches all addresses that begin 172.16. Also, OSPF reviews the **network** command with the most specific wildcard masks (wildcard masks with the most binary 0's) first, so an interface IP address beginning with 172.16.1 matches the command that references area 8.

2. D. ABRs, by definition, connect the backbone area to one or more nonbackbone areas. To perform this function, a router must have at least one interface assigned to the backbone area, and at least one interface assigned to a nonbackbone area.

3. B and C. First, for the two correct answers: **show ip ospf interface brief** explicitly lists all OSPF-enabled interfaces that are not passive. **show ip protocols** lists either the details of the configured **network** commands, or if configured using the **ip ospf area** command, it lists the interfaces on which OSPF is enabled. This command also lists the passive interfaces, so armed with interface IP address information, the list of OSPF-enabled nonpassive interfaces could be derived. Of the three wrong answers, **show ip ospf database** does not list enough detail to show the OSPF-enabled interfaces. **show ip route ospf** lists only routes learned with OSPF, so if no routes use a particular OSPF-enabled interface as an outgoing interface, this command would not indirectly identify the interface. Finally, an interface may be OSPF-enabled but with no neighbors reachable on the interface, so the **show ip ospf neighbor** command may not identify all OSPF-enabled interfaces.

4. B and C. On a LAN, the non-DR routers form fully adjacent neighborships with only the DR and BDR, giving R1 two neighbors in the FULL state. The other two neighbors settle into the 2WAY state.

5. C and D. The **show ip ospf interface** command displays a router's OSPF Hello Interval setting for each enabled interface. The other listed commands do not display the timer. Also, OSPF routers do need to have matching Hello timers to become neighbors, so the neighborship would fail.

6. B and D. The **area 0 authentication** command tells R1 to use simple text password authentication on all interfaces in area 0 unless overridden by an interface subcommand. So, R1 must have configured the **ip ospf authentication message-digest** on its Fa0/0 interface, enabling MD5 authentication instead. The other correct answer is the command that correctly configures the MD5 authentication key. Of the two incorrect answers that list an authentication key, **ip ospf authentication-key** defines the clear-text key, and the other is not a valid IOS command.

7. E. Table 5-5 in Chapter 5 lists the issues. For OSPF, Router IDs must be unique; the interfaces must not be passive; the dead timers must match; and the primary IP addresses must be in the same subnet, with the same subnet mask. However, the process IDs, found on the **router ospf** *process-id* command, do not have to match.

8. A. Frame Relay is a Layer 2 service and as such does not participate in customer routing protocols. Because the design uses a separate subnet per PVC, and one point-to-point subinterface per PVC/subnet, OSPF will use a point-to-point network type. That means that the two routers on either end of a PVC will become neighbors, and become fully adjacent, meaning the central site router will have 100 fully adjacent neighborships.

Chapter 6

1. D. As an ABR connected to areas 0 and 2, ABR2 will have LSDB entries for both area 0 and area 2. In Area 0, ABR2 learns Type 1 LSAs from the four routers internal to area 0, plus ABR1, and plus 1 for the area 0 Type 1 LSA ABR2 creates for itself. In area 2, ABR2 learns 1 each for the five routers internal to area 2, plus the 1 Type 1 LSA ABR2 created for itself inside area 2. The total is 12.

2. E. OSPF creates a Type 2 LSA for a subnet when the router interface connected to the subnet calls for the election of a designated router (DR), and at least two routers have discovered each other and elected a DR. Then, the DR creates and floods the Type 2 LSA. IOS by default does not elect a DR on point-to-point topologies. It does on router LAN interfaces. One answer states that one router only exists in the subnet, so it does not actually find a second router and elect a DR. In the other case, a DR and BDR have been elected, but the router described in the answer is the BDR, not the DR. So, none of the other answers is correct.

3. C. Each ABR, by definition, creates a single Type 3 LSA to represent a subnet known in one area to be advertised into another area. Assuming 10.100.0.0 is a subnet in area 0, both ABR1 and ABR2 would advertise a Type 3 LSA into area 100. The **show ip ospf database summary** command specifically lists type 3 network summary LSAs.

4. C. The Database Description (DD) packet lists a short LSA header but not the entire LSA. The Link State Request (LSR) packet asks the neighbors for a copy of an LSA. The Link State Update (LSU) holds the LSAs. LSAck simply acknowledges received LSAs, and Hello is used for neighbor discovery and neighbor state maintenance.

5. B and D. Because the subnet was stable before R5 arrived, the other routers will have elected a DR and BDR. OSPF does not preemptively elect a new DR nor BDR, so R5 will be neither (DROther). As a result, R5's messages to the DR will be sent to the 224.0.0.6 all-DR-routers multicast address, and the DR's messages directed to R5 will be sent to the 224.0.0.5 all-SPF-router address.

6. E. R1, internal to area 1, can use LSAs only in the area 1 LSDB. R2's Type 1 LSA exists only in area 2's LSDB. The Type 2 LSA for subnet 10.1.1.0/24, if one exists, also only exists in area 2's LSDB. R1 will use ABR1's Type 1 LSA in area 1 to calculate the possible intra-area routes inside area 1, but R1 will use ABR1's Type 1 LSA in area 1. Finally, the Type 3 LSA, created for 10.1.1.0/24, and flooded into area 1, is also needed to calculate the metric.

7. A and B. OSPF builds the SPF tree based on the topology information Type 1 and Type 2 LSAs. Changes therefore require another SPF run. Changes to the other LSA types do not require an SPF calculation.

8. A and B. Because none of the interfaces have a **bandwidth** command configured, the only commands that can influence the OSPF cost are the **auto-cost reference-bandwidth** router subcommand and the **ip ospf cost** interface subcommand. To give the output shown in the question, either the interface cost could be set directly on all three interfaces listed. Alternatively, the reference-bandwidth could be set (in router

configuration mode) to cause one of the interface costs to be as shown in the output, with the other two interfaces having their costs set directly.

For the wrong answers, the **ip ospf cost interface s0/0/0.1** router subcommand does not exist—instead, it is an interface subcommand. An auto-cost of 64700, used as the numerator in the ref-bw/bandwidth cost calculation, does not result in any of the three listed interface costs.

For the two correct answers, with a default bandwidth of 1544 (Kbps) on the serial subinterfaces, a reference bandwidth of 1000 (Mbps) implies the math 1,000,000 / 1544, for an Interface cost of 647. With a default bandwidth of 100,000 Kbps (100 Mbps) on Fa0/0, a reference bandwidth of 2000 (MBps) implies math of 2,000 / 100 = 20.

9. A, B, and C. OSPF uses Types 1, 2, and 3 for calculating routes internal to the OSPF domain. OSPF uses types 4, 5, and 7 for external routes redistributed into the OSPF domain, as discussed in Chapter 9, "Basic IGP Redistribution."

Chapter 7

1. C. The output lists all R1's routes for subnets within the range of 10.1.0.0–10.1.255.255, whose prefix lengths are longer than /16. One answer lists subnet 10.2.2.0/24, which is not in this range, so the output cannot be used to confirm nor deny whether the subnet was filtered. R1's route for 10.1.2.0/24 is an intra-area route by virtue of not listing an IA code by the route; Type 3 LSA filtering only filters Type 3 LSAs, which routers use to calculate interarea routes, so the output tells us nothing about any filtering of 10.1.2.0/24. The output shows a single interarea route for 10.1.3.0/24, so at least one ABR has flooded a Type 3 LSA for this route. Additionally, the output confirms that at least one ABR flooded a type 3 LSA for 10.1.3.0/24, or the output would not show an IA route for 10.1.3.0/24. So, the type 3 LSA for 10.1.3.0/24 was not filtered by both ABRs.

2. C. When referenced from a distribute list, OSPF filters routes from being added to that router's IP routing table but has no impact on the flow of LSAs. As such, neither A nor B is correct. An OSPF **distribute-list** command does attempt to filter routes from being added to the IP routing table by OSPF, so the two answers that mention the IP routing table might be correct. Sequence number 5 matches prefixes from 10.1.2.0–10.1.2.255, with prefix lengths between 25–27, and denies (filters) those prefixes. So, the prefix list will match 10.1.2.0/26 with the first line, with a deny action. The 10.1.2.0/24 subnet does not match the first line of the prefix list, but it does match the third line, the match all line, with a permit action. Because 10.1.2.0/26 is matched by a deny clause, this route is indeed filtered, so it is not added to R1's IP routing table. 10.1.2.0/24, matched with a permit clause, is allowed and would be in the IP routing table.

3. A. When referenced from an **area filter-list** command, OSPF filters Type 3 LSAs created on that router, preventing them from being flooded into area 1 (per the configuration command). As an ABR, R1 would calculate intra-area routes to these area 0 subnets, so this filtering will have no effect on R1's routes. Sequence number 5

matches prefixes from 10.1.2.0–10.1.2.255, with prefix lengths between 25–27, and denies (filters) those prefixes. So, the prefix list will match 10.1.2.0/26 with the first line, with a deny action. The 10.1.2.0/24 subnet does not match the first line of the prefix list because the prefix length does not match, but it does match the third line, the match all line, with a permit action. By matching subnet 10.1.2.0/26 with a deny action, the filter-list does prevent R1 from flooding a Type 3 LSA for that subnet. By matching 10.1.2.0/24 with a permit action, R1 does not filter the Type 3 LSA for that subnet.

4. B and D. The **area range** command does not cause a failure in neighborships. Because at least one intra-area subordinate subnet of 10.1.0.0/16 exists in R1, R1 both creates a summary route for 10.1.0.0/16 and stops advertising LSAs for the (three) subordinate subnets. By default, the metric of the summary is the metric of the lowest-metric component subnet.

5. D. The **show ip ospf database summary** command lists only Type 3 LSAs. The **summary-address** command creates Type 5 LSAs on ASBRs, ruling out one answer. The output does not specify whether the LSA was created as a summary route; all references to the word "summary" refer to Type 3 Summary LSAs. If created by an **area range** command, the metric defaults to be the best metric of all subordinate subnets, but it may also be explicitly set, ruling out another of the possible answers. In short, this LSA may represent a route summarized by the area range command, but that fact cannot be proved or disproved by the output as shown..

6. B. Without the **always** parameter, the **default-information originate** command generates an LSA for a default route, with prefix 0.0.0.0/0, but only if its own IP routing table has a route for 0.0.0.0/0. It does not flag another LSA as being used as a candidate default route.

7. C and D. Both types of NSSA stubby areas allow the redistribution of external routes into the area, but these routes are advertised as Type 7 LSAs. As a totally NSSA area, the ABR should flood no Type 5 LSAs into the area and flood no Type 3 LSAs into the area, except for the Type 3 LSAs used to advertise the default route into the area. As such, a router internal to a totally stubby are should see zero Type 5 LSAs, and a small number of Type 3 LSAs for the default route(s) advertised by the ABR(s).

8. B. The **stub** keyword means either a stub area or totally stubby. The **no-summary** command means the area is totally stubby.

Chapter 8

1. D. The answer with **area 0 virtual-link 4.4.4.4 cost 3** is incorrect because the show command output lists a transit area of 1, but the answer's **area** parameter refers to area 0 as the transit area. (There is also no **cost** parameter on the **area virtual-link** command.) The RID of the router on the other end of the virtual link, 4.4.4.4 per the **show** command output, does not have to be pingable for the virtual link to work. The cost of the virtual link is 3, but that cost is calculated as the cost to reach the other router through the transit area, so the command output listed with the question can-

not be used to predict Fa0/0's OSPF interface cost alone. However, because the output lists area 1 as the transit area, and because the neighbor RID is listed as 4.4.4.4, R1 will use the area 1 LSDB entries to calculate the cost to reach 4.4.4, a process that will include the area 1 Type 1 LSA for RID 4.4.4.4.

2. B. The **area virtual-link** command defines the virtual link, with the transit area—the area through which the virtual link passes—listed as the first parameter. The other parameter is the RID of the other router. Two of the wrong answers are not IOS commands.

3. D. Of the four types listed, only point-to-multipoint nonbroadcast does not use a DR but does require the static definition of neighbors.

4. C. Of the four types listed, only point-to-multipoint does not use a DR and dynamically discovers neighbors.

5. A and C. For routers to use their OSPF routes in a multipoint design, each router needs mapping to each other router in the Frame Relay subnet. In this case, R3–R10 all need **frame-relay map** commands to define the mapping to other routers with which they do not have a PVC. This network type requires static definition of neighbors, but the neighbor relationships match the PVC topology, so R3–R10 need only two **neighbor** commands. This OSPF network type does not use a DR, so the **ip ospf priority** commands have no effect and would be unnecessary.

Chapter 9

1. D. The three incorrect answers list typical reasons for using route redistribution. The correct answer—the least likely reason among the answers for using route redistribution—lists a problem for which an OSPF virtual link is often used. Route redistribution could be attempted to solve a problem with a discontiguous OSPF area, but the redistribution completely changes the LSAs that would have otherwise been known and could have negative impacts on route summaries and cause routing loops, and have other problems as well.

2. B and D. For a router to redistribute routes between two routing protocols, the router must have both routing protocols configured, have a working link into each routing domain, and configure **redistribute** commands under each routing process. The **redistribute** command, issued in routing protocol configuration mode, pulls routes into that routing process, from another routing process as referenced on the **redistribute** command.

3. B and C. Because the metrics come from a different routing protocol than EIGRP, the metric must be set. The metric must be set with five components; EIGRP will then use those components as it would for an internal route. The metric components may be set as listed in the two correct answers, plus using a route-map as referenced by the **redistribute** command.

4. C. This output is the external data section of a detailed view of an EIGRP topology table entry for an external route. This output confirms that this route was redistributed into EIGRP. If R1 were the redistributing router, the output would include the phrase "(this system)"; this example does not include that notation. The output means that on the router that did the redistribution, the route was redistributed from OSPF process 1, and the OSPF metric was 64. R1's metric is not based on the OSPF metric of the route.

5. B. The **redistribute ospf** command will attempt to redistribute OSPF routes and connected routes from interfaces on which OSPF is enabled. The metric components include 1000 Kbps (or 1 Mbps), 100 tens-of-microseconds (or 1000 microseconds), 10 for the loading, 1 for the reliability, and 1500 for MTU. The EIGRP version of the **redistribute** command does not include a subnets option.

6. A and C. Because the routes come from OSPF and feed into OSPF, the metrics can be set with the usual tools, or the metric can default. When taking routes from OSPF into another OSPF process, the default metric is taken from the source route's OSPF cost. Alternatively, the metric can be set for all routes, regardless of the route source, using the **default-metric** OSPF subcommand. The **metric transparent** keywords cannot be used for an OSPF **redistribute** command.

7. D. This command lists the output of Type 4 Summary ASBR LSAs. The LSID identifies the redistributing ASBR (9.9.9.9). The advertising router is the ABR that created and flooded the LSA (3.3.3.3), and the metric is the ABR's best metric route to reach the ASBR.

8. D. Routers add internal and external costs for E1 routes and use only external costs for E2 routes, so the cost for the route through R22 will always be lower. However, for a given prefix/length, OSPF always prefers intra-area routes first, then interarea, then E1, and finally, E2, all regardless of metric.

Chapter 10

1. E. Because OSPF does not use hop count as a metric, the information about the number of hops is not available in OSPF routes in the IP routing table. The other answers list items that can be matched with the route map **match** subcommand.

2. A. The deny clauses in the route map mean that the route map will filter routes matched by that clause. The permit or deny action of the referenced ACLs just defines whether the route is matched. So, routes permitted by ACL "two" will be matched and then filtered due to the route-map clause deny action. Routes denied by ACL "one" simply do not match the route map clause numbered 10; such routes may or may not be redistributed depending on the next two clauses. Clause number 100 does not have a **match** command, meaning it matches all routes not otherwise matched, with a permit action, allowing these routes to be redistributed.

3. A and C. The problem states that R1 has learned OSPF intra-area routes for 10.1.1.0/24, so **show ip route** will display that subnet. As an intra-area route based on a Type 2 LSA, the **show ip ospf topology** command lists the summary of the LSAs, including the 10.1.1.0 subnet number for that Type 2 LSA. However, because the re-distribution filtering discards subnet 10.1.1.0/24, this value will not be included in the EIGRP topology table.

4. B. The **external 2** parameters on the **redistribute** command act as matching logic; only routes from the source routing protocol (in this case OSPF 2) that match this ex-tra logic will be considered for redistribution by this **redistribute** command. The **set metric-type type-1** route-map subcommand sets the route type as it is injected into the destination routing protocol (in this case OSPF 1); this logic is not used for matching the source routes. The routes permitted by ACL 1 will be redistributed, but only those that are also E2 routes from the (source) OSPF 2 domain. The redistribute function will not change the attributes of routes inside a single routing domain, but only in the destination routing domain (OSPF 1), so the configuration has no effect on the OSPF 2 routes that remain in OSPF 2.

5. C. EIGRP, by default, sets a different AD for internal (90) and external (170) routes. The rest of the answers are accurate regarding default settings.

6. A. All the answers list reasonable options in some cases, but the only feature listed that is useful with all three routing protocols is the route tag feature. RIPv2 does not support the concept of differentiating between internal and external routes, so the two answers that suggest setting administrative distance (AD) based on the route type (internal or external) could not be used in all three routing domains, as required by the question. All three routing protocols support setting route tags and setting the AD per route; however, because RIPv2 cannot match based on the route type (inter-nal/external), the option to set the route tags is the only option that applies to all three routing domains.

7. D. AD can be used to prevent the domain loop problem with two routing domains by making each routing protocol's AD for internal routes be better (lower) than the other routing protocol's AD for external routes. RIP uses AD 120 for all routes, with no dis-tinction of internal or external. As such, OSPF's internal default AD settings of 110 meet the requirement that OSPF's internal AD (110) is better than RIP's external (120). However, RIP's default of 120 is not better than OSPF's default for externals (110), so the **distance ospf external 180** command changes that setting to meet both require-ments. The three wrong answers, while syntactically valid, do not help meet the re-quirements.

8. E. Route tags are unitless integers that can be given to a route and even passed be-tween different routing protocols by routers that perform redistribution.

Chapter 11

1. A and C. PBR supports processing packets on an interface, for the inbound direction only. The referenced route map causes PBR to attempt policy routing of packets that match a permit clause in the route map.

2. B and E. Packets created by Telnet use TCP, so the packet will match ACL 101 with a permit action. So, PBR will match the only route map clause shown in the configuration, with that permit route map clause listing a **set** command. The **set** command lists S0/0/1 as the outgoing interface, and without a **default** parameter. So, Router R1 will first attempt to forward the packet based on the **set** command (interface S0/0/1), but if the interface is down, then try to forward based on the IP routing table (interface S0/1/1).

3. D. The output from the **show ip policy** command shows the interfaces on which PBR has been enabled, and the name of the route map enabled for PBR on each interface. For the purposes of this question, the output tells us the interfaces on which PBR has been enabled. Two answers mention packets exiting the interface, so these answers cannot be correct, because PBR applies to packets entering an interface. For the two interfaces that mention inbound packets, one suggests that all packets will be forwarded per the PBR configuration; some may not be forwarded per PBR, depending on the configuration of the route map. The correct answer specifically mentions that PBR will consider all packets with PBR, which is the more accurate statement about PBR operations.

4. A and B. The IP SLA feature focuses on IP traffic, so IOS does not include Novell's older IPX protocol as part of IP SLA. IP SLA uses SNMP MIBs to store statistics, but it does not use SNMP as an operation.

5. C. The three lines shown create the operation number (first command), define the operation (second command), and start the operation (third command). All commands are correct. After the operation is started, IP SLA stores the data in the RTTMON MIB–no additional configuration necessary.

6. D. The up timers on the tracking object defines how long to wait, when in a down state, after seeing the IP SLA object transition to an OK state. Similarly, the down timer defines how long to wait, when in an OK state, after seeing the IP SLA object move to a down state, before moving the tracking object to a down state.

Chapter 12

1. B and E. The private IPv4 address space consists of Class A network 10.0.0.0, Class B networks 172.16.0.0–172.31.0.0, and the 256 Class C networks that begin 192.168.

2. B. ICANN and IANA manage the assignment of public IPv4 address space such that large address blocks (often called CIDR blocks) exist in a particular geography or

are assigned to particular ISPs. As such, Internet routers can more easily create summary routes to help keep the routing table small in the Internet. 200.1.2.0/24 would likely also be allocated to some registrar, ISP, or customer in Asia. Because of the large route summaries, in this case possibly a summary for 200.0.0.0/8, routers in North America would not see an increase in the size of their routing tables.

3. A. The router in ASN 22, R22, advertises the BGP update with (at least) 22 in the AS_Path Path Attribute (PA). When R1 advertises the route to R2, also in ASN 11, R1 does not add an ASN. As a result, R2's AS_Path has at least ASN 22 and not ASN 11.

4. A and C. The public range of 16-bit BGP ASNs is 1 through 64,495.

5. D. The question asks which answers are true about the eBGP peer but also not true about an iBGP peer. Both iBGP and eBGP use TCP port 179. An eBGP peer uses a different ASN than the local router, by definition, making that answer incorrect. The correct answer refers to the fact that an eBGP peer adds its own ASN to the BGP AS_Path PA before sending routing information to another router, whereas iBGP peers do not.

6. A. Although using BGP does avoid some static configuration at the Enterprise and the ISP, the primary reason to consider using BGP in the Enterprise is to influence and react to Path Attributes for the purpose of choosing the best path. Typically, engineers do not redistribute BGP routes into the IGP due to scalability problems. And although it may be interesting to monitor the size of the Internet BGP table, it is not a primary motivation for choosing to use BGP on a router.

7. C and D. The terms "homed" makes reference to a single homed ISP, and "multi-homed" to multiple ISPs. The terms "single" and "dual" refer to the number of connections to each ISP.

Chapter 13

1. B and C. The **router bgp** command lists the local ASN, and the **neighbor remote-as** command lists the neighbor's ASN. Because the neighbor relationship uses the IP addresses on the common link, the routers do not need to identify the update source interface, because each will default to use their S0/0 interfaces (in this case) as the update source.

2. D. Three of the commands list valid commands. The **neighbor 2.2.2.2 multihop 2** command is syntactically incorrect; it should be **neighbor 2.2.2.2 ebgp-multihop 2**.

3. D. The **show ip bgp** command lists the BGP neighbor state in the last column of output, listing the literal state, unless in an established state. In that state, the output lists the number of prefixes learned from the neighbor, so a numeric value implies an established state.

4. A and D. The output lists R2's local ASN as ASN 11, a value that is configured in the **router bgp** *asn* command. The line for neighbor 1.1.1.1 lists that router's ASN as 1, so a **neighbor 1.1.1.1 remote-as 1** command should exist on R2 instead of the **neighbor 1.1.1.1 remote-as 11** command. The state for neighbor 1.1.1.1 lists "Idle (Admin)," implying that the **neighbor 1.1.1.1 shutdown** command has been configured. The other answer lists a nonexistent command.

5. A. The BGP Update message lists a set of PAs, plus any prefixes/lengths that use those PAs. It can also list withdrawn routes in the same Update message as newly advertised routes. It can also list multiple prefixes in a single Update message.

6. C. The "Known via" text refers to the local router's (R1's) **router bgp** command, which identifies the local router's ASN. The rest of the output does not identify the neighboring ASN, nor the rest of the AS_Path details. It does list that the route is external, with the text "type external", and the AS Hops (which is the AS_Path length).

7. A. The third character in each line for each router is either blank, meaning the route is an eBGP route, or an "i," meaning an iBGP-learned route. The contents of the AS_Path can be determined (1, 2, 3, 4), but the answer about AS_Path does not suggest 4 ASNs. The best route for each prefix has a ">" in the second character, and this route does not.

8. D. The **network** command will take the route from the IP routing table and put the equivalent into the BGP table, if that exact route exists. The output does not show a route for 130.1.16.0/20, so the **network 130.1.16.0 mask 255.255.240.0** command does not match a specific route. The other answer with a **network** command is syntactically incorrect. Redistribution without aggregation would redistribute the three routes, but all three subordinate routes would be advertised into eBGP. By also using BGP route summarization, a single route for 130.1.16.0/20 can be advertised.

Chapter 14

1. C. R1 needs to be configured with **router bgp 1**, **neighbor 2.2.2.2 remote-as 1**, and **neighbor 2.2.2.2 update-source loopback1**. The **neighbor 2.2.2.2 ibgp-multihop 2** and **neighbor 2.2.2.2 ibgp-mode** commands are simply unsupported commands. The **neighbor 1.1.1.1 remote-as 1** command has correct syntax and is used as a command in R2's configuration but not on R1. The **neighbor 2.2.2.2 remote-as 2** command has correct syntax but with the wrong ASN (2 instead of 1).

2. D. The small letter "i" in the third character position implies the route was learned with iBGP. Of the five lines, four have an "i" in the third column.

3. B and C. The line reading "1.1.1.1 from 2.2.2.2..." implies the BGP RID of the neighbor is 1.1.1.1, with neighbor ID–the IP address on the local router's **neighbor** command–of 2.2.2.2. The end of the output shows that the route is internal (iBGP learned) and is best, so both the > and i will be displayed for this route by the **show ip bgp** command. Finally, the output does not identify the local ASN, although it does list the AS_Path of the route (1, 2, 3, 4).

4. B. By default, when a router advertises an iBGP route, it leaves the Next-Hop PA unchanged. By default, R2's next hop for routes learned from I2 will be I2's IP address used on the R2–I2 neighbor relationship.

5. A and C. The Enterprise core routers need to know which exit point (R1 or R2) is best; the correct answers supply those routes to the routers internal to the company. Note that redistribution from BGP into the IGP is not recommended, but it does defeat this particular problem.

6. B. The show ip bgp neighbors 2.2.2.2 advertised-routes command does list the post-outbound-filter BGP Update; however, the user did not issue a **clear** command, so the filter has not yet taken effect. As such, the output still lists the original three prefixes as if the filter had not yet been applied.

7. B, D, and E. The neighbor distribute-list out command refers to an ACL, but for the ACL to match on both prefix and prefix length, the ACL must be an extended ACL. The neighbor filter-list command refers to an AS-path filter and cannot match based on prefix/length.

8. A and B. The router resets the BGP neighborship when performing a hard reset of the peer. See Table 14-3 in the chapter for a list of several variations of the **clear** command and whether they perform a hard or soft reset.

Chapter 15

1. B. Weight and Local_Pref were created for the purpose of giving engineers tools to influence the BGP best path choice. AS_Path was created for loop avoidance, but AS_Path length can also be manipulated (for instance, with AS_Path prepend) to influence the best path choice. Although the Origin PA can be changed by configuration for the purpose of influencing the best path decision, the intent of this PA is to identify the source from which the route was introduced into BGP. Additionally, the best path algorithm considers the Origin PA after the other PAs listed in the answers, making Origin the least useful of these answers for influencing path choice.

2. A. Of the items listed in the question, Weight is the first one considered in the best path algorithm, with a bigger weight being better. As a result, Route 1 is the better route of the two.

3. B. Of the items listed in the question, Weight is the first one considered in the best path algorithm, and it is a tie. The next item considered, Local Preference, uses bigger-is-better logic, so Route 2 will be considered best.

4. B and D. Weight, a Cisco-proprietary feature of BGP on Cisco routers, cannot be transmitted in a BGP Update, so setting Weight on an outbound route map at the ISPs will have no effect. Also, the goals call for setting Weight for all routes from an ISP to the same number, so creating a prefix list to match a subset of reachable prefixes, in this case all class C networks, is not useful. However, two methods of configuring Weight do exist: the **neighbor weight** command and configuring an inbound route map with a **set weight** command in the route map.

5. B and C. The line reading 1.1.1.1 from 2.2.2.2... implies the BGP RID of the neighbor is 1.1.1.1, with neighbor ID–the IP address on the local router's **neighbor** command–of 2.2.2.2. The end of the output shows that the route is internal (iBGP learned), and the output lists the word "best," so the **show ip bgp** command will display both the > and i for this route. Finally, the output does not identify the local ASN, although it does list the AS_Path of the route (1, 2, 3, 4).

6. B. The output shows the results of AS_Path prepending. The repetitive 1's cannot mean that the route has been advertised into and out of the same ASN repeatedly because loop prevention would have prevented such an advertisement. With AS_Path prepending, the neighboring ASN typically adds its own ASN to the end of the AS_Path (as listed on the left of the output).

7. C. The command lists the administrative distance as the first number inside the square brackets and the MED values as the second number in brackets. The AD of 20 implies an eBGP route instead of iBGP. The output says nothing about the Weight or AS_Path length.

Chapter 16

1. D. Inside a quartet, any leading 0s can be omitted, and one sequence of one or more quartets of all 0s can be replaced with "::". The correct answer replaces the longer three-quartet sequence of 0s with ::.

2. C. The name of the prefix generally represents the group to which the prefix is given, with the exception of the term *global routing*. IANA assigns a prefix to a registry (registry prefix). The registry may assign a subset of that range as a prefix to an ISP (ISP prefix). That ISP then subdivides that range of addresses into prefixes and assigns a prefix to one of its customers (site prefix, also called global routing prefix). The Enterprise network engineers then further subdivides the range, often with prefix length 64, into subnet prefixes.

3. A and C. IPv6 supports stateful DHCP, which works similarly to IPv4's DHCP protocol to dynamically assign the entire IP address. Stateless autoconfiguration also allows for the assignment by finding the prefix from some nearby router and calculating the Interface ID using EUI-64 format. Stateless DHCP simply supplies the DNS server IP addresses, and NDP supplies Layer 2 mapping information.

4. D. Stateless autoconfiguration only helps a host learn and form its own IP address, but it does not help the host learn a default gateway. Stateless RS is not a valid term or feature. Neighbor Discovery Protocol (NDP) is used for several purposes, including the same purpose as ARP in IPv4, plus to learn configuration parameters such as a default gateway IP address.

5. D. Global unicast addresses begin with 2000::/3, meaning the first three bits match the value in hex 2000. Similarly, unique local addresses match FD00::/8, and link local addresses match FE80::/10 (values that begin with FE8, FE9, FEA, and FEB hex). Multicast IPv6 addresses begin with FF00::/8, meaning the first two hex digits are F.

6. B. When created automatically, link local addresses begin FE80::/64, because after the prefix of FE80::/10, the device builds the next 54 bits as binary 0s. Statically assigned link local addresses simply need to confirm to the FE80::/10 prefix. As a result, only two answers are candidates with a beginning quartet of FE80. Of these, only one has only hex 0s in the second, third, and fourth quartets, making answer B the only valid answer.

7. A and C. The **ipv6 address** command does not list an **eui-64** parameter, so R1 does not form its global unicast address using the EUI-64 format. However, it does form its link local address using EUI-64. The **show ipv6 interface brief** command lists both the global unicast and link local addresses in its output.

8. A. The group addresses listed in the output are the all IPv6 hosts address (FF02::1), the all IPv6 routers address (FF02::2), and the solicited node address that is based on R1's global unicast address (FF02::1:FF:12:3456). Also, R1's global unicast address is listed correctly in answer B, but the "[EUI]" notation implies that R1 derived the interface ID portion using EUI-64 conventions.

Chapter 17

1. A, B, and D. RIP-2 and RIPng both use UDP, both use Distance Vector logic, and both use the same metric, with the same maximum (15) and same metric that means infinity (16). RIPng does not perform automatic route summarization because IPv6 has no concept of a classful network. RIPng also uses the built-in IPv6 authentication mechanisms, rather than a RIP-specific authentication such as RIP-2.

2. B. That the configuration will be copied/pasted into a router means that the order of the commands matters. In this case, that the **ipv6 rip one enable** command precedes the **ipv6 address** command on interface f0/0 means that IOS will reject the first of these commands, therefore not enabling RIPng on F0/0. The correct order listed under S0/0/0 means that RIPng will be enabled on S0/0/0. As a result, RIPng on R1 will advertise about S0/0/0's connected IPv6 prefixes, and send Updates on S0/0/0, but will do nothing related for F0/0.

3. D. Because the question states that no IPv4 configuration exists, EIGRP for IPv6 cannot derive a 32-bit EIGRP router ID. Before EIGRP will work, R1 needs to define an EIGRP router ID (using the **eigrp router-id** command) and enable EIGRP using the **no shutdown** router subcommand.

4. B. EIGRP uses the link local address as the next hop for routing protocols. Based on R2's MAC address, R2's link local address on F0/0 will be FE80::1311:11FF:FE11:1111. This value is derived by splitting the MAC, inserting FFFE, and flipping bit 7, making the initial hex 11 become hex 13.

5. A and C. OSPFv3 supports multiple OSPF instances per interface, whereas OSPFv2 does not. Also, each version requires a different set of requirements be met before becoming neighbors, most notably that OSPFv3 does not require neighboring OSPFv3 routers to be in the same subnet.

6. C. Because the question states that no IPv4 configuration exists, OSPFv3 cannot derive a 32-bit OSPF router ID. Before OSPFv3 works, R1 needs to define an OSPF router ID (using the OSPF **router-id** command).

7. A. The **redistribute** command does not have a **subnets** option for IPv6 because OSPFv3 has no concept of IPv6 classful networks nor their subnets. As configured, the **redistribute** command redistributes only EIGRP-learned routes. If the **include-connected** parameter had been included, the connected route for 2000:0:0:1::/64 would have also been redistributed. Local routes are never redistributed.

8. B. The only configurable item after the interface that does not first list a keyword is the administrative distance parameter.

Chapter 18

1. C. Native IPv6 makes the most sense when the IPv6 deployment is pervasive, with traffic loads heavy or at least steady. Point-to-point tunnels work best when IPv6 is needed in only a subset of sites but also when the traffic should be somewhat regular or with higher volume. Multipoint tunnels also work well when IPv6 is needed in a subset of sites, but it is more appropriate when the traffic is more occasional and lower volume. Finally, NAT-PT is useful when an IPv4-only host needs to communicate with an IPv6-only host.

2. D. Native IPv6 makes the most sense when the IPv6 deployment is pervasive, with traffic loads heavy or at least steady.. Point-to-point tunnels work best when IPv6 is needed in only a subset of sites, but also when the traffic should be somewhat regular or with higher volume. Multipoint tunnels also work well when IPv6 is needed in a subset of sites, but it is more appropriate when the traffic is more occasional and lower volume. Finally, NAT-PT is useful when an IPv4-only host needs to communicate with an IPv6-only host.

3. E. Dual stacks means that the host runs both IPv4 and IPv6. A host must run both if the host is to send packets of each protocol. The host may use a multipoint tunnel, but the other three answers list features applicable to routers, but not hosts.

4. B. A manually configured tunnel explicitly defines the destination IPv4 address, as does a GRE IPv6 tunnel. The other two types listed in the answer do not. Additionally, a manually configured tunnel uses mode **ipv6ip**, whereas GRE tunnels use mode **gre**.

5. C. IOS defaults to use GRE encapsulation mode on tunnel interfaces, so the **tunnel mode** command is not required. The mode will default to GRE. The **tunnel source** and **tunnel destination** commands are required.

6. B and D. The two point-to-point tunneling methods—manually configured tunnel and GRE—support IPv6 IGPs. The two multipoint tunneling methods—automatic 6to4 and ISATAP—do not.

7. A. An automatic 6to4 tunnel does not use a **tunnel destination** command on the tunnel interface; ISATAP tunnels also do not use this command. However, automatic 6to4 tunnels use IPv6 addresses that begin 2002::/16 and have the tunnel's source IPv4 address imbedded as the second and third octets of the IPv6 address, whereas ISATAP tunnels do not. Because C0A5:101 hex equals 192.168.1.1 in dotted decimal, this configuration represents the almost completed configuration for an automatic 6to4 tunnel.

8. A and D. ISATAP uses a modified EUI-64 format, which adds the IPv4 address, in hex, into quartets 7 and 8. Automatic 6to4 tunnels use address range 2002::/16, with the next two quartets (second and third quartets) used to store the hex version of an IPv4 address.

9. D. The combination of the configured eui-64 parameter on the **ipv6 address** command, and the tunnel mode of **isatap**, tells the router to use modified EUI-64 rules. These rules start with the configured 64 bit prefix (2000::/64 in this case), adding 0000:5EFE as the fifth and sixth quartets. The last two quartets are taken from the **tunnel source** command's referenced IPv4 address. In this case, 192.168.1.1 converts to C0A8:0101, making the last answer correct.

Chapter 19

1. C. IPsec tunnels make for more secure communications, including encryption and authentication. However, it does not support IGP communications across the tunnel.

2. A and C. An IPsec tunnel would be useful to allow the packet to pass over the Internet and into the Enterprise. The GRE tunnel would only be needed if an IGP is also needed, and for this design, an IGP is not required. Instead, a floating static default route would work fine, with the static route sending traffic over the IPsec tunnel but only when the private leased line fails.

3. D. The ATM details, like VPI/VCI, will be configured under the ATM interface. PPP (including CHAP) and Layer 3 details will be configured under the dialer interface.

4. C. The NAT configuration acts only on packets permitted by a referenced ACL. As a result, the ACL can permit packets destined for the Internet, performing NAT on those packets. The ACL also denies packets going to the Enterprise, meaning that the router does not apply NAT to those packets.

5. B. As for the correct answer, the process of routing a packet out a GRE tunnel interface triggers the GRE encapsulation action. As for the incorrect answers: There is no **tunnel gre** *acl* command. There is no IPsec tunnel interface. Finally, one answer refers to logic that would describe a router's logic when determining whether to encapsulate a packet into an IPsec tunnel.

Conversion Tables

This appendix lists two conversion tables for reference when studying:

- Hex-to-decimal
- Decimal-to-binary

Use these tables for learning; however, such tables will not be available on the exam.

Table B-1 *Hex-to-Decimal Conversion Table*

Hex	Decimal
0	0
1	1
2	2
3	3
4	4
5	5
6	6
7	7
8	8
9	9
A	10
B	11
C	12
D	13
E	14
F	15

Table B-2 *Binary-to-Decimal Conversion Table*

Decimal Value	Binary Value	Decimal Value	Binary Value	Decimal Value	Binary Value	Decimal Value	Binary Value
0	00000000	32	00100000	64	01000000	96	01100000
1	00000001	33	00100001	65	01000001	97	01100001
2	00000010	34	00100010	66	01000010	98	01100010
3	00000011	35	00100011	67	01000011	99	01100011
4	00000100	36	00100100	68	01000100	100	01100100
5	00000101	37	00100101	69	01000101	101	01100101
6	00000110	38	00100110	70	01000110	102	01100110
7	00000111	39	00100111	71	01000111	103	01100111
8	00001000	40	00101000	72	01001000	104	01101000
9	00001001	41	00101001	73	01001001	105	01101001
10	00001010	42	00101010	74	01001010	106	01101010
11	00001011	43	00101011	75	01001011	107	01101011
12	00001100	44	00101100	76	01001100	108	01101100
13	00001101	45	00101101	77	01001101	109	01101101
14	00001110	46	00101110	78	01001110	110	01101110
15	00001111	47	00101111	79	01001111	111	01101111
16	00010000	48	00110000	80	01010000	112	01110000
17	00010001	49	00110001	81	01010001	113	01110001
18	00010010	50	00110010	82	01010010	114	01110010
19	00010011	51	00110011	83	01010011	115	01110011
20	00010100	52	00110100	84	01010100	116	01110100
21	00010101	53	00110101	85	01010101	117	01110101
22	00010110	54	00110110	86	01010110	118	01110110
23	00010111	55	00110111	87	01010111	119	01110111
24	00011000	56	00111000	88	01011000	120	01111000
25	00011001	57	00111001	89	01011001	121	01111001
26	00011010	58	00111010	90	01011010	122	01111010
27	00011011	59	00111011	91	01011011	123	01111011
28	00011100	60	00111100	92	01011100	124	01111100
29	00011101	61	00111101	93	01011101	125	01111101
30	00011110	62	00111110	94	01011110	126	01111110
31	00011111	63	00111111	95	01011111	127	01111111

Table B-2 *Binary-to-Decimal Conversion Table*

Decimal Value	Binary Value	Decimal Value	Binary Value	Decimal Value	Binary Value	Decimal Value	Binary Value
128	10000000	160	10100000	192	11000000	224	11100000
129	10000001	161	10100001	193	11000001	225	11100001
130	10000010	162	10100010	194	11000010	226	11100010
131	10000011	163	10100011	195	11000011	227	11100011
132	10000100	164	10100100	196	11000100	228	11100100
133	10000101	165	10100101	197	11000101	229	11100101
134	10000110	166	10100110	198	11000110	230	11100110
135	10000111	167	10100111	199	11000111	231	11100111
136	10001000	168	10101000	200	11001000	232	11101000
137	10001001	169	10101001	201	11001001	233	11101001
138	10001010	170	10101010	202	11001010	234	11101010
139	10001011	171	10101011	203	11001011	235	11101011
140	10001100	172	10101100	204	11001100	236	11101100
141	10001101	173	10101101	205	11001101	237	11101101
142	10001110	174	10101110	206	11001110	238	11101110
143	10001111	175	10101111	207	11001111	239	11101111
144	10010000	176	10110000	208	11010000	240	11110000
145	10010001	177	10110001	209	11010001	241	11110001
146	10010010	178	10110010	210	11010010	242	11110010
147	10010011	179	10110011	211	11010011	243	11110011
148	10010100	180	10110100	212	11010100	244	11110100
149	10010101	181	10110101	213	11010101	245	11110101
150	10010110	182	10110110	214	11010110	246	11110110
151	10010111	183	10110111	215	11010111	247	11110111
152	10011000	184	10111000	216	11011000	248	11111000
153	10011001	185	10111001	217	11011001	249	11111001
154	10011010	186	10111010	218	11011010	250	11111010
155	10011011	187	10111011	219	11011011	251	11111011
156	10011100	188	10111100	220	11011100 ·	252	11111100
157	10011101	189	10111101	221	11011101	253	11111101
158	10011110	190	10111110	222	11011110	254	11111110
159	10011111	191	10111111	223	11011111	255	11111111

Route Exam Updates

Over time, reader feedback allows Cisco Press to gauge which topics give our readers the most problems when taking the exams. To assist readers with those topics, the authors created new materials clarifying and expanding upon those troublesome exam topics. As mentioned in the introduction, the additional content about the exam is contained in a PDF document on this book's companion website, at http://www.ciscopress.com/title/9781587202537.

This appendix is intended to provide you with updated information if Cisco makes minor modifications to the exam upon which this book is based. When Cisco releases an entirely new exam, the changes are usually too extensive to provide in a simple update appendix. In those cases, you might need to consult the new edition of the book for the updated content.

This appendix attempts to fill the void that occurs with any print book. In particular, this appendix does the following:

- Mentions technical items that might not have been mentioned elsewhere in the book

- Covers new topics if Cisco adds new content to the exam over time

- Provides a way to get up-to-the-minute current information about content for the exam

Always Get the Latest at the Companion Website

You are reading the version of this appendix that was available when your book was printed. However, given that the main purpose of this appendix is to be a living, changing document, it is important that you look for the latest version online at the book's companion website. To do so:

Step 1   Browse to http://www.ciscopress.com/title/9781587202537.

Step 2   Select the Appendix option under the More Information box.

Step 3   Download the latest "Appendix C" document.

> **Note**   Note that the downloaded document has a version number. Comparing the version of this print Appendix C (Version 1.0) with the latest online version of this appendix, you should do the following:
>
> ■   Same version—Ignore the PDF that you downloaded from the companion website.
>
> ■   Website has a later version—Ignore this Appendix C in your book and read only the latest version that you downloaded from the companion website.

Technical Content

The current version of this appendix does not contain any additional technical coverage.

Index

A

ABR (area border routers), 143
  interarea routes, 210–211
  intra-area routes, 210–211
  OSPF
    route filtering, 226–230
    route summarization, 232–235
    virtual links, 260–262

ACK (acknowledgement) messages
  EIGRP, 61, 65
  LSAck messages, 200

ACL (access control lists)
  EIGRP route filtering, 102–105
  route maps, referencing ACL from, 112

active timers, EIGRP convergence process, 87

AD (Administrative Distance), route redistribution with multiple redistribution points
  preventing domain loops via per-route AD settings, 350–354
  preventing domain loops with AD, 346–349

AD (Advertised Distance), building EIGRP IP routing tables, 69–72

administrative Weight (BGP Path Control), influencing, 500–501

aggregation, Internet routing, 392–393

areas, 143
  interarea routes
    ABR, 210–211
    OSPF route selection, 206–210
  intra-area routes
    ABR, 210–211
    OSPF route selection, 205–206
  OSPF database exchange process, flooding throughout an area, 203–204

AS External LSA (link state advertisements), 180

AS_Path
  AS_Path Prepend command
    BGP Path Control, 517–519
    increasing length via, 517–519
  BGP PA, 494
  Weight (BGP Path Control), influencing, 508–511

AS_SEQ path attribute, BGP ASN, 397–399

ASBR (Autonomous System Border Routers)
  ASBR Summary LSA (link state advertisements), 179
  OSPF route summarization, 235–236

ASN (autonomous system numbers), BGP ASN
  AS_SEQ path attribute, 397–399
  public/private ASN, 400–402

D

J - K - L

M

P

U

V

W - X - Y - Z

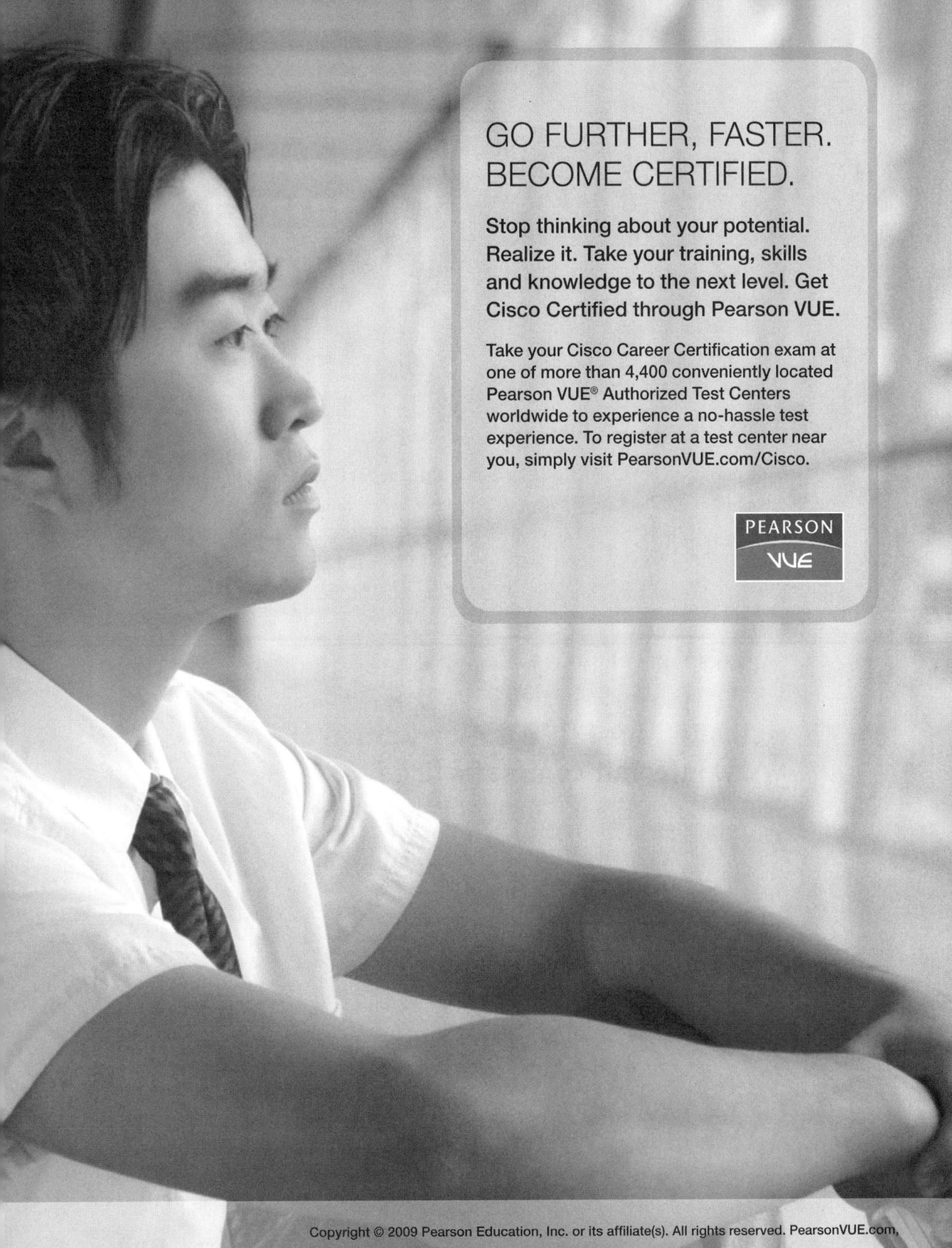

GO FURTHER, FASTER.
BECOME CERTIFIED.

Stop thinking about your potential.
Realize it. Take your training, skills
and knowledge to the next level. Get
Cisco Certified through Pearson VUE.

Take your Cisco Career Certification exam at
one of more than 4,400 conveniently located
Pearson VUE® Authorized Test Centers
worldwide to experience a no-hassle test
experience. To register at a test center near
you, simply visit PearsonVUE.com/Cisco.

PEARSON
VUE

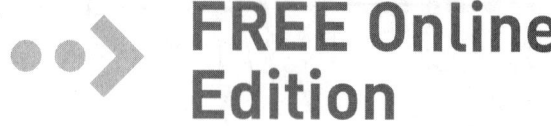

FREE Online Edition

Your purchase of **CCNP ROUTE 642-902 Official Certification Guide** includes access to a free online edition for 45 days through the Safari Books Online subscription service. Nearly every Cisco Press book is available online through Safari Books Online, along with more than 5,000 other technical books and videos from publishers such as Addison-Wesley Professional, Exam Cram, IBM Press, O'Reilly, Prentice Hall, Que, and Sams.

SAFARI BOOKS ONLINE allows you to search for a specific answer, cut and paste code, download chapters, and stay current with emerging technologies.

Activate your FREE Online Edition at
www.informit.com/safarifree

> **STEP 1:** Enter the coupon code: CMNJZAA.

> **STEP 2:** New Safari users, complete the brief registration form. Safari subscribers, just log in.

If you have difficulty registering on Safari or accessing the online edition, please e-mail customer-service@safaribooksonline.com